JN270354

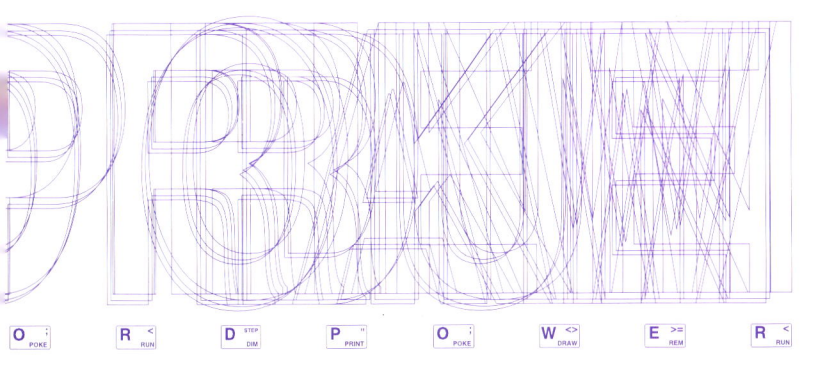

ワードパワー英英和辞典

編集主幹 島岡丘

増進会出版社
Oxford University Press

# Word Power

## Fully-bilingual Dictionary

Z-kai

ワードパワー英英和辞典
Wordpower Fully-bilingual Dictionary
©2002 株式会社 増進会出版社
Zoshinkai Publishers, Inc
First Edition 2002

© Oxford University Press 2000
This second edition of Oxford Wordpower Dictionary originally published in English in 2000 is
published by arrangement with Oxford University Press.

2000年に英語で出版された『オックスフォード・ワードパワー辞典』第2版は,
オックスフォード大学出版局により出版された.

# 刊行のことば

『ワードパワー英英和辞典』は**新しいタイプの学習辞典**です.全世界で定評のある *Oxford Wordpower Dictionary*(オックスフォード大学出版局発行)の原文そのままを使い,その翻訳をすると同時に,見出し語に対応する訳語を付けた**英英和辞典**です.そのほか,日本語話者が英語の学習上知っておくべき英語の特徴や日英語の違いなど必要な情報を選び,コラム記事の形で掲載していますので,**読む辞典**の役割も持っています.

この辞典は,単に英英辞典に日本語訳を併記しただけではありません.**日本語訳は英語の定義や例文を正しく理解する補助手段として活用できるようになっています.**

本辞典は**英英辞典の弱点を克服した**ものと言えます.英英辞典を使っても英語の定義自体などに新語句があってよく理解できない,という切実な問題がこれまではあったかと思いますが,英語の原文の直後に付けた訳文を参照することによって,学習者自身の解釈が正しかったとか,ああ,なるほどそういう意味だったのだ,と確認することができ,より着実に英語力を身に付けることができます.

本辞典はまた**英和辞典の弱点を克服した**ものとも言えます.従来の英和辞典には,いきなり日本語に訳すために,その語が本来持っているニュアンスが消えてしまうという問題点がありましたが,見出し語の定義を,その訳をヒントにしながら**よりよく理解できる**ので,その語が本来持つ意味を確実に把握することができます.

本辞典には約37000語の見出し語がありますが,その定義には基本語彙2500語を用いていますので,あらかじめどのような語が定義語によく使われているかをまとめて覚えておくとよいでしょう.それによって,英単語間のネットワークが分かり,英語力が一段と高まるでしょう.例えば次のような表現が定義でよく用いられますので,本辞典を使う際の参考にしてください.

---

**\* 名詞の定義でよく使われる言葉:**
a piece of ~(1つの~), a kind of ~(一種の~), a part of ~ (一種の~), a set of ~(一組の~); something(もの), object(物体), thing(もの); substance(物質), structure(構造[物]), liquid(液体), container(入れ物); person(人,人称), animal(動物), plant(植物), fish(魚), bird(鳥); time(時間), place(場所), relation(関係), furniture(家具), device(装置)

**\* 動詞の定義でよく使われる言葉:**
use(使う), do(する), make(作る,させる), mean(意味する); think(思う), feel(感じる), plan(計画する), act(行動する); say(言う), state(述べる), carry(運ぶ)

**\* 形容詞・副詞の定義でよく使われる言葉:**
having ~(~の性質などを持っている), like ~(~のような[に])

**\* その他:**
you(一般の人), used as ~(~として使われる), ~ that(that 以下の節が~を修飾する)

---

本辞典が皆さんの英語学習に新たな扉を開く一助となることを願ってやみません.
なお,本辞典の刊行に至るまで,Z会出版編集部の藤原敏晃部長と吉田晴奈さんにはことのほかお世話になりました.厚く御礼申し上げます.

平成14年2月

島岡　丘

# 編集委員一覧

### [編集主幹]

聖徳大学教授
筑波大学名誉教授（言語学博士）　　島岡　丘

### [編集委員]

| | |
|---|---|
| 東京女子大学名誉教授 | 小林　祐子 |
| 神戸松蔭女子学院短期大学講師 | 宮本　明人 |
| 茨城キリスト教大学講師 | レパヴーマリ |
| 茨城キリスト教大学短大部助教授 | 東海林宏司 |
| 筑波大学附属駒場中高等学校教諭 | 久保野雅史 |
| 筑波大学附属高等学校教諭 | 山本　良一 |
| 茨城県立竜ヶ崎第一高等学校教諭 | 山田　一雄 |

### [編集協力]

乾　　隆
岡田あずさ
近藤　育子
清水　真紀
風呂迫元武
山西　敏博
湯澤　伸夫

### [翻訳・編集]

(株)サン・フレア

# 本辞典の構成 V

- 見出し語 (37,000語)
- 発音記号 [→P.XI]
- 英文定義 [→P.VII]
- 定義訳
- 重要語
- 定義と例文の区切り
- 品詞表示 [→P.VI]
- 訳例 (太字) [→P.VIII]
- 例文 (イタリック)
- 重要なコロケーション (太字) [→P.X]

**★achieve** /ətʃíːv/ 動他 ▶定義1 to complete sth by hard work and skill ～に労力を費やしてまた技能によって完成させる➡**～を成し遂げる, 達成する, 果たす** ‖ *They have achieved a lot in a short time.* 彼らは短時間で多くの事をやり遂げた. ▶定義2 to gain sth, usually by effort or skill ～を, 通常は努力または技能によって得る➡**～を獲得する, 勝ち取る, もたらす** ‖ *You have achieved the success you deserve.* あなたは努力に値する成功を勝ち取った.

**★achievement** /ətʃíːvmənt/ 名 C U ▶定義 something that you have done successfully, especially through hard work or skill 特に労力を費やし, または技能によって, 無事にやり遂げた物事➡**業績, 偉業** ‖ *She felt that winning the gold medal was her greatest achievement.* 彼女は金メダルの獲得が自分にとって最大の成果であると感じた. *He enjoys climbing mountains because it gives him **a sense of achievement**.* 彼が山登りを楽しんでいるのは, 達成感を味わえるからだ.

# VI 記号・略語一覧

| 記号・略語 | 意味 |
|---|---|
| 略 | 省略形 |
| 名 | 名詞 |
| 代 | 代名詞 |
| 動 | 動詞 |
| 形 | 形容詞 |
| 副 | 副詞 |
| 接 | 接続詞 |
| 前 | 前置詞 |
| 冠 | 冠詞 |
| 間 | 間投詞 |
| 英 | イギリス英語 |
| 米 | アメリカ英語 |
| 自 | 自動詞 |
| 他 | 他動詞 |
| C | 可算 |
| U | 不可算 |
| 単 | 単数形 |
| 複 | 複数形 |
| 現分 | 現在分詞 |
| 過分 | 過去分詞 |
| 現 | 現在時制 |
| 過 | 過去時制 |
| 三単 | 三人称・単数 |
| 正式 | 改まった表現 |
| 略式 | 口語的表現 |
| (古) | 古風・古典的 |
| (比喩) | 比喩的 |
| (文) | 文語 |
| (名詞の前だけ) | 限定用法のみ. 名詞を修飾する |
| (名詞の前は不可) | 叙述用法のみ. 補語として使用する |
| ☛参, ⇒ | 参照 |
| ☛参 ～ の注 | ～の注記を参照 |
| ⇔ | 反意語 |
| ☛類 | 類義語 |
| ★ | 重要語 |
| sth, sb | something, somebody |

## 本辞典の効果的活用法 VII

　本辞典は，各英単語に対して，単なる日本語の対応語句を与えるという役割を超え，あなたの英語力の向上を助けるパートナーになることを目指して編集されました．本辞典は，基本的に次の3ステップで活用してください．

　①「英文定義を読む」
→②（英文定義の意味で，分からないところがあったら）「定義訳を読む」
→③「日本語の対応語句を訳例で確認する」

※英文定義の訳は，あくまでも補助ですので，英文定義と訳例だけで理解ができるようになったら，読み飛ばしましょう．

　これを繰り返せば，訳語だけが載っている英和辞典を使うのに比べて，格段の差が現れるでしょう．具体的な使い方を以下に示しますので，是非参考にしてください．

## I. 基本的な活用法

### 1. 英文定義を活用しよう！

#### ➤ Case 1 beautiful
→ beautiful =「美しい」ではない

> **\*beautiful** /bjúːtɪfəl/ 形 ▶定義 very pretty or attractive; giving pleasure to the senses 非常にきれいなまたは魅力的な；五感に喜びをもたらす→**美しい，きれいな；楽しませる，心地良い** ‖ *The view from the top of the hill was really beautiful.* 丘の頂上からの眺めは本当にきれいだった．*What a beautiful day - the weather's perfect!* 何てすてきな日でしょう － 天気は最高です．*He has a beautiful voice.* 彼は美しい声を持っている．*A beautiful perfume filled the air.* 心地良い香りがあたり一面に立ちこめていた．*a beautiful woman* 美しい女

　英語を使いこなす上で重要なのは，見出し語が日本語のどの語と対応しているかということだけでなく，その語が持つ本来の意味です．beautiful が，単に「美しい」という意味ではないことは，定義を読めば一目瞭然です．英和辞典のどの訳語を見ても意味がぴんと来ないということは，だれしも経験していると思います．そんなとき，語本来の定義が分かっていれば，訳語のバリエーションを自分で出すことができます．例えば「訳例」に載っている以外の，「おいしい」などという訳語も beautiful soup という用例に出会ったときに自然と出てくるでしょう．

**効能: その語本来の語感がつかめ，英語→日本語という1対1対応の思い込みから抜け出せる．語を自由自在に扱える．**

#### ➤ Case 2 regime
→ regime と government の違い

> **\*regime** /rɪʒíːm/ 名 **C** ▶定義 a method or system of government, especially one that has not been elected in a fair way 政府，特に公正な選挙で選ばれなかった政府の体制→**政治制度, 政治形態, 政権, 政府, 管理体制**

# VIII 本辞典の効果的活用法

訳語を読んだだけでは,語の正確な意味が取れないことがあります.例えば regime の場合,英和辞典では,単に「政治制度,政権」という訳語が掲載されています.しかし,これでは government と regime の意味の違いは分かりません.定義まで読むことで,語のニュアンスや類義語との正確な意味の違いをつかむことができます.

**効能: 訳語では理解できなかった意味の細かな違いまできちんと押さえられる.**


## 2. 訳例を活用しよう！

### ➢ Case 3 genetics
→ 日本語の相当語句は？

> **genetics** /dʒənétɪks/ 名 U ▶定義 the scientific study of the way that the development of living things is controlled by qualities that have been passed on from parents to children 両親から子供へと受け継がれる資質によって,生き物の成長がどのように支配されるかを,科学的に研究する学問→ **遺伝学**

英語の定義を読んで,概念は大まかに分かったものの,日本語ではさて何と言うのか,知りたい場合があります.そういうときには,「訳例」が役立ちます.(特に名詞に効果的です.)例えば genetics では,定義で 'scientific study', 'development of living things', 'passed on from parents to children' などのキーワードから概念をつかみ,訳例の「遺伝学」という語で理解は完成するでしょう.本辞典では,定義と訳例の両方を載せることにより,あいまいな部分を残しません.

**効能: 各単語について,定義と訳語の両方向からアプローチすることで,語の理解は万全.**


## 3. コラムを活用しよう！

### ➢ Case 4 hang
→ 会話で使える便利な表現

語の理解は,定義と訳例で万全ですが,さらに発展情報(語法や背景知識)をコラムから得ることができます.右に挙げた例のように,コラムでは,日本人学習者の視点に立って,言語構造の違いや文化的差異により,理解が不十分だったり誤解しやすかったりするトピックを重点的に取り上げています.5つのカテゴリー(①音声とつづり字 ②日本語 VS 英語 ③語法 ④社

> **▶コミュニケーション**
>
> 「頑張って」に当たる英語表現
>
> 　日本では特に若い人たち同士,別れ際のあいさつに「頑張って」とよく言います.英米では,Take it easy, Don't work too hard, Have fun などと,むしろ頑張るなと言って別れる方が多いのです.とはいえ,英語(特にアメリカ英語)にも「頑張れ」に似た意味の Hang in there! という表現があります.これは問題を抱えて頑張っている人に対する明るいくだけた声援と言えるでしょう.

## 本辞典の効果的活用法　IX

会・文化⑤コミュニケーション）に分類していますので，興味のあるカテゴリーから読んでみるのもよいでしょう．※P. XIVにコラム一覧があります．

**効能: 文法や文化の面からも，日本との違いを知ることで，総合的な英語力を高める．**

## II. ワンランク上の活用法

### 1. Active Vocabulary を増やす

> **Case 5　accompany**
> → 易しい言い換え

> ★**accompany** /əkʌ́mp(ə)ni/ 動 ⓒ (現分 **accompanying**; 三単現 **accompanies**; 過, 過分 **accompanied**) ▶定義1　to go together with sb/sth ～に伴う→～に付いていく，一緒に行く，付き添う ∥ *He went to America accompanied by his wife and three children.* 彼は妻と3人の子供を連れてアメリカへ行った． *Massive publicity accompanied the film's release.* その映画が封切りになる時，大規模な宣伝がなされた． ▶定義2　accompany sb (on sth) to play music for a singer or another instrument 歌手やほかの楽器に合わせて音楽を演奏する→～の伴奏をする ∥ *She accompanied him on the guitar.* 彼女はギターで彼の伴奏をした．

単に日本語の意味を見つけるだけでなく，英語のより簡単な表現に出会えることが，本辞典ではよくあります．上の accompany の例でも定義1は，日本語では「付き添う」という訳語が与えられていますが，実際に話したり文章を書く際は，accompany という難しい語を使わなくても，go together with という表現で代用できる場合があります．このように定義も，「使える英語」である場合が多いので，是非積極的に覚えてください．

**効能: 英文定義を活用することにより，発信に役立つ語彙力を身に付ける．**

> **Case 6　applaud**
> → 関連表現

> **applaud** /əplɔ́ːd/ 動 ▶定義1　Ⓒ ⓒ to hit your hands together noisily (clap) in order to show that you like sb/sth ～が気に入ったことを表すために，両手を大きな音を立ててたたく（拍手する）→～に拍手する，拍手を送る ∥ *The audience applauded loudly.* 聴衆は盛んに拍手した． *The team was applauded as it left the field.* そのチームはフィールドを去る時に拍手を送られた．

本辞典では，定義はすべて2500語の基本語のみでなされていますが，その2500語以外の単語で言い換えている箇所があります．定義文中で括弧でくくられて青字になっている箇所（上例では clap）がそれに当たります．

# x 本辞典の効果的活用法

　これを利用すれば, applaud の意味を調べることができるだけでなく, hit your hands together noisily が clap という語で言い換えられるという知識も得られます. これらの語は, 当然見出し語とかかわりが深い語句ですから, 関連語句の知識が増えます.

**効能: 定義の中で, 関連語句の知識を増やせる.**

## 2. コロケーションの知識を身に付ける

### ➤ Case 7  life
→ 語と語のつながり

> **\*life** /láɪf/ 图 (褁 **lives** /láɪvz/) ▶定義3 **❸ ⓤ** the state of being alive as a human being 人間として生きている状態→**命, 人命** ‖ *Would you **risk** your **life** to protect your property?* 財産を守るために命をかけますか. *Doctors fought all night to **save** her **life**.* 医師たちは彼女の命を救うため徹夜で闘った. ▶定義4 **❸ ⓤ** the period during which sb/sth is alive or exists 〜が生きている, または存在している期間→**一生, 生涯, 人生, 寿命, 耐用期間** ‖ *I've lived in this town **all** my **life**.* 私は生まれてからずっとこの町に住んでいる.

　例文の中で, 重要なコロケーション (語と語の結び付き) は, イタリック体で太字にして示してあります.
　上の例のように risk one's life, save one's life, all one's life などの表現が載せられていて, life という単語がどのような語と共によく使われるかが, 一目瞭然です.

**効能: コロケーションの知識を身に付けることで, 発信力がアップ.**


　以上, いくつかの実例を挙げて, 本辞典の活用法を紹介してきましたが, まずは英文定義を読むことから始めましょう. その後, 自分自身で使い方のバリエーションを広げていってください. 最初は時間がかかっても, 英語に触れ理解しようと努めた経験は, あなたの中で蓄積され, 最終的には英語力を格段に向上させることでしょう. 学習が進み, この辞典では物足りなくなったときには, さらに語彙数の多い, またはレベルの高い英英辞典に進んでください. 1人でも多くの方に, はるかな英語の世界への足掛かりとして, 本辞典を活用していただければ幸いです.

## 英語の発音一覧

### 母音（長母音・短母音・二重母音・弱母音）

| | 前 舌 | | | | 奥 舌 | | |
|---|---|---|---|---|---|---|---|
| iː | meet/miːt/ | | | uː | pool/puːl/ | | 高 位 |
| i | happy/hǽpi/ | | | u | usual/júːʒuəl/ | | |
| ɪ | mitt/mɪt/ | | | ʊ | pull/pʊl/ | | |
| ɪər | hear/hɪər/ | | | ʊər | tour/tʊər/ | | |
| éɪ | May/méɪ/ | | | óʊ | no/nóʊ/ | | 中 位 |
| e | bed/bed/ | ə | sofa/sóʊfə/ | ʌ | bus/bʌs/ | | |
| eər | chair/tʃeər/ | əːr | bird/bəːrd/ | | | | |
| | | | | ɔːr | door/dɔːr/ | | 低 位 |
| æ | bat/bæt/ | áɪ | night/náɪt/ | ɑːr | car/kɑːr/ | | |
| | | áʊ | cow/káʊ/ | ɑ | hot/hɑt/ | | |

注：/iː/と/i/, /uː/と/u/はそれぞれ同じ音質ですが，強弱が異なります．
　　弱い/i/と/u/は語末と母音の前にあるとき用いられます．
　　/ə/は特に弱い母音なので，弱母音またはあいまい母音と言います．

### 子音（唇音・舌先音・前舌ー奥舌音）

| 唇 音 | 舌 先 音 | | 前舌ー奥舌音 | |
|---|---|---|---|---|
| map/**m**æp/ | night/náɪ**t**/ | | si**ng**/sɪŋ/ | [鼻音] |
| peace/**p**iːs/ | time/táɪ**m**/ | chime/tʃáɪm/ | bank/bæŋ**k**/ | 閉じる |
| bean/**b**iːn/ | dice/dáɪs/ | joke/dʒóʊk/ | bag/bæ**g**/ | （閉鎖音） |
| fall/**f**ɔːl/ | thin/θɪn/ | say/séɪ/ | ship/ʃɪp/ | (ugh/ʌx/) | こする |
| van/**v**æn/ | this/ðɪs/ | zoo/zuː/ | measure /méʒər/ | | （摩擦音） |
| | light/láɪt/ | | | well/wel/ | 近づく |
| when/(h)wen/ | | right/ráɪt/ | yes/jes/ | | （接近音） |

注：主に動かす発音器官は唇と舌先と前舌ー奥舌です．
　　/l/は舌先を歯茎に付けて，/r/は舌先をつけずに発音します．

| | | | |
|---|---|---|---|
| /i/ | | | /u/ |
| /e/ | | | /o/ |
| | | /a/ | |

母音域

## XII 英語の発音解説

### 1. アルファベット26字とその発音

現在,世界で広く使われている英語はアルファベットの26種の文字を使います.各文字の名称を発音記号と実際の英語に近いカタカナ表記で以下に示します.

| | | | |
|---|---|---|---|
| **A** | /éɪ | エイ/ | (エーと長く伸ばさず,出だしを強く言います) |

注: /éɪ/は二重母音と言います.二重母音は出だしが強く長く発音するので,/éɪ/のようにアクセント記号を付けてあります.

| | | | |
|---|---|---|---|
| **B** | /bi: | ビー/ | (唇をしっかりと閉じてから発音します) |
| **C** | /si: | スィー/ | (日本語のシーではなく,スィーと発音します) |
| **D** | /di: | ディー/ | (舌先だけを歯茎に付けると発音しやすくなります) |
| **E** | /i: | イー/ | (出だしに力を入れ唇を左右に引いて言いましょう) |
| **F** | /ef | エゥ°/ | (/fゥ°/は/v ヴ/の無声音です.下唇を上歯に添えて出します) |
| **G** | /dʒi: | ヂュイー/ | (「チ」の有声音で唇を丸めて言います) |
| **H** | /éɪtʃ | エイチュ/ | (出だしを強く言います.最後の/tʃ/は/dʒ/の無声音です) |
| **I** | /áɪ | アイ/ | (出だしは強く終わりはあいまいに言います) |
| **J** | /dʒéɪ | ヂェイ/ | (Gと同じく唇を丸めてから言います) |
| **K** | /kéɪ | ケイ/ | (出だしが強いので息も共に出します) |
| **L** | /el | エゥ/ | (lは舌先を歯茎に付け,舌の両側から「ウ」の感じで声を出します) |
| **M** | /em | エム/ | (「エム」の最後は両唇を閉じたままにします) |
| **N** | /en | エンヌ/ | (終わりには舌先が歯茎に付いたままになります) |
| **O** | /óʊ | オウ/ | (唇を丸めて言うことに注目します) |
| **P** | /pi: | ピー/ | (両唇を閉じて息をためてから勢いよく言います) |
| **Q** | /kju: | キュー/ | (日本語の急などとほぼ同じで構いません) |
| **R** | /ɑːr | アー/ | (「ア」よりも口の奥の方で発音します) |

注: /r/はオプションのrです.アメリカ英語のrは母音の後でも発音しますが,イギリス英語のrは発音しません.ただし,母音に挟まれていると,ラ行音のように発音します.

| | | | |
|---|---|---|---|
| **S** | /es | エス/ | (/s/の後に母音を付けないようにします) |
| **T** | /ti: | ティー/ | (舌先を歯茎にしっかりと付けて息をためてから勢いよく言います) |
| **U** | /ju: | ユウー/ | (唇を十分丸めて発音します) |
| **V** | /vi: | ヴィー/ | (上の歯に下唇をそえて言います) |
| **W** | /dʌ́bljuː | ダブリュー/ | (lの前にヌを付けるつもりで言うとlらしく発音できます) |
| **X** | /eks | エックス/ | (子音が連続しても一息で発音します) |
| **Y** | /wáɪ | ウワイ/ | (出だしは唇を十分丸めて言います) |
| **Z** | /zed/zi: | ズェド/ズィー/ | (「スィー」を有声にして言います) |

### [英音と米音の違い]

本辞典は発音記号を,英音,米音の順で掲載しています.英音と米音の差があるときは,;(セミコロン)で区別しています.

# 英語の発音解説 XIII

アルファベットでイギリス英語 英 とアメリカ英語 米 と違いがあるのは次の3種です.
1. **O** は /英 óʊ/ 米 óʊ/　本辞典の扱い: /oʊ/で統一
2. **R** は /英 ɑː 米 ɑːr/　本辞典の扱い: /ɑːr/で統一
3. **Z** は /英 zed 米 ziː/　本辞典の扱い: /zed ; ziː/

アルファベットにない英米音の差は次のように表しています.
1. **hot**　　は /英 hɔt　米 hɑ(ː)t/　　　　　　本辞典の扱い: /hɑt/で統一
2. **drama**　は /英 drɑ́ːmə, drǽmə　米 drǽmə/　本辞典の扱い: /drɑ́ːmə, drǽmə/で統一
3. **god**　　は /英 gɔd　米 gɔːd, gɑd/　　　　本辞典の扱い: /gɔ(ː)d, gɑd/

注: 正確には, 英音の/ɔ/と/ɔː/とは舌の位置が異なります. 現代英語では/ɔː/の場合は, 奥舌の位置が中位になっています. 詳しくは発音辞典 *The Daniel Jones English Pronunciation* (CUP, 1997) などを参照してみてください.

## 2. 英語の母音と子音

英語には日本語の中にない音がいくつか含まれています. 次のような対語が発音記号の手掛かりなので, 区別することが必要です.

| | |
|---|---|
| /θ/ | think (考える), thank (感謝する), sympathy (同情) などの発音記号に見られます. この発音が難しい場合は, 「ス」を弱く言うとこの音に聞こえます. 舌先を両歯に挟むようにして発音します. |
| /ð/ | this (これは), that (あれは), the (その), these (これらは) などの発音記号に見られます. この発音が難しい場合は「ズ」を弱く言うとこの音に聞こえます. |
| /ʃ/ | ship (船) の出だしのshに当たる音です. 「シュ」に近い音です. |
| /æ/ | 「エア」の感じで言い, 「エヤ」にならないよう注意します. |
| /ʌ/ | bus (バス), sun (太陽) = son (息子) などの母音に当たる音です. |
| /iː/と/ɪ/, /uː/と/ʊ/ | leave (離れる) /liːv/ : live (住んでいる) /lɪv/<br>注: leave/liveの区別は長短の区別ではなく, 音の質の区別です. pool[puːl]/pull[pʊl]の区別も同様に音の質で区別します. liveの/ɪ/は日本語の「エ」に近く聞こえる「イ」です. pullの/ʊ/は「オ」に近く聞こえる「ウ」です. |
| /ɔː/と/əːr/ | walk (歩く) /wɔːk/ : work (働く) /wəːrk/ |
| /ɑːr/と/əːr/ | farm (農場) /fɑːrm/ : firm (会社, しっかりとした) /fəːrm/ |
| /æ/と/ʌ/ | bad (悪い) /bæd/ : bud (つぼみ) /bʌd/ |
| /l/と/r/ | light (光, 軽い) /láɪt/ : right (権利, 正しい, 右) /ráɪt/<br>注: /l/は舌先を歯茎に付けて発音します. /r/は唇を丸め舌先をどこにも付けずに発音します. |
| /θ/と/s/ | think (考える) /θɪŋk/ : sink/sɪŋk/ (沈む)<br>注: /θ/は舌先を上の歯とこすり合うようにまた弱めに発音します. |
| /ð/と/z/ | breathe (呼吸する) /briːð/ : breeze (そよ風) /briːz/<br>注: /ð/は/θ/と同じ構えで発音します. /ð/は/θ/の有声音です. |
| /ʃ/と/s/ | she (彼女[は, が]) /ʃiː/ : sea (海) /siː/<br>注: /ʃ/は/tʃ/, /dʒ/, /ʒ/, /r/と同様に唇を丸めて発音すると, 英語らしくなります. |

# XIV コラム一覧

## カテゴリー1　音声とつづり字

| | |
|---|---|
| **ABC** | ABC のアクセント |
| **ability** | 語尾が -ity ならアクセント位置は予測できる |
| **alphabet** | alphabet の発音の英米の差 |
| **and** | and の発音は an と同じ？ |
| **between** | between を2つに分けると→ ○ be-tween , × bet-ween |
| **blackboard** | blackboard と black board |
| **book** | oo は[ʊウ]？ |
| **can** | can の強弱 |
| **class** | class の cl- の発音 |
| **decide** | decide と decision とは母音が違う |
| **develop** | develop のアクセント位置 |
| **dictionary** | dictionary の発音は英音と米音で異なる |
| **English** | English を二分すると？ |
| **intonation** | John に呼び掛けるときの口調 |
| **like** | I would like... の言い方 |
| **name** | name の発音は e の規則による |
| **nice** | nice の c 規則と語法 |
| **separate** | separate と ate 規則 |
| **south-east** | South-east は South と east とどちらが強い？ |
| **spring** | Spring has come. の言い方 |
| **student** | Japanese のアクセント位置 |
| **tea** | tea の出だしの帯気音 |
| **tennis** | テニスを英語らしく発音しよう |
| **transistor** | transistor はどこを強く読む？ |
| **Yes** | Yes や No の言い方とそれぞれの意味 |

## カテゴリー2　日本語 vs 英語

| | |
|---|---|
| **and** | 2語を and でつなぐ言い方 |
| **apartment** | apart と「アパート」 |
| **bang** | 擬声語いろいろ |
| **beer** | イギリスの beer のいろいろ |
| **boss** | boss と「ボス」 |
| **bring** | 「持っていく」が bring になる場合 |
| **cider** | cider と「サイダー」は別な飲み物 |
| **classic** | 「クラシック」の意味 |
| **come** | 「行く」が come になる場合 |
| **cook** | cook と「料理する」 |
| **copy** | copy と「コピー」 |
| **cunning** | cunning と「カンニング」 |
| **drug** | drugstore と「薬屋」は違う？ |
| **feminist** | 「フェミニスト」の日本語特有の意味 |
| **finger** | 指を使った数え方の違い |
| **green** | 「青信号」の色 |
| **guarantee** | 「ギャラ」の語源 guarantee |
| **handle** | handle と「ハンドル」 |
| **homework** | homework と assignment |
| **hot** | hot は「辛い」と「熱い」 |
| **lip** | lip と「口」 |
| **mansion** | mansion と「マンション」 |
| **moody** | moody と「ムーディー」 |
| **pick** | 「ピックアップする」は pick out |
| **plastic** | プラスチック？ビニール？ |
| **print**[2] | print と handout の違い |
| **rice** | rice と「ご飯」 |
| **shoulder** | 「肩凝り」日英比較 |
| **sign** | 「サイン」の2つの意味 |
| **smart** | smart は「頭が良い」 |
| **squat** | いろいろな座り方 |
| **style** | style は「型」のこと |

## カテゴリー3　語法

| | |
|---|---|
| **about** | about/around と nearly/almost |
| **breakfast** | breakfast の語源と意味 |
| **cc** | 容積単位の cc は何の略 |
| **cent** | centimetre, centigrade, percent, century |
| **discuss** | discuss about... とは言えない |
| **do** | I did kiss her. は動詞を強調しない |
| **doctor** | ear, nose, throat で耳鼻科 |
| **get** | get on/off と get in/out |
| **hear** | hear と listen の違い |
| **here** | Here you are. と Here it is. の違い |
| **if** | if のイメージは二者択一 |
| **information** | information は不可算名詞 |
| **look** | look at と look on |

# コラム一覧

| | |
|---|---|
| medicine | drink medicine と言わない理由 |
| millimetre | millimetre, million と mile の関係 |
| mind[2] | 動名詞をとる動詞は megafeps |
| must | イメージは「絶対…しろ」または「絶対…だ」 |
| no[1] | no more/less は「差がゼロ」 |
| not | 部分否定の意味 |
| on | on は「接している」 |
| over | 多義語 over の意味の展開 |
| picture | a picture of my father playing golf |
| play | 試合は game, match, bout |
| quite | quite, rather, pretty などの違い |
| remember | remember...ing と remember that SV |
| remind | remind someone that SV も忘れずに |
| responsible | those responsible と a responsible man の違い |
| see | see と look の違い |
| seem | seem to は断定を避ける助動詞 |
| shall | 法令文の shall と意志 |
| skyscraper | 空をこする (scrape) 摩天楼 |
| still | still と yet の違い |
| street | on/in the street の英米差 |
| sure | sure と certain |
| trend | trend that SV は不可, trend of 名詞 ...ing を使う |
| what | How far is it？と What is the distance？ |
| would | 過去の習慣の would は状態動詞をとらない |

### 🌐 カテゴリー4　社会・文化

| | |
|---|---|
| breakfast | おいしい英国の朝ご飯 |
| Christmas | クリスマス |
| company | 会社の役職名 |
| dinner | クリスマスディナーは昼食？ |
| grade | 成績の付け方 |
| Halloween | ハロウィーン |
| holiday | 英米の祝祭日 |
| name[2] | 人名と呼び名の一覧表 |
| parliament | 英米の議会 |
| politically correct | 差別を避ける言い方 |
| pound | ポンド |
| Protestant | Protestant と Catholic の違い |
| school | 学校のいろいろ |
| service | morning service |
| shoe | 靴は衣類の一部 |
| spank | 子供への仕置き |
| superstition | 英米の迷信 |
| tea | 英国のティータイム |
| teacher | 先生のいろいろ |
| temperature | 摂氏と華氏 |
| ticket | 切符の種類 |
| valentine | バレンタインデー |

### 💬 カテゴリー5　コミュニケーション
#### a. 会話で使える便利な表現

| | |
|---|---|
| Congratulations | 英語の「おめでとう」の使い方 |
| excuse | エチケット違反には excuse me |
| hang | 「頑張って」に当たる英語表現 |
| happy | 「よかったね」に当たる英語表現 |
| pardon | 会話で「繰り返して」と頼むとき |
| pleasure | 「いいですとも」に当たる快諾表現 |
| problem | 相手の気持ちを楽にする応答 |
| something | 「とか何とか」に当たる英語表現 |
| sorry[2] | 「すみません」と thank you |

#### b. 注意が必要な身振り

| | |
|---|---|
| circle[2] | 「丸めた指」の日英比較 |
| close | 「他言無用」を表す身振り |
| crook | 「手招き」動作の日英比較 |
| pat | 「自画自賛」の身振り |
| point[2] | 「自分を指す」動作の日英比較 |
| raise | 「上げたまゆ」は「あきれた」ときの表情 |
| rap[2] | 「けんか」を表す身振りの日英比較 |
| shake | 握った手を上下させるのが「握手」 |
| shrug | 「すくめた肩」は無関心・無力のしぐさ |
| snap | どんなとき「指を鳴らす」か |
| tap | 頭がおかしい人を表す身振りの日英比較 |

**A, a**¹ /éɪ/ 名 C (複 **A's**; **a's** /éɪz/) ▶定義 1 the first letter of the English alphabet 英語アルファベットの第1文字→a(A)が表す音, a(A)の文字, a(A)の字形のもの ‖ *'Andy' begins with (an) 'A'.* AndyはAで始まる. ▶定義 2 the highest grade given for an exam or piece of work 試験や課題に対して与えられた最も良い成績→A, 優, 最高級のもの ‖ *I got an 'A' for my essay.* エッセーでAを取った.

★**a**² /ə 強形 éɪ/ (または **an** /ən 強形 æn/) 不冠
▶anは母音の前で用いる.

▶定義 1 one 1つの→1人の ‖ *A cup of coffee, please.* コーヒー1杯お願いします. *We've got an apple, a banana and two oranges.* 私たちは, リンゴを1個, バナナを1本, オレンジを2個買った. ▶定義 2 used when you talk about one example of sth for the first time ～の例を初めて挙げるときに用いて→ある, 1つの, 1人の ‖ *I saw a dog chasing a cat this morning. The cat climbed up a tree.* 今朝, 犬が猫を追い掛けるのを見た. その猫は木に登った. *Have you got a dictionary (= any dictionary)?* 辞書(= どんな辞書でもいいのですが)を持っていますか. ▶定義 3 used for saying what kind of person or thing sb/sth is ～がどんな種類の人が入るかを述べるために用いて→1人の, 1つの ‖ *He's a doctor.* 彼は医者だ. *She's a Muslim.* 彼女はイスラム教徒である. *You are a clever boy.* 君は賢い少年だ. *'Is that an eagle?' 'No, it's a falcon.'*「あれはワシですか」「いいえ, タカです」▶定義 4 (used with prices, rates, measurements) each (価格, 単位, 数量と用いて) それぞれに→～に付き, ～ごとに ‖ *I usually drink two litres of water a day.* 1日に大抵水を2リットル飲む. *twice a week* 週に2回 *He was travelling at about 80 miles an hour.* 彼は時速約80マイルで進んでいた. ▶定義 5 used with some expressions of quantity 数量を表す表現と共に用いて ‖ *a lot of money* 多額のお金 *a few cars* 数台の車 ▶定義 6 used when you are talking about a typical example of sth ～の典型的な例について話すときに用いて→どの～も, どれも, ～というものは ‖ *An elephant can live for up to eighty years.* 象の寿命は80年だ. ☛ 次の例文のように, 複数形の主語で同じ意味を表すこともできる. *Elephants can live for up to eighty years.* 象の寿命は80年だ.
▶不定冠詞についての説明は, 巻末の「文法早見表」を参照.

**the AA** /éɪ éɪ/ 略 ▶定義 (in Britain) the Automobile Association; an organization for drivers. If you are a member of the AA and your car breaks down, they will send sb to help you. (英国で)英国自動車協会; 自動車のドライバーの団体. 会員であれば, 車が故障した場合に, 助けてくれる人を派遣してもらえる→AA ‖ *My car wouldn't start so I called the AA.* 車が動かなくなったので, AAを呼んだ.

**aback** /əbæk/ 副
句動詞 take sb aback ⇒ TAKE

★**abandon** /əbændən/ 動 他 ▶定義 1 to leave sb/sth that you are responsible for, usually permanently 自分が責任を負っている～を, 通常は永久に手放す→～を捨てる, 見捨てる, 去る ‖ *The bank robbers abandoned the car just outside the city.* 銀行強盗たちは, 街を出た所で車を乗り捨てた. ▶定義 2 to stop doing sth without finishing it or without achieving what you wanted to do ～をやり終えないで, またはやりたいと思っていた～を成し遂げないうちにやめる→～をあきらめる, 断念する, 中止する ‖ *The search for the missing sailors was abandoned after two days.* 行方不明の船員の捜索は, 2日後に打ち切られた. — **abandonment** 名 U→放棄, 断念

**abashed** /əbǽʃt/ 形 ▶定義 feeling guilty and embarrassed because of sth that you have done 自分がしてしまった～のために罪悪感を感じ, 戸惑う→～に恥じ入って, 当惑した, 赤面した ‖ *'I'm sorry', said Ali, **looking abashed**.*「ごめんなさい」と, アリはきまり悪そうに言った.

**abattoir** /ǽbətwɑːr/ 英 = **SLAUGHTERHOUSE**

**abbey** /ǽbi/ 名 C ▶定義 a large church together with a group of buildings where religious communities of men (monks) or women (nuns) live or used to live 一定の戒律に従って共同生活をする男子(修道士)または女子(修道女)が住む, またはかつて住んでいた建物群が附随している大規模な教会→大修道院, 大寺院

# abbr

**abbr**(または **abbrev**) 略 abbreviation→**略語, 短縮**

**abbreviate** /əbríːvièɪt/ 動 他 ▶定義 to make sth shorter, especially a word or phrase 特に単語または句を短くする→**短縮する, 省略する** ‖ 'Kilometre' is usually abbreviated to 'km'. kilometre は普通 km と略される. ☞参 **abridge**

**abbreviation** /əbrìːviéɪʃ(ə)n/ 名 C ▶定義 a short form of a word or phrase 単語または句の簡略形→**略語, 省略, 短縮** ‖ In this dictionary 'sth' is the abbreviation for 'something'. この辞書では, sth は something の略語である.

**ABC** /éɪbiːsíː/ 名 [単数扱い] ▶定義 **1** the alphabet; the letters of English from A to Z アルファベット; A から Z の英語の文字→**アルファベット** ▶定義 **2** the simple facts about sth 〜についての基本的な事→**初歩, 入門, いろは** ‖ an ABC of Gardening ガーデニングの基礎

> ▶音声とつづり字
>
> ABC のアクセント
>
> 　3つのアルファベット文字が連続すると, 2番・3番・1番の順で強弱が決まります. BBC（British Broadcasting Corporation, 英国放送協会）, CNN（Cable News Network）なども同様に, 一番最後が最も強く, 最初はやや強く, 途中が一番弱くなります. 英語話者がNHKを言うときも, Kが強くNがその次に強く, Hは一番弱くなります. これを発音記号で書くと, [èn.eɪʃ.kʰéɪ]のようになります.

**abdicate** /ǽbdɪkèɪt/ 動 ▶定義 **1** 自 to give up being King or Queen 王または女王であることをやめる→**退位する** ‖ The Queen abdicated in favour of her son (= her son became king). 女王は自分の息子のために退位した(= 息子が王になった). ▶定義 **2** 他 to give sth up, especially power or a position 特に権力や地位を捨てる→**〜を放棄する, 正式に捨てる** ‖ to abdicate responsibility (= to refuse to be responsible for sth) 責任を放棄する(= 〜に対する責任を負うことを断る) — abdication /ǽbdɪkéɪʃ(ə)n/ 名 C U→**退位, 放棄**

**abdomen** /ǽbdəmən, æbdóʊ-, ǽbdòʊ-/ 名 C ▶定義 a part of your body below the chest, in which the stomach is contained 身体の一部分で, 胸の下にあり, 胃がある部分→**腹部** — abdominal /æbdάmənl/ 形 →**腹部の**

**abduct** /æbdʌ́kt, əb-/ 動 他 ▶定義 to take hold of sb and take him/her away illegally 〜を拘束し, 不法に連れ去る→**〜を誘拐する, かどわかす** ‖ He has been abducted by a terrorist group. 彼はテロ集団に誘拐された. — abduction 名 C U→**誘拐**

**abet** /əbét/ 動 他 (**abetting**; **abetted**)
成句 aid and abet ⇒ **AID**²

**abhor** /əbhɔ́ːr, æb-/ 動 他 (**abhorring**; **abhorred**) ▶定義 to hate sth very much 〜をひどく嫌う→**〜を嫌悪する, 憎悪している, 忌み嫌う** ‖ All civilized people abhor the use of torture. 文明人のだれもが拷問には嫌悪感を抱いている.

**abhorrence** /əbhɔ́(ː)rəns, -hάr-/ 名 U ▶定義 a strong feeling of hate; disgust ひどく嫌う気持ち; 嫌気→**嫌悪(感), 憎悪** ‖ Protesters expressed their **abhorrence of** war. 抗議者たちは戦争に対する嫌悪感を表した.

**abhorrent** /əbhɔ́(ː)rənt, -hάr-/ 形 ▶定義 that makes you feel hate or disgust 嫌悪感や嫌気を催させる→**嫌悪感を抱かせる, 憎悪されている, 相反する** ‖ The idea of slavery is **abhorrent to** us nowadays. 現在では奴隷制度は人々にひどく嫌がられている.

**abide** /əbáɪd/ 動
成句 can't/couldn't abide sb/sth/doing sth ▶定義 to hate sb/sth; to not like sb/sth at all 〜をひどく嫌う; 〜が全く気に入らない→**〜が我慢できない, 〜に耐えられない**
句動詞 abide by sth ▶定義 to obey a law, etc; to do what sb has decided 法律などに従う; 〜が決めた事をする→**〜を守る, 遵守する; 〜に従う**

★**ability** /əbíləti/ 名 C U (複 **abilities**) ▶定義 (an) ability to do sth the mental or physical power or skill that makes it possible to do sth 〜を行うことを可能にする精神力, 体力, 技術→**能力, 手腕, 力量** ‖ an ability to make decisions 決断力 A person of his ability will have no difficulty getting a job. 彼ほどの能力がある人なら, 就職するのに苦労はしないだろう.

> ▶音声とつづり字
>
> 語尾が -ity ならアクセント位置は予測できる
>
> 　abilityのアクセント位置は, -ityの直前にあ

ることを知っておくと便利です. -tion, -sion, -logyなどの接尾辞の場合も同様です.
例: -ity: curious > curiósity(好奇心)
responsible > responsibility(責任)
-tion: operate > operátion(作戦)
decide > decísion(決定)
-sion: invade > invásion(侵略)
-logy: type > typical > typólogy
(典型的な > 類型学)

**ablaze** /əbléɪz/ 形(名詞の前は不可) ▶定義 burning strongly; completely on fire 激しく燃え上がっている; 徹底的に燃えている→燃えている, 燃え上がっている ∥ Soldiers used petrol to **set** the building **ablaze**. 兵士たちはガソリンを使って, その建物を炎上させた.

*__able__ /éɪbl/ 形 ▶定義 1 be able to do sth(法助動詞で) to have the ability, power, opportunity, time, etc to do sth ～を行う能力, 体力, 機会, 時間などを持っている→～することができる, ～する能力がある ∥ Will you be able to come to a meeting next week? 来週の会合に来られますか. I was able to solve the problem quickly. 私はその問題を短時間で解くことができた. Many men don't **feel able** to express their emotions. 自分の感情を表現できないと思っている男性が多い.

▶次のような受動態の文では, can または could を使い, be able は使わない: The arrangement can't be changed. (その協定は変更することができない.) 法助動詞についての説明は, 巻末の「文法早見表」を参照.

▶定義 2 clever; doing your job well 賢い; 仕事が良くできる→有能な, 立派な, 見事な ∥ one of the ablest/most able students in the class そのクラスで最も優秀な生徒の1人 an able politician 有能な政治家 — **ably** /éɪbli/ 副 →有能に, 上手に, 立派に

**able-bodied** 形 ▶定義 physically healthy and strong; having full use of your body 肉体的に健康で強じんな; 体を十分に使っている→健康で丈夫な, 頑健な

**abnormal** /æbnɔ́ːrm(ə)l/ 形 ▶定義 different from what is normal or usual, in a way that worries you or that is unpleasant 心配させたり不快に感じさせたりすることで, 普通またはいつもの状態とは異なっている→異常な, 特異な, 普通でない ∥ abnormal weather conditions 異常気象 ⇔ **normal** — abnormally 副 →異常に, 異常なほど ∥ abnormally high temperatures 並外れて高い温度

**abnormality** /æbnəːrmǽləti/ 名 ℂ Ⓤ (複) **abnormalities** ▶定義 something that is not normal, especially in a person's body 特に人体が, 正常な状態ではないこと→特異なもの, 異常, 変則 ∥ He was born with an abnormality of the heart. 彼は心臓に異常を持って生まれた.

**aboard** /əbɔ́ːrd/ 副 前 ▶定義 on or onto a train, ship, aircraft or bus 電車, 船, 飛行機, バスなどに乗る, または乗り込む→(～に)乗って ∥ We climbed aboard the train and found a seat. 私たちは電車に乗り込み, 席を見つけた. Welcome aboard this flight to Caracas. カラカス行きの当便にご搭乗いただき, ありがとうございます.

**abode** /əbóʊd/ 名 [単数扱い] (文) ▶定義 the place where you live 住んでいる所→住居, 家, 住まい

成句 **(of) no fixed abode/address** ⇒ **FIXED**

**abolish** /əbɑ́lɪʃ/ 動 他 ▶定義 to end a law or system officially 法律や制度を公式にやめる→～を廃止する, 撤廃する ∥ When was capital punishment abolished here? ここでは死刑制度がいつ廃止されたのですか.

**abolition** /æbəlíʃ(ə)n/ 名 Ⓤ ▶定義 the act of ending a law or system officially 法律や制度を公式にやめること→廃止, 撤廃 ∥ the abolition of slavery in the US アメリカの奴隷制度廃止

**abominable** /əbɑ́m(ə)nəb(ə)l/ 形 ▶定義 very bad; shocking ぞっとするような; とてもひどい→嫌悪感を抱かせる, 憎悪を引き起こす, 憎むべき — abominably /-əbli/ 副 →とてもひどく, 嫌になるほど

**Aboriginal** /æbərídʒ(ə)n(ə)l/ (または **Aborigine** /æbərídʒ(ə)ni/) 名 ℂ ▶定義 a member of the race of people who were the original inhabitants of Australia オーストラリアの先住民族→アボリジニ, オーストラリア原住民 — Aboriginal 形 →アボリジニの ∥ Aboriginal traditions アボリジニの伝統

**abort** /əbɔ́ːrt/ 動 他 ▶定義 1 to end sth before it is complete ～を完成しないうちにやめる→～を中止する, 中断する ∥ The company aborted the project when they realized it was costing too much. その会社は，コストがかかりすぎることが分かって，このプロジェクトを中止した．▶定義2 to make a baby (foetus) die before it is born 胎児を生まれる前に死なせてしまう→ ～を中絶する，流産させる

**abortion** /əbɔ́ːʃ(ə)n/ 图 ❻❻ ▶定義 a medical operation that causes a baby to die inside its mother before it is fully developed 胎児が十分成長しないうちに母胎で死なせてしまう手術→ 妊娠中絶，堕胎(だたい)，流産させること ‖ to have an abortion 妊娠中絶をする Abortion is illegal in that country. 中絶はその国では違法である．

▶ miscarriage と比較．

**abortive** /əbɔ́ːrtɪv/ 形 ▶定義 not completed successfully; failed 無事に完了していない；失敗した→ 失敗に終わった，不成功の，水泡に帰した ‖ He made two abortive attempts to escape from prison. 彼は脱獄を2度試みたが，失敗に終わった．

**abound** /əbáʊnd/ 動 ⓐ ▶定義1 to exist in large numbers 数多く存在する→ たくさんいる・ある ‖ Animals abound in the forest. その森には動物がたくさんいる． Rumours abound about the actor's arrest. その俳優の逮捕が取りざたされている．▶定義2 abound with sth to contain large numbers of sth ～を数多く含んでいる→ 富む，満ちている ‖ The lake abounds with fish. その湖には魚が豊富にいる．

★**about**¹ /əbáʊt/ 副 ▶定義1 (特に 米 **around**) a little more or less than; approximately 少し多い，または少ない；おおよそ→ およそ，約～，～くらい ‖ It's about three miles from here to the city centre. ここから街の中心まで約3マイルある． I got home at about half past seven. 7時半ころに帰宅した．▶定義2 略式 almost; nearly ほぼ；もう少しで→ ほとんど，そろそろ ‖ Dinner's just about ready. 夕食はもうすぐですよ．▶定義3 (または **around**) in many directions or places 多くの方向または場所に→ 辺りを，あちこち(～して回る) ‖ I could hear people moving about upstairs. 人々が上の階をあちこち動き回っているのが聞こえた． Don't leave your clothes lying about all over the floor. 洋服を床のあちこちに散らかしたままにしないで．▶定義4 (または **around**) (used after certain verbs) without doing anything in particular (特定の動詞の後に)特に何もしないで→ 何もせずに，ぼんやりと ‖ The kids spent most evenings **sitting about**, bored. その子供たちは，ほぼ毎晩，ただ座っているだけで退屈していた．▶定義5 (または **around**) present in a place; existing ある場所にいる；存在している→ 近くに，辺りに，あちこちに ‖ It was very late and there were few people about. とても遅い時間だったので，辺りに人はほとんどいなかった． There isn't much good music about these days. 近ごろはいい音楽があまりない．

成句 be about to do sth ▶定義 to be going to do sth very soon ～をすぐにもしようとしている→ (まさに)～しようとしている，(ちょうど)～するところだ ‖ The film's about to start. その映画はちょうど始まるところだ． I was just about to explain when she interrupted me. まさに説明しようとしていた矢先に彼女が私の話を遮った．

> ▶語法
>
> about/around と nearly/almost
>
> aboutの原義は，The dog was running about me. (犬は私の周りを駆け回った)のように aroundと同様に「～の周囲・周辺」です．したがって，about/around fiftyは「50の辺り・前後」の意味になり，50を上回っても下回っても構いません．一方，nearly や almost の意味は「あと少しで～になるところ」ですから，50を上回ることはありません．

★**about**² /əbáʊt/ 前 ▶定義1 on the subject of ～の主題で→ ～について，～のことで，～に関する ‖ Let's talk about something else. 何かほかの事について話しましょう． What's your book about? あなたの本は何について書いてあるのですか． He told me **all about** his family. 彼は自分の家族のことをすべて私に話した． I don't like it, but there's nothing I can do about it. それが好きでもないし，それに関してできる事もない．▶定義2 (または **around**) in many directions or places; in different parts of sth 多くの方向または場所に；～のさまざまな部分で→ ～をあちこち(…して回る)，～の方々を ‖ We wandered about the town for an hour or two. 私

たちはその街を1,2時間歩き回った. *Lots of old newspapers were scattered about the room.* たくさんの古新聞が部屋中に散らかっていた. ▶定義3 in the character of sb/sth 〜の性質・特徴として→〜の身ало に, 周辺に, 〜には ‖ *There's something about him that I don't quite trust.* 彼にはどこかあまり信用できないところがある. *I like the food, the climate, and everything else about this country.* 私はこの国の食べ物, 気候, その他何でも気に入っている.

成句 how/what about...? ▶定義1 (used when asking for information about sb/sth or for sb's opinion or wish) (〜に関する情報, または…の意見や希望を尋ねるときに用いて)→〜についてどうですか, 〜についてどう思いますか ‖ *How about Ruth? Have you heard from her lately?* ルースのことを何か知っていますか. 最近, 彼女から便りがありましたか. *I'm going to have chicken. What about you?* 私はチキンにします. あなたは何にされますか. ▶定義2 (used when making a suggestion) (提案をするとき)→〜してはどうですか ‖ *What about going to a film tonight?* 今晩, 映画に行くというのはどうでしょう.

**about-turn**(米 **about-face**) 名 C ▶定義 a complete change of opinion, plan or behaviour 意見, 計画, 態度などを全く変えること→回れ右, 180度の転換, 急な変更 ‖ *The government did an about-turn over tax.* 政府は税金に関する方針を180度転換した. ☞参 **U-turn**

★**above** /əbʌv/ 前 ▶定義1 in a higher place より高い所に→〜より上に, 〜より高く, 〜の上方に ‖ *The people in the flat above make a lot of noise.* そのアパートの上の階に住んでいる人たちは, 非常に大きな音を立てる. *The coffee is in the cupboard above the sink.* コーヒーは流しの上の戸棚にある. ▶定義2 in an earlier part (of sth written) (書かれた〜の)より前の部分に→前述の, 上記の, 先に ‖ *Contact me at the above address/the address above.* 上記の住所に連絡してください. ⇔ **below**. ただし, 次の例文のように, **below** は名詞の前には置けない. *Contact me at the address below.* 下記の住所に連絡してください. ▶定義3 more than a number, amount, price, etc ある数, 量, 価格などより多い→〜以上で, 〜より多く, 〜を超えて ‖ *children aged 11 and above* 11歳以上の子供 *A score of 70 and above will get you a grade B.* 70点以上の点数なら評価はBだ. *You must get above 50% to pass.* 合格するには50パーセントを超えないと駄目だ. *above-average temperatures* 平均を上回る温度 ⇔ **below** ☞参 **over** ▶定義4 with a higher position in an organization, etc 組織などの中でより高い地位に→〜より上で, 〜より優れて, 〜より勝って ‖ *The person above me is the department manager.* 私の上司は部長だ. ⇔ **below** ▶定義5 too proud to do sth その〜をするには自尊心が許さない→〜することを恥じる ‖ *He seems to think he's above helping with the cleaning.* 彼は, 自分が掃除を手伝うような人間ではないと思っているようだ.

成句 **above all** ▶定義 (used to emphasize the main point) most importantly (大事な点を強調するために用いて) 極めて重要なことに→とりわけ, まず第1に, 中でも ‖ *Above all, stay calm!* とにかく落ち着いて.

(be) **above board** ▶定義 (used especially about a business deal, etc) honest and open (特にビジネス上の取り引きなどについて) 正直でガラス張りの→公正な, 公明正大な

**abrasive** /əbréɪsɪv, -zɪv/ 形 ▶定義1 rough and likely to scratch 粗く, こすれそうな→摩滅させる, 研磨用の ‖ *Do not use abrasive cleaners on the bath.* 研磨剤の入った洗剤をふろ場に使わないでください. ▶定義2 (used about a person) rude and rather aggressive (人について) 粗野で, かなり攻撃的な→いらいらさせる, しゃくに障る, 不愉快な

**abreast** /əbrést/ 副 ▶定義 abreast (of sb/sth) next to or level with sb/sth and going in the same direction 〜の隣または同じ高さにあり, 同じ方向に進んでいる→(横に)並んで, 並行して ‖ *The soldiers marched two abreast.* その兵隊は2列縦隊で行進した.

成句 **be/keep abreast of sth** ▶定義 to have all the most recent information about sth 〜についての最新情報をすべて持っている→〜に後れないでいる, 〜の最新の事情に通じている

**abridge** /əbrídʒ/ 動 他 ▶定義 to make sth (usually a book) shorter by removing parts of it 〜

(通常は本)の一部を削って短くする→**要約する、縮約する** ▶参 **abbreviate**

**\*abroad** /əbrɔ́ːd/ 副 ▶定義 in or to another country or countries ほかの国で、またはほかの国へ→**外国で、海外に** ‖ *They found it difficult to get used to living abroad.* 彼らは外国での生活に慣れるのは大変だと分かった. *My mother has never been abroad.* 母は海外に行ったことがない. *She often **goes abroad** on business.* 彼女は仕事でよく海外へ行く.

**abrupt** /əbrʌ́pt/ 形 ▶定義1 sudden and unexpected 突然で予期していない→**急な、不意の、突然の** ‖ *an abrupt change of plan* 計画の急な変更 ▶定義2 seeming rude and unfriendly 無礼で不親切に見える→**無愛想な、ぶっきらぼうな** ― abruptly 副 →**突然に、不意に** ― abruptness 名 Ⓤ →**突然、唐突さ、ぶっきらぼう**

**abscess** /ǽbses, -səs/ 名 Ⓒ ▶定義 a swelling on or in the body, containing a poisonous yellow liquid (pus) 体の表面または体内にでき、有毒な黄色い液(膿(うみ))を含んだはれ物→**膿瘍(のうよう)**

**abscond** /əbskɑ́nd, æb-/ 動 ⓘ 正式 ▶定義 abscond (from sth) (with sth) to run away from a place where you should stay, sometimes with sth that you should not take いるべき場所から、時には取ってはいけない〜を持って、逃げ出す→**逃亡する、姿をくらます、〜を持ち逃げする** ‖ *to abscond from prison* 脱獄する *She absconded with all the company's money.* 彼女は会社の金を全部持ち逃げした.

**absence** /ǽbs(ə)ns/ 名 ▶定義1 Ⓒ Ⓤ a time when sb is away from somewhere; the fact of being away from somewhere 〜がある場所から離れているとき；ある場所から離れていること→**不在、留守、欠席** ‖ *Frequent absences due to illness meant he was behind with his work.* 病気でしばしば休んだため、彼は自分の仕事が遅れてしまった. *I have to make all the decisions in my boss's absence.* 上司が不在のときは、私がすべて決断しなければならない. ▶定義2 Ⓤ the fact of sth/sb not being there; lack 〜がその場所にないかいないこと；欠乏→**〜がないこと、欠如** ‖ *In the absence of a doctor, try to help the injured person yourself.* 医者がいないので、けが人はあなたが助けてあげてください. ⇔ **presence**

**\*absent** /ǽbs(ə)nt/ 形 ▶定義1 absent (from sth) not present somewhere ある場所にいない→**不在の、居合わせない、欠席の** ‖ *He was absent from work because of illness.* 彼は病気のために仕事を休んだ. ⇔ **present** ▶定義2 thinking about sth else; not paying attention ほかのことについて考えている；注意を払っていない→**ぼんやりした、放心状態の** ‖ *an absent stare* ぼんやりとした目付き ― absently 副 →**ぼんやりして、うっかりして**

**absentee** /ǽbs(ə)ntíː/ 名 Ⓒ ▶定義 a person who is not in the place where he/she should be いるべき場所にいない人→**欠席者、欠勤者、不在者**

**absenteeism** /ǽbs(ə)ntíːz(ə)m/ 名 Ⓤ ▶定義 the problem of workers or students often not going to work or school 勤め人が職場や学生が学校にほとんど行かないという問題→**(正当な理由のない)欠席の常習、長期(無断)欠勤**

**absent-minded** 形 ▶定義 often forgetting or not noticing things, because you are thinking about sth else ほかの〜について考えているために、物事をよく忘れたり気付かなかったりする→**上の空の、ぼんやりした、忘れっぽい** ➡類 **forgetful** ― absent-mindedly 副 →**上の空で、ぼんやりして**

**absolute** /ǽbsəlùːt, ーー/ 形 ▶定義1 complete; total 完全な；全くの→**絶対的な、徹底した** ‖ *The whole trip was an absolute disaster.* その旅行は全部大失敗だった. *None of the political parties had **an absolute majority** (= more votes, etc than all the other parties together).* 絶対多数(= ほかの政党すべてを合わせても、それを上回る票数などがある)の政党はなかった. ▶定義2 not measured in comparison with sth else 何かほかの〜と比較して計算したのではない→**絶対的な、絶対の** ‖ *Spending on the Health Service has increased **in absolute terms**.* 公共医療への支出の絶対額が増加した.

**\*absolutely** 副 ▶定義1 /ǽbsəlùːtli, ーー, (強調) ーーー/ completely; totally 徹底的に；全面的に→**完全に、全く** ‖ *It's absolutely freezing outside!* 外は凍てつくようなものすごい寒さだ. *I absolutely refuse to believe that.* それは絶対に信じたくない. *He made absolutely no effort (= no effort at* all) to help me. 彼は私を全く助けようとはしなかった. ▶定義2 /ǽbsəlúːtli/ (used when you are agreeing with sb) yes; certainly (〜に同意するとき)そうだ; 確かに→**その通り, そうだとも** ‖ 'It is a good idea, isn't it?' 'Oh, absolutely!' 「いい考えでしょう」「ああ, 絶対そうです」

**absolve** /əbzálv, -sálv, -zɔ́(ː)lv/ 動他 ▶定義 absolve sb (from/of sth) to say formally that sb does not have to take responsibility for sth 〜に対する責任を…が負う必要がないと正式に言う→**〜を放免する, 解放する, 免除する** ‖ The driver was absolved of any blame for the train crash. その運転手は電車の衝突事故のすべての責任を免れた.

★**absorb** /əbsɔ́ːb, -zɔ́ːb/ 動他 ▶定義1 absorb sth (into sth) to take in and hold sth (a liquid, heat, etc) 〜(液体, 熱など)を取り込んで保持する→**〜を吸収する, 吸い込む, 吸い取る** ‖ a drug that is quickly absorbed into the bloodstream 血液内にすぐに吸収される薬 Black clothes absorb the sun's heat. 黒い服は太陽の熱を吸収する. ▶定義2 to take sth into the mind and understand it 〜を頭に入れて理解する→**〜を取り入れる, 自分のものにする, 吸収する** ‖ I found it impossible to absorb so much information so quickly. それほど多くの情報をそんなに早く自分のものにすることは不可能だと分かった.

▶定義3 absorb sth (into sth) to take sth into sth larger, so that it becomes part of it 〜をより大きな…に取り込み, その一部となるようにする→**〜を吸収する, 〜を合併する** ‖ Over the years many villages have been absorbed into the city. 何年もの間に, 多くの村がその町に合併された. ▶定義4 to hold sb's attention completely or interest sb very much 〜の注意力を完全に保つ, または〜に関心を強く持たせる→**〜を夢中にさせる, 〜に没頭させる** ‖ History is a subject that absorbs her. 歴史は彼女を夢中にさせる科目である. ▶定義5 to reduce the effect of a sudden violent knock, hit, etc 突然の強打, 激しい衝突などの影響を少なくする→**〜を吸収する, 〜を(吸収して)和らげる** ‖ The front of the car is designed to absorb most of the impact of a crash. 車の前部は衝撃をほとんど吸収するように設計されている. ━ absorption /əbsɔ́ːpʃ(ə)n, -zɔ́ː-/ 名 ❶→吸収, 熱中, 合併

**absorbed** /əbsɔ́ːbd, -zɔ́ːbd/ 形 ▶定義 absorbed (in sth) giving all your attention to sth 〜にすべての注意を傾けている→**〜に夢中の, 熱中した** ‖ He was absorbed in his work and didn't hear me come in. 彼は仕事に没頭していて, 私が入ってきたのが聞こえなかった.

**absorbent** /əbsɔ́ːbənt, -zɔ́ːbənt/ 形 ▶定義 able to take in and hold liquid 液体を取り込んで保持できる→**吸収性の, 吸収力のある** ‖ an absorbent cloth 吸収性のある布地

**absorbing** /əbsɔ́ːbɪŋ, -zɔ́ːbɪŋ/ 形 ▶定義 holding all your interest and attention すべての関心と注意をひいている→**夢中にさせる, とても面白い, 興味の尽きない** ‖ an absorbing book 夢中にさせられる本

**abstain** /əbstéɪn, æb-/ 動自 ▶定義1 正式 abstain (from sth/doing sth) to stop yourself from doing sth that you enjoy 楽しみとしている〜をやめる→**控える, 慎む, 避ける** ‖ The doctor said I should abstain from (drinking) alcohol until I'm better. その医者は私に, 回復するまで飲酒は控えるように言った. ☛ 名 abstinence ▶定義2 (in a vote) to say that you are not voting either for or against sth (投票について)〜に対して賛成にも反対にも投票しないと言う→**棄権する** ‖ Two people voted in favour, two voted against and one abstained. 2人が賛成, 2人が反対, 1人が棄権だった. ☛ 名 abstention

**abstention** /æbsténʃ(ə)n, əb-/ 名 ❶ ▶定義 the act of not voting either for or against sth 賛成にも反対にも投票しないこと→**棄権**

**abstinence** /ǽbstənəns/ 名 ❶ 正式 ▶定義 stopping yourself from having or doing sth that you enjoy 楽しみとしている〜を持ったり行ったりするのをやめること→**節制, 禁欲** ‖ The doctor advised total abstinence from alcohol. その医者は断酒を勧めた. ☛ 動 abstain

**abstract**¹ /ǽbstrækt/ 形 ▶定義1 existing only as an idea, not as a physical thing 実体としてではなく, 概念としてのみ存在する→**抽象的な** ‖ It is hard to imagine an abstract idea like 'eternity'. 「永遠」のような抽象的な概念を考えるのは難しい. ⇔ **concrete** ▶定義2 (used about art) not showing people and things as they really look (美術について)実際に見える様子と同じように人や物を描いていない→**抽象主**

8　abstract²

義(派)の‖ *an abstract painting* 抽象画

**abstract²** /ǽbstrækt/ 图 C ▶定義1 an example of abstract art 抽象的な絵画の一例→**抽象美術作品,抽象絵画** ▶定義2 a short piece of writing that tells you the main contents of a book, speech, etc 書物,演説などの重要な内容を短く書き表したもの→**摘要,要約,抜粋**

成句 **in the abstract** ▶定義 only as an idea, not in real life 概念としてあるだけで,実生活の中にはない→**抽象的に,理論上**

**absurd** /əbsə́ːrd, -zə́ːrd, æb-/ 形 ▶定義 not at all logical or sensible; ridiculous 全く論理的または賢明でない; ばかげている→**不合理な,理屈に合わない,おかしな** ‖ *It would be absurd to spend all your money on one book.* 1冊の本に持っている金を全部かけるなんてばかげている. *Don't be absurd! I can't possibly do all this work in one day.* ばかな事を言わないでください. この仕事全部を1日でなんてどうしたってできません.— absurdity 图 C U (複 absurdities)→**不合理,不条理,ばかげていること** — absurdly 副→**ばかばかしいほど,不合理に**

**abundance** /əbʌ́ndəns/ 图 [U, 単数扱い] ▶定義 a very large quantity of sth 非常にたくさんの→**多量,多数,豊富** ‖ *These flowers grow here in abundance.* これらの花はこの地に大量に育つ. *There is an abundance of wildlife in the forest.* 森には野生の生き物がたくさんいる.

**abundant** /əbʌ́ndənt/ 形 ▶定義 existing in very large quantities; more than enough 非常にたくさんある; 必要以上に→**豊富な,有り余るほどの,豊かな** ‖ *abundant supplies of food* 豊富な食料の供給 — abundantly 副→**豊富に,多量に,非常に**

**abuse¹** /əbjúːz/ 動他 ▶定義1 to use sth in a bad or dishonest way ～を間違った,あるいは不正な方法で使う→**～を乱用する,悪用する** ‖ *The politician was accused of abusing his position in order to become rich.* その政治家は,金持ちになるために自分の立場を悪用したとして告発された. ▶定義2 to say rude things to sb ～に無礼な事を言う→**～をののしる,侮辱する,罵倒(ばとう)する** ▶定義3 to treat sb badly, often violently ～に対してひどく,しばしば乱暴な扱いをする→**～を虐待する,酷使する** ‖ *The girl had been sexually abused.* その少女は性的虐待を受けていた.

**abuse²** /əbjúːs/ 图 ▶定義1 C U using sth in a bad or dishonest way ～を間違った,あるいは不正な方法で使うこと→**乱用,悪用,誤用** ‖ *an abuse of power* 権力の乱用 *the dangers of drug abuse* 麻薬乱用の危険 ▶定義2 U rude words, used to insult another person 他人を侮辱するために使われる失礼な言葉→**ののしり,悪口,毒舌** ‖ *The other driver leaned out of the car and hurled abuse at me.* もう一方の運転手が車から乗り出して, 私を罵倒(ばとう)した. *racial abuse* 人種に関する悪口 ▶定義3 U bad, usually violent treatment of sb ～に対するひどい,通常は乱暴な扱い→**虐待,酷使** ‖ *He subjected his children to verbal and physical abuse.* 彼は自分の子供たちを言葉と暴力で虐待した. *a victim of sexual abuse* 性的虐待の犠牲者

**abusive** /əbjúːsɪv, -zɪv/ 形 ▶定義 using rude language to insult sb ～を侮辱するために失礼な言葉を使っている→**口汚い,悪態をつく,ののしりの** ‖ *an abusive remark* 口汚い発言

**abysmal** /əbízm(ə)l, æ-/ 形 ▶定義 very bad; of very poor quality とてもひどい; 質の非常に悪い→**全くひどい,ひどく悪い** — abysmally 副→**全くひどく**

**abyss** /əbís/ 图 C ▶定義 a very deep hole that seems to have no bottom 底がなさそうに見える非常に深い穴→**底なしの穴,深淵(しんえん),奈落(ならく)**

**academic¹** /ækədémɪk/ ▶定義1 connected with education, especially in schools and universities 特に学校,大学で,教育に関連している→**学園の,学校の,大学の** ‖ *The academic year begins in September.* 学年は9月に始まる. ▶定義2 connected with subjects of interest to the mind rather than technical or practical subjects 技術的あるいは実用的な主題よりも,知的に興味ある主題の学科に関連している→**学問的な,学究的な,理論的な** ‖ *academic subjects such as History* 歴史のような学術的主題 ⇔ **non-academic** ▶定義3 not connected with reality; not affecting the facts of a situation 現実とは関連のない; ある状況に関する事実には影響を及ぼさない→**非現実的な,実用的でない,現**

実離れの ‖ *It's academic which one I prefer because I can't have either of them.* 私がどちらを選んでも現実には大差がない.なぜなら,どちらにしても手に入れることはできないのだから. — **academically** /-k(ə)li/ 副 ➡学問的に,学究的に,理論的に

**academic**[2] /ˌækədémɪk/ 名 C ▶定義 a person who teaches and/or does research at a university or college 大学で教えたり研究したりする人➡**大学生,大学教師,学者**

**academy** /əkǽdəmi/ 名 C (複 **academies**) ▶定義1 a school for special training 専門的な訓練のための学校➡**専門学校,高等教育機関** ‖ *a military academy* 陸軍士官学校 ▶定義2 (または **Academy**) an official group of people who are important in art, science or literature 芸術,科学,文学などの分野で重要な位置を占める人々が所属する公式団体➡**学士院,学会,芸術院** ‖ *the Royal Academy of Arts* 英国王立美術院

**accelerate** /əksélərèɪt, æk-/ 動 自他 ▶定義 to go faster; to make sth go faster or happen more quickly より速く行く;～をより速く進める,または実現させる➡**(～を)加速する,促進する,～の時期を早める** ‖ *The driver slowed down for the bend then accelerated away.* 運転手はカーブの所でスピードを落とし,それから加速して走り去った. *The government plans to accelerate the pace of reform.* 政府は改革のペースを上げようと計画している. — **acceleration** /ɪksèləréɪʃ(ə)n, æk-/ 名 U ➡**加速,促進,加速度**

**accelerator** /əksélərèɪtər, æk-/ 名 C ▶定義 the control in a vehicle that you press with your foot in order to make it go faster 乗り物の速度を上げるために足で押さえる制御装置➡**加速装置,アクセル(ペダル)** ← S7 ページのさし絵

★**accent** /ǽksənt/ 名 ▶定義1 C U a particular way of pronouncing words that is connected with the country, area or social class that you come from 出身地[国],地域,社会階層などに関連する,言葉の特有な発音法➡**なまり** ‖ *He speaks with a strong Scottish accent.* 彼は強いスコットランドなまりで話す. ▶定義2 C the greater force that you give to a particular word or part of a word when you speak 話すときにある特別な単語や単語の一部に加えるほかより強い力➡**アクセント,強勢** ‖ *In the word 'because' the accent is on the second syllable.* because という単語ではアクセントが第2音節にある. ▶定義3 C (in writing) a mark, usually above a letter, that shows that it has to be pronounced in a certain way (文書で) 特定の方式で発音することを表す記号,通常は文字の上に付ける➡**アクセント記号,アクセント符号** ▶定義4 [C, 通常は単数] the particular importance that is given to sth ～に対して置かれた特別な重み➡**重点,強調,特色** ‖ *In all our products the accent is on quality.* 我が社の製品は,すべて質に重点を置いている.

**accentuate** /æksént∫uèɪt, ək-/ 動 他 ▶定義 to make sth easier to notice ～を気付きやすくする➡**～を強調する,際立たせる,目立たせる** ‖ *She uses make-up to accentuate her beautiful eyes.* 彼女はきれいな目を強調するような化粧をする.

★**accept** /əksépt, æk-/ 動 ▶定義1 自他 to agree to take sth that sb offers you ～がさし出す…を受け取ることに同意する➡**(～を)受け取る,受理する** ‖ *Please accept this small gift.* ちょっとしたプレゼントですが受け取ってください. *Do I have to pay in cash or will you accept a cheque?* 現金で支払わないといけませんか.小切手でもいいですか. *Why won't you accept my advice?* 私の忠告を受け入れたらどうですか. ▶定義2 自他 to say yes to sth or to agree to sth ～に対して承諾する,または同意する➡**(～を)受け入れる,受諾する** ‖ *Thank you for your invitation. I am happy to accept.* ご招待くださってありがとう.喜んで伺います. *He asked her to marry him and she accepted.* 彼は彼女に結婚を申し込んだら,彼女は受け入れた. *She has accepted the job.* 彼女はその仕事を引き受けた. ▶定義3 他 to admit or recognize that sth unpleasant is true 快く思わない～が真実であると認める,または認識する➡**(～に)しぶしぶ同意する,仕方なく服する,～を引き受ける** ‖ *They refused to accept responsibility for the accident.* 彼らはその事故の責任を負うことを拒んだ. ▶定義4 他 to allow sb to join a group, etc ～が集団などに参加することを許す➡**～を受け入れる,迎え入れる** ‖ *The university has accepted me on the course.* 大学は私がその課程を取ることを認めてくれた.

**acceptable** /əkséptəb(ə)l, æ-/ 形 ▶定義1 that

can be allowed 許される→**受け入れられる, 容認できる, 許容できる** ‖ *One or two mistakes are acceptable but no more than that.* 1つや2つの誤りならいいが, それ以上となると認められない. ▶定義2 good enough; satisfactory 十分である; 満足できる→**結構な, 無難な** ‖ *We hope that you will consider our offer acceptable.* 私たちの申し出を喜んでいただけるといいのですが. ⇔ **unacceptable** — acceptability /ɪkˌsɛptəˈbɪləti, ɪk-/ 名 U →**受け入れられること, 受容性, 容認度** — acceptably /ɪkˈsɛptəb(ə)li, æk-/ 副 →**受け入れられるように, 無難に**

**acceptance** /əkˈsɛptəns, æk-/ 名 C U ▶定義 the act of accepting or being accepted 受け入れること, または受け入れられること→**容認, 受諾, 賛成** ‖ *His ready acceptance of the offer surprised me.* その申し出を彼が即座に受け入れたのには驚いた. *He quickly gained acceptance in the group (= the other people thought of him as equal to them).* 彼はそのグループですぐに認められた(= ほかのメンバーが彼も自分たちと同じであると見なした). *The new methods have received widespread acceptance.* その新しい方法は広く受け入れられている.

**access**[1] /ˈækses/ 名 U ▶定義1 access (to sth) a way of entering or reaching a place ある場所に入る, または近付く方法→**接近方法** ‖ *Access to the garden is through the kitchen.* 庭へは台所を通って出られる. ▶定義2 access (to sth) the chance or right to use or have sth 〜を利用または所有する機会や権利→**〜を利用する機会, 権利** ‖ *Do you have access to a personal computer?* パソコンを利用できる状態にありますか. ▶定義3 access (to sb) permission, especially legal or official, to see sb 〜に会うための, 特に法的または公的な許可→**面会の権利** ‖ *They are divorced, but he has regular access to the children.* 彼らは離婚しているが, 彼には子供に定期的に会える権利がある.

**access**[2] /ˈækses/ 動 他 ▶定義 to find information on a computer コンピューター上で情報を探す→**〜にアクセスする, データの読み込み・書き込みを行う** ‖ *Click on the icon to access a file.* ファイルにアクセスするには, そのアイコンをクリックしてください.

**accessible** /əkˈsɛsəb(ə)l, æk-/ 形 ▶定義1 possible to be reached or entered 近付くことができる, または入ることができる→**行くことができる, 接近できる, 行きやすい** ‖ *The island is only accessible by boat.* その島はボートでしか行けない. ▶定義2 easy to get, use or understand 入手, 利用, あるいは理解がしやすい→**入手できる, 利用可能な, 分かりやすい** ‖ *This television programme aims to make history more accessible to children.* このテレビ番組は, 子供にとって歴史がより分かりやすくなることを目的としている. ⇔ **inaccessible** — accessibility /ɪkˌsɛsəˈbɪləti, æk-/ 名 U →**行きやすさ, 接近できること, 入手できること** ‖ *Computers have given people greater accessibility to information.* コンピューターのお陰で情報がとても入手しやすくなった.

**accession** /əkˈsɛʃ(ə)n, æk-/ 名 U ▶定義 the act of taking a very high position, especially as ruler of a country or head of sth 特に一国の統治者または〜の長など, 非常に高い地位に就こうとする行為→**継承, 即位, 就任**

**accessory** /əkˈsɛs(ə)ri, æk-/ 名 C (複) accessories) ▶定義1 an extra item that is added to sth and is useful or attractive but not of great importance 〜に付け加える特別なもので, 役に立ったり魅力的であったりするが, それほど重要というわけではないもの→**付属品, 小物類** ‖ *The car has accessories such as an electronic alarm.* その車には電子アラームなどの付属品がある. ▶定義2 [通常は複数]a thing that you wear or carry that matches your clothes, for example a piece of jewellery, a bag, etc 宝石, バッグなどのように, 衣服に合わせて身に着けたり携帯したりするもの→**アクセサリー, 装飾品** ▶定義3 an accessory (to sth) (in law) a person who helps sb to do sth illegal (法律で)〜が違法な…を実行するのを助ける人→**従犯者**

\***accident** /ˈæksəd(ə)nt/ 名 C ▶定義 an unpleasant event that happens unexpectedly and causes damage, injury or death 予期せずに起き, 損害, 負傷者, 死者を発生する好ましくない出来事→**事故, 災難, 不測の出来事** ‖ *I hope they haven't had an accident.* 彼らが事故に遭っていなければよいのですが. *a car accident* 自動車事故 *a fatal accident (= when sb is killed)* 死亡事故(= 〜が死ぬ場合) *I didn't mean to kick*

*you, it was an accident.* あなたをけ飛ばすつもりはありませんでした. 偶然だったのです.
成句 **by accident** ▶定義 by chance; without intending to 偶然に; 意図せずに→**偶然に, たまたま** ‖ *I knocked the vase over by accident as I was cleaning.* 掃除をしている時に, 誤って花びんをひっくり返してしまった.

**accidental** /æksədéntl/ 形 ▶定義 happening by chance; not planned 偶然に起きる; 予定されていない→**偶然の, 思い掛けない, 不慮の** ‖ *Police do not know if the explosion was accidental or caused by a bomb.* その爆発は事故なのか, あるいは爆発物が原因なのか, 警察では分からない. — **accidentally** /-tli/ 副 →**偶然に, 思い掛けず, たまたま** ‖ *She accidentally took the key to the office home with her, so nobody could get in.* 彼女がたまたま事務所のかぎを持って帰宅したため, だれも中に入れなかった.

**accident-prone** 形 ▶定義 often having accidents よく事故に遭う→**事故に遭いやすい, 事故を起こしがちな**

**acclaim** /əkléɪm/ 動他 ▶定義 to express a very high opinion of sth/sb 〜をとても高く評価する→**〜を熱狂的に歓迎する, 賞賛する, 褒めたたえる** ‖ *a **highly acclaimed** new film* 絶賛されている新しい映画 *The novel has been acclaimed as a modern classic.* その小説は現代の古典であると賞賛されている. — **acclaim** 名 U →**喝さい, 賞賛, 歓呼** ‖ *The film received widespread critical acclaim.* その映画は幅広く評論家の絶賛を浴びた.

**acclimatize**(または**-ise**)/əkláɪmətaɪz/ 動自他 ▶定義 acclimatize (yourself/sb/ sth) (to sth) to get used to a new climate, a new situation, etc so that it is not a problem any more 新しい気候, 環境などに慣れ, それがもはや問題ではなくなる→**〜に慣れる, 慣らす; 順応する** — **acclimatization**(または**-isation**) /əklàɪmətaɪzéɪʃ(ə)n/ 名 U →**順応** — **acclimatized**(または**-ised**)形 →**〜に慣れた, 慣らされた, 順応した**

**accolade** /ǽkəleɪd, ˌ-ˈ-/ 名 C ▶定義 a comment, prize, etc that you receive that shows people's high opinion of sth you have done 自分のした〜に対して受ける周りからの高い評価や賞など→**賞賛, 賛辞, 名誉**

**accommodate** /əkɑ́mədèɪt/ 動他 ▶定義 1 to have enough space for sb/sth, especially for a certain number of people 〜, 特に一定の人数を入れる空間が十分ある→**〜を宿泊させる, 収容できる** ‖ *Each apartment can accommodate up to six people.* それぞれの部屋には6人まで宿泊できる. ▶定義 2 to provide sb with a place to stay, live or work 〜に宿泊, 生活, 務めなどの場所を提供する→**〜を調達する, 泊める** ‖ *During the conference, you will be accommodated in a nearby hotel.* 会議の期間中, 近くのホテルに宿泊することになります. ▶定義 3 正式 to do or provide what sb wants or needs 〜が望んだり必要としたりする物事を実行または提供する→**〜の便宜を図る, 〜の願いを入れる**

**accommodating** /əkɑ́mədèɪtɪŋ/ 形 ▶定義 (used about a person) agreeing to do or provide what sb wants (人について)〜が望む物事を実行または提供することに賛同している→**親切な, 好意的な, 融通の利く** ‖ *My boss is very accommodating when I need time off work.* 私が休みを必要とするとき, 上司はとても好意的に取り計らってくれる.

***accommodation** /əkɑ̀mədéɪʃ(ə)n/ 名 U ▶定義 a place for sb to live or stay 〜が住む, または滞在する場所→**宿泊設備, 収容施設** ‖ *We lived in rented accommodation before buying this house.* 私たちは, この家を購入する前は借家に住んでいた. *The price of the holiday includes flights and accommodation.* 旅行代金には航空運賃と宿泊代が含まれている.

➤ accommodation は不可算名詞なので, 'I will help you to find an accommodation.' とは言わず, 'I will help you to find somewhere to live.' (住む所を探すのを手伝いましょう.) と言う.

**accompaniment** /əkʌ́mp(ə)nɪmənt/ 名 C ▶定義 something that goes together with another more important thing ほかのもっと重要な事に伴うもの→**伴うもの, 付随して生じるもの, 付属物** ‖ *He only drinks wine as an accompaniment to food.* 彼は食事のときにしかワインを飲まない.

***accompany** /əkʌ́mp(ə)ni/ 動 他 (現分 **accompanying**; 三単現 **accompanies**; 過, 過分 **accompanied**) ▶定義 1 to go together with

sb/sth ～に伴う→～に付いていく, 一緒に行く, 付き添う ‖ *He went to America accompanied by his wife and three children.* 彼は妻と3人の子供を連れてアメリカへ行った. *Massive publicity accompanied the film's release.* その映画が封切りになる時, 大規模な宣伝がなされた.
▶定義2 accompany sb (on sth) to play music for a singer or another instrument 歌手やほかの楽器に合わせて演奏する→～の伴奏をする ‖ *She accompanied him on the guitar.* 彼女はギターで彼の伴奏をした.

**accomplice** /əkámpləs, əkʌ́m-/ 图 C ▶定義 an accomplice (to/in sth) a person who helps sb to do sth bad, especially a crime 何かの悪巧み, 特に罪を犯すのを手助けする人→共犯者, 共謀者 ‖ *She was charged with being an accomplice to the murder.* 彼女はその殺人の共犯者として告発された.

**accomplish** /əkámplɪʃ, -kʌ́m-/ 動 ⓗ ▶定義 to succeed in doing sth difficult that you planned to do 実行しようと計画していた難しい～をやり遂げる→～を成し遂げる, 成功させる, 達成する ‖ *I managed to accomplish my goal of writing ten letters in an evening.* 一晩で手紙を10通書くという目標を何とか達成した.

**accomplished** /əkámplɪʃt, əkʌ́m-/ 形 ▶定義 highly skilled at sth ～の技能が高度に優れている→熟達した, 熟練した, たんのうな ‖ *an accomplished actor* 熟練した俳優

**accomplishment** /əkámplɪʃmənt, əkʌ́m-/ 图 ▶定義1 ⓤ the act of completing sth successfully ～を最後までやり遂げること→完成, 遂行, 達成 ‖ *the accomplishment of a plan* 計画の遂行 ▶定義2 C something difficult that sb has succeeded in doing or learning ～がやり遂げた, または身に付けたことで一般には難しいこと→功績, 業績, 成果

**accord**¹ /əkɔ́ːrd/ 图 C ▶定義 an agreement, especially between countries 特に国家間で結ばれる合意事項→協定, 協約, 合意 ‖ *the Helsinki accords on human rights* 人権に関するヘルシンキ合意

成句 in accord ▶定義 in agreement about sth ～について同意している→～について一致している

of your own accord ▶定義 without being forced or asked 強制されたり要求されたりしないで→自発的に, 自分から進んで, 自然に ‖ *He wasn't sacked from his job - he left of his own accord.* 彼は解雇されたのではない ― 自分から辞めたのだった.

**accord**² /əkɔ́ːrd/ 動 正式 ▶定義1 ⓗ to give sth to sb ～に…を与える→～を与える, 授ける, 示す ▶定義2 ⓘ accord (with sth) to match; to agree with ～と釣り合う; ～に矛盾なく合っている→一致する, 調和する

**accordance** /əkɔ́ːrd(ə)ns/ 图
成句 in accordance with sth ▶定義 in a way that follows or obeys sth ～に従って, または～を守って→～に従って, ～通りに ‖ *to act in accordance with instructions* 指示に従って行動する

**accordingly** /əkɔ́ːrdɪŋli/ 副 ▶定義1 in a way that is suitable 適当な方法で→それ相応に, 状況に応じて ‖ *I realized that I was in danger and acted accordingly.* 私は危険を感じたので, しかるべく行動した. ▶定義2 正式 therefore; for that reason その結果; その理由で→それゆえに, したがって

*__according to__ /əkɔ́ːrdɪŋ tə, (母音の前) tu/ 前 ▶定義1 as stated by sb; as shown by sth ～によって述べられた通りに; ～が示すように→～によれば ‖ *According to Mick, it's a brilliant film.* ミックによると, それはすばらしい映画だそうだ. *More people now have a high standard of living, according to the statistics.* 統計によれば, 現在, 生活水準の高い人が増えたそうだ. ▶定義2 in a way that matches, follows or depends on sth ～と釣り合う, ～に従う, ～に基づく方法で→～に応じて, ～に比例して, ～に従って ‖ *Everything went off **according to plan** (= as we had planned it).* 万事, 計画通りに運んだ(= 自分たちが計画した通りに) *The salary will be fixed according to age and experience.* 給与は年齢と経験に応じて決まるだろう.

**accordion** /əkɔ́ːrdiən/ 图 C ▶定義 a musical instrument that you hold in both hands and play by pulling the two sides apart and then pushing them together, while pressing the keys and/or buttons with your fingers 両手で抱えて持ち, 両端を引き離したり押し縮めたりしながら, 指で鍵盤(けんばん)やボタンを押して

演奏する楽器➜アコーディオン,手風琴 ☛参 **piano** の注 ☛ **music** のさし絵

**accost** /əkɔ́(:)st, əkɑ́st/ [動][他] ▶定義 to go up and talk to a stranger in a way that is rude or frightening 見知らぬ人に近寄り,失礼な,または怖がらせるような態度で話し掛ける➜**～に近寄って話し掛ける,～を呼び止める**

***account**[1] /əkáʊnt/ [名] [C] ▶定義1 somebody's report or description of sth that has happened 発生した～についての報告または記述➜**説明,報告,記事** ‖ *She gave the police a full account of the robbery.* 彼女はその強盗事件のことを警察に詳細に説明した. ▶定義2 ([略] **a/c**) the arrangement by which a bank looks after your money for you 銀行が利用者の金を利用者に代わって管理するための仕組み➜**預金口座,預金(残高),取り引き関係** ‖ *to open/close an account* 口座を開く·閉じる *I have an account with/at Barclays.* 私はバークレーズ銀行に口座を持っている. *I paid the cheque into my bank account.* その小切手を自分の銀行口座に払い込んだ.

➤ cheque(小切手)で物を購入するときは, current account(当座預金)の口座を使う.貯金は, deposit account(定期預金口座), savings account(普通の預金口座)のどちらにもできる.

▶定義3 [通常は複数] a record of all the money that a person or business has received or paid out 個人または企業が受け取った,または支払ったすべての金額に関する記録➜**計算(書),勘定(書),請求書** ‖ *If you are self-employed you have to* ***keep*** *your own* ***accounts****.* 自営業の場合,自分で帳簿をつけなければならない. ▶定義4 an arrangement with a shop, etc that allows you to pay for goods or services at a later date 商品やサービスの費用を後日支払うことを認める,店などとの約束➜**付け,掛け売り** ‖ *Most customers* ***settle/pay*** *their* ***account*** *in full at the end of each month.* ほとんどの顧客は毎月末にまとめて勘定を清算している.

[成句] **by all accounts** ▶定義 according to what everyone says だれもが言うことによると➜**だれに聞いても,どの報道を見ても** ‖ *By all accounts, she's a very good doctor.* だれに聞いても,彼女はとてもいい医者だと言う.

**by your own account** ▶定義 according to what you say yourself 本人自身が言うことによると➜**本人の言うところによると** ‖ *By his own account, Peter was not very good at his job.* ピーターは,本人の言うところによると,仕事があまり良くできなかったそうだ.

**on account of** ▶定義 because of ～の理由で➜**～のために** ‖ *Our flight was delayed on account of bad weather.* 私たちが乗った飛行機は,天候不良のために遅れた.

**on no account; not on any account** ▶定義 not for any reason どんな理由でもあり得ない➜**決して～ない** ‖ *On no account should you walk home by yourself.* 自分一人で歩いて帰宅するようなことは絶対にしてはならない.

**take account of sth; take sth into account** ▶定義 to consider sth, especially when deciding or judging sth 特に～について決断や判断を下すときに,よく考える➜**～を考慮に入れる,斟酌(しんしゃく)する,重視する** ‖ *We'll take account of your comments.* 私たちはあなたの批評を考慮に入れるつもりだ. *We'll take your comments into account.* 私たちはあなたの批評を考慮に入れるつもりだ.

**account**[2] /əkáʊnt/ [動]

[成句] **account for sth** ▶定義1 to explain or give a reason for sth ～を説明する,または理由を示す➜**～の訳を説明する,釈明をする** ‖ *How can we account for these changes?* これらの変更はどのように説明できるのでしょう. ▶定義2 to form the amount that is mentioned 言及されている数量の一部を成す➜**～を占める** ‖ *Sales to Europe accounted for 80% of our total sales last year.* 昨年のヨーロッパ向けの売上高は,総売上高の80パーセントを占めていた.

**accountable** /əkáʊntəb(ə)l/ [形] ▶定義 expected to give an explanation of your actions, etc; responsible 自分の行動などについての説明が求められる; 責任がある➜**～を説明する義務がある,責任がある** ‖ *She is too young to* ***be held accountable*** *for what she did.* 彼女の年齢では,まだ自分の行動に対する責任能力がない.
— **accountability** /-əbíləti/ [名] [U] ➜**釈明の義務があること,責任**

**accountancy** /əkáʊnt(ə)nsi/ [名] [U] ▶定義 the work or profession of an accountant 会計に関

する仕事または職業➜**会計(職), 会計事務, 経理**

**accountant** /əkáʊntənt/ [名] [C] ▶定義 a person whose job is to keep or examine the financial accounts of a business, etc 企業などの財務管理または監査を仕事とする人➜**会計係, 会計士**

**accumulate** /əkjúːm(j)əlèɪt/ [動] ▶定義1 [他] to collect a number or quantity of sth over a period of time 時間をかけて～の数量をたくさん集める➜**～をためる, 蓄積する, 積み上げる** ‖ *Over the years, I've accumulated hundreds of books.* 私は長い年月の間に数百冊の本を集めた. ▶定義2 [自] to increase over a period of time 時間がたつうちに増える➜**たまる, 積もる, 集まる** ‖ *Dust soon accumulates if you don't clean the house for a week or so.* 1週間ほど家の掃除をしないと, すぐにほこりがたまる. — accumulation /əkjùːm(j)əléɪʃ(ə)n/ [名] [C] [U]➜**蓄積, 蓄財, 蓄積したもの**

***accurate** /ǽkjərət/ [形] ▶定義 exact and correct; without mistakes 厳密で正しい; 間違いのない➜**正確な, 周到な, 精密な** ‖ *He managed to give the police an accurate description of the robbers.* 彼は, 強盗について警察にどうにか正確に説明することができた. *That clock isn't very accurate.* その時計はあまり正確ではない. ⇔ **inaccurate** — accuracy /ǽkjərəsi/ [名] [U]➜**正確さ, 的確さ, 精密さ** ⇔ **inaccuracy** — accurately [副]➜**正確に, 間違いなく, 精密に** ‖ *It is difficult to estimate the age of these bones accurately.* これらの骨の年齢を正確に割り出すのは難しい.

**accusation** /æ̀kjəzéɪʃ(ə)n, -kju-/ [名] [C] [U] ▶定義 a statement saying that sb has done sth wrong ～が悪い事をしたと言うこと➜**非難, 告発**

***accuse** /əkjúːz/ [動] [他] ▶定義 accuse sb (of sth/doing sth) to say that sb has done sth wrong or broken the law ～が悪い事をした, または法を犯したと言う➜**～を告発する, 非難する, 責める** ‖ *I accused her of cheating.* 私は彼女がごまかしをしていると責めた. *He was accused of murder and sent for trial.* 彼は殺人罪で告訴され, 裁判にかけられた.

**the accused** /əkjúːzd/ [名] [C] ([複] **the accused**) ▶定義 (used in a court of law) the person who is said to have broken the law (法廷で用いて) 法を犯したとされている者➜**被告人, 被告**

**accusing** /əkjúːzɪŋ/ [形] ▶定義 showing that you think sb has done sth wrong ～が悪い…をしたと思っていることを示している➜**非難するような, とがめるような** ‖ *He gave me an accusing look.* 彼は非難に満ちた目付きで私を見た. — accusingly [副]➜**非難するように**

**accustom** /əkʌ́stəm/ [動] [他] ▶定義 accustom yourself/sb/sth to sth to make yourself/sb/sth get used to sth 自分自身または～を…に慣れるようにする➜**～を慣らす, 習慣づける, なじませる** ‖ *It took me a while to accustom myself to working nights.* 私は夜勤に慣れるまでしばらく時間がかかった.

**accustomed** /əkʌ́stəmd/ [形] ▶定義1 accustomed to sth if you are accustomed to sth, you are used to it and it is not strange for you. ～に慣れて違和感を感じなくなる➜**～に慣れる** ‖ *She's accustomed to travelling a lot in her job.* 彼女は仕事であちこち旅行することに慣れている. *It took a while for my eyes to get accustomed to the dark room.* 暗い部屋に目が慣れるまで少し時間がかかった. ▶定義2 [正式] usual; regular➜**いつもの; 例の**

**ace** /éɪs/ [名] [C] ▶定義1 a playing card which has a single shape on it. An ace has either the lowest or the highest value in a game of cards. トランプで印が1つしか付いていないカード. ゲームでは最も高いか最も低い価値がある➜**(トランプの) 1の札, エース** ‖ *the ace of spades* スペードのエース ☛参 **card** の注とさし絵 ▶定義2 (in tennis) the first hit of the ball (service) that the person playing against you cannot hit back (テニスで) 対戦相手が打ち返すことができない第1打のボール (サービス)➜**サービスエース, それで得た1点** ‖ *to serve an ace* サービスエースを取る

***ache**[1] /éɪk/ [名] [C] [U] ▶定義 a pain that lasts for a long time 長く続く痛み➜**痛み, うずき** ‖ *to have toothache/earache/stomach-ache* 歯・耳・胃が痛い

➤ ache はしばしば複合語で使われる. イギリス英語では, 通常, 次の例文のように a や an を付けない: *I've got toothache.* (私はずっと歯が痛いんです.) ただし, headache の場合は a を付けて使う: *I've got a bad headache.* (ひどい頭痛がしています.) アメリカ英語では, 特

に非常に激しい痛みについて話すときにはaやanを付けることが多い: *I have an awful toothache.*（歯がとても痛いです。）

**ache**² /éɪk/ 動 ⾃ ▶定義 to feel a continuous pain 継続的な痛みを感じる→**痛む, うずく** ‖ *His legs ached after playing football.* フットボールをした後, 彼の足は痛んだ. *She was aching all over.* 彼女は体中痛みを感じていた.

*★**achieve** /ətʃíːv/ 動 ⾃他 ▶定義 **1** to complete sth by hard work and skill ～に努力を費やしてまた技能によって完成させる→**～を成し遂げる, 達成する, 果たす** ‖ *They have achieved a lot in a short time.* 彼らは短時間で多くの事をやり遂げた. ▶定義 **2** to gain sth, usually by effort or skill ～を, 通常は努力または技能によって得る→**～を獲得する, 勝ち取る, もたらす** ‖ *You have achieved the success you deserve.* あなたは努力に値する成功を勝ち取った.

*★**achievement** /ətʃíːvmənt/ 名 ⒸⓊ ▶定義 something that you have done successfully, especially through hard work or skill 特に労力を費やし, または技能によって, 無事にやり遂げた物事→**業績, 偉業** ‖ *She felt that winning the gold medal was her greatest achievement.* 彼女は金メダルの獲得が自分にとって最大の成果であると感じた. *He enjoys climbing mountains because it gives him a sense of achievement.* 彼が山登りを楽しんでいるのは, 達成感を味わえるからだ.

**Achilles' heel** /əkíliːz híːl/ 名 Ⓒ ▶定義 a weak point or fault in sb/sth ～の弱みまたは短所→**唯一の弱点, アキレス腱（けん）, 弁慶の泣き所**

*★**acid**¹ /ǽsəd/ 名 ⒸⓊ ▶定義 (in chemistry) a liquid substance that can dissolve metal and may burn your skin or clothes. Acids have a pH value of less than 7. (化学で) 金属を溶解でき, 人間の皮膚や衣服を焼くことができる液体. 7より小さいpH値を持つ→**酸** ‖ *sulphuric acid* 硫酸　☞参 **alkali, base**

**acid**² /ǽsəd/ 形 ▶定義 **1** (used about a fruit, etc) with a sour taste (果物などについて) 酸っぱい味がする→**酸っぱい, 酸味のある** ▶定義 **2** (または **acidic** /əsídɪk, æ-/) containing an acid 酸を含んでいる→**酸性の, 酸の** ‖ *an acid solution* 酸性の溶液　☞参 **alkaline**

**acidity** /əsídəti, æ-/ 名 ⓊⒸ ▶定義 the quality of being acid 酸を含むという性質→**酸性度, 酸味** ‖ *to measure the acidity of soil* 土壌の酸性度を測定する

**acid rain** 名 Ⓤ ▶定義 rain that has chemicals in it from factories, etc and that causes damage to trees, buildings and rivers 工場などから排出された化学物質を含む雨で, 木々, 建物, 河川に損害を引き起こす→**酸性雨**

**acknowledge** /əknálɪdʒ, æk-/ 動 ⾃他 ▶定義 **1** to accept or admit that sth is true or exists ～が真実である, または存在すると受け入れる, あるいは認める→**～を認める, 承認する** ‖ *He acknowledged (the fact) that he had made a mistake.* 彼は自分が間違えたこと（事実）を認めた. *He is acknowledged to be the country's greatest writer.* 彼はその国最高の作家であると認められている. ▶定義 **2** to show that you have seen or noticed sb/sth or received sth ～を見た, または気が付いた, あるいは～を受け取ったことを示す→**～に謝意を表す, ～を受け取ったことを知らせる, 応答する** ‖ *The manager sent a card to all the staff to acknowledge their hard work.* そのマネージャーはスタッフ全員に熱心な仕事振りに感謝するカードを送った.

**acknowledgement** /əknálɪdʒmənt, æk-/ 名 ▶定義 **1** ⓊⒸ the act of showing that you have seen or noticed sb/sth ～を見た, または気が付いたことを示すこと→**承認, 認知, 自認** ‖ *The president gave a smile of acknowledgement to the photographers.* その社長はカメラマンたちに気付いてほほえんだ. ▶定義 **2** ⒸⒸ a letter, etc that says that sth has been received or noticed ～を受け取った, または知らされたことを述べる手紙など→**受取通知書, 領収書, 礼状** ‖ *I haven't received (an) acknowledgement of my job application yet.* 就職の応募書類を受理したという通知がまだ来ていない. ▶定義 **3** Ⓒ a few words of thanks that an author writes at the beginning or end of a book to the people who have helped him/her 作者が本の初めか終わりに書く, 協力してくれた人々に対する感謝の短い言葉→**感謝, お礼, 謝辞**

**acne** /ǽkni/ 名 Ⓤ ▶定義 a skin disease that usually affects young people. When you have acne you get a lot of spots on your face and neck. 通常は若者がかかる皮膚の病気. その皮

皮膚の病気にかかると、顔や首に吹き出物がたくさんできる→にきび

**acorn** /éɪkɔːrn/ 名 C 定義 the small nut that grows on a tree (an oak), and that grows in a base shaped like a cup 木(ナラやカシ)になる小さな木の実。椀(わん)のような形のからの中で生長する→ドングリ

**acoustic** /əkúːstɪk/ 形 定義1 connected with sound or the sense of hearing 音または聴覚に関連している→音の, 音響の, 聴覚の ▶定義2 (of a musical instrument) not electric (楽器で)電気を使っていない→アコースティックの, アンプを用いない ‖ an acoustic guitar アコースティックギター ☛ music のさし絵

**acoustics** /əkúːstɪks/ 名 [複数扱い] 定義 the qualities of a room, etc that make it good or bad for you to hear music, etc in 音楽などの聞こえ方の良し悪しを決める部屋などの特質→音響効果 ‖ The theatre has excellent acoustics. その劇場の音響効果は優れている.

**acquaintance** /əkwéɪntəns/ 名 定義1 C a person that you know but who is not a close friend 見知りではあるが親しい友人ではない人→知人, 知り合い ▶定義2 U acquaintance with sb/sth a slight knowledge of sb/sth 〜に関して少しだけ知っていること→面識, なじみ, 心得

**acquainted** /əkwéɪntɪd/ 形 正式 ▶定義1 acquainted with sth knowing sth 〜を知っている→〜を知っている, 分かっている ‖ I went for a walk to get acquainted with my new neighbourhood. 私は新たな近所の様子を知ろうと散歩に出た. ▶定義2 acquainted (with sb) knowing sb, but usually not very closely 〜を知っているが, 通常はあまり親しくない→〜と知り合いである

**acquiesce** /ækwiés/ 動 自 (文) 定義 acquiesce in/to sth to accept sth without argument, although you may not agree with it 同意できるとは限らないが, 議論をせずに〜を認める→〜に黙って従う, 不本意ながら同意する ― **acquiescence** /ækwiés(ə)ns/ 名 U →黙認, 黙従, 甘受

**acquire** /əkwáɪər/ 動 他 正式 ▶定義 to obtain or buy sth 〜を得る, または購入する→〜を獲得する, 手に入れる, 習得する ‖ She acquired an American accent while living in New York. 彼女はニューヨークに住んでいる間にアメリカ式のアクセントを身に付けた. He's acquired a reputation for being difficult to work with. 彼は一緒に仕事をしづらいという評判を得てしまっている. The company has acquired shares in a rival business. その会社は競合他社の株を手に入れた.

**acquisition** /ækwɪzíʃ(ə)n/ 名 正式 ▶定義1 U the act of obtaining or buying sth 〜を得る, または購入する行為→獲得, 入手, 習得 ‖ a study of language acquisition in children 子供の言語習得に関する研究 ▶定義2 C something that you have obtained or bought 手に入れたり, または購入したもの→獲得物, 取得物, 掘り出し物 ‖ This sculpture is the museum's latest acquisition. この彫刻はその博物館が最近入手したものである.

**acquit** /əkwít/ 動 他 (**acquitting**; **acquitted**) ▶定義1 acquit sb (of sth) to state formally that a person is not guilty of a crime その人が有罪ではないと正式に宣言する→〜を無罪とする, 〜が無罪を宣告する ‖ The jury acquitted her of murder. 陪審員は彼女の殺人容疑について無罪の評決をした. ⇔ **convict** ▶定義2 正式 acquit yourself... to behave in the way that is mentioned 言及されているように行動する→振る舞う ‖ He acquitted himself well in his first match as a professional. 彼はプロとしての最初の試合で立派に振る舞った. ― **acquittal** /əkwít(ə)l/ 名 C U →無罪(放免), 不起訴, 免除

**acre** /éɪkər/ 名 C 定義 a measure of land; 0.405 of a hectare 面積の単位; 0.405 ヘクタールに相当する→エーカー ‖ a farm of 20 acres/a 20-acre farm 20エーカーの農地

**acrobat** /ækrəbæt/ 名 C 定義 a person who performs difficult movements of the body, especially in a show which travels to different towns (a circus) 特に各地を興行して回るショー(サーカス)で, 難しい動きをする人→曲芸師, 軽業師, アクロバット

**acrobatic** /ækrəbætɪk/ 形 ▶定義 performing or involving difficult movements of the body 難しい身体動作をする, またそれに関係している→アクロバットの, 曲芸の, 軽業的な ‖ an acrobatic dancer 身軽なダンサー an acrobatic leap 軽業

的なジャンプ — acrobatically /-k(ə)li/ 副 →ア
クロバットのように,身軽に

**acrobatics** /ˌækrəbǽtɪks/ 名 U ▶定義 (the art of performing) difficult movements of the body (舞台芸術で)難しい身体動作→アクロバット,曲芸,軽業

**acronym** /ǽkrənìm/ 名 C ▶定義 an acronym (for sth) a short word that is made from the first letters of a group of words 語群を構成する各語の頭文字を組み合わせて作った短い単語→頭字語 ‖ *TEFL is an acronym for Teaching English as a Foreign Language.* TEFL は Teaching English as a Foreign Language (外国語としての英語教育)の頭字語である.

★**across** /əkrɔ́(ː)s/ 前 副 ▶定義1 from one side of sth to the other ～の一方から他方へ→(～を)横切って,渡って,横断して ‖ *The stream was too wide to jump across.* その小川は跳び越えるには幅が広すぎた. *He walked across the field.* 彼は野原を横切って歩いた. *A smile spread across his face.* ほほえみが彼の満面に広がった. *The river was about 20 metres across.* その川は幅約20メートルです. *The bank has 800 branches across (= in all parts of) the country.* その銀行は全国に(= すべての地域に)支店が800ある. ▶定義2 on the other side of sth ～の反対側に→～の向こう側に ‖ *There's a bank just across the road.* 道路のちょうど向こう側に銀行がある. *The house across the road from us is for sale.* 道路を挟んで私たちの反対側にある家が売りに出ている.

▶次の例文のようにacrossまたはoverを使って,「反対側に,反対側へ」の意味を表すことができる: *I ran across/over the road.*(私は道路を走って横断した.)ただし,高さのあるものを越える場合は,通常overを使う: *I can't climb over that wall.*(私はあの塀をよじ登って乗り越えることができない.)「部屋」を横切るときは,通常acrossを使う: *I walked across the room to the door.*(私は部屋を横切ってドアの所まで歩いていった.)

成句 **across the board** ▶定義 involving or affecting all groups, members, cases, etc すべての集団,構成員,場合などを含む,またはそれらに影響を及ぼす→全体に及ぶ,全面的に,一律に

**acrylic** /əkrílɪk/ 名 C U ▶定義 an artificial material that is used in making clothes and paint 衣類や絵の具を作るときに使う人工的な原料→アクリルペイント,アクリルの樹脂,アクリルの繊維

★**act**¹ /ækt/ 動 ▶定義1 ⓘ act (on sth) to do sth; to take action ～を行う; 行動する→～に従って行動する,行う,実行する ‖ *The doctor knew he had to act quickly to save the child.* その医者は,子供を救うために迅速に行動しなければならないと分かっていた. *I'm always giving my brother advice but he never acts on (= as a result of) it.* 私はいつも弟に忠告をしているが,彼がその通りに(= 忠告を受け入れて)したためしがない. ▶定義2 ⓘ act as sth to perform a particular function ある特別な機能を実行する→～の役を務める,～の働きをする ‖ *The man we met on the plane to Tokyo was kind enough to act as our guide.* 東京行きの飛行機で出会ったその男性は,親切にも私たちのガイドを務めてくれた. *The elephant's trunk acts as a nose, a hand and an arm.* 象の鼻は,鼻,手,腕としての役割をする. ▶定義3 ⓘ to behave in the way that is mentioned 言及されているように行動する→振る舞う,振りをする ‖ *Stop acting like a child!* 子供みたいなまねはやめなさい. *Although she was trying to act cool, I could see she was really upset.* 彼女は冷静に振る舞おうとしていたが,本当は動転しているのが私には分かった. *He hasn't really hurt himself - he's just acting!* 彼は本当はけがなどしていない — そう見せ掛けているだけだ. *Ali's acting strangely today - what's wrong with him?* 今日のアリの様子は変だね — どこか具合が悪いのだろうか. ▶定義4 ⓘ ⓘ to perform in a play or film 演劇または映画で演じる→～を演じる,上演する ‖ *I acted in a play at school.* 学校で行った劇に出演した.

★**act**² /ækt/ 名 C ▶定義1 a thing that you do 行う事→行動,行い,行為 ‖ *In a typical act of generosity they refused to accept any money.* 彼らは特に気前の良さを示そうとして,一銭の金も受け取ろうとしなかった. *to commit a violent act* 暴力的な行為をする

▶actとactionは同じ意味を表す場合がある: *It was a brave act/action.*(それは勇敢な行為だった.)actの次には次の例文のようにofが続くことがある: *It was an act of bravery.*(そ

**acting**¹

れは勇敢な行為だった.) activityは習慣的に行う事について用いる: *I like outdoor activities such as walking and gardening.* (私は散歩やガーデニングのような屋外の活動が好きだ.)

▶定義2 (しばしば **Act**) one of the main divisions of a play or opera 演劇またはオペラの主要な区分の1つ→**幕** ‖ *How many scenes are there in Act 4?* 第4幕には場面がいくつありますか. ▶定義3 a short piece of entertainment, especially as part of a show 特にショーの一部として行う短い余興→**出し物** ‖ *Did you enjoy the clowns' act?* ピエロの余興は面白かったですか. ▶定義4 (しばしば **Act**) a law made by a government 政府が制定した法→**法律, 条令, 決議** ‖ *The government passed an act forbidding the keeping of guns.* 政府は銃器の所持を禁止する法律を通過させた. ▶定義5 behaviour that hides your true feelings 本心を隠す行動→**見せ掛け, 振り, 芝居** ‖ *She seems very happy but she's just putting on an act.* 彼女はとても幸せそうに見えるが, 単なる見せ掛けにすぎない.

成句 **a hard act to follow** ⇒ **HARD**¹

**be/get in on the act** ▶定義 become involved in an activity that is becoming popular 評判になりつつあることにかかわることになる→**〜に加わる, 分け前にあずかろうと加わる, 一口乗る**

**get your act together** ▶定義 to organize yourself so that you can do sth properly 〜を適切に行えるように自分の状態を整える→**態勢を整える** ‖ *If he doesn't get his act together he's going to lose his job.* きちんとやれる態勢ができていないのなら, 彼は職を失うことになるだろう.

**in the act (of doing sth)** ▶定義 while doing sth, especially sth wrong 特に悪い〜をしている間に→**〜している最中に** ‖ *He was looking through the papers on her desk and she caught him in the act.* 彼女の机の上にある書類を彼が調べているところを, 彼女に見つかった.

**acting**¹ /ˈæktɪŋ/ 形 ▶定義 doing the job mentioned for a short time 言及されている仕事を短期間行っている→**代理の, 臨時の, 代行する** ‖ *James will be the acting director while Henry is away.* ヘンリーがいない間, ジェームズが臨時所長を務めることになっている.

**acting**² /ˈæktɪŋ/ 名 Ⓤ ▶定義 the art or profession of performing in plays or films 演劇や映画で演じる技術, または演じるという職業→**演技, 芝居をやること**

★**action** /ˈækʃ(ə)n/ 名 ▶定義1 Ⓤ doing things, often for a particular purpose 多くの場合, ある目的のために物事を行うこと→**行動, 活動, 実行** ‖ *Now is the time for action.* 今こそ行動する時だ. *If we don't take action quickly it'll be too late!* 迅速に行動しないと間に合いませんよ. ⇔ **inaction** ▶定義2 Ⓒ something that you do 行う物事→**行い, 振る舞い** ‖ *The doctor's quick action saved the child's life.* その医者の素早い措置によって, 子供の命が助かった. *They should be judged by their actions, not by what they say.* 彼らはその発言よりも行動で評価されるべきだ. **参** **act**² の注 ▶定義3 [単数扱い] the most important events in a story or play 物語や劇の中で最も重要な出来事→**筋** ‖ *The action takes place in London during the Second World War.* その話の中心となる出来事は第2次世界大戦中のロンドンで起きる. ▶定義4 Ⓤ exciting things that happen 興奮させるような出来事→**重要な活動, 活発な活動** ‖ *There's not much action in this boring town.* こんな退屈な街ではうまい話があまりない. *I like films with lots of action.* 私はアクションの多い映画が好きです. *an action-packed film* アクション映画 ▶定義5 Ⓤ fighting in a war 戦争で戦うこと→**戦闘, 交戦** ‖ *Their son was killed in action.* 彼らの息子は戦死した. ▶定義6 [単数扱い] the effect that one substance has on another ある物質がほかの物質に及ぼす効果→**作用, 影響, 機能** ‖ *They're studying the action of alcohol on the brain.* 彼らはアルコールが脳に及ぼす影響について研究している. ▶定義7 Ⓒ Ⓤ the process of settling an argument in a court of law 論争を法廷で解決するという措置→**訴訟** ‖ *He is going to take legal action against the hospital.* 彼は病院を相手取って法的手段に訴えようとしている.

成句 **in action** ▶定義 in operation; while working or doing sth 運転中である; 〜を作動または実施している最中である→**活動中で, 作動中で, 交戦中で** ‖ *We shall have a chance to see their new team in action next week.* 私たちは来週, 彼らの新しいチームが活動している様子を見る

機会があるだろう．

**into action** ▶定義 into operation 実施する→〜を実行に移す，活動させる ‖ *We'll put the plan into action immediately.* 私たちはその計画を直ちに実行に移すつもりだ．

**out of action** ▶定義 not able to do the usual things; not working いつもの事ができない；作動していない→活動できない，動かない，故障中の ‖ *The coffee machine's out of action again.* コーヒーの自動販売機がまた故障している．

**activate** /ǽktəvèɪt/ 動他 ▶定義 to make sth start working 〜を作動させる→作動させる，始動させる ‖ *A slight movement can activate the car alarm.* ちょっとした動きでも車の警告音が作動する．

★**active** /ǽktɪv/ 形 ▶定義 **1** involved in activity; lively 活動に参加する；元気の良い→**活動的な，元気な，積極的な** ‖ *My grandfather is very active for his age.* 私の祖父は年齢の割には非常に元気である．*I have a very active social life.* 私は人との付き合いがとても多い生活をしている．*I was at the meeting but I didn't* **take an active part** *in the discussion.* 私はその会合に出席していたが，議論には積極的に参加しなかった．⇔ **inactive** ▶定義 **2** that produces an effect; that is in operation 効果を生み出している；作動中である→**現役の，活動中の，有効な** ‖ *an active volcano* (= one that can still erupt) 活火山 (= まだ噴火する可能性がある) ▶定義 **3** used about the form of a verb or a sentence when the subject of the sentence performs the action of the verb 主語が動詞の表す動作を行う文において，その動詞や文の形態を指して→**能動の，能動態の** ‖ *In the sentence 'The dog bit him', the verb is active.* The dog bit him. という文の動詞は能動態である．

▶次のような言い方もできる: 'The verb is in the active.' (その動詞は能動態です．) passive を参照．

**activist** /ǽktɪvɪst/ 名 C ▶定義 a person who takes action to cause political or social change, usually as a member of a group 政治的または社会的変化を引き起こすために，通常は団体の一員として，行動を取る人→**行動主義者，活動家，行動隊員** ‖ *a protest by environmental activists* 環境問題の活動家による抗議

★**activity** /æktívəti/ 名 ( 複 **activities** )

▶定義 **1** ❶ a situation in which there is a lot of action or movement 動作あるいは動きが多い状況→**活動的なこと，活躍，活力** ‖ *The house was full of activity on the morning of the wedding.* 結婚式の日の朝，その家は活気にあふれていた．⇔ **inactivity** ▶定義 **2** C something that you do, usually regularly and for enjoyment 通常は習慣的に楽しみとして，行う物事→**活動，運動，行事** ‖ *The hotel offers a range of leisure activities.* そのホテルはいろいろなレジャーの催しを提供している．●参 **act²** の注

★**actor** /ǽktər/ 名 C ▶定義 a man or woman whose job is to act in a play, film or on television 演劇，映画，テレビなどで演じることを職業としている男性または女性→**俳優，役者**

**actress** /ǽktrəs/ 名 C ▶定義 a woman whose job is to act in a play, film or on television 演劇，映画，テレビなどで演じることを職業としている女性→**女優**

★**actual** /ǽktʃu(ə)l/ 形 ▶定義 real; that happened 現実の；実際に起きた→**実際の，現実に生じた，事実上の** ‖ *The actual damage to the car was not as great as we had feared.* その車が実際に受けた損傷は，私たちが心配したほど大きくなかった．*They seemed to be good friends but* **in actual fact** *they hated each other.* 彼らは良い友達同士に見えたが，実は互いに憎み合っていた．

★**actually** /ǽktʃu(ə)li/ 副 ▶定義 **1** really; in fact 本当に；実際に→**現実に，本当のところ** ‖ *You don't actually believe her, do you?* あなたは本当のところは彼女のことを信じていないのでしょうね．*I can't believe that I'm actually going to America!* 現実にアメリカへ行くことになるなんて信じられない．▶定義 **2** although it may seem strange 奇異に思えるかもしれないが→**実は，実を言うと，まさかと思うかもしれないが** ‖ *He actually expected me to cook his meal for him!* 実は彼は，私に食事を作ってもらいたいと思っていた．

▶ actually は，次の例文のように，会話の中で他人の注意をひく，または穏やかに訂正するためによく使われる: *Actually, I wanted to show you something. Have you got a minute?* (実はあなたにお見せしたかったものがあるんです．

ちょっとだけお時間よろしいですか．) We aren't married, actually.(実は私たち結婚していないのです．) I don't agree about the book. I think it's rather good, actually.(私はその本については同意していません．でも実のところ，かなりいいと思っています．) 英語では，actuallyに「現在では」の意味はないので，代わりにcurrently, at present, at the momentなどを使う: He's currently working on an article about China.(彼は現在，中国に関する記事に取り組んでいます．) I'm studying for my exams at present.(今，私は試験勉強をしているところです．)

**acupuncture** /ǽk(j)əpʌ̀ŋ(k)tʃər/ 名 U ▶定義 a way of treating an illness or stopping pain by putting thin needles into parts of the body 細い針を体の各部に刺して病気を治療したり痛みを抑えたりする方法→**針療法，針術**

**acute** /əkjúːt/ 形 ▶定義1 very serious; very great 非常に重大な；とても大変な→**深刻な，ひどい，きつい** ‖ *an acute shortage of food* 深刻な食糧不足 *acute pain* 激痛 ▶定義2 (used about an illness) becoming dangerous very quickly (病気について)急速に危険な状態になる→**急性の** ‖ *acute appendicitis* 急性虫垂炎・盲腸 ▶chronic と比較．

▶定義3 (used about feelings or the senses) very strong (知覚や感覚について)とても強い→**鋭い，鋭敏な，すぐに反応する** ‖ *Dogs have an acute sense of smell.* 犬は鋭敏な臭覚を持っている．*acute hearing* 鋭い聴覚 ▶定義4 showing that you are able to understand things easily 物事をすぐに理解できることを示している→**鋭い，鋭敏な** ‖ *The report contains some acute observations on the situation.* その報告書には状況に対する鋭い所見がいくつか含まれている．— **acutely** 副 →**鋭く，鋭敏に，痛切に**

**acute angle** 名 C ▶定義 an angle of less than 90° 90度より小さい角度→**鋭角**

**AD** /èɪ díː, ǽnoʊ dάmənài, -ni/ 略 ▶定義 from the Latin 'anno domini'; used in dates for showing the number of years after the time when Jesus Christ was born ラテン語の anno domini の略；その日付が，イエスキリストが生誕した時より後の年であることを表すために使われる→西暦〜年，紀元〜年 ‖ *AD 44* 紀元44年 ☞参 **BC**

**ad** /ǽd/ 名 略式 = **ADVERTISEMENT** ‖ *I saw your ad in the local paper.* あなたの広告を地方紙で見ました．

**adage** /ǽdɪdʒ/ 名 C ▶定義 a well-known phrase expressing sth that is always true about people or the world 人や世間について常に真実である〜を表した，よく知られた言葉→**ことわざ，格言，金言**

**adamant** /ǽdəmənt, -mænt/ 形 正式 ▶定義 very sure; refusing to change your mind とてもしっかりした；考えを変えようとしない→**断固とした，動じない，絶対に譲ろうとしない** — **adamantly** 副 →**断固として，頑強に**

*★**adapt** /ədǽpt/ 動 ▶定義1 自 他 adapt (yourself) (to sth) to change your behaviour because the situation you are in has changed 置かれた状況が変わったために態度を変更する→**〜に順応する，慣れる，なじむ** ‖ *He was quick to adapt (himself) to the new system.* 彼は新しいシステムに慣れるのが速かった．▶定義2 他 adapt sth (for sth) to change sth so that you can use it in a different situation 〜を変更し，別の状況でも使えるようにする→**〜を改作する，改造する** ‖ *The bus was adapted for disabled people.* そのバスは障害者向けに改良された．*The teacher adapts the coursebook to suit the needs of her students.* その教師は生徒の必要に応じて教科書を書き直している．

**adaptable** /ədǽptəb(ə)l/ 形 ▶定義 able to change to suit new situations 新たな状況に合わせられるように変わることができる→**順応できる，適応できる，融通の利く**

**adaptation** /ædəptéɪʃ(ə)n/ 名 ▶定義1 C a play or film that is based on a novel, etc 小説などを基にして作られた演劇や映画→**翻案物** ▶定義2 U the state or process of changing to suit a new situation 新たな状況に合わせられるように変えること，またはその過程→**適応，順応**

**adapted** /ədǽptəd/ 形 ▶定義 having all the necessary qualities to do sth 〜を行うために必要な資質をすべて持っている→**〜に適している，向いている** ‖ *Chickens are poorly adapted for flight.* 鶏は飛ぶには向いていない．

**adaptor** (または **adapter**) /ədǽptər/ 名 C ▶定義1 a device that allows you to connect more than one piece of electrical equipment to an electricity supply point (socket) 2つ以上の電気器具を電源(ソケット)に接続できるようにする装置→二また・三ツまたプラグ ▶定義2 a device for connecting pieces of electrical equipment that were not designed to be fitted together 相互に接続するように作られていない電気器具を接続するための装置→統合調整装置,アダプター

★**add** /æd/ 動 ▶定義1 📖 🕮 add (sth) (to sth) to put sth together with sth else, so that you increase the size, number, value, etc ~をほかの…と合わせて,その大きさ,数,価値などを増やす→(~を)加える,付け足す,追加する ‖ I added a couple more items to the shopping list. 私は買いリストにもう2,3点追加した. The noise of the crowd added to the excitement of the race. 観客の騒々しい声によって,そのレースの興奮がさらに増した. ▶定義2 📖 🕮 to put numbers or amounts together so that you get a total 数または量を合わせて合計を得る→(~を)足す,加算する ‖ If you **add** 3 and 3 **together**, you get 6. 3足す3は6です. **Add** $8 **to** the total, to cover postage and packing. その合計に8ドルを足すと,郵便料金と小包代を賄える. Ronaldo cost more than all the other players added together. ロナルドにかかる費用はほかの選手全員の費用を合計した額よりも多かった. Don't ask me to work it out - I can't add. 私に合計を出せなどと言わないで - 足し算ができないのだから. ⇔**subtract**
▶2つの数値を足すときに,次の例文のようにplusという語を用いる場合が多い: 2 plus 2 is 4. (2足す2は4です.)

▶定義3 🕮 to say sth more さらに~を言う→~と言い足す,言い添える,付け加えて言う・書く ‖ 'By the way, please don't tell anyone I phoned you,' she added. 「ところで,あなたに電話をしたことはだれにも言わないでください」と彼女は付け加えた.

句動詞 add sth on (to sth) ▶定義 to include sth ~を含める→~を付け足す ‖ 10% will be added on to your bill as a service charge. 請求金額にサービス料として10パーセントが加算される.

add up ▶定義 to seem to be a true explanation 正しい説明であるように見える→つじつまが合う,意味が通じる,筋が通っている ‖ I'm sorry, but your story just doesn't add up. 残念ですが,あなたのお話は筋が通っていませんね.

add (sth) up ▶定義 to find the total of several numbers いくつかの数値の合計を出す→合計する,加算する ‖ The waiter hadn't added up the bill correctly. そのウェーターは勘定を正しく合計できなかった.

add up to sth ▶定義 to have as a total 合計として得る→合計~になる ‖ How much does all the shopping add up to? 買い物の合計はいくらになりますか.

**added** /ˈædəd/ 形 ▶定義 in addition to what is usual; extra 通常の~に加えられた;余分の→付加された,それに加えた,さらなる ‖ milk with added vitamins ビタミンが添加された牛乳

**added to** 前 ▶定義 in addition to sth; as well as ~に加えて;~はもちろん→その上,さらに

**adder** /ˈædər/ 名 C ▶定義 a small poisonous snake 小形の毒蛇→クサリヘビ

**addict** /ˈædɪkt/ 名 C ▶定義 a person who cannot stop taking or doing sth harmful 有害な~を行ったり体に取り入れたりすることをやめられない人→常用者,中毒者,~に染まった人 ‖ a drug addict 麻薬中毒者 — addicted /əˈdɪktɪd/ 形 addicted (to sth)→常用して,~の中毒になって,~にふけって ‖ He is addicted to heroin. 彼はヘロイン中毒. ☛類 hooked on — addiction 名 C U →常用,中毒,熱中 ‖ the problem of teenage drug addiction 10代の麻薬中毒問題

**addictive** /əˈdɪktɪv/ 形 ▶定義 difficult to stop taking or doing 使ったり行ったりすることをやめるのが困難である→中毒性の,習慣となる,癖になってやめられない ‖ a highly addictive drug 中毒性の強い麻薬 an addictive game やめられないゲーム

★**addition** /əˈdɪʃ(ə)n/ 名 ▶定義1 U adding sth, especially two or more numbers ~に,特に2つか3つの数値を足すこと→追加,足し算,加算 ☛参 subtraction ▶定義2 C an addition (to sth) a person or thing that is added to sth ~に追加される人またはもの→追加分,増加分

成句 in addition (to sth) ▶定義 as well as ~も同様に→その上,さらに,~に加えて ‖ She speaks five foreign languages in addition to English. 彼女は英語に加えて5か国語を話せる.

**additional** /ədíʃ(ə)nl/ 形 ▶定義 added; extra 追加された; 余分の → **追加の, 付加的な, 特別に余分な** ‖ *a small additional charge for the use of the swimming pool* プールの利用に対する少額の割り増し料金 — **additionally** /-ʃ(ə)n(ə)li/ 副 → **さらに(加えて), その上**

**additive** /ǽdətɪv/ 名 C ▶定義 a substance that is added to sth in small amounts for a special purpose 特別な目的で〜に少量加える物質 → **添加物, 付加物** ‖ *food additives (= to add colour or flavour)* 食品添加物(= 色や香りを付けるために加える)

\***address**[1] /ədrés, ǽdres/ 名 C ▶定義 1 the number of the building and the name of the street and place where sb lives or works 〜の家や職場がある建物の番地や, 通り, 土地の名前 → **住所, あて先, 所在地** ‖ *Let me give you my home/business address.* 私の自宅・職場の住所をお教えしましょう. *She no longer lives at this address.* 彼女はもうこの住所には住んでいない. *Please inform the office of any change of address.* 住所に変更があれば事務所に知らせてください. *an address book (= a small book that you keep the addresses of people you know in)* 住所録(= 知人の住所を記録する小さいノート) ▶定義 2 a series of words and/or numbers that tells you where you can find sb/sth using a computer コンピューターで〜の居場所を特定するために使われる一連の語や数字 → **アドレス, 番地** ‖ *What's your e-mail address?* あなたの電子メールアドレスは. ▶定義 3 a formal speech that is given to an audience 聴衆に向かって行われる正式なスピーチ → **演説, (正式な)あいさつ(の言葉), 講演**

**address**[2] /ədrés/ 動 他 ▶定義 1 address sth (to sb/sth) to write the name and address of the person you are sending a letter, etc to 手紙などの送り先となる名前と住所を書く → **〜にあて名を書く, 上書きする** ‖ *The parcel was returned because it had been wrongly addressed.* その小包は, あて先が違っていたので送り返された. ▶定義 2 to make an important speech to an audience 重要なスピーチを聴衆に向けて行う → **〜に話し掛ける, 〜で演説する, 講演する** ▶定義 3 正式 address (yourself to) sth to try to deal with a problem, etc 問題などに対処しようとする → **〜に(本気で)取り組む, 〜を検討する** ‖ *The government is finally addressing the question of corruption.* 政府はようやく汚職の問題に取り組みつつある. ▶定義 4 address sb as sth to talk or write to sb using a particular name or title 特定の名前や肩書きで〜に話し掛けたり何かを書いたりする → **〜に(敬称を使って)呼び掛ける** ‖ *She prefers to be addressed as 'Ms'.* 彼女はMsで呼ばれる方が好きだ. ▶定義 5 正式 address sth to sb make a comment, etc to sb 〜に意見などを述べる → **〜を述べる, 言う, 申し入れる** ‖ *Would you kindly address any complaints you have to the manager?* 何か不満があれば, 部長におっしゃってください.

**adept** /ədépt/ 形 ▶定義 adept (at sth) very good or skilful at sth 〜がとても上手な, または巧みな → **熟練した, 精通した** ⇔ **inept**

**adequate** /ǽdɪkwət/ 形 ▶定義 1 enough for what you need 必要なだけある → **十分な, ちょうどの** ‖ *Make sure you take an adequate supply of water with you.* 十分な量の水を必ず持って行くようにしなさい. ▶定義 2 just good enough; acceptable 十分である; 容認できる → **何とか満足できる程度の, まずまずの, 平凡な** ‖ *Your work is adequate but I'm sure you could do better.* 君の仕事はまずまずの出来だが, 君ならもっと良くできるはずだ. ⇔ **inadequate** — **adequacy** /ǽdɪkwəsi/ 名 U → **妥当性, 適切さ, 申し分のなさ** — **adequately** 副 → **適切に, 十分に, まずまず** ‖ *The mystery has never been adequately explained.* そのなぞについては今まできちんと説明されたことがない.

**adhere** /ədhíər, æd-/ 動 自 正式 ▶定義 1 adhere (to sth) to stick firmly to sth 〜にしっかりくっつく → **〜に付着する, 粘着する, 固着する** ‖ *Make sure that the paper adheres firmly to the wall.* その紙が壁にしっかり張り付いているかどうか確かめなさい. ▶定義 2 adhere to sth to continue to support an idea, etc; to follow a rule 特定の考え方などを支持し続ける; 規則に従う → **〜を遵守する, 固守する, 信奉する**

**adherent** /ədhíərənt, æd-/ 名 C ▶定義 somebody who supports a particular idea 特定の考え方を支持する人 → **〜の支持者, 信奉者, 味方** — **adherence** 名 U → **固持, 執着, 信奉**

**adhesive**¹ /ədhíːsɪv, æd-, -zɪv/ 名 C ▶定義 a substance that makes things stick together 物を張り合わせることができる物質 → 接着剤, 粘着性物質 ‖ *a fast-drying adhesive* 速乾性のある接着剤

**adhesive**² /ədhíːsɪv, æd-, -zɪv/ 形 ▶定義 that can stick, or can cause two things to stick together; sticky くっつくことができる, または2つの物を張り合わせることができる; ねばねばする → 粘着性の, 付着する, べとつく ‖ *He sealed the parcel with adhesive tape.* 彼は粘着テープで小包の封をした.

**ad hoc** /ˌæd hák/ 形 ▶定義 made or done suddenly for a particular purpose 特定の目的のために急きょ作られた, または行われた → 特別の, この目的のためだけの, その場限りの ‖ *They set up an ad hoc committee to discuss the matter.* 彼らはその問題を討議するために特別委員会を設立した. *Staff training takes place occasionally* **on an ad hoc basis**. スタッフの訓練は場当たり的に時たま行われている.

**adjacent** /ədʒéɪs(ə)nt/ 形 ▶定義 adjacent (to sth) situated next to or close to sth ～の隣または近くにある → ～に近接した, 隣接した, 近隣の ‖ *There was a fire in the adjacent building.* 近隣の建物で火事があった. *She works in the office adjacent to mine.* 彼女は私の職場の近くにある事務所で働いている.

**adjectival** /ˌædʒɪktáɪv(ə)l/ 形 ▶定義 that contains or is used like an adjective 形容詞を含んでいる, または形容詞のように使われている → 形容詞の, 形容詞的な ‖ *The adjectival form of 'smell' is 'smelly'.* smell の形容詞形は smelly である.

★**adjective** /ˌædʒɪktɪv/ 名 C (文法) ▶定義 a word that tells you more about a noun 名詞のことについてさらに説明する語 → 形容詞 ‖ *The adjective 'reserved' is often applied to British people.* 「控えめな」という形容詞はイギリス人に対してよく用いられる. *What adjective would you use to describe my sister?* 私の姉を形容する言葉にはどのようなものがありますか.

**adjoining** /ə(d)dʒɔ́ɪnɪŋ/ 形 ▶定義 next to or nearest to sth ～の隣または最も近くである → 隣の, 隣り合った ‖ *A scream came from the adjoining room.* 隣の部屋から悲鳴が聞こえてきた.

**adjourn** /ədʒə́ːrn/ 動 自 他 ▶定義 to stop a meeting, a trial, etc for a short time and start it again later 会議, 裁判などを少しの間中止し, 後で再開する → (～を)延期する, 休会する, 中断する ‖ *The meeting adjourned for lunch.* その会合は昼食を取るため, 中断された. *The trial was adjourned until the following week.* その裁判は次週に延期された. — adjournment 名 C → 休会, 休廷, 延期

**adjudicate** /ədʒúːdɪkèɪt/ 動 自 他 (文) ▶定義 to act as an official judge in a competition or to decide who is right when two people or groups disagree about sth 競技会で公式審判を務める, または～について2人あるいは2組が合意しないときにどちらが正しいかを決める → ～に裁定を下す; 宣告する, 審査員を務める

**adjudicator** /ədʒúːdɪkèɪtər/ 名 C ▶定義 a person who acts as a judge, especially in a competition 主にコンクールで審判・審査を務める人 → 審判員, 審査員

★**adjust** /ədʒʌ́st/ 動 ▶定義 **1** 他 to change sth slightly, especially because it is not in the right position 特に～が適切な状態にないため, それを少し変更する → ～を調節する, 整備する ‖ *The brakes on my bicycle need adjusting.* 私の自転車のブレーキは調整が必要だ. *The seat can be adjusted to different positions.* その座席はいろいろな位置に調節できる. ▶定義 **2** 自 adjust (to sth) to get used to new conditions or a new situation 新たな条件や環境に慣れる → ～に順応する, なじむ ‖ *She found it hard to adjust to working at night.* 彼女は夜勤に慣れるのは大変だと分かった. — adjustment 名 C U → 調整, 精算, 適応 ‖ *We'll just* **make** *a few* **minor adjustments** *and the room will look perfect.* ほんの少し手を加えると, その部屋は完ぺきに見えるでしょう.

**adjustable** /ədʒʌ́stəbl/ 形 ▶定義 that can be adjusted 調整することができる → 調整可能な, 調節のできる, 整えられる ‖ *an adjustable mirror* 調節可能な鏡

**ad lib** /ˌæd líb/ 形 副 ▶定義 done or spoken without preparation 事前の準備なしに実行された, または話された → アドリブの, 即興の; アドリブで, 即興で ‖ *She had to speak ad lib because* *she couldn't find her notes.* 彼女はメモが見つからなかったので，アドリブで話さなければならなかった． — **ad lib** 動 自 (**ad libbing; ad libbed**) ➡~をアドリブで言う，即興的に歌う・演奏する・しゃべる ‖ *The singer forgot the words so he had to ad lib.* その歌手は歌詞を忘れたため，即興で歌うしかなかった．

**admin** = ADMINISTRATION

**administer** /ədmínəstər/ 動 他 正式 ▶定義1 to control or manage sth ~を支配する，または管理する ➡~を管理する，運営する，治める，実施する ▶定義2 to give sb sth, especially medicine ~に…を，特に薬を与える ➡~を与える，施す，投与する，実施する

**administration** /ədmìnəstréɪʃ(ə)n/ 名 ▶定義1 (または **admin** /ædmɪn/) ❶the control or the act of managing sth, for example a system, an organization or a business システム，組織，会社など，~の管理，またはそれらを運営すること ➡管理，運営，監督 ‖ *The administration of a large project like this is very complicated.* このような大規模なプロジェクトの管理はとても複雑である．*A lot of the teachers' time is taken up by admin.* 教員の勤務時間の多くは管理業務に取られている．▶定義2 (または **admin** /ædmɪn/) [単数扱い]the group of people or part of a company that organizes or controls sth 会社で~を組織化または管理する人々，またはそのような部門 ➡経営，経営陣 ‖ *the hospital administration* 病院経営 *She works in admin, on the second floor.* 彼女は3階(アメリカでは2階)の管理部門で働いている．▶定義3 (しばしば **the Administration**) ❷the government of a country, especially the US 一国の，特に米国の政府 ➡内閣，政府，政権 ‖ *the Clinton Administration* クリントン政権

**administrative** /ədmínəstrətɪv, -strèɪ-/ 形 ▶定義 connected with the organization of a country, business, etc, and the way in which it is managed 国，企業などの組織やその管理方法に関連する ➡管理(上)の，経営(上)の，行政(上)の ‖ *London is still the most important administrative centre in Britain.* ロンドンは今でもイギリスの行政の中心地として最も重要な場所である．

**administrator** /ədmínəstrèɪtər/ 名 C ▶定義 a person whose job is to organize or manage a system, a business, etc システム，企業などの組織化や管理を仕事とする人 ➡管理者，経営者，行政官

**admirable** /ǽdm(ə)rəb(ə)l/ 形 正式 ▶定義 that you admire; excellent 高く評価している；優れた ➡賞賛に値する，あっぱれな，見事な **admirably** /-əb(ə)li/ 副 ➡見事に，すばらしく ‖ *She dealt with the problem admirably.* 彼女はその問題に見事に対処した．

**admiral** /ǽdm(ə)rəl/ 名 C ▶定義 the most important officer in the navy 海軍で最上位の将校 ➡海軍大将，海軍将官，提督

**admiration** /ædməréɪʃ(ə)n/ 名 U ▶定義 **admiration (for/of sb/sth)** a feeling of liking and respecting sb/sth very much ~が大変気に入り，尊敬する気持ち ➡賞賛，感嘆，感服 ‖ *I have great admiration for what he's done.* 私は彼がやった事に大いに感心している．

*__admire__ /ədmáɪər/ 動 他 ▶定義 **admire sb/sth (for sth/doing sth)** to respect or like sb/sth very much; to look at sb/sth with pleasure ~を大変尊敬する，または気に入る；~を満足して見る ➡~を賞賛する，感嘆する，見とれる ‖ *Everyone admired the way he dealt with the problem.* 彼がその問題に対処した方法についてだれもが感嘆した．*I've always admired her for being such a wonderful mother.* 彼女があれほどすばらしい母親であることに私はいつも感心している．*We stopped at the top of the hill to admire the view.* 私たちは丘の頂上で立ち止まり，そこからの眺めに見とれていた．

**admirer** /ədmáɪərər/ 名 C ▶定義 a person who admires sb/sth ~を賞賛する人 ➡崇拝者賞賛者，ファン ‖ *I've always been a great admirer of her books.* 私はずっと彼女の本の大ファンだ．

**admiring** /ədmáɪərɪŋ/ 形 ▶定義 feeling or expressing admiration 感心している，または賞賛を表している ➡感心した，敬服の念に満ちた，うっとりした — **admiringly** 副 ➡感心して，賞賛して，うっとりして

**admission** /ədmíʃ(ə)n/ 名 ▶定義1 C U **admission (to sth)** the act of allowing sb to enter a school, club, public place, etc ~が学校，クラブ，公共の場所などに入るのを許すこと ➡入れること，入場，入学許可 ‖ *Admissions to British universities have increased by 15% this year.* イ

ギリシャの大学に入学が許可された人数は,今年15パーセント増えた. ☛参 **entrance** ▶定義**2** ❶the amount of money that you have to pay to enter a place ある場所に入るために払わねばならない金→**入場料, 入会金, 入学金** ‖ *The museum charges half-price admission on Mondays.* その博物館の入場料は,月曜日は半額になる. ▶定義**3** ❻ a statement that admits that something is true ある物事が真実であると認める陳述→**承認, 自白, 告白** ‖ *admission office* (AOと略)面談方式入学許可

*★**admit** /ədmít/ 動 (**admitting**; **admitted**) ▶定義**1** ❸❹admit sth; admit to sth/doing sth; admit (that...) to agree that sth unpleasant is true or that you have done sth wrong 不愉快な事が真実であると認める,または悪い事をしたことを認める→**(〜を)認める, 自白する** ‖ *He refused to admit to the theft.* 彼は盗みを働いたことを認めようとしなかった. *You should admit your mistake.* 君は自分の誤りを認めるべきだ. *After trying four times to pass the exam, I finally **admitted defeat**.* その試験の合格を目指して4度挑戦したが,ついに負けを認めた. *I have to admit (that) I was wrong.* 私は自分が間違っていたと認めざるを得ない. *She admitted having broken the computer.* 彼女はそのコンピューターを壊したことを白状した. ⇔ **deny** ▶定義**2** ❹admit sb/sth (into/to sth) to allow sb/sth to enter; to take sb into a place 〜が入るのを許す; 〜をある場所に入れる→**入場を認める, 〜を入れる, 通す** ‖ *He was admitted to hospital with suspected appendicitis.* 彼は盲腸の疑いで入院した.

**admittance** /ədmít(ə)ns/ 名 ❶正式 ▶定義 being allowed to enter a place; the right to enter ある場所に入るのを許されること; 入る権利→**入場, 立ち入り, 入場許可** ‖ *The journalist tried to gain admittance to the minister's office.* そのジャーナリストは大臣室への入室許可を取り付けようとした.

**admittedly** /ədmítɪdli/ 副 ▶定義 it must be admitted (that...) 〜であると認められるべきである→**人々が認める通り, 確かに, 明らかに** ‖ *The work is very interesting. Admittedly, I do get rather tired.* その仕事はとても面白いが,私がかなり疲れているのも事実だ.

**adolescence** /ædəlésns/ /ædə(ə)lésns/ 名 ❶ ▶定義 the period of a person's life between being a child and becoming an adult, between the ages of about 13 and 17 一生涯で子供から大人になる,大体13歳から17歳までの時期→**青年期, 青春期, 思春期** ☛参 **teenager**

**adolescent** /ædəlésnt/ /ædə(ə)lésnt/ 名 ❻ ▶定義 a young person who is no longer a child and not yet an adult, between the ages of about 13 and 17 もう子供でもなく大人にもなりきっていない,13歳から17歳くらいまでの若者→**思春期の少年 少女, 青年期の人, 未熟な若者** ‖ *the problems of adolescents* 青年期の問題 *an adolescent daughter* 思春期の娘

**adopt** /ədɑ́pt/ 動 ▶定義**1** ❸❹ to take a child into your family and treat him/her as your own child by law よその子供を自分の家族に加え,法律上,自身の子供として扱う→**〜を養子にする, 引き取る** ‖ *They couldn't have children so they adopted.* 彼らは子供が生まれなかったので,養子を取った. *They're hoping to adopt a child.* 彼らは養子を取ることを望んでいる. ▶定義**2** ❹to take and use sth 〜を選んで使う→**〜を採用する, 選ぶ** ‖ *What approach did you adopt when dealing with the problem?* その問題に対処する時,どのような方法を採ったのですか. — **adopted** 形→**養子になった, 帰化するために選んだ(国)** ‖ *an adopted child* 養子 — **adoption** 名 ❻❹養子縁組, 採用, 取り入れること ‖ *The number of adoptions has risen in the past year (= the number of children being adopted).* 養子縁組の数はここ1年で増えている (= 養子として引き取られる子供の数).

**adoptive** /ədɑ́ptɪv/ ▶定義 (used about parents) having legally taken a child to live with them as part of their family (親について) よその子供を合法的に引き取り,家族の一員として共に生活している→**養子関係の** ‖ *the baby's adoptive parents* その赤ん坊の養父母

**adorable** /ədɔ́ːrəb(ə)l/ ▶定義 (used about children or animals) very attractive; lovely (子供や動物について) とても引き付ける力のある; 愛らしい→**かわいい, すてきな**

**adore** /ədɔ́ːr/ 動 ❹ ▶定義**1** to love and admire sb/sth very much 〜をとても強く愛し賞賛する→**〜にあこがれる, 〜を敬愛する, 敬慕している**

‖ *Kim adores her older sister.* キムは自分の姉にあこがれている. ▶定義2 to like sth very much 〜を非常に好む→〜が大好きである‖ *She adores children* 彼女は子供が大好きだ. — **adoration** /ædəréiʃ(ə)n/ 名 Ⓤ ▶定義 熱愛, 思慕, 愛慕 — **adoring** 形 →崇拝する, 熱愛する‖ *his adoring fans* 彼に心酔しているファンたち

**adorn** /ədɔ́ːm/ 動 Ⓞ ▶定義 adorn sth (with sth) to add sth in order to make a thing or person more attractive or beautiful ある物や人をより魅力的に,または美しく見せるために〜を加える→〜を飾る, 美しくする

**adrenalin** /ədrén(ə)lən/ 名 Ⓤ ▶定義 a substance that your body produces when you are very angry, frightened or excited and that makes your heart go faster 強い怒り,恐怖,興奮を感じているときに体が分泌し,脈拍を速める物質→アドレナリン

**adrift** /ədríft/ 形 (名詞の前は不可) ▶定義 (used about a boat) not tied to anything or controlled by anyone (舟などについて)何にも結び付けられていない, だれにも操縦されていない→漂って, 漂流して

*★**adult** /ædʌlt, ədʌ́lt/ 名 Ⓒ ▶定義 a person or animal that is fully grown 十分に成長した人間または動物→成人, 大人, 成長した動植物‖ *This film is suitable for both adults and children.* この映画は大人にも子供にも向いている. — **adult** 形 →成人の, 成長した, 成人向きの

**adultery** /ədʌ́lt(ə)ri/ 名 Ⓤ 正式 ▶定義 sex between a married person and sb who is not his/her wife/husband 既婚者とその夫または妻でない人との間の性的関係→浮気, 姦通, 不義, 不倫‖ *to commit adultery* 不義を働く

**adulthood** /ədʌ́lthʊd/ 名 Ⓤ ▶定義 the time in your life when you are an adult 人の一生において成人である時期→成人期

**advance**¹ /ədvɑ́ːns; -vǽns/ 動 ▶定義1 Ⓘ to move forward 前に進む→進む, 前進する, 侵攻する‖ *The army advanced towards the city.* 軍隊はその街へ向かって進撃した. ⇔ **retreat** ▶定義2 Ⓘ Ⓣ to make progress or help sth make progress 進歩する, または〜が進歩するのを助ける→〜を進める, 前進させる, 向上する‖ *Our research has not advanced much recently.* 私たちの研究は最近あまり進んでいない.

**advance**² /ədvɑ́ːns; -vǽns/ 名 ▶定義1 [Ⓒ, 通常は単数]forward movement 前へ進むこと→前進, 進行, 進出‖ *the army's advance towards the border* 国境への進軍 ⇔ **retreat** ▶定義2 Ⓒ Ⓤ progress in sth 〜における前進→進歩, 向上, 発達‖ *advances in computer technology* コンピューター技術の進歩 ▶定義3 Ⓒ an amount of money that is paid to sb before the time when it is usually paid いつも支払われる時期よりも前に〜に支払われる金→前貸し(の金), 前払い(の金), 前金

成句 **in advance (of sth)** ▶定義 before a particular time or event ある時期や事より前に→前もって, あらかじめ予想より早く‖ *You should book tickets for the concert well in advance.* コンサートのチケットは早目に予約した方がいいですよ.

**advance**³ /ədvɑ́ːns; -vǽns/ 形 (名詞の前だけ) ▶定義 that happens before sth 〜に先立って起こる→前もっての, 事前の, あらかじめの‖ *There was no advance warning of the earthquake.* その地震の事前警告は何もなかった.

*★**advanced** /ədvɑ́ːnst; -vǽnst/ 形 ▶定義1 of a high level 高い水準→上級の, 上級者用の, 高等な‖ *an advanced English class* 英語の上級クラス ▶定義2 highly developed 高度に発達している→進んだ, 進歩した‖ *a country that is not very advanced industrially* 産業があまり発展していない国

**Advanced level** = A LEVEL

*★**advantage** /ədvɑ́ːntɪdʒ; -vǽn-/ 名 ▶定義1 Ⓒ an advantage (over sb) something that may help you to do better than other people ほかの人よりも良くできるよう手助けしてくれること→優位, 優越, 有利な立場‖ *Her experience gave her a big advantage over the other people applying for the job.* 彼女には経験があったので, その職に応募する上でほかの人よりも有利だった. *Living abroad means he **has the advantage of** being fluent in two languages.* 海外で生活していることは, 2か国語にたんのうであるという強みを持つことになる. *Some runners try to gain an unfair advantage by taking drugs.* 走者の中には, 薬物を服用するという不正を行って勝とうとする者がいる. ▶定義2 Ⓒ Ⓤ something that helps you or that will bring you a

good result その人の役に立つもの，または良い結果をもたらすようなもの➡**利点,利益,好都合** ‖ *the advantages and disadvantages of a plan* ある計画の長所と短所 *The traffic is so bad here that **there is no advantage in** having a car.* この辺りは交通事情がひどすぎるので，車を持つ利点はない. ⇔ **disadvantage**

**成句 take advantage of sb/sth** ▶定義1 to make good or full use of sth 〜をよく，または十分に利用する➡**〜を活用する,生かす** ‖ *We should take full advantage of these low prices while they last.* これらの価格の低い状況が続いている間に，それを十分に利用した方が良い.

▶定義2 to make unfair use of sb or of sb's kindness, etc in order to get what you want 自分が望むものを手に入れるために，(他)人の親切などを不当に利用する➡**〜につけ込む乗じる,〜を欺く** ‖ *You shouldn't let him take advantage of you like this.* このように彼に付け入らせてはいけない.

**advantageous** /ˌædvənˈteɪdʒəs/ 形 ▶定義 that will help you or bring you a good result その人の役に立つような，または良い結果をもたらすような➡**有利な,都合の良い**

**advent** /ˈædvənt, -vent/ 名[単数扱い] ▶定義1 正式 the fact of sb/sth arriving 〜が現れること➡**到来,出現,登場** ▶定義2 **Advent** (in the Christian year) the four weeks before Christmas (キリスト教の暦年で)クリスマスの前の4週間➡**(キリストの)降臨,降臨節,待降節**

**adventure** /ədˈventʃər/ 名 ⓒ ⓤ ▶定義 an experience or event that is very unusual, exciting or dangerous 非日常的ではらはらするような，または危険を伴った経験や出来事➡**冒険(心),冒険的な行動,予期せぬ出来事** ‖ *She left home to travel, hoping for excitement and adventure.* 彼女は刺激と冒険を求めて旅に出た. *Our journey through the jungle was quite an adventure!* ジャングルを通り抜ける私たちの行程は，まさに冒険そのものだった.

**adventurous** /ədˈventʃərəs, æd-/ 形 ▶定義1 (used about a person) liking to try new things or have adventures (人について)新しい物事を試したり冒険したりすることが好きな➡**冒険好きな,大胆な** ‖ *I'm not an adventurous cook - I like to stick to recipes I know.* 私は冒険的な料理人ではない－慣れたレシピ通りに作るのが

---

**advertise** 27

好きだ. ▶定義2 involving adventure 危険を伴う➡**冒険的な,危険な,勇気の要る** ‖ *For a more adventurous holiday try mountain climbing.* 休日をもっと冒険に満ちたものにするために，登山に挑戦しましょう.

***adverb** /ˈædvɜːrb/ 名 ⓒ ▶定義 a word that adds more information about place, time, manner, cause or degree to a verb, an adjective, a phrase or another adverb 動詞，形容詞，句，ほかの副詞を修飾して，場所，時，方法，原因，程度などの情報を添える言葉➡**副詞** ‖ *In 'speak slowly', 'extremely funny', 'arrive late' and 'I know her well', 'slowly', 'extremely', 'late' and 'well' are adverbs.* speak slowly, extremely funny, arrive late, I know her well では，それぞれ slowly, extremely, late, well が副詞である.

**adversary** /ˈædvərsəri; -ˌseri/ 名 ⓒ (複 **adversaries**) 正式 ▶定義 an enemy, or an opponent in a competition 敵または競争相手➡**敵,敵対者,対抗者**

**adverse** /ædˈvɜːrs, -/ 形 正式 ▶定義 making sth difficult for sb 〜にとって…を困難にさせている➡**〜に反対の,敵意のある,有害な** ‖ *Our flight was cancelled because of adverse weather conditions.* 私たちが乗る便は悪天候のためキャンセルになった. ⇔ **favourable** ☛参 **unfavourable** — adversely 副 ➡**不利に,反対に,ひどく**

**adversity** /ædˈvɜːrsəti, əd-/ 名 ⓒ ⓤ (複 **adversities**) 正式 ▶定義 difficulties or problems 困難または問題➡**逆境,不運,不幸**

***advert** /ˈædvɜːrt, əd-/ 名 英略式 = **ADVERTISEMENT**

***advertise** /ˈædvərtaɪz/ 動 ▶定義1 自 他 to put information in a newspaper, on television, on a picture on the wall, etc in order to persuade people to buy sth, to interest them in a new job, etc 人々に〜を買う気にさせたり，新しい職に関心を持たせたりするために，新聞，テレビ，壁に張るポスターなどに情報を載せる➡**(〜を)広告する,宣伝する,公示する** ‖ *a poster advertising a new type of biscuit* 新しい種類のビスケットを宣伝するポスター *The job was advertised in the local newspapers.* その仕事は地方

紙で広告された. *It's very expensive to advertise on television.* テレビに広告を打つのは非常に金がかかる. ▸定義2 [自]advertise for sb/sth to say publicly in a newspaper, on a sign, etc that you need sb to do a particular job, want to buy sth, etc ある仕事をしてくれる〜や, ある…を購入したいことなどを, 新聞や掲示などで公に知らせる➜**広告を出す** ‖ *The shop is advertising for a part-time sales assistant.* その店はパートの販売アシスタント募集の広告を出している. — advertising [名] [U]➜**広告, 広告すること, 広告業** ‖ *The magazine gets a lot of money from advertising.* その雑誌は広告によって大きく稼いでいる. *an advertising campaign* 広告キャンペーン

***advertisement** /ədvə́ːrtəsmənt; æ̀dvərtáɪz-/ (または [略式] **advert**; **ad**) [名] [C] ▸定義 a piece of information in a newspaper, on television, a picture on a wall, etc that tries to persuade people to buy sth, to interest them in a new job, etc 人々に〜を買う気にさせたり, 新しい職に関心を持たせたりするために,新聞,テレビ,壁に張るポスターなどに載せた情報➜**広告, 宣伝, 告示** ‖ *an advertisement for a new brand of washing powder* 新製品の粉末洗剤の広告 *to put an advertisement in a newspaper* 新聞に広告を掲載する

***advice** /ədváɪs/ [名] [U] ▸定義 an opinion that you give sb about what he/she should do 何をすべきかについて〜に与える意見➜**忠告, 助言, アドバイス** ‖ *She **took** her doctor's **advice** and gave up smoking.* 彼女は医者の忠告に従ってたばこをやめた. *Let me **give** you some **advice**...* ちょっとアドバイスさせてください.

➤ advice は不可算名詞なので, an advice, some advices とは言わず, 次のように言う: *a piece of advice* (一言の忠告) : *a lot of advice* (数多くの助言)

**advisable** /ədváɪzəb(ə)l/ [形][正式] ▸定義 that is a good thing to do; sensible 行うことが良いとされる; 分別のある➜**勧められる, 賢明な, 当を得た** ‖ *It is advisable to reserve a seat.* 座席を予約した方がいい. ⇔ **inadvisable**

***advise** /ədváɪz/ [動] ▸定義1 [自][他] advise (sb) (to do sth); advise (sb) (against sth/against doing sth) to tell sb what you think he/she should do 〜にするべきだと思うことを言う➜**〜を忠告する, 〜するように勧める, 〜しないように戒める** ‖ *I would strongly advise you to take the job.* 私なら君にその仕事を引き受けるように強く勧めるよ. *They advised us not to travel on a Friday.* 彼らは私たちに金曜日には旅行しないよう忠告した. *The newspaper article advised against eating too much meat.* その新聞記事は肉を食べすぎないようにと忠告していた. *He did what the doctor advised.* 彼は医者が助言したことを実行した. *She advises the Government on economic affairs.* 彼女は経済問題に関して政府に助言している. ▸定義2 [他][正式] to officially tell sb sth; to inform sb 〜に…を公式に言う; 〜に知らせる➜**〜を通知する**

**adviser** ([米]**advisor**) /ədváɪzər/ [名] [C] ▸定義 a person who gives advice to a company, government, etc 会社や政府などに助言をする人➜**助言者, 顧問, 相談相手** ‖ *an adviser on economic affairs* 経済問題の顧問

**advisory** /ədváɪz(ə)ri/ [形] ▸定義 giving advice only; not having the power to make decisions 助言だけをする; 決定権を持っていない➜**助言を与える, 忠告の, 顧問の**

**advocate**[1] /ǽdvəkèɪt/ [動][他][正式] ▸定義 to recommend or say that you support a particular plan or action 特定の計画や行動を支持することを勧める, または支持していると言う➜**〜を支持する, 擁護する, 主張する**

**advocate**[2] /ǽdvəkət/ [名] [C] ▸定義1 an advocate (of sth) a person who supports a particular plan or action, especially in public ある計画や行動を, 特に公的に, 支持する人➜**支持者, 擁護者, 主張者** ▸定義2 a lawyer who defends sb in a court of law 法廷で〜を弁護する弁護士➜**弁護士**

**aerial**[1] /éəriəl/ ([米]**antenna**) [名] [C] ▸定義 a long metal stick on a building, car, etc that receives radio or television signals ラジオやテレビの信号を受信する, 建物, 車などに取り付けられている長い金属製の棒➜**アンテナ**

**aerial**[2] /éəriəl/ [形] ▸定義 from or in the air 空からの, または空中での➜**飛行機からの, 空からの** ‖ *an aerial photograph of the town* その街の航空写真

**aerobics** /eəróʊbɪks/ [名] [U] ▸定義 physical exercises that people do to music 音楽に合わせて行う運動→エアロビクス ‖ *I do aerobics* twice a week to keep fit. 私は健康のために週２回エアロビクスをします. ☞ S1 ページのさし絵

**aerodynamics** /èəroʊdaɪnǽmɪks/ 名[Ⓤ, 複数扱い] ▶定義 the scientific study of the way that things move through the air 物体が空中を通過する状態についての科学的な研究→空気力学, 航空力学 — aerodynamic 形→空気力学の, 航空力学の, 空気抵抗の少ない ‖ the aerodynamic design of a racing car レーシングカーの空気力学的設計

*★**aeroplane** /éərəplèɪn/（または **plane**; 米 **airplane**) 名 Ⓒ ▶定義 a vehicle with wings and one or more engines that can fly through the air １つまたは複数のエンジンを備え, 空を飛べる乗り物→飛行機 ‖ the noise of an aeroplane flying overhead 頭上を飛んでいる飛行機の騒音

**aerosol** /éərəsɒ̀l, -sɔ̀(ː)l/ 名 Ⓒ ▶定義 a container in which a liquid substance is kept under pressure. When you press a button the liquid comes out in a fine spray. 圧縮した液体を保つ容器. ボタンを押すと, その液体が細かい霧状で噴き出す→噴霧器 ☞ **spray** のさし絵

**aesthetic** /iːsθétɪk/（米 または **esthetic** /esθétɪk, ɪs-/) 形 ▶定義 concerned with beauty or art 美または芸術に関連している→美の, 美的な, 審美眼のある ‖ *The columns are there for purely aesthetic reasons (= only to look beautiful).* その柱は美的な理由だけで（＝美しく見せるためだけに）そこにある. — aesthetically (米 または esthetically) /-k(ə)li/ 副→美的に, 芸術的に ‖ *The design is **aesthetically pleasing** as well as practical.* そのデザインは実用的にも美的にも優れている.

**afar** /əfɑ́ːr/ 副（文）
成句 from afar ▶定義 from a long distance away 遠く離れた距離から→遠くから, 遠巻きにして

*★**affair** /əféər/ 名 ▶定義 1 Ⓒ an event or situation 出来事または状況→事件, 事柄, 事変 ‖ *The whole affair has been extremely unpleasant.* その事件全体が極めて不愉快なものだった.
▶定義 2 **affairs**[複数扱い] important personal, business, national, etc matters 個人, 企業, 国などにとって重要な問題→業務, 問題 ‖ *the minister for foreign affairs* 外務大臣 *current affairs (= the political and social events that are happening at the present time)* 時事問題（＝現在起こっている政治的, 社会的な出来事) ▶定義 3 [単数扱い] something private that you do not want other people to know about 他人に知られたくない個人的な事→（個人的な）関心事, 問題 ‖ *What happened between us is my affair. I don't want to discuss it.* 私たちの間に起きた事は私の問題だから, それについて議論したくない.
▶定義 4 Ⓒ a sexual relationship between two people, usually when at least one of them is married to sb else ２人の間の性的関係. 通常, 少なくともどちらか一方がほかの～と結婚している→浮気, 情事, 不倫 ‖ *She's **having an affair with** her boss.* 彼女は上司と不倫している.
成句 state of affairs ⇒ **STATE**¹

*★**affect** /əfékt/ 動 ⓥ ▶定義 1 make sb/sth change in a particular way; to influence sb/sth ある特定の形に～を変化させる; ～に影響を及ぼす→～に影響を与える, 作用する, 跳ね返る ‖ *Her personal problems seem to be affecting her work.* 彼女の個人的な問題が仕事に影響を及ぼしているようだ. *This disease affects the brain.* この病気は脳を侵す. ☞参 **influence** の注 ▶定義 2 to make sb feel very sad, angry, etc ～を非常に悲しませたり怒らせたりするどする→～で感動させる, 心を動かす ‖ *The whole community was affected by the terrible tragedy.* その惨劇のため, 地域全体が悲しみに包まれた.
▶次の例文に見られるように, affectは動詞, effectは名詞である: *Smoking can affect your health.*（喫煙は健康に影響を及ぼす可能性がある.) *Smoking can have a bad effect on your health.*（喫煙は健康に悪影響を及ぼす可能性がある.)

**affected** /əféktəd/ 形 ▶定義 (used about a person or his/her behaviour) not natural or sincere （人またはその行動について）自然のまま, あるいは心からのものではない→見せ掛けの, 気取った, わざとらしい ⇔ **unaffected** — affectation /æ̀fektéɪʃ(ə)n/ 名 Ⓒ Ⓤ →振りをすること, 見せ掛け, 気取り

*★**affection** /əfékʃ(ə)n/ 名 Ⓒ Ⓤ ▶定義 (an) affection (for/towards sb/sth) a feeling of loving or liking sb/sth ～を愛する, または好む

気持ち→**愛情, 好意, 愛着** ‖ *Mark felt great affection for his sister.* マークは妹にとても愛着を感じていた.

**affectionate** /əfékʃ(ə)nət/ 形 ▶定義 showing that you love or like sb very much ～をとても愛している, または好きであることを示している→**愛情のこもった, 情愛の深い, 優しい** ‖ *a very affectionate child* 非常に優しい子供 — **affectionately** 副 →**愛情を込めて, 優しく**

**affiliate** /əfílièɪt/ 動他 (通常は受動態で) ▶定義 affiliate sth (to sth) to connect an organization to a larger organization ある組織をより規模の大きい組織に結合させる→**～を提携させる, 合併させる, 会員にする, 配属させる** ‖ *Our local club is affiliated to the national association.* 私たちの地元のクラブは中央の協会の支部になっている. — **affiliated** 形 →**系列の, 合併した, 提携した** — **affiliation** /əfìliéɪʃ(ə)n/ 名 **CU** →**加入, 加盟, 提携**

**affinity** /əfínəti/ 名 **CU** (複 **affinities**) ▶定義1 (an) affinity (for/with sb/sth) a strong feeling that you like and understand sb/sth, usually because you feel similar to him/her/it in some way ～を好み, 理解しているという強い気持ち. 通常, その～に何らかの点で似ていると感じるという理由で→**～への親近感, 好感, 強い好み** ‖ *He had always had an affinity for wild and lonely places.* 彼は荒涼とした寂しい場所にいつも親近感を抱いていた. ▶定義2 (an) affinity (with sb/sth); (an) affinity (between A and B) a similar quality in two or more people or things 複数の人または物事の間にある似よった資質→**類似点, 共通性, 親近性**

**affirm** /əfə́ːm/ 動他 正式 ▶定義 to say formally or clearly that sth is true or that you support sth strongly ～が真実である, または～を強く支持していると, 正式に, あるいははっきりと言う→**～を断言する, 主張する, 肯定する** — **affirmation** /æfəméɪʃ(ə)n/ 名 **CU** →**断言, 主張, 肯定**

**affirmative** /əfə́ːrmətɪv/ 形 正式 ▶定義 meaning 'yes' 同意を意味している→**肯定の, 是認する** ‖ *an affirmative answer* 肯定的な返事

▶次のような言い方もできる: *an answer in the affirmative*(肯定の答え)

⇔ **negative**

**afflict** /əflíkt/ 動他 (通常は受動態で) 正式 ▶定義 afflict sb/sth (with sth) to cause sb/sth to suffer pain, sadness, etc ～を痛い目に遭わせたり悲しませたりする→**～を苦しめる, 悩ませる** ‖ *He had been afflicted with a serious illness since childhood.* 彼は子供のころから重い病気に苦しんでいた. — **affliction** 名 **CU** →**苦悩, 苦痛, 苦しみの種**

**affluent** /æfluənt/ 形 ▶定義 having a lot of money たくさんの金を持っている→**裕福な, 豊かな, 富裕な** ‖ *Hugh comes from a very affluent family.* ヒューはとても裕福な家の出だ. — **affluence** 名 **U** →**富, 裕福, 財** ‖ *Increased exports have brought new affluence.* 輸出の増加によって, ますます豊かになった.

★**afford** /əfɔ́ːrd/ 動他 (通常は can, could, be able to の後で) afford sth/to do sth ▶定義1 to have enough money or time to be able to do sth ～が行えるだけの金や時間がある→**～の余裕がある, ～しても困らない** ‖ *We couldn't afford a television in those days.* 当時はテレビを買う余裕がなかった. *I've spent more money than I can afford.* 私は出せる額以上の金を費やした.
▶定義2 to not be able to do sth or let sth happen because it would have a bad result for you 悪い結果が生じるであろうから～をすることができない, または実現させられない→**～しても差し支えない** ‖ *The other team was very good so we couldn't afford to make any mistakes.* 相手チームの調子がいいので, ミスは1つも許されなかった. — **affordable** 形 →**入手可能な, 手ごろな, 余裕を持って乗り越えられる** ‖ *affordable prices* 手ごろな価格

**affront** /əfrʌ́nt/ 名 **C** ▶定義 an affront (to sb/sth) something that you say or do that is insulting to sb/sth ～を侮辱するような発言または行為→**侮辱, 無礼な言動**

**afield** /əfíːld/ 副
成句 **far afield** ⇒ **FAR**²

**afloat** /əflóʊt/ 形 (名詞の前は不可) ▶定義1 on the surface of the water; not sinking 水面に浮かんで; 沈んでいない→**浮かんで, 漂って** ‖ *A life jacket helps you stay afloat if you fall in the water.* 救命胴衣は, 海に落ちた場合に水面に浮いているのに役立つ. ▶定義2 (used about a business, an economy, etc) having enough money to survive (会社, 組織などについて) 生き残るために必要な資金がある ➔借金しないで, 経営できる, 負債のない

**afoot** /əfút/ 形 (名詞の前は不可) ▶定義 being planned or prepared 計画または準備されている ➔進行中で, 計画中で, 起こって

\***afraid** /əfréɪd/ 形 (名詞の前は不可) ▶定義1 afraid (of sb/sth); afraid (of doing sth/to do sth) having or showing fear; frightened 恐れる気持ちがある, または示している; 怖がっている ➔～を恐れて, 怖がって, ～するのを恐れて ‖ *Are you afraid of dogs?* あなたは犬が怖いですか. *Ben is afraid of going out after dark.* ベンは暗くなってから出掛けるのを怖がる. *I was too afraid to answer the door.* 私はあまりにも恐ろしくて玄関に出られなかった. ▶定義2 afraid (that...); afraid (of doing sth) worried about sth ～について心配している ➔～するのを恐れて, ～ではないかと心配する ‖ *We were afraid that you would be angry.* 私たちはあなたが怒るのではないかと心配した. *to be afraid of offending sb* ～を傷付けるのを恐れる ▶定義3 afraid for sb/sth worried that sb/sth will be harmed, lost, etc ～が傷付けられたり失われたりするのではないかなどと心配している ➔～について心配して ‖ *When I saw the gun I was afraid for my life.* 銃を見た時, 命を落とすのかと心配になった.

▶ afraid, frightened と比較. 次の例文のように, afraid は名詞の後にしか用いることができないが, frightened は名詞の前後どちらにも用いることができる: *a frightened animal* (おびえた動物) *The animal was afraid/frightened.* (その動物はびくびくしていた・おびえていた.)

成句 **I'm afraid (that...)** ▶定義 used for saying politely that you are sorry about sth ～について残念に思っているということを丁寧に言うときに用いられて ➔(残念ながら) ～ではないかと思う, どうやら～のようです, 申し上げにくいのですが ‖ *I'm afraid I can't come on Sunday.* 残念ながら日曜日には伺えません. *'Is the factory going to close?' 'I'm afraid so.'* 「その工場は閉鎖するのですか」「どうやらそのようですよ」 *'Is this seat free?' 'I'm afraid not/it isn't.'* 「この席は空いていますか」「あいにくふさがっています」

**afresh** /əfréʃ/ 副 正式 ▶定義 again, in a new way 再び, 新しい方法で ➔再び, 新たに, 改めて～し直す ‖ *to start afresh* 新たに始まる

**African American** 名 C ▶定義 an American citizen whose family was originally from Africa アメリカの国民で, 一族の祖先がアフリカの出身である人 ➔アフリカ系アメリカ人 — African American 形 ➔アフリカ系アメリカ人の

**Afro-Caribbean** /ǽfroʊ, -rə kærəbíːən, kəríbiən/ 名 C ▶定義 a person whose family came originally from Africa, and who was born or whose parents were born in the Caribbean 一族の祖先がアフリカの出身で, 本人またはその両親がカリブ海で生まれた人 ➔アフリカ系カリブ人 — Afro-Caribbean 形 ➔アフリカ系カリブ人の

\***after** /ɑ́ːftər, ǽf-/ 前 接 副 ▶定義1 later than sth; at a later time ～よりも遅くに; もっと後の時間に ➔～の後, ～してから, ～過ぎに ‖ *Ian phoned just after six o'clock.* イアンは6時を過ぎてすぐに電話した. *the week after next* 再来週 *I hope to arrive some time after lunch.* 昼食後の時間に着くようにしたいと思っています. *They arrived at the station after the train had left.* 彼らは電車が出た後に駅に着いた. *After we had finished our dinner, we went into the garden.* 私たちは夕食が済んでから庭に出た. *I went out yesterday morning, and **after that** I was at home all day.* 私は昨日の朝外出し, その後はずっと家にいた. *That was in April. Soon after, I heard that he was ill.* あれは4月のことだった. その後間もなく彼が病気であると聞いた.

▶次の例文のように, 文末には afterwards を使う方が一般的である: *We played tennis and went to Angela's house afterwards.* (私たちはテニスをして, その後でアンジェラの家に行った.)

▶定義2 ...after... repeated many times or continuing for a long time 何度も繰り返して, または長い間続いて ➔～の次も ‖ **day after day** *of hot weather* 来る日も来る日も続く暑さ *I've told the children time after time not to do that.* 私は子供たちにそれをしないよう何度も繰り返し言った. ▶定義3 following or behind sb/sth ～に続いて, またはその後に ➔～の後から, ～の次に, ～に次いで ‖ *Shut the door after you.* 入ったら・出たらドアを閉めてください. *C comes* after B in the alphabet. アルファベットでCはBの次に来る. ▶定義4 looking for or trying to catch or get sb/sth ～を捜している、または捕まえたりあるいは手に入れたりしようとしている→～を追って、～を捜して、～を求めて ‖ The police were after him. 警察は彼を追っていた. Nicky is after a job in advertising. ニッキーは広告関係の仕事を探している. ▶定義5 because of sth ～の理由で→～だから、～したのだから、～の結果 ‖ After the way he behaved I won't invite him here again. 彼がそのように振る舞ったのだから、私は二度と彼をここに招きません. ▶定義6 used when sb/sth is given the name of another person or thing ～にほかの人のまたは物の名前が与えられたときに用いられて→～に倣って、～風の、～にちなんで ‖ We called our son William after his grandfather. 私たちは息子のことを彼の祖父にちなんでウィリアムと呼んだ. 成句 after all ▶定義1 used when sth is different in reality to what sb expected or thought ～が期待した、または考えていたものと実際には異なっているときに用いられて→結局、やはり ‖ So you decided to come after all! (= I thought you weren't going to come) ああ、やはり来ることにしたのですね(= 私はあなたが来ないだろうと思っていた). ▶定義2 used for reminding sb of a certain fact ～にある事実を思い出させるために用いられて→そうは言っても、何と言っても、だって～だから ‖ She can't understand. After all, she's only two. 彼女には理解できないのです.何と言ってもまだ2歳ですから.

**after-effect** 名 C ▶定義 an unpleasant result of sth that comes some time later しばらくしてから出てくる～の好ましくない結果→余波、後遺症、悪影響

**aftermath** /ɑ́:ftərmæθ; ǽf-/ 名 [単数扱い] ▶定義 a situation that is the result of an important or unpleasant event 重要な、または好ましくない出来事の結果が生んだ状況→余波、結果、落とし子

***afternoon** /ɑ̀:ftəmú:n; ǽf-/ 名 C U ▶定義 the part of a day between midday and about six o'clock 1日のうちで正午から午後6時くらいまでの時間→午後 ‖ I'll see you tomorrow afternoon. 明日の午後にお会いしましょう. What are you doing this afternoon? 今日の午後は何をする予定ですか. I studied all afternoon. 私は午後ずっと勉強した. I usually go for a walk **in the afternoon**. 私はいつも午後に散歩をする. He goes swimming every afternoon. 彼は毎日午後は泳ぎに行く. She arrived at four o'clock in the afternoon. 彼女は午後4時に到着した. Tom works two afternoons a week. トムは週2回午後に働いている. Are you busy **on Friday afternoon**? 金曜日の午後は忙しいですか.

▶特定の日の午後について話しているときは、on Monday afternoon（月曜日の午後に）, on Tuesday afternoon（火曜日の午後に）, on Wednesday afternoon（水曜日の午後に）などという言い方をする. しかし、1日のうちの午後という時間帯に～をするということを一般的に述べる場合は、in the afternoon（午後に）と言う.

成句 good afternoon ▶定義 used when you see sb for the first time in the afternoon ～に午後に初めて会ったときに用いられて→こんにちは ☞ Afternoon とだけ言うことも多い. 'Good afternoon, Mrs Davies.' 'Afternoon, Jack.' 「デーヴィス先生、こんにちは」「こんにちは、ジャック」 **morning** の注を参照.

**aftershave** /ɑ́:ftərʃèɪv; ǽf-/ 名 C U ▶定義 a liquid with a pleasant smell that men put on their faces after shaving 男性がひげをそった後に顔に付ける、良い香りのする液体→アフターシェーブローション

**afterthought** /ɑ́:ftərθɔ̀:t; ǽf-/ 名 [C,通常は単数] ▶定義 something that you think of or add to sth else at a later time 後から考えた、またはほかの～に付け加えるもの→考え直し、後になってからの思い付き、付け足したもの、追想

***afterwards** /ɑ́:ftərwərdz; ǽf-/ (米 または **afterward**) 副 ▶定義 at a later time 後になって→後で、その後、以後 ‖ He was taken to hospital and died shortly afterwards. 彼は病院に運ばれたが、その後間もなく亡くなった. Afterwards, I realized I'd made a terrible mistake. 後になって、私はひどい間違いをしていたことに気付いた.

***again** /əgén, əgéɪn/ 副 ▶定義1 once more; another time もう一度; もう1回→再び、また、さらに ‖ Could you say that again, please? もう一度言ってくださいませんか. She's out at *the moment, so I'll phone again later.* 彼女は今いないので, 私が後からもう一度電話します. *Don't ever do that again!* 二度とそんな事をしてはいけませんよ. ▶定義2 in the place or condition that sb/sth was in before ～が以前にいた場所または状態に➔元の場所へ, 元の状態に, 元のように ‖ *It's great to be home again.* また故郷に戻れたなんて何とすばらしいことだ. *I hope you'll soon be well again.* あなたが早く元通りに元気になることを願っています. ▶定義3 in addition to sth ～に加えて➔その上, さらに加えて, さらにまた ‖ *'Is that enough?' 'No, I'd like half as much again, please.'* (= one-and-a-half times the original amount)「それで足りますか」「いや, あと半分下さい」(= 元の量の1.5倍)

成句 again and again ▶定義 many times 何回も➔何度も何度も, 再三再四 ‖ *He said he was sorry again and again, but she wouldn't listen.* 彼は「すみません」と何度も言ったが, 彼女は耳を貸そうとしなかった.

then/there again ▶定義 used to say that sth you have just said may not happen or be true 言ったばかりの～が起こらない, または真実ではないかもしれないと言う場合に用いられて➔しかしまた, そうではなくて, またその一方で ‖ *She might pass her test, but then again she might not.* 彼女は試験に合格するかもしれないが, そうではなくて合格しないかもしれない.

yet again ⇒ YET

★**against** /əgéɪnst/ 前 ▶定義1 being an opponent to sb/sth in a game, competition, etc, or an enemy of sb/sth in a war or fight 試合, 競争などで～の敵手である, または戦争や戦闘で～の敵である➔～に対する, ～を相手に, ～に対抗して ‖ *We played football against a school from another district.* 私たちはほかの地区の学校を相手にフットボールの試合をした. ▶定義2 not agreeing with or supporting sb/sth ～に同意していない, または支持していない➔～に反対して, ～に逆らって, ～に敵対して ‖ *Are you for or against the plan?* あなたはその計画に賛成ですか反対ですか. *She felt that everybody was against her.* 彼女はだれもが自分に反感を抱いていると思っていた. ⇔ **for** ▶定義3 what a law, rule, etc says you must not do 法, 規則などがしてはいけないと定めていること➔～に反して, ～に背いて, ～に違反して ‖ *It's against the law to buy cigarettes before you are sixteen.* 16歳にならないうちにたばこを買うのは法律違反だ. ▶定義4 to protect yourself from sb/sth ～から自分自身を守る➔～から身を守るために, ～に備えて, ～しないように ‖ *Take these pills as a precaution against malaria.* マラリア予防のためにこの薬を飲みなさい. ▶定義5 in the opposite direction to sth ～と反対の方向に➔～と反対方向へ, ～に逆らって ‖ *We had to cycle against the wind.* 私たちは風に逆らって自転車をこがなければならなかった. ▶定義6 touching sb/sth for support 支えるために～に触れている➔～にもたれて, ～に寄り掛かって ‖ *I put the ladder against the wall.* 私ははしごを壁に立て掛けた.

★**age**¹ /éɪdʒ/ 名 ▶定義1 ⓒ Ⓤ the length of time that sb has lived or that sth has existed ～が生きてきた, または～が存在した時間の長さ➔年齢, 年 ‖ *Ali is seventeen years of age.* アリは17歳です. *She left school at the age of sixteen.* 彼女は16歳で学校を卒業した. *Children of all ages will enjoy this film.* あらゆる年齢の子供たちがこの映画を楽しむだろう. *He needs some friends of his own age.* 彼には同じ年の友達が必要だ.

▶ある人の年齢を尋ねる場合, 普通, 次のように言う: *How old is she?*(彼女は何歳ですか.)これに対する答えは, 例えば: *She's eighteen.*(18歳です.)または: *She's eighteen years old.*(18歳です.)となる. しかし: *She's eighteen years.* とは言わない. 年齢について話すときの表現には, ほかにも次のようなものがある: *I'm nearly nineteen.*(私はもうすぐ19歳になります.) *a girl of eighteen*(18歳の女の子) *an eighteen-year-old girl*(18歳の女の子) *The robber is of medium height and aged about 16 or 17.*(その強盗は中背で, 年齢は16歳か17歳.)

▶定義2 ⓒ Ⓤ a particular period in sb's life ～の一生における特定の期間➔時期, 年ごろ, 世代 ‖ *a problem that often develops in middle age* 中年期に多発する問題 *Her sons will look after her in her old age.* 彼女の息子たちは, 彼女が年を取ったときに世話をするだろう. ▶定義3 Ⓤ

**age²**

the state of being old 年を取っているという状態→**高齢, 老齢** ‖ *a face lined with age* 年を取ってしわの寄った顔 *The doctor said she **died of old age**.* 医者は彼女が高齢のために亡くなったと言った. ●参 **youth** ▶定義4 ◉a particular period of history 歴史上のある特定の時期→**時代, 時期, 世** ‖ *the computer age* コンピューター世代 *the history of art through the ages* 全時代を通じての美術史, 美術通史 ▶定義5 **ages**[複数扱い] 略式 a very long time 非常に長い時間→**長い間, 長時間** ‖ *We had to wait (for) ages at the hospital.* 私たちは病院で長時間待たなければならなかった. *It's ages since I've done any exercise.* 運動するのは本当に久し振りだ.

成句 **the age of consent** ▶定義 the age at which sb can legally agree to have sex 法律上, ~が性的関係を持つことに同意することができる年齢→**承諾年齢**

**come of age** ▶定義 to become an adult in law 法律上, 成年者になる→**成人する, 成年に達する** ‖ *My father gave me a watch when I came of age.* 父は私が成人した時に腕時計をくれた.

**feel your age** ⇒ **FEEL¹**

**under age** ▶定義 not old enough by law to do sth 法律上, ~をする年齢には達していない→**未成年で**

**age²** /éɪdʒ/ 動⊜⊕ (現分 **ageing** または **aging**; 過, 過分 **aged** /éɪdʒd/) ▶定義 to become or look old; to cause sb to look old 年を取る, または年を取って見える; ~を年取ったように見せる→**年を取る, 老ける; ~を老けさせる** ‖ *My father seems to have aged a lot recently.* 私の父は最近めっきり老けたように見える. *I could see her illness had aged her.* 私は彼女が病気のせいで老けたのだと分かった. *an ageing aunt* 年老いたおば

**aged** ▶定義1 /éɪdʒd/ 形 (名詞の前は不可) of the age mentioned 言及された年齢の→**~歳の, ~歳で** ‖ *The woman, aged 26, was last seen at Victoria Station.* 26歳のその女性は, 最後にビクトリア駅で目撃された. ▶定義2 **the aged** /éɪdʒəd/ [複数扱い] very old people 非常に年を取っている人々→**老人, 高齢者**

**age group** 名 ◉ ▶定義 people of about the same age ほぼ同じ年齢の人々→**(ある特定の)年齢集団, 同年齢層** ‖ *This club is very popular with the 20-30 age group.* このクラブは20歳から30歳の人々にとても人気がある.

\***agency** /éɪdʒ(ə)nsi/ 名 ◉ (複 **agencies**) ▶定義1 a business that provides a particular service 特定のサービスを提供する会社→**代理店, 取次店, 特約店** ‖ *an advertising agency* 広告代理店 ▶定義2 米 a government department 政府の一部門→**政府機関, 庁, 局**

**agenda** /ədʒéndə/ 名 ◉ ▶定義 a list of matters that need to be discussed or dealt with 議論または対処が必要とされている問題の一覧表→**協議事項(のリスト), 懸案事項, 議事録** ‖ *The first item **on the agenda** at the meeting will be security.* その会議の最初の議題はセキュリティーについてだろう. *The government have **set an agenda** for reform over the next ten years.* 政府は, 今後10年かけて行う改革についての懸案事項を設定した.

\***agent** /éɪdʒ(ə)nt/ 名 ◉ ▶定義1 a person whose job is to do business for a company or for another person 会社や他人に代わって取り引きすることを仕事とする人→**代理人, 代理店, 特約店** ‖ *Our company's agent in Rio will meet you at the airport.* リオにある私たちの会社の代理人が, あなたと空港でお会いします. *Most actors and musicians have their own agents.* 多くの俳優や音楽家は各自の代理人を抱えている. *a travel agent* 旅行代理店 *an estate agent* 不動産業者 ▶定義2 = **SECRET AGENT**

**aggravate** /ǽɡrəveɪt/ 動⊕ ▶定義1 to make sth worse or more serious ~をもっと悪くする, または一層重大にする→**~を悪化させる, ~をさらに重くする** ▶定義2 略式 to make sb angry or annoyed ~を怒らせる, または悩ませる→**~を怒らせる, いら立たせる, ~に迷惑を掛ける** — **aggravation** /ǽɡrəveɪʃ(ə)n/ 名 ◉◉→**悪化, 激化, 立腹**

**aggregate** /ǽɡrɪɡət, -ɡeɪt/ 名

成句 **on aggregate** ▶定義 in total 合計で→**総計すると, 通算で** ‖ *Our team won 3-1 on aggregate.* 私たちのチームは総計で3対1で勝った.

**aggression** /əɡréʃ(ə)n/ 名 ◉ ▶定義1 angry feelings or behaviour that make you want to attack other people 他人を攻撃したいと思わせるような怒りの気持ち, またはそのような行動→**攻撃性, 敵対心** ‖ *People often react to this* kind of situation with fear or aggression. 人はこの種の状況に対し、怒りや敵対心を抱いて反応することが多い. ▶定義2 the act of starting a fight or war without reasonable cause 筋の通った理由もないのに闘いや戦争を始めること→**攻撃, 侵略**

★**aggressive** /əgrésɪv/ 形 ▶定義1 ready or likely to fight or argue 闘いや議論をいつでもする, あるいは今にもしそうな→**攻撃的な, けんか好きな, 侵略的な** ‖ *an aggressive dog* 攻撃的な犬 *Some people get aggressive after drinking alcohol.* お酒を飲むとけんかっ早くなる人がいる. ▶定義2 using or showing force or pressure in order to succeed 成功するために力や圧力を使ったり示したりしている→**積極的な, 精力的な, 活動的な** ‖ *an aggressive salesman* 押しの強いセールスマン — **aggressively** 副 →攻撃的に, 積極的に ‖ *The boys responded aggressively when I asked them to make less noise.* その少年たちは, 私が少し静かにしてくれるよう頼んだ時に, 攻撃的に言い返してきた.

**aggressor** /əgrésər/ 名 ◉ ▶定義 a person or country that attacks sb/sth or starts fighting first ～を攻撃する, または最初に戦いを始める人や国→**攻撃者(攻撃国), 侵略者(侵略国)**

**aggrieved** /əgríːvd/ 形 正式 ▶定義 upset or angry 腹を立てて, または怒って→**怒った, 憤慨した**

**agile** /ǽdʒaɪl; ǽdʒəl/ 形 ▶定義 able to move quickly and easily すぐに簡単に移動できる→**素早い, 機敏な, 頭の回転の速い** ‖ *Monkeys are extremely agile.* 猿は非常に機敏だ. — **agility** /ədʒíləti/ 名 ◉ →**素早さ, 頭の回転の速さ, 機敏** ‖ *This sport is a test of both physical and mental agility.* このスポーツは心身両面の機敏さを試している.

**agitate** /ǽdʒəteɪt/ 動 ◉ ▶定義 **agitate (for/against sth)** to make other people feel very strongly about sth so that they want to help you achieve it ～を達成するのを助けたいという気持ちになるように, ほかの人々にそれについてかなり強く共鳴させる→**人々を扇動する, 世論をかき立てる, 世論を喚起する** ‖ *to agitate for reform* 改革を求めて世論をかき立てる

**agitated** /ǽdʒəteɪtəd/ 形 ▶定義 worried or excited 心配して, または興奮して→**動揺した, 興奮した** — **agitation** /ædʒətéɪʃ(ə)n/ 名 ◉ →**動**

# agony 35

**揺, 興奮, 扇動**

**AGM** /èɪ dʒi: ém/ 略 特に 英 Annual General Meeting→**年次総会**

**agnostic** /ægnɑ́stɪk/ 名 ◉ ▶定義 a person who is not sure if God exists or not 神が存在しているかどうか確信がない人→**不可知論者**

★**ago** /əgóʊ/ 副 ▶定義 in the past; back in time from now 過去に; 今からさかのぼった時点で→**～前に** ‖ *Patrick left ten minutes ago (= if it is twelve o'clock now, he left at ten to twelve).* パトリックは10分前に出発した(= 現在12時ならば, 彼は11時50分に出発した) *That was a long time ago.* あれは随分前のことだった. *How long ago did this happen?* これはどのくらい前に発生したのですか.

▶ ago は, 過去形と共に用いられ, 現在完了形と共には用いられない: *I arrived in Britain three months ago.* (私は3か月前にイギリスに到着した.) ago, before と比較. ago は「今より前」の意味であり, before は「その時より前」(過去のある特定の時点より前)を意味する: *Anne married Simon two years ago. She left her first husband six months before (= six months before she married Simon).* (アンはサイモンと2年前に結婚した. 彼女は6か月前に最初の夫のもとから去っていた(= 彼女がサイモンと結婚する6か月前に).)

**agonize**(または**-ise**) /ǽgənaɪz/ 動 ◉ ▶定義 to worry or think about sth for a long time ～について長い間悩む, または考える→**～について苦悩する, 思い悩む, ひどく苦しむ** ‖ *to agonize over a difficult decision* 難しい決断について苦悩する

**agonized**(または**-ised**) /ǽgənaɪzd/ 形 ▶定義 showing extreme pain or worry 極度の痛み, または悩みを現している→**苦悩した, 苦しみの** ‖ *an agonized cry* 苦悩に満ちた叫び

**agonizing**(または**-ising**) /ǽgənaɪzɪŋ/ 形 ▶定義 causing extreme worry or pain 極度の悩み, または痛みを引き起こしている→**～を苦しめる, ～に苦痛を与える, 苦悩させる** ‖ *an agonizing choice* つらい決断 *an agonizing headache* 死ぬほどつらい頭痛

**agony** /ǽgəni/ 名 ◉ ◉ (複 **agonies**) ▶定義 great pain or suffering 強い痛み, または苦し

み→苦痛,痛み,苦悶（くもん）‖ to be/scream in agony 苦しみもだえる・苦痛で泣き叫ぶ

**agoraphobia** /ˌæɡ(ə)rəˈfoʊbiə/ 名 Ⓤ ▶定義 fear of being in public places where there are a lot of people 人が大勢集まる公の場所にいるのを怖がること→広場恐怖症 ― **agoraphobic** 形→広場恐怖症の

★**agree** /əˈɡriː/ 動 ▶定義1 ❶ agree (with sb/sth); agree (that...) to have the same opinion as sb/sth ～と…について同じ意見を持っている→賛成する,意見が一致する,同意する ‖ 'I think we should talk to the manager about this.' 'Yes, I agree.'「この事をマネージャーに話すのが良いと思います」「ええ,同感です」I agree with Paul. 私はポールに賛成です. Do you agree that we should travel by train? 私たちが電車で旅行することに賛成ですか. I'm afraid I don't agree. 残念ながら私は同意しません. ⇔ **disagree**

▶ I agree.（同意します）, I don't agree.（同意しません）という言い方はするが, I am agree. や I am not agree. とは言わないことに注意する. 後者は間違った表現である.

▶定義2 ❸ agree (to sth/to do sth) to say yes to sth ～に肯定の返事をする→～に応じる,～を承諾する,～することを認める ‖ I asked my boss if I could go home early and she agreed. 私が上司に早く帰宅してもよいかどうか尋ねたところ,承知してくれた. Alkis has agreed to lend me his car for the weekend. アルキスは週末に私に車を貸すことを承諾してくれた. ⇔ **refuse** ▶定義3 ❸ ❶ agree (to do sth); agree (on sth) to make an arrangement or decide sth with sb ～と取り決めをする,または～を決める→意見が一致して～に決まる,～で話がまとまる ‖ They agreed to meet again the following day. 彼らは翌日もう一度会うことに決めた. Can we agree on a price? 値段の話をつけることができるだろうか. We agreed a price of £500. 私たちは値段について500ポンドで話がまとまった. ▶定義4 ❸ agree with sth to think that sth is right ～が正しいと思う→～に賛成の意を表す ‖ I don't agree with experiments on animals. 私は動物を使った実験に賛成しかねます. ▶定義5 ❸ to be the same as sth ～と同じである→～と符合する,一致する ‖ The two accounts of the accident do not agree. その事故についての2件の報告は一致していない.

成句 **not agree with sb** ▶定義 (used about food) to make sb feel ill (食べ物について)～の具合を悪くさせる

**agreeable** /əˈɡriːəb(ə)l/ 形 ▶定義1 pleasant; nice 気持ちの良い;快い→感じの良い,愛想の良い,愛きょうのある ⇔ **disagreeable** ▶定義2 正式 ready to agree 同意できる→賛成の,同意している,乗り気で ‖ If you are agreeable, we would like to visit your offices on 21 May. あなたが同意してくださるなら,私たちは5月21日にあなたのオフィスに伺いたいと思います. ― **agreeably** /-əb(ə)li/ 副→快く,気持ち良く,楽しく ‖ I was agreeably surprised by the film. 私はその映画が案外良いのに驚いた.

★**agreement** /əˈɡriːmənt/ 名 ▶定義1 ❶ the state of agreeing with sb/sth ～に同意している状態→一致,同意,調和 ‖ She nodded her head in agreement. 彼女は同意してうなずいた. We are totally **in agreement with** what you have said. 私たちはあなたが言った事にすっかり同意している. ⇔ **disagreement** ▶定義2 ❸ a contract or decision that two or more people have made together 複数の人が互いに結んだ契約,または共に決めた決定事項→契約,協定,協約 ‖ Please sign the agreement and return it to us. その契約書に署名して,当方にお返しください. The leaders **reached an agreement** after five days of talks. 指導者たちは5日間の話し合いの後,合意に達した. We never **break an agreement**. 私たちは協定を破ったりしない.

★**agriculture** /ˈæɡrɪkʌltʃər/ 名 Ⓤ ▶定義 keeping animals and growing crops for food; farming 食用に動物を飼ったり農作物を育てたりすること;農耕→農業,農芸,農学 ‖ the Minister of Agriculture 農務大臣 ― **agricultural** /ˌæɡrɪˈkʌltʃ(ə)rəl/ 形→農業の,農業に関する,農学の

**ah** /ɑː/ 間 ▶定義 used for expressing surprise, pleasure, understanding, etc 驚き,喜び,了解などを表すために用いられて→ああ,おや,あっ ‖ Ah, there you are. ああ,そこにいたのですか.

**aha** /ɑːˈhɑː/ 間 ▶定義 used when you suddenly find or understand sth 突然～を見つけた,または～が分かったときに用いられて→ああ,ほう,分か

った ‖ Aha! Now I understand. ああ、やっと分かったよ.

**\*ahead** /əhéd/ 副形 ahead (of sb/sth) ▶定義 1 in front of sb/sth ～の前に[の] ➔ 前方に,行く手に,先に立って ‖ I could see the other car about half a mile ahead of us. 私たちの半マイル先を行くもう1台の車が見えた. The path ahead looked narrow and steep. これから先の道は狭くて険しそうに見えた. Look straight ahead and don't turn round! まっすぐ前を見て、振り返らないようにしなさい. ▶定義 2 before or more advanced than sb/sth ～よりも前に、または先立って ➔ ～より先に,～より勝って,優れて ‖ Inga and Nils arrived a few minutes ahead of us. インガとニルスは私たちよりも数分先に着いた. London is about five hours ahead of New York. ロンドンはニューヨークよりも約5時間進んでいる. The Japanese are **way ahead** of us in their research. 日本はその研究ではこちらよりもはるかに進んでいる. ▶定義 3 into the future 未来に向かって ➔ 先に,前途に,前もって ‖ He's got a difficult time ahead of him. 彼の前途には困難が待ち受けている. We must **think ahead** and make a plan. 私たちは、事前に考えて計画を立てておかなければならない. ▶定義 4 winning in a game, competition, etc ゲーム、試合などで勝っている ➔ 先行して,勝ち越して ‖ The goal **put** Italy 2-1 **ahead** at half-time. そのゴールが決まり、ハーフタイムの時点でイタリアが2対1でリードした. ☛参 behind

成句 ahead of your time ▶定義 so modern that people do not understand you とても新しいため、人々が理解できない ➔ 時代の先端を行っている

streets ahead ⇒ **STREET**

**aid**¹ /éɪd/ 名 ▶定義 1 ❶ help 助け ➔ 助力,援助,救援 ‖ to walk **with the aid of** a stick つえの助けを借りて歩く He had to **go to the aid of** a child in the river. 彼は川へ子供を助けに行かなければならなかった. ☛参 first aid ▶定義 2 ❻ a person or thing that helps you 助けてくれる人または物 ➔ 助力者,援助者,補助器具 ‖ a hearing aid 補聴器 dictionaries and other study aids 辞書やそのほかの学習補助教材 ▶定義 3 ❶ money, food, etc that is sent to a country or to people in order to help them 援助を目的としてある国や人々に送られる金や食糧など ➔ 救援物資 ‖ We sent aid to the earthquake victims. 私たちは地震の被災者に救援物資を送った. economic aid 経済援助

成句 **in aid of sb/sth** ▶定義 in order to collect money for sb/sth, especially for a charity 〜のために、特に慈善事業として、募金することを目的として ➔ ～の助けになるように、〜の助けとして ‖ a concert in aid of Children in Need 困っている子供たちを助けるためのコンサート

**aid**² /éɪd/ 動他 正式 ▶定義 to help sb/sth ～を助ける ➔ ～を援助する,助力する,促進する ‖ Sleep aids recovery from illness. 睡眠は病気からの回復を早める.

成句 **aid and abet** ▶定義 to help sb to do sth that is not allowed by law ～が法で許されていない…を行うのを手伝う ➔ 現場ほう助する,人をそそのかして・扇動して～を犯させる

**aide** /éɪd/ 名 ❻ ▶定義 a person who helps sb important in the government, etc; an assistant 政府などで重要な立場にある～を助ける人; 補佐 ➔ 補佐官,側近

**Aids** (または **AIDS**) /éɪdz/ 名 ❶ ▶定義 an illness which destroys the body's ability to fight infection 体が持っている感染症と闘う力を破壊する病気 ➔ エイズ ‖ He was HIV positive for three years before developing full-blown Aids. 彼は、エイズが発症するまでの3年間は HIV 陽性だった. to contract Aids エイズにかかる the Aids virus エイズウイルス

➤ Aids は Acquired Immune Deficiency Syndrome (後天性免疫不全症候群) の略である.

**ailing** /éɪlɪŋ/ 形 ▶定義 not in good health; weak 良い健康状態ではない; 弱々しい ➔ (長期にわたって)病んでいる,(慢性的に)病的な状態にある,(長い間)苦しんでいる ‖ an ailing economy 慢性的な経済不振

**ailment** /éɪlmənt/ 名 ❻ 正式 ▶定義 any illness that is not very serious あまり重くはない病気 ➔ 病気,持病,不快

**\*aim**¹ /éɪm/ 名 ▶定義 1 ❻ something that you intend to do; a purpose するつもりあるいは成し遂げようとする物事; 目的 ➔ 目的,目標,意図 ‖ Our aim is to open offices in Paris and Rome *before the end of the year.* 目標は年末までにパリとローマに事務所を開設することです. *His only aim in life is to make money.* 彼の人生における唯一の目的は，お金もうけだ. ▶定義2 ❶the act of pointing sth at sb/sth before trying to hit him/her/it with it ～を撃とうとする前に，…を～に向けること→ねらい，的，照準 ‖ *She picked up the gun, took aim and fired.* 彼女は銃を取り上げ，ねらいを定めて撃った. *Jo's aim was good and she hit the target.* ジョーのねらいは良かったので，標的に命中した.

★**aim**² /éɪm/ 動 ▶定義1 ⓐ aim to do sth; aim at/for sth to intend to do or achieve sth ～をするつもりである，または達成しようと思っている→～を目指す，～しようと志す，～の獲得・達成を意図する ‖ *We aim to leave after breakfast.* 私たちは朝食が済んだら出発しようと思っている. *The company is aiming at a 25% increase in profit.* その会社は利益の25パーセント増を目指している. *You should always aim for perfection in your work.* あなたは仕事で常に完全を目指すのがよい. ▶定義2 ⓑ aim sth at sb/sth to direct sth at a particular person or group ～を特定の人または集団に向ける→～に向けて発する，～を向ける ‖ *The advertising campaign is aimed at young people.* その広告キャンペーンは若者向けである. ▶定義3 ⓒ aim (sth) (at sb/sth) to point sth at sb/sth before trying to hit him/her/it with it ～を撃とうとする前に，…を～に向ける→～をねらう，ねらいをつける，～に向ける ‖ *She aimed (the gun) at the target and fired.* 彼女は標的をねらい(銃を)，撃った.

成句 be aimed at sth/doing sth ▶定義 to be intended to achieve sth ～を達成するように向けられている→～するように意図されている ‖ *The new laws are aimed at reducing heavy traffic in cities.* 新しい法律は，都市における激しい交通量を緩和するように意図したものである.

**aimless** /éɪmləs/ 形 ▶定義 having no purpose 目的を持っていない→目的のない，当てのない ‖ *an aimless discussion* 目的のない話し合い — **aimlessly** 副 →目的もなく，当てもなく，漫然と

**ain't** /éɪnt/ 略式 AM NOT, IS NOT, ARE NOT, HAS NOT, HAVE NOT の短縮形

☛ ain't は不適切な英語と見なされている.

★**air**¹ /eər/ 名 ▶定義1 ❶the mixture of gases that surrounds the earth and that people, animals and plants breathe 地球を取り囲んでおり，人間，動物，植物が吸って生きている気体の混合物→空気，大気 ‖ *the pure mountain air* 山の澄んだ空気 *Open a window - I need some fresh air.* 窓を開けてください — 新鮮な空気が吸いたいので. *The air was polluted by smoke from the factory.* 空気は工場の排煙で汚染された. ▶定義2 ❶the space around and above things 事物の周りや上方の空間→空，空中，外気 ‖ *to throw a ball high into the air* ボールを空高く投げ上げる *in the open air* (= outside) 戸外で(= 外で) ▶定義3 ❶travel or transport in an aircraft→航空機での旅行または輸送 ‖ *to travel by air* 飛行機で旅行する *an air ticket* 航空券 ▶定義4 [単数扱い] an air (of sth) the particular feeling or impression that is given by sb/sth ～から受ける特別な感情または印象→外見，雰囲気，様子 ‖ *She has a confident air.* 彼女は自信に満ちた様子だ.

成句 a breath of fresh air ⇒ BREATH
clear the air ⇒ CLEAR³
in the air ▶定義 probably going to happen soon 間もなく起こりそうである→広まって，近々起こりそうである ‖ *A feeling of change was in the air.* 何かが起こりそうな予感があった.
in the open air ⇒ OPEN¹
on (the) air ▶定義 sending out programmes on the radio or television ラジオまたはテレビで番組を放送している→放送中で，放送されて ‖ *This radio station is on the air 24 hours a day.* このラジオ局は1日24時間放送している.
vanish, etc into thin air ⇒ THIN¹

**air**² /eər/ 動 ▶定義1 ⓐ to put clothes, etc in a warm place or outside in the fresh air to make sure they are completely dry; to become dry in this way 衣類などを，完全に乾かすために暖かい場所や戸外の新鮮な空気の中に出す；そのようにして乾く→～を外気に当てる，～を空気に当てて乾かす ‖ *Put the sheets on the washing line to air.* シーツを物干しに掛けて乾かしなさい. ▶定義2 ⓑ to make a room, etc fresh by letting air into it; to become fresh in this way 部屋などに空気を入れてさわやかにする；そのようにしてさわやかになる→換気する ‖ *Open the* window to air the room. 窓を開けて部屋を換気しなさい. ▶定義3 ⓭ to tell people what you think about sth ～について考えている事を人々に知らせる→～を公表する,課題にのせる,見せびらかす ‖ The discussion gave people a chance to air their views. その話し合いは,人々に自分の見解を発表する機会を与えた.

**air bag** 名 C ▶定義 a safety device in a car that fills with air if there is an accident. It protects the people sitting in the front. 事故が起きたときに空気で膨らむ,車内に備えられた安全装置. 前に座っている人を保護する→エアバッグ

**airbase** /éərbèɪs/ 名 C ▶定義 an airport for military aircraft 軍用機のための空港→空軍基地,航空基地,軍港

**airborne** /éərbɔ̀ːm/ 形 ▶定義 flying in the air 空中を飛んでいる→飛行中の,空輸の,空気で運ばれる

**air conditioning** 名 U ▶定義 the system that keeps the air in a room, building, etc cool and dry 部屋,建物などの中の空気を涼しく,湿気のない状態に保つ装置→空気調節装置,冷暖房装置 ― **air-conditioned** 形→空気調整している,エアコン付きの ‖ air-conditioned offices エアコン付きのオフィス

\***aircraft** /éərkrɑ̀ːft, -kræ̀ft/ 名 C (複 **aircraft**) ▶定義 any vehicle that can fly in the air, for example a plane 空中を飛ぶことができる乗り物. 例えば飛行機→航空機

**aircraft carrier** 名 C ▶定義 a ship that carries military aircraft and that has a long flat area where they can take off and land 軍用機を運んだり離着陸できる長く平らな区域を持つ船→航空母艦, 空母

**airfield** /éərfìːld/ 名 C ▶定義 an area of land where aircraft can land or take off. An airfield is smaller than an airport. 航空機が離着陸できる場所. airfield は airport よりも小規模のもの→飛行場,離着陸場

**air force** 名 [C, 単数または複数形の動詞と共に] ▶定義 the part of a country's military organization that fights in the air 一国の軍隊のうち,空中で戦闘する組織→空軍 ☞参 **army, navy**

**air hostess** (または **hostess**) 名 C ▶定義 a woman who looks after the passengers on a plane 飛行機の乗客を世話する女性→スチュワーデス,エアホステス,キャビンアテンダント,客室乗務員 ☞類 **stewardess** ☞参 **air steward**

## airstrip 39

**airing cupboard** 名 C ▶定義 a warm cupboard that you put clothes, etc in to make sure they are completely dry after being washed 衣類などを,洗濯した後に完全に乾かすために入れる暖かい戸棚→(衣類の)乾燥用戸棚

**airless** /éərləs/ 形 ▶定義 not having enough fresh air 新鮮な空気が十分にない→風通しの悪い,空気のよどんだ ‖ The room was hot and airless. その部屋は暑くて空気がよどんでいた.

**airline** /éərlàɪn/ 名 C ▶定義 a company that provides regular flights for people or goods in aircraft 人々や貨物のために,飛行機による定期便を提供している会社→航空会社

**airliner** /éərlàɪnər/ 名 C ▶定義 a large plane that carries passengers 乗客を運ぶ大型の飛行機→(大型の)定期旅客機

**airmail** /éərmèɪl/ 名 U ▶定義 the system for sending letters, packages, etc by plane 飛行機で手紙や小包などを送る制度→航空郵便, エアメール ‖ I sent the parcel (by) airmail. 私はその小包を航空便で送った.

**airplane** /éərplèɪn/ 米 = AEROPLANE

\***airport** /éərpɔ̀ːrt/ 名 C ▶定義 a place where aircraft can land and take off and that has buildings for passengers to wait in 航空機が離着陸し,乗客が待つための建物がある場所→空港,飛行場

**air raid** 名 C ▶定義 an attack by military aircraft 軍用機による攻撃→空襲

**airsick** /éərsìk/ 形 ▶定義 feeling sick or vomiting as a result of travelling on a plane 飛行機で旅行した結果として,気分が悪い,または吐いている→飛行機に酔った ☞参 **carsick, seasick, travel-sick**

**airspace** /éərspèɪs/ 名 U ▶定義 the part of the sky that is above a country and that belongs to that country by law 一国の上空にあり,法律上,その国に属している空の部分→領空

**air steward** 名 C ▶定義 a man who looks after the passengers on a plane 飛行機の乗客の世話をする男性→スチュワード,乗客係,キャビンアテンダント,客室乗務員 ☞参 **air hostess**

**airstrip** /éərstrìp/ (または **landing strip**) 名 C ▶定義 a narrow piece of land where aircraft can take off and land 航空機が離着陸できる細長い土地→滑走路

**airtight** /éərtàɪt/ 形 ▶定義 that air cannot get into or out of 空気が出入りできない→気密の

**air traffic controller** 名 ⓒ ▶定義 a person whose job is to organize routes for aircraft, and to tell pilots by radio when they can land and take off 航空機の航路を管理し,航空機がいつ離着陸してよいかを無線でパイロットに知らせることを仕事としている人→航空交通管制官,空港管制官

**airy** /éəri/ 形 ▶定義 having a lot of fresh air inside 内側にたくさんの新鮮な空気がある→風通しの良い,広々とした

**aisle** /áɪl/ 名 ⓒ ▶定義 a passage between the rows of seats in a church, theatre, etc 教会や劇場などの座席の列の間にある通り道→通路

**ajar** /ədʒɑ́ːr/ 形 (名詞の前は不可) ▶定義 (used about a door) slightly open (戸について) 少し開いている→少し開いて,半開きで

**akin** /əkín/ 形 ▶定義 akin to sth similar to sth ～に似ている→～に似通って,類似して,同種の

**a la carte** /ɑ̀ː lə kɑ́ːrt/ 形 副 ▶定義 (used about a meal in a restaurant) where each dish on the list of available dishes (menu) has a separate price and there is not a fixed price for a complete meal (レストランでの食事について) 注文に応じられる料理の一覧表（メニュー）に載っている1つ1つの料理にそれぞれ値段が付いており,セットされた食事に対する決まった値段がない→アラカルトで,（定食でなく）献立表による,好みの料理を選んで

★**alarm**¹ /əlɑ́ːm/ 名 ▶定義 1 ❶a sudden feeling of fear or worry 突然起きる恐れや不安の気持ち→恐怖,不安,驚き ‖ *She jumped up in alarm.* 彼女は驚いて跳び上がった. ▶定義 2 [単数扱い] a warning of danger 危険の警告→警報 ‖ *A small boy saw the smoke and raised the alarm.* 小さな男の子が煙を見て,急を知らせた. ▶定義 3 ⓒa machine that warns you of danger, for example by ringing a loud bell 例えば大きな音のベルが鳴るなど,危険を警告する装置→警報器,自動警報装置 ‖ *The burglars set off the alarm when they broke the window.* 泥棒は,窓を割った時に警報装置を鳴らしてしまった. *The fire/burglar alarm went off in the middle of the night.* 火災感知機・盗難報知機が夜中に鳴り出した. ▶定義 4 ⓒ = ALARM CLOCK 成句 a false alarm ⇒ FALSE

**alarm**² /əlɑ́ːm/ 動 他 ▶定義 to make sb/sth feel suddenly frightened or worried ～を突然怖がらせる,または不安にさせる→～を怖がらせる,はっとさせる,不安がらせる

**alarm clock** (または **alarm**) 名 ⓒ ▶定義 a clock that you can set to make a noise at a particular time to wake you up 特定の時間にベルを鳴らして起こすようにセットできる時計→目覚まし時計 ‖ *She set the alarm clock for half past six.* 彼女は目覚まし時計を6時半にセットした. ☛ clock のさし絵

**alarmed** /əlɑ́ːrmd/ 形 ▶定義 alarmed (at/by sth) feeling frightened or worried 怖がっている,または心配させられている→驚いて,心配して

**alarming** /əlɑ́ːrmɪŋ/ 形 ▶定義 that makes you frightened or worried 怖がらせる,または心配させる→恐るべき,驚くほどの,～を不安にさせる — **alarmingly** 副 →驚くほど,不安にさせるほど

**alas** /əlɑ́ːs, əlǽs/ 間 正式 ▶定義 used for expressing sadness about sth ～について悲しみを表現するために用いられて→ああ悲しいことに,哀れにも,ああ悲しや

**albeit** /ɔːlbíːət, æl-/ 接 正式 ▶定義 although ～だけれども→～とはいえ,～ではあるが,～にもかかわらず,～であろうとも ‖ *He finally agreed to come, albeit unwillingly.* 彼はとうとう来ることに同意した. 嫌々ながらではあったが.

**albino** /ælbíːnoʊ, -báɪ-/ 名 ⓒ (複 **albinos**) ▶定義 a person or animal with very white skin, white hair and pink eyes 真っ白な皮膚,白い毛,ピンク色の目を持った人または動物→アルビノ,白子

**album** /ǽlbəm/ 名 ⓒ ▶定義 1 a collection of songs on one CD, cassette, etc 曲集を1枚のCD,カセットなどに収録したもの→アルバム,全集,曲集 ‖ *The band are about to release their third album.* そのバンドは3枚目のアルバムを発表しようとしている. ☛ 参 single ▶定義 2 a book in which you can keep stamps, photographs, etc that you have collected 収集した切手,写真などを保管できる帳面→アルバム

★**alcohol** /ǽlkəhɔ(ː)l, -hɑl/ 名 ⓤ ▶定義 1 the colourless liquid in drinks such as beer and wine that can make you drunk ビールやワインなどの酒類に含まれる,酔わせることのできる無色の液体→**アルコール,酒精** ▶定義**2** drinks such as beer, whisky, wine, etc that contain alcohol ビール,ウイスキー,ワインなどのように,アルコール分を含む飲み物→**アルコール飲料,酒**

**alcoholic**¹ /ælkəhɔ́(:)lɪk, -hál-/ 形 ▶定義 containing alcohol アルコール分を含んでいる→**アルコールを含んだ,アルコール性の** ‖ *alcoholic drinks* アルコール飲料 ⇔ **non-alcoholic**
▶アルコールを含まない飲み物は soft drink (清涼飲料,ソフトドリンク)とも呼ばれる.

**alcoholic**² /ælkəhɔ́(:)lɪk, -hál-/ 名 C ▶定義 a person who cannot stop drinking large amounts of alcohol アルコール飲料を大量に飲むのをやめられない人→**アルコール依存症患者,アルコール中毒患者**
▶アルコール飲料を全く飲まない人は teetotaller と呼ばれる.

**alcoholism** /ǽlkəhɔ(:)lɪz(ə)m/ 名 U ▶定義 a medical condition that is caused by regularly drinking a large amount of alcohol and not being able to stop 大量のアルコール飲料を習慣的に飲み,それをやめることができないために起きる,病的状態→**アルコール中毒,アルコール依存症**

**alcove** /ǽlkoʊv/ 名 C ▶定義 a small area in a room where one part of the wall is further back than the rest of the wall 部屋の壁の一部がほかよりも引っ込んでいる小さな空間→**床の間,アルコーブ,小部屋**

**ale** /éɪl/ 名 U C ▶定義 a type of beer ビールの一種→**エール**

**alert**¹ /ələ́ːrt/ 形 ▶定義 alert (to sth) watching, listening, etc for sth with all your attention 全神経を傾けて〜を見たり聞いたりしている→**〜に油断のない,用心深い,敏感な** ‖ *Security guards must be alert at all times.* 警備員はいつでも油断なく警戒していなければならない. *to be alert to possible changes* 起こりそうな変化に対して用心深い

**alert**² /ələ́ːrt/ 名 C ▶定義 a warning of possible danger あり得る危険の警告→**警戒警報** ‖ *a bomb alert* 空襲警報

成句 **on the alert (for sth)** ▶定義 ready or prepared for danger or an attack 危険や攻撃に対して用意または準備ができている→**〜を油断なく見張って,〜に対して油断なく警戒・待機して**

**alert**³ /ələ́ːrt/ 動 他 ▶定義 alert sb (to sth) to warn sb of danger or a problem 〜に危険や問題を警告する→**〜に注意を喚起する,〜に警報を出す**

**A level**(または 正式 **Advanced level**) 名 C ▶定義 an exam that schoolchildren in England, Wales and Northern Ireland take when they are about eighteen. You usually take A levels in two or three subjects and you need good results (grades) if you want to go to university. イングランド,ウェールズ,北アイルランドの生徒が 18 歳ころに受ける試験.大学へ進みたければ,通常,A レベルの試験を2,3科目受け,良い成績(点数)を取る必要がある→**A レベルの試験** ‖ *How many A levels have you got?* A レベルの試験を何科目取りましたか. *I'm doing my A levels this summer.* 私は今年の夏に A レベルの試験を受けるつもりです.
▶GCSE と比較.

**algae** /ǽldʒi/ 名[複数扱い,単数または複数形の動詞と共に] ▶定義 very simple plants that grow mainly in water 主に水中で育つ,非常に単純な植物→**藻(も),藻(そう)類**

**algebra** /ǽldʒəbrə/ 名 U ▶定義 a type of mathematics in which letters and symbols are used to represent numbers 数を表すために文字と記号が使われる数学の一分野→**代数(学)**

**alias**¹ /éɪliəs, -ljəs/ 名 C ▶定義 a false name, for example one that is used by a criminal 偽りの名前.例えば,犯人によって使われるもの→**偽名,別名** ‖ *Castorri is known to the police under several aliases.* カストーリはいくつかの偽名で警察に知られている.

**alias**² /éɪliəs, -ljəs/ 副 ▶定義 used for giving sb's false name 〜の別名を名乗るために用いられて→**別名で,またの名を** ‖ *Norma Jean Baker, alias Marilyn Monroe* ノーマ ジーン ベイカー,またの名をマリリン モンロー

**alibi** /ǽləbàɪ/ 名 C (複 **alibis**) ▶定義 an alibi (for sth) a statement by sb that says you were in a different place at the time of a crime and so cannot be guilty of the crime 犯罪が起きた時にほかの場所にいたため,その罪を犯すこと

はあり得ないという、第三者の陳述→**アリバイ、現場不在証明** ‖ *He had a good alibi for the night of the robbery.* 彼には、強盗事件があった夜の絶対的なアリバイがあった.

**alien**[1] /éɪliən, -ljən/ 名 C ▶定義1 a creature that comes from another planet ほかの惑星から来た生き物→**異星人、宇宙人、エイリアン** ▶定義2 [正式] a person who comes from another country ほかの国から来た人→**外国人、居留外国人**

**alien**[2] /éɪliən, -ljən/ 形 ▶定義1 of another country; foreign ほかの国の; 外国の→**よその、外国の** ‖ *an alien land* 異国の地 ▶定義2 alien (to sb) very strange and completely different from your normal experience とても奇妙で、普通に経験する事とは全く異なる→**～になじまない、～と相いれない、対立した**

**alienate** /éɪliənèɪt, -ljən-/ 動他 ▶定義1 to make people feel that they cannot share your opinions any more これ以上、自分と意見を合わせることができないと人々に感じさせる→**～を遠ざける、離反させる** ‖ *The Prime Minister's new policies on defence have alienated many of his supporters.* 防衛に関する首相の新しい政策は、支持者を離反させた. ▶定義2 alienate sb (from sb/sth) to make sb feel that he/she does not belong somewhere or is not part of sth ～に、どこにも属していない、または～の一部ではないと感じさせる→**～から疎遠にする、疎外する** — alienation /èɪliənéɪʃ(ə)n, -ljən-/ 名 U→**疎んじること、疎遠、疎外(感)**

**alight**[1] /əláɪt/ 形 ▶定義 on fire; burning 燃えている; 焼けている→**燃えて、火がともって** ‖ *A cigarette set the petrol alight.* たばこからガソリンに火がついた.

▶次の例文のように、alight は名詞の後でのみ用いられるが、burning は名詞の前で使うことができる: *The whole building was alight.* (その建物全体が燃えていた.) *a burning building* (燃えている建物)

**alight**[2] /əláɪt/ 動自 (文) ▶定義 alight (from sth) to get off a bus, train, etc バス、電車などを降りる→**～から降りる、下車する**

**align** /əláɪn/ 動他 ▶定義1 align sth (with sth) to arrange things in a straight line or so that they are parallel to sth else 物を直線上に整列させる、またはそれらがほかの～と平行になるようにする→**～を一列に並べる、一直線に並べる、整列させる** ‖ *to align the wheels of a car* 自動車の車輪の方向をそろえさせる ▶定義2 align yourself with sb to say that you support the opinions of a particular group, country, etc 特定の集団、国などの意見を支持していると言う→**～と協調する、連帯する、提携する**

**alignment** /əláɪnmənt/ 名 ▶定義1 ❶arrangement in a straight line or parallel to sth else 直線上に、またはほかの～と平行になるように整列させること→**整列、一列に並んでいること、一直線にすること** ▶定義2 C U an agreement between political parties, countries, etc to support the same thing 同じ事を支持するために政党、国などの間で交わされる合意→**同盟、提携、連合**

**alike** /əláɪk/ 形副 (名詞の前に不可) ▶定義1 very similar 非常に類似した→**似ている、同様な、一様で** ‖ *The two children are very alike.* その2人の子供はとてもよく似ている. ▶定義2 in the same way 同じ方法で→**同様に、同等に** ‖ *We try to treat women and men alike in this company.* この会社では、女性も男性も同等に扱おうとしています. *The book is popular with adults and children alike.* その本は、大人にも子供にも同じように人気がある.

**alimony** /ǽləmə̀ni, -mòʊni/ 名 U ▶定義 money that you have to pay by law to your former wife or husband after getting divorced 法律によって、離婚した後に前妻または前夫に支払わなければならない金→**別居手当、離婚手当、アリモニー**

★**alive** /əláɪv/ 形 ▶定義1 not dead; living 死んでいない; 生きている→**生きている、息をしている** ‖ *The young woman was still alive when the ambulance reached the hospital.* その若い女性は、救急車が病院に着いた時、まだ生きていた. *The quick action of the doctors kept the child alive.* その医者たちの迅速な行動が、その子を死なせずに済んだ.

▶次の例文のように、alive は名詞の後でのみ用いられるが、living は名詞の前で使うことができる: *Are her parents still alive?* (彼女の両親は今もご健在ですか.) *Does she have any living relatives?* (彼女にはご健在の親戚(しんせき)がだれかいますか.)

▶定義2 continuing to exist 存在し続けている→**存続して, 有効で, 弱まることなく保たれて** ‖ *Many old traditions are very much alive in this area of the country.* その国のこの地域では, 多くの古い伝統が残っている. ▶定義3 full of life 生気に満ちている→**生き生きとした, 活発な, 元気な** ‖ *In the evening the town really **comes alive**.* 夕方になると, その街は本当に活気に満ちてくる.

**alkali** /ǽlkəlài/ 名 ⓒⓊ ▶定義 a chemical substance that can burn skin when it is dissolved in water. An alkali has a pH value of more than 7. 水に溶けると皮膚をやけどさせる化学物質. 7 より大きい pH 値を持つ→**アルカリ**
☛参 **acid, base** — alkaline 形→**アルカリ性の, アルカリを含んだ**

★**all**¹ /ɔːl/ 形代 ▶定義1 the whole of a thing or of a period of time ある物事の全部, またはある期間の全体→**全体, 全部, すべて** ‖ *All (of) the food has gone.* すべての食べ物がなくなった. *They've eaten all of it.* 彼らはそれを全部食べてしまった. *They've eaten it all.* 彼らはそれを全部食べてしまった. *This money is all yours.* この金はすべて君のものだ. *All of it is yours.* そのすべては君のものだ. *all week/month/year* 一週間中・一か月中・一年中 *He worked hard all his life.* 彼は一生, 熱心に働き続けた. ▶定義2 every one of a group ある集団に属する1人1人または個々のもの→**〜の全員, 全部** ‖ *All (of) my children can swim.* 私の子供たちは全員泳ぐことができる. *My children can all swim.* 私の子供たちは全員泳ぐことができる. *She's read all (of) these books.* 彼女はこれらの本をすべて読了した. *She's read them all.* 彼女はそれらをすべて読了した. *The people at the meeting all voted against the plan.* その会合に出ていた人々は全員, その計画に反対票を投じた. *All of them voted against the plan.* 彼ら全員がその計画に反対票を投じた. ▶定義3 everything that; the only thing that 〜のすべての物事; 〜の唯一の物事→**すべて, 一切, 万事** ‖ *I wrote down all I could remember.* 私は思い出せるすべての事を書き留めた. *All I've eaten today is one banana.* 今日私が食べた物は, バナナ1本だけだ.

成句 above all ⇒ **ABOVE**
after all ⇒ **AFTER**

all² 43

for all ▶定義1 in spite of 〜にもかかわらず→**〜にもかかわらず, 〜ではあるけれども** ‖ *For all her wealth and beauty, she was never very happy.* 彼女は, その富と美しさにもかかわらず, あまり幸せではなかった. ▶定義2 used to show that sth is not important or of no interest or value to you 〜が重要でない, 興味をひかない, 価値がないことを示すために用いられて→**〜に関する限り, ほとんど〜がないから** ‖ *For all I know, he's probably remarried by now.* 私の知る限り, おそらく彼は今ごろはもう再婚しているだろう.

in all ▶定義 in total 合計で→**全部で, 全体で** ‖ *There were ten of us in all.* 私たちは全員で10人だった.

not all that... ▶定義 not very あまり〜でない→**それほど, そんなに** ‖ *The film wasn't all that good.* その映画はそれほど良くなかった.

(not) at all ▶定義 in any way いかなる点でも→**少しも(〜でない), 全然(〜でない)** ‖ *I didn't enjoy it at all.* 私はそれが少しも楽しめなかった.
▶ある物事に対して人から感謝されたとき, それに対する返事として not at all (どういたしまして) と言う.

★**all**² /ɔːl/ 副 ▶定義1 completely; very 完全に; 非常に→**全く, すっかり, ひどく** ‖ *He has lived all alone since his wife died.* 彼は, 妻が亡くなってから独りぼっちで生活している. *I didn't watch that programme - I forgot all about it.* 私はその番組を見なかった — それについてはすっかり忘れていたので. *They got all excited about it.* 彼らはその事ですっかり興奮した. ▶定義2 (in sport) for each side (スポーツで) どちらの側にとっても→**双方とも, 両方とも** ‖ *The score was two all.* 得点は両方とも2点だった.

成句 all along ▶定義 from the beginning 初めから→**ずっと, いつも** ‖ *I knew you were joking all along.* 私は, 君がずっと冗談を言っているのを知っていた.

all the better, harder, etc ▶定義 even better, harder, etc than before 以前よりも一層良い, 大変だ, など→**(かえって) 余計に, ますます** ‖ *It will be all the more difficult with two people missing.* それは, 2人足りなければ, ますます難しくなるだろう.

**Allah** /ǽlə, ɑːláː/ ▶定義 the Muslim name for God　イスラム教の神の名前　→アラー

**allay** /əléɪ/ 動他 正式 ▶定義 to make sth less strong　～を少し弱める　→～を鎮める, 軽減する, 和らげる

**the all-clear** 名 [単数扱い] ▶定義 a signal telling you that a situation is no longer dangerous　状況がもう危険ではないことを知らせる信号　→警報解除の合図・信号

**allege** /əlédʒ/ 動他 正式 ▶定義 to say that sb has done sth wrong, but without having any proof that this is true　～が何か悪い事をしたが, それに間違いないという証拠が何もないと言う　→（証拠なしに）～を主張する, 断言する ‖ *The woman alleged that Williams had attacked her with a knife.* その女性は, ウィリアムズがナイフで彼女を襲ったと主張した. — **allegation** /æligéɪʃ(ə)n/ 名 C →（証拠のない）主張, 申し立て ‖ *to make allegations of police corruption* 警察の汚職について申し立てをする — **alleged** /əlédʒd/ 形 (名詞の前だけ) →申し立てられた, 疑いをかけられた, 断定された — **allegedly** /əlédʒədli/ 副 →申し立てによると, 伝えられるところでは ‖ *The man was allegedly shot while trying to escape.* 伝えられるところによると, その男は逃げようとする間に撃たれた.

**allegiance** /əlíːdʒəns/ 名 U 正式 ▶定義 support for a leader, government, belief, etc; loyalty　指導者, 政府, 信念などに対する支持; 忠義　→忠誠, 忠節, 忠実 ‖ *Many people switched allegiance and voted against the government.* 多くの人が忠誠をひるがえして, 政府に反対する票を投じた.

**allergic** /əlɚːrdʒɪk/ 形 ▶定義 **1** allergic (to sth) having an allergy　アレルギーを持っている　→アレルギー体質で ‖ *I can't drink cow's milk. I'm allergic to it.* 私は牛乳が飲めません, それに対してアレルギーがあるのです. ▶定義 **2** caused by an allergy　アレルギーによって引き起こされる　→アレルギーによる, アレルギーの ‖ *an allergic reaction to house dust* 家庭内のほこりに対するアレルギー反応

**allergy** /ǽlɚdʒi/ 名 C (複 **allergies**) ▶定義 an allergy (to sth) a medical condition that makes you ill when you eat, touch or breathe sth that does not normally make other people ill　普通にはほかの人々には具合が悪くなることがない～でも, ある人にはそれを食べたり触れたり吸ったりすると具合を悪くさせる, 病的状態　→アレルギー ‖ *an allergy to cats/shellfish/pollen* 猫・貝・花粉に対するアレルギー

**alleviate** /əlíːvièɪt/ 動他 ▶定義 to make sth less strong or bad　～を少し弱める, または良くする　→～を和らげる, 緩和する, 軽減する ‖ *The doctor gave me an injection to alleviate the pain.* その医者は, 痛みを和らげるために注射をしてくれた. — **alleviation** /əlìːvieɪʃ(ə)n/ 名 U →緩和, 軽減

**alley** /ǽli/ (または **alleyway** /ǽliwèɪ/) 名 C ▶定義 a narrow passage between buildings　建物の間にある狭い道　→狭い裏道, 路地

**alliance** /əláɪəns/ 名 C ▶定義 an agreement between groups, countries, etc to work together and support each other　集団, 国などの間で結ばれた, 協同して相互に支援する協定　→同盟, 提携, 協定 ‖ *The two parties formed an alliance.* 2つの党派が同盟を結んだ. ☜参 **ally**

**allied** 形 ▶定義 **1** /ǽlaɪd/ (used about organizations, countries, etc) having an agreement to work together and support each other　（組織, 国などについて）協同して相互に支援する協定を結んでいる　→同盟した　▶定義 **2** /əláɪd/ allied (to sth) connected with; existing together with　～と結び付いている; ～と共に存在している　→連合した, 提携した, 関係した ‖ *The newspaper is closely allied to the government.* その新聞は政府と密接に関係している.

**alligator** /ǽləgèɪtɚr/ 名 C ▶定義 a large reptile with a long tail and a big mouth with sharp teeth. Alligators live in the lakes and rivers of America and China.　長い尾と, 鋭い歯のある大きな口を持つ大型のは虫類. アメリカや中国の湖, 川に住む　→アリゲーター・ワニ（広義） ☜参 **crocodile**

**all-in** 形 ▶定義 including everything　すべてを含んでいる　→全部を含めた, すべて込みの, 全面的な ‖ *an all-in price* すべて織り込みの価格

**allocate** /ǽləkèɪt/ 動他 ▶定義 allocate sth (to/for sb/sth) to give sth to sb as his/her share or to decide to use sth for a particular purpose　～を…に分け前として与える, または特定の目的のために～を使うことに決める　→～

を割り当てる, 分配する, ～を充てる ‖ *The government has allocated half the budget for education.* 政府は予算の半分を教育に割り当てた. — **allocation** /æ̀ləkéɪʃ(ə)n/ [名] [C] [U] ➜割り当て, 分配, 配置

**allot** /əlát/ [動][他] (**allotting**; **allotted**) ▶定義 allot sth (to sb/sth) to give a share of work, time, etc to sb/sth 仕事, 時間などの分担を～に与える ➜**～を割り当てる, 配分する, 分配する** ‖ *Different tasks were allotted to each member of the class.* 別々の課題が, そのクラスの１人１人に割り当てられた. *We all finished the exam in the allotted time.* 私たちは全員, 割り当てられた時間内でその試験を終えた.

**allotment** /əlátmənt/ [名] [C] [英] ▶定義 a small area of land in a town that you can rent for growing vegetables on 野菜の栽培のために借りることのできる, 町の中にある小さな土地➜**市民菜園**

**all out** [形][副] ▶定義 using all your strength, etc すべての力を使っている➜**全力を挙げての, 全面的な** ‖ *an all-out effort* 全力を挙げての努力

***allow** /əláʊ/ [動][他] ▶定義1 allow sb/sth to do sth; allow sth to give permission for sb/sth to do sth or for sth to happen ～が…をすることに, または～が起きることに許可を与える➜**～するのを許す, 許可する, 認める** ‖ *Children under twenty are not allowed to buy alcohol.* 20歳未満の子供はアルコール飲料を買うことが許されていない. *I'm afraid we don't allow people to bring dogs into this restaurant.* 申し訳ありませんが, このレストランに犬を連れ込むことは禁止されています. *Photography is not allowed inside the cathedral.* その大聖堂の中では写真撮影が許されていない.

➤ allow, permit, letと比較. allowは改まった英語でも口語的な英語でも用いられる. 受身形のbe allowed toは, とりわけよく使われる. permitは改まった単語で, 通常, 文語でのみ用いる. letは口語的な単語で, 話し言葉で非常によく使われる. allow sb to do sth（～が…をするのを許す）ではtoを付けるが, let sb do sthではtoを付けない. letは受動態で用いることができない：*Visitors are not allowed/ permitted to smoke in this area.*（来訪者はこの区域で喫煙してはいけない.）*Smoking is not allowed/ permitted.*（喫煙は許されていない.）*I'm not allowed to smoke in my bedroom.*（私は寝室での喫煙を許されていない.）*My dad won't let me smoke in my bedroom.*（私のお父さんは, 私が寝室でたばこを吸うのを許さないだろう.）

▶定義2 to give permission for sb/sth to be or go somewhere ～がある場所にいる, または行くことに許可を与える➜**～を許す, 許可する** ‖ *No dogs allowed.* 犬の連れ込み禁止. *I'm only allowed out on Friday and Saturday nights.* 私は金曜と土曜の夜だけ外出が許されている. ▶定義3 allow sb sth to let sb have sth ～に…を持たせる➜**支給する, 与える** ‖ *My contract allows me four weeks' holiday a year.* 契約によって, 私は１年に４週間の休暇が与えられる. ▶定義4 allow sb/sth to do sth to make it possible for sb/sth to do sth ～が…を行うことができるようにする➜**～させておく, ～するのに任せる** ‖ *Working part-time would allow me to spend more time with my family.* パートタイムの勤務にすると, 家族とより長い時間過ごせるようになるだろう. ▶定義5 allow sth (for sb/sth) to provide money, time, etc for sb/sth 金, 時間などを～に用意する➜**～を見込む, ～の余裕を見る, 取っておく** ‖ *You should allow about 30 minutes for each question.* １問に約30分を見込んだ方が良いだろう.

[句動詞] allow for sb/sth ▶定義 to think about possible problems when you are planning sth and include extra time, money, etc for them ～を計画するときに起こり得る問題について考え, そのために余分の時間, 金などを含める➜**～を考慮に入れる, ～のため余裕を取っておく** ‖ *The journey should take about two hours, allowing for heavy traffic.* その旅行は, 激しい交通量を考慮すると, 約２時間かかるだろう.

**allowance** /əláʊ(ə)ns/ [名] [C] ▶定義1 an amount of sth that you are allowed 認められている一定量➜**許容量** ‖ *Most flights have a 20kg baggage allowance.* 大半のフライトは20キロまでの手荷物を許可している. ▶定義2 an amount of money that you receive regularly to help you pay for sth that you need 必要とする～に対して支払うのを援助するための, 定期的に受け取る金➜**手当, 経費**

### all right

**成句 make allowances for sb/sth** ▶定義 to judge a person or his/her actions in a kinder way than usual because he/she has a particular problem or disadvantage 特別な問題あるいは不利な事を抱えている人のため、いつもよりも寛大にその人またはその行動を判断する→**〜を考慮に入れる，斟酌（しんしゃく）する，大目に見る**

**all right**(または略式 **alright**) 間副形(名詞の前は不可) ▶定義1 good enough; OK 結構である；良い→**申し分のない，満足な，差し支えない** ‖ *Is everything all right?* すべては問題ないでしょうか． ▶定義2 safe; not hurt; well 無事で；けがをしていない；元気な→**体調の良い，元気に，大丈夫な** ‖ *I hope the children are all right.* 私はその子供たちが元気であることを願っている． *Do you feel all right?* 大丈夫ですか． ▶定義3 showing you agree to do what sb has asked; OK 〜が頼んだ事をするのに同意していることを表している；分かった→**よろしい，了解した，承知した** ‖ *'Can you get me some stamps?' 'Yes, all right.'*「切手を何枚か取ってきてくれませんか」「はい，分かりました」

▶ほかの人から〜に対して感謝されたとき，またはほかの人が自分がした〜について謝ったとき，That's all right. と言う: *'Thanks for the lift home.' 'That's (quite) all right.'*(「車で家まで送ってくれてありがとう．」「いいえ，どういたしまして．」) *'I'm so sorry I'm late.' 'That's all right. We haven't started yet anyway.'*(「遅れてすみません．」「大丈夫ですよ．まだ始めていませんから．」)

**all-round** 形(名詞の前だけ) ▶定義 able to do many different things well; good in many different ways 多種多様な事を上手にすることができる；さまざまな方面で優れている→**多芸の，多才の，万能の** ‖ *a superb all-round athlete* すばらしい万能選手 *The school aims at the all-round development of the child.* 学校は子供の多方面にわたる成長を目指している．

**all-rounder** 名 C ▶定義 a person who can do many different things well 多種多様な事を上手にすることができる人→**万能選手，オールラウンドプレーヤー，器用な人**

**allude** /əlúːd/ 動 自 正式 ▶定義 allude to sb/sth to speak about sb/sth in an indirect way 〜について間接的な方法で話す→**それとなく言う，ほのめかす，遠回しに言及する** — **allusion** /əlúːʒ(ə)n/ 名 C U ▶**ほのめかし，当てこすり，遠回しな言及** ‖ *He likes to make allusions to the size of his salary.* 彼は自分の給料の額をそれとなく言うのが好きだ．

**ally** /ǽlaɪ/ 名 C (複 **allies**) ▶定義1 a country that has an agreement to support another country, especially in a war 特に戦争で，ほかの国を援助する協定を結んでいる国→**同盟国，盟邦** ‖ *France and its European allies* フランスとそのヨーロッパの同盟国 ☞参 **alliance** ▶定義2 a person who helps and supports you, especially when other people are against you 特に反対している人たちがいるときに，その反対されている人を援助し支持する人→**味方，協力者，盟友** ‖ *the Prime Minister's political allies* 首相の政治上の盟友

**almighty** /ɔːlmáɪti/ 形 ▶定義1 having the power to do anything 何でもできる力を持っている→**全能の** ‖ *Almighty God* 全能の神 ▶定義2 (名詞の前だけ) 略式 very great 非常に偉大な→**ひどい，ものすごい，強力な** ‖ *Suddenly we heard the most almighty crash.* 突然，私たちの上なくすさまじい大音響が聞こえた．

**almond** /ɑ́ːmənd/ 名 C ▶定義 a flat pale nut 平たく薄い木の実→**アーモンド，その木・実** ☞ **nut** のさし絵

*★**almost** /ɔ́ːlmoʊst/ 副 ▶定義 very nearly; not quite ほとんど真に；全くではなく少し足りない→**ほとんど，大抵，もう少しで** ‖ *By nine o'clock almost everybody had arrived.* 9時までに，ほとんど全員が到着していた． *Careful! I almost fell into the water then!* 気を付けて．あの時，私はもう少しで川・海に落ちるところだった． *The film has almost finished.* その映画はほぼ終わっている． *She almost always cycles to school.* 彼女はほとんどいつも自転車で学校へ行く． *There's almost nothing left.* ほとんど何も残っていない． *Almost all the students passed the exam.* ほとんどの学生がその試験に合格した．

*★**alone** /əlóʊn/ 形副 ▶定義1 without any other person ほかのだれとも一緒ではない→**1人で，単独で，独りぼっちで** ‖ *The old man lives alone.* その老人は独りぼっちで暮らしている． *Are you alone? Can I speak to you for a moment?*

あなたは1人でいるのですか。ちょっとお話ししてもいいですか. *I don't like walking home alone after dark.* 私は暗くなってから1人で歩いて帰宅したくない.

▶ alone と lonely はどちらも, ほかの人と一緒にいるのではないことを意味している. lonely (米 lonesome) は, それが悲しいと感じていることを意味するが, alone は通常, うれしいとも悲しいとも表していない. alone は名詞の前で使うことができない. また, on your own や by yourself を使って, alone の意味を表すことができる. こちらの表現の方が口語的であり, 話し言葉で非常によく使われる.

▶定義2 (名詞または代名詞の後で) only 〜だけ → ただ〜だけで, 〜のみで ‖ *You alone can help us.* あなただけが私たちを助けることができるのです. *The rent alone takes up most of my salary.* 賃借料だけで給料の大半を占めている.

成句 **go it alone** ▶定義 to start working on your own without the usual help 通例の援助を受けないで自分だけで活動を始める → 独力でやり遂げる, 独りでやる・行う

**leave sb/sth alone** ⇒ **LEAVE**¹

**let alone** ⇒ **LET**

\***along** /əlɔ́(ː)ŋ, əlɑ́ŋ/ 前 副 ▶定義1 from one end to or towards the other end of sth 〜の一方の端からもう一方の端へ, またはもう一方の端に向かって → 〜に沿って, 〜伝いに, 〜を通って ‖ *I walked slowly along the road.* 私は道に沿ってゆっくり歩いた. *David looked along the corridor to see if anyone was coming.* デーヴィッドはだれかがやって来るかどうかを見るため, 廊下をずっと先まで眺めた. ▶定義2 on or beside sth long 長い〜の上に, またはそれと並んで → 〜の上をずっと, 〜に沿って(端から端まで)ずっと, 〜をずっと行ったところに ‖ *Wild flowers grew along both sides of the river.* 野生の花が川の両側に沿って育った. *Our house is about halfway along the street.* 私たちの家はその通りの中間辺りにある. ▶定義3 forward 前方へ → (どんどんと)先へ, (止まらずに)前へ, 進んで ‖ *We moved along slowly with the crowd.* 私たちは群衆と共にゆっくり前に歩いていった. ▶定義4 略式 with sb 〜と一緒に → 〜を伴って, 連れて, 持って ‖ *We're going for a walk. Why don't you* **come along** *too?* 私たちはこれから散歩に出掛けます. あなたも一緒に行きませんか.

成句 **all along** ⇒ **ALL**²

**along with sb/sth** ▶定義 together with sb/sth 〜と一緒に → 〜と一緒に, 協力して, 〜に加えて

**go along with sb/sth** ▶定義 to agree with sb's ideas or plans 〜の考えまたは計画に同意する → 〜に同調する, 賛成する, 協力する

**alongside** /əlɔ́(ː)ŋsàid, əlɑ́ŋ-/ 前 副 ▶定義1 next to sb/sth or at the side of sth 〜の隣に, または〜のわきに → 〜のそばに, 傍らに, 〜と並んで ▶定義2 together with sb/sth 〜と一緒に → 〜と共に, 一緒に ‖ *the opportunity to work alongside experienced musicians* 経験豊かな音楽家と一緒に仕事をする機会

**aloof** /əlúːf/ 形 ▶定義1 not friendly to other people; distant ほかの人々に対して好意的ではない; 隔てのある → よそよそしい, 冷淡な, 冷ややかな ‖ *Her shyness made her seem aloof.* 彼女は内気なので, よそよそしく見えた. ▶定義2 **aloof (from sb/sth)** not involved in sth; apart 〜にかかわっていない; 離れて → 〜から距離を置いて, 遠ざかって, 〜の仲間に加わらない

**aloud** /əláυd/ (または **out loud**) 副 ▶定義 in a normal speaking voice that other people can hear; not silently ほかの人が聞こえるくらいの普通の話し声で; 沈黙しないで → 声を出して, 口に出して ‖ *to read aloud from a book* 本の一部を音読する

\***alphabet** /ǽlfəbèt, -bət/ 名 C ▶定義 a set of letters in a fixed order that you use when you are writing a language 1つの言語で書き表すときに使う文字を, 一定の順序で並べた一連の文字 → アルファベット, ABC, 字母 ‖ *There are 26 letters in the English alphabet.* 英語のアルファベットには26文字ある.

---

▶音声とつづり字

alphabet の発音の英米の差

アメリカ英語とイギリス英語との違いに注意しましょう. アルファベット26文字のうち, 米音と英音の違いがあるのは次の3種です.

     O       R       Z

米音: [óυ オゥ] [ɑr アァ] [ziː ズィ]
英音: [ə́υ エゥ] [ɑː アー] [zed ゼッド]

**alphabetical** /ælfəbétɪk(ə)l/ 形 ▶定義 arranged in the same order as the letters of the alphabet アルファベットの文字と同じ順序に配列された→**アルファベット順の, ABC 順の** ‖ *The names are listed in alphabetical order.* 名前はアルファベット順に記載されている. — **alphabetically** /-k(ə)li/ 副 →**アルファベット順に, ABC 順に**

**alpine** /ǽlpaɪn/ 形 ▶定義 of or found in high mountains 高い山の, または高い山で見られる→**高山の, 高山性の, 高山帯に生える** ‖ *alpine flowers* 高山植物

\***already** /ɔːlrédi/ 副 ▶定義 **1** used for talking about sth that has happened before now or before a particular time in the past 現在, または過去のある時より前に起こった~について話すときに用いられて→**もう, 既に, それまでに** ‖ *'Would you like some lunch?' 'No, I've already eaten, thanks.'* 「お昼でも食べませんか」「いや, 私はもう頂きました. ありがとう」 *We got there at 6.30 but Marsha had already left.* 私たちはそこに6時半に着いたが, マーシャは既に出発していた. *Sita was already awake when I went into her room.* 私がシーターの部屋に入った時, 彼女はとっくに目を覚ましていた. ▶定義 **2** (used in negative sentences and questions for expressing surprise) so early; as soon as this (否定文や疑問文で驚きを表すときに用いて) そんなに早く; これほどすぐに→**もう, 早くも, そんなに早く** ‖ *Have you finished already?* もう済んでしまったのですか. *Surely you're not going already!* まさか, もうお帰りになるのではないでしょう.

**alright** /ɔːlráɪt/ 略式 = **ALL RIGHT**

\***also** /ɔ́ːlsoʊ/ 副 (動詞の否定形と用いない) ▶定義 in addition; too 加えて; その上→**~もまた, さらに, 同様に** ‖ *He plays several instruments and also writes music.* 彼はいくつもの楽器を演奏し, さらに作曲もする. *Bring summer clothing and also something warm to wear in the evenings.* 夏服に加えて, 晩に何かはおれるあったかい衣類も持ってきなさい. *The food is wonderful, and also very cheap.* その食べ物はすばらしく, また, とても安い.

▶ too と as well は also よりも口語的で, 話し言葉で非常によく使われる. also は通常, 本動詞の前, または is, are, were などの後ろに置かれる: *He also enjoys reading.* (彼は読書も楽しむ.) *He has also been to Australia.* (彼はオーストラリアに行ったことがある. 彼はオーストラリアにも行ったことがある.) *He is also intelligent.* (彼は頭が良い. 彼は頭も良い.) too と as well は通常, 句または文の最後に置く: *I really love this song, and I liked the first one too/as well.* (私はこの歌が大好きだが, 最初の歌も好きだった.)

**成句** not only...but also ⇒ **ONLY**

**altar** /ɔ́ːltər/ 名 Ⓒ ▶定義 a high table that is the centre of a religious ceremony 宗教的な儀式の中心となる背の高い台→**祭壇, 供物台, 聖餐 (せいさん) 台**

**alter** /ɔ́ːltər/ 動 自 他 ▶定義 to make sth different in some way, but without changing it completely; to become different ~を何らかの点で異なるようにするが, 完全には変えてしまわない; 違うようにする→**~を (一部) 変える, ~を作り変える; 改造する** ‖ *We've altered our plan, and will now arrive at 7.00 instead of 8.00.* 私たちは計画を変更したので, 8時ではなく7時に着くことになる. *The village seems to have altered very little in the last twenty years.* その村は, ここ20年の間にほとんど変わっていないように見える.

**alteration** /ɔ̀ːltəréɪʃ(ə)n/ 名 Ⓒ Ⓤ ▶定義 (an) alteration (to/in sth) a small change in sb/sth ~における小さな変更→**(一部の) 変更, 修正, 手直し** ‖ *We want to make a few alterations to the house before we move in.* 私たちは, 入居する前にその家を少し改造したい.

**alternate¹** /ɔ́ːltərnət, ɔ́ːltər-/ 形 ▶定義 **1** (used about two types of events, things, etc) happening or following regularly one after the other (2種類の出来事, 物事などについて) 規則的に代わるがわる起きている, または引き続き起こっている→**交互に起きる, 交替の, 代わるがわるの** ‖ *There will be alternate periods of sun and showers tomorrow.* 明日は, 交互に太陽が出たり雨が降ったりする時間があるでしょう.

▶定義 **2** one of every two 2つごとに1つの→**1つおきの, 互い違いの** ‖ *He works alternate weeks* (= he works the first week, he doesn't work the second week, he works again the third week, etc). 彼は1週おきに働いている (=

1週目に働き, 2週目は働かないで, 3週目にまた働く, というように)— alternately 副 ➔代るがわる, 交互に, 互い違いに ‖ The bricks were painted alternately white and red. そのれんがは1つおきに白と赤に塗られていた.

**alternate**[2] /ɔ́ːltəmèɪt, ɔːltɚ-/ 動 ▶定義 1 自 alternate with sth; alternate between A and B (used about two types of events, things, etc) to happen or follow regularly one after the other (2種類の出来事, 物事などについて)規則的に代わるがわる起きる, または引き続いて起こる ➔ ~と交替する, ~を交互にする, 交互に来る ‖ Busy periods in the hospital alternate with times when there is not much to do. 病院の忙しい時期とそれほど忙しくない時期は交互にやって来る. She seemed to alternate between hating him and loving him. 彼女は, 彼を大嫌いになったり大好きになったり揺れ動いているようだった. ▶定義 2 他 alternate A with B to cause two types of events or things to happen or follow regularly one after the other 2種類の出来事や物事を規則的に代わるがわる起こす, または引き続いて起こさせる ➔ ~を交替にする, 交互にする, 互い違いにする ‖ He alternated periods of work with periods of rest. 彼は仕事をする時期と休む時期を交互に取った. — alternation /ɔ̀ːltɚnéɪʃ(ə)n/ 名 C U ➔交互(にすること), (2者間の)交替, 1つおき

**alternative**[1] /ɔːltɚ́ːmətɪv/ 形 (名詞の前だけ) ▶定義 1 that you can use, do, etc instead of sth else ほかの~の代わりに使ったり行ったりすることができる ➔ 代わりの, 代用の ‖ The motorway was closed so we had to find an alternative route. その高速道路は閉鎖されていたので, 私たちはそれに代わる道を探さなければならなかった. ▶定義 2 different to what is usual or traditional いつもの, または従来のものとは異なる ➔ 新しい, 代替~, 伝統的ではない ‖ alternative medicine 代替薬 — alternatively 副 ➔ その代わり, 二者択一的に, あるいは

**alternative**[2] /ɔːltɚ́ːmətɪv/ 名 C ▶定義 an alternative (to sth) one of two or more things that you can choose between 選択できる対象である複数の物事のうちの1つ ➔ 選択すべきもの, 選択(肢), ~に代わるもの ‖ What can I eat as an alternative to meat? 肉の代わりに何を食べることができますか. There are several alternatives open to us at the moment. 今のところ, 私たちには選択肢がいくつか与えられている.

★**although** /ɔːlðóʊ/ 接 ▶定義 1 in spite of the fact that ~という事実にもかかわらず ➔ ~であるけれども, ~にもかかわらず ‖ Although she was tired, she stayed up late watching television. 彼女は疲れていたにもかかわらず, 遅くまで起きてテレビを見ていた. ▶定義 2 and yet; but しかしそれでも; けれども ➔ ~であるけれども, たとえ~でも ‖ I love dogs, although I wouldn't have one as a pet. 私は犬が大好きだが, ペットとして飼おうとは思わない.

▶ though と although は同じであるが, 文末では though しか使うことができない: She knew all her friends would be at the party. She didn't want to go, though. (彼女は友達全員がパーティーに出ることを知っていた. でも自分は行きたくなかった.) even though は強調を表すために用いることができる: She didn't want to go, although/though/ even though she knew all her friends would be there. (彼女は, 友達全部がそこに行くことを知っていたけれども・たとえ知っていたとしても, 彼女自身は行きたくなかった.)

**altitude** /ǽltət(j)ùːd/ 名 ▶定義 1 [単数扱い]the height of sth above sea level ~の海水面からの高さ ➔ 高度, 海抜, 標高 ‖ The plane climbed to an altitude of 10000 metres. その飛行機は高度1万メートルまで上昇した. ▶定義 2 [通常は複数]a place that is high above sea level 海水面より上の高い所 ➔ 高所, 高地, 高台 ‖ You need to carry oxygen when you are climbing at high altitudes. 高所を登るときには, 酸素を持っていく必要がある.

**alto** /ǽltoʊ/ 名 C (複 **altos**) ▶定義 the lowest normal singing voice for a woman, the highest for a man; a woman or man with this voice 普通の歌声で最も低い女声, 最も高い男声; そのような声を持った女性または男性 ➔ アルト, アルト声部, アルト歌手

★**altogether** /ɔ̀ːltəgéðɚ/ 副 ▶定義 1 completely 完全に ➔ 全く, すっかり ‖ I don't altogether agree with you. 私はあなたに完全に同意しているというわけではない. At the age of 55 he stopped working altogether. 彼は55歳の時に

働くことをすっかりやめた. *This time the situation is altogether different.* 今回は状況が全く違う. ▶定義2 including everything; in total すべてを含めて; 総計で→**全部で,全体で,合計で** ‖ *How much money will I need altogether?* 合計でいくら必要になるのですか. *Altogether there were six of us.* 私たちは全員で6人だった. ▶定義3 when you consider everything; generally すべてを考慮すると, 一般→**全体的に見て,要するに,概して** ‖ *Altogether, this town is a pleasant place to live.* 全体的に見れば,この町は住みやすい所だ.

▶ altogether は all together と同じではない. all together は「すべての物事または人が一緒に」という意味を表す: *Put your books all together on the table.* (あなたの本を全部テーブルに置きなさい.) *Let's sing. All together now!* (歌を歌いましょう.さあ,みんな一緒に.)

**aluminium** /ˌæljəˈmɪniəm/ (米 **aluminum** /əˈluːmənəm/) (元素記号 Al) 名 U ▶定義 a light silver-coloured metal that is used for making cooking equipment, etc 調理用具などを作るために使われる,銀色の軽い金属→**アルミニウム** ‖ *aluminium foil* アルミホイル,アルミ箔(はく)

★**always** /ˈɔːlweɪz, -wəz/ 副 ▶定義1 at all times; regularly あらゆる時に; いつも→**いつでも,常に,始終** ‖ *I always get up at 6.30.* 私はいつも6時半に起きる. *Why is the train always late when I'm in a hurry?* 私が急いでいるときに,なぜ必ず電車が遅れるのだろうか. ▶定義2 all through the past until now 過去から今までずっと→**(今まで)ずっと,もともと,前々から** ‖ *Tony has always been shy.* トニーは前からずっとはにかみ屋だ. *I've always liked music.* 私は前々から音楽が好きです. ▶定義3 for ever 永久に→**いつまでも,永遠に** ‖ *I shall always remember this moment.* 私はこの瞬間をいつまでも忘れはしない. ▶定義4 (進行形だけと用いて) again and again, usually in an annoying way 通常,迷惑なやり方で,何度も何度も→**いつも~ばかりしている,絶えず~している,始終~している** ‖ *She's always complaining about something.* 彼女は絶えず何かについて不満ばかり言っている. ▶定義5 used with 'can' or 'could' for suggesting sth that sb could do, especially if nothing else is possible 特にほかに何も可能性がない場合に~ができる…を示すときに, can または could と共に用いられて→**(必要なときは)いつでも,とにかく,少なくとも** ‖ *If you haven't got enough money, I could always lend you some.* お金が足りないときには,いつでも私が少し貸してあげよう.

▶ always は通常,文頭に置かず,本動詞の前,または is, are, were などの後ろに置く: *He always wears those shoes.* (彼はいつもその靴を履いている.) *I have always wanted to visit Egypt.* (私はエジプトを訪れたいとずっと思っていた.) *Fiona is always late.* (フィオナはいつも遅刻する.) ただし,人にある事をするように言うときには, always が文頭に来ることもある: *Always stop and look before you cross the road.* (道路を渡る前には,必ず立ち止まってよく見なさい.)

**Alzheimer's disease** /ˈɑːltshaɪmərz dɪziːz, ˈælts-/ 名 [単数扱い] ▶定義 a disease that affects the brain and makes you become more and more confused as you get older 脳を侵し,年を取るにつれてだんだん意識が混乱してくる病気→**アルツハイマー症,アルツハイマー病**

**a.m.** /ˌeɪ ˈem/ 略 ▶定義1 (米 **A.M.**) before midday 正午より前→**午前** ‖ *10 a.m.* (= *10 o'clock in the morning*) 午前10時 (= 朝の10時) ▶定義2 **AM** one of the systems of sending out radio signals 無線信号を出すシステムの1つ→**振幅変調, AM 放送**

**am** ⇒ **BE**¹

**amalgamate** /əˈmælɡəmeɪt/ 動 自 他 ▶定義 (used especially about organizations, groups, etc) to join together to form a single organization, group, etc (特に組織, 集団などについて) 一緒に合わせて, 1つの組織, 集団になる→**~を合併する,合同する,融合する** — **amalgamation** /əˌmælɡəˈmeɪʃ(ə)n/ 名 C U →**融合, 合併, 合同**

**amass** /əˈmæs, əˈmæs/ 動 他 ▶定義 to collect or put together a large quantity of sth 大量の~を集める,または寄せ集める→**~を積む,集める,蓄積する** ‖ *We've amassed a lot of information on the subject.* 私たちはそのテーマに関する情報をたくさん集めた.

**amateur**¹ /ˈæmətər, -t(j)ʊər, ˌæməˈtɜːr/ 名 C ▶定義1 a person who takes part in a sport or an activity for pleasure, not for money as a job あるスポーツや活動に, 仕事で金を得るためではなく楽しみとして参加する人→**アマチュア, 素人** ‖ *Only amateurs can take part in the tournament.* そのトーナメントにはアマチュアだけが参加できる. ⇔ **professional**　▶定義2 (usually used when being critical) a person who does not have skill or experience when doing sth (通常, 批判的なときに用いて) 〜をする場合に技術や経験がない人→**未熟者, 未経験者, 生かじりの人**

**amateur**² /ǽmətər, -t(j)ùər, æmətə́ːr/ 形 ▶定義1 done, or doing sth, for pleasure (not for money as a job) 〜を楽しみで (仕事で金を得るためではなく) 行われた, または行っている→**アマチュアの, 素人の** ‖ *an amateur production of a play* 素人の芝居作り *an amateur photographer* アマチュア写真家 ⇔ **professional**　▶定義2 (または **amateurish** /-rɪʃ/) done without skill or experience 技術や経験がなくて行われた→**未熟な, 素人臭い, 下手な** ‖ *The painting was an amateurish fake.* その絵は下手なにせ物だった.

★**amaze** /əméɪz/ 動他 ▶定義 to surprise sb very much; to be difficult for sb to believe 〜を非常に驚かせる; 〜にとって信じ難い→**〜をびっくりさせる, 驚嘆させる, 仰天させる** ‖ *Sometimes your behaviour amazes me!* 君の行動には時々びっくりさせられるよ. *It amazes me that anyone could be so stupid!* だれもがそんなに愚かになれるとは, ほとほとあきれる.

★**amazed** /əméɪzd/ 形 ▶定義 amazed (at/by sb/sth); amazed (to do sth/that...) very surprised とても驚いている→**びっくりした, 驚嘆した** ‖ *I was amazed by the change in his attitude.* 私は彼の態度の変わりようにはびっくりした. *She was amazed to discover the truth about her husband.* 彼女は夫にまつわる事実が分かって驚嘆した.

**amazement** /əméɪzmənt/ 名 U ▶定義 a feeling of great surprise 強い驚きの気持ち→**驚愕, 驚嘆 (きょうがく), 仰天** ‖ *He looked at me in amazement.* 彼は驚いて私を見た. *To my amazement, I passed the test easily.* 驚いたことに, 私はテストに楽々と合格した.

★**amazing** /əméɪzɪŋ/ 形 ▶定義 very surprising and difficult to believe; incredible とても驚くべきことで信じ難い; 信じられない→**びっくりするような, 驚嘆すべき, 見事な** ‖ *She has shown amazing courage.* 彼女は驚くほどの勇気を見せた. *I've got an amazing story to tell you.* あなたに聞かせたい, びっくりするような話があるのです. — **amazingly** 副 →**驚嘆するほど, 驚くほど, 驚嘆すべきことに**

**ambassador** /æmbǽsədər, əm-/ 名 C ▶定義 an important person who represents his/her country in a foreign country 外国において自国を代表するという重要な役目を持つ人→**大使** ‖ *the Spanish Ambassador to Britain* 駐英スペイン大使

▶ ambassador は embassy (大使館) で生活し仕事をする. consul も参照.

**amber** /ǽmbər/ 名 U ▶定義1 a hard clear yellow-brown substance used for making jewellery or objects for decoration 宝石類や装飾品を作るために使われ, 硬くて光沢のある黄みがかった茶色の物質→**こはく** ▶定義2 a yellow-brown colour 黄みがかった茶色 (主にイギリス. アメリカなどは yellow)→**こはく色** ‖ *The three colours in traffic lights are red, amber and green.* 交通信号の3つの色は, 赤, こはく色, 緑だ. — **amber** 形 →**こはくの, こはくのような, こはく色の**

**ambiguity** /æmbəgjúːəti/ 名 C U (複 **ambiguities**) ▶定義 the possibility of being understood in more than one way; sth that can be understood in more than one way 2つ以上の意味に理解される可能性; 2つ以上の意味に理解される可能性がある〜→**あいまいさ, 多義性, あいまいな表現**

**ambiguous** /æmbígjuəs/ 形 ▶定義 having more than one possible meaning 2つ以上の意味に取れる→**あいまいな, 多義的な, 不明確な** — **ambiguously** 副 →**どっちつかずに, あいまいに**

★**ambition** /æmbíʃ(ə)n/ 名 ▶定義1 C ambition (to do/be sth); ambition (of doing sth) something that you very much want to have or do 手に入れたい, または実行したいと強く思っていること→**強い望み, 抱負, 夢** ‖ *It has always been her ambition to travel the world.* 世界を旅行することは彼女の前々からの強い望みだ. *He finally achieved his ambition of becoming a doctor.* 彼は医者になるという夢をとうとう実現した. ▶定義2 U a strong desire to be suc-

## ambitious

cessful, to have power, etc 成功したい, 権力を得たい, などという強い欲求→**大望, 野心, 野望** ‖ *One problem of young people today is their lack of ambition.* 今日の若者が抱える問題の1つは, 野心がないことである.

**\*ambitious** /æmbíʃəs/ 形 ▶定義 **1** ambitious (to be/do sth) having a strong desire to be successful, to have power, etc 成功したい, 権力を得たい, などという強い欲求を持っている→**大望を抱いた, 野心のある, 〜を熱望している** ‖ *I'm not particularly ambitious - I'm content with my life the way it is.* 私はとりわけ大望を抱いているわけではない ― あるがままの人生に満足している. *We are ambitious to succeed.* 私たちは成功したいと熱望している. ▶定義 **2** difficult to achieve or do because it takes a lot of work or effort 多くの仕事や努力を必要とするため, 成し遂げたり実行したりするのが難しい→**野心的な, 大掛かりの, 意欲的な** ‖ *The company have announced ambitious plans for expansion.* その会社は野心的な拡張計画を発表した.

**ambivalent** /æmbívələnt/ 形 ▶定義 having or showing a mixture of feelings or opinions about sth or sb 〜または…について入り交じった気持ちや意見を持っている, または示している→**〜に対して相反する感情の, 矛盾する感情を持つ, はっきりしない** ― ambivalence 名 ⓒ Ⓤ 〜**に対する相反する感情, 矛盾する感情, 両面価値・感情**

**\*ambulance** /ǽmbjələns/ 名 ⓒ ▶定義 a special vehicle for taking ill or injured people to and from hospital 病人やけが人を病院へ, または病院から運ぶための特別な乗り物→**救急車** ‖ *the ambulance service* 救急サービス

**ambush** /ǽmbʊʃ/ 名 ⓒ Ⓤ ▶定義 a surprise attack from a hidden position 隠れた位置から不意に襲撃すること→**待ち伏せして奇襲すること, 待ち伏せ** ‖ *He was killed in an enemy ambush.* 彼は敵の待ち伏せに遭って殺された. *The robbers were waiting in ambush.* その強盗たちは待ち伏せしていた. ― ambush 動 他 **〜を待ち伏せする, 待ち伏せして襲う, 待ち伏せさせる**

**amen** /ɑːmén, eɪ-, (聖歌で) ɑ́ːmén/ 間 ▶定義 a word used at the end of prayers by Christians and Jews キリスト教徒やユダヤ人たちが祈りの最後に唱える言葉→**アーメン**

**amenable** /əmíːnəb(ə)l/ ▶定義 happy to accept sth 〜を喜んで受け入れる→**〜に自ら進んで従う, 従順な, 受け入れる** ‖ *I'm amenable to any suggestions you may have.* 何かご提案があれば, 私は喜んで受け入れます.

**amend** /əménd/ 動 他 ▶定義 to change sth slightly in order to make it better 〜をより良くするために, 少し変更する→**〜を修正する, 改正する**

**amendment** /əméndmənt/ 名 ▶定義 **1** ⓒ a part that is added or a small change that is made to a piece of writing, especially to a law 文書, 特に法律に関して追加された部分, または加えられた小さな変更→**改正箇所, 修正箇所, 改善点** ▶定義 **2** Ⓤ an act of amending sth 〜を改正すること→**改正, 修正, 改善**

**amends** /əméndz/ 名 [複数扱い]
成句 **make amends** ▶定義 to do sth for sb, that shows that you are sorry for sth bad that you have done before 〜のために…をして, 以前にやった悪い〜を申し訳なく思っていることを示す→**償いをする, 埋め合わせをする**

**amenity** /əmíːnəti, əmé-/ 名 ⓒ (複 **amenities**) ▶定義 something that makes a place pleasant or easy to live in その場所を気持ち良くしたり住みやすくしたりする物→**生活を楽しく快適・便利にする物, 文化施設, 娯楽設備** ‖ *Among the town's amenities are two cinemas and a sports centre.* その街の娯楽設備の中には, 2つの映画館とスポーツセンターがある.

**\*American** /əmérəkən/ 形 ▶定義 from or connected with the US 米国の出身である, または米国と関連している→**アメリカの, アメリカ人の, アメリカ式の** ‖ *Have you met Bob? He's American.* ボブに会ったことがありますか. 彼はアメリカ人です. *an American accent* アメリカ式のアクセント ― American 名 ⓒ →**アメリカ人, 米国人** ‖ *Millions of Americans visit Britain each year.* 毎年, 数百万人のアメリカ人がイギリスを訪れる.

**American football** (米 **football**) 名 Ⓤ ▶定義 a game played in the US by two teams of eleven players with a ball that is not round. The players wear hard hats (**helmets**) and other protective clothing and try to carry the ball to the end of the field. アメリカで, 1チームが11

人から成る2チームの間で、丸くないボールを使って行われる競技。競技者は防護用の帽子（ヘルメット）とそのほかの防護服を身に着け、ボールをフィールドの端まで運ぼうとする→アメリカンフットボール

**American Indian** = NATIVE AMERICAN

**amiable** /éimiəbl/ 形 ▶定義 friendly and pleasant 好意的で感じの良い→愛想の良い、気立ての良い、素直な — amiably /-əbli/ 副→愛想良く、優しく、感じ良く

**amicable** /ǽmɪkəbl/ 形 ▶定義 made or done in a friendly way, without argument 友好的に、対立的な議論なしになされた、または行われた→友好的な、平和的な — amicably 副→友好的に、平和的に、仲良く

**amid** /əmíd/（または **amidst** /əmídst/）前 (文) ▶定義 in the middle of; among 〜の真ん中に、〜の中で→〜のさなかに、〜の中に、〜に囲まれて

**amiss** /əmís/ 形 副 ▶定義 wrong; not as it should be 誤った、あるべきではない→間違って、具合悪く、不適当な ‖ When I walked into the room I could sense that something was amiss. 私は歩いてその部屋に入った時、何かおかしいところがあると感じた.

成句 **not come/go amiss** ▶定義 to be useful or pleasant 役に立つ、または好ましい状態である→うまくいく、良いようになる ‖ Things are fine, although a bit more money wouldn't come amiss. もう少し金があっても悪いことはあるまい.

**take sth amiss** ▶定義 to be upset by sth, perhaps because you have understood it in the wrong way おそらく〜を間違って理解したために、それによって気分を害する→〜を誤解して気を悪くする、〜に腹を立てる、〜を誤解して悪く取る ‖ Please don't take my remarks amiss. 私の所見を悪く取らないでください.

**ammunition** /ˌæmjəníʃ(ə)n/ 名 U ▶定義1 the supply of bullets, etc that you need to fire from a weapon 武器から発砲するために必要な銃弾などの供給物→弾薬 ‖ The troops surrendered because they had run out of ammunition. その軍隊は弾薬が尽きたため降伏した. ▶定義2 facts or information that can be used against sb/sth 〜に対抗して使われる事実または情報→攻撃手段、攻撃材料、防衛手段

**amnesia** /æmníːziə, -ʒə/ 名 U ▶定義 loss of memory 記憶をなくすこと→記憶喪失、健忘症

**amnesty** /ǽmnəsti/ 名 C (複 **amnesties**) ▶定義1 a time when a government forgives political crimes 政府が政治犯を許すとき→恩赦、特赦、大赦 ‖ The government has announced an amnesty for all political prisoners. 政府は政治犯全員に対する恩赦を発表した. ▶定義2 a time when people can give in illegal weapons without being arrested 人々が逮捕されないで違法な武器を引き渡せる期間→免責期間

\***among** /əmʌ́ŋ/（または **amongst** /əmʌ́ŋst/）前 ▶定義1 surrounded by; in the middle of 〜に囲まれている；〜の中央に→〜の中に、〜の間に、〜に混じって ‖ I often feel nervous when I'm among strangers. 私は見知らぬ人たちの中にいると、しばしば不安になる. I found the missing letter amongst a heap of old newspapers. 古新聞の山の中に紛失した手紙はあった. ☛参 **between** の注とさし絵 ▶定義2 in or concerning a particular group of people or things ある特定の集団の人々または物事の中で、あるいはそれらに関して→〜の間で協力して、お互いに、〜同士で ‖ Discuss it **amongst yourselves** and let me know your decision. それについてあなたたちの間で話し合いをして、決まった事を私に知らせてください. There is a lot of anger among students about the new law. 新しい法律について学生の間では大いに怒りを呼んでいる.

**Among other things**, the drug can cause headaches and sweating. その薬は特に頭痛と発汗を引き起こす可能性がある. ▶定義3 to each one (of a group)（その集団の）各々に→〜の間で、〜の各々に ‖ On his death, his money will be divided among his children. 彼が亡くなれば、彼の金は子供たちの間で分けられることになるだろう.

**amoral** /eɪmɔ́(ː)r(ə)l, -már-/ 形 ▶定義 (used about people or their behaviour) not following any moral rules; not caring about right or wrong（人またはその行動について）道徳的な基準に全く則していない；善か悪かを気にしていない→善悪を区別しない、道徳と無関係な、道徳観念のない ☛参 **moral**, **immoral**

\***amount¹** /əmáʊnt/ 名 C ▶定義1 the amount of

**amount²**

sth is how much of it there is; quantity the amount of sth は、~の量がどのくらいあるかということを表す; 量➡**量, 額** ‖ *I spent an enormous amount of time preparing for the exam.* 私はその試験の準備に膨大な時間を費やした. *I have a certain amount of sympathy with her.* 私は彼女にある程度同情している. *a large amount of money* 多額の金 ▶定義2 total or sum of money 金の総計または合計➡**総量総額, 合計** ‖ *You are requested to pay the full amount within seven days.* 7日以内に全額支払っていただくことになっています.

**amount²** /əmáʊnt/ 動 自 amount to sth ▶定義1 to add up to; to total 合計~となる; 総計する➡**総計~になる, ~に達する, 上る** ‖ *The cost of the repairs amounted to £5000.* 修理費は5000ポンドに上った. ▶定義2 to be the same as ~と同じである➡**~とほぼ等しい, ~も同然だ, 結局~になる** ‖ *Whether I tell her today or tomorrow, it amounts to the same thing.* 私が彼女に話すのが今日であろうが明日であろうが, 結局同じことだ.

**amp** /æmp/ 名 C ▶定義1 (または 正式 **ampere** /ǽmpèər, -pìər/) a unit for measuring electric current 電流を測定する単位 ➡**アンペア** ▶定義2 = AMPLIFIER

**ample** /ǽmpl, ǽ-/ 形 ▶定義1 enough or more than enough 十分ある, または十分以上ある➡**余るほど十分な, 豊富な, たっぷりの** ‖ *We've got ample time to make a decision.* 私たちには決断を下すための時間がたっぷりある. *I'm not sure how much the trip will cost, but I should think £500 will be ample.* その旅行にいくら費用がかかるかよく分からないが500ポンドあれば十分だと思う. ▶定義2 large 大きい➡**豊かな, 広大な, 広々とした** ‖ *There is space for an ample car park.* 広大な駐車場用の土地がある. ― **amply** /ǽmpli/ 副 ➡**十分に, たっぷり, 詳細に**

**amplifier** /ǽmpləfàɪər/ (または 略式 **amp**) 名 C ▶定義 a piece of electrical equipment for making sounds louder or signals stronger 音声を大きくしたり信号を強くしたりするための電子機器➡**増幅器, アンプ**

**amplify** /ǽmpləfàɪ/ 動 他 (現分 **amplifying**; 三単現 **amplifies**; 過, 過分 **amplified**) ▶定義1 to increase the strength of a sound, using electrical equipment 電子機器を使って音声の強さを増す➡**~を増幅する** ▶定義2 to add details to sth in order to explain it more fully ~をもっと十分に説明するために, 詳細を付け加える➡**~を詳しく説明する, 敷えんする, ~をさらに詳述する** ― **amplification** /æmpləfəkéɪʃ(ə)n/ 名 U ➡**増幅, 詳しい説明, 敷えん**

**amputate** /ǽmpjətèɪt/ 動 自 他 ▶定義 to cut off a person's arm, leg, etc for medical reasons 人の手, 足などを治療上の理由で切断する➡**~を切断する** ‖ *His leg was so badly injured that it had to be amputated from the knee down.* 彼の足はとてもひどいけがをしていたので, ひざから下を切断しなければならなかった. ― **amputation** /æmpjətéɪʃ(ə)n/ 名 C U ➡**(手・足などの)切断(手術)**

*__amuse__ /əmjúːz/ 動 他 ▶定義1 to make sb laugh or smile; to seem funny to sb ~を笑わせたりほほえませたりする; ~にとって面白く見える➡**~を面白がらせる, 楽しませる, 笑わせる** ‖ *Everybody laughed but I couldn't understand what had amused them.* だれもが笑っていたが, 私には彼らが何を面白がっているのか理解することができなかった. ▶定義2 to make time pass pleasantly for sb; to stop sb from getting bored ~に楽しく時間を過ごさせる; ~が退屈しないようにする➡**~を楽しむ, ~に楽しく時間を過ごさせる, ~を慰める** ‖ *I did some crosswords to amuse myself on the journey.* 私は旅行中にクロスワードパズルをして楽しんだ. *I've brought a few toys to amuse the children.* 私は子供たちを楽しませるために少しおもちゃを買った.

*__amused__ /əmjúːzd/ 形 ▶定義 thinking that sth is funny and wanting to laugh or smile ~が面白いと思い, 笑いたい, またはほほえみたいと思っている➡**~を面白がって, 楽しんで** ‖ *I was amused to hear his account of what happened.* 私は, 何が起こったのかについての彼の説明を聞いて面白がった.

成句 **keep sb/yourself amused** ▶定義 to do sth in order to pass time pleasantly and stop sb/yourself getting bored 楽しく時間を過ごし, ~・自分を退屈させないようにするため, …を行う➡**~・自分を楽しませる**

*__amusement__ /əmjúːzmənt/ 名 ▶定義1 U the

feeling caused by sth that makes you laugh or smile, or by sth that entertains you 人を笑わせたりほほえませたりする～によって，または人を楽しませる～によって引き起こされる感情➔楽しさ, 愉快, 面白み ‖ *Much to the pupils' amusement, the teacher fell off his chair.* その先生がいすから落ちたので，生徒たちは大変面白がった. ▶定義2 ❻ something that makes time pass pleasantly; an entertainment 楽しく時間を過ごせる物事; 娯楽➔慰み, 気晴らし, 娯楽 ‖ *The holiday centre offers a wide range of amusements, including golf and tennis.* その行楽地は，ゴルフやテニスを含めて遊技施設を幅広く提供している.

**amusement arcade** = ARCADE(2)

*****amusing** /əmjúːzɪŋ/ 形 ▶定義 causing you to laugh or smile 人を笑わせたりほほえませたりする➔～を面白がらせるような, 楽しくさせる, 愉快な ‖ *He's a very amusing person and he makes me laugh a lot.* 彼はとても愉快な人で，私をよく笑わせてくれる. *The story was quite amusing.* その話はとても面白かった.

**an** ⇒ A²

**anaemia** (米 **anemia**)/əníːmiə/ 名 ❶ ▶定義 a medical condition in which there are not enough red cells in the blood 血液中に赤血球が十分にないという病的状態➔貧血(症)— anaemic 形➔貧血(症)の

**anaesthetic**(米 **anesthetic**)/ænəsθétɪk/ 名 ❻ ❶ ▶定義 a substance that stops you feeling pain, for example when a doctor is performing a medical operation on you 医者が手術をするときなどに，患者が痛みを感じないようにするための物質➔麻酔薬, 麻酔剤, 緩和剤 ‖ *You'll need to be **under anaesthetic** for the operation.* 手術を受けるときには麻酔をかける必要があるでしょう. *The dentist gave me a **local anaesthetic** (= one that only affects part of the body and does not make you unconscious).* その歯医者は，私に局部麻酔(=体の一部分だけに作用し，意識を失わせることのない麻酔)をかけた. *Did you have a **general anaesthetic** (= one that makes you unconscious) for your operation?* 手術の時に全身麻酔(=意識を失わせる麻酔)をかけられましたか.

**anaesthetist**(米 **anesthetist**)/ənésθətɪst; æníːs-/ 名 ❻ ▶定義 a person with the medical training necessary to give anaesthetic to patients 患者に麻酔薬を投与するために必要な医療の訓練を受けた人➔麻酔士, 麻酔医

**anaesthetize**(または **-ise**, 米 **anesthetize**) /ənésθətàɪz; æníːs-/ 動 他 ▶定義 to give an anaesthetic to sb ～に麻酔薬を投与する➔～に麻酔をかける

**anagram** /ǽnəgræm/ 名 ❻ ▶定義 a word or phrase that is made by arranging the letters of another word or phrase in a different order ある語句の文字を違う順序に並べ換えて作られた別の語句➔アナグラム, つづり換え ‖ *'Worth' is an anagram of 'throw'.* WorthはthrowのアナグラムaLlある.

**analogous** /ənǽləgəs/ 形 正式 ▶定義 **analogous (to/with sth)** similar in some way; that you can compare ある程度似ている; 比較することができる➔～に類似した, 相似の, 似た

**analogy** /ənǽlədʒi/ 名 ❻ (複 **analogies**) ▶定義 **an analogy (between A and B)** a comparison between two things that shows a way in which they are similar 2つの物事を比較し，両者の似ている点を明らかにすること➔類似, 似た点, 似かより ‖ *You could make an analogy between the human body and a car engine.* 人体と車のエンジンは似ていることが分かるでしょう.

成句 **by analogy** ▶定義 by comparing sth to sth else and showing how they are similar ～をほかの…と比較し，両者がどれほど似ているかを示すことによって➔～と比較して, 類推によって, ～から類推して

*****analyse**(米 **analyze**)/ǽn(ə)làɪz/ 動 他 ▶定義 to look at or think about the different parts or details of sth carefully in order to understand or explain it ～を理解したりまたは説明するために，さまざまな部分や詳細を注意深く見る，あるいは考える➔～を分析する, 分解して検討する, 解明する ‖ *The water samples are now being analysed in a laboratory.* その水のサンプルは，現在，研究室で分析中である. *to analyse statistics* 統計を分析する *She analysed the situation and then decided what to do.* 彼女はその状況を分析してから，すべき事を決めた.

## analysis

**analysis** /ənǽləsəs/ 名 (複 **analyses** /-siːz/)
▶定義1 ⓒⓊ the careful examination of the different parts or details of sth ～のさまざまな部分や詳細を注意深く調査すること→分析, 分解, 検討 ‖ *Some samples of the water were sent to a laboratory for analysis.* その水のサンプルの一部は, 分析するために研究室へ送られた.
▶定義2 ⓒ the result of a careful examination of sth ～を注意深く調査した結果→分析結果 ‖ *Your analysis of the situation is different from mine.* その状況についてのあなたの分析結果と私のとは異なっている.

**analyst** /ǽnəlɪst/ 名 ⓒ ▶定義 a person whose job is to examine sth carefully as an expert 専門家として～を注意深く調査することを仕事としている人→分析者, アナリスト, 解説者, 評論家 ‖ *a food analyst* 食品分析者 *a political analyst* 政治評論家

**analytical** /æn(ə)lítɪk(ə)l/ (または **analytic** /ìn(ə)lítɪk/) 形 ▶定義 using careful examination in order to understand or explain sth ～を理解または説明するために注意深く調査している→分析の, 分解の, 分析的な

**anarchic** /ænɑ́ːrkɪk, ə-/ 形 ▶定義 without rules or laws 規則や法がない状態の→無秩序の, 混乱した, 無政府状態の

**anarchism** /ǽnərkɪz(ə)m, ənɑ́ːr-/ 名 Ⓤ ▶定義 the political belief that there should be no government or laws in a country 国に政府や法があるべきではないとする政治的な信条→無政府主義, アナーキズム — **anarchist** 名 ⓒ →無政府主義者, アナーキスト

**anarchy** /ǽnərki/ 名 Ⓤ ▶定義 a situation in which people do not obey rules and laws; a situation in which there is no government in a country 人々が規則や法に従わないという状況; 国に政府がない状態→無政府状態, 無秩序, 混乱 ‖ *While the civil war went on, the country was in a state of anarchy.* 内戦が続いている間, その国は無政府状態だった.

**anatomy** /ənǽtəmi/ 名 (複 **anatomies**)
▶定義1 Ⓤ the scientific study of the structure of human or animal bodies 人間や動物の体の構造についての科学的な研究→解剖学
▶定義2 ⓒ the structure of a living thing 生物の構造→解剖学的構造, 組織, 構造 ‖ *the anatomy of the frog* カエルの構造 — **anatomical** /ænətɑ́mɪk(ə)l/ 形→解剖的の, 解剖学の, 構造上の

**ancestor** /ǽnsestər/ 名 ⓒ ▶定義 a person in your family who lived a long time before you 家族の中で, 自分よりもずっと前に生きていた人→祖先, 先祖 ‖ *My ancestors settled in this country a hundred years ago.* 私の祖先は100年前にこの国に移住した. ☞参 **descendant**

**ancestry** /ǽnsestri/ 名 ⓒⓊ (複 **ancestries**)
▶定義 all of a person's ancestors その人のすべての祖先→家系, 家柄, 血筋 ‖ *He is of Irish ancestry.* 彼はアイルランドの家系である.

**anchor**¹ /ǽŋkər/ 名 ⓒ ▶定義 a heavy metal object at the end of a chain that you drop into the water from a boat in order to stop the boat moving 船が動くのを止めるために船から水中へ下ろす, 鎖の端に付いた重い金属の物体→錨(いかり)

**anchor**² /ǽŋkər/ 動 ▶定義1 自他 to drop an anchor; to stop a boat moving by using an anchor 錨(いかり)を下ろす; 錨を使って船が動くのを止める→～を錨で止める, 停泊する, 投錨(びょう)する ▶定義2 他 to fix sth firmly so that it cannot move ～をしっかり固定させて動けないようにする→～を固定する, 固くつなぎ止める, 固着する

**ancient** /éɪnʃ(ə)nt/ 形 ▶定義1 belonging to a period of history that is thousands of years in the past 数千年前の歴史上の時代に属している→古代の, 大昔の, 古来の ‖ *ancient civilizations* 古代文明 *an ancient tradition* 古い伝統
▶定義2 very old 非常に年を取った→老齢の ‖ *I can't believe he's only 30 - he looks ancient!* 彼がまだ30歳とは信じられない － とても老けて見えるのに.

**\*and** /ən(d), n; 強形 æn(d)/ 接 ▶定義1 (used to connect words or parts of sentences) also; in addition to (文の中の単語または要素を結ぶために用いて) また; ～に加えて→～と…, そして, および ‖ *a boy and a girl* 男の子と女の子 *Do it slowly and carefully.* それをゆっくりまた注意深くしなさい. *We were singing and dancing all evening.* 私たちは一晩中歌ったり踊ったりしていた. *Come in and sit down.* 入って座りなさい.

▶2つの物事が密接につながっている場合

は、a などを繰り返す必要はない: *a knife and fork*（ナイフとフォーク）*my father and mother*（私の父と母）

▶定義2 (used when you are saying numbers in sums) in addition to; plus（計算で数を言うときに用いて）〜に加えて; プラスして➔**〜と…, 〜に加えて** ‖ *Twelve and six is eighteen.* 12足す6は18.

▶大きな数を言うときには、hundred の後に and が用いられる: *We say 2264 as two thousand, two hundred and sixty-four.*（2264 は千が2つと百が2つとそして64という言い方をする。）

▶定義3 used between repeated words to show that sth is increasing or continuing 〜が増えている、または続いていることを表すために繰り返される単語と単語の間で用いられて➔**〜も…も, ますます, どんどん** ‖ *The situation is getting worse and worse.* 状況はますます悪化している. *I shouted and shouted but nobody answered.* 私が叫んでも叫んでも、だれも答えなかった. ▶定義4 used instead of 'to' after certain verbs, for example 'go', 'come', 'try' go, come, try など、ある種の動詞の後で to の代わりに用いられて➔**〜するように** ‖ *Go and answer the door for me, will you?* 私の代わりに玄関に行って出てくれませんか. *Why don't you come and stay with us one weekend?* いつか週末に来て私たちの家に泊まったらどうですか. *I'll try and find out what's going on.* 私は何が起きるのか見てこよう.

### ▶音声とつづり字

#### and の発音は an と同じ?

and は語句や文をつなぐ働きを持ちますが、普通弱く発音します. and が弱く発音されると [ənd]，'nd [nd]，'n [n] などのように母音が弱まったり、全くなくなったり、また最後の [d] が聞こえなくなったりします.「バター付きパン」の発音は *bread'n'butter* のようになってしまいます.

Jack and Betty をカタカナで書くと「ジャックとベティー」となりますが、英語の発音に近く書くと「ヂェアックッ゛ン ベーリィ」のようになります. アメリカ英語では語中の t はラ行音になることも覚えておきましょう.

---

### ▶日本語 vs 英語

#### 2語を and でつなぐ言い方

2語を and を使ってつなぐ言い方は、英語ではポピュラーですが、日本語と順序が逆になるものが多いです.「行ったり来たり」は come and go,「昼も夜も」は night and day,「出たり入ったり」は in and out. 人の名前を挙げるときも、日本語では「私」は先でも後でも構いませんが、英語では *...and I* のように,「私」は必ず最後に持ってきます.

**anecdote** /ǽnɪkdòʊt/ 名 C ▶定義 a short interesting story about a real person or event 実在の人物や実際にあった出来事についての短くて面白い話➔**逸話, 秘話**

**anemia, anemic** 米 = ANAEMIA, ANAEMIC

**anesthetic** 米 = ANAESTHETIC

**anew** /ən(j)úː/ 副 (文) ▶定義 again; in a new or different way 再び; 新しい、または別の方法で➔**新たに, 別に, もう一度** ‖ *I wish I could start my life anew!* 人生を再出発できたらいいのに.

**angel** /éɪndʒ(ə)l/ 名 C ▶定義1 a spirit who is believed to live in heaven with God. In pictures angels are usually dressed in white, with wings. 神と共に天国に住んでいると信じられている妖精（ようせい）. 絵画では、通常、翼を付けて白衣を着ている➔**天使** ▶定義2 a person who is very kind とても親切な人➔**天使のような人, 清らかな人, 優しい人**

**angelic** /ændʒélɪk/ 形 ▶定義 looking or acting like an angel 天使のように見える、またはそのように振る舞っている➔**天使の（ような）, 愛らしい, 無垢（むく）な** — **angelically** /-k(ə)li/ 副 ➔**天使のように**

★**anger**[1] /ǽŋɡər/ 名 U  ▶定義 the strong feeling that you have when sth has happened or sb has done sth that you do not like 〜が起きたとき、または人が自分の気に入らない〜をしたときに抱く強い感情➔**怒り, 立腹** ‖ *He could not hide his anger at the news.* 彼はその知らせを聞いて怒りを隠せなかった. *She was shaking with anger.* 彼女は怒りに震えていた.

**anger**[2] /ǽŋɡər/ 動 他 ▶定義 to make sb become angry 〜を怒らせる➔**〜を怒らせる, 立腹させる**

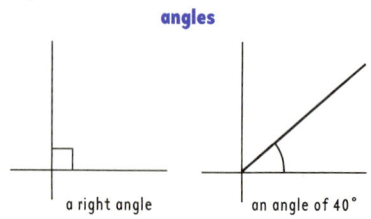

angles
a right angle / an angle of 40°

**★angle**¹ /ǽŋgl/ 名 C ▶定義 1 the space between two lines or surfaces that meet, measured in degrees 接している２本の線，または２つの面の間の空間．単位は度→**角度，角** ‖ *a right angle (= an angle of 90°)* 直角(= 90度の角) *at an angle of 40°* 40度の角を成して *The three angles of a triangle add up to 180°.* 三角形の３つの角を合計すると180度になる．▶定義 2 the direction from which you look at sth ～を見る方向→**角度，観点，見方** ‖ *Viewed from this angle, the building looks bigger than it really is.* この角度から見ると，その建物は実際よりも大きく見える．

成句 **at an angle** ▶定義 not straight まっすぐではない→**斜めに，傾いて，角度を付けて**

**angle**² /ǽŋgl/ 動 ▶定義 1 自 他 to put sth in a position that is not straight; to be in this position ～をまっすぐではない位置に置く；そのような位置にある→**～を斜めに動かす，～をある角度に置く，～に向ける** ‖ *Angle the lamp towards the desk.* ランプを机の方に向けてください．
▶定義 2 他 **angle sth (at/to/towards sb)** to show sth from a particular point of view; to aim sth at a particular person or group ある特定の視点から～を見せる；～を特定の人または集団に向ける→**～を(…向けに)書く，提示する** ‖ *The new magazine is angled at young professional people.* その新しい雑誌は専門職に就いている若者に向けて書かれている．

句動詞 **angle for sth** ▶定義 to try to make sb give you sth, without asking for it in a direct way 直接的な方法では頼まないで，～がくれるようにさせようとする→**～を遠回しに求める，～が欲しそうな素振りを見せる，～を得るために小細工をする** ‖ *She was angling for an invitation to our party.* 彼女は私たちのパーティーへの招待状が欲しそうな素振りを見せていた．

**angler** /ǽŋglər/ 名 C ▶定義 a person who catches fish as a hobby 魚釣りを趣味としてする人→**釣りをする人，釣り人，釣り師** ☞参 **fisherman**

**Anglican** /ǽŋglɪkən/ 名 C ▶定義 a member of the Church of England or of a related church in another English-speaking country 英国国教会の，または英語を話すほかの国にある関連する教会の会員→**英国国教徒** ― Anglican 形→**英国国教会の**

**angling** /ǽŋglɪŋ/ 名 U ▶定義 fishing as a sport or hobby 娯楽や趣味としての魚釣り→**釣り，魚釣り，釣り術** ‖ *He goes angling at weekends.* 彼は週末になると釣りに出掛ける．☞参 **fishing**

**Anglo-** /ǽŋgloʊ/ (複合語で) ▶定義 connected with England or Britain (and another country or countries) イングランドまたは英国(およびほかの国)と関連している→**イングランド(と～)の，英国(と～)の，英語(と～)の** ‖ *Anglo-American relations* 英米間の関係

**Anglo-Saxon** /ǽŋgloʊ sǽks(ə)n/ 名 ▶定義 1 C a person whose family originally came from England 一族の祖先がイングランド出身である人→**アングロサクソン人，アングロサクソン系の人** ▶定義 2 C a person who lived in England before the Norman Conquest (1066) ノルマン人のイングランド征服(1066年)より前にイングランドに住んでいた人→**アングロサクソン族** ▶定義 3 (または **Old English**) U the English language before about 1150 1150年ころより前の英語→**アングロサクソン語，古(期，代)英語** ― Anglo-Saxon 形→**アングロサクソン人の，アングロサクソン語の，英国系の**

**★angry** /ǽŋgri/ 形 (**angrier**; **angriest**) ▶定義 **angry (with sb) (at/about sth)** feeling or showing anger 怒りを感じている，または表している→**怒った，腹を立てた** ‖ *Calm down, there's no need to get angry.* 落ち着きなさい．怒る必要は何もありませんよ． *My parents will be angry with me if I get home late.* 私が遅く帰宅したら，両親は怒るだろう． *He's always getting angry about something.* 彼はいつも何かに対して腹を立てている．― angrily 副→**怒って，憤慨して**

**anguish** /ǽŋwɪʃ/ 名 Ⓤ (文) ▶定義 great mental pain or suffering 心の強い苦痛、または苦しみ→**苦痛, 苦悩, 苦悶（くもん）** — anguished 形→苦悩した, 苦痛に満ちた, 苦悶の

**angular** /ǽŋgjələr/ 形 ▶定義 with sharp points or corners 先または角のとがった →**角張った, 角のある**

*****animal** /ǽnəm(ə)l/ 名 Ⓒ ▶定義 a living creature that can move and feel. 'Animal' is sometimes used to talk about only creatures with warm blood (mammals). 動いたり感じたりすることができる生き物. animal は、温血の生物（ほ乳動物）だけを話題にするときに用いられる場合がある→**動物, ほ乳動物** ‖ *the animal kingdom* 動物界 *Humans are social animals.* 人間は社会的動物である. *farm animals* 家畜 *He studied the animals and birds of Southern Africa.* 彼は南アフリカの動物と鳥について研究した. ☛ C1 ページのさし絵

**animated** /ǽnəmèɪtəd/ 形 ▶定義1 interesting and full of energy 興味を起こさせ、元気一杯である→**活気のある, 生き生きとした, 活発な** ‖ *an animated discussion* 活発な議論 ▶定義2 (used about films) using a process or method which makes pictures or models appear to move (映画について) 絵や模型が動いているように見せる工程や方法を使っている→**アニメーションの, アニメーションとして製作・表現された** ‖ *an animated cartoon* アニメーション

**animation** /ænəméɪʃ(ə)n/ 名 Ⓤ ▶定義1 the state of being full of energy and enthusiasm 元気一杯で熱中している状態→**活気, 元気, 生気** ▶定義2 the method of making films, computer games, etc with pictures or models that appear to move 動いているように見える絵や模型を使って、映画、コンピューターゲームなどを製作する方法→**アニメーション製作, 動画の製作** ‖ *computer animation* コンピューターのアニメーションの製作

*****ankle** /ǽŋk(ə)l/ 名 Ⓒ ▶定義 the part of your body where your foot joins your leg 足のももからすねとその先をつないでいる身体の部分→**足首, くるぶし, 足関節** ‖ *The water only came up to my ankles.* 水は私の足首までしかなかった. ☛ C5 ページのさし絵

**annex** /ənéks, ǽneks/ 動 ⓣ ▶定義 to take control of another country or region by force ほかの国や地域を力ずくで支配する→**～を併合する** — annexation /ænekséɪ(ə)n/ 名 Ⓒ Ⓤ →併合, 付加, 添付

**annexe** (特に 米 **annex**) /ǽneks, -ɪks/ 名 Ⓒ ▶定義 a building that is joined to a larger one より大きな建物につながった建物→**（大きな建物の）増築部分, 別館, 新館**

**annihilate** /ənáɪələɪt/ 動 ⓣ ▶定義 to destroy or defeat sb/sth completely ～を完全に滅ぼす、または負かす→**～を全滅させる, 壊滅させる, 打ち負かす** — annihilation /ənàɪəléɪʃ(ə)n/ 名 Ⓤ →全滅, 壊滅, 絶滅

**anniversary** /ænəvə́ːrs(ə)ri/ 名 Ⓒ (複 **anniversaries**) ▶定義 a day that is exactly a year or a number of years after a special or important event 特別な、または重要な出来事からちょうど1年あるいは何年も経過した日→**記念日, 記念祭, ～周年記念** ‖ *the hundredth anniversary of the country's independence* その国の独立100周年記念祭 *a wedding anniversary* 結婚記念日 ☛参 **birthday**

**annotated** /ǽnəteɪtəd/ 形 ▶定義 (used about a book, etc) with notes added to it that explain and give extra information about the contents (本などについて) 書かれた内容について説明したり追加の情報を与えたりする注釈が本に加えられている→**注釈の付いた, 注解のある**

*****announce** /ənáʊns/ 動 ⓣ ▶定義1 to make sth known publicly and officially ～を公にまた公的に知らせる→**～を発表する, 公表する, 公告する** ‖ *They announced that our train had been delayed.* 当局は私たちの電車が遅れていると発表した. *The winners will be announced in next week's paper.* 勝者は来週の新聞で発表されるだろう. ▶定義2 to say sth in a firm or serious way ～を決然と、または本気で言う→**～を知らせる, 示す, 告げる** ‖ *She stormed into my office and announced that she was leaving.* 彼女は私の事務所に飛び込んできて、辞めると告げた.

*****announcement** /ənáʊnsmənt/ 名 ▶定義1 Ⓒ a statement that tells people about sth ～について人々に知らせる声明→**広告, お知らせ, 通知（状）** ‖ *Ladies and gentlemen, I'd like to make an announcement.* 皆さん、発表いたします. ▶定義2 [単数扱い] an act of telling people about sth ～について人々に知らせること→発表, 公表, アナウンス

**announcer** /ənáunsər/ 名 C ▶定義 a person who introduces or gives information about programmes on radio or television ラジオやテレビの番組を紹介したり, それについての情報を知らせたりする人→アナウンサー

★**annoy** /ənɔ́i/ 動他 ▶定義 to make sb angry or slightly angry ～を怒らせる, または少し怒らせる→～をいらいらさせる, 悩ます, いら立たせる ∥ *It really annoys me when you act so selfishly.* あなたが自分本位に行動すると, 私は本当にいらいらするよ. *Close the door if the noise is annoying you.* 騒音に悩まされているなら, 戸を閉めなさいよ.

**annoyance** /ənɔ́iəns/ 名 ▶定義1 ❶the feeling of being annoyed いらいらしているという気持ち→いら立ち, 腹立たしさ, いら立たしさ ▶定義2 ❷something that annoys sb ～をいらいらさせる物事→うるさいもの, 頭痛の種, 不快な思いをさせるもの

★**annoyed** /ənɔ́id/ 形 ▶定義 feeling angry or slightly angry 怒っている, または少し怒っていると感じている→いらいらして, 腹を立てて ∥ *I shall be extremely annoyed if he turns up late again.* 彼がまた遅れて現れたら, 私はひどく腹が立つだろう. *She's annoyed with herself for making such a stupid mistake.* 彼女はそのようなばかげた間違いをした自分に腹を立てている. *He's annoyed that nobody believes him.* 彼はだれも自分を信じてくれないことにいらいらしている.

★**annoying** /ənɔ́iiŋ/ 形 ▶定義 making you feel angry or slightly angry 怒らせている, または少し怒らせている→～をいら立たせるような, うるさい, 迷惑な ∥ *It's so annoying that there's no phone near here!* この近くに電話がないとは, 実にいら立たしい. *His most annoying habit is always arriving late.* 彼の最も困った癖は, いつも遅れて来ることだ.

★**annual**¹ /ǽnjuəl/ 形 ▶定義1 happening or done once a year or every year 年に1度または毎年起きている, あるいは行われる→年1回の, 毎年の, 例年の ∥ *the company's annual report* その企業の年報 *an annual festival* 毎年行われる祭

り ▶定義2 for the period of one year 1年の期間の→1年間の, 1年分の ∥ *What's the average annual salary for a nurse?* 看護婦の平均年収はいくらですか. *the annual sales figures* 年間売上高 ― **annually** 副 ▶毎年, 年ごとに, 年に1度

**annual**² /ǽnjuəl/ 名 C ▶定義 a book, especially one for children, that is published once each year 年に1度出版される本で, 特に子供向けのもの→年報, 年鑑, 年刊書 ∥ *the 1999 Football Annual* 1999年版フットボール年鑑

**anomalous** /ənɑ́mələs/ 形 ▶定義 different from what is normal 普通の状態とは異なる→異常な, 異例の, 変則的な ∥ *In a few anomalous cases, these drugs have made people ill.* 数件の異例の症例においては, これらの薬によって人々の具合が悪くなった.

**anomaly** /ənɑ́məli/ 名 C (複 **anomalies**) ▶定義 sth that is different from what is normal or usual 普通またはいつもの状態とは異なる～→異常, 異例, 変則 ∥ *We discovered an anomaly in the sales figures for August.* 私たちは8月の売上高に異変を見つけた.

**anon** /ənɑ́n/ 形 anonymous ▶定義 used to show that we don't know who did a piece of writing だれが作品を書いたのか分からないことを示すために用いられる→作者不明の

**anonymity** /æ̀nənímɪti/ 名 U ▶定義 the situation where a person's name is not known 人の名前が分からない状況→匿名 無名

**anonymous** /ənɑ́nəməs/ 形 ▶定義1 (used about a person) whose name is not known or made public (人について)その名前が分からない, または公にされていない→匿名の, 名を明かさない ∥ *An anonymous caller told the police that a robbery was going to take place.* 強盗事件が起こるだろうという匿名の電話が警察にあった. ▶定義2 done, written, etc by sb whose name is not known or made public 名前が分からない, または公にされていない人によって行われた, 書かれた, など→匿名の, 名前のない, 作者不明の ∥ *He received an anonymous letter.* 彼は匿名の手紙を受け取った. ― **anonymously** 副 ▶匿名で, 名もなく

**anorak** /ǽnəræk/ 名 C 英 ▶定義1 a short coat with a covering for your head that protects you from rain, wind and cold 雨, 風, 寒さから体を守り, 頭にかぶるフードが付いている短い上

着→アノラック,防寒用上着 ☛ C6 ページのさし絵 ▶定義2 (俗語) a person who enjoys learning boring facts うんざりするような事を覚えるのを楽しむ人→**どんくさいやつ,ダサい野郎,面白くもない男** ‖ *He's a real anorak - he can name every player in the World Cup.* 彼は全く面白くもないやつだ ー ワールドカップの出場選手を全員言えるなんて.

**anorexia** /ǽnəréksiə/ (または **anorexia nervosa** /ǽnəréksiə nərvóusəə/) 名 ❶ ▶定義 an illness, especially affecting young women. It makes them afraid of being fat and so they do not eat. 特に若い女性がかかる病気.太ることを恐れて食事をしないようになる→**拒食症,神経性無食欲症** ー **anorexic** 形名 ❻→**拒食症にかかった,食欲不振の,拒食症患者**

★**another** /ənʌ́ðər/ 形代 ▶定義1 one more person or thing of the same kind 同じ種類の人がもう1人,またはものがもう1つ→**もう1人(の),もう1つ(の),さらに一つ (の)** ‖ *Would you like another drink?* もう1杯いかがですか. *They've got three children already and they're having another.* 彼らは既に子供が3人いるが,もう1人生まれる予定だ. ▶定義2 a different thing or person 別のものまたは人→**別の(もの),ほかの(人),異なった(もの)** ‖ *I'm afraid I can't see you tomorrow. Could we arrange another day?* 残念ながら明日はお会いできません.ほかの日に調整できないでしょうか. *If you've already seen that film, we can go and see another.* その映画はもう見たのなら,ほかのを見に行ってもいいよ.
成句 one after another/the other ⇒ **ONE**¹
yet another ⇒ **YET**

★**answer**¹ /ǽnsər, ǽn-/ 動自他 ▶定義1 to say or write sth back to sb who has asked you sth or written to you 〜について質問した,または手紙を書いてきた…に対し,〜を言って,あるいは書いて返す→**〜に答える,解答する,返事をする** ‖ *I asked her what the matter was but she didn't answer.* 私は彼女にどうしたのか尋ねたが,答えなかった. *I've asked you a question, now please answer me.* 私はあなたに質問したのですから,さあ答えてください. *Answer all the questions on the form.* その用紙にあるすべての質問に答えなさい. *He hasn't answered my letter yet (= written a letter back to me).* 彼はまだ私の手紙に返事をくれない(= 返事の手紙を私に出していない). *When I asked him how much he earned, he answered that was none of my business.* 私が彼にいくら稼いでいるのか尋ねると,私に関係のないことだ,と答えた. *'No!' he answered angrily.*「いいえ」と彼は怒った調子で答えた.

➤ answer と reply は,質問や手紙などに対して話したり書いたりすることを表すときに最もよく使われる動詞である: *I asked him a question but he didn't answer.* (私は彼に質問をしたが,答えなかった.) *I sent my application but they haven't answer yet.* (私は応募用紙を送ったが,まだ返事が来ない.) answer の場合は, answer a person, answer a question, answer a letter のように to を付けないが, reply の場合は, reply to a letter のように to を付けることに注意する. respond は,この意味では answer や reply ほどよく使われず,より改まった表現である: *Applicants must respond within seven days.* (志願者は7日以内に返答しなければならない.)「望まれた通りに反応する」という意味で使われる方が一般的である: *Despite all the doctor's efforts the patient did not respond to treatment.* (医者の尽力にもかかわらず,患者には治療の効果が現れなかった.)

▶定義2 to do sth as a reply 返事として〜をする→**応答する,返事をする,応対する** ‖ *Can you answer the phone (= pick up the receiver) for me, please?* 私の代わりに電話に出て(= 受話器を取って)くれませんか. *I rang their doorbell but nobody answered.* 私が呼び鈴を鳴らしても,だれも出てこなかった.

句動詞 **answer back** ▶定義 to defend yourself against sth bad that has been written or said about you 自分について書かれたり言われたりした良くない〜に対して自分を守る→**自己弁護する,〜に抗弁する**

**answer (sb) back** ▶定義 to reply rudely to sb 〜に不作法に言い返す→**〜に口答えする,激しく言い返す**

**answer for sb/sth** ▶定義1 to accept responsibility for sth/sb 〜に対する責任を引き受ける→**〜の責任を取る,〜を償う** ‖ *Somebody will have to answer for all the damage that has been* caused. 与えてしまった損害はすべてだれかが償わなければならないだろう. ▶定義2 to speak in support of sb/sth ～を支持して話す→～を保証する, 請け合う

*__answer__² /ά:nsər; ǽn-/ 名 ⓒ an answer (to sb/sth) ▶定義1 something that you say, write or do as a reply 返事として言う, 書く, 行う事→**答え, 返事, 回答** ‖ *The answer to your question is that I don't know.* ご質問の答えは, 私には分からない, ということです. *They've made me an offer and I have to __give__ them __an answer__ by Friday.* 向こうから私に申し入れがあり, 金曜日までに回答しなければならない. *I wrote to them two weeks ago and I'm still waiting for an answer.* 私は2週間前に彼らに手紙を出したのですが, 今もまだ返事を待っています. *I knocked on the door and waited but there was no answer.* ドアをノックして待ったが応答がなかった. ▶定義2 a solution to a problem 問題の解決法→**解決策, いい方法** ‖ *I didn't have any money so the only answer was to borrow some.* 私はお金を全く持っていなかったので, いくらか借りるしか方法がなかった. ▶定義3 a reply to a question in a test or exam テストや試験の問題に対する答え→**解答, 答え** ‖ *My answer to question 5 was wrong.* 5番の問題への私の答えは間違っていた. *How many answers did you get right?* 何問正しく答えられましたか. ▶定義4 the correct reply to a question in a test or exam テストや試験の問題に対する正しい答え→**正答, 正解** ‖ *What was the answer to question 4?* 問題4の正解は何でしたか.

成句 in answer (to sth) ▶定義 as a reply (to sth) (～に対する)答えとして→～に答えて, ～に応じて

__answerable__ /ά:nsərəbl; ǽn-/ ▶定義 answerable to sb (for sth) having to explain and give good reasons for your actions to sb; responsible to sb 自分の行為について～に説明し, 適切な理由を挙げなければならない→～に責任のある

__answering machine__ (医 __answer-phone__ /ά:nsərfòun; ǽn-/) 名 ⓒ ▶定義 a machine that answers the telephone and records messages from the people who call 電話に応答し, かけた人からの伝言を録音する機械→**留守番電話, 留守電** ‖ *I rang him and left a message on his answering machine.* 私は彼に電話をかけ, 留守番電話に伝言を残した.

__ant__ /ænt/ 名 ⓒ ▶定義 a very small insect that lives in large groups and works very hard 大きな群れを成して生活し極めて勤勉に働く, 非常に小さい昆虫→**アリ** ☞ **insect** のさし絵

__antagonism__ /æntǽgənìz(ə)m/ 名 ⓒ ⓤ ▶定義 antagonism (towards sb/sth); antagonism (between A and B) a feeling of hate and of being against sb/sth ～に対する嫌悪感や反抗する気持ち→**対立, 敵対関係, 敵意** — antagonistic /æntægənístik/ 形 ▶対立する, 敵対する, ～に敵意のある

__antagonize__(または **-ise**) /æntǽgənàɪz/ 動 ⓣ ▶定義 to make sb angry or to annoy sb ～を怒らせる, または～をいらいらさせる→**～に敵意・反感を抱かせる, ～を怒らせる, 敵に回す**

__Antarctic__¹ /æntά:r(k)tɪk/ 形 ▶定義 connected with the coldest, most southern parts of the world 世界で最も寒く, 最も南にある地域に関連している→**南極の, 南極地方の** ‖ *an Antarctic expedition* 南極探検(隊) ☞参 **Arctic**

__the Antarctic__² /æntά:r(k)tɪk/ 名 [単数扱い] ▶定義 the most southern part of the world 世界で最も南にある地域→**南極地方** ☞参 **the Arctic** ☞ **earth** のさし絵

antelope

__antelope__ /ǽnt(ə)lòup/ 名 ⓒ (復 **antelope** または **antelopes**) ▶定義 an African animal with horns and long, thin legs that can run very fast 角と, 非常に速く走る細長い足を持ったアフリカの動物→**アンテロープ, レイヨウ**

__antenatal__ /æntɪnéɪtl/ 形 ▶定義 connected with the care of pregnant women 妊婦の安全に関連している→**出産前の, 出生前の, 妊娠期間中の** ‖ *an antenatal clinic* 妊産婦診療所 *antenatal care* 妊娠期間中の注意

__antenna__ /ænténə/ 名 ⓒ ▶定義1 (復 __antennae__ /-ni:/) one of the two long thin parts on the heads of insects and some animals that live in shells. Antennae are used for feeling things with. 昆虫や殻の中に住む動物の頭に付いてい

る2本の細長い器官のうちの1本. 触れて物を知覚するために使われる→**触角** ☞類 **feelers** ☞ **insect** のさし絵　▶定義2　(復 **antennas**) 米 = AERIAL¹

**anthem** /ǽnθəm/ 名 ⓒ ▶定義 a song, especially one that is sung on special occasions 歌, 特に特別な機会に歌われるもの→**聖歌, 賛美歌, 祝歌** ‖ the national anthem (= the special song of a country) 国歌 (= 国にとって特別な歌)

**anthology** /ænθɑ́lədʒi/ 名 ⓒ (復 **anthologies**) ▶定義 a book that contains pieces of writing or poems, often on the same subject, by different authors 別々の作者による著作や詩を, しばしば同じ主題のものを, 数編含んでいる本→**アンソロジー, 詞華集, 選集** ‖ an anthology of love poetry 恋愛詩選集

**anthropology** /ænθrəpɑ́lədʒi/ 名 Ⓤ ▶定義 the study of human beings, especially their origin, development, customs and beliefs 人類の, 特に起源, 発達, 慣習, 信仰についての研究→**人類学** ― anthropological /ænθrəpəlɑ́dʒɪk(ə)l/ 形→**人類学の, 人類学上の**

**antibiotic** /æntɪbaɪɑ́tɪk/ 名 ⓒ ▶定義 a medicine which is used for destroying bacteria and curing infections 細菌を壊滅させ, 感染症を治療するために使われる薬→**抗生物質**

**antibody** /ǽntɪbɑdi/ 名 ⓒ (復 **antibodies**) ▶定義 a substance that the body produces to fight disease 病気と闘うために身体が作り出すもの→**抗体**

**anticipate** /æntísəpèɪt/ 動 他 ▶定義 to expect sth to happen and prepare for it 〜が起こることを予期し, その準備をする→**〜を予想する, 期待する, 見越す** ‖ to anticipate a problem 問題が起きることを予期する I anticipate that the situation will get worse. 私は状況が悪化するだろうと予想している.

**anticipation** /æntìsəpéɪʃ(ə)n/ 名 Ⓤ ▶定義1 the state of expecting sth to happen (and preparing for it) 〜が起こることを期待して(その準備をして)いる状態→**予期, 予想, 期待** ‖ The government has reduced tax **in anticipation of** an early general election. 政府は早期に総選挙があることを見越して減税した. ▶定義2 excited feelings about sth that is going to happen これから起こる〜のことで興奮している気持ち→**先手を打つこと, 機先を制すること, 先手** ‖ They queued outside the stadium **in excited anticipation**. 彼らは期待で胸を躍らせながら競技場の外に列を作った.

**anticlimax** /æntɪklάɪmæks/ 名 ⓒ Ⓤ ▶定義 an event, etc that is less exciting than you had expected or than what has already happened 期待していたほど, または既に起こった事ほどわくわくさせるようなものではない出来事など→**がっかりさせる結末, 竜頭蛇尾, しりすぼみ** ‖ When the exams were over we all had a sense of anticlimax. 試験が終わった時, 私たちは皆あっけなさを感じた.

**anticlockwise** /æntɪklɑ́kwaɪz/ (米 **counterclockwise**) 副形 ▶定義 in the opposite direction to the movement of the hands of a clock 時計の針の動きとは反対の方向に→**反時計回りの, 左回りに, 時計の針と反対に** ‖ Turn the lid anticlockwise/in an anticlockwise direction. そのふたを時計の針と反対方向に回しなさい. ⇨ **clockwise**

**antics** /ǽntɪks/ 名 [複数扱い] ▶定義 funny, strange or silly ways of behaving こっけいな, 奇妙な, ばかげた振る舞い→**ひょうきんなしぐさ, ふざけた行為, おどけたしぐさ**

**antidote** /ǽntɪdòʊt/ 名 ⓒ ▶定義1 a medical substance that is used to prevent a poison or a disease from having an effect 毒または病気が影響を及ぼすのを防ぐために使われる医薬品→**解毒剤, 解毒薬** ‖ an antidote to snake bites 蛇にかまれた傷の解毒剤　▶定義2 anything that helps you to deal with sth unpleasant 不愉快な〜に対処するのを助けるもの→**〜の対策, 解消法, 解決方法**

**antipathy** /æntípəθi/ 名 ⓒ Ⓤ ▶定義 antipathy (to/towards sb/sth) a strong feeling of not liking sb/sth; dislike 〜を好きではないという強い気持ち; 嫌悪→**反感, 嫌悪(感), 敵対心**

**antiperspirant** /æntɪpə́ːrsp(ə)rənt/ 名 ⓒ Ⓤ ▶定義 a liquid that you use to reduce sweating, especially under your arms 特にわきの下の, 発汗を抑えるために使う液体→**発汗抑制剤**

**antiquated** /ǽntɪkwèɪtəd/ 形 ▶定義 old-fashioned and not suitable for the modern world 旧式で, 現代の世界には適していない→**時代後れの, 古風な**

**antique** /æntíːk/ 形 ▶定義 very old and therefore unusual and valuable 大変古く, そのために珍しくて価値がある→骨董(こっとう)品の, 古くて価値のある, 時代を経た ‖ an antique vase/table 古くて価値のある花びん・テーブル antique furniture/jewellery 骨董品の家具・宝石 ― antique 名 C →骨董品, アンティーク, 時代物 ‖ an antique shop (= one that sells antiques) 古美術店 (= 骨董品を売る店) That vase is an antique. あの花びんは骨董品である.

**antiquity** /æntíkwəti/ 名 (複 antiquities) ▶定義 1 ❶ the ancient past, especially the times of the Ancient Greeks and Romans 太古の昔, 特に古代ギリシャ・ローマの時代→古代, 大昔, (特にギリシャ・ローマの)古典時代 ▶定義 2 [C, 通常は複数]a building or object from ancient times 古代からの建物や物 →古代の遺物, 古代の文物, 古美術品 ‖ Greek/Roman antiquities 古代ギリシャ・ローマの遺跡 ▶定義 3 ❶ the state of being very old or ancient 大変古い, または古びている状態→古さ, 古色, 古雅

**anti-Semitism** /ˌænti sémətɪz(ə)m/ 名 ▶定義 unfair treatment of Jewish people ユダヤ人に対する不公平な扱い方→反ユダヤ主義, 反ユダヤ感情, 反ユダヤ運動 ― anti-Semitic /ˌænti səmétɪk/ 形 →反ユダヤ主義の反ユダヤ人の, ユダヤ人排斥の

**antiseptic** /ˌæntɪséptɪk/ 名 C U ▶定義 a liquid or cream that prevents a cut, etc from becoming infected 切り傷などに病原菌が感染するのを防ぐ液体やクリーム→消毒薬, 殺菌剤, 抗菌剤 ‖ Put an antiseptic/some antiseptic on that scratch. そのかすり傷に消毒薬を(少し)付けておきなさい. ― antiseptic 形 →殺菌効果のある, 消毒の, 抗菌の ‖ antiseptic cream 消毒用のクリーム

**antisocial** /ˌæntisóʊʃ(ə)l/ 形 ▶定義 1 harmful or annoying to other people ほかの人々にとって有害な, または迷惑な→はた迷惑な ‖ antisocial behaviour 反社会的な行動 ▶定義 2 not liking to be with other people ほかの人々と一緒にいるのが好きではない→非社交的な, 社交嫌いの, 利己的な

**antithesis** /æntíθəsəs/ 名 C U (複 antitheses /æntíθəsiːz/) 正式 ▶定義 1 the opposite of sth 〜の正反対の事物→正反対(の事物) ‖ Love is the antithesis of hate. 愛は憎しみの正反対である. ▶定義 2 a difference between two things 2つの物事の違い→完全な相違, 対照, 対比

**antler** /ǽntlər/ 名 [C, 通常は複数] ▶定義 a horn on the head of an adult male animal (a stag) 成長した動物の雄(雄ジカ)の頭に生えている角→枝角 ‖ a pair of antlers 一対の枝角 ☛ deer のさし絵 ☛ elk のさし絵

**anus** /éɪnəs/ 名 C ▶定義 the hole through which solid waste substances leave the body 固形の排せつ物が身体の外へ出るときに通る穴→肛門 ☛ C5 ページのさし絵

**anxiety** /æŋzáɪəti/ 名 C U (複 anxieties) ▶定義 a feeling of worry or fear, especially about the future 特に将来についての, 不安や恐れという気持ち→心配, 不安, 懸念 ‖ a feeling/state of anxiety 不安な気持ち・状態 There are anxieties over the effects of unemployment. 失業による影響が懸念されている.

*★**anxious** /ǽŋ(k)ʃəs/ 形 ▶定義 1 anxious (about/for sb/sth) worried and afraid 心配であり恐れている→〜を心配して, 不安で, 気にして ‖ I'm anxious about my exam. 私は試験のことが心配だ. I began to get anxious when they still hadn't arrived at 9 o'clock. 彼らが9時になってもまだ到着していなかったとき, 私は不安になり始めた. an anxious look/expression 心配そうな顔付き・表情 ▶定義 2 causing worry and fear 心配や恐れを引き起こしている→不安な, 不安にさせる ‖ For a few anxious moments we thought we'd missed the train. 私たちはその電車に乗り損なったと思い, 少しの間不安になった. ▶定義 3 anxious to do sth; anxious for sth wanting sth very much 〜をとても強く求めている→〜を切望して, 願って, 熱心で ― anxiously 副 →心配して, 気にして, 切望して

★**any** /éni/ 形 代 副 ▶定義 1 (used instead of some in negative sentences and in questions) (否定文や疑問文で some の代わりに用いて)→何も, 少しも, 何か, どれか, 少しでも ‖ We didn't have any lunch. 私たちは少しも昼食を取らなかった. I speak hardly any (= almost no) Spanish. 私はスペイン語をほとんど(= ほとんど全く)話しません. Do you have any questions? 何か質問はありませんか. I don't like any of his books. 私は彼の本のどれも好きではない. ☞参 some の注 ▶定義2 used for saying that it does not matter which thing or person you choose どのものまたは人を選んでも問題ではないと言うために用いられて→どれでも,何でも,だれでも‖ Take any book you want. どれでも欲しい本を取りなさい. Come round any time - I'm usually in. いつでも来てください－私は大抵いますから. I'll take any that you don't want. あなたが欲しくないものを何でも引き取ります. ▶定義3 (used in negative sentences and questions) at all; to any degree (否定文や疑問文で用いて)少しも; いくらかの程度に→少しも,全然,少しは,いくらか,多少‖ I can't run any faster. 私はこれ以上速く走ることはできない. Is your father any better? あなたのお父さんは少しは良くなりましたか.

成句 any moment/second/minute/day (now) ▶定義 very soon すぐに→いつ何時,今にも,今すぐにも,近々,もうそろそろ‖ She should be home any minute now. 彼女はそろそろ家にいるころだ.

*  **anybody** /énɪbɑ̀di, -bədi/ (または **anyone**) 代 ▶定義1 (usually in questions or negative statements) any person (通常,疑問文と否定文で)→だれか,だれも‖ I didn't know anybody at the party. 私はそのパーティーに出ている人をだれも知らなかった. Is there anybody here who can speak Japanese? ここにいる人の中で日本語を話せる人はだれかいますか. Would anybody else (= any other person) like to come with me? ほかにだれか(= ほかのどの人でも)私と一緒に行きませんか.

➤ somebody と anybody の違いは, some と any の違いと同じである. some, somebody の注を参照.

▶定義2 any person, it does not matter who どの人でも,それがだれでも問題ではない→だれでも,どの人も‖ Anybody (= all people) can learn to swim. だれでも(= すべての人)泳ぐことができるようになる. Can anybody come, or are there special invitations? だれでも伺ってよいのですか,それとも特別な招待状があるのですか.

*  **anyhow** /énɪhàʊ/ 副 ▶定義1 (または **anyway**) (used to add an extra point or reason) in any case(特別な点や理由を追加するために用いて) どんな場合でも→とにかく,どのみち,いずれにせよ‖ I don't want to go out tonight, and anyhow I haven't got any money. 私は今夜出掛けたくないし,とにかくお金を全く持っていない. ▶定義2 (または **anyway**) (used when saying or writing sth which contrasts in some way with what has gone before); nevertheless (以前にあった物事と何らかの点で対照となる～を言うとき,または書くときに用いて)それにもかかわらず→とはいうものの,それでもやはり‖ I don't think we'll succeed, but anyhow we can try. 私は自分たちが成功するとは思っていないが,それでも挑戦することだけはできる. I'm afraid I can't come to your party, but thanks anyhow. 残念ながらあなたのパーティーには伺えません. でも,どうもありがとう. ▶定義3 (または **anyway**) (used for correcting sth you have just said and making it more accurate) at least (自分が言ったばかりの～を訂正し,もっと正確に表すために用いて)少なくとも→ともかくも,せめて,いずれにせよ‖ Everybody wants to be rich - well, most people anyhow. だれでも金持ちになりたいと思っている － 少なくともほとんどの人はね. ▶定義4 (または **anyway**) used after a pause in order to change the subject or go back to a subject being discussed before 話題を変える,または前に話されていた話題に戻すために,一呼吸おいた後に用いられる→ともかく,それはそうとして‖ Anyhow, that's enough about my problems. How are you? ともかく,私の問題についてはそれで十分です. あなたの方はいかがですか. ▶定義5 in a careless way; with no order ぞんざいな方法で; 秩序がなく→いいかげんに,でたらめに,ぞんざいに

*  **anyone** /énɪwʌ̀n/ = ANYBODY
   **anyplace** /énɪplèɪs/ 米 = ANYWHERE
*  **anything** /énɪθɪŋ/ 代 ▶定義1 (usually in negative sentences and in questions) one thing (of any kind) (通常,否定文や疑問文で)(どんな種類の中からでも)１つのもの→何か,何も,どれも‖ It was so dark that I couldn't see anything at all. とても暗かったので,全く何も見えなかった. There isn't anything interesting in the newspaper today. 今日は新聞に何も面白い事が書いていない. Did you buy anything? 何か買

## anyway

いましたか. *'I'd like a kilo of apples please.'* *'Anything else?'* (= any other thing?)「リンゴを１キロ下さい」「ほかに何か(= 何かほかのものは)どうですか」

➤ something と anything の違いは, some と any の違いと同じである. some の注を参照.

▶定義2 any thing or things: it does not matter what あらゆるもの; それが何でも問題ではない→何でも, どんなものでも, どれでも ‖ *I'm very hungry - I'll eat anything!* 私はとてもおなかがすいている — 何でも食べられるでしょう. *I'll do anything you say.* あなたのおっしゃる事なら何でもします.

成句 **anything but** ▶定義 not at all 少しも〜でない→少しも〜ない, 〜どころではない ‖ *Their explanation was anything but clear.* 彼らの説明は明瞭(めいりょう)なんてもんじゃなかった.

**anything like sb/sth** ▶定義 at all similar to sb/sth; nearly 〜に少しは似ている; ほとんど→少しは, 〜に似たもの ‖ *She isn't anything like her sister, is she?* 彼女は彼女の妹にちっとも似ていないですよね. *This car isn't anything like as fast as mine.* この車などは私の車の速さに到底及ばない.

**as happy, quick, etc as anything** 口語 ▶定義 very happy, quick, etc とてもうれしい, 素早い, など→とても〜, 例えようもなく, めっぽう

**like anything** ⇒ LIKE²

**not come to anything** ⇒ COME

★**anyway** /éniwèi/ = ANYHOW

★**anywhere** /éni(h)wèər, -(h)wər/ (米 または **anyplace**) 副 ▶定義1 (usually in negative sentences or in questions) in, at or to any place (通常, 否定文や疑問文で) どの場所でも, またはどの場所へも→どこかに, どこかへ, どこへも, どこにも ‖ *I can't find my keys anywhere.* かぎがどこにも見当たらない. *Is there a post office anywhere near here?* この近くのどこかに郵便局がありますか. *You can't buy the book anywhere else* (= in another place). その本はここ以外に他のところでは (= ほかの場所で) 買えません.

➤ somewhere と anywhere の違いは, some と any の違いと同じである. some の注を参照.

▶定義2 any place; it does not matter where あらゆる場所; それがどこでも問題ではない→どこにでも, どこへでも ‖ *You can sit anywhere you like.* どこでも好きな所に座って構いません.

★**apart** /əpá:rt/ 副 ▶定義1 away from sb/sth or each other; not together 〜から, または互いから離れて→〜と離れて, 隔たって, 異にして ‖ *The doors slowly slid apart.* 戸がゆっくりと開いた. *Stand with your feet apart.* 足を開いて立ちなさい. *The houses are ten metres apart.* それらの家は１０メートル離れている. *I'm afraid our ideas are too far apart.* 私たちの考えがあまりにも掛け離れているのが心配だ. ▶定義2 into pieces ばらばらになって→ばらばらに, ずたずたに ‖ *The material was so old that it just fell/came apart in my hands.* その材料はとても古かったので, 私の手の中でばらばらになってしまった.

成句 **take sth apart** ▶定義 to separate sth into pieces 〜を部分に分ける→〜を分解する, ばらばらにする ‖ *He took the whole bicycle apart.* 彼はその自転車全体を分解した.

**tell A and B apart** ▶定義 to see the difference between A and B AとBの違いが分かる→〜を識別する, 区別する, 個々の区別を付ける ‖ *It's very difficult to tell the twins apart.* 双子を見分けるのはとても難しい.

★**apart from** (特に 米 **aside from**) 前 ▶定義1 except for 〜を除いては→〜は別にして, 〜はさておき, 〜以外に ‖ *I've answered all the questions apart from the last one.* 私は最後の質問以外はすべての質問に答えた. *There's nobody here apart from me.* ここには私のほかにだれもいない. ▶定義2 as well as; in addition to 〜はもちろん; 〜に加えて→〜である上に, 〜に加えて ‖ *Apart from music, she also loves sport and reading* 彼女は音楽に加えて, スポーツと読書も大好きだ.

**apartheid** /əpá:rt(h)àit, -(h)eit/ 名 Ⓤ ▶定義 the former official government policy in South Africa of separating people of different races and making them live apart 異なる人種を隔離し別々に生活させるという, 南アフリカの政府がかつて取っていた公式の政策→アパルトヘイト, 人種隔離制度・政策

**apartment** /əpá:rtmənt/ 名 Ⓒ ▶定義1 特に 米 = FLAT²(1) ▶定義2 a set of rooms rented for a holiday 休日に賃貸される一組の部屋→(保養地などの短期間滞在用の)(複数の部屋から

成る)貸室 ‖ *a self-catering apartment* 自炊できる貸室

▶日本語 vs 英語

apart と「アパート」

apart は「(時間的・距離的・部分的・質的に)分かれて」が原義で,副詞や形容詞(後置修飾)として用いられます.日本語のアパートは「複数の住戸に仕切られた1棟の賃貸共同住宅」を意味する名詞で,アメリカ英語ではapartment house(イギリス英語ではblock of flats)と言います.その中の1戸を指すときは,apartment/flat という表現を使います.

**apartment block** 名 C 特に 困 ▶定義 a large building containing several apartments 多くのアパートを含んでいる大きな建物→アパート群,団地

**apathetic** /æpəθétɪk/ 形 ▶定義 lacking interest or desire to act 行動することへの関心または意欲に欠けている→無関心な,無気力な,冷淡な,無感動な ‖ *Many students are apathetic about politics.* 多くの学生は政治に対して無関心だ.

**apathy** /ǽpəθi/ 名 U ▶定義 the feeling of not being interested in or enthusiastic about anything 何事に対しても関心がない,または熱心ではないという気持ち→無関心,無気力,冷淡,無感動 ‖ *There is widespread apathy towards the elections.* 選挙に対する無関心が広がっている.

**ape**¹ /éɪp/ 名 C ▶定義 a type of animal like a large monkey with no tail or only a very short tail 尾のない,または非常に短い尾を持つ大型の猿のような動物の一種→猿,類人猿 ‖ *Chimpanzees and gorillas are apes.* チンパンジーとゴリラは類人猿である.

**ape**² /éɪp/ 動 他 ▶定義 to copy sb/sth, especially in a ridiculous way ~を,特にこっけいに,まねる→~をまねる,(笑われるような下手な)~の物まねをする ‖ *The children were aping the teacher's way of walking.* その子供たちは先生の歩き方をふざけてまねていた.

**aperitif** /əpèrətíːf, -tíːf/ 名 C ▶定義 an alcoholic drink that you have before a meal 食事の前に飲むアルコールの入った飲み物→食前酒,アペリティフ,アペリチ(ー)フ

**apiece** /əpíːs/ 副 ▶定義 each それぞれに→各々に,各個に,各人に ‖ *Coates and Winterbotham scored a goal apiece.* コーツとウィンターボサムはそれぞれに1点を入れた.

**apologetic** /əpɑ̀lədʒétɪk/ 形 ▶定義 feeling or showing that you are sorry for sth you have done 自分がした~に対して申し訳ないと感じている,またはそれを表している→~に対して謝罪する,謝罪の,おわびの,弁解の ‖ *He was most apologetic about his son's bad behaviour.* 彼は自分の息子のひどい振る舞いについて大変申し訳なく思っていた. *I wrote him an apologetic letter.* 私は彼におわびの手紙を書いた.—
**apologetically** /-k(ə)li/ 副 →謝罪して,わびるように,弁解して

*★**apologize** (または -ise) /əpɑ́lədʒàɪz/ 動 自 ▶定義 apologize (to sb) (for sth) to say that you are sorry for sth that you have done (~に)自分がした…に対して申し訳なく思っていると言う→~のことで謝る,わびる,謝罪する ‖ *You'll have to apologize to your teacher for being late.* あなたは遅刻したことを先生に謝らなければならないでしょう.

▶謝るときに実際に言う言葉は,通常,I'm sorry.(どうもすみません.)である.

*★**apology** /əpɑ́lədʒi/ 名 C U (複 **apologies**) ▶定義 (an) apology (to sb) (for sth) a spoken or written statement that you are sorry for sth you have done, etc (~に)自分がした…などに対して申し訳なく思っていると言った,または書かれた言葉→わび,謝罪 ‖ *Please accept our apologies for the delay.* 遅れたことに対する私たちの謝罪を聞き入れてください. *a letter of apology* おわびの手紙

**apostrophe** /əpɑ́strəfi/ 名 C ▶定義 1 the sign (') used for showing that you have left a letter or letters out of a word as in 'I'm', 'can't' or 'we'll' I'm, can't, we'llなどに見られるように,単語の中の1文字または複数の文字を省略したことを表すために用いられる記号(')→アポストロフィー ▶定義 2 the sign (') used for showing who or what sth belongs to as in 'John's chair', 'the boy's room' or 'Russia's President'. John's chair, the boy's room, Russia's Presidentなどに見られるように,~がだれに,または何に属しているかを表すため

**appal** (米 **appall**) /əpɔ́ːl/ 動 他 (**appalling**; **appalled**) (通常は受動態で) ▶定義 to shock sb very much ～に強い衝撃を与える ➡～をぞっとさせる, ぎょっとさせる — appalling /əpɔ́ːlɪŋ/ 形 ➡ぞっとさせる, 恐ろしい, ぎょっとするような — appallingly 副 ➡ひどく, 恐ろしく, ぞっとするほど

**apparatus** /æpəréɪtəs; -ræt-/ 名 U ▶定義 the set of tools, instruments or equipment used for doing a job or an activity 仕事や活動をするために用いられる一組の道具, 器具, 装置 ➡器具一式, 機械, 装置

**apparent** /əpǽr(ə)nt, əpéər-/ 形 ▶定義 1 (名詞の前だけ) that seems to be real or true but may not be 真実である, または本当であるように見えるが, そうでないかもしれない ➡見掛け(だけ)の, 上辺の, 外見上の ▶定義 2 apparent (to sb) clear; easy to see 明らかな; 見えやすい ➡明白な, 明瞭(めいりょう)な, はっきりと理解できる ‖ It quickly became apparent to us that our teacher could not speak French. 先生がフランス語を話せないことは私たちにもすぐに明らかになった.

**apparently** /əpǽr(ə)ntli, əpéər-/ 副 ▶定義 according to what people say or to how sth appears, but perhaps not true 人々が言うこと, または～の見え方によると…だが, それは本当ではないかもしれない ➡(実際はともかく)見たところでは(～らしい), 外見上は, どうも～らしい ‖ Apparently, he's already been married twice. どうも彼は今までに2度結婚したことがあるらしい. He was apparently undisturbed by the news. 彼はその知らせに悩まされなかったようだった.

★**appeal**¹ /əpíːl/ 動 自 ▶定義 1 appeal to sb (for sth); appeal for sth to make a serious request for sth you need or want very much 必要としている, または強く求めている～を真剣に要請する ➡～を懇願する, 求める, 訴える ‖ Relief workers in the disaster area are appealing for more help and supplies. 被災地の救助隊員たちは, より一層の援助と物資を求めている. She appealed to the kidnappers to let her son go. 彼女は誘拐犯に息子を解放するよう訴えた. ▶定義 2 appeal (to sb) to be attractive or interesting to sb ～にとって魅力のある, または面白い ➡～の心に訴える, 気に入る, 受ける ‖ The idea of living in the country doesn't appeal to me at all. 田舎で生活するという考えは, 私の好みに全く合わない. ▶定義 3 appeal to sth to influence sb's feelings or thoughts so that he/she will do sth you want 自分が求めている～を…が行うように, その～の気持ちや考えに影響を及ぼす ➡～に訴える ‖ We aim to appeal to people's generosity. 私たちは人々の寛大さに訴えようとしている. ▶定義 4 appeal (against/for sth) to ask sb in authority to make or change a decision 権力を持っている～に決定することを, または決定を変更することを求める ➡抗議する, 控訴する, 上告する ‖ He decided to appeal against his conviction. 彼は有罪判決を不服として上訴することにした. The player fell down and appealed for a penalty. その選手は転倒し, 反則であると抗議した.

★**appeal**² /əpíːl/ 名 ▶定義 1 C a serious request for sth you need or want very much 必要としている, または強く求めている～を真剣に要請すること ➡懇願, 頼み, 訴え, 要求 ‖ The police have made an urgent appeal for witnesses to come forward. 警察は目撃者は名乗り出てくれるよう緊急に求めた. ▶定義 2 C an appeal to sth a suggestion that tries to influence sb's feelings or thoughts so that he/she will do what you want 自分が求めている～を…が行うように, その～の気持ちや考えに影響を及ぼそうとする 示唆 ➡訴えること, 訴え, アピール ▶定義 3 C a formal request to sb in authority to change a decision 権力を持っている～に決定の変更を正式に求めること ➡抗議, 控訴, 上告 ▶定義 4 U the attraction or interesting quality of sth/sb ～の魅力的な, または面白い性質 ➡心を引き付ける力, 魅力, 人気

**appealing** /əpíːlɪŋ/ 形 ▶定義 1 attractive or interesting 魅力のある, または面白い ➡心を動かす, 魅力的な, 興味をそそる ‖ The idea of lying on a beach sounds very appealing! 浜辺に寝そべるという考えはとても魅力的だね. ▶定義 2 showing that you need help, etc 助けなどを必要としていることを表している ➡訴えるような, 哀れを誘う ‖ an appealing look 訴えるような目付き — appealingly 副 ➡魅力的に,

訴えるように

\***appear** /əpíər/ 動 ❸ ▶定義1 appear to be/do sth; appear (that)... to seem 〜であるように思われる→〜のように見える, 思える, 〜らしい ‖ *She appears to be very happy in her job.* 彼女は仕事に大変満足しているように見える. *It appears that you were given the wrong information.* あなたは間違った情報を与えられたようです. ☞ 形 apparent ▶定義2 to suddenly be seen; to come into sight 急に目に見える; 視界に入ってくる→現れる, 姿を表す, 見えてくる ‖ *The bus appeared from round the corner.* バスが角を曲がって現れた. ⇔ **disappear** ▶定義3 to begin to exist 存在し始める→出現する, 登場する, 発生する ‖ *The disease is thought to have appeared in Africa.* その病気はアフリカで発生したと考えられている. ▶定義4 to be published or printed 発行される, または出版される→世に出る, 掲載される ‖ *The article appeared in this morning's paper.* その記事は今朝の新聞に出ていた. ▶定義5 to perform or speak where you are seen by a lot of people たくさんの人々に見られる場所で演じる, または話す→出演する ‖ *to appear on television/in a play* テレビに・芝居に出演する

\***appearance** /əpíərəns/ 名 ▶定義1 ❶the way that sb/sth looks or seems 〜の見えている様子→外観, 外見, 見掛け ‖ *A different hairstyle can completely change your appearance.* 違う髪型にすると見た目を全く変えることができる. *He gives the appearance of being extremely confident.* 彼は自分をとても自信ありげに見せている. ▶定義2 [単数扱い]the coming of sb/sth 〜が来ること→現れること, 出現, 登場 ‖ *the appearance of television in the home in the 1950s* 1950年代における家庭へのテレビの登場 ▶定義3 ❸an act of appearing in public, especially on stage, television, etc 公に, 特に舞台, テレビなどに, 姿を現すこと→出演, 出席

**appendicitis** /əpèndəsáɪtəs/ 名 ❶ ▶定義 an illness in which your appendix becomes extremely painful and usually has to be removed 虫垂・盲腸が非常に痛くなり, 通常は除去しなければならないような病気→虫垂炎, 盲腸炎

**appendix** /əpéndɪks/ 名 ❸ ▶定義1 ( 複 **appendixes**) a small organ inside your body near your stomach. In humans, the appendix has no real function. 体内で腸の近くにある小さな器官. 人間の場合, 実質的な機能は持っていない→虫垂 ▶定義2 ( 複 **appendices** /-dəsìːz/) a section at the end of a book, etc that gives extra information 追加の情報を与えるための, 本などの終わりにあるセクション→付録, 補遺, 追加

**appetite** /ǽpətàɪt/ 名 ❸ ❶ ▶定義 a strong desire for sth, especially food 〜, 特に食べ物への欲求→食欲, 〜に対する欲望, 欲求 ‖ *Some fresh air and exercise should give you an appetite (= make you hungry).* 少し新鮮な空気に当たり運動すれば食欲がきっとわく(= おなかがすく)でしょう. *He has a great appetite for work/life.* 彼は仕事・人生に対して意欲が旺盛(おうせい)である. *loss of appetite* 食欲不振 成句 whet sb's appetite ⇒ **WHET**

**appetizer**(または **appetiser**) /ǽpətàɪzər/ 特に 米 = **STARTER**

**appetizing**(または **appetising**) /ǽpətàɪzɪŋ/ 形 ▶定義 (used about food, etc) that looks or smells attractive; making you feel hungry(食べ物などについて) 見た目にも匂いも魅力的である; 空腹を感じさせている→食欲をそそる, おいしそうな ‖ *an appetizing smell* おいしそうなにおい

**applaud** /əplɔ́ːd/ 動 ▶定義1 ❸ ❶ to hit your hands together noisily (**clap**) in order to show that you like sb/sth 〜が気に入ったことを表すために, 両手を大きな音を立ててたたく(拍手する)→〜に拍手する, 拍手を送る ‖ *The audience applauded loudly.* 聴衆は盛んに拍手した. *The team was applauded as it left the field.* そのチームはフィールドを去る時に拍手を送られた. ▶定義2 ❶ (通常は受動態で) to express approval of sth 〜を承認することを表す→〜を賞賛する, 支持する ‖ *The decision was applauded by everybody.* その決定は全員の拍手によって承認された.

**applause** /əplɔ́ːz/ 名 ❶ ▶定義 the noise made by a group of people hitting their hands together (**clapping**) to show their approval and enjoyment 承認や喜びを表すために人々の集団が両手をたたく(拍手する)ことによって出る大きな音→拍手, 拍手喝さい, 賞賛, 拍手による承認

‖ Let's all give a big **round of applause** to the cook! その料理人に全員で大きな拍手を送りましょう。

\***apple** /ǽpl/ 名 C U ▶定義 a hard, round fruit with a smooth green, red or yellow skin 緑、赤、あるいは黄色の滑らかな皮のある、固くて丸い果物→**リンゴ** ‖ *apple juice* リンゴジュース ☞ C3 ページのさし絵

**appliance** /əpláɪəns/ 名 C ▶定義 a piece of equipment for a particular purpose in the house 家の中にある、特定の目的のための装置→**器具、装置、設備** ‖ *washing machines and other domestic appliances* 洗濯機とそのほかの家庭用電気器具

**applicable** /ǽplɪkəb(ə)l, əplík-/ 形 (名詞の前は不可) ▶定義 **applicable** (**to sb/sth**) that concerns sb/sth; relevant to sb/sth ～に関係する；～に関連がある→**～に適用される、当てはまる、適切な** ‖ *This part of the form is only applicable to married women.* 書類のこの部分は既婚の女性だけに当てはまる.

**applicant** /ǽplɪkənt/ 名 C ▶定義 a person who makes a formal request for sth (**applies for sth**), especially for a job, a place at a college, university, etc ～、特に職、大学などへの入学などを正式に依頼する(～に申し込む)人→**志願者、応募者、申し込み者** ‖ *There were over 200 applicants for the job.* その職に 200 人以上の応募者がいた.

**application** /ǽplɪkéɪʃ(ə)n/ 名 ▶定義 1 C U (**an**) **application** (**to sb**) (**for sth**) a formal written request, especially for a job or a place in a school, club, etc 特に職、学校への入学、クラブへの入会への、書面による正式な依頼→**～への申し込み、出願、申請** ‖ *Applications for the job should be made to the Personnel Manager.* その職への応募は人事部長あてにしてください. *To become a member, fill in the application form.* 会員になる場合は、申し込み用紙に記入してください. ▶定義 2 C U the practical use (of sth) (～の)実際的な利用→**適用、応用、利用** ▶定義 3 U hard work; effort 勤勉；努力→**打ち込むこと、専念、専心**

**applied** /əpláɪd/ 形 ▶定義 (used about a subject) studied in a way that has a practical use (ある分野について)実際に役立つように研究される→**応用の** ⇔ **pure**

\*apply /əpláɪ/ 動 (現分 **applying**; 三単現 **applies**; 過, 過分 **applied**) ▶定義 1 自 **apply** (**to sb**) (**for sth**) to ask for sth in writing ～を書面で求める→**～に申し込む、申請する、志願する** ‖ *I've applied to that company for a job.* 私はあの会社に求職している. *She's applying for a place at university.* 彼女は大学に出願している.
▶定義 2 自 **apply** (**to sb/sth**) to concern or involve sb/sth ～に関係する、または関連する→**～に当てはまる、適合する** ‖ *This information applies to all children born after 1997.* この情報は 1997 年より後に生まれた子供すべてに当てはまる. ▶定義 3 他 **apply sth** (**to sth**) to make practical use of sth ～を実際的に利用する→**～を適用する、応用する、利用する** ‖ *new technology which can be applied to solving problems in industry* 産業界の問題を解決するために適用できる新技術 ▶定義 4 他 (通常は受動態で) to use a word, a name, etc to describe sb/sth ～を描写するために言葉、名前などを用いる→**～を…に当てはめる、付ける** ‖ *I don't think the term 'music' can be applied to that awful noise.* 私は、あのひどい音に「音楽」という言葉は当てはまらないと思う. ▶定義 5 他 **apply sth** (**to sth**) to put or spread sth onto sth ～を…に…を付ける、または塗る→**～を…に加える、当てる、あてがう、～を…に塗る** ‖ *Apply the cream to the infected area twice a day.* そのクリームを感染した所に 1 日に 2 回塗ってください. ▶定義 6 **apply yourself/sth** (**to sth/doing sth**) to make yourself give all your attention to sth ～に自分のすべての注意を向けさせる→**～を…に向ける注ぐ、～に熱中する** ‖ *to apply your mind to sth* ～に専心する

**appoint** /əpɔ́ɪnt/ 動 他 ▶定義 1 **appoint sb** (**to sth**) to choose sb for a job or position ～をある職、または地位に選ぶ→**～を任命する、指名する** ‖ *The committee have appointed a new chairperson.* その委員会は新しい議長を指名した. *He's been appointed (as) assistant to Dr Beale.* 彼はビール博士の助手に任命された.
▶定義 2 正式 **appoint sth** (**for sth**) to arrange or decide on sth ～を取り決める、または決定する→**～を指定する、決める**

\***appointment** /əpɔ́ɪntmənt/ 名 ▶定義 1 C U an

**appointment (with sb)** an arrangement to see sb at a particular time ～とある特定の時間に会う約束→(面会の)約束,予約 ‖ *I have an appointment with Dr Sula at 3 o'clock.* スーラ博士と3時に会う約束がある. *I'd like to* **make an appointment** *to see the manager.* マネージャーにお会いする約束をしたいのですが. *I realized I wouldn't be able to keep the appointment so I cancelled it.* 私はその約束を守れないであろうことが分かったので,取り消した. *Visits are by appointment only (= at a time that has been arranged in advance).* ご予約の上に(=あらかじめ取り決められた時間に)お越しください. ▶定義2 **C**a job or a position of responsibility 責任のある職または地位→役職,官職,地位,任務 ‖ *a temporary/permanent appointment* 一時的な・常設の役職 ▶定義3 **U** appointment (to sth) the act of choosing sb for a job ～をある職に選ぶこと→任命,選任,使命

**appraisal** /əpréɪz(ə)l/ **C U** 正式 ▶定義 a judgement about the value or quality of sb/sth ～の価値または質についての判断→評価,分析,鑑定,値踏み,見積もり

**appraise** /əpréɪz/ 動 他 正式 ▶定義 to judge the value or quality of sb/sth ～の価値または質について判断する→～を評価する,鑑定する,査定する,値踏みする,見積もる

**appreciable** /əprí:ʃ(i)əbl/ 形 ▶定義 noticeable or important 人目をひく,または重要な→(容易に)感知できるほどの,目に見えるほどの,評価可能な,かなりの,相当の

★**appreciate** /əprí:ʃièɪt/ 動 ▶定義1 ⊕to enjoy sth or to understand the value of sb/sth ～を享受する,または～の価値を理解する→～を鑑賞する,味わう,高く評価する,～の真価を認める ‖ *My boss doesn't appreciate me.* 上司は私を評価してくれていない. *I don't appreciate good coffee - it all tastes the same to me.* 私はおいしいコーヒーが分からない － 私にはどれも同じ味がする. ▶定義2 ⊕to understand a problem, situation, etc 問題,状況などを理解する→～を正しく理解する,認識する,察する ‖ *I appreciate your problem but I'm afraid I can't help you.* あなたの問題は分かりますが,残念ながらお助けすることができません. ▶定義3 ⊕to be grateful for sth ～を有り難く思う→～を有り難く思う,～に感謝する ‖ *Thanks very much. I really appreciate your help.* どうもありがとうございます.ご助力に感謝します. ▶定義4 ⊜ to increase in value 価値が増大する→価値が上がる,相場が上がる,値上がりする

**appreciation** /əprì:ʃiéɪʃ(ə)n/ 名 **U** ▶定義1 understanding and enjoyment of the value of sth ～の価値の理解と享受→評価,理解(力),(真価を)認めること,鑑賞(力),～を味わうこと ‖ *I'm afraid I have little appreciation of modern architecture.* 残念ながら私は現代建築をほとんど理解できない. ▶定義2 the feeling of being grateful for sth ～を有り難く思っているという気持ち→～への感謝,感謝・賞賛の表明 ‖ *We bought him a present to show our appreciation for all the work he had done.* 私たちは,彼が成し遂げたすべての仕事に感謝を込めてプレゼントを買った. ▶定義3 understanding of a situation, problem, etc 状況,問題などの理解→正しい認識,理解 ▶定義4 an increase in value 価値の増大→高騰,騰貴,値上がり,増加

**appreciative** /əprí:ʃ(i)ətɪv; -ʃièɪtɪv/ 形 ▶定義1 feeling or showing pleasure or admiration 喜びや賞賛を感じている,または表している→～を鑑賞する,目の高い,鑑識眼のある ‖ *an appreciative audience* 耳の肥えた聴衆 ▶定義2 appreciative (of sth) grateful for sth ～を有り難く思っている→～に感謝している,感謝の ‖ *He was very appreciative of our efforts to help.* 彼は私たちが助けようとした努力にとても感謝していた.

**apprehensive** /ӕprɪhénsɪv/ 形 ▶定義 worried or afraid that sth unpleasant may happen 不愉快な～が起こるかもしれないと心配している,または恐れている→～を懸念して,心配して,恐れて,気遣う ‖ *I'm feeling apprehensive about tomorrow's exam.* 明日の試験のことを心配している. — apprehension /-ʃ(ə)n/ 名 **C U** →懸念,気遣い,心配,恐れ,危惧(きぐ),憂慮

**apprentice** /əpréntəs/ 名 **C** ▶定義 a person who works for low pay, in order to learn the skills needed in a particular job ある特定の仕事に必要とされる技術を身に付けるために,安い賃金で働く人→徒弟,見習い,でっち奉公,年季奉公人 ‖ *an apprentice electrician/chef/plumber* 電気技師・シェフ・配管工の見習い

**apprenticeship** /əpréntəsʃɪp/ ▶定義
the state or time of being an apprentice 徒弟である状態、またはその時期 →徒弟・見習いであること, 徒弟・見習い期間 ‖ He served a two-year apprenticeship as a carpenter. 彼は大工の見習いを2年務めた.

*****approach***[1]** /əpróʊtʃ/ ▶定義1 to come near or nearer to sb/sth 〜の近くに来る、またはもっと近くに来る →〜に近付く、アプローチする, 接近する ‖ The day of the exam approached. 試験の日が近付いた. When you approach the village you will see a garage on your left. その村に近付くと,左側に自動車修理工場が見えます. ▶定義2 to begin to deal with a problem, a situation, etc 問題、状況などに対処し始める →〜に取り組む、着手する、〜の処理・解決に取り掛かる ‖ What is the best way to approach this problem? この問題に取り組む最良の方法は何でしょうか. ▶定義3 to speak to sb usually in order to ask for sth 通常〜を頼むために、…に話し掛ける →〜に接近する、話を持ちかける、交渉する、申し入れをする ‖ I'm going to approach my bank manager about a loan. 銀行の支店長に貸し付けについて交渉するつもりだ.

**approach**[2] /əpróʊtʃ/ ▶定義1 a way of dealing with sb/sth 〜に対処する方法 →取り組み方、研究方法、アプローチ、手引き ‖ Parents don't always know what approach to take with teenage children. 親はいつも10代の子供にどのような対応の仕方をすればよいのか分からない. ▶定義2 [単数扱い] the act of coming nearer (to sb/sth) (〜の)もっと近くに来ること →近付くこと、接近 ‖ the approach of winter 冬の接近 ▶定義3 a request for sth 〜の依頼 →近付くこと、接近、申し出、言い寄り、申し入れ ‖ The company has made an approach to us for financial assistance. その会社は当方に財政援助の打診をした. ▶定義4 a road or path leading to sth 〜に通じる道または通路 →〜へ近付く道、通じる道、通路、〜の入り口 ‖ the approach to the village その村に通じる道

**approachable** /əpróʊtʃəbl/ ▶定義1 friendly and easy to talk to 友好的で話し掛けやすい →近付きやすい, 気さくな, 付き合いやすい ▶定義2 (名詞の前は不可) that can be reached 達することができる →接近できる, 近寄れる ☞類 accessible

*****appropriate***[1]** /əpróʊpriət/ ▶定義 appropriate (for/to sth) suitable or right for a particular situation, person, use, etc ある特定の状況、人、使い方などに適している、または合っている →〜にとって適切な, ふさわしい, 妥当な, 正しい ‖ The matter will be dealt with by the appropriate authorities. その件は該当の当局が対処するだろう. I don't think this film is appropriate for children. 私はこの映画が子供向きではないと思う. ⇔ inappropriate — appropriately 副 →ふさわしく, 適切に, 適切なやり方で

**appropriate**[2] /əpróʊprieɪt/ ▶定義 to take sth to use for yourself, usually without permission 通常は許可なしに、〜を取って自分のために使う →〜を(不法に)私物化する, 着服する, 盗用する

*****approval*** /əprúːv(ə)l/ ▶定義 feeling, showing or saying that you think sth is good; agreement 〜が良いと思うと感じる, 表す, あるいは言うこと; 同意 →是認, 賛成, (正式な)承認, 認可 ‖ Everybody gave their approval to the proposal. だれもがその提案に賛成した.

*****approve*** /əprúːv/ ▶定義1 approve (of sb/sth) to be pleased about sth; to like sb/sth 〜を喜ぶ; 〜が気に入る →〜を良いと認める, 是認する, 賛成する, 良く思う ‖ His father didn't approve of him becoming a dancer. 彼のお父さんは彼がダンサーになることを認めなかった. Her parents don't approve of her friends. 両親は彼女の友達のことを良く思っていない. ⇔ disapprove ▶定義2 to agree formally to sth or to say that sth is correct 〜に正式に同意する、または〜が正しいと言う →〜を(正式に)認可する, 承認する ‖ We need to get an accountant to approve these figures. 私たちは会計士にこれらの数値を承認させる必要がある.

**approving** /əprúːvɪŋ/ ▶定義 showing support or admiration for sth 〜への支持または賞賛を表している →賛成の, 是認した, 満足げな ‖ 'I agree entirely,' he said with an approving smile. 「私は全面的に賛成します」と,彼は満足げな笑みを浮かべて言った. — approvingly 副 →賛成して, 満足げに, うなずくように, 是認・賛意を表して

**approx** 略(文) approximate; approximately→おおよその, 近似の, およそ, ほぼ

**\*approximate** /əprάksəmət/ 形 ▶定義 almost correct but not completely accurate ほぼ正確であるが, 完全に正しくはない→おおよその, 近似の ‖ *The approximate time of arrival is 3 o'clock.* おおよその到着時刻は3時である. *I can only give you an approximate idea of the cost.* 私はその費用についておおよそのことしか言えない.

**\*approximately** /əprάksəmətli/ 副 ▶定義 about; roughly およそ;概略で→およそ, 約～, ほぼ ‖ *It's approximately fifty miles from here.* ここから約50マイルある.

**approximation** /əprὰksəméiʃ(ə)n/ 名 C ▶定義 a number, answer, etc which is nearly, but not exactly, right ほとんど合っているが厳密に言うと正確ではない数, 答えなど→概算, 推定(額・値), 近似値

**Apr** April→4月 ‖ *2 Apr 1993* 1993年4月2日

**apricot** /ǽprəkɑ̀t, éi-/ 名 C ▶定義 a small, round, yellow or orange fruit with a large seed (stone) inside 中に大きな種(核)がある, 黄色またはオレンジ色の小さくて丸い果物→アプリコット, アンズ(の実) ← C3 ページのさし絵

**\*April** /éiprəl/ 名 U C (略 **Apr**) ▶定義 the fourth month of the year, coming after March 3月の次に来る, 1年の4番目の月→4月

▶文中での月の表し方については, January の例と注を参照.

**April Fool's Day** 名 [単数扱い] ▶定義 1 April 4月1日→エイプリルフール(の日), 万愚節

▶この日には, ばかな話を作り上げてそれが本当であると他人に信じ込ませるなどして, 人々が互いにいたずらをするのが伝統となっている. そのような話を信じた人がいると, その人が April Fool(エイプリルフール)と呼ばれる.

**apron** /éipr(ə)n/ 名 C ▶定義 a piece of clothing that you wear over the front of your usual clothes in order to keep them clean, especially when cooking 特に料理のときに, いつもの服を汚さないようにするために前に着ける衣類→エプロン, 前掛け ← **overall** のさし絵

**apt** /ǽpt/ 形 ▶定義 1 suitable in a particular situation ある状況に適している→適切な, 適当な, ふさわしい ‖ *I thought 'complex' was an apt description of the book.*「複雑で理解しにくい」というのがその本にふさわしい説明であると思った. ▶定義 2 **apt to do sth** often likely to do sth しばしば～をしそうである→～する傾向がある, ～しがちな, ～しやすい, ～しそうである

**aptitude** /ǽptət(j)ùːd/ 名 U C ▶定義 **aptitude (for sth/for doing sth)** natural ability or skill 持って生まれた能力または器用さ→～についての才能, 素質, 適性 ‖ *She has an aptitude for learning languages.* 彼女には語学を習得する才能がある.

**aptly** /ǽptli/ 副 ▶定義 in an appropriate way; suitably 適切な方法で; ふさわしく→適切に, 巧みに, うまく ‖ *The winner of the race was aptly named Alan Speedy.* そのレースの勝者はいみじくも「アラン スピーディー」という名前だった.

**aquarium** /əkwéəriəm/ 名 C (複 **aquariums** または **aquaria** /-riə/) ▶定義 1 a glass container filled with water, in which fish and water animals are kept 水中で魚や水生動物を飼育するガラスの容器→水槽, ガラス鉢, 人工池, アクアリウム ▶定義 2 a building where people can go to see fish and other water animals 人々が魚やそのほかの水生動物を見に行くことができる建物→水族館

**Aquarius** /əkwéəriəs/ 名 C U ▶定義 the eleventh sign of the zodiac, the Water Carrier 黄道十二宮の11番目である水瓶(みずがめ)座→水瓶座, 宝瓶(ほうへい)宮

**aquatic** /əkwǽtik, -wάt-/ 形 ▶定義 living or taking place in, on or near water 水の中, 上, あるいはその近くに住んでいる, または起こっている→水生の, 水中・水上に住む, 水の, 水中・水上で行う ‖ *aquatic plants* 水草 *windsurfing and other aquatic sports* ウインドサーフィンとそのほかの水上スポーツ

**\*Arab** /ǽrəb/ 名 C ▶定義 a member of a people who lived originally in Arabia and who now live in many parts of the Middle East and North Africa 元はアラビアに住んでいたが, 今は中東や北アフリカの多くの地域に住んでいる民族の一員→アラブ人, アラビア人, アラブ民族 ― **Arab** 形 →アラブ人の, アラビアの, アラブ民族の ‖ *Arab countries* アラブ諸国

**\*Arabic** /ǽrəbik/ 名 [単数扱い] ▶定義 the language of Arab people アラブ人の言語→**アラビア語**

**arable** /ǽrəbl/ 形 ▶定義 (in farming) connected with growing crops for sale, not keeping animals (農耕で)動物を飼育するのではなく,売るための作物を育てることに関連している→**耕作に適した,耕作用の,耕作作物の,耕地の,耕地でとれた** ‖ *arable land/farmers* 耕作地・耕作民

**arbitrary** /ɑ́ːrbətr(ə)ri; -trèri/ 形 ▶定義 not seeming to be based on any reason or plan どのような理由または計画にも基づいていないように見える→**任意の,無作為な,恣意(しい)的な,勝手な,気まぐれな** ‖ *The choice of players for the team seemed completely arbitrary.* そのチームの選手の選び方は全くの気まぐれに見えた.— **arbitrarily** 副 →**恣意的に,任意に,勝手に,独断に**

**arbitrate** /ɑ́ːrbətrèɪt/ 動 自他 ▶定義 to settle an argument between two people or groups by finding a solution that both can accept 2人または2つの集団がどちらも受け入れられる解決策を見つけることによって,両者の議論に決着を付ける→**～を仲裁する,調停する** — **arbitration** /ɑ̀ːrbətréɪʃ(ə)n/ 名 Ⓤ→**仲裁,調停,裁定**

**arc** /ɑːrk/ 名 Ⓒ ▶定義 a curved line, part of a circle 曲線, 円の一部分→**円弧, 弧, 弓形**

**arcade** /ɑːrkéɪd/ 名 Ⓒ ▶定義 **1** a large covered passage or area with shops along one or both sides 片側または両側に店が並んでいる,屋根の付いた広い通りまたは区域→**アーケード** ‖ *a shopping arcade* 商店街 ☞ C8 ページのさし絵
▶定義 **2** (または **amusement arcade**) a large room with machines and games that you put coins into to play コインを入れて動く機械やゲームのある広い部屋→**ゲームセンター**

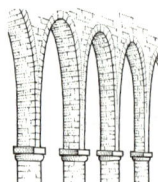
**arch**

**arch**¹ /ɑːrtʃ/ 名 Ⓒ ▶定義 **1** a curved structure with straight sides, often supporting a bridge or the roof of a large building, or it may be above a door or window 両側にまっすぐな部分がある湾曲した構造で, しばしば橋や大きな建物の屋根を支えている, または戸や窓の上部にかかっている場合もある→**アーチ,迫持(せりもち),アーチ門** ☞参 **archway** ▶定義 **2** the curved part of the bottom of your foot 足の裏の湾曲した部分→**土踏まず**

**arch**² /ɑːrtʃ/ 動 自他 ▶定義 to make a curve 湾曲を作る→**～をアーチ状にする, 弓形にする, アーチ形に曲げる, アーチを付ける**

**archaeological** (米 **archeological**) /ɑ̀ːrkiəlɒ́dʒɪk(ə)l/ 形 ▶定義 connected with archaeology 考古学に関連している→**考古学の,考古学的な,考古学上の**

**archaeologist** (米 **archeologist**) /ɑ̀ːrkiɑ́lədʒɪst/ 名 Ⓒ ▶定義 an expert in archaeology 考古学の専門家→**考古学者**

**archaeology** (米 **archeology**) /ɑ̀ːrkiɑ́lədʒi/ 名 Ⓤ ▶定義 the study of the past, based on objects or parts of buildings that are found in the ground 地中から見つかった物や建物の一部を基にした, 過去についての研究→**考古学**

**archaic** /ɑːrkéɪɪk/ 形 ▶定義 very old-fashioned; no longer used とても旧式である; もはや使われていない→**古風な,旧式の,すたれた,古語の**

**archbishop** /ɑːrtʃbíʃəp/ 名 Ⓒ ▶定義 a priest with a very high position, in some branches of the Christian Church, who is responsible for all the churches in a large area of a country 一国の広い範囲にあるすべての教会に対して責任を持っている, キリスト教の教会の一部の支部で非常に高い地位にある聖職者→**(カトリックの)大司教, (ギリシャ正教・英国国教会の)大主教, (プロテスタントの)大監督** ‖ *the Archbishop of Canterbury* (= *the head of the Church of England*) カンタベリー大主教(= 英国国教会の長) ☞参 **bishop**

**archer** /ɑ́ːrtʃər/ 名 Ⓒ ▶定義 a person who shoots pieces of wood or metal with a sharp point (**arrows**) through the air by pulling back a tight string on a curved piece of wood (**a bow**) and letting go. In past times this was done in order to kill people, but it is now done as a sport. 湾曲した木(弓)にぴんと張った弦を手元に引いてから手を離すことによって, 先のとがった木や金属(矢)を空中に放つ人. 昔は, これが人を殺すために行われたが, 今ではスポーツとして行われている→**弓の射手, アーチェリー選手, 弓術家**

**archery** /á:rtʃ(ə)ri/ 名 U ▶定義 the sport of shooting arrows 矢を射るスポーツ→**アーチェリー, 洋弓術**

*__architect__ /á:rkətèkt/ 名 C ▶定義 a person whose job is to design buildings 建物を設計することを仕事としている人→**建築家, 設計士, 設計者**

**architectural** /à:rkətéktʃ(ə)rəl/ 形 ▶定義 connected with the design of buildings 建物の設計に関連している→**建築上の, 建築学の, 建築的な構造・設計・組織を持った, 建築に関する**

**architecture** /á:rkətèktʃər/ 名 U ▶定義 1 the study of designing and making buildings 建物の設計と建設についての研究→**建築, 建築学, 建築術** ▶定義 2 the style or design of a building or buildings 建物や建物群の様式または設計→**建築様式, 建築方法, 建築物** ‖ *modern architecture* 現代建築

**archives** /á:rkaɪvz/ 名 [複数扱い] (または **archive** C) ▶定義 a collection of historical documents, etc which show the history of a place or an organization; the place where they are kept ある場所や組織の歴史を示す歴史的文書などが集まったもの; それらが保管されている所→**公文書, 古文書, 記録文書, 公文書保管所, 文書局** ‖ *archive material on the First World War* 第1次世界大戦に関する公文書保管所の資料

**archway** /á:rtʃwéɪ/ 名 C ▶定義 a passage or entrance with an arch over it 上部にアーチのある通り, または入り口→**アーチのある通路, アーチ道, 拱道(きょうどう), アーチのある門**

**Arctic**¹ /á:rkṭɪk/ 形 ▶定義 1 connected with the region around the North Pole (the most northern point of the world) 北極(世界で最も北にある地点)周辺の地域に関連している→**北極の, 北極地方の, 北極付近の** ☛参 **Antarctic** ▶定義 2 **arctic** extremely cold 非常に寒い→**極寒の, 極寒用の, 耐寒用の**

**the Arctic**² /á:rkṭɪk/ 名 [単数扱い] ▶定義 the area around the North Pole 北極周辺の地域→**北極地方** ☛参 **the Antarctic**

**the Arctic Circle** 名 [単数扱い] ▶定義 a line that we imagine going around the cold area at the top of earth; the line of latitude 66°30′N 地球の極点にある寒い地域の周りに引いてあるとする想像上の線; 緯度66度30分の線→**北極圏, 北極圏限界線** ☛ **earth** のさし絵

**ardent** /á:rdnt/ 形 ▶定義 showing strong feelings, especially a strong liking for sb/sth 特に～に対する強い好みなど, 強い気持ちを表している→**熱心な, 熱狂的な, 情熱的な, 熱烈な** ‖ *He was an ardent supporter of the Government.* 彼はその政府の熱心な支持者だった. — **ardently** 副 ▶**熱心に, 激しく, 熱烈に**

**arduous** /á:rdjuəs; -dʒu-/ 形 ▶定義 full of difficulties; needing a lot of effort 困難が一杯である; 多大な努力を必要としている→**困難な, つらい, 骨の折れる, きつい** ‖ *an arduous journey* 困難に満ちた旅 *arduous work* 骨の折れる仕事

**are** ⇒ **BE**

*__area__ /éəriə/ 名 ▶定義 1 C a part of a town, a country or the world 街, 国, 世界の一部分→**地域, 地方, 地帯** ‖ *Housing is very expensive in the Tokyo area.* 東京圏では住宅が非常に高い. *The wettest areas are in the West of the country.* 最も雨の多い地域は, その国の西部である. *built-up areas (= where there are a lot of buildings)* 市街地(= 建物がたくさんある所) *Forests cover a large area of the country.* 森林がその国の広い地域を覆っている. ☛参 **district** の注 ▶定義 2 C U the size of a surface, that you can calculate by multiplying the length by the width 長さに幅を掛けて算出できる表面の大きさ→**面積** ‖ *The area of the office is 35 square metres.* その事務所の面積は35平方メートルである. *The office is 35 square metres in area.* その事務所は面積が35平方メートルである. ☛参 **volume** ▶定義 3 C a space used for a particular activity 特定の活動に使われる空間→**区域, 場所, 空間** ‖ *The restaurant has a non-smoking area.* そのレストランには禁煙コーナーがある. ▶定義 4 C a particular part of a subject or activity あるテーマ, または活動中の特定の部分→**領域, 範囲, 分野** ‖ *Training is one area of the business that we could improve.* この会社で研修は, 改善できる一つの分野だろう.

**arena** /ərí:nə/ 名 C ▶定義 1 an area with seats around it where public entertainments (sporting events, concerts, etc) are held 公共の催し物(スポーツ競技, コンサートなど)が行われる, 周囲に座席が並んでいる場所→**競技場, 闘技場, 演技場**

**aren't** ARE NOT の短縮形

▶定義2 an area of activity that concerns the public 一般の人々に関係のある活動が行われる場所→場,舞台,世界,活動の領域,～界

**arguable** /áːrgjuəbl/ 形 ▶定義1 probably true; that you can give reasons for おそらく本当である；賛成する理由を挙げることができる→論証できる,もっともな,正しい,論じ得る ‖ *It is arguable that all hospital treatment should be free.* 病院の治療をすべて無料にするべきであるというのはもっともだ. ▶定義2 probably not true; that you can give reasons against おそらく本当ではない；反対する理由を挙げることができる→(不確かで)議論の余地がある,疑わしい,異論のある — **arguably** /-əbli/ 副 ▶定義 理由のあることだが,異論のあるところだが,おそらく,多分 ‖ *'King Lear' is arguably Shakespeare's best play.*「リア王」がおそらくシェークスピアの最高の劇であろう.

★**argue** /áːrgjuː/ 動 ▶定義1 自 argue (with sb) (about/over sth) to say things, often angrily that show that you do not agree with sb about sth ～と…について意見が一致しないことを表すような言葉を,しばしば怒って,言う→議論する,論じる,言い争う ‖ *The couple next door are always arguing.* 隣の夫婦はいつも言い争いをしている. *I never argue with my husband about money.* お金のことでうちの夫と決して言い争いをしないわ. ☞参 **fight**¹(4), **quarrel**² ▶定義2 自他 argue that...; argue (for/against sth) to give reasons that support your opinion about sth ～についての自分の意見を裏付ける理由を挙げることができる→～に賛成・反対の意見を述べる,～だと論じる,主張する ‖ *He argued against buying a new computer.* 彼は新しいコンピューターを買うことに反対の意見を述べた.

★**argument** /áːrgjəmənt/ 名 ▶定義1 C U an argument (with sb) (about/over sth) an angry discussion between two or more people who disagree with each other 互いに意見の合わない2人またはそれ以上の人の間での怒りを含んだ議論→議論,論争,口論,言い争い ‖ *Sue had an argument with her father about politics.* スーは政治のことで父親と議論した. *He accepted the decision without argument.* 彼はその決定を異議なく受け入れた.
▶quarrelは通常,argumentほど深刻ではないものを指す.
▶定義2 C the reason(s) that you give to support your opinion about sth ～についての自分の意見を裏付けるために挙げることができる理由→論,論点,論拠,主張 ‖ *What are the arguments for/against lower taxes?* 減税に賛成・反対する論拠は何ですか.

**argumentative** /àːrgjəméntətɪv/ 形 ▶定義 often involved in or enjoying arguments しばしば議論にかかわっている,またはそれを楽しんでいる→議論好きな,理屈っぽい,論争的な

**arid** /ǽrəd/ 形 ▶定義 (used about land or climate) very dry; with little or no rain (土地や気候について)とても乾燥している；ほとんど,または全く雨が降らない→(異常に)乾燥した,不毛の,湿気のない

**Aries** /éəriːz/ 名 C U ▶定義 the first of the twelve signs of the zodiac, the Ram 黄道十二宮の1番目である牡羊座→牡羊座,白羊宮

**arise** /əráɪz/ 動 自 (過 **arose** /əróʊz/; 過分 **arisen** /ərízn/) ▶定義 to begin to exist; to appear 存在し始める；現れる→起こる,生じる,現れる,生まれる ‖ *If any problems arise, let me know.* 何か問題が生じたら,私に知らせてください.

**aristocracy** /ǽrəstákrəsi/ 名 [C, 単数または複数形の動詞と共に] (複 **aristocracies**) ▶定義 the people of the highest social class who often have special titles 最も高い社会階級の中の,しばしば特別な肩書きを持つ人々→貴族,貴族階級,上流階級 ☞類 **nobility**

**aristocrat** /ǽrəstəkræt, ərís-/ 名 C ▶定義 a member of the highest social class, often with a special title しばしば特別な肩書きを持っている,最も高い社会階級の一員→貴族,貴族階級の人,上流階級の人 — **aristocratic** /ǽrəstəkrǽtɪk, ərìs-/ 形 ▶貴族の,貴族階級の,貴族的な

**arithmetic** /əríθmətɪk/ 名 U ▶定義 the kind of mathematics which involves counting with numbers (adding, subtracting, multiplying and dividing) 数字を使った計算(加算,減算,乗算,除算)にかかわる数学の部類→算数,算術 ‖ *I'm not very good at mental arithmetic.* 私は暗算があまり得意ではない.

★**arm**¹ /áːrm/ 名 C ▶定義1 the long part at each

side of your body connecting your shoulder to your hand 身体の両側にあり、肩と手をつないでいる長い部分➔腕,上肢,手,かいな ‖ *He was carrying a newspaper under his arm.* 彼は新聞を小わきに抱えて持っていた. ☛ C5 ページのさし絵 ▶定義2 the part of a piece of clothing that covers your arm; a sleeve 衣服で、腕を覆う部分; そで➔そで ‖ *He had a hole in the arm of his jumper.* 彼のジャンパーのそでには穴が開いていた. ▶定義3 the part of a chair where you rest your arms いすで、腕を置く部分➔ひじ掛け

成句 arm in arm ▶定義 with your arm folded around sb else's arm 自分の腕をほかの〜の腕に巻き付けて➔腕を組んで ‖ *The two friends walked arm in arm.* その2人の友達は腕を組んで歩いた. ☛ S6 ページのさし絵

cross/fold your arms ▶定義 to cross your arms in front of your chest 胸の前で両腕を組み合わせる➔腕組みをする ‖ *She folded her arms and waited.* 彼女は腕組みをして待っていた. *James was sitting with his arms crossed.* ジェームズは腕組みをして座っていた. ☛ S6 ページのさし絵

twist sb's arm ⇒ **TWIST**¹
with open arms ⇒ **OPEN**¹

**arm**² /ɑːm/ 動 ⊜ ⊕ ▶定義 to prepare sb/yourself to fight by supplying or getting weapons 武器を供給したり手に入れることによって、〜・自分に戦う準備をさせる➔武装させる,防備する,戦闘準備をする ☛参 **armed, arms**

**armaments** /ɑ́ːməmənts/ 名 [複数扱い] ▶定義 weapons and military equipment 武器および軍事用の装備➔軍備,軍事力,軍隊,兵器

**armband** /ɑ́ːmbænd/ 名 ⊙ ▶定義1 a piece of material that you wear around your arm 腕に巻き付ける物➔腕章 ‖ *The captain of the team wears an armband.* そのチームのキャプテンは腕章を付けている. ▶定義2 a plastic ring filled with air which you can wear on each of your arms when you are learning to swim 泳ぎを覚えているときに両腕に付けられる空気の入ったプラスチック製の輪➔(腕に付ける)浮き袋,腕巻き浮き輪

**armchair** /ɑ́ːmtʃeər/ 名 ⊙ ▶定義 a soft comfortable chair with sides which support your arms 両側に腕を支える物が付いている、柔らかくて座り心地の良いいす➔ひじ掛けいす ☛ C7 ページのさし絵

**armed** /ɑːmd/ 形 ▶定義 carrying a gun or other weapon; involving weapons 銃やそのほかの武器を携えている; 武器にかかわっている➔武装した,武器を身に付けた,武器による ‖ *All the terrorists were armed.* テロリストは全員武装していた. *armed robbery* 武装した強盗 *the armed forces (= the army, navy and air force)* 軍隊 (=陸軍, 海軍, 空軍) ⇔ **unarmed**

**armful** /ɑ́ːmfʊl/ 名 ⊙ ▶定義 the amount that you can carry in your arms 両腕で運ぶことができる量➔腕一杯,一抱え

**armhole** /ɑ́ːmhoʊl/ 名 ⊙ ▶定義 the opening in a piece of clothing where your arm goes through 衣服で、腕が通る開口部➔そでぐり,そで付け,アームホール

**armistice** /ɑ́ːməstəs/ 名 ⊙ ▶定義 an agreement between two countries who are at war that they will stop fighting 交戦中の2国間で結ばれた、戦いをやめるという協定➔休戦,停戦

**armour** /ɑ́ːrmər/ (米 **armor**) 名 ⊕ ▶定義 clothing, often made of metal, that soldiers wore in earlier times to protect themselves 昔、兵隊が体を保護するために身に着けた、しばしば金属でできている服➔よろいかぶと,かっちゅう ‖ *a suit of armour* よろいかぶと一式

**armoured** /ɑ́ːrmərd/ (米 **armored**) 形 ▶定義 (used about a vehicle) covered with metal to protect it in an attack (乗り物について) 攻撃から保護するために金属で覆っている➔装甲した

**armpit** /ɑ́ːmpɪt/ 名 ⊙ ▶定義 the part of the body under the arm at the point where it joins the shoulder わきの下で肩とつながっている身体の部分➔わきの下 ☛ C5 ページのさし絵

**arms** /ɑːmz/ 名 [複数扱い] ▶定義1 weapons, especially those that are used in war 武器,特に戦争で使われる物➔武器,兵器,武力 ‖ *a reduction in nuclear arms* 核兵器の削減 ▶定義2 = **COAT OF ARMS**

成句 up in arms ▶定義 protesting angrily about sth 〜について怒って異議を唱えている➔憤慨して,反旗をひるがえして ‖ *The workers were up in arms over the news that the factory was going to close.* その労働者たちは、工場が閉

鎖されるという知らせに対して激しく抗議した.

**＊army** /άːmi/ 名[C, 単数または複数形の動詞と共に] (複 **armies**) ▶定義1 the military forces of a country which are trained to fight on land 陸上で戦うよう訓練された, 一国の軍事力 → 陸軍 ‖ the British Army イギリス陸軍 She **joined the army** at the age of eighteen. 彼女は18歳で陸軍に入隊した. The army is/are advancing towards the border. 陸軍は国境に向かって前進している. an army officer 陸軍将校 →参 **air force, navy** ▶定義2 a large number of people, especially when involved in an activity together 特にある活動に一緒に参加するときの, 大勢の人々 → 大群, 大勢

**A-road** 名 C 英 ▶定義 a main road, usually not as wide as a motorway 通常は高速道路ほど幅広くない主要道路 → A級道路, 幹線道路

**aroma** /əróumə/ 名 C ▶定義 a smell, especially a pleasant one 香り, 特に心地良いもの → 香気, 芳香, 香り

**arose** /əróuz/ **ARISE** の過去形

**＊around** /əráund/ 副 前 ▶定義1 (または **about**) in or to various places or directions さまざまな場所や方向で, またはそれらの方へ → ～のあちこちに, 方々に, ～中 ‖ This is our office - David will show you around (= show you the different parts of it). これが私たちの事務所です－デーヴィッドがあなたをご案内します (= あなたに事務所内のいろいろな場所をお見せします). They wandered around the town, looking at the shops. 彼らは, 店々を見ながらその街のあちこちをぶらぶら歩いた. ▶定義2 moving so as to face in the opposite direction 正反対の方向に動いている → 曲がって, 向きを変えて, ぐるりと ‖ Turn around and go back the way you came. 向きを変えて, もと来た道を戻りなさい. ▶定義3 on all sides; forming a circle すべての面に; 円形を作っている → ～の周りに, ～を囲んで, 取り巻いて ‖ The park has a wall all around. その公園には一面に塀がある. Gather around so that you can all see. ちゃんと見えるように周りに集まりなさい. We sat down around the table. 私たちはテーブルを囲んで座った.

▶定義1, 2, 3の意味では, around の代わりに round を使うことができる.

▶定義4 (または **about**) near a place ある場所の近くに → ～の近くに, ～の辺りに ‖ Is there a bank around here? この近くに銀行はありますか. ▶定義5 (または **about**) present or available 存在している, または利用できる → 存在して, 活動して, (物が)出回っている, 手に入る ‖ I went to the house but there was nobody around. 私はその家に行ったがだれもいなかった. ▶定義6 (または **about**) approximately およそ → 約, 大体, ～くらい, ～ころ ‖ I'll see you around seven (= at about 7 o'clock). 7時ころお会いしましょう (= 7時くらいに). ▶定義7 (または **about**) used for activities with no real purpose 実際の目的がない活動に対して用いられる → 何もしないで, ぼやっと, ぶらぶらと, のんびりと ‖ 'What are you doing?' 'Nothing, just lazing around.' 「何をしているのですか」「何もしていません. ただのんびりしているだけです」

**arouse** /əráuz/ 動 他 ▶定義 to cause a particular reaction in people ある特定の反応を人々に引き起こさせる → ～を喚起する, 刺激する, 駆り立てる, 目覚めさせる ‖ to arouse sb's curiosity/interest ～の好奇心・興味をかき立てる — arousal 名 U → 目覚め, 喚起, 覚醒(かくせい)

**arr** 略 arrives → 到着する ‖ arr York 07.15 7時15分ヨーク着

**＊arrange** /əréɪndʒ/ 動 ▶定義1 他 to put sth in order or in a particular pattern ～を順番に並べる, またはある特定の型にする → ～をきちんと並べる, 整える, 配置する, そろえる ‖ The books were arranged in alphabetical order. それらの本はアルファベット順に並べられていた. Arrange the chairs in a circle. いすを円形に並べなさい. She arranged the flowers in a vase. 彼女はその花を花びんに生けた. ▶定義2 自 他 arrange (for) sth; arrange to do sth; arrange (sth) with sb to make plans and preparations so that sth can happen in the future ～が将来起きるように計画を立て準備をする → ～を取り決める, 計画する, 準備する, 手はずを整える, 手配する ‖ We're arranging a surprise party for Aisha. 私たちはアイーシャをびっくりさせるパーティーの準備をしている. She arranged to meet Stuart after work. 彼女は仕事の後でスチュアートに会う手はずを整えた. She arranged for her mother to look after the baby. 彼女は母親に赤ん坊を見てもらうよう手配した.

**\*arrangement** /əréɪndʒmənt/ 名 ▶定義 1 [ C, 通常は複数] plans or preparations for sth that will happen in the future 将来起きるような〜の計画または準備 → **準備, 手はず, 計画, 用意, 手配** ‖ *Come round this evening and we'll* **make arrangements for** *the party.* 今晩来てください. そうしたら(一緒に)パーティーの準備をしましょう. ▶定義 2 C U an agreement with sb to do sth 〜と…をする約束 → **協定, 取り決め, 打ち合わせ, 申し合わせ** ‖ *They* **have an arrangement** *to share the cost of the food.* 彼らは食費を分担するという取り決めをしている. *We both need to use the computer so we'll have to* **come to some arrangement**. 私たちはどちらもコンピューターを使う必要があるので, 何らかの話をつけなければならないだろう. ▶定義 3 C a group of things that have been placed in a particular pattern ある特定の型に並べられた物の集まり → **きちんと並べられた物, 配置された物, 整理した物** ‖ *a flower arrangement* 生け花

**array** /əréɪ/ 名 C ▶定義 a large collection of things, especially one that is impressive and is seen by other people たくさんの物の集まり, 特に印象的で他人から見られる物 → **整然と並んだ物, 大勢の人の勢ぞろい, たくさんの物(の陳列)**

**arrears** /ərɪ́ərz/ 名 [複数扱い] ▶定義 money that sb owes that he/she should have paid earlier 〜がもっと早くに支払うべきだった借りている金 → **未払いの金, 未払金, 滞納金**

成句 **be in arrears; fall/get into arrears** ▶定義 to be late in paying money that you owe 借りている金の支払いが遅れている → **遅れている, 未払いである, 滞る** ‖ *I'm in arrears with the rent.* 私は家賃の支払いが遅れている.

**be paid in arrears** ▶定義 to be paid for work after you have done the work 仕事が完了した後にそれに対して支払われる → **後から支払われる** ‖ *You will be paid monthly in arrears.* 賃金は毎月1回の後払いになります.

**\*arrest**[1] /ərést/ 動 他 ▶定義 when the police arrest sb, they take him/her prisoner in order to question him/her about a crime 警察が〜を逮捕すると, 犯罪について質問するためにその〜を留置する → **逮捕する, 検挙する, 拘束する**

**\*arrest**[2] /ərést/ 名 C ▶定義 the act of arresting sb 〜を逮捕すること → **逮捕, 検挙** ‖ *The police* **made** *ten* **arrests** *after the riot.* 警察は暴動の後で10名を逮捕した. *The wanted man is now* **under arrest** *(= has been arrested).* その指名手配中の者は現在拘留されている(= 逮捕されている).

**\*arrival** /əráɪv(ə)l/ 名 ▶定義 1 U reaching the place to which you were travelling 向かっている場所に着くこと → **到着, 到達** ‖ *On our arrival we were told that our rooms had not been reserved.* 私たちは到着するとすぐに, 部屋が予約されていないと言われた. ▶定義 2 C people or things that have arrived 到着した人々または物 → **到着した人, 到着した物, 着荷** ‖ *We brought in extra chairs for the late arrivals.* 私たちは遅く着く人たちのために余分にいすを持ってきた.

**\*arrive** /əráɪv/ 動 自 ▶定義 1 arrive (at/in...) to reach the place to which you were travelling 向かっていた場所に着く → **到着する, 着く** ‖ *We arrived home at about midnight.* 私たちは真夜中近くに家に着いた. *What time does the train arrive in Newcastle?* その電車は何時にニューキャッスルに到着しますか. *They arrived at the station ten minutes late.* 彼らは10分遅く駅に着いた.

▶ arrive inは街, 国などの名前と共に用い, arrive atは場所, 建物などと共に用いることに注意する.

▶定義 2 to come or happen 来る, または起こる → **来る, 到来する** ‖ *The day of the wedding had finally arrived.* 結婚式の日がいよいよやって来た.

句動詞 **arrive at** ▶定義 to reach sth 〜に達する → **〜に到達する, 達する** ‖ *We finally arrived at a decision.* 私たちはとうとう1つの結論に達した.

**arrogant** /ǽrəgənt/ 形 ▶定義 thinking that you are better and more important than other people 自分がほかの人々よりも優れていて偉いと思っている → **ごう慢な, 横柄な, 思い上がった, 尊大な** — **arrogance** 名 U → **ごう慢, 横柄, 思い上がり, 尊大さ** — **arrogantly** 副 → **ごう慢に, 横柄に**

**arrow** /ǽroʊ/ 名 C ▶定義 1 a thin piece of wood or metal, with one pointed end and feathers at the other end, that is shot by pulling back the string on a curved piece of wood (**a bow**) and letting go 一方の端はとがっており, もう一方には羽根が付いている細長い木または金属の棒

**arsenic** /ɑ́ːrs(ə)nɪk/ 図 ❶ ▶定義 a type of very strong poison 非常に強力な毒の一種➡ひ素

**arson** /ɑ́ːrs(ə)n/ 図 ❶ ▶定義 the crime of setting fire to a building on purpose 建物に故意に火をつけるという犯罪➡放火(罪)

**arsonist** /ɑ́ːrs(ə)nɪst/ 図 ❻ ▶定義 a person who deliberately sets fire to a building 建物に故意に火をつける人➡放火犯人

*****art** /ɑ́ːrt/ 図 ▶定義 1 ❶the activity or skill of producing things such as paintings, designs, etc; the objects that are produced 絵画、デザインなどの作品を生み出す活動、またはそのような技術; 生み出された作品➡美術, 芸術作品, 美術品 ‖ *an art class* 美術のクラス *modern art* 現代美術 *I've never been good at art.* 私には美術の才能が全くなかった. ☞参 **work of art** ▶定義 2 ❶a skill or sth that needs skill 技術, または技術を必要とする〜➡技術, 技巧, 手腕, 〜術, こつ ‖ *There's an art to writing a good letter.* 上手な手紙を書くには技術が要る. ▶定義 3 **the arts** [複数扱い] activities which involve creating things such as paintings, literature or music 絵画, 文学, 音楽などの作品を作り出すことにかかわる活動➡芸術 ▶定義 4 **arts** [複数扱い] subjects such as history or languages that you study at school or university 学校や大学で学ぶ, 歴史, 言語などの科目➡人文科学, 教養科目, 一般教育科目 ▶通常, sciences (または science subjects) (自然科学) に対して arts (または arts subjects) (人文科学) と言う.

**artefact** /ɑ́ːrtɪfækt/ 図 ❻ ▶定義 an object that is made by a person 人によって作られた物➡加工品, 人造物, 人工品

**artery** /ɑ́ːrtəri/ 図 ❻ (複 **arteries**) ▶定義 one of the tubes which take blood from the heart to other parts of the body 心臓から身体のほかの部分へ血を運ぶ血管の1つ➡動脈 ☞参 **vein**

**arthritis** /ɑːrθráɪtəs/ 図 ❶ ▶定義 a disease which causes swelling and pain in the places where your bones are connected (**joints**), where you bend your arms, fingers, etc 骨と骨がつながっていて腕や指などが曲がる所(関節)に, はれと痛みを引き起こす病気➡関節炎

**artichoke** /ɑ́ːrtɪtʃòʊk/ 図 ❻ ▶定義 a green vegetable with a lot of thick pointed leaves. You can eat the bottom part of the leaves and its centre. 先のとがった厚い葉がたくさん付いている青菜. 葉の付け根の部分と中央部が食べられる➡アーティチョーク, チョウセンアザミ ☞ C3ページのさし絵

*****article** /ɑ́ːrtɪkl/ 図 ❻ ▶定義 1 an object, especially one of a set 物, 特にまとまった物の中の1つ➡品物, 物, (同種のものの)1個, 1つ ‖ *articles of clothing* 衣料品 ▶定義 2 a piece of writing in a newspaper or magazine 新聞や雑誌に書かれたもの➡記事, 論説, 論文 ▶定義 3 (文法) the words 'a/an' (**the indefinite article**) or 'the' (**the definite article**) a/an (不定冠詞)や the (定冠詞)という単語➡冠詞 ▶冠詞についての説明は, 巻末の「文法早見表」を参照.

**articulate**¹ /ɑːrtíkjələt/ 形 ▶定義 good at expressing your ideas clearly 自分の考えを明確に表現するのが上手である➡考えをはっきり述べることができる, はきはきしている ⇔**inarticulate**

**articulate**² /ɑːrtíkjəlèɪt/ 動 ❶ ❷ ▶定義 to say sth clearly or to express your ideas or feelings 〜を明確に言う, または自分の考えや感情を表現する➡〜を明瞭(めいりょう)に発音する, 話す, 〜を明確に表現する, はっきり述べる

**articulated** /ɑːrtíkjəlèɪtəd/ 形 医 ▶定義 (used about a large vehicle such as a lorry) made of two sections which are joined together (トラックのような大きな乗り物について)つながっている2つの部分から成っている➡連結式の

*****artificial** /ɑ̀ːrtəfíʃ(ə)l/ 形 ▶定義 not genuine or natural but made by people 純粋または天然ではなく, 人によって作られた➡人工の, 人工的な, 人造の, 模造の ‖ *artificial flowers* 造花 — **artificially** 副 ➡人工的に, 不自然に, わざとらしく

**artificial intelligence** 図 ❶ ▶定義 (the study of) the way in which computers can be made to copy the way humans think コンピューターが人間の考える方法をまねるように作られる方法(の研究)➡人工知能

**artillery** /ɑːrtíl(ə)ri/ 図 ❶ ▶定義 large, heavy guns that are moved on wheels; the part of the army that uses them 車輪を付けて移動する大型で重い大砲; それらを使う軍隊の部門→**大砲, 火砲, 砲, (移動式)ミサイル発射機, 砲兵隊**

*__artist__ /áːrtɪst/ 名 C ▶定義 somebody who produces art, especially paintings or drawings 芸術, 特に絵画またはスケッチを生み出す人→**芸術家, 画家, 絵かき**

__artistic__ /ɑːrtístɪk/ 形 ▶定義 1 connected with art 芸術に関連している→**芸術の, 美術の, 芸術家の** ‖ *the artistic director of the theatre* その劇場の芸術監督 ▶定義 2 showing a skill in art 芸術の技量を見せている→**芸術的な, 風雅な, 趣のある, 技巧の優れた** — __artistically__ /-k(ə)li/ 副 →**芸術的に, 芸術的に見れば**

__artistry__ /áːrtɪstri/ 名 U ▶定義 the skill of an artist 芸術家の技量→**芸術的才能, 芸術的想像力, 芸術家としての腕前, 芸術性**

__artwork__ /áːrtwəːrk/ 名 ▶定義 1 U photographs, drawings, etc that have been prepared for a book or magazine 本や雑誌のために用意された写真, スケッチなど→**さし絵, イラスト, 図版, 写真** ‖ *a piece of artwork* 1 枚のさし絵 ▶定義 2 C a work of art, especially one in a museum or an exhibition 芸術作品, 特に美術館や展覧会に出ている物→**美術品, 芸術作品**

*__as__ /əz; 強形 æz/ 接 前 副 ▶定義 1 while sth else is happening ほかの〜が起こっている間に→**〜のとき, 〜しながら, 〜につれて** ‖ *The phone rang just as I was leaving the house.* 私が家を出ようとしたちょうどその時に電話が鳴った. *As she walked along the road, she thought about her father.* 彼女は, 道に沿って歩きながら父親のことを考えた. ▶定義 2 __as...as__ used for comparing people or things 人またはものを比較するために用いられて→**〜と同じくらい, 同様に** ‖ *Todor's almost as tall as me.* トドールは私とほぼ同じ背の高さだ. *Todor's almost as tall as I am.* トドールは私とほぼ同じ背の高さだ. *It's not as cold as it was yesterday.* 昨日ほど寒くない. *I'd like an appointment __as soon as possible__.* 私はできるだけ早く予約したい. *She earns __twice as much as__ her husband.* 彼女は夫の2倍稼いでいる. *I haven't got as many books as you have.* 私はあなたほどたくさんの本を持っていない. ▶定義 3 used for talking about sb/sth's job, role or function 〜の仕事, 役割, 機能などについて話すときに用いられて→**〜とし**て ‖ *He works as a train driver.* 彼は電車の運転手として働いている. *Think of me as your friend, not as your boss.* 私のことを上司ではなく友達だと思いなさい. *You could use this white sheet as a tablecloth.* この白いシーツをテーブルクロスとして使うことができるでしょう. ▶定義 4 in a particular way, state, etc; like ある特定の方法, 状態などで; 〜のように→**〜と同様に, 〜のように, 〜するやり方で, 〜の通りに** ‖ *Please do as I tell you.* 私の言う通りにしてください. *Leave the room __as it is__. Don't move anything.* 部屋はそのままにしておきなさい. 何も動かしてはいけません. ▶定義 5 used at the beginning of a comment about what you are saying 自分が言っている事についての論評の始めに用いられて→**〜ではあるが, 〜だけれども, 〜ながらも** ‖ *__As you know__, I've decided to leave at the end of the month.* ご存じの通り, 私は月末に出発することにしました. ▶定義 6 because 〜だから→**〜なので, 〜だから, 〜ゆえに** ‖ *I didn't buy the dress, as I decided it was too expensive.* そのドレスは値段が高すぎると思ったので買わなかった.

成句 __as for__ ▶定義 used when you are starting to talk about a different person or thing 別の人または物事について話し始めるときに用いられて→**〜はというと, 〜について言えば, 〜に関する限りでは** ‖ *Gianni's upstairs. As for Andreas, I've no idea where he is.* ジャーンニは2階にいます. アンドレアスについては, どこにいるのか私には分かりません.

__as if; as though__ ▶定義 used for saying how sb/sth appears 〜がどのように見えているかを述べるために用いられて→**あたかも〜であるかのように, まるで〜みたいに** ‖ *She looks as if/though she's just got out of bed.* 彼女はまるでベッドから起きてきたばかりのように見える.

__as it were__ ▶定義 used for saying that sth is only true in a certain way ある点においてのみ〜が真実であると言うために用いられて→**いわば, 言ってみれば** ‖ *She felt, as it were, a stranger in her own house.* 彼女は自分の家にいながらいわば他人であるかのように感じていた.

__as of; as from__ ▶定義 starting from a particular time ある特定の時間から始まっている→**〜(特**

定の日付)から、~以後、~以降 ‖ *As from next week, Tim Shaw will be managing this department.* 来週からティム ショーがこの部門を管理·運営します.

**as to** ▶定義 about a particular thing; concerning ~に関して→~については、~に関して ‖ *I was given no instructions as to how to begin.* 私はどうやって始めたらいいのかについて教わらなかった.

**ASA** /éɪsə/ 略 ▶定義 used for indicating the speed of a camera film カメラのフィルムの感度を示すために用いられて→フィルム感度基準

**asap** /èɪ es eɪ píː; éɪsæp/ 略 as soon as possible→できるだけ早く

**asbestos** /æsbéstəs, æz-/ 名 Ⓤ ▶定義 a soft grey material that does not burn and is used to protect against heat それ自身では燃えずに熱から保護するために用いられる,灰色の柔らかい物質→石綿、アスベスト

**ascend** /əsénd/ 動 自他 正式 ▶定義 to go up 上がる→登る、上がる、上昇する、高くなる ⇔ **descend** — ascending 形→上昇する、だんだん大きくなる、上方に向かう ‖ *The questions are arranged in ascending order of difficulty (= the most difficult ones are at the end).* その問題は難易順に並んでいる(= 最も難しい問題が最後に来る).

**ascent** /əsént/ 名 Ⓒ ▶定義1 the act of climbing or going up 登る、または上がること→登ること、上昇 ‖ *the ascent of Everest* エベレスト登頂 ▶定義2 a path or hill leading upwards 上の方へ行く道または坂→上り道、上り坂 ‖ *There was a steep ascent before the path became flat again.* 道が再び平たんになる前に急な上り坂があった. ⇔ **descent**

**ascertain** /æsərtéɪn/ 動 他 正式 ▶定義 to find sth out ~を見つけ出す→~を確かめる、突き止める、~だと確認する

**ascribe** /əskráɪb/ 動 他 ▶定義 ascribe sth to sb/sth to say that sth was written by or belonged to sb; to say what caused sth ~が…によって書かれた、または~が…のものであると言う; 何が~を引き起こしたかを述べる→~を…に帰する、~のせいにする、~によって生じたものと見なす ‖ *Many people ascribe this play to Shakespeare.* 多くの人はこの戯曲はシェークスピアの作であると考えている.

***ash** /æʃ/ 名 ▶定義1 Ⓤ(または **ashes**[複数扱い]) the grey or black powder which is left after sth has burned ~が燃えた後に残る灰色または黒の粉→灰、燃え殻、火山灰 ‖ *cigarette ash* たばこの灰 *the ashes of a fire* (火事の後の)灰じん ▶定義2 **ashes**[複数扱い] what is left after a dead person has been burned 死体を焼いた後に残る物→遺灰、遺骨 ▶定義3 Ⓒ a type of forest tree that grows in cool countries 冷寒の地に生育する森林樹の一種→トネリコ(材)

***ashamed** /əʃéɪmd/ 形 (名詞の前は不可) ▶定義 ashamed (of sth/sb/yourself); ashamed that...; ashamed to do sth feeling guilty or embarrassed about sb/sth or because of sth you have done ~について、または自分がした~のために、気がとがめている、あるいはきまりの悪い思いをしている→~したことを恥じて、恥ずかしがっている、恥ずかしくて~したくない、~するのが気が引ける ‖ *She was ashamed of her old clothes.* 彼女は自分の古い服を恥ずかしく思っていた. *How could you be so rude? I'm ashamed of you!* どうしてそんなに失礼な事ができるのですか. あなたにはあきれてしまいます. *She felt ashamed that she hadn't helped him.* 彼女は彼を助けなかったことを恥じていた. ⇔ **unashamed**

**ashore** /əʃɔːr/ 副 ▶定義 onto the land from the sea, a river, etc 海、川などから陸上へ→岸に、浜に、陸に ‖ *The passengers went ashore for an hour while the ship was in port.* その船が港に停泊している間、乗客たちは1時間陸に上がった.

**ashtray** /æʃtreɪ/ 名 Ⓒ ▶定義 a small dish for collecting the powder (ash) made when a cigarette burns たばこに火がついているときにできる粉(灰)を集めておくための小皿→灰皿

**Asian** /éɪʃən; -ʒən/ 名 Ⓒ ▶定義 a person from Asia or whose family was originally from Asia アジア出身の人、またはその祖先がアジア出身の人→アジア人 — Asian 形→アジアの、アジア人の、アジア風の

**aside** /əsáɪd/ 副 ▶定義1 on or to one side; out of the way 片側に、または片側へ; 道から離れて→わきに、傍らに、少し離れて ‖ *We stood aside to let the man go past.* 私たちはわきに寄ってその男を先に行かせた. ▶定義2 to be kept separately, for a special purpose 特別な目的のために別にして取っておく→**別にして,取っておいて,わきへ** ‖ I try to **set aside** a little money each month. 私は毎月少しの金を取っておこうとしている.

**aside from** 前 特に 米 = APART FROM

\***ask** /ɑːsk; æsk/ 動 ▶定義**1** 自他 ask (sb) (about sb/sth); ask sb sth to put a question to sb in order to find out some information 何らかの情報を得るために~に質問をする→**~を尋ねる,問う,聞く** ‖ We need to **ask about** tickets. 私たちはチケットについて問い合わせる必要がある. Can I **ask** you a question? 質問してよろしいですか. **Ask** him how old he is. 彼に何歳か聞きなさい. She **asked if** I wanted tea or coffee. 彼女は私が紅茶かコーヒーが飲みたいかと尋ねた. 'What's the time?' he **asked**.「何時ですか」と彼は尋ねた. He **asked** what the time was. 彼は何時であるかを尋ねた. He **asked** me the time. 彼は時間を尋ねた. ▶定義**2** 自他 ask (sb) for sth; ask sth (of sb); ask sb to do sth to request that sb gives you sth or does sth for you ~が自分に…をくれるように,または自分に~をしてくれるように頼む→**~を頼む,求める,請う** ‖ She sat down and **asked for** a cup of coffee. 彼女は座ってからコーヒーを頼んだ. Don't **ask** Joe for money - he hasn't got any. ジョーに金を無心してはいけない − 彼は全く持っていないから. You are **asking** too much of him - he can't possibly do all that! あなたは彼に求めすぎです − 彼にはそれを全部なんてとてもできません. Ring this number and **ask for** Mrs Khan. この番号に電話をして,カーンさんを呼び出してもらいなさい. I **asked** him if he would drive me home. 私は彼に家まで車で送ってほしいと頼んだ. I **asked** him to drive me home. 私は彼に家まで車で送ってほしいと頼んだ. ▶定義**3** 自他 to request permission to do sth ~をする許可を求める→**~をさせてほしいと頼む** ‖ I'm sure she'll let you go if you **ask**. あなたが頼めば彼女はきっと行かせてくれると思います. He **asked** to use our phone. 彼は電話を使わせてほしいと頼んだ. We **asked** if we could go home early. 私たちは早く帰らせてくれるかどうか尋ねた. ▶定義**4** 他 ask sb (to sth) to invite sb ~を誘う→**~を招待する,誘う,呼ぶ,招く** ▶定義**5** 他 to say the price that you want for sth ~に対して欲しい値段を言う→**~を**

aspect 83

**請求する,要求する,求める** ‖ How much are they **asking for** their car? 彼らは車がいくらだと言っているのですか.

成句 **ask for trouble/it** ▶定義 to behave in a way that will almost certainly cause you problems 問題をほぼ確実に起こすようなやり方で振る舞う→**自ら災難を招く,自業自得である,身から出たさびだ** ‖ Driving when you're tired is just **asking for trouble**. 疲れているときに運転するととんだことになる.

**if you ask me** ▶定義 if you want my opinion 私の意見を求めるならば→**言わせてもらえば,私に言わせれば,私の考えでは**

句動詞 **ask after sb** ▶定義 to ask about sb's health or to ask for news of sb ~の健康状態について尋ねる,または~にとって新しい出来事を聞く→**~を尋ねる,~は元気かと尋ねる,~の容体を聞く** ‖ Tina **asked after** you today. 今日,ティナがあなたは元気ですかと聞いていましたよ.

**askew** /əskjuː/ 副形 (名詞の前は不可) ▶定義 not in a straight or level position まっすぐな,または水平な位置にない→**斜めの,傾いて,曲がって,ゆがんで**

\***asleep** /əsliːp/ 形 (名詞の前は不可) ▶定義 not awake; sleeping 目が覚めていない; 眠っている→**眠って** ‖ The baby is **fast/sound asleep**. その赤ん坊はぐっすり眠っている. It didn't take me long to **fall asleep** last night. 昨夜は寝入るのに時間がかからなかった.

▶asleepは名詞の後でのみ用いることに注意する. sleepingは名詞の前で用いる: a sleeping child(眠っている子供)

☞参 **sleep²** の注

**asparagus** /əspǽrəgəs/ 名 U ▶定義 a plant with long green or white parts (**stems**) that you can cook and eat as a vegetable 野菜として調理し食べることができる,緑色または白の長い部分(茎)がある植物→**アスパラガス** ☞ C3 ページのさし絵

\***aspect** /ǽspekt/ 名 C ▶定義 one of the qualities or parts of a situation, idea, problem, etc ある状況,考え,問題などの性質の1つ,または一部分→**局面,側面,見地,見方** ‖ What are the main **aspects** of your job? あなたの主な仕事は何ですか.

**asphalt** /ǽsfɔːlt/ 名 U 定義 a thick black substance that is used for making the surface of roads 道路の表面を作るために使われる黒くてどろっとした物→アスファルト

**asphyxiate** /æsfíksièɪt, əs-/ 動 自 他 定義 to make sb unable to breathe or to be unable to breathe 〜が呼吸できないようにする，または呼吸できない状態である→窒息(死)させる，窒息(死)する ‖ *He was asphyxiated by the smoke while he was asleep.* 彼は眠っている間に煙で窒息死した．— **asphyxiation** /əsfìksiéɪʃ(ə)n/ 名 U→窒息(状態)，気絶，仮死状態

**aspire** /əspáɪər/ 動 自 正式 定義 aspire to sth/to do sth to have a strong desire to have or do sth 〜を所有する，または行うことを強く望む気持ちがある→〜に対して野心を抱く，〜することを熱望する，切望する ‖ *an aspiring actor* 向上心に燃えている俳優 — **aspiration** /æspəréɪʃ(ə)n/ 名 C U→野心，大望，熱望，抱負，向上心

**aspirin** /ǽsp(ə)rən/ 名 C U 定義 a drug used to reduce pain and a high temperature 痛みや高熱を抑えるために使われる薬→アスピリン，アスピリン錠剤

**ass** /æs/ = DONKEY

**assailant** /əséɪl(ə)nt/ 名 C 正式 定義 a person who attacks sb 〜を襲う人→攻撃者，襲撃者，加害者

**assassin** /əsǽs(ə)n/ 名 C 定義 a person who kills a famous or important person for money or for political reasons 金のため，または政治的な理由で，有名人や地位の高い人を殺す人→暗殺者，刺客 — **assassinate** /əsǽs(ə)nèɪt/ 動 他→暗殺する ☞参 kill の注 — **assassination** /əsæs(ə)néɪʃ(ə)n/ 名 C U→暗殺，暗殺事件

**assault** /əsɔ́ːlt/ 名 C U 定義 assault (on sb/sth) a sudden attack on sb/sth 〜への突然の襲撃→猛攻撃，急襲，強襲，非難 — **assault** 動 他→〜を襲う，暴行を働く，激しく非難する ‖ *He was charged with assaulting a police officer.* 彼は警官に暴行を働いたとして告発された．

**assemble** /əsémb(ə)l/ 動 定義 1 自 他 to come together or bring sb/sth together in a group 集める，または〜を1つのグループにまとめる→集まる，〜を集める，集合させる，召集する ‖ *I've assembled all the information I need for my essay.* 私はエッセーに必要な情報をすべて集めた． 定義 2 他 to fit the parts of sth together 〜の部品をはめ込む→〜を組み立てる，組み合わせて〜を作る ‖ *We spent hours trying to assemble our new bookshelves.* 私たちは何時間もかけて新しい本棚を組み立てようとした．

**assembly** /əsémbli/ 名 (複 **assemblies**) 定義 1 C a large group of people who come together for a particular purpose ある特定の目的のために集まっている大勢の人々→集まり，集会，会合 ‖ *school assembly* (= *a regular meeting for all the students and teachers of a school*) 学校集会 (= 学校の生徒と先生の全員が参加する定期的な会合) 定義 2 U the action of fitting the parts of sth together 〜の部品を組み立てること→組み立て，組み立て作業

**assembly line** 名 C 定義 a line of people and machines in a factory that fit the parts of sth together in a fixed order 工場で〜の部品を一定の順序で組み立てる，一列に並んだ人や機械→流れ作業工程，流れ作業列，組み立て作業ライン

**assent** /əsént, æ-/ 名 U 正式 定義 assent (to sth) official agreement to sth 〜への公式の同意→同意，賛成，賛同，承認 ‖ *The committee gave their assent to the proposed changes.* その委員会は提案された変更内容を承認した．— **assent** 動 自 assent (to sth)→〜に同意する，賛成する

**assert** /əsə́ːrt/ 動 他 定義 1 to say sth clearly and firmly 〜をはっきり，きっぱりと言う→〜を断言する，言い張る，はっきり述べる 定義 2 to behave in a determined and confident way to make people listen to you or to get what you want 自分の言うことに耳を傾けさせるために，または自分の望むものを得るために，決然と自信に満ちた態度で振る舞う→〜を主張する，行使する ‖ *You ought to assert yourself more.* あなたはもっと自分を主張するべきです. *to assert your authority* 権力を行使する

**assertion** /əsə́ːrʃ(ə)n/ 名 定義 1 C a statement that says you strongly believe that sth is true 〜が本当であることを強く信じているという主張→断言，断定 定義 2 U the action of showing, using or stating sth strongly 〜を強く示す，行使する，述べること→誇示

**assertive** /əsə́ːrtɪv/ 形 定義 expressing your opinion clearly and firmly so that people listen to you or do what you want 自分の言うことに耳を傾けさせるために、または自分の望むものを得るために、自分の意見をはっきり、きっぱりと言っている→自己主張の強い、断定的な、自信に満ちた、独断的な ― **assertively** 副→断固たる態度で、断定的に、自信に満ちた様子で ― **assertiveness** 名 U→断固たる態度、きっぱりしていること、断定すること、自己主張すること

**assess** /əsés/ 動他 ▶定義1 to judge or form an opinion about sth ～について評価したり意見をまとめる→～を評価する、判断する、見極める ‖ *It's too early to assess the effects of the price rises.* 価格上昇の影響を判断するには時期尚早である. ▶定義2 assess sth (at sth) to guess or decide the amount or value of sth ～の金額や価値を推測する、または判断する→～を査定する、評価する、算定する ‖ *to assess the cost of repairs* 修理費を算定する ― **assessment** 名 C U→査定、評価、算定、見積もり、判断 ‖ *I made a careful assessment of the risks involved.* 私はそれに伴って起きる危険を注意深く見積もった.

**asset** /ǽset/ 名 C ▶定義1 an asset (to sb/sth) a person or thing that is useful to sb/sth ～の役に立つ人または物事→価値のあるもの・人、貴重なもの・人、強み、利点、宝 ‖ *She's a great asset to the organization.* 彼女はその会社にとって貴重な人材だ. ▶定義2 [通常は複数]something of value that a person, company, etc owns 人、会社などが所有している、価値のあるもの→資産、財産

**assign** /əsáin/ 動他 ▶定義1 assign sth to sb/sth to give sth to sb for a particular purpose ある特定の目的のために～を…に与える→～を割り当てる ‖ *We have assigned 20% of our budget to the project.* 私たちは予算の20パーセントをそのプロジェクトに割り当てた. ▶定義2 assign sb to sth to give sb a particular job to do ～にある特定のやるべき仕事を与える→～を任命する、選任する、課題を出す

**assignment** /əsáinmənt/ 名 C U ▶定義 a job or type of work that you are given to do 行うべく与えられた仕事、または仕事の種類→課題、割り当て、任務、仕事、宿題 ‖ *The reporter disappeared while on (an) assignment in the war zone.* その記者は交戦地帯で任務に就いている間に姿を消した.

## associate² 85

**assimilate** /əsíməlèit/ 動 ▶定義1 自 assimilate sb/sth (into sth) to become or allow sb/sth to become part of a country, a social group, etc ～がある国、社会集団などの一部になる、またはそうなることを認める→～に同化する、同化させる、融合させる、似たものに変化させる ▶定義2 他 to learn and understand sth ～を学び理解する→～を吸収する、理解する、我が物とする ‖ *to assimilate new facts/information/ideas* 新しい事実・情報・考えを吸収する ― **assimilation** /əsìməléiʃ(ə)n/ 名 U→理解、同化、融合

**assist** /əsíst/ 動 自 他 正式 ▶定義 assist (sb) in/with sth; assist (sb) in doing sth to help ～を助ける→～を助ける、手伝う、援助する ‖ *Volunteers assisted in searching for the boy.* ボランティアたちはその少年を捜すのを手伝った.

**assistance** /əsístəns/ 名 U 正式 ▶定義 help or support 助け、または支え→手助け、援助、助力 ‖ *financial assistance for poorer families* 貧しい家族への金銭的援助 *She shouted for help but nobody came to her assistance.* 彼女は助けを求めて叫んだが、だれも助けに来なかった.

\***assistant** /əsístənt/ 名 C ▶定義1 a person who helps sb in a more important position より高い地位にある～を助ける人→助手、補佐役、アシスタント ‖ *the assistant manager* アシスタントマネージャー ▶定義2 (米 clerk) a person who sells things to people in a shop 店で人に物を売る人→店員 ‖ *a shop/sales assistant* 店員・販売員

**Assoc**(または **assoc**)略 association→協会

\***associate**¹ /əsóuʃiət, -si-/ 名 C ▶定義 a person that you meet and get to know through your work 仕事を通じて会い、知り合う人→仲間、同僚、仕事仲間 ‖ *a business associate* 同僚

\***associate**² /əsóuʃièit, -si-/ 動 ▶定義1 他 associate sb/sth (with sb/sth) to make a connection between people or things in your mind 心の中で人と人、または物事と物事を関連づける→～を連想する、～を結び付けて考える、～で…を思い出す ‖ *I always associate the smell of the sea with my childhood.* 私は海の香りがするといつも子供のころを思い出す. ▶定義2 自 associate with sb to spend time with sb ～と共に時を過ごす→～と交際する、付き合う、提携する ▶定義3 他 associate yourself with sth to say that you support sth or agree with sth ～を支持している，または～に同意していると言う→～を…に関係させる，～を…に連合させる，～を仲間に加える ⇔ **disassociate**

**association** /əsòusiéiʃ(ə)n, -ʃi-/ 名 ▶定義1 Ｕ joining or working with another person or group ほかの人または集団と共に参加する，あるいは働くこと→交際，交友，結合，共同，連合 ‖ *We work **in association with** our New York office.* 私たちはニューヨークの事務所で協同で仕事をしている． ▶定義2 Ｃ a group of people or organizations who work together for a particular purpose ある特定の目的のために一緒に働いている人々または組織の集まり→協会，組合 ‖ *the National Association of Language Teachers* 全国語学教師協会 ▶定義3 Ｃ Ｕ the act of connecting one person or thing with another in your mind 心の中である人や物事を別の人や物事を関連づけること→連想

**assorted** /əsɔ́ːrtəd/ 形 ▶定義 of different types; mixed さまざまな種類の；取り混ぜた→組み合わせた，各種の，幾多な ‖ *a bowl of assorted fruit* 果物を盛り合わせた鉢

**assortment** /əsɔ́ːrtmənt/ 名 Ｃ ▶定義 a group of different things or different types of the same thing; a mixture さまざまなもの，または同じものの異なる種類のものの集まり；入り交じったもの→各種取りそろえたもの，組み合わせ，各種詰め合わされたもの ‖ *You'll find a wide assortment of gifts in our shop.* 私どもの店では贈答品を幅広く取りそろえております．

**Asst**(または**asst**) 略 assistant→助手

*****assume** /əsjúːm; əsúːm/ 動 他 ▶定義1 to accept or believe that sth is true even though you have no proof; to expect sth to be true たとえ証拠がなくても，～が真実であることを認める，または信じる；～が真実であることを期待する→～を…であると仮定する，決めてかかる，当然のことと思い込む，想定する ‖ *I assume that you have the necessary documents.* 私はあなたが必要な書類を持っているものと思っている． *Everyone assumed Ralph was guilty.* だれもがラルフは有罪だと決めてかかった． *Everyone assumed Ralph to be guilty.* だれもがラルフは有罪だと決めてかかった． ▶定義2 to pretend to have or be sb/sth ～を持っている，または～である振りをする→（態度・ポーズなど）を取る，装う，帯びる，～の振りをする ‖ *to assume a false name* 偽名を語る ▶定義3 to begin to use power or to have a powerful position 権力を行使する，または影響力のある立場を持つことを始める→～を引き受ける，責任を負う ‖ *to assume control of sth* ～の支配権を奪い取る

**assumption** /əsʌ́m(p)ʃ(ə)n/ 名 ▶定義1 Ｃ something that you accept is true even though you have no proof たとえ証拠がなくても真実であると認めている物事→仮定，推定，仮説，想定，前提 ‖ *We'll work **on the assumption that** guests will be hungry when they arrive.* お客様は到着した時に空腹であると想定して仕事をしましょう．*It's unfair to **make assumptions about** a person's character before you know them.* その人をよく知らないうちに性格を決めてかかるのは良くないことだ． *a reasonable/false assumption* もっともな仮説・間違った仮説 ▶定義2 Ｕ **the assumption of sth** the act of taking power or of starting an important job 権力を持つこと，または重要な仕事を始めること→引き受けること，就任

**assurance** /əʃúərəns, əʃɔ́ː-/ 名 ▶定義1 Ｃ a promise that sth will certainly happen or be true ～がきっと起こる，または真実であるという約束→保証，確約，請け合い ‖ *They gave me **an assurance that** the work would be finished by Friday.* 彼らはその仕事が金曜日までに終わると私に保証した． ▶定義2 （または **self-assurance**）Ｕ the belief that you can do or succeed at sth; confidence ～ができる，または成功するという確信；自信→自信，確信

**assure** /əʃúər, əʃɔ́ːr/ 動 他 ▶定義1 to promise sb that sth will certainly happen or be true, especially if he/she is worried ～がきっと起こる，または真実であると，特に～が心配している場合に，その～に約束する→～を保証する，確約する，自信を持って言う，請け合う ‖ *I assure you that it is perfectly safe.* それは絶対に安全であると保証します．*Let me assure you of my full support.* 私が全面的に支援することを確約いたします． ▶定義2 to make sth sure or certain ～を確実にする，または確かめる→～を確実にする，安全にする ‖ *The success of the new product assured the survival of the company.* 新製品の

成功によってその会社の存続が確実になった.

**assured** /əfúərd, əfɔ́ːrd/ (または **self-assured**)
形 ▶定義 believing that you can do sth or succeed at sth; confident ～ができる，または成功すると信じている；自信がある→**自信のある，確信している，自信たっぷりの** ‖ *The doctor had a calm and assured manner.* その医者は冷静で自信に満ちた態度だった．

**asterisk** /ǽstərɪsk/ 名 C ▶定義 the sign (*) that you use to make people notice sth in a piece of writing 文書の中で人に～を気付かせるために用いる記号(*)→**星印，アステリスク**

**asthma** /ǽsmə; ǽz-/ 名 U ▶定義 a medical condition that makes breathing difficult 呼吸を困難にする病的状態→**ぜん息**

**asthmatic** /æsmǽtɪk; æz-/ 名 C ▶定義 a person who has asthma ぜん息を持っている人→**ぜん息患者** — asthmatic 形→**ぜん息の，ぜん息を患っている，ぜん息持ちの**

**astonish** /əstánɪʃ/ 動 他 ▶定義 to surprise sb very much ～を非常に驚かせる→**～を(非常に)驚かす，びっくりさせる** ‖ *She astonished everybody by announcing her engagement.* 彼女は婚約を発表してみんなをびっくりさせた．— astonished 形→**(非常に)驚いて，びっくりして** ‖ *I was astonished by the decision.* 私はその決定にびっくりした．

**astonishing** /əstánɪʃɪŋ/ 形 ▶定義 very surprising とても驚くべき，驚かすような，驚くべき，びっくりするような，目覚しい — astonishingly 副→**驚くほど，驚いたことに**

**astonishment** /əstánɪʃmənt/ 名 U ▶定義 very great surprise 非常に大きな驚き→**驚き，びっくり** ‖ *He dropped his book in astonishment.* 彼は驚いて本を落とした．

**astound** /əstáʊnd/ 動 他 (通常は受身態で) ▶定義 to surprise sb very much ～を非常に驚かせる→**びっくり仰天させる，非常に驚かせる，～の肝をつぶさせる** ‖ *We were astounded by how well he performed.* 私たちは彼があまりにもうまく演じたことに非常に驚いた．

**astounded** /əstáʊndəd/ 形 ▶定義 feeling or showing great surprise 大きな驚きを感じている，または表している→**びっくり仰天した，非常に驚いた** ‖ *We sat in astounded silence.* 私たちは驚きのあまり黙って座っていた．

**astounding** /əstáʊndɪŋ/ 形 ▶定義 causing sb to feel extremely surprised ～をとても驚かせている→**びっくり仰天するような，驚くべき** ‖ *an astounding success* 驚くべき成功

**astray** /əstréɪ/ 副
成句 **go astray** ▶定義 to become lost or be stolen 道に迷う，または盗まれる→**道に迷う，道を誤る，(物が)行方不明になる，紛失する**
**lead sb astray** ⇒ **LEAD**¹

**astride** /əstráɪd/ 副 前 ▶定義 with one leg on each side of sth ～の両側に片足ずつかけて→**またがって，両足を広げて** ‖ *to sit astride a horse* 馬にまたがる

**astrologer** /əstrɑ́lədʒər/ 名 C ▶定義 a person who is an expert in astrology 占星術を専門とする人→**占星術師，占星家**

**astrology** /əstrɑ́lədʒi/ 名 U ▶定義 the study of the positions and movements of the stars and planets and the way that some people believe they affect people and events 星や惑星の位置と動きの研究と，それらが人や出来事に及ぼすと一部の人が考えている影響の仕方の研究→**占星術，占星学** ☞参 **horoscope**, **zodiac**

**astronaut** /ǽstrənɔ̀ːt/ 名 C ▶定義 a person who travels in a spacecraft 宇宙船で旅する人→**宇宙飛行士**

**astronomer** /əstrɑ́nəmər/ 名 C ▶定義 a person who studies astronomy 天文学を研究する人→**天文学者**

**astronomical** /æ̀strənɑ́mɪk(ə)l/ 形 ▶定義1 connected with astronomy 天文学に関連している→**天文の，天文学の，天文学上の** ▶定義2 extremely large 極端に大きい→**天文学的な，とてつもなく多い，けた外れに大きい** ‖ *astronomical house prices* 住宅の天文学的な価格

**astronomy** /əstrɑ́nəmi/ 名 U ▶定義 the scientific study of the sun, moon, stars, etc 太陽，月，星などについての科学的研究→**天文学**

**astute** /əst(j)úːt; æs-/ 形 ▶定義 very clever; good at judging people or situations とても賢い；人や状況を判断するのがうまい→**機敏な，抜け目のない，賢い，ずるい**

**asylum** /əsáɪləm/ 名 U ▶定義 protection that a government gives to people who have left their own country for political reasons 政治的な理由で自分の国を出た人々に対して政府が与える保

護→保護, 亡命, 避難, 庇護(ひご) ‖ to give sb political asylum ～の政治的亡命を受け入れる

\***at** /ət; 強形 æt/ 前 ▶定義1 used to show where sb/sth is or where sth happens ～がいる・～がある場所, または～が起こる場所を表すために用いられて→～に, ～で, ～において, ～の所に ‖ at the bottom/top of the page そのページの一番下・一番上 He was standing at the door. 彼は戸口に立っていた. Change trains at Chester. チェスターで電車を乗り換えなさい. We were at home all weekend. 私たちは週末はずっと家にいた. Are the children at school? その子供たちは学校に来ていますか. 'Where's Peter?' 'He's at Sue's.' (= at Sue's house)「ピーターはどこにいますか」「スーの所にいます」(= スーの家に) ▶定義2 used to show when sth happens ～が起こる時を表すために用いられて→～に, ～から, ～で ‖ I start work at 9 o'clock. 私は9時から仕事を始める. at the weekend 週末に at night 夜に at Easter イースターの時期に She got married at 18 (= when she was 18). 彼女は18歳で(= 彼女が18歳の時に)結婚した. ▶定義3 in the direction of sb/sth ～の方向に→～を, ～に, ～を目掛けて, ～に向かって ‖ What are you looking at? 何を見ているのですか. He pointed a gun at the policeman. 彼は銃を警官に向けた. Don't shout at me! こちらに向かってどならないで. ▶定義4 because of sth ～の理由で→～で, ～のため, ～を見て, ～を聞いて ‖ I was surprised at her behaviour. 私は彼女の振る舞いに驚いた. We laughed at his jokes. 私たちは彼の冗談を聞いて笑った. ▶定義5 used to show what sb is doing or what is happening ～がしている事, または起こっている事を表すために用いられて→～に従事して, ～の最中で ‖ They were **hard at work**. 彼らは熱心に仕事をしていた. The two countries were **at war**. その2国は交戦中だった. ▶定義6 used to show the price, rate, speed, etc of sth ～の値段, 割合, 速度などを表すために用いられて→～で, ～の割合で ‖ We were travelling at about 50 miles per hour. 私たちは時速約50マイルで進んでいた. ▶定義7 used with adjectives that show how well sb/sth does sth ～がどのくらいうまく…をするかを表す形容詞と共に用いられて→～は, ～が, ～に関しては, ～において ‖ She's not very **good at** French. 彼女はフランス語があまり得意ではない.

**ate** EAT の過去形

**atheism** /éɪθìːz(ə)m/ 名 Ⅱ ▶定義 the belief that there is no God 神は存在しないという考え→無神論 ― **atheist** 名 C ●無神論者

**athlete** /ǽθliːt/ 名 C ▶定義 a person who can run, jump, etc very well, especially one who takes part in sports competitions, etc 走ったり跳んだりすることがとても上手にできる人, 特にスポーツの競技会などに参加する人→運動選手, スポーツマン, 競技者

**athletic** /æθlétɪk/ 形 ▶定義1 connected with athletes or athletics→運動選手や運動競技に関連している ‖ athletic ability 運動能力 ▶定義2 (used about a person) having a fit, strong, and healthy body (人について)健康で強くふさわしい身体を持っている→スポーツマンらしい, 筋骨たくましい, 運動選手らしい

**athletics** /æθlétɪks/ 名 Ⅱ ▶定義 sports such as running, jumping, throwing, etc 走る, 跳ぶ, 投げるなどのスポーツ→(戸外)運動競技, 陸上競技

**atishoo** /ətʃúː, ətíʃuː/ 間 ▶定義 used to represent the sound that you make when you suddenly blow air out of your nose (sneeze) 鼻から空気を突然出す(くしゃみをする)ときに立てる音を表すために用いられて→ハクション, ハックション

**atlas** /ǽtləs/ 名 C (複 **atlases**) ▶定義 a book of maps →地図帳 ‖ a road atlas of Europe ヨーロッパの道路地図帳

\***atmosphere** /ǽtməsfɪər/ 名 ▶定義1 [C, 通常は単数] **the atmosphere** the mixture of gases that surrounds the earth or any other star, planet, etc 地球やほかの星, 惑星などを取り囲んでいる気体の混合物→大気 ‖ the earth's atmosphere 地球の大気 ▶定義2 [単数扱い] the air in a place ある場所の空気→空気 ‖ a smoky atmosphere かすんだ空気 ▶定義3 [単数扱い] the mood or feeling of a place or situation ある場所や状況の雰囲気, または感じ→雰囲気, ムード, 周囲の状況 ‖ The atmosphere of the meeting was relaxed. その会合の雰囲気は和やかだった.

**atmospheric** /ætməsférɪk, -sfɪər-/ 形 ▶定義1 connected with the earth's atmosphere 地球の大気に関連している→大気の(中), 空気の ▶定義2 creating a particular feeling or emotion

特別な感じや感情を生み出している→独特の雰囲気のある, ムードのある, 雰囲気に富む ‖ *atmospheric music* ムード音楽

**atom** /ǽtəm/ 名 C ▶定義 the smallest part into which an element can be divided 元素が分割され得る最小の要素→原子 ☞参 molecule

**atomic** /ətɑ́mɪk/ 形 ▶定義 of or concerning an atom or atoms 1つまたは複数の原子の, あるいはそれらに関連している→原子の, 原子力の, 原子爆弾の ‖ *atomic physics* 原子物理学 ☞参 nuclear

**atomic bomb** (または **atom bomb**) 名 C ▶定義 a bomb that explodes using the energy that is produced when an atom or atoms are split 1つまたは複数の原子が分裂するときに生じるエネルギーを使って爆発する爆弾→原子爆弾

**atomic energy** 名 U ▶定義 the energy that is produced when an atom or atoms are split. Atomic energy can be used to produce electricity. 1つまたは複数の原子が分裂するときに生じるエネルギー. 発電のために使われる場合がある→原子力, 原子エネルギー

**atrocious** /ətróʊʃəs/ 形 ▶定義 extremely bad 極度に悪い→残虐な, 悲惨な, 極悪な, ぞっとするような ‖ *atrocious weather* ひどい天気 ― *atrociously* 副 →残虐に, ひどく, とんでもなく, 猛烈に

**atrocity** /ətrɑ́səti/ 名 C U (複 **atrocities**) ▶定義 形 (an action of) very cruel treatment of sb/sth ～への非常に冷酷な扱い(をすること)→残虐さ, 悲惨さ, 非道, 残虐な行為, 凶行 ‖ *Both sides were accused of committing atrocities during the war.* どちらの側も戦争中に残虐行為を働いたことで批難された.

\***attach** /ətǽtʃ/ 動 他 ▶定義 1 attach sth (to sth) to fasten or join sth to sth ～を…にしっかり固定する, または取り付ける→～をはり付ける, 取り付ける, 結び付ける, 接着する ‖ *I attached a label to each bag.* 私はそれぞれのバッグにラベルをはり付けた. ⇔ detach ▶定義 2 (通常は受動態で) attach sb/sth to sb/sth to make sb/sth join or belong to sb/sth ～を…に結び付ける, または所属させる→～を…に配属する, 所属させる, 付属させる, 参加させる ‖ *The research centre is attached to the university.* その研究センターは大学に付属している. ▶定義 3 attach sth to sb/sth to think that sth has a particular quality ～がある特定の性質を持っていると考える→～を…に認める, 与える, 帰する, ～が…にあるものと考える ‖ *Don't attach too much importance to what they say.* 彼らが言うことをあまり重要視してはいけません.

成句 (with) no strings attached; without strings ⇒ **STRING**¹

**attached** /ətǽtʃt/ 形 attached to sb/sth ▶定義 liking sb/sth very much ～が大変気に入っている→～に愛着を持っている, ～に愛情を持っている, ～に傾倒している

**attachment** /ətǽtʃmənt/ 名 ▶定義 1 C something that you can fit on sth else to make it do a different job 違う仕事をさせるためにほかの～に取り付けられる物→付属(部)品, 付属物 ‖ *an electric drill with a range of attachments* 一連の付属品が付いている電気ドリル ▶定義 2 C U attachment (to/for sb/sth) the feeling of liking sb/sth very much ～が大変気に入っているという気持ち→愛着, 愛情, 傾倒, 忠誠 ‖ *emotional attachment* 愛着

\***attack**¹ /ətǽk/ 名 ▶定義 1 C U (an) attack (on sb/sth) trying to hurt or defeat sb/sth by using force 暴力を振るって～を傷付けたり打ち負かそうとすること→攻撃, 襲撃 ‖ *The town was under attack from all sides.* その街は四方八方から攻撃を受けた. ▶定義 2 C U (an) attack (on sb/sth) an act of saying strongly that you do not like or agree with sb/sth ～が気に入らない, または同意していないと強く言うこと→非難 ‖ *an outspoken attack on government policy* 政府の政策に対する遠慮のない非難 ▶定義 3 C a short period when you suffer badly from a disease, medical condition, etc ある病気や病的状態などにひどく苦しむ短い期間→発作, 発病 ‖ *an attack of asthma/flu/nerves* ぜん息の発作・流感の発病・ヒステリーの発作 ▶定義 4 C the act of trying to score a point in a game of sport スポーツの試合で得点を入れようとすること→攻撃

\***attack**² /ətǽk/ 動 ▶定義 1 自 他 to try to hurt or defeat sb/sth by using force 暴力を振るって～を傷付けたり打ち負かそうとする→～を攻撃する, 襲う ‖ *The child was attacked by a dog.* その子供は犬に襲われた. ▶定義 2 他 to say strongly that you do not like or agree with sb/sth ～が気に入らない, または同意していないと強く言う→

~を非難する ‖ *Steffi attacked Guy's right-wing political views.* ステフィーはガイの右翼的な政治見解を非難した. ▶定義3 ⓗ to damage or harm sb/sth ~に損害を与える,または傷付ける → ~を襲う,侵す,痛める,駄目にする ‖ *a virus that attacks the nervous system* 神経系を侵すウイルス ▶定義4 ⓐⓗ to try to score a point in a game of sport スポーツの試合で得点を入れようとする → 攻撃する,得点しようとする ‖ *This team attacks better than it defends.* このチームは守るよりも攻撃する方がうまい.

**attacker** /ətǽkər/ ⓒ ▶定義 a person who tries to hurt sb using force 暴力を振るって~を傷付けようとする人 → 襲撃者,攻撃者 ‖ *The victim of the assault didn't recognize his attackers.* その襲撃の被害者は襲撃者たちに覚えがなかった.

**attain** /ətéɪn/ 動ⓗ ▶定義 to succeed in getting or achieving sth, especially after a lot of effort 特に多大な努力をした後で,~を得る,または達成することに成功する → ~を達成する獲得する,成し遂げる

**attainable** /ətéɪnəbl/ 形 ▶定義 that can be achieved 達成され得る → 達成可能な,成し遂げられる ‖ *realistically attainable targets* 現実的に達成可能な目標

**attainment** /ətéɪnmənt/ 名 ▶定義1 ⓤ the act of achieving sth ~を達成すること → 獲得,達成,到達 ‖ *the attainment of the government's objectives* 政府の目標の達成 ▶定義2 ⓒ a skill or sth you have achieved 獲得した技術または~ → 学識,技能,技芸

★**attempt**[1] /ətém(p)t/ 動ⓗ ▶定義 attempt (to do) sth to try to do sth that is difficult 困難な~をしようとする → ~を試みる,企てる ‖ *She was accused of attempted murder (= she didn't succeed).* 彼女は殺人未遂で(=成功しなかった)告発された. *Don't attempt to make him change his mind.* 彼の考えを変えさせようとしないでください.

★**attempt**[2] /ətém(p)t/ 名ⓒ ▶定義1 an attempt (to do sth/at doing sth) an act of trying to do sth ~をしようとすること → 試み,企て,努力 ‖ *The thief made no attempt to run away.* その泥棒は逃げ出そうとしなかった. *I failed the exam once but passed at the second attempt.* 私は1度試験に失敗したが,2度目で合格した. *They failed in their attempt to reach the North Pole.* 彼らは北極に到達しようという試みに失敗した. ▶定義2 an attempt (on sb/sth) trying to attack or beat sb/sth ~を攻撃または打ち負かそうとすること → ねらうこと,襲撃,攻撃 ‖ *an attempt on sb's life (= to kill sb)* ~の命をねらうこと(=~を殺す)

**威句** a last-ditch attempt ⇒ **LAST**[1]

★**attend** /əténd/ 動 ▶定義1 ⓗ to go to or be present at a place ある場所に行く,または出席する → ~に出席する,参列する,通う ‖ *Do you attend church regularly?* 教会に規則的に通っていますか. *The children attend the local school.* その子供たちは地元の学校に通っている. ▶定義2 ⓘⓗ 正式 attend to sb/sth to give your care, thought or attention to sb/sth or look after sb/sth ~に注意,配慮,関心などを向ける,または~の世話をする → ~に注意を払う,留意する,傾聴する,~の世話をする,応対する,精を出す ‖ *Please attend to this matter immediately.* この問題にすぐに注意を払ってください.

**attendance** /əténd(ə)ns/ 名 ▶定義1 ⓤ being present somewhere どこかに出席していること → 出席,参加,参列 ‖ *Attendance at lectures is compulsory.* 講義への出席は義務である. ▶定義2 ⓒⓤ the number of people who go to or are present at a place ある場所に行く,または出席する人の数 → 出席者数,参加者数,参会者数 ‖ *There was a poor attendance at the meeting.* その会合には出席者がわずかだった.

**attendant**[1] /əténdənt/ 名ⓒ ▶定義 a person whose job is to serve or help people in a public place 公共の場所で人々に応対したり助けたりすることを仕事としている人 → 係員,案内係,接客係 ‖ *a car park attendant* 駐車場の係員

**attendant**[2] /əténdənt/ 形 (名詞の前だけ) 正式 ▶定義 that goes together with or results from sth ~と同時に起こる,または~の結果として生ずる → ~に伴う,付随する,付帯の ‖ *unemployment and all its attendant social problems* 失業とそれに付随する社会的な問題

★**attention**[1] /ətén∫(ə)n/ 名ⓤ ▶定義1 watching, listening to or thinking about sb/sth carefully ~を注意深く見ること,聞くこと,あるいは考えること → 注意,注目,留意 ‖ *I shouted in order to* *attract* her **attention**. 私は彼女の注意をひくために叫んだ. *Shy people hate to be **the centre of attention** (= the person that everybody is watching).* 内気な人は注目の的(= みんながじっと見ている人)になるのを嫌がる. *to hold sb's attention (= to keep them interested in sth)* 〜の注意を引き付ける(= 〜に興味を持たせておく) ▶定義 2 special care or action 特別な世話または行動 →**配慮, 考慮, 世話, 手当て** ‖ *The hole in the roof needs urgent attention.* 屋根の穴は緊急に手入れが必要だ. *to require **medical attention*** 治療を必要とする ▶定義 3 a position in which a soldier stands up straight and still 軍人が直立して静止している姿勢 →**気を付けの姿勢, 直立不動の姿勢** ‖ *to stand/come to attention* 気を付けの姿勢で立つ・気を付けの姿勢を取る 成句 catch sb's attention/eye ⇒ **CATCH**¹ draw (sb's) attention to sth ⇒ **DRAW**¹ pay attention ⇒ **PAY**¹

**attention**² /əténʃ(ə)n/ 間 ▶定義 used for asking people to listen to sth carefully 人々に〜を注意深く聞くことを求めるために用いられて →**皆様に申し上げます, お知らせいたします, ちょっとお聞きください**

**attentive** /əténtɪv/ 形 ▶定義 attentive (to sb/sth) watching, listening to or thinking about sb/sth carefully 〜を注意深く見ている, 聞いている, あるいは考えている →**注意深い, よく耳を傾ける, 油断のない, 〜に対して心を配る, よく気の利く** ‖ *The hotel staff were very attentive to our needs.* そのホテルの従業員は私たちが必要とするものに対してよく心を配ってくれた. ⇔ **inattentive** — attentively 副 →**注意深く, 丁寧に** ‖ *to listen attentively to sth* 〜を注意深く聞く

**attic** /ǽtɪk/ 名 C ▶定義 the space or room under the roof of a house 家の屋根の下にある空間または部屋 →**屋根裏, 屋根裏部屋** ☞参 loft

*****attitude** /ǽtət(j)ùːd/ 名 C ▶定義 an attitude (to/towards sb/sth) the way that you think, feel or behave 考えたり感じたり振る舞ったりする仕方 →**考え方, 気持ち, 心構え, 態度, 姿勢** ‖ *People's attitude to marriage is changing.* 結婚に対する人々の考え方は変化している. *She has a very positive attitude to her work.* 彼女は自分の仕事に対してとても積極的な姿勢を取っている.

**attorney** /ətɔ́ːmi/ 米 = **LAWYER**

*****attract** /ətrǽkt/ 動 他 ▶定義 1 to cause sth to go to sth or give attention to sth 〜を…へ行かせる, または〜に注意させる →**〜を…に引き付ける, 魅惑する, (注意などを)ひく** ‖ *I waved to attract the waiter's attention.* 私はウエーターの注意をひくために手を振った. *Moths are attracted to light.* ガは光に引き寄せられる. *The new film has attracted a lot of publicity.* その新しい映画は大評判になっている. ▶定義 2 (通常は受動態で) to cause sb to like sb/sth 〜に…を好きにさせる →**〜が…に引き付けられる, 関心がある** ‖ *She's attracted to older men.* 彼女は年上の男性にひかれる.

**attraction** /ətrǽkʃ(ə)n/ 名 ▶定義 1 U a feeling of liking sb/sth 〜を好きだという気持ち →**魅力, 魅惑, 引き付ける力** ‖ *sexual attraction* 性的魅力 ▶定義 2 C sth that is interesting or enjoyable 面白い, または楽しめる〜 →**引き付けるもの, 呼び物, アトラクション** ‖ *The city offers all kinds of tourist attractions.* その都市にはあらゆる種類の観光名所がある.

*****attractive** /ətrǽktɪv/ 形 ▶定義 1 that pleases or interests you; that you like 喜ばせる, または興味を持たせるような; 好むような →**興味をそそる, 人を引き付ける, 面白い, 楽しい** ‖ *an attractive part of the country* その国の興味深い地方 *an attractive idea* 魅力的な考え ▶定義 2 (used about a person) beautiful or nice to look at (人について) 美しい, または見るのが快い →**魅力的な, 愛きょうのある** — attractively 副 →**魅力的に, 人目をひくように, 目に付くように** — attractiveness 名 U →**魅力的なこと, 魅力, 人目をひくこと, 引き付けること**

**attribute**¹ /ətríbjuːt/ 動 他 ▶定義 attribute sth to sb/sth to believe that sth was caused or done by sb/sth 〜が…によって引き起こされた, または行われたと信じる →**〜を…のせいにする, 〜を…に帰する, 〜が…にあると考える** ‖ *Mustafa attributes his success to hard work.* ムスタファは自分の成功が懸命な働きによるものと考えている. *a poem attributed to Shakespeare* シェークスピアの作とされている詩

**attribute**² /ǽtrɪbjùːt/ 名 C ▶定義 a quality of sb/sth; a feature 〜の性質; 特徴 →**属性, 特質, 特性** ‖ *physical attributes* 物理的な特性

**atypical** /eɪtípɪk(ə)l, ə-/ 形 正式 ▶定義 not typi-

cal of a particular type, group, etc ある特定の種類, 集団などの特徴を示していない→**典型的ではない, 代表的ではない, 型にはまらない, 異常な, 変則(的)な** || *atypical behaviour* 型にはまらない行動 ⇔ **typical**
► **untypical**と比較.

**aubergine** /óubərdʒìːn/ (特に 米**eggplant**) 名 **C U** ▶定義 a long vegetable with dark purple skin 濃い紫色の皮のある細長い野菜→**ナス** ☛ C3 ページのさし絵

**auburn** /ɔ́ːbəm/ 形 ▶定義 (used about hair) reddish-brown (毛髪について) 赤みがかった茶色の→**赤褐色の, とび色の**

**auction**¹ /ɔ́ːkʃ(ə)n/ 名 **C U** ▶定義 a public sale at which items are sold to the person who offers to pay the most money 最高額を払うと申し出た人に品物が売られる公の販売→**競売, 競り売り, オークション** || *The house was sold at/by auction.* その家は競売で売られた.

**auction**² /ɔ́ːkʃ(ə)n/ 動 他 ▶定義 auction sth (off) to sell sth at an auction ～を競売で売る→**～を競売にかける, 競売で売る**

**auctioneer** /ɔ̀ːkʃ(ə)níər/ 名 **C** ▶定義 a person who organizes the selling at an auction 競売をとりまとめる人→**競売人, 競り売り人**

**audible** /ɔ́ːdəbl/ 形 ▶定義 that can be heard 聞くことができる→**聞こえる, 聞き取ることができる, 可聴の** || *Her speech was barely audible.* 彼女の言葉はほとんど聞き取れなかった. ⇔ **inaudible** — **audibly** /-əbli/ 副 →聞こえるように, 聞き取れるほどに

*****audience** /ɔ́ːdiəns/ 名 **C** ▶定義 1 [単数または複数形の動詞と共に] all the people who are watching or listening to a play, concert, speech, the television, etc 演劇, 音楽会, 演説, テレビなどを見たり聴いたりしているすべての人々→**聴衆, 観衆, 観客, 視聴者, 聴取者** || *The audience was/were wild with excitement.* 観客は興奮して熱狂していた. *There were only about 200 people in the audience.* 聴衆はたった200人ほどだった. ▶定義 2 a formal meeting with a very important person 非常に高い地位にある人と正式に会うこと→**公式会見, 謁見, 接見** || *He was granted an audience with the President.* 彼は大統領との謁見を許された.

**audio** /ɔ́ːdiou/ 形 ▶定義 connected with the recording of sound 音声の録音に関連している→**音声の, 音の再生の** || *audio equipment* オーディオ装置 *audio tape* 音声テープ

**audio-visual** 形 ▶定義 using both sound and pictures 音声と画像を両方使っている→**視聴覚の**

**audit** /ɔ́ːdət/ ▶定義 1 名 **C** an official examination of the present state of sth, especially of a company's financial records ～, 特に企業の財務記録の現状についての公式検査→**会計監査, 会計検査, 監査, 検査** || *to carry out an audit* 会計監査を行う ▶定義 2 動 他 to attend a lecture etc not as a regular student→**正規の学生としてでなく授業などを聴講する** || *He was allowed to audit the professor's class.* 彼はその教授のクラスに聴講することを許された.

**audition**¹ /ɔːdíʃ(ə)n/ 名 **C** ▶定義 a short performance by a singer, actor, etc to find out if he/she is good enough to be in a play, show, etc 劇, ショーなどに出演できるだけの力があるかどうかを見極めるための, 歌手, 俳優などによる短時間の演奏や演技→**オーディション審査, 採用試技**

**audition**² /ɔːdíʃ(ə)n/ 動 自 他 ▶定義 audition (sb) (for sth) to do or to watch sb do an audition オーディションを行う, または～がオーディションをするのを見る→**オーディションを受ける, ～にオーディションを行う, ～にオーディションを受けさせる** || *I auditioned for a part in the play.* 私はその劇のある役のオーディションを受けた.

**auditor** /ɔ́ːdətər/ 名 **C** ▶定義 a person whose job is to examine a company's financial records 企業の財務記録を検査することを仕事としている人→**会計監査人, 監査役, 会計検査官, 公認会計士**

**auditorium** /ɔ̀ːdətɔ́ːriəm/ 名 **C** (複 **auditoriums** または **auditoria**) ▶定義 the part of a theatre, concert hall, etc where the audience sits 観客が座る劇場, コンサートホールなどの一部→**観客席, 聴衆席**

**Aug** 略 August→**8月** || *10 Aug 1957* 1957年8月10日

**augur** /ɔ́ːgər/ 動
成句 **augur well/ill for sb/sth** 正式 ▶定義 to be a good/bad sign of what will happen in the future 将来起こる事の良い・悪い兆候である→

〜にとって良い・悪い兆しとなる，〜の良い・悪い前兆である

**August** /ɔ́:ɡəst/ 名 ❶ ❻ (略式 **Aug**) ▶定義 the eighth month of the year, coming after July 7月の次に来る，1年の8番目の月→**8月**
▶文中での月の表し方については，Januaryの例と注を参照．

**aunt** /ά:nt; ænt/ (または 略式 **auntie**; **aunty** /ά:nti; ǽnti/) 名 ❻ ▶定義 the sister of your father or mother; the wife of your uncle 父親また母親の姉妹；伯父・叔父の妻→**伯母，叔母** ∥ *Aunt Ellen* エレンおばさん

**au pair** /òʊ péər/ 名 囲 ❻ ▶定義 a person, usually a girl, from another country who comes to live with a family in order to learn the language. An au pair helps to clean the house and looks after the children. 言語を学ぶために，ある家族と共に生活する外国から来る人で，通常は女の子．家の掃除や子供の世話を手伝う→**オーペア，オペア**

**aura** /ɔ́:rə/ 名 ❻ 略式 ▶定義 the quality that sb/sth seems to have 〜が持っているように見える性質→**特有の雰囲気，独特の雰囲気，感じ**

**aural** /ɔ́:rəl/ 形 ▶定義 connected with hearing and listening 聞こえることと聴くことに関連している→**聴覚の，耳の，聞き取り能力の** ∥ *an aural comprehension test* 聴解力テスト ☞参 **oral**

**auspices** /ɔ́:spəsìz/ 名 [複数扱い]
成句 **under the auspices of sb/sth** ▶定義 with the help and support of sb/sth 〜の助けと支持を得て→**〜の後援で，〜の賛助で，〜の主催で**

**auspicious** /ɔ:spíʃəs/ 形 ▶定義 that seems likely to be successful in the future 将来成功しそうに見えている→**さい先の良い，見通しの明るい，吉兆な** ∥ *She made an auspicious start to her professional career when she won her first race.* 彼女は最初の競争に勝ち，プロとしてさい先の良いスタートを切った． ⇔ **inauspicious**

**austere** /ɔ:stíər/ 形 ▶定義 1 very simple; without decoration とても質素な；装飾のない→**簡素な，飾り気のない，質素な** ▶定義 2 (used about a person) very strict and serious (人について) 非常に厳しくて深刻な→**厳格な，厳しい，厳粛な** ▶定義 3 not having anything that makes your life more comfortable 生活をより快適にする物を何も持っていない→**耐乏の，質素な，禁欲的な** ∥ *The nuns lead simple and austere lives.* その尼僧たちは質素で禁欲的な生活を送っている． — **austerity** /ɔ:stérəti/ 名 ❶ →**厳格さ，厳粛，質素，耐乏，緊縮，耐乏生活**

**authentic** /ɔ:θéntɪk, ə-/ 形 ▶定義 1 that you know is real or genuine 明らかに真実である，または本物である→**本物の，真正な** ∥ *an authentic Van Gogh painting* ヴァン ゴッホの本物の絵 ▶定義 2 true or accurate 本当の，あるいは正確な→**正確な，信頼できる，確実な，忠実な** ∥ *an authentic model of the building* その建物に忠実な模型 — **authenticity** /ɔ̀:θentísəti/ 名 ❶ →**本物であること，真正であること，信頼性，確実性**

**author** /ɔ́:θər/ 名 ❻ ▶定義 a person who writes a book, play, etc 本, 戯曲などを書く人→**著者，作者，作家** ∥ *a well-known author of detective novels* よく知られた推理小説作家 — **authorship** 名 ❶ →**著者名，原作者，著述業，出所，根源**

**authoritarian** /ɔ:θɔ̀(:)rətéəriən, ə-; -θὰr-/ 形 ▶定義 not allowing people the freedom to decide things for themselves 人々に物事を自分で決める自由を認めていない→**権威主義の，権威主義的な，独裁主義の** ∥ *authoritarian parents* 権威主義的な親

**authoritative** /ɔ:θɔ́:rətèɪtɪv; -θάrɪtèɪtɪv/ 形 ▶定義 1 having authority; demanding or expecting that people obey you 権力を持っている；自分に従うことを人々に要求，または期待している→**命令的な，強権的な，横柄な，独裁的な** ∥ *an authoritative tone of voice* 命令的な口調 ▶定義 2 that you can trust because it/he/she has a lot of knowledge and information たくさんの知識や情報を持っているから信用できる→**権威のある，信頼できる** ∥ *They will be able to give you authoritative advice on the problem.* 彼らはあなたにその問題について信頼できる助言をすることができるだろう．

**authority** /ɔ:θɔ́:rəti, -θά-/ 名 (復 **authorities**)
▶定義 1 ❶ the power and right to give orders and make others obey 命令をしたり他人に従わせたりする権力や権利→**権力，権限，支配** ∥ *Children often begin to question their parents' authority at a very early age.* 子供たちはまだ幼いころに，親の権力に疑問を持つことがしばしばある． *You must get this signed by a person in authority (= who has a position of power).* これ

## 94 authorize

には権限のある(=権限のある立場の)人に署名してもらわなければなりません. ▶定義2 ❶**au-thority (to do sth)** the right or permission to do sth ～をする権利または許可→**権限,職権,権能,許可** ‖ *The police* **have the authority** *to question anyone they wish.* 警察は,質問したい人がいればだれにでも質問できる権限を持っている. *He was sacked for using a company vehicle* **without authority**. 彼は無断で会社の車を使ったために首になった. ▶定義3 ❻(しばしば複数形で) a person, group or government department that has the power to give orders, make official decisions, etc 命令をする,公式の決定をするなどの権力を持つ人,集団,あるいは政府の省庁→**当局,官憲,官庁** ‖ *I have to report this to the authorities.* 私は当局にこれを報告しなければならない. ▶定義4 ❶a quality that sb has which makes it possible to influence and control other people ～が持っている,他人に影響を及ぼして左右することができるような性質→**権威,威信,威光** ‖ *He spoke with authority and everybody listened.* 彼は権威を持って話したのでだれもが耳を傾けた. ▶定義5 ❻**an authority (on sth)** a person with special knowledge 特別な知識を持っている人→**権威,大家** ‖ *He's an authority on criminal law.* 彼は刑法の権威である.

**authorize** /ɔ́ːθəraɪz/ (または**-ise**) 動他 ▶定義 to give official permission for sth or for sb to do sth ～が…をすることを公式に許可する→**～に権限を与える,～を公認する,認可する** ‖ *He authorized his secretary to sign letters in his absence.* 彼は秘書に自分の不在時に手紙に署名する権限を与えた. — authorization(または-isation)/ɔ̀ːθəraɪzéɪʃ(ə)n/ 名 ❶→**許可,認可,権限,権利,委任,許可証**

**autistic** /ɔːtístɪk/ 形 ▶定義 having a serious mental illness which makes it very difficult to form relationships with other people 他人と関係を作り上げることを非常に困難にする重い精神病を持っている→**自閉症の,自閉的な**

**autobiography** /ɔ̀ːtəbaɪɑ́grəfi, -toʊ-/ 名 ❻ ❶ (複 **autobiographies**) ▶定義 the story of a person's life written by that person 人の生活について,本人によって書かれた話→**自伝,自叙伝,自伝文学** ☛参 **biography** — autobiographical /ɔ̀ːtəbaɪəgrǽfɪk(ə)l, ɔ̀ːtoʊ-/ 形→**自伝の,自叙伝の,自伝風の,自伝体の**

**autograph** /ɔ́ːtəgræ̀f; -grɑ̀ːf/ 名 ❻ ▶定義 the signature of a famous person 有名な人の署名→**署名,サイン** ‖ *The players stopped outside the stadium to* **sign autographs**. その選手たちはサインをするために競技場の外で立ち止まった. — autograph 動他 →**～にサインする,自署する** ‖ *The whole team have autographed the football.* そのチーム全員がフットボールのボールにサインした.

**automate** /ɔ́ːtəmeɪt/ 動他(通常は受動態で) ▶定義 to make sth operate by machine, without needing people ～を,人が不要な機械によって操作させる→**～を自動化する,オートメーション化する,機械化する,オートメーションで製造する**

★**automatic**¹ /ɔ̀ːtəmǽtɪk/ 形 ▶定義1 (used about a machine) that can work by itself without direct human control (機械について)人による直接的な操作がなくても,それ自体で作動できるような→**自動の,自動的な,自動装置の,無人の** ‖ *an automatic washing machine* 自動洗濯機 ▶定義2 done without thinking 考えずに行われている→**機械的な,無意識の,習慣的な,反射的な** ▶定義3 always happening as a result of a particular action or situation ある特定の行動または状況の結果として必ず起こる→**自動的に起こる,必然的な,自然の成り行きの** ‖ *All the staff have an automatic right to a space in the car park.* 職員であれば全員,空いている駐車場を使う権利がある. — automatically /-k(ə)li/ 副 →**自動的に,無意識に,機械的に** ‖ *The lights will come on automatically when it gets dark.* その明かりは外が暗くなると自動的につく.

**automatic**² /ɔ̀ːtəmǽtɪk/ 名 ❻ ▶定義 an automatic machine, gun or car 自動の機械,銃,車など→**自動装置の機械,自動操作装置,自動けん銃,自動ピストル,オートマチック車** ‖ *This car is an automatic (= has automatic gears).* この車はオートマチック車だ(=自動変速装置が付いている).

**automation** /ɔ̀ːtəméɪʃ(ə)n/ 名 ❶ ▶定義 the use of machines instead of people to do work 仕事をするために人ではなく機械を使うこと→**自動操作,自動制御,自動化,オートメーション,機械使用**

**automobile** /ɔ́ːtəmoʊbiːl, ⸺⸺/ 特に米 =**CAR(1)**

**autonomy** /ɔːtɑ́nəmi/ 名 ❶ ▶定義 the right of a person, an organization, a region, etc to govern or control his/her/its own affairs 人，組織，地域などがそれ自体のことを決定したり管理したりする権利→自治，自治権 — autonomous /ɔːtánəməs/ 形 自治権を有している，自治を行っている，独立した ‖ *The people in this region want to be completely autonomous.* この地域の人々は完全に独立することを望んでいる．

**autopsy** /ɔ́ːtəpsi, -tɑ́p-/ 名 C (複 **autopsies**) ▶定義 an examination of a dead body to find out the cause of death 死因を調べるための死体の検査→検死，検死解剖

\*__autumn__ /ɔ́ːtəm/ (米 通常は **fall**) 名 C U ▶定義 the season of the year that comes between summer and winter 1年の中で夏と冬の間に来る季節→秋，秋季 ‖ *In autumn the leaves on the trees begin to fall.* 秋には木々の葉が落ち始める．— autumnal /ɔːtʌ́mn(ə)l/ 形 →秋の，秋らしい，秋に咲く，秋に実る

**auxiliary** /ɔːɡzíljəri, -zíl(ə)ri/ 形 (名詞の前だけ) ▶定義 giving extra help 補助している→補助の，予備の，補足の ‖ *auxiliary nurses/troops/staff* 補助の看護婦・援軍・補助職員

**auxiliary verb** 名 C (文法) ▶定義 a verb (for example be, do or have) that is used with a main verb to show tense, etc or to form questions 時制などを表したり疑問文を作るために本動詞と共に用いられる動詞（例えば be, do, have など)→法助動詞

**avail** /əvéɪl/ 名 U
成句 of little/no avail ▶定義 not helpful; having little or no effect 役に立たない；効果がほとんど，または全くない→ほとんど・全く役に立たない
to little/no avail ▶定義 without success 成功しないで→無益に，かいもなく ‖ *They searched everywhere, but to no avail.* 彼らは至る所を捜したが，見つからなかった．

**availability** /əvèɪləbíləti/ 名 U ▶定義 the state of being available 利用できる状態→利用できること，役に立つこと，入手可能であること，有効性，有用性，入手の可能性 ‖ *You will receive the colour you order, subject to availability (= if it is available).* 入手できる可能性があれば（= それが入手できるならば），注文された色をお受け取りになれるでしょう．

\*__available__ /əvéɪləbl/ 形 ▶定義 1 available (to sb) (used about things) that you can get, buy, use, etc (物事について) 手に入れる，買う，使う

などのことができるような→～に利用できる，手に入る，入手できる，役に立つ ‖ *This information is easily available to everyone at the local library.* この情報は地元の図書館でだれでも簡単に入手できる．*Refreshments are available at the snack bar.* 簡単な食事はスナックバーでできる．▶定義 2 (used about people) free to be seen, talked to, etc (人について) 手が空いていて，会う，話すなどができる→(忙しくないので) ～してもらえる，(手が空いて) ～することができる，忙しくない，～に応ずる暇がある ‖ *The minister was not available for comment.* その大臣はコメントに応じる暇がなかった．

**avalanche** /ǽvəlæ̀ntʃ, -lɑ̀ːn(t)ʃ/ 名 C ▶定義 a very large amount of snow that slides quickly down the side of a mountain 山の斜面を急速に滑り落ちてくる大量の雪→雪崩 ‖ *Two skiers are still missing after yesterday's avalanche.* 2人のスキーヤーは昨日の雪崩があってからいまだに行方不明である．

**the avant-garde** /ɑ̀ːvɑːn(t)ɡɑ́ːrd, æ̀vɑː(ŋ)ɡɑ́ːd; F avɑ̃ɡard/ 名 [単数扱い] ▶定義 extremely modern works of art, music or literature, or the artists who create these 非常に現代的な美術，音楽，文学などの作品，あるいはそのようなものを生み出す芸術家→前衛芸術，アバンギャルド，前衛芸術家，前衛派 — avant-garde 形 →前衛的な，前衛派の，アバンギャルドの，最先端の

**Ave** 略 Avenue→～街 ‖ *26 Elim Ave* エルム街26番地

**avenge** /əvéndʒ/ 動 他 ▶定義 avenge sth; avenge yourself on sb to punish sb for hurting you, your family, etc in some way 自分や自分の家族などを傷付けたことに対して～を何らかの方法で罰する→～に復讐（ふくしゅう）する，仕返しをする，あだを討つ ‖ *He wanted to avenge his father's murder.* 彼は父親が殺害されたことに対して復讐したいと思っていた．*He wanted to avenge himself on his father's murderer.* 彼は父親を殺した者に対して復讐したいと思っていた．☞参 revenge

**avenue** /ǽvən(j)ùː/ 名 C ▶定義 1 (略 **Ave**) a wide street, especially one with trees or tall buildings on each side 広い通りのことで，特に両側に木々や背の高い建物が並んでいるもの→

大通り, 本通り, 大街路, ～街, 並木道 ‖ *I live on Tennyson Avenue.* 私はテニスン大通りに住んでいる. ☛参 road の注 ▶定義2 a way of doing or getting sth ～を行う, または得る方法→**手段, 方法, 道** ‖ *We must explore every avenue open to us (= try every possibility).* 自分たちに可能なあらゆる手段を尽くさなければならない(=あらゆる可能性を試みる).

★**average**¹ /ǽv(ə)rɪdʒ/ 名 ▶定義1 ●the number you get when you add two or more figures together and then divide the total by the number of figures you added 複数の数字を足し, 足した数字の個数で合計を割って得られる数→**平均, 平均値** ‖ *The average of 14, 3 and 1 is 6 (= 18 divided by 3 is 6).* 14と3と1の平均は6である(=18 を3で割ると6). *He has scored 93 goals at an average of 1.55 per game.* 彼は93点のゴール, 1試合平均1.55ゴールを決めた.

▶定義2 〔単数扱い, ❶〕the normal standard, amount or quality 普通の基準, 量, 質など→**標準, 普通, 並み** ‖ *On average, I buy a newspaper about twice a week.* 平均して私は週に約2回, 新聞を買っている.

★**average**² /ǽv(ə)rɪdʒ/ 形 ▶定義1 (名詞の前だけ) (used about a number) found by calculating the average¹(1) (数について) average¹(1) を計算することによって得られる→**平均の, 平均した** ‖ *What's the average age of your students?* あなたの生徒の平均年齢は何歳ですか. ▶定義2 normal or typical 普通の, または典型的な→**並みの, 普通の** ‖ *children of above/below average intelligence* 普通の知能以上・以下の子供

**average**³ /ǽv(ə)rɪdʒ/ 動 ▶定義 to do, get, etc a certain amount as an average ある量を平均として行う, 得るなど→**平均して～する, 平均して～を得る** ‖ *If we average 50 miles an hour we should arrive at about 4 o'clock.* 平均時速50マイルで行けば, 4時ころに着くはずだ.

句動詞 average out (at sth) ▶定義 to result in an average (of sth) 結果として(～の)平均になる→**平均すると(～に)なる, 結局平均～に達する**

**averse** /əvə́ːrs/ 形 正式 ▶定義 averse to sth (often with a negative) against or not in favour of sth (しばしば否定語と共に)～に反対して, または賛成していない→**～が嫌いな, ～に気が進まない, 反対の** ‖ *He is not averse to trying out new ideas.* 彼は新しいアイデアを試してみるのを嫌がらない.

**aversion** /əvə́ːrʒ(ə)n, -ʃ(ə)n/ 名 ● ▶定義1 〔通常は単数〕an aversion (to sb/sth) a strong feeling of not liking sb/sth ～が好きではないという強い気持ち→**～を忌み嫌うこと, 嫌気, 気が進まないこと, 反感** ‖ *Some people have an aversion to spiders.* クモを忌み嫌う人がいる.

▶定義2 a thing that you do not like 好きではない物事→**忌み嫌うもの, 嫌なもの**

**avert** /əvə́ːrt/ 動 他 ▶定義 to prevent sth unpleasant 不快な～を防ぐ→**～を防ぐ, 回避する, 避ける** ‖ *The accident could have been averted.* その事故は防ぐことができただろうに.

**aviary** /éɪviəri; -vièri/ 名 ● (複 **aviaries**) ▶定義 a large cage or area in which birds are kept 鳥が飼われている大きなかご, または空間→**大きな鳥のおり, 鳥小屋, (大規模な)鳥類飼育場**

**aviation** /èɪviéɪʃ(ə)n/ 名 ❶ ▶定義 the designing, building and flying of aircraft 航空機の設計, 製造, 飛行→**航空, 飛行, 航空技術, 航空学**

**avid** /ǽvɪd/ 形 ▶定義1 very enthusiastic about sth (usually a hobby) ～に対してとても(通常は趣味)熱狂的な→**どん欲な, 熱心な** ‖ *an avid collector of antiques* 骨董(こっとう)品の熱心な収集家 ▶定義2 avid for sth wanting to get sth very much ～をとても強く得たいと思っている→**～を熱望している, 渇望している** ‖ *Journalists crowded round the entrance, avid for news.* 新聞記者たちはニュースを求めて入り口付近に押し寄せた. ― **avidly** 副 →**どん欲に, 熱心に, 渇望して, むさぼるように** ‖ *He read avidly as a child.* 彼は子供のように熱心に読んだ.

**avocado** /àːvəkáːdoʊ, æv-/ 名 ● (複 **avocados**) ▶定義 a tropical fruit that is wider at one end than the other, with a hard green skin and a large seed (**stone**) inside 一方の端がもう一方よりも幅広く, 緑色の硬い皮があり, 中には大きな種(核)がある熱帯地方の果物→**アボカド** ☛ C3 ページのさし絵

★**avoid** /əvɔ́ɪd/ 動 他 ▶定義1 avoid (doing sth) to prevent sth happening or to try not to do sth ～が起こるのを防ぐ, または～をしないようにする→**～することを避ける, ～しないようにする, ～の発生・実現を防止する** ‖ *He always tried to* *avoid an argument if possible.* 彼はいつもできる限り議論を避けようとした. *She has to avoid eating fatty food.* 彼女は脂っこい食べ物を取らないようにしなければならない. ▶定義2 to keep away from sb/sth 〜から遠ざけておく→〜を避ける, よける, 逃れる ‖ *I leave home at 7 o'clock in order to avoid the rush hour.* 私はラッシュアワーを避けるために7時に家を出ている. — **avoidance** 名 U →避けること, 回避, 忌避, 控えること

**avoidable** /əvɔ́ɪdəb(ə)l/ 形 ▶定義 that can be prevented; unnecessary 防ぐことができるような; 不必要な →避けられる, 回避可能な ⇔ **unavoidable**

**await** /əwéɪt/ 動 他 正式 ▶定義 to wait for sb/sth 〜を待つ→〜を待つ, 待ち受ける, 待ち構える ‖ *We sat down to await the arrival of the guests.* 私たちは座ってお客様の到着を待ち受けた.

**awake**¹ /əwéɪk/ 動 (過 **awoke** /əwóʊk/; 過分 **awoken** /əwóʊk(ə)n/ 自 他 ▶定義 to wake up; to make sb/sth wake up 目が覚める; 〜を起こす→目覚める, 起きる, 起こす ‖ *I awoke to find that it was already 9 o'clock.* 私が目が覚めるともう9時だった. *A sudden loud noise awoke us.* 突然の大きな物音で私たちは目が覚めた. ☞ **wake up**の方が awake よりも一般的である.

★**awake**² /əwéɪk/ 形 (名詞の前は不可) ▶定義 not sleeping 眠っていない→目が覚めて, 眠らずに ‖ *I was sleepy this morning but I'm wide awake now.* 今朝私は眠たかったが, 今はしっかり目が覚めている. *They were so tired that they found it difficult to stay awake.* 彼らはとても疲れていたので, 起きているのは難しかった. *I hope our singing didn't keep you awake last night.* 昨夜私たちが歌っていたために, あなたが眠れなかったのではないといいのですが. ⇔ **asleep**

**awaken** /əwéɪk(ə)n/ 動 ▶定義1 自 他 (文)to wake up; to make sb/sth wake up 目が覚める; 〜を起こす→〜を目覚めさせる, 目覚める ‖ *We were awakened by a loud knock at the door.* 私たちは戸を強くノックする音で目が覚めた. ☞ wake upの方が awaken よりもずっと一般的である. ▶定義2 他 正式 to produce a particular feeling, attitude, etc in sb 〜にある特定の感情, 態度などを生じさせる→〜が呼び起こされる, 〜がよみがえる, 〜を喚起する ‖ *The film awakened memories of her childhood.* その映画は彼女の子供のころの記憶をよみがえらせた.

句動詞 **awaken sb to sth** ▶定義 to make sb notice or realize sth for the first time 〜に…を初めて気付かせる, または認識させる→〜を目覚めさせる, 〜に…を気付かせる, 自覚させる ‖ *The letter awakened me to the seriousness of the situation.* その手紙を読んで私は状況の深刻さに気付いた.

**awakening** /əwéɪk(ə)nɪŋ/ 名 [単数扱い] ▶定義1 the act of starting to feel or understand sth; the start of a feeling, etc 〜を感じ始める, または理解し始めること; ある気持ちなどの始まり→目覚め, 覚醒(かくせい), 芽生え ‖ *the awakening of an interest in the opposite sex* 異性への関心の芽生え ▶定義2 a moment when sb notices or realizes sth for the first time 〜が初めて…に気付いたり認識したりする瞬間→自覚, 認識 ‖ *It was a rude (= unpleasant) awakening when I suddenly found myself unemployed.* 自分が失業していることに突然気付いたのは激しいショック(= 不快)だった.

★**award**¹ /əwɔ́ːrd/ 名 C ▶定義1 a prize, etc that sb gets for doing sth well 〜が良くできたことに対して…が得る賞など→賞, 賞品 ‖ *This year the awards for best actor and actress went to two Americans.* 今年の主演男優賞と主演女優賞は2人のアメリカ人に贈られた. ▶定義2 an amount of money given to sb as the result of a court decision 法廷での判決の結果として〜に与えられる金額→裁定額 ‖ *She received an award of £5000 for damages.* 彼女は損害賠償として5000ポンドの裁定額を受け取った.

★**award**² /əwɔ́ːrd/ 動 他 ▶定義 award sth (to sb) to give sth to sb as a prize, payment, etc 〜に…を賞, 金銭などとして与える→〜を…に与える, 授与する, 裁定して与える ‖ *She was awarded first prize in the gymnastics competition.* 彼女は体操の競技会で1等賞をもらった. *The court awarded £10000 each to the workers injured in the accident.* 裁判所はその事故で負傷した労働者1人1人に1万ポンドの賠償金を与えた.

★**aware** /əwéər/ 形 ▶定義1 aware (of sb/sth); aware (that) knowing about or realizing sth; conscious of sb/sth 〜について知っている, ま

98 awareness

たは分かっている；〜に気付いている→〜だと知って，分かって，〜に気付いて‖ I am well **aware** of the problems you face. 私にはあなたが直面している問題がよく分かっている. I suddenly **became aware** that someone was watching me. 私はだれかが私を見ていることに突然気付いた. There is no other entrance, **as far as I am aware**. 私の知る限りではほかに入り口はありません. ⇔ **unaware** ▶定義2 interested and informed 興味があり情報に通じている→見聞の広い，〜に通じている，〜の知識がある‖ Many young people are very politically aware. 政治意識の非常に高い若者たちが多い.

**awareness** /əwéəməs/ 発 ● ▶定義 knowledge, consciousness or interest 知識，意識，興味など→〜に気付いていること，自覚すること，認識，意識‖ People's awareness of healthy eating has increased in recent years. 近年，健康的な食事に対する人々の認識が高まっている.

**awash** /əwɔ́(ː)ʃ, -wɑ́ʃ/ 形 (名詞の前は不可) ▶定義 awash (with sth) covered with water; flooded 水に覆われている；水浸しになっている→波にぬれて，水浸しで，浸水して‖ (比喩)The city was awash with rumours. 街中うわさが広まっていた.

★**away** /əwéɪ/ 副形 ☞参 give away, take away などの句動詞 ▶定義1 away (from sb/sth) to a different place or in a different direction ほかの場所へ，または別の方向に→あちらへ，離れて，向こうへ，離れて別の方向に‖ Go away! I'm busy! あちらへ行って．私は忙しいのだから. I asked him a question, but he just looked away. 私は彼に質問をしたが，彼はただ目をそらしただけだった. ▶定義2 away (from sth) at a particular distance from a place ある場所から特定の距離に→〜から離れて，遠くへ‖ The village is two miles away from the sea. その村は海から2マイル離れている. My parents live five minutes away. 私の両親は5分で行ける所に住んでいる. ▶定義3 away (from sth) (used about people) not present; absent（人について）いない；不在の→不在で，留守で，欠席で‖ My neighbours are away on holiday at the moment. 私の近所の人たちは今は休暇で留守にしている. Aki was away from school for two weeks with measles. アキは

麻疹（はしか）で2週間学校を休んだ. ▶定義4 in the future 将来→(時間的に)〜から離れて‖ Our summer holiday is only three weeks away. 私たちの夏休みはもう3週間後だ. ▶定義5 into a place where sth is usually kept 〜がいつも置かれている場所に→安全な場所に，元の場所へ‖ Put your books away now. 自分の本を今すぐしまいなさい. They cleared the dishes away (= off the table). 彼らは食器を片付けた(＝テーブルから) ☞ 対比 **throw sth away**(＝〜をごみ箱に捨てる) ▶定義6 continuously, without stopping 止まらないで連続して→(休みなく)ずっと，絶え間なく，どんどん，せっせと‖ They chatted away for hours. 彼らは何時間もずっとしゃべり続けた. ▶定義7 (used about a football, etc match) on the other team's ground (サッカーなどの試合について)相手チームのグラウンドで→遠征地での，相手チームのグラウンドで行われる，相手の本拠地での‖ Our team's playing away on Saturday. 私たちのチームは土曜日に相手チームの本拠地で試合がある. an away match/game 遠征試合・ロードゲーム ⇔ **(at) home** ▶定義8 until sth disappears 〜が消え去るまで→消え去って，なくなって，弱まって‖ The crash of thunder slowly died away. 雷鳴はだんだんと収まった. He's given most of his money away. 彼は有り金のほとんどをくれてやった.

成句 **do away with sb/sth** ▶定義 to get rid of sb/sth 〜を取り除く→〜を除く，廃止する，やめる，殺す‖ The government are going to do away with the tax on fuel. 政府は燃料への税金を廃止するつもりだ.

**right/straight away** ▶定義 immediately; without any delay 直ちに；少しも遅れることなく→すぐに，直ちに，今すぐ‖ I'll phone the doctor right away. 私がすぐに先生に電話します.

**awe** /ɔ́ː/ 発 ● ▶定義 feelings of respect and either fear or admiration 尊敬と，恐れまたは感嘆の合わさった気持ち→畏敬，畏怖，尊敬と恐れの気持ち

成句 **be in awe of sb/sth** ▶定義 to admire sb/sth and be slightly frightened of him/her/it 〜を尊敬し，少し恐れを抱く→恐れ敬う‖ As a young boy he was very much in awe of his uncle. 彼は少年だった頃，自分のおじに強い畏敬の念を抱いていた.

**awe-inspiring** 形 ▶定義 causing a feeling of

respect and fear or admiration 尊敬と, 恐れまたは感嘆の合わさった気持ちを引き起こしている→畏敬の念を抱かせる, 荘厳な

**awesome** /ɔ́ːs(ə)m/ 形 ▶定義1 impressive and sometimes frightening 印象的で時にはぎょっとさせることもある→畏敬の念を抱かせる, 恐ろしい, すさまじい ‖ *an awesome task* すさまじい仕事 ▶定義2 米 (俗語) very good; excellent とても良い; 優れている→すばらしい, 優れた, すごい, とてもいい

*__awful__ /ɔ́ːf(ə)l/ 形 ▶定義1 very bad or unpleasant とてもひどい, または不快である→ひどい, 大変悪い, 不快な ‖ *We had an awful holiday. It rained every day.* ひどい休暇だった. 毎日雨が降っていたのだから. *I feel awful - I think I'll go to bed.* 具合が悪いのです — だから寝ることにします. *What an awful thing to say!* 何てひどい事を言うのですか. ▶定義2 terrible; very serious 恐ろしい; とても深刻な→恐ろしい, すさまじい, 恐怖を覚えさせる ‖ *I'm afraid there's been some awful news.* 残念だが恐ろしいニュースがいくつも続いている. ▶定義3 (名詞の前だけ) 略式 very great とても大きな→大変な, ものすごい ‖ *We've got an awful lot of work to do.* 私たちはやるべき仕事をものすごくたくさん抱えている.

**awfully** /ɔ́ːfli/ 副 略式 ▶定義 very; very much 非常に; とても多く→非常に, とても, すごく, ひどく ‖ *I'm awfully sorry.* 大変失礼しました.

**awkward** /ɔ́ːkwəd/ 形 ▶定義1 difficult to deal with 取り扱うのが難しい→厄介な, やりにくい, 困った, 使いにくい, 扱いにくい ‖ *That's an awkward question.* それは困った問題だ. *You've put me in an awkward position.* あなたのせいで私は厄介なことになった. *an awkward customer* 扱いにくい顧客 *The box isn't heavy but it's awkward to carry.* その箱は重くないが運びにくい. ▶定義2 not convenient, difficult 都合が良くない, 難しい→都合が悪い, 具合の悪い, 不便な ‖ *My mother always phones at an awkward time.* 私の母はいつも都合の悪いときに電話をする. *This tin-opener is very awkward to clean.* この缶切りはきれいにするのがとても難しい. ▶定義3 embarrassed or embarrassing 当惑した, または当惑させるような→気まずい思いをする, 当惑した, 落ち着かない, どぎまぎした ‖ *I often feel awkward in a group of people.* 私は集団の中にいるとしばしば落ち着かないことがある. *There was an awkward silence.* 気まずい沈黙があった. ▶定義4 not using the body in the best way; not elegant or comfortable 身体を最もうまく動かしていない; 上品ではない, または心地良くない→不器用な, ぎこちない, 下手な, 無様な ‖ *I was sitting with my legs in an awkward position.* 私は足を無様に構えて座っていた. — **awkwardly** 副 →不器用に, 無様に, 戸惑って, きまり悪そうに — **awkwardness** 名 Ⓤ →ぎこちなさ, 戸惑い, 間の悪さ, 無様

**awoke** AWAKE¹ の過去形
**awoken** AWAKE¹ の過去分詞形

**awry** /ərái/ 副 形 (名詞の前は不可) ▶定義 wrong, not in the way that was planned; untidy 違っている, 計画された通りではない; ずさんな→予定が狂った, 間違った, 不適切な, 不首尾で

**axe**¹ (特に 米 **ax**) /æks/ 名 Ⓒ ▶定義 a tool with a wooden handle and a heavy metal head with a sharp edge, used for cutting wood, etc 木製の柄と, 鋭利な刃の付いた金属の重い頭部からできている道具で, 木を切るなどのために使われる→おの, まさかり ☞ **garden** のさし絵

**axe**² (特に 米 **ax**) /æks/ 動 Ⓒ ▶定義1 to remove sb/sth 〜を取り除く→〜を解雇する ‖ *Hundreds of jobs have been axed.* 何百人もが職を失った. ▶定義2 to reduce sth by a great amount 〜を大量に減らす→〜に大なたを振るう, 〜を切る, 減らす, 削減する ‖ *School budgets are to be axed.* 学校の予算が削減されることになっている. ☞ この動詞は特に新聞で用いられる.

**axis** /ǽksəs/ 名 Ⓒ (複 **axes** /ǽksiːz/) ▶定義1 a line we imagine through the middle of an object, around which the object turns ある物体の中心を通っており, その周りをその物体が回っているとする想像上の線→軸, 回転軸, 中心軸 ‖ *The earth rotates on its axis.* 地球は地軸を中心に回転している. ☞ **earth** のさし絵 ▶定義2 a fixed line used for marking measurements on a diagram (graph) 図 (グラフ) に測定値を記すために用いられる固定された線→軸, 軸線 ‖ *the horizontal/vertical axis* 水平軸・垂直軸

**axle** /ǽks(ə)l/ 名 Ⓒ ▶定義 a bar that connects a pair of wheels on a vehicle 乗り物の車輪の対をつなぐ棒→車軸

# B b

**B, b**[1] /biː/ 名 C (複 **B's**; **b's**) ▶定義 the second letter of the English alphabet 英語アルファベットの第2文字▶b(B)が表す音,b(B)の文字,b(B)の字形のもの ‖ *'Billy' begins with (a) 'B'*. Billy は B で始まる.

**b**[2] /biː/ 略 **born** ⇒生まれ ‖ *J S Bach, b 1685* JS バッハ, 1685 年生まれ

**BA** /ˌbiː ˈeɪ/ 略 Bachelor of Arts ▶定義 the degree that you receive when you complete a university or college course in an arts subject 大学で(人)文学部の課程を修了した学生が授与される称号➡文学士(号) ☛参 **BSc, MA**

**baa** /bɑː; bæː/ 名 [単数扱い] ▶定義 the sound that a sheep makes 羊が出す声➡メェー

**B & B** /ˌbiː ən ˈbiː/ 略 =BED AND BREAKFAST

**babble**[1] /bæbl/ 名 [単数扱い] ▶定義 1 the sound of many voices talking at the same time たくさんの話し声が同時に聞こえる時の音➡ざわめき, 喧噪(けんそう), がやがやいう声 ‖ *I could hear a babble of voices coming from downstairs.* 下の階からざわめきが聞こえた.
▶定義 2 the sound of water running over stones 石の上を流れる水の音➡せせらぎ(の音)

**babble**[2] /bæbl/ 動 自 ▶定義 1 to talk quickly or in a way that is difficult to understand 速くまたは理解するのが困難な方法で話す➡ぺちゃくちゃしゃべる, たわ言を言う ▶定義 2 to make the sound of water running over stones 石の上を流れる水音を立てる➡さらさらと音を立てる, さらさら流れる

**babe** /beɪb/ 名 C ▶定義 1 特に 米 (俗語) used when talking to sb, especially a girl or young woman ～に, 特に少女や若い女性に, 話し掛けるときに用いて➡女の子, かわいこちゃん ‖ *It's OK, babe.* 大丈夫だよ, かわいこちゃん.
▶定義 2 (俗語) an attractive young woman 魅力的な若い女性➡かわいい人 ▶定義 3 (古) a baby 赤ん坊➡赤ん坊, 赤ちゃん

*****baby** /beɪbi/ 名 C (複 **babies**) ▶定義 1 a very young child 非常に幼い子供➡赤ん坊, 赤ちゃん ‖ *I'm going to **have a baby**.* 赤ちゃんがもうじき生まれます. *She's **expecting a baby** early next year.* 彼女は来年の早い時期に出産する予定です. *When's the baby **due**? (= when will it be born?)* 出産の予定日はいつですか(= いつ生まれるの). *a baby boy/girl* 男の・女の赤ちゃん
▶定義 2 a very young animal or bird 非常に若い動物または鳥➡赤ちゃん ▶定義 3 米 (俗語) a person, especially a girl or young woman, that you like or love あなたが好きなまたは愛する人, 特に少女や若い女性➡恋人, 女の子, 女房, 意中の人

**baby boom** 名 [通常は単数] ▶定義 a time when more babies are born than usual, for example after a war 通常よりも多くの赤ん坊が生まれる時期, 例えば戦後➡ベビーブーム

**baby boomer** 名 C ▶定義 a person born during a baby boom ベビーブームの間に生まれた人➡ベビーブーム時代に生まれた人, ベビーブーム世代の人(特に 1945～65 年に生まれた人)

**baby carriage** 米 = PRAM

**babyish** /beɪbiɪʃ/ 形 ▶定義 suitable for or behaving like a baby 赤ん坊にふさわしい, または赤ん坊のように振る舞う➡赤ん坊染みた, 大人気ない ‖ *This book is a bit too babyish for Faruk now.* この本はファルークが今読むにはちょっと赤ん坊染みている.

**babysit** /beɪbisɪt/ 動 自 (**babysitting**; 過, 過分 **babysat**) ▶定義 to look after a child for a short time while the parents are out 両親が出掛けている短い間, 子供の面倒を見る➡親の不在中に子守りをする, ベビーシッターをする ‖ *We have friends who babysit for us if we go out in the evening.* 夕方出掛けるのなら, ベビーシッターをしてくれる友達がいます. — **babysitter** 名 C ➡子守りをする人, ベビーシッター

**bachelor** /bætʃ(ə)lər/ 名 C ▶定義 1 a man who has not yet married まだ結婚していない男性➡独身の男, 未婚の男
▶現在では, single が結婚していない男または女を表す最も一般的な語である: *a single man/woman* (独身の男・女)
▶定義 2 a person who has a first university degree 大学の最初の学位を持つ人➡学士 ‖ *a Bachelor of Arts/Science* 文・理学士

*****back**[1] /bæk/ 名 C ▶定義 1 the part of a person's or animal's body between the neck and the bottom 人または動物の体の首としりの間の部分➡背中, 背(腰も含む) ‖ *Do you sleep **on your back** or on your side?* あなたはあおむけに寝ま

back to front     inside out

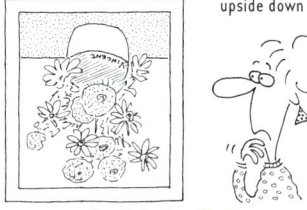

upside down

The painting is **upside down**.

# back³ 101

(の片隅)にあって,くつろいで映画を楽しめなかった.
**back to front** ▶定義 with the back where the front should be 前であるべきものが後ろにあって→**後ろ前に,前後を逆にして** ‖ *Wait a minute - you've got your jumper on back to front.* ちょっと待って － 君はセーターを後ろ前に着ているよ. ☞参 **way¹(3)**
**behind sb's back** ▶定義 without sb's knowledge or agreement 〜の知らない所で,または…の同意なしに→**ひそかに,陰で** ‖ *They criticized her behind her back.* 彼らは陰で彼女を批判していた. ⇔ **to sb's face**
**get off sb's back** 略式 ▶定義 to stop annoying sb, for example when you keep asking him/her to do sth 人を困らせるのをやめる,例えば〜に…をすることを頼み続けたりするとき→**〜を困らせるのをやめる** ‖ *I've told her I'll do the job by Monday, so I wish she'd get off my back!* その仕事を月曜日までに仕上げると,彼女に言ったので,もう私を困らせないでほしい.
**know sth like the back of your hand** ⇒ **KNOW¹**
**a pat on the back** ⇒ **PAT²**
**turn your back on sb/sth** ▶定義 to refuse to be involved with sb/sth 〜にかかわることを拒否する→**〜に背を向ける,〜から逃げる,〜を見捨てる** ‖ *He turned his back on his career and went to live in the country.* 彼は自分の職業を見捨てて,田舎に行って暮らした.

★**back²** /bæk/ 形 ▶定義 **1** (名詞の前だけ) furthest from the front 前から最も遠い→**後ろの,奥の,裏の** ‖ *Have you locked the back door?* 裏口にかぎをかけましたか. *the back row of the theatre* 劇場の後ろの列 *back teeth* 奥歯 ▶定義 **2** owed from a time in the past 過去のある時から借りている→**滞った,未納の** ‖ *back pay/rent/taxes* 未払い賃金・滞っている家賃・未納の税金
成句 **take a back seat** ▶定義 to allow sb to play a more important or active role than yourself in a particular situation ある特定の状況で,自分よりも重要なまたは影響のある役割を〜に果たさせる→**目立たない立場になる,一線を退く,消極的である**

★**back³** /bæk/ 副 ▶定義 **1** in or to a place or state

すか,それとも横向きですか. *She was standing with her back to me so I couldn't see her face.* 彼女は私に背を向けて立っていたので,顔は見えなかった. *A camel has a hump on its back.* らくだは背中にこぶがある. ▶定義 **2** the part or side of sth that is furthest from the front 前から最も離れている〜の部分または側面→**後ろ,背後,裏面** ‖ *I sat at the back of the class.* 私は教室の後ろに座った. *The answers are in the back of the book.* 答えはその本の後ろにあります. *Write your address on the back of the cheque.* 小切手の裏に住所を書いてください. ▶定義 **3** the part of a chair that supports your upper body when you sit down 座ったときに上半身を支えるいすの部分→**背,背もたれ** ‖ *He put his coat over the back of the chair.* 彼はいすの背にコートを掛けた.
成句 **at/in the back of your mind** ▶定義 if sth is at the back of your mind, it is in your thoughts but is not the main thing that you are thinking about もし sth is at the back of your mind (もし〜が頭の片隅にあれば),その〜は頭の中にはあるが,今考えている事の主要事ではない→**心の奥底に,頭の中にある** ‖ *With next week's exam at the back of my mind, I couldn't relax and enjoy the film.* 来週の試験のことが頭

that sb/sth was in before ～が前にあった[いた]場所または状態に[へ] →元の所へ[に・で], 元いた所に, 元の所に ‖ *I'm going out now - I'll be back* about six o'clock. 私はもう出掛けるよ—6時ころには戻ってくる. *It started to rain so I came back home.* 雨が降り出したので, 私は家に戻った. **Go back** to sleep. (まだ起きる時間ではないから,)もっと寝ていなさい. *Could I have my pen back, please?* 私のペンを返してもらえませんか. *I've got to take these books back to the library.* これらの本を図書館に返さなければならない. ▶定義2 away from the direction you are facing or moving in 自分が向いている, または向かっている方向から離れて→**後ろに[へ], 後方に[へ], 下がって** ‖ *She walked away without looking back.* 彼女は後ろを振り返らずに歩いていってしまった. *Could everyone move back a bit, please?* 皆さん, 少し下がってもらえますか. ⇔ forward ▶定義3 away from sth; under control ～から離れて; 管理されて→**抑えて, 遅らせるように** ‖ *The police were unable to keep the crowds back.* 警察は群衆を押し戻せなかった. *She tried to hold back her tears.* 彼女は涙をこらえようとした. ▶定義4 in return or in reply お返しに, または答えて→**お返しに(～する), (し)返す** ‖ *He said he'd phone me back in half an hour.* 彼は30分後に折り返し電話をすると言った. ▶定義5 in or into the past; ago 過去に[へ]; 以前に→**さかのぼって, 以前に, 今から～前に** ‖ *I met him a few years back, in Madrid.* 2, 3年前にマドリードで彼に会った. **Think back** to your first day at school. 学校の初めての日を振り返って考えてみなさい. 成句 **back and forth** ▶定義 from one place to another and back again, all the time いつも, ある場所から他へ, そしてまた戻り→**前後に, (繰り返し)あちらこちらに, 行ったり来たり** ‖ *Travelling back and forth to work takes up quite a bit of time.* 職場への往復は, かなり時間を取る.

*back⁴ /bæk/ 動 ▶定義1 🗎 🗎 to move backwards or to make sth move backwards 後ろに動く, または～を後ろに動かす→**後退する, 逆行する; 後退させる, バックさせる** ‖ *I'll have to back into that parking space.* あの駐車スペースにバックして入らなければならないだろう. *He backed the car into the parking space.* 彼は車をバックさせて駐車場に入った. ▶定義2 🗎 to face sth at the back その背後で～に面している→**～を背にする, 裏が～に面する** ‖ *Many of the colleges back onto the river.* 多くの大学は川を背にしている. ▶定義3 🗎 to give help or support to sb/sth ～を助ける, または支える→**～を後援する, 援助する, 支持する** ‖ *We can go ahead with the scheme if the bank will agree to back us.* もし銀行が我々を援助することに賛同すれば, その計画を進められる. ▶定義4 🗎 to bet money that a particular horse, team, etc will win in a race or game 特定の馬, チームなどがレースや試合で勝つことに金をかける→**～にかける** ‖ *Which horse are you backing in the 2 o'clock race?* 2時のレースでどの馬にかけるのですか.

句動詞 **back away (from sb/sth)** ▶定義 to move backwards because you are afraid, shocked, etc 怖い, ショックを受けたなどのために, 後退する→**(～から)後ずさりする, しりごみする** ‖ *He began to back slowly away from the snake.* 彼は蛇からゆっくりと後ずさりし始めた.

**back down** ▶定義 to stop saying that you are right 自分が正しいと言うのをやめる→**(元の主張・要求などから)後退する, 譲歩する** ‖ *I think you are right to demand an apology. Don't back down now.* あなたが謝罪を要求するのは正しいと思う. 今譲歩してはいけない.

**back out (of sth)** ▶定義 to decide not to do sth that you had promised to do すると約束した～をしないことに決める→**約束を破る, 手を引く** ‖ *You promised you would come with me. You can't back out of it now!* あなたは私と一緒に来ると約束した. 今更手は引けないよ.

**back sb/sth up** ▶定義 to support sb; to say or show that sth is true ～を支える; ～が真実だと言うまたは示す→**～を援助する, 支持する; (主張など)を証明する, 裏付ける** ‖ *I'm going to say exactly what I think at the meeting. Will you back me up?* 私は打ち合わせで, 自分が思う通りの事を言うつもりです. 私を援護してくれますか. *All the evidence backed up what the woman had said.* 証拠がすべてその女性の言った事を裏付けた.

**back (sth) up** ▶定義 to move backwards, especially in a vehicle 後ろに動く, 特に乗り物

で→〜を後退させる,バックさせる ‖ *Back up a little so that the other cars can get past.* ほかの車が通れるように少し下がってください.

**back sth up** ▶定義 (computing) to make a copy of a computer program, etc in case the original one is lost or damaged(コンピューター)原物・オリジナルがなくなったりまたは損傷した場合に備えて,コンピュータープログラムなどのコピーを作る→バックアップをとる,コピーする

**back bench** /bæk bentʃ/ 名[C,通常は複数]英 ▶定義 a seat in the House of Commons for an ordinary member of Parliament 下院にある普通の国会議員のための席→後方席,平議員席 ‖ *to sit on the back benches* 平議員席に座る — **back-bencher** 名 C →平議員

**backbone** /bǽkbòun/ 名 ▶定義1 C the row of small bones that are connected together down the middle of your back 背中の中央部にあるつながった小さな骨の列→背骨 ☞類 **spine** ☞ C5ページのさし絵 ▶定義2 [単数扱い] the most important part of sth 〜の最も重要な部分→主力,重要要素 ‖ *Agriculture is the backbone of the country's economy.* 農業は国の経済の主力だ.

**backcloth** /bǽkklɔ̀:θ/ = **BACKDROP**

**backdate** /bǽkdèɪt/ 動他 ▶定義 to make a document, cheque or a payment take effect from an earlier date 文書,小切手,または支払いを,ずっと早い日付から有効にする→(実施時期など)をさかのぼらせる ‖ *The pay rise will be backdated to 1 April.* 昇給は,4月1日にさかのぼって実施されるだろう.

**backdrop** /bǽkdrɑp/ (または **backcloth**) 名 C ▶定義 a painted piece of material that is hung behind the stage in a theatre as part of the scenery 劇場の舞台の後ろに背景の一部としてつり下げられている描かれたものの1つ→背景幕,背景

**backer** /bǽkər/ 名 C ▶定義 a person, organization or company that gives support to sb, especially financial support 〜に支援,特に経済的支援を与える人,組織,または会社→後援者,支持者,スポンサー

**backfire** /bǽkfàɪər/ 動自 ▶定義 to have an unexpected and unpleasant result, often the opposite of what was intended しばしば意図したものとは反対の,予期しない,嫌な結果を得る→思い掛けない結果となる,失敗に終わる

\***background** /bǽkgràʊnd/ 名 ▶定義1 [単数扱い]the part of a view, scene, picture, etc which is furthest away from the person looking at it 見ている人から最も遠くにある眺め,景色,絵などの部分→背景,遠景 ‖ *You can see the mountains in the background of the photo.* その写真の背景に山々が見える. ⇨ **foreground** ▶定義2 [単数扱い] a position where sb/sth can be seen/heard, etc but is not the centre of attention 〜が見える・聞こえるが,注意の中心ではない位置→目立たない所,背後,陰 ‖ *The film star's husband prefers to stay in the background.* その映画スターの夫は,目立たないでいることを好む. *All the time I was speaking to her, I could hear a child crying in the background.* 彼女と話をしている間中,後ろで子供が泣いているのが聞こえた. *I like to have background music when I'm studying.* 私は勉強をするときに音楽を流しておくのが好きだ. ▶定義3 [単数扱い, U]the facts or events that are connected with a situation ある状態に関連している事実または出来事→背景,遠因,社会的状況 ‖ *The talks are taking place against a background of increasing tension.* 緊迫の度合いを増している社会的状況に対して,会談が開かれている. *I need some background information.* 予備知識が必要だ. ▶定義4 C the type of family and social class you come from and the education and experience you have 人が育った家族や社会的階級の種類,また受けた教育や経験→経歴,(教養・家族・交友などの)背景,素性 ‖ *We get on very well together in spite of our different backgrounds.* 私たちは生まれ育ちが異なるにもかかわらず,非常にうまくやっている.

**backhand** /bǽkhæ̀nd/ 名[単数扱い] ▶定義 a way of hitting the ball in tennis, etc that is made with the back of your hand facing forward テニスなどで,手の甲を前に向けてボールを打つ方法→バックハンド(ストローク) ⇔ **forehand**

**backing** /bǽkɪŋ/ 名 U ▶定義 help or support to do sth, especially financial support 〜をすることへの助力,または支援,特に経済的な支援→後援,支持 ‖ *financial backing* 経済的支援

**backlash** /bǽklæʃ/ 名[単数扱い] ▶定義 a strong reaction against a political or social event or development 政治的または社会的な出来事や発展に反対する強い反応→**激しい反発, 激しい反動**

**backlog** /bǽklɔ̀ːg/ 名[C, 通常は単数] ▶定義 an amount of work, etc that has not yet been done and should have been done already まだ終わっていないが, 既に終わっていなければならない仕事などの量→**さばき切れない仕事(の山), やり残し, 未処理分, 残務** ‖ *Because I've been off sick, I've got a backlog of work to catch up on.* 病気で休んでいたので, 後れを取り戻さなければならない未処理の仕事がたまっている.

**backpack**¹ /bǽkpæk/ 名 C ▶定義 a large bag, often on a metal frame, that you carry on your back when travelling しばしば金属製の枠の付いている, 旅をするときに背中に担ぐ大きなバッグ→**バックパック** ☞類 **rucksack** ☞ **bag** のさし絵

**backpack**² /bǽkpæk/ 動 自 ▶定義 to go walking or travelling with your clothes, etc in a backpack バックパックに服などを入れて徒歩旅行をする, または旅行をする→**バックパックを背負って徒歩旅行・登山をする**

▶ go backpacking は, バックパックを背負って旅行をして過ごすことを表すときに用いられる: *We went backpacking round Europe last summer.* (私たちは昨年の夏バックパックを背負ってヨーロッパを旅した.)

— **backpacker** /bǽkpækər/ 名 C →**バックパックを背負って旅行する人**

**backside** /bǽksàɪd/ 名 C 略式 ▶定義 the part of your body that you sit on; your bottom 座ると下に触れる身体の部分; しり→**しり, 臀部(でんぶ)**

**backstage** /bǽksteɪdʒ/ 副 ▶定義 in the part of a theatre where the actors get dressed, wait to perform, etc 俳優が衣装を着たり出番を待つなどする劇場の一部分で→**楽屋で[へ], 舞台裏で[へ]**

**backstroke** /bǽkstroʊk/ 名 U ▶定義 a style of swimming that you do on your back 背中を下にして泳ぐ方法→**背泳ぎ, 背泳** ‖ *Can you do backstroke?* 背泳ぎができますか. ☞ S1 ページのさし絵

**backtrack** /bǽktræk/ 動 自 ▶定義1 to go back the same way you came 来た道と同じ道を帰る→**もと来た道を戻る** ‖ *We got lost in the wood and had to backtrack.* 私たちは森で道に迷い, もと来た道を戻らなければならなかった.

▶定義2 **backtrack (on sth)** to change your mind about a plan, promise, etc that you have made 既に決めた計画や約束などについて気が変わる→**(意見・声明・約束・政策などを)撤回する, 取り消す, ご破算にする** ‖ *Unions forced the company to backtrack on its plans to close the factory.* 組合は会社に工場閉鎖の計画の取り消しを余儀なくさせた.

**back-up** /bǽkʌp/ 名 ▶定義1 U extra help or support that you can get if necessary 必要なら受けられる臨時の助力や支援→**支援, バックアップ** ‖ *The police officer requested urgent back-up from the rest of the team.* 警察官は, ほかの仲間の緊急支援を要請した. ▶定義2 C (computing) a copy of a computer disk that you can use if the original one is lost or damaged (コンピューター) 元のコンピューターディスクがなくなったり, 破損したときに使えるコンピューターディスクのコピー→**バックアップ** ‖ *Always make a back-up of your files.* いつもファイルのバックアップを作りなさい.

*****backward** /bǽkwərd/ 形 ▶定義1 (名詞の前だけ) directed towards the back 後ろに向けられた→**後ろ向きの, 後方への, 戻りの** ‖ *a backward step/glance* 後ろへの1歩・振り返ってちらりと見ること ⇔ **forward** ▶定義2 slow to develop or learn 発達するまたは習得することが遅い→**後れた** ‖ *Our teaching methods are backward compared to some countries.* 我が国の教授方法は幾つかの国に比べて後れている.

**backwards** /bǽkwərdz/ (または **backward**) 副 ▶定義1 towards a place or a position that is behind 後ろの場所や位置に向かって→**後方に, 後ろ向きに** ‖ *Could everybody take a step backwards?* 皆さん, 後ろへ1歩下がってもらえますか. ▶定義2 in the opposite direction to usual 通常と反対の方向に→**逆に, 後ろから** ‖ *Can you say the alphabet backwards?* アルファベットを後ろから言えますか. ⇔ **forwards**

成句 **backward(s) and forward(s)** ▶定義 first in one direction and then in the other, all the time まずある方向にそしてほかの方向に, それ

をずっと→行ったり来たり, 前後に ‖ *The dog ran backwards and forwards, barking loudly.* その犬は大声でほえながら前後に走った.

**backwater** /bǽkwɔ̀ːtər/ 名 C 定義 a place that is away from where most things happen and so it is not affected by new ideas or outside events 多くの事が起こる場所から離れていて, そのために新しい思想や外部の出来事の影響を受けない所→孤立・沈滞した場所, へき地, 文化の後れた社会

**backyard** /bǽkjɑ̀ːrd/ 名 C 定義1 英 an area behind a house, usually of concrete or stone, with a wall or fence around it 家の後ろ側にある, 通常コンクリートまたは石でできた, 壁またはフェンスで囲まれた場所→裏庭, バックヤード 定義2 米 the whole area behind the house including the grass area and the garden 芝生が植えられている部分や草花が植えられている庭を含む, 家の裏側全体の場所→裏庭

**bacon** /béɪk(ə)n/ 名 U 定義 thin pieces of salted or smoked meat from the back or sides of a pig 豚の背中または横腹から取った肉を塩漬けまたは燻製 (くんせい) にしたものの薄い1切れ→ベーコン ☛参 meat の注

**bacteria** /bæktíəriə/ 名 [複数扱い] 定義 very small living things that can only be seen with special equipment (a microscope). Bacteria exist in large numbers in air, water, soil, plants and the bodies of people and animals. Some bacteria cause disease. 特別な器具 (顕微鏡) だけで見られる非常に小さな生き物. bacteria は, 空気, 水, 土壌, 植物, また人や動物の体の中に大量に存在する. 中には病気を引き起こすものもある→バクテリア, 細菌 ☛参 virus

\***bad** /bæd/ 形 ( **worse** /wɔːrs/, **worst** /wɔːrst/)
定義1 not good; unpleasant 良くない; 不快な→**悪い; 不快な, 嫌な** ‖ *Our family's had a bad time recently.* 最近, 私の家族は嫌な経験をした. *bad weather* 悪天候 *I'm afraid I've got some bad news for you.* あなたに悪い知らせがあります. 定義2 of poor quality; of a low standard 質の良くない; 低い基準の→**(質・内容などが) 悪い, 粗悪な, 不十分な** ‖ *Many accidents are caused by bad driving.* 多くの事故は, ひどい運転によって引き起こされる. *Some of the company's problems are the result of bad management.* 会社の問題のいくつかは, 間違った経営の結果だ. 定義3 bad (at sth/at doing sth) not able to do sth well or easily; not skilful or reliable ～をうまくまたは簡単にできない; 熟練していない, または信頼できない→**下手な, 未熟な, (～が) 苦手で** ‖ *a bad teacher/driver/cook* 未熟な教師・運転手・料理人 *I've always been bad at sport.* 私はずっと運動が苦手だ. 定義4 serious; severe 真剣な; 深刻な→**ひどい, 有害な, 悪い** ‖ *The traffic was very bad on the way to work.* 仕事に向かう途中, 交通の流れが非常に悪かった. *She went home with a bad headache.* 彼女はひどい頭痛で家に帰った. *That was a bad mistake!* それはひどい間違いだった. 定義5 (used about food) not fresh or fit to eat; rotten (食べ物について) 新鮮でない, または食べるに適さない; 腐った→**腐った, 傷んだ, 悪くなった** ‖ *These eggs will* ***go bad*** *if we don't eat them soon.* これらの卵はすぐに食べないと腐るだろう. 定義6 (used about parts of the body) not healthy; painful (体の部分について) 健康でない; 痛む→**病気の, 具合の悪い** ‖ *He's always had a bad heart.* 彼はずっと心臓の具合が悪い. *Keith's off work with a bad back.* キースは背中が痛くて仕事を休んでいる. 定義7 (used about a person or behavio(u)r) not good; morally wrong (人または行動について) 善くない; 道徳的に間違っている→**悪い, 不良な, 不正な, 不道徳な, 行儀の悪い** ‖ *He was not a bad man, just rather weak.* 彼は悪いやつではなかった, ただいくぶん弱かったのだ. 定義8 (名詞の前は不可) bad for sb/sth likely to damage or hurt sb/sth bad for sb/sth ～に損害を与えそうな, または傷付けそうな→**(～にとって) 悪い, 有害な** ‖ *Sugar is bad for your teeth.* 砂糖は歯に有害だ. 定義9 bad (for sth/to do sth) difficult or not suitable 難しい, または適しない→**不適当な, 都合の悪い** ‖ *This is a bad time to phone - everyone's out to lunch.* 今は電話をするには不適当な時間だ － 皆昼食に出ている.

成句 not bad 略式 定義 quite good かなり良い→**なかなか良い, まんざら悪くない, 結構いける** ‖ *'What was the film like?' 'Not bad.'*「その映画はどうでしたか」「結構いけるよ」

too bad 略式 定義 used to show that nothing can be done to change a situation ある状況を

変えるために,何もできる事がないことを示すために用いて→(〜であるとは)残念だ,気の毒だ,ついてないね‖ *'I'd much rather stay at home.' 'Well that's just too bad. We've said we'll go.'* 「私は家にいる方がいい」「おや,それは残念だね.私たちは行くと言ってしまった」

**baddy** (または **baddie**) /bædi/ 名 C (複 **baddies**) 略式 ▶定義 a bad person in a film, book, etc 映画,本などに登場する悪い人→悪玉,悪漢 ⇔ goody

*__badge__ /bædʒ/ 名 C ▶定義 a small piece of metal, cloth or plastic with a design or words on it that you wear on your clothing 服に付ける,模様または言葉が書かれた金属,布,プラスチック製の小さな物→バッジ,記章,肩章‖ *The players all have jackets with the club badge on.* すべての選手はクラブのバッジを付けた上着を持っています.

badger

**badger** /bædʒər/ 名 C ▶定義 an animal with black and white lines on its head that lives in holes in the ground and comes out at night 地中の穴に住み,夜になると出てくる,頭に黒と白の線がある動物→アナグマ

**bad language** 名 U ▶定義 words that are used for swearing ののしるときに使われる言葉→下品な・汚い言葉(遣い)‖ *You'll get into trouble if you use bad language.* もし下品な言葉を使うと,困ったことになりますよ.

**badly** /bædli/ 副 (**worse** /wɜːrs/, **worst** /wɜːrst/)
▶定義1 in a way that is not good enough; not well 十分に良くはない方法で; 上手でない→悪く,まずく,下手に‖ *'Can you speak French?' 'Only very badly.'* 「フランス語を話せますか」「非常に下手ですが」 *She did badly in the exams.* 彼女の試験の結果は悪かった.
▶定義2 seriously; severely 真剣に; 深刻に→ひどく‖ *He was badly hurt in the accident.* 彼は事故でひどいけがをした. ▶定義3 very much 非常に→非常に,大変,とても‖ *He badly needed a holiday.* 彼は休みをとても必要としていた.

成句 **badly off** ▶定義 poor; not having enough of sth 貧しい; 十分な〜を持っていない→貧乏な,(暮らしに)困っている,(暮らし向きが)悪い; (〜が)不足している‖ *They don't seem too badly off - they have smart clothes and a nice house.* 彼らはあまり困っているように見えない - こぎれいな身なりで,すてきな家を持っている. ⇔ **well off**

**badminton** /bædmɪnt(ə)n/ 名 U ▶定義 a game for two or four people in which players hit a type of light ball with feathers (**shuttlecock**) over a high net, using a piece of equipment (**a racket**), which is held in the hand 手に握った道具(ラケット)を使って,羽の付いた軽いボール(シャトル)を,高いネット越しに打ち合う,2人または4人で行うゲーム→バドミントン

**bad-tempered** 形 ▶定義 often angry or impatient よく怒る,または我慢できない→機嫌の悪い,意地の悪い,気難しい‖ *a bad-tempered old man* 気難しい老人

**baffle** /bæfl/ 動 他 ▶定義 to be impossible to understand; to confuse sb very much 理解することは不可能である; 〜を非常に混乱させる→困惑させる,当惑させる,まごつかせる‖ *His illness baffled the doctors.* 彼の病気は医者を困惑させた. — **baffled** 形 →困惑した,当惑した‖ *The instructions were so complicated that I was absolutely baffled.* その使用説明書はあまりにも複雑だったので,全く参った. — **baffling** 形 →どうしてよいか分からない,当惑させる‖ *I find it baffling how people can enjoy computer magazines.* 人々がどうしてコンピューター雑誌を楽しめるのか私には分からない.

*__bag__[1] /bæg/ 名 ▶定義1 Ca container made of paper or thin plastic that opens at the top 上部が開く紙または薄いプラスチックでできた入れ物→袋,手提げ‖ *She brought some sandwiches in a plastic bag.* 彼女はビニール袋に入ったサンドイッチを持ってきた. ▶定義2 Ca strong container made from cloth, plastic, leather, etc, usually with one or two handles, used to carry things in when trave(l)ling, shopping, etc 旅行や買い物などをするときに物を運ぶために使われる,布,プラスチック,革などでできた丈夫な容器,通常は1つまたは2つの取っ手が付いている→バッグ,かばん‖ *a shopping bag* 買い物袋 *Have you packed your bags yet?* もうかばんに詰めましたか. *She took her purse out of her bag* (= *handbag*). 彼女はバッグ(=ハンドバッグ)から財布を取り出した. ▶定義3 ❻ the amount contained in a bag 1袋に入っている量→1袋の量‖ *She's eaten a whole bag of sweets!* 彼女はお菓子を1袋丸ごと食べてしまった. *a bag of crisps/sugar/flour* ポテトチップス・砂糖・小麦粉1袋 ☞ **container** のさし絵 ▶定義4 **bags** [複数扱い] folds of skin under the eyes, often caused by lack of sleep しばしば睡眠不足のためにできる,目の下のしわ→たるみ‖ *I've got terrible bags under my eyes.* 目の下にひどいたるみができた. ▶定義5 **bags** [複数扱い] 英 **bags (of sth)** a lot (of sth); plenty (of sth) たくさん(の～); 多く(の～)→たくさん‖ *There's no hurry, we've got bags of time.* 急ぐことはない,時間はたくさんあるから.

**bag**² /bæg/ 動他 (**bagging**; **bagged**) 略式 ▶定義 to try to get sth for yourself so that other people cannot have it ほかの人々が持てないように,～を自分のために手に入れようとする→(他人のもの)を黙って持っていく,(席など)をうまく確保する,手に入れる‖ *Somebody's bagged the seats by the pool!* だれかがプールのそばの席を取った.

**bagel** /béɪg(ə)l/ 名 ❻ ▶定義 a type of bread roll in the shape of a ring 輪の形に巻かれたパンの一種→ベーグル ☞ **bread** のさし絵

*****baggage** /bǽgɪdʒ/ 名 Ⓤ ▶定義 bags, suitcases, etc used for carrying a person's clothes and things on a journey 旅行中,服や品々を運ぶために使われるバッグ,スーツケースなど→旅行荷物,手荷物(類)‖ **excess baggage** (= *baggage weighing more than the airline's permitted limit*) 超過手荷物(=航空会社が許可した上限よりも重い手荷物) *I went to wait for my suitcase at* **baggage reclaim** (= *the area in an airport where luggage goes after being taken off a plane*). スーツケースが出てくるのを待ちに手荷物受取所(=飛行機から降ろされた荷物が出てくる空港内の場所)へ行った. ☞類 **luggage**

**baggy** /bǽgi/ 形 ▶定義 (used about a piece of clothing) big; hanging loosely on the body (衣類について)大きな; 体にゆったりとしている→

**bags**

suitcase — handle, handle
backpack (英 または rucksack)
bumbag (米 fanny pack) — strap
handbag (米 purse) — strap, buckle, flap
briefcase
basket — handle
carrier bag (英 または carrier)
holdall — pocket

だぶだぶの, ぶくぶくの, ぶかぶかの ‖ *a baggy pullover* だぶだぶのプルオーバー

**bagpipes** /bǽgpaɪps/ [名] [複数扱い] ▶定義 a musical instrument, popular in Scotland, that is played by blowing air through a pipe into a bag and then pressing the bag so that the air comes out of other pipes スコットランドで人気のある楽器, 吹き込まれる空気がパイプを通って袋に入り, その空気を圧縮しほかのパイプから出ていくようにして演奏される➜**バグパイプ** ☛参 **piano** の注

**bail**[1] /béɪl/ [名] [U] ▶定義 money that sb agrees to pay if a person accused of a crime does not appear in front of the court on the day he/she is called. When bail has been arranged, the accused person can go free until that day. 罪で告訴された～が呼ばれている日に法廷に現れないときに, その人が支払うことを合意する金. これが用意されると, 被告人はその日まで自由になる➜**保釈金** ‖ *She was **released on bail** of £2000.* 彼女は 2000 ポンドの保釈金で釈放された. *The judge **set bail** at £10000.* 裁判官は1万ポンドの保釈金を言い渡した. *The judge felt that he was a dangerous man and **refused** him **bail**.* 裁判官は彼が危険だと感じて, 彼の保釈を却下した. *She was **granted bail**.* 彼女は保釈を許された.

**bail**[2] /béɪl/ [動] [他] ▶定義 to release sb on bail 保釈金で～を釈放する➜**保釈を許す**

[句動詞] **bail sb out** ▶定義1 to obtain sb's freedom by paying money to the court 裁判所に金を支払うことによって, ～の自由を手に入れる➜**～を保釈させる, ～を保釈してもらう** ‖ *Her parents went to the police station and bailed her out.* 彼女の両親は警察署に行き, 彼女を保釈してもらった. ▶定義2 to rescue sb or sth from a difficult situation (especially by providing money) 難しい状況から～または…を救い出す (特に金を与えて) ➜**(資金提供をして)～を救済する** ‖ *If you get into trouble don't expect me to bail you out again!* もしあなたが困ったことになっても, また私があなたを救うと期待するな.

**bailiff** /béɪləf/ [名] [C] ▶定義 an officer whose job is to take the possessions and property of people who cannot pay their debts 負債を支払えない人々の所有物と財産を差し押さえることを仕事とする役人➜**執行吏**

**bait** /béɪt/ [名] [U] ▶定義1 food or sth that looks like food that is put onto a hook to catch fish, or to catch animals or birds 魚を釣るために釣り針に付ける, または動物や鳥を捕まえるために置いておく食べ物または食べ物のような～➜**えさ, おびき寄せるもの** ▶定義2 something that is used for persuading or attracting sb ～を説得する, または引き付けるために用いられるもの➜**誘惑物, おとり, わな** ‖ *Free offers are often used as bait to attract customers.* 無料のプレゼントは客を引き寄せるおとりとしてよく使われる.

***bake** /béɪk/ [動] [自] [他] ▶定義1 to cook in an oven in dry heat オーブンを使って天火で調理する➜**焼く** ‖ *I could smell bread baking in the oven.* オーブンでパンが焼けるにおいがした. *On his birthday she baked him a cake.* 彼女は彼の誕生日にケーキを焼いてあげた. ☛参 **cook** の注 ▶定義2 to become or to make sth hard by heating it ～を熱して固くなる, または固くする➜**焼ける, 焼く, 焼き固まる** ‖ *The hot sun baked the earth.* 熱い太陽が地面を焼いた.

**baker** /béɪkər/ [名] ▶定義1 [C] a person who bakes bread, cakes, etc to sell in a shop 店で売るためにパン, ケーキなどを焼く人➜**パン屋, パン焼き職人** ▶定義2 **the baker's** [単数扱い] a shop that sells bread, cakes, etc パン, ケーキなどを売る店➜**パン屋** ‖ *Get a loaf at the baker's.* パン屋でパンの一山を買いなさい.

**bakery** /béɪk(ə)ri/ [名] [C] ([複] **bakeries**) ▶定義 a place where bread, cakes, etc are baked to be sold パン, ケーキなどが売られるために焼かれる場所➜**製パン所, パン屋**

**baking** /béɪkɪŋ/ [形] ▶定義 very hot 非常に暑い➜**焼け付くような** ‖ *The workers complained of the baking heat in the office in the summer.* 勤労者たちは, 夏の事務所の焼け付くような暑さに不満を言った.

***balance**[1] /bǽləns/ [名] ▶定義1 [単数扱い] (a) **balance (between A and B)** a situation in which different or opposite things are of equal importance, size, etc 異なるまたは反対のものが, 重要さ, 大きさなどで同等な状態➜**均衡, 釣り合い** ‖ *The course provides a good balance between academic and practical work.* その課

程は,学問的な課題と実務的な課題とのバランスがよく取れている. *Tourism has upset **the delicate balance of nature** on the island.* 観光事業は,その島の自然の微妙な均衡を狂わせた. ▶定義2 ⓤ the ability to keep steady with an equal amount of weight on each side of the body 体のそれぞれの側に等しい重量を掛けて,安定を保つ能力➡平衡(感覚) ∥ *to **lose** your **balance*** 体の平衡を失う *It's very difficult to **keep** your **balance** when you start learning to ski.* スキーの習い始めには,平衡を保つことがとても難しい. *You need a good **sense of balance** to ride a motor bike.* オートバイに乗るには優れた平衡感覚が必要だ. ▶定義3 **the balance** [ⓒ,単数扱い] the amount that still has to be paid; the amount that is left after some has been used, taken, etc まだ支払われなければならない量;いくらか使われたり,取られたりなどした後に残された量➡残り,余り ∥ *You can pay a 10% deposit now, with the balance due in one month.* 今10パーセントの手付け金を払って,残りを1か月以内に払う,ということでもいいですよ. *to check your **bank balance** (= to find out how much money you have in your account)* 銀行の残高を確認する(= 預金口座にいくらあるか分かる) ▶定義4 ⓒ (専門用語) an instrument used for weighing things 物の重さを量るために使われる道具➡天秤ばかり

感句 **in the balance** ▶定義 uncertain 不確かな➡不安定な,未確定の,どっちつかずの ∥ *Following poor results, the company's future hangs in the balance.* お粗末な結果によって,その会社の将来は不安定だ.

**(catch/throw sb) off balance** ▶定義 (to find or put sb) in a position that is not safe and from which it is easy to fall 安全でなく,落ちやすい場所に(~を見つけるまたは置く)➡平衡を失って,心の平静を失って ∥ *A strong gust of wind caught me off balance and I nearly fell over.* 一陣の強い突風で私は平衡を失い,もう少しで倒れるところだった.

**on balance** ▶定義 having considered all sides, facts, etc すべての面,事実などを考慮して➡すべてを考慮すると,結局のところ ∥ *On balance, I've had a pretty good year.* 結局のところ,自分にとってなかなか良い年だった.

**strike a balance (between A and B)** ⇒ **STRIKE**²

---

## balanced 109

\***balance**² /bǽləns/ 動 ▶定義1 ⓘⓣ to be or to put sb/sth in a steady position so that the weight of him/her/it is not heavier on one side than on the other 重さが一方よりももう一方が重い,ということがない安定した位置に~がある,またはそのような位置に置く➡~の釣り合いを保つ・取る,~を均衡・調和させる ∥ *I had to balance on the top step of the ladder to paint the ceiling.* 天井を塗るために,はしごの最上段で平衡を保たなければならなかった. *Carefully, she balanced a glass on top of the pile of plates.* 注意深く,彼女はグラスを皿の山の上にバランス良く置いた. ▶定義2 ⓘⓣ to have equal totals of money spent and money received 費やした金と受け取った金を等しい合計にする➡~の差引勘定をする,~の収支を合わせる,~の清算をする ∥ *I must have made a mistake - the accounts don't balance.* 間違いをしたに違いない ― 収支明細が合わない. *She is always very careful to balance her weekly budget.* 彼女はいつも非常に慎重に自分の週間予算の精算をする. ▶定義3 ⓘⓣ **balance (sth) (out) (with sth)** to have or give sth equal value, importance, etc in relation to other parts ほかの部分との関係において,価値,重要性などが等しい~を持つ,または~に等しい価値,重要性などを与える➡帳じりが合う,帳じりを合わせる ∥ *The loss in the first half of the year was balanced out by the profit in the second half.* 上半期の損失は,下半期の収益で帳じりが合った. ▶定義4 ⓣ **balance sth against sth** to consider and compare one matter in relation to another ~をほかの…との関係において考え,比べる➡~を比較する,対照する ∥ *In planning the new road, we have to balance the benefit to motorists against the damage to the environment.* 新しい道路の計画においては,運転者への利益と環境への被害を比較しなければならない.

**balanced** /bǽlənst/ 形 ▶定義 keeping or showing a balance so that different things, or different parts of things exist in equal or correct amounts 異なる物または異なる部分が,等しいまたは正しい量になるように,均衡を保っているまたは示している➡均衡のある,調和・釣り合いの取れた ∥ *I like this newspaper because it gives a balanced view.* この新聞は偏らない見方をするので

好きだ. ***A balanced diet** plays an important part in good health.* バランスの取れた食事は健康に重要な役割を果たす. ⇔ **unbalanced**

**balance of payments** 名 [単数扱い] ▶定義 the difference between the amount of money one country receives from other countries from exports, etc and the amount it pays to them for imports and services in a particular period of time 一定の期間に, ある国が輸出などによってほかの国々から受け取る金額と, 輸入やサービスに対してそれらの国々に支払う金額の差→国際収支

**balance of power** 名 [単数扱い] ▶定義1 a situation in which political power or military strength is divided between two countries or groups of countries 政治的な力または軍事力が, 2つの国または複数の国から成る2つの集団の間で分けられている状態→勢力の均衡 ▶定義2 the power that a smaller political party has when the larger parties need its support because they do not have enough votes on their own 複数の大きな政党が十分な得票数を持っていないために支援を必要とするとき, 小さな政党の持つ力→均衡を左右する力, 決定力

**balance sheet** 名 ● ▶定義 a written statement showing the amount of money and property that a company has, and how much has been received and paid out 会社が持つ資金と財産の量, および, いくら受け取りいくら支払ったかを示す決算報告書→貸借対照表, バランスシート

**balcony**

*balcony /bælkəni/ 名 ●(複 **balconies**) ▶定義1 a platform built on an upstairs outside wall of a building, with a wall or rail around it 建物の上階の壁面の外に設けられた台で, 周りには壁や手すりが付いている→バルコニー, 露台 ☛参 **patio, terrace, veranda** ▶定義2 特に 米 an area of seats upstairs in a theatre 劇場の上階にある席の区域→2階桟敷, 階上席

*bald /bɔːld/ 形 ▶定義1 (used about people) having little or no hair on your head (人について) 頭にほとんど, または全く毛がない→はげた, 髪のない || *I hope I don't **go bald** like my father did.* 父のようにはげないといいんだが. *He has a **bald patch** on the top of his head.* 彼は頭のてっぺんにはげがある. ☛ **hair** のさし絵 ▶定義2 (used about sth that is said) simple; without extra words (言及される〜について) 単純な; 余計な言葉なしに→飾り気のない, 素っ気ない, 有りのままの || *the bald truth* 有りのままの事実

**balding** /bɔ́ːldɪŋ/ 形 ▶定義 starting to lose the hair on your head 頭の毛を失い始めた→はげかかっている, 髪が薄くなり出した || *a balding man in his fifties* 50代で髪が薄くなり出した人

**bale** /béɪl/ 名 ● ▶定義 a large quantity of sth pressed tightly together and tied up 一緒にして, きつく押してくくられた大量の〜→梱(こり), 俵 || *a bale of hay/cloth/paper* 干し草・布・紙の梱

**balk** /bɔːk/ 特に 米 = **BAULK**

*ball /bɔːl/ 名 ● ▶定義1 a round object that you hit, kick, throw, etc in games and sports ゲームやスポーツで, 打つ, ける, 投げるなどする丸い物→ボール, 球 || *a tennis/golf/rugby ball* テニス・ゴルフ・ラグビーボール *a football* フットボール ☛ **pool**, S1 ページのさし絵 ▶定義2 a round object or a thing that has been formed into a round shape 丸い物または丸く形づくられている物→球形の物, 球体, (体の) 丸く膨らんだ部分 || *a ball of wool* 毛糸の玉 *The children threw **snowballs** at each other.* 子供たちは雪玉を投げ合った. *We had meatballs and pasta for dinner.* 私たちは夕食にミートボールとパスタを食べた. ▶定義3 one throw, kick, etc of the ball in some sports スポーツでボールを1回投げること, 1回けることなど→投球, 打球, けった球 || *That was a great ball from the defender.* それは, その守備の選手からの見事な送球だった. ▶定義4 a large formal party at which people dance 人々が踊る大きな正式な宴→大舞踏会

▶定義 5 (俗語) = **TESTICLE**
成句 **be on the ball** 語式 ▶定義 to always know what is happening and be able to react to or deal with it quickly 常に何が起きているかを知っていて, 迅速に対応または対処できる→抜け目がない, 有能だ, 機敏だ, 注意深い, 最新情報に通じている ‖ *With so many new developments, you really have to be on the ball.* とても多くの新開発について, あなたは本当に最新情報に通じていなければならない.

**set/start the ball rolling** ▶定義 to start sth (an activity, conversation, etc) that involves or is done by a group 集団でかかわる, または行う〜(活動, 会話など)を始める→始める, 口火を切る ‖ *I told a joke first, to set the ball rolling.* 私はまず冗談を言ってから始めた.

**ballad** /bǽləd/ 图 C ▶定義 a long song or poem that tells a story, often about love しばしば愛についての, 物語を語る長い歌や詩→バラード, 民間伝承の物語詩, 感傷的な恋歌

**ball bearing** 图 C ▶定義 one of a number of metal balls put between parts of a machine to make them move smoothly 機械の部品を滑らかに動かせるように, 部品の間に置かれた, たくさんの金属製ボールの1つ→ボールベアリング(の球), 玉軸受け

**ballerina** /bæ̀lərí:nə/ 图 C ▶定義 a woman who dances in ballets バレエを踊る女性→バレリーナ, 女性のバレエダンサー

**ballet** /bǽleɪ, -́-/ 图 ▶定義 1 U a style of dancing that tells a story with music but without words 言葉は使わないで音楽に乗せて物語を伝える, 踊りの一形式→バレエ ‖ *He wants to be a ballet dancer.* 彼はバレエのダンサーになりたいのです. ▶定義 2 C a performance or work that consists of this type of dancing この種のダンスから成る演技または作品→バレエ劇(曲)

**ball game** 图 C ▶定義 1 any game played with a ball ボールを使って行われるゲーム→球技 ▶定義 2 米 a baseball match→野球の試合
成句 **a (whole) new/different ball game** ▶定義 something completely new or different 完全に新しいまたは異なるもの→全く新しい状況・事態 ‖ *I'm used to working outside, so sitting in an office all day is a whole new ball game for me.* 私は外で働くことに慣れているので, 一日中事務所で座っていることは私にとって全く新しいことだ.

**balloon** /bəlú:n/ 图 C ▶定義 1 a small coloured object that you blow air into and use as a toy or for decoration 空気を吹き込んでおもちゃまたは飾りとして使う, 小さな色の付いた物→(ゴム)風船 ‖ *to blow up/burst/pop a balloon* 風船を膨らませる・破裂させる・ポンと鳴らす ▶定義 2 (または **hot-air balloon**) a large balloon made of material that is filled with gas or hot air so that it can fly through the sky, carrying people in a basket underneath it ガスや熱い空気を満たした材料でできている大きな風船で, それによって下に付いたかごの中の人を運びながら, 空を飛べる→気球, 熱気球

**ballot** /bǽlət/ 图 C U ▶定義 a secret written vote 他人に知られないで書かれた投票→無記名投票 ‖ *The union will hold a ballot on the new pay offer.* 組合は, 新しい賃金の提案について無記名投票を行うだろう. *The committee are elected by ballot every year.* 委員は毎年無記名投票で選ばれる. — **ballot** 動 他 **ballot sb (about/on sth)**→(〜について…に)(無記名)投票を求める ‖ *The union is balloting its members on strike action.* 組合は組合員にストライキ実施についての投票を求めている.

**ballot box** 图 ▶定義 1 C the box into which people put the piece of paper with their vote on 人々が投票内容を書いた用紙を入れる箱→投票箱 ▶定義 2 **the ballot box** [単数扱い] the system of voting in an election 選挙で投票する方式→無記名投票 ‖ *People will express their opinion through the ballot box.* 人々は無記名投票によって意見を表明するだろう.

**ballpark** /bɔ́:lpɑ̀:k/ 图 C ▶定義 a place where baseball is played 野球が行われる場所→野球場
成句 **in the ballpark** 語式 ▶定義 (used about figures or amounts) that are within the same limits (数字または量について)限度と同等以内である→まあそんなところで, 概算で ‖ *All the bids for the contract were in the same ballpark.* その契約についての入札価格は, おおよそ同じだった.

**a ballpark figure/estimate** ▶定義 a number, amount, etc that is approximately correct おお

## ballpoint

よそ正しい数字,量など→概算 ‖ *We asked the builders for a ballpark figure, to give us an idea of how much it would cost.* 私たちは、いくらかかるかをつかむため、建築業者に概算を尋ねた.

**ballpoint** /bɔ́:lpɔ̀ɪnt/ (または **ballpoint pen**) 名 C ▶定義 a pen with a very small metal ball at the end that rolls ink onto paper 先端に、回って紙の上にインクを出す非常に小さな金属製の球体の付いたペン→ボールペン ☞参 biro

**ballroom** /bɔ́:lru:m, -rʊm/ 名 C ▶定義 a large room used for dancing on formal occasions 正式な行事で踊るのに使われる大きな部屋→舞踏室・場、ダンス室・場

**ballroom dancing** 名 U ▶定義 a formal type of dance in which couples dance together using particular steps and movements 特定の歩調や動きで、男女一組が共に踊る正式な舞踏の一種→社交ダンス

**baloney** /bəlóʊni/ 名 U 米 (口語) ▶定義 nonsense; lies ばかげた事；うそ→たわ言、だぼら ‖ *Don't give me that baloney!* そんなたわ言を私に言うな.

**bamboo** /bæ̀mbú:/ 名 C U ▶定義 a tall tropical plant of the grass family. Young bamboo plants (bamboo shoots), can be eaten and the hard parts of the plant are used for making furniture, etc. イネ科の背の高い熱帯性植物. 若いタケ(竹の子)は食べられ、堅い部分は家具などを作るために使われる→タケ ‖ *a bamboo chair* 竹製のいす ☞ C2ページのさし絵

*****ban** /bæn/ 動 (**banning**; **banned**) ▶定義 *ban sth; ban sb (from sth/from doing sth)* to officially say that sth is not allowed, often by law しばしば法律によって、~が許されていないと公式に言う→~を禁止する ‖ *The government has banned the import of products from that country.* 政府はその国からの製品の輸入を禁止している. *He was fined £500 and banned from driving for a year.* 彼は500ポンドの罰金を科せられ、1年間運転を禁止された. ― ban 名 C *a ban (on sth)*→(~の)禁止 ‖ *There is a ban on smoking in this office.* このオフィスは禁煙だ. *to impose/lift a ban* 禁止する・解禁する

**banal** /bənɑ́:l, bənǽl/ 形 ▶定義 not original or interesting 独創的でない、面白くない→陳腐な、平凡な、ありふれた ‖ *a banal comment* ありふれた論評

*****banana** /bənɑ́:nə; -nǽnə/ 名 C ▶定義 a curved fruit with yellow skin that grows in hot countries 暑い国で生育する、黄色い皮の曲がった果物→バナナ ‖ *a bunch of bananas* バナナの1房 ☞ C3ページのさし絵

*****band** /bænd/ 名 C ▶定義 **1** [単数または複数形の動詞と共に] a small group of musicians who play popular music together, often with a singer or singers しばしば1人または2人以上の歌手と共に、ポピュラー音楽を演奏する小さな楽団→バンド、楽団、楽隊 ‖ *a rock/jazz band* ロック・ジャズバンド *He plays the drums in a band.* 彼はバンドでドラムを演奏している. *The band has/have announced that it/they is/are going to split up.* そのバンドは解散すると発表した. ▶定義 **2** [単数または複数形の動詞と共に] a group of people who do sth together or have the same ideas ~を一緒に行う、または同じ考えを持つ人々の集団→一団、一隊、一群 ‖ *A small band of rebels is/are hiding in the hills.* 反逆者の小さな一団が丘に隠れている. ▶定義 **3** a thin, flat, narrow piece of material used for fastening sth, or to put round sth ~を縛る、または~の回りに巻くために使われる、薄く平らで幅の狭い物→ひも、縄、輪、帯 ‖ *She rolled up the papers and put an elastic band round them.* 彼女は書類を丸めて輪ゴムを掛けた. ▶定義 **4** a line of colour or material on sth that is different from what is around it 周りにある物とは異なる~の色または素材の線→しま、筋 ‖ *She wore a red pullover with a green band across the middle.* 彼女は、腰の辺りに緑色のしまが入った赤いプルオーバーを着ていた. ▶定義 **5** = **WAVEBAND**

**bandage** /bǽndɪdʒ/ 名 C ▶定義 a long piece of soft white material that you tie round a wound or injury 傷やけがの回りに巻く、柔らかく白い素材の長い物→包帯 ― bandage 動 *bandage sth/sb (up)*→~に包帯をする ‖ *The nurse bandaged my hand up.* 看護婦は私の手に包帯を巻いた.

**bandit** /bǽndət/ 名 C ▶定義 a member of an armed group of thieves, who attack travellers 旅行者を襲う武装した盗人の集団の一員→盗賊、山賊、追いはぎ

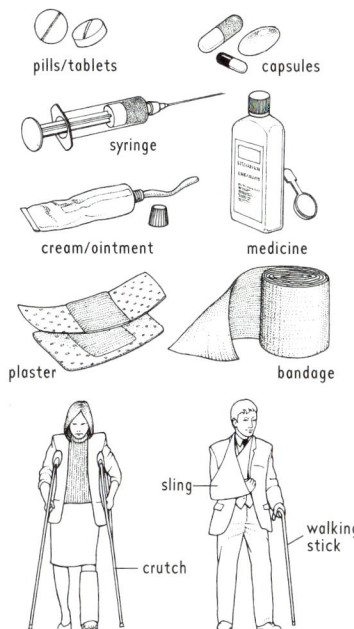

pills/tablets　capsules
syringe
cream/ointment　medicine
plaster　bandage
sling
walking stick
crutch

Her leg is **in plaster**.　His arm is **in a sling**.

**bandwagon** /bǽndwæɡən/ 名

成句 climb/jump on the bandwagon ▶定義 to copy what other people are doing because it is fashionable or successful 流行しているかまたは成功しているから、それをほかの人々がまねる→(政治運動・競争など)優勢な側に付く、時流に便乗する、流行に乗る

\***bang**¹ /bæŋ/ 動自他 ▶定義 1 to make a loud noise by hitting sth hard, to close sth or to be closed with a loud noise ～を強くたたいて大きな音を立てる、大きな音と共に～を閉めるまたは閉まる→ドンとたたく、(戸などが)ばたんと鳴る・閉まる、(戸などを)ばたんと鳴らす・閉める ∥ *Somewhere in the house, I heard a door bang.* 家のどこかで、扉がばたんと鳴る音が聞こえた. *He banged his fist on the table and started shouting.* 彼は握りこぶしでテーブルをドンとたたき、叫び始めた. ▶定義 2 to knock against sth by accident; to hit a part of the body against sth by accident うっかりして～をたたく; うっかりして体の一部を～に当てる→～にドンとぶつけ

# bang² 113

る; (頭・ひざなどを)ぶつける ∥ *Be careful not to bang your head on the ceiling. It's quite low.* 天井に頭をぶつけないように気を付けて、かなり低いから. *As I was crossing the room in the dark I banged into a table.* 暗闇(やみ)の中で部屋を通り過ぎようとしていたら、テーブルにぶつかった.

\***bang**² /bæŋ/ 名 C ▶定義 1 a sudden, short, very loud noise 突然の、短い、非常に大きな音→バタン、ドスン、ズドン、ガタンという音、衝撃音、大音響 ∥ *There was an enormous bang when the bomb exploded.* 爆弾が爆発したとき、ドスンというすごい音がした. ▶定義 2 a short, strong knock or hit, especially one that causes pain and injury 特に痛みとけがを引き起こす、短く、強い殴打または衝突→強打 ∥ *a nasty bang on the head* 頭へのひどい強打

成句 with a bang ▶定義 in a successful or exciting way 首尾良くまたは興奮を呼ぶようなやり方で→見事に、出し抜けに、いきなり ∥ *Our team's season started with a bang when we won our first five matches.* 私たちのチームは最初の5試合に勝ち、見事にシーズンを開始した.

▶日本語 vs 英語

擬声語いろいろ

【動物の鳴き声】meow, mew(猫) / bow-wow, whine(犬) / whinny(馬) / baa(羊) / roar(ライオン) / chatter(猿) / cock-a-doodle-doo(鶏) / cheep(ネズミ, ヒヨコ)

【衝撃, 破壊などの音】bang ズドン, バタン / bong ゴーン / crash ガラガラ, ガチャン / smash ガチャン, パシッ / slam バタン / slap ピシャ / clink チリン / click カチッ / snap パチ / splash(水)バシャ / plop(水)ドブン, ポチャン

【鐘, 警笛など】beep ブー / ding ゴーン, ジャーン / ding-dong ゴーンゴーン, キンコーン / honk ブーブー / jingle チリン

【その他】hiss シュー / frizzle(肉など)ジュージュー / swoosh サラサラ / rustle サラサラ, カサカサ / rattle ガタガタ / roar(風, 波, 雷)ゴーッ / puff プッ, フッ / pop ポン / swish ヒュッ / zing ヒューン / gleam キラッ / twinkle(星など)キラキラ

**bang**³ /bǽŋ/ 副 特に 英 略式 ▶定義 exactly; directly; right まさに; 直接に; まさしく→**まさに、ちょうど** ‖ *Our computers are bang up to date*. 我々のコンピューターはまさに最新式だ. *The shot was bang on target*. その一撃は見事に的に当たった.

成句 bang goes sth 略式 ▶定義 used for expressing the idea that sth is now impossible 〜は今, 不可能であるという考えを表現するために用いて→**(期待・機会などが)ご破算になる, パーになる** ‖ *'It's raining!' 'Ah well, bang goes our picnic!'* 「雨が降っているよ」「ああ, ピクニックはご破算だ」

**bang**⁴ /bǽŋ/ 間 ▶定義 used to sound like the noise of a gun, etc 銃などのような音に用いて→**バン, ズドン, ドスン, ガタン**

**banger** /bǽŋər/ 名 C 英 略式 ▶定義 1 a sausage→**ソーセージ** ▶定義 2 an old car that is in very bad condition とてもひどい状態の古い車→**騒音を出すおんぼろ車** ‖ *I'm tired of driving around in that old banger*. あのおんぼろ車でドライブするのは, うんざりだ. ▶定義 3 a small device (firework) that explodes with a short loud noise and is used for fun 短い大きな音を立てて爆発し, 楽しみのために使われる小さな装置(花火)→**爆竹**

**bangle** /bǽŋ(ə)l/ 名 C ▶定義 a circular metal band that is worn round the arm or wrist for decoration 飾りのために腕または手首にはめる, 円形の金属製のバンド→**腕輪** ☞ **jewellery** のさし絵

**bangs** /bǽŋz/ 米 = FRINGE¹(1)

**banish** /bǽnɪʃ/ 動 他 正式 ▶定義 1 to send sb away (especially out of the country), usually as a punishment 通常罰として, (特に国外へ)〜を追い出す→**〜を追放する, 流刑に処する** ‖ *They were banished from the country for demonstrating against the government*. 彼らは政府に反対してデモを行ったために, 国外へ追放された. ▶定義 2 to make sb/sth go away; to get rid of sb/sth 〜を追いやる; 〜を取り除く→**〜を追い払う, (心配などを)払いのける** ‖ *She banished all hope of winning from her mind*. 彼女は勝利の希望をすべて自分の気持ちから消し去った.

**banister** (または **bannister**) /bǽnəstər/ 名 C (しばしば複数形で) ▶定義 the posts and rail at the side of a staircase 階段の片側にある支柱または横棒→**手すり, 欄干** ‖ *The children loved sliding down the banister at the old house*. 子供たちは, その古い家の階段の手すりを滑り降りるのが好きだった.

**banjo** /bǽndʒoʊ/ 名 C (複 **banjos**) ▶定義 a musical instrument like a guitar, with a long thin neck, a round body and four or more strings 長く細い首, 丸い胴, それに4本以上の弦が付いている, ギターのような楽器→**バンジョー** ☞参 **piano** の注 ☞ **music** のさし絵

★**bank**¹ /bǽŋk/ 名 C ▶定義 1 an organization which keeps money safely for its customers; the office or building of such an organization. You can take money out, save, borrow or exchange money at a bank. 顧客のために金を安全に保管する機関; そのような機関の事務所や建物. そこで人は, 金銭の引き出し, 預金, 借り出し, 両替ができる→**銀行** ‖ *My salary is paid directly into my bank*. 私の給与は直接銀行に振り込まれる. *I need to go to the bank to get some money out*. いくらかのお金を引き出しに銀行に行く必要がある. *a bank account/loan* 銀行口座・ローン ▶定義 2 a store of things, which you keep to use later 後で使うために保管する物の蓄え→**〜貯蔵所, 〜バンク** ‖ *a databank* データバンク *a blood bank in a hospital* 病院内の血液銀行 ▶定義 3 the ground along the side of a river or canal 川や運河の側面に沿っている土地→**岸, 土手, 堤** ‖ *People were fishing along the banks of the river*. 人々は川岸で釣りをしていた. ▶定義 4 a higher area of ground that goes up or down at an angle, often at the edge of sth or dividing sth しばしば〜の端または〜を区切って, ある角度で下ったりまたは上ったり, より高くなった土地→**(道の両側や畑の境界の)盛り土, 仕切り** ‖ *There were grassy banks on either side of the road*. 道路の両側には草に覆われた盛り土があった. ▶定義 5 a mass of cloud, snow, etc 大量の雲や雪などを→**堆積(たいせき), 塊** ‖ *The sun disappeared behind a bank of clouds*. 太陽は厚い雲の背後に隠れた.

**bank**² /bǽŋk/ 動 自 ▶定義 bank (with/at ...) to have an account with a particular bank 特定の銀行に口座を持つ→**銀行に預ける, 預金する** ‖

*I've banked with Lloyds for years.* 私は, 何年もロイズ銀行に預金している.

**bank on sb/sth** ▶定義 to expect and trust sb to do sth, or sth to happen ～をすること, または起こることを…が期待し当てにする→～を当てにする, 頼みにする ‖ *Our boss might let you have the morning off but I wouldn't bank on it.* 上司は午前中の半休を取らせてくれるかもしれないが, 私は当てにはしない.

**banker** /bǽŋkər/ ▶定義 a person who owns or has an important job in a bank 銀行を所有する, または銀行で重要な地位にある人→銀行家, 銀行の役員, 銀行経営者

**bank holiday** ▶定義 a public holiday (not a Saturday or Sunday) 公の休日(土曜または日曜でない)→公休日

**banking** /bǽŋkɪŋ/ ▶定義 the type of business done by banks 銀行によって行われる種類の業務→銀行業, 銀行業務, 銀行経営 ‖ *She decided on a career in banking.* 彼女は職業を銀行業に決めた.

**banknote** /bǽŋknoʊt/ = **NOTE**¹(4)

***bankrupt** /bǽŋkrʌpt/ ▶定義 not having enough money to pay your debts 負債を支払うための十分な金を持っていない→倒産した, 支払い能力のない, 破産した ‖ *The company must cut its costs or it will go bankrupt.* 会社は支出を抑えなければならない, さもないと破産するだろう. — bankrupt 動他→～を破産させる ‖ *The failure of the new product almost bankrupted the firm.* 新製品の失敗で会社はほとんど破産に追い込まれた.

**bankruptcy** /bǽŋkrəp(t)si/ ▶定義 (複 **bankruptcies**) ▶定義 the state of being bankrupt 破産した状態→破産, 倒産, 破たん ‖ *The company filed for bankruptcy (= asked to be officially declared bankrupt) in 1999.* 会社は1999年に破産申告をした (= 公式に破産を宣言するよう頼んだ).

**bank statement** (または **statement**) ▶定義 a printed list of all the money going into or out of your bank account during a certain period 一定期間に銀行口座に入った, または出たすべての金額について印刷された一覧表→(銀行から預金者へ郵送される)銀行口座収支報告書

**banner** /bǽnər/ ▶定義 a long piece of cloth with words or signs on it, which can be hung up or carried on two poles つるされたりまたは2本の棒につるされるかあるいは運ばれる, 言葉や模様が書かれた長い布→のぼり, 横断幕 ‖ *The demonstrators carried banners saying 'Stop the War'.* デモ隊は「戦争をやめろ」と書かれた横断幕を掲げていた. ☞ **placard** のさし絵

**banquet** /bǽŋkwət/ ▶定義 a formal dinner for a large number of people, usually as a special event at which speeches are made 大勢の人々のための正式な夕食で, 通常スピーチが行われる特別な行事→宴会, 招宴

**banter** /bǽntər/ ▶定義 friendly comments and jokes 親しげな意見や冗談→冗談, からかい, 冷やかし, 軽口 — banter 動自→冷やかす, からかう, 冗談・軽口を言う

**baptism** /bǽptɪz(ə)m/ ▶定義 a ceremony in which a person becomes a member of the Christian Church by being held under water for a short time or having drops of water put onto his/her head. Often he/she is also formally given a name. 人を短時間水につける, または, 水滴をその人の顔に落とすことによって, キリスト教会の一員とする儀式. また, しばしば正式に名前が与えられる→洗礼(式), バプテスマ, 命名(式) ☞参 **christening** — baptize (または -ise) /bæptáɪz/ 動他→～に洗礼を施す ☞参 **christen**

**Baptist** /bǽptɪst/ ▶定義 (a member) of a Protestant Church that believes that baptism should only be for people who are old enough to understand the meaning of the ceremony and should be done by placing the person fully under water 洗礼はその儀式の意味が分かる年齢になってから, その人を完全に水につけて行うべきだと信じるプロテスタント教会の(一員)→バプテスト派信者, 浸礼協会員, バプテスト派の

***bar**¹ /bɑːr/ ▶定義 **1** a place where you can buy and drink (especially alcoholic) drinks and sometimes have sth to eat 飲み物(特にアルコール)を買って飲める, 時に食べる～もある場所→バー, 酒場 ‖ *a wine/coffee/snack bar* ワイン・コーヒー・スナックバー

▶英国では, アルコール飲料を飲めるバーは通常パブ, ホテル, レストランなどの一角にあり独立した建物にはない(ワインバーを除く).

## bar²

パブには2種類のバーがある。特別室は、一般席よりも快適である(また、しばしば値段がより高い).

▶定義2 a long, narrow, high surface where drinks are served 飲み物が出される長く、奥行きの狭い、高くなった面→カウンター、台 || *She went to the bar and ordered a drink.* 彼女はカウンターへ行き、飲み物を注文した. *We sat on stools at the bar.* 私たちはカウンターの腰掛けに座った. ▶定義3 **a bar (of sth)** a small block of solid material, longer than it is wide 硬い素材でできた長方形の小さな塊→棒、棒状の物 || *a bar of soap/chocolate* せっけん1個・板チョコ1枚 ▶定義4 a long, thin, straight piece of metal, often placed across a window or door, etc to stop sb from getting through it 長くて薄い、まっすぐな金属で、しばしば窓や扉などに交差して置かれ、〜がそこを通れないようにするもの→横木、かんぬき ▶定義5 **a bar (to sth)** a thing that prevents you from doing sth 〜をするのを妨げるもの→障害、妨げ || *Lack of education is not always a bar to success in business.* 教育の不足は、必ずしも仕事で成功するための妨げにはならない. ▶定義6 one of the short, equal units of time into which music is divided 音楽を短く、等しい時間に分けた単位の1つ→小節 || *If you sing a few bars of the song I might recognize it.* その歌の数小節を歌ってもらえば、おそらく私に分かるだろう.

成句 **behind bars** 略式 ▶定義 in prison 牢獄(ろうごく)内で→鉄格子の中で || *The criminals are now safely behind bars.* その犯罪者たちは今、安全に鉄格子の中にいる.

**bar²** /baːr/ 動 他 (**barring; barred**) ▶定義1 (通常は受動態で) to close sth with a bar or bars¹(4) 〜をかんぬきで閉じる→(戸・門に)かんぬきをかける、(戸・門を横木で)閉じる || *All the windows were barred.* すべての窓にはかんぬきがかけられていた. ▶定義2 to block a road, path, etc so that nobody can pass だれも通れないように、道路や小道などをふさぐ→ふさぐ、はばむ || *A line of police officers barred the entrance to the embassy.* 警官の列が大使館の入り口をふさいだ. ▶定義3 **bar sb from sth/from doing sth** to say officially that sb is not allowed to do, use or enter sth 〜が…をする、使う、または〜に入ることが許されていないと公式に言う→〜を除外する、締め出す、禁ずる || *He was barred from the club for fighting.* 彼はけんかをしたことでクラブから追放された.

**bar³** /baːr/ 前 ▶定義 except 除いて→〜を除いて、以外は || *All the seats were taken, bar one.* 1つを除いて、すべての席は取られていた.

**barbarian** /baːrˈbeəriən/ 名 C ▶定義 a wild person with no culture, who behaves very badly 教養のない、非常に下品に振る舞う、乱暴な人→野蛮人、未開人、粗野な人、無教養な人

**barbaric** /baːrˈbærɪk/ 形 ▶定義 very cruel and violent 非常に残忍で、暴力的な→野蛮人のような、野蛮な、残酷な、粗野な || *barbaric treatment of prisoners* 残酷な囚人の扱い — **barbarism** /ˈbɑːrbərɪz(ə)m/ 名 U ▶定義 野蛮、未開状態、野蛮な行為 || *acts of barbarism committed in war* 戦時に行われた野蛮な行為

**barbecue** /ˈbɑːrbɪkjuː/ (略 **BBQ**) 名 C ▶定義1 a metal frame on which food is cooked outdoors over an open fire 屋外でじか焼きで食べ物を調理する金属製の枠→バーベキュー用グリル、丸焼き台 ▶定義2 an outdoor party at which food is cooked in this way この方法で食べ物を調理する屋外のパーティー→バーベキューパーティー || *Let's have a barbecue on the beach.* 海岸でバーベキューパーティーをしよう. ◀参 **roast²**(2) — **barbecue** 動 他 →バーベキューにする、丸焼きにする || *barbecued steak* バーベキューされた肉

**barbed wire** /ˌbɑːrbd ˈwaɪər/ 名 U ▶定義 strong wire with sharp points on it とがった先の付いている丈夫な針金→有刺鉄線 || *a barbed wire fence* 有刺鉄線の柵(さく)

**barber** /ˈbɑːrbər/ 名 ▶定義1 C a man whose job is to cut men's hair and sometimes to shave them 男性の髪を切ったり、時にひげをそることを仕事にしている人→床屋、理髪師、理容師 ▶ **hairdresser** と比較.

▶定義2 **the barber's** [単数扱い] 医 a shop where men go to have their hair cut 男性が髪を切ってもらいに行く店→理髪店、床屋

**bar code** 名 C ▶定義 a pattern of thick and thin lines that is printed on things you buy. It contains information that a computer can read. 買う物に印刷されている, 太い線と細い線から成る模様. そこにはコンピューターが読み取れる情報が入っている➡バーコード

**\*bare** /beər/ 形 ▶定義1 (used about part of the body) not covered by clothing (体の部分について) 服で覆われていない➡**裸の, むき出しの** ‖ *bare arms/feet/shoulders* 露出した腕・足・肩 ☛参 **naked**, **nude** ▶定義2 without anything covering it or in it 覆う物のない, または中に何もない➡**むき出しの, (部屋などが) 空の, 家具のない, がらんとした** ‖ *They had taken the painting down, so the walls were all bare.* 彼らは塗装をはがしたので, 壁はすべてむき出しになっていた. ▶定義3 just enough; the most basic or simple ちょうど足りる; 最も基本的または単純な➡**最低限の, ぎりぎりの, ほんの, ただそれだけの** ‖ *You won't pass your exams if you just do the bare minimum.* ただ必要最低限の勉強だけだと, あなたは試験に合格しないだろう. *I don't take much luggage when I travel, just the bare essentials.* 旅行するときには必需品だけで, 私は多くの荷物は持っていかない.

成句 with your bare hands ▶定義 without weapons or tools 武器や道具なしで➡**素手で** ‖ *She killed him with her bare hands.* 彼女は素手で彼を殺した.

**barefoot** /béərfʊt/ 形副 ▶定義 with nothing (for example shoes, socks, etc) on your feet 足に何も履いていない (例えば, 靴, 靴下など)➡**はだしの, はだしで** ‖ *We walked barefoot along the beach.* 私たちははだしで海岸を歩いた.

**barely** /béərli/ 副 ▶定義 (used especially after 'can' and 'could' to emphasize that sth is difficult to do) only just; almost not (〜をすることが難しいことを強調するために, 特に can と could の後に用いて) ただ〜だけ; ほとんど〜ない➡**やっと, 辛うじて** ‖ *I was so tired I could barely stand up.* 私はとても疲れていたので, やっとのことで立ち上がった. *I earn barely enough money to pay my rent.* 私は辛うじて家賃を払えるくらい稼いでいる. ☛参 hardly

**bargain**¹ /báːrgən/ 名 C ▶定義1 something that is cheaper or at a lower price than usual 通常よりも安いまたは低い価格の物➡**安い買い物, 掘り出し物, 特売品, 買い得品** ‖ *At that price, it's an absolute bargain!* その値段なら, 絶対に買い得品だ. *I found a lot of bargains in the sale.* 特売でたくさんの掘り出し物を見つけた. ▶定義2 an agreement between people or groups about what each of them will do for the other or others 人々または集団の間での, 互いが相手のために何をするかについての合意➡**(売買)契約, 取り引き, 約束, 協定** ‖ *Let's make a bargain - I'll lend you the money if you'll help me with my work.* 契約を結びましょう ‐ 私の仕事を手伝ってくれたら, あなたにお金を貸すよ. *I lent him the money but he didn't keep his side of the bargain.* 私は彼に金を貸したが, 彼は約束を果たさなかった.

成句 into the bargain ▶定義 (used for emphasizing sth) as well; in addition; also (〜を強調するために用いて) 同様に; さらに; 〜もまた➡**その上, おまけに** ‖ *They gave me free tickets and a free meal into the bargain.* 彼らは入場無料の券をくれて, おまけに食事もおごってくれた.

strike a bargain (with sb) ⇒ **STRIKE**²

**bargain**² /báːrgən/ 動 自 ▶定義 bargain (with sb) (about/over/for sth) to discuss prices, conditions, etc with sb in order to reach an agreement that suits each person 互いに適した合意に到達するために, 〜と価格, 条件などについて話し合う➡**交渉する, 商談する, 値切る** ‖ *I'm sure that if you bargain with him, he'll drop the price.* もしあなたが彼と交渉すれば, 価格をきっと下げてくれますよ. *They bargained over the price.* 彼らは価格について交渉した.

句動詞 bargain for/on sth (通常否定文で) ▶定義 to expect sth to happen and be ready for it 〜が起きると期待して, その準備ができている➡**予期する, 勘定に入れる, 〜を当てにする** ‖ *When I agreed to help him I didn't bargain for how much it would cost me.* 彼を手伝うと承諾したとき, 私はどれほどの犠牲を払わなければならなくなるか予期していなかった.

**barge**¹ /bɑːrdʒ/ 名 C ▶定義 a long narrow boat with a flat bottom that is used for carrying goods or people on a canal or river 運河または川で品物や客を運ぶために使われる, 底の平らな細長い船➡**はしけ, だるま船, 平底の荷船**

**barge**² /bɑːrdʒ/ 動 自 他 ▶定義 to push people

out of the way in order to get past them 先へ進むために,人々を押しのける→どたばたと進む,ぶつかりながら進む,人を押しのけて進む‖ *He barged (his way) angrily through the crowd.* 彼は腹立たしげに群衆を押しのけて進んだ.

**baritone** /bǽrətòʊn/ 図 ⓒ ▶定義 a male singing voice that is fairly low; a man with this voice かなり低い,男の歌声; この声を持つ男性→バリトン,バリトン歌手

  ▶ baritone (バリトン) は, tenor (テノール) と bass (バス) の間.

**bark**¹ /bɑːrk/ 図 ▶定義 1 ❶ the hard outer covering of a tree 木の外側を覆う硬い物→樹皮,木の皮 ☞ C2 ページのさし絵 ▶定義 2 ⓒ the short, loud noise that a dog makes 犬の立てる短く大きな声→ほえる声 ‖ *The dog next door has a very loud bark.* 隣の犬は非常に大きな声でほえる.

★**bark**² /bɑːrk/ 動 ▶定義 1 ⓘ bark (at sb/sth) (used about dogs) to make a loud, short noise or noises (犬について) 大きな短い声を立てる→ほえる ▶定義 2 ⓘⓣ bark (sth) (out) (at sb) to speak to sb in a loud voice in an angry or aggressive way 怒って,または攻撃的な言い方で,～に大きな声で話す→どなって言う,かみ付くように言う‖ *The boss came in, barked out some orders and left again.* 上司は入ってきて,どなる調子でいくつか指令を出し,また出ていった.

**barley** /bɑ́ːrli/ 図 Ⓤ ▶定義 1 a plant that produces grain that is used for food or for making beer and other drinks 食べ物として,あるいはビールなどの飲み物を作るために使われる穀粒を産出する植物→大麦 ▶定義 2 the grain produced by this plant この植物から産出される穀粒→大麦の実 ☞ cereal のさし絵

**barmaid** /bɑ́ːrmeɪd/ 図 ⓒ ▶定義 a woman who serves drinks from behind a bar in a pub, etc パブ内のバーなどで,カウンターの向こう側から飲み物を客に出す女性→女性のバーテン

**barman** /bɑ́ːrmən/ 図 ⓒ (覆 **-men** /-mən/) (米 **bartender**) ▶定義 a man who serves drinks from behind a bar in a pub, etc パブ内のバーなどで,カウンターの向こう側から飲み物を客に出す男性→バーテン

**bar mitzvah** /bɑ̀ːr mítsvə/ 図 ⓒ ▶定義 a ceremony in the Jewish religion for a boy who is about 13 years old. After the ceremony, he is considered an adult. 13歳くらいの少年に対して行うユダヤ教の儀式.儀式の後,その少年は大人として認められる→バルミツバー ☛比 **bat mitzvah**

barn

**barn** /bɑːrn/ 図 ⓒ ▶定義 a large building on a farm in which crops or animals are kept 穀物や動物が保管されている農場の大きな建物→納屋,物置,家畜の小屋

**barometer** /bərɑ́mətər/ 図 ⓒ ▶定義 1 an instrument that measures air pressure and indicates changes in weather 気圧を計り,天候の変化を示す道具→気圧計,晴雨計 ▶定義 2 something that indicates the state of sth (a situation, a feeling, etc) ～の状態(状況,感情など)を示すもの→指標,尺度,バロメーター ‖ *Results of local elections are often a barometer of the government's popularity.* 地方選挙の結果は,しばしば政府の人気のバロメーターだ.

**baron** /bǽrən/ 図 ⓒ ▶定義 1 a man of a high social position in Britain; a nobleman 英国の高い社会的地位にある男性; 貴族→男爵 ▶定義 2 a person who controls a large part of a particular industry or type of business 特定の,産業または事業の大半を支配する人→大実業家,大立て者‖ *drug/oil barons* 麻薬王・石油王

**baroness** /bǽrənəs/ 図 ⓒ ▶定義 a woman of a high social position; the wife of a baron 高い社会的地位にある女性; 男爵の妻→女性の男爵; 男爵夫人

**barracks** /bǽrəks/ 図 [ⓒ,単数または複数形の動詞と共に] (覆 **barracks**) ▶定義 a building or group of buildings in which soldiers live 兵士が住んでいる建物または建物群→兵舎,営舎‖ *Guards were on duty at the gate of the barracks.* 護衛兵は兵舎の門で任務に就いていた.

**barrage** /bərɑ́ːʒ, -dʒ; bǽrɑ̀ːʒ/ 図 ⓒ ▶定義 1 a continuous attack on a place with a large number of guns 多数の銃による,ある場所への継続的な攻撃→(味方を援護するための)弾幕撃

▶定義2 a large number of questions, comments, etc, directed at a person very quickly 非常に速く, 1人の人に向けられた, たくさんの質問や意見など→〜の連続, 集中, 殺到 ‖ *The minister faced a barrage of questions from reporters.* 大臣は記者たちからの質問の連続に直面した.

**barrel** /bǽrəl/ 名 C ▶定義1 a large, round, wooden, plastic or metal container for liquids, that has a flat top and bottom and is wider in the middle 液体を入れるための, 大きくて丸い, 木製, プラスチック製, または金属製の容器で, 上と底が平らで, 真ん中が膨らんでいる→たる ‖ *a beer/wine barrel* ビール・ワインだる *The price of oil is usually given per barrel.* 石油の価格は通常1たるの単位で出される. ▶定義2 the long metal part of a gun like a tube through which the bullets are fired 銃の管のような長い金属製の部分で, そこを通って銃弾が発射される→銃身

**barren** /bǽrən/ 形 ▶定義1 (used about land or soil) not good enough for plants to grow on (土地または土壌について) 植物が育つのに不適な→**不毛の, 作物のできない** ▶定義2 (used about trees or plants) not producing fruit or seeds (木または植物について) 実や種を作らない→実のならない, 実を結ばない

**barricade** /bǽrəkèid, ˌ--´/ 名 C ▶定義 an object or line of objects that is placed across a road, entrance, etc to stop people getting through 人々が通っていくのを止めるために, 道や入り口などに横切って置かれた物または物の列→バリケード, 障害物 ‖ *The demonstrators put up barricades to keep the police away.* デモ隊は警官を近付けないようにバリケードを築いた. — barricade 動 他 →バリケードを築く, 〜をバリケードで防ぐ

句動詞 barricade yourself in ▶定義 to defend yourself by putting up a barricade バリケードを築いて自分を守る→バリケードを築いて閉じこもる ‖ *Demonstrators took over the building and barricaded themselves in.* デモ隊は建物を占拠し, バリケードを築いて閉じこもった.

\*barrier /bǽriər/ 名 C ▶定義1 an object that keeps people or things separate or prevents them moving from one place to another 人々や物を分けておく, または一方から他方に移動することを妨げるもの→柵(さく), 障壁, 防御壁 ‖ *The crowd were all kept behind barriers.* 群衆はみな柵の後ろに止めおかれた. *The mountains form a natural barrier between the two countries.* その山脈が2つの国の間に天然の壁を形づくっている. ☛参 **crash barrier** ▶定義2 a barrier (to sth) something that causes problems or makes it impossible for sth to happen 問題を起こす, または〜が起こることを不可能にするもの→**妨げ, 障害** ‖ *When you live in a foreign country, the language barrier is often the most difficult problem to overcome.* 外国で暮らすときには, しばしば言葉の壁は乗り越えることが最も難しい問題である.

**barring** /báːrɪŋ/ 前 ▶定義 except for; unless there is/are 〜を除く; 〜がない限り→〜がなければ ‖ *Barring any unforeseen problems, we'll be moving house in a month.* 予期しない問題がなければ, 私たちは1か月後に引っ越します.

**barrister** /bǽrəstər/ 名 C ▶定義 (in English law) a lawyer who is trained to speak for you in the higher courts (英国の法律で) 高等裁判所で被告のために発言する訓練を受けた弁護士→**法廷弁護士** ☛参 **lawyer** の注

**barrow** /bǽrou/ 名 C ▶定義1 英 a small thing on two wheels on which fruit, vegetables, etc are moved or sold in the street, especially in markets 果物や野菜などを載せて移動する, または通りで, 特に市場で売るために使う, 車輪が2つある小さな台車→**手押し車** ▶定義2 = WHEELBARROW

**bar staff** 名 [U, 複数形の動詞と共に] ▶定義 the people who serve drinks from behind a bar in a pub, etc パブのバーなどで, カウンターの向こう側から飲み物を差し出す人々→バーテンダー ‖ *The barstaff are very friendly here.* ここのバーテンダーたちはとても気さくだ. ☛参 **barmaid**, **barman**

**bartender** /báːrtèndər/ 米 = BARMAN

**barter** /báːrtər/ 動 自 他 ▶定義 barter sth (for sth); barter (with sb) (for sth) to exchange goods, services, property, etc for other goods, etc, without using money 品物, サービス, 財産などを, お金を使わないで, ほかの品々などと交換する→**物々交換する** ‖ *The farmer bartered his surplus grain for machinery.* 農民は余った穀物を機械と交換した. *The prisoners bartered* with the guards for writing paper and books. 囚人たちは守衛たちと物々交換で書く紙と本を手に入れた. — barter 名 ひ→物々交換

\*base¹ /béɪs/ 名 ⓒ ▶定義 1 the lowest part of sth, especially the part on which it stands or at which it is fixed or connected to sth ～の最も下の部分, 特に～の上に立っていたり, あるいは～が固定, または接続されている部分→土台, 基部, 基底, 根元 ‖ *the base of a column/glass/box* 柱の根元・グラスの底・箱の底 *I felt a terrible pain at the base of my spine.* 背骨の底部にひどい痛みを感じた. ▶定義 2 an idea, fact, etc from which sth develops or is made そこから～が発達する, または作られる考え, 事実など→基礎, 原理, 根拠, 根底, 基盤 ‖ *With these ingredients as a base, you can create all sorts of interesting dishes.* これらの食材を元にして, あらゆる種類の興味深い料理が作れる. *The country needs a strong economic base.* その国には強い経済的基盤が必要だ. ▶定義 3 a place used as a centre from which activities are done or controlled 活動が行われる, または管理する中心として使われる場所→基地, 根拠地, 本部 ‖ *This hotel is an ideal base for touring the region.* このホテルは, その地域を旅行するためには理想的な基地だ. ▶定義 4 a military centre from which the armed forces operate 武装した勢力が作戦を展開する軍事基地→基地, 根拠地, 本部 ‖ *an army base* 軍本部 ▶定義 5 (in baseball) one of the four points that a runner must touch (野球で) 走者が触れなければならない4つの地点の1つ→塁, ベース

\*base² /béɪs/ 動 ⓣ (通常は受動態で) ▶定義 base sb/sth in... to make one place the centre from which sb/sth can work or move around 1つの場所を～が働くまたは動き回る中心とする→基礎を置く, (会社などの)本拠を置く, (人などを)配置する ‖ *I'm based in New York, although my job involves a great deal of travel.* 私はニューヨークを本拠地にしている, もっとも仕事でたくさん旅をするけどね. *a Cardiff-based company* カーディフに本社をおく会社

句動 base sth on sth ▶定義 to form or develop sth from a particular starting point or source 特定の始点または源から～を形成する, または発達させる→～の基礎・根拠を…に置く, ～を…に基づかせる ‖ *This film is based on a true story.* この映画は実話に基づいている.

**baseball** /béɪsbɔ̀ːl/ 名 ⓤ ▶定義 a team game that is popular in the US in which players hit the ball with a bat and run round four points (bases). They have to touch all four bases in order to score a point (run). 選手がバットでボールを打ち4つの点(塁)を走って回る, 米国で人気のある団体試合. 1点取る(得点する)ためには4つのすべての塁に触れなければならない→野球

**basement** /béɪsmənt/ 名 ⓒ ▶定義 a room or rooms in a building, partly or completely below ground level 部分的にまたは完全に地面より下にある建物内の部屋→地階, (半)地下室 ‖ *a basement flat* 地階 ☛参 cellar

**bases** ▶定義 1 BASIS の複数形 ▶定義 2 BASE¹ の複数形

**bash¹** /bæʃ/ 動 略式 ▶定義 1 目 他 to hit sb/sth very hard ～を非常に強く打つ→～を強打する, 打ち壊す, 衝突する ‖ *I didn't stop in time and bashed into the car in front.* 止めるのが間に合わず, 正面の車に衝突した. ▶定義 2 他 to criticize sb/sth strongly ～を強く批判する→～を激しく非難する, こき下ろす, けなす ‖ *The candidate continued to bash her opponent's policies.* その候補者は対抗者の政策を激しく非難し続けた.

**bash²** /bæʃ/ 名 ⓒ ▶定義 1 a hard hit 強い打撃→強打 ‖ *He gave Alex a bash on the nose.* 彼はアレックスの鼻を強打した. ▶定義 2 略式 a large party or celebration 大きな宴会または祝典→にぎやかで, とても楽しいパーティー ‖ *Are you going to Gary's birthday bash?* ゲーリーの誕生パーティーに行きますか.

成句 have a bash (at sth/at doing sth) 英 (口語) ▶定義 to try 試みる→～をやってみる ‖ *I'll get a screwdriver and have a bash at mending the light.* ねじ回しを取ってきて, 電灯の修理をしてみるよ.

**bashful** /bæʃfəl/ 形 ▶定義 shy and embarrassed 人見知りで, 恥ずかしがる→はにかみやの, 内気の, 人見知りする

\*basic /béɪsɪk/ 形 ▶定義 1 forming the part of sth that is most necessary and from which other things develop ～の最も必要な部分を形成し, ほ

かの物がそこから発達する➡**基本的な,基礎の** ‖ *The basic question is, can we afford it?* 基本的な疑問は,我々にその余裕があるかどうかということだ. *basic information/facts/ideas* 基本的な情報・事実・考え ▶定義**2** of the simplest kind or level; including only what is necessary without anything extra 最も単純な種類の,または程度の;余分なものがなく必要なものだけを含んでいる➡**必要最小限の,基礎的な,簡素な** ‖ *This course teaches basic computer skills.* この講座では基礎的なコンピューター技術を教えます. *The basic pay is £200 a week - with extra for overtime.* 基本給は1週間200ポンド − 残業には割り増し給が付く.

*__basically__ /béɪsɪk(ə)li/ 副 ▶定義 used to say what the most important or most basic aspect of sb/sth is ~の最も重要な,または最も基本的な側面であることを言うために用いて➡**基本的に,根本的に** ‖ *The new design is basically the same as the old one.* 新しいデザインは基本的に古いものと同じだ.

**basics** /béɪsɪks/ 名[複数扱い] ▶定義 the simplest or most important facts or aspects of sth; things that you need the most ~の最も単純なまたは最も重要な事実や側面; 人が最も必要とするもの➡**基礎,基礎的な事** ‖ *So far, I've only learnt the basics of computing.* これまでに,私はコンピューター操作の基礎を学んだだけだ.

*__basin__ /béɪsn/ 名 ❻ ▶定義**1** = **WASHBASIN** ▶定義**2** a round open bowl often used for mixing or cooking food しばしば食べ物を混ぜる,または料理するために使われる,丸い開いた鉢➡**鉢,ボウル** ▶定義**3** an area of land from which water flows into a river 水が川に流れ込む地域➡**流域** ‖ *the Amazon Basin* アマゾン川流域

*__basis__ /béɪsɪs/ 名 (複 **bases** /béɪsi:z/) ▶定義**1** [単数扱い] the principle or reason which lies behind sth ~の背後にある原理や理由➡**基礎,論拠,根拠** ‖ *We made our decision __on the basis of__ the reports which you sent us.* お送りいただいた報告書に基づいて私たちは決断した. ▶定義**2** [単数扱い] the way sth is done or organized ~が行われる,または組織される方法➡**基準,方式** ‖ *They meet __on a regular basis__.* 彼らは定期的に会っている. *to employ sb __on a temporary/voluntary/part-time basis__* ~を臨時に・無償で・パートタイムで雇う ▶定義**3** ❻ a starting point, from which sth can develop ~が発達する始点➡**基礎,土台** ‖ *She used her diaries as a basis for her book.* 彼女は本を書く基礎として自分の日記を使った.

**bask** /bɑːsk; bæsk/ 動 ⓘ bask (in sth) ▶定義**1** to sit or lie in a place where you can enjoy the warmth 暖かい感じを楽しめる場所に座る,または横になる➡**暖まる,ひなたぼっこする** ‖ *The snake basked in the sunshine on the rock.* 蛇が岩の上でひなたぼっこしていた. ▶定義**2** to enjoy the good feelings you have when other people admire you, give you a lot of attention, etc ほかの人たちが自分を賞賛したり非常に注目したときに,良い気分を味わう➡**浴する** ‖ *The team was still __basking in the glory__ of winning the cup.* チームはまだ優勝の栄誉に浴していた.

*__basket__ /bɑ́ːskət; bǽs-/ 名 ❻ ▶定義**1** a container for carrying or holding things, made of thin pieces of material such as wood, plastic or wire that bends easily 細い材料,例えば簡単に曲がる木,プラスチック,針金でできた,物を運んだりしまっておくための入れ物➡**バスケット,かご,ざる** ‖ *a waste-paper basket* 紙くずかご *a shopping basket* 買い物かご *a clothes/laundry basket (in which you put dirty clothes before they are washed)* 洗濯物入れかご(汚れた服を洗う前に入れておく) ☛ **bag** のさし絵 ▶定義**2** a net that hangs from a metal ring high up at each end of a basketball court バスケットボールのコートの両端の高い所にある金属製の輪から垂れ下がっている網➡**ゴールの網** ☛ S1 ページのさし絵 ▶定義**3** a score of one, two or three points in basketball, made by throwing the ball through one of the nets バスケットボールで,ネットの1つにボールを投げ入れることによって,1,2または3点を得ること➡**ゴール,得点**

成句 put all your eggs in one basket ⇒ **EGG**¹

**basketball** /bɑ́ːskətbɔːl; bǽ-/ 名 Ⓤ ▶定義 a game for two teams of five players. There is a net (basket) fixed to a metal ring high up at each end of the court and the players try to throw a ball through the other team's net in order to score points (baskets). 5人の選手から成る,2つのチームで行う試合.コートの両端

の高い所にある金属製の輪に網（ゴール）が取り付けられていて，選手たちは点を得る（得点）ために相手チームのゴールにボールを投げ入れようとする→バスケットボール

**bass** /béɪs/ 名 ▶定義1 ❶ the lowest part in music 音楽の最低音部→バス，ベース ▶定義2 ❻ the lowest male singing voice; a singer with this kind of voice 最低音域の男性の歌声; このような声を持つ歌手→バス; バス歌手 ☞参 tenor, baritone ▶定義3 = DOUBLE BASS ▶定義4 ❻ (または **bass guitar**) an electric guitar which plays very low notes 非常に低い音調を弾く電気ギター→ベースギター ☞参 piano の注 — bass 形 (名詞の前だけ)→バス（用）の，低音の ‖ *a bass drum* バスドラム *Can you sing the bass part in this song?* この歌のバスの音域を歌えますか．

**bassoon** /bəsúːn, bæ-/ 名 ❻ ▶定義 a musical instrument that you blow which makes a very deep sound 吹くと非常に低い音が鳴る楽器→バスーン，ファゴット ☞参 piano の注 ☞ music のさし絵

bat

**bat**¹ /bæt/ 名 ❻ ▶定義1 a piece of wood for hitting the ball in sports such as table tennis, cricket or baseball スポーツ，例えば卓球，クリケット，野球でボールを打つための木材→バット，ラケット ‖ *a cricket bat* クリケットのバット ☞参 club, racket, stick ☞ S1 ページのさし絵 ▶定義2 a small animal, like a mouse with wings, which flies and hunts at night ネズミに似た，羽のある小動物で，夜に飛び狩りをする→こうもり

成句 **off your own bat** ▶定義 without anyone asking you or helping you だれにも頼まれないで，またはだれも手伝ってくれないで→自分の力で，自主的に，勝手に

**bat**² /bæt/ 動 ❸ (**batting**; **batted**) ▶定義 (used about one player or a whole team) to have a turn hitting the ball in sports such as cricket or baseball (1人の選手またはチーム全体について）スポーツ，例えばクリケットや野球でボールを打つ番になる→打席に立つ

成句 **not bat an eyelid**; 米 **not bat an eye** ▶定義 to show no surprise or embarrassment when sth unusual happens 変わった〜が起きたとき，驚きまたは困惑を見せない→少しも驚かない

**batch** /bætʃ/ 名 ❻ ▶定義 a number of things or people which belong together as a group 1つの集団として，共に属するたくさんの物または人々→1回分の量，1群，1団，1束 ‖ *The bus returned to the airport for the next batch of tourists.* バスは次の旅行者の1団のために空港に戻った．

**bated** /béɪtɪd/ 形
成句 **with bated breath** ▶定義 excited or afraid, because you are waiting for sth to happen 〜が起きるのを待っているため，興奮しているまたは怖がっている→息を殺して，かたずをのんで

\***bath**¹ /bɑːθ, bæθ/ 名 ▶定義1 ❻ (または **bathtub** /bæθtʌb/) a large container for water in which you sit to wash your body 体を洗うために座る湯を入れる大きな容器→浴槽，湯船 ‖ *Can you answer the phone? I'm in the bath!* 電話を取ってもらえませんか．今入浴中なので． ☞ C7 ページのさし絵 ▶定義2 [単数扱い] an act of washing the whole of your body when you sit or lie in a bath filled with water 水・湯で満たされた浴槽の中に座ってまたは横たわって，体中を洗う行為→水浴び，入浴 ‖ *to have a bath* 入浴する 特に 英 *Would you prefer to take a bath or a shower?* 入浴したいですか，それともシャワーを浴びますか． ▶定義3 **baths** /bɑːz; bæz/ [複数扱い] 英 (古) a public building where you can go to swim; a public place where people went in past times to have a wash or a bath 泳ぎに行く公の建物; 昔，体を洗ったり，入浴するために人々が行った公の場所→(屋内)プール; ふろ屋，温泉場 ‖ *Roman baths* ローマの公衆浴場

**bath**² /bɑːθ; bæθ/ 動 ▶定義1 ⓗ to give sb a bath →〜を入浴させる ‖ *bath the baby* 赤ん坊を入浴させる ▶定義2 ⓘ (古) to have a bath →入浴する

**bathe** /béɪð/ 動 ▶定義1 ⓗ to wash or put part of the body in water, often for medical reasons しばしば治療のため，体の一部を水の中で洗うまたは水につける→水で洗う，水につける ‖ *She bathed the wound with antiseptic.* 彼女は消毒剤で傷を洗った． ▶定義2 ⓘ (古) to swim in the sea or in a lake or river 海や湖,川で泳ぐ→**泳ぐ,泳ぎに行く** ☞参 **sunbathe**

**bathed** /béiðd/ 形(文) ▶定義 **bathed in sth**(名詞の前は不可) covered with sth ～で覆われた**(汗・涙などで)ぬれた,(光などで)あふれた** ‖ *The room was bathed in moonlight.* その部屋一杯に月明かりが注いでいた.

**bathrobe** /bǽːθroub; bǽːθ-/ = **DRESSING GOWN**

*****bathroom** /bǽːθrùːm -ròm; bǽːθ-/ 名 C ▶定義**1** a room where there is a bath, a place to wash your hands (a washbasin), and sometimes a toilet 浴槽,手を洗う所(洗面台),時にトイレがある部屋→**浴室,ふろ場** ☞ C7 ページのさし絵 ▶定義**2** 米 a room with a toilet トイレのある部屋→**浴室,(個人住宅の)トイレ** ☞参 **toilet** の注

**bathtub** = **BATH¹(1)**

**bat mitzvah** /bæt mítsvə/ 名 C ▶定義 a ceremony in the Jewish religion for a girl who is about 13 years old. 13歳くらいの少女に対して行うユダヤ教の儀式→**バトミツバー** ☞比

**bar mitzvah**

**baton** /bætɔn; bətán, bæ-/ 名 C ▶定義**1** = **TRUNCHEON** ▶定義**2** a short thin stick used by the leader of an orchestra オーケストラの指揮者によって使われる,短く細い棒→**指揮棒** ▶定義**3** a stick which a runner in a race (a relay race) passes to the next person in the team 競争(リレー競争)で走者が同じチームの次の走者に渡す棒→**バトン**

**batsman** /bǽtsmən/ 名 C (複 **-men** /-mən/) ▶定義 (in cricket) one of the two players who hit the ball to score points (runs). (クリケットで)点を得る(得点)ためにボールを打つ2人の選手のうちの1人→**打者**

**battalion** /bətǽljən/ 名 C ▶定義 a large unit of soldiers that forms part of a larger unit in the army 軍隊で大きな隊の一部を形成する,兵士の大きな組→**大隊**

**batter¹** /bǽtər/ 動 自 他 ▶定義 to hit sb/sth hard, many times 何度も～を強く打つ→**～を続け様に打つ,乱打する** ‖ *The wind battered against the window.* 風が窓に激しく吹き付けた. *He battered the door down.* 彼は扉をたたき壊した.

**batter²** /bǽtər/ 名 U ▶定義 a mixture of flour, eggs and milk used to cover food such as fish, vegetables, etc before frying them 食べ物,例え

ば魚,野菜などを少量の油で焼く前に,それを覆うために使われる小麦粉,卵,牛乳を混ぜた物→**こねもの,衣**

**battered** /bǽtərd/ 形 ▶定義 no longer looking new; damaged or out of shape もはや新しく見えない; 損傷した,または形の壊れた→**使い古された; つぶれた,壊れた** ‖ *a battered old hat* 型崩れした古い帽子

*****battery** /bǽtri; -təri/ 名 ( 複 **batteries**) ▶定義**1** C a device which provides electricity for a toy, radio, car, etc おもちゃ,ラジオ,車などに電気を供給する装置→**電池,バッテリー** ‖ *to recharge **a flat battery*** (= *no longer producing electricity*) 切れた(= もう電気を作らない)電池に充電する ☞ **light** のさし絵 ▶定義**2** C 英 a large number of very small cages in which chickens, etc are kept on a farm 農場で鶏などが入れておかれる,たくさんのとても小さなかご→**バタリ** ‖ *a battery hen/farm* バタリに入れられている雌鶏(めんどり)・養鶏農場 ☞参 **free-range** ▶定義**3** U the crime of attacking sb physically 身体的に～を攻撃する罪→**殴打** ‖ *He was charged with **assault and battery**.* 彼は暴行殴打で告発された.

*****battle¹** /bǽtl/ 名 ▶定義**1** C U a fight, especially between armies in a war 特に戦争中の軍隊同士の戦い→**戦闘,会戦,戦争** ‖ *the battle of Trafalgar* トラファルガーの海戦 *to die/be killed **in battle*** 戦争で死ぬ・殺される ▶定義**2** C *a battle (with sb) (for sth)* a competition, argument or fight between people or groups of people trying to win power or control 力または支配力を勝ち取ろうとする人々,または人々の集団の間で引き起こされる競争,論争,または戦い→**闘争,競争** ‖ *a legal battle for custody of the children* 子供たちの保護をめぐる法的闘争 ▶定義**3** [C, 通常は単数] *a battle (against/for sth)* a determined effort to solve a difficult problem or to succeed in a difficult situation 難問を解決するため,または難しい状況で成功するための断固とした努力→**闘争,戦い** ‖ *After three years she lost her battle against cancer.* 3年後,彼女はがんとの闘いに敗れた.

成句 *a losing battle* ⇒ **LOSE**

**battle²** /bǽtl/ 動 自 ▶定義 *battle (with/against*

sb/sth) (for sth); battle (on) to try very hard to achieve sth difficult or to deal with sth unpleasant or dangerous 難しい〜を達成しようと，あるいは不快なまたは危険な〜に対処しようと，必死で頑張る→**奮闘する** || *Mark is battling with his maths homework.* マークは数学の宿題と奮闘している．*The two brothers were battling for control of the family business.* 2人の兄弟は，家業の支配権を得ようと闘争していた．*Life is hard at the moment but we're battling on.* 今生活は大変だが，私たちは戦い続けている．

**battlefield** /bætlfi:ld/ (または **battleground** /bætlgraʊnd/) 名 ⓒ ▶定義 the place where a battle is fought 戦闘が行われる場所→**戦場，戦闘の場**

**battleship** /bætlʃɪp/ 名 ⓒ ▶定義 the largest type of ship used in war 戦争中に使われる最も大型の船→**戦艦**

**bauble** /bɔ́:bl/ 名 ⓒ ▶定義**1** a piece of cheap jewellery 1つの安いアクセサリー→**安物の装飾品・宝石，安ぴか物** ▶定義**2** a decoration in the shape of a ball that is hung on a Christmas tree クリスマスツリーにつるされる球形の飾り→**球飾り**

**baulk** (特に 困 **balk**) /bɔ:k/ 動 ⓘ ▶定義 baulk (at sth) to not want to do or agree to sth because it seems too difficult, dangerous or unpleasant 〜があまりに難しく，危険にまたは不快に思われるので，それをしたくないまたは同意したくない→**ためらう，躊躇（ちゅうちょ）する，しりごみする** || *She liked horses, but she baulked at trying to ride one.* 彼女は馬が好きだったが，乗馬をするのはためらっていた．

**bawl** /bɔ:l/ 動 ⓘⓒ ▶定義 to shout or cry loudly 大声で叫ぶ，または泣く→**わめく，どなる**

\***bay** /béɪ/ 名 ⓒ ▶定義**1** a part of the coast where the land goes in to form a curve 陸地が入り込んで曲線を描いている海岸の一部→**湾，入り江** || *the Bay of Bengal* ベンガル湾 *The harbour was in a sheltered bay.* 港は荒波を避けられる入り江にあった．▶定義**2** a part of a building, aircraft or area which has a particular purpose 特定の目的を持つ建物，飛行機，地域の一部→**(建物などの)区画，(飛行機の)隔室，倉** || *a parking/loading bay* 駐車場・荷物室

**成句** hold/keep sb/sth at bay ▶定義 to stop sb dangerous from getting near you; to prevent a situation or problem from getting worse 危険な〜が近付くのを止める；状況や問題が悪化するのを防ぐ→**〜を寄せ付けない，食い止める**

**bayonet** /béɪənət, -nét, bèɪənét/ 名 ⓒ ▶定義 a knife that can be fixed to the end of a gun 銃の先に固定できる短剣→**銃剣**

**bay window** 名 ⓒ ▶定義 a window in a part of a room that sticks out from the wall of a house 家の壁から突き出した部屋の一部にある窓→**出窓，張り出し窓**

**bazaar** /bəzá:r/ 名 ⓒ ▶定義**1** (in some eastern countries) a market (いくつかの東洋の国々で)市場→**市場，商店街** ▶定義**2** 医 a sale where the money that is made goes to charity 慈善に使われる金を作るための販売→**バザー**

**BBC** /bì: bi: sí:/ 略 the British Broadcasting Corporation ▶定義 one of the national radio and television companies in Britain 英国国営のラジオとテレビ会社の1つ→**BBC，英国放送協会** || *a BBC documentary* BBCのドキュメンタリー *watch a programme on BBC1* BBC1の番組を見る

**BBQ** 略 = **BARBECUE**

**BC** /bì: sí:/ 略 before Christ ▶定義 used in dates to show the number of years before the time when Christians believe Jesus Christ was born キリスト教徒がイエス キリストが誕生したと信じている年，それ以前の年数を示す日付に用いて→**紀元前** || *300 BC* 紀元前300年 ☛参 **AD**

\***be**¹ /bi, bɪ; 強形 bí:/ 動 ▶定義**1** ⓘ **there is/are** to exist; to be present 存在する；現存する→**いる，ある** || *I tried phoning them but there was no answer.* 私は彼らに電話をしたが，応答はなかった．*There are some people outside.* 外に何人かいる．*There are a lot of trees in our garden.* 私たちの庭にはたくさんの木がある．▶定義**2** ⓘ used to give the position of sb/sth or the place where sb/sth is situated 〜の位置，または〜が位置している場所を教えるために用いて→**いる，ある** || *Katrina's in her office.* カトリーナは自分の会社にいる．*Where are the scissors?* はさみはどこにありますか．*The bus stop is five minutes' walk from here.* バス停はここから歩いて5分の

所にある. *St Tropez is on the south coast.* サントロペは南海岸にある. ▶定義3 ❸ used to give the date or age of sb/sth or to talk about time 〜の日付や年齢を教える,または時間について話すときに用いて→**である** ‖ *My birthday is on April 24th.* 私の誕生日は4月24日です. *It's 6 o'clock.* 6時だ. *It was Tuesday yesterday.* 昨日は火曜日だった. *Sue'll be 21 in June.* スーは6月に21歳になる. *He's older than Miranda.* 彼はミランダより年上だ. *It's ages since I last saw him.* 最後に彼に会ってから,何年もたっている. ▶定義4 ❹ used when you are giving the name of people or things, describing them or giving more information about them 人々や物の名前を伝える,それらを描写する,あるいはより詳しい情報を与えるときに用いて→**である** ‖ *This is my father, John.* こちらは父のジョンです. *I'm Alison.* 私はアリソンです. *He's Italian. He's from Milan.* 彼はイタリア人です. ミラノ出身です. *He's a doctor.* 彼は医者だ. *What's that?* あれは何ですか. *A lion is a mammal.* ライオンはほ乳類だ. *'What colour is your car?' 'It's green.'* 「あなたの車は何色ですか」「緑だよ」 *How much was your ticket?* チケットはいくらでしたか. *The film was excellent.* その映画はすばらしかった. *She's very friendly.* 彼女はとても親切だ. *'How is your wife?' 'She's fine, thanks.'* 「奥さんはいかがですか」「元気だよ,ありがとう」 ▶定義5 ❺(完了形でのみ用いて)to go to a place (and return) ある場所に行く(そして戻る)→**行く,来る** ‖ *Have you ever **been to** Japan?* 日本へ行ったことがありますか.

➤ has, have gone と比較: *Julia's gone to the doctor's (= she hasn't returned yet).*(ジュリアは医者に行った(=まだ戻っていない).) *Julia's been to the doctor's today (=she has returned).*(ジュリアは今日医者に行った(=戻っている).)

成句 **be yourself** ▶定義 to act naturally 自然に振る舞う→**普段の自分でいる,有りのままでいる** ‖ *Don't be nervous; just be yourself and the interview will be fine.* 神経質になるなよ. 普段通りでいれば,面接はうまくいくよ.

**-to-be** (複合名詞を作るために用いて) ▶定義 future 未来の→**未来の,近い将来〜になる人** ‖ *his bride-to-be* 彼の未来の花嫁 *mothers-to-be (= pregnant women)* 未来の母親(= 妊娠している女性)

# beak 125

***be**² /bi, bɪ; 強形 biː/ 助 ▶定義1 used with a past participle to form the passive; used with a present participle to form the continuous tenses 受動態を作るために,過去分詞と用いて;進行形を作るために,現在分詞と用いて→**〜される;〜しているところだ** ☛ 巻末の「文法早見表」を参照. ▶定義2 **be to do sth** used to show that sth must happen or that sth has been arranged 〜が起こるはずである,または〜が準備されていることを示すために用いて→**〜するはずだ,〜するつもりだ,〜することになっている** ‖ *You are to leave here at 10 o'clock at the latest.* あなたは遅くとも10時にはここを出ることになっている. ▶定義3 **if sb/sth were to do sth** used to show that sth is possible but not very likely 〜は起こり得るが,あまりありそうにないことを示すために用いて→**仮に〜するとしたら** ‖ *If they were to offer me the job, I'd probably take it.* もし彼らが私に仕事をくれれば,おそらく私はそれを受けるだろう.

*beach /biːtʃ/ 名 ❻ ▶定義 an area of sand or small stones beside the sea 海のそばの砂または小石のある地帯→**浜辺,磯(いそ),波打ち際,ビーチ** ‖ *to sit **on the beach*** 浜辺に座る ☛ C8 ページのさし絵

**beacon** /ˈbiːk(ə)n/ 名 ❻ ▶定義 a fire or light on a hill or tower, often near the coast, which is used as a signal 信号として使われる,しばしば海岸の近くの丘または塔にある火や光→**かがり火,のろし,信号灯,灯台**

**bead** /biːd/ 名 ❻ ▶定義1 a small round piece of wood, glass or plastic with a hole in the middle for putting a string through to make jewellery, etc 装飾品などを作るための,糸を通す穴が真ん中に開いている,小さく丸い木,ガラス,またはプラスチック→**ビーズ,ガラス玉,数珠玉** ▶定義2 **beads** [複数扱い]a circular piece of jewellery (*a necklace*) made of beads ビーズで作られた円状の装飾品(ネックレス)→**首飾り** ☛ **jewellery** のさし絵 ▶定義3 a drop of liquid 液体の一滴→**滴** ‖ *There were **beads of sweat** on his forehead.* 彼は額に玉の汗をかいていた.

*beak /biːk/ 名 ❻ ▶定義 the hard pointed part of a bird's mouth 鳥の口の固くとがった部分→く

**beaker** ちばし ☛ C1 ページのさし絵
**beaker** /bíːkər/ 名 C ▶定義1 a plastic or paper drinking cup, usually without a handle 通常取っ手の付いていない、プラスチックまたは紙製の飲み物用コップ→(広口の)大型コップ ☛ **cup** のさし絵 ▶定義2 a glass container used in scientific experiments, etc for pouring liquids 科学的な実験などで使われる，液体をつぐためのガラス製の容器→ビーカー

**beam**¹ /biːm/ 名 C ▶定義1 a line of light 光の線→(太陽・月などの)光線, (ランプ・灯台・ヘッドライトの)光 ‖ *the beam of a torch* たいまつの光 *The car's headlights were **on full beam** (= giving the most light possible and not directed downwards).* 車のヘッドライトがまともに当たった(=最大限の光を当て，下に向けていない). *a laser beam* レーザー光線 ▶定義2 a long piece of wood, metal, etc that is used to support weight, for example in the floor or ceiling of a building 例えば建物の床または天井で，重量を支えるために使われている長い木，金属など→梁(はり), けた, 横木 ▶定義3 a happy smile 幸せな笑顔→(顔などの)輝き, 笑顔, 晴れやかさ

**beam**² /biːm/ 動 ▶定義1 自 **beam (at sb/sth)** to smile happily 楽しそうにほほえむ→にっこり笑う，顔をほころばせる ‖ *I looked at Sam and he beamed back at me.* 私がサムを見ると，彼は私ににっこりと笑顔を返した. ▶定義2 他 to send out radio or television signals ラジオまたはテレビの信号を送出する→(放送など)を向ける, 送る ‖ *The programme was beamed live by satellite to many different countries.* その番組は衛星により多くの国々に向けて生放送された. ▶定義3 自 to send out light and warmth 光と暖かさを送り出す→(太陽などが)輝く, 光・熱を発する ‖ *The sun beamed down on them.* 太陽が彼らを照らした.

✱**bean** /biːn/ 名 C ▶定義1 the seeds or seed containers (**pods**) from a climbing plant which are eaten as vegetables 野菜として食べられる，つる性の植物からとれる種または種の入れ物(さや)→豆 ‖ *soya beans* 大豆 *a tin of baked beans (= beans in a tomato sauce)* ベークドビーンズの缶詰(=トマトソースにつけられた豆) *green beans* さやいんげん ☛ C3 ページのさし絵 ▶定義2 similar seeds from other plants ほかの植物からとれる似たような種→豆, 実 ‖ *coffee beans* コーヒー豆

慣用 **full of beans/life** ⇒ **FULL**¹
**spill the beans** ⇒ **SPILL**

✱**bear**¹ /beər/ 名 C ▶定義 a large, heavy wild animal with thick fur and sharp teeth 厚い毛皮と鋭い歯を持つ，大きな，重い野生の動物→熊 ‖ *a polar/grizzly/brown bear* 北極熊・ハイイログマ・ヒグマ ☛参 **teddy bear**

✱**bear**² /beər/ 動 (過 **bore** /bɔːr/; 過分 **borne** /bɔːrn/)
▶定義1 他 (否定文または疑問文で can/could と用いて) to be able to accept and deal with sth unpleasant 不快な~を受け入れて，対処できる→~に耐える, ~を我慢・辛抱する ‖ *I can't bear spiders.* クモには耐えられない. *She couldn't bear the thought of anything happening to him.* 彼女は，彼に何かが起こるという思いには耐えられなかった. *How can you bear to listen to that music?* どうしてあの曲を聞くのを我慢できるの. *The pain was almost more than he could bear.* 痛みはもはや彼にはほとんど耐えられないほどだった. ☛類 **stand, endure** ▶定義2 他 **not bear sth/doing sth** to not be suitable for sth; to not allow sth ~に適さない; ~を許さない→~に適さない, ~に耐えられない ‖ *These figures won't bear close examination (= when you look closely you will find mistakes).* この数値は念入りな検討に耐えられないだろう(=細かく注意して見れば，間違いを見つけるだろう). *What I would do if I lost my job **doesn't bear thinking about** (= is too unpleasant to think about).* もし職を失ったら私はどうするかと考えることには耐えられない(=それについて考えることはあまりにも不愉快すぎる). ▶定義3 他 正式 to take responsibility for sth ~の責任を取る→~を持つ, 負担する ‖ *Customers will bear the full cost of the improvements.* 顧客は改良工事の全費用を負担するだろう. ▶定義4 他 to have a feeling, especially a negative feeling ある感情を持つ，特に否定的な感情→~を心に持つ, 抱く ‖ *Despite what they did, she **bears** no **resentment** towards them.* 彼らがした事にもかかわらず，彼女は彼らに何の怒りも抱いていない. *He's not the type to **bear a grudge** against anyone.* 彼は人に恨みを抱くようなタイプでは

ない. ▶定義5 ⓘ to support the weight of sth 〜の重さを支える➔〜を支える, 耐える‖ *Twelve pillars bear the weight of the roof.* 12本の柱が屋根の重みを支えている. ▶定義6 ⓘ 正式 to show sth; to carry sth so that it can be seen 〜を見せる; 〜が見られるように運ぶ➔〜を運ぶ, 持っていく‖ *The waiters came in bearing trays of food.* 給仕人たちが食べ物を載せた盆を持って入ってきた. *He still* **bears the scars** *of his accident.* 彼には事故の傷がある. *She* ***bore** a strong* ***resemblance** to her mother (= she looked like her).* 彼女は母親に非常によく似ていた (= 彼女は母親のようだった). ▶定義7 ⓘ (文) to give birth to children 子供を産む➔〜を産む, 出産する‖ *She bore him four children, all sons.* 彼女は彼との間に4人の子供をもうけた, 皆男の子だ.

　▶より一般的な表現は, She had four children. (彼女には4人の子供がいた.) ある人自身の誕生について述べるときには, be born を使う: *Robert was born in 1996.* (ロバートは1996年に生まれた.)

▶定義8 ⓘ to turn or go in the direction that is mentioned 言及された方向へ向く, または行く➔進む, 向かう‖ *Where the road forks, bear left.* 道が分岐している所で, 左に進め.

成句 bear the brunt of sb ▶定義 to suffer the main force of sth 〜のありったけの力を被る➔矢面に立つ‖ *Her sons usually bore the brunt of her anger.* 彼女の息子はいつも彼女の怒りの矢面に立たされた.

bear fruit ▶定義 to be successful; to produce results 成功する; 結果を生み出す➔実を結ぶ; (努力が)成果を上げる‖ *At last our hard work is beginning to bear fruit.* ついに, 我々の懸命な仕事が実を結び始めている.

bear in mind (that); bear/keep sb/sth in mind ⇒ **MIND**¹

bear witness (to sth) ▶定義 to show evidence of sth 〜の証拠を見せる➔〜を証言する, 〜の証拠・証人となる‖ *The burning buildings and empty streets bore witness to a recent attack.* 燃えている建物と通りにだれもいないことが, 起こったばかりの攻撃の証拠だった.

句動詞 bear down (on sb/sth) ▶定義1 to move closer to sb/sth in a frightening way ぎょっとさせるやり方で, 〜や…へ近付く➔〜にず

# bearing 127

んずん迫る, 〜を圧迫する, 〜に押し寄せてくる‖ *We could see the hurricane bearing down on the town.* 私たちは, その町へハリケーンがずんずん迫っていく様子を見ることができた. ▶定義2 to push down hard on sb/sth 〜を強く下へ押す➔〜を倒す, 〜に打ち勝つ

bear sb/sth out ▶定義 to show that sb is correct or that sth is true 〜が正しい, または…が真実であることを示す➔〜を支持する, 確証する‖ *The evidence bears out my theory.* その証拠は私の理論を確証している.

bear up ▶定義 to be strong enough to continue at a difficult time 困難なときでも続けられるほど強い➔頑張る, へこたれない‖ *How is he bearing up after his accident?* 彼は事故の後どのように頑張るのだろう.

bear with sb/sth ▶定義 to be patient with 〜に我慢する➔〜を我慢する, 〜に耐える‖ *Bear with me - I won't be much longer.* 少し待っていてください — すぐ終わりますから.

**bearable** /béərəbl/ 形 ▶定義 that you can accept or deal with, although unpleasant 不愉快だが, 受け入れられる, または対処できる➔我慢できる, 耐えられる‖ *It was extremely hot but the breeze made it more bearable.* 非常に暑かったが, そよ風が吹いていたのでその分しのげた. ⇔ **unbearable**

\***beard** /bíərd/ 名 ⓒ ⓤ ▶定義 the hair which grows on a man's cheeks and chin 男性のほおやあごに生える毛➔あごひげ‖ *I'm going to grow a beard.* 私はあごひげを伸ばすつもりだ.
　🖝参 **goatee, moustache** 🖝 **hair** のさし絵

**bearded** /bíərdid/ 形 ▶定義 with a beard ➔あごひげのある

**bearer** /béərər/ 名 ⓒ ▶定義 a person who carries or brings sth 〜を持っていく, または持ってくる人➔運ぶ者, 運搬人, 使者‖ *I'm sorry to be the bearer of bad news.* 残念だが悪い知らせを持ってきた.

**bearing** /béəriŋ/ 名 ▶定義1 [ⓤ, 単数扱い] (a) bearing on sth a relation or connection to the subject being discussed 議論されている主題との関係や関連➔関係, 関連‖ *Her comments had no* ***bearing** on our decision.* 彼女の意見は私たちの決定と全く関係がなかった. ▶定義2 [ⓤ, 単

数扱い] the way in which sb stands or moves ～が立つまたは動く方法➡️**態度, 振る舞い (独特の身振り・姿勢・歩き方など)** ‖ *a man of dignified bearing* 威厳ある態度の男性　▶定義3 **ⓒ** a direction measured from a fixed point using a special instrument (**a compass**) 特別な道具 (コンパス) を使って, ある固定された点から測られた方向➡️**方角, 方位, 方向**

成句 **get/find your bearings** ▶定義 to become familiar with where you are 自分がいる場所に精通するようになる➡️**自分の位置が分かる, 周囲の情勢が分かる**

**lose your bearings** ⇒ **LOSE**

**beast** /biːst/ 名 **ⓒ 正式** ▶定義 an animal, especially a large one 特に大きい動物 ➡️**獣** ‖ *a wild beast* 野獣

\***beat**¹ /biːt/ 動 (過 **beat**; 過分 **beaten** /bíːtn/)
▶定義1 **他** beat sb (at sth); beat sth to defeat sb; to be better than sth ～を打ち負かす; ～よりも良くなる➡️**～を負かす, ～に勝る** ‖ *He always beats me at tennis.* 彼はいつもテニスで私を負かす. *We're hoping to beat the world record.* 私たちは世界記録を破ることを願っている. *If you want to keep fit, you can't beat swimming.* もし健康を維持したいなら, 水泳に勝るものはない. ▶定義2 **自 他** to hit many times, usually very hard 通常非常に強く, 何度もたたく➡️**～を打つ, たたく** ‖ *The man was beating the donkey with a stick.* その男は棒でロバをたたいていた. *The rain was beating on the roof of the car.* 雨が車の屋根に打ち付けていた. ▶定義3 **自 他** to make a regular sound or movement 規則的な音を立てる, または動きをする➡️**(太鼓が) どんどん鳴る, (羽が) ばたばたする, (心臓が) 鼓動する** ‖ *Her **heart beat** faster as she ran to pick up her child.* 子供を抱き上げようと走ったとき, 彼女の心臓はいつもより速く鼓動した. *We could hear the drums beating in the distance.* 遠くで太鼓がどんどん鳴っているのが聞こえた. *The bird **beat its wings** (= moved them up and down quickly).* 鳥がその羽をばたばたさせた (= 羽を上下に速く動かした). ▶定義4 **他** to mix quickly with a fork, etc フォークなどで素早く混ぜる➡️**かき混ぜる** ‖ *Beat the eggs and sugar together.* 卵と砂糖をよくかき混ぜてください.

成句 **beat about the bush** ▶定義 to talk about sth for a long time without mentioning the main point 要点には触れずに, 長い時間～について話す➡️**遠回しに言う** ‖ *Stop beating about the bush and tell me how much money you need.* 遠回しに言うのはやめて, いくらお金が必要なのか言いなさい.

(it) **beats me** (口語) ▶定義 I do not know 私は知らない➡️**知らないよ** ‖ *It beats me where he's gone.* 彼がどこに行ったかなんて知らないよ. *'Why is she angry?' 'Beats me!'* 「彼女はどうして怒っているの」「知らないよ」

**off the beaten track** ▶定義 in a place where people do not often go 人々があまり行かない場所で➡️**普通でない, あまり知られていない**

句動詞 **beat sb/sth off** ▶定義 to fight until sb/sth goes away ～が逃げるまで戦う➡️**～を撃退する, 追い払う** ‖ *The thieves tried to take his wallet but he beat them off.* 泥棒たちが彼の財布を取ろうとしたが, 彼は撃退した.

**beat sb to sth** ▶定義 to get somewhere or do sth before sb else ほかの～より前に, どこかへ着くまたは…をする➡️**～より先に～に到着する, より先にやり遂げる** ‖ *She beat me back to the house.* 彼女は私より先に家に帰った. *I wanted to ring him first but Aisha beat me to it.* 私が最初に彼へ電話をしたかったが, アイーシャが先にかけた.

**beat sb up** ▶定義 to attack sb by hitting or kicking him/her many times ～を何度もたたいたりけったりして攻撃する➡️**～を打ちのめす, 散々殴り付ける** ‖ *He was badly beaten up outside the pub last night.* 彼は昨夜パブの外でひどく殴り付けられた.

**beat**² /biːt/ 名 ▶定義1 **ⓒ** a single hit on sth such as a drum or the movement of sth, such as your heart; the sound that this makes 例えば太鼓を1回打つこと, または, 例えば心臓の動き; それが立てる音➡️**一打ち, 鼓動; 打つ音, 動悸 (どうき)** ‖ *Her heart skipped a beat when she saw him.* 彼を見たとき, 彼女の鼓動は止まりそうになった. ▶定義2 [単数扱い] a series of regular hits on sth such as a drum, or of movements of sth; the sound that this makes 例えば太鼓を規則的に連続して打つこと, または～の動きの一続き; それが作る音➡️**打つこと**

[音], 鼓動; 動悸, 拍子 ‖ *the beat of the drums* 太鼓を打つ音 ☛参 **heartbeat** ▶定義3 **C** the strong rhythm that a piece of music has 曲における強いリズム→拍 ▶定義4 [単数扱い] the route along which a police officer regularly walks 警察官が定期的に歩く道筋→巡回・受け持ち区域 ‖ *Having more policemen on the beat helps reduce crime.* その巡回区域にもっと警官がいれば,犯罪減少に役立つ.

**beating** /bíːtɪŋ/ 名 ▶定義1 a punishment that you give to sb by hitting him/her ~に下す罰としてその~をたたくこと→むち打ち,せっかん ‖ *The boys got a beating when they were caught stealing.* 少年たちは盗んでいるところを捕まり,せっかんを受けた. ▶定義2 a defeat 負けたこと→敗北,散々な目に遭うこと

成句 **take a lot of/some beating** ▶定義 to be so good that it would be difficult to find sth better これ以上良い~を見つけるのが難しいほど良い→負かす・追い越すのが難しい ‖ *Mary's cooking takes some beating.* メアリーの料理はなかなか勝てない.

**beautician** /bjuːtíʃ(ə)n/ 名 **C** ▶定義 a person whose job is to improve the way people look with beauty treatments, etc 美容などによって,人々の外見を良くすることを仕事にする人→美容師

*****beautiful** /bjúːtɪfəl/ 形 ▶定義 very pretty or attractive; giving pleasure to the senses 非常にきれいなまたは魅力的な; 五感に喜びをもたらす→美しい,きれいな; 楽しませる,心地良い ‖ *The view from the top of the hill was really beautiful.* 丘の頂上からの眺めは本当にきれいだった. *What a beautiful day - the weather's perfect!* 何てすてきな日でしょう - 天気は最高です. *He has a beautiful voice.* 彼は美しい声を持っている. *A beautiful perfume filled the air.* 心地良い香りがあたり一面に立ちこめていた. *a beautiful woman* 美しい女

▶通常 beautiful は,女性や少女に用いられる.同じく女性と少女だけに用いられる pretty よりも意味が強い.男性は,handsome または good-looking と表現される.

— **beautifully** /bjúːtɪfəli/ 副 →美しく,鮮やかに ‖ *He plays the piano beautifully.* 彼はピアノを鮮やかに演奏する. *She was beautifully dressed.* 彼女は美しく着こなしていた.

*****beauty** /bjúːti/ 名 (複 **beauties**) ▶定義1 **U** the quality which gives pleasure to the senses; the state of being beautiful 五感に喜びを与える質; 美しい状態→美しさ,美 ‖ *I was amazed by the beauty of the mountains.* その山々の美しさに驚いた. *music of great beauty* とても美しい音楽 ▶定義2 **C** a beautiful woman 美しい女性→美しい人,美人 ‖ *She grew up to be a beauty.* 彼女は美人に成長した. ▶定義3 **C** a particularly good example of sth ~の特に良い模範→美点,良さ,長所 ‖ *Look at this tomato - it's a beauty!* このトマトを見て - 完ぺきだ.

**beauty spot** 名 **C** 英 ▶定義 a place in the countryside which is famous for its attractive scenery 田舎にある,魅力的な景色で有名な場所→名所,景勝地

beaver

**beaver** /bíːvər/ 名 **C** ▶定義 an animal with brown fur, a wide, flat tail and sharp teeth. It lives in water and on land and uses branches to build walls across rivers to hold back the water (*dams*). 茶色い毛の, 広く平らなしっぽと鋭い歯を持つ動物. 水中と陸上で暮らし, 木の枝を使って, 川の流れをせき止める(ダム)ために障壁を築く→ビーバー

**became** BECOME の過去形

*****because** /bɪkɔ́ːz, -káz/ 接 ▶定義 for the reason that ~という理由のために→なぜならば~だから(である), ~なので ‖ *They didn't go for a walk because it was raining.* 雨が降っていたので, 彼らは散歩に出掛けなかった.

*****because of** 前 ▶定義 as a result of; on account of ~の結果として; ~のために→~のせいで, ~の理由で ‖ *They didn't go for a walk because of the rain.* 雨のせいで, 彼らは散歩に出掛けなかった.

**beck** /bek/ 名

成句 **at sb's beck and call** ▶定義 always ready to obey sb's orders いつでも~の命令に従う用意ができている→~の言いなりになって

**beckon** /bék(ə)n/ 動 自 他 ▶定義 to show sb with a movement of your finger or hand that

## 130 become

you want him/her to come closer ～に近くに来てほしいことを,指または手の動きで示す→**手招きする,合図する** ‖ She beckoned me over to speak to her. 彼女は,私に彼女の所に来て話すように合図した.

**★become** /bɪkʌ́m/ 動 (過 **became** /bɪkéɪm/; 過分 **become**) ▶定義 to begin to be sth ～になり始める→**～になる,～の状態になる** ‖ Mr Saito became Chairman in 1998. 斎藤さんは 1998 年に会長になった. She wants to become a pilot. 彼女はパイロットになりたいと思っている. They became friends. 彼らは友達になった. She became nervous as the exam date came closer. 試験日が近付くと,彼女は神経質になった. He is becoming more like you every day. 彼は日増しにあなたに似てくる. ☞ この意味では,get も形容詞と共に用いられる. She got nervous as the exam date came closer. 試験日が近付くと,彼女は神経質になった. He's getting more like you every day. 彼は日増しにあなたに似てくる.これは会話では非常に一般的で,become よりは正式でない.

**(句動詞)** become of sb/sth ▶定義 to happen to sb/sth ～に起きる→**～はどうなる** ‖ What became of Alima? I haven't seen her for years! アリーマはどうなったのだろう.私はもう何年も彼女に会ったことがない.

**BEd** /bíːéd/ Bachelor of Education ▶定義 a degree in education for people who want to be teachers and do not already have a degree in a particular subject 教師になりたいがまだ特定の課目で学位を持っていない人々のためにある教育学の学位→**教育学学士**

**★bed¹** /bed/ 名 ▶定義**1** a piece of furniture that you lie on when you sleep 眠るとき,自分の体を横たえる家具→**ベッド,寝床** ‖ to make the bed (= to arrange the sheets, etc so that the bed is tidy and ready for sb to sleep in) 寝床の用意をする (= ベッドがきちんとなって～がいつでも眠れるように,シーツなどを整える) What time do you usually **go to bed**? 大抵何時に寝ますか. She was lying **on the bed** (= on top of the covers). 彼女はベッドで横になっていた (= 寝具の上で). When he rang I was already **in bed** (= under the covers). 彼が電話したとき,私は既に寝ていた (= 寝具の下で). It's late. It's **time for bed**. もう遅い.寝る時間だ. to get **into/out of bed** ベッドに入る・ベッドから出る ☞ C7 ページのさし絵

▶ 1 人用のベッドは single bed (シングルベッド),2 人用のベッドは double bed (ダブルベッド)と言われる.1 つの部屋に並べてある 2 つのシングルベッドは twin bed (ツインベッド)と言われる.ホテルでツインベッドがある部屋は,twin-bedded room (ツインルーム)と言われる.特に子供用の 2 つのシングルベッドで,一方の上に他方が組まれているものは bunk bed (2 段ベッド)と言われる.

▶定義**2** **-bedded** having the type or number of beds mentioned 言及された種類,または数

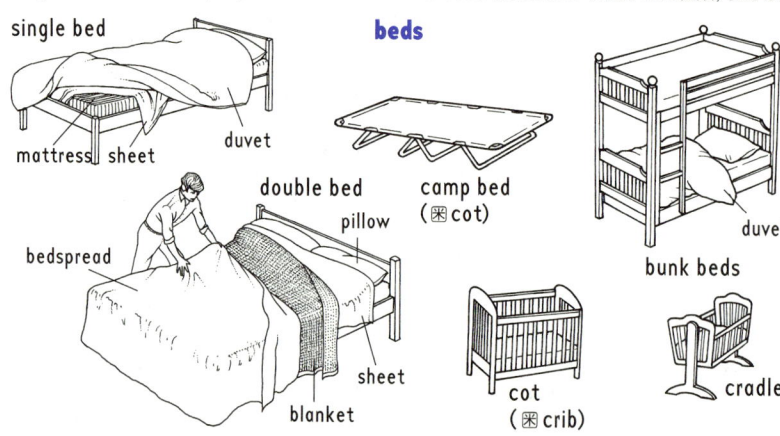

**beds**

single bed — mattress, sheet, duvet

double bed — bedspread, pillow, sheet, blanket

camp bed (英 cot)

bunk beds — duvet

cot (英 crib)

cradle

のベッドを持つ→~ベッド付きの ‖ *a twin-bedded room* ツインルーム ▶定義3 **C** the ground at the bottom of a river or the sea 川または海の底の土地→**川床, 水底** ‖ *the seabed* 海底 ▶定義4 = **FLOWER BED**

成句 **bed and breakfast; B & B** ▶定義 a place to stay in a private house or small hotel that consists of a room for the night and breakfast; a place that provides this 個人の家または小さなホテルに, 宿泊と朝食のために滞在すること; これを提供する場所→**朝食付き宿泊; 朝食付きの民宿・ホテル**

**go to bed with sb** 略式 ▶定義 to have sex with sb ~と性交をする→**~と寝る, ~と性的関係を持つ**

**bed**² /bed/ 動 ⓘ (**bedding**; **bedded**) ▶定義 to fix sth firmly in sth ~を…にしっかり固定する→**据え付ける, はめ込む, 積み重ねる**

句動詞 **bed down** ▶定義 to sleep in a place where you do not usually sleep いつもは寝る所でない場所で眠る→**寝床を作って寝る** ‖ *We couldn't find a hotel so we bedded down for the night in the van.* ホテルが見つからなかったので, その夜私たちは小型トラックの中に寝床を作って寝た.

**bedclothes** /bédklòʊðz/ (英 または **bedcovers**) 名 [複数扱い] ▶定義 the sheets, covers, etc that you put on a bed ベッドに掛けるシーツやカバーなど→**寝具, 夜具**

**bedding** /bédɪŋ/ 名 Ⓤ ▶定義 everything that you put on a bed and need for sleeping ベッドの上に掛ける, 眠るために必要なすべての物→**寝具**

**bedraggled** /bɪdrǽgld/ 形 ▶定義 very wet and untidy or dirty びっしょりぬれてだらしない, または汚れた→**(雨などで)ぐっしょりぬれた, (衣服や髪を)取り乱した, 汚れた, 薄汚い** ‖ *bedraggled hair* 乱れた髪

**bedridden** /bédrìdn/ 形 ▶定義 being too old or ill to get out of bed ベッドから起き上がるには年を取りすぎていて, または病気で→**寝たきりの**

*****bedroom** /bédru:m; -rʊm/ 名 **C** ▶定義 a room which is used for sleeping 眠るための部屋→**寝室** ‖ *You can sleep in the spare bedroom.* 予備の寝室で眠っていいよ. *a three-bedroom house* 3つの寝室がある家 ☛ C7 ページのさし絵

**bedside** /bédsàɪd/ 名 [単数扱い] ▶定義 the area that is next to a bed ベッドの隣の場所→**ベッドのそば, まくら元** ‖ *She sat at his bedside all night long.* 彼女は一晩彼のまくら元に座っていた. *A book lay open on the bedside table.* ベッドのそばのテーブルに本が開いて置いてあった. ☛ C7 ページのさし絵

**bedsit** /bédsìt/ (または **bedsitter**) 名 **C** 英 ▶定義 a rented room which is used for both living and sleeping 生活するためと眠るための両方に使われる賃貸の部屋→**ワンルームマンション, 貸間**

**bedspread** /bédsprèd/ 名 **C** ▶定義 an attractive cover for a bed that you put on top of the sheets and other covers シーツとほかのカバーの上に掛ける, ベッドを魅力的に見せるカバー→**ベッドカバー** ☛ **bed** のさし絵

**bedtime** /bédtàɪm/ 名 Ⓤ ▶定義 the time that you normally go to bed いつも寝床に就く時間→**就寝時間, 寝る時刻**

*****bee** /bi:/ 名 **C** ▶定義 a black and yellow insect that lives in large groups and that makes a sweet substance that we eat (**honey**) 大集団で生活していて, 人間が食べる甘い物(はちみつ)を作る, 黒と黄色の昆虫→**ハチ, ミツバチ**
▶多数のハチが一緒にいることは, swarm(群蜂(ぐんぽう))と言う. ハチがブンブンという音を出すことを buzz または hum と言う. ハチは怒ると sting(刺す)こともある. beehive も参照.

☛ **honeycomb** のさし絵 ☛ **insect** のさし絵

**beech** /bi:tʃ/ 名 ▶定義1 (または **beech tree**) **C** a large tree that produces small three-sided nuts 小さな三面体の木の実がなる大きな木→**ブナ, ブナの木** ▶定義2 Ⓤ the wood from this tree この木から取れる木材→**ブナ材**

*****beef** /bi:f/ 名 Ⓤ ▶定義 the meat from a cow 牛の肉→**牛肉** ‖ *a slice of roast beef* ローストビーフ1切れ ☛参 **meat** の注

**beefburger** /bí:fbɜ̀ːrɡər/ 名 **C** ▶定義 beef that has been cut up small and pressed into a flat round shape 細かく刻んで, 平たい円形に固められた牛肉→**ハンバーガー** ☛参 **hamburger**

**beefy** /bí:fi/ 形 ▶定義 having a strong body with big muscles たくましい筋肉の付いた強い体を持っている→**肉付きの良い, 筋骨たくましい**

**beehive** /bí:hàɪv/ (または **hive**) 名 **C** ▶定義 a

type of box that people use for keeping bees in 人々がミツバチを入れておくために使う, 箱の一種→ミツバチの巣箱

\*been /bɪn; biːn/ BE, GO¹ の過去分詞
▶ been は, be と go 両方の過去分詞として用いられる: *I've never been seriously ill.* (私は深刻な病気になったことがない.) *I've never been to Lisbon.* (私はリスボンへ行ったことがない.) gone もまた go の過去分詞である. 意味の違いに注意: *I'm cold because I've just been outside (= I'm here now).* (ついさっきまで外に出ていたので (= 今, 私はここにいる), 寒い.) *Jim's not here, I'm afraid - he's just gone out (= he's not here now).* (悪いけど, ジムはここにいないよ — ちょうど出掛けてしまったんだ (= 今, 彼はここにいない).)

**beep** /biːp/ 名 C ▶定義 **beep beep** a short high noise, for example made by the horn of a car 例えば自動車の警笛の音のような, 短く高い音 びーっと鳴る音 — beep 動 自 他 →びーっと鳴る, 鳴らす ‖ *I beeped my horn at the dog, but it wouldn't get off the road.* 犬に向かって警笛を鳴らしたが, 犬は道から離れようとしなかった.

**beeper** /ˈbiːpər/ 米 ⇒ BLEEPER

\*beer /bɪər/ 名 ▶定義 1 U a type of alcoholic drink that is made from grain 穀粒から作られるアルコール飲料の一種→ビール ▶定義 2 C a type or glass of beer ビールの一種または1杯→~ビール, 1 杯のビール

▶ lager (ラガー) は冷やして飲まれる, 明るい色のビール. bitter (ビター) は, 室温で飲まれる, 黒っぽいビール. shandy (シャンディー) はレモネードを混ぜたビール.

---

**▶日本語 vs 英語**

**イギリスの beer のいろいろ**

英国では beer の種類が多いですが, 日本語のビールに当たるものは英国でも冷やして飲まれる lager です. また英国では ale と言う場合がありますが, ほぼ同意語で用いられることが多いです. なお, 英国のパブでの one bitter は one pint of bitter のことになります.

---

**beetle** /ˈbiːtl/ 名 C ▶定義 an insect, often large, shiny and black, with a hard case on its back covering all its wings. There are many different types of beetle. しばしば大きく, 黒く光っていて背中に羽を覆う硬い殻のある昆虫. 多くの異なる種類がいる→甲虫 ☞ **insect** のさし絵

**beetroot** /ˈbiːtruːt/ (米 **beet**) 名 C U ▶定義 a dark red vegetable which is the root of a plant. Beetroot is cooked and can be eaten hot or cold. 植物の根である暗赤色の野菜. 調理して, 温めても冷やしても食べられる→ビートの根, 砂糖大根, 赤かぶ ☞ C3 ページのさし絵

**befall** /bɪˈfɔːl/ 動 自 (過 **befell** /bɪˈfel/; 過分 **befallen** /bɪˈfɔːlən/) (文) ▶定義 (used about sth bad) to happen to sb (悪い~について) …に起きる→~に降り懸かる, 起こる

\*before¹ /bɪˈfɔːr/ 前置 ▶定義 1 earlier than sb/sth; earlier than the time that ~よりも早い; ~の時間よりも早い→~の前に, ~より先に ‖ *You can call me any time before 10 o'clock.* 10 時前ならいつでも電話していいよ. *the week before last* 先々週 *They should be here before long (= soon).* 彼らはほどなく (= 間もなく) ここに来るはずだ. *Turn the lights off before you leave.* 出掛ける前に電気を消しなさい. ▶定義 2 in front of sb/sth (in an order) (順番で) ~の前に→~の前に, ~に優先して ‖ *'H' comes before 'N' in the alphabet.* アルファベットでは, H は N の前に来る. *A very difficult task lies before us.* 私たちの前にはとても難しい課題がある. *a company that puts profit before safety (= thinks profit is more important than safety)* 安全よりも利益を優先する (= 安全よりも利益が重要だと考える) 会社 ▶定義 3 正式 in a position in front of sb/sth ~の前の位置に→~の前に, ~の面前に, ~の前途に, ~の目前に ‖ *They knelt before the altar.* 彼らは祭壇の前にひざまずいた. *You will appear before the judge tomorrow.* 明日裁判官の前に出廷しなさい. ▶定義 4 rather than ~よりむしろ→(~する)よりむしろ ‖ *I'd die before I apologized to him!* 彼に謝るくらいなら, 死んだ方がましだ.

\*before²  /bɪˈfɔːr/ 副 ▶定義 at an earlier time; already 早い時間に; 既に→前に, 以前に, かつて ‖ *I think we've met somewhere before.* 私は以前どこかで会ったと思う. *It was fine yesterday but it rained the day before.* 昨日は天気が良

かったが,おとといは雨が降った.

**beforehand** /bɪfɔ́ːrhænd/ ▶定義 at an earlier time than sth ～よりも早いときに→**前もって,あらかじめ** ‖ *If you visit us, phone beforehand to make sure we're in.* 私たちを訪ねるのなら,あらかじめ電話して私たちがいることを確かめてください.

**befriend** /bɪfrénd/ 動 他 (文) ▶定義 to become sb's friend; to be kind to sb ～の友達になる;～に親切にする→**(弱い者や貧しい人の)友・味方になる,力になる**

**beg** /beg/ 動 自 他 (**begging**; **begged**) ▶定義1 beg (sb) for sth; beg sth (of/from sb); beg (sb) to do sth to ask sb for sth strongly, or with great emotion ～に…を強くまたは強い感情をもって頼む→**請う,頼む,懇願する** ‖ *He begged for forgiveness.* 彼は許しを請うた. *We begged him to lend us the money.* 私たちは彼に金を貸してくれるよう頼んだ. ☞類 **entreat, implore** ▶定義2 beg (for) sth (from sb) to ask people for food, money, etc because you are very poor 非常に貧しいので,人々に食べ物や金などを要求する→**施しを請う,こじきをする** ‖ *There are people begging for food in the streets.* 通りには食べ物を請う人々がいる.

成句 I beg your pardon 正式 ▶定義1 I am sorry. →**ごめんなさい,失礼しました** ‖ *I beg your pardon. I picked up your bag by mistake.* ごめんなさい.間違ってあなたのバッグを取りました. ▶定義2 used for asking sb to repeat sth because you did not hear it properly きちんと聞こえなかったために,～に…を繰り返してくれるよう頼むのに用いて→**恐れ入りますが,もう一度おっしゃってください(この場合は文末を上げて言う)**

**began** BEGIN の過去形

**beggar** /bégər/ 名 C ▶定義 a person who lives by asking people for money, food, etc on the streets 通りで人々に金,食べ物などを要求して生活している人→**こじき**

*****begin** /bɪgín/ 動 (現分 **beginning**; 過 **began** /bɪgǽn/; 過分 **begun** /bɪgʌ́n/) ▶定義1 自 他 to start doing sth; to do the first part of sth ～をし始める;～の最初の部分をする→**始める; 着手する** ‖ *Shall I begin or will you?* 私が始めますか,それともあなたが始めますか. *I began (= started reading) this novel last month and I still haven't finished it.* 私は先月この小説に取り掛かった(= 読み始めた)が,まだ終わっていない. *When did he begin his lesson?* 彼はいつ稽古(けいこ)を始めたの. *When do you begin work?* いつ仕事を始めるのですか. *We began writing to each other in 1980.* 私たちは1980年に文通を始めた. *The carpet is beginning to look dirty.* カーペットが汚れ始めている. ▶定義2 自 to start to happen or exist, especially from a particular time 特に特定の時間から起こり始める,または存在し始める→**始まる** ‖ *What time does the concert begin?* コンサートは何時に始まりますか. ▶定義3 自 begin (with sth) to start in a particular way, with a particular event, or in a particular place 特定の方法で,特定の出来事と共に,または特定の場所で始まる→**始まる** ‖ *My name begins with 'W' not 'V'.* 私の名前は,V ではなく,W で始まる. *The fighting began with an argument about money.* けんかは,金についての口論から始まった. *This is where the footpath begins.* ここがその小道の始まる所です.

▶ begin と start は,意味はとてもよく似ているが,start の方が略式の会話でより頻繁に使われる.いずれも to または -ing 形の動詞が後に続く: *The baby began/started crying/to cry.* (赤ん坊は泣き始めた.) begin や start 自体が -ing 形のときには,後に to が続かなければならない: *The baby was just beginning/starting to cry.* (赤ん坊はちょうど泣き始めたところだった.) いくつかの意味では,start だけが使われる: *I couldn't start the car.* (車を発進できなかった.) *We'll have to start (= leave) early if we want to be in Dover by 8 o'clock.* (8時までにドーバーに着きたいなら,私たちは早く出発し(= 出掛け)なければならないだろう.)

成句 to begin with ▶定義1 at first 最初に→**最初(のうち)は** ‖ *To begin with they were very happy.* 最初のうちは,彼らはとても幸せだった. ▶定義2 used for giving your first reason for sth or to introduce your first point ～についての1番目の理由を伝えるために,または1番目の考えを伝えるために用いて→**まず第1に** ‖ *We can't possibly go. To begin with it's too far and we can't afford it either.* 私たちはどうしても行かれない.まず第1に遠すぎるし,その余裕も

ない. — beginner [名] [C] ➜初心者, 初学者

***beginning** /bɪɡínɪŋ/ [名] [C] ▶定義 the first part of sth; the time when or the place where sth starts ～の最初の部分; ～が始まる時間や場所➜**最初, 初めの部分; 起源, 起こり** ‖ *I've read the article* ***from beginning to end.*** 私はその記事を最初から最後まで読んだ. *We're going away* ***at the beginning of*** *the school holidays.* 学校の休みの初めに, 私たちは出掛ける.

**begrudge** /bɪɡrʌ́dʒ/ [動] [他] begrudge (sb) sth ▶定義1 to feel angry or upset because sb has sth that you think that he/she should not have ～が持つべきでないと自分が思う…を持っているために, 怒る, またはうろたえる➜**～をねたむ** ‖ *He's worked hard. I don't begrudge him his success.* 彼はよく働いている. 私は彼の成功をねたまない. ▶定義2 to be unhappy that you have to do sth 自分が～をしなければならないことがうれしくない➜**～を出し渋る, 嫌がる** ‖ *I begrudge paying so much money in tax each month.* 月ごとにこんなにたくさんの税金を払うのは嫌だ.

**behalf** /bɪhɑ́ːf; -hǽf/ [名]

[成句] on behalf of sb; on sb's behalf ▶定義 for sb; as the representative of sb ～のために; ～の代理として➜**～のために; ～に代わって, ～を代表して** ‖ *Emma couldn't be present so her husband accepted the prize on her behalf.* エマは出席できなかったので, 夫が代わりに賞を受け取った. *I would like to thank you all on behalf of my colleagues and myself.* 私自身と私の同僚を代表して, 皆様方にお礼が言いたい.

***behave** /bɪhéɪv/ [動] ▶定義1 [自] behave well, badly, etc (towards sb) to act in a particular way 特定の方法で行動する➜**振る舞う** ‖ *Don't you think that Ellen has been behaving very strangely recently?* 最近エレンの行動はとても変だと思わないかい. *I think you behaved very badly towards your father.* あなたの父親に対する振る舞いは非常に悪かったと思うよ. *He* ***behaves as if/though*** *he was the boss.* 彼はあたかも自分がボスであるように振る舞う. ▶定義2 [自][他] behave (yourself) to act in the correct or appropriate way 正しいまたは適切な方式で行動する➜**行儀良くする** ‖ *I want you to behave yourselves while we're away.* 私たちが出掛けている間, あなたたちは行儀良くしていてね. ⇔ **misbehave** ▶定義3 **-behaved** (複合形容詞を作るために用いて) behaving in the way mentioned 言及された方法で振る舞っている➜**行儀が～な** ‖ *a well-behaved child* 行儀の良い子供 *a badly-behaved class* 行儀の悪いクラス

***behaviour** ([米] **behavior**) /bɪhéɪvjər/ [名] [U] ▶定義 the way that you act or behave 自分が行動するまたは振る舞う方法➜**振る舞い, 行儀, 態度** ‖ *He was sent out of the class for bad behaviour.* 彼は態度が悪いので教室を追い出された.

***behind** /bɪhάɪnd/ [前] [副] ▶定義1 in, at or to the back of sb/sth ～の後ろで[に・へ] ➜**～の後ろに[へ]** ‖ *There's a small garden behind the house.* 家の後ろに小さな庭がある. *The sun went behind a cloud.* 太陽は雲の後ろに隠れた. *You go on ahead. I'll follow on behind.* あなたが先に行ってくれ. 私は後に付いていく. *Look behind you before you drive off.* 走り出す前に後ろを見なさい. *He ran off but the police were close behind.* 彼は逃げたが, 警察はすぐ後ろに迫っていた. ▶定義2 behind (in/with) (sth) later or less good than sb/sth; making less progress than sb/sth ～よりも遅れて, または良くない; ～よりも進んでいない➜**遅れて, 劣って, 滞って** ‖ *The train is twenty minutes behind schedule.* 電車は定刻より20分遅れている. *Jane is behind the rest of the class in maths.* ジェーンは数学でクラスのほかの生徒より劣っている. *We are a month behind with the rent.* 私たちは家賃の支払いを1か月滞らせている. ☛参 **ahead** ▶定義3 supporting or agreeing with sb/sth ～を支える, またはそれらに同意する➜**～に味方して, ～を支持して, ～を後援して** ‖ *Whatever she decides, her family will be behind her.* 彼女が何を決めようとも, 彼女の家族は味方するだろう. ▶定義4 responsible for causing or starting sth ～を引き起こした, または始めたことについて責任がある➜**～の原因となって, ～の背後に, ～の陰に** ‖ *What is the reason behind his sudden change of opinion?* 彼が急に意見を変えた裏の理由は何だろう. ▶定義5 used to say that sth is in sb's past ～が…の過去に存在することを言うために用いて➜**～にとって過ぎ去って, 終わって** ‖ *It's time you* ***put*** *your* problems **behind you** (= forgot about them). あなたの問題を終わらせる（= それらについて忘れる）ときだ. ▶定義**6** in the place where sb/sth is or was ～がいるか、あるいはいた場所に→～の後に（残して、とどまって、など）‖ *Oh no! I've left the tickets* **behind** (= at home). あっ、いけない. チケットを置いてきてしまった（= 家に）.

**beige** /beɪʒ/ 形名 ❶ ▶定義 (of) a light brown colour 明るい茶色(の)→ベージュ色(の), 淡い灰褐色(の)

**being**¹ ⇒ BE

**being**² /bíːɪŋ/ 名 ▶定義**1** ❶ the state of existing; existence 存在している状態; 存在→生きていること, 存在 ‖ *When did the organization come into* **being**? その組織はいつできたの. ▶定義**2** ❻ a living person or thing 生きている人や物→人間, 生き物 ‖ *a human* **being** 人間

**belated** /bɪléɪtɪd/ 形 ▶定義 coming late 遅れて来て→遅れた ‖ *a* **belated** *apology* 遅まきの謝罪 ― **belatedly** 副 →遅れて, 遅まきながら ‖ *They have realized, rather* **belatedly**, *that they have made a mistake.* 彼らは、やや遅まきながら自分たちが間違いを犯したことに気付いた.

**belch** /beltʃ/ 動 ▶定義**1** ❺ to let gas out from your stomach through your mouth with a sudden noise 突然の音と共に、胃にある気体を口から出す→ゲップする ▶定義**2** ❻ to send out a lot of smoke, etc たくさんの煙などを送り出す→～を噴出する ‖ *The volcano* **belched** *smoke and ashes.* 火山は煙と灰を噴出した.
— **belch** 名 ❻→ゲップ, 噴出

**belie** /bɪláɪ/ 動 (現分 **belying**; 三単現 **belies**; 過, 過分 **belied**) ▶定義 to give an idea of sth that is false or not true 誤ったまたは事実ではない～についての考えを伝える→～を偽って示す・伝える ‖ *His smiling face* **belied** *his true feelings.* 彼の笑顔は、彼の本当の気持ちを偽っていた.

*****belief** /bɪlíːf/ 名 ▶定義**1** [単数扱い, ❶] **belief in sb/sth** a feeling that sb/sth is true, morally good or right, or that sb/sth really exists ～が真実であり、道徳的に良いまたは正しいという感情, または～が本当に存在するという感情→信じること, 信念, (～の存在の)確信 ‖ *She has lost her* **belief** *in God.* 彼女は神の存在に確信を失った. ☞参 **disbelief** ▶定義**2** [単数扱い, ❶]

# believe 135

正式 **belief (that...)** something you accept as true; what you believe 自分が真実として受け入れているもの; 信じていること→～という信念, 考え, 意見 ‖ *It's my* **belief** *that people are basically good.* 人間は基本的に善良だというのが私の信念である. *There is a general* **belief** *that things will soon get better.* 物事は間もなく良くなるだろうというのが一般的な意見だ. *Contrary to popular* **belief** (= in spite of what many people think) *the north of the country is not poorer than the south.* 一般的に考えられている事とは反対には(= 多くの人々が考えているにもかかわらず), その国の北部は南部よりも貧しくない. ▶定義**3** ❻ an idea about religion, politics, etc 宗教, 政治などについての考え→信仰, 信条 ‖ *Divorce is contrary to their religious* **beliefs**. 離婚は彼らの宗教的な信条に反する.

成句 **beyond belief** ▶定義 (in a way that is) too great, difficult, etc to be believed 信じるにはあまりに偉大すぎる, 難しすぎるなど(という見方で)→信じられないほどの[に] ‖ *The amount of money we owe has increased* **beyond belief**. 私たちが借りている金は信じられないほど増えている.

**believable** /bɪlíːvəb(ə)l/ 形 ▶定義 that can be believed 信じられる→信じられる, 信用できる ⇔ **unbelievable**

*****believe** /bɪlíːv/ 動 (進行形は不可) ▶定義**1** ❻ to feel sure that sth is true or that sb is telling the truth ～が真実である、または～が確かに本当の事を言っていると感じる→～を信じる, ～と(確信を持って)思う ‖ *He said he hadn't taken any money but I didn't* **believe** *him.* 彼は金を全く取らなかったと言ったが, 私は彼を信じなかった. *Nobody* **believes** *a word she says.* だれも彼女の言葉を信じない. ⇔ **disbelieve** ▶定義**2** ❻ **believe (that) ...** to think that sth is true or possible, although you are not certain 確信はないけれども, ～が真実または可能だと考える→～と思う, ～と考える ‖ *I* **believe** *they have moved to Italy.* 彼らはイタリアに移ったと思う. *'Does Pat still work there?' '***I believe so**.*'* 「パットはまだそこで働いているの」「そう思うよ」*The escaped prisoner is* **believed** *to be in this area.* 脱走した囚人はこの地域にいると思

## believer

われている. *Four people are still missing, believed drowned.* 4人がまだ見つかっていないが,溺死(できし)したと思われている. ▶定義3 **don't/can't believe sth** used to show anger or surprise at sth 〜への怒りや驚きを示すために用いて→**信じられない** ∥ *I can't believe (that) you're telling me to do it again!* 私にそれをもう一度するようにあなたが言うなんて,信じられない. ▶定義4 ● to have religious beliefs 宗教的信仰を持っている→信仰を持つ,信じる

▶この動詞は進行形では使われないが,現在分詞(= -ing 形)は一般に見られる: *Believing the house to be empty, she quietly let herself in.*(その家は空き家だと思ったので,彼女は静かに中に入った.)

成句 **believe it or not** ▶定義 it may be surprising but it is true 驚くかもしれないがほんとのことだ→**まさかと思うだろうが,うそのような話だが** ∥ *Believe it or not, English food can sometimes be quite good.* まさかと思うだろうが,英国の食べ物はしばしばかなりおいしい.

**give sb to believe/understand (that)** ▶定義 (しばしば受動態で) to give sb the impression or idea that sth is true 〜が事実だという印象または考えを…に与える→**〜と信じさせる,思わせる** ∥ *I was given to believe that I had got the job.* 私は仕事に就いたと周りに思われた.

句動詞 **believe in sb/sth** ▶定義 to be sure that sb/sth exists 〜が存在すると確信する→**〜の存在を信じる** ∥ *Do you believe in God?* あなたは神の存在を信じますか. *Most young children believe in Father Christmas.* ほとんどの幼い子供たちはサンタクロースの存在を信じている.

**believe in sb/sth; believe in doing sth** ▶定義 to think that sb/sth is good or right 〜が善いまたは正しいと考える→**〜を信頼する,信じる** ∥ *They need a leader they can believe in.* 彼らは信頼できる指導者を必要としている. *He doesn't believe in killing animals for their fur.* 彼は毛皮のために動物を殺すことが正しいとは信じていない.

**believer** /bɪlíːvər/ 名 C ▶定義 a person who has religious beliefs 宗教的信仰を持つ人→**信者**

成句 **be a (great/firm) believer in sth** ▶定義 to think that sth is good or right 〜が良いまたは正しいと信じる→**〜の(熱烈な)信奉者** ∥ *He is a great believer in getting things done on time.* 彼は,物事を時間通りに行うことの熱烈な信奉者だ.

**belittle** /bɪlítl/ 動 ● ▶定義 to make sb or the things he/she does, seem unimportant or not very good 〜または…のする事が,重要でないまたはあまり良くは思えないようにする→**〜を小さくする,〜を小さく見せる**

*bell /bel/ 名 C ▶定義1 a metal object, often shaped like a cup, that makes a ringing sound when it is hit by a small piece of metal inside it しばしばおわんの形をした金属製の物体で,中にある小さな金属片が当たると鳴り響く→**鈴,呼び鈴,鐘** ∥ *the sound of church bells* 教会の鐘の音 *Her voice came back clear as a bell.* 彼女の声が鐘の音のようにはっきりと伝わってきた. ☞ S7 ページのさし絵 ▶定義2 an electrical device that makes a ringing sound when the button on it is pushed; the sound that it makes ボタンが押されると,鳴り響くような音を出す電気装置;それが出す音→**ベル;ベルの音** ∥ *Ring the doorbell and see if they're in.* 戸口のベルを鳴らして,彼らがいるかどうかを確かめなさい.

成句 **ring a bell** ⇒ RING²

**bellow** /béloʊ/ 動 ▶定義1 ● ● **bellow (sth) (at sb)** to shout in a loud deep voice, especially because you are angry 特に怒っているせいで,大きな太い声で叫ぶ→**どなる,どなり声で言う** ▶定義2 ● to make a deep low sound, like an animal (a bull) 動物(雄牛)のように,太く低い音を出す→**大声で鳴く,ほえる** ― bellow 名 C→**鳴き声,ほえ声,どなり声**

**belly** /béli/ 名 C (複 **bellies**) ▶定義 the stomach or the front part of your body between your chest and your legs 腹部,または胸と足の間に位置する体の前の部分→**腹,腹部,胃腸**

**belly button** 略式 = NAVEL

*belong /bɪlɔ́(ː)ŋ, -láŋ/ 動 ● ▶定義1 **belong to sb** to be owned by sb 〜によって所有されている→**(〜の)ものである,所有物である** ∥ *Who does this pen belong to?* このペンはだれのものですか. *Don't take anything that doesn't belong to you.* 自分のものでない物は取ってはいけない. ▶定義2 **belong to sth** to be a member of a group or organization 集団や組織の一員である→**所属する, 属する** ‖ *Do you belong to any political party?* あなたはどこかの政党に属していますか. ▶定義**3** to have a right or usual place 正しいまたはいつもの位置にある→**ある, いる** ‖ *The plates belong in the cupboard over there.* 皿はそこの食器棚の中に置いてある. *It took quite a long time before we felt we belonged in the village (= until we felt comfortable).* 私たちがその村になじむまで(= 快適だと感じるまで), かなり長い時間がかかった.

**belongings** /bɪlɔ́ːŋɪŋz, -lɑŋ-/ 名 [複数扱い] ▶定義 the things that you own that can be moved, that is, not land and buildings 土地や建物ではない, 自分が所有する, 動かせる物→**所有物, 財産, 動産** ‖ *They lost all their belongings in the fire.* 彼らは火事ですべての財産を失った.

**beloved** /bɪlʌ́v(ə)d/ 形 正式 ▶定義 much loved 非常に愛された→**最愛の, いとしい** ‖ *They had always intended to return to their beloved Ireland.* 彼らはいつも, 愛するアイルランドに帰るつもりでいた.

➤ 名詞の前に beloved が来るときは, /bɪlʌ́vɪd/ と発音される.

\*ෆ**below** /bɪlóʊ/ 前 副 ▶定義 at or to a lower position or level than sb/sth 〜よりも低い位置またはレベルで[へ]→**〜より下に[へ], 〜の下に[へ]** ‖ *Do not write below this line.* この線の下には書かないでください. *The temperature fell below freezing during the night.* 夜中に気温は氷点下まで下がった. *Her marks in the exam were below average.* 彼女のテストの点数は平均より低かった. *I don't live on the top floor. I live on the floor below.* 私は最上階には住んでいない. 下の階に住んでいる. *temperatures of 30°C and below* 30度以下の温度 ☛参 **under** の注 ⇔ **above**

\*ෆ**belt**¹ /belt/ 名 C ▶定義**1** a thin piece of cloth, leather, etc that you wear around your waist 腰の回りに締める細い布, 皮など→**ベルト, 帯** ‖ *I need a belt to keep these trousers up.* このズボンがずり下がらないように, ベルトが必要だ. ☛ C6ページのさし絵 ☛参 **seat belt** ▶定義**2** a long narrow piece of rubber, cloth, etc in a circle, that is used for carrying things along or for making parts of a machine move 物を運ぶため, または機械の部品を動かすために使われる輪になった細長いゴム, 布など→**ベルト** ‖ *The suitcases were carried round on a conveyor belt.* スーツケースはベルトコンベヤーで運ばれていた. *the fan belt of a car (= that operates the machinery that cools a car engine)* 自動車のファンベルト(= 自動車のエンジンの冷却ファンを回転させる) ▶定義**3** an area of land that has a particular quality or where a particular group of people live 特定の質を持つ, または特定の人々の集団が住む土地の区域→**地帯** ‖ *the green belt around London (= an area of countryside where you are not allowed to build houses, factories, etc)* ロンドン周辺の緑地帯(= 家, 工場などを建てることが許されない田舎の地域) *the commuter belt* 通勤者の住んでいる地域, 住居地帯

成句 **below the belt** 略式 ▶定義 unfair or cruel 不正な, または残酷な→**ルール違反の, 不正な, 卑劣な** ‖ *That remark was rather below the belt.* その所見はかなり不当なものだった.

**tighten your belt** ⇒ **TIGHTEN**

**under your belt** 略式 ▶定義 that you have already done or achieved 既に行った, または達成した→**〜を達成済みで, 経験済みで, 完成させて** ‖ *She's already got four tournament wins under her belt.* 彼女は既に4つのトーナメントでの優勝を経験している.

**belt**² /belt/ 動 略式 ▶定義**1** 他 to hit sb hard 〜を強く打つ→**〜を激しく打つ, 〜をひっぱたく, 殴り付ける** ▶定義**2** 自 to run or go somewhere very fast 非常に速くどこかへ走るまたは行く→**疾走する, 突っ走る** ‖ *I was belting along on my bicycle.* 私は自転車で疾走していた.

句動詞 **belt sth out** ▶定義 to sing, shout or play sth loudly 〜を大きな声で歌う, 叫ぶ, または大きな音で演奏する→**〜を大声で歌う, 大きな音で演奏する** ‖ *In the restaurant, loudspeakers were belting out Spanish pop music.* レストランでは, スピーカーからスペインのポピュラー音楽が大きな音で流れていた.

**belt up**(俗語) ▶定義 used to tell sb rudely to be quiet 〜に静かにするよう, ぞんざいに言うときに用いて→**静かにする, 話をやめる** ‖ *Belt up! I can't think with all this noise.* 静かにしろ. こんなに騒々しかったら考えることができない.

**bemused** /bɪmjúːzd/ 形 ▶定義 confused and unable to think clearly 混乱して、はっきりと考えることができない→ぼーっとした、当惑した

\***bench** /bentʃ/ 名 ⓒ ▶定義1 a long wooden or metal seat for two or more people, often outdoors しばしば屋外にある、2人以上の人々のための木製または金属製の長い座席→ベンチ ‖ *a park bench* 公園のベンチ ▶定義2 (in the British parliament) the seats where a particular group of politicians sit (英国の議会で)特定の政治家の集団が座る座席→議席、議員席 ‖ *the Government front bench* 内閣の正面席 *the Labour back benches* 労働党の後方の議員席 ▶定義3 a long narrow table that people work at; for example, in a factory 仕事をする細長いテーブル; 例えば工場で→仕事台、作業台

**benchmark** /béntʃmɑːrk/ 名 ⓒ ▶定義 a standard that other things can be compared to ほかのものと比較できる標準→水準標準、基準 ‖ *These new safety features set a benchmark for other manufacturers to follow.* これらの新しい安全機能は、ほかのメーカーも従うべき基準になっている.

\***bend**¹ /bend/ 動 (過, 過分 **bent** /bent/) ▶定義1 Ⓣ to make sth that was straight into a curved shape まっすぐの~を曲がった形にする→~を曲げる ‖ *to bend a piece of wire into an S shape* 針金をS字型に曲げる *It hurts when I bend my knee.* ひざを曲げると痛い. ▶定義2 Ⓘ to be or become curved 曲がっている、または曲がったようになる→曲がる、たわむ ‖ *The road bends to the left here.* その道はここで左に折れている. ▶定義3 Ⓘ to move your body forwards and downwards 体を前方へそして下へ動かす→かがむ ‖ *He bent down to tie up his shoelaces.* 彼は靴ひもを結ぶために身をかがめた. ☞ S1 ページのさし絵

成句 **bend the rules** ▶定義 to do sth that is not normally allowed by the rules 普通は規則によって許されていない~をする→規則を曲げる

\***bend**² /bend/ 名 ⓒ ▶定義 a curve or turn, for example in a road 例えば道の、カーブや曲がり角→カーブ、曲がり ‖ *a sharp bend in the road* 道路の急カーブ

成句 **round the bend** 略式 ▶定義 crazy; mad 狂った; 正気でない→頭がおかしくなって ‖ *His behaviour is driving me round the bend* (= annoying me very much). 彼の振る舞いに私は頭がおかしくなりそうだ (= 私を非常に困らせる).

\***beneath** /bɪníːθ/ 前副 ▶定義1 in, at or to a lower position from sb/sth; under ~よりも低い位置に[で・へ]; ~の下に→~の下に[で] ‖ *The ship disappeared beneath the waves.* その船は波の下に消えた. *He seemed a nice person but there was a lot of anger beneath the surface.* 彼はすてきな人のように見えた、しかしその穏やかな表情下には深い怒りがあった. ☞参 **under** の注 ▶定義2 not good enough for sb ~にとってちょうど良いのではなくて→~にふさわしくない、~に劣って ‖ *She felt that cleaning for other people was beneath her.* 彼女は、人々のために掃除をすることが自分にふさわしくないと感じた.

**benefactor** /bénəfæktər/ 名 ⓒ ▶定義 a person who helps or gives money to a person or an organization 人または組織を援助する、または金を与える人→恩恵を施す人、後援者、寄贈者

**beneficial** /bènəfíʃ(ə)l/ 形 ▶定義 **beneficial (to sb/sth)** having a good or useful effect 良いまたは有用な効果のある→有益な、有利な ‖ *A good diet is beneficial to health.* 良い食事は健康のために有益だ.

\***benefit**¹ /bénəfɪt/ 名 ▶定義1 Ⓤⓒ an advantage or useful effect that sth has ~が持っている利点または有用な効果→利益、利点、得 ‖ *A change in the law would be to everyone's benefit.* 法の改正は皆の利益になるだろう. *I can't see the benefit of doing things this way.* 物事をこのようにする利点が私には分からない. *the benefits of modern technology* 近代技術の利点 ▶定義2 Ⓤ 英 money that the government gives to people who are ill, poor, unemployed, etc 病気のまたは貧しい、失業しているなどの人々に政府が与える金→給付金、扶助金 ‖ *child/sickness/housing benefit* 児童・疾病・住宅手当 *I'm not entitled to unemployment benefit.* 私は、失業手当を受ける権利がない. ▶定義3 [ⓒ、通常は複数] advantages that you get from your company in addition to the money you earn 稼ぐお金に加えて、自分が勤めている会社から得る利益→手当 ‖ *a company car and other benefits* 会社から支給

される車とそのほかの手当

成句 **for sb's benefit** ▶定義 especially to help, please, etc sb 特に〜を助ける，喜ばせるなどする➡**〜のために** ‖ *For the benefit of the newcomers, I will start again.* 初心者の方のために，もう一度始めます．

**give sb the benefit of the doubt** ▶定義 to believe what sb says although there is no proof that it is true 事実だと証明するものがないが，〜が言うことを信じる➡**疑わしい点は有利・好意的に解釈してやる**

**benefit**² /bénəfɪt/ 動 (**benefiting**; **benefited** または **benefitting**; **benefitted**) ▶定義 **1** 自 to produce a good or useful effect 良い，または有用な効果を生み出す➡**〜の役に立つ，ためになる** ‖ *The new tax laws will benefit people on low wages.* 新しい税法は低所得者にとって有益になるだろう．▶定義 **2** 自 benefit (from sth) to receive an advantage from sth 〜から利益を得る➡**利益を得る** ‖ *Small businesses have benefited from the changes in the law.* 小企業は法の改正により利益を得てきた．

**benevolent** /bənévələnt/ 形 正式 ▶定義 kind, friendly and helpful to others ほかの人に親切であり好意的で，その助けになる➡**優しい，情け深い** — **benevolence** 名 ⓤ➡**慈悲の心，善意**

**benign** /bɪnáɪn/ 形 ▶定義 **1** (used about people) kind or gentle (人について) 親切な，または優しい➡**親切な，優しい** ▶定義 **2** (used about a disease, etc) not dangerous (病気などについて) 危険でない⇔**malignant**

**bent**¹ **BEND**¹ の過去・過去分詞形

**bent**² /bent/ 形 ▶定義 **1** not straight まっすぐでない➡**曲がった** ‖ *Do this exercise with your knees bent.* ひざを曲げてこの運動をしなさい．*This knife is bent.* このナイフは曲がっている．

*It was so funny we were **bent double** with laughter.* それがあまりにもおかしかったので，私たちは身をよじるほど笑った．▶定義 **2** 叙 略式 (used about a person in authority) dishonest; corrupt (権力のある人について) 不正直な；わいろの利く➡**不正な，わいろで左右されやすい** ‖ *a bent policeman* わいろで左右されやすい警官

成句 **bent on sth/on doing sth** ▶定義 wanting to do sth very much; determined 〜をしたいと強く思っている；決心した➡**〜に熱心**

な；固く決心した ‖ *They seem bent on moving house, whatever the difficulties.* どんなに困難でも，彼らは引っ越しをすると固く決心しているようだ．

**bent**³ /bent/ 名 [単数扱い] ▶定義 a bent for sth/doing sth a natural skill at sth or interest in sth 〜に対する生まれながらの技量，または〜への興味➡**適性，好み** ‖ *She has a bent for music.* 彼女は音楽に向いている．

**bequeath** /bɪkwíːθ, -ð/ 動 他 正式 ▶定義 bequeath sth (to sb) to arrange for sth to be given to sb after you have died 死後，〜に…が与えられるように準備する➡**〜を遺言で譲る** ‖ *He bequeathed £1000 to his favourite charity.* 彼は自分の好きな慈善団体に1000ポンドを遺言で譲った．☛ leave の方がより一般的である．

**bequest** /bɪkwést/ 名 ⓒ 正式 ▶定義 something that you arrange to be given to sb after you have died 死後，〜に与えられるように準備した物➡**遺産，遺贈品，形見** ‖ *He left a bequest to each of his grandchildren.* 彼は孫たちのそれぞれに遺産を残した．

**bereaved** /bɪríːvd/ 形 ▶定義 **1** having lost a relative or close friend who has recently died 親戚(しんせき)または親友が最近死亡したため後に残された➡**死なれた** ▶定義 **2** **the bereaved** 名 [複数扱い] the people whose relative or close friend has died recently 親戚(しんせき)または親友を最近亡くした人々➡**遺族，近親を亡くした人たち**

**bereavement** /bɪríːvmənt/ 名 正式 ▶定義 **1** ⓤ the state of having lost a relative or close friend who has recently died 親戚(しんせき)または親友が最近死亡し，その人を失った状態➡**先立たれること，死別** ▶定義 **2** ⓒ the death of a relative or close friend➡**親戚(しんせき)または親友の死** ‖ *There has been a bereavement in the family.* その家族は，身内に不幸があった．

**beret** /béreɪ; bérèɪ/ 名 ⓒ ▶定義 a soft flat round hat 柔らかく，平たく，円い帽子➡**ベレー帽** ☛ **hat** のさし絵

\***berry** /béri/ 名 ⓒ ( 複 **berries**) ▶定義 a small soft fruit with seeds 種のある，小さく柔らかい果物➡**ベリー** ‖ *Those berries are poisonous.* それらのベリーには毒がある．*a raspberry/straw-*

berry/blueberry キイチゴ・イチゴ・ブルーベリー

**berserk** /bərsɚːrk, bər-, -zɚːrk, ̃/ 形 (名詞の前は不可) ▶定義 very angry; crazy 非常に怒った; 狂った→**狂暴な** ‖ *If the teacher finds out what you've done he'll* ***go berserk****.* あなたがした事を先生が見つけたら, 彼は怒り狂うだろう.

**berth** /bɚːrθ/ 名 C ▶定義1 a place for sleeping on a ship or train 船や電車内の眠るための場所→**寝台** ‖ *a cabin with four berths* 寝台が4つある船室 ▶定義2 a place where a ship can stop and stay 船が止まり, 停泊できる場所→**停泊場所**

**beset** /bɪsét/ (現分 **besetting**; 過, 過分 **beset**) 動 他 (文) ▶定義 to affect sb/sth in a bad way 〜に悪い方に影響する→**〜に付きまとう, 〜を悩ます** ‖ *The team has been beset by injuries all season.* そのチームはシーズン中ずっとけがに悩まされた.

***beside** /bɪsáɪd/ 前 ▶定義 at the side of, or next to sb/sth 〜のそばに, または隣に→**〜のそばに, 〜の隣に** ‖ *Come and sit beside me.* こちらに来て私の隣に座りなさい. *He kept his bag close beside him at all times.* いつでも彼はバッグを自分のすぐ隣に置いていた.

成句 **beside the point** ▶定義 not connected with the subject you are discussing 議論している主題に関連していない→**的を外れて**

**beside yourself (with sth)** ▶定義 not able to control yourself because of a very strong emotion とても強い感情のために自分を制御できない→**我を忘れて** ‖ *Emily was almost beside herself with grief.* エミリーは悲しみでほとんど我を忘れていた.

**besides** /bɪsáɪdz/ 前 副 ▶定義 in addition to or as well as sb/sth; also 〜に加えて, または〜と同様に; 〜もまた→**〜に加えて, さらにまた, その上〜のほかに** ‖ *There will be six people coming, besides you and David.* あなたとデーヴィッドのほかに, 6人来るだろう. *I don't want to go out tonight. Besides, I haven't got any money.* 今夜は出掛けたくない. おまけにお金もない.

**besiege** /bɪsíːdʒ/ 動 他 ▶定義1 to surround a place with an army ある場所を軍隊で囲む→**〜を包囲する** ▶定義2 (通常は受動態で) (used about sth unpleasant or annoying) to surround sb/sth in large numbers (不愉快なまたは悩ませる〜について) 〜を多数の…で囲む→**取り囲む, 〜に押し寄せる** ‖ *The actor was besieged by fans and reporters.* その俳優はファンと記者に取り囲まれた.

**besotted** /bɪsátəd/ 形 (名詞の前は不可) ▶定義 **besotted (with/by sb/sth)** so much in love with sb/sth that you cannot think or behave normally 普通に考えたり, または振る舞うことができないほど, 〜を強く愛する→**(酒・麻薬・恋などに)酔った, ぼうっとなった**

***best¹** /best/ 形 ▶定義 (good の最上級) of the highest quality or level; most suitable 最も高い品質または水準の; 最も適した→**最も良い, 最善の, 最上の** ‖ *His latest book is by far his best.* 彼の新しい本は, 彼の最高傑作だ. *I'm going to wear my best shirt to the interview.* 面接には一番良いシャツを着ていこうと思う. *Who in the class is* ***best at*** *maths?* クラスの中でだれが数学で一番ですか. ***It's best to*** *arrive early if you want a good seat.* 良い席を望むなら, 早く着くことが一番良い. *What's the best way to get to York from here?* ここからヨークへ行くためには, 何が最も良い方法ですか. *Who's your* ***best friend****?* あなたの一番の友人はだれですか.

成句 **your best bet** 略式 ▶定義 the most sensible or appropriate thing for you to do in a particular situation 特定の状況で行動する最も賢明な, または適切な事→**最善の策, 最も確実な事・方法** ‖ *There's nowhere to park in the city centre. Your best bet is to go in by bus.* 町の中心には駐車できる場所がない. バスで行くのが最善の策だ.

**the best/better part of sth** ⇒ **PART¹**

***best²** /best/ 副 ▶定義 (well の最上級) to the greatest degree; most 最大級に; 最も→**最も良く, 最も上手に, 一番** ‖ *He works best in the morning.* 彼は午前中に最もよく働く. *Which of these dresses do you like best?* これらの衣装の中で, どれが一番好きですか. *one of Britain's best-loved TV stars* 英国で最も愛されているテレビスターの1人

成句 **as best you can** ▶定義 as well as you can even if it is not perfectly たとえ完ぺきでなくとも, できるだけうまく→**できるだけ, できるだけうまく, どうにかこうにか**

**best**³ /best/ 名[単数扱い] ▶定義 **the best** the person or thing that is of the highest quality or level or better than all others 最も高い質または程度、またはほかのどれよりも良い人あるいは物→**最も良い物・部分・人, 最良, 最上, 最善** ‖ *When you pay that much for a meal you expect the best.* 食事にそれだけ払うなら、最上のものを期待する. *Even the best of us make mistakes sometimes.* 私たちのうちの最も優れた人でも時には間違う. *I think James is the best!* ジェームズが一番だと思う. *They are the best of friends.* 彼らは最良の友達だ. *The best we can hope for is that the situation doesn't get any worse.* 私たちが望めることはせいぜい、状況が悪化しないことだ. ☛参 **second-best**

成句 **all the best** 略式 ▶定義 used when you are saying goodbye to sb and wishing him/her success ～にさようならを言い、その人の成功を願うときに用いて→**ごきげんよう、さようなら、ご健康を祝して、手紙の結びの言葉としても用いられる** ‖ *All the best! Keep in touch, won't you?* さようなら。連絡を取り合おうね.

**at best** ▶定義 if everything goes as well as possible; taking the most hopeful view すべてが可能な限りうまくいったら; 最も希望的な見方をすると→**良くても、せいぜい** ‖ *We won't be able to deliver the goods before March, or, at best, the last week in February.* 私たちは製品を3月より前には出荷できないだろう、いや、良くて2月の最終週だ.

**at its/your best** ▶定義 in its/your best state or condition 最も良い有り様、または状態→**最も良い状態で[の], (桜の花などの)満開で** ‖ *This is an example of Beckett's work at its best.* これは最も良いときのベケットの作品の例です. *No one is at their best first thing in the morning.* 起きたばかりのときは、だれにとっても最高の状態ではない.

**be (all) for the best** ▶定義 to be good in the end even if it does not seem good at first 初めは良いと見えなくても、最後には良い→**結局は一番良い** ‖ *I didn't get the job, but I'm sure it's all for the best.* 仕事は得られなかったが、結局はそれで良かったのだと確信している.

**bring out the best/worst in sb** ▶定義 to show sb's best/worst qualities ～の最良・最悪の質を見せる→**～の性格を明らかにする・引き出す** ‖ *The crisis really brought out the best in Tony.* その危機のせいで本当にトニーの良いところが引き出された.

**do/try your best** ▶定義 to do all or the most that you can 自分ができる事をすべて、または最も多く行う→**全力・最善を尽くす**

**look your best** ▶定義 to look as beautiful or attractive as possible 可能な限り美しくまたは魅力的に見える→**一段立派に見える、よく見える**

**make the best of sth/a bad job** ▶定義 to accept a difficult situation and try to be as happy as possible 難しい状況を受け入れ、できる限り幸せでいようとする→**～を我慢してやっていく、何とかしのぐ**

**best man** 名[単数扱い] ▶定義 a man who helps and supports the man who is getting married (bridegroom) at a wedding 結婚式で結婚する男性(花婿)を助け、力になる男性→**花婿に付き添う男性** ☛参 **wedding**の注

**best-seller** 名 **C** ▶定義 a book or other product that is bought by large numbers of people 多くの人々に買われる本または製品→**ベストセラー** — **best-selling** 形→**ベストセラーの** ‖ *a best-selling novel* ベストセラーの小説

\***bet**¹ /bet/ 動 自 他 (現分 **betting**; 過, 過分 **bet** または **betted**) ▶定義 **1** **bet (sth) (on sth)** to risk money on a race or an event by trying to predict the result. If you are right, you win money. 競争または出来事の結果の予測を試みて、金をかける。もし正しければ金を勝ち取ることができる→**～をかける、かけ事をする** ‖ *I wouldn't bet on them winning the next election.* 私だったら、彼らが次の選挙で勝つことにかけたりしない. *I bet him £10 he couldn't stop smoking for a week.* 私は彼と、彼が1週間禁煙できないと10ポンドのかけをした. ☛類 **gamble, put money on sth** ▶定義 **2** (口語) used to say that you are almost certain that sth is true or that sth will happen ～が真実であるまたは…が起きる、と自分がほぼ確信している事を言うために用いて→**きっと～だと思う、断言する** ‖ *I bet he arrives late - he always does.* 彼はきっと遅れて到着するよ － いつもそうだから. *I bet you're worried about your exam, aren't you?* あなたは試験のことが心配なのだろう、違うかい.

## bet²

成句 you bet (口語) ▶定義 a way of saying 'Yes, of course!'「はい、もちろん」の意味の言い方→もちろん、そうだとも。‖ 'Are you coming too?' 'You bet (I am)!'「あなたも来るかい」「もちろん(行くよ)」

**bet²** /bét/ 名 C ▶定義1 an act of betting かける行為→かけ ‖ Did you **have a bet** on that race? あのレースにかけたのですか. to win/lose a bet かけに勝つ・負ける ▶定義2 an opinion 意見→意見、見当 ‖ My bet is that he's missed the train. 彼は電車に乗り損なっただろうというのが私の意見だ.

成句 your best bet ⇒ **BEST¹**
hedge your bets ⇒ **HEDGE²**

**betide** /bɪtáɪd/ 動
成句 woe betide sb ⇒ **WOE**

**betray** /bɪtréɪ/ 動 他 ▶定義1 to give information about sb/sth to an enemy; to make a secret known ～についての情報を敵に与える；秘密を知らせる→～を漏らす、密告する ‖ She betrayed all the members of the group to the secret police. 彼女はグループの全メンバーを秘密警察に密告した. He refused to betray their plans. 彼は彼らの計画を漏らすことを拒否した. to betray your country 母国を売る ☞参 traitor の注 ▶定義2 to hurt sb who trusts you, especially by not being loyal or faithful to him/her 特に不忠実または不誠実な事をして信じている人を傷付ける→～を裏切る、だます、背く ‖ If you take the money you'll **betray** her **trust**. その金を取ったら、あなたは彼女の信頼を裏切ることになる. When parents get divorced the children often **feel betrayed**. 両親が離婚するとき、子供たちはしばしば裏切られたと感じる. ▶定義3 to show a feeling or quality that you would like to keep hidden 隠しておきたい感情または特質を表す→～を(うっかり)さらけ出す、～がばれる、暴露する ‖ Her steady voice did not betray the emotion she was feeling. 彼女の落ち着いた声は、自分の感情をさらけ出すことがなかった. — betrayal /bɪtréɪ(ə)l/ 名 C U →裏切り、密告

***better¹** /bétər/ 形 ▶定義1 (good の比較級) better than sb/sth of a higher quality or level or more suitable than sb/sth ～よりも高い質や程度の、またはより適した→より良い、もっと良い ‖ I think her second novel was much better than her first. 私は、彼女の2番目の小説は最初のよりずっと良いと思う. He's far better at English than me. 彼は私よりもずっと英語がうまい. It's a long way to drive. It would be better to take the train. 運転していくには長い道のりだ。電車で行った方が良いだろう. You'd be better getting the train than driving. 運転していくより電車に乗った方が良いだろう. ▶定義2 (well の比較級) less ill; fully recovered from an illness 病状がより軽い；病気から完全に回復した→良くなって；全快して ‖ You can't go swimming until you're better. 良くなるまで泳ぎには行けませんよ.

***better²** /bétər/ 副 ▶定義 (well の比較級) in a better way; to a greater or higher degree より良い方法で；程度がより良くまたは高く→もっと良く、より上手に、もっとうまく ‖ I think you could have done this better. あなたはこれをもっとうまくできたと思うよ. Sylvie speaks English better than I do. シルヴィーは私より上手に英語を話す.

成句 (be) better off ▶定義1 to be in a more pleasant or suitable situation より好ましい、または都合の良い状況である→～の方が良い、好ましい ‖ You look terrible. You'd be better off at home in bed. ひどい様子だ。家で寝た方が良い. ▶定義2 (well off の比較級) with more money より多くお金を持つ→以前より裕福になる ‖ We're much better off now I go out to work too. 今は私も働きに出ていて、私たちは以前よりずっと裕福だ.

the best/better part of sth ⇒ **PART¹**
you, etc had better ▶定義 you should; you ought to あなたはすべきだ；あなたはしなければならない→～すべきだ、～するのが良い ‖ I think we'd better go before it gets dark. 私たちは暗くなる前に行くべきだと思う. You'd better take a pen and paper - you might want to take notes. ペンと紙を持っていった方が良い － ひょっとしてメモを取りたくなるかもしれないから.

know better (than that/than to do sth) ⇒ **KNOW¹**
think better of (doing) sth ⇒ **THINK**

***better³** /bétər/ 名 [単数扱い] ▶定義 something that is of higher quality より質の高いもの→よ

り良いもの, もっと良い事 ‖ *The hotel wasn't very good. I must say we'd expected better.* そのホテルはあまり良くなかった. もっと良い所だと私たちは期待したのだが.

**成句** get the better of sb/sth ▶定義 to defeat or be stronger than sb/sth 〜を負かす, またはそれよりも強い→(議論などに)勝つ, (敵・相手などを)負かす ‖ *When we have an argument she always gets the better of me.* 私たちが口論すると, いつも彼女が勝つ.

**betting shop** 名 C ▶定義 a shop where you can go to put money on a race or an event レースやイベントなどに金をかけられる店→私設馬券売り場, かけ屋, ノミ屋 ☞参 **bookmaker's**

### between/among

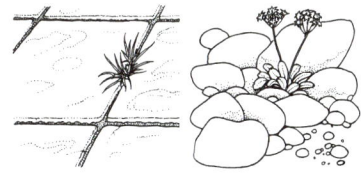

a plant growing **between** the slabs    a plant growing **among** the rocks

\***between** /bɪtwíːn/ 前副 ▶定義1 between A and B; in between in the space in the middle of two things, people, places etc 2つの物, 人々, 場所などの間の空間に→〜の間に[で・を・の], 〜の中間に[で・を・の] ‖ *I was sitting between Sam and Charlie.* 私は, サムとチャーリーの間に座っていた. *a village between Cambridge and Ely* ケンブリッジとイーリーの間の村 *She was standing **in between** the desk **and** the wall.* 彼女は机と壁の間に立っていた. ▶定義2 between A and B; in between (used about two amounts, distances, ages, times, etc) at a point that is greater or later than the first and smaller or earlier than the second; somewhere in the middle (2つの量, 距離, 年齢, 時間などについて)最初の物よりも大きいまたは遅い, 2番目の物よりも小さいまたは早い時点で; 中間のどこか→〜の間に[で・を・の], 〜の中間に[で・を・の] ‖ *They said they would arrive between 4 and 5 o'clock.* 彼らは4時から5時の間に到着するだろうと言った. *They've got this shirt in size 10 and size 16, but nothing in between.* あの店には, このシャツのサイズ10と16はあるが, その間のサイズのものはない. ▶定義3 from one place to another and back again ある場所からほかの場所へ, そしてまた戻る→〜の間を結んで ‖ *There aren't any direct trains between here and Manchester.* こことマンチェスターを結ぶ直通列車はない. ▶定義4 involving or connecting two people, groups or things 2人, 2つの集団または物事を巻き込む, あるいはそれらに関連した→〜の間に[で], 〜に関係する ‖ *There's some sort of disagreement between them.* 彼らの間にはある種の意見の相違がある. *There may be a connection between the two crimes.* その2つの犯罪には関連があるかもしれない. ▶定義5 choosing one and not the other (of two things) (2つのものから)もう一方のものではなく, 1つを選ぶ→〜のうちから1つを ‖ *to choose between two jobs* 2つの仕事から1つを選ぶ *What's the difference between 'some' and 'any'?* some と any の違いは何ですか. ▶定義6 by putting together the actions, efforts, etc of two or more people 2人またはそれ以上の人々の行動, 努力などを合わせて→〜の力を合わせて, 〜が共同で ‖ *Between us we saved up enough money to buy a car.* 私たちは力を合わせて, 車を買えるだけの金をためた. ▶定義7 giving each person a share それぞれの人に分け前を与えて→〜の間で[に] ‖ *The money was divided equally between the two children.* 金は2人の子供の間で均等に分けられた. *We ate all the chocolates between us.* 私たちでチョコレートをすべて食べた.

▶ between は通常2人または2つの物に用いられる: *sitting between her mother and father* (彼女の母と父の間に座って) *between the ages of 12 and 14* (12歳と14歳の間) しかし, between は, 特に(上の)定義7の意味では, 人々または物が独立した個として見なされる場合には, 2人より多い人々または2つより多い物についても用いられる: *We drank a bottle of wine between the three of us.* (私たちは3人でワインを1本飲んだ.) among は, 独立した個としてよりはむしろ集団として見なされている3人以上, 3つより多い物について, いつも用いられる: *You're among friends here.* (ここであなたは友達の中にいる.)

## beverage

> ▶音声とつづり字
>
> betweenを2つに分けると→○be-tween, ×bet-ween
>
> between の語形成は, be < by (= の間に) + tween (= two) の2つの要素から成り立っています. 日本語では tw がつながることがないので, bet-ween と解釈しがちですが, これは誤りです. 英語は子音連結になる傾向があり, twin, twinkle, twenty などに見られるように tw- は1つの子音連結となります. tw- を英語らしく発音するためには t の後に w を発音するのではなく, t を言うときに既に w の特徴である円唇を伴って発音し, また w も t の無声音の影響で無声化して発音すると良いでしょう.

**beverage** /bév(ə)rɪdʒ/ 名 C (文) ▶定義 a drink 飲み物→飲み物, 飲料

**beware** /bɪwéər/ 動 自 (命令形と不定詞だけで) ▶定義 **beware (of sb/sth)** (used for giving a warning) to be careful (警告を与えるために用いて) 気を付ける→**注意する, 用心する, 警戒する** ‖ *Beware of the dog!* (= *written on a sign*) 犬に注意. (= 標識に書かれて) *We were told to beware of strong currents in the sea.* 私たちは, 海中の強い潮流に用心するよう言われた.

**bewilder** /bɪwíldər/ 動 他 ▶定義 to confuse and surprise 混乱させ, 驚かせる→**〜をまごつかせる, うろたえさせる, 当惑させる** ‖ *I was completely bewildered by his sudden change of mood.* 彼の気分が突然変わったので, 私は完全にうろたえてしまった. — bewildered 形→**うろたえた, 当惑した** ‖ *a bewildered expression* 当惑した表情 — bewildering 形→**うろたえさせるような, まごつかせるような** ‖ *a bewildering experience* 当惑するような経験 — bewilderment 名 U→**当惑, うろたえ** ‖ *to stare at sb in bewilderment* 当惑して〜をじっと見る

**bewitch** /bɪwítʃ/ 動 他 ▶定義 to attract and interest sb very much 〜を強く引き付けて興味を持たせる→**魅惑する, うっとりさせる**

***beyond** /bɪjónd, -jánd/ 前 副 ▶定義1 on or to the other side of 〜のもう1つの側に[へ]→**〜の向こうに[へ], 〜を越えた所に[へ]** ‖ *beyond the distant mountains* 遠くの山々の向こうへ *We could see the mountains and the sea beyond.* 山々と海が向こうに見えた. ▶定義2 further than; later than 〜より遠い; 〜より遅い→**〜を越えて; 〜を過ぎて** ‖ *Does the motorway continue beyond Birmingham?* その自動車道路は, バーミンガムの先へ続きますか. *Most people don't go on working beyond the age of 65.* ほとんどの人々は, 65歳を過ぎてまで働き続けない. ▶定義3 more than sth 〜よりも多い→**〜を越えて, 〜以上に, 〜の及ばない** ‖ *The house was far beyond what I could afford.* その家は私には全く手が届かなかった. *I haven't heard anything beyond a few rumours.* いくつかのうわさ以外には何も聞かなかった. ▶定義4 used to say that sth is not possible 〜が可能ではないと言うために用いて→**〜を越えて, 〜以上に, 〜の及ばない** ‖ *The car was completely beyond repair* (= *too badly damaged to repair*). その車は全く修理できない (= 修理するには損傷しすぎた) 状態だった. *The situation is beyond my control.* その状況は私の手には負えない. ▶定義5 too far or too advanced for sb/sth 〜にとって, あまりに遠い, または進んだ→**〜の理解・能力を超えて** ‖ *The activity was beyond the students' abilities.* その活動は生徒たちの能力を超えていた.

成句 **be beyond sb** 略式 ▶定義 to be impossible for sb to understand or imagine 〜にとって理解するまたは想像することが不可能な→**〜には理解できない, 分からない** ‖ *Why she wants to go and live there is quite beyond me.* なぜ彼女がそこに行って暮らしたいのか, 私には全く理解できない.

**bias**¹ /báɪəs/ 名 (複 **biases**) ▶定義1 C U a strong feeling of favour towards or against one group of people, or on one side in an argument, often not based on fair judgement or facts 人の, 一集団または口論している一方への好意, 反感などの, しばしば公正な判断や事実に基づかずに感じる強い感情→**先入観, 偏見, 偏向** ‖ *a bias against women drivers* 女性運転手に対する先入観 *The BBC has been accused of political bias.* BBC は政治的偏向で非難されたことがある. ▶定義2 [C, 通常は単数] an interest in one thing more than others; a special ability ほかのものよりも, ある1つのものに持つ興味; 特別な能力→**(心の) 傾向, 好み, 性癖** ‖ *a course with a strong scientific bias* 強い科学的偏重のある講座

**bias**[2] /báɪəs/ [動][他]( **biasing**; **biased** または **biassing**; **biassed**) ▶定義 to influence sb/sth, especially unfairly; to give an advantage to one group, etc 特に不公正に〜に影響を及ぼす; ある1つの集団などを有利にする➜**〜に偏見を持たせる; 〜を一方に偏らせる** ‖ *Good newspapers should not be biased towards a particular political party.* 良い新聞は特定の政党に偏るべきではない. — **biased** [形]➜**偏見のある, ひいきしている** ‖ *a biased report* 偏った報告書

**bib** /bɪb/ [名] [C] ▶定義 a piece of cloth or plastic that a baby or small child wears under the chin to protect its clothes while it is eating 赤ん坊または幼い子供が食事中に, 衣服を守るためにあごの下に着ける布またはビニール➜**よだれ掛け**

**the Bible** /báɪbl/ [名] [C] ▶定義 the book of great religious importance to Christian and Jewish people キリスト教徒やユダヤ教徒にとって宗教的に極めて重要な本➜**聖書, バイブル** — **biblical** /bíblɪk(ə)l/ [形]➜**聖書の, 聖書から出た**

**bibliography** /bìbliɑ́grəfi/ [名] [C] ([複] **bibliographies**) ▶定義1 a list of the books and articles that a writer used when he/she was writing a particular book or article 作家が特定の本または記事を書いているときに使用した本と記事の一覧表➜**引用文献目録, 参照書目録** ▶定義2 a list of books on a particular subject 特定の主題についての本の一覧表➜**関係書目録**

**bicentenary** /bàɪsentíːnəri/ [名] [C]([複] **bicentenaries**) ([米] **bicentennial** /bàɪsenténiəl/) ▶定義 the day or the year two hundred years after sth happened or began 〜が起きてから, または始まってから, 200年後の日または年➜**200年(記念)祭** ‖ *the bicentenary of the French Revolution* フランス革命200年記念祭

**biceps** /báɪsèps/ [名] [C]([複] **biceps**) ▶定義 the large muscle at the front of the upper part of your arms 上腕部前方の大きな筋肉➜**力こぶ, 二頭筋**

**bicker** /bíkər/ [動][自] ▶定義 to argue about unimportant things ささいな事で議論する➜**口論する** ‖ *My parents are always bickering about money.* 私の両親はいつも金のことで口論している.

***bicycle** /báɪsɪk(ə)l/ (または **bike**) [名] [C] ▶定義 a vehicle with two wheels, which you sit on and ride by moving your legs 人がその上にまたがって座り, 足を動かして乗る, 2つの車輪が付いた乗り物➜**自転車** ☛参 **bike** の注. **cyclist** とは自転車に乗る人である. ☛ S7 ページのさし絵

**bid**[1] /bɪd/ [動] (**bidding**; 過, 過分 **bid**) [自][他] ▶定義 **bid (sth) (for sth)** to offer to pay a particular price for sth, especially at a public sale where things are sold to the person who offers most money (**an auction**) 特に最も多くの金額を申し出た人に品物が売られる競売(オークション)で, 〜に支払う特定の金額を申し出る➜**〜の値を付ける・申し出る** ‖ *I wanted to buy the vase but another man was* ***bidding against*** *me.* その花びんを買いたかったが, ほかの男が私に競り勝とうとしていた. *Somebody bid £5000 for the painting.* だれかがその絵に5000ポンドの値を付けた.

**bid**[2] /bɪd/ [名] [C] ▶定義1 **a bid (for sth); a bid (to do sth)** an effort to do, obtain, etc sth; an attempt 〜をしたり得たりするなどのための努力; 試み➜**努力; 試み** ‖ *His bid for freedom had failed.* 自由を得ようとする彼の努力は失敗した. *Tonight the Ethiopian athlete will* ***make a bid*** *to break the world record.* 今夜, エチオピアの選手が世界記録更新を試みるだろう. ▶定義2 an offer by a person or a business company to pay a certain amount of money for sth 〜に特定の金額を支払うという, 個人または一企業による申し出➜**付け値, 指し値, 入札** ‖ *Granada mounted a hostile* ***takeover bid*** *(= when one company tries to buy another company) for Forte.* グラナダがフォルトに敵対的株式公開買付を仕掛けた(= ある会社が他社を買収しようとするとき). *At the auction we* ***made a bid*** *of £100 for the chair.* 競売で, 私たちはそのいすに100ポンドの値を付けた. ▶定義3 特に [米] = **TENDER**[2] — **bidder** [名] [C]➜**競り手, 入札者** ‖ *The house was sold to the highest bidder (= the person who offered the most money).* その家は最高入札者(= 最も高い金額を申し出た人)に売られた.

**bide** /báɪd/ [動]

[成句] **bide your time** ▶定義 to wait for a good opportunity 良い機会を待つ➜**好機を待つ, 時節の到来を待つ** ‖ *I'll bide my time until the situation improves.* 状況が好転するまで, 機が熟するのを待つよ.

**bidet** /bɪdéɪ, bɪdét; bíːdeɪ/ 名 C ▶定義 a large bowl in the bathroom that you can sit on in order to wash your bottom しりを洗うために腰掛ける浴室にある大きな器→ビデ

**biennial** /baɪéniəl/ 形 ▶定義 happening once every two years 2年に1度起きる→2年ごとの, 2年に1回の

*****big** /bíg/ 形 (**bigger**; **biggest**) ▶定義 **1** large; not small 大きい; 小さくない→大きい, 大型の ‖ *a big house/town/salary* 大きな家・大きな町・高給 *This dress is too big for me.* この服は私には大きすぎる. ▶定義 **2** great or important 偉大な, または重要な→偉大な, 重要な, ものすごい ‖ *They had a big argument yesterday.* 彼らは昨日ものすごい口論をした. *That was the biggest decision I've ever had to make.* それは, これまで私が行った最も重大な決断だった. *some of the big names in Hollywood* ハリウッドの有名人の何人か ▶定義 **3** (名詞の前だけ) 略式 older →年上の ‖ *a big brother/sister* 兄・姉

▶ big と large は, いずれも大きさや数について話すときに用いられる. large はより正式だが, 通常, 人を描写するためには用いられない: *a big/large house* (大きな家) *a baby* (大きな赤ん坊). great は多くの場合, 人やものの重要性, 性質などについて話すときに用いられる: *a great occasion/musician* (大きな行事・偉大な音楽家) また, 不可算名詞と用いて a lot of (たくさんの) の意味を持つ: *great happiness/care/sorrow* (多大な幸福・心配・悲しみ) また, 大きさ, 質などの形容詞を強調するためにも用いられる. great¹(4) を参照.

成句 **Big deal!** 略式 ▶定義 used to say that you think sth is not important or interesting 〜が重要でない, または面白くないと, 自分が考えていることを言うために用いて→(皮肉で)すごいね, そりゃ大したもんだ. ‖ *'Look at my new bike!' 'Big deal! It's not as nice as mine.'* 「私の新しい自転車を見て」「すごいね. 私のほどすてきではないけど」

**a big deal/no big deal** 略式 ▶定義 something that is (not) very important or exciting 非常に [あまり] 重要, または刺激的な [ではない] もの→大したもの・人, 大したことないもの・人 ‖ *Birthday celebrations are a big deal in our family.* 我が家の誕生日の祝いは大したものだ. *A 2% pay increase is no big deal.* 賃金の2パーセント増は大したことではない.

**give sb a big hand** ⇒ **HAND**¹

**bigamy** /bígəmi/ 名 U ▶定義 the crime of being married to two people at the same time 同時に2人と結婚する罪→重婚, 重婚罪 — **bigamist** 名 C ▶重婚者

**big-head** 略式 名 C ▶定義 a person who thinks he/she is very important or clever because of sth he/she has done 自分がした事で, 自分がとても重要または賢いと思っている人→うぬぼれの強い人, うぬぼれ屋 — **big-headed** 形→うぬぼれの強い, うぬぼれた

**big mouth** 略式 名 C ▶定義 a person who talks too much and cannot keep a secret しゃべりすぎて秘密を守れない人→おしゃべりな人, 秘密を守れない人

**bigot** /bígət/ 名 C ▶定義 a person who has very strong and unreasonable opinions and refuses to change them or listen to other people とても強くしかも不合理な意見を持ち, それを変えたりまたは他人の話を聞くことを拒否する人→頑固な偏見を持つ人, 偏狭な人, 屈屈者 ‖ *a religious/racial bigot* 宗教的・民族的偏狭者 — **bigoted** 形→頑固な, 偏狭な, 屈屈な — **bigotry** /bígətri/ 名 U→頑固な偏見, 偏狭, 偏屈

**the big time** 名 [単数扱い] ▶定義 success; fame 成功; 名声→(芸能・スポーツ・政治などにおける) トップの座, 一流 ‖ *This is the role that could help her make it to the big time in Hollywood.* この役こそが, 彼女をハリウッドでトップの座に就かせる助けになるだろう.

**big time**¹ 副 特に 困 (俗語) ▶定義 very much とてもたくさん→とても, 非常に ‖ *You screwed up big time, Wayne!* 君はひどい間違いをしたね, ウェイン.

**big-time**² 形 (名詞の前だけ) ▶定義 important or famous 重要なまたは有名な→一流の, 大物の ‖ *a big-time drug dealer/politician* 大物の麻薬売人・政治屋

*****bike** /báɪk/ 名 C ▶定義 a bicycle or a motorbike 自転車またはオートバイ→自転車, オートバイ ‖ *Hasan's just learnt to ride a bike.* ヘイサンズはちょうど自転車の乗り方を覚えたところだ.

▶自転車やオートバイで行くときには, go on a/your bike または by bike と言う. 動詞

の ride や cycle も使える．
☛ S7 ページのさし絵

**bikini** /bəkíːni/ 图 ⓒ ▶定義 a piece of clothing, in two pieces, that women wear for swimming 女性が泳ぐときに着る，2 つに分かれた水着→ビキニ ☛ C6 ページのさし絵

**bilingual** /baɪlíŋgw(ə)l/ 形 ▶定義1 having or using two languages 2 つの言語を身に付けている，または使っている→2 言語による，2 言語で記述された ‖ *a bilingual dictionary* 2 言語で書かれた辞書 ☛参 **monolingual** ▶定義2 able to speak two languages equally well 2 つの言語を同等にうまく話せる→2 言語を話す ‖ *Our children are bilingual in English and Spanish.* 私たちの子供たちは，英語とスペイン語の 2 言語を話す．

*****bill**¹ /bɪl/ 图 ▶定義1 ⓒ (米 **check**) a piece of paper that shows how much money you owe for goods or services 商品やサービスについて，いくら借りがあるかを示す用紙→請求書，勘定書 ‖ *an electricity bill* 電気代の請求書 *Can I have the bill, please?* (= in a restaurant) 勘定書をもらえますか．(= レストランで) *to pay a bill* 勘定を払う ▶定義2 ⓒ 米 = **NOTE**¹(4) ‖ *a ten-dollar bill* 10 ドル札 ▶定義3 ⓒ a plan for a possible new law 可能な新法の案→**法案，議案** ‖ *The bill was passed/defeated.* その法案は可決された・否決された．▶定義4 [単数扱い] the programme of entertainment offered in a show, concert, etc ショー，コンサートなどで提供される娯楽の催し物→プログラム，出し物 ‖ *Which bands are **on the bill** at the festival?* その祭典にはどの楽団が出ますか．▶定義5 ⓒ a bird's beak 鳥のくちばし→くちばし ☛ C1 ページのさし絵
成句 foot the bill ⇒ **FOOT**²

**bill**² /bɪl/ 動他 (通常は受動態で) ▶定義 **bill sb/sth as sth** to describe sb/sth to the public in an advertisement, etc 〜について公に広告などに書く→印刷物で発表・告知する，番組に組む ‖ *This young player is being billed as 'the new Pele'.* この若い選手は「新ペレ」と発表されている．

**billboard** /bɪ́lbɔːrd/ 图 (英 または **hoarding**) ⓒ ▶定義 a large board near a road where advertisements are put 広告が掲載されている，道のそばの大きな板→広告板，掲示板，看板

**billfold** /bɪ́lfòʊld/ 米 = **WALLET**

**billiards** /bɪ́ljərdz/ 图 Ⓤ ▶定義 a game played on a big table covered with cloth. You use a long stick (*a cue*) to hit three balls against each other and into pockets at the corners and sides of the table. 布で覆われた大きな台の上で行われるゲーム．長い棒(キュー)を使って1つの球を打ち，2つの球に当てて，台の角と横にあるポケットに入れる→ビリヤード，玉突き ‖ *to have a game of/play billiards* ビリヤードをする ☛ billiard がほかの名詞の前に来るときには，s が付かないことに注意する．*a billiard table* ビリヤード台 ☛参 **snooker**, **pool**¹(5)

*****billion** /bɪ́ljən/ 图 ▶定義 1000000000 ‖ *billions of dollars* 数十億ドル
▶数えているとき，billion には s を付けないで使うことに注意する: *three billion yen* (30億円)．かつて billion は，「100 万の 100 万倍」の意味で使われた．現在ではこれを trillion (兆) と言う．数についての説明は，巻末の数についての特別項目を参照．

**billow** /bɪ́loʊ/ 動 ⓘ ▶定義1 to fill with air and move in the wind 空気を満たし，風の中で動く→膨らむ，吹き上がる ‖ *curtains billowing in the breeze* そよ風に揺れるカーテン ▶定義2 to move in large clouds through the air 大気中を大きな雲のように動く→大波が立つ，うねる ‖ *Smoke billowed from the chimneys.* 煙突から煙がもくもくと出ていた．

**bin** /bɪn/ 图 ⓒ ▶定義1 a container that you put rubbish in ごみを入れておく容器→ごみ箱 ‖ *to throw sth in the bin* 〜をごみ箱に投げ入れる *a* *litter bin* くず入れ（困 waste basket）*The dustmen come to empty the bins on Wednesdays.* 清掃員はいつも水曜日にごみ箱を空にしにやって来る. ▶定義2 a container, usually with a lid, for storing bread, flour, etc 通常ふたの付いた, パン, 小麦粉などを貯蔵しておくための容器→**ふた付きの大箱, 貯蔵箱** ‖ *a bread bin* パンの貯蔵箱

**binary system** /báɪnəri sìstəm/ 名［単数扱い］（専門用語）▶定義 a system of numbers using only the numbers 0 and 1. It is used especially with computers. 数字の0と1だけを使う数の体系. 特にコンピューターで使われる→**2進法**

**bind**¹ /báɪnd/ 動他（過, 過分 **bound** /báʊnd/）
▶定義1 bind sb/sth (to sb/sth); bind A and B (together) to tie or fasten with string or rope 糸やひもで縛るまたは固定する→**〜を縛る, くくり付ける, 結ぶ** ‖ *They bound the prisoner's hands behind his back.* 彼らは囚人を後ろ手に縛った. ▶定義2 bind A to B; bind A and B (together) to unite people, organizations, etc so that they live or work together more happily or with better effect 人々や組織などがより幸せに, またはより良い効果を出すよう, 共に生活するまたは働けるように, それらを結び付ける→**結び付ける, 団結させる** ‖ *The two countries are bound together by a common language.* その2国は, 1つの共通の言語で結び付いている. ▶定義3 bind sb (to sth) to force sb to do sth by making him/her promise to do it or by making it his/her duty to do it 〜に…を行うと約束させて, または人がものを行うことを義務として, 〜に…を行うよう強制する→**〜を束縛する, 〜に義務を負わせる, 強制する** ‖ *to be bound by a law/an agreement* 法律・協定によって束縛されている *The contract binds you to completion of the work within two years.* あなたには, 契約により2年以内に仕事を完了させる義務がある. ▶定義4（通常は受動態で）to fasten sheets of paper into a cover to form a book 本を作るために, 紙の束を表紙に固定する→**(原稿など)を製本する, (本)を装丁する** ‖ *The book was bound in leather.* その本は皮で装丁された.

**bind**² /báɪnd/ 名［単数扱い］困 略式 ▶定義 something that you find boring or annoying; a nuisance つまらない, またはいらいらさせると思う物事; 厄介なもの→**嫌な事, 退屈なもの; 苦境** ‖ *I find housework a real bind.* 家事は実に煩わしいものだと思う.

**binding**¹ /báɪndɪŋ/ 形 ▶定義 making it necessary for sb to do sth he/she has promised or to obey a law, etc 約束した〜をすること, または法などに従うことが, …にとって必要な事にして→**束縛する, 拘束力がある, 義務となる** ‖ *This contract is legally binding.* この契約には法的拘束力がある.

**binding**² /báɪndɪŋ/ 名 ▶定義1 ● a cover that holds the pages of a book together 本のページを1つにまとめる覆い→**表紙, 表装** ▶定義2 ● ● material that you fasten to the edge of sth to protect or decorate it 〜を守るまたは飾るために, その端に固定する素材→**(衣類の)縁取り材料** ▶定義3 **bindings**［複数扱い］(used in skiing) a device that fastens a ski boot to a ski (スキーで用いて)スキー靴をスキー板に固定する仕掛け→**ビンディング** ☞ **ski** のさし絵

**binge**¹ /bɪndʒ/ 名 ● 略式 ▶定義 a period of eating or drinking too much 食べすぎたり飲みすぎる時間→**(酒の入った)どんちゃん騒ぎ, したい放題(の振る舞い)** ‖ *to go on a binge* どんちゃん騒ぎする

**binge**² /bɪndʒ/ 動自（現分 **bingeing** または **binging**）略式 ▶定義 binge (on sth) to eat or drink too much, especially without being able to control yourself 特に自分を抑えることができずに, 食べすぎるまたは飲みすぎる→**〜を過食する** ‖ *When she's depressed she binges on chocolate.* 彼女は落ち込むと, チョコレートを食べすぎる.

**bingo** /bíŋɡoʊ/ 名 ● ▶定義 a game in which each player has a different card with numbers on it. The person in charge of the game calls numbers out and the winner is the first player to have all the numbers on their card called out. それぞれの参加者が, 数字の書かれた異なるカードを持つゲーム. ゲームの担当者が数字を読み上げる. そして勝者は読み上げられたすべての数字が自分のカードに最も早かった参加者になる→**ビンゴ(ゲーム)**

**binoculars** /baɪnɔ́kjələr, bə-; -nák-/ 名［複数扱い］▶定義 an instrument with two glass parts (lenses) which you look through in order to

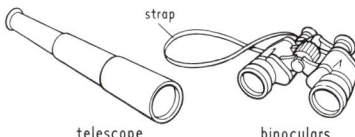

telescope　binoculars

make objects in the distance seem nearer 遠くにある物が近くにあるように見せる2つのガラス(レンズ)が付いた器具→**双眼鏡, オペラグラス** || *a pair of binoculars* 双眼鏡1個 ☛参 **telescope**

**biochemistry** /bàɪoʊkéməstri/ 名 U ▶定義 the study of the chemistry of living things 生物についての化学の研究→**生化学**

**biodegradable** /bàɪoʊdɪɡréɪdəb(ə)l/ 形 ▶定義 that can be absorbed back into the earth naturally and so not harm the environment 自然の作用で地中に吸収される, そのため環境に害のない→**無害物質に還元できる** ⇔ **non-biodegradable**

**biogas** /báɪəɡæs/ 名 U ▶定義 gas produced by natural waste, that can be used as fuel 自然の廃棄物から作られるガス, 燃料として使うことができる→**生物ガス**

**biographer** /baɪɑ́ɡrəfər/ 名 C ▶定義 a person who writes the story of sb else's life ほかの〜の人生航路を書く人→**伝記作者**

**biography** /baɪɑ́ɡrəfi/ 名 C U (複 **biographies**) ▶定義 the story of a person's life written by sb else ほかの〜によって書かれたある個人がたどった生涯→**伝記** || *a biography of Napoleon* ナポレオンの伝記 *I enjoy reading science fiction and biography.* 私はSFと伝記を読むのが好きだ. ☛参 **autobiography** — **biographical** /bàɪəɡrǽfɪk(ə)l/ 形→伝記の, 伝記体の

**biological** /bàɪəlɑ́dʒɪk(ə)l/ 形 ▶定義1 connected with the scientific study of animals, plants and other living things 動物, 植物, そのほかの生物についての科学的学問に関連した→**生物学(上)の** || *biological research* 生物学的研究 ▶定義2 involving the use of living things to destroy or damage other living things ほかの生物を破壊する, またはそれらに害を与える生物の利用にかかわる→**生物学(上)の** || *biological weapons* 生物兵器

**biology** /baɪɑ́lədʒi/ 名 U ▶定義 the scientific study of living things 生物についての研究→**生物学, 生態学** ☛参 **botany, zoology** — **biologist** 名 C →生物学者

**birch** /bɜːrtʃ/ 名 ▶定義1 (または **birch tree**) C a type of tree with smooth thin branches 滑らかな, 細い枝を持つ木の一種→**カバの木** ▶定義2 U the wood from this tree この木からとれる木材→**カバ材**

\***bird** /bɜːrd/ 名 C ▶定義 a creature with feathers and wings which can (usually) fly (通常は)飛ぶことができる, 羽と翼を持つ生物→**鳥** ☛ C1 ページのさし絵

▶ birds が飛ぶことを fly, 鳴くことを sing と言う. nest(巣)を作り, 卵を生むことは lay eggs と言う.

成句 kill two birds with one stone ⇒ **KILL**¹

**bird of prey** 名 C ▶定義 a bird that kills and eats other animals and birds ほかの動物や鳥を殺して食べる鳥→**猛禽(もうきん)**

**birdwatcher** /bɜ́ːrdwɒtʃər, -ɑ̀tʃə/ 名 C ▶定義 a person who studies birds in their natural surroundings 自然環境の中で鳥について学ぶ人→**野鳥観察者** ☛ 正式な用語は, ornithologist. — **birdwatching** 名 U →野鳥観察

**biro**™ /báɪroʊ/ 名 C (複 **biros**) ▶定義 a type of pen in which ink comes out of a small metal ball at the end 先端の金属製の玉からインクが出てくるペンの一種→**ボールペン** ☛参 **ballpoint**

\***birth** /bɜːrθ/ 名 ▶定義1 C U being born; coming out of a mother's body 生まれること; 母親の体から出てくること→**誕生, 出生; 出産** || *It was a difficult birth.* 難産でした. *The baby weighed 3 kilos at birth* (= when it was born). その赤ん坊の体重は, 出産時(= 生まれたとき)3キロだった. *What's your date of birth?* (= *the date on which you were born*) 誕生日(= 生まれた日)はいつですか. ▶定義2 U the country you belong to 自分が属する国→**生まれ** || *She's always lived in England but she's German by birth.* 彼女はずっとイギリスに住んでいるが, 生まれはドイツ人だ. ▶定義3 [単数扱い] the beginning of sth 〜の始まり→**出現, 起源, 発祥** || *the birth of an idea* ある思想の出現

成句 give birth (to sb) ▶定義 to produce a baby 赤ん坊を産む→**〜を産む** || *She gave birth* *to her second child at home.* 彼女は家で2番目の子供を産んだ.

**birth certificate** 图 ❻ ▶定義 an official document that states the date and place of a person's birth and the names of his/her parents 人が生まれた日付と場所, 両親の名前を記した公式の文書→**出生証明書**

**birth control** 图 ❶ ▶定義 ways of limiting the number of children you have 自分の子供の数を制限する方法→**産児制限, 避妊** ☛参 **contraception, family planning**

\***birthday** /báːθdeɪ/ 图 ❻ ▶定義 the day in each year which is the same date as the one when you were born 自分が生まれた日と同じ日付の1年に1度の日→**誕生日** ‖ *My birthday's on November 15th.* 私の誕生日は, 11月15日だ. *my eighteenth birthday* 私の18歳の誕生日 *a birthday present/card/cake* 誕生日祝いのプレゼント・カード・ケーキ

▶ anniversary は, birthday と同じではない. それは, 重要な過去の出来事があった日と同じ日付の1年に1度の日である: *our wedding anniversary* (私たちの結婚記念日) *the anniversary of the end of the war* (終戦記念日) 人の誕生日には, Happy Birthday! (誕生日おめでとう)と言う. よく知っている人にはカードかまたはプレゼントを贈る. (英国では) 18歳の誕生日は, 法的に成人となる重要な日である.

**birthmark** /báːθmàːrk/ 图 ❻ ▶定義 a red or brown mark on a person's body that has been there since he/she was born 生まれたときからずっと人の体に付いている, 赤または茶色の印→**(生まれつきの)あざ, ほくろ**

**birthplace** /báːθpleɪs/ ▶定義 1 ❻ the house or town where a person was born 人が生まれた家または町→**出生地, 生まれ故郷** ▶定義 2 [単数扱い] the place where sth began 〜が始まった場所→**発祥の地** ‖ *Greece is the birthplace of the Olympic Games.* ギリシャはオリンピックの発祥地だ.

**birth rate** 图 ❻ ▶定義 the number of babies born in a particular group of people during a particular period of time 特定の期間, 特定の人々の集団に生まれた赤ん坊の数→**出生率**

\***biscuit** /bískət/ (米 **cookie**) 图 ❻ ▶定義 1 a type of small cake that is thin, hard and usually sweet 薄く, 固く, 普通甘い小さな洋菓子の一種→**ビスケット** ‖ *a chocolate biscuit* チョコレートビスケット *a packet of biscuits* ビスケットの1包み ☛ **cake** のさし絵 ▶定義 2 米 a type of small simple cake that is not sweet 甘くない, 小さい, 飾り気のない焼きパンの一種→**小型パン, スコーン**

**bisexual** /baɪsékʃəl/ 形 ▶定義 sexually attracted to both men and women 性的に男性と女性の両方にひかれる→**両性愛の, 両性にひかれる** ☛参 **heterosexual, homosexual**

**bishop** /bíʃəp/ 图 ❻ ▶定義 a priest with a high position in some branches of the Christian Church, who is responsible for all the churches in a city or a district キリスト教教会のいくつかの支部の中で高い地位にある聖職者, 1つの町または地区のすべての教会について責任がある→**(カトリックの)司教, (英国国教会などの)主教** ☛参 **archbishop**

\***bit**¹ /bɪt/ 图 ▶定義 1 **a bit** [単数扱い] slightly, a little わずかに, 少しの→**少し, 少々, いくらか** ‖ *I was a bit annoyed with him.* 私は少し彼にむっとしていた. *I'm afraid I'll be a little bit late tonight.* 残念ながら, どうも今夜は少し遅くなりそうだ. *Could you be a bit quieter, please?* もうちょっと静かにしていただけますか. ▶定義 2 **a bit** [単数扱い] a short time or distance 短い時間または距離→**少しの時間, わずかな距離** ‖ *Could you move forward a bit?* 少し前の方に動いていただけますか. *I'm just going out for a bit.* 私はちょうど少しの間出掛けるところだ. ▶定義 3 **a bit** [単数扱い] 略式 a lot たくさん→**たくさん(の〜), 多量(の〜)** ‖ *It must have rained quite a bit during the night.* 夜中にかなり雨が降ったに違いない. ▶定義 4 ❻ **a bit of sth** a small piece, amount or part of sth 〜の小片, 少量の〜, または〜の小さい部分→**小片, 少量, かけら, 一部分** ‖ *There were bits of broken glass all over the floor.* 床中にガラスの細かな破片があった. *Could you give me a bit of advice?* 私に少し助言を頂けませんか. *Which bit of the film did you like best?* その映画のどの場面が一番好きでしたか. ▶定義 5 ❻ (computing) the smallest unit of information that is stored in a computer's memory (コンピ

ューター)コンピューターのメモリに保存されている情報の最小単位→ビット ▶定義6 ❻ a metal bar that you put in a horse's mouth when you ride it 馬に乗るときに、馬の口に入れる金属製の棒→はみ ☛ horse のさし絵

成句 bit by bit ▶定義 slowly or a little at a time ゆっくりと、または一度に少し→少しずつ、徐々に ‖ *Bit by bit we managed to get the information we needed.* 少しずつ、私たちはどうにかして必要な情報を得た.

a bit much 略式 ▶定義 annoying or unpleasant いらいらさせる、または不愉快な→あんまりな、ひどい ‖ *It's a bit much expecting me to work on Sundays.* 私が毎日曜日に働くだろうと思うなんて、あんまりだ.

a bit of a 略式 ▶定義 rather a いくぶん→多少、いくらか ‖ *I've got a bit of a problem...* いくらか問題があって...

bits and pieces 略式 ▶定義 small things of different kinds 異なる種類の小さな物事→こまごました物、半端物 ‖ *I've finished packing except for a few bits and pieces.* いくらかのこまごましたものを除いて、荷造りを終えた.

do your bit 略式 ▶定義 to do your share of sth; to help with sth 自分の分担の〜をする; 〜を手伝う→本分を尽くす、できる範囲内での寄付・奉仕をする ‖ *It won't take long to finish if we all do our bit.* 私たち皆が本分を尽くせば、それほど時間はかからないだろう.

not a bit ▶定義 not at all 全く〜でない→少しも〜でない ‖ *The holiday was not a bit what we had expected.* その休日は、私たちが期待したものでは全くなかった.

to bits ▶定義1 into small pieces 細かい断片に→粉々に、ばらばらに ‖ *She angrily tore the letter to bits.* 彼女は怒ってその手紙をびりびりに引き裂いた. ▶定義2 very; very much とても; 非常に→とても、非常に、大変 ‖ *I was thrilled to bits when I won the competition.* その競争に勝ったとき、私はとてもぞくぞくした.

**bit**² BITE¹ の過去形

**bitch**¹ /bɪtʃ/ 動 自 略式 ▶定義 bitch (about sb/sth) to say unkind and critical things about sb, especially when he/she is not there 特に〜がいないときに、その〜について思いやりのない、けちを付けることを言う→文句・不平・悪口を言う ‖ *She's not the kind of person who would bitch about you behind your back.* 彼女は陰であなたの悪口を言うような人ではない.

**bitch**² /bɪtʃ/ 名 ❻ ▶定義 a female dog 雌の犬→雌犬

**bitchy** /bɪtʃi/ 形 ▶定義 talking about other people in an unkind way 思いやりのない言い方で、ほかの人々について話している→意地悪な、怒りっぽい、機嫌の悪い ‖ *a bitchy remark* 意地悪な論評

\***bite**¹ /báɪt/ 動 過 **bit** /bɪt/; 過分 **bitten** /bítn/)
▶定義1 自 他 bite (into sth); bite (sb/sth) to cut or attack sb/sth with your teeth 歯で〜を切る、または攻撃する→かむ、かみ付く ‖ *Don't worry about the dog - she never bites.* その犬を怖がらないで − 決してかまないよ. *The cat bit me.* その猫が私をかんだ. *He picked up the bread and bit into it hungrily.* 彼は飢えた様子でそのパンを拾い上げ、食い付いた. ☛ **lick** のさし絵 ▶定義2 自 他 (used about some insects and animals) to push a sharp point into your skin and cause pain (いくつかの虫や動物について)鋭い先を皮膚に刺し、痛みを起こす→〜をかむ、刺す ‖ *He was bitten by a snake/mosquito /spider.* 彼は蛇にかまれた・蚊・くもに刺された.
➤ wasps (スズメバチ), bees (ミツバチ) や jellyfish (クラゲ) は bite (かむ) ことはない. これらは、sting (刺す) ことがある.

▶定義3 自 to begin to have an unpleasant effect 不愉快な効果を生じ始める→(厳しい)効果を示す、(不愉快な結果を)生む ‖ *In the South the job losses are starting to bite.* 南部では失業の不快な影響が出始めている.

成句 bite sb's head off ▶定義 to answer sb in a very angry way とても怒った様子で〜に答える→〜にけんか腰で答える・言う

\***bite**² /báɪt/ 名 ▶定義1 ❻ a piece of food that you can put into your mouth 口に入れられる、食べ物の一塊→一かじり、一口 ‖ *She took a big bite of the apple.* 彼女はリンゴを大きく一口かじった. ▶定義2 ❻ a painful place on the skin made by an insect, snake, dog, etc 虫に刺されたり、蛇、犬などにかまれてできた皮膚の痛い所→かみ傷、刺し傷 ‖ *I'm covered in mosquito bites.* 蚊の刺し傷だらけだ. ▶定義3 [単数扱い] 略式 a small meal; a snack 少量の食事; 軽食→

## bitten

軽い食事, (一口の)食べ物 ‖ Would you like a **bite to eat** before you go? 行く前に軽く食事を取りませんか.

**bitten** BITE¹ の過去分詞形

**\*bitter¹** /bítər/ 形 ▶定義1 caused by anger or hatred 怒りや嫌悪によって引き起こされて, 〜が原因となって→**敵意のある, 痛烈な** ‖ a bitter quarrel 痛烈な口論 ▶定義2 **bitter (about sth)** (used about a person) very unhappy or angry about sth that has happened because you feel you have been treated unfairly (人について)自分が不当に扱われたと感じるために, 起きた〜について非常に不満なまたは怒って→**苦い思いをして, ひがんだ, 怒って** ‖ She was very bitter about not getting the job. 彼女は仕事が得られなかったことに, とても苦い思いをした. ▶定義3 causing unhappiness or anger for a long time; difficult to accept 長い間不幸や怒りをもたらしている; 受け入れ難い→**つらい, 厳しい, 耐え難い** ‖ Failing the exam was **a bitter disappointment** to him. 試験に落ちたことは, 彼にとっては耐え難いショックだった. I've learnt **from bitter experience** not to trust him. 痛烈な経験から, 彼を信用しないことを学んだ. ▶定義4 having a sharp, unpleasant taste; not sweet 鋭い, 不愉快な味のする; 甘くない→**苦い** ‖ bitter coffee 苦いコーヒー ▶定義5 (used about the weather) very cold (天気について) とても寒い→**身を切るような, 厳しい** ‖ a bitter wind 身を切るような風 ― **bitterness** 名 Ｕ ▶定義 anger and unhappiness as a result of sth bad happening 悪い〜が起きた結果としての怒りや不幸→**苦しさ, 悲痛, つらさ**

**bitter²** /bítər/ 名 Ｕ 英 ▶定義 a type of dark beer that is popular in Britain 英国で人気のある黒ビールの一種→**ビター** ‖ A pint of bitter, please. ビターを1パイント下さい.

**bitterly** /bítərli/ 副 ▶定義1 (used for describing strong negative feelings or cold weather) extremely (強い否定的な感情または極端に寒い気候を描写するために用いて)極度に→**ひどく, 苦々しく, 痛烈に, 身を切るように** ‖ bitterly disappointed/resentful ひどく失望した・憤慨した a bitterly cold winter/wind ひどく寒い冬・身を切るような冷たい風 ▶定義2 in an angry and disappointed way 怒り, 落胆した様子で→**苦々しく, 敵意に満ちて** ‖ 'I've lost everything,' he said bitterly. 「私はすべてを失った」と彼は苦々しく言った.

**bitty** /bíti/ 形 ▶定義 made up of lots of parts which do not seem to be connected 関連しているようには見えない, たくさんの部分から成る→**寄せ集めの, 断片的な, まとまりのない** ‖ Your essay is rather bitty. あなたの論文は, いろいろな寄せ集めにすぎない.

**bizarre** /bəzá:r/ 形 ▶定義 very strange とても奇妙な→**奇怪な, 風変わりな** ‖ The story had a most bizarre ending. その話の結末はこの上なく奇妙だった.

**bk** (複) **bks** 略 book → **本**

**\*black¹** /blæk/ 形 ▶定義1 of the darkest colour, like night or coal 夜や石炭のような最も暗い色の→**黒い** ▶定義2 belonging to a race of people with dark skins 暗い色の肌を持つ人種に属している→**黒人の** ‖ the black population of Britain 英国の黒人人口 black culture 黒人文化 ▶定義3 (used about coffee or tea) without milk or cream (コーヒーまたは紅茶について)ミルクまたはクリームを入れない→**ブラックの, ミルクなしの** ‖ black coffee with sugar 砂糖入りのブラックコーヒー ▶定義4 very angry 非常に怒った→**怒った, 腹を立てた, 機嫌の悪い** ‖ to give sb **a black look** むっとして〜を見る ▶定義5 (used about a situation) without hope; depressing (ある状況について)望みのない; がっかりさせる→**陰うつな, 暗たんとした** ‖ The economic outlook for the coming year is rather black. 来るべき年の経済の見通しはかなり暗たんとしている. ▶定義6 funny in a cruel or unpleasant way 残酷または不愉快な方法でおかしな→**冷笑的な, 毒のある** ‖ The film was **a black comedy**. その映画は毒のある喜劇だった.

成句 **black and blue** ▶定義 covered with blue, brown or purple marks on the body (bruises) because you have been hit by sb/sth 〜に打たれて, 体が青, 茶, または紫色の印(打撲傷)で覆われた→**青あざのできるほど(の), 青黒くあざになった**

**black and white** ▶定義 (used about television, photographs, etc) showing no colours except black, white and grey (テレビ, 写真などについて)黒, 白, 灰色以外の色を見せない→**白黒の**

**black**[2] /blæk/ 名 ▶定義1 ① the darkest colour, like night or coal 夜や石炭のような最も暗い色→黒, 黒色 ‖ *People often **wear black** (= black clothes) at funerals.* 人々は葬式でしばしば黒(=黒い服)を着る. ▶定義2 (通常 **Black**) ⓒ a person who belongs to a race of people with dark skins 暗い色の肌をした人種に属する人→黒人 — blackness 名 ① →黒さ, 暗黒, 黒人であること

成句 be in the black ▶定義 to have some money in the bank 銀行にいくらか金を持っている→(営業が)黒字である, もうかっている ⇔ **be in the red**

in black and white ▶定義 in writing or in print 書いた, または印刷した→印刷して, 文書で ‖ *I won't believe we've got the contract till I see it in black and white.* 契約を書面で見るまで, 私たちがその契約を取ったなんて信じられない.

**black**[3] /blæk/ 動

句動詞 black out ▶定義 to lose consciousness for a short time 短時間意識を失う→(一時的に)意識を失う, 失神する

**blackberry** /blǽkb(ə)ri; -beri/ 名 ⓒ (複 **blackberries**) ▶定義 a small black fruit that grows wild on bushes 茂みに野生する, 小さな黒い果物→クロイチゴ, ブラックベリー ☞ C3 ページのさし絵

**blackbird** /blǽkbə̀ːrd/ 名 ⓒ ▶定義 a common European bird. The male is black with a yellow beak and the female is brown. 一般的なヨーロッパの鳥. 雄は黒く, 黄色いくちばしを持ち, 雌は茶色である→クロウタドリ, ムクドリモドキ

**blackboard** /blǽkbɔ̀ːrd/ (米 **chalkboard**) 名 ⓒ ▶定義 a piece of dark board used for writing on with chalk, which is used in a class チョークで書くための暗い色の板で, 教室で使われる→黒板 注: 白いものは whiteboard とも言う.

> ▶音声とつづり字
>
> blackboard と black board
>
> blackboard を bláckbòard と第1音節に強勢を置いて発音すると, 教室で使われる「黒板」の意味になり, 板の色は問題にしていません. しかし black board のように2語として書き, また blàck bóard のように発音すると「黒い板」という意味になり, チョークなどで書くための板ということは意味しません.

類例: sléeping càr (寝台車)/sléeping báby (眠っている子供), móving vàn (荷物運搬車)/mòving ván (動いているバン), Énglish tèacher (英語の先生)/Ènglish téacher (イギリス人の先生), wóman dòctor (婦人科医)/wòman dóctor (女性医師)

**blackcurrant** /blǽkkʌ̀rənt; -kə̀ːr(ə)nt/ 名 ⓒ ▶定義 a small round black fruit that grows on bushes 茂みに生育する, 小さく丸く黒い果物→クロフサスグリ(の実)

**blacken** /blǽk(ə)n/ 動 他 ▶定義1 to make sth black ～を黒くする→～を黒く・暗くする ▶定義2 to make sth seem bad, by saying unpleasant things about it それについて好ましくない事を言って, ～を悪く思わせる→(人格・名誉などを)汚す, 悪く言う ‖ *to blacken sb's name* ～の名を汚す

**black eye** 名 ⓒ ▶定義 an area of dark-coloured skin around sb's eye where he/she has been hit 殴られたときに, ～の目の周りにできる, 黒っぽい皮膚の部分→青あざ ‖ *He got a black eye in the fight.* 彼はけんかで目の周りに青あざを作った.

**blackhead** /blǽkhèd/ 名 ⓒ ▶定義 a small spot on the skin with a black centre 中央が黒い, 皮膚にできた小さな点→にきび

**blacklist** /blǽklɪst/ 名 ⓒ ▶定義 a list of people, companies, etc who are considered bad or dangerous 悪いまたは危険だと見なされている人々, 会社などの一覧表→ブラックリスト, 要注意人物一覧表 ‖ *to be on sb's blacklist* ～のブラックリストに載る — blacklist 動 他 →～をブラックリストに載せる ‖ *She was blacklisted by all the major Hollywood studios.* 彼女は, ハリウッドの大手映画会社すべてのブラックリストに載せられた.

**black magic** 名 ① ▶定義 a type of magic that is used for evil purposes 邪悪な目的で用いられる魔法の一種→黒魔術

**blackmail** /blǽkmèɪl/ 名 ① ▶定義 the crime of forcing a person to give you money or do sth for you, usually by threatening to make known sth which they want to keep secret 通常, 人が秘密にしておきたい～を知られるようにすると

脅して、人に金を出させる、または〜をすることを強要する犯罪→**恐喝、ゆすり** — **blackmail** 動他 **blackmail sb (into doing sth)** →〜から金などをゆすり取る、〜をゆすって…させる — **blackmailer** 名ⓒ→**恐喝者、ゆすりを働く者**

**black market** 名 [通常は単数] ▶定義 the buying and selling of goods or foreign money in a way that is not legal 合法的でないやり方で、品物または外貨を売買すること→**闇(やみ)市場、闇取り引き** ‖ *to buy/sell sth* **on the black market** 〜を闇取り引きで売る・買う

**blackout** /blǽkàut/ 名ⓒ ▶定義1 a period of time during a war, when all lights must be turned off or covered so that the enemy cannot see them 敵に見つからないようにすべての明かりが消される、または覆われなければならない、戦争中の期間→**灯火管制** ▶定義2 a period when you lose consciousness for a short time 短時間意識を失っている時間→**一時的視覚・意識・記憶喪失** ‖ *to have a blackout* 一時的に意識喪失する

**blacksmith** /blǽksmìθ/ 名ⓒ ▶定義 a person whose job is to make and repair things made of iron 鉄で物を作ったり直すことを仕事にしている人→**鍛冶(かじ)屋、鉄工、馬蹄(てい)工**

**bladder** /blǽdər/ 名ⓒ ▶定義 the part of your body where waste liquid (urine) collects before leaving your body 体から出る前に、廃液(尿)が集まる体の部分→**膀胱(ぼうこう)** ☞ C5 ページのさし絵

*****blade** /bléɪd/ 名ⓒ ▶定義1 the flat, sharp part of a knife, etc ナイフなどの平たく、鋭い部分→**刃、刀身** ☞ **garden, penknife, scissors** のさし絵 ▶定義2 one of the flat, wide parts that turn round very quickly on an aircraft, etc 飛行機などの、非常に速く回転する、平らで幅広い部品の1つ→**(プロペラの)羽根** ▶定義3 a long, thin leaf of grass 草の長く薄い葉→**葉、葉身** ‖ *a blade of grass* 1枚の草の葉

*****blame**[1] /bléɪm/ 動他 ▶定義1 **blame sb (for sth); blame sth on sb/sth** to think or say that a certain person or thing is responsible for sth bad that has happened 起きてしまった良くないことについて、ある人または物に責任があると考えるまたは言う→**〜のせいにする、責任を負**わせる ‖ *The teacher blamed me for the accident.* 教師はその事故を私のせいにした. *Some people blame the changes in the climate on pollution.* ある人々は気候の変化を汚染のせいにしている. ▶定義2 **not blame sb (for sth)** to think that sb is not wrong to do sth; to understand sb's reason for doing sth 〜が…をするのは悪くないと考える; 〜が…をする理由を理解する→**責めない、とがめない** ‖ *I don't blame you for feeling fed up.* いらいらされるのも無理はないですよ.

成句 **be to blame (for sth)** ▶定義 to be responsible for sth bad 悪い〜に責任がある→**責任・罪がある、非難に値する** ‖ *The police say that careless driving was to blame for the accident.* 警官は、その事故が不注意な運転のせいだったと言う.

**shift the blame/responsibility (for sth) (onto sb)** ⇒ **SHIFT**[1]

**blame**[2] /bléɪm/ 名Ⓤ ▶定義 **blame (for sth)** responsibility for sth bad 悪い〜への責任→**責任、責め、非難** ‖ *The government must* **take the blame** *for the economic crisis.* 政府は、経済危機についての責任を取らなければならない. *The report* **put the blame on** *rising prices.* その報告書は価格の上昇を非難した. *Why do I always* **get the blame**? なぜいつも私が責められるのですか.

**blameless** /bléɪmləs/ 形(文) ▶定義 not guilty; that should not be blamed 罪のない; 責められるべきでない→**潔白な、罪がない、非難するところのない** ‖ *He insisted that his wife was blameless and hadn't known about his crimes.* 妻は潔白であり、自分の罪については知らなかったと彼は主張した.

**bland** /blænd/ 形 ▶定義1 ordinary or not very interesting 普通の、または面白くない→**個性・面白味・迫力のない、魅力のない** ‖ *a rather bland style of writing* かなり面白味のない文体 ▶定義2 (used about food) mild or lacking in taste (食べ物について) 軽いまたは味のない→**味のない、刺激のない** ▶定義3 not showing any emotion 感情を示さない→**感情を出さない、物柔らかな、穏やかな** — **blandly** 副→**個性なく、穏やかに**

*****blank**[1] /blǽŋk/ 形 ▶定義1 empty, with nothing written, printed or recorded on it 空の、何も書

れていない,印刷または記録されていない→白紙の,書き入れていない,空の ‖ *a blank video/cassette/piece of paper/page* 録画されていないビデオ・録音されていないカセット・白紙・何も書かれていないページ ▶定義2 without feelings, understanding or interest 感情,理解,または興味のない→**無表情な,うつろな,無関心な** ‖ *a blank expression on his face* 彼の生気のない表情 *My mind **went blank** when I saw the exam questions (= I couldn't think properly or remember anything).* 試験問題を見たとき,頭が真っ白になった(= 適切に考えられない,または何も覚えていない). — blankly 副 →ぼんやりして ‖ *She stared at me blankly, obviously not recognizing me.* 彼女は,明らかに私だとは分からずに,私を漠然と注視した.

**blank**² /blæŋk/ 名 C ▶定義 an empty space 空いている場所→**空所,空欄,空白** ‖ *Fill in the **blanks** in the following exercise.* 以下の練習問題の空所を埋めなさい.(比喩) *I couldn't remember his name - my mind was a complete blank.* 彼の名前が思い出せなかった — 頭の中が真っ白だったのだ.

成句 draw a blank ⇒ **DRAW**¹

**blank cheque** 名 C ▶定義 a cheque that has been signed but that has an empty space so that the amount to be paid can be written in later 署名はされているが,後で支払い金額を書き込めるように空所のある小切手→**白地小切手**

\***blanket**¹ /blæŋkət/ 名 C ▶定義1 a cover made of wool, etc that is put on beds to keep people warm ベッドの上に掛けて人を暖める,羊毛などでできた覆い→**毛布** ☞ **bed** のさし絵 ▶定義2 a thick layer or covering of sth 〜の薄い層または…を覆う物→**一面を覆う物,一面の〜** ‖ *a blanket of snow* 一面の雪 — blanket 動 他 blanket sth (in/with sth) →〜を覆う ‖ *The countryside was blanketed in snow.* 田園地方は雪で覆われていた.

成句 a wet blanket ⇒ **WET**¹

**blanket**² /blæŋkət/ 形 ▶定義 (名詞の前だけ) affecting everybody or everything すべての人や物に影響する→**総括的な,全面的な,一斉の** ‖ *There is a **blanket ban** on journalists reporting the case.* 記者たちがその事件について報道することは全面的に禁止されている.

**blare** /bleər/ 動 自 他 ▶定義 blare (sth) (out) to make a loud, unpleasant noise 大きく,不快な音を立てる→**やかましく鳴らす[鳴る],騒がしい音を立てる** ‖ *Car horns were blaring in the street outside.* 外の通りでは,車の警笛がやかましく鳴っていた. *The loudspeaker blared out pop music.* スピーカーからポピュラー音楽がやかましく流れていた. — blare 名 [U,単数扱い]→**やかましい音** ‖ *the blare of a siren* サイレンのやかましい音

**blasphemy** /blǽsfəmi/ 名 U ▶定義 writing or speaking about God in a way that shows a lack of respect 敬いの気持ちに欠けたやり方で,神について書くまたは話すこと→**神への不敬,冒涜(ぼうとく)** — blasphemous /blǽsfəməs/ 形 →**不敬な,冒涜的な**

**blast**¹ /blɑːst; blæst/ 名 C ▶定義1 an explosion, especially one caused by a bomb 爆発,特に爆弾によって起きるもの→**爆発,爆破** ▶定義2 a sudden strong current of air 空気の突然の強い流れ→**突風,一陣の風** ‖ *a blast of cold air* 冷たい突風 ▶定義3 a loud sound made by a musical instrument, etc 楽器などによって立てられる大きな音→**吹き鳴らすこと,けたたましい音** ‖ *The driver gave a few blasts on his horn.* 運転手は警笛を2,3度,けたたましく鳴らした.

**blast**² /blɑːst; blæst/ 動 他 ▶定義1 to make a hole, a tunnel, etc in sth with an explosion 爆発によって,〜に穴やトンネルなどを作る→**〜を爆破する,〜を爆破して…にする** ‖ *They blasted a tunnel through the mountainside.* 彼らは爆破して山腹にトンネルを作った. ▶定義2 to criticize sth very strongly 〜をとても激しく批判する→**〜を激しく非難する,こき下ろす** ‖ *Union leaders last night blasted the government's proposals.* 組合の役員たちは,昨夜政府の提案を激しく非難した.

句動詞 blast off ▶定義 (used about a spacecraft) to leave the ground; to take off (宇宙船について)地面を離れる;離陸する→**発射される**

**blast-off** 名 U ▶定義 the time when a spacecraft leaves the ground 宇宙船が地面を離れる時→**発射,ロケットの打ち上げ**

**blatant** /bléɪtnt/ 形 ▶定義 very clear or obvious 非常にはっきりしたまたは明白な→**見え透いた,**

露骨な‖ *a blatant lie* 見え透いたうそ ☛ この単語は，批判的な意味で用いられる．— **blatantly** 副 →紛れもなく，露骨に，あからさまに

**blaze**¹ /bléɪz/ 名 ●定義1 A large and often dangerous fire 大きく，しばしば危険な火事→炎，火事 ‖ *It took firefighters four hours to put out the blaze.* 消防士たちがその火事を消すのに4時間かかった．▶定義2 [単数扱い] **a blaze of sth** a very bright show of light or colour 光または色のとても鮮やかな様子→燃え立つような色彩，強い輝き，まばゆさ ‖ *In the summer the garden was a blaze of colour.* 夏，その庭は燃え立つような色彩に満ちていた．*The new theatre(-er) was opened in* **a blaze of publicity** *(= the media gave it a lot of attention).* 評判がぱっと広まるなか(= マスメディアが非常に注目した)，新しい劇場はオープンした．

**blaze**² /bléɪz/ 動 ▶定義1 to burn with bright strong flames 明るく，強い炎と共に燃える→燃え立つ，燃え上がる ▶定義2 **blaze (with sth)** to be extremely bright; to shine brightly 極度に明るい；明るく輝く→あかあかと輝く，きらめく，(目が)怒りに燃える ‖ *I woke up to find that the room was blazing with sunshine.* 目が覚めると，部屋は日の光で輝いていた．(比喩) *'Get out!' she shouted, her eyes blazing with anger.* 「出ていって」と，彼女は怒りに燃えた目で叫んだ．

**blazer** /bléɪzər/ 名 ●定義 a jacket, especially one that has the colours or sign (**badge**) of a school, club or team on it ジャケット，特に学校，クラブ，チームの色または印(バッジ)の付いたもの→ブレザー ‖ *a school blazer* 学校の制服としてのブレザー ☛ C6 ページのさし絵

**bleach**¹ /bliːtʃ/ 動 他 ▶定義 to make sth white or lighter in colour by using a chemical or by leaving it in the sun 化学薬品を用いて，または日光にさらして，〜を白くする，または色を明るくする→〜を漂白する，脱色する

**bleach**² /bliːtʃ/ 名 ● U ▶定義 a strong chemical substance used for making clothes, etc whiter or for cleaning things 衣服などをより白くするため，または物の汚れを落とすために用いられる強い化学物質→漂白剤，脱色剤

**bleak** /bliːk/ 形 ▶定義1 (used about a situation) bad; not encouraging or hopeful (状況について)悪い；励みにならない，または希望のない→(将来などが)わびしい，(見通しなどが)暗い ‖ *a bleak future for the next generation* 次の世代の暗い未来 ▶定義2 (used about a place) cold, empty and grey (場所について)冷たく何もなくて灰色の→吹きさらしの，荒れた，荒涼とした ‖ *the bleak Arctic landscape* 荒涼とした北極の風景 ▶定義3 (used about the weather) cold and grey (天気について)冷たくて灰色の→冷たい，寒々とした ‖ *a bleak winter's day* 寒々とした冬の日 — **bleakly** 副 →荒涼と，わびしく — **bleakness** 名 U →荒涼，わびしさ，暗さ

**bleary** /blíəri/ 形 ▶定義 (used about the eyes) red, tired and unable to see clearly (目について)赤く，疲れて，はっきり見られない→目がかすんだ，ぼんやりした ‖ *We were all rather bleary-eyed after the journey.* 私たちはみんな，旅の後でいくぶん目がかすんでいた．— **blearily** 副 →目がかすんで，ぼんやりと

**bleat** /bliːt/ 動 ▶定義1 自 to make the sound of a sheep 羊の鳴き声を立てる→メーと鳴く ▶定義2 自他 to speak in a weak or complaining voice 小さい声，または不満そうな声で話す→泣き言を言う，哀れな声で〜を言う — **bleat** 名 C →メーという鳴き声

★**bleed** /bliːd/ 動 自 (過，過分 **bled** /bled/) ▶定義 to lose blood 血を失う→出血する，血を流す — **bleeding** 名 U →出血 ‖ *He wrapped a scarf around his arm to stop the bleeding.* 出血を止めるために，彼は腕にスカーフを巻いた．

**bleep**¹ /bliːp/ 名 ● ▶定義 a short, high sound made by a piece of electronic equipment 電気機器が鳴らす短く，高い音→ピーという音

**bleep**² /bliːp/ 動 ▶定義1 自 (used about machines) to make a short high sound (機械について)短く高い音を立てる→ピーという音を出す ‖ *Why is the computer bleeping?* どうしてそのコンピューターはピーピー鳴っているの．▶定義2 (米 または **beep**) 他 to attract a person's attention using an electronic machine 電気機器を使って人の注意を引き付ける→〜をピーという信号音・ポケットベルで呼び出す ‖ *Please bleep the doctor on duty immediately.* 直ちに当番医をポケベルで呼び出してください．

**bleeper** /blíːpər/ (米 **beeper**) 名 ● ▶定義 a small piece of electronic equipment that bleeps to let a person (for example a doctor) know when sb is trying to contact him/her 〜が彼・彼女(例えば医者)に連絡を取ろうとしていることを知らせるために、ピーと鳴る小さな電子機器→ポケットベル ☞類 **pager**

**blemish** /blémɪʃ/ 🅒 ▶定義 a mark that spoils the way sth looks 〜の外観を台なしにする印→汚れ, 傷, 染み — blemish 動(比喩)→〜を損なう, 汚す ‖ *The defeat has blemished the team's perfect record.* その敗北は、チームの全勝記録を汚した.

**blend**¹ /blend/ 動 ▶定義 1 ⓗ blend A with B; blend A and B (together) to mix 混ぜる→〜を混ぜる, 混ぜ合わせる, 混合する ‖ *First blend the flour and the melted butter together.* まず小麦粉と溶かしたバターを混ぜ合わせます. ▶定義 2 ⓘ blend (in) with sth to combine with sth in an attractive or suitable way 魅力的または適切なやり方で〜を結合する→調和する ‖ *The new room is decorated to blend in with the rest of the house.* 新しい部屋は、家のほかの部分と調和するように装飾されている. ▶定義 3 ⓘ blend (into sth) to match or be similar to the surroundings sb/sth is in 〜が住んでいる[存在している]環境と合っている、または似ている→混ざり合う, 溶け合う ‖ *These animals' ability to blend into their surroundings provides a natural form of defence.* これらの動物の環境に溶け込む能力は、自然の防衛手段になっている.

**blend**² /blend/ 🅒 ▶定義 a mixture 混合物→混合物, 混ぜ合わせた茶・コーヒーなど ‖ *He had the right blend of enthusiasm and experience.* 彼は情熱と経験をうまく併せ持っていた.

**blender** /bléndər/ (英 **liquidizer**) 🅒 ▶定義 an electric machine that is used for making food into liquid 食べ物を液状にするための電気器械→ミキサー ☞ **mixer** のさし絵

**bless** /bles/ 動 ⓗ (過, 過分 **blessed** /blest/) ▶定義 to ask for God's help and protection for sb/sth 〜のために神の救いと保護を求める→〜を祝福する, 〜のために神の恵み・加護を祈る 成句 be blessed with sth/sb ▶定義 to be lucky enough to have sth/sb 幸運にも〜を持つことができる→〜に恵まれている, (良いもの)を持っている ‖ *The West of Ireland is an area blessed with many fine sandy beaches.* アイルランド西部は多くの良い砂浜に恵まれている. Bless you! ▶定義 what you say to a person who has a cold and has just made a noise through his/her nose (sneezed) 風邪を引いていて、ちょうど鼻から音を出した(くしゃみをした)人に言う事→神のご加護を、お大事に

**blessed** /blésɪd/ 形 ▶定義 1 having God's help and protection 神の救いや保護を受けている→祝福された, 恵まれた, 神聖な ‖ *the Blessed Virgin Mary* 聖母マリア ▶定義 2 (in religious language) lucky; fortunate (宗教用語で) 幸運な; 恵まれた→幸いなる ‖ *Blessed are the pure in heart.* 心の清らかなる者は幸いなり. ▶定義 3 正式 giving great pleasure すばらしい喜びを与える→楽しい, 喜ばしい ‖ *The cool breeze brought blessed relief from the heat.* 暑さの中、冷たいそよ風が喜ばしい安堵(あんど)をもたらした.

**blessing** /blésɪŋ/ 🅒 ▶定義 1 a thing that you are grateful for or that brings happiness 感謝している、または幸福をもたらすもの→神の恵み, 祝福 ‖ *It's a great blessing that we have two healthy children.* 2人の健康な子供がいるのは偉大な神の恵みだ. *Not getting that job was a blessing in disguise* (= something which seems unlucky but turns out to be a good thing). あの仕事に就かなかったことは、不幸に見えて実は有り難いものであった(= 不運に思えるが、後で良い結果になること). ▶定義 2 [通常は単数]approval or support 承認あるいは支持→賛成, 励まし ‖ *They got married without their parents' blessing.* 双方の両親に賛成されないまま、彼らは結婚した. ▶定義 3 [通常は単数](a prayer asking for) God's help and protection 神の救いと加護(を求める祈り)→神の恩恵・祝福(を求めること) ‖ *The priest said a blessing.* 司祭は祝福を述べた.

**blew** **BLOW**¹ の過去形

★**blind**¹ /blaɪnd/ 形 ▶定義 1 unable to see 見ることができない→盲目の, 目の見えない ‖ *a blind person* 盲人 *to be completely/partially blind* 全盲・半盲 ☞ 人については、時に blind よりもむしろ partially sighted または visually impaired と表現される. ▶定義 2 blind (to sth) not wanting to notice or understand sth 〜に気付こうと、または理解しようと望まない→見る目がない, 〜に気付かない, 〜が分からない ‖ *He* was completely blind to her faults. 彼は彼女の欠点に全く気付かなかった. ▶定義3 without reason or thought 理由または考えなしに➡思慮のない, 理性の失われた ‖ He drove down the motorway in *a blind panic*. 彼は, どうにもない激しいパニック状態で高速道路を車で走った. ▶定義4 impossible to see round 周りを見ることができない➡見通しの悪い ‖ You should never overtake on *a blind corner*. 見通しの悪い曲がり角で, 追い越してはいけない. — blindly 副 ➡盲目的に — blindness 名 ❶ ➡目が見えないこと, 目が不自由なこと, 無分別, 無知

成句 turn a blind eye (to sth) ▶定義 to pretend not to notice sth bad is happening so that you do not have to do anything about it それについて何もしなくて良いように, 悪い〜が起きていることに気付かない振りをする➡見て見ぬ振りをする

**blind**² /bláɪnd/ 動 他 ▶定義1 to make sb unable to see 〜を見ることができないようにする➡〜の目をくらませる, 失明させる ‖ Her grandfather had been blinded in an accident (= permanently). 彼女のおじいさんは事故で失明した(= 永久に). Just for a second I was blinded by the sun (= for a short time). 一瞬太陽で目がくらんだ(= 短時間). ▶定義2 blind sb (to sth) to make sb unable to think clearly or behave in a sensible way 〜が明瞭(めいりょう)に考える, または分別を持って行動することをできなくさせる➡〜の分別を失わせる

**blind**³ /bláɪnd/ 名 ▶定義1 ❶ a piece of cloth or other material that you pull down to cover a window 窓を覆うために引き下げる, 布またはほかの素材でできたもの➡ブラインド, 日よけ ☛ curtain のさし絵 ▶定義2 the blind 名 [複数扱い] people who are unable to see 見ることができない人々➡盲人

**blind date** 名 ❶ ▶定義 an arranged meeting between a man and a woman who have never met before to see if they like each other enough to begin a romantic relationship それまで互いに面識のない男女を会わせて, 恋愛関係を始めるほど互いを好きかどうかを見る, 準備された出会い➡ブラインドデート, 見合い

**blindfold** /bláɪndfəʊld/ 名 ❶ ▶定義 a piece of cloth, etc that is used for covering sb's eyes 〜の目を覆うために使われる布など➡目隠し布 — blindfold 動 他 ➡〜を目隠しする

**blind spot** 名 ❶ ▶定義1 the part of the road just behind you that you cannot see when driving a car 車を運転しているときに, ちょうど自分の後ろになって見えない道の部分➡死角 ▶定義2 if you have a blind spot about sth, you cannot understand or accept it 〜について盲点があると, それを理解する, または受け入れることができない➡盲点, 当人の気付かない弱点

**blink** /blɪŋk/ 動 ▶定義1 自 他 to shut your eyes and open them again very quickly 素早く目を閉じてまた開く➡まばたきする, ぱちくりする ‖ Oh dear! You blinked just as I took the photograph! あら, まあ. 私が写真を撮った瞬間に, あなたまばたきしたわ. ☛参 wink ▶定義2 自 (used about a light) to come on and go off again quickly (光について)光り, 再びすぐに消える➡ちらつく, またたく — blink 名 ❶ ➡またたき, かすかなきらめき, 閃光(せんこう)

**blip** /blɪp/ 名 ❶ ▶定義1 a light flashing on the screen of a piece of equipment, sometimes with a short high sound 時には短く高い音と共に, 機器の画面上でぱっとつく光➡(レーダーの)光点, 映像 ▶定義2 a small problem that does not last for long 長くすまは続かない小さな問題➡(一時的な)変化・停滞

**bliss** /blɪs/ 名 ❶ ▶定義 perfect happiness 完全な幸福➡至福, 無上の喜び — blissful /-fʊl, -f(ə)l/ 形 ➡この上なく幸せな, 喜びに満ちた — blissfully /-fʊli, -f(ə)li/ 副 ➡この上なく幸福に, 喜びに満ちて

**blister**¹ /blɪstər/ 名 ❶ ▶定義 a small painful area of skin that looks like a bubble and contains clear liquid. Blisters are usually caused by rubbing or burning. 透明な液体を内包し, 泡のように見える, 皮膚の小さな, 痛みを感じる所. 水ぶくれは, 通常こすったり, やけどによりできる➡火ぶくれ, 水ぶくれ, (手足の)まめ

**blister**² /blɪstər/ 動 自 他 ▶定義1 to get or cause blisters 水ぶくれになる, または水ぶくれを起こす➡水ぶくれになる, 〜を火・水ぶくれにする ▶定義2 to swell and crack or to cause sth to do this はれて割れる, または〜にこれを起こさせる➡ぶつぶつができる, 〜にぶつぶつを作る ‖ The paint is starting to blister. 塗料にぶつぶつ

ができ始めている.

**blistering** /blístərɪŋ/ 形 ▶定義 very strong or extreme とても強い,または過激な→**猛烈な** ‖ *the blistering midday heat* 真昼の猛暑 *The runners set off at a blistering pace.* 走者たちは猛烈な速さで走り出した.

**blitz** /blɪts/ 名 C ▶定義 a blitz (on sth) a sudden effort or attack on sb/sth 〜への突然の企て,または攻撃→**電撃戦,奇襲** ‖ *The police are planning a blitz on vandalism.* 警察は,今起きている破壊活動への奇襲を計画している.

**blizzard** /blízərd/ 名 C ▶定義 a very bad storm with strong winds and a lot of snow 強風と大雪を伴う,とてもひどいあらし→**ブリザード,大吹雪,暴風雪** ☞参 **storm** の注

**bloated** /blóʊtɪd/ 形 ▶定義 unusually large and uncomfortable because of liquid, food or gas inside 中に液体,食べ物,または気体があるために,異常に大きくて心地良くない→**むくんだ,膨れ上がった** ‖ *I felt a bit bloated after all that food.* それを全部食べた後少しおなかが膨らんだ気がした.

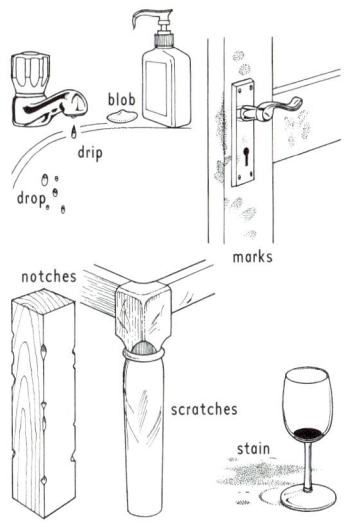

**blob** /blɑb/ 名 C ▶定義 a small piece of a thick liquid 濃い液体のほんの少量→**一滴,球状の小さい塊** ‖ *a blob of paint/cream/ink* 塗料・クリーム・インクの一滴

**bloc** /blɑk/ 名 [C,単数または複数形の動詞と共に] ▶定義 a group of countries that work closely together because they have the same political interests 同じ政治的な利害を持っているために,共に密接に働く国々の集団→**ブロック,圏**

***block**¹ /blɑk/ 名 C ▶定義 1 a large, heavy piece of sth, usually with flat sides 通常平たい側面を持った,〜の大きく,重い一片→**大きな塊** ‖ *a block of wood* 一片の大きな木材 *huge concrete blocks* 巨大なコンクリートブロック ▶定義 2 a large building that is divided into separate flats or offices 別々のアパートまたは事務所に分けられている大きな建物→**1棟** ‖ *a block of flats* アパートの1棟 ☞参 **apartment block**, **office block** ▶定義 3 a group of buildings in a town which has streets on all four sides 四方面を通りに囲まれた,町の中にある1つの建物の集まり→**ブロック,街区** ‖ *The restaurant is three blocks away.* そのレストランは3ブロック先にある. ▶定義 4 a quantity of sth or an amount of time that is considered as a single unit 1つの単位と見なされている,〜の量または時間の長さ→**一組,一そろい** ‖ *The class is divided into two blocks of fifty minutes.* 授業は,50分ごとの2組に分けられている. ▶定義 5 [通常は単数] a thing that makes movement or progress difficult or impossible 物の動きや進展を難しくまたは不可能にするもの→**障害物,邪魔物** ‖ *a block to further progress in the talks* 交渉の進展の障害物 ☞参 **roadblock**

成句 **have a block (about sth)** ▶定義 to be unable to think or understand sth properly 〜を適切に考える,または理解することができない→**思考が停止する,頭が働かない,苦手である** ‖ *I had a complete **mental block**. I just couldn't remember his name.* 頭が全然働かなかった.彼の名前すら思い出せなかった.

*****block**² /blɑk/ 動 他 ▶定義 1 block sth (up) to make it difficult or impossible for sb/sth to pass 〜が通過することを難しくまたは不可能にする→**〜をふさぐ,封鎖する** ‖ *Many roads are completely blocked by snow.* 多くの道路が雪で完全に封鎖されている. ▶定義 2 to prevent sth from being done ～がなされることを妨げる→～を妨げる, 妨害する‖ *The management tried to block the deal.* 経営陣はその取り引きを妨害しようとした. ▶定義3 to prevent sth from being seen by sb ～によって…が見られることを妨げる→～を遮る‖ *Get out of the way, you're blocking the view!* そこをどいてくれ, 君は視界を遮っている.

句動詞 **block sth off** ▶定義 to separate one area from another with sth solid 頑丈な～で, ある地域をほかから分離する→(障害物を置いて)～を遮る, 遮断する‖ *This section of the motorway has been blocked off by the police.* 自動車道路のこの区域は警察によって遮断されている.

**block sth out** ▶定義 to try not to think about sth unpleasant 不快な～について考えないようにする→～が入らない・見えないようにする, ～を締め出す‖ *She tried to block out the memory of the crash.* 彼女は, その衝突の記憶を忘れようとした.

**blockade** /blɑkéɪd/ 名 ⓒ ▶定義 a situation in which a place is surrounded by soldiers or ships in order to prevent goods or people from reaching it 商品または人々を到着させないように, 兵士や船によってある場所を取り囲む状況→(道路・港湾などの)封鎖, 遮断 — blockade 動 ⓗ →～を封鎖する, 遮断する

**blockage** /blɑ́kɪdʒ/ 名 ⓒ ▶定義 a thing that is preventing sth from passing; the state of being blocked ～が通過することを防ぐ物; 封鎖されている状態→妨害物, 障害物; 封鎖, 妨害‖ *a blockage in the drainpipe* 排水管のつまり *There are blockages on some major roads.* いくつかの主要道路が封鎖されている.

**blockbuster** /blɑ́kbʌstər; blɔ́k-/ 名 ⓒ ▶定義 a book or film with an exciting story which is very successful and popular 非常に大当たりして人気のある, とても面白い話の本または映画→大ヒット作

**block capital** 名 [ⓒ, 通常は複数] ▶定義 a big letter such as 'A' (not 'a') A(aではなく)のような, 大きな文字→活字体の大文字‖ *Please write your name in block capitals.* あなたのお名前を大文字で書いてください.

**bloke** /blóʊk/ 名 ⓒ 英 (俗語) ▶定義 a man 男の人→男, やつ‖ *He's a really nice bloke.* 彼は本当にすてきな男だ.

**blond**(または **blonde**) /blɒnd; blænd/ 名 ⓒ 形 ▶定義 (a person) with fair or yellow hair 金髪または黄色い髪を持つ(人)→ブロンド・金髪(の人)‖ *Most of our family have blond hair.* 私たちの家族はほとんどが金髪だ.

▶女性について描写するときには, blonde のつづりが用いられる: *She's tall, slim and blonde.* (彼女は, 背が高くほっそりして金髪だ.) 名詞は, 通常女性についてのみ用いられ, blonde とつづられる: *She's a blonde.* (彼女は金髪の人だ.) brunette も参照.

*****blood** /blʌd/ 名 ⓤ ▶定義 the red liquid that flows through your body 体の中を流れる赤い液体→血, 血液‖ *The heart pumps blood around the body.* 心臓は体中に血を押し出す.

☛参 **bleed**

成句 **in your blood** ▶定義 a strong part of your character 性格の強い部分→本気で何かをすること‖ *A love of the countryside was in his blood.* 彼は田舎が心底好きだった.

**in cold blood** ⇒ **COLD**¹
**shed blood** ⇒ **SHED**²
**your (own) flesh and blood** ⇒ **FLESH**

**bloodbath** /blʌ́dbɑːθ, -bæθ/ 名 [単数扱い] ▶定義 an act of violently killing many people 多くの人々を暴力的に殺す行為→大量殺人, 大虐殺

**blood-curdling** 形 ▶定義 very frightening 非常に怖い→ぞっとさせる‖ *a blood-curdling scream* 身の毛もよだつ叫び声

**blood donor** 名 ⓒ ▶定義 a person who gives some of his/her blood for use in medical operations 手術で使えるように, 自分の血液を一部提供する人→献血者, 供血者

**blood group**(または **blood type**) 名 ⓒ ▶定義 any of several different types of human blood 人間の血液の, いくつかの異なる種類のいずれか→血液型‖ *'What blood group are you?' 'O.'* 「あなたの血液型は何ですか」「O型です」

**bloodless** /blʌ́dləs/ 形 ▶定義1 without killing or violence 殺人, または暴力なしで→無血の, 血を流さない, 流血の惨事のない‖ *a bloodless coup* 無血クーデター ▶定義2 (used about a part of the body) very pale (体の一部について)とても青ざめた→青ざめた, 血の気のない

**blood pressure** 名 U ▶定義 the force with which the blood travels round the body 血が体を巡るための力→血圧 ‖ to have high/low blood pressure 血圧が高い・低い

**bloodshed** /blˈʌdʃèd/ ▶定義 the killing or harming of people 人々を殺すことまたは傷付けること→流血, 殺人, 虐殺 ‖ Both sides in the war want to avoid further bloodshed. その戦争で双方ともが,それ以上の流血を避けたいと思う.

**bloodshot** /blˈʌdʃɑ̀t/ 形 ▶定義 (used about the white part of the eyes) full of red lines, for example when sb is tired (目の白い部分について)赤い線がたくさんある,例えば〜が疲れているときに→充血した, 血走った

**blood sport** 名 C ▶定義 a sport in which animals or birds are killed 動物や鳥が殺されるスポーツ→動物を殺すスポーツ

**bloodstain** /blˈʌdstèin/ 名 C ▶定義 a mark or spot of blood on sth 〜に付いた血の印または点→血痕(けっこん) ― bloodstained 形 →血痕(けっこん)の付いた, 血まみれの

**bloodstream** /blˈʌdstrìːm/ 名 [単数扱い] ▶定義 the blood as it flows through the body 体を通って流れる血→血流, 血液 ‖ drugs injected straight into the bloodstream 血流に直接注射された薬

**bloodthirsty** /blˈʌdθə̀ːrsti/ 形 ▶定義 wanting to use violence or to watch scenes of violence 暴力を使いたい,または暴力的な場面を見たい→血に飢えた, 流血・殺生を好む, 残忍な

**blood transfusion** 名 C ▶定義 the process of putting new blood into a person's body 新しい血液を人体に入れる過程→輸血

**blood vessel** 名 C ▶定義 any of the tubes in your body which blood flows through 血液が通り抜けて循環する,体内の管→血管 ☞参 **vein**, **artery**, **capillary**

**bloody** /blˈʌdi/ 形 (**bloodier**; **bloodiest**) ▶定義1 involving a lot of violence and killing 多くの暴力と殺害に関係する→血生臭い, むごい, 残酷な ‖ a bloody war 血生臭い戦争 ▶定義2 covered with blood 血で覆われた→血まみれの, 血に汚れた ‖ a bloody knife 血まみれのナイフ ▶定義3 または 副 英 (俗語) a swear word used for emphasizing a comment or an angry statement 意見または怒りながら言うことを強調するために用いられるののしりの言葉→いまいましい, べらぼうな, ひどい ‖ The bloody train was late again this morning. あのいまいましい電車は今朝もまた遅れた. What a bloody stupid thing to say! 何てひどくばかげた事を言うのだ！ We had a bloody good time. べらぼうに良い時間を過ごした. ☜ 多くの人々は,この言葉を不快に思う.

**bloody-minded** 形 英 略式 ▶定義 (used about a person) deliberately difficult; not helpful (人について)わざと気難しくしている;助けにならない→わざと意地悪する, つむじ曲がりの ― bloody-mindedness 名 U →わざと意地悪すること, つむじ曲がりなこと

**bloom**¹ /bluːm/ 名 C ▶定義 a flower 花→(観賞用の)花
成句 **in bloom** ▶定義 with its flowers open 花が開いて→咲いて ‖ All the wild plants are in bloom. 全部の野生植物が咲いている.

**bloom**² /bluːm/ 動 自 ▶定義 to produce flowers 花を作る→花が咲く, 花をつける, 開花する ‖ This shrub blooms in May. この潅木(かんぼく)は,5月に花をつける.

**blossom**¹ /blˈɑsəm/ 名 C U ▶定義 a flower or a mass of flowers, especially on a fruit tree in the spring 1輪の花または一面の花, 特に春に見られる果樹の一面の花々→(木・庭木などの)花 ‖ The apple tree is **in blossom**. リンゴの木が咲いている. ☞ C2ページのさし絵

**blossom**² /blˈɑsəm/ 動 自 ▶定義1 (used especially about trees) to produce flowers (特に木について)花を作る→花をつける・開く ▶定義2 **blossom (into sth)** to become more healthy, confident or successful より健康になる, 自信を持つ, または成功する→実って〜となる, 成功する, 魅力的になる ‖ This young runner has blossomed into a top-class athlete. この若い走者は才能を開花させて, 一流のスポーツ選手になった.

**blot**¹ /blɑt/ 名 C ▶定義1 a spot of sth, especially one made by ink on paper; a stain 〜の点, 特に紙の上にインクで作られたもの; 汚れ→染み, 汚れ ▶定義2 **a blot on sth** a thing that spoils your happiness or other people's opinion of you 自分の幸福,または自分についての他人の評価を損なうもの→(人格・名声など

の)汚点,傷,美観を損なうもの

**blot²** /blɑt/ **動他 (blotting; blotted)** ▶定義1 to make a spot or a mark on sth, especially ink on paper ~に点や印を付ける,特に紙にインクで→**~に染みを付ける,~を汚す** ▶定義2 to remove liquid from a surface by pressing soft paper or cloth on it 柔らかい紙または布で押さえて,液体を表面から取り去る→**~を吸い取る**

句動詞 blot sth out ▶定義 to cover or hide sth ~を覆うまたは隠す→**~を覆い隠す,見えなくする,(文字などを)消す,抹消する** ‖ *Fog blotted out the view completely.* 霧が完全に視界を遮った. *She tried to blot out the memory of what happened.* 彼女はその出来事についての記憶を消そうとした.

**blotch** /blɑtʃ/ **名 C** ▶定義 a temporary mark or an area of different colour on skin, plants, material, etc 皮膚,植物,素材などに付いた一時的な印,または異なる色の部分→**染み,出来物** ‖ *The blotches on her face showed that she had been crying.* 彼女の顔の染みは,彼女が泣いていたことを示していた. ― blotchy(または blotched)形→**染み・出来物だらけの**

**blotting paper** 名 U ▶定義 soft paper that you use for drying wet ink after you have written sth on paper 紙に~を書いた後,ぬれたインクを乾かすために使う柔らかい紙→**吸い取り紙**

*****blouse** /blaʊz, -s/ **名 C** ▶定義 a piece of clothing like a shirt, that women wear 女の人が着る,シャツのような衣服→**ブラウス** ☞ C6ページのさし絵

blow/suck

blowing  sucking

*****blow¹** /bloʊ/ **動 (過 blew** /bluː/; **過分 blown** /bloʊn/) ▶定義1 **自他** (used about wind, air, etc) to be moving or to cause sth to move(風,空気などについて)動いている,または~を動かす→**吹く,~を吹き動かす,吹き飛ばす** ‖ *A gentle breeze was blowing.* そよ風が穏やかに吹いていた. ▶定義2 **自** to move because of the wind or a current of air 風または大気の流れによって動く→**吹かれる,吹かれて動く,はためく** ‖ *The balloons blew away.* 風船が吹き飛んでいった. *My papers blew all over the garden.* 私の書類が庭中に飛び散った. ▶定義3 **自** to send air out of the mouth 空気を口から外に送り出す→**息を吐く,息を吹き掛ける** ‖ *The policeman asked me to blow into the breathalyser.* 警官は私に酒気検知器に息を吹き掛けるように言った. ▶定義4 **他** to make or shape sth by blowing air out of your mouth 口から空気を送り出して~を作る,または形にする→**~を吹いて作る** ‖ *to blow bubbles/smoke rings* シャボン玉・煙の輪を吹いて作る *to blow (sb) a kiss* (= *to kiss your hand and pretend to blow the kiss towards sb*)(~に)投げキスをする (= 自分の手にキスをして,そのキスを~に向けて吹き飛ばす振りをする) ▶定義5 **自他** to produce sound from a musical instrument, etc by blowing air into it 空気を吹き込んで,楽器などの音を出す→**~を吹き鳴らす** ‖ *The referee's whistle blew for the end of the match.* 試合終了を告げる審判の笛が鳴った. *He blew a few notes on the trumpet.* 彼はトランペットで音階を2,3度吹き鳴らした. ▶定義6 **他 略式** to waste an opportunity 機会を無駄にする→**~をふいにする,棒に振る** ‖ *I think I've blown my chances of promotion.* 私は出世の機会をふいにしてしまったと思う. *You had your chance and you blew it.* あなたにはチャンスがあったが棒に振った. ▶定義7 **他 略式** blow sth (on sth) to spend or waste a lot of money on sth ~に大金を費やす,または無駄に使う→**~を浪費する,派手に使う** ‖ *She blew all her savings on a trip to China.* 彼女は中国旅行ですべての貯金を派手に使った. ▶定義8 **自他** (used about a thin piece of wire (a fuse) in an electrical system) to stop working suddenly because the electric current is too strong; to make sth do this (電流が強すぎるために突然,電気系統の細い電線(ヒューズ)の作動が止まることについて) ~にこの事をさせる→**飛ぶ; 飛ばす** ‖ *A fuse has blown.* ヒューズが飛んだ. *I think the kettle's blown a fuse.* 湯沸かしがヒューズを飛ばしたと思う.

成句 blow your nose ▶定義 to clear your nose

by blowing strongly through it into a piece of cloth (handkerchief) 布(ハンカチ)の中に強く息を吹き込んで鼻をきれいにする→鼻をかむ☞ **sneeze** のさし絵

[句動詞] blow over ▶定義 to disappear without having a serious effect 深刻な影響を与えることもなく,消える→(あらしが)静まる,(うわさ・悩みなどが)消える‖ *The scandal will soon blow over.* そのスキャンダルは間もなく消えるだろう.

blow up ▶定義1 to explode or to be destroyed in an explosion 爆発する,または爆発で壊される→爆発する,〜を爆破する‖ *The car blew up when the door was opened.* 車のドアが開けられたとき,その車は爆発した. ▶定義2 to start suddenly and strongly 突然,強烈に始まる→(あらしなどが)起こる,始まる‖ *A storm blew up in the night.* その夜あらしが吹き荒れた. *A huge row blew up about money.* お金のことで大きな騒ぎが突然起こった. ▶定義3 [略式] to become very angry 非常に怒る→怒る,〜をしかりとばす,どなりつける‖ *The teacher blew up when I said I'd forgotten my homework.* 私が宿題を忘れたと言うと,先生は怒った.

blow sth up ▶定義1 to make sth explode or to destroy sth in an explosion 〜を爆発させる,または…を爆発で壊す→〜を爆破する‖ *The terrorists tried to blow up the plane.* テロリストたちは飛行機を爆破しようとした. ▶定義2 to fill sth with air or gas 〜を空気または気体で満たす→〜を膨らませる‖ *to blow up a balloon* 風船を膨らませる ▶定義3 to make a photograph bigger 写真を大きくする→引き伸ばす

*__blow__² /blóu/ [名] [C] ▶定義1 a hard hit from sb's hand, a weapon, etc 〜の手,武器などによる強い一撃→強打,殴打‖ *She aimed a blow at me.* 彼女は私をねらって強打しようとした. ▶定義2 a blow (to sb/sth) a sudden shock or disappointment 突然の衝撃や失望→(精神的)打撃,痛手,災難‖ *It was a blow when I didn't get the job.* その仕事を得られなかったのは痛手だった. ▶定義3 an act of blowing 吹く行為→鼻をかむこと‖ *Give your nose a blow!* 鼻をかみなさい.

[成句] a blow-by-blow account, description, etc (of sth) ▶定義 an account, etc of an event that gives all the exact details of it あらゆる正確な詳細が記述されている,ある出来事についての報告書など→細部にわたる詳細な報告書,説明など

come to blows (with sb) (over sth) ▶定義 to start fighting or arguing (about sth) (〜についての)戦いまたは口論を…と始める→(〜のことで)殴り合いを始める

deal sb /sth a blow; deal a blow to sb /sth ⇒ **DEAL**¹

**blow-dry** [動] [他] (過,過分 **blow-dried**) ▶定義 to dry and shape sb's hair by holding a machine that produces hot air (a hairdryer) in your hand, and a brush 熱風を作り出す器械(ヘアドライヤー)とブラシを手に持ち,〜の髪を乾かし整える→〜をヘアドライヤーで整髪する,ブローする

**blown BLOW**¹ の過去分詞形

**blowout** /blóuaut/ [名] [C] [略式] ▶定義1 a burst tyre; a puncture 破裂したタイヤ; パンク→パンク‖ *We had a blowout on the motorway.* 高速道路でパンクした. ▶定義2 a very large meal at which people eat too much; a large party or social event 人々が食べすぎる,とても量の多い食事; 大きな宴会または社交的行事→ごちそう,大宴会

*__blue__¹ /blu:/ [形] ▶定義1 having the colour of a clear sky when the sun shines 太陽が輝いているときの晴れた空の色をした→青い,青色の‖ *His eyes were bright blue.* 彼の目は明るい青色だった. *light/dark blue* 明るい青色・紺色 ▶定義2 [略式] (often used in songs) sad (しばしば歌で用いて)悲しい→憂鬱(ゆううつ)な,悲しげな

[成句] black and blue ⇒ **BLACK**¹
once in a blue moon ⇒ **ONCE**

*__blue__² /blu:/ [名] ▶定義1 [C] [U] the colour of a clear sky when the sun shines 太陽が輝いているときの晴れた空の色→青,青色‖ *a deep blue* 濃い青色 *dressed in blue* (= blue clothes) 青(= 青い服)を着た ▶定義2 the blues [複数扱い,単数または複数形の動詞と共に] a type of slow sad music ゆっくりとした悲しい音楽の一種→ブルース‖ *a blues singer* ブルース歌手 ▶定義3 the blues [複数扱い] [略式] a feeling of great sadness; depression 大きな悲しみの感情; 憂鬱(ゆううつ)→憂鬱,憂鬱症‖ *to have the* *blues* 憂鬱になる

**成句** out of the blue ▶定義 suddenly; unexpectedly 突然; 予期せず→出し抜けに, 青天のへきれき, いきなり ‖ *I didn't hear from him for years and then this letter came out of the blue.* 彼からは何年も音さたがなかったところに, いきなりこの手紙が来た.

**blue-collar** 形 ▶定義 doing or involving physical work with the hands rather than office work 事務の仕事よりも手を使った肉体的な仕事をする, またはそれに関係する→ブルーカラーの, 肉体労働の ☞参 **white-collar**

**blueprint** /blúːprìnt/ 名 C ▶定義 a photographic plan or a description of how to make, build or achieve sth ～をどのように作るか, 建てるか, 達成するかについての非常に緻密な計画または描写→青写真, 設計図, 計画

**bluff**¹ /blʌf/ 動 自 他 ▶定義 to try to make people believe that sth is true when it is not, usually by appearing very confident 通常とても自信があるように見せることで, ～が事実ではないのに事実だと人々に信じさせようとする→はったりをかける, はったりをかけて～させる ‖ *They tried to bluff their parents into believing there was no school that day.* 彼らははったりをかけて, その日は学校が休みだと両親に信じさせようとした.

**成句** bluff your way in, out, through, etc sth ▶定義 to trick sb in order to get into, out of a place, etc ある場所などに入る, または出るために～をだます→はったりで切り抜ける ‖ *We managed to bluff our way into the stadium by saying we were journalists.* 私たちは記者だとはったりを言って, 何とか球場に入ることに成功した.

**bluff**² /blʌf/ 名 U C ▶定義 making sb believe that you will do sth when you really have no intention of doing it, or that you know sth when, in fact, you do not know it 実際にはするつもりがないのに～をする, または実際には知らないのに～を知っていると, …に信じさせること→こけおどし, はったり

**成句** call sb's bluff ⇒ **CALL**¹

**bluish** (または **blueish**) /blúːɪʃ/ 形 略式 ▶定義 slightly blue わずかに青い→青みがかった, 青っぽい ‖ *bluish green* 青みがかった緑

**blunder**¹ /blʌ́ndər/ 名 C ▶定義 a stupid mistake ばかげた間違い→へま, (大)失敗, 間違い ‖ *I'm afraid I've made a terrible blunder.* ひどいへまをしてしまったようだ.

**blunder**² /blʌ́ndər/ 動 自 ▶定義 to make a stupid mistake ばかげた間違いをする→へまをする, (大)失敗をする

**句動詞** blunder about, around, etc ▶定義 to move in an uncertain or careless way, as if you cannot see where you are going まるで自分がどこへ向かっているのか分からないかのように, おぼつかないまたは不注意な様子で動く→まごつく, まごまごして歩く ‖ *We blundered about in the dark, trying to find the light switch.* 私たちは, 電気のスイッチを探そうと暗闇 (やみ) の中をまごつき歩いた.

**blunt** /blʌnt/ 形 ▶定義 **1** (used about a knife, pencil, tool, etc) without a sharp edge or point (ナイフ, 鉛筆, 道具などについて) 鋭い端や先がない→切れない, なまくらの, とがっていない ‖ *blunt scissors* なまくらのはさみ ⇔ **sharp** ▶定義 **2** (used about a person, comment, etc) very direct; saying what you think without trying to be polite (人, 論評などについて) とても直接的な; 礼儀正しくいようと心掛けないで, 思う事を言う→ぶっきらぼうな, 素っ気ない ‖ *I'm sorry to be so blunt, but I'm afraid you're just not good enough.* 無遠慮な言い方で悪いが, 君が至らなかっただけだと思う. — blunt 動 他 →(ナイフなどを)鈍くする, (感覚・意思などを)鈍らせる — bluntly 副 →ぶっきらぼうに, 遠慮なく, 無作法に — bluntness 名 U →鈍さ, 鈍感, 無遠慮

**blur**¹ /bləːr/ 名 [C, 通常は単数] ▶定義 something that you cannot see clearly or remember well はっきりと見えない, またはよく覚えていないもの→ぼんやりしたもの, ぼやけたもの ‖ *Without my glasses, their faces were just a blur.* 眼鏡なしでは彼らの顔はただぼやけたものにすぎなかった.

**blur**² /bləːr/ 動 自 他 (**blurring**; **blurred**) ▶定義 to become or to make sth less clear ～がはっきりしなくなる, または～をはっきりさせない→ぼやける, かすむ, ～をぼんやりさせる, (涙が)～を曇らせる ‖ *The words on the page blurred as tears filled her eyes.* 彼女の目は涙で潤み, そのページの言葉がはっきりと見えなかった. — blurred 形 →ぼんやりした, ぼやけた

**blurt** /bləːrt/ 動
【句動詞】 blurt sth out ▶定義 to say sth suddenly or without thinking 突然にまたは考えなしに～を言う→～を口走る,出し抜けに言い出す‖ *We didn't want to tell Mum but Ann blurted the whole thing out.* 私たちはママには言いたくなかったが,アンが出し抜けに全部話した.

**blush** /blʌʃ/ 動 ⓘ ▶定義 to become red in the face, especially because you are embarrassed or feel guilty 特に恥ずかしい思いをしてまたは罪を感じて,顔が赤くなる→赤面する,顔を赤らめる‖ *She blushed with shame.* 彼女は恥ずかしくて赤面した. — **blush** 名 [Ⓒ, 通常は単数]→赤面,顔を赤くすること

**blusher** /blʌʃər/ 名 Ⓤ Ⓒ ▶定義 a coloured cream or powder that some people put on their cheeks to give them more colour 人々がほおに色を足すために付ける色の付いたクリームまたは粉→ほお紅

**blustery** /blʌstəri/ 形 ▶定義 (used to describe the weather) with strong winds (天気を描写するために用いて) 強い風のある→(天候が)荒れた,(風が)吹きすさぶ‖ *The day was cold and blustery.* その日は,寒くて風が吹きすさんでいた.

**BO** /biː óu/ 略 body odour→体臭,わきが

**boar** /bɔːr/ 名 Ⓒ (複 **boar** または **boars**)
▶定義1 a male pig 雄の豚→(去勢しない)雄豚
▶定義2 a wild pig 野性の豚→イノシシ ☞参 **pig** の注

*****board**[1] /bɔːrd/ ▶定義1 Ⓒ a long, thin, flat piece of wood used for making floors, walls, etc 床,壁などを作るために使われる,長く薄い平らな木材→板‖ *The old house needed new floorboards.* その古い家には新しい床板が必要だった. ▶定義2 Ⓒ a thin flat piece of wood, etc used for a particular purpose 特定の目的に用いられる,薄く平らな木材→盤,台‖ *an ironing board* アイロン台 *a surfboard* サーフボード *a noticeboard* 掲示板 *board games (= games you play on a board)* ボードゲーム (= 盤上で行うゲーム) ▶定義3 [Ⓒ, 単数または複数形の動詞と共に] a group of people who control an organization, company, etc 組織,会社などを管理,運営する人々の集団→委員会,評議員会,(官庁などの)省・庁・局・部‖ *The board of directors is/are meeting to discuss the firm's future.* 重役たちは,会社の将来について議論するために会議をしている. *a board meeting* 役員会議 ▶定義4 Ⓤ the meals that are provided when you stay in a hotel, etc ホテルなどに滞在しているときに提供される食事→食事,賄い‖ *The prices are for a double room and **full board** (= all the meals).* その価格は,ダブルルームで全食付き (= すべての食事) の場合だ.

【成句】 above board ⇒ **ABOVE**
across the board ⇒ **ACROSS**
on board ▶定義 on a ship or an aircraft 船または飛行機上で→乗り込んで,搭乗・乗船・乗車して,機内・船内・車内で‖ *All the passengers were safely on board.* すべての乗客は無事乗船した.

**board**[2] /bɔːrd/ 動 ⓘ ⓣ ▶定義 to get on a plane, ship, bus, etc 飛行機,船,バスなどに乗る→乗り込む,搭乗・乗船・乗車する‖ *We said goodbye and boarded the train.* 私たちはさよならを言って列車に乗り込んだ. *Lufthansa flight LH120 to Hamburg is now boarding (= ready to take passengers) at Gate 27.* ハンブルグ行きのルフトハンザ航空 LH120便は,現在27番ゲートで搭乗手続きをしています (= 乗客を迎える準備ができた).

【句動詞】 board sth up ▶定義 to cover with boards[1](1) boards[1](1)で覆う→～に板を張る,板で囲う‖ *Nobody lives there now - it's all boarded up.* あそこには今だれも住んでいない - 全体が板で囲まれている.

**boarder** /bɔ́ːrdər/ 名 Ⓒ 英 ▶定義1 a child who lives at school and goes home for the holidays. 学園に住んでいて,休暇に帰宅する子供→寮生 ▶定義2 a person who pays to live at sb's house 金を払って～の家に住む人→下宿生 ☞参 **lodger**

**boarding card** 名 Ⓒ ▶定義 a card that you must show in order to get on a plane or ship 飛行機または船に乗るために提示しなければならないカード→搭乗券,乗船券

**boarding house** 名 Ⓒ ▶定義 a private house where you can pay to stay and have meals for a period of time 金を払って一定期間滞在し食事を取る個人の家→下宿屋

**boarding school** 名 Ⓒ ▶定義 a school that schoolchildren live at while they are studying, going home only in the holidays 生徒たちは勉

強している間そこで暮らし,休暇のときだけ家に帰る学校→**寄宿学校**

**boardroom** /bɔ́ːrdrùːm, -rùm/ 名 ⓒ ▶定義 the room where the group of people in charge of a company or organization (the board of directors) meets 会社または組織の責任者の集団(重役)が会う部屋→**(重役会・理事会の)会議室**

**boast** /bóʊst/ 動 ▶定義 1 ⓘ to talk with too much pride about sth that you have or can do 自分が持つまたはできる～について,過度の自慢を持って話す→**自慢する,鼻に掛ける** ∥ *I wish she wouldn't boast about her family so much.* 彼女が自分の家族のことをあまり自慢しないとよいのだが. ▶定義 2 ⓣ (used about a place) to have sth that it can be proud of (場所について)誇れる～を持っている→**～があるのを自慢にする,誇りとして～を持つ** ∥ *The town boasts over a dozen restaurants.* その町には10軒以上のレストランがあることを誇りにしている. — boast 名 ⓒ →**自慢,鼻に掛けること**

**boastful** /bóʊstfəl, -f(ə)l/ 形 ▶定義 (used about a person or the things that he/she says) showing too much pride (人または人が言うことについて)あまりに誇らしげな→**自慢げな,自画自賛の**

**boats**

rowing boat (英 rowboat)
oar
paddle
canoe (または Kayak)
life jacket
dinghy

\***boat** /bóʊt/ 名 ⓒ ▶定義 1 a small vehicle that is used for travelling across water 水域を渡るために使われる小さな乗り物→**ボート,小舟** ∥ *The cave can only be reached by boat/ in a boat.* その洞窟(どうくつ)にはボートでのみ行ける. *a rowing/fishing/motor boat* 手こぎのボート・釣り船・モーターボート ▶定義 2 any ship あらゆる船→**船,汽船** ∥ *When does the next boat to France sail?* 次のフランス行きの船はいつ出航しますか.

成句 rock the boat ⇒ **ROCK²**

**bob** /bɑb/ 動 (**bobbing**; **bobbed**) ⓘ ⓣ ▶定義 to move quickly up and down; to make sth do this 素早く上下に動く;～をそうさせる→**ひょいと動く,ぴょこんとお辞儀をする;～を上下にひょいと動かす** ∥ *The boats in the harbour were bobbing up and down in the water.* 港の船は水面を上下に動いていた. *She bobbed her head down below the top of the wall.* 彼女は塀のてっぺんより下に,ひょいと頭を引っ込めた.

句動詞 bob up ▶定義 to appear suddenly from behind or under sth ～の後ろまたは下から突然現れる→**ひょいと現れる** ∥ *He disappeared and then bobbed up again on the other side of the pool.* 彼は姿を消すと,プールの向こう側からまたひょいと現れた.

**bobsleigh** /bɑ́bslèɪ/ (米 **bobsled** /bɑ́bsled/) 名 ⓒ ▶定義 a racing vehicle for two or more people that slides over snow along a track 競技用の進路に沿って雪の上を滑る,2人以上の人のための競技用の乗り物→**ボブスレー** ☛参 **sleigh, sledge, toboggan**

**bode** /bóʊd/ 動

成句 bode well/ill (for sb/sth) ▶定義 to be a sign that sb/sth will have a good/bad future ～に良いまたは悪い未来があるという印である→**(～にとって)良い・悪い前兆である,縁起が良い・悪い**

**bodily¹** /bɑ́dɪli/ 形 ▶定義 of the human body; physical 人間の体の;肉体的な→**身体上の,肉体上の** ∥ *First we must attend to their bodily needs (= make sure that they have a home, enough to eat, etc).* まず私たちは彼らが身体的に必要とするものに注意しなければならない(= 彼らが家を持っているか,十分に食べ物があるかなどを確認する).

**bodily²** /bɑ́dɪli/ 副 ▶定義 by taking hold of the body 体をつかんで→**体ごとそっくり,丸ごと** ∥ *She picked up the child and carried him bodily from the room.* 彼女はその子を持ち上げて部屋

から連れ出した.

**\*body** /bádi/ 名 (複 **bodies**) ▶定義1 ● the whole physical form of a person or animal 人または動物の肉体全体→**体, 肉体, 身体** ‖ *the human body* 人間の体 ▶定義2 ● the part of a person that is not his/her legs, arms or head 足, 腕, 頭以外の人の体の部分→**胴体** ‖ *She had injuries to her head and body.* 彼女は頭と胴体にけがをした. ▶定義3 ● a dead person 死んだ人→**死体, 遺体** ‖ *The police have found a body in the canal.* 警察は運河で死体を発見した. ▶定義4 [●,単数または複数形の動詞と共に] a group of people who work or act together, especially in an official way 特に公式に, 一緒に働くまたは行動する人々の集団→**一団, 一群, 集まり, 団体** ‖ *The governing body of the college meets/meet once a month.* その大学の運営団体は, 月に1度会合を開く. ▶定義5 [単数扱い] the main part of sth ～の主要な部分→**本体, 主要部** ‖ *We agree with the body of the report, although not with certain details.* その報告書の一部の詳細事項には同意しないが, 主要な点には同意する. ▶定義6 ●正式 an object →**物体** ‖ *The doctor removed a foreign body from the child's ear.* 医者は, その子供の耳から異物を取り除いた.

成句 **in a body** ▶定義 all together 皆一緒に→**一団となり, 全員そろって**

**bodybuilding** /bádɪbɪldɪŋ/ 名 ● ▶定義 making the muscles of the body stronger and larger by exercise 運動で体の筋肉をより強く, またより大きくすること→**ボディービル** — **bodybuilder** 名 ●→**ボディービルをする人**

**bodyguard** /bádɪgɑːrd/ 名 ● ▶定義 a person or group of people whose job is to protect sb ～を守ることを仕事とする人または人々の集団→**ボディーガード, 護衛**

**body language** 名 ● ▶定義 showing how you feel by the way you move, stand, sit, etc, rather than by what you say 口で言うよりもむしろ, 動く, 立つ, 座るなどの手段で自分がどう感じているかを示すこと→**ボディーランゲージ, 身振り言語** ‖ *I could tell by his body language that he was scared.* 彼の身振りで彼が怖がっているのが分かった.

**body odour** 名 ● (略 **BO**) ▶定義 the unpleasant smell from a person's body, especially of sweat 特に汗の, 人の体の不愉快なにおい→**体臭, わきが**

**bodywork** /bádiwɜːrk/ 名 ● ▶定義 the main outside structure of a vehicle, usually made of painted metal 通常塗装された金属でできた, 乗り物の外側の主な構造部→**車体**

**bog** /bɔ(ː)g, bɑg/ 名 ● ▶定義 an area of ground that is very soft and wet とても柔らかで湿気のあるぬれている土地の区域→**沼地, 湿地, 泥沼** ‖ *a peat bog* 泥炭地

**bogey** /bóugi/ 名 ● ▶定義1 something that causes fear, often without reason しばしば理由なく, 恐怖を起こさせるもの→**お化け, 幽霊** ▶定義2 略式 a piece of the sticky substance (mucus) that forms inside your nose 鼻の中で作られる, ねばねばした物質(鼻汁)→**鼻汁, 鼻くそ**

**bogged down** 形 ▶定義1 (used about a vehicle) not able to move because it has sunk into soft ground (乗り物について)柔らかい地面に沈んだために動けない→**泥沼にはまって, 身動きが取れない** ▶定義2 (used about a person) not able to make any progress (人について)全く進めない→**身動きが取れない** ‖ *We got bogged down in a long discussion and didn't have time to make any decisions.* 我々は長い討論にはまり込み, 決定をする時間がなかった.

**boggle** /bág(ə)l/ 動 自 ▶定義 to be unable to imagine sth; impossible to imagine or believe ～を想像することができない; 想像または信じることが不可能である→**しりごみする, ためらう, 仰天する** ‖ *'What will happen if his plan doesn't work?' 'The mind boggles!'* 「彼の計画がうまくいかなかったら, どうなるのだろう」「そんな事は到底考えられない」☞参 **mind-boggling**

**boggy** /bɔ́(ː)gi, bɑ́gi/ 形 ▶定義 (used about land) soft and wet, so that your feet sink into it (土地について)柔らかくて湿気があるため足が沈む→**湿地の, 沼地の, 沼沢の多い**

**bogus** /bóugəs/ 形 ▶定義 pretending to be real or genuine 実在しているまたは本物であるという振りをする→**偽りの, いんちきの** ‖ *a bogus policeman* にせ警官

**\*boil¹** /bɔ́ɪl/ 動 ▶定義1 自 (used about a liquid) to reach a high temperature where bubbles rise to the surface and the liquid changes to a gas (液

## boil²

体について)泡が表面まで上り,液体が気体に変わるときの高い温度に達する→**沸騰する,沸く** ‖ *Water boils at 100°C.* 水は摂氏100度で沸騰する. *The kettle's boiling.* やかんが沸騰している. ▶定義2 to heat a liquid until it boils and let it keep boiling 液体を沸騰するまで熱して,沸騰させ続ける→**～を沸騰させる,沸かす** ‖ *Boil all drinking water for five minutes.* すべての飲料水を5分間沸騰させなさい. ▶定義3 to cook (sth) in boiling water 沸騰した水の中で(～を)調理する→**煮える,ゆだる,～を煮る,ゆでる** ‖ *Put the potatoes on to boil, please.* ジャガイモを煮てください. *to boil an egg* 卵をゆでる ▶定義4 (used about a person) to feel very angry(人について)とても怒っている→**かっとなる,激昂(げっこう)する** ‖ *She was boiling with rage.* 彼女は激怒していた.

**句動詞** **boil down to sth** ▶定義 to have sth as the most important point ～を最も重要な点として持つ→**詰まる所～だ,～を要約する** ‖ *What it all boils down to is that you don't want to spend too much money.* 詰まる所,あなたはあまり金を使いたくないということだね.

**boil over** ▶定義1 (used about a liquid) to boil and flow over the sides of a pan(液体について)沸騰して,なべの外に流れ出す→**吹き・煮えこぼれる** ‖ *You let the soup boil over.* スープが吹きこぼれているよ. ▶定義2 (used about an argument or sb's feelings) to become more serious or angry(議論または～の感情について)さらに深刻になる,または怒る→**収拾がつかなくなる,暴動になる,かんかんに怒る**

**boil²** /bɔɪl/ ▶定義1 [単数扱い] a period of boiling; the point at which a liquid boils 沸騰している期間; 液体が沸騰する点→**沸騰状態,沸騰点** ‖ *You'll have to give those shirts a boil to get them clean.* これらのシャツをきれいにするには煮沸しなければならないだろう. ▶定義2 a small, painful swelling under your skin, with a red or yellow top 表面が赤いまたは黄色い,皮膚の下の小さな痛いはれ物→**はれ物,おでき**

**boiler** /bɔɪlə/ ▶定義 a container in which water is heated to provide hot water or heating in a building or to produce steam in an engine お湯を供給する,建物を暖める,またはエンジンで蒸気を作るために,水が温められる容器→**ボイラー,蒸気がま**

**boiler suit** (米 **coveralls**) ▶定義 a piece of clothing that you wear over your normal clothes to protect them when you are doing dirty work 汚れた仕事をするときに,普段着を守るためにその上に着る服→**作業服,カバーオール**

**boiling** /bɔɪlɪŋ/ (または **boiling hot**) ▶定義 very hot とても熱い→**煮え立っている,猛烈に熱い・暑い** ‖ *Open a window - it's boiling hot in here.* 窓を開けてくれ － ここは猛烈に暑い. *Can I open a window? I'm boiling.* 窓を開けてもいいですか. ひどく暑いので.

**boiling point** ▶定義 the temperature at which a liquid starts to boil 液体が沸騰し始める温度→**沸点**

**boisterous** /bɔɪst(ə)rəs/ ▶定義 (used about a person or behaviour) noisy and full of energy (人または行動について用いて)うるさくて,精力に満ちあふれた→**荒々しい,陽気で騒々しい** ‖ *Their children are very nice but they can get a bit too boisterous.* 彼らの子供たちはとてもかわいいが,多少うるさすぎる.

★**bold** /bóʊld/ ▶定義1 (used about a person or his/her behaviour) confident and not afraid(人またはその行動について)自信があり,恐れていない→**大胆な** ‖ *Not many people are bold enough to say exactly what they think.* 思った通りの事を言えるほど大胆な人は多くない. ▶定義2 that you can see clearly はっきり見てとれる→**際立った,目に付く** ‖ *bold, bright colours* 際立った,明るい色彩 ▶定義3 (used about printed letters) in thick, dark type(印刷された文字について)太く,濃い種類の→**肉太の** ‖ *Make the important text bold.* 重要な文を肉太にしなさい. ― **bold** →**肉太** ‖ *The important words are highlighted **in bold**.* 重要な単語は肉太で目立つようになっています. ― **boldly** →**大胆に,厚かましく** ― **boldness** →**大胆さ,厚かましさ**

**bollard** /bɔ́lɑːd/ ▶定義 a short thick post that is used to stop motor vehicles from going into an area that they are not allowed to enter 入ることが許されていない場所に自動車が入らないように使われる短くて太い柱→**保安柱**

**bolshie**(または **bolshy**) /bóʊlʃi/ 略式 ▶定義 (used about a person) bad-tempered and often refusing to do what people ask him/her to do（人について）意地悪で，人々がしてほしいと頼むことをしばしば拒否する➜**非協力的な，頑強に反抗する**

**bolster** /bóʊlstər/ [動][他] ▶定義 bolster sb/sth (up) to support or encourage sb/sth; to make sth stronger ～を支えたりまたは励ます; ～を強くする➜**～を支持する，強化する** ‖ *His remarks did nothing to bolster my confidence.* 彼の意見は何も私の自信を強めはしなかった.

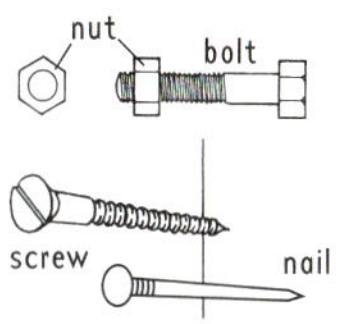


**bolt**[1] /bóʊlt/ [名][C] ▶定義1 a small piece of metal that is used with another piece of metal (a nut) for fastening things together 複数の物を一緒に留めるために，別の金属部品（ナット）と共に使われる小さな金属部品➜**ボルト** ▶定義2 a bar of metal that you can slide across the inside of the door in order to fasten it 扉をしっかりと締めるために，扉の内側に滑り込ませる金属製の棒➜**かんぬき，留め金**

**bolt**[2] /bóʊlt/ [動] ▶定義1 [自] (used especially about a horse) to run away very suddenly, usually in fear（特に馬について）通常怖がって，突然逃げ出す➜**（馬が驚いて）手綱を振り切って走り出す，（人が）逃げ出す** ▶定義2 [他] bolt sth (down) to eat sth very quickly とても速く～を食べる➜**～を丸のみにする，～を大急ぎで食べる・飲む** ‖ *She bolted down a sandwich and dashed out of the house.* 彼女はサンドイッチを大急ぎで食べると，家の外に駆け出した. ▶定義3 [他] to fasten one thing to another using a bolt[1](1) bolt[1](1)を使って，ある物を別の物に固定する➜**ボルトで固定する・締める** ‖ *All the tables have been bolted to the floor so that nobody can steal them.* だれにも盗めないように，すべてのテーブルは床にボルトで固定されている. ▶定義4 [他] to fasten a door, etc with a bolt[1](2) bolt[1](2)で扉などを固定する➜**かんぬきで締める** ‖ *Make sure that the door is locked and bolted.* 扉にかぎがかかって，かんぬきで締まっていることを確認しなさい.

**bolt**[3] /bóʊlt/ [副]

[成句] bolt upright ▶定義 sitting or standing very straight とてもまっすぐに座ってまたは立って➜**まっすぐに，背筋を伸ばして**

***bomb**[1] /bɑm/ [名] ▶定義1 [C] a container that is filled with material that will explode when it is thrown or dropped, or when a device inside it makes it explode 投げたり，落したりすると爆発する材料で満たされた容器，または中の装置がそれ自体を爆発する容器➜**爆弾** ‖ *Fortunately, the car bomb failed to* ***go off****.* 幸運にも，自動車に仕掛けた爆弾は爆発しないで済んだ. ▶定義2 **the bomb**［単数扱い］nuclear weapons 核兵器➜**核爆弾，原子爆弾** ‖ *How many countries have the bomb now?* 現在，核兵器を保有している国はいくつありますか. ▶定義3 **a bomb**［単数扱い］[略式] a lot of money ➜**大金** ‖ *That car must have cost you a bomb!* あの車には大金がかかっただろう.

**bomb**[2] /bɑm/ [動] ▶定義1 [他] to attack a city, etc with bombs 爆弾で町などを攻撃する➜**～を爆撃する，～を爆弾で破壊する** ‖ *Enemy forces have bombed the bridge.* 敵の軍隊が橋を爆撃した. ▶定義2 [自][英][略式] bomb along, down, up, etc to move along very fast in the direction mentioned, especially in a vehicle 特に乗り物で，言及された方向にとても速く動く➜**素早く動く，猛スピードでぶっ飛ばす** ‖ *He was bombing along at 100 miles an hour when the police stopped him.* 彼は時速100マイルで飛ばしていたら警官が停車させた.

**bombard** /bɑmbɑ́ːrd/ [動][他] ▶定義 to attack a place with bombs or guns 爆弾または銃で，ある場所を攻撃する➜**砲撃する，爆撃する** ‖ *They bombarded the city until the enemy surrendered.* 彼らは敵が降伏するまで町を爆撃した.（比喩）*The reporters bombarded the minister with questions.* 記者たちは大臣を質問攻めにした. — bombardment [名][C][U]➜**砲撃，爆撃，質問攻め** ‖ *The main radio station has* ***come under*** *enemy* ***bombardment****.* 主要なラジオ局は敵の爆撃にさらされた.

**bomb disposal** [名][U] ▶定義 the removing or exploding of bombs in order to make an area safe 安全にするために，爆弾をある地域から撤去するまたは爆発させること➜**不発弾処理** ‖ *a bomb disposal expert* 不発弾処理の専門家

**bomber** /bɑ́mər/ [名][C] ▶定義1 a type of plane

## 170　bombshell

that drops bombs 爆弾を落とす飛行機の一種→**爆撃機** ▶定義2 a person who makes a bomb explode in a public place 公の場所で爆発させる人→**爆弾を仕掛けた者,爆弾事件の犯人**

**bombshell** /bάmʃèl/ 名 [C,通常は単数] ▶定義 an unexpected piece of news, usually about sth unpleasant 通常不愉快な〜について、予期しない知らせ→**突発事件,人を驚かすような事・人** ‖ *The chairman **dropped a bombshell** when he said he was resigning.* 会長は辞任すると申し出て、人々を驚かせた.

**bona fide** /bóʊnə fáɪdi, -fáɪd/ 形 ▶定義 real or genuine 事実のまたは本物の→**真実の,誠実な,善意の** ‖ *This car park is for the use of bona fide customers only.* この駐車場は当店のお客さまだけがご利用できます.

**bond** /bάnd/ 名 ▶定義1 C something that joins two or more people or groups of people together, such as a feeling of friendship 2人以上の人々または集団を結び付けるもの、例えば友情→**結び付き,きずな,団結** ‖ *Our two countries are united by bonds of friendship.* 私たちの2つの国は、友情のきずなで結ばれています.
▶定義2 C a certificate that you can buy from a government or company that promises to pay you interest on the money you have given 政府または会社から買った証書で利子を本人に支払うと約束したもの→**(借金などの)証文,債権** ‖ *government bonds* 国債

\*\***bone**¹ /bóʊn/ 名 ▶定義1 C one of the hard parts inside the body of a person or animal that are covered with muscle, skin, etc 人または動物の体内にある,筋肉,皮膚などで覆われている硬い部分の1つ→**骨** ‖ *He's broken a bone in his hand.* 彼は手の骨を折った. *This fish has got a lot of bones in it.* この魚にはたくさんの骨がある. ▶定義2 U the substance that bones are made of 骨が作られている物質→**骨質**

成句 **have a bone to pick with sb** ▶定義 to have sth that you want to complain to sb about 〜に文句を言いたい…がある→**〜に苦情・文句がある**

**make no bones about (doing) sth** ▶定義 to do sth in an open honest way without feeling nervous or worried about it 神経質になったり気に病んだりせずに、公然と正直に〜をする→**平気で〜する,〜を率直に認める** ‖ *She made no bones about telling him exactly what she thought about him.* 彼女は彼について思う事をそのまま率直に本人に話した.

**bone**² /bóʊn/ 動 他 ▶定義 to take the bones out of sth 〜から骨を取り出す→**〜の骨を取る** ‖ *to bone a fish* 魚の骨を取る

**bone-dry** 形 ▶定義 completely dry 完全に乾いた→**からからに乾いた,干からびた** ‖ *Give that plant some water - it's bone-dry.* あの植物に水をやりなさい － 干からびている.

**bone marrow**(または **marrow**) 名 U ▶定義 the soft substance that is inside the bones of a person or animal 人または動物の骨の内側にある柔らかい物質→**骨の髄**

**bonfire** /bάnfàɪər/ 名 C ▶定義 a large fire that you build outside to burn rubbish, as part of a festival, etc 祭りの一環などとして、ごみを燃やすために外で起こす大きな火→**(祝いの)大かがり火,(野天の)たき火**

**Bonfire Night** 名 C ▶定義 in Britain, the night of 5 November 英国で11月5日の夜→**たき火の夜**
▶この日英国の人々は、17世紀にガイ フォークスが国会を爆破しようとして失敗したことを祝って、花火を打ち上げ、かがり火の上でguy(ガイ)と呼ばれる人形を燃やす.

**bonkers** /bάŋkərz/ 形 (俗語) ▶定義 crazy; mad 狂った; 正気でない→**頭がおかしい** ‖ *I'd go bonkers if I worked here full-time.* ここで全時間勤務したら頭がおかしくなる.

**bonnet** /bάnət/ (米 **hood**) 名 C ▶定義1 the front part of a car that covers the engine エンジンを覆う車の前方の部分→**ボンネット** ☛ S7ページのさし絵 ▶定義2 a type of hat which covers the sides of the face and is fastened with strings under the chin 顔の側面を覆い、あごの下でひもを結ぶ帽子の一種→**男子・兵士用縁なし帽**

**bonus** /bóʊnəs/ 名 C (複 **bonuses**) ▶定義1 a payment that is added to what is usual 通常のものに追加される給与→**賞与,ボーナス** ‖ *All our employees receive an annual bonus.* 当社の全社員は年に一度ボーナスを受け取る. ▶定義2 something good that you get in addition to what you expect 期待するものに加えて得る良

いもの→おまけ，思い掛けない良い事・贈り物 ‖ *I enjoy my job, and having my own office is **an added bonus**.* 仕事は楽しいし，おまけに自分の事務所も持っている．

**bony** /bóuni/ 形 ▶定義 so thin that you can see the shape of the bones 骨の形が分かるほどとても細い→骨のような，骨張った，やせた ‖ *long bony fingers* 長い骨張った指

**boo** /bu:/ 間 名 C (複 **boos**) ▶定義1 a sound you make to show that you do not like sb/sth 〜が好きではないことを示すために出す声→ブーという声，ブーイング ‖ *The minister's speech was met with boos from the audience.* 大臣の演説は聴衆からブーイングされた．▶定義2 a sound you make to frighten or surprise sb 〜を怖がらせるまたは驚かすために出す声→わっ ‖ *He jumped out from behind the door and said 'boo'.* 彼は扉の後ろから飛び出して「わっ」と言った．— boo 動 自他 →「ぶー」と言う，あざける，やじる

**boob** /bu:b/ 名 C (俗語) ▶定義1 a woman's breast 女性の胸→おっぱい，乳房 ▶定義2 a silly mistake ばかげた間違い→ばかげた間違い，間抜け，とんま — boob 動 自 →ばかげた間違いをする ‖ *I'm afraid I've boobed again.* またばかげた間違いをしてしまったようだ．

**booby prize** /bú:bi praɪz/ (または **wooden spoon**) 名 C ▶定義 a prize that is given as a joke to the person or team that comes last in a competition 大会で最下位になった人またはチームに冗談で与えられる賞→最下位賞，ブービー賞

**booby trap** /bú:bi træp/ 名 C ▶定義 a device that will kill, injure or surprise sb when he/she touches the object that it is connected to つながっている物に〜が触ると，その〜を殺す，傷付ける，または驚かす仕掛け→間抜け落とし，擬装爆弾 — booby-trap 動 他 →〜に間抜け落とし・擬装爆弾を仕掛ける

\***book**¹ /bʊk/ ▶定義1 C a written work that is published as printed pages fastened together inside a cover, or in electronic form 表紙に挟まれて一緒に束ねられた書かれたもので，印刷されたページとしてまたは電子形式で出版される→本，書物，著作 ‖ *I'm reading a book on astrology.* 私は，占星術の本を読んでいるところです．*She's writing a book about her life abroad.* 彼女は，海外での彼女の生活についての本を書いている．*Do you have any books by William Golding?* ウィリアム ゴールディングの著作を持っていますか．*hardback/paperback books* ハードカバーの本・ペーパーバック ▶定義2 C a number of pieces of paper, fastened together inside a cover, for people to write or draw on 人々が文字を書き込んだり絵をかくために，表紙に挟んで束ねられた多くの紙→帳面，ノート ‖ *Please write down all the new vocabulary in your exercise books.* すべての新しい単語を練習帳に書いてください．*a notebook* ノート *a sketch book* スケッチブック ▶定義3 C a number of things fastened together in the form of a book 本の形に束ねられたたくさんの物→本のようにとじた物，とじ込み，1冊 ‖ *a book of stamps* 1つづりの切手 *a chequebook* 小切手帳 ▶定義4 **books**[複数扱い] the records that a company, etc, keeps of the amount of money it spends and receives 会社などが使うまたは受け取る金額を記した記録→帳簿 ‖ *We employ an accountant to **keep the books**.* 帳簿をつける会計係を雇う．

成句 be in sb's good/bad books 略式 ▶定義 to have sb pleased/angry with you 自分について〜を喜ばせる・怒らせる→〜に気に入られている・嫌われている ‖ *He's been in his girlfriend's bad books since he forgot her birthday.* 彼は恋人の誕生日を忘れて以来，彼女から嫌われている．

by the book ▶定義 exactly according to the rules 規則通りに従って→規則通りに，正式に，きちんと ‖ *A policeman must always do things by the book.* 警官は常に規則通りに物事を行わなければならない．

(be) on sb's books ▶定義 (to be) on the list of an organization 組織の名簿に(載っている)→〜の一員として登録されている ‖ *The employment agency has hundreds of qualified secretaries on its books.* 職業紹介所には，数百人の資格を持った秘書が登録されている．

➤ 音声とつづり字

ooは[ʊ ウ]？

つづり字の oo は主として[ʊ ウ](book, cook, foot, look, ...)かまたは[u: ウー](cool,

## 172　book²

> food, fool, pool, school, ...と発音します. 一般に無声破裂音のt, kの前では[oʊ]になり, 有声音の前では[u: ウー]になることが多いです. roomやroofは[oʊ], [u: ウー]のいずれもあります.
>
> ooはそれ以外の次のような発音もあるので注意が必要です: brooch[bróʊtʃ], flood[flʌd], blood[blʌd], cooperate[koʊ.áp.ə.rèɪt]

*book² /bʊk/ 動 ▶定義1 他 略式 to arrange to have or do sth at a particular time 特定の時間に〜を持つ, または行うように手はずを整える→予約する ‖ *Have you booked a table, sir?* テーブルのご予約はなさいましたか. *to book a seat on a plane/train/bus* 飛行機・電車・バスの席を予約する *I've booked a hotel room for you/I've booked you a hotel room.* ホテルの部屋を予約させていただきました. *I'm sorry, but this evening's performance is fully booked (= there are no seats left).* 申し訳ありませんが, 今晩の上演はすべて予約済みです(= 席は残っていません). ▶定義2 他 略式 to officially write down the name of a person who has done sth wrong 悪い事をした人の名前を公式に書く→名前をリストに記載する ‖ *The police booked her for (= charged her with) dangerous driving.* 警官は危険な運転で彼女の名前を記入した(= 告訴した). *The player was booked for a foul and then sent off for arguing.* その選手はファウルを記録され, その事で言い争って退場させられた.

句動詞 book in ▶定義 to say that you have arrived at a hotel, etc, and sign your name on a list ホテルなどに到着し, 名簿に自分の名前を記入する→(ホテルで)記帳する, チェックインする

book sb in ▶定義 to arrange a room for sb at a hotel, etc in advance 〜のために, あらかじめホテルなどに部屋を用意する→〜の部屋を予約する ‖ *I've booked you in at the George Hotel.* ジョージホテルにお部屋を予約しておきました.

**bookcase** /bʊ́kkeɪs/ 名 C ▶定義 a piece of furniture with shelves to keep books on 本を保管しておくための, 棚の付いた家具→本箱, 本棚 ☞ C7ページのさし絵

**bookie** /bʊ́ki/ 略式 = BOOKMAKER

**booking** /bʊ́kɪŋ/ 名 C U ▶定義 the arrangement you make in advance to have a hotel room, a seat on a plane, etc ホテルの部屋, 航空機の座席などを取るために前もってする準備→予約 ‖ *Did you manage to make a booking?* 何とかご予約は取れましたか. *No advance booking is necessary.* ご予約の必要はありません.

**booking office** 名 C ▶定義 an office where you buy tickets 切符を買う事務所→切符売り場, 出札所

**bookkeeping** /bʊ́kkiːpɪŋ/ 名 U ▶定義 keeping the accounts of the money that a company, etc, spends or receives 会社などが使うまたは受け取る金の額を管理すること→簿記

**booklet** /bʊ́klət/ 名 C ▶定義 a small thin book, usually with a soft cover, that gives information about sth 通常柔らかい表紙の付いた, 〜についての情報を与える小さな薄い本→小冊子, パンフレット

**bookmaker** /bʊ́kmeɪkər/ (または 略式 **bookie**) 名 ▶定義1 C a person whose job is to take bets on horse races, etc 競馬などのかけに応じることを仕事にする人→かけ屋, ノミ屋 ▶定義2 **bookmaker's**[単数扱い]a shop, etc where you can bet money on a race or an event レースや出来事に金をかけることができる店など→かけ屋, ノミ屋 ☞参 betting shop

**bookmark** /bʊ́kmɑːrk/ ▶定義1 a narrow piece of card, etc that you put between the pages of a book so that you can find the same place again easily 容易にまた同じ場所を見つけられるように本の間に挟んでおく細いカードなど→しおり ▶定義2 a file from the Internet that you have stored on your computer 自分のコンピューターに保存してあるインターネットからのファイル→ブックマーク

**bookseller** /bʊ́ksɛlər/ 名 C ▶定義 a person whose job is selling books 本を売ることを仕事とする人→書籍販売人, 本屋

**bookshop** /bʊ́kʃɑp/ (米 **bookstore**) 名 C ▶定義 a shop that sells books 本を売る店→本屋, 書店 ☞参 library

**bookstall** /bʊ́kstɔːl/ (米 **news-stand**) 名 C ▶定義 a type of small shop, which is open at the front, selling newspapers, magazines and books, for example on a station 例えば駅で, 新聞, 雑誌, 本を売っている, 正面が開いている小さな店→雑誌・新聞売り場, キヨスク, 販売スタ

**bookworm** /búkwə̀ːm/ 名 C ▶定義 a person who likes reading books very much 本を読むことが大好きな人→**本の虫**

**boom**¹ /buːm/ 名 C ▶定義1 a period in which sth increases or develops very quickly 〜がとても速く増える,または発展する期間→**急速な増加,急成長,ブーム** ‖ *There was a boom in car sales in the 1980s.* 1980年代には自動車販売の急成長があった. ▶定義2 [通常は単数]a loud deep sound 大きな太い音→**ぶーんと鳴る音,とどろき,響く音** ‖ *the boom of distant guns* 遠くで聞こえる大砲のとどろき

**boom**² /buːm/ 動 ▶定義1 自他 boom (sth) (out) to make a loud deep sound 大きな太い音を立てる→**とどろく,うなりを立てる,大きな響く声で話す** ‖ *The loudspeaker boomed out instructions to the crowd.* 拡声器が群衆に大きな響く声で指示を出していた. ▶定義2 自 to grow very quickly in size or value 大きさや価値がとても速く増大する→**急増する,急成長する** ‖ *Business is booming in the computer industry.* コンピューター業界では事業が急成長している.

**boomerang** /búːməræŋ/ 名 C ▶定義 a curved piece of wood that returns to you when you throw it in a particular way 特定の方法で投げると自分の所に戻ってくる,曲がりのある木片→**ブーメラン**

**boon** /buːn/ 名 C ▶定義 a thing that is very helpful and that you are grateful for とても役に立ち,それに感謝するもの→**(〜にとって)有り難い物,恩恵,利益**

**boost**¹ /buːst/ 動 他 ▶定義 to increase sth in number, value or strength 〜の数,価値,強さなどを増す→**〜を増加する,増進する,(価格・電圧など)を上げる** ‖ *If we lower the price, that should boost sales.* もしその価格を下げれば,売り上げは増えるはずだ. *The good exam result boosted her confidence.* 試験の結果が良かったので,彼女は自信を強めた.

**boost**² /buːst/ 名 C ▶定義 something that encourages people; an increase 人々を激励するもの; 増加→**盛り上げるもの,景気付けるもの;増加,増進** ‖ *The fall in the value of the pound has led to a boost in exports.* ポンドの下落は輸出の増加につながった. *The president's visit gave a boost to the soldiers' morale.* 大統領の訪問が兵士の士気を高めた.

**\*boot**¹ /buːt/ 名 C ▶定義1 a type of shoe that covers your foot completely and sometimes part of your leg 足のくるぶしから下を完全に覆い,時にはそれより上の部分も覆う,靴の一種→**ブーツ,長靴** ‖ *ski boots* スキーブーツ *walking/climbing boots* ウォーキング・登山用ブーツ *football boots* サッカーシューズ ☞ **shoe**, **ski**のさし絵 ▶定義2 (米 **trunk**) the part of a car where you put luggage, usually at the back 荷物を入れておく車の部分,通常は後方にある→**乗用車の荷物入れ,トランク** ☞ S7ページのさし絵

**boot**² /buːt/ 動 略式 ▶定義1 他 to kick sth/sb hard 〜を強くける→**け飛ばす** ‖ *He booted the ball over the fence.* 彼は柵(さく)の向こうへボールをけり飛ばした. ▶定義2 自他 to make a computer ready for use when it is first switched on コンピューターのスイッチを初めて入れると,すぐ使えるようにコンピューターを準備させる→**ブートする**

**句動詞** boot sb/sth out ▶定義 to force sb/sth to leave a place 〜に場所から去るよう強制する→**〜から力ずくでほうり出す,首にする** ‖ *The boys were booted out of the club for fighting.* 少年たちはけんかをしたため,クラブからほうり出された.

**booth** /búːθ; -ð/ 名 C ▶定義 a small enclosed place with thin walls that divide it from the rest of the room or area 部屋の中または区域の中でほかの部分から分けられた,薄い壁で囲まれた狭い場所→**ブース,仕切り席** ‖ *a phone booth* 公衆電話ボックス

**booty** /búːti/ 名 U ▶定義 things that are taken by thieves or captured by soldiers in a war 泥棒に取られた,または戦争中に兵士に押収された品物→**戦利品,分捕り品,もうけ**

**booze**¹ /buːz/ 名 U 略式 ▶定義 alcohol アルコール→**酒**

**booze**² /buːz/ 動 自 略式 ▶定義 to drink a lot of alcohol 大量のアルコールを飲む→**大酒を飲む** ‖ *He went out boozing with some friends on Saturday.* 彼は土曜日に何人かの友達と大酒を飲みに出掛けた.

**booze-up** 名 C 英 略式 ▶定義 an occasion

when people drink a lot of alcohol 人々が大量のアルコールを飲む機会→酒盛り,どんちゃん騒ぎ

**\*border**[1] /bɔ́:rdər/ 名 ◎ ▶定義**1** a line that divides two countries, etc; the land close to this line 2つの国などを分ける線;この線に近い土地→**国境,境界,国境地帯** ‖ *The refugees escaped* ***across/over the border****.* 難民たちは国境を越えて逃げた. *the Moroccan border* モロッコの国境地帯 *the border between France and Italy* フランスとイタリアの国境 *Italy's border with France* イタリアのフランスとの国境地帯

▶2つの国または州を分ける線について話すとき, border, frontier(国境)を使う. 自然な境界について話すとき, 通常 border を使う: *The river forms the border between the two countries.*(川が2つの国の間に国境を形づくっている.)通常 boundary は, より小さな地域を分ける線について用いられる: *the county boundary*(郡の境界線)

▶定義**2** a band or narrow line around the edge of sth, often for decoration 〜の周りのへりを囲む帯や狭い線, しばしば飾るためのもの→**縁取り,飾り縁** ‖ *a white tablecloth with a blue border* 青の縁取りが付いた白いテーブルクロス

**border**[2] /bɔ́:rdər/ 動 ◎ ▶定義 to form a border to an area; to be on the border of an area ある地域に境界を作る; ある地域の境界にある→**〜に境を接する,〜に面する,〜を縁取る** ‖ *The road was bordered with trees.* その道は木々で縁取られていた.

句動詞 border on sth ▶定義**1** to be almost the same as sth 〜とほとんど同じである→**まるで〜の状態である** ‖ *The dictator's ideas bordered on madness.* その独裁者の思考はまるで狂気染みたものだった. ▶定義**2** to be next to sth 〜の隣にある→**〜に近い** ‖ *Our garden borders on the railway line.* 私たちの庭は鉄道線路に近い.

**borderline** /bɔ́:rdərlàɪn/ 名 [単数扱い] ▶定義 the line that marks a division between two different cases, conditions, etc 2つの異なる事例, 条件などの間を分ける線→**境界線,どっちつかずの状態** ‖ *He's* ***a borderline case*** *- he may pass the exam or he may fail.* 彼は境界線にいる ― 試験に通るかもしれないし落ちるかもしれない.

**\*bore**[1] /bɔ́:r/ 動 ▶定義**1** 他 to make sb feel bored, especially by talking too much 特にしゃべりすぎることによって, 〜を退屈に感じさせる→**〜をうんざりさせる,退屈させる** ‖ *I hope I'm not boring you.* 退屈させていないとよいのですが.

▶定義**2** 自他 to make a long deep hole with a tool 道具を使って長く深い穴を開ける→**〜を開ける,掘る,くりぬく** ‖ *This drill can bore (a hole) through solid rock.* このドリルは硬い岩を(穴を)掘ることができる. ▶定義**3** **BEAR**[2] の過去形

**bore**[2] /bɔ́:r/ 名 ▶定義**1** ◎ a person who talks a lot in a way that is not interesting 面白くない言い方で多くしゃべる人→**うんざりさせる人,退屈させる人** ▶定義**2** [単数扱い] 略式 something that you have to do that you do not find interesting 興味は持てないだろうが, しなければならない事→**つまらない物事** ‖ *It's such a bore having to learn these lists of irregular verbs.* これらの不規則動詞の一覧表を覚えなければならないなんて, つまらないことだ.

**bored** /bɔ́:rd/ 形 ▶定義 **bored (with sth)** feeling tired and perhaps slightly annoyed because sth is not interesting or because you do not have anything to do 〜が面白くないために, または何もする事がないために, 退屈して, 多分少しいらいらしている感じ→**退屈した,うんざりした** ‖ *I'm bored with eating the same thing every day.* 毎日同じ物を食べることにうんざりする. *The children* ***get bored*** *on long journeys.* 子供たちは長旅にうんざりしている. *He gave a bored yawn.* 彼は退屈であくびをした. *The play was awful - we were* ***bored stiff*** *(= extremely bored).* ひどい劇だった ― 私たちはとても退屈した(= すっかり退屈した).

▶する事がない, またはしている事が面白くないとき, bored(退屈)する. このように感じさせるのは boring(退屈な)人や物事である.

**boredom** /bɔ́:rdəm/ 名 ◎ ▶定義 the state of being bored 退屈した状態→**退屈,退屈なこと** ‖ *I sometimes eat out of boredom.* 私は, 時々退屈さのあまり食べる.

**boring** /bɔ́:rɪŋ/ 形 ▶定義 not at all interesting; dull 全く面白くない; 単調な→**退屈な,うんざりさせるような** ‖ *a boring film/job/speech/man*

退屈な映画・仕事・演説・男 ☛参 **bored** の注

\*__born__[1] /bɔːm/ 動 ▶定義 be born to come into the world by birth; to start existing 誕生によってこの世に来る; 存在し始める→**生まれる** ‖ *Where were you born?* あなたはどこで生まれましたか. *I was born in London, but I grew up in Leeds.* 私はロンドンで生まれましたが, リーズで育ちました. *I'm going to give up work after the baby is born.* 赤ん坊が生まれたら, 仕事はあきらめるつもりです. *The idea of free education for all was born in the nineteenth century.* すべての人への教育の自由の思想は, 19世紀に生まれました. *His unhappiness was __born out of__ a feeling of frustration.* 彼の不幸は挫折（ざせつ）感から生じたものだった.

__born__[2] /bɔːm/ 形 ▶定義 1 having a natural ability to do sth ~をするための生まれつきの能力がある→**生まれながらの, 天性の** ‖ *She's a born leader.* 彼女は生まれながらの指導者だ. ▶定義 2 -born (複合形容詞を作るために用いて) born in the place or state mentioned 言及された場所または状態で生まれた→**生まれが~の** ‖ *This Kenyan-born athlete now represents Denmark.* このケニア生まれの選手は今はデンマークを代表している.

__born-again__ 形 (名詞の前だけ) ▶定義 having found new, strong religious belief 新たに, 強い宗教的信条を見つけた→**生まれ変わった, 信仰を新たにした** ‖ *a born-again Christian* 信仰を新たにしたキリスト教徒

__borne__ /bɔːm/ **BEAR**[2] の過去分詞形

__borough__ /bʌroʊ, bʌ́rə/ 名 C ▶定義 a town, or an area inside a large town, that has some form of local government ある種の地方政府を持つ, 大きな町の中の町や地域→**自治区, 自治町村**

\*__borrow__ /bɔ́(ː)roʊ, bár-/ 動 自 他 borrow (sth) (from/off sb/sth) ▶定義 1 to take or receive sth from sb/sth that you intend to give back, usually after a short time 通常は短い期間の後, 返すつもりの~を…から手に入れる, または受け取る→**~を借りる, 借用する** ‖ *I had to borrow from the bank to pay for my car.* 車の代金を払うために, 銀行から借りなければならなかった. *We'll have to borrow a lot of money to buy a car.* 私たちは車を買うために, 多くの金額を借りなければならないだろう. *Could I borrow your pen for a minute?* 少しの間, お持ちのペン

**borrow/lend**

She's **lending** her son some money.

He's **borrowing** some money from his mother.

を借りられますか. *He's always borrowing off his mother.* 彼はいつも母親から借りている. *I borrowed a book from the library.* 私は図書館から本を借りた.

➤ 反対語の lend と混同しないように注意する.

▶定義 2 to take sth and use it as your own; to copy sth ~を取って自分のもののように使う; ~をまねる→**~を借りる, 盗用する, 模倣する** ‖ *That idea is borrowed from another book.* あの考えはほかの本から借用されている.

__borrower__ /bɔ́(ː)roʊər, bár-/ 名 C ▶定義 a person who borrows sth ~を借りる人→**借り手, 借用者**

__bosom__ /búzəm/ 名 ▶定義 1 [単数扱い] 正式 a person's chest, especially a woman's breasts 人の胸, 特に女性の胸→**胸** ‖ *She clutched the child to her bosom.* 彼女はその子供を胸にしっかり抱き締めた. ▶定義 2 C a woman's breast 女性の胸→**乳房**

成句 in the bosom of sth ▶定義 close to; with the protection of 近くに; ~の保護で→**(親しい人)と一緒に[で]** ‖ *He was glad to be back in the bosom of his family.* 彼は家族だんらんの中に戻れてうれしかった.

__bosom friend__ 名 C ▶定義 a very close friend とても親しい友→**親友**

\*__boss__[1] /bɔ(ː)s, bɑs/ 名 C 略式 ▶定義 a person whose job is to give orders to others at work; an employer; a manager 職場でほかの人に指示することが仕事の人; 雇用者; 経営者→**上司, 上役, 親分** ‖ *I'm going to ask the boss for a day off work.* 私は上司に1日休みを頼むつもりだ.

*OK. You're the boss (= you make the decisions).* 了解. あなたが親分だ(= あなたが決定する).

**➤日本語 vs 英語**

boss と「ボス」

日本語の「ボス」は「親父, やくざの親分」などのマイナスイメージがありますが, 英語では単に「上司」の意味で気楽に使われ, マイナスイメージはありません. また, Hello, Boss. のように呼び掛けにも使われます. また, boss は動詞としても用いられ, boss about/around～で「～を切り盛りする, 意のままに動かす」という意味を表します. また, bossy とすると形容詞になり, 「親分らしく振る舞う」の意味で用います.

**boss**² /bɔ(:)s, bɑs/ [動][他] ▸定義 boss sb (about/around) to give orders to sb, especially in an annoying way 特にうるさく, ～に命令を与える ➜ **あごで使う, こき使う** ‖ *I wish you'd stop bossing me around.* 私をあごで使うのはやめてほしい.

**bossy** /bɔ́(:)si, bɑ́si/ [形] ▸定義 liking to give orders to other people, often in an annoying way しばしばうるさく, ほかの人に命令を与えることが好きで ➜ **威張り散らす, 親分風を吹かせる** ‖ *Don't be so bossy!* そんなに威張り散らすな. — bossily [副] ➜ **威張り散らして** — bossiness [名] [U] ➜ **威張った態度, ボスづら, 親分風**

**botanist** /bɑ́tnɪst/ [名] [C] ▸定義 a person who studies plants 植物を研究する人 ➜ **植物学者**

**botany** /bɑ́tni/ [名] [U] ▸定義 the scientific study of plants 植物の科学的研究 ➜ **植物学** ☛参 **biology**, **zoology** — botanical /bətǽnɪk(ə)l/ [形] ➜ **植物の, 植物学上の** ‖ *botanical gardens (= a type of park where plants are grown for scientific study)* 植物園(= 科学的研究のために植物が育てられている公園の一種)

**botch** /bɑtʃ/ [動][他] ▸定義 botch sth (up) to do sth badly; to make a mess of sth ～を下手に行う; ～を台なしにする ➜ **～をやり損なう, 無様に繕う** ‖ *I've completely botched up this typing, I'm afraid.* 私は完全にタイプをやり損なってしまったようだ.

***both** /bóʊθ/ [形][代][副] ▸定義1 the two; the one as well as the other その2つ; 他と同様にそれも ➜ **両方の～とも, どちらの～も** ‖ *Both women were French.* どちらの女性もフランス人だった. *Both the women were French.* その両方の女性はフランス人だった. *Both of the women were French.* その女性たちは2人ともフランス人だった. *I liked them both.* 私は両方とも好きだった. *We were both very tired.* 私たちは2人ともとても疲れた. *Both of us were tired.* 私たちは2人とも疲れた. *I've got two sisters. They both live in London/Both of them live in London.* 私には2人の姉妹がいる. その2人ともロンドンに住んでいる.

➤ the both women や my both sisters とは言わないことに注意する.

▸定義2 both...and...; not only...but also... ➜ **～も…も; ～だけでなく…も** ‖ *Both he and his wife are vegetarian.* 彼も彼の妻も菜食主義者だ.

***bother**¹ /bɑ́ðər/ [動] ▸定義1 [他] to disturb, annoy or worry sb ～を不安にさせる, いらいらさせる, または心配させる ➜ **～を悩ます, うるさがらせる, 迷惑を掛ける** ‖ *I'm sorry to bother you, but could I speak to you for a moment?* お邪魔してすみませんが, 少し話してよいですか. *Don't bother Geeta with that now - she's busy.* 今そんな事でジータを煩わせてはいけません — 彼女は忙しいのです. ☛類 **trouble** ▸定義2 [自] bother (to do sth/doing sth); bother (about/with sth) (通常否定文で) to make the effort to do sth ～を行う努力をする ➜ **わざわざ～する** ‖ *'Shall I make you something to eat?' 'No, don't bother - I'm not hungry.'* 「何か食べる物を作りましょうか」「お手間を取るには及びません — おなかはすいていません」 *He didn't even bother to say thank you.* 彼はありがとうさえ言わなかった. *Don't bother waiting for me - I'll catch you up later.* 私を待たないで結構です — 後から追い付きます. *Don't bother about the washing-up. I'll do it later.* 汚れた食器を洗うなんて面倒な事しなくていいよ. 後で私がするから.

[成句] can't be bothered (to do sth) ▸定義 used to say that you do not want to spend time or energy doing sth ～をして時間または労力を費やしたくないことを言うために用いて ➜ **する気にならない, わざわざ～したくない** ‖ *I can't be* *bothered to do my homework now. I'll do it tomorrow.* 今宿題をする気にならない。明日しよう．

**not be bothered (about sth)** ▶定義 特に 英略式 to think that sth is not important 〜が重要ではないと考える→〜を思い悩まない，わざわざ〜しない ∥ *'What would you like to do this evening?' 'I'm not bothered really.'* 「今晩は何をしたい」「別にどうでもいいわ」

**bother²** /bάðər/ 名 U ▶定義 trouble or difficulty 問題または困難→面倒，厄介，騒ぎ ∥ *Thanks for all your help. It's saved me a lot of bother.* いろいろ手伝ってくれてありがとう．大分面倒が省けた．

**bothered** /bάðərd/ 形 ▶定義 worried about sth 〜について心配している→悩んでいる，うるさがっている ∥ *Sam doesn't seem too bothered about losing his job.* サムは失業したことでくよくよ悩んでいるようには見えない．

*★**bottle¹** /bάtl/ 名 C ▶定義1 a glass or plastic container with a narrow neck for keeping liquids in 液体を入れておくための，細い首のあるガラスまたはプラスチック製の容器→びん，ボトル ∥ *a beer bottle* ビールびん *an empty bottle* 空びん ▶定義2 the amount of liquid that a bottle can hold ボトルに入れておける液体の量→びん1本の量 ∥ *a bottle of beer* ビール1本 ☞ **container** のさし絵

**bottle²** /bάtl/ 動 他 ▶定義 to put sth into bottles 〜をボトルの中に入れる→〜をびんに入れる・詰める・貯蔵する ∥ *After three or four months the wine is bottled.* 3，4か月後にワインはびんに詰められる．*bottled water (= that you can buy in bottles)* びん詰の水（＝びんに入って買える）

句動詞 **bottle sth up** ▶定義 to not allow yourself to express strong emotions 強い感情を表現することを自分に許さない→〜を無理に抑える ∥ *You'll make yourself ill if you keep your feelings bottled up.* 感情を無理に抑え続けると病気になるよ．

**bottle bank** 名 C ▶定義 a large container in a public place where people can leave their empty bottles so that the glass can be used again (recycled) ガラスびんをもう一度使える（再利用）ように，人々が空びんを置いていく，公共の場所にある大きな容器→空びん回収箱

**bottleneck** /bάtlnèk/ 名 C ▶定義1 a narrow piece of road that causes traffic to slow down or stop 交通を減速させるまたは止めさせる，道路の狭い部分→道幅の狭い箇所 ▶定義2 something that slows down progress, especially in business or industry 特に仕事または産業において，進展を遅くさせるもの→障害，ネック

*★**bottom¹** /bάtəm/ 名 ▶定義1 [C，通常は単数] the lowest part of sth 〜の最も低い部分→最下部，下の方の部分 ∥ *The house is **at the bottom** of a hill.* その家は丘のふもとにある．*I think I've got a pen **in the bottom** of my bag.* 私のバッグの底の方にペンがあったと思う．*The sea is so clear that you can see the bottom.* その海はとても澄んでいるので，海底が見える．▶定義2 C the flat surface on the outside of an object, on which it stands 物自体がその上に立つ，物の外側の平らな表面→底，裏底 ∥ *There's a label **on the bottom** of the box.* 箱の裏底にラベルが張ってある．▶定義3 [単数扱い] the far end of sth 〜の遠い端→突き当たり，一番奥 ∥ *The bus stop is **at the bottom** of the road.* バス停はその道の突き当たりにある．▶定義4 [単数扱い] the lowest position in relation to other people, teams, etc ほかの人々，チームなどとの関係において最も低い位置→びり，末席 ∥ *She started **at the bottom** and now she's the Managing Director.* 彼女は下積みから始めて，今では専務取締役だ．▶定義5 C the part of your body that you sit on 体を載せる体の一部→しり ∥ *He fell over and landed on his bottom.* 彼はつまずいて転び，しりもちをついた．☞ C5ページのさし絵 ▶定義6 **bottoms** [複数扱い] the lower part of a piece of clothing that is in two parts 上下2つの部分に分かれている衣服の下の部分→ズボン ∥ *pyjama bottoms* パジャマのズボン *track suit bottoms* トラックスーツ（陸上選手の保温着）のズボン

成句 **be at the bottom of sth** ▶定義 to be the cause of sth 〜の原因である→〜の原因である，〜に責任がある ∥ *I'm sure Molly Potter is at the bottom of all this.* これはすべてモリー ポッターに責任があるのは確かだ．

**from the (bottom of your) heart** ⇒ **HEART**

**get to the bottom of sth** ▶定義 to find out

the real cause of sth ～の真の原因を見つける→～の真相・原因を突き止める

**bottom²** /bάtəm/ 形 ▶定義 in the lowest position 最も低い場所で→最下部の, 底の ‖ *the bottom shelf* 一番下の棚 *I live on the bottom floor.* 私は一番下の階に住んでいる.

**bottomless** /bάtəmləs/ 形 ▶定義 very deep; without limit とても深い; 制限のない→底なしの, 非常に深い;(資源が)無限の

**bottom line** 名 [単数扱い] ▶定義1 **the bottom line** the most important thing to consider when you are discussing or deciding sth, etc ～を論じている, または決定するときなどに, 考慮すべき最も重要な事→(物事の)本質, 肝心かなめのところ ‖ *A musical instrument should look and feel good, but the bottom line is how it sounds.* 楽器は見た目も感触も良くあるべきだが, 肝心かなめはどのような音が響くかだ. ▶定義2 the final profit or loss that a company has made in a particular period of time 特定期間内に会社が出した最終利益または損失→収益額, 損失額, 損益 ▶定義3 the lowest price that sb will accept for sth ～について…が受け入れる最低の価格→最低額

**bough** /báʊ/ 名 C ▶定義 one of the main branches of a tree 木の主な枝の1つ→大枝

**bought** /bɔːt/ **BUY¹**の過去・過去分詞形

**boulder** /bóʊldər/ 名 C ▶定義 a very large rock とても大きな岩→巨礫(きょれき)

**boulevard** /bʊ́ləvὰːrd, búːlə-/ 名 C ▶定義 a wide street in a city often with trees on each side しばしば両側に木々が植えられている, 都市の広い通り→大通り, 広い並木道

**bounce** /báʊns/ 動 ▶定義1 自他 (used about a ball, etc) to move away quickly after it has hit a hard surface; to make a ball do this (ボールなどについて)硬い表面にぶつかった後, 速く遠くへ動く; ボールをそうさせる→弾む, バウンドする; ～を弾ませる, バウンドさせる ‖ *The stone bounced off the wall and hit her on the head.* その石は壁にバウンドして, 彼女の頭を打った. *A small boy came down the street, bouncing a ball.* 小さな男の子がボールを弾ませながら, 通りをやって来た. ▶定義2 自 to jump up and down continuously 上下に絶え間なく跳ねる→跳ね回る, 弾むように動く・進む ‖ *The children were bouncing on their beds.* 子供たちはベッドの上で跳ね回っていた. ☛ **hop** のさし絵 ▶定義3 自他 (used about a cheque) to be returned by a bank without payment because there is not enough money in the account (小切手について)口座に十分な金がないために銀行から戻される→不渡りで戻る — **bounce** 名 C ▶定義 弾み, 跳ね返り, 弾力性

句動詞 **bounce back** ▶定義 to become healthy, successful or happy again after an illness, a failure, or a disappointment 病気, 失敗または失望の後に, 再び健康になる, 成功する, または幸せになる→立ち直る

**bouncy** /báʊnsi/ 形 ▶定義1 that bounces well or that can make things bounce よく弾む, または物体を弾ませることができる→よく弾む, 弾力性のある ‖ *a bouncy ball/surface* よく弾むボール・弾力性のある表面 ▶定義2 (used about a person) full of energy; lively (人について)エネルギーに満ちた; 生き生きとした→元気のいい, 生き生きとした ‖ *She's a very bouncy person.* 彼女はとても生き生きとした人だ.

**bound¹** /báʊnd/ 形 ▶定義1 **bound to do sth** certain to do sth ～をすることが確かな→確実に～するはずである, きっと～する ‖ *You've done so much work that you're bound to pass the exam.* あなたはそんなによく勉強したのだから, きっと試験に合格する. ▶定義2 (名詞の前は不可) having a legal or moral duty to do sth ～をする法的なまたは道徳的な義務を持つ→義務・責任がある, 拘束・束縛された ‖ *The company is bound by UK employment law.* その会社は英国の雇用法に従う義務がある. *She felt bound to refuse the offer.* 彼女はその申し出を断る義務があると感じた. ▶定義3 **bound (for...)** travelling to a particular place 特定の場所へ旅する→～行きの, ～へ行こうとしている ‖ *a ship bound for Australia* オーストラリア行きの船

成句 **bound up with sth** ▶定義 very closely connected with sth ～ととても密接に関連した→～と密接な関係がある, 深くかかわっている

**bound²** /báʊnd/ 動 自 ▶定義 to run quickly with long steps 大きな歩幅で速く走る→跳ねる, 跳び上がる ‖ *She bounded out of the house to meet us.* 彼女は私たちに会うために家から飛

び出した. — bound 名 ●→弾み,跳ね返り,バウンド ‖ *With a couple of bounds he had crossed the room.* ふた跳びで彼は部屋を横切った.

**bound**³ BIND¹ の過去・過去分詞形

\***boundary** /báʊnd(ə)ri/ 名 ● (覆 **boundaries**) ▶定義 a real or imagined line that marks the limits of sth and divides it from other places or things 〜の限界を印し,それをほかの場所などから分ける,実在するまたは仮想の線→境界,境界線,限界 ‖ *The main road is the boundary between the two districts.* その主要道路が2つの地域の境界線だ. *Scientists continue to push back the boundaries of human knowledge.* 科学者たちは人間の知識の限界を押し広げ続けている. ☛参 **border** の注

**boundless** /báʊndləs/ 形 ▶定義 having no limit 限界のない→無限の,限りのない ‖ *boundless energy* 無限のエネルギー

**bounds** /báʊndz/ 名 [複数扱い] ▶定義 limits that cannot or should not be passed 越えられない,または越えるべきではない限度→限界,限度,範囲 ‖ *Price rises must be kept within reasonable bounds.* 値上げは妥当な範囲に抑えられなければばらない.

成句 **out of bounds** ▶定義 not to be entered by sb 〜が入れない→出入禁止区域に ‖ *This area is out of bounds to all staff.* この区域は全職員出入禁止です.

**bouquet** /boʊkéɪ, buː-/ 名 ● ▶定義 a bunch of flowers that is arranged in an attractive way 魅力的な方法で整えられた花束→花束,ブーケ

**bourbon** /báːrbən/ 名 ● Ⓤ ▶定義 a type of strong alcoholic drink (**whisky**) that is made mainly in the US 主に米国で作られる強いアルコール飲料(ウイスキー)の一種→バーボン

**the bourgeoisie** /bùərʒwɑːzíː/ 名 [単数扱い,単数または複数形の動詞と共に] ▶定義 a class of people in society who are interested mainly in having more money and a higher social position 主により多くの金とより高い社会的地位を持つことに関心ある人々の社会的階級→中産階級 — **bourgeois** /búərʒwɑ̀ː/ 形 →中産階級の,ブルジョア根性の,俗物の,保守的な ‖ *bourgeois attitudes/ideas/values* 中産階級の態度・思考・価値観

**bout** /báʊt/ 名 ● ▶定義 1 a short period of great activity 短期間の大きな活動→一区切り,一仕事, 一働き ‖ *a bout of hard work* 一区切りの大変な仕事 ▶定義 2 a period of illness 病気の期間→発作,一区切り ‖ *I'm just recovering from a bout of flu.* ちょうど風邪が治りかけているところだ.

**boutique** /buːtíːk/ 名 ● ▶定義 a small shop that sells fashionable clothes or expensive presents おしゃれな服または高価な贈り物を売る小さな店→ブティック

**bovine** /bóʊvaɪn, -viːn/ 形 (専門用語) ▶定義 connected with cows 牛に関連した→ウシ科の,牛の(ような) ‖ *bovine diseases* 牛の病気

\***bow**¹ /báʊ/ 動 ▶定義 1 ㊀ ㊉ bow (sth) (to sb) to bend your head or the upper part of your body forward and down, as a sign of respect 敬意を表す印として,頭または上半身を前に倒す→お辞儀する,頭を下げる,腰をかがめる ‖ *The speaker bowed to the guests and left the stage.* 講演者は観客にお辞儀をしてから舞台から退場した. *He bowed his head respectfully.* 彼は恭しく頭を下げた. ▶定義 2 ㊀ **bow to sb/sth** to accept sth 〜を受け入れる→(嫌々)従う,屈服する ‖ *I do not think the unions should bow to pressure from the Government.* 組合は政府の圧力に屈服するべきではないと思う.

句動詞 **bow out (of sth /as sth)** ▶定義 to leave an important position or stop taking part in sth 重要な地位を去る,または〜に参加していることをやめる→お辞儀をして出ていく,手を引く,引退する ‖ *After a long and successful career, she has decided to bow out of politics.* 長くすばらしい政界での生活後,彼女は政界を引退することを決心した. *He finally bowed out as chairman after ten years.* 10年後,彼はついに会長を引退した.

**bow**² /báʊ/ 名 ● ▶定義 1 an act of bowing¹(1) bowing¹(1) の行為→お辞儀 ‖ *The director of the play came on stage to **take a bow**.* その芝居の監督は舞台に現れてお辞儀をした.
▶定義 2 the front part of a ship 船の前の部分→船首,艦首,へさき ☛参 **stern**

**bow**³ /bóʊ/ 名 ● ▶定義 1 a knot with two loose roundish parts and two loose ends that you use when you are tying shoes, etc 靴などを結ぶときに使う,2つの垂れ下がった円い輪の部分と2つの垂れ下がった端のある結び目→ちょ

う結び ‖ *He tied his laces in a bow.* 彼は靴ひもをちょう結びにした. ☞ **loop** のさし絵 ▶定義2 a weapon for shooting arrows. A bow is a curved piece of wood that is held in shape by a tight string. 矢を射るための武器, ぴんと張ったひもで湾曲を保った木→弓 ▶定義3 a long thin piece of wood with string stretched across it that you use for playing some musical instruments 楽器を演奏するために使う, 絃(げん)が強く張られている細長い木→弓 ‖ *a violin bow* バイオリンの弓 ☞ **music** のさし絵

★**bowel** /báu(ə)l/ 图[ⓒ, 通常は複数] ▶定義 one of the tubes that carries waste food away from your stomach to the place where it leaves your body 食物を胃から体内から排せつされる場所まで運ぶ管の１つ→腸

**bowl** **bowl**¹ /bóul/ 图ⓒ ▶定義1 a deep round dish without a lid that is used for holding food or liquid 食べ物や液体を入れておくために使われる, ふたのない底の深い円い皿→鉢, 茶わん, ボール ‖ *a soup bowl* スープ茶わん ▶定義2 the amount of sth that is in a bowl ボールに入った~の量→鉢・わん１杯の量 ‖ *I usually have a bowl of cereal for breakfast.* 私は通常朝食に１杯のシリアルを食べる. ▶定義3 a large plastic container that is used for washing dishes, washing clothes, etc 皿を洗う, 衣服を洗うなどのために使われる大きなプラスチックの入れ物→洗いおけ

**bowl**² /bóul/ 動⊜⊝ ▶定義 (in cricket) to throw the ball in the direction of the person with the bat (クリケットで)バットを持った人の方にボールを投げる→投球する

句動詞 **bowl sb over** ▶定義1 to knock sb down when you are moving quickly とても速く動いているときに~を倒す→ぶつかって~を転倒させる, 突き飛ばす ▶定義2 to surprise sb very much in a pleasant way とても愉快なやり方で~をとても驚かせる → ~をびっくりさせる ‖ *I was absolutely bowled over by the beautiful scenery.* 私はその美しい景色に全くびっくりした.

**bow legs** /báu lègz/ 图[複数扱い] ▶定義 legs that curve out at the knees ひざの所で外側に曲がった脚→O脚, がにまた ― **bow-legged** /báulègɪd, -gd/ 形 O脚の, がにまたの

**bowler** /bóulər/ 图ⓒ ▶定義1 (または **bowler hat**, 米 **derby**) a round hard black hat, usually worn by men 通常男性がかぶる, 丸く硬い黒い帽子→山高帽子 ☞ **hat** のさし絵 ▶定義2 (in cricket) the player who throws (**bowls**) the ball in the direction of the person with the bat (クリケットで)バットを持つ人の方向にボールを投げる(投球する)選手→投手

**bowling** /bóulɪŋ/ 图ⓤ ▶定義 a game in which you roll a heavy ball down a special track (a **lane**) towards a group of wooden objects (**pins**) and try to knock them all down 特別な軌道(レーン)で木製の的(ピン)の集まりに向けて重い球を転がして, 的を全部倒そうと試みるゲーム→ボウリング ‖ *to go bowling* ボウリングをしに行く

**bowls** /bóulz/ 图ⓤ ▶定義 a game in which you try to roll large wooden balls as near as possible to a smaller ball 小さな球のできるだけ近くに大きな木製の球を転がすゲーム→ボウルズ ‖ *to play bowls* ボウルズをする

**bow tie** /báu tài/ 图ⓒ ▶定義 a tie in the shape of a bow³(1), that is worn by men, especially on formal occasions 特に正式な場で, 男性が身に着けるbow³(1)の形のネクタイ→ちょうネクタイ ☞ C6 ページのさし絵

★**box**¹ /bɑks/ 图 ▶定義1 ⓒa square or rectangular container for solid objects. A box often has a lid. 硬い物を入れるための正方形または長方形の容器. しばしばふたがある→箱 ‖ *a cardboard box* ボール箱 *a shoebox* 靴箱 ☞ **container** のさし絵 ▶定義2 ⓒ a box and the things inside it 箱とその中にある物→１箱の分量 ‖ *a box of chocolates/matches/tissues* チョコレート・マッチ・ティッシュペーパー１箱 ▶定義3 ⓒ an empty square or rectangular space on a form in which you have to write sth 人が~を書き込まなければならない, 用紙上の空の正方形または長方形→解答欄, 四角(形) ‖ *Write your full name in the box below.* 下の空欄に姓名を書きなさい. ▶定義4 ⓒ a small enclosed area that is used for a particular purpose 特定の目的のために使われる小さな囲まれた区域→仕切った場所, ボックス ‖ *a telephone box* 電話ボックス the witness box (= in a court of law) 証人席(= 法廷で) ▶定義5 **the box**[単数扱い] 医 略式 television →テレビで何がありますか. *What's on the box tonight?* 今晩テレビで何がありますか.

\***box**² /báks/ 動 ▶定義1 国他 to fight in the sport of boxing スポーツとしてのボクシングで戦う→ボクシングをする ▶定義2 他 to put sth into a box 〜を箱の中に置く→〜を箱に入れる ‖ *a boxed set of CDs* 箱に入ったCD 一式

句動詞 **box sb/sth in** ▶定義 to prevent sb from getting out of a small space 〜が小さな場所から出ることを妨げる→〜を妨害する、〜を自由に行動できなくする ‖ *Someone parked behind us and boxed us in.* だれかが私たちの後ろに駐車して、私たちを動けなくした.

**boxer** /báksər/ 名 C ▶定義 a person who does boxing as a sport スポーツとしてボクシングを行う人→ボクサー、ボクシングの選手

**boxer shorts**(または **boxers**) 名 [複数扱い] ▶定義 shorts that men use as underwear 男性が下着として着用するパンツ→ボクサーショーツ、トランクス

**boxing** /báksɪŋ/ 名 U ▶定義 a sport in which two people fight by hitting each other with their hands inside large gloves 大きなグローブをはめた手で、2人が互いを殴って戦うスポーツ→ボクシング、拳闘(けんとう) ‖ *the world middleweight boxing champion* 世界ミドル級ボクシングチャンピオン *boxing gloves* ボクシングのグローブ ☞ S1 ページのさし絵

\***Boxing Day** 名 C 医 ▶定義 the day after Christmas Day; 26 December クリスマスの翌日; 12月26日→クリスマスの贈り物の日 ▶イングランドおよびウェールズでは、この日は公休日である.

**box number** 名 C ▶定義 a number used as an address, especially in newspaper advertisements 特に新聞広告で、住所として使われる番号→広告番号, 私書箱番号

**box office** 名 C ▶定義 the place in a cinema, theatre, etc where the tickets are sold 映画館、劇場などの中でチケットが売られている場所→切符売り場

\***boy** /bɔ́ɪ/ 名 C ▶定義 a male child or a young man 男の子供または若い男→少年, 男の子, 青年 ‖ *They've got three children - two boys and a girl.* 彼らには3人の子供がいる － 男の子2人と女の子1人だ. *I used to play here when I was a boy.* 私は少年のころ、ここで遊んだものだ.

**boycott** /bɔ́ɪkàt/ 動 他 ▶定義 to refuse to buy things from a particular company, take part in an event, etc because you strongly disapprove of it それについての強い不満があるために、特定の会社から物を買うことや行事に参加することなどを拒否する→〜をボイコットする、〜に対し不買同盟を結ぶ、排斥する ‖ *Several countries boycotted the Olympic Games in protest.* 数か国が抗議してオリンピックをボイコットした. — **boycott** 名 C →ボイコット, 不買同盟 ‖ *a boycott of the local elections* 地方選挙のボイコット

**boyfriend** /bɔ́ɪfrènd/ 名 C ▶定義 a man or boy with whom a person has a romantic and/or sexual relationship 人が恋愛の関係、そして・または性的な関係を持つ男性または少年→ボーイフレンド, 男友達, 恋人

**boyhood** /bɔ́ɪhùd/ 名 U ▶定義 the time of being a boy 少年でいるとき→少年時代, 少年期 ‖ *My father told me some of his boyhood memories.* 父は少年時代の思い出をいくつか私に語った.

**boyish** /bɔ́ɪɪʃ/ 形 ▶定義 like a boy 少年のような→少年のような、男の子のような ‖ *a boyish smile* 少年のようなほほえみ

**Boy Scout** = SCOUT(1)

\***bra** /bráː/ 名 C ▶定義 a piece of clothing that women wear under their other clothes to support their breasts 女性が胸を支えるためにほかの衣服の下に身に着ける衣類→ブラジャー

**brace**¹ /bréɪs/ 名 ▶定義1 C a metal frame that is fixed to a child's teeth in order to make them straight 歯をまっすぐにするために子供の歯に付ける金属の枠→歯列矯正器 ▶定義2 **braces** (医 **suspenders**)[複数扱い] a pair of straps that go over your shoulders to hold your trousers up ズボンを持ち上げておくために肩に掛けられた2本のひも→ズボンつり, サスペンダー

**brace**² /bréɪs/ 動 他 ▶定義 brace sth /yourself (for sth) to prepare yourself for sth unpleasant 不愉快な〜について覚悟しておく → 〜に備える、〜の覚悟をする ‖ *You'd better brace yourself* for some bad news. いくつかの悪い知らせについて覚悟をしておいた方が良い.

\*__bracelet__ /bréɪslət/ 名 ⓒ ▶定義 a piece of jewellery, for example a metal chain or band, that you wear around your wrist or arm 手首や腕に巻き付ける装飾品, 例えば金属製の鎖やバンド→ブレスレット, 腕輪 ☞ __jewellery__ のさし絵

__bracing__ /bréɪsɪŋ/ 形 ▶定義 making you feel healthy and full of energy 健康で精力に満ちているように感じさせる→(空気などが)身を引き締めるような, すがすがしい ‖ *bracing sea air* すがすがしい海の空気

__bracket__¹ /brǽkət/ 名 ⓒ ▶定義1 [通常は複数] (特に 米 __parenthesis__) one of two marks, ( ) or [ ], that you put round extra information in a piece of writing 文書中の追加情報の前後に置く ( ) または [ ] の印の1つ→括弧, 角括弧 ‖ *A translation of each word is given __in brackets__.* それぞれの単語の訳は括弧に入れてあります.
▶定義2 __age, income, price, etc. bracket__ prices, ages, etc which are between two limits 2つの制限の間にある価格, 年齢など→同じ階層の人たち, 同じグループ, 同じ集団 ‖ *to be in a high income bracket* 高所得者の枠内にいる
▶定義3 a piece of metal or wood that is fixed to a wall and used as a support for a shelf, lamp, etc 壁に固定されて, 棚, 照明などの支えとして使われる, 金属または材木の一片→腕木, 腕金, ブラケット

__bracket__² /brǽkət/ 動 他 ▶定義1 to put brackets¹(1) round a word, number, etc brackets¹(1) を単語, 数字などの前後に置く→～を括弧でくくる ▶定義2 __bracket A and B (together); bracket A with B__ to think of two or more people or things as similar in some way 2人以上の人または2つ以上の物をいくつかの意味で同じだと考える→一まとめに扱う, 同じに扱う

__brag__ /bræɡ/ 動 自 (__bragging; bragged__) ▶定義 __brag (to sb) (about/of sth)__ to talk too proudly about sth ～について過度に誇らしげに話す→自慢する, 見えを張る, ほらを吹く ‖ *She's always bragging to her friends about how clever she is.* 彼女はいつも友達にいかに自分が賢いかを自慢する.

__braid__ /breɪd/ 名 ▶定義1 Ⓤ thin coloured rope that is used to decorate military uniforms, etc 軍服などを装飾するのに使われる色の付いた細いひも→組みひも, モール ▶定義2 米 = __PLAIT__ ☞ __hair__ のさし絵

__Braille__ /breɪl/ 名 Ⓤ ▶定義 a system of printing, using little round marks that are higher than the level of the paper they are on and which blind people can read by touching them 盲人がそれに触れることで読める, 紙の上に盛り上がった小さな円い印を使った, 印刷の方式→点字(法) ‖ *The signs were written __in Braille__.* 表示は点字で書かれていた.

\*__brain__ /breɪn/ 名 ▶定義1 ⓒ the part of your body inside your head that controls your thoughts, feelings and movements 思考, 感情, 動作を管理する, 頭の中にある体の部分→脳, 脳髄 ‖ *He suffered serious brain damage in a road accident.* 彼は交通事故で脳に深刻な損傷を負った. *a brain surgeon* 脳外科医 ☞ C5 ページのさし絵 ▶定義2 ⓒⓊ the ability to think clearly; intelligence 明確に考える能力; 知性→頭脳, 知力; 知性 ‖ *She has a very quick brain and learns fast.* 彼女は頭の巡りがとても速く, 覚えが速い. *He hasn't got the brains to be a doctor.* 彼は医者としての頭脳を持っていない. ▶定義3 ⓒ 略式 a very clever person とても賢い人→優れた頭脳の持ち主 ‖ *He's one of the best brains in the country.* 彼はその国で最も優れた頭脳を持つ1人だ. ▶定義4 __the brains__ [単数扱い] the person who plans or organizes sth ～を計画する, または組織する人→知的指導者, ブレーン ‖ *She's the real brains in the organization.* 彼女はその組織の真の知的指導者だ.

成句 __have sth on the brain__ 略式 ▶定義 to think about sth all the time ～についてずっと考える→～が頭から離れない ‖ *I've had that song on the brain all day.* 一日中あの歌が頭から離れなかった.

__rack your brains__ ⇒ __RACK__²

__brainchild__ /bréɪntʃaɪld/ 名 [単数扱い] ▶定義 the idea or invention of a particular person 特定の人の考えまたは発明→新しい考え, 新構想 ‖ *The music festival was the brainchild of a young teacher.* その音楽祭はある若い教師の発案だった.

__brain-dead__ 形 ▶定義1 having serious brain damage and needing a machine to stay alive

脳に深刻な損傷を負い,生きているために機械を必要とする➡脳死(状態)の ▶定義2 略式 unable to think clearly; stupid 明確に考えられない; 愚かな➡頭を使っていない,愚かな ‖ *He's brain-dead from watching too much TV.* 彼はテレビの見すぎで頭が鈍くなっている.

**brainless** /bréɪnləs/ 形 略式 ▶定義 very silly; stupid とてもばかな; 愚かな➡頭の悪い,愚かな

**brainstorm**¹ /bréɪnstɔːm/ 名 ⒞ ▶定義1 a moment of sudden confusion 瞬間的な突然の混乱➡(突然の)精神錯乱 ‖ *I had a brainstorm in the exam and couldn't answer any questions.* 試験で精神錯乱し,どの問題にも答えられなかった.
▶定義2 米 = BRAINWAVE

**brainstorm**² /bréɪnstɔːm/ 動 ⾃ 他 ▶定義 to solve a problem or make a decision by thinking of as many ideas as possible in a short time 短時間にできるだけ多くの案を考えることによって,問題を解決する,または決定する➡ブレーンストーミングをする ‖ *We'll spend five minutes brainstorming ideas on how we can raise money.* どのようにしてお金を集められるかについて,私たちはこれから5分間のブレーンストーミングを行います.

**brainwash** /bréɪnwɒ(ː)ʃ, -wɑːʃ/ 動 他 ▶定義 brainwash sb (into doing sth) to force sb to believe sth by using strong mental pressure 強い精神的圧力を使って,~に…を信じるよう強制する➡洗脳する,洗脳して~させる ‖ *Television advertisements try to brainwash people into buying things that they don't need.* テレビ広告は人々を洗脳して必要のない物を買わせようとする.— **brainwashing** 名 Ⓤ ➡洗脳,思想改造教育

**brainwave** /bréɪnweɪv/ (米 **brainstorm**) 名 ⒞ 略式 ▶定義 a sudden clever idea 突然の賢い考え➡突然ひらめいた名案 ‖ *If I have a brainwave, I'll let you know.* もし名案がひらめいたら,あなたに知らせるよ.

**brainy** /bréɪni/ 形 略式 ▶定義 intelligent 知的な➡頭のいい,利口な

**braise** /bréɪz/ 動 他 ▶定義 to cook meat or vegetables slowly in a little liquid in a covered dish 覆いをした皿の中で,少しの液体の中でゆっくりと肉または野菜を調理する➡(肉や野菜)を油でいためて密閉したなべで蒸し煮する

\***brake**¹ /bréɪk/ 名 ⒞ ▶定義1 the part of a vehicle that makes it go slower or stop 乗り物の一部で減速させるかまたは止めるもの➡ブレーキ,ブレーキペダル ‖ *She put her foot on the brake and just managed to stop in time.* 彼女はブレーキペダルに足を乗せ,どうにか間に合って止めた. ☛ S7 ページのさし絵 ▶定義2 something that makes sth else slow down or stop ほかの~を減速させるまたは止めるもの➡ブレーキ ‖ *The Government must try to put a brake on inflation.* 政府はインフレにブレーキをかける努力をしなければならない.

**brake**² /bréɪk/ 動 ⾃ ▶定義 to make a vehicle go slower or stop by using the brakes ブレーキを使って,乗り物を減速させるまたは止める➡ブレーキをかける ‖ *If the driver hadn't braked in time, the car would have hit me.* もし運転手がブレーキをかけるのが間に合わなかったら,車は私にぶつかっていただろう.

**bran** /brǽn/ 名 Ⓤ ▶定義 the brown outer covering of grains that is left when the grain is made into flour 穀物から小麦粉を作るときに残される,穀物の茶色い外側の覆い➡もみ殻,ふすま,ぬか

\***branch**¹ /brάːntʃ; brǽntʃ/ 名 ⒞ ▶定義1 one of the main parts of a tree that grows out of the thick central part (trunk) 太い中央の部分(幹)から生えている,木の主要な部分のうちの1つ➡枝 ☛ C2 ページのさし絵 ▶定義2 an office, shop, etc that is part of a larger organization 大きな組織の一部である事務所,店などの➡支店,支社,支部,支局 ‖ *The company I work for has branches in Paris, Milan and New York.* 私が働いている会社はパリとミラノとニューヨークに支店がある. ▶定義3 a part of an academic subject 学問的な主題の一部➡部門,分科 ‖ *Psychiatry is a branch of medicine.* 精神医学は医学の一部門です.

**branch**² /brάːntʃ; brǽntʃ/ 動
句動詞 **branch off** ▶定義 (used about a road) to leave a larger road and go off in another direction (道について)大きな道を離れてほかの方向へ行く➡分岐する,本道・本線から分かれる ‖ *A bit further on, the road branches off to the left.* さらに少し行くと,その道は左に分岐している.

**branch out (into sth)** ▶定義 to start doing sth new and different from the things you usually do 新しくて,自分が日ごろしている事とは異なる～をし始める→事業・商売の間口を広げる,興味の幅を広げる ‖ *The band has recently branched out into acting.* その楽団は最近芝居の方にも活動の幅を広げた.

★**brand**¹ /brænd/ 名 C ▶定義1 the name of a product that is made by a particular company 特定の会社によって作られる製品の名前→**ブランド,銘柄** ‖ *a well-known brand of coffee* よく知られたコーヒーの銘柄 ▶定義2 a particular type of sth ～の特定の種類→種類,品種 ‖ *a strange brand of humour* 独特のユーモア

**brand**² /brænd/ 動他 ▶定義1 to mark an animal with a hot iron to show who owns it だれが所有するかを示すために,熱せられた鉄で動物に印を付ける→～に焼印を押す ▶定義2 **brand sb (as sth)** to say that sb has a bad character so that people have a bad opinion of him/her 性格が良くないのでその人の評判が悪いと言う→～に汚名を着せる,烙印(らくいん)を押す ‖ *She was branded as a troublemaker after she complained about her long working hours.* 彼女が長時間労働に不満を言った後,周りからもんちゃくを起こす人という烙印が押された.

**brandish** /brǽndɪʃ/ 動他 ▶定義 to wave sth in the air in an aggressive or excited way 攻撃的にまたは興奮した様子で,～を空中で振る→～を振り回す ‖ *The robber was brandishing a knife.* 強盗はナイフを振り回していた.

**brand new** 形 ▶定義 completely new 完全に新しい→真新しい,新品の

**brandy** /brǽndi/ 名 C U (複 **brandies**) ▶定義 a strong alcoholic drink that is made from wine ワインから造られる強いアルコール飲料→ブランデー

**brash** /bræʃ/ 形 ▶定義 too confident and direct 自信過剰で直接的な→生意気な,せっかちな ‖ *Her brash manner makes her unpopular with strangers.* 彼女は生意気な態度のため初めて会う人に評判が悪い. — **brashness** 名 U →生意気,せっかち

**brass** /brɑːs; bræs/ 名 ▶定義1 U a hard yellow metal that is a mixture of two other metals (copper and zinc) 2つの別の金属(銅と亜鉛)が混ぜられた,硬く黄色い金属→真鍮(しんちゅう),黄銅 ‖ *brass buttons on a uniform* 制服の真鍮のボタン ▶定義2 [単数扱い,単数または複数形の動詞と共に] the group of musical instruments that are made of brass 真鍮でできた楽器の集団→金管楽器(部) ‖ *the brass section in an orchestra* オーケストラの金管楽器部

**brat** /bræt/ 名 C ▶定義 a child who behaves badly and annoys you 行儀が悪く,人を困らせる子供→小僧,がき

**bravado** /brəváːdou/ 名 U ▶定義 a confident way of behaving that is intended to impress people, sometimes as a way of hiding a lack of confidence 時には自信がないことを隠す手段として,自信があるところを人々に印象づけようと意図して振る舞うこと→虚勢,空威張り

★**brave**¹ /breɪv/ 形 ▶定義1 ready to do things that are dangerous or difficult without showing fear 恐れを見せずに,危険なまたは難しい事をする用意ができている→勇敢な,勇気のある,大胆な ‖ *the brave soldiers who fought in the war* 戦争で戦った勇敢な兵士たち '*This may hurt a little, so try and be brave,*' *said the dentist.* 「これは少し痛いかもしれないから,勇気を出して」と歯医者が言った. ▶定義2 needing or showing courage 勇気を必要とする,または示す→(行動が)勇気を必要とする,勇気を示す ‖ *a brave decision* 勇気ある決断 ☞類 **gallant** — **bravely** 副 →勇敢にも,勇ましく ‖ *The men bravely defended the town for three days.* その男たちは勇敢にも3日間町を守った.

**brave**² /breɪv/ 動他 ▶定義 to face sth unpleasant, dangerous or difficult without showing fear 恐れを見せずに,不愉快な,危険な,または難しい～に直面する→～に勇敢に立ち向かう,ものともしない ‖ *She braved the rain and went out into the street.* 彼女は雨をものともせずに,通りへと出ていった.

**bravery** /bréɪv(ə)ri/ 名 U ▶定義 actions that are brave 勇敢な行為→勇敢さ,勇ましさ,勇敢な行為 ‖ *After the war he received a medal for bravery.* 戦後,彼は勇敢な行動に対して勲章を受けた.

**bravo** /bráːvou, -´-/ 間 ▶定義 a word that people shout to show that they have enjoyed sth that sb has done, for example a play 〜がした…, 例えば芝居を楽しんだことを示そうとして人々が叫ぶ言葉→**ブラボー, うまいぞ, でかしたぞ**

**brawl** /brɔːl/ 名 C ▶定義 a noisy fight among a group of people, usually in a public place 通常公共の場所で, 人々の集団の間での騒々しい戦い→**騒々しいけんか, 大騒ぎ** — brawl 動 自 →**けんかする, どなり立てる** ‖ *We saw some football fans brawling in the street.* 私たちは, 何人かのサッカーファンが路上で騒々しくけんかしているのを見た.

**brawn** /brɔːn/ 名 U ▶定義 physical strength 肉体的な力→**筋力, 腕力** ‖ *To do this kind of job you need more brawn than brain (= you need to be strong rather than clever).* この種の仕事をするには, 頭脳よりも腕力が必要だ(= 賢くなるよりも強くなる必要がある). — brawny 形 →**筋肉のたくましい, 強壮な, 屈強な** ‖ *He folded his brawny arms across his chest.* 彼は胸の前で筋肉のたくましい腕を組んだ.

**brazen** /bréɪz(ə)n/ 形 ▶定義 without embarrassment, especially in a way which shocks people 特に人々に衝撃を与えて, ばつの悪い思いをしない→**厚かましい** ‖ *Don't believe a word she says - she's a brazen liar!* 彼女が言う事を信じるな － 彼女は厚かましいうそつきだ. — brazenly 副 →**厚かましく(も)** ‖ *He brazenly admitted he'd been having an affair.* 彼は厚かましくも情事があったと認めた.

**Brazil nut** 名 C ▶定義 a nut that we eat with a very hard shell とても硬い殻の付いている, 私たちが食べる木の実→**ブラジルナットの実** ☞ **nut** のさし絵

**breach**¹ /briːtʃ/ 名 ▶定義 1 C U breach (of sth) an act that breaks an agreement, a law, etc 契約, 法律などを破る行為→**不履行, 違反** ‖ *Giving private information about clients is a breach of confidence.* 顧客の個人的な情報を提供することは, 信任に違反することだ. *The company was found to be **in breach of contract**.* その会社が契約違反していることが分かった. ▶定義 2 C a break in friendly relations between people, groups, etc 人々, グループなどの間の友好的関係が壊れること→**仲たがい, 不和** ‖ *The incident caused a breach between the two countries.* その出来事は 2 国間に不和を招いた. ▶定義 3 C an opening in a wall, etc that defends or protects sb/sth 〜を守るまたは保護する壁などの穴→**裂け目, 突破口** ‖ *The waves made a breach in the sea wall.* 波が防波堤に裂け目を作った.

**breach**² /briːtʃ/ 動 他 ▶定義 1 to break an agreement, a law, etc 契約, 法律などを破る→**〜を破る, 破棄する** ‖ *He accused the Government of breaching international law.* 彼は国際法に違反したと政府を告訴した. ▶定義 2 to make an opening in a wall, etc that defends or protects sb/sth 〜を守るまたは保護する壁などに穴を開ける→**〜に破れ目を作る, 破る**

**bread**

French bread
bagel
roll
slice
croissant
crust
loaf of bread

*****bread** /bred/ 名 U ▶定義 a type of food made from flour and water mixed together and baked in an oven. Another substance (yeast) is usually added to make the bread rise. 小麦粉と水を混ぜてオーブンで焼いて作る食べ物の一種. 通常は膨らませるためにほかの材料(イースト)が加えられる→**パン** ‖ *a piece/slice of bread* パン 1 切れ

▶ *a loaf of bread* (パン一塊)は, 1 つに形づくられて焼かれたパンである. *wholemeal bread* (全麦パン)は, 穀粒全部を含む小麦粉から作られたパンである.

☞ C4 ページのさし絵

**breadcrumbs** /brédkrʌmz/ 名 [複数扱い] ▶定義 very small bits of bread that are used in cooking 料理に使われる, パンのとても小さな片→**パン粉, (パンの)くず**

*****breadth** /bredθ/ 名 ▶定義 1 C U the distance between the two sides of sth 〜の 2 つの側の間の距離→**幅, 広さ** ‖ *We measured the length and breadth of the garden.* 私たちはその庭の奥行きと幅を測った. ▶定義 2 U the wide

## breadwinner

variety of things, subjects, etc that sth includes ～が含み持つ,物,テーマなどの多彩さ→**広がり, 範囲** || *I was amazed by the breadth of her knowledge.* 彼女の知識の広さに驚いた. ☞ 形 **broad**

**成句** the length and breadth of sth ⇒ **LENGTH**

**breadwinner** /brédwɪnər/ 名 [C, 通常は単数]
▶定義 the person who earns most of the money that his/her family needs 家族が必要とするお金の大部分を稼ぐ人→**大黒柱, 一家の稼ぎ手** || *When his dad died, Steve became the breadwinner.* 彼の父親が死んだ時, スティーヴは一家の稼ぎ手になった.

***break**¹ /bréɪk/ 動 (過 **broke** /bróʊk/; 過分 **broken** /bróʊk(ə)n/) ▶定義1 自他 to separate, or make sth separate, into two or more pieces 2つ以上に分かれる, または～を分ける→**壊れる, 割れる, 折れる; ～を壊す, 割る, 折る** || *She dropped the vase onto the floor and it broke.* 彼女は花びんを床に落としたら, 割れた. *He broke his leg in a car accident.* 彼は自動車事故で足を折った. ☞ **chip** のさし絵 ▶定義2 自他 (used about a machine, etc) to stop working; to stop a machine, etc working (機械などについて) 作動するのを止める; 機械などが作動するのを止める→**故障する, 壊れる; ～を故障させる, 壊す** || *The photocopier has broken.* コピー機が壊れた. *Be careful with my camera - I don't want you to break it.* 私のカメラに気を付けて - 壊さないでね. ▶定義3 他 to do sth that is against the law, or against what has been agreed or promised 法律, または合意や約束されたことに反する～をする→**～を破る, ～に違反する** || *to break the law/rules/speed limit* 法律・規則・速度制限を破る *Don't worry - I never break my promises.* 心配するな - 私は決して約束を破らない. ▶定義4 自他 to stop doing sth for a short time ～をすることを短時間やめる→**中断する, 仕事を一休みする** || *Let's break for coffee now.* さてちょっと休んでコーヒーを飲もう. *We decided to break the journey and stop for lunch.* 私たちは旅を中断して, 昼食に立ち寄ることにした. ▶定義5 他 to make sth end ～を終わらせる→**終わらせる, 中断する** || *Once you start smoking it's very difficult to break the habit.* 一度たばこを吸い始めると, その習慣をやめるのはとても難しい. *Suddenly, the silence was broken by the sound of a bird singing.* 突然, 静寂は鳥の鳴き声で破られた. ▶定義6 自 to begin 始まる→**急に現れる, 始まる, 突然起こる** || *The day was breaking as I left the house.* 私が家を出た時, 夜が明けるところだった. *We ran indoors when the storm broke.* あらしが突然襲ってきた時, 私たちは家の中へ駆け込んだ. *When the story broke in the newspapers, nobody could believe it.* その話が突然新聞で明らかになった時, だれもそれを信じられなかった. ▶定義7 自 (used about a wave) to reach its highest point and begin to fall (波について) 最も高い位置に到達し落ち始める→**砕ける, 割れる** || *I watched the waves breaking on the rocks.* 波が岩に砕けるのを見た. ▶定義8 自 (used about the voice) to change suddenly (声について) 突然変わる→**(声の)調子が変わる, 声変わりする** || *Most boys' voices break when they are 13 or 14 years old.* ほとんどの少年の声は, 13歳か14歳の時に声変わりする. *His voice was breaking with emotion as he spoke.* 話しているうちに彼の声は感情的に変わっていた.

▶ break を含む成句については, 名詞, 形容詞などの項を参照. 例えば break even は even の項にある.

**句動詞** **break away (from sb/sth)** ▶定義1 to escape suddenly from sb who is holding you 自分を押さえている～から突然逃げる→**突然立ち去る, 逃げる** ▶定義2 to leave a political party, state, etc in order to form a new one 新しいものを作るために政党, 国などを去る→**独立する, 離脱する, 脱退する**

**break down** ▶定義1 (used about a vehicle or machine) to stop working (乗り物または機械について) 動くのが止まる→**壊れる, 故障する** || *Akram's car broke down on the way to work this morning.* 今朝, 出勤途中にアクラムの車は故障した. ▶定義2 (used about a system, discussion, etc) to fail (制度, 議論などについて) 失敗する→**失敗に終わる** || *Talks between the two countries have completely broken down.* 2か国間の交渉は完全に失敗に終わった. ▶定義3 to lose control of your feelings and start crying 自分の感情の抑制ができなくなり,

泣き始める→取り乱す,精神的に参る ‖ *He broke down in tears when he heard the news.* その知らせを聞いた時,彼は取り乱して泣いた.

**break sth down** ▶定義 1 to destroy sth by using force 力ずくで〜を壊す→**〜を打ち壊す,解体する,押し倒す・開ける** ‖ *The police had to break down the door to get into the house.* 警察はその家に入るために扉を壊さなければならなかった. ▶定義 2 to make a substance separate into parts or change into a different form in a chemical process 物質を部分に分ける,または化学的工程で異なる形に変える→**〜を分解する,〜の化学成分を変える** ‖ *Food is broken down in our bodies by the digestive system.* 食物は体内で消化器系統によって分解される.

**break in** ▶定義 to enter a building by force, usually in order to steal sth 通常は〜を盗むために,力ずくで建物に入る→**押し入る,侵入する**

**break in (on sth)** ▶定義 to interrupt when sb else is speaking ほかの〜が話している時に遮る→**〜に口を挟む,〜を邪魔する** ‖ *The waiter broke in on our conversation to tell me I had a phone call.* ウエーターが私たちの会話に口を挟んで,私に電話がかかっていると言った.

**break into sth** ▶定義 1 to enter a place that is closed 閉まっている場所に入る→**〜に侵入する,入り込む** ‖ *Thieves broke into his car and stole the radio.* 泥棒は彼の車に侵入しラジオを盗んだ.(比喩) *The company is trying to break into the Japanese market.* その会社は日本市場に入り込もうとしている. ▶定義 2 to start doing sth suddenly 〜を突然し始める→**突然〜し出す** ‖ *to break into song/a run* 突然歌い出す・走り出す

**break off** ▶定義 to suddenly stop doing or saying sth 突然〜をすることまたは言うことをやめる→**〜を急にやめる,中断する,急に話をやめる** ‖ *He started speaking and then broke off in the middle of a sentence.* 彼は話し始めたが,それから急に文の途中で話をやめた.

**break (sth) off** ▶定義 to remove a part of sth by force; to be removed in this way 力ずくで〜の一部を取り去る;この方法で取り去られる→**〜をもぎ取る,ちぎり取る** ‖ *Could you break off another bit of chocolate for me?* 少しチョコレートを折り取って,また私に下さいますか.

**break sth off** ▶定義 to end a relationship suddenly 突然関係を終わらせる→**〜を急に断つ,終わらせる,絶交する** ‖ *After a bad argument, they decided to **break off** their **engagement**.* ひどい口論の後,彼らは婚約を解消することに決めた.

**break out** ▶定義 (used about fighting, wars, fires, etc) to start suddenly(けんか,戦争,火事などについて)突然始まる→**起こる,突発する,発生する**

**break out in sth** ▶定義 to suddenly have a skin problem 突然皮膚に問題が起こる→**突然出る,発しんする** ‖ *to break out in spots/a rash* にきび・発しんが突然出る

**break out (of sth)** ▶定義 to escape from a prison, etc 刑務所などから逃げる→**逃げ出す,脱出する**

**break through (sth)** ▶定義 to manage to get past sth that is stopping you 止めようとする〜をどうにかして通り抜ける→**〜を(強引に)通り抜ける,突破する** ‖ *The protesters were trying to break through the line of police.* 抗議者たちは警官の列を突破しようとしていた.

**break up** ▶定義 1 (used about events that involve a group of people) to end or finish (人々の集団のかかわる出来事について)終わるまたは終了する→**終わりになる,解散する** ‖ *The meeting broke up just before lunch.* その会議は昼食の直前に終わった. ▶定義 2 英 to start school holidays 学校の休日が始まる→**休暇に入る** ‖ *When do you break up for the summer holidays?* いつ夏休みに入りますか.

**break up (with sb)** ▶定義 to end a relationship with a wife, husband, girlfriend or boyfriend 妻,夫,ガールフレンドやボーイフレンドとの関係を終わらせる→**終わりになる,破たんする,別れる** ‖ *She's broken up with her boyfriend.* 彼女はボーイフレンドと別れた.

**break (sth) up** ▶定義 to separate into parts 複数の部分に分ける→**ばらばらになる,崩れる,分割される** ‖ *The ship broke up on the rocks.* 船は岩にぶつかってばらばらになった.

**break sth up** ▶定義 to end an event by separating the people who are involved in it かかわっている人々を引き離すことによって,あ

## break²

る出来事を終わらせる→**解散させる, 終わらせる** || *The police arrived and broke up the fight.* 警察が到着し, けんかを終わらせた.

**break with sth** ▶定義 to end a relationship or connection with sb/sth ～との関係または繋がりを終わらせる→**～との関係を断つ, ～と手を切る** || *to break with tradition/the past* 伝統・過去と決別する

★**break²** /bréɪk/ 名 C ▶定義 1 a place where sth has been broken ～が壊れている場所→**破損, 裂け目, 破損箇所** || *a break in a pipe* パイプの割れ目 ▶定義 2 an opening or space in sth ～の中の開いた場所または空間→**中断, とぎれ** || *Wait for a break in the traffic before you cross the road.* 道路を横切る前に往来がとぎれるのを待ちなさい. ▶定義 3 a short period of rest 短い期間の休み→**休み, 休憩, 短い休暇** || *We worked all day without a break.* 私たちは一日中休みなしに働いた. *to take a break* 休みを取る ☞参 **interval** の注 ▶定義 4 **break (in sth); break (with sb/sth)** a change from what usually happens or an end to sth 通常起きる事とは変わった事, または～の終わり→**変わり目, 変化, 断絶** || *The incident led to a break in diplomatic relations.* その事件は外交関係の断絶につながった. *She wanted to make a complete break with the past.* 彼女は過去と完全に決別したかった. ▶定義 5 略式 a piece of good luck 幸運→**チャンス, 運** || *to give sb a break (= to help sb by giving him/her a chance to be successful)* ～にチャンスを与える (= 成功するチャンスを与えて～を助ける)

成句 **break of day** ▶定義 the time when light first appears in the morning; dawn 朝最初に日光が現れる時間; 夜明け→**夜明け**

**give sb a break** ▶定義 1 used to tell sb to stop saying things that are annoying or not true いらいらさせること, または事実ではない事を言うことをやめるように～に言う→**いいかげんにしてくれ, もうたくさんだ** || *Give me a break and stop nagging, OK!* もうたくさんだ, がみがみ言うのはやめてくれ, いいか. ▶定義 2 特に 米 to be fair to sb ～に公正である→**(もう一度)チャンスをくれ**

**breakage** /bréɪkɪdʒ/ 名 [C, 通常は複数] ▶定義 something that has been broken 壊れているもの→**破損物, 破損高, 賠償高** || *Customers must pay for any breakages.* 顧客は破損物の代金を払わなければならない.

**breakaway** /bréɪkəweɪ/ 形 (名詞の前だけ) ▶定義 (used about a political group, an organization, or a part of a country) that has separated from a larger group or country (政党, 組織, 国の一部について) より大きい集団または国から分かれた→**分離した, 脱退した** — **breakaway** 名 C →分離, 脱退

**breakdown** /bréɪkdàʊn/ 名 C ▶定義 1 a time when a vehicle, machine, etc stops working 乗り物, 機械などが作動しなくなるとき→**(突然の)故障, 破損** || *I hope we don't have a breakdown on the motorway.* 高速道路上で故障がないことを願う. ▶定義 2 the failure or end of sth ～の失敗または終わり→**挫折 (ざせつ), 中断, 崩壊** || *The breakdown of the talks means that a strike is likely.* 交渉の決裂によってストライキがありそうだ. ▶定義 3 = **NERVOUS BREAKDOWN** ▶定義 4 a list of all the details of sth ～のすべての詳細の一覧→**内訳** || *I would like a full breakdown of how the money was spent.* そのお金がどのように使われたかについての全内訳が欲しい.

★**breakfast** /brékfəst/ 名 C U ▶定義 the meal which you have when you get up in the morning 朝起きた時に取る食事→**朝食** || *to have breakfast* 朝食を取る *What do you usually have for breakfast?* あなたは通常朝食に何を食べますか. *to eat a big breakfast* 朝食をたくさん食べる

> ▶語法
>
> **breakfast** の語源と意味
>
> breakfast 名 朝食 動 朝食を食べる
>
> fast には「速い」や「断食」の意味があり, 語源的には不変永続・固定の概念を表す語彙 (ごい) です. *Go fast.* はもともと「同じ状態で進む」が「速さを弱めずに進む」になり「速い, 速く」の意味が出てきました. 一方,「断食」は「固く守る, 節制する」の意味から生じました. 一晩中の断食を初めて break (破る) のが朝食です. この意味の fast は動詞語尾の en を付けて, *Fasten your seatbelt.* (シートベルトを締めてください) のように用いられます.

## ▶社会・文化

**おいしい英国の朝ご飯**

伝統的な英国の朝食は English breakfast と呼ばれ, シリアル, 卵とベーコン, ソーセージ, 焼いたトマト, ヨーグルト, トーストとマーマレード, フルーツジュースと紅茶かコーヒーから成ります. ロールパン, 果物とコーヒーなどから成る continental breakfast は, 英国以外のヨーロッパスタイルの朝食を指します.

**成句** bed and breakfast ⇒ **BED¹**

**break-in** 名 C ▶定義 the act of entering a building by force, especially in order to steal sth 特に~を盗む目的で, 力ずくで建物に入る行為→**侵入, 家宅・住居侵入** ‖ *The police say there have been several break-ins in this area.* 警察はこの地域でいくつかの家宅侵入があったと言う.

**breakneck** /bréɪknèk/ 形(名詞の前だけ) ▶定義 very fast and dangerous とても速く危険な→**(斜面・速度など)非常に危険な** ‖ *He drove her to the hospital at breakneck speed.* 彼は猛スピードで彼女を病院まで送った.

**breakthrough** /bréɪkθruː/ 名 C ▶定義 a breakthrough (in sth) an important discovery or development 重要な発見または開発→**大躍進, 飛躍的進歩, (難問の)解明** ‖ *Scientists are hoping to make a breakthrough in cancer research.* 科学者たちはがんの研究で飛躍的な進歩を遂げたいと願っている.

**break-up** /bréɪkʌp/ 名 C ▶定義1 the end of a relationship between two people 2人の間の関係の終わり→**絶縁, 絶交, 解消** ‖ *the break-up of a marriage* 離婚 ▶定義2 the separation of a group or organization into smaller parts 1つの集団または組織を小さな部分に分けること→**分解, 分割, 解体** ‖ *the break-up of the Soviet Union* ソビエト連邦の崩壊

***breast** /brest/ 名 C ▶定義1 one of the two soft round parts of a woman's body that can produce milk 乳を作ることができる, 女性の体の2つの柔らかく丸い部分の一方→**乳房** ▶定義2 a word used especially in literature for the top part of the front of your body, below the neck 首より下の体の前面の最上部, 特に文学作品で使われる言葉→**胸** ▶定義3 the front part of the body of a bird 鳥の体の前面の部分→**胸, 胸肉** ☞ C1 ページのさし絵

**breastfeed** /bréstfiːd/ 動 自 他 (過, 過分 **breastfed**) ▶定義 to feed a baby with milk from the breast 赤ん坊に乳房からの乳を与える→**母乳で育てる**

**breaststroke** /bréststròʊk/ 名 U ▶定義 a style of swimming on your front in which you start with your hands together, push both arms forward and then move them out and back through the water 初めは両手をそろえて, 水の中で両手を前に伸ばしてから外側後方へ動かす, 体の前面を下にして泳ぐ方法→**平泳ぎ** ‖ *to do (the) breaststroke* 平泳ぎをする ☞参 backstroke, butterfly, crawl ☞ S1 ページのさし絵

***breath** /breθ/ 名 ▶定義1 U the air that you take into and blow out of your lungs 肺に吸い込んで, そして外へ吐き出す空気→**息** ‖ *to have bad breath* (= breath which smells unpleasant) 息が臭い (= 不快なにおいがする息) ▶定義2 C an act of taking air into or blowing air out of your lungs 空気を吸い込む, または肺から吐き出す行動→**呼吸, 息** ‖ *Take a few deep breaths before you start running.* 走り始める前に数回深呼吸をしなさい.

**成句** a breath of fresh air ▶定義 the clean air which you breathe outside, especially when compared to the air inside a room or building 特に部屋や建物の中の空気と比べて, 戸外で呼吸するきれいな空気→**新鮮な空気** ‖ *Let's go for a walk. I need a breath of fresh air.* 散歩しましょう. 私には新鮮な空気が必要だ. (比喩) *James's happy face is like a breath of fresh air in that miserable place.* ジェームズの幸せそうな顔は, あの惨めな場所で一服の清涼剤のようだ.

catch your breath ⇒ **CATCH¹**

get your breath (again/back) ▶定義 to rest after physical exercise so that your breathing returns to normal 呼吸が通常通りに戻るように, 運動の後に休む→**(息違いが)元に戻る**

hold your breath ▶定義 to stop breathing for a short time, for example when you are swimming or because of fear or excitement 例えば泳いでいるとき, または恐れや興奮のため

に、短時間息を止める→**息を止める、かたずをのむ、息をこらす** ‖ *We all held our breath as we waited for her reply.* 私たちは皆かたずをのんで彼女の答えを待った.

**(be/get) out of/short of breath** ▶定義 (to be/start) breathing very quickly, for example after physical exercise 例えば運動の後に、とても速い呼吸を(している・始める)→**息が切れて**

**say sth, speak, etc under your breath** ▶定義 to say sth very quietly, usually because you do not want people to hear you 通常人に聞かれたくないために、とても静かに言う→**小声で言う・話す、ひそひそと言う・話す**

**take your breath away** ▶定義 to surprise sb very much 〜を非常に驚かす→**〜をはっとさせる** ‖ *The spectacular view took our breath away.* 壮大な眺めに私たちははっとした. ☞ 形 breathtaking

**take a deep breath** ⇒ **DEEP**¹

**with bated breath** ⇒ **BATED**

**breathalyse** (米 **breathalyze**) /bréθəlàɪz/ 動他 ▶定義 to test the breath of a driver with a special machine (a breathalyser) to measure how much alcohol he/she has drunk どのくらいアルコールを飲んだかを測るための特別な器械(飲酒探知器)で運転手の息を検査する→**飲酒・酒気探知器で調べる**

***breathe** /briːð/ 動自他 ▶定義 to take air, etc into your lungs and blow it out again 空気などを肺に取り入れて、再び吐き出す→**呼吸する、息をする** ‖ *Breathe out as you lift the weight and breathe in as you lower it.* ウエートを持ち上げながら息を吐き、下げながら息を吸いなさい. *I hate having to breathe (in) other people's cigarette smoke.* 私は他人のたばこの煙を吸い込まなくてはならないなんて嫌だ. — **breathing** 名 U→**呼吸、息遣い** ‖ *heavy/irregular breathing* 重い・不規則な息遣い *These deep breathing exercises will help you relax.* この深呼吸運動はあなたをリラックスさせるでしょう.

成句 **not breathe a word (of/about sth) (to sb)** ▶定義 to not tell sb about sth that is secret 秘密の〜について…に言わない→**〜を漏らさない、口に出さない** ‖ *If you breathe a word of this to my mother, I'll never speak to you again!* この事を母に漏らしたら、二度と君とは口をきかないよ.

**breather** /bríːðər/ 名 C 略式 ▶定義 a short rest 短い休み→**一休み** ‖ *to have/take a breather* 一休みする

**breathless** /bréθləs/ 形 ▶定義1 having difficulty breathing 呼吸することが困難な→**息を切らした、あえいだ** ‖ *I was hot and breathless when I got to the top of the hill.* 丘の頂上に着いた時、私は暑くて息を切らしていた. ▶定義2 not able to breathe because you are so excited, frightened, etc とても興奮している、怖がっているなどのために、息をすることができない→**息もつけないほどの、張り詰めた、緊迫した** ‖ *to be breathless with excitement* 興奮して息もつけない — **breathlessly** 副→**息を切らして、かたずをのんで**

**breathtaking** /bréθtèɪkɪŋ/ 形 ▶定義 extremely surprising, beautiful, etc 非常に驚いた、美しいなど→**はらはらさせる、はっとさせるような** ‖ *breathtaking scenery* はっとするような景色

**breath test** 名 C ▶定義 a test by the police on the breath of a driver to measure how much alcohol he/she has drunk どのくらいアルコールを飲んだかを測る、警察が行う運転手の息の検査→**(飲酒・酒気検知器による)飲酒・酒気検査**

**breed**¹ /briːd/ 動 (過, 過分 **bred** /bred/) ▶定義1 自 (used about animals) to have sex and produce young animals (動物について)性交を行って幼い動物を産む→**子を産む、繁殖する** ‖ *Many animals won't breed in zoos.* 多くの動物は動物園では繁殖しないだろう. ☞類 **mate** ▶定義2 他 to keep animals or plants in order to produce young from them それらから子・苗を作るために、動物または植物を保管する→**〜を飼育する、繁殖させる** ‖ *These cattle are bred to produce high yields of milk.* これらの牛は大量の牛乳を生産するために飼育されている. ▶定義3 他 to cause sth 〜を引き起こす→**(良くない物事)を発生させる、引き起こす** ‖ *This kind of thinking breeds intolerance.* この種の考え方は偏狭を引き起こす. — **breeding** 名 U→**繁殖、孵化(ふか)、飼育**

**breed**² /briːd/ 名 C ▶定義 a particular variety of an animal 動物の特定の種類→**品種、種類** ‖ *a breed of cattle/dog* 牛・犬の品種

**breeder** /bríːdər/ 名 C ▶定義 a person who

breeds animals or plants 動物または植物を繁殖させる人➔畜産家, 養魚・養鶏業者, 育種業者 ‖ *a dog breeder* 犬の飼育家

**breeding ground** 名 C ▶定義1 a place where wild animals go to breed 野生動物が繁殖しに行く場所➔繁殖地 ▶定義2 a place where sth can develop ～が発達できる場所➔(悪・病気などの)温床 ‖ *a breeding ground for crime* 犯罪の温床

**breeze**¹ /briːz/ 名 C ▶定義 a light wind 軽い風➔そよ風, 弱い風, 微風 ‖ *A warm breeze was blowing.* 暖かいそよ風が吹いていた.

**breeze**² /briːz/ 動 自 ▶定義 breeze along, in, out, etc to move in a confident and relaxed way 自信を持ちくつろいだ様子で動く➔楽々とする, すっと入ってくる, さっと出ていく ‖ *He just breezed in twenty minutes late without a word of apology.* 彼は, 20分遅れの謝罪の言葉もなく, ただすっと入ってきた.

**breezy** /bríːzi/ 形 ▶定義1 with a little wind 弱い風の吹いた➔そよ風の吹く, 風通しの良い, さわやかな ▶定義2 happy and relaxed 幸せでくつろいだ➔快活な, 元気の良い ‖ *You're bright and breezy this morning!* 今朝のあなたは朗らかで元気ね.

**brevity** /brévəti/ 名 U ▶定義 the state of being short or quick 短いまたは速い状態➔短さ, 簡潔さ ☛ 形 **brief**

**brew** /bruː/ 動 ▶定義1 他 to make beer ビールを造る➔～を醸造する ▶定義2 他 to make a drink of tea or coffee by adding hot water お湯を加えて紅茶またはコーヒーを作る➔～をいれる ‖ *to brew a pot of tea* ポットに紅茶をいれる ▶定義3 自 (used about tea) to stand in hot water before it is ready to drink (紅茶について)飲む準備ができるまでお湯の中に置く➔飲める状態にある ‖ *Leave it to brew for a few minutes.* 飲める状態になるように数分間置いておきなさい.
成句 be brewing ▶定義 (used about sth bad) to develop or grow (悪い～について)発達するまたは育つ➔(陰謀などが)たくらまれている, (あらし・戦争などが)起こりかけている ‖ *There's trouble brewing.* 問題が持ち上がりかけている.

**brewery** /brúː(ə)ri/ 名 C (複 **breweries**) ▶定義 a place where beer is made ビールが造られる場所➔醸造所

**bribe** /bráɪb/ 名 C ▶定義 money, etc that is given to sb such as an official to persuade him/her to do sth to help you that is wrong or dishonest 悪いまたは不正な～を自分のためにしてくれるよう説き伏せるために, …に, 例えば役人に与える金銭など➔賄賂(わいろ) ‖ *to accept/take bribes* 賄賂を受け取る ― **bribe** 動 他 bribe sb (with sth) ➔～を(…で)買収する, ～に(…の)賄賂を使う ‖ *They got a visa by bribing an official.* 彼らは役人を買収して入国許可証を手に入れた. ― **bribery** /bráɪb(ə)ri/ 名 U ➔賄賂をもらうこと, 汚職

**bric-a-brac** /brík ə bræk/ 名 U ▶定義 small items of little value, for decoration in a house 家の中を飾るための, あまり価値のない小さい品➔古物, 骨董(こっとう)品 ☛ C8ページのさし絵

★**brick** /brɪk/ 名 C U ▶定義 a hard block of baked clay that is used for building houses, etc 家などを建てるために使われる, 焼いた粘土でできた堅い塊➔れんが ‖ *a lorry carrying bricks* れんがを運ぶトラック *a house built of red brick* 赤れんがで建てられた家 ☛ C7ページのさし絵

**bricklayer** /bríklèɪər/ 名 C ▶定義 a person whose job is to build walls with bricks れんがで壁を造ることを仕事にする人➔れんが職人

**brickwork** /bríkwɜ̀ːrk/ 名 U ▶定義 the part of a building that is made of bricks れんがでできた建物の部分➔れんが造りの構築物, れんが積み(工事)

**bridal** /bráɪdl/ 形 (名詞の前だけ) ▶定義 connected with a bride 花嫁に関連した➔花嫁・新婦の, 婚礼の

★**bride** /bráɪd/ 名 C ▶定義 a woman on or just before her wedding day 結婚式の日またはその直前の女性➔花嫁, 新婦 ‖ *a bride-to-be* (= a woman whose wedding is soon) 未来の花嫁 (= 間もなく結婚する女性) ☛参 **wedding** の注

★**bridegroom** /bráɪdgruːm, -grʊm/ (または **groom**) ▶定義 名 C a man on or just before his wedding day 結婚式の日またはその直前の男性➔花婿, 新郎 ☛参 **wedding** の注

**bridesmaid** /bráɪdzmèɪd/ 名 C ▶定義 a woman or girl who helps a woman on her wedding day (the bride) 結婚式の日の女性(花嫁)を助ける女性または少女➔花嫁に付き添う(未婚の)女性

☛参 wedding の注

**★bridge¹** /brɪdʒ/ 名 ▶定義1 C a structure that carries a road or railway across a river, valley, road or railway 川、谷、道、または鉄道を越えて、道や鉄道を伸ばす建造物→橋 ‖ *a bridge over the River Danube* ドナウ川に架かる橋 ▶定義2 [単数扱い] the high part of a ship where the captain and the people who control the ship stand 船長と船を管理する人々が立つ、船の高い部分→ブリッジ、船・艦橋 ▶定義3 U a card game for four people 4人で行うトランプゲーム→ブリッジ

**bridge²** /brɪdʒ/ 動他 ▶定義 to build a bridge over sth ～に架かる橋を建てる→橋を架ける

成句 bridge a/the gap ▶定義 to fill a space between two people, groups or things or to bring them closer together 2人、2つの集団または物の間のすきまを埋める、あるいはそれらを互いに近付ける→溝・ギャップを埋める、～の橋渡しをする ‖ *Baby food bridges the gap between milk and solid food.* 離乳食は、ミルクから固形食への橋渡しをする.

**bridle** /ˈbraɪdl/ 名 C ▶定義 the leather straps that you put on a horse's head so that you can control it when you are riding it 乗馬しているときに、馬を制御できるように馬の頭にはめる皮のひも→馬ろく ☛ horse のさし絵

**★brief¹** /briːf/ 形 ▶定義 short or quick 短いまたは速い→短時間の、簡潔な ‖ *a brief description* 簡潔な描写 *Please be brief. We don't have much time.* 手短にしてください. あまり時間がありません. ☛ 名 brevity

成句 in brief ▶定義 using only a few words 数語だけを使って→要するに、手短に ‖ *In brief, the meeting was a disaster.* 要するに、会議は散々なものだった.

**brief²** /briːf/ 名 C ▶定義 instructions or information about a job or task 仕事や任務についての指示または情報→指示、任務 ‖ *He was given the brief of improving the image of the organization.* 彼は組織の印象を改善する任務を与えられた.

**brief³** /briːf/ 動他 ▶定義 to give sb information or instructions about sth ～に…についての情報または指示を与える→～に要点を話す、事前に必要な指示・情報を与える、(出発直前の飛行士)に指令を与える ‖ *The minister has been fully briefed on what questions to expect.* 大臣は予想される質問について事前に十分な情報を与えられていた.

**briefcase** /ˈbriːfkeɪs/ 名 C ▶定義 a flat case that you use for carrying papers, etc, especially when you go to work 特に職場へ行くときに、書類などを運ぶために用いる平らなかばん→ブリーフケース、書類かばん ☛ bag のさし絵

**briefing** /ˈbriːfɪŋ/ 名 C U ▶定義 instructions or information that you are given before sth happens ～が起こる前に与えられる指示または情報→簡潔な指令、(事前の)状況・概要説明、打ち合わせ ‖ *a press/news briefing (= where information is given to journalists)* 記者への状況説明(= 記者に情報が与えられる場)

**briefly** /ˈbriːfli/ 副 ▶定義1 for a short time; quickly 短い間に; 速く→簡単に、手短に ‖ *She glanced briefly at the letter.* 彼女はさっと手紙に目を通した. ▶定義2 using only a few words 数語だけを使って→手短・簡単に言えば ‖ *I'd like to comment very briefly on that last statement.* 最後の陳述について、手短に述べたい.

**briefs** /briːfs/ 名 [複数扱い] ▶定義 pants for men or women 男性または女性用のパンツ→短いパンツ、ブリーフ、パンティー ☛ a pair of briefs と言うことに注意する.

**brigade** /brɪˈɡeɪd/ 名 C ▶定義1 a unit of soldiers in the army 軍隊の兵士の一組→旅団 ▶定義2 a group of people who work together for a particular purpose 特定の目的のために共に働く人々の集団→(軍隊のように組織された)団体、隊 ‖ *the fire brigade* 消防団

**brigadier** /ˌbrɪɡəˈdɪər/ 名 C ▶定義 an important officer in the army 軍隊の重要な士官→准将(じゅんしょう)、旅団長

**★bright** /braɪt/ 形 ▶定義1 having a lot of light 多くの光を持つ→輝いている、明るい、まぶしい ‖ *a bright, sunny day* 明るく晴れた日 *eyes bright with happiness* 幸せに輝いた目 ▶定義2 (used about a colour) strong and easy to see (色について)はっきりしていて見やすい→鮮やかな、さえた ‖ *a bright yellow jumper* 鮮やかな黄色のジャンパー ⇔ soft ▶定義3 clever, or able to learn things quickly 賢い、または物事を速く覚えられる→利口な、頭のいい ‖ *a bright child* 利

口な子供 a **bright idea** うまい考え ▶定義4 likely to be pleasant or successful 楽しそうな, または成功しそうな→輝かしい, 明るい, 有望な ‖ *The future looks bright.* 未来は明るそうだ. ▶定義5 happy; cheerful 幸せな; 陽気な→晴れやかな, 朗らかな, 快活な — **brightly** 副→輝いて, 明るく, 鮮やかに ‖ *brightly-coloured clothes* 鮮やかな色の服— **brightness** 名 ❶→明るさ 輝き, 晴れやかさ

成句 **look on the bright side** ⇒ **LOOK**¹

**brighten** /bráɪt(ə)n/ 動 自 他 ▶定義 **brighten (sth) (up)** to become brighter or happier; to make sth brighter より明るくまたは幸せになる; 〜をより明るくする→明るくなる, 晴れやかになる; 〜を明るくする, 輝かせる ‖ *His face brightened when he saw her.* 彼女を見た時, 彼の顔は明るくなった. *to brighten up sb's day (= make it happier)* 〜の 1 日を楽しいものにする (= より幸せにする)

*****brilliant** /brɪ́ljənt/ 形 ▶定義1 having a lot of light; very bright 多くの光を持つ; とても明るい→光り輝く, きらびやかに輝いている; 鮮明な ‖ *brilliant sunshine* 光り輝く日差し ▶定義2 very clever, skilful or successful とても賢い, 巧みな, または成功した→極めて優秀な, すばらしい, 立派な ‖ *a brilliant young scientist* 極めて優秀な若い科学者 *That's a brilliant idea!* それはすばらしい考えだ. ▶定義3 略式 very good とても良い→見事な, すばらしい ‖ *That was a brilliant film!* あれはすばらしい映画だった. — **brilliance** 名 ❶→光り輝くこと, 華々しさ, 優れた才気 — **brilliantly** 副→きらきらと, きらびやかに, すばらしく

**brim**¹ /brɪm/ 名 C ▶定義1 the top edge of a cup, glass, etc 茶わん, コップなどの最上部の端→縁, へり ‖ *The cup was full to the brim.* 茶わんは縁まで一杯だった. ▶定義2 the bottom part of a hat that is wider than the rest ほかより広くなっている, 帽子の下の部分→つば ☞ **hat** のさし絵

**brim**² /brɪm/ 動 自 (**brimming**; **brimmed**) ▶定義 **brim (with sth)** to be full of sth 〜で一杯である→あふれそうになる ‖ *His eyes were brimming with tears.* 彼の目には涙があふれていた.

句動詞 **brim over (with sth)** ▶定義 (used about a cup, glass, etc) to have more liquid than it can hold (茶わん, コップなどについて) それに入る以上の液体を入れる→(〜で) あふれる, (〜に) 満ちている ‖ *The bowl was brimming over with water.* おわんは水であふれていた. (比喩) *to be brimming over with health/happiness* 健康・幸せに満ちている

### bring/fetch/take

**Bring** the newspaper.

**Fetch** the newspaper.

**Take** the newspaper.

*****bring** /brɪŋ/ 動 他 (過, 過分 **brought** /brɔːt/) ▶定義1 to carry or take sb/sth to a place with you 自分のいる場所に〜を運ぶ, または持ってくる→〜を連れてくる ‖ *Is it all right if I bring a friend to the party?* パーティーに友達を連れてきてもよいですか. *Could you bring us some water, please?* 私たちに水を頂けますか. (比喩) *He will bring valuable skills and experience to the team.* 彼は価値ある技術と経験をチームにもたらすだろう. *My sister went to Spain on holiday and brought me back a T-shirt.* 妹は休暇でスペインに行き, 私にTシャツを買って帰った. ▶定義2 to move sth somewhere 〜をどこかへ動かす→〜へ持ってくる, 〜から持ち出す ‖ *She brought the book down off the shelf.* 彼女はその本を棚から下ろした. *Louis brought a photo out of his wallet and showed it to us.* ルイスは財布から写真を出して, 私たちに見せてくれた.

## 194　bring

▶定義3 to cause or result in sth ～を引き起こす，または～の結果になる→～を導く，もたらす ‖ *The sight of her brought a smile to his face.* 彼女を見ると彼は笑みを浮かべた．*Money doesn't always bring happiness.* お金は必ずしも幸せをもたらさない．▶定義4 to cause sb/sth to be in a certain place or condition ～をある場所または状態に置く→～を(…する)気にさせる，～をある状態に至らせる ‖ *Their screams brought people running from all directions.* 彼らの叫び声に，四方八方から人々が走ってきた．*Add water to the mixture and bring it to the boil.* 混合物に水を加えて沸騰させなさい．*An injury can easily **bring** an athlete's career **to an end**.* けがは選手生命を簡単に終わらせることがある．▶定義5 bring yourself to do sth to force yourself to do sth 自分に～をすることを強いる→～する気になる ‖ *The film was so horrible that I couldn't bring myself to watch it.* その映画は恐ろしくて，見る気になれなかった．

▶ bring を含む成句については，名詞，形容詞などの項を参照．例えば bring up the rear は rear の項にある．

### ▶日本語 vs 英語

「持っていく」が bring になる場合

bring と take の使い分けは，come と go の使い分けと同様です．日本語の「持って(連れて)くる」は，話し手のいる場所への移動に用いられます．一方，英語の bring は，話し手または聞き手のいる場所への移動に用いられます．したがって，聞き手のいる場所への移動の場合，日本語では「持って(連れて)いく」となりますが，英語では bring を用いることになります．

**句動詞** bring about ▶定義 to cause sth to happen ～を起こさせる→(変化・事故など)を引き起こす，もたらす ‖ *to bring about changes in people's lives* 人々の生活に変化をもたらす

bring sth back ▶定義1 to cause sth that existed before to be introduced again 以前存在した～を再び導入させる→～を復活させる，回復させる ‖ *Nobody wants to bring back the days of child labour.* だれも年少者労働の時代を復活させようとは思わない．▶定義2 to cause sb to remember sth ～に…を思い出させる→～を思い出させる ‖ *The photographs brought back memories of his childhood.* 写真が彼の子供時代を思い出させた．

bring sb/sth down ▶定義 to defeat sb/sth; to make sb/sth lose a position of power ～を打ち負かす；～に権力のある地位を失わせる→**～を打ち倒す，破滅させる** ‖ *to bring down the government* 政府を打倒する

bring sth down ▶定義 to make sth lower in level ～の程度を低くする→～を下げる ‖ *to bring down the price of sth* ～の価格を下げる

bring sth forward ▶定義1 to move sth to an earlier time ～をより早い時間へ動かす→～の日取りを繰り上げる，(時計)を進める ‖ *The date of the meeting has been brought forward by two weeks.* 会議の日取りは2週間繰り上げられた．⇔ put sth back ▶定義2 to suggest sth for discussion ～を審議に提案する→～を持ち出す，提起する，提出する

bring sb in ▶定義 to ask or employ sb to do a particular job 特定の仕事をするために，～に頼むまたは～を雇う→～を(…してもらうように)参加させる ‖ *A specialist was brought in to set up the new computer system.* 新しいコンピューターシステムを設置するために専門家が迎えられた．

bring sth in ▶定義 to introduce sth ～を導入する→～を導入する，取り入れる ‖ *The government have brought in a new law on dangerous dogs.* 政府は危険な犬に関する新法を導入した．

bring sth off ▶定義 to manage to do sth difficult 難しい～をどうにかして行う→～を成し遂げる ‖ *The team brought off an amazing victory.* チームはびっくりするような勝利をもぎ取った．

bring sth on ▶定義 to cause sth ～を引き起こす→～を引き起こす ‖ *Her headaches are brought on by stress.* 彼女の頭痛はストレスによるものだ．

bring sth out ▶定義 to produce sth or cause sth to appear ～を作る，または～を出現させる→～を世間に出す，生産する，出版する ‖ *When is the company bringing out its next new model?* 会社はいつ次の新型を発表するのですか．

bring sb round ▶定義 to make sb become

conscious again→〜の意識を回復させる‖ *I splashed cold water on his face to try to bring him round.* 彼の意識を回復させるために,私は顔に冷水を掛けた.

bring sb round (to sth) ▶定義 to persuade sb to agree with your opinion 自分の意見に同意するよう〜を説得する→〜の考えを(…へ)変えさせる,説得する‖ *After a lot of discussion we finally brought them round to our point of view.* 討議を重ねた末,ついに彼らを私たちの見解に同調させた.

bring sth round to sth ▶定義 to direct a conversation to a particular subject 会話を特定の主題に向かわせる→〜を…の方に向けさせる‖ *I finally brought the conversation round to the subject of money.* 私はついに話題をお金に向けさせた.

bring sb up ▶定義 to look after a child until he/she is adult and to teach him/her how to behave 子供が大人になるまで面倒を見て,その子供に振る舞い方を教える→〜を育てる,しつける‖ *After her parents were killed the child was brought up by her uncle.* 両親が殺された後,その子供はおじに育てられた. *a well-brought-up child* よくしつけられた子供

bring sth up ▶定義1 to be sick so that food that you have swallowed comes back out of your mouth; to vomit 気分が悪くて飲み込んだ食べ物が口の外へ戻る;戻す→〜を吐き出す,戻す ▶定義2 to introduce sth into a discussion or conversation 〜を討議や会話に持ち込む→〜を持ち出す‖ *I intend to bring the matter up at the next meeting.* 私は次の会議でこの問題を持ち出すつもりだ.

**brink** /brɪŋk/ 图 [単数扱い] ▶定義 the brink (of sth) if you are on the brink of sth, you are almost in a very new, exciting or dangerous situation もしあなたが 'on the brink of sth' であるなら,あなたはもう少しで非常に新しい,刺激的な,または危険な状態になる→〜の寸前で,今にも〜しそうで,〜にひんして‖ *Just when the band were **on the brink** of becoming famous, they split up.* ちょうど有名になる寸前に,そのバンドは解散した.

**brisk** /brɪsk/ 形 ▶定義1 quick or using a lot of energy; busy 速い,または活力を大いに使った;忙しい→活発な,元気の良い‖ *They set off at a brisk pace.* 彼らは元気な足取りで出発した. *Trading has been brisk this morning.* 今朝の取り引きは活発だった. ▶定義2 confident and practical; wanting to get things done quickly 自信があり実践的な;物事をさっさとしたがる→きびきびした,威勢がよい — **briskly** 副 →活発に,きびきびと— **briskness** 图 Ⓤ →活発

**bristle**¹ /brísl/ 图 Ⓒ ▶定義1 a short thick hair 短く太い毛→堅い毛,剛毛‖ *The bristles on my chin hurt the baby's face.* 私のあごの剛毛が赤ん坊の顔を傷付けた. ▶定義2 one of the short thick hairs of a brush ブラシの短く太い毛の1本→堅い毛,剛毛

**bristle**² /brísl/ 動 Ⓘ ▶定義1 (used about hair or an animal's fur) to stand up straight because of fear, anger, cold, etc (髪または動物の毛皮について)恐れ,怒り,寒さなどのためにまっすぐに立つ→逆立つ ▶定義2 bristle (with sth) (at sb/sth) to show that you are angry 怒っていることを示す→(〜に)怒る,気色ばむ,態度を硬化する

句動詞 bristle with sth ▶定義 to be full of sth 〜が一杯である→〜が林立する,(不快なものが)充満する

**Brit** /brɪt/ 图 Ⓒ 略式 ▶定義 a British person 英国人→英国人

\***Britain** /brítn/ =GREAT BRITAIN ☞参 **United Kingdom** の注

\***British** /brítɪʃ/ 形 ▶定義1 of the United Kingdom (=Great Britain and Northern Ireland) 連合王国(=グレートブリテン島と北アイルランド)の→英国の,英国人の‖ *British industry* 英国の産業 *to hold a British passport* 英国のパスポートを持っている ▶定義2 the British [複数扱い] the people of the United Kingdom 連合王国の人々→英国人

**the British Isles** 图 [複数扱い] ▶定義 Great Britain and Ireland with all the islands that are near their coasts グレートブリテン島とアイルランド島,およびこれらの2つの島の近隣にあるすべての島々→英国諸島 ☞ 英国諸島は地理的区分であり,政治的区分ではないことに注意する.

**Briton** /brítn/ 图 Ⓒ ▶定義 a person who comes from Great Britain グレートブリテン島出身の人→ブリトン人,英国人

**brittle**

▶普通この語は新聞で、または古代ブリテン島の住民について述べるときにのみ用いる: *Three Britons killed in air crash.* (機体の墜落で英国人3名が死亡した。) *the Ancient Britons* (古代ブリトン人). それ以外の場合には a British man, a British woman と言う.

**brittle** /brítl/ 形 ▶定義 hard but easily broken 硬いが壊れやすい→砕けやすい, 折れやすい, もろい‖ *The bones become brittle in old age.* 年を取ると骨はもろくなる.

**broach** /bróʊtʃ/ 動 他 ▶定義 to start talking about a particular subject, especially one which is difficult or embarrassing 特定の主題, 特に難しいまたは気まずい思いをすることについて話し始める→〜を切り出す‖ *How will you broach the subject of the money he owes us?* 彼が私たちに借りているお金のことを、あなたはどのように切り出すつもりですか.

**B-road** 名 C ▶定義 (in Britain) a road that is not as wide or important as a motorway or a main road (A-road) (英国で)高速道路や主要な道路(A-road)ほど広くない, または重要でない道→Bロード‖ *We drove the whole way on B-roads.* 私たちは全行程、Bロードをドライブした.

★**broad** /brɔːd/ 形 ▶定義**1** wide 広い→幅の広い, 広々とした, 心の広い‖ *a broad street/river* 広い通り・広大な川 *broad shoulders* たくましい肩 *a broad smile* おおらかな笑顔

▶ある物の一方と他方の間の距離について述べるときには, broad より wide の方が多く用いられる: *The gate is four metres wide.* (その門は幅4メートルだ。)

⇔ **narrow** ☞ 名 **breadth** ▶定義**2** including many different people or things 多くの異なる人々または物を含む→幅広い‖ *We sell a broad range of products.* 私たちは幅広い商品を販売する. ▶定義**3** without a lot of detail; general 詳細があまりない; 概略の→大雑把な, 大要の‖ *I'll explain the new system in broad terms.* 新しいシステムについて大雑把に説明します. ▶定義**4** (used about the way sb speaks) very strong (〜の話し方について)とても強い→露骨な, 丸出しの‖ *She has a broad Somerset accent.* 彼女はひどいサマセットなまりがある.

成句 (**in**) **broad daylight** ▶定義 during the day, when it is easy to see 見えやすい昼間のうちに→真っ昼間に‖ *He was attacked in broad daylight.* 彼は真っ昼間に襲われた.

**broad bean** 名 C ▶定義 a type of large flat green bean that can be cooked and eaten 料理して食べることができる、大きく平たい緑色の豆の一種→そら豆

★**broadcast** /brɔ́ːdkɑːst, -kæst/ 動 自 他 (過, 過分 **broadcast**) ▶定義 to send out radio or television programmes ラジオまたはテレビの番組を送り出す→〜を放送・放映する‖ *The Olympics are broadcast live around the world.* オリンピックは世界中に生放送される. ― **broadcast** 名 C →放送‖ *The next news broadcast is at 9 o'clock.* 次のニュースの放送は9時だ.

**broadcaster** /brɔ́ːdkɑːstər, -kæstər/ 名 C ▶定義 a person who speaks on the radio or on television ラジオやテレビで話す人→放送者

**broaden** /brɔ́ːd(ə)n/ 動 自 他 ▶定義 **broaden (sth) (out)** to become wider; to make sth wider 広くなる; 〜を広くさせる→広くなる, 広がる; 〜を広げる, 〜を広める‖ *The river broadens out beyond the bridge.* その川は橋の向こうで広くなる. (比喩) *Travel broadens the mind (=it makes you understand other people better).* 旅は見聞を広める(=ほかの人々についてより深く理解させる).

**broadly** /brɔ́ːdli/ 副 ▶定義**1** (used to describe a way of smiling) with a big, wide smile (ほほえみを描写するときに用いて)顔全体がほほえみに満ちた→にこやかに‖ *He smiled broadly as he shook everyone's hand.* 彼は皆と握手しながら、にこやかにほほえんだ. ▶定義**2** generally 概して→大体, 大雑把に‖ *Broadly speaking, the scheme will work as follows...* 大筋では、その計画は以下のように進められる.

**broad-minded** 形 ▶定義 happy to accept beliefs and ways of life that are different from your own 自分自身のものとは異なる信条や生き方を喜んで受け入れる→寛大な, 心の広い, 偏見のない⇔ **narrow-minded**

**broccoli** /brάk(ə)li/ 名 U ▶定義 a thick green plant with green or purple flower heads that can be cooked and eaten 調理して食べられる、緑または紫色の頭状花が付いた、ずんぐりした緑色の植物→ブロッコリー ☞ C3 ページのさし絵

**brochure** /bróʊʃʊər, -ʃər/ 名 C ▶定義 a small

book with pictures and information about sth 〜についての写真と情報が載っている小さな本→(営業用の)パンフレット,小冊子

**broil** /brɔ́il/ 動他 特に 米 =GRILL²(1)

**broke¹** BREAK¹ の過去形

**broke²** /bróuk/ 形 (名詞の前は不可) 略式 ▶定義 having no money お金を持っていない→無一文で, 破産して ‖ *I can't come out tonight - I'm absolutely broke.* 今晩は出掛けられない － 完全に無一文なのだ.

**broken¹** BREAK¹ の過去分詞形

*****broken²** /bróuk(ə)n/ 形 ▶定義1 damaged or in pieces; not working 傷付いた, または粉々の; 働かない→壊れた, 砕けた; 故障した ‖ *The washing machine's broken.* その洗濯機は壊れている. *Watch out! There's broken glass on the floor.* 気を付けろ. 床に割れたガラスがある. *a broken leg* 折れた足 *How did the window get broken?* どうして窓が割れたの. ☞**chip** のさし絵 ▶定義2 (used about a promise or an agreement) not kept (約束や契約について) 守られない→破られた ▶定義3 not continuous; interrupted 続かない; 中断された→断続的な, とぎれがちの ‖ *a broken line* 破線 *a broken night's sleep* とぎれがちな夜の睡眠 ▶定義4 (used about a foreign language) spoken slowly with a lot of mistakes (外国語について) 多く間違えながらゆっくりと話される→片言の, 不完全な ‖ *to speak in broken English* 片言の英語を話す

**broken-down** 形 ▶定義1 in a very bad condition 非常に悪い状態で→打ち砕かれた, 健康を損ねた, 衰弱した ‖ *a broken-down old building* 老朽化した建物 ▶定義2 (used about a vehicle) not working (乗り物について) 動かない→故障した ‖ *A broken-down bus was blocking the road.* 故障したバスが道をふさいでいた.

**broken-hearted** =HEARTBROKEN

**broken home** 名 C ▶定義 a family in which the parents do not live together, for example because they are divorced 例えば離婚したために, 両親が一緒に暮らさない家族→崩壊した家庭 ‖ *Many of the children came from broken homes.* その子供たちの多くは崩壊した家庭の出だ.

**broker** /bróukər/ 名 C ▶定義 a person who buys and sells things, for example shares in a business, for other people 例えば会社の株をほかの人々のために売買する人→ブローカー, 仲買人 ‖ *an insurance broker* 保険の仲買人

**brolly** /bráli/ 名 C (後 **brollies**) 英 略式 = UMBRELLA

**bronchitis** /brɑŋkáitəs/ 名 U ▶定義 an illness of the tubes leading to the lungs (**bronchial tubes**) that causes a very bad cough ひどいせきが出る, 肺に伸びる管 (気管支) の病気→気管支炎

**bronze** /branz/ 名 ▶定義1 ❶ a reddish-brown metal that is made by mixing tin with another metal (**copper**) スズをほかの金属 (銅) と混ぜて作られる, 赤みがかった茶色の金属→ブロンズ, 青銅 ▶定義2 ❶ the colour of bronze ブロンズの色→ブロンズ色, 赤みがかった茶色 ▶定義3 =BRONZE MEDAL — bronze 形→ブロンズ色の, ブロンズ製の

**bronzed** /branzd/ 形 ▶定義 having skin that has been turned brown, in an attractive way, by the sun 太陽によって魅力的に茶色になった肌をした→日に焼けた

**bronze medal** 名 C ▶定義 a round piece of bronze that you get as a prize for coming third in a race or a competition 競走や競技で3位になったときに賞品としてもらう, 円いブロンズの製品→銅メダル ☞参 **gold medal, silver medal**

**brooch** /bróutʃ/ 名 C ▶定義 a piece of jewellery with a pin at the back that women wear on their clothes 女性が服に付ける, 後ろにピンの付いた装飾品→ブローチ ☞ **jewellery** のさし絵

**brood¹** /bruːd/ 動 自 ▶定義1 brood (on/over/about sth) to worry, or to think a lot about sth that makes you worried or sad 自分自身を悩ませたりまたは悲しませることについて大いに心配する, または考える→じっと考え込む, くよくよする ‖ *to brood on a failure* 失敗についてくよくよする ▶定義2 (used about a female bird) to sit on her eggs (雌の鳥について) 卵の上に座る→卵を抱く

**brood²** /bruːd/ 名 C ▶定義 all the young birds that belong to one mother 1羽の母鳥に属するすべての幼い鳥→一度にかえったひな

**broody** /brúːdi/ 形 ▶定義1 (used about a woman) wanting to have a baby (女性について) 赤ん坊を欲しがっている→子供を欲しがる ▶定義2 (used about a female bird) ready to have or sit on eggs(雌の鳥について)卵を持つ, または抱く用意のできた➡️卵を抱きたがっている,巣に付きたがる‖ *a broody hen* 卵を抱きたがっている雌鶏(めんどり)

**brook** /brúk/ 名 C ▶定義 a small flow of water (stream) 小さな水の流れ(小川)➡️小川

**broom** /brúːm, brʊ́m/ 名 C ▶定義 a brush with a long handle that you use for removing (sweeping) dirt from the floor 床からごみを取り去る(掃く)ために使う, 長い柄の付いたはけ➡️ほうき ☛ **brush** のさし絵

**broomstick** /brúːmstìk, brʊ́m-/ 名 C ▶定義 the handle of a broom➡️ほうきの柄

**Bros** 略 Brothers ➡️(会社の名前に用いて)~兄弟商会‖ *Wentworth Bros Ltd* ウェントワース兄弟商会

**broth** /brɔ́(ː)θ, brɑ́θ/ 名 U ▶定義 thin soup 薄いスープ➡️(肉でだしを取った)薄いスープ‖ *chicken broth* チキンスープ

**brothel** /brɔ́(ː)θəl, brɑ́θ-/ 名 C ▶定義 a place where men can go and pay to have sex with a woman (a prostitute) 男性が金を払って女性(売春婦)と性交できる場所➡️売春宿

★**brother** /brʌ́ðər/ 名 C ▶定義1 a man or boy who has the same parents as another person もう1人と同じ両親を持つ男性または男の子 兄, 弟, 兄弟‖ *Michael and Jim are brothers.* マイケルとジムは兄弟だ. *Michael is Jim's brother.* マイケルはジムの兄弟だ. *a younger/older brother* 弟・兄 ☛参 **half-brother**, **stepbrother**.

▶「兄弟と姉妹の両方」を意味する一般的な英単語はないことに注意する. *Have you got any brothers and sisters?* (兄弟か姉妹がいますか.) sibling (兄弟姉妹)は, とても正式な単語である.

▶定義2 a man who is a member of a Christian religious community キリスト教社会の一員である男性➡️信者仲間, 同一の教会員, 修道士 ▶定義3 略式 a man who you feel close to because he is a member of the same society, group, etc as you 自分と同じ社会, 集団などにいるために親近感を感じる男性➡️同胞, 同僚, 仲間, 同級生

**brotherhood** /brʌ́ðərhʊ̀d/ 名 ▶定義1 U a feeling of great friendship and understanding between people 人々の間で, 強い友情を感じ理解し合っていること➡️兄弟の愛情, 親交, 同胞のよしみ‖ *the brotherhood of man (=a feeling of friendship between all the people in the world)* 人類愛(=世界中のすべての人々の間に友情を感じること) ▶定義2 [C, 単数または複数形の動詞と共に]an organization which is formed for a particular, often religious, purpose 特定の目的のために, しばしば宗教的な目的で, 形成される組織➡️団体, 組合, 仲間

**brother-in-law** 名 C (複 brothers-in-law) ▶定義1 the brother of your husband or wife 夫または妻の兄弟➡️義兄, 義弟 ▶定義2 the husband of your sister 姉妹の夫➡️義兄, 義弟

**brotherly** /brʌ́ðərli/ 形 ▶定義 showing feelings of love and kindness that you would expect a brother to show 兄弟に期待されるような愛と優しさの感情を示す➡️兄弟の(ような), 兄弟にふさわしい, 親しい‖ *brotherly love/advice* 兄弟愛・優しさのこもった助言

**brought** BRING の過去・過去分詞形

**brow** /bráʊ/ 名 C ▶定義1 [通常は複数] =EYEBROW ▶定義2 =FOREHEAD ▶定義3 [単数扱い]the top part of a hill 丘の頂上部分➡️(険しい坂の)頂上, 崖(がけ)の縁‖ *Suddenly a car came over the brow of the hill.* 突然車が丘の頂上にやって来た.

**brown**¹ /bráʊn/ 名形 ▶定義1 C U (of) the colour of earth or wood 地面や材木の色(の)➡️茶色(の), 褐色(の)‖ *brown eyes/hair* 茶色い目・髪 *the yellows and browns of the trees in autumn* 秋の木の紅葉 *You don't look nice in brown (=in brown clothes).* あなたは茶色(=茶色い服)が似合わない. ▶定義2 having skin that the sun has made darker 太陽が黒くした肌を持つ➡️褐色の, 日に焼けた‖ *Although I often sunbathe, I never seem to go brown.* 私はよく日光浴するが, 決して日焼けしないようだ.

**brown**² /bráʊn/ 動 自他 U ▶定義 to become or make sth become brown 茶色くなる, または~を茶色くする➡️褐色・茶色になる, 日に焼ける; ~を褐色・茶色にする, 日焼けさせる‖ *Brown the meat in a frying pan.* フライパンで肉を茶色に焼きなさい.

**brownie** /bráʊni/ 名 C ▶定義1 Brownie a young girl who is a member of the junior part of the Girl Guides organization ガールガイド(少

女団)の幼年団の一員で年少の女の子➡ガールガイド, 見習いの幼年団員 (8〜11歳) ▶定義 2 a type of heavy chocolate cake that often contains nuts しばしばナッツが入った, こってりしたチョコレートケーキの一種➡ナッツ入りのチョコレートケーキ

**brown paper** 名 ❶ ▶定義 strong, thick paper used for putting round packages, etc 小包などの周りに巻いて使われる丈夫な厚い紙➡(茶色の)包装紙 ‖ *I wrapped the books in brown paper and tied the package with string.* 本を包装紙でくるみ, その包みをひもで縛った.

**browse** /bráʊz/ 動 ▶定義 1 ❺ to spend time pleasantly, looking round a shop, without a clear idea of what you are looking for 探している物についてのはっきりした考えもなしに, 店を見て回り, 楽しく過ごす➡ゆっくり見て回る ‖ *I spent hours browsing in the local bookshop.* 私は地元の本屋を何時間もゆっくり見て回った. ▶定義 2 ❺ browse through sth to look through a book or magazine without reading every part or studying it carefully すべてを読む, または注意深く勉強することをしないで, 本や雑誌に目を通す➡拾い読みする, 立ち読みする ‖ *I enjoyed browsing through the catalogue but I didn't order anything.* 私はカタログを拾い読みして楽しんだが, 何も注文しなかった. ▶定義 3 ❻ (computing) to look for and read information on a computer (コンピューター) コンピューターで情報を探して読む➡資料を探索する, (インターネットのホームページを)閲覧する ‖ *I've just been browsing the Internet for information on Iceland.* 私はアイスランドについての情報をインターネットで閲覧していたところです. —browse 名 [単数扱い]➡拾い読み, 立ち読み, (商品の)物色

**browser** /bráʊzər/ 名 ❻ ▶定義 (computing) a computer program that lets you look at words and pictures from other computer systems by receiving information through telephone wires (コンピューター) 電話線を通して情報を受け取ることによって, ほかのコンピューターシステムからの言葉や写真を見せるコンピューターのプログラム➡ブラウザ, 閲覧ソフト ‖ *an Internet browser* インターネットの閲覧ソフト

*****bruise** /bruːz/ 名 ❻ ▶定義 a blue, brown or purple mark that appears on the skin after sb has fallen, been hit, etc 〜が転んだり, ぶつかったりなどした後に皮膚に現れる青い, 茶色い, または紫色の印➡打撲傷, 打ち身, あざ ☛ 目の回りのあざは black eye と言う. —bruise 動 ❶ ❻ ➡あざになる, 打った跡が付く, 傷む; 〜にあざを付ける, 〜に打撲傷を与える, 傷める ‖ *I fell over and bruised my arm.* 私はつまずいて転び, 腕にあざができた. *Handle the fruit carefully or you'll bruise it.* 果物を注意して扱いなさい, さもないと傷を付けてしまいますよ. *I've got the sort of skin that bruises easily.* 私の肌はあざができやすい.

**brunette** /bruːnét/ 名 ❻ ▶定義 a white woman with dark brown hair 黒褐色の髪の白人女性➡ブルネットの女性, (髪が)黒褐色の人 ☛参 **blond**

**brunt** /brʌnt/ 名
成句 bear the brunt of sth ⇒ **BEAR²**

brushes — hairbrush, nail brush, brush, dustpan, brush/broom, paintbrushes, toothbrush

*****brush¹** /brʌʃ/ 名 ▶定義 1 ❻ an object that is used for cleaning things, painting, tidying your hair, etc 物をきれいにする, 色を塗る, 髪を整えるためなどに使われるもの➡ブラシ, はけ ‖ *I took a brush and swept the snow from the path.* 私はブラシを手に取り, 道の雪を掃いた. *a toothbrush* 歯ブラシ *a paintbrush* ペンキ用のはけ *a hairbrush* ヘアブラシ ▶定義 2 [単数扱い] an act of cleaning, tidying the hair, etc with a brush ブラシできれいにする, 髪を整えるなどの行為➡ブラシ・はけをかけること, 絵筆を使うこと ‖ *The floor needs a brush.* 床にブラシがけをする必要がある.

成句 (have) a brush with sb/sth ▶定義 (to have or almost have) an unpleasant meeting with sb/sth ~との不愉快な出会い(をする、またはしそうになる)➔ ~と軽い接触(をする)、~との小競り合い(をする) ‖ *My only brush with the law was when I was stopped for speeding.* 私が法に抵触したのは、速度違反で止められた時だけだ.

★**brush**[2] /brʌʃ/ 動 ▶定義 1 他 to clean, tidy, etc sth with a brush ブラシで~をきれいにする、整えるなど➔ ~にブラシをかける、磨く ‖ *Make sure you brush your teeth twice a day.* 1日に2回確実に歯を磨きなさい. *Brush your hair before you go out.* 出かける前に髪にブラシをかけなさい. ☛参 clean[2]の注 ▶定義 2 自他 to touch sb/sth lightly when passing 通り過ぎるときに~に軽く触る➔ かする; ~をかする、~をかすって通る ‖ *Her hand brushed his cheek.* 彼女の手が彼のほおをかすった. *Leaves brushed against the car as we drove along the narrow road.* 私たちが狭い道を車で行った時、葉が車をかすった.

句動詞 brush sb/sth aside ▶定義 1 to refuse to pay attention to sb/sth ~に注意を払うことを拒む➔ ~を無視する ‖ *She brushed aside the protests and continued with the meeting.* 彼女は抗議を無視して会議を続けた. ▶定義 2 to push past sb/sth ~を押しのけて進む➔ ~を払いのける ‖ *He hurried through the crowd, brushing aside the reporters who tried to stop him.* 彼を立ち止まらせようとする記者たちを払いのけながら、彼は人込みの中を急いだ.

brush sth off (sth)/away ▶定義 to remove sth with a brush or with the hand, as if using a brush ブラシで、またはブラシを使っているかのように手で~を取り去る➔ ~を払いのける・払い落とす ‖ *I brushed the dust off my jacket.* 私はジャケットのほこりを払い落とした.

brush sth up/brush up on sth ▶定義 to study or practise sth in order to get back knowledge or skill that you had before and have lost 以前持っていたが失ってしまった知識や技術を取り戻すために~を勉強する、または練習する➔ ~をやり直す、勉強し直す ‖ *She took a course to brush up her Spanish.* 彼女はスペイン語の勉強をし直すために講座を取った.

**brush-off** 名
成句 give sb the brush-off ▶定義 to refuse to be friendly to sb ~に好意的であることを拒む➔ ~にすげなく断る ‖ *I'd ask her to go out with me but I'm scared she'd give me the brush-off.* 彼女にデートをしてくれるよう頼みたいが、彼女がすげなく断るのではと怖い.

**brusque** /bruːsk, brʊsk; brʌsk/ 形 ▶定義 using very few words and sounding rude 言葉をあまり使わず、無礼に聞こえる➔ ぶっきらぼうな、愛想ない ‖ *He gave a brusque 'No comment!' and walked off.* 彼はぶっきらぼうに「何も言う事はない」と言って立ち去った. — brusquely 副➔ ぶっきらぼうに

**Brussels sprout** /ˌbrʌs(ə)lz ˈspraʊt/ (または **sprout**) 名 [C, 通常は複数] ▶定義 a small round green vegetable that looks like another vegetable (a cabbage), but is much smaller ほかの野菜(キャベツ)に似ているがはるかに小さい、小さく丸い緑色の野菜➔芽キャベツ ☛ C3ページのさし絵

**brutal** /ˈbruːtl/ 形 ▶定義 very cruel and/or violent とても残酷な、そして・または暴力的な➔ 残忍な、野蛮な ‖ *a brutal murder* 残忍な殺人 *a brutal dictatorship* 残忍な独裁政権 — brutally 副➔ 残酷に、野獣のように ‖ *He was brutally honest and told her that he didn't love her any more.* 彼は残酷にも率直にもう愛していないと彼女に言った.

**brutality** /bruːˈtæləti/ 名 C U (複 **brutalities**) ▶定義 very cruel and violent behaviour とても残酷で暴力的な振る舞い➔ 残忍性、野蛮さ、残忍・野蛮な行為

**brute**[1] /bruːt/ 名 C ▶定義 1 a cruel, violent man 残酷で暴力的な男➔ けだもの、野獣、人でなし ▶定義 2 a large strong animal 大きくて強い動物➔ 野獣、けだもの ‖ *That dog of theirs is an absolute brute.* 彼らの犬は全くの野獣だ.

**brute**[2] /bruːt/ 形 ▶定義 using strength to do sth rather than thinking about it ~を行うために、考えるよりも体力を使う➔ 理性のない、粗暴な ‖ *I think you'll have to use brute force to get this window open.* この窓を開けるには腕力を使わなければならないと思うよ.

**BSc** /ˌbiː es ˈsiː/ 略 Bachelor of Science ▶定義 the degree that you receive when you complete a university or college course in a science subject 総合大学または単科大学で、科学の課程を修了したときに受ける学位➔ 理学士号 ☛参 **BA, MSc**

**BSE** /ˌbiː es ˈiː/ (または 略式 **mad cow disease**)

名 ❶ ▶定義 bovine spongiform encephalopathy; a disease of cows which affects their brains and usually kills them 牛伝染性海綿状脳症；脳を侵し通常死に至らしめる牛の病気➡狂牛病 ☞参 CJD

**BST** /ˌbiː es ˈtiː/ British Summer Time ▶定義 the system used in Britain between March and October, when clocks are put one hour earlier than Greenwich Mean Time 3月から10月の間，時計をグリニッジ標準時よりも1時間早める英国の制度➡英国夏時間

**BTEC** /ˈbiːtek/ 名 ❸ ▶定義 an exam for young people who have left secondary school and are training in commercial or technical subjects 中学校を卒業して，商業科目または技術科目の訓練を受けている子供たちのための試験➡BTEC ‖ *She's doing a BTEC in design.* 彼女はデザインのBTECを受けている．

**bubbles**

bubble　sparkling
fizzy　still

*****bubble**[1] /ˈbʌb(ə)l/ 名 ❸ ▶定義 a ball of air or gas, in liquid or floating in the air 液体中の，または空中を漂う，空気または気体の球➡泡，あぶく，気泡 ‖ *We knew where there were fish because of the bubbles on the surface.* 水面の泡で，私たちは魚がどこにいるかを知った．

**bubble**[2] /ˈbʌb(ə)l/ 動 ⓘ ▶定義 **1** to produce bubbles or to rise with bubbles 泡を作る，または泡と共に上る➡泡立つ，沸騰する，ぶくぶくわく ‖ *Cook the pizza until the cheese starts to bubble.* チーズが泡立つまでピザに火を通しなさい． *The clear water bubbled up out of the ground.* 澄んだ水が地面からぶくぶくとわいた．▶定義 **2 bubble (over) (with sth)** to be full of happy feelings 幸せな感情で一杯になる➡満ちあふれる

**bubble bath** 名 ❶ ▶定義 a liquid that you can add to the water in a bath to produce a mass of white bubbles 大量の白い泡を作り出すために，浴槽の湯に加える液体➡(芳香と泡を立てる)入浴剤

**bubblegum** /ˈbʌb(ə)lɡʌm/ 名 ❶ ▶定義 a sticky sweet that you eat but do not swallow and that can be blown into bubbles out of the mouth 食べるが飲み込まないで，口から吹いて風船を作ることができる，ねばねばした甘い食べ物➡風船ガム ☞参 **chewing gum**

**bubbly** /ˈbʌb(ə)li/ 形 ▶定義 **1** full of bubbles 泡が一杯の➡泡の多い，泡立つ ▶定義 **2** (used about a person) happy and full of energy (人について)幸せで活力に満ちた➡はつらつとした，元気な，陽気な

**buck**[1] /bʌk/ 名 ❸ ▶定義 **1** 困 略式 a US dollar ➡米ドル ‖ *Could you lend me a few bucks?* 数ドル貸してもらえませんか．▶定義 **2** (複 **buck** または **bucks**) the male of certain types of animal (rabbits and deer) ある種の動物(ウサギとシカ)の雄➡雄 ☞参 **deer**の注

成句 **pass the buck** ⇒ **PASS**[1]

**buck**[2] /bʌk/ 動 ⓘ ▶定義 (used about a horse) to jump into the air or to kick the back legs in the air (馬について)空中に跳ぶ，または後ろ足を空中にけり上げる➡背を曲げて跳ねる，跳ね上がる

句動詞 **buck (sb/sth) up** ▶定義 略式 to feel or to make sb feel better or happier 気分が良くなるまたは幸せに感じる，あるいは～にそのように感じさせる➡元気を出す，励ます ‖ *Drink this - it'll buck you up.* これを飲みなさい － 元気が出るよ． *Unless you buck your ideas up (=become more sensible and serious), you'll never pass the exam.* 考えを改めないと(＝もっと分別をもち真剣にならないと)，試験には絶対受からないよ．

*****bucket** /ˈbʌkɪt/ 名 ❸ ▶定義 **1** a round, open container, usually made of metal or plastic, with a handle, that is used for carrying sth ～を運ぶために使う，通常金属またはプラスチック製の，取っ手の付いた円くてふたのない容器➡バケツ，手おけ ▶定義 **2** (または **bucketful**) the amount that a bucket contains バケツに入る量➡バケツ・手おけ1杯の量 ‖ *How many buckets of*

# 202 buckle¹

bucket, polish, duster, mop, rubber gloves, cloth, sponge

water do you think we'll need? バケツ何杯分の水が私たちには必要だと思いますか.
**成句 a drop in the bucket** ⇒ **DROP²**

**buckle¹** /bʌ́k(ə)l/ 名 C ▶定義 a piece of metal or plastic at the end of a belt or strap that is used for fastening it ベルトや肩ひもの端にあり, それらを止めるのに使われる金属またはプラスチック製の物→締め金, バックル, 飾り留め具 ☞ **bag, shoe**のさし絵

**buckle²** /bʌ́k(ə)l/ 動 自 他 ▶定義 1 to fasten or be fastened with a buckle バックルで留める, または留められる→(バックル・締め金で)締まる; 〜を(バックル・締め金で)締める ▶定義 2 to bend because of heat, force, weakness, etc 熱, 力, 弱さなどのために曲がる→曲がる, たわむ; 〜を曲げる, たわめる ‖ Some railway lines buckled in the heat. いくつかの鉄道線路が熱で曲がった.

**bud** /bʌd/ 名 C ▶定義 a small lump on a tree or plant that opens and develops into a flower or leaf 開いて花や葉に育つ, 木や植物の小さな硬い塊→芽, つぼみ ‖ rosebuds バラのつぼみ ☞ C2ページのさし絵
**成句 nip sth in the bud** ⇒ **NIP**

**Buddhism** /búːdɪz(ə)m, búd-/ 名 U ▶定義 an Asian religion that was started in India by Buddha インドで仏陀によって始められたアジアの宗教→仏教

**Buddhist** /búːdɪst, búd-/ 名 C ▶定義 a person whose religion is Buddhism 仏教を信仰する人→仏教徒— Buddhist 形 ▶定義 仏教の, 仏教徒の ‖ a Buddhist temple 仏教の寺

**budding** /bʌ́dɪŋ/ 形 ▶定義 wanting or starting to develop and be successful 発展し成功したがっている, またはし始めている→世に知られ始めた, 新進の ‖ Have you got any tips for budding young photographers? 新進の若い写真家たちについて, 何か情報がありますか.

**buddy** /bʌ́di/ 名 C (複 **buddies**) 略式 ▶定義 a friend, especially a male friend of a man 友達, 特に男性にとっての男性の友達→仲間, 相棒, 親友

**budge** /bʌdʒ/ 動 自 他 ▶定義 1 to move or make sth move a little 少し動く, または〜を少し動かす→(ちょっと)動く, 身動きする; 〜を(ちょっと)動かす ‖ I tried as hard as I could to loosen the screw but it simply wouldn't budge. ねじを緩めようと力一杯頑張ったが, 全く動かなかった. We just couldn't budge the car when it got stuck in the mud. 車が泥にはまり, 私たちは少しも動かすことができなかった. ▶定義 2 to change or make sb change a firm opinion 堅固な意見を変える, 〜に変えさせる→意見・態度を変える; 〜の意見・態度を変えさせる ‖ Neither side in the dispute is prepared to budge. 口論している両者とも意見を変えるつもりがない.

**budgerigar** /bʌ́dʒ(ə)rɪɡɑːr/ (または 略式 **budgie**) 名 C ▶定義 a small, brightly-coloured bird that people often keep as a pet in a cage しばしばペットとしてかごの中で飼う, 小さな鮮やかな色の鳥→セキセイインコ

*****budget¹** /bʌ́dʒət/ 名 C U ▶定義 1 a plan of how to spend an amount of money over a particular period of time; the amount of money that is mentioned 特定の期間内に, ある金額をどのように使うかについての計画; 言及されたその金額→予算, 予算案 ‖ What's your monthly budget for food? 毎月の食費の予算はいくらですか. a country's defence budget 国の防衛予算 The work was finished on time and **within budget**. その仕事は時間通りに予算内で完了した. The builders are already 20%**over budget**. 建設業者は既に予算を2割超過している. ▶定義 2 (または **Budget**) a statement by a government saying how much money it plans to spend on particular things in the next year and how it plans to collect money 翌年にいくら特定のものにお金を使うかの予定で, どのようにお金を集め

る予定であるかを政府が示す文書➜**予算案** ‖ *Do you think taxes will go up in this year's budget?* 今年の予算案では税金が上がると思いますか.

**budget**[2] /bʌ́dʒət/ [動][自][他] ▶定義 budget (sth) (for sth) to plan carefully how much money to spend on sth ～にお金をいくら使うかを慎重に計画する➜**予算を立てる; ～を割り当てる, 予算に組む** ‖ *The government has budgeted £10 billion for education.* 政府は, 教育に100億ポンドの予算を組んだ.

**budget**[3] /bʌ́dʒət/ [形][略式] ▶定義 (used in advertisements) very cheap (広告で用いて) とても安い➜**安い, 徳用な** ‖ *budget holidays* お得な休暇

**budgie** /bʌ́dʒi/ [略式] =**BUDGERIGAR**

**buff** /bʌf/ [名] [C][略式] ▶定義 a person who knows a lot about a particular subject and is very interested in it 特定の主題についてよく知っており, その事にとても興味を持っている人➜**～狂, ～ファン, ～通** ‖ *a film/computer buff* 映画・コンピューターおたく

**buffalo** /bʌ́fəlòʊ/ [名] [C] ([複] **buffalo** または **buffaloes**) ▶定義 a large wild animal that looks like a cow with long curved horns 長い曲がった角を持つ, 牛に似た大きな野性の動物➜**バッファロー, バイソン, 水牛** ‖ *a herd of buffalo* バッファローの群れ

**buffer** /bʌ́fər/ [名] [C] ▶定義1 a thing or person that reduces the unpleasant effects of sth or prevents violent contact between two things, people, etc ～の不快な影響を減らす, または2つの物, 2人などの間の激しい接触を防ぐ物や人➜**和らげてくれる物・人** ‖ *UN forces are acting as a buffer between the two sides in the war.* 国連軍は, 戦争中の双方の間の緩衝材として働いている. ▶定義2 a flat round piece of metal with a spring behind it that is on the front or back of a train or at the end of a railway track. Buffers reduce the shock when sth hits them. 電車の前や後ろまたは鉄道線路の最後にある, 裏にばねの付いた平たくて円い金属. ～がこれにぶつかるとき, その衝撃を減じる➜**緩衝器, 緩衝装置**

**buffet**[1] /bəféɪ, buː-; búfèɪ/ [名] [C] ▶定義1 a meal (usually at a party or a special occasion) at which food is placed on a long table and people serve themselves (通常パーティーまたは特別な場で) 食べ物が長いテーブルの上に置いてあり, 人々が自分で取る食事➜**立食料理** ‖ *Lunch was a cold buffet* 昼食は冷たい立食料理だった. *a buffet lunch* 立食料理の昼食 ▶定義2 part of a train where passengers can buy food and drinks; a cafe at a station 乗客が飲食物を買える列車の部分; 駅の軽食堂➜**ビュッフェ**

**buffet**[2] /bʌ́fət/ [動][他] ▶定義 to knock or push sth in a rough way from side to side ～を左右に乱暴にたたく, または押す➜**～を打つ, 打ちのめす, もてあそぶ** ‖ *The boat was buffeted by the rough sea.* 船は荒波にもまれていた.

**bug**[1] /bʌg/ [名] ▶定義1 [C] 特に [米] any small insect 小さな虫➜**虫, 昆虫** ▶定義2 [C] an illness that is not very serious and that people get from each other あまり深刻でない, 人々の間で感染する病気➜**ばい菌, 病原菌, ウイルス** ‖ *I don't feel very well - I think I've got the bug that's going round.* あまり気分が良くない – 蔓延(まんえん)している菌をもらったようだ. ▶定義3 [C] something wrong in a system or machine, especially a computer 特にコンピューターで, システムまたは機械の悪い所➜**バグ, 誤り, 故障** ‖ *There's a bug in the software.* そのソフトウェアにバグがある. ▶定義4 通常は **the-...bug** [単数扱い] [略式] a sudden interest in sth ～への突然の興味➜**～熱** ‖ *They've been bitten by the golf bug.* 彼らはゴルフ熱に取り付かれている. ▶定義5 [C] a very small device (microphone) that is hidden and secretly records people's conversations 隠されてこっそりと人の会話を録音する, とても小さな装置 (マイクロホン)➜ **盗聴器**

**bug**[2] /bʌg/ [動][他] (**bugging**; **bugged**) ▶定義1 to hide a very small device (microphone) somewhere so that people's conversations can be recorded secretly 人々の会話がこっそり録音されるように, とても小さな装置 (マイクロホン) をどこかに隠しておく➜**～に盗聴器を仕掛ける** ‖ *Be careful what you say. This room is bugged.* 気を付けて話しなさい. この部屋には盗聴器が仕掛けられている. ▶定義2 [略式] to annoy or worry sb ～をいらいらさせる, または心配させる➜**～を悩ます, 苦しめる** ‖ *It bugs him that he's not as successful as his brother.* 彼は自分が弟ほど成功していないことで悩んでいる.

**buggy** /bʌ́gi/ ([複] **buggies**) [英] =**PUSHCHAIR**

***build**[1] /bɪld/ [動] (過, 過分 **built** /bɪlt/) ▶定義1 [他]

## build²

to make sth by putting pieces, materials, etc together 部品，材料などを組み立てて〜を作る➔〜を建てる，建設する，造る ‖ *They've built a new bridge across the river.* 彼らは川に新しい橋を建設した． *The house is built of stone.* その家は石で造られている． ▶定義2 ❸to use land for building on 建設するために土地を使う➔建てる，(家が)建つ ‖ *There's plenty of land to build on around here.* この辺りには家を建てられる土地がたくさんある． ▶定義3 ⓜto develop or increase sth 〜を開発する，または増やす➔〜を築き上げる，(人格など)を形成する ‖ *The government is trying to build a more modern society.* 政府はより現代的な社会を築き上げようとしている． *This book claims to help people to build their self-confidence.* この本は人々が自信を付けるのに役立つと断言している．

句動詞 build sth in/on; build sth into/onto sth ▶定義 to make sth a part of sth else 〜をほかの…の一部にする➔〜を…の一部とする，〜に組み込む，〜に作り付けにする ‖ *They've made sure that a large number of checks are built into the system.* システムに多くの照合機能が組み込まれていることを，彼らは確認した． *We're planning to build two more rooms onto the back of the house.* 私たちは家の後ろに2部屋を建て増しするつもりだ．

build on sth ▶定義 to use sth as a base from which you can make further progress そこからさらに発展するための基礎として〜を使う➔〜に基礎を置く，〜を基に事を進める ‖ *Now that we're beginning to make a profit, we must build on this success.* 今や私たちは利益を出し始めているのだから，この成功を基に進まなければならない．

build sth on sth ▶定義 to base sth on sth 〜の基礎を…に置く➔〜の基礎を…に置く，〜を…に基づかせる ‖ *a society built on the principle of freedom and democracy* 自由と民主主義に基礎を置いた社会

build up (to sth) ▶定義 to become greater in amount or number; to increase 量または数が多くなる；増える➔増える ‖ *The traffic starts to build up at this time of day.* この時間になると交通量は増え始める．

build sth up ▶定義1 to make sth seem more important or greater than it really is 〜を実際よりも重要に，または大きく見せる➔宣伝して〜にする，〜の評判を高める ‖ *I don't think it's a very serious matter, it's just been built up in the newspapers.* ただ新聞で問題にされてしまっただけのことで，私はそれほど深刻な事だとは思わない． ▶定義2 to increase or develop sth over a period ある期間にわたって，〜を増やすまたは発達させる➔発達させる，増強する，(健康などが)増進する ‖ *You'll need to build up your strength again slowly after the operation.* 手術の後，ゆっくりと体力を回復させる必要があるだろう．

**build²** /bɪld/ 名 ❸ ⓤ ▶定義 the shape and size of sb's body 〜の体の形と大きさ➔体格，体付き ‖ *She has a very athletic build.* 彼女はとてもがっしりとした体をしている．

▶ build と figure を比較すると，build は通常，体力と筋肉に関連した大きさを表し，男性と女性のどちらにも用いられる．figure は通常，体型を，特にそれが魅力的かどうかを表し，通常は女性についてのみ用いられる．

**builder** /bíldər/ 名 ❸ ▶定義 a person whose job is to build houses and other buildings 家とそのほかの建物を建てることを職業とする人➔建設業者

**★building** /bíldɪŋ/ 名 ▶定義1 ❸ a structure, such as a house, shop or school, that has a roof and walls 屋根と壁のある建造物，例えば家，店舗，学校➔建物，建造物，ビル ‖ *There are a lot of very old buildings in this town.* この町にはとても古い建物がたくさんある． ▶定義2 ⓤthe process or business of making buildings 建物を造る過程，またはその仕事➔建てること，建造 ‖ *building materials* 建築資材 *the building industry* 建設業

**building site** 名 ❸ ▶定義 an area of land on which a building is being built 建物が建設されている土地の区画➔建設用地

**building society** 名 ❸ 英 ▶定義 an organization like a bank with which people can save money and which lends money to people who want to buy a house 人々がお金を貯蓄でき，また家を買いたい人々にお金を貸す，銀行のような組織➔住宅金融組合

**build-up** 名 [❸, 通常は単数] ▶定義1 a build-up (of sth) an increase of sth over a period ある期間にわたる〜の増加➔増加，強化，増強 ‖ *The build-up of tension in the area has made war* *seem more likely.* その地域の緊張の高まりにより,戦争がさらに起こりそうに思われる. ▶定義2 **a build-up (to sth)** a period of preparation or excitement before an event 行事の前の準備または興奮した騒ぎの期間➔**宣伝, 売り込み, 前評判** ‖ *The players started to get nervous in the build-up to the big game.* 選手たちは大きな試合への前評判で神経質になり始めていた.

**-built** /bɪlt/ ▶定義 (複合形容詞を作るために用いて) having a body with the shape and size mentioned 言及された形と大きさの体を持つ➔**〜の体格の** ‖ *a tall well-built man* 背の高い立派な体格の男

**built-in** 形 ▶定義 that is a part of sth and cannot be removed 〜の一部で取り除くことができない➔**はめ込みの, 作り付けの** ‖ *built-in cupboards* 作り付けの食器棚

**built-up** 形 ▶定義 covered with buildings 建物で覆われた➔**建て込んだ** ‖ *a built-up area* 建て込んだ地域

**bulb** /bʌlb/ 名 C ▶定義1 (または **light bulb**) the glass part of an electric lamp that gives out light 電灯の, 光を出すガラスの部分➔**電球** ‖ *The bulb's gone (=it no longer works) in this lamp.* この電灯の電球が切れた. (= もはや光らない). ☛ **light**のさし絵 ▶定義2 the round root of certain plants 特定の植物の丸い根➔**球根, 球茎, 鱗(りん)茎** ‖ *a tulip bulb* チューリップの球根 ☛ C2ページのさし絵

**bulbous** /bʌ́lbəs/ 形 ▶定義 fat, round and ugly 太く丸くて醜い➔**球根の形をした, 球根状の** ‖ *a bulbous red nose* 赤いだんご鼻

**bulge**[1] /bʌldʒ/ 名 C ▶定義 a round lump that sticks out on sth 〜から突き出した丸い塊➔**膨らみ, 出っ張り** ☛ **bump**のさし絵

**bulge**[2] /bʌldʒ/ 動 自 ▶定義1 to stick out in a lump from sth that is usually flat 通常は平らな物からこぶ状に突き出す➔**出っ張る** ‖ *My stomach is starting to bulge. I must get more exercise.* 腹が出っ張り始めている. もっと運動しなければ. ▶定義2 **bulge (with sth)** to be full of sth 〜で一杯になる➔**膨れる** ‖ *His bags were bulging with presents for the children.* 彼のかばんは子供たちへの贈り物で膨れていた.

**bulging** /bʌ́ldʒɪŋ/ 形 ▶定義1 sticking out 突き出した➔**出っ張った** ‖ *He had a thin face and rather bulging eyes.* 彼は顔が細く, 目がやや出っ張っていた. ▶定義2 very full 非常に一杯の➔**膨らんだ** ‖ *She came home with bulging carrier bags.* 彼女は膨らんだ買い物袋を持って帰宅した.

**bulk** /bʌlk/ 名 ▶定義1 **the bulk (of sth)** [単数扱い] the main part of sth; most of sth 〜の主要な部分; 〜のほとんど➔**大部分, 大半** ‖ *The bulk of the work has been done, so we should finish this week.* 仕事の大半は終わっているので, おそらく今週中には完了するだろう. ▶定義2 U the size, quantity or weight of sth large 大きな物の寸法, 量, 重さ➔**容積, かさ, 巨大さ, 巨体** ‖ *The cupboard isn't especially heavy - it's its bulk that makes it hard to move.* その食器棚は特に重くはない — 動かすのを難しくしているのはその容積だ. *He slowly lifted his vast bulk out of the chair.* 彼は大きな体をゆっくりといすから持ち上げた.

成句 **in bulk** ▶定義 in large quantities 多い量で➔**大量に, 大口で** ‖ *If you buy in bulk, it's 10% cheaper.* 大口で買えば10パーセント安い.

**bulky** /bʌ́lki/ 形 ▶定義 large and heavy and therefore difficult to move or carry 大きくて重く, そのために動かすには運ぶことが難しい➔**かさ張った, 大きい, 扱いにくい** ‖ *a bulky parcel* かさ張る小包

**bull** /bʊl/ 名 C ▶定義1 an adult male of the cow family ウシ科の成長した雄➔**雄牛** ☛ 参 **cow**の注とさし絵 ▶定義2 the male of certain other animals (**the whale** and **the elephant**) ほかのいくつかの動物 (鯨と象) の雄➔**雄**

**bulldog** /bʊ́ldɒ(ː)g, -dɑ̀g/ 名 C ▶定義 a strong dog with short legs, a large head and a short, thick neck 短い足, 大きな頭, 短く太い首を持つ強い犬➔**ブルドッグ**

**bulldoze** /bʊ́ldòʊz/ 動 他 ▶定義 to make ground flat or knock down a building with a bulldozer ブルドーザーで地面を平らにする, または建物を倒す➔**(土地を)ブルドーザーでならす, (建物などを)ブルドーザーで除去してならす** ‖ *The old buildings were bulldozed and new ones were built.* その古い建物はブルドーザーで除去してならされ, 新しいものが建てられた.

**bulldozer** /bʊ́ldòʊzər/ 名 C ▶定義 a large, powerful vehicle with a broad piece of metal at the front, used for clearing ground or knocking down buildings 地面をきれいにする，または建物を倒すために使われる，前方に幅の広い金属が付いた，大きくて力強い乗り物➔ブルドーザー

\***bullet** /búlət/ 名 C ▶定義 a small metal object that is fired from a gun 銃から発射される，小さい金属製の物 弾丸，小銃弾 ‖ *The bullet hit her in the arm.* 弾丸が彼女の腕に当たった． *a bullet wound* 弾丸による傷

**bulletin** /búlətn/ 名 C ▶定義1 a short news report on TV or radio; an official statement about a situation テレビやラジオの短いニュース報道；状況についての公式な声明➔ニュース速報；(官庁の)公報，告示 ‖ *The next **news bulletin** on this channel is at nine o'clock.* このチャンネルの次のニュース速報は９時です． ▶定義2 a short newspaper that a club or an organization produces クラブや組織が作る小さな新聞➔(学会などの)会報，紀要，(会社の)社報 ‖ *As a member of the fan club, she receives a monthly bulletin.* ファンクラブの一員として，彼女は毎月会報を受け取る．

**bulletin board** 米=NOTICEBOARD

**bulletproof** /búlətprùːf/ 形 ▶定義 made of a strong material that stops bullets from passing through it 弾丸が通り抜けるのを止める強い材料でできた➔防弾の

**bullfight** /búlfàɪt/ 名 C ▶定義 a traditional public entertainment, especially in Spain, Portugal and Latin America, in which an animal (a bull) is fought and often killed 特にスペイン，ポルトガル，南米で行われる，動物(雄牛)と戦ってしばしばそれを殺す，伝統的な一般大衆の娯楽➔闘牛 — **bullfighter** 名 C ➔闘牛士 — **bullfighting** 名 U ➔闘牛

**bullion** /búljən/ 名 U ▶定義 bars of gold or silver 金または銀の棒➔金・銀の延べ棒 ‖ *The dollar price of gold bullion has risen by more than 10%.* 金の延べ棒のドル建て価格は１０パーセント以上上がった．

**bull's-eye** /búlzàɪ/ 名 C ▶定義 the centre of a round object (target) that you shoot or throw things at in certain sports, or a shot that hits this 特定のスポーツで，撃つまたは物を投げ付ける円い物(的)の中心，またはそれに命中する一打ち➔(的の)金的, 金的を射た射撃・矢

**bully**¹ /búli/ 名 C (複 **bullies**) ▶定義 a person who uses his/her strength or power to hurt or frighten people who are weaker 自分の強さまたは力で，自分より弱い人々を傷付けたり脅かしたりする人➔弱い者いじめをする人，がき大将，いじめっ子

**bully**² /búli/ 動 他 (現分 **bullying**; 三単現 **bullies**; 過, 過分 **bullied**) ▶定義 bully sb (into doing sth) to use your strength or power to hurt or frighten sb who is weaker or to make them do sth 自分の強さまたは力で，自分より弱い者を傷付けたり脅したりする，あるいは何かをさせる➔~をいじめる，脅す，~に威張り散らす ‖ *Don't try to bully me into making a decision.* 私を脅して決めさせようとするな．— **bullying** 名 U ➔威張り散らすこと，いじめ ‖ *Bullying is a serious problem in many schools.* いじめは多くの学校で深刻な問題だ．

**bum** /bʌm/ 名 C 略式 ▶定義1 英the part of your body on which you sit; bottom 座ったときに下になる体の部分; 臀部(でんぶ)➔おしり ▶定義2 特に 米an insulting word for a person who lives on the street 路上で暮らす人への侮べつ的な言葉➔浮浪者 ▶定義3 特に 米a lazy or useless person 怠惰なまたは役に立たない人➔怠け者，無能な人，能なし

**bumbag** /bʌ́mbæg/ (米**fanny pack**) 名 C 略式 ▶定義 a small bag worn around the waist to keep money, etc in お金などを入れておくために，腰の回りに着ける小さなバッグ➔ウエストポーチ ☞ bag のさし絵

**bump**¹ /bʌmp/ 動 ▶定義1 自 bump against/into sb/sth to hit sb/sth by accident when you are moving 動いているとき偶然に~にぶつかる➔どんと突き当たる，衝突する ‖ *She bumped into a lamp post because she wasn't looking where she was going.* 彼女は前方を見ていなかったので，街灯の柱にぶつかった． ▶定義2 他 bump sth (against/on sth) to hit sth against or on sth by accident 偶然に~を…にぶつける➔~をどんと突き当てる，ぶつける ‖ *I bumped my knee on the edge of the table.* 私はひざをテーブルの端にぶつけた． ▶定義3 自 to move along over a rough surface でこぼこした表面の上を動く➔がたがたと進む ‖ *The car bumped along the track to the farm.* 車は農場への小道をがたがたと進んだ．

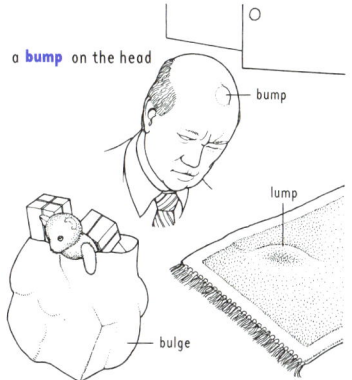

a **bump** on the head
a bag **bulging** with presents　a **lump** under the rug

**句動詞** bump into sb ▶定義 to meet sb by chance 偶然〜に会う→〜にひょっこり会う ‖ *I bumped into an old friend on the bus today.* 今日バスの中で旧友にひょっこり会った.

bump sb off (俗語) ▶定義 to murder sb 〜を殺す→〜を殺す, ばらす

bump sth up 略式 ▶定義 to increase or make sth go up 〜を増やす, または上げる→(価格・給料など)を上げる ‖ *All this publicity will bump up sales of our new product.* このすべての宣伝によって当社の新製品の販売は増えるだろう.

**bump**² /bʌmp/ 图 C ▶定義 1 the action or sound of sth hitting a hard surface 〜が硬い面にぶつかる行為または音→ばたん・どすんと当たること・音, 衝撃 ‖ *She fell and hit the ground with a bump.* 彼女はどすんと地面に倒れた. ▶定義 2 a lump on the body, often caused by a hit しばしばぶつかったためにできる, 体のこぶ→こぶ ▶定義 3 a part of a surface that is higher than the rest of it 表面のほかの部分より高くなっている部分→凹凸 ‖ *There are a lot of bumps in the road, so drive carefully.* その道には凹凸がたくさんあるので, 注意して運転しなさい.

**bumper**¹ /bʌ́mpər/ 图 C ▶定義 the bar fixed to the front and back of a motor vehicle to protect it if it hits sth 〜にぶつかった場合に車を守るために, 車の前後に取り付けられた横棒→バンパー

**bumper**² /bʌ́mpər/ 形 ▶定義 larger than usual 通常よりも大きい→巨大な, 大量の ‖ *The unusually fine weather has produced a bumper har-vest this year.* 今年は格別に天候が良かったので, 大量の収穫があった.

**bumpy** /bʌ́mpi/ 形 ▶定義 not flat or smooth 平らでない, または滑らかでない→でこぼこな, がたがたする ‖ *a bumpy road* でこぼこ道 *Because of the stormy weather, it was a very bumpy flight.* あらしのために, 飛行機がとてもがたがた揺れた. ⇨**smooth**

**bun** /bʌn/ 图 C ▶定義 1 a small round sweet cake 小さく丸くて甘い洋菓子→甘い丸パン ‖ *a currant bun* ブドウパン ☛ **cake**のさし絵 ▶定義 2 a small soft bread roll 小さく柔らかい巻いたパン→ロールパン, 丸いパン ‖ *a hamburger bun* ハンバーガーの丸パン ▶定義 3 hair fastened tightly into a round shape at the back of the head 頭の後ろに丸くきちんとまとめられた髪→束髪(そくはつ) ‖ *She wears her hair in a bun.* 彼女は束髪にしている. ☛ **hair**のさし絵

**bunch**¹ /bʌntʃ/ 图 ▶定義 1 C a number of things, usually of the same type, fastened or growing together 通常同じ種類の, 一緒に束ねられたり生えているたくさんの物→房, 束 ‖ *He bought her a bunch of flowers for her birthday.* 彼は彼女の誕生日の祝いに花束を買った. *a bunch of bananas/grapes* バナナ・ブドウの1房 *a bunch of keys* かぎの束 ▶定義 2 **bunches** [複数扱い] long hair that is tied on each side of the head 頭の左右で結ばれた長い髪→束ねた髪 ☛ **hair**のさし絵 ▶定義 3 [C, 単数または複数形の動詞と共に] 略式 a group of people 人々の集団→一団, 一味, 仲間 ‖ *My colleagues are the best bunch of people I've ever worked with.* 私の同僚たちは, 私がこれまで一緒に働いた中で最高の仲間だ.

**bunch**² /bʌntʃ/ 動自他 ▶定義 bunch (sth/sb) (up/together) to stay together in a group; to form sth into a group or bunch 集団で一緒にいる; 〜で集団または束を作る→束になる, 一団になる; 〜を束にする, 一団に集める ‖ *The runners bunched up as they came round the final bend.* 最終コーナーに差し掛かった時, 走者たちは一団になった. *He kept his papers bunched together in his hand.* 彼は, 自分のレポートを束にして, 手にしていた.

**bundle**¹ /bʌ́ndl/ 图 C ▶定義 a number of things tied or folded together 一緒に縛られたり包まれ

たくさんの物→束,巻いた物,包み ‖ *a bundle of letters with an elastic band round them* 輪ゴムでまとめられた手紙の束

**bundle**² /bándl/ 動他 ▶定義1 bundle sth (up) to make or tie a number of things together たくさんの物を一緒にする,または縛る→〜を束ねる,くくる,包みにする ‖ *I bundled up the old newspapers and threw them away.* 私は古新聞を束ねて捨てた. ▶定義2 to put or push sb or sth quickly and in a rough way in a particular direction 〜または…を素早く,特定の方向に乱暴に置くまたは押す→〜をせき立てる,追い立てる,〜に押し込む ‖ *He was arrested and bundled into a police car.* 彼は逮捕され,パトカーに押し込まれた.

**bung**¹ /bʌŋ/ 名 C ▶定義 a round piece of wood or rubber that is used for closing the hole in some types of container (a barrel or a jar) ある種の容器(たるまたはびん)の穴を閉じるために使われる,丸い木またはゴム→栓,たる口

**bung**² /bʌŋ/ 動他 英 略式 ▶定義 to put or throw sth somewhere in a rough or careless way 乱暴にまたは不注意に〜をどこかへ置くまたは投げる→〜をほうり投げる,乱暴に置く・押す ‖ *We bunged the suitcases into the car and drove away.* 私たちはスーツケースを車に投げ込むと,出発した.

**bungalow** /báŋɡəlòu/ 名 C ▶定義 a house that is all on one level, without stairs 階段のない,平屋の家→バンガロー

**bunged up** 形 略式 ▶定義 blocked, so that nothing can get through 閉鎖されて何も通り抜けられない→詰まった ‖ *I feel terrible - I've got a cold and my nose is all bunged up.* 気分がひどく悪い—風邪を引いて鼻が完全に詰まっている.

**bungee jumping** /bʌ́ndʒi dʒʌ̀mpiŋ/ 名 U ▶定義 a sport in which you jump from a high place, for example a bridge, with a thick elastic rope tied round your feet 太いゴムの綱を足に巻いて橋などの高い場所から飛び降りるスポーツ→バンジージャンプ

**bungle** /báŋɡ(ə)l/ 動自他 ▶定義 to do sth badly or fail to do sth 〜を下手にする,または〜をし損なう→しくじる;〜を下手にやる,しくじる ‖ *a bungled robbery* 強盗未遂

**bunk** /bʌŋk/ 名 C ▶定義1 a bed that is fixed to a wall, for example on a ship or train 船や列車などで壁に固定されたベッド→寝台 ▶定義2 (または **bunk bed**) one of a pair of single beds built as a unit with one above the other 一方が他方の上に組まれている,2つで一組になったシングルベッドの1つ→2段ベッド ☛参 bedの注とさし絵

成句 **do a bunk** 英 略式 ▶定義 to run away or escape; to leave without telling anyone 逃げる,または避難する;だれにも告げずに去る→逃げる,ずらかる

**bunker** /báŋkər/ 名 C ▶定義1 a strong underground building that gives protection in a war 戦争中に人を防護する頑丈な地下の建造物→掩蔽壕(えんぺいごう) ▶定義2 a hole filled with sand on a golf course ゴルフコース上にある砂で満たされたくぼみ→バンカー

**bunny** /báni/ 名 C (複 **bunnies**) ▶定義 (used by and to small children) a rabbit (幼児がまたは幼児に用いて)ウサギ→ウサ(ギ)ちゃん

**buoy**¹ /bɔ́i/ 名 C ▶定義 a floating object, fastened to the bottom of the sea or a river, that shows the places where it is dangerous for boats to go 海または川の底に固定され浮いていて,船が進むと危険な場所を示す物→ブイ,浮標

**buoy**² /bɔ́i/ 動他 buoy sb/sth (up) ▶定義1 to keep sb happy and confident 〜を幸せにし,自信を持たせる→〜を元気づける,支持する ‖ *His encouragement buoyed her up during that difficult period.* 彼の励ましは,難しい時期にあった彼女を元気づけた. ▶定義2 to keep sth at a high level 〜を高い位置に保つ→(価格など)を高くしておく ‖ *Share prices were buoyed by news of a takeover.* 買収のニュースで,株価は高止まりした.

**buoyant** /bɔ́i(ə)nt/ 形 ▶定義1 (used about a material) floating or able to float (物について)浮く,または浮くことができる→浮力のある ▶定義2 happy and confident 幸せで自信のある→楽天的な,快活な,うきうきした ‖ *The team were in buoyant mood after their win.* チームは勝利の後でうきうきしていた. ▶定義3 (used about prices, business activity, etc) staying at a high level or increasing, so that people make more money (価格,事業活動などについて)高い水準にあるまたは増えることで,人々はより多く

稼いでいる→上向きの,上昇傾向にある‖ *Despite the recession, the property market remained buoyant.* 不景気にもかかわらず,不動産市場はまだ上昇傾向にあった. ― buoyancy /-(ə)nsi/ 名 ❶→浮力,上昇傾向,楽天的な性質‖ *the buoyancy of the German economy* ドイツ経済の上昇傾向

\*burden¹ /bə́ːrdn/ 名 ❻ ▶定義 1 something that is heavy and difficult to carry 重くて運ぶことが難しいもの→重い荷物,重荷 ▶定義 2 a responsibility or difficult task that causes a lot of work or worry たくさんの仕事または心配をもたらす,責任または難しい課題→重荷,負担,義務‖ *Having to make all the decisions is a terrible burden for me.* すべての決断をしなければならないことは,私にとってひどく重荷だ. *I don't want to be a burden to my children when I'm old.* 年を取ったとき,子供たちの重荷になりたくない.

burden² /bə́ːrdn/ 動 ⑯ ▶定義 burden sb/yourself (with sth) to give sb/yourself a responsibility or task that causes a lot of work or worry たくさんの仕事または心配をもたらす,責任または課題を~または自分自身に与える→~に(重い)荷を負わせる

bureau /bjúərou, ╯/ 名 ❻ (複 bureaux または bureaus /-rouz/) ▶定義 1 特に 米 one of certain government departments ある政府機関の部門の1つ→局‖ *the Federal Bureau of Investigation* 連邦捜査局 ▶定義 2 an organization that provides information 情報を提供する組織→事務局,事務所‖ *a tourist information bureau* 観光案内所 ▶定義 3 英 a writing desk with drawers and a lid 引き出しとふたの付いた書き物机→引き出し付きの大きい机

bureaucracy /bjuərάkrəsi/ 名 (複 bureaucracies) ▶定義 1 ⓤ (often used in a critical way) the system of official rules that an organization has for doing sth, that people often think is too complicated (しばしば批判的に用いて) あまりにも複雑だとしばしば考えられている,組織体が~を行うための公式の規則の仕組み→(官僚制度に見られるような)煩雑な手続き,お役所仕事‖ *Getting a visa involves a lot of unnecessary bureaucracy.* ビザの取得には多くの不必要な煩雑な手続きを伴う. ▶定義 2 ❻ⓤ a system of government by a large number of officials who are not elected; a country with this system 選挙

で選ばれていない多数の役人による政治の組織体系; この組織体系を持つ国→官僚主義,官僚制度,官僚政治;官僚国家 ― bureaucratic /bjùərookrǽtɪk/ 形 ▶定義 connected with a bureaucracy, especially when it follows official rules too closely 官僚主義に関連した,特にあまりにも厳密な公式の規則を伴うとき→官僚的な,官僚政治の‖ *You have to go through a complex bureaucratic procedure if you want to get your money back.* もしお金を取り戻したければ,複雑な官僚的手続きを踏まなければならない.

bureaucrat /bjúərəkræt/ 名 ❻ ▶定義 (often used in a critical way) an official in an organization or government department (しばしば批判的に用いて) 組織または政府の部門の役人→官僚,官吏

bureau de change /F byro də ʃɑ̃ːʒ/ 名 ❻ (複 bureaux de change) 英 ▶定義 an office at an airport, in a hotel, etc where you can change the money of one country to the money of another country ある国の通貨をほかの国の通貨に替えられる,空港やホテルなどにある店→両替所・店

burger /bə́ːrɡər/ =HAMBURGER(1)

-burger /bə́ːrɡər/ (複合語で) ▶定義 1 a hamburger with sth else on top ほかの~が上にのったハンバーガー→~バーガー‖ *a cheeseburger* チーズバーガー ▶定義 2 something that is cooked like and looks like a hamburger, but is made of sth else ハンバーガーのように調理されたまたはそのように見えるが,ほかの~でできた物→~バーガー‖ *a veggie burger* ベジバーガー

burglar /bə́ːrɡlər/ 名 ❻ ▶定義 a person who enters a building illegally in order to steal 盗みを犯すために不法に建物に入る人→(押し込み)強盗‖ *The burglars broke in by smashing a window.* 強盗は窓を割って押し入った. ☛参 thief の注 ― burgle /bə́ːrɡl/ 動 ⑯→押し入って盗む‖ *Our flat was burgled while we were out.* 私たちが出掛けている間にアパートに泥棒が入った.

burglar alarm 名 ❻ ▶定義 a piece of equipment, usually fixed on a wall, that makes a loud noise if a thief enters a building 通常壁に取り付けられた,泥棒が建物に入ると大きな音を出す装置→盗難報知機

burglary /bə́ːrɡləri/ 名 ❻ⓤ (複 burglaries)

▶定義 the crime of entering a building illegally in order to steal 盗みを犯すために不法に建物に入る犯罪 →**押し込み強盗** ‖ *There was a burglary next door last week.* 先週隣の家に押し込み強盗があった. *He is in prison for burglary.* 彼は不法目的侵入罪で刑務所に入っている.

**burial** /bérial/ 名 C U ▶定義 the ceremony when a dead body is put in the ground (buried) 遺体が地中に置かれる(埋められる)儀式 →**埋葬** ‖ *The burial took place on Friday.* 埋葬は金曜日に行われた. ☞参 **funeral** の注

**burly** /bə́:rli/ 形 ▶定義 (used about a person or his/her body) strong and heavy (人または人体について)強く重い →**たくましい, 頑丈な, 屈強な**

*****burn**¹ /bə:rn/ 動 (過, 過分 **burnt** /bə:rnt/ または **burned** /bə:rnd/) ▶定義 1 他 to destroy, damage or injure sb/sth with fire or heat ～を火または熱で壊す, 損なう, または痛める →**～を燃やす, ～を焼き焦がす, ～にやけどさせる** ‖ *We took all the rubbish outside and burned it.* 私たちはごみをすべて外に出して燃やした. *It was a terrible fire and the whole building was burnt to the ground (=completely destroyed).* それはひどい火事で, 建物は全焼した(=完全に崩壊した). *If you get too close to the fire you'll burn yourself.* 火に近付きすぎると, やけどするよ. *The people inside the building couldn't get out and they were all burnt to death.* 建物の中にいた人々は外に出られず皆焼死した. ▶定義 2 自 to be destroyed, damaged or injured by fire or heat 火または熱で壊れる, 損なわれる, または痛められる →**燃える, 焼ける, 焦げる, 日に焼ける** ‖ *If you leave the cake in the oven for much longer, it will burn.* ケーキをオーブンにずっと入れたままにしておくと, 焦げてしまうよ. *I can't spend too much time in the sun because I burn easily.* 私は日焼けしやすいので, 日なたで長時間過ごせない. *They were trapped by the flames and they burned to death.* 彼らは炎に遮られて焼死した. ▶定義 3 他 to produce a hole or mark in or on sth by burning 燃やして～に穴または跡を作る →**～を焦がして穴を開ける, 焦がして～にする** ‖ *He dropped his cigarette and it burned a hole in the carpet.* 彼はたばこを落とし, じゅうたんを焦がして穴を開けた. ▶定義 4 自 to be on fire 火のついた →**燃える** ‖ *Firemen raced to the burning building.* 消防士たちは燃えている建物へ急いだ. ▶定義 5 他 to use sth as fuel ～を燃料として使う →**～を燃やす, 燃料とする** ‖ *an oil-burning lamp* 石油ランプ ▶定義 6 自 to produce light 光を作る →**輝く, 光を放つ** ‖ *I don't think he went to bed at all - I could see his light burning all night.* 彼は全く寝ていないと思う―一晩中彼の部屋の明かりがついているのが見えた.

▶定義 7 自 to feel very hot and painful とても熱くて痛みを感じる →**燃えるように感じる, 火照る** ‖ *You have a temperature, your forehead's burning.* あなたは熱がある, 額が火照っている.

▶定義 8 自 **burn (with sth)** to be filled with a very strong feeling とても強い感情に満たされている →**かっとなる, 興奮する, (～しようと)熱中する** ‖ *She was burning with indignation.* 彼女は憤りでかっとなっていた.

成句 sb's ears are burning ⇒ **EAR**

句動詞 **burn down** ▶定義 (used about a building) to be completely destroyed by fire (建物について)火事で完全に壊された →**全焼する** ‖ *The fire could not be brought under control and the school burned down.* 火の勢いは収まらず, 学校は全焼した.

**burn sth down** ▶定義 to completely destroy a building by fire 建物を火事で完全に壊す →**～を全焼させる, 焼き尽くす** ‖ *The house was burnt down in a fire some years ago.* その家は数年前に火事で全焼した.

**burn (sth) off** ▶定義 to remove sth or to be removed by burning 燃やして～を取り除くまたは取り除かれる →**～を焼き払う, 焼き尽くす**

**burn sth out** (通常は受動態で) ▶定義 to completely destroy sth by burning ～を燃やして完全に壊す →**～を焼き尽くす, ～の中をすっかり焼く** ‖ *the burnt-out wreck of a car* 焼き尽くされた車の残骸(ざんがい)

**burn yourself out** (通常は受動態で) ▶定義 to work, etc, until you have no more energy or strength 活力または体力がなくなるまで, 働くなど →**燃え尽きる, 精力を使い果たす, あごを出す** ‖ *I've been studying so hard recently I feel completely burned out.* 最近私はとても熱心に勉強していたので, 完全に精力を使い果たしたようだ.

**burn (sth) up** ▶定義 to destroy or to be destroyed by fire or strong heat 火事または強

い熱で壊す，または壊される➡焼き尽くす，燃え尽きる ‖ *The space capsule burnt up on its re-entry into the earth's atmosphere.* 宇宙カプセルは地球の大気圏への再突入の際に燃え尽きた．

**burn**² /bəːm/ 🔲 ⓒ ▶定義 damage or an injury caused by fire or heat 火や熱による損傷またはけが➡やけど，焼け焦げ，(ひりひりして痛い)日焼け ‖ *He was taken to (the) hospital with minor burns.* 彼は軽いやけどで病院に運ばれた．*There's a cigarette burn on the carpet.* じゅうたんにたばこの焼け焦げがある．

**burning** /bə́ːmɪŋ/ 🔲 (名詞の前だけ) ▶定義 1 (used about a feeling) extremely strong (感情について)極めて強い➡激しい，強烈な ‖ *a burning ambition/desire* 激しい野望・欲望 ▶定義 2 very important or urgent とても重要なまたは緊急な➡重大な，火急の，緊急の ‖ *a burning issue/question* 緊急の問題 ▶定義 3 feeling very hot とても熱く感じている➡焼け付くような，燃えるような ‖ *the burning sun* 焼け付くような太陽

**burp** /bəːp/ 🔲 ▶定義 to make a noise with the mouth when air rises from the stomach and is forced out 空気が胃から外へ押し出されるときに，口から音を出す➡げっぷをする ‖ *He sat back when he had finished his meal and burped loudly.* 彼は食事を終えると深く座って大きなげっぷをした．— burp 🔲 ⓒ ➡げっぷ

**burrow**¹ /bʌ́roʊ, bə́ːr-/ 🔲 ⓒ ▶定義 a hole in the ground made by certain animals, for example rabbits, in which they live ある種の動物，例えばウサギが地面に掘り，そこで暮らす穴➡(野ウサギ，キツネなどの)穴，巣

**burrow**² /bʌ́roʊ, bə́ːr-/ 🔲 ▶定義 to dig a hole in the ground, to make a tunnel or to look for sth トンネルを作るまたは〜を探すために，地面に穴を掘る➡穴を掘る，掘り進む ‖ *These animals burrow for food.* これらの動物は食べ物を探して穴を掘る．(比喩) *She burrowed in her handbag for her keys.* 彼女はハンドバッグの中のかぎを探した．

**bursar** /bə́ːrsər, -sɑːr/ 🔲 ⓒ ▶定義 the person who manages the financial matters of a school, college or university 学校，総合大学，または単科大学の経理を管理する人➡経理部長

**bursary** /bə́ːrs(ə)ri/ 🔲 ⓒ (複 **bursaries**) ▶定義 a sum of money given to a specially chosen student to pay for his/her studies at a college or university 単科大学または総合大学の学費を支払うために，特別に選ばれた学生に与えられるお金➡奨学金

\***burst**¹ /bəːrst/ 🔲 (過, 過分 **burst**) ▶定義 1 🔲 🔲 to break open suddenly and violently, usually because there is too much pressure inside; to cause this to happen 通常，内部に圧力がかかりすぎたために，突然激しく壊れて開く；これを引き起こす➡破裂する，爆発する；〜を破裂させる，破る ‖ *The ball burst when I kicked it.* 私がボールをけったら破裂した．*You'll burst that tyre if you blow it up any more.* それ以上空気を入れたら，そのタイヤを破裂させてしまうよ．(比喩) *If I eat any more I'll burst!* これ以上食べたら，おなかがはち切れる．*If it rains much more, the river will burst its banks.* もしもっとたくさん雨が降れば，川の堤防は決壊するだろう．▶定義 2 🔲 burst into, out of, through, etc to move suddenly in a particular direction, often using force しばしば力ずくによって，特定の方向へ突然動く➡急に現れる，勢いよく出る ‖ *She burst into the manager's office and demanded to speak to him.* 彼女は部長の部屋に飛び込むと，彼に話をしたいと言った．

成句 **be bursting (with sth)** ▶定義 to be very full of sth 〜でとても一杯になる➡(〜で)はち切れそうだ，一杯である ‖ *I packed so many clothes that my suitcase was bursting.* とてもたくさんの服を詰め込んだので，スーツケースははち切れそうだった．*She was bursting with pride when she won the race.* 競技に勝った時，彼女は優越感で一杯だった．

**be bursting to do sth** ▶定義 to want to do sth very much とても〜をしたい➡〜したくてたまらない ‖ *I'm bursting to tell someone the news but it's a secret.* その情報をだれかに話したくてたまらない，でもそれは秘密だ．

**burst (sth) open** ▶定義 to open or make sth open suddenly or violently 突然または激しく開く，または〜を開かせる➡ぱっと開く，ぱっと開ける ‖ *Suddenly the doors burst open and five police officers rushed in.* 突然扉が開き，5人の警官が突入してきた．

句動詞 **burst in on sb/sth** ▶定義 to interrupt sb/sth by arriving suddenly 突然来て〜の邪魔

をする→(話など)に割り込む, ~の邪魔に入る, ~のところへ突然現れる ‖ *The police burst in on the gang as they were counting the money.* ギャングたちが金を数えていたところへ, 突然警官が現れた.

burst into sth ▶定義 to start doing sth suddenly 突然~をし始める→突然~の状態になる ‖ *On hearing the news she burst into tears (=started crying).* その知らせを聞いて, 彼女は突然泣き出した(=泣き始めた). *The lorry hit a wall and burst into flames (=started burning).* そのトラックは壁にぶつかって, 突然炎に包まれた(=燃え始めた).

burst out ▶定義1 to start doing sth suddenly 突然~をし始める→突然~の状態になる ‖ *He looked so ridiculous that I burst out laughing.* 彼がとてもおかしな格好をしていたので, 私は突然笑い出した. ▶定義2 to say sth suddenly and with strong feeling 突然, とても感情的に~を言う→突然~と言い出す ‖ *Finally she burst out, 'I can't stand it any more!'* ついに彼女は「私はもう我慢できない」と言い出した.

**burst**² /bəːrst/ 動 ● ▶定義1 a short period of a particular activity, that often starts suddenly しばしば突然始まる, 特定の活動の短い期間→突発, 激発, (感情などの)ほとばしり ‖ *a burst of energy/enthusiasm/speed* 活力・情熱の発露, 突然の猛スピード *a burst of applause/gunfire* どっと起こる喝采・突然の発砲 *He prefers to work in short bursts.* 彼は短時間に猛烈に働く方が好きだ. ▶定義2 an occasion when sth bursts or explodes; a crack or hole caused by this ~が破裂するまたは爆発する状況; これによってできた割れ目または穴→破裂, 爆発; 破裂箇所 ‖ *a burst in a water pipe* 水道管の破裂箇所

*****bury** /béri/ 動 ⓒ (現分 **burying**; 三単現 **buries**; 過, 過分 **buried**) ▶定義1 to put a dead body in the ground 死体を地中に置く→~を葬る, 埋葬する ‖ *She wants to be buried in the village graveyard.* 彼女はその村の墓地に埋葬されることを望んでいる. ▶定義2 to put sth in a hole in the ground and cover it ~を地面の穴に入れて覆う→~を埋める, 隠す ‖ *Our dog always buries its bones in the garden.* うちの犬はいつも骨を庭に隠す. ▶定義3 (通常は受動態で) to cover or hide sth/sb ~を覆う, または隠す→~を葬り去る, 忘れる, ~に没頭する ‖ *At last I found the photograph, buried at the bottom of a drawer.* ついに私は, 引き出しの底に忘れていた写真を見つけた. (比喩) *Aisha was buried in a book and didn't hear us come in.* アイーシャは本に没頭していて, 私たちが入ってきたのも気付かなかった.

*****bus** /bʌs/ 名 ● (複 **buses**) ▶定義 a big public vehicle which takes passengers along a fixed route and stops regularly to let people get on and off 決まった道に沿って乗客を運び, 定期的に止まって人々を乗り降りさせる公共の大きな乗り物→バス ‖ *Where do you usually get on/off the bus?* 普段はどこでバスに乗りますか・バスを降りますか. *We'll have to hurry up if we want to catch the 9 o'clock bus.* 9時のバスに乗りたいなら急がなければなりません. *We'd better run or we'll miss the bus.* 走った方が良い, そうしないとバスに乗り遅れる.

▶ bus driver (バスの運転手) がお金 (fare (運賃)) を受け取り ticket (切符) をくれるか, あるいは運賃を集める conductor (車掌) がいることもある. bus stop (バス停) ではバスに乗り降りでき, またほとんどのバスの経路の始点は bus station (バスターミナルビル) にある. バスで旅行する場合, travel on the bus または by bus と言うことに注意する: '*How do you get to work?' 'On the bus.*' (「あなたはどうやって職場へ行くの」「バスで」)

*****bush** /bʊʃ/ 名 ▶定義1 ⓒ a plant like a small, thick tree with many low branches たくさんの低い枝が付いた, 低い茂った木のような植物→低木, 潅木(かんぼく), やぶ, 茂み ‖ *a rose bush* バラの茂み *The house was surrounded by thick bushes.* その家は生い茂る低木で囲まれていた. ▶定義2 (しばしば **the bush**) Ⓤ wild land that has not been cleared, especially in Africa and Australia 特にアフリカやオーストラリアで, 切り開かれていない野生の土地→未開拓の土地, 奥地 成句 **beat about the bush** ⇒ **BEAT**¹

**bushy** /bʊ́ʃi/ 形 ▶定義 growing thickly ぎっしりと生えて→もじゃもじゃの, 低木の茂った, やぶの多い ‖ *bushy hair/eyebrows* もじゃもじゃの毛・まゆ

**busier, busiest, busily** ⇒ **BUSY**¹

*****business** /bíznəs/ 名 ▶定義1 Ⓤ buying and selling as a way of earning money; commerce お金を稼ぐ手段として売買すること; 商業→商

売, 取り引き, 実業(界) ‖ *She's planning to **set up in business** as a hairdresser.* 彼女は美容師として独立する計画を立てている. *I'm going to **go into business** with my brother.* 私は兄と一緒に仕事を始めるつもりだ. *They are very easy to **do business with**.* その人たちはとても取り引きしやすい. ▶定義2 ❶the work that you do as your job 自分が職業としてする仕事→**仕事, 職務, 勤め** ‖ *The manager will be away **on business** next week.* 部長は来週出張でいないだろう. *a business trip* 出張 ▶定義3 ❶the number of customers that a person or company has had 人または会社が持っている顧客数→**営業(状態), 景気** ‖ *Business has been good for the time of year.* その時期の景気は良かった. ▶定義4 ❻ a firm, a shop, a factory, etc which produces or sells goods or provides a service 商品を作るまたは売る, あるいはサービスを提供する会社, 店, 工場など→**店, 会社, 企業, 事業所** ‖ *She aims to **start a business** of her own.* 彼女は自分の会社を始めるつもりだ. *Small businesses are finding it hard to survive at the moment.* 現在のところ, 小さな企業にとって生き残りが難しくなっている. ▶定義5 ❶something that concerns a particular person 特定の人に関するもの→**関係する事項, かかわり合い, (〜する) 権利** ‖ *The friends I choose are my business, not yours.* 私の友達を選ぶことは私の権利だ, 君のではない. *Our business is to collect the information, not to comment on it.* 私たちの仕事は情報を集めることで, それについて意見を言うことではない. *'How much did it cost?' 'It's **none of your business**!' (=I don't want to tell you. It's private.)* 「それはいくらしたの」「あなたにはかかわり合いのない事だ」(=あなたに言いたくない. それは個人的な事だ.) ▶定義6 ❶important matters that need to be dealt with or discussed 取り扱われる, または論議される必要のある重要な事柄→**用事, 用件, 議事** ‖ *First we have some unfinished business from the last meeting to deal with.* まず, 前回の会議で終わらなかった案件がいくつかあります. ▶定義7 [単数扱い]a situation or an event, especially one that is strange or unpleasant 特に変わったまたは不愉快な状況または出来事→**厄介な事, (漠然と)事柄** ‖ *The divorce was an awful business.* 離婚はひどく厄介なものだった. *I found the whole business very depress-ing.* それは全く憂鬱(ゆううつ)な事だった.

成句 **get down to business** ▶定義 to start the work that has to be done 行われるべき仕事を始める→**(大事な)仕事・用件に取り掛かる, 本論に入る** ‖ *Let's just have a cup of coffee before we get down to business.* 仕事に取り掛かる前に, ちょっとコーヒーを飲もう.

**go out of business** ▶定義 to have to close because there is no more money available それ以上使えるお金がないために閉めなければならない→**倒産・破産する, 廃業する** ‖ *The shop went out of business because it couldn't compete with the new supermarket.* その店は新しいスーパーマーケットに対抗できなかったために廃業した.

**have no business to do sth/doing sth** ▶定義 to have no right to do sth 〜をする権利を持たない→**〜する権利・資格がない** ‖ *You have no business to read/reading my letters without asking me.* 私に無断で私の手紙を読む権利はあなたにはない.

**mind your own business** ⇒ **MIND**²
**monkey business** ⇒ **MONKEY**

**businesslike** /bíznəslàɪk/ 形 ▶定義 dealing with matters in a direct and practical way, without trying to be friendly 友好的になろうとせずに, 直接的かつ実務的に物事を取り扱う→**事務的な, 実際的な, ドライな** ‖ *She has a very businesslike manner.* 彼女の態度はとても事務的だ.

**businessman** /bíznəsmæn/ 名 ❻ (複 **-men** /-mèn/) ▶定義1 a man who works in business, especially in a top position 特に最も上の地位にある, 実業界で働く男性→**実業家** ▶定義2 a man who is skilful at dealing with money お金の扱いが上手な男性→**実務家, 商売がうまい人**

**business studies** 名 ❻ ❶ ▶定義 the study of how to control and manage a company 会社の管理と経営の方法についての研究→**経営実務研究** ‖ *a course in business studies* 経営実務研究の課程

**businesswoman** /bíznəswùmən/ 名 ❻ (複 **-women** /-wìmən/) ▶定義1 a woman who works in business, especially in a top position 特に最も上の地位にある, 実業界で働く女性→**女性の実業家** ▶定義2 a woman who is skilful at dealing with money お金の扱いが上手な女性→**女性の実務家, 商売がうまい人**

**busk** /bʌsk/ 動 自 ▶定義 to sing or play music in the street so that people will give you money 人々からお金をもらうために, 路上で歌うまたは音楽を演奏する→**大道芸をする**

**busker** /bʌ́skər/ 名 C ▶定義 a street musician 辻(つじ)音楽師→**大道芸人** ☞C8ページのさし絵

**bust**[1] /bʌst/ 動 (過, 過分 **bust** または **busted**) 略式 ▶定義 1 他 to break or damage sth so that it cannot be used 使えなくなるように, ～を壊すまたは損傷を与える→**～を破壊する, 破裂させる** ▶定義 2 他 to arrest sb ～を逮捕する→**～を逮捕する** ‖ *He was busted for possession of heroin.* 彼はヘロイン所持で逮捕された.

**bust**[2] /bʌst/ 形 (名詞の前は不可) 略式 ▶定義 broken or not working 壊れた, または動かない→**壊れて** ‖ *The zip on these trousers is bust.* このズボンのチャックが壊れている.

成句 **go bust** 略式 ▶定義 (used about a business) to close because it has lost so much money (商売について)多額の損失を出したために廃業する→**倒産・破産する** ‖ *During the recession thousands of businesses went bust.* 不景気の期間に, 数千社が倒産した.

**bust**[3] /bʌst/ 名 C ▶定義 1 a model in stone, etc of a person's head, shoulders and chest 石などでできた, 人の頭と肩と胸の模型→**胸像** ▶定義 2 a woman's breasts; the measurement round a woman's chest 女性の胸; 女性の胸回りの寸法→**胸, バスト; 胸回り** ‖ *This blouse is a bit too tight around the bust.* このブラウスは胸回りが少しきつい. ▶定義 3 略式 an unexpected visit by the police in order to arrest people for doing sth illegal 不法行為をしている人々を逮捕するための, 警官による不意の訪問→**逮捕, 手入れ** ‖ *a drugs bust* 麻薬の手入れ

**bustle**[1] /bʌ́s(ə)l/ 動 ▶定義 1 自 他 to move in a busy, noisy or excited way; to make sb move somewhere quickly 忙しい, 騒々しい, または興奮した方法で動く; ～をどこかへ速く移動させる→**せわしなく動き回る, あたふたと急ぐ; ～をせき立てる** ‖ *He bustled about the kitchen making tea.* 彼は紅茶をいれながら台所をせわしなく動き回った. *They bustled her out of the room before she could see the body.* 彼女が死体を見る前に, 彼らは彼女を部屋の外へ追い立てた. ▶定義 2 自 bustle (with sth) to be full of people, noise or activity 人々, 騒音, または活気で一杯である→**(～で)あふれている** ‖ *The streets were bustling with shoppers.* 通りは買い物客であふれていた.

**bustle**[2] /bʌ́s(ə)l/ 名 U ▶定義 excited and noisy activity 興奮した騒々しい行動→**活気, 喧噪(けんそう), ざわめき** ‖ *She loved the bustle of city life.* 彼女は町の生活の活気を愛していた.

**bust-up** 名 C 略式 ▶定義 an argument 口げんか→**騒々しい口論** ‖ *He had a bust-up with his boss over working hours.* 彼は労働時間のことで上司と派手に言い争った.

*★**busy**[1] /bízi/ 形 (**busier**; **busiest**) ▶定義 1 busy (at/with sth); busy (doing sth) having a lot of work or tasks to do; not free; working on sth するべき仕事または職務がたくさんある; 暇がない; ～に従事している→**忙しい, ～で忙しい, ～するのに忙しい** ‖ *Mr Khan is busy until 4 o'clock but he could see you after that.* カーン氏は4時まで忙しいですが, その後でならあなたにお会いできます. *Don't disturb him. He's busy.* 彼の邪魔をするな, 今忙しいから. *She's busy with her preparations for the party.* 彼女はパーティーの準備で忙しい. *We're busy decorating the spare room before our visitors arrive.* 私たちは, お客が到着する前に予備の客用寝室の飾り付けをするのに忙しい. ▶定義 2 (used about a period of time) full of activity and things to do (ある期間について)すべき活動と事柄がたくさんある→**多忙な** ‖ *I've had rather a busy week.* かなり多忙な1週間だった. ▶定義 3 (used about a place) full of people, movement and activity (ある場所について)人々, 動き, 活動で一杯である→**にぎやかな, 混雑している** ‖ *The town centre was so busy that you could hardly move.* 中心街はほとんど身動きできないくらい混雑していた. ▶定義 4 特に 米 (used about a telephone) being used (電話について)使われている→**話し中で** ‖ *The line's busy at the moment. I'll try again later.* 現在話し中だ. 後でまたかけてみる. —**busily** 副→**忙しそうに, せっせと** ‖ *When I came in she was busily writing something at her desk.* 私が入っていった時, 彼女は机でせっせと何かを書いていた.

成句 **get busy** ▶定義 to start working 仕事を始

める➔**仕事に取り掛かる** ‖ *We'll have to get busy if we're going to be ready in time.* 時間通りに間に合わせるつもりならば、仕事に取り掛からなければならないでしょう.

**busy**² /bízi/ 動詞 (現分 **busying**; 三単現 **busies**; 過, 過分 **busied**) ▶定義 busy yourself with sth; busy yourself doing sth to keep yourself busy; to find sth to do ~で、~をすることで自分を忙しくする; する～を見つける➔**~で忙しい、~するのに忙しい**

**busybody** /bízibàdi/ 名 C (複 **busybodies**) ▶定義 a person who is too interested in other people's private lives 他人の個人的生活に過度に興味を持つ人➔**お節介な人、出しゃばりな人**

★**but**¹ /bət, 強形 bʌt/ 接 ▶定義 **1** used for introducing an idea which contrasts with or is different from what has just been said 言われた事と対照的な、または異なる考えを切り出すために用いて➔**しかし、だが、けれども** ‖ *The weather will be sunny but cold.* 天気は晴れるだろう、しかし寒いだろう. *Theirs is not the first but the second house on the left.* 彼らの家は左側の1番目ではなく、2番目だ. *James hasn't got a car but his sister has.* ジェームズは車を持っていない、だが姉は持っている. ▶定義 **2** however; and yet しかしながら; それでも➔**でも、けれども** ‖ *She's been learning Italian for five years but she doesn't speak it very well.* 彼女はイタリア語を5年間習っている、でも上手に話せない. *I'd love to come but I can't make it till 8 o'clock.* 是非伺いたいが、8時までは無理です. ▶定義 **3** used when you are saying sorry for sth ~についてわびを言うときに用いて➔**~ですが、けれども** ‖ *Excuse me, but is your name David Harries?* 失礼ですが、あなたはデーヴィッド ハリスさんですか. *I'm sorry, but I can't stay any longer.* すみませんが、私はこれ以上とどまることができません. ▶定義 **4** used for introducing a statement that shows that you are surprised or annoyed or that you disagree 驚いている、いらいらしている、または反対意見だという見解を示すために用いて➔**それにしても、まあ、いやはや** ‖ *'Here's the book you lent me.' 'But it's all dirty and torn!'* 「君が貸してくれた本だ」「それにしても、ひどく汚れて破れているな」*But that's not possible!* 何と、そんな事は無理だ.

成句 but then ▶定義 however; on the other hand しかしながら; 他方では➔**それにしても、そうとはいえ、その反面** ‖ *We could go swimming. But then perhaps it's too cold.* 私たちは泳ぎに行こうと思えば行ける. しかし, 多分寒すぎるだろう. *He's brilliant at the piano. But then so was his father (=however, this is not surprising because...).* 彼のピアノはすばらしい. それにしても彼の父親もそうだった(=しかしながらそれは驚くことではない, なぜなら...).

★**but**² /bət, 強形 bʌt/ 前 ▶定義 except 除いた➔**~を除いて、~のほかは** ‖ *I've told no one but you about this.* あなた以外にはだれにもこの事を話していない. *We've had nothing but trouble with this washing machine!* この洗濯機は故障ばかりしている.

成句 but for sb/sth ▶定義 except for or without sb/sth ~を除いて, または~なしで➔**~がなければ** ‖ *We wouldn't have managed but for your help.* あなたの助けがなかったら, 私たちは成し遂げられなかっただろう.

★**butcher**¹ /bútʃər/ 名 C ▶定義 **1** a person who sells meat 肉を売る人➔**肉屋** ‖ *The butcher cut me four lamb chops.* 肉屋は羊肉のチョップを4つ切ってくれた. *She went to the butcher's for some sausages.* 彼女はソーセージを買いに肉屋へ行った.

➤ the butcher は肉屋を経営する人で, the butcher's が肉屋であることに注意する.

▶定義 **2** a person who kills a lot of people in a cruel way 残酷な方法で多くの人々を殺す人➔**(残忍な)殺人者、無用の血を流す者**

**butcher**² /bútʃər/ 動 他 ▶定義 to kill a lot of people in a cruel way 残酷な方法で多くの人々を殺す➔**残忍に殺す、惨殺・虐殺する**

**butchery** /bútʃ(ə)ri/ 名 U ▶定義 cruel killing 残酷な殺人➔**大量殺人、虐殺**

**butler** /bʌ́tlər/ 名 C ▶定義 a person who works in a very large house, whose main duty is to organize and serve food and wine 大きな屋敷で働き、食事やワインを準備し給仕することを主な仕事とする人➔**執事、使用人頭**

**butt**¹ /bʌt/ 動 他 ▶定義 to hit sb/sth with the head ~を頭でぶつ➔**~を頭で突く・押す、角で突く**

句動詞 butt in (on sb/sth) ▶定義 to interrupt sb/sth or to join in sth without being asked ~

# 216 butt²

を邪魔する，または頼まれていないのに〜に加わる➡口を差し挟む，干渉する，出しゃばる ‖ *I'm sorry to butt in but could I speak to you urgently for a minute?* 口を挟んですみませんが，至急あなたと少しお話できますか．

**butt²** /bʌt/ 名 C ▶定義1 the thicker, heavier end of a weapon or tool 武器または道具の太くて重い末端➡太い方の端，(銃の)台じり，(釣りざおの)手元 ‖ *the butt of a rifle* ライフルの床尾 ▶定義2 a short piece of a cigarette which is left when it has been smoked たばこを吸った後に残る短い部分➡吸差し ▶定義3 特に 困 略式 the part of your body that you sit on; your bottom 座ったとき，下にある体の部分；しり➡しり ‖ *Get up off your butt and do some work!* しりを上げて仕事をしろ．▶定義4 a person who is often laughed at or talked about in an unkind way しばしば不人情に笑われるまたは語られる人➡的 ‖ *Fat children are often the butt of other children's jokes.* 太った子供たちはしばしばほかの子供たちのからかいの的になる．▶定義5 the act of hitting sb with your head 〜をあなたの頭でぶつ行為➡頭で突くこと，頭突き

*****butter¹** /bʌ́tər/ 名 U ▶定義 a soft yellow fat that is made from cream and used for spreading on bread, etc or in cooking クリームから作られ，パンなどに塗ったり料理に使われる，柔らかくて黄色い脂肪分➡バター ‖ *Do you prefer butter or low-fat spread?* バターと低脂肪スプレッドのどちらが好きですか．*First, melt a little butter in the pan.* 最初に，少量のバターを平なべに溶かします．☞ C4ページのさし絵

**butter²** /bʌ́tər/ 動 他 ▶定義 to spread butter on bread, etc パンなどにバターを塗る➡〜にバターを塗る ‖ *I'll cut the bread and you butter it.* 私がパンを切るから，あなたはバターを塗って．*hot buttered toast* バターを塗った温かいトースト

**butterfly** /bʌ́tərflài/ 名 ▶定義1 C ( 複 **butterflies**) an insect with a long, thin body and four brightly coloured wings 長く細い体と4つの鮮やかな色の羽を持つ昆虫➡チョウ ‖ *Caterpillars develop into butterflies.* 毛虫はチョウに成長する．☞ **insect**のさし絵 ▶定義2 [単数扱い] a style of swimming in which both arms are brought over the head at the same time, and the legs move up and down together 両手を同時に頭の上に運び，両足をそろえて上下に動かす泳法➡バタフライ泳法

成句 **have butterflies (in your stomach)** 略式 ▶定義 to feel very nervous before doing sth 〜をする前にとても神経質になる➡あがる，どきどきする

**buttermilk** /bʌ́təmìlk/ 名 U ▶定義 the liquid that is left when butter is separated from milk バターが牛乳から分離されたときに残る液体➡バターミルク

**buttock** /bʌ́tək/ 名 [C, 通常は複数] ▶定義 one of the two parts of your body which you sit on 座ったときに下にある体の，2つで一組の部分の1つ➡しり

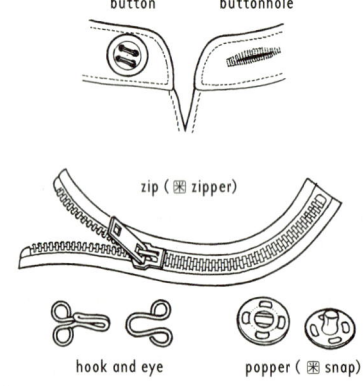

button　　buttonhole

zip ( 米 zipper)

hook and eye　　popper ( 米 snap)

*****button** /bʌ́tn/ 名 C ▶定義1 a small, often round, piece of plastic, wood or metal that you use for fastening your clothes 服を留めるために使う，小さくてしばしば円い，プラスチック，木，または金属➡ボタン ‖ *One of the buttons on my jacket has come off.* 上着のボタンが1つ取れた．*This blouse is too tight - I can't fasten the buttons.* このブラウスは少しきつい―ボタンが掛けられない．▶定義2 a small part of a machine, etc that you press in order to operate sth 〜を操作するために押す機械などの小さい部品➡押しボタン ‖ *Press the button to ring the bell.* ベルを鳴らすにはそのボタンを押しなさい．*To dial the same number again, push the 'redial' button.* 同じ番号にもう一度電話をかけるには，「再ダイヤル」ボタンを押しなさい．*Which button turns the volume down?* どのボタンで音量

を下げられますか. *To print a file, simply click on the 'print' button.* ファイルを印刷するには,「印刷」ボタンをクリックするだけでよい. *Double click the right mouse button.* マウスの右ボタンをダブルクリックしなさい. ☛ **handle**, **telephone** のさし絵

**buttonhole** /bʌ́tnhòul/ 🔢 🄲 ▶定義1 a hole in a piece of clothing that you push a button through in order to fasten it ボタンを掛けるための衣服の穴→ボタンの穴, ボタンホール ☛ **button** のさし絵 ▶定義2 医 a flower worn in the buttonhole of a coat or jacket コートや上着のボタン穴に付ける花→花, 花房

\***buy**¹ /báɪ/ 動他 (過, 過分 **bought** /bɔ́ːt/) ▶定義 buy sth (for sb); buy sb sth to get sth by paying money for it お金を払って～を手に入れる→買う ‖ *I'm going to buy a new dress for the party.* 私はそのパーティーのために新しいドレスを買うつもりだ. *We bought this book for you in London.* 私たちはあなたのためにこの本をロンドンで買った. *Can I buy you a coffee?* コーヒーを君におごっていいかい. *He bought the car from a friend.* 彼は友達からその車を買った. *Did you buy your car new or second-hand?* 新車を買われたのですか, それとも中古車を買われたのですか. *He bought the necklace as a present for his wife.* 彼は妻への贈り物にネックレスを買った.

成句 buy time ▶定義 to do sth in order to delay an event, a decision, etc ある出来事や決定などを遅らせるために～をする→時間稼ぎをする ‖ *He took a few days' holiday in order to buy some time before giving them his final decision.* 彼らに最終決定を下すまでの時間稼ぎに, 彼は数日休みを取った.

句動詞 buy sb off 略式 ▶定義 to pay sb money, especially dishonestly, to stop him/her from doing sth you do not want him/her to do 自分がしてほしくない事を～がするのを止めるために, 特に不正に, お金を払う→～を買収する ‖ *The construction company tried to buy off the opposition by offering them discounts on the properties they were planning to build.* 建設会社は, 建設を予定している建物の割引を申し出て, 反対派を買収しようとした.

buy sb out ▶定義 to pay sb for his/her share in a house, business, etc in order to get full control of it yourself 家, 会社などのすべてを自分で支配するために, ～の持分の代金をその人に支払う→～を買い取る, ～から株・権利を買い取る ‖ *After the divorce, she bought him out and kept the house for herself.* 離婚の後, 彼女は彼から家を買い取り自分のものにした.

**buy**² /báɪ/ 🔢 🄲 ▶定義 an act of buying sth or a thing that you can buy ～を買う行為, または自分が買える物→買い物 ‖ *I think your house was a very good buy (=worth the money you paid).* あなたの家はとても良い買い物だった (=あなたが支払ったお金の価値がある) と思う.

**buyer** /báɪər/ 🔢 🄲 ▶定義1 a person who is buying sth or may buy sth ～を買っている, または～を買うかもしれない人→買い手 ‖ *I think we've found a buyer for our house!* 私たちの家の買い手が見つかったようだ. ▶定義2 a person whose job is to choose and buy goods to be sold in a large shop 大きな店で売るための商品を選んで買うことを仕事にする人→仕入れ係, バイヤー

**buyout** /báɪàut/ 🔢 🄲 ▶定義 the act of buying enough or all of the shares in a company in order to get control of it ある会社を支配するために, その会社の株を十分なだけまたはすべてを買う行為→(事業の)買収, 買い占め

**buzz**¹ /bʌ́z/ 動 ▶定義1 自 to make the sound that bees, etc make when flying ハチなどが飛んでいるときに立てる音を立てる→ぶんぶんいう, ぶんぶん飛ぶ ‖ *A large fly was buzzing against the windowpane.* 大きなハエが窓ガラスに向かってぶんぶんと飛んでいた. ▶定義2 自 buzz (with sth) to be full of excitement, activity, thoughts, etc 興奮, 活気, 思考で一杯である→ざわめく, がやがやいう, 忙しく動き回る ‖ *Her head was buzzing with questions that she wanted to ask.* 彼女の頭の中は尋ねたい質問で一杯だった. *The room was buzzing with activity.* 部屋は活気でざわめいていた. ▶定義3 自他 to call sb by using an electric bell, etc 電気的な呼び鈴などを使って～を呼ぶ→呼ぶ; ～にブザーで合図をする ‖ *The doctor will buzz for you when he's ready.* 準備ができたら, 医者はあなたにブザーで合図をします.

**buzz**² /bʌ́z/ 🔢 ▶定義1 🄲 the sound that a bee, etc makes when flying ハチなどが飛んでいるときに立てる音→ぶんぶんいう音 ‖ *the buzz of* *insects* 昆虫のぶんぶんいう音 ▶定義2 [単数扱い] the low sound made by many people talking at the same time 多くの人々が同時に話すことで立つ低い音→**がやがやいう声，ざわめき** ‖ *I could hear the buzz of conversation in the next room.* 隣の部屋でがやがやという話し声がした．▶定義3 [単数扱い] 略式 a strong feeling of excitement or pleasure 興奮や喜びの強い感情→**興奮，わくわくすること** ‖ *a buzz of expectation* 期待でわくわくすること *Flying on Concorde gave him a real buzz.* 彼はコンコルドで飛んで本当に興奮した．*She gets a buzz out of shopping for expensive clothes.* 彼女は高い洋服の買い物をするときわくわくする．

**buzzer** /bʌ́zər/ 名 C ▶定義 a piece of equipment that makes a buzzing sound ブーという音を出す器具→**ブザー** ‖ *Press your buzzer if you know the answer to a question.* 質問の答えが分かったらブザーを押しなさい．

**buzzword** /bʌ́zwɜːrd/ 名 C ▶定義 a word or phrase, especially one connected with a particular subject, that has become fashionable and popular 流行して有名になった単語や言葉，特に特定の主題に関連したもの→**流行となった専門・業界用語** ‖ *Self-organization is the current buzzword.* 自己組織化は今はやりの専門用語だ．

*★**by** /báɪ/ 前置 ▶定義1 beside; very near ～のそばに; とても近い→**～のそばに[の・を]** ‖ *Come and sit by me.* こちらへ来て，私のそばに座りなさい．*We stayed in a cottage by the sea.* 私たちは海辺の小別荘に滞在した．*The shops are close by.* それらの店は近くにある．▶定義2 past 過ぎて→**～(のそば)を通り過ぎて** ‖ *He walked straight by me without speaking.* 彼は黙ったまま私のそばをまっすぐ歩いて通り過ぎた．*We stopped to let the ambulance get by.* 救急車を通過させるために，私たちは停止した．▶定義3 not later than; before ～よりも後ではない; 前の→**～までに** ‖ *I'll be home by 7 o'clock.* 私は7時までには帰宅するだろう．*He should have telephoned by now/by this time.* 彼が電話をしてきてもよいころだ．▶定義4 (通常 the を伴わないで) during a period of time; in particular circumstances ある期間の間; 特定の状況で→**～の間** ‖ *By day we covered about thirty miles and by night we rested.* 私たちは昼間は約30マイル旅し，夜は休んだ．*The electricity went off so we had to work by candlelight.* 電気が消えたので，ろうそくの明かりで働かなければならなかった．▶定義5 used after a passive verb for showing who or what did or caused sth 受動態の動詞の後に用いて，～の原因となった人や物を示す→**～によって，～で** ‖ *She was knocked down by a car.* 彼女は車にぶつけられて倒れた．*The event was organized by local people.* その行事は地元の人々によって準備された．*I was deeply shocked by the news.* 私はその知らせにとてもショックを受けた．*Who was the book written by?/Who is the book by?* その本はだれによって書かれましたか・この本はだれによるものですか．▶定義6 through doing or using sth; by means of sth ～をするまたは使うことを通して; ～によって→**～によって** ‖ *You can get hold of me by phoning this number.* この番号に電話すれば，私を捕まえられる．*Will you be paying by cheque?* 小切手でお支払いなさいますか．*The house is heated by electricity.* 家は電気で暖房されている．*'How do you go to work?' 'By train, usually.'*「どのようにして職場に行きますか」「電車で，通常は」*by bus/car/plane/bicycle* バスで・車で・飛行機で・自転車で *We went in by the back door.* 私たちは後ろの扉から中に入った．▶定義7 as a result of sth; due to sth ～の結果として; ～のために→**～の結果** ‖ *I got on the wrong bus by mistake/accident.* 誤って・たまたま，私は間違ったバスに乗った．*I met an old friend by chance.* 私は偶然旧友に会った．▶定義8 according to sth; with regard to sth ～によれば; ～に関して→**～によって，～で** ‖ *It's 8 o'clock by my watch.* 私の時計では今8時だ．*By law you have to attend school from the age of five.* 法律によって，5歳から学校に通わなければならない．*She's French by birth.* 彼女は生まれはフランス人だ．*He's a doctor by profession.* 彼の職業は医者だ．▶定義9 used for multiplying or dividing 掛け算または割り算に用いて→**～で(掛けて，割って)** ‖ *4 multiplied by 5 is 20.* 4を5で掛けると20だ．*6 divided by 2 is 3.* 6を2で割ると3だ．▶定義10 used for showing the measurements of an area ある地域の大きさを表すために用いて→**掛ける** ‖ *The table is six feet by three feet (=six feet long and three feet wide).* そ

のテーブルは6フィート掛ける3フィートだ(=長さ6フィート, 幅3フィートだ). ▶定義11 (しばしば the を伴って) in the quantity or period mentioned 言及された量または期間で→〜を単位として ‖ *You can rent a car by the day, the week or the month.* 車を日, 週, 月単位で借りることができます. *Copies of the book have been sold by the million.* その本は百万冊単位で売れた. *They came in one by one.* 彼らは1人ずつ入ってきた. *Day by day she was getting better.* 日ごとに彼女は良くなっていた. ▶定義12 to the amount mentioned 言及された量まで→〜だけ, 〜の程度まで ‖ *Prices have gone up by 10 per cent.* 価格は10パーセント上がった. *I missed the bus by a few minutes.* 私は数分遅れでバスを逃した. ▶定義13 (used with a part of the body or an article of clothing) holding (体の一部分または衣服の1点について) つかんでいる→〜を ‖ *He grabbed me by the arm.* 彼は私の腕をつかんだ.
**成句** by and large ⇒ **LARGE**
by the way ⇒ **WAY**¹

**bye** /báɪ/ (または **bye-bye** /bàɪbáɪ/) **間略式** ▶定義 goodbye さようなら→ではまた, じゃあね ‖ *Bye! See you tomorrow.* じゃあね. 明日会おう.

**by-election** 名 C ▶定義 an election to choose a new Member of Parliament for a particular town or area (a constituency). It is held when the former member has died or left suddenly. 前任者が亡くなったり突然辞任したときに行われる, 特定の町または地域(選挙区)で新しい国会議員を選ぶための選挙→補欠選挙 ☛参 **general election**

**bygone** /báɪɡɒ(ː)n, -ɡɔ̀ːn/ 形 (名詞の前だけ) ▶定義 that happened a long time ago ずっと以前に起きた→過去の ‖ *a bygone era* 過去の時代

**bygones** /báɪɡɒ(ː)nz, -ɡɔ̀ːnz/ 名 [複数扱い]
**成句** let bygones be bygones ▶定義 to decide to forget disagreements or arguments that happened in the past 過去に起きた意見の不一致または口論を忘れようと決める→**過去の事は過去の事としておく, 過ぎた事は水に流す**

**bypass**¹ /báɪpɑːs; -pæs/ 名 C ▶定義1 a road which traffic can use to go round a town, instead of through it 往来する車が, 町の中を通り抜ける代わりに, その周りを回っていくために利用できる道→**バイパス, 自動車用迂回(うかい)路** ☛参 **ring road** ▶定義2 (medical) an operation on the heart to send blood along a different route so that it does not go through a part which is damaged or blocked (医学)損傷したりふさがった部分を通らずに, ほかの経路で血液を送るための心臓手術→**バイパス** ‖ *a triple bypass operation* 3箇所のバイパス手術 *heart bypass surgery* 心臓のバイパス手術

**bypass**² /báɪpɑːs; -pæs/ 動 他 ▶定義 to go around or to avoid sth using a bypass バイパスを使って, 周りを回るまたは〜を避ける→**〜を迂回(うかい)する, 回避する** ‖ *Let's try to bypass the city centre.* 町の中心部を迂回してみよう. (比喩) *It's no good trying to bypass the problem.* 問題を回避しようとすることは良くない.

**by-product** /báɪprɒ̀dəkt/ 名 C ▶定義1 something that is formed during the making of sth else ほかの〜を作っている間に形成されるもの→**副産物** ▶定義2 something that happens as the result of sth else ほかの〜の結果として生じるもの→**(思い掛けない)副次的結果**

**bystander** /báɪstæ̀ndər/ 名 C ▶定義 a person who is standing near and sees sth that happens, without being involved in it 起きる〜を, それに巻き込まれずに, 近くに立って見ている人→**傍観者, 局外者, 見物人** ‖ *Several innocent bystanders were hurt when the two gangs attacked each other.* 2人のギャング同士が戦った時, 数人の罪のない見物人がけがをした.

**byte** /báɪt/ 名 C ▶定義 (computing) a unit of information that can represent one item, such as a letter or a number. A byte is usually made up of a series of eight smaller units (bits). (コンピューター) 文字や数字のような1つのものを表す情報の単位. 1バイトは, 通常さらに小さな単位(ビット)が8つ連続して構成されている→**バイト**

**byword** /báɪwə̀ːrd/ 名 [通常は単数] ▶定義1 *a byword for sth* a person or a thing that is a typical or well-known example of a particular quality 特定の属性の典型的なまたはよく知られた人または物→**典型的な例, 代名詞** ‖ *A limousine is a byword for luxury.* リムジンはぜいたく品の典型的な例だ. ▶定義2 特に 米 a word or phrase that is often used しばしば使われる単語または言葉→**決まり文句, ことわざ**

# C c

**C, c**[1] /si:/ 名 C (複 **C's**; **c's**) ▶定義 the third letter of the English alphabet 英語アルファベットの第3文字→c (C) が表す音, c (C) の文字, c (C) の字形のもの ‖ *'Car' begins with (a) 'C'.* Car は C で始まる.

**c**[2] /si:/ 略 ▶定義**1** **C** Celsius; centigrade 摂氏; 摂氏の→摂氏〜度 ‖ *Water freezes at 0°C.* 水は摂氏0度で凍る. ▶定義**2** (before dates) about; approximately (日付の前で) 約; おおよそ→〜ころ ‖ *c 1770* 1770年ころ

**cab** /kæb/ 名 C ▶定義**1** 特に 米 =TAXI[1] ‖ *Let's take a cab/go by cab.* タクシーに乗ろう・タクシーで行こう. ▶定義**2** the part of a lorry, train, bus, etc where the driver sits トラック, 列車, バスなどの運転手が座る部分→運転席, (列車の) 機関手室

**cabaret** /kǽbərèɪ, -´-/ 名 C U ▶定義 entertainment with singing, dancing, etc in a restaurant or club レストランやクラブでの, 歌や踊りなどを伴った余興→(キャバレーの) ショー

*****cabbage** /kǽbɪdʒ/ 名 C U ▶定義 a large round vegetable with thick green, dark red or white leaves 緑, 濃赤色または白の厚い葉を持つ大きな丸い野菜→キャベツ, キャベツの葉 ‖ *Cabbages are easy to grow.* キャベツは栽培しやすい. *Do you like cabbage?* キャベツは好きですか. ☞ C3 ページのさし絵

**cabin** /kǽbən/ 名 C ▶定義**1** a small room in a ship or boat, where a passenger sleeps 船やボートの乗客が眠るための小部屋→船室, キャビン ▶定義**2** the part of a plane where the passengers sit 飛行機の客席がある部分→旅客室 ▶定義**3** a small wooden house; a hut 小さな木の家; 小屋→小屋 ‖ *a log cabin* 丸太小屋 ☞ C8 ページのさし絵

**cabinet** /kǽb(ə)nət/ 名 C ▶定義**1** a cupboard with shelves or drawers, used for storing things 棚や引き出しのある戸棚で, 物を保管するために使われる→収納家具, 飾り棚, キャビネット ‖ *a medicine cabinet* (洗面所の) 戸棚 *a filing cabinet* 書類棚 ☞ S4 ページのさし絵 ▶定義**2** (または **the Cabinet**) [単数または複数形の動詞と共に] the most important ministers in a government, who have regular meetings with the Prime Minister 首相と定期的に会議をしている政府の主要な大臣たち→内閣, 閣僚 ‖ *The Cabinet is/are meeting today to discuss the crisis.* 今日, 閣僚が集まってその危機について議論することになっている.

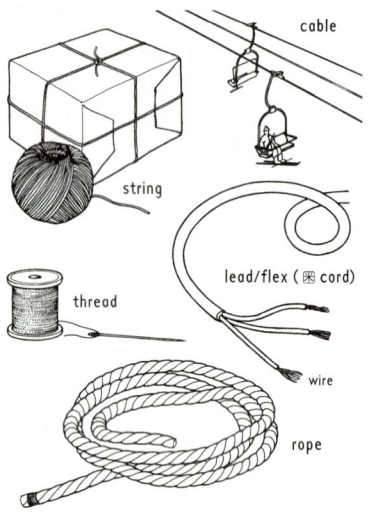

**cable** /kéɪb(ə)l/ 名 ▶定義**1** C a thick strong metal rope 太く頑丈な金属のロープ→太綱 (ふとづな), 鋼索 ▶定義**2** C U a set of wires covered with plastic, etc, for carrying electricity or signals 電気や信号を伝えるための, プラスチックなどで覆ったワイヤーの束→ケーブル, ケーブル線 ‖ *underground/overhead cables* 地下・高架ケーブル *a telephone cable* 電話線 *two metres of cable* 2メートルのケーブル ☞ C8 ページのさし絵 ▶定義**3** = CABLE TELEVISION

**cable car** 名 C ▶定義 a vehicle like a box that hangs on a moving metal rope (cable) and carries passengers up and down a mountain 動く金属索 (ケーブル) からつり下げられた箱形の乗り物で, 乗客を山頂やふもとに運ぶ→ケーブルカー, ロープウエー ☞ C8 ページのさし絵

**cable television** 名 U ▶定義 a system of sending out television programmes along wires instead of by radio signals テレビ番組を無線信号ではなく電線で送信する仕組み→ケーブルテ

レビ, 有線テレビ

**cackle** /kǽk(ə)l/ 動自 ▶定義 to laugh in a loud, unpleasant way 大声で, 不快な笑い方をする➔甲高い声で笑う, きゃっきゃっと笑う — **cackle** 名 C ▶甲高い笑い声

**cactus** /kǽktəs/ 名 C (複 **cactuses** または **cacti** /kǽktàɪ/) ▶定義 a type of plant that grows in hot, dry areas, especially deserts. A cactus has a thick central part (stem) and sharp points (prickles) but no leaves. 暑く乾燥した地域, 特に砂漠に生える植物の一種. 太い中心部分 (茎) と鋭い針 (とげ) があるが, 葉はない➔サボテン ☛ C2 ページのさし絵

**cadet** /kədét/ 名 C ▶定義 a young person who is training to be in the army, navy, air force or police 陸軍, 海軍, 空軍または警察に入るため訓練を受けている若者➔士官候補生, 士官学校生, 警察学校生

**cadge** /kædʒ/ 動自他 略式 ▶定義 cadge (sth) (from/off sb) to try to persuade sb to give or lend you sth ～を説得して…をもらったり, 借りたりしようとする➔(～に)(…を) ねだる, せびる, たかる ∥ He's always trying to cadge money off me. 彼はいつも私に金をせびる.

**Caesarean** (または**-rian**; 米 または **cesarean**) /sɪzéəriən/ 名 C ▶定義 a medical operation in which an opening is cut in a mother's body in order to take out the baby when a normal birth would be impossible or dangerous 通常の出産が不可能か危険な場合に, 赤ちゃんを取り出すために母体を切開する手術➔帝王切開 ∥ to have a Caesarean 帝王切開で出産する

▶この手術は Caesarean section, またはアメリカ英語では C-section と呼ばれることがある.

★**cafe** /kæféɪ, kə-; kǽfèɪ, -fi/ 名 C ▶定義 a small restaurant that serves drinks and light meals 飲み物と軽い食事を出す小さな食堂➔軽食堂, 喫茶店

▶英国において, 通常 cafe ではアルコール飲料を出さず, pub や bar で出す.

☛ C8 ページのさし絵

**cafeteria** /kæ̀fətíəriə/ 名 C ▶定義 a restaurant, especially one for staff or workers, where people collect their meals themselves and carry them to their tables 特に職員や労働者のための食堂で, 自分で食事を取りに行ってテーブルで運ぶ➔社員食堂, カフェテリア (セルフサービス式の簡易食堂) ☛参 **canteen**

**caffeine** /kǽfiːn/ 名 U ▶定義 the substance found in coffee and tea that makes you feel more awake and full of energy コーヒーや紅茶に含まれる物質で, 意識をはっきりさせ活力をみなぎらせる➔カフェイン ☛参 **decaffeinated**

★**cage** /kéɪdʒ/ 名 C ▶定義 a box made of bars or wire, or a space surrounded by wire or metal bars, in which a bird or animal is kept so that it cannot escape 棒材や針金で作られた箱, または針金や金属棒で囲まれた空間で, 逃げられないように鳥や動物を入れておく➔かご, おり ∥ a birdcage 鳥かご — **cage** 動他 ▶～をかご・おりに入れる — **caged** /kéɪdʒd/ 形 ▶かご・おりに入れられた ∥ He felt like a caged animal in the tiny office. 彼はその狭い事務所で, おりに閉じ込められた動物になった気がした.

**cagey** /kéɪdʒi/ 形 略式 ▶定義 cagey (about sth) not wanting to give information or to talk about sth ～について情報を与えたがらない, または話したがらない➔(～について) 用心深い, 自分の意見を表に出さない; 抜け目ない

**cagoule** /kəgúːl/ 名 C ▶定義 a long jacket with a covering for the head (hood) that protects you from the rain or wind 雨や風から保護するために頭を覆う物 (フード) が付いた長い上着➔カグール, アノラック ☛ C6 ページのさし絵

cakes

★**cake**¹ /kéɪk/ 名 ▶定義 1 C U a sweet food made by mixing flour, eggs, butter, sugar, etc together and baking the mixture in the oven 小麦粉, 卵, バター, 砂糖などを混ぜ合わせて, オーブンで焼いて作る甘い食べ物➔ケーキ, 洋菓子 ∥ to make/bake a cake ケーキを作る・焼く a wedding cake ウエディングケーキ a piece/

**cake²**

slice of birthday cake バースデーケーキ1切れ Would you like some more cake? ケーキをもう少しいかがですか. ▶定義2 ❷a mixture of other food, cooked in a round, flat shape 小麦粉や砂糖以外の食物を混ぜ合わせて円い平らな形に調理した物→(野菜, 魚などの)平らで円い形の食べ物, だんご ‖ fish/potato cakes 魚のコロッケ・ポテトケーキ

成句 **have your cake and eat it** ▶定義 to enjoy the advantages of sth without its disadvantages; to have both things that are available 〜の不利益を受けずにその利点だけを楽しむ; 手に入れることのできる両方のものを手にする→あちらもこちらもうまくやる ‖ You can't go out every night and pass your exams. You can't have your cake and eat it. 毎晩遊びに出掛けていると, 試験には受かりませんよ. あちらもこちらもうまくやることはできませんから.

**a piece of cake** ⇒ **PIECE¹**

**cake²** /kéɪk/ 動他 (通常は受動態で) ▶定義 cake sth (in/with sth) to cover sth thickly with a substance that becomes hard when it dries 乾くと固まる物質で〜を厚く覆う→〜を(…で)厚く塗る, 〜を固める ‖ boots caked in mud 泥が厚くこびり付いたブーツ

**calamity** /kəlǽməti/ 名 ❻ ❿ (複 **calamities**) ▶定義 a terrible event that causes a lot of damage or harm 多くの損害, または被害を引き起こすひどい出来事→災難, 大災害, 不幸

*★**calculate** /kǽlkjəlèɪt/ 動他 ▶定義1 to find sth out by using mathematics; to work sth out 数学を使用して〜の答えを出す; 〜を算定する→〜を計算する, 算出する; 見積もる ‖ It's difficult to calculate how long the project will take. そのプロジェクトの期間がどのくらいになるかを算定するのは難しい. ▶定義2 to consider or expect sth 〜について考える, または予想する→〜をあらかじめ考慮する, 判断する, 〜と推定する ‖ We calculated that the advantages would be greater than the disadvantages. 不利益より利益の方が大きいだろうと私たちは判断した.

成句 **be calculated to do sth** ▶定義 to be intended or designed to do sth 〜をするように意図された→〜するようにできている, 〜しそうである ‖ His remark was clearly calculated to annoy me. 彼の一言は明らかに私を怒らせることを意図したものだった.

**calculating** /kǽlkjəlèɪtɪŋ/ 形 ▶定義 planning things in a very careful way in order to achieve what you want, without considering other people ほかの人々のことを考慮することなく, 自分の望む事を達成するためにとても入念に計画を立てる→計算高い ‖ Her cold, calculating approach made her many enemies. 冷たい打算的なやり方のせいで彼女は多くの敵を作った.

**calculation** /kæ̀lkjəléɪʃ(ə)n/ 名 ▶定義1 ❻ ❿ finding an answer by using mathematics 数学を使って答えを見つけること→計算(すること), 計算の結果 ‖ I'll have to do a few calculations before telling you how much I can afford. ちょっと計算しないといくら出せるか言えない. Calculation of the exact cost is impossible. 正確な経費を計算することは不可能だ. ▶定義2 ❿ 正式 careful planning in order to achieve what you want, without considering other people ほかの人々のことを考慮することなく, 自分の望む事を達成するために入念に練られた計画→打算, もくろみ ‖ His actions were clearly the result of deliberate calculation. 彼の行動は明らかに意図的な打算の結果だった.

**calculator** /kǽlkjəlèɪtər/ 名 ❻ ▶定義 a small electronic machine used for calculating figures 数を計算するために使われる小さな電子機械→小型計算器, 電卓 ‖ a pocket calculator ポケット計算器, 電卓

**caldron** 特に 米 = **CAULDRON**

*★**calendar** /kǽləndər/ 名 ❻ ▶定義1 a list that shows the days, weeks and months of a particular year 特定の年の日, 週, 月を示す一覧表→カレンダー, 暦

▶ calendar はよく壁に掛けられていて, 時には絵や写真が付いた月ごとのページに分かれているものもある. diary は携帯できる小さなノートで, 日付の横の空欄に予定などを書き込める.

☛ S4 ページのさし絵 ▶定義2 a system for dividing time into fixed periods and for marking the beginning and end of a year 時間を一定の期間に分割するため, また1年の始まりと終わりを示すための仕組み→暦法 ‖ the Muslim calendar イスラム暦 ▶定義3 a list of dates and events in a year that are important in a particular area of activity 特定の活動分野において重要な，1年間の日付と行事の一覧表➜**年中行事予定表，予定表** ‖ *Wimbledon is a major event in the sporting calendar.* スポーツ界の年中行事予定表ではウィンブルドン大会は大きなイベントだ．

**calendar month** = MONTH(1)
**calendar year** = YEAR(1)

**calf** /kɑːf; kæf/ 名 ❻ ( 複 **calves** /kɑːvz; kævz/ )
▶定義1 a young cow 若い牛➜**子牛** ☞参 **cow**の注とさし絵

➤子牛の肉は veal と呼ばれる．meat の注を参照．

▶定義2 the young of some other animals, for example elephants 一部のほかの動物，例えば象の子供➜**(象，鯨，アザラシ，カバなど大型動物の) 子** ▶定義3 the back of your leg, below your knee ひざから下の後ろ側➜**ふくらはぎ** ‖ *I've strained a calf muscle.* ふくらはぎの筋肉を痛めてしまった． ☞ C5 ページのさし絵

**calibre** ( 米 **caliber**) /ˈkælɪbər/ 名 [ 単数扱い，❶ ] ▶定義 the quality or ability of a person or thing 人や物の質または能力➜**力量，度量，器量，特質** ‖ *The company's employees are of (a) high calibre.* その会社の社員は有能だ．

★**call¹** /kɔːl/ 動 ▶定義1 ❸❻ call (out) to sb; call (sth) (out) to say sth loudly or to shout in order to attract attention 注意をひくために～を大きな声で言う，または叫ぶ➜**大声で呼ぶ，叫ぶ，大声で言う** ‖ *'Hello, is anybody there?' she called.* 「こんにちは，だれかいますか」と彼女は大きな声で言った．*He called out the names and the winners stepped forward.* 彼が大声で名前を呼ぶと，勝者たちが進み出た．*I could hear a man calling his dog.* 男が飼い犬を大声で呼んでいるのが聞こえた． ▶定義2 ❸❻ = **RING²**(1) ‖ *Who's calling, please?* どちら様ですか．*I'll call you tomorrow.* 明日電話します．*We're just in the middle of dinner. Can I call you back later?* 私たちは今ちょうど食事中です．後ほどかけ直してもよろしいですか． ▶定義3 **be called** to have as your name ～という名前を持っている➜**～と呼ばれる，～という名前だ** ‖ *His wife is called Silvia.* 彼の妻はシルビアという名だ．*What was that village called?* その村は何という名前だったのですか． ▶定義4 ❻ to name or describe a person or thing in a certain way ある方法で人や物を名付ける，あるいは言い表す➜

**名付ける，呼ぶ** ‖ *They called the baby Freddie.* 彼らはその赤ん坊をフレディーと名付けた．*It was very rude to call her fat.* 彼女を「でぶ」と呼ぶのはとても失礼だった．*Are you calling me a liar?* 私をうそつき呼ばわりするのですか．

▶定義5 ❻ to order or ask sb to come to a certain place 特定の場所に来るように～に命令する，あるいは頼む➜**～を呼び出す，招く，召喚する** ‖ *Can you call everybody in for lunch?* 昼食のために皆を呼び入れてくれませんか．*I think we had better call the doctor.* 医者を呼んだ方がいいと思う． ▶定義6 ❻ to arrange for sth to take place at a certain time ～がある決められた時刻に行われるように手配する➜**～を召集する，指令する** ‖ *to call a meeting/an election/a strike* 会議を召集する・選挙の実施を発表する・ストライキの指令を発する ▶定義7 ❸ call (in/round) (on sb/at...) to make a short visit to a person or place 人あるいは場所を短時間訪問する➜**(～に) 立ち寄る，(～を) ちょっと訪ねる** ‖ *I called in on Mike on my way home.* 帰宅途中に私はマイクの所に立ち寄った．*We called at his house but there was nobody in.* 私たちは彼の家に立ち寄ったが，だれもいなかった．

▶定義8 ❸ call at... (used about a train, etc) to stop at the places mentioned (列車などについて) 言及された場所で止まる➜**停車する** ‖ *This is the express service to London, calling at Manchester and Birmingham.* この列車はロンドン行きの急行です．マンチェスターとバーミンガムに停車します．

成句 bring/call sb/sth to mind ⇒ **MIND¹**
call it a day 略式 ▶定義 to decide to stop doing sth ～をすることをやめようと決める➜**切り上げる，おしまいにする** ‖ *Let's call it a day. I'm exhausted.* この辺で終わりにしよう．とても疲れた．

call sb's bluff ▶定義 to tell sb to actually do what he/she is threatening to do (believing that he/she will not risk doing it) 人が脅していることを実際にやれと～に言う (あえて実行することはないだろうと考えて)➜**やれるものならやってみろと挑む，けしかける**

call sb names ▶定義 to use insulting words about sb ～に対して侮辱する言葉を使う➜**悪口**

## 224　call²

を言う, ののしる

**call the shots/tune** 略式 ▶定義 to be in a position to control a situation and make decisions about what should be done 事態を統制し, するべき事を決断する立場にある→**命ずる, 指図する**

句動詞 **call by** 略式 ▶定義 to make a short visit to a place or person as you pass 通り掛かりに場所や人をちょっと訪問する→**立ち寄る, ちょっと訪ねる** || *I'll call by to pick up the book on my way to work.* 仕事に行く途中にちょっと寄ってその本を受け取ります.

**call for sb** 英 ▶定義 to collect sb in order to go somewhere together 一緒にどこかへ行くために〜を連れに行く→**〜を迎えに行く** || *I'll call for you when it's time to go.* 出掛ける時間になったら迎えに行きます.

**call for sth** ▶定義 to demand or need sth 〜を要求する, または必要とする→**〜が必要だ, 〜に値する** || *The crisis calls for immediate action.* その危機に対して即刻行動を起こさなければならない. *This calls for a celebration!* これはお祝いをしなくては.

**call sth off** ▶定義 to cancel sth 〜を取り消す→**〜を中止する, キャンセルする** || *The football match was called off because of the bad weather.* 悪天候のためフットボールの試合は中止された.

**call sb out** ▶定義 to ask sb to come, especially to an emergency 特に緊急事態の際〜に来るように頼む→**〜を出動させる, 召集する, 呼び出す** || *We had to call out the doctor in the middle of the night.* 私たちは真夜中に医者を呼ばなければならなかった.

**call sb up** ▶定義 **1** 特に 米 to telephone sb 〜に電話をかける→**〜に電話する** || *He called me up to tell me the good news.* 彼は私に良いニュースを伝えるため電話をしてきた. ▶定義 **2** to order sb to join the army, navy or air force 陸軍, 海軍または空軍に入隊するように〜に命令する→**〜を(軍隊に)召集する, 徴兵する** || *All men under 30 were called up to fight in the war.* 30歳以下の男子はすべて戦争のために召集された.

**call sth up** ▶定義 to look at sth that is stored in a computer コンピューターに保存された〜を見る→**〜をコンピューターで呼び出す, 検索する** || *The bank clerk called up my account details on screen.* 銀行員は私の預金の明細を画面に呼び出した.

★**call²** /kɔːl/ 名 ▶定義 **1** (または **phone call**) ⓒ an act of telephoning or a conversation on the telephone 電話をかけること, 電話での会話→**電話で話すこと, 電話の呼び出し** || *Were there any calls for me while I was out?* 出掛けている間に私に電話がありませんでしたか. *I'll give you a call at the weekend.* 週末にあなたに電話します. *to make a local call* 市内電話をかける *a long-distance call* 長距離電話 ▶定義 **2** ⓒ a loud sound that is made to attract attention; a shout 注意をひくための大きな音; 叫び声→**大声, 呼び声, 鳴き声** || *a call for help* 助けを求める叫び声 *That bird's call is easy to recognize.* あの鳥の鳴き声は容易に分かる. ▶定義 **3** ⓒ a short visit, especially to sb's house 特に人の家への短い訪問→**ちょっと立ち寄ること** || *We could pay a call on Dave on our way home.* 私たちは帰宅中にデーヴの家へ立ち寄ることができた. *The doctor has several calls to make this morning.* その医師は今日の午前中に数件の往診をしなければならない. ▶定義 **4** ⓒ a request, demand for sth 〜に対する要望, 要求など→**〜を要求すること** || *There have been calls for the President to resign.* 大統領の辞任が要求されている. ▶定義 **5** ⓒ Ⓤ **call for sth** a need for sth 〜の必要性→**〜を必要とすること** || *The doctor said there was no call for concern.* 医師は心配する必要はないと言った.

成句 **at sb's beck and call** ⇒ **BECK**

**(be) on call** ▶定義 to be ready to work if necessary 必要ならば仕事をする用意ができている→**いつでも呼び出しに応じられる, 待機している** || *Dr Young will be on call this weekend.* この週末はヤング医師が待機します.

**CALL³** /kɔːl/ 略 computer-assisted language learning→**コンピューター援用言語学習**

**call box** = TELEPHONE BOX

**caller** /kɔ́ːlər/ 名 ⓒ ▶定義 a person who telephones or visits sb 〜に電話をかけている人, または〜を訪問している人→**訪問者**

**callous** /kǽləs/ 形 ▶定義 not caring about the suffering of other people ほかの人々の苦しみを

気に掛けない→冷淡な, 無情な

**\*calm¹** /kɑːm/ 形 ▶定義1 not excited, worried or angry; quiet 興奮したり, 心配したり, 怒ったりしていない; 静かな→落ち着いた, 穏やかな ‖ Try to **keep calm** - there's no need to panic. 冷静に－うろたえる必要はありません. She spoke in a calm voice. 彼女は物静かな声で話した. The city is calm again after last night's riots. 昨夜の暴動の後, その都市は再び平穏に戻った.
▶定義2 without big waves 大きな波のない→穏やかな ‖ a calm sea 穏やかな海 ⇔ **rough**
▶定義3 without much wind あまり風のない→静かな, 穏やかな ‖ calm weather 穏やかな天候
— calmly 副→静かに, 穏やかに — calmness 名 Ư→平静, 静かなこと, 穏やかな様子

**calm²** /kɑːm/ 動 自他 ▶定義 calm (sb/sth) (down) to become or to make sb quiet or calm ～が静かに, または平静になる・させる→落ち着く, 落ち着かせる, なだめる ‖ Calm down! Shouting at everybody won't help. 落ち着きなさい. 皆に向かってどなってもどうにもなりません. I did some breathing exercises to calm my nerves. 私は神経を静めるためにちょっと深呼吸をした.

**calm³** /kɑːm/ 名 C Ư ▶定義 a period of time or a state when everything is peaceful すべてが平和な期間または状態→安らかな一時, 静けさ ‖ After living in the city, I enjoyed the calm of country life. 都会での生活の後, 私は田舎暮らしの静けさを楽しんだ.

**Calor gas**™ /kǽlər gæs/ 名 Ư ▶定義 gas that is kept in special bottles and used for cooking, heating, etc 専用のびんに詰められたガスで, 料理や暖房などに使われる→キャラーガス (家庭用ブタンガス)

**calorie** /kǽl(ə)ri/ 名 C ▶定義 a unit for measuring the energy value of food 食品のエネルギー値を計る単位→カロリー ‖ A fried egg contains about 100 calories. 目玉焼きは約100カロリーある. a low-calorie drink/yoghurt/diet 低カロリー飲料・低カロリーヨーグルト・低カロリー食品

**calves** CALF の複数形

**camcorder** /kǽmkɔːrdər/ 名 C ▶定義 a camera that you can carry around and use for recording pictures and sound on a video cassette 持ち運びできて, ビデオカセットに画像や音を記録できるカメラ→ポータブルビデオカメラ

**came** COME の過去形

camel

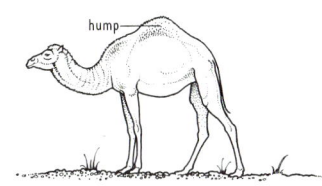

**\*camel** /kǽm(ə)l/ 名 C ▶定義 an animal that lives in the desert and has a long neck and either one or two large masses of fat (humps) on its back. It is used for carrying people and goods. 砂漠に住む動物で長い首を持ち, 背中に1つか2つの大きな脂肪の塊 (こぶ) を持つ. 人や物を運ぶために利用される→ラクダ

**cameo** /kǽmiòʊ/ 名 C ( 複 **cameos**) ▶定義1 a small part in a film or play that is usually played by a famous actor 一般に有名な俳優によって演じられる映画や劇の一部→名場面, 見せ場 ‖ Sean Connery plays a cameo role as the dying king. ショーン コネリーがひん死の王として短いが印象的なシーンを演じている. ▶定義2 a piece of jewellery that has a design in one colour and a background in a different colour 地の色と異なる色で模様がデザインされた装身具→カメオ, カメオ細工

camera

**\*camera** /kǽm(ə)rə/ 名 C ▶定義 a piece of equipment that you use for taking photographs or moving pictures 写真や映画を撮るために使う装置→カメラ, 写真機, テレビカメラ ‖ I need *a new film for my camera.* カメラに新しいフィルムを入れなければならない. *a video/television camera* ビデオカメラ・テレビカメラ

**cameraman** /kǽm(ə)rəmæ̀n, -mən/ 🔷 🅒 (複 **-men** /-mən, -mèn/) ▶定義 a person whose job is to operate a camera for a film or a television company 映画やテレビ会社でカメラを操作することを仕事とする人→カメラマン, 撮影技師 ☞参 **photographer**

**camouflage** /kǽməflà:ʒ, -dʒ/ 🔷 🅤 ▶定義1 materials or colours that soldiers use to make themselves and their equipment difficult to see 兵士が自分自身と装備をほかから見えにくくするために用いる材料や色→カムフラージュ, 偽装, 迷彩, 迷彩服 ▶定義2 the way in which an animal's colour or shape matches its surroundings and makes it difficult to see 動物の色や形が周囲と一致し, その動物を見えにくくしている様→擬態, 保護色 ‖ *The polar bear's white fur provides effective camouflage against the snow.* ホッキョクグマの白い毛皮は雪に対して効果的な保護色になる. ― **camouflage** 🔶 🅔 →～をカムフラージュする, 偽装する, ～に迷彩を施す

**camp**¹ /kæmp/ 🔷 🅒 🅤 ▶定義 a place where people live in tents or simple buildings away from their usual home 人々が普段住んでいる家から離れてテントや簡単な建物で生活する場所→キャンプ場, 野営地 ‖ *a refugee camp* 難民キャンプ *The climbers set up camp at the foot of the mountain.* 登山者たちは山のふもとにキャンプ場を設営した.

★**camp**² /kæmp/ 🔶 🅔 ▶定義 **camp (out)** to sleep without a bed, especially outside in a tent ベッドなしで, 特に屋外のテントの中で眠る→野営する, 野宿する ‖ *We camped next to a river.* 私たちは川のそばで野営した. ☞ **go camping** は楽しみのためにキャンプする場合に用いる普通の表現. *They went camping in France last year.* 彼らは去年フランスにキャンプに行った.

★**campaign**¹ /kæmpéɪn/ 🔷 🅒 ▶定義1 a plan to do a number of things in order to achieve a special aim 特定の目的を達成するためにいくつかの事をする計画→一連の作戦; 運動, キャンペーン ‖ *to launch an advertising/election campaign* 宣伝活動・選挙運動を開始する ▶定義2 a planned series of attacks in a war 戦争における計画的な一連の攻撃→軍事行動, 作戦行動; 戦闘

★**campaign**² /kæmpéɪn/ 🔶 🅔 ▶定義 **campaign (for/against sb/sth)** to take part in a planned series of activities in order to make sth happen or to prevent sth ～を起こすために, または防ぐために, 計画された一連の行動に参加する→(～の・～に反対の)運動をする, キャンペーンをする ‖ *Local people are campaigning for lower speed limits in the town.* 地元住民は街中の速度制限を下げるための運動をしている. ― **campaigner** 🔷 🅒 →運動をする人, 活動家 ‖ *an animal rights campaigner* 動物愛護活動家

**camp bed** (米 **cot**) 🔷 🅒 ▶定義 a light, narrow bed that you can fold up and carry easily 簡単に運べる, 軽く幅の狭いベッド→簡易ベッド, 折り畳み式ベッド ☞ **bed** のさし絵

**camper** /kǽmpər/ 🔷 🅒 ▶定義1 a person who stays in a tent on holiday 休暇にテントに泊まる人→キャンプする人, キャンパー ▶定義2 (米 または **camper van**) a motor vehicle in which you can sleep, cook, etc while on holiday 休暇に出掛けている間, 中で眠ったり, 料理をしたりできる自動車→キャンピングカー, (キャンプ用)トレーラー

**camping** /kǽmpɪŋ/ 🔷 🅤 ▶定義 sleeping or spending a holiday in a tent テントで眠ったり, 休暇を過ごしたりすること→キャンプ, キャンプ生活 ‖ *Camping is cheaper than staying in hotels.* キャンプはホテルに泊まるより安い. *to go on a camping holiday* 休暇にキャンプに行く

**campsite** /kǽmpsàɪt/ 🔷 🅒 ▶定義 a place where you can stay in a tent テントに泊まることのできる場所→キャンプ場, 野営地

**campus** /kǽmpəs/ 🔷 🅒 🅤 (複 **campuses**) ▶定義 the area of land where the main buildings of a college or university are 単科大学や総合大学の主な建物がある敷地→キャンパス, 大学構内 ‖ *the college campus* 大学のキャンパス

★**can**¹ /k(ə)n 強形 kæn/ 法助動詞 (否定形 **cannot** /kǽnɑt, kənɑ́t, kænʌ́t, kǽnət/ 短縮形 **can't** /kɑ:nt; kænt/; 過去形 **could** /kəd 強形 kʊd/; 否定形 **could not** 短縮形 **couldn't** /kʊdnt, kʊdnt/ ) ▶定義1 used for showing that it is possible for sb/sth to do sth or that sb/sth has the ability to do sth ～が何かをすることが可能であることを

表す場合, または〜が何かをする能力があることを表す場合に用いる→〜できる ‖ *Can you ride a bike?* 自転車に乗れますか. *He can't speak French.* 彼はフランス語を話せない.

➤ can には不定詞形と分詞形はない. 未来時制と完了時制を作るには, be able to を使う: *He's been able to swim for almost a year.* (彼が泳ぎを覚えてからほぼ1年になる.) could have は人が何かをする能力があったのに, それをしなかった場合に用いる: *She could have passed the exam but she didn't really try.* (彼女は試験に合格できただろうに, 努力をしなかった.)

▶定義2 used to ask for or give permission 許可を求める場合や許可を与える場合に用いる→〜してもよい, 差し支えない ‖ *Can I have a drink, please?* 飲み物を頂けますか. *He asked if he could have a drink.* 彼は飲み物をもらえないか尋ねた.

➤過去の一般的な許可について話している場合, could が用いられる: *I could do anything I wanted when I stayed with my grandma.* (おばあさんの所にいた時はやりたい事は何でもできた.) 1回だけの特定の場合について話している場合には could は用いない: *They were allowed to visit him in hospital yesterday.* (彼らは昨日, 彼を見舞うことを許可された (見舞いに行くことができた).)

▶定義3 used to ask sb to do sth 〜に…をしてくれるように頼む場合に用いる→〜してくれますか, 〜してくれませんか ‖ *Can you help me carry these books?* これらの本を運ぶのを手伝ってくれませんか. ▶定義4 used for offering to do sth 〜をすることを申し出る場合に用いる→〜しましょうか ‖ *Can I help at all?* お手伝いしましょうか.

➤法助動詞の詳細については, 巻末の「文法早見表」を参照.

▶定義5 used to talk about sb's typical behaviour or of a typical effect 〜に典型的な行動や影響について言う場合に用いる→〜するものだ, 〜なものだ ‖ *You can be very annoying.* あなたにはとてもいらいらする. *Wasp stings can be very painful.* スズメバチに刺されるととても痛いものだ. ▶定義6 used in the negative for saying that you are sure sth is not true 否定形で〜が真実でないと確信していると言う場合に用

## can³ 227

いる→〜であるはずがない, あり得ない ‖ *That can't be Maria - she's in London.* マリアであるはずがない − 彼女はロンドンにいるのだから. *Surely you can't be hungry. You've only just had lunch.* まさかおなかがすいているはずはないだろう. 昼食を食べたばかりなのだから.

▶定義7 used with the verbs 'feel', 'hear', 'see', 'smell', 'taste' feel, hear, see, smell, taste などの動詞と共に用いて→〜を感じている, 〜が聞こえて・見えている, 〜のにおいがする, 〜の味がする

➤これらの動詞は進行形では用いない. 特定の瞬間に見ている事や聞いている事を言いたい場合に can を用いる: *I can smell something burning.* (何かが焦げているにおいがする.) I'm smelling... とは言わない.

### ▶音声とつづり字

#### can の強弱

can は助動詞なので, 普通の発音は母音があいまいになるいわゆる弱形語 (weak form word) で [kən クン²] のように発音します. しかし, 文頭と特に文末では強形になり, [kʰæn ケアン²] のように発音します. canが弱形のとき後続音によって変化することが多いです.

また, n は, I can[m] make it. (私でやれる) では, mの影響で[m]になり, I can[ŋ] go. (行ける) では, gの影響で[ŋ] になります.

★**can**² /kæn/ 名  ▶定義1 a metal or plastic container that is used for holding or carrying liquid 液体を入れたり運ぶために使われる金属やプラスチックの容器→缶 ‖ *an oil can* 油の缶 *a watering can* じょうろ ▶定義2 a metal container in which food or drink is kept without air so that it stays fresh 食品や飲料を空気が遮断された状態にし, 新鮮さを保つための金属容器→缶, 缶詰 ‖ *a can of sardines* イワシの缶詰 *a can of beer* 缶ビール ☞ **container** のさし絵

➤食品が入った缶の場合はイギリス英語では通常 tin を用いる. can は飲料に用いる.

**can**³ /kæn/ 動 他 (**canning**; **canned**) ▶定義 to put food, drink, etc into a can in order to keep it fresh for a long time 長期間新鮮に保つために食品, 飲料などを缶に詰める→〜を缶詰にする ‖

*canned fruit* 缶詰の果物

**★canal** /kənǽl/ 名 C ▶定義1 a deep cut that is made through land so that boats or ships can travel along it or so that water can flow to an area where it is needed ボートや船が通行できるようにするため、または水が必要な地域まで流れるようにするために地面に掘った深い溝→運河, 水路, 掘り割り ‖ *the Panama Canal* パナマ運河 ▶定義2 one of the tubes in the body through which food, air, etc passes 食物, 空気などが通過する体内の管の1つ→(導)管, 脈管

**canary** /kənéəri/ 名 C (複 **canaries**) ▶定義 a small yellow bird that sings and is often kept in a cage as a pet (美しい声で)さえずる黄色の小鳥で、ペットとしてかごで飼われることが多い→カナリア

**★cancel** /kǽns(ə)l/ 動他 (**cancelling**; **cancelled**; 米 **canceling**; **canceled**) ▶定義1 to decide that sth that has been planned or arranged will not happen 既に計画されてしまった、または手配しておいた～を行わないと決める→～を取り消す, 中止する ‖ *All flights have been cancelled because of the bad weather.* 悪天候のためすべての便が中止になりました. ☛参 **postpone** ▶定義2 to stop sth that you asked for or agreed to 頼んだ～や同意した～をやめる→～を取り消す, 無効にする, 解約する, キャンセルする ‖ *to cancel a reservation* 予約をキャンセルする *I wish to cancel my order for these books.* これらの本の注文を取り消したい.

句動詞 cancel (sth) out ▶定義 to be equal or have an equal effect 同等になる、または同等の効果がある→埋め合わす, ～を相殺する, ～を帳消しにする ‖ *What I owe you is the same as what you owe me, so our debts cancel each other out.* 私が借りている金は, あなたに貸した額と同じなのだから, 貸し借りはなしです.

**cancellation** /kǽns(ə)léɪʃ(ə)n/ 名 C U ▶定義 the act of cancelling sth ～を取り消すこと→取り消し, 解除 ‖ *We had to make a last-minute cancellation.* 私たちは土壇場でキャンセルしなければならなかった.

**cancer** /kǽnsər/ 名 C U ▶定義1 a very serious disease in which lumps grow in the body 体内にしこりができる非常に重い病気→がん, がん腫 ‖ *She has lung cancer.* 彼女は肺がんにかかっている. *He died of cancer.* 彼はがんで亡くなった. ▶定義2 **Cancer** the fourth sign of the zodiac, the Crab 黄道十二宮の4番目である蟹(かに)座→蟹座, 巨蟹(きょかい)宮

**cancerous** /kǽnsərəs/ 形 ▶定義 (used especially about a part of the body or sth growing in the body) having cancer (特に体の一部や, 体に生じた～について)がんにかかっている→がんの, がんのような ‖ *a cancerous growth* がん腫 *cancerous cells* がん細胞

**candid** /kǽndəd/ 形 ▶定義 saying exactly what you think; frank 考えている事をそっくりそのまま言う, 率直な→遠慮のない, ざっくばらんな ☛ 名 candour — **candidly** 副→率直に, 遠慮なく

**candidacy** /kǽndədəsi/ 名 U ▶定義 being a candidate 候補者であること→立候補(資格)

**★candidate** /kǽndədèɪt, -dət/ 名 C ▶定義1 a person who makes a formal request to be considered for a job or wants to be elected to a particular position ある仕事に就けるよう考慮してほしいと正式に要求する人, または特定の地位に選出されたいと望む人→候補者, 立候補者 ‖ *We have some very good candidates for the post.* その職にぴったりの候補者が何人かいる. ▶定義2 a person who is taking an exam 試験を受ける人→志願者, 受験者

**candle** /kǽndl/ 名 C ▶定義 a round stick of solid oil or fat (**wax**) with a piece of string (**a wick**) through the middle that you can burn to give light 中心に糸(芯(しん))を通した固形の油や脂(ろう)の丸い棒で, 燃やして明かりにする→ろうそく ‖ *to light/blow out a candle* ろうそくに火をつける・ろうそくを吹き消す

**candle**
flame
wick
candle
candlestick
wax

**candlelight** /kǽndllàɪt/ 名 U ▶定義 light that comes from a candle ろうそくから発せられる光→ろうそくの明かり ‖ *They had dinner by candlelight.* 彼らはろうそくの明かりで食事をした.

**candlestick** /kǽndlstìk/ 名 C ▶定義 an object for holding a candle or candles 1本のまたは複数のろうそくを立てるためのもの→燭(しょく)台, ろうそく立て ☛ **candle** のさし絵

**candour** (米 **candor**) /kǽndər, -dɔ̀ːr/ 名 U ▶定義 the quality of being honest; saying exactly what you think 正直であること; 考えている事をそっくりそのまま言うこと→率直さ, 誠実さ, 公平, 公正 ☛ 形 **candid**

**candy** /kǽndi/ 名 C U (複 **candies**) 米 = **SWEET²(1)** ‖ *You eat too much candy.* あなたはキャンデーを食べすぎだ.

**cane** /kéɪn/ 名 ▶定義1 C U the long central part of certain plants (bamboo or sugar) that is like a tube and is used as a material for making furniture, etc ある種の植物(竹やサトウキビ)の管のように長い中心部分で, 家具などを作る材料として使われる→茎, 籐(とう)類 ‖ *sugar cane* サトウキビ *a cane chair* 籐いす ▶定義2 C a stick that is used to help sb walk 〜が歩くのを補助するために使われる棒→つえ, ステッキ

**canine** /kéɪnaɪn/ 形 ▶定義 connected with dogs 犬に関連した→イヌ科の, 犬の

**canister** /kǽnəstər/ 名 C ▶定義 a small round metal container 丸い小型の金属容器→缶; 金属製の筒, ボンベ ‖ *a gas canister* ガスボンベ

**cannabis** /kǽnəbəs/ 名 U ▶定義 a drug made from a plant (hemp) that some people smoke for pleasure, but which is illegal in many countries 一部の人々が快楽のために吸う, 植物(大麻)から作られる薬物で, 多くの国では違法→大麻, カンナビス

**cannibal** /kǽnəb(ə)l/ 名 C ▶定義 a person who eats other people ほかの人間を食べる人々→食人者, 人食い人種 — **cannibalism** /kǽnəb(ə)lìz(ə)m/ 名 U→人食い(の風習), 共食い, カニバリズム

**cannon** /kǽnən/ 名 C (複 **cannon** または **cannons**) ▶定義1 a large gun on a ship, army vehicle, aircraft, etc 船, 軍用車, 航空機などの大型の火砲→大砲, 機関砲 ▶定義2 a large, simple gun that was used in past times for firing large stone or metal balls (cannon balls) 昔, 大きな石や金属の球(球形砲弾)を発射するために使われた大型の単純な砲→カノン(砲)

**cannot** /kǽnɑt, kənɑ́t, kǽnət/ **CAN¹** の否定形

**canoe** /kənúː/ 名 C ▶定義 a light, narrow boat for one or two people that you can move through the water using a flat piece of wood (a paddle) 1人用または2人乗りの軽く幅の狭いボートで, 平らな木片(パドル)を使って水面を移動できる→カヌー, 丸木舟 ☛参 **kayak** ☛ **boat** のさし絵 — **canoe** 動 自 (現分 canoeing; 三単現 canoes; 過, 過分 canoed) →カヌーをこぐ, カヌーで行く ‖ *They canoed down the river.* 彼らはカヌーで川を下った. ☛ カヌーに乗って時を過ごすことを言う場合は, go canoeing と言う方が普通. *We're going canoeing on the river tomorrow.* 明日は川にカヌー遊びに行く予定だ.

**canon** /kǽnən/ 名 C ▶定義 a Christian priest who works in a large church (cathedral) 大きな教会(大聖堂)で働くキリスト教の聖職者→司教座聖堂参事会員

**canopy** /kǽnəpi/ 名 C (複 **canopies**) ▶定義 a cover that hangs or spreads above sth 〜の上につり下がった, または広がった覆い→天蓋(てんがい), 天蓋のように覆う物, 天蓋のようなひさし ‖ *The highest branches in the rainforest form a dense canopy.* 熱帯雨林の最も高い所にある枝は厚い天蓋のようだ. *a parachute canopy* パラシュートの傘

**can't** **CANNOT** の短縮形

**canteen** /kæntíːn/ 名 C ▶定義 the place in a school, factory, office, etc where the people who work there can get meals 学校, 工場, 会社などの中にある, 従業員や学生が食事を取れる場所→大食堂, 学食 ‖ *the staff canteen* 社員食堂 ☛参 **cafeteria**

**canter** /kǽntər/ 動 自 ▶定義 (used about a horse and its rider) to run fairly fast but not very (馬と馬に乗る人について) 比較的速いが, 速足というほどでもない速度で走る→緩い駆け足で走る, キャンターで走る ‖ *We cantered along the beach.* 海岸で緩い駆け足で馬を走らせた. — **canter** 名 [単数扱い] →緩い駆け足, キャンター(で走ること) ☛参 **gallop**, **trot**

**canvas** /kǽnvəs/ 名 ▶定義1 U a type of strong cloth that is used for making sails, bags, tents, etc 帆, 袋, テントなどを作るために使われる丈夫な布→ズック, キャンバス地 ▶定義2 C a piece of strong cloth for painting a picture on 絵をかくための丈夫な布→カンバス, 画布

**canvass** /kǽnvəs/ 動 ▶定義1 ❸⓾ canvass (sb) (for sth) to try to persuade people to vote for a particular person or party in an election or to support sb/sth 選挙で特定の人や政党に投票するように、または～を支持するように人を説得しようとする→**選挙運動をする** ‖ *to canvass for votes* 投票するように勧誘する *He's canvassing for the Conservative Party.* 彼は保守党を支持して運動している. *The Prime Minister is trying to canvass support for the plan.* 首相はその計画の支持を求めて説得しようとしている. ▶定義2 ⓾ to find out what people's opinions are about sth ～についての人々の意見を調べる→**世論調査をする, 念入りに調べる**

**canyon** /kǽnjən/ 名 ❸ ▶定義 a deep valley with very steep sides 両側が非常に急勾配(こうばい)の深い谷→**深い峡谷, 大峡谷**

★**cap**¹ /kæp/ 名 ❸ ▶定義1 a soft hat that has a part sticking out at the front (peak) 突き出した部分(ひさし)が前部にある柔らかい帽子→**(縁なしの)帽子** ‖ *a baseball cap* 野球帽 ☛ **hat** のさし絵 ▶定義2 a soft hat that is worn for a particular purpose 特定の目的のためにかぶる柔らかい帽子→**帽子, 帽子状の物** ‖ *a shower cap* シャワーキャップ ▶定義3 a hat that is given to a player who is chosen to play for his/her country 国のために試合をするよう選ばれた選手に与えられる帽子→**(代表チームの)選手帽** ‖ *He won his first cap against France.* 彼は対フランス戦の代表選手に初めて選ばれた. ▶定義4 a covering for the end or top of sth ～の端や先端の覆い→**ふた, キャップ, 口金** ‖ *Please put the cap back on the bottle.* びんにもう一度ふたをしてください. ☛参 **top**¹ の注 ☛ **container** のさし絵

**cap**² /kæp/ 動 ⓾ (**capping**; **capped**) ▶定義1 to cover the top of sth ～の先端を覆う→**～にふたをする, キャップを付ける; 上部を覆う** ‖ *mountains capped with snow* 頂上に雪を頂いた山 ▶定義2 to limit the amount of money that can be spent on sth ～に使うことのできる金額を制限する→**～の上限を設定する** ▶定義3 to follow sth with sth bigger or better より大きい、またはより良い～でほかの…の後に続く→**(人のする事・言う事)の上手(うわて)をいく, ～をしのぐ** ▶定義4 (sport) to choose a player to represent his/her country (スポーツ) 国を代表する選手を選ぶ→**(選手帽を与えて)代表チームに加える** 成句 **to cap it all** ▶定義 as a final piece of bad luck 不運続きの最後の出来事として→**挙げ句の果てに** ‖ *I had a row with my boss, my bike was stolen, and now to cap it all I've lost my keys!* 上司と口論になり, 自転車を盗まれ, 挙げ句の果てにかぎまでなくした.

**capability** /kèɪpəbíləti/ 名 ❸ ⓤ (優 **capabilities**) ▶定義 capability (to do sth/of doing sth) the quality of being able to do sth 何かができるという特性→**能力, 才能** ‖ *Animals in the zoo have lost the capability to catch/of catching food for themselves.* 動物園の動物たちは自分でえさを捕まえる能力をなくしている. *I tried to fix the computer, but it was beyond my capabilities.* 私はコンピューターを修理しようとしたが, 手に負えなかった.

★**capable** /kéɪpəb(ə)l/ 形 ▶定義1 capable of (doing) sth having the ability or qualities necessary to do sth 何かをするために必要な能力や性質がある→**～できて, 可能で** ‖ *He's capable of passing the exam if he tries harder.* もっと努力すれば, 彼には試験に合格する力がある. *That car is capable of 180 miles per hour.* あの車は時速180マイルを出すことができる. *I don't believe that she's capable of stealing.* 彼女は盗みのできるような人ではないと思う. ▶定義2 having a lot of skill; good at doing sth 多くの技術を持っている; 何かをするのが上手な→**有能な, 腕利きの** ‖ *She's a very capable teacher.* 彼女は非常に有能な教師だ. ⇔ **incapable** — **capably** 副→**立派に, 上手に**

**capacity** /kəpǽsəti/ 名 (優 **capacities**) ▶定義1 [単数扱い] ⓤ the amount that a container or space can hold 容器や空間が収容することのできる量→**容量, 収容力, 定員** ‖ *The tank has a capacity of 1000 litres.* そのタンクの容量は1000リットルだ. *The stadium was filled to capacity.* スタジアムは満員だった. ▶定義2 [単数扱い] a capacity (for sth/for doing sth); a capacity (to do sth) the ability to understand or do sth ～を理解したり行ったりする能力→**才能, 理解力, 力量** ‖ *That book is beyond the capacity of young children.* あの本は小さい子供には理解できない. *a capacity for hard* *work/for learning languages* 勤勉に努力できる資質・語学の才能 ▶定義3 ❻the official position that sb has ～の公的な地位→**資格, 立場** ‖ *In his capacity as chairman of the council...* 会議の議長としての立場で… ▶定義4 ［単数扱い，❶］the amount that a factory or machine can produce 工場や機械が生産できる量→**(最大)生産力, 産出力** ‖ *The power station is working at full capacity.* 発電所はフル稼働している.

**cape** /kéɪp/ 名 ❻ ▶定義1 a piece of clothing with no sleeves that hangs from your shoulders 肩に掛けるそでなしの衣類→**ケープ, 肩マント** ☛参 **cloak** ▶定義2 a piece of high land that sticks out into the sea 海に突き出した高い土地→**岬, ～岬** ‖ *the Cape of Good Hope* 喜望峰

\***capital**[1] /kǽp(ə)t(ə)l/ 名 ▶定義1 (または **capital city**) ❻the town or city where the government of a country is 一国の政府がある町または市→**首都, 首府** ‖ *Madrid is the capital of Spain.* マドリードはスペインの首都だ. ▶定義2 ❶an amount of money that you use to start a business or to put in a bank, etc so that you earn more money (interest) on it それを元手にして，さらに金(利子)をもうけられるように，事業を始めたり，または銀行に預けたりするために使われる金額→**資本金, 資金, 元金** ‖ *When she had enough capital, she bought a shop.* 十分な資金ができると，彼女は店を買った. ▶定義3 (または **capital letter**) ❻the large form of a letter of the alphabet アルファベットの文字の大きい形→**大文字** ‖ *Write your name in capitals.* 名前を大文字で書きなさい. ▶定義4 ❻a place that is well-known for a particular thing 特定の物事のためによく知られている場所→**中心地, 名所, メッカ** ‖ *Niagara Falls is the honeymoon capital of the world.* ナイアガラの滝は世界のハネムーンのメッカだ.

**capital**[2] /kǽp(ə)t(ə)l/ 形 ▶定義1 connected with punishment by death 死による罰に関連した→**死刑に値する, 死刑の** ‖ *a capital offence (= a crime for which sb can be sentenced to death)* 極刑に値する罪(= ～が死刑判決を受けるような犯罪) ▶定義2 (used about letters of the alphabet) written in the large form (アルファベットの文字について) 大きな形で書かれた→**大文字で書かれた, 大文字の** ‖ *'David' begins with a capital 'D'.* David は大文字の D で始まる.

---

**capsule** 231

**capital investment** 名 ❶ ▶定義 money that a business spends on buildings, equipment, etc 事業で建物や機器などに費やされる金→**設備投資, 資本投資**

**capitalism** /kǽp(ə)t(ə)lìz(ə)m/ 名 ❶ ▶定義 the economic system in which businesses are owned and run for profit by individuals and not by the state 国ではなく個人が企業を所有し, 利潤のための経営をする経済体制→**資本主義, 資本主義制度** ☛参 **communism, Marxism, socialism** — **capitalist** 名 ❻形 →**資本主義者(の), 資本家(の), 資本主義の, 資本を保有する**

**capitalize** (または **-ise**) /kǽp(ə)t(ə)làɪz/ 動 句動 capitalize on sth ▶定義 to use sth to your advantage ～を自分にとって有利に使う→**～を利用する, ～に乗ずる** ‖ *We can capitalize on the mistakes that our rivals have made.* 我々はライバルのミスに付け込むことができる.

**capital punishment** 名 ❶ ▶定義 punishment by death for serious crimes 重大な犯罪に対する死による刑罰→**死刑, 極刑** ☛参 **death penalty** 比較 **corporal punishment**

**capitulate** /kəpítʃəlèɪt/ 動 ❺ 正式 ▶定義 to stop fighting and accept that you have lost; to give in to sb 戦いをやめ敗北を認める; ～に屈服する→**降伏する, 抵抗をやめる; 従う** — **capitulation** /kəpìtʃəléɪʃ(ə)n/ 名 ❻ ❶ →**降伏, 屈服すること**

**capricious** /kəprí∫əs, -prí-/ 形 ▶定義 changing behaviour suddenly in a way that is difficult to predict 突然, 予期することができないやり方で行動を変える→**気まぐれな, 移り気な** ‖ *a capricious actor* 気まぐれな俳優

**Capricorn** /kǽprɪkɔ̀ːrn/ 名 ❻ ❶ ▶定義 the tenth sign of the zodiac, the Goat 黄道十二宮の 10 番目である山羊座→**山羊座, 磨羯(まかつ)宮**

**capsize** /kǽpsaɪz, ˌ-ˈ-/ 動 ❺ ❺ ▶定義 (used about boats) to turn over in the water (船について) 水の中でひっくり返る→**転覆する, ～を転覆させる** ‖ *The canoe capsized.* カヌーがひっくり返った. *A big wave capsized the yacht.* 大波でヨットが転覆した.

**capsule** /kǽpsəl, -suːl; -sjʊl/ 名 ❻ ▶定義1 a very small closed tube of medicine that you swallow 薬が密封された非常に小さい円筒で, 飲み込む

ためのもの➡カプセル ☛ **bandage** のさし絵 ▶定義2 a container that is closed so that air, water, etc cannot enter 空気や水などが入らないように密封された容器➡カプセル, 小さな容器

**Capt** 略 Captain ▶定義 a rank in the British and American armies 英国と米国の軍隊の一階級➡大尉, 海軍大佐

★**captain**¹ /kǽptən/ 名 C ▶定義1 the person who is in command of a ship or an aircraft 船や航空機で指揮を取る人➡船長, 艦長, 機長 ▶定義2 a person who is the leader of a group or team 集団やチームの指揮者➡キャプテン, 主将; 長 ‖ *Who's (the) captain of the French team?* フランスチームのキャプテンはだれですか. ▶定義3 an officer at a middle level in the army or navy 陸軍や海軍の中位階級の人➡陸軍大尉, 海軍大佐

**captain**² /kǽptən/ 動 他 ▶定義 to be the captain of a group or team 集団やチームのキャプテンになる➡〜の主将になる, 〜を統率する, 指揮する

**caption** /kǽpʃ(ə)n/ 名 C ▶定義 the words that are written above or below a picture, photograph, etc to explain what it is about さし絵, 写真などの上や下に書かれた, それが何を表しているかを説明するための言葉➡キャプション, 短い説明文

**captivate** /kǽptəvèɪt/ 動 他 ▶定義 to attract and hold sb's attention 〜の注意を引き付けて放さない➡〜の心を奪う, 〜をとりこにする, うっとりさせる — **captivating** 形➡うっとりさせるような, 魅惑的な

**captive**¹ /kǽptɪv/ 形 ▶定義 kept as a prisoner; (used about animals) kept in a cage, etc 囚人として捕われている; (動物について) おりなどに閉じ込められている➡捕虜の, 閉じ込められた, 捕らえられた ‖ (比喩) *a captive audience* (= listening because they cannot leave) 捕われの聴衆 (= 去ることができないので嫌でも聞いている)

成句 **hold sb captive** ▶定義 to keep sb as a prisoner and not allow him/her to escape 〜を囚人として捕まえておいて逃げ出せないようにする➡〜を捕虜にしておく

**take sb captive** ▶定義 to catch sb and hold him/her as your prisoner 〜を捕まえて囚人として閉じ込めておく➡〜を捕虜にする ☛ hold sb prisoner, take sb prisoner の用法も可.

**captive**² /kǽptɪv/ 名 C ▶定義 a prisoner 捕われた人➡捕虜, 捕らえられた者

**captivity** /kæptívəti/ 名 U ▶定義 the state of being kept in a place that you cannot escape from 脱出できない場所に閉じ込められている状態➡監禁状態, 束縛状態, 捕われの身 ‖ *Wild animals are often unhappy in captivity.* 野生動物は, 閉じ込められた状態では不適切である場合が多い.

**captor** /kǽptər, -tɔːr/ 名 C ▶定義 a person who takes or keeps a person as a prisoner 人を囚人として捕まえる, または閉じ込めておく人➡捕らえる人, 逮捕する人

**capture**¹ /kǽptʃər/ 動 他 ▶定義1 to take a person or animal prisoner 人や動物を捕われの身にする➡〜を捕らえる, 捕虜にする, 逮捕する ‖ *The lion was captured and taken back to the zoo.* ライオンは捕らえられて動物園に戻された. ▶定義2 to take control of sth 〜を支配する➡〜を占領する, 攻略する ‖ *The town has been captured by the rebels.* 街は反逆者に占領されている. *The company has captured 90% of the market.* その会社は市場の90パーセントを支配している. ▶定義3 to make sb interested in sth 〜に…への興味を持たせる➡(人の心・注意など)を捕らえる, 引き付ける ‖ *The story captured the children's imagination/interest/attention.* その物語は子供たちの想像力をかき立てた・興味を引き付けた・注目を集めた.

▶定義4 to succeed in representing or recording sth in words, pictures, etc 〜を言葉, 絵などで表現したり記録したりすることに成功する➡〜をうまく表現する ‖ *This poem captures the atmosphere of the carnival.* この詩はカーニバルの雰囲気をよく捕らえている. *The robbery was captured on video.* 強盗の様子がビデオにしっかりと映っていた.

**capture**² /kǽptʃər/ 名 U ▶定義 the act of capturing sth or being captured 〜を捕らえること, または捕らえられること➡捕獲, 生け捕り, 逮捕

★**car** /kɑːr/ 名 C ▶定義1 (特に 米 **automobile**) a road vehicle with four wheels that can carry a small number of people 少数の人を乗せる4つ

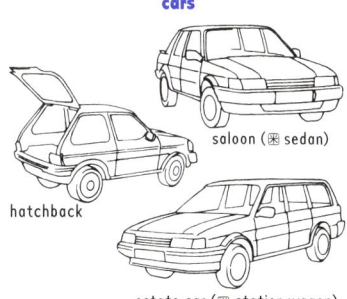

cars

hatchback

saloon (米 sedan)

estate car (米 station wagon)

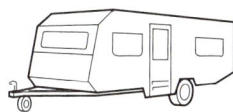

caravan

の車輪のある陸上の乗り物➔**車, 自動車, 乗用車** ‖ *a new/second-hand car* 新車・中古車 *Where can I park the car?* どこに駐車できますか. *They had a car crash.* 彼らは自動車の衝突事故に遭った. *to get into/out of a car* 車に乗る・車から降りる

➤ go in the car または by car は車で行く. 動詞 drive も用いられる: *I come to work in the car/by car.*（私は車で通勤している.）*I drive to work.*（私は車で通勤している.）

☞ S7 ページのさし絵 ▶定義**2** 英 a section of a train that is used for a particular purpose 列車で特定の目的に使われる部分➔**車両, 〜車** ‖ *a dining/sleeping car* 食堂車・寝台車 ▶定義**3** 英 = CARRIAGE(1)

**carafe** /kərɑ́ːf, -rǽf/ 图 ❻ ▶定義 a glass container like a bottle with a wide neck, in which wine or water is served 広首のびんのようなガラス容器で, これでワインや水を出す➔**(食卓に置く) ガラスの水差し, カラフ** ☞ jug のさし絵

**caramel** /kǽrəm(ə)l, -mèl/ 图 ▶定義**1** Ⓤ burnt sugar that is used to add flavour and colour to food 食品に風味と色を加えるために用いられる焦がした砂糖➔**カラメル** ▶定義**2** ❻Ⓤ a type of sticky sweet that is made from boiled sugar, butter and milk 煮詰めた砂糖, バター, ミルクから作られる柔らかい菓子➔**キャラメル**

**carat** ( 米 **karat**) /kǽrət/ 图 ❻ ▶定義 a unit for measuring how pure gold is or how heavy jewels are 金の純度や宝石の重さを計る単位➔**カラット** ‖ *a 20-carat gold ring* 20 カラットの金の指輪

★**caravan** /kǽrəvæ̀n/ 图 ❻ ▶定義**1**（米**trailer**) a large vehicle that is pulled by a car. You can sleep, cook, etc in a caravan when you are travelling or on holiday. 自動車で引っ張る大型の乗り物. 旅行や休暇のときにはこの中で眠ったり, 料理したりできる➔**移動住宅, トレーラーハウス** ☞ go caravanning は休暇にトレーラーハウスを使うこと. ▶定義**2** a group of people and animals that travel together, for example across a desert 例えば砂漠などを横断して旅する人と動物の一団➔**隊商, キャラバン (隊)**

**carbohydrate** /kɑ̀ːrbəhάidreit/ 图 ❻Ⓤ ▶定義 one of the substances in food, for example sugar, that gives your body energy 食物, 例えば砂糖などに含まれる物質で体にエネルギーを与える物➔**炭水化物, 含水炭素** ‖ *Athletes need a diet that is high in carbohydrate.* スポーツ選手には炭水化物を多く含む食事が必要だ. *Bread and rice contain carbohydrates.* パンと米には炭水化物が含まれている.

**carbon** /kάːrbən/ 图 Ⓤ (元素記号 **C**) ▶定義 a chemical substance that is found in all living things, and also in diamonds, coal, petrol etc すべての生物, またダイヤモンド, 石炭, ガソリンなどにも含まれる化学物質➔**炭素**

**carbon copy** 图 ❻ ▶定義**1** a copy of a letter, etc that was made using special paper (**carbon paper**) 手紙などを特別な紙 (カーボン紙) を使って写したもの➔**(カーボン紙を使った) 写し** ▶定義**2** an exact copy of sth 〜の正確な写し➔**そっくりな物, うり二つ**

**carbon dioxide** /kɑ̀ːrbən daiάksaid/ 图 Ⓤ (元素記号 $CO_2$) ▶定義 a gas that has no colour or smell that people and animals breathe out of their lungs 人や動物の肺から吐き出される無色, 無臭の気体➔**二酸化炭素, 炭酸ガス**

**carbon monoxide** /kɑ̀ːrbən mənάksaid/ 图 Ⓤ (元素記号 **CO**) ▶定義 a poisonous gas. Motor vehicles produce a lot of carbon monoxide. 有毒な気体. 自動車によって大量に生成される→一酸化炭素

**carbon paper** 名 U ▶定義 thin paper with a dark substance on one side that you put between two sheets of paper to make a copy of what you are writing 片面に黒い物質が付いた薄い紙で, 2枚の紙の間に挟んで書いている内容の写しを作成する→カーボン紙

**car boot sale** 名 C ▶定義 an outdoor sale where people sell things they do not want from the back of their cars 車の後部で, 不用になった物を売る屋外の売り出し→トランクセール, ガレージセール

**carburettor** (米 **carburetor**) /kɑ́ːrb(j)ərétər, -rèɪtər/ 名 C ▶定義 the piece of equipment in a car's engine that mixes petrol and air ガソリンと空気を混合させるための自動車のエンジンにある装置→気化器, キャブレター

**carcass** /kɑ́ːrkəs/ 名 C ▶定義 the dead body of an animal 動物の死体→(動物の)死骸(しがい), 屠殺(とさつ)体 ☞参 corpse

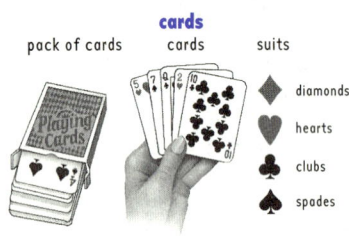

pack of cards / cards / suits
diamonds / hearts / clubs / spades
jack / queen / king / ace / joker

*****card** /kɑːrd/ 名 ▶定義1 U thick rigid paper 厚く硬い紙→厚紙, カード ▶定義2 C a piece of card or plastic that has information on it 情報が記載されたカードやプラスチック→カード, 券 ‖ *Here is my business card in case you need to contact me.* 私に連絡するときのために名刺を差し上げます. *a membership/identity/credit card* 会員証・身分証明証・クレジットカード

▶定義3 C a piece of card with a picture on it that you use for sending a special message to sb 特別の伝言を〜に送るために使う絵の付いたカード, はがき ‖ *a Christmas/birthday card* クリスマスカード・バースデーカード *a get-well card* (= *one that you send to sb who is ill*) お見舞いのカード (= 病気の〜に送るカード) ▶定義4 (または **playing card**) C one of a set of 52 small pieces of card with shapes or pictures on them that are used for playing games ゲームをするために使う, 図柄や絵の付いた52枚一組の小さなカードの1枚→トランプ(の札) ‖ *a pack of cards* 一組のトランプ ▶定義5 **cards** [複数扱い] games that are played with cards トランプで行うゲーム→トランプ遊び ‖ *Let's play cards.* トランプをやろう. *Let's have a game of cards.* トランプで遊ぼう. *I never win at cards!* 私はトランプで勝ったことがない.

▶ a pack of cards (一組のトランプ) は, 赤2組 (hearts (ハート) と diamonds (ダイヤ)) と黒2組 (clubs (クラブ) と spades (スペード)) の four suits (4組) に分かれている. 各組ごとに, ace (エース), king (キング), queen (クイーン), jack (ジャック) と2から10の数字が付いた9種類のカードがある. トランプを始める前にトランプを混ぜることを shuffle, 切ることを cut, そして配ることを deal と言う.

成句 **on the cards**; 米 **in the cards** 略式 ▶定義 likely to happen 起こりそうな→多分〜らしい ‖ *Their marriage break-up has been on the cards for some time now.* 彼らの結婚の破たんはしばらく前から予想が付いていた.

*****cardboard** /kɑ́ːrdbɔ̀ːrd/ 名 U ▶定義 very thick paper that is used for making boxes, etc 箱などを作るために使われる非常に厚い紙→ボール紙, 厚紙, 段ボール ‖ *The goods were packed in cardboard boxes.* 品物は段ボール箱に詰められていた.

**cardiac** /kɑ́ːrdiæ̀k/ 形 正式 ▶定義 connected with the heart 心臓に関連した→心臓の, 心臓病の ‖ *cardiac surgery* 心臓外科 *a cardiac arrest* (= *when the heart stops temporarily or permanently*) 心(拍)停止 (= 心臓が一時的にまたは永久に停止するとき)

**cardigan** /kɑ́ːrdɪgən/ 名 C ▶定義 a piece of

clothing like a woollen jacket, that fastens at the front ウールの上着のような衣服で、前で留める→**カーディガン** ☛ C6 ページのさし絵 ☛参 **sweater** の注

**cardinal** /káːrd(ə)n(ə)l/ 形 ● ▶定義1 a priest at a high level in the Roman Catholic church ローマカトリック教会の高位の聖職者→**枢機卿（すうきけい）** ▶定義2 （または **cardinal number**）a whole number, for example 1, 2, 3 that shows quantity 例えば 1, 2, 3 のような量を表す整数→**基数** ☛参 **ordinal**

★**care**¹ /keər/ 名 ▶定義1 ❶ care (for sb) looking after sb/sth so that he/she/it has what he/she/it needs for his/her/its health and protection ～の面倒を見て、健康や保護のためにその～が必要なものを与えること→**（～の）世話、介護、保護；監督** ‖ *All the children in their care were healthy and happy.* 彼らが面倒を見ている子供たちは皆健康で幸福だった． *This hospital provides free medical care.* この病院では医療が無料だ． *She's in intensive care (= the part of the hospital for people who are very seriously ill).* 彼女は集中治療室にいる（= 病院にある重傷患者のための場所）． *skin/hair care products* スキンケア・ヘアケア用製品 ▶定義2 ❶ care (over sth/in doing sth) thinking about what you are doing so that you do it well or do not make a mistake 自分がやっている事について気を付けて、うまくできるように、または間違いがないようにすること→**（～に対する）注意、用心、努力** ‖ *You should take more care over your homework.* もっと注意深く宿題をやらなくてはいけない． *This box contains glasses - please handle it with care.* この箱にはコップが入っています － 注意して取り扱ってください． ▶定義3 ❶ something that makes you feel worried or unhappy 人を心配させたり不幸にするもの→**心配、気懸かり、気苦労、不安** ‖ *Since Charlie retired he doesn't have a care in the world.* チャーリーは引退したので、もう何の気苦労もない． *It was a happy life, free from care.* それは何の心配もない幸福な人生だった．

成句 **in care** ▶定義 (used about children) living in a home which is organized by the government or the local council, and not with their parents (子供について) 政府や市町村議会などが用意する家に住み、両親と一緒に住んでいない→孤児で、施設で暮らしている ‖ *They were taken into care after their parents died.* 両親の死後、彼らは施設に入れられた．

**take care (that.../to do sth)** ▶定義 to be careful 注意する→**（～するよう）気を付ける** ‖ *Goodbye and take care!* さようなら、気を付けて． *Take care that you don't spill your tea.* お茶をこぼさないように注意しなさい． *He took care not to arrive too early.* 彼はあまり早く到着しないように気を遣った．

**take care of sb/sth** ▶定義 to deal with sb/sth; to organize or arrange sth ～に対処する；～を準備したり手配したりする→**～を処理する；～を責任を持って引き受ける** ‖ *I'll take care of the food for the party.* パーティーの料理は私が手配します．

**take care of yourself/sb/sth** ▶定義 to keep yourself/sb/sth safe from injury, illness, damage, etc; to look after sb/sth 自分自身または～をけがや病気、損害などから安全に守る；～の面倒を見る→**体に気を付ける、～に気を配る、～を大事にする；～の世話をする** ‖ *My mother took care of me when I was ill.* 私が病気の時には母が面倒を見てくれた． *She always takes great care of her books.* 彼女はいつも本をとても大事にしている．

★**care**² /keər/ 動 自 他 ▶定義 care (about sb/sth) to be worried about or interested in sb/sth ～について心配する、または興味を持つ→**（～を）気遣う、気に掛ける、（～に）関心を持つ** ‖ *Money is the thing that she cares about most.* 金こそ彼女が一番関心を持っているものだ． *He really cares about his staff.* 彼はスタッフのことを本当に気に掛けている． *I don't care what you do.* あなたが何をしようと私は興味ない．

成句 **I, etc couldn't care less** 略式 ▶定義 it does not matter to me, etc at all. 私（その他）は全く関心がない→**全然構わない、気にも掛けない** ‖ *I couldn't care less what Barry thinks.* バリーがどう思おうと私は全く関心がない．

**who cares?** 略式 ▶定義 nobody is interested; it is not important to anyone. だれも興味がない；それはだれにとっても重要でない→**どうでもいい、構わない** ‖ *'I wonder who'll win the match.' 'Who cares?'* 「だれが試合に勝つのだろうか」

「知るもんか」

**would you care for.../to do sth** 形式 ▶定義 a polite way to ask if sb would like sth or would like to do sth 〜が…を欲しいか、または…をしたいか尋ねる場合の丁寧な言い方 → **〜はいかがですか、〜なさいますか**

句動詞 **care for sb** ▶定義 to look after sb 〜の面倒を見る → **〜の世話をする** ‖ *Who cared for her while she was ill?* 彼女が病気の時はだれが看病をしたのですか.

**care for sb/sth** ▶定義 to like or love sb/sth 〜を好む、愛する → **〜が好き、〜を気に入る** ‖ *She still cares for Liam although he married someone else.* リアムはほかの人と結婚したのに、彼女はまだ彼を愛している. *I don't care for that colour very much.* その色はあまり好きではない.

\***career**[1] /kəríər/ 名 C ▶定義**1** the series of jobs that sb has in a particular area of work 〜が特定の職業分野で行う一連の仕事 → **(生涯のまたは専門的な)職業; 職歴, 経歴** ‖ *Sarah is considering a career in engineering.* サラはエンジニアリングを生涯の仕事にしようかと考えている. *a successful career in politics* 成功した政治家としての経歴 ▶定義**2** the period of your life that you spend working 仕事をしている人生の期間 → **経歴, 履歴** ‖ *She spent most of her career working in India.* 彼女は生涯の大部分をインドで働いた.

**career**[2] /kəríər/ 動 自 ▶定義 to move quickly and in a dangerous way 急いで, 危険な様子で移動する → **疾走する, 暴走する** ‖ *The car careered off the road and crashed into a wall.* 車は道路を外れて暴走し, 壁に衝突した.

**carefree** /kéərfrí:/ 形 ▶定義 with no problems or worries 問題や心配事のない → **のんきな, 気楽な, 楽しい**

\***careful** /kéərf(ə)l/ 形 ▶定義**1** careful (of/with sth); careful (to do sth) thinking about what you are doing so that you do not have an accident or make mistakes, etc 自分のやっている事について注意を払い, 事故に遭ったり間違いなどを起こさないようにする → **注意深い, 用心深い, 慎重な** ‖ *Be careful! There's a car coming.* 気を付けて. 車が来るよ. *Please be very careful of the traffic.* 交通に十分注意してください. *Be careful with that knife - it's very sharp.* そのナイフに気を付けて — とても鋭いから. *That ladder doesn't look very safe. Be careful you don't fall.* そのはしごはあまり安全そうではない. 落ちないように気を付けて. *I was careful not to say anything about the money.* お金のことには触れないように気を遣った. *a careful driver* 慎重な運転手 ▶定義**2** giving a lot of attention to details to be sure sth is right 〜が間違いないということを確認するために細部に多くの注意を払う → **念入りな, 入念な, 丁寧な** ‖ *I'll need to give this matter some careful thought.* この件についてはじっくり考えなくてはならないだろう. *a careful worker* 丁寧な仕事をする人 — **carefully** /kéərf(ə)li/ 副 → **注意深く, 慎重に, 念入りに** ‖ *Please listen carefully. It's important that you remember all this.* よく聞いてください. これを全部覚えることがとても大切です.

\***careless** /kéərləs/ 形 ▶定義**1** careless (about/with sth) not thinking enough about what you are doing so that you make mistakes 自分のやっている事についてよく考えないため, 誤りを犯す → **不注意な, 軽率な** ‖ *Jo's very careless.* ジョーはとても不注意だ. *The accident was caused by careless driving.* その事故は不注意な運転が原因だった. ▶定義**2** resulting from a lack of thought or attention to detail 考えまたは細部への注意が不足した結果として → **ぞんざいな, 不正確な, 不完全な** ‖ *a careless mistake* 不注意な間違い — **carelessly** 副 → **不注意に, 軽率に, ぞんざいに** ‖ *She threw her coat carelessly on the chair.* 彼女はコートをぞんざいにいすの上にほうり投げた. — **carelessness** 名 U → **不注意なこと, 軽率, むとんちゃく**

**carer** /kéərər/ (米 **caregiver** /kéərgìvər/) 名 C ▶定義 a person who regularly looks after sb who is unable to look after himself/herself because of age, illness, etc 高齢や病気などのため自分の面倒を見られない〜を定期的に世話する人 → **介護者**

**caress** /kərés/ 動 他 ▶定義 to touch sb/sth in a gentle and loving way 〜に優しく愛情をもって触れる → **〜を優しくなでる, 愛撫(ぶ)する** — **caress** 名 C → **愛撫, 抱擁**

**caretaker** /kéərtèikər/ (米 **janitor**) 名 C ▶定義 a person whose job is to look after a large building, for example a school or a block of flats 例えば学校やアパートなどの, 大きな建物の管理を仕事とする人→管理人, 守衛, 用務員

**cargo** /káːrgoʊ/ 图 ⓒⓊ (❀ **cargoes**: 困 または **cargos**) ▶定義 the goods that are carried in a ship or aircraft 船や航空機で運ばれる品物→船荷, 積み荷, 貨物 ‖ *Luggage is carried in the cargo hold of the plane.* 手荷物は飛行機の荷物室に積み込まれる. *a cargo ship* 貨物船

**the Caribbean** /kærəbíːən, kəríbiən/ 图 [単数扱い] ▶定義 the area in the Caribbean Sea where the group of islands called the West Indies are situated 西インド諸島と呼ばれる群島があるカリブ海の一帯→カリブ海 — Caribbean 形→カリブ海の, カリブ人の

**caricature** /kǽrɪkət(j)ʊ̀ər, -tʃʊ̀ər/ 图 ⓒ ▶定義 a picture or description of sb that makes his/her appearance or behaviour funnier and more extreme than it really is 〜の外見や行動を実際よりもこっけいに, おおげさにかいた絵や言葉による描写→風刺画・文, 戯画, カリカチュア ‖ *Many of the people in the book are caricatures of the author's friends.* その本の登場人物の多くは, 著者の友人を戯画化したものだ.

**caring** /kéərɪŋ/ 形 ▶定義 showing that you care about other people ほかの人々への気遣いを示す→愛情深い, 気遣う, 思いやりのある ‖ *We must work towards a more caring society.* もっと思いやりのある社会を目指して努力しなければならない.

**carnation** /kɑːnéɪʃ(ə)n/ 图 ⓒ ▶定義 a white, pink or red flower with a pleasant smell 良い香りのする白, ピンクまたは赤い色の花→カーネーション ☞ C2 ページのさし絵

**carnival** /káːmɪv(ə)l/ 图 ⓒ ▶定義 a public festival that takes place in the streets with music and dancing 道路で催される歌や踊りのある民衆の祝祭→カーニバル, 謝肉祭, お祭り ‖ *the carnival in Rio* リオのカーニバル

**carol** /kǽrəl/ 图 ⓒ ▶定義 a Christian religious song that people sing at Christmas 人々がクリスマスに歌うキリスト教の宗教歌→祝歌, 聖歌, 賛美歌, キャロル

**carousel** /kæ̀rəsél, -zél, ˙˙˙/ 图 ⓒ ▶定義 1 困 =MERRY-GO-ROUND ▶定義 2 a moving belt at an airport that carries luggage for passengers to collect 空港で乗客が回収する荷物を載せる動くベルト→手荷物引き渡し用ベルトコンベヤー, カルーセル

**car park** (❀ **parking lot**) 图 ⓒ ▶定義 an area or building where you can leave your car 車を止めておくことのできる区域または建物→駐車場 ‖ *a multi-storey car park* 立体駐車場

**carpenter** /káːrp(ə)ntər/ 图 ⓒ ▶定義 a person whose job is to make things from wood 木材から物を作ることを仕事にしている人→大工, 大工職人 ☞参 **joiner**

**carpentry** /káːrpəntri/ 图 Ⓤ ▶定義 the skill or work of a carpenter 大工の技術または仕事→大工職, 大工仕事, 木工品

**carpet** /káːrpət/ 图 ▶定義 1 ⓒⓊ (a piece of) thick material that is used for covering floors and stairs 床や階段を覆うために使われる厚手の生地 (の 1 枚) →カーペット, じゅうたん ‖ *a fitted carpet (= one that is cut to the exact shape of a room)* 床全面を覆うじゅうたん (=部屋の形通りに裁断されたじゅうたん) ‖ *a square metre of carpet* 1 平方メートルのカーペット ☞参 **rug** ▶定義 2 ⓒ a thick layer of sth that covers the ground 地面を覆う〜の厚い層→一面の広がり ‖ *The fields were under a carpet of snow.* 野原は厚い雪のじゅうたんに覆われていた. — carpeted 形 じゅうたんを敷いた, 厚く覆われた ‖ *All the rooms are carpeted.* すべての部屋はじゅうたん敷きだ.

**carriage** /kǽrɪdʒ/ 图 ⓒ ▶定義 1 (または **coach**, 困 **car**) one of the separate parts of a train where people sit 列車の個々に分けられる部分で, 乗客が座る場所→客車, 車両 ‖ *a first-class carriage* 1 等車 ▶定義 2 (または **coach**) a vehicle with wheels that is pulled by horses 馬が引く, 車輪のある乗り物→馬車, 4 輪馬車

**carriageway** /kǽrɪdʒwèɪ/ 图 ⓒ 困 ▶定義 one of the two sides of a motorway or main road on which vehicles travel in one direction only 高速道路または主要道路の, (上りと下り, 内回りと外回りなど) 2 つの路線のうちの 1 つで, 車両は一方向のみに進む→車道, 車線 ‖ *the southbound carriageway of the motorway* 高速道路の南行きの車線 ☞参 **dual carriageway**

**carrier** /kǽriər/ 图 ⓒ ▶定義 1 (in business) a company that transports people or goods (商業

で用いて)人や物を輸送する会社→運送業者, 運輸会社 ‖ *the Dutch carrier, KLM* オランダの航空会社, KLM ▶定義2 a military vehicle or ship that is used for transporting soldiers, planes, weapons, etc 兵士, 航空機, 武器などを輸送するための軍用車両または船→輸送車, 輸送船 ‖ *an aircraft carrier* 航空母艦 ▶定義3 a person or animal that can give an infectious disease to others but does not show the signs of the disease 伝染性の病気をほかに移すことがあるが, 病気の兆候は示さない人または動物→(病原体の)保有者, 保菌者 ‖ *Some insects are carriers of tropical diseases.* ある種の虫は熱帯病を媒介する. ▶定義4 英 =CARRIER BAG

**carrier bag** (英 または **carrier**) ▶定義 a plastic or paper bag for carrying shopping 買った物を持ち運ぶためのビニールや紙の袋→買物袋 ☞ *bag* のさし絵

*__carrot__ /kǽrət/ ▶定義1 a long thin orange vegetable that grows under the ground 地下で生長する細長いだいだい色の野菜→ニンジン ‖ *A pound of carrots, please.* ニンジンを1ポンド下さい. *grated carrot* 擦りおろしたニンジン ☞ C3ページのさし絵 ▶定義2 something attractive that is offered to sb in order to persuade him/her to do sth 説得して何かをさせるために~に差し出される魅力的なもの→説得の手段, 褒美 ‖ *The management have offered them the carrot of a £500 bonus if they agree to work extra hours.* 管理職は500ポンドのボーナスを褒美として提示して, 彼らに残業することを求めた.

*__carry__ /kǽri/ 動 (現分 **carrying**; 三単現 **carries**; 過, 過分 **carried**) ▶定義1 to hold sb/sth in your hand, arms or on your back while you are moving from one place to another ある場所からほかへ移動する間, ~を手・腕で持つ, または背負う→~を運ぶ, 持っていく ‖ *Could you carry this bag for me? It's terribly heavy.* このバッグを持っていただけますか. ひどく重いのです. *She was carrying a rucksack on her back.* 彼女はリュックサックを背負っていた.

▶衣服, 宝石などを身に着ける場合には wear を用い, carry は用いない: *He was wearing a black jacket.* (彼は黒い上着を着ていた.)

▶定義2 to have sth with you as you go somewhere どこかへ行くときに~を持っていく→~を持ち歩く, 携行する ‖ *I never carry much money with me when I go to London.* 私はロンドンに行くときは, 決して大金を持ち歩かないようにします. *Do the police carry guns in your country?* あなたの国では警官が銃を携帯していますか. ▶定義3 to transport sb/sth from one place to another ~をある場所からほかへ輸送する→~を運ぶ, 運送する ‖ *A train carrying hundreds of passengers crashed yesterday.* 昨日, 何百人もの乗客を乗せた列車が衝突した. *Strong winds carried the boat off course.* 強い風のため船は航路をそれた. ▶定義4 to have an infectious disease that can be given to others, usually without showing any signs of the disease yourself 一般に自分自身は病気の兆候を示していないのに, ほかに移るような伝染性の病気にかかっている→~の保菌者である, 感染者である ‖ *Rats carry all sorts of diseases.* ネズミはあらゆる病気を持っている. ▶定義5 (通常は受動態で) to officially approve of sth in a meeting, etc, because the largest number of people vote for it 最大多数の人が投票したという理由で, 会議などで正式に~を承認する→(主張)を通す, (会議などを)通過させる, 可決する ‖ *The motion was carried by 12 votes to 9.* その動議は12対9で可決された. ▶定義6 (used about a sound) to reach a long distance (音について)遠くまで届く→(音などが)通る, 達する ‖ *You'll have to speak louder if you want your voice to carry to the back of the room.* 部屋の後ろまで聞こえるように, もっと大きな声で話さなければいけません.

成句 **be/get carried away** ▶定義 to be so excited that you forget what you are doing 何をしているのか忘れるほど興奮する→夢中になる, 我を忘れる ‖ *I got so carried away watching the race that I forgot how late it was.* レースに夢中になっていて時間が遅いことを忘れていた.

**carry weight** ▶定義 to have influence on the opinion of sb else ほかの~の意見に影響を持つ→説得力がある, 納得させる力がある ‖ *Nick's views carry a lot of weight with our manager.* ニックの意見は支配人に対して大きな影響力を持っている.

句動詞 **carry it/sth off** ▶定義 to succeed in

doing sth difficult 困難な〜をうまくやり遂げる→〜をうまく切り抜ける, 成し遂げる ‖ *He felt nervous before he started his speech but he carried it off very well.* 彼はスピーチの前はあがっていたが, 非常にうまくやり遂げた.

**carry on (with sth/doing sth)** ▶定義 to continue 続ける→〜し続ける, 進める ‖ *They ignored me and carried on with their conversation.* 彼らは私を無視して話し続けた. *She intends to carry on studying after the course has finished.* 彼女はその課程を終了した後も勉強を続けるつもりだ.

**carry on sth** ▶定義 to do an activity ある活動を行う→〜をする, 行う ‖ *to carry on a conversation/a business* 会話をする・経営する

**carry out sth** ▶定義 1 to do sth that you have been ordered to do 命令された〜を行う→〜を実行する, 遂行する, 果たす ‖ *The soldiers carried out their orders without question.* 兵士たちは黙って命令を遂行した. ▶定義 2 to do a task, repair, etc 仕事, 修理などをする→〜を行う, 実施する ‖ *to carry out tests/an investigation* テストをする・調査を行う

**carrycot** /kǽrikɑt/ 名 C ▶定義 a small bed, like a box with handles, that you can carry a baby in 持ち手の付いた箱のような小型ベッドで, 赤ちゃんを入れて運ぶ→(赤ちゃん用)携帯ベッド ☞ **pram** のさし絵

**carry-on** 名 C 特に 困 ▶定義 a small piece of luggage that you can take onto a plane with you 航空機内に持ち込める小さな手荷物→**機内持ち込み手荷物**

**carsick** /kɑ́ːrsɪk/ 形 ▶定義 feeling sick or vomiting as a result of travelling in a car 車で移動することが原因で気分が悪くなる, 吐き気を催す→乗り物に酔った, 車酔いの ‖ *to get/feel/be carsick* 車に酔う ☞参 **airsick, seasick, travel-sick**

**cart**[1] /kɑːrt/ 名 C ▶定義 a vehicle with wheels that is used for transporting things 物を運ぶための車輪の付いた運搬具→**小型運搬車, 手押し車**

**cart**[2] /kɑːrt/ 動 他 略式 ▶定義 to take or carry sth/sb somewhere, often with difficulty しばしば骨を折って, 〜をどこかへ運ぶ, 持っていく→〜を(無理に)運ぶ, (扱いにくい物)〜を運ぶ ‖ *We left our luggage at the station because we didn't want to cart it around all day.* 一日中持ち歩きたくなかったので, 私たちは手荷物を駅に預けた.

**cartilage** /kɑ́ːrt(ə)lɪdʒ/ 名 C U ▶定義 a strong substance in the places where your bones join 骨の関節部にある丈夫な物質→**軟骨(組織)**

**carton** /kɑ́ːrtn/ 名 C ▶定義 a small container made of cardboard or plastic 厚紙やプラスチック製の小さな容器→**カートン, ボール箱, 紙パック** ‖ *a carton of milk/orange juice* 牛乳・オレンジジュース1パック ☞ **container** のさし絵

**cartoon** /kɑːrtúːn/ 名 C ▶定義 1 a funny drawing, especially in a newspaper or magazine 特に新聞や雑誌などに掲載されるこっけいな絵→**漫画, 戯画** ▶定義 2 a film that tells a story by using moving drawings instead of real people and places 実際の人や場所の代わりに, 動画を使って物語を表現する映画→**アニメーション, 漫画映画**

**cartoonist** /kɑːrtúːnɪst/ 名 C ▶定義 a person who draws cartoons 漫画をかく人→**漫画家**

**cartridge** /kɑ́ːrtrɪdʒ/ 名 C ▶定義 1 a small tube that contains explosive powder and a bullet. You put a cartridge into a gun when you want to fire it. 爆薬と弾丸が入った小型の筒. 発射するときに銃に入れる→**弾薬筒, 薬きょう** ▶定義 2 a closed container that holds sth that is used in a machine, for example film for a camera, ink for printing, etc. Cartridges can be removed and replaced when they are finished or empty. カメラのフィルム, 印刷インクなど機械に使用する〜を入れる密閉容器. 使い終わったり空になったら, 取り外して交換できる→**カートリッジ, (フィルムの)パトローネ**

**carve** /kɑːrv/ 動 ▶定義 1 自 他 **carve (sth) (out of sth)** to cut wood or stone in order to make an object or to put a pattern or writing on it 物を作るため, または模様を付けたり文字を書いたりするために, 木材や石を切る→**(〜を)(…に)彫る, 彫刻する** ‖ *The statue is carved out of marble.* その像は大理石で作られている. *He carved his name on the desk.* 彼は机に自分の名前を彫った. ▶定義 2 他 to cut a piece of cooked meat into slices 調理した肉を薄く切る→**〜を切り分ける** ‖ *to carve a chicken* チキンを切り分ける

## carving

**carving** /kάːrvɪŋ/ 名 C U ▶定義 an object or design that has been carved 彫られた物または図案→**彫刻, 彫り物** ‖ There are ancient carvings on the walls of the cave. 洞窟(どうくつ)の壁に古代の彫刻がある.

**cascade¹** /kæskéɪd/ 名 C ▶定義1 water that flows down the side of a mountain, etc (a waterfall) 山の斜面などを流れ落ちる水(滝)→**小さな滝** ▶定義2 a large quantity of sth that falls or hangs down 落下したり垂れ下がったりする大量の~→**滝状の物** ‖ a cascade of blond hair 豊かに流れるような金髪

**cascade²** /kæskéɪd/ 動 自 ▶定義 to fall or hang down, especially in large amounts or in stages 特に大量に, または段階状に落ちる, または垂れ下がる→**滝のように落ちる, 滝のように流れる** ‖ Water cascaded from the roof. 水が屋根から滝のように流れ落ちた.

★**case** /kéɪs/ 名 ▶定義1 C a particular situation or example of sth 個々の状況, または~の実例→**場合; 実例, 事例** ‖ In some cases, people have had to wait two weeks for a doctor's appointment. 場合によっては, 医師の予約を取るのに2週間待たなければならないこともあった. Most of us travel to work by tube - or, in Jim's case, by train and tube. 私たちの多くは地下鉄で通勤している — あるいは, ジムの場合は列車と地下鉄で. Cases of the disease are very unusual in this country. その症例はこの国では非常にまれである. ▶定義2 **the case** [単数扱い] the true situation 実際の状態→**真相, 事実, 実情** ‖ The man said he worked in Cardiff, but we discovered later that this was not the case. 男はカーディフで働いていると言ったが, 後にそれは事実とは違うことが分かった. ▶定義3 C a crime or legal matter 犯罪または法律上の事例→**ケース, 事例, 事件** ‖ The police deal with hundreds of murder cases a year. 警察は1年に何百件もの殺人事件を扱う. The case will come to court in a few months. 2,3か月でその事件は裁判になるだろう. ▶定義4 [C, 通常は単数] the facts and reasons that support one side in a discussion or legal matter 議論または法律上の事例で一方を裏書きする事実や根拠→**根拠; 訴訟事実** ‖ She tried to **make a case for** shorter working hours, but the others disagreed. 彼女は労働時間の短縮を主張したが, 皆は同意しなかった. ▶定義5 C (特に複合語で) a container or cover for sth ~の容器やカバー→**ケース, ~入れ** ‖ a pencil case 筆入れ a pillowcase まくらカバー a bookcase 本箱 She put her glasses back in the case. 彼女は眼鏡をケースにしまった. ▶定義6 =**SUITCASE** ‖ Would you like me to carry your case? あなたのスーツケースを運びましょうか.

成句 **(be) a case of sth/doing sth** ▶定義 a situation in which sth is needed ある~が必要とされる状況→**~の問題で, ~次第で** ‖ There's no secret to success in this business. It's just a case of hard work. この商売で成功する秘けつなどはありません. 努力次第です.

**in any case** ▶定義 whatever happens or has happened; anyway 何が起ころうとも, または起こったとしても; とにかく→**いずれにせよ** ‖ I don't know how much tickets for the match cost, but I'm going in any case. その試合のチケットがいくらするのか知らないけれど, いずれにせよ行くつもりだ.

**in case** ▶定義 because sth might happen ある~が起こる可能性があるため→**~するといけないので, 万一に備えて** ‖ I think I'll take an umbrella in case it rains. 雨が降るかもしれないから, 傘を持っていこう. I wasn't intending to buy anything but I took my cheque book **just in case**. 何も買うつもりはなかったが, 一応小切手帳を持っていった.

**in case of sth** 正式 ▶定義 if sth happens もしある~が起こったら→**~の場合には, ~の用心に; ~が起こったら** ‖ In case of fire, break this glass. 火災の場合には, このガラスを破ってください.

**in that case** ▶定義 if that is the situation そういう状況ならば→**その場合は, もしそうならば** ‖ 'I'm busy on Tuesday.' 'Oh well, in that case we'll have to meet another day.' 「私は火曜日は忙しい」「そうか, それならば会うのは別の日にしなければ」

**prove your/the case/point** ⇒ **PROVE**

**case study** 名 C ▶定義 a detailed study of a person, group, situation, etc over a period of time 人, 集団, 状況などについての一定期間にわたる詳しい研究→**事例研究, ケーススタディー**

**cash**¹ /kæʃ/ 名 U ▶定義1 money in the form of coins or notes and not cheques, plastic cards, etc 小切手やプラスチックのカードなどではなく，硬貨や紙幣の形態の金→**現金** ‖ *Would you prefer me to pay in cash or by cheque?* 現金と小切手どちらにしましょうか. *How much cash have you got with/on you?* 今, 現金をいくら持っていますか.

➤ cash は硬貨と紙幣の場合に用いる. change は硬貨のみに用いる.

▶定義2 略式 money in any form あらゆる形態の金→**お金** ‖ *I'm a bit short of cash this month so I can't afford to go out much.* 今月はちょっとお金が足りないので，あまり外出できない. ☞ **money** のさし絵

**cash**² /kæʃ/ 動他 ▶定義 to exchange a cheque, traveller's cheque, etc for coins and notes 小切手，トラベラーズチェックなどを硬貨と紙幣に換える→**〜を現金に換える, 換金する** ‖ *I'm just going to the bank to cash a cheque.* これからちょっと銀行に行って小切手を現金に換えてきます.

句動詞 cash in (on sth) ▶定義 to take advantage of a situation 状況の利点を生かす→**(〜で)もうける, (〜に)付け込む**

**cashback** /kǽʃbæk/ 名 U ▶定義1 an offer of money as a present that is made by some banks, companies selling cars, etc in order to persuade customers to do business with them 顧客が取り引きをしてくれるように勧めるため，贈り物として金を払うこと. 一部の銀行や自動車販売会社などが行う→**キャッシュバック**

▶定義2 a system in some shops (supermarkets), which allows the customer to take money out of his/her bank account at the same time as paying for the goods with a special card (cash card) 一部の店 (スーパー) のシステムで，特別のカード (キャッシュカード) で品物の支払いをすると同時に，客が自分の銀行口座から金を引き出せる仕組み→**キャッシュバック**

**cash card** (米 ATM card) 名 C ▶定義 a plastic card given by a bank to its customers so that they can get money from a special machine (cash machine) in or outside a bank 銀行の中や外の特別な機械 (現金自動預け払い機) から金を受け取れるように，銀行が顧客に与えるプラスチックのカード→**キャッシュカード** ☞参

cheque card, credit card

**cash desk** 名 C ▶定義 the place in a large shop where you pay for things 大型店にある，品物の支払いをする場所→**レジ, 勘定台**

**cashew** /kǽʃuː, kæʃúː/ (または **cashew nut**) 名 C ▶定義 a small curved nut that we eat 小さくて弓形の食用の木の実→**カシューナッツ** ☞ **nut** のさし絵

**cash flow** 名 [単数扱い] ▶定義 the movement of money into and out of a business as goods are bought and sold 商品が売買される際の商売上の金の出入り→**収支** ‖ *The company had cash-flow problems and could not pay its bills.* その会社の収支には問題があり，請求書の支払いができなかった.

**cashier** /kæʃíər/ 名 C ▶定義 the person in a bank, shop, etc that customers pay money to or get money from 客が金を支払ったり受け取ったりする，銀行や店などの係→**出納係, 会計係; レジ**

**cash machine** (または **cash dispenser**; **cashpoint**, 米 または **ATM** /èi tiː ém/) 名 C ▶定義 a machine inside or outside a bank that you can get money from at any time of day by putting in a special card (cash card) 銀行の中または外にある機械. 特別のカード (キャッシュカード) を挿入して１日のうちいつでも金を入手できる→**自動現金預け払い機**

**cashmere** /kǽʃmìər/ 名 U ▶定義 a type of wool that is very fine and soft 非常に細く柔らかい種類の毛糸→**カシミア**

**casino** /kəsíːnoʊ/ 名 C ( 複 **casinos**) ▶定義 a place where people play roulette and other games in which you can win or lose money 人々がルーレットなどのゲームをして金を得たり失ったりする場所→**カジノ, とばく場**

**cask** /kɑːsk; kæsk/ 名 C ▶定義 a large wooden container in which alcoholic drinks, etc are stored アルコール飲料などを保存するための大型の木製容器→**たる, 貯蔵だる**

**casserole** /kǽsəròʊl/ 名 ▶定義1 C U a type of food that you make by cooking meat and vegetables in liquid for a long time in the oven スープに入った肉と野菜をオーブンで長時間調理して作る食べ物→**キャセロール, シチュー** ‖

chicken casserole チキンキャセロール ▶定義2
❻ a large dish with a lid for cooking casseroles in キャセロールを調理するためのふた付きの大きななべ→キャセロール(なべ), 蒸し焼きなべ ☞ pan のさし絵

*cassette /kəsét, kæ-/ 名 ❻ ▶定義 a small flat case with tape inside that you use for recording and playing music and other sounds 音楽やほかの音を録音したり, 再生したりするために使う, テープが中に入った小さく平らなケース→カセット, カセットテープ ‖ to put on/play/listen to a cassette カセットをかける・かける・聴く

▶ tape は cassette と同じ意味の語. カセットの頭に戻ることを rewind(巻き戻す)と言う. 前へ進めることを fast forward(早送りする)と言う. ☞参 video

**cassette recorder** 名 ❻ ▶定義 a machine that you use for recording and playing cassettes カセットに録音したり, 再生したりするための機械→カセットレコーダー

**cast**¹ /kɑːst; kæst/ 動 (過, 過分 **cast**) ▶定義1 ⓒ (しばしば受動態で) to choose an actor for a particular role in a play, film, etc 劇や映画の特定の役に俳優を選ぶ→〜に役を割り当てる, 配役を決める ‖ She always seems to be cast in the same sort of role. 彼女はいつも同じような役を割り当てられるようだ. ▶定義2 ⓒ to throw a fishing line or net into the water 釣り糸や網を水に投げる→(釣り糸を)投げ込む, (網を)打つ

成句 **cast doubt on sth** ▶定義 to make people less sure about sth 人々が〜に対してあまり信頼を持てないようにする→疑いをかける, 不審に思わせる ‖ The newspaper report casts doubt on the truth of the Prime Minister's statement. 新聞の報道は首相の陳述の真偽に疑いを投げかけている.

**cast an eye/your eye(s) over sb/sth** ▶定義 to look at sb/sth quickly 〜を素早く見る→〜にざっと目を通す, 一瞥(べつ)する

**cast light on sth** ▶定義 to help to explain sth 〜を明らかにするのに役立つ→手掛かりになる, ヒントを与える ‖ Can you cast any light on the problem? この問題を解決する手掛かりが何かありますか.

**cast your mind back** ▶定義 to make yourself remember sth 〜を思い出す→以前のことを思い出す ‖ She cast her mind back to the day she met her husband. 彼女は夫と出会った日のことを思い出した.

**cast a shadow (across/over sth)** ▶定義 to cause an area of shade to appear somewhere どこかに影の部分を出現させる→(〜に)影を落とす, 影ができる ‖ (比喩) The accident cast a shadow over the rest of the holiday (= stopped people enjoying it fully). その事故は休日の残りの日々に影を落とした(= 休日を十分に楽しめなくした).

**cast a/your vote** ▶定義 to vote 投票する→評決する, 投票で支持する ‖ The MPs will cast their votes in the leadership election tomorrow. 下院議員は明日, 首脳部を選出する選挙を行う.

句動詞 **cast around/about for sth** ▶定義 to try to find sth 〜を見つけようとする→あちこち探し回る, あれこれ方策を考える ‖ Jack cast around desperately for a solution to the problem. ジャックはその問題を解決しようと必死にあれこれ考えた.

**cast**² /kɑːst; kæst/ 名 [ⓒ, 単数または複数形の動詞と共に] ▶定義 all the actors in a play, film, etc 劇または映画などの俳優たち全員→配役, キャスト ‖ The entire cast was/were excellent. 出演した俳優の全員がすばらしかった.

**castaway** /kǽstəwèɪ; kǽst-/ 名 ❻ ▶定義 a person who is left alone somewhere after his/her ship has sunk 船が沈没した後, 1人でどこかに取り残された人→難破漂流した人, 難船者

**caste** /kɑːst; kæst/ 名 ❻ ⓤ ▶定義 a social class or group based on your position in society, how much money you have, family origin, etc; the system of dividing people in this way 社会的地位, 財産, 家柄などに基づいた社会階級または集団; 人々をこのように分ける制度→身分, カースト; 階級制 ‖ Hindu society is based on a caste system. ヒンズー教社会はカースト制に基づいている.

**cast iron** 名 ⓤ ▶定義 a hard type of iron 硬い鉄の一種→鋳鉄(ちゅうてつ)

**cast-iron** 形 ▶定義 made of cast iron 鋳鉄で作られた→鋳鉄製の ‖ (比喩) a cast-iron alibi (= one that people cannot doubt) どうにも覆せない

アリバイ(= 人々が疑うことのできないもの)

**castle** /kάːs(ə)l; kǽs(ə)l/ 名 C ▶定義 a large building with high walls and towers that was built in the past to defend people against attack 昔、人々を攻撃から防御するために建てられた、高い壁と塔のある大きな建物→城, 城郭 ‖ *a medieval castle* 中世の城 *Edinburgh Castle* エディンバラ城

**cast-off** 名 [C, 通常は複数] ▶定義 a piece of clothing that you no longer want and that you give to sb else or throw away もう必要がないのでほかの〜にやるか、または捨てる衣服→古着, もう着なくなった服 ‖ *When I was little I had to wear my sister's cast-offs.* 小さいころは姉のお下がりを着なければならなかった.

**castrate** /kǽstreɪt; ˈ--/ 動 他 ▶定義 to remove part of the sexual organs of a male animal so that it cannot produce young 子供ができないように雄の動物の性器の一部を切除する→去勢する ☛参 **neuter**² ─ **castration** /kæstréɪʃ(ə)n/ 名 U ▶去勢

**casual** /kǽʒuəl/ 形 ▶定義 1 relaxed and not worried; not showing great effort or interest くつろいだ状態で心配していない; 大きな努力や関心を示さない→打ち解けた, のんきな; むとんちゃくな, おざなりの, 何気ない ‖ *I'm not happy about your casual attitude to your work.* 私は仕事に対する君のおざなりな態度が不満だ. *It was only a casual remark so I don't know why he got so angry.* 何気ない言葉だったのに彼がなぜあんなに怒ったのか分からない.

▶定義 2 (used about clothes) not formal (衣服について)正式でない→略装の, カジュアルな, 普段着の ‖ *I always change into casual clothes as soon as I get home from work.* 私は仕事から帰宅するとすぐに普段着に着替える.

▶定義 3 (used about work) done only for a short period; not regular or permanent (仕事について)短期間だけ行う; 定期的または永続的でない→臨時の, 不定期の ‖ *Most of the building work was done by casual labour.* 多くの建築作業は自由労働者によって行われた. *a casual job* 臨時の仕事 ─ **casually** /kǽʒuəli/ 副 ▶偶然に, 不用意に, 普段着で ‖ *She walked in casually and said, 'I'm not late, am I?'* 彼女は何気なく入ってきて言った.「遅刻していないわよね」 *Dress casually, it won't be a formal party.* 普段着でおいでください, 格式張ったパーティーではありませんから.

**casualty** /kǽʒuəlti/ 名 (複 **casualties**) ▶定義 1 ❶ a person who is killed or injured in a war or an accident 戦争や事故で死亡または負傷した人→死傷者, 犠牲者 ‖ *After the accident the casualties were taken to hospital.* 事故後, 死傷者は病院に運ばれた. ▶定義 2 ❶ a person or thing that suffers as a result of sth else ほかの〜が原因で被害を受ける人や物→被害者, 損害 ‖ *Many small companies became casualties of the economic crisis.* 多くの中小企業が経済危機の犠牲となった. ▶定義 3 (または **casualty department**, 米 **emergency room**; **ER**) U the part of a hospital where people who have been injured in accidents are taken for immediate treatment 事故の負傷者が病院での応急処置のために運搬される場所→緊急医療室, 救急病棟

**\*cat** /kæt/ 名 C ▶定義 1 a small animal with soft fur that people often keep as a pet よくペットとして飼われる柔らかい毛皮を持つ小型動物→猫 ▶定義 2 a wild animal of the cat family ネコ科の野生動物→ネコ科 ‖ *the big cats* (= *lions, tigers, etc*) 大型のネコ科動物 (= ライオン, トラなど)

▶ kitten は子猫. tom は雄猫. purr はうれしいときに猫が出す低く静かな声. miaow は purr より大きい声.

**catalogue** (米 **catalog**) /kǽt(ə)lɒ(ː)ɡ, -lὰɡ/ 名 C ▶定義 1 a list of all the things that you can buy, see, etc somewhere ある場所で買ったり見たりできる物すべての一覧表→カタログ, 目録 ▶定義 2 a series, especially of bad things 特に悪い事の連続→(連続して起こる)不運, 一連の不幸 ‖ *a catalogue of disasters/errors/injuries* 災害・誤り・けがの連続 ─ **catalogue** 動 他 →〜の目録を作る, 〜を目録に載せる ‖ *She started to catalogue all the new library books.* 彼女は図書館の新しい本の目録を作り始めた.

**catalytic converter** /kὰtəlítɪk kənvˈəːrtər/ 名 C ▶定義 a device used in motor vehicles to reduce the damage caused to the environment by poisonous gases 有毒ガスによって引き起こされる環境破壊を削減するために自動車で使用する装置→触媒コンバーター

**catapult**

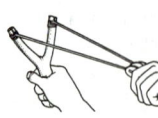

**catapult¹** /kǽtəpʌlt, -pʊlt/ (米 **slingshot**) 名 C ▶定義 a Y-shaped stick with a piece of elastic tied to each side that is used by children for shooting stones 両側にゴムひもを結び付けたY字形の棒で, 子供たちが石を飛ばすために使う→パチンコ

**catapult²** /kǽtəpʌlt, -pʊlt/ 動 他 ▶定義 to throw sb/sth suddenly and with great force ～を突然, 強く投げる→～を発射する, 勢いよく投げ出す ‖ *When the car crashed the driver was catapulted through the windscreen.* 車が衝突した時ドライバーは, フロントガラスを破って外へ投げ出された. (比喩) *The success of his first film catapulted him to fame.* 初作映画の成功で彼はあっと言う間に有名になった.

**cataract** /kǽtərækt/ 名 C ▶定義 a white area that grows over the eye as a result of disease 病変のため次第に目を覆うように広がる白い部分→(水晶体の)濁った部分, 白内障

**catarrh** /kətɑ́ːr/ 名 U ▶定義 a thick liquid that forms in the nose and throat when you have a cold 風邪を引いたときに鼻とのどで分泌される濃厚な液体→鼻水, たん, カタル

**catastrophe** /kətǽstrəfi/ 名 C ▶定義 1 a sudden disaster that causes great suffering or damage 大きな被害や損害をもたらす突然の災害→大災害, 大惨事 ‖ *major catastrophes such as floods and earthquakes* 洪水や地震といった大災害 ▶定義 2 an event that causes great difficulty, disappointment, etc 大きな困難や失望などを引き起こす出来事→不幸, 災難; 破滅 ‖ *It'll be a catastrophe if I fail the exam again.* また試験に落ちたらもうおしまいだ. ― **catastrophic** /kætəstrɑ́fɪk/ 形 ▶破滅的な, 悲劇的な ‖ *The war had a catastrophic effect on the whole country.* 戦争は国全体に壊滅的な影響を残した.

★**catch¹** /kætʃ/ 動 (過, 過分 **caught** /kɔːt/) ▶定義 1 他 to take hold of sth that is moving, usually with your hand or hands 動いている～を通常片手または両手でつかむ→～をつかむ, 捕まえる, 捕らえる ‖ *The dog caught the ball in its mouth.* 犬は口でボールを受け止めた. ▶定義 2 他 to capture sb/sth that you have been following or looking for 追い掛けていたり, 捜していた～を捕まえる→～を捕らえる, ～に追い付く, ～を見つけ出す ‖ *Two policemen ran after the thief and caught him at the end of the street.* 2人の警官が窃盗犯を追い掛け, 通りの外れで捕まえた. *to catch a fish* 魚をとる ▶定義 3 他 to notice or see sb doing sth bad ～が悪い事をしていることに気付く, 見る→見つける, 目撃する, 押さえる ‖ *I caught her taking money from my purse.* 彼女が私の財布から金を取るところを目撃した. ▶定義 4 他 to get on a bus, train, plane, etc バス, 列車, 飛行機などに乗る→～に乗る, 間に合う, ～を捕まえる ‖ *I caught the bus into town.* 私は街へ行くバスに乗った. ⇨ **miss** ▶定義 5 他 to be in time for sth; not to miss sb/sth ～の時間に間に合う; ～を逃さない→～に間に合う, ～を逃さない ‖ *We arrived just in time to catch the beginning of the film.* 私たちはちょうど映画が始まる時間に着いた. *I'll phone her now. I might just catch her before she leaves the office.* 今すぐ彼女に電話します. 彼女が会社を出る前に間に合うかもしれません. ▶定義 6 自 to become or cause sth to become accidentally connected to or stuck in sth ～が偶然に…につながる, またははまり込む→引っ掛かる, 巻き込まれる ‖ *His jacket caught on a nail and ripped.* 彼の上着はくぎに引っ掛かって裂けた. *If we leave early we won't get caught in the traffic.* 早々出発すれば, 交通渋滞に巻き込まれることはないだろう. ▶定義 7 他 to hit sb/sth ～を打つ→～に当たる, 命中する ‖ *The branch caught him on the head.* 木の枝は彼の頭に当たった. ▶定義 8 他 to get an illness 病気になる→(伝染病)に感染する, (病気)にかかる ‖ *to catch a cold/flu/measles* 風邪・インフルエンザ・麻疹(はしか)にかかる ▶定義 9 他 to hear or understand sth that sb says ～が言った事が聞こえる, または理解する→～を聞いて分かる, 見て分かる, ～を感じ取る, とらえる ‖ *I'm sorry, I didn't quite catch what you said. Could you repeat it?* すみません, あなたのおっしゃった事がよく聞き取れませんでした. もう一度繰り返してくださいませんか.

成句 **catch sb's attention/eye** ▶定義 to make sb notice sth ～に…に気付かせる→～の注意をひく, 目をひく ‖ *I tried to catch the waiter's eye* *so that I could get the bill.* 勘定書をもらうために，私はウエーターにこちらに気付かせようとした．

**catch your breath** ▶定義1 to rest after physical exercise so that your breathing returns to normal 呼吸が平静に戻るように，運動の後で休憩する➡**息を整える，一休みする** ‖ *I had to sit down at the top of the hill to catch my breath.* 息を整えるため，丘の頂上で腰を下ろさなければならなかった． ▶定義2 to breathe in suddenly because you are surprised 驚いて急に息を吸い込む➡**(はっとして)息をのむ**

**catch your death (of cold)** ▶定義 to get very cold とても寒くなる➡**凍える** ‖ *Don't go out without a coat - you'll catch your death!* コートなしで出掛けないで — 凍えてしまいますよ．

**catch fire** ▶定義 to start burning, often accidentally しばしば偶発的に，燃え始める➡**火がつく，燃え出す，出火する** ‖ *Nobody knows how the building caught fire.* なぜそのビルから出火したのかだれにも分からない．

**catch sb red-handed** ▶定義 to find sb just as he/she is doing sth wrong 〜がちょうど悪い事をしているところを見つける➡**悪事の現場を見つける，〜を現行犯で捕らえる** ‖ *The police caught the burglars red-handed with the stolen jewellery.* 警察は盗んだ宝石を持っていた強盗を現行犯で捕らえた．

**catch sight of/a glimpse of sb/sth** ▶定義 to see sb/sth for a moment 〜を一瞬見る➡**〜をちらりと見る，一瞥(べつ)する，一目見る** ‖ *We waited outside the theatre, hoping to catch a glimpse of the actress.* 女優の姿を一目でも見ようと私たちは劇場の外で待った．

**catch the sun** ▶定義1 to shine brightly in the sunlight 日差しの中で明るく輝く➡**日が当たる，日を受ける，日光できらめく** ‖ *The panes of glass flashed as they caught the sun.* 窓ガラスが日を受けてきらりと光った． ▶定義2 to become burned or brown in the sun 日光で日焼けする，または小麦色になる➡**日に焼ける，日光浴をする** ‖ *Your face looks red. You've really caught the sun, haven't you?* 顔が赤いよ．本当にたっぷり日に焼けたんだね．

句動詞 **catch on** 語式 ▶定義1 to become popular or fashionable 人気が出る，または流行になる➡**受ける，はやる** ‖ *The idea has never really caught on in this country.* その思想はこの国では真に受け入れられることはなかった． ▶定義2 to understand or realize sth 〜を理解する，または了解する➡**分かる，のみ込む，悟る** ‖ *She's sometimes a bit slow to catch on.* 彼女は時々のみ込みがいくらか遅いことがある．

**catch sb out** ▶定義 to cause sb to make a mistake by asking a clever question 巧妙な質問をして〜を誤らせる➡**〜にぼろを出させる，引っ掛ける** ‖ *Ask me anything you like - you won't catch me out.* 何でも聞いてくれ — 引っ掛けられはしないよ．

**catch up (with sb); catch sb up** ▶定義 to reach sb who is in front of you 自分の前にいる〜に到達する➡**(〜に)追い付く** ‖ *Sharon's missed so much school she'll have to work hard to catch up with the rest of the class.* シャロンは随分学校を休んだので，クラスの皆に追い付くには一生懸命勉強しなくてはならないだろう． *Go on ahead, I'll catch you up in a minute.* 先に行ってください，すぐに追い付きますから．

**catch up on sth** ▶定義 to spend time doing sth that you have not been able to do for some time しばらくできなかった〜をして時を過ごす➡**(遅れ・不足を)取り戻す** ‖ *I'll have to go into the office at the weekend to catch up on my work.* 遅れている仕事をするため週末に出勤しなければならない．

**be/get caught up in sth** ▶定義 to be or get involved in sth, usually without intending to 普通は意図せずに，〜に巻き込まれる➡**〜と掛かり合いになる，〜の巻き添えを食う** ‖ *I seem to have got caught up in a rather complicated situation.* かなり込み入った状況に巻き込まれてしまったようだ．

**catch**² /kætʃ/ ▶定義1 an act of catching sth, for example a ball 例えばボールなど，〜を捕らえること➡**捕球，取ること，受けること** ▶定義2 the amount of fish that sb has caught 〜が捕まえた魚の量➡**漁獲高，捕獲量** ‖ *The fishermen brought their catch to the harbour.* 漁師たちはとった魚を港に運んできた． ▶定義3 a device for fastening sth and keeping it closed 〜を留めて閉じておくための装置➡**留め金，ホ**

ック; 掛け金 ‖ *I can't close my suitcase - the catch is broken.* スーツケースが閉まらない － 留め金が壊れているから. *a window catch* 窓の掛け金 ▶定義**4** a hidden disadvantage or difficulty in sth that seems attractive 一見魅力的に見える～に隠された不利や難点→落とし穴, わな ‖ *It looks like a good offer but I'm sure there must be a catch in it.* それは良い申し出のように思えるが, 絶対に落とし穴があるはずだ.

**catchment area** /kǽtʃmənt èəriə/ 图 C ▶定義 the area from which a school gets its students, a hospital gets its patients, etc 学校が生徒を, または病院が患者を確保する一定の地域→通学圏, 学区, 通院範囲

**catchphrase** /kǽtʃfrèɪz/ 图 C ▶定義 a phrase that becomes famous for a while because it is used by a famous person 有名人が用いたために, しばらくの間有名になる文句→うたい文句, キャッチフレーズ

**catchy** /kǽtʃi/ 形 ▶定義 (used about a tune or song) easy to remember (曲や歌について) 覚えやすい→楽しくて覚えやすい, 人の心を捕らえやすい

**categorical** /kæ̀təgɔ́(:)rɪk(ə)l, -gɑ́r-/ 形 ▶定義 very definite 非常に明確な→絶対的な ‖ *The answer was a categorical 'no'.* 答えは無条件の「否」だった. — **categorically** /-k(ə)li/ 副 →絶対的に, 無条件に, 明確に ‖ *The Minister categorically denied the rumour.* 大臣はそのうわさをきっぱりと否定した.

**categorize** (または **-ise**) /kǽtɪɡəràɪz/ 動 他 ▶定義 to divide people or things into groups; to say that sb/sth belongs to a particular group 人や物をグループに分ける; ～が特定のグループに属していると言う→～を類別する, 分類する

***category** /kǽtəɡ(ə)ri; -ɡɔ̀(:)ri/ 图 C (複 **categories**) ▶定義 a group of people or things that are similar to each other 互いに似た人々や物の集まり→部類, 部門, 範疇 (はんちゅう) ‖ *This painting won first prize in the junior category.* この絵は青少年部門で第1位になった. *These books are divided into categories according to subject.* これらの本は題目に従って分類されている.

**cater** /kéɪtər/ 動 自 ▶定義**1** *cater for sb/sth;*

*cater to sth* to provide what sb/sth needs or wants ～が必要とする, または要求するものを提供する →～の (要求に) 応じる, 要求を満たす ‖ *We need a hotel that caters for small children.* 小さな子供に対応してくれるホテルを探している. *The menu caters to all tastes.* メニューは万人の好みを満たしている. ▶定義**2** to provide and serve food and drink at an event or in a place that a lot of people go to 催し物, または多くの人が集まる場所へ料理と飲み物を提供し配ぜんする→料理を賄う, 食事などを供する ‖ *Our firm caters for the 5000 staff and visitors at the festival.* 当社はその催しでスタッフと来訪者合わせて5000人分の食事を供する.

**caterer** /kéɪtərər/ 图 C ▶定義 a person or business that provides food and drink at events or in places that a lot of people go to 催し物, または多くの人が集まる場所へ料理と飲み物を提供する人や会社→仕出し屋, 宴会業者, サービス係

**catering** /kéɪtərɪŋ/ 图 U ▶定義 the activity or business of providing food and drink at events or in places that a lot of people go to 催し物や多くの人が集まる場所へ料理と飲み物を提供すること, またはその会社→仕出し(業), ケータリング ‖ *the hotel and catering industry* ホテル・仕出し業界 *Who's going to **do the catering** at the wedding?* 結婚式の料理の手配はだれがしますか.

**caterpillar** /kǽtərpɪlər/ 图 C ▶定義 a small hairy animal with a long body and a lot of legs, which eats the leaves of plants. A caterpillar later becomes an insect with large, often colourful wings (*a butterfly* or *a moth*). 長い体と多数の足を持つ毛の生えた小型の動物で, 植物の葉を食べる. 後に大きな, しばしば色とりどりの羽を持つ昆虫 (チョウやガ) になる→イモムシ, 毛虫 ☞ **insect** のさし絵

**cathedral** /kəθíːdr(ə)l/ 图 C ▶定義 a large church that is the most important one in a district 教区の中で最も重要な, 大きな教会→大聖堂, 司教座聖堂, カテドラル

**Catholic** /kǽθ(ə)lɪk/ =ROMAN CATHOLIC — **Catholicism** /kəθɒ́ləsɪz(ə)m/ = ROMAN CATHOLICISM

**cattle** /kǽtl/ 图 [複数扱い] ▶定義 male and female cows, for example on a farm 例えば農場

などの牡牛と牝牛→**牛, 畜牛** ‖ *a herd of cattle (= a group of them)* 牛の群 ☞参 **cow** の注

**caught** **CATCH**¹ の過去・過去分詞形

**cauldron** (特に 米 **caldron**) /kɔ́:ldr(ə)n/ 名 C
▶定義 a large, deep, metal pot that is used for cooking things over a fire 火にかけて物を調理するために使用される大型で深い金属の容器→**大なべ, 大がま**

**cauliflower** /kɔ́(:)lıflàυəァ, kάl-/ 名 C U ▶定義 a large vegetable with green leaves and a round white centre that you eat when it is cooked 緑の葉と丸い白い芯(しん)のある大型の野菜で、調理して食べる→**カリフラワー** ☞ C3 ページのさし絵

★**cause**¹ /kɔ:z/ 名 ▶定義 1 C a thing or person that makes sth happen 〜を引き起こす物や人→**原因, 種, もと** ‖ *The police do not know the cause of the accident.* 警察はその事故の原因が分からない. *Smoking is one of the causes of heart disease.* 喫煙は心臓病の原因の1つだ. ▶定義 2 U cause (for sth) reason for feeling sth or behaving in a particular way 〜を感じる、または特定の行動を取る理由→**(〜の) 訳, 正当な理由, 根拠, 動機** ‖ *The doctor assured us that there was no cause for concern.* 心配する必要はないと医者は請け合った. *I don't think you have any real cause for complaint.* あなたが不平を言う理由はないはずです.

▶定義 3 C an idea or organization that a group of people believe in and support 人々の集まりが信じる、または支持する考えや組織→**主義, 主張, 目標, 大義(名分)** ‖ *We are all committed to the cause of racial equality.* 我々は皆、人種的平等に専念している.

成句 a lost cause ⇒ **LOST**²

be for/in a good cause ▶定義 to be worth doing because it will help other people ほかの人々の助けになるため、行う価値がある→**信じる価値がある, 支援する価値がある, するだけの理由がある**

★**cause**² /kɔ:z/ 動他 ▶定義 to make sth happen 〜を引き起こす→**〜の原因となる, 〜を (結果として) 引き起こす, もたらす** ‖ *The fire was caused by an electrical fault.* その火災は漏電が原因だった. *High winds caused many trees to fall during the night.* 強風のため夜間に多くの樹木が倒れた. *Is your leg causing you any pain?* 足は痛みますか.

**cavalry** 247

**caustic** /kɔ́:stık/ 形 ▶定義 1 (used about a substance) able to burn or destroy things by chemical action (物質について) 化学作用によって物を燃焼させたり破壊したりできる→**苛性(かせい)の, 焼灼(しょうしゃく)性の, 腐食性の**

▶定義 2 critical in a cruel way 冷酷に批判する→**辛辣(しんらつ)な, 痛烈な** ‖ *a caustic remark* 辛辣な批評

**caution**¹ /kɔ́:ʃ(ə)n/ 名 ▶定義 1 ❶great care, because of possible danger 危険のおそれがあるために払われる細心の注意→**用心, 警戒** ‖ *Any advertisement that asks you to send money should be treated with caution.* 金を送れという広告には慎重に対処しなければならない.

▶定義 2 C a spoken warning that a judge or police officer gives to sb who has committed a small crime 軽犯罪を犯した〜に裁判官または警察官が与える口頭による訓戒→**警告, 注意, 諭旨**

**caution**² /kɔ́:ʃ(ə)n/ 動他 ▶定義 1 caution (sb) against sth to warn sb not to do sth 〜に…をしないように警告する→**(人に)〜しないように警告を与える, 注意する** ‖ *The President's advisers have cautioned against calling an election too early.* 大統領の顧問は早期に選挙を行わない方が良いと忠告した. ▶定義 2 to give sb an official warning 〜に公式の警告を与える→**警告する, 注意する** ‖ *Dixon was cautioned by the referee for wasting time.* ディクソンは遅延行為で審判に警告を受けた.

**cautionary** /kɔ́:ʃ(ə)n(ə)ri; -ə̀ri/ 形 ▶定義 giving a warning 警告を与える→**警告的な, 注意を促すような** ‖ *The teacher told us a cautionary tale about a girl who cheated in her exams.* 先生は、試験でカンニングをした女子生徒について戒めになる話をした.

★**cautious** /kɔ́:ʃəs/ 形 ▶定義 taking great care to avoid possible danger or problems 起こり得る危険や問題を避けるために細心の注意を払う→**用心深い, 注意深い, 慎重な** ‖ *I'm very cautious about expressing my opinions in public.* 公に意見を表明することについて、私はとても慎重だ.

— **cautiously** 副 →**用心して, 慎重に**

**cavalry** /kǽv(ə)lri/ 名 [単数扱い, 単数または複数形の動詞と共に] ▶定義 the part of the army that fought on horses in the past; the part of the modern army that uses heavily protected vehicles 昔，馬上で戦った軍隊の一部隊；重装備で保護された車両を使用する現代の軍隊の一部隊→騎兵隊；装甲機動部隊，ヘリ機動部隊

**cave¹** /kéɪv/ 图 C 定義 a large hole in the side of a cliff or hill, or under the ground 崖(がけ)や丘の斜面，または地下の大きな穴→洞窟(どうくつ)，ほら穴，横穴 ‖ *When it started to rain, we ran to shelter in a cave.* 雨が降り出した時，雨宿りのためほら穴に駆け込んだ．

**cave²** /kéɪv/ 動
句動詞 **cave in** ▶定義1 to fall in 内側に落ちる→崩れ落ちる，陥没する，へこむ ‖ *The roof of the tunnel had caved in and we could go no further.* トンネルの天井が崩れ落ちていてそれ以上進めなかった． ▶定義2 to suddenly stop arguing or being against sth 突然ある〜に反論，または反対することをやめる→屈服する，降参する ‖ *He finally caved in and agreed to the plan.* 彼はついに屈服してその計画に同意した．

**cavern** /kǽvərn/ 图 C 定義 a large, deep hole in the side of a hill or under the ground; a big cave 丘の斜面または地下の大きな深い穴；大きな洞窟(どうくつ)→大洞窟

**caviar** (または **caviare**) /kǽviɑːr, -- / 图 U ▶定義 the eggs of a large fish (**a sturgeon**) that we eat. Caviar is usually very expensive. 食用の大型魚(チョウザメ)の卵．通常は非常に高価→キャビア

**cavity** /kǽvəti/ 图 C (複 **cavities**) ▶定義 an empty space inside sth solid 内部の空の空間→空洞，穴，中空 ‖ *a cavity in a tooth* 虫歯 *a wall cavity* 壁の穴

**CBI** /sìː biː áɪ/ 略 the Confederation of British Industry ▶定義 an employer's association 経営者団体→英国産業連合

**cc** /sìː síː/ 略 cubic centimetre(s) →立方センチメートル ‖ *a 1200cc engine* 1200cc のエンジン

> ▶語法
>
> **容積単位の cc は何の略**
>
> 1 cm³ を 1 cc とも呼ぶのは，小学校の算数で学習します．しかし，なぜ cc なのでしょうか．cm³(立方センチメートル)を英語では cubic centimeter と読みます．その頭文字を取ったのが，ccなのです．ちなみに，cubicはcube(立方体)の形容詞形です．

**CCTV** /sìː sìː tìː víː/ 略 closed-circuit television→閉回路テレビ

**CD** /sìː díː/ (または **compact disc**) 图 C 定義 a small, round piece of hard plastic on which sound is recorded or information stored. You play a CD on a special machine (**CD player**). 音声が録音されたり情報が保存されている小さな円い硬質プラスチック盤．CDは専用の機械(CDプレーヤー)で再生する→コンパクトディスク，CD

**CD-ROM** /sìː diː rɑ́m/ ▶定義 a compact disc which has a lot of information recorded on it. The information cannot be changed or removed. 大量の情報が記録されたコンパクトディスク．情報は変更したり削除したりできない→CD ロム，CD 利用の読み出し専用記憶媒体

**cease** /síːs/ 動 自 他 正式 ▶定義 to stop or end 止まる，または終わる→やめる，停止する，中止する ‖ *Fighting in the area has now ceased.* その地域における戦いは今はやんでいる．*That organization has ceased to exist.* その組織はなくなった．

**ceasefire** /síːsfàɪər/ 图 C ▶定義 an agreement between two groups to stop fighting each other 互いに戦闘をやめるという2つの集団の間での合意→停戦，休戦，戦闘中止 ☞参 **truce**

**ceaseless** /síːsləs/ 形 ▶定義 continuing for a long time without stopping 止まることなく長期間続く→絶え間のない，不断の ― **ceaselessly** 副→絶え間なく，休みなく

**cede** /síːd/ 動 他 (文) ▶定義 to give land or control of sth to another country or person ほかの国または人に，土地や〜の支配権を与える→(権利など)を譲る，(領土)を割譲する，引き渡す

*★**ceiling** /síːlɪŋ/ 图 C ▶定義1 the top surface of the inside of a room 部屋の内側の頭上の壁→天井，天井板 ‖ *a room with a high/low ceiling* 天井の高い・低い部屋 ▶定義2 a top limit 最高限度→上限，シーリング ‖ *The Government has put a 10% ceiling on wage increases.* 政府は10パーセントの賃上げシーリングを設定した．

*★**celebrate** /séləbrèɪt/  動 自 他 ▶定義 to do sth to show that you are happy about sth that has

happened or because it is a special day 起こった出来事について喜びを表すため、または特別な日であるという理由で何かを行う→(~を)祝う、祝賀する ‖ *When I got the job we celebrated by going out for a meal.* 私がその仕事に就くことになった時、私たちは外で食事をして祝った。*Nora celebrated her 90th birthday yesterday.* 昨日ノラは90歳の誕生日のお祝いをした。— **celebratory** /sɑ́lébrətɔ̀ːri; -t(ə)ri/ 形 お祝いの、祝賀の ‖ *We went out for a celebratory meal after the match.* 試合の後、私たちはお祝いの食事に出掛けた。

**celebrated** /sélɪbrèɪtəd/ 形正式 定義 famous 有名な→名高い、高名な ‖ *a celebrated poet* 有名な詩人

**celebration** /sèlɪbréɪʃ(ə)n/ 名 CU 定義 the act or occasion of doing sth enjoyable because sth good has happened or because it is a special day 良い事があったため、または特別な日であるという理由で楽しい事をすること、またはそのような機会→お祝い、祝賀、祝賀会、祝典 ‖ *Christmas celebrations* クリスマスのお祝い / *I think this is an occasion for celebration!* これはお祝いをしなければ.

**celebrity** /sɑlébrəti/ 名 C ( 複 **celebrities**) 定義 a famous person 有名な人→著名人、名士 ‖ *a TV celebrity* テレビ界の有名人

**celery** /sél(ə)ri/ 名 U 定義 a vegetable with long green and white sticks that can be eaten without being cooked 緑と白色の長い茎を持つ野菜で、調理せずに食べられる→セロリ、オランダミツバ ‖ *a stick of celery* セロリ1本 ☞ C3 ページのさし絵

**celibate** /sélɪbət/ 形正式 定義 never having sexual relations, often because of religious beliefs しばしば信仰のため、決して性的関係を持たない→禁欲を誓った、独身を誓った — **celibacy** /sélɪbəsi/ 名 U →禁欲(生活)、独身(生活)

**cell** /sel/ 名 C 定義 1 the smallest living part of an animal or a plant 動物や植物の生物の最小単位→細胞、細胞組織 ‖ *The human body consists of millions of cells.* 人間の体は何百万という細胞から成り立っている。*red blood cells* 赤血球 定義 2 a small room in a prison or police station in which a prisoner is locked 囚人が監禁される、刑務所または警察署内の小さい部屋→独房、監禁室

**cellar** /sélər/ 名 C 定義 an underground room that is used for storing things 物を貯蔵するために使用する地下の部屋→地下室、地下貯蔵庫 ☞参 **basement** ☞ C7 ページのさし絵

**cellist** /tʃélɪst/ 名 C 定義 a person who plays the cello チェロを弾く人→チェロ奏者、チェリスト

**cello** /tʃélou/ 名 C ( 複 **cellos**) 定義 a large musical instrument with strings. You sit down to play it and hold it between your knees. 弦のある大型の楽器。演奏するときは座ってひざの間で支える→チェロ ☞参 **piano** の注 ☞ **music** のさし絵

**Cellophane**™ /séləfèɪn/ 名 U 定義 a transparent plastic material used for wrapping things 物を包むための透明なプラスチック材料→セロハン

**cellphone** /sélfòʊn/ (または **cellular phone**) = **MOBILE PHONE**

**cellular** /séljələr/ 形 定義 consisting of cells (1) 細胞から成り立っている→細胞の、細胞状の、細胞質の ‖ *cellular tissue* 細胞組織

*****Celsius** /sélsiəs, -fəs/ (または **centigrade**) 形 (略 C) 定義 the name of a scale for measuring temperatures, in which water freezes at 0° and boils at 100° 温度を測定する目盛りの名称で、水は0度で凍り、100度で沸騰する→摂氏、摂氏度 ‖ *The temperature tonight will fall to 7°C.* 今夜の気温は7度まで下がるだろう。☞「摂氏7度」は seven degrees Celsius と言う。**Fahrenheit** も参照.

**Celtic** /kéltɪk, sélt-/ 形 定義 connected with the people (**the Celts**) who lived in Wales, Scotland, Ireland and Brittany in ancient times, or with their culture 大昔にウェールズ、スコットランド、アイルランド、ブルターニュに住んでいた人々(ケルト人)と関連する、またはその文化と関連する→ケルトの、ケルト人の、ケルト語の

**cement**¹ /sɪmént/ 名 U 定義 a grey powder, that becomes hard after it is mixed with water and left to dry. It is used in building for sticking bricks or stones together or for making very hard surfaces. 灰色の粉末で、水と混合させてそのまま乾燥させると固まる。レンガや石を張り

## cement²

付ける,または非常に硬い表面を作ることにより,建築に使われる→**セメント, 接合剤**

**cement²** /sɪmént/ 動他 ▶定義1 to join two things together using cement, or a strong sticky substance セメントまたは強力な粘着物質を使って,2つの物を結合する→**〜を(セメントなどで)固める, 接着する** ▶定義2 to make a relationship, agreement, etc very strong 関係や協定を非常に強固にする→**きずなを作る,(友情,関係など)を固める** ‖ *This agreement has cemented the relationship between our two countries.* この協定によって2国間の関係が確固としたものになった.

**cemetery** /sémətri; -tèri/ 名 C (複 **cemeteries**) ▶定義 a place where dead people are buried, especially a place that does not belong to a church 死者を埋葬する場所,特に教会に所属しない場所→**共同墓地,(教会墓地でない)埋葬地** ☞参 **graveyard, churchyard**

**censor¹** /sénsər/ 動他 ▶定義 to remove the parts of a book, film, etc that might offend people or that are considered politically dangerous 本,映画などの,人々の感情を損なうおそれがある,または政治的に危険だと見なされる箇所を削除する→**〜を検閲する,(検閲して)削除する** ‖ *The soldier's letters home had to be censored.* 兵士が故郷にあてた手紙は検閲されなければならなかった. ― **censorship** 名 U ▶検閲, 検閲制度 ‖ *state censorship of radio and television programmes* ラジオとテレビ番組の国家による検閲

**censor²** /sénsər/ 名 C ▶定義 an official who censors books, films, etc 本,映画などを検閲する役人→**検閲官, 検閲係** ‖ *All films have to be examined by the board of film censors.* すべての映画は映画検閲委員会が審査する必要がある.

**censure** /sénʃər/ 動他 (文) ▶定義 to tell sb, in a strong and formal way, that he/she has done sth wrong 〜が不適切な事をしたと,その人に厳しく公式に言う→**〜を非難する, 酷評する, 譴責(けんせき)する** ‖ *The attorney was censured for not revealing the information earlier.* 代理人は早期に情報を開示しなかったことで譴責を受けた. ― **censure** 名 U ▶**非難, 酷評, 譴責, 不信任**

**census** /sénsəs/ 名 C (複 **censuses**) ▶定義 an official count of the people who live in a country, including information about their ages, jobs, etc その国に住む人の公式の人数で,年齢,職業などの情報を含む→**国勢調査, 人口調査**

\***cent** /sent/ 名 C (略 **c, ct**) ▶定義 a unit of money that is worth 100th part of a US dollar or of the main unit of money in some other countries 通貨単位で米ドルの100分の1,またはほかの国々の基本通貨単位の100分の1→**セント;1セント硬貨** ☞参 **per cent**

---

**▶語法**

**centimetre, centigrade, percent, century**

centの意味は100分の1です.したがって,1centimetreは「100分の1メートル」を表します.30℃(摂氏30度)のCは,この測定法の考案者Celsiusの頭文字であると共に,沸点(boiling point)と氷点(freezing point)の間を百等分した(centigrade)ことにも由来します.1centは1dollarの100分の1です.転じてcentは100も意味します.centuryが「100年」を表すのはこのためです.per centは「100につき」という比率を表します.ですからper centを複数形にしてはいけないのです.

---

**centenary** /sentíːn(ə)ri; sént(ə)nèri, senténəri/ 名 C (複 **centenaries**)(米 **centennial** /senténiəl/) ▶定義 the year that comes exactly one hundred years after an important event or the beginning of sth 重要な出来事から,または〜の始まりからちょうど100年後に来る年→**100周年, 100周年記念(祭)** ‖ *2001 is the centenary of Disney's birth.* 2001年はディズニーの生誕100周年だ.

**center** 米 = **CENTRE**

**centigrade** /séntəgrèɪd, sáːn-/ = **CELSIUS**

\***centimetre** (米 **centimeter**) /séntəmìːtər/ 名 C (略 **cm**) ▶定義 a measure of length. There are 100 centimetres in a metre. 長さの単位.1メートルは100センチメートル→**センチメートル, センチ**

\***central** /séntr(ə)l/ 形 ▶定義1 in the centre of sth 〜の中央の→**中央にある, 中心の** ‖ *a map of central Europe* ヨーロッパ中心部の地図 *Our flat is very central (= near the centre of the city and therefore very convenient).* 私たちのフラットは中心部にある (= 市の中心部に近いため,とても

便利). ▶定義2 most important; main 最も重要な; 主要な→**主流を成す, 中心を成す** ‖ *The film's central character is a fifteen-year-old girl.* その映画の主人公は15歳の少女だ. ▶定義3 (名詞の前だけ) having control over all other parts ほかの部分すべてを制御する→**中心的な, 中核の, 中央の** ‖ *central government (= the government of a whole country, not local government)* 中央政府(=国全体の政府で地方政府ではない) *the central nervous system* 中枢神経系

**central heating** 名 ❶ ▶定義 a system for heating a building from one main point. Air or water is heated and carried by pipes to all parts of the building. 建物の1箇所から全体を暖房するシステム. 空気または水を暖めてパイプで建物全体に運ばれる→**中央暖房(装置), セントラルヒーティング**

**centralize** (または **-ise**) /séntr(ə)làɪz/ 動 ⓤ (通常は受動態で) ▶定義 to give control of all the parts of a country or organization to a group of people in one place 国や組織のすべての支配を特定の一部の人々に与える→**〜を中央集権化する, 中心に集める** ‖ *Our educational system is becoming increasingly centralized.* 我々の教育システムはますます中央集権化している. — **centralization** (または **-isation**) /sèntr(ə)laɪzéɪ(ə)n, -lə-/ 名 ⓤ →**集中化, 中央集権化**

**centrally** /séntr(ə)li/ 副 ▶定義 in or from the centre 中心に, または中心から→**中心に, 中心となって, 中核として** ‖ *a centrally located hotel (= near the centre of the town)* 中心部にあるホテル(=街の中心部近くに)

*****centre**¹ (米 **center**) /séntər/ 名 ▶定義1 [ⓒ, 通常は単数] the middle point or part of sth 〜の中心点, または中心部→**中央, 真ん中** ‖ *I work in the centre of London.* 私はロンドンの中心部で働いている. *Which way is the town centre, please?* 街の中心はどちらですか. *She hit the target dead centre (= exactly in the centre).* 彼女は標的のちょうど真ん中に当てた. ☛参 **middle** の注 ▶定義2 ⓒ a building or place where a particular activity or service is based 特定の活動や事業の基盤が置かれている建物や場所→**中央施設, 中核, 総合地域施設, センター** ‖ *a sports/health/shopping centre* スポーツセンター・保健所・ショッピングセンター *This university is a centre of excellence for medical research.* この大学は卓越した医学研究の中核である. ▶定義3 ⓒ a place where sb/sth is collected together; the point towards which sth is directed 〜が集められている場所; 〜が向けられる点→**中心地, 密集地, 中核; 的(まと)** ‖ *major urban/industrial centres* 主要な都市の人口密集地・産業の中心地 *She always likes to be the centre of attention.* 彼女はいつも注目の的になりたがる. *You should bend your legs to keep a low centre of gravity.* 重心を低く保つには足を曲げなければならない. ▶定義4 [単数扱い, 単数または複数形の動詞と共に] a political position that is not extreme 過激ではない政治的立場→**中道派, 穏健派** ‖ *Her views are left of centre.* 彼女の考え方は左寄りだ.

**centre**² (米 **center**) /séntər/
句動詞 **centre on/around sb/sth** ▶定義 to have sb/sth as its centre 〜が中心にある→**〜に集中する, 集まる** ‖ *The life of the village centres on the church, the school and the pub.* 村の生活は教会, 学校, パブを中心としている.

**-centric** /séntrɪk/ (複合語で用いて) ▶定義 concentrating on or interested in the thing mentioned 言及されたものに集中する, または関心を持つ→**〜に中心を置いた, 〜中心の** ‖ *eurocentric policies (= concerned with Europe)* ヨーロッパ中心の政策(=ヨーロッパに関連した)

*****century** /séntʃ(ə)ri/ 名 ⓒ (複 **centuries**) ▶定義1 a particular period of 100 years that is used for giving dates 年代を言うのに用いられる特定の100年間→**世紀, 〜世紀** ‖ *We live in the 21st century (= the period between the years 2000 and 2099).* 私たちは21世紀に生きている(=2000年から2099年の期間). ▶定義2 any period of 100 years 任意の100年間→**100年** ‖ *People have been making wine in this area for centuries.* この地域では人々が何百年間もワインを造っている.

**ceramic** /səræmɪk/ 形 ▶定義 made of clay that has been baked 焼いた粘土で作られた→**陶製の, 陶磁器の, 陶芸の** ‖ *ceramic tiles* 陶製のタイル — **ceramic** 名 ⓒ →**陶磁器, 陶芸品, セラミックス** ‖ *an exhibition of ceramics by Picasso* ピカソの陶芸品の展覧会

**cereals**

wheat　rye　barley　millet

oats　maize (米 corn)　rice

★**cereal** /síːriəl/ 名 ●U ▶定義1 any type of grain that can be eaten or made into flour, or the grass that the grain comes from 食用，かつ粉にすることのできる穀物一般，または穀物が実る草木→**穀物，穀類；穀草類** ‖ *Wheat, barley and rye are cereals.* 小麦，大麦，ライ麦は穀物である． ▶定義2 a food that is made from grain, often eaten for breakfast with milk 穀物から作られた食品で，牛乳をかけて朝食で取ることが多い→**穀類加工食品（コーンフレーク，オートミールなど），シリアル** ‖ *a bowl of cereal* ボール1杯のシリアル ☞ C4 ページのさし絵

**cerebral** /sérəbr(ə)l/ 形 ▶定義 of the brain→**脳の，大脳の**

**ceremonial** /sèrəmóʊniəl/ 形 ▶定義 connected with a ceremony 儀式に関連した→**儀式(上)の，儀礼的な，儀式用の；正式・公式の** ‖ *a ceremonial occasion* 祭典行事 — **ceremonially** /-niəli/ 副 →**儀式として，儀式的に**

★**ceremony** /sérəməni; -mòʊni/ 名 ( 複 **ceremonies**) ▶定義1 ●a formal public or religious event 儀礼的な，公式または宗教的行事→**儀式，式典，式** ‖ *the opening ceremony of the Olympic Games* オリンピック大会の開会式 *a wedding ceremony* 結婚式 ▶定義2 ●formal behaviour, speech, actions, etc that are expected on special occasions 特別な機会に求められる正式の振る舞い，演説，行為など→**儀礼，礼儀** ‖ *The new hospital was opened with great ceremony.* 新しい病院の開院式が厳粛に行われた．

★**certain** /sə́ːrtn/ 形 ▶定義1（名詞の前は不可）certain (that...); certain (of sth) completely sure; without any doubts 本当に確信がある；全く疑いなく→**確かで，確信している，きっと～であると思っている** ‖ *She's absolutely certain that there was somebody outside her window.* 彼女は窓の外に絶対にだれかいると思った． *We're not quite certain what time the train leaves.* 列車が何時に出るのかはっきり知らない． *I'm certain of one thing - he didn't take the money.* 私は1つだけ確信している ― 彼は金を取らなかったということだ． ▶定義2 certain (that...); certain (to do sth) sure to happen or to do sth; definite 確実に起こる，または確実にある～をする；確定的な→**間違いなく～する，～するのは疑いがない；確実な，信頼できる** ‖ *It is almost certain that unemployment will increase this year.* 今年はほぼ間違いなく失業率が上昇するだろう． *The Director is certain to agree.* 理事はきっと同意するはずだ． *We must rescue them today, or they will face certain death.* 彼らを今日中に救助しなければならない，さもなければ彼らの死は確実だろう． ☞参 **sure** の注 ▶定義3（名詞の前だけ）used for talking about a particular thing or person without naming them 具体的には示さず特定のものや人に言及する場合に使われる→**ある（決まった），例の** ‖ *You can only contact me at certain times of the day.* 私に連絡が取れるのはある決まった時間だけです． *There are certain reasons why I'd prefer not to meet him again.* ある理由で，もう彼には会いたくない． ▶定義4（名詞の前だけ）some, but not very much あまり多くはないが，いくらかの→**多少の，いくらかの，ある程度の** ‖ *I suppose I have a certain amount of respect for Mr Law.* 私はロウ氏をいくらかは尊敬していると思う． ▶定義5 noticeable but difficult to describe 目に付くがそれを説明するのが難しい→**ある種の，何らかの** ‖ *There was a certain feeling of autumn in the air.* 大気にはある種の秋の気配が感じられた． ▶定義6 正式 used before a person's name to show that you do not know him/her 人の名前の前に付けて，その人を知らないことを示す→**ある，さる，～とかいう人** ‖ *I received a letter from a certain*

*Mrs Berry.* ベリー夫人という人から手紙をもらった.

**成句** **for certain** ▶定義 without doubt 疑いなく→**確かに間違いなく,きっと** || *I don't know for certain what time we'll arrive.* 何時に着くかはっきり分からない.

**make certain (that...)** ▶定義1 to do sth in order to be sure that sth else happens ほかの～が確実に起こるように何かをする→**確実にする, 必ず～するようにする** || *They're doing everything they can to make certain that they win.* 必ず勝てるように,彼らはできる事はすべてやっている. ▶定義2 to do sth in order to be sure that sth is true ～が本当であると確信するために何かをする→**（～を）確かめる,確認する** || *We'd better phone Akram before we go to make certain he's expecting us.* 行く前にアラムに電話して,私たちを待っていてくれているのか確認した方がいいと思う.

**certainly** /sə́ːrtnli/ 副 ▶定義1 without doubt; definitely 疑いなく;確実に→**確かに,きっと,必ず** || *The number of students will certainly increase after 2001.* 2001年以降は確実に生徒数が増えるだろう. ▶定義2 (used in answer to questions) of course (質問への答えに用いて) もちろん→**その通り,承知しました,いいですとも** || *'Do you think I could borrow your notes?' 'Certainly.'* 「あなたのノートをお借りできますか」「どうぞ」

**certainty** /sə́ːrtnti/ 名 (複 **certainties**) ▶定義1 ❶ the state of being completely sure about sth ～について絶対に確信していること→**確かさ,確信,確実性** || *We can't say with certainty that there is life on other planets.* ほかの惑星にも生物がいると断言することはできない. ⇔ **uncertainty** ▶定義2 ❷ something that is sure to happen 確実に起こる事→**確かな見込み,疑いのない事,必然的な事** || *It's now almost a certainty our team will win the league.* 我々のチームがリーグ優勝するのはもうほぼ確実だ.

*★**certificate** /sərtífikət/ 名 ❸ ▶定義 an official piece of paper that says that sth is true or correct ～が真実である,または間違いがないことを記述した公式の書類→**証明書,証明,証書** || *a birth/marriage/medical certificate* 出生証明書・結婚証明書・診断書

**certify** /sə́ːrtəfài/ 動 ⓗ (現分 **certifying**; 三単現 **certifies**; 過, 過分 **certified**) ▶定義1 to say formally that sth is true or correct ～が真実である,または正しいと正式に言う→**～を証明する,保証する** || *We need someone to certify that this is her signature.* これが彼女の署名だと証明してくれる人が必要だ. ▶定義2 to give sb a certificate to show that he/she has successfully completed a course of training for a particular profession 特定の職業の訓練課程を首尾良く終了したことを示す証明書を～に与える→**～に証明書・免許状を交付する,認定する** || *a certified accountant* 公認会計士

**cesarean** 米 =CAESAREAN

**cf** 略 compare→**比較する,参照する**

**CFC** /sìː ef síː/ 名 ❸ ⓤ ▶定義 chlorofluorocarbon; a type of gas found, for example, in cans of spray which is harmful to the earth's atmosphere クロロフルオロカーボン;例えばスプレー缶などに含まれる気体の一種で,地球の大気には有害な物質→**フロン(ガス)** ☞参 **ozone layer**

**Ch** 略 chapter→**章,重要な一区切り**

*★**chain**¹ /tʃéɪn/ 名 ▶定義1 ❸ ⓤ a line of metal rings that are joined together つなぎ合わせた金属製の環でできた綱→**鎖,チェーン;首飾り** || *a bicycle chain* 自転車のチェーン *She was wearing a silver chain round her neck.* 彼女は首に銀のネックレスをしていた. *a length of chain* 長い鎖 ☞ **jewellery, key, padlock**, S7ページのさし絵 ▶定義2 ❸ a series of connected things or people 関連のあるものや人々の一続き→**列,連鎖,一続き,連続** || *a chain of mountains/a mountain chain* 山並み・山脈 *The book examines the complex **chain of events** that led to the Russian Revolution.* その本は,ロシア革命を引き起こした一連の複雑な事件について考察している. *The Managing Director is at the top of the **chain of command**.* 常務取締役は指揮系統のトップだ. ▶定義3 ❸ a group of shops, hotels, etc that are owned by the same company 同じ会社が所有する店,ホテルなどのグループ→**連鎖店,チェーン(店)** || *a chain of supermarkets* スーパーマーケットのチェーン *a fast-food chain* ファーストフードのチェーン店

**chain**² /tʃéɪn/ 動 ⓗ ▶定義 chain sb/sth (to sth);

**chain** sb/sth (**up**) to fasten sb/sth to sth else with a chain 〜をほかの…に鎖でつなぐ→〜を鎖で(…に)つなぐ；(ドアなど)に鎖をかける，束縛する ‖ *The dog is kept chained up outside.* 犬は外に鎖でつながれて飼われている．

**chain-smoke** 動圓 ▶定義 to smoke continuously, lighting one cigarette after another 次々にたばこに火をつけて絶え間なく吸う→立て続けにたばこを吸う — **chain-smoker** 图 ⓒ→立て続けにたばこを吸う人，チェーンスモーカー

**chain store** 图 ⓒ ▶定義 one of a number of similar shops that are owned by the same company 同じ会社が所有する互いに類似した店の1つ→連鎖店，チェーン店

★**chair**¹ /tʃeər/ ▶定義 1 ⓒ a piece of furniture for one person to sit on, with a seat, a back and four legs 座部，背もたれ，4本の足のある1人掛けの家具→いす ‖ *a kitchen chair* 台所用のいす *an armchair* ひじ掛けいす ☞ C7 ページのさし絵 ▶定義 2 [単数扱い] the person who is controlling a meeting 会議を主宰する人→議長，司会者 ‖ *Please address your questions to the chair.* 質問は議長にしてください．▶定義 3 ⓒ the position of being in charge of a department in a university 大学の学部担当者の地位→大学教授の職 ‖ *She holds the chair of economics at London University.* 彼女はロンドン大学の経済学部教授だ．

**chair**² /tʃeər/ 動他 ▶定義 to be the chairman or chairwoman of a meeting 会議の議長をする→〜の議長を務める，司会をする ‖ *Who's chairing the meeting this evening?* 今夜はだれが議長ですか．

★**chairman** /tʃeərmən/ 图 ⓒ (複 **-men** /-mən/) ▶定義 1 the head of a company or other organization 会社やほかの組織の長→会長，社長，市長・知事の職，委員長 ▶定義 2 a person who controls a meeting 会議を主宰する人→議長，司会者 — **chairmanship** 图 [単数扱い]→議長・会長の地位［任務・期間］，議長・会長の才能［素質］

**chairperson** /tʃeərpɜːrs(ə)n/ 图 ⓒ (複 **-persons**) ▶定義 a person who controls a meeting 会議を主宰する人→議長，司会者

**chairwoman** /tʃeərwʊmən/ 图 ⓒ (複 **-women** /-wɪmən/) ▶定義 a woman who controls a meeting 会議を主宰する女性→(女性)議長，司会者

**chalet** /ʃæleɪ, -ˈ-/ 图 ⓒ ▶定義 a wooden house, especially one built in a mountain area or used by people on holiday 特に山地に建てられたり休日に使われたりする木造の家→シャレー(スイス山地の屋根の突き出た家)，シャレー風の別荘，バンガロー

**chalk**¹ /tʃɔːk/ 图 ▶定義 1 ⓤ a type of soft white rock 柔らかい白い岩→白亜(質)石灰岩 ‖ *chalk cliffs* 白亜の断崖(だんがい) ▶定義 2 ⓒⓤ a small stick of soft white or coloured rock that is used for writing or drawing 白または色の付いた石灰岩製の小さな棒で，文字や絵をかくのに使われる→チョーク，白墨

**chalk**² /tʃɔːk/ 動他圓 ▶定義 to write or draw sth with chalk チョークで〜を書く，または描く→(〜を)チョークで記す，(〜に)チョークを塗る ‖ *Somebody had chalked a message on the wall.* だれかが壁にチョークで伝言を書いた．

句動詞 **chalk sth up** ▶定義 to succeed in getting sth 〜を得ることに成功する→(得点・勝利など)を得る，達成する ‖ *The team has chalked up five wins this summer.* チームはこの夏5勝している．

**chalkboard** /tʃɔːkbɔːrd/ 米=BLACKBOARD

★**challenge**¹ /tʃæləndʒ/ 图 ⓒ ▶定義 1 something new and difficult that forces you to make a lot of effort 多くの努力を必要とする未知の困難→挑戦，やりがいのある仕事，努力目標，課題 ‖ *I'm finding my new job an exciting challenge.* 新しい仕事は刺激的でやりがいがあるとだんだん分かってきた．*The company will have to* **face** *many* **challenges** *in the coming months.* 会社はこの先数か月間に多くの難題に直面せざるを得ないだろう．*How will this government* **meet the challenge** *of rising unemployment?* この政府はどのように失業率上昇という難題に立ち向かうのか．▶定義 2 **a challenge** (**to sb**) (**to do sth**) an invitation from sb to fight, play, argue, etc against him/her 自分に対抗して戦う，競技する，議論するよう求める〜からの誘い→(〜に対する)(…しようという)挑戦，挑戦状，試合の申し込み ‖ *The Prime Minister should accept our challenge and call a new election now.* 首相は我々の抗議に応じて直ちに選挙を行うべきだ．

**challenge**² /tʃǽləndʒ/ 動 ❶ ▶定義1 challenge sb (to sth/to do sth) to invite sb to fight, play, argue, etc against you 自分に対抗して戦う、競技する、議論するよう誘う→〜に挑戦する、〜に（…を・…するように）挑む ‖ They've challenged us to a football match this Saturday. 彼らは私たちに今週の土曜日サッカーの試合を申し込んだ． ▶定義2 to question if sth is true, right, etc, or not 〜が真実か，正しいか，否かを問う→〜に異議を唱える，〜の正当性を疑う，〜を誤りだと主張する ‖ She hates anyone challenging her authority. 彼女は自分の権威に異議を唱える者を嫌う．

**challenger** /tʃǽləndʒər/ 名 ❷ ▶定義 a person who invites you to take part in a competition, because he/she wants to win a title or position that you hold 人が持っている選手権や地位を勝ち取りたいために，競技に参加するようその人を誘う者→（選手権）挑戦者

**challenging** /tʃǽləndʒɪŋ/ 形 ▶定義 forcing you to make a lot of effort 多くの努力を強要する→やりがいのある，挑戦的な ‖ a challenging job やりがいのある仕事

**chamber** /tʃéɪmbər/ 名 ❷ ▶定義1 an organization that makes important decisions, or the room or building where it meets 重要な決定をする組織，またはそうした組織が会議をする部屋や建物→議会，議院；会議場，会館 ‖ a council chamber 会議室 ▶定義2 a closed space in the body, a machine, etc 身体や機械などの閉じた空間→(機械の)室，空間；(生物体内の)小室，房，空洞 ‖ the four chambers of the heart 心臓の4つの心室 ▶定義3 a room that is used for a particular purpose 特別の目的に使用する部屋→特別室，間，部屋 ‖ a burial chamber 埋葬室

**chambermaid** /tʃéɪmbərmèɪd/ 名 ❷ ▶定義 a woman whose job is to clean and tidy hotel bedrooms ホテルの寝室を掃除し整とんすることを仕事とする女性→(ホテルの)部屋係の女性，客室係のメイド

**chamber music** 名 ❶ ▶定義 a type of music (classical music) that is written for a small group of instruments 小規模編成の楽器のために書かれた音楽(クラシック音楽)→室内楽

**champagne** /ʃæmpéɪn/ 名 ❷ ❶ ▶定義 a French white wine which has a lot of bubbles in it and is often very expensive 発泡性のフランス製白ワインで，通常は非常に高価→シャンパン，シャンパン色

\***champion**¹ /tʃǽmpiən/ 名 ❷ ▶定義1 a person, team, etc that has won a competition 競争に勝った人，またはチームなど→優勝者・チーム，選手権保持者，チャンピオン ‖ a world champion 世界チャンピオン a champion swimmer 水泳のチャンピオン ▶定義2 a person who speaks and fights for a particular group, idea, etc 特定の集団，思想などのために代弁し，戦う人→(主義・主張の)擁護者，闘士 ‖ a champion of free speech 言論の自由の擁護者

**champion**² /tʃǽmpiən/ 動 ❶ ▶定義 to support or fight for a particular group or idea 特定の集団や思想を支持する，またはそのために戦う→(主義・主張)のために戦う，〜を擁護する ‖ to champion the cause of human rights 人権という大義を守るために戦う

**championship** /tʃǽmpiənʃɪp/ 名 ❷ (しばしば複数形で) ▶定義 a competition or series of competitions to find the best player or team in a sport or game スポーツや競技で，最高の競技者やチームを見いだすための競争，または一連の競争→選手権(試合)，決勝戦 ‖ the World Hockey Championships ホッケー世界選手権

\***chance**¹ /tʃɑːns; tʃæns/ 名 ▶定義1 **a chance of (doing) sth; a chance (that...)** a possibility 可能性→(〜する・〜の)見込み，公算，成算，勝ち目 ‖ I think there's a good chance that she'll be the next Prime Minister. 彼女が次期首相になる公算が十分あると思う． to have a slim/an outside chance of success 成功の見込みはまずない・ごくわずかだ I think we **stand a good chance** of winning the competition. 競技に勝つ見込みはかなりあると思う． Is there any chance of getting tickets for tonight's concert? 今夜のコンサートのチケットが取れる可能性がありますか． ▶定義2 ❷ **chance (of doing sth/to do sth)** an opportunity 機会→(〜する)好機，チャンス ‖ If somebody invited me to America, I'd jump at the chance (= accept enthusiastically). もしだれかがアメリカに招いてくれたら，私はその好機に飛び付くだろう(=大喜びで受け入れる)． Be quiet and **give** her **a chance** to explain. 静かにして，彼女に説明する

機会を与えましょう. *I think you should tell him now. You may not **get** another **chance**.* 彼に今言うべきだと思う. もう二度とその機会がないかもしれないから. ☛参 **occasion** の注
▶定義3 ❻a risk 危険性➔**危険, 冒険, かけ** ‖ *We may lose some money but we'll just have to take that chance.* いくらか金を失う可能性があるが, かけてみるしかないだろう. *Fasten your seat belt - you shouldn't **take** (any) **chances**.* シートベルトを締めてください－危険です. *I didn't want to **take a chance** on anyone seeing me, so I closed the curtains.* 万一だれかに見られると嫌なので, 私はカーテンを閉めた.
▶定義4 ❶luck; the way that some things happen without any cause that you can see or understand 運; 人に分かったり, 理解できるような原因もなく, 何かが起こること➔**偶然, 巡り合わせ** ‖ *We have to plan every detail - I don't want to **leave** anything **to chance**.* 細かい点まですべて計画しなければならない－何1つ運任せにはしたくないから. *We met **by chance** (= we had not planned to meet) as I was walking down the street.* 私たちは通りを歩いていて偶然に出会った (= 会う予定はなかった).

成句 **by any chance** ▶定義 (used for asking sth politely) perhaps or possibly (~を丁寧に尋ねるときに用いて) 多分, またはおそらく➔**万一にも, ひょっとしたら** ‖ *Are you, **by any chance**, going into town this afternoon?* ひょっとして今日の午後, 街へ行かれますか.

**the chances are (that)…** 略式 ▶定義 it is probable that… の可能性がある➔**多分~であろう** ‖ *The chances are that it will rain tomorrow.* 多分明日は雨になるでしょう.

**no chance** 略式 ▶定義 there is no possibility of that happening その事が起こる可能性はない➔**ありっこない, そんなはずはない** ‖ *'Perhaps your mother will give you the money.' 'No chance!'* 「君のお母さんが金をくれるかもしれない」「そんな事ありっこない」

**on the off chance** ▶定義 in the hope that sth might happen, although it is not very likely あまり可能性はないが, ひょっとしたら~が起こるかもしれないと期待して➔**万一にも~と思って, ~を期待して** ‖ *I didn't think you'd be at home, but I just called in on the off chance.* 君が家にいるとは思わなかったけれど, ひょっとしたらと思って寄ってみたんだ.

**chance**² /tʃɑːns; tʃæns/ 動 ▶定義1 他 略式 **chance sth/doing sth** to risk sth ~を危険にさらす➔**~を運に任せてやってみる, (失敗を覚悟で) やってみる** ‖ *It might be safe to leave the car here, but I'm not going to **chance it**.* ここに車を止めておいても安全だとは思うが, 用心するに越したことはない. ▶定義2 自 正式 **chance to do sth** to do sth without planning or trying to do it 前もって計画したりやってみようと思ったりせずに~を行う➔**たまたま~する, 偶然~する** ‖ *I chanced to see the letter on his desk.* 私は偶然に彼の机の上の手紙を見てしまった.

**chance**³ /tʃɑːns; tʃæns/ 形 (名詞の前だけ) ▶定義 not planned あらかじめ計画されていたわけではない➔**偶然の, 思い掛けない** ‖ *a chance meeting* 偶然の出会い

**chancellor** /ˈtʃɑːns(ə)lər, tʃæn-/ 名 ❻ ▶定義1 the head of the government in some countries 一部の国における政府の長➔**(ドイツ・オーストリアの) 首相** ‖ *the German chancellor* ドイツ首相 ▶定義2 (または **Chancellor of the Exchequer**) 英the government minister who makes decisions about taxes and government spending 税や政府の歳出について決定する大臣➔**大蔵大臣**

**chandelier** /ˌʃændəˈlɪər/ 名 ❻ ▶定義 a large round frame with many branches for lights or candles, that hangs from the ceiling and is decorated with small pieces of glass 明かりやろうそくを固定するために枝状の物がたくさん出ている大型の円い枠で, 天井からつるされ, ガラスの小片で飾られている➔**シャンデリア**

*★**change**¹ /tʃeɪndʒ/ 動 ▶定義1 自他 to become different or to make sb/sth different; to alter 違うものになる, または~を違うものにする; 改める➔**変わる, 変化する; 変える, 変更する** ‖ *This town has changed a lot since I was young.* 私が若かったころと比べて, この街は大きく変わった. *Our plans have changed - we leave in the morning.* 計画を変更しました－午前中に出発します. *His lottery win has not changed him at all.* 富くじに当たっても彼は全く変わっていない. ▶定義2 自他 **change (sb/sth) to/into sth**; **change (from A) (to/into B)** to become a dif-

ferent thing; to make sb/sth take a different form 違ったものになる；～を違う形にする→～に変わる，～を(…に)変える，(Aから)(Bに)変化する，変ぼうする ‖ *The traffic lights changed from green to red.* 信号が青から赤に変わった．*They changed the spare bedroom into a study.* 彼らは予備の寝室を書斎に改装した．*The new job changed him into a more confident person.* 新しい職に就いてから彼は自信に満ちた人に変わった．▶定義3 ⓖ **change sth (for sth)** to take, have or use sth instead of sth else ほかの～の代わりにある…を取る，持つ，使う，など→～を(…に)取り替える，交換する，換える ‖ *Could I change this blouse for a larger size?* このブラウスを大きいサイズと交換できますか．*to change jobs* 転職する *to change a wheel on a car* 車のタイヤを交換する *to change direction* 方向転換する *Can I change my appointment from Wednesday to Thursday?* 予約を水曜日から木曜日に変更できますか．

▶定義4 ⓖ **to change sth (with sb)**(複数名詞と用いて) to exchange sth with sb, so that you have what he/she had, and he/she has what you had; to swap ～と，…を交換して，相手が持っていたものを自分が所有し，自分が持っていたものを相手が所有するようにする；交換する→～を(人と)取り替える，交換する，交易する ‖ *The teams change ends at half-time.* チームはハーフタイムにコートチェンジする．*If you want to sit by the window I'll change seats with you.* 窓際がよろしければ席を代わりましょう．

▶定義5 ⓐⓖ **change (out of sth) (into sth)** to take off your clothes and put different ones on 服を脱いで別の服を着る→着替える，服を取り替える ‖ *He's changed his shirt.* 彼はシャツを着替えた．*I had a shower and changed before going out.* 私は外出前にシャワーを浴びて着替えた．*She changed out of her work clothes and into a clean dress.* 彼女は仕事用の服を脱いで清潔なドレスに着替えた．

➤ *get changed* は「服を着替える」場合によく用いる: *You can get changed in the bedroom.* (寝室で着替えなさい．)

▶定義6 ⓖ to put clean things onto sb/sth ～に清潔な物を付ける→取り替える，替える ‖ *The baby's nappy needs changing.* 赤ちゃんのおむつを替えなければならない．*to change the bed* (= to put clean sheets on) ベッドのシーツを替える(＝清潔なシーツにする) ▶定義7 ⓖ **change sth (for/into sth)** to give sb money and receive the same amount back in money of a different type ～に金を与え，同じ金額を異なる種類の金で受け取る→(金)を(～に)両替する，崩す ‖ *Can you change a ten-pound note for two fives?* 10ポンド紙幣を5ポンド紙幣2枚に換えてくれませんか．*I'd like to change fifty pounds into US dollars.* 50ポンドを米ドルに換えたいのですが．▶定義8 ⓐⓖ to get out of one bus, train, etc and get into another 1つのバス，列車などから降りて別のバス，列車などに乗る→(～を)乗り換える，乗り継ぐ ‖ *Can we get to London direct or do we have to change (trains)?* 直行でロンドンへ行けますか，それとも(列車を)乗り換えなければなりませんか．

成句 **change hands** ▶定義 to pass from one owner to another 1人の所有者からほかへ渡る→持ち主が変わる

**change your mind** ▶定義 to change your decision or opinion 決心や意見を変える→考えが変わる，気が変わる，変心する ‖ *I'll have the green one. No, I've changed my mind - I want the red one.* 緑色のにします．いや，気が変わりました－赤いのにします．

**change/swap places (with sb)** ⇒ **PLACE**¹
**change the subject** ▶定義 to start talking about sth different 違う～について話し始める→話題を変える，話の方向を変える

**change your tune** 略式 ▶定義 to change your opinion or feelings about sth ～についての意見や感情を変える→調子，論調，態度を変える

**change your ways** ▶定義 to start to live or behave in a different and better way from before 以前とは違って良い生活をしたり，振る舞いをしたりするようになる→改心する，行動を改める

**chop and change** ⇒ **CHOP**¹

句動詞 **change over (from sth) (to sth)** ▶定義 to stop doing or using one thing and start doing or using sth else ある事をしたり，あるものを使うことをやめて，ほかの～をしたり使ったりする→(～から)(…に)切り替える，替える ‖ *The theatre has changed over to a com-*

*puterized booking system.* その劇場はコンピューター予約システムに切り替えた.

**★change²** /tʃeɪndʒ/ 名 ▶定義1 ⓒ ⓤ **change (into sth)** the process of becoming or making sth different 違う〜になる,または違う〜にする過程→(〜の・〜への)変化,変遷,変更,変動,修正 ‖ *There was little change in the patient's condition overnight.* 患者の病状は1晩ほとんど変わらなかった. *After two hot summers, people were talking about a change in the climate.* 暑い夏が2年続いたので,人々は気候が変わったと話している. ▶定義2 ⓒ **a change (of sth)** something that you take, have or use instead of sth else ほかの〜の代わりに取る,持つ,使うことのできるもの→(〜を)取り替えること,代替,交替,異動 ‖ *We must notify the bank of our change of address.* 住所の変更を銀行に知らせなければならない. *I packed my toothbrush and a change of clothes.* 歯ブラシと着替え用の服を詰めた. ▶定義3 ⓤ the money that you get back if you pay more than the amount sth costs 〜の価格より多く支払った場合に返ってくる金→釣り(銭),崩した金 ‖ *If a paper costs 60p and you pay with a pound coin, you will get 40p change.* 新聞の値段が60ペンスで,1ポンドの硬貨で支払えば,40ペンスのお釣りをもらえます. ▶定義4 ⓤ coins of low value 価値の低い硬貨→小銭,ばら銭 ‖ *He needs some change for the phone.* 彼は電話をかけるために小銭を欲しがっている. *Have you got change for a twenty-pound note? (= coins or notes of lower value that together make twenty pounds)* 20ポンド(札)が崩れますか. (= 合わせて20ポンドになる,より小さい硬貨や紙幣)

成句 **a change for the better/worse** ▶定義 a person, thing or situation that is better/worse than the one before 以前より良い・悪い人,物や状況→好転・悪化

**a change of heart** ▶定義 a change in your opinion or the way that you feel 意見の変化,または感じ方の変化→変心,転向,心変わり

**for a change** ▶定義 in order to do sth different from usual いつもとは違う〜をするために→気分転換に,時には,目先を変えて ‖ *I usually cycle to work, but today I decided to walk for a change.* いつもは自転車で仕事に行くが,今日は気分転換に歩くことにした.

**make a change** ▶定義 to be enjoyable or pleasant because it is different from what you usually do いつもする事とは違うので,楽しいまたは心地良い→(物事がうれしいことに)これまでと違う,気分転換になる

**changeable** /tʃeɪndʒəb(ə)l/ 形 ▶定義 likely to change; often changing 変化しそうな; 始終変化している→変わりやすい,移り気な; 変更可能な,可変の ‖ *English weather is very changeable.* 英国の天気はとても気まぐれだ.

**changeover** /tʃeɪndʒəʊvər/ 名 ⓒ ▶定義 a change from one system to another 1つのシステムからほかへの変更→切り替え,転換,改造

**changing room** 名 ⓒ ▶定義 a room for changing clothes in, for example before or after playing sport 例えば運動の前後に衣服を着替えるための部屋→更衣室,ロッカー室

**★channel¹** /tʃænl/ 名 ⓒ ▶定義1 a television station テレビ局→チャンネル,局 ‖ *Which channel is the film on?* その映画を放映しているのは何チャンネルですか. 参 **station¹(4)** ▶定義2 a band of radio waves used for sending out radio or television programmes ラジオやテレビの番組を送信するための無線波の周波数帯→周波数帯,チャンネル ‖ *terrestrial/satellite channels* 地上波・衛星チャンネル ▶定義3 a way or route along which news, information, etc is sent ニュース,情報などが送られる経路→経路,道筋,ルート ‖ *a channel of communication* 通信経路 *You have to order new equipment through the official channels.* 公式のルートで新しい装置を注文する必要がある. ▶定義4 an open passage along which liquids can flow 液体が流れることのできる覆いのない通路→溝,側溝 ‖ *a drainage channel* 排水路 ▶定義5 the part of a river, sea, etc which is deep enough for boats to pass through 川や海などの,小型船が通行することができるくらい深い部分→水路,可航水路,運河; 海峡 ▶定義6 **the Channel** (または **the English Channel**) the sea between England and France 英国とフランスの間の海→イギリス海峡,英仏海峡

**channel²** /tʃænl/ 動 他 ( **channelling**; **channelled**: 米 または **channeling**; **channeled**) ▶定義 to make sth move along a particular path or route ～を特定の通路や経路に沿って移動させる➡**～を水路で運ぶ,～を…に向ける,導く** ‖ *Water is channelled from the river to the fields.* 水は川から畑へ導かれる.(比喩)*You should channel your energies into something constructive.* あなたはそのエネルギーを建設的な物事に向けるべきだ.

**the Channel Tunnel** 名 [単数扱い] ▶定義 the tunnel under the sea that connects England and France 英国とフランスを結ぶ海底トンネル➡**英仏海峡トンネル,ドーバートンネル,ユーロトンネル**

**chant**¹ /tʃɑːnt; tʃænt/ 名 ▶定義1 ❻a word or phrase that is sung or shouted many times 繰り返して何度も歌われる,または叫ばれる言葉や言い回し➡**唱和,シュプレヒコール,スローガン** ‖ *A chant of 'we are the champions' went round the stadium.*「we are the champions(我々がチャンピオンだ)」という唱和が繰り返し競技場を巡った. ▶定義2 ❻Ⓤa usually religious song with only a few notes that are repeated many times 普通は宗教的な歌で,何回も繰り返されるほんのわずかな節(ふし)しか付いていないもの➡**聖歌,詠唱歌,単調な歌**

**chant**² /tʃɑːnt; tʃænt/ 動⾃他 ▶定義 to sing or shout a word or phrase many times 語や句を何回も歌う,または叫ぶ➡**～を詠唱する,唱和する** ‖ *The protesters marched by, chanting slogans.* 抗議する人々はスローガンを繰り返し叫びながら行進していった.

**chaos** /kéiɑs/ 名Ⓤ ▶定義 a state of great disorder; confusion 非常に無秩序な状態; 混乱➡**混とん,大混乱** ‖ *The country was in chaos after the war.* 戦後その国は大混乱に陥った. *The heavy snow has caused chaos on the roads.* 大雪のため道路は大混乱になっている.

**chaotic** /keiɑ́tik/ 形 ▶定義 in a state of chaos 混乱した状態で➡**混とんとした,大混乱の,無秩序な** ‖ *With no one in charge the situation became chaotic.* だれも担当者がいなかったので,大混乱になった.

**chap** /tʃæp/ 名 ❻ 特に 英略式 ▶定義 a man or boy 男または少年➡**(親しみを込めて)やつ; やあ,おい**

**chapel** /tʃǽp(ə)l/ 名 ❻Ⓤ ▶定義 a small building or room that is used by some Christians as a church or for prayer 一部のキリスト教徒が教会として,または祈りの場として使う小さな建物や部屋➡**礼拝堂・室,チャペル,(教会の)付属礼拝堂** ‖ *a Methodist chapel* メソジストの教会堂

**chaperone** /ʃǽpəròʊn/ 名 ❻ ▶定義 in the past, an older person, usually a woman, who went to public places with a young woman who was not married, to look after her and to make sure that she behaved correctly かつて,未婚の若い女性と社交の場所に行き,彼女が正しく振る舞うように彼女の面倒を見た,年配の人物(普通は女性)➡**介添え役中年女性,お目付役,付き添い** ― chaperone 動他➡**～のお目付役をする,～に付き添う**

**\*chapter** /tʃǽptər/ 名 ❻ ▶定義 one of the parts into which a book is divided 書物の中で分割された部分の1つ➡**章,第～章,重要な一区切り** ‖ *Please read Chapter 2 for homework.* 宿題として第2章を読んできてください. (比喩)*The last few years have been a difficult chapter in the country's history.* この数年は国の歴史において困難な時期だった.

**\*character** /kǽrɪktər/ 名 ▶定義1 [❻,通常は単数, Ⓤ] the qualities that make sb/sth different from other people or things; the nature of sb/sth ～をほかの人やものとは異なるようにしている特質; ～の性質➡**個性,性格,特性,特徴** ‖ *Although they are twins, their characters are quite different.* 彼らは双子だが,性格は全く違う. *These two songs are very different in character.* この2曲は特徴がかなり異なる. ▶定義2 Ⓤstrong personal qualities 強い個性➡**人格,人柄,精神力,気骨** ‖ *The match developed into a test of character rather than just physical strength.* その試合は体力よりむしろ,精神力の勝負となった. ▶定義3 Ⓤqualities that make sb/sth interesting ～を興味深くする特質➡**(強い)個性,(優れた・面白い)特徴** ‖ *Modern houses often seem to lack character.* 現代式の住宅は面白みがないことが多いようだ.

▶定義4 Ⓤthe good opinion that people have of you 人々がある人に対して持つ好意的な意見➡**評判,名声** ‖ *The article was a vicious attack on the President's character.* その記事は大統領の評判を傷付ける悪意ある攻撃だった.

▶定義5 ❻略式 an interesting, amusing, strange

or unpleasant person 興味深い, 面白い, 変わったまたは不快な人→個性の強い人, こっけいな人, 奇人, 変人 ‖ *Neil's quite a character - he's always making us laugh.* ニールは全く面白いやつだ － いつも私たちを笑わせている. *I saw a suspicious-looking character outside the bank, so I called the police.* 銀行の外で怪しげな人を見掛けたので, 警察に電話した. ▶定義6 ⓒ a person in a book, story, etc 書物や物語などの中に描かれる人物→登場人物, 配役, キャラクター ‖ *The main character in the film is a boy who meets an alien.* 映画の主役は異星人に出会う少年だ. ▶定義7 ⓒ a letter or sign that you use when you are writing or printing 筆記や印刷に使う文字や記号→(表意)文字, 符号, 記号 ‖ *Chinese characters* 漢字
成句 **in/out of character** ▶定義 typical/not typical of sb/sth ～に特有の・特有でない→～らしい・らしく, ～らしくない・なく ‖ *Emma's rude reply was completely out of character.* エマの無礼な返答は全く彼女らしくなかった.

**characteristic**[1] /ˌkærɪktərˈɪstɪk/ 名 ⓒ ▶定義 **a characteristic of (sb/sth)** a quality that is typical of sb/sth and that makes him/her/it different from other people or things ～に特有で, ほかのものから区別する性質 →～の特性, 特色, 特徴 ‖ *The chief characteristic of fish is they live in water.* 魚類の主な特徴は水中に住むということである.

**characteristic**[2] /ˌkærɪktərˈɪstɪk/ 形 ▶定義 **characteristic of (sb/sth)** very typical of sb/sth ～に非常に特徴的な→～に特有の, 特徴的な ‖ *The flat landscape is characteristic of this part of the country.* 平野がこの国のこの地域の特徴だ. ⇔ **uncharacteristic** — **characteristically** /-k(ə)li/ 副→特徴的に, 特質上 ‖ *'No' he said, in his characteristically direct manner.* いかにも彼らしく, 単刀直入に「駄目だ」と言った.

**characterize** (または **-ise**) /ˈkærɪktəraɪz/ 動 ⊕ 正式 ▶定義1 (しばしば受動態で) to be typical of sb/sth ～の特徴になる→～を特徴付ける, いかにも～らしい, ～によくある ‖ *the tastes that characterize Thai cooking* タイ料理独特の味 ▶定義2 **characterize sb/sth (as sth)** to describe what sb/sth is like ～の様子を説明する→～を (…であると) 描く, 評する ‖ *The President characterized the meeting as friendly and positive.* 大統領は, その会議は友好的かつ建設的だったと述べた.

**charade** /ʃəˈrɑːd; -ˈreɪd/ 名 ▶定義1 ⓒ a situation or event that is clearly false but in which people pretend to do or be sth 明らかに偽りなのに, 何かをしたり何かの振りをしたりする場面や出来事→見せ掛け, 見え透いたまねごと ‖ *They pretend to be friends but it's all a charade. Everyone knows they hate each other.* 彼らは友人の振りをしているが, すべて見せ掛けだ. 彼らがお互いに憎み合っていることは皆知っている.

▶定義2 **charades** ⓤ a party game in which people try to guess the title of a book, film, etc that one person must represent using actions but not words 1人が本や映画などのタイトルを言葉ではなく身振りで示し, ほかの人がそれを当てるパーティーゲーム→シャレード (ジェスチャーゲームの一種); そのジェスチャー, その語句

**charcoal** /ˈtʃɑːkəʊl/ 名 ⓤ ▶定義 a black substance that is produced from burned wood. It can be used for drawing or as a fuel. 焼いた木材から作られる黒い物質. 絵をかいたり燃料として使うことができる→木炭, 炭

★**charge**[1] /tʃɑːdʒ/ 名 ▶定義1 ⓒⓤ the price that you must pay for sth ～に対して支払う代価→料金, 使用料, 手数料, 経費 ‖ *The hotel makes a small charge for changing currency.* そのホテルでは両替時に手数料を少し取られる. *We deliver free of charge.* 無料で配達いたします. ☛参 **price**の注 ▶定義2 ⓒⓤ a statement that says that sb has done sth illegal or bad ～が違法行為, または不正行為をしたという陳述→非難, 告発, 告訴; (告発すべき)罪 ‖ *He was arrested on a charge of murder.* 彼は殺人罪で逮捕された. *The writer dismissed the charge that his books were childish.* 著者は彼の著書が幼稚だという非難を無視した. ▶定義3 ⓤ a position of control over sb/sth; responsibility for sb/sth ～を統率する立場; ～に対する責任→管理, 監督; 義務, 保護 ‖ *Who is in charge of the office while Alan's away?* アランがいない間, 事務所を管理するのはだれですか. *The assistant manager had to take charge of the team when the manager resigned.* 監督が辞任したので, 助

監督がチームを統率しなければならなかった. ▶定義4 ◉a sudden attack where sb/sth runs straight at sb/sth else 〜がほかの…に突進する突然の攻撃➡突撃, 急襲 ▶定義5 ◉the amount of electricity that is put into a battery or carried by a substance 電池に入れることのできる, または物質が帯びている電気の量➡充電, 電荷 ‖ *a positive/negative charge* 正・負電荷

成句 **bring/press charges (against sb)** ▶定義 to formally accuse sb of a crime so that there can be a trial in a court of law 〜の罪を正式に告発し, 裁判所で審理できるようにする➡(人を)**告発する, 起訴する**

reverse the charges ⇒ **REVERSE**[1]

**charge**[2] /tʃɑːrdʒ/ 動 ▶定義1 📧 ⓜ charge (sb/sth) for sth to ask sb to pay a particular amount of money 〜に特定の金額を支払うよう求める➡〜を(…に)**請求する, (支払い)を負担させる, (税など)を科す** ‖ *We charge £35 per night for a single room.* シングルルームで1晩35ポンドです. *They forgot to charge us for the drinks.* 彼らは飲み物の分を請求し忘れた.

☛参 **overcharge** ▶定義2 ⓜ charge sb (with sth) to accuse sb officially of doing sth which is against the law 違法な事をしたとして〜を正式に告発する➡〜を(…の罪で・・・のことで)**告訴する, 訴える** ‖ *Six men have been charged with attempted robbery.* 強盗未遂で6人の男が告発された. ▶定義3 📧 ⓜ to run straight at sb/sth, or in a particular direction, in an aggressive or noisy way 〜を目掛けて突進する, 特定の方向に, 攻撃的にまたは騒々しく走っていく➡**突進する, 駆け寄る, 突然勢いよく進む** ‖ *The bull put its head down ready to charge (us).* (私たちに向かって)突進しようとして雄牛は頭を下げた. *The children charged into the room.* 子供たちが部屋に駆け込んだ. ▶定義4 ⓜ to put electricity into sth 〜に電気を入れる➡〜を**充電する, 荷電する** ‖ *to charge a battery* 電池に充電する ☛参 **recharge**

**chariot** /ˈtʃæriət/ 🔤 ⓒ ▶定義 an open vehicle with two wheels that was pulled by a horse or horses in ancient times 古代の, 1〜数頭の馬に引かせた屋根のない2輪の乗り物➡**2輪馬車, 2頭立て馬車**

**charisma** /kəˈrɪzmə/ 🔤 ⓤ ▶定義 a powerful personal quality that some people have to attract and influence other people 一部の人が持つ, ほかの人々に影響を与える強力な個性➡**カリスマ(的な資質), 信服力, 権威** ‖ *The president is not very clever, but he has great charisma.* 社長はそれほど聡明(そうめい)なわけではないが, 強いカリスマ性を持っている.

— **charismatic** /ˌkærəzˈmætɪk/ 形 ➡**カリスマ的な, 信服力のある**

**charitable** /ˈtʃærətəb(ə)l/ 形 ▶定義1 kind; generous 親切な; 寛大な➡**慈悲深い, 情け深い** ‖ *Some people accused him of lying, but a more charitable explanation was that he had made a mistake.* 彼がうそをついたと非難した人もいるが, もっと寛大に考えれば彼は間違えただけだった. ▶定義2 connected with a charity 慈善(事業)と関連した➡**慈善の, 善意の**

★**charity** /ˈtʃærəti/ 🔤 (🔢 **charities**) ▶定義1 ⓒ ⓤ an organization that collects money to help people who are poor, sick, etc or to do work that is useful to society 貧困, 病気などの人を助けるために, または社会に有益な仕事をするために金を集める組織➡**慈善団体, 慈善事業** ‖ *We went on a sponsored walk to raise money for charity.* 慈善事業の金を募るために, 私たちは慈善クロスカントリー競歩に参加した. ▶定義2 ⓤ kindness towards other people ほかの人々に対する親切➡**博愛, 慈悲心, 思いやり, 同情** ‖ *to act out of charity* 博愛の精神から行動する

**charity shop** 🔤 ⓒ ▶定義 a shop that sells clothes, books, etc given by people to make money for charity 慈善の金を得るために, 人々が寄付した衣類, 本などを売る店➡**慈善の店, 中古店**

★**charm**[1] /tʃɑːrm/ 🔤 ▶定義1 ⓒ ⓤ a quality that pleases and attracts people 人々を喜ばせ引き付ける性質➡**魅力, 感じが良い** ‖ *The charm of the island lies in its unspoilt beauty.* その島の魅力は損なわれていない自然の美しさにある. *Barry found it hard to resist Linda's charms.* バリーはリンダの魅力に抗しきれなかった.

▶定義2 ⓒ something that you wear because you believe it will bring you good luck 幸運をもたらすと信じて身に付ける物➡**魔よけ, お守り** ‖ *a necklace with a lucky charm on it* 幸運のお

262　charm²

守りの付いたネックレス

**\*charm²** /tʃɑːm/ 動他 ▶定義1 to please and attract sb ～を喜ばせ引き付ける➔～を魅了する，うっとりさせる，誘惑する ‖ *Her drawings have charmed children all over the world.* 彼女の絵は世界中の子供たちを夢中にさせている．

▶定義2 to protect sb/sth as if by magic まるで魔法のように～を守る➔～を危害から守る，～を魔力のように取り除く，和らげる ‖ *He has led a charmed life, surviving serious illness and a plane crash.* 重病と飛行機事故から生還するとは，彼は不死身だ．

**charming** /tʃɑːmɪŋ/ 形 ▶定義 very pleasing or attractive 非常に心地良い，または魅力的な➔感じが良い，愛きょうがある，すばらしい，すてきな ‖ *a charming old church* 魅力的な古い教会 — **charmingly** 副➔感じ良く，すてきに

**charred** /tʃɑːd/ 形 ▶定義 burnt black by fire 火で黒く焦げた➔黒焦げになった，炭になった

**chart¹** /tʃɑːt/ 名 ▶定義1 ❶a drawing which shows information in the form of a diagram, etc 図表などの形態で情報を表す線描➔図表，～図，グラフ ‖ *a temperature chart* 温度グラフ *This chart shows the company's sales for this year.* この表は会社の今年の販売高を示している．
☛参 **pie chart, flow chart** ▶定義2 ❶a map of the sea or the sky 海または空の地図➔海図，水路図，航空図 ‖ *navigation charts* 航行図 ▶定義3 **the charts** [複数扱い] an official list of the songs or CDs, etc, that have sold the most in a particular week ある特定の週に最も売れた歌やCDなどの公式のリスト➔ヒットチャート，週間順位表

**chart²** /tʃɑːt/ 動他 ▶定義1 to follow or record sth carefully and in detail ～を注意深く詳細に追跡する，または記録する➔～を詳細に記録する，～の跡をたどる ‖ *This television series charts the history of the country since independence.* その連続テレビ番組は国の独立以降の歴史を詳しくたどっている．▶定義2 to make a map of one area of the sea or sky 海または空の1区域の地図を作る➔～を海図・空図に記す，図に作る ‖ *an uncharted coastline* 地図にない海岸線

**charter¹** /tʃɑːtər/ 名 ❶Ⓤ ▶定義1 a written statement of the rights, beliefs and purposes of an organization or a particular group of people 組織や特定の人々の集団の権利，信念，目的の書面による声明➔宣言，憲章，綱領 ‖ *The club's charter does not permit women to become members.* クラブの憲章では女性の入会は認められていない．▶定義2 the renting of a ship, plane, etc for a particular purpose or for a particular group of people 船，飛行機などを特定の目的で，または特定の集団に賃貸借すること➔貸し切り(契約)，チャーター ‖ *a charter airline* チャーター便

**charter²** /tʃɑːtər/ 動他 ▶定義 to rent a ship, plane, etc for a particular purpose or for a particular group of people 船，飛行機などを特定の目的で，または特定の集団に賃貸借する➔～をチャーターする，(飛行機，車など)を借り切る ‖ *As there was no regular service to the island we had to charter a boat.* その島への定期便はなかったので，船をチャーターしなければならなかった．

**chartered** /tʃɑːtərd/ 形 (名詞の前で) ▶定義 (used about people in certain professions) fully trained; having passed all the necessary exams (特定の職業の人々について) 十分に訓練された；必要な試験すべてに合格した➔免許を受けた，公認の ‖ *a chartered accountant* 公認会計士

**charter flight** 名 ❶ ▶定義 a flight in which all seats are paid for by a travel company and then sold to their customers, usually at a lower price than an ordinary (scheduled) flight 旅行会社が座席を買い占め，普通は通常の便(定期便)よりも低価格で客に販売される便➔チャーター便，チャーター機

**\*chase¹** /tʃeɪs/ 動 ▶定義1 ❶ chase (after) sb/sth to run after sb/sth in order to catch him/her/it ～を捕まえるために追い掛ける➔～を追う，追跡する，追い求める，狩る ‖ *The dog chased the cat up a tree.* 犬は猫を木の上に追い詰めた．*The police car chased after the stolen van.* パトカーが盗まれたワゴン車を追跡した．

▶定義2 ❶to run somewhere fast ある場所を速く走る➔走り回る，駆け回る，急ぐ ‖ *The kids were chasing around the park.* 子供たちが公園を駆け回っていた．

**\*chase²** /tʃeɪs/ 名 ❶ ▶定義 the act of following sb/sth in order to catch him/her/it ～を捕まえるために追い掛けること➔追跡，追撃，追求，追う

こと ‖ *an exciting car chase* はらはらする車の追跡場面

**成句 give chase** ▶定義 to begin to run after sb/sth in order to try to catch him/her/it 捕まえるために〜を追い掛け始める→**追う, 追跡する, 追撃する** ‖ *The robber ran off and the policeman gave chase.* 強盗が逃走し, 警官が追跡した.

**chasm** /kǽz(ə)m/ 名 C ▶定義 1 a deep hole in the ground 地面に開いた深い穴→**大きな亀裂(きれつ), 深い割れ目, 小峡谷** ▶定義 2 a wide difference of feelings, interests, etc between two people or groups 二者の感情や興味などの大きな違い→**亀裂, (感情, 意見などの)食い違い, 隔たり, 溝**

**chassis** /ʃǽsi, tʃǽsi/ 名 C ( 複 **chassis** /ʃǽsi, tʃǽsi/) ▶定義 the metal frame of a vehicle onto which the other parts fit 車両部分の金属の枠で, その上にほかの部品が取り付けられる→**車台, シャシー**

**chaste** /tʃéɪst/ 形 ( 古 ) ▶定義 1 not involving thoughts and feelings about sex 性についての考えや感情を伴わない→**純正な, みだらでない, きちんとした, 上品な** ‖ *She gave him a chaste kiss on the cheek.* 彼女は彼のほおに友情のキスをした. ▶定義 2 never having had a sexual relationship, or only with your husband/wife 性的関係を持ったことがない, または夫・妻とだけ性的関係を持つ→**純潔な, 貞節な; 汚れのない** — **chastity** /tʃǽstəti/ 名 U→**純潔, 貞節, 純正, 清純**

**chat**¹ /tʃǽt/ 動 自 (**chatting**; **chatted**) ▶定義 **chat (with/to sb) (about sth)** to talk to sb in a friendly, informal way 〜と親しみのあるくだけた調子で話す→**(〜と)(…について)おしゃべりする, 談笑する, 歓談する** ‖ *The two grandmothers sat chatting about the old days.* 2 人のおばあさんは腰を下ろして昔の事を語り合った.

**句動 chat sb up** 英 略式 ▶定義 to talk to sb in a friendly way because you are sexually attracted to him/her 性的魅力を感じて〜に親しげに話し掛ける→**〜に言い寄る, 〜を口説く**

**chat**² /tʃǽt/ 名 C U ▶定義 a friendly informal conversation 親しげな, くだけた会話→**おしゃべり, 談笑, 歓談** ‖ *I'll **have a chat** with Jim about the arrangements.* 準備についてジムとちょっと話し合ってみよう.

**chat show** 名 C ▶定義 a television or radio programme on which well-known people are invited to talk about themselves 有名人が招かれて自分自身について語るテレビ番組やラジオ番組→**対談番組, インタビュー番組, トークショー**

**chatter** /tʃǽtər/ 動 自 ▶定義 1 to talk quickly or for a long time about sth unimportant 取るに足らない事を早口に, または長い時間話す→**ぺちゃくちゃしゃべる, ぺらぺらしゃべる; 無駄話をする** ‖ *The children were laughing and chattering excitedly.* 子供たちは活発に笑いおしゃべりした. ▶定義 2 (used about your teeth) to knock together because you are cold or frightened (歯について)寒くて, またはおびえてぶつかり合う→**がちがち鳴る, がたがたと音を立てる** — **chatter** 名 U→**ぺちゃくちゃしゃべること, おしゃべり, がたがた・カタカタいう音**

**chatty** /tʃǽti/ 形 ▶定義 1 talking a lot in a friendly way 親しげにたくさん話す→**おしゃべりな, 話し好きの, 話しやすい** ▶定義 2 in an informal style くだけた調子の→**打ち解けた, くだけた** ‖ *a chatty letter* 打ち解けた調子の手紙

**chauffeur** /ʃóʊfər, ʃoʊfɜ́ːr/ 名 C ▶定義 a person whose job is to drive a car for sb else ほかの〜のために車を運転する職業の人→**お抱え運転手, 運転手** ‖ *a chauffeur-driven limousine* お抱え運転手が運転するリムジン — **chauffeur** 動 他→**〜のお抱え運転手を務める**

\*cheap¹ /tʃíːp/ 形 ▶定義 1 low in price, costing little money 価格が低い, ほとんど金がかからない→**安い, 安価な** ‖ *Oranges are cheap at the moment.* ちょうど今はオレンジが安い. *Computers are getting cheaper all the time.* コンピューターはどんどん安くなっていく. ☛類 **inexpensive** ⇔ **expensive** ▶定義 2 charging low prices 低い値段を付ける→**安い, 費用が少なくて済む, 低価格の** ‖ *a cheap hotel/restaurant* 安いホテル・レストラン ▶定義 3 low in price and quality and therefore not attractive 価格と質が低いため魅力的でない→**安っぽい, つまらない** ‖ *The clothes in that shop look cheap.* あの店の服は安っぽく見える.

**成句 dirt cheap** ⇒ **DIRT**

**cheap**² /tʃíːp/ 副 略式 ▶定義 for a low price 安価で→**安く, 安っぽく** ‖ *I got this coat cheap in the sale.* このコートは特売で安く買った.

## cheaply

成句 **be going cheap** 略式 ▶定義 be on sale at a lower price than usual 通常より安い価格で売る→**安く, 割引で**

**cheaply** /tʃiːpli/ 副 ▶定義 for a low price 安価で→**安く, 低価格で**

★**cheat**¹ /tʃiːt/ 動 ▶定義 1 ⓔ to trick sb, especially when that person trusts you; to deceive sb 特に~が信用しているときにだます; ~を欺く→**~をだます, 偽る, ごまかす** ‖ *The shopkeeper cheated customers by giving them too little change.* その店主はお釣りをごまかした. ▶定義 2 ⓔ **cheat (at sth)** to act in a dishonest or unfair way in order to get an advantage for yourself 自分の利益のために不誠実な, または不正な行動を取る→**~でごまかしをする, 不正行為・カンニングをする** ‖ *Paul was caught cheating in the exam.* ポールは試験でカンニングをして見つかった. *to cheat at cards* トランプでいかさまをする ▶定義 3 ⓔ **cheat (on sb)** to not be faithful to your husband, wife or regular partner by having a secret sexual relationship with sb else ほかの~と秘密の性的関係を持って, 夫, 妻, または決まったパートナーを裏切る→**(~に隠れて)浮気をする, 不倫をする**

句動詞 **cheat sb (out) of sth** ▶定義 to take sth from sb in a dishonest or unfair way 不誠実な, または不正なやり方で~から…を取る→**人から物をだまし取る, ~を巻き上げる** ‖ *They tried to cheat the old lady out of her savings.* 彼らは老婦人から貯金を巻き上げようとした.

**cheat**² /tʃiːt/ 名 ⓒ ▶定義 a person who cheats ごまかしをする人→**詐欺師, いかさま師**

★**check**¹ /tʃek/ 動 ▶定義 1 ⓔⓘ **check (sth) (for sth)** to examine or test sth in order to make sure that it is safe or correct, in good condition, etc ~の安全性, 正確さ, 具合の良し悪しなどを確認するために検査したり調べたりする→**~を点検する, 調査する, 確かめる** ‖ *Check your work for mistakes before you hand it in.* 答案を提出する前に間違いがないか確認しなさい. *The doctor X-rayed me to check for broken bones.* 医師は骨折しているかどうか調べるためレントゲンを撮った. ▶定義 2 ⓔⓘ **check (sth) (with sb)** to make sure that sth is how you think it is ~が思った通りかどうか確認する→(人に)(~を)確かめる, 問い合わせる, 照合する ‖ *You'd better check with Tim that it's OK to borrow his bike.* 自転車を借りてもいいかどうかティムに聞いた方がいいよ. *I'll phone and check what time the bus leaves.* 電話してバスが何時に出るか問い合わせてみます. ▶定義 3 ⓔ to stop or make sb/sth stop or go more slowly ~を止める, 止まらせる, またはゆっくりと進ませる→**~を阻止する, 抑止する, 妨害する, 遅らせる** ‖ *She almost told her boss what she thought of him, but checked herself in time.* 彼女は上司のことをどう思っているかもう少しで本人に口を滑らせそうになったが, 辛うじて思いとどまった. *Phil checked his pace as he didn't want to tire too early.* あまり早く疲れないようにフィルはペースを落とした. ▶定義 4 ⓔ 米 = **TICK**¹(2)

句動詞 **check in (at…); check into…** ▶定義 to go to a desk in a hotel or an airport and tell an official that you have arrived ホテルや空港でフロントやカウンターに行って係に自分の到着を告げる→**(~で・~に)宿泊手続きをする, 搭乗手続きをする, チェックインする**

**check sth off** ▶定義 to mark names or items on a list リストの名前や項目に印を付ける→**~に照合済みの印を付ける, 表にチェックする** ‖ *The boxes were all checked off as they were unloaded.* 箱は荷降ろしされた時にすべてチェックされた.

**check (up) on sb/sth** ▶定義 to find out how sb/sth is ~の様子を調べる→**~を調べる, 調査する, 確認する** ‖ *We call my grandmother every evening to check up on her.* 毎晩私たちは祖母に電話して様子を確認する.

**check up on sb/sth** ▶定義 to make sure that sb/sth is working correctly, behaving well, etc, especially if you think he/she/it is not ~が正しく作動しているか, 調子がいいかなどを, 特にそうでないと思われる場合に確認する→**~を詳しく調べる, 検査する, 点検する**

**check out (of…)** ▶定義 to pay your bill and leave a hotel 料金を払ってホテルを出る→**勘定を済ませて(~を)出る, チェックアウトする**

**check sb/sth out** ▶定義 1 to find out more information about sb/sth, especially to find out if sth is true or not 特にある事の真偽を確かめるために, ~についてさらに情報を見つける→~

を調べ上げる，確かめる ‖ We need to check out these rumours of possible pay cuts. 賃金カットのうわさが本当かどうかよく確認する必要がある． ▶定義2 特に 困 (俗語) to look at sth, especially to find out if you like him/her/it 特に気に入るかどうか知るために〜を見てみる→〜を調べる，確かめる ‖ I'm going to check out that new club tonight. 今夜その新しいクラブをのぞいてみよう．

\*check² /tʃek/ 图 ▶定義1 ⓒa check (on sth) a close look at sth to make sure that it is safe, correct, in good condition, etc 〜の安全性，正しさ，具合の良し悪しなどを確認するために詳しく調べること→調査，検査，照合 ‖ We carry out/do regular checks on our products to make sure that they are of high quality. 製品の定期検査を実施して品質確認している．I don't go to games, but I like to keep a check on my team's results. 試合を見には行かないけれど，ひいきのチームの結果を常にチェックするのが好きだ．

▶定義2 ⓒⓊa pattern of squares, often of different colours 普通は色の異なる四角形の模様→格子柄，チェック ‖ a check jacket チェックの上着 a pattern of blue and red checks 青と赤のチェック柄 ▶定義3 Ⓤthe situation in a particular game (chess), in which a player must move to protect his/her king 特定のゲーム（チェス）で，指し手が駒（こま）を動かして自分のキングを守らなければならない状態→王手，チェック ☛参 checkmate ▶定義4 困=CHEQUE ▶定義5 困=BILL¹(1) ▶定義6 困=TICK²(1) 成句 hold/keep sth in check ▶定義 to stop sth from advancing or increasing too quickly 〜が急激な進行や増加を止める→〜を食い止める，抑える，抑止する ‖ government measures to keep inflation in check インフレを抑える政府の対策

**checkbook** 困=CHEQUEBOOK

**checked** /tʃekt/ 形 ▶定義 with a pattern of squares 四角形の模様の→格子柄の，チェックの ‖ a red-and-white checked tablecloth 赤と白のチェックのテーブルクロス

**checkers** /tʃekərz/ 困=DRAUGHT¹(2)

**check-in** 图 ⓒ ▶定義1 the act of checking in at an airport 空港で搭乗手続きをすること→チェックイン ‖ Our check-in time is 10.30 am. 私たちのチェックインは午前10時30分です．

# cheeky 265

▶定義2 the place where you check in at an airport 空港の搭乗手続きをする場所→チェックインカウンター

**checking account** 困=CURRENT ACCOUNT

**checklist** /tʃeklɪst/ 图 ⓒ ▶定義 a list of things that you must do or have すべき事や所持品の一覧→（確認用の）照合表，一覧表，チェックリスト

**checkmate** /tʃekmeɪt/ 图 Ⓤ ▶定義 the situation in a particular game (chess), in which you cannot protect your king and so have lost the game 特定のゲーム（チェス）でキングを守れず，負けとなる→詰み，チェックメイト ☛参 check²(3)

**checkout** /tʃekaʊt/ 图 ⓒ ▶定義 the place in a large food shop (supermarket) where you pay 大型の食料品店（スーパーマーケット）の支払いをする場所→レジ，勘定カウンター

**checkpoint** /tʃekpɔɪnt/ 图 ⓒ ▶定義 a place where all people and vehicles must stop and be checked すべての通行人や車両が停止して検査を受ける場所→検問所，チェックポイント ‖ an army checkpoint 軍の検問所

**check-up** 图 ⓒ ▶定義 a general medical examination to make sure that you are healthy 健康を確認するための全身医療検査→健康診断，健診

**cheddar** /tʃedər/ 图 Ⓤ ▶定義 a type of hard yellow cheese 固くて黄色いチーズの一種→チェダーチーズ

\*cheek /tʃiːk/ 图 ▶定義1 ⓒeither side of the face below your eyes 目の下の部分→ほお ☛ C5 ページのさし絵 ▶定義2 ⓒⓊ困 rude behaviour; lack of respect 無礼な振る舞い; 敬意の欠如→生意気な言動，ずうずうしさ ‖ He's got a cheek, asking to borrow money again! 彼は厚かましい，また金を貸してくれと言うなんて．

成句 (with) tongue in cheek ⇒ TONGUE

**cheekbone** /tʃiːkbəʊn/ 图 ⓒ ▶定義 the bone below your eye 目の下の骨→ほお骨，頬骨（かんこつ）☛ C5 ページのさし絵

**cheeky** /tʃiːki/ 形 困 (cheekier; cheekiest) ▶定義 not showing respect; rude 敬意を示さない; 無礼な→礼儀知らずな，生意気な，ずうずうしい ‖ Don't be so cheeky! Of course I'm not fat! 失礼な事言わないで．もちろん私，太ってなんかいないわ．— cheekily 副→無礼な態度で，

ずうずうしく

**★cheer¹** /tʃɪər/ 動 ▶定義1 自他 to shout to show that you like sth or to encourage sb who is taking part in competition, sport, etc 何かが好きであることを示すために、または競技、スポーツなどに参加している〜を励ますために叫ぶ→〜に喝さいを送る、歓呼する、〜を声援する ‖ *Everyone cheered the winner as he crossed the finishing line.* 優勝者がゴールすると皆が喝さいを送った. ▶定義2 他 to make sb happy or more hopeful 〜を喜ばせる、または希望を持たせる→〜を元気づける、活気づける、励ます、慰める ‖ *They were all cheered by the good news.* 彼ら全員が良い知らせに活気づいた.

句動詞 cheer sb on ▶定義 to shout in order to encourage sb in a race, competition, etc レース、競技などで〜を励ますために叫ぶ→〜に喝さいを送る、〜を声援する ‖ *As the runners started the last lap the crowd cheered them on.* 走者たちが最後の1周に入ると、観衆が声援を送った.

cheer (sb/sth) up ▶定義 to become or to make sb happier; to make sth look more attractive 幸福になる、または〜を喜ばせる；〜がより魅力的に見えるようにする→元気になる、〜を元気づける、励ます；活気づける、明るくする ‖ *Cheer up! Things aren't that bad.* 元気を出して. そう悲観的になることはないよ. *A few pictures would cheer this room up a bit.* 数枚の絵があればこの部屋もいくらか明るくなるだろう.

**★cheer²** /tʃɪər/ 名 C ▶定義 a loud shout to show that you like sth or to encourage sb who is taking part in a competition, sport, etc 何かが好きであることを示すため、または競技、スポーツなどで競技している〜を応援するために上げる大声→喝さい、歓呼、声援 ‖ *The crowd **gave a cheer** when the president appeared.* 大統領が現れると群衆が喝さいを送った.

**★cheerful** /ˈtʃɪərfʊl, -f(ə)l/ 形 ▶定義 feeling happy; showing that you are happy 幸福に感じる；自分が幸福なことを示す→機嫌のいい、快活な、明るい、元気のいい ‖ *Caroline is always very cheerful.* キャロラインはいつもとても快活だ. *a cheerful smile* 快活な笑み ― **cheerfully** /-fʊli, -f(ə)li/ 副 →機嫌良く、快活に ― **cheerfulness**

名 U →機嫌がいいこと、快活なこと

**cheerio** /ˌtʃɪəriˈoʊ/ 間 英 略式 ▶定義 goodbye さようなら→じゃあまた、それじゃあ

**cheerleader** /ˈtʃɪərˌliːdər/ 名 C (特に米国で) ▶定義 one of a group of girls or women at a sports match who wear special uniforms and shout, dance, etc in order to encourage people to support the players スポーツの試合で特別のユニフォームを着て叫んだり踊ったりし、観衆が選手の応援に励むよう働き掛ける少女や女性から成る一団のメンバー→チアリーダー、(女性の)応援団員

**cheers** /tʃɪərz/ 間 略式 ▶定義1 used to express good wishes before you have an alcoholic drink アルコール飲料を飲む前に幸運を祈るために用いて→乾杯、健康を祝して ‖ *'Cheers,' she said, raising her wine glass.* 彼女は「乾杯」と言ってワイングラスを掲げた. ▶定義2 英 goodbye さようなら→じゃあね、ではまた ▶定義3 英 thank you ありがとう→どうも

**cheery** /ˈtʃɪəri/ 形 ▶定義 happy and smiling 幸福でほほえんでいる→上機嫌の、陽気な ‖ *a cheery remark/wave/smile* 陽気な言葉・陽気に手を振る・陽気な笑み ― **cheerily** 副 →上機嫌で、陽気に

**★cheese** /tʃiːz/ 名 ▶定義1 U a type of food made from milk. Cheese is usually white or yellow in colour and can be soft or hard. 牛乳から作る食品の一種. 色は通常白か黄で、柔らかい物も硬い物もある→チーズ、チーズ状のもの ‖ *a piece of cheese* チーズ1個 *a cheese sandwich* チーズサンドイッチ ☛ C4ページのさし絵 ▶定義2 C a type of cheese ある種類のチーズ→チーズ、チーズの種類 ‖ *a wide selection of cheeses* さまざまな種類のチーズ

**cheesecake** /ˈtʃiːzˌkeɪk/ 名 C U ▶定義 a type of cake that is made from soft cheese and sugar on a pastry or biscuit base, often with fruit on top ペーストリーやビスケットの台の上に柔らかいチーズと砂糖を(混ぜ合わせて)乗せたケーキの一種で、しばしば上に果実を飾る→チーズケーキ

**cheetah** /ˈtʃiːtə/ 名 C ▶定義 a large wild cat with black spots that can run very fast 黒い斑点(はんてん)のある大型のネコ科の野生動物で、走るのが非常に速い→チーター ☛ lion のさし絵

**chef** /ʃef/ 名 C ▶定義 a professional cook,

especially the head cook in a hotel, restaurant, etc プロの料理人, 特にホテル, レストランなどの料理長➡**コック長, シェフ, コック**

\***chemical**¹ /kémɪk(ə)l/ 形 ▶定義 connected with chemistry; involving changes to the structure of a substance 化学と関連した; 物質の構造の変化を伴う➡**化学の, 化学的な, 化学薬品の; 化学作用の** ‖ *a chemical reaction* 化学反応 ― **chemically** /-k(ə)li/ 副 ➡**化学的に, 化学作用によって, 化学的に見ると**

\***chemical**² /kémɪk(ə)l/ 名 C ▶定義 a substance that is used or produced in a chemical process 化学的工程で使用される, または生産される物質➡**化学物質, 化学製品・薬品** ‖ *Sulphuric acid is a dangerous chemical.* 硫酸は危険な化学物質だ. *chemical weapons/warfare* 化学兵器・戦争

\***chemist** /kémɪst/ 名 C ▶定義1 (または **pharmacist**, 米 **druggist**) a person who prepares and sells medicines 薬品を調合し販売する人➡**薬剤師, 薬屋** ▶定義2 **the chemist's** (米 **drugstore**) a shop that sells medicines, soap, camera film, etc 薬品, せっけん, 写真フィルムなどを売る店➡**薬局, 薬屋, ドラッグストア** ‖ *I got my tablets from the chemist's.* 薬局で錠剤を買った. ▶定義3 a person who is a specialist in chemistry 化学の専門家➡**化学者**

\***chemistry** /kémɪstri/ 名 U ▶定義1 the scientific study of the structure of substances and what happens to them in different conditions or when mixed with each other 物質の構造や, さまざまな条件や混合による物質の変化を研究する科学➡**化学** ‖ *We did an experiment in the chemistry lesson today.* 今日, 化学の授業で実験をした. ▶定義2 the structure of a particular substance 特定の物質の構造➡**化学的性質, 化学構造・作用**

\***cheque** (米 **check**) /tʃek/ 名 C U ▶定義 a piece of paper printed by a bank that you sign and use to pay for things 銀行で印刷される紙片で, 署名をして物の支払いに使用する➡**小切手** ‖ *She wrote out a cheque for £20.* 彼女は20ポンドの小切手を切った. *I went to the bank to cash a cheque.* 私は銀行に行って小切手を現金に換えた. *Can I pay by cheque?* 小切手で支払えますか. ☞ **money** のさし絵

**chequebook** (米 **checkbook**) /tʃékbʊk/ 名 C ▶定義 a book of cheques 小切手のとじ込み帳➡**小切手帳**

**cheque card** 名 C 英 ▶定義 a small plastic card that you show when you pay with a cheque as proof that your bank will pay the amount on the cheque 小切手で支払いをするときに提示する, 銀行が小切手の金額を支払う証明の小さなプラスチックのカード➡**チェックカード** ☞参 **cash card**, **credit card**

**cherish** /tʃérɪʃ/ 動 ▶定義1 to love sb/sth and look after him/her/it carefully ～を愛して大切に面倒を見る➡～**を大事にする, (愛情を込めて)世話をする** ‖ *The ring was her most cherished possession.* その指輪は彼女の一番大切なものだった. ▶定義2 to keep a thought, feeling, etc in your mind and think about it often 考え, 感情などを心に抱いて, それについてしばしば考える➡**(望み, 考え, 感情など)～を持ち続ける, 思い続ける, 胸に秘める** ‖ *a cherished memory* 胸に秘めた思い出

**cherry** /tʃéri/ 名 C (複 **cherries**) ▶定義1 a small round black or red fruit that has a stone inside it 中に種のある小さく丸い, 黒ずんだまたは赤い果実➡**サクランボ, 桜桃; サクランボ色, 鮮紅色** ☞ C3 ページのさし絵 ▶定義2 (または **cherry tree**) the tree that produces cherries サクランボのなる木➡**サクラの木**

**chess** /tʃes/ 名 U ▶定義 a game for two people that is played on a board with 64 black and white squares (**a chessboard**). Each player has sixteen pieces which can be moved according to fixed rules. 白黒64の市松模様の盤(チェス盤)上で2人でやるゲーム. 各指し手が16駒(こま)を持ち, 決まったルールに従って動かす➡**チェス, 西洋将棋** ‖ *Can you play chess?* チェスができますか.

\***chest** /tʃest/ 名 C ▶定義1 the top part of the front of your body 体の上半身前部➡**胸, 胸部** ☞ C5 ページのさし絵 ▶定義2 a large strong box that is used for storing or carrying things 物を保管したり運んだりするために使用される大型の頑丈な箱➡**大型の収納箱, ひつ** ☞ C7 ページのさし絵

成句 **get sth off your chest** 略式 ▶定義 to talk about sth that you have been thinking or worrying about ずっと考えていた事や心配して

268　chestnut

いた事を話す➔〜を打ち明ける, (心の)重荷を下ろす

**chestnut** /tʃés(t)nʌt/ 名 C ▶定義1 (または **chestnut tree**) a tree with large leaves that produces smooth brown nuts in shells with sharp points on the outside 大きな葉のある木で, 滑らかな茶色の実は, 外側に鋭利なとげのある殻に入っている➔クリ, クリの木, クリ材 ▶定義2 a smooth brown nut from the chestnut tree. You can eat some chestnuts. クリの木になる滑らかな茶色の実. 食用になるものもある➔クリ, クリの実; クリ色 ‖ *roast chestnuts* 焼きぐり ☞参 **conker** ☞ **nut** のさし絵

**chest of drawers** 名 C ▶定義 a piece of furniture with drawers in it that is used for storing clothes, etc 衣類などを保管するために使われる, 引き出しの付いた家具➔たんす, 整理だんす ☞ C7 ページのさし絵

*****chew** /tʃuː/ 動自他 ▶定義1 to break up food in your mouth with your teeth before you swallow it 飲み込む前に口の中で歯を使って食物を細かくする➔(〜を)かむ, かんで食べる ▶定義2 chew (on) sth to bite sth continuously with the back teeth 〜を奥歯で絶え間なくかむ➔〜をかみこなす, かみ砕く, 咀嚼(そしゃく)する ‖ *The dog was chewing on a bone.* 犬が骨をかみ砕いていた.

**chewing gum**(または **gum**) 名 U ▶定義 a sweet sticky substance that you chew in your mouth but do not swallow 甘い粘着性の物質で, 飲み込まないで口の中でかみ続ける➔チューインガム, ガム ☞参 **bubblegum**

**chewy** /tʃúːi/ 形 ▶定義 (used about food) difficult to break up with your teeth before it can be swallowed (食べ物について)飲み込めるように歯で細かくするのが難しい➔よくかむ必要のある, かみこなせない, 歯ごたえのある ‖ *chewy meat/toffee* 硬い肉・タフィー(キャンデーの一種)

**chic** /ʃiːk, ʃɪk/ 形 ▶定義 fashionable and elegant 高級で優雅な➔粋(いき)な, 上品な, あか抜けた, シックな ― chic 名 U➔粋, 上品さ

**chick** /tʃɪk/ 名 C ▶定義 a baby bird, especially a young chicken 鳥の子, 特に子の鶏➔ひな, ひな鳥, ひよこ ☞ **chicken** のさし絵

chickens

cock　　chick　　hen

*****chicken**¹ /tʃíkən/ 名 ▶定義1 C a bird that people often keep for its eggs and its meat 卵と肉をとるためによく飼育される鳥➔鶏, 鶏のひな, ひな鳥 ▶定義2 U the meat of this bird この鳥の肉➔鶏肉, チキン ‖ *chicken soup* チキンスープ ➤ chicken はこの鳥とその肉を指す一般的な語. cock (米 rooster) は雄鶏(おんどり). hen は雌鶏(めんどり). chick は鶏のひな.

成句 Don't count your chickens (before they're hatched) ⇒ **COUNT**¹

**chicken**² /tʃíkən/ 動
句動詞 chicken out (of sth) 略式 ▶定義 to decide not to do sth because you are afraid 恐れから何かをしないことに決める➔おじけづいて(〜を)やめる, (〜から)しりごみする ‖ *Mark chickened out of swimming across the river when he saw how far it was.* 川幅がいかに広いか見て, マークはおじけづいて川を泳いで横断することをやめた.

**chickenpox** /tʃíkənpɒks/ 名 U ▶定義 a disease, especially of children. When you have chickenpox you feel very hot and get red spots on your skin that make you want to scratch. 特に子供がかかる病気で, これにかかると高熱を出し, 皮膚にかゆみのある赤い斑点(はんてん)ができる➔水ぼうそう, 水痘

**chicory** /tʃíkəri/ (米 **endive**) 名 U ▶定義 a small pale green plant with bitter leaves that can be eaten cooked or not cooked 小さな薄緑色の植物で, 調理しても生でも食べられる苦味のある葉を持つ➔チコリー, キクニガナ, チコリの根

**chief**¹ /tʃiːf/ 形 (名詞の前だけ) ▶定義1 most important; main 最も重要な; 主要な➔主な, 最重要の, 中心となる ‖ *One of the chief reasons for his decision was money.* 彼が決定を下した主な理由の1つは金だった. ▶定義2 of the highest level or position 最高レベルの, または

最高位の→第1位の, 最高の ‖ *the chief executive of a company* 会社の代表取締役

**★chief**² /tʃiːf/ 名 C ▶定義1 the person who has command or control over an organization 組織の指揮権または管理権を持つ人→**支配者, 上長, 局[部・課・所]長** ‖ *the chief of police* 警察署長 ▶定義2 the leader of a tribe 部族の長→**族長, 酋長(しゅうちょう)**

**chiefly** /tʃiːfli/ 副 ▶定義 mainly; mostly 主に; 主として→**大部分, 第1に, 何よりも, 特に** ‖ *His success was due chiefly to hard work.* 彼が成功した主な理由は努力だ.

**chieftain** /tʃiːftən/ 名 C ▶定義 the leader of a tribe 部族の長→**族長, 酋長(しゅうちょう)** ‖ *a twelfth-century Scottish chieftain* 12世紀スコットランドの族長

**chiffon** /ʃɪfɑn, ⌒/ 名 U ▶定義 a very thin, transparent type of cloth used for making clothes, etc 衣服などを作るために用いる非常に薄い透ける布→**シフォン, 絹モスリン**

**chilblain** /tʃɪlbleɪn/ 名 C ▶定義 a painful red area on your foot, hand, etc that is caused by cold weather 寒気が原因で足や手などにできる赤くはれて痛みのある部分→**霜焼け, 凍瘡(とうそう)**

**★child** /tʃaɪld/ 名 C (複 **children** /tʃɪldrən/) ▶定義1 a young boy or girl who is not yet an adult まだ成人に達していない幼い少年や少女→**子供, 児童** ‖ *A group of children were playing in the park.* 子供たちのグループが公園で遊んでいた. *a six-year-old child* 6歳の子供 ▶定義2 a son or daughter of any age 年齢にかかわりなく息子または娘→**(親に対して)子, 子供, 子息, 子女** ‖ *She has two children but both are married and have moved away.* 彼女には2人の子供がいるが, 2人とも結婚して親元を離れてしまった.

▶ only child は兄弟や姉妹のいない子供, 一人っ子. adopt a child は実の子ではない子を引き取る(= 養子にする)(例えばその子供の両親が死亡している場合). foster child は一定期間自分の家族ではない家族に面倒を見てもらっている子供.

**childbirth** /tʃaɪldbɜːrθ/ 名 U ▶定義 the act of giving birth to a baby 子供を産むこと→**出産, 分べん, お産** ‖ *His wife died in childbirth.* 彼の妻はお産で亡くなった.

**childcare** /tʃaɪldkèər/ 名 U ▶定義 the job of looking after children, especially while the parents are at work 特に両親が仕事をしている間, 子供の面倒を見る仕事→**児童保護, 保育** ‖ *Some employers provide childcare facilities.* 雇用主が保育施設を提供している所もある.

**childhood** /tʃaɪldhùd/ 名 C U ▶定義 the time when you are a child 子供である期間→**子供時代, 幼年時代, 幼時** ‖ *Harriet had a very unhappy childhood.* ハリエットはとても不幸な子供時代を過ごした. *childhood memories* 子供のころの思い出

**childish** /tʃaɪldɪʃ/ 形 ▶定義 like a child 子供のような→**子供っぽい, 幼稚な; 大人気ない, ばかげた** — **childishly** 副 →**子供っぽく, 幼稚に**

▶ childlike は人や行動がどこか子供のようである場合に用いる: *His childlike enthusiasm delighted us all.* (彼の子供のような熱狂振りは, 私たち皆を大喜びさせた.) childish は大人の行動をばかげていると批判する場合に用いる: *Don't be so childish! You can't always have everything you want.* (子供っぽい事は言わないで. 欲しい物がいつもすべて手に入るわけではないのだ.)

**childless** /tʃaɪldləs/ 形 ▶定義 having no children 子供がいない→**子供のない, 子供に恵まれない**

**childlike** /tʃaɪldlàɪk/ 形 ▶定義 like a child 子供のような →**(良い意味で)子供らしい, 純真な, 無邪気な** ☞参 childish

**childminder** /tʃaɪldmàɪndər/ 名 C 英 ▶定義 a person whose job is to look after a child while his/her parents are at work 両親が働いている間, 子供の面倒を見ることを仕事とする人→**子供を預かる人, 保育士**

**children's home** 名 C ▶定義 an institution where children live whose parents cannot look after them 両親が面倒を見ることができない子供の住む施設→**養育院, 孤児院**

**chili** 米 = CHILLI

**chill**¹ /tʃɪl/ 名 ▶定義1 [単数扱い] an unpleasant cold feeling 不快な寒気→**悪寒, 冷え; 冷気, 冷え込み** ‖ *There's a chill in the air.* 肌寒い天気だ. (比喩) *A chill of fear went down my spine.* 背筋がぞっとした. ▶定義2 C 略式 an common illness that affects your nose and throat; a cold

**chill²**

鼻やのどを侵すありふれた病気；風邪→感冒，（風邪による）悪寒 ‖ *to catch a chill* 風邪を引く

**chill²** /tʃɪl/ 動自他 ▶定義 to become or to make sb/sth colder ～が冷たくなる，冷たくする→冷える；～を冷やす，寒がらせる ‖ *It's better to chill white wine before you serve it.* 白ワインは食卓に出す前に冷やした方がいい．

**chilli** (米 **chili**) /tʃɪli/ 名 C U (複 **chillies**: 米 **chilies**) ▶定義 a small green or red vegetable that has a very strong hot taste 非常に辛い小さな緑色または赤色の野菜→トウガラシ，トウガラシの実・木 ‖ *chilli powder* チリパウダー（粉末にしたチリトウガラシ）☞ C3 ページのさし絵

**chilling** /tʃɪlɪŋ/ 形 ▶定義 frightening 恐ろしい→ぞっとする，ぞくぞくする ‖ *a chilling ghost story* ぞくぞくする怪談

**chilly** /tʃɪli/ 形 (**chillier**; **chilliest**) ▶定義 (used about the weather but also about people) too cold to be comfortable (天候，または人々について) あまりに寒くて不快な→冷え冷えとした，薄ら寒い，ひんやりとした ‖ *It's a chilly morning. You need a coat on.* 今朝は冷える．コートを着なければいけないよ．*We got a very chilly reception* (= *unfriendly*). 私たちは非常に冷淡に迎えられた (= 不愛想に).

**chime** /tʃaɪm/ 動自他 ▶定義 (used about a bell or clock) to ring (鐘や時計について) 鳴る→鳴り響く，(鐘を) 打つ，鳴らす，(音で時刻を) 知らせる ― **chime** 名 C →一組の鐘，チャイム (の音)，時報

句動詞 **chime in (with sth)** 略式 ▶定義 to interrupt a conversation and add your own comments 会話を遮って自分が一言いい添える→（〜に）口を挟む，話に割り込む，相づちを打つ

**chimney** /tʃɪmni/ 名 C ▶定義 a pipe through which smoke or steam is carried up and out through the roof of a building 煙や蒸気が建物の屋根へと導かれ排出される管→煙突，煙突状の物 ☞ C7 ページのさし絵

**chimney sweep** 名 C ▶定義 a person whose job is to clean the inside of chimneys with long brushes 長いブラシで煙突の内部を掃除することを仕事とする人→煙突掃除人

**chimpanzee** /tʃɪmpænziː, -pən-/ (または 略式 **chimp** /tʃɪmp/ 名 C ▶定義 a small intelligent animal like a monkey but without a tail (*an ape*), which is found in Africa 猿に似た尾のない知能の高い小型動物（類人猿）で，アフリカに住む→チンパンジー

**chin** /tʃɪn/ 名 C ▶定義 the part of your face below your mouth 口より下の部分→あご，下あご，あご先 ☞ C5 ページのさし絵

**china** /tʃaɪnə/ 名 U ▶定義 1 white clay of good quality that is used for making cups, plates, etc 良質の白い粘土で，カップ，皿などを作るために使われる→陶土，カオリン ‖ *a china vase* 陶土製の花びん ▶定義 2 cups, plates, etc that are made from china 陶土から作られたカップ，皿など→磁器，陶磁器，瀬戸物；食器類

**chink** /tʃɪŋk/ 名 C ▶定義 a small narrow opening 小さく狭い開口部→裂け目，割れ目，すきま ‖ *Daylight came in through a chink between the curtains.* カーテンのすきまから日の光が漏れ入っていた．

**chintz** /tʃɪnts/ 名 U ▶定義 a shiny cotton cloth with a printed design, usually of flowers, which is used for making curtains, covering furniture, etc 光沢のある綿布で，普通は花などのプリント模様で，カーテンを作ったり家具のカバー用に使われる→チンツ，木綿さらさ

chips (米 French fries)　　crisps (米 chips)

**chip¹** /tʃɪp/ 名 C ▶定義 1 the place where a small piece of stone, glass, wood, etc has broken off sth 石，ガラス，木材などの小片が〜から欠けた箇所→欠けた箇所，欠けた傷 ‖ *This dish has a chip in it.* この皿は欠けている．▶定義 2 a small piece of stone, glass, wood, etc that has broken off sth 〜から欠けた石，ガラス，木材などの小片→かけら，切れ端，小片 ▶定義 3 (米 **French fry**) [通常は複数] a thin piece of potato that is fried in hot fat or oil 細切りのジャガイモを高温の脂または油で揚げたもの→フライドポテト，フレンチフライ ☞ C4 ページのさし絵

▶定義4 (または **potato chip**) 米 = CRISP²
▶定義5 = MICROCHIP ▶定義6 a flat round piece of plastic that you use instead of money when you are playing some games ある種のゲームをするときに，金の代わりに使われる平らで円いプラスチック片→(ポーカー，ルーレットなどの)数取り札，点棒，チップ

成句 **have a chip on your shoulder (about sth)** 略式 ▶定義 to feel angry about sth that happened a long time ago because you think it is unfair ずっと以前に起こった事について不公平だと怒る→恨みを抱いている，けんか腰である，怒りっぽい ‖ *My dad still has a chip on his shoulder about being thrown out of school.* 私の父は退学になったことについてまだ恨みを抱いている．

chipped　cracked　broken

**chip²** /tʃɪp/ 動他自 (**chipping**; **chipped**) ▶定義1 to break a small piece off the edge or surface of sth ～の縁または表面から小片が欠ける・を欠けさせる→(～を)割って取る，そぐ，削る ‖ *They chipped the paint trying to get the table through the door.* テーブルをドアから入れようとして，塗料がはげた．▶定義2 (in sport) to kick or hit a ball a short distance through the air (スポーツで)宙に短い距離のボールをける，または打つ→チップショットをける，打つ

句動詞 **chip in (with sth)** 略式 ▶定義1 to interrupt when sb else is talking ほかの～が話しているときに割り込む→口を出す，口を挟む

▶定義2 to give some money as part of the cost of sth ～の代価の一部として金を与える→金を提供する，金を出し合う ‖ *We all chipped in and bought him a present when he left.* 彼が去る時私たち皆が金を出し合って贈り物を買った．

**chip shop** (または **chippy** /tʃɪpi/) 名 C ▶定義 (in Britain) a shop that cooks and sells fish and chips and other fried food to take away and eat (英国で)持ち帰り用にフィッシュアンドチップスやそのほかの揚げ物を調理して販売する店→フィッシュアンドチップスの店

**chiropodist** /kərɒpədɪst, ʃə-, kaɪə-/ (米 **podia-**

chocolate　271

**trist**) 名 C ▶定義 a person whose job is to look after people's feet 人の足を治療する職業の人→足病医，フットドクター

**chirp** /tʃɜːrp/ 動自 ▶定義 (used about small birds and some insects) to make short high sounds (小鳥や一部の昆虫について)短い高い音を発する→(チュンチュンと)鳴く，さえずる

**chisel** /tʃɪz(ə)l/ 名 C ▶定義 a tool with a sharp end that is used for cutting or shaping wood or stone 木材や石を切るまたは彫るために用いる先端の鋭い道具→のみ，たがね；彫刻刀 ☞ **tool** のさし絵

**chivalry** /ʃɪv(ə)lri/ 名 U ▶定義 polite and kind behaviour by men which shows respect towards women 男性の女性に対する敬意を表す礼儀正しい振る舞い→騎士道(精神)，(女性や弱者への)親切 ─ **chivalrous** /ʃɪv(ə)lrəs/ 形→騎士道的な，騎士道の

**chive** /tʃaɪv/ 名 [C，通常は複数] ▶定義 a long thin green plant that tastes like onion and is used in cooking タマネギと似た味で調理に使われる細長い緑の植物→エゾネギ(の葉)，チャイブ

**chlorine** /klɔːriːn, -rən/ 名 U (元素記号 **Cl**) ▶定義 a greenish-yellow gas with a strong smell, that is used for making water safe to drink or to swim in 強い臭気のある黄緑色の気体で，飲料水，水泳用の水の消毒に用いる→塩素

**chock-a-block** /tʃæk ə blɒk/ 形 (名詞の前は不可) ▶定義 completely full 完全に一杯の→ぎっしり詰まった，一杯の ‖ *The High Street was chock-a-block with shoppers.* ハイストリートは買い物客でごった返していた．

**chocoholic** /tʃɒ(ː)kəhɒ(ː)lɪk, tʃɑːkəhɑːlɪk/ 名 C ▶定義 a person who loves chocolate and eats a lot of it チョコレートが大好きで大量に食べる人→チョコレート中毒者，チョコレートが異常に好きな人

*****chocolate** /tʃɒ(ː)k(ə)lət, tʃɑːk-/ 名 ▶定義1 U a sweet brown substance made from seeds (**cocoa beans**) that you can eat as a sweet or use to give flavour to food and drinks ある種子(カカオ豆)から作られる甘い茶色の食品で，菓子として食べたり，食品や飲料に風味を付けるために用いる→チョコレート，チョコレート粉末 ‖ *a bar of milk/plain chocolate* ミルク・ブラ

ックチョコレート1枚 *a chocolate milkshake* チョコレート味のミルクセーキ ▶定義2 ❻a small sweet that is made from or covered with chocolate チョコレートで作られた,またはチョコレートでくるんだ小さな菓子→**チョコレート1個, チョコレート菓子** ‖ *a box of chocolates* チョコレート1箱 ▶定義3 ❻❶a drink made from powdered chocolate with hot milk or water 粉末のチョコレートに熱いミルクや湯を加えて作った飲み物→**チョコレート飲料** ‖ *a mug of hot chocolate* マグ1杯のホットチョコレート ▶定義4 ❶a dark brown colour 濃い茶色→**チョコレート色, 焦げ茶色**

★**choice**¹ /tʃɔ́ɪs/ 图 ▶定義1 ❻a choice (between A and B) an act of choosing between two or more people or things 2人または2つ以上から選ぶこと→**選択, 選び取ること** ‖ *David was forced to make a choice between moving house and losing his job.* デーヴィッドは転居するか職を失うかの選択を余儀なくされた.

▶定義2 ❶the right or chance to choose 選択する権利や機会→**選択権, 選択の自由; えり好み** ‖ *There is a rail strike so we have no choice but to cancel our trip.* 鉄道のストがあるので,旅行を取りやめる以外ない. *to have freedom of choice* 選択の自由がある ☛類 **option** ▶定義3 ❻❶two or more things from which you can or must choose 選ぶことができる,または選ばなければならない2つ以上のもの→**選択の範囲・種類, 選択肢** ‖ *This cinema offers a choice of six different films every night.* この映画館では, 毎晩6本の映画から選んで見ることができる.

▶定義4 ❻a person or thing that is chosen 選択された人または物→**選ばれた人・物, 選出された人・物, えり抜き** ‖ *Barry would be my choice as team captain.* 私はバリーをチームの主将に選びたい. ☛動 **choose**

成句 **out of/from choice** ▶定義 because you want to; of your own free will ～したいため; 自らの自由意志で→**進んで, 好んで, 望んで** ‖ *I wouldn't have gone to America out of choice. I was sent there on business.* 自ら好んでアメリカへ行くことはなかっただろう. 私は仕事で行かされたのだ.

**choice**² /tʃɔ́ɪs/ 形 ▶定義 of very good quality 非常に良質の→**えりすぐった, 選び抜かれた, 高級な** ‖ *choice beef* 上等の牛肉

**choir** /kwáɪə*r*/ 图 [❻, 単数または複数形の動詞と共に] ▶定義 a group of people who sing together in churches, schools, etc 教会, 学校などで合唱する人のグループ→**聖歌隊, 合唱団**

★**choke**¹ /tʃóʊk/ 動 ▶定義1 ❶❻ **choke (on sth)** to be or to make sb unable to breathe because sth is stopping air getting into the lungs ～によって肺へ空気が流れることが妨げられ…が呼吸できない,または呼吸ができないようにする→**窒息する・させる, 息が詰まる, 息苦しくさせる, のどが詰まる・詰まらせる, むせる** ‖ *She was choking on a fish bone.* 彼女は魚の骨がのどにつかえてむせていた. *The smoke choked us.* 私たちは煙で息ができなかった. ☛参 **strangle** ▶定義2 ❻ (通常は受動態で) **choke sth (up) (with sth)** to fill a passage, space, etc, so that nothing can pass through 通路, 空間などを一杯にして何も通れないようにする→**～を(…で)ふさぐ, 詰まらせる** ‖ *The roads to the coast were choked with traffic.* 海岸へ行く道路は渋滞していた.

句動詞 **choke sth back** ▶定義 to hide or control a strong emotion 強い感情を隠す, または抑制する→**(感情)を抑える, こらえる** ‖ *to choke back tears/anger* 涙・怒りを抑える

**choke**² /tʃóʊk/ 图 ❻ ▶定義1 the device in a car, etc that controls the amount of air going into the engine. If you pull out the choke it makes it easier to start the car. エンジンに吸入される空気量を調整するため車などに付いている装置. これを引くと車を簡単に始動できる→**チョーク, (自動車の)空気吸入調節弁** ☛ S7 ページのさし絵 ▶定義2 an act or the sound of sb choking ～が息を詰まらせること, その声→**窒息, むせること, むせる声** ‖ *A tiny choke of laughter escaped her.* 彼女はかすかに笑い声を漏らした.

**cholera** /kálərə/ 图 ❶ ▶定義 a serious disease that causes stomach pains and vomiting and can cause death. Cholera is most common in hot countries and is carried by water. 腹痛や吐き気を伴う重病で死に至ることもある. 熱帯気候の国に多く, 水から伝染する→**コレラ**

**cholesterol** /kəléstərɔ̀(ː)l, -ròul, -ràl/ 图 ❶ ▶定義 a substance that is found in the blood, etc of people and animals. Too much cholesterol is thought to be a cause of heart disease. 人や動物の血液などに含まれる物質．多すぎると心臓病の原因になると考えられている➡コレステロール

\***choose** /tʃúːz/ 動自他 (過 **chose** /tʃóʊz/; 過分 **chosen** /tʃóʊz(ə)n/) ▶定義1 choose (between A and/or B); choose (A) (from B); choose sb/sth as sth to decide which thing or person you want out of the ones that are available 入手可能な中から，望むものまたは人を決定する➡（〜を）選ぶ，選択する，選び取る ‖ *Choose carefully before you make a final decision.* 最終決定をする前に慎重に選択してください． *Amy had to choose between getting a job or going to college.* エイミーは就職か大学進学かを選ばなければならなかった． *The viewers chose this programme as their favourite.* 視聴者はこの番組をお気に入りに選んだ． ▶定義2 choose (to do sth) to decide or prefer to do sth 〜をすることに決める，または選ぶ➡〜することを決める，〜する方を選ぶ，〜したいと思う，〜が欲しい ‖ *You are free to leave whenever you choose.* いつでも好きなときに出ていって構いません． *They chose to resign rather than work for the new manager.* 彼らは新しい支配人の下で働くよりも辞職する方を選んだ． ☞ 名 choice
成句 pick and choose ⇒ **PICK**¹

**choosy** /tʃúːzi/ 形略式 ▶定義 (used about a person) difficult to please（人について）喜ばすのが難しい➡好みにうるさい，えり好みする，気難しい

\***chop**¹ /tʃɑp/ 動他 (**chopping**; **chopped**) ▶定義 chop sth (up) (into sth) to cut sth into pieces with a knife, etc ナイフなどで〜を細かく切る➡〜を（…に）切り刻む，細かく切る ‖ *finely chopped herbs* 細かく刻んだ香草 *Chop the onions up into small pieces.* タマネギを細かく切ってください．
成句 chop and change ▶定義 to change your plans or opinions several times 計画や意見を数回変える➡〜をコロコロ変える，しょっちゅう変える
句動詞 chop sth down ▶定義 to cut a tree, etc at the bottom so that it falls down 木などを根元から切って倒す➡〜を切り倒す
chop sth off (sth) ▶定義 to remove sth from sth by cutting it with a knife or a sharp tool ナイフや鋭い道具で切って〜から…を取り除く➡〜を（…から）切り落とす，切り離す

**chop**² /tʃɑp/ 名 ⓒ ▶定義1 a thick slice of meat with a piece of bone in it 骨が付いた厚切りの肉➡骨付き肉，チョップ ☞参 **steak** ☞ C4 ページのさし絵 ▶定義2 an act of chopping sth 〜をたたき切ること➡たたき切り，ブツ切り；たたき切るように強く打つこと ‖ *a karate chop* 空手チョップ

**chopper** /tʃɑ́pər/ 名 ⓒ略式 =HELICOPTER

**chopping board** 名 ⓒ ▶定義 a piece of wood or plastic used for cutting meat or vegetables on 肉や野菜を切るために用いる木製やプラスチック製の板➡まな板，物切り台 ☞ **kitchen** のさし絵

**choppy** /tʃɑ́pi/ 形 ▶定義 (used about the sea) having a lot of small waves, slightly rough（海について）小波の多い，いくらか荒れた➡波立ち騒ぐ，三角波の立つ

**chopsticks** /tʃɑ́pstìks/ 名 [複数扱い] ▶定義 two thin sticks made of wood or plastic, that people in China, Japan, etc use for picking up food to eat 木製やプラスチック製の細い2本の棒で，中国や日本で食品を挟んで食べるために用いる➡箸（はし）

**choral** /kɔ́ːr(ə)l/ 形 ▶定義 (used about music) that is written for or involving a group of singers (a choir)（音楽について）グループの歌い手（合唱団）のために書かれた，またはそれに関連した➡合唱曲の，合唱の，合唱隊の

**chord** /kɔːrd/ 名 ⓒ ▶定義 two or more musical notes that are played at the same time 同時に演奏される2つ以上の音符➡和音，和弦，コード

**chore** /tʃɔːr/ 名 ⓒ ▶定義 a job that is not interesting but that you must do 面白くないがしなければならない仕事➡半端仕事，雑用；（家庭や農場の）毎日の仕事，決まりきった仕事 ‖ *household chores* 家事

**choreograph** /kɔ́(ː)riəgrɑ̀ːf, kɑ́r-; -græf/ 動他 ▶定義 to design and arrange the movements of a dance ダンスの動きをデザインし編成を考える➡〜の振り付けをする，（バレエ，ダンス）を編成する — choreographer 名 ⓒ➡振り付け師，バレエ編成家

**choreography** /kɔ̀(ː)riɑ́grəfi, kɑ̀r-/ 名 Ⓤ ▶定義 the arrangement of movements for a dance

performance ダンスの動きの取り決め➔振り付け, 舞踏法, 舞踏術

**chorus**¹ /kɔ́ːrəs/ 名 ▶定義1 ❻the part of a song that is repeated at the end of each verse 歌の各節の終わりの繰り返される部分➔合唱部分, 折り返し, コーラス, リフレイン ☛類 refrain ▶定義2 ❻a piece of music, usually part of a larger work, that is written for a large group of people (a choir) to sing 通常は大作の一部で, 大勢のグループ(合唱団)用に作られた曲➔合唱(曲), 合唱部 ▶定義3 ❻[単数または複数形の動詞と共に] a large group of people who sing together 一緒に歌う大勢のグループ➔合唱団, 合唱隊 ▶定義4 ❻[単数または複数形の動詞と共に] the singers and dancers in a musical show who do not play the main parts ミュージカルで主役以外を演じる歌い手と踊り手➔合唱舞踏団, コーラス ▶定義5 a chorus of sth [単数扱い] something that a lot of people say together 大勢の人々が一緒に言うこと➔一斉に発する言葉・声, 異口同音 ‖ *a chorus of cheers/criticism/disapproval* 一斉の歓呼・非難・反対

**chorus**² /kɔ́ːrəs/ 動 他 ▶定義 (used about a group of people) to sing or say sth together (人々の集団について)〜を一緒に歌う, または言う➔〜を合唱する, 声をそろえて言う, 異口同音に言う ‖ *'That's not fair!' the children chorused.*「そんなのずるい」と子供たちが一斉に声を上げた.

**chose** CHOOSE の過去形
**chosen** CHOOSE の過去分詞形
**Christ** /kráɪst/ (または **Jesus**; **Jesus Christ** /dʒíːzəs kráɪst, -z-/) 名 ▶定義 the man who Christians believe is the son of God and who established the Christian religion キリスト教徒により神の子であると信じられ, キリスト教を確立した人物➔キリスト, イエス, 救世主

**christen** /krís(ə)n/ 動 他 ▶定義1 to give a person, usually a baby, a name during a Christian ceremony in which he/she is made a member of the Church 教会の一員となるためのキリスト教の儀式において, 人, 普通は赤ん坊に名前を付ける➔〜に洗礼名を与える, 洗礼を施す ‖ *The baby was christened Simon Mark.* 赤ん坊はサイモン マークと命名された. ☛参 baptize ▶定義2 to give sb/sth a name 〜に名前を付ける➔名付ける, 命名する ‖ *People drive so dangerously on this stretch of road that they've christened it 'The Mad Mile'.* その道路はあまりに無謀運転が多いので, 「狂人の道」という名前が付いた.

**christening** /krís(ə)nɪŋ/ 名 ❻ ▶定義 the church ceremony in the Christian religion in which a baby is given a name 赤ん坊に名前を付けるキリスト教教会の儀式➔洗礼, 命名式 ☛参 baptism

*★**Christian** /krístʃən/ 名 ❻ ▶定義 a person whose religion is Christianity キリスト教を宗教とする人➔キリスト教徒, キリスト信者, クリスチャン ― Christian 形 ➔キリスト教徒の, キリスト教の

**Christianity** /krìstʃiǽnəti, -ti-/ 名 ❿ ▶定義 the religion that is based on the teachings of Jesus Christ イエス キリストの教えに基づく宗教➔キリスト教, キリスト教信仰

*★**Christmas** /krísməs/ 名 ▶定義1 ❻❿the period of time before and after 25 December 12月25日の前後の期間➔クリスマスの時期, クリスマス ‖ *Where are you spending Christmas this year?* 今年のクリスマス休暇はどこで過すのですか. ▶定義2 **Christmas Day** ❻a public holiday on 25 December. It is the day on which Christians celebrate the birth of Christ each year. 12月25日の祝日. 毎年キリスト教徒がキリストの生誕を祝う日➔クリスマス, キリスト降誕祭 ☛ Xmas は略式の英語で, Christmas をこう書くこともある.

---

▶社会・文化

**クリスマス**

Christmas は12月25日のキリストの誕生日ですが, 24日の Christmas Eve から1月1日の New Year's Day, または1月6日の Epiphany までを指すこともあります. 日本のように, イブに仲間たちとレストランなどで大騒ぎすることはあまりなく, 親類や知人を家に招いて比較的静かに過ごします. 多くの家庭では25日の午前は教会で礼拝し, 午後は家で過ごし, 七面鳥を焼いた Christmas dinner を食べます. イギリスではデザートにフルーツケーキの一種の Christmas pudding がよく出されます. 日ごろ離れている

家族や一族が family reunion (再会) する大切な機会でもあります.

**Christmas card** 名 C ▶定義 a card with a picture on the front and a message inside that people send to their friends and relatives at Christmas クリスマスに友人や親戚（しんせき）に送るカードで，表に絵が描かれ中にメッセージが書かれている→クリスマスカード

**Christmas carol** = CAROL

**Christmas cracker** = CRACKER(2)

**Christmas dinner** 名 C ▶定義 the traditional meal eaten on Christmas Day クリスマスの日に食べる伝統的な食事→クリスマスディナー（英国では七面鳥やクリスマスプディング，ミンスパイなどとワイン）‖ *We had a traditional Christmas dinner that year, with roast turkey, Christmas pudding and all the trimmings.* 私たちはその年は七面鳥のロースト，クリスマスプディング，そしてさまざまな付け合わせの伝統的クリスマスディナーを食べた．

**Christmas Eve** 名 C ▶定義 24 December, the day before Christmas Day 12月24日，クリスマスの前日→クリスマスイブ

**Christmas pudding** 名 C U ▶定義 a sweet dish made from dried fruit and eaten hot with sauce at Christmas dinner ドライフルーツで作る甘い食べ物で，温めてソースを掛けてクリスマスディナーの時に食べる→クリスマスプディング

**Christmas tree** 名 C ▶定義 a real or artificial tree, which people bring into their homes and cover with coloured lights and decorations at Christmas 天然木または人工の木で，クリスマスに家の中に運んで色の付いた電球や飾りで覆う→クリスマスツリー

**chrome** /króum/（または **chromium** /króumiəm/）名 U ▶定義 a hard shiny metal that is used for covering other metals ほかの金属を覆うために使用する固く光沢のある金属→クロム，クロム合金，クロムめっき

**chromosome** /króuməsoum, -mə-/ 名 C ▶定義 a part of a cell in living things that decides the sex, character, shape, etc that a person, an animal or a plant will have 生物の細胞の一部で，人や動物，植物の性別，特徴，形状などを決定する→染色体

---

chuck 275

**chronic** /kránɪk/ 形 ▶定義 (used about a disease or a problem) that continues for a long time（病気や障害について）長期間継続する→慢性の，慢性的な，長期にわたる‖ *There is a chronic shortage of housing in the city.* 市内では慢性的に住宅が不足している．

➤ acute と比較．

— **chronically** /-k(ə)li/ 副 →慢性的に，長期間にわたって

**chronicle** /kránɪk(ə)l/ 名 C (しばしば複数形で) ▶定義 a written record of historical events describing them in the order in which they happened 歴史的出来事を記述した記録で，出来事が起こった順序で記述される→年代記，編年史

**chronological** /krànəládʒɪk(ə)l, kròu-/ 形 ▶定義 arranged in the order in which the events happened 出来事が起こった順序で編成されている→年代順の，発生順の‖ *This book describes the main events in his life in chronological order.* この本には彼の人生の主な出来事が年代順に書かれている．— **chronologically** /-k(ə)li/ 副 →年代順に，発生順に

**chrysalis** /krísələs/（複 **chrysalises**) 名 C ▶定義 the form of an insect, (a butterfly or a moth), while it is changing into an adult inside a hard case, also called a chrysalis 昆虫（チョウ，ガなど）の成長過程の形態で，硬い殻（これも，chrysalis と呼ばれる）の中で成虫になるまでの期間→さなぎ，繭；準備期，過渡期 ☛ insect のさし絵

**chrysanthemum** /krəsǽnθəməm/ 名 C ▶定義 a large garden flower which is brightly coloured and shaped like a ball 球形で鮮やかな色をした大型の園芸用の花 キク，キクの花 ☛ C2 ページのさし絵

**chubby** /tʃʌ́bi/ 形 ▶定義 slightly fat in a pleasant way 感じ良くいくらか太っている→ふくよかな，ふっくらした‖ *a baby with chubby cheeks* ふっくらしたほおの赤ん坊

**chuck** /tʃʌk/ 動 他 略式 ▶定義 to throw sth in a careless way ～を無造作に投げる→～をほうる，ほうり投げる，ぽいと投げる，投げ捨てる‖ *You can chuck those old shoes in the bin.* その古い靴はごみ箱にほうり込んで構いません．

**句動詞** **chuck sth in** ▶定義 to give sth up ～をあ

きらめる→～をほうり出す, 中止する, 放棄する, やめる ‖ *He's chucked his job in because he was fed up.* 彼はうんざりして仕事を辞めた.

**chuck sb out (of sth)** ▶定義 to force sb to leave a place ～をある場所から去らせる→～を追い出す, つまみ出す ‖ *They were chucked out of the cinema for making too much noise.* 彼らは騒ぎすぎて, 映画館からつまみ出された.

**chuckle** /tʃʌk(ə)l/ 動自 ▶定義 to laugh quietly 静かに笑う→くすくす笑う, ほくそ笑む, 含み笑いをする ‖ *Bruce chuckled to himself as he read the letter.* ブルースは手紙を読みながら1人でくすくす笑った. — chuckle 名 C → くすくす笑うこと, 含み笑い

**chug** /tʃʌg/ 動自 (**chugging**; **chugged**) ▶定義 1 (used about a machine or engine) to make short repeated sounds while it is working or moving slowly (機械やエンジンについて) 作動中やゆっくり動いているときに短い連続的な音を出す→シュッシュッと音を立てる, ゆっくりした排気音を立てる ▶定義 2 **chug along, down, up, etc** to move in a particular direction making this sound そのような音を立てて特定の方向に進む→シュッシュッと音を立てて進む, ゆっくりした排気音を立てて進む ‖ *The train chugged out of the station.* 列車はシュッシュッと音を立てて駅を出た.

**chunk** /tʃʌŋk/ 名 C ▶定義 a large or thick piece of sth ～の大きい, または厚い塊→大きな塊, 厚切り ‖ *chunks of bread and cheese* チーズを添えたパンの厚切り

**chunky** /tʃʌŋki/ 形 ▶定義 1 thick and heavy 厚くて重い→厚ぼったい, どっしりした ‖ *chunky jewellery* どっしりした宝石類 ▶定義 2 (used about a person) short and strong (人について) 背が低くて丈夫な→ずんぐりした, がっちりした ‖ *He was a short man with chunky legs.* 彼は背が低く足ががっしりしていた. ▶定義 3 (used about food) containing thick pieces (食べ物について) 厚いかけらを含む→塊の入った, だまのある ‖ *chunky banana milkshake* 塊の入ったバナナミルクセーキ

\***church** /tʃɜːtʃ/ 名 ▶定義 1 C U a building where Christians go to pray, etc 祈る目的などでキリスト教徒が行く建物→教会, 教会堂 ‖ *Do you go to church regularly?* あなたは定期的に教会に行きますか.

▶教会の儀式 (礼拝) に行く場合には, in church, to church, at church のように, a や the なしで用いる: *Was Mrs Stevens at church today?* (今日スティーヴンズさんは礼拝に来ましたか.)

▶定義 2 **Church** C a particular group of Christians 特定の宗派のキリスト教徒→(独立した) 教派, ～教会 ‖ *the Anglican/Catholic/Methodist/Church* 英国国教・カトリック・メソジスト教会

▶定義 3 **(the) Church** [単数扱い] the ministers or the institution of the Christian religion キリスト教の聖職者または制度→聖職, 僧職; (全)キリスト教徒, キリスト教世界, (国家に対する) 教会, 教権 ‖ *the conflict between Church and State* 教会と国家の衝突

**churchgoer** /tʃɜːtʃˌɡəʊər/ 名 C ▶定義 a person who goes to church regularly 定期的に教会に行く人→(規則正しく) 教会に通う人, 礼拝によく行く人, 熱心な礼拝出席者

**the Church of England** (略 **C of E**) 名 [単数扱い] ▶定義 the Protestant Church, which is the official church in England, whose leader is the Queen or King 英国の公式の教会であるプロテスタント教会で, その長は女王または王→英国国教会, 英国聖公会 ☛参 **Anglican**

**churchyard** /tʃɜːtʃjɑːd/ 名 C ▶定義 the area of land that is around a church 教会の周囲の土地→(教会の) 中庭, 構内; (教会付属の) 墓地 ☛参 **cemetery, graveyard**

**churn** /tʃɜːn/ 動 ▶定義 1 自他 **churn (sth) (up)** to move, or to make water, mud, etc move around violently 水, 泥などが激しく動く, または水, 泥などをかき回す→沸き返る, 泡立つ; ～を攪拌 (かくはん) する, かき立てる, 沸き返らせる ‖ *The dark water churned beneath the huge ship.* 巨大な船の下で黒い水が激しく波立った. *Vast crowds had churned the field into a sea of mud.* 大勢の群衆に踏まれて野は泥の海に変わった.

▶定義 2 自 if your stomach churns or sth makes it churn, you feel sick because you are disgusted or nervous 胃がむかつく, または何かによってむかついたりする, 嫌悪感や不安から気分が悪くなる→吐き気がする, 気持ちが悪くなる ‖ *Reading about the murder in the paper made my stomach churn.* 新聞で殺人事件について読

んで, 胃がむかついた. ▶定義3 ❿ to make butter from milk or cream 牛乳やクリームからバターを作る→～を(攪(かく)乳器で), かき回す, かき回して作る

**句動詞** churn sth out 略式 ▶定義 to produce large numbers of sth very quickly 多数の～を非常に素早く作る→～を大量に作り出す, 粗製濫造する ‖ *Modern factories can churn out cars at an amazing speed.* 現代の工場は驚くべき速度で大量の車を製造できる.

**chute** /ʃuːt/ 🔢 ❻ ▶定義 a passage down which you can drop or slide things, so that you do not have to carry them 自ら運搬する手間を省くための, 物を落とすまたは流す輸送路→落とし樋(ひ), 滑降斜面路; レターシュート ‖ *a laundry/rubbish chute (from the upper floors of a high building)* 洗濯物・ダストシュート(高層ビルの上階からの) *a water chute (at a swimming pool)* ウォーターシュート(プールの)

**chutney** /ˈtʃʌtni/ 🔢 ❿ ▶定義 a thick sweet sauce that is made from fruit or vegetables. You eat chutney cold with cheese or meat. 果物や野菜から作る濃厚な甘いソース. 冷たいままチーズや肉と一緒に食べる→チャツネ

**CIA** /ˌsiː aɪ ˈeɪ/ 略 the Central Intelligence Agency ▶定義 the US government organization that tries to discover secret information about other countries 他国についての極秘情報を発見するための米国政府の組織→中央情報局

**ciabatta** /tʃəˈbɑːtə/ 🔢 ❿ ❻ ▶定義 a type of heavy Italian bread; a whole piece (loaf) of this イタリアの歯ごたえのあるパン; このパンの一塊→チャバッタ

**cider** /ˈsaɪdər/ 🔢 ❿ ▶定義1 英 an alcoholic drink made from apples リンゴから作るアルコール飲料→リンゴ酒 ‖ *dry/sweet cider* 辛口・甘口リンゴ酒 ▶定義2 米 a drink made from apples that does not contain alcohol リンゴから作るアルコールを含まない飲料→リンゴジュース

▶日本語 vs 英語

cider と「サイダー」は別な飲み物

　cider には「果汁を発酵させたリンゴ酒(hard cider)」と「果汁を発酵させないリンゴジュース(sweet cider)」があります. 通例, 英国では前者, 米国では後者の意味で用いられます. 一方, 日本語の「サイダー」とは「炭酸水に甘

味や香料を加えた清涼飲料水」(soda pop)のことです.

**cigar** /sɪˈɡɑːr/ 🔢 ❻ ▶定義 a roll of dried tobacco leaves that people smoke. Cigars are larger than cigarettes. 乾燥したたばこの葉を巻いた物で, これを吸う. cigarette より大きい→葉巻, シガー

**cigarette** /ˌsɪɡəˈret/ 🔢 ❻ ▶定義 tobacco in a tube of thin white paper that people smoke 薄い白い紙の筒に入ったたばこで, これを吸う→たばこ, 紙巻きたばこ ‖ *a packet of cigarettes* たばこ1箱

**cigarette lighter** (または **lighter**) 🔢 ❻ ▶定義 an object which produces a small flame for lighting cigarettes, etc たばこなどに火をつけるための小さな炎を出す物→ライター, たばこ用ライター

**cinder** /ˈsɪndər/ 🔢 ❻ ▶定義 a very small piece of burning coal, wood, etc 燃えている炭, 木材などの非常に小さいかけら→燃え殻, 消し炭, 灰

\***cinema** /ˈsɪnəmə/ 🔢 ▶定義1 ❻ 英 a place where you go to see a film 映画を見に行く場所→映画館 ‖ *What's on at the cinema this week?* その映画館では今週何をやっていますか.

▶アメリカ英語で映画を上映する建物のことは movie theater と言い, 映画館に映画を見に行くと言う場合は the movies を用いる: *There are five movie theaters in this town.* (この町には5つの映画館がある.) *Let's go to the movies this evening.* (今夜, 映画を見に行こう.)

▶定義2 ❿ films in general; the film industry 映画全般; 映画産業→(集合的に)映画, 映画芸術 ‖ *one of the great successes of British cinema* 大成功を収めたイギリス映画のうちの1本

**cinnamon** /ˈsɪnəmən/ 🔢 ❿ ▶定義 a sweet brown powder that is used for giving flavour to food 食品に風味を添えるために使われる甘い茶色の粉末→シナモン, 肉桂(にっけい)

**circa** /ˈsɜːrkə/ 前 (略 **c**) (文) ▶定義 (used with dates) about; approximately (日付と用いて) 約; 近似の→およそ, ～ころ ‖ *The vase was made circa 600 AD.* その花びんは西暦600年ころに作られた.

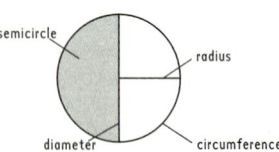

circle
semicircle / radius / diameter / circumference

\***circle**¹ /sə́ːrk(ə)l/ 名 ▶定義1 ❻a round shape like a ring 輪のような円い形→円, 円形, 丸 ‖ *The children were drawing circles and squares on a piece of paper.* 子供たちは紙に円と四角形を書いていた. *We all stood in a circle and held hands.* 私たちはみんな輪になって手をつないだ. ▶定義2 ❻a flat, round area 平らで円い領域→円, 円形の物 ‖ *She cut out a circle of paper.* 彼女は紙を円く切り抜いた. ☛ **shape** のさし絵 ▶定義3 ❻a group of people who are friends, or who have the same interest or profession 友人, または同じ興味を持つ人や同じ職業の人の集団→仲間, 団体, 〜界 ‖ *He has a large circle of friends.* 彼は交友範囲が広い. *Her name was well known in artistic circles.* 芸術界では彼女の名はよく知られていた. ▶定義4 **the (dress) circle** (困 **balcony**) [単数扱い] an area of seats that is upstairs in a cinema, theatre, etc 映画館, 劇場などの上階の席 →(半円形の)桟敷, 特等席 感句 a vicious circle ⇒ **VICIOUS**

\***circle**² /sə́ːrk(ə)l/ 動 ▶定義1 自他 to move, or to move round sth, in a circle 円形に動く, または〜の周りを円形に巡る→(〜を)回る, 旋回する ‖ *The plane circled the town several times before it landed.* 飛行機が着陸する前に町を数周旋回した. ▶定義2 他 to draw a circle round sth 〜の周りに円を書く→〜を丸で囲む, 〜に丸を付ける ‖ *There are three possible answers to each question. Please circle the correct one.* 各問いに3つの答えが用意されています. 正しいものに丸を付けなさい.

> ▶コミュニケーション
>
> 「丸めた指」の日英比較
>
> circle one's thumb and finger: 親指と人差し指で丸を作って, OK, よし, 万事順調, 完ぺきを合図するしぐさ. 一般に OK の O の字をかたどったものと言われます. 近年日本でも同じ意味に使われますが, もともとは日本ではお金の当て振りです. ただし OK の場合は高々と丸めた指を見せるのに対し, お金の場合はてのひらを上にして丸めた指を目立たないように低めに出すのが特徴です. 英米でお金を表すときは, 親指と他の指をこすり合わせて (rub one's fingers together) 札を数えるまねをします.

**circuit** /sə́ːrkət/ 名 ▶定義1 ❻a circular journey or track round sth 周遊の旅, または〜の周りの走路→回遊旅行, 巡回; 1周すること, 競争路, サーキット ‖ *The cars have to complete ten circuits of the track.* 車はコースを10周しなければならない. ▶定義2 ❻a complete circular path that an electric current can flow around 電流が流れる完全な環状の通路→回路, 回線 ▶定義3 [単数扱い] a series of sports competitions, meetings or other organized events that are regularly visited by the same people 同じ人々が定期的に訪れる一連のスポーツの競技会, 会議, またはほかの組織的な催し→巡回トーナメント, リーグ, 連盟, 巡回, 興業系統 ‖ *She's one of the best players on the tennis circuit.* 彼女はテニスリーグの最高の選手の1人だ.

\***circular**¹ /sə́ːrkjələr/ 形 ▶定義1 round and flat; shaped like a circle 円くて平らな; 円のような形の→円形の, 円い, 環状の ‖ *a circular table* 円いテーブル ▶定義2 (used about a journey, etc) moving round in a circle (旅行などについて) 周遊する→回遊の, 巡回の ‖ *a circular tour of Oxford* オックスフォード周遊旅行

**circular**² /sə́ːrkjələr/ 名 ❻ ▶定義 a printed letter, notice or advertisement that is sent to a large number of people 大勢の人々に送る印刷した手紙, 通知, 広告→回状, 回覧(板), (広告用の)散らし

**circulate** /sə́ːrkjəlèɪt/ 動 自他 ▶定義1 to go or be passed from one person to another 人から人へと渡る, または回される→流通する・させる, (新聞, 雑誌などが) 読まれる, 行き渡る, (うわさなどが) 広がる, 広める ‖ *Rumours were circulating about the Minister's private life.* 大臣の私生活に関するうわさが広まっていた. *We've circulated a copy of the report to each department.* 各部署に報告書を1部ずつ配布した. ▶定義2 (used about a substance) to move or make sth move round continuously (物質について) 円形に動き続ける、または〜をそのように動かす→**循環する・させる、円運動をする・させる** ‖ *Blood circulates round the body.* 血液は体内を循環する.

**circulation** /sɚːrkjəléɪʃ(ə)n/ 🔷 ▶定義1 ❶the movement of blood around the body 体内を循環する血液の動き→**(血液の) 循環, 血行, 血の巡り** ‖ *If you have bad circulation, your hands and feet get cold easily.* 血行が悪いと、すぐに手足が冷たくなる. ▶定義2 ❶the passing of sth from one person or place to another 〜がある人またはある場所からほかへ渡ること→**回覧, 伝達, 流布, 流通** ‖ *the circulation of news/information/rumours* ニュース・情報・うわさの流布 *Old five pence coins are no longer in circulation (= being used by people).* 旧5ペンス硬貨はもう流通して (= 人々に使われて) いない.

▶定義3 ❻the number of copies of a newspaper, magazine, etc that are sold each time it is produced 新聞、雑誌などが作られる度に売れる部数→**発行部数, 売れ行き** ‖ *This newspaper has a circulation of over a million.* この新聞の発行部数は100万部を超えている.

**circumcise** /sɚːrk(ə)msaɪz/ 🔷🔷 ▶定義 to cut off the skin at the end of a man's sexual organ (penis) or to remove part of a woman's sexual organs (clitoris), for religious or sometimes (in the case of a man) medical reasons 宗教上の理由, また時には (男性の場合) 医学上の理由から, 男性性器 (ペニス) の先端の皮膚を切り取る, または女性性器の一部 (クリトリス) を切除する→**〜に割礼を行う, 〜の包皮を切除する** — *circumcision* /sɚːrk(ə)mˈsɪʒ(ə)n/ 🔷 ❻❶→**割礼, 包皮環状切除**

**circumference** /sərkʌmf(ə)r(ə)ns/ 🔷 ❻❶ ▶定義 the distance round a circle or sth circular 円, または円形の〜の周囲の長さ→**円周, 周辺の長さ・距離** ‖ *The Earth is about 40000 kilometres in circumference.* 地球は円周が約4万キロメートルである. ☞参 **diameter**, **radius** ☞ **circle** のさし絵

★**circumstance** /sɚːrk(ə)mstəns, -stæns/ 🔷 ▶定義1 [❻, 通常は複数] the facts and events that affect what happens in a particular situation ある特定の状況下で起こる物事に影響する事実や出来事→**状況, 事情, 境遇** ‖ *Police said there were no **suspicious circumstances** surrounding the boy's death.* 少年の死に関して疑わしい点はないと警察は言った. *In normal circumstances I would not have accepted the job, but at that time I had very little money.* 普通の状況ならその仕事は受けなかっただろうが, その時は大変金に困っていた. ▶定義2 **circumstances** [複数扱い] 正式 the amount of money that you have 所持金の額→**経済状態, 暮らし向き** ‖ *The company has promised to repay the money when its financial circumstances improve.* 財政状態が改善したら, 金を返済すると会社は約束した.

成句 **in/under no circumstances** ▶定義 never; not for any reason 決して〜ない; どのような理由でも〜ない→**決して〜ない, どんな事があっても〜ない** ‖ *Under no circumstances should you enter my office.* どんな事があっても決して私のオフィスに入ってはならない.

**in/under the circumstances** ▶定義 as the result of a particular situation ある特定の状況の結果として→**こんな・そんな事情だから, 現状では** ‖ *My father was ill at that time, so under the circumstances I decided not to go on holiday.* その時は父が病気だったので, そういう事情を考えて休暇で出掛けるのをやめることにした. *It's not an ideal solution, but it's the best we can do in the circumstances.* 理想的な解決方法ではないが, 現状では最善の方法だ.

**circumstantial** /sɚːrk(ə)mstænʃ(ə)l/ 🔷 ▶定義 (used in connection with the law) containing details and information that strongly suggest sth is true but are not actual proof of it (法律について用いて) 何かが真実であることを強く示す事柄や情報を含んでいるが, 実際の証拠にはならないような→**状況的な, 付随的な** ‖ *circumstantial evidence* 状況証拠

★**circus** /sɚːrkəs/ 🔷 ❻ ▶定義 a show performed in a large tent by a company of people and animals 人や動物の一座が大きなテントで催す見せ物→**サーカス, 曲馬, 曲芸**

**CIS** /ˌsiː aɪ és/ 略 the Commonwealth of Independent States→**独立国家共同体** ☞参 **USSR**

**cistern** /sístəm/ 🔷 ❻ ▶定義 a container for storing water, especially one that is connected to a toilet 水をためる容器で，特にトイレに取り付けられたもの→**水槽，(水洗トイレの)貯タンク**

**cite** /sáɪt/ 動 他 正式 ▶定義 to mention sth or use sb's exact words as an example to support, or as proof of, what you are saying 自分が話している事の裏付けまたは証拠となる具体例として何かについて言及する，または～の言葉をそのまま用いる→**～を例証する，言及する，引用する，引き合いに出す** ‖ *She cited a passage from the President's speech.* 彼女は大統領の演説の一節を引用した．

\***citizen** /sítəz(ə)n/ 名 C ▶定義 1 a person who is legally accepted as a member of a particular country 特定の国の一員として法律上受け入れられている人→**国民，公民，人民，市民** ‖ *She was born in Japan, but became an American citizen in 1981.* 彼女は日本で生まれたが，1981年にアメリカ市民となった． ▶定義 2 a person who lives in a town or city 町や市に居住する人→**市民，町民，住民** ‖ *the citizens of Paris* パリ市民
◆参 **senior citizen**

**citizenship** /sítəz(ə)nʃɪp/ 名 U ▶定義 the state of being a citizen of a particular country 特定の国の市民であること→**市民権，公民権，公民の身分・資格；国籍** ‖ *After living in Spain for twenty years, he decided to apply for Spanish citizenship.* 20年間スペインに住んだ後，彼はスペインの市民権を申請する決心をした．

**citrus** /sítrəs/ 形 ▶定義 used to describe fruit such as oranges and lemons オレンジやレモンのような果物について言うときに用いて→**かんきつ類の**

\***city** /síti/ 名 (複 **cities**) ▶定義 1 C a large and important town 大きく主要な町→**市；都市，都会** ‖ *Venice is one of the most beautiful cities in the world.* ベニスは世界で最も美しい町の1つだ． *Many people are worried about housing conditions in Britain's inner cities (= the central parts where there are often social problems).* 英国の都心部(＝多くの場合社会問題を抱える中心部)の住宅事情について多くの人が悩んでいる． *the city centre* 市の中心部 ▶定義 2 **the City** [単数扱い] the oldest part of London, which is now Britain's financial centre ロンドンの最も古い地域で，現在は英国の金融の中心部→**シティー**

**civic** /sívɪk/ 形 ▶定義 officially connected with a city or town 市または町に公式に関連している→**市の，都市の，市民の，市立の** ‖ *civic pride (= feeling proud because you belong to a particular town or city)* 市民の誇り(＝特定の町や市に属していることを誇りに思う) *civic duties* 市民の義務 *the civic centre (= the area where the public buildings are in a town)* 官庁街，都心(＝都市の公共建物のある地域)

**civil** /sív(ə)l/ 形 ▶定義 1 (名詞の前だけ) connected with the people who live in a country ある国に住む人々に関連した→**市民の，公民の，国内の** ‖ *civil disorder (= involving groups of people within the same country)* 内乱(＝同じ国の内部でさまざまな人々の集団を巻き込む) ▶定義 2 (名詞の前だけ) connected with the state, not with the army or the Church 軍隊や教会ではなく国家に関連した→**一般人の，民間の，(軍に対して)文の，俗の** ‖ *civil engineering (= the designing and building of roads, railways, bridges, etc)* 土木工学(＝道路，鉄道，橋などの設計と建設) *a civil wedding (= not a religious one)* 民事婚(＝宗教儀式ではない) ▶定義 3 (名詞の前だけ) (in law) connected with the personal legal matters of ordinary people, and not criminal law (法律で)一般人の個人的な法律上の問題に関連したもので，刑法上の問題ではない→**民法の，民事の** ‖ *civil courts* 民事裁判所 ▶定義 4 polite, but not very friendly 礼儀正しいが，あまり親しげではない→**礼儀正しい，丁寧な** ‖ *I know you don't like the director, but do try and be civil to him.* あなたが理事のことを好きではないことは知っていますが，どうか彼に礼儀正しくするようにしてください．—**civilly** /sívə(l)li/ 副→**民法上，民事上；礼儀正しく，丁寧に**

\***civilian** /səvíljən/ 名 C ▶定義 a person who is not in the army, navy, air force or police force 陸軍，海軍，空軍または警察に所属してない人→**民間人，一般市民，文民** ‖ *Two soldiers and one civilian were killed when the bomb exploded.* 爆弾が爆発した時に，2人の兵士と1人の民間人が死亡した．

\***civilization** (または **civilisation**) /sìv(ə)laɪzéɪʃ(ə)n, -lə-/ ▶定義 1 C U a society which has its own highly developed culture and way of life 高度に発達した独自の文化と生活様式を持つ社会→**文明, 文化生活** ‖ *the civilizations of ancient Greece and Rome* 古代ギリシャとローマの文明 *Western civilization* 西洋文明 ▶定義2 ❶an advanced state of social and cultural development, or the process of reaching this state 社会的, 文化的に進んだ状態, またはそうした状態に達する過程→**文明化, 開化, 教化** ‖ *the civilization of the human race* 人類の開化 ▶定義3 ❶all the people in the world and the societies they live in considered as a whole 全体として見た世界の人々とその社会→**文明世界, 文明社会** ‖ *Global warming poses a threat to the whole of civilization.* 地球温暖化は文明社会全体への脅威である.

**civilize**(または **-ise**) /sív(ə)làɪz/ 動 ⓗ ▶定義 to make people or a society develop from a low social and cultural level to a more advanced one 人や社会を社会的, 文化的に低い段階からより進んだ段階に発展させる→**～を文明化する, 教化する, 啓蒙(けいもう)する**

*****civilized** (または **-ised**) /sív(ə)làɪzd/ 形 ▶定義1 (used about a society) well-organized; having a high level of social and cultural development (社会について) よく組織された; 社会的, 文化的発展段階が高度な→**文明化した, 文化の発達した, 教化された** ▶定義2 polite and reasonable 礼儀正しく道理をわきまえた→**教養のある, 上品な, 洗練された** ‖ *a civilized conversation* 洗練された会話

**civil rights**(または **civil liberties**) 名 [複数扱い] ▶定義 a person's legal right to freedom and equal treatment in society, whatever his/her sex, race or religion 性別, 人種, 宗教にかかわりなく, 個人が社会において自由と平等な扱いを受ける法的な権利→**市民権, 公民権** ‖ *the civil rights leader Martin Luther King* 公民権運動の指導者, マーティン ルーサー キング

**civil servant** 名 ❻ 特に 英 ▶定義 a person who works for the government's or State's own organization (**the civil service**) 政府または国家所有の組織 (政府官庁) のために働く人→**公務員, 文官**

**the civil service** 名 [単数扱い] ▶定義 all the government departments (except for the armed forces) and all the people who work in them す べての政府の部門 (軍関連は除く), およびそこで働くすべての人→**政府官庁, 行政機関; 公務員, 文官**

**civil war** 名 ❻ ❶ ▶定義 a war between groups of people who live in the same country 同じ国に住む人の間の戦争→**内戦, 内乱**

**CJD** /sìː dʒeɪ díː/ Creutzfeldt-Jakob disease ▶定義 a disease of the brain caused by eating infected meat 感染した肉を食べることでかかる脳の病気→**クロイツフェルト ヤコブ病, 狂牛病** ☞参 **BSE**

**cl** 略 centilitre(s)→センチリットル

**clad** /klæd/ 形 (名詞の前は不可) (古) ▶定義 dressed (in); wearing a particular type of clothing (～を) 身にまとった; 特定の衣服を身に着けた→**～を着た, ～に身を包んだ** ‖ *The children were warmly clad in coats, hats and scarves.* 子供たちはコート, 帽子, マフラーで暖かく身を包んでいた.

*****claim**¹ /kléɪm/ 動 ▶定義1 ⓗ **claim (that); claim (to be sth)** to say that sth is true, without having any proof 証拠なしに何かを真実だと言う→**であると主張する, 言い張る** ‖ *Colin claims the book belongs to him.* コリンはその本が自分のものだと言い張った. *The woman claims to be the oldest person in Britain.* その女性は自分が英国一長寿だと主張している. ▶定義2 ❸ ⓗ **claim (for sth)** to ask for sth from the government, a company, etc because you think it is your legal right to have it, or it belongs to you 法律上の権利があると考えて, または自分のものだと考えて, 政府や会社などに何かを求める→**～を要求する, 請求する; 所有権があると主張する** ‖ *The police are keeping the animal until somebody claims it.* 所有者が現れるまで警察がその動物を保護している. *Don't forget to claim for your travel expenses when you get back.* 戻ったら出張費を忘れずに請求してください. (比喩) *No one has claimed responsibility for the bomb attack.* 爆弾事件の犯行声明は出されていない. ▶定義3 ⓗ to cause death 死を引き起こす→**(人命)を奪う, 死の原因となる** ‖ *The earthquake claimed thousands of lives.* 地震で何千人もの人命が失われた.

*****claim**² /kléɪm/ 名 ❻ ▶定義1 **a claim (that)** a

## claimant

statement that sth is true, which does not have any proof 証拠なしに何かを真実だと言う主張 → (〜であるという)主張, 言い張ること, 断言 ‖ *I do not believe the Government's claim that they can reduce unemployment by the end of the year.* 今年の終わりまでに失業者を減らすことができるという政府の主張は信じられない．

▶定義2 **a claim (to sth)** the right to have sth 〜を持つ権利 → (〜を要求する)権利, 資格, (自分のものとしての)要求, (所有権などの)主張 ‖ *You will have to prove your claim to the property in a court of law.* その財産についての所有権を法廷で争うことになるだろう． ▶定義3 **a claim (for sth)** a demand for money that you think you have a right to, especially from the government, a company, etc 特に政府や会社などに対して, 権利があると考えて金を請求すること → 請求, 支払い要求 ‖ *to make an insurance claim* 保険金の支払いを要求する． *After the accident he decided to put in a claim for compensation.* 事故後, 彼は賠償金を請求することにした．

成句 stake a/your claim ⇒ **STAKE**²

**claimant** /kléɪm(ə)nt/ 名 C ▶定義 a person who believes he/she has the right to have sth 自分が〜を受ける権利があると信じている人 → 主張者, 要求者, (賠償などの)原告 ‖ *The insurance company refused to pay the claimant any money.* 保険会社は保険金の支払いを拒否した．

**clairvoyant** /kleərvɔ́ɪ(ə)nt/ 名 C ▶定義 a person who some people believe has special mental powers and can see what will happen in the future 特別な精神的な力で未来に起こることが見えると, 一部の人から信じられている人 → 千里眼, 透視力を持つ人, 予知能力者

**clam**¹ /klæm/ 名 C ▶定義 a type of shellfish that can be eaten 食用の貝の一種 → ハマグリ, 二枚貝 ☞ **shellfish** のさし絵

**clam**² /klæm/ 動 (**clamming**; **clammed**)

句動詞 **clam up (on sb)** 略式 ▶定義 to stop talking and refuse to speak especially when sb asks you about sth 特に〜が何かについて尋ねたときに, 話すのをやめて話すことを拒否する → (〜に)突然口をつぐむ, 黙ってしまう, 黙秘する

**clamber** /klǽm(b)ər/ 動 自 ▶定義 **clamber up, down, out etc** to move or climb with difficulty, usually using both your hands and feet 一般に両手足を使って苦労して動く, または登る → よじ登る, はい登る ‖ *She managed to clamber up the over the wall.* 彼女は何とか壁によじ登った．

**clammy** /klǽmi/ 形 ▶定義 cold, slightly wet and sticky in an unpleasant way 冷たく, やや湿っていてべとつくような, 不快な感じ → 冷たくてべとべとする, じとじとする ‖ *clammy hands* じっとりした手

**clamour** (米 **clamor**) /klǽmər/ 動 自 ▶定義 **clamour for sth** to demand sth in a loud or angry way 大声で, または怒ったように〜を要求する → 〜をやかましく要求する, 強く要求する ‖ *The public are clamouring for an answer to all these questions.* これらの質問すべての回答を民衆が大声で要求している． — **clamour** (米 **clamor**) 名 [単数扱い] → 大きな叫び, 喧嘩(けんそう), (不平, 抗議, 要求などの)叫び ‖ *the clamour of angry voices* 怒号を上げての要求

**clamp**¹ /klæmp/ 名 C
▶定義1 a tool that you use for holding two things together very tightly ２つの物をしっかりと合わせて固定するために用いる道具 → かすがい, 締め金 ▶定義2 (または **wheel clamp**) 英 a metal object that is fixed to the wheel of a car that has been parked illegally, so that it cannot drive away 違法駐車した車の車輪にはめて, 走り去れないようにする金属製の器具 → 車輪クランプ, 車輪止め

**clamp**² /klæmp/ 動 他 ▶定義1 **clamp A and B (together); clamp A to B** to fasten two things together with a clamp かすがいなどで２つの物を一緒に固定する → 〜を(かすがいなどで)締める, A を B に留める ‖ *The metal rods were clamped together.* 金属ロッドがかすがいで留められていた． *Clamp the wood to the table so that it doesn't move.* テーブルに木材をかすがいで打ち込んで動かないようにしなさい．

▶定義2 to hold sth very firmly in a particular position 〜を特定の位置に非常にしっかりと固定する → きつく締める・留める, 固定させる ‖

*Her lips were clamped tightly together.* 彼女は唇をぎゅっと結んだ. ▶定義3 to fix a metal object to the wheel of a vehicle that has been parked illegally, so that it cannot move 違法駐車した車の車輪に金属製の器具をはめて動けないようにする→～に車輪クランプを付けて動けなくする, 車輪クランプをはめる ‖ *Oh no! My car's been clamped.* 参った. 車に車輪クランプをはめられてしまった.

句動詞 **clamp down on sb/sth** 略式 ▶定義 to take strong action in order to stop or control sth 何かを中止する, または統制するために強い行動に出る→～を取り締まる, 締め付ける, 弾圧する ‖ *The police are clamping down on people who drink and drive.* 警察は飲酒運転を厳しく取り締まっている.

**clampdown** /klǽmpdàʊn/ 名 C ▶定義 strong action to stop or control sth 何かを中止する, または統制するための強い行動→取り締まり, 締め付け, 弾圧 ‖ *a clampdown on tax evasion* 脱税の取り締まり

**clan** /klǽn/ 名 [C, 単数または複数形の動詞と共に] ▶定義 a group of families who are related to each other, especially in Scotland 特にスコットランドの, 血縁関係にある複数の家族→(スコットランド高地人の)氏族; 一族, 一門

**clandestine** /klændéstən/ 形 正式 ▶定義 secret and often not legal 秘密の, しばしば違法な→内々の, 秘密の, 人目に付かない ‖ *a clandestine meeting* 秘密の会議

**clang** /klǽŋ/ 動 自他 ▶定義 to make or cause sth metal to make a loud ringing sound 金属製の～が大きく響く音を立てる・立てさせる→ガーン・カチン・ガランと鳴る, 鳴らす, 金属的な音を立てる ‖ *The iron gates clanged shut.* 鉄の門がガチャンと閉まった. — **clang** 名 C →ガーン・カチン・ガランという音

**clank** /klǽŋk/ 動 自他 ▶定義 to make or cause sth metal to make a loud unpleasant sound 金属製の～が大きく不快な音を立てる・立てさせる→ガチャン・チャリン・カチンと鳴る, 鳴らす ‖ *The lift clanked its way up to the seventh floor.* エレベーターは大きな金属音を立てて8階へ上がった. — **clank** 名 C →ガチャン・チャリン・カチンという音

★**clap**¹ /klǽp/ 動 (**clapping**; **clapped**) ▶定義1 自他 to hit your hands together many times, usually to show that you like sth 手を何回も打ち合わせ, 通常何かが気に入ったことを示す→手をたたく, 拍手する ‖ *The audience clapped as soon as the singer walked onto the stage.* 歌手が舞台に登場するや否や観客が拍手した. ▶定義2 他 to put sth onto sth quickly and firmly ～を…の上に素早くしっかりと載せる→～をポンと置く, (体の部分に)当てる ‖ *'Oh no, I shouldn't have said that,' she said, clapping a hand over her mouth.* 「嫌だ, 口を滑らしたわ」と言って, 彼女は口にさっと手を当てた.

**clap**² /klǽp/ 名 C ▶定義1 a sudden loud noise 突然の大きな音→パチパチ, バリバリ, ピシャリという音, 破裂音 ‖ *a clap of thunder* 大きな雷鳴 ▶定義2 an act of clapping 拍手すること→拍手

**clarification** /klæ̀rəfɪkéɪʃ(ə)n/ 名 U ▶定義 an act of making sth clear and easier to understand ～を明確にし, より理解しやすくすること→説明, 解明, 明白にすること ‖ *We'd like some clarification of exactly what your company intends to do.* あなたの会社がやろうとしていることを明快に説明していただきたい. ☞参 **clarity**

**clarify** /klǽrəfàɪ/ 動 他 (現分 **clarifying**; 三単現 **clarifies**; 過, 過分 **clarified**) ▶定義 to make sth become clear and easier to understand ～を明確にし, より理解しやすくする→～を明らかにする, 明快にする, 説明する ‖ *I hope that what I say will clarify the situation.* 私の話で状況を明白に理解してもらえればいいのですが. ☞参 形 **clear**

**clarinet** /klæ̀rənét, -nət/ 名 C ▶定義 a musical instrument that is made of wood. You play a clarinet by blowing through it. 息を吹き込んで演奏する, 木製の楽器→クラリネット ☞参 **piano** の注 ☞ **music** のさし絵

**clarity** /klǽrəti/ 名 U ▶定義 the quality of being clear and easy to understand 明確で理解しやすいこと→明快さ, 明確さ, 明せき ‖ *clarity of expression* 説明の明快さ ☞参 **clarification**

**clash**¹ /klǽʃ/ 動 ▶定義1 自 **clash (with sb) (over sth)** to fight or disagree seriously about sth ～について争う, または大きく意見が食い違う→(～について)(…と)対立する, ぶつかる, 衝突する ‖ *A group of demonstrators clashed with police outside the Town Hall.* 市役所の外でデモ隊の一

団が警察と衝突した. ▶定義2 ⓔ clash (with sth) (used about two events) to happen at the same time (2つの出来事について)同時に起こる→(〜と)かち合う,(日時が)重なる ‖ *It's a pity the two concerts clash. I wanted to go to both of them.* 2つのコンサートがかち合うのは残念だ. 両方に行きたかったのに. ▶定義3 ⓔ clash (with sth) (used about colours, etc) to not match or look nice together (色などについて)合わない,または一緒になると見栄えが良くない→(〜と)釣り合わない,調和しない ‖ *I don't think you should wear that tie - it clashes with your shirt.* そのネクタイは着けない方がいいわ — シャツと合わないから. ▶定義4 ⓔ ⓤ (used about two metal objects) to hit together with a loud noise; to cause two metal objects to do this (2つの金属物について)大きな音を立ててぶつかり合う; 2つの金属物をそのようにぶつける→ガチャンとぶつかる・ぶつける, ガチャンと音がする ‖ *Their swords clashed.* 彼らの剣が金属音を立ててぶつかった.

**clash**² /klæʃ/ 🔊 ⓒ ▶定義1 a fight or serious disagreement 争い, または意見の大きな相違→衝突, 対立, 小競り合い ‖ *a clash between police and demonstrators* 警察とデモ隊の衝突 ▶定義2 a big difference 大きな違い→衝突, 対立, 不一致, 不調和 ‖ *a clash of opinions* 意見の衝突 *There was a personality clash between the two men (= they did not get well on together or like each other).* 2人の男の間には性格の不一致があった(= 2人はうまくいかなかった, または互いに好きではなかった). ▶定義3 a loud noise, made by two metal objects hitting each other 金属製の物がぶつかり合って立てる大きな音→ガチャンという音, ジャンジャンという音

**clasp**¹ /klɑːsp; klæsp/ 🔊 ⓒ ▶定義 an object, usually of metal, which fastens or holds sth together 普通は金属製で, 〜を固定するまたは結合させるために使われる→留め金, 締め金, バックル ‖ *the clasp on a necklace/brooch/handbag* ネックレス・ブローチ・ハンドバッグの留め金

**clasp**² /klɑːsp; klæsp/ 🔊 ⓥ ▶定義 to hold sb/sth tightly 〜をしっかりと捕まえる→〜を握りしめる, 抱き締める, 留める ‖ *Kevin clasped the child in his arms.* ケヴィンは子供を腕にしっかりと抱き締めた.

★**class**¹ /klɑːs; klæs/ 🔊 ▶定義1 [ⓒ, 単数または複数形の動詞と共に] a group of students who are taught together 一緒に授業を受ける生徒の集まり→学級, 組, クラス ‖ *Jane and I are in the same class at school.* ジェーンと私は学校で同じクラスだ. *The whole class is/are going to the theatre tonight.* 今夜クラスの全員が劇場へ行く. ▶定義2 ⓒ ⓤ a lesson 授業→授業時間, 講義, 講習 ‖ *Classes begin at 9 o'clock in the morning.* 授業は午前9時に始まる. *We watched an interesting video in class (= during the lesson) yesterday.* 昨日私たちは授業で(= 授業中に), 面白いビデオを見た. ▶定義3 ⓤ ⓒ the way people are divided into social groups; one of these groups 人々を社会的集団に分ける方法; こうした集団の1つ→(階級)制度, 階層, 身分 ‖ *The idea of class still divides British society.* 階級という考え方がいまだに英国社会を分断している. *class differences* 階級の差 [単数または複数形の動詞と共に] ▶定義4 ⓒ (専門用語) a group of animals, plants, words, etc of a similar type 同じような種類の動物, 植物, 単語などのグループ→分類, 種類,(生物の)綱(こう) ‖ *There are several different classes of insects.* 昆虫は数種に分類される. ▶定義5 ⓤ 略式 high quality or style 高品質または高度な様式→優秀, 卓越, 優雅, 上品 ‖ *Pele was a football player of great class.* ペレは卓越したサッカー選手だった. ▶定義6 ⓒ (複合形容詞を作るために用いて) of a certain level of quality あるレベルの品質の→〜級, 〜等, 水準, ランク ‖ *a first-class carriage on a train* 列車の1等車 ▶定義7 ⓒ 英 (複合形容詞を作るために用いて) a mark that you are given when you pass your final university exam 大学の最終試験に合格すると得られる評価→優等試験の合格等級 ‖ *a first-/second-/third-class degree* 第1・2・3級の学位

▶音声とつづり字

class の cl- の発音

classは日本語ではクラスになります. 英語らしく発音するにはclの発音を[ku-ra-s]にならないよう工夫することが必要です. 子音1+子音2を子音連結として発音するには,

子音2の発音の構えを子音1の前に持っていくと発音しやすいでしょう．つまり，classの場合は[l]を[k]の前に持っていき，まず舌先を歯茎に付け，舌先が歯茎から離れないようにして，kを発音します．

**class²** /klɑːs; klæs/ 動 他 ▶定義 class sb/sth (as sth) to put sb/sth in a particular group or type ～を特定のグループや種類に分ける→～を(…に)分類する，～に等級を付ける ‖ Certain animals and plants are now classed as 'endangered species'. 一部の動物や植物は現在「絶滅危惧(きぐ)種」に分類されている．

**classic¹** /klǽsɪk/ 形 (通常は名詞の前だけ) ▶定義 1 typical 典型的な→模範的な，標準的な ‖ It was a classic case of bad management. これは悪い経営の見本だ． ▶定義 2 (used about a book, play, etc) important and having a value that will last (本，演劇などについて)重要で長いこと変わらない価値を持った→古典の，古典的な，一流の，名作の ‖ the classic film 'Gone With The Wind' 名作映画「風と共に去りぬ」

▶日本語 vs 英語

「クラシック」の意味

　音楽の「クラシック」は和製英語です．英語ではこのタイプの音楽を classical music と言います．それには古典音楽，古典風音楽の両方が含まれます．ところで，英語の classic は「歴史のある質の高いもの」という意味です．バッハの作品は本当の classic と言えますが，ほんの2，3年前に作曲されたものは，「古さ」という点で classic とは言えません．

**classic²** /klǽsɪk/ 名 ▶定義 1 ❶a famous book, play, etc which has a value that will last 長年月にわたって変わらない価値を持った有名な本，演劇など→古典，名作，一流の作品 ‖ All of Charles Dickens' novels are classics. チャールズ ディケンズの小説はすべて名作である．

▶定義 2 **Classics** ❶the study of ancient Greek and Roman language and literature 古代ギリシャとローマの言語と文学の研究→(古典)文学，古典語

**classical** /klǽsɪk(ə)l/ 形 (通常は名詞の前だけ) ▶定義 1 (used about music) serious and having a value that lasts (音楽について)本格的で長い間にわたって変わらない価値を持った→古典の，クラシックの，古典派の ‖ I prefer classical music to pop. 私はポピュラー音楽よりクラシックが好きだ． ☛参 **jazz, pop, rock** ▶定義 2 traditional, not modern 伝統的で現代的でない→古典的な，伝統的な，正統派の，クラシックの ‖ classical ballet クラシックバレエ ▶定義 3 connected with ancient Greece or Rome 古代ギリシャとローマに関連した→古代ギリシャ・ローマの，古典文学の，古典語の ‖ classical architecture 古代ギリシャ・ローマ建築 — **classically** /-k(ə)li/ 副 →古典的に，伝統的に

**classified** /klǽsəfàɪd/ 形 ▶定義 officially secret 公的に秘密の→機密扱いの，極秘の ‖ classified information 極秘情報

**classified advertisement** (英 略式 **classified ad**; **small ad**) 名 [通常は複数] ▶定義 a small advertisement that you put in a newspaper if you want to buy or sell sth, employ sb, find a flat, etc ～を売買したいまたは…を雇いたいとき，アパートを探しているときなどに，新聞に載せる小さな広告→項目別広告，三行広告，求人・求職広告

**classify** /klǽsəfàɪ/ 動 他 (現分 **classifying**; 三単現 **classifies**; 過，過分 **classified**) ▶定義 classify sb/sth (as sth) to put sb/sth into a group with other people or things of a similar type ～を，同類の人や物と一緒に1つのグループに入れる→～を(…と)分類する，類別する，等級に分ける，区分する ‖ Would you classify it as an action film or a thriller? その映画をアクションとスリラーのどちらに分類しますか． — **classification** /klæ̀səfɪkéɪʃ(ə)n/ 名 ❶ ❶ →分類，区分 ‖ the classification of the different species of butterfly 異なる種のチョウの分類

**classmate** /klɑ́ːsmèɪt; klǽs-/ 名 ❶ ▶定義 a person who is in the same class as you at school or college 学校や大学で同じクラスの人→同級生，クラスメート

**classroom** /klɑ́ːsrùːm, rùm; klǽs-/ 名 ❶ ▶定義 a room in a school, college, etc where lessons are taught 学校，大学などで授業を行う部屋→教室，講義室

**classy** /klɑ́ːsi; klǽ-/ 形 (**classier**; **classiest**) 略式 ▶定義 of high quality or style; expensive and fashionable 高品質の、または一流の; 高価で高級な→**高級な, 上品な, 上等な, 粋(いき)な** ‖ *a classy restaurant* 高級レストラン

**clatter** /klǽtər/ 動自他 ▶定義 to make or cause sth hard to make a series of short loud repeated sounds 硬い〜によって短く大きな連続音を発生させる→**カタカタ・ガタガタ・ガチャガチャと鳴る, 鳴らす** ‖ *The horses clattered down the street.* 馬がひづめの音を立てて通りを行った. — clatter 名 [通常は単数] →**カタカタ・ガタガタ・ガチャガチャという音**

**clause** /klɔ́ːz/ 名 C ▶定義1 one of the sections of a legal document that says that sth must or must not be done すべき事やすべきでない事を述べた法律文書の項の1つ→**条項, 個条** ▶定義2 （文法）a group of words that includes a subject and a verb. A clause is usually only part of a sentence. 主語と述語を含む語の集合. 通常は文の一部→**節, 文節** ‖ *The sentence, 'After we had finished eating, we watched a film on the video,' contains two clauses.* 「食事を終えてから，ビデオで映画を見た」という文は2つの節から成り立っている.

**claustrophobia** /klɔ̀ːstrəfóubiə/ 名 U ▶定義 fear of being in a small or enclosed space 狭いまたは閉ざされた空間にいることの恐怖→**閉所恐怖症, 密室恐怖**

**claustrophobic** /klɔ̀ːstrəfóubik/ 形 ▶定義1 extremely afraid of small, enclosed spaces 狭い閉ざされた空間を極端に恐れる→**閉所恐怖症の, 密室恐怖の** ‖ *I always feel claustrophobic in lifts.* 私はいつもエレベーターでは閉所恐怖症に襲われる. ▶定義2 used about sth that makes you feel afraid in this way そのような恐怖を感じさせる〜について→**閉所恐怖症を起こさせるような, 狭苦しい** ‖ *a claustrophobic little room* 閉所恐怖症になりそうな狭い部屋

**claw**¹ /klɔ́ː/ 名 C ▶定義1 one of the long curved nails on the end of an animal's or a bird's foot 動物や鳥の足の先にある長い曲がったつめの1つ→**(猫・ワシ・タカなどの)かぎつめ, かぎつめのある足, かぎつめ形の物** ☜ C1 ページのさし絵 ▶定義2 one of a pair of long, sharp fingers that certain types of shellfish and some insects have. They use them for holding or picking things up. 一部の甲殻類や昆虫が持つ一組の長く鋭い指状の器官．これを用いて物をつかむ，またはつついて取る→**(カニ, エビなどの)はさみ** ‖ *the claws of a crab* カニのはさみ

**claw**² /klɔ́ː/ 動自他 ▶定義 claw (at) sb/sth to scratch or tear sb/sth with claws or with your fingernails 〜をかぎつめや指のつめでひっかく，または引き裂く→**(〜を)つめでひっかく, かきむしる, つめでひっかいて〜する** ‖ *The cat was clawing at the furniture.* 猫が家具をひっかいていた．

**clay** /kléi/ 名 U ▶定義 heavy earth that is soft and sticky when it is wet and becomes hard when it is baked or dried 湿っているときは柔らかく粘着性で，焼いたり乾燥させたりすると固くなる重い土→**粘土, 土, 泥** ‖ *clay pots* 粘土のつぼ

★**clean**¹ /klíːn/ 形 ▶定義1 not dirty 汚れていない→**清潔な, きれいな; 洗濯・掃除してある** ‖ *The whole house was beautifully clean.* 家中がとても清潔だった. *Cats are very clean animals.* 猫はとてもきれい好きな動物だ. ▶定義2 (used about humour) not about sex, etc; not dirty (ユーモアについて) 性などに関連しない; 不快でない→**みだらでない, 下品でない, 品のいい** ‖ *clean joke* （性的でない）趣味のいいジョーク ⇨ 定義1, 2 **dirty** ▶定義3 having no record of offences or crimes 違反や犯罪の前科がない→**潔白な, 違反していない, 前科のない** ‖ *a clean driving licence* 違反記録のない運転免許証

成句 **a clean sweep** ▶定義 a complete victory in a sports competition, election, etc that you get by winning all the different parts of it スポーツ競技や選挙などで，すべての面で勝つ完全な勝利→**完勝, 全勝, 総なめ** ‖ *The Russians made a clean sweep of all the gymnastics events.* すべての体操競技でロシアが完勝した. ☞ 名 **cleanliness**

★**clean**² /klíːn/ 動 ▶定義1 他 to remove dirt, dust and marks from sth 〜から汚れ，ほこり，跡を取り除く→**〜をきれいにする, 清潔にする, 〜の手入れをする, (歯)を磨く** ‖ *to clean the windows* 窓を掃除する *Don't forget to clean your teeth!* 歯を磨くのを忘れないで.

➤ clean は物から汚れを取り除く場合に用いる一般的な語. wash は水と普通はせっけんを用いて汚れを取り除く. wipe は湿った布で表

面をふく. dust は乾いた布で表面をふく. brush は短い柄の付いたブラシで汚れを取り除く. sweep は長い柄の付いたブラシを床などに使う.

▶定義2 自他 to make the inside of a house, office, etc free from dust and dirt 家や事務所などの内部の汚れやほこりを取り除く→(〜を)掃除する, 清掃する ‖ *Mr Burrows comes in to clean after office hours.* バローズさんが営業時間後に掃除をしに来た. ☛ do the cleaning は clean の代わりによく用いられる. *I do the cleaning once a week.* 私は週に1回掃除をする.

句動詞 clean sth out ▶定義 to clean the inside of sth 〜の中をきれいにする→きれいに掃除する, すっかり掃除する ‖ *I'm going to clean out all the cupboards next week.* 来週すべての戸棚の中をきれいに掃除するつもりだ.

clean (sth) up ▶定義 to remove all the dirt from a place that is particularly dirty 特に汚れた場所からすべての汚れを取り除く→(〜を)きれいに掃除する, 片付ける, 大掃除する ‖ *I'm going to clean up the kitchen before Mum and Dad get back.* 母さんと父さんが帰ってくる前に, 台所をきれいに片付けるつもりだ. *Oh no, you've spilt coffee on the new carpet! Can you clean it up?* 嫌だ, 新しいカーペットにコーヒーをこぼしたのね. すっかりきれいにできるの. ☛参 **dry-clean**, **spring-clean**

**clean**³ /kliːn/ 副 略式 ▶定義 completely 完全に→全く, すっかり ‖ *I clean forgot it was your birthday.* あなたの誕生日をすっかり忘れていた.

成句 come clean (with sb) (about sth) 略式 ▶定義 to tell the truth about sth that you have been keeping secret 秘密にしていた事について真実を話す→(〜に)(…のことを)白状する, 本音を吐く, 打ち明ける ‖ *She decided to come clean with Martin about her relationship with Tom.* 彼女はトムとの関係についてマーティンに打ち明ける決心をした.

go clean out of your mind ▶定義 to be completely forgotten 完全に忘れられる→すっかり忘れる, きれいに忘れる

**cleaner** /ˈkliːnər/ 名 ▶定義1 ●a person whose job is to clean the rooms and furniture inside a house or other building 仕事として, 家やほかの建造物内の部屋と家具を掃除する人→掃除人, 清掃作業員, 清掃係 ‖ *an office cleaner* 会社の清掃作業員 ▶定義2 ●a substance or a special machine that you use for cleaning sth 〜をきれいにするために用いる物質や特別の機械→洗剤, クリーナー, 掃除機 ‖ *liquid floor cleaners* 床用液体洗剤 *a carpet cleaner* カーペット用洗剤 ☛参 **vacuum cleaner** ▶定義3 **the cleaner's** =**DRY-CLEANER'S**

**cleanliness** /ˈklɛnlinəs/ 名 Ⓤ ▶定義 being clean or keeping things clean きれいなこと, または物をきれいにしておくこと→清潔, きれいなこと; きれい好き ‖ *High standards of cleanliness are important in a hotel kitchen.* ホテルの厨房(ちゅうぼう)には高水準の清潔さが重要だ.

**cleanly** /ˈkliːnli/ 副 ▶定義 easily or smoothly in one movement 1つの動きで簡単に, または滑らかに→手際良く, きれいに, 楽々と, 見事に ‖ *The knife cut cleanly through the rope.* ナイフでロープをすぱっと切った.

**cleanse** /klɛnz/ 動 他 ▶定義 to clean your skin or a wound 皮膚や傷口をきれいにする→〜を清潔にする, 洗う, 浄化する ☛参 **ethnic cleansing**

**cleanser** /ˈklɛnzər/ 名 Ⓒ ▶定義 a substance that you use for cleaning your skin, especially your face 肌, 特に顔をきれいにするために用いる物質→洗顔料

**clean-shaven** 形 ▶定義 (used about men) having recently shaved (男性について) ひげをそったばかりの→ひげをきれいにそった, ひげのない

★**clear**¹ /klɪər/ 形 ▶定義1 easy to see, hear or understand 簡単に見える, 聞こえる, 理解できる→はっきりした, くっきりした, 明瞭(めいりょう)な ‖ *His voice wasn't very clear on the telephone.* 彼の声は電話ではあまりはっきり聞き取れなかった. *She gave me clear directions on how to get there.* 彼女はそこへ行く順路を分かりやすく教えてくれた. ▶定義2 **clear (about/on sth)** sure or definite; without any doubts or confusion 確信のある, 明確な; 疑いや混乱のない→(〜について)はっきりと分かって, 確かな, 確信がある ‖ *I'm not quite clear about the arrangements for tomorrow.* 明日の予定についてはまだよく分からない. ☛ 動 **clarify** ▶定義3 **clear (to sb)** obvious 明らかな→(〜にとって)明白な,

はっきりした, 分かりきった ‖ *There are clear advantages to the second plan.* 第2の計画には明白な利点がある. *It was clear to me that he was not telling the truth.* 彼が真実を話していないことが私にははっきり分かった.
▶定義 **4** easy to see through 簡単に見通せる→澄んだ, 透き通った, 透明な ‖ *The water was so clear that we could see the bottom of the lake.* 水がとても澄んでいたので, 湖の底が見えた.
▶定義 **5** clear (of sth) free from things that are blocking the way 妨げる物のない→障害物のない, 開けた, 空いた ‖ *The police say that most roads are now clear of snow.* 大部分の道路にはもう雪はないと警察は言っている.
▶定義 **6** free from marks 跡のない→きれいな, 傷のない, 純粋の ‖ *a clear sky (= without clouds)* 晴れ渡った空(= 雲のない) *a clear skin (= without spots)* きれいな肌(= 染みのない)
▶定義 **7** free from guilt 罪がない→潔白な, やましいところのない ‖ *It wasn't your fault. You can have a completely clear conscience.* あれはあなたのせいではなかった. あなたには何もやましいところはありません.

成句 **make yourself clear; make sth clear/plain (to sb)** ▶定義 to speak so that there can be no doubt about what you mean 意図した事を疑いの余地がないように話す→はっきり言う, はっきりさせる ‖ *'I do not want you to go to that concert,' said my mother. 'Do I make myself clear?'*「そのコンサートには行かせたくないの」と母は言った.「ちゃんと分かったの」 *He made it quite clear that he was not happy with the decision.* その決定が気に入らないと彼ははっきりと言った.

★**clear**² /klɪər/ 副 ▶定義 **1** = CLEARLY(1) ‖ *We can hear the telephone loud and clear from here.* ここからでも電話の音が大きくはっきりと聞こえる. ▶定義 **2** clear (of sth) away from sth; not touching sth ～から離れて;～に触らずに→(～から)離れて, ～に近付かないで, (～の)邪魔にならずに ‖ *stand clear of the doors (= on a train)* ドアの前から離れて立つ(= 列車で)

成句 **keep/stay/steer clear (of sb/sth)** ▶定義 to avoid sb/sth because he/she/it may cause problems 問題を起こすかもしれないので, ～を避ける→(～に)近付かない, (～を)避けている, (～と)かかわらない ‖ *It's best to keep clear of the town centre during the rush hour.* ラッシュ時は街の中心部を避けるのが一番いい.

★**clear**³ /klɪər/ 動 ▶定義 **1** 他 to remove sth that is not wanted or needed 要らない～や不用な～を取り除く→～を片付ける, きれいにする, 排除する ‖ *to clear the roads of snow/to clear snow from the roads* 道路から雪を取り除く・道路を除雪する *It's your turn to clear the table (= to take away the dirty plates, etc after a meal).* あなたがテーブルを片付ける番ですよ(= 食事の後で汚れた皿を片付ける). ▶定義 **2** 自 (used about smoke, etc) to disappear (煙などについて)消える→晴れる, 消え去る ‖ *The fog slowly cleared and the sun came out.* ゆっくりと霧が晴れて太陽が出た. ▶定義 **3** 自 (used about the sky, the weather or water) to become free of clouds, rain, or mud (空, 天候, 水などについて)雲, 雨, または泥がなくなる→晴れる, 晴れ上がる, (雨が)上がる, 澄む ‖ *After a cloudy start, the weather will clear during the afternoon.* 朝のうちは曇っていますが, 午後には晴れるでしょう. ▶定義 **4** 他 **clear sb (of sth)** to provide proof that sb is innocent of sth ～が無実であるという証拠を提供する→～から(…の)疑いを晴らす, ～の潔白を証明する ‖ *The man has finally been cleared of murder.* その男の殺人の容疑がついに晴れた.
▶定義 **5** 他 to jump over or get past sth without touching it ～に触れずに飛び越える, または通り過ぎる→～に触れずに通過する, (障害物など)をきれいに飛び越える ▶定義 **6** 他 to give official permission for a plane, ship, etc to enter or leave a place 航空機や船舶などに, 立ち入りまたは出発の許可を正式に与える→～の出入港, 離着陸などの承認を与える ‖ *At last the plane was cleared for take-off.* やっとその飛行機の離陸が認められた. ▶定義 **7** 他 **clear sth (with sb)** to get official approval for sth to be done ～を行うための正式の承認を得る→～の認可を求める, 許可を求める ‖ *I'll have to clear it with the manager before I can refund your money.* お金を払い戻す前に, 支配人の許可を得なければならないでしょう. ▶定義 **8** 自 (used about a cheque) to go through the system that moves money from one account to another (小切手について)金をある口座から別の口座へ移す過程を通る→

現金化される ‖ *The cheque will take three days to clear.* 小切手を清算するのに3日かかります.

**成句** clear the air ▶定義 to improve a difficult or tense situation by talking honestly about worries, doubts, etc 心配や疑いなどについて誠実に話し, 困難な状況または張り詰めた状況を改善する→疑惑を晴らす, 緊張をほぐす, 場の雰囲気を明るくする ‖ *I'm sure if you discuss your feelings with her it will help to clear the air between you.* 自分の気持ちについて彼女と話し合えば, あなたたちの間の緊張はほぐれると思いますよ.

clear your throat ▶定義 to cough slightly in order to make it easier to speak 話しやすくするために軽くせきをする→せき払いをする

**句動詞** clear off **略式** ▶定義 used to tell sb to go away ～に去るように言う場合に用いて→あっちへ行け, 去れ

clear sth out ▶定義 to tidy sth and throw away things that you do not want ～を整とんして必要のない物を捨てる→～を片付ける, 整理する

clear up ▶定義 (used about the weather or an illness) to get better (天候や病気について) 良くなる→回復する, 晴れる, 治る, 快方に向かう ‖ *We can go out for a walk if it clears up later on.* もし後で晴れたら散歩に出掛けられます. *The doctor told him to stay at home until his cold cleared up.* 医師は彼に風邪が治るまで家にいるようにと言った.

clear (sth) up ▶定義 to make sth tidy ～を整とんする→整理する, きちんと片付ける ‖ *Make sure you clear up properly before you leave.* きちんと片付けたことを確かめてから, 出ていきなさい.

clear sth up ▶定義 to find the solution to a problem, cause of confusion, etc 問題や混乱の原因などの解決方法を見つける→～を解く, 解き明かす, 解決する, 明らかにする ‖ *There's been a slight misunderstanding but we've cleared it up now.* ちょっとした誤解があったが, もう解決した.

**clearance** /klíərəns/ **名** **U** ▶定義 **1** the removing of sth that is old or not wanted 古い～や必要ない…を取り除くこと→除去, 撤去, 一掃; 片付け, 整理 ‖ *The shop is having a clearance sale (= selling things cheaply in order to get rid of them).* その店では在庫一掃セールをやっている (= 物を処分するために安く売る). ▶定義 **2** the distance between an object and something that is passing under or beside it, for example a ship or vehicle ある物の, その下やそばを通過する物, 例えば船や乗り物などとの距離→間隔, ゆとり, すきま ‖ *There was not enough clearance for the bus to pass under the bridge safely.* バスが陸橋の下を安全に通過できるだけの余裕がなかった. ▶定義 **3** official permission for sb/sth to do sth ～が何かをすることを認める正式の許可→承認; 通関手続き, 離着陸許可, 秘密情報の使用許可 ‖ *She was given clearance to work at the nuclear research establishment.* 彼女は原子力研究施設で働く許可を得た.

**clear-cut** **形** ▶定義 definite and easy to see or understand 明確で見やすい, または分かりやすい→輪郭のはっきりした, くっきりした; 明快な, 疑いの余地のない

**clear-headed** **形** ▶定義 able to think clearly, especially if there is a problem 特に問題が生じたときに, 明せきに考えられる→頭脳明せきな, 頭のさえた, 洞察力のある

**clearing** /klíərɪŋ/ **名** **C** ▶定義 a small area without trees in the middle of a wood or forest 林や森の中で樹木の生えていない小さな場所→(森林の) 開拓地, 林間の空き地

**clearly** /klíərli/ **副** ▶定義 **1** in a way that is easy to see, hear or understand 簡単に見える, 聞こえる, 理解できるように→はっきりと, 明らかに, 明瞭 (めいりょう) に ‖ *It was so foggy that we couldn't see the road clearly.* 霧がとても深くて道路がはっきり見えなかった. ▶定義 **2** in a way that is not confused 混乱しないやり方で→明確に, はっきりと ‖ *I'm so tired that I can't think clearly.* 疲れきっているので, はっきりものが考えられない. ▶定義 **3** without doubt; obviously 疑いなく; 明確に→明らかに, 明白に ‖ *She clearly doesn't want to speak to you any more.* 明らかに彼女はもうあなたとは話したくないのです.

**clear-sighted** **形** ▶定義 able to understand situations well and to see what might happen in the future 状況をよく理解し, 将来起こりそうな事が分かる→判断力がある, 先見の明のある

**cleavage** /klíːvɪdʒ/ **名** **C** **U** ▶定義 the space between a woman's breasts 女性の胸の間の空

間→(胸の)谷間, くぼみ

**clef** /klef/ 名 ● ▶定義 (in music) a sign (𝄞, 𝄢) at the beginning of a line of written music that shows the area of sound that the notes are in (音楽で)楽譜の先頭の記号(ト音記号, ヘ音記号)で, 音符がある音の範囲を示す→音部記号 ‖ *the bass/treble clef* 低音部・高音部記号

**clementine** /klémənti:n, -tàɪn/ 名 ● ▶定義 a type of small orange 小型のオレンジの一種→クレメンタイン

**clench** /klentʃ/ 動 他 ▶定義 to close or hold tightly しっかりと閉じる, または持つ→(手など)を握りしめる, ぎゅっとつかむ; (歯)を食いしばる ‖ *She clenched her fists and looked as if she was going to hit him.* 彼女はこぶしを握りしめ, 今にも彼をたたきそうな様子だった.

**clergy** /klə́:rdʒi/ 名 [複数扱い] ▶定義 the people who perform religious ceremonies in the Christian church キリスト教の教会で宗教的儀式を行う人々→聖職者, 牧師たち ‖ *a member of the clergy* 聖職者の一員

**clergyman** /klə́:rdʒimən/ 名 (複 **-men** /-mən/) ▶定義 a male member of the clergy 聖職者の男性→聖職者, 牧師

**clergywoman** /klə́:rdʒiwùmən/ 名 ● (複 **-women** /-wìmən/) ▶定義 a female member of the clergy 聖職者の女性→女性聖職者, 女性牧師

**clerical** /klérɪk(ə)l/ 形 ▶定義 1 connected with the work of a clerk in an office 事務所の事務員の仕事と関連した→事務の, 事務員の ‖ *clerical work* 事務の仕事 ▶定義 2 connected with the clergy 聖職者と関連した→聖職者の, 聖職の, 牧師の

★**clerk** /klɑ:k; klə:rk/ 名 ● ▶定義 1 a person whose job is to do written work or look after records or accounts in an office, bank, court of law, etc 事務所, 銀行, 裁判所などで書記の仕事や, 記録や計算書を扱う仕事をする人→事務員, 行員, (官庁, 法廷の)職員, 書記 ▶定義 2 (または **sales clerk**) 米 = SHOP ASSISTANT

★**clever** /klévər/ 形 ▶定義 1 able to learn, understand or do sth quickly and easily; intelligent ～を素早く容易に学ぶ・理解する, または実行することができる; 頭の良い→頭が良い, 頭の回転が速い, 賢い, 才気のある, 利口な; 器用な, 巧みな ‖ *a clever student* 頭の良い生徒 *How clever of you to mend my watch!* 私の時計を直してくれたなんて, 何て器用なんだろう. ▶定義 2 (used about things, ideas, etc) showing skill or intelligence (物, 考えなどについて)巧みさや知性を示す→巧妙な, うまい, 思い付きのいい ‖ *a clever device* 巧妙な仕掛け *a clever plan* うまい計画 — **cleverly** 副 →利口に, 器用に; 巧妙に — **cleverness** 名 ● →利口なこと, 器用さ, 巧妙さ

**cliche** /klı:ʃéɪ; klí:ʃeɪ/ 名 ● ▶定義 a phrase or idea that has been used so many times that it no longer has any real meaning or interest 何回も用いられたために, もはや実際の意味や興味が失われた句や考え→陳腐な決まり文句, ありふれた表現, 陳腐な考え, 月並みなもの

**click**¹ /klɪk/ 動 ▶定義 1 自 他 to make a short sharp sound; to cause sth to do this 短く鋭い音を立てる; ～にそのような音を立てさせる→カチッと鳴る・鳴らす, カチッと音がして～する, カチッと鳴らして～する ‖ *The door clicked shut.* ドアがカチリと閉まった. *He clicked his fingers at the waiter.* 彼はウエーターに向かって指を鳴らした. ▶定義 2 自 他 **click (on sth)** (computing) to press one of the buttons on a mouse (コンピューター)マウスのボタンを押す→(～を)クリックする ‖ *To open a file, click on the menu.* ファイルを開くには, メニューをクリックします. *Position the pointer and **double click** the left-hand mouse button (= press it twice very quickly).* ポインターを合わせて, マウスの左ボタンをダブルクリックします (= 非常に素早く2回押す). ▶定義 3 自 英 略式 (used about two people) to become friendly immediately (2人の人について)すぐに親しくなる→意気投合する, 気が合う, うまが合う ‖ *We met at a party and just clicked.* 私たちはパーティーで出会ってすぐに意気投合した. ▶定義 4 自 略式 (used about a problem, etc) to become suddenly clear or understood (問題などについて)突然明白になる, または理解できる→突然分かる, ぴんと来る, つじつまが合う ‖ *Once I'd found the missing letter, everything **clicked into place**.* 抜けている文字が分かったら, すべてが解けた.

**click**² /klɪk/ 名 ● ▶定義 1 a short sharp sound 短く鋭い音→カチッという音 ‖ *the click of a switch* スイッチのカチッという音 ▶定義 2

(computing) the act of pressing the button on a computer mouse (コンピューター) コンピューターのマウスのボタンを押すこと➜クリック

**\*client** /kláɪənt/ 名 C ▶定義1 somebody who receives a service from a professional person, for example a lawyer 例えば弁護士などの専門家から業務提供を受ける人➜(弁護士の)依頼人, (公的機関に)相談する人, 顧客 ▶定義2 (computing) one of a number of computers that is connected to a special computer (server) that stores shared information (コンピューター) 共有する情報を保存した特別のコンピューター(サーバー)に接続された複数のコンピューターのうちの1台➜クライアント

▶ client は店やレストランの客には用いないので注意する. 店やレストランの客には customer を用いる. clientele は clients と customers の両方を意味する全般的で正式な語.

**clientele** /klìːəntél, klàɪən-/ 名 U ▶定義 all the customers, guests or clients who regularly go to a particular shop, hotel, organization, etc 特定の店, ホテル, 組織などへ定期的に行くすべての顧客, 客または依頼人➜顧客たち, 常連, 訴訟依頼人たち ☛ customers または guests よりも正式な語.

**\*cliff** /klíf/ 名 C ▶定義 a high, very steep area of rock, especially one next to the sea 高く非常に険しい岸壁, 特に海に面した場所➜崖(がけ), 絶壁, 断崖(だんがい) ☛ C8 ページの挿し絵

**\*climate** /kláɪmət/ 名 C ▶定義1 the normal weather conditions of a particular region 特定地域の通常の天候状態➜気候, 風土, (気候から見た)地方 ∥ a dry/humid/tropical climate 乾燥した気候・湿潤な気候・熱帯性気候 ▶定義2 the general opinions, etc that people have at a particular time 人々が特定の時期に抱く世間一般の意見など➜風潮, 思潮; 気風, 雰囲気, 精神的風土 ∥ What is the current **climate of opinion** regarding the death penalty? 死刑に関する現在の世論はどのようなものですか. the political climate 政治情勢

**climatic** /klaɪmǽtɪk/ 形 ▶定義 connected with the climate(1) climate(1) と関連した➜気候の, 風土的な

**climax** /kláɪmæks/ 名 C ▶定義 the most important and exciting part of a book, play, piece of music, event, etc 本, 演劇, 音楽, 出来事などの最も重要で刺激的な部分➜山場, クライマックス; 頂点, 最高潮 ∥ The novel **reaches a dramatic climax** in the final chapter. 小説は最終章で劇的なクライマックスを迎える. ―climax 動 自➜最高潮に達する, 山場に達する

**\*climb**¹ /kláɪm/ 動 ▶定義1 自 他 climb (up) (sth) to move up towards the top of sth 〜の頂上に向かって移動する➜(〜を)登る, よじ登る, (〜を)上がる ∥ to climb a tree/mountain/rope 木に登る・山に登る・ロープをよじ登る She climbed the stairs to bed. 彼女は階段を上がって寝室に行った. to climb up a ladder はしごを登る ▶定義2 自 to move, with difficulty or effort, in the direction mentioned 言及された方向に苦労して, または努力して移動する➜(手足を使ってはうように)進む, 何とか進む; もぐり込む ∥ I managed to climb out of the window. 私は何とか窓から外に出た. ▶定義3 自 to go up mountains, etc as a sport スポーツとして山などに登る➜登山をする, 登攀(とうはん)する ☛ go climbing は楽しみのために登山することを表す普通の表現. I go climbing in the Alps most summers. 私は夏には大抵アルプスに登山に行く. ▶定義4 自 to rise to a higher position 高い位置に昇る➜上昇する, 立ち昇る, 上がる ∥ The plane climbed steadily. 飛行機は着実に高度を上げた. The road climbed steeply up the side of the mountain. 道は急な登りになって山の斜面を上がっていった. (比喩) The value of the dollar climbed against the pound. ドルはポンドに対して上昇した.

成句 climb/jump on the bandwagon ⇒ **BANDWAGON**

句動詞 climb down (over sth) 略式 ▶定義 to admit that you have made a mistake; to change your opinion about sth in an argument 自分が間違いを犯したことを認める; 議論で〜に対する意見を変える➜(〜について)非を認める, 引き下がる, (主張など)を捨てる

**climb²** /kláɪm/ 名 C ▶定義 an act of climbing or a journey made by climbing 登ること, または登る行程➜登り, よじ登り, 登り坂, 登山 ∥ The monastery could only be reached by a three-hour climb. 修道院へ行くには3時間山を登る以外なかった.

**climbdown** /kláımdàʊn/ 名 C ▶定義 an act of admitting you have been wrong; a change of opinion in an argument 自分が悪いと認めること, または議論で意見を変えること➡**非を認めること, 撤回, 譲歩** ‖ *a government climbdown* 政府の譲歩

**climber** /kláımər/ 名 C ▶定義 a person who climbs mountains as a sport スポーツとして山に登る人➡**登山家, 登山者**

**clinch** /klɪntʃ/ 動他 略式 ▶定義 to finally manage to get what you want in an argument or business agreement 議論や商談の取り決めで, ついに何とか自分が望むものを手に入れる➡**(取り引き, 議論など)をまとめる, 〜の決着を付ける, 〜に片を付ける** ‖ *to clinch a deal* 商談をまとめる

**cling** /klɪŋ/ 動自 (過, 過分 **clung** /klʌ́ŋ/) ▶定義 1 cling (on) to sb/sth; cling together to hold on tightly to sb/sth 〜にしっかりと捕まる➡**すがり付く, しがみ付く, (ぴったりと)くっつく** ‖ *She clung to the rope with all her strength.* 彼女は力を振り絞ってロープにしがみ付いた. *They clung together for warmth.* 彼らは抱き合って暖め合った. ▶定義 2 cling (on) to sth to continue to believe sth, often when it is not reasonable to do so しばしばそうすることが理性的には言えないのに, 〜を信じ続ける➡**固執する, 執着する** ‖ *They were still clinging to the hope that the girl would be found alive.* 彼らは, 少女が無事発見されるという希望にまだすがり付いていた. ▶定義 3 cling to sb/sth to stick firmly to sth 〜にしっかりとくっつく➡**ぴったり付く, 粘着する, くっついて離れない** ‖ *Her wet clothes clung to her.* ぬれた服が彼女の体にはり付いた. ― clingy 形➡**くっつく, まとい付く, ねばり付く, 体にぴったりした** ‖ *a clingy child (= that does not want to leave its parents)* 親にまとい付く子供 (= 両親から離れたがらない子供) *a clingy sweater* ぴったりしたセーター

**cling film** 名 U ▶定義 thin transparent plastic used for covering food to keep it fresh 食品を新鮮に保つために用いる薄い透明のプラスチック➡**(食品保存用の) ラップ**

**clinic** /klɪ́nɪk/ 名 C ▶定義 1 a small hospital or a part of a hospital where you go to receive special medical treatment 特別の治療を受けるために行く小さな病院, または病院の一部➡**診療所, 診療科, 個人病院, 専門病院** ‖ *He's being treated at a private clinic.* 彼は個人病院で治療を受けている. *an ante-natal clinic* 妊産婦診療所 ▶定義 2 a time when a doctor sees patients and gives special treatment or advice 医師が患者を診察して, 特定の治療や忠告をする時間➡**診療時間, 診察** ‖ *Dr Greenall's clinic is from 2 to 4 on Mondays.* グリーノール医師の診療時間は毎週月曜日2時から4時までです.

**clinical** /klɪ́nɪk(ə)l/ 形 ▶定義 1 connected with the examination and treatment of patients at a clinic or hospital 診療所や病院での患者の検診, 治療に関連した➡**臨床の, 病床の** ‖ *Clinical trials of the new drug have proved successful.* 新薬の臨床試験は成功だった. ▶定義 2 (used about a person) cold and not emotional (人について) 冷たく感情のない➡**第三者的な, 冷ややかな**

**clinically** /klɪ́nɪk(ə)li/ 副 ▶定義 1 according to medical examination 医学上の検査によると➡**臨床的に, 臨床上** ‖ *to be clinically dead* 臨床的には死亡している ▶定義 2 in a cold way; without showing any emotion 冷たく; 全く感情を表さずに➡**第三者的に, 冷ややかに**

**clink** /klɪŋk/ 名 [単数扱い] ▶定義 the short sharp ringing sound that objects made of glass, metal, etc make when they touch each other ガラス製や金属製の物が互いに触れ合ったときに立てる短くて鋭い響く音➡**チリン・カチンという音** ‖ *the clink of glasses* グラスがぶつかるカチンという音 ― clink 動自他➡**チリン・カチンと鳴る [鳴らす]**

**clip** /klɪp/ 名 C ▶定義 1 a small object, usually made of metal or plastic, used for holding things together 普通は金属やプラスチック製で, 物をまとめて挟むために用いる小さな用具➡**クリップ, 書類ばさみ, 留め金具** ‖ *a paper clip* (金属製) 紙ばさみ *a hairclip* ヘアピン ▶定義 2 a small section of a film that is shown so that people can see what the rest of the film is like 映画の短い一部分で, 残りの部分がどのようなものか知らせるために見せる➡**(切り取った) 映画フィルムの一部, フィルムクリップ** ☛参 **trailer** ▶定義 3 略式 a quick hit with the hand 手で素早く打つこと➡**ぶん殴ること, ひっぱたくこと** ‖ *She gave the boy a clip round the ear.* 彼女は少年の耳の辺りをひっぱたいた. ▶定義 4 an act of cutting sth ～を切ること➔切り抜くこと, 切り抜き, 刈ること

**clip**² /klɪp/ 動 (**clipping**; **clipped**) ▶定義1 自他 to be fastened with a clip; to fasten sth to sth else with a clip クリップで留められる; ～をほかの…にクリップで固定する➔クリップで留められる, ～をクリップで留める ‖ *Clip the photo to the letter, please.* その写真を手紙にクリップで留めてください. ▶定義2 他 to cut sth, especially by cutting small parts off 特に一部を少し切り離すことで, ～を切る➔～を刈る, 刈り込む, 切り抜く, 切り取る ‖ *The hedge needs clipping.* 生け垣を刈り込む必要がある. ▶定義3 他 to hit sb/sth quickly ～を素早く打つ➔～をぶん殴る, ひっぱたく, ～にぶつかる ‖ *My wheel clipped the pavement and I fell off my bike.* 車輪が歩道にぶつかり, 私は自転車から落ちた.

**clippers** /klípərz/ 名 [複数扱い] ▶定義 a small metal tool used for cutting things, for example hair or fingernails 例えば髪やつめなどの物を切るために使う小さな金属製の道具➔(木・針金などを切る)はさみ, バリカン, つめ切り ‖ *a pair of nail clippers* つめ切り ☛ **scissors** のさし絵

**clipping** /klípɪŋ/ 英 = CUTTING¹(1)

**clique** /kliːk, klɪk/ 名 C ▶定義 a small group of people with the same interests who do not want others to join their group 同じ興味を持つ人々の排他的な小さな集まり➔派閥, 徒党

**clitoris** /klítərəs, klaɪ-/ 名 C ▶定義 the small part of the female sex organs which becomes larger when a woman is sexually excited 女性器の小さな部分で, 女性が性的に興奮すると大きくなる➔陰核, クリトリス

**cloak** /klóʊk/ 名 ▶定義1 C a type of loose coat without sleeves that was more common in former times そでなしのゆったりしたコートで, 昔はよく見られた➔(そでなしの)外套(がいとう), マント ☛参 **cape** ▶定義2 [単数扱い] a thing that hides sth else ほかの～を隠すためのもの➔覆い; 仮面, 偽装, 口実 ‖ (比喩) *a cloak of mist* 辺りを包み込む霧

**cloakroom** /klóʊkruːm, -rʊm/ 名 C ▶定義 a room near the entrance to a building where you can leave your coat, bags, etc 建物の入り口近くの部屋で, コートやバッグなどを置いておくことができる➔(ホテル, 劇場などの)携帯品一時預かり所, クローク

**clobber** /klάbər/ 動 他 英 略式 ▶定義 to hit sb hard ～を強く打つ➔～を容赦なくたたく, 打ちのめす, 殴り倒す

★**clock**¹ /klάk/ 名 C ▶定義1 an instrument that shows you what time it is 何時であるかを示す器具➔(携帯用でない)時計, 掛け時計, 置き時計 ‖ *an alarm clock* 目覚まし時計 *a church clock* 教会の時計 ☛参 **watch** ▶定義2 an instrument in a car that measures how far it has travelled 走行距離を測定する車の計器➔走行距離計 ‖ *My car has only 10000 miles on the clock.* 走行距離計によると私の車は1万マイルしか走っていない.

成句 **against the clock** ▶定義 to do sth fast in order to finish it before a certain time 特定の時間までに終わらせるために～を速く行う➔時計と競争で, 全速力で; 締め切り・期限に追われて ‖ *It was a race against the clock to get the building work finished on time.* 建築作業を時間通りに終わらせるのは, 時間との戦いだった.

**around/round the clock** ▶定義 all day and all night 昼も夜も一日中➔丸一日, 昼夜兼行で, 24時間ぶっ通しで ‖ *They are working round the clock to repair the bridge.* 橋を修理するため彼らは昼も夜もぶっ通しで働いた.

**put the clock/clocks forward/back** ▶定義 to change the time, usually by one hour, at the beginning/end of summer 夏の始め・終わりに通常は1時間, 時間を変更する➔(夏時間・冬時間のある地域で)時計の針を進める・遅らせる

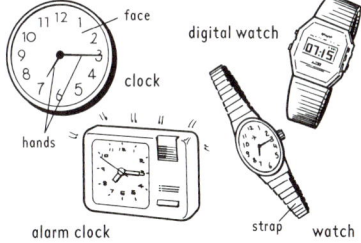

face / digital watch / clock / hands / alarm clock / strap / watch

**clock**² /klάk/ 動

句動詞 **clock in/on; clock off** ▶定義 to record the time that you arrive at or leave work, especially by putting a card into a type of clock 特に時計型の機械にカードを挿入して, 出勤または退社時刻を記録する➔(タイムレコーダーで)出

勤時刻を記録する; 退社時刻を記録する

**clock sth up** ▶定義 to achieve a certain number or total 特定の数や合計に達する→記録する, 達成する ‖ *Our car clocked up over 2000 miles while we were on holiday.* 私たちの車の走行距離は休暇中に2000マイルを超えた.

**clockwise** /klɑ́kwàːrz/ 副形 ▶定義 in the same direction as the hands of a clock 時計の針と同じ方向に→時計回りの[に], 右回りの[に] ‖ *Turn the handle clockwise.* ハンドルを右に回しなさい. *to move in a clockwise direction* 時計回りに動く ⇔ 英 **anticlockwise**, 米 **counter-clockwise**

**clockwork** /klɑ́kwəːrk/ 名 Ⓤ ▶定義 a type of machinery found in certain toys, etc that you operate by turning a key 一部のおもちゃに入っている機械装置の一種で, ねじを回して操作する→ぜんまい仕掛け, 時計仕掛け ‖ *a clockwork toy* ぜんまい仕掛けのおもちゃ *The plan went like clockwork* (= smoothly and without any problems). 計画はすらすらと滞りなく進行した(= 円滑に問題なく).

**clog**¹ /klɔ(ː)g, klɑg/ 名 Ⓒ ▶定義 a type of shoe made completely of wood or with a thick wooden base すべて木製の, または厚い木製の底の付いたタイプの靴→木靴

**clog**² /klɔ(ː)g, klɑg/ 動 (**clogging**; **clogged**) 自他 ▶定義 clog (sth) (up) (with sth) to block or become blocked ふさぐ, またはふさがれる→(~を)邪魔する, 妨害する, 詰まる, 詰まらせる, ふさがる ‖ *The drain is always clogging up.* この下水はいつも詰まってしまう. *The roads were clogged with traffic.* 道路は渋滞していた.

**clone** /klóun/ 名 Ⓒ ▶定義 an exact copy of a plant or animal that is produced from one of its cells by scientific methods 科学的手段によって自身の細胞の1つから作られる植物や動物の正確な複製→クローン, コピー生物; そっくりなもの —clone 動 →クローンとして発生させる・発生する, クローンを作る, そっくりに作る ‖ *A team from the UK were the first to successfully clone an animal.* 英国のチームが動物のクローンを作ることに最初に成功した.

★**close**¹ /klóuz/ 動 自他 ▶定義 **1** to shut 閉める, 閉まる→(~を)閉じる, 閉ざす, ふさぐ ‖ *The door closed quietly.* ドアが静かに閉まった. *to close a door/window* ドア・窓を閉める *Close your eyes - I've got a surprise.* 目をつぶって — びっくりさせるものがあるんだ. ▶定義**2** to be, or to make sth, not open to the public ~が一般の人々に開かれていない, または開かない→閉鎖する, ~の営業を停止する, 閉じる, 休業する, 閉店する ‖ *What time do the shops close?* 閉店時間は何時ですか. *The police have closed the road to traffic.* 警察が道路の交通を遮断してしまった. ▶定義**3** to end or to bring sth to an end 終わる, または終わらせる→終わる, ~を終える, 完了する, 打ち切る ‖ *The meeting closed at 10pm.* 会議は午後10時に終わった. *Detectives have closed the case on the missing girl.* 刑事たちは少女行方不明事件の捜査を打ち切った. ⇔ **open**

> ▶コミュニケーション
>
> 「他言無用」を表す身振り
>
> **close one's lips with a zipper**: 立てた親指, または親指と人差し指の指先を唇に沿って端から端まで動かすしぐさ. 唇をファスナーで留めるまねをして, 他言無用を合図するときに使います. くだけた会話(特にアメリカ英語)で, だれにも言うんじゃないと, 秘密厳守を命じるとき, しぐさの代わりに You'd better zip your mouth (lip) と言ったりもします.

句動詞 **close (sth) down** ▶定義 to stop all business or work permanently at a shop or factory 店や工場ですべての営業や操業を永久にやめる→(~を)閉鎖する, 閉店する ‖ *The factory has had to close down.* 工場は閉鎖を余儀なくされた. *Health inspectors have closed the restaurant down.* 保健所の検査官がそのレストランを営業停止にした.

**close in (on sb/sth)** ▶定義 to come nearer and gradually surround sb/sth, especially in order to attack 特に攻撃するために, ~に近付き徐々に取り囲む→(~を)包囲する, (~に)迫る, 迫ってくる ‖ *The army is closing in on the enemy troops.* 軍は敵の軍勢を包囲しつつある.

**close sth off** ▶定義 to prevent people from entering a place or an area 人々がある場所や範囲内に入ることを防止する→~を閉鎖する, 閉め

出す ‖ *The police closed off the city centre because of a bomb alert.* 爆弾に対する警戒体制で、警察は市の中心部を閉鎖した.

*__close__² /klóuz/ 图 [単数扱い] ▶定義 the end, especially of a period of time or an activity 特にある期間や活動の終わり→**終結, 最後, 終末, 締め切り** ‖ *the close of trading on the stock market* 株式市場の取り引き終了 ⇔ **open**

成句 **bring sth/come/draw to a close** ▶定義 to end 終わらせる, 終わる→**～を終わりにする, 終了する・させる, 終わりに近付く** ‖ *The chairman brought the meeting to a close.* 議長が会議を閉会した. *The guests began to leave as the evening drew to a close.* 夜が終わりに近付くにつれて, 客が帰り始めた.

*__close__³ /klóus/ 形副 ▶定義 1 (名詞の前は不可) **close (to sb/sth); close (together)** near 近くの[に]→**(～に)接近した[して], ごく近い・近く, 間隔の詰まった, 密な・密に, ぴったり(と)** ‖ *Is our hotel close to the beach?* 私たちが泊まるホテルは海岸の近くですか. *The tables are quite close together.* テーブル同士がとても近い. *to follow close behind someone* だれかのすぐ後から付いていく *I held her close (= tightly).* 彼女をきつく(＝しっかりと)抱いた.

▶定義 2 (used about a friend, etc) known very well and liked (友人などについて) よく知っていて好きな→**親しい, 親密な, 気心の知れた** ‖ *They invited only close friends to the wedding.* 彼らは親しい友人だけを結婚式に招いた.

▶定義 3 near in a family relationship 親族関係が近い→**近親の, (血縁関係が)近い** ‖ *a close relative* 近い親戚(しんせき) ▶定義 4 (used about a competition, etc) only won by a small amount (競争などについて) わずかな差で勝った→**互角の, ほとんど優劣のない** ‖ *a close match* 接戦 ☞参 **near**¹ の注 ▶定義 5 careful; thorough 注意深い; 綿密な→**細心の, 精密な, 周到な** ‖ *On close examination, you could see that the banknote was a forgery.* 綿密に調べれば, その紙幣が偽造された物だと分かるだろう. ▶定義 6 (used about the weather, etc) heavy and with little movement of air (天候などについて) どんよりして空気がほとんど動かない→**蒸し暑い, うっとうしい, 風通しの悪い** ‖ *It's so close today that there might be a storm.* 今日はとても蒸し暑いので, もしかしたらあらしになるかもしれない.

—**closely** 副→**接近して, ぴったりと; 綿密に, 詳しく; 親しく** ‖ *to watch sb closely* ～をじっくりと見る *The insect closely resembles a stick.* その虫は棒にそっくりだ. —**closeness** 图 ❶→**接近, 近似; 親密さ; 精密さ; 密着, 密集**

成句 **a close shave/thing** ▶定義 a bad thing that almost happened 今にも起こりそうだった悪いこと→**間一髪の危機脱出, 九死に一生を得ること, 辛うじて助かること** ‖ *I wasn't injured, but it was a close shave.* 私はけがはしなかったが, 危ないところだった.

**at close quarters** ▶定義 at or from a position that is very near 非常に近い位置で・位置から→**接近して, 肉薄して**

**close by (sb/sth)** ▶定義 at a short distance from sb/sth ～から近距離で→**(～の)すぐ近くに, すぐそばに** ‖ *She lives close by.* 彼女はすぐ近くに住んでいる.

**close/near/dear to sb's heart** ⇒ **HEART**

**close on** ▶定義 nearly; almost もう少しで; ほとんど→**～に近い, およそ** ‖ *He was born close on a hundred years ago.* 彼はほぼ100年前に生まれた.

**close up (to sb/sth)** ▶定義 at or from a very short distance to sb/sth ～と非常に近距離で[から]→**(～の)間近で, すぐそばで, 密着して; 詳しく観察して** ‖ *You can't tell it's a forgery until you look at it close up.* すぐそばで見ない限りそれがにせ物だとは分からない.

**come close (to sth/to doing sth)** ▶定義 to almost do sth ほとんど～しそうな→**今にも～しそうになる, もう少しで～する** ‖ *We didn't win but we came close.* 勝てなかったが, あと一歩だった.

**close**⁴ /klóus/ 图 ❻ ▶定義 part of the name of a street 通りの名前の一部→**～通り, ～小路** ‖ *5 Devon Close* デヴォン小路5番地

*__closed__ /klóuzd/ 形 ▶定義 not open; shut 開いていない; 閉じた→**閉ざされた, 閉鎖した, 非公開の, 排他的な** ‖ *Keep your mouth closed.* 口を閉じていなさい. *The supermarket is closed.* スーパーマーケットは閉店している. ⇔ **open**

**closed-circuit television** ( 略 **CCTV** ) 图 ❻ ❶ ▶定義 a type of television system used inside a building, for example a shop, to protect it from crime 例えば店などで犯罪から防護するために建物内で使用されるテレビシステム→閉回路テレビ, 有線テレビ

**closet** /klɔ́zət, klά-/ 图 ⓒ 特に 困 ▶定義 a large cupboard that is built into a room 部屋に作り付けの大型の戸棚→クロゼット, 収納室, 戸棚, 押し入れ

**close-up** /klóusʌ̀p/ 图 ⓒ ▶定義 a photograph or film of sb/sth that you take from a very short distance away 非常に近い距離から撮影した〜の写真または映画→接写, 大写し, クローズアップ ‖ *Here's a close-up of Mike.* これがマイクのアップです.

**closing time** 图 ⓒ ▶定義 the time when a shop, pub, etc closes 店やパブなどが閉まる時間→閉店時間, 終業時間, 看板

**closure** /klóuʒər/ 图 ⓒⓊ ▶定義 the permanent closing, for example of a business 例えば商売などを永久にやめること→閉鎖, 廃業, 閉店 ‖ *The firm is threatened with closure.* その会社は廃業の恐れがある.

**clot**¹ /klɑt/ 图 ⓒ ▶定義 a lump formed by blood as it dries 血液が乾いてできる塊→凝血, 血塊; どろっとした塊 ‖ *They removed a blood clot from his brain.* 彼らは脳から血栓を取り除いた.

**clot**² /klɑt/ 動 ⾃他 (**clotting**; **clotted**) ▶定義 to form or cause blood to form thick lumps 血液がどろっとした塊になる, または塊にする→凝血する・させる, (血などが) 固まる ‖ *a drug that stops blood from clotting during operations* 手術中に血液が凝固することを防止する薬品

★**cloth** /klɔ(ː)θ, klɑθ/ 图 (覆 **cloths** /klɔ́əðz, -θs, klά-/) ▶定義 1 Ⓤ a material made of cotton, wool, etc that you use for making clothes, curtains, etc 綿, 羊毛などから作られた物で, 衣類, カーテンなどを作るのに用いる→布, 布地, 生地, 織物 ‖ *a metre of cloth* 1 メートルの生地. ▶定義 2 ⓒ a piece of material that you use for a particular purpose 特定の目的に用いる1枚の布切れ→テーブル掛け, ふきん, ぞうきん ‖ *a tablecloth* テーブルクロス *Where can I find a cloth to wipe this water up?* この水をふき取るためのぞうきんはどこにありますか. ☞ **bucket** のさし絵

**clothe** /klóuð/ 動 他 ▶定義 to provide clothes for sb 〜に衣服を与える→着せる, 覆う, (衣服) をあてがう ‖ *to feed and clothe a child* 子供に食物と衣類を与える

**clothed** /klóuðd/ 形 ▶定義 **clothed (in sth)** dressed; wearing sth (衣服を) 着た; 〜を身に着けている→〜を着た, 身に着けた ‖ *He was clothed in leather from head to foot.* 彼は頭のてっぺんから足の先まで革製の衣類に身を包んでいた.

★**clothes** /klóu(ð)z/ 图 [複数扱い] ▶定義 the things that you wear, for example trousers, shirts, dresses, coats, etc 身に着ける物, 例えばズボン, シャツ, ドレス, コートなど→衣服, 衣類, 洋服 ‖ *Take off those wet clothes.* ぬれた服を脱ぎなさい. *She was wearing new clothes.* 彼女は新しい服を着ていた. ☞参 **garment**
▶ clothes は常に複数形. 身に着ける 1 つの物を示す場合は an item/piece/article of clothing のように言う: *A kilt is an item of clothing worn in Scotland.* (キルトはスコットランドの衣服です.)

**clothes line** 图 ⓒ ▶定義 a thin rope that you hang clothes on so that they can dry 衣類を乾かすためにつるす, 細い綱→物干し綱

**clothes peg** (困 **clothes pin**) ⇒ **PEG**¹(3)

★**clothing** /klóuðɪŋ/ 图 Ⓤ ▶定義 the clothes that you wear, especially for a particular activity 特に特定の活動をするために身に着ける衣類→衣服, 衣類, 衣料品 ‖ *You will need waterproof/outdoor/winter clothing.* 防水・野外用・冬向きの衣類が必要でしょう. ☞ clothing は clothes より正式な語.

**clotted cream** 图 Ⓤ 英 ▶定義 a type of thick rich cream 濃厚でこってりしたクリームの一種→固形クリーム (脂肪分の高いクリーム)

★**cloud**¹ /klάud/ 图 ▶定義 1 ⓒⓊ a mass of very small drops of water that floats in the sky and is usually white or grey 微細な水滴の集まりで, 空に浮かび, 通常は白色や灰色→雲 ‖ *The sun disappeared behind a cloud.* 太陽が雲に隠れた. *A band of thick cloud is spreading from the west.* 厚い雲の帯が西から広がりつつある. ▶定義 2 ⓒ a mass of smoke, dust, sand, etc 煙, ほこり, 砂などの塊→雲状の物, もくもくと沸き立つ物 ‖ *Clouds of smoke were pouring from the burning building.* 燃える建物から煙がもくもくと吹き出していた.

**成句** every cloud has a silver lining ▶定義 even a very bad situation has a positive or hopeful side 非常に悪い状況であっても前向きさ、または希望の持てる面がある→どんな雲にも銀の裏打ちがされている, 憂いの反面には喜びもある

under a cloud ▶定義 with the disapproval of the people around you 周りの人々の非難を受けて→容疑を受けて; 面目を失って, 嫌われて‖ *She left her job under a cloud because she'd been accused of stealing.* 彼女は盗みで告発されて非難の中, 仕事を辞めた.

**cloud**² /kláυd/ 動 ▶定義 1 ⊜ to become or make sth difficult to see through 透かして〜を見ることが難しくなる, または難しくする→曇る・曇らせる, 濁る・濁らせる‖ *His eyes clouded with tears.* 彼は涙で目が潤んだ.

▶定義 2 ⊜ to make sth less clear or easy to understand 〜を明白でなくならせる, または分かりにくくする→〜をあいまいにする, 鈍らせる, ぼやけさせる‖ *Her personal involvement in the case was beginning to **cloud her judgement**.* 自分がその件に個人的にかかわっていたため, 彼女の判断力は鈍くなりかけていた. ▶定義 3 ⊜ to make sth less enjoyable; to spoil 〜をつまらなくする; 損なう→〜を曇らせる, 暗くする, 〜に暗い影を投げ掛ける‖ *Illness has clouded the last few years of his life.* 彼の人生の最後の数年間は病気のため暗いものになった.

**句動詞** cloud over ▶定義 (used about the sky) to become full of clouds (空について)雲で一杯になる→曇る, 雲に覆われる

**cloudburst** /kláυdbə̀ːrst/ 图 ❻ ▶定義 a sudden heavy fall of rain 突然の大雨→不意の豪雨, 土砂降り

**cloudless** /kláυdləs/ 形 ▶定義 (used about the sky, etc) clear; without any clouds (空などについて)晴れた; 雲のない→晴れ渡った, 快晴の

**cloudy** /kláυdi/ 形 ▶定義 1 (used about the sky, etc) full of clouds (空などについて)雲で一杯の→曇った, 曇りの, 雲が多い ▶定義 2 (used about liquids, etc) not clear (液体などについて)澄んでいない→濁った, 透明でない‖ *cloudy water* 濁った水

**clout** /kláυt/ 图 略式 ▶定義 1 ❻ a hard hit, usually with the hand 通常は手で強く打つこと→殴ること, たたくこと‖ *to give someone a clout* 人を強くたたく ▶定義 2 ❶ influence and power 影響力と権力→(特に政治的な)影響力, 勢力‖ *He's an important man - he has a lot of clout in the company.* 彼は重要な男だ − 社内に大きな影響力を持っている.

**clove** /klóυv/ 图 ❻ ▶定義 1 the small dried flower of a tropical tree, used to give a special flavour in cooking 熱帯産の樹木に咲く小型の花を乾燥した物で, 料理に特別な風味を加えるために用いる→クローブ, チョウジ ▶定義 2 one of the small separate sections of a vegetable root (garlic) 野菜の根(ニンニク)の独立した小さな部分→(ニンニクなどの)小鱗茎(りんけい), (ニンニクなどの)一片

**clover** /klóυvər/ 图 ❻ ▶定義 a small plant with pink or white flowers and leaves with three parts to them 白またはピンクの花と三つ葉の葉を持つ小型の植物→クローバー, シロツメクサなどの総称 ☞ C2ページのさし絵

▶クローバーの葉は時には四つ葉のものもあり, これを見つけると非常に幸運だと考えられている.

**clown**¹ /kláυn/ 图 ❻ ▶定義 1 a person who wears funny clothes and a big red nose and does silly things to make people (especially children) laugh こっけいな服を着て大きな赤い鼻を付け, ひょうきんな事をして人々(特に子供たち)を笑わせる人→道化師, ピエロ ▶定義 2 a person who makes jokes and does silly things to make the people around him/her laugh ジョークを言いばかばかしい事をして周りの人々を笑わせる人→おどけ者, 道化のような人‖ *At school, Jan was always the class clown.* ジャンは学校ではいつもクラスのひょうきん者だった.

**clown**² /kláυn/ 動 ⊜ ▶定義 clown (about/around) to act in a funny or foolish way こっけいな, またはばかげた振る舞いをする→おどける, ふざける‖ *Stop clowning around and get some work done!* ふざけるのはやめて, 仕事をしなさい.

★**club**¹ /kláb/ 图 ▶定義 1 ❻ a group of people who meet regularly to share an interest, do sport, etc; the place where they meet 趣味を共有し, スポーツをするために定期的に集まる人々のグループ; このような人々が集まる場所→クラブ, (同好)会, サークル; クラブ室‖ *to join a club* クラブに入る *to be a member of a club* クラブの

## club²

会員である *a tennis/football/golf club* テニス・サッカー・ゴルフクラブ ▶定義2（または **nightclub**）❹a place where you can go to dance and drink late at night 夜遅くダンスをしたり飲みに出掛ける場所→ナイトクラブ ▶定義3 ❹a heavy stick, usually with one end that is thicker than the other, used as a weapon 重い棒で，通常は一方の端がほかより太く，武器として用いる→こん棒，警棒 ▶定義4 ❹a long stick that is specially shaped at one end and used for hitting a ball when playing golf 一方の端が特別の形に作られた長い棒で，ゴルフでボールを打つために用いる→ゴルフクラブ ☞S1ページのさし絵 ☞参 bat, racket, stick ▶定義5 clubs [複数扱い] the group (suit) of playing cards with black three-leafed shapes on them 黒い三つ葉の印の付いたトランプの札の組（札）→クラブの組札 ‖ *the two/ace/queen of clubs* クラブの2・エース・クイーン ☞参 card の注とさし絵 ▶定義6 ❹one of the cards from this suit このような組の札→クラブ（の札） ‖ *I played a club.* 私はクラブの札を出した．

**club²** /klʌb/ 動 (**clubbing**; **clubbed**) ▶定義1 ⓗto hit sb/sth hard with a heavy object 〜を重い物で強く打つ→〜を（こん棒などで）打つ，懲らしめる ▶定義2 ❺ **go clubbing** to go dancing and drinking in a club クラブにダンスをしたり飲みに行く→ナイトクラブに行く，ナイトクラブで遊ぶ ‖ *She goes clubbing every Saturday.* 彼女は毎週土曜日にナイトクラブに行く．

句動詞 **club together (to do sth)** ▶定義 to share the cost of sth, for example a present 〜，例えば贈り物などの費用を分け合って出す→（〜するために）資金を出し合う；（共同の目的に）協力する ‖ *We clubbed together to buy him a leaving present.* 私たちは金を出し合って彼のために別れの贈り物を買った．

**cluck** /klʌk/ 名 ❹ ▶定義 the noise made by a chicken 雌鶏（めんどり）が立てる音→コッコッと鳴く声，雌鶏の鳴くような声 — **cluck** 動 ⓘ →コッコッと鳴く，雌鶏の鳴くような声で（承認，不満などを）表す

**clue** /kluː/ 名 ❹ ▶定義 **a clue (to sth)** a piece of information that helps you solve a problem or a crime, answer a question, etc 問題や犯罪を解決する，または質問に答える助けとなる情報→手掛かり，糸口，ヒント ‖ *The police were looking for clues to his disappearance.* 警察は彼の行方不明についての手掛かりを捜していた． *the clues for solving a crossword puzzle* クロスワードパズルを解くためのヒント

成句 **not have a clue** 略式 ▶定義 to know nothing about sth 〜について何も知らない→全く知らない，見当が付かない

**clued-up** /kluːd ʌp/ （米 または **clued-in**）形 ▶定義 **clued-up (on sth)** knowing a lot about sth 〜について多くを知っている→（〜について）よく知っている，熟知している ‖ *I'm not really clued-up on the technical details.* 私は技術的な細かい事は実はあまりよく知らない．

**clueless** /kluːləs/ 形 略式 ▶定義 not able to understand; stupid 理解できない；愚かな→無知な，無能な ‖ *I'm absolutely clueless about computers.* 私はコンピューターのことは全く分からない．

**clump** /klʌmp/ 名 ❹ ▶定義 a small group of plants or trees, growing together 固まって生えている植物や樹木の小さな集まり→木立，（低木の）やぶ，茂み

**clumsy** /ˈklʌmzi/ 形 (**clumsier**; **clumsiest**) ▶定義1 (used about a person) careless and likely to knock into, drop or break things（人について）不注意で物にぶつかる，または物を落とすことで壊したりしやすい→不器用な，ぎこちない，下手な，動きの鈍い ‖ *She undid the parcel with clumsy fingers.* 彼女は不器用に小包をほどいた． ▶定義2 (used about a comment, etc) likely to upset or offend people （コメントなどについて）人々を嫌な気分にさせる，または感情を損なう事をしがちな→（弁解，表現などが）下手な，まずい，気の利かない ‖ *He made a clumsy apology.* 彼は下手な言い訳をした． ▶定義3 large, difficult to use, and not attractive in design 大きくて使いにくく，デザインも魅力的でない→不格好な，使いにくい，扱いにくい ‖ *a clumsy piece of furniture* 不格好で使いにくい家具 — **clumsily** 副 →ぎこちなく，不器用に，使いにくく — **clumsiness** 名 ⓤ →不器用，ぎこちなさ

**clung** CLING の過去・過去分詞形

**cluster¹** /ˈklʌstər/ 名 ❹ ▶定義 a group of people, plants or things that stand or grow close together 固まって立っている人々や, 固まって生えている植物または物の集まり→**群, 集団, 一団, 群生** ‖ *a cluster of schoolchildren* 小学生の一団

**cluster**² /klʌ́stər/ 動
句動詞 **cluster around sb/sth** ▶定義 to form a group around sb/sth ～の周りに集団を作る→**～の周りに群がる, 集まる, 密集する** ‖ *The tourists clustered around their guide.* 旅行者たちがガイドの周りに集まった.

**clutch**¹ /klʌtʃ/ 動他 ▶定義 to hold sth tightly, especially because you are in pain, afraid or excited 特に痛みを感じる・恐れる, または興奮することで～をしっかりとつかむ→**～をしっかり握る, 握りしめる, ～にすがり付く** ‖ *He clutched his mother's hand in fear.* 彼はおびえて母の手をしっかりつかんだ.

句動詞 **clutch at sth** ▶定義 to try to take hold of sth ～をつかもうとする→**～にすがろうとする, ～を捕まえようとする** ‖ *She clutched at the money but the wind blew it away.* 彼女は金をつかもうとしたが, 風に吹き飛ばされた.

**clutch**² /klʌtʃ/ 名 ▶定義1 ❻the part of a vehicle, etc that you press with your foot when you are driving in order to change the speed (gear); the part of the engine that it is connected to 車などの部品で, 運転中に速度(ギア)を変えるために足で踏む; それが連結されているエンジンの部分→**クラッチペダル, クラッチ** ‖ *to press/release the clutch* クラッチを踏む・放す ☞ S7 ページのさし絵 ▶定義2 **clutches** [複数扱い] power or control over sb ～に対する力や支配→**支配力, 手中, 魔手** ‖ *He fell into the enemy's clutches.* 彼は敵の手中に落ちた.

**clutter**¹ /klʌ́tər/ 名 ❶ ▶定義 things that are where they are not wanted or needed and make a place untidy 望ましくない, または不必要な場所にあって, そこを散らかしている物→**散らかっている物, 乱雑, 混乱** ‖ *Who left all this clutter on the floor?* 床をこんなに散らかしたのはだれですか. — **cluttered** 形→**散らかした, 散らかった, 乱雑な** ‖ *a cluttered desk* 散らかった机

**clutter**² /klʌ́tər/ 動他 ▶定義 **clutter sth (up)** to cover or fill sth with lots of objects in an untidy way ～をたくさんの物で乱雑に覆う, または埋める→**～を取り散らかす, 乱す, ごった返す** ‖ *Don't leave those books there - they're clutter-ing up the table.* 本をそこに置かないで － テーブルが散らかるから.

**cm** 略 centimetre(s)→**センチメートル, センチ**

**Co** ▶定義1 company→**会社, 商会** ‖ *W Smith & Co* Wスミス商会 ▶定義2 county ‖ **(英国, アイルランドの) 州, (米国の) 郡** ‖ *Co Down* ダウン州

**c/o** ▶定義 (used for addressing a letter to somebody who is staying at another person's house) care of (よその家に滞在している人に手紙を出す場合に用いる)→**気付, ～方** ‖ *Andy Kirkham, c/o Mrs Potter* ポッター様方, アンディー カークハム様

***coach**¹ /kóʊtʃ/ 名 ❸ ▶定義1 a person who trains people to compete in certain sports ある種のスポーツ競技のために選手を訓練する人→**コーチ, 指導員** ‖ *a tennis coach* テニスのコーチ ▶定義2 英a comfortable bus used for long journeys 長距離の旅行に使われる快適なバス→**長距離(観光)バス** ‖ *It's cheaper to travel by coach than by train.* 列車で旅行するより長距離バスの方が安い. ▶定義3 = **CARRIAGE**(1) ▶定義4 a large vehicle with four wheels pulled by horses, used in the past for carrying passengers 馬が引く4輪の大型の乗り物で, 昔, 乗客を運ぶために使われた→**4輪大型馬車, 乗り合い馬車, (国王用の)公式馬車** ☞参 **carriage**, **car**

**coach**² /kóʊtʃ/ 動自他 ▶定義 **coach sb (in/for sth)** to train or teach sb, especially to compete in a sport or pass an exam 特にスポーツ競技のため, または試験に合格させるために～を訓練する, または教える→**～に(…の)コーチをする, (～を)指導する, 指導して合格させる** ‖ *She is being coached for the Olympics by a former champion.* 彼女はオリンピック出場のために前チャンピオンから指導を受けている.

***coal** /kóʊl/ 名 ▶定義1 ❶a type of black mineral that is dug (mined) from the ground and burned to give heat 地中から掘り出し(採掘), 熱を得るために燃やす黒色の鉱物の一種→**石炭, (燃料用に砕いた)石炭** ‖ *a lump of coal* 石炭1個 *a coal fire* 石炭の火 ▶定義2 **coals** [複数扱い] burning pieces of coal 燃えている石炭→**燃えさし, おき** ☞ **fireplace** のさし絵

**coalition** /kòʊəlíʃ(ə)n/ 名 [❻, 単数または複数形の動詞と共に] ▶定義 a government formed by two or more political parties working together 行動を共にする複数の政党から成る政府 ➡ **連立（政府）；連合，合同** ‖ *a coalition between the socialists and the Green Party* 社会主義者と緑の党の連立

**coal mine**（または **pit**）名 C ▶定義 a place, usually underground, where coal is dug from the ground 通常は地下にある，石炭を地中から掘り出す場所 ➡ **炭鉱，炭坑，炭山** ☞参 **colliery**

**coal miner**（または **miner**）名 C ▶定義 a person whose job is to dig coal from the ground 地中から石炭を掘り出す仕事をする人 ➡ **炭坑夫，採炭夫**

**coarse** /kɔːrs/ 形 ▶定義 1 consisting of large pieces; rough, not smooth 大きなかけらから成る；粗い，滑らかでない ➡ **きめの粗い，ごわごわした，粗大な** ‖ *coarse salt* 粗塩 *coarse cloth* 織りの粗い布地 ⇔ **fine** ▶定義 2 (used about a person or his/her behaviour) rude, likely to offend people; having bad manners（人やその行動について）無礼な，人の感情を損ないがちな；行儀が悪い ➡ **粗野な，下品な；みだらな** ‖ *His coarse remarks about women offended her.* 彼の女性に対する無礼な言葉が彼女を怒らせた． — **coarsely** 副 ▶定義 粗く，粗野に，下品に ‖ *Chop the onion coarsely* (= into pieces which are not too small). タマネギを粗く（= あまり細かくなく）切ってください．*He laughed coarsely.* 彼は下品に笑った．

**coarsen** /kɔ́ːrs(ə)n/ 動 自他 ▶定義 to become or to make sth coarse 粗雑になる，または〜を粗雑にする ➡ **粗野になる・する，ざらざらになる・する**

★**coast**¹ /kóʊst/ 名 C ▶定義 the area of land that is next to or close to the sea 海に面した，または海に近い陸地 ➡ **海岸，沿岸** ‖ *After sailing for an hour we could finally see the coast.* 1時間ほど帆走すると，やっと海岸が見えた．*Scarborough is on the east coast.* スカーバラは東海岸にある．

**coast**² /kóʊst/ 動 自 ▶定義 1 to travel in a car, on a bicycle, etc (especially down a hill) without using power 動力を使わずに車や自転車などで（特に丘を下って）走る ➡ **滑走する，惰力で走る** ▶定義 2 to achieve sth without much effort あまり努力をせずに〜を成し遂げる ➡ **苦労せずにや**っていく，苦労せずに進歩・出世する ‖ *They coasted to victory.* 彼らはやすやすと勝った．

**coastal** /kóʊstəl/ 形 ▶定義 on or near a coast 海に面した，海岸に近い ➡ **海岸(沿い)の，沿岸の，近海の** ‖ *coastal areas* 沿岸地域

**coastguard** /kóʊstgɑːrd/ 名 C ▶定義 a person or group of people whose job is to watch the sea near the coast in order to help people or ships that are in danger or to stop illegal activities 危険に陥った人々や船舶を救助するため，または違法行為を阻止するために，海岸近くの海を監視する仕事をする人や組織 ➡ **沿岸警備隊(員)**

**coastline** /kóʊstlaɪn/ 名 C ▶定義 the edge or shape of a coast 海岸の縁または形状 ➡ **海岸線** ‖ *a rocky coastline* 岩の多い海岸線

★**coat**¹ /kóʊt/ 名 C ▶定義 1 a piece of clothing that you wear over your other clothes to keep warm when you are outside 屋外で寒くないようにほかの衣類の上に着る衣服 ➡ **コート，外套(がいとう)** ‖ *Put your coat on - it's cold outside.* コートを着なさい — 外は寒いから．☞参 **overcoat, raincoat** ☞ C6 ページのさし絵 ▶定義 2 the fur or hair covering an animal's body 動物の体を覆っている毛皮や毛 ➡ **(獣の)外被，被毛** ‖ *a dog with a smooth coat* 滑らかな毛並みの犬 ▶定義 3 a layer of sth covering a surface 表面を覆う層 ➡ **皮，殻，(被)覆，外被物** ‖ *The walls will probably need two coats of paint.* 壁はおそらくペンキを2度塗りする必要があるだろう．

**coat**² /kóʊt/ 動 他 ▶定義 coat sth (with/in sth) to cover sth with a layer of sth 〜を何かの層で覆う ➡ **〜を(…で)覆う，塗る，かぶせる** ‖ *biscuits coated with milk chocolate* ミルクチョコレートでくるまれたビスケット

**coat hanger** = **HANGER**

**coating** /kóʊtɪŋ/ 名 C ▶定義 a thin layer of sth that covers sth else 〜を覆う薄い層 ➡ **塗り，上塗り，(食物の)衣** ‖ *wire with a plastic coating* プラスチックで被覆された電線

**coat of arms**（または **arms**）名 C ▶定義 a design that is used as the symbol of a family, a town, a university, etc 一家，町，大学などのシンボルとして使われる図案 ➡ **(盾形の)紋章**

**coax** /kóʊks/ 動 他 ▶定義 coax sb (into/out of sth/doing sth); coax sth out of/from sb to persuade sb gently 〜を優しく説得する ➡ **〜を**

おだてて…させる,…をやめさせる,なだめすかして人から〜を手に入れる ‖ *The child wasn't hungry, but his mother coaxed him into eating a little.* 子供はおなかがすいていなかったが,母親はなだめすかして少し食べさせた. *At last he coaxed a smile out of her.* 彼はようやく彼女をほほえませた.

**cobble** /kάb(ə)l/ 動

句動詞 cobble sth together ▶定義 to make sth or put sth together quickly and without much care 手早くあまり注意せずに〜を作る,またはくっつける→〜をつぎはぎで作り上げる,ざっと仕上げる

**cobbler** /kάblər/ 图 C (古) ▶定義 a person who repairs shoes 靴を修繕する人→靴の修繕屋

**cobbles** /kάb(ə)lz/ (または **cobblestones** /kάb(ə)lstòunz/) 图 [複数扱い] ▶定義 small rounded stones used (in the past) for covering the surface of streets 路面を覆うために(昔)用いられた小さい丸い石→丸石,玉石 —**cobbled** 形→丸石を敷いた,丸石で舗装した

**cobra** /kóubrə/ 图 C ▶定義 a poisonous snake that can spread out the skin at the back of its neck. Cobras live in India and Africa. 首の後ろの皮を広げることのできる毒蛇.インドとアフリカに生息する→コブラ

**cobweb** /kάbwèb/ 图 C ▶定義 a net of threads made by a spider in order to catch insects クモが虫を捕まえるために糸で作る網→クモの巣; (人を陥れる)わな

**cocaine** /koukéin, kəkéin/ (または 略式 **coke**) 图 U ▶定義 a dangerous drug that some people take for pleasure but which is difficult to stop using (addictive) 一部の人が快楽のために使う危険な薬物だが,使用をやめるのは難しい(中毒性)→コカイン

**cock**[1] /kάk/ 图 C ▶定義 1 (米 **rooster**) an adult male chicken 成長した雄の鶏→雄鶏(おんどり) ☞参 **chicken** の注とさし絵 ▶定義 2 an adult male bird of any type あらゆる種類の成長した雄の鳥→鳥の雄

**cock**[2] /kάk/ 動 他 ▶定義 to hold up a part of the body 体の一部を上に上げる→〜をぴんと立てる,上に向ける ‖ *The horse cocked its ears on hearing the noise.* 物音を聞いて馬は耳をぴんと立てた.

句動詞 cock sth up 英 (俗語) ▶定義 to do something very badly and spoil sth 非常にまずい事をして〜を駄目にする→しくじる,台なしにする ☞参 **cock-up**

**cock-a-doodle-doo** /kὰkədùːdldúː/ [単数扱い] ▶定義 the noise made by an adult male chicken (cock) 成熟した雄鶏(おんどり)の鳴き声→コケコッコー

**cockerel** /kάk(ə)rəl/ 图 C ▶定義 a young male chicken 若い雄の鶏→(1歳未満の)若い雄鶏(おんどり)

**cockney** /kάkni/ ▶定義 1 C a person who was born and grew up in the East End of London ロンドンのイーストエンドで生まれ育った人→ロンドン子,イーストエンドの労働者階級の人 ▶定義 2 U the way of speaking English that is typical of people living in this area この地域に住む人々に特徴的な英語の話し方→ロンドンなまり,コクニー ‖ *a cockney accent* ロンドンなまり

**cockpit** /kάkpɪt/ 图 C ▶定義 1 the part of a plane where the pilot sits 飛行機のパイロットが座る場所→操縦席・室,コックピット ▶定義 2 the part of a racing car where the driver sits レーシングカーのドライバーが座る場所→操縦席,運転席

**cockroach** /kάkròutʃ/ (困 **roach**) 图 C ▶定義 a large dark brown insect, usually found in dirty or slightly wet places 汚れた場所や湿り気を帯びた場所によくいる大型の焦げ茶色の昆虫→ゴキブリ,アブラムシ ☞ **insect** のさし絵

**cocktail** /kάktèɪl/ 图 C ▶定義 1 a drink made from a mixture of alcoholic drinks and fruit juices アルコール飲料とフルーツジュースを混ぜて作る飲み物→カクテル ▶定義 2 a mixture of small pieces of food that is served cold 小さく切った食べ物をあえた料理で,冷やして出される→(前菜としての)カクテル,オードブル ‖ *a prawn cocktail* エビのカクテル

**cock-up** 图 C (俗語) ▶定義 something that was badly done; a mistake that spoils sth まずい行い; 〜を駄目にする誤り→へま,失敗 ☞参 **cock**[2]

**cocoa** /kóukou/ 图 ▶定義 1 U a dark brown powder made from the seeds of a tropical tree and used in making chocolate 熱帯産の樹木の

実から作られる焦げ茶色の粉末で，チョコレートを作るために用いられる➜**ココア, ココアの粉末** ▶定義2 [C][U]a hot drink made from this powder mixed with milk or water; a cup of this drink この粉末を牛乳や湯と混ぜて作る温かい飲み物；この飲み物1杯➜**ココア** ‖ *a cup of cocoa* ココア1杯

**coconut** /kóʊkənʌ̀t/ [名][C][U] ▶定義 a large tropical fruit with a hard, hairy shell 繊維質で覆われた硬い殻を持つ大型の熱帯の果実➜**ココナッツ, ココヤシの実** ☛ C3 ページのさし絵

**cod** /kɑd/ [名][C][U]（[複] **cod**）▶定義 a large sea fish that lives in the North Atlantic that you can eat 北大西洋に住む大型の海水魚で食用となる➜**タラ, タラの肉**

**code**[1] /kóʊd/ [名] ▶定義1 [C][U]a system of words, letters, numbers, etc that are used instead of the real letters or words to make a message or information secret 語，文字，数字などの体系で，伝言や情報を秘密にするために本物の文字や語の代わりに用いる➜**暗号** ‖ *They managed to break/crack the enemy code (= find out what it means).* 彼らは何とか敵の暗号を解いた・解読した（= 意味が分かった）. *They wrote letters to each other* ***in code****.* 彼らはお互いに暗号で手紙を書いた. ☛参 **decode** ▶定義2 [C]a group of numbers, letters, etc that is used for identifying sth ～を識別するために用いる番号や文字などの集まり➜**符号, 記号, コード** ‖ *What's the code (= the telephone number) for Stockholm?* ストックホルムの番号（= 電話番号）は何番ですか. ☛参 **bar code** ▶定義3 [C]a set of rules for behaviour 行動する際の規則➜**おきて, 規約, 規定；慣例** ‖ *a code of practice (= a set of standards agreed and accepted by a particular profession)* 合意基準（= 特定の職業で同意され受け入れられる基準）*the Highway Code (= the rules for driving on the roads)* 道路交通規則集（= 道路で運転する際の規則）

**code**[2] /kóʊd/ [動][他] ▶定義1（または **encode**）to put or write sth in code[1](1) ～を暗号にする，または暗号で書く➜**～を暗号にする, 暗号化する** ‖ *coded messages* 暗号で書かれたメッセージ ⇔ **decode** ▶定義2 to use a particular system for identifying things 物を識別するために特定の体系を使う➜**～を符号［コード］化する, 記号［コード］で分類する** ‖ *The files are colour-coded: blue for Europe, green for Africa.* ファイルは色で分類されている. 例えばヨーロッパは青で，アフリカは緑というように.

**coerce** /koʊə́ːrs/ [動][他][正式] ▶定義 coerce sb (into sth/doing sth) to force sb to do sth, for example by threatening him/her 例えば脅迫などによって，～に強いて何かをさせる➜**～を強制して…させる, 強要する, 強いる** — coercion /koʊə́ːrʒ(ə)n, -ʃ(ə)n/ [名][U]➜**強制, 威圧, 弾圧政治**

**coexist** /kòʊɪgzíst/ [動][自] ▶定義 to live or be together at the same time or in the same place as sb/sth ～と同じ時に，または同じ場所に住む，あるいは存在する➜**同時に存在する, 共存する；（２国が）平和共存する** — coexistence [名][U]➜**共存,（２国間の）平和共存**

**C of E** /síː ə(v) íː/ [略]Church of England➜**英国国教会, 英国聖公会**

***coffee** /kɔ́(ː)fi, kɑ́fi/ [名] ▶定義1 [U]the cooked beans (coffee beans) of a tropical tree, made into powder and used for making a drink 熱帯産の樹木の豆（コーヒー豆）を煎（い）ったもので，粉末にして飲み物を作るのに用いる➜**コーヒー, コーヒー豆** ‖ *Coffee is the country's biggest export.* コーヒーはその国の最大の輸出品である. *coffee beans* コーヒー豆 ▶定義2 [U] a drink made by adding hot water to this powder この粉末に湯を加えて作った飲み物➜**コーヒー** ‖ *Would you prefer tea or coffee?* コーヒーと紅茶のどちらにしますか. *a cup of coffee* コーヒー1杯 ▶定義3 [C]a cup of this drink この飲み物1杯➜**コーヒー1杯** ‖ *Two coffees please.* コーヒーを２杯下さい. ☛ C4 ページのさし絵

➤ black coffee はミルク抜きのコーヒー，white coffee はミルクを入れたコーヒー，decaffeinated coffee はカフェイン抜きのコーヒー. weak/strong coffee は薄い・濃いコーヒー，instant coffee はびん詰で売られ，カップにコーヒーの粉末を入れて熱い湯や牛乳を注いで作る. fresh coffee はひき立てのコーヒー豆からコーヒーポットで作る.

**coffee bar**（または **coffee shop**）[名][C][英] ▶定義 a place in a hotel, a large shop, etc, where simple food, coffee, tea and other drinks without alcohol are served ホテル，大きな商店

などにあって, 簡単な食べ物, コーヒー, 紅茶, アルコール抜きの飲み物が出される場所→喫茶店, 喫茶軽食堂, 軽食のできるコーヒー店

**coffee pot** 名 C ▶定義 a container in which coffee is made and served コーヒーを作ってつぐための容器→コーヒーポット, コーヒー沸かし ☛ C4 ページのさし絵

**coffee table** 名 C ▶定義 a small low table for putting magazines, cups, etc, on 雑誌, カップなどを置くための小さな低いテーブル→コーヒーテーブル ☛ C7 ページのさし絵

**coffin** /kɔ́(:)fən, káf-/ 名 C (米 **casket**) ▶定義 a box in which a dead body is buried or burned (cremated) 遺体を埋葬または焼却(火葬)するための箱→棺, ひつぎ ☛参 funeral の注

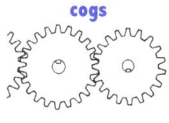

cogs

**cog** /kɔ(:)g, kɑg/ 名 C ▶定義 one of a series of teeth on the edge of a wheel that fit into the teeth on the next wheel and cause it to move 輪の縁にある一連の歯の1つで, 次の輪の歯とかみ合ってその輪を動かす→(歯車の)歯, 歯車

**cognac** /kánjæk, kóu-/ 名 ▶定義1 U a type of strong alcoholic drink (brandy) that is made in France フランス製の強いアルコール飲料の一種(ブランデー)→コニャック, 高級ブランデー ▶定義2 C a glass of this drink この飲み物1杯→コニャック1杯

**cohabit** /kouhǽbət/ 動 自 正式 ▶定義 (used about a couple) to live together as if they are married (一組の男女について)結婚しているように一緒に暮らす→同棲(どうせい)する, (男女が)同居する

**coherent** /kouhíər(ə)nt/ 形 ▶定義 clear and easy to understand 明白で理解しやすい→筋の通った, 首尾一貫した, 理路整然とした ⇔ **incoherent** ― coherence 名 U ▶筋が通っていること, 首尾一貫性 ― coherently 副 →首尾一貫して, 理路整然と

**cohesion** /kouhí:ʒ(ə)n/ 名 U ▶定義 the ability to stay or fit together well 一緒にうまくやる, または調和する能力→つながり, まとまり, 団結, 結束 ‖ *What the team lacks is cohesion - all the players play as individuals.* チームに欠けているのは団結だ ― 選手全員が個人としてプレーしている.

## coincidence 303

**coil**¹ /kɔ́ɪl/ 動 他 ▶定義 to make sth into a round shape ～を円い形にする→(～を)ぐるぐる巻く, 巻き付ける; とぐろを巻く, 円くなる ‖ *a snake coiled under a rock* 岩の下でとぐろを巻いている蛇

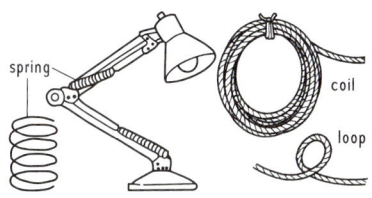

spring / coil / loop

**coil**² /kɔ́ɪl/ 名 C ▶定義 a length of rope, wire, etc that has been made into a round shape 円い形になったある長さのロープ, 針金など→巻いた物, 輪, 1巻き, 巻き毛 ‖ *a coil of rope* ロープ1巻き

★**coin**¹ /kɔ́ɪn/ 名 C ▶定義 a piece of money made of metal 金属製の貨幣→硬貨, 鋳貨, コイン ‖ *a pound coin* 1ポンド硬貨 ☛ **money** のさし絵

**coin**² /kɔ́ɪn/ 動 他 ▶定義 to invent a new word or phrase 新しい語や句を作る→(新語など)を作り出す, 生み出す ‖ *Who was it who coined the phrase 'a week is a long time in politics'?* 「政治の世界では1週間は長い」という言葉を作り出したのはだれだったのだろう.

**coincide** /kòuənsáɪd/ 動 自 coincide (with sth) ▶定義1 (used about events) to happen at the same time as sth else (出来事について)ほかの出来事と同時に起こる→(～と)同時期に起こる, 重なる ‖ *The Queen's visit is timed to coincide with the country's centenary celebrations.* 女王の訪問はその国の建国100年祭の時期に合わせられた. ▶定義2 to be exactly the same or very similar 全く同じ, または非常に似たものである→(～に)一致する, 合致する, 符合する ‖ *Our views coincide completely.* 私たちの意見は全く同じだ.

**coincidence** /kouínsəd(ə)ns, -dèns/ 名 C U ▶定義 two or more similar things happening at the same time by chance, in a surprising way よく似た複数の事が, 思い掛けない形で偶然同時に起こること→同時発生, 偶然の一致 ‖ *We hadn't planned to meet, it was just coincidence.*

私たちは会うことを予定していなかったのに、全くの偶然だった.

**coincidental** /kouìnsədéntl/ 形 ▶定義 resulting from two similar or related events happening at the same time by chance 2つの類似した、または関連した出来事が偶然、同時に起こる結果として→一致した, 符号する, 同時に起こる, 偶然の一致の ─ **coincidentally** /-tli/ 副 →一致して, 同時に, 偶然の一致で

**coke** /kóuk/ 名 Ⓤ ▶定義1 a solid black substance produced from coal and used as a fuel 石炭から作られ、燃料として用いられる固形の黒色の物質→コークス ▶定義2 = COCAINE

**Col** 略 Colonel→(空軍・陸軍・海兵隊の)大佐

**cola** /kóulə/ 名 Ⓒ Ⓤ ▶定義 a brown, sweet cold drink that does not contain alcohol; a glass or can of this アルコールを含まない茶色の甘く冷たい飲み物; この飲み物コップ1杯または1缶→コーラ(1杯), コーラ1缶

**colander** /kʌ́ləndər, kɑ́l-/ 名 Ⓒ ▶定義 a metal or plastic bowl with a lot of small holes in it that is used for removing water from food that has been boiled or washed 小さな穴がたくさん開いた金属またはプラスチックのボウルで、食品をゆでた後、または洗った後水を切るために用いる→水切り器, 水切り(ボウル) ☞ kitchen のさし絵

*__cold__¹ /kóuld/ 形 ▶定義1 having a low temperature; not hot or warm 温度が低い; 暑くない, 暖かくない→寒い, 冷たい, 低温の ‖ *I'm not going into the sea, the water's too cold.* 私は海には入らない, 水が冷たすぎるから. *Shall I put the heating on? I'm cold.* 暖房をつけてもいいですか. 寒いのです.

▶ cold, hot, cool, warmと比較. cold は cool よりも低い温度を表し、不快なほど低い温度を表す場合もある: *a terribly cold winter* (ひどく寒い冬). cool は「やや温度が低い」を意味し、温度が低くて快適であることを表す場合がある: *It's terribly hot outside but it's nice and cool in here.* (外はひどく暑いが、ここは涼しくて快適だ.) hot は warm より高い温度を表し、不快なほど高い温度を表す場合もある: *I can't drink this yet, it's too hot.* (これは熱すぎてまだ飲めません.) warm は「やや温度が高い」を意味し、温度が高くて快適であることを表す場合もある: *Come and sit by the fire, you'll soon get warm again.* (火のそばに来て座りなさい、またすぐに暖まりますよ.)

▶定義2 (used about food or drink) not heated or cooked; having become cold after being heated or cooked (食べ物や飲み物について) 加熱されていない、または調理されていない; 加熱や調理の後で冷たくなった→冷やした, 冷たくした, 冷えた, 冷たい; 冷めた ‖ *a cold drink* 冷たい飲み物 *Have your soup before it gets cold.* 冷めないうちにスープを飲みなさい. ▶定義3 (used about a person or sb's behaviour) very unfriendly; not showing kindness, understanding, etc (人やその行動について) 非常に非友好的な; 親切や理解などを示さない→冷たい, 冷淡な, よそよそしい, 冷酷な, 無情な ‖ *She gave him a cold, hard look.* 彼女は冷たく厳しい目付きで彼を見た.

成句 **cold turkey** ▶定義 suddenly and completely, without getting used to sth gradually 〜に徐々に慣れるのではなく突然、完全に→きっぱり(絶つなど), 突然, 準備なしで ‖ *I gave up smoking cold turkey.* 私はきっぱりとたばこをやめた.

**get/have cold feet** 略式 ▶定義 to become/be afraid to do sth 何かをすることを恐れる→いざというときにためらう, おじけづく ‖ *She started to get cold feet as her wedding day approached.* 結婚式の日が近付くにつれて彼女はためらい始めた.

**in cold blood** ▶定義 in a cruel way and without pity 残酷に哀れみなしで→冷酷に, 平然として ‖ *to kill sb in cold blood* 平然と人を殺す

*__cold__² /kóuld/ 名 ▶定義1 [単数扱い, Ⓤ] lack of heat; low temperature; cold weather 熱の不足; 低温; 寒い天候→冷たさ, 寒さ, 冷気 ‖ *We walked home in the snow, shivering with cold.* 寒さに震えながら、私たちは雪の中を歩いて帰った. *Come on, let's get out of the cold and go indoors.* さあ、寒い所にいないで中に入ろう.

▶定義2 Ⓒ Ⓤ a common illness of the nose and throat. When you have a cold you have a sore throat and often cannot breathe through your nose. 鼻とのどのありふれた病気. この病気にかかるとのどが痛み、鼻から呼吸できなくなることがよくある→風邪, 感冒 ‖ *I think I'm getting a* cold. 風邪を引きそうだ. *Wear some warm clothes when you go out or you'll **catch cold**.* 外に出るときは暖かい服を着ないと風邪を引きますよ.

**cold-blooded** 形 ▶定義1 having a blood temperature that changes with the temperature of the surroundings 血液の温度が周囲の温度と共に変化する→(動物が)冷血の, 変温の ‖ *Reptiles are cold-blooded.* 爬虫(はちゅう)類は変温動物である. ☛参 **warm-blooded** ▶定義2 cruel; having or showing no pity 残酷な; 哀れみのない, または哀れみを示さない→冷酷な, 冷淡な, 血も涙もない ‖ *cold-blooded killers* 冷酷な殺人者たち

**cold-hearted** 形 ▶定義 unkind; showing no kindness, understanding, etc 不親切な; 親切心や理解などを示さない→冷淡な, 無情な

**coldly** /kóuldli/ 副 ▶定義 in an unfriendly way; in a way that shows no kindness or understanding 非友好的に; 親切や理解を示さずに→冷ややかに, 冷淡に, よそよそしく

**coldness** /kóuldnəs/ 名 Ⓤ ▶定義 the lack of warm feelings; unfriendly behaviour 温かい感情がないこと; 非友好的な振る舞い→冷ややかさ, 冷淡, よそよそしさ

**colic** /kάlɪk/ 名 Ⓤ ▶定義 pain in the stomach area, which especially babies get 特に赤ん坊の腹部の痛み→(幼児の)激しい腹痛; 疝痛(せんつう), 差し込み

**collaborate** /kəlǽbərèɪt/ 動 ⓔ ▶定義1 collaborate (with sb) (on sth) to work together (with sb), especially to create or produce sth 特に〜を創造する, または制作するために(…と)一緒に作業する→(〜と)(〜を)共同作業する, 共同研究する, 協力する ‖ *She collaborated with another author on the book.* 彼女はほかの作家と共著でその本を書いた. ▶定義2 collaborate (with sb) to help the enemy forces who have taken control of your country 自国を占領した敵の軍隊を助ける→(占領軍, 敵国に)協力する ☛ この場合は非難を示す. ― collaboration /kəlæbəréɪʃ(ə)n/ 名 Ⓤ →協力, 合作, 共著, 共同研究 ― collaborator 名 Ⓒ →協力者, 共編者, 合作者

**collage** /kəlά:ʒ, kɔ:-, kou-/ 名 Ⓒ Ⓤ ▶定義 a picture made by fixing pieces of paper, cloth, photographs, etc onto a surface; the art of making a picture like this 紙, 布, 写真などの断片を表面にはり付けて作る絵; このような絵を創作する芸術→コラージュ, コラージュの作品; コラージュ技法

★**collapse**¹ /kəlǽps/ 動 ⓔ ▶定義1 to fall down or break into pieces suddenly 突然倒れる, またはばらばらに壊れる→崩れる, つぶれる, 崩壊する ‖ *A lot of buildings collapsed in the earthquake.* 地震で多くの建物が崩壊した. ▶定義2 (used about a person) to fall down, usually because you are very ill, and perhaps become unconscious (人について)一般に体調が非常に悪い事が原因で倒れ, 意識不明になる場合もある→倒れる, 卒倒する, 衰弱する ‖ *The winner collapsed at the end of the race.* レースの最後で優勝者が卒倒した. ▶定義3 (used about a business, plan, etc) to fail suddenly or completely (事業, 計画などについて)突然または完全に失敗する→つぶれる, 失敗する, 挫折(ざせつ)する ‖ *The company collapsed, leaving hundreds of people out of work.* 会社がつぶれ, 何百人という人々が職を失った. ▶定義4 to fold sth or be folded into a shape that uses less space 場所を取らない形に〜を畳む, または畳まれる→〜を折り畳む, 折り畳める

**collapse**² /kəlǽps/ 名 ▶定義1 Ⓒ Ⓤ the sudden or complete failure of sth, such as a business, plan, etc 事業, 計画などの突然の, または完全な失敗→挫折(ざせつ), 崩壊, つぶれること ‖ *The peace talks were on the brink/verge of collapse.* 和平交渉は決裂寸前だ. ▶定義2 [単数扱い, Ⓤ] (used about a building) a sudden fall (建物について)突然倒れること→倒壊, 崩壊, 陥没 ‖ *the collapse of the motorway bridge* 高速道路の橋の倒壊 ▶定義3 [単数扱い, Ⓤ] (used about a person) a medical condition when a person becomes very ill and suddenly falls down (人について)医学上の症状で, 体調が非常に悪くなって突然倒れる→虚脱; 衰弱; 卒倒

**collapsible** /kəlǽpsəb(ə)l/ 形 ▶定義 that can be folded into a shape that makes sth easy to store 〜を保管しやすい形に畳める→折り畳みの, 折り畳み式の ‖ *a collapsible bed* 折り畳み式ベッド

★**collar**¹ /kάlər/ 名 Ⓒ ▶定義1 the part of a shirt, coat, dress, etc that fits round the neck and is

**collar** often folded over シャツ, コート, ドレスなどの首の回りに沿う部分で, 大抵は折り返される~えり, カラー ‖ *a coat with a fur collar* 毛皮のえりの付いたコート ☞ **lace** のさし絵 ☞参 **dog collar**, **blue-collar**, **white-collar** ▶定義2 a band of leather that is put round an animal's neck (especially a dog or cat) 動物 (特に犬や猫) の首に付ける革の帯→首輪

**collar**² /kɑ́lər/ 動 他 略式 ▶定義 to catch hold of sb who does not want to be caught 捕まりたくない~を捕まえる→~を捕らえる, ~のえり首をつかむ, (話をするため) 引き止める ‖ *The police officer collared the thief.* 警官が窃盗犯を捕まえた.

**collarbone** /kɑ́lərbòun/ 名 C ▶定義 one of the two bones that connect your chest bones to your shoulder 胸骨を肩に連結している骨→鎖骨 ☞ C5 ページのさし絵

**collateral** /kəlǽt(ə)rəl, kɑl-/ 名 C ▶定義 property or sth valuable that you agree to give if you cannot pay back money that you have borrowed 借金を返済できない場合に提供することを同意した所有物または金銭的価値のある~→担保, 担保物件

\***colleague** /kɑ́liːg/ 名 C ▶定義 a person who works at the same place as you 自分と同じ場所で働いている人→同僚, (職場の) 仲間

\***collect**¹ /kəlékt/ 動 ▶定義1 他 to bring a number of things together いくつかの物をまとめる→~を集める, 回収する, 寄せ集める ‖ *All the exam papers will be collected at the end.* 試験用紙は最後にすべて回収します. ▶定義2 他 to get and keep together a number of objects of a particular type over a period of time as a hobby 趣味として一定の期間, 特定の種類の物を集めて持っている→~を収集する, 集める ‖ *He used to collect stamps.* 彼は以前, 切手を集めていた.
▶定義3 他 to ask for money from a number of people 何人もから金を募る→(~を) 徴収する, 募る ‖ *to collect for charity* 義えん金を募る *The landlord collects the rent at the end of each month.* 家主は毎月月末に家賃を徴収する.
▶定義4 自 to come together; to gather 一緒になる; 集まる→集結する, 群がる ‖ *A crowd collected to see what was going on.* 何が起こっているのかを見ようと群衆が群がった. ▶定義5 他 特に 英 to go and get sb/sth from a particular place; to pick sb/sth up 特定の場所に行って~を連れて, 取ってくる; ~を拾う→~を連れに行く, 迎えに行く; 取りに行く, 取ってくる ‖ *to collect the children from school* 学校に子供たちを迎えに行く ▶定義6 他 **collect yourself/sth** to get control of yourself, your feelings, thoughts, etc 自分自身, 感情, 考えなどを抑制する→心を落ち着ける, 気を取り直す, (自制心など) を取り戻す, (考え) をまとめる ‖ *She collected herself and went back into the room as if nothing had happened.* 彼女は心を落ち着かせて, 何事もなかったかのように部屋に戻った. *I tried to collect my thoughts before the exam.* 私は試験の前に考えをまとめようとした.

**collect**² /kəlékt/ 形 副 困 ▶定義 (used about a telephone call) to be paid for by the person who receives the call (電話について) 電話を受けた人が料金を払う→受信人払いの [で], コレクトコールの [で] ‖ *a collect call* 受信人払いの通話 *She called me collect.* 彼女は私にコレクトコールを掛けてきた. ☞ イギリス英語では **make a reverse-charge call** または **reverse the charges** と言う.

**collected** /kəléktəd/ 形 ▶定義 calm and in control of yourself, your feelings, thoughts, etc 冷静で, 自分自身, 感情, 考えなどを抑制している→落ち着いた, 冷静な ‖ *She felt cool, calm and collected before the interview.* インタビュー前, 彼女は落ち着いており平静で自制心を保っていた.

\***collection** /kəlékʃ(ə)n/ 名 ▶定義1 C a group of objects of a particular type that sb has collected as a hobby ~が趣味で集めた特定の種類の物の集まり→収集物, 採集物, 収蔵物, コレクション ‖ *a stamp collection* 切手のコレクション ▶定義2 C U the act of getting sth from a place or from people 場所や人々から~を得ること→集めること, 収集, 採集, 回収 ‖ *rubbish collections* ごみの回収 ▶定義3 C a group of people or things 人々や物の集まり→堆積 (たいせき), 山と積まれた物, 群, 群衆 ‖ *a large collection of papers on the desk* 机の上に山積みになった書類 ▶定義4 C a number of poems, stories, letters, etc published together in one book まとめて1冊の本として出版された多数の詩, 物語, 手紙など→~集, 作品集, 選集 ‖ *a collection of modern poetry* 現代詩集 ▶定義5 C the act of asking for money from a number of people (for charity, in church, etc) 何人もの人々に（慈善のため教会などで）金を募ること→**募金, 献金, 寄付金** ‖ *a collection for the poor* 貧しい人々のための募金　▶定義6 ❹a variety of new clothes or items for the home that are specially designed and sold at a particular time 特定の時期に特別にデザインされ販売されるさまざまな新しい服や家庭用品→**新作（発表会）,（服飾の）コレクション** ‖ *Armani's stunning new autumn collection* アルマーニのすばらしい秋の新作

**collective**[1] /kəléktɪv/ 形 ▶定義 shared by a group of people together; not individual 人が集団で共有する；個人でない→**集合的な, 集団的な, 共同の, 団体の** ‖ *collective responsibility* 共同責任　— **collectively** 副 →**集合的に, 共同で, 一まとめにして** ‖ *We took the decision collectively at a meeting.* 私たちは会議の総意として決定した．

**collective**[2] /kəléktɪv/ 名 [❻, 単数または複数形の動詞と共に] ▶定義 an organization or business that is owned and controlled by the people who work in it そこで働く人々が所有し管理する組織や企業→**集団, 共同体; 共産主義社会, 集団農場**

**collector** /kəléktər/ 名 ❻（しばしば複合語で）▶定義 a person who collects things as a hobby or as part of his/her job 趣味または仕事の一部として物を集める人→**収集家, 採集人; 集金人, 取り立て人** ‖ *a stamp collector* 切手の収集家　*a ticket/rent/tax collector* 改札係・家賃徴収人・収税吏

*★**college** /kálɪdʒ/ 名 ▶定義1 ❻❶an institution where you can study after you leave school (at the age of 16)（16歳で）学校を出た後に勉強できる機関→**（単科）大学; 専修学校,（特殊）専門学校, 大学予備校, 高校** ‖ *an art college* 美術学校　*a sixth-form college (= an institution where pupils aged 16 to 18 can prepare for A Levels)* 第6学年カレッジ（＝16〜18歳の生徒がAレベル試験の準備をする所）*She's studying Spanish at the college of further education (= a college that is not a university where people who have left school can study).* 彼女は継続教育の学校でスペイン語を学んでいる（＝総合大学ではない学校で, 学校を出た人々が勉強できる所）．

▶学生として college や university に出席している場合は, the を付けない: *He's at college in York.*（彼はヨークの大学に行っている．）*She's going to college in October.*（彼女は10月から大学に通う．）ただし, そのほかの理由で行く場合は, the を付ける: *I went to an art exhibition at the college last night.*（私は昨晩, 大学の展覧会に行った．）

▶定義2 ❻(in Britain) one of the separate institutions into which certain universities are divided（英国で）一部の総合大学の分割された機関の1つ→**(Oxford, Cambridge などの大学を構成し自治体として独立した) カレッジ** ‖ *King's College, London* ロンドン大学キングズカレッジ　▶定義3 ❻(in the US) a university, or part of one, where students can study for a degree（米国で）総合大学, またはその一部で, 学生が単位を取得するために学ぶことができる→**大学, 学部**

**collide** /kəláɪd/ 動 ❺ ▶定義 **collide (with sb/sth)** to crash; to hit sb/sth very hard while moving 衝突する；動いているときに〜に激しくぶつかる→**(〜と) 衝突する, (強く) ぶつかり合う** ‖ *He ran along the corridor and collided with his teacher.* 彼は廊下を走っていて, 先生とぶつかった．

**colliery** /káljəri, -ièri/ 名 ❻（複 **collieries**）特に英 ▶定義 a coal mine and its buildings 炭坑とその建物→**炭鉱**

**collision** /kəlíʒ(ə)n/ 名 ❻❶ ▶定義 a crash; an occasion when things or people collide 衝突；物や人が衝突するとき→**衝突, 激突, ぶつかること** ‖ *It was a **head-on collision** and the driver was killed instantly.* それは正面衝突で運転者は即死だった．

成句 **be on a collision course (with sb/sth)** ▶定義1 to be in a situation which is certain to end in a disagreement or argument 意見の相違や議論になって終わることが確実な状況にある→**(〜との) 対立が避けられない, 必ず衝突する** ‖ *I'm not surprised they're arguing - they've been on a collision course over money all week.* 彼らが論争していることには驚かない — 彼らは金をめぐって今週ずっと衝突が避けられない状況にあったのだから．　▶定義2 to be moving in a direction which is certain to cause a crash 必ず衝突する方向に動いている→**衝突進**

路にいる, 衝突必至である ‖ *The ship was on a collision course with an iceberg.* 船は氷山との衝突を回避できない航路を進んでいた.

**colloquial** /kəlóukwiəl/ 形 ▶定義 (used about words, phrases, etc) used in spoken conversation, not in formal situations (語, 句などについて)改まった状況ではなく, 会話で用いて→口語(体)の, 話し言葉の, 日常会話の; くだけた ― **colloquially** /-kwiəli/ 副 →口語で, 会話で

**collusion** /kəlúːʒ(ə)n/ 名 U 正式 ▶定義 secret agreement, especially in order to do sth dishonest 特に何か不誠実な事をするための秘密の取り決め→共謀, 談合 ‖ *The drugs were brought into the country with the collusion of customs officials.* 税関の役人との共謀で, 薬物が国内に持ち込まれた.

**cologne** /kəlóun/ 名 U = EAU DE COLOGNE

**colon** /kóulən/ 名 C ▶定義 the mark (:) used before a list, an explanation, an example, etc 例えば一覧, 説明, 例示などの前に使われる(:)の記号→コロン

**colonel** /kə́ːml/ 名 C ▶定義 an officer of a high level in the army 軍の高位の士官→(空軍・陸軍・海兵隊の)大佐

**colonial** /kəlóuniəl, -njəl/ 形 ▶定義 connected with or belonging to a country that controls another country (colony) 他国(植民地)を支配する国に関連した, または所属する→植民地(風)の; 古めかしい ‖ *Spain used to be a major colonial power.* スペインはかつて, 植民地支配の一大勢力だった.

**colonialism** /kəlóuniəlìz(ə)m, -njəl-/ 名 U ▶定義 the practice by which a powerful country controls another country or countries, in order to become richer 強大な国がさらに富を得るためにほかの国(々)を支配すること→植民地主義, 植民政策

**colonist** /kálənɪst/ 名 C ▶定義 a person who goes to live in a country that has become a colony 植民地になっている国に行って住む人→入植者, 海外移住民, 植民地開拓者

**colonize** (または -**ise**) /kálənàɪz/ 動 他 ▶定義 to take control of another country or place and make it a colony ほかの国や場所を支配して植民地にする→〜を植民地として開拓する, 植民地化する, 〜を移住させる ― **colonization** (または -**isation**) /kàlənaɪzéɪʃ(ə)n; -nə-/ 名 U →植民地化, 入植

**colony** /káləni/ 名 C ( 複 **colonies**) ▶定義1 a country or area that is ruled by another, more powerful country より強大な他国に支配される国または地域→植民地; 属領, 海外領土 ▶定義2 [単数または複数形の動詞と共に] a group of people who go to live permanently in another country but keep their own habits and traditions ほかの国に行き永住するが, 自分たちの習慣や伝統は維持している人々の集団→居留民, 〜人街 ▶定義3 a group of the same type of animals, insects or plants living or growing in the same place 同じ場所に生息する, または生育する同じ種類の動物, 昆虫, 植物などの集まり→群落, 集団, 群生, コロニー; 群体 ‖ *a colony of ants* アリの群落

**color** 米 = COLOUR

**colossal** /kəlás(ə)l/ 形 ▶定義 extremely large 非常に大きい→巨大な, 途方もなく大きい ‖ *a colossal building* 巨大なビル *a colossal amount of money* ばく大な金額

★**colour**¹ ( 米 **color**) /kʌ́lər/ 名 ▶定義1 C U the fact that sth is red, green, yellow, blue, etc 〜が赤, 緑, 黄, 青などであるということ→色(彩), 色調 ‖ *'What colour is your car?' 'Red.'* 「あなたの車は何色ですか」「赤です」 *What colours do the Swedish team play in?* スウェーデンチームのユニフォームは何色ですか. *a dark/deep colour* 暗い・濃い色 *a bright colour* 鮮やかな色 *a light/pale colour* 明るい・薄い色 *Those flowers certainly give the room a bit of colour.* 花を飾ったら部屋が実に明るくなる.

▶「〜色だ」と言う場合, A thing is a certain colour. と言い, It has a colour. とは言わない.

▶定義2 U the use of all the colours, not just black and white 黒と白だけでなくすべての色を使用すること→カラー, (形容詞的に)色付きの ‖ *All the pictures in the book are in colour.* その本のさし絵はすべてカラーだ. *a colour television* カラーテレビ ▶定義3 U a red or pink colour in your face, particularly when it shows how healthy you are or that you are embarrassed 赤やピンクの顔色, 特に健康や気恥ずかしさを示す顔色→顔色, 血色; (顔の)赤らみ, 赤面, 紅潮 ‖ *You look much better now, you've got a bit more colour.* 具合が良くなったようだね, 顔色が良くなったよ. *Colour flooded her face when she thought of what had happened.* 起った事を思い出して, 彼女の顔はかっと赤くなった. ▶定義4 ❶interesting or exciting details 面白い, または興奮させるような細部→**精彩, 生気, 生き生きしていること, 個性, 味** ‖ *It's a busy area, full of activity and colour.* ここはにぎやかで華やかな繁華街です.

成句 off colour ▶定義 ill 具合が悪い→元気がない, 顔色が悪い, 気分が優れない

with flying colours ⇒ FLYING

★**colour**² ( 米 color) /kʌ́lər/ 動 他 ▶定義1 to put colour on sth, for example by painting it 例えばペンキを塗って~に色を付ける→**~に着色する, 色を塗る, ~を染める** ‖ *Colour the picture with your crayons.* クレヨンで絵に色を塗りなさい. *The area coloured yellow on the map is desert.* 地図の黄色く塗られている部分は砂漠です.

▶定義2 to influence thoughts, opinions, etc 考え, 意見などに影響を及ぼす→**~を潤色する, 粉飾する; ~に (悪) 影響を与える, ゆがめる** ‖ *You shouldn't let one bad experience colour your attitude to everything.* 嫌な経験を1回したからといって, それがあなたの姿勢すべてに影響することがあってはいけない.

句動詞 colour sth in ▶定義 to fill a shape, a picture, etc with colour using pencils, paint, etc 鉛筆, 塗料などを使って形, 絵などを色で塗りつぶす→**色を付ける, 色を塗り込む** ‖ *The children were colouring in pictures of animals.* 子供たちは動物の絵に色を塗っていた.

**colour-blind** 形 ▶定義 unable to see certain colours, especially red and green 特定の色, 特に赤と緑が分からない→**色盲の**

**coloured** /kʌ́lərd/ ( 米 **colored**) 形 ▶定義1 having colour or a particular colour 色の付いた, または特定の色の→**着色した, 彩色してある; ~色の** ‖ *a coffee-coloured dress* コーヒー色のドレス *brightly-coloured lights* 鮮やかな色の明かり

▶定義2 (used about a person) belonging to a race that does not have white skin (人について) 白い肌でない人種に属する→**有色の, 有色人種の** ☛ この語は現在では侮辱的だと見なされる. 特定の人種に属する人のことを言う場合には, 必要に応じて black, Asian 等を用いる.

**colourful** ( 米 **colorful**) /kʌ́lərfʊl, -f(ə)l/ 形 ▶定義1 with bright colours; full of colour 鮮やかな色の; 色彩豊かな→**色彩に富んだ, 多彩な, 華やかな, 派手な** ‖ *a colourful shirt* 派手なシャツ

▶定義2 full of interest or excitement 興味や刺激に富んだ→**精彩のある, はつらつとした, 生き生きとした** ‖ *a colourful story* 生き生きとした物語 *He has a rather colourful past.* 彼の過去はなかなか精彩に富んでいる.

**colouring** ( 米 **coloring**) /kʌ́lərɪŋ/ 名 ▶定義1 ❶ the colour of a person's hair, skin, etc 人の髪や肌などの色→**血色, 顔色, (肌・目・髪などの) 色** ‖ *to have fair/dark colouring* 色白で金髪・肌が浅黒く黒髪である ▶定義2 C ❶ a substance that is used to give a particular colour to sth, especially food ~, 特に食物に特定の色を付けるために使われる物質→**着色料, 着色剤**

**colourless** ( 米 **colorless**) /kʌ́lərləs/ 形 ▶定義1 without any colour 色のない→**無色の, 色の付いていない** ‖ *a colourless liquid, like water* 水のように無色の液体 ▶定義2 not interesting or exciting; dull 面白くない, または刺激のない; 退屈な→**精彩を欠いた, つまらない, 特色のない**

**colour scheme** 名 C ▶定義 the way in which colours are arranged, especially in a room 特に室内の色を配合するやり方→**色彩設計, (室内装飾の) 配色**

**colt** /kóʊlt/ 名 C ▶定義 a young male horse 若い雄馬→**雄の子馬 (4~5歳までの), 若駒 (わかごま)**

★**column** /kάləm/ 名 C ▶定義1 a tall solid vertical post made of stone, supporting or decorating a building or standing alone 石でできた背

の高い頑丈な垂直の柱で，建物を支える・装飾する，または独立して立っている→柱，円柱，支柱 ‖ *Nelson's Column is a monument in London.* ネルソン記念碑はロンドンの記念建造物だ． ▶定義2 something that has the shape of a column 柱のような形をした物→柱[円柱]状の物，柱状部 ‖ *a column of smoke (= smoke rising straight up)* 煙の柱（＝まっすぐ立ち昇る煙） ▶定義3 one of the vertical sections into which a printed page, especially in a newspaper, is divided 印刷物のページ，特に新聞の縦に分割された欄の１つ→（新聞・雑誌などの）縦の欄，段 ▶定義4 a piece of writing in a newspaper or magazine that is part of a regular series or always written by the same writer 新聞や雑誌の記事で，連載の一部またはいつも同じ著者が書くもの→特約定期寄稿欄，コラム（の記事）‖ *the travel/gossip column* 旅行・ゴシップ欄 ▶定義5 a series of numbers written one under the other 縦に並んだ数字の列→縦の列，縦の表 ‖ *to add up a column of figures* 数字の列の合計を出す ▶定義6 a long line of people, vehicles, etc, one following behind another 後ろに続く人や乗り物などの長い列→行列，隊列 ‖ *a column of troops* 軍隊の隊列

**columnist** /kάləm(n)ɪst/ 名 C ▶定義 a journalist who writes regular articles in a newspaper or magazine 新聞や雑誌に定期的に記事を書くジャーナリスト→特約寄稿家，特別欄担当者，コラムニスト ‖ *a gossip columnist* ゴシップ欄担当執筆者

**coma** /kóʊmə/ 名 C ▶定義 a deep unconscious state, often lasting for a long time and caused by serious illness or injury 深い無意識の状態で，大抵は長期間続き重い病気やけがが原因で引き起こる→昏睡（こんすい）（状態）

**comatose** /kóʊmətòʊs, kάm-/ 形 ▶定義1 略式 deeply asleep ぐっすり眠っている→眠りこける，眠くてたまらない；無気力な，だるい ‖ *He had drunk a bottle of vodka and was comatose.* 彼はウオッカを１びん飲んで眠りこけていた． ▶定義2 (medical) deeply unconscious; in a coma （医学）深い無意識状態の；昏睡（こんすい）状態の→昏睡状態の，昏睡性の

\***comb**¹ /kóʊm/ 名 ▶定義1 C a flat piece of metal or plastic with teeth that you use for making your hair tidy 歯のある金属やプラスチックの小さな板で，髪を整えるために用いる→くし，くし状のもの ▶定義2 [C, 通常は単数] an act of combing the hair 髪をくしでとかすこと→くしけずること，髪をすくこと ‖ *Give your hair a comb before you go out.* 外出する前にくしで髪をとかしなさい．

**comb**² /kóʊm/ 動 他 ▶定義1 to make your hair tidy using a comb くしを使って髪を整える→～をくしけずる，くしですく，(髪)をくしでとかす ▶定義2 comb sth (for sb/sth) to search an area carefully ある範囲を注意深く捜す→(場所)を(～を求めて)徹底的に捜す，くまなく捜索する ‖ *Police are combing the woodland for the murder weapon.* 警察は殺人の凶器を捜して林をくまなく捜索している．

**combat**¹ /kάmbæt, kám-, -bət/ 名 C U ▶定義 a fight, especially in war 特に戦争での戦い→戦闘，闘争，戦うこと ‖ *unarmed combat (= without weapons)* 丸腰の（＝武器を持たない）戦い

**combat**² /kəmbæt, kάmbæt, kám-/ 動 他 ▶定義 to fight against sth; to try to stop or defeat sth ～に対抗して戦う；～を止めるまたは打ち負かそうとする→～と戦う，～に立ち向かう，～を撲滅・除去しようと務める ‖ *to combat terrorism* テロリズムと戦う *new medicines to combat heart disease* 心臓病を治療するための新薬

**combatant** /kəmbæt(ə)nt, kάmbət(ə)nt/ 名 C ▶定義 a person who takes part in fighting, especially in war 特に戦争で戦闘に参加する人→戦闘員；戦う人，闘士，格闘者

\***combination** /kὰmbənéɪʃ(ə)n/ 名 C U ▶定義 a number of people or things mixed or joined together; a mixture 混合された，または結合された複数の人や物；混合→結合，組み合わせ，取り合わせ，配合；連合，連盟，連携 ‖ *The team manager still hasn't found the right combination of players.* チーム監督は選手の適切な組み合わせがまだ見つからないでいる． *On this course, you may study French in combination with Spanish or Italian.* この課程では，スペイン語かイタリア語のいずれかをフランス語と組み合わせて学べます．

\***combine**¹ /kəmbάɪn/ 動 ▶定義1 自 他 combine (with sb/sth) to join or mix two or more things together 複数の物を結合または混合する➡(〜を)結合する, 合併する・させる, 連合する・させる, 結び付く・結び付ける ‖ *The two organizations combined to form one company.* 2つの組織が合併して1つの会社になった. *Bad planning, combined with bad luck, led to the company's collapse.* まずい計画が不運と結び付いて, 会社は倒産した. ▶定義**2** 🌐 **combine A and/with B** to do or have two or more things at the same time 同時に複数の事をする, または複数の物を所有する➡(A と B)を兼ね備える, 兼ねる, 併せ持つ, 兼業する ‖ *This car combines speed and reliability.* この車はスピードと信頼性を兼ね備えている.

**combine**² /kámbaɪn/ (医 または **combine harvester**) 🔊 ● ▶定義 a large farm machine that both cuts corn and separates the grain from the rest of the plant 大型の農業用機械で, 穀物を刈り, 同時に殻粒をほかの穂から取り離す➡コンバイン, 刈り取り脱穀機 ☞参 **harvest**

**combined** /kámbaɪnd/ 形 ▶定義 done by a number of people joining together, resulting from the joining of two or more things 何人かの人が一緒になって行われる, 2つ以上の物を結合した結果として➡結合された, 合同の, 共同の, 連合の; 化合した ‖ *The combined efforts of the emergency services prevented a major disaster.* 多くの救急機関の協力によって大きな被害を防いだ.

**combustion** /kəmbʌ́stʃ(ə)n/ 🔊 Ⓤ ▶定義 the process of burning 燃える過程➡燃焼, (有機体の)酸化

*****come** /kʌm/ 動 🈁 (過 **came** /kéɪm/; 過分 **come**)
▶定義**1** to move to or towards the person who is speaking or the place that sb is talking about 話している人, または〜が話題にしている場所に, またはその方向に移動する➡(話し手の方へ)来る, (こちらへ)やって来る, (相手の方へ)行く ‖ *Come here, please.* こちらに来てください. *Come and see what I've found.* ここに来て私が見つけた物を見て. *I hope you can come to my party.* 私のパーティーに来てほしいのですが. *They're coming to stay for a week.* 彼らは1週間滞在しに来る予定だ. *The children came running into the room.* 子供たちが部屋に駆け込んできた. ▶定義**2** **come (to...)** to arrive somewhere or reach a particular place or time どこかに到着する, または特定の場所や時刻に達する➡やって来る, 着く, 届く, 到達する ‖ *What time are you coming home?* 何時に家に帰ってきますか. *Has the newspaper come yet?* 新聞はもう来ましたか. *After a few hours in the jungle, we came to a river.* ジャングルを数時間歩くと, 川に着いた. *Her hair comes down to her waist.* 彼女の髪は腰まで届く. *The water in the pool came up to our knees.* 池の水は私たちのひざまでの深さだった. *The time has come to say goodbye.* 別れの時がやって来た.

▶定義**3** to be in a particular position in a series 一続きのものの中で特定の位置にある➡巡ってくる, 到来する, (順序に従って)出てくる, 現れる, 来る ‖ *March comes after February.* 3月は2月の次に来る. *Charlie came second in the exam.* チャーリーは試験で2番になった. *I can't wait to find out what comes next in the story.* 物語の続きが待ちきれない. ▶定義**4** **come in sth** to be available 手に入る➡入手できる, 売り出される, 売っている, 買える ‖ *This blouse comes in a choice of four colours.* このブラウスは4色から選べる. *Do these trousers come in a larger size?* このズボンの大きいサイズはありますか.

▶定義**5** to be produced by or from sth 〜によって, または〜から産み出される➡産出される, 作られる, 〜から取る, 採集する ‖ *Wool comes from sheep.* 羊毛は羊から取る. ▶定義**6** to become open or loose 開くまたは緩む➡開く, 外れる, ほどける ‖ *Your blouse has come undone.* ブラウスのボタンが外れていますよ. *Her hair has come untied.* 彼女の髪がほどけた.

▶定義**7** **come to do sth** used for talking about how, why or when sth happened 〜がどのようにして, なぜ, いつ起こったか言うときに用いて➡(結果として)〜になる, 結局〜ということになる ‖ *How did you come to lose your passport?* どんな状況でパスポートをなくしたのですか. ▶定義**8** **come to/into sth** to reach a particular state 特定の状況になる➡〜になる, という結果になる ‖ *We were all sorry when the holiday came to an end.* 私たちは皆休暇が終わるとがっかりした. *The military government came to power in a coup d'état.* クーデターで軍事政府が政権を握った.

## come

▶ come を含むこのほかの成句については,名詞,形容詞などの項を参照.例えば come to a head は head の項にある.

### ▶日本語 vs 英語

「行く」が come になる場合

　come と go の使い分けは,日本語の「来る・行く」とは異なります.日本語の「来る」は,話し手のいる場所への移動に用いられます.一方,英語の come は,話し手または聞き手のいる場所への移動に用いられます.したがって,聞き手のいる場所への移動の場合,日本語では「君の家に行く」となりますが,英語では I'll come to your house. となります.「今行きます」を I'm coming. と言うのも同様です.

**成句** come and go ▶定義 to be present for a short time and then go away 短時間だけ現れて消える→行ったり来たりする,つかの間である ‖ *The pain in my ear comes and goes.* 耳の痛みが出たり消えたりする.

come easily/naturally to sb ▶定義 to be easy for sb to do ～にとって簡単にできる→たやすくできる,難しくない ‖ *Apologizing does not come easily to her.* 彼女はなかなか謝らない.

come to nothing; not come to anything ▶定義 to fail; to not be successful 失敗する;成功しない→無駄になる,ろくなことにならない,徒労に終わる ‖ *Unfortunately, all his efforts came to nothing.* 残念ながら,彼の努力はすべて無駄になった.

how come...? **略式** ▶定義 why or how なぜ,またはどのように→どうして,一体なぜ ‖ *How come you're back so early?* どうしてこんなに早く戻ってきたのですか.

to come (名詞の後で) ▶定義 in the future 将来の→未来の,来るべき ‖ *You'll regret it in years to come.* 何年後かにその事を後悔するでしょう.

when it comes to sth/to doing sth ▶定義 when it is a question of sth ～のこととなると→～(のこと)となると,～については ‖ *When it comes to value for money, these prices are hard to beat.* 金額に見合う価値ということになると,この価格に対抗できる物はない.

**句動詞** come about ▶定義 to happen 起こる→生じる,ということになる ‖ *How did this situation come about?* どうしてこういう状況になったのですか.

come across/over (as sth) ▶定義 to make an impression of a particular type 特定の印象を与える→理解される,(相手に)～という印象を与える ‖ *Elizabeth comes across as being rather shy.* エリザベスはどちらかといえば内気な印象を与える.

come across sb/sth ▶定義 to meet or find sb/sth by chance ～に偶然会う,または見つける→～に偶然出くわす,偶然見つけ出す,(考えなどが)浮かぶ ‖ *I came across this book in a second-hand shop.* 古本屋で偶然この本を見つけた. ☛類 **encounter**

come along ▶定義 **1** to arrive or appear 到着する,または現れる→やって来る,現れる ‖ *An old man was coming along the road.* 老人が道路をこちらにやって来た. ▶定義 **2** = **COME ON(2)** ▶定義 **3** = **COME ON(3)**

come apart ▶定義 to break into pieces ばらばらに壊れる→ばらばらに割れる,分解する ‖ *This old coat is coming apart at the seams.* この古いコートは縫い目の所から裂け始めている.

come away (from sth) ▶定義 to become loose or unfastened 緩む,または外れる→取れる,はがれる,離れる ‖ *The wallpaper is coming away from the wall in the corner.* 壁紙が壁の隅からはがれかけている.

come away with sth ▶定義 to leave a place with a particular opinion or feeling 特定の意見や感情を抱いてある場所から去る→(感情,印象など)を抱いて離れる,立ち去る ‖ *We came away with a very favourable impression of Cambridge.* 私たちはとても良い印象を抱いてケンブリッジを後にした.

come back ▶定義 **1** to return 戻る→帰る,戻ってくる ‖ *I don't know what time I'll be coming back.* 何時に帰れるか分かりません. ▶定義 **2** to become popular or fashionable again 再び人気が出るまたは流行する→(流行などが)復活する,返り咲く ‖ *Flared trousers are coming back again.* フレア形のズボンがまたはやり出している.

come back (to sb) ▶定義 to be remembered 思い出される→(～に)よみがえる,思い出す ‖

*When I went to Italy again, my Italian started to come back to me.* またイタリアに行ったら、イタリア語を思い出してきた.

**come before sb/sth** ▶定義 to be more important than sb/sth else ほかの〜より重要である➡〜**に先立つ, 〜の上位にある, 〜に優先する** ‖ *Mark feels his family comes before his career.* マークは出世よりも家族の方が大事だと思っている.

**come between sb and sb** ▶定義 to damage the relationship between two people 2人の関係を駄目にする➡〜**の仲を裂く, (2者のことに)干渉する** ‖ *Arguments over money came between the two brothers.* 金に関する言い争いで2人の兄弟の仲は険悪になった.

**come by sth** ▶定義 to manage to get sth 何とか〜を得る➡〜**を手に入れる** ‖ *Fresh vegetables are hard to come by in the winter.* 冬には新鮮な野菜がなかなか手に入らない.

**come down** ▶定義1 to fall down 落下する➡**倒れる, 落ちる** ‖ *The power lines came down in the storm.* あらしで送電線が垂れ下がった.

▶定義2 (used about an aircraft or spacecraft) to land (航空機や宇宙船について)着陸する➡**降りる, 着陸する, 不時着する** ‖ *The helicopter came down in a field.* ヘリコプターが畑に不時着した. ▶定義3 (used about prices) to become lower (価格について)低下する➡**安くなる, (値が)下落する, 下がる, (値段を)負ける** ‖ *The price of land has come down in the past year.* 前年、地価は下落した.

**come down to sth/to doing sth** 略式 ▶定義 to be able to be explained by a single important point 1つの重要な点によって説明できる➡〜**に帰着する, 結局〜になる, 〜という結果になる** ‖ *It all comes down to having the right qualifications.* 結局は適性があるかどうかという問題だ.

**come down with sth** ▶定義 to become ill with sth 何らかの病気になる➡**(病気に)かかる** ‖ *I think I'm coming down with flu.* どうやら流感にかかったようだ.

**come forward** ▶定義 to offer help 助けを申し出る➡**求めに応じて立つ, 買って出る, 志願する** ‖ *The police are asking witnesses to come forward.* 警察は目撃者は名乗り出るように求めている.

**come from...** ▶定義 to live in or have been born in a place ある場所に住む, またはある場所で生まれた➡〜**の出身である, 〜の生まれである, 〜の出である** ‖ *Where do you come from originally?* もともとご出身はどちらですか.

**come from (doing) sth** ▶定義 to be the result of sth 〜の結果である➡〜**の結果として生じる, 〜のせいである** ‖ *'I'm tired.' 'That comes from all the late nights you've had.'* 「疲れた」「夜更かしばかりしていたせいですよ」

**come in** ▶定義1 to enter a place ある場所に入る➡**入ってくる, 入場する** ‖ *Come in and sit down.* 中に入ってお掛けください. ▶定義2 (used about the tides of the sea) to move towards the land and cover the beach (海の潮について)陸の方向に移動して海岸を覆う➡**(潮が)満ちてくる, 差してくる** ☞参 tide¹ ▶定義3 to become popular or fashionable 人気が出る, または流行する➡**はやる** ‖ *Punk fashions came in in the seventies.* パンクファッションは70年代に流行した. ▶定義4 (used about news or information) to be received (ニュースや情報について)受け取る➡**入ってくる, 届く** ‖ *Reports are coming in of fighting in Beirut.* ベイルートの戦闘の報告が入ってきています.

**come in for sth** ▶定義 to receive sth, especially sth unpleasant 〜, 特に不快な〜を受け取る➡**(非難などを)受ける, 被る** ‖ *The government came in for a lot of criticism.* 政府は大変な批判の矢面に立った.

**come of sth/of doing sth** ▶定義 to be the result of sth➡〜**の結果として起こる** ‖ *We've written to several companies asking for help but nothing has come of it yet.* 数社に手紙を書いて支援を求めたが、いまだに何の返事もない.

**come off** ▶定義1 to be able to be removed 取り除くことができる➡**取れる, 外れる, 取り外せる** ‖ *Does the hood come off?* フードは取り外せますか. ▶定義2 略式 to be successful 成功する➡**うまくいく** ‖ *The deal seems unlikely to come off.* 取り引きはうまくいきそうにない. ▶定義3 略式 (後に副詞を伴って) to be in a good, bad, etc situation as a result of sth 何かの結果として良い状況や悪い状況などになる➡**結果が〜となる** ‖ *Unfortunately, Dennis came off worst in the fight.* 残念ながら、デニスはその

けんかで負けた．

come off (sth) ▶定義1 to fall off sth 〜から落ちる→(〜から)落下する, 転ぶ ‖ Kim came off her bicycle and broke her leg. キムは自転車で転んで足の骨を折った． ▶定義2 to become removed from sth 〜から外れる→(〜から)取れる, 外れる, 離れる ‖ One of the legs has come off this table. このテーブルの脚が1本取れた．

come off it (口語) ▶定義 used to say that you do not believe sb/sth or that you strongly disagree with sb 〜の言うこと・〜を信じない, または人に強く反対するときに用いて→ばかなことを言うな, いいかげんにしろ ‖ 'I thought it was quite a good performance.' 'Oh, come off it - it was awful!' 「とてもいい演技だと思った」「ばかを言わないで − あれはひどかったわ」

come on ▶定義1 to start to act, play in a game of sport, etc スポーツの試合などで登場する, またはプレーを始める→出場する, 登場する ‖ The audience jeered every time the villain came on. 悪役が登場する度に観客がやじった． The substitute came on in the second half. 後半に控えの選手が登場した． ▶定義2 (または come along) to make progress or to improve 進歩する, または向上する→上達する, うまくなる, 良くなる ‖ Your English is coming on nicely. あなたの英語はかなり上達しています． ▶定義3 Come on! (または Come along!) used to tell sb to hurry up, try harder, etc 〜に急ぐように言う, またはもっと頑張るように言うときなどに用いる→さあ(行こう), さあ早く, しっかり, 頑張って, いいかげんにしろ ‖ Come on or we'll be late! さあ急ごう, じゃないと遅れるよ． ▶定義4 to begin 始まる→襲ってくる, やって来る ‖ I think I've got a cold coming on. どうやら風邪を引いた[引きかけている]ようだ．

come out ▶定義1 to appear; to be published 現れる; 出版される→出てくる, (書物などが)発表される ‖ The rain stopped and the sun came out. 雨がやんで太陽が出てきた． The report came out in 1998. その報告書は, 1998年に発表された． ▶定義2 to become known 知られる→(物事が)知れる, 分かる, はっきりする, 明らかになる ‖ It was only after his death that the truth came out. 彼の死後, 初めて真実が明らかになった． ▶定義3 (used about a photograph, etc) to be produced successfully (写真などについて)うまく出来上がる→(写真が)はっきりと(鮮明に)写る, (〜に)写っている ‖ Only one of our photos came out. 私たちの撮った写真は1枚しか写っていなかった．

come out (of sth) ▶定義 to be removed from sth 〜から取り除かれる→取れる, 落ちる ‖ Red wine stains don't come out easily. 赤ワインの染みはなかなか落ちない．

come out against sth ▶定義 to say in public that you do not like or agree with sth 〜が好きでない, または同意できないと公言する→〜に反対を表明する, 反対する ‖ The Prime Minister came out against capital punishment. 首相は死刑に反対であることを表明した．

come out in sth ▶定義 to become covered in spots, etc 発疹(はっしん)などで覆われる→(吹き出物など)で覆われる, 発疹が出る ‖ Heat makes him come out in a rash. 彼は暑いと発疹が出る．

come out with sth ▶定義 to say sth unexpectedly 不意に何かを言う→〜を口に出す, 話す ‖ The children came out with all kinds of stories. 子供たちはいきなりさまざまな物語を話し始めた．

come over = **COME ACROSS/OVER**

come over (to...) (from...) ▶定義 to visit people or a place a long way away 遠く離れた人や場所を訪ねる→(〜から)(…へ)はるばる(わざわざ)やって来る ‖ They've invited us to come over to Australia for a holiday. 休暇にオーストラリアへ来るように招待された．

come over sb ▶定義 (used about a feeling) to affect sb (感情について)〜に影響を与える→(感情などが)〜を襲う ‖ A feeling of despair came over me. 私は絶望感に襲われた．

come round ▶定義1 (used about an event that happens regularly) to happen (定期的に起こる出来事について)起こる→やって来る, 巡ってくる, 回ってくる ‖ The end of the holidays always comes round very quickly. 休暇の終わりはいつもとても早くやって来る． ▶定義2 (または come to) to become conscious again 再び意識を取り戻す→意識を回復する, 気が付く ⇔ **pass out**

come round (to...) ▶定義 to visit a person or place not far away 遠くはない人や場所を訪ね

る→立ち寄る ‖ *Do you want to come round for lunch on Saturday?* 土曜日に昼食を食べに来ませんか.

come round (to sth)▶定義 to change your opinion so that you agree with sb/sth 自分の意見を変えて，〜に同意する／(〜に)同調する，同意する ‖ *They finally came round to our way of thinking.* 彼らはやっと私たちの考えに同意した.

come through ▶定義 (used about news, information, etc) to arrive (ニュース，情報などについて) 到着する→届く，入る，伝わる ‖ *The football results are just coming through.* サッカーの結果がちょうど入ってきている.

come through (sth)▶定義 to escape injury or death in a dangerous situation, illness, etc 危険な状況，病気などのけがや死を免れる→(病気，危機などを)切り抜ける，持ちこたえる ‖ *to come through an enemy attack* 敵の攻撃を切り抜ける

come to = **COME ROUND(2)**

come to sth ▶定義 **1** to equal or total a particular amount 特定の量と等しくなる，合計が特定の量になる→合計〜になる，〜になる ‖ *The bill for the meal came to £35.* 食事代は，35ポンドかかった. ▶定義 **2** to result in a bad situation 結果が悪い状況になる→結局〜ということになる，失敗する ‖ *We will sell the house to pay our debts if we have to but we hope it won't come to that.* 必要となれば家を売って借金を払うつもりだが，そうはならないことを願っている.

come under ▶定義 to be included in a particular section, department, etc 特定の区分や部門などに含まれる→〜の項目に入る，〜に分類される，編入される ‖ *Garages that sell cars come under 'car dealers' in the telephone book.* 車を売る自動車サービスステーションは，電話帳の「自動車販売業者」の項目に載っている.

come up ▶定義 **1** to happen or be going to happen in the future 起こる，または将来起こる→生じる，(問題などが)起こる，(身に)降り懸かる ‖ *Something's come up at work so I won't be home until late tonight.* 仕事で問題が起こったので，今夜は遅くまで帰れないだろう. ▶定義 **2** to be discussed or mentioned 議論または言及される→議論に上る，注目される，話題になる ‖ *The subject of religion came up.* 宗教問題が議論に上った. ▶定義 **3** (used about the sun and moon) to rise (太陽と月について) 昇る→(太陽，

# comedy 315

月が)出る ▶定義 **4** (used about a plant) to appear above the soil (植物について) 土の上に出てくる→芽を出す

come up against sb/sth ▶定義 to find a problem or difficulty that you have to deal with 自分で対処しなければならない問題や困難にぶつかる→(困難，反対など)に直面する，ぶつかる ‖ *I had to stop when I came up against a high fence.* 高い塀が立ちはだかって止まらなければならなかった.

come up to sth ▶定義 to be as good as usual or as necessary 通常のレベルを満たした，または必要なレベルと同じの→劣らない，(水準など)に達する ‖ *This piece of work does not come up to your usual standard.* この作品はあなたのいつもの水準には達していない.

come up with sth ▶定義 to find an answer or solution to sth 〜の答えや解決策を見つける→(解決策など)を考え出す，見つけ出す，思い付く ‖ *Engineers have come up with new ways of saving energy.* 技術者たちは新しい省エネ方法を考え出した.

**comeback** /kámbæk/ 🔊 ⒸI ▶定義 a return to a position of strength or importance that you had before 以前と同じ力や重要性のある立場に戻ること→復帰，カムバック ‖ *The former world champion is hoping to make a comeback.* 元世界チャンピオンは復帰を望んでいる.

**comedian** /kəmíːdiən/ (または **comic**) 🔊 ⒸI ▶定義 a person whose job is to entertain people and make them laugh, for example by telling jokes 例えばジョークを言って人々を楽しませ，笑わせることを仕事とする人→喜劇俳優，コメディアン ☛ 女性の comedian は comedienne と呼ばれることもある.

**comedown** /kámdàʊn/ 🔊 [ⒸI, 通常は単数] 略式 ▶定義 a loss of importance or social position 重要性や社会的地位を失うこと→(地位・名誉などの)失墜，失望，落ちぶれること ‖ *It's a bit of a comedown for her having to move to a smaller house.* 前よりも小さな家に引っ越さなければならないことは，彼女にとっては少々屈辱的であった.

**comedy** /kámədi/ 🔊 (® **comedies**) ▶定義 **1** ⒸI an amusing play, film, etc that has a happy ending ハッピーエンドで終わる楽しい劇や映画→**喜劇** ☞参 **tragedy** ▶定義2 ❶the quality of being amusing or making people laugh 愉快さや人々を笑わせる特質→**喜劇的要素・出来事・場面, おかしみ**

**comet** /kɑ́mɪt/ 名 C ▶定義 an object in space that looks like a bright star with a tail and that moves around the sun 尾のある明るい星のような天体で, 太陽の周りを回っている→**彗星 (すいせい), ほうき星**

\***comfort**¹ /kʌ́mfərt/ 名 ▶定義1 ❶the state of having everything your body needs, or of having a pleasant life 体が必要とする物をすべて持っている, または快適な生活をしている状態→**快適, 安楽; 満足** ‖ *Most people expect to live in comfort in their old age.* 多くの人々は老後は安楽な暮らしをしたいと思っている. *to travel in comfort* 快適に旅行する ▶定義2 ❶the feeling of being physically relaxed and in no pain 肉体的にくつろいでいて苦痛がないこと→**快適, 心地良さ, 居心地の良いこと** ‖ *This car has been specially designed for extra comfort.* この車は極上の快適さを追求して特別に設計されている. ⇔ **discomfort** ▶定義3 ❶help or kindness to sb who is suffering 苦しんでいる人に対する援助や親切→**慰め, 慰安, 安らぎ** ‖ *I tried to offer a few words of comfort.* 私は二言三言慰めの言葉を掛けようとした. ▶定義4 **be a comfort (to sb)** [単数扱い] a person or thing that helps you when you are very sad or worried 深く悲しんでいる人, または心配している人を助ける人や物→**慰めとなる人・物** ‖ *You've been a real comfort to me.* あなたは私にとって本当に慰めになりました. ▶定義5 C something that makes your life easier or more pleasant 生活を容易にする, または快適にするもの→**生活を快適にするもの; 楽しみ** ‖ *the comforts of home* 家にいるようなくつろいだ気持ちにさせてくれる設備

**comfort**² /kʌ́mfərt/ 動 他 ▶定義 to try to make sb feel less worried or unhappy 人の心配や不幸を減らそうとする→**～を慰める, なだめる, 安心させる** ‖ *to comfort a crying child* 泣いている子供をなだめる

\***comfortable** /kʌ́mfərtəb(ə)l/ 形 ▶定義1 (または 略式 **comfy**) that makes you feel physically relaxed and in no pain; that provides you with everything your body needs 肉体的にくつろいで苦痛のない状態にする; 体が必要とする物をすべて与える→**快適な, 気持ちの良い, 心地良い, 楽な** ‖ *a comfortable temperature (= not too hot or too cold)* 快適な温度 (= 暑すぎず寒すぎない) *Sit down and make yourselves comfortable.* 座って楽にしてください. *a comfortable pair of shoes* 履き心地の良い靴 ⇔ **uncomfortable** ▶定義2 not having or causing worry, difficulty, etc 心配や困難などがない, または生じさせない→**不安・疑問を感じない, くつろげる, 落ち着ける** ‖ *He did not feel comfortable in the presence of so many women.* 大勢の女性がいたので彼は落ち着かなかった. ▶定義3 having or providing enough money for all your needs 必要をすべて満たすために十分な金がある, またはそれだけの金を与える→**(収入などが) 十分な, 経済的にゆとりのある** ‖ *They are not wealthy but they're quite comfortable.* 彼らは裕福ではないが, 経済的に十分なゆとりがある. —**comfortably** 副 →**快適に, 心地良く, くつろいで, (経済的に) 不自由なく** ‖ *Jon was sitting comfortably in the armchair.* ジョンはひじ掛けいすにくつろいで座っていた. *You can't live comfortably on such low wages.* こんなに安い賃金では不自由なく暮らすことはできない.

**comic**¹ /kɑ́mɪk/ 形 ▶定義 that makes you laugh; connected with comedy 人を笑わせる; 喜劇に関係した→**こっけいな, おかしい; 喜劇の** ‖ *a comic scene in a play* 劇のこっけいな場面

**comic**² /kɑ́mɪk/ 名 C ▶定義1 =**COMEDIAN** ▶定義2 (特に 米 **comic book**) a magazine for children that tells stories through pictures 絵を通して物語を表現する子供用の雑誌→**漫画本**

**comical** /kɑ́mɪk(ə)l/ 形 ▶定義 that makes you laugh; funny 笑わせる; おかしい→**こっけいな** —**comically** /-k(ə)li/ 副 →**こっけいに**

**comic strip** (または **strip cartoon**) 名 C ▶定義 a short series of pictures that tell a funny story, for example in a newspaper 例えば新聞などでこっけいな話を表す短い一続きの絵→**(新聞, 雑誌などの) 続き漫画**

**coming** /kʌ́mɪŋ/ 名 C ▶定義 the moment when sth new arrives or begins 新しい～が到着する, または始まる瞬間→**到来, 出現, 来訪** ‖ *The coming of the computer meant the loss of many* *jobs.* コンピューターの出現によって多くの職が失われた. ― **coming** 形→来るべき, 次の‖ *We've got a lot of plans for the coming year.* 私たちには来年の計画がたくさんある.

**comma** /kámə/ 名 ❻ ▶定義 the mark (,) used for dividing parts of a sentence or items in a list 文やリストの項目を分割するために用いる (,) の記号→コンマ

*★**command**¹ /kəmǽnd; -mάːnd/ 動 ▶定義 1 ⊜ ⊕ 正式 command (sb to do sth) to tell or order sb to do sth 人に何かをするように言う, 命じる→ (〜に…するように) 命令する, 号令を下す‖ *I command you to leave now!* 今すぐ立ち去れと命令します. ▶定義 2 command sb/sth ⊕ to control or be in charge of sb/sth 〜を支配する, または責任を持つ→〜を指揮する, 率いる, 統率する‖ *to command a ship/regiment/army* 船・連隊・軍隊の指揮を取る ▶定義 3 ⊕ to deserve and get sth 〜に値し, それを得る→ (同情, 尊敬など) を集める, 起こさせる‖ *The old man commanded great respect.* その老人は大変尊敬されていた.

*★**command**² /kəmǽnd; -mάːnd/ 名 ▶定義 1 ❻ an order 命令→命令, 指図, 言い付け‖ *The captain's commands must be obeyed without question.* 船長の命令には何の疑問も持たずに黙って従わなければならない. ▶定義 2 ⓤ control over sb/sth 〜に対する支配→指揮, 制御; 制御力, 支配権‖ *Who is in command of the expedition?* この遠征隊のリーダーはだれですか. *to take command of a situation* 状況を統制する ▶定義 3 [単数扱い] the state of being able to do or use sth well 何かがうまくできること, または使えること→自由に駆使する力, 使いこなせること‖ *She has a good command of French.* 彼女はフランス語を自由に使いこなせる.

成句 **at/by sb's command** 正式 ▶定義 because you were ordered by sb 〜に命令されたために→〜の命令で, 〜に命じられて‖ *At the command of their officer the troops opened fire.* 将校の命令で軍隊は射撃を開始した.

**be at sb's command** ▶定義 to be ready to obey sb 〜に進んで従う→〜にいつでも喜んで従う‖ *I'm completely at your command.* 何なりとご用を言い付けてください.

**commandeer** /kὰməndíər/ 動 ▶定義 to take control or possession of sth for military or police use 軍用または警察用に〜を支配する, または所有する→〜を (軍用, 公用などに) 徴用する, 徴発する

**commander** /kəmǽndər, -mάːn-/ 名 ❻ ▶定義 1 a person who controls or is in charge of a military organization or group 軍の組織や集団を指揮する人, または管理する人→指揮官, 司令官 ▶定義 2 医 an officer at a fairly high level in the navy 海軍のかなり高い地位の武官→海軍中佐

**commanding** /kəmǽndɪŋ; -mάːn-/ 形 ▶定義 1 in charge or having control of sb/sth 〜を管理する, または指揮する→命令する, 支配する, 指揮している‖ *Who is your commanding officer?* あなたの指揮官はだれですか. ▶定義 2 strong or powerful 強い, または力のある→堂々とした, 威厳のある‖ *to speak in a commanding tone of voice* 威圧するような声で話す

**commandment** (または **Commandment**) /kəmάːn(d)mənt; -mǽn(d)-/ 名 ❻正式 ▶定義 one of the ten important laws that Christian people should obey キリスト教徒が従うべき10の重要な戒律の1つ→モーセの十戒の1つ; 神のおきて, 戒律

**commando** /kəmάːndoʊ; -mǽn-/ 名 ❻ (複 **commandos**) ▶定義 one of a group of soldiers who is trained to make sudden attacks in enemy areas 敵陣で急襲を仕掛けるために訓練された兵士の集団→奇襲隊 (員), 特殊部隊, ゲリラ隊 (員)

**commemorate** /kəmémərèɪt/ 動 ⊕ ▶定義 to exist or take place in order to make people remember a special event 人々が特別の出来事を思い出すために存在する, または催される→〜を記念する, 〜の記念となる; 祝する, 記念式を挙行する; (死者) を悼む‖ *a statue commemorating all the soldiers who died in the last war* 先の戦争で亡くなった兵士すべてを記念する像 ― **commemoration** /kəmèməréɪ(ə)n/ 名 ❻ⓤ→記念, 記念式, 記念品, 祝賀‖ *The concerts were held in commemoration of the 200th anniversary of Mozart's death.* モーツァルトの没後200年を記念してコンサートが催された.

**commence** /kəméns/ 動 ⊜ ⊕ 正式 ▶定義 commence sth/doing sth to start or begin 始まる, 始める→ (〜を) 開始する, (〜に) 着手する

―**commencement** 名 ●Ⓤ→開始, 始まり; (大学・高校などの) 卒業式, 学位授与式

**commend** /kəménd/ 動他 正式 ▶定義 to say officially that sb/sth is very good いいと正式に言う→**〜を賞賛する, 褒める** ‖ *Dean was commended for his excellent work.* ディーンはすばらしい作品を賞賛された.

**commendable** /kəméndəb(ə)l/ 形 正式 ▶定義 that people think is good 人々が良いと考える→**立派な, 感心な** ‖ *She acted with commendable honesty and fairness.* 彼女は賞賛に値するほど誠実に公正に行動した.

***comment**[1] /káment/ 名 ●Ⓒ Ⓤ ▶定義 comment (on sth) something that you say or write that gives your opinion or feeling about sth 物事についての意見や感情を伝えるために言ったり書いたりすること→**(〜についての) 論評, 意見, 評言, 批評, 解説, コメント** ‖ *The chancellor was not available for comment.* 大蔵大臣はコメントを控えた. *I heard someone make a rude comment about my clothes.* だれかが私の洋服について失礼な事を言うのが聞こえた. ☛参 **observation, remark**

成句 **no comment** ▶定義 used in reply to a question when you do not want to say anything at all 何も言いたくないときに質問への答えとして用いて→**何も申し上げられません, ノーコメント** ‖ *'Mr President, how do you feel about these latest developments?' 'No comment.'* 「大統領, 最近の状況についてどうお考えですか」「ノーコメント」

**comment**[2] /káment/ 動 自他 ▶定義 comment (on sth) to say what you think or feel about sth 物事について考えている事や感じている事を言う→**(〜を) 論評する, 批評する, 意見として述べる, 解説する** ‖ *Several people commented on how ill David looked.* デーヴィッドの具合がとても悪そうだと数人の人が言っていた.

**commentary** /káment(ə)ri; -tèri/ 名 ( 複 **commentaries**) ▶定義1 ●Ⓤ a spoken description on the radio or television of sth as it is happening ラジオやテレビで起こっている事を口頭で説明すること→**実況解説** ‖ *a sports commentary* スポーツの実況放送 ▶定義2 ●a written explanation or discussion of sth such as a book or play 本や劇などの内容の説明や論を書いたもの →**論評, 批評** ▶定義3 ●something that shows what sth is like 〜がどんな風か示すもの→**典型となるもの, 見本, 実例** ‖ *This drug scandal is a sad commentary on the state of the sport.* この薬物スキャンダルはスポーツ界の現状を示す悲しむべき実例だ.

**commentate** /káməntèit/ 動 自 ▶定義 **commentate (on sth)** to give a spoken description on the radio or television of sth as it is happening ラジオやテレビで起こっている事を口頭で説明する→**(〜について) 実況する, 解説をする**

**commentator** /káməntèitər/ 名 ● ▶定義1 a person who commentates on sth 〜について解説する人→**解説者, 評論者** ‖ *a sports commentator* スポーツの解説者 ▶定義2 a person who gives his/her opinion about sth on the radio, on television or in a newspaper ラジオ, テレビまたは新聞で物事についての自分の意見を述べる人→**(時事) 解説者, 評論家** ‖ *a political commentator* 政治評論家

**commerce** /kámərs/ 名 Ⓤ ▶定義 the business of buying and selling things 物を売買する商売→**商業, 通商, 貿易**

***commercial**[1] /kəmɔ́ːrʃ(ə)l/ 形 ▶定義1 connected with buying and selling goods and services 品物やサービスの販売に関連した→**商業(上)の, 通商(上)の, 貿易の** ‖ *commercial law* 商法 ▶定義2 making or trying to make money 金をもうける, またはもうけようとする→**営利的な, 商業的な, 営利本位の** ‖ *Although it won a lot of awards, the film was not a commercial success.* その映画は多くの賞を受賞したが, 商業的には成功しなかった. ▶定義3 selling sth or sold in large quantities to the public 〜を一般大衆に大量に売る, またはそのように売られる→**商業ベースの, 大量生産の, 市販の** ‖ *commercial airlines* 民間航空 *commercial products* 市販製品 —**commercially** /-ʃ(ə)li/ →**商業的に, 営利目的で, 商業的に見て** ‖ *The factory was closed down because it was no longer commercially viable.* 商業的見地からもはや存続不可能なので, 工場は閉鎖された.

**commercial**[2] /kəmɔ́ːrʃ(ə)l/ 名 Ⓒ ▶定義 an advertisement on television or the radio テレビやラジオの広告→**広告放送, コマーシャル** ‖ *a* *commercial break* (= a space between television programmes when commercials are shown) コマーシャルによる中断 (= コマーシャルが放送されるテレビ番組の間の時間)

**commercialism** /kəmə́ːrʃ(ə)lìzə)m/ ▶定義 the attitude that making money is more important than anything else ほかの事より金をもうけることの方が重要だという姿勢→**商業主義、営利主義、もうけ本位**

**commercialize** (または **-ise**) /kəmə́ːrʃ(ə)làɪz/ ▶定義 to try to make money out of sth, even if it means spoiling it 何かを損なうことになろうとも、それによって金をもうけようとする→**(しばしば悪い意味で) 〜を商業化する、営利化する、商品化する** ∥ *Christmas has become very commercialized over recent years.* 近年クリスマスは非常に商業的になってしまった. ― **commercialization** (または **-isation**) /kəmə̀ːrʃ(ə)ləzéɪʃ(ə)n; -laɪ-/ ▶**商業化(すること)、商品化(すること)、営利目的**

**commiserate** /kəmízərèɪt/ ▶定義 commiserate (with sb) (on/over/for sth) to feel sorry for and show understanding towards sb who is unhappy or in difficulty 不幸な、または困難な状況にある〜に同情して理解を示す→**(〜を) (…について・・・のことで) ふびんに思う、哀れむ; 哀悼の意を示す** ∥ *I commiserated with Debbie over losing her job.* 私は職を失ったデビーに同情した.

**commission**¹ /kəmíʃ(ə)n/ ▶定義 **1** (しばしば **Commission**) [C, 単数または複数形の動詞と共に] an official group of people who are asked to find out about sth ある事柄について調べることを任せられた人の公式の集団→**(調査、管理などを委託された) 委員会、委員会の人たち** ∥ *A Commission was appointed to investigate the causes of the accident.* 事故の原因を調査するための委員(会)が任命された. ▶定義 **2** money that you get for selling sth 〜を売って得る金→**手数料、歩合、コミッション** ∥ *Agents get 10% commission on everything they sell.* 代理店は販売した物すべてについて、10パーセントの手数料を取る. ▶定義 **3** money that a bank, etc charges for providing a particular service 銀行などが特定のサービスに課す料金→**手数料** ▶定義 **4** a formal request to an artist, writer, etc to produce a piece of work 芸術家、作家などへの作品制作の正式の要求→**依頼、注文、委任、委託** ∥ *He received a commission to write a play for the festival.* 彼はそのフェスティバルのために劇を書いてほしいという依頼を受けた.

**commission**² /kəmíʃ(ə)n/ ▶定義 commission sb (to do sth); commission sth (from sb) to ask an artist, writer, etc to do a piece of work 芸術家、作家などに作品を依頼する→**(芸術作品を)注文する、(制作を)依頼する、(〜に)(…を)委託する** ∥ *to commission an architect to design a building* 建築家にビルの設計を依頼する

**commissioner** /kəmíʃ(ə)nər/ ▶定義 the head of the police or of a government department in some countries 一部の国の警察や政府省庁の長→**(税務・警察などの)監督官; 理事、長官、局長**

*****commit** /kəmít/ (**committing; committed**) ▶定義 **1** to do sth bad or illegal 悪い〜や違法な〜をする→**(罪、過失など)を犯す** ∥ *to commit a crime* 犯罪を犯す *to commit suicide* 自殺する ▶定義 **2** commit sb/yourself (to sth/to doing sth) to make a definite agreement or promise to do sth 〜をするというはっきりした同意や約束をする→**〜を引き受ける、約束する** ∥ *I can't commit myself to helping you tomorrow.* 明日お手伝いできると確約はできません. ▶定義 **3** commit yourself (on sth) to make a decision or give an opinion publicly so that it is then difficult to change it あとで変更が難しくなるように決断や意見の公表をする→**自分の考え・立場を明らかにする、明言する** ∥ *I'm not going to commit myself on who will win the election.* だれが選挙に勝つか明言するつもりはない. ☛参 **noncommittal** ▶定義 **4** 正式 to decide to use money or time in a certain way 金や時間をある特定の用途に使うことを決定する→**(人、経費など)を〜のために割くと約束する** ∥ *The government has committed £2 billion to education.* 政府は教育に、20億ポンドを支出することを決定した. ▶定義 **5** 正式 commit sb to sth to send sb to a prison, mental hospital, etc 〜を刑務所、精神病院などへ送る→**〜を(施設など)に引き渡す、送る、収容する**

**commitment** /kəmítmənt/ ▶定義 **1** commitment (to sth) being prepared to give a lot of your time and attention to sth because you believe it is right or important ある事が正しい、または重要だと考えてその事に多くの時間を使い注意を傾ける準備ができていること➡献身, 傾倒, かかわり合い ‖ *I admire Gary's commitment to protecting the environment.* ゲーリーの環境保護への献身には感心する. ▶定義2 ❻❶a promise or agreement to do sth; a responsibility 〜をするという約束や同意; 責任➡(果たすと言った)約束, 責任 ‖ *When I make a commitment I always stick to it.* 私は約束した事は常に守る. *Helen now works fewer hours because of family commitments.* 家族の世話があるので, ヘレンは今は勤務時間が短い.

**committed** /kəmítəd/ 形 ▶定義 committed (to sth) prepared to give a lot of your time and attention to sth because you believe it is right or important ある事が正しい、または重要だと信じてその事に多くの時間を使い注意を傾ける準備ができている➡(〜に)傾倒している, 専心して ‖ *The company is committed to providing quality products.* 会社は良質の製品を提供することに専心している.

★**committee** /kəmíti/ 名 [❻, 単数または複数形の動詞と共に] ▶定義 a group of people who have been chosen to discuss sth or decide sth 〜を議論する, または決定するために選ばれた人々の集団➡委員会, 委員(全員) ‖ *to be/sit on a committee* 委員会の一員である *The planning committee meets/meet twice a week.* 立案委員会は週に2回開かれる.

**commodity** /kəmɑ́dəti/ 名 ❻ ( 複 **commodities**) ▶定義 a product or material that can be bought and sold 売買できる製品や材料➡商品, 生産物 ‖ *Salt was once a very valuable commodity.* 塩はかつては非常に価値のある商品だった.

★**common**¹ /kɑ́mən/ 形 ▶定義1 happening or found often or in many places; usual しばしば, または多くの場所で起こるまたは見つかる; 一般的な➡普通の, ありふれた ‖ *Pilot error is the commonest/most common cause of plane crashes.* パイロットのミスは飛行機事故の最も一般的な原因である. *The daisy is a common wild flower.* ヒナギクはありふれた野の花だ. ▶定義2 common (to sb/sth) shared by or belonging to two or more people or groups; shared by most or all people 複数の人や集団が共有する・に所属する; 大部分の, またはすべての人々が共有する➡共同の, 共通の; 公共の, 公共の ‖ *This type of behaviour is common to most children of that age.* このような振る舞いは, その年齢の多くの子供に一般的だ. *We have a common interest in gardening.* 私たちには園芸という共通の趣味がある. ▶定義3 (名詞の前だけ) not special; ordinary 特別でない; 普通の一般の, 平凡な, 並みの ‖ *The officers had much better living conditions than the common soldiers.* 士官たちは兵士よりずっと良い生活をしていた. ▶定義4 英略式 having or showing a lack of education 教育が不足して, または教育の不足を表して➡通俗な, 品のない ‖ *Don't speak like that. It's common!* そんな話し方をしてはいけません. 下品ですよ. ⇔ 定義1, 3 **uncommon**

成句 be common/public knowledge ⇒ **KNOWLEDGE**

**common**² /kɑ́mən/ 名 ❻ ▶定義 an area of open land that anyone can use だれでも使える出入り自由の土地➡共有地, 公有地

成句 have sth in common (with sb/sth) ▶定義 to share sth with sb/sth else ほかの人や物と何かを共有する➡〜を共通に持つ, 共通点がある ‖ *to have a lot in common with sb* 〜と多くの共通点を持つ

in common with sb/sth 正式 ▶定義 in the same way as sb/sth else; like sb/sth ほかの人や物と同じで; 〜のように➡〜と共通して; 〜と同じように ‖ *This company, in common with many others, is losing a lot of money.* この会社も, 多くの会社と同じように多額の損失を出している.

**common ground** 名 ❶ ▶定義 beliefs, interests, etc that two or more people or groups share 複数の人々や集団が共有する信念, 興味など➡(議論などの)共通点, 一致した見解

**common law** 名 ❶ ▶定義 laws in England that are based on decisions that judges have made, not laws that were made by Parliament 英国の法律で, 議会で制定されるものではなく裁判官の決定に基づくもの➡普通法, 慣習法, コ

**commonly** /kάmənli/ 副 ▶定義 normally; usually 典型的に; 一般に→**一般に, 通常, よく**

**commonplace** /kάmənplèɪs/ 形 ▶定義 not exciting or unusual; ordinary 刺激的でない、または珍しくない; 普通の→**ありふれた, 平凡な** ‖ *Foreign travel has become commonplace in recent years.* 最近では外国旅行は特別な事ではなくなった.

**common room** 名 ⓒ ▶定義 a room in a school, university, etc where students or teachers can go to relax when they are not in class 学校や大学などの, 授業中以外に生徒や教師がくつろぐために行く部屋→**(学校などの) 談話室, 休憩室, 教員控え室**

**the Commons** /kάmənz/ = THE HOUSE OF COMMONS ☞参 Parliament の注

**common sense** 名 ⓤ ▶定義 the ability to make good sensible decisions or to behave in a sensible way 適切な分別のある決定をする, または分別のある振る舞いをする能力→**良識, 常識**

**the Commonwealth** /kάmənwèlθ/ 名 [単数扱い] ▶定義 the group of countries that once formed the British Empire and that work together in a friendly way かつて大英帝国を形成し, 体友好的に協力している国々→**イギリス連邦, 英連邦**

**commotion** /kəmóʊʃ(ə)n/ 名 [単数扱い, ⓤ] ▶定義 great noise or excitement 大きな騒音または興奮→**騒動, 興奮, 喧噪 (けんそう), 騒ぎ立てること**

**communal** /kəmjúːnl, kάmjənl/ 形 ▶定義 shared by a group of people 人々の集団が共有する→**共同の, 共用の** ‖ *a communal kitchen* 共同の台所

**commune** /kάmjuːn/ 名 [ⓒ, 単数または複数形の動詞と共に] ▶定義 a group of people, not from the same family, who live together and share their property and responsibilities 同じ家族ではない人々の集団で, 一緒に住み, 所有物や責任を共有する→**生活共同体, コミューン**

*****communicate** /kəmjúːnəkèɪt/ 動 ▶定義1 ⓘ ⓣ to share and exchange information, ideas or feelings with sb 情報, 考え, または感情などを〜と分かち合い交換する→**(〜を) 伝達する, 通信する; 通じ合う, 理解し合う** ‖ *Parents often have difficulty communicating with their teenage children.* 親は10代の子供となかなか理解し合えないことが多い. *Our boss is good at communicating her ideas to the team.* 私たちの上司は部下に考えを伝えるのがうまい. ▶定義2 ⓣ 正式 (通常は受動態で) to pass a disease from one person or animal to another 1人の人や1匹の動物からほかへ病気を移す→**〜を感染させる, 伝染させる** ▶定義3 ⓘ to lead from one place to another ある場所からほかへつながる→**(別の部屋などと) 通じる, 連絡する** ‖ *two rooms with a communicating door* ドアでつながっている2つの部屋

*****communication** /kəmjùːnəkéɪʃ(ə)n/ 名 ▶定義1 ⓤ the act of sharing or exchanging information, ideas or feelings 情報, 考え, 感情などを分け合う, または交換すること→**通信, 交信, 文通, 伝達, 連絡, 意志疎通** ‖ *Radio is the only means of communication in remote areas.* 遠く離れた地域では無線が唯一の連絡手段だ. *We are in regular communication with our head office in New York.* 私たちはニューヨーク本社と常に連絡を取っている. ▶定義2 **communications** [複数扱い] the methods that are used for travelling to and from a place or for sending messages between places ある場所に [から] 移動する, または複数の場所で伝言をやり取りするために用いる手段→**交通機関・手段, 交通網, 連絡手段, 通信手段; 報道機関** ‖ *The telephone lines are down so communications are very difficult.* 電話線が切れて, 連絡を取るのが非常に難しい. ▶定義3 ⓒ 正式 a message 伝言→**(伝達された) 情報, 通知, ニュース, 通信文** ‖ *a communication from head office* 本社からの通知

**communicative** /kəmjúːnɪkətɪv, -nəkèɪ-/ 形 ▶定義 willing and able to talk and share ideas, etc 考えなどを進んで話し分かち合える→**話し好きな, (情報) 伝達の** ‖ *Paolo has excellent communicative skills.* パオロは人と話すのがとてもうまい.

**communion** /kəmjúːnjən/ 名 ⓤ ▶定義1 正式 the sharing of thoughts or feelings 考えや感情を分かち合うこと→**共有, 交わり** ▶定義2 **Communion** a Christian church ceremony in which people share bread and wine 人々がパン

とワインを分け合うキリスト教の儀式→聖餐(せいさん)(式), 聖体拝領

**communiqué** /kəmjúːnəkèɪ, -́--́/ 名 **C** (文) ▶定義 an official statement, especially from a government, a political group, etc 特に政府, 政治団体などの公式の声明→**公式発表, 声明, 公報, コミュニケ**

**communism** /kάmjənìz(ə)m/ 名 **U** ▶定義 the political system in which the state owns and controls all factories, farms, services etc and aims to treat everyone equally 政治の仕組みで, 国がすべての工場, 農場, 公共事業などを所有して管理し, すべての人を平等に扱うことを目指す→**共産主義(体制)** ←参 Marxism, socialism, capitalism

**communist**(または **Communist**) /kάmjənɪst/ 名 **C** ▶定義 a person who believes in or supports communism; a member of the Communist Party 共産主義を信じる, または支持する人; 共産党の一員→**共産主義者; 共産党員** ―communist(または Communist) 形 →**共産主義(者)の, 共産党の** ‖ communist sympathies 共産党の支持者

\***community** /kəmjúːnəti/ 名 (複 **communities**) ▶定義 **1 the community**[単数扱い] all the people who live in a particular place, area, etc when considered as a group 1つの集団として考えた場合の, 特定の場所や地域などに住むすべての人々→**地域社会, (市町村)自治体, 地域住民; 一般社会** ‖ Recent increases in crime have disturbed the whole community. 最近の犯罪増加によって地域社会全体に不安が広がっている. ▶定義 **2** [**C**, 単数または複数形の動詞と共に] a group of people who have sth in common 共通の～を所有している集団→**共同体, 社会(集団), 団体, ～界** ‖ the Asian community in Britain 英国のアジア人社会 the business community 実業界 ▶定義 **3** **U** the feeling of belonging to a group in the place where you live 自分が住んでいる場所の集団に属しているという意識→**共同体意識, 連帯感, 結び付き** ‖ There is a strong sense of community in the neighbourhood. この近隣の人たちには強い連帯感がある.

**community centre** 名 **C** ▶定義 a building that local people can use for meetings, classes, sports, etc 地域の人々が会議, 講習, スポーツなどに使う建物→**コミュニティーセンター, 市民文化会館**

**commute** /kəmjúːt/ 動 **自** ▶定義 to travel a long distance from home to work every day 毎日家から仕事先まで長距離を通う→**長距離通勤・通学する** ‖ A lot of people commute to London from nearby towns. 多くの人々が近郊の町からロンドンに通勤している. ―commuter 名 **C** →**通勤者, 長距離通勤者**

**compact** /kəmpǽkt, kάmpækt/ 形 ▶定義 small and easy to carry 小さくて持ち運ぶのが簡単な→**小型の** ‖ a compact camera コンパクトカメラ(小型の自動式カメラ)

**compact disc** = CD

**companion** /kəmpǽnjən/ 名 **C** ▶定義 a person or animal with whom you spend a lot of time or go somewhere 長い時間一緒に過ごしたり一緒にどこかへ行く人や動物→**仲間, 友** ‖ a travelling companion 旅の道連れ

**companionship** /kəmpǽnjənʃɪp/ 名 **U** ▶定義 the pleasant feeling of having a friendly relationship with sb and not being alone 人と友好的な関係を保っていて1人ではないという快い感情→**(親密な)交友関係, 仲間付き合い, 交わり**

\***company** /kÁmp(ə)ni/ 名 (複 **companies**) ▶定義 **1** [**C**, 単数または複数形の動詞と共に] a business organization selling goods or services 品物やサービスを売る事業組織→**会社, 商会, ～社** ‖ The company is/are planning to build a new factory. その会社は新しい工場の建設を計画している.

▶会社の名前を書くときは, company は大文字で始まる. 省略形は Co: the Walt Disney Company (ウォルト ディズニー社) Milton & Co (ミルトン商会)

▶定義 **2** [**C**, 単数または複数形の動詞と共に] a group of actors, singers, dancers, etc 俳優, 歌手, ダンサーなどの集団→**一座, 劇団; 一行, 一隊** ‖ a ballet company バレエ団 the Royal Shakespeare Company ロイヤルシェークスピア劇団 ▶定義 **3** **U** being with a person 人と一緒であること→**一緒にいること** ‖ I always enjoy Rachel's company. レイチェルと一緒にいるといつも楽しい. Jeff is very good company (= pleasant to be with). ジェフと付き合うのは楽しい(= 一緒にいるのが楽しい). ▶定義 **4** **U** visitor or visitors 訪問者、または複数の訪問者→客, 来客 ‖ *Sorry, I wouldn't have called if I'd known you had company.* すみません、あなたに来客があると知っていたら電話をかけなかったのですが.

### ▶社会・文化

**会社の役職名**

会社の社長を英語では president と言いますが、くだけた感じで言うときには boss も使われます。また重役は executive, 部長は department chief, 課長は section chief, 係長は unit chief と呼ばれることが多いです.

**成句** keep sb company ▶定義 to go or be with sb so that he/she is not alone だれかが1人にならないようにその人と一緒に行く、またはいる→同行する、付き添う ‖ *She was nervous so I went with her to keep her company.* 彼女が緊張していたので、私は彼女に付き添っているため一緒に行った.

part company ⇒ **PART**²

**comparable** /kámp(ə)rəb(ə)l/ 形 ▶定義 comparable (to/with sb/sth) of a similar standard or size; that can be compared with sth 同じような水準の、または大きさの; ほかの～と比べることができる→(～に)相当する、匹敵する、(～と)同等の、同種の、類似の;(～と)比較できる ‖ *The population of Britain is comparable to that of France.* 英国の人口はフランスと同じくらいだ. *A comparable flat in my country would be a lot cheaper.* 同じようなフラットなら私の国ではずっと安いだろう.

**comparative**¹ /kəmpǽrətɪv/ 形 ▶定義 1 that compares things of the same kind 同種の～を比べる→比較上の、比較による、比較に基づいた ‖ *a comparative study of systems of government* 政府組織の比較研究 ▶定義 2 compared with sth else or with what is usual or normal ほかの～、または普通のものや標準的なものと比べて→ほかと比較しての、相対的な、かなりの ‖ *He had problems with the written exam but passed the practical exam with comparative ease.* 彼は筆記試験では問題があったが、実技試験は比較的たやすく合格した. ▶定義 3（文法）(used about the form of an adjective or adverb) expressing a greater amount, quality, size, etc

### compare 323

（形容詞や副詞の形について）より多くの量、高い質、大きいサイズなどを表現する→比較級の ‖ *'Hotter' and 'more quickly' are the comparative forms of 'hot' and 'quickly'.* hotter と more quickly は hot と quickly の比較級である.

**comparative**² /kəmpǽrətɪv/ 名 ⓒ（文法）▶定義 the form of an adjective or adverb that expresses a greater amount, quality, size, etc より多くの量、高い質、大きいサイズなどを表す形容詞または副詞の形→比較級 ‖ *'Bigger' is the comparative of 'big'.* bigger は big の比較級である.

**comparatively** /kəmpǽrətɪvli/ 副 ▶定義 when compared with sth else or with what is usual; fairly ほかのもの、または普通のものと比較した場合に; かなり→比較的、いくぶん ‖ *The disease is comparatively rare nowadays.* その病気は現在では比較的まれだ.

*****compare** /kəmpéər/ 動 ▶定義 1 ⓣ compare A and B; compare A with/to B to consider people or things in order to see how similar or how different they are 人々や物について考慮して、どの程度似ているか、または異なっているかを見る→～を比較する、対照する ‖ *I'm quite a patient person, compared with him.* 私は彼と比べればとても忍耐強い. *Compared to the place where I grew up, this town is exciting.* 私が育った場所と比べると、この町は刺激的だ. *When the police compared the two letters, they realized that they had been written by the same person.* 警察は2通の手紙を比較して、同一人物が書いたものであることを見抜いた. ▶定義 2 ⓣ compare A to B to say that sb/sth is similar to sb/sth else ～がほかの…と似ていると言う→～を…に例える ‖ *When it was built, people compared the stadium to a spaceship.* スタジアムが建設された時、人々は宇宙船に例えた.

▶定義 3 ⓘ compare (with/to sb/sth) to be as good as sb/sth ～と同じくらい良い→～と肩を並べる、～に匹敵する、比べられる ‖ *Her last film was brilliant but this one simply doesn't compare.* 彼女のこの前の映画はすばらしかったが、今回のものは比較にもならない. *There is nothing to compare with the taste of bread fresh from the oven.* オーブンから出した焼き立ての

パンの味に勝るものは何もない.

**成句 compare notes (with sb)** ▶定義 to discuss your opinions, ideas, experiences, etc with sb else 意見, 考え, 経験などをほかの〜と議論する→意見・情報を交換する, 感想を述べ合う ‖ *At the beginning of term we met and compared notes about the holidays.* 学期の初めに私たちは会って休暇の感想を述べ合った.

*★**comparison** /kəmpǽrəs(ə)n/ 名 **C U** ▶定義 an act of comparing; a statement in which people or things are compared 比較すること; 人々や物を比較して述べること→比較, 対象, 比べること ‖ *Put the new one and the old one side by side, **for comparison**.* 新しい物と古い物を並べて, 比較しなさい. *It's hard to **make comparisons** between two athletes from different sports.* 異なるスポーツの選手を比較することは難しい.

**成句 by/in comparison (with sb/sth)** ▶定義 when compared 比較して→比べて, 比べると ‖ *In comparison with many other people, they're quite well off.* ほかの多くの人と比べると彼らはかなり裕福だ.

**compartment** /kəmpɑ́ːrtmənt/ 名 **C** ▶定義 **1** one of the separate sections into which some larger parts of a train (**carriages**) are divided 列車の広い部分 (客車) を仕切って独立させた室の1つ→仕切り客室, コンパートメント ‖ *a first-class compartment* 1等客室 ▶定義 **2** one of the separate sections into which certain containers are divided ある種の容器の分割された独立した部分の1つ→区画, 仕切り, 仕切った部分 ‖ *The drugs were discovered in a secret compartment in his suitcase.* 彼のスーツケースの隠れた仕切りから麻薬が発見された.

*★**compass** /kʌ́mpəs/ 名 **C** ▶定義 **1** an instrument for finding direction, with a needle that always points north 常に北を指す針の付いた, 方向を知るための道具→コンパス, 方位磁石, 羅針盤 ‖ *They had to find their way back to the camp using a map and a compass.* 彼らは地図とコンパスを使ってキャンプへ戻らなければならなかった. ▶定義 **2 compasses** [複数扱い] a V-shaped instrument that is used for drawing circles 円を書くために用いるV字形の道具→(製図用) コンパス, 両脚規 ‖ *a pair of compasses* コンパス一組

**compassion** /kəmpǽʃ(ə)n/ 名 **U** ▶定義 **compassion (for sb)** understanding or pity for sb who is suffering 苦しんでいる人に対する理解または哀れみ→(〜への) 哀れみ, 同情, 思いやり ‖ *to have/feel/show compassion* 同情する — **compassionate** /-ʃ(ə)nət, -eɪt/ 形→哀れみ深い, 思いやりのある

**compatible** /kəmpǽtəb(ə)l/ ▶定義 **compatible (with sb/sth)** suitable to be used together, or to live or exist together 一緒に使うのに適した, または一緒に住んだり存在するのに適した→両用の, 両立できる, 互換性がある, 共存できる ‖ *These two computer systems are not compatible.* これら2つのコンピューターシステムには互換性がない. *Lee's diet is not compatible with his active lifestyle.* リーの食餌 (しょくじ) 療法は彼の行動的な生活様式とは合わない. ⇨ **incompatible** — **compatibility** /kəmpæ̀təbíləti/ 名 **U**→適性, 両立性, 互換性

**compatriot** /kəmpǽtriət, -péɪt-/ 名 **C** ▶定義 a person who comes from the same country as you 自分と同じ国の出身者→同国人, 同胞

**compel** /kəmpél/ 動 **他** (**compelling**; **compelled**) 正式 ▶定義 **compel sb to do sth** to force sb to do sth 〜に強制して何かをさせる→〜に無理やり…させる, 〜を…するように強いる, 〜を強要する ‖ *I felt compelled to tell her what I really thought of her.* 私が彼女のことを本当にどう思っているか, 彼女に言わざるを得ないと感じた.

**compelling** /kəmpélɪŋ/ 形 ▶定義 that forces or persuades you to do or to believe sth 何かをするように, または信じるように強制したり説得する→説得力のある, 信じざるを得ないような ‖ *compelling evidence* 信じざるを得ない証拠 ☛ 名 **compulsion**

**compensate** /kɑ́mpənsèɪt/ 動 ▶定義 **1 自 compensate (for sth)** to remove or reduce the bad effect of sth 何かの悪い影響を取り除く, または減らす→(〜を) 相殺する, (損失を) 埋め合わせる, 償う, 補う ‖ *His willingness to work hard compensates for his lack of skill.* 進んで努力する彼の姿勢が技能の不足を補っている. ▶定義 **2 自 他 compensate (sb) (for sth)** to pay sb money because you have injured him/her or lost or damaged his/her property 〜にけがを負わせ

る，あるいは〜の所有物をなくすまたは損なうことをしたために…に金を払う→(〜を)償う，(〜に)(…の)補償をする，賠償する ‖ *The airline sent me a cheque to compensate for losing my luggage.* 航空会社が手荷物を紛失した補償として小切手を送ってきた．

**compensation** /kàmpənséɪʃ(ə)n/ 名 ▶定義1 U compensation (for sth) money that you pay to sb because you have injured him/her or lost or damaged his/her property 〜にけがを負わせる，あるいは〜の所有物をなくすまたは損なうことをしたために人に払う金→補償金，賠償金 ‖ *I got £5000 (in) compensation for my injuries.* 私はけがの補償金として5000ポンドを受け取った．▶定義2 C U a fact or action that removes or reduces the bad effect of sth 〜の悪い影響を取り除く，または減らす事実または行動→償い，代償，埋め合わせ(をすること) ‖ *City life can be very tiring but there are compensations (= good things about it).* 都市生活はとても疲れることもあるが，それを埋め合わせるものもある(= 良い事もある)．

**compère** /kámpeər/ 名 C 英 ▶定義 a person who entertains the audience and introduces the different performers in a show ショーで観客を楽しませ，異なる演技者を紹介する人→(テレビ，舞台，ショーなどの)司会者 ― compère 動 他 →(テレビ，舞台，ショーなど)の司会をする ‖ *Who compèred the show?* そのショーの司会者はだれでしたか．

*__compete__ /kəmpíːt/ 動 自 ▶定義 compete (in sth) (against/with sb) (for sth) to try to win or achieve sth, or to try to be better than sb else 〜を勝ち取ろうとするまたは達成しようとする，あるいはほかの人よりうまくやろうとする→(〜で)(…と)(〜をかけて)競争する，(競技などに)参加する ‖ *The world's best athletes compete in the Olympic Games.* オリンピックには世界最高のスポーツ選手が参加する．*We'll be competing against seven other teams for the trophy.* 私たちはトロフィーを目指して7チームと競い合う．*As children, they always used to compete with each other.* 子供のころ，彼らはいつも張り合っていた．*Supermarkets have such low prices that small shops just can't compete.* スーパーマーケットの価格はとても安いので，小さな商店はとてもかなわない．

**competence** /kámpət(ə)ns/ 名 U ▶定義 the fact of having the ability or skill that is needed for sth 〜に必要な能力や技能を持っていること→能力，適性，(〜する)力 ‖ *She quickly proved her competence in her new position.* 彼女には新しい職にふさわしい能力があることがすぐに分かった．⇔ **incompetence**

**competent** /kámpət(ə)nt/ 形 ▶定義1 having the ability or skill needed for sth 〜に必要な能力や技能がある→有能な，能力がある，適任の ‖ *a highly competent player* 非常に力のある選手 *She is competent at her job.* 彼女は仕事が良くできます．⇔ **incompetent** ▶定義2 good enough, but not excellent 十分に良いが，優秀ではない→十分な，まずまずの，要求にかなう ‖ *The singer gave a competent, but not particularly exciting, performance.* その歌手の公演はまずまずだったが，特にすばらしいとは言えなかった．
―**competently** 副 →有能に，立派に，十分に

*__competition__ /kàmpətíʃ(ə)n/ 名 ▶定義1 C an organized event in which people try to win sth 人々が何かを勝ち取ろうとする組織された催し→競技会，試合，コンテスト，コンクール ‖ *to go in for/enter a competition* 競技会に参加する *They hold a competition every year to find the best young artist.* 最も優れた若い芸術家を選ぶために毎年コンテストが行われる．*He came second in an international piano competition.* 彼は国際ピアノコンクールで2位になった．

▶定義2 U a situation where two or more people or organizations are trying to achieve, obtain, etc the same thing or to be better than sb else 複数の人々や組織が，同じ物事を達成したり同じ物を入手しようとする，またはほかの人よりうまくやろうとしている状況→競争(すること)，競り合い，張り合い ‖ *He is in competition with three other people for promotion.* 彼は昇進をめぐって3人と張り合っている．*There was fierce competition among the players for places in the team.* チーム内でのポジションをめぐって選手同士の激しい競争があった．

▶定義3 **the competition** [単数扱い，単数または複数形の動詞と共に] the other people, companies, etc who are trying to achieve the same as you 自分と同じ事を達成しようとしているほ

かの人々，会社など→**競争相手，競争者，競合する企業** ‖ *If we are going to succeed, we must offer a better product than the competition.* 成功しようと思ったら，競合する他社よりも良い製品を提供しなければならない．

**competitive** /kəmpétətɪv/ 形 ▶定義1 involving people or organizations competing against each other 互いに競い合う人々や組織に関連した→**競争の，競争による，競争的な** ‖ *The travel industry is a highly competitive business.* 旅行業はとても競争が激しい仕事だ．*competitive sports* 競技 ▶定義2 able to be as successful as or more successful than others ほかと同じ程度に，またはほかよりもうまくいく→**競争できる，競争力のある，匹敵する** ‖ *They are trying to make the company competitive in the international market.* 彼らは国際市場で競争力のある企業を目指している．*Our prices are highly competitive (= as low as or lower than those of the others).* 我が社の価格は非常に競争力がある（＝他社の価格と同じくらい安い，または他社より安い）．▶定義3 (used about people) wanting very much to win or to be more successful than others (人々について) 非常に強く勝ちたいと思う，またはほかより成功したいと思う→**負けず嫌いの，競争心の強い** ‖ *She's a very competitive player.* 彼女はとても負けず嫌いの選手だ．— competitively 副 →**競争して，匹敵して，競争好きで** ‖ *Their products are competitively priced.* その製品は競争力のある価格だ．— competitiveness 名 ⓤ→**競争的なこと，競合心，競争力**

**competitor** /kəmpétətər/ 名 ⓒ ▶定義 a person or organization that is competing against others 互いに競争している人や組織→**競争相手，競争者，競技の参加者** ‖ *There are ten competitors in the first race.* 第1レースには10人の参加者がいる．*Two local companies are our main competitors.* 現地の2つの会社が我が社の主な競争相手である．

**compilation** /kɑ̀mpəléɪʃ(ə)n/ 名 ▶定義1 ⓒ a collection of pieces of music, writing, film, etc that are taken from different places and put together 異なる所から音楽，著作，映画などを集めて一緒にしたもの→**編集物，編纂（へんさん）物** ‖ *A compilation CD of the band's greatest hits* バンドのベストヒット曲を集めて編集したCD ▶定義2 ⓤ the act of compiling sth 〜を編集することを→**編集，編纂**

**compile** /kəmpáɪl/ 動 他 ▶定義 to collect information and arrange it in a list, book, etc 情報を集めて目録や本などに編成する→**〜を編集する，編纂（へんさん）する，(編集のために) 集める** ‖ *to compile a dictionary/a report/a list* 辞書・報告書・目録を編集する

**complacent** /kəmpléɪs(ə)nt/ 形 ▶定義 feeling too satisfied with yourself or with a situation, so that you think that there is no need to worry 自分自身や状況に過度に満足して，何も心配する必要がないと感じること→**自己満足した** ‖ *He had won his matches so easily that he was in danger of becoming complacent.* 彼はやすやすと試合に勝ったので，自己満足に陥るおそれがあった．— complacency /kəmpléɪs(ə)nsi/ 名 ⓤ→**自己満足**— complacently 副 →**自己満足して**

\***complain** /kəmpléɪn/ 動 自 ▶定義1 complain (to sb) (about sth/that...) to say that you are not satisfied with or happy about sth 〜について満足していない，または喜んでいないと言う→**(〜に) (…について・…だと) 不平を言う，愚痴をこぼす，文句を言う** ‖ *People are always complaining about the weather.* 人々はいつも天気について愚痴をこぼしている．*We complained to the hotel manager that the room was too noisy.* 私たちはその部屋の騒音がかなりひどいとホテルの支配人に文句を言った．☛参 **grumble, protest** の注 ▶定義2 正式 complain of sth to say that you have a pain or illness 痛みがある，または病気だと言う→**(病苦を) 訴える，〜が痛いと言う** ‖ *He went to the doctor, complaining of chest pains.* 彼は胸が痛いと言って医者に行った．

\***complaint** /kəmpléɪnt/ 名 complaint (about sth); complaint (that...) ▶定義1 ⓒ a statement that you are not satisfied with sth 〜について満足していないと言うこと→**不平，不満，愚痴，苦情** ‖ *You should make a complaint to the company that made the machine.* その機械を製造した会社に苦情を言うべきだ．▶定義2 ⓤ the act of complaining 不平を言うこと→**不満を言うこと，愚痴を言うこと，苦情を訴えること** ‖ *I wrote a letter of complaint to the manager about the*

*terrible service I had received.* ひどいサービスについて私は支配人に苦情を訴える手紙を書いた. *Jim's behaviour never gave the teachers **cause for complaint**.* ジムの振る舞いは教師たちから見て文句の付けようがないものだった.
▶定義3 an illness or disease 不健康や疾患→病気,体の不調‖*a heart complaint* 心臓疾患

**complement**¹ /kámpləmənt/ 名 ▶定義1 a thing that goes together well with sth else ほかの~とよく合うもの→ぴったり合うもの‖*A cream sauce is the perfect complement to this dessert.* このデザートにはクリームソースがぴったりです. ▶定義2 the total number that makes a group complete ある集まりを完全なものにする合計数→(必要な)全数,全量;定員‖*Without a full complement of players, the team will not be able to take part in the match.* 必要な人数の選手がそろわなければ,チームは試合に参加できない. ▶定義3 (文法) a word or words, especially a noun or adjective, used after a verb such as 'be' or 'become' and describing the subject of that verb be や become のような動詞の後に用いる1つまたは複数の語,特に名詞や形容詞で,その動詞の主語を説明する→補語‖*In 'He's friendly' and 'He's a fool', 'friendly' and 'fool' are complements.* He's friendly と He's a fool では, friendly と fool が補語です.

**complement**² /kámpləmənt/ 動 ▶定義 to go together well with~→~とよく合う‖*The colours of the furniture and the carpet complement each other.* 家具とじゅうたんの色がよく合っている.

**complementary** /kàmpləmént(ə)ri/ 形 ▶定義 going together well with sb/sth; adding sth which the other person or thing does not have ~とよく合う;一方の人や物にない~を補う→(互いに)補い合う,相補的な,ぴったり合う‖*They work well together because their skills are complementary: he's practical and she's creative.* 技能を互いに補い合えるので,彼らは一緒にうまく働いている.彼は実際的で,彼女は創造的だ.

*★**complete**¹ /kəmplíːt/ 形 ▶定義1 having or including all parts; with nothing missing すべての部分を持っている,または含んでいる;欠けているものがない→全部の,完ぺきな,完全な‖*I gave a complete list of the stolen items to the police.* 私は盗まれた物すべてのリストを警察に提出した. *The book explains the complete history of the place.* その本にはその地域のすべての歴史が書かれている. ▶定義2 (名詞の前は不可) finished or ended 完了した,または終わった→完成して,出来上がって,まとまっていて‖*The repair work should be complete by Friday.* 修理は金曜日までに終えなければならない. ⇔定義1,2 **incomplete** ▶定義3 **complete (with sth)** including sth extra, in addition to what is expected 当然あるものに加えて,追加の~を含んでいる→(~が)完備した,~付きの‖*The computer **comes complete** with instruction manual and printer.* そのコンピューターには入門マニュアルとプリンターが付いている.
▶定義4 (名詞の前だけ) as great as possible; total; in every way 可能な限りたくさんの;全くの;あらゆる点で→徹底した,完全な,全面的な‖*It was a complete waste of time.* 完全に時間の無駄だった. *The room is a complete mess.* 部屋は完全にめちゃくちゃだ. —**completeness** 名 ∪→完全,完全であること

*★**complete**² /kəmplíːt/ 動 ▶定義1 to make sth whole ~を完全にする→~を完全なものにする,(数,量)を満たす,全部そろえる‖*We need two more players to complete the team.* チームのメンバーをそろえるには選手があと2人必要だ.
▶定義2 to finish sth; to bring sth to an end ~を仕上げる;~を終わらせる→~を完成させる‖*When the building has been completed, it will look impressive.* その建物が完成すれば,印象的なものになるだろう. *He completed his teacher training course in June 1997.* 彼は1997年6月に教職課程を修了した. ▶定義3 to write all the necessary information on sth (for example a form) ~(例えば書式)に必要な情報をすべて書く→(申し込み用紙など)に記入する,書き込む‖*Please complete the following in capital letters.* 以下に大文字で記入してください.

**completely** /kəmplíːtli/ 副 ▶定義 in every way; fully; totally すべての点で;十分に;全く→完全に,完ぺきに,徹底的に,すっかり‖*The building was completely destroyed by fire.* その建物は火災で完全に焼失した.

**completion** /kəmplíːʃ(ə)n/ 名 ∪ 正式 ▶定義 the

act of finishing sth or the state of being finished 〜を完了すること，または完了した状態→**完成, 完了** ‖ *You will be paid on completion of the work.* 仕事が終わり次第，賃金が支払われます. *The new motorway is due for completion within two years.* 新しい高速道路は2年以内に完成することになっている.

★**complex**[1] /kɑmpléks, kəm-/ 形 ▶定義 made up of several connected parts and often difficult to understand; complicated いくつかの関連した部分から成り立ち，しばしば分かりづらい；複雑な→**複合の，込み入った，入り組んだ** ‖ *a complex problem/subject* 複雑な問題・主題

**complex**[2] /kɑmpléks/ 名 C ▶定義1 a group of connected things, especially buildings 関連した物，特に建物の集まり→**総合ビル, 総合施設; 複合体** ‖ *a shopping/sports complex* ショッピング・スポーツ総合施設 ▶定義2 a complex (about sth) a mental problem that makes sb worry a lot about sth 〜が何かについて大いに悩む原因となる精神上の問題→**コンプレックス；(あることについての)固定観念，強迫観念** ‖ *He's got a complex about his height.* 彼は身長に関してコンプレックスを抱いている. *an inferiority complex* 劣等感

**complexion** /kəmplékʃ(ə)n/ 名 C ▶定義1 the natural colour and quality of the skin on your face 自然な顔の肌の色と質→**肌の色，顔色，血色** ‖ *a dark/fair complexion* 色黒の・色白の肌 *a healthy complexion* 健康そうな顔色 ▶定義2 [通常は単数] the general nature or character of sth 〜の全般的な性質や特徴→**外観，様子** ‖ *These announcements put a different complexion on our situation.* この発表によって私たちの状況は異なった様相を呈する.

**complexity** /kəmpléksəti/ 名 (複 **complexities**) ▶定義1 ❶ the state of being complex and difficult to understand 複雑で理解するのが難しい状態→**複雑さ，複雑で難解なこと** ‖ *an issue of great complexity* 非常に複雑な問題 ▶定義2 ❷ one of the many details that make sth complicated 〜を複雑にしている多くの項目の1つ→**複雑なもの，入り組んだもの** ‖ *I haven't time to explain the complexities of the situation now.* 今は複雑な状況を1つ1つ説明している時間はありません.

**compliant** /kəmplái(ə)nt/ 形 正式 ▶定義 compliant (with sth) working or done in agreement with particular rules, orders, etc 特定の規則，命令などに従って働く，または行われる→**(〜に)従った，準拠した** ‖ *All new products must be compliant with EU specifications.* 新しい製品はすべてEUの仕様に準拠していなければならない. — **compliance** 名 U ➡ 従うこと，準拠 ‖ *A hard hat must be worn at all times in compliance with safety regulations.* 安全規則に従って常にヘルメットを着用しなければならない.

★**complicate** /kɑ́mpləkèit/ 動 他 ▶定義 to make sth difficult to understand or deal with 〜を理解するまたは対処することを難しくする→**〜を複雑にする，分かりにくくする** ‖ *Let's not complicate things by adding too many details.* あまり細かい事まで考えて物事をややこしくするのはやめましょう. — **complicated** 形 →**複雑な，込み入った，分かりにくい** ‖ *a novel with a very complicated plot* とても込み入った筋の小説

**complication** /kɑ̀mpləkéiʃ(ə)n/ 名 C ▶定義1 something that makes a situation hard to understand or to deal with 状況を分かりにくくするまたは対処しづらくするもの→**複雑な事柄; 複雑化, 混乱** ‖ *Unless there are any unexpected complications, I'll be arriving next month.* 予測不能の問題が起こらない限り，私は来月には着きます. ▶定義2 a new illness that you get when you are already ill 既に病気のときにかかる新たな病気→**合併症, 余病, 併発(症)** ‖ *Unless he develops complications, he'll be out of hospital in a week.* 合併症が出ない限り，1週間で退院できるでしょう.

**complicity** /kəmplísəti/ 名 U 正式 ▶定義 the fact of being involved with sb else in a crime ほかの〜と一緒に犯罪にかかわること→**共謀, 共犯**

**compliment**[1] /kɑ́mpləmənt/ 名 ▶定義1 C a compliment (on sth) a statement or action that shows admiration for sb 〜に対する賞賛を示す言葉や行為→**賛辞, 褒め言葉** ‖ *People often pay her compliments on her piano playing.* 彼女はよくピアノの演奏を褒められる. ▶定義2 **compliments** [複数扱い] 正式 used to say that you like sth or to thank sb for sth 〜を好きだと言うとき，または〜に対して…に感謝するときに用いて→**(表敬の)言葉** ‖ *Tea and* *coffee are provided with the compliments of the hotel management (= without charge).* ホテル側のサービスでお茶とコーヒーが出された (= 無料で).

**compliment**² /kάmpləmènt/ 動 ◐ ▶定義 compliment sb (on sth) to say that you think sb/sth is very good ～を非常に良いと思っていると言う→～を(…について)褒める, 賞賛する, 敬意を表する ‖ *She complimented them on their smart appearance.* 彼女は彼らの洗練された格好を賞賛した.

**complimentary** /kὰmpləmént(ə)ri/ 形 ▶定義 1 showing that you think sb/sth is very good ～を非常に良いと思っていると示す→賞賛の, 敬意を表する ‖ *He made several complimentary remarks about her work.* 彼は彼女の仕事について二言三言賞賛の言葉を述べた. ▶定義 2 given free of charge 無料で与えられる→招待の, 優待の, 無料の ‖ *a complimentary theatre ticket* 劇場の優待券

**comply** /kəmplάɪ/ 動 ◐ (現分 **complying**; 三単現 **complies**; 過, 過分 **complied**) 正式 ▶定義 comply (with sth) to obey an order or request 命令や要求に従う→(～に)応じる, 準拠する, よりどころとする ‖ *All office buildings must comply with the fire and safety regulations.* オフィスビルはすべて防火規則と安全規則に従わなければならない.

**component** /kəmpóʊnənt, kámpòʊ-/ 名 ● ▶定義 one of several parts of which sth is made ～が構成されているいくつかの部分の1つ→構成要素, 成分, 部品, (ステレオなどの)コンポ ‖ *The human eye has two main components.* 人間の目は2つの主要な部分から成り立っている. *the components of a machine/system* 機械の部品・システムの構成要素 ― component 形 →構成している, 構成要素を成す, 成分の ‖ *the component parts of an engine* エンジンを構成している部品

**compose** /kəmpóʊz/ 動 ▶定義 1 ◐ to be the parts that together form sth 合わせて～を形成する部分となる→～を構成する, 組み立てる ‖ *the parties that compose the coalition government* 連立政府を構成する政党 ▶定義 2 ⊜ ◐ to write music 音楽を作る→(～を)作曲する ‖ *Mozart composed forty-one symphonies.* モーツァルトは41の交響曲を作曲した. ▶定義 3 ◐ to produce a piece of writing, using careful thought 注意深く考えながら文章を書く→(詩, 文など)を作る, 創作する ‖ *I sat down and composed a letter of reply.* 私は座って返事の手紙を書いた. ▶定義 4 ◐ to make yourself, your feelings, etc become calm and under control 自分自身や自分の感情などを落ち着かせて抑制する→気を静める, (気持ちなど)を整理する, (表情など)を和らげる ‖ *The news came as such a shock that it took me a while to **compose myself**.* そのニュースはあまりに衝撃的だったので, 私は気を落ち着かせるのにしばらく時間がかかった.

**composed** /kəmpóʊzd/ 形 ▶定義 1 composed of sth made or formed from several different parts, people, etc いくつかの異なる部分, 人々などから作られるまたは形成される→～から成る, 構成されて ‖ *The committee is composed of politicians from all parties.* 委員会はすべての政党の政治家から構成されている. ▶定義 2 calm, in control of your feelings 冷静で, 感情を抑制している→落ち着いた, 沈着な ‖ *Although he felt very nervous, he managed to appear composed.* 彼は非常に神経質になっていたが, 何とか表面的には冷静さを保った.

**composer** /kəmpóʊzər/ 名 ● ▶定義 a person who writes music 音楽を作る人→作曲家, 作曲者

**composite** /kəmpάzət, kəm-/ 形 ▶定義 consisting of different parts or materials 異なる部分や材料から成る→混成の, 合成の, 混合の ― composite 名 ● →合成物, 混合物

**composition** /kὰmpəzíʃ(ə)n/ 名 ▶定義 1 ❶ the parts that form sth; the way in which the parts of sth are arranged ～を形成する部分; ～の部分の配列のされ方→構成(すること), 組み立てる(こと); 構成物, 合成物, 混合物; 配置, 構成, 組成 ‖ *the chemical composition of a substance* ある物質の化学組成 *the composition of the population* 人口構成 ▶定義 2 ❷ a piece of music that has been written by sb ～が書いた一編の音楽→(一編の)楽曲, 曲 ‖ *Chopin's best-known compositions* ショパンの有名な曲 ▶定義 3 ❶ the act or skill of writing a piece of music or text 音楽や文章を書くこと, またはその技能→作曲, 作文, 作詩; 創作(すること) ‖ *She studied both musical* *theory and composition.* 彼女は音楽理論と作曲の両方を学んだ．▶定義4 ❸a short piece of writing done at school, in an exam, etc 授業や試験などで書く短い作品→**作文, 小論文, (学科としての)作文法** ‖ *Write a composition of about 300 words on one of the following subjects.* 次のうち1つの主題について300語程度の作文を書きなさい．

**compost** /kámpɔ̀st; -pòʊst/ 名 Ⓤ ▶定義 a mixture of dead plants, old food, etc that is added to soil to help plants grow 枯れた植物や古い食物などの混合物で，土壌に加えて植物の生育を助ける→**堆肥(たいひ), コンポスト**

**composure** /kəmpóʊʒər/ 名 Ⓤ ▶定義 the state of being calm and having your feelings under control 冷静で感情を抑制していること→**平静, 落ち着き, 落ち着いていること** ‖ *The goalkeeper couldn't regain his composure after his mistake.* ミスをした後，そのゴールキーパーは冷静さを取り戻せなかった．

**compound**¹ /kámpaʊnd/ 名 Ⓒ ▶定義1 something that consists of two or more things or substances combined together 互いに結合し合った，2つまたは複数の物や物質から成るもの→**合成物, 混合物; 化合物** ‖ *a chemical compound* 化合物 ▶定義2 (文法) a word or phrase consisting of two or more parts that combine to make a single meaning 1つの意味を作るために結合された，2つまたは複数の部分から成る語や句→**複合語, 合成語** ‖ *'Car park' and 'bad-tempered' are compounds.* car park と bad-tempered は複合語である．▶定義3 an area of land with a group of buildings on it, surrounded by a wall or fence 建物が集まって建つ土地の1つの区域で，壁や塀で囲まれた場所→**(壁, 塀などで囲まれた)構内, 敷地内**

**compound**² /kəmpáʊnd, kámpaʊnd/ 動 他 ▶定義 to make sth such as a problem worse 問題などをより悪化させる→**(困難など)をひどくする, (問題など)を大きくする**

**comprehend** /kàmprɪhénd/ 動 他 正式 ▶定義 to understand sth completely ~を完全に理解する→**~を(十分に)理解する, 把握する** ‖ *She's too young to comprehend what has happened.* 彼女はあまりに幼かったので起こったことを完全には理解できなかった．

**comprehensible** /kàmprɪhénsəb(ə)l/ 形 ▶定義 easy to understand 理解しやすい→**理解できる, 分かりやすい** ‖ *The book is written in clear, comprehensible language.* その本ははっきりとした分かりやすい言葉で書かれている．⇔ **incomprehensible**

**comprehension** /kàmprɪhénʃ(ə)n/ 名 ▶定義1 Ⓤ 正式 the ability to understand 理解する能力→**理解力; 理解** ‖ *The horror of war is beyond comprehension.* 戦争の恐怖は理解を絶する．⇔ **incomprehension** ▶定義2 ⒸⓊ an exercise that tests how well you understand spoken or written language 話し言葉や書き言葉の理解力を試す練習→**(言語能力の)試験, 練習** ‖ *a listening comprehension* 聞き取りテスト

**comprehensive**¹ /kàmprɪhénsɪv/ 形 ▶定義1 including everything or nearly everything that is connected with a particular subject 特定の主題に関連する，すべてまたはほとんどすべてを含んでいる→**包括的な, 総合的な, 幅広い, 広範囲の** ‖ *a guide book giving comprehensive information on the area* その地域についての幅広い情報を載せたガイドブック ▶定義2 囡(used about education) educating children of all levels of ability in the same school (教育について)同じ学校であらゆるレベルの能力の子供を教育する→**総合教育の, 総合の** ‖ *a comprehensive education system* 総合教育システム

**comprehensive**² /kàmprɪhénsɪv/ (または **comprehensive school**) 名 Ⓒ 囡 ▶定義 a secondary school in which children of all levels of ability are educated あらゆる能力レベルの子供が教育を受ける中等学校→**総合中等学校** ‖ *I went to the local comprehensive.* 私は地元の総合中等学校に通った．

**comprehensively** /kàmprɪhénsɪvli/ 副 ▶定義 completely; thoroughly 完全に; 徹底的に→**包括的に, 総合的に, 広範囲に**

**compress** /kəmprés/ 動 他 ▶定義 compress sth (into sth) to make sth fill less space than usual 通常より少ない空間を~が占めるようにさせる→**~を(…に)圧縮する, 押し縮める, 押し詰めて小さくする** ‖ *Divers breathe compressed air from tanks.* ダイバーたちはタンクの圧縮空気を吸う．*He found it hard to compress his ideas into a single page.* 彼は自分の考えを1ペ

ージに要約しようとしたが難しかった. ― compression /kəmpréʃ(ə)n/ 名 **①**→圧縮, 押し縮めること

**comprise** /kəmpráɪz/ 動 他 ▶定義1 to consist of; to have as parts or members 〜から成る; 部分や構成員として持つ→〜を含む, から成り立つ ‖ *a house comprising three bedrooms, kitchen, bathroom and a living room* 寝室3つ, 台所, 浴室, 居間から成る家 ▶定義2 to form or be part of sth 〜を形成する, またはその一部となる→(部分として)〜を含む, (部分から全体)を構成する, 〜を占める ‖ *Women comprise 62% of the staff.* 女性はスタッフの62パーセントを占めている.

**compromise**¹ /kámprəmàɪz/ 名 **① ①** ▶定義 a compromise (between/on sth) an agreement that is reached when each person gets part, but not all, of what he/she wanted それぞれの人が望む物のすべてではなく一部を得るときに達成される合意→妥協, 歩み寄り, 折衷(案) ‖ *to reach a compromise* 妥協する *Both sides will have to be prepared to **make compromises**.* 両者が妥協案で折り合うことを考えなければならないだろう.

**compromise**² /kámprəmàɪz/ 動 ▶定義1 **自** compromise (with sb) (on sth) to accept less than you want or are aiming for, especially in order to reach an agreement 特に合意に達するために, 望むまたは目指している物事より低い程度を受け入れる→(〜と)(…について)妥協する, 歩み寄る, 折り合う ‖ *Unless both sides are prepared to compromise, there will be no peace agreement.* 両者に妥協の意志がなければ, 和平交渉は成立しないだろう. *The company never compromises on the quality of its products.* 会社は製品の品質に関しては決して妥協しない. ▶定義2 **他** compromise sb/sth/yourself to put sb/sth/yourself in a bad or dangerous position, especially by doing sth that is not very sensible 特にあまり分別があるとは言えない〜をすることによって, …または自分自身を悪い立場や危険な立場に置く→(名誉, 信用など)を危うくする, 傷付ける, 損なう, 〜の評判を落とす ‖ *He compromised himself by accepting money from them.* 彼らから金を受け取ったことで, 彼は自分の信用を損なった.

**compulsion** /kəmpʌ́lʃ(ə)n/ 名 ▶定義1 **①** the act of forcing sb to do sth or being forced to do sth 〜に強いて…をさせること, または…をするように強いられること→強制, 強制する[される]こと ‖ *There is no compulsion to take part. You can decide yourself.* 参加は強制ではありません. 自分で決めてください. ☞ compel ▶定義2 **⊙**a strong desire that you cannot control, often to do sth that you should not do; an urge しばしば, してはいけない事をしたいという抑制できない強い欲求; 衝動→強い欲望, 抑え難い衝動 ‖ *Tony sometimes felt a strong compulsion to tell lies.* トニーは時々そう言いたくてたまらなくなった.

**compulsive** /kəmpʌ́lsɪv/ 形 ▶定義1 (used about a bad or harmful habit) caused by a strong desire that you cannot control (悪い, または有害な習慣について)抑制できない強い欲求による→衝動的な, 欲望に駆られた ‖ *compulsive eating* 食べずにはいられないこと ▶定義2 (used about a person) having a bad habit that he/she cannot control (人について)抑制できない悪い習慣を持っている→常習的な, 我慢できない, (〜が)…しないではいられない ‖ *a compulsive gambler/shoplifter* ギャンブルをやめられない人・常習的な万引き犯 ▶定義3 so interesting or exciting that you cannot take your attention away from it とても面白くて, または刺激的で注意をそらすことができない→夢中にさせる ‖ *This book makes compulsive reading.* この本は読み始めたらやめられない. ― compulsively 副→強制的に, 是非を言わせず

***compulsory** /kəmpʌ́ls(ə)ri/ 形 ▶定義 that must be done, by law, rules, etc; obligatory 法律, 規則などによってやらなければならない; 必須(ひっす)の→強制的な, 義務的な, 必修の ‖ *Maths and English are compulsory subjects on this course.* 数学と英語はこの課程の必修科目です. *It is compulsory to wear a hard hat on the building site.* 建築現場ではヘルメットをかぶる規則になっています. ☞ やる必要がないものは, non-compulsory (非強制的な), voluntary (自発的な) または optional (任意の) と表現する.

**compute** /kəmpjúːt/ 動 他 正式 ▶定義 to calculate sth 物を計算する→(数, 量など)を算定する, 見積もる

## computer

**computer** /kəmpjúːtər/ 名 C ▶定義 an electronic machine that can store, find and arrange information, calculate amounts and control other machines 情報を保存, 検索, 配列し, 量を計算し, ほかの機械を制御できる電子機器→コンピューター, 電子計算機 ‖ *The bills are all done by computer.* 請求書はすべてコンピューターで処理される. *a computer program* コンピュータープログラム *a home/personal computer* ホームコンピューター・パーソナルコンピューター *computer software/games* コンピューターソフトウェア・コンピューターゲーム *First of all, the details are fed into a computer.* まず第1に, 項目をコンピューターに入力します. ☞ S5 ページのさし絵

**computerize**(または **-ise**) /kəmpjúːtəraɪz/ 動 他 ▶定義 to use computers to do a job or to store information 仕事をするためまたは情報を保存するためにコンピューターを使う→〜をコンピューターで処理する, コンピューター化する, 電算化する ‖ *The whole factory has been computerized.* 工場全体がコンピューター化されている. *We have now computerized the library catalogue.* 今では図書館の目録がコンピューター化されています. ― **computerization** (または **-isation**) /kəmpjùːtəraɪzéɪʃ(ə)n/ 名 U →コンピューター化(すること)

**computer-literate** 形 ▶定義 able to use a computer コンピューターを使える→コンピューターの知識がある, コンピューターに熟達した

**computing** /kəmpjúːtɪŋ/ 名 U ▶定義 the use of computers コンピューターを使うこと→コンピューターで処理・計算すること ‖ *She did a course in computing.* 彼女はコンピューターの課程を取った.

**Con** (または **Cons**) 略 ▶定義 (in British politics) Conservative→(英国の政治で) 保守党員

**con**¹ /kɑn/ 動 他 (**conning**; **conned**) 略式 ▶定義 con sb (into doing sth/out of sth) to cheat sb, especially in order to get money 特に金を得るために〜をだます→〜をペテンに掛ける, ごまかす, だまして〜させる, 〜をだまし取る ‖ *He conned her into investing in a company that didn't really exist.* 彼は彼女をだまして実際には存在しない会社に投資させた. *The old lady was conned out of her life savings.* 老婦人は一生かけてためた老後の蓄えをだまし取られた.

**con**² /kɑn/ 名 C ▶定義 略式 a trick, especially in order to cheat sb out of some money 特に〜から金をだまし取るためのごまかし→信用詐欺, ペテン

**成句 the pros and cons** ⇒ **PRO**

**concave** /kɑ́nkèɪv/ ▶定義 having a surface that curves towards the inside of sth, like the inside of a bowl 椀(わん)の内側のように〜の内側に湾曲した面を持つ→凹面の, 凹形の, くぼんだ ☞参 convex

**conceal** /kənsíːl/ 動 他 正式 ▶定義 conceal sth/sb (from sb/sth) to hide sb/sth; to prevent sb/sth from being seen or discovered 〜を隠す; 〜を見られたり発見されないようにする→〜を(…から)隠しておく, 秘密にする ‖ *She tried to conceal her anger from her friend.* 彼女は友達に怒りを見せないようにした. ― **concealment** 名 U →隠すこと, 隠れている状態 ‖ *the concealment of the facts of the case* その事件に関する事実の隠蔽(いんぺい)

**concede** /kənsíːd/ 動 他 正式 ▶定義 1 to admit that sth is true although you do not want to そうしたくないが, 〜が真実であることを認める→〜を(しぶしぶ)事実と認める ‖ *When it was clear that he would lose the election, he conceded defeat.* 落選が確定すると, 彼はしぶしぶ敗北を認めた. *She conceded that the problem was mostly her fault.* その問題の大部分は自分の落ち度によるものだと彼女はしぶしぶ認めた.

▶定義 2 concede sth (to sb) to allow sb to take sth although you do not want to そうしてほしくないが, 〜が…を取ることを許可する→(権利, 特権など)を(〜に)与える, 譲る; (得点など)を与える, (論点など)を譲歩する ‖ *They lost the war and had to concede territory to their enemy.* 彼らは戦争に負けて領土を敵に譲らなければならなかった. ☞ concession

**conceit** /kənsíːt/ 名 U ▶定義 too much pride in yourself and your abilities and importance 自分自身および自分の能力や重要度についての大きすぎる誇り→うぬぼれ, 自負心 ― **conceited** 形 →うぬぼれの強い, 思い上がった ‖ *He's so conceited - he thinks he's the best at everything!* 彼はうぬぼれが強い - 何でも自分が1番だと思っている.

**conceivable** /kənsíːvəb(ə)l/ 形 ▶定義 possible to imagine or believe 想像するまたは信じることが可能な→考えられる, ありそうな ‖ *I made every conceivable effort to succeed.* 私は成功するために思い付く限りの努力をした. ⇔ **inconceivable** ― conceivably /-əb(ə)li/ 副 →考えられるところでは, ひょっとすると ‖ *She might just conceivably be telling the truth.* ひょっとすると彼女は本当の事を言っているだけかもしれない.

**conceive** /kənsíːv/ 動 ▶定義1 他 正式 to think of a new idea or plan 新しい案や計画を考える→〜を思い付く, 考え出す ‖ *He conceived the idea for the novel during his journey through India.* 彼はインドを旅行中にその小説の案を思い付いた. ▶定義2 自他 正式 conceive (of) sb/sth (as sth) to think about sb/sth in a particular way; to imagine 〜について特定のやり方で考える; 想像する→〜を…だと考える, 〜を理解する, 認識する ‖ *He started to conceive of the world as a dangerous place.* 彼は世界を危険な場所だと考えるようになった. ▶定義3 自 他 to become pregnant 妊娠する→(子を)身ごもる ☛ 名 conception

*__concentrate__ /kɑ́ns(ə)ntrèɪt/ 動 自他 ▶定義1 concentrate (sth) (on sth/doing sth) to give all your attention or effort to sth 〜にすべての注意と努力を注ぐ→〜を(…に)集中する, 専念する, 全力を注ぐ ‖ *I need to concentrate on passing this exam.* この試験に合格することに専念する必要がある. *I tried to concentrate my thoughts on the problem.* その問題に考えを集中しようとした. ▶定義2 to come together or to bring people or things together in one place 集まる, または人々や物を1箇所に集める→一点に集まる・集める, 集中する・させる, 集結する・させる ‖ *Most factories are concentrated in one small area of the town.* 多くの工場は町の1つの狭い地域に集中している.

**concentrated** /kɑ́ns(ə)ntrèɪtəd/ 形 ▶定義1 showing determination 決意を示す→一心な; 集中した ‖ *With one concentrated effort we can finish the work by tonight.* みんなで集中してやれば, 今夜仕事を終えることができる. ▶定義2 made stronger by the removal of some liquid (ある量の)液体を取り除くことで濃くなった→濃縮した, 濃厚な ‖ *This is concentrated orange juice. You have to add water before you drink it.* これは濃縮オレンジジュースです. 水を加えて飲んでください. ⇔ **dilute**

*__concentration__ /kɑ̀ns(ə)ntréɪʃ(ə)n/ 名 ▶定義1 **U** concentration (on sth) the ability to give all your attention or effort to sth 〜にすべての注意と努力を注ぐ能力→(〜への)集中(力), 専念 ‖ *This type of work requires total concentration.* このような仕事には全面的な集中力が必要だ. *Don't **lose** your **concentration** or you might make a mistake.* 集中力をなくさないように, さもないとミスをしますよ. ▶定義2 **C** concentration (of sth) a large amount of people or things in one place 1箇所に集まった大量の人々や物→(〜の)集中, 集積; 濃縮, 濃度 ‖ *There is a high concentration of chemicals in the drinking water here.* ここの飲料水は化学物質の濃度が高い.

**concentration camp** 名 **C** ▶定義 a prison (usually a number of buildings inside a high fence) where political prisoners are kept in very bad conditions 政治犯がひどい悪条件下で捕らえられている監禁所(通常は高い塀の内部にいくつかの建物が集まっている)→強制収容所

**concentric** /kənséntrɪk, kɑ̀n-/ 形 ▶定義 (used about circles of different sizes) having the same centre point (異なる大きさの円について)同じ中心を持っている→同心の, 同中心の; 同心円を成す

*__concept__ /kɑ́nsept/ 名 **C** ▶定義 the concept (of sth/that...) an idea; a basic principle 考え; 基本的原理→概念, 観念, 考え; 構想, 発想 ‖ *It is difficult to **grasp** the **concept** of eternity.* 永遠という概念を理解するのは難しい. ― **conceptual** /kənséptʃuəl/ 形 →概念の, 概念的な

**conception** /kənsépʃ(ə)n/ 名 **C U** ▶定義1 (a) conception (of sth) an understanding of how or what sth is 〜がどのようであるか, または何であるか理解すること→概念, 認識, 考え, 想像(力) ‖ *We have no real conception of what people suffered during the war.* 戦争中の人々の苦しみは私たちには想像がつかない. ▶定義2 the process of forming an idea or a plan 考えや計画を形づくる過程→構想, 着想, 考案, 思い付き ▶定義3 the moment when a woman or female animal becomes pregnant 女性や雌の動物が妊娠する時→受胎, 妊娠 ☛ 動 conceive

\***concern**¹ /kənsə́ːm/ 動 ● ▶定義 1 to affect or involve sb/sth ～に影響する, または関連する→～に関係している, ～の利害に関係する, 重要である‖ *This does not concern you. Please go away.* これはあなたには関係ありません. あちらに行ってください. *It is important that no risks are taken where safety is concerned.* 安全面に関する限りではリスクを冒さないことが重要である. ▶定義 2 to be about sth ～に関する→～に関係する, ～についてのことである‖ *The main problem concerns the huge cost of the project.* 主要な問題はプロジェクトの膨大な経費についてである. ▶定義 3 to worry sb ～を心配させる→～を案じさせる‖ *What concerns me is that we have no long-term plan.* 私が気懸かりなのは長期的な計画がないことだ. ▶定義 4 concern yourself with sth to give your attention to sth ～に注意を向ける→～にかかわる, 携わる‖ *You needn't concern yourself with the hotel booking. The travel agent will take care of it.* ホテルの予約をする必要はありません. それは旅行代理店が手配します.

成句 be concerned in sth ▶定義 to have a connection with or be involved in sth ～と関連する, またはかかわる→～に関与する‖ *She was concerned in a drugs case some years ago.* 彼女は数年前に麻薬事件に関与した.

be concerned with sth ▶定義 to be about sth ～に関する→～に関連する, ～についてのことである‖ *Tonight's programme is concerned with the effects of the law on ordinary people.* 今夜の番組は一般の人々に対する法律の効力についてです.

\***concern**² /kənsə́ːm/ 名 ▶定義 1 ● ⓤ concern (for/about/over sb/sth); concern (that...) a feeling of worry; sth that causes worry 心配の感情; 心配を引き起こす～→心配, 懸念, 気遣い‖ *The safety officer assured us that there was no cause for concern.* 安全管理の職員は何も心配はないと請け合った. *My main concern is that we'll run out of money.* 私の主な心配はお金が足りなくなりそうだということだ. ▶定義 2 ● something that is important to you or that involves you 自分にとって重要な事, または自分に関係した事→関心事, 重大事‖ *Financial matters are not my concern.* 私は財政問題には関心がない. ▶定義 3 ● a company or business 会社または事業→会社, 企業; 事業, 商売‖ *a large industrial concern* 大(製造)会社

成句 a going concern ⇒ GOING²

**concerned** /kənsə́ːmd/ 形 ▶定義 concerned (about/for sth); concerned (that...) worried and feeling concern about sth ～について心配し気懸かりな→(～について)心配な, (ということを)案じて, 気遣って‖ *If you are concerned about your baby's health you should consult a doctor immediately.* 赤ん坊の健康状態が心配ならば, すぐに医者に診せるべきだ. ⇔ **unconcerned**

**concerning** /kənsə́ːmɪŋ/ 前 ▶定義 about; on the subject of ～について; ～に関して→～に関連する‖ *She refused to answer questions concerning her private life.* 彼女は私生活に関する質問には断固として答えなかった.

\***concert** /kάnsərt/ 名 ● ▶定義 a performance of music 音楽の公演→音楽会, 演奏会, コンサート‖ *The band is on tour doing concerts all over the country.* そのバンドは全国コンサートツアー中だ. ☛参 recital

成句 in concert (with sb/sth) 正式 ▶定義 working together with sb/sth ～と一緒に作業して→(～と)協力して

**concerted** /kənsə́ːrtəd/ 形 ▶定義 done by a group of people working together 協力した人々の集団によって行われる→協調した, 一致した‖ *We must all make a concerted effort to finish the work on time.* 全員が一致協力して時間通りに仕事を終えなければならない.

**concertina** /kὰnsərtíːnə/ 名 ● ▶定義 a musical instrument that you hold in your hands and play by pressing the ends together and pulling them apart 手に持って両端を押し付けたり引き離したりして演奏する楽器→コンチェルティーナ, コンサーティーナ ☛ 小さな accordion (アコーディオン)のような楽器 ☛参 piano の注 ☛ music のさし絵

**concerto** /kəntʃéərtoʊ/ 名 ● (複 concertos) ▶定義 a piece of music for an orchestra with one instrument playing an important part (solo) オーケストラ用の楽曲で, 1つの楽器が重要な

パート(ソロ)を演奏する➡**協奏曲, コンチェルト** ‖ *Mozart's second piano concerto* モーツァルトの第2ピアノ協奏曲

**concession** /kənséʃ(ə)n/ 名 ▶定義1 ❻Ⓤ(a) concession (to sb/sth) something that you agree to do in order to end an argument 議論を終わらせるために, すると同意した事➡**譲歩, 折り合い** ‖ *Employers have been forced to **make concessions** to the union.* 雇用者側は組合に譲歩せざるを得なかった. 動 concede ▶定義2 ❻ a lower price for certain groups of people 特定の人の集団向けの安い価格➡**(特定の客への)料金割引** ‖ *Concessions are available for students and pensioners.* 学生と年金受給者には割引制度があります.

**concessionary** /kənséʃ(ə)n(ə)ri, -èri/ 形 ▶定義 having a lower price for certain groups of people 特定の人の集団に安い価格で➡**割引の** ‖ *a concessionary fare* 割引料金

**conciliation** /kənsìliéiʃ(ə)n/ 名 Ⓤ ▶定義 the process of ending an argument or disagreement 議論や不和を終わらせる過程➡**和解, 調停; なだめること** ‖ *All attempts at conciliation have failed and civil war seems inevitable.* 和解の試みはすべて失敗に終わり, 内戦は避けられそうにない.

**conciliatory** /kənsíliət(ə)ri; -tɔ̀ːri/ 形 ▶定義 that tries to end an argument or disagreement 議論や不和を終わらせようとする➡**懐柔的な, なだめるような** ‖ *a conciliatory speech/gesture* なだめるような話し方・身振り

**concise** /kənsáis/ 形 ▶定義 giving a lot of information in a few words; brief 少ない言葉で多くの情報を与える; 簡潔な➡**簡明な, 手短な, 簡潔な** ‖ *He gave a clear and concise summary of what had happened.* 彼は何が起こったかをはっきりと簡潔にまとめて話した. ─ concisely 副➡**簡潔に, 簡明に** ─ conciseness 名 Ⓤ➡**簡潔(なこと)**

**conclude** /kənklúːd/ 動 ▶定義1 ❿ conclude sth from sth to form an opinion as the result of thought or study 考えたり研究した結果, ある見解をまとめる➡**~から…だと結論を下す, 断定する** ‖ *From the man's strange behaviour I concluded that he was drunk.* 私は, 男の奇妙な振る舞いから, 彼は酔っているのだと断定した.

▶定義2 ⾃他 正式 to end or to bring sth to an end 終わる, または~を終わらせる➡**(~を)終わりにする, 完結する, (~を)締めくくる** ‖ *The Prince concluded his tour with a visit to a charity concert.* 皇太子はチャリティーコンサートへの訪問でご旅行を締めくくられた. ▶定義3 ⾃ conclude sth (with sb) to formally arrange or agree to sth ~を正式に取り決める, または~に同意する➡**(条約など)を(~と)結ぶ, 締結する** ‖ *conclude a business deal/treaty* 取り引きをまとめる・条約を結ぶ

*★**conclusion** /kənklúːʒ(ə)n/ 名 ▶定義1 ❻ the conclusion (that…) an opinion that you reach after thinking about sth carefully ~を注意深く考えた末の意見➡**結論, 断定, 決定** ‖ *After trying to phone Bob for days, I **came to the conclusion** that he was on holiday.* 何日も電話でボブを捕まえようとした末に, 私は彼が休暇中だという結論に達した. *Have you **reached any conclusions** from your studies?* 研究の結果から何か結論が出ましたか. ▶定義2 [❻, 通常は単数] 正式 an end to sth ~の終わり➡**結末, 結び** ‖ *Let us hope the peace talks **reach a successful conclusion**.* 和平交渉が良い結末になることを期待したい. ▶定義3 ❿ an act of arranging or agreeing to sth formally ~を正式に取り決めること, または~に同意すること➡**(条約, 取り引きなどの)締結** ‖ *The summit ended with the conclusion of an arms-reduction treaty.* サミットは軍備縮小条約を締結して終了した.

成句 **a foregone conclusion** ⇒ **FOREGONE**
**in conclusion** ▶定義 finally; lastly 最後に; 終わりに➡**結論として, 要するに**
**jump to conclusions** ⇒ **JUMP**¹

**conclusive** /kənklúːsɪv/ 形 ▶定義 that shows sth is definitely true or real ~が明らかに真実または事実であることを示す➡**決定的な, 確実な** ‖ *The blood tests gave conclusive proof of Robson's guilt.* 血液検査はロブソンの有罪を示す決定的な証拠となった. ⇔ **inconclusive** ─ conclusively 副➡**決定的に, 確実に**

**concoct** /kənkɑ́kt/ 動 他 ▶定義1 to make sth unusual by mixing different things together 異なる物を混合して珍しい物を作る➡**(材料を混ぜ合わせてスープ, 飲み物など)を作る, 調合する** ▶定義2 to make up or invent sth (an excuse, a story, etc) (言い訳, 物語など) を作り上げたりでっち上げる➡〜をでっち上げる, ねつ造する, (計画, 陰謀など) を仕組む — concoction /kənkákʃ(ə)n/ 名 ❻ ➡混合して作った物, 混合飲料, 調合薬

**concourse** /kánkɔːrs/ 名 ❻ ▶定義 a large hall or space inside a building such as a station or an airport 駅や空港などの建物内にある大きなホールまたは空間 ➡中央ホール, コンコース

**concrete**¹ /kánkriːt/ 形 ▶定義 real or definite; not only existing in the imagination 本物の, または明確な; 想像の中だけに存在するのではない ➡具体的な, 有形の; 現実の, 実際の ‖ Can you give me a concrete example of what you mean? 言いたい事を具体的な例を挙げて説明してください. ⇔ abstract — concretely 副 ➡具体的に, 具体的に言うと

**concrete**² /kánkriːt/ 名 ❶ ▶定義 a hard substance made from cement mixed with sand, water, small stones (gravel), etc, that is used in building セメントに砂, 水, 小石 (砂利) などを混ぜて作る硬い物質で, 建築物に使われる ➡コンクリート ‖ a modern office building of glass and concrete ガラスとコンクリートの現代的なオフィスビル a concrete floor/bridge コンクリートの床・橋

**concrete**³ /kánkriːt/ 動他 ▶定義 concrete sth (over) to cover sth with concrete 〜をコンクリートで覆う ➡〜にコンクリートを塗る, 〜をコンクリートで固める

**concur** /kənkə́ːr, kɑn-/ 動⾃ (concurring; concurred) 正式 ▶定義 to agree 同意する ➡(意見などが) 一致する, 合意に達する

**concurrent** /kənkə́ːr(ə)nt, kɑn-; -kə́ːr-/ 形 ▶定義 existing or happening at the same time as sth else ほかの〜と同時に存在する, または起こる ➡同時発生の, 同時に起こる, 共に作用する — concurrently 副 ➡同時に, 共に ‖ The semi-finals are played concurrently, so it is impossible to watch both. 準決勝戦は同時に行われるので, 両方を見ることはできない.

**concuss** /kənkʌ́s/ 動他 (通常は受動態で) ▶定義 to injure sb's brain by hitting his/her head 頭を殴って〜の脳に損傷を与える ➡〜に脳震盪 (しんとう) を起こさせる ‖ I was slightly concussed when I fell off my bicycle. 私は自転車から落ちた時に軽い脳震盪を起こした. — concussion /kənkʌ́ʃ(ə)n/ 名 ❶ ➡脳震盪

*****condemn** /kəndém/ 動他 ▶定義1 condemn sb/sth (for/as sth) to say strongly that you think sb/sth is very bad or wrong 〜が非常に悪い, または間違っていると強く言う ➡〜を (…のことで…として) 強く非難する, とがめる, (厳しく) 責める ‖ A government spokesman condemned the bombing as a cowardly act of terrorism. 政府のスポークスマンは爆撃を卑劣なテロだと強く非難した. ▶定義2 condemn sb (to sth/to do sth) to say what sb's punishment will be; to sentence sb 〜の罰が何であるかを言う; 〜に刑を宣告する ➡〜に (有罪の) 判決を下す, 〜に (…を・…するように) 宣告する; 〜を (…に・…するように) 運命づける, 追い込む ‖ The murderer was condemned to death. その殺人者は死刑を宣告された. (比喩) Their poor education condemns them to a series of low-paid jobs. 教育が不十分なため, 彼らは低賃金の職にしか就けない. ▶定義3 condemn sth (as sth) to say officially that sth is not safe enough to use 〜が使われるには十分に安全ではないと正式に言う ➡(品物) を不良品と定める ‖ The building was condemned as unsafe and was demolished. その建物は危険だと断定され取り壊された.

**condemnation** /kɑ̀ndemnéɪʃ(ə)n/ 名 ❻ ❶ ▶定義 the act of condemning sth; a statement that condemns 〜を非難すること; 非難の言明 ➡非難; 罪の宣告 ‖ The bombing brought condemnation from all around the world. その爆撃は世界中から強い非難を浴びた.

**condensation** /kɑ̀ndenséɪʃ(ə)n/ 名 ❶ ▶定義 small drops of liquid that are formed when warm air touches a cold surface 暖かい空気が冷たい面に触れた時に形成される液体の小さい滴 ➡(気体から液体への) 凝縮, 凝結; (水蒸気などの) 水滴, 結露

**condense** /kəndéns/ 動 ▶定義1 ⾃他 to change or make sth change from gas to liquid 〜が気体から液体に変わる, または変える ➡凝縮する・させる, 凝結する・させる ‖ Steam condenses into water when it touches a cold surface. 水蒸気が冷たい面に触れると凝縮して水になる. ☛参 evaporate ▶定義2 他 condense sth (into sth) to make smaller or shorter so that it fills less space 小さくまたは短くしてスペースを取らないようにする→〜を(…に)要約する, 短縮する ‖ *We'll have to condense these three chapters into one.* この3章を1章に短縮しなければならない.

**condescend** /kɑ̀ndɪsénd/ 動 ⓐ ▶定義1 condescend (to sb) to behave towards sb in a way that shows that you think you are better or more important than him/her; to patronize sb 自分の方が優れている, または重要だと思っているような態度を〜に対して取る; 〜に対して庇護(ひご)者振る→威張って〜する, (相手を)見下した振る舞いをする, 恩に着せる, わざと親切にする ▶定義2 condescend (to do sth) to do sth that you believe is below your level of importance 自分の偉さより劣ると思っている事をする→身を落として〜する ‖ *Celia only condescends to speak to me when she wants me to do something for her.* シーリアは何かしてもらいたいときだけ, 下手に出て私に話し掛ける.
— condescending 形→わざと親切にする, 人を見下したような ‖ *a condescending smile* おもねるような笑み — condescension /kɑ̀ndɪsénʃ(ə)n/ 名 Ⓤ→恩着せがましさ, へつらい

***condition**¹ /kəndíʃ(ə)n/ 名 ▶定義1 [Ⓤ, 単数扱い] the state that sb/sth is in 〜の有り様→状態, 調子; 健康状態, 体調 ‖ *to be in poor/good/excellent condition* 不調で・好調で・絶好調で *He looks really ill. He is certainly not in a condition to drive home.* 彼はとても具合が悪そうだ. 自分で運転して家に帰れるような状態ではないのは確かだ. ▶定義2 Ⓒsomething that must happen so that sth else can happen or be possible ほかの〜が起こるまたは可能であるために, 起こらなければならない事→条件, 必要条件, 制約 ‖ *One of the conditions of the job is that you agree to work on Sundays.* この仕事の条件の1つは, あなたが日曜日の仕事に同意するということです. *He said I could borrow his bike on one condition - that I didn't let anyone else ride it.* 1つの条件をのめば彼は私に自転車を貸してくれると言った - それは私以外にはだれも乗せないということだった. ▶定義3 **conditions**[複数扱い] the situation or surroundings in which people live, work or do things 人々が生活し, 働きまたは物事をする境遇や環境→状況, 事情 ‖ *The prisoners were kept in terrible conditions.* 囚人たちはひどい状況に置かれていた. *poor living/housing/working conditions* 劣悪な生活状況・住宅事情・労働環境 ▶定義4 Ⓒa medical problem that you have for a long time 人が長い間持っている医学的な問題→(身体の)異常, 病気 ‖ *to have a heart/lung condition* 心臓・肺が悪い
成句 **on condition (that...)** ▶定義 only if 〜であるとすれば→〜という条件で, もし〜ならば ‖ *I agreed to help on condition that I got half the profit.* 利益の半分をもらえるという条件で援助することに同意した.

**on no condition** 正式 ▶定義 not for any reason どのような理由であっても→どんな条件でも〜ない, どんな事があっても〜ない ‖ *On no condition must the press find out about this.* どんな事があっても, この事が報道関係者に漏れてはならない.

**out of condition** ▶定義 not physically fit 体の状態が良くない→調子が悪い, 体調が良くない

**condition**² /kəndíʃ(ə)n/ 動 ⓐ ▶定義 to affect or control the way that sb/sth behaves 〜の行動に影響する, またはこれを制御する→〜を決定する, 慣らす ‖ *Boys are conditioned to feel that they are stronger than girls.* 少年たちは, 彼らが少女たちよりも強いと考えるように慣らされている.

***conditional** /kəndíʃ(ə)n(ə)l/ 形 ▶定義1 conditional (on/upon sth) that only happens if sth else is done or happens first ほかの〜が行われたとき, または最初に起こったときにのみ起こる→(〜という)条件付きの, 〜次第の ‖ *My university place is conditional on my getting good marks in the exams.* 私の大学生としての身分は, 試験で良い点数を取ることに懸かっている.
⇔ **unconditional** ▶定義2 (文法) describing a situation that must exist before sth else can happen. A conditional sentence often contains the word 'if'. ほかの〜が起こる前に存在しなければならない状況を述べる. 条件文には多くの場合 if の語が含まれる→条件を表す ‖ *'Unless you study, you won't pass the exam'* is a conditional sentence. 「勉強しなければ, 試験に合格できませんよ」は条件文である.

▶条件文についての説明は, 巻末の「文法早見表」を参照.

**conditioner**

— conditionally /-ʃ(ə)n(ə)li/ 副 ▶条件付きで, 暫定的に

**conditioner** /kəndíʃ(ə)nər/ 名 C U ▶定義 a substance that keeps sth in a good condition 〜を良い状態に保つ物質→クリーム, コンディショナー; 柔軟仕上げ剤 ‖ *Do you use conditioner on your hair?* 髪にリンスを使っていますか.

**condolence** /kəndóul(ə)ns, kɑn-/ 名 [複数扱い, U] ▶定義 an expression of how sorry you feel for sb whose relative or close friend has just died 肉親や親しい友人が亡くなったばかりの〜に, 残念に思っていることを示すこと→悔やみ, 弔辞 ‖ *offer your condolences* お悔やみを言う *a message of condolence* お悔やみの言葉

**condom** /kɑ́ndəm, kʌ́n-/ (または 略式 **rubber**) 名 C ▶定義 a thin rubber covering that a man wears over his sexual organ during sex to prevent the woman from becoming pregnant or as protection against disease 男性が性交中に性器に着ける薄いゴムの覆いで, 女性が妊娠することを防ぐためまたは病気の予防として用いる→コンドーム

**condominium** /kɑ̀ndəmíniəm/ ( または 略式 **condo** /kɑ́ndou/) 名 C 米 ▶定義 a flat or block of flats owned by the people who live in them 住人によって所有されるフラット, またはフラットの入った建物→分譲アパート・マンション

**condone** /kəndóun/ 動 他 ▶定義 to accept or agree with sth that most people think is wrong 多くの人々が間違っていると考える〜を受け入れる, またはこれに同意する→容赦する, (罪, 違反など) を許す ‖ *I can never condone violence - no matter what the circumstances are.* 私は暴力は絶対に許せません—どんな状況であろうとも.

**conducive** /kənd(j)úːsɪv/ 形 正式 ▶定義 *conducive (to sth)* helping or making sth happen 〜が起こることを助ける, または〜を起こす→(〜の) 助けとなる, 促す ‖ *This hot weather is not conducive to hard work.* この暑い天候はきつい仕事には向かない.

**conduct**[1] /kəndʌ́kt/ 動 他 ▶定義 1 正式 to organize and do sth, especially research 特に研究などを組織化して行う→〜を行う, 実施する, 管理する ‖ *to conduct tests/a survey/an inquiry* 試験・調査・調査を行う ▶定義 2 to stand in front of an orchestra and direct the musicians オーケストラの前に立って音楽家たちに指示する→〜を指揮する ▶定義 3 正式 *conduct yourself well, badly, etc* to behave in a particular way 特定の振る舞い方をする→振舞う, 身を処する ▶定義 4 to allow heat or electricity to pass along or through sth 熱や電気を〜に沿って, または〜を通って伝えることができる→(熱, 電気など) を伝える, 伝導する ‖ *Rubber does not conduct electricity.* ゴムは電気を通さない.

**conduct**[2] /kɑ́ndʌkt/ 名 U ▶定義 1 a person's behaviour 人の行動→行い, 行為 ‖ *His conduct has always been of the highest standard.* 彼の品行はいつも最高の水準だ. *a code of conduct* (= a set of rules for behaviour) 行動規範 (= 行動の規則) ▶定義 2 正式 *conduct of sth* the act of controlling or organizing sth 〜を制御または組織すること→管理, 運営, 経営 ‖ *She was criticized for her conduct of the bank's affairs.* 彼女は銀行業務の遂行について批判された.

**conductor** /kəndʌ́ktər/ 名 C ▶定義 1 a person who stands in front of an orchestra and directs the musicians オーケストラの前に立って音楽家たちを指揮する人→指揮者 ▶定義 2 米 a person whose job is to collect money from passengers on a bus or to check their tickets バスで乗客から運賃を集めたり乗車券を確認することを仕事とする人→(バスなどの) 車掌 ▶定義 3 英 =GUARD'(5) ▶定義 4 a substance that allows heat or electricity to pass through or along it 熱や電気を通す, または伝えることができる物質→伝導体, 導体, 導線

**cone** /kóun/ 名 C ▶定義 1 a shape or object that has a round base and a point at the top 円形の底面ととがった頂点を持つ形または物体→円錐 (えんすい) 形, 円錐 (体) ‖ *traffic cones* (セーフティー) コーン (道路の工事区間などに置く円錐形の標識) *an ice cream cone* アイスクリームのコーン ☛ 形 **conical** ☛ **cube** のさし絵 ▶定義 2 the hard fruit of some trees (pine and fir) 一部の樹木 (マツ, モミ) の堅い果実→球果, 松かさ ☛ C2 ページのさし絵 ☛ 参 **conifer**

**confectionery** /kənfékʃ(ə)n(ə)ri/ 名 U ▶定義 sweets, cakes, chocolates, etc 菓子, ケーキ, チョコレートなど→菓子類

**confederation** /kənfèdəréɪʃ(ə)n/ 名 C U ▶定義 an organization of smaller groups which have joined together 小グループが一緒になった組織→**連合, 同盟** ‖ *a confederation of independent republics* 独立共和国連合

**confer** /kənfə́ːr/ 動 (**conferring**; **conferred**) ▶定義1 自 confer (with sb) (on/about sth) to discuss sth with sb before making a decision 決定する前に〜と…について議論する→(〜と)(…について)相談する, 協議する, 打ち合わせる ‖ *The President is conferring with his advisers.* 大統領は顧問たちと協議している. ▶定義2 他(文) confer sth (on sb) to give sb a special right or advantage 〜に特別の権利または利点を与える→(勲章・学位・名誉など)を(人に)授与する, 贈る

\***conference** /kɑ́nf(ə)rəns/ 名 ● ▶定義 a large official meeting, often lasting several days, at which members of an organization, profession, etc meet to discuss important matters 通常は数日間続く大規模な公式の会合で, ある組織や職業などに属する人々が重要な事柄について議論する→**会議, 協議会** ‖ *an international conference on global warming* 地球温暖化に関する国際会議

\***confess** /kənfés/ 動 自 他 ▶定義 confess (to sth/to doing sth); confess (sth) (to sb) to admit that you have done sth bad or wrong 自分が悪い事または誤った事をしたと認める→**告白する, 白状する, 打ち明ける; (〜を)認める** ‖ *The young woman confessed to the murder of her boyfriend/to murdering her boyfriend.* その若い女性は恋人を殺害したことを認めた. *They confessed to their mother that they had spent all the money.* 彼らは金を全部使ってしまったと母親に打ち明けた. ☛参 own up (to sth) はあまり正式でない言い方.

**confession** /kənféʃ(ə)n/ 名 ● ▶定義 an act of admitting that you have done sth bad or wrong 自分が悪い事または誤った事をしたと認めること→**告白, 自白, 白状** ‖ *The police persuaded the man to make a full confession.* 警察は男を説得してすべてを白状させた.

**confetti** /kənféti/ 名 ▶定義 small pieces of coloured paper that people throw over a man and woman who have just got married 結婚したばかりの男女に人々が投げ掛ける色紙の細片→**紙吹雪**

**confide** /kənfáɪd/ 動 他 ▶定義 confide sth to sb to tell sb sth that is secret 〜に秘密を話す→(秘密など)を〜に打ち明ける, 告白する ‖ *She did not confide her love to anyone - not even to her best friend.* 彼女は自分の恋をだれにも話さなかった − 親友にさえも.

回動詞 confide in sb ▶定義 to talk to sb that you trust about sth secret or private 信用している〜に秘密または個人的な事を話す→**〜に秘密を打ち明ける**

\***confidence** /kɑ́nfəd(ə)ns/ 名 ❶ ▶定義1 confidence (in sb/sth) trust or strong belief in sb/sth 〜に対する信頼, または強い信念→**信用(すること), 信任, 信頼** ‖ *The public is losing confidence in the present government.* 国民は現在の政府に対する信頼を失いつつある. *I have every confidence in Emily's ability to do the job.* 私は, エミリーにはその仕事をする能力があると全面的に信頼している. ▶定義2 the feeling that you are sure about your own abilities, opinion, etc 自分の能力, 意見などについて確信を持っているという気持ち→**自信, 確信** ‖ *I didn't have the confidence to tell her I thought she was wrong.* 私は自信がなかったので彼女に間違っているとは言えなかった. *to be full of confidence* 自信満々で *'Of course we will win,' the team captain said with confidence.* 「もちろん私たちが勝ちます」とチームの主将は自信を持って言った. ☛参 **self-confidence** ▶定義3 a feeling of trust in sb to keep sth a secret 〜が秘密を守ってくれると信頼する気持ち→**信頼(すること)** ‖ *The information was given to me in strict confidence.* 私を全面的に信頼してその情報は明かされた. *It took a while to win/gain her confidence.* 彼女の信頼を得るまでにしばらくかかった.

**confidence trick** 名 ● ▶定義 a way of getting money by cheating sb 〜をだまして金を手に入れる方法→**信用詐欺, 詐欺**

\***confident** /kɑ́nfəd(ə)nt/ 形 ▶定義 confident (of sth/that...); confident (about sth) feeling or showing that you are sure about your own abilities, opinions, etc 自分の能力, 意見などに確信を持っている, またはそれを示す→**(〜を・〜だと)確信して; 自信を持った, 確信に満ちた** ‖ *Kate feels confident of passing/that she* *can pass the exam.* ケートは試験に合格する自信がある. *to be confident of success* 成功すると確信する *You should feel confident about your own abilities.* 自分の能力に自信を持たなければいけません. *Dillon has a very confident manner.* ディロンはとても自信に満ちた態度だ. ☛参 self-confident — confidently 副 ➔自信を持って, 確信して ∥ *She stepped confidently onto the stage and began to sing.* 彼女は自信を持って舞台に歩み出て歌い始めた.

**confidential** /kànfədénʃ(ə)l/ 形 ▶定義 secret; not to be shown or told to other people 秘密の; ほかの人々に見せない, または話さない➔秘密の, 内密の, 機密の ∥ *The letter was marked 'private and confidential'.* 手紙には「親展」と記されていた. — confidentiality /kànfədenʃiǽləti/ 名 U ➔秘密性, 機密性, 秘密であること — confidentially /-ʃ(ə)li/ 副 ➔内密に, 内緒で

**confine** /kənfáɪn/ 動 他 ▶定義 1 confine sb/sth (in/to sth) to keep a person or animal in a particular, usually small, place 人や動物を特別の場所, 通常は狭い場所に入れておく➔~を(…に)閉じ込める, 監禁する ∥ *The prisoners are confined to their cells for long periods at a time.* 囚人たちは一度に長い間監房に閉じ込められる. ▶定義 2 confine sb/sth/yourself to sth to stay within the limits of sth ~の制限内にとどまる➔~を…に限る, とどめる, 制限する ∥ *Please confine your questions to the topic we are discussing.* 質問は議論に関連したものだけにしてください.

**confined** /kənfáɪnd/ 形 ▶定義 (used about a space) very small (空間について) 非常に小さい➔狭い, 限られた

**confinement** /kənfáɪnmənt/ 名 U ▶定義 being kept in a small space 小さな空間に入れておかれること➔閉じ込めること, 監禁, 幽閉 ∥ *be kept in solitary confinement* (= *in a prison*) 独房 (= 刑務所の) に監禁される

**confines** /kánfaɪnz/ 名 [複数扱い] 正式 ▶定義 the limits of sth ~の限界➔境界(線), 限界 ∥ *Patients are not allowed beyond the confines of the hospital grounds.* 患者は病院構内の外に出ることは許されていない.

★**confirm** /kənfə́ːm/ 動 他 ▶定義 1 to say or show that sth is true; to make sth definite ~が本当だと言う, または示す; ~を明確にする➔~を確証する, ~を(本当だと)確かめる ∥ *Seeing the two of them together confirmed our suspicions.* 2人が一緒にいるのを見て私たちの疑いが強まった. *Can you confirm that you will be able to attend?* 確かに出席できますか. ▶定義 2 to accept sb as a full member of a Christian Church in a special ceremony 特別の儀式で~をキリスト教会の完全な一員と認める➔~に堅信式[礼]を施す, 堅信する ∥ *He was confirmed at the age of thirteen.* 彼は13歳で堅信礼を受けた. — confirmation /kɒnfərméɪʃ(ə)n/ 名 U C ➔確証, 確認; 堅信礼 ∥ *We are waiting for confirmation of the report.* 我々はその報告が確認されるのを待っている.

**confirmed** /kənfə́ːmd/ 形 (名詞の前だけ) ▶定義 fixed in a particular habit or way of life 特定の習慣や生活様式に固定された➔習慣を変えようとしない, 常習的な ∥ *a confirmed bachelor* 結婚しないことに慣れきった男

**confiscate** /kánfəskèɪt/ 動 他 ▶定義 to take sth away from sb as a punishment 罰として~から…を取り上げる➔~を没収する, 押収する ∥ *Any cigarettes found in school will be confiscated.* 校内でたばこが見つかったら没収します. — confiscation /kànfəskéɪʃ(ə)n/ 名 C U ➔没収, 押収

★**conflict**¹ /kánflɪkt/ 名 C U ▶定義 1 (a) conflict with sb/sth (over sth) a fight or an argument 戦いまたは議論➔争い, 戦闘; 論争 ∥ *an armed conflict* 武力衝突 *The new laws have brought the Government into conflict with the unions over pay increases.* 新法によって, 政府は賃上げをめぐって労働組合と争いになった.

▶定義 2 a difference between two or more ideas, wishes, etc 複数の考え, 望みなどの違い➔葛藤(かっとう), 対立 ∥ *Many women have to cope with the conflict between their career and their family.* 多くの女性は職業と家族という相反することに対処しなければならない. *a conflict of interests* 利害の対立

**conflict**² /kənflíkt/ 動 他 ▶定義 A and B conflict; A conflicts with B to disagree with or be different from sb/sth ~と意見が一致しない, または~と異なる➔相いれない, 矛盾する, 対立する ∥ *The statements of the two witnesses con-*

flict. 2人の証人の証言は矛盾している. *John's statement conflicts with yours.* ジョンの言うことはあなたとは違っている. *conflicting results* 矛盾する結果

**conform** /kənfɔ́ːm/ 動⾃ conform (to sth) ▶定義1 to obey a rule or law 規則や法律に従う→(規則, 法を) 守る ‖ *This building does not conform to fire regulations.* この建物は防火規則に従っていない. ▶定義2 to behave in the way that other people and society expect you to behave ほかの人々または社会が求めるようなやり方で振る舞う→(習慣, 基準などに) 適合する, 順応する, 慣れる ‖ *Children are under a lot of pressure to conform when they first start school.* 子供たちは初めて学校に上がった時は, 順応するために多くのプレッシャーを負う. — conformity /kənfɔ́ːməti/ 名 ❶→服従, 準拠; 適合, 順応

**conformist** /kənfɔ́ːmɪst/ 名 C ▶定義 a person who behaves in the way that people are expected to behave by society 社会から求められるやり方で振る舞う→(法律, 習慣などに) よく従う人, 体制順応的な人 ⇔ non-conformist

**confront** /kənfrʌ́nt/ 動⽥ ▶定義1 confront sth; confront sb with sb/sth to think about, or to make sb think about, sth that is difficult or unpleasant 困難な事または不快な事を考える, または〜に考えさせる→〜に直面する・させる, 向き合う ‖ *to confront a problem/difficulty/issue* 障害, 困難, 問題に向き合う *When the police confronted him with the evidence, he confessed.* 警察が証拠を突き付けると, 彼は自白した. ▶定義2 to stand in front of sb, for example because you want to fight him/her 例えば〜と戦いたいために…の前に立つ→〜に立ち向かう ‖ *The unarmed demonstrators were confronted by a row of soldiers.* 武器を持たないデモ参加者に兵士の隊列が立ち向かった.

**confrontation** /kɑ̀nfrʌntéɪʃ(ə)n/ 名 C ❶ ▶定義 a fight or an argument 戦いまたは議論→対立, 衝突, 対決

★**confuse** /kənfjúːz/ 動⽥ ▶定義1 (通常は受動態で) to make sb unable to think clearly or to know what to do 〜がはっきり考えることまたはなすべき事を, 理解できないようにする→〜を混乱させる ‖ *He confused everybody with his pages of facts and figures.* 彼が書いた正確な詳細は皆を混乱させた. ▶定義2 confuse A and/with B to mistake sb/sth for sb/sth else 〜をほかの…と間違える→〜を混同する, 取り違える ‖ *I often confuse Lee with his brother. They look very much alike.* 私はリーと彼の兄をよく間違える. 2人はとてもよく似ている.

▶定義3 to make sth complicated 〜を複雑にする→分かりにくくする, あいまいにする ‖ *The situation is confused by the fact that so many organizations are involved.* 多くの組織がかかわっているため状況は混乱している.

★**confused** /kənfjúːzd/ 形 ▶定義1 not able to think clearly はっきりと考えられない→混乱した, 困惑した ‖ *When he regained consciousness he was dazed and confused.* 意識を取り戻した時, 彼はぼうっとして混乱していた.

▶定義2 difficult to understand 理解するのが難しい→あいまいな, 分かりにくい ‖ *The article is very confused - I don't know what the main point is.* その記事はとてもあいまいだ — 要点が何なのか分からない. — confusedly /-(ə)dli/ 副→混乱して; 乱雑に

★**confusing** /kənfjúːzɪŋ/ 形 ▶定義 difficult to understand 理解するのが難しい→混乱させる(ような) ‖ *Her instructions were contradictory and confusing.* 彼女の指示は矛盾していて混乱させられる. — confusingly 副 →混乱させるように

★**confusion** /kənfjúːʒ(ə)n/ 名 ❶ ▶定義1 the state of not being able to think clearly or not understanding sth 〜をはっきり考えられない, または理解できない状態→混乱, 困惑 ‖ *He stared in confusion at the exam paper.* 彼は困惑して試験用紙を見詰めた. *There is still a great deal of confusion as to the true facts.* 真実は混乱していてまだよく分からない.

▶定義2 a state of disorder 無秩序な状態→混乱, 乱雑 ‖ *Their unexpected visit threw all our plans into confusion.* 彼らが突然訪ねてきたので, 私たちの計画はすべてめちゃくちゃになってしまった. ▶定義3 the act of mistaking sb/sth for sb/sth else 〜をほかの…と間違えること→混同 (すること), 取り違え ‖ *To avoid confusion, all luggage should be labelled with your name and destination.* 取り違えないよう

に手荷物にはすべて自分の名前と行き先の札を付けなければなりません.

**congeal** /kəndʒíːl/ 動自他 ▶定義 (used about a liquid) to become solid; to make a liquid solid (液体について) 固体になる; 液体を固体にする→凝結する, 凍る, 固まる; ～を凝結させる, 凍らせる, 固める ‖ *congealed blood* 固まった血液

**congenial** /kəndʒíːnjəl/ 形正式 ▶定義 pleasant 快い→楽しい, 気持ちの良い ‖ *We spent an evening in congenial company.* 私たちは気の合った仲間と夜を過ごした.

**congenital** /kəndʒénətl, kən-/ 形 ▶定義 (used about a disease) beginning at and continuing since birth (病気について) 誕生時に発病してそれ以来継続している→生まれつきの, 先天的な

**congested** /kəndʒéstəd, kən-/ 形 ▶定義 so full of sth that nothing can move ～が一杯で何も動かせない→密集した, 混雑した, 過密の ‖ *The streets of London are congested with traffic.* ロンドンの通りは交通渋滞していた. — **congestion** /kəndʒéstʃ(ə)n/ 名 U 定義 →密集, 混雑, 過密 ‖ *severe traffic congestion* ひどい交通渋滞

**conglomerate** /kənglám(ə)rət/ 名 C ▶定義 a large firm made up of several different companies いくつかの異なる子会社から成る大規模企業→複合企業, コングロマリット

**conglomeration** /kənglàməréɪʃ(ə)n, kàn-/ 名 C ▶定義 a group of many different things that have been brought together 多くの異なる物が一緒になった集団→密集体; 集会

*__congratulate__ /kəngrætʃəleɪt/ 動他 ▶定義 congratulate sb (on sth) to tell sb that you are pleased about sth he/she has done; to praise sb その人がした事についてうれしく思っていると～に告げる; ～を賞賛する→～に祝いの言葉を述べる ‖ *I congratulated Sue on passing her driving test.* 私は, スーが運転免許試験に合格したことにおめでとうと言った.

*__congratulations__ /kəngrætʃəleɪʃ(ə)nz/ 名 [複数扱い] ▶定義 used for telling sb that you are pleased about sth he/she has done ～に告げるときに用いて→祝いの言葉, 祝辞; おめでとう ‖ *Congratulations on the birth of your baby boy!* 男の子の誕生, おめでとう.

▶コミュニケーション
英語の「おめでとう」の使い方
　Congratulations! は, 出産・結婚・入学・昇進など, 特別に何かすばらしい事が起きた人への祝いの言葉として使われ, 日本語の「おめでとう」のように誕生日, 新年など祝日のあいさつには使われません. Congratulations への応答は Thank you と言います. 何に対する祝辞かは, Congratulations on your graduation など, 前置詞 on の後に示します. 特におめでとうを強調したいとき, Many congratulations! と言うこともあります.

**congregate** /káŋgrɪgèɪt/ 動自 ▶定義 to come together in a crowd or group 集まって群衆や集団になる→集まる, 集合する

**congregation** /kàŋgrɪgéɪʃ(ə)n/ 名 [C, 単数または複数形の動詞と共に] ▶定義 the group of people who attend a particular church 特定の教会に出席する人々の集団→(礼拝に集まる) 会衆, 信徒たち

*__congress__ /káŋgrəs/; -gres/ 名 C ▶定義1 a large formal meeting or series of meetings 大規模な正式の会合または一連の会合→会議, 評議会, 大会 ‖ *a medical congress* 医学学会　▶定義2 **Congress** the name in some countries (for example the US) for the group of people who are elected to make the laws 一部の国 (例えば米国) で, 法律を作るために選出された人々の集団の名称→国会, 議会

▶ US Congress (米国議会) は Senate (上院) と House of Representatives (下院) から成る.

**congressional** /kəngréʃənl, kən-/ 形 ▶定義 connected with a congress or Congress 会議または国会と関連した→会議の; 国会の

**conical** /kánɪk(ə)l, kóʊ-/ 形 ▶定義 having a round base and getting narrower towards a point at the top 底面が円形で, 先端に向けて細くなる→円錐 (えんすい) の, 円錐形の ● 名 **cone**

**conifer** /kánəfər, kóʊ-/ 名 C ▶定義 a tree with short, very thin leaves (needles) that stay green all through the year and that has hard brown fruit (cones) 短く非常に細い葉 (針状葉) を持つ樹木で, 常緑で, 硬い茶色の実 (球果) をつける→針葉樹, 球果植物 (マツ, モミ, スギなど) — **coniferous** /kánəfərəs, kóʊ-/ 形→針葉樹の, 球果

**conjecture** /kəndʒéktʃər/ 動自他 正式 ▶定義 to guess about sth without real proof or evidence 実際の証明や証拠なしに〜について推測する→(〜と)推測する, 憶測でものを言う — conjecture 名 ©Ⓤ→推測, 推量, 憶測

**conjugate** /kándʒəgèrt/ 動他 ▶定義 to give the different forms of a verb 動詞を異なる形にする→(動詞)を活用[変化]させる — conjugation /kàndʒəgéɪʃ(ə)n/ 名 ©Ⓤ→(動詞の)活用[変化], (動詞の)活用[変化]形

**conjunction** /kəndʒʌ́n(k)ʃ(ə)n/ 名 © ▶定義 a word that is used for joining other words, phrases or sentences ほかの語, 句, 文を結び付けるために用いる語→接続詞 ‖ *'And', 'but' and 'or' are conjunctions.* and, but, or は接続詞である.
成句 **in conjunction with sb/sth** ▶定義 together with sb/sth 〜と一緒に→〜と共に, 〜と合同して; 〜と関連して

**conjure** /kándʒər, kʌ́n-/ 動自 ▶定義 to do tricks by clever, quick hand movements, that appear to be magic 手際の良い素早い手の動きで魔法のようなトリックを行う→手品で出す, 魔法のように(作り)出す, 消す・追い払う — conjuring 名 Ⓤ→手品, 奇術
句動 **conjure sth up** ▶定義1 to cause an image to appear in your mind 心にイメージを浮かび上がらせる→〜を思い描く, 心に思い浮かべる ‖ *Hawaiian music conjures up images of sunshine, flowers and sandy beaches.* ハワイアン音楽を聞くと太陽の光, 花々, 砂浜が目の前に浮かんでくる. ▶定義2 to make sth appear quickly or suddenly 〜を素早くまたは突然出現させる→〜を瞬く間に作る ‖ *Mum can conjure up a meal out of almost anything.* お母さんはどんな物からでもあっと言う間にご飯を作れる.

**conjuror**(または **conjurer**) /kándʒərər, kʌ́n-/ 名 © ▶定義 a person who does clever tricks that appear to be magic 魔法のような手際の良いトリックをする人→手品師, 奇術師 ☛参 **magician**

**conker** /kάŋkər/ 英略式 (または **horse chestnut**) 名 © ▶定義 the seed of the horse chestnut tree, used in a children's game (**conkers**) セイヨウトチノキの実で, 子供の遊び(コンカーズ)に使われる→トチの実; トチの実遊び, コンカーズ(ひもに通したトチの実を振って相手の実を割をつける英国の子供の遊び)

★**connect** /kənékt/ 動 ▶定義1 自他 **connect (sth) (up) (to/with sth)** to be joined to sth; to join sth to sth else 〜に結合された; 〜をほかの…に結合させる→〜を(…に)つなぐ, 連結する, 接続する; つながる ‖ *The tunnels connect (up) ten metres further on.* トンネルは10メートル先でつながっている. *The printer is connected to the computer.* プリンターがコンピューターに接続されている *This motorway connects Oxford with Birmingham.* この高速道路はオックスフォードとバーミンガムを結んでいる. ☛参 **disconnect** ▶定義2 他 **connect sb/sth (with sb/sth)** to have an association with sb/sth else; to realize or show that sb/sth is involved with sb/sth else ほかの〜と関係を持つ; 〜がほかの…と関連していることに気付く, または示す→〜を(…と)結び付けて考える, 連想する, 関連づける ‖ *There was no evidence that she was connected with the crime.* 彼女がその犯罪に関係していたという証拠はなかった. ▶定義3 自 **connect (with sth)** (used about a bus, train, plane, etc) to arrive at a particular time so that passengers can change to another bus, train, plane, etc (バス, 列車, 飛行機などについて)乗客が別のバス, 列車, 飛行機などに乗り換えられるように特定の時間に到着する→(〜と)連絡する, 接続する ‖ *a connecting flight* 連絡する便

★**connection** /kənékʃ(ə)n/ 名 ▶定義1 © **a connection between A and B**; **a connection with/to sth** an association or relationship between two or more people or things 複数の人々や物の関連や関係→関係, 関連, つながり, 交流 ‖ *Is there any connection between the two organizations?* 2つの組織は関係があるのですか. *What's your connection with Brazil? Have you worked there?* ブラジルとの結び付きは何ですか. あちらで働いていたことがあるのですか. ▶定義2 © a place where two wires, pipes, etc join together 2本の電線やパイプなどが結び付けられている場所→接続, 連結部 ‖ *The radio doesn't work. There must be a loose connection somewhere.* 無線が故障している. どこかで接続が緩んでいるに違いない. ▶定義3 © a bus, train, plane, etc that leaves soon after another arrives ほかの1台が到着した直後に出発するバス, 列車, 飛行機など➡**乗り継ぎ, 連絡, 接続(便)** ‖ *Our bus was late so we missed our connection.* 私たちが乗ったバスが遅れたので, 乗り換えのバスが出てしまった.

成句 **in connection with sb/sth** 正式 ▶定義 about or concerning 〜について, 〜に関連する ➡**〜に関して, 〜に関する** ‖ *I am writing to you in connection with your application.* お申し込みの件についてお返事いたします.

**in this/that connection** 正式 ▶定義 about or concerning this/that これ・あれについて, または関連して➡**これ・それと関連して, この・その点に関して**

**connive** /kənáɪv/ 動自 ▶定義 **connive at sth**; **connive (with sb) (to do sth)** to work secretly with sb to do sth that is wrong; to do nothing to stop sb doing sth wrong 悪い〜をするために…とひそかに協力する; 〜が悪い…をするのを止める努力をしない➡**(〜と) 共謀する; 見て見ぬ振りをする, 黙認する** ‖ *The two parties connived to get rid of the president.* 2つの派が共謀して社長を追放した.

**connoisseur** /kànəsə́:r/ 名 C ▶定義 a person who knows a lot about art, good food, music, etc 芸術, おいしい食事, 音楽などについてよく知っている人➡**目利き, 鑑定家, 通**

**connotation** /kànətéɪʃ(ə)n/ 名 C ▶定義 an idea expressed by a word in addition to its main meaning 言葉の主な意味以外に表された考え➡**言外の意味, 含蓄, 含意** ‖ *'Spinster' means a single woman but it has negative connotations.* spinster は独身の女性を意味するが, 言外に否定的な意味が込められている.

*★**conquer** /kάŋkər/ 動他 ▶定義 **1** to take control of a country or city and its people by force, especially in a war 特に戦争において, 武力で国や都市とそこに住む人々を支配する➡**〜を征服する, 征伐する, 武力で奪う** ‖ *Napoleon's ambition was to conquer Europe.* ナポレオンの野心はヨーロッパ征服だった. (比喩) *The young singer conquered the hearts of audiences all over the world.* その若い歌手は世界中の観客の心をとりこにした. ▶定義 **2** to succeed in controlling or dealing with a strong feeling, problem, etc 強い感情や問題などをうまく抑える, またはこれらにうまく対処する➡**克服する, 〜に打ち勝つ** ‖ *She's trying to conquer her fear of flying.* 彼女は飛行機恐怖症を克服しようとしている.

**conqueror** /kάŋkərər/ 名 C ▶定義 a person who has conquered (1) sth 〜を征服した人➡**征服者, 戦勝者**

**conquest** /kάnkwèst, kάŋ-/ 名 ▶定義 **1** C U an act of conquering sth 〜を征服すること➡**征服, 克服** ‖ *the Norman conquest (= of England in 1066)* ノルマン人の征服 (=1066年のイングランド征服) *the conquest of Mount Everest* エベレストの征服 ▶定義 **2** C an area of land that has been taken in a war 戦争で奪われた土地➡**占領地, 征服地**

**conscience** /kάnʃ(ə)ns/ 名 C U ▶定義 the part of your mind that tells you if what you are doing is right or wrong 自分のしている事が正しい事か間違った事かを教えてくれる自分の心の部分➡**良心, 判断力, 道徳観念** ‖ *a clear/a guilty conscience* やましくない・やましい心

成句 **have sth on your conscience** ▶定義 to feel guilty because you have done sth wrong 悪い〜をしたためにやましく感じる➡**〜をやましく思う, 後ろめたく思う, 〜に気がとがめる**

**conscientious** /kànʃiénʃəs/ 形 ▶定義 **1** (used about people) careful to do sth correctly and well (人について) 正しく良い〜をするように心掛ける➡**良心的な, 誠実な, まじめな** ‖ *He's a conscientious worker.* 彼は良心的に働いている. ▶定義 **2** (used about actions) done with great care and attention (行動について) 十分に配慮して注意深く行われる➡**念入りな, 慎重な** ‖ *conscientious work* 念入りな仕事 ― **conscientiously** 副 ➡**良心的に; 念入りに, 注意深く**

**conscientious objector** 名 C ▶定義 a person who refuses to join the army, etc because he/she believes it is morally wrong to kill other people 人を殺すのは道義的に間違っていると信じて, 軍隊などに入ることを拒否する人➡**良心的兵役拒否者**

*★**conscious** /kάnʃəs/ 形 ▶定義 **1** able to see, hear, feel, etc things; awake 物事を見る, 聞く, 感じることなどができる; 目が覚めている➡**意識がある, 気が付いている** ‖ *The injured driver was still conscious when the ambulance*

*arrived.* 救急車が到着した時負傷した運転者はまだ意識があった. ⇔ **unconscious** ▶定義2
**conscious (of sth/that...)** noticing or realizing that sth exists; aware of sth 〜が存在することに気付いている;〜を意識している→(〜に・〜ということに)気付いて,(〜を)自覚して,感付いて,悟って ‖ *She didn't seem conscious of the danger.* 彼女は危険を意識していないようだった. *Bill suddenly became conscious that someone was following him.* ビルはだれかが後を付けていることに不意に気付いた. ▶定義3 that you do on purpose or for a particular reason 意図的に,または特定の理由があって行う→**意識的な,故意の,わざとらしい** ‖ *We made a conscious effort to treat both children equally.* 私たちは意識して2人の子供を平等に扱おうと努力した.
☛参 deliberate は同様の意味で用いられる. ― **consciously** 副 →意識して,意識的に

\***consciousness** /kánʃəsnəs/ 名 ▶定義1 **❶** the state of being able to see, hear, feel, etc 〜を見る,聞く,感じることなどができる状態→**意識(があること),正気** ‖ *As he fell, he hit his head and **lost consciousness**.* 落下した時,彼は頭を打って意識を失った. *She **regained consciousness** after two weeks in a coma.* 2週間の昏睡(こんすい)状態の後,彼女は意識を取り戻した. ▶定義2 [❶, 単数扱い] **consciousness (of sth)** the state of realizing or noticing that sth exists 〜が存在していることを悟っている,または気付いていることを悟っている状態→**知覚,認識,感付いていること** ‖ *There is (a) growing consciousness of the need to save energy.* 省エネルギーの必要性に対する認識が高まりつつある.

**conscript**¹ /kənskrípt/ 動 他 ▶定義 to make sb join the army, navy or air force 〜を陸軍,海軍または空軍に入隊させる→**〜を徴兵する,兵に取る** ― **conscription** 名 ❶ →**徴兵(制度),徴用**

**conscript**² /kánskrıpt/ 名 ❷ ▶定義 a person who has been conscripted 徴兵された人→**徴収兵** ☛参 **volunteer**¹(2)

**consecrate** /kánsəkrèıt/ 動 他 ▶定義 to state formally in a special ceremony that a place or an object can be used for religious purposes 場所や物を宗教的な目的のために使用できることを,特別の儀式で正式に述べる→**(教会・場所・物など)を奉献する,神聖にする** ― **consecration** /kànsəkréıʃ(ə)n/ 名 ❷ ❶ →**奉献,神聖化**

### consequent 345

**consecutive** /kənsék(j)ətıv/ 形 ▶定義 coming or happening one after the other 後から続いてやって来る,または起こる→**連続した,一連の** ‖ *This is the team's fourth consecutive win.* これでチームは4連勝した. ― **consecutively** 副 →**連続して,引き続いて**

**consensus** /kənsénsəs/ 名 [ 単数扱い, ❶ ] ▶定義 **(a) consensus (among/between sb) (on/about sth)** agreement among a group of people 大勢の人の同意 →**(人の間の)(〜についての)総意,合意,コンセンサス** ‖ *to **reach a consensus*** 合意に達する *There is no consensus among experts about the causes of global warming.* 地球温暖化の原因について専門家の意見は一致していない.

**consent**¹ /kənsént/ 動 ⾃ ▶定義 **consent (to sth)** to agree to sth; to allow sth to happen 〜に同意する;〜を起こさせておく→**(〜に)同意する,承諾する**

**consent**² /kənsént/ 名 ❶ ▶定義 agreement; permission 同意;許可→**同意,承諾** ‖ *The child's parents had to give their consent to the operation.* 子供の両親は手術に同意せざるを得なかった.

成句 **the age of consent** ⇒ **AGE**¹

\***consequence** /kánsıkwəns/ 名 ▶定義1 ❷ something that happens or follows as a result of sth else ほかの〜の結果として起こる出来事,または結果として続いて起こる出来事→**結果,影響** ‖ *Many people may lose their jobs **as a consequence of** recent poor sales.* 最近の落ち込んだ売り上げの結果から,多くの人が職を失うことになるだろう. ▶定義2 ❶ 正式 importance 重要性→**重要さ** ‖ *It is of no consequence.* それは重要ではない.

**consequent** /kánsıkwənt/ 形 正式 (名詞の前だけ) ▶定義 following as the result of sth else 結果として続く→**結果の; 必然の** ‖ *The lack of rain and consequent poor harvests have led to food shortages.* 雨が降らなかったのと,それによる凶作で食糧不足が発生した. ― **consequently** 副 →**結果として,したがって** ‖ *She didn't work hard enough, and consequently failed the exam.* 彼女はあまり一生懸命勉強しなかったので,その結果試験は不合格だった.

**conservation** /kɑ̀nsərvéɪʃ(ə)n/ 名 U ▶定義1 the protection of the natural world 自然界を保護すること→(自然などの)保護, 保全 ‖ *Conservation groups are protesting against the plan to build a road through the forest.* 自然保護団体が森を通り抜ける道路の建設計画に抗議している. ▶定義2 not allowing sth to be wasted, damaged or destroyed ～が浪費される, 傷付けられる, または破壊されることを許さないこと→(資源などの)節約 ‖ *the conservation of energy* エネルギーの節約 ☛動 conserve

**conservationist** /kɑ̀nsərvéɪʃ(ə)nɪst/ 名 C ▶定義 a person who believes in protecting the natural world 自然界を保護することを信条としている人→環境保全論者, 資源保護論者

**conservatism** /kənsɔ́ːrvətìzə)m/ 名 U ▶定義1 the disapproval of new ideas and change 新しい考えや変化を受け入れないこと→保守性, 保守主義 ▶定義2 usually **Conservatism** the beliefs of the Conservative Party 通常はConservatism. 保守党の信念→保守党の主義・政策

\***conservative**[1] /kənsɔ́ːrv(ə)tɪv/ 形 ▶定義1 not liking change; traditional 変化を好まない; 伝統的な→保守的な, 古臭い ▶定義2 (**Conservative**) connected with the British Conservative Party 英国保守党と関連した→保守党の ‖ *Conservative voters* 保守党に投票する人 ▶定義3 (used when you are guessing how much sth costs) lower than the real figure or amount (～の値段を推測する場合に用いて)実際の数値や量より少ない→控えめな ‖ *Even a conservative estimate would put the damage at about £4000 to repair.* 控えめに見積もっても損害を修復するには4000ポンドほどかかるだろう. ―**conservatively** 副→保守的に; 控えめに

**conservative**[2] /kənsɔ́ːrv(ə)tɪv/ 名 C ▶定義1 a person who does not like change 変化を好まない人→保守的な人, 保守主義者, 慎重な人 ▶定義2 (usually **Conservative**) a member of the British Conservative Party (通常はConservative) 英国保守党の一員→保守党員

**Conservative Party** 名 C ▶定義 one of the main political parties in Britain. The Conservative Party supports a free market and is opposed to the state controlling industry. 英国の主要な政党の1つ. 保守党は自由市場を支持し, 国家による産業の管理には反対している →保守党 ☛参 Labour Party, Liberal Democrats

**conservatory** /kənsɔ́ːrvətɔ̀ːri, -tòːri/ 名 C (複 **conservatories**) ▶定義 a room with a glass roof and walls often built onto the outside of a house 多くの場合家屋の外に付属して建てられ, 屋根と壁がガラス製の部屋→温室, コンサバトリー

**conserve** /kənsɔ́ːrv/ 動 他 ▶定義 to avoid wasting sth ～を無駄にしない→～を保存する, (資源など)を節約する ‖ *to conserve water* 水を節約する ☛名 conservation

\***consider** /kənsídər/ 動 他 ▶定義1 consider sb/sth (for/as sth); consider doing sth to think about sth carefully, often before making a decision 多くの場合結論を出す前に, ～について慎重に考える→～をよく考える, 熟考する, 検討する ‖ *She had never considered nursing as a career.* 彼女は今まで, 仕事としての看護について真剣に考えたことがなかった. *We're considering going to Spain for our holidays.* 私たちは休暇にスペインへ行くことを考えている.
▶定義2 consider sb/sth (as/to be) sth; consider that... to think about sb/sth in a particular way ～について特定の考えを抱く→～を…と見なす, ～と思う ‖ *He considered the risk (to be) too great.* 彼は危険が大きすぎると考えた. *He considered that the risk was too great.* 彼は危険が大きすぎると考えた. *Jane considers herself an expert on the subject.* ジェーンは自分がその問題についての専門家だと思っている.
▶定義3 to remember or pay attention to sth, especially sb's feelings ～, 特に…の感情を覚えている, またはそれを気に掛ける→～を思いやる, 考慮に入れる ‖ *I can't just move abroad. I have to consider my family.* 私はすぐに海外に引っ越すわけには行かない. 家族のことを考えなければならない.

\***considerable** /kənsíd(ə)rəb(ə)l/ 形 ▶定義 great in amount or size 量が多いまたはサイズが大きい→かなりの, 相当な ‖ *A considerable number of people preferred the old building to the new one.* かなり多くの人々が新しい建物よりも古

い建物を好んだ. —**considerably** /-əb(ə)li/ 副 ▶かなり, なかなか ‖ *This flat is considerably larger than our last one.* このフラットは私たちがこれまで住んでいたものよりかなり広い.

**considerate** /kənsíd(ə)rət/ 形 ▶定義 careful not to upset people; thinking of others 人の感情をかき乱さないように注意する; 他人のことを考える→**思いやりのある, 気が利く, 気が回る** ‖ *It was very considerate of you to offer to drive me home.* 車で家まで送ると言ってくださって, ご親切にありがとうございました. ⇔ **inconsiderate**

★**consideration** /kənsìdəréɪʃ(ə)n/ 名 ▶定義1 ❶正式 an act of thinking about sth carefully or for a long time ~について慎重にまたは長い間考えている行為→**よく考えること, 考慮, 検討** ‖ *I have given some consideration to the idea but I don't think it would work.* その案についてよく考えてみたが, うまくいくとは思えない. ▶定義2 ❸ something that you think about when you are making a decision 人が決定をしている際に考慮する事柄→**考慮する事柄, 問題点** ‖ *If he changes his job, the salary will be an important consideration.* 彼が転職するのなら, 給料のことが重要な理由になるだろう. ▶定義3 ❶ **consideration (for sb/sth)** the quality of thinking about what other people need or feel ほかの人が必要とする事または感じている事について考慮する性質→**(~に対する) 思いやり, 思慮, (気持ちを) 察すること, 気の付くこと** ‖ *Most drivers show little consideration for cyclists.* 多くの運転者は自転車に乗る人の立場をほとんど考えていない.

熟語 **take sth into consideration** ▶定義 to think about sth when you are forming an opinion or making a decision 意見をまとめるまたは決定する際に~について考える→**~を考慮する, 考えに入れる, 斟酌 (しんしゃく) する**

**considering** /kənsíd(ə)rɪŋ/ 前接 ▶定義 (used for introducing a surprising fact) when you think about or remember sth (驚くべき事を話すときに用いて) ~について考えて, または思い出して→**~にしては** ‖ *Considering you've only been studying for a year, you speak English very well.* 1年しか勉強していないにしては, あなたは英語を話すのがとても上手です.

**consign** /kənsáɪn/ 動 ⊕ 正式 ▶定義 **consign sb/sth to sth** to put or send sb/sth somewhere, especially in order to get rid of him/her/it 特に追い払うために~をある場所に配置する, または送る→**~を…に引き渡す, 送る, 片付ける** ‖ *I think I can consign this junk mail straight to the bin.* この不用な郵便物はこのままごみ箱に捨てていいだろう.

**consignment** /kənsáɪnmənt/ 名 ❸ ▶定義 goods that are being sent to sb/sth ~に送られる品物→**送り荷** ‖ *a new consignment of books* 書籍の新規委託貨物

★**consist** /kənsíst/ 動 (進行形は不可)

句動詞 **consist in sth** ▶定義 to have sth as its main point 主要部として~を含む→**主に~から成る** ‖ *Her job consisted in welcoming the guests as they arrived.* 彼女の主な仕事は到着した客を迎えることだ.

**consist of sth** ▶定義 to be formed or made up of sth ~から形成される, または作られる→**~から成る, ~から構成される** ‖ *The band consists of a singer, two guitarists and a drummer.* そのバンドのメンバーは歌手1人, ギタリスト2人, そしてドラマー1人だ.

▶この動詞は進行形では用いられないが, 現在分詞 (= -ing 形) としてはよく用いられる: *It's a full-time course consisting of six different modules.* (これは6単位から成る全日制の課程です.)

**consistency** /kənsíst(ə)nsi/ 名 (複 **consistencies**) ▶定義1 ❶ the quality of always having the same standard, opinions, behaviour, etc 常に水準, 意見, 行動などが同じである性質→**一貫性, 矛盾がないこと** ‖ *Your work lacks consistency. Sometimes it's excellent but at other times it's full of mistakes.* あなたの仕事には一貫性がありません. すばらしい出来の場合もあれば, 間違いだらけの場合もあります. ⇔ **inconsistency** ▶定義2 ❸ ❶ how thick or smooth a liquid substance is 液体の濃度や滑らかさ→**濃度, 密度, 粘度** ‖ *The mixture should have a thick, sticky consistency.* その混合物は高濃度で高粘度になるはずだ.

**consistent** /kənsíst(ə)nt/ 形 ▶定義1 always having the same opinions, standard, behav-

**consolation**

iour, etc; not changing 意見,水準,行動が常に同じような;変化しない→一貫性のある,矛盾のない ▶定義2 **consistent (with sth)** agreeing with or similar to sth 〜に一致する,または〜と似ている→調和する,両立する ‖ *I'm afraid your statement is not consistent with what the other witnesses said.* あなたの陳述はほかの証人の言うこととは矛盾しているようですが. ⇔ **inconsistent** — consistently 副→首尾一貫して,矛盾なく ‖ *We must try to maintain a consistently high standard.* 私たちは一貫して高い水準を維持できるように努めなければならない.

**consolation** /kɑ̀nsəléɪʃ(ə)n/ 名 C U ▶定義 a thing or person that makes you feel better when you are sad; a comfort 悲しいときに気持ちをいやしてくれる物または人;慰安→慰め,慰めとなるもの ‖ *It was some consolation to me to know that I wasn't the only one who had failed the exam.* 試験に落ちたのは私1人だけではないと知って,少し慰めになった.

**console** /kənsóʊl/ 動 他 ▶定義 to make sb happier when he/she is very sad or disappointed; to comfort sb ひどく悲しんでいる〜または落胆している〜を喜ばす;〜を慰める→〜を元気づける

**consolidate** /kənsɑ́lədèɪt/ 動 自 他 ▶定義 to become or to make sth firmer or stronger 〜が堅固または強固になる,あるいは〜を堅固または強固にする→固まる,強固になる;〜を固める,強化する ‖ *We're going to consolidate what we've learnt so far by doing some revision exercises today.* 今日は復習の練習問題をやって,これまでに学んだ事をしっかりと身に付けます. — consolidation /kənsɑ̀lədéɪʃ(ə)n/ 名 U→強化

**consonant** /kɑ́ns(ə)nənt/ 名 C ▶定義 any of the letters of the English alphabet except a, e, i, o, and u a, e, i, o, u 以外の英語アルファベット文字→子音,子音字 ‖ *The letters 't', 'm', 's' and 'b' are all consonants.* t, m, s, b の文字はすべて子音である. ◆参 vowel

**consortium** /kənsɔ́ːrtiəm, -ʃ(i)əm/ 名 C (複 **consortiums** または **consortia** /-tiə/) ▶定義 a group of companies that work closely together for a particular purpose 特定の目的のために共に働く会社の集合→共同企業体,コンソーシアム

**conspicuous** /kənspíkjuəs/ 形 ▶定義 easily seen or noticed 簡単に見える,または気付く→はっきり見える,目立つ,際立って見える;顕著な ⇔ **inconspicuous** — conspicuously 副→目立って,顕著に

**conspiracy** /kənspírəsi/ 名 C U (複 **conspiracies**) ▶定義 a secret plan by a group of people to do sth bad or illegal 悪い〜や違法な〜を行うために複数の人がひそかに立てる計画→陰謀,共謀 ‖ *a conspiracy against the president* 社長に対する陰謀

**conspirator** /kənspírətər/ 名 C ▶定義 a member of a group of people who are planning to do sth bad or illegal 悪い〜や違法な〜を計画する人々→共謀者,陰謀者

**conspire** /kənspáɪər/ 動 自 ▶定義1 **conspire (with sb) (to do sth)** to plan to do sth bad or illegal with a group of people 集団で悪事や違法行為を計画する→(〜と)共謀する,陰謀を企てる,(〜することを)たくらむ ‖ *A group of terrorists were conspiring to blow up the plane.* テロリストのグループは飛行機の爆破をたくらんでいた. ▶定義2 **conspire (against sb/sth)** (used about events) to seem to work together to make sth bad happen (出来事について) 悪い〜を一緒に起こさせているように思える→(事件などが)重なる,相次ぐ ‖ *When we both lost our jobs in the same week, we felt that everything was conspiring against us.* 2人とも同じ週に失業した時は,すべてが私たちにとって悪い方に動いているように感じた.

**constable** /kɑ́nstəb(ə)l, kʌ́n-/ =POLICE CONSTABLE

**constabulary** /kənstǽbjʊləri; -bjəlèri/ 名 C (複 **constabularies**) ▶定義 the police force of a particular area 特定の地域の警察隊→(1管区の)警察隊,警察官(全体) ‖ *the West Yorkshire Constabulary* 西ヨークシャー警察

*__constant__ /kɑ́nst(ə)nt/ 形 ▶定義1 happening or existing all the time or again and again 常に,または何度も繰り返し起こるまたは出現する→継続的な,絶えず続く ‖ *The constant noise gave me a headache.* 騒音が絶え間なく続いたので頭痛がした. ▶定義2 that does not change 変化しない→不変の,一定の;1つの事を守り通す,忠実な,堅実な ‖ *You use less petrol if you drive at a constant speed.* 一定の速度で走ればあなたは

ガソリンを節約できます.

**constantly** /kánst(ə)ntli/ 副 ▶定義 always; again and again 常に; 何度も繰り返して→**絶えず, いつも** ‖ *The situation is constantly changing.* 状況は絶えず変化している.

**constellation** /kànstəléɪʃ(ə)n/ 名 C ▶定義 a group of stars that forms a pattern and has a name 一定の形に並んでいて, 名前を持つ星の集まり→**星座**

**consternation** /kànstəméɪʃ(ə)n/ 名 U ▶定義 a feeling of shock or worry 衝撃または心配の感情→**ショック, 仰天, 大きな不安** ‖ *We stared at each other in consternation.* 私たちはひどく驚いてお互いを見詰め合った.

**constipated** /kánstəpèɪtəd/ 形 ▶定義 not able to empty waste from your body 体内の老廃物を排せつできない→**便秘している, 便秘の** ― **constipation** /kànstəpéɪʃ(ə)n/ 名 U→**便秘** ‖ *to suffer from/have constipation* 便秘している

**constituency** /kənstítʃuənsi/ 名 C (複 **constituencies**) ▶定義 a district and the people who live in it that a politician represents 政治家が代表する地区とそこに住む人々→**選挙区, 選挙民**

**constituent** /kənstítʃuənt/ 名 C ▶定義 1 one of the parts that form sth ～を構成する部分の1つ→**成分, (構成)要素** ‖ *Hydrogen and oxygen are the constituents of water.* 水素と酸素が水を構成している. ▶定義 2 a person who lives in the district that a politician represents 政治家が代表する地区に住む人→**選挙区民, 選挙人, 有権者**

**constitute** /kánstət(j)ùːt/ 動 他 正式 (進行形は不可) ▶定義 1 to be one of the parts that form sth ～を構成する一部である→**～を構成する, ～の一部を成す** ‖ *Women constitute a high proportion of part-time workers.* 女性がパート労働者の高い比率を占めている. ▶定義 2 to be considered as sth; to be equal to sth ある～だと見なされる; ある～に等しい→**～となる, ～を表す, ～と言える** ‖ *The presence of the troops constitutes a threat to peace.* 軍隊の存在は平和への脅威である.

▶この動詞は進行形では用いられないが, 現在分詞(=-ing形)ではよく用いられる: *Management has to fix a maximum number of hours as constituting a day's work.* (経営者側は1日の最大労働時間を決めなければならない.)

**constitution** /kànstət(j)úːʃ(ə)n/ 名 ▶定義 1 C the basic laws or rules of a country or organization 国や組織の基本的な法律や規則→**憲法, 法令, 規約** ‖ *the United States constitution* 合衆国憲法 ▶定義 2 U the way the parts of sth are put together; the structure of sth ～の各部分が結合されている様子; ～の構造→**構成, 構造, 組織** ‖ *the constitution of DNA* DNAの構造

**constitutional** /kànstət(j)úːʃ(ə)n(ə)l/ 形 ▶定義 connected with or allowed by the constitution of a country, etc 国などの法律に関連した, またはこれによって許可される→**憲法(上)の, 合憲の** ‖ *It is not constitutional to imprison a person without trial.* 裁判なしで人を刑務所に入れるのは憲法に反する.

**constrain** /kənstréɪn/ 動 他 正式 ▶定義 constrain sb/sth (to do sth) to limit sb/sth; to force sb/sth to do sth ～を制限する; ～に強制的にある事をさせる→**～を束縛する, 抑制する; ～に無理に…させる, ～を強制する** ‖ *The company's growth has been constrained by high taxes.* 会社の成長は高い税によって抑えられてきた.

**constraint** /kənstréɪnt/ 名 C U ▶定義 something that limits you; a restriction 人を制限する物; 制約→**制約, 束縛, 強制** ‖ *There are always some financial constraints on a project like this.* このようなプロジェクトには財政上の制約が付き物だ.

**constrict** /kənstríkt/ 動 自 他 ▶定義 1 to become or make sth tighter, narrower or less より窮屈, 狭小, 少量になる; ～を窮屈に, 狭く, または少なくする→**(～を)圧縮する, (～を)締め付ける, 制限する** ‖ *She felt her throat constrict with fear.* 彼女は恐怖で息が詰まりそうだった. *The valve constricts the flow of air.* バルブが空気の流れを制限する. ▶定義 2 to limit a person's freedom to do sth 人が～をする自由を制限する→**(～を)抑制する, 束縛する** ― **constriction** 名 C U→**圧縮, 締め付け**

**construct** /kənstrʌ́kt/ 動 他 ▶定義 to build or make sth ～を建てる, または作る→**～を建設する, 作る** ‖ *Early houses were constructed out of* *mud and sticks.* 昔の家は泥と棒切れから作られた. ☛ construct は build より正式な語.

**construction** /kənstrʌ́kʃ(ə)n/ 名 ▶定義1 **①**the act or method of building or making sth ～を建設したり作ること, またはその方法→建造, 建設(作業) ‖ *A new bridge is now under construction.* 新しい橋は現在建設中である. *He works in the construction industry.* 彼は建設業界で働いている. ▶定義2 **⊜正式** something that has been built or made; a building 建設または作成された物; 建物→建造物, 建築物 ‖ *The new pyramid was a construction of glass and steel.* 新しいピラミッドはガラスと鋼鉄の建造物である. ▶定義3 **⊜**the way that words are used together in a phrase or sentence 句や文での語の組み立てられ方→(文・語句の)組み立て, 構文; (語句の)解釈 ‖ *a grammatical construction* 文法的構造

**constructive** /kənstrʌ́ktɪv/ 形 ▶定義 useful or helpful 役立つまたは助けになる→建設的な, 有益な ‖ *constructive suggestions/criticisms/advice* 建設的な提案・批判・忠告 — **constructively** 副 →建設的に, 前向きに

**construe** /kənstrúː/ 動他正式 ▶定義 **construe sth (as sth)** to understand the meaning of sth in a particular way ～の意味を特定の見方で理解する→～を(…と)解釈する, (～という)意味に取る ‖ *Her confident manner is often construed as arrogance.* 彼女の自信にあふれた態度はしばしばごう慢だと受け取られる. ☛参 **misconstrue**

**consul** /kɑ́ns(ə)l/ 名 **⊜** ▶定義 an official who works in a foreign city helping people from his/her own country who are living or visiting there 外国の都市で働く役人で, そこに住んでいるまたは旅行している自国の人を援助する→領事 ☛参 **ambassador** — **consular** /kɑ́nsjʊlər, -s(ə)lər/ 形 →領事(館)の

**consulate** /kɑ́ns(ə)lət, -sjʊ-/ 名 **⊜** ▶定義 the building where a consul works 領事が働く建物 →領事館 ☛参 **embassy**

**consult** /kənsʌ́lt/ 動 ▶定義1 **⊕ consult sb/sth (about sth)** to ask sb for some information or advice, or to look for it in a book, etc ～に情報や忠告を求める, または本などで調べる→意見を聞く, 助言を求める, (辞書など)を調べる ‖ *If the symptoms continue, consult your doctor.* 症状が続くようなら, 医師に診てもらいなさい. ▶定義2 **⊜ consult with sb** to discuss sth with sb ～と…について議論する→相談する, 話し合う ‖ *Harry consulted with his brothers before selling the family business.* 家業を売却する前にハリーは兄弟と話し合った.

**consultancy** /kənsʌ́ltənsi/ 名 ▶定義1 **⊜**a company that gives expert advice on a particular subject 特定の問題について専門的な助言を与える会社→コンサルタント会社 ▶定義2 **⓾**expert advice that sb is paid to provide on a particular subject 特定の問題について～が有料で提供する専門的助言→専門的意見

**consultant** /kənsʌ́lt(ə)nt/ 名 **⊜** ▶定義1 a person who gives advice to people on business, law, etc 商売や法律などについて助言を与える人→顧問, コンサルタント ‖ *a firm of management consultants* 経営コンサルタント会社 ▶定義2 **医** a hospital doctor who is a specialist in a particular area of medicine 医学の特定の分野における専門家である病院の医師 →顧問医, 立ち会い医, 主任専門医 ‖ *a consultant psychiatrist* 顧問精神科医

**consultation** /kɑ̀ns(ə)ltéɪʃ(ə)n/ 名 **⊜⓾** ▶定義1 a discussion between people before a decision is taken 決定を下す前に行う議論→(専門家の)会議, 協議(会), 審議(会) ‖ *Diplomats met for consultations on the hostage crisis.* 外交官が集まって人質事件について協議した. *The measures were introduced without consultation.* その法案は審議を経ずに提出された. ▶定義2 正式 meeting sb to get information or advice, or looking for it in a book 情報や助言を得るために～に会うこと, または書物で調べること→相談, 諮問, (書物などの)参照, 参考 ‖ *a consultation with a doctor* 医師による診察

**consume** /kənsjúːm, -súːm/ 動他正式 ▶定義1 to use sth such as fuel, energy or time 燃料, エネルギー, 時間などの～を使う→～を消費する, 使う ‖ *This car consumes a lot of petrol.* この車はガソリンをたくさん食う. ▶定義2 to eat or drink sth ～を食べるまたは飲む→～を食べる・飲む, 摂取する ‖ *Wrestlers can consume up to 10000 calories in a day.* レスラーは1日に1万カロリーも摂取する. ☛ 名 **consumption** ▶定義3 (used about fire) to destroy sth (火につ

いて)〜を破壊する→〜を焼き尽くす,全焼させる ▶定義4 (used about an emotion) to affect sb very strongly (感情について)〜に非常に強い影響を与える→(感情が)心に食い入る,〜の心を奪う ‖ *She was consumed by grief when her son was killed.* 彼女は息子が死んだ時,悲嘆に暮れて憔悴(しょうすい)してしまった.

★**consumer** /kənsjúːmər, -súːm-/ 名 C ▶定義 a person who buys things or uses services 物を買う人またはサービスを利用する人→消費者

**consuming** /kənsjúːmɪŋ, -súːm-/ 形 (名詞の前だけ) ▶定義 that takes up a lot of your time and attention 多くの時間と集中力を使う →(感情などが)焼き尽くすような,激しい,強い ‖ *Sport is her consuming passion.* 彼女はスポーツに対して強い情熱を持っている.

**consummate**¹ /kánsəmət, kənsámət/ 形 (名詞の前だけ) 正式 ▶定義 extremely skilled; a perfect example of sth 非常に熟練した;〜の完ぺきな模範の→完全な,申し分のない,円熟した ‖ *a consummate performer/professional* 熟練した演奏家・最高の専門家

**consummate**² /kánsəmèɪt/ 動他 正式 ▶定義 to make a marriage or relationship complete by having sex 性交をすることにより結婚または関係を完全なものにする →(結婚)を完全にする — **consummation** /kànsəméɪʃ(ə)n/ 名 C U →(性交による)結婚の成立

**consumption** /kənsám(p)ʃ(ə)n/ 名 U ▶定義1 the amount of fuel, etc that sth uses 〜が使用する燃料などの量→消費量 ‖ *a car with low fuel consumption* 低燃費の車 ▶定義2 the act of using, eating, etc sth 〜を使用するまたは食べるなどの行為→消費,消耗,体内摂取 ‖ *The meat was declared unfit for human consumption (= for people to eat).* その肉は食用には(= 人が食べるためには)適さないと公表された. ☛ 動 consume

**cont**(または**contd**) 略 continued→続く ‖ *cont on p 91* 91ページに続く

★**contact**¹ /kántækt/ 名 ▶定義1 U contact (with sb/sth) meeting, talking to or writing to sb else 〜に会う,〜と話す,または〜に手紙を書くこと →(〜との)交際,連絡 ‖ *They are trying to make contact with the kidnappers.* 彼らは誘拐犯と接触しようとしている. *We keep in contact with our office in New York.* 私たちはニューヨークの事務所との連絡を絶やさない. *It's a pity to lose contact with old schoolfriends.* 学生時代の旧友たちと連絡が取れなくなるのは残念だ. ▶定義2 U contact (with sb/sth) the state of touching sb/sth 〜と接触すること(〜と)連絡を取ること,交際すること,かかわりを持つこと ‖ *This product should not come into contact with food.* この製品は食品に触れないようにすべきです. ▶定義3 C a person that you know who may be able to help you 知人で自分を助けてくれるかもしれない人→コネ,縁故 ‖ *business contacts* 商売上のコネ

**contact**² /kántækt/ 動他 ▶定義 to telephone or write to sb 〜に電話したり手紙を書く→〜に連絡する,接触する ‖ *Is there a phone number where I can contact you?* あなたに連絡ができる電話番号はありますか.

**contact lens** 名 C ▶定義 a small piece of plastic that fits onto your eye to help you to see better 目に装着する小さなプラスチック片で,物がよく見えるようになる→コンタクトレンズ ☛ **glasses** のさし絵

**contagious** /kəntéɪdʒəs/ 形 ▶定義 (used about a disease) that you can get by touching sb/sth (病気について)〜に接触することによって感染する→(接触)伝染性の,伝染病を感染させる ‖ *Smallpox is a highly contagious disease.* 天然痘は伝染性の高い病気である. (比喩) *Her laugh is contagious.* 彼女の笑いにはつい釣られてしまう. ☛参 **infectious** の注 — **contagion** /kəntéɪdʒ(ə)n/ 名 U→接触伝染,(接触)伝染病

★**contain** /kəntéɪn/ 動他 (進行形は不可) ▶定義1 to have sth inside or as part of itself 〜を内部に持つ,または一部として持つ→包含する,〜が入っている,組み込まれている ‖ *Each box contains 24 tins.* それぞれの箱には24缶ずつ入っている. ▶定義2 to keep sth within limits; to control sth 〜を制限内に保つ;〜を制御する→〜を抑える,食い止める ‖ *efforts to contain inflation* インフレを抑制するための努力 *She found it hard to contain her anger.* 彼女には怒りを抑えるのが難しかった.

▶この動詞は進行形では用いられないが,現在分詞(= -ing形)ではよく用いられる: *petrol containing lead* (鉛を含むガソリン)

## container

**containers**

*(illustrations labeled: box, box, matchbox, packet (米 pack), packet (米 package), sachet, packet, straw, carton, carton, tub, tube, cap/top, top, bag, bag, lid, top, spray, top, cork, lid, tin/can (米 can), can, can, bottle, jar)*

➤ contain はその内部に別の物を持つ物体について話す場合に用いる: *a jar containing olives* (オリーブの入ったびん) *This film contains violent scenes.* (この映画には暴力的な場面が含まれている。) include は～が全体の一部を形成している場合，または何かに属している場合を示すのに用いる: *a team of seven people including a cameraman and a doctor* (カメラマンと医師を含む7人のチーム) *The price of the holiday includes accommodation.* (その休暇の価格には宿泊料金も含まれている。)

**＊container** /kəntéɪnər/ 名 ❶ ▶定義 1 a box, bottle, packet, etc in which sth is kept ～を入れる箱，びん，かごなど➔**容器，入れ物** ‖ *a plastic container* プラスチック容器 ▶定義 2 a large metal box that is used for transporting goods by sea, road or rail 海上，道路，鉄道などで品物を輸送するために使用する大型の金属の箱➔**コンテナ** ‖ *a container lorry/ship* コンテナトラック・コンテナ船

**contaminate** /kəntǽmənèɪt/ 動他 ▶定義 to add a substance which will make sth dirty or harmful ～を汚したり有害にする物質を加える➔**～を汚染する，汚す** ‖ *The town's drinking water was contaminated with poisonous chemicals.* 町の飲料水は有害な化学物質で汚染された．— **contamination** /kəntæ̀mənéɪʃ(ə)n/ 名 ❶ ➔ **汚染，汚濁**

**contemplate** /kάntəmplèɪt/ 動他 ▶定義 1 to think carefully about sth or the possibility of doing sth ～について，または…を行う可能性について慎重に考える➔**熟考する，検討する** ‖ *Before her illness she had never contemplated retiring.* 病気になる前は，彼女は引退について真剣に考えたことがなかった． ▶定義 2 to look at sb/sth, often quietly or for a long time しばしば静かにまたは長い時間，～を見る➔**凝視する** — **contemplation** /kὰntəmpléɪʃ(ə)n, -təm-/ 名 ❶ ➔ **黙想，熟考，凝視**

**＊contemporary**[1] /kəntémp(ə)r(ə)ri; -rèri/ 形 ▶定義 1 belonging to the same time as sb/sth else ～と同じ時期に属する➔**同時代の，当時の** ‖ *The programme includes contemporary film footage of the First World War.* 番組には第1次世界大戦当時の映画フィルムが含まれている．

▶定義2 of the present time; modern 現在の; 現代の→**現代の** ‖ *contemporary music/art/society* 現代音楽・芸術・社会

**contemporary**² /kəntémp(ə)r(ə)ri; -rèri/ 图 ❷ (複 **contemporaries**) ▶定義 a person who lives or does sth at the same time as sb else ほかの〜と同じ時期に, 生きるまたは…をする人→**同時代の人**

**contempt** /kəntémpt/ 图 ❶ ▶定義 contempt (for sb/sth) the feeling that sb/sth does not deserve any respect or is without value 〜が尊敬に値しない, または価値がないと思うこと→**(〜に対する)軽べつ, 軽視** ‖ *The teacher treated my question with contempt.* 教師は私の質問を軽くあしらった. — **contemptuous** /kəntémptʃuəs/ 形→**軽べつ的な** ‖ *The boy just gave a contemptuous laugh when I asked him to be quiet.* 私が静かにするように言うと, 少年はばかにしたように笑った.

**contend** /kənténd/ 動 ▶定義1 ❸ contend with/against sb/sth to have to deal with a problem or a difficult situation 問題または困難な状況に対処しなければならない→**〜に立ち向かう** ‖ *She's had a lot of problems to contend with.* 彼女には取り組まねばならない問題がたくさんあった. ▶定義2 ⊕ 正式 to say or argue that sth is true 〜が真実であると言う, または主張する→**力説する** ‖ *The young man contended that he was innocent.* 若者は自分が無実だと主張した. ▶定義3 ❸ contend (for sth) to compete against sb to win or gain sth 勝利または〜を得ることを目指して…と競争する→**競う, 張り合う** ‖ *Two athletes are contending for first place.* 2人の選手は優勝を目指して競い合っている.

**contender** /kənténdər/ 图 ❷ ▶定義 a person who may win a competition 競争で勝つ可能性のある人→**競争相手, ライバル** ‖ *There are only two serious contenders for the leadership.* 本当にリーダーの座を競っているのは2人だけだ.

★**content**¹ /kəntént/ 形 (名詞の前は不可) ▶定義 content (with sth); content to do sth happy or satisfied with what you have or do 自分が持っている物または自分がする事を楽しんでいる, または満足している→**(〜に・〜して)満足して, 十分で** ‖ *I don't need a new car - I'm perfectly content with the one I've got.* 新しい車は必要ない—今持っている物に十分満足しているから.

★**content**² /kάntent/ 图 ▶定義1 contents [複数扱い] the thing or things that are inside sth 〜の内部にある物→**中身** ‖ *Add the contents of this packet to a pint of cold milk and mix well.* この包みの中身を1パイントの冷たい牛乳に加えてよくかき混ぜてください. ▶定義2 [単数扱い] the main subject, ideas, etc of a book, article, television programme, etc 本, 記事, テレビ番組などの主題, 主旨など→**趣旨, テーマ, 内容** ‖ *The content of the essay is good, but there are too many grammatical mistakes.* 小論文の趣旨はいいが, 文法上の誤りが多すぎます. ▶定義3 [単数扱い] the amount of a particular substance that sth contains 〜に含まれる特定の物質の量→**含有量** ‖ *Many processed foods have a high sugar content.* 多くの加工食品は砂糖の含有量が多い.

**content**³ /kɑntént/ 图 [単数扱い] 成句 to your heart's content ⇒ **HEART**

**content**⁴ /kəntént/ 動 ⊕ ▶定義 content yourself with sth to accept sth even though it was not exactly what you wanted 本当に望んだ物ではなくても〜を受け入れる→**妥協する, 〜で我慢する** ‖ *The restaurant was closed, so we had to content ourselves with a sandwich.* そのレストランが閉まっていたので, 私たちはサンドイッチで我慢しなければならなかった.

**contented** /kənténtəd/ 形 ▶定義 happy or satisfied 喜んで, または満足して→**満足そうな, 幸福そうな** ‖ *The baby gave a contented chuckle.* 赤ん坊は満足そうに笑った. — **contentedly** 副→**満足そうに, 満足した様子で**

**contention** /kəntén∫(ə)n/ 图 ▶定義1 ❶ 正式 arguing; disagreement 議論すること; 不和→**口論, 争い** ▶定義2 ❷ 正式 your opinion; sth that you say is true 意見; 真実だと主張する〜→**主張** ‖ *The government's contention is that unemployment will start to fall next year.* 政府は来年には失業者が減少し始めると主張している.

成句 **in contention (for sth)** ▶定義 having a chance of winning a competition 競争に勝つチャンスがある→**(〜をめぐって)争って, 競って** ‖ *Four teams are still in contention for the cup.* 今も4チームが優勝カップを目指して争っている.

**contentious** /kəntén∫əs/ 形 ▶定義 likely to

cause argument 議論になりそうな→**議論を呼ぶ** ‖ *a contentious issue* 異論のある問題

**contentment** /kəntént mənt/ 名 U ▶定義 a feeling of happy satisfaction 幸福で満足した気持ち→**満ち足りていること**

*****contest**[1] /kάntest/ 名 C ▶定義 a competition to find out who is the best, strongest, most beautiful, etc 最も優れた人, 強い人, 美しい人などを決める競争→**競技, 競争, コンテスト, コンクール** ‖ *I've decided to enter that writing contest.* 私はその作文コンクールに応募することを決めた. *The by-election will be a contest between the two main parties.* その補欠選挙は2大政党間の争いになるだろう.

**contest**[2] /kəntést/ 動 他 ▶定義 1 to take part in a competition or try to win sth 競争に参加する, または〜を勝ち取ろうとする→**〜を競う, 争う** ‖ *Twenty-four teams will contest next year's World Cup.* 来年のワールドカップでは24チームが競う. ▶定義 2 to say that sth is wrong or that it was not done properly 〜が間違っているとまたは正しく行われなかったと言う→**異議を唱える** ‖ *They contested the decision, saying that the judges had not been fair.* 裁判官が公正でなかったと言って, 彼らは決定に異議を唱えた.

**contestant** /kəntéstənt/ 名 C ▶定義 a person who takes part in a contest コンテストに参加する人→**競技者, 競争相手, (競技会などの)出場者, 参加者** ‖ *Four contestants appear on the quiz show each week.* クイズショーには毎週4人の参加者が出場する.

*****context** /kάntekst/ 名 C U ▶定義 1 the situation in which sth happens or that caused sth to happen 〜が起こる, または…を起こす原因となる状況→**背景, 状況** ‖ *To put our company in context, we are now the third largest in the country.* 状況を考えて正しく判断すると, 当社は現在国内第3位の規模である. ▶定義 2 the words that come before or after a word, phrase or sentence that help you to understand its meaning 語, 句または文の前や後に来る語で, その語・句・文の意味を理解するのに役立つ→**文脈, 脈絡, (文の)前後関係, コンテクスト** ‖ *You can often guess the meaning of a word from its context.* 語の意味は文脈から推測できることが多い. *Taken out of context, his comment made no sense.* 前後関係を切り離すと, 彼のコメントは意味をなさなかった.

*****continent** /kάnt(ə)nənt/ 名 ▶定義 1 C one of the seven main areas of land on the Earth 地球上の7つの主要な陸地の1つ→**大陸** ‖ *Asia, Africa and Antarctica are continents.* アジア, アフリカ, 南極は大陸である. ▶定義 2 **the Continent** [単数扱い] 英 the main part of Europe not including the British Isles イギリス諸島以外のヨーロッパの主要部分→**ヨーロッパ大陸**

**continental** /kὰnt(ə)néntl/ 形 ▶定義 1 connected with or typical of a continent 大陸に関連した, または大陸に典型的な→**大陸の, 大陸風の, 大陸性の** ‖ *Moscow has a continental climate: hot summers and cold winters.* モスクワは大陸性気候で, 夏は暑く冬は寒い. ▶定義 2 英 connected with the main part of Europe not including the British Isles イギリス諸島以外のヨーロッパの主要部分と関連した→**ヨーロッパ大陸式・風の** ‖ *continental holidays* 大陸式の休暇

**contingency** /kəntíndʒ(ə)nsi/ 名 C ( 複 **contingencies** ) ▶定義 a possible future situation or event 起こり得る将来の状況や出来事→**(予期される)事件, 万一の出来事** ‖ *We'd better make contingency plans just in case something goes wrong.* 万一問題が起こったときのために緊急時の計画を立てておく方がよい. *We've tried to prepare for every possible contingency.* 起こり得るすべての緊急事態に備えようとした.

**contingent** /kəntíndʒ(ə)nt/ 名 [C, 単数または複数形の動詞と共に] ▶定義 1 a group of people from the same country, organization, etc who are attending an event 行事に参加している人の集まりで, 同じ国や組織に属する人々→**代表団, 派遣団** ‖ *the Irish contingent at the conference* 会議のアイルランド代表団 ▶定義 2 a group of armed forces forming part of a larger force より大きな軍隊の一部を成す軍隊の一団→**分遣隊, 分艦隊**

**continual** /kəntínjuəl/ 形 ▶定義 happening again and again 何回も起こる→**頻繁に起こる, 継続的な** ‖ *His continual phone calls started to annoy her.* 彼が何回も電話してくるので, 彼女はいら立ち始めた. ☛参 **incessant** — **continually**

副 →継続的に, 頻繁に

**continuation** /kəntìnjuéɪʃ(ə)n/ 名 [単数扱い, ❶] ▶定義 something that continues or follows sth else; the act of making sth continue 継続する, または~に続いて起こる物事; ~を継続させること→続けること, 連続 ‖ *The team are hoping for a continuation of their recent good form.* チームは最近の良いコンディションが続くことを願っている. *Continuation of the current system will be impossible.* 現在のシステムを継続させることは不可能だ.

\***continue** /kəntínju:/ 動 ▶定義1 ⓔ to keep happening or existing without stopping 止まることなく起こる, または存在し続ける→続く, 存続する ‖ *If the pain continues, see your doctor.* 痛みが続くようなら医師に診てもらいなさい. ▶定義2 ⓔⓜ continue (doing/to do sth); continue (with sth) to keep doing sth without stopping やめることなく~を続ける→~を継続する, 持続する ‖ *They ignored me and continued their conversation.* 彼らは私を無視して話し続けた. *He continued working/to work late into the night.* 彼は夜遅くまで働き続けた. *Will you continue with the lessons after the exam?* 試験の後も勉強を続けるつもりですか. ▶定義3 ⓔⓜ to begin to do or say sth again after you had stopped 中断した後, 再び~を始めるまたは言う→再開する ‖ *The meeting will continue after lunch.* 会合は昼食後に再開します. ▶定義4 ⓔⓜ to go further in the same direction 同じ方向にさらに進む→進み続ける ‖ *The next day we continued our journey.* 次の日も私たちは旅を続けた.

**continued** /kəntínju:d/ 形 ▶定義 going on without stopping 止まることなく続く→続く, 連続している ‖ *There are reports of continued fighting near the border.* 国境付近では戦闘が続いているといううわさだ.

**continuity** /kɑ̀nt(ə)n(j)ú:əti/ 名 ⓤ ▶定義 the fact of continuing without stopping or of staying the same 止まらずに続くこと, または変わらないこと→連続(性), 継続, 切れ目がないこと ‖ *The pupils will have the same teacher for two years to ensure continuity.* 授業内容がとぎれないように, 生徒たちは2年間同じ教師に教わる.

\***continuous** /kəntínjuəs/ 形 ▶定義 happening or existing without stopping 止まることなく起こるまたは存在する→連続的な, 切れ目のない, とぎれない ‖ *There was a continuous line of cars stretching for miles.* 車の列が何マイルもとぎれずに続いていた. — continuously 副 →連続的に, 切れ目なく ‖ *It has rained continuously here for three days.* 当地では3日間ずっと雨が降り続いている.

**the continuous tense**(または **the progressive tense**)名 ⓒ (文法) ▶定義 the form of a verb such as 'I am waiting', 'I was waiting' or 'I have been waiting' which is made from a part of 'be' and a verb ending in '-ing' and is used to describe an action that continues for a period of time I am waiting, I was waiting, I have been waiting のような動詞の形で, be の一部と -ing で終わる動詞から作られ, 一定期間続く動作を表す場合に用いる→進行形

▶進行形についての説明は, 巻末の「文法早見表」を参照.

**contort** /kəntɔ́:rt/ 動 ⓔⓜ ▶定義 to move or to make sth move into a strange or unusual shape ~が動いて奇妙な形や普通でない形になる, または~を動かしてそのような形に変える→ねじ曲がる, ゆがむ; ~をねじ曲げる, ゆがめる ‖ *His face contorted/was contorted with pain.* 彼は痛みに顔をゆがめた. — contortion 名 ⓒ→ねじれ, ゆがみ

**contour** /kɑ́ntʊər/ 名 ⓒ ▶定義1 the shape of the outer surface of sth ~の表面の形→外形, 輪郭 ‖ *I could just make out the contours of the house in the dark.* 暗がりで家の輪郭だけが見て取れた. ▶定義2 (または **contour line**) a line on a map joining places of equal height 地図で同じ高さの地点を結んだ線→等高線

**contraception** /kɑ̀ntrəsépʃ(ə)n/ 名 ⓤ ▶定義 the ways of preventing a woman from becoming pregnant 女性が妊娠することを防ぐ方法→避妊(法) ‖ *a reliable form of contraception* 確実な避妊法 ☛参 **birth control**, **family planning**

**contraceptive** /kɑ̀ntrəséptɪv/ 名 ⓒ ▶定義 a drug or a device that prevents a woman from becoming pregnant 女性が妊娠することを防ぐ薬や道具→避妊薬, 避妊具 — contraceptive 形 →避妊(用)の

\***contract**[1] /kɑ́ntrækt/ 名 ⓒ ▶定義 a written legal

agreement 書面による法律上の同意→**契約(書), 約定** ‖ They **signed** a three-year **contract with** a major record company. 彼らは大きなレコード会社と３年の契約を結んだ. a temporary contract 仮契約

**contract**[2] /kəntrǽkt/ 動 ▶定義1 ⊜ ⊕ to become or to make sth smaller or shorter ～が小さくまたは短くなる, ～を小さくまたは短くする→**縮む･める, 収縮する･させる** ‖ Metals contract as they cool. 金属は冷えると収縮する. ⇔ **expand** ▶定義2 ⊕ to get an illness or disease, especially a serious one 病気, 特に重病になる→**(病気)にかかる, 罹患(りかん)する** ‖ to contract pneumonia 肺炎にかかる ▶定義3 ⊜ ⊕ to make a written legal agreement with sb to do sth ～を行うことについて…で書面で法的に同意する→**(～を)契約する** ‖ His firm has been contracted to supply all the furniture for the new building. 彼の会社は新しいビルの家具をすべて提供する契約をしている.

句動詞 contract sth out (to sb) ▶定義 to arrange for work to be done by sb outside your own company 社外の～に仕事をしてもらう手配をする→**(～に)(仕事)を請け負わせる, 下請けに出す**

**contraction** /kəntrǽkʃ(ə)n/ 名 ▶定義1 ⓤ the process of becoming or of making sth become smaller or shorter ～が小さくまたは短くなること, ～を小さくまたは短くすること→**短縮, 収縮, 縮小** ‖ the expansion and contraction of a muscle 筋肉の弛緩(しかん)と収縮 ▶定義2 ⓒ a strong movement of the muscles that happens to a woman as her baby is born 出産時に女性に見られる筋肉の激しい動き→**(子宮の)収縮, 陣痛** ▶定義3 ⓒ a shorter form of a word or words 語の短い形→**短縮形, 縮約形** ‖ 'Mustn't' is a contraction of 'must not'. mustn't は must not の短縮形です.

**contractor** /kántræktər/ 名 ⓒ ▶定義 a person or company that has a contract to do work or provide goods or services for another company 他社のために働くことまたは品物やサービスを提供することを契約した人または会社→**請負人, 請負業者**

**contractual** /kəntrǽktʃuəl/ 形 ▶定義 connected with or included in a contract 契約と関連した, 契約に含まれる→**契約の, 契約上の**

**contradict** /kàntrədíkt/ 動 ⊕ ▶定義 to say that sth is wrong or not true; to say the opposite of sth ～が間違っている, または真実でないと言う; ～と反対の事を言う→**否定する, 否認する** ‖ These instructions seem to contradict previous ones. この指示は前のものとは矛盾しているようだ.

**contradiction** /kàntrədíkʃ(ə)n/ 名 ⓒ ⓤ ▶定義 a statement, fact or action that is opposite to or different from another one ある物とは反対または異なる言明, 事実, 行動→**矛盾, 不一致, 反論** ‖ There were a number of contradictions in what he told the police. 彼が警察に話したことにはいくつかの矛盾点があった. This letter is **in** complete **contradiction to** their previous one. この手紙には前のものとは正反対の事が書いてある.

**contradictory** /kàntrədíkt(ə)ri/ 形 ▶定義 being opposite to or not matching sth else ほかの～と反対の, または一致しない→**矛盾した, 相反する** ‖ Contradictory reports appeared in the newspapers. 新聞に矛盾する報告が掲載された.

**contraflow** /kántrəflòu/ 名 ⓒ ▶定義 the system that is used when one half of a wide road is closed for repairs, and traffic going in both directions has to use the other side 広い道路の半分が修理のため閉鎖された場合に使われるシステムで, 双方向の交通をもう一方の側で行わなければならない→**片側通行**

**contralto** /kəntrǽltou/ 名 ⓒ ⓤ ▶定義 the lowest female singing voice; a woman with this voice 女性の歌声の最も低い声域; このような声の女性→**コントラルト, コントラルト歌手**

**contraption** /kəntrǽpʃ(ə)n/ 名 ⓒ ▶定義 a strange or complicated piece of equipment 奇妙で複雑な装置→**奇妙な仕掛け, 珍奇な機械** ‖ The first aeroplanes were dangerous contraptions. 最初の飛行機は危険で奇妙な機械だった.

**contrary**[1] /kántrəri; -trèri/ 形 ▶定義1 (名詞の前だけ) completely different; opposite 全く違う; 反対の→**逆の** ‖ I thought it was possible, but she took the contrary view. 私は可能だと思ったが, 彼女の見解は全く反対だった. ▶定義2 **contrary to** completely different from; opposite to; against ～の反対で→**～に反して** ‖ Contrary **to** popular **belief** (= to what many people *think), not all boxers are stupid.* 一般的な思い込み(= 多くの人が考えている事)に反して,すべてのボクサーが愚かなわけではない.

**contrary**² /kάntrəri; -trèri/ 名
成句 **on the contrary** ▶定義 the opposite is true; certainly not 反対の事が事実で;とんでもない→**それどころか,とんでもない** ‖ *'You look as if you're not enjoying yourself.' 'On the contrary, I'm having a great time.'* 「何だかつまらなそうですね」「とんでもない,大いに楽しんでいます」
**to the contrary** 正式 ▶定義 saying the opposite 反対の内容で[の]→ **それと反対に[の],逆に[の]** ‖ *Unless I hear anything to the contrary, I shall assume that the arrangements haven't changed.* 予定変更の知らせがなければ,取り決めは変更されていないということだろう.

***contrast**¹ /kάntræst; -træst/ 名 ▶定義 1 ⓤ comparison between two people or things that shows the differences between them 2者の違いを示すような2人の人または2つの物の比較→**対照(すること),対比** ‖ *In contrast to previous years, we've had a very successful summer.* これまでの年と比較して,この夏は大変うまくいった. ▶定義 2 ⓒⓤ (a) contrast (to/with sb/sth); (a) contrast (between A and B) a clear difference between two things or people that is seen when they are compared 比較したときに分かる2つの物または2人の人の明らかな違い→**大きな差異,相違** ‖ *There is a tremendous contrast between the climate in the valley and the climate in the hills.* 渓谷の気候と丘陵の気候は大きく異なる. ▶定義 3 ⓒ something that is clearly different from sth else when the two things are compared 2つのものを比べたときに他方の〜と明らかに違うもの→**正反対のもの,対照的なもの** ‖ *This house is quite a contrast to your old one!* この家はあなたの古い家とは全くの別物だ.

***contrast**² /kəntάːst; -træst/ 動 ▶定義 1 ⓗ contrast (A and/with B) to compare people or things in order to show the differences between them その違いを示すために人々または物を比較する→**〜を対照する,対比する** ‖ *The film contrasts his poor childhood with his later life as a millionaire.* 映画は彼の貧しい子供時代を,後年の富豪時代と対比している. ▶定義 2 ⓘ contrast with sb/sth to be clearly different when compared 比較したときに明らかに異なる→**〜に対照して引き立つ・目立つ,〜と良い対照を成す** ‖ *This comment contrasts sharply with his previous remarks.* このコメントは彼の前の意見とは鋭い対照を成している.

**contravene** /kὰntrəvíːn/ 動 ⓗ 正式 ▶定義 to break a law or a rule 法律や規則を破る→**〜に違反する,反する,〜を犯す** — **contravention** /kὰntrəvénʃ(ə)n/ 名 ⓒⓤ→**違反(行為)**

***contribute** /kəntríbjuːt/ 動 contribute (sth) (to/towards sth) ▶定義 1 ⓘⓗ to give a part of the total, together with others 皆と一緒に全体の一部を与える→**〜に寄付する,〜を寄贈する,〜に貢献する,寄与する** ‖ *Would you like to contribute towards our collection for famine relief?* 飢餓救済の募金にご協力いただけませんか. *The research has contributed a great deal to our knowledge of cancer.* その研究は私たちのがんについての知識に大いに寄与した. ▶定義 2 ⓘ to be one of the causes of sth 〜の原因の1つとなる→**一因となる** ‖ *It is not known whether the bad weather contributed to the accident.* 悪天候が事故の一因になったかどうかは分からない. ▶定義 3 ⓘⓗ to write articles for a magazine or newspaper 雑誌または新聞に記事を書く→**〜に(…を)寄稿する,記事を寄せる**

**contribution** /kὰntrɪbjúːʃ(ə)n/ 名 ⓒ ▶定義 a contribution (to/toward sth) something that you give, especially money or help, or do together with other people 特に金や援助など人が与える物,またはほかの人と協力して行う事→**寄付(金),寄贈(物);貢献,寄与** ‖ *If we all **make a small contribution**, we'll be able to buy Ray a good present.* 皆が少しずつお金を出し合えば,レイに良いプレゼントを買えるでしょう.

**contributor** /kəntríbjətər/ 名 ⓒ ▶定義 a person who contributes to sth 〜に寄与する人→**貢献者,寄付者**

**contributory** /kəntríbjət(ə)ri; -tɔ̀ːri/ 形 ▶定義 helping to cause or produce sth 〜を引き起こしたり生み出す助けとなる→**一因となる,一助となる** ‖ *Alcohol was a contributory factor in her death.* アルコールは彼女の死の一因だった.

**contrive** /kəntráɪv/ 動 ⓗ ▶定義 1 to manage to do sth, although there are difficulties 困難があ

っても何とか～を行う➔どうにか～をする, 何とかうまく～をする, 見事に～する ‖ *If I can contrive to get off work early, I'll see you later.* 何とか早くに仕事を終えられたら, 後で会いましょう. ▶定義2 to plan or invent sth in a clever and/or dishonest way 巧妙で不正なやり方で～を計画する, または発明する➔**～をたくらむ; ～を考案する** ‖ *He contrived a scheme to cheat insurance companies.* 彼は保険会社をだます計略を考え出した.

**contrived** /kəntráɪvd/ 形 ▶定義 hard to believe; not natural or realistic 信じ難い; 自然でない, または現実的でない➔**不自然な** ‖ *The ending of the film seemed rather contrived.* その映画の結末はかなり不自然だった.

***control**¹ /kəntróʊl/ 名 ▶定義1 ❶ control (of/over sb/sth) power and ability to make sb/sth do what you want ～に自分が望む事をさせる力と能力➔**(～に対する)支配(力)** ‖ *Rebels managed to **take control** of the radio station.* 反逆者たちはうまくラジオ局を支配下に収めた. *Some teachers find it difficult to **keep control** of their class.* 一部の教師はクラスを監督するのが難しいと思っている. *He **lost control** of the car and crashed.* 彼は車を制御できなくなり衝突した. *I was late because of circumstances **beyond my control**.* 私にはどうにもできない事情によって遅刻しました. ▶定義2 ❻Ⓤ (a) control (on/over sth) a limit on sth; a way of keeping sth within certain limits ～に対する制限; ～を一定の制限内に置く方法➔**抑制, 制御, 統制, 規制** ‖ *price controls* 物価統制 *The faults forced the company to review its **quality control** procedures.* その欠陥のため会社は品質管理手順を見直さなければならなくなった. ▶定義3 ❻ one of the parts of a machine that is used for operating it 機械を操作するために使用する部分➔**制御装置, 操縦装置** ‖ *the controls of an aeroplane/a TV* 飛行機の操縦装置・テレビの調整用つまみ *a control panel* 制御盤 ▶定義4 [単数扱い] the place from which sth is operated or where sth is checked ～が操作される場所, または～が検査される場所➔**制御室, 管制室** ‖ *We went through passport control and then got onto the plane.* 私たちはパスポートコントロールを通って飛行機に乗った.

成句 **be in control (of sth)** ▶定義 to have the power or ability to deal with sth ～に対処する力または能力を持つ➔**～を管理している, 支配している** ‖ *The police are again in control of the area following last night's violence.* 昨夜の暴力事件の後, 警察は再び地域を掌握している.

**be/get out of control** ▶定義 to become impossible to deal with 対処できない・できなくなる➔**制しきれない, 統制できなくなる, 手に負えなくなる** ‖ *The demonstration got out of control and fighting broke out.* デモが秩序が保たれなくなり暴力ざたが発生した.

**under control** ▶定義 being dealt with successfully うまく対処している➔**～の管理下にある, 掌握している, 制御している** ‖ *It took several hours to bring the fire under control.* 消火には数時間かかった.

*****control**² /kəntróʊl/ 動 ⓥ (**controlling; controlled**) ▶定義1 to have power and ability to make sb/sth do what you want ～に自分が望む事をさせる力と能力を持つ➔**(～を)支配する, 管理する, 監督する** ‖ *One family controls the company.* 1つの家が会社を支配している. *Police struggled to control the crowd.* 警察は群衆を統制するのに苦労した. *I couldn't control myself any longer and burst out laughing.* 私はこらえきれずにとうとう大笑いした. ▶定義2 to keep sth within certain limits ～を一定の制限内に保つ➔**(～を)制限する, 規制する** ‖ *measures to control price rises* 物価上昇を抑制する方策 — **controller** 名 ❻➔**支配者, 管理する人, 制御する人; 制御手段** ‖ *air traffic controllers* 航空管制官

**controversial** /kɑ̀ntrəvə́ːrʃ(ə)l, -siəl/ 形 ▶定義 causing public discussion and disagreement 公の議論と意見の相違を引き起こす➔**論争の的になる, 議論の余地のある** ‖ *a controversial issue/decision/plan* 議論の的になる問題・決定・計画

**controversy** /kɑ́ntrəvə̀ːrsi, kəntrɑ́vəsi/ 名 ❻Ⓤ (複 **controversies**) ▶定義 public discussion and disagreement about sth ～についての公の議論と意見の相違➔**議論の的, 論争, 議論** ‖ *The plans for changing the city centre caused a great deal of controversy.* 市の中心部を変更する計画は大きな議論を引き起こした.

**conurbation** /kɑ̀nərbéɪʃ(ə)n/ 名 ❻ ▶定義 a very

large area of houses and other buildings where towns have grown and joined together 街が成長し合併してできた, 住宅とそのほかの建造物がある広い地域→**大都市圏, 広域都市圏**

**convalesce** /kὰnvəlés/ 動⾃ ▶定義 to rest and get better over a period of time after an illness 病気の後で一定期間休息を取り回復させる→**病後療養する** ― **convalescence** /kὰnvəlés(ə)ns/ 名[単数扱い, **U**]→**病後療養期; 病み上がり** ― **convalescent** /kὰnvəlés(ə)nt/ 形→**回復期の, 病み上がりの**

**convene** /kənvíːn/ 動⾃他 正式 ▶定義 to come together or to bring people together for a meeting, etc 会合などのために集まってくる, または人を集める→**(〜を)召集する, 召喚する;(会が)開かれる,(人が)会合する**

**convenience** /kənvíːnjəns/ 名 ▶定義1 **U** the quality of being easy, useful or suitable for sb 〜にとって容易, 有益または適切であること→**便利, 好都合(なこと), 都合のいいとき・機会, 便宜** ‖ *a building designed for the convenience of disabled people* 障害のある人々の利便を考えて設計されたビル *For convenience, you can pay for everything at once.* 都合がいいように, すべてまとめてお支払いいただけます. ▶定義2 **C** something that makes things easier, quicker or more comfortable 物事をより容易に, 速く, または快適にするもの→**便利な物, 便利な設備, 衣食住の便;(文明の)利器** ‖ *houses with all the modern conveniences (= central heating, hot water, etc)* 近代設備(= セントラルヒーティング, 給湯など)がすべて整った家 ▶定義3 **C** 英 a public toilet →**公衆トイレ**

**convenience food** 名 **C U** ▶定義 food that you buy frozen or in a box or can, that you can prepare very quickly and easily 冷凍食品または箱詰めや缶詰の食品で, 非常に速く簡単に調理できる→**インスタント食品**

\***convenient** /kənvíːnjənt/ 形 ▶定義1 suitable or practical for a particular purpose; not causing difficulty 特定の目的に適した, または役に立つ; 不便を掛けない→**便利な, 都合が良い** ‖ *I'm willing to meet you on any day that's convenient for you.* いつでもあなたのご都合の良い日にお会いしましょう. *It isn't convenient to talk at the moment, I'm in the middle of a meeting.* 今はちょっと都合が悪くて話せません. 会議の最中なのです. ⇔ **inconvenient** ▶定義2 close to sth; in a useful position 〜に近い; 便利な場所にある→**近くで; 便利な** ‖ *Our house is convenient for the shops.* 我が家は商店が近くて便利だ. ― **conveniently** 副 →**便利に, 都合良く**

**convent** /kάnvənt/ 名 **C** ▶定義 a place where women (nuns) live in a religious community 女性(修道女)が宗教的共同生活をする場→**(女子)修道院,(女子)修道会** ☛参 **monastery**

**convention** /kənvén∫(ə)n/ 名 ▶定義1 **C U** a traditional way of behaving or of doing sth 伝統的な行動様式, または〜をする伝統的方法→**慣習,(世間の)仕来り, 慣行; 因習** ‖ *A speech by the bride's father is one of the conventions of a wedding.* 花嫁の父のあいさつは結婚式の慣習の1つだ. *The film shows no respect for convention.* その映画は慣習を無視している. ▶定義2 **C** a large meeting of the members of a profession, political party, etc; a conference 同業者や政党などによる大規模な会合; 会議→**代表者会議, 協議会, 大会, 党大会** ‖ *the Democratic Party Convention* 民主党大会 ▶定義3 **C** a formal agreement, especially between different countries 特に国家間の正式な同意→**条約, 協定, 協約** ‖ *the Geneva Convention* ジュネーブ条約

**conventional** /kənvén∫(ə)n(ə)l/ 形 ▶定義 always behaving in a traditional or normal way 常に伝統的なまたは標準的な振る舞いをする→**慣習に従った, 因習的な; 型にはまった, 平凡な** ‖ *conventional attitudes* 型にはまった態度 *I quite like him but he's so conventional (= boring, because of this).* 彼のことはとても好きだが, 平凡すぎる(= そのために退屈である). ⇔ **unconventional** ― **conventionally** /-∫(ə)n(ə)li/ 副 →**慣習的に, 仕来り通りに; 月並みに, 平凡に**

**converge** /kənvə́ːrdʒ/ 動⾃ ▶定義 converge (on sb/sth) (used about two or more people or things) to move towards each other or meet at the same point from different directions (複数の人や物について)互いに向かって動く, または別の方向から来て同じ点で出会う→**一点に集まる, 集中する, 集合する** ‖ *Fans from all over the country converge on the village during the annual music festival.* 毎年の音楽祭には国中からファンがその村に集まる.

**conversant** /kənvˊɚːrs(ə)nt/ 形 正式 ▶定義 **conversant with sth** knowing about sth; familiar with sth ～について知っている; ～に慣れている→～に精通して, 親しんで ‖ *All employees should be conversant with basic accounting.* 従業員はすべて会計の基礎に精通していなければならない.

★**conversation** /kὰnvərséɪʃ(ə)n/ 名 ❻ ❶ ▶定義 a talk between two or more people 複数の人が交わす話→**会話, 対話, 談話** ‖ *I had a long conversation with her about her plans for the future.* 私は将来の計画について彼女と長時間話し合った. *His job is his only topic of conversation.* 彼が話す話題は仕事のことばかりだ.

成句 **deep in thought/conversation** ⇒ **DEEP**¹

**converse** /kənvˊɚːrs/ 動 ⓐ 正式 ▶定義 to talk to sb; to have a conversation ～に話す; 会話する→**談話を交わす, 語り合う**

**conversely** /kənvˊɚːrsli/ 副 正式 ▶定義 in a way that is opposite to sth ～の反対で→**逆に, 正反対に** ‖ *People who earn a lot of money have little time to spend it. Conversely, many people with limitless time do not have enough money to do what they want.* 大金を稼ぐ人はその金を使う時間がほとんどない. 反対に時間が無制限にある人は大抵, したい事をするだけの金がない.

**conversion** /kənvˊɚːrʒ(ə)n, -ʃ(ə)n/ 名 (**a**) **conversion (from sth) (into/to sth)** ▶定義 1 ❻ ❶ the act or process of changing from one form, system or use to another 1つの形, 形式, 利用法などからほかへ変化すること, またはその過程→**転換, 転化, 転用; 改造, 改装** ‖ *a conversion table for miles and kilometres* マイルとキロメートルの変換表 ▶定義 2 ❻ ❶ becoming a member of a different religion 異なる宗教の信者になる→**改宗, 回心**

**convert**¹ /kənvˊɚːrt/ 動 ⓐ ⓞ ▶定義 1 **convert (sth) (from sth) (into/to sth)** to change from one form, system or use to another 1つの形, 形式, 利用法などからほかへ変わる・変える→**(～を)(…から)(～へ)転換する, 転用する, 改造する, 改装する** ‖ *a sofa that converts into a double bed* ダブルベッドとしても使えるソファー *How do you convert pounds into kilos?* ポンドをキロに変換するにはどうしますか. ▶定義 2 **convert (sb) (from sth) (to sth)** to change or to persuade sb to change to a different religion 異なる宗教に変わる, または説得して～を異なる宗教に変えさせる→**(～から)(…に)改宗する, ～を(…から)(～に)改宗させる** ‖ *As a young man he converted to Islam.* 若い時に彼はイスラム教に改宗した. *to convert people to Christianity* 人々をキリスト教に改宗させる

**convert**² /kάnvəːrt/ 名 ❻ ▶定義 **a convert (to sth)** a person who has changed his/her religion 宗教を変えた人 → **(～への)改宗者**

**convertible**¹ /kənvˊɚːrtəb(ə)l/ 形 ▶定義 able to be changed into another form 別の形に変えることができる→**変えられる, 転換できる** ‖ *convertible currencies (= those that can be exchanged for other currencies)* 兌換(だかん)貨幣(= ほかの通貨に変えられる通貨)

**convertible**² /kənvˊɚːrtəb(ə)l/ 名 ❻ ▶定義 a car with a roof that can be folded down or taken off 折り畳むまたは取り外すことができる屋根の付いた車→**コンバーチブル**

**convex** /kɑnvéks, kənvéks/ 形 ▶定義 having a surface that curves towards the outside of sth, like an eye 目のように～の外に向かって湾曲した面を持つ→**凸状の, 凸面の** ‖ *a convex lens* 凸面レンズ ☛参 **concave**

**convey** /kənvéɪ/ 動 ⓞ ▶定義 1 **convey sth (to sb)** to make ideas, thoughts, feelings, etc known to sb 案, 考え, 感情などを～に知らせる→**～を(…に)伝える, 伝達する** ‖ *The film conveys a lot of information but in an entertaining way.* その映画は多くの情報を, 楽しめる形で伝えてくれる. *Please convey my sympathy to her at this sad time.* この悲しい時にお悔やみを彼女に伝えてください. ▶定義 2 正式 to take sb/sth from one place to another, especially in a vehicle 特に乗り物で～をある場所から別の場所へ運ぶ→**～を運搬する, 運送する, 運ぶ**

**conveyor belt** 名 ❻ ▶定義 a moving belt that carries objects from one place to another, for example in a factory 例えば工場などで物をある場所から別の場所へ運ぶ動くベルト→**ベルトコンベヤー**

**convict**¹ /kənvíkt/ 動 ⓞ ▶定義 **convict sb (of sth)** to say officially in a court of law that sb is guilty of a crime 法廷で～が有罪であると正式に言う→**～を(…の罪で)有罪と宣告する, ～を有罪**

と決する ‖ *He was convicted of armed robbery and sent to prison.* 彼は武装強盗で有罪の判決を受け刑務所に送られた. ⇨**acquit**

**convict**² /kánvɪkt/ 名 ● ▶定義 a person who has been found guilty of a crime and put in prison 有罪を宣告され刑務所に入れられた人→**罪人,囚人,有罪の宣告を受けた人**

**conviction** /kənvíkʃ(ə)n/ 名 ▶定義1 ● Ⓤ the action of finding sb guilty of a crime in a court of law 法廷で〜が有罪であると決定すること→**有罪の判決** ‖ *He has several previous convictions for burglary.* 彼は過去に何回か不法侵入で有罪になっている. ▶定義2 ● a very strong opinion or belief 非常に確固とした意見や信念→**確信,信念,強く信じること** ‖ *religious convictions* 宗教的信念 ▶定義3 Ⓤ the feeling of being certain about what you are doing 自分のしている事に確信があること→**自信,(自分に対する)確信,自信** ‖ *He played without conviction and lost easily.* 彼は自信を持たずにプレーして,あっさりと負けた.

*****convince** /kənvíns/ 動 ⓗ ▶定義1 convince sb (of sth/that...) to succeed in making sb believe sth 〜に…を信じさせることに成功する→**〜を(…だと)納得させる,説得する** ‖ *She convinced him of the need to go back.* 彼女は引き返すことが必要だと彼を説得した. *I couldn't convince her that I was right.* 彼女は私が正しいということを納得しなかった. ▶定義2 convince sb (to do sth) to persuade sb to do sth 〜を説得して…をさせる→**(〜するように)…を納得させる,〜するように…を説得する** ‖ *The salesman convinced them to buy a new cooker.* セールスマンは彼らに新しい調理器具をうまく売り付けた.

*****convinced** /kənvínst/ 形 (名詞の前は不可) ▶定義 completely sure about sth 〜について完全に確信している→**信念のある,確信を抱いた,自信のある** ‖ *He's convinced of his ability to win.* 彼は自分に勝つ力があると確信している.

*****convincing** /kənvínsɪŋ/ 形 ▶定義1 able to make sb believe sth 〜に…を信じさせることができる→**説得力のある; もっともらしい** ‖ *Her explanation for her absence wasn't very convincing.* 彼女の欠席理由はあまり説得力がなかった. ▶定義2 (used about a victory) complete; clear (勝利について) 完全な; 明白な→**圧倒的な**

# cook¹ 361

‖ *a convincing win* 圧倒的な勝利 — **convincingly** 副 →**納得がいくように,なるほどと思わせるように**

**convoy** /kánvɔɪ/ 名 ● Ⓤ ▶定義 a group of vehicles or ships travelling together 一緒に移動する車両または船舶の集団→**車両部隊,船団; 護衛艦,警護艦** ‖ *a convoy of lorries* トラックの集団 *warships travelling in convoy* 船団を作って進む軍艦

**convulse** /kənvʌ́ls/ 動 ⓐ ⓗ ▶定義 to make sudden violent movements that you cannot control; to cause sb to move in this way 抑制できない急な激しい動きをする; 〜にそのような動きをさせる→**激しく震動する・させる,けいれんする・させる** ‖ *He was convulsed with pain.* 彼は痛みに身を震わせた.

**convulsion** /kənvʌ́lʃ(ə)n/ 名 [●, 通常は複数] ▶定義 a sudden violent movement that you cannot control 抑制できない急な激しい動き→**激しい震動,けいれん** ‖ *Children sometimes have convulsions when they are ill.* 子供は病気のときにけいれんを起こすことがある.

**coo** /kuː/ 動 ⓐ ▶定義1 to make a soft low sound like a bird (a dove) 鳥(ハト)のような静かな低い音を立てる→**クークーと鳴く,(ハトのように)クークーと言う** ▶定義2 to speak in a soft, gentle voice 低く優しい声で話す→**優しくささやく** ‖ *He went to the cot and cooed over the baby.* 彼はベッドに近付いて赤ん坊に優しく話し掛けた.

*****cook¹** /kʊk/ 動 ▶定義1 ⓐ ⓗ to prepare food for eating by heating it 食品を加熱して食べられるようにする→**(〜を)(火で)料理する,調理する,(食事)を作る** ‖ *My mother taught me how to cook.* 母が私に料理の仕方を教えてくれた. *The sauce should be cooked on low heat for twenty minutes.* ソースは弱火で20分間煮込みます. *He cooked us a meal.* 彼が私たちに食事を作ってくれた. ▶定義2 ⓐ (used about food) to be prepared for eating by being heated (食べ物について)加熱されて食べられるようになる→**(火で)料理される,煮える,焼ける,火が通る** ‖ *I could smell something cooking in the kitchen.* 台所で何かが煮えているにおいがした.

▶食品はさまざまな方法で調理される. boilingはなべで湯を使う. fryingはフライパンで

熱した油や脂を使う. grilling はグリルで食品を上から加熱する. toast bread はグリルやトースターでパンをカリカリしたキツネ色に焼く. bake はケーキやパンをオーブンで焼く. roast はオーブンで肉やジャガイモを焼く.

### ▶日本語 vs 英語

**cook と「料理する」**

日本語の「料理する」は, 火を通さず食卓に出すことも表現できますが, 英語の cook は食材に火を通すことで食べられるように加工されて初めて成立する行為です.

**句動詞** cook sth up **略式** ▶定義 to invent sth that is not true 真実でない〜をねつ造する→〜をごまかす, でっち上げる ‖ She cooked up an excuse for not arriving on time. 彼女は遅刻した言い訳をでっち上げた.

**cook**² /kʊk/ 名 C ▶定義 a person who cooks 料理をする人→料理人, コック ‖ My sister is an excellent cook. 私の姉は料理がうまい.

**cookbook** /kókbʊk/ = COOKERY BOOK

★**cooker** /kókər/ 名 C ▶定義 a large piece of kitchen equipment for cooking using gas or electricity. It consists of an oven, a flat top on which pans can be placed and often a device which heats the food from above (a grill). ガスや電気を使用して調理するための大型の台所設備. オーブン, なべなどを置ける平らな部分, そして多くは食品を上から加熱する装置（グリル）から成る→料理用こんろ, レンジ, オーブン ☞ C7ページのさし絵

**cookery** /kók(ə)ri/ 名 U ▶定義 the skill or activity of preparing and cooking food 食物を準備して料理する技術, またはその行為→料理, 料理法 ‖ Chinese/French/Italian cookery 中華・フランス・イタリア料理

**cookery book** (または **cookbook**) 名 C ▶定義 a book that gives instructions on cooking and how to cook individual dishes (recipes) 料理の方法と特定の料理の作り方（レシピ）を教える本→料理の本

**cookie** /kóki/ 米 = BISCUIT

★**cooking** /kókɪŋ/ 名 U ▶定義1 the preparation of food for eating 食物を食べられるように準備すること→料理（すること）, 調理 ‖ Cooking is one of her hobbies. 料理は彼女の趣味の1つだ.

▶ do the cooking は食品を調理する場合に一般的に用いる表現: In our house, I do the cleaning and my husband does the cooking. (我が家では私が掃除をして夫が料理をする.)

▶定義2 food produced by cooking 調理して出来上がる食物→料理 ‖ He missed his mother's cooking when he left home. 家を離れた時, 彼は母の料理が懐かしかった.

★**cool**¹ /kuːl/ 形 ▶定義1 fairly cold; not hot or warm 程よく冷たい・寒い; 暑く［熱く］も, 暖かく［温かく］もない→涼しい, (程よく) 冷たい ‖ It was a cool evening so I put on a pullover. 涼しい夕方だったので, 私はセーターを着た. What I'd like is a long cool drink. 私が欲しいのは深いグラスに注いだ冷たい飲み物だ. ☞参 cold¹の注 ▶定義2 calm; not excited or angry 冷静な; 興奮したり怒っていない→平静な, 落ち着いた, 慌てない ‖ She always manages to remain cool under pressure. 彼女はプレッシャーを受けてもいつもうまく平静を保てる. ▶定義3 unfriendly; not showing interest 親しげでない; 興味を示さない→冷淡な, よそよそしい; 熱意のない, 無関心な ‖ When we first met, she was rather cool towards me, but later she became friendlier. 初めて会った時彼女はよそよそしかったが, そのうち親しげになった. ▶定義4 (俗語) very good or fashionable とても良い, または流行の→すばらしい, すてきな, 格好いい ‖ Those are cool shoes you're wearing! とても格好いい靴を履いているね.

★**cool**² /kuːl/ 動 ▶定義1 自 他 cool (sth/sb) (down/off) to lower the temperature of sth; to become cool¹(1) 〜の温度を下げる; 少し冷たく［寒く］なる→冷える, 〜を冷やす, 涼しくなる, 〜を涼しくする ‖ Let the soup cool (down). スープを冷ましなさい. After the game we needed to cool off. 試合の後で涼まなければならなかった. A nice cold drink will soon cool you down. 冷たい飲み物を飲めばすぐに涼しくなりますよ. ▶定義2 自 (used about feelings) to become less strong (感情について) それほど強くなくなる→静まる, 冷静になる

**句動詞** cool (sb) down/off ▶定義 to become or make sb calmer 〜が冷静になる, 〜を冷静にさせる→静まる, 静める, 落ち着く, 落ち着かせる

**cool**³ /kuːl/ 名 [単数扱い] ▶定義 **the cool** a cool temperature or place; the quality of being cool 涼しい温度または場所; 涼しいこと→涼しい場所・時; 涼味, 程よい冷気, 涼しさ ‖ *We sat in the cool of a cafe, out of the sun.* 私たちは太陽を避けて涼しい喫茶店に座った.

成句 **keep/lose your cool** ▶定義 to stay calm/to stop being calm and become angry, nervous, etc 冷静でいる・冷静さを失って怒る, 神経質になるなどする→落ち着いている・興奮する, かっとなる, 慌てる

**cooling-off period** 名 C ▶定義 a period of time when sb can think again about a decision that he/she has made ～が自分のした決定についてもう一度考えることができる期間→冷却期間, 購入契約撤回[クーリングオフ]期間

**coolly** /kúːli/ 副 ▶定義 in a calm way; without showing much interest or excitement 冷静に; 興味や関心をあまり示さずに→落ち着いて; 冷淡に, よそよそしく ‖ *At first she was very angry; then she explained the problem coolly.* 最初彼女はとても怒っていたが, 後で冷静に問題を説明してくれた.

**coolness** /kúːlnəs/ 名 U ▶定義 the quality or state of being cool 冷たいこと, 冷静なこと→冷静さ, 冷淡さ ‖ *the coolness of the water* 水の冷たさ *his coolness under stress* ストレスを受けても彼が平然としていること *their coolness towards strangers* 彼らのよそ者に対する冷淡さ

**coop** /kuːp/ 動
句動詞 **coop sb/sth up (in sth)** ▶定義 to keep sb/sth inside a small space ～を狭い場所に閉じ込める→～を閉じ込める, (かご, おりなどに)入れる ‖ *The children were cooped up indoors all day because the weather was so bad.* とても天気が悪かったので子供たちは一日中屋内に閉じ込められていた.

**cooperate**(医 または **co-operate**) /koυápərèɪt/ 動 自 cooperate (with sb/sth) ▶定義 **1** to work with sb else to achieve sth ～と一緒に働いて…を成し遂げる→(～と)協力する, 協同する, 協力して～する ‖ *Our company is cooperating with a Danish firm on this project.* このプロジェクトで当社はデンマークの会社と協力している.

▶定義 **2** to be helpful by doing what sb asks you to do ～に頼まれた事をして役に立つ→力を合わせる, 協力的になる, 力を貸す ‖ *If everyone cooperates by following the instructions, there will be no problem.* 皆が指示に従って力を合わせれば, 何の問題もないだろう.

**cooperation**(医 または **co-operation**) /koυàpəréɪʃ(ə)n/ 名 U ▶定義 **1** cooperation (with sb) working together with sb else to achieve sth ～と一緒に働いて…を成し遂げること→協力, 共同, 提携 ‖ *Schools are working in close cooperation with parents to improve standards.* 学校は保護者と密接に協力し合って教育水準を上げることを目指している. ▶定義 **2** help that you give by doing what sb asks you to do ～に頼まれた事をして役に立つこと→協力, 支援, 援助 ‖ *The police asked the public for their cooperation in the investigation.* 警察は市民に捜査に協力するよう求めた.

**cooperative**¹(医 または **co-operative**) /koυáp(ə)rətɪv/ 形 ▶定義 **1** done by people working together 人々が共に働いて成し遂げる→協力して, 協調的な, 共同の ‖ *a cooperative business venture* 共同ベンチャー事業 ▶定義 **2** helpful; doing what sb asks you to do 助けとなる; ～に頼まれた事をする→協力的な, 助けとなる ‖ *My firm were very cooperative and allowed me to have time off.* 私の会社はとても協力的で, 仕事を休むことを認めてくれた. ⇔ **uncooperative**

**cooperative**²(医 または **co-operative**) /koυáp(ə)rətɪv/ 名 C ▶定義 a business or organization that is owned and run by all of the people who work for it そこで働くすべての人が所有し経営する事業や組織→生協, 生活協同組合(の売店), 共同組織 ‖ *a workers' cooperative* 労働者の生活協同組合

**coordinate**¹(医 または **co-ordinate**) /koυɔ́ːrd(ə)nət, -nèɪt/ 動 他 ▶定義 to organize different things or people so that they work together 共同し合えるように異なる人または物をまとめ上げる→～を調整する, 調和させる, まとめる ‖ *It is her job to coordinate the various departments.* さまざまな部門をまとめるのが彼女の仕事だ.

**coordinate**²(医 **co-ordinate**) /koυɔ́ːrd(ə)nət, -nèɪt/ 名 C ▶定義 one of the two sets of numbers and/or letters that are used for finding the position of a point on a map 地図上の地点を見つけるために使用する2組の番号と・または文字のうちの1つ→地図で地点を示すための数字や文字; 座標

**coordination**(医 または **co-ordination**) /koʊɔ́ːrd(ə)néɪʃ(ə)n/ 名 U ▶定義1 the organization of different things or people so that they work together 共同し合えるように異なる物または人をまとめ上げること→調整、調和させること、協力、まとめること ▶定義2 the ability to control the movements of your body properly 体の動きを適切に制御する力→(運動器官の)連動、協調; 共同作用 ‖ *Children's coordination improves as they get older.* 子供の運動器官の連動は成長するにつれて向上する.

**coordinator**(医 または **co-ordinator**) /koʊɔ́ːrd(ə)nèɪtər/ 名 C ▶定義 a person who is responsible for organizing different things or people so that they work together 共同し合えるように異なる物または人をまとめることを担当する人→調整役、まとめ役、責任者、コーディネーター

**cop**¹ /kɑp/(または **copper**) 名 C 略式 ▶定義 a police officer 警察官→警官、巡査

**cop**² /kɑp/ 動 (**copping**; **copped**) 略式
句動詞 **cop out (of sth)** ▶定義 to avoid sth that you should do, because you are afraid or lazy 恐れるまたは怠惰であるためにやるべき~を避ける→手を引く、すっぽかす ‖ *She was going to help me with the cooking but she copped out at the last minute.* 彼女は私の料理を手伝ってくれる予定だったが、土壇場ですっぽかした.

**cope** /koʊp/ 動 自 ▶定義 **cope (with sb/sth)** to deal successfully with a difficult matter or situation 困難な問題や状況にうまく対処する→(~に)うまく対処する、(~を)うまく切り抜ける ‖ *She sometimes finds it difficult to cope with all the pressure at work.* 彼女は時には仕事のプレッシャーすべてに対処することが難しいと感じる.

**copious** /koʊpiəs/ 形 ▶定義 in large amounts; plentiful 大量の; 豊富な→非常に多い、ばく大な、豊かな ‖ *She made copious notes at the lecture.* 彼女は講義で非常にたくさんノートを取った.
— **copiously** 副 →大量に、豊かに

**cop-out** 名 C 略式 ▶定義 a way of avoiding sth that you should do やるべき~を避ける方法→逃げ道、口実

**copper** /kɑ́pər/ 名 ▶定義1 U a common reddish-brown metal よく見られる赤茶色の金属→銅 ‖ *water pipes made of copper* 銅製の配水管 ▶定義2 C 英 a coin of low value made of brown metal 茶色の金属から作られる低額の硬貨→銅貨、1ペニー硬貨 ‖ *I only had a few coppers left.* 銅貨が2、3個しか残っていなかった. ▶定義3 = COP¹

**copse** /kɑps/ 名 C ▶定義 a small area of trees or bushes 木々またはやぶが生えた狭い範囲→雑木林、低木林、茂み

**copulate** /kɑ́pjəleɪt/ 動 自 正式 ▶定義 (used especially about animals) to have sex (特に動物について)交尾する→交尾する、交接する — **copulation** /kɑ̀pjəléɪʃ(ə)n/ 名 U →交尾、種付け

★**copy**¹ /kɑ́pi/ 名 C (複 **copies**) ▶定義1 something that is made to look exactly like sth else ほかの~と全く同じに見えるように作られたもの→写し、複写、コピー ‖ *I kept a copy of the letter I wrote.* 私は自分が書いた手紙の写しを保管しておいた. *the master copy (= the original piece of paper from which copies are made)* 原本(= 写しが作られた元の書類) *to make a copy of a computer file* コンピューターのファイルのコピーを作る ☛参 **photocopy** ▶定義2 one book, newspaper, record, etc of which many have been printed or produced 数多く印刷または制作された本、新聞、レコードなどの1つ→~部、冊、通 ‖ *I managed to buy the last copy of the book left in the shop.* 私は書店に残っていたその本の最後の1冊を何とか買うことができた.

> ▶日本語 vs 英語
>
> copy と「コピー」
>
> 　英語の copy には、日本語のコピーと同じ意味の「複写」という意味もありますが、機械での複写を言うときには特に photocopy を用います。また copy は「冊」という意味で用いられることが多く、a copy of the Bible(聖書1冊)のように表現します。

★**copy**² /kɑ́pi/ 動 (現分 **copying**; 三単現 **copies**; 過、過分 **copied**) ▶定義1 to make sth exactly the same as sth else ~をほかの…と全く同じにする→~を複写する、~の写しを取る、~を写す、コピーする ‖ *The children copied pictures from* *a book.* 子供たちは本の絵を写した. *It is illegal to copy videos.* ビデオのコピーを取るのは違法だ. ▶定義2 ⓘ **copy sth (down/out)** to write down sth exactly as it is written somewhere else どこかほかの場所に書かれている通り正確に〜を書き取る→〜をそっくり写す, 写し取る, 模写する ‖ *I copied down the address on the brochure.* 私はパンフレットの住所を書き写した. *I copied out the letter more neatly.* 私は手紙をきちんと清書した. ▶定義3 ⓘ = PHOTO-COPY ▶定義4 ⓘ to do or try to do the same as sb else; to imitate ほかの〜と同じ事をする, またはしようとする; まねする→〜をまねる, 模倣する, 手本とする ‖ *She copies everything her friends do.* 彼女は何でも友達のする事をまねする. ▶定義5 ⓘ **copy (from sb)** to cheat in an exam or test by writing what sb else has written ほかの〜の書いたものを書き写して, 試験やテストでカンニングする→(カンニングなどをして)写し取る, カンニングをする ‖ *He was caught copying from another student in the exam.* 彼は試験でほかの生徒の答案をカンニングして見つかった.

**copyright** /kápiràɪt/ 🔣 ⓒ ⓤ ▶定義 the legal right to be the only person who may print, copy, perform, etc a piece of original work, such as a book, a song or a computer program 本, 歌またはコンピュータープログラムなどの原物を, 印刷, 複写, または演奏などできる唯一の人であるという法律上の権利→著作権, 版権

**coral** /kɔ́(ː)r(ə)l/ 🔣 ⓤ ▶定義 a hard red, pink or white substance that forms in the sea from the bones of very small sea animals 非常に小さい海洋生物の骨から海中で形成される, 赤, ピンクまたは白の硬い物体→さんご ‖ *a coral reef (= a line of rock in the sea formed by coral)* さんご礁 (= さんごが形成する海中の岩の列)

**cord** /kɔːrd/ 🔣 ▶定義1 ⓒ ⓤ (a piece of) strong, thick string (1本の) 丈夫で太いひも→綱, ひも ▶定義2 ⓒ ⓤ 特に 困 (a piece of) wire covered with plastic; flex プラスチックで被覆された (1本の) 針金; コード→(電気, 電話などの) コード ☛ **cable** のさし絵 ▶定義3 **cords** [複数扱い] trousers made of a thick soft cotton cloth (**corduroy**) 厚くて柔らかい綿布 (コーデュロイ) から作られたズボン→コーデュロイ[コール天]のズボン

**cordial** /kɔ́ːrdʒəl; -diəl/ 🔣 ▶定義 pleasant and friendly 愛想が良く親しげな→誠心誠意の, 温かい, 心のこもった ‖ *a cordial greeting/smile* 心のこもったあいさつ・ほほえみ — **cordially** /-dʒəli; -diəl-/ 🔣 →心を込めて, 心から

**cordless** /kɔ́ːrdləs/ 🔣 ▶定義 without a cord (2) cord (2) のない→コードのない, コードレスの, 充電式の ‖ *a cordless phone/kettle/iron* コードレス電話機・湯沸かし・アイロン

**cordon**¹ /kɔ́ːrdn/ 🔣 ⓒ ▶定義 a line or ring of police or soldiers that prevents people from entering an area 人々がある範囲に入ることを阻止する警官や兵士の列や輪→非常線

**cordon**² /kɔ́ːrdn/ 🔣
**句動詞 cordon sth off** ▶定義 to stop people entering an area by surrounding it with a ring of police or soldiers 人々がある範囲に入るのを阻止するため, 警官や兵士の輪で囲む→〜に非常線を張る, 〜の交通を遮断する ‖ *The street where the bomb was discovered was quickly cordoned off.* 爆弾が発見された通りは速やかに交通が遮断された.

**corduroy** /kɔ́ːrdərɔ̀ɪ/ 🔣 ⓤ ▶定義 thick soft cotton cloth with lines on it, used for making clothes あぜのある厚くて柔らかい綿布で, 衣服を作るために用いる→コーデュロイ, コール天 ‖ *a corduroy jacket* コーデュロイ[コール天]の上着

**core** /kɔːr/ 🔣 ▶定義1 ⓒ the hard centre of certain fruits, containing seeds ある種の果実の堅い中心部で種が入っている→芯(しん), 果心 ‖ *an apple core* リンゴの芯 ▶定義2 [単数扱い] the central or most important part of sth 〜の中心, または最も重要な部分→核心, 心臓部 ‖ *the core curriculum (= the subjects that all pupils have to study)* コアカリキュラム (= 生徒全員が学ばなければならない科目) *What's the core issue here?* ここで最も重大な問題は何ですか. ▶定義3 ⓒ the central part of a planet 惑星の中心部→中心核 ‖ *the earth's core* 地球の中心核 成句 **to the core** ▶定義 completely; in every way 完全に; あらゆる点で→徹底的に ‖ *The news shook him to the core (= shocked him very much).* その知らせは彼を心の底まで揺さぶった (= 彼に大きな衝撃を与えた).

**cork** /kɔːrk/ 🔣 ▶定義1 ⓤ a light soft material

which comes from the outside of a type of tree ある種の樹木の外側から取れる軽くて柔らかい物質→**コルク** ‖ *cork floor tiles* コルク製の床用タイル ▶定義**2** **⊙**a round piece of cork that you push into the end of a bottle to close it, especially a bottle of wine びんの先端に押し込んでふさぐための丸いコルクで、特にワインのびんに使用される→**コルク栓** ☞ **container** のさし絵

**corkscrew** /kɔ́ːrkskrùː/ 名 **⊙** ▶定義 a tool that you use for pulling corks (2) out of bottles びんからコルク(cork (2))を抜くための道具→**コルク栓抜き**

★**corn** /kɔːrn/ 名 ▶定義**1** **⓾** 特に 奧 any plant that is grown for its grain, such as wheat; the seeds from these plants 穀物を穫るために育てられる小麦などの植物; これらの植物の種子→**穀物, 穀類, 小麦** ‖ *a field of corn* 穀物畑, 麦畑 *a corn field* 穀物畑, 麦畑 ▶定義**2** **⓾**米 = **MAIZE** ☞ **cereal**のさし絵 ▶定義**3** **⊙**a small, painful area of hard skin on the toe 足指にできる小さく痛みのある皮膚の硬くなった部分→**魚の目, 豆**

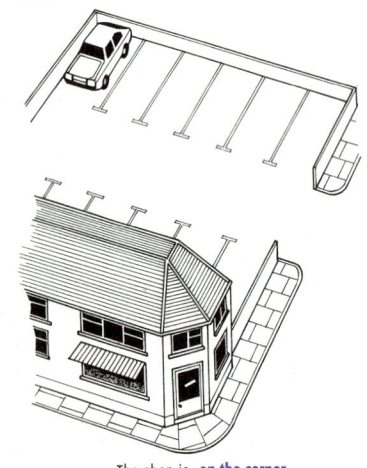

**corner**
The car is **in the corner**.

The shop is **on the corner**.

★**corner**¹ /kɔ́ːrnər/ 名 **⊙** ▶定義**1** a place where two lines, edges, surfaces or roads meet 2つの線, 縁, 面または道路が出会う箇所→**角, 隅, 曲がり角, 街角** ‖ *Put the lamp in the corner of the room.* ランプを部屋の隅に置いてください. *Write your address in the top right-hand corner.* 右上に住所を書きなさい. *The shop is on the corner of Wall Street and Long Road.* その店はウォール街とロング街の交わる角にある. *He went round the corner at top speed.* 彼は最高速度で角を曲がった. ▶定義**2** a quiet or secret place or area 静かで奥まった場所や地域→**奥地, 人目に付かない場所** ‖ *a remote corner of Scotland* スコットランドの奥地 ▶定義**3** a difficult situation from which you cannot escape 逃れることができない困難な状況→**苦境, 苦しい立場, 窮地** ‖ *to get yourself into a corner* 自分自身を窮地に追い込む ▶定義**4** (used in football) a free kick from the corner of the field (サッカーで用いて) フィールドのコーナーからのフリーキック→**コーナーキック**

成句 **cut corners** ▶定義 to do sth quickly and not as well as you should ～を手早くあまり丁寧でなく行う→**手を抜く, 安易な方法を採る**

**(just) round the corner** ▶定義 very near 非常に近い→**すぐそこに** ‖ *There's a phone box just round the corner.* すぐそこに電話ボックスがあります.

★**corner**² /kɔ́ːrnər/ 動 他 ▶定義**1** to get a person or an animal into a position from which he/she/it cannot escape 人や動物を逃れられない場所に追い込む→**～を隅に追い詰める, 窮地に陥れる** ‖ *He cornered me at the party and started telling me all his problems.* 彼はパーティーで私を隅に追い詰めて, 自分の悩み事をすべて話し始めた. ▶定義**2** to get control in a particular area of business so that nobody else can have any success in it 事業で特定の分野を支配して他者がその分野で成功できないようにする→**～を買い占める, 独占する** ‖ *That company's really cornered the market in health foods.* その会社は健康食品の市場を実質的に支配している.

**cornflakes** /kɔ́ːrnflèɪks/ 名 [複数扱い] ▶定義 food made of small pieces of dried corn and eaten with milk for breakfast 乾燥した穀物の薄片から作られる食品で, 牛乳をかけて朝食に食べる→**コーンフレーク**

**cornflour** /kɔ́ːrnflàʊər/ 名 **⓾** ▶定義 very fine

flour often used to make sauces, etc thicker ソースにとろみを付けるためによく使われる非常に細かい穀粉→コーンフラワー, コーンスターチ

**corn on the cob** 名 U ▶定義 corn that is cooked with all the yellow grains still on the inner part and eaten as a vegetable 黄色い実が芯(しん)に付いたまま調理して野菜として食べる穀物→軸付きトウモロコシ

**corny** /kɔ́ːmi/ 形 略式 ▶定義 too ordinary or familiar to be interesting or amusing ありふれて見慣れているので興味または面白味が感じられない→陳腐な, ありきたりの, 古臭い ‖ *a corny joke* 陳腐なジョーク

**coronary**[1] /kɔ́(ː)rən(ə)ri, kɔ́r(ə)nèri/ 形 ▶定義 connected with the heart 心臓に関連した→心臓の

**coronary**[2] /kɔ́(ː)rən(ə)ri, kɔ́r(ə)nèri/ 名 C (複 **coronaries**) ▶定義 a type of heart attack 心臓発作の一種→冠状動脈血栓症

**coronation** /kɔ̀(ː)rənéiʃ(ə)n/ 名 C ▶定義 an official ceremony at which sb is made a king or queen 〜を王や女王にするための公的儀式→戴冠(たいかん)式, 即位式

**coroner** /kɔ́(ː)rənər, kár-/ 名 C ▶定義 a person whose job is to find out the causes of death of people who have died in violent or unusual ways 暴力的または不自然な死に方をした人の死因を突き止めることを仕事とする人→検死官

**Corp** 略 困 Corporation→社団法人, 株式[有限責任]会社 ‖ *West Coast Motor Corp* ウエストコースト自動車会社

**corporal** /kɔ́ːrp(ə)rəl/ 名 C ▶定義 a person at a low level in the army or air force 陸軍または空軍の下位の人→伍長(ごちょう)(最下位の下士官)

**corporal punishment** 名 U ▶定義 the punishment of people by hitting them, especially the punishment of children by parents or teachers 人をたたくことによる罰, 特に両親や教師による子供に対する罰→体罰, 体刑 ☞参 **capital punishment**

**corporate** /kɔ́ːrp(ə)rət/ 形 ▶定義 of or shared by all the members of a group or organization グループや組織全員の, または全員が共有する→法人組織の, 会社の, 団体の, 共同の, 集合的な ‖ *corporate responsibility* 共同責任

**corporation** /kɔ̀ːrpəréiʃ(ə)n/ 名 C, 単数または複数形の動詞と共に ▶定義1 a large business company 大きな企業→会社, 株式[有限責任]会社; 法人, 社団法人 ‖ *multinational corporations* 多国籍企業 ‖ *the British Broadcasting Corporation* イギリス放送協会 ▶定義2 英 a group of people elected to govern a particular town or city 特定の町や市を統治するために選出された人の集団→都市自治体, 市政機関

**corps** /kɔːr/ 名 C, 単数または複数形の動詞と共に (複 **corps** /kɔːrz/) ▶定義1 a part of an army with special duties 特別な任務を帯びた軍隊の一部→軍団, 兵団, 部隊, 〜隊 ‖ *the medical corps* 衛生隊 ▶定義2 a group of people involved in a special activity 特別な活動に従事する人の集団→団体, 団, 班 ‖ *the diplomatic corps* 外交団

**corpse** /kɔːrps/ 名 C ▶定義 a dead body, especially of a person 特に人の死体→死体, 遺体, 死骸(しがい) ☞参 **carcass**

★**correct**[1] /kərékt/ 形 ▶定義1 with no mistakes; right or true 誤りがない; 正しい, または真実の→間違いのない, 正確な, 正当な, 正解 ‖ *Well done! All your answers were correct.* よくできました. 全問正解です. *Have you got the correct time, please?* 正確な時間が分かりますか. ▶定義2 (used about behaviour, manners, dress, etc) suitable, proper or right (行動, 作法, 服装などについて)適切な, きちんとしている, または正しい→(動作, 服装などが)正式な, 礼儀にかなった, 品行方正な ‖ *What's the correct form of address for a vicar?* 牧師さんにはどう呼び掛けるのが正しいですか. ⇔定義1, 2 **incorrect** — correctly 副 →正確に, 正しく — correctness 名 U →正確, 正しいこと

★**correct**[2] /kərékt/ 動 他 ▶定義1 to make a mistake, fault, etc right or better 誤りや欠点などを正しく, またはより良くする→〜を訂正する, 修正する, 直す ‖ *to correct a spelling mistake* スペリングの間違いを訂正する *to correct a test (= mark the mistakes in it)* テストを採点する (= 間違いに印を付ける) ▶定義2 to tell sb what mistakes he/she is making or what faults he/she has 〜が犯した誤り, または欠点を指摘する→訂正する, 誤りだと言う, 〜をたしなめる ‖ *He's always correcting me when I'm talking to people.* 私が人と話しているときに彼はいつも私の揚げ足を取る. — correction 名 C, U →修正, 校

正, 懲らしめ ‖ *Some parts of the report needed correction.* レポートには修正が必要な部分がある.

**corrective** /kəréktɪv/ 形 ▶定義 intended to make sth right that is wrong 間違った〜を正しくすることを意図した➡矯正的な,調整的な,誤りを正す ‖ *to take corrective action* 矯正策をとる

**correlate** /kɔ́(ː)rəlèɪt, kár-/ 動自他 ▶定義 to have or to show a relationship or connection between two or more things ２つのまたは複数のものの間に関連または結び付きがある,またはそうした関連または結び付きを示す➡相互に関連がある,〜を互いに関連づける — correlation /kɔ̀(ː)rəléɪʃ(ə)n, kàr-/ 名 C U ➡相互関係,相関性 ‖ *There is a correlation between a person's diet and height.* その人の日常の食事と身長との間には関連がある.

**correspond** /kɔ̀(ː)rəspánd, kàr-/ 動自 ▶定義1 correspond (to/with sth) to be the same as or equal to sth; to match 〜と同じである,または等しい; 一致する ➡(〜に)一致する ‖ *Does the name on the envelope correspond with the name inside the letter?* 封筒のあて名と手紙の中の名前は一致していますか. ▶定義2 正式 correspond (with sb) to write letters to and receive them from sb 〜に手紙を書き,その人から返事を受け取る➡(〜と)文通する,手紙で連絡を取り合う ‖ *They corresponded for a year before they got married.* 彼らは結婚する前に１年間文通をした.

**correspondence** /kɔ̀(ː)rəspánd(ə)ns, kàr-/ 名 ▶定義1 U 正式 the act of writing letters; the letters themselves 手紙を書くこと; その手紙➡文通,通信 ‖ *There hasn't been any correspondence between them for years.* 彼らは何年間も手紙のやり取りをしていない. ▶定義2 C U a close connection or relationship between two or more things ２つのまたは複数の物の間の密接な結び付きまたは関連➡関連性,一致 ‖ *There is no correspondence between the two sets of figures.* ２組の数字には何の関連もない.

**correspondent** /kɔ̀(ː)rəspánd(ə)nt, kàr-/ 名 C ▶定義1 a person who provides news or writes articles for a newspaper, etc, especially from a foreign country 新聞などに,特に海外からニュースを配信するまたは記事を書く人➡(新聞,放送などの)通信員,特派員,担当記者,レポーター ‖ *our Middle East correspondent, Andy Jenkins* 当社の中東特派員, アンディー ジェンキンズ ▶定義2 a person who writes letters to sb 〜に手紙を書く人➡文通する人

**corresponding** /kɔ̀(ː)rəspándɪŋ, kàr-/ 形(名詞の前だけ) ▶定義 related or similar to sth 〜に関連した,または似ている➡対応する,一致する,相当する ‖ *Sales are up 10% compared with the corresponding period last year.* 昨年の同期間と比較して販売高が10パーセント上昇している.
— correspondingly 副 ➡相応して,同様に

★**corridor** /kɔ́(ː)rədər, kár-, -dɔ̀ːr/ 名 C ▶定義 a long narrow passage in a building or train, with doors that open into rooms, etc 建物や列車内の長く細長い通路で,ドアで部屋などに通じる➡廊下,回廊

**corroborate** /kərábərèɪt/ 動他 正式 ▶定義 to support a statement, idea, etc by providing new evidence 言明,考えなどを新しい証拠を提出して支持する➡(意見など)を補強する,裏付ける,確証する ‖ *The witness corroborated Mr Patton's statement about the night of the murder.* 証人は,殺人のあった夜についてのパットン氏の陳述を裏付けた. — corroboration /kərɑ̀bəréɪʃ(ə)n/ 名 U ➡確実にすること,裏付け

**corrode** /kəróʊd/ 動自他 ▶定義 (used about metals) to become weak or to be destroyed by chemical action; to cause a metal to do this (金属について)化学作用によってもろくなる,または壊れる; 金属をそのような状態にする➡腐食する,さびつく; 〜を腐食させる,さびつかせる ‖ *Parts of the car were corroded by rust.* 車の部品がさびで腐食していた. — corrosion /kəróʊʒ(ə)n/ 名 U ➡腐食(作用),さび — corrosive /kəróʊsɪv/ ➡腐食性の,さびつかせる

**corrugated** /kárəgèɪtəd/ 形 ▶定義 (used about metal or cardboard) shaped into folds (金属または厚紙について)ひだを付けられた➡波形の,うね状の

**corrupt**[1] /kərʌ́pt/ 形 ▶定義 doing or involving illegal or dishonest things in exchange for money, etc 金銭などの交換に違法または不誠実な事をしたり,そのような事に関係する➡汚職の,わいろの,不正な,腐敗した ‖ *corrupt officials who accept bribes* わいろを受け取る腐敗した

役人 corrupt business practices 不正な業務上の慣行

**corrupt**[2] /kərʌ́pt/ 動他 ▶定義 to cause sb/sth to start behaving in a dishonest or immoral way 〜に不誠実な、または不道徳な振る舞いをさせる➔〜を堕落させる，腐敗させる ‖ *Too many people are corrupted by power.* あまりにも多くの人々が権力によって堕落する．

**corruption** /kərʌ́pʃ(ə)n/ 名 Ⓤ ▶定義 1 dishonest or immoral behaviour or activities 不誠実または不道徳な行動や活動➔堕落，汚職 ‖ *There were accusations of corruption among senior police officers.* 警察上層部の腐敗が告発された．▶定義 2 the process of making sb/sth corrupt 〜を堕落させる過程➔堕落させること，腐敗させること

**corset** /kɔ́ːrsət/ 名 Ⓒ ▶定義 a piece of clothing that some women wear pulled tight around their middle to make them look thinner やせて見えるように，一部の女性が胴や腰をきつく締めるため身に着ける衣類➔コルセット

**cosmetic**[1] /kɑzmétɪk/ 名[通常は複数] ▶定義 a substance that you put on your face or hair to make yourself look more attractive より魅力的に見えるように顔や髪に付けるもの➔化粧品 ☛参 make-up

**cosmetic**[2] /kɑzmétɪk/ 形 ▶定義 1 used or done in order to make your face or body more attractive 顔や体をより魅力的にするために使われる，または行われる➔化粧用の，美容の ‖ *cosmetic products* 化粧品 *cosmetic surgery* 美容整形 ▶定義 2 done in order to improve only the appearance of sth, without changing it in any other way 〜の外見だけを改良するために行われ，それ以外のやり方では変更しない➔ぼろ隠しの，外見を取り繕う，表面的な ‖ *changes in government policy which are purely cosmetic* 単なる上辺だけの政策変更

**cosmic** /kɑ́zmɪk/ 形 ▶定義 connected with space or the universe 宇宙空間や宇宙に関連した➔宇宙の; 広大無辺な，大規模の

**cosmopolitan** /kɑ̀zməpɑ́lətn/ 形 ▶定義 1 containing people from all over the world 世界中の人々から成る➔全世界的な，国際的な ‖ *a cosmopolitan city* 国際都市 ▶定義 2 influenced by the culture of other countries 他国の文化の影響を受けた➔国際的感覚の，視野の広い，コスモポリタンの ‖ *a cosmopolitan and sophisticated young woman* 国際感覚にあふれて洗練された若い女性

**the cosmos** /kɑ́zmə(ː)s; -məs/ 名[単数扱い] ▶定義 the universe 宇宙➔宇宙，万有，天地万物，世界

★**cost**[1] /kɔ(ː)st, kɑst/ 名 ▶定義 1 Ⓒ Ⓤ the money that you have to pay for sth 〜に対して支払わなければならない金銭➔費用，経費；値段，価格 ‖ *The cost of petrol has gone up again.* ガソリンの価格がまた上がった．*The hospital was built at a cost of £10 million.* その病院は1千万ポンドの費用で建設された．*The damage will have to be repaired regardless of cost.* 費用がどれだけかかっても損傷を修復しなければならないだろう．☛参 price の注 ▶定義 2 [単数扱い，Ⓤ] what you have to give or lose in order to obtain sth else 別の〜を得るために与える，または失わなければならないもの➔代償，犠牲，損失 ‖ *He achieved great success but only at the cost of a happy family life.* 彼は大きな成功を収めたが，それは幸福な家庭生活を犠牲にして得られたものである．▶定義 3 **costs**[複数扱い] the amount of money that the losing side has to pay to the winning side in a court of law 法廷で敗訴した側が勝訴した側に支払わなければならない金額➔訴訟費用 ‖ *a £250 fine and £100 costs* 250ポンドの罰金と100ポンドの訴訟費用

成句 **at all costs/at any cost** ▶定義 using whatever means are necessary to achieve sth 〜を成し遂げるために必要な手段を何でも使って➔どんな犠牲を払っても，何としても ‖ *We must win at all costs.* 何としても勝たなければならない．

**cover the cost (of sth)** ⇒ **COVER**[1]

**to your cost** ▶定義 in a way that is unpleasant or bad for you 人にとって不快なまたは悪いように➔ひどい経験をして，損をして ‖ *Life can be lonely at university, as I found out to my cost.* つらい経験を通して私が知ったように，大学生活は孤独なこともある．

★**cost**[2] /kɔ(ː)st, kɑst/ 動他(過，過分 **cost**) ▶定義 1 to have the price of 〜の価格である➔(金額)がかかる，値段が〜する，〜を要する ‖ *How much does a return ticket to London cost?* ロン

ドンまでの往復切符はいくらですか. *We'll take the bus - it won't cost much.* バスで行こう — その方が安いから. 略式 *How much did your car cost you?* あなたの車はいくらしましたか. ▶定義2 to make you lose sth 〜を失わせる→なくす ‖ *That one mistake cost him his job.* 1つの過ちで彼は職を失った.

成句 **cost the earth/a fortune** ▶定義 to be very expensive 非常に高価である→途方もなく金がかかる

**co-star** /koʊstɑːr/ 動 (**co-starring; co-starred**)
▶定義1 ⊕ (used about a film, play, etc) to have two or more famous actors as its stars (映画, 劇などについて)スターとして複数の有名な俳優が出る→(スター)を共演させる ‖ *a film co-starring Leonardo di Caprio and Kate Winslett* レオナルド ディカプリオとケート ウィンスレット共演の映画 ▶定義2 ⊕ (used about actors) to be one of two or more stars in a film, play, etc (俳優について)映画, 劇などの複数のスターのうちの1人になる→共演する ‖ *Kate Winslett co-stars with Leonardo di Caprio in the film.* ケート ウィンスレットはその映画でレオナルド ディカプリオと共演している. — co-star →共演者 ‖ *His co-star was Marilyn Monroe.* 彼の共演者はマリリン モンローだった.

**costly** /kɔ́(ː)stli, kɑ́st-/ 形 (**costlier; costliest**)
▶定義1 costing a lot of money; expensive 多くの金がかかる; 高価な→金のかかる, ぜいたくな ‖ *a costly repair bill* 多額の修理代の請求書 ▶定義2 involving great loss of time, effort, etc 多くの時間, 労力などを失うような→多くの犠牲を払う, 高くつく ‖ *a costly mistake* 手痛い誤り

**costume** /kɑ́st(j)uːm/ 名 ⊕ ⓤ ▶定義1 a set or style of clothes worn by people in a particular country or in a particular historical period 特定の国や特定の時代に人々が身に着けた衣服または衣服の様式→(時代, 地方などに特有の)服装, 衣装 ‖ *17th century costume* 17世紀の衣装 *Welsh national costume* ウェールズの民族衣装 ▶定義2 clothes that an actor, etc wears in order to look like sth else 俳優などが別の〜に似せるために着る衣類 →(演劇などに用いる)衣装, ふん装 ‖ *One of the children was dressed in a pirate's costume.* 子供たちの1人が海賊にふ

んしていた. *The last rehearsal of the play will be done in costume.* 劇の最後のリハーサルは衣装を着けて行います. ▶定義3 困 =SWIMSUIT

**cosy** /kóuzi/ 形 (**cosier; cosiest**) (米 **cozy**)
▶定義 warm and comfortable 暖かくて快適な→居心地の良い, 暖かい雰囲気の ‖ *The room looked cosy and inviting in the firelight.* 火明かりで部屋は居心地良く魅力的に見えた.

**cot** /kɑt/ (米 **crib**) 名 ⓒ ▶定義1 a bed with high sides for a baby 側面が高い赤ん坊用のベッド→小児用ベッド ▶定義2 困 =CAMP BED ☞ **bed** のさし絵

**cottage** /kɑ́tɪdʒ/ 名 ⓒ ▶定義 a small and usually old house, especially in the country 特に田舎の, 小さく, 普通は古い家→田舎家, 小家屋, 農家, 小屋

**cottage cheese** 名 ⓤ ▶定義 a type of soft white cheese in small wet lumps 柔らかく白いチーズの一種で小さな湿り気のある塊になっている→カッテージチーズ

*****cotton** /kɑ́tn/ 名 ⓤ ▶定義1 a natural cloth or thread made from the thin white hairs of the cotton plant 綿の細く白い毛から作られる天然の布または糸→綿布, 綿織物, 木綿, 綿糸, 木綿糸 ‖ *a cotton shirt* 綿のシャツ ☞ **knit** のさし絵
▶定義2 困 =COTTON WOOL

**cotton wool** 名 ⓤ ▶定義 a soft mass of cotton, used for cleaning the skin, cuts, etc 肌または切り傷などを清潔にするために使用する綿の柔らかな塊→脱脂綿

**couch¹** /kaʊtʃ/ 名 ⓒ ▶定義 a long seat, often with a back and arms, for sitting or lying on 座ったり横になったりするための長い座席で, 通常は背もたれとひじ掛けがある→寝いす, ソファー, カウチ ‖ *They were sitting on the couch in the living room.* 彼らは居間のカウチに座っていた.

**couch²** /kaʊtʃ/ 動 ⊕ (通常は受動態で) 正式
▶定義 to express a thought, idea, etc in the way mentioned 特定のやり方で考えまたは案などを表現する→〜を言い表す, 述べる ‖ *His reply was couched in very polite terms.* 彼の答えは非常に丁寧な言葉で述べられた.

*****cough¹** /kɔ(ː)f, kɑf/ 動 ▶定義1 ⊕ to send air out of your throat and mouth with a sudden loud noise, especially when you have a cold, have sth in your throat, etc 特に風邪を引いたときやたのどに〜が詰まったときに, 急に大きな音を

出してのどと口から空気を吐く→**せきをする,せき払いをする** ‖ *Cigarette smoke makes me cough.* 私はたばこの煙でせきが出る. ● **sneeze**のさし絵 ▶定義2 ⓾ cough (up) sth to send sth out of your throat and mouth with a sudden loud noise 急に大きな音を出して~をのどと口から出す→**せきをして~を吐き出す,せきをして~を戻す** ‖ *When I started coughing (up) blood I called the doctor.* せき込んで血を吐いたので私は医者を呼んだ.

句動詞 cough (sth) up 略式 ▶定義 to give money when you do not want to 与えたくないが金を与える→**しぶしぶ支払う,嫌々ながら渡す** ‖ *Come on, cough up what you owe me!* さあ,貸した金を返してくれ.

**cough²** /kɔ(ː)f, kɑf/ 名 ⓒ ▶定義1 an act or the sound of coughing せきをすること,またはその音→**せき,せき払い** ‖ *He gave a nervous cough before he started to speak.* 彼は話す前に神経質そうにせき払いした. ▶定義2 an illness or infection that makes you cough a lot ひどくせきが出る病気または感染症→**せきの出る病気** ‖ *Kevin's got a bad cough.* ケヴィンはひどいせきに悩んでいる.

★**could** /kəd 強形 kʊd/ 法助動詞(否定形 **could not**; 短縮形 **couldn't** /kədnt, kʊdnt/) ▶定義1 used for saying that sb had the ability or was allowed to do sth ~が…をする能力があった,または~をすることを許可されたと言うときに用いて→**(~することが)できた,~しようと思えばできた,~することを許されていた,~してもよかった** ‖ *I could run three miles without stopping when I was younger.* 若いころには私は休まずに3マイル走ることができた. *Elena said we could stay at her house.* エレナは我々が彼女の家に泊まってもいいと言った.

▶ was/were able to または managed to はたまたま過去のある時(1回だけ)に何かが可能であった場合に用いる: *The firemen were able to/managed to rescue the children.* (消防士は子供を助けることができた.) 否定文では could not も用いることができる: *The firemen couldn't rescue the children.* (消防士は子供を助けることができなかった.)

▶定義2 used for saying that sth may be or may have been possible ~の可能性がある,または可能性があったと言う場合に用いて→**かもしれない,だったかもしれない** ‖ *I could do it now if you like.* あなたが望むなら今やってもいいんですよ. *She could be famous one day.* 彼女はいつか有名になるかもしれない. *He could have gone to university but he didn't want to.* 彼は大学へ行けたのに行きたがらなかった. *You could have said you were going to be late!* (= I'm annoyed that you didn't) 遅れると言ってくれればよかったのに(= 言ってくれなかったので私はいらいらした). ▶定義3 used for asking permission politely 丁寧に許可を求める場合に用いて→**~していいですか,~してもよろしいですか** ‖ *Could I possibly borrow your car?* 車を貸していただけますか. ▶定義4 used for asking sb politely to do sth for you ~に…をしてくれるように丁寧に頼む場合に用いて→**~してくれませんか,~していただけますか** ‖ *Could you open the door? My hands are full.* ドアを開けてくれませんか.両手がふさがっているので.

▶ 法助動詞についての説明は,巻末の「文法早見表」を参照.

▶定義5 used for making a suggestion 提案する場合に用いて→**~してもいい,~するのはどうですか** ‖ *'What do you want to do tonight?' 'We could go to the cinema or we could just stay in.'* 「今夜は何をしたい」「映画に行ってもいいし,家にいてもいい」 ▶定義6 used with the verbs 'feel', 'hear', 'see', 'smell', 'taste' feel, hear, see, smell, taste の動詞と共に用いて→**感じられた,聞こえた,見えた,においがした,味がした**

▶ これらの動詞は進行形では使われない.過去のある時点に見えたり聞こえたりしたという場合にcouldを用いる: *We could hear/see children playing outside.* (子供たちが外で遊んでいる声が聞こえた・遊んでいるのが見えた.) (We were hearing... とは言わない.)

★**council**(または **Council**) /káʊns(ə)l/ 名 [ⓒ, 単数または複数形の動詞と共に] ▶定義1 a group of people who are elected to govern an area such as a town or county 町や郡などの地域を統治するために選挙で選ばれた人々の集まり→**地方議会,市議会,町議会** ‖ *The city council has/have decided to build a new road.* 市議会は新しい道路の建設を決定した. *a council house* (= one that a council owns and lets to people who do *not have much money)* 公営住宅(= 地方議会が所有し, あまり裕福でない人に貸す住宅) *My dad's on the local council.* 父さんは地方議会議員だ. ▶定義2 a group of people chosen to give advice, manage affairs, etc for a particular organization or activity 特定の組織や活動のために, 助言するまたは仕事を処理するために選ばれた人々の集まり➡**評議会, 協議会, 審議会** || *the Arts Council* 芸術協会

**councillor** /káʊns(ə)lər/ 名 C ▶定義 a member of a council 評議会の一員➡**評議員, 顧問官, 議員** || *to elect new councillors* 新しい評議員を選ぶ

**counsel**¹ /káʊns(ə)l/ 動 他 ( **counselling**; **counselled**: 米 **counseling**; **counseled**)
▶定義1 to give professional advice and help to sb with a problem 問題のある~に専門的助言または援助を与える➡**~に(専門的に)忠告する, ~の相談に乗る** ▶定義2 (文)to tell sb what you think he/she should do; to advise ~にするべき事を告げる; 忠告する➡**~を勧める, ~するよう助言する** || *Mr Dean's lawyers counselled him against making public statements.* ディーン氏の弁護士は公式の発言はしない方がいいと忠告した.

**counsel**² /káʊns(ə)l/ 名 U ▶定義1 (文)advice 忠告➡**助言, 勧告** ▶定義2 a lawyer who speaks in a court of law 裁判所で意見を述べる弁護士➡**法廷弁護士, 弁護人(団)** || *the counsel for the defence/prosecution* 被告側弁護人·検察側弁護人

**counselling**(米**counseling**) /káʊns(ə)lɪŋ/ 名 U
▶定義 professional advice and help given to people with problems 問題を抱えた人に与えられる専門的助言または援助➡**指導, 相談, カウンセリング** || *Many students come to us for counselling.* 多くの生徒が私たちの所に相談に来る.

**counsellor**(米**counselor**)/káʊns(ə)lər/ 名 C
▶定義 a person whose job is to give advice 助言を与えることを仕事とする人➡**カウンセラー, 相談員, 顧問** || *a marriage counsellor* 結婚カウンセラー

\*count¹ /káʊnt/ 動 ▶定義1 他 to say numbers one after another in order 数を順に1つずつ言う➡**数える, 数え上げる** || *Close your eyes and count (up) to 20.* 目をつぶって20まで数えてください. ▶定義2 他 count sth to calculate the total number or amount of sth ~の合計数や合計量を計算する➡**~を数える, 合計する, 算出する** || *The teacher counted the children as they got on the bus.* 教師はバスに乗る子供たちを数えた.
▶定義3 他 to include sb/sth when you are calculating an amount or number 量や数を数えるときに~を含める➡**~を勘定[数]に入れる, ~の1つと見なす** || *There were thirty people on the bus, not counting the driver.* 運転手を除いてバスには30人乗っていた. ▶定義4 自 count (for sth) to be important or valuable 重要である, または価値がある➡**重要である, 大切である, (~ほどの)重要性·意味を持つ** || *I sometimes think my opinion counts for nothing at work.* 仕事場では私の意見は何の価値もないのではないかと考えることがある. ▶定義5 自 count (as sth) to be valid or accepted 有効である, または受け入れられる➡**(~として)有効である, 認められる** || *The referee had already blown his whistle so the goal didn't count.* 審判は既に笛を吹いていたのでゴールは無効だ. *Will my driving licence count as identification?* 運転免許証は身分証明書として認められますか. ▶定義6 自他 to consider sb/sth in a particular way ~をある特定のやり方で考える➡**(~を)…と見なす, ~と思う, ~と認める, ~として扱う** || *You should count yourself lucky to have a good job.* 良い仕事に就けて幸運だと考えなくてはいけない. *On this airline, children over 12 count/are counted as adults.* この航空会社では12歳以上の子供は大人扱いだ.
**成句** Don't count your chickens (before they're hatched) ▶定義 used to say that you should not be too confident that sth will be successful because sth might still go wrong ~がまだうまくいかない可能性もあるのだから, うまくいくと自信を持ちすぎてはいけないと言うときに用いて➡**捕らぬ狸(たぬき)の皮算用をしてはいけない**

**句動詞** count against sb ▶定義 to be considered as a disadvantage 不利と見なされる➡**~の不利になる, 不利な条件となる** || *Do you think my age will count against me?* 年齢のせいで私に不利になると思いますか.

count on sb/sth ▶定義 to expect sth with confidence; to depend on sb/sth 自信を持って

〜を期待する; 〜に頼る➡〜を当てにする, 頼りにする ‖ *Can I count on you to help me?* あなたの助けを当てにしていいですか.

**count sb/sth out** ▶定義1 to count things slowly, one by one 物を1つずつゆっくりと数える➡(物や金)をゆっくり数えて出す, 〜の数をすっかり数える ‖ *She carefully counted out the money into my hand.* 彼女は慎重に金を数えて私の手に乗せた. ▶定義2 略式 to not include sb/sth 〜を含めない➡〜を数に入れない, 除外する, 除く ‖ *If you're going swimming, you can count me out!* もし泳ぎに行くのなら私は数に入れないでください.

**count**² /káʊnt/ 名 C ▶定義1 [通常は単数]an act of counting or a number that you get after counting 数えること, または数えた結果の数➡**計算, 勘定, 総数, 総計** ‖ *At the last count*, there were nearly 2 million unemployed. 最新の統計では失業者が2百万人近くいた. *On the count of three, all lift together.* 3つ数えたら, みんなで持ち上げよう. ▶定義2 [通常は複数]a point that is made in a discussion, argument, etc 議論や論争などで出てくる事項➡**問題点, 論点, 争点** ‖ *I proved her wrong on all counts.* 私はすべての点で彼女が間違っていると証明した.

成句 **keep/lose count (of sth)** ▶定義 to know/not know how many there are of sth 〜がいくつあるか知っている・知らない➡(〜の)数を覚えている・(〜の)数を忘れる, (〜の)数を数えきれなくなる ‖ *I've lost count of the number of times he's told that joke!* 彼がそのジョークを何回言ったか分からなくなってしまった.

**countable** /káʊntəb(ə)l/ 形 (文法) ▶定義 that can be counted 数えられる➡**可算の** ‖ *'Chair' is a countable noun, but 'sugar' isn't.* chairは可算名詞だが, sugarはそうではない. *Countable nouns are marked [C] in this dictionary.* この辞書では可算名詞には C が付けられている. ⇔ **uncountable**

▶可算名詞についての説明は巻末の「文法早見表」を参照.

**countdown** /káʊntdàʊn/ 名 C ▶定義 the act of saying numbers backwards to zero just before sth important happens 重要な〜が開始する直前に, 数を0まで逆に言うこと➡**秒読み, カウントダウン** ‖ *the countdown to the lift-off of a rocket* ロケット発射の秒読み (比喩) *The countdown to this summer's Olympic Games has started.* この夏のオリンピックまでのカウントダウンが始まった.

**counter**¹ /káʊntər/ 名 C ▶定義1 a long, flat surface in a shop, bank, etc where customers are served 店, 銀行などの長くて平らな面で, ここで客に応対する➡**カウンター, 勘定台, 売り台** ‖ *The man behind the counter in the bank was very helpful.* 銀行のカウンターの男性はとても助けになった. ▶定義2 a small object (usually round and made of plastic) that is used in some games to show where a player is on the board ある種のゲームで使われる小片(通常は円いプラスチック製)で, プレーヤーが盤のどこにいるかを示す➡**チップ, カウンター** ▶定義3 an electronic device for counting sth 〜を数えるための電子装置➡**計数器, カウンター**

**counter**² /káʊntər/ 動 自 他 ▶定義1 to reply or react to criticism 批判に答える, または反応する➡**(〜に)反論する, 反証を挙げる** ‖ *He countered our objections with a powerful defence of his plan.* 彼は自分の計画を強力に擁護して, 私たちの異議に反論した. ▶定義2 to try to reduce or prevent the bad effects of sth 〜の悪影響を減らそうとするまたは回避しようとする➡**(〜に)立ち向かう, 対抗する** ‖ *The shop has installed security cameras to counter theft.* 盗みに対抗するため店は防犯カメラを設置した.

**counter**³ /káʊntər/ 副 ▶定義 **counter to sth** in the opposite direction to sth 〜と反対の方向に➡**正反対に, 逆に** ‖ *The results of these experiments run counter to previous findings.* これらの実験の結果はこれまでの研究結果とは正反対である.

**counteract** /kàʊntərǽkt/ 動 他 ▶定義 to reduce the effect of sth by acting against it 〜に対抗してその影響を弱める➡**(反作用で)〜を和らげる, 〜を中和する, 妨げる, 打ち消す** ‖ *measures to counteract traffic congestion* 交通渋滞を緩和する手段

**counter-attack** 名 C ▶定義 an attack made in reaction to an enemy or opponent's attack 敵や反対者の攻撃に反応して行う攻撃➡**逆襲, 反撃, 反論** — **counter-attack** 動 自 他 ➡**(〜に)逆襲する, 反論する**

**counter-clockwise** 困 = ANTICLOCKWISE

**counterfeit** /káʊntərfɪːt/ 形 ▶定義 not genuine, but copied so that it looks like the real thing 本物ではなく,実物に似せて複製した→偽造の,模造の,にせの ‖ *counterfeit money* にせ金

**counterfoil** /káʊntərfɔɪl/ 名 C ▶定義 the part of a cheque, ticket, etc that you keep when you give the other part to sb else 小切手や入場券などの一部を~に渡したとき手元に残る部分→半券,控え

**counterpart** /káʊntərpɑ̀ːrt/ 名 C ▶定義 a person or thing that has a similar position or function in a different country or organization 異なる国や組織で同じような地位または機能を持つ人や物→相当する人・物,対応物,対称物,(対等の)相手方 ‖ *the French President and his Italian counterpart* (= *the Italian President*) フランス大統領とイタリア側の同等の人物(=イタリア大統領)

**counter-productive** 形 ▶定義 having the opposite effect to the one you want 意図したものと逆の効果を持つ→逆効果の,逆の結果を招く,裏目に出る ‖ *It can be counter-productive to punish children.* 子供を罰するのは逆効果になることもある.

**countless** /káʊntləs/ 形 (名詞の前だけ) ▶定義 very many 非常に多い→数えきれない,無数の,ばく大な ‖ *I've tried to phone him countless times but he's not there.* 彼に数えきれないほど電話したが,彼はいない.

*__country__ /kʌ́ntri/ 名 (複 **countries**) ▶定義1 C an area of land with its own people, government, etc それ自身の国民,政府を有する領土→国,国土,国家;故国 ‖ *France, Spain and other European countries* フランス,スペイン,そのほかのヨーロッパ諸国 *There was snow over much of the country during the night.* その国のほとんどの地域で夜に雪が降った.

▶ state は1つの政府が統治する組織化された国の共同体としての国.政府そのものを意味する場合もある: *a politically independent state* (政治上の独立国家) *the member states of the EU* (EU加盟国) *You get a pension from the state when you retire.* (引退したら国から年金がもらえる.) *state education* (公教育). land はより正式で文語的な語: *Explorers who set out to discover new lands* (新天地を発見するために出発した探検家たち)

▶定義2 **the country** [単数扱い] the people who live in a country ある国に住む人々→国民 ‖ *a survey to find out what the country really thinks* 国民の本音を知るための調査 ▶定義3 **the country** [単数扱い] land which is away from towns and cities 街や都市から離れた地域→田舎,地方 ‖ *Do you live in a town or in the country?* 街にお住まいですか,それとも田舎にお住まいですか.

▶ countryside は,やはり街から離れた地域を意味するが,そこにある丘や川,木々などの自然を強調する語: *beautiful countryside* (美しい田園地帯) *the destruction of the countryside by new roads* (新しい道路によって田園地帯が破壊されること). scenery の注も参照.

▶定義4 ❶ an area of land ある範囲の土地→地域,地方,地帯,土地 ‖ *We looked down over miles of open country.* 私たちは何マイルも続く開けた平野を見下ろした. *hilly country* 丘の多い地域 ☛類 terrain ▶定義5 = COUNTRY AND WESTERN

**country and western** 名 U ▶定義 a type of popular music based on traditional music from southern and western US 米国南部と西部の伝統的音楽を起源とする大衆音楽の一種→カントリーミュージック

**countryman** /kʌ́ntrimən/ 名 C (複 **-men** /-mən/) ▶定義 a person from your own country (1) 同国の人 (country (1))→同国人,同郷の人 ‖ *The Italian Castorri beat his fellow countryman Rossi in the final.* イタリア人カストーリが決勝で同国のロッシを破った.

**the countryside** /kʌ́ntrisàɪd/ 名 [U, 単数扱い] ▶定義 land which is away from towns and cities, where there are fields, woods, etc 街や都市から離れた野や森などのある地域→田舎,田園,地方 ‖ *From the hill there is a magnificent view of the surrounding countryside.* 丘から辺りの広大な田園地帯が見える. ☛参 country の注

**county** /káʊnti/ 名 C (複 **counties**) ▶定義 an area in Britain, Ireland or the US which has its own local government 英国,アイルランド,米

国で独自の地方政府を持つ地域 →(英国, アイルランドの)州, (米国の)郡 ‖ *the county of Nottinghamshire* ノッティンガムシャー州 *Orange County, California* カリフォルニア州, オレンジ郡

➤ province, state¹(4) と比較.

**coup** /kuː/ 名 C ▶定義1 (または **coup d'état** /kuː deɪtάː/) a sudden, illegal and often violent change of government 突然, 非合法的に, しばしば暴力を使って政府が変わること→クーデター, 武力政変 ‖ *a coup to overthrow the President* 大統領を追放するクーデター *an attempted coup (= one which did not succeed)* クーデター未遂(=成功しなかったクーデター)

▶定義2 a clever and successful thing to do 手際良く成功すること→大当たり, 大成功 ‖ *Getting that promotion was a real coup.* その昇進は本当に大成功だった.

★**couple**¹ /kʌ́p(ə)l/ 名[C, 単数または複数形の動詞と共に] ▶定義 two people who are together because they are married or in a relationship 結婚や恋愛によって結び付いた2人→カップル, 夫婦, 恋人同士 ‖ *a married couple* 結婚しているカップル *Is/Are that couple over there part of our group?* あそこにいるカップルも私たちのグループですか. ☞参 pair

成句 **a couple of people/things** ▶定義1 two people/things 2人・2つの物→2人の, 2つの, 一対の ‖ *I need a couple of glasses.* グラスが2個必要だ. ▶定義2 a few 少しの→2, 3(人)の, 数個[人]の, いくつかの ‖ *I last saw her a couple of months ago.* 最後に彼女を見たのは2, 3か月前だ.

**couple**² /kʌ́p(ə)l/ 動 他 (通常は受動態で) ▶定義 to join or connect sb/sth to sb/sth else 〜を別の…に結び付ける→(2つのもの)をつなぐ, 連結する, 合わせる ‖ *The fog, coupled with the amount of traffic on the roads, made driving very difficult.* 霧がかかりさらに道路は交通量が多いため, 運転はとても難しかった.

**coupon** /kúːpɑ̀n/ 名 C ▶定義1 a small piece of paper which you can use to buy goods at a lower price, or which you can collect and then exchange for goods より安い価格で品物を買うことができる, または集めて品物と交換できる紙片→クーポン券, 割引券, 優待券, 景品券 ‖ *a coupon worth 10% off your next purchase* 次の買い物が10パーセント割引になるクーポン

▶定義2 a printed form in a newspaper or magazine which you use to order goods, enter a competition, etc 品物を注文するまたはコンテストに応募することができる, 新聞や雑誌の申し込み用紙→切り取り申し込み券, 応募用紙, (資料などの)請求券

★**courage** /kə́ːrɪdʒ; kʌ́r-/ 名 U ▶定義 the ability to control fear in a situation that may be dangerous or unpleasant; bravery 危険または不快な状況で恐怖を抑制できる能力; 勇敢さ→勇気, 度胸, 強い精神力 ‖ *It took real courage to go back into the burning building.* 燃えるビルに引き返すには真の勇気が必要だった. *She showed great courage all through her long illness.* 彼女は長い病気の間, ずっと強い精神力を示した. — courageous /kəréɪdʒəs/ 形 →勇気のある, 大胆な, 精神的に強い

成句 **pluck up courage** ⇒ **PLUCK**¹

**courgette** /kʊərʒét/ (特に 米 **zucchini**) 名 C ▶定義 a long vegetable with dark green skin that is white inside 皮が濃緑色で中身が白い細長い野菜→ズッキーニ ☞ C3ページのさし絵

**courier** /kúəriər/ 名 C ▶定義1 a person whose job is to carry letters, important papers, etc, especially when they are urgent 手紙または重要な書類などを, 特に緊急の場合に運ぶことを仕事とする人→特使, 密使; 宅配業者, 配達人 ‖ *The package was delivered by motorcycle courier.* 小包はバイク便で届けられた. ▶定義2 a person whose job is to look after a group of tourists 旅行者たちの世話を仕事とする人→(団体旅行の)添乗員, 案内人, ガイド

★**course** /kɔːrs/ 名 ▶定義1 C *a course (in/on sth)* a complete series of lessons or studies 稽古(けいこ)や勉強のすべての課程→課程, 科目, 講習, 講座, 講義, コース ‖ *I've decided to enrol on a computer course.* コンピューターコースに登録することにした. *I'm going to take/do a course in self-defence.* 護身の講習を受けるつもりだ. ▶定義2 C U the route or direction that sth, especially an aircraft, ship or river, takes 〜, 特に航空機, 船, 川などのとる経路または方向→進路, 針路, 航(空)路, 水路 ‖ *The hijackers forced the captain to change course and head* *for Cuba.* ハイジャック犯は機長に進路を変更してキューバへ向かうよう強要した. **to be on/off course** (= going in the right/wrong direction) 進路通り・進路を外れる(= 正しい・間違った方向へ進む)(比喩)*I'm on course* (= making the right amount of progress) *to finish this work by the end of the week.* 週末までにはこの仕事を順調に終えられる見込みだ(= 予定通りの分量で進んでいる). *The road follows the course of the river.* 道路は川に沿って走っている. ▶定義3 (または **course of action**) ❻a way of dealing with a particular situation 特定の状況に対処する方法→**方針, 方向, 策, 行動** ‖ *In that situation resignation was the only course open to him.* あの状況では彼にできる事は辞任することだけだった. ▶定義4 [単数扱い]the development of sth over a period of time 時間経過による~の進展→**経過, 進行, 推移** ‖ *events that changed the course of history* 歴史の流れを変えた出来事 *In the normal course of events* (= the way things normally happen) *such problems do not arise.* 自然の成り行き(= 普通の状況)ではそのような問題は発生しない. ▶定義5 ❻the first, second, third, etc separate part of a meal 食事の1品目, 2品目, 3品目などの個々の料理→**(食事の) 1品, 1皿, コース** ‖ *a three-course lunch* 3品料理の昼食 *I had chicken for the main course.* メインコースにチキンを食べた. ▶定義6 ❻an area where golf is played or where certain types of race take place ゴルフをする場所, またはある種の競争が行われる場所→**(ゴルフ, 競争, 競技の) コース, 走路, トラック** ‖ *a golf course* ゴルフコース *a racecourse* 競馬場 ▶定義7 ❻a course (of sth) a series of medical treatments 一連の治療→**クール, (治療の)一定期間, 治療単位, 一定期間に飲むべき一連の薬** ‖ *The doctor put her on a course of tablets.* 医師は彼女に一定期間, 錠剤による治療を施した.

成句 **be on a collision course (with sb/sth)** ⇒ **COLLISION**

**in the course of sth** ▶定義 during sth ~の最中に→**~の間に, ~中に** ‖ *He mentioned it in the course of conversation.* 彼は会話の最中にそれについて触れた.

**in the course of time** ▶定義 when enough time has passed; eventually 十分な時間がたったら; やがては→**そのうちに, 時がたつにつれて, いつかは**

**in due course** ⇒ **DUE**¹
**a matter of course** ⇒ **MATTER**¹
**of course** ▶定義 naturally; certainly 当然, 確かに→**もちろん, 言うまでもなく** ‖ *Of course, having children has changed their lives a lot.* もちろん, 子供が産まれて彼らの生活は大きく変わった. *'Can I use your phone?' 'Of course (you can).'*「電話をお借りできますか」「もちろん(いいですよ)」*'You're not annoyed with me, are you?' 'Of course (I'm) not.'*「私のことをうるさいとは思っていませんよね」「もちろん(思っていません)」

**coursebook** /kɔ́ːrsbùk/ 图 ❻ ▶定義 a book for studying from that is used regularly in class 授業で定期的に使われる学習するための本→**教科書, 教本**

★**court**¹ /kɔːrt/ 图 ▶定義1 ❻❶a place where legal trials take place and crimes, etc are judged 裁判が行われ犯罪などが裁かれる場所→**裁判所, 法廷** ‖ *A man has been charged and will appear in court tomorrow.* 男は告発されており, 明日出廷する. *Bill's company are refusing to pay him so he's decided to take them to court.* 会社が給料を支払わないので, ビルは訴訟に持ち込むことにした. ▶定義2 **the court**[単数扱い]the people in a court, especially those taking part in the trial 法廷にいる人, 特に裁判に参加する人→**裁判官, 判事** ‖ *Please tell the court exactly what you saw.* 見た事を正確に裁判官に話してください. ▶定義3 ❻❶an area where certain ball games are played 一部の球技が行われる場所→**コート** ‖ *a tennis/squash/badminton court* テニス・スカッシュ・バドミントンコート

▶ **pitch**¹と比較.

**court**² /kɔːrt/ 動 ⓘ ▶定義1 to try to gain sb's support by paying special attention to him/her ~に特別の配慮をすることで支持を得ようとする→**(賞賛, 支持など)を求める, 得ようと務める, ~の機嫌を伺う** ‖ *Politicians from all parties will be courting voters this week.* 今週あらゆる党の政治家が有権者の支持を求めるだろう. ▶定義2 to do sth that might have a very bad effect 非常に悪い影響があるかもしれない~をする→**(良くな**

い事)を招く,自ら(良くない事)に陥る ‖ *Britain is courting ecological disaster if it continues to dump waste in the North Sea.* 北海に廃棄物投棄を続けるならば,英国は自ら環境破壊を招くようなものだ.

**courteous** /kə́ːrtiəs/ ▶形 ▶定義 polite and pleasant, showing respect for other people 礼儀正しく愛想が良く,ほかの人への尊敬を示す→礼儀正しく思いやりのある,丁重な,親切な⇔**discourteous** — courteously 副→礼儀正しく,丁重に

**courtesy** /kə́ːrtəsi/ 名 (複 **courtesies**) ▶定義 1 ❶ polite and pleasant behaviour that shows respect for other people ほかの人への尊敬を示す,礼儀正しく愛想の良い振る舞い→礼儀正しさ,礼儀正しい言動,丁重,親切 ‖ *She didn't even have the courtesy to say that she was sorry.* 彼女はすみませんという礼儀すらわきまえていなかった. ▶定義 2 ❷正式 a polite thing that you say or do when you meet people in formal situations 正式な場で人に会ったときの礼儀正しい言動→いんぎんな行為・言葉,丁重な行為・言葉 ‖ *The two presidents exchanged courtesies before their meeting.* 2人の社長は会議の前にあいさつの言葉を交わした.

成句 (by) courtesy of sb 正式 ▶定義 with the permission or because of the kindness of sb 〜の許可を得て,または好意によって→〜の好意によって(無料で),〜の提供によって ‖ *These pictures are being shown by courtesy of BBC TV.* これらの映像はBBCテレビのご好意で提供されています.

**court martial** 名 ❷ ▶定義 a military court that deals with matters of military law; a trial that takes place in such a court 軍法の問題を扱う軍の法廷;そのような法廷で行われる裁判→軍法会議(の公判) ‖ *His case will be heard by a court martial.* 彼の問題は軍法会議に掛けられるだろう. — court-martial 動 他→〜を軍法会議に掛ける

**court of law**=COURT¹(1)

**courtship** /kɔ́ːrtʃip/ 名 ❷ ❶ (古) ▶定義 the relationship between a man and a woman before they get married 結婚する前の男性と女性の関係→求愛,交際,求愛行動

**courtyard** /kɔ́ːrtjɑːrd/ 名 ❷ ▶定義 an area of ground, without a roof, that has walls or buildings around it, for example in a castle or between houses or flats 例えば城内,または家と家,アパートとアパートの間で壁や建物に囲まれた屋根のない場所→中庭,内庭,坪庭

★**cousin** /kʌ́z(ə)n/ (または **first cousin**) 名 ❷ ▶定義 the child of your aunt or uncle 伯母・叔母または伯父・叔父の子供→いとこ ‖ *Paul and I are cousins.* ポールと私はいとこ同士だ.

➤ cousinは男女両方のいとこに用いる. second cousinはいとこの子供(またいとこ).

**cove** /kóuv/ 名 ❷ ▶定義 a small area of the coast where the land curves round so that it is protected from the wind, etc 海岸の狭い地域で,陸地が曲線を描いているために風などを防いでいる→(湾内の)入り江,小湾 ‖ *a sandy cove* 砂浜になった入り江

★**cover¹** /kʌ́vər/ 動 他 ▶定義 1 cover sb/sth (up/over) (with sth) to put sth on or in front of sth to hide or protect it 〜を…の上や前に置いてそれを隠すまたは保護する→〜を(…で)覆う,〜に…をかぶせる ‖ *Could you cover the food and put it in the fridge?* 食べ物に覆いをして冷蔵庫に入れてくれますか. *She couldn't look any more and covered her eyes.* 彼女は見るに堪えず目を覆った. *I covered the floor with newspaper before I started painting.* 私はペンキを塗る前に床に新聞を敷いた. (比喩)*Paula laughed to cover (= hide) her embarrassment.* ポーラは照れ隠しに笑った. ⇔ **uncover** ▶定義 2 cover sb/sth in/with sth to be on the surface of sth; to make sth do this 〜の表面にある;〜をほかの…の表面に付ける→〜を塗る,はる,覆う ‖ *A car went through the puddle and covered me with mud.* 車が水たまりを通り抜け,私は泥だらけになった. *Graffiti covered the walls.* 壁は落書きだらけだった. *The eruption of the volcano covered the town in a layer of ash.* 火山の噴火によって町はうっすらと灰に覆われた. ▶定義 3 to fill or spread over a certain area 一定の範囲を満たす,または広がる→〜に及ぶ,わたる ‖ *The floods cover an area of about 15000 square kilometres.* 洪水は約15000平方キロの地域に及んだ. ▶定義 4 to include or to deal with sth 〜を含める,または対処する→〜を含む,扱う,取り上げる ‖ *All the papers covered the election in depth.* すべての新聞が選挙を詳しく扱っていた. *The* course covered both British and European history. その講座は英国と欧州両方の歴史を取り上げた. ▶定義5 to travel a certain distance 一定の距離を移動する→(距離)を行く, 踏破する, 走破する ‖ We covered about 500 kilometres that day. 私たちはその日, 約500キロを走破した. ▶定義6 to be enough money for sth ～のために十分な金がある→(金銭が)～に足りる, ～を十分賄う, ～の支払いに十分である ‖ We'll give you some money to cover your expenses. 出費を賄うためいくらか金を出しましょう. ▶定義7 cover sb/sth against/for sth to protect sb/sth by insurance ～を保険によって保護する→～に保険を掛ける, ～を(保険で)補償する ‖ The insurance policy covers us for any damage to our property. 財産の損害はすべて保険で賄える. ▶定義8 cover (for sb) to do sb's job while he/she is away from work 仕事に出られない～の仕事をする→(～の)代わりを務める, 代行をする ‖ Matt's phoned in sick so we'll have to find someone to cover (for him). マットが病気だと電話してきたので, (彼の)代わりを見つけなければならない.

成句 cover the cost (of sth) ▶定義 to have or make enough money to pay for sth ～に支払う十分な金を持つ, または作る→～の支払いに十分である, ～を賄う ‖ We made so little money at our school dance that we didn't even cover the cost of the band. 学校のダンスパーティーの収入はほんのわずかだったので, バンドの費用も賄えなかった.

句動詞 cover (sth) up ▶定義 to prevent people hearing about a mistake or sth bad 誤りまたは悪い～が人々の耳に入らないようにする→(悪事, ミスなど)を隠す, もみ消す ‖ The police have been accused of trying to cover up the facts of the case. 事件の事実を隠蔽(いんぺい)しようとしたとして警察は告発されている.

cover up for sb ▶定義 to hide a person's mistakes or crimes in order to protect him/her 人を守るためにその人の誤りまたは罪を隠す→～をかばう, (人のために)取り繕う ‖ His wife covered up for him to the police. 彼の妻は警察から彼をかばった.

★**cover**² /kʌ́vər/ 图 ▶定義1 Ⓒsomething that is put on or over sth, especially in order to protect it 特に保護するために～の上に置くまたはかぶせるもの→覆い, カバー, ふた ‖ a plastic cover for a computer コンピューター用のプラスチックのカバー a duvet cover 羽毛掛け布団 ▶定義2 Ⓒthe outside part of a book or magazine 本や雑誌の外側→表紙 ‖ I read the magazine from cover to cover (= from beginning to end). 私はその雑誌を全部読んだ(= 最初から最後まで). ▶定義3 Ⓤ cover (against sth) insurance against sth, so that if sth bad happens you get money or help in return 何か悪い～が起こったときに, 代わりに金または援助を得るための～に対する保険→(～に対する)保険, 保険による担保, 保証(金) ‖ The policy **provides cover** against theft. 保険は窃盗に対しても保証している. ▶定義4 Ⓤ protection from the weather, damage, etc; shelter 天候または損害などからの保護; 避難所→保護; 隠れ場所, 遮るもの, 遮蔽(しゃへい)物 ‖ When the storm started we had to **take cover** in a shop doorway. あらしがやって来た時私たちは店の入り口に避難しなければならなかった. When the gunfire started everyone **ran for cover**. 砲撃が始まった時皆が身を隠す場所を求めて走った. ▶定義5 **the covers** [複数扱い] the sheets, etc on a bed ベッドのシーツなど→寝具(シーツ, 毛布, 布団など), (寝具用の)上掛け ▶定義6 Ⓒ Ⓤ a cover (for sth) something that hides what sb is really doing ～が実際にしている事を隠すもの→隠れみの ‖ The whole company was just a cover for all kinds of criminal activities. 会社全体があらゆる犯罪行為の全くの隠れみのだった. police officers working **under cover** 内密で捜査をしている警官 ▶定義7 Ⓤ doing sb's job for him/her while he/she is away from work 仕事に出られない～の仕事を代わりにすること→代わりを務めること, 代理 ‖ Joanne's off next week so we'll have to arrange cover. ジョアンは来週休みを取るので代わりを手配しなければならない.

成句 under (the) cover of sth ▶定義 hidden by sth ～に隠れて→～に紛れて, ～を隠れみのにして ‖ They attacked under cover of darkness. 彼らは闇(やみ)に紛れて攻撃した.

**coverage** /kʌ́vərɪdʒ/ 图 Ⓤ ▶定義1 the act or amount of reporting on an event in newspapers, on television, etc 新聞やテレビなどで出来

事を報道すること，またはそうした報道の量→**報道(量)，取材(規模)，放送範囲・量** ‖ *TV coverage of the Olympic Games was excellent.* オリンピック大会のテレビ放送はすばらしかった．　▶定義2 the amount or quality of information included in a book, magazine, etc 本や雑誌などの情報の量または質→**掲載(内容)，取り扱う範囲・量** ‖ *The grammar section provides coverage of all the most problematic areas.* 文法の節では最も問題の多い分野についてすべて取り上げている．

**coveralls** /kÁvərɔ̀ːlz/ 图 =**OVERALL²(2)**

**covered** /kÁvərd/ 形 ▶定義1 covered in/with sth having a layer or a large amount of sth on sb/sth ～の上に…の層または大量の～がある→**～に覆われた，～まみれの** ‖ *She was covered in mud/sweat/dust.* 彼女は泥・汗・ほこりまみれだった．*nuts covered with chocolate* チョコレートでくるまれたナッツ ▶定義2 having a cover, especially a roof 特に屋根のある，覆い→**屋根付きの，覆いの付いた** ‖ *a covered shopping centre* 屋根のあるショッピングセンター

**covering** /kÁvərɪŋ/ 图 ❻ ▶定義 something that covers the surface of sth ～の表面を覆うもの→**覆い，カバー** ‖ *There was a thick covering of dust over everything.* すべてが厚いほこりに覆われていた．

**covering letter** 图 ❻ ▶定義 a letter that you send with a package, etc that gives more information about it 小包などと共に送る手紙で，送る物について知らせるためのもの→**添え手紙，添え書き** ‖ *To apply for the job, send your CV with a covering letter.* 仕事に応募したい方は，履歴書に手紙を添えてお送りください．

**covert** /kÁvərt/ 形 ▶定義 done secretly ひそかに行う→**秘密の，内密の，隠れた** ‖ *a covert police operation* 内密の警察捜査 ― **covertly** 副 →**ひそかに，内密に，隠れて**

**cover-up** 图 ❻ ▶定義 an act of preventing sth bad or dishonest from becoming known 悪い～または不誠実な…を隠す行為→**隠すこと，もみ消し** ‖ *Several newspapers have claimed that there has been a government cover-up.* 新聞数紙は，政府がもみ消したと主張している．

**covet** /kÁvət/ 動 他 正式 ▶定義 to want to have sth very much (especially sth that belongs to sb else) ～(特にほかの…が所有している～)を強く欲しがる→**～をむやみに欲しがる，切望する，熱望する**

**\*cow** /káʊ/ 图 ❻ ▶定義1 a large female animal that is kept on farms to produce milk 牛乳を得るために農場で飼育される大型の雌の動物→**雌牛，乳牛** ‖ *to milk a cow* 乳牛の乳をしぼる *a herd of cows* 雌牛の群

　▶ cowはしばしば雌と雄両方について用いる．bullは雄だけを表す語．oxは繁殖できない雄で，昔は重い荷を引くために使われた．calfは子牛．cattleは複数のcowが集まっている場合に用いる．meatの注を参照．

　▶定義2 the adult female of certain large animals, for example elephants 象など，一部の大型動物の雌の成体→**(象，サイ，アザラシ，鯨などの)雌**

**coward** /káʊərd/ 图 ❻ ▶定義 a person who has no courage and is afraid in dangerous or unpleasant situations 勇気がなく，危険または不快な状況を恐れる人→**おくびょう者，卑怯(ひきょう)者，弱虫** ‖ *I hate going to the dentist's because I'm a terrible coward.* 私はひどいおくびょう者なので，歯医者に行くのが大嫌いだ．― **cowardly** 形 →**おくびょうな，意気地のない**

**cowardice** /káʊərdəs/ 图 ❶ ▶定義 a lack of courage; behaviour that shows that you are afraid 勇気がないこと；恐れていることを示す振る舞い→**おくびょう，意気地なし**

**cowboy** /káʊbɔ̀ɪ/ 图 ❻ ▶定義1 a man whose job is to look after cows (usually on a horse) in certain parts of the US 米国の一部の地域で(通常は馬に乗って)牛の世話をすることを仕事とする男性→**カウボーイ，牛飼い，牧童**　▶定義2 英略式 a person in business who is not honest or who does work badly 商売において誠実でない人，または仕事をきちんとしない人→**悪質な業者，やっつけ仕事をする人** ‖ *a cow-*

boy builder やっつけ仕事をする建設業者

**cower** /káuər/ 動 ▶定義 to move back or into a low position because of fear 恐れのため退く，または姿勢を低くする→後ずさりする，縮こまる，すくむ ‖ *The dog cowered under the table when the storm started.* あらしがやって来ると犬はおびえてテーブルの下に隠れた．

**coy** /kɔ́i/ 形 ▶定義1 pretending to be shy or innocent 内気または無垢(むく)な振りをする→かまとと，おしとやか振った ‖ *She lifted her head a little and gave him a coy smile.* 彼女はわずかに顔を上げて彼に向かってわざと恥ずかしそうにほほえんだ．▶定義2 not wanting to give information about sth or to answer questions that tell people too much about you ～について の情報を教えたがらない，または自分自身についての詳しい質問に答えたがらない→秘密主義の ‖ *Don't be coy, tell me how much you earn.* 隠さないで，いくら稼いでいるのか教えてください．— **coyly** 副 →恥ずかしそうに，内気そうに

**cozy** 米 =COSY

**crab** /kræb/ 名 C U ▶定義 a sea animal with a flat shell and ten legs. The front two legs have long curved points (pincers) on them. Crabs move sideways; the meat from a crab 扁平(へんぺい)な殻と10本の足のある海洋動物．前部の2本の足は先端が長く湾曲している(はさみ)．横に歩く．この動物の肉→カニ，カニに似た甲殻類，カニの肉 ☛ **shellfish** のさし絵

★**crack**¹ /kræk/ 動 ▶定義1 C U to break or to make sth break so that a line appears on the surface, but without breaking into pieces 表面に筋ができるように～が割れる，ただし，ばらばらにはならない，またはこのように～を割る→ひびが入る，割れ目ができる，パチンと割れる；～にひびを入れる，～をパチンと割る ‖ *Don't put boiling water into that glass - it'll crack.* 熱湯をそのコップに入れないように － ひびが入るから．*The stone cracked the windscreen but didn't break it.* 石でフロントガラスにひびが入ったが，割れはしなかった．☛ **chip** のさし絵 ▶定義2 C to break sth open ～を割って開く→～を割る，砕く，割って～する ‖ *Crack two eggs into a bowl.* 卵2個をボウルに割り入れます．▶定義3 C U to make a sudden loud, sharp sound; to cause sth to make this sound 突然大きな鋭い音を立てる；～にこのような音を立てさせる→鋭い音を発する，パーンと鳴る；～に鋭い音を出させる，～をパーンと鳴らす ‖ *to crack a whip/your knuckles* むちをピシッと・指関節をパチッと鳴らす ▶定義4 C to hit a part of your body against sth; to hit somebody with sth ～に体の一部をぶつける；人を…で打つ→～をぶつける，ぴしゃりと打つ・たたく ‖ *She stood up and cracked her head on the cupboard door.* 彼女は立ち上がった時に食器戸棚のドアに頭をぶつけた．*She cracked the thief over the head with her umbrella.* 彼女は傘で泥棒の頭を打った．▶定義5 C to no longer be able to deal with pressure and so lose control 重圧に耐えられなくなり抑制を失う→くじける，(精神的に)弱る，参る ‖ *He cracked under the strain of all his problems.* 彼はさまざまな問題による緊張に耐えきれなくなった．▶定義6 C (used about sb's voice) to suddenly change in a way that is not controlled (～の声について)突然抑制できなくなって変わる→(声が)かすれる，上ずる，調子が変わる ‖ *Her voice cracked as she spoke about her parent's death.* 両親の死について話しているうちに彼女の声が不意に上ずった．▶定義7 C 略式 to solve a problem 問題を解決する→～を解く，解読する，(犯罪組織など)を暴く ‖ *to crack a code* 暗号を解読する *The police have cracked an international drug-smuggling ring.* 警察は国際的麻薬密輸組織を押さえた．▶定義8 C to tell or make a joke ジョークを言う→冗談を言う，ジョークを飛ばす ‖ *Stop cracking jokes and do some work!* 冗談ばかり言っていないで仕事をしなさい．

成句 **get cracking** 英 略式 ▶定義 to start doing sth immediately ～を直ちに始める→さっと取り掛かる，てきぱきとやる ‖ *I have to finish this job today so I'd better get cracking.* この仕事を今日終えなければならないので，早く取り掛かろう．

句動詞 **crack down (on sb/sth)** ▶定義 (used about people in authority) to start dealing strictly with bad or illegal behaviour (権力のある人について)不正または違法行為に対して厳格に対処する→(～を)厳重に取り締まる，(～に)断固たる措置を取る，弾圧する ‖ *The police have started to crack down on drug dealers.* 警察は

麻薬密売人の取り締まりを開始した.

**crack up** ▶定義1 略式 to be unable to deal with pressure and so lose control and become mentally ill 重圧に対処できずに自制力を失い精神の病気になる→**精神的に参る** ‖ *He cracked up when his wife left him.* 妻が去った時に彼は精神的に参ってしまった. ▶定義2 （俗語）to suddenly start laughing, especially when you should be serious 特にまじめな場で急に笑い出す→**(こらえられず)吹き出す**

★**crack**² /kræk/ 名 ▶定義1 C a line on the surface of sth where it has broken, but not into pieces 〜が壊れたが, ばらばらにはならないときに表面にできる筋→**ひび, 割れ目** ‖ *a pane of glass with a crack in it* ひびが入った窓ガラス （比喩） *They had always seemed happy together, but then cracks began to appear in their relationship.* 彼らはいつも一緒で幸福そうだったが, やがて彼らの関係にひびが入り始めた. ☛ **chip** のさし絵 ▶定義2 C a narrow opening 細い開口部→**すきま, 亀裂(きれつ), 裂け目** ‖ *a crack in the curtains* カーテンのすきま ▶定義3 C a sudden loud, sharp sound 突然の大きな鋭い音→**発射音, 爆音, パチッ, ピシャリ, パーン(などという音)** ‖ *There was a loud crack as the gun went off.* 銃が発射された時に大きな鋭い音がした. ▶定義4 C a hard hit on a part of the body 体の一部を強く打つこと→**鋭い一撃** ‖ *Suddenly a golf ball gave him a nasty crack on the head.* 突然ゴルフボールが彼の頭に勢いよくぶつかった. ▶定義5 C 略式 an amusing, often critical, comment; a joke 面白く, しばしば批判的な論評; ジョーク→**警句, 皮肉, 気の利いた受け答え, 機知に富む冗談** ‖ *She made a crack about his bald head and he got angry.* 彼女が彼のはげ頭について冗談を言ったので彼は怒った.

▶定義6 U a dangerous and illegal drug that some people take for pleasure and cannot then stop taking 一部の人が快楽のために摂取する危険な違法薬物で, 使用をやめられなくなる→**麻薬, クラック**

成句 **the crack of dawn** ▶定義 very early in the morning 朝とても早く→**夜明け, 日の出, 早朝**

**have a crack (at sth/at doing sth)** 略式 ▶定義 to try to do sth 〜をしようとする→**〜を試みる** ‖ *I'm not sure how to play but I'll have a crack at it.* どうやったらいいのかよく分かりませんが, やってみます.

**crack**³ /kræk/ 形 ▶定義 (used about soldiers or sports players) very well-trained and skilful (兵士やスポーツ選手について) 非常によく訓練され巧みな→**優秀な, 一流の, 卓越した** ‖ *crack troops* 精鋭部隊 *He's a crack shot (= very accurate at shooting) with a rifle.* 彼はライフルの名手だ(= 射撃が非常に正確).

**crackdown** /ˈkrækdaʊn/ 名 C ▶定義 action to stop bad or illegal behaviour 不正行為や違法行為を止める行動→**取り締まり, 摘発, 手入れ** ‖ *Fifty people have been arrested in a police crackdown on street crime.* 町の犯罪に対する警察の取り締まりで50人が逮捕された.

**cracker** /ˈkrækər/ 名 C ▶定義1 a thin dry biscuit that is often eaten with cheese 薄い乾燥したビスケットで, よくチーズと一緒に食べる→**クラッカー** ☛ **cake** のさし絵 ▶定義2 （または **Christmas cracker**) a cardboard tube covered in coloured paper and containing a small present. Crackers are pulled apart by two people, each holding one end, at Christmas parties. They make a loud noise as they break. 色紙で包まれ中に小さな贈り物が入ったボール紙の筒. クリスマスパーティーで2人の人がそれぞれ端を持って引いて引き裂く. 壊れるときに大きな音を立てる→**クラッカー** ▶定義3 英 略式 a very good example of sth 〜のとても良い例→**大したもの, 逸品, 面白くてすてきなもの** ‖ *That story he told was a real cracker.* 彼が話した物語は本当に面白かった.

**crackle** /ˈkræk(ə)l/ 動 自 ▶定義 to make a series of short, sharp sounds 連続した短く鋭い音を立てる→**パチパチ音を立てる, パリパリ鳴る** ‖ *The radio started to crackle and then it stopped working.* ラジオがガリガリ言い出し, そして鳴らなくなってしまった. — **crackle** 名 [単数扱い]→**短く鋭い音, パチパチいう音** ‖ *the crackle of dry wood burning* 乾いたまきが燃えるパチパチという音

**cradle**¹ /ˈkreɪdl/ 名 C ▶定義 a small bed for a baby. Cradles can often be moved from side to side. 赤ん坊用の小型ベッド. 通常は横に揺らすことができる→**揺りかご, 小児用ベッド** ☛ **bed** のさし絵

**cradle²** /kréɪdl/ 動 他 ▶定義 to hold sb/sth carefully and gently in your arms ～を腕に注意深く優しく抱く→～を抱くように持つ, そっと持つ, 揺すってあやす

**craft** /krɑːft; kræft/ 名 ▶定義1 ⓒ ⓤ a job or activity for which you need skill with your hands 手先の器用さが必要な仕事または活動→工芸, 手工芸, 職人の仕事 ∥ *an arts and crafts exhibition* 芸術と工芸の展示会 *I studied craft and design at school.* 私は学校で工芸とデザインを学んだ. ☛参 **handicraft** ▶定義2 ⓒ any job or activity for which you need skill 技能を必要とする仕事または活動→技能, 技巧, 技術, 技(わざ) ∥ *He regards acting as a craft.* 彼は演技を技能だと考えている. ▶定義3 ⓒ (複 **craft**) a boat, aircraft or spacecraft 小型船, 航空機, 宇宙船→船舶, ～船

**craftsman** /krɑ́ːftsmən/ 名 ⓒ (複 **-men** /-mən/) ▶定義 a person who makes things skilfully, especially with his/her hands 特に手で物を巧みに作る人→(熟練した)職人, 熟練工

**craftsmanship** /krɑ́ːftsmənʃɪp/ 名 ⓤ ▶定義 the skill used by sb to make sth of high quality with his/her hands 手で高品質の～を作るために…が使用する技術→職人の技能, 熟練

**crafty** /krɑ́ːfti; kræft-/ 形 ▶定義 clever at getting or achieving things by using unfair or dishonest methods 不正な, または不誠実な手段で物を得たり成し遂げたりするのがうまい→悪賢い, ずるい, 狡猾(こうかつ)な ― **craftily** 副 →悪賢く, 狡猾に

**crag** /kræg/ 名 ⓒ ▶定義 a steep, rough rock on a hill or mountain 丘や山の急勾配(こうばい)でごつごつした岩→ごつごつした岩, 険しい岩山, 絶壁

**craggy** /krǽgi/ 形 ▶定義1 having a lot of steep rough rock 急勾配(こうばい)でごつごつした岩が多い→岩でごつごつして, 岩だらけの ▶定義2 (used about a man's face) strong and with deep lines, especially in an attractive way (男性の顔について)特に魅力的なほど, たくましく, 深いしわがある→いかつい, ごつごつした, 強そうな

**cram** /kræm/ 動 (**cramming**; **crammed**) ▶定義1 他 to push people or things into a small space 人々または物を狭い空間に押し込む→～を(無理に)詰め込む, ぎっしり詰める, 一杯にする ∥ *I managed to cram all my clothes into the bag but I couldn't close it.* 私は何とか洋服を全部かばんに詰め込んだが, かばんが閉まらなかった. *We only spent two days in Rome but we managed to cram a lot of sightseeing in.* ローマには2日間しか滞在しなかったが, できるだけ多くの観光地を見て回った. ▶定義2 自 to move, with a lot of other people, into a small space 大勢の人と一緒に狭い空間に移動する→押し寄せる, (どっと)詰め掛ける, (大勢が)乗り込む ∥ *He only had a small car but they all managed to cram in.* 彼は小さな車しか持っていなかったが, 何とか全員が乗り込んだ. ▶定義3 自 to study very hard and learn a lot in a short time before an exam 試験の前に一生懸命勉強し短時間で多くを覚え込む→詰め込み勉強をする, 一夜漬けの勉強をする ∥ *She's cramming for her exams.* 彼女は試験のために詰め込み勉強をしている.

**crammed** /kræmd/ 形 ▶定義 very or too full ぎっしり詰まった, または詰め込みすぎの→一杯に詰まった, 無理に詰め込んだ, 一杯の, 満員の ∥ *That book is crammed with useful information.* その本には役に立つ情報がぎっしり詰まっている.

**cramp** /kræmp/ 名 ⓤ ▶定義 a sudden pain that you get in a muscle, that makes it difficult to move 動けなくなるような筋肉の急な痛み→こむら返り, (筋肉の)けいれん, 引きつり

**cramped** /kræm(p)t/ 形 ▶定義 not having enough space 十分な空間がない→狭苦しい, 窮屈な ∥ *The flat was terribly cramped with so many of us living there.* 大勢が住んでいて, フラットはとても狭苦しかった.

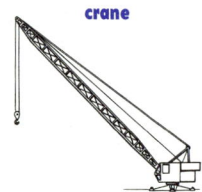
**crane**

**crane¹** /kreɪn/ 名 ⓒ ▶定義 a large machine with a long metal arm that is used for moving or lifting heavy objects 重い物を動かすまたは持ち上げるための, 長い金属の腕のある大型機械→クレーン, 起重機

**crane**² /kreɪn/ 動 自 他 ▶定義 to stretch your neck forward in order to see or hear sth ～を見るまたは聞くために首を前に伸ばす➔**前に乗り出す, 身を乗り出す** ‖ *We all craned forward to get a better view.* もっとよく見ようと皆が首を伸ばした.

**crank** /kræŋk/ 名 C ▶定義 a person with strange ideas or who behaves in a strange way 奇妙な考えを持っている人, または奇妙な行動を取る人➔**風変わりな人, 変人, 変わり者** ‖ *Lots of cranks phoned the police confessing to the murder.* 大勢の変人が警察に電話して殺人の告白をした.

**cranny** /krǽni/ 名 C (複 **crannies**) ▶定義 a small opening in a wall, rock, etc 壁や岩などの小さな開口部➔**割れ目, 裂け目, すきま**
成句 every nook and cranny ⇒ **NOOK**

**crap** /kræp/ 名 U (俗語) ▶定義 a very rude word meaning nonsense or rubbish ばかげたことまたは下らないことを意味する, 非常に下品な言葉➔**下らぬ事・物; くそ** ☛ 多くの人がこの語を不快だと感じる.

★**crash**¹ /kræʃ/ 動 ▶定義1 自 他 to have an accident in a vehicle; to drive a vehicle into sth 乗り物に乗っていて事故に遭う; 乗り物を～に衝突させる➔**ぶつかる, 衝突する, 衝突事故に遭う;(乗り物を)ぶつける** ‖ *He braked too late and crashed into the car in front.* ブレーキをかけたが遅すぎて彼は前の車に衝突した. ▶定義2 自 to hit sth hard, making a loud noise 大きな音を立てて～を強く打つ➔**ガチャンとぶつかる** ‖ *The tree crashed to the ground.* 木が大きな音を立てて地面に倒れた. ▶定義3 自 to make a loud noise 大きな音を立てる➔**激しい音を立てる** ‖ *I could hear thunder crashing outside.* 外で雷のすさまじい音がした. ▶定義4 自 (used about money or business) to suddenly lose value or fail (金や商売について)突然に価値を失う, または失敗する➔**(事業などが)失敗する, つぶれる** ▶定義5 自 (used about a computer) to suddenly stop working (コンピューターについて)突然動作しなくなる➔**(システムが)故障する, クラッシュする** ‖ *We lost the data when the computer crashed.* コンピューターがクラッシュしてデータを失った.

★**crash**² /kræʃ/ 名 C ▶定義1 a sudden loud noise made by sth breaking, hitting sth, etc ～が壊れる, または…を打ったりするときなどの突然の大きな音➔**すさまじい音, ガラガラ, ガシャン** ‖ *I heard a crash and ran outside.* 大きな音がしたので外に飛び出した. ▶定義2 an accident when a car or other vehicle hits sth and is damaged 車などの乗り物が～にぶつかって破損する事故➔**衝突事故, 交通事故** ‖ *a car/plane crash* 自動車・飛行機事故 ▶定義3 (used about money or business) a sudden fall in the value or price of sth (金や商売について)～の価値または価格の急落➔**(相場, 事業などが)つぶれること, 暴落, 倒産** ‖ *the Stock Market crash of 1987* 1987年の株式市場の暴落 ▶定義4 a sudden failure of a machine, especially a computer 機械, 特にコンピューターの突然の故障➔**(システムの)故障, クラッシュ**

**crash**³ /kræʃ/ 形 ▶定義 done in a very short period of time 非常に短い期間で行う➔**大急ぎの, 集中的** ‖ *She did a **crash course** in Spanish before going to work in Madrid.* 彼女は仕事でマドリードに行く前に, スペイン語の集中講座で学んだ.

**crash barrier** 名 C ▶定義 a fence that keeps people or vehicles apart, for example when there are large crowds or between the two sides of the road 例えば大群衆が集まるとき, または道路の2方向など, 人や乗り物を隔てる仕切り➔**防護柵(さく), ガードレール, 中央分離帯**

**crash helmet** 名 C ▶定義 a hard hat worn by motorbike riders, racing drivers, etc オートバイの運転者やレーシングドライバーなどがかぶる安全帽➔**ヘルメット** ☛ hat のさし絵.

**crash-land** 動 自 ▶定義 to land a plane in a dangerous way in an emergency 緊急時に飛行機を危険な方法で着陸させる➔**胴体着陸する, 強行着陸する, 不時着する** ― **crash-landing** 名 C ➔**胴体着陸, 不時着** ‖ *to make a crash-landing* 胴体着陸する

**crass** /kræs/ 形 ▶定義 stupid, showing that you do not understand sth 愚かな, ～を理解していないことを示す➔**鈍い, ひどい無知の** ‖ *It was a crass comment to make when he knew how upset she was.* 彼女が動転していることを彼は分かっていたのに, あんな事を言うなんてひどく愚かだ.

**crate** /kréɪt/ 名 C ▶定義 a large box in which goods are carried or stored 品物を運ぶまたは保管するための大型の箱→梱包(こんぽう)用の箱,枠箱

**crater** /kréɪtər/ 名 C ▶定義1 a large hole in the ground 地面の大きな穴→(爆弾,砲弾,地震などによる)穴,クレーター ‖ *The bomb left a large crater.* 爆弾で大きな穴が開いた. *craters on the moon* 月面のクレーター ▶定義2 the hole in the top of a mountain through which hot gases and liquid rock are forced (a volcano) 熱いガスや溶岩が噴出する山(火山)の頂にできた穴→噴火口 ☞ volcano のさし絵

**cravat** /krəvæt/ 名 C ▶定義 a wide piece of cloth that some men tie around their neck and wear inside the collar of their shirt 一部の男性が首に巻き,シャツのえりの内側に付ける幅広の布→アスコットタイ

**crave** /kréɪv/ 動 自 他 ▶定義 crave (for) sth to want and need to have sth very much 〜を非常に強く欲しがり必要とする→(〜を)しきりに欲しがる,切望する ‖ *Sometimes I really crave for some chocolate.* 時々チョコレートが欲しくてたまらなくなる.

**craving** /kréɪvɪŋ/ 名 C ▶定義 a strong desire for sth 〜に対する強い欲求→切望,熱望 ‖ *When she was pregnant she used to have cravings for all sorts of peculiar food.* 彼女は妊娠中に奇妙な食べ物ばかり食べたくなったものだった.

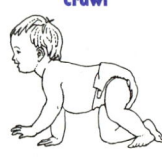
crawl

**crawl¹** /krɔːl/ 動 自 ▶定義1 to move slowly with your body on or close to the ground, or on your hands and knees 体を地面に付けるまたは近付けて,または手とひざで,ゆっくり進む→はう,腹ばいで進む,ほふく前進する ‖ *Their baby has just started to crawl.* 彼らの赤ん坊ははいはいを始めたところだ. *An insect crawled across the floor.* 虫が床をはった. ▶定義2 (used about vehicles) to move very slowly (乗り物について)非常にゆっくりと動く→のろのろ走る,ゆっくり進む ‖ *The traffic crawls through the centre of town in the rush hour.* ラッシュ時には車は街の中心をのろのろと通り抜ける. ▶定義3 略式 crawl (to sb) to be very polite or pleasant to sb in order to be liked or to gain sth 好かれるためまたは〜を得るために,…に非常に礼儀正しくまたは快く接する→へつらう,こびる,ぺこぺこする ‖ *He only got promoted because he crawled to the manager.* 彼が昇進したのは支配人に取り入ったからにすぎない.

成句 **be crawling with sth** ▶定義 to be completely full of or covered with unpleasant animals 不快な生物で一杯の,または覆われた→〜がうようよいる,うじゃうじゃしている,(虫などが)わいている ‖ *The kitchen was crawling with insects.* 台所には虫がうようよしていた. (比喩) *The village is always crawling with tourists at this time of year.* 1年のこの時期は村には旅行者が大勢いる.

**crawl²** /krɔːl/ 名 ▶定義1 [単数扱い] a very slow speed 非常にゆっくりとした速度→徐行,のろのろ進むこと ‖ *The traffic slowed to a crawl.* 車の流れはスピードを落としてのろのろ通行になった. ▶定義2 (しばしば **the crawl**) [単数扱い, U] a style of swimming which you do on your front. When you do the crawl, you move first one arm and then the other over your head, turn your face to one side so that you can breathe and kick up and down with your legs. うつぶせで進む泳法. まず一方の腕を頭上に動かして次に他方を動かし,呼吸できるように顔を一方に向け,足で上下にける→クロール,クロール泳法 ☞ S1ページのさし絵

**crayon** /kréɪɑn, -ən/ 名 C U ▶定義 a soft, thick, coloured pencil that is used for drawing or writing, especially by children 特に子供が絵や文字をかくために使う柔らかい太い色鉛筆→クレヨン — **crayon** 動 自 他 →(〜を)クレヨンでかく,クレヨンで塗る

**craze** /kréɪz/ 名 C a craze (for sth) ▶定義1 a strong interest in sth, that usually only lasts for a short time 〜に対する強い興味で,通常は短期間しか続かない→(一時的)熱狂,熱中,(一時的)大流行 ‖ *There was a craze for that kind of music last year.* 去年はその種の音楽が大流行した. ▶定義2 something that a lot of people are very interested in 大勢の人々が強い興味を示すもの→流行,はやり ‖ *Pocket TVs are the latest craze among teenagers.* 最近,ティーン

エージャーの間でポケットテレビ熱がすごい.

**\*crazy** /kréɪzi/ 形 (**crazier**; **craziest**) 略式
▶定義1 very silly or foolish 非常に愚かな,またはばかげた→正気とは思えない,狂気染みた,どうかしている,気が変な ‖ *You must be crazy to turn down such a wonderful offer.* そんなすばらしい申し出を断るなんて正気とは思えない.
▶定義2 very angry 非常に怒った→激怒した,かっとなる ‖ *She **goes crazy** when people criticize her.* 彼女は批判されるとかっとなる.
▶定義3 **crazy about sb/sth** liking sb/sth very much ~がとても好きで→~に夢中な,大好きな,ほれている ‖ *He's always been crazy about horses.* 彼はいつも馬に夢中になっている.
▶定義4 showing great excitement 強い興奮を示す→熱狂的な,夢中な ‖ *The fans **went crazy** when their team scored the first goal.* ひいきのチームが最初の得点を上げるとファンは熱狂した. — crazily 副→狂気のように,かっとなって,熱狂して — craziness 名 Ⓤ→愚かさ,激怒,熱狂

**creak** /kri:k/ 動 ▶定義 to make the noise of wood bending or of sth not moving smoothly 木材が曲がる,または~の動きが滑らかでないような音を出す→きしむ,キーキー・ギーギーと鳴る ‖ *The floorboards creaked when I walked across the room.* 部屋を歩くと床板がきしんだ. — creak 名 Ⓒ→きしむ音,きしみ — creaky 形→きしむ,キーキー鳴る ‖ *creaky stairs* キーキーときしむ階段

**\*cream**¹ /kri:m/ 名 ▶定義1 Ⓤ the thick yellowish-white liquid that rises to the top of milk 牛乳の上層にできる濃厚な黄白色の液体→クリーム,乳脂 ‖ *coffee with cream* クリームを入れたコーヒー *whipped cream* (= *cream that has been beaten*) ホイップクリーム (= かき混ぜたクリーム) ☛ C4ページのさし絵
▶定義2 Ⓒ Ⓤ a substance that you rub into your skin to keep it soft or as a medical treatment 肌を柔らかくするために,または治療のために肌に塗り込むもの→(化粧用・医療用)クリーム ‖ (an) *antiseptic cream* 消毒用塗り薬 ☛ **bandage**のさし絵 ▶定義3 **the cream** [単数扱い]the best part of sth or the best people in a group ~の最良の部分,または集団の中の最良の人々→精選された物・人

**cream**² /kri:m/ 形名 Ⓤ ▶定義 (of) a yellowish-white colour 黄白色(の)→クリーム色(の)

---

create 385

**cream**³ /kri:m/ 動
句動詞 **cream sb/sth off** ▶定義 to take away the best people or part from sth for a particular purpose 特別の目的のために,~から最良の人々または部分を抜き取る→~を精選する,抜擢(ばってき)する,引き抜く ‖ *The big clubs cream off the country's best young players.* 大規模なクラブがその国の最高の若手選手たちを引き抜く.

**creamy** /krí:mi/ 形 (**creamier**; **creamiest**)
▶定義1 containing cream; thick and smooth like cream クリームを含んだ;クリームのように濃厚で滑らかな→クリーム状の,クリーミーな,滑らかで柔らかい ‖ *a creamy sauce* 濃厚で滑らかなソース ▶定義2 having a light colour like cream クリームのような薄い色の→クリーム色の,黄白色の ‖ *creamy skin* クリーム色の肌

**crease**¹ /kri:s/ 名 Ⓒ ▶定義1 an untidy line on paper, material, a piece of clothing, etc that should not be there 紙,材料,布などの不要な乱れた筋→しわ ‖ *Your shirt needs ironing, it's full of creases.* シャツにアイロンをかけた方がいい,しわくちゃだから. *When I unrolled the poster, there was a crease in it.* ポスターを広げたら,しわが付いていた. ▶定義2 a tidy straight line that you make in sth, for example when you fold it 例えば折り畳むときに~に付けるきちんとしたまっすぐな線→折り目 ‖ *He had a sharp crease in his trousers.* 彼のズボンにはくっきりと折り目が付いている.

**crease**² /kri:s/ 動 Ⓘ Ⓣ ▶定義 to get creases; to make sth get creases しわが付く;~にしわを付ける→しわが寄る,折り目が付く;~にしわを寄せる,折り目を付ける ‖ *Hang up your jacket or it will crease.* 上着を掛けておかないと,しわになりますよ. *Crease the paper carefully down the middle.* 紙の真ん中に丁寧に折り目を付けてください.

**\*create** /kriéɪt/ 動 Ⓣ ▶定義 to cause sth new to happen or exist 新しい~を引き起こすまたは出現させる→~を創造する,創設する,創立する,生み出す,引き起こす ‖ *a plan to create new jobs in the area* その地域に新しい職を生み出す計画 *He created a bad impression at the interview.* 彼はインタビューで悪い印象を与えた.

**creation** /kriéɪʃ(ə)n/ 名 ▶定義1 ❶the act of causing sth new to happen or exist 新しいものを引き起こすことまたは出現させること→**創造,創作,創設,創立** ‖ *the creation of new independent states* 新しい独立国家の創造 ▶定義2 (通常は **the Creation**) [単数扱い] the act of making the whole universe, as described in the Bible 聖書に書かれているように全世界を創造すること→**天地創造,創世** ▶定義3 ❻something new that sb has made or produced ～が作り出すまたは生み出す新しい…→**創作物,作品,(知力,想像力の)産物** ‖ *This dish is a new creation - I didn't use a recipe.* この料理は新しく創作した物です － レシピは使いませんでした.

**creative** /kriéɪtɪv/ 形 ▶定義1 using skill or imagination to make or do new things 新しい物を作るまたは新しい事を行うために技能や想像力を使って→**創造的な,創造力のある,創意に富んだ,独創的な** ‖ *She's a fantastic designer - she's so creative.* 彼女はすばらしいデザイナーだ － 非常に独創的だ. ▶定義2 connected with producing new things 新しい物を生み出すことに関連した→**創作の,創作活動の,創造の,創造的な** ‖ *His creative life went on until he was well over 80.* 彼の創作生活は80歳を優に超えるまで続いた. ― **creatively** 副 →**創造的に,創造力豊かに**

**creativity** /krìːeɪtívəti/ 名 ❶ ▶定義 the ability to make or produce new things using skill or imagination 技能や想像力を使って新しい物を作り出すまたは生み出す能力→**創造性,独創力,創造的なこと** ‖ *We want teaching that encourages children's creativity.* 子供たちの創造力を伸ばす授業を望んでいる.

**creator** /kriéɪtər/ 名 ❻ ▶定義 a person who makes or produces sth new 新しい～を作り出すまたは生み出す人→**創造者,創作者** ‖ *He was the creator of some of the best-known characters in literature.* 彼は文学において最もよく知られた登場人物を生み出した.

\***creature** /kríːtʃər/ 名 ❻ ▶定義 a living thing such as an animal, a bird, a fish or an insect, but not a plant 動物,鳥,魚,昆虫などの生物,植物は含まれない→**生き物,動物** ‖ *sea creatures* 海洋生物

**crèche** /kréɪʃ, kreʃ/ 名 ❻ ▶定義 a place where small children are looked after while their parents are working, shopping, etc 両親が仕事や買い物などをしている間,幼い子供の面倒を見る場所→**保育所,託児所**

**credentials** /krɪdénʃ(ə)lz/ 名 [複数扱い] ▶定義1 the qualities, experience, etc that make sb suitable for sth ～を…に対して適性があるとする素質または経験など→**資質,資格,適性** ‖ *He has the perfect credentials for the job.* 彼にはその仕事に就くのに申し分ない資質がある. ▶定義2 a document that is proof that you have the training, education, etc necessary to do sth, or proof that you are who you say you are ～を行うために必要な訓練や教育などを受けたと証明する書類,または本人であると証明する書類→**資格・成績証明書,信用証明書,人物証明書**

**credibility** /krèdəbíləti/ 名 ❶ ▶定義 the quality that sb has that makes people believe or trust him/her 人の持っている特質で,その人をほかの人に信用または信頼させるもの→**信じ得ること,信用性,信憑(しんぴょう)性,確実性** ‖ *The Prime Minister had lost all credibility and had to resign.* 首相は信頼を完全に失い,辞任せざるを得なかった.

**credible** /krédəb(ə)l/ 形 ▶定義1 that you can believe 信じられる→**信頼できる** ‖ *It's hardly credible that such a thing could happen without him knowing it.* 彼の知らないところでそんな事が起こるなんてほとんど信じられない. ⇔ **incredible** ▶定義2 that seems possible ありそうに思える→**確かな,可能性のある,実行できそうな** ‖ *We need to think of a credible alternative to nuclear energy.* 核エネルギーに代わる実用可能なエネルギーを考える必要がある.

\***credit**[1] /krédət/ 名 ▶定義1 ❶a way of buying goods or services and not paying for them until later 商品またはサービスを購入して後で支払いをする方式→**クレジット,信用掛け,付け** ‖ *I bought the television on credit.* テレビをクレジットで買った. ▶定義2 ❻❶a sum of money that a bank, etc lends to sb 銀行などが～に貸すある額の金→**貸付金,融資** ‖ *The company was not able to get any further credit and went bankrupt.* 会社はそれ以上融資を受けられず倒産した. ▶定義3 ❶having money in an account at a bank 銀行の口座に金があること→**預金,預金額** ‖ *No bank charges are made if your account* *remains in credit.* 口座に預金がある限り銀行手数料はかかりません. ▶定義4 ❹a payment made into an account at a bank 銀行の口座への支払い→**振り込み, 入金, 預け入れ** ∥ *There have been several credits to her account over the last month.* 先月彼女の口座には数回の入金があった. ⇔ **debit** ▶定義5 ❶an act of saying that sb has done sth well ～が…をうまくやったと言うこと→**賞賛** ∥ *He got all the credit for the success of the project.* プロジェクト成功の名誉はすべて彼のものだった. *I can't take any credit; the others did all the work.* 私の手柄ではありません, 皆のお陰です. *She didn't do very well but at least give her credit for trying.* 彼女はあまりうまくできなかったが, 少なくともやるだけはやったと認めよう. ▶定義6 [単数扱い] *a credit to sb/sth* a person or thing that you should be proud of 誇りに思うべき人や物→**(～の)名誉となる人・物, 誉(ほま)れ** ∥ *She is a credit to her school.* 彼女は学校の名誉だ. ▶定義7 **the credits** [複数扱い] the list of the names of the people who made a film or TV programme, shown at the beginning or end of the film 映画やテレビ番組を制作した人の名前の一覧で, 映画の最初か最後に表示される→**クレジット(タイトル)** ▶定義8 ❹米 a part of a course at a college or university, that a student has completed successfully 学生が終了して及第した大学の課程→**(履修)単位, 履修証明**

成句 *do sb credit* ▶定義 (used about sb's qualities or achievements) to be so good that people should be proud of him/her (～の資質や功績について)人が名誉に思うくらい非常に優れている→**～の名誉となる, ～に面目を施させる** ∥ *His courage and optimism do him credit.* 彼の勇気と楽観主義はすばらしい.

*(be) to sb's credit* ▶定義 used for showing that you approve of sth that sb has done, although you have criticized him/her for sth else ほかの～では批判したが, その…がした～を是認することを示す場合に用いて→**～の名誉となるように, 感心にも, 立派なことに** ∥ *The company, to its credit, apologized and refunded my money.* 会社は感心にも謝罪して, 私に返金してくれた.

*have sth to your credit* ▶定義 to have finished sth that is successful 見事な～を成し遂げる→**名誉となる事をする, ～という功績を残** す, ～を成し遂げる ∥ *He has three best-selling novels to his credit.* 彼はもう既に3冊のベストセラー小説を出している.

**credit**[2] /krédɪt/ 動 他 ▶定義1 to add money to a bank account 銀行口座に金を追加する→**～を口座に振り込む, 預金する, 入金する** ∥ *Has the cheque been credited to my account yet?* 小切手はもう私の口座に記入されましたか. ▶定義2 *credit sb/sth with sth; credit sth to sb/sth* to believe or say that sb/sth has a particular quality or has done something well ～に特別な資質がある, または何かをうまくやったと信じる, またはそう言う→**～が(性質, 能力など)を持っていると信じる** ∥ *Of course I wouldn't do such a stupid thing - credit me with a bit more sense than that!* もちろん私はそんなばかな事はしません － 私にはもう少し分別があることを信じてください. ▶定義3 (特に否定文と疑問文で) to believe sth ～を信じる→**～を信じる, ～だと思う** ∥ *I simply cannot credit that he has made the same mistake again!* 彼がまた同じ誤りを犯したなんてとても信じられない.

**creditable** /krédɪtəb(ə)l/ 形 ▶定義 of a quite good standard that cannot be criticized, though not excellent 優秀ではないが, かなり良い水準で批判できない→**賞賛に値する, 立派な, かなりの, なかなかの** ∥ *It was a creditable result considering that three players were injured.* 3人の選手が負傷したことを考えれば立派な結果だった.

**credit card** 名 ❹ ▶定義 a small plastic card that allows sb to get goods or services without using money. You usually receive a bill once a month for what you have bought. 金を使わずに～が商品またはサービスを購入できる小さなプラスチックのカード. 購入した物の請求書は普通月に1度受け取る→**クレジットカード** ∥ *Can I pay by credit card?* クレジットカードで支払いができますか. ☞参 **cash card**, **cheque card** ☞ **money**のさし絵

**creditor** /krédətər/ 名 ❹ ▶定義 a person or company from whom you have borrowed money 人が金を借りた相手の人, または会社→**債権者, 貸し主, 融資者**

**creed** /kriːd/ 名 ❹ ▶定義 a set of beliefs or principles (especially religious ones) that strongly influence sb's life ～の人生に強い影響を与える一連の信念や原理(特に宗教的なもの)➡信念,信条,主義

**creek** /kriːk/ 名 C ▶定義1 米 a narrow piece of water where the sea flows into the land 海が陸地に入り込む狭い水の流れ➡小さな入り江,小湾,～浦 ▶定義2 英 a small river; a stream 小さな川;流れ➡小川,支流,細流,クリーク

**creep**¹ /kriːp/ 動 自 (過,過分 **crept** /krept/) ▶定義1 to move very quietly and carefully so that nobody will notice you だれにも気付かれないように非常に静かに注意深く動く➡そっと歩く,忍び足で進む,こそこそ歩く ‖ *She crept into the room so as not to wake him up.* 彼女は彼を起こさないように忍び足で部屋に入った. ▶定義2 to move forward slowly ゆっくり前進する➡のろのろ進む,徐行する,徐々に進む ‖ *The traffic was only creeping along.* 交通はのろのろとしか進まなかった.

成句 make your flesh creep ⇒ **FLESH**

句動詞 creep in ▶定義 to begin to appear 現れ始める➡いつの間にか～する,忍び寄る,知らぬ間に入り込む ‖ *All sorts of changes are beginning to creep into the education system.* いつの間にか教育制度にあらゆる変化が起こり始めている.

**creep**² /kriːp/ 名 C 略式 ▶定義 a person that you do not like because they try too hard to be liked by people in authority 権威のある人に一生懸命取り入ろうとするので嫌われている人➡おべっか使い,ごますり,嫌な人

成句 give sb the creeps 略式 ▶定義 to make sb feel frightened or nervous ～をおびえさせたり不安にさせたりする➡～をぞっとさせる,身の毛がよだつ,気味が悪い ‖ *There's something about him that gives me the creeps.* 彼にはどこか不気味なところがある.

**creeper** /kriːpər/ 名 C ▶定義 a plant that grows up trees or walls or along the ground 木や壁に絡まる,または地面をはう植物➡つる性植物,ツタ類

**creepy** /kriːpi/ 形 略式 ▶定義 that makes you feel nervous or frightened 不安にさせたりおびえさせる➡ぞっとする,身の毛のよだつ,気味の悪い

**cremate** /krɪˈmeɪt, ˈkriːmeɪt/ 動 他 ▶定義 to burn the body of a dead person as part of a funeral service 葬儀の一部として死者の体を焼く➡～を火葬にする — **cremation** /krɪˈmeɪʃ(ə)n/ 名 C U ➡火葬 ☞参 **funeral**の注

**crematorium** /ˌkriːməˈtɔːriəm/ 名 C ▶定義 a building in which the bodies of dead people are burned 死者の体が焼かれる建物➡火葬場

**Creole** (または **creole**) /ˈkriːoʊl/ 名 ▶定義1 C a person who was born in the Caribbean whose family originally came from Europe and Africa カリブ地域で生まれた人で,一族はヨーロッパとアフリカの出身➡クレオール人,ヨーロッパ人と黒人の混血児 ▶定義2 C a person whose relatives (**ancestors**) were among the first Europeans to live in the Caribbean and South America, or among the first French or Spanish people to live in the southern states of the US 親族(祖先)がカリブ地域と南アメリカへ移住した最初のヨーロッパ人,または米国南部の州に移住した最初のフランス人またはスペイン人➡クレオール人,西インド諸島や中南米などに移住した白人の子孫,メキシコ湾沿岸諸州のフランスやスペイン系移民の子孫 ‖ *the Creole cooking of New Orleans* ニューオーリンズのクレオール料理 ▶定義3 C U a language that was originally a mixture of a European language and a local, especially African, language 元来はヨーロッパの言語と現地,特にアフリカの言語が混合した言語➡クレオール語

**crept** **CREEP**¹の過去・過去分詞形

**crescendo** /krəˈʃendoʊ/ 名 C (複 **crescendos**) ▶定義 a noise or piece of music that gets louder and louder 徐々に大きくなる騒音または音楽➡クレッシェンド

**crescent** /ˈkresnt/ 名 C ▶定義1 a curved shape that is pointed at both ends, like the moon in its first and last stages 満ち欠けの始まりと終わりの月のように,両端がとがった湾曲した形➡三日月形 ☞ **shape**のさし絵 ▶定義2 a street that is curved 湾曲した通り➡三日月形の街路・家並み

**cress** /kres/ 名 U ▶定義 a small plant with very small green leaves that does not need to be cooked and is eaten in salads and sandwiches 非常に小さい緑の葉のある小型の植物で,調理の必要がなくサラダやサンドイッチにして食べ

**crest** /krest/ 名 C ▶定義1 a group of feathers on the top of a bird's head 鳥の頭頂にある羽の集まり→とさか, 冠毛 ● C1ページのさし絵 ▶定義2 the top of a hill 丘の頂→丘の頂上, 山頂 ▶定義3 the white part at the top of a wave 波の先端の白い部分→波頭(なみがしら), (波の)峰

**crestfallen** /kréstfɔːl(ə)n/ 形 ▶定義 sad or disappointed 悲しい, または失望した→がっかりした, 元気のない, 意気消沈した

**crevasse** /krivǽs/ 名 C ▶定義 a deep crack in a very thick layer of ice 非常に厚い氷の層の深い割れ目→クレバス, (氷河の深い)割れ目

**crevice** /krévəs/ 名 C ▶定義 a narrow crack in a rock, wall, etc 岩や壁などの狭い割れ目→(狭く深い)裂け目, 亀裂(きれつ)

*__crew__ /kruː/ 名 [C, 単数または複数形の動詞と共に] ▶定義1 all the people who work on a ship, aircraft, etc 船, 航空機などで働く人全員→(全)乗組員, 乗務員 ▶定義2 a group of people who work together 共に働く人々の集まり→(作業員や従業員の)一団, 仲間, チーム‖ *a camera crew* (= people who film things for television, etc) カメラクルー(= テレビなどのために撮影する人々)

**crib**¹ /krɪb/ 特に 米 = COT

**crib**² /krɪb/ 動 自 他 (**cribbing**; **cribbed**) ▶定義 crib (sth) (from/off sb) to copy sb else's work and pretend it is your own ほかの〜の作品をまねして自分のものである振りをする→ (〜を)(…から)盗用する, 盗作する

**crick** /krɪk/ 名 [単数扱い] ▶定義 a pain in your neck, back, etc that makes it difficult for you to move easily 動くのが困難になるような首や背中などの痛み→筋違い, (筋肉の)けいれん, 引きつり — crick 動 他 →〜の筋を違える, 〜にけいれんを起こす‖ *I've cricked my neck.* 首の筋を違えた.

**cricket** /krɪkət/ 名 ▶定義1 U a game that is played with a bat and ball on a large area of grass by two teams of eleven players バットとボールで行うゲームで, 広い芝生の上で11人から成る2組で行う→クリケット

▶クリケットでは, bowler(投手)がボールをbatsman(打者)に向かって投げ, batsmanがこれをbat(バット)で打ち, 次にpitch(ピッチ)の端から端まで走ってrun(得点)を獲得する.

▶定義2 C an insect that makes a loud noise by rubbing its wings together 羽をこすり合わせて大きな音を出す昆虫→コオロギ

**cricketer** /krɪkətər/ 名 C ▶定義 a person who plays cricket クリケットをする人→クリケット競技者

*__crime__ /kraɪm/ 名 ▶定義1 C something which is illegal and which people are punished for, for example by being sent to prison 刑務所に送られるなどの罰を受けるような違法行為→犯罪, (法律上の)罪‖ *to commit a crime* 犯罪を犯す ▶定義2 U illegal behaviour or activities 違法行為または活動→犯罪, 悪事, 違反行為‖ *There has been an increase in car crime recently.* 最近車による犯罪が増加している. *to fight crime* 犯罪と戦う ▶定義3 (通常は **a crime**) [単数扱い] something that is morally wrong 道徳的に悪い事→罪, 罪悪, 悪い事‖ *It is a crime to waste food when people are starving.* 飢えている人がいるのに食物を無駄にするのは罪です.

*__criminal__¹ /krɪmənəl/ 名 C ▶定義 a person who has done something illegal 違法な事をした人→犯罪者, (法律上の)罪人, 犯人

*__criminal__² /krɪmənəl/ 形 ▶定義1 (名詞の前だけ) connected with crime 犯罪と関連した→犯罪の, 犯罪的な, 犯罪を犯している; 刑事上の‖ *Deliberate damage to public property is a **criminal** offence.* 公共物を故意に破壊することは犯罪行為だ. *criminal law* 刑法 ▶定義2 morally wrong 道徳的に悪い→罪悪の, けしからぬ, 嘆かわしい, 法外な‖ *a criminal waste of taxpayers' money* 納税者の金のけしからぬ浪費

**crimson** /krɪmz(ə)n/ 形 名 U ▶定義 (of) a dark red colour 濃い赤色(の)→深紅色(の), 真っ赤(な)

**cringe** /krɪndʒ/ 動 自 ▶定義1 to feel embarrassed 気恥ずかしく感じる→恥ずかしい, 照れ臭い, きまり悪い‖ *awful family photographs which make you cringe* 気恥ずかしくなるようなひどい家族写真 ▶定義2 to move away from sb/sth because you are frightened おびえて〜から離れる→すくむ, 後ずさりする, 縮こまる‖ *The dog cringed in terror when the man raised his arm.* 男が腕を上げると犬はおびえて後ずさりした.

**crinkle** /krɪŋk(ə)l/ 動 自 他 ▶定義 crinkle (sth)

(up) to have, or to make sth have, thin folds or lines in it ～に薄い折り目または筋が付く，または付ける➜しわが寄る；しわを寄せる ‖ *He crinkled the silver paper up into a ball.* 彼は銀紙をくしゃくしゃに丸めた. — crinkly /kríŋk(ə)li/ [形]➜縮んだ，波状の ‖ *crinkly material* 縮れた生地

**cripple** /kríp(ə)l/ [動][他] ▶定義 to damage sth badly ～をひどく損傷させる➜**～を損なう，壊す，まひさせる** ‖ *The recession has crippled the motor industry.* 景気後退で自動車産業が大打撃を受けた.

**crippling** /kríp(ə)lɪŋ/ [形] ▶定義 that causes very great damage or has a very bad effect 非常に大きな損害を引き起こす，または非常に悪い影響を与える➜**壊滅的な，破壊的な，大打撃を与える** ‖ *They had crippling debts and had to sell their house.* 彼らはばく大な借金を抱え，家を売る以外なかった.

**crisis** /kráɪsəs/ [名] [C] [U] ([複] **crises** /-sìːz/) ▶定義 a time of great danger or difficulty; the moment when things change and either improve or get worse 大きな危険や困難の時；物事が変化し良くなるか悪くなるかという瞬間➜**危機，局面，瀬戸際，転換期** ‖ *the international crisis caused by the invasion* 侵略によって発生した国際危機 *a friend you can rely on in times of crisis* 苦しいときに頼りになる友人

**crisp**[1] /krɪsp/ [形] ▶定義1 pleasantly hard and dry 心地良く固く乾いている➜**パリパリ・カリカリした，しけていない** ‖ *Store the biscuits in a tin to keep them crisp.* ビスケットがしけないように缶に入れておきなさい. ▶定義2 firm and fresh or new しっかりして新鮮な，または新しい➜**出来立ての，しゃきっとした，ぱりっとした，張りのある** ‖ *a crisp salad/apple* 新鮮なサラダ・リンゴ *a crisp cotton dress* ぱりっとした綿の衣服 ▶定義3 (used about the air or weather) cold and dry (空気や天候について) 寒くて乾燥した➜**身が引き締まるような，さわやかな，すがすがしい** ‖ *a crisp winter morning* 身が引き締まるような冬の朝 ▶定義4 used about the way sb speaks) quick, clear but not very friendly (～の話し方について) 早口で明瞭(めいりょう)だが，あまり親しげでない➜**てきぱきした，きびきびした，歯切れのいい** ‖ *a crisp reply* 歯切れのいい応答 — crisply [副] ➜**きびきびと，歯切れ良く** ‖ *'I disagree,' she said crisply.* 「反対です」と彼女ははっきり言った. — crispy [形][略式] = **CRISP**[1](**1**,**2**)

**crisp**[2] /krɪsp/ ([米]**chip**; **potato chip**) [名] [C] ▶定義 a very thin piece of potato that is fried in oil, dried and then sold in packets. Crisps usually have salt or another flavouring on them. ジャガイモの薄片を油で揚げて乾燥させたもので，袋に入れて販売される. 通常は塩などの調味料で味付けされている➜**ポテトチップ** ‖ *a packet of crisps* ポテトチップ1袋 ☛ **chip** のさし絵

**criss-cross** /krískrɔ̀(ː)s, -krɑ̀s/ [形] (名詞の前だけ) ▶定義 with many straight lines that cross over each other 交差する直線がたくさんある➜**縦横に線が引かれた，縦横に走る，十字に交差している** ‖ *a criss-cross pattern* 縦横に線が引かれた模様 — criss-cross [動][自][他] ➜ **(～に)縦横に線を引く，(～を)縦横に交差させる** ‖ *Many footpaths criss-cross the countryside.* 田園には多くの小道が交差して通っている.

**criterion** /kraɪtíəriən/ [名] [C] ([複] **criteria** /-riə/) ▶定義 the standard that you use when you make a decision or form an opinion about sb/sth 決定を下すときまたは～についての意見を形成するときに用いる基準➜**基準，標準，尺度** ‖ *What are the criteria for deciding who gets a place on the course?* その課程をだれが担当するか決める基準は何ですか.

**critic** /krítɪk/ [名] [C] ▶定義1 a person who says what is bad or wrong with sb/sth ～についてどこが悪いか，または誤っているかを言う人➜**批評する人，批判者** ‖ *He is a long-standing critic of the council's transport policy.* 彼は審議会の交通政策について長年にわたって批判してきた. ▶定義2 a person whose job is to give his/her opinion about a play, film, book, work of art, etc 劇，映画，本，芸術作品などについて自分の意見を言うことを仕事とする人➜**批評家，評論家；鑑定家** ‖ *a film/restaurant/art critic* 映画・レストラン・美術評論家

***critical** /krítɪk(ə)l/ [形] ▶定義1 critical (of sb/sth) saying what is wrong with sb/sth ～について悪い点を言う➜**(～に)批判的な，(～の)あら捜しをする，(～を)酷評する** ‖ *The report was very critical of safety standards on the railways.* 報告書は鉄道の安全基準について厳しく批判してい

た. ▶定義2 (名詞の前だけ) describing the good and bad points of a play, film, book, work of art, etc 劇, 映画, 本, 芸術作品などについて良い点や悪い点を述べる→批評の, 評論の, 批評眼のある‖ *a critical guide to this month's new films* 今月の新作映画の批評ガイド ▶定義3 dangerous or serious 危険な, または重大な→**危機的な, 際どい, 危ない, 危篤な**‖ *The patient is **in a critical condition**.* 患者は危篤状態だ. ▶定義4 very important; at a time when things can suddenly become better or worse とても重要な; 物事が突然良い方にまたは悪い方に向かうとき→**決定的な, 極めて重大な, 局面を左右する**‖ *The talks between the two leaders have **reached a critical stage**.* 2人の指導者の会談は決定的な局面に差し掛かった. — critically /-ɪk(ə)li/ 副 →批評的に; 際どく, 決定的に‖ *a critically ill patient* 危篤状態の患者 *a critically important decision* 局面を左右する重要な決断

\*criticism /krítəsìz(ə)m/ 名 ▶定義1 ◉Ⓤ (an expression of) what you think is bad about sb/sth ～について悪いと思う点 (の表現) →**批判, 非難, あら捜し, けなすこと**‖ *The council has **come in for** severe **criticism** over the plans.* 審議会は計画についての厳しい批判に直面している. ▶定義2 Ⓤ the act of describing the good and bad points of a play, film, book, work of art, etc 劇, 映画, 本, 芸術作品などについて良い点や悪い点を述べること→**批判, 評論; 鑑定**‖ *literary criticism* 文学評論

\*criticize (または -ise) /krítəsàɪz/ 動自他 ▶定義 criticize (sb/sth) (for sth) to say what is bad or wrong with sb/sth ～について悪い点や間違った点を言う→**(～を) (…のことで) 批判する, 非難する, 酷評する, ～のあら捜しをする**‖ *The doctor was criticized for not sending the patient to hospital.* その医師は患者を病院に送らなかったことで非難された.

critique /krɪtíːk/ 名 ◉ ▶定義 a piece of writing that describes the good and bad points of sb/sth ～の良い点と悪い点を述べた文章→**批評 (文), 評論**

croak /króʊk/ 動自 ▶定義 to make a harsh low noise like a particular animal (a frog) ある種の動物 (カエル) のように耳障りな低い声を出す→**(カエルが) ガーガー鳴く, (カラスが) カアカア鳴く, しわがれた声を出す** — croak 名 ◉→ガーガー

# crook 391

一鳴く声, しわがれ声

crochet /króʊfeɪ; -, -fi/ 名 Ⓤ ▶定義 a way of making clothes, cloth, etc by using wool or cotton and a needle with a hook at one end 毛糸または綿糸と, 一方の先にかぎの付いた針を使って衣類や布などを作る方法→**かぎ針編み, クロシェ編み** — crochet 動自他 (過, 過分 crocheted /-feɪd/) → (～を) かぎ針編みで編む ☛参 knit

crockery /krák(ə)ri/ 名 Ⓤ ▶定義 cups, plates and dishes カップ, 浅皿, 深皿→**瀬戸物, 陶磁器類** ☛参 cutlery

crocodile /krákədàɪl/ 名 ◉ ▶定義 a large reptile with a long tail and a big mouth with sharp teeth. Crocodiles live in rivers and lakes in hot countries. 長い尾と鋭い歯のある口を持つ爬虫 (はちゅう) 類. 暑い国の川や湖に住む→**クロコダイル, (大型の) ワニ** ☛参 alligator

croissant /F krwɑsɑ̃/ 名 ◉ ▶定義 a type of bread roll, shaped in a curve, that is often eaten with butter for breakfast 曲がった形のロールパンで, 多くはバターを付けて朝食に食べる→**クロワッサン** ☛ bread のさし絵

crony /króʊni/ 名 ◉ (複 cronies) 略式 ▶定義 (often used in a critical way) a friend (しばしば批判的に用いて) 友人→**悪友, 旧友, 仲間**

crook /krʊk/ 名 ◉ ▶定義1 略式 a dishonest person; a criminal 不正直な人; 犯罪者→**いかさま師, ペテン師, 泥棒, 悪党** ▶定義2 a bend or curve in sth ～の曲がった部分または曲線→**湾曲部, 屈曲部; 曲がった物**‖ *the crook of your arm* (= the inside of your elbow) 曲げた腕の内側 (= ひじの内側)

> ▶コミュニケーション
>
> 「手招き」動作の日英比較
>
> crook one's finger: てのひらを上にし, 軽く握った指のうち, 人差し指だけを相手の方に2, 3度曲げ伸ばして見せる手招きのしぐさ. 日本の「手招き」に比べて無遠慮な動作とされます. 言葉で Come here と人を呼び付けるのに近い意味を持ちます. 日本の手招きは, てのひらを下にし, 4本の指を軽くそろえて相手に向けて2, 3度上下させる動作ですが, 英米の Go away のしぐさに似ているため,

## 392 crooked

招きの合図が全く逆の「あっちへ行け」の合図に誤解されやすいとも言われます.

**crooked** /krókəd/ 形 ▶定義1 not straight or even まっすぐでない, または平らでない→曲がっている, 屈曲した, ゆがんだ ‖ *That picture is crooked.* その絵は曲がっている. *crooked teeth* 歯並びの悪い歯 ▶定義2 略式 not honest 誠実でない→不正直な, 不正な; 心の曲がった, ひねくれた ‖ *a crooked accountant* 不正直な会計士

*__crop__¹ /krɑp/ 名 ▶定義1 ⓒ all the grain, fruit, vegetables, etc of one type that a farmer grows at one time 農夫が一度に育てる1種類の穀物, 果物, 野菜などのすべて→(特定の)作物, 収穫物, 農作物 ‖ *a crop of apples* リンゴの収穫 ▶定義2 [ⓒ, 通常は複数] plants that are grown on farms for food 食用のため農場で育てられる植物→全作物, 農産物 ‖ *Rice and soya beans are the main crops here.* 米と大豆がここの主な農産物だ. ▶定義3 [単数扱い] a number of people or things which have appeared at the same time 同時に現れた多くの人または物→群, 集まり ‖ *the recent crop of movies about aliens* 最近, 続々と出てくる異星人についての映画

**crop²** /krɑp/ 動 (**cropping**; **cropped**) ▶定義1 ⓗ to cut sth very short ～を非常に短く切る→～を刈り込む, ～の先端を切る ‖ *cropped hair* 刈り込んだ髪 ▶定義2 ⓘ to produce a crop¹(1) 作物(crop¹(1))を産出する→(作物が)できる, 作付けする

句動詞 **crop up** ▶定義 to appear suddenly, when you are not expecting it 予期していないときに急に現れる→突然生じる, (問題などが)持ち上がる, 不意に現れる ‖ *We should have finished this work yesterday but some problems cropped up.* この仕事は昨日終わっているはずだったのだが, 突然問題が起こった.

**cropper** /krɑpər/ 名
成句 **come a cropper** 略式 ▶定義1 to fall over or have an accident 落ちる, または事故に遭う→どしんと落ちる ▶定義2 to fail 失敗する→大失敗をする, 散々な目に遭う, 落ちぶれる

*__cross__¹ /krɔ(ː)s, krɑs/名 ⓒ ▶定義1 a mark that you make by drawing one line across another (× or x). The sign is used for showing the position of sth, for showing that sth is not correct, etc. 1本の線をもう1本と交差させて書いた印(+ または×). この印は～の位置を示したり, ～が正しくないことなどを示すために使われる→十字(形), 十字記号, バツ印 ‖ *I drew a cross on the map to show where our house is.* 私は自分の家の場所を示すため地図に十字の印を書いた. *Incorrect answers were marked with a cross.* 間違った答えにはバツ印が付いていた. ☞**tick**のさし絵 ▶定義2 (または **the Cross**) the two pieces of wood in the shape of a cross on which people were killed as a punishment in former times, or something in this shape that is used as a symbol of the Christian religion 十字形をした2本の木材で, 昔はこの上で人が罰として殺された. またはこのような形をした物でキリスト教の象徴として用いられる→十字架, はりつけ台, 十字形の紋章 ‖ *She wore a gold cross round her neck.* 彼女は首に金の十字架をぶら下げていた. ☞参 **crucifix** ▶定義3 [通常は単数] a cross (between A and B) something (especially a plant or an animal) that is a mixture of two different types of thing (特に植物または動物の) 2種類の異なった物の混合→(異種)交配, 雑種, 交配種, 中間物 ‖ *a fruit which is a cross between a peach and an apple* モモとリンゴを交配した果物 ▶定義4 (in sports such as football) a kick or hit of the ball that goes across the front of the goal (サッカーのようなスポーツで) ゴール前を横切って飛ぶ, けったり打ったりしたボール→クロスパス

成句 **noughts and crosses** ⇒ **NOUGHT**

*__cross__² /krɔ(ː)s, krɑs/ 動 ▶定義1 ⓘ ⓗ **cross (over) (from sth/to sth)** to go from one side of sth to the other ～の一方から他方へ動く→(～を)横切る, 横断する, 渡る ‖ *to cross the road* 道路を横断する *Where did you cross the border?* どこで国境を越えましたか. *Which of the runners crossed the finishing line first?* 最初にゴールを切ったのはどちらのランナーですか. ▶定義2 ⓘ (used about lines, roads, etc) to pass across each other (線や道路などについて) 互いに交わる→交差する, 互いに出会う ‖ *The two roads cross just north of the village.* 2本の道路は村のすぐ北で交わっている. ▶定義3 ⓗ to put sth across or over sth else ～を別の…と交差させて, または別の～の上に置く→～を

架ける, 渡す, 組み合わせる, 交差させる ‖ *to cross your arms* 腕を組む ☛ S6ページのさし絵 ▶定義4 ⓘ to make sb angry by refusing to do what he/she wants you to do 〜がしてほしいと望むことを断って怒らせる→〜に逆らう, (人の計画, 意図など)を妨げる, 邪魔する ‖ *He's an important man. It could be dangerous to cross him.* 彼は重要な男だ. 彼に逆らうのは危険かもしれない. ▶定義5 ⓘ cross sth with sth to produce a new type of plant or animal by mixing two different types 2つの異なる種を組み合わせて新しい植物または動物を作り出す→〜を…と交配させる, 掛け合わせる ‖ *If you cross a horse with a donkey, you get a mule.* 馬とロバを掛け合わせるとラバが生まれる. ▶定義6 ⓘ ⓘ (in sports such as football and hockey) to pass the ball across the front of the goal (サッカーやホッケーのようなスポーツで) ゴール前を横切ってボールをパスする→クロスパスする, クロスパスを出す

成句 **cross my heart (and hope to die)** (口語) ▶定義 used for emphasizing that what you are saying is true 自分の言葉が本当であると強調するために用いて→十字を切って誓う, 神にかけて誓う

**cross your fingers; keep your fingers crossed** ⇒ **FINGER**¹

**cross your mind** ▶定義 (used about a thought, idea, etc) to come into your mind (考え, 案などについて)心に浮かぶ→思い付く, (心を)よぎる ‖ *It never once crossed my mind that she was lying.* 彼女がうそをついているなんて夢にも思わなかった.

句動詞 **cross sth off (sth)** ▶定義 to remove sth from a list, etc by drawing a line through it 線を引いて〜をリストなどから削除する→〜を(…から)線で消す, 抹消する ‖ *Cross Dave's name off the guest list - he can't come.* 客のリストからデーヴの名前を消してください — 彼は来られないから.

**cross sth out** ▶定義 to draw a line through sth that you have written because you have made a mistake, etc 間違えたりしたときに, 書いた〜の上に線を引く→〜を線を引いて消す ‖ *to cross out a spelling mistake* 間違ったスペルを線で消す

**cross**³ /krɔ(ː)s, krɑs/ 形 略式 ▶定義 cross (with sb) (about sth) angry or annoyed 怒った, いらいらした→怒りっぽい, 不機嫌な, 苛立った ‖ *I was really cross with her for leaving me with all the work.* 仕事を全部押し付けられたので, 私は彼女に本当に腹が立った. ☛ cross は angry よりくだけた語. — **crossly** 副 →腹を立てて, いら立って, 不機嫌に ‖ *'Be quiet,' Dad said crossly.* 「静かにしなさい」と父さんは不機嫌に言った.

**crossbar** /krɔ́(ː)sbɑːr, krɑ́s-/ 名 ⓒ ▶定義1 the piece of wood over the top of a goal in football, etc フットボールなどのゴールの上部にある木製の棒→クロスバー, ゴールの横木 ▶定義2 the metal bar that joins the front and back of a bicycle 自転車の前後を連結する金属棒→(自転車の)上パイプ, ハンドルとサドルをつなぐ心棒 ☛ S7ページのさし絵

**cross-country** 形副 ▶定義 across fields and natural land; not using roads or tracks 野や自然の地形を横切る; 道路や走路を使わない→山野を横断する[して], クロスカントリーの[で] ‖ *We walked about 10 miles cross-country before we saw a village.* 野を越えて10マイルほど歩くと村が見えた.

**cross-examine** 動 ⓘ ▶定義 to ask sb questions in a court of law, etc in order to find out the truth about sth 〜について真実を知るために法廷などで…に質問する→〜に反対尋問を行う; 鋭く追求する ‖ *The witness was cross-examined for two hours.* 証人は2時間にわたる尋問を受けた. — **cross-examination** 名 ⓒ ⓤ →反対尋問, (厳しい)追及

**cross-eyed** 形 ▶定義 having one or both your eyes looking towards your nose 一方または両方の目が鼻の方を見ている→内斜視の

**crossfire** /krɔ́(ː)sfɑɪər, krɑ́s-/ 名 ⓤ ▶定義 a situation in which guns are being fired from two or more different directions 複数の方向から銃が発射されている状況→十字砲火, 一斉射撃・攻撃 ‖ *The journalist was killed in crossfire.* そのジャーナリストは十字砲火で死亡した. (比喩) *When my parents argued, I sometimes got* ***caught in the crossfire***. 両親が口論するときには私が板挟みになることもあった.

**crossing** /krɔ́(ː)sɪŋ, krɑ́s-/ 名 ⓒ ▶定義1 a place where you can cross over sth 〜を横切ることの

できる場所→**交差点, 横断歩道, 十字路** ‖ *You should cross the road at the pedestrian crossing.* 道路を渡るときは横断歩道を使うべきだ. *a border crossing* 国境検問所 ▶定義2（英 **level crossing**) a place where a road and a railway line cross each other 道路と線路が互いに交差する場所→**踏切** ▶定義3 a journey from one side of a sea or river to the other 海や川の一方から他方へ渡ること→**渡航, 渡河, 横断** ‖ *We had a rough crossing.* 我々の渡航は大荒れだった.

**cross-legged** /krɔ́(:)s légəd, krɑ̀s-/ 形副 ▶定義 sitting on the floor with your legs pulled up in front of you and with one leg or foot over the other 足を体の前へ引き付け, 一方の脚または足を他方の上に載せて床に座って→**足を組んだ[で], あぐらをかいた[て]** ‖ *to sit cross-legged* あぐらをかいて座る ☜ S6ページのさし絵

**cross purposes** 成句
成句 **at cross purposes** ▶定義 a state of confusion between people who are talking about different things but think they are talking about the same thing 異なる事を話しているのに, 同じ事を話していると考えている人々の間の混乱状態→**互いに食い違って, 誤解して, とんちんかんで**

**cross-reference** 名 C ▶定義 a note in a book that tells you to look in another place in the book for more information 本の注で, さらに情報を得るためにほかの箇所を参照するもの→**(他箇所)参照, (同一書中の)相互参照**

**crossroads** /krɔ́(:)sròʊdz, krɑ̀s-/ 名 C (複 **crossroads**) ▶定義 a place where two or more roads cross each other 2つまたは複数の道路が互いに交差する場所→**十字路, 交差点, 辻(つじ)** ‖ *When you come to the next crossroads turn right.* 次の交差点を右に曲がってください. ☜ **roundabout**のさし絵

**cross section** 名 C ▶定義1 a picture of what the inside of sth would look like if you cut through it 切断したときに～の内部がどう見えるかを示した絵→**断面図, 横断面** ‖ *a cross section of the human brain* 人間の脳の断面図 ▶定義2 a number of people, etc that come from the different parts of a group, and so can be considered to represent the whole group ある一集団の異なる部分から来た多数の人々などで, その集団全体を表すと考えられる人→**代表的な一面, (社会などの)断面, 見本, 典型例** ‖ *The families we studied were chosen to represent a cross section of society.* 調査対象の家族は社会の断面を表すように選ばれた.

**crosswalk** /krɔ́(:)swɔ̀:k, krɑ́s-/ 米=**PEDESTRIAN CROSSING**

★**crossword** /krɔ́(:)swə̀:rd, krɑ́s-/ (または **crossword puzzle**) 名 C ▶定義 a word game in which you have to write the answers to questions (**clues**) in square spaces, which are arranged in a pattern 質問(かぎ)の答えを, あるパターンによって並べられた升目に書き込む言葉遊び→**クロスワード(パズル)** ‖ *Every morning I try to do the crossword in the newspaper.* 毎朝私は新聞のクロスワードを解こうとする.

**crotch** /krɑtʃ/ (または **crutch**) 名 C ▶定義 the place where your legs, or a pair of trousers, join at the top 脚またはズボンが上部でつながった箇所→**(人体の)また, (ズボンなどの)またの部分**

**crouch** /kraʊtʃ/ 動 自 ▶定義 **crouch (down)** to bend your legs and body so that you are close to the ground 地面に近付くように脚と体を曲げる→**かがむ, しゃがむ, うずくまる** ‖ *He crouched down behind the sofa.* 彼はソファーの後ろにかがみ込んだ. ☜ **kneel**のさし絵

**crow**¹ /kroʊ/ 名 C ▶定義 a large black bird that makes a loud noise 大きな声で鳴く大型の黒い鳥→**カラス**
成句 **as the crow flies** ▶定義 (used for describing distances) in a straight line (距離を表すために用いて)直線で→**直線距離では, 一直線に** ‖ *It's a kilometre as the crow flies but three kilometres by road.* 直線距離では1キロですが, 道路を行けば3キロです.

**crow**² /kroʊ/ 動 自 ▶定義1 to make a loud noise like a male chicken (**cock**) makes 雄鶏(おんどり)のような大きな声を上げる→**(雄鶏が)鳴く; 歓声を上げる** ▶定義2 略式 to speak very proudly about sth; to boast ～について非常に誇らしげに話す; 自慢する→**大得意になる, 勝ち誇る**

**crowbar** /kroʊbɑ̀:r/ 名 C ▶定義 a long iron bar that is used for forcing sth open ～をこじ開けるために用いる長い鉄製の棒→**バール, かなてこ**

★**crowd**¹ /kraʊd/ 名 ▶定義1 [C, 単数または複数

形の動詞と共に] a large number of people in one place 1箇所に集まった大勢の人々 → **群衆, 人込み, 大勢, 観衆** ‖ *The crowd was/were extremely noisy.* 群衆は非常に騒々しかった. *He pushed his way through the crowd.* 彼は人込みをかき分けて進んだ. *I go shopping early in the morning to avoid the crowds.* 私は混雑を避けて午前中早くに買い物に行く. ▶定義2 **the crowd** [単数扱い] ordinary people 普通の人々 →**(一般)大衆, 民衆** ‖ *He wears weird clothes because he wants to **stand out from the crowd**.* 彼は普通の人より目立ちたくて妙な服を着ている.

▶定義3 [**C**, 単数または複数形の動詞と共に] 略式 a group of people who know each other お互いを知っている人々の集まり→**仲間, 連中, グループ** ‖ *John, Linda and Barry will be there - all the usual crowd.* ジョン, リンダ, バリーが行くだろう - いつもの仲間みんなだ.

\***crowd**² /kráʊd/ 動 ▶定義1 ⓐ **crowd around/round (sb)** (used about a lot of people) to stand in a large group around sb/sth (大勢の人々について)〜の周りに大勢で立つ→**群がる, 集まる, (人が)殺到する** ‖ *Fans crowded round the singer hoping to get his autograph.* サインをもらおうとファンが歌手の周りに押し寄せた.

▶定義2 ⓑ (used about a lot of people) to fill an area (大勢の人々について) ある範囲を埋める→**〜に群がる, 詰め掛ける, 〜を一杯にする** ‖ *Groups of tourists crowded the main streets.* メインストリートは旅行者の団体で一杯だった. (比喩) *Memories crowded her mind.* 彼女の心に思い出が押し寄せた.

句動詞 **crowd into sth; crowd in** ▶定義 to go into a small place and make it very full 狭い場所に入り込んで一杯にする→**〜に押し掛ける, 押し寄せる** ‖ *Somehow we all crowded into their small living room.* 私たちは皆何とか狭い居間に入り込んだ.

**crowd sb/sth into sth; crowd sb/sth in** ▶定義 to put a lot of people into a small place 狭い場所に大勢の人を入れる→**〜を(…に)押し込む, 詰め込む, 一杯にする** ‖ *Ten prisoners were crowded into one small cell.* 10人の囚人が1つの狭い監房に詰め込まれた.

**crowd sth out; crowd sb out (of sth)** ▶定義 to completely fill a place so that nobody else can enter ほかにだれも入れないようにある場所を完全に一杯にする→**(満員のため)締め出す, 押し出す** ‖ *Students crowd out the cafe at lunchtimes.* 昼食時にはカフェは学生で満員になる. *Smaller companies are being crowded out of the market.* 市場が独占され中小企業が締め出されつつある.

**crowded** /kráʊdəd/ 形 ▶定義 full of people 人で一杯の→**込み合った, 混雑した, 満員の** ‖ *a crowded bus* 満員のバス *people living in poor and crowded conditions* 貧しく, 狭い場所でひしめき合って暮らす人々

**crown**¹ /kráʊn/ 名 ▶定義1 ⓒ a circle made of gold and jewels, that a king or queen wears on his/her head on official occasions 王や女王が正式の場でかぶる金や宝石で作られた環→**王冠, 冠** ▶定義2 **the Crown** [単数扱い] the state as represented by a king or queen 王や女王の地位→**王位, 帝位, 王権, 主権** ‖ *an area of land belonging to the Crown* 国王の所有地 ▶定義3 [単数扱い] the top of your head or of a hat 頭や帽子の先端→**(頭の)脳天, (帽子の)山, (丸みを帯びたもの)最も高い部分** ☛ **hat** のさし絵 ▶定義4 [単数扱い] the top of a hill 丘の頂→**山頂, 頂上, てっぺん**

**crown**² /kráʊn/ 動 ▶定義1 to put a crown on the head of a new king or queen in an official ceremony 公式の儀式で新しい王や女王に王冠をかぶせる→**〜を王位に就かせる, 王冠を頂かせる** ‖ *Elizabeth was crowned in 1952.* エリザベスは1952年に王位に就いた. (比喩) *the newly crowned British champion* 新しい英国チャンピオン ▶定義2 (しばしば受動態で) **crown sth (with sth)** to have or put sth on the top of sth 〜の上に…がある, または〜を載せる→**〜の頂を(…で)覆う, てっぺんに(〜を)載せる, てっぺんに付ける** ‖ *The mountain was crowned with snow.* 山の頂は雪に覆われていた. (比喩) *Her years of hard work were finally crowned with success.* 長年の彼女の苦労はやっと成功によって報われた.

**crowning** /kráʊnɪŋ/ 形 (名詞の前だけ) ▶定義 the best or most important 最良の, または最も重要な→**頂点の, 最高の, この上ない, 極上の** ‖ *Winning the World Championship was the crowning moment of her career.* 世界チャンピ

オンの獲得は彼女の生涯での絶頂期だった.

**crucial** /krú:ʃ(ə)l/ 形 ▶定義 crucial (to/for sth) extremely important; vital 極めて重要な; なくてはならない→**非常に重大な, 必須(ひっす)の, 欠くことのできない; 命にかかわる** ‖ *Early diagnosis of the illness is crucial for successful treatment.* 治療の成功には病気を早期に診断することが欠かせない. — **crucially** /-ʃ(ə)li/ 副 →**重大に, 決定的に**

**crucifix** /krú:sɪfɪks/ 名 C ▶定義 a small model of a cross with a figure of Jesus on it キリストの像が付いた小さな十字架の模型→**キリスト受難の像, はりつけ像**

**crucifixion** /krù:sɪfíkʃ(ə)n/ 名 C U ▶定義 the act of crucifying sb ～を十字架に架けること→**はりつけ** ‖ *the Crucifixion of Christ* キリストの処刑

**crucify** /krú:sɪfàɪ/ 動 他 (現分 **crucifying**; 三単現 **crucifies**; 過, 過分 **crucified**) ▶定義 to kill sb by nailing or tying him/her to a cross ～を十字架にくぎ付けにしてまたは縛り付けて殺す→**～をはりつけにする, 十字架に架けて処刑する**

**crude** /kru:d/ 形 ▶定義 1 simple and basic, without much detail, skill, etc 精巧さまたは巧みさなどがあまりなく, 単純で基本的な→**大まかな, 粗い** ‖ *The method was crude but very effective.* その方法は単純だが, 非常に効果的だった. *She explained how the system worked in crude terms.* 彼女は大雑把にシステムの働き方を説明した. ▶定義 2 referring to sex or the body in a way that would offend many people 多くの人々を不快にするようなやり方で性や体に言及する→**粗野な, 下品な, 露骨な, みだらな** ‖ *He's always telling crude jokes.* 彼はいつも下品なジョークを言っている. ▶定義 3 in its natural state, before it has been treated with chemicals 化学処理をする前の天然の状態の→**精製・精錬していない, 加工していない, 天然のままの** ‖ *crude oil* 原油 — **crudely** 副 →**下品に, 露骨に, 粗яに; 天然のままで** ‖ *a crudely drawn face* 大まかにかかれた顔

*****cruel** /krú:əl/ 形 (**crueller**; **cruellest**) ▶定義 causing physical or mental pain or suffering to sb/sth ～に肉体的または精神的苦痛・苦しみを引き起こす→**残酷な, 過酷な, 冷酷な, 悲惨な** ‖ *I think it's cruel to keep animals in cages.* 動物をおりに入れるのは残酷だと思う. *a cruel punishment* 厳しい罰 — **cruelly** /krú:əli/ 副 →**過酷に, 厳しく, 残酷に**

*****cruelty** /krú:əlti/ 名 (複 **cruelties**) ▶定義 1 ❶ cruelty (to sb/sth) cruel behaviour 残酷な振る舞い→**(～に対する)虐待, 残酷さ, むごさ, 無慈悲** ‖ *cruelty to children* 子供に対する虐待 ▶定義 2 [C, 通常は複数] a cruel act 残酷な行為→**残虐行為, 虐待行為** ‖ *the cruelties of war* 戦争の悲惨さ

**cruise**¹ /kru:z/ 動 自 ▶定義 1 to travel by boat, visiting a number of places, as a holiday 休暇として船でいくつかの場所を訪ねながら旅行する→**(船で)周遊する, 船旅をする, 巡航する** ‖ *to cruise around the Caribbean* カリブ海を巡る船旅をする ▶定義 2 to stay at the same speed in a car, plane, etc 車や飛行機などが同じ速度を維持する→**巡航・経済速度で進む[飛ぶ・走る]** ‖ *cruising at 80 kilometres an hour* 時速80キロの巡航速度で進む.

**cruise**² /kru:z/ 名 C ▶定義 a holiday in which you travel on a ship and visit a number of different places 船で旅行していくつかの異なる場所を訪ねる休暇→**(船の)周遊旅行, 船旅, 巡洋航海** ‖ *They're planning to go on a cruise.* 彼らは船旅を計画している.

**cruiser** /krú:zər/ 名 C ▶定義 1 a large fast ship used in a war 戦争で使われる大型の高速船→**巡洋艦, 巡洋戦艦** ▶定義 2 a motor boat which has room for people to sleep in it 人々が眠るための空間のあるモーターボート→**クルーザー, レジャー用モーターボート**

**crumb** /krʌm/ 名 C ▶定義 a very small piece of bread, cake or biscuit パン, ケーキ, ビスケットなどの非常に小さなかけら→**(パンなどの)くず, かけら; パン粉** ☞ **cake** のさし絵

**crumble** /krʌ́mb(ə)l/ 動 自 他 ▶定義 crumble (sth) (up) to break or make sth break into very small pieces ～が非常に小さなかけらに砕ける, またはそのようなかけらに砕く→**粉々になる, くずになる; ～を粉々にする, 細かくちぎる** ‖ *The walls of the church are beginning to crumble.* 教会の壁が崩れかけている. *We crumbled up the bread and threw it to the birds.* 私たちはパンを細かくちぎって鳥に投げた. (比喩) *Support for the government is beginning to crumble.* 政

府に対する支持が崩れかけている. — crumbly [形]➜**砕けやすい, もろい** ‖ *This cheese has a crumbly texture.* このチーズはもろい.

**crumple** /krʌ́mp(ə)l/ [動][自][他] ▶定義 crumple (sth) (into sth); crumple (sth) (up) to be pressed or to press sth into an untidy shape ～が圧力によって乱雑な形になる, またはそのような形にする➜**しわくちゃになる, つぶれる; ～をしわくちゃにする, つぶす** ‖ *The front of the car crumpled when it hit the wall.* 壁にぶつかって車の前部がつぶれた. *She crumpled the letter into a ball and threw it away.* 彼女は手紙をくしゃくしゃに丸めて投げ捨てた.

**crunch**[1] /krʌntʃ/ [動] ▶定義1 [他] crunch sth (up) to make a loud noise when you are eating sth hard 硬い～を食べるときに大きな音を立てる➜**～をバリバリ・ポリポリかむ, 音を立ててかみ砕く** ‖ *to crunch an apple* 音を立ててリンゴをかみ砕く. ▶定義2 [自] to make a loud noise like the sound of sth being crushed ～がつぶれるときのような大きな音を立てる➜**バリバリ砕ける, ざくざく砕ける, ざくざくと音を立てて～する** ‖ *We crunched through the snow.* 私たちは雪の中をざくざくと音を立てて進んだ. — crunchy [形]➜**バリバリいう, ざくざくと音がする** ‖ *a crunchy apple* かむとガリガリと音がするリンゴ

**crunch**[2] /krʌntʃ/ [名] [単数扱い] ▶定義 an act or noise of crunching バリバリと砕けること, またはその音➜**ガリガリかみ砕くこと・音, ざくざくと踏むこと・音** ‖ *There was a loud crunch as he sat on the box of eggs.* 彼が卵の箱の上に座ったので卵が割れる大きな音がした.

[成句] if/when it comes to the crunch ▶定義 if/when you are in a difficult situation and must make a difficult decision 困難な状況で困難な決断をしなければならないときに➜**いざというときには, ピンチのときには** ‖ *If it comes to the crunch, I'll stay and fight.* いざとなったら私はとどまって戦う.

**crusade** /kruːséɪd/ [名] [C] ▶定義1 a fight for sth that you believe to be good or against sth that you believe to be bad 自分が正しいと信じる～のため, または間違っていると思う～に対抗しての戦い➜**擁護・撲滅運動** ‖ *Mr Khan is leading a crusade against drugs in his neighbourhood.* カーン氏は地域の麻薬撲滅運動を先導している. ▶定義2 **Crusade** one of the wars fought in Palestine by European Christians against Muslims in the Middle Ages 中世にパレスチナで, ヨーロッパのキリスト教徒がイスラム教徒と戦った諸戦の１つ➜**十字軍, 聖戦** — crusader [名] [C]➜**十字軍戦士, 改革運動家**

**crush**[1] /krʌʃ/ [動][他] ▶定義1 to press sb/sth hard so that he/she/it is broken, damaged or injured 壊れる, 損傷するまたは負傷するほど強く～を圧迫する➜**～を押しつぶす, ぺしゃんこにする, 押し砕く, 踏みつぶす** ‖ *Most of the eggs got crushed when she sat on them.* 彼女が上に座った時にほとんどの卵がつぶれた. *He was crushed to death by a lorry.* 彼はトラックにひき殺された. ▶定義2 crush sth (up) to break sth into very small pieces or a powder ～を非常に細かいかけらや粉に砕く➜**～を粉々にする, 砕いて～にする, ばらばらにする** ‖ *Crush the garlic and fry in oil.* ニンニクをみじん切りにして油で揚げます. ☛ **squeeze** のさし絵 ▶定義3 to defeat sb/sth completely ～を完全に打ち負かす➜**～を打ち負かす, 打ちひしぐ, 鎮圧する, 打倒する** ‖ *The army was sent in to crush the rebellion.* 反逆者を鎮圧するため軍隊が送られた.

**crush**[2] /krʌʃ/ [名] ▶定義1 [単数扱い] a large group of people in a small space 狭い空間内の大勢の人々➜**大群衆, 雑踏, 混雑, 押し合い** ‖ *There was such a crush that I couldn't get near the bar.* ひどく混雑していてカウンターの近くへ行けなかった. ▶定義2 [C][略式] a crush (on sb) a strong feeling of love for sb that only usually lasts for a short time 通常は短期間しか続かない, ～に対する強い愛情➜**のぼせ上がり, 首ったけになる, 夢中** ‖ *Maria **had a** huge **crush** on her teacher.* マリアは先生に夢中だった.

**crushing** /krʌ́ʃɪŋ/ [形] (名詞の前だけ) ▶定義 that defeats sb/sth completely; very bad ～を完全に打ち負かすような; 非常に悪い➜**打ちひしぐような, 決定的な打撃の, 壊滅的な, 圧倒的な** ‖ *a crushing defeat* 壊滅的な敗北

**crust** /krʌst/ [名] [C][U] ▶定義1 the hard part on the outside of a piece of bread, a pie, etc パンやパイなどの外側の硬い部分➜**パンの耳, パイの皮** ☛ **bread** のさし絵 ▶定義2 a hard layer on the outside of sth ～の外側の硬い層➜**硬い表面, 外皮, 凍結雪面** ‖ *the earth's crust* 地殻

**crusty** /krΛsti/ 形 ▶定義1 having a hard crust (1) 硬い表面(crust (1))を持つ→**表面が固くなった,皮殻質の,外皮のような** ‖ *crusty bread* 固くなったパン ▶定義2 略式 bad-tempered and impatient 機嫌が悪く短気な→**怒りっぽい,気難しい,無愛想な** ‖ *a crusty old man* 気難しい老人

**crutch** /krΛtʃ/ 名 C ▶定義1 a type of stick that you put under your arm to help you walk when you have hurt your leg or foot 脚や足にけがをしたときに,わきの下に挟んで歩くときの補助にするつえの一種→**松葉づえ** ‖ *She was **on crutches** for two months after she broke her ankle.* 彼女は足首を骨折して2か月間松葉づえを使った.

➤ walking stick と比較.

☞ **bandage** のさし絵 ▶定義2 = CROTCH

**crux** /krΛks, krʊks/ 名 [単数扱い] ▶定義 the most important or difficult part of a problem 問題の最も重要な,または困難な部分→**要点,急所,核心,ポイント** ‖ *The **crux of the matter** is how to stop this from happening again.* 問題の核心はどうやって再発を防ぐかだ.

**★cry¹** /kraɪ/ 動 (現分 **crying**; 三単現 **cries**; 過,過分 **cried**) ▶定義1 自 to make a noise and produce tears in your eyes, for example because you are unhappy or have hurt yourself 声を立てて目から涙を流す,例えば悲しいときまたはけがをしたときなど→**(声を上げて)泣く,大声で泣く** ‖ *The baby never stops crying.* 赤ん坊はなかなか泣きやまない. *The child was crying for (= because she wanted) her mother.* 子供は母親を求めて(=母親に来てほしいと)泣いていた. ▶定義2 自 他 cry (out) to shout or make a loud noise 叫ぶ,または大きな声を出す→**大声で叫ぶ,どなる,(～を求めて)叫ぶ** ‖ *We could hear someone crying for help.* だれかが助けを求めて叫んでいるのが聞こえた. *'Look,' he cried, 'There they are.'* 「見て.彼らがあそこにいる」と彼は叫んだ.

成句 **a shoulder to cry on** ⇒ **SHOULDER¹**

**cry your eyes out** ▶定義 to cry a lot for a long time 長い間泣く→**目を泣きはらす,激しく泣く,さめざめと泣く**

句動詞 **cry out for sth** ▶定義 to need sth very much ～を強く必要とする→**～を大いに必要とする,大いに求める** ‖ *Birmingham is crying out for a new transport system.* バーミンガムには新しい交通システムが是非とも必要だ.

**★cry²** /kraɪ/ 名 (複 **cries**) ▶定義1 C a shout or loud high noise 叫び,または大きな高い音→**叫び(声),悲鳴,歓声,(鳥獣の)鳴き声** ‖ *the cries of the children in the playground* 運動場の子供たちの歓声 *We heard Adam give a cry of pain as the dog bit him.* 犬にかまれてアダムが痛くて叫ぶのを聞いた.(比喩) *Her suicide attempt was really **a cry for help**.* 彼女の自殺未遂は本当は助けを求める叫びだった. ▶定義2 [単数扱い] an act of crying¹(1) 泣くこと→**声を上げて泣くこと,号泣,泣き叫ぶこと** ‖ *After a good cry I felt much better.* 思い切り泣いたら気分が良くなった.

成句 **a far cry from sth/from doing sth** ⇒ **FAR¹**

**crying** /kraɪɪŋ/ 形 (名詞の前だけ) ▶定義 (used to talk about a bad situation) very great (悪い状況について言う場合に)非常に大きい→**緊急の,ひどく悪い,甚だしい,捨てておけない** ‖ *There's a crying need for more doctors.* 緊急に医師がさらに必要だ. *It's **a crying shame** that so many young people can't find jobs.* 多くの若者が仕事を見つけられないのはひどく残念なことだ.

**crypt** /krɪpt/ 名 C ▶定義 a room that is under a church, where people were sometimes buried in the past 教会の下にあり昔は人が葬られたこともあった部屋→**(聖堂の)地下室,地下聖堂**

**cryptic** /krɪptɪk/ 形 ▶定義 having a hidden meaning that is not easy to understand; mysterious 理解しにくい隠れた意味がある;神秘的な→**なぞめいた,隠れた,秘密の,難解な** ‖ *a cryptic message/remark* なぞめいた伝言・言葉 — **cryptically** /-k(ə)li/ 副 →**なぞめいて,秘密で,神秘的に**

**crystal** /krɪstl/ 名 ▶定義1 C a regular shape that some mineral substances form when they become solid 一部の鉱物が固体になったときに形成される規則正しい形→**結晶(体)** ‖ *salt crystals* 塩の結晶 ▶定義2 U a clear mineral that can be used in making jewellery 宝石を作るときに用いられる透明な鉱物→**水晶;水晶製品・細工** ▶定義3 U very high-quality glass 非常に高品質のガラス→**クリスタルグラス,カットグラス** ‖ *a crystal vase* クリスタルグラスの花びん

**crystal ball** 名 C ▶定義 a glass ball in which

some people say you can see what will happen in the future 未来に起こる事が見えると言われているガラス球➜**(占い用の)水晶球**

**crystal clear** [形] ▶定義1 (used about water, glass, etc) that you can see through perfectly (水やガラスなどについて)完全に見通せる➜**透明な, 透き通った, (水晶のように)非常に澄んだ** ▶定義2 very easy to understand 非常に理解しやすい➜**明白な, 明せきな, 分かりやすい, 疑いの余地のない** ‖ *The meaning is crystal clear.* 意味は非常に明白だ.

**cu** [略] cubic➜**立方の** ‖ *a volume of 3 cu ft* 3立方フィートの体積

**cub** /kʌb/ [名] [C] ▶定義1 a young bear, lion, etc ➜**(クマ, ライオンなどの)子, 幼獣** ☛ **lion**のさし絵 ▶定義2 **the Cubs**[複数扱い]the part of the Boy Scout organization that is for younger boys 年少の少年のためのボーイスカウト組織の一部➜**カブスカウト, (ボーイスカウトの)年少隊** ▶定義3 **Cub**(または**Cub Scout**) [C]a member of the Cubs カブスカウトの一員➜**カブスカウト, 年少隊の1人**

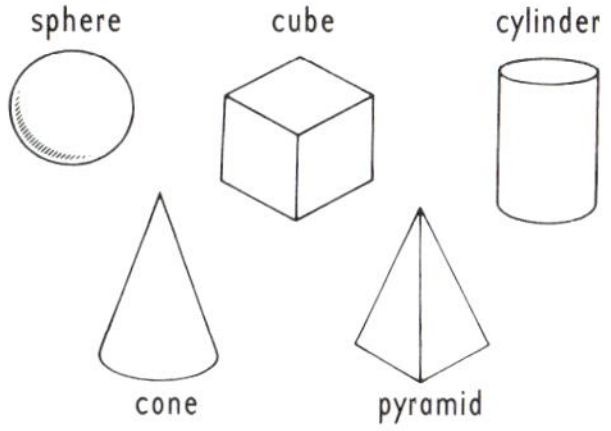


**cube**[1] /kjuːb/ [名] [C] ▶定義1 a solid shape that has six equal square sides 6つの合同な正方形を面に持つ立体形➜**立方体, 正六面体, 立方形の物** ▶定義2 the number that you get if you multiply a number by itself twice 同数を2回掛けたときに得られる数➜**3乗, 立方** ‖ *the cube of 5 ($5^3$) is 125 (= 5 x 5 x 5).* 5の3乗($5^3$)は125(=5×5×5).

**cube**[2] /kjuːb/ [動][他] (通常は受動態で) ▶定義 to multiply a number by itself 同数を2回掛ける➜**〜を3乗する** ‖ *Four cubed ($4^3$) is 64 (= 4 x 4 x 4).* 4を3乗($4^3$)すると64(=4×4×4).

**cubic** /kjúːbɪk/ [形] ▶定義 a measure of volume expressed as a cube[1](2) cube[1](2)で表される体積[容積]の単位➜**立方の** ‖ *If a box is 4cm long, 4cm wide and 4cm high, its volume is 64 cubic centimetres.* 長さ4 cm, 幅4 cm, 高さ4 cmの箱の体積は64立方センチメートルである. *The lake holds more than a million cubic metres of water.* その湖は100万立方メートルを超える水量がある.

**cubicle** /kjúːbɪk(ə)l/ [名] [C] ▶定義 a small room that is made by separating off part of a larger room 広い部屋の部分を分割して作った小さな部屋➜**(仕切りのある)個人用小室, 小部屋, 小ボックス, 更衣室** ‖ *There are cubicles at the swimming pool for changing your clothes.* プールには着替えのために仕切られた小部屋がある.

**cuckoo** /kúːkùː, kʊ́-/ [名] [C] ▶定義 bird which makes a sound like its name and which leaves its eggs with another bird's eggs in its nest cuckooの名前通りの声で鳴く鳥で, 卵をほかの鳥の巣にその鳥自身の卵と一緒に残す➜**カッコウ**

**cucumber** /kjúːkʌmbər/ [名] [C] [U] ▶定義 a long, thin vegetable with a dark green skin that does not need to be cooked 調理する必要がない濃緑色の皮の細長い野菜➜**キュウリ** ☛ C3ページのさし絵

**cuddle** /kʌ́dl/ [動][自][他] ▶定義 to hold sb/sth closely in your arms 〜を腕にしっかりと抱く➜**(〜を)抱き締める, 抱擁する, 抱き合う** ‖ *The little girl was cuddling her favourite doll.* 幼い少女はお気に入りの人形を抱き締めていた. —**cuddle** [名] ➜**抱き締めること, 抱擁** ‖ *He **gave** the child **a cuddle** and kissed her goodnight.* 彼は子供を抱き締めておやすみのキスをした.

[句動詞] **cuddle up (to/against sb/sth); cuddle up (together)** ▶定義 to move close to sb and sit or lie in a comfortable position 〜のそばに寄って楽な姿勢に座ったりまたは横になったりする➜**(〜に)ぴったり寄り添う, 寄り添って座る・寝る** ‖ *They cuddled up together for warmth.* 彼らは暖め合うためにぴったりと寄り添った.

**cuddly** /kʌ́dli/ [形] ▶定義 soft and pleasant to hold close to you しっかりと抱くと柔らかくて心地良い➜**抱き締めたいような, 思わず抱き締めたくなる, とてもかわいい** ‖ *a cuddly toy* 抱き締めたくなるおもちゃ

**cue** /kjuː/ [名] [C] ▶定義1 a word or movement that is the signal for sb else to say or do sth, especially in a play 特に劇で, 〜に…を言ったり

または振る舞うように、合図する言葉またはしぐさ→**キュー，合図，指示** || *When Julia puts the tray on the table, that's your cue to come on stage.* ジュリアが盆をテーブルに置いたら、それがあなたが舞台に出る合図です．▶定義2 an example of how to behave 振る舞い方の一例→**手掛かり，(行動を教える)きっかけ，手本となる合図** || *I'm not sure how to behave at a Japanese wedding, so I'll **take** my **cue from** the hosts.* 日本式の結婚式でどう振る舞ったらいいのか分からないので，主人役の合図を手本にするつもりだ．▶定義3 a long, thin wooden stick used to hit the ball in some games that are played on a special table (snooker and billiards) 特別な卓台で行うゲームの一種(スヌーカーとビリヤード)でボールを打つために使用する細長い木製の棒→**(玉突きの)キュー，突き棒** ☛ pool, S1ページのさし絵

成句 **(right) on cue** ▶定義 at exactly the moment expected ぴったり予期された時間に→**ちょうどいい時に，適時に，タイミング良く** || *Just as I was starting to worry about Stan, he phoned right on cue.* スタンのことが心配になり始めた時に、ちょうど良く彼が電話してきた．

**cuff** /kʌf/ 名 C ▶定義1 the end part of a sleeve, which often fastens at the wrist そでの先端部分で，多くは手首で留める→**カフス，そで口** ☛ C6ページのさし絵 ▶定義2 **cuffs** [複数扱い] =HANDCUFFS ▶定義3 a light hit with the open hand 開いた手で軽くたたくこと→**平手打ち，ピシャリと打つこと**

成句 **off the cuff** ▶定義 (used about sth you say) without thought or preparation before that moment (話している～について)事前の考えまたは準備なしで→**即座に，即興で；形式張らないで，非公式の** || *I haven't got the figures here, but, off the cuff, I'd say the rise is about 10%.* ここには数字がありませんが、大雑把に言って上昇率は約10パーセントでしょう．

**cufflink** /kʌflɪŋk/ 名 [通常は複数] ▶定義 one of a pair of small objects used instead of a button to fasten a shirt sleeve together at the wrist シャツのそでを手首の所で留めるためにボタンの代わりに用いる2組の小物の1つ→**カフスボタン**

**cuisine** /kwɪˈziːn/ 名 U 正式 ▶定義 the style of cooking of a particular country, restaurant, etc 特定の国やレストランなどの料理の様式→**(独特の)料理，料理法** || *Italian cuisine* イタリア料理 ☛ cooking はあまり正式でない語．

**cul-de-sac** /kʌl dɪ sæk, kɔːl-, ˌ--ˈ-/ 名 C (複 **cul-de-sacs**) ▶定義 a street that is closed at one end 一方が行き止まりの通り→**袋小路，行き止まり；行き詰まり，窮地**

**culinary** /kʌlən(ə)ri, kjuː-; -nèri/ 形 正式 ▶定義 connected with cooking 料理と関連した→**料理(用)の，台所(用)の**

**cull** /kʌl/ 動 ⓣ ▶定義1 to kill a number of animals in a group to prevent the group from becoming too large 群が大きくなりすぎないように、群の中の何匹かの動物を殺す→**～をえり抜いて殺す，淘汰(とうた)する，間引く** ▶定義2 to collect information, ideas, etc, from different places いろいろな場所から情報または考えなどを集める→**～をえり抜く，選び取る，抜粋する** || *I managed to cull some useful addresses from the Internet.* 私はインターネットから役に立つアドレスを何とか選び出した．— **cull** 名 C (複 **culls**) **選択，淘汰，間引き** *a deer cull* シカの淘汰

**culminate** /kʌlməneɪt/ 動 ⓘ 正式 ▶定義 **culminate in sth** to reach a final result 最終結果に到達する→**ついに～となる，結果的に～となる；実を結ぶ** || *The team's efforts culminated in victory in the championships.* チームの努力がついに実を結んで選手権で優勝した．— **culmination** /kʌlməneɪʃ(ə)n/ 名 [単数扱い]→**結末，終わり，結実，成果；頂点，全盛** || *The joint space mission was the culmination of years of research.* 共同の宇宙飛行は長年の研究のたまものだった．

**culpable** /kʌlpəb(ə)l/ 形 正式 ▶定義 responsible for sth bad that has happened 起こった悪い～に責任がある→**過失のある，とがめられるべき，有罪の**

**culprit** /kʌlprət/ 名 C ▶定義 a person who has done sth wrong 悪い～をした人→**犯人，犯罪者，容疑者，刑事被告人**

**cult** /kʌlt/ 名 C ▶定義1 a type of religion or religious group, especially one that is considered unusual 宗教または宗教団体の一種で特に異常と見なされるもの→**新興宗教(教団)，えせ宗教，狂信的宗教(団体)** ▶定義2 a person or thing that has become popular with a particular group of people 特定の集団の人々から人気を得た人またはもの➜崇拝の的; 流行, 熱狂, ～熱 ‖ *cult movies* カルト映画(一部の人々から熱狂的な支持を受ける映画)

**cultivate** /kʌ́ltəvèɪt/ [動][他] ▶定義1 to prepare and use land for growing plants for food or to sell 食料または商品として植物を育てるために土地を整えて使う➜**～を耕す, 耕作する, 開墾する** ‖ *to cultivate the soil* 土地を耕す ▶定義2 to grow plants for food or to sell 食料または商品として植物を育てる➜**～を栽培する, 植え育てる** ‖ *Olives have been cultivated for centuries in Mediterranean countries.* 地中海諸国では何世紀にもわたってオリーブが栽培されている. ▶定義3 to try hard to develop a friendship with sb 一生懸命～との友情を育てようとする ➜**(友情など)をはぐくむ, 深める, ～に交際を求める, ～と親しくなろうとする** ‖ *He cultivated links with colleagues abroad.* 彼は海外の同僚とのつながりを深めようとした. — cultivation /kʌ̀ltəvéɪʃ(ə)n/ [名] [U] ➜**耕作, 作物の栽培**

**cultivated** /kʌ́ltəvèɪtəd/ [形] ▶定義1 well educated, with good manners 教育が高く行儀の良い➜**教養のある, 知性のある, 洗練された** ▶定義2 (used about land) used for growing plants for food or to sell (土地について)食料または商品として植物を育てるために使われる➜**耕された, 耕地の, 農地の** ▶定義3 (used about plants) grown on a farm, not wild (植物について)野生ではなく農場で育てられている➜**栽培された, 栽培で改良された**

***cultural** /kʌ́ltʃ(ə)rəl/ [形] ▶定義1 connected with the customs, ideas, beliefs, etc of a society or country 社会または国の習慣, 考え, 信念などと関連した➜**文化の, 精神文明の** ‖ *The country's cultural diversity is a result of taking in immigrants from all over the world.* その国の文化が多様なのは世界中から移民を受け入れたためである. ☛参 **multicultural** ▶定義2 connected with art, music, literature, etc 美術, 音楽, 文学などと関連した➜**文化的な, 教養的な, 人文の, 修養の** ‖ *The city has a rich cultural life, with many theatres, concert halls and art galleries.* 多くの劇場やコンサートホール, 画廊のあるその市には豊かな文化生活がある. — culturally /-rəli/ [副] ➜ **文化的に, 教養上**

***culture** /kʌ́ltʃər/ [名] ▶定義1 [C] [U] the customs, ideas, beliefs, etc of a particular society, country, etc 特定の社会または国などの習慣, 考え, 信念など➜**文化, 精神文明** ‖ *the language and culture of the Aztecs* アステカ族の言語と文化 *people from many different cultures* 多くの異なる文化圏から来た人々 ▶定義2 [U] art, literature, music, etc 美術, 文学, 音楽など➜**教養, 人文, 修養, 洗練** ‖ *London has always been a centre of culture.* ロンドンはいつも文化の中心だった.

**cultured** /kʌ́ltʃərd/ [形] ▶定義 well-educated, showing a good knowledge of art, music, literature, etc 教育があり, 美術や音楽, 文学などの十分な知識があることを示す➜**教養のある, 洗練された, 文化のある**

**culture shock** [名] [U] ▶定義 a feeling of confusion, etc that you may have when you go to live in or visit a country that is very different from your own 自国とは全く違う国に住んだとき, または訪れたときに感じる混乱など➜**カルチャーショック**

**cumbersome** /kʌ́mbərsəm/ [形] ▶定義1 heavy and difficult to carry, use, wear, etc 重くて運ぶ, 使うまたは身に着けるのが困難な➜**扱いにくい, 厄介な, 邪魔な, 不格好な** ▶定義2 (used about a system, etc) slow and complicated (制度などについて)時間がかかり複雑な➜**煩わしい, 面倒な, 手間のかかる** ‖ *cumbersome legal procedures* 煩わしい法律上の手続き

**cumulative** /kjúːmjələtɪv, -lèɪ-/ [形] ▶定義 increasing steadily in amount, degree, etc 量または程度などが着実に増加する➜**累積する, 累加する, 累積的な** ‖ *a cumulative effect* 累積効果

**cunning** /kʌ́nɪŋ/ [形] ▶定義 clever in a dishonest or bad way 不誠実な, または悪いやり方で巧妙な➜**狡猾(こうかつ)な, 悪賢い, ずるい** ‖ *He was as cunning as a fox.* 彼はキツネのようにずる賢かった. *a cunning trick* 悪賢い策略 ☛類 **sly**, **wily** — cunning [名] [U] ➜**狡猾, 抜け目なさ, ずるさ** — cunningly [副] ➜**狡猾に, 悪賢く, 抜け目なく**

**➤日本語 vs 英語**

cunning と「カンニング」

日本語の「カンニング」は英語では cheating になります.「試験でカンニングする」は,

## 402　cup¹

cheat in[困 on]an examination と言います. なお, 英語の cunning は「狡猾(こうかつ)さ, ずるさ」という意味です.

cup and saucer / mug / beaker / plastic cup/beaker / wine glass / beer glass

\*cup¹ /kʌp/ 名 C ▶定義 1 a small container usually with a handle, used for drinking liquids 普通は取っ手の付いた小さな容器で, 液体を飲むために用いる→**カップ, 茶わん; カップ１杯分** ‖ *a teacup* ティーカップ *a cup of coffee* カップ１杯のコーヒー ▶定義 2 (in sport) a large metal cup given as a prize; the competition for such a cup (スポーツで) 賞として与えられる大きな金属の杯; このような杯を争う競争→**優勝カップ, 優勝杯(争奪戦)** ‖ *Our team won the cup in the basketball tournament.* バスケットボールのトーナメントで私たちのチームが優勝杯を獲得した. *the World Cup* 世界選手権大会 ☞ **medal** のさし絵 ▶定義 3 an object shaped like a cup カップのような形の物→**杯状の物** ‖ *an eggcup* ゆで卵立て

成句 **not sb's cup of tea** ▶定義 not what sb likes or is interested in 〜が好むものまたは興味を持つものでない→**好みでない, 性に合わない, 趣味ではない, 得意ではない** ‖ *Horror films aren't my cup of tea.* ホラー映画は私の好みではない.

**cup²** /kʌp/ 動 他 (**cupping; cupped**) ▶定義 to form sth, especially your hands, into the shape of a cup; to hold sth with your hands shaped like a cup 〜, 特に両手をカップの形にする; カップ状にした両手で〜を持つ→**(両手)を丸める, 両手を杯状にして〜をすくう, 〜を支える, 覆う** ‖ *I cupped my hands to take a drink from the stream.* 私は両手を丸めて小川の水をすくって飲んだ.

\***cupboard** /kʌ́bərd/ 名 C ▶定義 a piece of furniture, usually with shelves inside and a door or doors at the front, used for storing food, clothes, etc 通常は内部に棚があり前部にドアがある家具で, 食品や衣類などを保管するために用いる→**食器戸棚, 戸棚, 押入れ** ☞ C7ページのさし絵

**cupful** /kʌ́pfʊl/ 名 C ▶定義 the amount that a cup will hold カップ１杯の量→**カップ１杯(の量), 計量カップ１杯分(1/2 パイント = 約 240cc)** ‖ *two cupfuls of water* 水カップ２杯

**curable** /kjʊərəb(ə)l/ 形 ▶定義 (used about a disease) that can be made better (病気について) 良くなることができる→**治癒できる, 治療できる, 治せる, 治る** ⇔ **incurable**

**curator** /kjʊəréɪtər, kjúːr-/ 名 C ▶定義 a person whose job is to look after the things that are kept in a museum 博物館に保管されている物の管理を仕事とする人→**館長, 主事, 管理者**

**curb¹** /kəːrb/ 動 他 ▶定義 to limit or control sth, especially sth bad 〜, 特に悪い〜を制限するまたは制御する→**〜を抑制する, 抑える** ‖ *He needs to learn to curb his anger.* 彼は怒りを抑えることを学ぶ必要がある.

**curb²** /kəːrb/ 名 C ▶定義 1 a curb (on sth) a control or limit on sth 〜に対する制御または制限→**抑制, 拘束** ‖ *a curb on local government spending* 地方自治体の歳出の抑制 ▶定義 2 特に 困 = **KERB**

**curdle** /kə́ːrdl/ 動 自 他 ▶定義 (used about liquids) to turn sour or to separate into different parts; to make something do this (液体について

て)酸っぱくなる,または異なる部分に分離する;物をこのような状態にする➔(牛乳が)凝乳になる,固まる,凝結する;～を凝乳にする,凝固させる ‖ *I've curdled the sauce.* ソースが分離してしまった. ☛参 **blood-curdling**

**★cure**¹ /kjʊər/ 動 ⓤ ▶定義 **1** cure sb (of sth) to make sb healthy again after an illness 病気の～を再び健康にする➔(病人)を治す,いやす,回復させる,～の(病気・悪腫)を治す・直す ‖ *The treatment cured him of cancer.* その治療で彼のがんは治った. ▶定義 **2** to make an illness, injury, etc end or disappear 病気やけがなどを治す,またはなくす➔(病気やけが)を治療する,治す,取り除く ‖ *It is still not possible to cure the common cold.* いまだに普通の風邪の治療は不可能だ. (比喩)*The plumber cured the problem with the central heating.* その配管工はセントラルヒーティングの故障を直した. ▶定義 **3** to make certain types of food last longer by drying, smoking or salting them 乾燥,燻製(くんせい),または塩漬けにして,ある種の食品を長持ちさせる➔～を保存処理する,保存する ‖ *cured ham* 燻製のハム

**cure**² /kjʊər/ 名 ⓒ a cure (for sth) ▶定義 **1** a medicine or treatment that can cure an illness, etc 病気などを治すことのできる薬または治療➔治療薬,治療法 ‖ *There is no cure for this illness.* この病気には治療法がない. ▶定義 **2** a return to good health; the process of being cured 健康状態に戻ること;治癒の過程➔治ること,回復,療養,治癒 ‖ *The new drug brought about a miraculous cure.* 新薬によって奇跡的な回復がもたらされた.

**curfew** /kɜ́ːrfjuː/ 名 ⓒ ▶定義 **1** a time after which people are not allowed to go outside their homes, for example during a war 例えば戦争中などで,それ以降の外出が禁止される時間➔(戒厳令下の)(夜間)外出禁止時間,(夜間)外出禁止令 ‖ *The government imposed a dusk-to-dawn curfew.* 政府は終夜(夕暮れから夜明けまで)外出禁止令を敷いた. ▶定義 **2** 困 a time when children must arrive home in the evening 子供が夜,家に帰らなければならない時間➔門限時間,門限 ‖ *She has a ten o'clock curfew.* 彼女の門限は10時だ.

**curiosity** /kjʊ̀əriɑ́səti/ 名 (複 **curiosities**) ▶定義 **1** ⓤ a desire to know or learn 知りたいまたは学びたいと思う欲求➔好奇心,興味,関心;詮索(せんさく)好き,物好き ‖ *I was full of curiosity about their plans.* 私は彼らの計画が知りたくてたまらなった. *Out of curiosity, he opened her letter.* 好奇心から,彼は彼女の手紙を開封した. ▶定義 **2** ⓒ an unusual and interesting person or thing 変わっていて興味深い人または物➔珍しい物,珍奇な人・物,変わった人;骨董(こっとう)品 ‖ *The museum was full of historical curiosities.* 博物館には歴史的な珍しい物がたくさんあった.

**★curious** /kjʊ́əriəs/ 形 ▶定義 **1** curious (about sth); curious (to do sth) wanting to know or learn sth ～について知りたがるまたは学びたがる➔好奇心の強い,(～に)強い興味を持つ;知りたがりの,詮索(せんさく)好きな ‖ *They were very curious about the people who lived upstairs.* 彼らは上の階の住人のことをしきりに知りたがっていた. *He was curious to know how the machine worked.* 彼はその機械の仕組みに強い興味を持った. ▶定義 **2** unusual or strange 普通でない,または奇妙な➔珍しい,珍奇な,不思議な,奇異な ‖ *It was curious that she didn't tell anyone about the incident.* 彼女がその出来事をだれにも話さないのが不思議だった. — **curiously** 副 ➔物珍しそうに,物好きに;奇妙にも,不思議なことに

**curl**¹ /kɜːrl/ 動 ▶定義 **1** ⓘ ⓤ to form or to make sth form into a curved or round shape ～が曲がったまたは丸い形になる,または～をそうした形にする➔丸くなる,カールする;～を丸める,カールさせる,縮らせる ‖ *Does your hair curl naturally?* あなたの巻き毛は生まれつきですか. ▶定義 **2** ⓘ to move round in a curve 曲線を描いて動く➔曲がりくねる,湾曲する,渦巻く,らせん状になる ‖ *The snake curled around his arm.* 蛇が彼の腕に巻き付いた. *Smoke curled up into the sky.* 煙が渦巻きながら空に昇った.

句動詞 curl up ▶定義 to pull your arms, legs and head close to your body 腕,脚,頭を体に引き寄せる➔体を丸める,丸くなる,縮こまる ‖ *The cat curled up in front of the fire.* 猫は暖房器の前で丸くなった.

**curl**² /kɜːrl/ 名 ⓒ ▶定義 **1** a piece of hair that curves round 丸まった髪の束➔巻き毛,カール ‖ *Her hair fell in curls round her face.* 彼女の髪が

カールして顔にかかっていた. ▶定義2 a thing that has a curved round shape 丸まった形の物→らせん状の物, 渦巻き状の物 ‖ a curl of blue smoke 青い煙の渦

**curler** /kə́ːrlər/ 名 ▶定義 a small plastic or metal tube that you roll your hair around in order to make it curly 髪をカールさせるために巻き付ける小さなプラスチックまたは金属の筒→カーラー, カールクリップ

**curly** /kə́ːrli/ 形 ▶定義 full of curls; shaped like a curl カールの多い; カールのような形の→巻き毛の, カールした; 渦巻き状の ‖ curly hair 巻き毛 ⇔straight ☞ hair のさし絵

**currant** /kʌ́r(ə)nt; kʌ́ːrənt/ 名 C ▶定義1 a very small dried grape used to make cakes, etc ケーキなどを作るための非常に小さい干しブドウ→(小粒の種なし)干しブドウ, カラント ▶定義2 (しばしば複合語で) one of several types of small soft fruit 数種の小さく柔らかい果実の一種→スグリ ‖ blackcurrants クロフサスグリ

*★**currency** /kʌ́r(ə)nsi; kʌ́ːrən-/ 名 (複 **currencies**) ▶定義1 C U the system or type of money that a particular country uses 特定の国が用いる貨幣体系または種類→通貨, (現在通用している)貨幣 ‖ The currency of Argentina is the austral. アルゼンチンの通貨はアウストラルである. foreign currency 外貨 a weak/strong/stable currency 弱い・強い・安定した通貨 ▶定義2 U the state of being believed, accepted or used by many people 多くの人々が信じる, 受け入れるまたは使用していること→通用(していること), 流通, 普及, 流布, 流行 ‖ The new ideas soon **gained currency**. 新しい考え方はすぐに広まった.

*★**current**¹ /kʌ́r(ə)nt; kʌ́ːrənt/ 形 ▶定義1 of the present time; happening now 現在の; 今起こっている→現在の, 今の, 現時点での, 最新の ‖ current fashions/events 最新のファッション・最近の事件 ▶定義2 generally accepted; in common use 一般に受け入れられた; 一般に使われる→現在通用[流通]している, 現在行われている, 流行している ‖ Is this word still current? この言葉は今も使われていますか.

**current**² /kʌ́r(ə)nt; kʌ́ːrənt/ 名 ▶定義1 C a continuous flowing movement of water, air, etc 水や空気などの連続して流れる動き→流れ, 流動; 気流, 潮流; 風潮, 時流 ‖ to swim **against/with the current** 流れに逆らって・乗って泳ぐ(比喩) a current of anti-government feeling 反政府感情の風潮 ▶定義2 U the flow of electricity through a wire, etc 電線などを通る電気の流れ→電流

**current account** (米 **checking account**) 名 C ▶定義 a bank account from which you can take out your money when you want, with a cheque book or cash card 小切手帳またはキャッシュカードで必要なときに金を引き出せる銀行口座→当座預金(口座)

**current affairs** 名 [複数扱い] ▶定義 important political or social events that are happening at the present time 現在起こっている重要な政治または社会の出来事→時事(問題), 時局

**currently** /kʌ́r(ə)ntli; kʌ́ːrəntli/ 副 ▶定義 at present; at the moment 現在は; ちょうど今→今のところ, 現在, 目下 ‖ He is currently working in Spain. 彼は現在, スペインで働いている. ☞参 **actually** の注

**curriculum** /kərík jələm/ 名 C (複 **curriculums** または **curricula** /-lə/) ▶定義 all the subjects that are taught in a school, college or university; the contents of a particular course of study 学校, 大学で教える全科目; 特定の学習課程の内容→カリキュラム, 教育[教科]課程, 履修課程 ‖ Latin is not **on the curriculum** at our school. ラテン語は私たちの学校のカリキュラムにはない. ☞参 **syllabus**

**curriculum vitae** /kərík jələm víːtaɪ/ =**CV**

**curry** /kʌ́ri; kʌ́ːri/ 名 C U (複 **curries**) ▶定義 an Indian dish of meat, vegetables, etc containing a lot of spices usually served with rice 多くの香辛料が入ったインドの肉や野菜などの料理で, 通常はご飯と共に出される→カレー(料理) ‖ a hot/mild curry 辛口・甘口カレー — **curried** 形→カレー味の, カレー粉で調理した ‖ curried chicken カレー味のチキン

**curry powder** 名 U ▶定義 a fine mixture of strongly flavoured spices that is used to make curry 風味の強い香辛料を混合した細かい粉末で, カレーを作るために用いる→カレー粉

**curse**¹ /kəːrs/ 名 C ▶定義1 a word used for expressing anger; a swear word 怒りを表すために用いる語; ののしりの言葉→ののしり, 悪態, 不敬な言葉 ▶定義2 a word or words expressing a wish that sth terrible will happen to sb ～にひどい…が降り懸かるようにという願いを表す言葉→のろい,のろいの言葉‖ *The family seemed to be under a curse (= lots of bad things happened to them).* その一家はのろわれているようだった(= 悪い事がたくさん起こった). ▶定義3 something that causes great harm 大きな害を引き起こすもの→災い,災いのもと,不幸の種,大害‖ *the curse of drug addiction* 麻薬中毒の大害

**curse**² /kə:rs/ 動 ▶定義1 🈩 🈶 curse (sb/sth) (for sth) to swear at sb/sth; to use rude language to express your anger ～をののしる;無礼な言葉を使って怒りを表す→(～を)ののしる,(～に)悪態をつく,不敬な言葉を使う‖ *He dropped the box, cursing himself for his clumsiness.* 彼は箱を落とし,自分の不器用さに悪態をついた. ▶定義2 🈶 to use a magic word or phrase against sb because you wish him/her harm 災いを望んで～に対して魔法の言葉や表現を使う→～をのろう,～にのろいを掛ける,～に災いあれと願う‖ *She cursed his family.* 彼女は彼の家族にのろいを掛けた.

**cursor** /kə:rsər/ 名 🅒 ▶定義 (computing) a small sign on a computer screen that shows the position you are at (コンピューター) コンピューター画面上の小さな印で,現在の位置を示す物→カーソル ☞ S5ページのさし絵

**cursory** /kə:rs(ə)ri/ ▶定義 quick and short; done in a hurry 素早く短い;急いでなされた→急ぎの,せっかちな,ぞんざいな,大まかな‖ *a cursory glance* 素早い一瞥(べつ)

**curt** /kə:rt/ 形 ▶定義 short and not polite 短くて礼儀正しくない→ぶっきらぼうな,素っ気ない;簡略な‖ *She gave him a curt reply and slammed the phone down.* 彼女は彼に素っ気なく応えて受話器をたたき付けた. ― curtly 副 →ぶっきらぼうに,素っ気なく ― curtness 名 🅤 →ぶっきらぼう,無愛想

**curtail** /kərtéil/ 動 🈺 正式 ▶定義 to make sth shorter or smaller; to reduce ～を短く,または小さくする;縮小する→～を短縮する,切り詰める,短く切り上げる,削減する‖ *I had to curtail my answer as I was running out of time.* 時間がなくなりかけたので,答えを切り詰めなければならなかった. ― curtailment 名 🅒🅤 →短縮,削減,抑制

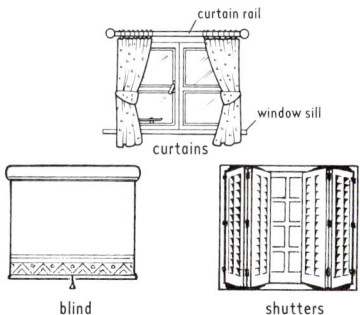

\*__curtain__ /kə:rtn/ 名 🅒 ▶定義1 (米 または drape) a piece of material that you can move to cover a window, etc 動かして窓などを覆う生地→カーテン;幕,どんちょう‖ *Could you **draw the curtains**, please? (= Could you open/close the curtains)* カーテンを引いてくれませんか(= カーテンを開けて・閉めてくれませんか). *The curtain goes up at 7pm (= in a theatre, the play begins).* 幕は午後7時に開く(= 劇場で劇が始まる). ▶定義2 a thing that covers or hides sth ～を覆うまたは隠す物→カーテン状の物,覆う物,遮る物‖ *a curtain of mist* 霧の幕

**curtsy** (または **curtsey**) /kə:rtsi/ 名 🅒 (複 **curtsies** または **curtseys**) ▶定義 a movement made by a woman as a sign of respect, done by bending the knees, with one foot behind the other 女性が尊敬の印として示す動作で,両ひざを曲げ一方の足を後ろに引く→女性のおじぎ,女性の会釈 ― curtsy(または curtsey)動 🈩 →おじぎをする,会釈する

\*__curve__¹ /kə:rv/ 名 🅒 ▶定義 a line that bends round 湾曲した線→曲線,曲線状の物‖ *a curve on a graph* グラフの曲線 ☞ lineのさし絵

**curve**² /kə:rv/ 動 🈩🈶 ▶定義 to bend or to make sth bend in a curve ～が曲線状に曲がる,または～をそのように曲げる→湾曲する,曲線を描く;～を湾曲させる‖ *The bay curved round to the south.* その湾は南に向かって湾曲している. *a curved line* 曲線 ☞ lineのさし絵

**cushion**¹ /kúʃ(ə)n/ 名 🅒 ▶定義1 a bag filled with

soft material, for example feathers, which you put on a chair, etc to make it more comfortable 例えば羽などの柔らかい物が詰まった袋で, 快適になるようにいすなどに置く➜**クッション, 座布団** ☛ ベッドに置く cushion は pillow (まくら). ▶定義2 something that acts or is shaped like a cushion クッションとして機能する物, またはクッションのような形の物➜**クッション状の物, 衝撃などを和らげる物, 緩衝物** ‖ *A hovercraft rides on a cushion of air.* ホバークラフトは空気のクッションに乗っている.

**cushion²** /kʊ́ʃ(ə)n/ [動][他] ▶定義1 to make a fall, hit, etc less painful 落下, 衝突などの苦痛を少なくする➜**(衝撃)を和らげる, 緩和する, ～のクッション代わりとなる** ‖ *The snow cushioned his fall.* 落下した彼の衝撃は雪のお陰で和らげられた. ▶定義2 to reduce the unpleasant effect of sth ～の不快な影響を減らす➜**～を保護する, 守る, (苦しみなど)を取り除く** ‖ *She spent her childhood on a farm, cushioned from the effects of the war.* 彼女は子供時代を農場で過ごして, 戦争の影響から守られた.

**cushy** /kʊ́ʃi/ [形][略式] ▶定義 too easy, needing little effort (in a way that seems unfair to others) ほとんど努力が必要なく簡単すぎる (ほかの人には不公平に思えるほど)➜**楽な, 気楽な, 朝飯前の** ‖ *a cushy job* 朝飯前の仕事

**custard** /kʌ́stərd/ [名][U] ▶定義 sweet yellow sauce made from milk, eggs and sugar. In Britain it is eaten hot or cold with sweet dishes. 牛乳, 卵, 砂糖から作る甘い黄色のソース. 英国では温めてまたは冷たいままで甘い料理と共に食べる➜**カスタードソース** ☛ C4ページのさし絵

**custodian** /kʌstóʊdiən/ [名][C] ▶定義1 [正式] a person who looks after sth, especially a museum, library, etc ～, 特に博物館または図書館などの管理をする人➜**(公共建造物の)管理人, 保管者** ▶定義2 [米] =CARETAKER

**custody** /kʌ́stədi/ [名][U] ▶定義1 the legal right or duty to take care of sb/sth ～の世話をする法律上の権利または義務➜**保護, 監督, 後見** ‖ *After the divorce, the mother **had custody of** the children.* 離婚後は母親が子供の親権者となった. ▶定義2 the state of being guarded, or kept in prison temporarily, especially by the police 特に警察によって監視されている状態, または刑務所に一時的に収監されている状態➜**拘留, 留置, 監禁** ‖ *The man was **kept in custody** until his trial.* 男は公判まで拘置された.

***custom** /kʌ́stəm/ [名] ▶定義1 [C][U] a way of behaving which a particular group or society has had for a long time 特定の集団または社会が長いこと維持してきた振る舞い➜**慣習, 習慣, 風習, 慣例** ‖ *It's the custom in Britain for a bride to throw her bouquet to the wedding guests.* 花嫁がブーケを結婚式の客に投げるのは英国の慣習だ. *according to **local custom*** 地元の風習に従えば ☛参 **habit** の注 ▶定義2 [単数扱い] [正式] something that a person does regularly 人が規則正しく行う事➜**(個人の)習慣, 習慣的行為** ‖ *It's my custom to drink tea in the afternoon.* 午後にお茶を飲むのは私の習慣だ. ▶定義3 [U] [英] commercial activity; the practice of people buying things regularly from a particular shop, etc 商業活動; 人が特定の店などから定期的に物を買うこと➜**(商店などの)愛顧, お得意, 引き立て** ‖ *The local shop lost a lot of custom when the new supermarket opened.* 新しいスーパーが開店した時に, 近所の商店は多くの得意客を失った. ☛参 **customs**

**customary** /kʌ́stəm(ə)ri; -mèri/ [形] ▶定義 according to custom; usual 習慣に従った; 通常の➜**習慣的な, 通例の, 慣例の** ‖ *Is it customary to send cards at Christmas in your country?* あなたの国ではクリスマスにカードを送る習慣がありますか.

***customer** /kʌ́stəmər/ [名][C] ▶定義1 a person who buys goods or services in a shop, restaurant, etc 店やレストランなどで品物またはサービスを買う人➜**顧客, 常連, 得意先, 取引先** ‖ *The shop assistant was serving a customer.* 店員が客に応対していた. ☛参 **client** ▶定義2 [略式] (特定の形容詞の後で) a person 人➜**(～な)人, (～な)やつ** ‖ *a tough/an awkward/an odd/ customer* 荒っぽい・扱いにくい・変なやつ

***customs** (または **Customs**) /kʌ́stəmz/ [名] [複数扱い] ▶定義 the place at an airport, etc where government officials check your luggage to make sure you are not bringing goods into the country illegally 空港などの場所で, 政府の役人が手荷物を検査して物を国内に違法に持ち込まないように確認する所➜**税関** ‖ *a customs offi-*

*cer* 税関職員 ☞参 **excise**

\***cut**[1] /kʌt/ 動 (現分 **cutting**; 過, 過分 **cut**)
▶定義1 自他 to make an opening, wound or mark in sth using a sharp tool, for example a pair of scissors or a knife はさみやナイフのような鋭い道具などを使って〜に開口部, 傷口または印などを付ける→(〜を)切る, 傷付ける, けがをする;(刃物などが)切れる ‖ *Be careful not to cut yourself on that broken glass!* その割れたガラスでけがをしないように気を付けなさい. *This knife doesn't cut very well.* このナイフはあまり良く切れない. ▶定義2 他 cut sth (from sth) to remove sth or a part of sth, using a knife, etc ナイフなどを使って〜または…の一部を取り除く→〜を切り離す, 切り取る, 切断する, 摘み取る ‖ *She cut two slices of bread (from the loaf).* 彼女はパンを2切れ(塊から)切った. ▶定義3 他 cut sth (in/into sth) to divide sth into pieces with a knife, etc ナイフなどで〜を小片に分ける→〜を(…に)切り分ける, 切って分配する ‖ *She cut the cake into eight (pieces).* 彼女はケーキを8つ[8切れ]に切った. *He cut the rope in two.* 彼はロープを半分に切った.
▶定義4 他 to make sth shorter by using scissors, etc はさみなどを使って〜を短くする→〜を短く切る, 刈る, 刈り込む ‖ *I cut my own hair.* 私は自分で髪を切る. *to have your hair cut (= at the hairdresser's)* 髪を切る(= 美容院で) *to cut the grass* 草を刈る ▶定義5 他 to make or form sth by removing material with a sharp tool 鋭い道具で材料を取り除いて〜を作るまたは形づくる→〜を切って作る, 切って形を整える, 彫る, 刻む ‖ *She cut a hole in the card and pushed the string through.* 彼女は厚紙に穴を開けてひもを通した. *They cut a path through the jungle.* 彼らはジャングルに道を切り開いた.
▶定義6 他 to reduce sth or make it shorter; to remove sth 〜を減らす, または〜を短くする; 〜を取り除く→〜を削減する, 切り詰める, 短縮する; 〜を削除する, カットする ‖ *to cut taxes/costs/spending* 税・経費・出費を切り詰める *Several violent scenes in the film were cut.* 映画のいくつかの暴力的な場面がカットされた. ▶定義7 他 (computing) to remove a piece of text from the screen (コンピューター) 画面から本文を取り除く→〜を削除する, 消去する ‖ *Use the **cut and paste** buttons to change the order of the paragraphs.* カットアンドペースト(切り取り・はり付け)ボタンを使って段落の順序を変えなさい. ▶定義8 自 cut across, along, through, etc (sth) to go across, etc sth, in order to make your route shorter 道筋を短くするために〜を横切ったりする→近道する, 通り抜ける, 突っ切る ‖ *It's much quicker if we cut across the field.* 野原を横切ればずっと速い. ▶定義9 他 (口語) to stop sth 〜を止める→〜をやめる, 絶つ, 停止する, 中止する ‖ *Cut the chat and get on with your work!* おしゃべりをやめて仕事を進めなさい. ▶定義10 他 to deeply offend sb or hurt his/her feelings 〜の感情を大きく損なう, または感情を傷付ける→心を傷付ける, 心をえぐる, 〜を苦しめる ‖ *His cruel remarks cut her deeply.* 彼の冷酷な言葉は彼女を深く傷付けた.

▶ cutを含むこのほかの成句については名詞, 形容詞などの項を参照. 例えばcut cornersはcornerにある.

句動詞 **cut across sth** ▶定義 to affect or be true for different groups that usually remain separate 通常は別個の異なる集団に影響する, またはそのような集団にとって真実となる→〜に広く及ぶ, 〜を越える, 超越する ‖ *The question of aid for the earthquake victims cuts across national boundaries.* 地震の被災者に対する援助の問題は国境を越える.

**cut sth back; cut back (on sth)** ▶定義 to reduce sth 〜を削減する→(〜を)切り詰める, 切り下げる, 縮小する ‖ *to cut back on public spending* 政府の支出を削減する

**cut sth down** ▶定義1 to make sth fall down by cutting it 〜を切って倒す→〜を切り倒す, 伐(き)る ‖ *to cut down a tree* 木を切り倒す ▶定義2 to make sth shorter 〜を短くする→〜を切り詰める, 省略する ‖ *I have to cut my essay down to 2000 words.* 私は小論文を2000語に切り詰めなければならない.

**cut sth down; cut down (on sth)** ▶定義 to reduce the quantity or amount of sth; to do sth less often 〜の量を削減する; 〜をする頻度を減らす→(〜を)減らす, (たばこ, 酒, 食物などの量を)減らす ‖ *You should cut down on fatty foods.* 脂っこい食物の量を減らさなければなら

**cut in (on sb/sth)** ▶定義 to interrupt sb/sth ～を遮る→(話などを)遮る,(～に)口を出す,割り込む‖ *She kept cutting in on our conversation.* 彼女は私たちの会話に割り込んでばかりいた.

**cut sb off**(しばしば受動態) ▶定義 to stop or interrupt sb's telephone conversation ～の電話の会話をやめさせるまたは遮る→(通話中の人)の電話を切る‖ *We were cut off before I could give her my message.* 彼女に伝言を告げる前に電話が切れた.

**cut sb/sth off**(しばしば受動態) ▶定義 to stop the supply of sth to sb ～への…の供給を止める→～を絶つ,遮断する,止断する‖ *The electricity/gas/water has been cut off.* 電気・ガス・水道が止められた.

**cut sth off** ▶定義 to block a road, etc so that nothing can pass 何も通れないように道路などをふさぐ→遮断する,封鎖する,通行止めにする‖ *We must cut off all possible escape routes.* 考えられるすべての逃走経路を封鎖しなければならない.

**cut sth off (sth)** ▶定義 to remove sth from sth larger by cutting より大きい～から…を切って取り除く→～を(…から)切り離す,切り落とす,切り取る‖ *Be careful you don't cut your fingers off using that electric saw.* その電動のこぎりで指を切り落とさないように気を付けて.

**cut sb/sth off (from sb/sth)**(しばしば受動態で) ▶定義 to prevent sb/sth from moving from a place or contacting people outside ～がある場所から移動したり外部の人と接触できないようにする→～を(…から)遮断する,包囲する,封鎖する,孤立させる‖ *The farm was cut off from the village by heavy snow.* 農場は大雪のため村から孤立した.

**cut sth open** ▶定義 to open sth by cutting ～を切って開く→～を切り開く,切り傷が開く‖ *She fell and cut her head open.* 彼女は転落して頭を切った.

**cut sth out** ▶定義1 to remove sth or to form sth into a particular shape by cutting 切って～を取り除く,または特定の形に作る→～を切り抜く,切り取る‖ *He cut the job advertisement out of the newspaper.* 彼は新聞から求人広告を切り抜いた. ▶定義2 to not include sth ～を含めない→～を除外する,省略する,省く‖ *Cut out the boring details!* 退屈な細部は省略しなさい. ▶定義3 特に 困略式 to stop saying or doing sth that annoys sb ～をいら立たせる…を言ったりまたはすることをやめる→(話,騒ぎなど)をやめる‖ *Cut that out and leave me alone!* いいかげんにしてほっておいてくれ. ▶定義4 略式 to stop doing or using sth ～をするまたは使うことをやめる→～をやめる,絶つ‖ *You'll only lose weight if you cut out sweet things from your diet.* 食事で甘い物を取るのをやめれば体重が減りますよ.

**be cut out for sth; be cut out to be sth** ▶定義 to have the qualities needed to do sth; to be suitable for sth/sb ～をするために必要な資質がある;～に適切である→～に・～するのに向いている,適性がある‖ *You're not cut out to be a soldier.* あなたは兵士には向かない.

**cut sth up** ▶定義 to cut sth into small pieces with a knife, etc ナイフなどで～を小片に切る→～を切り刻む,細かく切る,ばらばらに切る

★**cut**[2] /kʌt/ 名 ⓒ ▶定義1 an injury or opening in the skin made with a knife, etc ナイフなどによる皮膚のけがまたは開いた傷→切り傷,切り口,裂傷‖ *He had a deep cut on his forehead.* 彼の額には深い傷口がある. ▶定義2 an act of cutting 切ること→切り付け,切断,切り取り,散髪,刈り取り‖ *to have a cut and blow-dry (= at a hairdresser's)* 髪を切ってドライヤーで整えてもらう(= 美容院で) ▶定義3 a cut (in sth) a reduction in size, amount, etc 大きさまたは量などを縮小すること→削減,切り詰め,引き下げ,切断,停止,削除‖ *a cut in government spending* 政府の支出の削減 *a power cut (= when the electric current is stopped temporarily)* 停電(= 電流が一時的に止まるとき) ▶定義4 a piece of meat from a particular part of an animal 動物の特定の部位の肉→肉片,切り身‖ *cheap cuts of lamb* 子羊の安い肉 ▶定義5 略式 a share of the profits from sth, especially sth dishonest ～,特に不正な～から得る利益の分配→(もうけ,略奪などの)分け前,取り分 ☞参 **short cut**

**cutback** /ˈkʌtbæk/ 名 ⓒ ▶定義 a reduction in amount or number 量または数を減らすこと→縮小,削減‖ *The management were forced to* *make cutbacks in staff.* 経営者側は人員を削減せざるを得なかった.

**cute** /kjuːt/ 形 ▶定義 attractive; pretty 魅力的な; かわいい→かわいらしい、きれいな、かれんな ‖ *Your little girl is so cute!* 娘さんは本当にかわいらしい. *a cute smile* かれんな笑み

**cutlery** /kʌ́tləri/ 名 ▶定義 the knives, forks and spoons that you use for eating food 食事をするために用いるナイフ, フォーク, スプーン→食卓用金物 ☞参 **crockery**

**cutlet** /kʌ́tlət/ 名 C ▶定義 a small, thick piece of meat, often with bone in it, that is cooked しばしば骨付きの調理された小さく厚い肉の一片→カツレツ

**cut-off** 名 C ▶定義 the level or time at which sth stops ～が停止する段階または時刻→期限, 締め切り, 限界 ‖ *The cut-off date is 12 May. After that we'll end the offer.* 締め切り日は5月12日です. それ以降は特価提供を終了します.

**cut-price** (米 **cut-rate**) 形 ▶定義 sold at a reduced price; selling goods at low prices 値下げして販売される; 低価格で品物を販売する→割引値段の, 特価の; 特売の, 割引セールの ‖ *cut-price offers* 割引で提供 *a cut-price store* 特価店

**cutters** /kʌ́tərz/ 名 [複数扱い] ▶定義 a tool that you use for cutting through sth, for example metal 例えば金属などを切るために用いる道具→切断器, 裁断器, 切削工具, カッター ‖ *a pair of wire cutters* ワイヤーカッター

**cut-throat** 形 ▶定義 caring only about success and not worried about hurting anyone 成功だけを考え, 人を傷付けることを気に掛けない→(競争などが)激しい, 厳しい, 苛烈な, 殺人的な ‖ *cut-throat business practices* 苛烈な業務慣行

**cutting**¹ /kʌ́tɪŋ/ 名 C ▶定義 1 (米 **clipping**) a piece cut out from a newspaper, etc 新聞などから切り抜いた部分→切り抜き ‖ *press cuttings* 新聞の切り抜き ▶定義 2 a piece cut off from a plant that you use for growing a new plant 新しい植物を育てるのに使うために, 植物から切り取った部分→(さし木用の)切り枝, 切り穂, さし穂

**cutting**² /kʌ́tɪŋ/ 形 ▶定義 (used about sth you say) unkind; meant to hurt sb's feelings (話す物事について)不親切な; ～の感情を傷付ける

ことを意図した→痛烈な, 辛辣(しんらつ)な, 皮肉な ‖ *a cutting remark* 辛辣な言葉

**CV** /sìː víː/ (米 **résumé**) 名 [単数扱い] ▶定義 curruculum vitae; a formal list of your education and work experience, often used when you are trying to get a new job しばしば新しい仕事を得る際に使う学歴と職業経験の正式の一覧→履歴書, 経歴書

**cwt** 略 a hundred weight ▶定義 a measure of weight, about 50.8 kg 重さの単位, 約50.8kg→ハンドレッドウェート

**cyanide** /sáɪənàɪd, -nəd/ 名 U ▶定義 a poisonous chemical 有毒な化学物質→シアン化物, 青酸カリ, 青酸ナトリウム

**cybercafe** /sáɪbərkæfèɪ, -kə-; -fiː/ 名 C ▶定義 a cafe with computers where customers can pay to use the Internet 客が料金を払ってインターネットを使用できるコンピューターのある喫茶店→インターネットカフェ, 電脳喫茶

**cyberspace** /sáɪbərspèɪs/ 名 U ▶定義 a place that is not real, where electronic messages exist while they are being sent from one computer to another 現実ではない空間で, 電子的メッセージが1台のコンピューターからほかのコンピューターへ送られる間に存在する場所→サイバースペース, コンピューターネットワークによって形成される三次元空間

★**cycle**¹ /sáɪk(ə)l/ 名 C ▶定義 1 a series of events, etc that happen again and again in the same order 同じ順序で何回も起こる一連の出来事など→循環, 一巡, 周期 ‖ *the life cycle* of a frog カエルの生活環 ▶定義 2 a bicycle or motor cycle 自転車またはオートバイ→自転車, オートバイ, 単車 ‖ *a cycle shop* 自転車店 ☞類 **bike**

**cycle**² /sáɪk(ə)l/ 動 ▶定義 to ride a bicycle 自転車に乗る→自転車で行く, サイクリングをする ‖ *He usually cycles to school.* 彼は普通, 自転車で学校へ行く. ☞ go cycling は楽しみのために自転車に乗ることを言う一般的な語. *We go cycling most weekends.* 私たちは週末は大抵サイクリングをする.

**cyclic** /sáɪklɪk, sík-/ (または **cyclical** /sáɪklɪk(ə)l, sík-/) 形 ▶定義 following a repeated pattern 繰り返しのパターンに従った→循環の, 循環する, 周期的な

**cyclist** /sáɪklɪst, sík-/ 名 C ▶定義 a person who rides a bicycle 自転車に乗る人→自転車に乗る人, 自転車で行く人

**cyclone** /sáɪkloʊn/ 名 C ▶定義 a violent wind that moves in a circle causing a storm 環状に移動しながらあらしを引き起こす烈風→サイクロン; 熱帯性・温帯性低気圧, 大暴風 ☞参 **storm** の注

**cylinder** /sílɪndər/ 名 C ▶定義1 an object shaped like a tube 筒のような形をした物→円筒, 円柱, 円筒形の物 ☞ **cube** のさし絵 ▶定義2 a tube-shaped part of an engine, for example in a car 車などのエンジンの筒形の部分→シリンダー, 気筒 — **cylindrical** /səlíndrɪk(ə)l/ 形→円筒(形)の, 円柱(状)の

**cymbal** /símb(ə)l/ 名 [C, 通常は複数] ▶定義 one of a pair of round metal plates used as a musical instrument. Cymbals make a loud ringing sound when you hit them together or with a stick. 楽器として使われる一組の円い金属板の一方. 互いに打ち合わせる, または棒で打つと大きく響く音を立てる→シンバル ☞ **music** のさし絵

**cynic** /sínɪk/ 名 C ▶定義 a person who believes that people only do things for themselves, rather than to help others 人は他人を助けるためより自分のためだけに行動すると信じている人→皮肉屋, 冷笑家, (〜の誠実さを)軽べつする人 ‖ *Don't be such a cynic. He did it to help us, not for the money.* そんなに皮肉な考え方をしないで. 彼はお金のためでなく, 私たちを助けるためにそうしたのです. — **cynical** /sínɪk(ə)l/ 形→冷笑的な, 皮肉な ‖ *a cynical remark* 皮肉な言葉 — **cynically** /-k(ə)li/ 副→冷笑的に, 皮肉に — **cynicism** /sínəsɪz(ə)m/ 名 U→冷笑, 皮肉(な言動・考え方)

**Cyrillic** /sərílɪk/ 名 U ▶定義 the alphabet that is used in languages such as Russian ロシア語などの言語で使われるアルファベット→キリル文字, キリルアルファベット, スラブ文字

**cyst** /sɪst/ 名 C ▶定義 a swelling or a lump filled with liquid in the body or under the skin 体内または皮膚の下の液体がたまってできたはれ物またはこぶ→嚢胞(のうほう), 膿(うみ)がたまった水疱, 膿腫(のうしゅ), 膿を持ったはれ物

# D d

**D, d**¹ /diː/ 名 C (複 **D's**; **d's**) ▶定義 the fourth letter of the English alphabet 英語アルファベットの第4文字→d(D)が表す音, d(D)の文字, d(D)の字形のもの ‖ *'David' begins with (a) 'D'.* Davidは, Dで始まる.

**d**² 略 died→亡くなった ‖ *W A Mozart, d 1791* W. A. モーツァルト 1791 年没

**dab**¹ /dæb/ 動 自他 (**dabbing**; **dabbed**) ▶定義 to touch sth lightly, usually several times 通常は数回, 〜を軽く触れる→軽くたたく ‖ *He dabbed the cut with some cotton wool.* 彼は傷口に脱脂綿をそっと当てた.

句動詞 **dab sth on/off (sth)** ▶定義 to put sth on or to remove sth lightly 〜を軽く当てる, またはそっと取り除く→〜を手早く取り除く, 払い落とす ‖ *to dab some antiseptic on a wound* 傷口に消毒液をざっと塗る

**dab**² /dæb/ 名 C ▶定義1 a light touch 軽く触れること→軽くたたくこと ‖ *She gave her eyes a dab with a handkerchief.* 彼女はさっとハンカチを目に当てた. ▶定義2 a small quantity of sth that is put on a surface 表面に塗られた少量の〜→(バター・塗料などの)一塗り(の量) ‖ *a dab of paint/perfume* ペンキの一塗り・少量の香水

**dabble** /dǽb(ə)l/ 動 ▶定義1 自 to become involved in sth in a way that is not very serious あまりまじめではないやり方で〜に関係するようになる→(面白半分に)ちょっと手を出す, かじる ‖ *to dabble in politics* 政治にちょっと手を出す ▶定義2 他 to put your hands, feet, etc in water and move them around 手足などを水に入れて, あちこちに動かす→〜をばたつかせる, ばちゃばちゃさせる ‖ *We sat on the bank and dabbled our toes in the river.* 私たちは岸に座り, 川の中でつま先をぱちゃぱちゃさせた.

*****dad** /dæd/ 名 C 略式 ▶定義 father お父さん→お父さん, パパ, 親父 ‖ *Is that your dad?* あの人があなたのお父さんなの. *Come on, Dad!* 急いで, パパ.

*****daddy** /dǽdi/ 名 C (複 **daddies**) 略式 ▶定義 (used by children) father (子供たちが用いて)お父さん→お父さん, パパ ‖ *I want my daddy!* お父さんに会いたいよ.

**daffodil** /dǽfədìl/ 名 C ▶定義 a tall yellow flower that grows in the spring 春に咲く,背の高い黄色い花→**ラッパズイセン** ☞ C2ページのさし絵

**daft** /dɑːft; dæft/ 形 略式 ▶定義 silly; foolish→**ばかな;愚かな** ‖ *Don't be daft.* ばかな事をするな. *a daft idea* ばかげた考え

**dagger** /dǽɡər/ 名 C ▶定義 a type of knife used as a weapon, especially in past times 特に昔,武器として使われた短刀の一種→**短剣,短刀** ☞ spearのさし絵

★**daily**¹ /déɪli/ 形 副 ▶定義 done, made or happening every day 毎日行われる,作られる,または起こる→**毎日の,日常の** ‖ *a daily routine/delivery/newspaper* 毎日の決まった仕事・毎日の配達・日刊新聞 *Our airline flies to Japan daily.* 私どもの航空便は,毎日日本に飛びます.

**daily**² /déɪli/ 名 C (複 **dailies**) 略式 ▶定義 a newspaper that is published every day except Sunday 日曜日を除き,毎日発行される新聞→**日刊紙**

**dainty** /déɪnti/ 形 ▶定義 **1** small and pretty 小さくてかわいらしい→**優美な,きゃしゃな,繊細な** ‖ *a dainty lace handkerchief* 繊細なレースのハンカチ ▶定義 **2** (used about a person's movements) very careful in a way that tries to show good manners (人の身振りについて)行儀の良さを示そうとする様子,とても気を遣って→**優美な,上品な** ‖ *Veronica took a dainty bite of the giant hot dog.* ベロニカは大きなホットドックを上品に一口食べた.—**daintily** 副 →**優美に,上品に**

**dairy**¹ /déəri/ 名 C (複 **dairies**) ▶定義 **1** a place on a farm where milk is kept and butter, cheese, etc are made 農場で,牛乳が貯蔵されて,バター,チーズなどが作られる所→**乳製品製造所,牛乳加工所** ▶定義 **2** a company which sells milk, butter, eggs, etc 牛乳,バター,卵などを売る会社→**牛乳・乳製品販売店**

**dairy**² /déəri/ 形 (名詞の前だけ) ▶定義 **1** made from milk 牛乳で作られた→**乳製品の** ‖ *dairy products/produce* (= *milk, butter, cheese, etc*) 酪農製品 (= 牛乳,バター,チーズなど) ▶定義 **2** connected with the production of milk 牛乳の生産に関係する→**牛乳加工所の** ‖ *dairy cattle* 乳牛 *a dairy farm* 酪農場

**daisy** /déɪzi/ 名 C (複 **daisies**) ▶定義 a small white flower with a yellow centre, which usually grows wild in grass 通常は野生で草原に生える,中心の黄色い小さな白い花→**デージー,ヒナギク** ☞ C2ページのさし絵

**dam** /dæm/ 名 C ▶定義 a wall built across a river to hold back the water and form a lake (reservoir) behind it 水をせき止めてその後ろに湖(貯水池)を造るために,川を横切って建てられた壁→**ダム,せき** — **dam** 動 他 →**〜をダムでせき止める,〜にダムを造る**

★**damage**¹ /dǽmɪdʒ/ 名 ▶定義 **1** U damage (to sth) harm or injury caused when sth is broken or spoiled 〜が壊される,または傷んだ場合に生じる害または損害→**損害,被害,害** ‖ *Earthquakes can cause terrible damage in urban areas.* 地震は,都市部にひどい損害を引き起こしかねない. *It will take weeks to repair the damage done by the vandals.* 破壊者たちによってなされた損害の修復には,数週間かかるだろう. ▶定義 **2 damages** [複数扱い] money that you can ask for if sb damages sth of yours or hurts you 〜が自分の…に損害を与えたり,または自分にけがをさせた場合に要求できるお金→**損害賠償金(額)** ‖ *Mrs Rees, who lost a leg in the crash, was awarded damages of £100000.* 衝突事故で片足を失ったリース夫人に,10万ポンドの損害賠償金が支払われた.

★**damage**² /dǽmɪdʒ/ 動 他 ▶定義 to spoil or harm sth, for example by breaking it 例えば〜を壊すことによって,台なしにするまたは害する→**〜に損害を与える,〜を傷付ける** ‖ *The roof was damaged by the storm.* 屋根はあらしで傷付いた.—**damaging** 形 →**損害を与える,不利な,有害な** ‖ *These rumours could be damaging to her reputation.* これらのうわさは,彼女の評判を傷付けるかもしれない.

**dame** /deɪm/ 名 C **Dame** 英 ▶定義 a title given to a woman as an honour because of sth special that she has done ある女性が行った特別な〜によって,名誉の印としてその女性に与えられる称号→**デイム(ナイトに叙せられた女性の敬称.男性の Sir に相当する)** ‖ *Dame Agatha Christie* デイム アガサ クリスティ

**damn**¹ /dæm/ 動 自 他 (俗語) ▶定義 a swear word that people use to show that they are angry 怒っていることを表すために人々が使う，口汚いののしりの言葉→**こん畜生，くそっ，しまった** ‖ *Damn (it)! I've left my money behind.* しまった，お金を忘れた．

**damn**² /dæm/（または **damned**）形副（俗語）
▶定義1 (a swear word that people use for emphasizing what they are saying) very (話していることを強調するために人々が使う，口汚いののしりの言葉) とても→**ひどく，とても，全く** ‖ *Read it! It's a damn good book.* 読んでみてよ，すごくいい本だよ．▶定義2 a swear word that people use to show that they are angry 怒っていることを表すために人々が使う，口汚いののしりの言葉→**いまいましい，いやらしい，ひどい** ‖ *Some damn fool has parked too close to me.* くそいまいましいばかが，ぼくの車に寄せすぎて駐車してる．

**damn**³ /dæm/ 名
成句 **not give a damn (about sb/sth)**（俗語）
▶定義 not care at all→**全く気にしない** ‖ *I don't give a damn what he thinks about me.* 彼が私をどう思っていようと，私は全く気にしない．

**damning** /dǽmɪŋ/ 形 ▶定義 that criticizes sth very much ～をひどく酷評する→**非常に批判的な** ‖ *There was a damning article about the book in the newspaper.* その本についての非常に厳しい記事が新聞に載った．

★**damp**¹ /dæmp/ 形 ▶定義 a little wet 少しぬれた→**湿った，じめじめした** ‖ *The house had been empty and felt rather damp.* その家はずっと空き家で，かなり湿った感じだった．— damp 名 **U**→**湿気，水気** ‖ *She hated the damp and the cold of the English climate.* 彼女は，イギリスの気候のじめじめした寒さが嫌いだった．● 参 wet の注

**damp**² /dæmp/ 動 他 **damp sth (down)**
▶定義1 to make a fire burn less strongly or stop burning 火力を弱める，または火を消す→**～を弱める，～を消す** ‖ *He tried to damp (down) the flames.* 彼は炎を小さくしようとした．
▶定義2 to make sth less strong or urgent ～の強さまたは緊急の度合いを弱める→(**熱意など**)**をそぐ，**(**気力**)**をくじく，抑える** ‖ *He tried to damp down their expectations in case they failed.* 失敗した場合の用心に，彼はみんなの期待を抑えようと努めた．

**dampen** /dǽmpən/ 動 他 ▶定義1 to make sth less strong or urgent ～の強さまたは緊急の度合いを弱める→(**希望など**)**をくじく，そぐ，抑える** ‖ *Even the awful weather did not dampen their enthusiasm for the trip.* 悪天候でさえも，彼らの旅行への熱意をそぐことはなかった．
▶定義2 to make sth a little wet ～を少しぬらす→**～を湿らせる** ‖ *He dampened his hair to try to stop it sticking up.* 彼は，立っている髪をなで付けようと，髪を湿らせた．

★**dance**¹ /dɑːns; dæns/ 名 ▶定義1 **C** a series of steps and movements which you do to music 音楽に合わせて行う一連のステップと動き→**踊り，ダンス** ▶定義2 **U** dancing as a form of art or entertainment 芸術または娯楽の一形式としての踊り→**踊り，ダンス** ‖ *She's very interested in modern dance.* 彼女はモダンダンスにとても興味がある．▶定義3 **C** (古) a social meeting at which people dance with each other 人々が2人ずつ踊る社交的な集まり→**ダンスパーティー，舞踏会** ‖ *My parents met at a dance.* 私の両親は，ダンスパーティーで知り合った．

★**dance**² /dɑːns; dæns/ 動 ▶定義1 **自他** to move around to the rhythm of music by making a series of steps 一連のステップを踏んで，音楽のリズムに合わせて動き回る→**踊る，ダンスをする** ‖ *I can't dance very well.* 私はあまりうまく踊れない．*to dance the samba* サンバを踊る
▶定義2 **自** to jump and move around with energy 勢いよく飛び跳ねて，動き回る→(**喜び・痛みなどで**)**飛び跳ねる，小躍りする** ‖ *She was dancing up and down with excitement.* 彼女は興奮して小躍りしていた．

**dancer** /dǽːnsər; dǽn-/ 名 **C** ▶定義 a person who dances, often as a job 通常は仕事として，踊る人→**踊り子，ダンサー** ‖ *a ballet dancer* バレエダンサー *She's a good dancer.* 彼女はダンスが上手だ．

**dandelion** /dǽnd(ə)làɪən, -di-/ 名 **C** ▶定義 a small wild plant with a bright yellow flower 鮮やかな黄色い花の咲く，小さな野生の植物→**タンポポ** ● C2ページのさし絵

**dandruff** /dǽndrəf/ 名 **U** ▶定義 small pieces of dead skin in the hair, that look like white powder 白い粉のように見える，髪の間にある，死んだ皮膚の小さな片→(**頭の**)**ふけ**

**\*danger** /déɪndʒər/ 图 ▶定義 1 ❶ ⓒ the chance that sb/sth may be hurt, killed or damaged or that sth bad may happen ～が傷付けられる、殺される、または損害を受けるかもしれない、あるいは悪い事が起きるかもしれない可能性→**危険、危険な状態** ‖ *When he saw the men had knives, he realized his life was in danger.* 男たちがナイフを持っているのを見て、彼は自分の命が危険にさらされていることに気付いた. *The men kept on running until they thought they were out of danger.* 男たちは、危険を脱したと思うところまで走り続けた. *If things carry on as they are, there's a danger that the factory may have to close.* 事態がそのまま進行していったら、工場は閉鎖の危機に陥るかもしれない.

▶定義 2 ❷ a danger (to sb/sth) a person or thing that can cause injury, pain or damage to sb ～に危害を加える、苦しめる、または損害を与えるおそれのある人または物事→**(～にとって)危険な人・物、脅威、障害物** ‖ *Drunk drivers are a danger to everyone on the road.* 酒に酔った運転手は、道路にいるすべての人にとって危険な人物だ.

**\*dangerous** /déɪndʒərəs/ 形 ▶定義 likely to cause injury or damage 危害や損害を与えるおそれがある→**危険な、危ない** ‖ *a dangerous animal/road/illness* 危険な動物・道路・病気 *Police warn that the man is highly dangerous.* その男は極めて危険であると、警察は警告している. ― dangerously 副 →**危険なほど、危なく** ‖ *He was standing dangerously close to the cliff edge.* 彼は危険なほど崖(がけ)のへり近くに立っていた.

**dangle** /dǽŋg(ə)l/ 動 ⾃⽥ ▶定義 to hang freely; to hold sth so that it hangs down in this way 自然にぶら下がっている; 自然にぶら下がるように～を持つ→**ぶら下がる、ぶらぶら揺れる; ～をぶら下げる、ぶらぶら揺らす** ‖ *She sat on the fence with her legs dangling.* 彼女は柵(さく)に座り、足をぶらぶら揺らしていた. *The police dangled a rope from the bridge and the man grabbed it.* 警察は橋からロープを垂らし、男はそれをぎゅっとつかんだ.

**dank** /dæŋk/ 形 ▶定義 wet, cold and unpleasant 湿って寒く不愉快な→**湿っぽい、薄ら寒い**

**\*dare¹** /deər/ 動 ▶定義 1 ⾃ (通常は否定文で) dare (to) do sth to have enough courage to do sth ～をするのに十分な勇気がある→**あえて**～する, 思い切って～する, ～する勇気・ずうずうしさがある ‖ *Nobody dared (to) speak.* だれも口をきく勇気がなかった. *I daren't ask her to lend me any more money.* もっとお金を貸してほしいと、彼女に頼むずうずうしさは私にはない. *We were so frightened that we didn't dare (to) go into the room.* とてもおびえていたので、私たちはあえて部屋には入らなかった.

▶否定形は、dare not (通常は daren't /deənt/) または do not/does not (= don't/doesn't) dare である. 過去時制では、did not (didn't) dare となる.

▶定義 2 ⾒ dare sb (to do sth) to ask or tell sb to do sth in order to see if he/she has the courage to do it それをする勇気があるかどうかを確かめるために、～に…をするように頼む、または言う→**(人に)(できるものならやってみろと)挑む、挑戦・挑発する** ‖ *Can you jump off that wall? Go on, I dare you!* あの壁から飛び降りることができるか. さあ、やれるものならやってみろ. *He dared his friend to put a mouse in the teacher's bag.* 彼は友達に、先生のかばんにネズミを入れてみろよと言った.

成句 **don't you dare** ▶定義 used for telling sb very strongly not to do sth ～に…をしないようにと、とても強く言うために用いて→**～したら承知しないよ** ‖ *Don't you dare tell my parents about this!* この事を私の両親に言ったら承知しないよ.

**how dare you** ▶定義 used when you are angry about sth that sb has done ～がやってしまった…に怒っているときに用いて→**よくも・厚かましくも・ずうずうしくも～できたものだ** ‖ *How dare you speak to me like that!* よくも私に向かってそんな口がきけるわね.

**I dare say** ▶定義 used when you are saying sth is possible 可能性がある～について言うときに用いて→**おそらく・多分～であろう** ‖ *'I think you should accept the offer.' 'I dare say you're right.'* 「君はその申し出を受けるべきだと思う」「多分あなたが正しいのでしょうね」

**\*dare²** /deər/ 图 [ ⓒ, 通常は単数 ] ▶定義 something dangerous that sb asks you to do, to see if you have the courage to do it あなたにそれをする勇気があるかどうかを見るため

に，〜が行うよう要求した危険な事➡あえてすること，挑戦 ‖ *'Why did you try to swim across the river?' 'For a dare.'*「どうして川を泳いで渡ろうとしたの」「挑戦を受けたから」

**daredevil** /déədèvl/ 名 C ▶定義 a person who likes to do dangerous things 危険な事をすることが好きな人➡向こう見ずな人，命知らずの人

**daring** /déərɪŋ/ 形 ▶定義 involving or taking risks; brave 危険にかかわることまたは危険を冒すこと；勇敢な➡大胆な，向こう見ずな，勇敢な ‖ *a daring attack* 勇敢な攻撃 — **daring** 名 U ➡大胆なこと，大胆不敵，向こう見ず ‖ *The climb required skill and daring.* 登山には，技術と大胆さが必要だった．

*****dark**[1] /dɑːrk/ 形 ▶定義 **1** with no light or very little light 光がない，またはかすかな光があるだけの➡暗い，闇(やみ)の ‖ *It was a dark night, with no moon.* 月の出ていない闇夜だった．*What time does it get dark in winter?* 冬は，何時に暗くなりますか．▶定義 **2** (used about a colour) not light; nearer black than white (色について)明るくない；白よりは黒に近い➡濃い，黒ずんだ ‖ *dark blue* 濃紺 ⇔ **light**, **pale** ▶定義 **3** 特に 英 (used about a person's hair, skin or eyes) brown or dark; not fair (人の髪, 肌, 目について) 茶色または黒色；金髪色白ではない➡黒みがかった，黒っぽい髪の，肌の浅黒い ‖ *She was small and dark with brown eyes.* 彼女は背が低く，黒っぽい髪，茶色の目をしていた．▶定義 **4** (名詞の前だけ) hidden and frightening; mysterious 隠されていて人をぎょっとさせるような；神秘的な➡隠された，秘密の，あいまいな ‖ *He seemed friendly, but there was a dark side to his character.* 彼は親しみやすく見えるが，その性格には隠された側面があった．▶定義 **5** (名詞の前だけ) sad; without hope 悲しい；希望のない➡暗い，陰うつな，悲観的な ‖ *the dark days of the recession* 不景気で陰うつな時代

*****dark**[2] /dɑːrk/ 名 [単数扱い] **the dark** ▶定義 the state of having no light 光がない状態➡闇(やみ)，暗がり ‖ *He's afraid of the dark.* 彼は暗闇が怖い．*Why are you sitting alone in the dark?* なぜ暗いところに1人で座っているの．

成句 **before/after dark** ▶定義 before /after the sun goes down in the evening 夕暮れの太陽が沈む前・後➡暗くならないうちに，夕方までに；暗くなってから，夜になってから

**(be/keep sb) in the dark (about sth)** ▶定義 (be/keep sb) in a position of not knowing about sth 〜について知らない状態 (〜がその状態である・〜をその状態にしておく)➡〜を秘密にしておく；〜について知らないでいる ‖ *Don't keep me in the dark. Tell me!* 私に秘密にしないで，話してください．

**darken** /dɑ́ːrk(ə)n/ 動 自 他 ▶定義 to become or to make sth darker 〜が暗くなる，または〜を暗くする➡暗く・黒くなる；〜を暗く・黒くする ‖ *The sky suddenly darkened and it started to rain.* 空が突然暗くなり，雨が降り出した．

**dark glasses** = SUNGRASSES

**darkness** /dɑ́ːrknəs/ 名 U ▶定義 the state of being dark 暗い状態➡暗さ，暗闇(やみ)，暗黒 ‖ *We sat in total darkness, waiting for the lights to come back on.* 再び明かりがつくのを待ちながら，私たちは真っ暗闇の中に座っていた．

**darkroom** /dɑ́ːrkrùːm, -rùm/ 名 C ▶定義 a room that can be made completely dark so that film can be taken out of a camera and photographs can be produced there フィルムをカメラから取り出して写真を現像するために，真っ暗にできる部屋➡暗室

**darling** /dɑ́ːrlɪŋ/ 名 C ▶定義 a word that you say to sb you love 愛する〜に呼び掛ける言葉➡あなた，お前

**darn** /dɑːrn/ 動 自 他 ▶定義 to repair a hole in clothes by sewing across it in one direction and then in the other 一方向にそして次には別の方向に穴の全体にわたって縫って，衣服の穴を繕う➡(ほころび・穴などを)繕う，かがる ‖ *I hate darning socks.* 靴下を繕うのは嫌だ．

**dart**[1] /dɑːrt/ 名 ▶定義 **1** C an object like a small arrow. It is thrown in a game or shot as a weapon. 小さな矢のような物．ゲームで，または武器として投げられる➡投げ矢，投げやり ‖ *The keeper fired a tranquillizer dart into the tiger to send it to sleep.* トラを眠らせるために，飼育係は鎮静剤を付けた投げやりをトラ目掛けて放った．▶定義 **2 darts** U a game in which you throw darts at a round board with numbers on it (**a dartboard**) 数字が書かれた円い盤(ダートボード)に投げ矢を投げるゲーム➡ダーツ，投げ矢遊び

**dart**² /dɑːrt/ 動 自他 ▶定義 to move or make sth move suddenly and quickly in a certain direction ある方向へ突然素早く動く,または〜を動かす→さっと動く,突進する;(視線など)を投げ掛ける ‖ *A rabbit darted across the field.* ウサギはさっと野原を横切った. *She darted an angry glance at me.* 彼女は怒って私をじろりとにらんだ.

**dash**¹ /dæʃ/ 名 ▶定義 1 [単数扱い]an act of going somewhere suddenly and quickly 突然素早く,どこかへ向かう行動→突進(すること),突撃 ‖ *Suddenly the prisoner made a dash for the door.* 突然,囚人はドアに突進した. ▶定義 2 [C, 通常は単数]a small amount of sth that you add to sth else ほかの〜に追加する,少量の…→少量,(少量の)混ぜ物 ‖ *a dash of lemon juice* レモン汁少々 ▶定義 3 Ca small horizontal line (-) used in writing, especially for adding extra information 特に補足情報を追加するために,文中で使われる短い横線→ダッシュ(-の記号) ☛参 **hyphen**

**dash**² /dæʃ/ 動 ▶定義 1 自to go somewhere suddenly and quickly 突然素早くどこかへ行く→(短い距離を)突進する ‖ *We all dashed for shelter when it started to rain.* 雨が降り出した時,私たちは皆雨宿りの場所を目掛けて突進した. *I must dash - I'm late.* すぐ行かないと － 時間に遅れているので. ▶定義 2 自他 to hit sth with great force; to throw sth so that it hits sth else very hard 強い力で〜を打つ; ほかの〜にとても強く当たるように…を投げる→(波などが)打ち付ける,たたき付ける; 〜をたたき付ける,投げ付ける ‖ *She dashed her racket to the ground.* 彼女は自分のラケットを地面にたたき付けた.

成句 **dash sb's hopes (of sth/of doing sth)** ▶定義 to completely destroy sb's hopes of doing sth 〜をしたいという…の希望を完全に打ち砕く→希望をくじく・打ち砕く,(人を)がっかりさせる ‖ *The accident dashed his hopes of becoming a pianist.* その事故は,ピアニストになりたいという彼の夢を打ち砕いた.

句動詞 **dash sth off** ▶定義 to write or draw sth very quickly 〜をとても素早く書く→(手紙・絵など)をさっと書き上げる ‖ *I dashed off a note to my boss and left.* 私は上司あてにメモをさっと書いて,出た.

### date 415

**dashboard** /dǽʃbɔːrd/ 名 C ▶定義 the part in a car in front of the driver where most of the switches, etc are ほとんどのスイッチなどがある,自動車の運転席の正面の部分→(自動車・飛行機などの)ダッシュボード,計器盤 ☛ S7ページのさし絵

★**data** /déɪtə, dάː-, dǽtə/ 名 [U, 複数扱い] ▶定義 facts or information 事実または情報→資料,データ,情報 ‖ *to gather/collect data* 情報を集める *data capture/retrieval (= ways of storing and looking at information on a computer)* データの取り込み・検索(＝コンピューター上に情報を蓄えて見る方法)

**database** /déɪtəbèɪs, dάː-, dǽtə-/ 名 C ▶定義 a large amount of data that is stored in a computer and can easily be used, added to, etc コンピューターに蓄えられ,簡単に利用,追加などができる,ばく大な量のデータ→データベース

★**date**¹ /déɪt/ 名 ▶定義 1 Ca particular day of the month or year その月またはその年の特定の日→日付,年月日 ‖ *What's the date today?/What date is it today?/What's today's date?* 今日は何日ですか. *What's your date of birth?* あなたの生年月日はいつですか. *We'd better fix a date for the next meeting.* 次の会議の日取りを決めた方が良いでしょう. ▶定義 2 [単数扱い]a particular time 特定の日時→(物事の起こる)日時,日取り ‖ *We can discuss this at a later date.* これについては後日話し合いましょう. ☛参 **sell-by date** ▶定義 3 Can arrangement to meet sb, especially a boyfriend or girlfriend 〜,特にボーイフレンドまたはガールフレンドと会う予定→会う約束,(異性との)デート ‖ *Shall we make a date to have lunch together?* 昼食を一緒にしませんか. *I've got a date with Roxanne on Friday night.* 金曜日の夜に,ロクサンとデートがある. ☛参 **blind date** ▶定義 4 Ca small, sweet, dark brown fruit that comes from a tree which grows in hot countries 熱帯の国々に育つ木からとれる,小さくて甘い暗褐色の果実→ナツメヤシの実 ☛ C3ページのさし絵

成句 **out of date** ▶定義 1 not fashionable; no longer useful 流行後れの; もはや役に立たない→時代後れの,旧式の ‖ *out-of-date meth-*

ods/machinery 時代後れの方式・旧式の機械 ▶定義2 no longer able to be used もはや使用できない→**期限切れの** ‖ *I must renew my passport. It's out of date.* 私のパスポートを更新しなければならない. 期限が切れている.

to date 正式 ▶定義 until now 今まで→**現在までに** ‖ *We've had very few complaints to date.* 現在までのところ, 苦情はほとんどない.

up to date ▶定義1 completely modern 完全に最新の→**最新(式)の** ‖ *The new kitchen will be right up to date, with all the latest gadgets.* 新しい台所は完全に最新式で, すべて最新の器機が備えられます. ▶定義2 with all the latest information; having done everything that you should すべて最新の情報で; すべき事はすべてしていて→**最新情報の入った;(仕事などが)仕上がって** ‖ *In this report we'll bring you up to date with the latest news from the area.* この番組では, 地域の最新ニュースと共に最新情報を皆様にお届けします.

\*__date__² /déɪt/ 動 ▶定義1 ⓗ to discover or guess how old sth is ～がどのくらい古いかを見いだす, または推定する→**～の年代を定める・突き止める** ‖ *The skeleton has been dated at about 3000 BC.* その骸骨(がいこつ)は, 紀元前3000年ころのものと推定された. ▶定義2 ⓗ to write the day's date on sth ～にその日の日付を書く→**(手紙などに)日付を入れる** ‖ *The letter is dated 24 March, 2000.* その手紙は, 2000年3月24日付だ. ▶定義3 ⓘⓗ to seem, or to make sb/sth seem, unfashionable 時代後れに見える, または～を時代後れに見えるようにする→**時代・流行後れになる, 古臭くなる; ～を時代・流行後れにする, 古臭くする** ‖ *We chose a simple style so that it wouldn't date as quickly.* すぐ流行後れにならないように, 私たちはシンプルなスタイルを選んだ.

句動詞 date back to...; date from... ▶定義 to have existed since... ～以来存在している→**(ある時代に)さかのぼる;(ある時代から)始まる** ‖ *The house dates back to the seventeenth century.* この家は17世紀に建てられたものである. *photographs dating from before the war* 戦前に撮られた写真

__dated__ /déɪtɪd/ 形 ▶定義 unfashionable 時代後れの→**時代・流行後れの, 旧式の** ‖ *This sort of jacket looks rather dated now.* このタイプの上着は今ではかなり流行後れに見える.

\*__daughter__ /dɔ́ːtər/ 名 ⓒ ▶定義 a female child 女の子供→**娘** ‖ *I have two sons and one daughter.* 私には2人の息子と1人の娘がいる. *Janet's daughter is a doctor.* ジャネットの娘は医者だ.

__daughter-in-law__ 名 ⓒ (複 __daughters-in-law__) ▶定義 the wife of your son 息子の妻→**嫁**

__daunt__ /dɔ́ːnt/ 動 ⓗ (通常は受動態で) ▶定義 to frighten or to worry sb by being too big or difficult 大きすぎる, またはあまりに難しいために, ～をおびえさせる, または心配させる→**～を威圧する,(決心などを)くじく, ひるませる** ‖ *Don't be daunted by all the controls - in fact it's a simple machine to use.* どの制御装置にもひるむことはないよ － 実際には簡単に使える機械なのだから. — __daunting__ 形→**(仕事などが)やる気をなくさせる, 困難な** ‖ *a daunting task* 困難な任務

__dawdle__ /dɔ́ːdl/ 動 ⓘ ▶定義 to go somewhere very slowly とてもゆっくりどこかへ行く→**ぶらぶら歩く** ‖ *Stop dawdling! We've got to be there by two.* ぶらぶら歩くな. 2時までに着かなくてはならないのだ.

__dawn__¹ /dɔ́ːn/ 名 ▶定義1 ⓤⓒ the early morning, when light first appears in the sky 早朝, 最初の光が空に現れる時→**夜明け, 暁, あけぼの** ‖ *before/at dawn* 夜明け前に・明け方に *Dawn was breaking (= it was starting to get light) as I set off to work.* 私が職場に向かう時, 夜が明けようとしていた(= 明るくなり始めるところだった). ▶定義2 [単数扱い] the beginning 始まり→**(事の)始まり, 兆し** ‖ *the dawn of civilization* 文明の誕生

成句 the crack of dawn ⇒ __CRACK__²

__dawn__² /dɔ́ːn/ 動 ⓘ ▶定義1 正式 to begin to grow light, after the night 夜の後に, 光が増し始める→**夜が明ける, 空が白む** ‖ *The day dawned bright and cold.* 明るく寒い夜明けがきた. (比喩) *A new era of peace is dawning.* 新しい平和な時代が始まる. ▶定義2 dawn (on sb) to become clear (to sb) (～に)明らかになる→**(事実などが)(人に)分かり始める** ‖ *Suddenly it dawned on her. 'Of course!' she said. 'You're Mike's brother!'* 突然彼女には分かった. 「もちろん」と

彼女は言った.「あなたはマイクの兄弟ね」

\***day** /déɪ/ 名 定義1 ⒞a period of 24 hours. Seven days make up a week. 24 時間の期間. 7日で1週間となる→日, 1日 ‖ 'What day is it today?' 'Tuesday.' 「今日は何曜日ですか.」「火曜日です」 We went to Italy for ten days. 私たちはイタリアに10日間行った. We're meeting again the day after tomorrow/in two days' time. 明後日にまたお会いしましょう. The next/following day I saw Mark again. その翌日, またマークに会った. I'd already spoken to him the day before/the previous day. その前日, 私は彼に既に話していた. I have to take these pills twice a day. 私は, これらの丸薬を1日2回飲まなくてはならない. I work six days a week. Sunday's my day off (= when I do not work). 私は週6日働いています. 日曜日が休み(= 私が働かない日)です. 定義2 ⒞Ⓤthe time when the sky is light; not night 空が明るい間; 夜でない→昼間, 日中 ‖ The days were warm but the nights were freezing. 日中は暖かかったが, 夜は凍るような寒さだった. It's been raining all day (long). 一日中雨が降った. Owls sleep **by day** (= during the day) and hunt at night. フクロウは昼間(= 日中)眠り, 夜間に獲物を狩る. 定義3 ⒞the hours of the day when you work あなたが1日に働く時間→1日の労働時間 ‖ She's expected to work a seven-hour day. 彼女は1日に7時間働くことを期待されている. 定義4 ⒞(または **days**)a particular period of time in the past 過去における特定の期間→時代, 時世 ‖ in Shakespeare's day シェークスピアの時代に There weren't so many cars in those days その当時は, それほどたくさんの車はなかった.

成句 **at the end of the day** ⇒ **END**[1]
**break of day** ⇒ **BREAK**[2]
**call it a day** ⇒ **CALL**[1]

**day by day** 定義 every day; as time passes 毎日; 時が過ぎると共に→日に日に, 日ごとに ‖ Day by day, she was getting a little bit stronger. 日に日に, 彼女は少しずつ強くなっていった.

**day in, day out** 定義 every day, without any change 何の変化もなしに, 毎日→来る日も来る日も, 明けても暮れても ‖ He sits at his desk working, day in, day out. 来る日も来る日も, 彼は机に向かって仕事をする.

**day-to-day** 定義 happening as a normal part of each day; usual 日々の当たり前のこととして起こる; いつも→日々の, 毎日の, 日常の

**from day to day; from one day to the next** 定義 within a short period of time 短い期間内に→日々, その日その日で; 翌日にはもう, (少し)先には ‖ Things change so quickly that we never know what will happen from one day to the next. 物事があまりにも速く変化するので, 私たちにはその日その日で何が起こるのか全く分からない.

**have a field day** ⇒ **FIELD DAY**
**it's early days (yet)** ⇒ **EARLY**

**make sb's day** 略式 定義 to make sb very happy ～をとても幸せにさせる→～にとってうれしい日とする, ～をとても喜ばす

**one day; some day** 定義 at some time in the future 未来のいつかに→いつか, いつの日にか, そのうちに ‖ Some day we'll go back and see all our old friends. そのうちに私たちは帰って, 昔なじみの友人たちみんなに会うだろう.

**the other day** 定義 a few days ago; recently 2, 3日前に; 最近→先日, この間 ‖ I bumped into him in town the other day. 先日, 町で彼に偶然出会った.

**the present day** ⇒ **PRESENT**[1]

**these days** 定義 in the present age; nowadays 今の時代に; このごろは→近ごろは, 最近は

**daybreak** /déɪbreɪk/ 名 Ⓤ 定義 the time in the early morning when light first appears; dawn 早朝の光が最初に現れる時; 夜明け→夜明け

**daydream** /déɪdriːm/ 名 ⒞ 定義 thoughts that are not connected with what you are doing; often pleasant scenes in your imagination 今している事とは関連のない考え; 空想の, しばしば楽しい場面→(楽しい)空想, 夢想, 白昼夢 ‖ The child stared out of the window, lost in a daydream. その子供は窓の外をじっと見詰め, 空想にふけった. — **daydream** 動 ⒤ 空想にふける ‖ Don't just sit there daydreaming - do some work! そこにただ座って空想にふけっているのはやめて - 何か仕事をしなさい.

**daylight** /déɪlaɪt/ 名 Ⓤ 定義 the light that there is during the day 日中の光→日光, 昼間, 日中 ‖ The colours look quite different in

**daylight**. 日光の下では、色がとても違って見える. *daylight hours* 昼間の時間
成句 **broad daylight** ⇒ **BROAD**

**day return** 名 ⓒ 因 ▶定義 a train or bus ticket for going somewhere and coming back on the same day. It is cheaper than a normal return ticket. 同じ日に、ある場所へ行って戻ってくるための電車、またはバスの切符. 普通の往復切符よりも安い→当日往復割引切符

**daytime** /déɪtàɪm/ 名 Ⓤ ▶定義 the time when it is light; not night 明るい時間; 夜ではない→昼間、日中 ‖ *These flowers open in the daytime and close again at night.* これらの花は、日中開花して夜間はまた閉じる. *daytime TV* 昼間のテレビ

**daze** /déɪz/ 名
成句 **in a daze** ▶定義 unable to think or react normally; confused 正常に考えるまたは反応することができない; 困惑した→困惑して、混乱して

**dazed** /déɪzd/ 形 ▶定義 unable to think or react normally; confused 正常に考えるまたは反応することができない; 困惑した(ショック・打撃などで)気が遠くなった、ぼうっとなった; 困惑した ‖ *He had a dazed expression on his face.* 彼はぼうっとした顔をしていた.

**dazzle** /dǽz(ə)l/ 動 他 (通常は受動態で)
▶定義1 (used about a bright light) to make sb unable to see for a short time (明るい光について)短時間、~の目を見えなくさせる→~の目をくらませる、目を回させる ‖ *She was dazzled by the other car's headlights.* 彼女は対向車のヘッドライトで目がくらんだ. ▶定義2 to impress sb very much ~にとても強い印象を与える→(技術・特質・美などが)~を圧倒する、感嘆させる ‖ *He had been dazzled by her beauty.* 彼は彼女の美しさに目を奪われていた. — **dazzling** 形 →目のくらむような、まぶしい ‖ *a dazzling light* まぶしい光

★**dead**¹ /déd/ 形 ▶定義1 no longer alive もう生きていない→死んだ、死んでいる、(植物が)枯れた ‖ *My father's dead. He died two years ago.* 私の父はいない. 2年前に死んだ. *Police found a dead body under the bridge.* 警察は橋の下で死体を発見した. *The man was shot dead by a masked gunman.* その男性は、覆面をして鉄砲を持った男に射殺された. *dead leaves* 枯れ葉
☛ 名 **death** 動 **die** ▶定義2 no longer used; finished もはや使用されない; 終わりになった→(物が)使われていない、すたれた ‖ *Latin is a dead language.* ラテン語は死語である. ⇨ **living**
▶定義3 (名詞の前は不可) (used about a part of the body) no longer able to feel anything (身体の一部分について)もはや何も感じられない→感覚のない、まひした ‖ *Oh no, my foot's gone dead. I was sitting on it for too long.* 嫌だ、足がしびれた. 足を曲げて長く座りすぎた. ▶定義4 (名詞の前は不可) (used about a piece of equipment) no longer working (設備の1つについて)もはや機能しない→機能しない、用をなさない ‖ *I picked up the telephone but the line was dead.* 受話器を取ったが、電話は通じていなかった. *This battery's dead.* この電池は寿命が切れている. ▶定義5 without movement, activity or interest 動き、活動、または興味がない→活気・活動のない、静まり返った、つまらない、退屈な ‖ *This town is completely dead after 11 o'clock at night.* この街は、夜の11時を過ぎると完全に静まり返る. ▶定義6 (名詞の前だけ) complete or exact 完全な、または正確な→全くの、完全な ‖ *a dead silence/calm* 完全な静けさ *The arrow hit the dead centre of the target.* 矢は、的のど真ん中に当たった.

成句 **a dead end** ▶定義1 a street that is only open at one end 片一方からだけ行き来できる道→行き止まり、袋小路 ▶定義2 a point, situation, etc from which you can make no further progress それ以上進展させられない段階、状況など→(仕事などの)行き詰まり、窮地 ‖ *a dead-end job* (= one that offers no chance of promotion) 将来性のない職 (= 昇進の機会が提供されないもの)

**drop dead** ⇒ **DROP**¹

**dead**² /déd/ **the dead** 名 [複数扱い]
▶定義 people who have died 死んだ人々→死者 ‖ *A church service was held in memory of the dead.* 死者を追悼して、礼拝式が行われた.
成句 **in the dead of night** ▶定義 in the middle of the night, when it is very dark and quiet とても暗くて静かな、真夜中に→真夜中に

**dead**³ /déd/ 副 ▶定義 completely, exactly or very→全く、正確に、非常に ‖ *The car made a strange noise and then stopped dead.* 車は変

な音を立て,そしてぱったりと止まった. *He's dead keen to start work.* 彼は仕事を非常に始めたがっている.

**deaden** /déd(ə)n/ 動他 ▶定義 to make sth less strong, painful, etc ～の強さ, 痛みなどを少なくする→～を弱くする, 和らげる ‖ *They gave her drugs to try and deaden the pain.* 彼らは彼女に麻薬を与えて, 痛みを和らげようとした.

**dead heat** 名 C ▶定義 the result of a race when two people, etc finish at exactly the same time 2人などがまさに同時に終えた競技の結果→同着(のレース), 引き分け(の試合)

**deadline** /dédlàin/ 名 C ▶定義 a time or date before which sth must be done or finished その前に～がなされて, または完成されていなければならない時間, または日→(原稿・仕事などの)締め切り(時間), 最終期限 ‖ *I usually set myself a deadline when I have a project to do.* やるべき研究課題があるとき, 私は大抵自分自身で締め切りを設定する. *A journalist is used to having to meet deadlines.* ジャーナリストは, 締め切りを守ることには慣れている.

**deadlock** /dédlàk/ 名[単数扱い, U] ▶定義 a situation in which two sides cannot reach an agreement 2者が合意に到達できない状況→(交渉などの)行き詰まり ‖ *Talks have reached (a) deadlock.* 会談はこう着状態になった. *to try to break the deadlock* 行き詰まりを打開しようとする

**deadly** /dédli/ 形副 (**deadlier**; **deadliest**) ▶定義 1 causing or likely to cause death 死を引き起こす, または引き起こしそうな→致命的な, 命にかかわる ‖ *a deadly poison/weapon/disease* 命取りになる毒物・凶器・致命的な病気 ▶定義 2 very great; complete とても重大な; 完全な→すごい, 命懸けの ‖ *They're deadly enemies.* 彼らは不倶戴天(ふぐたいてん)の敵だ. ▶定義 3 completely; extremely 完全に; 極端に→ひどく, 極度に ‖ *I'm not joking. In fact I'm deadly serious.* 私は冗談を言っているのではない. 実際, 大まじめだ. ▶定義 4 extremely accurate, so that no defence is possible とても正確なので, 防御することは不可能だ→(ねらいが)正確な ‖ *That player is deadly when he gets in front of the goal.* あの選手は, ゴール前にたどり着ければ, 正確にシュートを決める.

**deadpan** /dédpæn/ 形 ▶定義 without any expression on your face or in your voice 顔または声に, 何の感情も表さないで→(感情を隠して)ポーカーフェースの, 無表情な ‖ *He told the joke with a completely deadpan face.* 彼は全く無表情で, その冗談を言った.

★**deaf** /déf/ 形 ▶定義 1 unable to hear anything or unable to hear very well 全く耳が聞こえない, またはほとんど耳が聞こえない→耳が聞こえない, 耳の不自由な, 耳が遠い ‖ *You'll have to speak louder. My father's a bit deaf.* もっと大きな声で話す必要があります. 父は少し耳が遠いのです. *to go deaf* 耳が聞こえなくなる ▶定義 2 **the deaf** 名[複数扱い] people who cannot hear 耳が聞こえない人々→耳の不自由な人々 ▶定義 3 **deaf to sth** not wanting to listen to sth ～を聞きたいと思っていない→聞こうとしない, ～に耳を傾けない, 耳を貸さない ‖ *I've told her what I think but she's deaf to my advice.* 私が考えている事を彼女に話したのだが, 彼女は私の忠告を聞こうとしない. ― **deafness** 名 U →耳が聞こえないこと, (人の言葉に)耳を貸さないこと

**deafen** /déf(ə)n/ 動他 (通常は受動態で) ▶定義 to make sb unable to hear by making a very loud noise とても大きな騒音を立てて, ～を聞こえなくさせる→～の耳を聞こえなくする, 耳をつんざく ‖ *We were deafened by the loud music.* 騒々しい音楽で, 私たちの耳が聞こえなくなった. ― **deafening** 形 →耳をつんざくような ‖ *deafening music* 耳をつんざくような音楽

★**deal**¹ /díːl/ 動 (過, 過分 **dealt** /délt/) ▶定義 1 自他 **deal (sth) (out); deal (sth) (to sb)** to give cards to players in a game of cards トランプ遊びをする人に札を配る→カードを配る; ～を配る ‖ *Start by dealing seven cards to each player.* 競技者たちに7枚ずつカードを配って, ゲームを始めなさい. ▶定義 2 自 **deal (in sth); deal (with sb)** to do business, especially buying and selling goods 商売をする, 特に商品の売買を行う→(品物を)商う, 扱う; (会社・人と)取り引きする ‖ *He deals in second-hand cars.* 彼は中古車を商っている. *Our firm deals with customers all over the world.* 我々の会社は, 世界中の顧客と取り引きしている. ▶定義 3 自他 略式 to buy and sell illegal drugs 違法な麻薬の売買をする→麻薬を扱う, 麻薬を密売する

## 420 deal²

**成句** deal sb/sth a blow; deal a blow to sb/sth ▶定義1 to hit sb/sth ~を打つ→~に打撃を与える ‖ He was dealt a nasty blow to the head in the accident. 彼は事故で頭部をひどく打った. ▶定義2 to give sb a shock, etc ~に衝撃などを与える→~に精神的打撃を与える ‖ This news dealt a terrible blow to my father. このニュースは父にとって大きなショックだった.

**句動詞** deal sth out ▶定義 to give sth to a number of people ~を複数の人に与える→~を分配する, 分ける ‖ The profits will be dealt out among us. 利益は我々の間で分配される.

deal with sb ▶定義 to treat sb in a particular way; to handle sb 特定のやり方で~を扱う; ~をうまく扱う→~を扱う, 待遇する ‖ He's a difficult man. Nobody quite knows how to deal with him. 彼は気難しい. 彼とどう接したらよいのか, だれにもよく分からない.

deal with sth ▶定義1 to take suitable action in a particular situation in order to solve a problem, complete a task, etc; to handle sth 問題を解決する, または仕事を完成するなどのために, 特定の状況の下で適切な行動を取る; ~をうまく扱う→~を処理する, ~に対処する, 対応する ‖ My secretary will deal with my correspondence while I'm away. 私の留守中は, 私の秘書が私への連絡に対応する. ▶定義2 to have sth as its subject ~を主題として取り上げる→~を扱う, 論じる ‖ This chapter deals with letter-writing. この章では, 手紙の書き方を取り上げます.

★**deal²** /diːl/ 🅑 🅒 ▶定義1 an agreement or arrangement, especially in business 特に仕事上の, 契約, または協定→取り引き, 契約 ‖ We're hoping to **do a deal** with an Italian company. イタリアの会社と取り引きをしたいと思っています. Let's **make a deal** not to criticize each other's work. お互いの仕事を批判しないという取り引きをしよう. 'I'll help you with your essay if you'll fix my bike.' 'OK, **it's a deal!**' 「私の自転車を直してくれたら, 君の論文を手伝うよ」「よし, それで決まりだ.」 ▶定義2 the way that sb is treated ~が扱われているやり方→取り扱い, 待遇 ‖ With high fares and unreliable services, rail users are **getting a raw deal**. 高い運賃といいかげんな運行状況で, 列車の利用者はひどい扱いを受けている. The new law aims to give pensioners **a fair deal**. 新しい法律は, 年金受給者を公平に扱うことをねらいとしている. ▶定義3 the action of giving cards to players in a card game トランプ遊びで, 競技者に札を配る行為→トランプを配ること, 配る番

**成句** a big deal/no big deal ⇒ **BIG**

a good/great deal (of sth) ▶定義 a lot (of sth) たくさん(の~)→相当な量(の~), 非常にたくさん(の~) ‖ I've spent a great deal of time on this report. 私はこの報告書にとても長い時間を費やした.

**dealer** /díːlər/ 🅒 ▶定義1 a person whose business is buying and selling things 物の売買を仕事としている人→業者, 販売人, ~商 ‖ a dealer in gold and silver 金銀の業者 a drug dealer 麻薬の売人 ▶定義2 the person who gives the cards to the players in a game of cards トランプ遊びで, 札を競技者に配る人→札を配る人, 親

**dealing** /díːlɪŋ/ 🅒 ▶定義1 dealings [複数扱い] relations, especially in business 特に商売上の, 関係→取り引き, 商取引 ‖ We had some dealings with that firm several years ago. あの会社とは数年前にいくつか取り引きがあった. ▶定義2 🅤 buying and selling 売買→取り引きのやり方 ‖ share dealing 株の売買

**dealt** DEAL¹ の過去・過去分詞形

★**dear¹** /dɪər/ 🅕 ▶定義1 used at the beginning of a letter before the name or title of the person you are writing to あなたがあてて書いている人の名前または肩書きの前の, 手紙の書き出しに用いて→親愛なる~様, 拝啓 ‖ Dear Sarah, ... 親愛なるサラ様, ... Dear Sir or Madam, ... 拝啓... ▶定義2 dear (to sb) loved by or important to sb ~の愛する, または大切な→親愛な, いとしい, 大切な, 貴重な ‖ It was a subject that was very dear to him. それは彼にとって非常に大事な問題だった. She's one of my dearest friends. 彼女は私の最も大切な友人の1人です. ▶定義3 🇬🇧 expensive 高価な→(商品が)高価な, 高い ‖ How can people afford to smoke when cigarettes are so dear? たばこの値段がこんなに高いというのに, どうして人々は吸う余裕があるのだろうか.

**成句** close/dear/near to sb's heart ⇒

**dear**² /díər/ 副 ▶定義 1 used for expressing disappointment, sadness, surprise, etc 失望、悲しみ、驚きなどを表すために用いて→おや、まあ | *Dear me! Aren't you ready?* まあ、準備できていないの. ▶定義 2 (古) used when speaking to sb you know well よく知っている~に話し掛けるときに用いて→あなた、かわいい子、いい子 | *Would you like a cup of tea, dear?* あなた、お茶はいかがですか.

**dearly** /díərli/ 副 ▶定義 1 very much 非常に→非常に、とても | *I'd dearly like to go there again.* そこにまた行きたいと強く思っている. ▶定義 2 正式 in a way that causes damage or suffering, or costs a lot of money 損害または苦難をもたらす、あるいは多額のお金がかかる方法で→大きな犠牲を払って、高いものについて | *I've already paid dearly for that mistake.* あの間違いのために、私は既に大きな犠牲を払っている.

**dearth** /dəːrθ/ 名 [単数扱い] ▶定義 a dearth (of sb/sth) a lack of sth; not enough of sth ~の欠如; ~が十分にないこと→(~の)不足、欠如 | *There's a dearth of young people in the village.* その村には若者が足りない.

★**death** /deθ/ 名 ▶定義 1 ⓒⓊ the end of sb/sth's life; dying ~の生命の終わり; 死ぬこと→死、死ぬこと | *There were two deaths and many other people were injured in the accident.* その事故では2人が死亡し、大勢の人が負傷した. *The police do not know the **cause of death**.* 警察は死因が分からない. *There was no food and people were **starving to death**.* 食糧がなく、人々は餓死した. ☞ 形 **dead** 動 **die** ▶定義 2 Ⓤ the end (of sth) (~の)終わり→終わり、消滅 | *the death of communism* 共産主義の終焉(しゅうえん)

感句 catch your death ⇒ **CATCH**¹
a matter of life and/or death ⇒ **MATTER**¹
put sb to death (通常は受動態で) 正式 ▶定義 to kill sb as a punishment, in past times 過去において、罰として~を殺す→~を殺す、死刑にする
sick to death of sb/sth ⇒ **SICK**¹
sudden death ⇒ **SUDDEN**

**deathly** /déθli/ 形副 ▶定義 like death 死のような→死んだような、死を思わせる; 死んだように | *There was a deathly silence.* 死のような沈黙があった.

**death penalty** 名 [単数扱い] ▶定義 the legal punishment of being killed for a crime 犯罪を犯して処せられる、殺されるという法的な処置→死刑 ☞参 **capital punishment**

**death toll** 名 ⓒ ▶定義 the number of people killed in a disaster, war, accident, etc 災害、戦争、事故などで亡くなった人々の数→死亡者数、死亡者名簿

**debase** /dɪbéɪs/ 動他 (通常は受動態で) 正式 ▶定義 to reduce the quality or value of sth ~の品質または価値を落とす→~の品質・価値・人格・評判を落とす, (硬貨の)質を落とす

**debatable** /dɪbéɪtəb(ə)l/ 形 ▶定義 not certain; that you could argue about 確かではない; 議論し得る→疑わしい; 議論の余地がある | *It's debatable whether people have a better lifestyle these days.* 最近、人々の生活が良くなっているかどうかは、疑わしい.

**debate**¹ /dɪbéɪt/ 名 ▶定義 1 ⓒ a formal argument or discussion of a question at a public meeting or in Parliament 公開の場または議会での、問題についての正式な論争または討議→討論会、ディベート ▶定義 2 Ⓤ general discussion about sth expressing different opinions ~についていろいろな意見を述べる、一般の議論→討論、議論、論争 | *There's been a lot of debate about the cause of acid rain.* 酸性雨の原因については、多くの議論がなされてきた.

**debate**² /dɪbéɪt/ 動 ▶定義 1 自他 to discuss sth in a formal way or at a public meeting ~を正式に、または公の場で討論する→討論・討議する; ~を討論・討議する ▶定義 2 他 to think about or discuss sth before deciding what to do 何を行うか決める前に~について考える、または討議する→~を熟考する、慎重に考える | *They debated whether to go or not.* 彼らは行くかどうかを慎重に考えた.

**debit**¹ /débət/ 名 ⓒ ▶定義 an amount of money paid out of a bank account 銀行口座から支払われるお金の総額→借り方記入額, (口座からの)引き落とし ⇔ **credit**¹ ☞参 **direct debit**

**debit**² /débət/ 動他 ▶定義 to take an amount of money out of a bank account, etc usually as a payment; to record this 通常は支払いとして、

銀行口座などからお金を引き出す；これを記録する→引き落とす；(ある金額)を(人の口座の)借り方に記入する

**debris** /dəbríː, deɪ-, déɪbriː; déɪbriː, déb-/ 名 ❶ ▶定義 pieces from sth that has been destroyed, especially in an accident 特に事故で，破壊された～の断片→残骸(ざんがい)，がれき

*__debt__ /det/ 名 ▶定義 1 ❻ an amount of money that you owe to sb ～に借りているお金の総額→借金，負債 ‖ *She borrowed a lot of money and she's still paying off the debt.* 彼女は多額のお金を借り，いまだに返済している． ▶定義 2 ❶ the state of owing money 金を借りている状態→借金のある状態，借金状態 ‖ *After he lost his job, he got into debt.* 失業してから，彼は借金をした． ▶定義 3 [❻, 通常は単数] 正式 something that you owe sb, for example because he/she has helped or been kind to you 例えば人があなたを助けて，または親切にしていてくれるので，あなたがその～から恩恵を受けていること→義理，恩義，借り ‖ *In his speech he acknowledged his debt to his family and friends for their support.* 演説で彼は，家族と友人たちの支援のお陰であることを感謝した．

成句 __be in/out of debt__ ▶定義 to owe/not owe money お金を借りている・いない→借金している；借金をしていない

__be in sb's debt__ 正式 ▶定義 to feel grateful to sb for sth that he/she has done for you 自分のためにしてくれた～のために…に感謝する→～に恩義がある

**debtor** /détər/ 名 ❻ ▶定義 a person who owes money 金を借りている人→債務者，借り主

**début** (または **debut**) /déɪbjuː, déb-/ 名 ❻ ▶定義 a first appearance in public of an actor, etc 俳優などが，初めて公の場に出ること→デビュー，初出演，初舞台 ‖ *She __made__ her __début__ in London in 1959.* 彼女は1959年にロンドンでデビューした．

**Dec** 略 December→12月 ‖ *5 Dec 1999* 1999年12月5日

**decade** /dɪkéɪd, -əd, dékeɪd/ 名 ❻ ▶定義 a period of ten years 10年の期間→10年間

**decadence** /dékəd(ə)ns/ 名 ❶ ▶定義 behaviour, attitudes, etc that show low moral standards 道徳的基準の低さを示す振る舞い，態度など→堕落，衰退，退廃 ― __decadent__ /dékəd(ə)nt/ 形→衰退した，退廃的な ‖ *a decadent society* 退廃した社会

**decaffeinated** /diːkǽfənèɪtəd/ 形 ▶定義 (used about coffee or tea) with most or all of the substance that makes you feel awake and gives you energy (**caffeine**) removed (コーヒーまたは紅茶について)眠気を覚まし活力を与える物質(カフェイン)を大部分，またはすべて取り除いた→カフェイン抜きの

**decapitate** /dɪkǽpətèɪt/ 動 他 正式 ▶定義 to cut off a person's head 人の首を切り落とす→(刑罰で)首をはねる

*__decay__[1] /dɪkéɪ/ 動 自 ▶定義 1 to become bad or be slowly destroyed 悪くなる，またはゆっくりと損なわれていく→腐る，腐敗する，朽ちる ‖ *the decaying carcass of a dead sheep* 腐敗した羊の死体 ☛類 __rot__ ▶定義 2 to become weaker or less powerful 弱体化する，または勢力が衰える→(社会・制度などが)衰える，衰退する ‖ *His business empire began to decay.* 彼の巨大企業組織も衰退し始めた． ― __decayed__ 形→腐った，朽ちた，虫歯の ‖ *a decayed tooth* 虫歯

**decay**[2] /dɪkéɪ/ 名 ❶ ▶定義 the process or state of being slowly destroyed ゆっくりと損なわれていく過程，または状態→腐敗，腐食 ‖ *tooth decay* 虫歯 *The old farm was in a terrible state of decay.* その古い農場は，ひどい荒れ様だった．

**the deceased** /dɪsíːst/ 名 [単数扱い] 正式 ▶定義 a person who has died, especially one who has died recently 特に最近，亡くなった人→故人 ‖ *Many friends of the deceased were present at the funeral.* 故人の友人が多数，葬儀に参列した． ― __deceased__ 形→(最近)死去した，故～

**deceit** /dɪsíːt/ 名 ❶ ▶定義 dishonest behaviour; trying to make sb believe sth that is not true 不正直な振る舞い；事実ではない～を…に信じさせようとすること→欺く・だますこと，欺まん，詐欺(行為) ‖ *Their marriage eventually broke up because she was tired of his lies and deceit.* 彼女が夫のうそと欺まんにうんざりしたために，結婚は結局破局した．

**deceitful** /dɪsíːtfʊl, -f(ə)l/ 形 ▶定義 dishonest; trying to make sb believe sth that is not true 不正直な；事実ではない～を…に信じさせようと

する➜うそつきな, 人をだます, 不正直な ― deceitfully /-fʊli, -f(ə)li/ [副] ➜偽って ― deceitfulness [名] [U] ➜不正直

***deceive** /dɪsíːv/ [動][他] ▶定義 deceive sb/yourself (into doing sth) to try to make sb believe sth that is not true 事実ではない～を…に信じさせようとする➜～をだます, 欺く ‖ *He deceived his mother into believing that he had earned the money, not stolen it.* その金は自分が稼いだもので盗んだのではないと, 彼は母親をだまして信じ込ませた. *You're deceiving yourself if you think there's an easy solution to the problem.* その問題に対する簡単な解決策があると思っているのなら, それはあなたの思い違いだ. ☛ [名] deception, deceit

***December** /dɪsémbər/ [名] [U] [C] ([略] Dec) ▶定義 the twelfth month of the year, coming after November 11月の次に来る, 1年の12番目の月➜12月 ☛ 文中での月の表し方については, January の例と注を参照.

**decency** /díːs(ə)nsi/ [名] [U] ▶定義 moral or correct behaviour 道徳的または礼節にかなった振る舞い➜(言葉･振る舞い･服装などが)きちんとしていること, 礼儀正しさ ‖ *She **had the decency to** admit that it was her fault.* それは自分の誤りだと認める礼節を, 彼女はわきまえていた.

**decent** /díːs(ə)nt/ [形] ▶定義1 being of an acceptable standard; satisfactory 容認できる水準の; 満足できる➜かなり良い, 満足できる ‖ *All she wants is a decent job with decent wages.* 彼女の望みは, 満足できる給料がもらえるような, 満足できる仕事だけである. ▶定義2 (used about people or behaviour) honest and fair; treating people with respect (人々または振る舞いについて) 正直で公正な; 敬意を持って人々に接する➜(社会的に)きちんとした, まともな, 礼儀をわきまえた ▶定義3 not likely to offend or shock sb ～に不快感またはショックを与えそうもない➜(身なり･振る舞いが)ちゃんとした, 見苦しくない, 適切な ‖ *I can't come to the door, I'm not decent (= I'm not dressed).* ドアの外に出られません. ちゃんとした格好をしていない (= 服を着ていない) ので. ⇔ **indecent** ― decently [副] ➜見苦しくなく, きちんと

**deception** /dɪsépʃ(ə)n/ [名] [C] [U] ▶定義 making sb believe or being made to believe sth that is not true 事実ではない～を…に信じさせること, あるいは信じさせられること➜だますこと, ごまかし(行為), ペテン ‖ *He had obtained the secret papers **by deception**.* 彼はだまして, 秘密文書を手に入れた. ☛ [動] deceive

**deceptive** /dɪséptɪv/ [形] ▶定義 likely to give a false impression or to make sb believe sth that is not true 誤った印象を与えそうな, 事実ではない～を…に信じさせそうな➜人を欺く･惑わすような, 当てにならない ‖ *The water is deceptive. It's much deeper than it looks.* 水は人を欺く. 見掛けよりもずっと深い. ― deceptively [副] ➜人を欺くように, 惑わすように, 一見したところでは ‖ *She made the task sound deceptively easy.* 彼女は, その仕事を一見したところでは簡単そうに思わせた.

**decibel** /désəbèl, -bəl/ [名] [C] ▶定義 a measurement of how loud a sound is 音量を計る単位➜デシベル(音の強さの単位)

***decide** /dɪsáɪd/ [動] ▶定義1 [自][他] decide (to do sth); decide against (doing) sth; decide about/on sth; decide that... to think about two or more possibilities and choose one of them 2つまたはそれより多い可能性について検討し, それらのうち1つを選ぶ➜～しようと決心する, ～を決める, (最終的に)～と判断する ‖ *There are so many to choose from - I can't decide!* 選択肢がたくさんありすぎる ― 私には決められない. *We've decided not to invite Isabel.* 私たちはイザベルを招待しないことに決めた. *She decided against borrowing the money.* 彼女はお金を借りないことに決めた. *They decided on a name for the baby.* 彼らは赤ちゃんの名前を決めた. *He decided that it was too late to go.* 彼は, 行くには遅すぎると判断した. *The date hasn't been decided yet.* 日にちはまだ決まっていない. ▶定義2 [他] to influence sth so that it produces a particular result 特定の結果が生じるように, ～に影響を与える➜～を決定する, 決める ‖ *Your votes will decide the winner.* あなたの投票が受賞者を決める. ▶定義3 [他] to cause sb to make a decision➜～に決心させる ‖ *What finally decided you to leave?* 何がきっかけになって, あなたは出発する決心をしたのですか. ☛ [名] decision [形] decisive

D

## 424 decided

> **▶音声とつづり字**
>
> decide と decision とは母音が違う
>
> decide + ion の場合は d が摩擦音の s[z] になり、e の前の母音 i が[aɪ]から[ɪ]になります。これを母音短縮化現象とも言います。この現象は次のように広範囲で認められます。
>
> 例: admire[aɪ] > admiration[ə]
> crisis[aɪ] > critical[ɪ]
> describe[aɪ] > description[ɪ]
> divide[aɪ] > division[ɪ]
> deep[iː] > depth[e]
> wide[aɪ] > width[ɪ]
> pronounce[aʊ] > pronunciation[ʌ]
> south[aʊ] > southern[ʌ]
> type[aɪ] > typical[ɪ]

**decided** /dɪsáɪdəd/ 形 ▶定義 clear; definite 明らかな; 確かな➡**明らかな、はっきりとした、決定的な** ‖ *There has been a decided improvement in his work.* 彼の作品には、明らかな進歩が見られる. ⇔**undecided** — **decidedly** ➡はっきりと、明確に

**deciduous** /dɪsídʒuəs/ 形 ▶定義 (used about a tree) of a type that loses its leaves every autumn (樹木について)秋になると葉を落とす種類の➡**落葉性の** ☛参 **evergreen**

**decimal**¹ /dés(ə)məl/ 形 ▶定義 based on or counted in units of ten 10 を単位として基礎を置いて、または数えて➡**10進法の** ‖ *decimal currency* 10進制通貨

**decimal**² /dés(ə)məl/ 名 C ▶定義 part of a number, written after a kind of full stop (**decimal point**) 一種のピリオド(小数点)の後に書かれる、数値の一部分➡**小数** ‖ *Three quarters expressed as a decimal is 0.75.* 4分の3を小数で表すと、0.75である.

**decipher** /dɪsáɪfər/ 動 他 ▶定義 to succeed in reading or understanding sth that is not clear 明瞭(めいりょう)でない~を読む、または理解することに成功する➡**(暗号など)を解読する、~を判読する** ‖ *It's impossible to decipher his handwriting.* 彼の書いた字を判読することは不可能だ.

★**decision** /dɪsíʒ(ə)n/ 名 ▶定義 1 C U *a decision (to do sth); a decision on/about sth; a decision that...* a choice or judgement that you make after thinking about various possibilities いろいろな可能性について考えた後に行う選択または判断➡**決定(すること)、決心、解決** ‖ *Have you made a decision yet?* もう決心はついたのですか. *I realize now that I made the wrong decision.* 今になって、自分が間違った決定をしたことが分かる. *There were good reasons for his decision to leave.* 出発するという彼の決定には、もっともな理由があった. *I took the decision that I believed to be right.* 私は、自分で正しいと信じる決断をした. ▶定義 2 U being able to decide clearly and quickly 明瞭(めいりょう)で迅速に決断できる➡**決断力、果断** ‖ *We are looking for someone with decision for this job.* 私たちは、この仕事のために決断力のある人を探している. ☛動 **decide**

**decisive** /dɪsáɪsɪv/ 形 ▶定義 1 making sth certain or final 確実なまたは最終的な~にする➡**決定的な、決め手となる** ‖ *the decisive battle of the war* その戦争での天下分け目の戦い ▶定義 2 having the ability to make clear decisions quickly 明瞭(めいりょう)な決定を速やかに下す能力のある➡**断固とした、決断力のある** ‖ *It's no good hesitating. Be decisive.* ためらうのは良くない。決断力を持ちなさい. ⇔**indecisive** ☛動 **decide** — **decisively** ➡決定的に、断固として — **decisiveness** 名 U ➡決定的・明白なこと、断固とした態度

**deck** /dek/ 名 C ▶定義 1 one of the floors of a ship or bus 船またはバスの床➡**(船の)デッキ、甲板、(バス・電車などの)階** ▶定義 2 米 = **PACK**¹(6) ‖ *a deck of cards* トランプ一組

**成句 on deck** ▶定義 on the part of a ship which you can walk on outside 船の一部、人が歩き回れる外側で➡**甲板へ、甲板へ出て** ‖ *I'm going out on deck for some fresh air.* 私は新鮮な空気を吸いに甲板に行きます.

**deckchair** /déktʃeər/ 名 C ▶定義 a chair that you use outside, especially on the beach. You can fold it up and carry it. 屋外、特に浜辺で使ういす. 折り畳んで持ち運べる➡**デッキチェア**

★**declaration** /dèkləréɪʃ(ə)n/ 名 ▶定義 1 C U an official statement about sth ~についての公式な声明➡**宣言、声明、布告** ‖ *In his speech he made a strong declaration of support for the* *rebels.* 彼は演説の中で,反逆者を支持すると力強く宣言した. *a declaration of war* 宣戦布告 ▶定義2 ❸a written statement giving information on goods or money you have earned, on which you have to pay tax 税金を支払わなければならない,商品またはあなたが稼いだ金についての情報を記した文書→(税関・税務署での)申告,申告書 ‖ *a customs declaration* 税関の申告書

\*declare /dɪkléər/ 動他 ▶定義1 to state sth publicly and officially or to make sth known in a firm, clear way ~を公に正式に述べる,または~を断固とした,明らかな方法で知られるようにする→~を宣言する,布告する,公表する ‖ *to declare war on another country* 他国へ宣戦布告する *I declare that the winner of the award is Joan Taylor.* 受賞者はジョーン テイラーであることを発表します. ▶定義2 to give information about goods or money you have earned, on which you have to pay tax 税金を支払わなければならない商品またはあなたが稼いだ金についての情報を与える→税関で(課税品)の申告をする,(所得税など)を申告する ‖ *You must declare all your income on this form.* あなたは,この書類にすべての収入を申告しなければなりません.

decline¹ /dɪkláɪn/ 動 ▶定義1 自to become weaker, smaller or less good 弱く,少なく,または悪くなる→衰える,減少する,低下する ‖ *declining profits* 減少する利益 *The standard of education has declined in this country.* この国では,教育水準が低下している. ▶定義2 自他 正式 to refuse, usually politely 通常は礼儀正しく,断る→(丁重に)断る,辞退する; ~を断る,辞退する ‖ *Thank you for the invitation but I'm afraid I have to decline.* お招きは有り難いのですが,残念なことにお断りしなければなりません.

decline² /dɪkláɪn/ 名 ❸Ⓤ ▶定義 (a) decline (in sth) a process or period of becoming weaker, smaller or less good 弱く,少なく,または悪くなる過程,あるいは期間→衰退(期),減少,低下 ‖ *a decline in sales* 売り上げの減少 *As an industrial power, the country is in decline.* その国は,工業大国としては衰退している.

decode /dɪkóʊd/ 動他 ▶定義 to find the meaning of a secret message (*code*) 秘密の伝言(暗号)の意味を解読する→(暗号文)を普通文にする,解読・翻訳する ⇔ **encode**

## decorative 425

decoder /dɪkóʊdər/ 名 ❸ ▶定義 a device that changes electronic signals into a form that can be understood 電気信号を理解できる形に変換する装置→デコーダー,復号器 ‖ *a satellite/video decoder* 衛星・ビデオデコーダー

decompose /dìːkəmpóʊz/ 動自他 ▶定義 to slowly be destroyed by natural chemical processes 自然の化学変化によって徐々に損なわれていく→腐敗する,変質する; ~を腐敗させる,変質させる ‖ *The body was so badly decomposed that it couldn't be identified.* その死体は腐敗がひどかったため,身元を明らかにできなかった.

décor /déɪkɔːr, dék-; dékɔːr, dɪ-/ 名 [Ⓤ,単数扱い] ▶定義 the style in which the inside of a building is decorated 建物内部が装飾されている様式→室内装飾,舞台装置

\*decorate /dékərèɪt/ 動 ▶定義1 他 decorate sth (with sth) to add sth in order to make a thing more attractive to look at 見た目をより魅力的なものにするために,~を加える→~を飾る,装飾する ‖ *Decorate the cake with cherries and nuts.* サクランボとナッツで,ケーキを飾ってください. ▶定義2 自他 特に 英 to put paint and/or coloured paper onto walls, ceilings and doors in a room or building 部屋または建物内の壁や天井,ドアにペンキを塗る,そして・または色刷りの紙を張る→~の内装をする ― decorator 名 ❸ ▶定義 a person whose job is to paint and decorate houses and buildings 家と建物の塗装と内装を仕事とする人→内装・外装業者,室内装飾家・業者,インテリアデザイナー

decoration /dèkəréɪʃ(ə)n/ 名 ▶定義1 ❸Ⓤ something that is added to sth in order to make it look more attractive 見た目をより魅力的なものにするために,~に加えられるもの→装飾,飾り付け ▶定義2 Ⓤthe process of decorating a room or building; the style in which sth is decorated 部屋または建物を装飾する過程; ~が装飾されている様式→内装,外装 ‖ *The house is in need of decoration.* その家は内装する必要がある.

decorative /dék(ə)rətɪv/ 形 ▶定義 attractive or pretty to look at 見た目が魅力的,またはすてきな→飾り・装飾用の,飾りになる ‖ *The cloth had* a decorative lace edge. そのテーブルクロスには、レースの縁飾りが付いていた.

**decoy** /díːkɔɪ, dɪkɔ́ɪ/ 名 C ▶定義 a person or object that is used in order to trick sb/sth into doing what you want, going where you want, etc ～をだまして自分が望んでいることをさせる、または自分が望んでいる場所へ行かせるなどのために使われる、人または物体→おとり役、(鳥を)おびき寄せるおとり、デコイ ― decoy 動 他 → ～をおとりで誘う

*__decrease__[1] /dɪkríːs, díːkriːs/ 動 自 他 ▶定義 to become or to make sth smaller or less ～が小さくまたは少なくなる、あるいはそうさせる→減る、低下する；～を減らす、～を低下させる ‖ Profits have decreased by 15%. 利益は15パーセント減少した. Decrease speed when you are approaching a road junction. 道路の合流地点に近付いたら、速度を落としなさい. ⇔ **increase**

*__decrease__[2] /díːkriːs, dɪkríːs/ 名 C U ▶定義 (a) decrease (in sth) the process of becoming or making sth smaller or less; the amount that sth is reduced by ～が小さくまたは少なくなる、あるいはそうさせる過程；～が減少した量→減少、縮小；減少量 ‖ a 10% decrease in sales 売り上げの10パーセントの減少

**decree** /dɪkríː/ 名 C ▶定義 an official order given by a government, a ruler, etc 政府、統治者などによって与えられる公式の命令→法令、政令、布告 ― decree 動 他 (過、過分 decreed) → (法令によって)～を命じる、布告する

**decrepit** /dɪkrépət/ 形 ▶定義 (used about a thing or person) old and in very bad condition or poor health (物または人について)古くてひどい状態である、または老齢で健康が思わしくない→老朽化した、(老齢で)衰えた

**dedicate** /dédɪkèɪt/ 動 他 ▶定義 **1** dedicate sth to sth to give all your energy, time, efforts, etc to sth すべての精力、時間、努力などを～に注ぐ→(主義・目的・活動などのために)～をささげる、(余暇など)をつぎ込む ‖ He dedicated his life to helping the poor. 彼はその生涯を貧しい人々の援助にささげた. ▶定義 **2** dedicate sth to sb to say that sth is specially for sb ～が特別に人のためのものであると言う→(著作・曲など)をささげる、献呈する ‖ He dedicated the book he had written to his brother. 彼は自著を自分の兄［弟］にささげた.

**dedicated** /dédɪkèɪtəd/ 形 ▶定義 giving a lot of your energy, time, efforts, etc to sth that you believe to be important 自分が大切だと信じる物に多大な精力、時間、努力などを注ぐ→(活動などに)打ち込んでいる、献身的な、ひたむきな ‖ dedicated nurses and doctors 献身的な看護婦と医者たち

**dedication** /dèdɪkéɪʃ(ə)n/ 名 ▶定義 **1** U wanting to give your time and energy to sth because you feel it is important それが大切だと思うので、～に時間と精力を注ぎたいと願っている→献身、専念 ‖ I admire her dedication to her career. 自分の職業に対する彼女の専念振りには感心する. ▶定義 **2** C a message at the beginning of a book or piece of music saying that it is for a particular person 本または楽曲がある特定の人のためだと述べている、冒頭のメッセージ→献呈、献呈の言葉

**deduce** /dɪd(j)úːs/ 動 他 ▶定義 to form an opinion using the facts that you already know 自分が既に知っている事実を使って、考えをまとめる→演繹(えんえき)する、推測する ‖ From his name I deduced that he was Polish. 名前から、彼はポーランド人だと推測した. ☛ 名 **deduction**

**deduct** /dɪdʌ́kt/ 動 他 ▶定義 deduct sth (from sth) to take sth such as money or points away from a total amount 総計から物、例えばお金または点数を引く→(お金、点数などを)差し引く、控除する ‖ Marks will be deducted for untidy work. マークスは、ずさんな仕事をしたので減給される.

**deduction** /dɪdʌ́kʃ(ə)n/ 名 C U ▶定義 **1** something that you work out from facts that you already know; the ability to think in this way 自分が既に知っている事実から考え出したもの；このように考える能力→演繹(えんえき)、推論 ‖ It was a brilliant piece of deduction by the detective. その刑事の推論は見事だった. ☛ 動 **deduce** ▶定義 **2** deduction (from sth) taking away an amount or number from a total; the amount or number taken away from the total 総計から量または数を引くこと；総計から差し引かれた量または数→差し引き、控除；控除額 ‖ What is your total income after deductions? (= when *tax, insurance, etc are taken away*) 控除後(=税金,保険料などが差し引かれた後)の手取り収入はいくらですか. ☞ **動** deduct

**deed** /diːd/ **名 C** ▶定義1 **正式** something that you do; an action あなたが行うもの; 行動→(意図的な)行い,行為,行動,実行 ‖ *a brave/good/evil deed* 勇敢な行為・善行・悪事 ▶定義2 a legal document that shows that you own a house or building 家または建物を所有していることを示す法的な文書→(正式に署名,押印している)証書,権利書

**deem** /diːm/ **動 他 正式** ▶定義 to have a particular opinion about sth ～について特定の意見を持つ→～を…と思う,見なす ‖ *He did not even deem it necessary to apologize.* 彼は謝罪が必要だとさえ考えなかった.

★**deep**¹ /diːp/ **形** ▶定義1 going a long way down from the surface 表面から長く下がっていって→深い,奥深い ‖ *to dig a deep hole* 深い穴を掘る *That's a deep cut.* あれは深い傷だ. *a coat with deep pockets* 深いポケットの付いたコート ☞ **名** depth ● **shallow** のさし絵 ▶定義2 going a long way from front to back 前から後まで長く行って→奥行きのある,奥深い ‖ *deep shelves* 奥行きのある棚 ▶定義3 measuring a particular amount from top to bottom or from front to back 上から下までまたは前から後までの特定の量を測って→深さが～の,奥行きが～の ‖ *The water is only a metre deep at this end of the pool.* プールのこちらの端では,水深はたった1メートルだ. *shelves 40 centimetres deep* 奥行き40センチの棚 ▶定義4 (used about sounds) low (音について) 低い→低い,太い ‖ *a deep voice* 低い声 ▶定義5 (used about colours) dark; strong (色について) 濃い; 強い→濃い; 強烈な ‖ *a deep red* 濃い赤 ▶定義6 (used about an emotion) strongly felt (感情について) 強く感じて→痛切な,深刻な ‖ *He felt a very deep love for the child.* 彼はその子供に深い愛情を感じた. ▶定義7 (used about sleep) not easy to wake from (睡眠について) 簡単には覚めない→深い ‖ *I was in a deep sleep and didn't hear the phone ringing for ages.* 私は深く眠っていたので,長い間電話が鳴っていることに気付かなかった. ▶定義8 dealing with difficult subjects or details; thorough 難解な主題または詳細を扱う; 徹底的な→深遠な,難解な,(人が)深く考える ‖ *His books show a deep understanding of human nature.* 彼の本は,人間性に対する深い理解を示している. ― **the deep 名** →海 ‖ *in the deep of the night* (= *in the middle of the night*) 真夜中に (= 夜の真ん中に) *the deep* (= *a literary way of referring to the sea*) 海 (= 海を述べる文学的表現) ― **deeply 副** →深く,激しく,非常に ‖ *a deeply unhappy person* とても不幸な人 *to breathe deeply* 深呼吸する

**成句** **deep in thought/conversation** ▶定義 thinking very hard or giving sb/sth your full attention とても熱心に考えている,あるいは～に最大限の注意を払っている→考え・話に夢中になって

**take a deep breath** ▶定義 breathe in a lot of air, especially in preparation for doing something difficult 特に困難なものを行う準備として,多量の空気を吸い込む→深呼吸をする ‖ *He took a deep breath then walked on stage.* 彼は深呼吸をすると,舞台に向かった.

★**deep**² /diːp/ **副** ▶定義 a long way down or inside sth ～の下に,または内部に向かって長く→深く,(かなり)深い所で ‖ *He gazed deep into her eyes.* 彼は彼女の目の奥をじっと見入った. *He dug his hands deep into his pockets.* 彼は手をポケットに深く突っ込んだ.

**成句** **deep down** ▶定義 in what you really think or feel 本当に考えた,または感じることでは→心の底では,実際は ‖ *I tried to appear optimistic but deep down I knew there was no hope.* 私は楽観的に見えるように努めたが,心の底では見込みがないことは分かっていた.

**dig deep** ⇒ **DIG**¹

**deepen** /ˈdiːp(ə)n/ **動 自 他** ▶定義 to become or to make sth deep or deeper 深くまたはより深くなる,あるいは～を深くまたはより深くする→深くなる,深まる; ～を深くする,深める ‖ *The river deepens here.* 川はここで深くなる.

**deep-freeze** = **FREEZER**

**deep-rooted** (または **deep-seated**) **形** ▶定義 strongly felt or believed and therefore difficult to change 強く思われているまたは信じられているので,変えることが難しい→(感情・偏見などが)深く根ざした,根強い ‖ *deep-rooted fears* 根強い恐怖

**deer**
antlers / doe / stag

**deer** /dɪər/ 名 C (複 deer) ▶定義 a large wild grass-eating animal. The male has large horns shaped like branches (antlers). 大きな野生の草食動物.雄には枝のような形の大きな角（枝角）がある→シカ

▶雄ジカは buck, または特に角が完全に生えそろったものは stag と呼ばれる.雌ジカは doe で,子ジカは fawn である. venison はシカの肉である.

**deface** /dɪféɪs/ 動 他 ▶定義 to spoil the way sth looks by writing on or marking its surface 表面に書いたり傷を付けたりして～の外観を損なう→（落書きなどで）～の外観を損なう,～の表面を汚す・傷付ける

**default**¹ /dɪfɔ́ːlt/ 名 [単数扱い] ▶定義 (computing) a course of action taken by a computer when it is not given any other instruction (コンピューター)指示が与えられないときに,コンピューターが取る行動方針→省略時解釈,省略値,デフォルト値

成句 **by default** ▶定義 because nothing happened, not because of successful effort 何も起こらないので,頑張った成果としてではなく→規定事項（特別な変更が加わらない限りそのまま生じること）により ‖ *They won by default, because the other team didn't turn up.* 相手チームが現れなかったので,彼らは不戦勝となった.

**default**² /dɪfɔ́ːlt/ 動 自 ▶定義 1 **default (on sth)** to not do sth that you should do by law 法律によってあなたがやるべき事をしない→（義務などの）怠慢,（債務などの）不履行,（料金などの）滞納 ‖ *If you default on the credit payments (= you don't pay them), the car will be taken back.* クレジットの支払いを滞納する(= 支払わない)と,その車は返品されます. ▶定義 2 (computing) **default (to sth)** to take a particular course of action when no other command is given (コンピューター)命令が与えられないときに,特定の行動方針を取る→省略値・デフォルト値を取る

*****defeat**¹ /dɪfíːt/ 動 他 ▶定義 1 to win a game, a fight, a vote, etc against sb; to beat sb 人を相手に,試合,戦い,投票などに勝つ;～を打ち負かす→～を負かす;打ち破る ‖ *The army defeated the rebels after three days of fighting.* 3日間の戦闘の後,軍隊は反逆者たちを打ち破った. *In the last match France defeated Wales.* 最後の試合で,フランスはウェールズを負かした.

▶定義 2 to be too difficult for sb to do or understand ～が行う,または理解するには難しすぎる→～を当惑させる ‖ *I've tried to work out what's wrong with the car but it defeats me.* 車のどこが悪いのか見つけようとしたが,私には歯が立たない. ▶定義 3 to prevent sth from succeeding ～の成功を妨げる→（希望・計画など）をくじく,挫折(ざせつ)させる ‖ *The local residents are determined to defeat the council's building plans.* 地域住民は,議会の建設計画を挫折させることを固く決意している.

**defeat**² /dɪfíːt/ 名 ▶定義 1 C an occasion when sb fails to win or be successful against sb else ～が勝つことに,またはほかの～よりも成功していることに失敗する場合→打ち負かされること,敗北,負け ‖ *This season they have had two victories and three defeats.* 今シーズン,彼らは2勝3敗だった. ▶定義 2 U the act of losing or not being successful 失うまたは成功していない行為→失敗,挫折(ざせつ) ‖ *She refused to admit defeat and kept on trying.* 彼女は失敗を認めることを拒み,挑戦し続けた.

**defeatism** /dɪfíːtɪz(ə)m/ 名 U ▶定義 the attitude of expecting sth to end in failure ～が失敗に終わることを予期する態度→敗北主義

**defeatist** /dɪfíːtɪst/ 形 ▶定義 expecting not to succeed 成功しないことを予期する→敗北主義(者)の ‖ *a defeatist attitude/view* 敗北主義的な態度・意見 — **defeatist** 名 →敗北主義者 ‖ *Don't be such a defeatist, we haven't lost yet!* そんな敗北主義者になるな.まだ私たちは負けたわけではない.

**defecate** /défəkèɪt/ 動 自 正式 ▶定義 to get rid of waste from the body; to go to the toilet 排せ

つ物を体外に出す; トイレに行く➡**排便する; トイレに行く**

**defect**[1] /díːfekt, dɪfékt/ 名 C ▶定義 sth that is wrong with or missing from sb/sth ～が具合の悪い、または～に欠けている物➡**欠点, 欠陥** ‖ *a speech defect* 言語障害 *defects in the education system* 教育制度の欠陥 — defective /dɪféktɪv/ 形➡**欠点・欠陥のある, 不完全な**

**defect**[2] /dɪfékt/ 動 自 ▶定義 to leave your country, a political party, etc and join one that is considered to be the enemy 自分の国、政党などから離れて、敵であると見なされている所に参加する➡**離反して相手側に走る, 亡命する** — defection 名 C U ➡**離反, 脱会, 離党, 亡命**

★**defence**(米 **defense**) /dɪféns/ 名 ▶定義**1**
❶ something you do or say to protect sb/sth from attack, bad treatment, criticism, etc 攻撃、ひどい扱い、非難などから～を守るために、するまたは言う事➡**防御, 防衛, 守備** ‖ *Would you fight in defence of your country?* 自国を守るためにあなたは戦いますか. *When her brother was criticized she leapt to his defence.* 自分の兄[弟]が非難された時、彼女はすぐにかばった. *I must say in her defence that I have always found her very reliable.* 彼女を弁護して言いますが、彼女はいつもとても信頼のおける人です. ☛参 self-defence ▶定義**2** ❷ *a defence (against sth)* something that protects sb/sth from sth, or that is used to fight against attack ～から…を防御するもの、または攻撃に対して戦うために使われるもの➡**防御物, 防御手段・方法・能力** ‖ *the body's defences against disease* 病気に対する身体的防御 ▶定義**3** ❶ the military equipment, forces, etc for protecting a country 国を守るための軍備、兵力など➡**防衛～, 防御施設** ‖ *Spending on defence needs to be reduced.* 防衛費は削減される必要がある. ▶定義**4** ❶ (in law) an argument in support of the accused person in a court of law (法律で)法廷で被告人を援護するための弁論➡**弁護, 弁明** ‖ *His defence was that he was only carrying out orders.* 彼の答弁は、命令を実行しただけだ、というものだった. ▶定義**5** *the defence* [単数扱い, 単数または複数形動詞と共に] (in law) the lawyer or lawyers who are acting for the accused person in a court of law (法律で)法廷で被告人のために活動する弁護士または弁護団➡**被告側, 被告弁護団** ‖ *The defence claims/claim that many of the witnesses were lying.* 被告側は、目撃者の多くがうそをついていたと主張している. ☛参 the prosecution ▶定義**6** 通常は *the defence* [単数扱い, ❶] (in sport) action to prevent the other team scoring; the players who try to do this (スポーツで)相手チームの得点を妨げるための行動; これをしようとする選手➡**守備, 守備側, ディフェンス** ‖ *She plays in defence.* 彼女は守備についている.

**defenceless** /dɪfénsləs/ 形 ▶定義 unable to defend yourself against attack 攻撃から自分自身を守れない➡**無防備の, 防御できない, 無力な**

★**defend** /dɪfénd/ 動 ▶定義**1** 他 defend sb/sth/yourself (against/from sb/sth) to protect sb/sth from harm or danger 危害または危険から～を守る➡**～を守る, 防ぐ** ‖ *Would you be able to defend yourself if someone attacked you in the street?* 通りで襲われたら、あなたは自分の身を守れますか. ▶定義**2** 他 defend sb/sth/yourself (against/from sb/sth) to say or write sth to support sb/sth that has been criticized 批判されている～を支援するために、何かを言うまたは書く➡**(人・思想など)を擁護する, 支持する** ‖ *The minister went on television to defend the government's policy.* 大臣は政府の政策を擁護するために、テレビに出演した. ▶定義**3** 他 (in law) to speak for sb who is accused of a crime in a court of law (法律で)犯罪で告訴されている人のために、法廷で話す➡**～を弁護する** ▶定義**4** 自 他 (in sport) to try to stop the other team or player scoring (スポーツで)相手チームまたはそこの選手が得点するのを止めようとする➡**～を守る, 守備する** ‖ *They defended well and managed to hold onto their lead.* 彼らは巧みに守備して、何とかリードを守りきった. ▶定義**5** 他 to take part in a competition that you won before and try to win it again 以前に勝利し、再び勝とうとして競技会に参加する➡**(タイトル)を防衛する** ‖ *She successfully defended her title.* 彼女はタイトルの防衛に成功した. *He is the defending champion.* 彼はタイトルを防衛したチャンピオンだ.

**defendant** /dɪfénd(ə)nt/ 名 C ▶定義 a person

who is accused of a crime in a court of law 法廷において犯罪で告訴されている人→被告

**defender** /dɪféndər/ 名 C ▶定義 a person who defends sb/sth, especially in sport 特にスポーツにおいて、～を防御する人→選手権保持者, 防御者, 弁護者

**defense** 米 = DEFENCE

**defensive**¹ /dɪfénsɪv/ 形 ▶定義 1 that protects sb/sth from attack 攻撃から～を防御する…→防御の, 防衛の, 守備の ‖ *The troops took up a defensive position.* 軍隊は防御的な陣形をとった. ⇔ **offensive** ▶定義 2 showing that you feel that sb is criticizing you 人に批判されていると, あなたが感じていることを示す→(行動・言葉・態度などが)守勢な, 弁護的な ‖ *When I asked him about his new job, he became very defensive and tried to change the subject.* 彼に新しい仕事のことを尋ねたら, とても言い訳がましくなって話題を変えようとした.

**defensive**² /dɪfénsɪv/ 名
成句 **on the defensive** ▶定義 acting in a way that shows that you expect sb to attack or criticize you ～があなたを攻撃する, または批判すると予期していることを表すやり方で行動する→防御態勢をとって, 自己弁護をして ‖ *My questions about her past immediately put her on the defensive.* 過去について尋ねると, 彼女は急に言い訳がましいことを言い始めた.

**defer** /dɪfə́ːr/ 動 ⊕ (**deferring**; **deferred**)
正式 ▶定義 to leave sth until a later time 後まで～をほうっておく→～を延ばす, 延期する ‖ *She deferred her place at university for a year.* 彼女は大学での勉学を1年間延期した.

**deference** /défərəns/ 名 U ▶定義 polite behaviour that you show towards sb/sth, usually because you respect him/her 通常, 相手に敬意を感じているので, ～に向かって示す礼儀正しい振る舞い→敬意, 尊敬
成句 **in deference to sb/sth** ▶定義 because you respect and do not wish to upset sb ～を尊敬しており, その人を怒らせたくないために→～を考慮・尊重して, ～に敬意を払って ‖ *In deference to her father's wishes, she didn't mention the subject again.* 自分の父の意向を尊重して, 彼女はもうその話題には触れなかった.

**defiance** /dɪfáɪəns/ 名 U ▶定義 open refusal to obey sb/sth ～に従うことへのあからさまな拒否→(権威などに対する)公然たる反抗, 挑戦, (命令などの)無視 ‖ *an act of defiance* 挑戦的な行動 ‖ *He continued smoking in defiance of the doctor's orders.* 医者の命令を無視して, 彼はたばこを吸い続けた. ☛ 動 **defy**

**defiant** /dɪfáɪənt/ 形 ▶定義 showing open refusal to obey sb/sth ～に従うことへのあからさまな拒否を示して→反抗的な, 挑戦的な ☛ 動 **defy** — **defiantly** 副 ▶反抗的に, 挑戦的に

**deficiency** /dɪfíʃənsi/ 名 (複 **deficiencies**) **deficiency (in/of sth)** ▶定義 1 C U the state of not having enough of sth; a lack 物が十分にない状態; 不足→不足, 欠乏 ‖ *a deficiency of vitamin C* ビタミンC不足 ▶定義 2 C a fault or a weakness in sb/sth ～の欠陥または弱点→不完全(なもの), 欠陥, 不備 ‖ *The problems were caused by deficiencies in the design.* 問題は, 設計の不備から生じていた.

**deficient** /dɪfíʃ(ə)nt/ 形 ▶定義 1 **deficient (in sth)** not having enough of sth 物が十分にない→(～が)不足した, 欠乏した ‖ *food that is deficient in minerals* ミネラルが不足している食物 ▶定義 2 not good enough or not complete 十分には良くない, または完全でない→不完全な, 不備な

**deficit** /défəsɪt/ 名 C ▶定義 the amount by which the money you receive is less than the money you have spent 受け取る金額が使った金額より少ないことによる総計→(～の)不足(額), 欠損, 赤字 ‖ *a trade deficit* 貿易赤字

**define** /dɪfáɪn/ 動 ⊕ ▶定義 1 to say exactly what a word or idea means 言葉または概念が意味するものを正確に言う→～を定義する, ～の意味を明確にする ‖ *How would you define 'happiness'?* 「幸福」をどのように定義しますか. ▶定義 2 to explain the exact nature of sth clearly ～の正確な本質を明解に説明する→～の性質・立場などを明らかにする, 説明する ‖ *We need to define the problem before we can attempt to solve it.* その問題を解決しようとする前に, 私たちはその本質を明らかにする必要がある.

***definite** /déf(ə)nət/ 形 ▶定義 1 fixed and unlikely to change; certain 確固としていて, 変わりそうにない; 確かな→(はっきりと)限定された, 一

定の; 確かな ‖ *I'll give you a definite decision in a couple of days.* 数日後に,確答をします. ⇔ **indefinite** ▶定義2 clear; easy to see or notice 明確な; 分かりやすい,または気付きやすい→**明確な, 明らかな** ‖ *There has been a definite change in her attitude recently.* 最近, 彼女の態度は明らかに変化している.

**the definite article** 名 C ▶定義 (文法) the name used for the word 'the' 単語の the に用いられている名称→**定冠詞** ☛参 **indefinite article**

▶定冠詞についての説明は,巻末の「文法早見表」を参照.

**definitely** /déf(ə)nətli/ 副 ▶定義 certainly; without doubt 確実に; 疑いなく→**確かに; 間違いなく** ‖ *I'll definitely consider your advice.* あなたの助言を必ず考慮します.

**definition** /dèfəníʃ(ə)n/ 名 C U ▶定義 a description of the exact meaning of a word or idea 言葉または概念の正確な意味の説明→**定義, 意味を明らかにすること**

**definitive** /dɪfínətɪv/ 形 ▶定義 in a form that cannot be changed or that cannot be improved 変更できない,または改良できない形で→**決定的な,最終的な** ‖ *This is the definitive version.* これは最終版だ. *The definitive performance of Hamlet* ハムレット公演の決定版 — **definitively** 副 →**決定的に,最終的に**

**deflate** /dɪfléɪt/ 動 ▶定義1 自他 to become or to make sth smaller by letting the air or gas out of it 空気またはガスが抜けて小さくなる,あるいは~を小さくする→**(気球などが)しぼむ; ~を空気・ガスを抜いてしぼませる** ‖ *The balloon slowly deflated.* 風船はゆっくりとしぼんでいった. ⇔ **inflate** ▶定義2 他 to make sb feel less confident, proud or excited ~の自信, 誇り, または興奮を弱める→**(自信など)を失わせる, くじく, ~をしょげさせる** ‖ *I felt really deflated when I got my exam results.* 試験の結果を受け取った時, 私は本当に自信をなくした.

**deflect** /dɪflékt/ 動 ▶定義1 自他 to change direction after hitting sb/sth; to make sth change direction in this way ~にぶつかって方向を変える; この方法で~の方向を変えさせる→**それる, 曲がる; ~をそらす, 変える, 曲げる** ‖ *The ball deflected off a defender and into the goal.* ボールは守備の選手をそれて,ゴールに入

った. ▶定義2 他 to turn sb's attention away from sth ~の注意を…からそらす→**(批判・注意など)をそらす,かわす,~を(関心・目的などから)そらす** ‖ *Nothing could deflect her from her aim.* 何も,彼女の関心を目標からそらすことはできなかった.

**deflection** /dɪflékʃ(ə)n/ 名 C U ▶定義 a change of direction after hitting sb/sth ~にぶつかって方向を変えること→**(進路などが)それること,(計器の)振れ**

**deforestation** /dɪfɔ̀(:)rəstéɪʃ(ə)n, -fàr-/ 名 U ▶定義 cutting down trees over a large area 広範囲にわたって木々を伐採すること→**森林伐採**

**deform** /dɪfɔ́:rm/ 動 他 ▶定義 to change or spoil the natural shape of sth ~の自然な形を変える, または損なう→**~を変形させる,不格好にする**

**deformed** /dɪfɔ́:rmd/ 形 ▶定義 having a shape that is not normal because it has grown wrongly 異常に成長したため,正常な形をしていない→**奇形の,変形した**

**deformity** /dɪfɔ́:rməti/ 名 (複 **deformities**) C U ▶定義 the condition of having a part of the body that is an unusual shape because of disease, injury, etc 病気, けがなどで, 身体の一部が正常な形ではない状態→**奇形, (身体の)奇形した部分** ‖ *The drug caused women to give birth to babies with severe deformities.* その薬のせいで,重度の奇形の赤ん坊たちが産まれた.

**defraud** /dɪfrɔ́:d/ 動 他 ▶定義 defraud sb (of sth) to get sth from sb in a dishonest way 不正直なやり方で,人から何かを得る→**~からだまし取る,横領する** ‖ *He defrauded the company of millions.* 彼はその会社から何百万ポンドもだまし取った.

**defrost** /dɪfrɔ́(:)st/ 動 ▶定義1 他 to remove the ice from sth ~から氷を取り除く→**(冷蔵庫など)の霜取りをする, 霜・氷・曇りを取る** ‖ *to defrost a fridge* 冷蔵庫の霜取りをする ▶定義2 自他 (used about frozen food) to return to a normal temperature; to make food do this (冷凍食品について)常温に戻る; 食品をこの状態にする→**解凍される,解氷する; ~を解凍する** ‖ *Defrost the chicken thoroughly before cooking.* 調理する前に, 鶏肉を完全に解凍しなさい. ☛参 **de-ice**

## deft

**deft** /deft/ 形 ▶定義 (used especially about movements) skilful and quick (特に動きについて) 熟練していて素早い → 手先が器用な, 巧みな — **deftly** 副 → 器用に, 巧みに

**defunct** /dɪfʌŋ(k)t/ 形 ▶定義 no longer existing or in use もう存在していない, または使われていない → 故人となった, 消滅した, 廃止になった

**defuse** /diːfjúːz/ 動他 ▶定義1 to remove part of a bomb so that it cannot explode 爆発できなくするために, 爆弾の一部を取り除く → (爆弾など)から信管を抜く ‖ *Army experts defused the bomb safely.* 軍隊の専門家が無事にその爆弾から信管を抜いた. ▶定義2 to make a situation calmer or less dangerous 状況を沈静化させる, または危険を少なくさせる → (緊張・怒りなど)を和らげる, 〜から危険を取り除く ‖ *She defused the tension by changing the subject.* 話題を変えることで, 彼女は緊張を和らげた.

**defy** /dɪfáɪ/ 動他 (現分 **defying**; 三単現 **defies**; 過, 過分 **defied**) ▶定義1 to refuse to obey sb/sth 〜に従うことを拒否する → 〜に反抗する, 〜を無視する, 侮る ‖ *She defied her parents and continued seeing him.* 彼女は両親に反抗し, 彼に会い続けた. ☛ 形 **defiant** 名 **defiance** ▶定義2 **defy sb to do sth** to ask sb to do sth that you believe to be impossible 不可能だと自分が思う物事を人にするように要求する → (〜してみろと)…に挑む ‖ *I defy you to prove me wrong.* 私が悪いと証明できるならしてみなさい. ▶定義3 to make sth impossible or very difficult 〜を不可能に, またはとても困難にする → (物事が)(解決・理解・想像など)を拒む, 絶する ‖ *It's such a beautiful place that it defies description.* そこはとても美しい所で, 言葉では言い表せない.

**degenerate**¹ /dɪdʒénəreɪt/ 動自 ▶定義 to become worse, lower in quality, etc 質などが悪くなる, 低下する → 退化する, 堕落する ‖ *The calm discussion degenerated into a nasty argument.* 平穏な討論が, 悪意に満ちた口論へと堕落した. — **degeneration** /dɪdʒènəréɪʃ(ə)n/ 名 Ü → (品位・価値・評価などの)低下, 堕落

**degenerate**² /dɪdʒén(ə)rət/ 形 ▶定義 having moral standards that have fallen to a very low level とても低い水準に落ちた道徳的基準を持って → 退化した, 堕落した

**degradation** /dègrədéɪʃ(ə)n/ 名 Ü ▶定義1 the action of making sb be less respected; the state of being less respected 〜への敬意を薄くさせる行為; 敬意が払われていない状態 → 格下げ, 降格, (地位などの)低落 ‖ *the degradation of being in prison* 入獄しているという不名誉 ▶定義2 causing the condition of sth to become worse 〜の状態を悪化させる → (品質・価値などの)下落, 低下, 劣悪化 ‖ *environmental degradation* 環境の悪化

**degrade** /dɪgréɪd/ 動他 ▶定義 to make people respect sb less 人々の〜への敬意を薄くさせる → 〜の品位・価値・評価を落とす, 〜の地位・身分などを下げる ‖ *It's the sort of film that really degrades women.* この映画は, 本当に女性を侮辱するたぐいのものだ. — **degrading** 形 → 品位を落とすような, 屈辱的な, 卑しい

*__degree__ /dɪgríː/ 名 ▶定義1 Ⓒ a measurement of temperature 温度の測定 → 度 ‖ *Water boils at 100 degrees Celsius (100°C).* 水は摂氏100度 (100℃)で沸騰する. *three degrees below zero/minus three degrees (-3°)* 零下3度・マイナス3度(-3℃) ▶定義2 Ⓒ a measurement of angles 角度の測定 → 度 ‖ *a forty-five degree (45°) angle* 45度(45°)の角度 *An angle of 90 degrees is called a right angle.* 90度の角度で, 直角と呼ばれる. ▶定義3 Ⓒ Ü (used about feelings or qualities) a certain amount or level (感情または特質について) 一定の量または程度 → 程度 ‖ *There is always a degree of risk involved in mountaineering.* 登山には常にある程度の危険が伴う. *I sympathize with her to some degree.* 私はある程度彼女に同情する. ▶定義4 Ⓒ an official document gained by successfully completing a course at university or college 総合大学または単科大学での課程を首尾良く修了するときに授与される公式文書 → 学位, 称号 ‖ *She's got a degree in Philosophy.* 彼女は哲学の学位を持っている. *to do a Chemistry degree* 化学の学位を取る

▶英国では, 総合大学の課程を修了し合格した際に取得する資格として, degree (学位) は一般的である. 違う種類の単科大学では, diploma (卒業証書) を目指して勉強することもできる. その課程は, 学位課程よりも短く実践的なこともある. 英国の総合大学での学位

の最高点はfirstで、続いてtwo-one, two-two, third, pass, failである.

**dehydrate** /dɪháɪdreɪt/ 動 ▶定義1 他(通常は受動態で)to remove all the water from sth 〜からすべての水分を取り除く→**〜を脱水する, 乾燥させる** ∥ *Dehydrated vegetables can be stored for months.* 乾燥野菜は、何か月も保存できる. ▶定義2 自他 to lose too much water from your body 身体から限度を超えた水分が失われる→**脱水状態になる** ∥ *If you run for a long time in the heat, you start to dehydrate.* 暑さの中で長時間走ると、脱水状態になり始める. — **dehydration** /dìːhaɪdréɪʃ(ə)n/ 名 ❶→**脱水, 乾燥, 脱水症** ∥ *Several of the runners were suffering from severe dehydration.* 走者のいく人かは、重い脱水症になった.

**de-ice** /dìáɪs/ 動 他 ▶定義 to remove the ice from sth 〜から氷を取り除く→**〜を除氷する, 〜に除氷装置を施す** ∥ *The car windows need de-icing.* 車の窓の氷を取り除く必要がある.
☞参 **defrost**

**deign** /déɪn/ 動 ▶定義 deign to do sth to do sth although you think you are too important to do it それをするには自分は社会的地位が高すぎると思っているけれども、〜をする→**もったいなくも〜してくださる, 恥を忍んで〜する** ∥ *He didn't even deign to look up when I entered the room.* 私が部屋に入っても、彼は顔も上げてくださらなかった.

**deity** /díːəti, déɪ-/ 名 ❸ (複 **deities**) 正式 ▶定義 a god→**神**

**dejected** /dɪdʒéktəd/ 形 ▶定義 very unhappy, especially because you are disappointed 特に落胆したために、とてもふさいでいる→**落胆した, 意気消沈した** ∥ *The fans went home dejected after watching their team lose.* ひいきのチームが負けるのを見た後、ファンはがっかりして家に帰った. — **dejectedly** 副→**意気消沈して, すごすごと** — **dejection** 名 ❶→**落胆, 意気消沈**

★**delay**¹ /dɪléɪ/ 動 ▶定義1 他 to make sb/sth slow or late 〜を緩慢にさせる, または遅れさせる→**(悪天候・事故などが)〜を遅らせる, 遅延させる** ∥ *The plane was delayed for several hours because of bad weather.* 悪天候のために、飛行機は数時間遅れた. ▶定義2 自他 delay (sth/doing sth) to decide not to do sth until a later time 〜をもっと後になるまで行わないと決める→**〜を延期する, 延ばす** ∥ *I was forced to delay the trip until the following week.* 私は次の週まで旅行を延期せざるを得なかった.

**delay**² /dɪléɪ/ 名 ❸ ❶ ▶定義 a situation or period of time where you have to wait 待たなければならない状況または期間→**遅れ, 延期, 遅延(時間)** ∥ *Delays are likely on the roads because of heavy traffic.* 道が混んでいるため、遅れることになりそうだ. *If you smell gas, report it without delay (= immediately).* ガス臭い場合は、直ちに通報しなさい.

**delegate**¹ /déləɡət, -ɡèɪt/ 名 ❸ ▶定義 a person who has been chosen to speak or take decisions for a group of people, especially at a meeting 特に会議の場で、人々の集団を代表して発言するまたは決定するために選ばれた人→**代表, 代議員, 使節(個人)**

**delegate**² /déləɡèɪt/ 動 自他 ▶定義 to give sb with a lower job or position a particular task to do 自分の部下や、自分より下の地位の人に特定の任務を与える→**(任務・権限など)を委任する, 任命して〜させる** ∥ *You can't do everything yourself. You must learn how to delegate.* 自分1人で何もかもはできない. 人に任せることを学ぶべきだ.

**delegation** /dèləɡéɪʃ(ə)n/ 名 ▶定義1 [❸, 単数または複数形の動詞と共に]a group of people who have been chosen to speak or take decisions for a larger group of people, especially at a meeting 特に会議の場で、大きな人々の集団を代表して、発言するまたは決定をするために選ばれた人々の一団→**代表団, 派遣団** ∥ *The British delegation walked out of the meeting in protest.* 英国の代表団は、抗議のために会議の席から立ち去った. ▶定義2 ❶ giving sb with a lower job or position a particular task to do 自分の部下や、自分より下の地位の人に特定の任務を与えること→**(任務・権限などの)委任, 代表任命(派遣)**

**delete** /dɪlíːt/ 動 他 ▶定義 to remove sth that is written 書かれたものを取り除く→**(文章などから)(語などを)削除する** — **deletion** /dɪlíːʃ(ə)n/ 名 ❸ ❶→**削除, 削除箇所**

★**deliberate**¹ /dɪlíb(ə)rət/ 形 ▶定義1 done on purpose; planned 故意に行う; 計画された→**故**

**deliberate²** 意の, たくらんだ, 計画的な ‖ *Was it an accident or was it deliberate?* それは偶然でしたか, それとも計画的でしたか. ☞類 **intentional** ▶定義2 done slowly and carefully, without hurrying 慌てずに, ゆっくり注意深く行う→(行動・言葉・考えが)慎重な, (〜に)注意深い, 落ち着いた ‖ *She spoke in a calm, deliberate voice.* 彼女は平静で落ち着いた声で話した.

**deliberate²** /dɪlíbərèɪt/ 動 自 他 正式 ▶定義 to think about or discuss sth fully before making a decision 決定を下す前に, 〜について十分に考える, または議論する→熟慮・熟考する, 相談する; 〜を熟慮・熟考する, 討議する ‖ *The judges deliberated for an hour before announcing the winner.* 勝者を発表する前に, 審判たちは1時間討議した.

**★deliberately** /dɪlíb(ə)rətli/ 副 ▶定義1 on purpose; intentionally 故意に; 意図して→わざと, 故意に ‖ *I didn't break it deliberately, it was an accident.* わざと壊したのではありません, 事故だったのです. ☞類 **purposely** ▶定義2 slowly and carefully, without hurrying 慌てずに, ゆっくりと注意深く→慎重に, よく考えた上で, ゆっくりと

**deliberation** /dɪlìbəréɪʃ(ə)n/ 名 正式 ▶定義1 C U discussion or thinking about sth in detail 〜を細部にわたって討論すること, または考えること→熟考, 審議 ‖ *After much deliberation I decided to reject the offer.* 熟慮の末, 私はその申し出を断ることに決めた. ▶定義2 U the quality of being very slow and careful in what you say and do 言動がとてもゆっくりで注意深いという特性→慎重さ, 落ち着き ‖ *He spoke with great deliberation.* 彼はとても慎重に話した.

**delicacy** /délɪkəsi/ 名 ( 複 **delicacies**) ▶定義1 U the quality of being easy to damage or break 傷付きやすい, または壊れやすいという特性→壊れやすさ, 弱さ, きゃしゃなこと ▶定義2 U great care; a gentle touch 大変注意を払うこと; 丁寧に触れること→(問題などが)微妙なこと, デリケートなこと; 慎重さを要すること ‖ (比喩)*Be tactful! It's a matter of some delicacy.* 気を付けてものを言いなさい. それは微妙な問題ですよ. ▶定義3 C a type of food that is considered particularly good とりわけすばらしいと見なされる食べ物の種類→珍味, ごちそう, おいしいもの ‖ *Try this dish, it's a local delicacy.* この料理を食べてみてください, この地方のごちそうです.

**★delicate** /délɪkət/ 形 ▶定義1 easy to damage or break 傷付きやすい, または壊れやすい→敏感な, 精巧な, 壊れやすい ‖ *delicate skin* 敏感肌 *the delicate mechanisms of a watch* 腕時計の精巧な機械仕掛け ▶定義2 frequently ill or hurt よく病気になる, またはけがをする→虚弱な, か弱い ‖ *He was a delicate child and often in hospital.* 彼は体の弱い子供で, 度々入院した. ▶定義3 (used about colours, flavours, etc) light and pleasant; not strong (色, 味などについて)薄くて感じのいい; 濃くない→(色・香りなどが)かすかな, ほのかな, (食べ物・味などが)あっさりしておいしい; どぎつくない ‖ *a delicate shade of pale blue* 淡青色の柔らかい色調 ▶定義4 needing skilful treatment and care 巧みな取り扱いと注意を必要とする→(問題などが)微妙な, 扱いにくい, 細心の注意を要する ‖ *Repairing this is going to be a very delicate operation.* この修理は, 細心の注意を要する作業になります. — **delicately** 副 →優雅に, 繊細に, よく気を配って ‖ *She stepped delicately over the broken glass.* 彼女は注意深く, 割れたガラスをまたいで歩いた.

**delicatessen** /dèlɪkətésn/ 名 C ▶定義 a shop that sells special, unusual or foreign foods, especially cold cooked meat, cheeses, etc 特に調理済の冷たい肉, チーズなど, あるいは特製の, 珍しい, または外国の食品を販売する店→デリカテッセン, 総菜屋

**★delicious** /dɪlíʃəs/ 形 ▶定義 having a very pleasant taste or smell とても心地良い味または香りのする→(非常に)おいしい, 香りの良い ‖ *This soup is absolutely delicious.* このスープは本当においしい.

**delight¹** /dɪláɪt/ 名 ▶定義1 U great pleasure; joy 大きな喜び; 躍り上がるほどのうれしさ→大喜び, うれしさ ‖ *She laughed with delight as she opened the present.* 贈り物を開けた時, 彼女は躍り上がるほど喜んで笑った. ▶定義2 C something that gives sb great pleasure 〜に大きな喜びを与えるもの→(非常な)喜び・楽しみとなるもの, 大変うれしいもの ‖ *The story is a delight to read.* この物語は本当に面白いです

よ. — **delightful** /-fʊl, -f(ə)l/ 形 →(物事が)とてもうれしい, 楽しい, 愉快な ‖ *a delightful view* 心が浮き立つ眺め — **delightfully** /-fʊli, -f(ə)li/ 副 →楽しく, 愉快に, 快く

\***delight**² /dɪláɪt/ 動 他 ▶定義 to give sb great pleasure ～に大きな喜びを与える→～を喜ばせる, 楽しませる, うれしがらせる ‖ *She delighted the audience by singing all her old songs.* 彼女は自分の懐かしい歌を残らず歌って, 聴衆を喜ばせた.

句動詞 **delight in sth/in doing sth** ▶定義 to get great pleasure from sth ～から大きな喜びを得る→～を喜ぶ; ～をして喜ぶ ‖ *He delights in playing tricks on people.* 彼は人々にいたずらをして大いに楽しんでいる.

**delighted** /dɪláɪtəd/ 形 ▶定義 **delighted (at/with/about sth); delighted to do sth/that...** extremely pleased とても喜んでいる→(人が)(非常に)喜んでいる, (とても)うれしがっている ‖ *She was delighted at getting the job/that she got the job.* 彼女は仕事が決まって大変喜んだ. *They're absolutely delighted with their baby.* 彼らは子供が生まれたことを本当に喜んだ.

**delinquency** /dɪlíŋkwənsi/ 名 U 正式 ▶定義 bad or criminal behaviour, especially among young people 特に若者が犯す, 悪いまたは犯罪的な行為→(未成年の)非行, 犯罪

**delinquent** /dɪlíŋkwənt/ 形 正式 ▶定義 (usually used about a young person) behaving badly and often breaking the law (通常は若者について)素行が悪く, しばしば法を犯す→非行の, 反社会的な — **delinquent** 名 C →法律違反者, 非行少年・少女 ‖ *a juvenile delinquent* 未成年犯罪者

**delirious** /dɪlíəriəs/ 形 ▶定義 **1** speaking or thinking in a crazy way, often because of illness 多くは病気のために, 異常な様子で話しているまたは考えている→(高熱などで)精神が錯乱して, うわごとを言う ▶定義 **2** extremely happy この上なく幸せな→(喜びで)興奮した, 有頂天の ‖ *I was absolutely delirious when I passed the exam.* 試験に合格した時は, 本当に有頂天だった. — **deliriously** 副 →精神が錯乱して, 我を忘れるほど

\***deliver** /dɪlívər/ 動 ▶定義 **1** 自 他 to take sth (goods, letters, etc) to the place requested or to the address on it ～(品物, 手紙など)を依頼

## delta 435

された場所, またはそこに記載された住所に届ける→～を配達する, 届ける ‖ *Your order will be delivered within five days.* ご注文の品物は, 5日以内にお届けします. *We deliver free within the local area.* 地区内は, 無料で配達します. ▶定義 **2** 他 to help a mother to give birth to her baby 妊婦が子供を産む助けをする→(妊婦)に分べんさせる, (赤ん坊)を取り上げる ‖ *to deliver a baby* 赤ん坊を取り上げる ▶定義 **3** 他 正式 to say sth formally 正式に～を言う→(意見など)を述べる, (演説など)をする, (評決など)を申し渡す ‖ *to deliver a speech/lecture/warning* 演説をする・講義をする・警告を申し渡す ▶定義 **4** 自 **deliver (on sth)** 略式 to do or give sth that you have promised 約束した事をする, または与える→約束を果たす, 実行する, うまくやり遂げる ‖ *The new leader has made a lot of promises, but can he deliver on them?* 新しい指導者は多くの約束をしたが, やり遂げることができるのだろうか.

成句 **come up with/deliver the goods** ⇒ **GOODS**

**delivery** /dɪlív(ə)ri/ 名 (複 **deliveries**) ▶定義 **1** U the act of taking sth (goods, letters, etc) to the place or person who has ordered it or whose address is on it ～(品物, 手紙など)を, それが依頼された, または住所が記載されている, 場所または人に届ける行為→配達, 配送, 引き渡し ‖ *Please allow 28 days for delivery.* 配送には28日かかりますので, ご了承ください. *a delivery van* 配送用貨物自動車 ▶定義 **2** C an occasion when sth is delivered ～が配達される機会→配達, (郵便などの)～の便 ‖ *Is there a delivery here on Sundays?* ここでは, 日曜日の配達はありますか. ▶定義 **3** C something (goods, letters, etc) that is delivered 配達されるもの(品物, 手紙など)→配達品 ‖ *The shop is waiting for a new delivery of apples.* その店では, リンゴが届けられるのを待っている. ▶定義 **4** C the process of giving birth to a baby 赤ん坊を産む過程→出産, 分べん ‖ *an easy delivery* 安産

**delta** /déltə/ 名 C ▶定義 an area of flat land shaped like a triangle where a river divides into smaller rivers as it goes into the sea 川が海に

436　delude

流れ込む過程で小さな川に分岐する, 三角形のような形をした平たんな土地→(河口の)三角州, デルタ

**delude** /dɪlúːd/ 動他 ▶定義 to make sb believe sth that is not true 事実ではない事をだれかに信じさせる→(誤った情報などで)〜を欺く, 誤解させる, 勘違いさせる ∥ *If he thinks he's going to get rich quickly, he's deluding himself.* すぐに金持ちになれると思っているのなら, 彼は勘違いしている. ☞ 名 delusion

**deluge**[1] /dél(j)uːdʒ/ 名 ⓒ ▶定義 1 a sudden very heavy fall of rain; a flood 突然の豪雨; 洪水→豪雨, 土砂降り; 大洪水, 氾濫 (はんらん) ▶定義 2 a deluge (of sth) a very large number of things that happen or arrive at the same time 一度に起こるまたは到着する, とても多くの物事→どっと押し寄せるもの, (〜の)殺到 ∥ *The programme was followed by a deluge of complaints from the public.* その番組の後, 一般の人々からの苦情が殺到した.

**deluge**[2] /dél(j)uːdʒ/ 動他 ▶定義 (通常は受動態で) to send or give sb/sth a very large quantity of sth, all at the same time 〜にとても大量の物を一度に送る, または与える→〜に殺到させる ∥ *They were deluged with applications for the job.* 彼らの元に, その仕事に対する応募が殺到した.

**delusion** /dɪlúːʒ(ə)n/ 名 ⓒ ⓤ ▶定義 a false belief 誤った思い込み→惑わす[される]こと, 錯覚, 思い違い ∥ *He seems to be **under the delusion** that he's popular.* 自分は人気があると, 彼は思い違いをしているようだ. ☞ 動 delude

**de luxe** /dɪlʌ́ks, -lúks, -lúːks/ 形 ▶定義 of extremely high quality and more expensive than usual 非常に質が高く, そして通常よりも値段が高い→高級な, 豪華な ∥ *a de luxe hotel* 豪華なホテル

**delve** /delv/ 動 自 ▶定義 delve into sth to search inside sth 〜の内部を探す→探求する, 詮索(せんさく)する ∥ *She delved into the bag and brought out a tiny box.* 彼女はかばんの中をくまなく探し, 小さな箱を取り出した. (比喩) *We must delve into the past to find the origins of the custom.* その風習の起源を知るためには, 過去を深く探求する必要がある.

＊**demand**[1] /dɪmɑ́ːnd; -mǽnd/ 名 ▶定義 1 ⓒ a demand (for sth/that...) a strong request or order that must be obeyed 従わなければならない強い要求または命令→(〜の・〜という)要求, 請求 ∥ *a demand for changes in the law* 法改正の要求 *I was amazed by their demand that I should leave immediately.* 私は即刻立ち去るべきだという彼らの要求に驚いた. ▶定義 2 **demands** [複数扱い] something that sb makes you do, especially sth that is difficult or tiring だれかに特に困難なまたは疲れることをさせられること→負担 ∥ *Running a marathon **makes huge demands** on the body.* マラソンをすることは, 身体に大きな負担をかける. ▶定義 3 [ⓤ, 単数扱い] demand (for sth/sb) the desire or need for sth among a group of people 人々の集団の間での, 物への欲求または必要性→(〜の)需要 ∥ *We no longer sell that product because there is no demand for it.* 需要がないので, あの商品はもう販売しない.

成句 **in demand** ▶定義 wanted by a lot of people 多くの人々に欲しがられている→需要のある, 人気のある, 引っ張りだこの ∥ *I'm in demand this weekend - I've had three invitations!* 私は今週末は引っ張りだこだ － 3 箇所から招待されているのだから.

**on demand** ▶定義 whenever you ask for it 要求のあるときはいつでも→請求・要求され次第 ∥ *This treatment is available from your doctor on demand.* あなたから要求があればいつでも, 医者はこの治療法で治療します.

＊**demand**[2] /dɪmɑ́ːnd; -mǽnd/ 動他 ▶定義 1 demand to do sth/that...; demand sth to ask for sth in an extremely firm or aggressive way とても断固としたまたは攻撃的な態度で, 〜を要求する→(権利として)〜を要求する, (必要なもの)を請求する ∥ *I walked into the office and demanded to see the manager.* 私は事務所に入り, 支配人に会わせるように言った. *She demanded that I pay her immediately.* 彼女は私に, すぐに支払うよう要求した. *Your behaviour was disgraceful and I demand an apology.* あなたの行為はとてもひどいものでした. 私に謝っていただきたい. ▶定義 2 to need sth 〜を必要とする→〜を要する, (緊急に)必要とする ∥ *a sport that demands skill as well as strength* 体力と同様に技能も要する競技

**demanding** /dɪmáːndɪŋ; -mǽnd-/ 形 ▶定義1 (used about a job, task, etc) needing a lot of effort, care, skill, etc(仕事, 務めなどについて) 多大な労力, 注意, 技能などを必要とする→**手間のかかる, 骨の折れる, きつい** ‖ *It will be a demanding schedule - I have to go to six cities in six days.* これはきつい日程だ－6日間で6都市に行かなくてはならない. ▶定義2 (used about a person) always wanting attention or expecting very high standards of people(人について)常に注目されていたい, あるいは人々にとても高い水準を期待している→**(人が)要求の多い, 自分本位の, 注文の多い** ‖ *Young children are very demanding.* 幼い子供は, とても手がかかる. *a demanding boss* 要求の多い上司

**demise** /dɪmáɪz/ 名 [単数扱い] ▶定義1 the end or failure of sth ～の終わり, または失敗→**終焉(しゅうえん), 終了, 停止** ‖ *Poor business decisions led to the company's demise.* お粗末な経営判断により, 会社は活動停止となった. ▶定義2 (文) the death of a person 人の死→**逝去, 死亡, 崩御**

*****democracy** /dɪmɑ́krəsi/ 名 (複 **democracies**) ▶定義1 ❶ a system in which the government of a country is elected by the people 国家の政府が国民によって選ばれる制度→**民主主義, 民主政治, 民主制** ▶定義2 ❷ a country that has this system この制度を持つ国家→**民主主義国, 民主社会** ▶定義3 ❶ the right of everyone in an organization, etc to be treated equally and to vote on matters that affect them 平等に取り扱われ, 自分たちに影響を及ぼす事柄については投票して決するという, 団体などに属するすべての人が持つ権利→**社会的平等, 民主的精神** ‖ *There is a need for more democracy in the company.* その会社には, もっと社会的平等が必要だ.

**democrat** /démǝkræt/ 名 ❷ ▶定義1 a person who believes in and supports democracy 民主主義を信じ, 支持する人→**民主主義者, 平等論者** ▶定義2 **Democrat** a member or supporter of the Democratic Party of the US アメリカ合衆国の民主党の会員または支持者→**民主党員, 民主党支持者** ☛参 **Republican**

*****democratic** /dèməkrǽtɪk/ 形 ▶定義1 based on the system of democracy 民主主義の制度に基づいた→**民主主義の, 民主政治の** ‖ *democratic elections* 民主主義の選挙 *a democratic government* 民主政治の政府 ▶定義2 having or supporting equal rights for all people すべての人に平等の権利がある, または平等の権利を支持する→**民主的な, (社会的に)平等な** ‖ *a democratic decision (= made by all the people involved)* 民主的な決定 (= 関係するすべての人によってなされた) ― **democratically** /-k(ə)li/ 副 →**民主的に, 民主主義的に, 民主制で** ‖ *a democratically elected government* 民主的に選出された政府

**the Democratic Party** 名 [単数扱い] ▶定義 one of the two main political parties of the US アメリカ合衆国の二大政党の1つ→**民主党**
▶もう1つの主要政党は, the Republican Party(共和党).

**demolish** /dɪmɑ́lɪʃ/ 動 ❶ ▶定義 to destroy sth, for example a building 物, 例えば建物, を破壊する→**～を取り壊す, (粉々に)破壊する** ‖ *The old shops were demolished and a supermarket was built in their place.* 古い何軒かの店が取り壊され, その跡地にスーパーが建設された. (比喩) *She demolished his argument in one sentence.* 彼女は彼の主張を一言で粉砕した. ― **demolition** /dèməlíʃ(ə)n, dìː-/ 名 ❻ ❶ →**取り壊し, 破壊, 粉砕**

**demon** /díːmən/ 名 ❷ ▶定義 an evil spirit 邪悪な霊→**悪魔, 鬼, 鬼神**

*****demonstrate** /démənstrèɪt/ 動 ▶定義1 ❶ **demonstrate sth (to sb)** to show sth clearly by giving proof 証拠を提示して, ～を明瞭(めいりょう)に示す→**(理論・学説など)を証明する, 実証する, 明らかにする** ‖ *Using this chart, I'd like to demonstrate to you what has happened to our sales.* この図表を使って, 売り上げに何が起きているのか明らかにしたいと思います. ▶定義2 ❺ ❶ **demonstrate sth (to sb)** to show and explain to sb how to do sth or how sth works ～をどう扱うか, または～がどのように機能するかを人に示して説明する→**(実物を見せて)～を説明する, 実演してみせる** ‖ *The crew demonstrated the use of lifejackets just after take-off.* 乗務員は離陸直後に救命胴衣の使用法を実演してみせた. *I'm not sure what you mean - could you demonstrate?* あなたのおっしゃる意味がよく分かりません － 実際にやっ

てみていただけますか. ▶定義3 🗐 demon-strate (against/for sb/sth) to take part in a public protest for or against sb/sth ～に賛成または反対する公の抗議行動に参加する→(～支持の・～反対の)示威運動をする, デモをする ‖ Enormous crowds have been demonstrating against the government. ばく大な数の人々が, 政府反対のデモをした.

*__demonstration__ /dèmənstréɪʃ(ə)n/ ▶定義1 🖸 🗵 something that shows clearly that sth exists or is true ～が存在している, または正しいということを明確に示すもの→証明, 実証 ‖ This accident is a clear demonstration of the system's faults. この事故は, 制度の不備を明らかに実証している. ▶定義2 🖸 🗵 an act of showing or explaining to sb how to do sth or how sth works ～をどう扱うか, または物がどのように機能するかを人に示す, または説明する行為→実演, 実物説明 ‖ The salesman gave me a demonstration of what the computer could do. 販売員は, コンピューターで何ができるかを実演してくれた. ▶定義3 🖸 a demon-stration (against/for sb/sth) a public protest for or against sb/sth ～に賛成, または反対する公の抗議行動→(～賛成の・～反対の)デモ, 示威行動 ‖ demonstrations against a new law 新法反対のデモ

__demonstrative__ /dɪmɑ́nstrətɪv/ 形 ▶定義 (used about a person) showing feelings, especially loving feelings, in front of other people (人について) 人々の前で感情, 特に愛情を表す→感情・愛情をあらわに示す, 感情的な

__demonstrator__ /démənstrèɪtər/ 名 🖸 ▶定義 a person who takes part in a public protest 公の抗議行動に参加する人→デモ参加者, 示威運動者

__demoralize__ (または -ise) /dɪmɔ́(ː)r(ə)làɪz/ 動 他 ▶定義 to make sb lose confidence or the courage to continue doing sth ～をやり続ける自信または勇気を…から失わせる→～の士気をくじく, やる気・自信・希望を失わせる ‖ Repeated defeats demoralized the team. 重なる敗北で, チームの士気が失われた. — demoralization (または -isation) /dɪmɔ̀(ː)r(ə)laɪzéɪʃ(ə)n, -lə-/ 名 🗵 → 士気喪失, 意気消沈 — demoralizing (または demoralising) 形→士気・やる気・自信・希望を失

わせる ‖ Constant criticism can be extremely demoralizing. 常に批判されていると, 本当に士気が失われる.

__demure__ /dɪmjʊ́ər/ 形 ▶定義 (used especially about a girl or young woman) shy, quiet and polite (特に, 少女または若い女性について) 内気で物静かで礼儀正しい→おとなしい, 控えめな, 慎み深い

__den__ /den/ 名 🖸 ▶定義1 the place where certain wild animals live, for example lions ある種の野生動物, 例えばライオンが住む場所→住みか, 巣穴, (動物園の)おり ▶定義2 a secret place, especially for illegal activities 特に違法な活動のための, 秘密の場所→(犯罪者などの)隠れ家, 巣窟(そうくつ), アジト ‖ a gambling den とばく部屋

__denial__ /dɪnáɪ(ə)l/ ▶定義1 🖸 a statement that sth is not true ～が事実ではないという申し立て→否定の申し立て ‖ The minister issued a denial that he was involved in the scandal. 大臣は, その醜聞への関与を否定する声明を出した. ▶定義2 🖸 🗵 (a) denial (of sth) refusing to allow sb to have or do sth 人が～を持つまたは行うことを拒否すること→拒絶, 拒否 ‖ a denial of personal freedom 個人の自由の拒否 ▶定義3 🗵 a refusal to accept that sth unpleasant or painful has happened 不愉快な, またはつらい～が起きたことを受け入れることを拒否すること→否定, 打ち消し, 否認 ‖ He's been in denial ever since the accident. その事故以来ずっと彼は否認している. ← 動 deny

__denim__ /dénəm/ 名 🗵 ▶定義 a thick cotton material (often blue) that is used for making clothes, especially trousers (jeans) 衣服, 特にズボン(ジーンズ), を作るために使われる, 厚手の綿素材(青であることが多い)→デニム(厚手の綿布), デニム地 ‖ a denim jacket デニム地の上着

__denomination__ /dɪnὰmənéɪʃ(ə)n/ 名 🖸 ▶定義 one of the different religious groups that you can belong to 人が所属する, 異なった宗教集団の1つ→宗派, 教派

__denote__ /dɪnóʊt/ 動 他 ▶定義 to mean or be a sign of sth ～を意味する, または～の印である→～を表す, 意味する ‖ In algebra the sign x always denotes an unknown quantity. 代数学では, 記号xは常に未知数を表す.

**denounce** /dɪnáʊns/ 動 他 ▶定義 to say publicly that sth is wrong; to be very critical of a person in public 〜が間違っていると公に言う；人に対して人前で非常に批判的である→**(公然と)〜を非難する,責める,弾劾する** ‖ *The actor has been denounced as a bad influence on young people.* その俳優は，若者に悪影響を及ぼしたと非難されている．☛ 名 denunciation

**dense** /dens/ 形 ▶定義1 containing a lot of things or people close together 多数の物または人々が密集して入っている→**密集した,込み合った** ‖ *dense forests* うっそうとした森 *areas of dense population* 人口が密集した地域 ▶定義2 difficult to see through 見通すことが難しい→**(霧・雲などが)濃い, (物質が)高密度の, 見通しが悪い** ‖ *dense fog* 濃霧 ▶定義3 略式 not intelligent; stupid 知的でない；愚かな→**頭の悪い, 飲み込みの遅い** — densely 副 →**密集して, ぎっしりと, 濃く** ‖ *densely populated areas* 人口が密集した地域

**density** /dénsəti/ 名 (複 **densities**) ▶定義1 ❶ the number of things or people in a place in relation to its area ある地域内に存在する物または人々の数→**密度, 密集(状態)** ‖ *There is a high density of wildlife in this area.* この地域には, 野生生物が密集している. ▶定義2 ❶ ❶ (専門用語) the relation of the weight of a substance to its size 物質の重さと大きさの関係→**密度, 濃度, 比重** ‖ *Lead has a high density.* 鉛は密度が高い.

**dent**[1] /dent/ 名 ❶ ▶定義 a place where a flat surface, especially metal, has been hit and damaged but not broken 特に金属の, 平らな表面がたたかれ, 壊れはしないが損なわれてしまった部分→**(小さな)へこみ, くぼみ** ‖ *This tin's got a dent in it.* この缶にはへこみがある.

**dent**[2] /dent/ 動 他 ▶定義 to damage a flat surface by hitting it but not breaking it 平らな表面をたたいて, 壊しはしないが損害を与える→**〜をへこませる, 損なう** ‖ *I hit a wall and dented the front of the car.* 壁に衝突して, 車の前をへこませた.

**dental** /déntl/ 形 ▶定義 connected with teeth 歯に関係する→**歯の, 歯科の** ‖ *dental care/treatment* 歯の手入れ・歯の治療

*★**dentist** /déntɪst/ 名 ▶定義1 ❶ a person whose job is to look after people's teeth 人々の歯の手入れをするのを仕事とする人→**歯科医, 歯医者** ▶定義2 **the dentist's** [単数扱い] the place where a dentist works 歯科医が働く場所→**歯科医院** ‖ *I have to go to the dentist's today.* 今日, 歯医者さんに行かなければならない.

**dentures** /déntʃərz/ = **FALSE TEETH**

**denunciation** /dɪnʌ̀nsiéɪʃ(ə)n/ 名 ❶ ❶ ▶定義 an expression of strong disapproval of sb/sth in public 公然と〜への強い非難を表すこと→**公然の非難, 弾劾, 告発** ☛ 動 denounce

*★**deny** /dɪnáɪ/ 動 他 (現分 **denying**; 三単現 **denies**; 過, 過分 **denied**) ▶定義1 deny sth/doing sth; deny that... to state that sth is not true; to refuse to admit or accept sth 〜が事実ではないと述べる；〜を認める, または受け入れることを拒む→**〜を否定・否認する, 〜ではないと言う** ‖ *In court he denied all the charges.* 彼は法廷で, すべての容疑を否認した. *She denied telling lies/that she had told lies.* 彼女は, うそをついていないと言った. ⇔ **admit** ▶定義2 正式 deny sb sth; deny sth (to sb) to refuse to allow sb to have sth 人が〜を持つことを許さない→**(要求など)を拒絶する, (人に要求されたもの・与えるべきもの)を与えない** ‖ *She was denied permission to remain in the country.* 彼女は, その国に引き続き滞在する許可を得られなかった. ☛ 名 denial

**deodorant** /dióʊdərənt/ 名 ❶ ❶ ▶定義 a chemical substance that you put onto your body to prevent bad smells 不快なにおいを防ぐために身体に付ける化学物質→**防臭剤, 制汗剤, デオドラント**

**dep** 略 departs→**〜発** ‖ *dep London 15.32* 15時32分ロンドン発

**depart** /dɪpáːrt/ 動 自 正式 ▶定義 to leave a place, usually at the beginning of a journey 通常は旅の初めに, ある場所から離れる→**出発する, たつ** ‖ *Ferries depart for Spain twice a day.* スペイン行きの連絡船は, 1日に2回出港する. *The next train to the airport departs from platform 2.* 次の空港行き列車は, 2番ホームから出発します. ☛ 名 departure ☛参 **leave**[1]の注

*★**department** /dɪpáːrtmənt/ 名 ❶ (略 **Dept**) ▶定義1 one of the sections into which an organization for example, a school or a busi-

ness, is divided 組織(例えば学校,企業)が複数の部門に分けられている,その1つ→**部門,(組織・会社などの)部,課,(大学の)学部** ‖ *the Modern Languages department* 現代言語学部 *She works in the accounts department.* 彼女は会計課で働いている. ▶定義**2** a division of the government responsible for a particular subject; a ministry 特定の分野に対して責任を持つ政府の部門;省→**(米)省,(英)局,課** ‖ *the Department of Health* 保健局

**departmental** /dɪpɑːrtméntl, dìːpɑːt-/ 形 ▶定義 concerning a department 部門に関する→**部門(別)の,各部・課・省・局の** ‖ *There is a departmental meeting once a month.* 月に1度,部門別会議がある.

**department store** 名 C ▶定義 a large shop that is divided into sections selling different types of goods さまざまな商品を販売する売り場に分かれている,大規模な小売店→**デパート,百貨店**

*__departure__ /dɪpɑːrtʃər/ 名 C U ▶定義 **1** leaving or going away from a place ある場所から離れること,または立ち去ること→**出発(すること),発車** ‖ *Helen's sudden departure meant I had to do her job as well as mine.* ヘレンの突然の出発は,私が自分の仕事に加えて彼女の分までやらなくてはならないことを意味した. *Passengers should check in at least one hour before departure.* ご搭乗のお客様は,少なくとも出発の1時間前には搭乗手続きをお済ませください. ☛ 動 depart ▶定義**2** a departure (from sth) an action which is different from what is usual or expected 通常とは,または期待されていることとは違う行動→**(伝統・習慣からの)離脱,逸脱** ‖ *a departure from normal practice* 通常の習慣からの離脱

*__depend__ /dɪpénd/ 動
成句 **that depends; it (all) depends** ▶定義 (単独で,または文頭で用いて) used to say that you are not certain of sth until other things have been considered ほかの事柄を考慮に入れるまでは,～に確信が持てないことを言うために用いて→**場合による,その時の事情による,ケースバイケースだ** ‖ *'Can you lend me some money?' 'That depends. How much do you want?'* 「少しお金を貸してくれませんか」「事情によりますよ.いくら借りたいのですか」 *I don't know whether I'll see him. It depends what time he gets here.* 彼に会えるかどうか分からない.彼が何時に着くかによる.

句動詞 **depend on sb/sth** ▶定義 to be able to trust sb/sth to do sth; to rely on sb/sth ～が何かをすると当てにできる;～に頼る→**～を頼りにする,(援助など)を当てにする** ‖ *If you ever need any help, you know you can depend on me.* 助けが必要なときはいつでも私を頼ってください. *You can't depend on the trains. They're always late.* 電車は当てにならない.いつも時間に遅れる. *I was depending on getting the money today.* 私は,今日お金が入るのを当てにしていた.

**depend on sb/sth (for sth)** ▶定義 to need sb/sth to provide sth ～が…を提供してくれることを必要とする→**(援助など)に頼る,依存する** ‖ *Our organization depends on donations from the public.* 我々の組織は,一般からの寄付に頼っている.

**depend on sth** ▶定義 to be decided or influenced by sb/sth ～によって決められる,または影響される→**～次第である,～による** ‖ *His whole future depends on these exams.* 彼のすべての将来は,これらの試験に懸かっている.

**dependable** /dɪpéndəb(ə)l/ 形 ▶定義 that can be trusted; reliable 信頼できる;頼りになる→**信頼できる,頼りになる,当てになる** ‖ *The bus service is very dependable.* バスの便はとても正確だ.

**dependant** (特に 米 **dependent**) /dɪpéndənt/ 名 C ▶定義 a person who depends on sb else for money, a home, food, etc お金,住居,食物などをほかの人に頼っている人→**扶養家族,居候** ‖ *insurance cover for you and all your dependants* 本人および扶養家族全員に対する保険の補償範囲

**dependence** /dɪpénd(ə)ns/ 名 U ▶定義 **dependence on sb/sth** the state of needing sb/sth ～を必要とする状況→**頼ること,依存** ‖ *The country wants to reduce its dependence on imported oil.* その国は,輸入石油への依存を減らしたいと願っている.

**dependency** /dɪpénd(ə)nsi/ 名 U ▶定義 the state of being dependent on sb/sth; the state of being unable to live without sth, especially a drug ～に依存している状態; 何か, 特に麻薬, なしでは暮らせない状態 ➡依存, 従属; 麻薬中毒 (症)

\***dependent** /dɪpénd(ə)nt/ 形 ▶定義1 dependent (on sb/sth) needing sb/sth to support you ～の援助を必要としている➡(～に)頼っている, (～の)世話になっている ‖ *The industry is heavily dependent on government funding.* その産業は, 政府の資金援助に大きく依存している. *Do you have any dependent children?* 独り立ちしていない子供たちはいますか. ▶定義2 dependent on sb/sth influenced or decided by sth ～の影響を受ける, または～によって決まる➡～次第の, ～に左右される ‖ *The price you pay is dependent on the number in your group.* あなたが支払う値段は, グループの人数によります. ⇔ **independent**

**depict** /dɪpíkt/ 動他 ▶定義1 to show sb/sth in a painting or drawing 絵画または線描で～を表す➡～を絵で示す, 描く, 描写する ‖ *a painting depicting a country scene* 田園の風景を描いた絵画 ▶定義2 to describe sb/sth in words 言葉で～を描写する➡(言葉で)～を描く, 叙述する ‖ *The novel depicts rural life a century ago.* この小説は, 1世紀前の田園生活を描いている.

**deplete** /dɪplíːt/ 動他 ▶定義 to reduce the amount of sth so that there is not much left 残りがほとんどないように, ～の量を減らす➡(資金・勢力など)を激減・消耗させる, (資源など)を使い果たす ‖ *We are depleting the world's natural resources.* 私たちは, 世界の天然資源を激減させている. ― depletion /dɪplíːʃ(ə)n/ 名 Ｕ ➡使い果たすこと, 枯渇, 消耗

**deplorable** /dɪplɔ́ːrəb(ə)l/ 形 正式 ▶定義 morally bad and deserving disapproval 道徳的に悪く, 非難されるべき➡嘆かわしい, 非難すべき, ひどい ‖ *They are living in deplorable conditions.* 彼らはひどい状況で生活している. ― deplorably /-əbli/ 副 ➡嘆かわしく, ひどく

**deplore** /dɪplɔ́ːr/ 動他 正式 ▶定義 to feel or say that sth is morally bad ～が道徳的に悪いと感じる, または言う➡～を遺憾に思う, 非難する ‖ *I deplore such dishonest behaviour.* そのような不誠実な振る舞いを遺憾に思う.

**deploy** /dɪplɔ́ɪ/ 動他 ▶定義1 to put soldiers or weapons in a position where they are ready to fight 兵または武器を, いつでも戦闘できる場所に配置する➡配置する, (兵器を)配備する ▶定義2 to use sth in a useful and successful way ～を有効にうまく活用する➡(資金など)を効果的に運用する ― deployment 名 Ｕ ➡(軍隊の)配置, (兵器の)配備 ‖ *the deployment of troops* 軍隊の配備

**deport** /dɪpɔ́ːrt/ 動他 ▶定義 to force sb to leave a country because he/she has no legal right to be there 滞在する法的な権利がないので, ～を強制的に国外に出す➡(外国人)を国外に追放する, 退去させる ‖ *A number of illegal immigrants have been deported.* 多数の不法移民が国外に追放された. ― deportation /dìːpɔːrtéɪʃ(ə)n/ 名 Ｃ Ｕ ➡国外追放・退去

**depose** /dɪpóʊz/ 動他 ▶定義 to remove a ruler or leader from power 統治者または指導者を権力の座から追放する➡～を退位させる, 権力の座から退ける, 解任する ‖ *There was a revolution and the dictator was deposed.* 革命が起こり, 独裁者は権力の座から退けられた.

**deposit**¹ /dɪpázət/ 動他 ▶定義1 to put sth down somewhere ～をある場所に置く➡～を置く ‖ *He deposited his bags on the floor and sat down.* 彼は床にかばんを置き, 座った. ▶定義2 (used about liquid or a river) to leave sth lying on a surface, as the result of a natural or chemical process (液体または河川について) 自然または化学作用によるプロセスを経た結果, ～が表面に残される➡～を堆積(たいせき)させる, 沈殿させる ‖ *mud deposited by a flood* 洪水で堆積された泥 ▶定義3 to put money into an account at a bank 銀行の口座にお金を入れる➡～を預金する, 入金する ‖ *He deposited £20 a week into his savings account.* 彼は毎週20ポンドを自分の預金口座に預金した. ▶定義4 deposit sth (in sth); deposit sth (with sb/sth) to put sth valuable in an official place where it is safe until needed again 貴重な物をまた必要なときまで安全な公的な場所に置く➡～を預ける ‖ *Valuables can be deposited in the hotel safe.* 貴重品は, ホテルの金庫に預けられます.

**deposit**² /dɪpázət/ 名 Ｃ ▶定義1 a deposit (on sth) a sum of money which is the first payment for sth, with the rest of the money to be paid later 物に対して最初に支払われる金額,残金は後で支払われる→**手付け金,頭金** ‖ *Once you have paid a deposit, the booking will be confirmed.* 手付け金が支払われた時点で,予約が確認されます. ▶定義2 a deposit (on sth)[通常は単数]a sum of money that you pay when you rent sth and get back when you return it without damage 物を借りるときに支払い,それを無傷で返却すれば戻ってくる金額→**保証金** ‖ *Boats can be hired for £5 an hour, plus £20 deposit.* 1時間あたり5ポンド,それと保証金20ポンドでボートを借りられる. ▶定義3 a sum of money paid into a bank account 銀行口座に入金された金額→**預金,積立金** ▶定義4 a substance that has been left on a surface or in the ground as the result of a natural or chemical process 自然または化学作用によるプロセスを経た結果,表面または地中に残された物質→**堆積(たいせき)物,沈殿物,埋蔵物** ‖ *mineral deposits* 鉱床

**deposit account** 名 🅒 医 ▶定義 a type of bank account where your money earns interest. You cannot take money out of a deposit account without arranging it first with the bank. 預けたお金に利子がつく,銀行口座の一種. 前もって銀行に手配しないと,預金を引き出せない→**通知預金口座**

**depot** /dépoʊ; díːp-/ 名 🅒 ▶定義1 a place where large numbers of vehicles (buses, lorries, etc) are kept when not in use 多数の乗り物(バス,トラックなど)が,使用されないときに置かれている場所→**(バス・鉄道などの)車庫** ▶定義2 a place where large amounts of food, goods or equipment are stored 多量の食品,商品,または器具が貯蔵されている場所→**倉庫,貯蔵所** ▶定義3 米 a small bus or railway station 小さなバスの停留所または鉄道の駅→**(小さな)駅**

**depreciate** /dɪpríːʃieɪt/ 動 🅐 ▶定義 to become less valuable over a period of time ある期間を過ぎて価値が下がる→**価値が下がる** ‖ *New cars start to depreciate the moment they are on the road.* 新車は,道路に出た瞬間から価値が下がり始める. — **depreciation** /dɪpriːʃiéɪʃ(ə)n/ 名 🅒 🅤 →**価値の低下,軽視,侮り,(会計)減価償却**

**depress** /dɪprés/ 動 🅐 ▶定義1 to make sb unhappy and without hope or enthusiasm 人を ふさぎこませ,希望または熱意を失わせる→**~を落胆させる,意気消沈させる** ‖ *The thought of going to work tomorrow really depresses me.* 明日は仕事に行くと思うと,気がめいる. ▶定義2 (used about business) to cause sth to become less successful(商売について)物事がうまくいかなくなる原因となる→**~を不況・不景気にする,(価格・需要など)を低下させる** ‖ *The reduction in the number of tourists has depressed local trade.* 旅行者の減少により,地元の商売は不振になった. ▶定義3 正式 to press sth down on a machine, etc 機械などに付いている~を押し下げる→**(レバーなど)を押し下げる,(ボタンなど)を押す** ‖ *To switch off the machine, depress the lever.* 機械のスイッチを切るには,レバーを押し下げてください. — **depressing** 形 →**気のめいるような,意気消沈させる,憂鬱(ゆううつ)な** ‖ *The thought of growing old alone is very depressing.* 1人で老いていくことを考えると,とても気がめいる. — **depressingly** 副 →**憂鬱に,気のめいるほど**

**depressed** /dɪprést/ 形 ▶定義1 very unhappy, often for a long period of time しばしば長期間にわたって,とてもふさぎ込んでいる→**落胆した,気がめいった** ‖ *He's been very depressed since he lost his job.* 職を失ってから,彼はとても気落ちしている. ▶定義2 (used about a place or an industry) without enough businesses or jobs(場所または産業について)十分な仕事または職がない→**不景気の,不振の**

★**depression** /dɪpréʃ(ə)n/ 名 ▶定義1 🅤a feeling of unhappiness that lasts for a long time. Depression can be a medical condition and may have physical signs, for example being unable to sleep, etc. 長期間続く不幸な気分. うつ病は医療が必要な健康状態で,身体的な兆候,例えば眠れないなど,を伴うこともあり得る→**憂鬱(ゆううつ),落胆,うつ病** ‖ *clinical/postnatal depression* 臨床的うつ病・産後うつ病 ▶定義2 🅒🅤a period when the economic situation is bad, with little business activity and many people without a job 事業活動はほとんどなく,失業者の多い,経済状況が悪い時期→**(長期に及ぶ深刻な)不景気,不況** ‖ *The country was in the grip of (an) economic depression.*

その国は，経済危機に見舞われていた．
▶定義3 ❷a part of a surface that is lower than the parts around it その周囲よりも低くなっている地表の一部→**くぼみ, くぼ地, 低地** ‖ *Rainwater collects in shallow depressions in the ground.* 雨水は地面の浅いくぼみにたまる．

**deprive** /dɪpráɪv/ 動⓲ ▶定義 deprive sb/sth of sth to prevent sb/sth from having sth; to take away sth from sb 〜が…を持つことを妨げる; 〜から…を取り上げる→**(人に)〜を享受させない；(物・権利・地位などを)〜から奪う, 奪い去る** ‖ *The prisoners were deprived of food.* 囚人たちは食事を取り上げられた．— **deprivation** /dèprəvéɪʃ(ə)n, diːpraɪ-/ 名 ⓾→**剥奪(はくだつ)(された状態), 奪取, 喪失**

**deprived** /dɪpráɪvd/ 形 ▶定義 not having enough of the basic things in life, such as food, money, etc 生活に基本的なもの, 例えば食べ物, お金など, が十分ではない→**恵まれない, 困窮した, 貧しい** ‖ *He came from a deprived background.* 彼は恵まれない生い立ちだ．

**Dept** 略 department→**部門** ‖ *the Sales Dept* 販売部門

*★**depth** /depθ/ 名 ▶定義1 ❷⓾the distance down from the top to the bottom of sth 〜の最上部から底部までの距離→**深さ, 深度** ‖ *The hole should be 3cm in depth.* その穴はおそらく3センチの深さだろう． ▶定義2 ❷⓾the distance from the front to the back of sth 〜の前面から背面までの距離→**奥行き** ‖ *the depth of a shelf* 棚の奥行き ☛ **length** のさし絵 ▶定義3 ⓾the amount of emotion, knowledge, etc that a person has 人が持っている感情, 知識などの量→**(人格・知識・考えなどの)深さ, 深遠** ‖ *He tried to convince her of the depth of his feelings for her.* 彼は彼女に対する思いの深さを信じてもらおうとした． ▶定義4 ❷[通常は複数]the deepest, most extreme or serious part of sth 物の最も深い, 最も極端な, または最も深刻な部分→**最も深い・強烈な・厳しい部分, 奥まった所, どん底** ‖ *in the depths of winter (= when it is coldest)* 真冬(最も寒い時)に ☛ 形 **deep** 成句 **in depth** ▶定義 looking at all the details; in a thorough way すべての細部をよく見ること; 徹底的なやり方で→**詳細に; 徹底して, 広範囲にわたって** ‖ *to discuss a problem in depth* 徹底的に問題を議論する

**out of your depth** ▶定義1 英in water that is too deep for you to stand up in 深すぎて自分の背が立たない水中で→**背が立たない深さで** ▶定義2 in a situation that is too difficult for you 自分には難しすぎる状況で→**理解できない, 能力の及ばない** ‖ *When they start discussing politics I soon get out of my depth.* 彼らが政治について議論し始めると, すぐに私は理解できなくなる．

**deputation** /dèpjətéɪʃ(ə)n/ 名[❷, 単数または複数形の動詞と共に] ▶定義 a group of people sent to sb to act or speak for others ほかの人々の代わりに行動するまたは話すために, 人の所へ送られた集団→**代表(委員)団**

**deputize**(または **-ise**) /dépjətàɪz/ 動⓲ ▶定義 deputize (for sb) to act for sb in a higher position, who is away or unable to do sth 自分より高い地位にいる, 不在である, または〜をすることができない人の代わりに行動する→**代理をする・務める**

*★**deputy** /dépjəti/ 名 ❷(複 **deputies**) ▶定義 the second most important person in a particular organization, who does the work of his/her manager if the manager is away ある組織で2番目に重要な地位にあり, 上司が不在の場合はその仕事を行う人→**代理(人), 副〜** ‖ *the deputy head of a school* 副校長

**derail** /dɪréɪl/ 動⓲ ▶定義 to cause a train to come off a railway track 列車を線路から外れさせる→**〜を脱線させる**

**derailment** /dɪréɪlmənt/ 名 ❷⓾ ▶定義 an occasion when sth causes a train to come off a railway track 列車が線路から外れることを何かが引き起こした場合→**脱線**

**deranged** /dɪréɪndʒd/ 形 ▶定義 thinking and behaving in a way that is not normal, especially because of mental illness 特に精神病のために, 普通ではない様子で考え, 振る舞うこと→**錯乱した, 発狂した**

**derby** /dáːrbi; dáːr/ 名 ❷(複 **derbies**) ▶定義1 英a race or sports competition 競走またはスポーツの試合→**〜競技, 〜レース** ‖ *a motorcycle derby* オートバイレース ▶定義2 英 **the Derby** a horse race which takes place every year at Epsom エプソムで毎年開催される競馬→**ダービー**

一競馬 ▶定義3 🏴= BOWLER(1)

**derelict** /dérəlɪkt/ 形 ▶定義 no longer used and in bad condition もう使用されないで、ひどい状態にある→(建物などが)遺棄・放棄された ‖ *a derelict house* 見捨てられた家

**deride** /dɪráɪd/ 動他 ▶定義 to say that sb/sth is ridiculous; to laugh at sth in a cruel way ～がばかげていると言う; ～をあざけって笑う→～をばかにする; ～を嘲笑(ちょうしょう)する — **derision** /dɪríʒ(ə)n/ 名 Ⓤ ▶あざけり, あざ笑い, 嘲笑 ‖ *Her comments were met with derision.* 彼女の意見は嘲笑された. — **derisive** /dɪráɪsɪv, -zɪv/ 形 →あざける・ばかにするような, 嘲笑的な ‖ *'What rubbish!' he said with a derisive laugh.*「何て下らない」彼はあざ笑いながら言った.

**derisory** /dɪráɪsəri, -zə-/ 形 ▶定義 too small or of too little value to be considered seriously まじめに考慮するには、あまりにも小さいまたは価値がない→取るに足りない, 嘲笑(ちょうしょう)されるほどの ‖ *Union leaders rejected the derisory pay offer.* 組合の幹部たちは, 取るに足りないほどの賃金の申し出を拒絶した.

**derivation** /dèrəvéɪʃ(ə)n/ 名 Ⓒ Ⓤ ▶定義 the origin from which a word or phrase has developed 言葉または句が発展してきた源→語源, 起源

**derivative** /dɪrívətɪv/ 名 Ⓒ ▶定義 a form of sth (especially a word) that has developed from the original form 本来の形から発展してきた物 (特に言葉)の形→派生したもの, 派生語 ‖ *'Sadness' is a derivative of 'sad.'* sadnessは, sadの派生語である.

**derive** /dɪráɪv/ 動 ▶定義1 他 正式 derive sth from sth to get sth (especially a feeling or an advantage) from sth ～から…(特に感情または利益)を得る→(～から)…を引き出す, 得る, 見いだす ‖ *I derive great satisfaction from my work.* 私は仕事から大きな満足感を得ている. ▶定義2 自他 (used about a name or word) to come from sth; to have sth as its origin (名前または言葉について)～から来る; 源としての～を持つ→(～から)出る, 派生する; (～に)由来する ‖ *The town derives its name from the river on which it was built.* その町の名前は, 川に接して町が作られたので, その川の名前に由来している.

**derogatory** /dɪrágət(ə)ri; -tɔ̀ːri/ 形 ▶定義 expressing a lack of respect for, or a low opinion of sth ～への尊敬が欠如している, または低く評価していることを表している→(言葉などが)軽べつ的な, (名誉・価値などを)傷付けるような ‖ *derogatory comments about the standard of my work* 私の仕事の水準を傷付けるような意見

**descend** /dɪsénd/ 動 自他 正式 ▶定義 to go down to a lower place; to go down sth 低い場所へ下る→下る, 降りる; ～を下げる ‖ *The plane started to descend and a few minutes later we landed.* 飛行機は下降し始め, 数分後に着陸した. *She descended the stairs slowly.* 彼女はゆっくりと階段を降りた. ⇔**ascend**
成句 **be descended from sb** ▶定義 to have sb as a relative in past times ～を過去における身内とする→～の子孫である, ～の系統を引く ‖ *He says he's descended from a Russian prince.* 彼は, 自分がロシアの王子の子孫だと言う.

**descendant** /dɪsénd(ə)nt/ 名 Ⓒ ▶定義 a person who belongs to the same family as sb who lived a long time ago 遠い昔に生きた人と同じ家系に属する人→子孫, 末裔(まつえい) ‖ *Her family are descendants of one of the first Englishmen to arrive in America.* 彼女の一族は, アメリカに最初に着いた英国人の1人の子孫だ. 参 ancestor

**descent** /dɪsént/ 名 ▶定義1 Ⓒ a movement down to a lower place 低い場所に下る動き→降りる・下ること, 下降, 低下 ‖ *The pilot informed us that we were about to begin our descent.* 操縦士は, 機体が下降し始めるところだと知らせた. ▶定義2 Ⓤ a person's family origins 一族の源→家系, 血統 ‖ *He is of Italian descent.* 彼はイタリア系だ.

★**describe** /dɪskráɪb/ 動 他 ▶定義 describe sb/sth (to/for sb); describe sb/sth (as sth) to say what sb/sth is like, or what happened ～がどのようなものであるか, または何が起きたかを言う→～の様子を述べる, ～を描写する, 説明する ‖ *Can you describe the bag you lost?* あなたがなくしたかばんの特徴を説明してくれませんか. *It's impossible to describe how I felt.* 私がどのように感じたかを言い表すことは不可能だ. *The thief was described as tall, thin, and aged about twenty.* 泥棒は背が高く, やせ形で,

年齢は20歳前後であると述べられた.

**description** /dɪskrípʃ(ə)n/ 名 ▶定義1 C U a picture in words of sb/sth or of sth that happened 人や物,または起きた物事についての言葉による生き生きとした描写 ➔**叙述,描写** ‖ *The man gave the police a detailed description of the burglar.* その男は警察に強盗の様子を詳しく話した. ▶定義2 C a type or kind of sth ～の型式または種類 ➔**種類,(商品の)銘柄** ‖ *It must be a tool of some description, but I don't know what it's for.* これはある種の道具に違いないのだが,何に使うものか私には分からない.

**descriptive** /dɪskríptɪv/ 形 ▶定義 that describes sb/sth, especially in a skilful or interesting way 特に巧みな,または興味深いやり方で,～を描写する ➔**生き生きと描写する** ‖ *a piece of descriptive writing* 生き生きと描写された一編の作品 *She gave a highly descriptive account of the journey.* 彼女はその旅行をとても生き生きと描写して報告した.

**desert**¹ /dɪzə́ːrt/ 動 ▶定義1 U to leave sb/sth, usually for ever 普通永遠に,～から去る ➔**(家族・地位・立場など)を見捨てる,(見捨てて)去る** ‖ *Many people have deserted the countryside and moved to the towns.* 多くの人が田舎を捨て,町に移った. ▶定義2 自 U (used especially about sb in the armed forces) to leave without permission (特に軍隊に所属する人について)許可なく立ち去る ➔**職務を捨てる,部署を離れる,脱走する;(持ち場・職場)を捨てる,～から脱走する** ‖ *He deserted because he didn't want to fight.* 彼は戦闘したくなかったので脱走した. ― desertion 名 C U ➔**(家族など)を見捨てること,職場放棄,脱走**

**desert**² /dézərt/ 名 C U ▶定義 a large area of land, usually covered with sand, that is hot and has very little water and very few plants 通常は砂に覆われている,暑くて水と植物はほとんどない,広大な土地 ➔**砂漠,荒野**

**deserted** /dɪzə́ːrtɪd/ 形 ▶定義 empty, because all the people have left すべての人々が去ってしまったため,人気のない ➔**人の住まない,さびれ果てた,とてもすいている** ‖ *a deserted house* 空き家

**deserter** /dɪzə́ːrtər/ 名 C ▶定義 a person who leaves the armed forces without permission 許可なく軍隊を離れた人 ➔**脱走兵**

**desert island** 名 C ▶定義 an island, especially a tropical one, where nobody lives だれも住んでいない島,特に熱帯の島 ➔**無人島**

**deserve** /dɪzə́ːrv/ 動 U (進行形は不可) ▶定義 to earn sth, either good or bad, because of sth that you have done 自分がした事に対して,良いものにせよ悪いものにせよ,何かを受け取る ➔**～をされる,～に値する** ‖ *We've done a lot of work and we deserve a break.* 私たちはたくさん仕事をしたので,休んで当然だ. *He deserves to be punished severely for such a crime.* 彼はそのような犯罪を犯したのだから,厳しく処罰されて当然だ.

▶この動詞は進行形では使われないが,現在分詞(= -ing形)を見ることは一般的である: *There are other aspects of the case deserving attention.*(その事例については,注目すべき別の見方がある.)

**deservedly** /dɪzə́ːrv(ə)dli/ 副 ▶定義 in a way that is right because of what sb has done ～が行った物事の報いとして正当であるように ➔**当然,正当に** ‖ *He deservedly won the Best Actor award.* 当然彼は,最優秀男優賞を勝ち取った.

**deserving** /dɪzə́ːrvɪŋ/ 形 ▶定義 deserving (of sth) that you should give help, money, etc to 援助,金銭などを与えるべき ➔**(特に経済的に)援助すべき,(奨学金などの)援助に値する** ‖ *This charity is a most deserving cause.* この慈善事業は,最も援助すべきものだ.

**design**¹ /dɪzáɪn/ 名 ▶定義1 U the way in which sth is planned and made or arranged 物の設計から作成,または配置のされ方 ➔**デザイン,意匠,図案** ‖ *Design faults have been discovered in the car.* その車にはデザイン上の失敗があることが分かった. ▶定義2 U the process and skill of making drawings that show how sth should be made, how it will work, etc ～の作り方,作動の仕方などを表した図面を作成する過程とその技術 ➔**デザイン,意匠術,設計技術** ‖ *to study industrial design* 工業デザインを勉強する *graphic design* グラフィックデザイン ▶定義3 C a design (for sth) a drawing or plan that shows how sth should be made, built, etc 物の作成方法,建築方法などを表した図面または設計図 ➔**設計図,計画** ‖ *The architect showed us* *her design for the new theatre.* 建築家は,私たちに新しい劇場の設計図を見せた. ▶定義4 [C] a pattern of lines, shapes, etc that decorate sth ～を装飾する,線,形などによる模様➜**模様,柄** ‖ *a T-shirt with a geometric design on it* 幾何学模様のTシャツ ☛類 **pattern**

***design**² /dɪzáɪn/ [動] ▶定義1 [自][他] to plan and make a drawing of how sth will be made 物がどのように作成されるかを計画して図面を作成する➜**デザインする; ～をデザイン・設計する** ‖ *to design cars/dresses/houses* 車を設計する・ドレスをデザインする・家を設計する ▶定義2 [他] to invent, plan and develop sth for a particular purpose 一定の目的のために～を考案し,計画して開発する➜**～の計画を立てる,もくろむ,～を(…の用途に)充てる** ‖ *The bridge wasn't designed for such heavy traffic.* その橋は,そのような激しい交通量を考えて設計されたのではない.

**designate** /dézɪgnèɪt/ [動][他] (しばしば受動態で) [正式] ▶定義1 designate sth as sth to give sth a name to show that it has a particular purpose 特定の目的を持っていることを示すために,～に名目を与える➜**～を指定する,選定する** ‖ *This has been designated (as) a conservation area.* ここは保護管理地区に指定されている. ▶定義2 designate sb (as) sth to choose sb to do a particular job or task 特定の仕事または任務を行う人を選ぶ➜**～を任命する,指名する** ‖ *Who has she designated (as) her deputy?* 彼女は,自分の代理にだれを指名したのですか. ▶定義3 to show or mark sth ～を表す,または示す➜**～を明確に示す,明示する** ‖ *These arrows designate the emergency exits.* これらの矢印は,非常口を明示する.

**designer** /dɪzáɪnər/ [名][C] ▶定義 a person whose job is to make drawings or plans showing how sth will be made 物がどのように作られるかを示す図面または設計図を作成することを仕事とする人➜**デザイナー,設計者** ‖ *a fashion/jewellery designer* 服飾・宝石デザイナー *designer jeans (= made by a famous designer)* デザイナージーンズ(= 有名デザイナーによって作られた)

**desirable** /dɪzáɪərəb(ə)l/ [形] ▶定義1 wanted, often by many people; worth having 通常は多くの人によって,求められている; 持つに値する➜**望ましい,好ましい** ‖ *Experience is desirable but not essential for this job.* この仕事には,経験があることは望ましいが絶対に必要なものではない. ▶定義2 sexually attractive 性的に魅力的な➜**性的魅力のある,セクシーな** ⇔ **undesirable**

**desire**¹ /dɪzáɪər/ [名][C][U] (a) desire (for sth/to do sth) ▶定義1 the feeling of wanting sth very much; a strong wish ～を強く望む気持ち; 強い願望➜**(強い)願い,願望,欲望** ‖ *the desire for a peaceful solution to the crisis* 危機に対する平和的な解決への願い *I have no desire to visit that place again.* 私は,あの場所をまた訪れたいとは思わない. ▶定義2 the wish for a sexual relationship with sb ～と性的な関係を持ちたいという願望➜**性欲**

**desire**² /dɪzáɪər/ [動][他] ▶定義1 [正式] (進行形は不可) to want; to wish for 望む; ～を願望する➜**～を望む,願う,(～しようと)欲する** ‖ *They have everything they could possibly desire.* 彼らは,望み得るものはすべて持っている. *The service in the restaurant left a lot to be desired (= was very bad).* そのレストランのサービスには,遺憾なことが多い(= とても悪い). ▶定義2 to find sb/sth sexually attractive ～に性的な魅力を見つける➜**(性的に)～を求める**

➤この動詞は進行形では使われないが,現在分詞(= -ing形)を見ることは一般的である: *Not desiring another argument, she turned away.* (それ以上,議論を続けたくなかったので,彼女は顔を背けた.)

***desk** /desk/ [名][C] ▶定義1 a type of table, often with drawers, that you sit at to write or work 通常は引き出しが付いていて,ものを書くまたは仕事するために向かう,テーブルの一種➜**机** ‖ *The pupils took their books out of their desks.* 生徒たちは机から本を取り出した. *He used to be a pilot but now he has* ***a desk job*** *(= he works in an office).* 彼はかつてパイロットであったが,現在はデスクワークをしている(= 彼は事務所で働いている). ▶定義2 a table or place in a building where a particular service is provided 特定のサービスを提供している,建物内のテーブルまたは場所➜**(ホテル・会社などの)受付,フロント** ‖ *an information desk* 案内所 *Take your suitcases and tickets to the check-in*

**desktop** /désktàp/ 名 C ▶定義1 the top of a desk 机の上→**机上, 卓上** ▶定義2 a computer screen on which you can see symbols (icons) showing the programs, information, etc that are available to be used 使用可能なプログラムや情報などを示した記号(アイコン)が表示されているコンピューター画面→**デスクトップ(「机の上」を表した, GUI 環境の基本画面)** ▶定義3 (または **desktop computer**) a computer that can fit on a desk 机の上に置くのに適したコンピューター→**デスクトップコンピューター** ☞参 **laptop**

**desktop publishing** (略 DTP) 名 U ▶定義 the use of a small computer and a machine for printing, to produce books, magazines and other printed material 小型コンピューターと印刷用の機械を使って, 本, 雑誌, そのほかの印刷物を作り出すこと→**デスクトップパブリッシング(出版作業をコンピューターとレーザープリンターを用いて行う出版方式)**

**desolate** /désələt, déz-/ 形 ▶定義1 (used about a place)empty in a way that seems very sad(場所について)とても悲しく見えるほど空虚→**荒れ果てた, 住む人もない** ∥ desolate wasteland 住む人もない荒地 ▶定義2 (used about a person) lonely, very unhappy and without hope(人について)孤独でとても不幸で希望のない→**(人・生活などが)孤独な, 寂しい, 惨めな** ― desolation /dèsəléɪʃ(ə)n, dèz-/ 名 U →**荒廃, 孤独** ∥ a scene of desolation. 荒れ果てた風景 He felt utter desolation when his wife died. 妻が死んだ時, 彼は孤独を痛感した.

**despair**¹ /dɪspéər/ 名 U ▶定義 the state of having lost all hope すべての望みを失った状態→**絶望, 失望, 断念** ∥ I felt like giving up **in despair**. 私は絶望して, やめたくなった. ― despairing 形 →**(すっかり)絶望している, 絶望的な** ∥ a despairing cry 絶望の叫び ☞参 **desperate**

**despair**² /dɪspéər/ 動 自 ▶定義 despair (of sb/sth) to lose all hope that sth will happen ~が起きるという, すべての望みを失う→**絶望する, あきらめる** ∥ We began to despair of ever finding somewhere to live. 私たちは, 住む所なんて絶対に見つからないと思い始めた.

**despatch** /dɪspætʃ/ = **DISPATCH**

**desperate** /désp(ə)rət/ 形 ▶定義1 out of control and ready to do anything to change the situation you are in because it is so terrible 自分のいる状況があまりにもひどいので, それを変えるためにはどんな事でも制しきれないほどに進んでやる気のある→**必死の, 自暴自棄の** ∥ She became desperate when her money ran out. お金が尽きた時, 彼女は自暴自棄になった. ▶定義2 done with little hope of success, as a last thing to try when everything else has failed ほかのすべての事が失敗したとき, 最後の試みとして, 成功の望みはほとんどなくて行われた→**(状況が)絶望的な, 最終手段の** ∥ I made a desperate attempt to persuade her to change her mind. 彼女を説得して考えを変えさせようと必死に試みた. ▶定義3 desperate (for sth/to do sth) wanting or needing sth very much ~がとても欲しい, または必要とする→**(物・機会などが)欲しくてたまらない, (~したくて)仕方がない** ∥ Let's go into a cafe. I'm desperate for a drink. コーヒー店に入ろう. 飲み物が欲しくてたまらない. ▶定義4 terrible, very serious ひどい, とても重大な→**ひどい, 甚だしい, すさまじい** ∥ There is a desperate shortage of skilled workers. 熟練労働者の不足が甚だしい. ― desperately 副 →**必死に, ひどく** ∥ She was desperately (= extremely) unlucky not to win. 勝たなかったとは, 彼女もひどく(= 極めて)運が悪かった. ― desperation /dèspəréɪʃ(ə)n/ 名 U →**自暴自棄, やけ**

**despicable** /dɪspíkəb(ə)l, déspɪk-/ 形 ▶定義 very unpleasant or evil とても不愉快な, または邪悪な→**卑しむべき, 見下げ果てた, 卑劣な** ∥ a despicable act of terrorism テロの卑劣な行為

**despise** /dɪspáɪz/ 動 他 ▶定義 to hate sb/sth very much ~をとても嫌悪する→**~を大嫌いになる** ∥ I despise him for lying to me. 彼は私にうそをついたので, 大嫌いだ.

**despite** /dɪspáɪt/ 前 ▶定義 without being affected by the thing mentioned 言及された事に影響されることなく→**~にもかかわらず** ∥ Despite having very little money, they enjoy life. お金がほとんどないにもかかわらず, 彼らは人生を楽しんでいる. The scheme went ahead despite public opposition. 社会の反対にもかかわらず,

その計画は進行した. ☛類 **in spite of**

**despondent** /dɪspάnd(ə)nt/ 形 ▶定義 despondent (about/over sth) without hope; expecting no improvement 望みのない; 進歩を期待していない→失望した, 落胆した, 意気消沈した ‖ *She was becoming increasingly despondent about finding a job.* 彼女は仕事を見つけることに次第に失望していった. — **despondency** /dɪspάnd(ə)nsi/ 名 Ⓤ ▶失望, 落胆, 意気消沈

**dessert** /dɪzə́ːrt/ 名 Ⓒ Ⓤ ▶定義 something sweet that is eaten after the main part of a meal 主な食事の後に食べる甘いもの→デザート ‖ *What would you like for dessert - ice cream or fresh fruit?* デザートは, アイスクリームと新鮮な果物のどちらになさいますか.
☛参 **pudding, sweet**

**dessertspoon** /dɪzə́ːrtspùːn/ 名 Ⓒ ▶定義 a spoon used for eating sweet food after the main part of a meal 主な食事の後に甘いものを食べるために使われるスプーン→デザートスプーン

**destabilize** /dìːstéɪbəlàɪz/ 動 ⑪ ▶定義 to make a system, government, country, etc become less safe and successful 制度, 政府, 国などの安全と成功の度合いを低くさせる→(政治的に)~を不安定にする, 動揺させる ‖ *Terrorist attacks were threatening to destabilize the government.* テロリストの攻撃は, 政府を動揺させるための脅しだった. ☛参 **stabilize**

**destination** /dèstənéɪʃ(ə)n/ 名 Ⓒ ▶定義 the place where sb/sth is going ~が向かっている場所→目的地, 行き先, 届け先 ‖ *I finally reached my destination two hours late.* 2時間遅れてやっと目的地に着いた. *popular holiday destinations like the Bahamas* バハマのような, 人気のある行楽地

**destined** /déstənd/ 形 ▶定義1 destined for sth/to do sth having a future that has been decided or planned at an earlier time 早い時期に決められた, または計画された, 将来を持っている→~の運命の, ~する運命で ‖ *I think she is destined for success.* 彼女は成功する運命だと思う. *He was destined to become one of the country's leading politicians.* 彼はその国の指導的な政治家たちの1人になる運命だった.

▶定義2 destined for... travelling towards a particular place 特定の目的地に向かっている→(乗り物などが)~行きで, 行きの ‖ *I boarded a bus destined for New York.* 私はニューヨーク行きのバスに乗った.

**destiny** /déstəni/ 名 (複 **destinies**) ▶定義1 the things that happen to you in your life, especially things that you cannot control 特に自分では制御できない, 人生に起こる出来事→運命, 宿命 ‖ *She felt that it was her destiny to be a great singer.* 偉大な歌手になることが彼女の宿命なのだ, と彼女は感じた. ▶定義2 ❶ a power that people believe controls their lives; fate 人々が人生を支配すると信じている力; 運命→運命の神, 運命(の力)

**destitute** /déstətjùːt/ 形 ▶定義 without any money, food or a home お金, 食糧, または住居なしに→貧窮した— **destitution** /dèstətjúːʃ(ə)n/ 名 Ⓤ ▶貧窮, 貧困

★**destroy** /dɪstrɔ́ɪ/ 動 ⑪ ▶定義1 to damage sth so badly that it can no longer be used or no longer exists もはや使用できないように, またはもはや存在できないように, ~をひどく破壊する→~を破壊する ‖ *The building was destroyed by fire.* 建物は火災で焼失した. *The defeat destroyed his confidence.* 敗北によって, 彼の自信は打ち砕かれた. ▶定義2 to kill an animal, especially because it is injured or dangerous 特にそれがけがをしているまたは危険であるので, 動物を殺す→~を殺す, 始末する, 処分する ‖ *The horse broke its leg and had to be destroyed.* その馬は足を骨折し, 処分されなければならなかった.

**destroyer** /dɪstrɔ́ɪər/ 名 Ⓒ ▶定義1 a small ship that is used when there is a war 戦争のときに使われる小型の船→駆逐艦 ▶定義2 a person or thing that destroys sth ~を破壊する人または物→破壊者, 破壊する人・物

★**destruction** /dɪstrʌ́kʃ(ə)n/ 名 Ⓤ ▶定義 the action of destroying sth ~を破壊する行為→破壊(すること・されること), 破滅, 滅亡 ‖ *The war brought death and destruction to the city.* 戦争により, その市に死と破壊がもたらされた. *the destruction of the rainforests* 熱帯雨林の破壊

**destructive** /dɪstrʌ́ktɪv/ 形 ▶定義 causing a lot of harm or damage 多大な危害または損害をもたらす→破壊的な, 破壊を招く, 有害な ‖ *destruc-*

*tive weapons* 破壊兵器 *the destructive effects of drink and drugs* 飲酒と麻薬の有害な影響

**detach** /dɪtǽtʃ/ [動][他] ▶定義 detach sth (from sth) to separate sth from sth it is connected to つながっている～から…を分離する ➜**～を取り外す, 分離する, 切り離す** ‖ *Detach the form at the bottom of the page and send it to this address...* そのページの下に付いている書式を切り離し, 次の住所に送ってください. ⇔ **attach**

**detachable** /dɪtǽtʃəb(ə)l/ [形] ▶定義 that can be separated from sth it is connected to つながっている～から分離できる ➜**取り外せる, 分離できる** ‖ *a coat with a detachable hood* 取り外し可能なフード付きコート

**detached** /dɪtǽtʃt/ [形] ▶定義1 (used about a house) not joined to any other house (家について) どの家とも接続されていない ➜**一戸建ての, 独立した** ▶定義2 not being or not feeling personally involved in sth; without emotion ～に個人的にかかわっていない, またはそうは思っていない; 感情なしに ➜**(利害などに)超然とした, (意見・判断などが)公平な, 私心のない**

**detachment** /dɪtǽtʃmənt/ [名] ▶定義1 [U] the fact or feeling of not being personally involved in sth ～に個人的にかかわっていないという事実, または思い ➜**(利害などに)超然としていること, 公平, 無関心** ▶定義2 [C] a group of soldiers who have been given a particular task away from the main group 本隊から離れて, 特別の任務を与えられた兵士の一団 ➜**分遣隊, 分遣艦隊**

***detail**[1] /dɪtéɪl; díːteɪl/ [名] [C] [U] ▶定義 one fact or piece of information 1つの事実または情報 ➜**細部, 細目** ‖ *Just give me the basic facts. Don't worry about the details.* 基本的な事実だけを教えてください. 細かい点は気にしないでください. *On the application form you should give details of your education and experience.* 申し込み用紙には, 学歴と職務経験を詳細に記述した方が良い. *The work involves close attention to detail.* その仕事は, 細部にわたって厳密な注意を払う必要がある. — detailed [形] ➜**詳細な, 詳細にわたる, 詳しく述べた, 詳しく説明した** ‖ *a detailed description* 詳細な記述

[成句] go into detail(s) ▶定義 to talk or write about the details of sth; to explain sth fully ～の詳細について述べる, または書く; ～を十分に説明する ➜**詳しく述べる, 細部にわたる** ‖ *I can't go into detail now because it would take too long.* 時間がかかりすぎるでしょうから, 今詳しく述べることはできない.

in detail ▶定義 including the details; thoroughly 細部も含めている; 徹底的に ➜**(丹念に)細部にわたって, 詳細に, 詳しく** ‖ *We haven't discussed the matter in detail yet.* その問題について, 私たちはまだ細部にわたって議論していない.

**detail**[2] /díːteɪl/ [動][他] ▶定義 to give a full list of sth; to describe sth completely ～のすべての明細を与える; ～を完全に描写する ➜**細目を挙げる; 詳述する** ‖ *He detailed all the equipment he needed for the job.* 彼はその仕事に必要なすべての技能を詳しく述べた.

**detain** /dɪtéɪn/ [動][他] ▶定義 to stop sb from leaving a place; to delay sb ～がその場から立ち去るのを止める; ～を引き止める ➜**～を引き止める, 待たせておく** ‖ *A man has been detained by the police for questioning (= kept at the police station).* 男は尋問のために警察に引き止められていた (= 警察署に拘留されていた). *Don't let me detain you if you're busy.* お忙しいなら, お引き止めはしません. ☛参 **detention**

**detect** /dɪtékt/ [動][他] ▶定義 to notice or discover sth that is difficult to see, feel, etc 見る, 感じることなどが困難な～に気付く, または発見する ➜**(人の悪事・秘密など)を見つけ出す, 発見する, ～に気付く** ‖ *I detected a slight change in his attitude.* 私は, 彼の態度のかすかな変化に気付いた. *Traces of blood were detected on his clothes.* 彼の衣服に血の痕跡 (こんせき) が発見された. — detection [名] [U] ➜**発見, 看破, 発覚** ‖ *The crime escaped detection (= was not discovered) for many years.* その犯罪は何年間も発覚を免れた (= 気付かれなかった).

***detective** /dɪtéktɪv/ [名] [C] ▶定義 a person, especially a police officer, who tries to solve crimes 犯罪の解明に努める人, 特に警察官 ➜**刑事, 探偵**

**detective story** [名] [C] ▶定義 a story about a crime in which sb tries to find out who the guilty person is その中で人が犯人を見つけ出そうとする, 犯罪に関する小説 ➜**推理・探偵小説**

**detector** /dɪtéktər/ [名] [C] ▶定義 a machine that is used for finding or noticing sth ～を発見す

D

る, または感知するために使用される機械 →**探知機, 検出器** ‖ *a smoke/metal/lie detector* 火災報知機・金属探知機・うそ発見機

**detention** /dɪténʃ(ə)n/ 名 ᴜ ᴄ ▶定義1 the act of stopping a person leaving a place, especially by keeping him/her in prison 特に拘置所に拘留することによって, 人がある場所から立ち去ることを止める行為 →**留置, 拘留, 拘禁** ‖ *They were kept in detention for ten days.* 彼らは10日間拘留された. ▶定義2 the punishment of being kept at school after the other schoolchildren have gone home ほかの生徒たちが帰宅した後, 学校に引き止められる罰 →**放課後の居残り** ☜ detain

**deter** /dɪtə́:r/ 動 ⊕ (**deterring**; **deterred**) ▶定義 deter sb (from doing sth) to make sb decide not to do sth, especially by telling him/her that it would have bad results 特にそれが悪い結果をもたらし得ると話して, ~をしないと…に決心させる →**~に(…をすることを)やめさせる, 思いとどまらせる, ~を妨げる** ‖ *The council is trying to deter visitors from bringing their cars into the city centre.* 市議会は, 観光客が市の中心部へ車を乗り入れることを阻止しようとしている. ☜ 名 deterrent

**detergent** /dɪtə́:rdʒ(ə)nt/ 名 ᴄ ᴜ ▶定義 a chemical liquid or powder that is used for cleaning things 物を洗うために使われる, 液状または粉末の化学製品 →**合成・中性洗剤**

**deteriorate** /dɪtíəriəreɪt/ 動 ⊜ ▶定義 to become worse より悪くなる →**(状態・質などが)悪化する, 低下する, 悪化して~になる** ‖ *The political tension is deteriorating into civil war.* 政治的緊張は内戦に向かって悪化しつつある. — **deterioration** /dɪtìəriəréɪʃ(ə)n/ 名 ᴄ ᴜ → **(状態・質などの)悪化, 低下**

*****determination** /dɪtə̀:rmənéɪʃ(ə)n/ 名 ᴜ ▶定義1 determination (to do sth) the quality of having firmly decided to do sth, even if it is very difficult たとえそれが非常に困難であっても, ~をしようと固く心に決める性質 →**(~しようという)決意, 決心, 決断力** ‖ *her determination to win* 勝とうという彼女の決意 *You need great determination to succeed in business.* 事業を成功するには, 本当の意味での決断力が必要だ.

▶定義2 正式 the process of deciding sth officially 正式に~を決定する過程 →**(物事の)決定, 確定, 判定** ‖ *the determination of future government policy* 将来の政治政策の決定

**determine** /dɪtə́:rmən/ 動 ⊕ ▶定義1 正式 to discover the facts about sth ~についての事実を発見する →**(原因など)を特定する, 究明する** ‖ *We need to determine what happened immediately before the accident.* 事故の直前に何が起きたのかを究明する必要がある. ▶定義2 to make sth happen in a particular way or be of a particular type 何かが特定の方法で起こるように, または特定の種類であるようにさせる →**(物事が原因となって)~を決定する, 支配する, ~に決定的な影響を与える** ‖ *The results of the tests will determine what treatment you need.* 検査の結果により, あなたに必要な治療法が決まります. *Age and experience will be determining factors in our choice of candidate.* 私たちが候補者を選択するに当たって, 年齢と経験が決定的な要因となる. ▶定義3 正式 to decide sth officially ~を正式に決定する →**~を決定する, 取り決める, (日取りなど)を予定する** ‖ *A date for the meeting has yet to be determined.* 会議の日取りは, まだ予定されていない.

*****determined** /dɪtə́:rmənd/ 形 ▶定義 determined (to do sth) having firmly decided to do sth or to succeed, even if it is difficult たとえそれが困難であっても, ~をする, または成功すると固く決心している →**(~することを)固く決心した, 断固とした** ‖ *He is determined to leave school, even though his parents want him to stay.* たとえ両親が学校にとどまってほしいと望んでも, 彼は退学することを決意した. *She's a very determined athlete.* 彼女はとても意志の強い運動選手だ.

**determiner** /dɪtə́:rmənər/ 名 ᴄ (文法) ▶定義 a word that comes before a noun to show how the noun is being used その名詞がどのような使われ方をしているかを示すために, 名詞の前に付けられる単語 →**決定詞, 限定詞** ‖ *'Her', 'most' and 'those' are all determiners.* her, most, those はすべて, 決定詞である.

**deterrent** /dɪtér(ə)nt, -tə́:r-/ 名 ᴄ ▶定義 something that should stop you doing sth 人が~をしていることを止めるはずのもの →**引き止めるもの, 阻止するもの** ‖ *Their punishment will* *be a deterrent to others.* 彼らを罰することは、ほかの者たちへの制止となる。● deter — deterrent 形 ➤ (物事が) 妨げる, 抑止する, 制止する

**detest** /dɪtést/ 動他 ▶定義 to hate or not like sb/sth at all 〜を嫌悪する, または少しも好きではない ➤ 〜をひどく嫌う, 憎む ‖ *They absolutely detest each other.* 彼らは完全に憎み合っている.

**detonate** /dét(ə)nèɪt/ 動自他 ▶定義 to explode or to make a bomb, etc explode 爆発する, または爆弾などを爆発させる ➤ 爆発する; (大音響と共に) 〜を爆発させる

**detour** /dɪtúər; díːtʊər/ 名 C ▶定義 1 a longer route from one place to another that you take in order to avoid sth/sb or in order to see or do sth ある場所から別の場所へ人が行くとき, 〜を避けるために, あるいは〜を見るまたは行うために, 長くなった道筋 ➤ 回り道, 遠回り ‖ *Because of the accident we had to make a five-kilometre detour.* 事故のせいで, 5キロもの回り道をしなければならなかった. ▶定義 2 米 = DIVERSION(2)

**detract** /dɪtrǽkt/ 動自 ▶定義 detract from sth to make sth seem less good or important ものの良さまたは重要性が, より少なくなったように感じさせる ➤ (価値・名声などを) 落とす, 損なう ‖ *These criticisms in no way detract from the team's achievements.* これらの批判は, 決してチームの業績を損なうものではない.

**detriment** /détrəmənt/ 名
成句 to the detriment of sb/sth ▶定義 harming or damaging sb/sth 〜を傷付けている, または損なっている ➤ 〜を損なうほど, 〜に損害を与えて ‖ *Doctors claim that the changes will be to the detriment of patients.* 医者たちは, その変更が患者に不利益になると主張する. — detrimental /dètrəméntl/ 形 ➤ (〜に) 有害な, 損失となる ‖ *Too much alcohol is **detrimental to** your health.* お酒の飲みすぎは健康に悪い.

**deuce** /d(j)úːs/ 名 U ▶定義 a score of 40 points to each player in a game of tennis テニスの試合で, 双方の選手が40点を得点すること ➤ ジュース

**devalue** /dìːvǽljuː/ 動他 ▶定義 1 to reduce the value of the money of one country in relation to the value of the money of other countries ほかの国々の通貨価値との関連で, ある国の通貨の価値を下げる ➤ (通貨の) 平価を切り下げる ‖ *The pound has been devalued against the dollar.* ドルに対するポンドの平価が切り下げられた. ▶定義 2 to reduce the value or importance of sth 〜の価値または重要性を下げる ➤ 〜の価値を低下させる, (人・作品など) をけなす ‖ *The refusal of the top players to take part devalues this competition.* 上位の選手たちが参加を拒否したことで, この競技会の価値は低下する. — devaluation /dìːvæljuéɪʃ(ə)n/ 名 U ➤ 平価切下げ

**devastate** /dévəstèɪt/ 動他 ▶定義 1 to destroy sth or damage it badly 〜を破壊する, または〜をひどく損なう ➤ (町・地域など) を荒廃させる, 徹底的に破壊する, 〜に大損害を与える ‖ *a land devastated by war* 戦争で荒廃した国土 ▶定義 2 to make sb extremely upset and shocked 〜を極度に動揺させ, 衝撃を与える ➤ 〜を打ちのめす, ぼう然とさせる, 圧倒する ‖ *This tragedy has devastated the community.* この悲惨な出来事は, 大衆をぼう然とさせた. — devastation /dèvəstéɪʃ(ə)n/ 名 U ➤ 破壊, 荒廃 (状態), 廃墟 (はいきょ) ‖ *a scene of total devastation* 完全に荒廃した風景

**devastated** /dévəstèɪtəd/ 形 ▶定義 extremely shocked and upset 極度に衝撃を受けて動揺して ➤ 打ちのめされた, ぼう然とした, 圧倒された ‖ *They were devastated when their baby died.* 赤ん坊が死んだ時, 彼らは打ちのめされた.

**devastating** /dévəstèɪtɪŋ/ 形 ▶定義 1 that destroys sth completely 〜を完全に破壊する ➤ 破壊的な, 荒廃させる, 壊滅的な ‖ *a devastating explosion* 破壊的な爆発 ▶定義 2 that shocks or upsets sb very much 〜に非常に衝撃を与える, または動揺させる ➤ 手厳しい, 痛烈な, 圧倒的な ‖ *The closure of the factory was a devastating blow to the workers.* 工場の閉鎖は, 労働者にとって痛烈な打撃だった.

*__develop__ /dɪvéləp/ 動 ▶定義 1 自他 to grow slowly, increase, or change into sth else; to make sb/sth do this ゆっくりと発育する, 増える, またはほかのものに変化する; 〜にこれをさせる ➤ 発達する, 発展する, 成長・発育する; 〜を発達させる, 進展させる ‖ *to develop from a child into an adult* 子供から大人へと成長する *a scheme to help pupils develop their natural talents* 生徒が生来の素質を発達させるために役立

## 452　developed

つ計画 *Scientists have developed a drug against this disease.* 科学者たちは、この病気の治療薬を改良してきた. *Over the years, she's developed her own unique singing style.* 何年もかけて、彼女は自分独自の歌い方を作り上げてきた. ▶定義2 to begin to have a problem or disease; to start to affect sth 問題が起こり始める、または病気が発症し始める；～に影響し始める→(問題・困難などが)現れてくる、(新事実が)明らかになる、(病気が)発症する；波及してくる ‖ *to develop cancer/Aids* がん・エイズを発症する *Trouble is developing along the border.* 国境周辺で、問題が生じてきている. ▶定義3 to make an idea, a story, etc clearer or more detailed by writing or talking about it more さらにそれについて書くまたは話すことで、考え、話などをより明瞭(めいりょう)にまたは詳細にする→(主題・議論など)を展開する、(考え・計画)を練る、詳しく述べる ‖ *She went on to develop this theme later in the lecture.* 彼女は講義の後半でこの主題を展開した. ▶定義4 to make pictures or negatives from a piece of film by using special chemicals 特別な化学薬品を使って、1本のフィルムから写真またはネガを作る→～を現像する ‖ *to develop a film* フィルムを現像する ▶定義5 to build houses, shops, factories, etc on a piece of land ある土地に、複数の住宅、店舗、工場などを建設する→～を開発する、(宅地など)を造成する ‖ *This site is being developed for offices.* この用地は、事業所向けに開発されている.

### ▶音声とつづり字

#### develop のアクセント位置

語は音節から成ります.音節は英語では母音で終わるもの(開音節)のほかに母音+子音で終わるもの(閉音節)があります.develop は音節に分けると de-vel-op と3つになります.最後から2つ目の音節は子音+母音+子音の閉音節構造です.一般に終わりから2番目の音節が閉音節だと、音節は重く感じられ、アクセントもそこに置かれます.同様に終わりから2番目の音節が二重母音だと、やはりその音節は重く感じられ、アクセントを呼び込みます.

比較: appéndix(付録) bronchítis [áɪ] (気管支炎)

**developed** /dɪvéləpt/ ▶定義 of a good level or standard 良い水準または標準の→発達した, 先進の, 成熟した ‖ *a highly developed economy* 高度に発展した経済

**developer** /dɪvéləpər/ (または **property developer**) ▶定義 a person or company that builds houses, shops, etc on a piece of land ある土地に、複数の住宅、店舗などを建設する人または会社→開発者, 宅地造成・開発業者

**developing** /dɪvéləpɪŋ/ ▶定義 (used about a poor country) that is trying to develop or improve its economy (貧しい国について)経済の発展または向上を図っている→発展途上の, 発展・発達中の ‖ *developing country* 発展途上国 *the developing world* 発展途上国全体

*****development** /dɪvéləpmənt/ ▶定義1 the process of becoming bigger, stronger, better etc, or of making sb/sth do this より大きく、強く、良くなどとなる、または～をこのようにさせる過程→発達, 発展, 進展 ‖ *the development of tourism in Cuba* キューバの観光事業の発展 *a child's intellectual development* 子供の知的発達 ▶定義2 the process of creating sth more advanced; a more advanced product ～をより進ませる過程；より進んだ製品→開発, 改良；開発・改良の結果・成果, 新製品, 新発明 ‖ *She works in **research and development** for a drug company.* 彼女は製薬会社で研究開発の仕事をしている. *the latest developments in space technology* 宇宙工学の最新の成果 ▶定義3 a new event that changes a situation 状況を変える新しい出来事→新しい事態, 新情勢 ‖ *This week has seen a number of new developments in the Middle East.* 今週になって中東ではかなりの新しい事態が起こった. ▶定義4 a piece of land with new buildings on it; the process of building on a piece of land 複数の新しい建物が建っている、ある土地；ある土地に建設する過程→開発・造成した土地, 住宅団地, (土地・地域の)開発, 造成 ‖ *a new housing development* 新たな住宅開発 *The land has been bought for development.* その土地は、開発用に購入された.

**deviate** /díːvièɪt/ ▶定義 deviate (from

sth) to change or become different from what is normal or expected 通常のまたは予想していたものとは違ったものに変わる、またはなる→(車・道路などが)(~から)それる、(人・行為などが)(計画・規範などから)それる‖ He never once deviated from his original plan. 彼は本来の計画から逸脱したことが一度もない.

**deviation** /diːviˈeɪʃ(ə)n/ 名 C U ▶定義 a difference from what is normal or expected, or from what is approved of by society 通常のまたは予想していたもの、あるいは社会に良いと認められるものとの相違→(基準・規範・計画などからの)逸脱‖ sexual deviation 性的逸脱 a deviation from our usual way of doing things 通常の物事のやり方からの逸脱

★**device** /dɪˈvaɪs/ 名 C ▶定義1 a tool or piece of equipment made for a particular purpose 特定の目的のために作られた道具または装置→(機械的)仕掛け,考案物‖ a security device which detects any movement どんな動きも感知する防犯装置 labour-saving devices such as washing machines and vacuum cleaners 洗濯機と掃除機のような、省力化の道具 ☛参 tool の注 ▶定義2 a clever method for getting the result you want 望む結果を手に入れるための巧みな方法→工夫,計画,策略‖ Critics dismissed the speech as a political device for winning support. 評論家たちはその演説を、支持を勝ち取るための政治的手段であるとして無視した.

**devil** /ˈdevl/ 名 C ▶定義1 the Devil the most powerful evil being, according to the Christian, Jewish and Muslim religions キリスト教、ユダヤ教とイスラム教によると、最も勢力のある邪悪な存在→魔王,サタン ☛参 Satan ▶定義2 an evil being; a spirit 邪悪な存在; 霊魂→悪魔,魔神 ▶定義3 (口語) a word used to show pity, anger, etc when you are talking about a person 人について話しているとき、同情、怒りなどを表すために用いられる言葉→悪魔のような人,~の鬼,~なやつ‖ The poor devil died in hospital two days later. その哀れなやつは2日後に病院で死んだ. Those kids can be little devils sometimes. この子供たちも、時には子悪魔のようになることがある.

成句 be a devil ▶定義 used to encourage sb to do sth that he/she is not sure about doing 人が行うことをためらっていることを、その人が行うように勇気づけるために用いて→思い切ってやってみろ,さあ頑張れ‖ Go on, be a devil - buy both of them. さあ - 2つとも買ってしまえ.

speak/talk of the devil ▶定義 used when the person who is being talked about appears unexpectedly 話題にされていた人が思い掛けず現れるときに用いて→うわさをすれば影

**devious** /ˈdiːviəs/ 形 ▶定義 clever but not honest or direct 利口ではあるが誠実でない、または率直でない→狡猾(こうかつ)な‖ I wouldn't trust him - he can be very devious. 彼を信用できない - 彼にはとても狡猾なところがある. a devious trick/plan ずる賢いたくらみ・よこしまな計画 — **deviously** 副→不正に,よこしまに

**devise** /dɪˈvaɪz/ 動他 ▶定義 to invent a new way of doing sth 何かを行う新しい方法を考え出す→~を考案する,発明・工夫する‖ They've devised a plan for keeping traffic out of the city centre. 彼らは、車を市の中心部に入れないための計画を考え出した.

**devoid** /dɪˈvɔɪd/ 形 正式 ▶定義 devoid of sth not having a particular quality; without sth 特定の資質を持たない; ~なしで→(~に)欠けている‖ devoid of hope/ambition/imagination 希望・野心・想像力に欠けている

**devolution** /ˌdiːvəˈluːʃ(ə)n; diː-/ 名 U ▶定義 the movement of political power from central to local government 中央から地方自治体への、政治的な権限の移動→委任,移管,委譲

**devote** /dɪˈvəʊt/ 動他 ▶定義 devote yourself/sth to sb/sth to give a lot of time, energy, etc to sb/sth ~に多大な時間、労力などを注ぐ→~にささげる,向ける,充てる‖ She gave up work to devote herself full-time to her music. すべての時間を音楽に専念するために、彼女は仕事を辞めた. Schools should devote more time to science subjects. 学校は理科系の科目にもっと時間を充てるべきだ.

**devoted** /dɪˈvəʊtɪd/ 形 ▶定義 devoted (to sb/sth) loving sb/sth very much; completely loyal to sb/sth ~をとても愛している; ~に完全に忠実な→献身的な,熱心な,愛情をささげた‖ Neil's absolutely devoted to his wife. ニールは妻を本当に熱愛している.

**devotee** /ˌdevəˈtiː/ 名 C ▶定義 a devotee (of

**454　devotion**

sb/sth) a person who likes sb/sth very much ～がとても好きな人→(熱烈な)愛好家, ファン, 信奉者 ‖ *Devotees of science fiction will enjoy this new film.* SFファンにとって, この新作映画は面白いものだ.

**devotion** /dɪvóuʃ(ə)n/ 名 U ▶devotion (to sb/sth) ▶定義1 great love for sb/sth ～に対する深い愛→(～への)深い愛情, 熱愛 ‖ *a mother's devotion to her children* 子供への母親の深い愛情 ▶定義2 the act of giving a lot of your time, energy, etc to sb/sth 多大な時間, 労力などを～に注ぐ行為→(～への)献身, 専心, 傾倒 ‖ *devotion to duty* 職務に対する献身振り ▶定義3 very strong religious feeling とても強い宗教心→信心, 信仰, 帰依

**devour** /dɪváuər/ 動他 ▶定義1 to eat sth quickly because you are very hungry とても空腹であるため, ～を素早く食べる→～をむさぼり食う, ～をがつがつ平らげる ▶定義2 to do or use sth quickly and completely 何かを素早く徹底的に行う, または使う→～をむさぼるように読む, 夢中になって見る・聞く ‖ *Lisa devours two or three novels a week.* リーサは週に2, 3冊の小説をむさぼり読む.

**devout** /dɪváut/ 形 ▶定義 very religious とても信心深い→信心深い, 敬虔(けいけん)な, 信仰心の厚い ‖ *a devout Muslim family* イスラム教を深く信仰している家族 — **devoutly** 副 →敬虔に, 信心深く

**dew** /d(j)uː/ 名 U ▶定義 small drops of water that form on plants, leaves, etc during the night 夜間に植物, 葉などの上に生じる小さな水滴→露

**dexterity** /dekstérəti/ 名 U ▶定義 skill at doing things, especially with your hands 特に手で, 物事を行う優れた技量→(手先の)器用さ, 巧妙さ, 敏捷(びんしょう)さ

**diabetes** /dàɪəbíːtiːz, -təs/ 名 U C ▶定義 a serious disease in which a person's body cannot control the level of sugar in the blood 身体が血液中の糖の水準を制御できない, 重い病気→糖尿病

**diabetic**¹ /dàɪəbétɪk/ 名 C ▶定義 a person who suffers from diabetes 糖尿病を患っている人→糖尿病患者

**diabetic**² /dàɪəbétɪk/ 形 ▶定義 connected with diabetes or diabetics 糖尿病または糖尿病患者に関する→糖尿病(患者)の, 糖尿病患者用の ‖ *diabetic chocolate (= safe for diabetics)* 糖尿病患者用のチョコレート(= 糖尿病患者に安全な)

**diagnose** /dáɪəgnòus, -z, ˌ-ˈ-/ 動他 ▶定義 diagnose sth (as sth); diagnose sb as/with sth to find out and say exactly what illness a person has or what the cause of a problem is 人がかかっている病気が何であるかまたは問題の原因が何であるかを探し出して正確に言う→～を(…と)診断する ‖ *His illness was diagnosed as bronchitis.* 彼の病気は, 気管支炎と診断された. *I've been diagnosed as (a) diabetic/with diabetes.* 私は糖尿病と診断されている. *After a couple of minutes I diagnosed the trouble - a flat battery.* 数分後に, 私は故障の原因が分かった － 電池が切れていたのだ.

**diagnosis** /dàɪəgnóusəs, -əg-/ 名 C U (複) **diagnoses** /-sìːz/ ▶定義 the act of saying exactly what illness a person has or what the cause of a problem is 人がかかっている病気が何であるかまたは問題の原因が何であるかを正確に言う行為→診断, 診断書, (問題点などの)指摘, 究明 ‖ *to make a diagnosis* 診察をする

**diagonal** /daɪǽgənl, -ǽgnəl/ 形 ▶定義 (used about a straight line) joining two sides of sth at an angle that is not 90° or vertical or horizontal (直線について)～の2辺を, 90度ではない, または垂直ではない, または水平ではない角度で結んでいる→対角線の, 斜めの ‖ *Draw a diagonal line from one corner of the square to the opposite corner.* 正方形の1つの角から相対する角へ, 対角線を引きなさい. ☞ **line**のさし絵 — **diagonally** /-nli, -nəli/ 副 →斜めに, 対角線の方向に

**diagram** /dáɪəgræm/ 名 C ▶定義 a simple picture that is used to explain how sth works or what sth looks like 物がどのように機能するか, または物がどう見えるのかを説明するために用いられる, 単純な図→図, 図形, グラフ ‖ *a diagram of the body's digestive system* 体の消化器系の図

**dial**¹ /dáɪ(ə)l/ 名 C ▶定義1 the round part of a clock, watch, control on a machine, etc that shows a measurement of time, amount, temperature, etc 時間, 量, 温度などの測定値を示す, 時計, 腕時計, 機械の制御装置などにある円形の

部品→文字盤,目盛り盤,指針盤 ‖ *a dial for showing air pressure* 空気圧を示す目盛り盤 ▶定義2 the round control on a radio, cooker, etc that you turn to change sth ～を変えるために人が回す,ラジオ,レンジなどに付いている円形の制御装置→ダイヤル ▶定義3 the round part with holes in it on some older telephones that you turn to call a number. 番号に電話するために人が回す,旧式の電話に付いている,複数の穴が開いた円形の部品→ダイヤル

**dial**² /dáɪ(ə)l/ 動 自 他 (**dialling**; **dialled**: 米 **dialing**; **dialed**) ▶定義 to push the buttons or move the dial on a telephone in order to call a telephone number 電話番号に電話するために,電話のボタンを押す,またはダイヤルを回す→電話をかける,～に電話をかける,ダイヤルを回す ‖ *You can now dial direct to Singapore.* 今はシンガポールに直通電話をかけられます. *to dial the wrong number* 間違い電話をする

**dialect** /dáɪəlèkt/ 名 C U ▶定義 a form of a language that is spoken in one part of a country 国の一部の地域で話される言葉の形態→方言,地方語 ‖ *a local dialect* 現地の方言

*__dialogue__ (米 **dialog**) /dáɪəlɔ̀(ː)g, -lɑ̀g/ 名 C U ▶定義1 (a) conversation between people in a book, play, etc 本,芝居などの中での人間同士の会話→会話,対話体 ‖ *This movie is all action, with very little dialogue.* この映画はアクションばかりで,ほとんど会話がない. *On the tape you will hear a short dialogue between a shop assistant and a customer.* そのテープには,店員と客との短い会話があります. ▶定義2 (a) discussion between people who have different opinions 違う意見を持つ人々の間の論議→意見の交換,対話,対談 ‖ *(a) dialogue between the major political parties* 主要政党間の会談

**diameter** /daɪǽmətər/ 名 C ▶定義 a straight line that goes from one side to the other of a circle, passing through the centre 中心を通って,円の一端から相対する端へ進む直線→直径,差し渡し ☞参 **radius**, **circumference** ☞ **circle** のさし絵

*__diamond__ /dáɪ(ə)mənd/ 名 C U ▶定義1 C U a hard, bright precious stone which is very expensive and is used for making jewellery. A diamond usually has no colour. とても高価で装身具を作るために用いられる,硬くて光り輝く宝石.普通,無色である→ダイヤモンド ▶定義2 C a flat shape that has four sides of equal length and points at two ends 等しい長さの4つの辺と2つのとがった先端を持つ,平たい形→ダイヤモンド形,ひし形 ☞ **shape** のさし絵 ▶定義3 **diamonds**[複数扱い]the group (suit) of playing cards with red shapes like diamonds(2) on them 赤い diamonds(2) のような形が描かれた,トランプの集団(組)→ダイヤの組札 ‖ *the seven of diamonds* ダイヤの7の札 ☞参 **card** の注とさし絵 ▶定義4 C one of the cards from this suit この組の札の1枚→ダイヤの札 ‖ *I haven't got any diamonds.* 私はダイヤの札を1枚も持っていない. ▶定義5 U celebrating the 60th anniversary of sth ～の60周年の記念を祝うこと→60周年の祝い ‖ *This year's their diamond wedding.* 今年は彼らのダイヤモンド婚式だ. ☞参 **silver**, **golden**

**diaper** /dáɪ(ə)pər/ 米 = **NAPPY**

**diaphragm** /dáɪəfræm/ 名 C ▶定義1 the muscle between your lungs and your stomach that helps you to breathe 人が呼吸することを助ける,肺と胃の間にある筋肉→横隔膜 ▶定義2 a thin piece of rubber that a woman puts inside her body before having sex to stop her having a baby 子供ができないように性交の前に,女性が体内に入れる薄いゴム片→ペッサリー

**diarrhoea** (米 **diarrhea**) /dàɪəríːə; -ríːə/ 名 U ▶定義 an illness that causes you to get rid of waste material (**faeces**) from your body very often and in a more liquid form than usual 通常よりも流動的になった排せつ物(糞便(ふんべん))をかなり頻繁に排出することを引き起こす病気→下痢

*__diary__ /dáɪ(ə)ri/ 名 C (複 **diaries**) ▶定義1 a book in which you write down things that you have to do, remember, etc やるべき事柄,覚えておかなければならない事などを記した帳面→手帳 ‖ *I'll just check in my diary to see if I'm free that weekend.* その週末が空いているかどうか,ちょっと手帳を調べてみます. ☞参 **calendar** の注 ▶定義2 a book in which you write down what happens to you each day 日々自分に起きたことを記す帳面→日記,日誌 ‖ *Do you* *keep a diary*? 日記をつけていますか.

**dice** /dáɪs/ 名 C (複 **dice**) ▶定義 a small square object with a different number of spots (from one to six) on each side, used in certain games ある種のゲームに使われる,それぞれの面に違う数の点(1から6)の付いた,小さな立方体→**さいころ** ‖ *Throw the dice to see who goes first.* さいころを振って,だれが最初に行くかを決めよう.

**dictate** /díkteɪt, -´-/ 動 ▶定義1 自他 dictate (sth) (to sb) to say sth aloud so that sb else can write or type it ほかの人がそれを書き取れるように,またはタイプできるように,~を大きな声で言う→**口述する,~を口述筆記してもらう** ‖ *to dictate a letter to a secretary* 秘書に手紙を書き取らせる ▶定義2 自他 dictate (sth) (to sb) to tell sb what to do in a way that seems unfair 不当に思えるやり方で,人に何かするように告げる→**押し付ける** ‖ *Parents can't dictate to their children how they should run their lives.* 親は子供に,どのように子供が人生を送るべきかを押し付けることはできない. ▶定義3 他 to control or influence sth ~を支配する,または~に影響を与える→**~を決定する,~に影響する** ‖ *The kind of house people live in is usually dictated by how much they earn.* 人々がどのような家に住むかは,通常,彼らがいくら稼ぐかによって決定される.

**dictation** /dɪkteɪʃ(ə)n/ 名 C U ▶定義 spoken words that sb else must write or type ほかの人が書くまたはタイプしなければならない,話された言葉→**書き取り,ディクテーション** ‖ *We had a dictation in English today (= a test in which we had to write down what the teacher said).* 今日は英語のディクテーション(= 教師が言った事を書き取らなければならない試験)があった.

**dictator** /dɪkteɪtər, -´--/ 名 C ▶定義 a ruler who has total power in a country, especially one who rules the country by force 国のすべての権力を掌握する統治者,特に暴力で国を支配する者→**独裁者,専制者** — dictatorship 名 C U → **独裁政治,独裁国家** ‖ *a military dictatorship* 軍事独裁政治

*__dictionary__ /díkʃ(ə)nri, -ʃ(ə)nəri; -nèri/ 名 C (複 **dictionaries**) ▶定義1 a book that contains a list of the words in a language in the order of the alphabet and that tells you what they mean, in the same or another language ある言語の言葉をアルファベット順に記載し,同じまた違う言語でそれらの意味が分かるようになっている本→**辞書,辞典,字引** ‖ *to look up a word in a dictionary* 辞書で言葉を調べる *a bilingual/monolingual dictionary* 2言語による辞典・1言語による辞典 ▶定義2 a book that lists the words connected with a particular subject and tells you what they mean ある特定の主題に関連した言葉を記載していて,それらの意味を人に教える本→**用語辞典,専門分野の辞書・辞典・事典** ‖ *a dictionary of idioms* 成句辞典 *a medical dictionary* 医学事典

> ▶ 音声とつづり字
>
> dictionary の発音は英音と米音で異なる
>
> 多音節語では英音は第1アクセントだけですが,米音には第1アクセントのほかに第2アクセントが付きます.
>
> | | 英音 | 米音 |
> |---|---|---|
> | dictionary | [dík.ʃ(ə).n.ri] | [dík.ʃ(ə).nèr.i] |
> | secondary | [sék.ən.dri] | [sék.ən.dèr.i] |

**did** DO の過去形
**didn't** DID NOT の短縮形

*__die__ /dáɪ/ 動 (現分 **dying**; 三単現 **dies**; 過,過分 **died**) ▶定義1 自他 die (from/of sth) to stop living 生きていることを停止する→**死ぬ,枯れる** ‖ *My father died when I was three.* 父は,私が3歳の時に亡くなった. *Thousands of people have died from this disease.* この病気で何千人もの人が死んだ. *to die of hunger* 飢えのために死ぬ *to die for what you believe in* 信じるもののために死ぬ *to die a natural/violent death* 自然死する・非業の死を遂げる ☞ 形 **dead** 名 **death** ▶定義2 自 to stop existing; to disappear 存在することを止める; 消滅する→**(火・光などが)消える,(愛情などが)冷める,(制度などが)滅びる** ‖ *The old customs are dying.* 古い慣習は,消えつつある. *Our love will never die.* 私たちの愛は決して冷めない.

**成句 be dying for sth/to do sth** (口語) ▶定義 to want sth/to do sth very much ~がとても欲しい,~をとてもやりたい→**~が欲しくてたま**

らない、~したくてたまらない ‖ *I'm dying for a cup of coffee.* コーヒーが飲みたくてたまらない.

**die hard** ▶定義 to change or disappear only slowly or with difficulty ただただゆっくりと、または困難を伴って変化するまたは消滅する→(慣習・考えなどが)なかなかなくならない、なかなか消えない ‖ *Old attitudes towards women die hard.* 女性への古い考え方はなかなか消えない.

**to die for** 略式 ▶定義 if you think that sth is to die for, you really want it and would do anything to get it もし何かについて to die for であると人が思うなら、その人はそれを本当に欲していて、それを手に入れるためには何でもするかもしれない→(そのために死んでもいいほど)すてきな、とてもすばらしい ‖ *They have a house in town that's to die for.* 彼らは街に家を持っているが、それはすばらしい家だ.

**die laughing** ▶定義 to find sth very funny ~がとても面白いと分かる→笑いこける ‖ *I thought I'd die laughing when he told that joke.* 彼がその冗談を言った時、私は笑いこけるだろうなと思った.

句動詞 **die away** ▶定義 to slowly become weaker before stopping or disappearing 止まるまたは消滅する前に、ゆっくりと弱くなる→(音が)徐々に小さくなる、(光などが)暗くなる、(風などが)少しずつ弱くなる ‖ *The sound of the engine died away as the car drove into the distance.* 車が走り去るにつれて、エンジンの音が徐々に聞こえなくなった.

**die down** ▶定義 to slowly become less strong ゆっくりと弱くなる→(音などが)小さくなる、静まる、(風などが)衰える、(興奮などが)冷める ‖ *Let's wait until the storm dies down before we go out.* あらしが静まるまで、外出するのは待とう.

**die off** ▶定義 to die one by one until there are none left だれもいなくなるまで、1人ずつ死ぬ→次々と死ぬ、死に絶える

**die out** ▶定義 to stop happening or disappear 起こらなくなる、または消滅する→死に絶える、絶滅する、(慣習・考えなどが)すたれる ‖ *The use of horses on farms has almost died out in this country.* この国では、農場での馬の使用はほとんどすたれた.

**diesel** /díːz(ə)l, -s(ə)l/ 名 ▶定義 1 ❶a type of heavy oil used in some engines instead of petrol ある種のエンジンで石油の代わりに用いられる重油の一種→ディーゼル燃料 ‖ *a diesel engine* ディーゼルエンジン *a taxi that runs on diesel* ディーゼル燃料で走るタクシー ▶定義 2 ❷a vehicle that uses diesel ディーゼル燃料を使用する乗り物→ディーゼル車、ディーゼル機関車、ディーゼル機関船 ‖ *My new car's a diesel.* 私の新車は、ディーゼル車だ.

☞参 **petrol**

\***diet**¹ /dáɪət/ ▶定義 1 ❻❶the food that a person or animal usually eats 人または動物が普段食べている食物→日常の食物、常食 ‖ *They live on a diet of rice and vegetables.* 彼らは米と野菜を常食している. *I always try to have a healthy, balanced diet (= including all the different types of food that our body needs).* 私は常に、健康的でバランスの取れた食事 (= 身体が必要とするさまざまな種類の食物をすべて含んでいる) を取るように努めている. *Poor diet is a cause of ill health.* 粗末な食事は、不健康の原因となる. ▶定義 2 ❻certain foods that a person who is ill, or who wants to lose weight is allowed to eat 病気の人、または減量したい人が食べることを許される、ある種の食物→(治療・減量のための)ダイエット、規定食、食餌 (しょくじ) 療法 ‖ *a low-fat diet* 低脂肪食 *a sugar-free diet* 無糖食 ― **dietary** /dáɪətèri; -t(ə)ri/ 形 ▶飲食物の、食事の、規定食の ‖ *dietary habits/requirements* 食習慣・必須 (ひっす) の食物

成句 **be/go on a diet** ▶定義 to eat only certain foods or a small amount of food because you want to lose weight 減量したいので、特定の食物または少量の食事しか取らない→ダイエット・食餌 (しょくじ) 療法・食事制限をしている・する

**diet**² /dáɪət/ 動 ⊜ ▶定義 to try to lose weight by eating less food or only certain kinds of food 食事を少なく、またはある種の食物しか食べないで、減量しようとする→ダイエットをする、食餌 (しょくじ) 療法・制限をする ‖ *You've lost some weight. Have you been dieting?* 少しやせましたね. ダイエットをしているのですか.

**differ** /dífər/ 動 ⊜ ▶定義 1 **differ (from sb/sth)** to be different 異なっている→異なる、違う ‖ *How does this car differ from the more expensive model?* この車は、もっと高価なモデルとどのように違うのですか. ▶定義 2 **differ (with**

sb) (about/on sth) to have a different opinion 異なる意見を持つ→**意見が異なる, 意見が合わない, 一致しない** || *I'm afraid I differ with you on that question.* 残念ながら, 私はこの問題についてはあなたと考えが違うようです.

★**difference** /dífərəns/ 名 ▶定義1 ⒞ⓊⓊ a difference (between A and B) the way that people or things are not the same or the way that sb/sth has changed 人々または物事が同じではない点, あるいは〜が変わった点→**相違(点), 差異** || *What's the difference between this computer and that cheaper one?* このコンピューターと, あの値段の安いものとの違いは何ですか. *From a distance it's hard to* **tell the difference** *between the twins.* 遠くからだと, 双子の違いを見分けることは難しい. ▶定義2 ⒞Ⓤ difference (in sth) (between A and B) the amount by which people or things are not the same or by which sb/sth has changed 人々または物事が同じではない, または〜が変わっている程度→**差, 差額** || *There's an age difference of three years between the two children.* その2人の子供たちには, 3歳の年齢差がある. *There's very little difference in price since last year.* 昨年から物価の変動はほとんどない. *We gave a 30% deposit and must* **pay the difference** *when the work is finished* (= the rest of the money). 我々は30パーセントの手付け金を支払っており, 仕事が終了した時には差額(= 残りの金額)を支払わなければならない.

▶定義3 ⒞ a disagreement that is not very serious あまり深刻ではない意見の相違→**意見の相違, 不和** || *All couples* **have their differences** *from time to time.* どの夫婦にも, 時には意見の相違がある. *There was* **a difference of opinion** *over how much we owed.* 私たちがいくら払うかについて, 意見の違いがあった.

成句 **make a, some, etc difference (to sb/sth)** ▶定義 to have an effect (on sb/sth) (〜に)影響を及ぼす→**変化をもたらす, 相違を生ずる, 影響する** || *Marriage made a big difference to her life.* 結婚は彼女の人生に大きな変化をもたらした.

**make no difference (to sb/sth); not make any difference** ▶定義 to not be important (to sb/sth); to have no effect (〜にとって)重要でない; 少しも影響しない→**全く変わりはない, 少しも重要でない** || *It makes no difference to us if the baby is a girl or a boy.* 私たちは, 赤ん坊が男の子でも女の子でも構わない.

**split the difference** ⇒ **SPLIT**¹

★**different** /dífərənt/ 形 ▶定義1 different (from/to sb/sth) not the same 同じでない→**違った, 異なった, 別の** || *The play was different from anything I had seen before.* その芝居は, それまでに見たどんなものとも違っていた. *The two houses are very different in style.* 2軒の家は, 様式が非常に違っている. *You'd look completely different with short hair.* 短い髪型だと, あなたは全く別人のようだ. *When Ulf started school in this country, the other kids were cruel to him because he was different.* ウルフがこの国で学校に行き始めた時, 彼が皆と違うのでほかの子供たちは彼につらく当たった. ⇔ **similar**
▶アメリカ英語では, different than も使われる.

▶定義2 separate; individual 別々の; 個々の→**さまざまな, 種々の, いろいろな** || *This coat is available in three different colours.* このコートは, 3色ご用意してあります. — **differently** 副 →**(〜と)異なって, 違って, それぞれに** || *I think you'll feel differently about it tomorrow.* 明日になれば, あなたはそれについて違うように感じると思う.

**differentiate** /dífərénʃièit/ 動 ▶定義1 ⒤Ⓣ differentiate between A and B; differentiate A (from B) to see or show how things are different 物事がどのように違うかが分かる, または示す→**見分ける; 〜を見分ける, 識別する** || *It is hard to differentiate between these two types of seed.* これらの2種類の種を見分けるのは難しい. ▶定義2 Ⓣ differentiate sth (from sth) to make one thing different from another あるものを他とは違ったものにする→**〜との違いとなる, 区別する特徴となる** || *The coloured feathers differentiate the male bird from the plain brown female.* 色の付いた羽毛が, 地味な茶色の羽毛の雌鳥と雄鳥との違いだ. ▶定義3 Ⓣ to treat one person or group differently from another 1人または1つの集団に対して, 他とは異なる扱いをする →**〜を差別する** || *We don't differentiate between the two groups - we treat everybody alike.* 私たちは, 2つのグループを差別していま

せん － だれでも皆同じように扱っています．
☞類 **distinguish**

**\*difficult** /dífɪk(ə)lt, -kʌlt/ 形 ▶定義 **1** difficult (for sb) (to do sth) not easy to do or understand 行うまたは理解することが容易ではない→**難しい，困難な** ‖ *a difficult test/problem* 難しい試験・問題 ‖ *I find it difficult to get up early in the morning.* 早起きは難しいと，私は思う． ‖ *It was difficult for us to hear the speaker.* 私たちには講演者の話がよく聞こえなかった． ‖ *I'm in a difficult situation. Whatever I do, somebody will be upset.* 私は難しい状況にいる．どんな事をしてもだれかが怒る． ▶定義 **2** (used about a person) not friendly, reasonable or helpful (人について) 愛想が良くない，思慮分別がない，または力になってくれない→**気難しい，扱いにくい** ‖ *a difficult customer* 扱いにくい客

**\*difficulty** /dífɪk(ə)lti/ 名 (複 **difficulties**) ▶定義 **1** ❶❷ difficulty (in sth/in doing sth) a problem; a situation that is hard to deal with 問題; 取り扱いが困難な状況→**困難な点，障害** ‖ *I'm sure you won't have any difficulty getting a visa for America.* あなたの米国へのビザの取得には何の問題もないと確信しています． ‖ *We had no difficulty selling our car.* 私たちは，車の売却には少しも苦労しなかった． ‖ *We found a hotel without difficulty.* ホテルは楽に見つかった． ‖ *With difficulty, I managed to persuade Alice to lend us the money.* やっとのことで私たちにお金を貸してくれるよう，アリスを何とか説得した． ‖ *I could see someone in difficulty in the water so I went to help them.* だれかがおぼれているのが見えたので，私は救助に向かった． ‖ *If you borrow too much money you may get into financial difficulties.* お金を借りすぎると，財政的な苦境に陥るかもしれない． ▶定義 **2** ❶ how hard sth is to do or to deal with 〜を行うまたは取り扱うことの難しさ→**難しさ，困難** ‖ *The questions start easy and then increase in difficulty.* 質問は易しいものから始まり，段々と難度が上がっていく．

**diffident** /dífɪdənt/ 形 ▶定義 not having confidence in your own strengths or abilities 自分の体力または能力に自信を持っていない→**内気な，おずおずした** ‖ *He has a very diffident manner.* 彼はとても遠慮がちな態度だ． — **diffidence** 名 ❶→遠慮がちなこと，気後れ，自信のなさ

# dig¹ 459

dig
spade

**dig¹** /dɪɡ/ 動⾃他 (現分 **digging**; 過，過分 **dug** /dʌɡ/) ▶定義 to move earth and make a hole in the ground 土を動かして，地面に穴を作る→**土・穴を掘る，〜を掘る，掘り起こす** ‖ *The children are busy digging in the sand.* 子供たちは砂地で穴掘りに熱中している． *to dig a hole* 穴を掘る

成句 **dig deep** ▶定義 to try harder, give more, go further, etc than is usually necessary 普段必要とされているよりも熱心にやってみる，より多く与える，もっと先まで行くなど→**いつもよりもっと** ‖ *Charities for the homeless are asking people to dig deep into their pockets in this cold weather.* ホームレスへの慈善事業は，この寒さの中で人々にもっと多くのお金を寄付してくれるように頼んでいる．

**dig your heels in** ▶定義 to refuse to do sth or to change your mind about sth 〜をすること，または〜についての考えを変えることを拒む→**頑として譲らない，自分の立場に固執する** ‖ *The union dug its heels in and waited for a better pay offer.* 組合は頑として譲らず，もっと多額の賃金の申し出を待った．

句動詞 **dig (sth) in; dig sth into sth** ▶定義 to push or press (sth) into sb/sth (ものを)〜に入れる，または押し付ける→**〜を…に突き立てる，〜に食い込む** ‖ *My neck is all red where my collar is digging in.* えりが食い込んでいる首のところが真っ赤になっている． ‖ *He dug his hands deep into his pockets.* 彼は両手をポケットの奥深く突っ込んだ．

**dig sb/sth out (of sth)** ▶定義 **1** to get sb/sth out of sth by moving the earth, etc that covers him/her/it それを覆っていた土などをどけて，〜を…から取り出す→**(〜から)…を取り出す，掘り出す** ‖ *Rescue workers dug the survivors out of the rubble.* 救助隊員たちは，がれきの山から生存者たちを引き出した． ▶定義 **2** to get or find sb/sth by searching 〜を探して手に入れる，または見つけ出す→**〜を探し出す，見つけ出す** ‖

*Bill went into the attic and dug out some old photos.* ビルは屋根裏部屋へ行き, 数枚の古い写真を見つけ出した.

**dig sth up** ▶定義1 to remove sth from the earth by digging 地面を掘って地中から～を取り出す→～を掘り出す, 掘り当てる ‖ *to dig up potatoes* ジャガイモを掘り出す ▶定義2 to make a hole or take away soil by digging 地面を掘って穴を作る, または土を取り除く→(土地を)掘り起こす ‖ *Workmen are digging up the road in front of our house.* 作業員たちは, 私たちの家の前の道路を掘り起こしている. ▶定義3 to find information by searching or studying 調査または研究によって情報を見つけ出す→(新事実などを)見つける, 探り当てる ‖ *Newspapers have dug up some embarrassing facts about his private life.* 新聞は彼の私生活に関する厄介な事実を探り当てた.

**dig²** /dɪɡ/ 名 ▶定義1 ●a hard push 強く押すこと→(体の部分を)つつくこと, 小突き, 突き ‖ *to give sb a dig in the ribs* (= *with your elbow*) 人の横腹を(= ひじで)突く ▶定義2 ●something that you say to upset sb 人を動揺させるために言う事→(～に対する)嫌味 ‖ *The others kept making **digs** at him because of the way he spoke.* 彼の話し方のせいで, ほかの人々が彼に嫌味を言い続けた. ▶定義3 ●an occasion or place where a group of people try to find things of historical or scientific interest in the ground in order to study them それらを研究するために, 人々の集団が歴史的または科学的に興味深いものを地中に発見する, 機会または場所→(考古学上の)発掘(作業), 発掘物 ‖ *an archaeological dig* 考古学上の発掘

*****digest** /daɪdʒést, də-/ 動他 ▶定義1 to change food in your stomach so that it can be used by the body 体が利用できるように, 食物を胃の中で変える→～を消化する ‖ *I'm not going to go swimming until I've digested my lunch.* お昼ご飯がこなれるまで, 私は泳ぎには行かない. ▶定義2 to think about new information so that you understand it fully 十分に理解するように, 新しい情報について考える→(知識・考え・意味など)をよく理解する, 吸収する, 会得する ‖ *The lecture was interesting, but too much to digest all at once.* その講義は興味深いものだったが, 一度に全部を理解するには内容が多すぎた.

**digestion** /dədʒéstʃ(ə)n, daɪ-/ 名 ●Ｕ ▶定義 the process of changing food in your stomach so that it can be used by the body 体が利用できるように, 食物を胃の中で変える過程→消化, 消化作用, 消化力 — **digestive** /dədʒéstɪv, daɪ-/ 形 →消化の, 消化を助ける, 消化力のある ‖ *the digestive system* 消化器系

**digit** /dídʒət/ 名 ●Ｃ ▶定義 any of the numbers from 0 to 9 0から9までの, いずれかの数字→数字, 0から9までのアラビア数字 ‖ *a six-digit telephone number* 6けたの電話番号

**digital** /dídʒətl/ 形 ▶定義1 using an electronic system that uses the numbers 1 and 0 to record sound or store information, and that gives high-quality results 音を録音するまたは情報を保存するために0と1の数値を使い, 高品質な結果を得られる, 電子システムを使っている→デジタル(式)の ‖ *a digital recording* デジタル録音 ▶定義2 showing information by using numbers 数字を使って情報を表示している→(通信・信号・録音などが)数字で表示する, デジタル(式)の ‖ *a digital watch* デジタル腕時計 ☞ **clock** のさし絵

**dignified** /dígnəfàɪd/ 形 ▶定義 behaving in a calm, serious way that makes other people respect you ほかの人々に尊敬させるような, 落ち着いたまじめな様子で振る舞っている→威厳のある, 堂々とした, 品位のある ‖ *dignified behaviour* 威厳のある態度 ⇔ **undignified**

**dignity** /dígnəti/ 名 ●Ｕ ▶定義1 calm, serious behaviour that makes other people respect you ほかの人々が尊敬するような, 落ち着いたまじめな態度→威厳, 荘重さ ‖ *to behave **with dignity*** 毅然(きぜん)として振る舞う ▶定義2 the quality of being serious and formal まじめで改まっている様子→荘厳さ, 厳粛さ, 気高さ, 尊厳 ‖ *the quiet dignity of the funeral service* 葬儀の静かな気品

**digress** /daɪgrés, də-/ 動自 正式 ▶定義 to stop talking or writing about the main subject under discussion and start talking or writing about another less important one 論議の主要なテーマについて話しているまたは書いていることをやめて, 別の重要性の低いテーマについて話し始めるまたは書き始める→(話などが)わき道にそれ

る, 脱線する — digression /daɪgréʃ(ə)n, də-/ [名] [C] [U] ➜ (話などが)わき道にそれること, 脱線, 余談

**dike** = DYKE

**dilapidated** /dəlǽpədèɪtəd/ [形] ▶定義 (used about buildings, furniture, etc) old and broken (建物, 家具などについて)古くて壊れている➜ **ぼろぼろになった, 壊れかかった, 見る影もない** —dilapidation /dəlæ̀pədéɪʃ(ə)n/ [名] [U] ➜ **荒廃, 崩壊, 破損**

**dilemma** /dəlémə, daɪ-/ [名] [C] ▶定義 a situation in which you have to make a difficult choice between two or more things 2つまたはそれより多い物の中から難しい選択をしなくてはならない状況➜ **ジレンマ, 板挟み, 窮地** ‖ *Doctors **face** a moral **dilemma** of when to keep patients alive artificially and when to let them die.* 医者たちは患者をいつまで人工的に生かし, いつ死に至らしめるかという, 倫理的な窮地に直面している. *to be **in a dilemma*** ジレンマに陥る

**dilute** /daɪlúːt, də-/ [動] [他] ▶定義 dilute sth (with sth) to make a liquid weaker by adding water or another liquid 水またはほかの液体を加えて, 液体を薄める➜ **(〜で)…を薄める** — dilute [形] ➜ **薄めた, 希釈した**

**dim**[1] /dɪm/ [形] (**dimmer**; **dimmest**) ▶定義1 not bright or easy to see; not clear 明るくない, または見えにくい; 明瞭(めいりょう)でない➜ **薄暗い, (姿・形などが)ぼんやりした, (記憶・考えなどが)あいまいな** ‖ *The light was too dim to read by.* 明かりが暗すぎて読めなかった. *a dim shape in the distance* 遠くのぼんやりした形 *My memories of my grandmother are quite dim.* 祖母についての思い出は, とてもあいまいだ. ▶定義2 [略式] not very clever; stupid あまり利口ではない; 愚鈍な➜ **頭が鈍い; 間抜けな** ‖ *He's a bit dim.* 彼は少し頭が鈍い. ▶定義3 [略式] (used about a situation) not hopeful (状況について)望みのない➜ **(見通しが)暗い, 悲観的な** ‖ *The prospects of the two sides reaching an agreement look dim.* 双方が合意に達する見通しは悲観的なようだ. — dimly [副] ➜ **薄暗く, ぼんやりと, かすかに**

**dim**[2] /dɪm/ [動] [自] [他] (**dimming**; **dimmed**) ▶定義 to become or make sth less bright or clear 〜が暗くまたは不明瞭(めいりょう)になる; 〜を暗くまたは不明瞭にする➜ **薄暗くなる, あいまいになる; 〜を薄暗くする, あいまいにする** ‖ *The lights dimmed.* 明かりが薄暗くなった. *to dim the lights* 明かりを薄暗くする

**dime** /dáɪm/ [名] [C] ▶定義 a coin used in the US and Canada that is worth ten cents 10セントの価値がある, 米国およびカナダで使われる硬貨➜ **ダイム, 10セント硬貨**

**dimension** /dəménʃ(ə)n/ [名] ▶定義1 [C] [U] a measurement of the length, width or height of sth 〜の長さ, 幅, または高さの寸法➜ **寸法** ▶定義2 **dimensions** [複数扱い] the size of sth including its length, width and height 長さ, 幅と高さを含む, 〜の大きさ➜ **大きさ, 面積, 容積, 規模** ‖ *to measure the dimensions of a room* 部屋の大きさを測る (比喩) *The full dimensions of this problem are only now being recognized.* この問題全体の大きさが, ようやく今認識され始めている. ▶定義3 [C] something that affects the way you think about a problem or situation 問題または状況についての考え方に影響を及ぼすもの➜ **局面, 側面, 要因** ‖ *to add a new dimension to a problem/situation* 問題・状況に新たな要素を付け加える ▶定義4 **-dimensional** /-ʃ(ə)n(ə)l/ (複合形容詞を作るために用いて) having the number of dimensions mentioned 言及された数の次元を持っている➜ **〜次元の** ‖ *a three-dimensional object* 三次元の物体

**diminish** /dəmínɪʃ/ [動] [自] [他] [正式] ▶定義 to become or to make sth smaller or less important; decrease 〜が小さくなるまたは重要でなくなる, あるいは〜を小さくするまたは重要性を低くする; 減少する➜ **減少する, 小さくなる; 〜を減らす, 小さくする** ‖ *The world's rainforests are diminishing fast.* 世界の熱帯雨林は, 急速に減少している. *The bad news did nothing to diminish her enthusiasm for the plan.* 悪い知らせも, 彼女の計画に対する熱意を少しも減らすことはなかった.

**diminutive** /dəmínjətɪv/ [形] [正式] ▶定義 much smaller than usual 普通よりもとても小さい➜ **小さい, 小型の, 小柄の**

**dimple** /dímp(ə)l/ [名] [C] ▶定義 a round area in the skin on your cheek, etc, which often only appears when you smile ほほえんだときだけによく現れる, ほおなどの皮膚の円形の部分➜

えくぼ

**din** /dín/ 图 [単数扱い] ▶定義 a lot of unpleasant noise that continues for some time しばらくの間続く，大きな不快な騒音→(じゃんじゃん・がんがん響く)うるさい音，騒音

**dine** /dáin/ 動 自 正式 ▶定義 to eat a meal, especially in the evening 特に晩に，食事をする→食事をする，ディナーを取る ‖ *We dined at an exclusive French restaurant.* 私たちは高級フランス料理店で食事をした．
句動詞 **dine out** ▶定義 to eat in a restaurant レストランで食べる→外食する，ディナーに招待されて出掛ける

**diner** /dáinər/ 图 C ▶定義 1 a person who is eating at a restaurant レストランで食事をしている人→食事をする人，ディナーの客 ▶定義 2 米 a restaurant that serves simple, cheap food 簡単で安い食事を出すレストラン→(道路沿いにある食堂車風の)簡易食堂

**dinghy** /díŋɡi/ 图 C (複 **dinghies**) ▶定義 1 a small boat that you sail 人が操縦する小さな船→ディンギー(競走用の小型ヨット) ← 参 **yacht** ▶定義 2 a small open boat, often used to take people to land from a larger boat 屋根のない小さな船，しばしば人々を大型船から陸地へ連れていくために用いられる→小ボート，救命ボート ← **boat** のさし絵

**dingy** /díndʒi/ 形 ▶定義 dirty and dark 汚くて暗い→(衣類・建物・場所などが)薄汚い，すすけた，くすんだ色の ‖ *a dingy room/hotel* 薄汚い部屋・ホテル

**dining room** 图 C ▶定義 a room where you eat meals 食事をする部屋→(家・ホテルなどの)食堂，ダイニングルーム ← C7 ページのさし絵

★**dinner** /dínər/ 图 ▶定義 1 C U the main meal of the day, eaten either at midday or in the evening 1 日のうちの主要な食事，真昼か晩のいずれかに食べられる→ディナー(1 日のうちでの主要な食事) ‖ *Would you like to **go out for/to dinner** one evening?* いつか晩に，外でディナーをいかがですか． *I never eat a big dinner.* 私は豪勢なディナーを決して食べない． *What's for dinner, Mum?* ママ，ディナーは何． ▶定義 2 C a formal occasion in the evening during which a meal is served 食事が供され，夜に催される正式な行事→晩餐(ばんさん)会，夕食会，祝宴 ‖ *The club is holding its annual dinner next week.* 当クラブは例年の晩餐会を来週催します．

▶社会・文化
**クリスマスディナーは昼食？**
「ディナー」と言うと日本では夕食を指しますが，英語では昼食を指す場合もあります．特に北部地方に住む人や労働者たちは，昼食を dinner と言い，夕食を supper あるいは tea と呼びます．したがって，「クリスマスディナー」Christmas dinner は昼に食べます．中流階級以上の人たちは，夕食を dinner と言い，寝る前に食べる軽い夜食を supper と言います．

**dinner jacket** ( 米 **tuxedo**) 图 C ▶定義 a black or white jacket that a man wears on formal occasions. A dinner jacket is usually worn with a special tie (a bow tie). 正式な場で男性が着る，黒または白の上着．通常は特別なネクタイ(ちょうネクタイ)を付けて着用される→タキシード

**dinosaur** /dáinəsɔ̀:r/ 图 C ▶定義 one of a number of very large animals that disappeared from the earth (became extinct) millions of years ago 何百万年も前に地球から姿を消した(絶滅した)，何種類かのとても大きな動物の 1 つ→恐竜(古生物) ‖ *dinosaur fossils* 恐竜の化石 ← C8 ページのさし絵

**Dip** 略 diploma→修了証書

**dip**² /díp/ 動 (**dipping**; **dipped**) ▶定義 1 他 **dip sth (ino sth); dip sth (in)** to put sth into liquid and immediately take it out again 〜を液体の中に入れ，すぐにまた取り出す→〜をちょっと浸す，さっとつける ‖ *Julie dipped her toe into the pool to see how cold it was.* どれくらい冷たいかを見るために，ジュリーはプールにつま先をちょっとつけた． ▶定義 2 自 to go down or make sth go down to a lower level 低い水準に下がる，または〜を下げる→(物・値段などが)下がる，(太陽などが)沈む，(道路などが)急に下り坂になる ‖ *The road suddenly dipped down to the river.* 突然，道路が川に向かって下り坂になった． *The company's sales have dipped disastrously this year.* 今年の会社の売り上げは，悲惨なほどに下降している．

**句動詞** **dip into sth** ▶定義1 to use part of an amount of sth that you have 手持ちの〜の一部を使う➔**(貯金などに)手を付ける** ‖ *Tim had to dip into his savings to pay for his new suit.* ティムは新しいスーツの支払いのために、貯金の一部に手を付けなければならなかった. ▶定義2 to read parts, but not all, of sth 〜の全部ではなく、一部を読む➔**〜をちょっと調べる、〜にざっと目を通す** ‖ *I've only dipped into the book. I haven't read it all the way through.* その本にざっと目を通しただけです。全体を通して読んではいません.

**dip**³ /dɪp/ 名 ▶定義1 Ⓒa fall to a lower level, especially for a short time 特に短期間に、より低い水準へ落ちること➔**(物や数量の)低下、下降** ‖ *a dip in sales/temperature* 売り上げ・気温の低下 ▶定義2 Ⓒan area of lower ground より低くなった地面の区域➔**沈下、くぼみ、傾斜** ‖ *The cottage was in a dip in the hills.* 小屋は、丘のくぼみにあった. ▶定義3 略式 a short swim 短時間泳ぐこと➔**一泳ぎ** ‖ *We went for a dip before breakfast.* 朝食前に、私たちは一泳ぎに行った. ▶定義4 ⒸⓊa thick sauce into which you dip biscuits, vegetables, etc before eating them 食べる前に、ビスケット、野菜などをちょっと浸す濃厚なソース➔**ディップ、ソース** ‖ *a cheese/chilli dip* チーズディップ・チリディップ

**diphtheria** /dɪfθíəriə, dɪp-/ 名 Ⓤ ▶定義 a serious disease of the throat that makes it difficult to breathe 呼吸することを難しくさせる、のどの重い病気➔**ジフテリア**

**diphthong** /dífθɔ(:)ŋ, dɪp-, -θɑŋ/ 名 Ⓒ ▶定義 two vowel sounds that are pronounced together to make one sound, for example the /aɪ/ sound in 'fine' 1つの音を作るために一緒に発音される2つの母音の音、例えば fine の /aɪ/ の音➔**二重母音**

**diploma** /dəplóʊmə/ 名 Ⓒ ▶定義 a diploma (in *sth*) a certificate that you receive when you complete a course of study, often at a college 多くは単科大学で、人が学習課程を終えるときに受ける修了証明書➔**卒業証書、修了証書、(学部・学科の)学位記** ‖ *I'm studying for a diploma in hotel management.* 私はホテル経営の修了証書を目指して勉強している. ☛参 **degree** の注

**diplomacy** /dəplóʊməsi/ 名 Ⓤ ▶定義1 the activity of managing relations between different countries 異なる国々の間の関係を管理する活動➔**外交(交渉)** ‖ *If diplomacy fails, there is a danger of war.* 外交が失敗すると、戦争の危険がある. ▶定義2 skill in dealing with people without upsetting or offending them 人々を怒らせるまたは機嫌を損ねることなく、うまく扱う能力➔**駆け引き、外交的手腕** ‖ *He handled the tricky situation with tact and diplomacy.* 彼は機転と駆け引きのうまさで、油断のならない事態に対処した.

**diplomat** /dípləmæt/ 名 Ⓒ ▶定義 an official who represents his/her country in a foreign country 外国で、自分の国を代表する役人➔**外交官** ‖ *a diplomat at the embassy in Rome* ローマにある大使館の外交官

**diplomatic** /dìpləmǽtɪk/ 形 ▶定義1 connected with diplomacy(1) diplomacy (1) に関連した➔**外交の、外交上の** ‖ *to break off diplomatic relations* 外交関係を断絶する ▶定義2 skilful at dealing with people 人々を扱う能力にたけている➔**駆け引きのうまい、外交的手腕のある** ‖ *He searched for a diplomatic reply so as not to offend her.* 彼女の機嫌を損ねないように、彼はそつのない返事を探した. — **diplomatically** /-k(ə)li/ 副 ➔**外交上、外交的に、外交手腕をもって**

**dire** /dáɪər/ 形 正式 ▶定義 very bad or serious; terrible とても悪い、または深刻な; ひどい➔**(必要・危機などが)差し迫った、(事態などが)重大な、深刻な、ものすごい** ‖ *dire consequences/poverty* 深刻な結果・貧困

**成句** **be in dire straits** ▶定義 to be in a very difficult situation とても難しい状況である➔**非常に困難な状況にある、ひどい窮境にある** ‖ *The business is in dire straits financially.* 事業は財政的に非常に困難な状況にある.

★**direct**¹ /dərékt, daɪ-/ 形 副 ▶定義1 with nobody/nothing in between; not involving anyone/anything else 間にだれも・何も入らない; ほかのだれも・何も絡まない➔**直接的な、途中に介在するもののない、直接** ‖ *The British Prime Minister is* **in direct contact with** *the US President.* イギリスの首相はアメリカ大統領に直接連絡を取っている. *a direct attack on the capital* 首都への直接攻撃 *As a* **direct result** *of the new road, traffic jams in the centre have been reduced.* 新しい道路による直接的な成果

として, 中心部の交通渋滞が緩和された. *You should protect your skin from direct sunlight.* 直射日光から肌を守るべきだ. ▶定義2 going from one place to another without turning or stopping; straight 迂回(うかい)する, または止まることなく, ある場所から別の場所へ行くこと; まっすぐな→**まっすぐな, 直行・直通の, 一直線に** || *a direct flight to Hong Kong* 香港への直行便 *This bus goes direct to London.* このバスは, ロンドンに直行する. ▶定義3 saying what you mean; clear 意図している事をそのまま言う; 明快な→**率直な, 単刀直入な, 正直に** || *Politicians never give a direct answer to a direct question.* 政治家は, 単刀直入な質問に対して単刀直入な答えを出すことは決してしない. *She sometimes offends people with her direct way of speaking.* 彼女は時々, 率直なものの言い方で人を怒らせる. ⇔定義1, 2, 3 **indirect** ▶定義4 (名詞の前だけ) complete; exact 完全な; 正確な→**全くの, そのものずばりの, 明白な** || *What she did was in direct opposition to my orders.* 彼女がした事は私の指示と全く反対だった.

★**direct**[2] /dərékt, dai-/ 動 他 ▶定義1 **direct sth to/towards sb/sth; direct sth at sb/sth** to point or send sth towards sb/sth or in a particular direction 〜を…にまたはある特定の方向に, 向けるまたは送る→**(物・言葉・努力など)を〜に向ける, 注ぐ, (郵便物など)を〜あてに送る** || *In recent weeks the media's attention has been directed towards events abroad.* 最近の何週間か, マスコミの注目は海外の出来事に向けられている. *The advert is directed at young people.* その広告は若者向けだ. *The actor directed some angry words at a photographer.* その俳優はカメラマンに対して怒りの言葉を浴びせた. ▶定義2 to manage or control sb/sth 〜を管理するまたは監督する→**(活動・人・組織など)を指揮する, 指導する, 管理・監督する** || *A policeman was in the middle of the road, directing the traffic.* 交通整理をするために, 警察官が道路の真ん中にいた. *to direct a play/film* 芝居・映画を監督する ▶定義3 **direct sb (to...)** to tell or show sb how to get somewhere 〜にある場所への行き方を教える, または示す→**〜に(…への道を)教える** || *I was directed to an office at the end of the corridor.* 廊下の端にある事務所へ案内された. ●参 **lead**[1](1) の注 ▶定義4 正式 to tell or order sb to do sth →**〜に…するよう指示する, 命じる** || *Take the tablets as directed by your doctor.* 医者の指示通りに錠剤を服用しなさい.

**direct debit** 名 C U ▶定義 an order to your bank that allows sb else to take a particular amount of money out of your account on certain dates ほかの〜が特定の日に特定の額のお金を自分の口座から引き出すことを許す, 銀行への指示→**口座引き落とし, 自動振替**

★**direction** /dərékʃ(ə)n, dai-/ 名 ▶定義1 C U the path, line or way along which a person or thing is moving, looking, pointing, developing, etc 人または物が移動したり, 見たり, 向かったり, 発達したりしている道, 線または方法→**方向, 方角, (活動などの)方面** || *A woman was seen running in the direction of the station.* 女の人が駅の方に走っていくのが見えた. *We met him coming in the opposite direction.* 私たちは彼が反対の方向から来るのに出会った. *I think the new speed limit is still too high, but at least it's a step in the right direction.* 新しい制限速度は依然として速すぎるものの, 少なくとも正しい方向への第一歩だと思う. *I think the wind has changed direction.* 風向きが変わったと思う. *I've got such a hopeless sense of direction - I'm always getting lost.* 私はどうしようもない方向音痴だ - いつも道に迷ってばかりいる. ▶定義2 C U a purpose; an aim 目的; 目標→**(活動などの)傾向, 目標, 目的** || *I want a career that gives me a (sense of) direction in life.* 私は人生の目標(の感覚)を与えてくれるような一生の仕事を得たい. ▶定義3 [通常は複数] information or instructions about how to do sth or how to get to a place 〜のやり方, またはある場所への行き方についての情報または指示→**指示, 指図, (薬・道具などの)使用法** || *I'll give you directions to my house.* 我が家への道順をお教えしましょう. ▶定義4 U the act of managing or controlling sth 〜を管理するまたは監督する行為→**監督, 指揮, 指導** || *This department is under the direction of Mrs Walters.* この部門は, ウォルターズ夫人の監督下にある.

**directive** /dəréktɪv, dai-/ 名 C ▶定義 an official order to do sth 〜を行うようにという公式の命令→**指示, 命令, 指令書** || *an EU directive on* *safety at work* 職場の安全性に関するEUの指令書

**directly**¹ /dəréktli, daɪ-/ 副 ▶定義1 in a direct line or way 一直線に,または直接的なやり方で→**まっすぐに,直接に,じかに** ‖ *The bank is directly opposite the supermarket.* 銀行はスーパーのちょうど反対側にある. *He refused to answer my question directly.* 彼は私の質問に直接答えることを拒否した. *Lung cancer is directly related to smoking.* 肺がんは喫煙と直接関係がある. ⇔ **indirectly** ▶定義2 immediately; very soon→**直ちに; すぐに** ‖ *Wait where you are. I'll be back directly.* そこで待っていてください.すぐに戻りますから.

**directly**² /d(ə)rékli/ 接 ▶定義 as soon as→**～するとすぐに** ‖ *I phoned him directly I heard the news.* その知らせを聞くとすぐに,私は彼に電話した.

**direct object** 名 ⓒ (文法) ▶定義 a noun or phrase that is affected by the action of a verb 動詞の働きの影響を受ける名詞または句→**直接目的語** ‖ *In the sentence 'Anna bought a record', 'a record' is the direct object.* Anna bought a record の文章で,a record は直接目的語である. ☛参 **indirect object**
▶直接目的語についての説明は,巻末の「文法早見表」を参照.

\***director** /dəréktər, daɪ-/ 名 ⓒ ▶定義1 a person who manages or controls a company or organization 会社または組織を管理するまたは監督する人→**組織全体の)指導者,責任者,(会社の)重役,(官庁の)局長,長官** ‖ *the managing director of Rolls Royce* ロールスロイス社の専務取締役 *She's on the board of directors (= group of directors) of a large computer company.* 彼女は,コンピューター関係の大企業の取締役会(= 重役の集まり)の一員だ. ▶定義2 a person who is responsible for a particular activity or department in a company, a college, etc 会社,単科大学などで,特定の活動または部門に責任のある人→**管理職の人,管理者** ‖ *the director of studies of a language school* 語学学校の学校教育長 ▶定義3 a person who tells the actors, etc what to do in a film, play, etc 映画,芝居などで,俳優たちに何をするか指示する人→**監督,演出家** ‖ *a film/theatre director* 映画・舞台監督

**directory** /dərékt(ə)ri, daɪ-/ 名 ⓒ (複 **directories**) ▶定義 a list of names, addresses and telephone numbers in the order of the alphabet アルファベット順の,氏名,住所と電話番号の一覧→**人名簿,電話帳,住所録** ‖ *the telephone directory* 電話帳 *I tried to look up Joe's number but he's **ex-directory** (= he has chosen not to be listed in the telephone directory).* ジョーの電話番号を調べたが,彼の名前は電話帳に載っていない(= 彼は電話帳に載せないことを選択している).

**direct speech** 名 Ⓤ (文法) ▶定義 the actual words that a person said 人が言った,実際の言葉→**直接話法** ☛参 **indirect speech**
▶直接話法についての説明は,巻末の「文法早見表」を参照.

\***dirt** /də:rt/ 名 Ⓤ ▶定義1 a substance that is not clean, such as dust or mud 例えばほこりや泥などのような,清潔でない物質→**汚れ,ほこり,ごみ,汚物** ‖ *His face and hands were covered in dirt.* 彼の顔と手はすっかり汚れていた. ▶定義2 earth or soil 土または土壌→**泥,土** ‖ *a dirt track* (泥土を敷いた)オートバイの競走路 ▶定義3 damaging information about sb ～を傷付ける情報→**悪口,悪いうわさ** ‖ *The press are always trying to **dig up dirt** on the President's love life.* マスコミはいつも,大統領の性生活に関する悪いうわさを探し出そうとしている.

成句 **dirt cheap** ▶定義 extremely cheep 極めて安い→**非常に安い・安く,ばか安の**

\***dirty**¹ /dá:rti/ 形 (**dirtier; dirtiest**) ▶定義1 not clean 清潔でない→**汚い,汚れた,泥だらけの** ‖ *Your hands are dirty. Go and wash them!* 手が汚れている.洗ってきなさい. *Gardening is dirty work (= it makes you dirty).* 園芸は泥まみれになる仕事だ(= それは人を泥まみれにする). ⇔ **clean** ▶定義2 referring to sex in a way that may upset or offend people 人々をどぎまぎさせる,または怒らせる恐れのあるやり方で,性に言及している→**卑わいな,わいせつな,いやらしい** ‖ *to tell a dirty joke* 卑わいな冗談を言う ▶定義3 unpleasant or dishonest 不愉快な,または不正な→**(行為が)卑劣な,不正な,軽べつすべき** ‖ *He's a dirty player.* 彼は卑劣な選手だ. *He doesn't sell the drugs himself - he gets kids to **do his dirty work** for him.* 彼は自分では麻薬を

売らない － 彼の不正行為を子供たちにやらせている. — dirty 副 →**不正に, 卑劣に, みだらに**
感句 a dirty word ▶定義 an idea or thing that you do not like or agree with 自分が好きではない, または賛成できない考えまたは物事→**嫌われる考え・物, 禁句, 不信を抱かせる言葉** ‖ *Work is a dirty word to Frank.* 仕事という言葉はフランクには禁句だ.

play dirty 略式 ▶定義 to behave or to play a game in an unfair or dishonest way 不公平または不正なやり方で, 振る舞うまたはゲームをする →**卑怯(ひきょう)に振る舞う, 卑劣な・汚いことをする**

**dirty**[2] /dɚːti/ 動 自 他 (現分 **dirtying**; 三単現 **dirties**; 過, 過分 **dirtied**) ▶定義 to become or to make sth dirty ～が汚れる, または～を汚す→**汚れる; ～を汚す, ～を不潔にする, 汚らしくする** ⇔ **clean**

**disability** /dìsəbíləti/ 名 (複 **disabilities**) ▶定義 1 ❶ the state of being unable to use a part of your body properly, usually because of injury or disease 普通はけがまたは病気のために, 身体の一部を適切に使えない状態→**(身体)障害のあること, 無力** ‖ *physical/mental disability* 身体障害・精神障害 ▶定義 2 ❷ something that makes you unable to use a part of your body properly 身体の一部を適切に使えなくさせるもの→**身体障害, 障害, ハンディキャップ** ‖ *Because of his disability, he needs constant care.* 身体障害のため, 彼には常に介護が必要だ.

**disable** /dɪséɪb(ə)l/ 動 他 (通常は受動態で) ▶定義 to make sb unable to use part of his/her body properly, usually because of injury or disease 普通はけがまたは病気のために, ～の身体の一部を適切に使えなくさせる→**～の身体を不自由にする, ～を身体障害者にする** ‖ *Many soldiers were disabled in the war.* 多くの兵士が戦争で身体障害者になった.

**disabled** /dɪséɪb(ə)ld/ 形 ▶定義 1 unable to use a part of your body properly 身体の一部を適切に使えない→**身体障害の, 身体の不自由な** ‖ *A car accident left her permanently disabled.* 自動車事故により彼女は一生身体が不自由になった. ▶定義 2 **the disabled** 名 [複数扱い] people who are disabled 身体の不自由な人々→**身体障害者たち** ‖ *The hotel has improved facilities for the disabled.* そのホテルは, 身体障害者たちのために設備を改善した.

*__disadvantage__ /dìsədvάːntɪdʒ; -væn-/ 名 ❻ ▶定義 1 something that may make you less successful than other people ほかの人々より, 成功することを難しくさせるかもしれないもの→**不利な立場, 不利なこと, デメリット** ‖ *Your qualifications are good. Your main disadvantage is your lack of experience.* あなたの資格は申し分ない. 不利となる主な事は経験不足だ. ▶定義 2 something that is not good or that causes problems 良くない, または問題を引き起こすもの→**不利益, 不利, 不都合** ‖ *The main disadvantage of the job is the long hours.* その仕事の不都合な点は何と言っても, 労働時間の長さだ. *What are the advantages and disadvantages of nuclear power?* 原子力発電の長所と短所は何ですか. ⇔ **advantage**

感句 **put sb/be at a disadvantage** ▶定義 to put sb/be in a situation where he/she/you may be less successful than other people ほかの人々より成功することが難しいかもしれない状況に～を置く, あるいはいる→**不利な立場にいる; ～を不利な立場に置く** ‖ *The fact that you don't speak the language will put you at a disadvantage in France.* フランス語を話さないことは, フランスでは不利になるだろう.

**to sb's disadvantage** 正式 ▶定義 not good or helpful for sb ～に対して良くない, または役に立たない→**～の不利になるような[に]** ‖ *The agreement will be to your disadvantage － don't accept it.* その契約はあなたにとって不利になるだろう － 受け入れてはいけない.

**disadvantaged** /dìsədvάːntɪdʒd; -væn-/ 形 ▶定義 in a bad social or economic situation; poor 社会的または経済的に悪い状況で; 貧しい →**(社会的に)不利な, 恵まれない, 困窮している** ‖ *extra help for the most disadvantaged members of society* 社会で最も恵まれない人たちへの特別援助

**disadvantageous** /dìsædvəntéɪdʒəs/ 形 ▶定義 causing sb to be in a worse situation compared to other people ～をほかの人々と比べて悪い状況に置く原因となる→**(～にとって)不利な, 都合の悪い**

*__disagree__ /dìsəgríː/ 動 自 ▶定義 1 disagree

(with sb/sth) (about/on sth) to have a different opinion from sb/sth; to not agree 〜とは違う意見を持つ; 賛成しない➡(〜と)意見が合わない, (意見・決定などに)同意しない, (行動・提案などに)異議を唱える ‖ *Noel often disagrees with his father about politics.* ノエルは, 政治について父と意見が合わないことがよくある. *They strongly disagreed with my idea.* 彼らは私の考えに強く異議を唱えた. *'We have to tell him.' 'No, I disagree. I don't think we should tell him at all.'*「彼に話さなければならない」「いいや, そうは思わない. 彼に話すべきではないと思う」 ▶定義2 to be different 異なっている➡(言動, 計算などが)一致しない, 異なる ‖ *These two sets of statistics disagree.* この2組の統計値は, 一致しない. ⇔ **agree**

句動詞 disagree with sb ▶定義 (used about sth you have eaten or drunk) to make you feel ill; to have a bad effect on you (自分が食べた, または飲んだ〜について)気持ち悪くさせる, 悪い影響を及ぼす➡(〜の)体に合わない, (〜に)適さない, 害になる

**disagreeable** /dìsəgríːəb(ə)l/ 形 正式 ▶定義 unpleasant 不愉快な ⇔ **agreeable** — **disagreeably** /-əbli/ 副 ➡不快そうに, 嫌になるほど

**disagreement** /dìsəgríːmənt/ 名 C U ▶定義 disagreement (with sb) (about/on/over sth) a situation in which people have a different opinion about sth and often also argue 人々が〜について異なる意見を持ち, しばしば口論にもなる状況➡意見の相違, 不一致, 異論 ‖ *It's normal for couples to have disagreements.* 男女の意見が合わないのは, 普通の事です. *Mandy resigned after a disagreement with her boss.* 上司と意見の相違があった後, マンディーは辞職した. *The conference ended in disagreement.* 会議は意見の一致を見ないまま終了した. ⇔ **agreement**

**disallow** /dìsəláu/ 動 他 ▶定義 to not allow or accept sth 〜を許さない, または受け入れない➡〜を(公式に)認めない, 許可しない, 却下する ‖ *The goal was disallowed because the player was offside.* 選手がオフサイドだったので, 得点は認められなかった.

\***disappear** /dìsəpíər/ 動 自 ▶定義1 to become impossible to see or to find; vanish 見えなくなる, または見つけられなくなる; 消える➡見えなくなる, 消える, 姿を消す ‖ *He walked away and disappeared into a crowd of people.* 彼は歩き去り, 人込みの中に消えていった. *My purse was here a moment ago and now it's disappeared.* 私のお財布はちょっと前にはここにあったのに, 今はなくなってしまった. ▶定義2 to stop existing; vanish 存在しなくなる; 消える➡存在しなくなる, 消滅する, なくなる ‖ *Plant and animal species are disappearing at an alarming rate.* 動植物の種は, 驚くべき速度で消滅し続けている. ⇔ **appear** — **disappearance** 名 C U ➡失踪(しっそう), 消滅, 紛失 ‖ *The mystery of her disappearance was never solved.* 彼女の失踪のなぞは, 全く解明されなかった.

**disappoint** /dìsəpɔ́int/ 動 他 ▶定義 to make sb sad because what he/she had hoped for has not happened or is less good, interesting, etc than he/she had hoped 望んでいた事が実現しなかった, あるいは望んでいたものより良くなかった, または面白くなかったなどのために, 〜を悲しませる➡〜をがっかりさせる, 失望させる ‖ *I'm sorry to disappoint you but I'm afraid you haven't won the prize.* がっかりさせることになって申し訳ないけれど, 残念なことにあなたは賞を取れませんでした.

\***disappointed** /dìsəpɔ́intəd/ 形 ▶定義 disappointed (about/at sth); disappointed (in/with sb/sth); disappointed that... sad because you/sb/sth did not succeed or because sth was not as good, interesting, etc as you had hoped 自分・〜が成功しなかったので, あるいは〜が期待していたほどには良くなかった, または面白くなかったなどで, 悲しい➡がっかりして, 失望して ‖ *Lucy was deeply disappointed at not being chosen for the team.* ルーシーはチームに選ばれなかったことに, 心の底からがっかりした. *We were disappointed with our hotel.* 私たちが泊まったホテルにはがっかりした. *I'm disappointed in you. I thought you could do better.* あなたには失望しています. あなたはもっとうまくやれると思っていました. *They are very disappointed that they can't stay longer.* 滞在を延ばせないので, 彼らはとてもがっかりしている. *I was disappointed to hear that you can't come to the party.* あなたがパーティ

—に来られないと聞いて、がっかりしました.

**\*disappointing** /dìsəpɔ́ɪntɪŋ/ 形 ▶定義 making you feel sad because sth was not as good, interesting, etc as you had hoped ～が期待していたほどには良くなかった、または面白くなかったなどで、人を悲しくさせている→失望させる、がっかりさせる、期待外れの ‖ *It has been a disappointing year for the company.* 会社にとって、期待外れの1年だった. ― **disappointingly** 副→期待外れなことに、残念なことに

**\*disappointment** /dìsəpɔ́ɪntmənt/ 名 ▶定義 1 ⒞ the state of being disappointed がっかりしている状態→失望、落胆、期待外れ ‖ *To his great disappointment he failed to get the job.* 非常にがっかりしたことには、彼は仕事を得られなかった. ▶定義 2 ⒞ a disappointment (to sb) a person or thing that disappoints you 人をがっかりさせる人または物事→(人を)失望させるもの、案外つまらない人・事・物 ‖ *She has suffered many disappointments in her career.* 彼女は生涯、多くの失望を味わってきた.

**disapproval** /dìsəprúːv(ə)l/ 名 Ⓤ ▶定義 a feeling that sth is bad or that sb is behaving badly ～が悪い、または～が悪く振る舞っていると思う感情→不承知、不賛成、非難 ‖ *She shook her head in disapproval.* 彼女は賛成できずかぶりを振った.

**\*disapprove** /dìsəprúːv/ 動 自 ▶定義 disapprove (of sb/sth) to think that sb/sth is bad, foolish, etc ～が悪い、または愚かであるなどと思う→賛成しない、いけないと思う、(～を)非とする ‖ *His parents strongly disapproved of him leaving college before he had finished his course.* 彼が全課程を修了する前に大学を辞めることについて、両親は強く反対した. ― **disapproving** 形→不賛成の、不満げな、不満の ‖ *After he had told the joke there was a disapproving silence.* 彼が冗談を言った後、不満げな沈黙が広がった. ― **disapprovingly** 副→不賛成の様子で、不満げに、批判的に ‖ *David frowned disapprovingly when I lit a cigarette.* 私がたばこに火をつけると、デーヴィッドは不服そうに顔をしかめた.

**disarm** /dɪsάːrm, dɪz-/ 動 ▶定義 他 to take weapons away from sb ～から武器を奪い去る→～の武装を解除する、～から武器を取り上げる ‖ *The police caught and disarmed the terrorists.* 警察はテロリストを捕らえて武器を取り上げた. ▶定義 2 自 (used about a country) to reduce the number of weapons it has (国について)所有している武器の数量を減らす→(核)軍備を縮小・制限・撤廃する, (核)武装を解除する ▶定義 3 他 to make sb feel less angry ～の怒りを和らげる→～の怒り・敵意・警戒心を解く・和らげる, (批判など)を鎮める ‖ *Jenny could always disarm the teachers with a smile.* ジェニーはいつもほほえみで教師たちの怒りを和らげることができた.

**disarmament** /dɪsάːməmənt, dɪz-/ 名 Ⓤ ▶定義 reducing the number of weapons that a country has 国が所有する武器の数量を減らすこと→武装解除、軍備縮小、軍備撤廃 ‖ *nuclear disarmament* 核軍縮

**disassociate** =DISSOCIATE

**\*disaster** /dɪzǽstər, -zάːs-/ 名 ▶定義 1 ⒞ an event that causes a lot of harm or damage 多大な被害または損害をもたらす出来事→(突然の)災害、大惨事 ‖ *earthquakes, floods and other natural disasters* 地震、洪水およびほかの自然災害 ▶定義 2 ⒞Ⓤ a terrible situation or event 悲惨な状況または出来事→(大きな)不幸、災難 ‖ *Losing your job is unpleasant, but it's not a disaster.* 仕事を失うことは不愉快なことだが、悲惨と言うほどのことではない. *This year's lack of rain could spell disaster for the region.* 今年の雨不足は、その地域にとって災いになるかもしれない. ▶定義 3 ⒞Ⓤ 略式 a complete failure 完全な失敗→大失敗(である人・物事), 惨めなこと ‖ *The school play was an absolute disaster. Everything went wrong.* 学校劇は完全に大失敗だった. すべてがうまくいかなかった. ― **disastrously** 副→悲惨にも、破壊的に、ひどく(惨めに) ‖ *The plan went disastrously wrong.* その計画はひどく惨めに失敗した.

**disastrous** /dɪzǽstrəs; -zάːs-/ 形 ▶定義 terrible, harmful or failing completely ひどい、有害な、または完全に失敗した→大災害の、災難を生じる、悲惨な ‖ *Our mistake had disastrous results.* 私たちの誤りは、悲惨な結果をもたらした.

**disband** /dɪsbǽnd/ 動 自 他 ▶定義 to stop existing as a group; to separate 集団としての存在を終え(させ)る; ばらばらに分かれる→(組織などが)解散する; (組織など)を解散させる

**disbelief** /dìsbəlíːf/ 名 Ū ▶定義 the feeling of not believing sb/sth 〜を信じない気持ち→**信じ(ようとし)ないこと，不信，疑惑** ‖ *'It can't be true!' he shouted **in disbelief**.* 「そんなはずはない！」彼は信じられぬ思いで叫んだ．

**disbelieve** /dìsbəlíːv/ 動他 ▶定義 to think that sth is not true or that sb is not telling the truth 〜が本当ではない，または〜が本当の事を言っていないと思う→**〜を信じない，疑う** ‖ *I have no reason to disbelieve her.* 彼女を疑う理由はない． ⇔ **believe**

**disc** (特に 米 **disk**) /dɪsk/ 名 C ▶定義 **1** a round flat object 円形で平らなもの→**円盤，円盤状のもの，(月・太陽などの)円い平面の表面** ▶定義 **2** = **DISK** ▶定義 **3** one of the pieces of thin strong material (cartilage) between the bones in your back 背中の骨の間にある，薄くて堅固な物質 (軟骨)→**椎間板**

**discard** /dɪskɑ́ːrd, 〜/ 動他 正式 ▶定義 to throw sth away because it is not useful 〜が役に立たないので捨てる→**(不用のもの)を捨てる，処分する**

**discern** /dɪsə́ːrn, dɪz-/ 動他 ▶定義 to see or notice sth with difficulty 苦労して〜を見る，または〜に気付く→**(見えにくいもの)を見つける，(目以外の感覚で)認める，認識する** ‖ *I discerned a note of anger in his voice.* 彼の声に怒りが込められているのが分かった．— discernible 形→**識別できる，見分けられる** ‖ *The shape of a house was just discernible through the mist.* 霧の向こうに家の形が辛うじて見て取れた．

**discerning** /dɪsə́ːrnɪŋ, dɪz-/ 形 ▶定義 able to recognize the quality of sb/sth 〜の特性に気付くことができる→**(物事を)見抜く力のある，洞察力のある，違いの分かる** ‖ *The discerning music lover will appreciate the excellence of this recording.* 明敏な音楽愛好家なら，この録音が優れていることを高く評価することだろう．

**discharge**¹ /dɪstʃɑ́ːrdʒ, 〜/ 動他 ▶定義 **1** to send sth out (a liquid, gas, etc) 〜(液体，気体など)を送り出す→**〜を排出する，流出させる，(電気)を放電する** ‖ *Smoke and fumes are discharged from the factory.* 煙と排気ガスが工場から排出される．▶定義 **2** to allow sb officially to leave; to send sb away 〜が去ることを公式に許可する；〜を去らせる→**〜を解放する，釈放する，解雇する** ‖ *to discharge sb from hospital* 〜を退院させる ▶定義 **3** to do sth that you have to do やらなければならない〜をする→**(義務・職務など)を果たす，遂行する，(借金など)を支払う・返済する** ‖ *to discharge a duty/task* 義務・任務を果たす

**discharge**² /dístʃɑːrdʒ, 〜/ 名 C Ū ▶定義 **1** the action of sending sb/sth out or away 〜を送り出す，または去らせる行為→**排出，流出，解放，解雇** ‖ *The discharge of oil from the leaking tanker could not be prevented.* 漏れたタンカーからの石油の流出を妨げることはできなかった．*The wounded soldier was given a medical discharge.* その負傷兵は，傷病のため除隊となった．▶定義 **2** a substance that has come out of somewhere どこからか出てくる物質→**排出物，流出物，膿(うみ)** ‖ *yellowish discharge from a wound* 傷口から出た黄色っぽい膿

**disciple** /dɪsáɪp(ə)l/ 名 C ▶定義 a person who follows a teacher, especially a religious one 特に宗教上の，師に従う人→**弟子，門弟，信奉者**

**disciplinary** /dísəplən(ə)ri, -nèri/ 形 ▶定義 connected with punishment for breaking rules 規則を破ったことに対する処罰に関する→**しつけの，規律上の，懲戒の**

★**discipline**¹ /dísəplən/ 名 ▶定義 **1** Ū the practice of training people to obey rules and behave well 人々が規則に従い正しく振る舞うように養成する 訓練→**しつけ，鍛錬，修養** ‖ *A good teacher must be able to **maintain discipline** in the classroom.* 立派な教師は，教室内の規律を維持できなければならない．▶定義 **2** Ū the practice of training your mind and body so that you control your actions and obey rules; a way of doing this 自分の行動を制御して規則を守るように，自分の精神と肉体を鍛える訓練；これを行う方法→**鍛錬，修行，自制** ‖ *It takes a lot of **self-discipline** to study for three hours a day.* 1日に3時間勉強することは，かなりの自己鍛錬が必要だ．*Having to get up early every day is good discipline for a child.* 毎日早起きしなければならないことは，子供には良い鍛錬になる．▶定義 **3** C a subject of study; a type of sporting event 勉強の科目；スポーツ行事の種類→**学問 (分野)，学科，(スポーツなどの)種目** ‖ *Barry's a good all-round athlete, but the long jump is his strongest discipline.* バリーはすばらしい万能運

動選手だが, 走り幅跳びが彼の最も得意とする種目だ.

**discipline²** /dísəplən/ 動他 ▶定義1 to train sb to obey and to behave in a controlled way 穏やかな様子で従い, 振る舞うように〜を訓練する→〜を訓練する, しつける, 鍛える ‖ *You should discipline yourself to practise the piano every morning.* 毎朝ピアノの練習をするように, 自分を鍛えるべきだ. ▶定義2 to punish sb 〜を罰する→〜を罰する, 懲らしめる

**disc jockey**=DJ

**disclaim** /dɪskléɪm/ 動他 ▶定義 to say that you do not have sth; deny 〜を持っていないと言う; 否定する→(関係・責任など)を否定・否認する ‖ *to disclaim responsibility/knowledge* 責任を否定する・何も知らないと言う

**disclose** /dɪsklóʊz/ 動他 正式 ▶定義 to tell sth to sb or to make sth known publicly 〜を…に言う, または〜を公に知らしめる→(秘密・情報など)を明らかにする, 公表する, 暴露する ‖ *The newspapers did not disclose the victim's name.* 新聞は被害者の氏名を明らかにしなかった.

**disclosure** /dɪsklóʊʒər/ 名 C U ▶定義 making sth known; the facts that are made known 〜を知らしめること; 知らされた事実→(秘密・情報など)を暴くこと, 公表, (情報の)公開; 発覚した事柄, 打ち明け話 ‖ *the disclosure of secret information* 秘密情報の開示 *He resigned following disclosures about his private life.* 彼は私生活が暴露されたことで辞職した.

**disco** /dískoʊ/ 名 C (複 discos) (古) ▶定義 a place, party, etc where people dance to pop music 人々がポピュラー音楽に合わせて踊る場所, パーティーなど→ディスコ, ディスコパーティー, クラブ ‖ *Are you going to the school disco?* 学校で行われるディスコに行きますか. ☞参 club¹(2)

**discolour** (米 **discolor**) /dɪskʌ́lər/ 動自他 ▶定義 to change or to make sth change colour (often by the effect of light, age or dirt) 色が変わる, または〜の色を変える (しばしば光, 年月または汚れなどのために)→変色する, 色あせる; 〜を変色させる, 〜の色を汚す

**discomfort** /dɪskʌ́mfərt/ 名 ▶定義1 **U** a slight feeling of pain 軽い痛みを感じること→軽い痛み, (ちょっとした)不快 ‖ *There may be some discomfort after the operation.* 手術後に軽い痛みがあるかもしれません. ⇔ comfort ▶定義2 **U** a feeling of embarrassment 当惑した気持ち→(ちょっとした)不安, 戸惑い, しゅう恥 ‖ *I could sense John's discomfort when I asked him about his job.* ジョンに仕事のことを尋ねた時, ちょっと戸惑った様子を受けた.

**disconcert** /dɪskənsə́ːrt/ 動他 (通常は受動態で) ▶定義 to make sb feel confused or worried 〜を困惑させる, または心配させる→〜をまごつかせる, 面食らわせる, 不安にする ‖ *She was disconcerted when everyone stopped talking and looked at her.* 皆が話を止めて自分を見たので, 彼女は狼狽(ろうばい)した. — **disconcerting** 形→まごつかせる, 狼狽させる, 面食らわせる — **disconcertingly** 副→当惑・混乱させるように, まごつかせるほどに

**disconnect** /dɪskənékt/ 動他 ▶定義1 to stop a supply of water, gas or electricity going to a piece of equipment or a building 器具または建物へ流れている水, ガスまたは電気の供給を止める→〜への供給を止める ‖ *If you don't pay your gas bill your supply will be disconnected.* ガス料金をお支払いにならないと, 供給をお止めすることになります. ▶定義2 to separate sth from sth 〜を…から分離する→〜の接続を絶つ, 電源・スイッチを切る, 〜を切り離す ‖ *The brake doesn't work because the cable has become disconnected from the lever.* ケーブルがレバーから外れてしまったので, ブレーキが利かない.

**discontent** /dɪskəntént/ (または **discontentment** /dɪskənténtmənt/) 名 **U** ▶定義 the state of being unhappy with sth 〜に対して不満を持っている状態→不満, 不平 ‖ *The management could sense growing discontent among the staff.* 経営者側は, 職員の間に不満が高まりつつあることを感じた. — **discontented** 形→不満・不平のある ‖ *to be/feel discontented* 不満がある・不満を感じる

**discontinue** /dɪskəntínjuː/ 動他 正式 ▶定義 to stop sth or stop producing sth 〜をやめる, または〜の生産をやめる→(継続していたこと・生産など)をやめる, 中断する

**discord** /dískɔːrd/ 名 正式 **U** ▶定義 disagreement or argument 不一致または口論→不一致, 不和, 仲たがい

**discordant** /dɪskɔ́ːrd(ə)nt/ 形 ▶定義 that spoils a general feeling of agreement 全般的な調和の感じを損なう→**調和しない, 一致しない, 耳障りな** ‖ *Her criticism was the only discordant note in the discussion.* 彼女の批判は, その議論では耳障りな発言にすぎなかった.

**discount**[1] /dískàʊnt/ 名 ⓒ ⓤ ▶定義 a lower price than usual; reduction 通常よりも安い価格; 割引→**割引, 割引額・率** ‖ *Staff get 20% discount on all goods.* スタッフは全商品が20パーセント割引になる. *Do you give a discount for cash?* 現金で払ったら割り引いてもらえますか.

**discount**[2] /dískàʊnt, -´-/ 動 他 ▶定義 to consider sth not true or not important ～を事実でない, または重要でないと考える→**(人の話など)を割り引いて聞く, 軽視する** ‖ *I think we can discount that idea. It's just not practical.* あの案は無視できると思う. 全く現実的ではない.

**discourage** /dɪskə́ːrɪdʒ; -kʌ́r-/ 動 他 ▶定義 **discourage sb (from doing sth)** to stop sb doing sth, especially by making him/her realize that it would not be successful or a good idea 特に, それが成功しないまたは良い考えではないだろうと, 本人に悟らせて, ～をやめさせる→**～を思いとどまらせる, ～を妨げる, ～に…するのを思いとどまらせる** ‖ *I tried to discourage Jake from giving up his job.* 私はジェークに, 仕事を辞めるのを思いとどまらせようとした. *Don't let these little problems discourage you.* そんな小さな事であきらめてはいけない. ⇔ **encourage** — discouraged 形→**がっかりした, やる気をなくした, 落胆して** ‖ *After failing the exam again Paul felt very discouraged.* 再び試験に失敗して, ポールはとても落胆した. — discouraging 形→**落胆させる, がっかりさせる** ‖ *Constant criticism can be very discouraging.* 始終批判されると, 人はとても落ち込むものだ.

**discouragement** /dɪskə́ːrɪdʒmənt; -kʌ́r-/ 名 ⓒ ⓤ ▶定義 a thing that makes you not want to do sth; the action of trying to stop sb from doing sth ～をやりたくないと思わせるもの; ～が…をしているのをやめさせようとする行為→**抑止するもの, 思いとどまらせること, 妨害** ‖ *the government's discouragement of smoking* 政府による喫煙の阻止

*****discover** /dɪskʌ́vər/ 動 他 ▶定義1 to find or learn sth that nobody had found or knew before それまではだれも発見していなかった, または知らなかった～を発見する, または知る→**～を発見する, 見つけ出す** ‖ *Who discovered the lost city of Machu Picchu?* だれが失われた都市マチュピチュを発見したのですか. *Scientists are hoping to discover the cause of the epidemic.* 科学者たちは, 伝染病の原因を発見することを望んでいる. ▶定義2 to find or learn sth without expecting to or that sb does not want you to find 思い掛けずに～を, あるいは…が知られたくないと思っている～を発見する, または知る→**～ということを知る, 悟る, ～に気が付く** ‖ *I think I've discovered why the computer won't print out.* コンピューターがなぜ印刷しないか多分分かった. *The police discovered drugs hidden under the floor.* 警察は, 床下に隠されていた麻薬を見つけた. — discoverer 名 ⓒ→**発見者** ‖ *Parkinson's disease was named after its discoverer.* パーキンソン病という病名は, 発見者の名を取って付けられた.

**discovery** /dɪskʌ́v(ə)ri/ 名 ( 複 **discoveries** ) ▶定義1 ⓤ the act of finding sth ～を発見する行為→**発見, ～に気が付くこと, (新人の)発掘** ‖ *The discovery of X-rays changed the history of medicine.* X線の発見は, 医学の歴史を変えた. ▶定義2 ⓒ something that has been found 発見されたもの→**発見物** ‖ *scientific discoveries* 科学上の発見物

**discredit** /dɪskrédət/ 動 他 ▶定義 to make people stop respecting or believing sb/sth ～に対する人々の敬意または信頼を失わせる→**～の信用・評判を落とす, 信憑(しんぴょう)性を失わせる** ‖ *Journalists are trying to discredit the President by inventing stories about his love life.* マスコミは大統領の性生活に関する作り話をでっち上げて, 彼の評判を落とそうとする. — discredit 名 ⓤ→**不名誉, 不面目, 不信**

**discreet** /dɪskríːt/ 形 ▶定義 careful in what you say and do so as not to cause embarrassment or difficulty for sb ～を困惑させるまたは困らせないように, 言う事とする事に注意する→**分別・思慮のある, 慎重な, 口の堅い** ‖ *I don't want anyone to find out about our agreement, so please be discreet.* 私たちの取り決めについてだれにも知られたくないので, 慎重にお願いします. —

discreetly 副 →考え深く,慎重に,控えめに ☛名
discretion ⇔ **indiscreet**

**discrepancy** /dɪskrép(ə)nsi/ 名 C U
(複 **discrepancies**) ▶定義 a difference between two things that should be the same 同じであるべき2つの物の間の違い→**相違,矛盾,食い違い** ‖ *Something is wrong here. There is a discrepancy between these two sets of figures.* ここに何か誤りがある.これら2組の数字に矛盾がある.

**discretion** /dɪskréʃ(ə)n/ 名 U ▶定義 1 the freedom and power to make decisions by yourself 自分自身で決断を下す自由と能力→**行動・判断・選択の自由,自由裁量** ‖ *You must decide what is best. Use your discretion.* あなたは何が一番いいかを決めなければならない.あなたの判断に任せます. ▶定義 2 care in what you say and do so as not to cause embarrassment or difficulty for sb ～を困惑させるまたは困らせないように,言う事とする事に注意すること→**思慮分別,慎重さ,慎重な判断** ‖ *This is confidential but I know I can rely on your discretion.* これは秘密なのだが,あなたの思慮分別は信頼できると思う. ☛形 discreet
成句 **at sb's discretion** ▶定義 depending on what sb thinks or decides ～の考えまたは決断によって決まる→**～の自由裁量で,意のままに,計らいで** ‖ *Pay increases are awarded at the discretion of the director.* 賃上げは,重役の意のままに決められる.

**discriminate** /dɪskrímənèɪt/ 動 ▶定義 1 自 discriminate (against sb) to treat one person or group worse than others 1人または1集団の扱いが他に比べて劣る→**差別・冷遇する** ‖ *It is illegal to discriminate against any ethnic or religious group.* いかなる民族または宗教団体をも差別することは違法である. ▶定義 2 自他 discriminate (between A and B) to see or make a difference between two people or things 2人または2つの物事の違いが分かる,または区別する→**区別する,識別する;～を区別する,識別する** ‖ *The immigration law discriminates between political and economic refugees.* 移民法では,政治的難民と経済的難民を区別している.

**discrimination** /dɪskrìmənéɪʃ(ə)n/ 名 U
▶定義 1 discrimination (against sb) treating one person or group worse than others 1人または1集団を他に比べて劣る扱いをすること→**差別,差別待遇** ‖ *sexual/racial/religious discrimination* 性・人種・宗教差別 *Discrimination against disabled people is illegal.* 身体障害者に対する差別は違法である. ▶定義 2 正式 the state of being able to see a difference between two people or things 2人または2つの物事の間の違いが分かる状態→**区別,識別,識別する力** ‖ *discrimination between right and wrong* 正邪の区別

**discus** /dískəs/ 名 ▶定義 1 C a heavy round flat object that is thrown as a sport スポーツで投げられる,重い,平たい円形の物体→**(競技用の)円盤** ▶定義 2 **the discus** [単数扱い] the sport or event of throwing a discus as far as possible 円盤をできるだけ遠くまで投げる競技または種目→**円盤投げ競技**

*****discuss** /dɪskʌ́s/ 動 中 ▶定義 discuss sth (with sb) to talk or write about sth seriously or formally ～について,真剣にまたは正式に話すまたは書く→**～について話し合う,～を討論する,議論する** ‖ *I must discuss the matter with my parents before I make a decision.* 決定を下す前に,その問題について両親と話し合わなければならない.

> ▶語法
>
> discuss about... とは言えない
>
> 「～について議論する」という日本語や talk about... の影響を受けて,*We discussed about the problem. と言ってしまう誤りがあります.しかし discuss は他動詞ですから前置詞 about は不要です.ただし,名詞形 discussion の場合には,discussion about/on the plan のように前置詞が必要となります.

*****discussion** /dɪskʌ́ʃ(ə)n/ 名 C U ▶定義 the process of talking about sth seriously or deeply ～について,真剣にまたは深く話し合う過程→**議論,討論,話し合い** ‖ *After much discussion we all agreed to share the cost.* 長い話し合いの末,費用を分担することで全員が合意した. *We had a long discussion about art.* 私たちは芸術について,長時間論じ合った.
成句 **under discussion** ▶定義 being talked about 現在話し合われている→**審議中の・で,討議中の・で** ‖ *Plans to reform the Health Service are under discussion in Parliament.* 公共医療制度の

改正案は,国会で審議中だ.

**disdain** /dɪsdéɪn/ 名 ❶ ▶定義 the feeling that sb/sth is not good enough to be respected 〜が尊敬されるほどのものではないと思う気持ち➡軽べつ,尊大さ ‖ *Monica felt that her boss always **treated** her ideas **with disdain**.* モニカは,上司がいつも自分の案を見下して扱うように感じた. — disdainful /-fʊl, -f(ə)l/ 形 ➡見下した,横柄な — disdainfully /-fʊli, -f(ə)li/ 副 ➡軽べつ的に,尊大に

***disease** /dɪzíːz/ 名 ❻ ❶ ▶定義 an illness of the body in humans, animals or plants 人間,動物または植物の身体の病気➡病気,疾患 ‖ *an infectious/contagious disease* 感染症・接触伝染病 *These children **suffer from a** rare **disease**.* この子供たちは,珍しい病気にかかっている. *Rats and flies **spread disease**.* ネズミとハエが病気を蔓延(まんえん)させる. *Smoking causes heart disease.* 喫煙は心臓病を引き起こす. — diseased 形 ➡病気の,疾患のある,(社会などが)病んでいる ‖ *His diseased kidney had to be removed.* 彼の疾患のある腎臓(じんぞう)を除去しなければならなかった.

▶ illnessおよびdiseaseは,同じように用いられる.しかし病名が付き,特定の症状が認められる病気の様子を述べるためには,diseaseを用いる.diseaseは,細菌,ウイルスなどが原因になることがあり,それらは人から人へ伝染されることが多い.illnessは,病気であるときの一般的な状態と,健康でない期間を表すために用いられる.

**disembark** /dìsəmbάːrk/ 動 ❸ 正式 ▶定義 to get off a ship or an aircraft 船または飛行機から降りる➡降りる,上陸する,下船する ⇔ **embark** — disembarkation /dìsəmbɑːrkéɪʃ(ə)n/ 名 ❶ ➡陸揚げ,下船,上陸

**disenchanted** /dìsɪntʃάːntəd, -en-; -tʃǽnt-/ 形 ▶定義 having lost your good opinion of sb/sth 〜への好意的な評価をなくしてしまっている➡(〜に)幻滅した ‖ *Fans are already becoming disenchanted with the new team manager.* ファンは,チームの新監督に既に幻滅しつつある. — disenchantment 名 ❶ ➡幻滅,幻滅させられること

**disentangle** /dìsɪntǽŋg(ə)l, -en-/ 動 ❶ ▶定義 to free sb/sth that had become connected to sb/sth else in a confused and complicated way

# disgraceful 473

ほかの〜と,複雑で込み入った関係にあった…を解放する➡(ひも・髪などの)もつれをほどく,(もつれ・ごたごたから)〜を解き放つ,分離する,取り出す ‖ *My coat got caught up in some bushes and I couldn't disentangle it.* コートが低木に引っ掛かって,もつれをほどくことができなかった.(比喩) *Listening to the woman's story, I found it hard to disentangle the truth from the lies.* その女性の話を聞いていると,うそと本当をより分けるのが難しかった.

**disfigure** /dɪsfígjər; -gjər/ 動 ❶ ▶定義 to spoil the appearance of sb/sth 〜の外見を損なう➡〜を醜くする,〜の形を崩す,〜の美観を損なう ‖ *His face was permanently disfigured by the fire.* 彼の顔は,火事で一生消えない跡が付いた.

**disgrace**¹ /dɪsgréɪs/ 名 ▶定義 **1** ❶ the state of not being respected by other people, usually because you have behaved badly 通常は行いが悪いために,ほかの人々から敬意を払われない状態➡不名誉,不面目,不人気 ‖ *She left the company **in disgrace** after admitting stealing from colleagues.* 同僚から盗みを働いたことを認めた後,彼女は面目を失って退職した. ▶定義**2** [単数扱い] a disgrace (to sb/sth) a person or thing that gives a very bad impression and makes you feel sorry and embarrassed 非常に印象が悪く,がっかりさせてばつの悪い思いをさせる人または物➡恥・不名誉となる人・物,面汚し,恥さらし ‖ *The streets are covered in litter. It's a disgrace!* 道路は散らかったごみであふれている.実に恥ずかしいことだ. *Teachers who hit children are a disgrace to their profession.* 子供を殴る教師は,教職に対する面汚しだ.

**disgrace**² /dɪsgréɪs/ 動 ❶ ▶定義 to behave badly in a way that makes you or other people feel sorry and embarrassed ほかの人々をがっかりさせてばつの悪い思いをさせるようなやり方で,悪く振る舞う➡〜の不名誉・恥となる,名を汚す ‖ *My brother disgraced himself by starting a fight at the wedding.* 兄は結婚式でけんかを始めて,恥をさらした.

**disgraceful** /dɪsgréɪsfʊl, -f(ə)l/ 形 ▶定義 very bad, making other people feel sorry and embarrassed ほかの人々をがっかりさせてばつの悪い思いをさせるほど,とても悪い➡不名誉な,

不面目な, ひどい ‖ *The behaviour of the team's fans was absolutely disgraceful.* そのチームのファンの行動は全く恥ずべきものだった. — **disgracefully** /-fʊli, -f(ə)li/ 副 ➡不名誉にも, ひどく

**disgruntled** /dɪsɡrʌ́ntld/ 形 ▶定義 disappointed and annoyed がっかりして腹を立てて ➡不満な, 不愉快な, むっとした

**disguise**[1] /dɪsɡáɪz/ 動 他 ▶定義 disguise sb/sth (as sb/sth) to change the appearance, sound, etc of sb/sth so that people cannot recognize him/her/it 人々に気付かれないように, ~の外見, 音声などを変える ➡~を変装させる, 偽装させる ‖ *They disguised themselves as fishermen and escaped in a boat.* 彼らは漁師に変装し, ボートに乗って逃げた. (比喩)*His smile disguised his anger.* 彼はほほえみで怒りを隠した.

**disguise**[2] /dɪsɡáɪz/ 名 C U ▶定義 a thing that you wear or use to change your appearance so that nobody recognizes you だれにも気付かれないように, 人の外見を変えるために着るまたは使うもの ➡変装(用具), 仮装 ‖ *She is so famous that she has to go shopping **in disguise**.* 彼女はとても有名なので, 変装して買い物に行かなくてはならない. *The robbers were wearing heavy disguises so that they could not be identified.* 身元が分からないように, 強盗どもは凝った変装をしていた.

**disgust**[1] /dɪsɡʌ́st/ 名 U ▶定義 disgust (at sth) a strong feeling of not liking or approving of sth/sb that you feel is unacceptable, or sth/sb that looks, smells, etc unpleasant 容認できないと思う~, または不愉快な感じのする外見, においなどの~に対して, 好意を持てないあるいは容認できないと思う強い感情 ➡(むかむかするほどの)嫌悪, 嫌気 ‖ *The film was so bad that we walked out **in disgust**.* その映画はとてもひどかったので, 私たちはうんざりして席を立った. ***Much to my disgust**, I found a hair in my soup.* 大変うんざりするようなことだったが, スープに髪の毛が入っていた.

**disgust**[2] /dɪsɡʌ́st/ 動 他 ▶定義1 to cause a strong feeling of not liking or approving of sb/sth ~に対して好意を持てない, または容認できないと思う強い感情を引き起こす ➡~をむかむかさせる, うんざりさせる, ~の気持ちを悪くさせる ‖ *Cruelty towards animals absolutely disgusts me.* 動物に対する残虐な振る舞いには, 全くむかむかする. ▶定義2 to make sb feel sick ~の気分を悪くする ➡~に愛想を尽かせる, ~をむかむかさせる, うんざりさせる ‖ *The way he eats with his mouth open completely disgusts me.* 口を開けて食べる彼の食べ方には, 全くうんざりだ.

**disgusted** /dɪsɡʌ́stəd/ 形 ▶定義 disgusted (at/with sb/sth) not liking or approving of sb/sth at all ~に全く好意を持てない, または容認できない ➡うんざりした, むかむかした ‖ *We were disgusted at the standard of service we received.* 私たちは, サービスのひどさにうんざりした.

**disgusting** /dɪsɡʌ́stɪŋ/ 形 ▶定義 very unpleasant とても不愉快な ➡嫌悪を感じさせるような, 嫌な, むかむかさせる ‖ *What a disgusting smell!* 何て嫌なにおいなんだ.

**disgustingly** /dɪsɡʌ́stɪŋli/ 副 ▶定義1 (often used to show you are jealous of sb/sth) extremely (しばしば~をしっとしていることを示すために用いられて)極めて ➡とても, すごく, 大変 ‖ *Our neighbours are disgustingly rich.* 近所の人たちは, うらやむほど裕福だ. ▶定義2 in a way that you do not like or approve of or that makes you feel sick 人が好意を持てない, または是認できない, あるいは人の気分を害するやり方で ➡うんざり・むかむかさせるほどに, とてもひどく ‖ *The kitchen was disgustingly dirty.* その台所はとてもひどく汚れていた.

★**dish**[1] /dɪʃ/ 名 ▶定義1 C a round container for food that is deeper than a plate 取り皿より深い, 料理のための円形の入れ物 ➡盛り皿, 大皿, 深皿 ▶定義2 C a type of food prepared in a particular way ある特定の方法で準備された食べ物の一種 ➡(皿に盛られた)料理, 食べ物 ‖ *The **main dish** was curry. It was served with a selection of **side dishes**.* 主菜はカレーだった. よりすぐりの副菜を添えて出された. *Paella is a typical Spanish dish, made with rice and shellfish.* パエリアは, 米と甲殻類とで作られる, 典型的なスペイン料理である. ▶定義3 **the dishes**[複数扱い] all the plates, cups, etc that you use during a meal 食事中に使う, すべての皿, 茶碗(ちゃわん)など ➡皿類, 食器類 ‖ *I'll cook and you can wash the dishes.* 私が料理をしますから, あなたはお

皿を洗ってください. ▶定義4 = SATELLITE DISH

**dish²** /dɪʃ/ 動
[句動詞] dish sth out [略式] ▶定義 to give away a lot of sth たくさんの〜を気前良く与える→〜を(気前良く)与える, 配る‖ to dish out advice 助言を気前良く与える

dish sth up [略式] ▶定義 to serve food 料理を出す→料理を皿に盛る

**disheartened** /dɪshάːrt(ə)nd/ 形 ▶定義 sad or disappointed 悲しい, またはがっかりした→がっかりした, 失望・落胆した

**disheartening** /dɪshάːrt(ə)nɪŋ/ 形 ▶定義 making you lose hope and confidence; causing disappointment 人に希望と自信を失わせる; 失望させる→がっかりさせる, 失望・落胆させる ⇔ heartening

**dishevelled**( 米 **disheveled**) /dɪʃév(ə)ld/ 形 ▶定義 (used about a person's appearance) very untidy (人の外見について)とてもだらしない→(髪・服などが)乱れた, ぼさぼさの, (身なりが)だらしない

**dishonest** /dɪsάnəst/ 形 ▶定義 that you cannot trust; likely to lie, steal or cheat 信頼できない; うそ, 盗み, またはごまかしをするおそれがある→不正直な, 不誠実な, ずるい ⇔ honest ―
dishonestly 副 →不正直に, 不誠実にも, 不正に ―
dishonesty 名 ❶ →不正直, 不誠実, 不正行為 ⇔ honesty

**dishonour¹**( 米 **dishonor**) /dɪsάnər/ 名 [ ❶, 単数扱い] [正式] ▶定義 the state of no longer being respected, especially because you have done sth bad 特に悪い事をしたために, もはや尊敬されない状態→不名誉, 不面目, 恥‖ Her illegal trading has **brought dishonour on** the company. 彼女の違法な取り引きは, 会社に不名誉をもたらした. ⇔ honour ― dishonourable /-nərəb(ə)l/ 形 →不名誉な, 恥ずべき, 卑劣な ⇔ honourable

**dishonour²**( 米 **dishonor**) /dɪsάnər/ 動他 [正式] ▶定義 to do sth bad that makes people stop respecting you or sb/sth close to you 自分または自分に近い〜への人々の敬意を失わせる, 悪い事をする→〜の名誉を汚す, 〜に恥辱を与える

**dishwasher** /dɪ́ʃwɔ̀(ː)ʃər, -wɑ̀ʃ-/ 名 ⓒ ▶定義 a machine that washes plates, cups, knives, forks, etc 皿, 茶碗(ちゃわん), ナイフ, フォークなどを洗う機械→自動皿洗い機

**disjointed** 475

**disillusion** /dìsɪlúːʒ(ə)n/ 動他 ▶定義 to destroy sb's belief in or good opinion of sb/sth 〜に対する…の信頼または良い評価を打ち砕く→〜に幻想を捨てさせる, 幻滅を感じさせる, 〜の迷いを覚まさせる ― disillusion(または disillusionment) 名 ❶ →迷いから覚めること, 覚醒(せい), 幻滅‖ I feel increasing disillusion with the government. 私は政府に対する幻滅が募っていくのを感じている.

**disillusioned** /dìsɪlúːʒ(ə)nd/ 形 ▶定義 disappointed because sb/sth is not as good as you first thought 〜が初めに思っていたほどすばらしくないので, がっかりして→(〜に)幻滅した‖ She's disillusioned with nursing. 彼女は介護の仕事に幻滅している.

**disinfect** /dìsɪnfékt/ 動他 ▶定義 to clean sth with a liquid that destroys bacteria 細菌を死滅させる液体で〜を洗浄する→〜を消毒する, 殺菌する‖ to disinfect a wound 傷を消毒する ― disinfection 名 ❶ →消毒, 殺菌

**disinfectant** /dìsɪnféktənt/ 名 ⓒ ❶ ▶定義 a substance that destroys bacteria and is used for cleaning 細菌を死滅させ, 洗浄に用いられる物質→消毒液, 殺菌剤

**disintegrate** /dɪsíntəgrèɪt/ 動⾃ ▶定義 to break into many small pieces 多数の小片になる→ばらばらになる, 崩壊する, 分解する‖ The spacecraft exploded and disintegrated. その宇宙船は爆発してばらばらになった. ― disintegration /dɪsìntəgréɪʃ(ə)n/ 名 ❶ →ばらばらになること, ばらばらにすること, 崩壊, 分解‖ the disintegration of the empire 帝国の崩壊

**disinterested** /dɪsínt(ə)rəstəd; -t(ə)rèst-/ 形 ▶定義 fair, not influenced by personal feelings 公平で, 個人的な感情に影響されない→利害関係のない, 客観的な, 公平な‖ disinterested advice 客観的な助言 ☛参 uninterested. この単語は違う意味である.

**disjointed** /dɪsdʒɔ́ɪntəd/ 形 ▶定義 (used especially about ideas, writing or speech) not clearly connected and therefore difficult to follow (特に考え, 文章または話について)つながりが明瞭(めいりょう)ではなく, そのために話の流れに付いていくことが難しい→支離滅裂な, 脈絡のない, ちぐはぐな ― disjointedly 副 →支離滅裂に, ちぐは

**disk** /dɪsk/ 名 C ▶定義1 英=DISC ▶定義2 (computing) a flat piece of plastic that stores information for use by a computer(コンピューター)コンピューターで使うための情報を保存する, 平たい1枚のプラスチック→情報記録用ディスク ☞参 floppy disk, hard disk

**disk drive** 名 C ▶定義 (computing) a piece of electrical equipment that passes information to or from a computer disk(コンピューター)コンピューターのディスクへ, またはディスクから情報を流す, 電子装置の1台→ディスクドライブ, ディスク駆動装置 ☞ S5ページのさし絵

**diskette** /dɪskét/ = FLOPPY DISK

**dislike**¹ /dɪsláɪk/ 動 他 ▶定義 dislike (doing) sth to think that sb/sth is unpleasant ～が不愉快であると思う→～を好まない, 嫌う ‖ I really dislike flying. 私は飛行機に乗ることが本当に嫌いだ. What is it that you dislike about living here? どうしてここに住むのが嫌なのですか. ⇔ like

**dislike**² /dɪsláɪk/ 名 [ U, 単数扱い ] ▶定義 (a) dislike (of/for sb/sth) the feeling of not liking sb/sth ～が好きではない気持ち→嫌うこと, 嫌悪 ‖ She couldn't hide her dislike for him. 彼女は, 彼に対する嫌悪を隠すことができなかった. He seems to have a strong dislike of hard work. 彼は熱心に働くことへの強い嫌悪感があるように見える.

成句 **take a dislike to sb/sth** ▶定義 to start disliking sb/sth ～を嫌い始める→～を嫌いになる ‖ He took an instant dislike to his boss. 彼は即座に上司が嫌いになった.

**dislocate** /dísloʊkèɪt, dɪslóʊkeɪt/ 動 他 ▶定義 to put sth (usually a bone) out of its correct position ～(通常は骨)を正しい位置から外す→～を脱臼(だっきゅう)させる, (計画・機械など)を狂わせる, 混乱させる ‖ He dislocated his shoulder during the game. 彼は試合中に肩を脱臼した. — dislocation /dìsloʊkéɪʃ(ə)n, -lə-/ 名 C U →脱臼, 混乱, 狂い

**dislodge** /dɪslɑ́dʒ/ 動 他 ▶定義 dislodge sth (from sth) to make sb/sth move from its correct fixed position ～を正しく固定された位置から移動させる→～を取り除く, (敵など)を追い払う ‖ The strong wind dislodged several tiles from the roof. 強風により, 屋根から数枚のかわらがはがされた.

**disloyal** /dɪslɔ́ɪ(ə)l/ 形 ▶定義 disloyal (to sb/sth) not supporting your friends, family, country etc; doing sth that will harm them 自分の友人, 家族, 国などを支持していない; それらを損なう事をしている→忠実でない, 不実な, 不義な ‖ It was disloyal to your friends to repeat their conversation to Peter. 会話の内容をピーターに伝えたことは, 君の友人たちに対する裏切りだった. ⇔ loyal — disloyalty /-lɔ́ɪ(ə)lti/ 名 C U (複 disloyalties) →(～に対する)不誠実, 不実, 背信行為

**dismal** /dízm(ə)l/ 形 ▶定義1 causing or showing sadness; depressing 悲嘆を引き起こす, または表す; 憂鬱(ゆううつ)な→陰気な, 憂鬱な ‖ dismal surroundings 陰気な環境 ☞類 miserable ▶定義2 略式 of low quality; poor 質が悪い; 貧弱な→惨めな, ひどい ‖ a dismal standard of work ひどい作業水準

**dismantle** /dɪsmǽntl/ 動 他 ▶定義 to take sth to pieces; to separate sth into the parts it is made from ～を解体する; ～を元の部品にまで分解する→(機械など)を分解する, (部品など)を取り除く ‖ The photographer dismantled his equipment and packed it away. そのカメラマンは自分の道具を分解して片付けた.

**dismay** /dɪsméɪ, dɪz-/ 名 U ▶定義 a strong feeling of disappointment and sadness 失望と悲しみの強い感情→狼狽(ろうばい), 落胆, 失望 ‖ I realized **to my dismay** that I was going to miss the plane. うろたえてしまったことに, 私は飛行機に遅れそうになっていることに気付いた. — dismay 動 他 (通常は受動態で)→～を狼狽(ろうばい)させる, 落胆させる ‖ I was dismayed to hear that my old school had been knocked down. 母校が解体されたことを聞いて, 私は落胆した.

**dismember** /dɪsmémbər/ 動 他 ▶定義 to cut a dead body into pieces 死体をいくつかの部分に切断する→～の手足を切断する

**dismiss** /dɪsmís/ 動 他 ▶定義1 dismiss sb/sth (as sth) to decide not to think about sth/sb ～について考えないと決心する→(考えなど)を払いのける, 捨てる, 無視する, 否定する ‖ He dismissed the idea as nonsense. 彼はその考えを, 無意味なものとして無視した. ▶定義2 dismiss

**sb (from sth)** to order an employee to leave his/her job 従業員に仕事を辞めるように命じる →～を解雇する, 免職にする ‖ *He was dismissed for refusing to obey orders.* 彼は命令に従うことを拒否したため, 解雇された.

▶ fire と sack は, dismiss に比べてよりくだけた語である.

▶定義 **3** to send sb away ～を追い払う →～を去らせる, (クラス・集会など)を解散させる ‖ *The lesson ended and the teacher dismissed the class.* 授業が終わり, 教師はクラスを解散させた. ▶定義 **4** (used in law) to say that a trial or court case should not continue, usually because there is not enough evidence (法律で用いて)通常は証拠不十分のため, 裁判または訴訟を続行するべきではないと述べる →(訴えなど)を却下する, 棄却する ‖ *The case was dismissed.* その訴訟は棄却された.— dismissal /dɪsmís(ə)l/ 名 ❻ ❶ →解雇(通告), 解任, (考えなどの)放棄 ‖ *She was hurt at their dismissal of her offer of help.* 援助の申し出を彼らに断られて, 彼女は気分を害した. *a case of unfair dismissal* 不当解雇の事例

**dismissive** /dɪsmísɪv/ 形 ▶定義 **dismissive (of sb/sth)** saying or showing that you think that sb/sth is not worth considering seriously ～が真剣に検討するに値しないと考えていることを言うまたは示す →(～を)見下すような, 素っ気ない, 冷淡な ‖ *The boss was dismissive of all the efforts I had made.* 上司は, 私のあらゆる努力に対して冷淡だった.— dismissively 副 →見下すように, 素っ気なく

**dismount** /dɪsmáʊnt/ 動 ⾃ ▶定義 to get off sth that you ride (a horse, a bicycle, etc) 乗っている ～ (馬, 自転車など)から降りる →降りる ⇔ **mount**

**disobedient** /dìsəbíːdiənt/ 形 ▶定義 refusing or failing to obey 従うことを拒否している, または従い損ねている →服従しない, 従順でない, 違反する ⇔ **obedient** — disobedience 名 ❶ →不服従, 反抗, 違反

**disobey** /dìsəbéɪ/ 動 ⾃ 他 ▶定義 to refuse to do what you are told to do するように言われたことをするのを拒否する →(人・規則・命令などに)服従しない, 反抗する ‖ *He was punished for disobeying orders.* 彼は命令に従わなかったので罰せられた. ⇔ **obey**

**disorder** /dɪsɔ́ːrdər/ 名 ▶定義 **1** ❶ an untidy, confused or badly organized state 乱雑な, 混乱した, または不適切に組織された状態 →混乱, 乱雑 ‖ *His financial affairs are in complete disorder.* 彼の財政事情は, 完全に混乱している. ⇔ **order** ▶定義 **2** ❶ violent behaviour by a large number of people 多数の人々による暴力行為 →(社会的・政治的)無秩序, 混乱 ‖ *Disorder broke out on the streets of the capital.* 首都の街路で暴動が勃発（ぼっぱつ）した. ▶定義 **3** ❻ ❶ an illness in which the mind or part of the body is not working properly 心または身体の一部が適切に働かない病気 →(心身の)不調, 異常 ‖ *treatment for eating disorders such as anorexia* 例えば拒食症のような摂食障害に対する治療 *a kind of mental disorder* 精神障害の一種

**disordered** /dɪsɔ́ːrdərd/ 形 ▶定義 untidy, confused or badly organized 乱雑な, 混乱した, または不適切に組織された →秩序のない, 混乱した, (心身が)不調な

**disorderly** /dɪsɔ́ːrdərli/ 形 ▶定義 **1** (used about people or behaviour) out of control and violent; causing trouble in public (人々または行為について)制御できないで暴力的な; 人前で問題を引き起こす →(人・行為が)秩序を乱す, 無法の, 乱暴な ‖ *They were arrested for being drunk and disorderly.* 彼らは泥酔して大騒ぎをしたので逮捕された. ▶定義 **2** untidy 乱雑な →無秩序の, 乱雑な ⇔ **orderly**

**disorganization**(または**-isation**)/dɪsɔ̀ːrɡənaɪzéɪ(ə)n, -nə-/ 名 ❶ ▶定義 a lack of careful planning and order 綿密な計画と秩序の欠如 →秩序・組織の破壊, 混乱 ⇔ **organization**

**disorganized** /dɪsɔ́ːrɡənàɪzd/ (または **-ised**) 形 ▶定義 badly planned; not able to plan well 不適切に計画された; 上手に計画できない →無秩序な, 混乱した, でたらめな ⇔ **organized**

**disorientate** /dɪsɔ́ːriəntèɪt/ (特に 米 **disorient** /dɪsɔ́ːriənt/) 動 他 ▶定義 to make sb become confused about where he/she is 自分がどこにいるのかについて～をまごつかせる →～を道に迷わせる, ～に方向を見失わせる, ～の方向感覚を狂わせる ‖ *The road signs were very confusing and I soon became disorientated.* 道路標識が非常に紛らわしく, 私はすぐに道に迷ってしまった.— disorientation /dɪsɔ̀ːriəntéɪʃ(ə)n, -èn-/ 名 ❶ →道

に迷うこと,方向を見失うこと,方向感覚の喪失

**disown** /dɪsóun/ 動他 ▶定義 to say that you no longer want to be connected with or responsible for sb/sth もはや~にかかわりたくない、または~に関して責任を取りたくないと言う➔~を自分のものと認めない、~とのかかわりを否認する、~と縁を切る ‖ *When he was arrested, his family disowned him.* 彼が逮捕された時,家族は彼とのかかわりを否認した.

**disparage** /dɪspǽrɪdʒ/ 動他 正式 ▶定義 to talk about sb/sth in a critical way; to say that sb/sth is of little value or importance ~について批判的に述べる;~がほとんど価値がない,またはほとんど重要でないと言う➔~の評判を悪くする、~を軽んじる ― disparaging 形 ➔けなすような,軽んじるような,見くびるような ‖ *disparaging remarks* けなすような意見

**dispatch** (医 または **despatch**) /dɪspǽtʃ/ 動他 正式 ▶定義 to send sb/sth to a place ~をある場所に送る➔~を派遣する、~を発送する ‖ *Your order will be dispatched within 7 days.* ご注文の品は,7日以内に発送されます.

**dispel** /dɪspél/ 動他 (**dispelling**; **dispelled**) ▶定義 to make sth, especially a feeling or a belief, disappear ~、特に感情または信念を消滅させる➔~を追い散らす、(心配・恐怖など)を払いのける、(疑いなど)を晴らす ‖ *His reassuring words dispelled all her fears.* 彼の頼もしい言葉で,彼女の恐怖心はすっかり払いのけられた.

**dispensable** /dɪspénsəb(ə)l/ 形 ▶定義 not necessary 必要でない➔なくても済ませられる、(必ずしも)必要でない ‖ *I suppose I'm dispensable. Anybody could do my job.* 私がいなくても困らないと思う.だれでも私の仕事はできるだろう.
⇔ **indispensable**

**dispense** /dɪspéns/ 動他 正式 ▶定義 to give or provide people with sth 人々に~を与えるまたは供給する➔~を(人に)分配する、施す ‖ *a machine that dispenses hot and cold drinks* 温かい飲み物と冷たい飲み物を供給する機械
句動詞 **dispense with sb/sth** ▶定義 to get rid of sb/sth that is not necessary 必要でない~を取り除く➔~なしで済ます、~を不要にする ‖ *They decided to dispense with luxuries and live a simple life.* 彼らは,ぜいたくをしないで質素な生活をすることに決めた.

**dispenser** /dɪspénsər/ 名 C ▶定義 a machine or container from which you can get sth そこから~を得られる機械または容器➔ディスペンサー(日用品・食品・飲料などを一定量ずつ取り出せる容器)、自動販売機 ‖ *a cash dispenser at a bank* 銀行の現金自動支払機 *a soap dispenser* せっけんのディスペンサー

**disperse** /dɪspə́ːrs/ 動自他 ▶定義 to separate and go in different directions; to make sb/sth do this 分かれて別々の方向に行く;~をこのようにさせる➔(群集などが)散らばる、分散する;(群集など)を散らす、分散させる ‖ *When the meeting was over, the group dispersed.* 会議が終了すると,一同は解散した. *The police arrived and quickly dispersed the crowd.* 警官が到着し,素早く群集を散らせた.

**dispirited** /dɪspírətəd/ 形 ▶定義 having lost confidence or hope; depressed 自信または希望をなくした;憂鬱(ゆううつ)な➔意気消沈した、落胆した、元気のない

**displace** /dɪspléɪs/ 動他 ▶定義 1 to remove and take the place of sb/sth ~を取り去って、取って代わる➔~に取って代わる、押しのける、(地位にある人)を辞めさせる ‖ *She hoped to displace Seles as the top tennis player in the world.* 彼女は,世界最高のテニス選手であるセレシュに取って代わりたいと願っていた. ▶定義 2 to force sb/sth to move from the usual or correct place 通常のまたは正しい場所から、~を移動するように強要する➔~を動かす、移動させる、立ち退かせる ‖ *refugees displaced by the war* 戦争によって追われた難民

★**display**¹ /dɪspléɪ/ 動他 ▶定義 1 to put sth in a place where people will see it or where it will attract attention 人々が見る、または注目を集める場所に、~を置く➔~を見せる、展示する、陳列する ‖ *Posters for the concert were displayed throughout the city.* コンサートのポスターは,その都市の至る所に掲示されていた. ▶定義 2 to show signs of sth (for example a feeling or a quality) 何か(例えば感情または性質)の印を表す➔(性質・感情など)を表す、示す ‖ *She displayed no interest in the discussion.* 彼女は議論には何の関心も示さなかった.

★**display**² /dɪspléɪ/ 名 C ▶定義 1 an arrangement of things in a public place for people to see

人々に見せるために公共の場に物が配置されること➡見せること, 展示, 陳列 ‖ *a window display in a shop* 店のウインドーの展示 ▶定義2 a public event in which sth is shown in action 活動している〜を見せる, 公の催し物➡見せ物, ショー ‖ *a firework display* 花火大会 ▶定義3 behaviour that shows a particular feeling or quality 特定の感情または性質を表す振る舞い➡表示, 誇示 ‖ *a sudden display of aggression* 突然に攻撃性をあらわにすること ▶定義4 (computing) words, pictures, etc that can be seen on a computer screen (コンピューター) コンピューター画面に表示される言葉, 画像など➡(データの)表示

成句 on display ▶定義 in a place where people will see it and where it will attract attention 人々がそれを見るであろう, またそれが注目を集めるであろう場所に➡陳列されて, 展示中で ‖ *Treasures from the sunken ship were put on display at the museum.* 沈没船の宝物は, 美術館に展示された.

**displease** /dɪsplíːz/ 動他 正式 ▶定義 to annoy sb or to make sb angry or upset 〜をいらいらさせる, あるいは〜を怒らせるまたは動揺させる➡〜を不快にさせる, 怒らせる, いらいらさせる ― displeased 形 ➡(〜が)気に入らない, (〜に)腹を立てて ⇔ pleased

**displeasure** /dɪpléʒər/ 名 Ⓤ 正式 ▶定義 the feeling of being annoyed or not satisfied いらいらさせられる, または不満な感情➡不愉快, 不満, 立腹 ‖ *I wrote to express my displeasure at not having been informed sooner.* 私は, もっと早く知らせてくれなかったことへの不満を手紙に書いた.

**disposable** /dɪspóʊzəb(ə)l/ 形 ▶定義 made to be thrown away after being used once or for a short time 1度または短期間使用された後に, 捨てられるように作られた➡使い捨ての, 使い捨て式の ‖ *a disposable razor* 使い捨てのかみそり

**disposal** /dɪspóʊz(ə)l/ 名 Ⓤ ▶定義 the act of getting rid of sth or throwing sth away 〜を取り除く, または〜を捨てる行為➡処分, 処理 ‖ *the disposal of dangerous chemical waste* 危険な化学廃棄物の処分 *bomb disposal* 爆弾処理

成句 at sb's disposal ▶定義 available for sb to use at any time 〜がいつでも利用可能な➡〜の自由になって, 〜が勝手に使えて

# disqualify 479

**dispose** /dɪspóʊz/ 動

句動詞 dispose of sb/sth ▶定義 to throw away or sell sth; to get rid of sb/sth that you do not want 〜を捨てるまたは売る; 人が欲しがらない〜を処分する➡〜を処分する, (問題など)を処分する・片付ける, 〜に始末をつける

**disproportionate** /dɪsprəpɔ́ːrʃ(ə)nət/ 形 ▶定義 disproportionate (to sth) too large or too small when compared to sth else ほかの〜と比較すると, 大きすぎるまたは小さすぎる➡不釣り合いな, 不似合いな ‖ *Her salary is disproportionate to the amount of work she has to do.* 彼女の給料は, しなければならない仕事量に対して釣り合いが取れていない. ― disproportionately 副 ➡不釣り合いに

**disprove** /dɪsprúːv/ 動他 ▶定義 to show that sth is not true 〜が本当ではないことを示す➡(考え・理論など)の誤りを立証する, 〜に反証する, 〜の反証を挙げる

★**dispute**¹ /dɪspjúːt, díspjuːt/ 名 Ⓒ Ⓤ ▶定義 (a) dispute (between A and B) (over/about sth) a disagreement or argument between two people, groups or countries 2人, 2つの集団または2国間の意見の相違または口論➡論争, 議論, 口論 ‖ *There was some dispute between John and his boss about whose fault it was.* それがだれの責任なのか, ジョンと上司の間で少し議論があった. *a pay dispute* 賃金争議

成句 in dispute ▶定義 in a situation of arguing or being argued about 物事について論争している, または論争されている状態で➡論争中の, 紛争中で, 問題になって ‖ *He is in dispute with the tax office about how much he should pay.* 彼はいくら支払うべきかについて, 税務署と論争中だ.

**dispute**² /dɪspjúːt/ 動他 ▶定義 to argue about sth and to question if it is true or right 〜について議論し, それが事実なのかまたは正しいのかを問う➡〜について論争する, 〜に異議を唱える ‖ *The player disputed the referee's decision.* 選手は審判の判定に異議を唱えた.

**disqualify** /dɪskwɒ́lɪfaɪ/ 動他 (現分 **disqualifying**; 三単現 **disqualifies**; 過, 過分 **disqualified**) ▶定義 disqualify sb (from sth/doing sth); disqualify sb (for sth) to officially prevent sb from doing sth or taking part in sth, usually because he/she has broken a rule or law 通常はその人が法律または規則を犯したために、~が…をすることを、公式に妨げる➔~の資格を奪う, ~を失格とする, 不適任と判定する ‖ *He was disqualified from driving for two years.* 彼は2年間の運転免許停止となった. *The team were disqualified for cheating.* そのチームは, 不正により出場資格を失った. — **disqualification** /dɪskwɒləfɪkéɪʃ(ə)n/ 名 C U ➔ 資格剥奪(はくだつ), 無資格, 失格

**disregard** /dìsrɪɡáːrd/ 動他 ▶定義 to take no notice of sb/sth; to treat sth as unimportant ~に注目しない; ~を重要でないものとして扱う➔~に注意を払わない, ~を無視する, 軽んじる ‖ *These are the latest instructions. Please disregard any you received before.* 最新の使用説明書です. 以前に受け取られたものは, 無視してくださいますようお願いいたします. — **disregard** 名 [U, 単数扱い] disregard (for sb/sth)➔無視, 無関心, 軽視 ‖ *He rushed into the burning building with complete disregard for his own safety.* 自分自身の安全など全く意に介さず, 彼は燃えている建物に飛び込んだ.

**disrepair** /dìsrɪpéər/ 名 U ▶定義 the state of being in bad condition because repairs have not been made 手入れされていなかったため, ひどい状況にある状態➔(手入れ不足による)破損(状態), 荒廃 ‖ *Over the years the building fell into disrepair.* 数年の間に建物は荒廃していった.

**disreputable** /dɪsrɪpjətəb(ə)l/ 形 ▶定義 not to be trusted; well-known for being bad or dishonest 信頼されていない; 悪いまたは不正直であることがよく知られている➔評判の悪い, 不評の, 不名誉な ‖ *disreputable business methods* 評判の悪い仕事のやり方 ⇔ **reputable**

**disrepute** /dìsrɪpjúːt/ 名 U ▶定義 the situation when people no longer respect sb/sth 人々がもはや~に敬意を払わない状態➔不評, 悪評, 不名誉 ‖ *Such unfair decisions bring the legal system into disrepute.* そのような不公平な決定は, 法律制度に対する悪評を招く.

**disrespect** /dìsrɪspékt/ 名 U ▶定義 disrespect (for/to sb/sth) a lack of respect for sb/sth that is shown in what you do or say 人が言うまたはすることに表されている, ~に対する敬意の欠如➔無礼, 失礼 ⇔ **respect** — **disrespectful** /-fʊl, -f(ə)l/ 形➔敬意を払わない, 失礼な, 無礼な ⇔ **respectful** — **disrespectfully** /-fʊli, -f(ə)li/ 副➔失礼に(も), 無礼に(も)

**disrupt** /dɪsrʌ́pt/ 動他 ▶定義 to stop sth happening as or when it should そうすべきときに起きている~を止める➔(会議・交通など)を混乱させる, 中断させる ‖ *The strike severely disrupted flights to Spain.* ストライキにより, スペイン行きの航空便は容赦なく運航中止となった. — **disruption** 名 C U ➔混乱, 中断 — **disruptive** /dɪsrʌ́ptɪv/ 形➔混乱を引き起こす, 中断させる

**dissatisfaction** /dɪ(s)sætəsfǽkʃ(ə)n/ 名 U ▶定義 dissatisfaction (with/at sb/sth) the feeling of not being satisfied or pleased 満足していない, または喜んでいない気持ち➔不満, 不平 ‖ *There is some dissatisfaction among teachers with the plans for the new exam.* 新しい試験の計画について, 教師の間には多少の不満がある. ⇔ **satisfaction**

**dissatisfied** /dɪ(s)sǽtəsfàɪd/ 形 ▶定義 dissatisfied (with sb/sth) not satisfied or pleased 満足していない, または喜んでいない➔不満な, 不満そうな ‖ *complaints from dissatisfied customers* 不満を感じた顧客たちからの苦情 ⇔ **satisfied**

**dissect** /dɪsékt, daɪ-, dáɪsèkt/ 動他 ▶定義 to cut up a dead body, a plant, etc in order to study it 研究するために, 死体, 植物などを切り開く➔(人体・動植物)を解剖, 切開する, (理論・作品など)を検査する, (結果・言動など)を分析する — **dissection** 名 C U ➔(人体・動植物の)解剖, 解剖された部分, (理論・作品などの)精査

**dissent**[1] /dɪsént/ 名 U 正式 ▶定義 disagreement with official or generally agreed ideas or opinions 正式にまたは一般的に合意された考えまたは意見に対する異議➔意見の相違, 異議 ‖ *There is some dissent within the Labour Party on these policies.* それらの政策に関して, 労働党内で多少の意見の相違がある.

**dissent**[2] /dɪsént/ 動自 正式 ▶定義 dissent (from sth) to have opinions that are different to those that are officially held 公式に抱かれているものとは異なる意見を持つ➔異議を唱える, 同意しない — **dissenting** 形➔同意しない, 異議を

**dissertation** /dìsərtéɪʃ(ə)n/ 名 C ▶定義 a long piece of writing on sth that you have studied, especially as part of a university degree 特に総合大学の学位の一部として, 研究している〜に関する長い著作物 ➡ 論文, 学説, 学位論文 ☞参 **thesis**

**disservice** /dɪ(s)sə́ːrvəs/ 名 [U, 単数扱い]
成句 do (a) disservice to sb/sth ▶定義 to do sth that harms sb and the opinion other people have of him/her 〜と, ほかの人々が持っているその人に対する見解を, 傷付けるような…を行う ➡ 〜に害をなす, 〜にひどい仕打ちをする ‖ *The minister's comments do the teaching profession a great disservice.* その大臣の発言は, 教職に対して非常に害をなすものだ.

**dissident** /dísəd(ə)nt/ 名 C ▶定義 a person who strongly disagrees with and criticizes his/her government, especially in a country where it is dangerous to do this 特にこれを行うことが危険を伴う国で, 自国の政府に強く反対し批判する人 ➡ 反体制者, 異議を持つ人 ‖ *left-wing dissidents* 左翼の反体制者 ― **dissidence** 名 U ➡ (意見などの)相違, 不同意, 不賛成

**dissimilar** /dɪ(s)sím(ə)lər/ 形 ▶定義 **dissimilar (from/to sb/sth)** not the same; different 同じではない; 異なる ➡ 似ていない, 異なる ‖ *The situation you're in is not dissimilar to mine.* あなたの今の状況は, 私のとよく似ている. ⇔ **similar**

**dissociate** /dɪsóʊʃieɪt, -si-/ (または **disassociate** /dìsəsóʊʃieɪt, -si-/) 動 ▶定義 **dissociate sb/sth/yourself (from sth)** to show that you are not connected with or do not support sb/sth; to show that two things are not connected with each other 〜と関連がない, または支持していないことを示す; 2つの事柄はお互いに関連がないことを示す ➡ 〜を(…から)分離する, 引き離す, 分けて考える ‖ *She dissociated herself from the views of the extremists in her party.* 彼女は, 自分の所属する政党内の過激主義者たちの見解から, 自分自身を分けて考えた. ⇔ **associate**

**dissolve** /dɪzɑ́lv/ 動 自 他 ▶定義 (used about a solid) to become or to make sth become liquid (固体について)液体になる, または〜を液体にする ➡ 溶ける; 〜を溶かす, 溶解する ‖ *Sugar dissolves in water.* 砂糖は水に溶ける. *Dissolve two tablets in cold water.* 2錠を冷水で溶かしな

さい.

**dissuade** /dɪswéɪd/ 動 他 ▶定義 **dissuade sb (from doing sth)** to persuade sb not to do sth 〜に…をしないように説得する ➡ 〜に(…を)断念させる, 思いとどまらせる ‖ *I tried to dissuade her from spending the money, but she insisted.* 私は彼女にその金を使うことを断念させようとしたが, 彼女は言うことを聞かなかった. ⇔ **persuade**

★**distance**¹ /dístəns/ 名 ▶定義 **1** C U the amount of space between two places or things 2つの場所または物の間の空間の量 ➡ 距離, 道のり, 間隔 ‖ *The map tells you the distances between the major cities.* その地図を見ると, 主要都市の間の距離が分かります. *We can walk home from here, it's no distance (= it isn't far).* 私たちは, ここから家まで歩いて帰れます. 距離はありません (= 遠くはない). *The house is **within walking distance** of the shops.* その家は商店街から徒歩圏内にある. ▶定義 **2** [単数扱い] a point that is a long way from sb/sth 〜から離れた地点 ➡ 遠距離, 遠い地点 ‖ *At this distance I can't read the number on the bus.* この距離からだと, バスに付いている番号が読めない. *From a distance the village looks quite attractive.* 遠くから見ると, その村はとても魅力的に見える.

成句 **in the distance** ▶定義 far away 遠い ➡ 遠くに, 遠方に ‖ *I could just see Paul in the distance.* 遠くに辛うじてポールを見ることができた.

**keep your distance** ▶定義 to stay away from sb/sth 〜から遠くに離れて ➡ 〜とあまり親しくしない, 〜から遠ざかっている, 〜にあまり近付かない ‖ *Rachel's got a bad cold so I'm keeping my distance until she gets better.* レイチェルはひどい風邪を引いているので, 私は彼女が良くなるまであまり近付かないでいる.

**within striking distance** ⇒ **STRIKE**²

**distance**² /dístəns/ 動 他 ▶定義 **distance yourself from sb/sth** to become less involved or connected with sb/sth 〜とかかわっているまたは関連している状態が弱くなる ➡ 〜を(…から)遠くに置く, 遠ざける, 引き離す ‖ *She was keen to distance herself from the views of her colleagues.* 彼女は, 同僚たちの見解とは一線を引きたいと強く望んだ.

**distant** /dístənt/ 形 ▶定義1 a long way away in space or time 空間的または時間的に遠く離れた→遠い, 離れている ‖ *travel to distant parts of the world* 世界の遠い所へ旅する *in the not-too-distant future (= quite soon)* 遠すぎない将来に (= 近いうちに) ▶定義2 (used about a relative) not closely related (親戚(しんせき)について) 近い親戚でない→遠縁の ‖ *a distant cousin* 遠縁のいとこ ▶定義3 not very friendly あまり好意的でない→よそよそしい, 冷ややかな, 水臭い ‖ *He has a rather distant manner and it's hard to get to know him well.* 彼はかなりよそよそしいので, どんな人か知ることは難しい. ▶定義4 seeming to be thinking about sth else ほかの〜を考えているような→遠くを見るような, ぼんやりした, 上の空の ‖ *She had a distant look in her eyes and clearly wasn't listening to me.* 彼女の目はぼんやりしていて, 明らかに私の言うことを聞いていなかった.

**distaste** /distéɪst/ 名 [Ⓤ, 単数扱い] ▶定義 not liking sth; the feeling that sb/sth is unpleasant or offends you 〜が好きではないこと; 〜が不愉快である, または自分に不快な感じを与えると思う感情→嫌い, 嫌気, (軽い)嫌悪 ‖ *She looked around the dirty kitchen with distaste.* 彼女は嫌々ながら汚れた台所を見回した.

**distasteful** /distéɪstfəl, -f(ə)l/ 形 ▶定義 unpleasant or causing offence 不愉快な, または怒らせる→(仕事・出来事などが)不愉快な, 嫌な ‖ *a distasteful remark* 不愉快な批評

**distil** (米 **distill**) /distíl/ 動 Ⓤ (**distilling**; **distilled**) ▶定義 to make a liquid pure by heating it until it becomes a gas and then collecting the liquid that forms when the gas cools 液体が気体になるまで熱し, その気体が冷えたときにできる液体を集めることによって, その液体を純粋にする→〜を蒸留する, (ウイスキーなど)を蒸留して造る

**distillery** /distíl(ə)ri/ 名 Ⓒ (複 **distilleries**) ▶定義 a factory where strong alcoholic drink is made by the process of distilling 蒸留の過程により, アルコール度の高い酒が造られる工場→蒸留酒製造所・会社

*****distinct** /distíŋ(k)t/ 形 ▶定義1 clear; easily seen, heard or understood 明らかな; たやすく見える, 聞けるまたは理解できる→鮮明な, 明確な, はっきりした ‖ *There has been a distinct improvement in your work recently.* 最近のあなたの仕事振りは, 明らかに進歩している. *I had the distinct impression that she was lying.* 彼女がうそをついているというのははっきりした印象を受けた. ▶定義2 **distinct (from sth)** clearly different 明らかに異なる→(〜とは)別個の, 異なった ‖ *Her books fall into two distinct groups: the novels and the travel stories.* 彼女の著作は2つの異なった種類に分けられる. 小説と旅行記である. *This region, as distinct from other parts of the country, relies heavily on tourism.* この地域は国内のほかの地域とは異なり, 観光事業に大きく依存している. ⇔ 両方の定義 **indistinct**

*****distinction** /distíŋ(k)ʃ(ə)n/ 名 ▶定義1 Ⓒ Ⓤ (a) **distinction (between A and B)** a clear or important difference between things or people 物事または人々の間の明らかなまたは重要な相違→区別, 差別, 相違 ‖ *We must make a distinction between classical and popular music here.* ここでは, クラシック音楽とポピュラー音楽を区別しなくてはなりません. ▶定義2 Ⓒ Ⓤ the quality of being excellent; fame for what you have achieved 優秀であるという特性; 人が成し遂げた物事への名声→優秀さ, すばらしさ, 名誉 ‖ *a violinist of distinction* 優れたバイオリン奏者 ▶定義3 Ⓒ the highest mark that is given to students in some exam for excellent work 試験での優秀な成績に対して学生たちに与えられる最高の評価→優等 ‖ *James got a distinction in maths.* ジェームズは数学で優を取った.

成句 draw a distinction between sth and sth ⇒ **DRAW**¹

**distinctive** /distíŋ(k)tɪv/ 形 ▶定義 clearly different from others and therefore easy to recognize 他とは明らかに異なっていて, そのため見分けることが簡単な→(他との)違いを示す, 際立った, 特徴のある ‖ *The soldiers were wearing their distinctive red berets.* 兵士たちは, 特徴のある赤のベレー帽をかぶっていた. — **distinctively** 副 → 特徴的に, 区別して, 独特に

**distinctly** /distíŋ(k)tli/ 副 ▶定義1 clearly 明らかに→はっきりと, 明確に ‖ *I distinctly heard her say that she would be here on time.* 時間通りにここにいると彼女が言ったのを, 私ははっきりと聞いた. ▶定義2 very; particularly とても; 特に

➜確かに,紛れもなく,疑いようもなく ‖ *His behaviour has been distinctly odd recently.* 彼の行動は最近,確かに常軌を逸している.

***distinguish** /dɪstíŋ(g)wɪʃ/ [動] ▶定義1 [自][他] distinguish between A and B; distinguish A from B to recognize the difference between two things or people 2つの物事または2人の間の相違を見分ける ➜**〜を区別する,〜と見分ける,聞き分ける** ‖ *He doesn't seem able to distinguish between what's important and what isn't.* 彼は,重要な事とそうでない事が区別できないように見える. *People who are colour-blind often can't distinguish red from green.* 色盲の人はしばしば,赤を緑と区別できない. ☛類 **differentiate** ▶定義2 [他] distinguish A (from B) to make sb/sth different from others 〜を他とは違うものにする ➜**〜の特色・特徴を示す,特色づける,(物事が)〜を区別する** ‖ *distinguishing features (= things by which sb/sth can be recognized)* 他と区別する特徴(= それにより〜が見分けられるもの) *The power of speech distinguishes humans from animals.* 言語能力によって人間は動物と区別される. ▶定義3 [他] to see, hear or recognize with effort 努力して見る,聞くまたは認める ➜**〜をはっきりと認める,識別する,はっきりと聞こえる,はっきりと見える** ‖ *I listened carefully but they were too far away for me to distinguish what they were saying.* 注意深く聞いたが,遠すぎて彼らの言うことをはっきりと聞くことはできなかった. ▶定義4 [他] distinguish yourself to do sth which causes you to be noticed and admired 人に知られ高く評価される原因となる物・事を行う ➜**有名になる,目立つ** ‖ *She distinguished herself in the exams.* 彼女はその試験で有名になった.

**distinguishable** /dɪstíŋ(g)wɪʃəb(ə)l/ [形] ▶定義1 possible to recognize as different from sb/sth else ほかの〜とは違ったものとして見分けられる ➜**区別が付く,見分けられる** ‖ *The male bird is distinguishable from the female by the colour of its beak.* くちばしの色で,雄鳥は雌鳥と区別が付く. ▶定義2 possible to see, hear or recognize with effort 努力して見る,聞くまたは認めることができる ➜**はっきりと見える・聞こえる** ‖ *The letter is so old that the signature is barely distinguishable.* その手紙はとても古いので,その署名は辛うじて読める. ⇔ **indistinguishable**

**distinguished** /dɪstíŋ(g)wɪʃt/ [形] ▶定義 important, successful and respected by other people 重要で成功していて,ほかの人々に尊敬されている ➜**著名な,名高い,際立った** ‖ *a distinguished guest* 著名な客

**distort** /dɪstɔ́ːrt/ [動][他] ▶定義1 to change the shape or sound of sth so that it seems strange or is not clear 〜の形または音を変えて,それが奇妙に思えるまたは鮮明でないようにする ➜**(音)をひずませる,(形)を変形する,(顔・手足など)をゆがめる** ‖ *Her face was distorted with grief.* 彼女の顔は深い悲しみでゆがんでいた. ▶定義2 to change sth and show it falsely 〜を変えて,偽って示す ➜**(事実・考えなど)を歪曲(わいきょく)して伝える,曲げる,ゆがめる** ‖ *Foreigners are often given a distorted view of this country.* 外国人にはしばしば,この国についてゆがんだ見方が伝えられている. — distortion [名] [C][U] ➜**(事実などの)歪曲,ゆがめられた話,(物・画像・音などの)ゆがみ**

**distract** /dɪstrǽkt/ [動][他] ▶定義 distract sb (from sth) to take sb's attention away from sth 〜の注意を…からそらす ➜**〜をそらす,紛らす** ‖ *Could you stop talking please? You're distracting me from my work.* おしゃべりをやめていただけませんか.気が散って仕事ができません.

**distracted** /dɪstrǽktəd/ [形] ▶定義 unable to give your full attention to sth because you are worried or thinking about sth else ほかの〜が心配なので,またはそれについて考えているので,…にすべての注意を傾けることができない ➜**注意をそらした,集中していない**

**distraction** /dɪstrǽkʃ(ə)n/ [名] [C][U] ▶定義 something that takes your attention away from what you were doing or thinking about 行っていた事または考えていた事から人の注意をそらすもの ➜**気を散らすもの,注意をそらすもの,気晴らし** ‖ *I find it hard to work at home because there are so many distractions.* 気が散ってしまう事がたくさんあるので,家で仕事をすることは難しいと悟っている.

[成句] to distraction ▶定義 with the result that you become upset, excited, or angry and unable to think clearly 動揺する,興奮するまた

**distraught** /dɪstrɔ́ːt/ 形 ▶定義 extremely sad and upset 極度の悲しみと悩みを感じて→取り乱した, 気も狂わんばかりの

**distress**¹ /dɪstrés/ 名 Ⓤ ▶定義 **1** the state of being very upset or of suffering great pain or difficulty とても悲しんでいる, あるいはひどい苦痛または困難を被っている状態→苦痛, 苦悩, 悲しみ ‖ *She was **in** such **distress** that I didn't want to leave her on her own.* 彼女がひどく悩んでいたので, 私は彼女を1人にしておきたくなかった. ▶定義 **2** the state of being in great danger and needing immediate help 非常に危険で, 即座に助けを必要としている状態→危険な状態, 災難, 遭難 ‖ *The ship's captain radioed that it was **in distress**.* 船長は, 船が遭難していると無線連絡をした.

**distress**² /dɪstrés/ 動 他 ▶定義 to make sb very upset or unhappy ～をとても動揺させるまたは悲しませる→～を苦しめる, 悩ます, 悲しませる ‖ *Try not to say anything to distress the patient further.* これ以上患者を苦しめる事は言わないようにしてください. ― distressed 形→困惑した, 苦しんだ, 困窮した ‖ *She was too distressed to talk.* 彼女は困惑のあまり話すことができなかった. ― distressing 形→(人を)悲しませる, つらい, 悲惨な ‖ *a distressing experience/illness* 悲惨な経験・つらい病気

★**distribute** /dɪstríbjuːt/ 動 他 ▶定義 **1** distribute sth (to/among sb/sth) to give things to a number of people 何人かの人に～を与える→～を配る, 分配する, 配布する ‖ *Tickets will be distributed to all club members.* チケットは, クラブの全会員に配られます. *They distributed emergency food supplies to the areas that were most in need.* 最も必要とする地域に, 彼らは緊急食糧品を分配した. ▶定義 **2** to transport and supply goods to shops, companies, etc 店, 会社などに商品を輸送して供給する→～を配達・配送する, 流通させる, 販売する ‖ *Which company distributes this product in your country?* あなたの国では, どの会社がこの製品を販売しているのですか. ▶定義 **3** to spread sth equally over an area ある地域全体にわたって, ～を均等に散布する→～を分布させる, 配置する, 散布する ‖ *Make sure that the weight is **evenly distributed**.* その重量が均等に配分されていることを確認しなさい.

★**distribution** /ˌdɪstrəbjúːʃ(ə)n/ 名 ▶定義 **1** [単数扱い, Ⓤ] the act of giving or transporting sth to a number of people or places ～を何人かの人またはいくつかの場所に与える, または輸送する行為→(～への)配布, 分配, 配給 ‖ *the distribution of food parcels to the refugees* 難民への食糧の包みの配給 ▶定義 **2** [単数扱い, Ⓤ] the way sth is shared out; the pattern in which sth is found ～が分配される方法; ～が発見される型→分布, 分布区域, 配置 ‖ *a map to show the distribution of rainfall in Africa* アフリカの降雨が見られる区域を示す地図

**distributor** /dɪstríbjətər/ 名 Ⓒ ▶定義 a person or company that transports and supplies goods to a number of shops and companies いくつかの店と会社に商品を輸送, 供給する人または会社→(ある商品・地域などの)販売(代理)店, 流通業者, 卸し売り業者

★**district** /dístrɪkt/ 名 Ⓒ ▶定義 **1** a part of a town or country that is special for a particular reason or is of a particular type 特定の理由を持った, 特別なまたは特定の種類の, 町または国の一部→地方, 地帯, 地域 ‖ *rural districts* 田園地帯 *the financial district of the city* 市の金融街 ▶定義 **2** an official division of a town or country 町または国の公式の区分→地区, 区域, 管区 ‖ *the district council* 地方議会 *postal districts* 郵便業務の必要性から区分された区域

▶ district は町または国の一部で, 境界が確定されている場合がある: *the district controlled by a council* (地方議会に支配される地区). region はもっと広く, 通常は国の一部のみで境界が確定されていないこともあり得る: *the industrial regions of the country* (その国の工業地帯). area は最も一般的な用語で, district と region の両方の意味で使われる: *the poorer areas of a town* (町の貧困地区) *an agricultural area of the country* (その国の農業地帯). 町の地区について話しているとき, よく part を使う: *Which part of Paris do you live in?* (パ

リのどこに住んでいるのですか.)

**distrust** /dɪstrʌ́st/ 名[ 単数扱い] ▶定義 (a) distrust (of sb/sth) the feeling that you cannot believe sb/sth; a lack of trust ～を信じられない気持ち;信頼の欠如→**不信感,疑惑,邪推** ― distrust 動他→～を疑う,信用しない,邪推する ‖ *She distrusts him because he lied to her once before.* 以前1度うそをついたことがあるので,彼女は彼を信用していない.
▶ mistrust と比較.
― distrustful 形→疑う,信用しない,疑い深い

★**disturb** /dɪstə́ːrb/ 動他 ▶定義 1 to interrupt sb while he/she is doing sth or sleeping; to spoil a peaceful situation ～が…をしている,または寝ている最中に邪魔する;平穏な状況を台なしにする→**(人・休息・仕事など)を邪魔する,妨げる** ‖ *I'm sorry to disturb you but there's a phone call for you.* お邪魔してすみませんが,お電話が入っています. *Their sleep was disturbed by a loud crash.* 彼らは,すさまじいドシンという音で目が覚めた. ▶定義 2 to cause sb to worry ～に心配させる→**(人・心)をかき乱す,不安にする,心配させる** ‖ *It disturbed her to think that he might be unhappy.* 彼がふさいでいるのではないかと考えて,彼女は不安になった. ▶定義 3 to move sth or change its position ～を動かす,またはその位置を変える→**(形・場所)を乱す,乱雑にする** ‖ *I noticed a number of things had been disturbed and realized that there had been a burglary.* いくつかの物が乱雑にされているのに気付いて,泥棒に入られたことが分かった.

**disturbance** /dɪstə́ːrbəns/ 名 C U ▶定義 something that makes you stop what you are doing, or that upsets the normal condition of sth 人がしている事をやめさせる,または～の正常な状態を台なしにするもの→**(秩序・静寂などを)乱すこと,混乱,騒動,心の動揺** ‖ *They were arrested for causing a disturbance (= fighting) in the town centre.* 彼らは,町の中心部で騒動を起こした(= けんかをした)かどで逮捕された. *emotional disturbance* 情緒障害

**disturbed** /dɪstə́ːrbd/ 形 ▶定義 having mental or emotional problems 精神的または情緒的な問題を持っている→**心配している,悩んでいる,精神・情緒障害のある** ‖ *a school for disturbed young people* 精神障害のある青少年のための学校

**disturbing** /dɪstə́ːrbɪŋ/ 形 ▶定義 making you

## divan 485

worried or upset 人を心配または動揺させている→**(人を)動揺させる,不安にさせる** ‖ *I found the film about Aids very disturbing.* 私は,エイズに関する映画がとても人を動揺させるものだと分かった.

**disuse** /dɪsjúːs/ 名 U ▶定義 the state of not being used any more もう使われていない状態→**使われなくなること,不使用,廃止** ‖ *The farm buildings had been allowed to* ***fall into disuse***. 農場の建物は使われなくなった.

**disused** /dɪsjúːzd/ 形 ▶定義 not used any more もう使われていない→**もう使われていない,廃止された** ‖ *a disused railway line* もう使われていない鉄道線路

**ditch**[1] /dɪtʃ/ 名 C ▶定義 a long narrow hole that has been dug into the ground, especially along the side of a road or field for water to flow along 特に水が沿って流れるように道路または田畑のわきに沿った,地面に掘られた細長い溝→**用水路,排水路**
成句 *a last-ditch attempt* ⇒ **LAST**[1]

**ditch**[2] /dɪtʃ/ 動他 略式 ▶定義 to get rid of or leave sb/sth ～を取り除く,または～から離れる→**捨てる,人を見捨てる,(人・車など)を置き去りにする** ‖ *She ditched her old friends when she became famous.* 彼女は有名になると,古い友人たちを見捨てた.

**dither** /díðər/ 動自 ▶定義 to be unable to decide sth; to hesitate ～を決められない;ためらう→**(心が)揺れる,決めかねる,迷う** ‖ *Stop dithering and make up your mind!* 迷うのはやめて,決心しなさい.

**ditto** /dítou/ 名 C ▶定義 (represented by the mark (〃) and used instead of repeating the thing written above it) the same (記号 〃 で表され,上記の事柄を繰り返す代わりに用いて)同じ物事→**同上,同前** ― ditto 副→**同感,(私も)同じ(だ)** ‖ *'I'm starving.' 'Ditto (= me too).'* 「おなかがぺこぺこだ」「同感だ(= 私も)」

**divan** /dɪvǽn, dɑɪ-/ 名 C 英 ▶定義 a type of bed with only a thick base to lie on but no frame at either end 横になるための厚い台だけがあって,両側の枠がない,寝台の一種→**ディバン(壁際に置く背もたれ,ひじ掛けのない長いす・寝いす),寝いす,ソファーベッド**

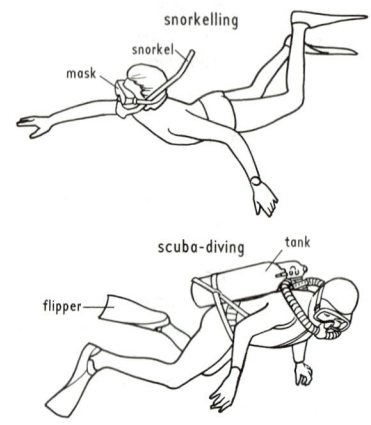

snorkelling
snorkel
mask

scuba-diving
tank
flipper

★**dive**¹ /dáɪv/ 動🅐 (過 **dived**: 米 または **dove** /dóʊv/; 過分 **dived**) ▶定義1 dive (off/from sth) (into sth); dive in to jump into water with your arms and head first 両腕と頭から先に水に飛び込む→飛び込む ∥ *In Acapulco, men dive off the cliffs into the sea.* アカプルコでは，男たちは絶壁から海に飛び込む. *A passer-by dived in and saved the drowning man.* 通行人が飛び込み，おぼれている男性を救助した. ☞S1ページのさし絵 ▶定義2 to swim under the surface of the sea, a lake, etc 海，湖などの水面下を泳ぐ→水に潜る，潜水する ∥ *people diving for pearls* 真珠を探すために潜水する人々 *I'm hoping to go diving on holiday.* 休日にはダイビングに行きたいと思っている. ▶定義3 to move quickly and suddenly downwards 突然素早く下方に移動する→(飛行機・鳥が)急降下する，(人・動物が)突進する，駆け込む ∥ *He dived under the table and hid there.* 彼はテーブルの下に駆け込み，そこに隠れた. *The goalkeeper dived to save the penalty.* ゴールキーパーは，ペナルティーキックを防ごうと突進した.

句動詞 dive into sth ▶定義 to put your hand quickly into a pocket or bag in order to find or get sth ～を見つける，または取るために，ポケットまたはかばんに素早く手を入れる→～に手を突っ込む，～を探る ∥ *She dived into her bag and brought out an old photograph.* 彼女はバッグを探って，古い写真を取り出した.

**dive**² /dáɪv/ 名🅒 ▶定義1 the act of diving into water 水に飛び込む行為→飛び込むこと，飛び込み，ダイビング ▶定義2 a quick and sudden downwards movement 素早い突然の下方への動き→(飛行機・鳥の)急降下，(人・動物の)突進，逃げ込み ∥ *Despite a desperate dive, the goalkeeper couldn't stop the ball.* 必死の突進にもかかわらず，ゴールキーパーはボールを止めることができなかった.

**diver** /dáɪvər/ 名🅒 ▶定義1 a person who swims under the surface of water using special equipment 特別の装置を使って，水面下を泳ぐ人→潜水する人，ダイバー ▶定義2 a person who jumps into water with his/her arms and head first 両腕と頭から先に水に飛び込む人→水に飛び込む人，ダイビング選手

**diverge** /dəvə́ːrdʒ, daɪ-/ 動🅘 diverge (from sth) ▶定義1 (used about roads, lines, etc) to separate and go in different directions (道路，線などについて) 分岐して違う方向に行く→分岐する，分かれる ∥ *The paths suddenly diverged and I didn't know which one to take.* 道が突然分かれ，私はどっちの道を行くのか分からなかった.
▶定義2 to be or become different 異なる，または違うものになる→(意見などが)互いに異なる，分かれる ∥ *Attitudes among teachers diverge on this question.* この問題に関して，教師の間で受け止め方が分かれる.

**diverse** /daɪvə́ːrs, də-, dáɪvəːrs/ 形 ▶定義 very different from each other お互いに非常に異なる→さまざまな，互いに異なった，多様な ∥ *people from diverse social backgrounds* さまざまな社会的な経歴を持つ人々 *My interests are very diverse.* 私の興味はとても多岐にわたっている.
☞名 diversity

**diversify** /dəvə́ːrsəfaɪ, daɪ-/ 動🅘他 (現分 **diversifying**; 三単現 **diversifies**; 過，過分 **diversified**)
▶定義 diversify (sth) (into sth) to increase or develop the number or types of sth ～の数または種類を増やす，または開発する→多様になる，多様化する，多角化して(新しい分野に)参入する ∥ *To remain successful in the future, the company will have to diversify.* 将来にわたって繁栄するためには，その会社は多角化しなければならない. *Latin diversified into several different languages.* ラテン語はいくつかの異なった言語へと

分化した. — **diversification** /dəvə̀ːrsəfəkéɪʃ(ə)n, daɪ-/ 名 C U →多様化, 多様性, 多角経営

**diversion** /dəvə́ːrʒ(ə)n, daɪ-, -ʃ(ə)n, dɪ-, -ʒ(ə)n/ 名 ▶定義1 C U the act of changing the direction or purpose of sth, especially in order to solve or avoid a problem 特に問題を解決するまたは避けるために, ~の方向または目的を変更する行為→わきへそらすこと, (方向などの)転換, (資金などの)流用 ‖ *the diversion of a river to prevent flooding* 洪水を防ぐために川の流れをわきへそらすこと *the diversion of government funds to areas of greatest need* 政府の資金を, 最も必要度の高い地域へ転用すること ▶定義2 C (米 **detour**) a different route which traffic can take when a road is closed 道路が閉鎖されている場合に, 交通できる別の道筋→迂回(うかい)路, 回り道 ‖ *For London, follow the diversion.* ロンドンへは, 迂回路を進みなさい. ▶定義3 C something that takes your attention away from sth 人の注意を~からそらすもの→注意をそらすもの, 陽動(作戦) ‖ *Some prisoners created a diversion while others escaped.* ほかの囚人たちが逃げている間, 何人かの囚人たちは人の注意をそらしていた.

**diversity** /dəvə́ːrsəti, daɪ-/ 名 U ▶定義 the wide variety of sth ~の広い多様性→**多様性, 相違(点)** ‖ *cultural and ethnic diversity* 文化的, 民族的多様性

**divert** /dəvə́ːrt, daɪ-/ 動 他 ▶定義 divert sb/sth (from sth) (to sth); divert sth (away from sth) to change the direction or purpose of sb/sth, especially to avoid a problem 特に問題を避けるために, ~の方向または目的を変える→(金など)を転用する, (流れなど)の向きを変える, (注意・批判など)をそらす ‖ *During the road repairs, all traffic is being diverted.* 道路が修復される間, すべての交通は迂回(うかい)させられている. *Government money was diverted from defence to education.* 政府の資金は, 防衛から教育に転用された. *Politicians often criticise each other to divert attention away from their own mistakes.* 政治家たちは, 自分たちの誤りから注意をそらせるために, しばしばお互いに相手を批判する.

★**divide**¹ /dəváɪd/ 動 ▶定義1 自 他 divide (sth) (up) (into sth) to separate into different parts 別の部分に分かれる, 分ける→**分かれる, 分離す**る; ~を分割する, 分ける ‖ *The egg divides into two cells.* 卵子が2つの細胞に分裂する. *The house was divided up into flats.* 家は階ごとに分けられた. ▶定義2 他 divide sth (out/up) (between/among sb) to separate sth into parts and give a part to each of a number of people ~をいくつかに分け, 何人かの人々に1つずつ与える→**~を分配する, 分ける, 分かち合う** ‖ *The robbers divided the money out between themselves.* 泥棒たちは, その金を分け合った. *When he died, his property was divided up among his children.* 彼が死んだ時, その財産は子供たちに分けられた. ▶定義3 他 divide sth (between A and B) to use different parts or amounts of sth for different purposes 異なる目的のために, ~の別個の部分または数量の一部を使う→**(時間など)を配分する, 割り当てる** ‖ *They divide their time between their two homes.* 彼らは2つの家庭に自分たちの時間を割り当てた. ▶定義4 他 to separate two places or things 2つの場所または2つの事を切り離す→**~を分離する, 隔てる** ‖ *The river divides the old part of the city from the new.* 川が, 旧市街地を新市街地から隔てている. ▶定義5 他 to cause people to disagree 人々の間に意見の不一致を引き起こす→**人を分裂させる, (人の)仲を裂く, ~の間に不一致を起こす** ‖ *The question of immigration has divided the country.* 移民の問題で国内の意見が分かれている. ▶定義6 他 divide sth by sth to calculate how many times a number will go into another number ある数を何倍すると別の数になるかを計算する→**~を…で割る** ‖ *10 divided by 5 is 2.* 10を5で割ると2である. ⇔ **multiply**

**divide**² /dəváɪd/ 名 C ▶定義 a divide (between A and B) a difference between two groups of people that separates them from each other 互いを区別する, 人々の2つの集団間の相違点→**(大きな)相違, 溝, 分裂** ‖ *a divide between the rich and the poor* 貧富の差

**divided highway** 米 =DUAL CARRIAGEWAY

**dividend** /dívədènd/ 名 C ▶定義 a part of a company's profits that is paid to the people who own shares in it (**shareholders**) 株式を保有する人々(株主)に支払われる, 企業の利益の

一部➡(株式の)配当(金), 利益配当(金)

**divine** /dəváɪn/ 形 ▶定義 connected with God or a god 創造主または神に関する➡神の, 神から授かった, 神聖な

**diving** /dáɪvɪŋ/ 名 ❶ ▶定義 the activity or sport of jumping into water or swimming under the surface of the sea, a lake, etc 水に飛び込むまたは海, 湖などの水面下を泳ぐ, 行為またはスポーツ➡潜水, ダイビング, 飛び込み

**diving board** 名 ❸ ▶定義 a board at the side of a swimming pool from which people can jump into the water そこから人々が水中に飛び込める, スイミングプールの側面にある板➡飛び込み板, 飛び込み台

**divisible** /dəvízəb(ə)l/ 形 ▶定義 that can be divided 分割できる➡分けられる, 分割できる, (数が)割り切れる ‖ *12 is divisible by 3.* 12は3で割り切れる.

*__division__ /dəvíʒ(ə)n/ 名 ▶定義 1 [❶, 単数扱い] division (of sth) (into sth); division (of sth) (between A and B) the separation of sth into different parts; the sharing of sth between different people, groups, places, etc ～を別々の部分に分けること; さまざまな人々, 集団, 場所などで～を共有すること➡分割, 分離, 分配 ‖ *There is a growing economic division between the north and south of the country.* 国の北部と南部の間で経済格差が増大している. *an unfair division of the profits* 利益の不当な分配 ▶定義 2 ❶ dividing one number by another ある数をほかの数で割ること➡割り算, 除法 ‖ *the teaching of multiplication and division* 掛け算と割り算の授業 ▶定義 3 ❸ a division (in/within sth); a division (between A and B) a disagreement or difference of opinion between sb/sth ～の間の意見の不一致または相違➡意見の相違, 不一致 ‖ *deep divisions within the Labour Party* 労働党内の深刻な意見の相違 ▶定義 4 ❸ a part or section of an organization 組織の部分または部門➡部分, 部門, 課 ‖ *the company's sales division* 会社の販売部門 *the First Division (= of the football league)* (サッカーリーグの)1部リーグ ▶定義 5 ❸ a line that separates sth; a border ～を分離する線; 境界線➡仕切り, 境界線 ‖ *The river marks the division between the two counties.* その川が2国間の境界線を示す.

**divisive** /dəváɪsɪv/ 形 正式 ▶定義 likely to cause disagreements or arguments between people 人々の間に意見の相違または論争を引き起こしそうな➡意見の相違を起こす, 不和を生む ‖ *a divisive policy* 意見の分かれる政策

*__divorce__¹ /dɪvɔ́ːrs/ 名 ❶ ❶ ▶定義 the legal end of a marriage 婚姻の法律的な終わり➡離婚 ‖ *to get a divorce* 離婚をする

*__divorce__² /dɪvɔ́ːrs/ 動 他 ▶定義 1 to legally end your marriage to sb ～との結婚を法律的に終わらせる➡～と離婚する, ～を離婚させる ‖ *My parents got divorced when I was three.* 私が3歳の時に, 両親は離婚した. *She divorced him a year after their marriage.* 結婚の1年後, 彼女は夫と離婚した. ▶定義 2 divorce sb/sth from sth to separate sb/sth from sth ～を…から分離する➡～を分離する, 絶縁する ‖ *Sometimes these modern novels seem completely divorced from everyday life.* 時々, これらの現代小説は日常生活から完全に遊離しているように思える. — divorced 形 ➡離婚した, 分離した

**divorcee** /dɪvɔːrséɪ, -síː, -ˈ-/ 名 ❸ ▶定義 a person who is divorced➡離婚した人(特に女性)

**divulge** /dəvʌ́ldʒ, daɪ-/ 動 他 正式 ▶定義 to tell sth that is secret 秘密の～を話す➡(秘密など)を漏らす, 暴露する ‖ *The phone companies refused to divulge details of their costs.* 電話会社は, 価格の詳細を漏らすことを拒絶した.

**Diwali** /dɪwɑ́ːli, -vɑ́ː-/ 名 [単数扱い] ▶定義 a festival in several Indian religions that takes place in October or November, in which people decorate their homes with lights いくつかのインドの宗教で10月または11月に行われる祭り, その時人々は自分の家を明かりで飾り付ける➡ディーワーリー(秋に行われるヒンドゥー教の灯明の祭り)

**DIY** /díː aɪ wáɪ/ 略 do it yourself ▶定義 the activity of making and repairing things yourself around your home 自分の家の周りの物を自分で作り修理する行為➡日曜大工 ‖ *a DIY expert* 日曜大工の達人

**dizzy** /dízi/ 形 ▶定義 1 feeling as if everything is turning round and that you might fall すべての物が回り, 自分が転ぶように感じている➡めまいがする, くらくらする ‖ *I feel/get dizzy in high places.* 私は高い所にいるとくらくらする. ▶定義 2 very great; extreme 非常に大きい; 極端

な→(場所などが)目がくらむような ‖ *the dizzy pace of life in London* 目がくらむような速さのロンドンでの生活 *The following year, the band's popularity reached **dizzy heights**.* 翌年、そのバンドの人気は目がくらむような高さにまで達した.— **dizziness** 名 Ⓤ→めまい

**DJ** /dìː dʒéɪ/(または **disc jockey**) 名 Ⓒ ▶定義 a person who plays records and talks about music on the radio or in a club ラジオまたはクラブで、レコードをかけて音楽について話す人→ディスクジョッキー

★**do**¹ /(子音の前) də, (母音の前) du 強形 duː/ 助
▶定義1 used with other verbs to form questions and negative sentences, also in short answers and short questions at the end of a sentence (question tags) 疑問文および否定文を作るためにほかの動詞と共に用いられ、同様に短い答えと文末に来る短い疑問文(付加疑問文)でも用いられる→(疑問文・否定文を作る), (疑問文の答えで), (付加疑問文で) ☞ 巻末の「文法早見表」を参照. ▶定義2 used for emphasizing the main verb 主動詞を強調するために用いて→**本当に, 是非** ‖ *I can't find the receipt now but I'm sure I **did** pay the phone bill.* 今は領収書が見つからないのですが、本当に電話料金を払ったと言い切れます. ▶定義3 used to avoid repeating the main verb 主動詞を繰り返すことを避けるために用いて→(先行する動詞(句)の反復を避けて) ‖ *He earns a lot more than I **do**.* 彼は私より多く稼ぐ. *She's feeling much better than she **did** last week.* 彼女は先週よりかなり体調が良くなっている.

> ▶語法 📖
> **I did kiss her. は動詞を強調しない**
> doは動詞を強調する働きがある、という説明をよく目にしますが、これは誤解を招く言い方です. 正確には「文の内容が真実であること」を強調しているのです. この言い方は、聞き手が話し手の発話を信じてくれないときなどに用います. したがって, I did kiss her. は「(うそじゃなくて)本当にキスした!」という意味になります.「強烈にキスした」という意味ではありません.

★**do**² /duː/ 動 ▶定義1 Ⓣ to perform an action, activity or job 活動, 行動または仕事を行う→~をする, 果たす, 仕上げる ‖ *What are you **doing**?* 何をしているのですか. *What is the government **doing** about pollution (= what action are they taking)?* 政府は公害に対して何をしているのか(= どのような行動を取っているのか). *What do you **do** (= what is your job)?* 何をなさっていますか(= お仕事は何ですか). *Have you **done** your homework?* 宿題は済ませたのですか. *I **do** twenty minutes' exercise every morning.* 私は毎朝, 20分間運動をする. *to **do** the cooking/cleaning/ironing* 料理をする・掃除をする・アイロンをかける *to **do** judo/aerobics/windsurfing* 柔道をする・エアロビクスをする・ウインドサーフィンをする *What did you **do** with the keys (= where did you put them)?* かぎをどうしたのですか(= どこに置いたのですか). ▶定義2 Ⓘ to make progress or develop; to improve sth 進歩または発展する; ~が向上する ‖ *'How's your daughter **doing** at school?' 'She's **doing** well.'* 「娘さんは学校ではいかがですか」「うまくやっています」 *Last week's win has **done wonders for** the team's confidence.* 先週勝利したことは、そのチームが自信を付けることに驚くほど効果を上げた. *This latest scandal will **do nothing for** (= will harm) this government's reputation.* この最新のスキャンダルは、現在の政府の評判を損ねる(= 傷付ける)だろう. ▶定義3 Ⓣ to make or produce sth ~を作る, または生み出す→**~を作る, 翻訳する, 料理する** ‖ *The photocopier **does** 60 copies a minute.* そのコピー機は, 1分間に60枚のコピーをする. *to **do** a painting/drawing* 絵をかく・スケッチをする ▶定義4 Ⓣ to provide a service サービスを提供する→**~を扱う, もてなす** ‖ *Do you **do** eye tests here?* ここでは目の検査を行っていますか. ▶定義5 Ⓣ to study sth or find the answer to sth ~を勉強する, または~の答えを見つける→**~を勉強する, 学ぶ, (問題など)を解く** ‖ *to **do** French/a course/a degree* フランス語を勉強する・教科課程を学ぶ・学位を取る *I can't **do** question three.* 第3問が解けない. ▶定義6 Ⓣ to travel a certain distance or at a certain speed ある距離を行く, またはある速さで行く→(人・乗り物などが)~を行く, ~の速度で進む ‖ *This car **does** 120 miles per hour.* この自動車は, 時速

120マイルで走る. *I normally do about five miles when I go running.* ランニングするとき, 私はいつも5マイルくらい走る. ▶定義7 ⓤto have a particular effect 特定の結果を持つ→(害・益など)を与える, もたらす ‖ *A holiday will do you good.* 休暇はあなたの健康に良いだろう. *The storm did a lot of damage.* そのあらしは大きな損害をもたらした. ▶定義8 🇬🇧ⓤ to be enough or suitable 十分または適当である→必要を満たす, 間に合う, 役に立つ ‖ *If you haven't got a pen, a pencil will do.* ペンを持っていないのなら, 鉛筆で結構です.

成句 **be/have to do with sb/sth** ▶定義 to be connected with sb/sth →~と関係がある ‖ *I'm not sure what Paola's job is, but I think it's something to do with animals.* パオラの仕事が何なのか私には確かではないが, 動物に関係のある仕事だと思う. *'How much do you earn?' 'It's nothing to do with you!'* 「いくら稼いでいるのですか」「あなたには関係のないことです」

**could do with sth** ▶定義 to want or need sth ~が欲しい, または必要だ→~が欲しい, 必要である, あるとよい ‖ *I could do with a holiday.* 私は休暇が欲しい.

**how do you do?** ⇒ **HOW**

**make do with sth** ⇒ **MAKE**¹

句動詞 **do away with sth** ▶定義 to get rid of sth ~を取り除く→~を廃止・廃絶する, やめる, 破壊する ‖ *Most European countries have done away with their royal families.* ヨーロッパの大部分の国では, 王室を廃止している.

**do sb out of sth** ▶定義 to prevent sb having sth in an unfair way; to cheat sb 不正な方法で, ~が…を持つことを妨げる; ~をだます→(金・機会・職場などを)~からだまして取り上げる・奪う ‖ *They've done me out of my share of the money!* 彼らは私の取り分のお金をだまし取った.

**do sth up** ▶定義1 to fasten a piece of clothing 衣服を留める→(ボタン・靴ひも・衣服などを)を留める ‖ *Hurry up. Do up your jacket and we can go!* 急いで. 上着のボタンを掛けなさい, そうすれば出掛けられるのよ. ▶定義2 to repair a building and make it more modern 建物を修理して, より現代風にする→~の手入れをする, 修理する, 改装する ‖ *They're doing up the old cottage.* 彼らは古い別荘を改装しているところだ.

**do without (sth)** ▶定義 to manage without having sth ~なしで, 何とかする→~なしで済ます, やっていく ‖ *If there isn't any coffee left, we'll just have to do without.* コーヒーが少しも残っていないなら, なしで何とか済ませなければならないでしょう.

**do**³ /duː/ 名 ⓒ ( 複 **dos** /duːz/) 英 略式 ▶定義 a party or other social event パーティーまたはほかの社交的な出来事→宴会, パーティー, 催し ‖ *We're having a bit of a do to celebrate Tim's birthday.* ティムの誕生日を祝うちょっとしたパーティーがあります.

成句 **dos and don'ts** ▶定義 things that you should and should not do やるべき事とやるべきではない事→すべき事としてはならない事, 規則, 慣例 ‖ *the dos and don'ts of mountain climbing* 登山の規則

**docile** /dóʊsaɪl; dásəl/ 形 ▶定義 (used about a person or animal) quiet and easy to control (人・動物について)物静かで, 扱いやすい→従順な, おとなしい, 扱いやすい

**dock**¹ /dɑk/ 名 ▶定義1 ⓒⓤ an area of a port where ships stop to be loaded, repaired, etc 荷が積まれる, または修理されることなどが目的で, 船が停泊する港内の場所→船着き場, 埠頭(ふとう), 波止場, ドック ▶定義2 **docks** [複数扱い] a group of docks with all the buildings, offices, etc that are around them 周辺の建物, 事務所などをすべて含んだ, 複数の埠頭の一帯→港湾, 港湾施設, ドック地帯 ‖ *He works down at the docks.* 彼はドック地帯で働いている. ▶定義3 [ⓒ, 通常は単数] the place in a court of law where the person who is accused sits or stands 告訴されている人が座るまたは立つ, 司法裁判所内の場所→(刑事法廷の)被告席 ▶定義4 米 =**LANDINGSTAGE**

**dock**² /dɑk/ 動 ▶定義1 🇬🇧ⓤ (used about a ship) to sail into a port and stop at the dock (船について)入港してドックに停泊する→(船が)ドックに入る; (船を)ドックに入れる ‖ *The ship had docked/was docked at Lisbon.* その船はリスボンでドックに入った. ▶定義2 ⓤ to take away part of the money sb earns, especially as a punishment 特に罰として, ~が稼いだお金の一部を引く→(賃金など)を減らす, (一部)を差し引く, 人から(給料などを)さっ引く ‖ They've *docked £20 off my wages because I was late.* 私が遅刻したため,彼らは私の給料から20ポンドを差し引いた.

***doctor**[1] /dáktər/ [名] ([略] **Dr**) ▶定義1 [C] a person who has been trained in medicine and who treats people who are ill 医学の教育を受け,病気の人々を治療する人→**医者,医師** ‖ *Our family doctor is Dr Young.* 私たちの掛かり付けの医者は,ヤング先生です. *I've got a doctor's appointment at 10 o'clock.* 私は10時に医者の予約をしている.

➤ doctor(医者)はpatient(患者)をsee(診察する)またはtreat(治療する)と言う.また治療法またはmedicine(薬)をprescribe(処方する)こともある.これはprescription(処方せん)に書かれる.

▶定義2 **the doctor's**[単数扱い] the place where a doctor sees his/her patients; a doctor's surgery 医者が患者を診察する場所; 医師の診察室→**診療所,医院** ‖ *I'm going to the doctor's today.* 今日私は医者に行くつもりだ. ▶定義3 [C] a person who has got the highest degree from a university (doctorate) 総合大学から最高位の学位(博士号)を取得した人→**博士,博士号** ‖ *a Doctor of Philosophy* 博士号

> **➤語法**
>
> **ear, nose, throat で耳鼻科**
>
> 耳鼻咽喉(いんこう)科医は正式には otolaryngologist ですが, ear, nose, throat の頭文字を取って ENT doctor と呼ぶことが一般的です.眼科医の場合も, oculistよりもeye doctor が好まれます.

**doctor**[2] /dáktər/ [動][他] ▶定義1 to change sth that should not be changed in order to gain an advantage 有利な立場を得るために,変えるべきではない～を変える→**(文章など)を勝手に書き換える,～に手を加える,改ざんする** ‖ *The results of the survey had been doctored.* 調査結果は改ざんされていた. ▶定義2 to add sth harmful to food or drink 食物または飲料に有害な～を加える→**～に混ぜ物をする,薬を入れる,毒を盛る**

**doctorate** /dáktərət/ [名] [C] ▶定義 the highest university degree 総合大学での最高位の学位→**博士号**

**doctrine** /dáktrən/ [名] [C] [U] ▶定義 a set of beliefs that is taught by a church, political party, etc 教会,政党などで教えられる一連の信条→**教義,主義**

***document** /dákjəmənt/ [名] [C] ▶定義 an official piece of writing which gives information, proof or evidence 情報,証拠または根拠を示す,公式の文書→**文書,書類,証書** ‖ *Her solicitor asked her to read and sign a number of documents.* 事務弁護士は,彼女にいくつかの文書を読んで署名するように求めた.

**documentary** /dàkjəmént(ə)ri/ [名] [C] ([複] **documentaries**) ▶定義 a film or television or radio programme that gives facts or information about a particular subject 特定のテーマについての事実または情報を伝える,映画あるいはテレビまたはラジオの番組→**(映画・テレビなどの)記録作品,ドキュメンタリー** ‖ *Did you see that documentary on Sri Lanka?* スリランカに関するあのドキュメンタリーを見ましたか.

**doddle** /dádl/ [名][単数扱い] [英][略式] ▶定義 something that is very easy to do 非常に簡単に行えるもの→**簡単な仕事,とても簡単な事** ‖ *The exam was an absolute doddle!* 試験は全く簡単なものだった.

**dodge**[1] /dadʒ/ [動] ▶定義1 [自][他] to move quickly in order to avoid sb/sth ～を避けるために敏速に動く→**(～を)さっとよける,(～から)身をかわす** ‖ *I had to dodge between the cars to cross the road.* 道路を横切るために,車の間をさっとよけなければならなかった. ▶定義2 [他] to avoid doing sth that you should do すべき～を避ける→**(義務・困難など)をうまく逃れる,(質問など)をはぐらかす** ‖ *Don't try to dodge your responsibilities!* 責任逃れをしようとするな.

**dodge**[2] /dadʒ/ [名] [C] [略式] ▶定義 a clever way of avoiding sth ～を避けるためのずる賢いやり方→**(税金などの)ごまかし,言い逃れ,逃げ口上** ‖ *The man had been involved in a massive tax dodge.* その男は,巨額な税金逃れに関係していた.

**dodgy** /dádʒi/ [形] (**dodgier**; **dodgiest**) [英][略式] ▶定義 involving risk; not honest or not to be trusted 危険を伴う; 正直でない,または信頼されない→**危険な,ずるい,信頼のおけない** ‖ *a dodgy business deal* リスクの大きい商取引 *This meat* *looks a bit dodgy - when did we buy it?* この肉は少し傷んでいるように見えるよ－いつ買ったんだっけ.

**doe** /dóʊ/ 名 C ▶定義 the female of certain types of animal (deer and rabbits) 特定の種の動物(シカとウサギ)の雌→(シカ・ウサギなどの)雌 ☞参 deer の注とさし絵

**does** ⇒ DO

**doesn't** DOES NOT の短縮形

★**dog**¹ /dɔ́(:)g, dάg/ 名 C ▶定義 **1** an animal that many people keep as a pet, or for working on farms, hunting, etc ペットとして，あるいは農場または狩りなどで働かせるために，多くの人々が飼う動物→犬

▶ dog(犬) は bark(ほえる), growl(うなる), または whine(哀れっぽく鳴く) と言う. うれしがっている様子は wag(尾を振る) と表現する.

▶定義 **2** a male dog or other animal (fox) 犬またはほかの動物(キツネ)の雄→雄犬, (オオカミ・キツネなどの)雄

**dog**² /dɔ́(:)g, dάg/ 動 他 (**dogging**; **dogged**) ▶定義 to follow sb closely ぴったりと~の後に付いていく→~の後を追う，~を尾行する，(不幸・天災などが)~に付いて回る ‖ *A shadowy figure was dogging their every move.* はっきりしない人影が，彼らの一挙一動を追っていた. (比喩) *Bad luck and illness have dogged her career from the start.* 不運と病気が，彼女の仕事に最初から付きまとっていた.

**dog collar** 名 C 略式 ▶定義 a white collar that is worn by priests in the Christian church キリスト教の教会で聖職者が身に着ける白いえり→(首の後ろで留める)聖職者用カラー, (牧師の)白い立ちカラー

**dog-eared** 形 ▶定義 (used about a book or piece of paper) in bad condition with untidy corners and edges because it has been used a lot (本または紙について) 何度となく使われたために，角または縁がくちゃくちゃでひどい状態の→ページ・紙の隅が折れた

**dogged** /dɔ́(:)gəd, dάg-/ 形 ▶定義 refusing to give up even when sth is difficult ~が困難なときでも，あきらめることを拒んでいる→(人・行為が)不屈の，執拗(しつよう)な ‖ *I was impressed by his dogged determination to succeed.* 成功しようとする彼の不屈の決意に感銘を受けた. — **doggedly** 副→執拗に, 頑固に ‖ *She doggedly refused all offers of help.* 彼女は頑固に，すべての援助の申し出を拒んだ.

**dogma** /dɔ́(:)gmə, dάg-/ 名 C U ▶定義 a belief or set of beliefs that people are expected to accept as true without questioning 疑いのない事実として人々が受け入れると思われる信条または一連の信条→(教会などが定めた)教義, 信条

**dogmatic** /dɔ(:)gmǽtɪk, dɑg-/ 形 ▶定義 being certain that your beliefs are right and that others should accept them, without considering other opinions or evidence ほかの意見または証拠を考慮に入れないで，自分の考えが正しく，ほかの人はそれを受け入れるべきだと確信している→独断的な, 教条主義的な — **dogmatically** /-k(ə)li/ 副→独断的に, 教義的に

**dogsbody** /dɔ́(:)gzbὰdi, dάgz-/ 名 C (複 **dogsbodies**) 英 略式 ▶定義 a person who has to do the boring or unpleasant jobs that no one else wants to do and who is considered less important than other people ほかのだれもやりたがらない退屈な，または嫌な仕事をしなければならない人で，しかもほかの人々に比べて重要ではないと思われている人→雑用係, 下働き, 下っ端

**doldrums** /dɔ́(:)ldrəmz, dάl-/ 名 [複数扱い] 成句 **in the doldrums** ▶定義 **1** not active or busy 活気がない，または活発でない→(活動が)沈滞して, 不活発で ‖ *Business has been in the doldrums recently.* 最近，商売は落ち込んでいる. ▶定義 **2** sad or unhappy 悲しい，または不幸な→ふさぎ込んで

**dole**¹ /dóʊl/ 動 略式 句動詞 **dole sth out** ▶定義 to give sth, especially food, money, etc in small amounts to a number of people ~, 特に食物, お金などを少しずつ何人かの人々に与える→~を少しずつ分けてやる

**the dole**² /dóʊl/ 名 [単数扱い] 英 略式 ▶定義 money that the State gives every week to people who are unemployed 失業している人々に国が毎週支給するお金→失業手当 ‖ *I lost my job and had to go on the dole.* 私は職を失い，失業手当を受けなくてはならなかった.

**doleful** /dóʊlfʊl, -f(ə)l/ 形 ▶定義 sad or unhappy 悲しい，または不幸な→悲しみに沈ん

だ, 痛ましい, 陰うつな ‖ She looked at him with doleful eyes. 彼女は悲しみに沈んだ目で彼を見た. — **dolefully** /-fʊli, -f(ə)li/ 副 ➡悲しみに沈んで, 悲しげに

**doll** /dɑl, dɔːl/ 名 C ▶定義 a child's toy that looks like a small person or a baby 小さな人間または赤ん坊に似ている, 子供のおもちゃ➡人形

★**dollar** /dάlər/ 名 ▶定義 1 C (記号 $) a unit of money in some countries, for example the US, Canada and Australia いくつかの国々, 例えば米国, カナダ, オーストラリア, の貨幣単位➡ドル ☛ 1ドルは100セントである. ▶定義 2 C a note or coin that is worth one dollar 1ドルの価値を持つ紙幣または硬貨➡1ドル紙幣, 1ドル硬貨 ▶定義 3 **the dollar** [単数扱い] the value of the US dollar on international money markets 国際金融市場における米ドルの価値➡(貨幣制度としての)ドル, ドル相場

**dollop** /dάləp/ 名 C 略式 ▶定義 a lump of sth soft, especially food 特に食品の, 柔らかい〜の一塊➡(柔らかいものの)塊, スプーン1杯分, 少量 ‖ a dollop of ice cream アイスクリーム一塊

**dolphin** /dάlfɪn/ 名 C ▶定義 an intelligent animal that lives in the sea and looks like a large fish. Dolphins usually swim in large groups (**schools**). 海に生息し大きな魚に似ている, 知能の高い動物. 通常, 大きな集団(= 群れ)を成して泳ぐ➡イルカ

**domain** /doʊméɪn, də-/ 名 C ▶定義 an area of knowledge or activity 知識または活動の範囲➡(活動・関心・学問の)範囲, 分野 ‖ I don't know - that's outside my domain. 分かりません — それは私の専門外です. This issue is now in the public domain (= the public knows about it). この問題は今では一般的に既知の事柄です(= 一般の人々がこれについて知っている).

**dome** /dóʊm/ 名 C ▶定義 a round roof on a building 建物の上の丸い屋根➡ドーム, (半球状の)丸屋根, 丸天井 ‖ the dome of St Paul's in London ロンドンのセントポール大聖堂の丸屋根

★**domestic** /dəméstɪk/ 形 ▶定義 1 not international; only within one country 国際的ではない; 一国の中だけの➡国内の, 自国の ‖ domestic flights 国内便 domestic affairs/politics 国内の事件・国内政治 ▶定義 2 (名詞の前だけ) connected with the home or family 家庭または家族に関する➡家庭の, 家事の ‖ domestic chores/tasks 家事 the growing problem of **domestic violence** (= violence between members of the same family) 増大する家庭内暴力(= 同一家族の成員の間での暴力) domestic water/gas/electricity supplies 家庭への水道・ガス・電気の供給 ▶定義 3 (used about animals) kept as pets or on farms; not wild (動物について)ペットとして, または農場で飼われている; 野生ではない➡飼いならされた ‖ domestic animals such as cats, dogs and horses 猫, 犬または馬のような, 飼いならされた動物 ▶定義 4 (used about a person) enjoying doing things in the home, such as cooking and cleaning (人について)料理や掃除のような, 家の中の事をするのを楽しんでいる➡家庭的な, 家事が好きな

**domesticated** /dəméstɪkèɪtəd/ 形 ▶定義 1 (used about animals) happy being near people and being controlled by them (動物について)人のそばにいて, 人に管理されていることで幸せな➡家畜化した ▶定義 2 (used about people) able to do or good at cleaning the house, cooking, etc (人々について)家の掃除, 料理などができる, または得意な➡家事に慣れた, 家庭的な ‖ Men are expected to be much more domesticated nowadays. 今日では, 男性は以前よりも家庭的であることが期待される.

**dominance** /dάm(ə)nəns/ 名 U ▶定義 control or power 支配または権力➡支配, 統治, 優勢 ‖ Japan's dominance of the car industry 自動車業界での日本の優勢

**dominant** /dάm(ə)nənt/ 形 ▶定義 more powerful, important or noticeable than others 他よりもっと力強い, 重要なまたは顕著な➡支配的な, 権力を握った, 優位を占めている ‖ His mother was the dominant influence in his life. 母親は, 彼の人生を支配するほどの影響を及ぼした.

**dominate** /dάmənèɪt/ 動 ▶定義 1 自 他 to be more powerful, important or noticeable than others 他よりもっと力強い, 重要または顕著である➡支配する, 優勢である; 〜を支配する, 〜の優位に立つ ‖ The Italian team dominated throughout the second half of the game. 試合の後半戦は, イタリアチームが終始優位に進めた. She always tends to dominate the conversation. 彼女はいつも話し合いを仕切る傾向がある.

## 494　domineering

▶定義2 ⓤ(used about a building or place) to be much higher than everything else(建物または場所について)ほかのすべてより抜きんでて高い→~を見下ろす, ~にそびえたつ ‖ *The cathedral dominates the area for miles around.* 大聖堂は, 周囲何マイルにもわたった地域を見下ろしている. — **domination** /dὰmənéɪʃ(ə)n/ 名 ⓤ→支配, 統治, 優勢

**domineering** /dὰməníərɪŋ/ 形 ▶定義 having a very strong character and wanting to control other people とても激しい性格で, ほかの人々を支配したがっている→ごう慢な, 威圧的な, 威張り散らす

**dominion** /dəmínjən/ 名 正式 ▶定義1 ⓤ the power to rule and control 統治および支配する権力→統治権, 主権, 支配 ‖ *to have dominion over an area* 地域全体の統治権を握る ▶定義2 Ⓒ an area controlled by one government or ruler 1つの政府または1人の統治者に支配される地域→領土, 領地 ‖ *the dominions of the Roman empire* ローマ帝国の領土

**dominoes**

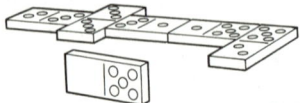

**domino** /dάmənòʊ/ 名 Ⓒ ( 複 **dominoes** ) ▶定義 one of a set of small flat pieces of wood or plastic, marked on one side with two groups of spots representing numbers, that are used for playing a game (dominoes) 片面には2組の数字を表す点が付いた, ゲーム(ドミノ)をするために使われる, 木またはプラスチックでできた小さくて平らなものの一組→ドミノ牌(はい), ドミノ

**donate** /dóʊneɪt, -´-/ 動 ⓣ ▶定義 **donate sth (to sb/sth)** to give money or goods to an organization, especially one for people or animals who need help ある団体, 特に援助を必要としている人々または動物のための団体に, お金または物を与える→~を寄付する, 寄贈する ‖ *She donated a large sum of money to Cancer Research.* 彼女はがん研究基金にばく大なお金を寄付した.

**donation** /doʊnéɪʃ(ə)n/ 名 Ⓒ ▶定義 money, etc that is given to a person or an organization such as a charity, in order to help people or animals in need 必要としている人々または動物を援助するために, 人または慈善団体のような組織に与えられるお金など→寄付金, 寄贈品

**done**¹ **DO**²の過去分詞形

★**done**² /dʌn/ 形 ( 名詞の前は不可 ) ▶定義1 finished 終えた→(人・物事が)済んだ, (人が)終えた, (人と)関係を絶った ‖ *I've got to go out as soon as this job is done.* この仕事が済み次第, 出掛けなければならない. ▶定義2 (used about food) cooked enough(食べ物について)十分調理されている→煮えた, 焼き上がった ‖ *The meat's ready but the vegetables still aren't done.* 肉の用意はできたのだが, 野菜がまだ煮えていない.

成句 **over and done with** ▶定義 completely finished; in the past 完全に終わった; 過去に→(嫌な事が)すっかり終わって, すっかり済んで, 今は大したことではない, もう済んだことで

**done**³ /dʌn/ 間 ▶定義 used for saying that you accept an offer 申し出を受けることを言うために用いて→よろしい, よしきた, 承知した ‖ *'I'll give you twenty pounds for it.' 'Done!'* 「それに20ポンドを出そう」「承知した」

**donkey**

**donkey** /dάŋki, dʌ́ŋ-, ＊dɔ́ːŋ-/ 名 Ⓒ ( または **ass**) ▶定義 an animal like a small horse, with long ears 長い耳を持つ, 小さな馬に似た動物→ロバ

成句 **donkey's years** 英 略式 ▶定義 a very long time とても長い時間→非常に長い間, 随分長い間 ‖ *They've been going out together for donkey's years.* 彼らは随分長い間, 交際している.

**donor** /dóʊnər, -nɔːr/ 名 Ⓒ ▶定義1 a person who gives blood or a part of his/her own body for medical use 医学的な使用のために, 自分の血液または身体の一部を提供する人→提供者, ドナー ‖ *a blood/kidney donor* 血液・腎臓(じんぞう)の提供者 ▶定義2 somebody who gives money or goods to an organization that helps people or animals 人々または動物を援助する団体に, お金または品物を寄付する人→寄付者, 寄贈者

**don't** ⇒ **DO**

**doodle** /dúːdl/ 動自 ▶定義 to draw lines, patterns, etc without thinking, especially when you are bored 特に退屈なときに、何も考えずに線、模様などを書く→**いたずら書きをする** — doodle 名 C→**いたずら書き**

**doom** /duːm/ 名 U ▶定義 death or a terrible event in the future which you cannot avoid 人には避けられない、将来起こる死または悲惨な出来事→**死, 運命, 悲運の予感** ‖ *a sense of impending doom* (= *that something bad is going to happen*) 差し迫った運命の(= 悪い事が起きようとしている)気配 *Don't listen to her. She's always full of doom and gloom* (= *expecting bad things to happen*). 彼女の言うことを聞くな. 彼女はいつもふさいで悲観してばかりいる(= 悪い事が起こることを予想している). — doomed 形→**(不幸な結果に)運命を定められた, 〜するように運命づけられた, 失敗・破滅する運命にある** ‖ *The plan was doomed from the start.* その計画は最初から失敗する運命にあった.

★**door** /dɔːr/ 名 C ▶定義 1 a piece of wood, glass, etc that you open and close to get in or out of a room, building, car, etc 部屋, 建物, 車などに入るまたは出るために開け閉めする, 木, ガラスなどの1枚→**ドア, 戸, 扉** ‖ *to open/shut/close the door* 戸を開ける・閉める・閉じる *to answer the door* (= *to open the door when sb knocks or rings the bell*) 応対に出る(= 〜がノックしたときやベルを鳴らしたとき, 戸を開ける) *Have you bolted/locked the door?* ドアの差し錠・かぎをかけましたか. *I could hear someone knocking on the door.* だれかがドアをノックしているのが聞こえた. *the front/back door* 玄関・裏口 *the fridge door* 冷蔵庫のドア ☛ S7ページのさし絵 ▶定義 2 the entrance to a building, room, car, etc 建物, 部屋, 車などの入り口→**戸口, 出入り口** ‖ *I looked through the door and saw her sitting there.* 戸口からのぞくと, 彼女がそこに座っているのが見えた.

成句 **(from) door to door** ▶定義 (from) house to house 家(から)家へ→**1軒ごとに, 戸口から戸口へ, (旅行などで)出発地から到着地まで** ‖ *The journey takes about five hours, door to door.* その旅行は, 出発地から到着地まで約5時間かかる. *a door-to-door salesman* (= *a person who visits people in their homes to try and sell them things*) 訪問販売員(= 商品を売ろうとするために, 人々を家まで訪ねる人)

**next door (to sb/sth)** ▶定義 in the next house, room, etc 隣の家, 部屋などに→**隣に[の], 非常に近い** ‖ *Do you know the people who live next door?* 隣に住んでいる人々を知っていますか.

**out of doors** ▶定義 outside 屋外に→**屋外で[に], 戸外で[に・へ], 野外で[へ]** ‖ *Shall we eat out of doors today?* 今日は戸外で食べませんか. ☞類 **outdoors** ⇔ **indoors**

**doorbell** /dɔ́ːrbèl/ 名 C ▶定義 a bell on the outside of a house which you ring when you want to go in 人が中に入りたいときに鳴らす, 家の外に付いているベル→**戸口のベル, ブザー**

**doormat** /dɔ́ːmæt/ 名 C ▶定義 1 a piece of material on the floor in front of a door which you can clean your shoes on before going inside 屋内に入る前に靴をきれいにする, 戸口の前の床に敷かれている1枚の生地→**(玄関前・部屋の前の)靴ぬぐい, ドアマット** ▶定義 2 略式 a person who allows other people to treat him/her badly without complaining 不平も言わないで, ほかの人々にひどい扱いをされるままの人→**ばかにされても文句も言わない人, 意気地なし**

**doorstep** /dɔ́ːrstèp/ 名 C ▶定義 a step in front of a door outside a building 建物の外の, 戸口の前の段→**戸口の段**

成句 **on your/the doorstep** ▶定義 very near to you あなたにとても近い→**(家の)近くに, 面前で** ‖ *The sea was right on our doorstep.* 海はちょうど我が家の目の前だった.

**doorway** /dɔ́ːrwèɪ/ 名 C ▶定義 an opening filled by a door leading into a building, room, etc 建物, 部屋などに通じている, 戸でふさがれた開口部→**戸口, 出入り口** ‖ *She was standing in the doorway.* 彼女は戸口に立っていた.

**dope**¹ /dóʊp/ 名 略式 ▶定義 1 U an illegal drug, especially cannabis or marijuana 違法な薬物で, 特に大麻またはマリファナ→**麻薬, (スポーツ選手などの違法な)興奮剤** ▶定義 2 C a stupid person 愚かな人→**ばか, 間抜け** ‖ *What a dope!* 何て間抜けなんだ.

**dope**² /dóʊp/ 動 他 ▶定義 to give a drug secretly to a person or animal, especially to make them sleep 特に眠らせるため, ひそかに人または動物

に麻薬を与える→(スポーツ選手・競走馬などに)に麻薬を与える, (食物・飲料)に麻薬・睡眠薬を混ぜる

**dopey** /dóupi/ 形 ▶定義1 tired and not able to think clearly, especially because of drugs, alcohol or lack of sleep 特に麻薬, 酒または睡眠不足などが理由で, 疲れていて明確に考えることができない→意識がもうろうとした, ぼーっとした ▶定義2 略式 stupid; not intelligent 愚かな; 頭が良くない→愚かな, 間抜けな

**dormant** /dɔ́ːmənt/ 形 ▶定義 not active for some time しばらくの間活動しない→(一時的に)活動を休止した, (動物が)冬・夏眠中の, (能力などが)潜在している ‖ *a dormant volcano* 休火山

**dormitory** /dɔ́ːmət(ə)ri; -tɔ̀ːri/ 名 C (複 **dormitories**) (または **dorm**) ▶定義1 a large bedroom with a number of beds in it, especially in a school, etc 特に学校などで, たくさんのベッドがある広い寝室→(寄宿舎・ユースホステルなどの)共同寝室 ▶定義2 米 a building at a college or university where students live 学生が住む, 単科大学または総合大学内の建物→学生寮, 寄宿舎

**dosage** /dóusɪdʒ/ 名 [C, 通常は単数] ▶定義 the amount of a medicine you should take over a period of time ある期間にわたって服用すべき薬の量→1回分の投薬量 ‖ *The recommended dosage is one tablet every four hours.* 4時間ごとに1錠を服用してください.

**dose**¹ /dóus/ 名 C ▶定義1 an amount of medicine that you take at one time 1回に服用する薬の量→1服, 服用量 ‖ *You should take a large dose of this cough medicine before going to bed.* 寝る前にこのせき止め薬の多量な1服を, 服用されると良いですよ. ☞参 **overdose** ▶定義2 an amount of sth, especially sth unpleasant ~, 特に嫌な~の量→(特に嫌な事の体験の)1回分, 一定量 ‖ *a dose of the flu* 1回引いた風邪 *I can only stand him in small doses.* 彼とは短い時間だけなら耐えられる.

**dose**² /dóus/ 動他 ▶定義 to give sb/yourself a medicine or drug ~または自分自身に医薬品または麻薬を与える→~を投薬する, 服用させる ‖ *She dosed herself with aspirin and went to work.* 彼女はアスピリンを飲み, 仕事に行った.

**doss** /dɑs/ 動 英 (俗語)

句動詞 **doss down** ▶定義 to lie down to sleep, without a proper bed まともなベッドなしで, 横になって寝る→(仮の場所で)寝る ‖ *Do you mind if I doss down on your floor tonight?* 今夜, 君のうちの床で寝ても構わないかな.

**doss about/around** ▶定義 to waste time not doing very much ほとんど何もせずに時間を無駄にする→何もしないで過ごす ‖ *We just dossed about in class yesterday.* 昨日私たちは授業中, ただ何もしないで過ごした.

★**dot**¹ /dɑt/ 名 C ▶定義1 a small, round mark, like a full stop 終止符と同様の小さな円い記号→点, ピリオド, 小数点, 玉の模様 ‖ *a white dress with black dots* 黒い水玉の白いドレス *The letters i and j have dots above them.* iとjの文字の上には, 点が付いている.

▶電子メールアドレスを言うとき, dot(ドット)を使う. ann@smithuni.co.ukと書かれたアドレスを, 「annアットsmithuniドットco ドットuk」と読むことがある.

▶定義2 something that looks like a dot 点のように見えるもの→小さい物, 小片, 少量 ‖ *He watched until the aeroplane was just a dot in the sky.* 飛行機が大空のほんの小さな点になるまで, 彼はじっと見ていた.

成句 **on the dot** 略式 ▶定義 at exactly the right time or at exactly the time mentioned 正しい時間ちょうどに, または言及された時間ちょうどに→時間通りに, きっかりに ‖ *Lessons start at 9 o'clock on the dot.* 授業は9時きっかりに始まる.

**dot**² /dɑt/ 動 (**dotting**; **dotted**) (通常は受動態で) ▶定義 to mark with a dot 点を印す→~に点を打つ, ~を点線で示す

成句 **be dotted about/around** ▶定義 to be spread over an area ある範囲に広がっている→~に点在する, ~を散在させる ‖ *There are restaurants dotted about all over the centre of town.* レストランは街の中心部の至る所に点在している.

**be dotted with** ▶定義 to have several things or people in or on it その中またはそこにいくつかの物または人々がいる→~に点在する ‖ *a hillside dotted with sheep* 羊が点在する丘の斜面

**dote** /dóut/ 動 自 ▶定義 **dote on sb/sth** to have or show a lot of love for sb/sth and think he/she/it is perfect ~にたっぷりの愛情を持って, または表して, その~が完ぺきだと思う→溺

愛(できあい)する,見境なくかわいがる ‖ *He's always doted on his eldest son.* 彼はずっと長男を溺愛してきた.— **doting** 形 ➔ 溺愛している,子ぼんのうな,親ばかの ‖ *doting parents* 親ばか

**dotted line** 名 ▶定義 a line of small round marks (dots) which show where sth is to be written on a form, etc 書式などで何かが書かれる場所を示す,小さな円い記号(点) ➔ **点線** ‖ *Sign on the dotted line.* 点線の上に署名をしてください. ☞ **line** のさし絵

*★**double**¹ /dʌ́b(ə)l/ 形 ▶定義 1 twice as much or as many (as usual) (通常の)量または数の2倍 ➔ **(数量・大きさ・価値などが)2倍の,倍の** ‖ *His income is double hers.* 彼の収入は彼女の2倍だ. *We'll need double the amount of wine.* 私たちには,2倍の量のワインが必要になるよ. ▶定義 2 having two equal or similar parts 2つの同等なまたは類似した部分を持っている ➔ **二重の,複(式)の,対になった** ‖ *double doors* 二重扉 *Does 'necessary' have (a) double 's'?* necessary には二連続のsがありますか. *My phone number is two four double three four (= 24334).* 私の電話番号は2,4,3が2つ,4(= 24334)です. ▶定義 3 made for or used by two people or things 2人または2つの物のために,あるいは2人または2つの物で使うように作られた ➔ **2人用の,2つ用の** ‖ *a double garage* 2台用の車庫 ☞参 **bed**¹ の注

*★**double**² /dʌ́b(ə)l/ 副 ▶定義 in twos or two parts 2つにまたは2つの部分に ➔ **二重に,2人で,対を成して** ‖ *When I saw her with her twin sister I thought I was seeing double.* 彼女とその双子の姉を一緒に見た時,二重に見えているのかと思った.

*★**double**³ /dʌ́b(ə)l/ 名 ▶定義 1 ❶ twice the (usual) number or amount (通常の)数または量の2倍 ➔ **2倍(の数量),2倍のもの** ‖ *When you work overtime, you get paid double.* 残業をすると,倍額が支払われる. ▶定義 2 ❷ a glass of strong alcoholic drink containing twice the usual amount 通常の量の2倍の酒が入った,グラス1杯の強い酒 ➔ **ダブル** ▶定義 3 ❷ a person who looks very much like another 別の人にとてもよく似ている人 ➔ **よく似た人,生き写し** ‖ *I thought it was you I saw in the supermarket. You must have a double.* スーパーで見掛けた人は,君だと思ったよ.君にとてもよく似た人がいるに違いないね. ▶定義 4 ❷ an actor who replaces another actor in a film to do dangerous or other special things 映画で,危険なまたはほかの特別な事を行うために,別の俳優の代わりをする俳優 ➔ **代役,替え玉** ▶定義 5 ❷ a bedroom for two people in a hotel, etc ホテルなどの2人用の寝室 ➔ **2人部屋,ツイン・ダブルルーム** ☞参 **single**²(3) ▶定義 6 **doubles** [複数扱い] (in some sports, for example tennis) with two pairs playing (いくつかのスポーツ,例えばテニスで)2組のペアの競技で ➔ **ダブルス(の試合)** ‖ *the Men's Doubles final* 男子ダブルスの決勝 ☞参 **single**²(4)

*★**double**⁴ /dʌ́b(ə)l/ 動 ▶定義 1 ❶ ⓗ to become or to make sth twice as much or as many; to multiply by two 〜の量または数が2倍になる,または2倍にする;2を掛ける ➔ **2倍になる,倍加・倍増する;〜を2倍にする** ‖ *The price of houses has almost doubled.* 住宅の価格は約2倍になった. *Think of a number and double it.* 数を思い浮かべ,それを2倍しなさい. ▶定義 2 ❶ double (up) as sth to have a second use or function 2つ目の用途または機能を持つ ➔ **二役を演じる・務める,兼ねる** ‖ *The small room doubles (up) as a study.* その小部屋は書斎も兼ねる.

**句動詞** **double (sb) up/over** ▶定義 (to cause sb) to bend the body (〜が)体を曲げる(原因となる) ➔ **〜の体を折り曲げさせる** ‖ *to be doubled up with pain/laughter* 痛みで・笑いで体を折り曲げる

**double bass** (または **bass**) 名 ❷ ▶定義 the largest musical instrument with strings, that you can play either standing up or sitting down 立ってまたは座って演奏できる,弦の付いた最も大きな楽器 ➔ **ダブルベース,コントラバス** ☞参 **piano** の注 ☞ **music** のさし絵

**double-breasted** 形 ▶定義 (used about a coat or jacket) having two rows of buttons down the front (コートまたは上着について)前面の下側にボタンが縦に2列に付いている ➔ **ダブルの,二重ボタンの**

**double-check** 動 ❶ ⓗ ▶定義 to check sth again, or with great care 〜をもう一度,または十分に注意して確かめる ➔ **再確認する,再点検する**

**double-cross** 動 ⓗ ▶定義 to cheat sb who

believes that he/she can trust you after you have agreed to do sth dishonest together あなたが不正な~を一緒にやると同意した後、あなたを信用できると信じている…をだます➡~を裏切る、だます

**double-decker** 名 C ▶定義 a bus with two floors 2つの階があるバス➡**2階建てバス**

**double Dutch** 名 U ▶定義 conversation or writing that you cannot understand at all 人が全く理解できない会話または文章➡**ちんぷんかんぷんな言葉・文章, ナンセンス** ‖ *The listening comprehension in the exam was really hard. It all sounded like double Dutch to me!* 聞き取りの試験は本当に難しかった。私にはすべてがちんぷんかんぷんだった。

**double figures** 名 U ▶定義 a number that is more than nine 9より多い数➡**2けた台(の数)** ‖ *Inflation is now in double figures.* インフレ率は現在2けた台だ。

**double glazing** 名 U ▶定義 two layers of glass in a window to keep a building warm or quiet 建物の温かさまたは静けさを保つために、2層になった窓ガラス➡**二重ガラス, 二重窓** — double-glazed 形➡二重ガラスの, 二重窓の

**doubly** /dʌ́b(ə)li/ 副 ▶定義 1 in two ways 2つのやり方で➡**二様に, 2つの点で** ‖ *He was doubly blessed with both good looks and talent.* 彼は外見の良さと才能という2つの点で恵まれていた。▶定義 2 more than usually 普通より多く➡**普段の倍** ‖ *I made doubly sure that the door was locked.* ドアにかぎがかかっているか、私は念には念を入れて確かめた。

★**doubt**¹ /dáʊt/ 名 C U ▶定義 doubt (about sth); doubt that...; doubt as to sth (a feeling of) uncertainty 不確実(の感情)➡**疑い, 疑惑, 不信** ‖ *If you have any doubts about the job, feel free to ring me and discuss them.* 仕事について疑問な点があれば、遠慮なく私に電話して、それについて話し合いましょう。*There's some doubt that Jan will pass the exam.* ジャンが試験に受かるかどうかは少し疑問だ。

成句 cast doubt on sth ⇒ **CAST**¹
give sb the benefit of the doubt ⇒ **BENEFIT**¹
in doubt ▶定義 not sure or definite はっきりしない、または確かでない➡**疑って, 不確かで, 迷って**
no doubt ▶定義 (used when you expect sth to happen but you are not sure that it will) probably (~が起こることを予想しているが、そうなるかどうか確信を持っていないときに用いて)多分➡**多分, おそらく** ‖ *No doubt she'll write when she has time.* 時間があれば、多分彼女は手紙を書くでしょう。
without (a) doubt ▶定義 definitely 明確に➡**疑いもなく, 確かに** ‖ *It was, without doubt, the coldest winter for many years.* 確かに、ここ何年もの間で最も寒い冬でした。

★**doubt**² /dáʊt/ 動 他 ▶定義 to think sth is unlikely or to feel uncertain (about sth) ~がありそうにないと思う、または(~について)疑わしいと感じる➡**~を疑う, 疑問に思う** ‖ *She never doubted that he was telling the truth.* 彼が真実を話しているということを、彼女は一度も疑ったことがなかった。*He had never doubted her support.* 彼は彼女の支持を疑ったことは決してなかった。

**doubtful** /dáʊtfəl, -f(ə)l/ 形 ▶定義 1 unlikely or uncertain ありそうもない、または疑わしい➡**疑わしい, あいまいな, 不確かな** ‖ *It's doubtful whether/if we'll finish in time.* 私たちが時間までに終わるかどうかは疑わしい。*It was doubtful that he was still alive.* 彼がまだ生きているかどうかは不確かだった。▶定義 2 doubtful (about sth/about doing sth) (used about a person) not sure (人について)確信していない➡**疑いを持っている, 迷っている** ‖ *He still felt doubtful about his decision.* 彼は自分の決断に、まだ迷いを感じていた。— doubtfully /-fʊli, -f(ə)li/ 副 ➡**疑わしげに, 疑問の余地があるが** ‖ *'I suppose it'll be all right,' she said doubtfully.* 「大丈夫だと思います」と、彼女は疑わしげに言った。

**doubtless** /dáʊtləs/ 副 ▶定義 almost certainly ほぼ確実に➡**おそらく, 多分, きっと** ‖ *Doubtless she'll have a good excuse for being late!* きっと彼女には、遅れていることへのうまい言い訳があるのよ。

**dough** /dóʊ/ 名 U ▶定義 1 a mixture of flour, water, etc used for baking into bread, etc パンなどを焼くための、小麦粉、水などを混ぜたもの➡**生地, こね粉** ▶定義 2 俗式 money お金➡**お金, 現ナマ**

**doughnut** (米 **donut**) /dóʊnət/ 名 C ▶定義 a small cake in the shape of a ball or a ring, made from a sweet dough cooked in very hot oil 甘い生地から作られ, 非常に熱い油で調理される, ボールまたは輪の形をした小さなケーキ→ドーナツ ☞ **cake**のさし絵

**dour** /dʊər, dáʊ(ə)r/ 形 ▶定義 (used about a person's manner or expression) cold and unfriendly (人の態度または表情について) 冷たくてよそよそしい→気難しい, 陰うつな

**douse** (または **dowse**) /dáʊs/ 動他 ▶定義1 douse sth (with sth) to stop a fire from burning by pouring liquid over it 液体を掛けて燃えている火を消し止める→(火)を消す ‖ *The firefighters managed to douse the flames.* 消防士たちは何とか火災を消し止めた. ▶定義2 douse sb/sth (in/with sth) to cover sb/sth with liquid ~を液体で覆う→~に(液体を)浴びせる, ~を(液体に)浸す ‖ *to douse yourself in perfume* (= wear too much of it) 香水を浴びせる (= 多すぎるほど付ける)

**dove**¹ /dʌv/ 名 C ▶定義 a type of white bird, often used as a sign of peace しばしば平和の象徴として用いられる, 白い鳥の一種→ハト

**dove**² /dóʊv/ 困 **DIVE**¹の過去形

**dowdy** /dáʊdi/ 形 ▶定義 (used about a person or the clothes he/she wears) not attractive or fashionable (人またはその人が着ている衣服について) 魅力的でない, または流行の物ではない→身なりのだらしない, (服装が) 野暮ったい, ぱっとしない

★**down**¹ /dáʊn/ 副前 ▶定義1 to or at a lower level or place; from the top towards the bottom of sth より低い水準または場所へ[で]; ~の最上部から最下部へ→下方へ[に], より低いところへ[に] ‖ *Can you get that book down from the top shelf?* 一番上の棚からあの本を取ってくれますか. *'Where's Mary?' 'She's down in the basement.'* 「メアリーはどこですか」「地下室です」 *Her hair hung down her back.* 彼女は髪を背中にたらしていた. *The rain was running down the window.* 雨が窓に流れ落ちていた. ▶定義2 along 沿って→(道路などに)沿って, (平面な地帯)の向こうへ[に], ~の端に ‖ *We sailed down the river towards the sea.* 私たちは海に向かって川を船で下った. *'Where's the nearest garage?' 'Go down this road and take the first turning on the right.'* 「一番近い自動車修理工場はどこですか」「この道をまっすぐ行って, 最初の角を右に

曲がりなさい」 ▶定義3 from a standing or vertical position to a sitting or horizontal one 立っているまたは垂直な姿勢から, 座っているまたは水平な姿勢へ→直立から水平方向へ, (立っているものを)横にして ‖ *I think I'll sit/lie down.* 座ろうと・横になろうと思います. ▶定義4 to or in the south 南へまたは南で→(地図上で)下に, 南に ‖ *We went down to Devon for our holiday.* 私たちは休暇のためデヴォンへ南下した. ▶定義5 used for showing that the level, amount, strength, etc of sth is less or lower ~の水準, 量, 強さなどがより少ないまたは下がっていることを表すために用いて→下がって, 低いレベルに, より劣悪な状態に ‖ *Do you mind if I turn the heating down a bit?* 暖房を少し弱めても構いませんか. ▶定義6 (文) on paper 紙に(書かれた)→紙に, 書面に ‖ *Put these dates down in your diary.* これらの日付を手帳に書き留めなさい. ▶定義7 down to sb/sth even including 取るに足らないものまでも含まれている→(上から下まで)すっかり, (~に)至るまでも ‖ *We had everything planned down to the last detail.* 私たちは詳細の最後の最後まですべてを計画していた.

成句 be down to sb ▶定義 to be sb's responsibility ~の責任である→~次第である, ~の責任・せいである ‖ *When my father died it was down to me to look after the family's affairs.* 父が死んだ時, 家族のことを面倒見るのは私の責任となった.

be down to sth ▶定義 to have only the amount mentioned left 言及された量だけが残っている→少なくなって~だけになっている ‖ *I need to do some washing - I'm down to my last shirt.* 少し洗濯をする必要がある - 最後のシャツだけになってしまったから.

down and out ▶定義 having no money, job or home お金, 仕事または家がなくて→落ちぶれて, 困窮して

down under 略式 ▶定義 (in) Australia→オーストラリア(で)

**down**² /dáʊn/ 動他 略式 ▶定義 to finish a drink quickly 急いで飲み終える→(飲食物)を平らげる, 飲み干す ‖ *She downed her drink in one* (= she drank the whole glass without stopping). 彼女は酒を一気に飲み干した (= グラスの中身を

全部中断することなく飲んだ).

**down**[3] /dáʊn/ 形 ▶定義1 sad 悲しい→落ち込んだ, 意気消沈した, 悲しい ‖ *You're looking a bit down today.* 今日は少し落ち込んでいるように見えます. ▶定義2 lower than before 以前より低い → 下 (方) に向かう, 下降する ‖ *Unemployment figures are down again this month.* 失業者数は今月もまた下がった.
▶定義3 (used about computers) not working (コンピューターについて) 作動しない→作動しないで, 動かないで, 故障した ‖ *I can't access the file as our computers have been down all morning.* 午前中一杯, コンピューターが動かないので, ファイルにアクセスできない.

**down**[4] /dáʊn/ 名 ❶ ▶定義 very soft feathers とても柔らかい羽毛→(鳥の)綿毛, ダウン ‖ *a duvet filled with duck down* アヒルの綿毛を詰めた羽布団

成句 ups and downs ⇒ **UP**

**down-and-out** 名 ❻ ▶定義 a person who has got no money, job or home お金, 仕事または家のない人→落ちぶれた人, 無一文の人

**downcast** /dáʊnkà:st, -kæ̀st/ 形 ▶定義1 (used about a person) sad and without hope (人について) 悲しくて望みがない→がっかりした, 意気消沈した ▶定義2 (used about eyes) looking down (目について) 下を見ている→(目が) 下を向いた, 伏し目の, (顔が) うつむいた

**downfall** /dáʊnfɔ̀:l/ 名 [単数扱い] ▶定義 a loss of a person's money, power, social position, etc; the thing that causes this 人がお金, 権力, 社会的地位などを失うこと; これを引き起こす物事→身の破滅 (の原因), 転落, 没落, 失脚 ‖ *The government's downfall seemed inevitable.* その政府の失脚は避けられないように思えた. *Greed was her downfall.* 強欲さが彼女の身の破滅を招いた.

**downgrade** /dáʊngrèɪd/ 動他 ▶定義 downgrade sb/sth (from sth) (to sth) to reduce sb/sth to a lower level or position of importance 〜を低い水準または重要度の低い位置まで下げる→〜を格下げする, 降格する, 左遷する ‖ *Tom's been downgraded from manager to assistant manager.* トムは, 支配人から副支配人に降格させられた.

**downhearted** /dàʊnhá:rtəd/ 形 ▶定義 sad 悲しい→落胆した, 沈んだ

**downhill** /dáʊnhíl, (副) ⌣́/ 形 副 ▶定義 (going) in a downward direction; towards the bottom of a hill 下方に (行って); 丘のふもとに向かって→下り坂の, 下方へ; 坂を下って ‖ *It's an easy walk. The road runs downhill most of the way.* 歩くのは楽ですよ. 道のほとんどが下り坂ですから. ⇔ **uphill**

成句 go downhill ▶定義 to get worse 悪くなる→(状況・健康などが) 悪くなる, 衰える ‖ *Their relationship has been going downhill for some time now.* 彼らの関係は, ここしばらく悪くなってきている.

**download** /dáʊnlòʊd/ 動他 ▶定義 to copy a computer file, etc from a large computer system to a smaller one 大きなコンピューターのシステムから小さなコンピューターのシステムに, コンピューターのファイルなどを複写する→(データ) をダウンロードする, 転送する

**downmarket** /dáʊnmà:rkət/ 形 副 ▶定義 cheap and of low quality 値段が安くて品質が悪い→低所得者向けの, 大衆向け, 安っぽい ‖ *a downmarket newspaper* 大衆向けの新聞

**downpour** /dáʊnpɔ̀:r/ 名 ❻ ▶定義 a heavy, sudden fall of rain 突然の豪雨→土砂降り, 豪雨

**downright** /dáʊnràɪt/ 形 (名詞の前だけ) ▶定義 (used about sth bad or unpleasant) complete (悪いまたは不快な物事について) 完全な→徹底的な, あきれるほどの ‖ *The holiday was a downright disaster.* 休日はあきれるほど散々なものだった. ― **downright** 副→徹底的に, 全く ‖ *The way he spoke to me was downright rude!* 彼の私への口のきき方は全く無礼だった.

**downside** /dáʊnsàɪd/ 名 [ ❻, 通常は単数] ▶定義 the disadvantages or negative aspects of sth 〜の不利なまたは否定的な側面→(物事の) 否定的な面, 下降, 悪化 ‖ *All good ideas have a downside.* すべての良い考えにも否定的な面がある.

**Down's syndrome** /dáʊnz sìndroʊm/ 名 ❶ ▶定義 a condition that a person is born with. People with this condition have a flat, wide face and lower than average intelligence. 生まれつきの病気. この病気の人々は幅の広い平べったい顔になり, 平均的な知能よりも低い→ダウン症 (候群)

**downstairs** /dàʊnstéərz (形) ⌒/ 副形 ▶定義 towards or on a lower floor of a house or building 家または建物の下の階へまたは下の階で→**階下の, 1階の; 階下へ[に・で]** ‖ *He fell downstairs and broke his arm.* 彼は階下に落ちて腕を骨折した. *Dad's downstairs, in the kitchen.* お父さんは1階, 台所にいます. *a downstairs toilet* 階下のトイレ⇔**upstairs**

**downstream** /dáʊnstrìːm/ 副 ▶定義 in the direction in which a river flows 川が流れる方向に→**流れを下って, 下流へ[に]** ‖ *We were rowing downstream.* 私たちは下流へこいでいた. ⇔**upstream**

**down-to-earth** 形 ▶定義 (used about a person) sensible, realistic and practical (人について)分別があり, 現実的で実際的な→**(人・行動が)現実的な, 地に足の着いた**

**downtrodden** /dáʊntrɑ̀dn/ 形 ▶定義 (used about a person) made to suffer bad treatment or living conditions by people in power, but being too tired, poor, ill, etc to change this (人について)権力を握る人々からひどい扱いまたはひどい生活状態に耐えることを強いられているが, 過度の疲れ, 貧困, 病気などであるためにこれを変えることができない→**虐げられた, 踏みにじられた**

**downturn** /dáʊntɜ̀ːm/ 名 [通常は単数] ▶定義 *a downturn (in sth)* a drop in the amount of business that is done; a time when the economy becomes weaker 行われる商売の量の下落; 経済がより弱くなるとき→**下降, 悪化** ‖ *a downturn in sales/trade/business* 売り上げ・取り引き・商売の悪化⇔**upturn**

★**downward** /dáʊnwərd/ 形副 (名詞の前だけ) ▶定義 towards the ground or a lower level 地面またはより低い水準に向かって→**下方への, 下向きの; 下の方へ, 下向きに** ‖ *a downward movement* 下方への動き — **downwards** /dáʊnwərdz/ 副 →**下の方へ, 下向きに** ‖ *She laid the picture face downwards on the table.* 彼女は, 絵の表を下に向けてテーブルに置いた. ⇔**upward(s)**

**dowry** /dáʊəri/ 名 ⓒ (複 **dowries**) ▶定義 an amount of money or property which, in some countries, a woman's family gives to the man she is marrying いくつかの国で, 結婚する女性の家族が相手の男性に与える, お金または財産の量→**(新婦の)持参金, (新婦の)財産**

**dowse** = DOUSE

**doz** 略 dozen→ダース, 12個

**doze**¹ /dóʊz/ 動 自 ▶定義 to sleep lightly and/or for a short time 浅くかつ・または短時間眠る→**うたた寝をする, 居眠りする** ‖ *He was dozing in front of the television.* 彼はテレビの前でうたた寝をしていた. — **doze** 名 [単数扱い] →**うたた寝, 居眠り**

句動詞 **doze off** ▶定義 to go to sleep, especially during the day 特に日中に, 寝てしまう→**ふと・思わず居眠りをしてしまう** ‖ *I'm sorry - I must have dozed off for a minute.* すみません — ちょっとうとうとしてしまったようです.

★**dozen** /dʌ́zn/ (略 **doz**) 名 ⓒ (複 **dozen**) ▶定義 twelve or a group of twelve 12または12の一組→**ダース, 12個** ‖ *A dozen eggs, please.* 卵を1ダースお願いします. *half a dozen (= six)* 半ダース(=6) *two dozen sheep* 2ダース(24匹)の羊

成句 **dozens (of sth)** 略式 ▶定義 very many 非常に多くの→**多数, かなりたくさん, 何十もの** ‖ *I've tried phoning her dozens of times.* 私は彼女に何十回も電話をかけてみた.

**dozy** /dóʊzi/ 形 ▶定義 **1** wanting to sleep; not feeling awake 眠りたい; 起きている気がしない→**眠い, 眠たくなるような** ‖ *The wine had made her rather dozy.* ワインのせいで彼女はかなり眠くなった. ▶定義 **2** 医 略式 stupid, not intelligent 愚かな; 頭が良くない→**愚かな, 頭の鈍い** ‖ *You dozy thing - look what you've done!* 間抜けめ — 自分がやった事を見なさい.

**Dr** 略 doctor→〜博士, 〜先生 ‖ *Dr Timothy Woodhouse* ティモシー ウッドハウス博士

**drab** /dræb/ 形 ▶定義 not interesting or attractive 面白くない, または魅力的でない→**面白みのない, 退屈な, さえない** ‖ *a drab grey office building* さえない灰色のオフィスビル

**draft**¹ /drɑːft; dræft/ 名 ⓒ ▶定義 **1** a piece of writing, etc which will probably be changed and improved; not the final version 多分変更されて良くなるであろう, 1つの著作物など; 最終版ではない→**草稿, 下書き** ‖ *the first draft of a speech/essay* 演説・論文の初稿 ▶定義 **2** a written order to a bank to pay money to sb 〜にお金を支払うよう, 銀行に対して書かれた指示→

**draft²**

為替手形, 小切手 || Payment must be made **by bank draft**. 支払いは銀行手形でなければならない. ▶定義3 英 = **DRAUGHT¹**(1)

**draft²** /drɑːft; dræft/ 動 ▶定義1 to make a first or early copy of a piece of writing 1つの書き物の最初の, または初期の原稿を作る → **~の草案を書く, 下書きをする, ~を起草する** || I'll draft a letter and show it to you before I type it. 手紙の下書きをして, それをタイプする前にあなたに見せます. ▶定義2 英(通常は受動態で) to force sb to join the armed forces 軍隊に参加するよう, ~を強制する → **~を徴集する, 召集する, 徴募する** || He was drafted into the army. 彼は軍隊に召集された.

**drafty** 英 = **DRAUGHTY**

★**drag¹** /dræg/ 動 (**dragging**; **dragged**) ▶定義1 他 to pull sb/sth along with difficulty ~を困難を伴って引っ張る → **(やっとのことで)~を引きずる, 引っ張る** || The box was so heavy we had to drag it along the floor. 箱はとても重かったので, 私たちは床の上を引きずらなくてはならなかった. ☞ **pull**のさし絵 ▶定義2 他 to make sb come or go somewhere ~を来させる, またはどこかへ行かせる → **~を(無理やり)引き込む, 引きずり込む, 引っ張り出す** || She's always trying to drag me along to museums and galleries, but I'm not interested. 彼女はいつも私を一緒に美術館や画廊に引っ張り出そうとするが, 私には興味がない. ▶定義3 **drag (on)** to be boring or to seem to last a long time うんざりさせる, または長時間続いているように思える → **(物・事が)ゆっくり進む, だらだら長引く** || The speeches dragged on for hours. いくつもの演説が何時間もだらだらと続いた. ▶定義4 他 (computing) to move sth across the screen of the computer using the mouse (コンピューター) マウスを使って, コンピューターの画面上の~を動かす → **~を(マウスで)ドラッグする** || Click on the file and drag it into the new folder. ファイルをクリックして, 新しいフォルダにドラッグしなさい.

句動詞 **drag sth out** ▶定義 to make sth last longer than necessary ~を必要以上に長く続かせる → **(会議などを)(不必要に)長引かせる** || Let's not drag this decision out - shall we go or not? この決断を長引かせるのはやめよう — 私たちは行くか, それとも行かないか.

**drag sth out (of sb)** ▶定義 to force or persuade sb to give you information 情報をあなたに与えるよう, ~を強制または説得する → **(人から)~を無理やり聞き出す, 引きずり出す**

**drag²** /dræg/ 名 ▶定義1 [単数扱い] 略式 a person or thing that is boring or annoying うんざりさせる, またはいらいらさせる人または物 → **退屈な人, うんざりする物事** || 'The car's broken down.' 'Oh no! What a drag!' 「車が壊れてしまった」「なんだって. 何てことだ」 ▶定義2 U women's clothes worn by a man, especially as part of a show, etc 特にショーなどの一部として, 男性に着られる女性の衣服 → **女装用の服** || men **in drag** 女装した男たち ▶定義3 C an act of breathing in cigarette smoke たばこの煙を吸う行為 → **たばこを吸うこと, 一服** || He took a long drag on his cigarette. 彼はゆっくりとたばこを吸った.

**dragon** /ˈdræɡ(ə)n/ 名 C ▶定義 (in stories) a large animal with wings, which can breathe fire (物語の中で) 火を吐くことができる, 翼のある大きな動物 → **ドラゴン, 竜**

★**drain¹** /dreɪn/ 名 C ▶定義 a pipe or hole in the ground that dirty water, etc goes down to be carried away 汚水などが運び去られるために流れ込む, 地中の管または穴 → **排水管, 排水溝, 下水路** ☞ C7ページのさし絵

成句 **a drain on sb/sth** ▶定義 something that uses up time, money, strength, etc 時間, お金, 力などを使い果たすもの → **~の枯渇・弱体・損失のもと, 流出, 消耗** || The cost of travelling is a great drain on our budget. その旅行費によって, 私たちは家計のほとんどを使い果たしてしまう.

**(go) down the drain** 略式 ▶定義 (to be) wasted 無駄で(ある) → **無駄になって, ふいになって** || All that hard work has gone down the drain. あんなに一生懸命働いたのに, すっかり無駄になった.

★**drain²** /dreɪn/ 動 ▶定義1 自他 to become empty or dry as liquid flows away and disappears; to make sth dry or empty in this way 液体が流れ去って消え, 空になるまたは乾く; そのようにして乾かす → **(容器などが)水分が取れる, 乾く; ~の水気を切る, 水分を取る** || The whole area will have to be drained before it can be used for farming. 農業に利用できるようになる前に, 区域全体の水が乾かなければならない. Drain the pasta and add the sauce. パスタの水気を切り, ソースを加えなさい. ▶定義2 🔵🌐 drain sth (from/out of sth); drain sth (away/off) to flow away; to make a liquid flow away; 液体を流れ去らせる →**はける, 排水される; 〜の排水をする, 〜から(水など)を除く** ‖ *The sink's blocked - the water won't drain away at all.* 洗面台が詰まっている − 水が全然はけない. *The plumber had to drain the water from the heating system.* 配管工は, 暖房装置から水を除かなければならなかった. (比喩) *He felt all his anger begin to drain away.* 彼はすべての怒りが引き始めるのを感じた. ▶定義3 🌐 to drink all the liquid in a glass, cup, etc グラス, カップなどの液体をすべて飲む →**(容器)を空にする, 飲み干す** ‖ *He drained his glass in one gulp.* 彼は一飲みでグラスを空にした. ▶定義4 🌐 drain sb/sth (of sth) to make sb/sth weaker, poorer, etc by slowly using all the strength, money, etc available 使用可能なすべての力, お金などをゆっくりと使っていくことにより, 〜を弱めたり貧しくしたりする →**〜を消耗させる, 使い果たす, 〜から(財産・力など)を奪う** ‖ *My mother's hospital expenses were slowly draining my funds.* 母の入院費用のため, 私の持ち金は徐々になくなっていった. *The experience left her **emotionally drained**.* その経験で彼女は感情的に疲れ果てていった.

**drainage** /dréɪnɪdʒ/ 🟦 🅾 ▶定義 a system used for making water, etc flow away from a place ある場所から水などを流し去らせるために使われる仕組み →**排水施設・設備, 排水, 水はけ**

**draining board** 🟦 🅲 ▶定義 the place in the kitchen where you put plates, cups, knives, etc to dry after washing them 台所で, 洗い終えた皿, カップ, ナイフなどを乾燥させるために置く場所 →**水切り(台)** ☛ C7 ページのさし絵

**drainpipe** /dréɪnpaɪp/ 🟦 🅲 ▶定義 a pipe which goes down the side of a building and carries water from the roof into a hole in the ground (drain) 建物の側面を下向きに伸びていて, 水を屋根から地中の穴(排水管)へ運ぶ管 →**排水管, 下水管** ☛ C7 ページのさし絵

**drama** /drάːmə, drǽmə/ 🟦 ▶定義1 🅲 a play for the theatre, radio or television 劇場, ラジオまたはテレビ用の芝居 →**劇** ‖ *a contemporary drama* 現代劇 ▶定義2 🅾 plays as a form of writing; the performance of plays 文学の形としての演劇; 演劇の公演 →**戯曲, 脚本, 演劇** ‖ *He wrote some drama, as well as poetry.* 彼は詩と同様に戯曲もいくつか書いた. ▶定義3 🅲 🅾 an exciting event; exciting things that happen 刺激的な出来事; 起こった刺激的な物事 →**劇的な事件, 劇的な状況** ‖ *a real-life courtroom drama* 現実の法廷での劇的な出来事

★**dramatic** /drəmǽtɪk/ 形 ▶定義1 noticeable or sudden and often surprising 人目をひくまたは突然で, しばしば意外な →**劇的な, 目覚しい** ‖ *a dramatic change/increase/fall/improvement* 目覚しい変化・増加・下落・進歩 ▶定義2 exciting or impressive 興奮させるような, または印象的な →**劇的な, 印象的な** ‖ *the film's dramatic opening scene* その映画の印象的な冒頭シーン ▶定義3 connected with plays or the theatre 芝居または演劇全体に関連した →**演劇の, 戯曲の, 脚本の** ‖ *Shakespeare's dramatic works* シェークスピアの戯曲作品 ▶定義4 (used about a person, a person's behaviour, etc) showing feelings, etc in a very obvious way because you want other people to notice you (人または人の言動などについて)ほかの人々に注目されたいので, とてもあからさまなやり方で感情などを表している →**芝居染みた, おおげさな, オーバーな** ‖ *Calm down. There's no need to be so dramatic about everything!* 落ち着きなさい. いちいち, そうおおげさにする必要はないよ. — **dramatically** /-k(ə)li/ 副 →**劇的に, 目覚しく**

**dramatist** /drǽmətɪst, drǽ-/ 🟦 🅲 ▶定義 a person who writes plays for the theatre, radio or television 劇場, ラジオまたはテレビのために脚本を書く人 →**劇作家, 脚本家**

**dramatize**(または **-ise**) /drǽmətaɪz, drǽ-/ 動 ▶定義1 🌐 to make a book, an event, etc into a play 本, 出来事などを芝居にする →**〜を劇にする, 脚色する** ‖ *The novel has been dramatized for television.* その小説はテレビのために脚色された. ▶定義2 🔵🌐 to make sth seem more exciting or important than it really is 〜を実際よりも刺激的にまたは重大に見えるようにする →**(出来事など)を誇張して伝える, おおげさに表現する** ‖ *The newspaper was accused of dramatizing the situation.* その新聞は, その状況を誇張したとして告発された. — **dramatization**(または

-isation) /drèmətaɪzéɪʃ(ə)n, drɑ̀ː-; -tə-/ 名 C U →劇化, 脚色, おおげさな扱い

**drank** DRINK¹ の過去形

**drape** /dréɪp/ 動 他 ▶定義1 **drape sth round/over sth** to put a piece of material, clothing, etc loosely on sth 布地, 衣服などを〜にふわっと置く → 〜を掛ける ∥ *He draped his coat over the back of his chair.* 彼はいすの背にコートを掛けた. ▶定義2 **drape sb/sth (in/with sth)** (通常は受動態で) to cover sb/sth (with cloth, etc) 〜を(布などで)覆う → 〜を覆う, 包む ∥ *The furniture was draped in dustsheets.* 家具はほこりよけカバーで覆われていた. ― drape 名 C 米 =CURTAIN

**drastic** /dræstɪk/ 形 ▶定義 extreme, and having a sudden very strong effect 極端で, とても強い影響を突然に及ぼす → 徹底的な, 思い切った, 抜本的な, 急激な ∥ *There has been a drastic rise in crime in the area.* その地域では犯罪が急激に増加している. ― **drastically** /-k(ə)li/ 副 →思い切って, 徹底的に, 抜本的に, 急激に

**draught**¹ /drɑːft; dræft/ 名 ▶定義1 (米 **draft**) C a flow of cold air that comes into a room 部屋に入ってくる冷たい空気の流れ → すきま風, 通風 ∥ *Can you shut the door? There's a draught in here.* ドアを閉めてもらえますか. ここにすきま風が入るのです. ▶定義2 **draughts** (米 **checkers**) U a game for two players that you play on a black and white board using round black and white pieces 白黒の盤上で円形の白と黒の駒を使って行う, 2人の競技者のためのゲーム → チェッカー ― **draughty** 形 → すきま風の入る

**draught**² /drɑːft; dræft/ 形 ▶定義 (used about beer, etc) served from a large container (a barrel) rather than in a bottle (ビールなどについて) びんではなく, それより大きな容器(たる)から出される → たる出しの, 生の ∥ *draught beer* 生ビール

**draughtsman** (米 **draftsman**) /drɑ́ːftsmən; dræfts-/ 名 C (複 -men /-mən/) ▶定義 a person whose job is to do technical drawings 技術的な絵をかくことが仕事である人 → 製図者, 製図工, デッサン家

★**draw**¹ /drɔː/ 動 (過 **drew** /druː/; 過分 **drawn** /drɔːn/) ▶定義1 自 他 to do a picture or diagram of sth with a pencil, pen, etc but not paint 〜の絵または図を絵の具ではなく, ペン, 鉛筆などでかく → (線画・図形を)かく, 線を引く ∥ *Shall I draw you a map of how to get there?* その場所への行き方の地図をかきましょうか. *I'm good at painting but I can't draw.* 油絵は得意なのだが, 線描は駄目だ. ▶定義2 自 to move in the direction mentioned 言及された方向に動く → ゆっくり移動する, 動く, (時が)近付く ∥ *The train drew into the station.* 列車は駅に入ってきた. *I became more anxious as my exams drew nearer.* 試験が近付くにつれ, 心配が募ってきた. ▶定義3 他 **draw sth out of/from sth** to pull sth/sb into a new position or in the direction mentioned 〜を新しい位置に, または言及された方向に引っ張る → 〜を引く, 引っ張る ∥ *She drew the letter out of her pocket and handed it to me.* 彼女はポケットから手紙を引っ張り出して, 私に手渡した. *to draw (= open or close) the curtains* カーテンを引く (= 開けるまたは閉める) *He drew me by the hand into the room.* 彼は私の手を引いて部屋に入れた. ▶定義4 他 **draw sth (from sth)** to learn or decide sth as a result of study, research or experience 研究, 調査または経験の結果, 〜を知るまたは判断する → (結論・教訓などを)引き出す, 得る ∥ *Can we draw any **conclusions** from this survey?* 私たちは, この調査から何か結論を導き出すことができるでしょうか. *There are important **lessons to be drawn** from this tragedy.* この悲劇から得られる重要な教訓がある. ▶定義5 他 **draw sth (from sb/sth)** to get or take sth from sb/sth 〜から…を得るまたは取る → (支持・慰めなどを)得る, (批判などを)受ける, (給料などを)受け取る ∥ *He draws the inspiration for his stories from his family.* 彼は, 自分の書く小説のヒントを家族から得る. ▶定義6 他 **draw sth (from sb); draw sb (to sb/sth)** to make sb react to or be interested in sb/sth 〜に…へ反応させる, または〜に対する興味を起こさせる → (人などを)引き寄せる, 引き付ける, (関心・興味などを)引く ∥ *The advertisement has drawn criticism from people all over the country.* その広告は, 全国の人々からの非難を招いた. *The musicians drew quite a large crowd.* その演奏家たちは, とても多くの人々の関心をひいた. ▶定義7 自 他 to finish a game, competition, etc with equal scores so that neither person or team wins 競技，試合などが同点で終わり，そのためどちらの人またはチームも勝利しない➡**引き分ける** ‖ *The two teams drew.* 両チームは引き分けた. *The match was drawn.* 試合は引き分けだった.

成句 bring sth/come/draw to an end ⇒ **END**'
draw (sb's) attention to sth ▶定義 to make sb notice sth ～に…に気付かせる➡**～の注意を…に向けさせる，～に…を指摘する** ‖ *The article draws attention to the problem of homelessness.* その記事は人々にホームレスの問題を喚起させる.

draw a blank ▶定義 to get no result or response 成果または反応が得られない➡**失敗する，不成功・無駄骨に終わる** ‖ *Detectives investigating the case have drawn a blank so far.* その事件を捜査中の刑事たちは，今のところ手掛かりをつかめないでいる.

draw a distinction between sth and sth ▶定義 to show how two things are different 2つの物事がどのように違っているかを示す➡**～を区別する，違いをはっきりさせる**

draw the line at sth ▶定義 to say 'no' to sth even though you are happy to help in other ways たとえほかの場合では喜んで助けるにしても，その～に対しては「否」と言う➡**一線を画す，(～までは)やらない** ‖ *I do most of the cooking but I draw the line at washing up as well!* 料理はほとんど私がするが，食器洗いまではやらないよ.

draw lots ▶定義 to decide sth by chance 偶然によって～を決定する➡**くじ(引き)で決める** ‖ *They drew lots to see who should stay behind.* 彼らは，だれが後に残るかを決めるためにくじを引いた.

句動詞 draw in ▶定義 to get dark earlier as winter arrives 冬になって，早く日が暮れる➡**(日が)短くなる，暮れる** ‖ *The days/nights are drawing in.* 日が短くなる・夕暮れが迫る.

draw out ▶定義 (used about days) to get longer in the spring (日々について)春に昼間の時間が長くなる➡**(日が)長くなる，延びる**

draw sth out ▶定義 to take money out of a bank account 銀行口座からお金を引き出す➡**(預金を)引き出す，(金)を下ろす** ‖ *How much money do I need to draw out?* いくらお金を下ろす必要がありますか.

draw up ▶定義 (used about a car, etc) to drive up and stop in front of or near sth (車などについて)車で着いて，～の前または近くで止める➡**(車などが)止まる，車を止める** ‖ *A police car drew up outside the building.* パトカーが建物の外で止まった.

draw sth up ▶定義 to prepare and write a document, list, etc 書類，一覧表などを準備して書く➡**(文書・案などを)作成する，～の草案を作る** ‖ *Our solicitor is going to draw up the contract.* 私たちの事務弁護士が，契約書を作成することになっている.

**draw**² /drɔː/ 名 ● ▶定義 **1** a result of a game or competition in which both players or teams get the same score so that neither of them wins 双方の選手またはチームが同得点でどちらも勝利を得ない，競技または試合の結果➡**引き分け，引き分け試合** ‖ *The match ended in a draw.* 試合は引き分けに終わった. ▶定義 **2** an act of deciding sth by chance by pulling out names or numbers from a bag, etc 袋などから名前または番号を引き，その偶然によって～を決定する行為➡**くじ(引き)，抽選** ‖ *She won her bike in a prize draw.* 彼女はくじ引きで自転車を当てた.

**drawback** /drɔ́ːbæk/ 名 ● ▶定義 a disadvantage or problem 不利な点または問題➡**不利な点，欠点，短所** ‖ *His lack of experience is a major drawback.* 彼の経験不足は大きな欠点だ.

*****drawer** /drɔ́ːər/ 名 ● ▶定義 a container which forms part of a piece of furniture such as a desk, that you can pull out to put things in 中に物を入れるために引き出せる，例えば机のような，家具の一部分である入れ物➡**引き出し** ‖ *There's some paper in the top drawer of my desk.* 私の机の一番上の引き出しに，何枚かの紙があります.

*****drawing** /drɔ́ːɪŋ/ 名 ● ▶定義 **1** Ⓒ a picture made with a pencil, pen, etc but not paint 絵の具ではなく，鉛筆，ペンなどでかかれた絵➡**線画，図形スケッチ** ☞参 **painting** の注 ▶定義 **2** Ⓤ the art of drawing pictures 絵をかく技術➡**(ペン・鉛筆などで)かくこと，デッサン** ‖ *She's good at drawing and painting.* 彼女はデッサンと油彩が上手だ.

**drawing pin** (米 **thumbtack**) 名 ● ▶定義 a

short pin with a flat top, used for fastening paper, etc to a board or wall 紙などを板または壁に留めるために使われる, 頭が平らな短いピン➔画びょう, 製図ピン ☛ **pin**, S4ページのさし絵

**drawing room** 名 ❻ (古) ▶定義 a living room, especially in a large house 特に大邸宅の, 居間 ➔居間, 応接間

**drawl** /drɔːl/ 動 自他 ▶定義 to speak slowly, making the vowel sounds very long 母音をとても長く発音しながら, ゆっくり話す➔(母音を伸ばして)ゆっくり・物憂げに話す, ゆっくりと発音する — **drawl** 名 [単数扱い]➔ゆっくりとした話し振り・言葉 ‖ *to speak with a drawl* ゆっくりとした話し振りで話す

**drawn**¹ **DRAW**¹ の過去分詞形

**drawn**² /drɔːn/ 形 ▶定義 (used about a person or his/her face) looking tired, worried or ill (人またはその顔について)疲れて, 心配そうに, または気分が悪そうに見えている➔(顔の)引きつった, やつれた, 悩んでいる ‖ *He looked pale and drawn after the long journey.* 長旅の後, 彼は青白くやつれて見えた.

**drawn-out** 形 ▶定義 lasting longer than necessary 必要以上に長く続いている➔(会議などが)長引いた, 長ったらしい ‖ *long drawn-out negotiations* 延々と続いた交渉

**dread**¹ /dred/ 動 他 ▶定義 to be very afraid of or worried about sth 〜をとても恐れる, または心配する➔(前途の危険など)をひどく恐れる, 怖がる, 心配する ‖ *I'm dreading the exams.* 私は試験をひどく心配している. *She dreaded having to tell him what had happened.* 何が起きたのかを彼に伝えなければならないことを, 彼女は恐れていた. *I dread to think what my father will say.* 父が何と言うかを考えると私は怖くなる. — **dreaded** 形➔恐れられている, 恐るべき, 恐ろしい

**dread**² /dred/ 名 [ ❶, 単数扱い ] ▶定義 great fear 大変な恐怖➔(将来の危険などに対する)恐怖, 心配, 不安 ‖ *He lived in dread of the same thing happening to him one day.* 彼は, 同じ事がいつか自分にも起きるのかということを心配しながら暮らした.

**dreadful** /drédfʊl, -f(ə)l/ 形 ▶定義 very bad or unpleasant とても悪い, または不快な➔恐ろしい, 怖い, ひどく悪い・嫌な ‖ *We had a dreadful journey - traffic jams all the way!* 私たちの旅行はひどかった − 至る所ずっと渋滞だった. *I'm afraid there's been a dreadful (= very serious) mistake.* 恐ろしい(= 非常に深刻な)誤りがあるのではないかと思う.

**dreadfully** /drédfʊli, -f(ə)li/ 副 ▶定義1 very; extremely とても; 極度に➔ひどく, とても ‖ *I'm dreadfully sorry, I didn't mean to upset you.* 誠に申し訳ない, あなたを怒らせるつもりはなかった. ▶定義2 very badly とても悪く➔ひどく悪く, ひどく不快に ‖ *The party went dreadfully and everyone left early.* パーティーはひどく不快なものになり, 皆は早く帰った.

**dreadlocks** /drédlɒks/ 名 [複数扱い] ▶定義 hair worn in long thick pieces, especially by some black people 特に一部の黒人たちがしている, 長くて太い複数の房に結った髪➔ドレッドロックス ☛ **hair** のさし絵

*****dream**¹ /driːm/ 名 ▶定義1 ❻a series of events or pictures which happen in your mind while you are asleep 睡眠中に心の中で起こる一連の出来事またはイメージ➔夢 ‖ *I had a strange dream last night.* 昨夜は奇妙な夢を見た. *That horror film has given me bad dreams.* あのホラー映画のせいで悪い夢を見た. ☛参 **nightmare** ▶定義2 ❻something that you want very much to happen, although it is not likely likely そうもないけれども, 起きてほしいととても強く願っている物事➔(心に描く将来の)夢, 理想 ‖ *His dream was to give up his job and live in the country.* 彼の夢は, 仕事を辞めて田舎に住むことだった. *My dream house would have a huge garden and a swimming pool.* 私の理想の家は, 広大な庭とプールがあるものだ. *Becoming a professional dancer was a dream come true for Nicola.* プロのダンサーになることは, ニコラにとってまるで夢のようだった. ▶定義3 [単数扱い] a state of mind in which you are not thinking about what you are doing 自分がしている事について何も考えていない精神状態➔夢想状態, 夢うつつ, 夢心地 ‖ *You've been in a dream all morning!* あなたは午前中ずっとぽーっとしてたよ.

*****dream**² /driːm/ 動 ( 過, 過分 **dreamed** /driːmd; dremt/ または **dreamt** /dremt/) ▶定義1 ❸ 他 dream (about sb/sth) to see or experience pictures and events in your mind while you are asleep 睡眠中に心の中で像と出来事を見る、または体験する→**夢を見る** ‖ *I dreamt about the house that I lived in as a child.* 私は、子供のころに住んでいた家の夢を見た. *I dreamed that I was running but I couldn't get away.* 走っても逃げきれない夢を見た. ☞参 **daydream** ▶定義2 ⊜ dream (about/of sth/doing sth) to imagine sth that you would like to happen 起きてほしい~を想像する→**夢見る、空想する、夢想にふける** ‖ *I've always dreamt about winning lots of money.* 私はいつも、お金をたくさん得ることを夢見てきた. ▶定義3 ⊜ dream (of doing sth/that...) to imagine that sth might happen ~が起きるかもしれないと想像する→**想像する、考えてみる** ‖ *I wouldn't dream of telling Stuart that I don't like his music.* スチュアートの音楽は嫌いだと、彼に言うことなど考えてもいない. *When I watched the Olympics on TV, I never dreamt that one day I'd be here competing!* オリンピックをテレビで見ていた時、いつかここで競技をするだろうとは夢にも思わなかった.

句動詞 dream sth up 略式 ▶定義 to think of a plan, an idea, etc, especially sth strange 計画、考えなど、特に一風変わった~を考え付く→**(とんでもない計画・口実など)を思い付く、考え出す** ‖ *Which of you dreamt up that idea?* 君たちのだれがあの考えを思い付いたの.

**dreamer** /dríːmər/ 名 ⓒ ▶定義 a person who thinks a lot about ideas, plans, etc which may never happen instead of thinking about real life 実生活について考える代わりに、決して実現しないかもしれない考え、計画などについてたっぷり考える人→**夢想家、空想家、夢見る人**

**dreamy** /dríːmi/ 形 ▶定義 looking as though you are not paying attention to what you are doing because you are thinking about sth else 別の~について考えているので、まるで今していることに対して注意を払っていないかのように見えている→**(人・考え・表情が)夢を見ているような、夢見がちな** ‖ *a dreamy look/expression* 夢見がちな様子・表情 — dreamily 副 →**夢見心地で、夢のように**

**dreary** /dríəri/ 形 (drearier; dreariest) ▶定義 not at all interesting or attractive; boring 全く面白くないまたは魅力的でない; 退屈な→**退屈な、つまらない** ‖ *His dreary voice sends me to sleep.* 彼の退屈な声を聞いていると、私は眠くなる.

**dredge** /dredʒ/ 動他 ▶定義 to clear the mud, etc from the bottom of a river, canal, etc using a special machine 特別な機械を使って、川、運河などの底から泥などを取り除く→**(港湾・河川)を浚渫(しゅんせつ)する、(底の泥)をさらい上げる**

句動詞 dredge sth up ▶定義 to mention sth unpleasant from the past that sb would like to forget ~が忘れたがっている不愉快な過去の...を述べる→**~を蒸し返す、持ち出す** ‖ *The newspaper had dredged up all sorts of embarrassing details about her private life.* その新聞は、彼女の私生活に関する厄介事をすべて事細かに持ち出した.

**dregs** /dregz/ 名 [複数扱い] ▶定義1 the last drops in a container of liquid, containing small pieces of solid waste 小さな固形のくずを含んでいる、液体を入れた容器内の最後の数滴→**(液体の底にたまる)おり、かす** ▶定義2 the worst and most useless part of sth ~の最もひどくて最も役に立たない部分→**役立たずのもの、くず** ‖ *These people were regarded as the dregs of society.* これらの人々は、社会のくずと見なされていた.

**drench** /drentʃ/ 動他 (通常は受動態で) ▶定義 to make sb/sth completely wet ~をすっかり濡らす→**~をずぶぬれにする、水に浸す** ‖ *Don't go out while it's raining so hard or you'll get drenched.* こんなひどい雨の中を出掛けるのはやめなさい、そうでないとずぶぬれになりますよ.

*****dress**¹ /dres/ 名 ▶定義1 ⓒ a piece of clothing worn by a girl or a woman. It covers the body from the shoulders to the knees or below. 少女または婦人に着用される衣服. 肩からひざまたはその下までの身体を覆う→**婦人服、ドレス、ワンピース** ☜ C6ページのさし絵 ▶定義2 ⓤ clothes for either men or women 男性または女性用の衣服→**服装、衣服** ‖ *formal/casual dress* 正装・普段着 *He was wearing Bulgarian national dress.* 彼はブルガリアの民族衣装を着ていた.

*****dress**² /dres/ 動 ▶定義1 ⊜他 to put clothes on sb or yourself ~または自分自身に服を着せる→**服を着る、身支度をする; ~に服を着せる、身ごし**

らえをさせる ‖ *He dressed quickly and left the house.* 彼は手早く身支度をして家を出た. *My husband dressed the children while I got breakfast ready.* 私が朝食の用意をしている間に, 夫が子供たちに服を着せた. *Hurry up, Simon! Aren't you dressed yet?* 早くして, サイモン. まだ身支度できてないの. ⇔**undress** ☞ dress よりも get dressed と言う方がより一般的である. ▶定義**2** ⓘ to put or have clothes on, in the way or style mentioned 言及された方法または型で衣服を着るまたは身に着けている→**(ある)服装をしている, 身なり・服装が~である** ‖ *to dress well/badly/casually* 身なりが立派な・良くない・くだけている *to be well dressed/badly dressed/casually dressed* 立派な・良くない・くだけた服装をしている ▶定義**3** ⓣ to put a clean covering on the place on sb's body where he/she has been hurt ~の体の痛んでいるところに清潔な覆いを当てる→**(傷)の手当てをする, ~に包帯をする** ‖ *to dress a wound* 傷の手当てをする
成句 **(be) dressed in sth** ▶定義 wearing sth→**~を着ている** ‖ *The people at the funeral were all dressed in black.* 葬式の参列者は全員黒い服を着ていた.
句動詞 **dress up** ▶定義**1** to put on special clothes, especially in order to look like sb/sth else 特にほかの~のように見せるために, 特別な衣服を身に着ける→**仮装する** ‖ *The children decided to dress up as pirates.* 子供たちは, 海賊の仮装をすることに決めた. ▶定義**2** to put on formal clothes, usually for a special occasion 通常は特別な行事のために, 礼服を身に着ける→**正装・盛装する** ‖ *You don't need to dress up for the party.* そのパーティーのために正装する必要はないよ.

**dresser** /drésər/ 图 特に 英 ▶定義 a piece of furniture with cupboards at the bottom and shelves above. It is used for holding dishes, cups, etc. 下部に戸棚と上部に棚の付いている家具. 皿, カップなどの収納に用いられる→**食器棚** ☞ C7ページのさし絵

**dressing** /drésɪŋ/ 图 ▶定義**1** ⓒ a covering that you put on a part of sb's body that has been hurt to protect it and keep it clean そこを保護し清潔に保つために, 傷付いている~の体の部分にかぶせる覆い→**傷の手当て用品(包帯・ガーゼ・こう薬など)** ▶定義**2** ⓒⓤ a sauce for food, especially for salads 特にサラダのための, 料理用のソース→**(サラダの)ドレッシング, (種々の, 仕上げ用)ソース**

**dressing gown**(または **bathrobe**, 米 **robe**) 图 ⓒ ▶定義 a piece of clothing like a loose coat with a belt, which you wear before or after a bath, before you get dressed in the morning, etc 入浴の前後, 朝, 身支度をする前などに着用する, ベルトの付いたゆったりしたコートのような衣服→**(パジャマの上などに羽織る)ガウン, 部屋着**

**dressing table** 图 ⓒ ▶定義 a piece of furniture in a bedroom, which has drawers and a mirror 引き出しと鏡が付いている, 寝室にある家具→**化粧台, 鏡台** ☞ C7ページのさし絵

**drew DRAW**¹の過去形

**dribble** /dríb(ə)l/ 動 ▶定義**1** ⓘ (used about a liquid) to move downwards in a thin flow; to make a liquid move in this way (液体について)細長い流れになって下方に落ちる; 液体をこのように動かす→**滴り落ちる, ぽたぽた落ちる, 落とす** ‖ *The paint dribbled down the side of the pot.* つぼの側面にペンキが滴り落ちた.
▶定義**2** ⓘ to allow liquid (saliva) to run out of the mouth 液体(だ液)が口から流れ落ちるままにする→**よだれを垂らす** ‖ *Small children often dribble.* 幼い子供はしばしばよだれを垂らす.
▶定義**3** ⓣ (used in ball games) to make a ball move forward by using many short kicks or hits (球技で用いて)ボールを何回も短い距離をける, または打って前に進める→**ドリブルする** ‖ *Ronaldo dribbled round the goalkeeper and scored.* ロナルドはドリブルでゴールキーパーを回り込み, 得点した.

**dried**¹ **DRY**²の過去・過去分詞形

**dried**² /dráɪd/ 形 ▶定義 (used about food) with all the liquid removed from it (食べ物について)水分をすべて取り除いた→**乾燥した, 干した** ‖ *dried milk* 粉ミルク *dried fruit* 乾燥果実

**drier**¹ 形 ⇒ **DRY**¹

**drier**² (または **dryer**) /dráɪər/ 图 ⓒ ▶定義 a machine that you use for drying sth ~を乾かすために使う機械→**乾燥機, ドライヤー** ‖ *a hair-drier* ヘアドライヤー

**drift**¹ /drɪft/ 動 ▶定義**1** to be carried or moved along by wind or water 風または水で運ばれる,

または動かされる→漂流する,漂う,流されていく ‖ *The boat drifted out to sea.* ボートは海へ流されていった. ▶定義2 to move slowly or without any particular purpose ゆっくりと,または特定の目的もなく動く→(人が)(当てもなくあちこち)動く,放浪・流浪する ‖ *He drifted from room to room.* 彼は部屋から部屋へと当てもなく動いた. *She drifted into acting almost by accident.* 彼女はほとんど偶然に女優になった. ▶定義3 (used about snow or sand) to be moved into piles by wind or water (雪または砂について)風または水によって動かされて積もる→吹きだまりになる,吹き積もる ‖ *The snow drifted up to two metres deep in some places.* 雪が吹き積もって2メートルになった所もある. 句動詞 **drift apart** ▶定義 to slowly become less close or friendly with sb 徐々に～との親密さまたは仲の良さがなくなってくる→(気持ちが)離れていく,(人が)互いに疎遠になる

**drift**² /drɪft/ 图 ▶定義1 ❻ a slow movement towards sth ～へ向かうゆっくりとした動き→傾向,動き,動向 ‖ *the country's drift into economic decline* 経済が衰退しつつある,その国の傾向 ▶定義2 [単数扱い] the general meaning of sth ～の大まかな意味→趣旨,大意,骨子 ‖ *I don't understand all the details of the plan but I get the drift.* その計画のすべての詳細を理解してはいないが,概略はつかんでいる. ▶定義3 ❻ a pile of snow or sand that was made by wind or water 風または水によって作られた,雪または砂の堆積(たいせき)→吹きだまり,漂流物,漂積物

**drill**¹ /drɪl/ 图 ▶定義1 ❻ a tool or machine that is used for making holes in things 物に穴を開けるために使われる道具または機械→きり,ドリル,穴開け器 ‖ *a dentist's drill* 歯科医のドリル ☞ **tool** のさし絵 ▶定義2 ❶ exercise in marching, etc that soldiers do 兵隊が行う,行進などの訓練→軍事教練,演習 ▶定義3 ❻ something that you repeat many times in order to learn sth ～を習得するために何回も繰り返す物事→反復訓練,練習,稽古(けいこ) ▶定義4 ❻❶ practice for what you should do in an emergency 緊急時に何をするべきかの訓練→(厳格な,集団的)訓練,演習 ‖ *a fire drill* 消防訓練

**drill**² /drɪl/ 動 ▶定義1 ❸❶ to make a hole in sth with a drill ドリルで～に穴を開ける→(～に)穴を開ける,(穴)を開ける ‖ *to drill a hole in sth* ～に穴を開ける *to drill for oil* 石油を採掘するために穴を開ける ▶定義2 ❶ to teach sb by making him/her repeat sth many times ～を何回も繰り返させて…に教える→～に繰り返し教え込む,～に反復練習させる

**drily** (または **dryly**) /dráɪli/ 副 ▶定義 (used about the way sb says sth) in an amusing way that sounds serious (～の…の言い方について)まじめに聞こえる,面白い言い方で→さりげなく,素っ気なく,皮肉的に ‖ *'I can hardly contain my excitement,' Peter said drily (= he was not excited at all).* 「興奮は抑えられないな」と,ピーターは皮肉っぽく言った(= 彼は全く興奮していなかった).

★**drink**¹ /drɪŋk/ 動 (過 **drank** /dræŋk/; 過分 **drunk** /drʌŋk/) ▶定義1 ❸❶ to take liquid into your body through your mouth 液体を口を通して体内に入れる→飲む;～を飲む ‖ *Would you like anything to drink?* 何か飲みますか. *We sat drinking coffee and chatting for hours.* 私たちは座ってコーヒーを飲み,何時間も雑談した. ▶定義2 ❸❶ to drink alcohol 酒を飲む→酒を飲む,酒飲みである ‖ *I never drink and drive so I'll have an orange juice.* 私は酒を飲んで運転することは絶対にしないので,オレンジジュースにします. *What do you drink - beer or wine?* 何を飲みますか － ビールですか,それともワインですか. *Her father used to drink heavily but he's teetotal now.* 彼女の父は昔は大酒飲みだったが,今では絶対禁酒主義を実践している.

句動詞 **drink to sb/sth** ▶定義 to wish sb/sth good luck by holding your glass up in the air before you drink 飲む前に自分のグラスを空中に差し上げて,～の幸運を祈る→～に乾杯する,～を祈って乾杯する ‖ *We all drank to the future of the bride and groom.* 私たちは花嫁と花婿の将来を祈って,全員で乾杯した. ☞参 **toast**²

**drink (sth) up** ▶定義 to finish drinking sth ～を飲み終わる→～を飲み干す,吸い上げる ‖ *Drink up your tea - it's getting cold.* お茶を全部飲みなさい － 冷めますよ.

★**drink**² /drɪŋk/ 图 ❻❶ ▶定義1 liquid for drinking 飲むための液体→飲み物,飲料 ‖ *Can I have a drink please?* すみませんが,飲み物をもらえますか. *a drink of milk* 1杯の牛乳 *soft drinks (=*

## drink-driver

*cold drinks without alcohol*) ソフトドリンク(= アルコールの入っていない冷たい飲み物) ▶定義2 alcoholic drink アルコール飲料→アルコール飲料, 酒 ‖ *He's got a drink problem.* 彼はアルコール中毒だ. *Shall we go for a drink?* 飲みに行きませんか.

**drink-driver** (または **drunk-driver**) ▶定義 a person who drives after drinking too much alcohol 酒を飲みすぎた後に運転する人→飲酒・酔っ払い運転をする人 — **drink-driving** ▶→飲酒・酔っ払い運転 ‖ *He was convicted of drink-driving and was banned for two years.* 彼は飲酒運転で有罪になり, 2年間の運転禁止になった.

**drinker** /drínkər/ ▶定義 a person who drinks a lot of sth, especially alcohol ~, 特にアルコール飲料をたくさん飲む人→飲む人, 酒飲み, 酒好き ‖ *a heavy drinker* 大酒飲み *I'm not a big coffee drinker.* 私はあまりコーヒーを飲まない.

**drinking** /dríŋkɪŋ/ ▶定義 drinking alcohol アルコール飲料を飲むこと→飲むこと, 飲酒 ‖ *Her drinking became a problem.* 彼女の飲酒が問題になってきた.

**drinking water** ▶定義 water that is safe to drink 飲んで安全な水→飲料水

**drip**¹ /drɪp/ 動 (**dripping**; **dripped**) ▶定義1 (used about a liquid) to fall in small drops (液体について)小さな滴となって落ちる→滴が落ちる, ぽたぽた落ちる ‖ *Water was dripping down through the roof.* 屋根を通して水が滴り落ちていた. ▶定義2 to produce drops of liquid 液体の滴を生み出す→(蛇口・ノズルなどが)滴を落とす; ~の滴を垂らす, 滴らせる ‖ *The tap is dripping.* 蛇口から水がぽたぽた垂れている. *Her finger was dripping blood.* 彼女の指から血が滴っていた.

**drip**² /drɪp/ ▶定義1 [単数扱い] the act or sound of water dripping 水が滴ること, またはその音→滴が落ちること, 滴り, ぽたぽた落ちる音 ▶定義2 a drop of water that falls down from sb/sth ~から落ちる水滴→滴, 水滴 ‖ *We put a bucket under the hole in the roof to catch the drips.* 水滴を受けるために, 私たちは屋根の穴の下にバケツを置いた. ☛ **blob** のさし絵 ▶定義3 a piece of medical equipment, like a tube, that is used for putting liquid food or medicine straight into a person's blood 流動食または薬を直接, 人の血管に入れるために使われる, 管に似た医療器具→点滴装置 ‖ *She's on a drip.* 彼女は点滴を受けている.

★**drive**¹ /draɪv/ 動 (過 **drove** /dróʊv/; 過分 **driven** /drív(ə)n/) ▶定義1 to control or operate a car, train, bus, etc 自動車, 列車, バスなどを操縦する, 運転する→車を運転する; (馬車)を御する, ~を運転する ‖ *Can you drive?* 車の運転はできますか. *to drive a car/train/bus/lorry* 車・列車・バス・トラックを運転する ▶定義2 to go or take sb somewhere in a car, etc 車などである場所へ行く, または~を連れていく→(車などで)行く, ドライブする; ~を車で送る・運ぶ, 乗せていく ‖ *I usually drive to work.* 私は大抵職場へ車で行く. *We drove Aisha to the airport.* 私たちは, アイーシャを空港まで車で送った. ▶定義3 to force people or animals to move in a particular direction 人々または動物を特定の方向に強制的に移動させる→(動物など)を追い立てる, 駆り立てる, 追い払う ‖ *The dogs drove the sheep into the field.* その犬たちが羊を牧草地へ追い立てた. ▶定義4 to force sth into a particular position by hitting it それを打って, ~を特定の位置に押しやる→(くぎ・くいなど)を打ち込む, (ねじなどを)締め込む ‖ *to drive a post into the ground* くいを地面に打ち込む ▶定義5 to cause sb to be in a particular state or to do sth ~を特定の状態にする, または~に…をさせる→人を(ある状態などに)追いやる, 追い込む, (人に)無理に~させる ‖ *His constant stupid questions drive me mad.* 彼のひっきりなしのばかげた質問で, 私は頭にきている. *to drive sb to despair* ~を絶望に追い込む ▶定義6 to make sb/sth work very hard ~を過酷に働かせる→~を過度に働かせる, 酷使する ‖ *You shouldn't drive yourself so hard.* そんなに働きすぎてはいけない. ▶定義7 to make a machine work, by giving it power 動力を与えて, 機械を作動させる→(水力・電力などで)(機械)を動かす ‖ *What drives the wheels in this engine?* このエンジンの回転盤は何で動いているのですか.

成句 **be driving at** 略式 ▶定義 to want to say sth; to mean ~を言いたい; 意味する→~をする・言うつもりだ, 意図する ‖ *I'm afraid I don't understand what you are driving at.* 残念ながら,

私にはあなたが何を言いたいのか分からない. **drive sth home (to sb)** ▶定義 to make sth clear so that people understand it 人々が理解できるように, ～を明らかにする→(知識など)を(徹底的に)たたき込む, 納得させる, しっかり理解させる

**句動詞** drive off ▶定義 (used about a car, driver, etc) to leave (車, 運転手などについて) 去る→(車が)走り去る, (人が)車で去っていく

drive sb/sth off ▶定義 to make sb/sth go away ～を立ち去らせる→～を追い払う‖ *They kept a large dog outside to drive off burglars.* 彼らは泥棒を追い払うために, 戸外に大型犬を飼っていた.

★**drive**² /dráɪv/ 名 ▶定義 **1** ⓒ a journey in a car 車を使った移動→ドライブ, (自動車などでの)旅行‖ *The supermarket is only a five-minute drive away.* そのスーパーは車でわずか5分行ったところです. *Let's **go for a drive**.* ドライブに行こう. ▶定義 **2** ⓒ a wide path or short road that leads to the door of a house 家の玄関に通じている幅広の小道または短い道路→(敷地内の)自動車道, 車回し, 私設車道‖ *We keep our car on the drive.* 私たちは車を私設車道に止めている. ☞ C7ページのさし絵 ▶定義 **3** ⓒ a street, usually where people live 通常は人々が住んでいる, 通り→(地名で)～通り‖ *They live at 23 Woodlands Drive.* 彼らは, ウッドランズ通り23番地に住んでいる. ▶定義 **4** ⓒ a big effort by a group of people in order to achieve sth ～に到達するための, 人々の集団による非常な努力→(ある目的のための)努力, 運動‖ *The company is launching a big sales drive.* その会社は, 販売キャンペーンを大々的に開始する. ▶定義 **5** Ⓤ the energy and determination you need to succeed in doing sth ～をうまく行うために必要な活力と決断力→活力, 意欲, やる気‖ *You need lots of drive to run your own company.* 自社を経営するためには, 強い意欲が必要だ. ▶定義 **6** ⓒ Ⓤ a strong natural need or desire 強い自然な欲求または欲望→(本能的な)衝動, 心理的誘引‖ *a strong sex drive* 強い性衝動 ▶定義 **7** ⓒ (in sport) a long hard hit (スポーツで) 長く強い当たり→(ボールの)長打, (ボールの)飛距離‖ *This player has the longest drive in golf.* この選手は, ゴルフで最長の飛距離を持っている. ▶定義 **8** ⓒ (computing) the part of a computer that reads and stores information (コンピューター) 情報を読んだり蓄えたりする, コンピューターの一部→ドライブ, 駆動装置‖ *a 224 MB hard drive* 224メガバイトのハードドライブ *a CD drive* CDドライブ ☞参 **disk drive** ▶定義 **9** ⓒ the equipment in a vehicle that takes power from the engine to the wheels エンジンからの動力を車輪に伝える, 乗り物内の装置→(動力の)伝導, 駆動(装置)‖ *a car with four-wheel drive* 4輪駆動車

**drive-by** 形 困(名詞の前だけ) ▶定義 (used about a shooting) done from a moving car (射撃について)動いている車からなされる→走行中の車からの‖ *drive-by killings* 走行中の車からの射殺

**drive-in** 名 ⓒ 困 ▶定義 a place where you can eat, watch a film, etc in your car 車の中にいながら, 食べたり映画を見たりできる場所→ドライブイン

**driven** **DRIVE**¹の過去分詞形

★**driver** /dráɪvər/ 名 ⓒ ▶定義 a person who drives a vehicle 乗り物を運転する人→運転手, ドライバー‖ *a bus/train driver* バス・列車の運転手

**drive-through** 名 ⓒ 特に 困 ▶定義 a restaurant, bank, etc where you can be served without getting out of your car 車から降りることなしにサービスを受けられるレストラン, 銀行など→ドライブスルー

★**driving**¹ /dráɪvɪŋ/ 名 Ⓤ ▶定義 the action or skill of controlling a car, etc 自動車などを操縦する行為または技術→運転, 運転の仕方‖ *She was arrested for dangerous driving.* 彼女は危険な運転をしたかどで逮捕された. *Joe's having **driving lessons**.* ジョーは運転の教習を受けている. *She works as a **driving instructor**.* 彼女は自動車教習の教官として働いている. *a **driving school*** 自動車教習所 *Did you pass your **driving test** first time?* 自動車運転免許試験を1回で合格しましたか. *How long have you had a **driving licence** (= an official piece of paper that says you are allowed to drive a car, etc)?* 自動車運転免許証 (= 車などの運転を許可されている旨を記した公式文書)を取ってどのくらいたちましたか.

**driving**² /dráɪvɪŋ/ 形 ▶定義 very strong とても強い→激しい, 精力的な, (雨・雪などが)吹き降りの‖

*driving rain* 激しい雨 *driving ambition* 強い野心 *Who's the driving force behind this plan?* だれがこの計画の推進力となっているのですか.

**drizzle** /drízl/ 名 ∪ ▶定義 light rain with very small drops とても細かな水滴の小雨 →霧雨, こぬか雨 — drizzle 動 自 →霧雨が降る ☛参 **weather**の注

**drone** /dróun/ 動 自 ▶定義 to make a continuous low sound 絶え間ない低い音を出す →(ハチ・飛行機などが)ブーンとうなる, ブーンという低い音を立てる ‖ *the sound of the tractors droning away in the fields* ブーンという低い音を立てながら牧草地に消えていったトラクターの音

句動詞 **drone on** ▶定義 to talk in a flat or boring voice 平板なまたは退屈な声で話す →単調にだらだらと話す, だらだらと続く ‖ *We had to listen to the chairman drone on about sales for hours.* 私たちは社長が売り上げについて何時間もだらだらと話すのを聞かなければならなかった. — drone 名 [単数扱い] →ブーンという音, 単調な話

**drool** /druːl/ 動 自 ▶定義 1 to let liquid (saliva) come out from the mouth, usually at the sight or smell of sth good to eat 通常はおいしそうな～を見てまたはにおいをかいで, 液体(だ液)を口から垂らす →よだれを垂らす ▶定義 2 drool (over sb/sth) to show in a silly or exaggerated way that you want or admire sb/sth very much ～をとても欲しているまたは賞賛していることを, ばかげたまたは誇張されたやり方で示す →大喜びする, はしゃぐ, ばかみたいに喜ぶ ‖ *teenagers drooling over photographs of their favourite pop stars* お気に入りのポピュラー音楽のスターの写真に大喜びしているティーンエージャーたち

**droop** /druːp/ 動 自 ▶定義 to bend or hang downwards, especially because of weakness or because you are tired 特に弱いため, または疲れているために, 下向きに曲がるまたは垂れる →(力なく)垂れる, うなだれる, (草木が)しおれる ‖ *The flowers were drooping without water.* 水がなくて, 花はしおれていた. — drooping 形 →垂れ下がった ‖ *a drooping moustache* 垂れ下がった口ひげ

drop

**\*drop**¹ /drɑp/ 動 (**dropping**; **dropped**) ▶定義 1 他 to let sth fall ～を落とす →～を落とす, 降らす, 投げ落とす ‖ *That vase was very expensive. Whatever you do, don't drop it!* あの花びんはとても高価な物だった. どんな事をしたって, 落としちゃいけない. ▶定義 2 自 to fall 落ちる →落ちる, 落下する ‖ *The parachutist dropped safely to the ground.* 落下傘兵は, 無事に地面に落下した. *At the end of the race she dropped to her knees exhausted.* レースの最後で, 彼女は疲れてがっくりひざを付いた. ▶定義 3 自 他 to become lower; to make sth lower より低くなる; ～をより低くさせる →下がる, 衰える; ～を低くする, 衰えさせる ‖ *The temperature will drop to minus 3 overnight.* 気温は夜のうちにマイナス3度に下がるでしょう. *They ought to drop their prices.* 彼らは値下げすべきだ. *to drop your voice (= speak more quietly)* 声を落とす(= もっと静かに話す) ▶定義 4 drop sb/sth (off) to stop your car, etc so that sb can get out, or in order to take sth out ～が降りられるように, または～を下ろせるように, 車などを止める →～を降ろす, ～を送り届ける ‖ *Drop me off at the traffic lights, please.* 信号の所で降ろしてください. *I'll drop the parcel at your house.* あなたの家に小包を送り届けます. ▶定義 5 他 drop sb/sth (from sth) to no longer include sb/sth in sth もはや～に…を含まない →～を抜かす, 外す, 除名する ‖ *Joe has been dropped from the team.* ジョーはチームから除名された. ▶定義 6 他 to stop doing sth ～をすることをやめる →～をやめる, 中止する, 放棄する ‖ *I'm going to drop geography next term (= stop studying it).* 次の学期は, 地理学をやめることにするよ(= それを勉強することをやめる).

成句 **drop dead** 略式 ▶定義 to die suddenly 突然死ぬ →急死する

**drop sb a line** 略式 ▶定義 to write a letter to sb ～に手紙を書く →～に一筆書き送る, 便りを書く ‖ *Do drop me a line when you've time.* 時間のあるときには, 是非お便り下さいね.

**[句動詞]** drop back; drop behind (sb) ▶定義 to move into a position behind sb else, because you are moving more slowly ほかの人よりもゆっくりと動くので, ほかの〜の後ろの位置へ動く→(速度が落ちて)後退する, 遅れる ‖ *Towards the end of the race she dropped behind the other runners.* レースの終盤で, 彼女はほかの走者より遅れた.

drop by; drop in (on sb) ▶定義 to go to sb's house on an informal visit or without having told him/her you were coming 気軽にまたは行くことを告げずに, 〜の家に訪問する→ちょっと立ち寄る, 不意に訪れる ‖ *We were in the area so we thought we'd drop in and see you.* 私たちはその地域にいたので, ちょっと立ち寄ってあなたに会おうと思った.

drop off [略式] ▶定義 to fall into a light sleep 浅い眠りに落ちる→(うとうと)眠ってしまう, 居眠りを始める ‖ *I dropped off in front of the television.* テレビの前で居眠りしてしまった.

drop out (of sth) ▶定義 to leave or stop doing sth before you have finished 終わらせる前に, している〜から離れる, またはしている〜を中断する→脱落する, 抜ける, 中途退学する ‖ *His injury forced him to drop out of the competition.* けがのせいで, 彼は試合から抜けざるを得なかった.

★**drop**² /dróp/ 名 ▶定義 **1** ◉a very small amount of liquid that forms a round shape 丸い形を作る, ごく少量の液体→滴, 滴り, 水滴 ‖ *a drop of blood/rain* 1 滴の血・雨　● **blob** のさし絵 ▶定義 **2** [◉, 通常は単数]a small amount of liquid 少量の液体→ほんの少しの量, 微量, ほんの数滴 ‖ *I just have a drop of milk in my coffee.* 私はコーヒーにミルクをほんの少し入れる. ▶定義 **3** [単数扱い]a fall to a smaller amount or level より少ない量または水準に落ちること→(量・質・価格などの)下落, 低下 ‖ *The job is much more interesting but it will mean a drop in salary.* 仕事は今までよりもずっと面白くなるが, 給料は減ることになる. *a drop in prices/temperature* 価格・気温の低下 ▶定義 **4** [単数扱い]a distance down from a high point to a lower point 高い位置からより低い位置までの下方への距離→垂直距離, 落ちる高さ, 落差 ‖ *a sheer drop of 40 metres to the sea* 海まで40メートルの絶壁 ▶定義 **5** drops[複数扱い] liquid medicine that you put into your eyes, ears or nose 目, 耳または

は鼻に入れる液状の薬→(目・耳・鼻に差す)滴薬, 点滴薬 ‖ *The doctor prescribed me drops to take twice a day.* 医者は, 1日に2回差す点滴薬を処方してくれた.

**[成句]** a drop in the ocean; [米] a drop in the bucket ▶定義 an amount of sth that is too small or unimportant to make any real difference to a situation 状況に実質的な変化をもたらすにはあまりにも少なすぎるまたは重要性がなさすぎる, 〜の量→大海の一滴, 焼け石に水, 取るに足らない量 ‖ *The money we made was a drop in the ocean compared to the amount we need.* 私たちが調達したお金は, 必要な金額に比べると大海の一滴にすぎなかった.

at the drop of a hat ▶定義 immediately; without having to stop and think about it 直ちに; 中断することもそれについて考えてみることも必要なく→待ってましたとばかり, ためらわずに

**drop-dead** 副 [略式] ▶定義 used before an adjective to emphasize how attractive sb/sth is 〜がいかに魅力的であるかを強調するために, 形容詞の前で用いて→目をみはらせるほど, はっとさせるほど ‖ *She's drop-dead gorgeous.* 彼女ははっとするほど魅力的だ.

**drop-out** 名 ◉ ▶定義 **1** a person who leaves school, university, etc before finishing his/her studies 課程を修了する前に学校, 総合大学などを辞める人→中途退学者 ▶定義 **2** a person who does not accept the ideas and ways of behaving of the rest of society 社会のほかの人たちの考えと振る舞い方を受け入れない人→(社会からの)離脱者, 逃避者

**droppings** /drópɪŋz/ 名 [複数扱い] ▶定義 waste material from the bodies of small animals or birds 小さな動物のまたは鳥の体から出る排せつ物→(鳥・動物の)落とし物, 糞(ふん)

**drought** /dráʊt/ 名 ◉ ◉ ▶定義 a long period without rain 雨の降らない長い期間→干ばつ, 日照り ‖ *Drought has affected many countries in Africa.* アフリカの多くの国を, 干ばつが襲っている.

**drove** DRIVE¹の過去形

★**drown** /dráʊn/ 動 ▶定義 **1** 自他 to die in water because it is not possible to breathe; to make sb die in this way 呼吸ができないので水中で死ぬ; 〜をこの方法で死なせる→おぼれ死ぬ, 水死

する; ～を溺死(できし)・水死させる ‖ *The girl fell into the river and drowned.* 少女は川に落ちておぼれ死んだ. *Twenty people were drowned in the floods.* 洪水で,20人が溺死した. ▶定義2 [他] **drown sb/sth (out)** (used about a sound) to be so loud that you cannot hear sb/sth else (音について)ほかの～が聞き取れないほど,とても騒々しい➜**(ほかの音)をかき消す** ‖ *His answer was drowned out by the music.* 彼の返事は音楽でかき消された.

**drowsy** /dráuzi/ [形] ▶定義 not completely awake; sleepy 完全には目が覚めていない; 眠い➜**眠い, 眠そうな, うとうとしている** ‖ *The heat made me feel drowsy.* 暖かくて眠気がした.—**drowsily** [副] ➜**眠そうに, うとうとと** — **drowsiness** [名] [U] ➜**眠気**

**drudgery** /drʌ́dʒ(ə)ri/ [名] [U] ▶定義 hard and boring work つらく退屈な仕事➜**(単調で嫌な)骨折り仕事, つまらぬ仕事**

***drug**[1] /drʌg/ [名] [C] ▶定義1 a chemical which people use to give them pleasant or exciting feelings. It is illegal in many countries to use drugs. 気持ちの良いまたは興奮する感じを得るために,人々が自分に用いる薬物. drugを用いることは多くの国で違法である➜**麻薬, 覚醒剤** ‖ *He doesn't drink or **take drugs**.* 彼は酒は飲まないし麻薬も打たない. *She suspected her son was **on drugs**.* 彼女は,息子が麻薬をやっているのではないかと疑った. *hard drugs such as heroin and cocaine* 例えばヘロインとコカインのような,中毒性の強い薬物 *soft drugs* 中毒性の弱い薬物 ▶定義2 a chemical which is used as a medicine 医薬品として用いられる薬物➜**薬, 薬剤, 薬品** ‖ *drug companies* 製薬会社 *Some drugs can only be obtained with a prescription from a doctor.* 薬品の中には,医師の処方せんがなければ手に入らないものもある.

**➤日本語 vs 英語**

**drugstoreと「薬屋」は違う?**

drugstore[米]は,薬や医薬品のほかに,日用雑貨(daily necessities)や食料品(groceries)などが売られている店を指し,最近日本でも同様の形態を取る店が増えています.アメリカでは,カウンターで簡単な食事ができるようになっている所が多くあります.薬のみを扱う「薬屋」はpharmacyです.イギリスのchemist's(shop)では薬のほか,主に香水やシャンプーなどが売られています.なお,dispensaryは病院内などの調剤室を指します.

**drug**[2] /drʌg/ [動][他] (**drugging**; **drugged**) ▶定義1 to give a person or animal a chemical to make him/her/it fall asleep or unconscious 人または動物を眠らせる,または意識を失わせるために,薬物を与える➜**～に麻酔をかける, ～に薬を飲ませて眠らせる, ～に麻薬・毒薬を飲ませる** ‖ *The lion was drugged before the start of the journey.* 旅に出る前に,ライオンは麻酔をかけられた. ▶定義2 to put a drug into food or drink 食物または飲料に薬を入れる➜**(飲食物)に薬物を入れる, 薬を混ぜる** ‖ *I think his drink was drugged.* 彼の飲み物には薬が混ぜられたのだと思う.

**drug addict** [名] [C] ▶定義 a person who cannot stop taking drugs 麻薬を打つことを止められない人➜**麻薬常習者** — **drug addiction** [名] [U] ➜**麻薬中毒**

**druggist** /drʌ́gɪst/ [米] = **CHEMIST(1)**

**drugstore** /drʌ́gstɔ̀ːr/ [米] = **CHEMIST(2)**

***drum**[1] /drʌm/ [名] [C] ▶定義1 a musical instrument like an empty container with plastic or skin stretched across the ends. You play a drum by hitting it with your hands or with sticks. 両端にプラスチックまたは革を張った,空の容器に似た楽器.手またはスティックでたたいて演奏する➜**太鼓, ドラム** ‖ *She plays the drums in a band.* 彼女はバンドでドラムを演奏している. ☛参 **piano**の注 ☛ **music**のさし絵 ▶定義2 a round container 円筒形の容器➜**太鼓の形をしたもの, 円筒形の容器, ドラム缶** ‖ *an oil drum* 石油缶

**drum**[2] /drʌm/ [動] (**drumming**; **drummed**) ▶定義1 [自] to play a drum ドラムを演奏する➜**太鼓・ドラムをたたく, ドラムを演奏する** ▶定義2 [自][他] to make a noise like a drum by hitting sth many times ～を何回もたたいて,太鼓のような物音を立てる➜**太鼓のような音を出す・立てる, どんどん・とんとんたたく; ～をたたいて太鼓のような音を立てる, ～でどんどん・とんとんたたく** ‖ *to drum your fingers on the table (= because you are annoyed, impatient, etc)* 指先でテーブルをとんとんたたく(= むっとしている,またはいらいらしている,ことなどが理由で)

**句動詞** drum sth into sb ▶定義 to make sb remember sth by repeating it many times 何回も繰り返して、〜に…を覚えさせる→(考え・規則など)を〜にたたき込む、やかましく教え込む ‖ *Road safety should be drummed into children from an early age.* 交通安全は、幼い時から子供たちにたたき込むべきだ.

drum sth up ▶定義 to try to get support or business 支持または取り引きを得ようとする→(鳴り物入りで)〜を呼び集める、(宣伝などによって)(商売など)を活気づける、(取り引き・支持など)を獲得する ‖ *to drum up more custom* もっと多くの顧客を獲得する

**drummer** /drÁmər/ 名 C ▶定義 a person who plays a drum or drums 1つまたは複数のドラム、太鼓を演奏する人→ドラマー、太鼓・ドラム奏者

**drumstick** /drÁmstìk/ 名 C ▶定義1 a stick used for playing the drums ドラム、太鼓の演奏に使われる棒→太鼓のばち、スティック ▶定義2 the lower leg of a chicken or similar bird that we cook and eat 調理して食べる、鶏またはそれに似た鳥の脚の下の部分→(調理した)鶏・アヒル・七面鳥の脚、脚の下半分

★**drunk**¹ /drÁŋk/ 形 (名詞の前は不可) ▶定義 having drunk too much alcohol お酒を飲みすぎている→酔っ払った、酔った ‖ *to get drunk* 酔っ払った ― drunk (または (古) drunkard) 名 C →酔っ払い、飲んだくれ ‖ *There were two drunks asleep under the bridge.* 橋の下で酔っ払いが2人寝ていた.

**drunk**² DRINK¹の過去分詞形

**drunken** /drÁŋk(ə)n/ 形 (名詞の前だけ) ▶定義1 having drunk too much alcohol お酒を飲みすぎている→酔った、酔っ払った、飲んだくれの ‖ *drunken drivers* 酔っ払い運転手 ▶定義2 showing the effects of too much alcohol 酒の飲みすぎによる影響を表している→酔った挙げ句の、酔った上での、酔っ払いたちの ‖ *drunken singing* 酔っ払いたちの歌声 ― drunkenly 副→酔って、酒の上で ― drunkenness 名 U →酔い、酔っていること、酒浸り

★**dry**¹ /drái/ 形 (drier; driest) ▶定義1 without liquid in it or on it; not wet その中または表面に水分のない→乾いた、乾燥した、水気のない ‖ *The washing isn't dry yet.* 洗濯物はまだ乾いていない. *The paint is dry now.* ペンキはもう乾いています. *Rub your hair dry with a towel.* 髪の毛をタオルでふいて乾かしなさい. ▶定義2 having little or no rain 雨がほとんど、または全く降らない→雨の降らない、日照り続きの ‖ *a hot, dry summer* 暑く、日照り続きの夏 *a dry climate* 雨の降らない気候 ⇔ 定義1, 2 wet ▶定義3 (used about hair or skin) not having enough natural oil (髪の毛または皮膚について)十分な量の自然の油分がない→乾燥した、潤いのない、パサパサした ▶定義4 (used about wine) not sweet (ワインについて)甘くない→甘くない、辛口の ▶定義5 (used about what sb says, or sb's way of speaking) amusing, although it sounds serious (〜の話した事、または〜の話し方について)まじめに聞こえるけれども、面白い→(冗談などが)さりげない、平静を装って言う、まじめな顔で言った ‖ *a dry sense of humour* さりげないユーモアのセンス ▶定義6 boring 退屈な→退屈な、無味乾燥な、面白くない ‖ *dry legal documents* 無味乾燥な法律文書 ▶定義7 without alcohol; where no alcohol is allowed 酒なしの; 酒が許可されていない場所の→(国・法などが)飲酒を禁じている、禁酒法実施の ‖ *Saudi Arabia is a dry country.* サウジアラビアは、禁酒の国である. ― dryness 名 U →乾燥(状態), さりげなさ, 無味乾燥

**成句** be left high and dry ⇒ HIGH¹

★**dry**² /drái/ 動 自 他 (現分 drying; 三単現 dries; 過, 過分 dried) ▶定義 to become dry; to make sth dry 乾燥する; 〜を乾かす→乾く, (水が)かれる; 〜を乾かす, 乾燥させる ‖ *I hung my shirt in the sun to dry.* シャツを乾かすために、外に干した. *to dry your hands on a towel* タオルで手をふく

**句動詞** dry (sth) out ▶定義 to become or make sth become completely dry 〜が完全に乾く、または〜を完全に乾燥させる→すっかり・完全に乾く、水分がすっかりなくなる; 〜をすっかり・完全に乾かす ‖ *Don't allow the soil to dry out.* 耕土を干上がらせてはいけない.

dry up ▶定義1 (used about a river, etc) to have no more water in it (川などについて)もう水がない→すっかり乾く、干上がる ▶定義2 to stop being available 入手できなくなる→(蓄え・力などが)なくなる、枯渇する、尽きる ‖ *Because of the recession a lot of building work has dried up.* 景気後退のせいで、多くの建設作業が枯渇した. ▶定義3 to forget what you were going to say, for example because you are very nervous

例えばとても神経質になっているので,言おうとしていた事を忘れる→話せなくなる,何を言いたいか忘れる‖ *When he came on stage and saw the audience, he dried up completely.* 舞台に上がり観客を見た時,何を言うつもりだったか,彼は全く忘れてしまった.
**dry (sth) up** ▶定義 to dry plates, knives, forks, etc with a towel after they have been washed 洗った後の皿,ナイフ,フォークなどをタオルでふく→〜をふく

**dry-clean** 動他 ▶定義 to clean clothes using special chemicals, without using water 水を使わないで,特別な化学薬品を使って衣服を洗う→〜をドライクリーニングする

**dry-cleaner's** (または **cleaner's**) 名 C ▶定義 the shop where you take your clothes to be cleaned 洗ってもらうために衣服を持っていく店→(ドライ)クリーニング店

**dry land** 名 U ▶定義 land, not the sea 海ではない,陸→(空・海洋に対して)陸地‖ *I was glad to be back on dry land again.* 再び陸地に戻れてうれしかった.

**DTP** /ˌdiː tiː ˈpiː/ 略 desktop publishing→デスクトップパブリッシング

**dual** /ˈd(j)úːəl/ 形 (名詞の前だけ) ▶定義 having two parts; double 2つの部分を持つ;二重の→2つの,2つの部分から成る,二重の‖ *to have dual nationality* 二重国籍を持つ

**dual carriageway** (米 **divided highway**) 名 C ▶定義 a wide road that has an area of grass or a fence in the middle to separate the traffic going in one direction from the traffic going in the other direction ある方向に行く交通と反対方向に行く交通を分離するために,中央に草または柵(さく)の地帯がある,幅の広い道路→中央分離帯のある幹線道路

**dub** /dʌb/ 動他 (**dubbing**; **dubbed**) ▶定義 1 to give sb/sth a new or amusing name (a nickname) 〜に新しいまたは面白い名前(あだ名)を付ける→(新聞などが)〜にあだ名を付ける,〜を…と呼ぶ‖ *Bill Clinton was dubbed 'Slick Willy'.* ビル クリントンは「口のうまいウィリー」とあだ名を付けられた. ▶定義 2 **dub sth (into sth)** to change the sound in a film so that what the actors said originally is spoken by actors using a different language 俳優たちが原作で言っていた台詞(せりふ)を異なる言語を使って俳優たちが話すように,映画で音声を変える→〜を吹き替える,〜に吹き替えの台詞を入れる‖ *I don't like foreign films when they're dubbed into English. I prefer subtitles.* 私は英語に吹き替えられた外国映画が好きではない.字幕の方が好きだ. ▶定義 3 to make a piece of music by mixing different pieces of recorded music together 別々に録音された音楽を一緒にして,1曲の音楽を作る→〜を多重録音する,ミキシングして曲を作る

**dubious** /ˈd(j)úːbiəs/ 形 ▶定義 1 **dubious (about sth/about doing sth)** not sure or certain 主観的にまたは客観的に,確信がない→疑わしく思う,決心がつかない,半信半疑で‖ *I'm very dubious about whether we're doing the right thing.* 私たちが正しい事をしているのかどうか,とても疑わしく思う. ▶定義 2 that may not be honest or safe 公正または安全でないかもしれない→疑わしい,はっきりしない,額面通りに受け取れない‖ *dubious financial dealings* 疑わしい金融取引 — **dubiously** 副→疑わしげに,怪しげに

**duchess** /ˈdʌtʃəs/ 名 C ▶定義 a woman who has the same position as a duke, or who is the wife of a duke 公爵と同じ地位を持つ,または公爵の妻である,女性→女公爵,公爵夫人

**\*duck¹** /dʌk/ 名 (複 **ducks** または **duck**) ▶定義 1 C a common bird that lives on or near water. Ducks have short legs, special (webbed) feet for swimming and a wide beak. 水上または水辺に生息するありふれた鳥.短い脚,泳ぐための特別な足(水かき),幅の広いくちばしを持つ→アヒル,カモ ▶定義 2 C a female duck アヒルの雌→雌のアヒル・カモ

► 雄のアヒルはdrake, 子供のアヒルはduckling と呼ばれる. アヒルの鳴き声はquackである.
▶定義3 ❶ the meat of a duck duck の肉→カモ・アヒルの肉 ‖ roast duck with orange sauce 焼いたカモ肉のオレンジソース添え

**duck**² /dʌk/ 動 ▶定義1 ⾃他 to move your head down quickly so that you are not seen or hit by sb/sth 〜に見られないまたは打たれないように, 頭を敏速に下に動かす→ひょいと身をかがめる, 頭をひょいと引っ込める; 〜をひょいと下げる ‖ The boys ducked out of sight behind a hedge. 少年たちは生垣の後ろの見えない所にひょいとかがんだ. I had to duck my head down to avoid the low doorway. 低い出入り口を避けるために, 頭をひょいと下げなければならなかった. ▶定義2 ⾃他 成句 duck (out of) sth to try to avoid sth difficult or unpleasant 困難なまたは不快な物事を避けようとする→(疑惑・責任など)をかわす, 逃れる ‖ She tried to duck out of apologizing. 彼女は謝らないで済まそうとした. The President is trying to duck responsibility for the crisis. 大統領は, その危機に対する責任をかわそうとしている. ▶定義3 他 to push sb's head under water for a short time, especially when playing 特に遊んでいるときに, 〜の頭を短い時間水中に押す→(ひょいと水に)〜をつける ‖ The kids were ducking each other in the pool. 子供たちはプールでお互いに沈め合っていた.

**duct** /dʌkt/ 名 C ▶定義 a tube that carries liquid, gas, etc 液体, 気体などを運ぶ管→管, 輸送管, 導管 ‖ They got into the building through the air duct. 彼らは通気管を通って建物内に入った. tear ducts (= in the eye) 涙管(= 目の中にある)

**dud** /dʌd/ 名 C 略式 ▶定義 a thing that cannot be used because it is not real or does not work properly 本物ではない, または適切に働かないために使用できないもの→役に立たないもの・人 ‖ a dud cheque/coin/firework 不渡り小切手・偽造硬貨・不発の花火

**dude** /d(j)uːd/ 名 C 特に 米 (俗語) ▶定義 a man 男→あいつ, 野郎

★**due**¹ /d(j)uː/ 形 ▶定義1 (名詞の前は不可) expected or planned to happen or arrive 起こるまたは到着することが予想されたまたは計画された→(〜する)予定で, はずで, 到着予定で ‖ The conference is due to start in four weeks' time. 会議は4週間後に始まる予定です. What time is the next train due (in)? 次の列車は何時の予定ですか. The baby is due in May. 赤ん坊は5月に生まれる予定です. ▶定義2 (名詞の前は不可) having to be paid 支払われなければならない→当然支払われるべき, (手形などが)満期の ‖ The rent is due on the fifteenth of each month. 家賃は毎月15日の支払いです. ▶定義3 due (to sb) that is owed to you because it is your right to have it あなたにはそれを持つ当然の権利があるので, あなたに当然負われるべき〜→(感謝・賞賛などが)〜に当然払われるべき, 当然与えられるべき ‖ Make sure you claim all the benefits that are due to you. あなたに与えられるべき利益をすべて要求していることを確かめなさい. ▶定義4 due to sb/sth caused by or because of sb/sth 〜が原因となって, または〜のせいで→〜の理由・原因で, 〜のためで ‖ His illness is probably due to stress. 彼の病気は多分ストレスが原因だ. ▶定義5 due for sth expecting sth or having the right to sth 〜を期待する, または〜に対して当然の権利を持つ→〜を受けることになっている, 〜の見込みである ‖ I think that I'm due for a pay rise. 私は当然, 給料が上がると思う. 成句 in due course ▶定義 at some time in the future, quite soon 将来のある時期に, 極めて近いうちに→やがて, 時期が来れば ‖ All applicants will be informed of our decision in due course. 応募者全員に, 後日決定を通知します.

**due**² /d(j)uː/ 副 ▶定義 (used before 'north', 'south', 'east' and 'west') exactly (north, south, east, west の前で用いて)正確に→真〜に, 正確に〜 ‖ The aeroplane was flying due east. 飛行機は真東に向けて飛行していた.

**due**³ /d(j)uː/ 名
成句 give sb his/her due ▶定義 to be fair to a person 人に対して公正である→(好ましくないものでも)正当に扱う, 公平に接する, 長所を長所として認める ‖ She doesn't work very quickly, but to give Sarah her due, she is very accurate. サラはあまり速く仕事をしないが, 公平に言えば, その仕事はとても正確だ.

**duel** /d(j)úːəl/ 名 C ▶定義 a formal type of fight with guns or other weapons which was used in the past to decide an argument between two men 2人の男のけんかに決着を付けるために昔行

## 518　duet

われた，けん銃またはそのほかの武器を使った正式な争い→**決闘，果たし合い**

**duet** /d(j)uːét/（または **duo**; 複 **duos**) 名 C
▶定義 a piece of music for two people to sing or play 2人で歌うまたは演奏するための曲→**二重唱・奏曲，デュエット** ☛参 solo

**duffel coat**（または **duffle coat**) /dʌ́f(ə)l kòut/
名 C ▶定義 a coat made of heavy woollen cloth with a covering for the head (a hood). A duffle coat has special long buttons (toggles). 頭を覆うもの(フード)の付いた，厚手のウール地で作られたコート．特別に長いボタン(トグル)が付いている→**ダッフルコート**

**dug** DIG¹ の過去・過去分詞形

**duke** /d(j)uːk/（または **Duke**) 名 C ▶定義 a man of the highest social position 社会的地位が最も高い男性→**公爵(貴族の最高位)** ☛参 duchess

＊**dull** /dʌl/ 形 ▶定義 1 not interesting or exciting; boring 面白くない，または刺激的でない；退屈な→**面白くない，平凡な，退屈な** ‖ Miss Potter's lessons are always so dull. ポッター先生の授業はいつもとても退屈だ．▶定義 2 not bright 輝いていない→**曇った，どんよりした，うっとうしい** ‖ a dull and cloudy day どんよりと曇った日 ▶定義 3 not loud, sharp or strong うるさく，鋭く，または強くない→**(色・音に)はっきりしない，鈍い，ぼんやりした** ‖ Her head hit the floor with a dull thud. 彼女はどすんと頭を床にぶつけた．a dull pain 鈍い痛み ⇔ **sharp** ― **dullness** 名 U → **退屈さ，不活発さ，鈍さ** ― dully 副 →**鈍く，のろく**

**duly** /d(j)úːli/ 副 正式 ▶定義 in the correct or expected way 正しいまたは期待されたやり方で→**適切に，正しく** ‖ We all duly assembled at 7.30 as agreed. あらかじめ決めた通り，7時30分ぴったりに全員が集まった．

**dumb** /dʌm/ 形 ▶定義 1 not able to speak 話すことができない→**口がきけない，ものを言わない** ‖ to be deaf and dumb 聾唖(ろうあ)である(比喩) They were **struck dumb** with amazement. 彼らはびっくりしてものも言えなかった．▶定義 2 略式 stupid 愚かな→**ばかな，間抜けな** ‖ What a dumb thing to do! 何て間抜けな事をするのだ．― dumbly 副 →**無言で，黙って** ‖ Ken did all the talking, and I just nodded dumbly. ケンがずっと話して，私はただ黙ってうなずいた．

**dumbfounded** /dʌmfáundəd, ⁀-/ 形 ▶定義 very surprised とても驚いた→**驚いて口もきけない，あぜんとした**

**dummy**

**dummy** /dʌ́mi/ 名 C
（複 **d u m m i e s**）
▶定義 1 a model of the human body used for putting clothes on in a shop window or while you are making clothes

店のウインドーでまたは衣服を作っている間，衣服を着せるために使われる人体の模型→**マネキン人形，人台** ‖ a tailor's dummy 仕立て屋の人台 ▶定義 2 略式 a stupid person 愚かな人→**ばか，間抜け** ‖ Don't just stand there like a dummy - help me! そこにばかみたいにただ立っているんじゃない － 私を手伝え．▶定義 3 米 **pacifier** a rubber object that you put in a baby's mouth to keep him/her quiet and happy 静めて喜ばせるために赤ん坊の口に入れる，ゴム製のもの→**おしゃぶり** ▶定義 4 something that is made to look like sth else but that is not the real thing ほかの〜に似せて作られているが，本物ではないもの→**模型，型見本** ‖ The robbers used dummy handguns in the raid. 強盗は襲撃の際に，模型のけん銃を使った．

**dump**¹ /dʌmp/ 動 他 ▶定義 1 to get rid of sth that you do not want, especially in a place which is not suitable 特に適切ではない場所に，要らない〜を処分する→**(ごみなど)を捨てる，処分する** ‖ Nuclear waste should not be dumped in the sea. 核廃棄物は，海中に投棄されるべきではない．(比喩) I wish you wouldn't keep dumping the extra work on me. 私に余分な仕事を押し付けたままにしないでほしい．▶定義 2 to put something down quickly or in a careless way 物を急いで，またはぞんざいに下に置く→**〜をどさっと投げ出す・降ろす・落とす，ぞんざいに降ろす** ‖ The children dumped their coats and bags in the hall and ran off to play. 子供たちは玄関にコートとかばんをどさっと降ろすと，走って遊びに行った．▶定義 3 略式 to get rid of sb, especially a boyfriend or girlfriend 〜，特に恋人から自由になる→**〜を捨てる，振る** ‖ Did you hear that Laura dumped Chris last night? 昨日の晩，ローラがクリスを振ったことを聞きましたか．

**dump**² /dʌmp/ 名 C ▶定義 1 a place where rubbish or waste material from factories, etc is left 工場などからのごみ、または廃棄物が置き去りにされる場所→ごみの山, ごみ捨て場 ‖ *a rubbish dump* ごみ捨て場 ▶定義2 話式 a place that is very dirty, untidy or unpleasant とても汚い, 乱雑な, または不愉快な場所→汚い場所 ‖ *The flat is cheap but it's a real dump.* そのアパートは安いけれど, 本当に汚い所だ. ☛類 tip

成句 **down in the dumps** ▶定義 unhappy or sad 惨めな, または悲しい→ふさぎ込んで, 落ち込んで

**dumpling** /dʌ́mplɪŋ/ 名 C ▶定義 a small ball of flour and fat (dough) that is cooked and usually eaten with meat 調理されて通常は肉と一緒に食べられる, 小麦粉と牛脂(こね粉)の小さな玉→ゆでだんご(肉の付け合わせやスープに入れたりする)

**dune** /d(j)uːn/(または **sand dune**) 名 C ▶定義 a low hill of sand by the sea or in the desert 海辺または砂漠にある低い砂の丘→砂丘

**dung** /dʌŋ/ 名 U ▶定義 waste material from the bodies of large animals 大型動物の体から出る排せつ物→(牛・馬などの)糞(ふん), くそ ‖ *cow dung* 牛の糞

**dungarees** /dʌ̀ŋɡəríːz/ ⇔ (困 **overalls**) 名 [複数扱い] ▶定義 a piece of clothing, similar to trousers, but covering your chest as well as your legs and with straps that go over the shoulders ズボンに似ているが脚と同様に胸も覆い, 両肩に掛けるひもの付いた衣服→(青デニムの)作業ズボン, ダンガリー, オーバーオール ‖ *a pair of dungarees* 1着のオーバーオール ☛ C6 ページのさし絵

**dungeon** /dʌ́ndʒ(ə)n/ 名 C ▶定義 an old underground prison, especially in a castle 特に城内の, 古い地下牢(ろう)→地下牢, 土牢

**duo** /d(j)úːoʊ/ 名 C ▶定義1 two people playing music or singing together 一緒に音楽を演奏するかもしくは歌う2人→二重唱・奏者 ▶定義2 = **DUET**

**dupe** /d(j)uːp/ 動 他 ▶定義 to lie to sb in order to make him/her believe sth or do sth ~に…を信じさせるまたは…を行わせるためにうそをつく→~をだます, 担ぐ, ~をだまして…させる ‖ *The woman was duped into carrying the drugs.* その女性はだまされて麻薬を運ばされた.

**duplicate**[1] /d(j)úːplɪkèɪt/ 動 他 ▶定義1 to make an exact copy of sth ~の正確な写しを作る→~の写しを取る, ~を複写・複製する ▶定義2 to do sth that has already been done 既に行われた~を行う→~を繰り返す, まねる ‖ *We don't want to duplicate the work of other departments.* 私たちはほかの部門の仕事をまねしたくない. — **duplication** /d(j)ùːplɪkéɪʃ(ə)n/ 名 U →複写, 複製, 複写・複製したもの

**duplicate**[2] /d(j)úːplɪkət/ 名 C ▶定義 something that is exactly the same as sth else ほかの~と全く同じもの→複写, 複製, 写し — **duplicate** 形 (名詞の前だけ)→そっくり同じの, 複写・複製の, 二重の ‖ *a duplicate key* 合いかぎ

成句 **in duplicate** ▶定義 with two copies (for example of an official piece of paper) that are exactly the same (例えば正式な書類の)全く同じ2通がある→正副2通にして ‖ *The contract must be in duplicate.* 契約書は正副2通でなければならない.

**durable** /d(j)úərəb(ə)l/ 形 ▶定義 that can last a long time 長期間耐えられる→長持ちする, 耐久性に優れた, 丈夫な ‖ *a durable fabric* 耐久性に優れた織物 — **durability** /d(j)ùərəbíləti/ 名 U →耐久性・力, 永続性

**duration** /d(j)ʊəréɪʃ(ə)n/ 名 U ▶定義 the time that sth lasts ~が続く時間→持続・存続時間, 期間 ‖ *Please remain seated for the duration of the flight.* 飛行中は席に座ったままでいてください.

**duress** /d(j)ʊərés/ 名 U ▶定義 threats or force that are used to make sb do sth ~に…を行わせるために用いられる脅迫または暴力→脅迫, 監禁 ‖ *He signed the confession under duress.* 彼は強迫されて供述書に署名した.

*★**during** /d(j)úərɪŋ/ 前 ▶定義 within the period of time mentioned 言及された期間内に→~の間中, ~の間ずっと ‖ *During the summer holidays we went swimming every day.* 夏休みの間中, 私たちは毎日泳ぎに行った. *Grandpa was taken very ill during the night.* おじいちゃんは夜の間ずっと, とても具合が悪かった.

▶ある事がいつ起きるかを言うためにduringを使い, ある事がどのくらい続くかを言うために for を使うことに注意: *I went shopping during my lunch break.*(私は昼食時間の間に, 買い物に行った.) *I was out for about 25 minutes.*(私は約25分間外出していた.)

**dusk** /dʌsk/ 名 U ▶定義 the time in the evening

when the sun has already gone down and it is nearly dark 日は既に落ちてほとんど暗い, 夕方の一時→**夕闇, たそがれ** ☞参 **dawn, twilight**

**\*dust**[1] /dʌ́st/ 名 Ü ▶定義 very small pieces of dry dirt, sand, etc in the form of a powder 粉状の, 乾燥した非常に小さなほこり, 砂など▶**ほこり, ちり, (もうもうと上がる)砂ぼこり** ‖ *a thick layer of dust* 厚く積もったほこり *chalk/coal dust* 白墨・石炭のちり *The tractor came up the track in a cloud of dust.* トラクターは, もうもうと立ち昇る砂ぼこりの中, 道をやって来た. *a speck (= small piece) of dust* 小片の(= 小さな一片)ほこり — **dusty** →**ちり・ほこりまみれの, ほこりっぽい** ‖ *This shelf has got very dusty.* この棚はすごくほこりっぽくなった.

**\*dust**[2] /dʌ́st/ 動 他 ▶定義 to clean a room, furniture, etc by removing dust with a cloth 布でほこりを払って, 部屋, 家具などを掃除する→**ちり払いをする; 〜のちり・ほこりを払う** ‖ *Let me dust those shelves before you put the books on them.* あなたが本を置く前に, 私がそれらの棚のほこりを払いましょう. ☞参 **clean**[2]の注

**dustbin** /dʌ́stbìn/ (米 **garbage can; trash can**) 名 C ▶定義 a large container for rubbish that you keep outside your house 家の外に置いておく, ごみを入れる大きな容器→**(大型のふた付き)ごみ容器, ごみ入れ缶** ☞ **bin**のさし絵

**duster** /dʌ́stər/ 名 C ▶定義 a soft dry cloth that you use for cleaning furniture, etc 家具などの掃除に使う, 柔らかくて乾いた布→**ほこりを払い取る布, ぞうきん** ☞ **bucket**のさし絵

**dustman** /dʌ́stmən/ 名 C (複 **-men** /-mən/) ▶定義 a person whose job is to take away the rubbish that people put in large containers outside the house (**dustbins**) 家の外にある大型の容器(ごみ容器)に捨てられたごみを持ち去ることが仕事の人→**ごみ収集人, 清掃業者**

**dustpan** /dʌ́stpæ̀n/ 名 C ▶定義 a flat container with a handle into which you brush dirt from the floor 床のごみを掃き入れる, 柄の付いた平らな入れ物→**ちり取り, ごみ取り** ‖ *Where do you keep your dustpan and brush?* ちり取りと小ほうきはどこに置いてあるのですか. ☞ **brush**のさし絵

**Dutch** /dʌ́tʃ/ 形 ▶定義 from the Netherlands オランダからの→**オランダの, オランダ人の, オランダ語の** ☞ 巻末の地名の項を参照.

**dutiful** /d(j)úːtifəl, -f(ə)l/ 形 ▶定義 happy to respect and obey sb 喜んで〜を尊敬し従う→**忠実な, 従順な, 礼儀正しい** ‖ *a dutiful son* 従順な息子

**\*duty** /d(j)úːti/ 名 (複 **duties**) ▶定義 **1** C Ü something that you have to do because people expect you to do it or because you think it is right それをすることを人々が期待しているので, あるいはそれは正しいと考えるので, 行わなければならない物事→**義務, 本分, 義理** ‖ *A soldier must do his duty.* 兵士は本分を尽くさなければならない. *a sense of moral duty* 道徳的義務の感覚 ▶定義 **2** C Ü the tasks that you do when you are at work 職場にいるときに人が行う務め→**職務, 任務** ‖ *the duties of a policeman* 警察官の任務 *Which nurses are on night duty this week?* 今週は看護婦さんはだれが夜勤ですか. ▶定義 **3** C a tax that you pay, especially on goods that you bring into a country 特に国内に持ち込んだ商品にかかる, 人が支払う税金→**税, 関税**

**成句 on/off duty** ▶定義 (used about doctors, nurses, police officers, etc) to be working/not working (医師, 看護婦, 警察官などについて) 仕事中で・仕事中ではない→**当直で, 勤務時間中で; 非番で, 勤務時間外で** ‖ *The porter's on duty from 8 till 4.* ポーターの勤務時間は, 8時から4時です. *What time does she go off duty?* 彼女は何時に勤務を終えますか.

**duty-free** 形 副 ▶定義 (used about goods) that you can bring into a country without paying tax (商品について) 税金を支払わずに, 国内に持ち込める→**税金・関税がかからない, 免税の; 免税で** ‖ *an airport duty-free shop* 空港の免税店 *How much wine can you bring into Britain duty-free?* 英国に免税で持ち込めるワインの量はどれくらいですか. ☞参 **tax-free**

**duvet** /duvéi, d(j)úːvèi/ 名 C ▶定義 a thick cover filled with feathers or another soft material that you sleep under to keep warm in bed ベッドの中で暖かさを保つために掛けて寝る, 羽毛またはほかの柔らかい素材を詰めた厚手の寝具→**キルトに羽毛を詰めた掛け布団, 羽毛掛け布団** ☞参 **eiderdown, quilt** ☞ **bed**のさし絵

**dwarf**[1] /dwɔ́ːrf/ 名 C (複 **dwarfs** または **dwarves** /dwɔ́ːrvz/) ▶定義 **1** a person, animal or plant that

**dwarf**² /dwɔːrf/ 動 ▶定義 (used about a large object) to make sth seem very small in comparison(巨大な物について)それと比べると、~をとても小さく見せる→~を(対照的に)小さく見せる ‖ *The skyscraper dwarfs all the other buildings around.* その超高層ビルは、周辺のすべてのビルを小さく見せる.

**dwell** /dwel/ 動 ⊜(過, 過分 **dwelt** /dwelt/ または **dwelled**)(古) 正式 ▶定義 to live or stay in a place ある場所に住むまたは滞在する→住む, 居住する

 句動詞 **dwell on/upon sth** ▶定義 to think or talk a lot about sth that it would be better to forget 忘れた方が良いに違いない~について、よく考えるまたは話す→~をくよくよ・つくづく考える、~にこだわる、~についてくどくど話す・書く ‖ *I don't want to dwell on the past. Let's think about the future.* 私は過去にこだわりたくない. 未来について考えよう.

**dweller** /dwélər/ 名 ⊜ (しばしば複合語で) ▶定義 a person or animal that lives in the place mentioned 言及された場所に住む人または動物 →居住者, 住人 ‖ *city-dwellers* 都会人

**dwelling** /dwélɪŋ/ 名 ⊜ 正式 ▶定義 the place where a person lives; a house 人が住む場所; 家→住居, 住宅

**dwindle** /dwíndl/ 動 ⊜ ▶定義 **dwindle (away)** to become smaller or weaker より小さく、または弱くなる→だんだん小さくなる、次第に減少する、重要でなくなる ‖ *Their savings dwindled away to nothing.* 彼らの貯金はだんだん少なくなり、しまいにはなくなってしまった.

**dye**¹ /daɪ/ 動 ⊕(現分 **dyeing**; 三単現 **dyes**; 過, 過分 **dyed**)▶定義 to make sth a different colour ~を別の色にする→~を染める, ~に色を付ける ‖ *Does she dye her hair?* 彼女は髪を染めているのですか. *I'm going to dye this blouse black.* このブラウスを黒に染めます.

**dye**² /daɪ/ 名 ⊜ ⊎ ▶定義 a substance that is used to change the colour of sth ~の色を変えるために使われる材料→染料

**dying** DIE の現在分詞形

# dyslexia  521

**dyke**(または **dike**)/daɪk/ 名 ⊜ ▶定義 **1** a long thick wall that is built to prevent the sea or a river from flooding low land 海または河川が低地に氾濫(はんらん)することを防ぐために建てられる、長く厚い壁→堤防, 土手 ▶定義 **2** 特に 医 a long narrow space dug in the ground and used for taking water away from land 地面に掘られた細長い溝で、土地から水を取り去るために使われる→水路, 溝

**dynamic** /daɪnǽmɪk/ 形 ▶定義 **1** (used about a person) full of energy and ideas; active(人について)活力と着想に満ちている; 活動的な→活動的な, 精力的な ▶定義 **2** (used about a force or power) that causes movement(勢いまたは動力について)運動を生じさせる→動的な, 動力の, 力学の — **dynamism** /dáɪnəmɪz(ə)m/ 名 ⊎→(人が)活動的なこと, 活力, 精力

**dynamite** /dáɪnəmàɪt/ 名 ⊎ ▶定義 **1** a powerful explosive substance 強力な爆発物→ダイナマイト ▶定義 **2** a thing or person that causes great excitement, shock, etc 大きな興奮または衝撃などを引き起こす物または人→強烈なショック・驚きを与えるもの, 衝撃的・物騒な人・物事 ‖ *His news was dynamite.* 彼の知らせは衝撃的だった.

**dynamo** /dáɪnəmòʊ/ 名 ⊜ (複 **dynamos**) ▶定義 a device that changes energy from the movement of sth such as wind or water into electricity ~、例えば風または水の動きから生じるエネルギーを電力に変える装置→発電機

**dynasty** /dáɪnəsti; dín-/ 名 ⊜ (複 **dynasties**) ▶定義 a series of rulers who are from the same family 同じ一族出身の統治者の一続き→王朝, 王家 ‖ *the Ming dynasty in China* 中国の明王朝

**dysentery** /dísntri; -tèri/ 名 ⊎ ▶定義 a serious disease which causes you to get rid of waste material from your body very often in liquid form (**to have diarrhoea**), and to lose blood 人の体から非常に頻繁に液状の排せつ物を出し(下痢を起こす), 血液を減らす原因となる, 重い病気→赤痢

**dyslexia** /dɪsléksiə/ 名 ⊎ ▶定義 a difficulty that some people have with reading and spelling ある人々が示す, 読むこととつづることの困難な状態→失語症 — **dyslexic** 名 ⊜ 形→失読症患者; 失語症の

# E e

**E, e**[1] /iː/ 图 ⓒ (複 **E's; e's**) ▶定義 the fifth letter of the English alphabet 英語アルファベットの第5文字→e(E)が表す音, e(E)の文字, e(E)の字形のもの ‖ *'Egg' begins with (an) 'E'*. EggはEで始まる.

**E**[2] east(ern)→東(の) ‖ *E Asia* 東アジア

**ea** 略 each→それぞれ, 銘々, 各

\***each** /iːtʃ/ 形代 ▶定義 every individual person or thing 個々の人または物→それぞれ, 銘々, 各 ‖ *Each lesson lasts an hour.* 各授業は1時間だ. *Each of the lessons lasts an hour.* 授業はそれぞれ1時間だ. *The lessons each last an hour.* 授業はそれぞれ1時間だ. *These T-shirts are £5 each.* これらのTシャツは1枚5ポンドだ.

### each other

He's looking at himself.

They're looking at **each other**.

\***each other** 代 ▶定義 used for saying that A does the same thing to B as B does to A BがAにしたのと同じ事をAがBにするというときに用いられて→互いに ‖ *Emma and Dave love each other very much* (= *Emma loves Dave and Dave loves Emma*). エマとデーブはとても愛し合っている(= エマはデーブを愛していて, デーブはエマを愛している). *We looked at each other.* 私たちは互いに顔を見合わせた.

\***eager** /íːɡər/ 形 ▶定義 **eager (to do sth); eager (for sth)** full of desire or interest; keen 欲望や興味で一杯の; 夢中の→しきりに~をしたがる; ~を切望する; 熱心な, 激しい, 強烈な ‖ *We're all eager to start work on the new project.* 我々は皆新しいプロジェクトで仕事を開始するのを心待ちにしている. *eager for success* 成功を熱望する —**eagerly** 副 →熱心に —**eagerness** 名 Ⓤ →熱望, 熱心さ

**eagle** /íːɡ(ə)l/ 图 ⓒ ▶定義 a very large bird that can see very well. It eats small birds and animals. 大変よく目の利く非常に大きな鳥で, 小鳥や小動物を食べる→ワシ

**EAP** /ìː eɪ píː/ 略 English for Academic Purposes →学術目的の英語

\***ear** /ɪər/ 图 ▶定義 **1** ⓒ one of the two parts of the body of a person or animal that are used for hearing 人または動物が音を聞くときに使う体の部分で, 2つあるうちの1つ→耳 ☞参 C1, C5ページのさし絵 ▶定義 **2** [単数扱い] **an ear (for sth)** an ability to recognize and repeat sounds, especially in music or language 特に音楽や言語において, 音を聞き分けてまねる能力→(~を)聞く力; 聴力, 聴覚 ‖ *Yuka has a good ear for languages.* ユカは言葉を聞き取る能力が高い. ▶定義 **3** ⓒ the top part of a plant that produces grain 穀粒を作る作物の一番上の部分→穂 ‖ *an ear of corn* 穀物の穂

**成句** **sb's ears are burning** ▶定義 used when a person thinks that other people are talking about him/her, especially in an unkind way 特に否定的な意味で, ほかの人が自分のことを話していると思ったときに用いて→だれかが(自分のことを)うわさしている

**play (sth) by ear** ▶定義 to play a piece of music that you have heard without using written notes 聞いたことのある曲を楽譜なしで演奏する→暗譜で演奏する ‖ *She can read music, but she can also play by ear.* 彼女は楽譜が読めるが, 譜を見ずに演奏することもできる.

**go in one ear and out the other** ▶定義 (used about information, etc) to be forgotten quickly (情報等について)すぐに忘れてしまう→聞いたそばから忘れる, 片方の耳から入って反対側の耳に抜ける ‖ *Everything I tell him seems to go in one ear and out the other.* 彼に何を言っても聞いたそばから忘れてしまうようだ.

**play it by ear** ▶定義 to decide what to do as things happen, instead of planning in advance 前もって計画を立てずに, 事が起きてからどうするかを決める→(下準備なしに)処理する, その場で対応する ‖ *We don't know what Alan's reaction will be, so we'll just have to play it by ear.* アランがどう反応するか分からないから, その場で対応するしかない.

**prick up your ears** ⇒ **PRICK**[1]

**earache** /íərèɪk/ 图 Ⓤ ▶定義 a pain in your ear→耳の痛み ‖ *I've got earache.* 耳痛がする.

☛参 ache の注

**eardrum** /íərdrʌm/ 名 C ▶定義 a thin piece of skin inside the ear that is tightly stretched and that allows you to hear sound 耳の内側にきつく張った薄い皮膜で、これで音を聞くことができる→**鼓膜**

**earl** /ə́:rl/ 名 C ▶定義 a British man of a high social position 英国の高い社会的地位にある男性→**伯爵**

**ear lobe** 名 C ▶定義 the round soft part at the bottom of your ear 耳の外部を形成する部分のうち、下部の丸みを帯びた柔らかいところ→**耳たぶ**

*__early__ /ə́:rli/ 形 副 (__earlier__; __earliest__) ▶定義 1 near the beginning of a period of time, a piece of work, a series, etc 一定の期間、1つの作品、一連の事柄などの最初の方に(ある)→**早い、初期の、早めの** ‖ *I have to get up early on weekday mornings.* 平日の朝は早起きしなければならない. *I think John's in his early twenties.* 私はジョンが20代初めだと思う. *The project is still in its early stages.* そのプロジェクトはまだ初期段階にある. ▶定義 2 before the usual or expected time いつものまたは予定された時間よりも前に→**早めに** ‖ *She arrived five minutes early for her interview.* 彼女はインタビューの時間よりも5分早めに到着した.

成句 **at the earliest** ▶定義 not before the date or time mentioned 述べられた日または時間より前ではない→**早くても** ‖ *I can repair it by Friday at the earliest.* 修理が終わるのは早くても金曜日だ.

**it's early days (yet)** ▶定義 used to say that it is too soon to know how a situation will develop 時期が早すぎて状況がどう変わるかまだ分からないときに用いて→**まだどうなるか分からない、結論を出すのは時期尚早だ**

**the early hours** ▶定義 very early in the morning in the hours after midnight→**午前0時を過ぎた非常に早い時間帯**

**an early/a late night** ⇒ **NIGHT**

**early on** ▶定義 soon after the beginning 始まって間もなく→**早くから** ‖ *He achieved fame early on in his career.* 彼は仕事を始めて早いうちから名声を得た.

**an early riser** ▶定義 a person who usually gets up early in the morning いつも朝早く起きる人→**早起き**

**earmark** /íərmɑ̀:rk/ 動 他 ▶定義 earmark sb/sth (for sth/sb) to choose sb/sth to do sth in the future 将来ある事をするために〜を選ぶ→**(〜のために)…を取っておく** ‖ *Everybody says Elena has been earmarked as the next manager.* 皆はエレナが間違いなく次のマネージャーだと言っている.

*__earn__ /ə́:rn/ 動 他 ▶定義 1 to get money by working 働いてお金を得る→**〜を稼ぐ、もうける** ‖ *How much does a dentist earn?* 歯医者ってどのくらい稼ぐの. *I earn £20000 a year.* 私は年間2万ポンド稼ぐ. *It's hard to earn a living as an artist.* 芸術家で食べていくのは難しい. ▶定義 2 to win the right to sth, for example by working hard よく働くなどして〜の権利を得る→**〜を得る、受ける、手に入れる** ‖ *The team's victory today has earned them a place in the final.* そのチームは今日の勝利で決勝戦への出場権を手に入れた. ▶定義 3 to get money as profit or interest on money you have in a bank, lent to sb, etc お金を銀行に預けたり、人に貸したりして利益や利子を得る→**〜をもうける、得る** ‖ *How much interest will my savings earn in this account?* この口座に預けた貯蓄預金の利子はどのくらいですか.

**earnest** /ə́:rnəst/ 形 ▶定義 serious or determined 真剣なまたは決然とした→**真剣な、熱心な、まじめな** ‖ *He's such an earnest young man - he never makes a joke.* 彼は非常にまじめな青年だ — 冗談も言わない. *They were having a very earnest discussion.* 彼らは非常に真剣に討論していた. —**earnestly** 副 →**まじめに、真剣に、熱心に**

成句 **in earnest** ▶定義 1 serious and sincere about what you are going to do これからしようとする事について真剣でまじめな→**まじめな[に]、本気で[の]** ‖ *He was in earnest about wanting to leave university.* 彼は大学を辞めたいと本気で考えていた. ▶定義 2 happening more seriously or with more force than before 以前よりも真剣にまたは力を入れて→**本格的に** ‖ *After two weeks work began in earnest on the project.* 2週間後からプロジェクトは本格的に始動した.

**earnings** /ə́:rniŋz/ 名 [複数扱い] ▶定義 the money that a person earns by working 働いて

得たお金→**所得, もうけ, 稼ぎ** ‖ *Average earnings have increased by 5%.* 平均所得は5パーセント増加した.

**earphones** /íərfòʊnz/ 名 [複数扱い] ▶定義 a piece of equipment that fits over or in the ears and is used for listening to music, the radio, etc 耳にかぶせ, または耳の中にはめて音楽, ラジオなどを聴くのに使う器具→**イヤホン, ヘッドホン**

**earring** /íəriŋ/ 名 C ▶定義 a piece of jewellery that is worn in or on the lower part of the ear 耳の下部に付ける装飾品→**イヤリング, 耳飾り** ‖ *Do these earrings clip on or are they for pierced ears?* これはイヤリングかしら, それともピアスかしら. ☛参 **jewellery**のさし絵

**earshot** /íərʃɑ̀t/ 名 U

成句 **(be) out of/within earshot** ▶定義 where a person cannot/can hear 聞こえない・聞こえる所にいる→**呼んでも聞こえない所に, 呼べば聞こえる所に** ‖ *Wait until he's out of earshot before you say anything about him.* 彼のことを話すのは, 彼に聞こえない所に行ってからにしなさい.

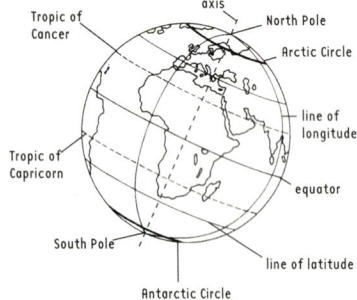

the earth
northern hemisphere
axis / North Pole / Arctic Circle / Tropic of Cancer / line of longitude / Tropic of Capricorn / equator / South Pole / line of latitude / Antarctic Circle
southern hemisphere

★**earth**¹ /ə:rθ/ 名 ▶定義**1** (または **the earth**; **the Earth**) [単数扱い] the world; the planet on which we live 世界; 私たちが住んでいる惑星→**地球, 世界** ‖ *life on earth* 地球上の生物 *The earth goes round the sun.* 地球は太陽の周りを回る. ▶定義**2** [単数扱い] the surface of the world; land 地球の表面; 土地→**地面, 大地** ‖ *The spaceship fell towards earth.* 宇宙船が地面に向けて落ちてきた. *I could feel the earth shake when the earthquake started.* 地震が起こると, 地面が揺れるのが分かった. ▶定義**3** ❶ the substance that plants grow in; soil 植物が育つ場所; 土壌→**土壌, 土** ‖ *The earth around here is very fertile.* この辺の土壌は非常に肥沃(ひよく)である. ☛参 **ground**の注 ▶定義**4** [❻, 通常は単数] (米 **ground**) a wire that makes a piece of electrical equipment safer by connecting it to the ground 電気器具を安全に使用するための地面につないで使う線→**アース**

成句 **charge/pay the earth** 略式 ▶定義 to charge/pay a very large amount of money→**大金を請求する・支払う** ‖ *Dan must have paid the earth for that new car.* ダンはあの新車に大金を支払ったに違いない.

**cost the earth/a fortune** ⇒ **COST**²

**how/why/where/who etc on earth** 略式 ▶定義 used for emphasizing sth or expressing surprise 強調したり, 驚きを表すのに用いて→(疑問詞の後において)**一体(全体)** ‖ *Where on earth have you been?* 一体どこに行ってきたのですか.

**earth**² /ə:rθ/ (米 **ground**) 動 他 ▶定義 to make a piece of electrical equipment safer by connecting it to the ground with a wire 安全に利用するために電気器具を電線で地面につなぐ→**アースする** ‖ *Make sure the plug is earthed.* プラグにアースするのを忘れないで.

**earthquake** /ə́:rθkwèɪk/ (または 略式 **quake**) 名 C ▶定義 violent movement of the earth's surface 地表が激しく揺れること→**地震**

**earthworm** /ə́:rθwə̀:rm/ 名 C ▶定義 a small, long, thin animal with no legs or eyes that lives in the soil 土の中にいる小さく, 細長い, 足や目がない動物→**みみず**

**ease**¹ /i:z/ 名 U ▶定義 a lack of difficulty 難しくないこと→**容易さ, 平易** ‖ *She answered the questions with ease.* 彼女は難なく質問に答えた. ☛形 **easy** ⇔ **unease**

成句 **(be/feel) at (your) ease** ▶定義 to be/feel comfortable, relaxed, etc 快適に, くつろいで→**落ち着く, 安心する** ‖ *They were all so kind and friendly that I felt completely at ease.* 彼らは皆とても親切で優しいので, 私は完全にくつろげた.

**ease**² /i:z/ 動 ▶定義**1** 自 他 to become or make sth less painful or serious 〜の痛みや深刻さが和らぐ, またはそれらを和らげる→**楽になる・す**

る, 和らぐ·和らげる ‖ *The pain should ease by this evening.* 痛みは今日の夕方までには和らぐだろう. *This money will ease their financial problems a little.* このお金で彼らの経済的困難も少し楽になるだろう. ☛ [形] easy ▶定義 2 [他] to move sth slowly and gently ～をゆっくりと静かに動かす ➜ **～をそっと動かす** ‖ *He eased the key into the lock.* 彼はそっとかぎ穴にかぎを差し込んだ.

[成句] **ease sb's mind** ▶定義 to make sb feel less worried ～の心配を和らげる ➜ **気持ちを楽にする, 和らげる** ‖ *The doctor tried to ease her mind about her son's illness.* 医者は, 息子の病気についての彼女の不安を和らげようとした.

[句動詞] **ease off** ▶定義 to become less strong or unpleasant 強さや不快さが弱まる ➜ **弱まる, 和らぐ** ‖ *Let's wait until the rain eases off.* 雨が収まるのを待とう.

**ease up** ▶定義 to work less hard 仕事の手を緩める ➜ **手を緩める, のんびりする** ‖ *Ease up a bit or you'll make yourself ill!* 少し仕事の手を緩めないと病気になるよ.

**easel** /iːz(ə)l/ [名] [C] ▶定義 a wooden frame that holds a picture while it is being painted かいている間絵を立てておく木製の枠 ➜ **画架, イーゼル, 台**

**easily** /iːz(ə)li/ [副] ▶定義 1 without difficulty 難なく ➜ **容易に, 簡単に, 楽に, すぐに** ‖ *I can easily ring up and check the time.* すぐに電話をかけて, 時間を調べられるよ. ▶定義 2 **easily the best, worst, nicest, etc** without doubt ➜ **(the best, worst, nicest のような最上級を強めて) 確かに, 疑いなく** ‖ *It's easily his best novel.* その小説は断然彼の最高傑作だ.

***east**[1] /iːst/ [名] [単数扱い] ([略] E) ▶定義 1 (または **the east**) the direction you look towards in order to see the sun rise; one of the four main directions that we give names to (**the points of the compass**) 日の出を見るとき向く方向; (方位磁針にもある) 4つの方角の1つ ➜ **東** ‖ *Which way is east?* 東はどちらだろう. *a cold wind from the east* 東からの冷たい風 *Which county is **to the east of** Oxfordshire?* オックスフォードシャーの東にあるのはどの州ですか. ☛参 **north** のさし絵 ▶定義 2 **the east** the part of any country, city, etc that is further to the east than the other parts 国や都市などの一部分で, ほかの地域よりも東にある地域 ➜ **東部** ‖ *Norwich is in the east of England.* ノリッジはイングランド東部にある. ▶定義 3 **the East** the countries of Asia, for example China and Japan 中国や日本などのアジアの国々 ➜ **東洋, アジア** ☛参 **the Far East, the Middle East**

**east**[2] /iːst/ (または **East**) [形][副] ▶定義 in or towards the east or from the east 東方へ·に, または東から ➜ **東の [に], 東部の, 東方の [へ], 東からの** ‖ *They headed east.* 彼らは東へ向かった. *the East Coast of America* アメリカ東海岸 *We live east of the city.* 私たちはその都市の東部に住んでいる. *an east wind* 東からの風

**eastbound** /iːstbàʊnd/ [形] ▶定義 travelling or leading towards the east 東に向かって旅する, または進む ➜ **東へ向かっている, 東回りの** ‖ *The eastbound carriageway of the motorway is blocked.* 高速道路の東回り路線は閉鎖されている.

***Easter** /iːstər/ [名] [U] ▶定義 a festival on a Sunday in March or April when Christians celebrate Christ's return to life; the time before and after Easter Sunday キリスト教徒がキリストの復活を祝う祭日で3月または4月の日曜日; 復活祭の日曜日を挟む期間 ➜ **復活祭** ‖ *the Easter holidays* 復活祭休み *Are you going away **at Easter**?* 復活祭の休みにはお出掛けしますか.

**Easter egg** [名] [C] ▶定義 an egg, usually made of chocolate, that you give as a present at Easter 復活祭の時に人に贈る卵で, 通常チョコレートでできている ➜ **イースターエッグ**

**easterly** /iːstərli/ [形] ▶定義 1 towards or in the east 東へ向けて, または東へ ➜ **東の, 東寄りの** ‖ *They travelled in an easterly direction.* 彼らは東の方角に向けて旅をした. ▶定義 2 (used about winds) coming from the east ➜ **(風について) 東から吹く** ‖ *cold easterly winds* 東からの冷たい風

***eastern** (または **Eastern**) /iːstərn/ [形] ▶定義 1 of, in or from the east of a place ある場所の東の, 東部にある, または東から ➜ **東の, 東からの** ‖ *Eastern Scotland* スコットランド東部 *the eastern shore of the lake* 湖の東岸 ▶定義 2 from or connected with the countries of the East 東洋諸国からの, またはそれに関連した ➜ **東洋の** ‖ *Eastern cookery (= that comes from Asia)* 東洋料理 (= アジアに由来する料理)

**eastward** /íːstwərd/(または **eastwards**) 形副
▶定義 towards the east 東に向けて➡**東向きに、東に向かって** ‖ *to travel in an eastward direction* 東に向かって旅をする *The Amazon flows eastwards.* アマゾン川は東に向かって流れる.

\*easy¹ /íːzi/ 形 (**easier; easiest**) ▶定義 1 not difficult 難しくない➡**易しい、簡単な、容易な** ‖ *an easy question* 易しい質問 *It isn't easy to explain the system.* そのシステムを説明するのは簡単ではない. *The system isn't easy to explain.* そのシステムの説明は簡単ではない. ⇔ **hard**
▶定義 2 comfortable, relaxed and not worried 快適で、落ち着いていて、心配のない➡**気楽な、安楽な、心地良い** ‖ *an easy life* 気楽な暮らし *My mind's easier now.* 気持ちが前より楽になった. ⇔ **uneasy** ☞ 名動 **ease**
成句 **free and easy** ⇒ **FREE¹**
**I'm easy** 略式 ▶定義 used to say that you do not have a strong opinion when sb offers you a choice 〜から選択の自由を与えられたときに、自分は強い意見がない場合に用いて➡**どちらでも構わない** ‖ *'Would you like to go first or second?' 'I'm easy.'* 「最初に行きたいの、それとも2番目がいいの」「どっちでもいいよ」

\*easy² /íːzi/ 副 (**easier; easiest**)
成句 **easier said than done**（口語）▶定義 more difficult to do than to talk about 口で言うよりも実行する方が難しい➡**言うは易く、行うは難し** ‖ *'You should get her to help you.' 'That's easier said than done.'*「彼女に手伝わせるべきだよ」「言うは易く、行うは難しさ」
**go easy on sb/on/with sth** 略式 ▶定義 1 to be gentle or less strict with sb 〜に優しくまたはあまり厳しくしない➡**〜を大事に扱う、加減して用いる、大目に見る** ‖ *Go easy on him; he's just a child.* 大目に見てあげなよ. 彼はまだ子供なんだから. ▶定義 2 to avoid using too much of sth 〜を使いすぎないようにする➡**〜を控えめに使う、控えめに食べる・飲む** ‖ *Go easy on the salt; it's bad for your heart.* 塩をとりすぎてはいけないよ. 心臓に悪いからね.
**take it/things easy** ▶定義 to relax and not work too hard or worry too much 落ち着いて、心配しすぎたり働きすぎたりしない➡**のんびり構える**

**easy chair** 名 C ▶定義 a large comfortable chair with arms ひじ掛けが付いた、大きくて楽に座れるいす➡**安楽いす**

**easy-going** 形 ▶定義 (used about a person) calm, relaxed and not easily worried or upset by what other people do（人について）おっとりして、落ち着いていて、他人のする事について簡単に気に病んだり、うろたえたりしない➡**のんびりした、おっとりした、(物事に)こだわらない** ‖ *Her parents are very easy-going. They let her do what she wants.* 彼女の両親はのんびりしている. 彼女のやりたいようにさせている.

\*eat /íːt/ 動 (過 **ate** /éɪt; et, éɪt/; 過分 **eaten** /íːtn/)
▶定義 1 自他 to put food into your mouth, then bite and swallow it 食べ物を口に入れて、かんで、飲み込む➡**(〜を)食べる** ‖ *Who ate all the biscuits?* ビスケットを全部食べたのはだれ. *Eat your dinner up, Joe (= finish it all).* 夕食を食べてしまいなさい、ジョー(= 全部済ませる). *She doesn't eat properly. No wonder she's so thin.* 彼女は適切に食事を取らない. あんなにやせているのも無理はない. ▶定義 2 自 to have a meal 食事を取る➡**食事をする** ‖ *What time shall we eat?* 何時に食事にしましょうか.
成句 **have sb eating out of your hand** ▶定義 to have control and power over sb 〜を管理、支配する➡**〜を言いなりにさせる**
**have your cake and eat it** ⇒ **CAKE¹**
句動詞 **eat sth away/eat away at sth** ▶定義 to damage or destroy sth slowly over a period of time 一定期間をかけてゆっくり〜を壊したり損なったりする➡**〜を侵食する、腐食する** ‖ *The sea had eaten away at the cliff.* その崖(がけ)は海によって侵食されていた.
**eat out** ▶定義 to have a meal in a restaurant レストランで食事をする➡**外食する** ‖ *Would you like to eat out tonight?* 今夜は外食しませんか.

**eater** /íːtər/ 名 C ▶定義 a person who eats in a particular way 特定の食べ方をする人➡**食べる人、食べるのが〜な人** ‖ *My uncle's a big eater (= he eats a lot).* 私のおじは大食漢だ(= たくさん食べる). *We're not great meat eaters.* 私たちはあまり肉を食べない.

**eau de cologne** /òʊ də kəlóʊn/（または **cologne**）名 U ▶定義 a type of pleasant smelling liquid (**perfume**) that is not very strong あまり強くなく、良い香りのする液体(香水)➡**オーデ**

**eaves** /iːvz/ 名 [複数扱い] ▶定義 the edges of a roof that stick out over the walls 壁から突き出している屋根の端→ひさし, 軒 ‖ *There's a bird's nest under the eaves.* 軒下に鳥の巣がある. ☞ C7 ページのさし絵

**eavesdrop** /íːvzdrɑ̀p/ 動 自 (**eavesdropping**; **eavesdropped**) ▶定義 eavesdrop (on sb/sth) to listen secretly to other people talking 人が話しているのをこっそり聞く→(〜の話を)盗み聴きする, こっそり聞く, 立ち聞きする ‖ *They caught her eavesdropping on their conversation.* 彼らは, 彼女が会話を盗み聴きしているところを捕まえた.

**ebb**¹ /eb/ 動 自 ▶定義 1 (used about sea water) to flow away from the land, which happens twice a day (海水について)海水が陸から離れて流れていく, 1日に2度起こる現象→(潮が)引く ☞類 go out ▶定義 2 ebb (away) (used about a feeling, etc) to become weaker (感情などについて)弱くなる→減退する, 衰える, 薄れる ‖ *The crowd's enthusiasm began to ebb.* 群衆の熱は冷め始めた.

**the ebb**² /eb/ 名 [単数扱い] ▶定義 the time when sea water flows away from the land 海水が陸から離れて流れていく時間→引き潮, 干潮
▶ 1日に2度変わる海水の流れのことをtide (潮)と言う. ebb tide (引き潮)の反対は, high tide (満ち潮)である.

成句 **the ebb and flow (of sth)** ▶定義 (used about a situation, noise, feeling, etc) a regular increase and decrease in the progress or strength of sth (状況, 騒音, 感情などについて)〜の進行や強さが定期的に強まったり, 弱まったりすること→(〜の)変動

**ebony** /ébəni/ 名 U ▶定義 a hard black wood 固く黒い木→黒檀(こくたん)

**eccentric** /ɪkséntrɪk, ek-/ 形 ▶定義 (used about people or their behaviour) strange or unusual (人々または人の行動について)変わっている, または普通でない→奇妙な, 変わった, 常軌を逸している, エキセントリックな ‖ *People said he was mad but I think he was just slightly eccentric.* 人々は彼が狂っていると言ったが, 私は少し変わっていただけだと思う. — **eccentric** 名 C → 変人, 奇人 ‖ *She's just an old eccentric.* 彼女はただの変わった老人だ. — **eccentricity** /èksentrísəti, -sən-/ 名 C U (複 **eccentricities**)

→風変わり, 常軌を逸していること

**echo**¹ /ékou/ 名 C (複 **echoes**) ▶定義 a sound that is repeated as it is sent back off a surface such as the wall of a tunnel トンネルの壁などの表面にぶつかって, 跳ね返ってくるために繰り返し聞こえる音→こだま, 山びこ, 反響 ‖ *I could hear the echo of footsteps somewhere in the distance.* どこか遠くで足音が響くのが聞こえた.

**echo**² /ékou/ 動 ▶定義 1 自 (used about a sound) to be repeated; to come back as an echo (音について)繰り返される; 音がこだまして返ってくる→こだまする, 鳴り響く ‖ *Their footsteps echoed in the empty church.* 彼らの足音はがらんとした教会に鳴り響いた. ▶定義 2 自 他 echo sth (back); echo (with/to sth) to repeat or send back a sound; to be full of a particular sound 音を繰り返させる, または跳ね返らせる; 特定の音で一杯になる→(〜を)反響させる, (〜と)反響する, (〜が)鳴り響く ‖ *The tunnel echoed back their calls.* トンネルに彼らの声が反響した. *The hall echoed with their laughter.* 講堂に彼らの笑い声がこだました. ▶定義 3 他 to repeat what sb has said, done or thought 〜が言った事, した事, 考えた事を繰り返す→〜をまねる, 繰り返す, 反映する ‖ *The child echoed everything his mother said.* その子供は母親が言った事を何でもおうむ返しに繰り返した. *The newspaper article echoed my views completely.* その新聞記事は私の意見を完全に反映していた.

**eclair** /ɪkléər/ 名 C ▶定義 a type of long thin cake, usually filled with cream and covered with chocolate 細長いケーキで, 普通, 中にクリームが入っていてチョコレートが掛けられている→エクレア ☞ cake のさし絵

**eclipse**

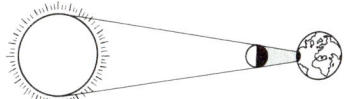

**eclipse**¹ /ɪklíps/ 名 C ▶定義 an occasion when the moon or the sun seems to completely or partly disappear, because one of them is passing between the other and the earth 月または太

陽が,一方が他方と地球の間に入り込むことによって,完全にまたは部分的に欠けて見える現象 →(太陽・月の)食(しょく) ‖ *a total/partial eclipse of the sun* 皆既日食・部分日食

**eclipse**[2] /ɪklíps/ 動他 ▶定義 (used about the moon etc) to cause an eclipse of the sun, etc (月などについて)日食などの原因となる →(ほかの天体)を食する

**eco-friendly** /ékoʊ fréndli, íːk-, -kə-/ 形 ▶定義 not harmful to the environment 環境に害を及ぼさない →環境に優しい ‖ *eco-friendly products/fuel* 環境に優しい製品・燃料

**ecologist** /ɪkɑ́lədʒɪst/ 名 C ▶定義 a person who studies or is an expert in ecology 生態学を学ぶ人,またはその専門家 →生態学者,環境学者

**ecology** /ɪkɑ́lədʒi/ 名 U ▶定義 the relationship between living things and their surroundings; the study of this subject 生物と環境の関係;それに関する学問 →生態,自然環境; 生態学,エコロジー ― ecological /ìːkəlɑ́dʒɪk(ə)l, èkə-/ 形 →生態の,環境の,生態学の ‖ *an ecological disaster* 環境災害 ― ecologically 副 →生態学的に,環境に関して

*__economic__ /ìːkənɑ́mɪk, èkə-/ 形 ▶定義 1 (名詞の前だけ) connected with the supply of money, business, industry, etc 金の供給,ビジネス,産業などに関連した →経済上の,経済的な ‖ *The country faces growing economic problems.* その国は拡大する経済問題に直面している.
▶定義 2 producing a profit 利益を生み出す →利益の上がる,もうかる ‖ *The mine was closed because it was not economic.* その鉱山は利益が上がらないために閉鎖された. ☞参 economical. この単語は違う意味である. ⇔ uneconomic ― economically /ìːkənɑ́mɪk(ə)li, ìːkə-/ 副 →経済的に ‖ *The country was economically very underdeveloped.* その国は経済的に大変遅れていた.

**economical** /ìːkənɑ́mɪk(ə)l, èkə-/ 形 ▶定義 that costs or uses less time, money, fuel, etc than usual 時間,金,燃料などが普通よりもかからない,または使わない →経済的な,節約する ‖ *an economical car to run* 経済的な走りの車 ☞参 economic. この単語は違う意味である. ⇔ uneconomical ― economically /èkənɑ́mɪk(ə)li, ìːkə-/ 副 →経済的に,節約して ‖ *The train service could be run more economically.* 電車の運行はもっと経済的にできるだろうに.

**economics** /ìːkənɑ́mɪks, èkə-/ 名 U ▶定義 the study or principles of the way money, business and industry are organized 金,ビジネス,産業の編成方法についての学問または原理 →経済学,経済状況 ‖ *a degree in economics* 経済学の学位 *the economics of a company* 会社の経済状況

**economist** /ɪkɑ́nəmɪst/ 名 C ▶定義 a person who studies or is an expert in economics 経済学を学ぶ人またはその専門家 →経済学者

**economize**(または **-ise**) /ɪkɑ́nəmaɪz/ 動 ▶定義 *economize (on sth)* to save money, time, fuel, etc; to use less of sth 金,時間,燃料などを節約する;~をなるべく使わないようにする →(~を)節約する,倹約する

*__economy__ /ɪkɑ́nəmi/ 名 (複 **economies**) ▶定義 1 (または **the economy**) C the operation of a country's money supply, commercial activities and industry 国の市場に出回る資金,商業活動,産業の運営 →経済 ‖ *There are signs of improvement in the economy.* 経済に回復の兆しがある. *the economies of America and Japan* 米国と日本の経済 ▶定義 2 C U careful spending of money, time, fuel, etc; trying to save, not waste sth 金,時間,燃料などを慎重に使うこと;~を抑えて,使いすぎないようにすること →節約,倹約 ‖ *Our department is **making economies** in the amount of paper it uses.* 私たちの部署では紙の使用量を節約している. *economy class (= the cheapest class of air travel)* エコノミークラス(= 飛行機の一番安い等級の席)

**ecstasy** /ékstəsi/ 名 C U (複 **ecstasies**) ▶定義 a feeling or state of great happiness 大きな幸福感,またはその状態 →無我夢中,有頂天,恍惚(こうこつ) ‖ *to be **in ecstasy*** 有頂天になる *She **went into ecstasies** about the ring he had bought her.* 彼女は彼が買ってくれた指輪に恍惚とした.

**ecstatic** /ɪkstǽtɪk, ek-/ 形 ▶定義 extremely happy 非常に幸せな →有頂天の,うっとりした

**ecu**(または **ECU**) /ékjuː, éɪ-/ 名 (複 **ecus**; **ecu**) C ▶定義 (until 1999) money used for business and commercial activities between member countries of the European Union. Ecu is short for (European Currency Unit).(1999年まで)欧

州連合(EU)加盟国の間で取り引きや商業活動に使われる金. European Currency Unit の略→エキュー, 欧州通貨単位

**eczema** /ɪɡzíːmə; éksɪmə/ 名 ⓤ ▶定義 a disease which makes your skin red and dry so that you want to scratch it 皮膚が赤くなって乾燥し, かゆくなる病気→湿疹(しっしん)

**ed** 略 edited by; edition; editor→〜によって編集された; 版; 編集長, 編集者, 編集責任者

**eddy** /édi/ 名 ⓒ (複 **eddies**) ▶定義 a circular movement of water, wind, dust, etc 水, 風, ほこりなどが円を描いて回ること→渦巻き

★**edge**¹ /edʒ/ 名 ⓒ ▶定義 **1** the place where sth, especially a surface, ends 〜, 特に表面が終わるところ→端, へり, 縁 ‖ the edge of a table テーブルの端 The leaves were brown and curling at the edges. 葉は茶色く, へりが丸まっていた. I stood at the water's edge. 私は水際に立っていた. ▶定義 **2** the sharp cutting part of a knife, etc ナイフなどの鋭く切れる部分→刃先, 刃

成句 **an/the edge on/over sb/sth** ▶定義 a small advantage over sb/sth 〜よりも少し有利な→〜より少し有利な, 少し勝っている ‖ She knew she had the edge over the other candidates. 彼女はほかの候補者よりも自分が少し有利なことを知っていた.

**(be) on edge** ▶定義 to be nervous, worried or quick to become upset or angry 神経質な, 心配した, または, すぐにうろたえたり, 怒ったりする→いらいらしている, いら立っている ‖ I'm a bit on edge because I get my exam results today. 今日試験の結果が分かるので, 私は少しぴりぴりしている.

**edge**² /edʒ/ 動 ▶定義 **1** 他 (通常は受動態で) edge sth (with sth) to put sth along the edge of sth else 〜をほかの…の縁に付ける→〜に(…で)縁を付ける, 〜を縁取る ‖ The cloth was edged with lace. その布はレースで縁取りされていた. ▶定義 **2** 自他 **edge (your way/sth) across, along, away, back**, etc to move yourself/sth somewhere slowly and carefully 自分・〜をほかの場所へゆっくり注意深く動かす→じりじり動く; 〜をじりじり動かす, そっとずらす, 〜を少しずつ動かす ‖ We edged closer to get a better view. 私たちはもっとよく見えるようにと少し近付いた. She edged her chair up to the window. 彼女はいすを窓の方へそろそろとずらした.

**edgeways** /édʒweɪz/ (または **edgewise** /-waɪz/) 副

成句 **not get a word in edgeways** ⇒ **WORD**¹

**edgy** /édʒi/ 形略式 ▶定義 nervous, worried or quick to become upset or angry 神経質な, 心配した, または, すぐにうろたえたり, 怒ったりする→いらいらした, とげとげしい ‖ You seem very edgy. What's bothering you? 君はとてもいらいらしているようだ. 何か悩みでもあるの.

**edible** /édəb(ə)l/ 形 ▶定義 good or safe to eat 食べてもよい, または安全な→食べられる, 食用の ‖ Are these mushrooms edible? これらのキノコは食べられますか. ⇔ **inedible**

**edifice** /édəfəs/ 名 ⓒ 正式 ▶定義 a large impressive building 大きくて印象的な建物→大建築

**edit** /édɪt/ 動 他 ▶定義 **1** to prepare a piece of writing to be published, making sure that it is correct, the right length, etc 正しく適当な長さにするなどして, 原稿を出版する準備をする→〜を編集する, 編纂(へんさん)する ▶定義 **2** to prepare a film, television or radio programme by cutting and arranging filmed material in a particular order 映画, テレビ, ラジオ番組などを, 収録したものを削ったり, 特定の順番に並べたりして準備する→〜を編集する ▶定義 **3** to be in charge of a newspaper, magazine, etc 新聞, 雑誌などの責任者である→〜を編集する

**edition** /ɪdíʃ(ə)n/ 名 ⓒ ▶定義 **1** the form in which a book is published; all the books, newspapers, etc published in the same form at the same time 本が出版される形態; 同時に同じ形で出版されるすべての本, 新聞など→版 ‖ a paperback/hardback edition ペーパーバック・ハードカバー版 the morning edition of a newspaper 新聞の朝刊 ▶定義 **2** one of a series of newspapers, magazines, television or radio programmes 一連の新聞, 雑誌, テレビまたはラジオ番組のうちの1つ→(新聞・雑誌などある版の)1冊, 1部, (連続番組の)1回分 ‖ And now for this week's edition of 'Panorama'... そしていよいよ今週の「パノラマ」です.

★**editor** /édətər/ 名 ⓒ ▶定義 **1** the person who is in charge of all or part of a newspaper, magazine, etc and who decides what should be included 新聞, 雑誌などの全責任, または一部の責任を負い, 何を載せるかを決定する人→編集長 ‖ *the financial editor*(新聞の)経済欄主任 *Who is the editor of 'The Times'?*「タイムズ」の編集長はだれですか. ▶定義2 a person whose job is to prepare a book to be published by checking for mistakes and correcting the text 誤りをチェックしたり, 文章を直したりして本を出版する準備をすることを仕事にする人→編集者 ▶定義3 a person whose job is to prepare a film, television programme, etc for showing to the public by cutting and putting the filmed material in the correct order 収録された映像を削ったり正しい順番に並べたりして, 映画, テレビ番組などを公開する準備をすることを仕事にする人→編集者

**editorial** /ˌèdətɔ́:riəl/ 名 ❻ ▶定義 an article in a newspaper, usually written by the head of the newspaper (editor), giving an opinion on an important subject 通常その新聞の長(編集長)によって書かれる新聞原稿で, 重要な問題について意見を述べたもの→社説, 論説

**educate** /édʒukèit/ 動 ⓗ ▶定義 to teach or train sb, especially in school 特に学校で, ~に教えたり, 訓練したりする→~を(…するように)教育する, 教化する ‖ *Young people should be educated to care for their environment.* 若者は環境を大事にするよう教育されるべきだ. *All their children were educated at private schools.* 彼らの子供は皆, 私立学校で教育を受けた.

**educated** /édʒəkèitəd/ 形 ▶定義 having studied and learnt a lot of things to a high standard 多くの事を高い水準で学び, 習った→教育を受けた, 教育・教養のある ‖ *a highly educated woman* 高度な教育を受けた女性

★**education** /ˌèdʒəkéiʃ(ə)n/ 名 [ ❻, 通常は単数, ⓤ ] ▶定義 the teaching or training of people, especially in schools 特に学校で, 人々を教えたり, 訓練したりすること→教育 ‖ *primary, secondary, higher, adult education* 初等・中等・高等・成人教育 *She received an excellent education.* 彼女は優れた教育を受けた. — **educational** /-ʃ(ə)n(ə)l/ 形 →教育的な, 教育のための, 教育上の ‖ *an educational toy/visit/experience* 教育的なおもちゃ・訪問・経験

**eel** /i:l/ 名 ❻ ▶定義 a long fish that looks like a snake 蛇に似た, 長い魚→うなぎ

**eerie** (または **eery**) /íəri; í:ri/ 形 ▶定義 strange and frightening 奇妙で怖い→気味の悪い, ぞっとするような ‖ *an eerie noise* 気味の悪い音 — **eerily** 副 →気味悪く — **eeriness** 名 ⓤ →気味悪さ

★**effect** /ɪfékt, e-/ 名 ❻ ▶定義1 ❻ ⓤ (an) effect (on sb/sth) a change that is caused by sth; a result ~が原因で起きる変化; 結果→(~への)影響, 効果 ‖ *the effects of acid rain on the lakes and forests* 酸性雨の湖や森への影響 *Her shouting had little or no effect on him.* 彼女の叫び声は, 彼にほとんどまたは何の効果も及ぼさなかった. *Despite her terrible experience, she seems to have suffered no ill effects.* 彼女は恐ろしい経験をしたにもかかわらず, 悪い影響は何も受けていないようだ. ☞参 **after-effect**, **side-effect** と **affect** の注 ▶定義2 ❻ ⓤ a particular look, sound or impression that an artist, writer, etc wants to create 芸術家, 作家などが創造しようとする特別な外観, 音, 印象→効果, 見せ掛け ‖ *How does the artist create the effect of moonlight?* 芸術家はどのように月光の効果を創造するのか. *He likes to say things just for effect (= to impress people).* 彼は見せ掛けだけの話をしたがる.(= 人々に印象づけるために). ▶定義3 **effects** [複数扱い] 正式 your personal possessions 個人的な所有物→身の回り品

成句 **come into effect** ▶定義 (used especially about laws or rules) to begin to be used (特に法律や規則などについて)用いられ始める→効力を発する, 施行される

**in effect** ▶定義1 in fact; for all practical purposes 実際に; すべての実際的な目的のために→実際に, 事実上 ‖ *Though they haven't made an official announcement, she is, in effect, the new director.* まだ公式には発表されていないが, 彼女は事実上の新取締役だ. ▶定義2 (used about a rule, a law, etc) in operation; in use (規則や法律などについて)実施されている; 使われている→効力のある, 有効の ‖ *The new rules will be in effect from next month.* 新しい規則は来月から効力を発する.

**take effect** ▶定義1 (used about a drug, etc) to begin to work; to produce the result you want (薬品などについて)作用し始める; 望んでいる結果を生じる→効く ‖ *The anaesthetic took*

effect immediately. 麻酔がすぐに効いた. ▶定義2 (used about a law, etc) to come into operation (法律などについて)実施され始める→効力を生じる ‖ *The ceasefire takes effect from midnight.* 停戦は夜の12時から効力を生じる.
to this/that effect ▶定義 with this/that meaning この・その意味で→**この・その趣旨で** ‖ *I told him to leave her alone, or words to that effect.* 私は彼に彼女を独りにしておくように,またはそのような意味の事を告げた.

*__effective__ /ɪféktɪv, e-/ 形 ▶定義1 successfully producing the result that you want 欲しい結果をうまく出す→**効果的な,有効な** ‖ *a medicine that is effective against the common cold* 普通の風邪に有効な薬 *That picture would look more effective on a dark background.* その絵は背景を暗くするとより効果的に見えるだろう. ⇔ **ineffective** ▶定義2 real or actual, although perhaps not official 多分正式ではないが,実際の,または現実の→**実際の,事実上の** ‖ *The soldiers gained effective control of the town.* その兵士たちは事実上,町を支配した. — **effectiveness** 名 ❶ →**有効,有効性**

__effectively__ /ɪféktɪvli, e-/ 副 ▶定義1 in a way that successfully produces the result you wanted 欲しい結果をうまく出すように→**有効に,効果的に** ‖ *She dealt with the situation effectively.* 彼女はその状況に効果的に対処した. ▶定義2 in fact; in reality 実際は; 現実には→**事実上** ‖ *It meant that, effectively, they had lost.* その事は事実上,彼らの負けを意味した.

__effeminate__ /ɪfémənət/ 形 ▶定義 (used about a man or his behaviour) like a woman (男性またはその行いについて)女のようだ→**めめしい,男らしくない**

*__efficient__ /ɪfíʃ(ə)nt/ 形 ▶定義 able to work well without making mistakes or wasting time and energy 間違ったり,時間や労力を無駄にせずにうまく働ける→**有能な,能力のある,能率的な,有効な** ‖ *Our secretary is very efficient.* 私たちの秘書は非常に有能だ. *You must find a more efficient way of organizing your time.* あなたはもっと有効な時間の管理法を見つけなければならない. ⇔ **inefficient** — **efficiency** /ɪfíʃ(ə)nsi/ 名 ❶ →**能力,有能さ,効率,能率** — **efficiently** 副 →**効率よく,有能に,有効に**

__effluent__ /éfluənt/ 名 ❶ ▶定義 liquid waste, especially chemicals produced by factories 液体の廃棄物,特に工場で作られる化学物質→**廃液,廃水**

*__effort__ /éfət/ 名 ❶ ▶定義1 the physical or mental strength or energy that you need to do sth; sth that takes a lot of energy ～をするのに必要な肉体的または精神的強さやエネルギー; 多くのエネルギーを要する～→**努力,骨折り** ‖ *They have put a lot of effort into their studies this year.* 彼らは今年,研究に非常に力を入れた. *He made no effort to contact his parents.* 彼は両親に連絡を取る努力を全くしなかった. ▶定義2 ❻ an effort (to do sth) something that is done with difficulty or that takes a lot of energy 困難を伴ってなされること,または多大なエネルギーを要すること→**(～しようとする)努力,試み,企て** ‖ *It was a real effort to stay awake in the lecture.* その講義の間起きているのはとても大変だった.

__effortless__ /éfətləs/ 形 ▶定義 needing little or no effort so that sth seems easy ～が簡単に思えるくらい,努力をほとんど,または全く必要としない→**やすやすとやってのけた,努力を要しない,楽な,簡単な** — **effortlessly** 副 →**楽々と,努力せずに**

__EFL__ /iː ef él/ 略 English as a Foreign Language→**外国語としての英語**

__eg__ /iː dʒíː, f(ə)r ɪgzá:mp(ə)l; -zǽm-/ 略 for example →**例えば** ‖ *popular sports, eg football, tennis, swimming* 人気のあるスポーツ,例えばサッカー,テニス,水泳

__egalitarian__ /ɪgæ̀lətéəriən/ 形 ▶定義 (used about a person, system, society, etc) following the principle that everyone should have equal rights (人,制度,社会などについて)すべての人が平等の権利を持つべきだという原則に従う→**平等主義の**

*__egg__¹ /eg/ 名 ▶定義1 ❻ an almost round object with a hard shell that contains a young bird, reptile or insect 鳥,は虫類,昆虫などの子供が入っている,硬い殻の付いたほぼ球状の物→**卵** ☛ **insect** のさし絵

# egg²

▶雌鳥は egg (卵) を lay (産む) と, hatch (かえる) までその卵を sit on (抱く) ことになる.

▶定義2 ●Ⓤ a bird's egg, especially one from a chicken, etc that we eat 鳥の卵, 特に鶏などの食用のもの➡卵, 鶏卵

▶ egg (卵) は, boil (ゆでる), fry (目玉焼きにする) ほかに, poach (落とし卵) や scramble (いり卵) にもできる.

▶定義3 ● (in women and female animals) the small cell that can join with a male seed (sperm) to make a baby (女性や雌の動物にある) 小さな細胞で, 男性 (または雄) の種 (精子) と結合して赤ん坊を作るもの➡卵子, 卵細胞

**成句** put all your eggs in one basket ▶定義 to risk everything by depending completely on one thing, plan, etc instead of giving yourself several possibilities いくつかの可能性を残さず, 1つの事・計画などに完全に依存して, すべての危険を冒す➡1つの事にすべてをかける, 1つの事業に資金全部をつぎ込む

**egg²** /eg/ 動

**句動詞** egg sb on (to do sth) ▶定義 to encourage sb to do sth that he/she should not do ～がすべきでない…をする気にさせる➡～を(…をするように)そそのかす, けしかける

**eggcup** /égkʌ̀p/ 名 ●▶定義 a small cup for holding a boiled egg ゆで卵を立てておく小さな器➡ゆで卵立て

**eggplant** /égplæ̀nt; -plɑ̀ːnt/ 特に米=AUBERGINE

**eggshell** /égʃèl/ 名 ●Ⓤ▶定義 the hard outside part of an egg 卵の硬い外側➡殻 ☞ egg のさし絵

**ego** /ígou, íːgou/ 名 ● ((複) egos) ▶定義 the (good) opinion that you have of yourself 自分について持っている (良い) 意見➡自我, エゴ, 自尊心 ‖ It was a blow to her ego when she lost her job. 彼女は仕事を失って, 自尊心を傷付けられた.

**egocentric** /ègouséntrɪk, ìːgou-/ 形 ▶定義 thinking only about yourself and not what other people need or want; selfish 自分のことばかり考えて, 他人が必要としている事を考えない; 自分勝手な➡自己中心的な, 自分本意の

**egoism** /égoʊìz(ə)m, íːgoʊ-/ (または **egotism** /égətìz(ə)m, íːgə-/) 名 Ⓤ ▶定義 thinking about yourself too much; selfishness 自分のことばかり考えすぎること; 自分勝手➡利己主義, 自分本意, 自分勝手 — **egoist** /égoʊɪst, íːgoʊ-/ (または **egotist** /íːgətɪst, égətɪst/) 名 ●➡利己主義者, 自分勝手な人 ‖ I hate people who are egoists. 自分勝手な人間は嫌いだ. — **egoistic** /ègoʊístɪk, íːgoʊ-/ (または **egotistical** /ègətístɪk(ə)l, íːgə-/) 形➡自分勝手な, 利己主義の

**eh** /(上昇調で) eɪ/ 間 因略式 ▶定義1 used for asking sb to agree with you ～に同意を求めるときに用いて➡～でしょ, だろう ‖ 'Good party, eh?' 「いいパーティーでしょ」 ▶定義2 used for asking sb to repeat sth ～に…を繰り返してほしいときに用いて➡何だって, えっ ‖ 'Did you like the film?' 'Eh?' 'I asked if you liked the film!' 「映画は気に入ったかい」「えっ」「映画は気に入ったかと聞いたんだ」

**Eid** (または **Id**) /iːd/ 名 ●▶定義 any of several Muslim festivals, especially one that celebrates the end of a month when people do not eat during the day (Ramadan) イスラム教の祭りのことをいい, 特に, 日中に断食をする月 (ラマダーン) の終わりを祝うもの➡イード (祭典), イードアルフィトル (断食明けの祭典)

**eiderdown** /áɪdə·dàʊn/ 名 ●▶定義 a covering for a bed filled with soft feathers (down), usually used on top of other coverings for the bed 柔らかい羽根 (羽毛) の詰まった, ベッドに掛ける布団で, 通常一番上に掛けられる➡羽布団 ☞参 duvet

*****eight** /eɪt/ 数 ▶定義1 8

▶文中での数詞の使い方については, six の項を参照.

▶定義2 eight- (複合形で用いて) having eight of sth 8つの～を持った➡8の, 8つの, 8個の, 8人の ‖ an eight-sided shape 八面体

*****eighteen** /èɪtíːn ⌢/ 数 ▶定義 18

▶文中での数詞の使い方については, six の項を参照.

**eighteenth** /èɪtíːnθ/ 代形副 ▶定義 18th➡18番目 (の, に), 第 18 (の, に) ☞参 sixth の例

**eighth¹** /eɪtθ/ 名 ●▶定義 the fraction 1/8; one of eight equal parts of sth 分数の8分の1; ～を8つに均分したときの1つ➡8分の1

**eighth²** /eɪtθ/ 代形副 ▶定義 8th➡8番目 (の, に), 第8 (の, に) ☞参 sixth の例

**eightieth** /éitiəθ/ 代形副 ▶定義 80th→80 番目(の,に),第 80(の,に) ☞参 **sixth** の例

**★eighty** /éiti/ 数 ▶定義 80
▶文中での数詞の使い方については,sixty の項を参照.

**★either¹** /áiðər, íː-/ 形代 ▶定義 **1** one or the other of two; it does not matter which 2つのうちの1つまたは他方;どちらかは問題でない→**どちらか一方(の)** ‖ *You can choose either soup or salad, but not both.* スープかサラダかどちらか1つを選べるが,両方は駄目だ. *You can ask either of us for advice.* 私たちのどちらにでも助言を求めてよい. *Either of us is willing to help.* 私たちのどちらでも喜んで手伝うよ.
▶定義 **2** both 両方とも→**どちらでも,どちらも** ‖ *It is a pleasant road, with trees on either side.* その道路は,木が両側にあって気持ち良い.

**★either²** /áiðər, íː-/ 副 ▶定義 **1** (2つの否定的表現の後に用いて) also また→**もまた~ない** ‖ *I don't like Pat and I don't like Nick much either.* 私はパットが好きではないし,ニックもあまり好きではない. *'I can't remember his name.' 'I can't either.'* 「彼の名前が思い出せない」「僕も思い出せない」
▶neither can I とも言う.肯定文への合意については,too を参照.
▶定義 **2** used for emphasizing a negative statement 否定文を強調するのに用いて→**それに~ない,その上~でもない** ‖ *The restaurant is quite good. And it's not expensive either.* そのレストランはとても良い.それに高くもないし.

**either³** /áiðər, íː-/ 接 ▶定義 either...or... used when you are giving a choice, usually of two things 通常2つの事について,選択するときに用いて→**~か…のどちらか(一方),~または…のどちらでも** ‖ *I can meet you either Thursday or Friday.* 私は木曜日か金曜日のどちらでも会えます. *Either you leave or I do.* 君が行かなければ,僕が行くよ. *You can either write or phone.* 手紙でも,電話でもいいよ.

**ejaculate** /ɪdʒǽkjəlèɪt/ 動 ▶定義 **1** 自 to send out liquid (semen) from the male sexual organ (penis) 男性性器(ペニス)から液体(精液)を送り出す→**射精をする** ▶定義 **2** 自他 (古) to say sth suddenly ~を突然言う→**(~と)突然叫び出す,出し抜けに言う** — **ejaculation** /ɪdʒìkjəléɪʃ(ə)n/ 名 C U ▶射精,突然の叫び

**eject** /ɪdʒékt/ 動 ▶定義 **1** 他 正式 (しばしば受動態で) eject sb (from sth) to push or send sb/sth out of a place (usually with force) ~を(通常力ずくで)ある場所から押し出す,または送り出す→**~を(…から)追い出す,追放する** ‖ *The protesters were ejected from the building.* 抗議する人々は,その建物から追い出された.
▶定義 **2** 自他 to remove a tape, disk etc from a machine, usually by pressing a button 通常ボタンを押して,機械からテープ,ディスクなどを出す→**出る,~を出す,取り出す** ‖ *To eject the CD, press this button.* CDを取り出すには,このボタンを押してください. *After recording for three hours the video will eject automatically.* 3時間録画すると,ビデオは自動的に出ます.
▶定義 **3** 自 to escape from an aircraft that is going to crash 墜落しようとする飛行機から逃げる→**緊急脱出する**

**eke** /iːk/ 動
句動 **eke sth out** ▶定義 to make a small amount of sth last a long time 少ない~が長持ちするようにする→**~を何とか持たせる**

**elaborate¹** /ɪlǽb(ə)rət/ 形 ▶定義 very complicated; done or made very carefully 非常に複雑な;非常に入念になされた,または作られた→**非常に精巧な,手の込んだ,念入りな** ‖ *an elaborate pattern* 非常に精巧な模様 *elaborate plans* 念入りな計画

**elaborate²** /ɪlǽbərèɪt/ 動 自 正式 ▶定義 elaborate (on sth) to give more details about sth ~についてより詳しく述べる→**(~について)詳細に述べる** ‖ *Could you elaborate on that idea?* その案の詳細を述べていただけませんか.

**elapse** /ɪlǽps/ 動 自 正式 ▶定義 (used about time) to pass (時間について) 過ぎる→**経過する**

**elastic¹** /ɪlǽstɪk/ 名 U ▶定義 material with rubber in it which can stretch ゴムでできた伸びる素材→**ゴム入り生地,ゴムひも,輪ゴム**

**elastic²** /ɪlǽstɪk/ 形 ▶定義 **1** (used about material, etc) that returns to its original size and shape after being stretched (素材などについて)伸ばした後,元の大きさや形に戻る→**弾力性のある** ▶定義 **2** that can be changed; not fixed 変えられる;固定されていない→**柔軟性のある,融通の利く** ‖ *Our rules are quite elastic.* 私たちの規

則はかなり柔軟性があります.

**elastic band** =RUBBER BAND

**elated** /ɪléɪtəd/ 形 ▶定義 very happy and excited 大変喜び,興奮した➔**意気盛んな,得意になった** ― elation /ɪléɪʃ(ə)n/ 名 Ⓤ ➔**意気揚々**

\***elbow**¹ /élboʊ/ 名 Ⓒ ▶定義1 the place where the bones of your arm join and your arm bends 腕の骨が接合し,腕が曲がる場所➔**ひじ** ☞ C5ページのさし絵 ▶定義2 the part of the sleeve of a coat, jacket, etc that covers the elbow コート,上着などのそでのひじを覆う部分➔**ひじの部分**

**elbow**² /élboʊ/ 動 ⊕ ▶定義 to push sb with your elbow➔**〜をひじで押す** ‖ She elbowed me out of the way. 彼女はひじで私を押しのけた. ☞ S6ページのさし絵

**elbow room** 名 Ⓤ ▶定義 enough space to move freely 自由に動けるだけの十分な空間➔**ゆとり,余地**

\***elder**¹ /éldər/ 形 (名詞の前だけ) ▶定義 older (of two members of a family) (家族で2人のうち)年上の➔**年上の,年長の** ‖ My elder daughter is at university now but the other one is still at school. 私の上の娘は今大学にいるが,もう1人はまだ高等学校にいる. an elder brother/sister 兄・姉

**elder**² /éldər/ 名 ▶定義1 [単数扱い] **the elder** the older of two people 2人のうちの年上の人➔**年長者,先輩** ‖ Who is the elder of the two? 2人のうちどちらが年上ですか. ▶定義2 **my, etc elder** [単数扱い] a person who is older than me, etc 自分などより年上の人➔**〜より年上の人** ‖ He is her elder by several years. 彼は彼女より何歳か年上だ. ▶定義3 **elders** [複数扱い] older people 年上の人々➔**年長者** ‖ Do children still respect the opinions of their elders? 子供たちはまだ年長者の意見を尊重していますか.

**elderly** /éldərli/ 形 ▶定義1 (used about a person) old (人について)年を取った➔**年配の,初老の,お年寄りの** ☞ old の丁寧な言い方. ▶定義2 **the elderly** [複数扱い] old people in general お年寄りの一般的名称➔**お年寄り** ‖ The elderly need special care in winter. お年寄りは冬には特に注意が必要だ. ☞参 old

\***eldest** /éldəst/ 形名 Ⓒ ▶定義 (the) oldest (of three or more members of a family) (3人以上の家族の中で)一番年上の(〜)➔**最年長の,最年長者** ‖ Their eldest child is a boy. 彼らの一番上の子供は男の子だ. John's got 4 boys. The eldest has just gone to university. ジョンには4人の男の子がいる.長男はちょうど大学に進学したところだ.

\***elect** /ɪlékt/ 動 ⊕ ▶定義1 **elect sb (to sth); elect sb (as sth)** to choose sb to have a particular job or position by voting for him/her 〜に投票して,特別な職業または地位に就かせるように選ぶ➔**〜を(…に)選出する,選ぶ** ‖ He was elected to Parliament in 1970. 彼は1970年に国会議員に選出された. The committee elected her as their representative. 委員会は彼女を代表に選んだ. ▶定義2 正式 **elect to do sth** to decide to do sth 〜をしようと決断する➔**〜することに決める**

\***election** /ɪlékʃ(ə)n/ 名 Ⓒ Ⓤ ▶定義 (the time of) choosing a Member of Parliament, President, etc by voting 国会議員,大統領などを投票で選ぶこと(時期)➔**選挙,選出** ‖ In America, presidential elections are held every four years. アメリカでは,大統領選挙が4年ごとに行われる. If you're interested in politics why not **stand for election** yourself? 政治に興味があるのなら,自分で選挙に立候補したらどうだい.

▶英国では, general election(総選挙)は約5年ごとに行われる.ほかに by-election(補欠選挙)が行われることがある.有権者は,それぞれの地域(constituency(選挙区))で candidate(候補者)名簿の中から1人を選ぶことになる.

**elector** /ɪléktər/ 名 Ⓒ ▶定義 a person who has the right to vote in an election 選挙で投票する権利を持っている人➔**有権者,選挙人** ☞ voter の方がより一般的. ― electoral /ɪléktər(ə)l, ìːlektóːrəl/ 形 ➔**選挙の,選挙人の** ‖ the electoral register/roll (= the list of electors in an area) 選挙人名簿(= ある地域の有権者の名簿)

**electorate** /ɪléktərət, -rèɪt-/ 名 [Ⓒ, 単数または複数形の動詞と共に] ▶定義 all the people who can vote in a region, country, etc ある地域,国などで投票できるすべての人➔**選挙民,選挙母体,有権者**

\***electric** /ɪléktrɪk/ 形 ▶定義1 producing or using electricity 電気を起こす,または使う➔**電気の,電動の** ‖ an electric current 電流 an electric kettle 電気湯沸かし ▶定義2 very exciting 非常に興奮

した➜感動的な, わくわくする, 電撃的な ‖ *The atmosphere in the room was electric.* その部屋は興奮した雰囲気だった.

***electrical** /ɪléktrɪk(ə)l/ [形] ▶定義 of or about electricity 電気の, または電気についての➜**電気の, 電気に関する** ‖ *an electrical appliance (= a machine that uses electricity)* 電気器具(= 電気を使う機械) *an electrical engineer (= a person who produces electrical systems and equipment)* 電気技師(= 電気システムや電気機器を作る人)

**the electric chair** [名][単数扱い] ▶定義 a chair used in some countries for killing criminals with a very strong electric current いくつかの国で使われている犯罪者を非常に強い電流で殺すいす➜**電気いす**

***electrician** /ɪlèktríʃ(ə)n, ìːlek-/ [名] [C] ▶定義 a person whose job is to make and repair electrical systems and equipment 電気システムや電気機器を作ったり, 修理したりする人➜**電気技師**

***electricity** /ɪlektrís(ə)ti/ [名] [U] ▶定義 a type of energy that we use to make heat, light and power to work machines, etc 熱, 光, 機械の動力などを生み出すのに使うエネルギーの一種➜**電気** ‖ *Turn that light off. We don't want to waste electricity.* 明かりを消しなさい. 電気を無駄遣いしたくないから.

➤ electricity (電気) は通常 power station (発電所) で generate (起こされる) ことになる. generator (発電機) や battery (電池) でも作ることができる.

**electric razor** = SHAVER

**electric shock** (または **shock**) [名] [C] ▶定義 a sudden painful feeling that you get if electricity goes through your body 電流が体内を流れたときに感じる, 突然の痛み➜**電撃, 感電**

**electrify** /ɪléktrəfàɪ/ [動][他] (現分 **electrifying**; 三単現 **electrifies**; 過, 過分 **electrified**) ▶定義 1 to supply sth with electricity ～に電流を供給する➜**～に電気をかける, 電気を通す, (鉄道など)を電化する** ‖ *The railways are being electrified.* 鉄道は電化されつつある. ▶定義 2 to make sb very excited ～を非常に興奮させる➜**～を感動させる, 興奮させる** ‖ *Ronaldo electrified the crowd with his pace and skill.* ロナルドはテンポよい話術で群衆を興奮させた.

**electrocute** /ɪléktrəkjùːt/ [動][他] ▶定義 to kill sb with electricity that goes through the body ～の体に電流を流して殺す➜**～を感電死させる, 電気いすで処刑する**—electrocution /ɪléktrəkjùːʃ(ə)n/ [名] [U]➜**感電死, 電気いすによる処刑**

**electrode** /ɪléktròʊd/ [名] [C] ▶定義 one of two points (terminals) where an electric current enters or leaves a battery, etc 電池などで電流が入ったり, 出ていく2箇所(端子)のうちの一方➜**電極**

***electronic** /ɪlèktránɪk/ [形] ▶定義 1 using electronics 電子工学を使う➜**電子工学の, エレクトロニクスの; 電子の** ‖ *electronic equipment* 電子装置 *This dictionary is available in electronic form (= on a computer disk).* この辞書は電子形式で(= コンピューターのディスク上で)利用できます. ▶定義 2 done using a computer コンピューターを使ってなされる➜**コンピューターによる** ‖ *electronic banking/shopping* 電子バンキング・電子ショッピング —electronically /-k(ə)li/ [副] ➜**電子的に, 電子工学的に, コンピューターを利用して**

**electronics** /ɪlèktránɪks/ [名] [U] ▶定義 the technology used to produce computers, radios, etc コンピューター, ラジオなどの製造に用いられる技術➜**電子工学, エレクトロニクス** ‖ *the electronics industry* エレクトロニクス産業

**elegant** /éləgənt/ [形] ▶定義 having a good or attractive style 良い, または魅力的な物腰の➜**優雅な, 上品な** ‖ *She looked very elegant in her new dress.* 彼女は新しいドレスを着て, とても優雅に見えた. *an elegant coat* 上品なコート —elegance /élɪgəns/ [名] [U]➜**上品, 優雅, 気品** —elegantly [副] ➜**上品に, 優雅に**

***element** /éləmənt/ [名] ▶定義 1 [C] one important part of sth ～の重要な一部➜**要素, 成分** ‖ *Cost is an important element when we're thinking about holidays.* 休日について考えるとき, 費用は重要な要素だ. ▶定義 2 [[C], 通常は単数] an element of sth a small amount of sth 少量の～➜**少しの～, ～気味** ‖ *There was an element of truth in what he said.* 彼の言った事には多少の真実があった. ▶定義 3 [C] people of a certain type ある種の人々➜**(構成)分子, ～派** ‖ *The criminal element at football matches causes a lot of trouble.* サッカーの試合にいる犯罪分子が多くの問題を引き

E

起こす. ▶定義4 ⓒone of the simple chemical substances, for example iron, gold, etc 単純な化学物質の1つ, 例えば, 鉄, 金など→元素 ▶定義5 ⓒthe metal part of a piece of electrical equipment that produces heat 熱を発生する電気機器の金属部品→抵抗線, 電熱線, 発熱部分 ▶定義6 the elements [複数扱い] (bad) weather (悪)天候→暴風雨, 自然の力 ‖ *to be exposed to the elements* 暴風雨にさらされる

成句 **in/out of your element** ▶定義 in a situation where you feel comfortable/uncomfortable あなたが快適に・不快に感じる状況→自分に適した・適していない環境にある ‖ *Bill's in his element speaking to a large group of people, but I hate it.* ビルは多くの人に話し掛けるとなると本領を発揮するが, 私は嫌いだ.

*****elementary** /èləmént(ə)ri/ 形 ▶定義1 connected with the first stages of learning sth ~を学ぶ最初の段階に関連した→初等の, 初歩の, 入門の ‖ *an elementary course in English* 英語の初級講座 *a book for elementary students* 初歩の学習者のための本 ▶定義2 basic; not difficult 基本の; 難しくない→基本的な, 簡単な ‖ *elementary physics* 基礎物理学

**elementary school** 名 ⓒ 米 ▶定義 a school for children aged six to eleven 6歳から11歳までの子供が通う学校→小学校

**elephant**

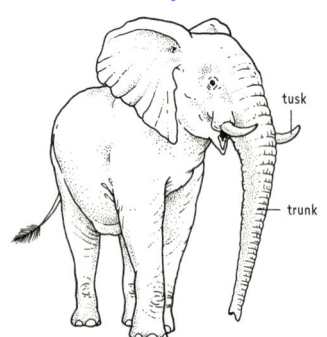

tusk

trunk

*****elephant** /éləfənt/ 名 ⓒ ▶定義 a very large grey animal with big ears, two long curved teeth (tusks) and a long nose (trunk) とても大きな灰色の動物で, 大きな耳, 2本の長く湾曲した歯(きば), そして長い鼻を持つ→象

**elevate** /éləvèit/ 動他 正式 ▶定義 to move sb/sth to a higher place or more important position ~をより高い場所, またはより重要な地位に動かす→~を昇進させる, 向上させる, 持ち上げる ‖ *an elevated platform* 床よりも高くなった教壇 *He was elevated to the Board of Directors.* 彼は重役に昇進した.

**elevation** /èləvéiʃ(ə)n/ 名 ▶定義1 ⓒ Ⓤ 正式 the process of moving to a higher place or more important position より高い場所, またはより重要な地位に移動する過程→向上, 昇格, 昇進 ‖ *his elevation to the presidency* 彼の社長昇格 ▶定義2 ⓒ the height of a place (above sea-level) (海面からの)場所の高さ→海抜, 高さ ‖ *The city is at an elevation of 2000 metres.* その町は海抜2000メートルにある.

**elevator** /éləvèitər/ 米 = LIFT²(1)

*****eleven** /ilév(ə)n/ 数 ▶定義 11

▶文中での数詞の使い方については, sixの項を参照.

**eleventh** /ilév(ə)nθ/ 代形副 ▶定義 11th→11番目(の, に), 第11(の, に) ☞参 sixthの例

**elf** /elf/ 名 ⓒ (複 **elves** /elvz/) ▶定義 (in stories) a small creature with pointed ears who has magic powers (物語の中で)耳のとがった, 魔法を使える小さな生き物→小妖精(ようせい)

**elicit** /ilísət/ 動他 正式 ▶定義 **elicit sth (from sb)** to manage to get information, facts, a reaction, etc from sb ~から情報, 事実, 反応などをどうにかして得る→~を(人から)聞き出す, 引き出す

**eligible** /élədʒəb(ə)l/ 形 ▶定義 **eligible (for sth/to do sth)** having the right to do or have sth ~をする, または持つ権利を有しているような→(~の・~する)資格がある ‖ *In Britain, you are eligible to vote when you are eighteen.* 英国では, 18歳になると投票権がある. ⇔**ineligible**

**eliminate** /ilímənèit/ 動他 ▶定義1 to remove sb/sth that is not wanted or needed 欲しくない, または必要のない~を取り去る→~を除去する, 排除する, 消去する ‖ *We must try and eliminate the problem.* 私たちは, その問題を消し去るように努力せねばならない. ▶定義2 (しばしば受動態で)to stop sb going further in a competition, etc 競争などで~が先に進むのを止め

る→～を敗退させる, 失格にする ‖ *The school team was eliminated in the first round of the competition.* その学校のチームは大会の初戦で敗退した. — **elimination** /ɪlìmənéɪʃ(ə)n/ 名 ❶ ▶定義 除去, 排除, 敗退, 失格

**élite** /eɪlíːt/ 名 [●, 単数または複数形の動詞と共に] ▶定義 a social group that is thought to be the best or most important because of its power, money, intelligence, etc その権力, 金, 知性などから, 最良または最も重要と考えられている社会的集団→エリート ‖ *an intellectual élite* 知的エリート *an élite group of artists* 芸術家のエリート集団

**élitism** /eɪlíːtìzm/ 名 ❶ ▶定義 the belief that some people should be treated in a special way ある人々が特別扱いされるべきだという考え方→エリート主義, エリート意識 — **élitist** /-tɪst, -, i-/ 名 ●形 →エリート主義者(の)

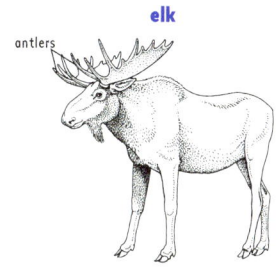
elk
antlers

**elk** /elk/ (米 **moose**) 名 ● ▶定義 a very large wild animal (deer) with large flat horns (antlers) 大きく平らな角(枝角)を持つ非常に大きな野生動物(シカの一種)→ヘラジカ

**elm** /elm/ (または **elm tree**) 名 ● ▶定義 a tall tree with broad leaves 背の高い広葉樹→楡(にれ)

**elongated** /iːlɔ́ːŋgèɪtəd/ 形 ▶定義 long and thin 長く, 細い→長く伸ばされた

**elope** /ɪlóup/ 動 ⓐ ▶定義 elope (with sb) to run away secretly to get married 結婚するためにこっそり逃げる→(～と)駆け落ちする

**eloquent** /éləkwənt/ 形 正式 ▶定義 able to use language and express your opinions well, especially when you speak in public 特に人前で話をするときに, 言葉を駆使して自分の意見をうまく表現できる→雄弁な, 表現力のある — **eloquence** 名 ❶ →雄弁(術) — **eloquently** 副 →

雄弁に, 弁舌さわやかに

\***else** /els/ 副 (any-, no-, some- の付いた語や疑問詞の後に用いて) ▶定義 another, different person, thing or place ほかの, ほかの人・事・場所→そのほかの, 別の, ほかの ‖ *This isn't mine. It must be someone else's.* これは私のものではない. だれかほかの人のものに違いない. *Was it you who phoned me, or somebody else?* 私に電話したのはあなたですか, それともだれかほかの人ですか. *Everybody else is allowed to stay up late.* ほかの人は皆遅くまで起きていることを許されている. *You'll have to pay. Nobody else will.* あなたはお金を払わなければならないだろう. ほかにだれも払わないだろうから. *What else would you like?* 何かほかに召し上がりますか. *I'm tired of that cafe - shall we go somewhere else for a change?* あのコーヒー店には飽きました - 気分転換に, どこかほかの所に行きませんか.

成句 **or else** ▶定義 otherwise; if not さもなければ, もし～でなければ→そうでないと, そうしないと ‖ *You'd better go to bed now or else you'll be tired in the morning.* もう寝た方がいいよ, そうしないと朝疲れるから. *He's either forgotten or else he's decided not to come.* 彼は忘れたか, さもなければ来ないことにしたのだ.

\***elsewhere** /éls(h)wèər, -´-/ 副 ▶定義 in or to another place ほかの場所で, またはほかの場所へ→ほかの場所で[へ] ‖ *He's travelled a lot - in Europe and elsewhere.* 彼はたくさん旅行している - ヨーロッパへも, ほかの場所へも.

**ELT** /iː el tíː/ 略 English Language Teaching→英語教育

**elude** /ɪlúːd/ 動 他 正式 ▶定義 1 to manage to avoid being caught 捕まらないようにする→～を逃れる, ～からうまく身をかわす ‖ *The escaped prisoner eluded the police for three days.* 脱獄者は3日間警察から逃れた. ▶定義 2 to be difficult or impossible to remember 思い出すのが難しい, またはできない→～に理解できない, 思い出せない ‖ *I remember his face but his name eludes me.* 彼の顔は覚えているが, 彼の名前が思い出せない.

**elusive** /ɪlúːsɪv, -zɪv/ 形 ▶定義 not easy to catch, find or remember 捕まえたり, 見つけたり, 思い

出すのが簡単でない→うまく逃げる，捕まえにくい，つかみどころのない，思い出せない

**elves** ELFの複数形

**'em** /əm/ 代略式 = THEM

**emaciated** /ɪméɪʃièɪtəd; -si-/ 形 ▶定義 extremely thin and weak because of illness, lack of food, etc 病気，食糧不足などのために極端に細く，弱い→やつれた，やせ衰えた — **emaciation** /ɪmèɪʃiéɪʃ(ə)n; -si-/ 名 U ▶衰弱，憔悴(しょうすい)

**e-mail** (または **email**) /íːmeɪl/ 名 ▶定義 1 ⓒ U a way of sending electronic messages and data from one computer to another あるコンピューターからほかのコンピューターへ電子的メッセージやデータを送る方法→電子メール, E メール ‖ *to send a message by e-mail* 電子メールでメッセージを送る ▶定義 2 ⓒ U a message or messages sent by e-mail 電子メールで送られるメッセージ→電子メール, E メール ‖ *I'll send you an e-mail tomorrow.* 明日君に電子メールを送るよ．— **e-mail** 動他 →～を電子メールで送る，～に電子メールを送る ‖ *I'll e-mail the information to you.* その情報を君に電子メールで送るよ．

**emancipate** /ɪmænsəpèɪt/ 動他 正式 ▶定義 to give sb the same legal, social and political rights as other people ～にほかの人々と同じ法的，社会的，政治的な権利を与える→～を解放する，釈放する — **emancipation** /ɪmænsəpéɪʃ(ə)n/ 名 U ▶解放，解放すること・されること

**embankment** /ɪmbæŋkmənt, em-/ 名 ⓒ ▶定義 a wall of stone or earth that is built to stop a river from flooding or to carry a road or railway 川の氾濫(はんらん)を防ぐため，または道路や鉄道を支えるために建てられた石や土でできた壁→堤防, 築堤, 土手

**embargo** /ɪmbáːrɡoʊ, em-/ 名ⓒ (複 **embargoes**) ▶定義 an official order to stop doing business with another country 他国との取り引きを中止する公の命令→禁輸, 通商禁止 ‖ *to impose an embargo on sth* ～を禁輸する *to lift/remove an embargo* 通商を解禁する

**embark** /ɪmbáːrk, em-/ 動自 ▶定義 to get on a ship 船に乗る→乗船する, 乗り込む ‖ *Passengers with cars must embark first.* 車に乗った乗客が先に乗船しなければならない. ⇔ **disembark** — **embarkation** /èmbɑːrkéɪʃ(ə)n, -bər-/ 名 ⓒ U →乗船, 搭乗, 乗り込むこと

句動詞 **embark on sth** 正式 ▶定義 to start sth (new) (新しく)～を始める→～に乗り出す，～を始める，～に従事する ‖ *I'm embarking on a completely new career.* 私は全く新しい職業を始めつつある．

**embarrass** /ɪmbærəs, em-/ 動他 ▶定義 to make sb feel uncomfortable or shy ～に居心地悪く，または恥ずかしく感じさせる→～に恥ずかしい思いをさせる，～を困惑させる，～にきまりの悪い思いをさせる ‖ *Don't ever embarrass me in front of my friends again!* 二度と私に友達の前で恥をかかせないで．*The Minister's mistake embarrassed the government.* 大臣の過ちに政府は困惑した．

**\*embarrassed** /ɪmbærəst, em-/ 形 ▶定義 feeling uncomfortable or shy because of sth silly you have done, because people are looking at you, etc ばかな事をしてしまったとか，人々が見ているなどの理由で，居心地悪く，または恥ずかしく感じる→きまりの悪い[気まずい]思いをした, 困惑した, どぎまぎした ‖ *I felt so embarrassed when I dropped my glass.* グラスを落として，とてもどぎまぎした．

**\*embarrassing** /ɪmbærəsɪŋ, em-/ 形 ▶定義 making you feel uncomfortable or shy 人を不快，または恥ずかしい気持ちにさせる→どぎまぎさせるような, 気まずい思いをさせる ‖ *an embarrassing question/mistake/situation* 気まずい質問・間違い・状況 — **embarrassingly** 副 →どぎまぎさせるように, 気まずい思いをさせて

**embarrassment** /ɪmbærəsmənt, em-/ 名 ▶定義 1 U the feeling you have when you are embarrassed どぎまぎしたときの感情→当惑，困惑, 気まずさ, ばつの悪さ ▶定義 2 ⓒ a person or thing that makes you embarrassed あなたを気まずくさせる人や物→当惑させる人・物, 邪魔, 厄介者

**embassy** /émbəsi/ 名 ⓒ (複 **embassies**) ▶定義 (the official building of) a group of officials (**diplomats**) and their head (**ambassador**), who represent their government in a foreign country 外国で政府を代表する役人(外交官)とその長(大使)の一団(のいる公の建物)→大使館
☛参 **consulate**

**embed** /ɪmbéd, em-/ 動他 (**embedding**; **embedded**) (通常は受動態で) ▶定義 to fix sth firmly and deeply (in sth else) ～を(ほかの…に)しっかりと, 深く固定する➔～を(…に)はめ込む, 埋める, 深く留める ‖ *The axe was embedded in the piece of wood.* おのはその木片に深く刺さっていた.

**ember** /émbər/ 名[ C, 通常は複数] ▶定義 a piece of wood or coal that is not burning, but is still red and hot after a fire has died 燃えてはいないが火が消えた後も赤く, 熱い, まきや石炭の一片➔(まき, 石炭などの)燃えさし, 燃え残り

**embezzle** /ɪmbézəl, em-/ 動他 ▶定義 to steal money that you are responsible for or that belongs to your employer 自分に責任のある, または雇用者に属する金を盗む➔～を使い込む, 横領する, 着服する ― embezzlement 名U➔横領, 使い込み

**emblem** /émbləm/ 名C ▶定義 an object or symbol that represents sth ～を象徴する物や印➔記章, 象徴, 印, エンブレム ‖ *The dove is the emblem of peace.* ハトは平和の象徴です.

**embody** /ɪmbάdi, em-/ 動他 (現分 **embodying**; 三単現 **embodies**; 過, 過分 **embodied**) 正式 ▶定義1 to be a very good example of sth ～の非常に良い例である➔～を具体的に表す, 具体化・具象化する, 擬人化する ‖ *To me she embodies all the best qualities of a teacher.* 私にとって, 彼女は最高の教師そのものだ. ▶定義2 to include or contain sth ～を含む, または入っている➔～を取り入れる, 包含する, 統合する ‖ *This latest model embodies many new features.* この最新型はたくさんの新しい機能を統合している. ― embodiment 名 C➔具体的表現, 化身, 権化 ‖ *She is the embodiment of a caring mother.* 彼女は思いやりのある母親そのものだ.

**embrace** /ɪmbréɪs, em-/ 動 ▶定義1 自他 to put your arms around sb as a sign of love, happiness, etc 愛情, 幸福などの表現として, ～の周りに腕を回す➔(～を)抱き締める, 抱擁する ▶定義2 他 正式 to include 含む➔～を含む, ～に及ぶ ‖ *His report embraced all the main points.* 彼の報告書は主な点をすべて含んでいた. ▶定義3 他 正式 to accept sth with enthusiasm ～を強い興味をもって受け入れる➔～を喜んで受け入れる, 快諾する ‖ *She embraced Christianity in her later years.* 彼女は晩年キリスト教に帰依した. ― embrace 名 C➔抱擁 ‖ *He held her in a warm embrace.* 彼は彼女を温かく抱擁した.

**embroider** /ɪmbrɔ́ɪdər, em-/ 動 ▶定義1 自他 to decorate cloth by sewing a pattern or picture on it 模様や絵を縫って布を飾る➔(～に)刺繍(ししゅう)する, (～を)縫い込む ▶定義2 他 to add details that are not true to a story to make it more interesting 話を面白くするために真実ではないことを付け加える➔～に尾ひれを付ける, ～を潤色する ― embroidery /-d(ə)ri/ 名U➔刺繍, 縫い取り, 尾ひれ, 潤色

**embryo** /émbrioʊ/ 名 C (複 **embryos** /-òʊz/) ▶定義 a baby, an animal or a plant in the early stages of development before birth 生まれる前の発達初期にある赤ん坊, 動物, 植物など➔胎児, 胚(はい) ☞参 **foetus** ― embryonic /ὲmbriάnɪk/ 形➔胎児の, 胚の, 未発達の

**emerald** /émərəld/ 名 C ▶定義 a bright green precious stone 明るい緑色をした宝石➔エメラルド ― emerald (または emerald green) 形➔エメラルド(鮮緑)色の, エメラルドグリーンの, エメラルドの ‖ *an emerald green dress* エメラルドグリーンのドレス

**emerge** /ɪmɚ́ːrdʒ/ 動自 emerge (from sth) ▶定義1 to appear or come out from somewhere どこからか現れる, または出てくる➔(～から)現れる, 出てくる ‖ *A man emerged from the shadows.* 1人の男が暗がりから現れた. (比喩) *The country emerged from the war in ruins.* その国は戦争の荒廃から立ち上った. ▶定義2 to become known 知られる➔(～から)明るみに出る, 明らかになる ‖ *During investigations it emerged that she was lying about her age.* 調査の過程で, 彼女が年齢を偽っていることが明らかになった. ― emergence /-dʒəns/ 名U➔出現, 発生 ‖ *the emergence of Aids in the 1980s* 1980年代のエイズの発生

★**emergency** /ɪmɚ́ːrdʒ(ə)nsi/ 名 C U (複 **emergencies**) ▶定義 a serious event that needs immediate action 即座の行動を必要とする深刻な出来事➔緊急事態, 緊急時 ‖ *In an emergency phone 999 for help.* 非常時には, 999に電話して助けを求めなさい. *The government has declared a state of emergency.* 政府は非常[緊急]事態を宣言した. *an emergency exit* 非常口

**emergency room** 米 = CASUALTY(3)

**emigrant** /émɪgrənt/ 名 C ▶定義 a person who has gone to live in another country 他国に行って暮らす人 →(他国への)移民, 出稼ぎ人, 出国者 ☛参 immigrant

**emigrate** /émɪgreɪt/ 動 自 ▶定義 emigrate (from...) (to...) to leave your own country to go and live in another 自分の国を去り, 他国へ行って暮らす (～から)(…へ)移住する ‖ *They emigrated from Ireland to Australia twenty years ago.* 彼らは20年前にアイルランドからオーストラリアへ移住した. — **emigration** /èməgréɪʃ(ə)n/ 名 C U → (他国への)移住, 移民, 出国 ☛参 immigrant, immigration, migrate

**eminent** /émənənt/ 形 正式 ▶定義 (used about a person) famous and important (人について) 有名で重要な → 著名な, 高名な ‖ *an eminent scientist* 著名な科学者

**eminently** /émənəntli/ 副 正式 ▶定義 very; extremely 非常に; 極度に → 著しく, 抜きんでて ‖ *She is eminently suitable for the job.* 彼女はその仕事に抜群の適性がある.

**emit** /ɪmít, e-/ 動 他 (**emitting**; **emitted**) 正式 ▶定義 to send out sth, for example a smell, a sound, smoke, heat or light におい, 音, 煙, 熱, 光などの～を放出する → ～を発する, 発散する ‖ *The animal emits a powerful smell when scared.* その動物は, 脅されると, 強烈なにおいを発する. — **emission** /ɪmíʃ(ə)n, e-/ 名 C U → 発散, 放射, 排出 ‖ *sulphur dioxide emissions from power stations* 発電所からの二酸化硫黄排出

*__emotion__ /ɪmóʊʃ(ə)n/ 名 C U ▶定義 a strong feeling such as love, anger, fear, etc 愛, 怒り, 恐れなどの強い感情 → 感情, 情緒, 興奮 ‖ *to control/express your emotions* 感情を抑制・表現する *His voice was filled with emotion.* 彼の声には感情があふれていた. *He showed no emotion as the police took him away.* 警察が彼を連れていったとき, 彼は何の感情も表さなかった.

*__emotional__ /ɪmóʊʃ(ə)n(ə)l/ 形 ▶定義1 connected with people's feelings 人々の感情に関連した → 感情的な, 情緒的な ‖ *emotional problems* 感情的な問題 ▶定義2 causing strong feelings 強い感情を引き起こす → 感動的な, 感情に訴える ‖ *He gave an emotional speech.* 彼は感動的なスピーチをした. ▶定義3 having strong emotions and showing them in front of people 強い感情を抱き, 人々の前でそれを示す → 感情的な, 感情的に振る舞う ‖ *She always gets very emotional when I leave.* 私が去るとき, いつも彼女は非常に感情的になる. — **emotionally** /-ʃ(ə)n(ə)li/ 副 → 感情的に, 情緒的に ‖ *She felt physically and emotionally drained after giving birth.* 彼女は出産後, 体力的にも感情的にも消耗しきった感じがした.

**emotive** /ɪmóʊtɪv/ 形 ▶定義 causing strong feelings 強い感情を引き起こす → 感情に訴える, 感動的な, 感情的な ‖ *emotive language* 情的言語, 感情に訴える言葉 *an emotive issue* 感情的な問題

**empathy** /émpəθi/ 名 C U ▶定義 empathy (with/for sb/sth); empathy (between A and B) the ability to imagine how another person is feeling and so understand his/her mood 他人がどう感じているかを想像して, その人の気持ちを理解する能力 → (～への・～間の)感情移入, 共感 ‖ *Some adults have (a) great empathy with children.* 子供への感情移入の強い大人がいる. — **empathize** (または -ise) /émpəθaɪz/ 動 自 **empathize (with sb/sth)** → (～に)共感する, 感情移入する ‖ *He's a popular teacher because he empathizes with his students.* 彼は生徒に共感するので, 人気がある教師だ.

**emperor** /émp(ə)rər/ 名 C ▶定義 the ruler of an empire 帝国の支配者 → 皇帝

*__emphasis__ /émfəsəs/ 名 C U ( 複 **emphases** /-siːz/) ▶定義1 emphasis (on sth) (giving) special importance or attention (to sth) (～に)特別に重きを置く, または注意を払うこと, そういった重き・注意 → 強調, 重要視 ‖ *There's a lot of emphasis on science at our school.* 私たちの学校では科学を非常に重要視している. *You should put a greater emphasis on quality rather than quantity when you write.* 書くときには, 量よりもむしろ質を重要視すべきだ. ▶定義2 the force that you give to a word or phrase when you are speaking; a way of writing a word to show that it is important 話すときに, ある言葉や句に置く強勢; ある言葉が重要だと分かるようにする書き方 → 強調, 強勢 ‖ *In the word 'photographer' the emphasis is on the second syllable.* 単語の photographer は第2音節に強

勢が置かれる. *I underlined the key phrases of my letter for emphasis.* 私は手紙の重要な句を強調するために下線を引いた. ☛類 **stress**¹

**\*emphasize** (または **-ise**) /émfəsaɪz/ 動他
▶定義 emphasize (that...) to put emphasis on sth ～を強調する→～を強調する, ～だと力説する ‖ *They emphasized that healthy eating is important.* 彼らは健康な食事が重要だと力説した. *They emphasized the importance of healthy eating.* 彼らは健康な食事の重要性を力説した. ☛類 **stress**²

**emphatic** /ɪmfǽtɪk, em-/ 形 ▶定義 said or expressed in a strong way 強く言われた, 表現された→強調された, 強い調子の, きっぱりとした ‖ *an emphatic refusal* 断固とした拒否 — **emphatically** /-k(ə)li/ 副 →強調して, 断固として

**empire** /émpaɪər/ 名 C ▶定義 1 a group of countries that is governed by one country 1つの国によって統治される複数の国→帝国 ‖ *the Roman Empire* ローマ帝国 ☛参 **emperor**, **empress** ▶定義 2 a very large company or group of companies 非常に大きな会社, または会社のグループ→巨大企業組織

**empirical** /ɪmpírɪk(ə)l, em-/ 形 正式 ▶定義 based on experiments and practical experience, not on ideas 概念でなく, 実験や実際の経験に基づいた→経験的な, 実験的な, 実証的な, 経験主義の ‖ *empirical evidence* 実証的証拠

**\*employ** /ɪmplɔ́ɪ, em-/ 動 他 ▶定義 1 employ sb (in/on sth); employ sb (as sth) to pay sb to work for you ～にお金を払い働いてもらう→～を(…に・…として)雇う, 雇用する ‖ *He is employed as a lorry driver.* 彼はトラック運転手として雇われている. *They employ 600 workers.* 彼らは600人雇っている. *Three people are employed on the task of designing a new computer system.* 新しいコンピューターシステムの開発に3人が雇われている. ☛参 **unemployed**
▶定義 2 正式 employ sth (as sth) to use 使う→～を(…として)使用する, 用いる ‖ *In an emergency, an umbrella can be employed as a weapon.* 緊急時には, 傘が武器として使われることもある.

**employee** /ɪmplɔ́(ɪ)iː, em-/ 名 C ▶定義 a person who works for sb ～のために働く人→雇われ人, 社員, 従業員, 使用人 ‖ *The factory has 500 employees.* この工場には500人の従業員がいる.

**employer** /ɪmplɔ́ɪər, em-/ 名 C ▶定義 a person or company that employs other people ほかの人々を雇う人, または会社→雇用者, 雇い主, 使用者

**employment** /ɪmplɔ́ɪmənt, em-/ 名 U ▶定義 1 the state of having a paid job 給料をもらう仕事がある状態→雇用, 雇われること, 仕事, 職業 ‖ *to be in/out of employment* 就職・失業している *This bank can give employment to ten extra staff.* この銀行には10名の臨時雇用がある. *It is difficult to find employment in the north of the country.* 国の北部で職を見つけるのは難しい.
☛参 **unemployment** と **work**¹ の注 ▶定義 2 正式 the use of sth ～を使うこと→使用する・されること ‖ *the employment of force* 武力の行使

**employment agency** 名 C ▶定義 a company that helps people to find work and other companies to find workers 人々の職探しや, ほかの会社の労働者探しを手伝う会社→職業紹介所, 職業安定所

**empower** /ɪmpáʊər, em-/ 動 他 正式 (通常は受動態で) ▶定義 to give sb power or authority (to do sth) ～に(…をするための)力や権威を与える→～に(…する)権限を与える, 権力を委任する — **empowerment** 名 U →権限委譲

**empress** /émprəs/ 名 C ▶定義 1 a woman who rules an empire 帝国を統治する女性→女帝 ▶定義 2 the wife of a man who rules an empire (emperor) 帝国を統治する男性(皇帝)の妻→皇后

**\*empty**¹ /ém(p)ti/ 形 ▶定義 1 having nothing or nobody inside it 中に何もない, またはだれもいない→空の ‖ *an empty box* 空き箱 *The bus was half empty.* バスには半分しか乗客がいなかった. ▶定義 2 without meaning or value 意味または価値のない→内容の乏しい, 無意味な, 空虚な ‖ *It was an empty threat (= it was not meant seriously).* こけおどしだった(= 本気ではなかった). *My life feels empty now the children have left home.* 今では子供たちも家を離れ, 私の生活はむなしい. — **emptiness** /ém(p)tinəs/ 名 U →空虚, 空っぽ, 無意味, 内容のないこと

**\*empty**² /ém(p)ti/ 動 (現 分 **emptying**; 三 単 現 **empties**; 過, 過分 **emptied**) ▶定義 1 他 empty sth (out/out of sth) to remove everything that is inside a container, etc 容器などの中にあるものをすべて取り去る→～を空にする, 中身を空け

る, 移す ‖ *I've emptied a wardrobe for you to use.* あなたが使えるようにと洋服ダンスを空けておきました. *Luke emptied everything out of his desk and left.* ルークは机の中を空にして, 去った. ▶定義2 [自] to become empty➜**空になる** ‖ *The cinema emptied very quickly once the film was finished.* 映画が終わると, 映画館はあっという間に空になった.

**empty-handed** [形] ▶定義 without getting what you wanted; without taking sth to sb 欲しいものを得ないで; ～を…に持っていかないで➜**手ぶらで, 何の収穫もない** ‖ *The robbers fled empty-handed.* 泥棒は空手で逃げた.

**EMU** /iː em júː, íːmjuː/ [略] Economic and Monetary Union (of the countries of the European Union)➜**(欧州連合加盟国の) 経済通貨同盟** ☛参 **euro**

**emulate** /émjəlèɪt/ [動][他][正式] ▶定義 to try to do sth as well as, or better than, sb ～と同じように, またはそれ以上に…をしようと努力する➜**～と張り合う, ～に負けまいと努力する, ～を見習って頑張る** ☛ 少し略式の表現は copy.

***enable** /ɪnéɪb(ə)l, en-/ [動][他] ▶定義 enable sb/sth to do sth to make it possible for sb/sth to do sth ～が…をすることを可能にする➜**～に…できるようにする, ～に…する力を与える** ‖ *The new law has enabled more women to return to work.* 新しい法律のお陰で仕事に復帰できる女性が増えた.

**enamel** /ɪnǽm(ə)l/ [名][U] ▶定義1 a hard, shiny substance used for protecting or decorating metal, etc 金属などを保護したり, 飾ったりするのに使われる硬い, 光沢のある物質➜**エナメル, ほうろう, (陶器の) うわ薬** ‖ *enamel paint* エナメル塗装 ▶定義2 the hard white outer covering of a tooth 歯の外側を覆う固くて白い物質➜**ほうろう質**

**enc** (または **encl**) [略] ▶定義 (used at the end of a business letter to show that there is sth else in the envelope with the letter) enclosed (ビジネスレターの最後に使われて, その封筒に手紙と一緒にほかの～が入っていることを示す)➜**同封**

**enchanted** /ɪntʃɑ́ːntəd, en-; -tʃǽnt-/ [形] ▶定義1 (in stories) affected by magic powers (物語の中で) 魔法の力の作用を受けた➜**魔法にかかった** ▶定義2 [正式] pleased or very interested 喜んだ, またはとても興味を持った➜**うっとりとした, 魅了された, 大いに喜んだ** ‖ *The audience was enchanted by her singing.* 聴衆は彼女の歌声に魅了された.

**enchanting** /ɪntʃɑ́ːntɪŋ, en-; -tʃǽnt-/ [形] ▶定義 very nice or pleasant; attractive 非常にすてきな, または好ましい; 魅力的な➜**うっとりさせる, 魅惑的な, 楽しい**

**encircle** /ɪnsə́ːrk(ə)l, en-/ [動][他][正式] ▶定義 to make a circle round sth; to surround ～の回りに円を作る; 囲む➜**～を取り囲む, 囲む** ‖ *London is encircled by the M25 motorway.* ロンドンはM25高速道路に囲まれている.

***enclose** /ɪnklóʊz, en-/ [動][他] ▶定義1 enclose sth (in sth) (通常は受動態で) to surround sth with a wall, fence, etc; to put one thing inside another ～を壁, 囲いなどで囲む; 1つのものをほかの中に入れる➜**～を囲む, ～に囲いをする** ‖ *The jewels were enclosed in a strong box.* 宝石は丈夫な箱の中に収められていた. *He gets very nervous in enclosed spaces.* 彼は閉ざされた空間にいると非常にいらいらしてくる. ▶定義2 to put sth in an envelope, package, etc with sth else ～をほかの…と一緒に封筒, 包みなどの中に入れる➜**～を同封する, 封入する** ‖ *Can I enclose a letter with this parcel?* この小包に手紙を同封できますか. ***Please find enclosed** a cheque for £100.* 100ポンドの小切手を同封いたしましたので, お受け取りください (商業文で用いる).

**enclosure** /ɪnklóʊʒər, en-/ [名][C] ▶定義1 a piece of land inside a wall, fence, etc that is used for a particular purpose 特別な目的のために使われる, 壁, 囲いなどの中の土地➜**囲い地** ‖ *a wildlife enclosure* 野生動物の囲い地 ▶定義2 something that is placed inside an envelope together with the letter 手紙と一緒に封筒の中に入れられた物➜**(手紙の) 同封物**

**encode** /ɪnkóʊd, en-/ = **CODE²(1)**

**encore¹** /ɑ́ŋkɔːr, -́-/ [間] ▶定義 called out by an audience that wants the performers in a concert, etc to sing or play sth extra コンサートなどで, 聴衆が演奏者, 役者, 歌手などに追加で～を歌って, または演奏してほしいと求めるときに叫ばれる言葉➜**アンコール**

**encore²** /ɑ́ŋkɔːr, -́-/ [名][C] ▶定義 a short, extra

performance at the end of a concert, etc コンサートなどの最後に追加で行われる短い演奏→アンコール曲, (アンコールに応じた)再演

**encounter**¹ /ɪnkáʊntər, en-/ 動他 ▶定義1 to experience sth (a danger, difficulty, etc)(危険, 困難など)を経験する→〜に遭遇する, 直面する ‖ *I've never encountered any discrimination at work.* 私は職場で差別に遭ったことはない. ☛類 meet with ▶定義2 正式 to meet sb unexpectedly; to experience or find sth unusual or new 予期せず〜に会う; 珍しい, または新しい〜を経験する, または見つける→〜に偶然会う, 出くわす ☛類 come across

**encounter**² /ɪnkáʊntər, en-/ 名 C ▶定義 an encounter (with sb/sth); an encounter (between A and B) an unexpected (often unpleasant) meeting or event 予期しない(しばしば嫌な)出会い, または出来事→(〜との・〜間の)出会い, 遭遇, 邂逅(かいこう) ‖ *I've had a number of **close encounters** (= situations which could have been dangerous) with bad drivers.* 私は悪い運転手に遭遇して何度も怖い思い(=危険と思われる経験)をした.

*__encourage__ /ɪnkə́ːrɪdʒ, -kʌ́r-/ 動他 ▶定義1 encourage sb/sth (in sth/to do sth) to give hope, support or confidence to sb 〜に希望, 支援, 自信を与える→〜の(…を)・〜を(…するように)励ます, 奨励する, 〜を勇気づける ‖ *The teacher encouraged her students to ask questions.* 先生は生徒たちに質問することを奨励した. ▶定義2 to make sth happen more easily 〜が簡単に起こるようにする→〜を奨励する, 助長する, 促進する ‖ *The government wants to encourage new businesses.* 政府は新しい事業を奨励したがっている. ⇔ **discourage** ― encouragement 名 C U 奨励, 激励, 促進, 励みになるもの ― encouraging 形 励みとなる, 元気づける, 奨励する

**encroach** /ɪnkróʊtʃ, en-/ 動自 正式 ▶定義 encroach (on/upon sth) to use more of sth than you should 〜をすべき以上に使う→(〜を)侵害する ‖ *I do hope that I am not encroaching too much upon your free time.* あなたの自由時間をあまり侵害していないとよいのですが.

**encyclopedia**(または **encyclopaedia**) /ɪnsàɪkləpíːdiə, en-/ 名 C (複 **encyclopedias**) ▶定義 a book or set of books that gives information about very many subjects, arranged in the order of the alphabet (= from A to Z) アルファベット順に(=AからZまで)並べられた, 非常に多くの項目について情報を与える1冊のまたは一組の本→百科事典

*__end__¹ /end/ 名 C ▶定義1 the furthest or last part of sth; the place or time where sth stops 〜の一番端の, または最後の部分; 〜が終わる場所または時間→最後, 終わり, 端 ‖ *My house is **at the end of** the street.* 私の家は, その通りの突き当りにある. *There are some seats **at the far end of** the room.* 部屋の向こうの端にいくつかのいすがある. *I'm going on holiday **at the end of** October.* 私は10月の終わりに休みを取る. *He promised to give me an answer by the end of the week.* 彼は週末までに返事をすると約束した. *She couldn't wait to hear the end of the story.* 彼女は話の最後を聞くまで待てなかった.
▶endはほかの名詞の前に用いられることがある: *the end house*(端の家), *the end seat*(端の席)
▶成句 in the end は, 時間を表し「最後に」を意味する: *We were too tired to cook, so in the end we decided to eat out.*(私たちは料理するには疲れすぎていたので, 結局外食することに決めた.) at the end of sth は, 本, 映画, 授業などの, 終わろうとしている最後の部分を示す: *At the end of the meal we had a row about who should pay for it.*(食事の後で, 私たちはだれがお金を払うかについて口論した.)
☛参 名 finish. レースや競争に関してのみ, end(最後)を意味するのに使われる. ▶定義2 正式 an aim or purpose ねらい, または目的→目的 ‖ *They were prepared to do anything to achieve their ends.* 彼らは目的達成のために何でもする用意があった. ▶定義3 a little piece of sth that is left after the rest has been used ほかが使われてしまった後に残った〜の一部→残り物, 切れ端, くず ‖ *a cigarette end* たばこの吸殻

成句 **at an end** 正式 ▶定義 finished or used up 終わった, または使い尽くされた→終わって, 尽きて ‖ *Her career is at an end.* 彼女の前途も終わりだ.

**at the end of your tether** ▶定義 having no more patience or strength もう我慢できない, ま

## end²

たは力が出ない→万策・忍耐が尽きて

**at the end of the day**(口語) ▶定義 used to say the most important fact in a situation ある状況の最も重要な事実を言うのに用いて→結局は、とどのつまりは ‖ *At the end of the day, you have to make the decision yourself.* 詰まる所、あなたは自分で決めなければならない.

**at a loose end** ⇒ **LOOSE¹**

**at your wits' end** ⇒ **WIT**

**bring sth/come/draw to an end** ▶定義 (to cause sth) to finish→(～を)終わらせる・(～が)終わる ‖ *His stay in England was coming to an end.* 彼の英国滞在は終わろうとしていた.

**a dead end** ⇒ **DEAD¹**

**end to end** ▶定義 in a line with the ends touching 端をつなげて列になって→端と端をつなげて ‖ *They put the tables end to end.* 彼らはテーブルをつなげた.

**in the end** ▶定義 at last; finally 最後に; とうとう→ついに、とうとう、結局のところ ‖ *He wanted to get home early but in the end it was midnight before he left.* 彼は早く家に帰りたかったが、結局出発する時には真夜中になっていた.

**make ends meet** ▶定義 to have enough money for your needs 必要なだけのお金を持っている→収支を合わせる、収入の範囲内でやっていく ‖ *It's hard for us to make ends meet.* 私たちにとって収入内で暮らすのは難しい.

**make sb's hair stand on end** ⇒ **HAIR**

**a means to an end** ⇒ **MEANS**

**no end of sth**(口語) ▶定義 too many or much; a lot of sth 多すぎる; たくさんの～→際限ないほどの、たくさんの ‖ *She has given us no end of trouble.* 彼女は途方もない迷惑を私たちに掛けてきた.

**odds and ends** ⇒ **ODDS**

**on end** ▶定義 (used about time) continuously (時間について) 継続して→立て続けに、続けて ‖ *He sits and reads for hours on end.* 彼は何時間もずっと座って、本を読む.

**put an end to sth** ▶定義 to stop sth from happening any more ～をそれ以上起こらないように止める→～を終わらせる、やめる

★**end²** /end/ 動自他 ▶定義 end (in/with sth) (to cause sth) to finish ～を終わらせる→(～が)終わる、～を終わらせる ‖ *The road ends here.* 道はここで行き止まりだ. *How does this story end?* この話はどんな風に終わるの. *The match ended in a draw.* 試合は引き分けに終わった. *I think we'd better end this conversation now.* この話はここでやめた方が良さそうです.

**句動詞 end up (as sth); end up (doing sth)** ▶定義 to find yourself in a place/situation that you did not plan or expect 気が付いたら予定または予期しなかった場所にいる・状況にいる→最後には(～に)なる、結局(～することに)なる ‖ *We got lost and ended up in the centre of town.* 私たちは道に迷い、最後には町の真ん中にいた. *She had always wanted to be a writer but ended up as a teacher.* 彼女はずっと作家になりたかったが、最後は教師になった. *There was nothing to eat at home so we ended up getting a takeaway.* 家には何も食べ物がなかったので、結局持ち帰りの料理を買うことになった.

**endanger** /ɪndéɪndʒər, en-/ 動他 ▶定義 to cause danger to sb/sth ～に危険をもたらす→～を危険にさらす ‖ *Smoking endangers your health.* 喫煙は健康に害を及ぼす.

**endangered** /ɪndéɪndʒərd, en-/ 形 ▶定義 (used about animals, plants, etc) in danger of disappearing from the world (**becoming extinct**) (動物、植物などについて) 世界から消える (絶滅する) 危険性がある→絶滅にひんした、絶滅寸前の ‖ *The giant panda is an endangered species.* ジャイアントパンダは絶滅寸前の生き物だ.

**endear** /ɪndíər, en-/ 動他 正式 ▶定義 endear sb/yourself to sb to make sb/yourself liked by sb ～または自分を…から好かれるようにする→～をかわいく思わせる、慕わせる ‖ *She managed to endear herself to everybody by her kindness.* 彼女は親切さで皆からどうにか慕われていた.
— endearing 形→愛らしい、かわいらしい
— endearingly 副→愛らしく、かわいらしく

**endeavour** (米 **endeavor**) /ɪndévər, en-/ 動自 正式 ▶定義 endeavour (to do sth) to try hard 懸命に努力する→(～しようと)(真剣に)努力する ‖ *She endeavoured to finish her work on time.* 彼女は仕事を時間通りに終わらせようと努力した.
— endeavour 名 C U→(懸命な)努力

★**ending** /éndɪŋ/ 名 C ▶定義 **1** the end (of a story, play, film, etc) (物語、劇、映画などの) 終わり→終わり、結末 ‖ *That film made me cry but I* was pleased that it had **a happy ending**. その映画を見て私は泣いたが、ハッピーエンドだったのでうれしかった. ▶定義2 (文法)the last part of a word, which can change 語の最後の部分で、変化する部分→**語尾** ‖ *When nouns end in -ch or -sh or -x, the plural ending is -es not -s.* 名詞で -ch、または -sh、または -x で終わるときには、その複数形の語尾は -s ではなく -es となる.

**endive** /éndaɪv/ 米 = CHICORY

*★**endless** /éndləs/ 形 ▶定義1 very large in size or amount and seeming to have no end 寸法または量が非常に大きく、際限がないように見える→**終わりのない、無限の、果てしのない** ‖ *The possibilities are endless.* 可能性は無限だ. ▶定義2 lasting for a long time and seeming to have no end 長い間続いて、終わりがないように見える→**無限の、切れ目のない、エンドレスの** ‖ *Our plane was delayed for hours and the wait seemed endless.* 我々の乗る飛行機が何時間も遅れて、際限なく待たされたように思えた.
☛類 **interminable** — endlessly 副→**制限なく、無限に**

**endorse** /ɪndɔ́ːrs, en-/ 動他 ▶定義1 to say publicly that you give official support or agreement to a plan, statement, decision, etc 計画、報告書、決定などへの正式な支持や同意を公に言う→**~を是認する、支持する、推奨する** ‖ *Members of all parties endorsed a ban on firearms.* どの党派の人たちも武器の禁止を支持した. ▶定義2 医(通常は受動態で)to add a note to the document which allows you to drive a vehicle (driving licence) to say that the driver has broken the law 車の運転を許可する書類(運転免許証)にその運転手が法律を破った旨の注釈を加える→**~に違反事項を記入する** — endorsement 名 C U→**裏書き、是認、支持**

**end product** 名 C ▶定義 something that is produced by a particular process or activity 特定の過程や活動によって生産されるもの→**最終生産物、最終結果**

**endurance** /ɪnd(j)úər(ə)ns, en-/ 名 U ▶定義 the ability to continue doing sth painful or difficult for a long period of time without complaining 痛みを伴う、または難しい~を長い期間不平を言わずにし続けられる能力→**忍耐、我慢、辛抱**

**endure** /ɪnd(j)úər, en-/ 動 正式 ▶定義1 他 to suffer sth painful or uncomfortable, usually without complaining 通常不平を言わずに、痛みを伴うまたは不快な~を受ける→**~を我慢する、辛抱する、堪え忍ぶ** ‖ *She endured ten years of loneliness.* 彼女は10年間の孤独に耐えた. ☛類 **bear** ▶定義2 自 to continue 続く→**持ちこたえる、持続する** ☛類 **last** — enduring 形→**永続的な、長く続く、不朽の**

*★**enemy** /énəmi/ 名 ( 複 **enemies**) ▶定義1 C a person who hates and tries to harm you あなたを嫌い、傷付けようとする人→**敵、敵対者** ‖ *They used to be friends but became **bitter enemies**.* 彼らはかつては友達だったが、憎い敵になった. *He has **made** several **enemies** during his career.* 彼は仕事をする中で数人の敵を作った. ☛名 **enmity** ▶定義2 **the enemy**[単数形または複数形の動詞と共に] the army or country that your country is fighting against あなたの国が戦っている相手の軍または国→**敵兵、敵軍、敵国** ‖ *The enemy is/are approaching.* 敵軍が近付いている. *enemy forces* 敵の軍隊

*★**energetic** /ènərdʒétɪk/ 形 ▶定義 full of or needing energy and enthusiasm エネルギーや情熱で一杯の、またはそれらを必要とする→**精力的な、活気に満ちた、元気な、エネルギッシュな** ‖ *Jogging is a very energetic form of exercise.* ジョギングは非常にエネルギッシュな運動だ. — energetically /-k(ə)li/ 副→**精力的に、元気一杯に、エネルギッシュに**

*★**energy** /énərdʒi/ 名 ( 複 **energies**) ▶定義1 U the ability to be very active or do a lot of work without getting tired 疲れずに非常に活動的でいたり、たくさんの仕事ができる能力→**精力、活力、活気、気力** ‖ *Children are usually **full of energy**.* 子供たちはいつも元気一杯なものだ. ▶定義2 U the power that comes from coal, electricity, gas, etc that is used for producing heat, driving machines, etc 石炭、電気、ガスなどから得られる力で、熱を作ったり、機械を動かすためなどに使われるもの→**エネルギー、エネルギー資源** ‖ *nuclear energy* 核エネルギー ▶定義3 **energies** [複数扱い] the effort and attention that you give to doing sth ~をするために払う努力や注意→**活動力、行動力、精力** ‖ *She devoted all her energies to helping the blind.* 彼女は、目の不自由な人を助けるために全精力を傾けた.

**enforce** /ɪnfɔ́ːrs, en-/ 動他 ▶定義 to make people obey a law or rule or do sth that they do not want to 人々を法律や規則に従わせたり、したがらない～をさせる→(法律など)を施行する，実行する，～を無理強いする，押し付ける，強制する ‖ *How will they enforce the new law?* 彼らはどのように新しい法律を施行するのだろう． — **enforced** 形→強制的な ‖ *enforced redundancies* 強制解雇 — **enforcement** 名 U →施行，執行，強制

**engage** /ɪnɡéɪdʒ, en-/ 動他 正式 ▶定義1 to interest or attract sb ～に興味を持たせる，または引き付ける→(人の注意・関心などを)ひく，人を引き込む ‖ *You need to engage the students' attention right from the start.* 生徒の注意を最初から引き付ける必要がある． ▶定義2 **engage sb (as sth)** to give work to sb ～に仕事を与える→～を(…として)従事させる，雇う ‖ *They engaged him as a cook.* 彼らは彼を料理人に雇った． ▶定義3 **engage (with sth)** to make parts of a machine fit together 機械の部品をはめ合わせる→～をかみ合わせる，(クラッチなどを)入れる ‖ *Engage the clutch before selecting a gear.* ギアを選択する前にクラッチを入れなさい．
句動詞 **engage in sth** ▶定義 to take part in sth ～に参加する→～に従事する，かかわる ‖ *I don't engage in that kind of gossip!* 私はそのようなうわさ話には加わらないよ．

★**engaged** /ɪnɡéɪdʒd, en-/ 形 ▶定義1 正式 **engaged (in/on sth)** (used about a person) busy doing sth (人について)～をするのに忙しい→～で忙しい，～に従事して，暇がない ‖ *They are engaged in talks with the Irish government.* 彼らはアイルランド政府との話し合いで忙しい． ▶定義2 **engaged (to sb)** having agreed to get married 結婚すると同意している→(～と)婚約している ‖ *We've just got engaged.* 私たちは婚約したばかりだ． *Susan is engaged to Jim.* スーザンはジムと婚約している． ▶定義3 (米 **busy**) (used about a telephone) in use (電話が)使われている→話し中で ‖ *I can't get through - the line is engaged.* 電話がつながらない — 話し中だ． ▶定義4 (used about a toilet) in use (トイレが)使われている→使用中で ⇔ **vacant**

**engagement** /ɪnɡéɪdʒmənt, en-/ 名 C ▶定義1 an agreement to get married; the time when you are engaged 結婚をする同意；婚約している期間→婚約 ‖ *He broke off their engagement.* 彼は婚約を破棄した． ▶定義2 正式 an arrangement to go somewhere or do sth at a fixed time; an appointment 決まった時間にどこかへ行く，または～をする予定；約束→約束，予約 ‖ *I can't come on Tuesday as I have a prior engagement.* 火曜日は先約があるので私は行けない．

**engagement ring** 名 C ▶定義 a ring, usually with precious stones in it, that a man gives to a woman when they agree to get married 結婚することに同意したときに男性が女性に与える指輪，通常宝石が付いている→婚約指輪

★**engine** /éndʒən/ 名 C ▶定義1 the part of a vehicle that produces power to make the vehicle move 乗り物の一部分で，その乗り物を動かすための動力を作る部分→エンジン，機関，発動機 ‖ *This engine runs on diesel.* このエンジンはディーゼルで動く． *a car/jet engine* 自動車の・ジェット機のエンジン ☞参 **motor** の注 ☞ **motorbike** のさし絵 ▶定義2 (または **locomotive**) a vehicle that pulls a railway train 電車を引っ張る車両→機関車

**engine driver** (または **train driver**, 米 **engineer**) 名 C ▶定義 a person whose job is to drive a railway engine 機関車の運転を仕事にする人→(鉄道の)機関士，運転士

★**engineer**¹ /èndʒəníər/ 名 C ▶定義1 a person whose job is to design, build or repair engines, machines, etc エンジン，機械などの設計，製造，または修理を仕事にする人→技術者，技師，エンジニア ‖ *a civil/chemical/electrical/mechanical engineer* 土木・化学・電気・機械技師 ▶定義2 米 = **ENGINE DRIVER**

**engineer**² /èndʒəníər/ 動他 正式 ▶定義 to arrange for sth to happen by careful secret planning 注意深く，秘密裏に計画して～が起きるように調整する→～を工作する，たくらむ，企てる ‖ *Her promotion was engineered by her father.* 彼女の昇進は，彼女の父親が陰で工作したものだった．

**engineering** /èndʒəníərɪŋ/ 名 U ▶定義 (the study of) the work that is done by an engineer 技師によって行われる仕事(その研究)→工学 ‖ *mechanical/civil/chemical engineering* 機械・土木・化学工学

**English**¹ /ínglıʃ/ 名 ▶定義1 ❶the language that is spoken in Britain, the US, Australia, etc 英国, 米国, オーストラリアなどで話されている言葉→**英語** || *Do you speak English?* 英語を話しますか. *I've been learning English for 5 years.* 私は5年間英語を学んでいる. ▶定義2 **the English** [複数扱い]the people of England 英国・イングランドの人々→**英国人, イングランド人**

**English**² /ínglıʃ/ 形 ▶定義 belonging to England, the English people, the English language, etc 英国, 英国人, 英語に属する→**英国の, 英国人の, 英語の, イングランドの** || *English history* イングランドの歴史 *the English countryside* イングランドの田舎

▶注意. スコットランドやウェールズの人々は British で, English ではない. the United Kingdom の注を参照.

---

▶音声とつづり字

English を二分すると?

書く場合と発音する場合とで異なることを示す適例. English や England などは文字上では Eng-lish, Eng-land ですが, 発音上は [gl-] と子音連結を構成するので, -glish, -gland のようになります. ただし, Scot-land は文字上の切れ目と音声上の切れ目が合致します. 日本語は「音楽」は [-gaku] でも [-ŋaku] でもよいですが, 英語では [g] と [ŋ] は, はっきり区別します.

---

**Englishman** /ínglıʃmən/ 名 ⓒ (複) **-men** /-mən/) ▶定義 a man who comes from England or whose parents are English 英国出身の, または両親が英国人の人→**英国人, イギリス人, イングランド人**

▶通常, I'm English. と言い, I'm an Englishman. とは言わない. 英国出身の女性を an Englishwoman と言うことも可能だが, これは一般的には使われない.

**engrave** /ıngréɪv, en-/ 動他 ▶定義 **engrave B on A; engrave A with B** to cut words or designs on metal, stone, etc 金属, 石などに文字や模様を刻む→**B を A に・A に B を彫る, 彫り込む** || *His name is engraved on the cup.* 彼の名前がカップに彫られている. *The cup is engraved with his name.* カップには彼の名前が彫られている.

**engraving** /ıngréɪvɪŋ, en-/ 名 ⓒ ⓤ ▶定義 a design that is cut into a piece of metal or stone; a picture made from this 金属や石の一片に刻まれている模様; それによって作られた絵→**版画**

**engrossed** /ıngróʊst, en-/ 形 ▶定義 **engrossed (in/with sth)** so interested in sth that you give it all your attention ある〜に非常に興味を持っていて, すべての注意をそれに傾ける→**(〜に)熱中した, 興味を奪われた, 夢中の** || *She was completely engrossed in her book.* 彼女はその本に完全に夢中になっていた.

**enhance** /ınhá:ns, en-; -hæns/ 動他 正式 ▶定義 to improve sth or to make sth look better 〜を向上させる, またはよく見せる→**(価値, 質などを)増す, 高める**

**enigma** /ınígmə, e-/ 名 ⓒ (複 **enigmas**) ▶定義 a person, thing or situation that is difficult to understand 理解するのが難しい人・事・状況→**なぞ, なぞの人, 不思議な物・事** ― **enigmatic** /èɪnɪgmǽtɪk/ 形 **不思議な, なぞの, 得体の知れない**

*****enjoy** /ındʒɔ́ı, en-/ 動他 ▶定義1 **enjoy sth/ enjoy doing sth** to get pleasure from sth 〜から喜びを得る→**〜を楽しむ** || *I really enjoyed that meal.* 食事は本当に楽しかった. *He enjoys listening to music while he's driving.* 彼は運転しながら音楽を楽しむ. ▶定義2 **enjoy yourself** to be happy; to have a good time 楽しい; 楽しい時間を過ごす→**愉快に過ごす, 楽しい思いをする** || *I enjoyed myself at the party last night.* 昨夜のパーティーは楽しかった.

**enjoyable** /ındʒɔ́ıəb(ə)l, en-/ 形 ▶定義 giving pleasure 喜びを与えるような→**楽しい, 愉快な, 面白い**

**enjoyment** /ındʒɔ́ımənt, en-/ 名 ⓤⓒ ▶定義 pleasure or a thing which gives pleasure 喜び, または喜びを与えるもの→**楽しむこと, 楽しみ** || *She gets a lot of enjoyment from teaching.* 彼女は教えることをとても楽しんでいる. *One of her main enjoyments is foreign travel.* 彼女の主な楽しみの1つは海外旅行だ.

**enlarge** /ınlá:rdʒ, en-/ 動自他 ▶定義 to make sth or to become bigger 〜を大きくする, または大きくなる→**〜を大きくする, 大きくなる, 広くする, 拡張する** || *I'm going to have this photo enlarged.* 私はこの写真を引き伸ばすつもりだ.

**句動詞** enlarge on sth ▶定義 to say or write more about sth ～についてもっと話す，またはもっと書く→～について詳しく述べる・書く

**enlargement** /ɪnlɑ́ːrdʒmənt, en-/ 🈩🅒🅤 ▶定義 making sth bigger or sth that has been made bigger ～を大きくすること，または大きくされた～→拡大，増大，拡張，引き伸ばした写真 ‖ *an enlargement of a photo* 写真を引き伸ばしたもの

**enlighten** /ɪnláɪtn, en-/ 🈩🈔🈪 ▶定義 to give sb information so that he/she understands sth better ～に情報を与えて，その人が…をより理解できるようにする→～に教えてよく分からせる，～を啓蒙（けいもう）する，啓発する，教化する

**enlightened** /ɪnláɪtnd, en-/ 🈘 ▶定義 having an understanding of people's needs, a situation, etc that shows a modern attitude to life 人々の欲求，状況などに対し，開けた生活傾向を示すような理解の仕方をする→理解のある，開けた，見識のある，啓蒙（けいもう）された，教化された

**enlist** /ɪnlíst, en-/ 🈩 ▶定義 to get help, support, etc 助け，支援などを得る→(力)を借りる，得る ‖ *We need to enlist your support.* 私たちはあなたの力を借りる必要がある. ▶定義2 🈒🈔 to join the army, navy or air force; to make sb a member of the army, etc 陸軍，海軍，または空軍に参加する；～を陸軍などの一員にする→入隊する；～を入隊させる ‖ *They enlisted as soon as war was declared.* 戦争が布告されると同時に，彼らは入隊した.

**enmity** /énməti/ 🈩🅤 ▶定義 the feeling of hatred towards an enemy 敵への憎悪の感情→**敵意，悪意，憎しみ**

**enormity** /ɪnɔ́ːrməti/ 🈩 [単数扱い] 🈢 ▶定義 the very great size, effect, etc of sth; the fact that sth is very serious ～の非常に大きな寸法，効果など；～が非常に深刻だという事実→途方もなく大きいこと ‖ *the enormity of a task/decision/problem* 途方もなく大きな仕事・決定・問題

★**enormous** /ɪnɔ́ːrməs/ 🈘 ▶定義 very big or very great 非常に大きな，偉大な→**巨大な，ばく大な** ‖ *an enormous building* 巨大な建物 *enormous pleasure* 非常な喜び — **enormously** 🈓→**ばく大に，非常に**

★**enough**¹ /ɪnʌ́f/ 🈘🈙 ▶定義1 as much or as many of sth as necessary 必要なだけの量・数の～→**必要なだけの，足りるだけの，十分な** ‖ *We've saved enough money to buy a computer.* 私たちはコンピュータを買うのに必要なだけの金をためた. *Not everybody can have a book - there aren't enough.* 皆が本を持てるわけではない — 十分にない. *If enough of you are interested, we'll arrange a trip to the theatre.* もし興味のある人が十分な数いれば，私たちは劇場へのツアーを用意しますよ. ▶定義2 as much or as many as you want 欲しいだけの量・数の→**十分な** ‖ *I've had enough of living in a city (= I don't want to live in a city any more).* もう都会での生活はたくさんだ（＝ もう都会では暮らしたくない）. *Don't give me any more work. I've got quite enough already.* これ以上私に仕事を与えないで．もうかなり十分あるから.

★**enough**² /ɪnʌ́f/ 🈓 (動詞，形容詞，副詞の後で) ▶定義1 to the necessary amount or degree; sufficiently 必要な量または程度に；十分に→**十分に，必要なだけ** ‖ *You don't practise enough.* あなたは十分に練習していない. *He's not old enough to travel alone.* 彼はまだ独りで旅をするには若すぎる. *Does she speak Italian well enough to get the job?* 彼女は仕事を取れるくらい上手にイタリア語を話しますか. ☛ **too**のさし絵 ▶定義2 quite, but not very かなり，しかし非常にではない→**随分と，～と言ってよいほどに** ‖ *She plays well enough, for a beginner.* 彼女は初心者にしては，かなり上手だ.

**成句** fair enough ⇒ **FAIR**¹

funnily, strangely, etc enough ▶定義 it is funny, etc that... ～はおかしいことだがなど→**おかしな・奇妙なことに** ‖ *Funnily enough, I thought exactly the same myself.* おかしなことに，私も全く同じ事を考えた.

sure enough ⇒ **SURE**

★**enquire**(または **inquire**) /ɪnkwáɪər, en-/ 🈩🈢 🈒🈔 ▶定義 enquire (about sb/sth) to ask for information about sth ～についての情報を求める→**(～について)聞く，尋ねる，調べる** ‖ *Could you enquire when the trains to Cork leave?* いつコーク行きの電車が出るか聞いていただけますか. *We need to enquire about hotels in Vienna.* 私たちはウィーンのホテルについて尋ねる必要がある.

**句動詞** enquire after sb ▶定義 to ask about

sb's health ～の健康について尋ねる→～の健康状態・安否を尋ねる, 見舞う

**enquire into sth** ▶定義 to study sth in order to find out all the facts すべての事実を見つけ出すために～を調べる→～を調査する, 調べる ‖ *The journalist enquired into the politician's financial affairs.* 記者はその政治家の財政状態を調べた.

**enquirer** /ɪnkwáɪərər, en-/ 名 C正式 ▶定義 a person who asks for information 情報を求める人→尋問者, 探求者

**enquiring** /ɪnkwáɪərɪŋ, en-/ 形 ▶定義 1 interested in learning new things 新しい事を学ぶことに興味のある→事実を求める, 好奇心のある, 探求心のある ‖ *We should encourage children to have an enquiring mind.* 我々は子供たちに探求心を持つことを奨励すべきだ. ▶定義 2 asking for information 情報を求める→詮索(せんさく)するような, 不審そうな ‖ *He gave me an enquiring look.* 彼は詮索するような目で私を見た. — enquiringly 副 ▶不審そうに, 詮索するように

*****enquiry** (または **inquiry**) /ɪnkwáɪəri, en-/ 名 (複 enquiries) ▶定義 1 ① 正式 an enquiry (about/concerning/into sb/sth) a question that you ask about sth ～について尋ねる質問→(～についての)質問, 尋問, 調査 ‖ *I'll make some enquiries into English language courses in Oxford.* オックスフォードでの英語講座について調べてみます. ▶定義 2 ① the act of asking about sth ～について尋ねる行為→質問, 探求 ‖ *After weeks of enquiry he finally found what he was looking for.* 数週間の探求の後, 彼はついに探していたものを見つけた. ▶定義 3 C enquiry (into sth) an official process to find out the cause of sth ～の原因を見つけ出すための公式な過程→(～の)調査, 取り調べ, 審問 ‖ *After the accident there was an enquiry into safety procedures.* その事故の後, 安全への取り組みに対する調査が行われた.

**enrage** /ɪnréɪdʒ, en-/ 動他正式 ▶定義 to make sb very angry ～を非常に怒らせる→～を激怒させる

**enrich** /ɪnrítʃ, en-/ 動他 ▶定義 1 to improve the quality, flavour, etc of sth ～の質, 風味などを向上させる→～を濃厚にする, 豊富にする, 豊かにする ‖ *These cornflakes are enriched with vitamins/are vitamin-enriched.* このコーンフレークはビタミンが増強されている. ▶定義 2 to make

sb/sth rich or richer→～を豊かにする ⇔ **impoverish**

**enrol** (米 **enroll**) /ɪnróʊl, en-/ 動 自他 (**enrolling**; **enrolled**) ▶定義 to become or to make sb a member of a club, school, etc クラブ, 学校などの一員になる, または～を一員にさせる→(～に)登録する, ～を入学させる, 会員にする ‖ *They enrolled 100 new students last year.* 彼らは昨年100名の新入生を受け入れた. 米 *I've enrolled on an Italian course.* 私はイタリア語の講座に登録した. — enrolment(米 enrollment) 名 ① →登録, 入学, 入会 ‖ *Enrolment for the course will take place next week.* その講座の登録は来週行われる.

**en route** /ɑ̃n rúːt/ 副 ▶定義 en route (from...)(to...); en route (for...) on the way; while travelling from/to a place 途上で; ある場所から・ある場所へ旅する間に→(～からの)(…への)道の途中で; (～へ)向かって ‖ *The car broke down when we were en route for Dover.* ドーバーに向かう途中で, 車が故障した.

**ensue** /ɪns(j)úː, en-/ 動自正式 ▶定義 to happen after (and often as a result of) sth else ほかの～に続いて(しばしばその結果として)起こる→続いて起こる, 起こる

**en suite** /ɑ̃n swíːt/ 形副 ▶定義 (used about a bedroom and bathroom) forming one unit (寝室と浴室について) 1つの組を構成する→一続きの[で], 付属して ‖ *The bedroom has a bathroom en suite.* この寝室には浴室が付いている.

**ensure** (米 **insure**) /ɪnʃʊ́r, en-, -ʃʊ́ər/ 動他 ▶定義 to make sure that sth happens or is definite ～が起きること, または～が確実なことを確かにする→～を確実にする, 確保する, 確かめる ‖ *Please ensure that the door is locked before you leave.* 出掛ける前にドアにかぎがかかっていることを確認してください.

**entail** /ɪntéɪl, en-/ 動他正式 ▶定義 to make sth necessary; to involve sth ～を必要とする; ～を含む→～を要する, 伴う ‖ *The job sounds interesting but I'm not sure what it entails.* その仕事は面白そうだが, それに何が伴うのかよく分からない.

**entangled** /ɪntǽŋg(ə)ld, en-/ 形 ▶定義 caught in sth else ほかのものに捕らえられて→絡まつ

## 550 enter

た, 巻き込まれた, 掛かり合いになった ‖ *The bird was entangled in the net.* その鳥は網に掛かっていた. (比喩) *I've got myself entangled in some financial problems.* 私はある経済的問題に巻き込まれている.

**★enter** /éntər/ 動 ▶定義1 ⊜⊖正式 to come or go into a place ある場所に来る, または入っていく →(〜に)入る, 加わる ‖ *Don't enter without knocking.* 入るときは必ずノックしてください. *They all stood up when he entered the room.* 彼が部屋に入ると彼らは皆立ち上がった.
☞ 名 entrance, entry
▶注意. enter は前置詞を付けずに用いられる. come into または go into の方が一般的.

▶定義2 ⊖ to become a member of sth, especially a profession or an institution 特に職業や団体など, 何かの一員になる →〜に加わる, 入会する, 入学する ‖ *She entered the legal profession in 1998.* 彼女は1998年に法曹界に入った. *to enter school/college/university* 学校・大学に入学する ☞ 名 entrant ▶定義3 ⊖ to begin or become involved in an activity, a situation, etc ある活動, 状況などを始める, またはそういう活動・状況にかかわる →〜に参加する ‖ *When she entered the relationship, she had no idea he was already married.* 彼女がその関係を始めた時, 彼が既に結婚しているとは全く思わなかった. *We have just entered a new phase in international relations.* 我々は国際関係の新しい局面に入ったところだ. ▶定義4 ⊜⊖ enter (for) sth; enter sb (in/for sth) to put your name or sb's name on the list for an exam, race, competition, etc 自分または〜の名前を, 試験, 競争, 競技などのリストに載せる →登録する ‖ *I entered a competition in the Sunday paper and I won £20!* 私はその日曜新聞のコンテストに登録して20ポンドを勝ち取った. ▶定義5 ⊖ enter sth (in/into/on/onto sth) to put names, numbers, details, etc in a list, book, computer, etc 名前, 番号, 詳細などを, リスト, 本, コンピューターなどに入れる →〜を(…に)入力する, 記入する ‖ *I've entered all the data onto the computer.* 私はすべてのデータをコンピューターに入力した. *Enter your password and press return.* パスワードを入れて, 改行キーを押してください.

句動詞 enter into sth ▶定義1 to start to think or talk about sth 〜について考え始めたり, 話し始める →〜に取り掛かる, 〜を論じ始める ‖ *I don't want to enter into details now.* 今は詳細を論じたくない. ▶定義2 to be part of sth; to be involved in sth 〜の一部になる; 〜にかかわる → 従事する, 中に入る ‖ *This is a business matter. Friendship doesn't enter into it.* これは仕事上のことだ. 友情の入り込む余地はない.

enter into sth (with sb) ▶定義 to begin sth 〜を始める →(〜との)…に取り掛かる ‖ *The government has entered into negotiations with the unions.* 政府は, 組合との交渉に取り掛かった.

**enterprise** /éntərpràɪz/ 名 ▶定義1 ⓒ a new plan, project, business, etc 新しい計画, 企画, 事業など →企て, 事業 ‖ *It's a very exciting new enterprise.* それは非常に刺激的な新事業だ. *a new industrial enterprise* 新しい産業事業 ▶定義2 Ⓤ the ability to think of new projects or create new businesses and make them successful 新しい企画を考える, または新しい事業を創造して成功させる能力 →進取の気象, 冒険心 ‖ *We need men and women of enterprise and energy.* 私たちは, 進取の気象と活力のある男性と女性を必要としている.

**enterprising** /éntərpràɪzɪŋ/ 形 ▶定義 having or showing the ability to think of new projects or new ways of doing things and make them successful 新しい企画や新しいやり方を考え, うまく成し遂げる能力がある, またはそのような能力を見せる →進取の気象に富んだ, 冒険心のある, 行動力のある ‖ *One enterprising farmer opened up his field as a car park and charged people to park there.* 1人の進取の気象に富んだ農夫が畑を駐車場にし, 駐車料金を取った.

**★entertain** /èntərtéɪn/ 動 ▶定義1 ⊖ entertain (sb) (with sth) to interest and amuse sb in order to please him/her 〜を喜ばせるために, その〜を面白がらせ, 楽しませる →〜を楽しませる, 面白がらせる ‖ *I find it very hard to keep my class entertained on a Friday afternoon.* 金曜の午後に私のクラスの生徒を楽しませておくのはとても難しいと分かった. ▶定義2 ⊜⊖ to welcome sb as a guest, especially to your home; to give sb food and drink 〜を特に自宅に, 客として歓迎する; 〜に食事や飲み物を与える →〜をもてなす, 招待する ‖ *They entertain a lot./They*

**entertainer** /èntərtéɪnər/ 名 C ▶定義 a person whose job is to amuse people, for example by singing, dancing or telling jokes 例えば歌ったり、踊ったり、冗談を言ったりして、人々を面白がらせるのを仕事にする人→楽しませる人、エンターテイナー、芸人 ‖ *a street entertainer* 大道芸人

**entertaining** /èntərtéɪnɪŋ/ 形 ▶定義 interesting and amusing 面白くて楽しい→楽しませる、面白い

*__entertainment__ /èntərtéɪnmənt/ 名 U C ▶定義 film, music, etc used to interest and amuse people 人々を面白がらせ、楽しませるための映画、音楽など→娯楽、楽しみ ‖ *There isn't much entertainment for young people in this town.* この町には若者の娯楽があまりない. *There's a full programme of entertainments every evening.* 毎晩たくさんの娯楽番組がある.

**enthral** (米 **enthrall**) /ɪnθrɔ́ːl, en-/ 動 他 (**enthralling**; **enthralled**) ▶定義 to hold sb's interest and attention completely 〜の興味や注意を完全に捕らえる→〜の心を奪う、〜を魅了する ‖ *He was enthralled by her story.* 彼は、彼女の話に心を奪われた. — **enthralling** 形 ▶魅惑的な、心を奪うような

*__enthusiasm__ /ɪnθj(j)úːziæz(ə)m, en-/ 名 U ▶定義 **enthusiasm (for/about sth/doing sth)** a strong feeling of excitement or interest in sth and a desire to become involved in it 〜に強く感じる興奮や興味、また、それにかかわりたいという欲求→(〜に・〜することに対する)熱中、熱心 ‖ *Jan showed great enthusiasm for the new project.* ジャンは新しい事業に強い情熱を示した.

**enthusiast** /ɪnθjúːziæst, -sɪ̀, en-/ 名 C ▶定義 a person who is very interested in an activity or subject ある活動や事柄に非常に興味のある人→熱狂者、ファン

*__enthusiastic__ /ɪnθj(j)ùːziǽstɪk, en-/ 形 ▶定義 **enthusiastic (about sth/doing sth)** full of excitement and interest in sth 〜に非常に興奮し、興味を持った→(〜に・〜することに)熱心な、熱中した、熱狂的な — **enthusiastically** /-k(ə)li/ 副 →熱心に、熱狂的に

**entice** /ɪntáɪs, en-/ 動 他 ▶定義 **entice sb (into sth/doing sth)** to persuade sb to do sth or to go somewhere by offering him/her something nice 何かすてきなものを提供して、〜に…するように、またはどこかへ行くように説得する→〜を誘う、〜をそそのかして(…させる)、誘惑する ‖ *Advertisements try to entice people into buying more things than they need.* 広告は、人々に必要以上の物を買わせようとする. — **enticement** 名 C U →誘惑

**enticing** /ɪntáɪsɪŋ, en-/ 形 ▶定義 attractive and interesting 魅力的な、また興味をひく→誘惑するような、心を誘う

*__entire__ /ɪntáɪər, en-/ 形 (名詞の前だけ) ▶定義 whole or complete 全体の、または完全な→全体の、まるまるの、全くの ‖ *He managed to read the entire book in two days.* 彼は2日でどうにかその本を全部読んだ.

▶ entire は whole よりも強い意味を持つ.

— **entirely** 副 →全く、すっかり ‖ *I entirely agree with you.* 私は全くあなたに同感だ. — **entirety** /ɪntáɪərti, en-/ 名 U →完全、全体 ‖ *We must consider the problem in its entirety (= as a whole).* 私たちはその問題を全体で(= 全体として)考えなければならない.

**entitle** /ɪntáɪtl, en-/ 動 他 ▶定義 **entitle sb (to sth)** (通常は受動態で) to give sb the right to have or do sth 〜に…を持つまたはする権利を与える→〜に(…の)権利を与える、資格を与える ‖ *I think I'm entitled to a day's holiday - I've worked hard enough.* 私は1日休みをもらう権利があると思う — 十分よく働いたのだから.

**entitled** /ɪntáɪtld, en-/ 形 ▶定義 (used about books, plays, etc) with the title (本、劇などについて) 題名のある→〜と題した ‖ *Duncan's first book was entitled 'Aquarium'.* ダンカンの処女作は「アクアリウム」という題名だった.

**entity** /éntəti/ 名 C (複 **entities**) ▶定義 something that exists separately from sth else and has its own identity ほかのものと別に存在し、自身の主体性を持つもの→実在、実体 ‖ *The kindergarten and the school are in the same building but they're really separate entities.* その幼稚園と学校は同じ建物の中にあるが、全く別の存在だ.

*__entrance__ /éntr(ə)ns/ 名 ▶定義 **1** C **the entrance (to/of sth)** the door, gate or opening where you go into a place ある場所に入る扉、門、または開口部→(〜への)入り口、玄関、戸口 ‖ *I'll meet* *you at the entrance to the theatre.* 劇場の入り口で会いましょう. ▶定義2 ❻entrance (into/onto sth) the act of coming or going into a place, especially in a way that attracts attention 特に注意をひく方法で, ある場所に入る行為→(〜に)入ること, (〜への)入場, 登場 ∥ *He made a dramatic entrance onto the stage.* 彼は舞台上に劇的な登場をした. ☞ entry も同じ意味で用いられる. ⇔ 定義1, 2 exit ▶定義3 ❶entrance (to sth) the right to enter a place ある場所に入る権利→〜に入る権利 ∥ *They were refused entrance to the disco because they were wearing shorts.* 彼らはショートパンツを履いていたので, ディスコへの入場を拒否された. *an entrance fee* 入場料 ☞ entry も同じ意味で用いられる. admission, admittance を参照. ▶定義4 ❶entrance (into/to sth) permission to join a club, society, university, etc クラブ, 団体, 大学などに入会・入学することを許すこと→(〜への)入学, 入会 ∥ *You don't need to take an entrance exam to get into university.* 君は大学入学のために入試を受ける必要はない. ☞参 admission

**entrant** /éntrənt/ 图 ❻ ▶定義 a person who enters a profession, competition, exam, university, etc ある職業に就いたり, コンクールに参加したり, 試験を受けたり, 大学などに入る人→新入生, 参加者, 新入社員

**entreat** /ɪntríːt, en-/ 動他 正式 ▶定義 to ask sb to do sth, often in an emotional way しばしば感情的に, 〜に…をしてくれるように頼む→〜に嘆願する, 折り入って頼む ☞類 beg

**entrust** /ɪntrʌ́st, en-/ 動他 正式 ▶定義 entrust A with B/entrust B to A to make sb responsible for sth 〜に…についての責任を持たせる→AにBを・BをAにゆだねる, 委任する ∥ *I entrusted Rachel with the arrangements for the party./I entrusted the arrangements for the party to Rachel.* レイチェルにパーティーの準備を任せた.

*\***entry** /éntri/ 图 ( 複 **entries**) ▶定義1 ❻the act of coming or going into a place ある場所に入る行為→入ること ∥ *The thieves forced an entry into the building.* 泥棒は建物に押し入った. ☞類 **entrance** ▶定義2 ❶entry (to/into sth) the right to enter a place ある場所に入る権利→(〜への)入場許可, 加入, 参加 ∥ *The immigrants were refused entry at the airport.* 移民たちは空港で入国を拒否された. *The sign says 'No Entry'.* 標識には「立ち入り禁止」と書いてある. *an entry visa* 入国査証 ☞類 **entrance**. **admission**, **admittance** を参照. ▶定義3 ❶the right to take part in sth or become a member of a group 〜に参加する, またはある集団の一員になる権利→参加, 加盟 ∥ *countries seeking entry into the European Union* 欧州連合加盟を目指している国々 ▶定義4 ❻a person or thing that is entered for a competition, etc コンテストなどに登録された人や物→参加者, 参加作品, 出品物 ∥ *There were fifty entries for the Eurovision song contest.* ユーロヴィジョンのソングコンテストに50組の参加があった. *The winning entry is number 45!* 優勝者は45番です. ▶定義5 ❻one item that is written down in a list, diary, account book, dictionary, etc 名簿, 手帳, 会計簿, 辞書などに書かれた1つの項目→記載事項, 項目, 記載, 記入, (辞書の)見出し(語) ∥ *an entry in a diary* 手帳への記入 *You'll find 'ice-skate' after the entry for 'ice'.* ice の項目の後に ice skate があります. ▶定義6 ❻ 困 a door, gate, passage, etc where you enter a building, etc 建物などに入る扉, 門, 廊下など→入り口, 戸口 ☞類 **entrance**

**envelop** /ɪnvéləp, en-/ 動他 正式 ▶定義 to cover or surround sb/sth completely (in sth) 〜を完全に(…の中に)覆うまたは囲む→〜を包む, 囲む, 覆う ∥ *The hills were enveloped in mist.* 丘は霧に覆われていた.

*\***envelope** /énvəlòup, ɔ́n-, ɑ́ːn-/ 图 ❻ ▶定義 the paper cover for a letter 紙製の手紙の覆い→封筒 ► 手紙を書いたら, 封筒に address(あて先を書く)そして, seal(封をする). そして切手を右上隅にはる.

☞参 **stamped/self-addressed envelope** ☞ S4 ページのさし絵

**enviable** /énviəb(ə)l/ 形 ▶定義 (used about sth that sb else has and that you would like) attractive(ほかの〜が持っている, また, 自分が欲しい〜について)魅力的な→うらやましい, うらやましがらせる ⇔ **unenviable** ☞ 動 名 **envy**

**envious** /énviəs/ 形 ▶定義 envious (of sb/sth) wanting sth that sb else has ほかの〜が持っている…を欲しがるような→(〜を)うらやましが

る, うらやましげな, ねたみ深い ‖ *She was envious of her sister's success.* 彼女は妹の成功をうらやんでいた. ●類 **jealous** ● 動名 **envy** — **enviously** 副 →うらやましげに, ねたんで

\***environment** /ɪnváɪərənmənt/ 名 ▶定義1 C U the conditions in which you live, work, etc 人が住んだり, 働いたりしている状況 →**環境, 境遇** ‖ *a pleasant working environment* 好ましい職場環境 ▶定義2 **the environment** [単数扱い] the natural world, for example the land, air and water, in which people, animals and plants live 人, 動物, 植物が生きる自然界, 例えば大地, 空気, 水→**環境** ‖ *We need stronger laws to protect the environment.* 環境を守るためのより強い法律が必要だ. ●参 S2ページ ●参 **surroundings** — **environmental** /ɪnvàɪərənméntl/ 形 →**環境の, 周囲(の事情)からの** ‖ *environmental science* 環境科学 — **environmentally** /-t(ə)li/ 副 →**環境的に** ‖ *These products are environmentally friendly.* これらの製品は環境に優しい.

**environmentalist** /ɪnvàɪərənméntlɪst/ 名 C ▶定義 a person who wants to protect the environment 環境を守ることを望む人 →**環境保護論者, 環境問題専門家**

**envisage** /ɪnvízɪdʒ, en-/ 動他 正式 ▶定義 to think of sth as being possible in the future; to imagine ～を将来可能だと考える; 想像する →**～を予測する, 予想する, 心に描く** ‖ *I don't envisage any problems with this.* これについては何の問題も予想できない.

**envoy** /énvɔɪ/ 名 C ▶定義 a person who is sent by a government with a message to another country 政府から他国に伝達事項と共に送られる人 →**使者, 使節, 公使**

\***envy**¹ /énvi/ 名 U ▶定義 envy (of sb); envy (at/of sth) the feeling that you have when sb else has sth that you want 自分が欲しい～をほかの…が持っているときに持つ感情 →**(～を)ねたむこと, うらやむこと, (～に対する)ねたみ, うらやみ, しっと, 羨望(せんぼう)** ‖ *It was difficult for her to hide her envy of her friend's success.* 友達の成功へのしっとを隠すことは彼女には難しかった.

成句 **be the envy of sb** ▶定義 be the thing that causes sb to feel envy ～にしっとを感じさせるようなものである →**～の羨望(せんぼう)の的だ** ‖ *The City's transport system is the envy of many of its European neighbours.* その都市の交通システムは, ヨーロッパの近隣諸国の多くの羨望の的だ. ●参 **enviable**, **envious**

**envy**² /énvi/ 動他 (現分 **envying**; 三単現 **envies**; 過, 過分 **envied**) ▶定義 envy (sb) (sth) to want sth that sb else has; to feel envy ほかの～が持っている…を欲しがる; ねたみを感じる →**(～に)(…を)・(～の)(…を)うらやむ, うらやましがる, ねたむ** ‖ *I've always envied your good luck.* 私はいつも君の幸運がうらやましかった. *I don't envy you that job* (= I'm glad that I don't have it). 君のあの仕事はうらやましくはないよ (= 自分がその仕事を持っていなくてよかった).

**epic** /épɪk/ 形 ▶定義 very long and exciting 非常に長く, 好奇心をそそる →**勇壮な, 壮大な, 叙事詩的な** ‖ *an epic struggle/journey* 壮大な戦い・旅 — **epic** 名 C →**叙事詩, 大作, 壮大な作品** ‖ *The film 'Glory' is an American Civil War epic.* 映画「グローリー」はアメリカ南北戦争を描いた大作だ.

**epidemic** /èpədémɪk/ 名 C ▶定義 a large number of people or animals suffering from the same disease at the same time 多数の人や動物が同じ病気に同時にかかること →**(病気の)流行, 流行病の発生, 蔓延(まんえん)**

**epilepsy** /épəlèpsi/ 名 U ▶定義 a disease of the brain that can cause a person to become unconscious (sometimes with violent movements that he/she cannot control) 人が気を失う脳の病気(時に抑えられない激しい震えを伴う) →**てんかん**

**epileptic** /èpəléptɪk/ 名 C ▶定義 a person who suffers from epilepsy てんかんにかかっている人 →**てんかん患者** — **epileptic** 形 →**てんかんの** ‖ *an epileptic fit* てんかんの発作

**epilogue** /épəlɔ̀(ː)g, -làg/ (米 **epilog**) 名 C ▶定義 a short piece that is added at the end of a book, play, etc and that comments on what has gone before 本, 演劇などの最後に追加される短い部分で, その前に起こった事について注釈するもの →**結びの言葉, エピローグ** ●参 **prologue**

**episode** /épəsòʊd/ 名 C ▶定義1 one separate event in sb's life, a novel, etc ～の生涯, 小説などの中での1つの独立した出来事 →**エピソード, 挿話的な出来事** ‖ *That's an episode in my*

### epitaph

*life I'd rather forget.* それは,私の人生で,どちらかといえば忘れてしまいたいエピソードだ.
▶定義2 one part of a television or radio story that is shown in several parts (a serial) 何回かにわたって見せられるテレビやラジオの話(連続物)の一部➡挿話,(連続ドラマ・小説の)1回分

**epitaph** /épətà:f, -tæf/ 名 ❻ ▶定義 words that are written or said about a dead person, especially words written on a stone where he/she is buried 死んだ人について書かれた,または言われた言葉,特にその人が葬られた墓石に書かれた言葉➡墓碑銘,碑文

**epitome** /ɪpítəmi/ 名 [単数扱い] ▶定義 the epitome (of sth) a perfect example of sth 〜の完ぺきな例➡(〜の)典型,縮図 ‖ *Her clothes are the epitome of good taste.* 彼女の服は趣味の良さを絵にかいたようだ.

**epitomize**(または **-ise**) /ɪpítəmàɪz/ 動⊕ ▶定義 to be typical of sth 〜の特色をよく示す➡〜の縮図である,典型である ‖ *This building epitomizes modern trends in architecture.* この建物は建築における現代の潮流の典型だ.

**epoch** /íːpɔk, -àk; épək/ 名 ❻ ▶定義 a period of time in history (that is important because of special events, characteristics, etc) (特別な出来事,特徴などのために重要な)歴史の中の一時期➡新紀元,新時代,重大な事件の起こった時代

*★**equal**¹ /íːkw(ə)l/ 形 ▶定義1 equal (to sb/sth) the same in size, amount, value, number, level, etc 大きさ,量,価値,数,程度などが同じ➡等しい,同等の ‖ *This animal is equal in weight to a small car.* この動物は小型車と同じくらいの重さだ. *They are equal in weight.* 彼らは重さが同じくらいだ. *They are of equal weight.* 彼らは同じくらいの重さだ. *Divide it into two equal parts.* それを二等分しなさい. ⇔ **unequal**
▶定義2 having the same rights or being treated the same as other people ほかの人々と同じ権利を持った,または,同じように扱われる➡平等の,対等の ‖ *This company has an equal opportunities policy (= gives the same chance of employment to everyone).* この会社は機会均等策を取っている(= 皆に同じ雇用機会を与える). ▶定義3 正式 equal to sth having the strength, ability etc to do sth 〜をするための強さ,能力などを持っている➡〜に耐えられる,〜する力量がある ‖ *I'm afraid Bob just isn't equal to the job.* ボブはその仕事に耐えられないだろう.

成句 be on equal terms (with sb) ▶定義 to have the same advantages and disadvantages as sb else ほかの〜と同じ有利な点と不利な点を持つ➡〜と同じ条件で,対等で

**equal**² /íːkw(ə)l/ 動⊕( **equalling; equalled**; 米 **equaling; equaled**) ▶定義1 (used about numbers, etc) to be the same as sth (数字などについて)〜と同じになる➡〜に等しい ‖ *44 plus 17 equals 61 is written: 44 + 17 = 61.*「44足す17は61」という式は44+17=61と書く.
▶定義2 to be as good as sb/sth 〜と同じくらい良い➡〜に匹敵する,劣らない ‖ *He ran an excellent race, equalling the world record.* 彼は世界記録に匹敵するすばらしいレースをした.

**equal**³ /íːkw(ə)l/ 名 ❻ ▶定義 a person who has the same ability, rights, etc as you do あなたと同じ能力,権利などを持つ人➡同等の人,平等に ‖ *to treat sb as an equal* 〜を同等に扱う

*★**equality** /ɪkwáləti/ 名 ❿ ▶定義 the situation in which everyone has the same rights and advantages 皆が同じ権利や有利性を持つ状況➡平等,同等 ‖ *racial equality (= between people of different races)* 人種的(= 異なる民族の間の)平等 ⇔ **inequality**

**equalize**(または **-ise**) /íːkw(ə)làɪz/ 動⊜ ▶定義 (sport) to reach the same number of points as your opponent (スポーツ)敵と同じ点数を取る➡同点になる,同等になる

*★**equally** /íːkwəli/ 副 ▶定義1 to the same degree or amount 同じ程度または量まで➡等しく,同様に ‖ *They both worked equally hard.* 彼らはどちらも同じようによく働いた. ▶定義2 in equal parts 等しい部分に➡等しく,平等に ‖ *His money was divided equally between his children.* 彼の金は子供たちの間で平等に分けられた. ▶定義3 正式(used when you are comparing two ideas or commenting on what you have just said) at the same time; but/and also (2つの案を比べるときや,言ったばかりのことに意見を述べるときに用いて)同時に; けれどもまた➡それと同様に,それと同時に ‖ *I do not think what he did was right. Equally, I can understand*

*why he did it.* 私は彼がした事を正しくないと思う. けれどもまた, なぜ彼がそれをしたのか理解できる.

**equate** /ɪkwéɪt/ 動他 ▶定義 equate sth (with sth) to consider one thing as being the same as sth else ある事柄をほかの事柄と同じと考え る→~を(…と)等しく見なす,同等視する ‖ *You can't always equate money with happiness.* いつも金を幸福と同一視できるわけではない.

**equation** /ɪkwéɪʒ(ə)n, -ʃ(ə)n/ 名 C ▶定義 (in mathematics) a statement that two quantities are equal (数学で)2つの量が同じであると述べること→等式, 方程式 ‖ *2x + 5 =11 is an equation.* 2x + 5= 11は方程式. 

**the equator** (または **the Equator**) /ɪkwéɪtər, í:kwèr-/ 名 [単数扱い] ▶定義 the imagined line around the earth at an equal distance from the North and South Poles 北極と南極から同じ距 離にある地球上の点を結んでできた仮想的な 線→赤道 ‖ *north/south of the Equator* 赤道の 北・南 *The island is on the equator.* その島は赤 道直下にある. ☞ **earth**のさし絵

**equestrian** /ɪkwéstriən/ 形 正式 ▶定義 connected with horse riding 乗馬に関連した→ 乗馬の, 馬術の

**equip** /ɪkwíp/ 動他 (**equipping**; **equipped**) equip sb/sth (with sth) ▶定義 **1** (通常は受動態 で) to supply sb/sth with what is needed for a particular purpose 特定の目的のために必要な ものを~に供給する→~に(…を)備え付ける, 装 備する ‖ *We shall equip all schools with new computers over the next year.* 来年にかけてすべ ての学校に新しいコンピューターを備え付けま しょう. *The flat has a **fully-equipped** kitchen.* そのフラット・アパートにはキッチンが完備され ている. ▶定義 **2** to prepare sb for a particular task 特定の任務のために~を準備させる→~に (…の)身支度をさせる, ~に(…を)身に付けさせる ‖ *The course equips students with all the skills necessary to become a chef.* その講座は受講者 に料理人になるために必要なすべての技術を身 に付けさせます.

\***equipment** /ɪkwípmənt/ 名 U ▶定義 the things that are needed to do a particular activity 特定 の活動に必要なもの→備品, 設備, 装備 ‖ *office/sports/computer equipment* 事務用品・ス ポーツ用具・コンピューター設備

▶ equipmentは不可算名詞であることに注意. 1つの品目について言うときには, a piece of equipmentとしなければならない: *a very useful piece of kitchen equipment*(非常に便 利な台所用品1つ)

**equivalent** /ɪkwívjəl(ə)nt/ 形 ▶定義 equivalent (to sth) equal in value, amount, meaning, importance, etc 価値, 量, 意味, 重要性などが等 しい→(~と)同等の, 同量の, (~に)同数の, 相当す る ‖ *The British House of Commons is roughly equivalent to the American House of Representatives.* 英国の下院は, おおよそ米国の 下院に相当する. ― equivalent 名 C→同等物, 当価値のもの, 同義語 ‖ *There is no English equivalent to the French 'bon appétit'.* フランス 語の bon appétit に相当する英語はない.

**er** /əːr/ 間 ▶定義 used in writing to show the sound that sb makes when he/she cannot decide what to say next 次に言う事が決まらない ときに~が発する音を書き表すのに用いて→えー, あのー

**era** /íərə/ 名 C ▶定義 a period of time in history (that is special for some reason) (ある理由のた めに特別な)歴史上のある期間→時代, 年代 ‖ *We are living in the era of the computer.* 私たちはコ ンピューターの時代に生きている.

**eradicate** /ɪrǽdəkèɪt/ 動他 正式 ▶定義 to destroy or get rid of sth completely ~を完全に 壊す, または排除する→~を根こそぎにする, 一掃 する, 根絶する ‖ *Scientists have completely eradicated some diseases, such as smallpox.* 科学者は, 天然痘など, いくつかの病気を完全に 根絶した. ― eradication /ɪrædəkèɪʃ(ə)n/ 名 U → 根絶, 絶滅, 一掃

**erase** /ɪréɪz, -s/ 動他 正式 ▶定義 to remove sth completely (a pencil mark, a recording on tape, a computer file, etc) (鉛筆の跡, テープ上の記録, コンピューターのファイルなど)を完全に取り去 る→~を消し去る, 消す ‖ (比喩) *He tried to erase the memory of those terrible years from his mind.* 彼はその恐ろしい数年間の記憶を頭から 消し去ろうとした. ☞ 鉛筆の跡を消す場合は, 通 常rub outと言う. ― eraser 特に 米 →消しゴム, 黒板ふき = **RUBBER**(2)

**erect**[1] /ɪrékt/ 形 ▶定義 **1** standing straight up ま

**erect²**

っすぐに立った→**直立した,まっすぐの** ‖ *He stood with his head erect.* 彼は気を付けの姿勢をした. ☛類 **upright** ▶定義**2** (used about the male sexual organ) hard and standing up because of sexual excitement (男性性器について)性的興奮のために堅く立った→**勃起(ぼっき)した**

**erect²** /ɪrékt/ 動他 正式 ▶定義 to build sth or to stand sth straight up ～を建てる,またはまっすぐ立てる→**～を建てる,直立させる,まっすぐにする** ‖ *to erect a statue* 彫像を立てる *Huge TV screens were erected above the stage.* 巨大なテレビ画面がステージの上に立てられた.

**erection** /ɪrékʃ(ə)n/ 名 ▶定義**1** ⓒ if a man has an erection, his sexual organ (penis) becomes hard and stands up because he is sexually excited 男性が erection の状態になると,性的興奮のために性器(ペニス)が堅くなり立ち上がる→**勃起(ぼっき)** ‖ *to get/have an erection* 勃起する ▶定義**2** ⓤ 正式 the act of building sth or standing sth straight up ～を建てる,またはまっすぐ立てること→**組み立て,建設,直立,起立**

**erode** /ɪróud/ 動他 (通常は受動態で) ▶定義 (used about the sea, the weather, etc) to destroy sth slowly (海,天気などについて)～をゆっくりと壊す→**～を侵食する** ‖ *The cliff has been eroded by the sea.* その絶壁は海に侵食されていた. ― **erosion** /ɪróuʒ(ə)n/ 名 ⓤ →**腐食,侵食,崩壊** ‖ *the erosion of rocks by the sea* 海による岩の侵食

**erotic** /ɪrάtɪk/ 形 ▶定義 causing sexual excitement 性的興奮を引き起こす→**性的刺激の強い,エロチックな,性愛を扱った** ‖ *an erotic film/poem/dream* エロチックな映画・詩・夢

**err** /əːr/ 動 正式 ▶定義 to be or do wrong; to make mistakes 間違う,または間違った事をする;過ちを犯す→**間違いをする,誤る,過ちを犯す**
成句 **err on the side of sth** ▶定義 to do more of sth than is necessary in order to avoid the opposite happening 反対のことが起こるのを避けるために,必要以上に～を行う→**～に失する,～すぎる** ‖ *It is better to err on the side of caution (= it is better to be too careful rather than not careful enough).* 慎重すぎる方が良い(=注意が足りないより,注意しすぎる方が良い).

**errand** /érənd/ 名 ⓒ (古) ▶定義 a short journey to take or get sth for sb, for example to buy sth from a shop 例えば店で～を買うなど,…のために～を手に入れるためのちょっとしたお出掛け→**お使い,使い走り**

**erratic** /ɪrǽtɪk/ 形 ▶定義 (used about a person's behaviour, or about the quality of sth) changing without reason; that you can never be sure of (人の行動や～の質について)理由もなく変わる;全く確かではない→**散漫な,突飛な,むら気な,不安定な** ‖ *Jones is a talented player but he's very erratic (= sometimes he plays well, sometimes badly).* ジョーンズは才能のある演奏家だが,大変むら気だ(=演奏の上手な時もあれば,下手な時もある). ― **erratically** /-k(ə)li/ 副 →**散漫に,突飛に,不規則に**

★**error** /érər/ 名 ▶定義**1** ⓒ 正式 a mistake 間違い→**誤り,間違い,過失,エラー** ‖ *The telephone bill was far too high due to a computer error.* コンピューターのエラーのために電話の請求金額がひどく高かった. *an error of judgement* 判断の誤り *to make an error* 間違いをする,犯す
► error は mistake より正式. error of judgement (判断の誤り), human error (人為的誤り) など error だけが使える表現がいくつかある.
▶定義**2** ⓤ the state of being wrong 間違った状態→**間違い** ‖ *The letter was sent to you in error.* その手紙は誤ってあなたに送られた. *The accident was the result of human error.* その事故は人為的誤りによるものだった.
成句 **trial and error** ⇒ **TRIAL**

**erupt** /ɪrʌ́pt/ 動自 ▶定義**1** (used about a volcano) to explode and throw out fire, rock that has melted (lava), smoke, etc (火山について)爆発して,火,溶けた岩(溶岩),煙などを噴出する→**噴火する,噴出する,爆発する** ▶定義**2** (used about violence, shouting, etc) to start suddenly (暴力,叫びなどについて)突然始まる→**どっと発生する,突発する** ‖ *The demonstration erupted into violence.* デモは突然暴動に変わった. ▶定義**3** (used about a person) to suddenly become very angry (人について)突然猛烈に怒る→**爆発する,激怒する** ‖ *George erupted when he heard the news.* ジョージはその知らせを聞くと激怒した. ― **eruption** 名 ⓒⓤ →**噴火,爆発,噴出** ‖ *a volcanic eruption* 火山の噴火

**escalate** /éskəleɪt/ 動自他 ▶定義**1** escalate

(sth) (into sth) (to cause sth) to become stronger or more serious より強く、または深刻になる・する→どんどん拡大する、激化する、強化する、エスカレートする、〜をエスカレートさせる ‖ *The demonstrations are escalating into violent protest in all the major cities.* デモは、すべての大都市で暴力的抗議にエスカレートしつつある。*The terrorist attacks escalated tension in the capital.* テロリストの攻撃が拡大し、首都では緊張が高まった。 ▶定義2 (to cause sth) to become greater or higher; to increase より大きく、高くなる、(〜を)より大きく、高くする；増える・増やす→拡大する、高騰する ‖ *The cost of housing has escalated in recent years.* 近年、住宅費は高騰した。— escalation /èskəléɪʃ(ə)n/ 图 ⓒⓊ→段階的拡大、強化、増大

**escalator** /éskəleɪtər/ 图 ⓒ ▶定義 a moving staircase in a shop, etc 店などにある動く階段→エスカレーター

**escapade** /éskəpeɪd, ˌ-ˈ-/ 图 ⓒ ▶定義 an exciting adventure that may be dangerous 危険を伴う刺激的な冒険→脱線的な行動、突飛な行為

★**escape**[1] /ɪskéɪp, es-/ 動 ▶定義1 ⓘ escape (from sb/sth) to manage to get away from a place where you do not want to be; to get free いたくない場所からどうにかして逃げる；自由になる→(〜から)逃げる、逃亡する、脱出する ‖ *Two prisoners have escaped.* 2名の囚人が逃亡した。*They managed to escape from the burning building.* 彼らは燃え盛るビルからどうにかして逃げた。 ▶定義2 ⓘⓣ to manage to avoid sth dangerous or unpleasant 危険な、または不快な〜をどうにかして避ける→(〜を)逃れる、免れる ‖ *The two men in the other car escaped unhurt in the accident.* その事故で、別の車に乗っていた2名の男性は無傷で逃れた。*David Smith escaped injury when his car skidded off the road.* 車が横滑りして道路から落ちたが、デーヴィッド スミスは負傷しないで済んだ。*to escape criticism/punishment* 非難・処罰を免れる ▶定義3 ⓣ to be forgotten or not noticed by sb 〜に忘れられる、または気付かれない→〜に忘れられる、〜の注意から外れる、(記憶・注意)から外れる ‖ *His name escapes me.* 彼の名前を思い出せない。*to escape sb's notice* 〜の目に留まらない ▶定義4 ⓘ (used about gases or liquids) to come or get out of a container, etc (気体または液体について)容器などの外に出る→漏れる、出る ‖ *There's gas escaping somewhere.* どこかでガスが漏れている。— escaped 形→逃れた、免れた ‖ *an escaped prisoner* 脱獄囚

★**escape**[2] /ɪskéɪp, es-/ 图 ▶定義1 ⓒⓊ escape (from sth) the act of escaping (1,2) escape (定義1、2)すること→(〜からの)逃亡、逃走、(〜を)免れること ‖ *There have been twelve escapes from the prison this year.* 今年は12名の脱獄囚がいた。*She had a narrow/lucky escape when a lorry crashed into her car.* トラックが彼女の車に追突した時、彼女は辛うじて・幸運にも脱出した。*When the guard fell asleep they were able to make their escape.* 看守が居眠りした時、彼らは逃亡することができた。 ☛参 fire escape ▶定義2 [Ⓤ、単数扱い]something that helps you forget your normal life 日常の生活を忘れさせるようなもの→現実逃避(の手段) ‖ *For him, listening to music is a means of escape.* 彼にとって、音楽鑑賞は現実逃避の手段だ。*an escape from reality* 現実からの逃避

**escort**[1] /ésko:rt/ 图 ⓒ ▶定義1 [単数または複数形の動詞と共に]one or more people or vehicles that go with and protect sb/sth, or that go with sb/sth as an honour 〜と一緒に行って守る、または栄誉として〜と共に行く、1人・1つまたは複数の人または乗り物→護衛者、付き添いの人物、護衛艦・機・車 ‖ *an armed escort* 武装した護衛 *He arrived under police escort.* 彼は警察の護衛の下で到着した。 ▶定義2 正式 a person who takes sb to a social event 〜を社交的行事に連れていく人→付き添い ▶定義3 a person, especially a woman, who is paid to go out socially with sb 〜と社交場に出掛けて報酬を得る人、特に女性→社交媛 ‖ *an escort agency* 社交場へ同伴する人を紹介する会社

**escort**[2] /eskó:rt/ 動 ⓣ ▶定義1 to go with sb as an escort(1) escort(1) として〜と共に出掛ける→〜を護衛する、警護する、護送する ‖ *The President's car was escorted by several police cars.* 大統領の車は数台のパトカーに護衛されていた。 ▶定義2 to take sb somewhere 〜をある場所に連れていく→〜に付き添う、〜を送り届ける ‖ *Philip escorted her to the door.* フィリップ

は彼女をドアまで送った.

**Eskimo** /éskəmòu/ (古) = **INUIT** ☞ イヌイットは, エスキモーと呼ばれるのを好まない.

**ESL** /éS エs eL/ 略 English as a Second Language→第2言語としての英語

**esp** 略 ▶定義1 especially→特に, 特別に ▶定義2 **ESP** /I: es pí:/ English for Specific/Special Purposes; the teaching of English to people who need it for a special reason, such as scientific study, engineering, etc 科学, 工学など特別の目的のために英語を必要とする人々に英語を教えること→特定・特殊目的の英語(教育)

**especial** /ɪspéʃ(ə)l, es-/ 形 (名詞の前だけ) 正式 ▶定義 not usual; special 普通でない; 特別な→特別な, 格別の ‖ *This will be of especial interest to you.* これにはあなたも特別な興味を持たれるでしょう.

★**especially** /ɪspéʃ(ə)li, es-/ 副 ▶定義1 more than other things, people, situations, etc; particularly ほかの物, 人々, 状況などよりも上で; 特に→特に, 特別に, とりわけ ‖ *She loves animals, especially dogs.* 彼女は動物, とりわけ犬が好きだ. *Teenage boys especially can be very competitive.* 10代の少年はとりわけ競争心旺盛(おうせい)だ. *He was very disappointed with his mark in the exam, especially as he had worked so hard for it.* 彼はとてもよく勉強したのでなおさら試験の点数にひどくがっかりした.
▶定義2 for a particular purpose or person 特別な目的や人のために→特別に, 特に ‖ *I made this especially for you.* 特にあなたのために, 私はこれを作りました. ☞ より略式の語に specially がある. ▶定義3 very (much) 非常に→とりわけ, 特に ‖ *It's not an especially difficult exam.* それは特別難しい試験ではない. *'Do you like jazz?' 'Not especially.'* 「ジャズは好きですか」「いや別に」

**espionage** /éspiənà:ʒ/ 名 U ▶定義 the act of finding out secret information about another country or organization ほかの国や組織についての秘密の情報を見つけ出す行為→スパイ行為, スパイ活動 ☞ 動 spy

**Esq** 略 特に 英 正式 ▶定義 Esquire; used when you are writing a man's name on an envelope 封筒に男性の名前を書くときに用いて→～殿, 様 ‖ *Edward Hales, Esq* エドワード ヘイルズ殿

▶古典的な言い回しで, 現在では Mr Edward Hales とする方が好まれている.

★**essay** /ései/ 名 C ▶定義 an essay (on/about sth) a short piece of writing on one subject 1つの主題について書かれた短い一編→(～についての)随筆, 評論, 作文, 小論, レポート ‖ *We have to write a 1000-word essay on tourism for homework.* 宿題で, 私たちは観光についての1000語の作文を書かねばならない.

**essence** /ésns/ 名 ▶定義1 ❶ the basic or most important quality of sth ～の基本的または最も重要な特質→本質, 神髄 ‖ *The essence of the problem is that there is not enough money available.* 問題の本質は十分な金がないことだ. *Although both parties agree in essence, some minor differences remain.* 双方の党派は本質的には合意しているが, いくつかの小さな相違点が残っている. ▶定義2 ❷ Ⓤ a substance (usually a liquid) that is taken from a plant or food and that has a strong smell or taste of that plant or food 植物や食物から取れる物質(通常は液体)で, その植物や食物の強いにおいや味を持つもの→エキス, 精, エッセンス ‖ *coffee/vanilla essence* コーヒー・バニラエッセンス

★**essential** /ɪsénʃ(ə)l/ 形 ▶定義 completely necessary; that you must have or do 完全に必要な; 持たなければ, またはしなければならない→欠くことのできない, (絶対に)必要な, 肝心な; 本質的な ‖ *essential medical supplies* 欠くことのできない医療品 *Maths is essential for a career in computers.* コンピューターの仕事に数学は欠かせない. *It is essential that all school-leavers should have a qualification.* 学業を離れた者は全員, 資格を持っている必要がある. — **essential** 名 [C, 通常は複数]→本質的要素, 不可欠なもの, 必需品, 要点 ‖ *food, and other essentials such as clothing and heating* 食べ物, および衣類や暖房などのそのほかの不可欠なもの

★**essentially** /ɪsénʃ(ə)li/ 副 ▶定義 when you consider the basic or most important part of sth; basically ～の基本的な, または最も重要な部分を考えると; 基本的に→本質的に, 本質的には, 本来は ‖ *The problem is essentially one of money.* その問題は本質的には金の問題だ.

★**establish** /ɪstǽblɪʃ, es-/ 動 ▶定義1 to start or create an organization, a system, etc 組織, 制度などを始める, または創造する→～を設立する,

創立する, 設置する, 制定する ‖ *The school was established in 1875.* その学校は1875年に創立された. *Before we start on the project we should establish some rules.* その事業を始める前に, いくつかの規則を制定しなければならない. ▶定義2 to start a formal relationship with sb/sth ~と公式な関係を始める→(関係・習慣など)を確立する, 樹立する ‖ *The government is trying to establish closer links between the two countries.* 政府はこの2国間により緊密な関係を確立しようとしている. ▶定義3 establish sb/sth (as sth) to become accepted and recognized as sth ~として受け入れられる, または認められるようになる→~を(…として)確立する, ~を(…の地位などに)就かせる, 認めさせる ‖ *She has been trying to establish herself as a novelist for years.* 彼女は数年間小説家としての地位を確立しようとしてきた. ▶定義4 to discover or find proof of the facts of a situation ある状況の事実を証明するものを発見する, または見つける→~を確証する, 立証する ‖ *The police have not been able to establish the cause of the crash.* 警察はその衝突の原因を立証することができていない.

\*__establishment__ /ɪstǽblɪʃmənt, es-/ 名 ▶定義1 **C 正式** an organization, a large institution or a hotel 組織, 大きな機関, またはホテル→機構, 社会的機関, 施設・会社・学校・病院・ホテルなど, 事務所 ‖ *an educational establishment* 教育機関, 学校 ▶定義2 **the Establishment**[単数扱い] the people in positions of power in a country, who usually do not support change ある国の権力の座にあり通常変化を歓迎しない人々→支配階級, 体制, 権力 ▶定義3 **U** the act of creating or starting a new organization, system, etc 新しい組織, 制度などを創造する, または始めること→設立, 創立, 設置, 制定 ‖ *the establishment of new laws on taxes* 新しい税法の制定

\*__estate__ /ɪstéɪt, es-/ 名 **C** ▶定義1 a large area of land in the countryside that is owned by one person or family ある個人または1家族が所有する地方の広い土地→地所, 私有地, 屋敷 ‖ *He owns a large estate in Scotland.* 彼はスコットランドに広い地所を持っている. ▶定義2 英 an area of land that has a lot of houses or factories of the same type on it 同じ型の家や工場がたくさん並んでいる土地→団地 ‖ *an industrial estate* (= where there are a lot of factories) 工業団地 (= たくさんの工場がある場所) *a housing estate* 住宅団地 ▶定義3 all the money and property that sb leaves when he/she dies 人が死んだときに残すすべての金や財産→遺産, 資産

__estate agent__(米 __realtor__; __real estate agent__) 名 **C** ▶定義 a person whose job is to buy and sell houses and land for other people 他人のために家や土地を売買することを仕事にする人→不動産業者, 不動産屋

__estate car__ (米 __station wagon__) 名 **C** ▶定義 a car with a door at the back and a long area for luggage behind the back seat 後部にドアがあり, 荷物を入れる広い場所が後部座席の後ろに付いた車→ステーションワゴン ☞ **car** のさし絵

__esteem__ /ɪstíːm, es-/ 名 **U 正式** ▶定義 great respect; a good opinion of sb 大変な尊敬; ~を良く思うこと→尊敬, 尊重

__esthetic__ 米 = AESTHETIC

\*__estimate__¹ /éstəmət/ 名 **C** ▶定義1 an estimate (of sth) a guess or judgement about the size, cost, etc of sth, before you have all the facts and figures すべての詳細が分かる前に出した, ~の大きさ, 費用などについての推測, または判断→見積もり, 見込み, 評価 ‖ *Can you give me a rough estimate of how many people will be at the meeting?* その打ち合わせに何人来るかおおよその見込みを教えてくれますか. *At a conservative estimate* (= the real figure will probably be higher), *the job will take six months to complete.* 控えめに見積もって(= 実際の数はおそらくもっと大きい), その仕事を完成するのに6か月かかるだろう. ▶定義2 an estimate (for sth/doing sth) a written statement from a person who is going to do a job for you, for example a builder or a painter, telling you how much it will cost あなたのためにある仕事をしてくれる人, 例えば建設業者や塗装業者などが渡す, 費用がいくらかかるかを知らせる書類→見積書 ‖ *They gave me an estimate for repairing the roof.* 彼らは屋根の修理の見積書をくれた. ☞参 **quotation**

成句 a ballpark figure/estimate ⇒ **BALLPARK**

\*__estimate__² /éstəmèɪt/ 動 他 ▶定義 estimate sth

(at sth); estimate that... to calculate the size, cost, etc of sth approximately, before you have all the facts and figures すべての詳細が分かる前に, ～の大きさ, 費用などを大まかに計算する ➡～を(…だと)～と見積もる, (大まかに)判断する ‖ *The police estimated the crowd at 10000.* 警察は群衆を1万人と見積もった. *She estimated that the work would take three months.* 彼女はその仕事には3か月かかるだろうと見積もった.

**estimation** /èstəméɪʃ(ə)n/ 名 ❶正式 ▶定義 opinion or judgement 意見や判断 ➡判断, 意見, 評価 ‖ *Who is to blame, in your estimation?* あなたの判断では, だれが責められるべきですか.

**estranged** /ɪstréɪndʒd/ 形 ▶定義1 no longer living with your husband/wife もはや夫・妻と一緒に暮らしていない ➡別居中の ‖ *her estranged husband* 彼女の別居中の夫 ▶定義2 estranged (from sb) no longer friendly or in contact with sb who was close to you 仲が良かった人ともう仲良くしたり, 連絡を取ったりしない ➡心が離れた, よそよそしい, 疎遠な ‖ *He became estranged from his family following an argument.* ある口論の後, 彼は家族と疎遠になった.

**estuary** /éstjʊəri/ -tʃuèri/ 名 C (複 **estuaries**) ▶定義 the wide part (mouth) of a river where it joins the sea 川の, 海に合流する広い部分(河口) ➡河口, 河口域

**etc** 略 etcetera ▶定義 and so on, and other things of a similar kind そのほかに同じような種類のものも ➡その他, ～など ‖ *sandwiches, biscuits, cakes, etc* サンドイッチ, ビスケット, ケーキなど

**eternal** /ɪtɜ́ːml/ 形 ▶定義1 without beginning or end; existing or continuing for ever 始まりも終わりもない; 永遠に存在する, または続く ➡永遠の, 永久の, 不朽の ‖ *Some people believe in eternal life (= after death).* 永遠の命(=死後の)を信じる人々もいる. ▶定義2 happening too often; seeming to last for ever あまりにもしばしば起きる; 永遠に続くように思える ➡果てしない, いつまでも続く ‖ *I'm tired of these eternal arguments!* 延々と続く議論にはうんざりだ. — **eternally** /-li/ 副 ➡永遠に, いつまでも, 永久に ‖ *I'll be eternally grateful if you could help me.* もし手伝ってくれたら, 一生恩に着るよ.

**eternity** /ɪtɜ́ːnəti/ 名 ▶定義1 ❶ time that has no end; the state or time after death 終わりのない時間; 死後の状態または時間 ➡永遠, 永久; 死の世界, 来世 ▶定義2 an eternity [単数扱い] a period of time that never seems to end 決して終わることがないように思われる一定の時間 ➡無限, 長い時間 ‖ *It seemed like an eternity before the ambulance arrived.* 救急車が到着するまでの時間が無限に長く思われた.

**ethical** /éθɪk(ə)l/ 形 ▶定義1 connected with beliefs of what is right or wrong 善か悪かの信条に関した ➡道徳上の, 倫理的な ‖ *That is an ethical problem.* それは倫理的な問題だ. ▶定義2 morally correct 道徳的に正しい ➡道徳的な ‖ *Although she didn't break the law, her behaviour was certainly not ethical.* 彼女は法を破ってはいないが, 彼女の行為は確かに道徳的でない.

**ethics** /éθɪks/ 名 ▶定義1 ❶ the study of what is right and wrong in human behaviour 人間の行動の善悪についての研究 ➡倫理学 ▶定義2 [複数扱い] beliefs about what is morally correct or acceptable 道徳的に何が正しく, 受け入れられるかについての信条 ➡道徳原理, 道義, 倫理, モラル ‖ *The medical profession has its own code of ethics.* 医者には独自の倫理規程がある.

**ethnic** /éθnɪk/ 形 ▶定義 connected with or typical of a particular race or religion ある特定の人種や宗教に関した, またはそれらに典型的な ➡人種的な, 民族的な, 人種・民族特有の ‖ *ethnic minorities* 少数民族(集団) *ethnic food/music/clothes* 民族料理・音楽・衣装

**ethnic cleansing** 名 ❶ ▶定義 the policy of forcing people of a certain race or religion to leave an area or country ある地域や国から, 特定の民族や宗教を持つ人々を追い出す政策 ➡民族浄化

**etiquette** /étɪkɛt/ 名 ❶ ▶定義 the rules of polite and correct behaviour 丁寧で正しい行いの規則 ➡エチケット, 礼儀作法 ‖ *social/professional etiquette* 社会的・職業的礼儀

**etymology** /ètəmɑ́lədʒi/ 名 ( 複 **etymologies**) ▶定義1 ❶ the study of the origins and history of words and their meanings 言葉とその意味の起源や歴史についての学問 ➡語源学 ▶定義2 C an explanation of the origin and history of a particular word 特定の言葉の起源や歴史の説

明→語源, 語源の説明

**euphemism** /júːfəmìz(ə)m/ 名 ❻ ❶ ▶定義 (using) a polite word or expression instead of a more direct one when you are talking about sth that is unpleasant or embarrassing 不快さやはきまりの悪い物事を話すときに, より直接的な表現を避けて使う丁寧な言葉や表現, またその表現を使うこと→えん曲語法, えん曲語句 ‖ *'Pass away' is a euphemism for 'die'.*「他界する」は「死ぬ」のえん曲語法だ.

**euphoria** /juːfɔ́ːriə/ 名 ❶ 正式 ▶定義 an extremely strong feeling of happiness 非常に強い幸福感→幸福感

**euro** /jóərou/ 名 ❻ ▶定義 (since 1999) a unit of money used in several countries of the European Union (1999年から)欧州連合に加盟する数か国で使われている通貨の単位→ユーロ ‖ *The price is given in dollars or euros.* 価格はドルとユーロで表示されています. ☛参 EMU

**Eurocheque** /jóəroutʃèk, -rə-/ 名 ❻ ▶定義 a cheque that can be used in many European countries 多くのヨーロッパ諸国で使える小切手→ユーロチェック

***European**[1] /jùərəpíːən/ 形 ▶定義 of or from Europe ヨーロッパの, またはヨーロッパからの→ヨーロッパの, 欧州の ‖ *European languages* ヨーロッパの言語

***European**[2] /jùərəpíːən/ 名 ❻ ▶定義 a person from a European country ヨーロッパの国から来た人→ヨーロッパ人, 欧州人

**the European Union** 名 [単数扱い] (略 **EU**) ▶定義 an economic and political association of certain European countries 特定のヨーロッパの国々が作る経済的・政治的な共同体→欧州[ヨーロッパ]連合

**euthanasia** /jùːθənéɪʒ(i)ə, -ziə/ 名 ❶ ▶定義 the practice (illegal in most countries) of killing without pain sb who wants to die because he/she is suffering from a disease that cannot be cured 不治の病に苦しみ死を望む人を, 痛みを伴わずに殺す行為(多くの国で不法)→安楽死

**evacuate** /ɪvǽkjuèɪt/ 動⓭ ▶定義 to move people from a dangerous place to somewhere safer; to leave a place because it is dangerous 危険な場所からより安全な場所へ人々を移動させる; 危険なためにある場所を去る→~を避難させる, 立ち退かせる, ~から避難する, ~を立ち退く ‖ *Thousands of people were evacuated from the war zone.* 交戦地帯から何千人もの人々が避難させられた. *The village had to be evacuated when the river burst its banks.* 川が堤防を決壊させた時, 村の人々は避難させられねばならなかった. — evacuation /ɪvǽkjuéɪʃ(ə)n/ 名 ❻ ❶ →避難, 撤退, 立ち退き

**evade** /ɪvéɪd/ 動⓭ ▶定義1 to manage to escape from or to avoid meeting sb/sth ~からどうにかして逃げる, または会うのを避ける→~を回避する, 免れる ‖ *They managed to evade capture and escaped to France.* 彼らはどうにかして追っ手を逃れて, フランスへ逃げた. ▶定義2 to avoid dealing with or doing sth ~を扱うこと, またはすることを避ける→~を回避する, はぐらかす, うまくかわす ‖ *to evade responsibility* 責任を回避する *I asked her directly, but she evaded the question.* 私は彼女に直接尋ねたが, 彼女は質問をはぐらかした. ☛ 名 evasion

**evaluate** /ɪvǽljuèɪt/ 動⓭ 正式 ▶定義 to study the facts and then form an opinion about sth 事実を学んだ上で~についての意見を組み立てる→~を評価する ‖ *We evaluated the situation very carefully before we made our decision.* 私たちは決定を下す前に, 注意深く状況を評価した. — evaluation /ɪvǽljuéɪʃ(ə)n/ 名 ❻ ❶ →評価, 値踏み

**evaporate** /ɪvǽp(ə)rèɪt/ 動⓮ ▶定義1 (used about a liquid) to change into steam or gas and disappear (液体について)蒸気や気体に変わり, 消える→蒸発する ‖ *The water evaporated in the sunshine.* 日に照らされて水は蒸発した. ☛参 **condense** ▶定義2 to disappear completely 完全に消える→消えてなくなる, 霧消する ‖ *All her confidence evaporated when she saw the exam paper.* 試験用紙を見た時, 彼女の自信はすべて消えてなくなった. — evaporation /ɪvǽp(ə)réɪʃ(ə)n/ 名 ❶ →蒸発, (希望などが)消えてなくなること

**evasion** /ɪvéɪʒ(ə)n/ 名 ❻ ❶ ▶定義1 the act of avoiding sth that you should do すべき~を避ける行為→逃れること, 回避, 忌避 ‖ *He has been sentenced to two years' imprisonment for **tax evasion**.* 彼は脱税で禁固2年の判決を受けた. *an evasion of responsibility* 責任の回避

## 562 evasive

▶定義2 a statement that avoids dealing with a question or subject in a direct way 質問や話題を直接扱うことを避ける申し立て→**言い逃れ,逃げ口上** ‖ *The President's reply was full of evasions.* 大統領の返答は言い抜けばかりだった. ☞⃞動 **evade**

**evasive** /ɪvéɪsɪv/ 形 ▶定義 trying to avoid sth; not direct 〜を避けようとする; 直接的でない→**回避する,言い逃れの** ‖ *Ann gave an evasive answer.* アンは言い逃れをした.

**eve** /iːv/ 名 C ▶定義 the day or evening before a religious festival, important event, etc 宗教的な祭り, 重要な行事などの前日, または前夜→**イブ, 前夜, 前日, 前夜祭** ‖ *Christmas Eve* クリスマスイブ *He injured himself on the eve of the final.* 彼は決勝戦の前日にけがをした.

★**even**¹ /íːv(ə)n/ 形 ▶定義1 flat, level or smooth 平らな, 凹凸のない, 滑らかな→**(表面が)平らな, 水平の, 滑らかな** ‖ *The game must be played on an even surface.* そのゲームは平らな面で行わねばならない. ▶定義2 not changing; regular 変わらない; 規則的な→**一様な, むらのない, 均一な, 落ち着いた** ‖ *He's very even-tempered - in fact I've never seen him angry.* 彼は非常に落ち着いている − 実際, 彼が怒っているのを見たことがない. ▶定義3 (used about a competition, etc) equal, with one side being as good as the other (競争などについて)同等の, 一方が他方と同じくらい良い→**同等な, 互角の** ‖ *The contest was very even until the last few minutes of the game.* 試合は最後の数分まで全く互角だった. ⇔定義1, 2, 3 **uneven** ▶定義4 (used about numbers) that can be divided by two (数字について) 2で割り切れる→**偶数の** ‖ *2, 4, 6, 8, 10, etc are even numbers.* 2, 4, 6, 8, 10などは偶数だ. ⇔ **odd**

成句 **be/get even (with sb)** 略式 ▶定義 to hurt or harm sb who has hurt or harmed you 自分を傷付けた, または害を及ぼした〜を傷付ける, または害を及ぼす→**〜に仕返しをする**

**break even** ▶定義 to make neither a loss nor a profit 損失も利益も生み出さない→**(商売・かけ事などで)損得なしに終わる**

★**even**² /íːv(ə)n/ 副 ▶定義1 used for emphasizing sth that is surprising 驚くような〜を強調するのに用いられて→**〜でさえ, すら** ‖ *It isn't very warm here even in summer.* ここは夏でさえあまり暑くない. *He didn't even open the letter.* 彼はその手紙を開けさえしなかった. ▶定義2 **even more, less, bigger, nicer, etc** used when you are comparing things, to make the comparison stronger 物事を比較するときに, 比較をより強調するのに用いて→**さらに〜, なお〜, 一層〜** ‖ *You know even less about it than I do.* それについてあなたは私よりもなお知らない. *It is even more difficult than I expected.* それは私が予測していたよりさらに難しい. *We are even busier than yesterday.* 昨日よりもさらに忙しい.

成句 **even if** ▶定義 used for saying that what follows 'if' makes no difference if の次に来る内容によって何の違いも起きないことを言うのに用いられて→**たとえ〜しても** ‖ *I wouldn't ride a horse, even if you paid me.* たとえ君がお金をくれても, 僕は馬に乗らないよ.

**even so** ▶定義 (used for introducing a new idea, fact, etc that is surprising) in spite of that; nevertheless (驚くような新しい考え, 事実などを紹介するために用いて) それにもかかわらず; しかしながら→**たとえそうでも** ‖ *There are a lot of spelling mistakes; even so it's quite a good essay.* つづりの間違いがたくさんあるが, それでも, なかなか良い作文だ.

**even though** ▶定義 although 〜だが, だけれども→**〜だがそれでも** ‖ *I like her very much even though she can be very annoying.* 彼女はとてもうるさいこともあるが, それでも私は彼女がとても好きだ. ☞⃞参 **although**の注

★**evening** /íːvnɪŋ/ 名 C U ▶定義 the part of the day between the afternoon and the time that you go to bed 1日のうちで, 日没と就寝時との間の時間帯→**夕方, 晩** ‖ *What are you doing this evening?* 今晩何をしますか. *We were out yesterday evening.* 昨日の晩, 私たちは出掛けていた. *I went to the cinema on Saturday evening.* 私は土曜日の夕方に映画を見に行った. *Tom usually goes swimming on Wednesday evenings.* トムは水曜日の夕方には大抵泳ぎに行く. *Most people watch television **in the evening**.* ほとんどの人は夕方テレビを見る. *an evening class (= a course of lessons for adults that takes place in the evening)* 夜間授業(= 夕

方に行われる成人のための連続講座)

**成句 good evening** ▶定義 used when you see sb for the first time in the evening 夕方に初めて~に会ったときに用いられて➡**今晩は** ☛ しばしば Evening とだけ言う．'Good evening, Mrs Wilson.' 'Evening, Mr Mills.'「今晩は，ウィルソンさん」「今晩は，ミルズさん」

\***evenly** /íːv(ə)nli/ 副 ▶定義 in a smooth, regular or equal way 滑らかな，規則的な，等しい方法で➡**平らに，一様に，むらなく，公平に，互角に** ‖ *The match was very evenly balanced.* その試合は非常に拮抗(きっこう)していた．*Spread the cake mixture evenly in the tin.* ブリキ製の容器にケーキミックスを平らに広げる．

\***event** /ɪvént/ 名 ❸ ▶定義 1 something that happens, especially sth important or unusual 起きる事柄，特に重要なまたは珍しい事➡**出来事，事件，行事** ‖ *a historic event* 歴史的出来事 *The events of the past few days have made things very difficult for the Government.* この数日間の出来事は，政府にとって事を非常に難しくした．
▶定義 2 a planned public or social occasion 計画された公のまたは社会的な催し➡**催し物，イベント** ‖ *a fund-raising event* 資金集めのイベント
▶定義 3 one of the races, competitions, etc in a sports programme スポーツの催し物で，その中の1つの競争，競技など➡**種目，1 試合** ‖ *The next event is the 800 metres.* 次の種目は800メートル走です．

**成句 at all events/in any event** ▶定義 whatever happens 何が起ころうも➡**とにかく，いずれにしても** ‖ *I hope to see you soon, but in any event I'll phone you on Sunday.* すぐに会えるといいな．いずれにしても日曜日に電話するよ．

**in the event of sth** 正式 ▶定義 if sth happens もし~が起きたら➡**~の場合には，際には** ‖ *In the event of fire, leave the building as quickly as possible.* 火事の際には，できるだけ素早くビルを離れなさい．

\***eventful** /ɪvéntfʊl, -f(ə)l/ 形 ▶定義 full of important, dangerous, or exciting things happening たくさんの重要な，危険な，または刺激的な事が起きた➡**出来事の多い，波乱に富んだ**

**eventual** /ɪvéntʃuəl/ 形 (名詞の前だけ) ▶定義 happening as a result at the end of a period of time or of a process 一定の期間や過程の最後に結果として起きる➡**いつかは起こり**得る，最終的な，結局の ‖ *It is impossible to say what the eventual cost will be.* 最終的な費用がいくらになるかを言うのは不可能だ．

\***eventually** /ɪvéntʃuəli/ 副 ▶定義 in the end; finally 最後に；最終的に➡**最後には，結局は** ‖ *He eventually managed to persuade his parents to let him buy a motor bike.* 彼は最後にはオートバイを買わせてくれるよう両親を説得した．
☛類 **finally**

\***ever**¹ /évər/ 副 ▶定義 1 (疑問文や否定文の中で，物事を比較するときに，また if の文中で用いて) at any time いつでも➡**いつか，今までに，今でも，どんな時でも，今までよりも** ‖ *Do you ever wish you were famous?* ああ有名人だったらと思うことはありますか．*Nobody ever comes to see me.* だれも決して私に会いに来ない．*She **hardly ever** (= almost never) goes out.* 彼女はめったに外出しない(= ほとんど~しない)．*Today is hotter **than ever**.* 今日は今までよりも暑い．*This is the best meal I have ever had.* これは今までのどの食事よりもおいしい．*If you ever visit England, you must come and stay with us.* いつかイングランドを訪ねる機会があったら，私たちの家に来て泊まりなさい．▶定義 2 (完了形の動詞を伴う疑問文に用いて) at any time up to now 今までのどんな時にも➡**今まで，かつて** ‖ *Have you ever been to Spain?* あなたは今までにスペインに行ったことがありますか．▶定義 3 used with a question that begins with 'when', 'where', 'who', 'how', etc, to show that you are surprised or shocked when, where, who, how などで始まる疑問文に用いて，驚いたまたはショックを受けたことを示す➡**一体** ‖ *How ever did he get back so quickly?* 一体どうやって彼はそんなに速く帰ってきたの．*What ever were you thinking about when you wrote this?* 一体何を考えてこれを書いたの．☛参 **whatever, whenever, however** など

**成句 (as) bad, good, etc as ever** ▶定義 (as) bad, good, etc as usual or as always 通常またはいつもと同じくらい悪い・良いなど➡**相変わらず，いつまでも，いつものように** ‖ *In spite of his problems, Andrew is as cheerful as ever.* 問題を抱えているにもかかわらず，アンドリューは相変わらず陽気だ．

ever after ▶定義 (used especially after at the end of stories) from that moment on for always (特に物語の最後に用いて)その瞬間からいつもずっと→**その後ずっと,その後ずっと** ‖ *The prince married the princess and they lived happily ever after.* 王子は王女と結婚して,その後ずっと幸せに暮らしました.

ever since... ▶定義 all the time from...until now ~から今までずっと→**~からずっと,~以来ずっと** ‖ *She has had a car ever since she was at university.* 彼女は大学生のころからずっと車を持っている.

ever so/ever such (a) 英略式 ▶定義 very 非常に→**非常に,とても** ‖ *He's ever so kind.* 彼はとっても親切だ. *He's ever such a kind man.* 彼はとっても親切な男だ.

for ever ⇒ **FOREVER(1)**

**ever-**² /évər/ (複合語で) ▶定義 always; continuously いつも;続けて→**常に~の,絶えず~の** ‖ *the ever-growing problem of pollution* 常に広がる汚染の問題

**evergreen** /évərgrìːn/ 名 C形 ▶定義 (a tree or bush) with green leaves all through the year 一年中緑の葉のついた(木や茂み)→**常緑の,常緑樹**
☞参 **deciduous**

**everlasting** /èvərlǽstɪŋ, -láːst-/ 形 正式 ▶定義 continuing for ever; never changing 永遠に続く;決して変わらない→**永遠の,不朽の** ‖ *everlasting life/love* 永遠の命・愛

*****every** /évri/ 形 ▶定義 **1** (単数名詞と共に用いて) all of the people or things in a group of three or more 3人・3つ以上から成るグループのすべての人々または物→**すべての,どの~も** ‖ *She knows every student in the school.* 彼女は学校のすべての生徒を知っている. *There are 200 students in the school, and she knows every one of them.* 学校には200名の生徒がいて,彼女はどの生徒も知っている. *I've read every book in this house.* 私はこの家のすべての本を読んだ. *You were out every time I phoned.* 私が電話をした時,あなたはいつも出掛けていた.
☞参 **everybody**の注 ▶定義 **2** all that is possible 可能な事すべて→**ありとあらゆる** ‖ *You have every chance of success.* あなたはありとあらゆる成功の機会を持っている. *She had every reason to be angry.* 彼女が怒るのも無理はなかった. ▶定義 **3** used for saying how often sth happens ~がどれだけしばしば起きるかを言うのに用いられて→**~ごとに,毎~** ‖ *We see each other every day.* 私たちは毎日会う. *Take the medicine every four hours (= at 8, 12, 4 o'clock, etc).* その薬を4時間ごとに飲みなさい(= 8時,12時,4時など). *I work every other day (= on Monday, Wednesday, Friday, etc).* 私は1日おきに働く(= 月曜,水曜,金曜など). *One in every three marriages ends in divorce.* 3組中1組の夫婦が離婚する.

*****everybody** /évribɑ̀di/ (または **everyone** /évriwʌ̀n/) 代 ▶定義 [単数形の動詞と共に]every person; all people どの人も;すべての人々→**だれでも皆,すべての人** ‖ *Is everybody here?* 皆さんここにいますか. *The police questioned everyone who was at the party.* 警察はパーティーにいた人すべてに質問した. *I'm sure everybody else (= all the other people) will agree with me.* ほかの人は皆(= ほかの人々すべて)私に同意すると確信している.
▶everyone は人々についてのみ用いられて,後に of が続くことはない. every one は「それぞれの人または物事」を意味し,しばしば of が続く: *Every one of his records has been successful.* (彼の記録はどれもすばらしかった.) **somebody** の注も参照.

**everyday** /évridèɪ/ 形 (名詞の前だけ) ▶定義 normal or usual 普通の,または通常の→**日常の,普段の,平凡な** ‖ *The computer is now part of everyday life.* コンピューターは今や日常生活の一部だ.

**everyplace** /évriplèɪs/ 米 = **EVERYWHERE**

*****everything** /évriθɪŋ/ 代 [単数形の動詞と共に] ▶定義 **1** each thing; all things それぞれの物;すべての物→**すべての物・事,何もかも** ‖ *Sam lost everything in the fire.* サムはその火事ですべてを失った. *Everything is very expensive in this shop.* この店は何もかも高い. *We can leave everything else (= all the other things) until tomorrow.* ほかのものは何もかも(= ほかのものすべて)明日まで残しておける. ▶定義 **2** the most important thing 最も重要な物・事→**最も大切な事・物・人** ‖ *Money isn't everything.* 金がすべてではない.

**everywhere** /évri(h)wèər/ 副 ▶定義 in or to

every place あらゆる場所で[へ] ➡どこでも, どこにも ‖ *I've looked everywhere, but I still can't find it.* 私は至る所を捜したが, まだそれは見つからない.

**evict** /ɪvíkt/ 動他 ▶定義 to force sb (officially) to leave the house or land which he/she is renting ～を(公式に)借りている家や土地から去らせる ➡～を立ち退かせる ‖ *They were evicted for not paying the rent.* 彼らは家賃を払わないので立ち退かされた. — **eviction** 名 C U ➡立ち退かせること, 立ち退き

★**evidence** /évəd(ə)ns/ 名 U ▶定義 **evidence (of/for sth); evidence that...** the facts, signs, etc that make you believe that sth is true ～が真実だと信じさせるような事実, 兆候など ➡(～の)証拠, 証言, 形跡 ‖ *There was no evidence of a struggle in the room.* 部屋には争った跡はなかった. *There was not enough evidence to prove him guilty.* 彼の有罪を証明する十分な証拠はなかった. *Her statement to the police was used in evidence against him.* 警察への彼女の証言は, 彼に不利な証拠として使われた. *The witnesses to the accident will be asked to give evidence in court.* 事故の目撃者は法廷で証言することを求められるだろう. *You have absolutely no evidence for what you're saying!* 君が言っている事は, 全く証拠がない.

▶ evidence は不可算であることに注意. 証拠の1つについて言う場合には, piece を使う: *One piece of evidence is not enough to prove somebody guilty.* (1つの証拠では人の有罪を証明するには十分でない.)

成句 **(to be) in evidence** ▶定義 that you can see; present in a place 見ることのできる; ある場所に存在する ➡はっきり見えて ‖ *When we arrived there was no ambulance in evidence.* 我々が着いた時には, 救急車は見当たらなかった.

**evident** /évəd(ə)nt/ 形 ▶定義 clear (to the eye or mind); obvious ➡(目または心に)明らかな; 明白な ‖ *It was evident that the damage was very serious.* 損害が非常に深刻なことは明らかだった.

**evidently** /évəd(ə)ntli/ 副 ▶定義 1 clearly; that can be easily seen or understood 明らかに; 簡単に見える, または理解できるような ➡明らかに, 明白に ‖ *She was evidently extremely shocked at the news.* 彼女はそのニュースを聞いて, 明らかに極度にショックを受けていた. ▶定義 2 according to what people say 人々のうわさによれば ➡どうやら(～らしい) ‖ *Evidently he has decided to leave.* どうやら彼は去ることに決めたらしい.

**evil**¹ /íːv(ə)l/ 形 ▶定義 morally bad; causing trouble or harming people 道徳的に悪い; 問題を起こす, または人々に害を及ぼす ➡邪悪な, 悪い, 有害な ‖ *In the play Richard is portrayed as an evil king.* 劇中では, リチャードは邪悪な王として描かれている.

**evil**² /íːv(ə)l/ 名 C U ▶定義 a force that causes bad or harmful things to happen 悪いまたは害のある事を引き起こす力 ➡悪, 邪悪 ‖ *The play is about the good and evil in all of us.* その劇は私たちすべての中にある善と悪についてである. *Drugs and alcohol are two of the evils of modern society.* 麻薬とアルコールは現代社会の2つの悪だ.

成句 **the lesser of two evils** ⇒ **LESSER**

**evoke** /ɪvóʊk/ 動他 正式 ▶定義 to produce a memory, feeling, etc in sb ～に記憶, 感情などを生み出す ➡～を呼び起こす, 引き起こす, 喚起する ‖ *For me, that music always evokes hot summer evenings.* 私には, その音楽はいつも暑い夏の夕方を喚起する. *Her novel evoked a lot of interest.* 彼女の小説は多大な興味を引き起こした.

**evolution** /èvəlúːʃ(ə)n, ìːv-/ 名 U ▶定義 1 the development of plants, animals, etc over many thousands of years from simple early forms to more advanced ones 数千年もかけて, 植物, 動物などが初期の単純な形からより進んだ形に発達すること ➡進化 ‖ *Darwin's theory of evolution* ダーウィンの進化論 ▶定義 2 the gradual process of change and development of sth ～の変化や発達の漸進的な過程 ➡発展, 進展 ‖ *Political evolution is a slow process.* 政治的進展はゆっくりした過程だ.

**evolve** /ɪválv/ 動 自他 正式 ▶定義 1 to develop or to make sth develop gradually, from a simple to a more advanced form 次第に単純なものからより高度な形に発達する, または発達させる ➡発展・発達・進展する, ～を発展・発達・進展させる ‖ *His style of painting has evolved gradually over* *the past 20 years.* 彼の画法は過去20年の間に次第に発展した. ▶定義2 ●evolve (from sth) (used about plants, animals, etc) to develop over many thousands of years from simple forms to more advanced ones(植物,動物などについて)数千年かけて単純な形からより高度な形へと発達する➔**進化する,発展する**

**ewe** /juː, (米方言) jóu/ 名 © ▶定義 a female sheep➔**雌の羊** ☞参 sheep の注 ☞ goat のさし絵

★**exact**[1] /ɪgzǽkt/ 形 ▶定義1 (completely) correct; accurate(完全に)正しい;正確な➔**正確な,精密な** ‖ *He's in his mid-fifties. Well, 56 to be exact.* 彼は50代半ばだ. ええと, 正確には56歳だ. *I can't tell you the exact number of people who are coming.* 来る人の正確な数は分からない. *She's the exact opposite of her sister.* 彼女は妹とは全く対照的だ. ▶定義2 able to work in a way that is completely accurate 完全に正確な方法で働ける➔**(人が)きちょうめんな** ‖ *You need to be very exact when you calculate the costs.* 費用の計算をするときは, 非常にきちょうめんになる必要がある. — **exactness** 名 ❶➔**正確さ**

**exact**[2] /ɪgzǽkt/ 動 他 正式 ▶定義 exact sth (from sb) to demand and get sth from sb ~を…に要求し, 得る➔**~を(…に)求める,要求する, 厳しく取り立てる**

**exacting** /ɪgzǽktɪŋ/ 形 ▶定義 needing a lot of care and attention; difficult たくさんの手間と注意が必要な;難しい➔**要求の厳しい,厳しい** ‖ *exacting work* 骨の折れる仕事

★**exactly** /ɪgzǽktli/ 副 ▶定義1 (used to emphasize that sth is correct in every way) just(~があらゆる点で正しい事を強調するために用いて)ちょうど➔**まさしく,ちょうど,全く** ‖ *You've arrived at exactly the right moment.* あなたたはちょうど良い時に到着されました. *I found exactly what I wanted.* まさしく私が欲しかったものを見つけた. ▶定義2 used to ask for, or give, completely correct information 完全に正しい情報を求める, または与えるときに用いられて➔**正確に(は)** ‖ *He took exactly one hour to finish.* 彼は1時間きっかりで終えた. ☞類 **precisely** ▶定義3 (口語) (used for agreeing with a statement) yes; you are right(意見に同意するために用いて)はい, そうです; あなたの言う通り➔**(まさに)その通り** ‖ *'I don't think she's old enough to travel on her own.' 'Exactly.'* 「彼女はまだ独りで旅ができる年齢じゃないと思う」「全くその通りだよ」

成句 **not exactly**(口語) ▶定義1 (used when you are saying the opposite of what you really mean) not really; not at all(実際に言いたい事と反対の事を言うときに用いられる)あんまり;決して~ない➔**必ずしも~ではない,少しも~ない** ‖ *He's not exactly the most careful driver I know.* 彼は必ずしも私の知る最も注意深い運転手ではない. ▶定義2 (used as an answer to say that sth is almost true)(~がほとんど真実だと答えるのに用いられる)➔**必ずしもそうではない** ‖ *'So you think I'm wrong?' 'No, not exactly, but…'* 「それでは, あなたは私が間違っていると思うのですか」「いいえ, そういう訳でもないのですが」

★**exaggerate** /ɪgzǽdʒərèɪt/ 動 自 他 ▶定義 to make sth seem larger, better, worse, etc than it really is ~を実際よりも大きく, 良く, 悪くなど見せる➔**(~を)おおげさに言う・見せる, 誇張する** ‖ *Don't exaggerate. I was only two minutes late, not twenty.* おおげさに言うなよ. 2分遅れただけで, 20分じゃないぞ. *The problems have been greatly exaggerated.* その問題は非常に誇張されてきた. — **exaggeration** /ɪgzædʒəréɪʃ(ə)n/ 名 © ❶➔**誇張, おおげさ** ‖ *It's rather an exaggeration to say that all the students are lazy.* すべての学生が怠慢だと言うのはかなり言いすぎだ.

★**exam** /ɪgzǽm/ (または 正式 **examination**) 名 © ▶定義 a written, spoken or practical test of what you know or can do 知っている事やできる事についての, 筆記, 口頭, または実技のテスト➔**試験** ‖ *an English exam* 英語の試験 *the exam results* 試験の結果 *to do/take/sit an exam* 試験を受ける *to pass/fail an exam* 試験に受かる・落ちる

▶ test は, 通常 exam ほど形式的ではなく, 通常 exam より短い.

★**examination** /ɪgzæmənéɪʃ(ə)n/ 名 ▶定義1 © ❶the act of looking at sth carefully, especially to see if there is anything wrong or to find the cause of a problem 特に何か悪いものがないか調べたり, 問題の原因を見つけたりするために, ~を注意深く見る行為➔**調査, 検査** ‖ *On close examination, it was found that the passport was* *false*. よく調べてみると、そのパスポートはにせ物だと分かった. *a medical examination* 健康診断 ▶定義2 ●正式 = EXAM

**＊examine** /ɪɡzǽmən/ 動他 ▶定義1 to consider or study an idea, a subject, etc very carefully 非常に注意深く、考えや主題を検討したり、研究する→〜を調べる、調査する、検討する ‖ *These theories will be examined in more detail later on in the lecture.* これらの理論は後でより詳しく、講義の中で検討します. ▶定義2 examine sb/sth (for sth) to look at sb/sth carefully in order to find out sth 〜を見つけ出すために…を注意深く見る→（〜について・〜を求めて）…を調べる ‖ *The detective examined the room for clues.* 探偵は手掛かりを求めて部屋を調べた. ▶定義3 正式 examine sb (in/on sth) to test what sb knows or can do 〜が知っている、またはできる事を試す→〜に（…の）試験をする ‖ *You will be examined on everything that has been studied in the course.* この講座で学んだすべての事について試験が課されます.

**examiner** /ɪɡzǽmənər/ 名 ● ▶定義 a person who tests sb in an exam 〜を試験で試す人→試験官

**＊example** /ɪɡzǽmp(ə)l; -zǽm-/ 名 ● ▶定義1 an example (of sth) something such as an object, a fact or a situation which shows, explains or supports what you say あなたの言うことを示す、説明する、または裏付ける物、事実、状況など→例、実例 ‖ *I don't quite understand you. Can you give me an example of what you mean?* あなたの言うことがよく分からない. 言いたい事の例を示せますか. *This is a typical example of a Victorian house.* これはビクトリア朝風家屋の典型的な例です. ▶定義2 an example (to sb) a person or thing or a type of behaviour that is good and should be copied 正しいために模倣すべき人、物、または行動→手本、模範、手本となる人・行為 ‖ *Joe's bravery should be an example to us all.* ジョーの勇気を私たち皆の手本にするべきだ.

成句 follow sb's example/lead ⇒ FOLLOW
for example（略 eg）▶定義 used for giving a fact, situation, etc, which explains or supports what you are talking about 言おうとする事を説明する、または裏付けるような事実、状況などを示すのに用いられて→**例えば** ‖ *In many countries, Italy, for example, family life is much more important than here.* 多くの国で、例えばイタリアでは、家族生活はここでよりずっと大切にされている.

set a(n) (good/bad) example (to sb) ▶定義 to behave in a way that should/should not be copied 模倣すべき・すべきでないような振る舞いをする→（〜の）（良い・悪い）手本となる ‖ *Parents should always take care when crossing roads in order to set a good example to their children.* 子供の良い手本となるように、親は道路を渡るときにはいつも気を付けるべきだ.

**exasperate** /ɪɡzǽːsp(ə)rèɪt; -zǽs-/ 動他 ▶定義 to make sb angry; to annoy sb very much 〜を怒らせる; 〜を非常に困らせる→〜を怒らせる、〜の腹を立てさせる ‖ *She was exasperated by the lack of progress.* 彼女は進展がないことに腹を立てた. — exasperating 形→腹立たしい ‖ *an exasperating problem* 腹立たしい問題 — exasperation /ɪɡzǽspərérʃ(ə)n; -zæːs-/ 名 Ｕ→憤激、激怒 ‖ *She finally threw the book across the room in exasperation.* 彼女はとうとう激怒して部屋の中で本を投げた.

**excavate** /ékskəvèɪt/ 動自他 ▶定義 to dig in the ground to look for old objects or buildings that have been buried for a long time; to find sth by digging in this way 長い間埋まった古い物や建物を探して地面を掘る; そのように掘って〜を見つける→（〜を）発掘する ‖ *A Roman villa has been excavated in a valley near the village.* 古代ローマの荘園がその村の近くの谷で発掘された. — excavation /èkskəvéɪʃ(ə)n/ 名 ● Ｕ→発掘、穴掘り ‖ *Excavations on the site have revealed Saxon objects.* その遺跡の発掘でサクソン人のものが出てきた.

**exceed** /ɪksíːd/ 動他 ▶定義1 to be more than a particular number or amount 特定の数字または量よりも多い→〜より大きい、多い、〜を超える ‖ *The weight should not exceed 20 kilos.* 重量は20キロを超えてはいけない. ▶定義2 to do more than the law, a rule, an order, etc allows you to do 法律、規則、命令などで許された以上のことをする→〜を越す、度を越える ‖ *He was stopped by the police for exceeding the speed limit (= driving faster than is allowed).* 彼は制限

速度を超えた(= 許されているよりも速く走ったために警察に止められた. ☞参 **excess**, **excessive**

**exceedingly** /ɪksíːdɪŋli/ 副 正式 ▶定義 very 非常に → **非常に, 極めて** ‖ *an exceedingly difficult problem* 極めて難しい問題

**excel** /ɪksél/ 動 (**excelling**; **excelled**) 正式
▶定義 1 ⓔ **excel (in/at sth/doing sth)** to be very good at doing sth ～をするのが非常に上手 → **(～に)秀でる, (～の点で)優れている, 抜きんでる** ‖ *Anne excels at sports.* アンはスポーツに秀でている. ▶定義 2 ⓔ **excel yourself** 英 to do sth even better than you usually do ～を通常よりもさらにうまくする → **いつもより良い, 勝る** ‖ *Rick's cooking is always good but this time he really excelled himself.* リックの料理はいつもうまいが, 今回のは本当にいつもよりましてうまかった.

**excellence** /éks(ə)ləns/ 图 Ⓤ ▶定義 the quality of being very good 非常に優れているという特質 → **優れていること, すばらしさ** ‖ *The head teacher said that she wanted the school to be a centre of academic excellence.* 校長は, その学校を優れた学問の中心地にしたいと言った.

*★**excellent** /éks(ə)lənt/ 形 ▶定義 very good; of high quality 非常に良い; 質の高い → **優れた, すばらしい** ‖ *He speaks excellent French.* 彼は見事にフランス語を話す. ― excellently 副 → **優れて, すばらしく, 立派に**

*★**except**¹ /ɪksépt/ 前 ▶定義 **except (for) sb/sth; except that...** not including sb/sth; apart from the fact that ～を含まない; ～という事実は別にして → **～を除いて, 以外は** ‖ *The museum is open every day except Mondays.* 博物館は月曜日を除く毎日開いている. *I can answer all of the questions except for the last one.* 最後の1つを除くすべての質問に答えられます. *It was a good hotel except that it was rather noisy.* いくらか騒がしいのを除けば, 良いホテルだった.

**except**² /ɪksépt/ 動 ⓗ 正式 ▶定義 **except sb/sth (from sth)** (しばしば受動態で) to leave sb/sth out; to not include sb/sth ～を取り去る; ～を含まない → **～を(…から)除く, 例外にする** ‖ *Nobody is excepted from helping with the housework.* だれも例外なく家事を手伝う. ― excepting

前 → **～を除いて, 以外は** ‖ *I swim every day excepting Sundays.* 日曜以外は毎日泳ぎます.

*★**exception** /ɪksépʃ(ə)n/ 图 Ⓒ ▶定義 a person or thing that is not included in a general statement 一般的な意味には含まれていない人や物事 → **例外** ‖ *Most of his songs are awful but this one is an exception.* 彼の歌はほとんどがひどいが, この歌は例外だ. *Everybody was poor as a student and I was no exception.* 学生はだれでも貧しく, 私も例外ではなかった.

成句 **make an exception (of sb/sth)** ▶定義 to treat sb/sth differently ～を違って扱う → **(～を)例外にする, 特別扱いする** ‖ *We don't usually allow children under 14 but we'll make an exception in your case.* 私たちは通常14歳未満の子供には許可しませんが, あなたの場合は特別です.

**with the exception of** ▶定義 except for; apart from ～を除いて; ～は別として → **～を除いては, ～のほかは** ‖ *He has won every major tennis championship with the exception of Wimbledon.* 彼はウィンブルドンを除いてすべての大きなテニス選手権で優勝した.

**without exception** ▶定義 in every case; including everyone/everything どのような場合にも; すべての人・すべての物を含んで → **例外なく** ‖ *Everybody without exception must take the test.* 例外なく全員がテストを受けなければならない.

**exceptional** /ɪksépʃ(ə)n(ə)l/ 形 ▶定義 very unusual; unusually good 非常に変わった; 著しく良い → **例外的な, まれな, 特に優れた** ‖ *You will only be allowed to leave early in exceptional circumstances.* 例外的な状況でのみ早く出ることが許されるでしょう. ― exceptionally /-ʃ(ə)n(ə)li/ 副 → **例外的に, 特に優れて** ‖ *The past year has been exceptionally difficult for us.* 昨年は私たちにとって特に大変な年だった.

**excerpt** /éksəːrpt/ 图 Ⓒ ▶定義 a short piece taken from a book, film, piece of music, etc 本, 映画, 曲などから取り出した短い一部分 → **抜粋, 引用**

**excess**¹ /ɪksés, ékses/ 图 [単数扱い] ▶定義 **an excess (of sth)** more of sth than is necessary or usual; too much of sth 必要な, または通常より多い～; 多すぎる～ → **(～の)過剰, 超過, 余分(な～)** ‖ *An excess of fat in your diet can lead to* heart disease. 食物中の余分な脂肪は心臓病の原因になります. **成句 in excess of** ▶定義 more than 〜より以上に→〜より多く，〜を超えて ‖ *Her debts are in excess of £1000.* 彼女の負債は1000ポンドを超えている. ☞ 動 exceed

**excess**² /ɪksés/ **形** (名詞の前だけ) ▶定義 more than is usual or allowed; extra 通常または許されたものより多い; 余分の→**余分の, 制限外の, 超過した** ‖ *Cut any excess fat off the meat.* 肉の余分な脂肪を落としなさい. ☞ 動 exceed

**excessive** /ɪksésɪv/ **形** ▶定義 too much; too great or extreme 多すぎる; 大きすぎるまたは極端すぎる→**過度の, 多すぎる, 法外な** ‖ *He was driving at excessive speed when he crashed.* 彼は衝突したとき途方もないスピードで運転していた. — excessively **副** →過度に, 法外に, 度を越して

*__exchange__*¹ /ɪkstʃéɪndʒ/ **名** ▶定義 1 **C U** giving or receiving sth in return for sth else 〜をほかの…のお返しとして与える，または受け取ること→**交換, やり取り** ‖ *a useful exchange of information* 有用な情報交換 *We can offer free accommodation __in exchange for__ some help in the house.* 家のことをいくらか手伝ってくれたら，ただで泊めてあげられる. ▶定義 2 **U** the relation in value between kinds of money used in different countries 異なる国で使われる数種類の通貨の間の価値の関係→**為替, 為替相場** ‖ *What's the __exchange rate__/__rate of exchange__ for dollars?* ドルの為替レートはいくらですか. *Most of the country's __foreign exchange__ comes from oil.* その国のほとんどの外国為替は石油から来ている. ☞ 参 Stock Exchange ▶定義 3 **C** a visit by a group of students or teachers to another country and a return visit by a similar group from that country 生徒や教師の一団が他国を訪問することと，その訪問先の国から同様の一団がお返しで訪問すること→**交換留学, 相互訪問** ‖ *She went on an exchange to Germany when she was sixteen.* 彼女は16歳の時に, 交換留学でドイツに行った. ▶定義 4 **C** an angry conversation or argument 怒った会話または論争→**口論** ‖ *She ended up having a __heated exchange__ with her neighbours about the noise the night before.* 彼女は結局，昨夜の騒音のことで近所の人たちと激しい口論をすることになってしまった.

---

## excitement 569

*__exchange__*² /ɪkstʃéɪndʒ/ **動 他** ▶定義 exchange A for B; exchange sth (with sb) to give or receive sth in return for sth else 〜をほかの…のお返しに与える, または受け取る→**A を B と交換する, 取り替える, (人と)〜を交換する, 交わす** ‖ *I would like to exchange this skirt for a bigger size.* このスカートをもっと大きいサイズのものと交換したいのですが. *Claire and Molly exchanged addresses with the boys.* クレアとモリーはその少年たちと住所を交換した. *They exchanged glances (= they looked at each other).* 彼らは互いに目くばせをした (= お互いを見た).

**excise** /éksaɪz/ **名 U** ▶定義 a government tax on certain goods that are produced or sold inside a country, for example tobacco, alcohol, etc たばこ, アルコールなど, 国内で生産あるいは販売される特定の製品にかけられる政府の税→**国内消費税, 物品税** ☞ 参 customs

**excitable** /ɪksáɪtəb(ə)l/ **形** ▶定義 easily excited 簡単に興奮する→**興奮しやすい, すぐかっとなる**

**excite** /ɪksáɪt/ **動 他** ▶定義 1 to make sb feel happy and enthusiastic or nervous 〜を幸せで熱中させたり, 神経質にさせたりする→**〜を興奮させる, 刺激する** ‖ *Don't excite the baby too much or we'll never get him off to sleep.* 赤ん坊を興奮させすぎないようにしなさい. さもないと寝かし付けられませんよ. ▶定義 2 to make sb react in a particular way 〜にある特別な反応をさせる→**〜を呼び起こす, 刺激する, そそる** ‖ *The programme excited great interest.* その番組は非常に興味をそそった.

*__excited__* /ɪksáɪtəd/ **形** ▶定義 excited (about/at/by sth) feeling or showing happiness and enthusiasm; not calm 幸せや情熱を感じる, または示す; 平静でない→**(〜に・で)興奮した, わくわくした** ‖ *Are you getting excited about your holiday?* 休日のことで興奮しているのですか. *We're all very excited at the thought of moving house.* 私たちは引っ越しのことを考えて, とてもわくわくしている. — excitedly **副** →興奮して, わくわくして

*__excitement__* /ɪksáɪtmənt/ **名 U** ▶定義 the state of being excited, especially because sth interesting is happening or will happen 特に面白い

物事が起きている、または起ころうとしているために、興奮した状態→**興奮, 動揺, わくわくすること** ‖ There was **great excitement** as the winner's name was announced. 優勝者の名前が発表された時、大きな動揺が起きた. The match was **full of excitement** until the very last minute. その試合は最後の瞬間まで興奮に満ちていた.

**★exciting** /ɪksáɪtɪŋ/ 形 ▶定義 causing strong feelings of pleasure and interest 喜びや興味の強い感情を起こすような→**興奮させる, わくわくするような, 刺激的な** ‖ That's very exciting news. それは非常にわくわくするようなニュースだ. Berlin is one of the most exciting cities in Europe. ベルリンはヨーロッパの最も刺激的な町の1つだ.

**exclaim** /ɪkskléɪm/ 動自他 ▶定義 to say sth suddenly and loudly because you are surprised, angry, etc 驚いたり, 怒ったりなどの理由で, ～を突然大声で言う→**(～と)叫ぶ** ‖ 'I just don't believe it!' he exclaimed. 「僕はそんな事は信じないよ」と彼は叫んだ.

**exclamation** /èksklәméɪ(ә)n/ 名 C ▶定義 a short sound, word or phrase that you say suddenly because of a strong emotion, pain, etc 強い感情, 痛みなどのために, 突然発する短い音声, 言葉, 語句→**叫び, 絶叫, 感嘆詞・間投詞** ‖ 'Ouch!' is an exclamation. 「あいたっ」は感嘆詞である.
☛類 interjection

**exclamation mark** (米 **exclamation point**) 名 C ▶定義 a mark (!) that is written after an exclamation 感嘆文の後に書かれる記号(!)→**感嘆符**

**★exclude** /ɪksklú:d/ 動他 (進行形は不可) ▶定義1 to leave out; not include 取り去る; 含まない→**～を排除する, 除外する, 入れない** ‖ The price excludes all extras such as drinks or excursions. その価格には, 飲み物や小旅行などの追加料金はどれも入っていない. ▶定義2 exclude sb/sth (from sth) to prevent sb/sth from entering a place or taking part in sth ～がある場所に入るのを, または…に参加するのを防ぐ→**～を(…から)締め出す, ～を(…に)入れない** ‖ Women are excluded from the temple. その寺は女人禁制だ. Jake was excluded from the game for cheating. ジェークはいかさまをするのでゲームから締め出された. ⇔ **include** ▶定義3 to decide that sth is not possible ～が可能でないと判断する→**～を除外する, 全く残さない** ‖ The police had **excluded the possibility** that the child had run away. 警察は, その子供が逃げたという可能性を排除していた.

**★excluding** /ɪksklú:dɪŋ/ 前 ▶定義 leaving out; without 取り去った; ～なしの→**～を除いて** ‖ Lunch costs £10 per person excluding drinks. 昼食は飲み物を除いて1人当たり10ポンドかかる. ⇔ **including**

**exclusion** /ɪksklú:ʒ(ә)n/ 名 U ▶定義 keeping or leaving sb/sth out ～を締め出しておくこと, または取り去ること→**除外, 排除, 締め出し**

**exclusive**¹ /ɪksklú:sɪv/ 形 ▶定義1 (名詞の前だけ) only to be used by or given to one person, group, etc; not to be shared 1人, 1つの集団などにのみ使われる, または与えられる; 共有されない→**独占的な, 専用の** ‖ This car is for the Director's exclusive use. この車は取締役専用です. Tonight we are showing an exclusive interview with the new leader of the Labour Party (= on only one television or radio station). 今夜は労働党の新党首との独占インタビューをお届けします(=1つのテレビまたはラジオ局だけで). ▶定義2 expensive and not welcoming people who are thought to be of a lower social class 高価で, 低い社会階級と考えられている人々は歓迎されないような→**高級な** ‖ an exclusive restaurant 高級レストラン a flat in an exclusive part of the city 町の高級住宅街にあるフラット・マンション ▶定義3 exclusive of sb/sth not including sb/sth; without ～を含まない; ～なしの→**～を除いて** ‖ Lunch costs £7 per person exclusive of drinks. 昼食は飲み物を除いて1人当たり7ポンドかかる.

**exclusive**² /ɪksklú:sɪv/ 名 C ▶定義 a newspaper story that is given to and published by only one newspaper 1つの新聞にだけ掲載され, 発行された新聞の記事→**独占記事, 特種**

**exclusively** /ɪksklú:sɪvli/ 副 ▶定義 only; not involving anyone/anything else ～だけ; ほかのだれも・何も含まない→**排他的に, 全く～だけ** ‖ The swimming pool is reserved exclusively for members of the club. そのプールはクラブの会員専用です.

**excrement** /ékskrəmənt/ 名 ❶ 正式 ▶定義 the solid waste material that you get rid of when you go to the toilet トイレに行ったときに出す固形の排出物→糞便(ふんべん), 大便 ☞類 faeces

**excrete** /ɪkskríːt/ 動 他 正式 ▶定義 to get rid of solid waste material from the body 体内から固形の排出物を出す→～を排出する

**excruciating** /ɪkskrúːʃiɛɪtɪŋ/ 形 ▶定義 extremely painful 非常に痛い→耐え難い, 激しい

**excursion** /ɪkskə́ːrʒ(ə)n, -ʃ(ə)n/ 名 ❶ ▶定義 a short journey or trip that a group of people make for pleasure 団体で楽しみに出掛ける短い旅行→観光旅行, 小旅行, 遠足 ‖ *to go on an excursion to the seaside* 海辺へ遠足に行く
☞参 travelの注

**excusable** /ɪkskjúːzəb(ə)l/ 形 ▶定義 that you can forgive 許すことのできる→許される, 申し訳の立つ ‖ *an excusable mistake* 許される過ち ⇔ **inexcusable**

★**excuse**¹ /ɪkskjúːs/ 名 ❶ ▶定義 an excuse (for sth/doing sth) a reason (that may or may not be true) that you give in order to explain your behaviour 自分の行為を説明するために言う(真実である場合も, 真実でない場合もある)理由→言い訳, 言い分, 口実 ‖ *There's no excuse for rudeness.* 無礼に対する言い訳はない. *He always finds an excuse for not helping with the housework.* 彼はいつも家事を手伝わない口実を見つける. *to make an excuse* 言い訳をする

★**excuse**² /ɪkskjúːz/ 動 他 ▶定義 **1** excuse sb/sth (for sth/for doing sth) to forgive sb for sth he/she has done wrong that is not very serious ～があまり深刻でない悪い…をしたのを許す→～を許す, 勘弁する, ～の…を・～が…するのを許す, 勘弁する ‖ *Please excuse the interruption but I need to talk to you.* お邪魔して申し訳ありませんが, あなたにお話しする必要があるのです. ▶定義 **2** to explain sb's bad behaviour and make it seem less bad ～の悪い行いを説明して, あまり悪く思われないようにする→～の言い訳をする, 弁解をする, ～の弁解になる ‖ *Nothing can excuse such behaviour.* 何ものも, このような行為に対する弁解にはならない.
▶定義 **3** excuse sb (from sth) to free sb from a duty, responsibility, etc 任務, 責任などから～を自由にする→～を(…から)免除する, ～に(…を)免ずる, ～に退席を許す ‖ *She excused herself (= asked if she could leave) and left the meeting early.* 彼女は退席を許してもらい(= 去ってよいかを尋ね), 打ち合わせの途中で出た.
▶ excuse me という表現は, だれかの邪魔をするときや, 自分が知らない人に話し掛けるときに使われる: *Excuse me, can you tell me the way to the station?* (失礼ですが, 駅までの道を教えていただけませんか.) 米国では, また場合によっては英国でも, 何かについて謝るときに用いられる: *Did I tread on your toe? Excuse me.* (つま先を踏みましたか. ごめんなさい.)

> ▶コミュニケーション
>
> エチケット違反には excuse me
>
> Excuse me は, 日本語の「失礼」「ごめんなさい」に当たる儀礼表現ですが, これが求められる範囲は, 日本の「失礼」より広いのが現状です. 乗り物で軽く体が触れても, 人前を通るときも, 話の途中で軽くせきをしても, Excuse me と言う必要があります. 子供が食卓を離れたいときは, "May I be excused?"(失礼していいですか)と断らなければ許してもらえません. 偶然一緒のテーブルに着いた人に対しても, 先に立つときは Would you excuse me?(連れがいる場合は excuse us)と断るのが礼儀とされています.

**execute** /éksɪkjùːt/ 動 他 ▶定義 **1** (通常は受動態で) execute sb (for sth) to kill sb as an official punishment 公式の罰として～を殺す→～を(…の罪で)処刑する ‖ *He was executed for murder.* 彼は殺人罪で処刑された. ▶定義 **2** 正式 to perform a task, etc or to put a plan into action 任務などを遂行する, または計画を実行に移す→～を実行する, 果たす — execution /èksɪkjúːʃ(ə)n/ 名 ❶ ❶ →処刑, 遂行, 実行

**executioner** /èksɪkjúːʃ(ə)nər/ 名 ❶ ▶定義 a person whose job is to execute criminals 犯罪人を処刑することを仕事にする人→死刑執行人

**executive**¹ /ɪgzékjətɪv/ 形 ▶定義 **1** (used in connection with people in business, government, etc) concerned with managing, making plans, decisions, etc (企業, 政府などの人々に関

## executive²

して用いて)経営,企画,決定などに携わる➡**管理の,経営の,経営にかかわっている,行政上の** ‖ *an executive director of the company* その会社の専務取締役 *executive decisions/jobs/duties* 経営的決定・責務・任務 ▶定義2 (used about goods, buildings, etc) designed to be used by important business people(製品,建物などについて)重要なビジネスマンに使われるように設計された➡**管理職向きの,高級な** ‖ *an executive briefcase* 高級書類かばん

**executive²** /ɪgzék(j)ətɪv/ 名 ▶定義1 ❹a person who has an important position as a manager of a business or organization 会社や組織の管理職として重要な地位にある人➡**役員,管理職,重役** ‖ *She's a senior executive in a computer company.* 彼女はコンピューター会社の首脳だ. ▶定義2 [単数扱い] the group of people who are in charge of an organization or a company 組織や会社の責任を負う人々の集団➡**経営陣**

**exemplary** /ɪgzémpləri/ 形 ▶定義 very good; that can be an example to other people 非常に良い; ほかの人への例になる➡**模範的な,立派な** ‖ *exemplary behaviour* 模範的な行い

**exemplify** /ɪgzémpləfàɪ/ 動 他 (現分 **exemplifying**; 三単現 **exemplifies**; 過, 過分 **exemplified**) ▶定義 to be a typical example of sth ～の典型的な例になる➡**～の例となる,～を例示する**

**exempt¹** /ɪgzém(p)t/ 形(名詞の前は不可) ▶定義 exempt (from sth) free from having to do sth or pay for sth ～をしなければならない,または～に料金を払わなければならないことから解放された➡**免除された,免れた** ‖ *Children under 16 are exempt from dental charges.* 16歳未満の子供は歯の治療費を免除されている.
— exemption /ɪgzém(p)ʃ(ə)n/ 名 ❹Ⓤ➡**免除**

**exempt²** /ɪgzém(p)t/ 動 他 正式 ▶定義 exempt sb/sth (from sth) to say officially that sb does not have to do sth or pay for sth ～が…をしなくてもよい,または…に料金を払わなくてもよいと公式に言う➡**～を(…から)免除する**

★**exercise¹** /éksərsàɪz/ 名 ▶定義1 Ⓤ physical or mental activity that keeps you healthy and strong あなたを健康に,強く保つような肉体的または精神的活動➡**運動,体操,鍛錬** ‖ *The doctor advised him to **take regular exercise**.* 医者は彼に定期的に運動するように勧めた. *Swimming is a good form of exercise.* 水泳は良い運動だ. ▶定義2 ❹ (しばしば複数形で) a movement or activity that you do in order to stay healthy or to become skilled at sth 健康でいるため,または～が上手になるためにする動きまたは活動➡**運動,体操,練習,稽古(けいこ)** ‖ *I do keep-fit exercises every morning.* 私は毎朝健康体操をしている. *breathing/stretching/relaxation exercises* 呼吸・屈伸・弛緩(しかん)運動 ▶定義3 ❹a piece of work that is intended to help you learn or practise sth ～の学習や練習の助けとなることを意図した作業➡**練習問題,課題** ‖ *an exercise on phrasal verbs* 句動詞の練習問題 ▶定義4 ❹ an exercise in sth an activity or a series of actions that have a particular aim 特定の目的を持った活動または一連の行動➡**(～する)活動,作業** ‖ *The project is an exercise in getting the best results at a low cost.* この事業は少ない費用で最善の結果を得る活動である. ▶定義5 Ⓤ正式 exercise of sth the use of sth, for example a power, right, etc 力,権利などを使うこと➡**～の行使,～を働かせること** ‖ *the exercise of patience/judgement/discretion* 忍耐・裁定・決定権の行使 ▶定義6 [❹, 通常は複数] a series of activities by soldiers to practise fighting 兵士が戦闘の練習をする一連の活動➡**演習** ‖ *military exercises* 軍事演習

★**exercise²** /éksərsàɪz/ 動 ▶定義1 ⓘ to do some form of physical activity in order to stay fit and healthy 元気に健康でいるために肉体的活動をする➡**運動する,鍛える** ‖ *It is important to exercise regularly.* 定期的に運動することが重要だ. ▶定義2 ⓣ to make use of sth, for example a power, right, etc 力,権利などを使う➡**～を行使する,(精神力など)を働かせる** ‖ *You should exercise your right to vote.* 投票権を行使すべきだ.

**exert** /ɪgzə́ːrt/ 動 他 ▶定義1 to make use of sth, for example influence, strength, etc, to affect sb/sth ～に影響を及ぼすために,影響力,力などを使う➡**～を行使する,出す,働かせる,及ぼす** ‖ *Parents exert a powerful influence on their children's opinions.* 両親は子供たちの意見に強い影響を及ぼす. ▶定義2 exert yourself to make a big effort 多大な努力をする➡**(大いに)努力する** ‖ *You won't make any progress if you don't* *exert yourself a bit more.* もう少し努力しないと,進歩はないよ.

**exertion** /ɪgzɔ́:ʃ(ə)n/ 名 **U C** ▶定義 using your body in a way that takes a lot of effort; sth that you do that makes you tired 多大な努力を要する方法で体を使うこと; 人がすることで,その人を疲れさせること➡**力を出すこと,努力,骨の折れる仕事,激しい活動** ‖ *At his age physical exertion was dangerous.* 彼の年齢では,激しい運動は危険だった. *I'm tired after the exertions of the past few days.* ここ数日の骨の折れる仕事で疲れてしまった.

**exhale** /eks(h)éɪl/ 動 自 正式 ▶定義 to breathe out so that the air leaves your lungs 空気が肺から出るように深く息を吐く➡**息を吐く** ⇔ **inhale**

**exhaust**¹ /ɪgzɔ́:st/ 名 ▶定義 **1 U** the waste gas that comes out of a vehicle, an engine or a machine 乗り物,エンジン,機械から出る排出ガス➡**排気ガス** ‖ *car exhaust fumes/emissions* 自動車の排気ガス ▶定義 **2 C** (または **exhaust pipe** 米 **tailpipe**) a pipe (particularly at the back of a car) through which waste gas escapes from an engine or machine エンジンや機械からそれを通して排気ガスが出ていく(特に車の後ろにある)管➡**排気管** ☞ S7ページのさし絵

*★**exhaust**² /ɪgzɔ́:st/ 動 他 ▶定義 **1** to make sb very tired ~を非常に疲れさせる➡**~をうんざりさせる,疲れ果てさせる** ‖ *The long journey to work every morning exhausted him.* 毎朝の長距離通勤で彼は疲れ果てていた. ▶定義 **2** to use sth up completely; to finish sth ~を完全に使い尽くす; ~を終わらせる➡**~を使い果たす,尽きさせる,空にする** ‖ *All the supplies of food have been exhausted.* すべての支給食糧は尽きてしまった. ▶定義 **3** to say everything you can about a subject, etc ある主題などについて自分の言えることをすべて言う➡**~について余すところなく述べる,~を論じ尽くす** ‖ *Well, I think we've exhausted that topic.* さて,もうその話題については語り尽くしたと思います.

*★**exhausted** /ɪgzɔ́:stəd/ 形 ▶定義 very tired 非常に疲れた➡**疲れきった,疲れ果てた**

*★**exhausting** /ɪgzɔ́:stɪŋ/ 形 ▶定義 making sb very tired ~を非常に疲れさせる➡**疲れさせる,消耗させる** ‖ *Teaching young children is exhausting work.* 小さい子供たちに教えるのは疲れる仕事だ.

**exhaustion** /ɪgzɔ́:stʃ(ə)n/ 名 **U** ▶定義 the state of being extremely tired 極度に疲れた状態➡**極度の疲労,疲労困憊(こんぱい)**

**exhaustive** /ɪgzɔ́:stɪv/ 形 ▶定義 including everything possible あり得るすべてのことを含む➡**徹底的な,完全な,余すところのない,網羅的な** ‖ *This list is certainly not exhaustive.* このリストは確かに完全ではない.

**exhibit**¹ /ɪgzíbət/ 名 **C** ▶定義 an object that is shown in a museum, etc or as a piece of evidence in a court of law 博物館などで見せられる物,または法廷で証拠の品として示される物➡**展示物,展示品,証拠物件**

**exhibit**² /ɪgzíbət/ 動 他 ▶定義 **1** to show sth in a public place for people to enjoy or to give them information 公の場所で,人々が楽しむためや人々に情報を与えるために~を見せる➡**~を展示する,示す,陳列する,出品する** ‖ *His paintings have been exhibited in the local art gallery.* 彼の絵は地元の画廊に展示されていた. ▶定義 **2** 正式 to show clearly that you have a particular quality, feeling. etc 自分が特別な性質,感情などを持っていることを明らかに示す➡**~を見せる,示す,表す** ‖ *The refugees are exhibiting signs of exhaustion and stress.* 難民は疲労とストレスの兆候を見せている.

*★**exhibition** /èksəbíʃ(ə)n/ 名 ▶定義 **1 C** a collection of objects, for example works of art, that are shown to the public 一般に公開されている,例えば美術作品などの収集物➡**展示(品),展覧会,展示会** ‖ *an exhibition of photographs* 写真展 *Her paintings will be on exhibition in London for the whole of April.* 彼女の絵は4月一杯ロンドンで展示される. ▶定義 **2 C** an occasion when a particular skill is shown to the public 特別な技能が公に見せられる機会➡**模範演技・演奏,公演** ‖ *We saw an exhibition of Scottish dancing last night.* 昨夜,私たちはスコットランド舞踊の公演を見た. ▶定義 **3** [単数扱い] 正式 the act of showing a quality, feeling, etc 特質,感情などを見せること➡**見せること,表現,発露,発揮** ‖ *The game was a superb exhibition of football at its best.* その試合はこの上なくラグビーのすばらしさを表現していた.

**exhibitor** /ɪgzíbətər/ 名 **C** ▶定義 a person, for

example an artist, a photographer, etc, who shows his/her work to the public 芸術家, 写真家など, 自分の作品を一般に見せる人→**出品者**

**exhilarate** /ɪgzílərèɪt/ 動他 (通常は受動態で) ▶定義 to make sb feel very excited and happy ～を非常に興奮させ, 幸せにする→**～をうきうきさせる, 陽気にする, 鼓舞する** ‖ *We felt exhilarated by our walk along the beach.* 海岸沿いを歩いていたら, うきうきしてきた. — exhilarating 形→(人を)うきうきさせるような, 陽気にするような — exhilaration /ɪgzìləréɪʃ(ə)n/ 名 ❶→**うきうきした気分, 陽気**

**exile** /éksaɪl, égz-/ 名 ▶定義 1 ❶ the state of being forced to live outside your own country (especially for political reasons) (特に政治的理由で) 自分の国の外で暮らすことを強いられている状態→**追放, 亡命, 流罪** ‖ *He went into exile after the revolution of 1968.* 彼は 1968年の革命の後, 亡命した. *They lived in exile in London for many years.* 彼らは長年ロンドンで亡命生活を送った. ▶定義 2 ❷ a person who is forced to live outside his/her own country (especially for political reasons) (特に政治的理由で) 自国の外で暮らすことを強いられている人→**亡命者, 追放された人** ◆参 refugee — exile 動他 (通常は受動態で)→**～を追放する, 流刑にする** ‖ *After the revolution the king was exiled.* 革命の後, 王は追放された.

*****exist** /ɪgzíst/ 動自 ▶定義 1 (進行形は不可) to be real; to be found in the real world; to live 実在する; 現実の世界で見つかる; 生きている→**存在する, 実在する, ある, 生きている** ‖ *Dreams only exist in our imagination.* 夢は想像の中にだけ存在する. *Fish cannot exist out of water.* 魚は水の外では生きられない. ▶定義 2 exist (on sth) to manage to live どうにかして生きる→**(～で)暮らしていく** ‖ *I don't know how she exists on the wage she earns.* 彼女が自分の稼ぎでどうやって暮らしているのか, 私には分からない.

**existence** /ɪgzíst(ə)ns/ 名 ▶定義 1 ❶ the state of existing 存在している状態→**存在, 実在** ‖ *This is the oldest human skeleton in existence.* これは現存する最古の人間の骸骨(がいこつ)です. *How did the universe come into existence?* 宇宙はどのようにして生まれたの. ▶定義 2 [単数扱い] a way of living, especially when it is difficult 特に困難な時の, 生き方→**生活, 暮らし振り** ‖ *They lead a miserable existence in a tiny flat in London.* 彼らはロンドンのちっぽけなアパートで惨めな暮らしをしている.

**existing** /ɪgzístɪŋ/ 形 (名詞の前だけ) ▶定義 that is already there or being used; present 既にそこにある, または使われているような; 現在の→**現在の, 既存の** ‖ *Under the existing law you are not allowed to work in this country.* 現行の法では, 君はこの国で働くことを許されていない.

*****exit**[1] /éksət, égz-/ 名 ❶ ▶定義 1 a door or way out of a public building or vehicle 公共の建物や乗り物の外に出る扉, または通路→**出口** ‖ *The emergency exit is at the back of the bus.* 非常口はバスの後部にあります. ▶定義 2 the act of leaving sth ～を離れる行為→**退出, 退室, 退場** ‖ *If I see her coming I'll make a quick exit.* 彼女が来るのを見たら, 私は素早く退出する. *an exit visa* (= *one that allows you to leave a country*) 出国査証 (= 国を出ることを許可するもの) ⇔ 定義 1, 2 **entrance** ▶定義 3 a place where traffic can leave a road or a motorway to join another road 交通がある道や高速道路を離れて, ほかの道に加わる場所→**出口** ‖ *At the roundabout take the third exit.* ロータリーで3番の出口に進みなさい.

**exit**[2] /éksət, égz-/ 動自 他 正式 ▶定義 to leave a place ある場所を去る→**出る, 退場する** ‖ *He exited through the back door.* 彼は後方の扉から出た. *I exited the database and switched off the computer.* 私はデータベースから抜けて, コンピューターのスイッチを切った.

**exonerate** /ɪgzánərèɪt/ 動他 正式 (しばしば受動態で) ▶定義 to say officially that sb was not responsible for sth bad that happened 起こった悪い～について…に責任がないと公式に言う→**～を免罪・免責にする, 免除する**

**exorbitant** /ɪgzɔ́ːrbət(ə)nt/ 形 正式 ▶定義 (used about the cost of sth) much more expensive than it should be (～の費用について) しかるべき値段よりずっと高い→**法外な, 途方もない**

**exotic** /ɪgzátɪk/ 形 ▶定義 unusual or interesting because it comes from a different country or culture 異なる国または文化から来ているために珍しい, または面白い→**異国風の, 風変わりで面白い, 異国情緒のある, エキゾチックな** ‖ *exotic* *plants/animals/fruits* 外来植物・外来動物・外国産の果物

**\*expand** /ɪkspǽnd/ **動 自他 ▶定義** to become or to make sth bigger ～がより大きくなる、または大きくする→**広がる、～を広げる、膨らむ、～を拡張する** ‖ *Metals expand when they are heated.* 金属は暖められると膨張する. *We hope to expand our business this year.* 今年私たちは事業を拡張したい. ⇔ **contract**

**句動詞** expand on sth **▶定義** to give more details of a story, plan, idea, etc 話、計画、案などの詳細を与える→**～について詳しく述べる**

**expanse** /ɪkspǽns/ **名 C ▶定義** a large open area (of land, sea, sky, etc) (大地、海、空などの)大きく開いた部分→**広がり** ‖ *I lay on my back and stared up at the vast expanse of blue sky.* 私はあおむけに寝て、広大に広がる青い空を見た.

**\*expansion** /ɪkspǽnʃ(ə)n/ **名 U ▶定義** the action of becoming bigger or the state of being bigger than before 以前より大きくなる行為、または大きくなった状態→**拡大、拡張** ‖ *The rapid expansion of the university has caused a lot of problems.* 大学の急速な拡大は多くの問題を起こした.

**expansive** /ɪkspǽnsɪv/ **形 正式 ▶定義** (used about a person) who talks a lot in an interesting way; friendly (人について)面白くたくさん話す; 友好的な→**打ち解けた、話し好きな、開けっ広げな**

**expatriate** /ekspéɪtriət, -trièɪt/ (または **略式 expat**) **名 C ▶定義** a person who lives outside his/her own country 自国の外で暮らす人→**国外追放者、国外移住者、亡命者** ‖ *American expatriates in London* ロンドンで暮らすアメリカ人移住者

**\*expect** /ɪkspékt/ **動 他 ▶定義1** to think or believe that sb/sth will come or that sth will happen ～が来る、または～が起きると考える、または信じる→**～を予期する、多分～と思う** ‖ *She was expecting a letter from the bank this morning but it didn't come.* 彼女は銀行から手紙が今朝来ると思っていたが、来なかった. *I expect that it will rain this afternoon.* 今日の午後は多分雨が降ると思う. *I know the food's not so good, but what did you expect from such a cheap restaurant? (= it's not surprising)* 食事はそれほどおいしくないと分かっているが、こんな安い食堂に何を期待していたのか. (= 驚くことではない) *She's expecting a baby in the spring (= she's pregnant).* 彼女は春に出産の予定だ. (= 妊娠している). ☛参 **wait**¹の注

**▶定義2** expect sth (from sb); expect sb to do sth to feel confident that you will get sth from sb or that he/she will do what you want ～を…から得られると、またはその人が自分の望むことをすると確信している→**(当然のこととして)～を(…に)期待する、求める、～に(当然のこととして)…してほしいと思っている** ‖ *He expects a high standard of work from everyone.* 彼はすべての人に高い水準の仕事を期待する. *Factory workers are often expected to work at nights.* 工場労働者はしばしば夜間労働を求められる.

**▶定義3 英** (進行形は不可) to think that sth is true or correct; to suppose ～を事実または正しいと考える; 仮定する→**～だと予測する、～を当然のことと思う** ‖ *'Whose is this suitcase?' 'Oh it's Maureen's, I expect.'* 「このスーツケースはだれのですか」「ああ、きっとモーリーンのだろう」 *'Will you be able to help me later on?' 'I expect so.'* 「後で手伝ってもらえますか」「大丈夫だと思います」

▶この動詞は進行形では使われないが、現在分詞(= -ing形)はよく見られる: *She flung the door open, expecting to see Richard standing there.* (彼女は、そこにリチャードが立っていると思い、扉を勢いよく開けた.)

**expectancy** /ɪkspékt(ə)nsi/ **名 U ▶定義** the state of expecting sth to happen; hope ～が起きることを予期している状態; 望み→**見込み、予期、期待** ‖ *a look/feeling of expectancy* 期待している様子・気持ち ☛参 **life expectancy**

**expectant** /ɪkspékt(ə)nt/ **形 ▶定義1** thinking that sth good will happen; hopeful 良い～が起こると考えている; 望みを持った→**期待している、予期している** ‖ *an expectant audience* 期待する聴衆 *expectant faces* 期待した顔 **▶定義2** pregnant 妊娠した→**妊娠している** ‖ *Expectant mothers need a lot of rest.* 妊婦にはたくさんの休憩が必要だ. — expectantly **副**→**期待して、待ち受けて**

**expectation** /èkspektéɪʃ(ə)n/ **名 正式 ▶定義1** **U** expectation (of sth) the belief that sth will happen or come ～が起きるまたは来ると信じること→**予期する・されること, 見込み, 期待** ‖ *The dog was sitting under the table in expectation of food.* 犬はえさを期待してテーブルの下に座っていた. ▶定義2 [**C**, 通常は複数]hope for the future 未来への望み→**期待, 期待される物・事** ‖ *They had great expectations for their daughter, but she didn't really live up to them.* 彼らは娘に多大な期待をしていたが, 彼女は実際にはそれにこたえなかった.

**成句** against/contrary to (all) expectation(s) ▶定義 very different to what was expected 期待されたのとは全く異なる→**期待に反して** ‖ *Contrary to all expectations, Val won first prize.* 全く期待に反して, ヴァルが優勝した.

not come up to (sb's) expectations ▶定義 to not be as good as expected 期待されたほど良くない→**期待に沿わない**

**expedient** /ɪkspíːdiənt/ 形正式 ▶定義 (used about an action) convenient or helpful for a purpose, but possibly not completely honest or moral (行動について)ある目的のために便利で役に立つが, おそらく完全には正直または道徳的でない→**便宜のよい, 好都合な, 得策の** ‖ *The government decided that it was expedient not to increase taxes until after the election.* 政府は, 選挙が終わるまでは増税しないのが得策だと判断した. — expediency /-ənsi/ 名 **U**→好都合, 便宜, 方便

**expedition** /èkspədíʃ(ə)n/ 名 **C** ▶定義1 a long journey for a special purpose 特別な目的のための長い旅→**探検, 遠征, 調査** ‖ *a scientific expedition to Antarctica* 南極大陸への科学探検 ▶定義2 a short journey that you make for pleasure 楽しみのために行う短い旅→**小旅行, 遠出** ‖ *a fishing expedition* 釣り旅行

**expel** /ɪkspél/ 動 (**expelling**; **expelled**) ▶定義1 to force sb to leave a country, school, club, etc 強制的に～を国, 学校, クラブなどから去らせる→**～を追放する, 追い出す** ‖ *The government has expelled all foreign journalists.* 政府はすべての外国人記者を追放した. *The boy was expelled from school for smoking.* その少年は喫煙したために退学処分になった. ▶定義2 to send sth out by force ～を力で送り出す→**～を**

排出する, 吐き出す ‖ *to expel air from the lungs* 肺から空気を吐き出す ☛ 名 expulsion

**expend** /ɪkspénd/ 動 正式 ▶定義 expend sth (on sth) to spend or use money, time, care, etc in doing sth ～をするのに, 金, 時間, 手間などをかけるまたは使う→**～を(…に)費やす, ～を消費する** ‖ *I have expended a lot of time and energy on that project.* 私はその事業に多くの時間と労力を費やした.

**expendable** /ɪkspéndəb(ə)l/ 形正式 ▶定義 not considered important enough to be saved 救うほど重要と考えられていない→**犠牲にしてもよい, 消耗してよい** ‖ *In a war human life is expendable.* 戦争では人間の命は使い捨てにされる.

**expenditure** /ɪkspéndɪtʃər/ 名 [**U**, 単数扱い] 正式 ▶定義 the act of spending money; the amount of money that is spent 金を消費する行為; 費やされる金額→**支出, 出費** ‖ *Government expenditure on education is very low.* 政府の教育に対する支出は非常に低い.

*★**expense** /ɪkspéns/ 名 ▶定義1 **C U** the cost of sth in time or money 時間や金で表す～の費用→**出費, 費用** ‖ *Running a car is a great expense.* 車を走らせるのは非常に費用がかかる. *The movie was filmed in Tahiti at great expense.* その映画はタヒチで多額の費用をかけて撮影された. ▶定義2 **expenses**[複数扱い]money that is spent for a particular purpose 特別な目的のために費やされる金→**費用, 経費** ‖ *You can claim back your travelling expenses.* 旅費の払い戻しを求められますよ.

**成句** at sb's expense ▶定義1 with sb paying; at sb's cost ～の支払いで; ～の出費で→**～の負担で** ‖ *My trip is at the company's expense.* 私は会社の負担で旅行している. ▶定義2 against sb, so that he/she looks silly ～が愚かに見えるように, その～に対して→**～をだしにして** ‖ *They were always making jokes at Paul's expense.* 彼らはいつもポールをだしにして冗談を言っていた.

at the expense of sth ▶定義 harming or damaging sth ～を傷付けて, または害を及ぼして→**～を犠牲にして** ‖ *He was a successful businessman, but it was at the expense of his family life.* 彼は成功した実業家だったが, それは家庭生活を犠牲にしてのことだった.

*★**expensive** /ɪkspénsɪv/ 形 ▶定義 costing a lot of money 多くの金がかかって→**高い, 高価な, 費用**

のかかる ‖ *Houses are very expensive in this area.* この地域では家はとても高価だ. ⇔ **inexpensive**, **cheap** —expensively 副 ➡️費用をかけて

***experience**¹ /ɪkspíəriəns/ 名 ▶定義1 ❶the things that you have done in your life; the knowledge or skill that you get from seeing or doing sth 人生の中であなたがした事; 〜を見たりしたりして得た知識や技能➡️経験, 経験による能力, 体験 ‖ *We all learn by experience.* 私たちは皆経験から学ぶ. *She has five years' teaching experience.* 彼女は5年間の教師の経験がある. *I know from experience what will happen.* 私は経験から, 何が起こるかが分かる.
▶定義2 ❷something that has happened to you (often something unusual or exciting) 人に起きた(しばしば珍しい、または刺激的な)こと➡️体験した事, 心に残った事 ‖ *She wrote a book about her experiences in Africa.* 彼女はアフリカで体験した事についての本を書いた.

**experience**² /ɪkspíəriəns/ 動 ⓣ ▶定義 to have sth happen to you; to feel 〜が自分に起こる; 感じる➡️〜を体験する, 経験する, 〜な目に遭う ‖ *It was the first time I'd ever experienced failure.* 私が失敗を経験したのは、それが初めてだった. *to experience pleasure/pain/difficulty* 喜び・痛み・困難を経験する

***experienced** /ɪkspíəriənst/ 形 ▶定義 having the knowledge or skill that is necessary for sth 〜に必要な知識や技能を持った➡️経験のある, 熟練した, 経験を積んだ ‖ *He's an experienced diver.* 彼はベテランのダイバーだ. ⇔ **inexperienced**

***experiment**¹ /ɪkspérəmənt/ 名 ⓒⓤ ▶定義 a scientific test that is done in order to get proof of sth or new knowledge 〜の証明, または新しい知識を得るために行う科学的試験➡️実験 ‖ *to carry out/perform/conduct/do an experiment* 実験をする *We need to prove this theory by experiment.* 私たちはこの理論を実験で証明する必要がある. —experimentally /-t(ə)li/ 副 ➡️実験的に, 実験によって

**experiment**² /ɪkspérəmènt/ 動 ⓘ ▶定義 experiment (on/with sth) to do tests to see if sth works or to try to improve it 〜が作動するか見るために, またはそれを改良しようとして試験を行う➡️(〜で)実験する, (〜を)試験する, 試してみる ‖ *Is it really necessary to experiment on animals?* 動物実験は本当に必要なのか. *We're experimenting with a new timetable this month.* 私たちは今月新しい時間割りを試している.

**experimental** /ɪkspèrəméntl/ 形 ▶定義 connected with experiments or trying new ideas 実験または新しい考えを試すことに関した➡️実験的な, 実験の, 実験に基づく, 実験用の ‖ *We're still at the experimental stage with the new product.* 新製品についてはまだ実験段階だ. *experimental schools* 実験的な学校

***expert** /ékspɚːrt/ 名 ⓒ ▶定義 an expert (at/in/on sth) a person who has a lot of special knowledge or skill 多くの特別な知識や技能を持った人➡️(〜の)専門家, 熟練者, ベテラン, 達人 ‖ *She's a leading expert in the field of genetics.* 彼女は, 遺伝学の分野では第一人者です. *a computer expert* コンピューターの専門家 *Let me try - I'm an expert at parking cars in small spaces.* 私にやらせて ― 私は狭い場所に駐車する達人だから. —expert 形 ➡️熟練した, 専門家の ‖ *He's an expert cook.* 彼はベテランの料理人だ. *I think we should get expert advice on the problem.* この問題については専門家の意見を仰ぐべきだと思う. —expertly 副 ➡️巧みに, 上手に

**expertise** /èkspɚːrtíːz, -s/ 名 ⓤ ▶定義 a high level of special knowledge or skill 高い水準の特別な知識や技能➡️専門知識, 専門技術, 熟練 ‖ *I was amazed at his expertise on the word processor.* 私は彼のワープロの技術に驚いた.

**expire** /ɪkspáɪɚr/ 動 ⓘ 正式 ▶定義 (used about an official document, agreement, etc) to come to the end of the time when you can use it or in which it has effect (公式文書, 合意などについて)それを使える, またはそれが有効な期間の終わりに来た➡️満期になる, 期限切れとなる, 終了する ‖ *My passport's expired. I'll have to renew it.* パスポートの期限が切れている. 更新しなければならない. ☛ より略式の言い方に run out がある.

**expiry** /ɪkspáɪəri/ 名 ⓤ ▶定義 the end of a period when you can use sth 〜を使える期間が終わること➡️期限切れ, 満了, 終了 ‖ *The expiry date on this yoghurt was 20 November.* このヨーグルトの賞味期限は11月20日だった.

**E**

***explain** /ɪkspléɪn/ [動][自][他] explain (sth) (to sb) ▶定義 1 to make sth clear or easy to understand ～を明らかに,または分かりやすくする➜(～を)(人に)説明する ‖ *She explained how I should fill in the form.* 彼女は用紙の記入方法を説明した. *I don't understand this. Can you explain it to me?* これが理解できません.私に説明してくれますか.

➤ Explain it to me と言うことに注意. Explain me it は誤り.

▶定義 2 to give a reason for sth ～の理由を与える➜**～が…の説明·理由になる,～を(人に)釈明する,弁明する,弁解する** ‖ *'This work isn't very good.' 'I wasn't feeling very well.' 'Oh, that explains it then.'* 「この作品はあまり良くないねえ」「あまり気分が良くなかったんです」「ああ,そういう訳か」 *The manager explained to the customers why the goods were late.* 部長は,なぜ製品が遅れたのかを顧客に釈明した.

[成句] explain yourself ▶定義 1 to give reasons for your behaviour, especially when it has upset sb 特にそれが～を慌てさせたときに,自分の行為についての理由を与える➜**自分の行為を弁明する** ▶定義 2 to say what you mean in a clear way 自分の意味するところを明確に言う➜**自分の考えをはっきり説明する**

[句動詞] explain sth away ▶定義 to give reasons why sth is not your fault or is not important ～がなぜ自分の過ちでないか,または重要でないかの理由を与える➜**～を説明して片付ける,うまく言い抜ける**

***explanation** /èksplənéɪʃ(ə)n/ [名] ▶定義 1 [C][U] an explanation (for sth) a statement, fact or situation that gives a reason for sth ～に理由を与える主張,事実または状況➜**(～の)説明,弁明,弁解** ‖ *He could not **give an explanation** for his behaviour.* 彼は自分の行いについて弁解できなかった. ▶定義 2 [C] a statement or a piece of writing that makes sth easier to understand ～をより分かりやすくするような主張や文章➜**説明となるもの,弁解の言葉** ‖ *That idea needs some explanation.* その案にはいくらか説明が必要だ.

**explanatory** /ɪksplǽnət(ə)ri; -tɔ̀ːri/ [形] ▶定義 giving an explanation 説明を与える➜**説明的な,説明するような** ‖ *There are some explanatory notes at the back of the book.* 本の後ろに注釈が付いている. *Those instructions are self-explanatory (= they don't need explaining).* その指示は自明だ(= 説明する必要がない).

**explicable** /ekspl íkəb(ə)l, ékspl ɪkə-/ [形] ▶定義 that can be explained 説明できるような➜**説明できる,解説できる** ‖ *Barry's strange behaviour is only explicable in terms of the stress he is under.* バリーの奇妙な振る舞いは,彼が感じているストレスによるとしか説明できない. ⇔ **inexplicable**

**explicit** /ɪksplísət/ [形] ▶定義 1 clear, making sth easy to understand 明らかな,～を分かりやすくするような➜**明白な,はっきりと言葉にした** ‖ *I gave you explicit instructions not to touch anything.* 何にも触らないようにはっきり命令しておいたはずだ. *She was quite explicit about her feelings on the subject.* 彼女はその事についての感情をかなりはっきりと言葉にした. ☛参 **implicit** ▶定義 2 not hiding anything 何も隠さない➜**露骨な,はっきりと·隠さずにものを言う** ‖ *Some of the sex scenes in that TV play were very explicit.* そのテレビドラマのセックスシーンの中には非常に露骨なものがあった.— explicitly [副]➜**はっきりと,明白に** ‖ *He was explicitly forbidden to stay out later than midnight.* 彼は夜12時以降に外出していることをはっきりと禁止されていた.

***explode** /ɪksplóʊd/ [動][自][他] ▶定義 to burst with a loud noise 大きな音を立てて破裂する➜**爆発する,～を爆発させる,破裂する,～を破裂させる** ‖ *The bomb exploded without warning.* 爆弾は警告もなく爆発した. *The army exploded the bomb at a safe distance from the houses.* 軍隊は,家々から離れた安全な場所で,その爆弾を爆発させた. (比喩) *My father exploded (= became very angry) when I told him how much the car would cost to repair.* 車を修理するのにいくらかかるか話した時,父は爆発した(= ひどく怒った). ☛[名] explosion

***exploit**[1] /ɪksplɔ́ɪt/ [動][他] ▶定義 1 to use sth or to treat sb unfairly for your own advantage 自分の利益のために,不公平に～を使ったり,…を扱ったりする➜**～を搾取する,利用する,食い物にする** ‖ *Some employers exploit foreign workers, making them work long hours for low pay.* 低い

賃金で長時間働かせて,外国人労働者を食い物にする雇用者がいる. ▶定義2 to develop sth or make the best use of sth ～を開発する,または～を最大限に利用する➔～を開発する,開拓する ‖ *This region has been exploited for oil for fifty years.* この地域では50年間石油開発が行われてきた. *Solar energy is a source of power that needs to be exploited more fully.* 太陽エネルギーはもっと全面的な開発が必要な動力源である. — exploitation /èksplɔɪtéɪʃ(ə)n/ 名 ❶➔搾取,開発,開拓 ‖ *They're making you work 80 hours a week? That's exploitation!* 彼らは君を週80時間も働かせているのですか.それは搾取だ.

**exploit**² /éksplɔɪt/ 名 ❻ ▶定義 something exciting or interesting that sb has done ～がした何か刺激的な,または面白い事～➔偉業,功績

**exploration** /èksplərétʃ(ə)n/ 名 ❻❶ ▶定義 the act of travelling around a place in order to learn about it ある場所を,そこについて学ぶために旅して回る行為➔(実地)調査,探検 ‖ *space exploration* 宇宙探査

**exploratory** /ɪksplɔ́ːrət(ə)ri; -tɔ̀ːri/ 形 ▶定義 done in order to find sth out ～を見つけ出すためになされた➔探検の,調査の,予備的な ‖ *The doctors are doing some exploratory tests to try and find out what's wrong.* 医者たちは,どこが悪いのかを見つけ出そうと予備試験をしている.

*★**explore** /ɪksplɔ́ːr/ 動 ❸ ❻ ▶定義 to travel around a place, etc in order to learn about it ある場所などを,それについて学ぶために旅して回る➔(未知の場所などを)探検する,調査する,(問題・可能性などを)探究する ‖ *They went on an expedition to explore the River Amazon.* 彼らはアマゾン川調査のため探検に出掛けた. *I've never been to Paris before - I'm going out to explore.* 僕はこれまでパリに行ったことがなかった － これから探検に出掛けるつもりです.(比喩)*We need to explore (= look carefully at) all the possibilities before we decide.* 私たちは決定する前に,あらゆる可能性を検討する(= 注意深く見る)必要がある.

**explorer** /ɪksplɔ́ːrər/ 名 ❻ ▶定義 a person who travels round a place in order to learn about it ある場所を,それについて学ぶために旅して回る人➔探検家,探検する人

*★**explosion** /ɪksplóʊʒ(ə)n/ 名 ❻ ▶定義1 突然で極めて激しい破裂➔爆発 ‖ *Two people were killed in the explosion.* その爆発で2人死んだ. ▶定義2 a sudden dramatic increase in sth ～の突然で劇的な増加➔爆発的増加・成長 ‖ *the population explosion* 人口の爆発的増加 ☞ 動 explode

**explosive**¹ /ɪksplóʊsɪv/ 形 ▶定義1 capable of exploding and therefore dangerous 爆発する可能性があり,危険な➔爆発の,爆発しそうな,爆発寸前の ‖ *Hydrogen is highly explosive.* 水素は非常に爆発しやすい. ▶定義2 causing strong feelings or having dangerous effects 強い感情を起こす,または危険な影響のある➔一触即発の,かっとなりやすい ‖ *The situation is explosive. We must do all we can to calm people down.* 一触即発の状況だ.何としても人々を落ち着かせなければならない.

**explosive**² /ɪksplóʊsɪv/ 名 ❻ ▶定義 a substance that is used for causing explosions 爆発を起こすために使われる物質➔爆薬,爆発物

*★**export**¹ /ɪkspɔ́ːrt/ 動 ❸ ❻ ▶定義1 to send goods, etc to another country, usually for sale 通常売るために,製品などを他国に送る➔～を輸出する ‖ *India exports tea and cotton.* インドは紅茶と綿を輸出する. ⇔ **import** ▶定義2 (computing) to move information from one program to another (コンピューター)情報をあるプログラムから他に移す➔(～を)エクスポートする

*★**export**² /ékspɔːrt/ 名 ▶定義1 ❶sending goods to another country for sale 売るために製品を他国へ送ること➔輸出 ‖ *Most of our goods are produced for export.* 我々の製品のほとんどは輸出用に生産されている. *the export trade* 輸出貿易 ▶定義2 [❻,通常は複数]something that is sent to another country for sale 売るために他国へ送られる物➔輸出品 ‖ *What are Brazil's main exports?* ブラジルの主な輸出品は何ですか. ⇔ **import** — exporter 名 ❻➔輸出業者,輸出国 ‖ *Japan is the largest exporter of electronic goods.* 日本は電子製品の最大輸出国だ. ⇔ **importer**

**expose** /ɪkspóʊz/ 動 ❻ ▶定義1 expose sth (to sb); expose sb/sth (as sth) to show sth that is usually hidden; to tell sth that has been kept secret 通常隠されている～を見せる; 秘密にさ

## 580 exposed

れていた~を話す➔~を(人に)・~を(…であると)暴露する, 暴く, 人目にさらす ‖ *She didn't want to expose her true feelings to her family.* 彼女は本当の気持ちを家族にさらしたくなかった. *The politician was exposed as a liar on TV.* その政治家はテレビでうそつきということが暴かれた. ▶定義2 **expose sb/sth to sth** to put sb/sth or yourself in a situation that could be difficult or dangerous ~または自分自身を, 難しいまたは危険な状況に置く➔**(日光・風雨・危険など)にさらす** ‖ *to be exposed to radiation/danger* 放射能・危険にさらされる ▶定義3 **expose sb to sth** to give sb the chance to experience sth ~に…を経験する機会を与える➔**人を~に触れさせる** ‖ *I like jazz because I was exposed to it as a child.* 私は子供の時にジャズに触れたので, ジャズが好きだ. ▶定義4 (in photography) to allow light onto the film inside a camera when taking a photograph (写真で) 写真を撮るときに, カメラの中で光をフィルムに当てる➔**(フィルム)を露光する, 露出する**

**exposed** /ɪkspóʊzd/ 形 ▶定義 (used about a place) not protected from the wind and bad weather (場所について) 風や悪い天候から守られていない➔**風雨にさらされた**

**exposure** /ɪkspóʊʒɚ/ 名 ▶定義1 **C** the act of making sth public; the thing that is made public ~を公にすること; 公にされたもの➔**暴露, 発覚, 露出** ‖ *The new movie has been given a lot of exposure in the media.* 新しい映画はメディアにたくさん取り上げられた. *The politician resigned because of the exposures about his private life.* その政治家は, 私生活が暴露されたために辞任した. ▶定義2 **U** being allowed or forced to experience sth ~を経験することを許されている, または強いられていること➔**身をさらすこと, さらされること** ‖ *Exposure to radiation is almost always harmful.* 放射能にさらされることは, ほとんどいつでも有害だ. *Television can give children exposure to other cultures from an early age.* テレビは, 子供たちに小さいころから異文化に触れる機会を与える. ▶定義3 **U** a harmful condition when a person becomes very cold because he/she has been outside in very bad weather とても天気の悪い日に外にいたために, 非常に寒くなる有害な状況➔**寒さや風雨に身をさらすこと・さらされること** ‖ *The climbers all died of exposure.* 登山者たちは皆寒さに身をさらされて死んだ. ▶定義4 **C** the amount of film that is used when you take one photograph 写真を撮るときに使われるフィルムの量➔**1コマ, 枚** ‖ *How many exposures are there on this film?* このフィルムは何枚撮りですか.

**★express**¹ /ɪksprés/ 動他 ▶定義1 to show sth such as a feeling or an opinion by words or actions 感情や意見などを言葉や行動で示す➔**~を表現する, 言い表す** ‖ *I found it very hard to express what I felt about her.* 私が彼女に感じた事を言い表すのはとても難しかった. *to express fears/concern about sth* ~についての恐怖・心配を表現する ▶定義2 **express yourself** to say or write your feelings, opinions, etc 自分の感情, 意見などを言ったり, 書いたりする➔**自分の考えを述べる** ‖ *I don't think she expresses herself very well in that article.* 彼女はその記事で自分の思っている事をあまりうまく表現していないと思う.

**express**² /ɪksprés/ 形 ▶定義1 going or sent quickly 速く行く, または送られるような➔**急行の, 速達の** ‖ *an express coach* 急行列車 *We'd better send the parcel express if we want it to get there on time.* もし時間通りに届けたいなら, 小包を速達で送った方が良いだろう. ▶定義2 (used about a wish, command, etc) clearly and definitely stated (望み, 命令などについて) はっきりと明確に述べられた➔**明白な, はっきりした** ‖ *It was her express wish that he should have the picture after her death.* 彼女の死後, 彼にその絵を持っていてほしいというのが彼女のたっての希望であった.

**express**³ /ɪksprés/ (または **express train**) 名 **C** ▶定義 a fast train that does not stop at all stations すべての駅には止まらない速い電車➔**急行**

**★expression** /ɪkspréʃ(ə)n/ 名 ▶定義1 **C U** something that you say that shows your opinions or feelings 言葉によって意見や感情を示しているもの➔**表現** ‖ *Freedom of expression is a basic human right.* 表現の自由は基本的人権だ. *an expression of gratitude/sympathy/anger* 感謝・同情・怒りの表現 ▶定義2 **C** the look on a person's face that shows what he/she is thinking or feeling 人の考えている，または感じている事を示す顔付き→**表情** ‖ *He had a puzzled expression on his face.* 彼は当惑した表情を浮かべていた． ▶定義3 **❸** a word or phrase with a particular meaning 特別な意味の言葉や語句→**言い回し，表現，語句** ‖ *'I'm starving' is an expression meaning 'I'm very hungry'.* I'm starving は「おなかがとてもすいた」という意味の言葉だ． *a slang/an idiomatic expression* 俗語的・慣用的表現

**expressive** /ɪksprésɪv/ 形 ▶定義 showing feelings or thoughts 感情や考えを示した→**表情に富む，表現力に富む** ‖ *That is a very expressive piece of music.* それは非常に表現力豊かな曲だ． *Dave has a very expressive face.* デーブは非常に表情豊かだ．— expressively 副→表情たっぷりに，意味ありげに

**expressly** /ɪksprésli/ 副 ▶定義1 clearly; definitely はっきりと；明確に→**はっきりと，明白に** ‖ *I expressly told you not to do that.* 私は君にそれをするなとはっきり言ったはずだ． ▶定義2 for a special purpose; specially 特別な目的のために，特別に→**わざわざ，特別に** ‖ *These scissors are expressly designed for left-handed people.* このはさみは，左利きの人用に特別に設計されている．

**expressway** /ɪksprésweɪ/ 米 = **MOTORWAY**

**expulsion** /ɪkspʌ́lʃ(ə)n/ 名 **❸ Ⓤ** ▶定義 the act of making sb leave a place or an institution ～をある場所または組織から去らせること→**排除，追放，除名** ‖ *There have been three expulsions from school this year.* 今年は3名の放校処分があった． ☞ 動 expel

**exquisite** /ékskwɪzət, ékskwɪzət/ 形 ▶定義 extremely beautiful and pleasing 極度に美しく，好ましい→**極めて見事な，非常に美しい，優雅な** ‖ *She has an exquisite face.* 彼女は非常に美しい顔をしている． *I think that ring is exquisite.* その指輪はとても見事だ．

**ext** 略 extension number of a telephone→**内線番号** ‖ *ext 3492* 内線番号3492

*★**extend** /ɪksténd/ 動 ▶定義1 Ⓤ to make sth longer or larger (in space or time) (空間や時間において)～をより長くまたは大きくする→**～を延長する，拡大する，拡張する，広げる** ‖ *Could you extend your visit for a few days?* 滞在を数日延長できませんか． *We're planning to extend the back of the house to give us more space.* もっと空間を取るために，家の裏を拡張しようと計画している． *Since my injury I can't extend this leg fully (= make it completely straight).* けがをして以来，足を完全に伸ばすこと (= 完全にまっすぐにすること) ができない． ▶定義2 **目 Ⓤ** to cover the area or period of time mentioned 言及されている地域または期間をカバーする→(～に) **わたる，及ぶ，広がる** ‖ *The desert extends over a huge area of the country.* 砂漠はその国の広大な地域に広がっている． *The company is planning to extend its operations into Asia.* 会社は事業をアジアに広げようと計画しているところだ． ▶定義3 Ⓤ 正式 to offer sth to sb ～を…に提供する→**～を…に及ぼす，施す** ‖ *to extend hospitality/a warm welcome/an invitation to sb* ～に親切にする・～を歓迎する・～を招待する

**extension** /ɪksténʃ(ə)n/ 名 **❸** ▶定義1 an extra period of time that you are allowed for sth ～について許された追加の期間→**延長** ‖ *I've applied for an extension to my work permit.* 労働許可の延長を申し込んだ． ▶定義2 a part that is added to a building 建物に追加される部分→**拡張箇所，建て増し部分** ‖ *They're building an extension on the hospital.* 彼らは病院の拡張工事をしている． ▶定義3 a telephone that is connected to a central phone in a house or to a central point (switchboard) in a large office building 家庭の中心の電話，または大きな事務所内の中心点(電話交換盤)につながれた電話→**内線** ‖ *What's your extension number?* 内線番号は何番ですか． *Can I have extension 4342, please?* 内線4342につないでもらえますか．

**extensive** /ɪksténsɪv/ 形 ▶定義 large in area or amount 面積または量の大きい→**広い，大規模の，大量の** ‖ *The house has extensive grounds.* その家には広い敷地がある． *Most of the buildings suffered extensive damage.* 建物のほとんどが，大きな被害を受けた．— extensively 副→**広く，広範囲にわたって**

*★**extent** /ɪkstént/ 名 Ⓤ ▶定義 the extent of sth the length, area, size or importance of sth ～の長さ，面積，大きさまたは重要性→**程度，範囲** ‖ *I was amazed at the extent of his knowledge.* 私は彼の知識の深さに驚いた． *The **full extent of***

the damage is not yet known. 被害の全容はまだ分かっていない. ▶定義 **成句 to a certain/to some extent** ▶定義 used to show that sth is only partly true 〜が部分的にのみ正しいことを示すのに用いられて→**ある程度** ‖ *I agree with you to a certain extent but there are still a lot of points I disagree with.* ある程度君に賛成だが, まだ同意できない点がたくさんある.

**to what extent** ▶定義 how far; how much どこまで; どのくらいたくさん→**どの程度** ‖ *I'm not sure to what extent I believe her.* 私は自分がどの程度彼女を信じているのか分からない.

**exterior**[1] /ɪkstíəriər/ 形 ▶定義 on the outside 外側の→**外部の, 外側の, 外面の** ‖ *the exterior walls of a house* 家の外壁 ⇔ **interior**

**exterior**[2] /ɪkstíəriər/ 名 C ▶定義 the outside of sth; the appearance of sb/sth 〜の外側; 〜の外見→**外観, 外部** ‖ *The exterior of the house is fine but inside it isn't in very good condition.* 家の外部は申し分ないが, 内部はあまり良い状態ではない. *Despite his calm exterior, Steve suffers badly from stress.* 外見は落ち着いているが, スティーヴはひどくストレスにさいなまれている.

**exterminate** /ɪkstə́ːmənèɪt/ 動 他 ▶定義 to kill a large group of people or animals 人や動物の大きな集団を殺す→**〜を絶滅させる, 根絶する, 皆殺しにする** ‖ *Once cockroaches infest a building, they are very hard to exterminate.* ゴキブリは一度はびこると, 駆除するのはとても難しい. — extermination /ɪkstə̀ːmənéɪʃ(ə)n/ 名 U →**絶滅, 皆殺し, 駆除**

★**external** /ekstə́ːml/ 形 ▶定義1 connected with the outside of sth 〜の外側に関した→**外部の, 外の** ‖ *The cream is for external use only (= to be used on the skin).* そのクリームは外用だ（＝皮膚に使われるべき）. ▶定義2 coming from another place ほかの場所から来る→**外からの, 外部の** ‖ *You will be tested by an external examiner.* 君は外部の試験官にテストされる. ⇔ **internal**

**extinct** /ɪkstíŋ(k)t/ 形 ▶定義1 (used about a type of animal, plant, etc) no longer existing (ある種の動物, 植物などについて) もはや存在しない→**絶滅した, 死に絶えた** ‖ *Tigers are nearly extinct in the wild.* 野生のトラはほとんど絶滅している. ▶定義2 (used about a volcano) no longer active (火山について) もはや活動していない→**活動を停止した** — extinction /ɪkstíŋ(k)ʃ(ə)n/ 名 U →**絶滅, 死滅, 消滅, 廃止** ‖ *The giant panda is in danger of extinction.* ジャイアントパンダは絶滅の危機にある.

**extinguish** /ɪkstíŋgwɪʃ/ 動 他 正式 ▶定義 to cause sth to stop burning 〜が燃えるのを止める→**〜を消す** ‖ *The fire was extinguished very quickly.* 火は非常に素早く消し止められた. ☛ より略式の表現に put out がある. — extinguisher = **FIRE EXTINGUISHER**

**extort** /ɪkstɔ́ːrt/ 動 他 正式 ▶定義 extort sth (from sb) to get sth by using threats or violence 脅しや暴力を用いて〜を得る→**〜を（人から）ゆすり取る, 〜を（人に）無理強いする** ‖ *The gang were found guilty of extorting money from small businesses.* ギャングは小さな会社から金をゆすり取った件で有罪になった. — extortion 名 U →**ゆすり, 強要**

**extortionate** /ɪkstɔ́ːrʃ(ə)nət, -nèɪt/ 形 ▶定義 (used especially about prices) much too high (特に価格について) あまりにも高い→**法外な**

★**extra**[1] /ékstrə/ 形副 ▶定義 more than is usual, expected, or than exists already 普通より, 予期されるより, または既に存在するものより多い→**余分の, 割り増しの** ‖ *I'll need some extra money for the holidays.* 休日に余分な金が必要になるだろう. '*What size is this sweater?' 'Extra large.*' 「このセーターのサイズはいくらですか」「エキストララージ［特大］です」 *'Is wine included in the price of the meal or is it extra?'* 「ワインは食事代に含まれているの. それとも追加料金なの」 *I tried to be extra nice to him yesterday because it was his birthday.* 昨日は彼の誕生日だったので, いつもより彼に優しくしようと努めた.

**extra**[2] /ékstrə/ 名 C ▶定義1 something that costs more, or that is not normally included 余計にかかる, または通常含まれていないもの→**割り増し料金, 割り増し料金の必要なもの** ‖ *Optional extras such as colour printer, scanner and modem are available on top of the basic package.* カラープリンター, スキャナー, モデムのような追加料金の必要なオプション品は, 基本パッケージと別にあります. ▶定義2 a person in a film, etc who has a small unimportant part, for example in a crowd 映画などに登場する,例えば群衆の中にいるような小さな重要でない役の人➔エキストラ

**extract**[1] /ɪkstrækt/ 動他 正式 ▶定義 to take sth out, especially with difficulty 特に困難を伴って,～を取り出す➔～を引き抜く,抜き取る,抽出する,引き出す ‖ *I think this tooth will have to be extracted.* この歯は抜かなければならないだろう. *I wasn't able to extract an apology from her.* 彼女から謝罪の言葉を引き出すことはできなかった.

**extract**[2] /ékstrækt/ 名 C ▶定義 a part of a book, piece of music, etc, that has often been specially chosen to show sth しばしば～を示すために特別に選ばれた,本や曲などの一部➔引用,抜粋 ‖ *The newspaper published extracts from the controversial novel.* 新聞は,議論の的となっている小説の抜粋を載せた.

**extraction** /ɪkstrækʃ(ə)n/ 名 正式 ▶定義 1 C U the act of taking sth out ～を取り出すこと➔引き抜き,抽出,抜き取り ‖ *extraction of salt from the sea.* 海水から塩を抽出すること *Dentists report that children are requiring fewer extractions.* 歯医者は子供たちが抜かねばならない歯の数が以前よりも減っていると報告している. ▶定義 2 U family origin 家族の起源➔血統,系統 ‖ *He's an American but he's of Italian extraction.* 彼はアメリカ人だが,イタリア系だ.

**extra-curricular** /ékstrə kərɪ́kjələr/ 形 ▶定義 not part of the normal course of studies (**curriculum**) in a school or college 学校や大学の正規の講座(カリキュラム)の一部でない➔課外の ‖ *The school offers many extra-curricular activities such as sport, music, drama, etc.* その学校は,スポーツ,音楽,演劇など多くの課外活動を提供している.

**extradite** /ékstrədaɪt/ 動他 ▶定義 to send a person who may be guilty of a crime from the country in which he/she is living to the country which wants to put him/her on trial for the crime 有罪かもしれない人を,住んでいる国から,その罪に関して法廷に出廷させたい国に送る➔～を引き渡す,送還する ‖ *The suspected terrorists were captured in Spain and extradited to France.* テロの容疑者はスペインで逮捕され,フランスに引き渡された. ― extradition /èkstrədɪ́ʃ(ə)n/ 名 C U ➔引き渡し,送還

### extreme 583

*****extraordinary** /ɪkstrɔ́ːrd(ə)n(ə)ri, èkstrəɔ́ːr-; -dnèri/ 形 ▶定義 1 very unusual 非常に変わった➔並外れた,風変わりな,非凡な ‖ *She has an extraordinary ability to whistle and sing at the same time.* 彼女は口笛を吹きながら歌うという風変わりな能力がある. ▶定義 2 not what you would expect in a particular situation; very strange ある特定の状況で普通期待することとは異なった;非常に奇妙な➔突飛な,異常な ‖ *That was extraordinary behaviour for a teacher!* それは教師としては異常な行為でした. ⇔ **ordinary** ― extraordinarily 副 ➔異常に,並外れて ‖ *He was an extraordinarily talented musician.* 彼は人並み外れた才能のある音楽家だった.

**extravagant** /ɪkstrǽvəgənt/ 形 ▶定義 1 spending or costing too much money あまりにも多くの金を費やす,金のかかる➔浪費する,ぜいたくな ‖ *He's terribly extravagant - he travels everywhere by taxi.* 彼はひどい浪費家だ ― どこへでもタクシーで行く. *an extravagant present* ぜいたくな贈り物 ▶定義 2 exaggerated; more than is usual, true or necessary おおげさな;普通以上の,実際以上の,または必要以上の➔度を越した,突飛な,むちゃな ‖ *The advertisements made extravagant claims for the new medicine.* 広告はその新薬について行き過ぎた主張をしていた. ― extravagance 名 C U ➔ぜいたく,浪費 ― extravagantly 副 ➔ぜいたくに,法外に

*****extreme** /ɪkstríːm/ 形 ▶定義 1 (名詞の前だけ) the greatest or strongest possible 可能な限り最大の,または最強の➔極度の ‖ *You must take extreme care when driving at night.* 夜運転するときには,極度の注意を払わなくてはならない. *extreme heat/difficulty/poverty* 極度の熱さ・困難・貧困 ▶定義 2 much stronger than is considered usual, acceptable, etc 普通の,受け入れられるものなどよりずっと強い➔過激な,極端な ‖ *Her extreme views on immigration are shocking to most people.* 移民についての彼女の極端な意見は,ほとんどの人にとって衝撃的だ. ▶定義 3 (名詞の前だけ) as far away as possible from the centre in the direction mentioned 述べられた方向で,中央からできる限り遠く離れた➔一番端の,先端の ‖ *There could be snow in the extreme north of the country.* 国の最北端で

は雪が降ることもあるだろう. *politicians on the extreme left of the party* 党の極左派の政治家 ☛参 **moderate**, **radical** — extreme ◪ ◉ 定義 極端なもの, 極度 ‖ *Alex used to be very shy but now she's gone to the opposite extreme.* アレックスは非常に恥ずかしがり屋だったが, 今では正反対だ.

**extremely** /ɪkstríːmli/ 副 ▶定義 very とても→極めて, 極端に ‖ *Listen carefully because this is extremely important.* これは極めて重要なので, 注意深く聞いてください.

**extreme sport** 名 ◉ ▶定義 a very dangerous sport or activity which some people do for fun ある人々が遊びでする非常に危険な運動または活動→過激なスポーツ, エクストリームスポーツ ‖ *The first day of the extreme sports championships featured white-water rafting.* 過激なスポーツ大会の初日は急流下りだった.

**extremist** /ɪkstríːmɪst/ 名 ◉ ▶定義 a person who has extreme political opinions 極端な政治的見解を持つ人→過激派, 過激主義者 ☛参 **moderate**, **radical** — extremism 名 ◎ →過激, 過激主義

**extremity** /ɪkstrémətɪ/ 名 ◉ ( 複 **extremities**) ▶定義 the part of sth that is furthest from the center ～の中心から最も遠い部分→先端, 末端

**extricate** /ékstrəkèɪt/ 動 他 ▶定義 to manage to free sb/sth from a difficult situation or position ～を困難な状況や位置からどうにかして自由にする→～を救出する, 助け出す ‖ *I finally managed to extricate myself from the meeting by saying that I had a train to catch.* 私は電車に間に合わないからと言って, やっと打ち合わせの席から脱出した.

**extrovert** /ékstrəvə̀ːrt/ 名 ◉ ▶定義 a person who is confident and full of life and who prefers being with other people to being alone 自信があって元気一杯の, 独りでいるよりほかの人々と一緒にいる方を好む人→社交家, 外向性の人 ⇔ **introvert**

**exuberant** /ɪɡzjúːb(ə)rənt; -zúː-/ 形 ▶定義 (used about a person or his/her behaviour) full of energy and excitement (人やその行為について) 活力や興奮で一杯の→活気のある, 元気な — exuberance 名 ◎ →活気, 元気

★**eye**¹ /áɪ/ 名 ◉ ▶定義1 one of the two organs of your body that you use to see with 見るのに使う身体の2つの器官のうちの1つ→目 ‖ *She opened/closed her eyes.* 彼女は目を開けた・閉じた. *He's got blue eyes.* 彼は青い目をしている. ☛ C5ページのさし絵

▶目を殴られると, 目の周りに **black eye** (あざ) ができる. 素早く両目を閉じてから, 開けることを, **blink** (まばたきする) と言う. 片方の目を速く閉じて, 開けることを, **wink** (ウインクする) と言う.

▶定義2 the ability to see sth ～を見る力→視力, 視覚, 眼力, 眼識 ‖ *He has sharp eyes* (= he can see very well). 彼は視力が良い (= とてもよく見ることができる). *She has an eye for detail* (= she notices small details). 彼女は細かいところに目が届く (= 細かいところに気が付く). ▶定義3 the hole at one end of a needle that the thread goes through 針の一方の端にある糸を通す穴→針の穴

成句 **an eye for an eye** ▶定義 used to say that you should punish sb by doing to him/her what he/she has done to sb else ある人がほかの人にした事を, そのままその人にすることで, 懲らしめるべきだと言うときに用いて→目には目を

**as far as the eye can see** ⇒ **FAR**²

**be up to your eyes in sth** 略式 ▶定義 to have more of sth than you can easily do or manage 簡単にはできないほど, またはどうにもできないほど～にかかわった→～に没頭している, 忙殺されている ‖ *I can't come out with you tonight - I'm up to my eyes in work.* 今夜は君と出掛けられない - 仕事にはまり込んでいるのだ.

**before sb's very eyes** ▶定義 in front of sb so that he/she can clearly see what is happening 何が起きているかがはっきりと分かるくらい, ～の面前で→～の見ている前で, 公然と

**cast an eye/your eye(s) over sb/sth** ⇒ **CAST**¹

**catch sb's attention/eye** ⇒ **CATCH**¹

**cry your eyes out** ⇒ **CRY**¹

**have (got) your eye on sb** ▶定義 to watch sb carefully to make sure that he/she does nothing wrong 何も悪い事をしないように～を注意深く見る→～を見張る

**have (got) your eye on sth** ▶定義 to be thinking about buying sth ～を買うことを考えてい

る→~に目を付ける ‖ *I've got my eye on a suit that I saw in the sales.* セールで見たスーツに目を付けている．

in the eyes of sb/in sb's eyes ▶定義 in the opinion of sb ～の意見で→～の見るところでは，～の考えでは ‖ *She was still a child in her mother's eyes.* 母親から見れば，彼女はまだ子供だった．

in the public eye ⇒ **PUBLIC**¹

keep an eye on sb/sth ▶定義 to make sure that sb/sth is safe; to look after sb/sth ～が安全であるようにする；～の面倒を見る→～を見張る，～から目を離さない ‖ *Please could you keep an eye on the house while we're away?* 私たちが出掛けている間，家を見ていてもらえますでしょうか．

keep an eye open/out (for sb/sth) ▶定義 to watch or look out for sb/sth ～を警戒する，または捜す→～を見張っている，目を皿のようにして捜す ‖ *I've lost my ring - could you keep an eye out for it?* 指輪をなくしました － 捜してもらえますか．

keep your eyes peeled/skinned (for sb/sth) ▶定義 to watch carefully for sb/sth ～を注意深く見る→～に気を付けている，目を光らせる，注意している ‖ *Keep your eyes peeled for the turning to the village.* 村への曲がり角に気を付けていて．

look sb in the eye ⇒ **LOOK**¹
the naked eye ⇒ **NAKED**
not bat an eye ⇒ **BAT**²
see eye to eye (with sb) ⇒ **SEE**
set eyes on sb/sth ⇒ **SET**¹
turn a blind eye ⇒ **BLIND**¹

with your eyes open ▶定義 knowing what you are doing 自分がしている事が分かっている→承知の上で ‖ *You went into the new job with your eyes open, so you can't complain now.* 承知の上で新しい仕事に就いたのだから，不平は言えないよ．

**eye**² /áɪ/ 動 他 (現分 **eyeing** または **eying**; 過, 過分 **eyed**) ▶定義 to look at sb/sth closely ～を注意深く見る→～をよく見る，じろじろ見る ‖ *She eyed him with suspicion.* 彼女は疑いの目で彼をじろじろ見た．

**eyeball** /áɪbɔ̀ːl/ 名 C ▶定義 the whole of your eye (including the part which is hidden inside the head) (頭部内に隠れた部分も含んで)目全体→眼球

**eyebrow** /áɪbràʊ/ 名 C ▶定義 the line of hair that is above your eye 目の上にある毛の線→まゆ毛，まゆ ☞ C5ページのさし絵

成句 raise your eyebrows ⇒ **RAISE**

**eye-catching** 形 ▶定義 (used about a thing) attracting your attention immediately because it is interesting, bright or pretty (物について)面白い，明るい，またはきれいなために，すぐに注意をひくような→人目をひく

**eyeglasses** /áɪɡlæ̀sɪz, -glæ̀s-/ 米 = **GLASSES**

**eyelash** /áɪlæ̀ʃ/ (または **lash**) 名 C ▶定義 one of the hairs that grow on the edges of your eyelids まぶたの端に生えた毛の1本→まつげ ☞ C5ページのさし絵

**eye level** 形 ▶定義 at the same height as sb's eyes when he/she is standing up ～が立ったときに，目と同じ高さにある→目の高さの ‖ *an eye-level grill* 目の高さの格子窓口

**eyelid** /áɪlɪ̀d/ (または **lid**) 名 C ▶定義 the piece of skin that can move to cover your eye 目を覆うために動かす皮膚の一部→まぶた ☞ C5ページのさし絵

成句 not bat an eyelid ⇒ **BAT**²

**eye-opener** 名 C ▶定義 something that makes you realize the truth about sth ～についての真実に気付かせるようなもの→はっとさせる事実，目をみはらせるような事 ‖ *That television programme about the inner cities was a real eye-opener.* スラム地区に関するテレビ番組にははっとさせられた．

**eyeshadow** /áɪʃæ̀doʊ/ 名 U ▶定義 colour that is put on the skin above the eyes to make them look more attractive 目の上の皮膚に乗せて，目をより魅力的に見せるための色→アイシャドー

**eyesight** /áɪsàɪt/ 名 U ▶定義 the ability to see 見る能力→視力 ‖ *good/poor eyesight* 良い・悪い視力

**eyesore** /áɪsɔ̀ːr/ 名 C ▶定義 something that is ugly and unpleasant to look at 醜く，見ると不快な物→目障り(な物) ‖ *All this litter in the streets is a real eyesore.* 通りに散乱したごみが本当に目障りだ．

**eyewitness** /áɪwɪ̀tnəs/ = **WITNESS**¹(1)

# F f

**F, f¹** /ef/ 名 C (複 **F's; f's**) ▶定義 the sixth letter of the English alphabet 英語アルファベットの第6文字→f(F)が表す音, f(F)の文字, f(F)の字形のもの ‖ *'Father' begins with (an) 'F'*. Father はFで始まる.

**F²** ▶定義 1 Fahrenheit→華氏 ‖ *Water freezes at 32°F.* 水は華氏32度 [32°F] で凍る. ▶定義 2 (または **fem**) female; feminine→女性, 雌, 女性の

**FA** /ˌef ˈeɪ/ 名 医 the Football Association→サッカー協会 ‖ *the FA Cup* FA杯

**fable** /ˈfeɪbl/ 名 C ▶定義 a short story that teaches a lesson (a moral) and that often has animals as the main characters 教訓(道徳)を教え, しばしば動物が主人公として登場する短い物語→寓(ぐう)話, 例え話 ‖ *Aesop's fables* イソップ物語

**fabric** /ˈfæbrɪk/ 名 ▶定義 1 C U (a type of) cloth or soft material that is used for making clothes, curtains, etc 衣類やカーテンなどを作るために使われる(ような種類の)布, または柔らかい生地→布地, 織物, 織地 ‖ *cotton fabrics* 綿織物 ▶定義 2 [単数扱い] the basic structure of a building or system 建物や組織の基本構造→枠組み, 骨組み, 構造, 組織 ‖ *The Industrial Revolution changed the fabric of society.* 産業革命によって社会の基本構造が変わった.

**fabulous** /ˈfæbjələs/ 形 ▶定義 1 very good; excellent 非常に良い; 優れた→すばらしい, すてきな, わくわくする ‖ *It was a fabulous concert.* それはすばらしいコンサートだった. ▶定義 2 very great 非常に際立った→途方もない, ものすごい, 驚くべき, とてつもない, 信じ難い ‖ *fabulous wealth/riches/beauty* ものすごい財産・巨万の富・驚くべき美しさ

**façade** (または **facade**) /fəˈsɑːd, fæ-/ 名 C ▶定義 1 the front wall of a large building that you see from the outside 外側から見える, 大きな建物の正面の壁→(建物の)正面, 前面, ファサード ▶定義 2 the way sb/sth appears to be, which is not the way he/she/it really is 実際の在り方とは異なる〜の見え方→外見, 上辺, 見掛け, 見せ掛け, 体裁 ‖ *His good humour was just a façade.* 彼の機嫌の良さは見せ掛けにすぎなかった.

**★face¹** /feɪs/ 名 C ▶定義 1 the front part of your head; the expression that is shown on it 頭部の前面の部分; そこに表れる表情→顔, 顔面, 顔付き, 顔色, 表情 ‖ *Go and wash your face.* 顔を洗ってきなさい. *She has a very pretty face.* 彼女はとてもかわいらしい顔をしている. *He came in with a smile on his face.* 彼は顔に笑みを浮かべて入ってきた. *Her face lit up (= showed happiness) when John came into the room.* ジョンが部屋に入ってくると, 彼女の顔は輝いた(= 幸せそうな表情をした). ▶定義 2 the front or one side of sth 〜の前面または一方の面→表面, 正面, 表側, (器具などの)使用面 ‖ *the north face of the mountain* その山の北面 *He put the cards face up/down on the table.* 彼はカードの表を上・下にしてテーブルに置いた. *a clock face* 時計の文字盤 ☞ **clock** のさし絵 ▶定義 3 **-faced** (複合形容詞を作るために用いて) having the type of face or expression mentioned 言及されたような顔や表情をしている→〜のような顔をした, 〜の顔の, 〜の表情の ‖ *red/round/sour-faced* 赤い・丸い・不機嫌な顔をした

成句 **face to face (with sb/sth)** ▶定義 close to and looking at sb/sth 〜に近付いて見ている→〜と近くで向かい合って, 面と向かって, 差し向かいで, 直面して

**keep a straight face** ⇒ **STRAIGHT¹**

**lose face** ⇒ **LOSE**

**make/pull faces/a face (at sb/sth)** ▶定義 to make an expression that shows that you do not like sb/sth 〜が好きではないという表情をする→嫌な顔をする, 顔をしかめる, 顔をゆがめる, しかめっ面をする ‖ *When she saw what was for dinner she pulled a face.* 彼女は夕食に出された物を見て顔をしかめた.

**make/pull faces** ▶定義 to make rude expressions with your face 顔に不作法な表情を浮かべる→こっけいな顔をする, 妙な顔をする, 嫌な顔をしてみせる ‖ *The children made faces behind the teacher's back.* 子供たちは先生の背後でこっけいな顔をした.

**save face** ⇒ **SAVE¹**

**to sb's face** ▶定義 if you say sth to sb's face, you do it when that person is with you 〜を言う場合, その相手の人と一緒にいるときに言う→〜に面と向かって, 直接, 公然と ‖ *I wanted to say that I was sorry to her face, not on the* *phone.* 私は彼女に電話ではなく，面と向かって謝りたかった． ⇔ **behind sb's back**

***face**[2] /féɪs/ [動][他] ▶定義**1** to have your face or front pointing towards sb/sth or in a particular direction 顔や体の前面を～に向ける，または特定の方向に向ける➜**～に顔を向ける，面する，向く，向かう** ‖ *The garden faces south.* その庭は南向きだ. *Can you all face the front, please?* どうぞ皆さん前を向いてください. ▶定義**2** to have to deal with sth unpleasant; to deal with sb in a difficult situation 不快な～を処理しなければならない; 困難な状況で～に対処しなければならない➜**～に真っ向から向かう，立ち向かう，対抗する，直面する，～を直視する，～と正面から話し合う** ‖ *I can't face another argument.* 私はさらに議論をする気はない. *He couldn't face going to work yesterday - he felt too ill.* 昨日彼はどうしても仕事に行くことができなかった－ひどく気分が悪かったのだ. ▶定義**3** to need attention or action from sb ～の注意や行動を必要とする➜**（困難，問題，危険などが）～に迫る，差し迫る，現れる，直面する** ‖ *There are several problems facing the government.* 政府に差し迫っている問題がいくつかある. *We are faced with a difficult decision.* 私たちは難しい決定を迫られている.

[成句] **let's face it** [略式] ▶定義 we must accept it as true それを真実として受け入れなければならない➜ **（嫌な事でも）事実は事実として認めよう，現実を直視しよう，大変だが頑張ろう** ‖ *Let's face it, we can't afford a holiday this year.* やむを得ない，私たちは今年休暇を取るのは無理だ.

[句動詞] **face up to sth** ▶定義 to accept a difficult or unpleasant situation and do sth about it 困難な，または不快な状況を受け入れ，それに対して～をする➜**現実を直視して～に立ち向かう，～に真っ正面から対抗する，～を受け入れる，認める** ‖ *She had to face up to the fact that she was wrong.* 彼女は自分が間違っていたという事実を受け入れなければならなかった.

**facecloth** /féɪsklɒ(ː)θ, -klɔ̀θ/ (または **flannel**) [名] [C] ▶定義 a small square towel that is used for washing the face, hands, etc 顔や手などを洗うために用いられる小さな四角いタオル➜**洗面用手ぬぐい，洗面用タオル**

**faceless** /féɪsləs/ [形] ▶定義 without individual character or identity １人１人の特性や個性がない➜**特徴のない，個性を欠いた，主体性のない** ‖ *faceless civil servants* 個性のない公務員

**facelift** /féɪslɪft/ [名] [C] ▶定義 a medical operation that makes your face look younger 顔を若く見せるための手術➜**顔のしわ取り手術，顔の若返り術，美容整形** ☛参 **plastic surgery**

**facet** /fǽsət/ [名] [C] ▶定義**1** one part or particular aspect of sth ～の一部またはある特定の局面➜**（物事の）面，側面，相，様相** ‖ *There are many facets to this argument (= points that must be considered).* この議論には多くの側面（= 考慮されるべき点）がある. ▶定義**2** one side of a precious stone 宝石の一面➜**（結晶体，宝石などの）小面，（ガラスの）切り子面，ファセット**

**facetious** /fəsíːʃəs/ [形] ▶定義 trying to be amusing about a subject or at a time that is not appropriate so that other people become annoyed ある話題について，またはふさわしくないときに面白くしようとしていて，そのためにほかの人が不快になる➜**ふざけた，こっけいな，おどけた，冗談の（つもりの）** ‖ *He kept making facetious remarks during the lecture.* 彼は講義の間ずっと，ふざけた事ばかり言い続けていた.
— **facetiously** [副] ➜**ふざけて，こっけいに，冗談のつもりで**

**face value** [名] [[U]，単数扱い] ▶定義 the cost or value that is shown on the front of stamps, coins, etc 切手や硬貨などの表面に示されている代価あるいは価値➜**額面（価格），券面額**

[成句] **take sb/sth at (its, his, etc) face value** ▶定義 to accept sb/sth as it, he, etc appears to be ～を見掛け通りに受け入れる➜**～を額面通りに受け取る，そっくり信用する** ‖ *Don't take his story at face value. There's something he hasn't told us yet.* 彼の話をそっくり信用してはいけない. まだ彼が私たちに話していない事があるから.

**facial** /féɪʃ(ə)l/ [形] ▶定義 connected with a person's face 人の顔に関連した➜**顔の，顔面の，顔に用いる，顔用の** ‖ *a facial expression* 顔の表情 *facial hair* 顔の毛

**facile** /fǽsàɪl; -əl/ [形] ▶定義 (used about a comment, argument, etc) not carefully thought out （論評や議論などについて）注意深く検討されていない➜**安易すぎる，深みのない，たやすく得られる，いいかげんな**

**facilitate** /fəsílətèɪt/ 動 中 正式 ▶定義 to make sth possible or easier ～を可能にする、または簡単にする→～を容易にする，促進する，助長する，促す

\***facility** /fəsíləti/ 名 (複 **facilities**) ▶定義 **1 facilities** [複数扱い] a service, building, piece of equipment, etc that makes it possible to do sth ～を行うことを可能にするサービス，建物，設備など→便，便宜，設備，施設，機関‖ *Our town has excellent sports facilities (= a stadium, swimming pool, etc).* 私たちの町には一流のスポーツ施設（＝競技場，プールなど）がある．

▶定義 **2** C an extra function or ability that a machine, etc may have 機械などに備わっている，追加の機能や性能→機能，手段‖ *This word processor has a facility for checking spelling.* このワープロにはスペルチェックの機能がある．

**facsimile** /fæksíməli/ 名 C U ▶定義 an exact copy of a picture, piece of writing, etc 絵や文書などの正確な複写→複製，複写，模写，コピー
→参 fax

\***fact** /fækt/ 名 ▶定義 **1** C something that you know has happened or is true 起こった，または真実であると分かっている物事→事実，実際，現実に起こった事‖ *It is a scientific fact that light travels faster than sound.* 光が音より高速に伝わるということは科学的事実である． *We need to know all the facts before we can decide.* 私たちは決定する前にすべての事実を知る必要がある． *I know **for a fact** that Peter wasn't ill yesterday.* 昨日，ピーターが本当に病気でなかったことを私は知っている． ***The fact that** I am older than you makes no difference at all.* 私の方があなたよりも年上であるという事実があるからといって変わる事は何もない． *You must **face facts** and accept that he has gone.* あなたは彼が去ったのだという事実に向き合い，受け入れなければならない． ▶定義 **2** U true things; reality 真実の事；真実性→本当の事，実際の事・真実・現実，事実であること‖ *The film is based on fact.* この映画は事実に基づいている． ⇔ **fiction**
成句 **as a matter of fact** ⇒ **MATTER**[1]
**the fact (of the matter) is (that)...** ▶定義 the truth is that... 真実は～だ→実は～だ，真相は～だ，実際は～だ‖ *I would love a car, but the fact is that I just can't afford one.* 私は車が大好きだが，実際は車を買う余裕がない．

**facts and figures** ▶定義 detailed information 詳しい情報→正確な情報，正確な詳細，明細‖ *Before we make a decision, we need some more facts and figures.* 決定する前に，詳しい情報がもう少し必要だ．

**a fact of life** ▶定義 something unpleasant that you must accept because you cannot change it 変えることができないので，受け入れなければならない不快な物事→人生の（避け難い）現実，現状‖ *Most people now see unemployment as just another fact of life.* 今では大多数の人が失業を人生の現実の1つにすぎないと見ている．

**the facts of life** ▶定義 the details of sexual behaviour and how babies are born 性行動と子供がどのようにして生まれるかについての詳細→生の実態，性に関する事実，性の知識

**hard facts** ⇒ **HARD**[1]

**in (actual) fact** ▶定義 **1** (used for emphasizing that sth is true) really; actually （～が真実であると強調するために用いて）本当に；実際に→実際に，事実上，実は，それどころか本当は‖ *I thought the lecture would be boring but in actual fact it was rather interesting.* その講義は退屈だろうと思っていたが，実際はむしろ面白かった．
▶定義 **2** used for introducing more detailed information より詳しい情報を持ち出す場合に用いられる→要するに，つまり，もっとはっきり言えば‖ *It was cold. In fact it was freezing.* 寒かった．それどころか凍りつきそうだった．

**factor** /fǽktər/ 名 C ▶定義 **1** one of the things that influences a decision, situation, etc 決定や状況などに影響する物事の1つ→要因，要素‖ *His unhappiness at home was a major factor in his decision to go abroad.* 家庭で不幸だったことが，彼が海外へ行く決心をした主な要因だった． ▶定義 **2** （専門用語）(in mathematics) a whole number (except 1) by which a larger number can be divided（数学で）それによってより大きい数を割り切れるすべての数（1を除く）→因数，約数‖ *2, 3, 4 and 6 are factors of 12.* 2，3，4，6は12の約数である．

\***factory** /fǽkt(ə)ri/ 名 C (複 **factories**) ▶定義 a building or group of buildings where goods are made in large quantities by machine 機械によって商品が大量に作られている建物，または建

物の集まり→**工場, 製造所, 製作所**

**factual** /fǽktʃuəl/ 形 ▶定義 based on or containing things that are true or real 真実や本当である物事に基づいた, またはそのような物事を含んでいる→**事実の, 事実についての, 実際の, 事実に基づく** ‖ *a factual account of the events* その出来事についての事実に基づく説明 ☞参 **fictional**

**faculty** /fǽk(ə)lti/ 名 ⓒ (複 **faculties**) ▶定義 1 one of the natural abilities of a person's body or mind 人の体や心の, 持って生まれた能力の1つ1つ→**能力, 機能** ‖ *the faculty of hearing/sight/speech* 聴覚機能・視覚機能・言語機能 ▶定義 2 (または **Faculty**) one department in a university, college, etc 総合大学や単科大学などの一学部→**学部** ‖ *the Faculty of Law/Arts* 法学部・教養学部 ☞ Faculty は, 総合大学や単科大学の学部の教授陣を表すこともあり, その場合は単数形または複数形の動詞と共に用いられる. *The Faculty has/have been invited to the meeting.* 教団はその会合に招かれた.

**fad** /fæd/ 名 ⓒ略式 ▶定義 a fashion, interest, etc that will probably not last long おそらく長くは続かないであろう流行や関心など→**一時的流行, 一時的熱狂, 気まぐれ, 気まぐれな熱中, 物好き**

\*****fade** /feɪd/ 動 ▶定義 1 自他 to become or make sth become lighter in colour or less strong or fresh 〜の色が薄くなる, 〜が弱まる, あるいは新鮮でなくなる, または〜をそのようにする→**薄れる, 色あせる, 衰える, しおれる, 〜を薄れさせる, 〜の色をあせさせる, 〜を衰えさせる, しおれさせる** ‖ *Jeans fade when you wash them.* ジーンズは洗うと色が落ちる. *Look how the sunlight has faded these curtains.* 日光によってこのカーテンがどれほど色あせたか見てください. ▶定義 2 自 **fade (away)** to disappear slowly (from sight, hearing, memory, etc) (視界, 聞こえる範囲, 記憶などから) ゆっくりと消える→**次第に消えていく, 見えなくなる, 薄れていく, 衰える** ‖ *The cheering of the crowd faded away.* 群衆の歓声が次第に消えていった. *The smile faded from his face.* 彼の顔から笑みが消えた.

**faeces** (米 **feces**) /fíːsɪz/ 名 [複数扱い] (専門用語) ▶定義 the solid waste material that you get rid of when you go to the toilet トイレに行ったときに排せつする固体の老廃物→**大便, 糞便 (ふんべん), 排せつ物**

---

**fail¹** 589

**fag** /fæg/ 名 英 ▶定義 1 ⓒ (俗語) a cigarette たばこ→**紙巻きたばこ** ▶定義 2 [単数扱い] 略式 a piece of work that you do not want to do やりたくない仕事→**面倒な仕事, 嫌な仕事, 骨折り仕事, 雑用** ‖ *I've got to wash the car. What a fag!* 車を洗わなければならない. 面倒だ.

**Fahrenheit** /fǽrənhaɪt, fǽ-/ 名 Ⓤ (略 **F**) ▶定義 the name of a scale which measures temperatures 温度を計る単位の名前→**華氏, 華氏温度** ‖ *Water freezes at 32° Fahrenheit (32°F).* 水は華氏32度[32°F]で凍る. ☞参 **Celsius**

\*****fail¹** /feɪl/ 動 ▶定義 1 自他 to not be successful in sth 〜に成功しない→**〜に失敗する, しくじる, うまくいかない, 〜できない** ‖ *She failed her driving test.* 彼女は運転免許試験に失敗した. *I feel that I've failed - I'm 25 and I still haven't got a steady job.* 私はしくじったような気がする — 25歳なのにいまだに安定した職に就いていないので. ☞参 **pass, succeed** ▶定義 2 他 to decide that sb is not successful in a test, exam, etc テストや試験などで〜が合格していないと決定する→**〜を落第させる, 不合格にする, 落とす** ‖ *The examiners failed half of the candidates.* 試験官は志願者の半数を不合格にした. ⇔ **pass** ▶定義 3 自 **fail to do sth** to not do sth 〜をしない→**〜し損なう, 〜できない, 〜しない, 〜をおこたる** ‖ *She never fails to do her homework.* 彼女は必ず宿題をする. ▶定義 4 自他 to not be enough or not do what people are expecting or wanting 十分でない, または人が期待している事や要求している事をしない→**〜が不作になる, 不足する; 〜に欠けている, 〜の役に立たない, 〜の期待を裏切る, 〜を失望させる, 見捨てる** ‖ *If the crops fail, people will starve.* 不作になると人々が飢える. *I think the government has failed us.* 政府は我々を失望させたと思う. ▶定義 5 自 (used about health, eyesight, etc) to become weak (健康や視力などについて) 弱くなる→**弱る, 衰える, 衰弱する** ‖ *His health is failing.* 彼の健康は衰えてきている. ▶定義 6 自 to stop working 機能することをやめる→**動かなくなる, 働かなくなる, 作用しなくなる, うまく機能しなくなる** ‖ *My brakes failed on the hill but I managed to stop the car.* 坂道でブレーキが利かなくなったが, 何とか車を止めた.

## 590 fail²

**fail²** /feɪl/ 名 C ▶定義 the act of not being successful in an exam 試験で合格しないこと→落第, 不合格, 失敗 ⇔ **pass**
成句 **without fail** ▶定義 always, even if there are difficulties たとえ困難があっても常に→間違いなく, きっと, 必ず, 例外なく, いつも ‖ *The postman always comes at 8 o'clock without fail.* 郵便配達はいつも必ず8時にやって来る.

**failing¹** /feɪlɪŋ/ 名 C ▶定義 a weakness or fault 弱み, または欠点→弱点, 短所, 欠点, 欠陥 ‖ *She's not very patient - that's her only failing.* 彼女はあまり忍耐強くない－それが唯一の欠点だ.

**failing²** /feɪlɪŋ/ 前 ▶定義 if sth is not possible ～が不可能ならば→～がない場合には, ～がないので ‖ *Ask Jackie to go with you, or failing that, try Anne.* ジャッキーに一緒に行ってくれるように頼みなさい. それが駄目ならアンに頼んでみなさい.

*****failure** /feɪljər/ 名 ▶定義1 U lack of success 成功しないこと→不成功, 失敗, しくじり, 落第, 不首尾 ‖ *All my efforts ended in failure.* 私の努力はすべて失敗に終わった. ▶定義2 C a person or thing that is not successful うまくいかない人または物事→失敗者, 落選者, 落第者, 失敗した企て, 失敗作, 不出来なもの ‖ *His first attempt at skating was a miserable failure.* 彼のスケート初体験は惨めな失敗だった. ⇔ 定義1, 2 **success** ▶定義3 C U failure to do sth not doing sth that people expect you to do するだろうと人が期待する～をしないこと→不履行, 怠慢, ～をしないこと, ～できないこと, ～し忘れること ‖ *I was very disappointed at his failure to come to the meeting.* 彼が会合に来なかったことに私はとても失望した. ▶定義4 C U an example of sth not working properly 正しく機能しない～の実例→機能不全, 故障, 停止, 衰え, 減退, 損傷 ‖ *She died of heart failure.* 彼女は心臓まひで亡くなった. *There's been a failure in the power supply.* 停電があった.

*****faint¹** /feɪnt/ 形 ▶定義1 (used about things that you can see, hear, feel, etc) not strong or clear (見る, 聞く, あるいは感じることなどができる物事について) 強くない, またははっきりしない→かすかな, ほのかな, ぼんやりした, 弱々しい ‖ *a faint light/sound* かすかな光・音 *There is still a faint hope that they will find more people alive.* 生存者がもっと見つかるのではないかというかすかな希望が, まだ残っている. ▶定義2 (used about people) almost losing consciousness; very weak (人について) ほとんど意識を失っている; 非常に弱い→気が遠くなって, めまいがして, 衰弱して, ふらふらして ‖ *I feel faint - I'd better sit down.* めまいがする－座った方が良さそうだ. ▶定義3 (used about actions, etc) done without much effort (行動などについて) あまり努力せずに行われた→気のない, やる気のない, 心のこもらない, 熱意のない, 弱々しい ‖ *He made a faint protest.* 彼は形だけの抗議をした.
成句 **not have the faintest/foggiest (idea)** ▶定義 to not know at all 全く知らない→全然分からない, 何一つ知らない, 皆目見当が付かない ‖ *I haven't the faintest idea where they've gone.* 彼らがどこへ行ったのか全く分からない.

**faint²** /feɪnt/ 動 自 ▶定義 to lose consciousness 意識を失う→気絶する, 失神する, 気が遠くなる, 気を失う

*****fair¹** /feər/ 形 副 ▶定義1 appropriate and acceptable in a particular situation 特定の状況において適切で容認できる→適正な[に], 正当な[に], 理にかなった[て], 規則にかなった[て] ‖ *That's a fair price for that house.* それはその家の価格として適正だ. *I think **it's fair to say that** the number of homeless people is increasing.* ホームレスの人々の数が増加していると言っても差し支えないと思う. ▶定義2 **fair (to/on sb)** treating each person or side equally, according to the law, the rules, etc 法律や規則などに従って, それぞれの人または側を平等に扱う→公正な[に], 公平な[に], 平等な[に] ‖ *That's not fair - he got the same number of mistakes as I did and he's got a better mark.* それは公平ではありませんよ－彼も私と同じ数だけ間違えたのに, 彼の方が点数がいいなんて. *It wasn't fair on her to ask her to stay so late.* そんなに遅くまでいるように求めるのは, 彼女に対して公正ではなかった. *a fair trial* 公正な裁判 ⇔ 定義1, 2 **unfair** ▶定義3 quite good, large, etc かなり良い, 大きいなど→かなりの, 相当な, いい線の, 十分にある ‖ *They have a fair chance of success.* 彼らには成功するチャンスが十分にある. ▶定義4 (used about the skin or hair) light in colour (肌や髪について) 色

が明るい→**色白の, 金髪の, ブロンドの** || *Chloe has fair hair and blue eyes.* クローイは金髪で青い目をしている. ▶定義5 (used about the weather) good, without rain (天気について) 良い, 雨が降らない→**晴れた, 晴天の, 好天の**

成句 **fair enough**(口語) ▶定義 used to show that you agree with what sb has suggested 〜が提案したことに同意することを表すために用いて→**結構だ, よし, もっともだ, 了解だ, オーケー**

**fair play** ▶定義 equal treatment of both/all sides according to the rules 規則に従って両方の側, またはすべての側を平等に扱うこと→**公正な扱い, 公明正大な態度, 正々堂々とした試合振り, フェアプレー** || *The referee is there to ensure fair play during the match.* 審判は, 試合中にフェアプレーが確実に行われるようにするためにいる.

**(more than) your fair share of sth** ▶定義 (more than) the usual or expected amount of sth 〜の通常の, または予想される量 (より多い)→**正当な分け前 (より多い), 当然受け取る物 (より大きい), 公平な分配 (より多い)** || *We've had more than our fair share of trouble this year.* 私たちにとって今年はあまりにも問題が多すぎた.

**fair**[2] /feər/ 名 ⓒ ▶定義1 (または **funfair**) a type of entertainment in a field or park. At a fair you can ride on machines or try and win prizes at games. Fairs usually travel from town to town. 野原や公園で催される娯楽の一種. ここで機械仕掛けの乗り物に乗ること, あるいはゲームをして賞品を取ることなどができる. 通常は, 町から町へと移動するものである→**移動遊園地, 縁日** ▶定義2 a large event where people, businesses, etc show and sell their goods 人々や会社などが自分たちの商品を展示して販売する大規模な催し物→**定期市, 品評会, 展示会, 博覧会** || *a trade fair* 産業博覧会 *the Frankfurt book fair* フランクフルト書籍見本市

**fairground** /féərɡràund/ 名 ⓒ ▶定義 a large outdoor area where fairs are held 移動遊園地が開かれる屋外の広い土地→**移動遊園地が開かれる場所**

**fair-haired** 形 ▶定義 with light-coloured hair; blonde 明るい色の髪をした; ブロンドの→**金髪の, 薄いとび色の髪の**

***fairly** /féərli/ 副 ▶定義1 in an acceptable way; in a way that treats people equally or according to the law, rules, etc 容認できるやり方で; 人を平等に, または法律や規則などに従って扱って→**公正に, 公平に, 公明正大に, 正々堂々と, 合法的に** || *I felt that the teacher didn't treat us fairly.* 私はその先生が私たちを公平に扱っていないと感じた. ⇔ **unfairly** ▶定義2 quite, not very かなり, あまり〜でない→**かなり, 相当に, 結構, なかなか, まあまあ, まずまず, 中くらいに, 並で, いくらか** || *He is fairly tall.* 彼はかなり背が高い. ☛参 **rather** の注

**fairness** /féərnəs/ 名 Ⓤ ▶定義 treating people equally or according to the law, rules, etc 人を平等に, または法律や規則などに従って扱うこと→**公正, 公平, 公明正大**

**fairy** /féəri/ 名 ⓒ (覆 **fairies**) ▶定義 (in stories) a small creature with wings and magic powers (物語で) 翼と魔法を持った小さな生き物→**妖精 (ようせい), 精**

**fairy tale** (または **fairy story**) 名 ⓒ ▶定義 a story that is about fairies, magic, etc 妖精 (ようせい) や魔法などについての物語→**妖精物語, おとぎ話, 童話**

***faith** /féiθ/ 名 ▶定義1 Ⓤ faith (in sb/sth) strong belief (in sb/sth); trust (〜に対する) 強い確信; 信頼→**信頼, 信用, 確信, 自信** || *I've got great/little faith in his ability to do the job.* 私は彼にその仕事をする能力があると強く信じている・ほとんど信じていない. *I have lost faith in him.* 私は彼への信頼を失った. ▶定義2 Ⓤ strong religious belief 強い宗教的信念→**信仰, 信心, 信教** || *I've lost my faith.* 私は信仰を失った. ▶定義3 ⓒ a particular religion 特定の宗教→**宗教, 信条, 教義, 教旨** || *the Jewish faith* ユダヤ教

成句 **in good faith** ▶定義 with honest reasons for doing sth 〜をするための信ずべき理由がある→**疑いなく, 誠実に, 誠意を持って** || *I bought the car in good faith. I didn't know it was stolen.* 私は何の疑いも抱かないでその車を買った. 盗難車とは知らなかった.

***faithful** /féiθful, -f(ə)l/ 形 **faithful (to sb/sth)** ▶定義1 always staying with and supporting a person, organization or belief; loyal 常に人, 組織, または信念などと共にあり, 支えている; 忠実な→**忠実な, 誠実な, 信義に厚い, 信心深い** ||

## 592　fake¹

*Peter has been a faithful friend.* ピーターは誠実な友人だった. *He was always faithful to his wife (= he didn't have sexual relations with anyone else).* 彼はいつも妻に対して誠実だった（＝ほかのだれとも性的関係を持たなかった）.
　■類 **loyal** ⇔ **unfaithful**　▶定義2 true to the facts; accurate 事実に忠実な; 正確な→**事実通りの, 正確な, 信じられる** ∥ *a faithful description* 正確な記述 — **faithfully** /-fʊli, -f(ə)li/ 副 →**忠実に, 誠実に, 正確に**
　▶ Yours faithfully は, 正式な手紙の結びに用いられる.
— **faithfulness** 名 Ⓤ →**忠実, 誠実, 貞節, 信義, 正確さ** ■参 **fidelity**

**fake**¹ /féɪk/ 名 Ⓒ ▶定義1 a work of art, etc that seems to be real or genuine but is not 真正である, または本物であるように見えるが, そうではない芸術作品など→**偽造品, 模造品, がん作, にせ物**　▶定義2 a person who is not really what he/she appears to be 実際は見掛けと異なる人→**いかさま師, 詐欺師, ペテン師, にせ者** — fake 形 →**にせの, 偽造の, 模造の, まやかしの** ∥ *a fake passport* 偽造パスポート

**fake**² /féɪk/ 動 ⓽ ▶定義1 to copy sth and try to make people believe it is the real thing 〜を模造し, それが本物であると人に信じさせようとする→**〜を偽造する, 模造する, ねつ造する, でっち上げる, 〜のにせ物を作る** ∥ *He faked his father's signature.* 彼は父親の署名を偽造した.
　▶定義2 to make people believe that you are feeling sth that you are not 自分が実際には感じていない〜を感じていると人に信じさせる→**〜の振りをする, 〜と見せ掛ける, 〜を装う** ∥ *I faked surprise when he told me the news.* 彼がそのニュースを私に話した時, 私は驚いた振りをした.

**falcon** /fɔ́ː(l)kən; fǽl-/ 名 Ⓒ ▶定義 a bird with long pointed wings that kills and eats other animals (**a bird of prey**). Falcons can be trained to hunt. ほかの動物を殺して食べる, 先のとがった長い翼のある鳥（猛禽（もうきん））. 狩りをするように訓練できる→**（タカ狩りに用いる）ハヤブサ, タカ**

\***fall** /fɔ́ːl/ 動 ⓘ （過 **fell** /fel/; 過分 **fallen** /fɔ́ːl(ə)n/）
　▶定義1 to drop down towards the ground 地面に向かって落ちる→**落ちる, 落下する, 転落する, (雨などが) 降る, 降りる, 抜け落ちる, (花, 葉などが) 散る** ∥ *He fell off the ladder onto the grass.* 彼ははしごから芝生の上に落ちた. *The rain was falling steadily.* 雨は絶え間なく降っていた.
　▶定義2 **fall (down/over)** to suddenly stop standing and drop to the ground 立っているのを突然やめて地面に倒れる→**倒れる, 転ぶ, 平伏する, 倒壊する, 崩れ落ちる** ∥ *She slipped on the ice and fell.* 彼女は氷の上で滑って転んだ. *The little boy fell over and hurt his knee.* その小さな少年は転んでひざにけがをした.　▶定義3 to hang down ぶら下がる→**垂れ下がる, 垂れる, 下がっている** ∥ *Her hair fell down over her shoulders.* 彼女の髪は肩に垂れていた.　▶定義4 to become lower or less 低くなる, または少なくなる→**下がる, 低下する, 減少する, 弱まる, 小さくなる, 衰える** ∥ *The temperature is falling.* 温度が下がっている. *The price of coffee has fallen again.* コーヒーの価格がまた下がった. ⇔ **rise**
　▶定義5 to be defeated 打破される→**(国家, 政府などが) 倒れる, 崩壊する, 勢力を失う, (要塞（ようさい）, 都市などが) 陥落する, 滅びる, 失脚する** ∥ *The Government fell because of the scandal.* 政府は汚職事件のため倒れた.　▶定義6 〈文〉to be killed (in battle) 殺される（戦いで）→**傷付いて倒れる, 戦死する, 死ぬ** ∥ *Millions of soldiers fell in the war.* その戦争で何百万という兵士が死んだ.　▶定義7 to change into a different state; to become 異なる状態に変化する; 〜になる→**〜になる, 陥る, 至る** ∥ *He fell asleep on the sofa.* 彼はソファーの上で眠りに落ちた. *They fell in love with each other in Spain.* 彼らはスペインで恋に落ちた. *I must get some new shoes - these ones are falling to pieces.* 新しい靴を買わなければならない — これはぼろぼろになりかけているので.　▶定義8 正式 to come or happen 来る, または起こる→**(ある日に) 当たる, 起こる, 生じる, ある, (夜, 季節などが) 来る, 訪れる** ∥ *My birthday falls on a Sunday this year.* 私の誕生日は今年は日曜日に当たる.　▶定義9 to belong to a particular group, type, etc 特定の集団や種類などに属する→**分類される, 分けられる, 分かれる, (ある範囲に) 入る** ∥ *Animals fall into two groups, those with backbones and those without.* 動物は, 背骨のある動物とない動物の2つのグループに分けられる.

**成句** fall flat ⇒ **FLAT**¹
fall/slot into place ⇒ **PLACE**¹
fall short (of sth) ⇒ **SHORT**¹

**句動詞** fall apart ▶定義 to break (into pieces) (ばらばらに)壊れる➡ばらばらになる, (壊れて)分解する, 崩壊する ‖ *My car is falling apart.* 私の車はばらばらになりかかっている.

fall back on sb/sth ▶定義 to use sb/sth when you are in difficulty 困難な状態にあるときに〜を利用する➡〜に頼る, 〜をよりどころとする, 当てにする ‖ *When the electricity was cut off we fell back on candles.* 停電になった時はろうそくが頼りだった.

fall for sb **略式** ▶定義 to be strongly attracted to sb; to fall in love with sb 〜に強く引き付けられる; 〜と恋に落ちる➡〜にほれ込む, 〜を好きになる, とても気に入る, 〜に夢中になる

fall for sth **略式** ▶定義 to be tricked into believing sth that is not true だまされて真実ではない〜を信じ込む➡〜に引っ掛かる, だまされる ‖ *He makes excuses and she falls for them every time.* 彼が言い訳をすると, それに毎回彼女はだまされる.

fall out (with sb) ▶定義 to argue and stop being friendly (with sb) (〜と)論争し, 親しくすることをやめる➡〜と仲たがいする, けんかする, 不和になる

fall through ▶定義 to fail or not happen 失敗する, または起こらない➡失敗に終わる, ご破算になる, 駄目になる, できなくなる ‖ *Our trip to Japan has fallen through.* 日本への旅行は駄目になった.

★**fall**² /fɔːl/ **名** ▶定義 **1 ⓒ** an act of falling down or off sth 落ちること, または〜から落ちること➡落下, 転落, 降下, 墜落 ‖ *She had a nasty fall from her horse.* 彼女は馬からひどい落ち方をした. ▶定義 **2 ⓒ** a fall (of sth) the amount of sth that has fallen or the distance that sth has fallen 落下した〜の量, または〜が落下した距離➡降雨量, 降雪量, 落差, 落下距離 ‖ *We have had a heavy fall of snow.* 大雪が降った. *a fall of four metres* 4メートルの落差 ▶定義 **3 ⓒ** a fall (in sth) a decrease (in value, quantity, etc) (価格, 量などの)減少➡低下, 下落, 低落, 減少, 降下 ‖ *There has been a sharp fall in the price of oil.* 石油の価格が急落した. ☛類 drop ⇔ rise ▶定義 **4** [単数扱い] the fall of sth a (political) defeat; a failure (政治的な)敗北; 失敗➡滅亡, 崩壊, 失墜, 堕落 ‖ *the fall of the Roman Empire* ローマ帝国の滅亡 ▶定義 **5 falls** [複数扱い] a large amount of water that falls from a height down the side of a mountain, etc; a waterfall 山腹などの高い所から落下する大量の水; 滝➡滝, ばく布, 落水 ‖ *Niagara Falls* ナイアガラの滝 ▶定義 **6 ⓒ** 米 = **AUTUMN**

**fallacy** /fǽləsi/ **名**(複 **fallacies**) **ⓒ Ⓤ** **正式** ▶定義 a false belief or a wrong idea 間違った信念, または誤った考え➡誤った考え, 誤った推論, 誤信 ‖ *It's a fallacy to believe that money brings happiness (= it's not true).* 金が幸福をもたらすというのは誤信である (= 真実ではない).

**fallen** **FALL**¹ の過去分詞形

**fallible** /fǽləb(ə)l/ **形** ▶定義 able or likely to make mistakes 間違いを犯し得る, または犯しそうな➡誤りに陥りがちな, 誤りのあり得る, 必ずしも正確でない, 完全無欠ではない ‖ *Even our new computerized system is fallible.* コンピューター化された新しいシステムでさえも誤りが発生する可能性がある. ⇔ **infallible**

**fallout** /fɔ́ːlàʊt/ **名 Ⓤ** ▶定義 dangerous waste that is carried in the air after a nuclear explosion 核爆発後の空気中に放出された危険な廃棄物➡放射性降下物, 降灰, 死の灰

★**false** /fɔːls/ **形** ▶定義 **1** not true; incorrect 真実でない, 不正確な➡偽りの, 虚偽の, 間違った, 誤った, 正しくない, 事実に反する ‖ *I think the information you have been given is false.* あなたが与えられた情報は偽りだと思います. *I got a completely false impression of him from our first meeting.* 私たちが初めて会った時, 私は彼について全く間違った印象を受けた. ⇔ **true** ▶定義 **2** not real; artificial 本物でない; 人工の➡人造の, 人工の, 作り物の ‖ *false hair/eyelashes/teeth* つけ毛・つけまつげ・義歯 ⇔ **real**, **natural** ▶定義 **3** not genuine, but made to look real in order to trick people 本物ではないが, 人をだますために本物に見えるように作られた➡にせの, 模造の, 偽造の ‖ *This suitcase has a false bottom.* このスーツケースは二重底になっている. *a false name/passport* 偽名・偽造パスポート ▶定義 **4** (used about sb's behaviour or expression) not sincere or honest (〜の振る舞

いや表情について)誠実または正直ではない→**不誠実な, 不正直な, 裏切りの, 偽りの, わざとらしい** ‖ *a false smile* 偽りの笑い *false modesty* 上辺だけの謙そん

**慣用** a false alarm ▶定義 a warning about a danger that does not happen 起こらない危険についての警告→**間違い・いたずら警報, にせ警報, 人騒がせ**

a false friend ▶定義 a word in another language that looks similar to a word in your own but has a different meaning 自分が使う言語にある言葉と似ているように見えるが, 異なる意味を持つ, 別の言語の言葉→**(よく似た)異義語**

under false pretences ▶定義 pretending to be or to have sth in order to trick people 人をだますために, ～の振りをする, または～を持っている振りをする→**～の振りをする, 身分を偽る, だまして** ‖ *She got into the club under false pretences - she isn't a member at all!* 彼女は身分を偽ってそのクラブに入り込んだ － 彼女はメンバーなどではない.

**false teeth** (または **dentures**) 名 [複数扱い] ▶定義 artificial teeth that are worn by sb who has lost his/her natural teeth 自然に生えた歯を失った～が付ける人工的な歯→**義歯, 入れ歯**

**falsify** /fɔ́ːlsəfaɪ/ 動他 (現分 **falsifying**; 三単現 **falsifies**; 過, 過分 **falsified**) 正式 ▶定義 to change a document, information, etc so that it is no longer true in order to trick sb ～をだますために, もはやそれが真実ではなくなるように文書や情報などを変更する→**～を変造する, 偽造する, 改ざんする, ～に不正に手を加える, ～をゆがめる, 偽る** ‖ *to falsify data/records/accounts* データ・記録・請求書を改ざんする

**falter** /fɔ́ːltər/ 動自 ▶定義1 to become weak or move in a way that is not steady 弱くなる, または安定していない状態で動く→**弱まる, 鈍る, 調子が悪くなる, 衰える, つまずく, ふらつく** ‖ *The engine faltered and stopped.* エンジンの調子がだんだん悪くなって, ついに停止した. ▶定義2 to lose confidence and determination 自信と決意を失う→**たじろぐ, ためらう, ひるむ, 弱気になる, くじける** ‖ *Sampras faltered and missed the ball.* サンプラスは弱気になり, ボールを外した.

\***fame** /feɪm/ 名 U ▶定義 being known or talked about by many people because of what you have achieved 達成したことによって, 多くの人々に知れ渡る, または話題に上ること→**名声, 高名, 有名, 名誉, 評判** ‖ *Pop stars achieve fame at a young age.* ポピュラー音楽のスターは若くして名声を得る. *The town's only claim to fame is that there was a riot there.* その町で有名な事と言えば暴動があったという事だけである.

**famed** /feɪmd/ 形 ▶定義 famed (for sth) well-known (for sth) (何かで) よく知られている→**有名な, 名高い** ‖ *Welsh people are famed for their singing.* ウェールズ人は歌がうまいので有名だ. **参** **famous**. famed よりも一般的な語である.

\***familiar** /fəmíljər/ 形 ▶定義1 familiar (to sb) well-known to you; often seen or heard and therefore easy to recognize 自分がよく知っている; よく見られる, または聞かれるので, 簡単にそれと分かる→**よく知られた, 見慣れた, 聞き慣れた, なじみのある, ありふれた** ‖ *to look/sound familiar* 見慣れている・聞き慣れている *Chinese music isn't very familiar to people in Europe.* 中国音楽はヨーロッパの人々にはあまり知られていない. *It was a relief to see a familiar face in the crowd.* 人込みの中に見慣れた顔を見つけてほっとした. ▶定義2 familiar with sth having a good knowledge of sth ～についてよく知っている→**熟知して, 精通して, 詳しい, 通じている** ‖ *People in Europe aren't very familiar with Chinese music.* ヨーロッパの人々は中国音楽にあまり詳しくない. ⇔定義1, 2 **unfamiliar** ▶定義3 familiar (with sb) (used about a person's behaviour) too friendly and informal (人の振る舞いについて) あまりにも親しげで打ち解けすぎる→**なれなれしい, 厚かましい, 無遠慮な** ‖ *I was annoyed by the waiter's familiar behaviour.* ウエーターの無遠慮な態度にいらいらした.

**familiarity** /fəˌmɪliǽrəti, -mìliǽr-/ 名 U ▶定義1 familiarity (with sth) having a good knowledge of sth ～についてよく知っていること→**精通, 熟知** ‖ *His familiarity with the area was an advantage.* その地域をよく知っていることは彼に有利だった. ▶定義2 being too friendly and informal あまりにも親しげで打ち解けすぎるこ

と➡なれなれしさ, 厚かましさ, 無遠慮, ずうずうしさ

**familiarize** (または **-ise**) /fəmíljəràɪz/ 動他
▶定義 familiarize sb/yourself (with sth) to teach sb about sth or learn about sth until you know it well ～に…について教える, またはよく分かるまで～について学ぶ➡～に慣れさせる, なじませる, 親しませる, 習熟する, ～を詳しく知る ‖ *I want to familiarize myself with the plans before the meeting.* 私は会議の前にその計画についてよく知っておきたい.

*__family__ /fǽm(ə)li/ 名 (複 **families**) ▶定義 **1** [C, 単数または複数形の動詞と共に] a group of people who are related to each other 互いに関係のある人々の集まり➡家族, 一家, 身内, 世帯 ‖ *I have quite a large family.* 私の家はかなりの大家族だ.

➤ family は, 「両親とその子供」(a nuclear family (核家族)) を意味する場合に用いられることもあれば, 祖父母, 伯母・叔母, 伯父・叔父などの親戚 (しんせき) (an extended family (拡大家族)) も含めて用いられることもある.
family を一単位として考える場合は, 単数の動詞と共に用いられる: *Almost every family in the village owns a television.* (その村のほとんどすべての家庭にテレビがある.) 家族の一員を個人として考える場合は, 複数形の動詞と共に用いられる: *My family are all very tall.* (私の家族は皆とても背が高い.) family をほかの名詞の前に用いて, 家族向けの, または家族全員で使える物を言う場合もある: *family entertainment* (家族向けの娯楽) *the family car* (家族向けの車)

▶定義 **2** C U children➡子供たち ‖ *Do you have any family?* お子さんはいますか. *We are planning to **start a family** next year (= to have our first baby).* 来年には子供を持つ (= 最初の子供をもうける) つもりである. *to bring up/raise a family* 子供を育てる ▶定義 **3** C a group of animals, plants, etc that are of a similar type 同じような種類の動物や植物などの集団➡科 ‖ *Lions belong to the cat family.* ライオンはネコ科に属する.

成句 run in the family ▶定義 to be found very often in a family ある家族において非常によく見られる➡家族に遺伝している, 血筋の, 血統の, 家系的である ‖ *Red hair runs in the family.* 赤毛はその一家に遺伝的なものである.

**family name** 名 C ▶定義 the name that is shared by members of a family; surname 家族の構成員によって共有される名前; 姓➡姓, 名字, 氏 ☞参 name の注

**family planning** 名 U ▶定義 controlling the number of children you have by using birth control 避妊することによって, 産む子供の数を制限する➡家族計画, 産児制限 ☞参 **contraception**

**family tree** 名 C ▶定義 a diagram that shows the relationships between different members of a family over a long period of time 長期間にわたる家族の1人1人の間の関係を示す図➡(家)系図, 系譜 ‖ *How far back can you trace your family tree?* 家系をどこまでさかのぼることができますか.

**famine** /fǽmən/ 名 C U ▶定義 a lack of food over a long period of time in a large area that can cause the death of many people 多くの人々の死亡の原因となり得るような, 広い地域での長期間にわたる食物の不足➡飢饉(ききん), 凶作, 食糧不足 ‖ *There is a severe famine in many parts of Africa.* アフリカの多くの地域で深刻な飢饉が発生している. *The long drought (= a lack or rain or water) was followed by famine.* 長い干ばつ (= 雨または水の不足) の後, 凶作となった.

**famished** /fǽmɪʃt/ 形 叙述式 (名詞の前は不可)
▶定義 very hungry 非常に空腹である➡ひどく腹のすいた, 腹ぺこで ‖ *When's lunch? I'm famished!* 昼食はいつ. 腹ぺこだよ.

*__famous__ /féɪməs/ 形 ▶定義 famous (for sth) well-known to many people 多くの人々によく知られている➡有名な, 名高い, 高名な ‖ *a famous singer* 有名な歌手 *Glasgow is famous for its museums and art galleries.* グラスゴーは博物館と美術館で有名である. ☞参 **infamous**, **notorious** は「悪いことで有名である」という意味を表す.

**famously** /féɪməsli/ 副 ▶定義 in a way that is famous 有名であるように➡よく知られて, 高名で, 名高く, 広く知られているように ‖ *the words he famously uttered just before he died*

## 596  fan¹

死の間際に彼が残したとして広く知られている言葉

**成句 get on/along famously** ▶定義 to have a very good relationship with sb, especially from the first meeting 特に最初に会った時から、〜ととても良い関係を持つ→意気投合する, 気が合う, うまが合う, とても仲良くやっている

fans

**★fan¹** /fæn/ 名 C ▶定義 1 somebody who admires and is very enthusiastic about a sport, a film star, a singer, etc スポーツ, 映画スター, 歌手などを賞賛し, 非常に熱狂的な人→**ファン, 熱心な愛好者, 熱烈な支持者** ‖ football fans サッカーファン He's a Van Morrison fan. 彼はヴァン モリソンのファンだ. fan mail (= letters from fans to the person they admire) ファンレター (= ファンから応援している人にあてた手紙) ▶定義 2 a machine with parts that turn around very quickly to create a current of cool or warm air 非常に速く回転して冷風または温風を生じる部品の付いた機械→**送風機, 扇風機, ファン** ‖ an electric fan 電気扇風機 a fan heater ファンヒーター ▶定義 3 an object in the shape of a half-circle made of paper, feathers, etc that you wave in your hand to create a current of cool air 手で振って涼しい風の流れを作り出す, 紙や羽などから作られた半円形の物→**うちわ, 扇, 扇子**

**fan²** /fæn/ 動 (**fanning; fanned**) ▶定義 1 to make air blow on sb/sth by waving a fan¹(3), your hand, etc in the air 空気中で扇 (fan¹(3)), 手などを振って〜に風を送る→**〜をあおぐ, 〜に風を送る, 〜をあおいで払う** ‖ She used a newspaper to fan her face. 彼女は新聞で顔をあおいだ. ▶定義 2 to make a fire burn more strongly by blowing on it 風を送ることによって火を強く燃え上がらせる→**(火)をあおる, 燃え立たせる** ‖ The strong wind really fanned the flames. 強風が現実に炎を燃え上がらせた.

**句動詞 fan out** ▶定義 to spread out 広がる→**扇形に広がる, 散開する** ‖ The police fanned out across the field. 警官たちは現場に広がっていった.

**fanatic** /fəˈnætɪk/ 名 C ▶定義 a person who is very enthusiastic about sth and may have extreme or dangerous opinions (especially about religion or politics) 〜に非常に熱狂的で, (特に宗教や政治について) 極端な, または危険な意見を持っているかもしれない人→**マニア, 狂信者, 熱狂的な支持者・愛好者** ‖ a religious fanatic 宗教の狂信者 She's a health-food fanatic. 彼女は健康食品の熱狂的愛好者である. ☞類 fiend, freak — **fanatical** /-k(ə)l/ (または **fanatic**) 形 →**狂信的な, 熱狂的な** ‖ He's fanatical about keeping things tidy. 彼は物がきちんと片付いていないと気がすまない. — **fanatically** /-k(ə)li/ 副 →**熱狂的に, 狂信的に** — **fanaticism** /-təsɪz(ə)m/ 名 C U →**熱狂, 狂信, 狂信的行為**

**fan belt** 名 C ▶定義 the belt that operates the machinery that cools a car engine 車のエンジンを冷却する機械類を駆動するベルト→**ファンベルト**

**fancy¹** /ˈfænsi/ 動 (現分 **fancying**; 三単現 **fancies**; 過, 過分 **fancied**) ▶定義 1 他 英略式 to like the idea of having or doing sth; to want sth or to want to do sth 〜を持つ, または行うという考えを好む; 〜を欲しがる, または〜をしたがる→**〜を好む, 望む, 気に入る, 〜が欲しい, したい** ‖ What do you fancy to eat? 何が食べたいですか. I don't fancy going out in this rain. この雨の中を出掛けたくない. ▶定義 2 他 英略式 to be sexually attracted to sb 〜に性的に引き付けられる→**〜に気がある, 性的魅力を感じる, ひかれている** ‖ Jack keeps looking at you. I think he fancies you. ジャックはあなたをずっと見ている. 彼はあなたに気があるのだと思うわ. ▶定義 3 他 **fancy yourself (as) sth** to think that you would be good at sth; to think that you are sth (although this may not be true) 自分は〜がうまいかもしれないと考える; 自分が〜であると考える (それが本当ではないかもしれないが) →**〜と思い込む, 〜であると空想する, 勝手に想像する, うぬぼれる, 〜の気になっている** ‖ He fancied himself (as) a poet. 彼は詩人のつもりでいた.

**fancy²** /ˈfænsi/ 形 ▶定義 not simple or ordinary 単純ではない, または普通ではない→**手の込ん**

だ, 凝った, 装飾的な, 派手な, 風変わりな, 突飛な ‖ *My father doesn't like fancy food.* 父は手の込んだ料理は好きではない. *I just want a pair of black shoes - nothing fancy.* 私は黒い靴が欲しいのです — ごく普通の.

**fancy**³ /fǽnsi/ 名

熟語 **take sb's fancy** ▶定義 to attract or please sb ～を引き付ける, または喜ばせる→～が…の気に入る ‖ *If you see something that takes your fancy I'll buy it for you.* 気に入った物が見つかったら買ってあげましょう.

**take a fancy to sb/sth** ▶定義 to start liking sb/sth ～を好きになる→～にひかれる, ほれる, ～が気に入る, 好きになる ‖ *I think that Laura's really taken a fancy to you.* ローラは本当にあなたにひかれていると思います.

**fancy dress** 名 U ▶定義 special clothes that you wear to a party at which people dress up to look like a different person (for example from history or a story) 人々が別の人物(例えば歴史上や物語の中の)に見えるようにふん装するパーティーに着ていく, 特別な衣服→仮装服, 風変わりな服, 奇抜な衣装 ‖ *It was a Hallowe'en party and everyone went in fancy dress.* ハロウィーンパーティーだったので, だれもが仮装していた.

**fanfare** /fǽnfèər/ 名 C ▶定義 a short loud piece of music that is used for introducing sb important, for example a king or queen 例えば王や女王などのように重要な～を紹介するために使われる, 大きな音の短い音楽→ファンファーレ, 華やかなトランペットなどの演奏

**fang** /fæŋ/ 名 C ▶定義 a long sharp tooth of a dog, snake, etc 犬や蛇などの長く鋭い歯→きば, 犬歯, (蛇の)毒歯, 毒牙(どくが) ☛ C1 ページのさし絵

**fanny pack** /fǽni pæk/ 米 = BUMBAG

**fantasize** (または **-ise**) /fǽntəsàɪz/ 動 自 他 ▶定義 to imagine sth that you would like to happen 起こってほしいと思っている～を想像する→～を夢想する, 空想する, 思い描く ‖ *He liked to fantasize that he had won a gold medal at the Olympics.* 彼は自分がオリンピックで金メダルを取ることを空想するのが好きだった.

**fantastic** /fæntǽstɪk, fən-/ 形 ▶定義 1 略式 very good; excellent 非常に良い; 優れた→とてもすばらしい, すてきな, すごい ‖ *She's a fantastic swimmer.* 彼女はすばらしく泳ぎがうまい. ▶定義 2 strange and difficult to believe 奇妙で信じ難い→奇想天外な, 風変わりな, 異様な, 空想的な, 現実離れした ‖ *a story full of fantastic creatures from other worlds* 想像の世界の奇妙な生き物がたくさん出てくる物語 ▶定義 3 略式 very large or great 非常に大きい, または際立った→途方もない, 法外な, ばく大な, 膨大な, とんでもない ‖ *A Rolls Royce costs a fantastic amount of money.* ロールスロイスはとんでもない値段だ. — **fantastically** /-k(ə)li/ 副 →とてもすばらしく, 異様に, 空想的に, 法外に, 途方もなく

**fantasy** /fǽntəsi, -zi/ 名 C U ( 複 **fantasies**) ▶定義 situations that are not true, that you just imagine 真実ではなく, 想像しているだけの状況→空想, 幻想, 夢想, ファンタジー ‖ *I have a fantasy about going to live in the Bahamas.* 私はバハマに行って暮らすことを夢想している. *They live in a world of fantasy.* 彼らは幻想の世界に住んでいる. ☛参 **imagination** の注

**fanzine** /fǽnzi:n/ 名 C ▶定義 a magazine that is written by and for people (**fans**) who like a particular sports team, singer, etc 特定のスポーツチーム, 歌手などを好む人(ファン)によって, そのような人のために書かれている雑誌→ファン雑誌, マニア雑誌

**FAQ** /èf eɪ kjú:/ 名 C ▶定義 a document on the Internet that contains the most frequently asked questions about a subject and the answers to these questions ある主題についてのよく聞かれる質問とそれに対する回答を載せた, インターネット上の文書→よくある質問, Q&A

***far**¹ /fɑ:r/ 形 ( **farther** /fɑ́:rðər/ または **further** /fɑ́:rðər/, **farthest** /fɑ́:rðəst/ または **furthest** /fɑ́:rðəst/) ▶定義 1 distant; a long way away 遠い; 遠く離れた→遠い, 遠くの, 離れた, はるかな, かなたの ‖ *Let's walk - it's not far.* 歩こう — そう遠くはないから. ▶定義 2 (名詞の前だけ) the most distant of two or more things 複数のもののうちで最も遠い→遠い方の, 遠くにある, 向こう側の ‖ *the far side of the river* 川の向こう側 ▶定義 3 (名詞の前だけ) a long way from the centre in the direction mentioned 中心から言及された方向へ遠く離れている→極端な, 極〜 ‖ *politicians from the far left of the party* その政党

の極左の政治家たち

**成句 a far cry from sth/from doing sth** ▶定義 an experience that is very different from sth/doing sth 〜とは、または〜をすることとは全く異なる体験 **➡大きな隔たり，大きな相違**

**★far²** /fɑːr/ 副 (**farther** /fɑ́ːrðər/ または **further** /fə́ːrðər/, **farthest** /fɑ́ːrðəst/ または **furthest** /fə́ːrðəst/) ▶定義 1 (at) a distance 遠く(に) ➡**はるかに，遠くへ，遠く離れて** ‖ *London's not far from here.* ロンドンはここから遠くない. *How far did we walk yesterday?* 昨日はどのくらい遠くまで歩いたでしょうか. *If we sit too far away from the screen I won't be able to see the film.* スクリーンからあまり遠い所に座ると，私は映画が見えません. *I can't swim as far as you.* 私はあなたほど長い距離を泳ぐことができない. *How much further is it?* どのくらい遠いですか.
▶ far は，この意味では通常，否定文と疑問文で用いられる．肯定文では a long way を用いる: *It's a long way from here to the sea.* (ここから海までは遠い.) 形の上では肯定であっても，否定の意味を持つ文もある．far はそのような文でも用いられる: *Let's get a bus. It's much too far to walk.* (バスに乗ろう．歩くにはあまりにも遠すぎるから.)

▶定義 2 very much 非常に ➡**(比較級の形容詞の前で)ずっと，大いに，はるかに** ‖ *She's far more intelligent than I thought.* 彼女は私が思っていたよりはるかに聡明(そうめい)だ. *There's far too much salt in this soup.* このスープはあまりにも塩気が多すぎる. ▶定義 3 (to) a certain degree ある程度(まで) ➡**〜まで，〜である限り，〜する限り** ‖ *How far have you got with your homework?* どこまで宿題をやりましたか. *The company employs local people as far as possible.* その会社はできる限り地元の人を雇っている. ▶定義 4 a long time 長い時間 ➡**ずっと，遅くまで，長いこと，はるかに，遠く** ‖ *We danced far into the night.* 私たちは夜更けまで踊った.

**成句 as far as** ▶定義 to the place mentioned but not further 言及された場所までだが，それを越えないで➡**〜まで，〜まで遠く** ‖ *We walked as far as the river and then turned back.* 私たちは川まで歩いてから引き返した.

**as/so far as** ▶定義 used for giving your opinion or judgement of a situation 意見，またはある状況についての判断を言う場合に用いられて➡**〜に関して言えば，〜する限りでは** ‖ *As far as I know, she's not coming, but I may be wrong.* 私が知っている限りでは彼女は来ないが，私が間違っているかもしれない. *As far as school work is concerned, he's hopeless.* 学校の勉強に限って言えば，彼は見込みがない. *As far as I'm concerned, this is the most important point.* 私の意見では，これが最も重要な点だ. *As far as I can see, the accident was John's fault, not Ann's.* 私の見るところでは，その事故の責任はジョンにあるのであり，アンではなかった.

**as far as the eye can see** ▶定義 to the furthest place you can see 見える最も遠い場所まで➡**目の届く限り，見渡す限り**

**by far** ▶定義 (used for emphasizing comparative or superative words) by a large amount (比較級または最上級の語を強調するために用いて) 多量に➡**はるかに，ずば抜けて，ずっと，断然** ‖ *Carmen is by far the best student in the class.* カーメンはクラスでもずば抜けて優秀な生徒だ.

**far afield** ▶定義 far away, especially from where you live or from where you are staying 特に住んでいる所から，または滞在している所から，遠く離れて➡**遠く離れて，ずっと遠くまで，はるか遠くへ** ‖ *We decided to hire a car in order to explore further afield.* 遠くまで探検するために，私たちは車を借りることにした.

**far from doing sth** ▶定義 instead of doing sth 〜をする代わりに…をする➡**〜するどころか，〜から程遠く，〜とは反対に** ‖ *Far from enjoying the film, he fell asleep in the middle.* 彼は映画を楽しむどころか，途中で眠ってしまった.

**far from sth** ▶定義 almost the opposite of sth; not at all 〜のほとんど逆で; 全く〜でない➡**少しも〜でない，決して〜でない** ‖ *He's far from happy (= he's very sad or angry).* 彼は少しも幸福ではない (= 彼は非常に悲しい，または腹を立てている).

**far from it** 略式 ▶定義 certainly not; just the opposite 全く違う; 正反対で➡**とんでもない，そんな事は絶対にない，その反対だ** ‖ *'Did you enjoy your holiday?' 'No, far from it. It was awful.'* 「休暇を楽しみましたか」「いいえ，とんでもない．ひどいものでした」

few and far between ⇒ **FEW**

**go far** ▶定義 **1** to be enough 十分である→たっぷりある, 足りる, (金などが) 価値が大きい, (食物などが) 長く持つ, 使いでがある, 大いに役立つ ‖ *This food won't go very far between three of us.* 私たち 3 人でこの食料では, あまり十分ではないだろう. ▶定義 **2** to be successful in life 人生で成功する→出世する, 成功する, うまくやる ‖ *Dan is very talented and should go far.* ダンはとても才能があるので, きっと成功するはずだ.

**go too far** ▶定義 to behave in a way that causes trouble or upsets other people 問題を起こす, またはほかの人を混乱させるような振る舞いをする→度が過ぎる, やりすぎる, 極端に走る ‖ *He's always been naughty but this time he's gone too far.* 彼はいつも行儀が悪かったが, 今回はやりすぎだ.

**so far** ▶定義 until now 今までは→今までのところ, これまでは, ここまで ‖ *So far the weather has been good but it might change.* 今までのところは天気が良かったが, 変わるかもしれない.

**so far so good** (口語) ▶定義 everything has gone well until now 今まではすべてがうまくいっている→これまでのところは順調だ, 今のところはうまくいっている

**faraway** /fáːrəwèi/ 形 ▶定義 **1** (文) a great distance away 長い距離を離れた→遠方の, 遠く離れた, かなたの, 遠くからの ‖ *He told us stories of faraway countries.* 彼は私たちに遠く離れた国の話をしてくれた. ▶定義 **2** (used about a look in a person's eyes) as if you are thinking of sth else (人の目付きについて) ほかの〜を考えているような→上の空で, ぼかんとした, 夢見るような ‖ *She stared out of the window with a faraway look in her eyes.* 彼女は夢見るような目で窓の外を見詰めていた.

**farce** /fɑːs/ 名 C ▶定義 **1** something important or serious that is not organized well or treated with respect うまくまとまっていない, または敬意を持って扱われないような重要な, あるいは重大な事→茶番 (的行為), 茶番劇, ばかばかしいこと, こっけいなまねごと ‖ *The meeting was a farce - everyone was shouting at the same time.* その会議は茶番だった － 皆が同時にどなっていただけだ. ▶定義 **2** a funny play for the theatre full of ridiculous situations ばかばかしい状況のたくさんある, 劇場用のこっけいな劇→茶番狂言, 笑劇, 道化芝居 ― **farcical** /fáːsɪk(ə)l/ 形→茶番の, 茶番染みた, ばかばかしい, 笑劇の, 笑わせる

*****fare**¹ /feər/ 名 C ▶定義 the amount of money you pay to travel by bus, train, taxi, etc バス, 列車, タクシーなどで移動するために支払う金額→運賃, 乗車賃, 料金 ‖ *What's the fare to Birmingham?* バーミンガムまでの料金はいくらですか. *Adults pay **full fare**, children pay **half fare**.* 大人は全額料金, 子供は半額料金です.

**fare**² /feər/ 動 自 正式 ▶定義 to be successful or not successful in a particular situation ある特定の状況で成功する, または成功しない→(人が) 暮らす, やっていく, 事が運ぶ ‖ *How did you fare in your examination (= did you do well or badly)?* 試験はどうでしたか (= うまくいきましたか, それとも失敗しましたか).

**the Far East** 名 [単数扱い] ▶定義 China, Japan and other countries in E and SE Asia 中国, 日本, および東アジアと東南アジアのほかの国々→極東, 極東諸国 ☞ **the Middle East**

**farewell** /fèəwél/ 間 (古) ▶定義 goodbye さようなら, さようなら, ごきげんよう, さらば ― **farewell** 名 C→別れのあいさつ, 告別, 別れ ‖ *He said his farewells and left.* 彼は別れのあいさつをして去った.

**far-fetched** 形 ▶定義 not easy to believe 信じるのが容易ではない→こじつけの, 不自然な, 無理な, 持って回った, 信じ難い ‖ *It's a good book but the story's too far-fetched.* それは良い本だが, 話があまりにも不自然だ.

*****farm**¹ /fɑːm/ 名 C ▶定義 an area of land with fields and buildings that is used for growing crops and keeping animals 作物を育て動物を飼育するために使われる田畑や建物のある土地→農場, 農園, 農地 ‖ *to work on a farm* 農場で働く *farm buildings/workers/animals* 農場の建物・農場労働者・家畜

*****farm**² /fɑːm/ 動 自 他 ▶定義 to use land for growing crops or keeping animals 作物を育てるまたは動物を飼育するために土地を使用する→〜を耕作する, 耕す, 農場を経営する, 農業をする ‖ *She farms 200 acres.* 彼女は 200 エーカーの土地を耕作している.

**farmer** /fáːmər/ 名 C ▶定義 a person who

**farmhouse** /fáːmhàus/ 名 C ▶定義 the house on a farm where the farmer lives 農場主が住む、農場内の家→農家、農場内の家屋、農園主の住居

**farming** /fáːmɪŋ/ 名 U ▶定義 managing a farm or working on it 農場を経営すること、またはそこで働くこと→農場経営、農業 ‖ *farming methods/areas* 農場経営法・農地

**farmyard** /fáːmjàːrd/ 名 C ▶定義 an outside area near a farmhouse surrounded by buildings or walls 農場の建物に近い、建物や壁に囲まれた屋外の区域→農場構内、農家の庭

**far-reaching** 形 ▶定義 having a great influence on a lot of other things ほかの多くの物事に大きな影響を与えている→遠くまで及ぶ、広範囲にわたる、将来にわたる ‖ *far-reaching changes* 広範囲に及ぶ変化

**far-sighted** 形 ▶定義1 being able to see what will be necessary in the future and making plans for it 将来に必要となることを予測でき、そのための計画を立てている→先見の明のある、先を見通した、思慮分別のある、卓見のある、賢明な ▶定義2 米 = LONG-SIGHTED

**fart** /fɑːrt/ 動 自 俗 ▶定義 to suddenly let gas from the stomach escape from your bottom しりから急に腹部のガスを放出する→放屁(ほうひ)する、おならをする — fart 名 C →屁(へ)、放屁、おなら

*****farther** /fáːrðər/ FAR の比較級 ☞参 **further** の注

*****farthest** /fáːrðəst/ FAR の最上級

*****fascinate** /fǽs(ə)nèɪt/ 動 他 ▶定義 to attract or interest sb very much ～をとても強く引き付ける、または関心を持たせる→～を魅了する、魅惑する、うっとりさせる、とりこにする、～の心を奪う、～の興味をそそる ‖ *Chinese culture has always fascinated me.* 中国文化は常に私を魅了してきた. — fascinating 形 →魅了する、魅惑的な、うっとりさせる、心を奪うような、すばらしい、とても美しい — fascination /fæs(ə)néɪʃ(ə)n/ 名 C U →魅惑、魅了、うっとりした状態、～に魅せられていること、心を奪われていること、魅力

**fascism** (または **Fascism**) /fǽʃɪz(ə)m/ 名 U ▶定義 an extreme (right-wing) political system 極端な(右翼の)政治体制→ファシズム、独裁的国家主義、極右的国家主義 — fascist (または Fascist) /fǽʃɪst, fǽʃ-/ 名 C 形 →国粋主義者、ファシズム信奉者、ファシスト、ファシズムの、ファシズム的な

*****fashion** /fǽʃ(ə)n/ 名 ▶定義1 C U the style of dressing or behaving that is the most popular at a particular time ある時期に最も人気のある服装や行動の様式→流行、はやりの型、時代の好み、人気、ファッション ‖ *What is **the latest fashion** in hairstyles?* 髪形の最新の流行は何ですか. *a fashion show/model/magazine* ファッションショー・ファッションモデル・ファッション雑誌 *Jeans are always **in fashion**.* ジーンズはいつも流行している. *I think hats will **come back into fashion**.* 私は帽子がまたはやると思う. *That colour is **out of fashion** this year.* 今年はその色ははやっていない. ▶定義2 [単数扱い] the way you do sth ～をするやり方→流儀、仕方、やり方、～風 ‖ *Watch him. He's been behaving **in a** very strange **fashion**.* 彼を見てごらん. とても奇妙な振る舞いをしている.

*****fashionable** /fǽʃ(ə)nəb(ə)l/ 形 ▶定義1 popular or in a popular style at the time その時期に人気がある、または人気がある型の→流行の、はやりの、当世風の、はやっている ‖ *a fashionable area/dress/opinion* 流行の場所・服・考え ▶定義2 considering fashion to be important 流行を重要であると見なしている→流行を追う、流行の先駆けをする、流行にこだわる、上流社会の、高級な、一流の ‖ *fashionable society* 上流社会 ⇔ **unfashionable, old-fashioned** — fashionably /-əbli/ 副 →流行を追って、当世風に、粋(いき)に、おしゃれに

*****fast**[1] /fɑːst; fæst/ 形 ▶定義1 able to move or act at great speed 非常な速さで動くことができる、または行動できる→速い、高速の、敏速な、素早い、すばしこい、性急な ‖ *a fast car/worker/runner/reader* スピードの出る車・仕事の速い人・走るのが速い人・読書の速い人 ☞参 **quick** の注 ▶定義2 (used about a clock or watch) showing a time that is later than the real time (時計や腕時計について) 実際の時刻より先の時刻を示している→進んでいる ‖ *The clock is five minutes fast.* その時計は5分進んでいる. ⇔ **slow** ▶定義3 (used about camera film) very sensitive to light, and therefore good for taking photographs in poor light or of things that are moving quickly (カメラのフィルムについて) 光に非常に敏感なので, あまり明るくない所で, または素早く動いている物を撮影するのに適した➔**高感度の, 高速撮影用の** ▶定義**4** (名詞の後だけ) firmly fixed しっかり固定された➔**しっかりした, しっかり取り付けた, しっかり定着した, (結び目などが) 固い, (色が) 簡単にあせない** ‖ *He made the boat fast (= he tied it to something) before he got out.* 彼は降りる前にボートをつないだ (= ボートを何かに結び付けた). *Do you think the colour in this T-shirt is fast (= will not come out when washed)?* このTシャツの色は落ちない (= 洗っても色があせない) と思いますか.

成句 fast and furious ▶定義 very fast and exciting 非常に速く, 興奮している➔**どっと, 勢いよく, 白熱化して, 盛り上がって**

hard and fast ⇒ **HARD**¹

**fast**² /fɑːst; fæst/ 副 ▶定義**1** quickly 速い➔**速い, 急速な, 素早い** ‖ *She ran very fast.* 彼女はとても速く走った. ▶定義**2** firmly or deeply しっかりと, または深く➔**しっかりと, 堅く, 堅固に; ぐっすりと** ‖ *Sam was fast asleep by ten o'clock.* サムは10時には熟睡していた. *Our car was stuck fast in the mud.* 私たちの車は泥に深くはまった.

**fast**³ /fɑːst; fæst/ 動 ⊜ ▶定義 to eat no food for a certain time, usually for religious reasons 通常は宗教上の理由で, ある一定の期間, 食物を食べない➔**断食する, 精進する, 絶食する** ‖ *Muslims fast during Ramadan.* イスラム教徒はラマダーンの期間は断食する. — fast 名 ⓒ➔**断食, 絶食, 断食期間**

*****fasten** /fɑ́ːsn; fǽsn/ 動 ▶定義**1** ⊜ ⓘ fasten sth (up) to close or join the two parts of sth; to become closed or joined 〜の2つの部分を閉じる, または結合する; 閉じられる, または結合される➔**〜をしっかり固定する, しっかり留める, くくり付ける, (ベルトなどを) 締める, しっかりと締まる,** ‖ *Please fasten your seat belts.* シートベルトをお締めください. *Fasten your coat up - it's cold outside.* コートのボタンを留めなさい — 外は寒いですよ. *My dress fastens at the back.* 私の服は後ろ開きです. ▶定義**2** ⓘ fasten sth (on/to sth); fasten A and B (together) to fix or tie sth to sth, or two things together 〜を…に, または2つの物を, 固定した

り結び付ける➔**〜を取り付ける, しっかり留める, 結合する, 結び合わせる** ‖ *Fasten this badge on your jacket.* このバッジを上着に付けてください. *How can I fasten these pieces of wood together?* これらの木片をどうやったら合わせられるのですか. ▶定義**3** ⓘ to close or lock sth firmly so that it will not open 開かないようにしっかりと〜を閉じる, またはかぎをかける➔**〜を閉める, (かぎなど) をかける, 戸締まりをする** ‖ *Close the window and fasten it securely.* 窓をきちんと閉めて, しっかりとかぎをかけなさい.

**fastener** /fɑ́ːsnər, fǽsnər/ (または **fastening** /fɑ́ːsnɪŋ; fǽsnɪŋ/) 名 ⓒ ▶定義 something that fastens things together 物を留め合わせる物➔**留め金具, 締め具, ファスナー, クリップ**

**fast food** 名 ⓤ ▶定義 food that can be served very quickly in special restaurants and is often taken away to be eaten in the street 専門の飲食店で非常に早く出され, しばしば持ち出して通りで食べられるような食べ物➔**ファーストフード** ‖ *a fast food restaurant* ファーストフード店

**fast forward** 動 ⓘ ▶定義 to make a videotape or a cassette go forward quickly without playing it ビデオテープやカセットを再生せずに高速で進める➔**〜を早送りする** — fast forward 名 ⓤ➔**早送り** ‖ *Press fast forward to advance the tape.* テープを進めるには早送りを押してください. *the fast-forward button* 早送りボタン ☞参 rewind

**fastidious** /fæstídiəs, fəs-/ 形 ▶定義 difficult to please; wanting everything to be perfect 喜ばせるのが難しい; すべてが完全であることを望んでいる➔**気難しい, 好みにうるさい, 潔癖な, 完全主義の**

*****fat**¹ /fæt/ 形 (fatter; fattest) ▶定義**1** (used about people's or animal's bodies) weighing too much; covered with too much flesh (人や動物の体について) 体重が重すぎる; 肉が付きすぎた➔**太った, 肥満した, 太らせた, 脂肪の多い** ‖ *You'll get fat if you eat too much.* 食べすぎると太りますよ. ⇔ thin

▶ 人が fat であると言うのは失礼である. plump, stout または overweight の方が丁寧な語.

▶定義**2** (used about a thing) thick or full (物に

ついて)厚い,またはぎっしり詰まった→**分厚い, 膨れた, 豊かな, たっぷりの** ‖ *a fat wallet/book* 金がたんまり入った札入れ・分厚い本

**\*fat²** /fæt/ 图 ▶定義 1 ❶the soft white substance under the skins of animals and people 動物や人の皮膚の下にある柔らかい白い物質→**皮下脂肪, 脂肪組織, 脂身** ‖ *I don't like meat with fat on it.* 私は脂身の多すぎる肉は好きではない. ☛ 形 fatty ▶定義 2 ❶❷the substance containing oil that we obtain from animals, plants or seeds and use for cooking 動物,植物,種子などからとれて料理に用いる, 油を含む物質→**脂, (食用)油脂, 脂肪** ‖ *Cook the onions in a little fat.* 少量の油でタマネギをいためます.

**\*fatal** /féɪtl/ 形 ▶定義 1 causing or ending in death 死の原因となる,または死で終わる→**致命的な, 命取りになる, 命にかかわる, 不治の** ‖ *a fatal accident/disease* 死亡事故・不治の病 ☛参 mortal ▶定義 2 causing trouble or a bad result 問題や悪い結果を引き起こしている→**破滅的な, 極めて重大な, 決定的な, 運命を決する** ‖ *She made the fatal mistake of trusting him.* 彼女は彼を信用するという決定的な誤りを犯した.
— fatally /-li/ 副→**致命的に, 運命的に, 決定的に, 取り返しのつかないほど** ‖ *fatally injured* 致命傷を負って

**fatality** /feɪtǽləti, fə-/ 图 ❷ (複 **fatalities**) ▶定義 a person's death caused by an accident, in war, etc 事故や戦争などを原因とする人の死→**不慮の死, 戦死, 死亡者** ‖ *There were no fatalities in the fire.* その火事での死亡者はなかった.

**\*fate** /feɪt/ 图 ▶定義 1 ❶the power that some people believe controls everything that happens 起こるすべての事を支配すると一部の人が信じる力→**運命, 運命の力, 宿命** ‖ *It was fate that brought them together again after twenty years.* 20年後に彼らが再会したのは運命だった.
▶定義 2 ❷your future; something that happens to you 自分の未来; 未来に自分に起こること→**(個人の)運命, 運, 不運, (物事の)成り行き, 結末** ‖ *Both men suffered the same fate - they both lost their jobs.* どちらの男も同じ不運に見舞われた — 2人とも失業したのだった. ☛類 fortune

**fateful** /féɪtfʊl, -f(ə)l/ 形 ▶定義 having an important effect on the future 未来に重要な影響を持っている→**運命的な, 運命を決する, 決定的な, 重大な** ‖ *a fateful decision* 重大な決意

**\*father¹** /fɑ́ːðər/ 图 ❷ ▶定義 1 a person's male parent 人の男親→**父, 父親, お父さん** ‖ *John looks exactly like his father.* ジョンは父親にそっくりだ. ▶定義 2 **Father** the title of certain priests 特定の聖職者の尊称→**神父, 司祭, 修道院長, 〜師** ‖ *Father O'Reilly* オライリー神父

**father²** /fɑ́ːðər/ 動 ⦿ ▶定義 to become a father 父となる→**〜の父親となる, (男が)子を持つ** ‖ *to father a child* 子供の父親となる

**Father Christmas** (または **Santa Claus**) 图 ❷ ▶定義 an old man with a red coat and a long white beard who, children believe, brings presents at Christmas 赤い上着を着て, 長い白いあごひげがあり, クリスマスに贈り物を持ってきてくれると子供たちが信じている老人→**サンタクロース**

**fatherhood** /fɑ́ːðərhʊd/ 图 ❶ ▶定義 the state of being a father 父親であること→**父であること, 父としての資格, 父権**

**father-in-law** 图 ❷ (複 **fathers-in-law**) ▶定義 the father of your husband or wife 夫または妻の父→**義理の父親, 義父, しゅうと**

**fatherly** /fɑ́ːðərli/ 形 ▶定義 like or typical of a father 父親らしい, または父親を象徴している→**父親のような, 父としての, 父親にふさわしい, 慈父のような** ‖ *Would you like a piece of fatherly advice?* 父親として1つ忠告しよう.

**fathom** /fǽðəm/ 動 ⦿ (通常は否定文で) ▶定義 to understand sth 〜を理解する→**〜を推測する, 見抜く, 理解する** ‖ *I can't fathom what he means.* 彼が何を言おうとしているのか分からない.

**fatigue** /fətíːg/ 图 ❶ ▶定義 1 the feeling of being extremely tired 非常に疲れている気分→**疲労, 疲れ** ‖ *He was suffering from mental and physical fatigue.* 彼は精神的にも肉体的にも疲れていた. ▶定義 2 weakness in metals caused by a lot of use 何度も使用することによって金属が弱くなること→**金属疲労** ‖ *The plane crash was caused by metal fatigue in a wing.* その飛行機の墜落は翼の金属疲労が原因で起こった.

**fatten** /fǽtn/ 動 ⦿ ▶定義 **fatten sb/sth (up)** to make sb/sth fatter 〜を太らせる→**〜を太らせ**

る, 肥やす, 大きくする, 厚くする, 増やす ‖ *He's fattening the pigs up for market.* 彼は市場に出すため豚を太らせている.

**fattening** /fǽtnɪŋ/ 形 ▶定義 (used about food) that makes people fat (食べ物について) 人を太らせるような→**太りやすい, 肥満になる** ‖ *Chocolate is very fattening.* チョコレートはとても太りやすい.

**fatty** /fǽti/ 形 (**fattier**; **fattiest**) ▶定義 (used about food) having a lot of fat in or on it (食べ物について) 内部や表面に多くの油がある→**脂肪を多く含む, 脂肪分の多い, 脂っこい, 油を多く使った**

**faucet** /fɔ́ːsət/ 米 = **TAP**²(1)

\***fault**¹ /fɔ́ː(l)lt/ 名 ▶定義 **1** Ⓒ something wrong or not perfect in a person's character or in a thing 人の性質や物の, 悪い点や完全でないところ→**欠点, 短所, 欠陥, 傷** ‖ *One of my faults is that I'm always late.* 私の欠点の１つは, いつも遅刻することです. ☞参 **mistake** の注 ▶定義 **2** Ⓤ responsibility for a mistake 誤りに対する責任→**過失の責任, 罪, せい, 落ち度** ‖ *It will be your own fault if you don't pass your exams.* 試験に合格できなければ, それは自分自身の責任です.

成句 **be at fault** ▶定義 to be wrong or responsible for a mistake 誤っている, または誤りに対する責任がある→**間違っている, 誤って, 落ち度のある, 罪がある, 〜のせいである, 〜に対して責任がある** ‖ *The other driver was at fault - he didn't stop at the traffic lights.* もう一方の運転者に責任があった − 彼は信号で停止しなかった.

**find fault (with sb/sth)** ⇒ **FIND**¹

**fault**² /fɔ́ːlt/ 動 他 ▶定義 to find sth wrong with sb/sth 〜について悪い…を見つける→**あらを捜す, 欠点を見つける, 〜を非難する, とがめる** ‖ *It was impossible to fault her English.* 彼女の英語は文句の付けようがなかった.

**faultless** /fɔ́ːltləs/ 形 ▶定義 without any mistakes; perfect 間違いが１つもない; 完ぺきな→**欠点のない, 欠陥のない, 完ぺきな, 申し分のない, 完全無欠な** ‖ *The pianist gave a faultless performance.* そのピアニストは完ぺきな演奏をした.

**faulty** /fɔ́ːlti/ 形 ▶定義 (used especially about electricity or machinery) not working properly (特に電気や機械について) 正しく機能していない→**欠陥のある, 不完全な, 調子の悪い** ‖ *a faulty switch* 調子の悪いスイッチ

**fauna** /fɔ́ːnə/ 名 Ⓤ ▶定義 all the animals of an area or a period of time ある地域, またはある時代のすべての動物→**動物相, 動物区系, ファウナ** ‖ *the flora and fauna of South America* 南アメリカの植物相と動物相 ☞参 **flora**

**faux pas** /fòu pάː; F fo pɑ/ 名 Ⓒ (複 **faux pas** /fóu pάː(z); F --/) ▶定義 something you say or do that is embarrassing or offends people 人を当惑させるような, または人を不快にさせるような言葉あるいは行い→**(社交上の) 失策, 失言, 非礼, 不品行, 不作法** ‖ *to make a faux pas* 失策を犯す

\***favour**¹ (米 **favor**) /féɪvər/ 名 ▶定義 **1** Ⓒ something that helps sb 〜を助ける事→**親切 (な行為), 好意, 願い, 尽力, 世話** ‖ *Would you do me a favour and post this letter for me?* すみませんが, この手紙を投かんしてくれませんか. *Could I ask you a favour?* お願いがあるのですが. *Are they paying you for the work, or are you doing it as a favour?* その仕事に対して彼らはお金を払っていますか, それともあなたの好意でやっているのですか. ▶定義 **2** Ⓤ favour (with sb) liking or approval 好みまたは承認→**好意, 好感, 人気, 引き立て, 愛顧, 支持, 賛成, 是認** ‖ *I'm afraid I'm out of favour with my neighbour since our last argument.* この間の言い争い以降, どうも私は近所の人から嫌われているようだ. *The new boss's methods didn't find favour with the staff.* 新しい上司のやり方は部下の支持を得られなかった.

成句 **in favour of sb/sth** ▶定義 in agreement with 〜に同意して→**〜に賛成して, 〜に味方して, 〜を支持して, 〜の方を選んで** ‖ *Are you in favour of private education?* 私学教育に賛成ですか.

**in sb's favour** ▶定義 to the advantage of sb 〜の有利に→**〜のために, 〜の利益となるように, 〜に好都合に** ‖ *The committee decided in their favour.* 委員会は彼らに有利な決定をした.

\***favour**² (米 **favor**) /féɪvər/ 動 他 ▶定義 **1** to support sb/sth; to prefer 〜を支持する; 〜を好む→**〜に賛成する, 味方する, 好意を示す, 〜を奨励する, 〜を好む** ‖ *Which suggestion do you favour?* どちらの提案を支持しますか. ▶定義 **2** to treat one person very well and so be unfair to others

1人を非常に厚遇し、そのためにほかの人に不公平になる→〜をえこひいきする、〜を偏愛する、〜に特に目をかける || *Parents must try not to favour one of their children.* 親は1人の子供だけをえこひいきしないようにしなければならない.

**favourable** (米 **favorable**) /féɪv(ə)rəb(ə)l/ 形
▶定義 1 showing liking or approval 好みや承認を示している→好意を持った、気に入られる、好意を得る、賛成の、〜に好意的の、承認の、承諾の || *He made a favourable impression on the interviewers.* 彼は面接官に良い印象を与えた.
▶定義 2 (often used about the weather) suitable or helpful (しばしば天候について)適切な、または助けになる→ちょうど良い、都合の良い、有利な、順調な || *Conditions are favourable for skiing today.* 今日はスキーに好都合な状況だ.
⇔ **unfavourable**, **adverse** — **favourably** (米 **favorably**) /-əbli/ 副 →好意的に、賛成して、有利に、都合良く、順調に

\***favourite**¹ (米 **favorite**) /féɪv(ə)rət/ 形 ▶定義 liked more than any other ほかの何よりも好まれている→一番好きな、お気に入りの、大好きな、得意な || *What is your favourite colour?* 一番好きな色は何ですか. *Who is your favourite singer?* 一番お気に入りの歌手はだれですか.

**favourite**² (米 **favorite**) /féɪv(ə)rət/ 名 C
▶定義 1 a person or thing that you like more than any others ほかの何よりも好きな人または物→お気に入り、特に好きな人・物 || *The other kids were jealous of Rose because she was the teacher's favourite.* ローズは先生のお気に入りだったので、ほかの子供たちは彼女に焼きもちを焼いた. ▶定義 2 favourite (for sth/to do sth) the horse, team, competitor, etc who is expected to win 勝つと期待されている馬、チーム、競争者など→本命、優勝候補、人気馬 || *Mimms is the hot favourite for the leadership of the party.* ミムズは党の指導者争いの大本命だ.
⇔ **outsider**

**favouritism** (米 **favoritism**) /féɪv(ə)rətɪz(ə)m/ 名 U ▶定義 giving unfair advantages to the person or people that you like best 最も気に入った人や人々に対して不当に有利な扱いをすること→えこひいき、偏愛、情実 || *The referee was accused of showing favouritism to the home side.* その審判はホームチームをひいきしたとして非難された.

**fawn**¹ /fɔːn/ 形 名 U ▶定義 (of) a light yellowish-brown colour 明るい黄色がかった茶色(の)→淡い黄褐色(の)

**fawn**² /fɔːn/ 名 C ▶定義 a young animal (deer) 若い動物(シカ)→(1歳未満の)子ジカ ☞参 **deer** の注

**fax**¹ /fæks/ 名 ▶定義 1 C U a copy of a letter, etc that you can send by telephone lines using a special machine 専用の機械を使って電話線で送信できる、手紙などの複写→ファックス || *They need an answer today so I'll send a fax.* 彼らは今日返事が必要なので、私はファックスを送るつもりだ. *They contacted us by fax.* 彼らはファックスで連絡してきた. ▶定義 2 C (または **fax machine**) the machine that you use for sending faxes ファックスを送信するために使用する機械→ファックス装置、ファクシミリ || *Have you got a fax?* ファックスがありますか. *What's your fax number?* ファックス番号を教えてください.

**fax**² /fæks/ 動 他 ▶定義 fax sth (to sb); fax sb (sth) to send sb a fax 〜にファックスを送信する→〜に…をファックスで送る || *We will fax our order to you tomorrow.* 注文書を明日ファックスでお送りします. *I've faxed her a copy of the letter.* 私は手紙のコピーを彼女にファックスで送った.

**faze** /feɪz/ 動 略式 ▶定義 to make sb worried or nervous 〜を心配させる、またはいらいらさせる→〜の心を騒がせる、〜を慌てさせる、動揺させる、困惑させる、困らせる || *He doesn't get fazed by things going wrong.* 彼は物事がうまくいかなくても慌てない.

**FBI** /ˌef biː ˈaɪ/ 略 米 Federal Bureau of Investigation ▶定義 the section of the US Justice Department which investigates crimes that are against the laws of the US as a whole, such as bank robbery and terrorism 銀行強盗やテロのような米国全体にかかわる法律に違反する犯罪を捜査する、米国司法省の部局→連邦捜査局

**FC** /ˌef ˈsiː/ 略 英 Football Club→サッカークラブ || *Everton FC* エヴァートン サッカークラブ

**FCO** /ˌef siː ˈəʊ/ 略 Foreign and Commonwealth

Office→外務連邦省, 外務省

\*__fear__¹ /fíɚ/ 名 ❻ ❶ ▶定義 the feeling that you have when sth dangerous, painful or frightening might happen 危険な, 苦しい, または恐ろしい事が起こりそうなときに抱く感情→**恐怖, 恐れ, おびえ, 不安, 心配, 懸念** ‖ *He was shaking with fear after the accident.* その事故の後, 彼は恐怖で震えていた. *People in this area live in constant fear of crime.* この地区の人々は常に犯罪におびえて暮らしている. *This book helped me overcome my fear of dogs.* この本は私の犬への恐怖心を克服させてくれた. *She showed no fear.* 彼女は不安を表に出さなかった. *My fears for his safety were unnecessary.* 彼が無事かどうかを心配する必要はなかった.

成句 **no fear** (口語) ▶定義 (used when answering a suggestion) certainly not (提案に答える場合に用いて) もちろん反対だ→**とんでもない, 大反対, (絶対に) 駄目だ**

\*__fear__² /fíɚ/ 動 ▶定義 1 ⓤ to be afraid of sb/sth or of doing sth 〜を恐れる, または〜をすることを恐れる→**〜を恐れる, 怖がる, ためらう** ‖ *We all fear illness and death.* 私たちは皆, 病と死を恐れている. ▶定義 2 ⓤ to feel that something bad might happen or might have happened 何か悪い事が起こるかもしれない, または起こったかもしれないと感じる→**〜を心配する, 気遣う, 恐れる, 不安に思う, 〜ではないかと危ぶむ** ‖ *The government fears that it will lose the next election.* 政府は次の選挙で敗北するのではないかと心配している. *Thousands of people are feared dead in the earthquake.* 何千人もの人々がその地震で亡くなったのではないかと思われる.

句動詞 **fear for sb/sth** ▶定義 to be worried about sb/sth 〜について心配する→**〜を心配する, 気遣う** ‖ *Parents often fear for the safety of their children.* 親はしばしば子供の安全について心配する.

__fearful__ /fíɚfəl, -f(ə)l/ 形 正式 ▶定義 1 fearful (of sth/doing sth); fearful that… afraid or worried about sth 〜について恐れる, または心配する→**〜を恐れて, 怖がって, 気遣って, 心配して, 不安がって** ‖ *You should never be fearful of starting something new.* 新しい事を始めるのを決して恐れてはいけない. *They were fearful that they would miss the plane.* 彼らは飛行機に乗り遅れるのではないかと心配した. ☛参 **frightened**, **scared** と **afraid** の注. これらの語の方がもっと一般的である. ▶定義 2 terrible ひどい→**すごい, ものすごい, 恐ろしい, つらい, 大変な, 激しい, 劣悪な** ‖ *the fearful consequences of war* 戦争の恐ろしい結果 — __fearfully__ /-fʊli, -f(ə)li/ 副 →**恐る恐る, びくびくして, 怖がって, ひどく, 恐ろしく** — __fearfulness__ 名 ⓤ →**不安, 心配, 恐れること, 恐ろしさ, 恐怖心**

__fearless__ /fíɚləs/ 形 ▶定義 never afraid 決して恐れない→**恐れを知らない, 大胆不敵な, 怖いもの知らずの** — __fearlessly__ 副 →**恐れずに, 大胆不敵に** — __fearlessness__ 名 ⓤ →**怖いもの知らず, 大胆不敵, 大胆さ**

__feasible__ /fíːzəb(ə)l/ 形 ▶定義 possible to do 実行できる→**実行可能な, うまくいきそうな, 無理のない** ‖ *a feasible plan* 実行可能な計画 — __feasibility__ /fíːzəbíləti/ 名 ⓤ →**実行できること, 実行可能性, 成否**

__feast__ /fíːst/ 名 ❻ ▶定義 a large, special meal, especially to celebrate sth 特に〜を祝うための, 特別な大規模な食事→**大宴会, 祝宴, ごちそう, 豪勢な食事** — __feast__ 動 🄐 **feast (on sth)**→**祝宴にあずかる, 大いに食べる, ごちそうになる, 〜を満喫する, 大いに楽しむ** ‖ *They feasted on exotic dishes.* 彼らは異国風の料理を大いに楽しんだ.

__feat__ /fíːt/ 名 ❻ ▶定義 something you do that shows great strength, skill or courage 際立った力, 技術, 勇気などを示す行為→**手柄, 偉業, 功績, 離れ業, 芸当, 妙技** ‖ *That new bridge is a remarkable feat of engineering.* あの新しい橋は工学技術の粋だ. *Persuading Helen to give you a pay rise was no mean feat* (= difficult to do). 給料を上げてくれるようにヘレンを説得するのは本当に大変だった (= そうするのが難しかった).

\*__feather__ /féðɚ/ 名 ❻ ▶定義 one of the light, soft things that grow in a bird's skin and cover its body 鳥の皮膚に生えて体を覆っている, 1 枚 1 枚の軽く柔らかい物→**羽, 羽毛** ☛ C1 ページのさし絵

\*__feature__¹ /fíːtʃɚ/ 名 ❻ ▶定義 1 an important or noticeable part of sth 〜の重要な, または目立つ部分→**特徴, 特色, 主要点** ‖ *Mountains and lakes are the main features of the landscape of Wales.*

**feature**² 山と湖がウェールズの風景の主な特色である. *Noise is a feature of city life.* 騒音は都市生活の1つの特徴だ. ▶定義2 a part of the face 顔の部分→顔の造作, 目鼻立ち, 容貌(ようぼう), 顔立ち, 顔付き ‖ *Her eyes are her best feature.* 彼女の顔の中で目が一番美しい. ▶定義3 a feature (on sth) a newspaper or magazine article or television programme about sth 〜についての新聞や雑誌の記事, またはテレビ番組→特別記事, (特集)記事・番組, 特別番組 ‖ *There's a feature on kangaroos in this magazine.* この雑誌にはカンガルーの特集記事がある. ▶定義4 (または **feature film**) a long film that tells a story 筋のある長い映画→長編劇映画, 主要作品, 特別作品 ― **featureless** 形→特徴のない, 特色のない, 面白くない, 平凡な ‖ *dull, featureless landscape* 退屈で特徴のない風景

**feature**² /fíːtʃər/ 動 ▶定義1 ⑯ to include sb/sth as an important part 〜を重要な部分として含む→〜を呼び物にする, 大きく扱う, 特集する, 特色にする, 主演させる ‖ *The film features many well-known actors.* その映画には有名な俳優がたくさん出演している. ▶定義2 ⑲ feature in sth to have a part in sth 〜のある部分を持つ→役割を演じる, 重要な役割を果たす, 役目を果たす, 含まれる ‖ *Does marriage feature in your future plans?* 結婚はあなたの将来の計画に含まれていますか. ☞類 **figure**

**Feb** 略 February→2月 ‖ *18 Feb 1993* 1993年2月18日

*****February** /fébjuəri, fébrə-; fébruəri, fébju-/ 名 ⓤ ⓒ (略 **Feb**) ▶定義 the second month of the year, coming after January 1月の次に来る, 1年の2番目の月→2月

▶文中での月の表し方については, January の例と注を参照.

**feces** 米 = FAECES

**fed** FEED¹ の過去・過去分詞形

**federal** /fédərəl/ 形 ▶定義1 organized as a federation 連邦として組織されている→連邦の, 連合の, 同盟の ‖ *a federal system of rule* 連邦制による統治 ▶定義2 connected with the central government of a federation 連邦の中央政府に関連している→連邦政府の, 連邦制の ‖ *That is a federal not a state law.* それは州法ではなく連邦法である.

**federation** /fèdəréɪʃ(ə)n/ 名 ⓒ ▶定義 a group of states, etc that have joined together to form a single group 連合して1つの集団を形成する州などの集まり→連合, 連盟, 同盟, 連合体, 連邦国家・政府

**fed up** 形武 (名詞の前は不可) ▶定義 **fed up (with/of sb/sth/doing sth)** bored or unhappy; tired of st 退屈で, または不幸で; 〜にうんざりしている→〜に飽き飽きして, 嫌になって, 食傷して ‖ *What's the matter? You look really fed up.* どうしたのですか. 実にうんざりしているように見えますが. *I'm fed up with waiting for the phone to ring.* 私は電話が鳴るのを待つのに嫌気が差している.

*****fee** /fíː/ 名 ⓒ ▶定義1 (通常は複数) the money you pay for professional advice or service from private doctors, lawyers, schools, universities, etc 専門的な忠告, または私営の医師, 弁護士, 学校, 大学などのサービスに対して支払う金→(専門職に払う)謝礼金, 報酬, 料金, 授業料, 会費 ‖ *We can't afford private school fees.* 私たちには私立校の授業料を払う余裕はない. *Most ticket agencies will **charge a** small **fee**.* 大抵の切符取次業者は少額の手数料を取る.

▶定義2 the cost of an exam, the cost of becoming a member of a club, the amount you pay to go into certain buildings, etc 試験の費用, クラブの会員になる経費, 特定の建物に入るために支払う料金など→受験料, 入会金, 入場料, 会費 ‖ *How much is the entrance fee?* 入場料はいくらですか. ☞参 **pay**² の注

**feeble** /fíːb(ə)l/ 形 ▶定義1 with no energy or power; weak 勢いや力がない; 弱い→弱った, 弱々しい, 衰弱した, かすかな ‖ *a feeble old man* 弱々しい老人 *a feeble cry* かすかな叫び声 ▶定義2 not able to make sb believe sth 〜に…を信じさせることができない→説得力の弱い, 内容の乏しい, 根拠が不十分な, 不足している ‖ *a feeble argument/excuse* 説得力のない議論・言い訳

*****feed**¹ /fíːd/ 動 (過, 過分 **fed** /féd/) ▶定義1 ⑯ **feed sb/sth (on) (sth)** to give food to a person or an animal 人や動物に食べ物を与える→〜に食べ物を与える, (赤ん坊に)授乳する, えさを与える ‖ *Don't forget to feed the dog.* 犬にえさをやるのを忘れないように. *I can't come yet. I* haven't fed the baby. まだ行けません. 赤ん坊に授乳していないので. *Some of the snakes in the zoo are fed (on) rats.* 動物園の蛇の一部は, えさとしてネズミを与えられている. ▶定義2 ⓔ feed (on sth) (used about animals or babies) to eat (動物や赤ん坊について) 食べる→(動物が) 物を食う, (赤ん坊が) 食事をする ‖ *What do horses feed on in the winter?* 馬は冬には何を食べるのですか. *Bats feed at night.* コウモリは夜にえさを食べる. ▶定義3 ⓣ feed A (with B); feed B into/to/through A to supply sb/sth with sth; to put sth into sth else ～に…を供給する; ～をほかの…の中へ入れる→～を送る, 送り込む, 提供する, 補給する, ～に油を差す ‖ *This channel feeds us with news and information 24 hours a day.* このチャンネルは1日24時間, ニュースと情報を放送している. *Metal sheets are fed through the machine one at a time.* 金属の薄板が1度に1枚ずつ, その機械に送り込まれる.

**feed**² /fiːd/ 名 ▶定義1 ⓒ a meal for an animal or a baby 動物や赤ん坊の食事→食事, 授乳, 1食分の食事 ‖ *When's the baby's next feed due?* その赤ん坊の次の食事はいつですか. ▶定義2 ⓤ food for animals 動物の食べ物→えさ, 飼料 ‖ *cattle feed* 牛の飼料

**feedback** /ˈfiːdbæk/ 名 ⓤ ▶定義 information or comments about sth that you have done which tells you how good or bad it is 自分がした～について, どの程度良いか悪いかを述べている情報または批評→反応, 意見, 感想, フィードバック ‖ *The teacher spent five minutes with each of us to **give** us **feedback on** our homework.* その先生は私たち1人ずつに5分取って, 宿題について批評してくれた.

★**feel**¹ /fiːl/ 動 (過, 過分 **felt** /felt/) ▶定義1 ⓛ (通常は形容詞と共に) to be in the state that is mentioned 言及されたような状態である→～であると感じる, ～の感じがする, 心地がする ‖ *to feel cold/sick/tired/happy* 寒い・気分が悪い・疲れた・幸福だと感じる *How are you feeling today?* 今日はご気分はいかがですか. *You'll feel better in the morning.* 朝には気分が良くなりますよ. ▶定義2 ⓛ used to say how something seems to you when you touch, see, smell, experience, etc it 触れる, 見る, においをかぐ, 体験するなどしたときに事物がどのように思わ

れたかを言う場合に用いられる→～の感じがする, 手触りが～と感じる, 思われる, 気がする ‖ *My new coat feels like leather but it's not.* 私の新しいコートは革のような手触りだが, 実際は革ではない. *He felt as if he had been there before.* 彼は前にそこに行ったことがあるような気がした. *My head feels as though it will burst.* 頭が破裂しそうな気がする. *I felt (that) it was a mistake not to ask her advice.* 彼女に助言を求めなかったのは間違いだったと思った.

▶この意味のfeelの主語には, it がしばしば用いられる: *It feels as if it is going to snow soon.* (もうすぐ雪になりそうだ.)

▶定義3 ⓣ to notice or experience sth physical or emotional 肉体的または感情的な～を認める, または体験する→～を感じる, 覚える, 感じ取る, 気付く, ～の感覚がある ‖ *I damaged nerves and now I can't feel anything in this hand.* 私は神経に損傷を受けたので, 今はこちらの手では何も感じられない. *I felt something crawling up my back.* 何かが背中をはい上がってくるのを感じた. *I don't feel any sympathy for Matt at all.* 私はマットに対して全く同情を感じない. *You could feel the tension in the courtroom.* 法廷の緊張感が感じ取れるはずだ. ▶定義4 ⓣ to touch sth in order to find out what it is like それがどのようなものであるかを知るために～に触る→～に触ってみる, 触れる, ～を触って調べる ‖ *Feel this material. Is it cotton or silk?* この生地に触ってみてください. 綿でしょうか, それとも絹でしょうか. *I felt her forehead to see if she had a temperature.* 熱があるかどうか, 彼女の額に触ってみた. ▶定義5 ⓘ feel (about) (for sb/sth) to try to find something with your hands instead of your eyes 目ではなく手で物を見つけようとする→～を手探りで探す, 手探りで進む ‖ *She felt about in the dark for the light switch.* 彼女は暗闇(やみ)で手探りで明かりのスイッチを探した. ▶定義6 ⓘ to be affected by sth ～に影響される→～に感じ入る, 衝撃を受ける, 心を動かされる, ～が身に染みる ‖ *Do you feel the cold in winter?* 冬には寒さがこたえますか. *She felt it badly when her mother died.* 彼女は母親が亡くなった時, 大きな衝撃を受けた.

成句 feel free (to do sth) 略式 ▶定義 used to

## 608 feel²

tell sb he/she is allowed to do sth ～に…をするのが許されていると言うときに用いられて➡**自由に～する, 遠慮なく～する** ‖ *Feel free to use the phone.* どうぞご自由に電話をお使いください.

**feel like sth/doing sth** ▶定義 to want sth or to want to do sth ～を欲しがる, または～をしたがる➡**～が欲しい, ～したい気がする** ‖ *Do you feel like going out?* 外出したいですか.

**feel your age** ▶定義 to realize that you are getting old, especially compared to other younger people around you 特に周りにいるほかの若い人々に比べて, 自分が年を取りつつあると気付く➡**年を取ったと感じる, 衰えを感じる**

**not feel yourself** ▶定義 to not feel healthy or well 健康状態または調子が良くない➡**気分が良くない, 体調が悪い, いつもの元気がない**

句動詞 **feel for sb** ▶定義 to understand sb's feelings and situation and feel sorry for him/her ～の感情や状況を理解して, 気の毒に感じる➡**～に同情する, 共鳴する, 哀れむ** ‖ *I really felt for him when his wife died.* 彼の妻が亡くなった時, 私は彼に本当に同情した.

**feel up to sth/to doing sth** ▶定義 to have the strength and the energy to do or deal with sth ～をする, または～に対処する体力や力がある➡**～できそうに思う, ～に耐えられる, ～に適している** ‖ *I really don't feel up to eating a huge meal.* たくさん食べられそうな気分ではとてもありません.

\***feel²** /fi:l/ 名 [単数扱い] ▶定義 1 the impression something gives you when you touch it; the impression that a place or situation gives you それを触ったときに, 物が与える印象; 場所や状況が与える印象➡**手触り, 肌触り, 感触, 雰囲気** ‖ *You can tell it's wool by the feel.* それは手触りでウールだと分かります. *The town has a friendly feel.* その町は友好的な雰囲気だ. ▶定義 2 an act of touching sth in order to learn about it ～について知るために触ること➡**触ること, 触って感じること, 手探り** ‖ *Let me have a feel of that material.* その生地に触らせてください.

**feelers** /fi:lərz/ 名 [複数扱い] ▶定義 the long thin parts at the front of an insect's head that it uses to feel things 昆虫が～を感じ取るために使う, 頭の前部にある細長い部分➡**触角** ☛類

antennae

\***feeling** /fi:lɪŋ/ 名 ▶定義 1 ⓒ a feeling (of sth) something that you feel in your mind or body 心や体で感じるもの➡**感覚, 触感, 知覚, 感じ, 意識** ‖ *a feeling of hunger/happiness/fear/helplessness* 空腹感・幸福感・恐怖感・無力感 *I've got a funny feeling in my leg.* 脚が変な感じがする.

▶定義 2 [単数扱い] a belief or idea that sth is true or is likely to happen ～が真実である, または～が起こりそうだという信念や考え➡**感じ, 印象, 予感** ‖ *I get the feeling that Ian doesn't like me much.* イアンは私をあまり好いていないという感じがする. *I have a nasty feeling that Jan didn't get our message.* ジャンは私たちのメッセージを受け取っていなかったのではないかという嫌な予感がする. ▶定義 3 ⓒ Ⓤ **feeling(s) (about/on sth)** an attitude or opinion about sth ～についての態度や意見➡**考え, 意見, 感想, 印象** ‖ *What are your feelings on this matter?* この問題について, あなたはどうお考えですか. *My own feeling is that we should postpone the meeting.* 私の考えでは, その会議を延期すべきだ. *Public feeling seems to be against the new road.* 市民の意見は, 新しい道路に反対のようだ. ▶定義 4 [ⓒ Ⓤ, 通常は複数] a person's emotions; strong emotion 人の感情; 強い感情➡**気持ち, 感動, 激情, 興奮** ‖ *I have to tell Jeff his work's not good enough but I don't want to hurt his feelings.* ジェフに彼の仕事の出来はあまり良くないと言わなければならないが, 彼の気持ちを傷付けたくない. *Let's practise that song again, this time with feeling.* もう一度その歌を練習しましょう. 今度は感情を込めて. ▶定義 5 ⓒ Ⓤ **(a) feeling/feelings (for sb/sth)** love or understanding for sb/sth ～への愛情または理解➡**愛情, 同情, 共感, 思いやり, 理解** ‖ *She doesn't have much (of a) feeling for music.* 彼女は音楽にあまり興味がない. *He still has feelings for his ex-wife.* 彼はまだ前の妻に未練がある. ▶定義 6 Ⓤ the ability to feel in your body 体で感知する能力➡**感覚, 知覚, 触覚** ‖ *After the accident he lost all feeling in his legs.* 事故の後, 彼は脚の感覚をすべて失った.

成句 **bad/ill feeling** ▶定義 unhappy relations between people 人々の間の不幸な関係➡**反感, 不信感, わだかまり** ‖ *The decision caused a lot of bad feeling at the factory.* その決定によって

工場には多くの反感が生じた.
**no hard feelings** ⇒ **HARD**¹

**feet FOOT**¹ の複数形

**feline** /fíːlàin/ 形 ▶定義 connected with an animal of the cat family; like a cat ネコ科の動物に関連している; 猫のような→**ネコ科の, 猫に似た, しなやかな, 優雅な, おとなしい, 人目を盗む, ずるい**

**fell**¹ /fel/ **FALL**¹ の過去形

**fell**² /fel/ 動他 ▶定義 to cut down a tree 木を切り倒す→**〜を切り倒す, 伐採する**

**fellow**¹ /félou/ 名 C ▶定義 1 a member of an academic or professional organization, or of certain universities 学究的または専門的な組織, あるいはある大学の一員→**(学術団体の)特別会員, (大学の)評議員, 理事, 教官, フェロー** ‖ *a fellow of the Royal College of Surgeons* 王立医科大学の評議員 ▶定義 2 a person who is paid to study a particular thing at a university 大学である事を研究するために支払いを受けている人→**特別研究員, フェロー** ‖ *Jill is a research fellow in the biology department.* ジルは生物学部の特別研究員だ. ▶定義 3 (古) a man **男, 人, 少年, やつ**

**fellow**² /félou/ 形 (名詞の前だけ) ▶定義 another or others like yourself in the same situation 同じ状況にある, 自分と似た人や人々→**仲間の, 同僚の, 同輩の, 同級の, 同行する** ‖ *Her fellow students were all older than her.* 彼女の学友はみんな彼女より年上だった. *fellow workers/passengers/citizens* 同僚・同乗者・同郷の市民

**fellowship** /féloufip/ 名 ▶定義 1 ❶ a feeling of friendship between people who share an interest 利害を共有する人々の間の友情→**仲間意識, 連帯感, 友情, 親交, 協力, 共同** ▶定義 2 ❷ a group or society of people who share the same interest or belief 利害または信念を共有する人々の集団や社会→**団体, 協会, 組合, 信徒集団, グループ** ▶定義 3 ❷ the position of a college or university fellow 単科大学や総合大学のフェローの地位→**評議員の地位, 特別研究員の地位**

**felt**¹ **FEEL**¹ の過去・過去分詞形

**felt**² /felt/ 名 U ▶定義 a type of soft cloth made from wool, etc which has been pressed tightly together 合わせて強く圧縮された羊毛などから作られる, 柔らかい布の一種→**フェルト, 毛せん** ‖ *a felt hat* フェルトの帽子

**felt-tip pen** (または **felt tip**) 名 C ▶定義 a type of pen with a point made of felt フェルトでできた先端を持つペンの一種→**フェルトペン, サインペン**

*****female**¹ /fíːmeil/ 形 ▶定義 1 being a woman or a girl 女性または少女である→**女の, 女性の, 女子の** ‖ *a female artist/employer/student* 女性芸術家・女性の雇い主・女子学生 ▶定義 2 being of the sex that produce eggs or give birth to babies 卵を産む, または子供を産む性である→**雌の** ‖ *a female cat* 雌猫 ▶定義 3 (used about plants and flowers) that can produce fruit (植物や花について) 果実を実らせることができるような→**雌性の, 雌株の, めしべだけを持つ**

**female**² /fíːmeil/ 名 C ▶定義 1 an animal that can produce eggs or give birth to babies; a plant that can produce fruit 卵を産む, または子供を産むことができる動物; 果実を実らせることができる植物→**雌, 雌性植物, 雌株** ▶定義 2 a woman or a girl 女性または少女→**女性, 女, 女子**
▶ female と male は, 生物学的性を言う場合にのみ用いられる. 女性と男性に特有だと思われる性質について言う場合は, feminine と masculine を用いる.

*****feminine** /fémənən/ 形 ▶定義 1 typical of or looking like a woman; connected with women 女性に特有の, または女性のように見える; 女性に関連した→**女性特有の, 女性用の, 女性の, 女の, 女性的な, 女らしい** ‖ *My daughter always dresses like a boy. She hates looking feminine.* 私の娘はいつも少年のような服装をしている. 女らしく見えることを嫌がっているのだ. ☛参 **masculine** と **female** の注 ▶定義 2 (略 **fem**) (文法) (in English) of the forms of words used to describe females (英語で) 女性を指す場合に用いられる語形の→**女性の, 女性形の** ‖ *'Lioness' is the feminine form of 'lion'.* lioness は lion の女性形である. ▶定義 3 (略 **fem**) (文法) (in grammar of some languages) belonging to a certain class of nouns, adjectives or pronouns (いくつかの言語の文法で) 名詞, 形容詞, または代名詞のある分類に属している→**女性の** ‖ *The German word for a flower is feminine.* ドイツ語の花という語は女性(名詞)だ. ☛参 **masculine**, **neuter** ―**femininity** /fèmənínəti/ 名 U →**女性で**

あること，女性の特質，女らしさ

**feminism** /fémənɪz(ə)m/ 名 U ▶定義 the belief that women should have the same rights and opportunities as men 女性が男性と同じ権利と機会を持つべきだという信念➡男女同権主義，女性解放論，女権拡張論，フェミニズム ― **feminist** /fémənɪst/ 名 ●形 ➡男女同権主義者(の)，女性解放論者(の)，フェミニスト(の)

### ▶日本語 vs 英語

#### 「フェミニスト」の日本語特有の意味

英語の feminist は「男女同権主義者」「女権拡張論者」を意味します．日本語の「フェミニスト」は，俗に「女性に対して優しい[甘い]男性」の意で使われますが，英語にはそのような意味はありません．日本語の「フェミニスト」に近い意味の語には，中世ヨーロッパの騎士道に由来する chivalrous 形 (婦人に優しい) や philogyny 名 (女好き) などがあります．

\*fence¹ /fens/ 名 C ▶定義 a line of wooden or metal posts joined by wood, wire, metal, etc to divide land or to keep in animals 土地を分割したり，動物を囲い込むための，木材，針金，金属などでつながれた木製または金属製の柱の列➡柵(さく)，垣根，囲い，垣，フェンス ● C7 ページのさし絵

成句 sit on the fence ⇒ SIT

**fence²** /fens/ 動 ▶定義1 ⊕ to surround land with a fence 土地を柵(さく)で囲む➡～に塀を巡らす，囲いを作る，～で囲いをする ▶定義2 ⊜ to fight with a long thin pointed weapon (a foil) as a sport 先のとがった細長い武器(フルーレ)でスポーツとして戦う➡剣を使う，フェンシングをする，フルーレを使う

句動詞 fence sb/sth in ▶定義1 to surround sb/sth with a fence ～を柵(さく)で囲う➡～を囲い込む，～に柵を巡らす ‖ They fenced in their garden to make it more private. 彼らは人目をさらに遠ざけるために，庭を柵で囲んだ．

▶定義2 to restrict sb's freedom ～の自由を制限する➡～を制限する，束縛する，拘束する ‖ She felt fenced in by so many responsibilities. あまりに多くの責任を負って，彼女は束縛されていると感じた．

**fence sth off** ▶定義 to separate one area from another with a fence ある区域を柵(さく)で他から隔てる➡～を囲いで仕切る，柵で防護する，～を囲いで封じ込 める

**fencing** /fénsɪŋ/ 名 U ▶定義 the sport of fighting with long thin pointed weapons (foils) 先のとがった細長い武器(フルーレ)で戦うスポーツ➡フェンシング，フルーレ競技，剣術

**fend** /fend/ 動

句動詞 **fend for yourself** ▶定義 to look after yourself without help from anyone else ほかのだれからの助けもなしに自分自身の面倒を見る➡自活する，独力でやっていく，自立する ‖ It's time Ben left home and learned to fend for himself. ベンはそろそろ家を出て自活することを覚える時期だ．

**fend sb/sth off** ▶定義 to defend yourself from sb/sth that is attacking you 襲ってくる～から自分自身を防御する➡～をかわす，そらす，受け流す，食い止める，防ぐ ‖ Politicians usually manage to fend off awkward questions. 政治家は大抵，都合の悪い質問をうまく受け流そうとする．

**fender** /féndər/ 名 C ▶定義1 米 = WING(4)
▶定義2 a low metal frame in front of an open fire that stops coal or wood falling out 裸火の前に置く，石炭やまきが外に落ちるのを防ぐための背の低い金属の枠➡炉格子，ストーブ囲い

**ferment¹** /fəmént/ 動 ⊜ ⊕ ▶定義 to change or make the chemistry of sth change, especially sugar changing to alcohol 特に砂糖がアルコールに変化するなど，～の化学的性質が変わる，またはそれを変える➡～を発酵する；～を発酵させる ‖ The wine is starting to ferment. ブドウ酒が発酵し始めている．

**ferment²** /fə́:mènt/ 名 U ▶定義 a state of political or social excitement and change 政治的または社会的な騒動と変化➡動乱，騒ぎ，動揺，政治的・社会的不安定 ‖ The country is in ferment and nobody's sure what will happen next. その国は不安定で，次に何が起こるかだれにも分からない．

**fern** /fə:n/ 名 C ▶定義 a green plant with no flowers and a lot of long thin leaves 花がつかず，細長い葉がたくさんある緑の植物➡シダ，シダ類 ● C2 ページのさし絵

**ferocious** /fəróʊʃəs/ 形 ▶定義 very aggressive and violent 非常に攻撃的で暴力的な➡どう猛

な, 凶暴な, 残忍な, 猛烈な, ひどい, ものすごい ‖ *a ferocious beast/attack/storm/war* どう猛な獣・凶暴な攻撃・猛烈なあらし・残忍な戦争 — ferociously 副 ➡どう猛に, 凶暴に, 残忍に, 激しく, ひどく, ものすごく

**ferocity** /fərɑ́səti/ 名 Ⓤ ▶定義 violence; cruel and aggressive behaviour 暴力; 残酷で攻撃的な行動➡どう猛さ, 残忍性, 凶暴さ, 凶暴な行為, 野蛮行為 ☛形 fierce

*__ferry__¹ /féri/ 名 Ⓒ (複 __ferries__) ▶定義 a boat that carries people, vehicles or goods across a river or across a narrow part of the sea 川や海の狭い部分を横切って, 人, 乗り物, または品物などを運ぶ船➡フェリー (ボート), 渡し船, 連絡船 ‖ *a car ferry* カーフェリー

**ferry**² /féri/ 動 他 (現分 __ferrying__; 三単現 __ferries__; 過, 過分 __ferried__) ▶定義 to carry people or goods in a boat or other vehicle from one place to another, usually for a short distance 人や品物を船などの乗り物で, ある場所からほかの場所へ, 通常は短距離を運ぶ➡~を船で渡す, ~で…を運ぶ ‖ *Could you ferry us across to the island?* その島まで私たちを乗せていただけますか. *We share the job of ferrying the children to school.* 私たちは分担して子供たちを学校へ車で送っている.

**fertile** /fə́ːtail; fə́ːtl/ 形 ▶定義 1 (used about land or soil) that plants grow well in (土地や土壌について) そこで植物がよく育つような➡肥えた, 肥沃(ひよく)な, 豊かな, 作物のよくできる ▶定義 2 (used about people, animals or plants) that can produce babies, fruit or new plants (人, 動物, または植物などについて) 子供, 果実, または新しい植物を生み出すことができるような➡繁殖力のある, 結実能力のある, よく実を結ぶ, 多産の ▶定義 3 (used about a person's mind) full of ideas (人の心について) 考えにあふれている➡創造力に富んだ, 創意に富む, 創造力豊かな ‖ *a fertile imagination* 豊かな創造力 ⇔ **infertile**. **sterile** を参照. — fertility /fərtíləti/ 名 Ⓤ ➡土地が肥えていること, 肥沃(ひよく), 多産, 繁殖力, 創造力の豊かさ ‖ *Nowadays women can take drugs to increase their fertility* (= their chances of having a child). 今日では女性は薬を飲んで受胎能力 (= 子供を持つ可能性) を高められる. ⇔ **infertility**

**fertilize** (または -**ise**) /fə́ːtlaiz/ 動 他 ▶定義 1 (専門用語) to put a male seed into an egg, a plant or a female animal so that a baby, fruit or a young animal starts to develop 赤ん坊, 果実または動物の子が発育し始めるように, 雄の種子を卵, 植物または雌の動物に入れる➡~を受精させる, 受胎させる, 受粉させる ▶定義 2 to put natural or artificial substances on soil in order to make plants grow better 植物をもっとよく生長させるために, 天然または人工の物質を土にまく➡~に肥料を与える, ~を肥沃(ひよく)にする — fertilization (または -isation) /fəːtlaizéɪʃ(ə)n; -lə-/ 名 Ⓤ ➡土地を肥やすこと, 受精, 受胎, 受粉

**fertilizer** (または -**iser**) /fə́ːtlaizər/ 名 Ⓒ Ⓤ ▶定義 a natural or chemical substance that is put on land or soil to make plants grow better 植物をもっとよく生長させるために土地や土壌にまかれる, 天然のまたは化学的な物質➡肥料, 化学肥料 ☛参 manure

**fervent** /fə́ːrv(ə)nt/ 形 ▶定義 having or showing very strong feelings about sth ~について非常に強い感情を持っている, または示している➡熱烈な, 熱心な, 強烈な, 熱狂的な ‖ *She's a fervent believer in women's rights.* 彼女は女性の権利の熱烈な信奉者である. *a fervent belief/hope/desire* 強い信念・希望・欲望 — fervently 副 ➡熱烈に, 熱心に, 強烈に

**fervour** (米 **fervor**) /fə́ːrvər/ 名 Ⓤ ▶定義 very strong feelings about sth; enthusiasm ~に対する非常に強い感情; 熱中➡熱烈, 熱情, 熱狂, 熱意

**fester** /féstər/ 動 自 ▶定義 1 (used about a cut or an injury) to become infected (傷やけがについて) 感染する➡膿(う)む, ただれる, 化膿(かのう)する ‖ *a festering sore/wound* 膿んでいるはれ物・傷 ▶定義 2 (used about an unpleasant situation, feeling or thought) to become more unpleasant because you do not deal with it successfully (不快な状況, 感情, または考えについて) うまく対処できなかったため, もっと不快になる➡(不満や怒りなどが) 高じる, 心にわだかまる, 悩む, 増幅する

*__festival__ /féstəv(ə)l/ 名 Ⓒ ▶定義 1 a series of plays, films, musical performances, etc often held regularly in one place しばしば1つの場所で定期的に催される一連の劇, 映画, 音楽の演奏

など→（定期的な）催し, 催し物のシーズン, ～祭, フェスティバル ‖ *the Cannes Film Festival* カンヌ映画祭 *a jazz festival* ジャズフェスティバル ▶定義2 a day or time when people celebrate sth (especially a religious event) 人々が～を祝う日または時（特に宗教的な催し）→**祝祭, 祭礼, 祝日, 祭日** ‖ *Christmas is an important Christian festival.* クリスマスはキリスト教の重要な祭礼である.

**festive** /féstɪv/ 形 ▶定義 happy, because people are enjoying themselves celebrating sth 人々が～を祝って楽しんでいるので幸福な→**お祭り気分の, お祝いの, 陽気な, 楽しい, 愉快な** ‖ *the festive season (= Christmas)* おめでたい季節（= クリスマス）

**festivity** /festívəti, fəs-/ 名 (複 **festivities**) ▶定義1 [複数扱い] happy events when people celebrate sth 人々が～を祝う楽しい催し→**祭典, 祭礼, 祝祭, 祝宴, 祝いの催し事** ‖ *The festivities went on until dawn.* 祝宴は夜明けまで続いた. ▶定義2 Ⓤ being happy and celebrating sth 幸福で～を祝っていること→**お祭り騒ぎ, お祭り気分, 祝いの喜び** ‖ *The wedding was followed by three days of festivity.* 結婚式の後は, 3日間お祭り騒ぎが続いた.

***fetch** /fetʃ/ 動他 ▶定義1 特に 英 to go to a place and bring back sb/sth ある場所に行き, ～を連れて・持って帰る→**～を取ってくる, 持ってくる, 取りに行く, 連れ帰る, 呼んでくる** ‖ *Shall I fetch you your coat?/Shall I fetch your coat for you?* コートを取ってきてあげましょうか. ☞ **bring** のさし絵 ▶定義2 (used about goods) to be sold for the price mentioned（品物について）言及された価格で売られる→**（ある値段で）売れる,（収益）をもたらす,（良い値）を呼ぶ** ‖ *'How much will your car fetch?' 'It should fetch about £900.'*「車をいくらで売るつもりですか」「大体900ポンドでしょうね」

**fête** /feɪt, fet/ 名 Ⓒ ▶定義 an outdoor event with competitions, entertainment and things to buy, often organized to make money for a particular purpose しばしばある特定の目的の金を作るために企画された, 競争, 娯楽, 露店などがある屋外の催し物→**慈善市, バザー, 祝宴, 祝祭, 祭り** ‖ *the school/village/church fête* 学校・村・教会のバザー

**fetus** 米 = FOETUS

**feud** /fjuːd/ 名 Ⓒ ▶定義 a feud (between A and B); a feud (with sb) (over sb/sth) an angry and serious argument between two people or groups that continues over a long period of time 長い期間にわたって続いている, 2者または2つの集団の間の怒りに満ちた重大な論争→**確執, いさかい, 不和, 争い** ‖ *a family feud (within a family or between two families)* 家族の確執（= 家族内の, または2つの家族の間の）— feud 動 自 →**反目する, 相争う**

**feudal** /fjúːdl/ 形 ▶定義 connected with the system of feudalism 封建制と関連している→**封建の, 封建制の, 封建時代の** ‖ *the feudal system* 封建制度

**feudalism** /fjúːdlìz(ə)m/ 名 Ⓤ ▶定義 the social system which existed in the Middle Ages in Europe, in which people worked and fought for a person who owned land and received land and protection from him in return 中世のヨーロッパに存在した社会体制で, 人々は土地を所有する人のために働き, 戦い, その代わりに土地所有者から土地と保護を与えられた→**封建制度**

**fever** /fíːvər/ 名 ▶定義1 ⒸⓊ a condition of the body when it is too hot because of illness 病気のために体が熱するときの体の状態→**発熱, 熱があること,（病気による）熱** ‖ *A high fever can be dangerous, especially in small children.* 高熱は, 特に幼い子供の場合には危険なこともある. ▶ 人の体温が非常に高い場合は, 普通, he/she has a temperature と言う.
▶定義2 [単数扱い] a fever (of sth) a state of nervous excitement 神経が興奮している状態→**興奮状態, 熱狂, 熱中**

**feverish** /fíːvərɪʃ/ 形 ▶定義1 suffering from or caused by a fever 熱が出ている, または熱によって起きている→**熱のある, 熱っぽい, 熱による, 熱病の** ‖ *a feverish cold/dream* 熱の出る風邪・熱にうなされて見た夢 ▶定義2（通常は名詞の前）showing great excitement 激しい興奮を示している→**興奮した, 熱狂的な, 大騒ぎの, 猛烈な** — feverishly 副 →**熱っぽく, 熱狂的に, 熱狂して, ひどく興奮して, 熱を出して,**

***few** /fjuː/ 形代（複数形の可算名詞, 複数形の動詞と用いて）▶定義1 not many 多くない→**ほとんどない, わずかしかない, 少ししかない, ごくわ**

ずかの ‖ *Few people live to be 100.* 100歳まで生きられる人はわずかしかいない. *There are fewer cars here today than yesterday.* ここは昨日より今日の方が車が少ない. *Few of the players played really well.* 本当にうまいのは選手のうちのごくわずかだ. ▶定義 **2 a few** a small number of; some 少数の, いくらかの→**少しはある, 少しの, 多少の, 2・3の, 少数の人・物, 少数** ‖ *a few people* 少数の人々 *a few hours/days/years* 数時間・数日・数年 *I'll meet you later. I've got a few things to do first.* 後で会いましょう. 先にしなければならない事が2，3あるので. *I knew a few of the people there.* 私はそこにいる人たちのうち，数人知っていた. ☛参照 **less** の注

成句 **few and far between** ▶定義 not happening very often; not common それほど頻繁には起こっていない; 一般的ではない→**ごくまれで, たまに, ごく少なく, 珍しい** ‖ *Pubs are a bit few and far between in this area.* この地域にはパブがあまりない.

**a good few; quite a few** ▶定義 quite a lot かなり多い→**かなり多数の, 非常に多くの, 相当数の** ‖ *It's been a good few years since I saw him last.* 私が最後に彼に会ってからかなりの年数になる.

**ff** 略 ▶定義 used to show that sth starts on a particular page or line and continues for several pages or lines more 〜があるページや行から始まり, さらに数ページまたは数行続くことを示すために用いられて→**〜ページ・行以下を見よ** ‖ *British Politics, p10ff* 英国の政治, 10ページ以下を見よ.

*★**fiancé** (女性形 **fiancee**) /fiɑ́ːnseɪ; fiːɑ̀ːnseɪ/ 名 C ▶定義 a person who has promised to marry sb 〜と結婚すると約束した人→**婚約者, フィアンセ** ‖ *This is my fiancée Liz. We got engaged a few weeks ago.* こちらは私の婚約者のリズです. 私たちは数週間前に婚約しました.

**fiasco** /fiǽskoʊ/ 名 C (複 **fiascos**; 米 または **fiascoes**) ▶定義 an event that does not succeed, often in a way that causes embarrassment しばしばきまり悪い思いをさせてしまい, 成功しない出来事→**(こっけいな結果で終わるような) 大失敗, 不面目な結果, 惨めな失敗** ‖ *Our last party was a complete fiasco.* この間のパーティーは完全な失敗だった.

**fib** /fɪb/ 名 C 略式 ▶定義 something you say that is not true 口にする, 本当ではない事→**ささいなうそ, たわいのない, 罪のないうそ** ‖ *Please don't tell fibs.* うそは言わないでください. ☛類 **lie** — **fib** 動 自 (**fibbing; fibbed**) →**ささいなうそをつく, たわいのないうそをつく**

▶ **fib** は, そのうそがあまり重大ではないと思われる場合に用いられる.

**fibre** (米 **fiber**) /fáɪbər/ 名 ▶定義 **1** U parts of plants that you eat which are good for you because they help to move food quickly through your body 食物の体内移動を速くするのを助けるので体に良い, 植物の食べられる部分→**繊維, 繊維質, 食物繊維** ‖ *Wholemeal bread is high in fibre.* 全粒小麦粉のパンには繊維が多く含まれている. ▶定義 **2** C U a material or a substance that is made from natural or artificial threads 天然または人工の糸から作られる素材や生地→**繊維, 生地, 繊維製品**

▶ natural (天然) 繊維には, 例えば綿や毛などがある. man-made (人工) 繊維または synthetic (合成) 繊維には, ナイロン, ポリエステルなどがある.

▶定義 **3** C one of the thin threads which form a natural or artificial substance 天然や人工の素材を形成する細い糸の1本1本→**繊維, ファイバー** ‖ *cotton/wood/nerve/muscle fibres* 綿繊維・木の目・神経繊維・筋肉繊維

**fibreglass** (米 **fiberglass**) /fáɪbərɡlɑ̀ːs; -ɡlæ̀s/ (または **glass fibre**) 名 U ▶定義 a material made from small threads of plastic or glass, used for making small boats, parts of cars, etc 小型船, 自動車部品などを作るために用いられる, プラスチックまたはガラスの細い線から作られた材料→**ファイバーグラス, グラスファイバー, 繊維ガラス**

**fickle** /fɪ́k(ə)l/ 形 ▶定義 always changing your mind or your feelings so you cannot be trusted 常に気が変わっている, または感情が変化しているので, 信頼されない→**気まぐれな, 移り気の, 変わりやすい** ‖ *a fickle friend* 移り気な友

*★**fiction** /fɪ́kʃ(ə)n/ 名 U ▶定義 stories, novels, etc which describe events and people that are not real 実在しない出来事や人々を描いた物語や小説など→**小説, 創作, フィクション** ‖ *I don't read much fiction.* 私は小説をあまり読まない.

⇔ **non-fiction**. **fact**を参照.
➤ fiction は literature (文学) の一形式である. drama, poetry を参照.

**fictional** /fíkʃ(ə)n(ə)l/ 形 ▶定義 not real or true; only existing in stories, novels, etc 現実または真実ではない; 物語や小説などの中だけに存在している→**虚構の, 架空の, 作り事の** ‖ *The book gave a fictional account of a doctor's life.* その本は架空の医師の人生を描いていた. ☛参 **factual**

**fictitious** /fɪktíʃəs/ 形 ▶定義 invented; not real 作られた; 現実でない→**架空の, 仮想の, 想像上の, 創作の** ‖ *The novel is set in a fictitious village called Paradise.* その小説は, パラダイスという架空の村が舞台である.

**fiddle**¹ /fídl/ 名 C 略式 ▶定義 1 =VIOLIN ▶定義 2 英 a dishonest action, especially one connected with money 特に金と関連した, 不誠実な行動→**詐欺, ペテン, ごまかし, いかさま** ‖ *a tax fiddle* 税金のごまかし

**fiddle**² /fídl/ 動 ▶定義 1 自 fiddle(about/around) (with sth) to play with sth carelessly, because you are nervous or not thinking 神経質であるため, または何も考えていないため, ～を気軽にもてあそぶ→**～をいじくる, いじる, もてあそぶ** ‖ *He sat nervously, fiddling with a pencil.* 彼は鉛筆をもてあそびながら, いらいらして座っていた. ▶定義 2 他 略式 to change the details or facts of sth (business accounts, etc) in order to get money dishonestly 不正に金を入手するために, ～ (業務上の計算書など) の細部や事実を変更する→**(数字などを) ごまかす, ～を不正な手段で得る** ‖ *She fiddled her expenses form.* 彼女は所要経費の用紙をごまかして記入した.

**fiddly** /fídli/ 形 略式 ▶定義 difficult to do or manage with your hands (because small or complicated parts are involved) (細かい, または複雑な部分が含まれているため) 行うことや手で扱うことが難しい→**扱いにくい, 厄介な, 面倒な, 煩わしい**

**fidelity** /fədéləti, faɪ-/ 名 U ▶定義 1 正式 fidelity (to sb/sth) the quality of being faithful, especially to a wife or husband by not having a sexual relationship with anyone else 特に妻や夫に対してほかのだれとも性的関係を持たないことによって, 誠実であること→**誠実, 貞節** ☛ faithfulness の方があまり堅苦しくない語である. ⇔ **infidelity** ▶定義 2 (used about translations, the reproduction of music, etc) the quality of being accurate or close to the original (翻訳, 音楽の再生などについて) 原物, 原音に忠実な, または近いこと→**正確さ, 忠実度, 原音に対して忠実な音の再生, 原物にそっくりなこと, 真に迫っていること, 迫真性** ☛参 **hi-fi**

**fidget** /fídʒət/ 動 自 ▶定義 fidget (with sth) to keep moving your body, hands or feet because you are nervous, bored, excited, etc 不安である, 退屈している, 興奮しているなどのために, 体, 手, あるいは足を動かし続ける→**もじもじする, そわそわする, いらいらする, 落ち着かない, 気をもむ, (無意識に) いじり回す** ‖ *She fidgeted nervously with her keys.* 彼女は神経質にかぎをもてあそんだ. — **fidgety** 形→**そわそわする, 落ち着きのない, 不安な, やきもきする**

★**field**¹ /fíːld/ 名 C ▶定義 1 an area of land on a farm, usually surrounded by fences or walls, used for growing crops or keeping animals in 通常は柵 (さく) や壁で囲まれ, 作物を育てたり動物を飼うために使われる, 農場の土地→**畑, 田畑, 牧草地, 耕作地** ▶定義 2 an area of study or knowledge 研究や知識の範囲→**分野, 領域, 範囲** ‖ *He's an expert in the field of economics.* 彼は経済分野の専門家である. *That question is outside my field (= not one of the subjects that I know about).* その質問は私の専門外です (= 私が知っている分野の1つではない). ▶定義 3 an area of land used for sports, games or some other activity スポーツ, 試合などの活動に利用される土地→**競技場, 運動場, 球場, グランド, フィールド, 戦地** ‖ *a football field* サッカーの競技場 *an airfield (= where aeroplanes land and take off)* 飛行場 (= 飛行機が離着陸する場所) *a battlefield* 戦場 ☛参 **pitch** ▶定義 4 an area affected by or included in sth ～に影響される, または含まれる範囲→**～の場, 界, 視野, 視界, 領域** ‖ *a magnetic field* 磁界 *It's outside my field of vision (= I can't see it).* それは私の視界に入っていない (= 私にはそれが見えない). ▶定義 5 an area of land where oil, coal or other minerals are found 石油や石炭などの鉱物がある土地→**(鉱物の) 産地, 採掘地帯, 埋蔵地, 産出地** ‖ *a coalfield* 炭田 *a North Sea oilfield* 北海油田

**field**² /fíːld/ 動 ▶定義1 🗐 🕮 (in cricket, baseball, etc) to (be ready to) catch and throw back the ball after sb has hit it (クリケット, 野球などで) 〜がボールを打った後, それを捕って投げ返す (準備ができている) → (打球を) さばく, 守備をする, 受け止める, 守備につく

▶一方のチームが fielding (守備についている) とき, もう一方のチームは batting (打撃をしている) と言う.

▶定義2 🕮 to choose a team for a game of football, cricket, etc サッカーやクリケットなどの試合のためにチームを選ぶ → 〜を試合に出す, 出場させる, 編成する ∥ New Zealand is fielding an excellent team for the next match. ニュージーランドは, 次の試合のために優秀なチームを編成している.

### field day 名

成句 have a field day ▶定義 to get the opportunity to do sth you enjoy, especially sth other people disapprove of 楽しめる〜, 特にほかの人が非難するような〜をする機会を得る → 思う存分楽しむ, 大いに楽しむ, 大はしゃぎする ∥ The newspapers always have a field day when there's a political scandal. 政治スキャンダルがあると, 新聞はいつも書きたい放題に書く.

### field event 名 C ▶定義 a sport, such as jumping and throwing, that is not a race and does not involve running 競走ではなく, 走ることを含まない, 跳んだり投げたりするようなスポーツ → フィールド競技, フィールド種目 ☛参 track event

### fieldwork /fíːldwə̀ːrk/ 名 U ▶定義 practical research work done outside school, college, etc 学校や大学などの外で行われる実際的な調査 → 実地調査, 現地調査, 実地研究, (生物学などの) 野外作業, 野外採集, (社会学などの) 現場訪問, フィールドワーク

### fiend /fíːnd/ 名 C ▶定義1 a very cruel person 非常に残酷な人 → 鬼・悪魔のような人, 冷酷な・残忍な人, 鬼畜 ▶定義2 略式 a person who is very interested in one particular thing ある1つの物事にとても興味を持っている人 → 凝り性, 〜狂, 〜マニア, 〜中毒, 〜の鬼 ∥ a health fiend 健康マニア ☛類 fanatic

### fiendish /fíːndɪʃ/ 形 ▶定義1 very unpleasant or cruel 非常に不快な, または残酷な → 鬼・悪魔のような, 極悪な, 冷酷な, 残忍な ▶定義2 略式 clever and complicated 賢明で複雑な → 手の込んだ, 巧妙な ∥ a fiendish plan 巧妙な計画 — fiendishly 副 → 鬼・悪魔のように, ひどく, 残酷に, 巧妙に

**\*fierce** /fíərs/ 形 ▶定義1 angry, aggressive and frightening 怒っており, 攻撃的で恐ろしい → どう猛な, 凶暴な, 荒々しい, 残忍な ∥ The house was guarded by fierce dogs. その家は猛犬によって守られていた. ▶定義2 very strong; violent 非常に強い; 暴力的な → すさまじい, 激しい, 強烈な, 荒れ狂う ∥ fierce competition for jobs 仕事を求める激しい競争 a fierce attack 強烈な攻撃 ☛名 ferocity — fiercely 副 → どう猛に, 激しく, 猛烈に, ひどく

**fiery** /fáɪəri/ 形 ▶定義1 looking like fire 火のように見えている → 火のような, 燃えるような, 燃え立つような ∥ She has fiery red hair. 彼女は燃えるような赤い髪をしている. ▶定義2 quick to become angry すぐに怒る → 激しやすい, 気の荒い, かんしゃくの強い, 気の短い ∥ a fiery temper 激しやすい気質

**\*fifteen** /fɪftíːn, ≠/ 数 ▶定義 15

▶文中での数字の使い方については, six を参照.

**fifteenth** /fɪftíːnθ, ≠/ 代形副 ▶定義 15th → 15番目の(に), 第15(の, に) ☛参 sixth の例

**\*fifth**¹ /fífθ/ 代形副 ▶定義 5th → 5番目(の, に), 第5(の, に) ☛参 sixth の例

**fifth**² /fífθ/ 名 C ▶定義 the fraction 1/5; one of five equal parts of sth 分数の1/5; 〜の均等な5個の部分の1つ → 5分の1

**fiftieth** /fíftiəθ/ 代形副 ▶定義 50th → 50番目(の, に), 第50(の, に) ☛参 sixth の例

**\*fifty** /fífti/ 数 ▶定義 50

▶文中での数字の使い方については, six を参照.

**fifty-fifty** 形副 ▶定義 equal or equally (between two people, groups, etc) (2人または2つの集団などの間で) 等しい, または等しく → 五分五分の[に], 半々の[に], 山分けで[に], 等分の[に] ∥ You've got **a fifty-fifty chance** of winning. 君の勝算は五分五分だ. We'll divide the money fifty-fifty. 金は山分けにしよう.

**fig**¹ /fíg/ 名 C ▶定義 (a type of tree with) a soft sweet fruit full of small seeds that grows in warm countries and is often eaten dried 暖かい国に生育し、しばしば乾燥させて食べる、小さな種が多く、柔らかくて甘い果実（を付ける木）→ イチジク、イチジクの木 ☞ C3 ページのさし絵

**fig²** 略 ▶定義1 figure, illustration 図、さし絵→ 図、図解、さし絵 ∥ *See diagram at fig 2.* 図 2 の図表を参照．▶定義2 figurative(ly) 比喩的な[に]→比喩で表して、比喩的に、象徴的に

★**fight¹** /fáɪt/ 動（過, 過分 **fought** /fɔːt/）▶定義1 自他 fight (against sb) to use physical strength, guns, weapons, etc against sb/sth ～に対して肉体的な力、銃、武器などを使う→～と戦う、戦いをする、争う、格闘する、けんかをする、戦争する ∥ *They gathered soldiers to fight the invading army.* 彼らは侵略軍と戦うために兵士を集めた． *My younger brothers were always fighting.* 私の弟たちはけんかばかりしていた． ▶定義2 自他 fight (against sth) to try very hard to stop or prevent sth ～を止める、または防ぐために非常に努力する→～と戦う、～を克服・阻止するために戦う、～に逆らう ∥ *to fight a fire/a decision/prejudice* 消火活動をする・決定に逆らう・偏見と戦う *to fight against crime/disease* 犯罪・病気と戦う ▶定義3 自 fight (for sth/to do sth) to try very hard to get or keep sth ～を得る、または維持するために非常に努力する→～のために戦う、奮闘する ∥ *to fight for your rights* 自分の権利のために戦う ▶定義4 自 fight (with sb) (about/over sth) to argue 議論する→論争する、激論する、口論する ∥ *It's not worth fighting about money.* 金の問題は議論するに値しない． ☞参 **argue**, **quarrel²** 句動詞 **fight back** ▶定義 to protect yourself with actions or words by attacking sb who has attacked you 自分を攻撃した～を行動や言葉で攻撃することによって自分を守る→反撃する、やり返す、抵抗する ∥ *If he hits you again, fight back!* また彼に殴られたら、やり返しなさい．

★**fight²** /fáɪt/ 名 ▶定義1 C a fight (with sb/sth); a fight (between A and B) the act of using physical force against sb/sth ～に対して肉体的な力を行使すること→格闘、乱闘、殴り合い、けんか ∥ *Don't get into a fight at school, will you?* 学校でけんかに加わってはいけませんよ． *Fights broke out between rival groups of fans.* ファンの中の対立するグループの間で乱闘が始まった．▶定義2 a fight (against/for sth) (to do sth) [単数扱い] the work done trying to destroy, prevent or achieve sth ～を破壊、防止、または達成しようとするために行われる努力→戦い、闘争、奮闘 ∥ *Workers won their fight against the management to stop the factory from closing down.* 労働者たちは、工場の閉鎖を経営者側にやめさせる戦いに勝った．▶定義3 特に 米 a fight (with sb/sth) (about/over sth) an argument about sth ～についての議論→論争、激論、口論 ∥ *I had a fight with my mum over what time I had to be home.* 私は門限をめぐって母と言い争いをした．▶定義4 ❶ the desire to continue trying or fighting 努力し続けたい、または戦い続けたいという欲求→闘志、戦意、気概、闘争心、ファイト ∥ *I've had some bad luck but I've still got plenty of fight in me.* 運が悪いこともあったが、まだ戦う気概は十分ある．

成句 **pick a fight** ⇒ **PICK¹**

**fighter** /fáɪtər/ 名 C ▶定義1（または **fighter plane**）a small fast military aircraft used for attacking enemy aircraft 敵の航空機を攻撃するために使われる、小型で高速の軍用機→戦闘機 ∥ *a fighter pilot* 戦闘機のパイロット *a jet fighter* ジェット戦闘機 ▶定義2 a person who fights in a war or in sport (a boxer) 戦争またはスポーツで戦う人（ボクサー）→戦士、闘士、武人、プロボクサー

**figurative** /fíɡ(j)ərətɪv/ 形（略 **fig**）▶定義 (used about a word or an expression) not used with its exact meaning but used for giving an imaginative description or a special effect （言葉や表現について）そのままの意味で用いられるのではなく、想像的な描写をする、または特別な効果を与えるために用いられて→比喩の、比喩的な、象徴的な、文字通りでない ∥ *'He exploded with rage' is a figurative use of the verb 'to explode'.*「彼は怒りで爆発した」というのは、動詞「爆発する」の比喩的な用法である．☞参 **literal**, **metaphor** — **figuratively** 副→比喩的に、象徴的に

★**figure¹** /fíɡə; -ɡjər/ 名 C ▶定義1 an amount (in numbers) or a price （数字で表した）量、または価格→数値、合計数、総額、価格、値段 ∥ *The unemployment figures are lower this month.* 失業者数は今月は減少した． *What sort of figure* are you thinking of for your house? 家に対していくらくらいの金額を考えているのですか.

▶定義2 a written sign for a number (0 to 9) 数（0から9）を表す書かれた文字→**数字, 数, 位, けた** ‖ *Write the numbers in figures, not words.* その数を言うのではなく, 数字で書きなさい. *He has a six-figure income/an income in six figures (= £100000 or more).* 彼の収入は6けたである (= 彼は6けたの収入がある (= 10万ポンド以上)). *Interest rates are now down to single figures (= less than 10%).* 今は金利が1けた (= 10パーセント未満) に下がっている. *double figures (= 10 to 99)* 2けたの数 (= 10〜99)

▶定義3 **figures** [複数扱い] 略式 mathematics 数学→**算数, 計算** ‖ *I don't have a head for figures (= I'm not very good with numbers).* 私には計算の能力がない (= 私は数字を扱うのがあまり得意ではない). ▶定義4 a well-known or important person よく知られた, または重要な人→**人物, 重要人物, 名士** ‖ *an important political figure* 政界の重要人物 ▶定義5 the shape of the human body, especially a woman's body that is attractive 人間の体, 特に魅力的な女性の体の形→**姿, 体形, 体付き, 容姿, スタイル, プロポーション, 風采 (ふうさい)** ‖ *She's got a beautiful slim figure.* 彼女はほっそりした美しいスタイルである. ☞参 build² の注 ▶定義6 a person that you cannot see very clearly or do not know あまりはっきりとは見えない, または知らない人→**人影, 人の姿** ‖ *Two figures were coming towards us in the dark.* 暗闇 (やみ) の中を2つの人影が私たちに向かってやって来るところだった. *There were two figures on the right of the photo that I didn't recognize.* その写真の右側に私の知らない人が2人写っていた. ▶定義7 (略 **fig**) a diagram or picture used in a book to explain sth 本の中で〜を説明するために使われる図やさし絵→**図解, 図表, さし絵** ‖ *Figure 3 shows the major cities of Italy.* 図3にはイタリアの主要都市が示されている.

成句 a ballpark figure/estimate ⇒ **BALLPARK**

facts and figures ⇒ **FACT**

in round figures/numbers ⇒ **ROUND¹**

**figure²** /fígər; -gjər/ 動 ▶定義1 自 figure (as sth) (in/among sth) to be included in sth; to be an important part of sth 〜に含まれる; 〜の重要な部分を成す→**〜に…として現れる, 登場する, かかわる, 出る, 目立つ, 重要な役割を演ずる** ‖ *Women don't figure much in his novels.* 彼の小説には女性はあまり登場しない. ☞類 **feature**

▶定義2 他 figure (that) 特に 米 to think or guess sth 〜を考える, または推測する→**〜と思う, 考える, 判断する** ‖ *I figured he was here because I saw his car outside.* 外で彼の車を見掛けたので, 彼はここにいると思った.

成句 **it/that figures** 略式 ▶定義 that is what I expected 予期した通りの→**思った通りだ, なるほど, やっぱり, それは当然だ, そうだろうな**

句動詞 **figure on sth/on doing sth** 特に 米 ▶定義 to include sth in your plans 〜を計画に含める→**〜を考慮に入れる, 見込む, 当てにする, 計画する, 予想する** ‖ *I figure on arriving in New York on Wednesday.* 私は水曜日にニューヨークに着くよう計画している.

**figure sb/sth out** ▶定義 to find an answer to sth or to understand sb 〜の答えを見つける, または〜を理解する→**〜を解く, 解決する, 見つけ出す, 考え付く, 理解する, 〜が分かる** ‖ *I can't figure out why she married him in the first place.* そもそも彼女がなぜ彼と結婚したのか, 私には分からない.

**figure of eight** (米 **figure eight**) 名 C (複 **figures of eight**) ▶定義 something in the shape of an 8 8の形をした物→**8の字形, (ロープの) 8字形結び**

**figure of speech** 名 C (複 **figures of speech**) ▶定義 a word or expression used not with its original meaning but in an imaginative way to make a special effect もともとの意味ではなく, 特別な効果を出すために想像的な方法で用いられる言葉や表現→**比喩的表現, 言葉のあや, 修辞的表現法, 物の例え**

★**file¹** /fáil/ 名 C ▶定義1 a box or a cover that is used for keeping papers together 紙をまとめておくために用いられる箱またはカバー→**とじ込み帳, フォルダー, ファイル, 書類ばさみ, 書類差し, 書類整理箱・棚** ☞ S4 ページのさし絵

▶定義2 a collection of information or material on one subject that is stored together in a computer or on a disk, with a particular name 特定の名前を付けてコンピューターまたはディスク

にまとめて保存されている，1つのテーマについての情報やデータの集まり➜**ファイル** ‖ *to open/close a file* ファイルを開く・閉じる *to create/delete/save/copy a file* ファイルを作成・削除・保存・コピーする ▶定義3 a file (on sb/sth) a collection of papers or information about sb/sth kept inside a file ファイルの中に保管された，～についての書類や情報の集まり➜**書類, 資料, 記録** ‖ *The police are now keeping a file on all known football hooligans.* 警察は現在，分かる範囲のサッカーのフーリガン全員の記録を保存している． ▶定義4 a metal tool with a rough surface used for shaping hard substances or for making surfaces smooth 硬い物を削る，または表面を滑らかにするために用いられる，表面がざらざらした金属製の道具➜**やすり** ‖ *a nail file* つめやすり

[成句] on file ▶定義 kept in a file ファイルに保管された➜**ファイルに記録されて, 整理されて, 保存されて, とじ込まれて** ‖ *We have all the information you need on file.* 私たちは，あなたが必要とする情報をすべてファイルに記録してあります．

in single file ▶定義 in a line, one behind the other 1列に，ある列の後ろに別の列が並んで➜**1列縦隊で, 1列縦隊に並んで**

the rank and file ⇒ RANK[1]

**file²** /fáɪl/ [動] ▶定義1 [他] file sth (away) to put and keep documents, etc in a particular place so that you can find them easily; to put sth into a file 簡単に見つけられるように，書類などを特定の場所に置いて保管する；～をファイルの中に入れる➜**～をとじ込む, 整理保存する, ファイルする** ‖ *I filed the letters away in a drawer.* 私はその手紙を引き出しに整理保管した． ▶定義2 [自] file in, out, past, etc to walk or march in a line 列になって歩く，または行進する➜**1列になって進む, 縦列で進む, 列を成して～に繰り込む** ‖ *The children filed out of the classroom.* 子供たちは1列になって教室から出ていった． ▶定義3 [他] file sth (away, down, etc) to shape sth hard or make sth smooth with a file やすりで，硬い～の形を作る，または～を滑らかにする➜**～をやすりで削る, (やすりで) 磨く, 研ぐ, ～にやすりをかける** ‖ *to file your nails* つめをやすりで磨く

***fill** /fɪl/ [動] ▶定義1 [自][他] fill (sth/sb) (with sth) to make sth full or to become full ～を一杯にする，または一杯になる➜**あふれる, 充満する; ～を満たす, 占める, 埋める, ～に詰める** ‖ *Can you fill the kettle for me?* やかんに一杯に水を入れてくれませんか． *The news filled him with excitement.* その知らせを聞いて彼の胸は興奮で一杯になった． *The room filled with smoke within minutes.* その部屋にはすぐに煙が充満した． ▶定義2 [他] to take a position or to use up your time doing sth 地位を得る，または～をして自分の時間を使い果たす➜**(地位) を占める, (役) を務める, (職務, 約束など) を果たす, (要求など) を満たす** ‖ *I'm afraid that teaching post has just been filled (= somebody has got the job).* どうやらその教員の職はちょうど埋まってしまったようだ (= だれかがその職を得た)．

[句動詞] fill sth in ([米] または **fill sth out**) ▶定義1 to complete a form, etc by writing information on it 情報を書き込んで用紙などを完成させる➜**～に必要事項を記入する, 空所を埋める, 書き込む** ‖ *Could you fill in the application form, please?* 応募用紙にご記入ください． ▶定義2 to fill a hole or space completely to make a surface flat 表面を平らにするために，穴やすきまなどを完全に埋める➜**ふさぐ, 充填 (じゅうてん) する, 埋める, 埋め立てる** ‖ *You had better fill in the cracks in the wall before you paint it.* ペンキを塗る前に，壁の割れ目をふさいだ方がいいですよ．

fill (sth) up ▶定義 to become or to make sth completely full ～が完全に一杯になる，または～を完全に一杯にする➜**満員になる, 満タンになる, ぎっしり詰まる, ～を一杯に満たす, 占める, 満員にする, ぎっしり詰める** ‖ *There weren't many people at first but then the room filled up.* 最初は人が多くなかったが，やがてその部屋が満員になった．

**fillet** ([米] **filet**) /fílət/ [名] [C][U] ▶定義 a piece of meat or fish with the bones taken out 骨を取り除いた一切れの肉または魚➜**ヒレ, 骨のない切り身**

**filling¹** /fílɪŋ/ [名] ▶定義1 [C] the material that a dentist uses to fill a hole in a tooth 歯科医が歯の穴を埋めるために使う材料➜**充填(じゅうてん)材, 詰め物** ‖ *a gold filling* 金の詰め物 ▶定義2 [C][U] the food inside a sandwich, pie, cake, etc サンドイッチ，パイ，ケーキなどの中の食べ物➜

F

詰め物, 中身, 具

**filling**² /fílɪŋ/ 形 ▶定義 (used about food) that makes you feel full (食べ物について) 満腹を感じさせるような→**満腹させる, 腹にたまる, 腹の足しになる, 食べごたえのある** ‖ *Pasta is very filling.* パスタはとてもおなかにたまる.

★**film**¹ /fílm/ 名 ▶定義1 （米 または **movie**） ●a story, play, etc shown in moving pictures at the cinema or on television 映画館やテレビで, 映像の中で描かれる物語, 劇など→**映画** ‖ *Let's go to the cinema - there's a good film on this week.* 映画館に行きましょう — 今週は良い映画をやっていますよ. *to* **watch** *a film on TV* テレビで映画を見る *to* **see** *a film at the cinema* 映画館で映画を見る *a horror/documentary/feature film* ホラー映画・ドキュメンタリー映画・長編映画 *a film director/producer/critic* 映画監督・制作者・批評家 ▶定義2 ⓤthe art or business of making films 映画を制作する技術または仕事→**映画制作技術, 映画産業, 映画界** ‖ *She's studying film and theatre.* 彼女は映画と演劇を学んでいる. *the film industry* 映画産業 ▶定義3 ⓤmoving pictures of real events 実際の出来事を描いた映像→**映画, 映像, フィルム** ‖ *The programme included film of the town one hundred years ago.* その番組には100年前の町の映像が含まれていた. ▶定義4 ⓒⓤa roll of thin plastic that you use in a camera to take photographs 写真を撮るためにカメラに入れて使う, 薄いプラスチックを巻いた物→**フィルム, 感光膜** ‖ *to have a film developed* フィルムを現像する *Fast film is better if there's not much light.* あまり明るくない場合は高感度フィルムの方が良い. ☞ **camera** のさし絵 ▶定義5 [通常は単数] a thin layer of a substance or material ある物質や材料の薄い層→**薄膜, 薄皮, 皮膜** ‖ *The oil forms a film on the surface of the water.* 油は水面で薄膜を作る.

★**film**² /fílm/ 動 ⓒⓘⓤ ▶定義 to record moving pictures of an event, story, etc with a camera 出来事, 物語などの映像をカメラで記録する→**〜を撮影する, 撮る, 映す, 映画化する, 映画になる, 映画を制作する** ‖ *A lot of westerns are filmed in Spain.* 数多くの西部劇がスペインで撮影されている. *The man was filmed stealing from the shop.* その男は店で盗みを働くところを映されていた.

**film star** 名 ⓒ ▶定義 a person who is a well-known actor in films 映画でよく知られた俳優である人→**映画スター**

**filter**¹ /fíltər/ 名 ⓒ ▶定義1 a device for holding back solid substances from a liquid or gas that passes through it 通過する液体や気体から固体をとどめるための装置→**ろ過器, ろ過装置, ろ紙, 水こし, フィルター** ‖ *a coffee filter* コーヒーフィルター *an oil filter* オイルフィルター ▶定義2 a piece of coloured glass used with a camera to hold back some types of light ある種の光を入れないためにカメラに用いられる色付きのガラス→**フィルター, ろ光器**

**filter**² /fíltər/ 動 ▶定義1 ⓣto pass a liquid through a filter 液体をフィルターに通す→**〜をこす, ろ過する, こして〜を取り除く** ‖ *Do you filter your water?* 水をろ過しますか. ▶定義2 ⓘ filter in, out, through, etc to move slowly and/or in small amounts ゆっくりと, または少量ずつ動く→**〜が漏れる, 染み出る, 浸透する, 徐々に移動する** ‖ *Sunlight filtered into the room through the curtains.* カーテンを通して日光が部屋に差していた. （比喩）*News of her illness filtered through to her friends.* 彼女の病気の知らせは友人たちの間に徐々に広まった.

句動詞 filter sb/sth out (of sth) ▶定義 to remove sth that you do not want from a liquid, light, etc using a special device or substance 特別な装置や物質を用いて, 不要な〜を液体, 光などから取り除く→**〜を…からこして取り除く, ろ過して除去する** ‖ *This chemical filters impurities out of the water.* この化学物質は, 水をろ過して不純物を取り除く. （比喩）*This test is designed to filter out weaker candidates before the interview stage.* このテストは, 面接の段階の前に力のない志願者を除外するためのものである.

**filth** /fílθ/ 名 ⓤ ▶定義1 unpleasant dirt 不快な汚れ→**汚れ, 不潔な物, 汚物, 不潔, 不浄** ‖ *The room was covered in filth.* その部屋は汚れきっていた. ▶定義2 sexual words or pictures that cause offence 〜の感情を害するような性的な言葉や写真→**わいせつな[下品な]言葉・写真, 卑わいな言葉・写真**

**filthy** /fílθi/ 形 (**filthier**; **filthiest**) ▶定義1 very dirty 非常に汚い→**不潔な, 汚れた** ▶定義2 (used about language, books, films, etc) connected with sex, and causing offence (言葉, 本, 映画などについて)性と関連し, 人の感情を害するような→**わいせつな, みだらな, 卑わいな, 下品な, 不道徳な**

**fin** /fín/ 名 C ▶定義 **1** one of the parts of a fish that it uses for swimming 魚が泳ぐために用いる器官の1つ→**ひれ, (アザラシ, ペンギンなどの)ひれ状器官** ☞ C1 ページのさし絵 ▶定義 **2** a flat, thin part that sticks out of an aircraft, a vehicle, etc to improve its balance and movement through the air or water 空中や水中でのバランスと動きを良くするための, 航空機や車両などから突き出た平たく薄い部分→**(航空機の)垂直安定板, (潜水艦などの)水平舵, (レーシングカーの)水平翼, (ロケットの)尾翼**

★**final¹** /fáɪnl/ 形 ▶定義 **1** (名詞の前だけ) last (in a series) (一続きのものの)最後の→**最終の, 最後の** ‖ *This will be the final lesson of our course.* これがこの課程の最後の授業です. *I don't want to miss the final episode of that serial.* この連続物の最後のエピソードを見逃したくない. ▶定義 **2** not to be changed 変更されない→**決定的な, 最終的な, 究極の, 変更できない** ‖ *The judge's decision is always final.* 裁判官の判決は常に最終的なものである. *I'm not lending you the money, and that's final!* あなたにお金は貸しません, この考えは変わりませんからね.

成句 **the last/final straw** ⇒ **STRAW**

★**final²** /fáɪnl/ 名 ▶定義 **❶** the last game or match in a series of competitions or sporting events 一連の競争やスポーツ大会の最後の試合または競技→**決勝, 決勝戦** ‖ *The first two runners in this race go through to the final.* この競走で2位までの走者が決勝に進む. ☞参 **semi-final** ▶定義 **2 finals** [複数扱い] the exams you take in your last year at university 大学の最終学年で受ける試験→**最終・卒業試験** ‖ *I'm taking my finals in June.* 私は6月に最終試験を受ける.

**finale** /fənǽli, fɪnǽ-/ 名 C ▶定義 the last part of a piece of music, an opera, a show, etc 楽曲, オペラ, ショーなどの最後の部分→**最終章, 終楽章, フィナーレ, 終局, 大団円, 大詰め**

**finalist** /fáɪnlɪst/ 名 C ▶定義 a person who is in the final²(1) of a competition 競争の決勝戦(final²(1))に進出する人→**決勝戦出場選手, 決勝戦進出者** ☞参 **semi-finalist**

**finalize** (または **-ise**) /fáɪnlàɪz/ 動他 ▶定義 to make firm decisions about plans, dates, etc 計画, 日取りなどについて, 揺るぎない決定をする→**最終決定をする, ~に決着を付ける, ~を最終的に承認する** ‖ *Have you finalized your holiday arrangements yet?* 休暇の計画はもう確定しましたか.

★**finally** /fáɪnli/ 副 ▶定義 **1** after a long time or delay 長い時間, または遅れの後で→**ついに, とうとう, ようやく, やっと, 結局** ‖ *It was getting dark when the plane finally took off.* 飛行機がやっと離陸した時には暗くなりかけていた. ☞類 **eventually** ▶定義 **2** used to introduce the last in a list of things 物事の一覧の最後を導入するために用いられて→**最後に, 終わりに当たって, 締めくくりとして** ‖ *Finally, I would like to say how much we have all enjoyed this evening.* 最後に, 私たちは皆, 今晩とても楽しい時を過ごせたと申し上げたいと思います. ☞類 **lastly** ▶定義 **3** in a definite way so that sth will not be changed ~が変更されないように明確に→**決定的に, 最終的に, きっぱりと, すっかり** ‖ *We haven't decided finally who will get the job yet.* だれがその仕事を担当するか, まだ最終的に決めていない.

★**finance¹** /fáɪnæns/ 名 ▶定義 **1 ❶** the money you need to start or support a business, etc 事業などを始める, または支えるために必要とする金→**資金, 財源** ‖ *How will you raise the finance to start the project?* そのプロジェクトを開始するための資金はどのように調達するつもりですか. ▶定義 **2 ❶** the activity of managing money 金を管理すること→**財務, 財政(学)** ‖ *Who is the new Minister of Finance?* 新しい財務大臣はだれですか. *an expert in finance* 財務の専門家 ▶定義 **3 finances** [複数扱い] the money a person, company, country, etc has to spend 人, 会社, 国などが使うために持っている金→**財力, 財政状態, 収入, 歳入** ‖ *What are our finances like at the moment?* (= how much money have we got?) 現在の私たちの財政状態はどうなっていますか (= 私たちは金をどれだけ持っていますか).

**finance²** /fənǽns, faɪnǽns/ 動他 ▶定義 to provide the money to pay for sth ～に支払うための金を提供する→～に金を融通する, 融資する, 資金を調達する, 金を出す ‖ *Your trip will be financed by the company.* 出張代は会社が負担します.

**financial** /fənǽnʃ(ə)l, faɪ-/ 形 ▶定義 connected with money 金に関連している→財政上の, 財務の, 金融上の, 財界の ‖ *The business got into financial difficulties.* 会社は財政困難に陥った.
— **financially** /-ʃ(ə)li/ 副 →財政的に, 財政的に

**finch** /fɪntʃ/ 名 C ▶定義 a small bird with a short strong beak 短く丈夫なくちばしを持つ小鳥→フィンチ, ヒワ・アトリ科の小鳥の総称

*★**find**¹ /fáɪnd/ 動 他 (過, 過分 **found** /fáʊnd/)
▶定義 1 to discover sth that you want or that you have lost after searching for it 欲しい～, またはなくした～を捜して見つけ出す→～を見つける, 発見する, 捜し出す ‖ *Did you find the pen you lost?* なくしたペンは見つかりましたか. *After six months she finally found a job.* 6か月後, 彼女はやっと職を見つけた. *Scientists haven't yet found a cure for colds.* 科学者たちはまだ風邪の治療法を発見していない. *I hope you find an answer to your problem.* その問題の答えが見つかるといいですね.

➤ find the time, find the money という言い方に注意: *I never seem to find the time to write letters these days.* (最近は手紙を書く時間も全く取れないようだ.) *We'd like to go on holiday but we can't find the money.* (休暇には出掛けたいが, 金がない.)

▶定義 2 to discover sth by chance 偶然, ～を見つける→～をふと見つける, ～に気付く, ～に出くわす ‖ *I've found a piece of glass in this milk.* このミルクにガラス片が入っているのを見つけた. *We went into the house and found her lying on the floor.* 私たちは家に入ると, 彼女が床に倒れているのを見つけた. *This animal can be found (= exists) all over the world.* この動物は世界中で見られる (= 存在する). ▶定義 3 to have an opinion about sth because of your own experience 経験から～についての意見を持つ→～を悟る, 認める, (経験から) 知る, (試みて) 分かる, 感じる ‖ *I find that book very difficult to understand.* 私はあの本を理解するのが難しいと思う. *We didn't find the film at all funny.* 私たちはその映画がおかしいとは全く感じなかった.

*How are you finding life as a student?* 学生生活はいかがですか. ▶定義 4 to suddenly realize or see sth 急に～に気付く, または～を見いだす→～を悟る, ～と分かる, 知る, 気付く ‖ *I got home to find that I'd left the tap on all day.* 家に帰ったら, 一日中水道を出しっ放しにしていたことが分かった. *Ben turned a corner and suddenly found himself in the port.* ベンは角を曲がると, 突然港に出た. ▶定義 5 to arrive somewhere naturally 自然にどこかに着く→～に達する, 届く, 行き着く, たどり着く ‖ *These birds **find their way** to Africa every winter.* これらの鳥は毎年冬にアフリカに行き着く.

成句 **find fault (with sb/sth)** ▶定義 to look for things that are wrong with sb/sth and complain about them ～の悪い点を探して, それについて不平を言う→～のあら・欠点を捜す, 文句を言う, ～を非難する ‖ *Monica wouldn't make a good teacher because she's always finding fault with people.* モニカはいつも人のあらばかり捜しているから, 良い教師にはなれないだろう.

**find your feet** ▶定義 to become confident and independent in a new situation 新しい状況で自信を持ち, 独立する→環境に慣れる, 独り立ちする, 社会的に自立する, 自分に自信を持つ ‖ *Don't worry if the job seems difficult at first - you'll soon find your feet.* 最初は仕事が難しく思えても心配しないように － すぐに慣れますよ.

句動詞 **find (sth) out** ▶定義 to get some information; to discover a fact 情報を得る; 事実を発見する→～を調査する, 探り出す, 見つけ出す, (答えなどを) 知る, 分かる ‖ *Have you found out how much the tickets cost?* そのチケットがいくらするか分かりましたか. *I later found out that Will had been lying to me.* ウィルが私にずっとうそをついていたことが後になって分かった.

**find sb out** ▶定義 to discover that sb has done sth wrong ～が悪い…をしたことを発見する→(不正, 罪などを) 見破る, (犯人を) 見つける, 正体を見抜く, 捜し出す ‖ *He had used a false name for years before they found him out.* 彼らが正体を見破るまで, 彼は何年間も偽名を使っていた.

**find**² /fáɪnd/ 名 C ▶定義 a thing or a person that has been found, especially one that is valuable or useful 見つけ出された物または人, 特に価値のある, または役に立つ物や人➜**発見, 注目される人, 掘り出し物, 逸材** ‖ *Archaeologists made some interesting finds when they dug up the field.* 考古学者たちは, その野を掘り起こした時に, いくつかの興味深い発見をした. *This new young player is quite a find!* この若い新人演奏家は逸材だ.

**finder** /fáɪndər/ [名] [C] ▶定義 a person or thing that finds sth ～を見つける人や物➜**発見者, 拾得者, 探知機**

**finding** /fáɪndɪŋ/ [名] [[C], 通常は複数] ▶定義 information that is discovered as a result of research into sth ～を調査した結果として発見された情報➜**発見した物, 調査結果, 研究成果, 結論, 答申, 所見** ‖ *the findings of a survey/report/committee* 調査結果・報告の結論・委員会の答申

***fine**[1] /fáɪn/ [形] ▶定義1 in good health, or happy and comfortable 良好な健康状態の, または幸福で快適な➜**元気な, 健康な, 快適な, 満足できる, 結構な** ‖ *'How are you?' '**Fine thanks.**'* 「お元気ですか」「ありがとう, 元気です」 *'Do you want to change places?' 'No I'm fine here, thanks.'* 「場所を変わりたいですか」「いいえ, ここで大丈夫です. ありがとう」 ▶定義2 all right; acceptable 結構な; 受け入れられる➜**十分な, 満足のいく, まあまあの, まずまずの** ‖ *'Do you want some more milk in your coffee?' 'No **that's fine**, thanks.'* 「コーヒーにもう少しミルクを入れますか」「これで結構です, ありがとう」 *Don't cook anything special - a sandwich will be fine.* 何も特別な物を作らないでくださいね – サンドイッチで十分です. *The hotel rooms were fine but the food was awful.* ホテルの部屋はまあまあだったが, 食事はひどかった.

➤定義1と2の意味は, 疑問文と否定文では用いない. したがって Are you fine? または This isn't fine. とは言えない.

▶定義3 (used about weather) bright with sunlight; not raining (天候について) 日光で明るい; 雨が降っていない➜**晴れた, 晴天の, 良い天気の, 雨でない** ‖ *Let's hope it stays fine for the match tomorrow.* 明日の試合まで天気が持つことを祈ろう. ▶定義4 (名詞の前だけ) of very good quality, beautiful, well-made 非常に高品質の, 美しい, 良くできた➜**立派な, すばらしい, きれいな, 見事な, 高級の, 優美な** ‖ *a fine piece of work* すばらしい作品 *fine detail/carving/china* 見事な細部装飾・彫刻・陶磁器 ▶定義5 very thin or narrow 非常に薄い, または細い➜**極薄の, 極細の, ほっそりした, 鋭い, とがった** ‖ *That hairstyle's no good for me - my hair's too fine.* その髪型は私には似合わない – 私の髪は細すぎるから. *You must use a fine pencil for the diagrams.* 図を書くにはとがった鉛筆を使わなければならない. ⇔ **thick** ▶定義6 made of very small pieces, grains, etc 非常に小さいかけらや粒などから作られている➜**細かい, きめの細かい, 精巧な** ‖ *Salt is finer than sugar.* 塩は砂糖より粒が細かい. ⇔ **coarse** ▶定義7 difficult to notice or understand 気付く, または理解するのが難しい➜**繊細な, 微妙な, 細部の** ‖ *I couldn't understand **the finer points** of his argument.* 彼の議論の微妙な点が分からなかった. *There's **a fine line between** being reserved and being unfriendly.* 控えめな態度と親密でない態度の間には微妙な一線がある.

***fine**[2] /fáɪn/ [名] [C] ▶定義 a sum of money that you have to pay for breaking a law or rule 法律や規則を破ったことに対して支払わなければならない金額➜**罰金, 科料** ‖ *a parking fine* 駐車違反の罰金 *You'll **get a fine** if you park your car there.* そこに車を止めると罰金を取られますよ. — fine [動][他] fine sb (for sth/doing sth) ➜**～に罰金を科す, 罰金を取る, 罰金として払う** ‖ *He was fined £50 for driving without lights.* 彼はライトをつけずに運転したために50ポンドの罰金を科せられた.

**finely** /fáɪnli/ [副] ▶定義1 into small pieces 小片に➜**細かく, 微細に, 細く** ‖ *The onions must be finely chopped for this recipe.* このレシピでは, タマネギを細かく刻まなければならない. ▶定義2 very accurately 非常に正確に➜**精密に, 微妙に, 繊細に, 精細に** ‖ *a finely tuned instrument* 精密に調整された計器

***finger**[1] /fíŋgər/ [名] [C] ▶定義 one of the five parts at the end of each hand 手の先端にある5本の部分のうちの1本1本➜**手の指** ‖ *little finger, ring finger, middle finger, forefinger (or index finger), thumb* 小指, 薬指, 中指, 人差し指, 親指 ☛ C5 ページのさし絵

➤ thumb (親指) は, 指の 1 本と考えられることもあれば, 別だと考えられることもある: *Hold the pen between your finger and thumb.* (指と親指でペンを持ちなさい.) 足の先端にある 5 本の部分は, toes と呼ばれる.

> **▶日本語 vs 英語**
>
> 指を使った数え方の違い
>
> 　数を数えるとき, 日本では人差し指から順番に立てていくか, 親指から折っていくかどちらかですが, 英語圏では逆に親指から立てていきます. 例えば「2」を表す場合, てのひらを上に向けたまま, 親指と人差し指が伸びた状態になっています.

**句動詞** cross your fingers; keep your fingers crossed ▶定義 to hope that sb/sth will be successful or lucky ～がうまくいく, または幸運であることを願う→**人差し指に中指を重ねる, 幸運を祈る (しぐさをする)** ‖ *I'll keep my fingers crossed for you in your exams.* 試験がうまくいくことを祈っています. *There's nothing more we can do now - just cross our fingers and hope for the best.* 今, 私たちにできることはもうない － 人差し指に中指を重ねて最善を祈ろう.

have green fingers ⇒ **GREEN**¹

snap your fingers ⇒ **SNAP**¹

**finger**² /fíŋgər/ **動** ▶定義 to touch or feel sth with your fingers 指で～に触れる, または探る→**～に指で触る, ～を指でいじる**

**fingermark** /fíŋgərmà:rk/ **名 C** ▶定義 a mark on sth made by a dirty finger 汚れた指で～に付けられた跡→**指跡, 指で触った跡, 指の汚れの跡**

**fingernail** /fíŋgənèɪl/ (または **nail**) **名 C** ▶定義 the thin hard layer that covers the outer end of each finger 指の先端を覆う硬くて薄い層→**(指の) つめ** ☞ C5 ページのさし絵

**fingerprint** /fíŋgərprìnt/ **名 C** ▶定義 the mark made by the skin of a finger, used for identifying people 指の皮膚によって付けられる跡で, 人を識別するために使われる→**指紋** ‖ *The burglar left his fingerprints all over the house.* 強盗は家中に指紋を残した. ☞ **footprint** のさし絵

**fingertip** /fíŋgərtìp/ **名 C** ▶定義 the end of a finger→**指先**

**成句** have sth at your fingertips ▶定義 to have sth ready for quick and easy use ～を素早く簡単に使えるように準備する→**～を用意している, すぐ使える, ～が手元にある, ～についてよく知っている** ‖ *They asked some difficult questions but luckily I had all the facts at my fingertips.* 彼らはいくつか難しい質問をしたが, 幸運にも私はあらゆる事実をよく知っていた.

★**finish**¹ /fíniʃ/ **動** ▶定義 1 **自 他** finish (sth/doing sth) to complete sth or reach the end of sth ～を完了する, または～の終わりに到達する→**～を終える, 済ます, 完了する, 完成させる, 終わる, 済む, 完成する** ‖ *What time does the film finish?* その映画は何時に終わりますか. *Haven't you finished yet? You've taken ages!* まだ終わらないのですか. いつまでかかっているの. *The Ethiopian runner won and the Kenyans finished second and third.* エチオピアの走者が優勝し, ケニア人が 2 位と 3 位に入った. *Finish your work quickly!* 早く仕事を終えなさい. *Have you finished typing that letter?* 手紙をタイプし終えましたか. ▶定義 2 **他** finish sth (off/up) to eat, drink or use the last part of sth ～の最後の部分を食べる, 飲む, または使う→**～をすっかり平らげる, 食べ終える, 飲み終える, 使い果たす, 使いきる** ‖ *Finish up your milk, Tony!* トニー, ミルク [牛乳] を飲んでしまいなさい. *Who finished off all the bread?* パンを全部食べたのはだれですか. ▶定義 3 **他** finish sth (off) to complete the last details of sth or make sth perfect ～の最後の細部を仕上げる, または～を完ぺきにする→**～に仕上げをする, 磨きをかける** ‖ *He stayed up all night to finish off the article he was writing.* 彼は徹夜をして, 書いていた記事を仕上げた. *He's just **putting the finishing touches to** his painting.* 彼はちょうど絵の仕上げをしているところだ.

**句動詞** finish sb/sth off **語式** ▶定義 to kill sb/sth; to be the thing that makes sb unable to continue ～を殺す; ～が何かを続けられないようにする物である→**～をやっつける, とどめを刺す, 参らせる, ～の命取りのものとなる** ‖ *The cat played with the mouse before finishing it off.* 猫はとどめを刺す前にネズミをもてあそんだ. *I was very tired towards the end of the race, and that last hill finished me off.* レースの終わり近くにはとても疲れていて, あの最後の丘で私は参

ってしまった．
finish with sb/sth ▶定義1 to stop needing or using sb/sth ～を必要とする，または使うのをやめる➔～の用がなくなる，～でおしまいにする，切り上げる ‖ *I'll borrow that book when you've finished with it.* あなたが読み終わったら，私がその本を借ります． ▶定義2 略式 to end a relationship with sb ～との関係を終わらせる➔～との付き合いをやめる，絶交する，手を切る，別れる ‖ *Sally's not going out with David any more - she finished with him last week.* サリーはもうデーヴィッドと付き合っていない － 彼女は先週彼と別れたのだ．

**finish**[2] /fíniʃ/ 名 ⓒ ▶定義1 the last part or end of sth ～の最後の部分，または終わり➔最後，終わり，終結，最終段階 ‖ *There was a dramatic finish to the race when two runners fell.* 2人の走者が転倒し，レースは劇的に終了した． *I enjoyed the film from start to finish.* 私はその映画を始めから終わりまで楽しんだ． ▶定義2 the last covering of paint, polish, etc that is put on a surface to make it look good 物を美しく見せるために表面に塗られる，ペンキやつや出しなどの最後の一塗り➔仕上げ，仕上がり，上塗り，つや出し

***finished** /fíniʃt/ 形 ▶定義1 （名詞の前は不可） finished (with sb/sth) having stopped doing sth, using sth or dealing with sb/sth ～をすること，～を使うこと，または～に対処することをやめている➔～を終わって，終えて，済んで，～と関係を絶って ‖ *'Are you using the computer?' 'Yes, I won't be finished with it for another hour or so.'* 「コンピューターを使っていますか」「はい，終わるまでにはあと1時間程度かかります」 ▶定義2 （名詞の前は不可） not able to continue 続けることができない➔望みを絶たれた，零落した，絶望的な，おしまいで ‖ *The business is finished - there's no more money.* 会社もおしまいだ － もう資金がない． ▶定義3 made; completed 作られた；完了した➔完成した，仕上がった，出来上がった，済んだ ‖ *the finished product/article* 完成した製品・仕上がった記事

**finite** /fáɪnaɪt/ 形 ▶定義 having a definite limit or a fixed size 明確な限度がある，または決まった大きさがある➔限りのある，限定された，制限された，有限の ‖ *The world's resources are finite.* 世界の資源には限りがある． ⇔ **infinite**

**fir** /fəːr/ （または **fir tree**） 名 ⓒ ▶定義 a tree with thin leaves (needles) that do not fall off in winter 冬にも落ちない細い葉（針状葉）のある木➔モミ，モミの木

**fir cone** 名 ⓒ ▶定義 the fruit of the fir tree モミの木の果実 ➔ モミの実，モミの球果

***fire**[1] /fáɪər/ 名 ▶定義1 ⓒ Ⓤ burning and flames, especially when it destroys and is out of control 特に破壊的で，制御できない場合の，火災と炎➔火，火炎，火事 ‖ *Firemen struggled for three hours to **put out the fire**.* 消防士たちは火を消すために3時間奮闘した． *It had been a dry summer so there were many forest fires.* ずっと乾燥した夏だったので，多くの山火事が発生した． *In very hot weather, dry grass can **catch fire** (= start burning).* 非常に暑い天候の場合は，枯れ草に火がつく（= 燃え出す）ことがある． *Did someone **set fire to** that pile of wood?* だれかこのまきの束に火をつけたのですか． *Help! The frying pan's **on fire**!* 助けて．フライパンが燃えている． ▶定義2 Ⓒ burning wood or coal used for warming people or cooking food 人を暖めたり，食品を調理するために用いられる，燃やすきや石炭 (暖房，調理用の) 火，炉火，炭火，たき火 ‖ *They tried to **light a fire** to keep warm.* 彼らは暖をとるために火をつけようとした． *It's cold - don't let the fire go out!* 寒い － 火が消えないようにしてください． ▶定義3 ⓒ a machine for heating a room, etc 部屋などを暖めるための機械➔暖房器，ヒーター ‖ *a gas/an electric fire* ガスヒーター・電気ヒーター ▶定義4 Ⓤ shooting from guns 銃を発射すること➔発射，発砲，射撃，銃火，砲火 ‖ *The soldiers came **under fire** from all sides.* 兵士たちは四方八方から砲火を浴びた． *I could hear gunfire in the distance.* 遠くで銃声が聞こえた．

成句 **get on/along like a house on fire** ⇒ **HOUSE**[1]

**open fire** ⇒ **OPEN**[2]

**come/be under fire** ▶定義 be strongly criticized 強く批判される➔非難を受ける，攻撃を受ける ‖ *The government has come under fire from all sides for its foreign policy.* 政府は外交政策についてあらゆる方面から非難を受けた．

**fire**[2] /fáɪər/ [動] ▶定義1 [自][他] fire (sth) (at sb/sth); fire (sth) (on/into sb/sth) to shoot bullets, etc from a gun or other weapon 銃やそのほかの武器から弾丸などを発射する➜**〜を発砲する, 発射する, 射撃する, 撃つ, 射る** ‖ *Can you hear the guns firing?* 銃を撃っているのが聞こえますか. *The soldiers fired on the crowd, killing twenty people.* 兵士は群衆に向かって発砲し, 20人が死亡した. *She fired an arrow at the target.* 彼女は的を目掛けて矢を射った. (比喩) *If you stop firing questions at me I might be able to answer!* 私に質問を浴びせるのをやめてくれれば, 答えられるのに. ▶定義2 [他] [略式] to remove an employee from a job 従業員を仕事から外す➜**〜を解雇する, 首にする** ‖ *He was fired for always being late.* 彼はいつも遅刻するので首になった. ▶定義3 [他] fire sb with sth to produce a strong feeling in sb 〜に強い感情を抱かせる➜**〜をかき立てる, 燃え立たせる, 起こさせる, たき付ける, (人の心) を動かす** ‖ *Her speech fired me with determination.* 彼女の演説を聴いて決意が固まった.

**fire alarm** [名] [C] ▶定義 a bell or other signal to warn people that there is a fire 人々に火事があることを警告するための, ベルやほかの信号➜**火災報知機, 火災警報**

**firearm** /fáɪərɑ̀ːrm/ [名] [C] ▶定義 a gun that you can carry 持ち運ぶことのできる銃➜**小火器**

**fire brigade** ([米] **fire department**) [名] [[C], 単数または複数形の動詞と共に] ▶定義 an organization of people trained to deal with fires 火災に対処するように訓練された人々の組織➜**消防隊, 消防団, 消火隊**

**-fired** /fáɪərd/ (複合語で) ▶定義 using the fuel mentioned 言及された燃料を使っている➜**〜を燃料とする, 〜を燃料に用いる** ‖ *gas-fired central heating* ガス燃料のセントラルヒーティング

**fire engine** [名] [C] ▶定義 a special vehicle that carries equipment for dealing with large fires 大規模な火災に対処するための装置を運ぶ専用の車両➜**消防車, 消防自動車**

**fire escape** [名] [C] ▶定義 a special staircase on the outside of a building that people can go down if there is a fire 火事の際に人が降りるための, 建物の外側にある専用の階段➜**非常階段, 火災避難装置, 避難設備**

**fire extinguisher** (または **extinguisher**) [名] [C] ▶定義 a metal container with water or chemicals inside that you use for stopping small fires 小規模な火事を消すために用いる, 水や化学薬品の入った金属製の容器➜**消火器**

**firefighter** /fáɪərfàɪtər/ [名] [C] ▶定義 a person whose job is to stop fires 火事を消すことを仕事とする人➜**消防士, 消防隊員**

**firelight** /fáɪərlàɪt/ [名] [U] ▶定義 the light that comes from a fire 火によって発生する明かり➜**火明かり, 炉火の明かり**

**fireman** /fáɪərmən/ ([複] **-men** /-mən/) = **FIREFIGHTER**

**fireplace**

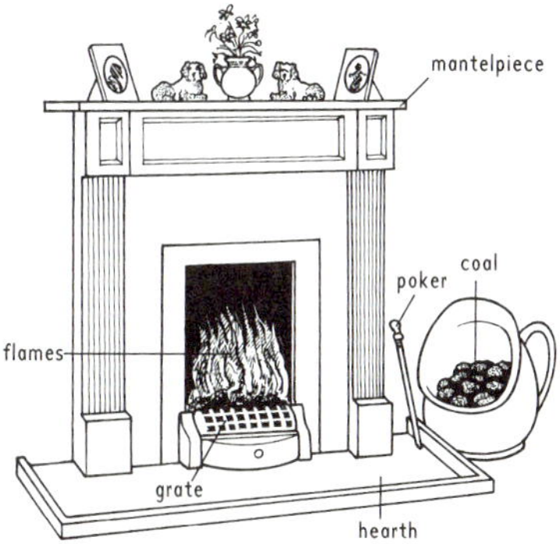


**fireplace** /fáɪərplèɪs/ [名] [C] ▶定義 the open place in a room where you light a fire 室内の, 火をつける開けた場所➜**暖炉, 壁炉, 炉床**

**fireside** /fáɪərsàɪd/ [名] [単数扱い] ▶定義 the part of a room beside the fire 部屋の中の炉火のそばの部分➜**暖炉のそば, 炉辺, 炉端** ‖ *Come and sit by the fireside.* 暖炉のそばに来て座りなさい.

**fire station** [名] [C] ▶定義 a building where firefighters wait to be called, and where the vehicles that they use are kept 消防士が通報を待ち, 彼らが使う車両が保管されている建物➜**消防署, 消防 (隊員) 詰め所**

**firewood** /fáɪərwʊ̀d/ [名] [U] ▶定義 wood used for burning on fires 火を燃やすために使われる木➜**まき, 薪**

626 firework

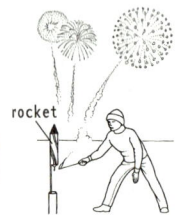

fireworks
rocket

**firework** /fáɪərwɚːrk/ 名 C ▶定義 a small object that burns or explodes with coloured lights and loud sounds, used for entertainment 娯楽として使われ、色の付いた光と大きな音と共に燃えたり爆発したりする小型の物→花火, 花火の打ち上げ

**firing squad** 名 C ▶定義 a group of soldiers who have been ordered to shoot and kill a prisoner 囚人を射殺するよう命令された兵士の集団→銃殺刑執行隊

*__firm__¹ /fɚːm/ 形 ▶定義 1 able to stay the same shape when pressed; quite hard 押されても同じ形を保つことができる; かなり堅い→堅い, 堅固な, 身の引き締まった ‖ a firm mattress 堅いマットレス firm muscles 引き締まった筋肉 ▶定義 2 strong and steady or not likely to change 強固で安定した, または変わりそうにない→しっかり固定された, ぐらつかない, 安定した, 力を込めた, 確固とした, 不変の ‖ She kept a firm grip on her mother's hand. 彼女は母親の手をしっかりと握っていた. a firm commitment/decision/offer 確固とした公約・揺るぎない決定・力強い申し出 ▶定義 3 firm (with sb) strong and in control 強固で管理されている→断固とした, 強硬な, 決然とした, 厳しい, しっかりした ‖ He's very firm with his children. 彼は子供たちにとても厳しい. You have to show the examiner that you have a firm grasp (= good knowledge) of grammar. 試験官に文法をしっかり把握していること (= よく知っていること) を示さなければなりません. ― firmly 副→堅く, 堅固に, 強く, しっかりと, 断固として ― firmness 名 U→硬さ, 堅固, 堅実, 断固とした態度, 厳しさ, 強さ

成句 **a firm hand** ▶定義 strong control or discipline 厳しい管理や規律→厳格な管理, 強力な指導, 厳しいしつけ ‖ Those children need a teacher with a firm hand. あの子供たちには厳しい指導をする教師が必要だ.

*__firm__² /fɚːm/ 名 [C, 単数または複数の動詞と共に] ▶定義 a business company 企業→会社, 商社, 商会, 商店 ‖ Which firm do you work for? どちらの会社にお勤めですか.

*__first__¹ /fɚːst/ 形 ▶定義 coming before all others; that has not happened before ほかのどれよりも先に来る; 以前に起こったことがない→第1の, 1番目の, 先頭の, 最初の, 初の ‖ She's expecting her first baby. 彼女にもうすぐ初めての子供が生まれる. the first half of the game 試合の前半 You've won first prize! あなたが1等賞です. What were your first impressions of this country when you arrived? この国に着いた時の第一印象はいかがでしたか. King Charles I (= King Charles the First) チャールズ王1世 (= 最初のチャールズ王) ☞参 one

成句 **at first glance/sight** ▶定義 when first seen or examined 最初に見られた, または調べられた時に→一見して, 最初, ちょっと見たところでは ‖ The task seemed impossible at first glance, but it turned out to be quite easy. 最初に見た時はその仕事は無理だと思われたが, とても簡単であることが分かった.

first/last thing ⇒ **THING**

*__first__² /fɚːst/ 副 ▶定義 1 before any others ほかの何よりも先に→一番先に, 第1位に, 最初に, 1等で ‖ Sue arrived first at the party. スーがパーティーに一番早くやって来た. Mike's very competitive - he always wants to **come first** when he plays a game. マイクはとても競争心が強い ― ゲームをするときはいつも1番になりたがる. Do you want to **go first** or second? 1等車にしますか, それとも2等車にしますか. ▶定義 2 before doing anything else ほかのどんな事をするよりも先に→まず, 最初に, 初めに, 一番先に ‖ I'll come out later. I've got to finish my homework first. 後から行きます. 先に宿題を済ませなければならないので. ▶定義 3 the time before all the other times; for the first time ほかのどの回よりも前の時; 初めて→最初に, 初めて ‖ Where did you first meet your husband? ご主人に初めて会ったのはどこでしたか. ▶定義 4 at the beginning 初めに→最初のころに, 始めたばかりの時期に ‖ When I first started my job I hated it. 仕事に就いたばかりのころは嫌でたまらなかった. ▶定義 5 used for introducing the first thing in a list 一覧の中の最初の物事を導入するために用いられて→第1に, 何よりも, 初め

に ‖ *There are several people I would like to thank: First, my mother.* 感謝したい人が何人かいます. まず第1に母です. ☛類 **firstly**

**成句 at first** ▶定義 at the beginning 初めは→**最初は, 初めのころは** ‖ *At first I thought he was joking, but then I realized he was serious.* 最初は彼が冗談を言っているのだと思ったが, そのうち真剣だと分かった.

**come first** ▶定義 to be more important to sb than anything else 〜にとってほかの何よりも大切である→**1番目である, 第1である, すべてに優先する, 最も重要である** ‖ *Although she enjoys her job, her family has always come first.* 彼女は仕事を楽しんでいるが, 常に家族が優先である.

**first and foremost** ▶定義 more than anything else; most importantly ほかの何よりも; 最も重要で→**真っ先に, まず何よりも, まず第1に** ‖ *He worked in television but he was a stage actor first and foremost.* 彼はテレビの仕事もしたが, まず何よりも舞台俳優であった.

**first come, first served** 略式 ▶定義 people will be dealt with, served, seen, etc strictly in the order in which they arrive 厳密に到着した順序で人々が対処されたり, サービスを受けたり, 見てもらえたりする→**先着順である, 早い者勝ちである** ‖ *Tickets can be bought here on a first come, first served basis.* チケットはここで先着順で購入できます.

**first of all** ▶定義 as the first thing (to be done or said) (される, または言われる) 最初の事として→**第1に, 初めに, 何よりも先に** ‖ *In a moment I'll introduce our guest speaker, but first of all, let me thank you all for coming.* これからゲストスピーカーをご紹介します. しかしその前にまず, 本日のご来場を感謝いたします.

**first off** 略式 ▶定義 before anything else ほかの何よりも先に→**第1に, まず, 初めに** ‖ *First off, let's decide who does what.* まず初めに, だれが何をするかを決めよう.

**head first** ⇒ **HEAD**¹

★**first**³ /fɜːrst/ 名代 ▶定義**1 the first** (複 **the first**) **C** the first person or thing, people or things 1番目の人や物 (単数または複数)→**第1(位)の人・物, 最初の人・物, 先頭の人・物** ‖ *Are we to be the first to arrive?* 私たちが最初に着いたのですか. *They enjoyed the holiday - their first for ten years.* 彼らは休暇を楽しんだ - 10年振りの

休暇だったのだ. ▶定義**2 a first** [単数扱い] an important event that is happening for the first time 初めて起こっている重要な出来事→**初めての事, 初の出来事** ‖ *This operation is a first in medical history.* この手術は医学の歴史上初めてのものである. ▶定義**3 C** 英 the highest mark given for a university degree 大学の学位として与えられる最高点→**優等, 第1級, 最優秀の成績** ‖ *He got a first in History.* 彼は歴史で優等を取った.

**成句 from the (very) first** ▶定義 from the beginning 最初から→**初めから, 当初から** ‖ *They hated each other from the first.* 彼らは初めからお互いを嫌っていた.

**first aid** 名 **U** ▶定義 medical help that you give to sb who is hurt or ill before the doctor arrives 医師が来るまでに, けがや病気の〜に施す医学上の援助→**応急手当て, 応急処置, 救急処置** ‖ *a first aid kit/course* 救急箱・応急処置のコース *to give sb first aid* 〜に応急処置を施す

**first class** 形副 ▶定義**1** excellent; of the best quality 優秀な; 最高品質の→**一級の[で], 一流の[で], 最高級の[で]** ‖ *a first-class player* 一流の演奏家 *This book is really first class.* この本は実にすばらしい. ▶定義**2** giving or using the best and most expensive type of service 最上で最も高価なサービスを提供している, または利用している→**1等の[で], 第1種郵便(英国では速達に準ずる扱い)の[で]** ‖ *He always travels first class.* 彼はいつも1等車で旅をする. *Ten first-class stamps, please.* 第1種の切手を10枚下さい.

**the first floor** 名 **C** ▶定義**1** 英 the floor of a building above the one on street level (**the ground floor**) 建物のある通りの高さ(1階)より1つ上の階→**2階** ‖ *I live in a flat on the first floor.* 私はアパートの2階に住んでいる. *a first-floor flat* 2階建てのアパート ▶定義**2** 米 the floor of a building on street level 建物のある通りと同じ高さの階→**1階**

**first gear** 名 **C** ▶定義 the lowest gear on a car, bicycle, etc 車や自転車などの1番下のギア→**(ギアの)第1段, ローギア** ‖ *To move off, put the car into first gear and slowly release the clutch.* 発進するには, ギアをローに入れて

ゆっくりとクラッチを放します.

**first-hand** /fɚːrst hǽnd/ 形副 ▶定義 (used about information, experience, a story, etc) heard, seen or learnt by yourself, not from other people (情報, 経験, 話などについて) ほかの人からでなく自分自身で聞いた, 見た, 知った→**直接的な[に], 実際に体験によって得た, 1次情報的で[で]** ‖ *He gave me a first-hand account of the accident (= he had seen it).* 彼は事故について実際に見た事を話してくれた (= 彼が事故を見た). *I've experienced the problem first-hand, so I know how you feel.* 私も実際に同じ問題を経験したことがあるので, あなたの気持ちが分かります.

**firstly** /fɚːrstli/ 副 ▶定義 used to introduce the first point in a list 一覧の中の最初の点を導入するために用いられて→**第1に, 何よりも, 最初に** ‖ *They were angry firstly because they had to pay extra, and secondly because no one had told them about it.* 彼らは, 第1に余分な金を払わなければならなかったことに, 第2にだれもそれを教えてくれなかったことに腹を立てた. ☛類 **first**

**first name** 名 C ▶定義 the first of your names that come before you family name 名前で姓の前に来る最初の名前→**名, 名前, ファーストネーム** ‖ *'What's Mr Munn's first name?' 'Robert, I think.'* 「マン氏の名前は何ですか」「ロバートだと思います」 ☛参 **name**¹ の注

**the first person** 名 [単数扱い] ▶定義**1** (文法) the words such as 'I', 'me', 'we', and the verb forms that go with them I, me, we などの語と, これらと共に用いる動詞の形→**一人称(形)** ‖ *'I am' is the first person singular of the verb 'to be'.* I am は, 動詞 to be の一人称単数形である. ▶定義**2** the style of telling a story as if it happened to you まるで自分自身に起こったことであるかのように物語を描写する形式→**一人称の物語形式, 一人称小説** ‖ *The author writes in the first person.* 著者は一人称形式で書いている.

**first-rate** 形 ▶定義 excellent; of the best quality 優秀な; 最高品質の→**第1級の, 一流の, 最上の**

**\*fish**¹ /fɪʃ/ 名 (複 **fish** または **fishes**) ▶定義**1** C an animal that lives and breathes in water and swims 水中に生息し, 呼吸し, 泳ぐ動物→**魚, 魚類** ‖ *How many fish have you caught?* 魚を何匹釣りましたか. *I went diving on holiday - it was fantastic to see so many different fishes (= types or species of fish).* 私は休日にダイビングに行った ー 本当にいろいろな魚 (= 魚の種類や種) をたくさん見るのはすばらしかった. ☛ C1 ページのさし絵

▶複数形としては fish の方が一般的である. fishes は, 異なる種類の魚について述べるときに用いられる.

▶定義**2** ❶ fish as food 食べ物としての魚→**魚, 魚肉, 魚料理** ‖ *We're having fish for dinner.* 私たちは夕食に魚料理を食べている. ☛ C4 ページのさし絵

▶英国では, fish and chip shop (フィッシュアンドチップス屋) で買う fish and chips (フィッシュアンドチップス) が, 一般的なファーストフードである.

**\*fish**² /fɪʃ/ 動 ❶ ▶定義**1** fish (for sth) to try to catch fish 魚を捕まえようとする→**魚をとる, 釣りをする, 釣る** ‖ *He's fishing for trout.* 彼はマスを釣っている. *They often go fishing at weekends.* 彼らは週末によく釣りに行く. ▶定義**2** fish (around) (in sth) (for sth) to search for sth in water or in a deep or hidden place 水中や, 深い, または隠れた場所で~を探す→**~を(手探りで)探す, 探る, 取り出そうとする** ‖ *She fished (around) for her keys in the bottom of her bag.* 彼女はバッグの底からかぎを取り出そうと探した.

句動詞 **fish for sth** ▶定義 to try to get sth you want in an indirect way 欲しい~を間接的に手に入れようとする→**それとなく引き出そうとする, それとなく手に入れようとする, 誘い出す** ‖ *to fish for an invitation* それとなく招待してもらおうとする

**fish sth out (of sth)** ▶定義 to take or pull sth out (of sth) especially after searching for it 特にそれを探した後で, (~から)…を取り出す, または引き出す→**~を引き上げる, 引っ張り出す, 取り出す, 探り出す** ‖ *After the accident they fished the car out of the canal.* 事故の後, 彼らは車を運河から引き上げた.

**fisherman** /fɪʃərmən/ 名 C (複 **-men** /-mən/) ▶定義 a person who catches fish either as a job or as a sport 仕事またはスポーツとして, 魚を

捕まえる人→漁夫, 漁師, 釣り人 ☛参 angler

**fishing** /fíʃɪŋ/ 🔲 🅄 ▶定義 catching fish as a job, sport or hobby 仕事, スポーツ, あるいは趣味として魚を捕まえること→漁(業), (魚)釣り‖ *Fishing is a major industry in Iceland.* 漁業はアイスランドの主要な産業である. ☛参 angling

**fishing rod** 🔲 🅒 ▶定義 a long thin stick with a long thread (line) and a hook on it for catching fish 魚をとるための, 長い糸(釣り糸)とその先にかぎの付いた細長い棒→釣りざお

**fishmonger** /fíʃmʌŋɡər, -mɑ̀ŋ-/ 🔲 英 ▶定義 1 🅒 a person whose job is to sell fish 魚を売ることを仕事とする人→魚屋, 魚売り ▶定義 2 **the fishmonger's** [単数扱い] a shop that sells fish 魚を売る店→魚屋

**fishy** /fíʃi/ 形 ▶定義 1 tasting or smelling like a fish 魚のような味がしている, またはにおいがしている→魚のような味・においの, 生臭い‖ *a fishy smell* 生臭いにおい ▶定義 2 略式 seeming suspicious or dishonest 疑わしい, または不誠実に思われる→怪しい, 疑わしい, いかがわしい, うさんくさい, まゆつばの‖ *The police thought the man's story sounded extremely fishy.* 警察はその男の話は非常に怪しいと考えた.

**fist** /fɪst/ 🔲 🅒 ▶定義 a hand with the fingers closed together tightly 指を堅く閉じ合わせた手→握りこぶし, げんこつ, 鉄拳(てっけん)‖ *She clenched her fists in anger.* 彼女は怒りで両こぶしを握りしめた.

★**fit¹** /fɪt/ 動 (**fitting**; **fitted**) ▶定義 1 🅑 🅄 to be the right size or shape for sb/sth ～にちょうど合う大きさ, または形である→～にぴったり合う, 適合する, ぴったりはめ込める, 収まる‖ *These jeans fit very well.* このジーンズはぴったり合う. *This dress doesn't fit me any more.* この服はもう私には合わない. *This key doesn't fit in the lock.* このかぎはその錠に合わない. ▶定義 2 🅄 fit (sb/sth) in/into/on/onto sth to find or have enough space for sb/sth ～のための十分な場所を見つける, または十分な場所がある→～を…に合わせる, ～を…に差し込む, ～を割り込ませる, ～の場所を確保する‖ *I can't fit into these trousers any more.* 私はこのズボンはもう履けない. *Can you fit one more person in the car?* 車にもう1人乗れますか. *I can't fit all these books onto the shelf.* これらの本の全部は棚に入りきらない. ▶定義 3 🅄 to put or fix sth in the right place 適切な場所に～を置く, または取り付ける→～をはめ込む, 取り付ける, 備え付ける, うまく納める‖ *The builders are fitting new windows today.* その建築業者は今日は新しい窓を取り付けている. *I can't fit these pieces of the model together.* この模型の部品をうまく組み立てられない. ▶定義 4 🅄 to be or make sb/sth right or suitable ～が正しい, または適切である, あるいはそのようにする→適する, ふさわしい, ～を…に適するようにする, 適合させる, ふさわしくする, 一致させる‖ *I don't think Ruth's fitted for such a demanding job.* 私はルースがそのような骨の折れる仕事に適任だとは思わない. *That description fits Jim perfectly.* その説明はジムにぴったり当てはまる.

**句動詞** fit sb/sth in; fit sb/sth in/into sth ▶定義 to find time to see sb or to do sth ～に会う, または～をする時間を見つける→日時を都合する, 時間を確保する, 暇を見つける, 予定を～に合わせる‖ *The doctor managed to fit me in this morning.* その医師は何とか今日の午前中に私を診る時間を取ろうとしてくれた. *You're tired because you're trying to fit too much into one day.* あなたは1日にあまりに多くの予定を入れすぎるから疲れるのです.

fit in (with sb/sth) ▶定義 to be able to live, work, etc in an easy and natural way with sb/sth) 簡単に自然に(～と共に)生活することや働くことなどができる→～に適応する, ～とうまくやっていく, 調和する‖ *The new girl found it difficult to fit in (with the other children) at school.* その新入生の女の子は, 学校で(ほかの子供たちと)うまくやっていくのは大変であることが分かった.

★**fit²** /fɪt/ 形 (**fitter**; **fittest**) ▶定義 1 fit (for sth/to do sth) strong and in good physical health (especially because of exercise) (特に運動をしているため)丈夫で, 体の健康状態が良い→体の調子が良い, (運動選手などの)コンディションが良い, 健康で, 元気で‖ *Swimming is a good way to keep fit.* 水泳は健康を保つのにいい方法だ. *My dad's almost recovered from his illness, but he's still not fit enough for work.* 私の父は病気からほぼ回復したが, まだ仕事ができるほどには元気になっていない. *She goes to* keep-fit classes. 彼女は体操教室に通っている. ⇔ unfit ▶定義2 fit (for sb/sth); fit to do sth good enough; suitable 十分に良い; 適切な→〜に適した, 適任の, ふさわしい, 〜する能力のある ‖ Do you think she is fit for the job? 彼女はその仕事に適任だと思いますか. These houses are not fit (for people) to live in. これらの家は(人が)住むにはふさわしくない.

**fit**³ /fɪt/ 图 ▶定義1 Ⓒ a sudden attack of an illness, in which sb loses consciousness and his/her body may make violent movements 〜が意識を失い, 体が激しく動くことがあるような, 突然の病気の発作→発作, 引き付け, けいれん ‖ to have fits 発作を起こす ▶定義2 Ⓒ a sudden short period of coughing, laughter, etc that you cannot control 自分で抑制できないような急な短い時間のせき込み, 笑いなど→発作的に〜すること, 一時的興奮, (感情の)激発 ‖ a fit of laughter/anger どっと笑うこと・かっとなること ▶定義3 [単数扱い] (通常は形容詞の後で) the way in which sth (for example a piece of clothing) fits 〜 (例えば衣服など) の合い方→合い具合, ちょうど良いこと, 適合性, 合致 ‖ a good/bad/tight/loose fit 体にちょうど合う・合わない・きつい・緩い

**fitness** /ˈfɪtnəs/ 图 Ⓤ ▶定義1 the condition of being strong and healthy 丈夫で健康な状態→健康, 元気であること, フィットネス ‖ Fitness is important in most sports. 健康であることは多くのスポーツで重要な事だ. ▶定義2 fitness for sth/to do sth the quality of being suitable 適性があること→適格, 適切, 適任, 適合(性), ふさわしいこと ‖ The directors were not sure about his fitness for the job. 重役たちは彼がその仕事に適任かどうか確信がなかった.

**fitted** /ˈfɪtəd/ 形 ▶定義 made or cut to fit a particular space and fixed there ある特定の場所に合うように作られたり切られたりしていて, そこに固定されている→ぴったり合うように作られた, 作り付けの, 家具・備品付きの ‖ a fitted carpet 床全面を覆ったじゅうたん a fitted kitchen (= one with fitted cupboards) ぴったり合うように作られた台所 (= 作り付けの食器戸棚のあるもの)

**fitting**¹ /ˈfɪtɪŋ/ 形 ▶定義1 [正式] right; suitable 適切な; ふさわしい→〜にぴったりの, ふさわしい, 適切な, 適当で, 適切で ‖ It would be fitting for the Olympics to be held in Greece, as that is where they originated. オリンピックは発祥の地であるギリシャで開催されるのがふさわしいであろう. ▶定義2 -fitting used in compounds to describe how clothes, etc fit 複合語として用いて, 衣服などの合い具合を言う→合い具合が〜な ‖ a tight-fitting dress きつい服 loose-fitting trousers 緩いズボン

**fitting**² /ˈfɪtɪŋ/ 图 [Ⓒ, 通常は複数] ▶定義 the things that are fixed in a building or on a piece of furniture but that can be changed or moved if necessary 建物や家具に固定されているが, 必要ならば変更したり移動したりできる物→家具類, 備品, 調度品, 付属器具類, 取り付け部品 ☞参 fixture

★**five** /faɪv/ 数 ▶定義1 5 ☞参 fifth (= 5th)
►文中での数字の使い方については, six を参照.
▶定義2 five- (複合語で) having five of the thing mentioned 言及された物事が5つある→5つの, 5〜の ‖ a five-day week 週5日制 a five-hour flight 5時間の飛行

**fiver** /ˈfaɪvər/ 图 Ⓒ [英略式] ▶定義 a five-pound note; £5 5ポンド紙幣; 5ポンド→5ポンド紙幣

★**fix**¹ /fɪks/ 動 ⑪ ▶定義1 to put sth firmly in place so that it will not move 動かないように〜をしっかりと適切な場所に付ける→〜を固定する, 取り付ける, 留める, 据え付ける ‖ Can you fix this new handle to the door? この新しい取っ手をドアに取り付けてくれませんか. (比喩) I found it difficult to keep my mind fixed on my work. 私は仕事に集中し続けるのが難しいことに気付いた.

▶定義2 to repair sth 〜を修理する→〜を直す, 修理する, 修繕する ‖ The electrician's coming to fix the cooker. 電気工がレンジを直しに来ることになっている. ☞類 repair ▶定義3 fix sth (up) to decide or arrange sth 〜を決める, または手配する→〜を定める, 決定する, 確定する, 整える ‖ We need to fix the price. 私たちは価格を決めなければならない. Have you fixed (up) a date for the party? パーティーの日取りは決めましたか. ▶定義4 fix sth (up) to get sth ready 〜を準備する→〜の手はずを整える, 〜を用意する, 準備する ‖ They're fixing up their spare room for the new baby. 彼らは生まれてくる赤ん坊のた

めに予備の部屋を整えている. ▶定義5 (通常は受動態で) 略式 to arrange the result of sth in a way that is not honest or fair 〜の結果を, 誠実ではない, または不公正なやり方で仕組む➡〜に不正工作をする, 〜を買収する ‖ *Fans of the losing team suspected that the match had been fixed.* 負けたチームのファンは, その試合が八百長だったのではないかと疑った. ▶定義6 fix sth (for sb) 特に 米 to prepare sth (especially food or drink) 〜 (特に食べ物や飲み物) を用意する➡〜を用意する, 準備する, 作る ‖ *Can I fix you a drink/a drink for you?* 飲み物を作りましょうか.

句動副 **fix sb up (with sth)** 略式 ▶定義 to arrange for sb to have sth 〜が…を持てるように手配する➡〜のために…を手配する, あてがう, 用意する, 世話する ‖ *I can fix you up with a place to stay.* 滞在する場所を用意できます.

**fix**² /fɪks/ 名 ▶定義1 Ⓒa solution to a problem, especially one that is easy or temporary 問題の, 特に簡単で一時的な問題の解決法➡応急の解決法, 近道の解決法, 緊急の調整, 解決策 ‖ *There's no **quick fix** to this problem.* この問題には近道の解決方法はない. ▶定義2 [通常は単数] 略式 a difficult situation 困難な状況➡苦境, 窮地, 苦しい立場 ‖ *I was **in a real fix** - I'd locked the car keys inside the car.* 本当に困ってしまった ― 車の中にキーを残したままロックしてしまったのだ. ▶定義3 [通常は単数] 略式 a result that is dishonestly arranged 不正に仕組まれた結果➡八百長, 不正工作, 買収

**fixation** /fɪkˈseɪʃ(ə)n/ 名 Ⓒ ▶定義 a fixation (with sth) an interest in sth that is too strong and not normal 〜への強すぎて普通ではない興味➡執着, 固執, 熱中 ‖ *I'm tired of James's fixation with football.* 私はジェームズのサッカーへの執着にうんざりしている.

**fixed** /fɪkst/ 形 ▶定義1 already decided 既に決定した➡決まった, 確定した, 不変の, 一定の ‖ *a fixed date/price/rent* 確定した日付・定価・一定の賃料 ⇔ **movable** ▶定義2 not changing 変化していない➡固定の, 固執した, 頑固な, 確固たる, 定着した, 凝り固まった ‖ *He has such fixed ideas that you can't discuss anything with him.* 彼にはそのような固定観念があるので, 議論の余地は全くありませんよ.

成句 **(of) no fixed abode/address** 正式 ▶定義 (with) no permanent place to live 決まって住む所のない➡住所不定の ‖ *Daniel Stephens, of no fixed abode, was found guilty of robbery.* 住所不定のダニエル スティーヴンズが強盗で有罪となった.

**fixture** /ˈfɪkstʃər/ 名 Ⓒ ▶定義1 a sporting event arranged for a particular day ある特定の日に予定されるスポーツ大会➡(期日の確定した) 大会, 恒例の試合 ‖ *to arrange/cancel/play a fixture* 恒例の大会の準備をする・恒例の大会を取り消す・恒例の大会で競技する ▶定義2 [通常は複数] a piece of furniture or equipment that is fixed in a house or building and sold with it 家や建物に取り付けられていて, 一緒に販売される家具または設備➡据え付け品, 備え付け家具, 備品, 付属設備 ‖ *Does the price of the house include fixtures and fittings?* 家の価格には備え付けの家具と調度品は含まれていますか. ☞参 **fitting**

**fizz** /fɪz/ 名 Ⓤ ▶定義 the bubbles in a liquid and the sound they make 液体の中の泡と, それが立てる音➡発砲, 発泡性飲料の泡, シューという音 ‖ *This lemonade's lost its fizz.* このレモネードは泡がなくなっている. ― fizz 動 ⓘ➡泡が立つ, 発泡する, シューシューと鳴る

**fizzle** /ˈfɪz(ə)l/ 動

句動副 **fizzle out** ▶定義 to end in a weak or disappointing way 力のない, あっけないやり方で終わる➡勢いがなくなる, (好調な出だしの後) 立ち消えになる, 途中で失敗に終わる, しりすぼみになる ‖ *The game started well but it fizzled out in the second half.* その試合は順調に始まったが, 後半は勢いがなくなった.

**fizzy** /ˈfɪzi/ 形 ▶定義 (used about a drink) containing many small bubbles of gas (飲み物について) 気体の細かい泡を多く含んでいる➡発泡性の, 泡立つ, 泡の多い

▶泡を含むワインやミネラルウォーターは, 通常 sparkling と呼ばれる. fizzy とは言わない.

☞ **bubble** のさし絵 ☞参 **still**

**fizzy drink** (米 **soda**) 名 Ⓒ ▶定義 a sweet non-alcoholic drink that contains many small bubbles 小さな泡を多く含み, アルコールを含まない甘い飲み物➡発泡性清涼飲料 ☞ C4 ページのさし絵

**fjord** /fjɔːrd, fiɔ́ːrd/ 名 C ▶定義 a long narrow piece of sea between cliffs, especially in Norway 特にノルウェーで、断崖（だんがい）の間に入り込んだ細長い海→**フィヨルド，峡湾**

**flabbergasted** /flǽbərɡæ̀stəd; -ɡɑ̀ːst-/ 形 略式 ▶定義 extremely surprised and/or shocked 非常に驚き，衝撃を受けた→**びっくり仰天した，面食らった**

**flabby** /flǽbi/ 形 ▶定義 having too much soft fat instead of muscle 筋肉ではなく柔らかい脂肪があまりにも多くある→**たるんだ，締まりがない，ぶよぶよの，ぜい肉の付いた** ‖ *a flabby stomach* たるんだ腹

★**flag**¹ /flǽɡ/ 名 C ▶定義 a piece of cloth with a pattern or picture on it, often tied to a pole (**flagpole**) or rope and used as a symbol of a country, club, etc or as a signal しばしばさお（旗ざお）やロープにつながれ，国やクラブなどの象徴として，または信号として用いられる，柄や絵の付いた布→**旗**

**flag**² /flǽɡ/ 動 自 (**flagging**; **flagged**) ▶定義 to become tired or less strong 疲れる，または弱る→**衰える，弱る，なえる，緩む，しおれる**
句動詞 **flag sb/sth down** ▶定義 to wave to sb in a car to make him/her stop 車に乗った～を止めるために，その～に向かって手を振る→**～を合図して止める，止まるように合図する** ‖ *to flag down a taxi* 手を振ってタクシーを止める

**flagrant** /fléɪɡr(ə)nt/ 形（名詞の前だけ）▶定義 (used about an action) shocking because it is done in a very obvious way and shows no respect for people, laws, etc (行動について) 非常にあからさまに行われ，人や法律などに敬意を示していないために衝撃的な→**目に余る，甚だしい，罪の意識のない，極悪の**

**flail** /fléɪl/ 動 自 他 ▶定義 to wave or move about without control 制御できずに揺れる，または動き回る→**（手足などを）激しく揺り動かす，振り回される，振り回す，激しく動く** ‖ *The insect's legs were flailing in the air.* 昆虫の足が宙で激しく動いていた．*Don't flail your arms about like that - you might hurt someone.* そんな風に腕を振り回すのはやめなさい－だれかにけがをさせるかもしれませんよ．

**flair** /fléər/ 名 ▶定義 1 (a) **flair for sth** [単数扱い] a natural ability to do sth well ～がうまくできる生まれつきの能力→**才能，素質，直感力，勘，天分** ‖ *She has a flair for languages.* 彼女には語学の才能がある．▶定義 2 ❶ the quality of being interesting or having style 人の関心をひく性質であること，または品格があること→**センスの良さ，趣味の良さ，スマートさ，あか抜けていること** ‖ *That poster is designed with her usual flair.* あのポスターは，彼女のいつものセンスの良さでデザインされている．

**flak** /flǽk/ 名 U 略式 ▶定義 criticism 批判→**非難，攻撃，文句，猛反対** ‖ *He'll get some flak for missing that goal.* 彼はゴールを外したことで多少文句を言われるだろう．

**flake**¹ /fléɪk/ 名 C ▶定義 a small thin piece of sth ～の小さくて薄いかけら→**薄片，一片，破片** ‖ *snowflakes* 雪片 *flakes of paint* ペンキのはげ落ちた破片

**flake**² /fléɪk/ 動 自 ▶定義 **flake (off)** to come off in flakes 薄片になって落ちる→**はげる，はげ落ちる，ひらひら落下する** ‖ *This paint is very old - it's beginning to flake (off).* このペンキはとても古い－はげ始めている．

**flamboyant** /flæmbɔ́ɪənt/ 形 ▶定義 1 (used about a person) acting in a loud, confident way that attracts attention (人について) 注意を集めるようなにぎやかで自信に満ちたやり方で振る舞っている→**派手な，華々しい，華麗な，大胆な** ‖ *a flamboyant gesture/style/personality* 派手な身振り・スタイル・個性 ▶定義 2 bright and easily noticed 明るく，簡単に目に付く→**派手な，鮮やかな，燃えるような，きらびやかな，けばけばしい** ‖ *flamboyant colours* けばけばしい色 — **flamboyance** 名 U →**華麗さ，派手さ，鮮やかさ，あくどさ** — **flamboyantly** 副→**華々しく，華麗に，派手に，鮮やかに**

★**flame** /fléɪm/ 名 C U ▶定義 an area of bright burning gas that comes from sth that is on fire 燃えている～から発生する，明るく燃えている気体の部分→**炎，火炎** ‖ *The flame of the candle flickered by the open window.* 窓が開いていたので，ろうそくの炎がちらちら揺れた．*The house was **in flames** when the fire engine arrived.* 消防車が着いた時には，その家は炎に包まれていた．*The piece of paper **burst into flames** in the fire (= suddenly began to burn strongly).* 紙片が火の中でぱっと燃え立った（=

突然激しく燃え出した). ☞ **candle, fireplace** のさし絵

**flaming** /fléimiŋ/ 形 (名詞の前だけ) ▶定義 **1** (used about anger, an argument, etc) violent (怒りや論争などについて) 激しい→**強烈な, 激しい, 激情に駆られた, 猛烈な** ‖ *We had a flaming argument over the bills.* 私たちは請求書をめぐって激しい議論になった. ▶定義 **2** burning brightly 明るく燃えている→**燃えるような, 燃え立つような, 炎のような, 炎に包まれた, 炎を上げている** ▶定義 **3** (俗語) used as a mild swear word 控えめなののしりの言葉として用いられて→**ばかばかしい, いまいましい, 下らない, とんでもない** ‖ *I can't get in - I've lost the flaming key.* 中に入れない － あのいまいましいかぎをなくしてしまったのだ. ▶定義 **4** (used about colours, especially red) very bright (色, 特に赤色について) 非常に鮮やかな→**燃えるような, 鮮やかな, 炎のような, 燃え立つように赤い** ‖ *flaming red hair* 炎のように赤い毛 *a flaming sunset* 燃えるような夕焼け空

**flamingo** /fləmíŋgou/ 名 C ▶定義 a large pink and red bird that has long legs and stands in water 長い足を持ち, 水の中に立つ, ピンクと赤色の大型の鳥→**フラミンゴ, ベニヅル**

**flammable** /flǽməb(ə)l/ 形 ▶定義 able to burn easily すぐに燃える→**可燃性の, 引火性の高い, 燃えやすい** ‖ inflammable は flammable と同じ意味を表すが, こちらの方が一般的な語である. ⇔ **non-flammable**

**flan** /flæn; F flɑ̃/ 名 C U ▶定義 a round open pie that is filled with fruit, cheese, vegetables, etc 果物, チーズ, 野菜などが詰められている, 上部が覆われていない円いパイ→**フラン, タルトの一種**

**flank**¹ /flæŋk/ 名 C ▶定義 **1** the side of an animal's body 動物の体のわき→**わき腹, 横腹, わき腹肉** ▶定義 **2** the parts of an army at the sides in a battle 戦闘で側面に位置する軍隊の一部→**(隊形などの) 側面, 翼**

**flank**² /flæŋk/ 動 (通常は受動態で) ▶定義 to be placed at the side or sides of 一側面, または複数の側面に配置されている→**～の側面に立つ, ～の横に位置する, ～の側面を守る, 固める, 攻撃する** ‖ *The road was flanked by trees.* その道路の両側には並木があった.

**flannel** /flǽnl/ 名 ▶定義 **1** U a type of soft woollen cloth 柔らかいウールの布の一種→**フランネル, フラノ, 本ネル** ▶定義 **2** = FACE-CLOTH

**flap**¹ /flæp/ 名 C ▶定義 a piece of material, paper, etc that is fixed to sth at one side only, often covering an opening ～の一方の側のみに取り付けられ, 通常は開口部を覆っている物や紙など→**垂れぶた, 垂れ縁, 折り返し** ‖ *the flap of an envelope* 封筒の折り返し ☞ **bag, tent** のさし絵

成句 **be in/get into a flap** 略式 ▶定義 to be in/get into a state of worry or excitement 心配や興奮の状態にある・なる→**はらはらしている・してくる, そわそわしている・してくる, 興奮している・してくる**

**flap**² /flæp/ 動 (**flapping**; **flapped**) ▶定義 **1** 自 他 to move (sth) up and down or from side to side, especially in the wind 特に風で, 上下や左右に動く, または (～を) そのように動かす→**ばたばた動く, はためく; ばたばた揺らす, 羽ばたかせる** ‖ *The sails were flapping in the wind.* 帆が風に揺れていた. *The bird flapped its wings and flew away.* 鳥は翼を羽ばたかせて飛び立った. ▶定義 **2** 自 to become worried or excited 心配する, または興奮する→**そわそわする, はらはらする, 慌てふためく** ‖ *Stop flapping - it's all organized!* そわそわしないで －すべてきちんと整っているのだから.

**flare**¹ /fleər/ 動 自 ▶定義 to burn for a short time with a sudden bright flame 急に明るい炎を出して, 短い間燃える→**めらめら燃える, ぱっと燃え上がる**

句動詞 **flare up** ▶定義 **1** (used about a fire) to suddenly burn more strongly (火について) 急に強く燃える→**燃え上がる, ぱっと燃え立つ** ▶定義 **2** (used about violence, anger, etc) to start suddenly or to become suddenly worse (暴力や怒りなどについて) 突然始まる, または急にひどくなる→**突発する, かっとなる, 激怒する, 荒くなる**

**flare**² /fleər/ 名 ▶定義 **1** [単数扱い] a sudden bright light or flame 突然の明るい光, または炎→**きらめき, 閃光 (せんこう), 発火, ゆらめく炎, ぱっと燃え上がる光** ▶定義 **2** C a thing that produces a bright light or flame, used especially as a signal 特に信号として用いられる, 明るい光や炎を発生させる物→**発光信号, 火炎信号, 照明弾**

**flared** /fleəd/ 形 ▶定義 (used about trousers and skirts) becoming wider towards the bottom (ズボンやスカートについて) すそに向かって広がっている→**フレアーの, すそが広がった, (ズボンが) ラッパになっている**

\***flash**¹ /flæʃ/ 動 ▶定義1 🄰 🄸 to produce or make sth produce a sudden bright light for a short time 突然の明るい光を短時間発生させる, または〜にそのような光を出させる→**ぴかっと光る, ひらめく, 発光する; 〜をひらめかせる, 発光させる, つける, 〜にぱっと照らす** ‖ *The neon sign above the door flashed on and off all night.* ドアの上のネオンが一晩中ついたり消えたりした. *That lorry driver's flashing his lights at us (= in order to tell us sth).* トラックの運転手は私たちに向かってライトを点滅させている (= 〜を知らせるために). ▶定義2 🄰 to move very fast 非常に速く動く→**さっと通る, 素早く通過する, ぱっと現れる, (考えなどが) ひらめく, よぎる** ‖ *I saw something flash past the window.* 何かが窓をぱっと横切るのが見えた. *Thoughts kept flashing through my mind and I couldn't sleep* さまざまな思いがずっと心をよぎって眠れなかった. ▶定義3 🄸 to show sth quickly 〜を素早く見せる→**〜をちらりと見せる, さっと出す** ‖ *The detective flashed his card and went straight in.* その刑事は身分証をさっと見せて, まっすぐ中に入っていった. ▶定義4 🄸 to send sth by radio, television, etc 無線やテレビなどで〜を送信する→**(情報, ニュースなど) を速報する, 瞬時に送る, 素早く伝える, 打電する** ‖ *The news of the disaster was flashed across the world.* その災害のニュースはあっと言う間に世界中に伝わった.

句動詞 **flash back** ▶定義 (used about a person's thoughts) to return suddenly to a time in the past (人の考えについて) 突然, 過去のある時に戻る→**過去の出来事をはっきりと思い出す, 突然過去が心によみがえる** ‖ *Something he said made my mind flash back to my childhood.* 彼が言った何かによって私の心は子供時代に突然戻った.

\***flash**² /flæʃ/ 名 ▶定義1 🄲 a sudden bright light that comes and goes quickly 素早く現れて消える, 突然の明るい光→**ひらめき, きらめき, 閃光 (せんこう)** ‖ *a flash of lightning* 稲光 ▶定義2 🄲 **a flash (of sth)** a sudden strong feeling or idea 突然の強い感情や考え→**(感情の) 突発, 興奮, ひらめき, 思い付き** ‖ *a flash of inspiration* 霊感のひらめき *The idea came to me in a flash.* 突然その考えがひらめいた. ▶定義3 🄲 🄸 a bright light that you use with a camera for taking photographs when it is dark; the device for producing this light 暗いときに写真を撮るためにカメラで用いる明るい光; そのような光を出す装置→**フラッシュ, フラッシュ装置** ☞ **camera** のさし絵

成句 **in/like a flash** ▶定義 very quickly 非常に速く→**急に, たちまち, あっと言う間に, すぐに, 一瞬のうちに**

**(as) quick as a flash** ⇒ **QUICK**¹

**flashback** /flǽʃbæk/ 名 🄲 🄸 ▶定義 a part of a film, play, etc that shows sth that happened before the main story 映画や劇などで, 中心となる物語の前に起こった〜を見せる部分→**フラッシュバック, 回想シーン**

**flashlight** /flǽʃlaɪt/ 米 = **TORCH(1)**

**flashy** /flǽʃi/ 形 **(flashier; flashiest)** ▶定義 attracting attention by being very big, bright and expensive 非常に大きく, 明るく, 高価であるために注目を集めている→**華美な, 華々しい, 派手な, 豪華けんらんの, けばけばしい** ‖ *a flashy sports car* 派手なスポーツカー

**flask** /flɑːsk; flæsk/ 名 🄲 ▶定義1 (または **Thermos**™) 英 a type of container for keeping a liquid hot or cold 液体を熱いまま, または冷たいままに保存するための容器→**魔法びん** ▶定義2 a bottle with a narrow neck that is used for storing and mixing chemicals in scientific work 科学的な作業において化学物質を保管したり混合したりするために用いられる, 首の細いびん→**フラスコ**

\***flat**¹ /flæt/ 形 副 **(flatter; flattest)** ▶定義1 smooth and level, with no parts that are higher than the rest 滑らかで水平で, 他より高い部分がない→**平らな [に], 平たい [く], 平たんな [に], 起伏のない, 平らに伏して** ‖ *The countryside in Essex is quite flat (= there are not many hills).* エセックスの田舎は全く平たんである (= あまり丘がない). *I need a flat surface to write this* *letter on.* この手紙を書くために平らな面が必要だ. *a flat roof* 陸屋根 *She lay flat on her back in the sunshine.* 彼女は日なたであおむけに寝転んだ. *He fell flat on his face in the mud.* 彼は泥の中にうつぶせにばったり倒れた. ▶定義2 not high or deep 高くない, または深くない→**平べったい, 浅い[く], 薄い[く]** ‖ *You need flat shoes for walking.* 歩くためにはかかとの低い靴が必要です. *a flat dish* 浅い皿 ▶定義3 without much interest or energy あまり興味や活気がない→**単調な[に], 平板な[に], 退屈な[に], 変化の乏しい, 面白みのない** ‖ *Things have been a bit flat since Alex left.* アレックスがいなくなってから生活が少し退屈だ. ▶定義4 (名詞の前だけ) (used about sth that you say or decide) that will not change; firm (言う, または決心する～について) 変更しないような; 確固とした→**きっぱりと(した), 断固と(した), ～にべもない・なく** ‖ *He answered our request with a flat 'No!'* 彼は私たちの求めに対し, きっぱりと「駄目だ」と答えた. ▶定義5 (in music) half a note lower than the stated note (音楽で) 指定された音よりも半音低い→**半音下げた・下げて, フラットの[で], 変音の** ☛参 **sharp** ▶定義6 (in music) lower than the correct note (音楽で) 正しい音より低い→**低すぎる, 低すぎて, ピッチが低い・低く** ‖ *That last note was flat. Can you sing it again?* その最後の音は低すぎました. もう一度歌ってください. *You're singing flat.* あなたの歌は音程が低くなっている. ☛参 **sharp** ▶定義7 (used about a drink) not fresh because it has lost its bubbles (飲み物について) 泡が消えているので新鮮ではない→**気の抜けた[て], 味のない** ‖ *Open a new bottle. That lemonade has gone flat.* 新しいびんを開けなさい. そのレモネードは気が抜けています. ▶定義8 医(used about a battery) no longer producing electricity; not working (バッテリーについて) もう電気を発生しない; 機能していない→**(バッテリーが)切れた[て], 上がった[て]** ‖ *We couldn't start the car because the battery was completely flat.* バッテリーが完全に上がっていたので車のエンジンがかからなかった. ▶定義9 (used about a tyre) without enough air in it (タイヤについて) 中に十分な空気が入っていない→**空気の抜けた[て], パンクした[て], ぺしゃんこになった** ‖ *This tyre looks flat - has it got a puncture?* このタイヤは空気が抜けているようだ － パンクしたのだろうか. ▶定義10 (used about the cost of sth) that is the same for everyone; that is fixed (～の費用について) 皆に同じような; 一定の→**均一の[に], 一律の[に], 定額の[に], 固定した** ‖ *We charge a flat fee of £20, however long you stay.* どれだけ滞在しても20ポンドの定額料金です. ▶定義11 (used for emphasizing how quickly sth is done) in exactly the time mentioned and no longer (～がどれほど速く行われたか強調するために用いて) 正確に言及された通りの時間で, それを超えない→**きっかり(の), ちょうど(の), フラットで[の]** ‖ *She can get up and out of the house in ten minutes flat.* 彼女は10分きっかりで起床して家を出ることができる.

成句 fall flat ▶定義 (used about a joke, a story, an event, etc) to fail to produce the effect that you wanted (冗談, 物語, 出来事などについて) 望んでいた効果を生み出さない→**受けない, 受けが悪い, 全く反応がない, 少しも効き目がない, 完全に失敗に終わる**

flat out ▶定義 as fast as possible; without stopping できるだけ速く; 止まらずに→**全速力で, 全力を尽くして, 休みなく, 中断せずに** ‖ *He's been working flat out for two weeks and he needs a break.* 彼は2週間休まずに働いているのだから, 休みが必要だ.

**flat**² /flæt/ 名 ▶定義1 ⓒ (特に 米 **apartment**) a set of rooms that is used as a home (usually in a large building) (通常は大きな建物の中にある) 家として使われる一そろいの部屋→**フラット, フラット式共同住宅, アパート** ‖ *Do you rent your flat or have you bought it?* お宅のフラットは賃貸ですか, 分譲ですか.

▶アメリカ英語では apartment が一般的である. イギリス英語では, 住むためではなく休暇などのために借りるフラットを apartment と言う: *We're renting an apartment in the South of France.* (私たちはフランス南部にアパートを借りている.)

フラットは landlord/landlady から rent (借りる) と言う. その landlord/landlady は, tenant である人にフラットを let (貸す) と言う. 借りた人が支払わなければならない金は, rent と呼ばれる. フラットは furnished (家具付き)

の場合も unfrnished (そうでない) 場合もある. block of flats は, たくさんのフラットが入っている現代的な背の高い建物のことである. フラットを自分と共有している人は flatmate と言う.

▶定義2 ❻ (記号 ♭) (in music) a note which is half a note lower than the note with the same letter (音楽で) 同じ名前の音よりも半音低い音 ➡フラット, 変音記号 ☛参 sharp ▶定義3 [単数扱い] the flat (of sth) the flat part or side of sth 〜の平らな部分または側面➡平面, 平たい部分, 平たい側 ‖ the flat of your hand 手のひら ▶定義4 ❻ 特に 米 a tyre on a vehicle that has no air in it 中に空気が入っていない乗り物のタイヤ➡空気の抜けたタイヤ, パンクしたタイヤ

**flatly** /flǽtli/ 副 ▶定義1 in a direct way; absolutely 直接; 絶対的に➡きっぱりと, はっきりと, 断固として ‖ He flatly denied the allegations. 彼はその申し立てをきっぱりと否定した. ▶定義2 in a way that shows no interest or emotion 興味や感情を表さないように➡活気なく, 単調に, 退屈そうに, 無味乾燥に

**flatten** /flǽtn/ 動自他 ▶定義 flatten (sth) (out) to become or make sth flat 〜が平らになる, または平らにする➡平たんになる・する, 平らに伏す, 平たくなる・する ‖ The countryside flattens out as you get nearer the sea. 海に近付くにつれて田園地帯は平たんになる. The storms have flattened crops all over the country. そのあらしで国中の作物がなぎ倒された.

**flatter** /flǽtər/ 動他 ▶定義1 to say nice things to sb, often in a way that is not sincere, because you want to please him/her or because you want to get an advantage for yourself 〜を喜ばせたい, または自分がメリットを得たいために, しばしば誠実でないやり方で, その〜にうまい事を言う➡〜におべっかを使う, おもねる, お世辞を言う, こびへつらう ▶定義2 flatter yourself (that) to choose to believe sth good about yourself although other people may not think the same ほかの人は同じように考えないかもしれないが, 自分自身についての良い〜を信じる方を選ぶ➡とうぬぼれる, 得意になる, 都合良く思い込む, 自負する, 心ひそかに

〜と信ずる ‖ He flatters himself that he speaks fluent French. 彼は流ちょうなフランス語を話せるとうぬぼれている. ▶定義3 (通常は受動態で) to give pleasure or honour to sb 〜に喜びまたは名誉を与える➡〜をうれしく思わせる, 光栄に感じさせる, 名誉に思わせる, 得意がらせる ‖ I felt very flattered when they gave me the job. 彼らがその仕事を与えてくれた時, 私はとても名誉に思った.

**flattering** /flǽtərɪŋ/ 形 ▶定義 making sb look or sound more attractive or important than he/she really is 〜を実際より魅力的, または重要に見せたり思わせたりしている➡実物より良く見せる, 見栄えのする

**flattery** /flǽtəri/ 名 Ⓤ ▶定義 saying good things about sb/sth that you do not really mean 〜について真意でない良い事を言うこと➡お世辞, ごますり, おべっか, へつらい

**flaunt** /flɔːnt/ 動他 ▶定義 to show sth that you are proud of so that other people will admire it ほかの人が賞賛するように, 自分が自慢に思っている〜を見せる➡〜を見せびらかす, 誇示する, ひけらかす

**flautist** /flɔːtɪst/ (米 **flutist**) 名 ❻ ▶定義 a person who plays a musical instrument that you blow into (a flute) 息を吹き込む楽器 (フルート) を演奏する人➡フルート奏者, フルーティスト

★**flavour**¹ (米 **flavor**) /fléɪvər/ 名 ❻ Ⓤ ▶定義1 the taste (of food) (食品の) 味➡味, 風味, 香味 ‖ Do you think a little salt would improve the flavour? もう少し塩を加えると味が良くなると思いませんか. ten different flavours of yoghurt ヨーグルトの10種類の味 yoghurt in ten different flavours 10種類の味のヨーグルト ▶定義2 [単数扱い] an idea of the particular quality or character of sth 〜の特別な質または特徴の感じ➡味わい, 趣, 気味, 雰囲気, 風情 ‖ This video will give you a flavour of what the city is like. このビデオを見ると, その都市がどんな雰囲気か分かるでしょう.

**flavour**² (米 **flavor**) /fléɪvər/ 動他 ▶定義 to give flavour to sth 〜に味を付ける➡〜に風味・香味を添える, 味付けする ‖ Add a little nutmeg to flavour the sauce. ソースに風味を添えるため, ナツメグを少々加えます. strawberry-flavoured milkshake イチゴ味のミルクセーキ

**flavouring** (米 **flavoring**) /fléɪvərɪŋ/ 名 C U
▶定義 something that you add to food or drink to give it a particular taste 特別な風味になるように食べ物または飲み物に加える物→香味料, 調味料, 薬味 ‖ *This orange juice contains no artificial flavourings.* このオレンジジュースには人工の香味料は含まれていない.

**flaw** /flɔː/ 名 C ▶定義1 a flaw (in sth) a mistake in sth that makes it not good enough or not function as it should それをあまり良くない状態にさせる, またはするべき機能をさせない, 〜にある誤り→欠陥, 不備な点, 欠点, 弱点, 穴 ‖ *There are some flaws in her argument.* 彼女の議論にはいくつか欠陥がある. ▶定義2 a mark or crack in an object that means that it is not perfect 完ぺきでないことを示す, 物体に付いた跡または傷→傷跡, 割れ目, ひび ▶定義3 a flaw (in sb/sth) a bad quality in sb's character 〜の性格の悪い特質→欠点, 弱み, 弱点, 短所 ‖ *His only real flaw is impatience.* 彼の本当の唯一の欠点は短気なことだ. — **flawed** 形 ▶欠陥のある, 傷のある, 欠点のある, 不備のある ‖ *I think your plan is flawed.* あなたの計画には不備があると思います.

**flawless** /flɔ́ːləs/ 形 ▶定義 perfect; with no faults or mistakes 完全な; 欠陥または誤りのない→傷のない, 欠点のない, 完ぺきな, 完全な, 非の打ち所のない ‖ *a flawless diamond* 傷のないダイヤモンド

**flea** /fliː/ 名 C ▶定義 a very small jumping insect without wings that lives on animals, for example cats and dogs. Fleas bite people and animals and make them scratch. 猫または犬のような動物の体に住む, 羽のない, 非常に小さくて跳ねる昆虫. 人または動物を刺し, そこをかゆくさせる→ノミ

**flea market** 名 C ▶定義 a market, often in a street, that sells old and used goods 古い物または中古品を売る, しばしば通りで開かれる市→蚤(のみ)の市, 古物市, フリーマーケット

**fleck** /flek/ 名 [C, 通常は複数] ▶定義 a very small mark on sth; a very small piece of sth 〜に付いた非常に小さい跡; 〜の非常に小さいかけら→斑点(はんてん), 斑紋(はんもん), そばかす, 小片, 滴 ‖ *After painting the ceiling, her hair was covered with flecks of blue paint.* 天井にペンキを塗った後, 彼女の髪は青いペンキの染みだらけになった.

**flee** /fliː/ 動 自 他 (過, 過分 **fled** /fled/) ▶定義 flee (to…/into…); flee (from) sb/sth to run away or escape from sth 〜から逃げ出す, または脱出する→(〜へ・〜から)逃げる, 逃れる, 逃避する, 〜を捨てる ‖ *The robbers fled the country with £100000.* その強盗は10万ポンドを手にその国から逃走した.

**fleet** /fliːt/ 名 [C, 単数または複数形の動詞と共に] ▶定義1 a group of ships or boats that sail together 共に航海する船または小舟の集団→艦隊, 船団, 船隊 ‖ *a fishing fleet* 漁船の船団 ▶定義2 a fleet (of sth) a group of vehicles (especially taxis, buses or aircraft) that are travelling together or owned by one person 共に移動している, または1人の人によって所有されている乗り物 (特にタクシー, バス, または航空機) の集団→(車)隊, 編隊, 一団, 全車両

*****flesh** /fleʃ/ 名 U ▶定義1 the soft part of a human or animal body (between the bones and under the skin) 人間または動物の体の (骨の間と皮膚の下の) 柔らかい部分→肉, 獣肉, 身 ☞ 食用にする動物の肉は meat と呼ばれる. ▶定義2 the part of a fruit or vegetable that is soft and can be eaten 果物または野菜の柔らかい食べられる部分→果肉, 葉肉, 身

成句 **your (own) flesh and blood** ▶定義 a member of your family 家族の一員→肉親, 身内, 同族

**in the flesh** ▶定義 in person, not on television, in a photograph, etc テレビまたは写真などではなく, 実物で→本物で, 直接本人に, 直々に, 目の当たりに見る, 実物で

**make your flesh creep** ▶定義 to make you feel disgusted and/or nervous 嫌悪感または不安を感じさせる→ぞっとさせる, おぞましがらせる, 鳥肌を立たせる ‖ *The way he smiled made her flesh creep.* 彼の笑い方に彼女はぞっとした.

**flew** FLY¹の過去形

**flex**¹ /fleks/ (特に 米 **cord**) 名 C U ▶定義 (a piece of) wire inside a plastic tube, used for carrying electricity to electrical equipment 電気機器に電気を伝えるために用いられる, プラスチックの管に入った針金 (の1本) → 電気のコード ☞ **cable** のさし絵

▶ flex (コード) の先端には plug (プラグ) があり, これを socket (コンセント) または power point (壁コンセント) に差し込む.

**flex**² /fleks/ 動 ⦿ ▶定義 to bend or move a leg, arm, muscle, etc in order to exercise it 運動させるために, 脚, 腕, 筋肉などを曲げたり動かしたりする → ~を曲げる, 動かす, 屈伸する, 収縮させる

**flexible** /fléksəb(ə)l/ 形 ▶定義1 able to bend or move easily without breaking 壊さずに簡単に曲げたり動かしたりできる → 柔軟な, 弾力性のある, たわみやすい, しなる ▶定義2 that can be changed easily 簡単に変更できるような → 柔軟性のある, 適応性のある, 従順な, 弾力的な ‖ flexible working hours 自由勤務時間制, フレックスタイム制 ⇔ **inflexible** — **flexibility** /flèksəbíləti/ 名 ⦿ → 柔軟さ, 柔軟性, 適応性, 融通性

flick

**flick** /flɪk/ 動 ▶定義1 ⦿ flick sth (away, off, onto, etc) to hit sth lightly and quickly with your finger or hand in order to move it 動かすために, ~を指または手で軽く素早くたたく → ~を軽く打つ, はじく, 軽く払いのける, 払い落とす ‖ She flicked the dust off her jacket. 彼女は上着のほこりを軽く払い落とした. Please don't flick ash on the carpet. じゅうたんの上に灰を払い落とさないでください. ▶定義2 ⦿ ⦿ flick (sth) (away, off, out, etc) to move, or to make sth move, with a quick sudden movement 急な素早い動きで動く, または~を動かす → 急に動く, ぐいっと動く; ~をさっと動かす, パチッと切り替える ‖ She flicked the switch and the light came on. 彼女がスイッチを入れると明かりがついた. — **flick** 名 ⦿ → 軽く打つこと, 払いのけること, ピシッと指ではじくこと, パチッという音

句動詞 **flick/flip through sth** ▶定義 to turn over the pages of a book, magazine, etc quickly without reading everything 全部は読まずに, 本または雑誌などのページを素早くめくる → ~を素早く読む, 斜め読みする, パラパラとめくる, ~にざっと目を通す

**flicker**¹ /flíkər/ 動 ⦿ ▶定義1 (used about a light or a flame) to keep going on and off as it burns or shines (光または炎について) 燃えるまたは輝くときに, ついたり消えたりし続ける → 明滅する, 点滅する, ちらちらする, 揺らめく ‖ The candle flickered and went out. ろうそくの炎が揺らめいて消えた. ▶定義2 (used about a feeling, thought, etc) to appear for a short time (感情または考えなどについて) 短い時間, 現れる → さっと浮かぶ, ひらめく, さっとよぎる ‖ A smile flickered across her face. 彼女の顔にかすかに笑みが浮かんだ. ▶定義3 to move lightly and quickly up and down 上下に軽く素早く動く → 揺れる, 震える, そよぐ, はためく, ひるがえる ‖ His eyelids flickered for a second and then he lay still. 彼のまぶたが一瞬震え, そして彼は動かなくなった.

**flicker**² /flíkər/ 名 [⦿, 通常は単数] ▶定義1 a light that shines on and off quickly 素早く輝いたり消えたりする光 → 明滅する光, 揺らぎ, 揺らめき, ちらつき ‖ the flicker of the television/flames テレビのちらつき・炎の揺らめき ▶定義2 a small, sudden movement of part of the body 体の一部の急で小さな動き → 震え, まばたき, ぴくぴく動くこと ▶定義3 a feeling of sth that only lasts for a short time 短い間しか続かない, ~に対する感情 → かすかな現れ, つかの間の感情, ひらめき, 兆し ‖ a flicker of hope/interest/doubt かすかな希望・興味・疑い

**flies** ⇒ **FLY**

*****flight** /flaɪt/ 名 ▶定義1 ⦿ a journey by air 飛行機による旅 → 飛行, 空の旅, 飛行機旅行, 宇宙旅行 ‖ to book a flight 飛行機を予約する a direct/scheduled/charter flight 直行便・定期便・チャーター便 They met **on a flight** to Australia. 彼らはオーストラリアへ向かう飛行機で出会った. a manned space flight to Mars 火星への有人宇宙飛行 ▶定義2 ⦿ an aircraft that takes you on a particular journey 特定の航路を行く航空機 → 飛行機の便, ある便の飛行機, 定期航空便, フライト ‖ Flight number 340 from London to New York is boarding now (= is ready for passengers to get on it). ロンドン発ニューヨーク行きの340便はただいま搭乗中です (= 乗客が乗り込む準備ができている).

▶定義3 ⦿ the action of flying 飛ぶこと → 飛行, 飛翔 (ひしょう), 飛行能力, 飛行による移動 ‖ It's unusual to see swans **in flight** (= when they are flying). 飛んでいる白鳥 (= 白鳥が飛んでいると

き）を見るのは珍しい. ▶定義4 [C]a number of stairs or steps going up or down 上りまたは下りの何段かの階段または段➜**階段の一続き, 階と階をつなぐ階段** ‖ *a flight of stairs* 一続きの階段 ▶定義5 [C][U]the action of running away or escaping from a dangerous or difficult situation 危険なまたは困難な状況から逃げ出すこと, あるいは脱出すること➜**避難, 逃走, 逃亡, 敗走, 脱出** ‖ *the refugees' flight from the war zone* 戦闘地域からの難民の脱出

**flimsy** /flímzi/ [形] ▶定義1 not strong; easily broken or torn 強くない; 簡単に壊れるまたは裂ける➜**もろい, 壊れやすい, 頑丈でない, 薄っぺらな** ‖ *a flimsy bookcase* 壊れやすい本箱 *a flimsy blouse* 薄っぺらなブラウス ▶定義2 weak; not making you believe that sth is true 弱い; ～が真実であるとは信じさせていない➜**薄弱な, 見え透いた, 説得力のない, 浅薄な, 取るに足りない** ‖ *He gave a* ***flimsy excuse*** *for his absence.* 彼は欠席したことについて見え透いた言い訳をした.

**flinch** /flɪntʃ/ [動][自] ▶定義1 flinch (at sth); flinch (away) to make a sudden movement backwards because of sth painful or frightening 痛いまたは恐ろしい～が原因で, 突然後ろに動く動作をする➜**(～に) ひるむ, たじろぐ, 身がすくむ** ‖ *She couldn't help flinching away as the dentist came towards her with the drill.* 歯医者がドリルを手に近付いてきたので, 彼女は思わず身をすくめた. ▶定義2 flinch from sth/doing sth to avoid doing sth because it is unpleasant 不快なので, ～をすることを避ける➜**～にためらう, しりごみする, 二の足を踏む, 恐れをなす** ‖ *She didn't flinch from telling him the whole truth.* 彼女は, 彼にすべての真実を話すことをためらわなかった.

**fling**[1] /flɪŋ/ [動][他] (過, 過分 **flung** /flʌŋ/) ▶定義 to throw sb/sth suddenly and carelessly or with great force ～を急にぞんざいに, または大きな力で投げる➜**～を投げ出す, ほうり出す, 投げ飛ばす, 投げ付ける** ‖ *He flung his coat on the floor.* 彼は上着を床にほうり投げた.

**fling**[2] /flɪŋ/ [名] [C] ▶定義 a short period of fun and pleasure 短い間の楽しみと快楽➜**したい放題, 羽目を外すこと, 勝手な振る舞い**

**flint** /flɪnt/ [名] ▶定義1 [U]very hard grey stone that produces small flames (sparks) when you hit it against steel 鋼に打ち付けると小さな炎（火花）を発生させる, 非常に硬い灰色の石➜**火打ち石, すい石, フリント** ▶定義2 [C]a small piece of flint or metal that is used to produce sparks (for example in a cigarette lighter) （例えばライターなどで）火花を発生させるために用いられる小さな火打ち石, または金属➜**ライターの石, 発火石**

**flip** /flɪp/ [動] (**flipping**; **flipped**) ▶定義1 [自][他]to turn (sth) over with a quick movement 素早い動きで（～を）ひっくり返す➜**～をさっと裏返す, ひっくり返す, 素早くめくる** ‖ *She flipped the book open and started to read.* 彼女はさっと本を開いて読み始めた. ▶定義2 [他]to throw sth into the air and make it turn over ～を空中に投げてひっくり返す➜**～を指ではじく, はじき上げる, ほうり上げる, ひょいと投げる** ‖ *Let's flip a coin to see who starts.* だれが最初にするか, コインを投げて決めよう. ▶定義3 [自] flip (out) （口語）to become very angry or excited ひどく怒る, または興奮する➜**怒り出す, かっとなる, 夢中になる, 熱狂する** ‖ *When his father saw the damage to the car he flipped.* 彼の父は車の損傷を見てかっとなった.

[句動詞] flick/flip through sth ⇒ **FLICK**

**flip-flop** ([米] **thong**) [名] ［通常は複数］▶定義 a simple open shoe with a thin strap that goes between your big toe and the toe next to it 足の親指とその隣の指の間に通す細いひもの付いた, 甲のない簡素な履物➜**革ひも付きサンダル, ゴム草履**

**flippant** /flíp(ə)nt/ （または [略式] **flip**）[形] ▶定義 not serious enough about things that are important 重要な物事に対して十分に真剣ではない➜**軽々しい, 軽薄な, 軽率な, 不まじめな**

**flipper** /flípər/ [名] [C] ▶定義1 a flat arm that is part of the body of some sea animals which they use for swimming 泳ぐために用いる, ある種の海洋動物の体の一部である平たい腕➜**ひれ状の前足, 水かき, ペンギンの翼** ‖ *Seals have flippers.* アザラシにはひれ足がある. ☛ **seal** のさし絵 ▶定義2 a rubber shoe shaped like an animal's flipper that people wear so that they can swim better, especially under water 特に水中で, 人がよりうまく泳げるようにするために履く, 動物のひれのような形をしたゴムの靴➜足

F

640　**flipping**

びれ，水かき，フリッパー ‖ *a pair of flippers* 一組の足びれ ☛ **dive** のさし絵

**flipping** /flípiŋ/ 形副（俗語）▶定義 used as a mild way of swearing 穏やかなののしり言葉として用いられて➔**ひどい，いまいましい，全く，ひどく** ‖ *When's the flipping bus coming?* いまいましいバスはいつになったら来るんだろう．

**flirt¹** /flɜ́ːrt/ 動自 ▶定義 flirt (with sb) to behave in a way that suggests you find sb attractive and are trying to attract him/her 魅力的な～を見つけ，その～の気をひこうとしていることをそれとなく示すような行動をする➔**いちゃつく，ふざける，戯れる，恋をもてあそぶ** ‖ *Who was that boy Irene was flirting with at the party?* アイリーンがパーティーでいちゃついていたあの男の子はだれですか．（比喩）*to flirt with death/danger/disaster* 死・危険・災難とたわむれる

句動詞 flirt with sth ▶定義 to think about doing sth (but not very seriously) ～をすることについて考える（しかし，あまり真剣ではなく）➔**～をもてあそぶ，面白半分に考える** ‖ *She had flirted with the idea of becoming a teacher for a while.* 彼女はしばらくは教師にでもなろうかと冗談半分に考えていた．

**flirt²** /flɜ́ːrt/ 名C ▶定義 a person who often flirts with people 人とよくいちゃつく人➔**浮気者，恋をもてあそぶ人**

**flit** /flít/ 動自 (**flitting**; **flitted**) ▶定義 flit (from A to B); flit (between A and B) to fly or move quickly from one place to another without staying anywhere for long どこにも長くとどまらずに，1つの場所から他へ素早く飛ぶ，または動く➔**すいすい飛ぶ，飛び回る，軽やかに移動する，行き交う** ‖ *She flits from one job to another.* 彼女は気軽に職を変える．

*****float¹** /flóʊt/ 動 ▶定義 1 自 to move slowly through air or water 空中または水上をゆっくりと動く➔**漂う，浮動する，浮遊する，流れる** ‖ *The boats were floating gently down the river.* 船はゆっくりと下流に向かって漂っていた．*The smell of freshly-baked bread floated in through the window.* 窓から焼き立てのパンの香りが漂ってきた．▶定義 2 自 float (in/on sth) to stay on the surface of a liquid and not sink 液体の表面にとどまって沈まない➔**浮く，浮かぶ** ‖ *Wood floats in water.* 木材は水に浮く．▶定義 3 他 to sell shares in a company or business for the first time 会社または事業の株を初めて売る➔**株券を発行する，初めて売り出す** ‖ *The company was floated on the stock market in 1999.* その会社は1999年に株式市場に上場した．▶定義 4 自他 (used in economics) to allow the value of a country's money to change freely according to the value of the money of other countries（経済学で用いて）一国の通貨価値を他国の通貨価値に従って自由に変化させる➔**変動相場制である，自由に変動する，～を変動相場制にする**

**float/sink**

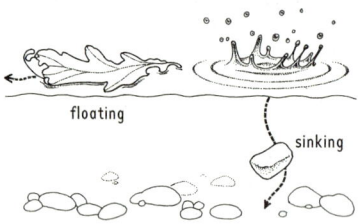

floating

sinking

**float²** /flóʊt/ 名 C ▶定義 1 a lorry or other vehicle that is decorated and used in a celebration that travels through the streets 装飾されていて，祝典で使われるトラックなどの通りを進む乗り物➔**山車（だし），台車** ‖ *a carnival float* カーニバルの山車 ▶定義 2 a light object used in fishing that moves on the water when a fish has been caught 釣りで用いられ，魚がかかると水面で動く軽い物➔**浮き** ▶定義 3 a light object used for helping people to learn to swim 人が泳ぎを覚えるのを助けるために使われる軽い物➔**水かき板，浮き袋**

**floating** /flóʊtiŋ/ 形 ▶定義 not fixed; not living permanently in one place 固定していない；1箇所に定住していない➔**浮動的な，定着しない，変動する，流動的な** ‖ *London's floating population* ロンドンの浮動人口

**flock¹** /flɑ́k/ 名 C ▶定義 1 a group of sheep or birds 羊または鳥の集団➔**群れ** ☛参 **herd** ▶定義 2 a large number of people 多数の人々➔**人の群れ，一団，一群，一行，群衆** ‖ *Flocks of tourists visit London every summer.* 毎年夏には大勢の旅行者がロンドンを訪れる．

**flock²** /flɑ́k/ 動自 ▶定義 (used about people) to

go or meet somewhere in large numbers (人について) 大勢でどこかに行く、またはどこかで会う→**集まる, 群がる, 押し寄せる, 大挙していく** ‖ *People are flocking to her latest exhibition.* 彼女の最新の展示会に続々と人が集まっている.

**flog** /flɔːg, flɑɡ/ 動他 (**flogging**; **flogged**) ▶定義1 (通常は受動態で) to hit sb hard several times with a stick or a long thin piece of leather (whip) as a punishment 罰として棒または細長い革ひも (むち) で〜を数回強く打つ→**〜を棒でたたく, むち打つ, 〜に体罰を与える** ▶定義2 英略式 to sell sth 〜を売る→**〜を売る, 売り込む, 売り付ける**

**flogging** /flɔːgɪŋ, flɑ́g-/ 名 C U ▶定義 the act of hitting sb several times with a long thin piece of leather (whip) or a stick as a punishment 罰として細長い革ひも (むち) または棒で〜を数回打つこと→**むち打ち, 棒たたき, 体罰**

*★**flood**[1] /flʌd/ 動自他 ▶定義1 to fill a place with water; to be filled or covered with water ある場所を水で満たす; 水で満たされる, または覆われる→**氾濫 (はんらん) する・させる, あふれる・させる, 浸水する・させる, 水浸しになる・する** ‖ *I left the taps on and flooded the bathroom.* 蛇口を開けたままにしておいたので, 浴室が水浸しになった. *The River Trent floods almost every year.* トレント川はほとんど毎年氾濫する.
▶定義2 flood in/into/out of sth to go somewhere in large numbers 大勢でどこかへ行く→**〜にどっと押し寄せる, 大挙していく, 殺到する, あふれる** ‖ *Since the television programme was shown, phone calls have been flooding into the studio.* そのテレビ番組が放映されてから, スタジオに電話が殺到している. ▶定義3 (used about a thought, feeling, etc) to fill sb's mind suddenly (考え, 感情などについて) 突然〜の心を満たす→**〜にあふれる・させる, 押し寄せる, 満たす, みなぎらせる** ‖ *At the end of the day all his worries came flooding back.* 1日の終わりに心配事すべてが彼の心に一気によみがえった.

*★**flood**[2] /flʌd/ 名 C ▶定義1 a large amount of water that has spread from a river, the sea, etc that covers an area which should be dry 乾燥しているはずの地帯を覆う, 川または海などから広がった大量の水→**洪水, 大水, 冠水** ‖ *Many people have been forced to leave their homes because of the floods.* 洪水のため, 多くの人々が自分の家から去らなければならなかった.
▶定義2 a flood (of sth) a large number or amount 多数または大量→**(〜の) 殺到, 充満, 多数の〜, 多量の〜** ‖ *She received a flood of letters after the accident.* 事故後, 彼女の元に手紙が殺到した.

**floodlight** /flʌ́dlàɪt/ 名 C ▶定義 a powerful light that is used for lighting places where sports are played, the outside of public buildings, etc スポーツが行われる場所, 公共の建物の外などを照らすために用いられる強力な照明→**投光照明(器), フラッドライト**

**floodlit** /flʌ́dlɪ̀t/ 形 ▶定義 lit by powerful lights (floodlights) 強力な照明 (投光照明) で照らされた→**投光照明器で照射された, ナイター照明された** ‖ *a floodlit hockey match* 投光照明を使って行われるホッケーの試合

*★**floor**[1] /flɔːr/ 名 ▶定義1 [C, 通常は単数] the flat surface that you walk on indoors 室内でその上を歩く平らな面→**床, 板の間, 床板** ‖ *Don't come in - there's broken glass **on the floor**!* 入ってはいけません － 床に割れたガラスが落ちています. *a wooden/concrete/marble floor* 木製・コンクリート・大理石の床 ☛参 **ground**の注
▶定義2 C all the rooms that are on the same level of a building 建物の同じ高さにあるすべての部屋→**階, フロア, ある階の部屋すべて** ‖ *My office is **on the second floor**.* 私のオフィスは3階にある.
▶英国では, ground floor が通りと同じ高さにある階 (1階) で, その上の階が first floor である. アメリカ英語では, first floor は通りと同じ高さにある階を指す.

▶定義3 [C, 通常は単数] the ground or surface at the bottom of the sea, a forest, etc 海, 森などの底の地面または表面→**底, 床, 下底, 海底, 地面** ‖ *the ocean/valley/cave/forest floor* 海底・谷底・洞窟 (どうくつ) の底・林床

**floor**[2] /flɔːr/ 動他 略式 ▶定義 to surprise or confuse sb completely with a question or a problem 質問または問題で〜を徹底的に驚かす, または困惑させる→**〜をやり込める, 閉口させる, 参らせる, まごつかせる, 困惑させる** ‖ *Some of the questions I was asked in the interview completely floored me.* 面接で尋ねられたいくつか

の質問に, 私はすっかりまごついてしまった.

**floorboard** /flɔ́ːrbɔ̀ːrd/ 名 C 定義 one of the long wooden boards used to make a floor 床を作るために用いられる長い木製の板の 1 枚 1 枚 → 床板

**flop**¹ /flɑp/ 動 自 (**flopping**; **flopped**) 定義 1 flop into, onto sth; flop (down/back) to sit or lie down in a sudden and careless way because you are very tired 非常に疲れたため, 急にぞんざいに座るまたは横になる → 〜にどさりと座り込む, ごろりと横になる, 寝転ぶ ‖ I was so tired that all I could do was flop onto the sofa and watch TV. 非常に疲れていたので, できる事と言えばソファーに寝転んでテレビを見ることだけだった. 定義 2 flop around, back, down, etc to move, hang or fall in a careless way without control 統制されずに気ままに動く, 垂れ下がるまたは倒れる → ばたばた動き回る, のそのそと不格好に歩く, ぶらぶら揺れる, どさりと倒れる ‖ I can't bear my hair flopping in my eyes. 髪が目にかかるのは我慢できない. 定義 3 (used about a book, film, record, etc) to be a complete failure with the public (本, 映画, レコードなどについて) 世間的に完全に失敗である → 失敗に終わる

**flop**² /flɑp/ 名 C 定義 (used about a film, play, party, etc) something that is not a success; a failure (映画, 演劇, パーティーなどについて) 成功ではないもの; 失敗 → 完全な失敗, 失敗作, 失敗に終わったもの ‖ Her first novel was very successful but her second was a flop. 彼女の最初の小説は大成功だったが, 2 作目は失敗作だった. a box-office flop 興業面での失敗

**floppy** /flɑ́pi/ 形 定義 soft and hanging downwards; not rigid 柔らかくて垂れ下がっている; 固くない → 柔らかい, だらりとした, 垂れ下がった, 締まりのない ‖ a floppy hat 型崩れした帽子

**floppy disk** (または **floppy** ( 複 **floppies**), **diskette**) 名 C 定義 a square piece of plastic that can store information from a computer コンピューターの情報を保存できる四角いプラスチック製品 → フロッピーディスク ‖ Don't forget to back up your files onto a floppy disk. フロッピーディスクにファイルのバックアップを取るのを忘れないように. ☛ 参 **hard disk** ☛ S5 ページのさし絵

**flora** /flɔ́ːrə/ 名 [複数扱い] 定義 all the plants growing in a particular area 特定の地域に生育しているすべての植物 → 植物相, 植物誌, フローラ ‖ He's studying the **flora and fauna** (= the plants and animals) of South America. 彼は南米の植物誌と動物誌 (= 植物と動物) を研究している. ☛ 参 **fauna**

**floral** /flɔ́ːrəl/ 形 定義 decorated with a pattern of flowers, or made with flowers 花の模様で装飾された, または花で作られた → 花柄の, 花模様の, 花の, 花のような, 花で覆われた, 花でできた

**florist** /flɔ́(ː)rɪst, flɑ́r-/ 名 定義 1 ● a person who has a shop that sells flowers 花を売る店を持っている人 → 花屋の主人 定義 2 **the florist's** [単数扱い] a shop that sells flowers 花を売る店 → 花屋

**flounder** /flávndər/ 動 自 定義 1 to find it difficult to speak or act (usually in a difficult or embarrassing situation) (通常は, 困難なまたは間の悪い状況で) 話したり行動したりするのが難しいと気付く → まごつく, もたつく, おろおろする, うろたえる ‖ The questions they asked her at the interview had her floundering helplessly. 面接で尋ねられた質問に彼女はどうしようもなく口ごもった. 定義 2 to have a lot of problems and be in danger of failing completely 多くの問題を抱え, 完全に失敗する危険がある → あがく, もがく, のたうつ, 苦労する ‖ By the late nineties, the business was floundering. 90 年代後半には事業は窮地に陥っていた. 定義 3 to move with difficulty, for example when trying to get out of some water, wet earth, etc 例えば水, ぬかるみなどから抜け出そうとするときに苦労して動く → もがく, もがきながら進む, のたうちまわる

*****flour** /fláuər/ 名 U 定義 a very thin powder made from wheat or other grain and used for making bread, cakes, biscuits, etc 小麦またはほかの穀物から作られ, パン, ケーキ, ビスケットなどを作るために用いられる非常に細かい粉末 → 小麦粉, メリケン粉 ☛ C4 ページのさし絵

**flourish**¹ /flɜ́ːrɪʃ; flʌ́r-/ 動 定義 1 自 to be strong and healthy; to develop in a successful way 丈夫で健康である; うまく発展する → 元気でいる, 繁茂する, 繁栄する, 隆盛を極める ‖ a flourishing business 繁盛している商売 定義 2 他 to wave sth in the air so that people will notice it 人が気付くように～を宙に振る➡️～を振る, 大きく振り回す, 打ち振る, 誇示する ‖ *He proudly flourished two tickets for the concert.* 彼は2枚のコンサートチケットを自慢げに見せびらかした.

**flourish**² /flʌrɪʃ, flɜːr-/ 🔢 ⓒ ▶定義 an exaggerated movement 誇張された動き➡️派手な身振り, おおげさな身振り, これ見よがしの態度, 見せびらかし ‖ *He opened the door for her with a flourish.* 彼は彼女のためにおおげさな身振りでドアを開けた.

**flout** /flaʊt/ 🔢 ⓘ ▶定義 to refuse to obey or accept sth ～に従うこと, または受け入れることを拒否する➡️～を無視する, ばかにする, 軽べつする, 鼻であしらう ‖ *to flout the rules of the organization* 組織の規則を無視する *to flout sb's advice* ～の忠告を鼻であしらう

★**flow**¹ /floʊ/ 🔢 [単数扱い] **a flow of sth/sb** ▶定義1 a steady, continuous movement of sth/sb ～の一定で継続した動き➡️流れ, 流れるような動き, 流動, 噴出 ‖ *Press hard on the wound to stop the flow of blood.* 出血を止めるため傷口を強く押さえなさい. ▶定義2 a supply of sth ～の供給➡️流入, 流出, 供給 ‖ *the flow of information between the school and the parents* 学校と親の間の情報のやり取り ▶定義3 the way in which words, ideas, etc are joined together smoothly 言葉または考えなどが滑らかにつながっている様子➡️よどみない流れ, 流れるような話, すらすらと流れ出ること ‖ *Once Charlie's in full flow, it's hard to stop him talking.* いったんチャーリーがとうとうと話し始めたら, 止めるのは難しい.

成句 **the ebb and flow (of sth)** ⇒ **EBB**²

★**flow**² /floʊ/ 🔢 ⓘ ▶定義1 to move in a smooth and continuous way (like water) (水のように)滑らかに継続して動く➡️流れる, 注ぐ, 流れるように動く ‖ *This river flows south into the English Channel.* この川は南へ流れてイギリス海峡に注ぐ. *a fast-flowing stream* 流れの速い小川 *Traffic began to flow normally again after the accident.* 事故後, 交通は再び通常通りに流れ始めた. ▶定義2 (used about words, ideas, actions, etc) to be joined together smoothly (言葉, 考え, 動作などについて)滑らかにつながっている➡️すらすら流れ出る, よどみなく流れる, わき出る, わき起こる ‖ *As soon as we sat down at the table,*

*the conversation began to flow.* テーブルに着くとすぐに会話がよどみなく進み出した. ▶定義3 (used about hair and clothes) to hang down in a loose way (髪または衣服について) 緩やかに垂れ下がる➡️垂れ下がる, すらりと垂れる, 優雅に垂れる ‖ *a long flowing dress* 丈の長い流れるようなドレス

**flow chart** (または **flow diagram**) 🔢 ⓒ ▶定義 a diagram that shows the connections between different stages of a process or parts of a system ある過程の異なる段階の間の, またはあるシステムの異なる部分の間の関連を示す図➡️流れ図, 作業工程図, フローチャート

★**flower**¹ /flaʊər/ 🔢 ⓒ ▶定義1 the coloured part of a plant or tree from which seeds or fruit grow 植物または木の, 種子または果実がなる色の付いた部分➡️花 ← C2ページのさし絵

▶ flower は数枚の petal (花びら) から成る. stem (茎) の先端の bud (つぼみ) から生長する.

▶定義2 a plant that is grown for its flowers 花が目的で育てられる植物➡️花, 花の咲く植物, 花を観賞する植物 ‖ *to grow flowers* 花を育てる

▶ flower を pick (摘む), 花びんに arrange (生ける) と言う. 特別な場合に贈られる, または届けられる花は bouquet (花束, ブーケ) と呼ばれる.

★**flower**² /flaʊər/ 🔢 ⓘ ▶定義 to produce flowers 花を生じる➡️花が咲く, 花をつける, 開花する ‖ *This plant flowers in late summer.* この植物は夏の終わりに花をつける.

**flower bed** 🔢 ⓒ ▶定義 a piece of ground in a garden or park where flowers are grown 花が育てられる庭または公園の土地➡️花壇 ← C7ページのさし絵

**flowerpot** /flaʊərpɒt/ 🔢 ⓒ ▶定義 a pot in which a plant can be grown 植物を育てることができる鉢➡️植木鉢

**flowery** /flaʊəri/ 🔢 ▶定義1 covered or decorated with flowers 花で覆われた, または飾られた➡️花が咲き乱れた, 花で飾った, 花模様の, 花柄の ‖ *a flowery dress/hat/pattern* 花柄のワンピース・花を飾った帽子・花模様 ▶定義2 (used about a style of speaking or writing) using long, difficult words when they are not necessary (話し方または文体について) 必要でないときに長

い難解な言葉を用いている→**美辞麗句**を連ねた, 美文調の, 華やかな, 飾り立てた

**flown** **FLY**¹ の過去分詞形

**fl oz** 略 fluid ounce(s)→液量オンス

**flu** /fluː/ (または 正式 **influenza**) 名 Ü ▶定義 an illness that is like a bad cold but more serious. You usually feel very hot and your arms and legs hurt. ひどい風邪に似ているがもっと重い病気. 通常は, 非常に熱っぽく腕と足が痛む→**インフルエンザ, 流感**

**fluctuate** /flʌ́ktʃueɪt/ 動 自 ▶定義 fluctuate (between A and B) (used about prices and numbers, or people's feelings) to change frequently from one thing to another (価格または数, あるいは〜の感情について) 1つのものから他へしばしば変わる→**変動する, 上下する, 揺れ動く, 動揺する** ‖ *The number of students fluctuates between 100 and 150.* 学生数は100人から150人の範囲で変動している. — **fluctuation** /flʌ̀ktʃuéɪʃ(ə)n/ 名 Ü Ç→変動, 上下, 動揺, 揺らぎ, 不安定

**fluent** /fluːənt/ 形 ▶定義 1 fluent (in sth) able to speak or write a foreign language easily and accurately 外国語をすらすらと正確に話す, または書くことができる→**流ちょうな, すらすらと話せる・書ける, 達者な** ‖ *After a year in France she was fluent in French.* フランスで1年過ごしたので, 彼女はフランス語が達者になった. ▶定義 2 (used about speaking, reading or writing) expressed in a smooth and accurate way (話す, 読む, または書くことについて) 滑らかで正確に表現された→**流ちょうな, 能弁な, 筆の立つ** ‖ *He speaks fluent German.* 彼は流ちょうなドイツ語を話す. — **fluency** /fluːənsi/ 名 Ü→流ちょうさ, 滑らかさ, 達者, すらすら話せる・書けること ‖ *My knowledge of Japanese grammar is good but I need to work on my fluency.* 私は日本語の文法の知識は十分にあるが, 滑らかに話せるように練習する必要がある. — **fluently** 副→流ちょうに, 滑らかに, すらすらと, 達者に

**fluff** /flʌf/ 名 Ü ▶定義 1 very small pieces of wool, cotton, etc that form into balls and collect on clothes and other surfaces 玉になり衣服またはほかの表面にたまる, 羊毛, 綿などの非常に小さいかけら→**けば, 毛玉, 綿毛, 綿ごみ, 綿ぼこ**

り ▶定義 2 the soft new fur on young animals or birds 幼い動物または鳥の新しい柔らかい毛→**うぶ毛**

**fluffy** /flʌ́fi/ 形 ▶定義 1 covered in soft fur 柔らかい毛で覆われた→**けばの, 綿毛の, うぶ毛の** ‖ *a fluffy kitten* 柔らかい毛の子猫 ▶定義 2 that looks or feels very soft and light 非常に柔らかく軽く見える, または感じるような→**ふわふわした, ふんわりした, 柔らかい** ‖ *fluffy clouds/towels* ふんわりした雲・ふわふわのタオル

**fluid**¹ /fluːɪd/ 名 Ç Ü ▶定義 a substance that can flow; a liquid 流れることができる物質; 液体→**流体, 流動体, 水分, 飲み物** ‖ *The doctor told her to drink plenty of fluids.* 医者は彼女に水分をたくさん取るように言った. *cleaning fluid* 液体洗剤

**fluid**² /fluːɪd/ 形 ▶定義 1 able to flow smoothly like a liquid 液体のように滑らかに流れることができる→**流動性 [体] の, 流動する, 流れるような, 流麗な** ‖ (比喩) *I like her fluid style of dancing.* 彼女の滑らかな踊り方が好きだ. ▶定義 2 (used about plans, etc) able to change or likely to be changed (計画などについて) 変更できる, または変更される可能性がある→**流動的な, 変わり得る, 不安定な, 決定的でない**

**fluid ounce** 名 Ç (略 **fl oz**) ▶定義 a measure of liquid; in Britain, 0.0284 of a litre; in the US, 0.0295 of a litre 液量の単位; 英国では0.0284リットル; 米国では0.0295リットル→**液量オンス**

▶度量衡についての説明は, 巻末の数についての特別項目を参照.

**fluke** /fluːk/ 名 [Ç, 通常は単数] 非正式 ▶定義 a surprising and lucky result that happens by accident, not because you have been clever or skilful 賢明だったから, または熟練していたからではなく, 偶然に起こる驚くべき幸運な結果→**まぐれ当たり, 幸運 (な偶然)** ‖ *The result was no fluke. The better team won.* 結果はまぐれではなかった. 優れていた方のチームが勝ったのだ.

**flung** **FLING**¹ の過去・過去分詞形

**fluorescent** /flɔːrésnt, flʊər-/ 形 ▶定義 1 producing a bright white light 明るい白色の光を発している→**蛍光性の, 蛍光を発する** ‖ *fluorescent lighting* 蛍光照明 ▶定義 2 very bright; seeming to shine 非常に明るい; 輝いているように見えている→**蛍光色の, 輝かしい** ‖ *fluorescent pink* *paint* 蛍光性のピンクのペンキ

**fluoride** /flɔ́ːràid, flúə-/ 名 U ▶定義 a chemical substance that can be added to water or toothpaste to help prevent bad teeth 虫歯の予防に役立つように水または練り歯磨き粉に加えられることがある化学物質→フッ化物

**flurry** /flʌ́ri; flə́ːri/ 名 C (復 **flurries**) ▶定義 1 a short time in which there is suddenly a lot of activity 突然多くの動きが発生する短い時間→突然の混乱, 動揺, 狼狽(ろうばい), 興奮 ‖ *a flurry of excitement/activity* 突然の興奮・行動 ▶定義 2 a sudden short fall of snow or rain 急に短時間降る雪または雨→にわか雪, にわか雨, 通り雨

**flush**¹ /flʌʃ/ 動 ▶定義 1 自 (used about a person or his/her face) to go red (人またはその顔について) 赤くなる→紅潮する, 赤面する, 火照る, 血が顔にさっと上る ‖ *Susan flushed and could not hide her embarrassment.* スーザンは真っ赤になり, きまり悪さを隠せなかった. ☞ blush の方が一般的な語である. ▶定義 2 他 to clean a toilet by pressing or pulling a handle that sends water into the toilet トイレに水を流すためのハンドルを押すか引くかして, トイレをきれいにする→~に水を流して洗う, トイレの水を流す ‖ *Please remember to flush the toilet.* トイレの水を流すのを忘れないでください. ▶定義 3 自 (used about a toilet) to be cleaned with a short flow of water (トイレについて) 短時間の水の流れできれいになる→一気に流れる, トイレに水が流れる, 洗い流される ‖ *The toilet won't flush.* トイレの水が流れない. ▶定義 4 他 **flush sth away, down,** etc to get rid of sth in a flow of water 水の流れで~を取り除く→~を水で洗い流す, 水で洗浄する ‖ *You can't flush tea leaves down the sink - they'll block it.* お茶の葉を流しに水で流してはいけません - 流しが詰まってしまいます.

**flush**² /flʌʃ/ 名 [C, 通常は単数] ▶定義 1 a hot feeling or red colour that you have in your face when you are embarrassed, excited, angry, etc 気恥ずかしいとき, 興奮したとき, 怒ったときなどの激しい気持ちまたは顔に出る赤らみ→感激, 興奮, 激怒, 赤面, 紅潮 ‖ *The cold wind brought a flush to our cheeks.* 冷たい風に当たってほおが赤くなった. *a flush of anger* 突然の怒り ▶定義 2 the act of cleaning a toilet with a quick flow of water; the system for doing this 素早い水の流れでトイレをきれいにすること; そのようにする仕組み→水洗(設備)

**flushed** /flʌʃt/ 形 ▶定義 with a hot red face 火照った赤い顔をした→顔を紅潮させて, 赤面した, 興奮した ‖ *You look very flushed. Are you sure you're all right?* 顔がとても赤いですよ. 本当に大丈夫ですか.

**fluster** /flʌ́stər/ 動 他 (通常は受動態で) ▶定義 to make sb feel nervous and confused (because there is too much to do or not enough time) (やる事が多すぎるため, または時間が十分にないため)~をいらいらさせる, あるいは混乱させる→~を慌てさせる, 取り乱させる, 狼狽(ろうばい)させる, 面食らわせる ‖ *Don't get flustered - there's plenty of time.* 慌てないで - 時間はたっぷりあります. — **fluster** 名 C ●慌てふためくこと, 混乱, 動揺, 狼狽 ‖ *I always get in a fluster before exams.* 私は試験前はいつも慌てふためく.

**flute** /fluːt/ 名 C ▶定義 a musical instrument like a pipe that you hold sideways and play by blowing over a hole at one side 横向きに持ち, 片側にある穴に息を吹き込んで演奏する, パイプのような楽器→フルート, 横笛 ☞参 **piano** の注 ☞ **music** のさし絵 — **flutist** /flúːtist/ 米 = **FLAUTIST**

**flutter**¹ /flʌ́tər/ 動 ▶定義 1 自他 to move or make sth move quickly and lightly, especially through the air 特に空中で, 素早く軽く動く, または~をそのように動かす→はためく, ~をはためかせる, ひるがえる・らせる, 羽ばたく・かせる ‖ *The flags were fluttering in the wind.* 旗が風ではためいていた. *The bird fluttered its wings and tried to fly.* 鳥が羽ばたいて飛ぼうとした. ▶定義 2 自 your heart or stomach flutters when you feel nervous and excited 不安なとき, または興奮したときに, 心臓または胃が激しく不規則に動く→動悸(どうき)がする, どきどきする, 胸が躍る, ときめく

**flutter**² /flʌ́tər/ 名 [C, 通常は単数] ▶定義 1 a quick, light movement 素早い軽い動き→はためき, 羽ばたき, 心臓などの不規則な動き, 異常な鼓動 ‖ *the flutter of wings/eyelids* 羽ばたき・まぶたがぴくぴくすること ▶定義 2 英 (俗語) a bet on a race, etc 競走などへのかけ→少額のかけ,

投機 ‖ I sometimes **have a flutter** on the horses. おれは時々馬にかけることがある.

**\*fly**¹ /fláɪ/ 動 (現分 **flying**; 三単現 **flies**; 過 **flew** /flu:/; 過分 **flown** /flóʊn/) ▶定義1 🚗 🈁 (used about a bird, insect, aircraft, etc) to move through the air (鳥, 昆虫, 航空機などについて)空中を移動する→飛ぶ, 舞う, 漂う, 〜を飛ばす, 放つ ‖ This bird has a broken wing and can't fly. この鳥は翼をけがしているので飛ぶことができない. Concorde can fly (across) the Atlantic in three hours. コンコルドは大西洋を(横断して)3時間で飛べる. ▶定義2 🚗 🈁 to travel or carry sth in an aircraft, etc 航空機などで旅行する, または〜を運ぶ→〜で飛ぶ, 飛行機で旅行する, 飛行機で行く, 〜を空輸する ‖ My daughter is flying (out) to Singapore next week. 私の娘は来週, 飛行機でシンガポールへ行く予定だ. Supplies of food were flown (in) to the starving people. 飢えに苦しむ人々の元に食糧品が飛行機で運ばれた. ▶定義3 🚗 🈁 (used about a pilot) to control an aircraft (パイロットについて) 航空機を操縦する→(飛行機を)飛ばす, 操縦する ‖ You have to have special training to fly a jumbo jet. ジャンボジェット機を操縦するためには特別な訓練を受けなければならない. ▶定義4 🚗 to move quickly or suddenly, especially through the air 特に空中を, 素早く, または急に動く→飛ぶ, 飛んでいく, 飛ぶように走る, 駆ける, 急いで行く, 急に動いて〜になる, 飛ぶように過ぎる, 急速に広まる ‖ A large stone **came flying** through the window. 大きな石が窓から飛び込んできた. I slipped and my shopping **went flying** everywhere. 足を滑らせたので, 買った品物があちこちに飛び散った. Suddenly the door **flew open** and Mark came running in. 突然ドアが開いてマークが駆け込んできた. (比喩) The weekend has just **flown by** and now it's Monday again. 週末は飛ぶように過ぎ, また月曜日になった.

▶定義5 🚗 🈁 to move about in the air; to make sth move about in the air 空中を動き回る; 空中で〜を動き回らせる→ひるがえる・がえす, 舞い上がる, 揚げる ‖ The flags are flying. 旗がひるがえっている. to fly a flag/kite 旗を揚げる・たこを揚げる ☞ 名 flight

成句 as the crow flies ⇒ **CROW**¹

**fly off the handle** 略式 ▶定義 to become very angry in an unreasonable way 道理をわきまえずに非常に腹を立てる→かっとなる, 自制心を失う

**let fly (at sb/sth)** ▶定義1 to shout angrily at sb 〜に向かって怒ってどなりつける→〜をののしる, 非難する, 暴言を吐く, 悪口を浴びせる ▶定義2 to hit sb in anger かっとなって〜を打つ→〜を殴る, たたく, 食って掛かる ‖ She let fly at him with her fists. 彼女はこぶしで彼を殴った.

**\*fly**² /fláɪ/ 名 C ▶定義1 (複 **flies**) a small insect with two wings 2枚の羽のある小さい昆虫→ハエ, イエバエ ‖ Flies buzzed round the dead cow. ハエが死んだ牛の周りをブンブン飛び回っていた. ☞ **insect** のさし絵 ▶定義2 (または **flies** [複数扱い]) an opening down the front of a pair of trousers that fastens with buttons or another device (**a zip**) and is covered with a narrow piece of material ボタンまたはそのほかの仕掛け(ファスナー)で締まり, 幅の狭い生地がかぶせられている, ズボンの前面の下向きに開くところ→ズボンの前チャック ☞ C6ページのさし絵

**flying** /fláɪŋ/ 形 ▶定義 able to fly 飛ぶことができる→飛べる, 空を飛ぶ, 飛行する ‖ flying insects 飛ぶことのできる昆虫

成句 **with flying colours** ▶定義 with great success; very well 大成功で; 非常にうまく→大勝利で, 大成功で, 見事に, 堂々と ‖ Martin passed the exam with flying colours. マーティンは見事に試験に合格した.

**get off to a flying start** ▶定義 to begin sth well; to make a good start 〜をうまく始める; 良いスタートを切る→順調な出だしである, 順調に始まる

**flying saucer** 名 C ▶定義 a round spacecraft that some people claim to have seen and that they believe comes from another planet 一部の人が見たことがあると主張し, ほかの惑星から来たと信じている円形の宇宙船→空飛ぶ円盤

**flying visit** 名 C ▶定義 a very quick visit とても大急ぎの訪問→ちょっと立ち寄ること, 慌ただしい訪問 ‖ I can't stop. This is just a flying visit. すぐに帰ります. ちょっと立ち寄っただけなので.

**flyover** /fláɪoʊvər/ (米 **overpass**) 名 C ▶定義 a

**FM** /èf ém/ 略 frequency modulation ▶定義 one of the systems of sending out radio signals 無線信号を送信する方式の1つ→**FM 放送**

**foal** /fóul/ 名 C ▶定義 a young horse 若い馬→**馬の子, 子馬** ☞参 **horse** の注

**foam¹** /fóum/ 名 U ▶定義1 (または **foam rubber**) a soft light rubber material that is used inside seats, cushions, etc 座席, クッションなどの内部に使われる, 柔らかく軽いゴム製の材料→**気泡ゴム, フォームラバー** ‖ *a foam mattress* フォームラバーのマットレス ▶定義2 a mass of small air bubbles that form on the surface of a liquid 液体の表面にできる小さな気泡の塊→**あぶく, 泡(まつ)** ‖ *white foam on the tops of the waves* 波頭の白い泡 ▶定義3 an artificial substance that is between a solid and a liquid and is made from very small bubbles 固体と液体の中間で, 非常に細かい泡からできている人工的な物質→**泡状の物質, 消化器の泡, フォーム** ‖ *shaving foam* ひげそり用フォーム

**foam²** /fóum/ 動 自 ▶定義 to produce foam 泡を生ずる→**泡立つ, 泡ができる, 泡を吹く** ‖ *We watched the foaming river below.* 私たちは泡立つ川を見下ろした.

**fob** /fɑb/ 動 (**fobbing**; **fobbed**)

句動詞 fob sb off (with sth) ▶定義1 to try to stop sb asking questions or complaining by telling him/her sth that is not true 真実でない～を言って, …が質問することまたは不平を言うことをやめさせようとする→**～をうまくはぐらかす, ごまかす, うまく避ける** ‖ *Don't let them fob you off with any more excuses.* これ以上言い訳をさせて彼らにごまかされないように.

▶定義2 to try to give sb something that he/she does not want ～が望まない物を与えようとする→**～をつかませる, 押し付ける** ‖ *Don't try to fob me off with that old car - I want a new one.* その古い車を押し付けようとしないでください－私は新車が欲しいのです.

**focal point** /fóuk(ə)l pɔ̀int/ 名 [単数扱い] ▶定義 the centre of interest or activity 興味または活動の中心→**焦点, 関心の中心, 活動の中心**

**focus¹** /fóukəs/ 動 自 他 (**focusing**; **focused** または **focussing**; **focussed**) focus (sth) (on sth) ▶定義1 to give all your attention to sth ～にすべての注意を向ける→**精神を集中させる, 注意を集中する, ～の焦点を合わせる, 重点的に取り扱う** ‖ *to focus on a problem* 問題に集中する

▶定義2 (used about your eyes or a camera) to change or be changed so that things can be seen clearly (目またはカメラについて)物がはっきりと見えるように変わる, または変える→**焦点・ピントが合う, 焦点・ピントを調整する; ～の焦点・ピントを合わせる** ‖ *Gradually his eyes focused.* 次第に彼の目の焦点が合った. *I focussed (the camera) on the person in the middle of the group.* 私はその集団の真ん中の人に(カメラの)ピントを合わせた.

**focus²** /fóukəs/ 名 [C, 通常は単数] ▶定義 the centre of interest or attention; special attention that is given to sb/sth 興味または注意の中心; ～に向けられる特別な注意→**中心, 焦点, 的** ‖ *The school used to be the focus of village life.* 学校はかつては村の生活の中心だった.

成句 in focus/out of focus ▶定義 (used about a photograph or sth in a photograph) clear/not clear (写真または写真の中の～について) 鮮明な・鮮明でない→**焦点が合っている・ずれている, ピントが合っている・ずれている, はっきりして・ぼんやりして** ‖ *This picture is so badly out of focus that I can't recognize anyone.* この写真はひどくぼけていて, だれも見分けられない.

**fodder** /fάdər/ 名 U ▶定義 food that is given to farm animals 農場の動物に与えられるえさ→**飼料, かいば**

**foe** /fóu/ 名 C (文) ▶定義 an enemy 敵→**敵, かたき, 敵対者**

**foetus** (米 **fetus**) /fíːtəs/ 名 C (複 **foetuses**; **fetuses**) ▶定義 a young human or animal that is still developing in its mother's body まだ母親の体内で発育中の幼い人間, または動物→**胎児**
▶ embryo は発育のもっと早期の段階にある.

**fog** /fɔ(ː)g, fɑg/ 名 U C ▶定義 thick white cloud that forms close to the land or sea. Fog makes it difficult for us to see. 陸または海の近くで発生する濃い白色の雲. これによって視界が悪くなる→**霧, 濃霧, もや** ‖ *Patches of dense fog are making driving dangerous.* 所々に濃い霧がかかっていて運転するのが危険だ. *Bad fogs are* common in November. 11月にはよくひどい霧が発生する.

➤ fog は mist より濃い. haze は暑さによって発生する. smog は公害によって起こる. weather の注を参照.

**foggy** /fɔ(ː)gi, fági/ 形 (**foggier**; **foggiest**) ▶定義 used to describe the weather when there is fog 霧がかかっているときの天候を述べるときに用いられて➡霧の(多い・深い), 霧がかかった

成句 not have the faintest/foggiest (idea) ⇒ **FAINT**¹

**foil**¹ /fɔil/ 名 ▶定義1 (または **tinfoil**) ❶ metal that has been made into very thin sheets, used for putting around food 非常に薄い板状に作られた金属で, 食品を包むために用いられる➡箔(はく), 金属の薄片, ホイル ‖ *aluminium foil* アルミ箔 ▶定義2 ❷ a long, thin, pointed weapon used in a type of fighting sport (fencing) 戦う形式のスポーツ(フェンシング)の一種で使われる, 細長く, 先のとがった武器➡フルーレ, フォイル

**foil**² /fɔil/ 動 ▶定義 to prevent sb from succeeding, especially with a plan; to prevent a plan from succeeding ～が, 特に計画について, うまくいくことを阻止する; 計画がうまくいくことを阻止する➡～をくじく, 失敗させる, 挫折(ざせつ)させる, 妨げて成功を無にする ‖ *The prisoners were foiled in their attempt to escape.* 囚人たちは脱走をしようとする試みを阻止された.

**foist** /fɔist/ 動

句動詞 foist sth on/upon sb ▶定義 to force sb to accept sth that he/she does not want ～にその～が望まない…を強制的に受け入れさせる➡～を押し付ける, 強制する, つかませる ‖ *Jeff had a lot of extra work foisted on him when his boss was away.* 上司の留守中に, ジェフに余分の仕事がたくさん押し付けられた.

★**fold**¹ /fóuld/ 動 ▶定義1 ❶ fold sth (up) to bend one part of sth over another part in order to make it smaller, tidier, etc ～を小さくしたり, きちんと片付けたりするために, その～の一部分を曲げて別の部分に重ねる➡～を折る, 折り重ねる・畳む・曲げる ‖ *He folded the letter into three before putting it into the envelope.* 彼は手紙を3つに折ってから封筒に入れた. *Fold up*

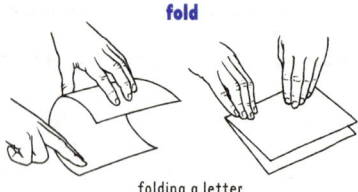

folding a letter

*your clothes neatly, please.* 衣類をきちんと畳んでください. ⇔ **unfold** ▶定義2 ❷ fold (up) to be able to be made smaller in order to be carried or stored more easily より簡単に運ぶ, または保管することができるように小さくできる➡折り畳める ‖ *This table folds up flat.* このテーブルは平たく折り畳める. *a folding bed* 折り畳み式ベッド ▶定義3 ❷ fold A in B; fold B round/over A to put sth around sth else ～をほかの…に巻く～～をくるむ, 包む, 覆う, 巻き付ける ‖ *I folded the photos in a sheet of paper and put them away.* 私は写真を紙に包んでしまった. ▶定義4 ❷ (used about a business, a play in the theatre, etc) to close because it is a failure (事業, 劇場での芝居などについて)失敗であるため終了する➡つぶれる, 失敗する, 終わりになる, 上演打ち切りになる

成句 cross/fold your arms ⇒ **ARM**¹

★**fold**² /fóuld/ 名 ❷ ▶定義1 the mark or line where sth has been folded ～が折られた跡または線➡折り目, 折りじわ ▶定義2 a curved shape that is made when there is more material, etc than is necessary to cover sth ～を覆うために必要な量より, 生地などが多い場合にできる湾曲した形➡ひだ, しわ ‖ *the folds of a dress/curtain* ワンピース・カーテンのひだ ▶定義3 a small area inside a fence where sheep are kept together in a field 牧草地で羊を集めておく柵(さく)の中の狭い空間➡おり, 囲い

**folder** /fóuldər/ 名 ❷ ▶定義1 a cardboard or plastic cover that is used for holding papers, etc 書類などを入れるために使われる厚紙またはプラスチックのカバー➡書類ばさみ, フォルダー ▶定義2 a collection of information or files on one subject that is stored in a computer or on a disk コンピューターまたはディスクに保存された, 1つのテーマについての情報またはファイルの集まり➡フォルダー

**foliage** /fóuliidʒ/ 名 ❶ 正式 ▶定義 all the leaves

of a tree or plant 木または植物のすべての葉→(群)葉, 葉群

**folk**¹ /fóuk/ 图 ▶定義1 (困 **folks**) [複数扱い] 略式 people in general 一般の人々→人々 ‖ *Some folk are never satisfied.* 満足することを知らない人たちもいる. ▶定義2 [複数扱い] a particular type of people ある特定の種類の人々→人々 ‖ *Old folk often don't like change.* 老人は大抵変化を好まない. *country folk* 田舎の人たち ▶定義3 **folks** [複数扱い] 略式 used as a friendly way of addressing more than one person 複数の人々に話し掛けるときの親しみを込めた言い方として用いられて→皆さん ‖ *What shall we do today, folks?* 皆さん, 今日は何をしましょうか. ▶定義4 **folks** [複数扱い] 略式 your parents or close relatives 両親または近い親戚(しんせき)→両親, 家族, 親類 ‖ *How are your folks?* ご家族の皆さんはお元気ですか. ▶定義5 🅤 music in the traditional style of a country or community 国または地域の伝統的な形式の音楽→民族音楽, フォーク ‖ *Do you like Irish folk?* アイルランドの民族音楽は好きですか.

**folk**² /fóuk/ 形 ▶定義 traditional in a community; of a traditional style 地域の伝統に従っている; 伝統的な形式の→民族的な, 民衆の, 民俗の, 民間(伝承)の ‖ *Robin Hood is an English folk hero.* ロビンフッドはイングランド民族の英雄である. *folk music* 民俗音楽 *a folk song* 民謡

**folklore** /fóuklɔːr/ 图 🅤 ▶定義 traditional stories and beliefs 伝統的な物語または信仰→民間伝承, 民俗, フォークロア

*****follow** /fálou/ 動 ▶定義1 🅐🅤 to come, go or happen after sb/sth ～の後から来る, 行く, または起こる→～の後に付いていく, 後に続く, ～の次に起こる ‖ *You go first and I'll follow (on) later.* あなたが先に行ってください. 私は後から行きます. *The dog followed her (around) wherever she went.* その犬は彼女の行く所ならどこへでも付いていった(付きまとった). *I'll have soup followed by spaghetti.* スープの後でスパゲッティを頂きます. ▶定義2 🅤 to go along a road, etc; to go in the same direction as sth 道などに沿って行く; ～と同じ方向に行く→～をたどる, ～に沿って進んでいく, ～と平行して走る, ～伝いに走る ‖ *Follow this road for a mile and then turn right at the pub.* この道を1マイル進んで, パブの角を右に曲がってください. *The road follows the river for a few miles.* 道路は数マイル, その川と平行に走っている. ▶定義3 🅤 to do sth or to happen according to instructions, an example, what is usual, etc 指示, 例, 慣例の事などに従って～をする, または起こる→～に倣う, 従う, 習う, ～を守る ‖ *When lighting fireworks, it is important to **follow the instructions** carefully.* 花火に火をつけるときは, 指示に正確に従うことが大切です. *The day's events followed the usual pattern.* その日の催しはいつものパターンだった. ▶定義4 🅐🅤 to understand the meaning of sth ～の意味を理解する→～に付いていく, ～をはっきり理解する, 頭でたどる ‖ *The children couldn't follow the plot of that film.* 子供たちはその映画の筋に付いていけなかった. ▶定義5 🅤 to keep watching or listening to sth as it happens or develops ～が起こる, または展開するのを見続ける, あるいは聞き続ける→見守る, ～に注目する, よく聞く, ～に注意深く耳を傾ける ‖ *The film follows the career of a young dancer.* その映画は若いダンサーの生涯を追っている. *Have you been following the tennis championships?* テニスの選手権をずっと見ていますか. ▶定義6 🅤 **follow (on) (from sth)** to be the logical result of sth; to be the next logical step after sth ～の論理的な結果である; その後の次の論理的な段階である→(～から)結果として生じる, ～という結果になる, (必然の)結果としてになる ‖ *It doesn't follow that old people can't lead active lives.* 老人は活動的な生活ができないということにはならない. *Intermediate Book One follows on from Elementary Book Two.*「初級2」の本の次に「中級1」の本が続く.

成句 **a hard act to follow** ⇒ **HARD**¹

**as follows** ▶定義 used for introducing a list 一覧を紹介するために用いられて→次のように, 次の通りに, 以下のように ‖ *The names of the successful candidates are as follows...* 当選した候補者の名前は以下の通りです.

**follow in sb's footsteps** ▶定義 to do the same job as sb else who did it before you 自分より前にその仕事をしたほかの～と同じ仕事をする→～の先例に倣う, ～を見習う, ～の志を継ぐ, 後を継ぐ ‖ *He followed in his father's footsteps and* *joined the army.* 彼は父に倣って陸軍に入隊した.

**follow sb's example/lead** ▶定義 to do what sb else has done or decided to do ほかの〜がした事，またはすると決めた事をする➡〜の例に倣う，〜を手本とする，〜の先導に従う，指図に従う

**follow suit** ▶定義 to do the same thing that sb else has just done ほかの〜がしたばかりの事と同じ事をする➡人のまねをする，人のやった通りにする，先例に従う

**follow your nose** ▶定義 to go straight forward まっすぐ前に進む➡まっすぐに行く，直進する ‖ *Turn right at the lights and after that just follow your nose until you get to the village.* 信号を右に曲がって，その後は村までまっすぐ進むだけです.

句動詞 **follow sth through** ▶定義 to continue doing sth until it is finished 〜が完了するまでし続ける➡〜を最後までやり通す，やり抜く，やり遂げる，仕上げる

**follow sth up** ▶定義**1** to take further action about sth 〜についてさらに行動を起こす➡引き続いて〜する，さらに〜を付け加える，〜の後に続けて…する ‖ *You should follow up your letter with a phone call.* 手紙を出した後で電話もかけなさい. ▶定義**2** to find out more about sth 〜についてもっと調べる➡〜を徹底的に究明する，どこまでも追求する，厳しく追跡する ‖ *We need to follow up the story about the school.* 私たちは，その学校についての話をさらに詳しく調べる必要がある.

**follower** /fálouər/ 名 C ▶定義 a person who follows or supports a person, belief, etc ある人，信念などに従う，または支持する人➡信奉者，支持者，弟子，信徒，熱心なファン

**following**¹ /fálouɪŋ/ 形 ▶定義**1** next (in time) (時間的に)次の➡次に続く，次に来る，翌〜 ‖ *He became ill on Sunday and died the following day.* 彼は日曜日に具合が悪くなり，次の日に亡くなった. ▶定義**2** that are going to be mentioned next 次に述べられることになっているような➡次の，以下の，下記の，後述の ‖ *Please could you bring the following items to the meeting...* 会合に以下の物を持参してください.

**following**² /fálouɪŋ/ 名 ▶定義**1** [単数扱い] a group of people who support or admire sth 〜を支持または賞賛する人々の集団➡支持者たち，信奉者たち，ファンの集まり ‖ *The Brazilian team has a large following all over the world.* ブラジルチームには世界中に多くのファンがいる.
▶定義**2 the following** [複数扱い] the people or things that are going to be mentioned next 次に述べられることになっている人々または物事➡下記のもの，次に述べる事，以下の事 ‖ *The following are the winners of the competition...* 次の人々がその競技の勝者です.

**following**³ /fálouɪŋ/ 前 ▶定義 after; as a result of 〜の後で; 〜の結果としての➡〜に次いで，〜に引き続いて，〜の後で ‖ *Following the riots many students have been arrested.* 暴動の後で，大勢の学生が逮捕された.

**follow-up** 名 C ▶定義 something that is done as a second stage to continue or develop sth 〜を継続または発展させる第2段階として行われる事➡追跡(調査)，続報，続編 ‖ *As a follow-up to the television series, the BBC is publishing a book.* そのテレビ番組のシリーズの続きとして，BBC は本を出版する予定だ.

**folly** /fáli/ 名 C U ( 複 **follies**) 正式 ▶定義 an act that is not sensible and may have a bad result 分別のない，悪い結果を招く可能性のある行動➡愚行，愚挙，ばかげた事 ‖ *It would be folly to ignore their warnings.* 彼らの警告を無視するとしたら愚かなことだ.

*****fond** /fand/ 形 ▶定義**1** (名詞の前には不可) **fond of sb/sth; fond of doing sth** liking a person or thing, or liking doing sth 人または物が気に入っている，または〜をすることが好きである➡〜を好んで，愛して，〜が気に入って，好きで ‖ *Elephants are very fond of bananas.* 象はバナナが大好きです. *I'm not very fond of getting up early.* 私は早起きはあまり好きではない. *Teachers often **grow fond** of their students.* 教師はしばしば生徒たちを大変好きになるものだ.
▶定義**2** (名詞の前だけ) kind and loving 親切で愛情に満ちた➡優しい，情け深い，好意的な ‖ *I have **fond memories** of my grandmother.* 私には祖母の温かい思い出がある.

**fondle** /fándl/ 動他 ▶定義 to touch sb/sth gently in a loving or sexual way 愛情を込めて，または性的に〜に優しく触れる➡〜を優しくなでる，愛撫(ぶ)する，かわいがる

**fondly** /fándli/ 副 ▶定義 in a loving way 愛情を

込めて→**優しく, 甘く, かわいがって, 温かく** ‖ *Miss Murphy will be fondly remembered by all her former students.* マーフィー先生のことは元生徒たち全員が懐かしく思い出すだろう.

**fondness** /fɑ́ndnəs/ 名 [U, 単数扱い] ▶定義 (a) fondness (for sb/sth) a liking for sb/sth ~に対する好み→(〜に対する)**愛情, 愛好, 愛着, 慈しみ, 溺愛(できあい)** ‖ *I've always had a fondness for cats.* 私は前からずっと猫が好きだ. *My grandmother talks about her schooldays with fondness.* 私の祖母は学生時代について懐かしそうに話す.

**\*food** /fuːd/ 名 ▶定義1 ❶ something that people or animals eat 人または動物が食べる物→**食べ物, 食物, 食料, 食糧** ‖ *Food and drink will be provided after the meeting.* 会議の後で食事と飲み物が出ます. *There is a shortage of food in some areas.* 一部の地域では食糧が不足している. ▶定義2 ❷ⓊA particular type of food that you eat 食べるためのある特定の種類の食品→**食べ物, 食品, 料理** ‖ *My favourite food is pasta.* 私の好きな食べ物はパスタです. *Have you ever had Japanese food?* 日本料理を食べたことがありますか. *baby food* ベビーフード *dog food* ドッグフード *health foods* 健康食品

**food poisoning** 名 Ⓤ ▶定義 an illness that is caused by eating food that is bad 悪くなった食物を食べたことによって引き起こされた病気→**食中毒, 食あたり**

**food processor** 名 Ⓒ ▶定義 an electric machine that can mix food and also cut food into small pieces 食品を混ぜることができ, 食品を細かく切ることもできる電気器具→**フードプロセッサー** ☞ **mixer** のさし絵

**foodstuff** /fúːdstʌ̀f/ 名 [Ⓒ, 通常は複数] ▶定義 a substance that is used as food 食べ物として用いられる物→**食料品, 食糧, 食材, 食品** ‖ *There has been a sharp rise in the cost of basic foodstuffs.* 基礎的な食料品の値段が急騰している.

**\*fool¹** /fuːl/ 名 Ⓒ ▶定義 a person who is silly or who acts in a silly way 愚かな人, または愚かに振る舞う人→**ばか者, 愚か者, 愚人** ‖ *I felt such a fool when I realized my mistake.* 誤りに気付いた時, 自分がひどい愚か者だと思った. ☞参 **April Fool**

成句 **make a fool of sb/yourself** ▶定義 to make sb/yourself look foolish or silly ~・自分自身をばかに, または愚かに見せる→**〜をばかにする, 笑い者にする, ばかなまねをする, 物笑いになる** ‖ *Barry got drunk and made a complete fool of himself.* バリーは酔って全くばかなまねをした.

**\*fool²** /fuːl/ 動 ▶定義1 ⓉⒶ fool sb (into doing sth) to trick sb ~をだます→**〜をだます, ごまかす, 担ぐ, だまして〜させる** ‖ *Don't be fooled into believing everything that the salesman says.* セールスマンにだまされて, 言うことをすべて信じてはいけません. ▶定義2 Ⓘ to speak without being serious 不まじめに話す→**冗談を言う, ふざける** ‖ *You didn't really believe me when I said I was going to America, did you? I was only fooling.* 私がアメリカへ行くと言った時本気にしなかったでしょう. 私はただ冗談を言っただけでしたからね.

句動詞 **fool about/around** ▶定義 to behave in a silly way 愚かに振る舞う→**ぶらつく, 無為に過ごす, 〜をもてあそぶ, いじくる** ‖ *Stop fooling around with that knife or someone will get hurt!* そのナイフをもてあそぶのはやめなさい. だれかがけがをしますよ.

**foolhardy** /fúːlhɑ̀ːrdi/ 形 ▶定義 taking unnecessary risks 不必要な危険を冒している→**無謀な, 向こう見ずな, 無鉄砲な**

**\*foolish** /fúːlɪʃ/ 形 ▶定義1 silly; not sensible 愚かな; 分別のない→**ばかな, ばかげた, 思慮のない, 非常識な** ‖ *I was foolish enough to trust him.* 彼を信用するなんて私が愚かだった. ▶定義2 looking silly or feeling embarrassed 愚かに見える, または気恥ずかしい思いをしている→**きまりの悪い, 面食らった, 当惑した** ‖ *I felt a bit foolish when I couldn't remember the man's name.* その男の名前を思い出せなかった時, 私は少しきまりの悪い思いをした. — **foolishly** 副→**愚かに(も), ばからしくも, むちゃに** ‖ *I foolishly agreed to lend him money.* 私は愚かにも彼に金を貸すことに同意した. — **foolishness** 名 Ⓤ→**愚かさ, 愚行, ばかげた事**

**foolproof** /fúːlpruːf/ 形 ▶定義 not capable of going wrong or being wrongly used 間違える, または誤って使用される可能性のない→**失敗の余地のない, 間違いようのない, だれでも扱える, 極めて簡単に操作できる** ‖ *Our security system is* *absolutely foolproof.* 私たちの安全システムは絶対確実です.

**\*foot**¹ /fʊt/ 名 ● (複 **feet** /fiːt/) ▶定義1 the lowest part of the body, at the end of the leg, on which a person or animal stands 足の先端にあり、そこで人または動物が立つ、体の最も下の部分→足 ‖ *People usually get to their feet (= stand up) for the national anthem.* 国歌が演奏されるときは通常、起立する(= 立ち上がる). *I usually go to school on foot (= walking).* 私は普通、徒歩で(= 歩いて)学校に行く. *I need to sit down - I've been on my feet all day.* 私は座りたい — 一日中立っていたので. *There's broken glass on the floor, so don't walk around in bare feet (= without shoes and socks).* 床に割れたガラスが落ちているので、素足で(= 靴や靴下を履かないで)歩き回らないように. *She sat by the fire and the dog sat at her feet.* 彼女は火のそばに座り、犬は彼女の足元に座った. *a foot brake/pedal/pump (= one that is operated by your foot)* 足ブレーキ・フットペダル・足踏み式ポンプ(= 足で操作されるもの) ☛ C5 ページのさし絵 ▶定義2 **-footed** (複合形容詞、複合副詞を作るために用いて) having or using the type of foot or number of feet mentioned 言及された種類または本数の足を持っている、あるいは使っている→足が〜の, 〜本足の ‖ *There are no left-footed players in the team.* このチームには利き足が左の選手はいない. *a four-footed creature* 4本足の生物 ▶定義3 the part of a sock, etc that covers the foot 靴下などの足を包む部分→足部, 足が入る部分 ▶定義4 **the foot of sth** the bottom of sth [単数扱い] 〜の基部→〜の足部, 下部, ふもと, 根元 ‖ *There's a note at the foot of the page.* ページの下の部分に注があります. *the foot of the stairs* 階段の最下部 *the foot of the bed* ベッドの足⇔**top** ▶定義5 (略 **ft**) a measurement of length; 30.48 centimetres 長さの単位; 30.48センチメートル→フィート ‖ *'How tall are you?' 'Five foot six (inches).'* 「身長はどのくらいですか」「5フィート6(インチ)です」 *a six-foot high wall* 高さ6フィートの壁
▶度量衡についての説明は、巻末の数についての特別項目を参照.

成句 **back on your feet** ▶定義 completely healthy again after an illness or a time of difficulty 病気または困難な時期の後で、再び完全に健康になる→元気になって, 回復して, 立ち直って

**be rushed/run off your feet** ▶定義 to be extremely busy; to have too many things to do 極度に忙しい; する事がたくさんありすぎる→人を忙しく働かせる, 駆けずり回らせる, せき立てる ‖ *Over Christmas we were rushed off our feet at work.* クリスマスの間中、私たちは仕事でとても忙しかった.

**fall/land on your feet** ▶定義 to be lucky in finding yourself in a good situation, or in getting out of a difficult situation 幸運にも良い状況にある、または困難な状態から抜け出す→難を免れる, うまく切り抜ける, 幸運に恵まれる ‖ *I really landed on my feet getting such a good job with so little experience.* 経験がほとんどないのにこんないい仕事に就けるなんて、私は本当に運が良かった.

**find your feet** ⇒ **FIND**¹
**get/have cold feet** ⇒ **COLD**¹
**get/start off on the right/wrong foot (with sb)** 略式 ▶定義 to start a relationship well/badly 関係をうまく・まずく始める→初めからうまくいく・いかない, 出足が順調・不調である ‖ *I seem to have got off on the wrong foot with the new boss.* 新しい上司との関係は初めからうまくいかなかったようだ.

**have one foot in the grave** 略式 ▶定義 to be so old or ill that you are not likely to live much longer 高齢または病気であるため、あまり長く生きられそうにない→棺おけに片足を突っ込んでいる, 死にかけている

**put your foot down** 略式 ▶定義 to say firmly that sth must (not) happen 〜が起こるに違いない(起こるはずがない)ときっぱりと言う→断固とした態度を取る, 断固として反対する ‖ *I put my foot down and told Andy he couldn't use our car any more.* 私は断固たる態度を取り、アンディーにもう私たちの車は使わせないと言った.

**put your foot in it** 略式 ▶定義 to say or do sth that makes sb embarrassed or upset 〜を戸惑わせる、またはうろたえさせるような〜を言う、あるいはする→へまをする, 失言する, へまな事を言って苦しい立場に陥る, どじを踏む

**put your feet up** ▶定義 to sit down and relax, especially with your feet off the floor and supported 特に足を床から上げて支えて，座ってくつろぐ→**楽にする，ゆったりと座って休む，一休みする，のんびりする** ‖ *I'm so tired that I just want to go home and put my feet up.* 私はとても疲れているので，とにかく家に帰ってのんびりしたい．

**set foot in/on sth** ⇒ **SET**¹

**stand on your own (two) feet** ▶定義 to take care of yourself without help; to be independent 援助なしで自分自身の面倒を見る; 独立している→**自立している，独立する，自主的に行動する**

**under your feet** ▶定義 in the way; stopping you from working, etc 邪魔になって; 仕事などをさせていない→**～の邪魔になって，足手まといで** ‖ *Would somebody get these children out from under my feet and take them to the park?* だれかこの子供たちが私の邪魔をするのをやめさせて，公園に連れていってくれませんか．

**foot**² /fút/ 動

成句 **foot the bill (for sth)** ▶定義 to pay (for sth) (～の代金を)払う→**(～の)勘定を持つ, (～を)支払う**

**footage** /fútɪdʒ/ 名 Ⓤ ▶定義 part of a film showing a particular event ある出来事を描いている映画の一部→**場面** ‖ *The documentary included footage of the assassination of Kennedy.* そのドキュメンタリーにはケネディ暗殺の場面が含まれていた．

\***football** /fútbɔ̀ːl/ 名 ▶定義**1** (または **soccer**)
Ⓤ a game that is played by two teams of eleven players who try to kick a round ball into a goal 丸いボールをゴールにけり込もうとする１チーム 11 人の２チームによって行われる試合→**サッカー** ‖ *a football pitch/match* サッカーの競技場・試合

➤米国では，American Football を指して football という語を使うので，サッカーには soccer が通常用いられる．

▶定義**2** Ⓒ the large round ball that is used in this game この試合で使われる丸い大きなボール→**サッカー用ボール**

\***footballer** /fútbɔ̀lər/ 名 Ⓒ ▶定義 a person who plays football サッカーをする人→**サッカー選手** ‖ *a talented footballer* 有能なサッカー選手

**football pools** (または **the pools**) 名 [複数扱い] ▶定義 a game in which people bet money on the results of football matches and can win large amounts of money サッカーの試合結果に金をかけて，大金を獲得できるゲーム→**サッカーくじ，サッカーとばく**

**foothold** /fúthòʊld/ 名 Ⓒ ▶定義 a place where you can safely put your foot when you are climbing 登っているときに安全に足を置くことができる場所→**足場，足掛かり** ‖ (比喩) *We need to get a foothold in the European market.* 私たちはヨーロッパ市場での足掛かりを得る必要がある．

**footing** /fútɪŋ/ 名 [単数扱い] ▶定義**1** being able to stand firmly on a surface 表面にしっかりと立てること→**確かな足元，足場，足掛かり** ‖ *Climbers usually attach themselves to a rope in case they lose their footing.* 万一足を滑らせたときのために，登山者は通常，体にロープを結び付ける．(比喩) *The company is now on a firm footing and should soon show a profit.* その会社は現在，基盤がしっかりしているので，間もなく利益を上げるはずである．▶定義**2** the level or position of sb/sth (in relation to sb/sth else) ～の(ほかの…と比較したときの)水準または地位→**地位，身分，資格，立場，関係，間柄** ‖ *to be on an equal footing with sb* ～と対等の立場にある

**footnote** /fútnòʊt/ 名 Ⓒ ▶定義 an extra piece of information that is added at the bottom of a page in a book 本のページの下の部分に加えられた追加の情報→**脚注**

**footpath** /fútpæ̀θ; -pɑ̀ːθ/ 名 Ⓒ ▶定義 a path for people to walk on 人が歩くための小道→**歩道，小道，細道，通り道** ‖ *a public footpath* 公道

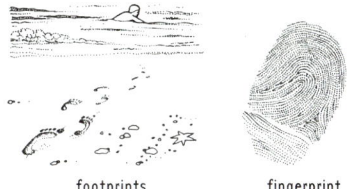

footprints　　fingerprint

**footprint** /fútprìnt/ 名 Ⓒ ▶定義 a mark that is left on the ground by a foot or a shoe 足または靴によって地面に残された跡→**足跡，足形** ☛参 **track**

**footstep** /fútstèp/ 名 C ▶定義 the sound of sb walking 〜が歩いている音➡**足音** ‖ *I heard his footsteps in the hall.* 廊下から彼の足音が聞こえた.
成句 follow in sb's footsteps ⇒ **FOLLOW**

**footwear** /fútwèər/ 名 U ▶定義 boots or shoes ブーツまたは靴➡**履物**

**\*for**¹ /fər, 強形 fɔːr/ 前 ▶定義 1 showing the person that will use or have sth 〜を使う,または持つことになっている人を表している➡**〜のための[に],〜あての,〜向けの,〜用の** ‖ *Here is a letter for you.* これはあなたあての手紙です. *He made lunch for them.* 彼は彼らのために昼食を作った. *It's a book for children.* それは子供向けの本です. ▶定義 2 in order to do, have or get sth 〜をする,持つ,または手に入れるために➡**〜のために,〜する(目的の)ために,〜を得ようとして,〜を求めて** ‖ *What's this gadget for?* この装置は何のためのものですか. *What did you do that for?* (= *Why did you do that?*) 何のためにそんな事をしたのですか(= なぜそんな事をしたのですか). *Do you learn English for your job or for fun?* 英語を学ぶのは仕事のためですか,それとも楽しみのためですか. *She asked me for help.* 彼女は私に助けを求めた. *Phone now for information.* 詳しくは今すぐ電話でお問い合わせください. *to go for a walk/swim/drink* 散歩に行く・泳ぎに行く・飲みに行く ▶定義 3 in order to help sb/sth 〜を助けるために➡**〜を治すために,〜を救うために,〜に役立つように,〜に良い** ‖ *What can I do for you?* あなたのために何かできる事がありますか. *You should take some medicine for your cold.* 風邪を治すために薬を飲むべきだ. *Doctors are fighting for his life.* 医師たちは彼の命を救うために闘っている. *shampoo for dry hair* 潤いのない髪向けのシャンプー ▶定義 4 in support of (sb/sth) (〜を)支持して➡**〜に賛成して,味方して,弁護して,擁護して** ‖ *Are you for or against shops opening on Sundays?* 日曜に商店が営業することに賛成ですか,反対ですか. ▶定義 5 meaning sth or representing sb/sth 〜を意味している,または〜を代表している➡**〜を表す,意味する,〜の代表として,〜の代わりに** ‖ *What's the 'C' for in 'BBC'?* BBC の C は何を表していますか. *What's the Russian for 'window'?* 「窓」を意味するロシア語は何ですか. *She plays hockey for England.* 彼女はイングランド代表としてホッケーをする. ▶定義 6 showing the place that sb/sth will go to 〜が行くことになっている場所を示している➡**〜に向かって,〜行きの,〜方面行きの,〜を目指して** ‖ *Is this the train for Glasgow?* これはグラスゴー行きの列車ですか. *They set off for the shops.* 彼らは店に向かって出発した. ▶定義 7 (showing a reason) as a result of (理由を示して) 〜の結果として➡**〜が理由で,〜が原因で,〜のために,〜の結果として** ‖ *Ben didn't want to come for some reason.* ベンはある理由で行きたくなかった. *He was sent to prison for robbery.* 彼は強盗の罪で刑務所に送られた. *I couldn't speak for laughing.* 私は笑いすぎて話すことができなかった. ▶定義 8 (showing the price or value of sth); in exchange for (〜の値段または価値を示して); 〜と交換に➡**〜の額の,〜と引き換えに,〜の報酬として,〜に付き** ‖ *I bought this car for £2000.* 私はこの車を2000ポンドで買った. *You get one point for each correct answer.* 正解1つに付き,1点を獲得できます. *I want to exchange this sweater for a larger one.* 私はこのセーターを大きいサイズのものと取り替えたい. *The officer was accused of giving secret information for cash.* その役人は機密情報を売り渡したとして告発された. ▶定義 9 showing a length of time 時間の長さを示している➡**〜の間,〜の期間ずっと,〜にわたって** ‖ *I'm going away for a few days.* 私は2,3日留守にします. *for a while/a long time/ages* しばらくの間・長い間・何年も *They have left the town **for good** (= they will not return).* 彼らは永久に町から去った (= 戻ってこないだろう). *He was in prison for 20 years (= he is not in prison now).* 彼は20年間刑務所に入っていた (= 今は刑務所に入っていない). *He has been in prison for 20 years (= he is still in prison).* 彼は20年間刑務所に入っている (= 今も刑務所にいる).

▶ since は,何かが始まった時を示すために,ある時点と共に用いられる: *He has been in prison since 1982.* (彼は1982年から刑務所に入っている.) ago も,何かが始まった時を示すために用いられる: *He went to prison 20 years ago.* (彼は20年前に刑務所に入った.)

▶定義 10 showing how many times sth has happened 〜が何回起こったかを示している➡〜回目に，〜度目に ‖ *I'm warning you for the last time.* 警告するのはこれが最後です．*I met him for the second time yesterday.* 昨日，彼に２度目に会った．▶定義 11 at a particular, fixed time ある特定の決まった時間に➡〜に，〜の時に ‖ *What did they give you for your birthday?* 彼らは誕生日に何をくれましたか．*Shall we have eggs for breakfast?* 朝食に卵を食べましょうか．*I'm going to my parents' for Christmas.* 私はクリスマスに両親の家へ行く．*The appointment is for 10.30.* 予約は10時30分です．▶定義 12 showing a distance 距離を示している➡〜の距離を，〜にわたって ‖ *He walked for ten miles.* 彼は10マイル歩いた．▶定義 13 (形容詞の後で) showing how usual, suitable, difficult, etc sb/sth is in relation to sb/sth else 〜が，ほかの…と比較してどのくらい普通か，適切か，困難かなどを示している➡〜の割には，〜にしては，〜に適した，〜に向いている ‖ *She's tall for her age.* 彼女は年の割には背が高い．*It's quite warm for January.* １月にしてはかなり暖かい．*It's unusual for Alex to be late.* アレックスが遅れるなんて珍しい．*I think Sandra is perfect for this job.* サンドラはこの仕事に最適だと思う．

成句 be (in) for it 英 話式 ▶定義 to be going to get into trouble or be punished 面倒な事に巻き込まれる，または罰せられることになる➡ひどい目に遭うことになる，罰を受けることになる，しかられることになる ‖ *If you arrive late again you'll be in for it.* また遅刻したら，しかられますよ．

for all ▶定義 in spite of 〜にもかかわらず➡たとえ〜であっても，〜であるとしても，〜であるけれども ‖ *For all his money, he's a very lonely man.* 彼は金持ちではあるけれども，非常に孤独な男だ．

for ever ⇒ **FOREVER**(1)

**for**² /fər, 強形 fɔːr/ 接 正式 ▶定義 because なぜならば➡なぜなら，理由は，というのは ‖ *The children soon lost their way, for they had never been in the forest alone before.* その子供たちはすぐに道に迷った．なぜなら，子供たちだけで以前にその森に入ったことがなかったからだ．

★**forbid** /fərbíd, fɔːr-/ 動 他 (現分 **forbidding**; 過 **forbade** または **forbad** /fərbǽd, fɔːr-/; 過分 **forbidden** /fərbídn, fɔːr-/) ▶定義 1 (通常は受動態

で) to not allow sth 〜を許可しない➡〜を禁じる，禁止する，許さない ‖ *Smoking is forbidden inside the building.* その建物の中は禁煙です．

▶定義 2 **forbid sb to do sth** to order sb not to do sth 〜に…をしないように命じる➡〜が…することを禁止する，許さない，〜に…をさせない ‖ *My parents forbade me to see Tim again.* 両親は私がもう一度ティムに会うことを禁じた．

**forbidding** /fərbídɪŋ, fɔːr-/ 形 ▶定義 looking unfriendly or frightening 友好的でない，または恐ろしそうに見えている➡近付き難い，人を寄せ付けない，陰険な，不気味な ‖ *The coast near the village is rather grey and forbidding.* その村の近くの海岸はかなり薄暗くて，人を寄せ付けない雰囲気だ．

★**force**¹ /fɔːrs/ 名 ▶定義 1 ❶ physical strength or power 物理的な強さ，または力➡勢い，威力，体力，腕力，暴力 ‖ *The force of the explosion knocked them to the ground.* 爆発の衝撃で彼らは地面に倒れた．*The police **used force** to break up the demonstration.* 警察は力ずくでそのデモを解散させた．▶定義 2 ❶ power and influence 力と影響➡影響力，説得力，効果，効力，強制力 ‖ *the force of public opinion* 世論の影響力 ▶定義 3 ❻ a person or thing that has power or influence 力または影響力を持っている人または物➡有力者，実力者，権力者，支配力，迫力 ‖ *Britain is no longer a major force in international affairs.* 英国はもはや国際情勢において大きな影響力を及ぼす国ではない．*Julia has been **the driving force** behind the company's success.* ジュリアが会社の成功を支えた中心人物であった．▶定義 4 ❻ a group of people who are trained for a particular purpose ある目的のために訓練された人々の集団➡集団，一団，一隊，団体，総勢 ‖ *a highly trained workforce* 高度の訓練を受けた従業員たち *the police force* 警官隊 ▶定義 5 [通常は複数] the soldiers and weapons that an army, etc has 軍隊などが所有する兵士と武器➡軍事力，戦力，兵力，武力，部隊 ‖ *the armed forces* 軍隊 ▶定義 6 ❻ ❶ (専門用語) a power that can cause change or movement 変化または動きを引き起こすことのできる力➡力 ‖ *the force of gravity* 重力

成句 bring sth/come into force ▶定義 to start

using a new law, etc; to start being used 新しい法律などを使い始める; 使われ始める➔~を施行する, 実施する, 効力を発する, 実施される ‖ *The government want to bring new anti-pollution legislation into force next year.* 政府は来年には新しい公害防止法を実施したいと考えている.

**force of habit** ▶定義 if you do sth from or out of force of habit you do it in a particular way because you have always done it that way in the past. ~をforce of habitから行うというのは, 今まで常にあるやり方で行ってきたため, そのやり方で行うということである➔習慣, 癖, 慣れ

**in force** ▶定義 **1** (used about people) in large numbers (人について) 多数で➔大勢で, 大挙して ‖ *The police were present in force at the football match.* サッカーの試合会場に警察官が大勢出ていた. ▶定義 **2** (used about a law, rule, etc) being used (法律または規則などについて) 使用されている➔実施されて, 施行されて, 有効で, 適用されて ‖ *The new speed limit is now in force.* 今は新しい速度制限が適用されている.

**join forces (with sb)** ▶定義 to work together in order to achieve a shared goal 共通の目的を達成するために共に働く➔(~と)力を合わせる, 協力する, 提携する ‖ *The two companies joined forces to win the contract.* その2つの会社は契約を獲得するため提携した.

\***force**² /fɔːrs/ 動 ⊕ ▶定義 **1** force sb (to do sth); force sb (into sth/doing sth) to make sb do sth that he/she does not want to do ~にその…がしたくない~をさせる➔~に…を強制する, 強いる, 強要する, 余儀なくさせる ‖ *She forced herself to speak to him.* 彼女は意を決して彼に話し掛けた. *The President was forced into resigning.* 大統領は辞任に追い込まれた. ▶定義 **2** to use physical strength to do sth or to move sth ~をするために, または~を動かすために体力を用いる➔力ずくで~をする, ~を押し進める, 押し込む ‖ *The window had been forced (open).* 窓がこじ開けられていた. *We had to force our way through the crowd.* 私たちは人込みを押し分けて進まなければならなかった. ▶定義 **3** to make sth happen when it will not happen naturally 自然に起こらないときに~を起こす➔無理に~をさせる, 無理に出す, 無理に作る ‖ *to force a smile/laugh* 作り笑いをする・無理に笑う *To force the issue, I gave him until midday to decide.* 強引に決着を付けるために, 私は彼に正午まで時間を与えた.

**forceful** /fɔːrsfʊl, -f(ə)l/ 形 ▶定義 having the power to persuade people 人を説得する力を持っている➔説得力のある, 力強い, 効果的な, 有効な ‖ *He has a very forceful personality.* 彼はとても印象に残る個性を持っている. *a forceful speech* 説得力のある演説

**forceps** /fɔːrsəps, -sèps/ 名 [複数扱い] ▶定義 a special instrument that looks like a pair of scissors but is not sharp. Forceps are used by doctors for holding things firmly. はさみに似ているが鋭利でない特別な道具. 医師が物をしっかりつかむために用いる➔ピンセット, 鉗子(かんし) ‖ *a pair of forceps* 鉗子1本

**forcible** /fɔːrsəb(ə)l/ 形 (名詞の前だけ) ▶定義 done using (physical) force (物理的な)力を使って行われる➔強制的な, 無理強いの, 力ずくの, 暴力的な ‖ *The police made a forcible entry into the building.* 警察はその建物に強制的に踏み込んだ. ― **forcibly** /fɔːrsəbli/ 副 ➔強制的に, 無理に, 力ずくで ‖ *The squatters were forcibly removed by the police.* 不法占拠者は警察によって強制的に追い出された.

**ford** /fɔːrd/ 名 ⊕ ▶定義 a place in a river where you can walk or drive across because the water is not deep 水が深くないため, 歩いてまたは車で渡れるような川の部分➔浅瀬, 渡り場, 歩いて渡れる所, 車で渡れる所

**fore** /fɔːr/ 名

成句 **be/come to the fore** ▶定義 to be in or get into an important position so that you are noticed by people 重要な地位にある, または人々に注目されるように重要な地位に就く➔重要な役割を演ずる, 注目を集める, 表に立って活躍する, 頭角を現す

**forearm** /fɔːrɑːrm/ 名 ⊕ ▶定義 the lower part of your arm 腕の下の方の部分➔前腕 ☞ C5ページのさし絵

**foreboding** /fɔːrbóʊdɪŋ/ 名 [ ⓤ, 単数扱い] ▶定義 a strong feeling that danger or trouble is coming これから危険または困難が降り懸かるという強い感じ➔(不吉な)予感, 虫の知らせ, 凶事の前兆 ‖ *She was suddenly filled with a sense* *of foreboding.* 彼女の胸は急に不吉な予感で一杯になった.

**forecast** /fɔ́ːrkæ̀st, -kæ̀st/ 動 他 (過, 過分 **forecast**) ▶定義 to say (with the help of information) what will probably happen in the future 将来おそらく起こるであろう事を(情報を活用して)言う➡~を予報する, 予測する, 予想する, 予言する ‖ *The Chancellor did not forecast the sudden rise in inflation.* 大蔵大臣はインフレの急激な進行は予測していなかった. *Rain has been forecast for tomorrow.* 明日の予報は雨だ. — forecast 名 C➡予報, 予測, 予想 ‖ *a sales forecast for the coming year* 来年の売上高予測 ☛参 **weather forecast**

**forecourt** /fɔ́ːrkɔ̀ːrt/ 名 C ▶定義 a large open area in front of a building such as a hotel or petrol station ホテルまたはガソリンスタンドなどの建物の正面にある広く開けた場所➡**前庭, 給油場**

**forefinger** /fɔ́ːrfɪ̀ŋɡər/ (または **index finger**) 名 C ▶定義 the finger next to the thumb 親指の隣の指➡**人差し指**

**forefront** /fɔ́ːrfrʌ̀nt/ 名 [単数扱い] ▶定義 the leading position; the position at the front 指導的な地位; 先頭の位置➡**最前線, 先頭, 第一線, 中心** ‖ *Our department is right at the forefront of scientific research.* 私たちの部門は科学研究のまさに最前線にいる.

**forego** = FORGO

**foregone** /fɔːrɡɔ́(ː)n, -ɡɑ́n, ≠/ 形
成句 **a foregone conclusion** ▶定義 a result that is or was certain to happen 起こることが確実である, または確実であった結果➡**初めから分かりきっている結論, 予測できる結末, 避けられない結果, 予測された結果**

**foreground** /fɔ́ːrɡrɑ̀ʊnd/ 名 [単数扱い]
▶定義 1 the part of a view, picture, photograph, etc that appears closest to the person looking at it 景色, 絵, 写真などの, 見ている人に最も近く見える部分➡**前景** ‖ *Notice the artist's use of colour **in the foreground** of the picture.* その絵の前景での画家の色使いに注目してください.
▶定義 2 a position where you will be noticed most 最も注目されるであろう位置➡**前面, 最前部, 表面, 最も目立つ位置** ‖ *He likes to be in the foreground at every meeting.* 彼はどの会合でも最前面を好む. ⇔ **background**

**forehand** /fɔ́ːrhæ̀nd/ 名 C ▶定義 a way of hitting the ball in tennis, etc that is made with the inside of your hand facing forward 手の内側を前に向けて行われる, テニスなどでのボールの打ち方➡**フォア(ハンド), 前打ち** ⇔ **backhand**

**forehead** /fɔ́rəd, fɔ́ːrhèd/ (または **brow**) 名 C ▶定義 the part of a person's face above the eyes and below the hair 人の顔の, 目より上で髪より下の部分➡**前頭部, (前)額部** ☛ C5 ページのさし絵

**foreign** /fɔ́ː(ː)rən, fɑ́ːr-/ 形 ▶定義 1 belonging to or connected with a country that is not your own 自分の国ではない国に属している, または関連する➡**外国の, 在外の, 外国産の, 外国風の** ‖ *a foreign country/coin/accent* 外国・外国の硬貨・外国風のなまり *to learn a foreign language* 外国語を習う ▶定義 2 (名詞の前だけ) dealing with or involving other countries ほかの国々を扱っている, または関係させている➡**対外的な, 外交の, 外国との** ‖ *foreign policy (= government decisions concerning other countries)* 外交政策(= ほかの国々に関する政府の決定事項) *foreign affairs/news/trade* 外交問題・外国ニュース・外国貿易 *the French Foreign Minister* フランスの外務大臣 ▶定義 3 (used about an object or a substance) not being where it should be (物体または物質について)あるべき所にはない➡**異質な, 外から入ってきた, 外来の, 有害な** ‖ *The X-ray showed up a foreign body (= object) in her stomach.* エックス線で彼女の胃の中の異質な物体(= 物)が見つかった.

**the Foreign and Commonwealth Office** (略 **FCO**) 名 [単数扱い, 単数または複数形の動詞と共に] ▶定義 the British government department that deals with relations with other countries ほかの国々との関係を扱う英国政府の省➡**外務連邦省, 英国外務省** ☛ 多くの人が今でもこの省を the Foreign Office という古い名称で呼んでいる.

**foreigner** /fɔ́ː(ː)rənər, fɑ́ːr-/ 名 C ▶定義 a person who belongs to a country that is not your own 自分の国ではない国に属する人➡**外国人**

**foreign exchange** 名 C U ▶定義 the system of buying and selling money from a different country; the place where it is bought and sold

異なる国の金を売買する制度; それが売買される場所→外国為替, 外国為替取引; 外国為替取引所

**the Foreign Secretary** 名 C ▶定義 the person in the government who is responsible for dealing with foreign countries 外国に対応する責任がある政府の人→外務大臣 ☛参 **Home Secretary**

**foremost** /fɔ́:mòʊst, -məst/ 形 ▶定義 most famous or important; best 最も有名な, または重要な; 最良の→主要な, 真っ先の, 主流を占める, 一流の ‖ *Laurence Olivier was among the foremost actors of the last century.* ローレンス・オリビエは20世紀最高の俳優の1人だった.
成句 first and foremost ⇒ **FIRST**²

**forename** /fɔ́:nèɪm/ 名 C 正式 ▶定義 your first name, that is given to you when you are born 生まれた時に与えられた名前→名, ファーストネーム ☛参 **name** の注

**forensic** /fərénsɪk, -zɪk/ 形 (名詞の前だけ) ▶定義 using scientific tests to find out about a crime 犯罪について調査するために科学的な検査を用いている→科学捜査の, 法医学の, 法医学的な ‖ *The police are carrying out forensic tests to try and find out the cause of death.* 警察は死因を解明しようと, 法医学的な検査を行っている.

**forerunner** /fɔ́:rʌ̀nər/ 名 C ▶定義 a forerunner (of sb/sth) a person or thing that is an early example or a sign of sth that appears or develops later 後になって現れる, または発展する~の先例または兆候である人あるいは物事→先駆者, 先駆け, 前触れ, 前兆 ‖ *Country music was undoubtedly one of the forerunners of rock and roll.* カントリーミュージックは明らかにロックンロールの先駆けの1つだった.

**foresee** /fɔ:sí:/ 動 他 (過 **foresaw** /fɔ:sɔ́:/; 過分 **foreseen** /fɔ:sí:n/) ▶定義 to know or guess that sth is going to happen in the future 将来~が起こりそうであることが分かる, または推測する→~を予知する, 予見する, 予感する, 見越す ‖ *Nobody could have foreseen the result of the election.* 選挙の結果を予測することはだれにもできなかっただろう. ☛参 **unforeseen**

**foreseeable** /fɔ:sí:əb(ə)l/ 形 ▶定義 that can be expected; that you can guess will happen 予測され得るような; 起こるだろうと推測できるような→予知できる, 予見できる, 予測できる ‖ *These problems were foreseeable.* これらの問題は予測できた. *The weather won't change in the foreseeable future (= as far ahead as we can see).* 天候は当面は変わらないだろう (= 先を見越すことができる限りでは).

**foresight** /fɔ́:rsàɪt/ 名 U ▶定義 the ability to see what will probably happen in the future and to use this knowledge to make careful plans 将来起こるであろう事を見通し, その知識を利用して慎重な計画を立てることができる能力→先見の明, 洞察力, 先を見る目 ‖ *My neighbour had the foresight to move house before the new motorway was built.* 私の隣人は, 新しい高速道路が建設される前に引っ越すだけの先見の明があった. ☛参 **hindsight**

**foreskin** /fɔ́:rskɪ̀n/ 名 C ▶定義 the piece of skin that covers the end of the male sexual organ 男性の生殖器の先端を覆っている皮膚→包皮

***forest** /fɔ́(:)rəst, fɑ́r-/ 名 C U ▶定義 a large area of land covered with trees 木々で覆われた広い範囲の土地→森(林), 山林, 森林地帯 ‖ *the tropical rainforests of South America* 南米の熱帯雨林 *a forest fire* 山火事
▶ forest は wood より大きい. jungle は世界の熱帯地域にある森林を指す.

**forestall** /fɔ:rstɔ́:l/ 動 他 ▶定義 to take action to prevent sb from doing sth or sth from happening ~が…をすることを防ぐため, または~が起こることを防ぐために行動を取る→~の機先を制する, 先手を取る, ~に先んじる, ~を出し抜く

**forestry** /fɔ́(:)rəstri, fɑ́r-/ 名 U ▶定義 the science of planting and taking care of trees in forests 森林の植樹と樹木の手入れについての科学→林学, 森林管理

**forethought** /fɔ́:rθɔ̀:t/ 名 U ▶定義 careful thought about, or preparation for, the future 将来に対する注意深い思慮, または準備→事前の考慮, 深慮, 配慮, 将来に対する用心

***forever** /fərévər, fɔ:-/ 副 ▶定義 1 (または **for ever**) for all time; permanently いつまでも; 永久に→永遠に, 永久に, いつまでも ‖ *I wish the holidays would last forever!* 休暇がいつまでも続けばいいのに. *I realized that our relationship had finished forever.* 私たちの関係は永遠に終わってしまったと悟った. ▶定義 2 (進行形で) very often; in a way which is annoying 非常にしばしば; いらいらさせるように→**絶えず, いつも, ひっきりなしに** ‖ *Our neighbours are forever having noisy parties.* 私たちの隣人はひっきりなしに騒々しいパーティーを開いている.

**foreword** /fɔ́ːrwə̀ːrd/ 名 C ▶定義 a piece of writing at the beginning of a book that introduces the book and/or its author 本またはその著者を紹介する, 本の冒頭の文章→**端書き, 序文, 前書き, 緒言**

**forfeit** /fɔ́ːrfət/ 動他 ▶定義 to lose sth or have sth taken away from you, usually because you have done sth wrong 通常は悪い~をしたために, …を失う, または…を取り上げられる→**~を失う, 喪失する, 没収される, 剥奪(はくだつ)される** ‖ *Because of his violent behaviour he forfeited the right to visit his children.* 暴力行為のため, 彼は子供たちを訪問する権利を剥奪された. — forfeit 名 C→没収, 喪失, 剥奪

**forgave** FORGIVE の過去形

**forge**¹ /fɔ́ːrdʒ/ 動他 ▶定義1 to make an illegal copy of sth ~の違法な複製を作る→**~を偽造する, 模造する, ねつ造する** ‖ *to forge a signature/banknote/passport/cheque* 署名・紙幣・パスポート・小切手を偽造する ☞参 **counterfeit** ▶定義2 to put a lot of effort into making sth strong and successful ~を強く成功させることに多大な努力を払う→**~を努力して進歩させる, 苦労して作り上げる, 築き上げる** ‖ *Our school has forged links with a school in Romania.* 私たちの学校はルーマニアの学校との関係を築き上げてきた.

句動詞 **forge ahead** ▶定義 to go forward or make progress quickly 前進する, または素早く進歩する→**リードする, 先頭に立つ, 急速に進歩する, 長足の進歩を遂げる** ‖ *I think it's now time to forge ahead with our plans to open a new shop.* 今こそ新しい店を開く計画を一気に進める時だと思う.

**forge**² /fɔ́ːrdʒ/ 名 C ▶定義 a place where objects are made by heating and shaping metal 金属を熱して形づくることによって物が作られる場所→**かじ場, 鉄工所**

**forgery** /fɔ́ːrdʒ(ə)ri/ 名 (複 **forgeries**) ▶定義1 ❶ the crime of illegally copying a document, signature, painting, etc 書類, 署名, 絵画などを違法に複製する犯罪→**偽造, 模造, ねつ造, 偽造罪**

---

### forget 659

▶定義2 ❷ a document, signature, picture, etc that is a copy of the real one 実物の複製である文書, 署名, 絵画など→**偽造物, 模造品, がん作, 偽造文書, にせ札**

*****forget** /fərɡét/ 動 (過 **forgot** /fərɡɑ́t/; 過分 **forgotten** /fərɡɑ́tn/) ▶定義1 他 forget (doing) sth to not be able to remember sth ~を覚えていることができない→**~を忘れる, 思い出せない, 失念する, ~したことを忘れる** ‖ *I've forgotten what I was going to say.* 私は言おうとしていた事を忘れてしまった. *I've forgotten her telephone number.* 彼女の電話番号を思い出せない. *He forgot that he had invited her to the party.* 彼は, 彼女をパーティーに招待したことを忘れていた. *I'll never forget meeting my husband for the first time.* 私は初めて夫に出会った時のことを決して忘れないだろう. ▶定義2 自他 forget (about) sth; forget to do sth to fail to remember to do sth that you ought to have done しておくべきだった~をすることを覚えていない→**~することを忘れる, 忘れて~をしていない, ~し忘れる, ~するのをおこたる** ‖ *'Why didn't you come to the party?' 'Oh dear! I completely forgot about it!'* 「なぜパーティーに来なかったのですか」「まあ, すっかり忘れていました」 *'Did you feed the cat?' 'Sorry, I forgot.'* 「猫にえさをやりましたか」「すみません, 忘れていました」 *Don't forget to do your homework!* 宿題をするのを忘れないで. ▶定義3 他 to fail to bring sth with you ~を持ってくるのを忘れる→**(持ってくるの)を忘れる, 置き忘れる, 忘れ物をする** ‖ *When my father got to the airport he realized he'd forgotten his passport.* 父は空港に着いた時に, パスポートを忘れたことに気付いた.

▶ 忘れてしまった物について話しているときに, それがどこにあるかを言いたい場合は, leave を用いる必要がある. *He forgot his passport at home.* と言うことはできない. *He left his passport at home.* と言わなければならない.

▶定義4 自他 forget (about) sb/sth; forget about doing sth to make an effort to stop thinking about sb/sth; to stop thinking that sth is possible ~について考えるのをやめようと努力する; ~が可能であると考えるのをやめる→

660 **forgetful**

〜を忘れようとする,意識的に忘れる,気にしない,無視する ‖ *Forget about your work and enjoy yourself!* 仕事のことは忘れて楽しみなさい. *'I'm sorry I shouted at you.' 'Forget it (= don't worry about it).'*「どなったりしてすみません」「もう忘れてください(= 気にしないでください)」

**forgetful** /fərgétfəl, -f(ə)l/ 形 ▶定義 often forgetting things しばしば物事を忘れている→忘れっぽい,忘れやすい,物覚えが悪い,物忘れする ‖ *My mother's nearly 80 and she's starting to get a bit forgetful.* 母は80歳に近いが,少し物忘れするようになってきている. ☛類 **absent-minded**

**forgivable** /fərgívəb(ə)l/ 形 ▶定義 that can be forgiven 許されることができるような→許される,大目に見られる

*__forgive__ /fərgív/ 動他 (過 **forgave** /fərgéiv/ ; 過分 **forgiven** /fərgív(ə)n/) ▶定義1 forgive sb/yourself (for sth/for doing sth) to stop being angry towards sb for sth that he/she has done wrong 〜が行った悪い…について,その〜に腹を立てるのをやめる→〜を許す,勘弁する,大目に見る,容赦する ‖ *I can't forgive his behaviour last night.* 彼の昨夜の振る舞いは許せない. *I can't forgive him for his behaviour last night.* 彼の昨夜の振る舞いは許せない. *I can't forgive him for behaving like that last night.* 彼が昨夜あのように振る舞ったことは許せない. ▶定義2 forgive me (for doing sth) used for politely saying sorry 丁寧に謝る場合に用いられて→(〜して)すみません,申し訳ありません,お許しください ‖ *Forgive me for asking, but where did you get that dress?* 失礼ですが,そのワンピースはどこで買ったのですか. — **forgiveness** 名 ❶→ 許すこと,許されること,容赦,勘弁 ‖ *He begged for forgiveness for what he had done.* 彼は自分がした事について,私に許しを請うた.

**forgiving** /fərgívɪŋ/ 形 ▶定義 ready and able to forgive 進んで許すことができる→快く許す,とがめ立てしない,寛大な,寛容な

**forgo** (または **forego**) /fɔːrgóu/ 動他 (過 **forwent** /fɔːrwént/; 過分 **forgone** /fɔːrgɔ́(ː)n, -gán/) 正式 ▶定義 to decide not to have or do sth that you want 望むものを持たない,またはしないと決める→〜をなしで済ませる,見合わせる,差し控える,あきらめる

**forgot** FORGET の過去形
**forgotten** FORGET の過去分詞形

*__fork__¹ /fɔːrk/ 名 ❻ ▶定義1 a small metal object with a handle and two or more points (**prongs**) that you use for lifting food to your mouth when eating 食べるときに食べ物を持ち上げて口に運ぶために用いる,柄と2つ以上の先端(先のとがった部分)のある小さな金属製の物→フォーク ‖ *a knife and fork* ナイフとフォーク ▶定義2 a large tool with a handle and three or more points (**prongs**) that you use for digging the ground 地面を掘るために用いる,柄と3つ以上の先端(先のとがった部分)のある大きな道具→くま手,またぐわ,農業用フォーク ‖ *a garden fork* 園芸用のくま手 ☛ **garden** のさし絵 ▶定義3 a place where a road, river, etc divides into two parts; one of these parts 道路または川などが2本に分かれる場所; そのような部分の1つ→分岐点,合流点,分かれ道,支流 ‖ *After about two miles you'll come to a fork in the road.* 2マイルほど進むと,分かれ道に出ます.

*__fork__² /fɔːrk/ 動自 ▶定義1 (used about a road, river, etc) to divide into two parts (道路または川などについて) 2つの部分に分かれる→分岐する,二またになる ‖ *Bear right where the road forks at the top of the hill.* 丘の頂上の道が分岐している所で右に曲がりなさい. ▶定義2 to go along the left or right fork of a road 道路の左または右の分岐路に沿って進む→分かれ道を曲がる,分岐点で左・右へ行く,左・右の分岐路を行く ‖ *Fork right up the hill.* 分岐路を右に進んで丘を登りなさい.

句動詞 **fork out (for sth)** 略式 ▶定義 to pay for sth when you do not want to 望んでいないときに〜に対して(お金を)支払う→〜を(…に)しぶしぶ手渡す,支払う,出費する ‖ *I forked out over £20 for that book.* 私はその本にしぶしぶ20ポンド以上支払った.

**forlorn** /fərlɔ́ːrn/ 形 ▶定義 lonely and unhappy; not cared for 孤独で不幸な; 面倒を見られていない→孤独な,哀れな,惨めな,見放された

*__form__¹ /fɔːrm/ 名 ▶定義1 ❻a particular type or variety of sth or a way of doing sth 〜の,または〜の仕方のある特定の型または種類→方式,方法,形態,形式 ‖ *Swimming is an excellent form of exercise.* 水泳は優れた運動方法です. *We* never eat meat **in any form**. 私たちは肉類は一切食べません. ▶定義2 ●**①**the shape of sb/sth 〜の形→体, 姿(態), 形状, 外観 || *The articles will be published **in book form**.* その記事は単行本として出版される予定です. ▶定義3 ●an official document with questions on it and spaces where you give answers and personal information 質問とその答え, または個人情報を書き込む空欄がある公式の書類→(申し込み)用紙, 書き込み用紙 || *an **entry form** for a competition* 競技の参加申し込み書 *to fill in an **application form*** 申し込み用紙に記入する ▶定義4 ●a class in a school 学校のクラス→学級, クラス, 学年

▶英国では, 中等学校の学年は, first form, second form, third form などと呼ばれていたが, 現在では Year 7 〜 Year 11 と呼ばれている. ただし, 最後の2学年(16〜18歳の生徒)は今でも the sixth form と呼ばれる.

▶定義5 ● (文法) a way of spelling or changing a word in a sentence 文中の単語をつづる方法, または変化させる方法→語形, 形式, 形態 || *the irregular forms of the verbs* 動詞の不規則変化形 *The plural form of mouse is mice.* mouse の複数形は mice である. ▶定義6 **①**the state of being fit and strong for a sports player, team, etc スポーツ選手またはチームなどが体調が良く, 健康である状態→コンディション, 体調, 健康状態 || *to be **in/out of form*** 調子が良い・悪い ▶定義7 **①**how well sb/sth is performing at a particular time, for example in sport or business スポーツまたは事業などで, ある特定の時に〜がどのくらいよく機能しているかということ→調子 || *to be **on/off form*** 調子が良い・悪い *On present form the Italian team should win easily.* 現在の調子では, イタリアチームが簡単に勝つはずだ.

**成句** true to form ⇒ **TRUE**

★**form**² /fɔːm/ 動 ▶定義1 **⊜①**to begin to exist or to make sth exist 出現し始める, または〜を出現させる→形を成す, 発生する, 現れる, 〜になる, 作り上げる || *A pattern was beginning to form in the monthly sales figures.* 月間売上高の数字に1つのパターンが現れ始めた. *These tracks were formed by rabbits.* これらの足跡はウサギのものだった. ▶定義2 **①**to make or organize sth 〜を作る, または組織する→〜を組

# formal 661

み立てる, 構成する, 結成する || *to form a government* 組閣する *In English we usually form the past tense by adding '-ed'.* 英語では通常, -ed を付けて過去形を作る. ▶定義3 **①**to become or make a particular shape ある形になる, または作る→〜を形づくる, 作り上げる, 〜になる, 整列させる || *The police formed a circle around the house.* 警察はその家の周りに円形に布陣した. *to form a line/queue* 行列・列を作る ▶定義4 **①**to be the thing mentioned 言及された物になる→〜の構成要素となる, 〜を成す, 構成する, 〜になる, 含まれる || *Seminars form the main part of the course.* セミナーはその課程の主要部分を成している. *The survey **formed part of** a larger programme of market research.* その調査は, より大規模な市場調査の計画の一環を成していた. ▶定義5 **①**to begin to have or think sth 〜を持ち始める, または考え始める→〜を形づくる, まとめる, 練り上げる || *I haven't formed an opinion about the new boss yet.* 新しい上司についての意見はまだ固まっていない. *to form a friendship* 友情を育てる

★**formal** /fɔːm(ə)l/ 形 ▶定義1 (used about language or behaviour) used when you want to appear serious or official and in situations in which you do not know the other people very well (言葉または行動について) まじめにまたは形式張って見えるようにしたいとき, あるいはほかの人々をあまりよく知らない場合に用いられて→格式張った, 儀礼的な, 改まった, 形式的な || *'Yours faithfully' is a formal way of ending a letter.* 「敬具」は手紙を締めくくるときの改まった言葉である. *She has a very formal manner - she doesn't seem to be able to relax.* 彼女はとても堅苦しい − くつろぐことができないようだ. *a formal occasion (= one where you must behave politely and wear the clothes that people think are suitable)* 改まった席 (= 礼儀正しく振る舞い, 皆が適切であると考える衣服を着用しなければならない場面)

▶この辞書では, 一部の語または句に **正式** または **略式** と書かれている. これは, ある状況に適した語を選ぶ際の助けとなるはずである. 正式な語と同じような意味に相当する, 略式の語または中間的な語がある場合が多い.

▶定義2 official 公式の→**正式の, 本式の, 正規の, 一定の形式の** ‖ *I shall make **a formal complaint** to the hospital about the way I was treated.* 私が受けた治療方法について, その病院に対し正式に苦情を申し立てます. ⇔**informal** — **formally** /-m(ə)li/ 副 →**儀礼的に, 堅苦しく, 形式的に, 正式に**

**formality** /fɔːmǽləti/ 名 (複 **formalities**)
▶定義1 ©an action that is necessary according to custom or law 慣習または法律に従って必要とされる行為→**儀礼的行為, 形式張った行為, 形式上の手続き** ‖ *There are certain formalities to attend to before we can give you a visa.* ビザを発給する前に, 正式な手続きがあります.

▶ある行為が **just a formality** (単なる formality にすぎない場合) とは, それが慣習または法律によって必要とされているが, そのほかの実際的な重要性または影響はないと一般に考えられていることを表す.

▶定義2 Ⓤ careful attention to rules of language and behaviour 言葉または振る舞い方の決まりに対して細心の注意を払うこと→**形式にこだわること, 形式偏重, 丁重さ, 堅苦しさ**

**format**¹ /fɔːmæt/ 名 © ▶定義 the shape of sth or the way it is arranged or produced ~の形, またはそれが整えられたり作り出される方法→**型, 判, 体裁, 方式, 形式** ‖ *It's the same book but in a different format.* それは同じ本ですが, 体裁が違います.

**format**² /fɔːmæt/ 動 (**formatting**; **formatted**)
▶定義1 (computing) to prepare a computer disk so that data can be recorded on it (コンピューター) データが記録できるように, コンピューターのディスクを準備する→**~をフォーマットする, 初期化する** ‖ *to format a disk* ディスクを初期化する ▶定義2 to arrange text on a page or a screen ページまたは画面の文字列を配置する→**~の体裁を整える, ~を形式に従って配置する** ‖ *to format a letter* 手紙の体裁を整える

**formation** /fɔːméɪʃ(ə)n/ 名 ▶定義1 Ⓤthe act of making or developing sth ~を作る, または発展させること→**構成, 編成, 組成, 成立, 形成** ‖ *the formation of a new government* 新政府の編成 ▶定義2 ©Ⓤa number of people or things in a particular shape or pattern ある形または型をした多数の人または物→**隊形, 布陣, 構造物, 構成物, 組成物** ‖ *rock formations* 岩層 *A number of planes flew over in formation.* 多くの飛行機が編隊を組んで飛んでいった. *formation dancing* フォーメーションダンス

**formative** /fɔːmətɪv/ 形 ▶定義 having an important and lasting influence (on sb's character and opinions) (~の性格または意見に対して) 重要で長く続く影響を持っている→**人格形成の, 発達の, 形を与える, 形成する** ‖ *A child's early years are thought to be the most formative ones.* 子供の幼児期は人格形成上, 最も重要な時期であると考えられている.

*****former** /fɔːmər/ 形 (名詞の前だけ) ▶定義 of an earlier time; belonging to the past より早い時の; 過去に属している→**以前の, 先の, かつての, 初期の, 昔の** ‖ *George Bush, the former American President* 米国の元大統領ジョージ・ブッシュ *In former times people often had larger families.* 昔はもっと大家族だった.

*****the former** /fɔːmər/ 名 [単数扱い] ▶定義 the first (of two people or things just mentioned) (言及されたばかりの2人の人または2つの物のうち) 最初の→**前者, 前の人・物, 初めに挙げられた人・物** ‖ *Of the two hospitals in the town - the General and the Royal - the former (= the General) has the better reputation.* その町の2つの病院 — 総合病院と国立病院 — では, 前者 (= 総合病院) の方が評判が良い. ☞参 **the latter**

*****formerly** /fɔːmərli/ 副 ▶定義 in the past; before now 過去に; 現在より前に→**以前は, 昔は, かつては, 先に** ‖ *the country of Myanmar (formerly Burma)* ミャンマーという国 (かつてはビルマ) *The hotel was formerly a castle.* そのホテルは以前は城だった.

▶ **used to be** は **was formerly** より一般的な言い方である: *The hotel used to be a castle.* (そのホテルは以前は城だった.)

**formidable** /fɔːmɪdəb(ə)l/ 形 ▶定義1 causing you to be quite frightened 人をかなり怖がらせている→**恐ろしい, 恐るべき, ぞっとするような** ‖ *His mother is a rather formidable lady.* 彼の母親はかなり怖い女性だ. ▶定義2 difficult to deal with; needing a lot of effort 対処するのが難しい; 多くの努力を必要としている→**手ごわい, 手に負えそうもない, 侮れない** ‖ *Reforming the educa-*

*tion system will be a formidable task.* 教育制度の改革は手ごわい仕事になるだろう.

**formula** /fɔːmjələ/ 名 C (複 **formulas** または **formulae** /-liː/) ▶定義1 (専門用語) a group of signs, letters or numbers used in science or mathematics to express a general law or fact 一般的な法則または事実を表すために科学または数学で用いられる記号, 文字または数字の集まり→**式, 公式** ‖ *What is the formula for converting miles to kilometres?* マイルをキロメートルに換算する公式はどのようなものですか.
▶定義2 a list of (often chemical) substances used for making sth; the instructions for making sth ～を作るために用いられる(しばしば化学的な)物質のリスト; ～を作るための指示→**処方, 処方せん, 製法, 調合法, 調理法** ‖ *The formula for the new vaccine has not yet been made public.* 新しいワクチンの製法はまだ公開されていない.
▶定義3 **a formula for (doing) sth** a plan of how to get or do sth ～を得る, または行うための方法→**一定の方式, ～の決まった方法, 定石, 定則** ‖ *What is her formula for success?* 彼女の成功の秘けつは何ですか. *Unfortunately, there's no magic formula for a perfect marriage.* 残念ながら, 完全な結婚への常道はない.

**formulate** /fɔːmjəleɪt/ 動他 ▶定義1 to prepare and organize a plan or ideas for doing sth ～を行う計画または案を準備し, まとめる→**～を組み立てる, まとめる, 練り上げる, 考え出す** ‖ *to formulate a plan* 計画をまとめる ▶定義2 to express sth (clearly and exactly) ～を(明確に正確に)表現する→**～を組織的に述べる, 明確に述べる, 系統立てて述べる, 公式化する** ‖ *She struggled to formulate a simple answer to his question.* 彼女は彼の質問に対して簡潔な答えを明確に述べようと努力した.

**fort** /fɔːt/ 名 C ▶定義 a strong building that is used for military defence 軍事上の防御のために使われる強固な建物→**とりで, 城砦(じょうさい), 要塞(ようさい)**

**forth** /fɔːθ/ 副
成句 **and so forth** ▶定義 and other things like those just mentioned ～と述べたばかりのものと同様のほかのもの→**～など, その他** ‖ *The sort of job that you'll be doing is taking messages, making tea and so forth.* あなたがする仕事は伝言を受けたり, お茶をいれたりすることなどです.

**fortnight** 663

**back and forth** ⇒ **BACK**³

**forthcoming** /fɔːθkʌmɪŋ, ˌ--ˈ-/ 形 ▶定義1 that will happen or appear in the near future 近い将来に起こる, または現れるような→**やがて来る, 間近に迫った, 今度の, 近々の** ‖ *Look in the local paper for a list of forthcoming events.* 近々行われる催しの一覧は地元紙を見てください.
▶定義2 (名詞の前は不可) offered or given 提供された, または与えられた→**手近に用意されている, 利用できる, すぐ使える, すぐに間に合う** ‖ *If no money is forthcoming, we shall not be able to continue the project.* 金が用意されなければ, 私たちはそのプロジェクトを続けられないだろう.
▶定義3 (名詞の前は不可) (used about a person) ready to be helpful, give information, etc (人について) 進んで助けになる, 情報を提供するなど→**すぐ手助けしてくれる, 協力的な, 何でも話す, 愛想のいい** ‖ *Kate isn't very forthcoming about her previous job, so I don't know what she did exactly.* ケートは前の仕事のことはあまり話さないので, 彼女が何をしていたのか, あまりよく分からない.

**forthright** /fɔːθraɪt/ 形 ▶定義 saying exactly what you think in a clear and direct way 考えている事をそのまま明確に直接的に言っている→**率直な, はっきりとした, ずばりと言う, 単刀直入な**

★**fortieth** /fɔːtiəθ/ 代形名 ▶定義 40th→**40番目(の, に), 第40(の, に)** ☞参 **sixth**¹ の例

**fortification** /fɔːtəfəkeɪʃ(ə)n/ 名 [C, 通常は複数] ▶定義 walls, towers, etc, built especially in the past to protect a place against attack 特に過去に, ある場所を攻撃から守るために作られた壁, 塔など→**とりで, 防塁, 要塞(ようさい), 防御施設**

**fortify** /fɔːtəfaɪ/ 動他 (現分 **fortifying**; 三単現 **fortifies**; 過, 過分 **fortified**) ▶定義 to make a place stronger and ready for an attack ある場所を強固にし攻撃に備える→**～を要塞(ようさい)化する, ～の防備を固める, ～に防御工事を施す** ‖ *to fortify a city* 都市を要塞化する

**fortnight** /fɔːtnaɪt/ 名 [C, 通常は単数] 英 ▶定義 two weeks 2週間→**2週間, 14日** ‖ *We're going on holiday for a fortnight.* 私たちは2週間の休暇に出掛ける. *School finishes in a* *fortnight/in a fortnight's time* (= two weeks from now). 学校は2週間後に(=今から2週間で)終わる.

**fortnightly** /fɔːrtnàɪtli/ 形副 ▶定義 (happening or appearing) once every two weeks 2週間ごとに1度(起こっている,または現れている)→2週間に1度の,2週間ごとの,隔週の,2週間に1度,2週間ごとに,隔週で ‖ *This magazine is published fortnightly.* この雑誌は隔週で発刊されている.

**fortress** /fɔːrtrəs/ 名 C ▶定義 a castle or other large strong building that it is not easy to attack 攻撃するのが容易でない,城またはほかの大型で頑丈な建物→要塞(ようさい)

**fortunate** /fɔːrtʃ(ə)nət/ 形 ▶定義 lucky 幸運な→運の良い,幸せな,縁起の良い,幸運をもたらす ‖ *It was fortunate that he was at home when you phoned.* あなたが電話した時に彼が家にいたのは幸運でした. ⇔ **unfortunate**

*__fortunately__ /fɔːrtʃ(ə)nətli/ 副 ▶定義 by good luck; luckily 運良く;幸運にも→運良く,幸運にも,幸いに,有り難いことには ‖ *Fortunately the traffic wasn't too bad so I managed to get to the meeting on time.* 幸運にも,交通渋滞はそれほどひどくなかったので,何とか時間通りに会議に出ることができた.

*__fortune__ /fɔːrtʃ(ə)n/ 名 ▶定義 1 C U a very large amount of money 非常に多くの金→大金,巨額の金,資産,財産,富 ‖ *I always spend a fortune on presents at Christmas.* 私はクリスマスにはいつも贈り物に相当お金をかける. *She went to Hollywood in search of fame and fortune.* 彼女は名声と富を求めてハリウッドに行った. ▶定義 2 U chance or the power that affects what happens in a person's life; luck 人生に起こる事に影響する機会または力;運→運,運命(の女神) ‖ *Fortune was not on our side that day* (= we were unlucky). その日は運が私たちに味方しなかった(=私たちは不運だった). ☛類 fate ▶定義 3 [C, 通常は複数] the things (both good and bad) that happen to a person, family, country, etc 人,家族,国などに起こる事(良い事と悪い事の両方)→運命,命運,宿命,人生[運命]の浮沈 ‖ *The country's fortunes depend on its industry being successful.* その国の将来は工業の成功に懸かっている. ▶定義 4 C what is going to happen to a person in the future 未来に人に起こりそうな事→運勢,運命 ‖ *Show me your hand and I'll try to tell your fortune.* 手を見せてください.運勢を占ってあげましょう.
☛類 fate, destiny

成句 cost the earth/a fortune ⇒ **COST**²

**fortune teller** 名 C ▶定義 a person who tells people what will happen to them in the future 人々に将来起こるであろう事を予測する人→占い師,易者

*__forty__ /fɔːrti/ 数 ▶定義 40
▶文中での数詞の使い方については,sixty を参照.
成句 **forty winks** 略式 ▶定義 a short sleep, especially during the day 特に日中の,短時間の睡眠→昼寝,うたた寝,一眠り

**forum** /fɔːrəm/ 名 C ▶定義 a forum (for sth) a place or meeting where people can exchange and discuss ideas 人々が意見を交換し議論できる場所または会合→公開討論会の会場,公共広場,公開討論会,フォーラム ‖ *Television is now an important forum for political debate.* 現在ではテレビが政治論争をする上で重要な公開討論の場である.

*__forward__¹ /fɔːrwərd/ 副 ▶定義 1 (または **forwards**) in the direction that is in front of you; towards the front, end or future 自分の前の方向へ;前,先,または未来へ向かって→前(方)へ,先へ,今後,将来に向かって ‖ *Keep going forward and try not to look back.* 前進し続けて振り返らないようにしなさい. ⇔ **back, backward(s)** ▶定義 2 in the direction of progress; ahead 進行方向へ;前へ→前進して,前進的に,進歩的に,進んで ‖ *The new form of treatment is a big step forward in the fight against Aids.* 新しい治療法はエイズとの闘いにおける大きな前進だ.
▶ forward は,bring, come, look, put など多くの動詞の後で用いられる.これらの意味については,各動詞の項を参照.
成句 backward(s) and forward(s) ⇒ **BACKWARDS**
put the clock/clocks forward/back ⇒ **CLOCK**¹

*__forward__² /fɔːrwərd/ 形 ▶定義 1 (名詞の前だけ) towards the front or future 前または未来に向かって→前方の,前部の,将来へ向けての,先の ‖ *forward planning* 将来の計画 ▶定義 2 having developed earlier than is normal or expected; advanced 通常または予想より早く進展してきている; 進んだ➜**早い, 早く進んでいる, はかどっている, 早く成長する** ⇔ **backward** ▶定義3 behaving towards sb in a way that is too confident or too informal ～に対して, 自信過剰な, またはくだけすぎる態度で振る舞っている➜**うぬぼれた, 生意気な, 厚かましい, 出しゃばりの, ずうずうしい, なれなれしい** ‖ *I hope you don't think I'm being too forward, asking you so many questions.* 質問ばかりするので厚かましいと思わないでくだされぱいいのですが.

**forward**[3] /fɔ́ːrwərd/ [動][他] ▶定義1 to send a letter, etc received at one address to a new address ある住所で受け取られた手紙などを新しい住所へ送る➜**～を転送する** ‖ *The post office is forwarding all our mail.* 郵便局が私たちの郵便物をすべて転送してくれている. ▶定義2 to help to improve sth or to make sth progress ～を向上させるのを助ける, または～を発展させる➜**～を進める, 促進する, 助長する, 助成する** ‖ *I'm trying to forward my career in publishing.* 私は出版業界で出世しようと努力している.

**forward**[4] /fɔ́ːrwərd/ [名] [C] ▶定義 an attacking player in a sport such as football サッカーなどのスポーツで攻撃をする選手➜**フォワード, 前衛**

**forwarding address** [名] [C] ▶定義 a new address to which letters, etc should be sent 手紙などが送られるべき新しい住所➜**回送先, 転送先 (住所)** ‖ *The previous owners didn't leave a forwarding address.* 前の所有者は転送先の住所を残さなかった.

**forward-looking** [形] ▶定義 thinking about or planning for the future; having modern ideas 将来について考えている, または計画している; 現代的な考えを持っている➜**前向きの, 将来を見極めた, 積極的な, 進取の**

**forwent** FORGO の過去形

**fossil** /fás(ə)l/ [名] [C] ▶定義 (part of) an animal or plant that lived thousands of years ago which has turned into rock 何千年も前に生きており, 岩石に変化した動物または植物 (の一部) ➜**化石**

**foster** /fɔ́(ː)stər, fás-/ [動][他] ▶定義1 特に [英] to take a child who needs a home into your family and to care for him/her without becoming the legal parent 家庭を必要とする子供を自分の家族に引き取り, 法律上の親にはならないで世話をする➜**～を養育する, 世話する, 里子として育てる, ～の里親になる** ‖ *to foster a homeless child* 家のない子を里子として育てる

➤ このような事をする人は foster-parent である. その子供は foster-child と言う. adopt を参照.

▶定義2 to help or encourage the development of sth (especially feelings or ideas) ～ (特に感情または考え) の発展を助ける, または促進する➜**～を育成する, 育てる, 助長する, 促進する** ‖ *to foster sb's friendship/trust* ～の友情・信頼を育てる

**fought** FIGHT[1] の過去・過去分詞形

**foul**[1] /fáʊl/ [形] ▶定義1 that smells or tastes disgusting 嫌なにおい, または味がするような➜**臭い, 悪臭のある, ひどい味の, むかつくような** ‖ *a foul-smelling cigar* 嫌なにおいの葉巻 *This coffee tastes foul!* このコーヒーはまずい. ▶定義2 特に [英] very bad or unpleasant 非常に悪い, または不快な➜**邪悪な, 卑劣な, 不正な, 荒れた, 不愉快な** ‖ *Careful what you say - he's **in a foul temper/mood**.* 言葉に気を付けて ― 彼はとても機嫌が悪いから. *The **foul weather** prevented our plane from taking off.* 悪天候のため私たちの飛行機は離陸できなかった. ▶定義3 (used about language) very rude; full of swearing (言葉について) 非常に無礼な; ののしりで一杯の➜**口汚い, 悪い, 下品な, みだらな** ‖ *foul language* 汚い言葉

[成句] **fall foul of sb/sth** ▶定義 to get in trouble with sb/sth because you have done sth wrong 悪い～をしたために, …と面倒な事態になる➜**～とごたごたを起こす, 争う, ～とかかわり合いになる** ‖ *At sixteen she fell foul of the law for the first time.* 16歳の時に彼女は初めて法の裁きを受けた.

**foul**[2] /fáʊl/ [動] ▶定義1 [自][他] (used in sports) to attack another player in a way that is not allowed (スポーツで用いて) 認められていない方法でほかの選手を攻撃する➜**反則を犯す, 反則をして～を妨害する, ～に反則 (行為を) する** ‖ *Shearer was fouled inside the box and the referee awarded his team a penalty.* シアラーがペナルティーエリアで反則を受け, 審判は彼の敵チームにペナルティーキックを与えた. ▶定義2

## 666　foul³

⓭ to make sth dirty (with rubbish, waste, etc) ～を(ごみ,くずなどで)汚くする➔～を汚す,汚くする‖ *Dogs must not foul the pavement.* 犬が歩道を汚してはいけない.

**句動詞** foul sth up (口語) ▶定義 to spoil sth ～を駄目にする➔～を台なしにする,めちゃめちゃにする,混乱させる,へまをやる‖ *The delay on the train fouled up my plans for the evening.* 列車が遅れたため,私のその晩の計画は台なしになった.

**foul³** /fáʊl/ 图 ● ▶定義 (used in sports) an action that is against the rules (スポーツで)ルールに反する行為➔ファウル,反則‖ *He was sent off for a foul on the goalkeeper.* 彼はゴールキーパーに対する反則で退場させられた.

**foul play** 图 ⓤ ▶定義 **1** violence or crime that causes sb's death ～の死を招くような暴力または犯罪➔凶行,暴行,暴力,殺人,犯罪‖ *The police suspect foul play.* 警察は殺人ではないかと疑っている. ▶定義 **2** action that is against the rules of a sport スポーツのルールに反する行為➔ファウル,反則

**found¹** FIND¹ の過去・過去分詞形

**found²** /fáʊnd/ 動 ⓣ ▶定義 **1** to start an organization, institution, etc 組織,制度などを始める➔～を起こす,創設する,創立する,設立する‖ *This museum was founded in 1683.* この博物館は1683年に設立された. ▶定義 **2** to be the first to start building and living in a town or country 街または国に建物を建てて住み始める最初である➔～を建設する,創建する,建国する‖ *Liberia was founded by freed American slaves.* リベリアは解放されたアメリカの奴隷たちによって建国された. ▶定義 **3** found sth (on sth) (通常は受動態で) to base sth on sth ～に…の基礎を置く➔～を…に基づいて作る,～の上に…を建てる,～を…の根拠とする‖ *The book was founded on real life.* その本は実生活に基づいていた.

*****foundation** /faʊndéɪʃ(ə)n/ 图 ● ▶定義 **1** [複数扱い] **foundations** a layer of bricks, etc under the surface of the ground that forms the solid base of a building 建物の堅固な基礎となる,地表の下のレンガなどの層➔基礎,土台,礎 ▶定義 **2** ● ⓤ the idea, principle, or fact on which sth is based ～の基礎となる考え,原理,または事実➔根拠,基盤,土台,よりどころ,出発点‖ *This coursebook aims to give students a solid foundation in grammar.* この教科書は,生徒の文法の基礎を固めることを目標としている. *That rumour is completely without foundation (= it is not true).* そのうわさには全く根拠がない(= 真実ではない). ▶定義 **3** ● an organization that provides money for a special purpose 特別な目的のためにお金を提供する組織➔財団,基金,団体‖ *The British Heart Foundation* 英国心臓財団 ▶定義 **4** ⓤ the act of starting a new institution or organization 新しい機関または組織を開始すること➔創設,創建,創立,設立

**founder** /fáʊndər/ 图 ● ▶定義 a person who starts a new institution or organization 新しい機関または組織を開始する人➔創設者,創立者,設立者,発起人

**founder member** 图 ● ▶定義 one of the original members of a club, organization, etc あるクラブ,組織などの最初のメンバーの1人1人➔創立会員,創立メンバー

**foundry** /fáʊndri/ 图 ● (複 **foundries**) ▶定義 a place where metal or glass is melted and shaped into objects 金属またはガラスが溶かされ,物に形づくられる場所➔鋳造所,鋳造場,鋳物工場,ガラス工場

*****fountain** /fáʊnt(ə)n/ 图 ● ▶定義 **1** a decoration (in a garden or in a square in a town) that sends a flow of water into the air; the water that comes out of a fountain 水流を空中に放出する(庭または町の広場にある)装飾物; 泉から出てくる水➔噴水,噴水池,泉,わき水 ☞ C8ページのさし絵 ▶定義 **2** a strong flow of liquid or another substance that is forced into the air 空中に噴出される液体またはほかの物質の勢いのある流れ➔噴流,流れ,吹き出すもの,ほとばしるもの‖ *a fountain of blood/sparks* 血しぶき・火花の噴水 ▶定義 **3** a person or thing that provides a large amount of sth 大量の～を提供する人または物➔(源)泉,起源,根源‖ *Ed's a fountain of information on football.* エドはサッカー情報の宝庫である.

**fountain pen** 图 ● ▶定義 a type of pen that you fill with ink インクを詰める方式のペン➔万年筆

*****four** /fɔːr/ 图 ▶定義 **1** 4

▶文中での数詞の使い方の例については, six を参照.

**▶定義2 four-** (複合形で) having four of the thing mentioned 言及された物が4つある➡**4つの, 4個の, 4人の** ‖ *four-legged animals* 4本足の動物

**成句 on all fours ▶定義** with your hands and knees to the ground; crawling 両手と両足を地面に付けて, はっている➡**四つんばいになって, はいながら, 四つ足で** ‖ *The children went through the tunnel on all fours.* 子供たちは四つんばいになってトンネルをくぐった.

**four-letter word** 名 C ▶定義 a swear word that shocks or offends people (often with four letters) 人を憤慨させる, または不快感を与えるような, (しばしば4文字から成る)ののしりの言葉➡**卑わい語, 4文字言葉**

\*fourteen /fɔːrtíːn, ^/ 代形 ▶定義 14
▶文中での数詞の使い方の例については, six を参照.

\*fourteenth /fɔːrtíːnθ, ^/ 代形副 ▶定義 14th➡**14番目(の, に), 第14(の, に)**

\*fourth /fɔːrθ/ 代形副 ▶定義 4th➡**4番目(の, に), 第4(の, に)**
▶4分の1には quarter を用いる: *a quarter of an hour (= fifteen minutes)* 4分の1時間 (=15分)

**four-wheel drive** 形 ▶定義 (used about a vehicle) having an engine that turns all four wheels (乗り物について)4輪すべてを回転させるエンジンを持っている➡**4輪駆動の, 4輪駆動方式の**

**fowl** /fául/ 名 C (複 fowl または fowls) ▶定義 a bird, especially a chicken, that is kept on a farm 農場で飼われる鳥, 特に鶏➡**鶏, 家禽(かきん)**

fox

\*fox /fɑks/ 名 C ▶定義 a wild animal like a small dog with reddish fur, a pointed nose and a thick tail 赤みを帯びた毛, とがった鼻, 太い尾を持つ, 小犬に似た野生動物➡**キツネ**

▶キツネは, sly (ずるい), または cunning (ずる賢い)と言われることが多い. 雌のキツネは vixen, 子供のキツネは cub と言う.

**foyer** /fɔ́iər, fɔ́i(j)eɪ; F fwaje/ 名 C ▶定義 an entrance hall in a cinema, theatre, hotel, etc where people can meet or wait 人々が会うまたは待つことができる, 映画館, 劇場, ホテルなどの玄関ホール➡**ロビー, ホワイエ, 休憩室**

**fraction** /frǽkʃ(ə)n/ 名 C ▶定義1 a small part or number 小さい部分, または少量➡**わずかな部分, 破片, 断片, 端数** ‖ *For a fraction of a second I thought the car was going to crash.* ほんの一瞬, 車が衝突するかと思った. ▶定義2 a division of a number 数を分割したもの➡**分数** ‖ *1/2 and 1/4 are fractions.* 1/2と1/4は分数である.

**fractionally** /frǽkʃ(ə)n(ə)li/ 副 ▶定義 to a very small degree; slightly 非常に少ない程度まで; わずかに➡**断片的に, ごく少量, ほんの少し, わずかに** ‖ *fractionally faster/taller/heavier* わずかに速い・背が高い・重い

**fracture** /frǽktʃər/ 名 C U ▶定義 a break in a bone or other hard material 骨またはほかの硬い物が折れること➡**骨折, 砕けること, 割れること, 破損, 破砕** ― fracture 動 自 他➡**骨折する, 壊れる, 割れる, 壊す, 割る** ‖ *She fell and fractured her ankle.* 彼女は転んで足首を骨折した. *A water pipe fractured and flooded the bathroom.* 水道管が破裂して, 浴室が水浸しになった.

**fragile** /frǽdʒàɪl; -əl/ ▶定義 easily damaged or broken 簡単に損傷を受ける, または壊れる➡**壊れやすい, 折れやすい, 割れやすい, もろい** ‖ *This bowl is very fragile. Please handle it carefully.* この鉢はとても割れやすいです. 注意して扱ってください.

**fragment**[1] /frǽgmənt/ 名 C ▶定義 a small piece that has broken off or that comes from sth larger 壊れた, または大きな〜から出てきた小片➡**破片, 断片, かけら** ‖ *The builders found fragments of Roman pottery on the site.* 建設業者は現場で古代ローマの陶器の破片を発見した. *I heard only a fragment of their conversation.* 私には彼らの会話の断片しか聞こえなかった.

**fragment**[2] /frǽgmənt/ 動 自 他 正式 ▶定義 to break (sth) into small pieces 粉々に壊れる, (〜

を）粉々に壊す➔ばらばらになる, 破片になる; ～をばらばらにする, 破片にする ‖ *The country is becoming increasingly fragmented by civil war.* その国は, 内戦によってますますばらばらになりつつある.

**fragrance** /fréɪgr(ə)ns/ 图 ❻ ❶ ▶定義 a pleasant smell 心地良い香り➔良い香り, 芳香, 香気

**fragrant** /fréɪgr(ə)nt/ 形 ▶定義 having a pleasant smell 心地良い香りを持っている➔良い香りの, 香気のある, 芳しい, かぐわしい

**frail** /fréɪl/ 形 ▶定義 weak or not healthy 弱い, または健康でない➔虚弱な, か弱い, もろい, 弱った ‖ *My aunt is still very frail after her accident.* 事故の後, おばはまだとても弱っている.

**frailty** /fréɪlti/ 图 ❻ ❶ (複 **frailties**) ▶定義 weakness of a person's body or character 人の体または性格の弱さ➔虚弱, もろさ, 意志薄弱, 弱点

★**frame**¹ /fréɪm/ 图 ❻ ▶定義1 a border of wood or metal that goes around the outside of a door, picture, window, etc ドア, 絵, 窓などの外側を囲む, 木または金属の縁➔縁, 枠, 額縁, フレーム ‖ *a window frame* 窓枠 ▶定義2 the basic strong structure of a piece of furniture, building, vehicle, etc which gives it its shape 家具, 建物, 乗り物などの, それらに形を与える基礎的で強固な構造物➔骨組み, 軸部, 車枠, 台枠, 機体骨 ‖ *the frame of a bicycle/an aircraft* 自転車・航空機の骨組み ☞ S7 ページのさし絵 ▶定義3 [通常は複数] a structure made of plastic or metal that holds the two pieces of glass (**lenses**) in a pair of glasses 眼鏡の2枚のガラス (レンズ) を支えるプラスチックまたは金属の構造物➔フレーム, 眼鏡の縁枠 ☞ **glasses** のさし絵 ▶定義4 [通常は単数] the basic shape of a human or animal body 人間または動物の体の基本的な形➔体格, 骨格, 体付き ‖ *He has a large frame but he's not fat.* 彼は体格が大きいが太ってはいない.

成句 **frame of mind** ▶定義 a particular state or condition of your feelings; the mood 感情のある状態または状況; 気分➔気持ち, 気分, 機嫌 ‖ *I'm not in the right frame of mind for a party. I'd prefer to be on my own.* 私はとてもパーティーに行くような気分ではありません. 1人でいたいのです.

**frame**² /fréɪm/ 動 ⓣ ▶定義1 to put a border around sth (especially a picture or photograph) (特に絵または写真) の周りに縁を付ける➔～を額に入れる, 枠にはめる, ～に枠を付ける, 縁を付ける ‖ *Let's have this photograph framed.* この写真を額に入れよう. ▶定義2 (通常は受動態で) to give false evidence against sb in order to make him/her seem guilty of a crime ～が有罪に見えるようにするため, その～に対する偽りの証拠を挙げる➔～にぬれぎぬを着せる, ～を罪に陥れる, はめる, わなに掛ける ‖ *The man claimed that he had been framed by the police.* その男は警察にぬれぎぬを着せられたと主張した. ▶定義3 正式 to express sth in a particular way あるやり方で～を表現する➔～を言う, 表す, 書き表す, 表現する ‖ *The question was very carefully framed.* 質問は非常に念入りに組み立てられていた.

**framework** /fréɪmwə̀ːrk/ 图 ❻ ▶定義1 the basic structure of sth that gives it shape and strength 形と強度を与える, ～の基本的な構造➔枠組み, 骨組み, 骨格 ‖ *A greenhouse is made of glass panels fixed in a metal framework.* 温室は金属の骨組みに固定されたガラス板でできている. (比喩) *the basic framework of society* 社会の基本的枠組み ▶定義2 a system of rules or ideas which help you decide what to do 何をするべきかを決める助けとなる規則または考えの体系➔基本となるもの, 構成, 構想, 骨子 ‖ *The plan may be changed but it will provide a framework on which we can build.* その計画は変更されるかもしれないが, その基本構想はそのまま使えるだろう.

**franc** /fræŋk/ 图 ❻ ▶定義 the unit of money that is used in France, Belgium, Switzerland and several other countries フランス, ベルギー, スイス, そのほか数か国で使用されている通貨の単位➔フラン

**franchise** /fræntʃàɪz/ 图 ▶定義1 ❻ ❶ official permission to sell a company's goods or services in a particular area 特定の地域で, ある会社の商品またはサービスを販売できる正式な許可➔販売権, 営業権, フランチャイズ ‖ *They have the franchise to sell this product in Cyprus.* 彼らはこの製品をキプロスで販売する権利を持っている. *Most fast-food restaurants are operated* *under franchise.* ほとんどのファーストフード店はフランチャイズに基づいて営業されている.

▶定義2 ❶正式 the right to vote in elections 選挙で投票する権利 ➡ 選挙権, 参政権

**frank** /fræŋk/ 形 ▶定義 showing your thoughts and feelings clearly; saying what you mean 自分の考えまたは感情をはっきりと示している; 自分の意図される事を言っている ➡ 率直な, ざっくばらんな, 隠し立てをしない, 腹を割った ‖ *To be perfectly frank with you, I don't think you'll pass your driving test.* 正直に言って, あなたが運転免許試験に受かるとは思わない. ― **frankly** 副 ➡ 率直に, ざっくばらんに, 隠し立てせずに, 腹蔵なく ‖ *Please tell me frankly what you think about my idea.* 私の考えをどう思うか, 率直に聞かせてください. ― **frankness** 名 ❶ ➡ 率直(さ), 正直, ざっくばらん

**frankfurter** /ˈfræŋkfɜːrtər/ (米 または **wiener**) 名 ❶ ▶定義 a type of small smoked sausage 小さな燻製(くんせい)のソーセージの一種 ➡ フランクフルトソーセージ

**frantic** /ˈfræntɪk/ 形 ▶定義1 extremely worried or frightened 非常に心配した, またはおびえた ➡ 気も狂わんばかりの, 半狂乱の, 取り乱した ‖ *The mother went frantic when she couldn't find her child.* 子供が見つからないので, 母親は半狂乱になった. *frantic cries for help* 助けを求める, 気も狂わんばかりの声 ▶定義2 very busy or done in a hurry 非常に忙しい, または急いで行われた ➡ 大急ぎの, 大慌ての, 大忙しの ‖ *a frantic search for the keys* 大慌てでかぎを探すこと *We're not busy at work now, but things get frantic at Christmas.* 私たちは今は仕事が忙しくないが, クリスマスには大忙しになる. ― **frantically** /-k(ə)li/ 副 ➡ 半狂乱で, 死に物狂いで, 大急ぎで, 大慌てで

**fraternal** /frəˈtɜːnl/ 形 正式 ▶定義 connected with the relationship that exists between brothers; like a brother 兄弟の間にある関係に関連した; 兄弟のように ➡ 兄弟の, 兄弟らしい, 兄弟のような ‖ *fraternal love/rivalry* 兄弟愛・兄弟間の競争

**fraternity** /frəˈtɜːnəti/ 名 (複 **fraternities**) ▶定義1 ❶ the feeling of friendship and support between people in the same group 同じ集団の人々の間の友情と助け合いの気持ち ➡ 友愛, 同胞愛 ▶定義2 ❷ a group of people who share the same work or interests 同じ仕事または興味を共有する人々の集団 ➡ 協同団体, 同業組合, 同業者仲間, 同人, (アメリカの大学内での) 同じ意識を持った男性集団 ‖ *the medical fraternity* 医師会

**fraud** /frɔːd/ 名 ▶定義1 ❷ ❶ (an act of) cheating sb in order to get money, etc illegally 金などを違法に得るために, ~をだますこと (だます行為) ➡ ペテン, 詐欺(行為), 不正手段 ‖ *The accountant was sent to prison for fraud.* その会計士は詐欺で刑務所に送られた. *Massive amounts of money are lost every year in credit card frauds.* クレジットカードの不正使用で, 毎年ばく大な金が失われる. ▶定義2 ❷ a person who tricks sb by pretending to be sb else ほかの~の振りをして…をだます人 ➡ 詐欺師, ペテン師

**fraudulent** /ˈfrɔːdʒələnt/ 形 正式 ▶定義 done in order to cheat sb; dishonest ~をだますために行われる; 不誠実な ➡ 詐欺的な, 詐欺(行為)の, 不正な ‖ *the fraudulent use of stolen cheques* 盗難小切手の不正使用

**fraught** /frɔːt/ 形 ▶定義1 fraught with sth filled with sth unpleasant 不快な~で一杯の ➡ ~に満ちた, ~をはらんだ, 伴う ‖ *a situation fraught with danger/difficulty* 危険・困難に満ちた状態 ▶定義2 (used about people) worried and nervous; (used about a situation) very busy so that people become nervous (人について) 心配で不安な, (状態について) 人がいらいらするほど非常に忙しい ➡ 心配して, 不安な, 緊張して, 緊迫した ‖ *Things are usually fraught at work on Mondays.* 月曜日の職場はいつも大忙しだ.

**fray** /freɪ/ 動 ⾃ 他 ▶定義1 if cloth, etc frays or becomes frayed, some of the threads at the end start to come apart 布などがそのようになった場合には, 端の糸の一部がほつれ始める ➡ 擦り切れ(させ)る, ほつれ(させ)る ‖ *This shirt is beginning to fray at the cuffs.* このシャツはそで口がほつれかけている. *a frayed rope* 擦り切れたロープ ▶定義2 if a person's nerves, etc fray or become frayed, he/she starts to get annoyed 人の神経などがそのようになった場合には, その人はいらいらし始める ➡ すり減る, いら立つ, ~をすり減らす, いら立たせる ‖ *Tempers began* to fray towards the end of the match. 試合が終わりに近付くと、冷静さが失われ始めた.

**freak**[1] /fríːk/ 名 C ▶定義1 略式 a person who has a very strong interest in sth ～に非常に強い興味を持っている人→**熱狂者, マニア, ファン, ～狂** ‖ *a fitness/computer freak* 健康マニア・コンピューターマニア ☞類 **fanatic** ▶定義2 a very unusual and strange event, person, animal, etc 非常に珍しい奇妙な出来事、人、動物など→**異常な・不思議な出来事, 異変, 奇人, 変人** ‖ *a freak accident/storm/result* 珍しい事故・異常なあらし・珍しい結果 *The other kids think Ally's a freak because she doesn't watch TV.* アリーはテレビを見ないので、ほかの子供たちは彼女を変人だと思っている.

**freak**[2] /fríːk/ 動 自他 略式 ▶定義 freak (sb) (out) to react very strongly to sth that makes you feel shocked, frightened, upset, etc 衝撃を受けさせる、怖がらせる、混乱させるなどのような～に非常に強く反応する→**ひどく興奮する, 異常な精神状態になる; ～をひどく興奮させる, 異常な精神状態にさせる** ‖ *She freaked out when she heard the news.* 彼女はニュースを聞いてひどく興奮した. *The film 'Psycho' really freaked me out.* 「サイコ」という映画は本当に怖かった.

**freckle** /frék(ə)l/ 名 C 通常は複数 ▶定義 a small brown spot on your skin 肌の小さい茶色の染み→**そばかす, 染み** ‖ *A lot of people with red hair have got freckles.* 赤毛の人の多くはそばかすがある. ☞参 **mole** — freckled 形→そばかすのある, 染みのある

\***free**[1] /fríː/ 形 ▶定義1 not in prison, in a cage, etc; not held or controlled 刑務所またはおりなどに入っていない; 拘束されていない、または抑制されていない→**自由な, 自由の身の, 監禁されていない, 束縛されていない** ‖ *The government set Mandela free in 1989.* 政府は1989年にマンデラを解放した. *There is nowhere around here where dogs can run free.* この辺りには犬を放せる場所はない. ▶定義2 free (to do sth) not controlled by the government, rules, etc 政府、規則などによって統制されていない→**自由な, 自由(主義)の, 独立した, 自主的な** ‖ *There is free movement of people across the border.* 人々は国境を自由に越えている. *free speech/press* 言論・報道の自由 ▶定義3 costing nothing 経費がかからない→**無料の, 無償の, 負担のない** ‖ *Admission to the museum is free/free of charge.* 博物館の入場は無料です. *Children under five usually travel free on trains.* 5歳未満の子供は、普通は無料で列車に乗れる. ▶定義4 not busy or being used 忙しくない、または使われていない→**暇な, 仕事から解放されて, 手が空いて, 使用可能な** ‖ *I'm afraid Mr Spencer is not free this afternoon.* 残念ながらスペンサー氏は今日の午後は空いていません. *I don't get much free time.* 私には自由時間があまりない. *Is this seat free?* この席は空いていますか. ▶定義5 free from/of sth not having sth dangerous, unpleasant, etc 危険であったり、不快であったりする～を持っていない→**～がない, ～から免れて, ～に悩まされない** ‖ *free of worries/responsibility* 心配・責任がない *free from pain* 痛みのない

成句 feel free ⇒ **FEEL**[1]

free and easy ▶定義 informal or relaxed くだけている、またはくつろいだ→**厳格でない, 打ち解けた, のんびりした, のんきな** ‖ *The atmosphere in our office is very free and easy.* 我が社の雰囲気はとてものんびりしています.

get, have, etc a free hand ▶定義 to get, have, etc permission to make your own decisions about sth ～について自分で決定する許可を得る、持つなど→**行動の自由を得る・持つ, 自由裁量権を得る・持つ**

of your own free will ▶定義 because you want to, not because sb forces you ～が強制したからではなく、自分が望むから→**自由意志で, 自分から進んで**

\***free**[2] /fríː/ 動 他 ▶定義1 free sb/sth (from sth) to let sb/sth leave or escape from a place where he/she/it is held 拘束されている場所から～を去らせる、または脱出させる→**～を解放する, 自由にする, 放す, 釈放する** ‖ *to free a prisoner* 囚人を釈放する *The protesters freed the animals from their cages.* 抗議者たちは動物をおりから出してやった. ▶定義2 free sb/sth of/from sth to take away sth that is unpleasant from sb ～から不快な…を取り去る→**～を取り除く, 免れさせる, ～から救う, 解放する** ‖ *The medicine freed her from pain for a few hours.* その薬によって彼女は数時間、痛みから解放され

た． ▶定義3 free sb/sth (up) for sth; free sb/sth (up) to do sth to make sth available so that it can be used; to put sb in a position in which he/she can do sth ～が使用できる状態にする；～を…が行える立場に置く→～を空ける，なくす，解消する，～が…できるようにする ‖ *If I cancel my trip, that will free me to see you on Friday.* 旅行を取り消せば，金曜日にあなたに会えます．

**free agent** 名 C ▶定義 a person who can do what he/she wants because nobody else has the right to tell him/her what to do 何をするべきかを指示する権利を持つ人がほかにだれもいないため，自分が望むことをできる人→**自由に行動できる人，自由行為者，自由契約選手**

**＊freedom** /frí:dəm/ 名 ▶定義1 ❶ the state of not being held prisoner or controlled by sb else 捕虜にされていない，またはほかの～に支配されていない状態→**自由（の身），自由であること，束縛のないこと** ‖ *The opposition leader was given his freedom after 25 years.* 反対派の指導者は25年後に自由を与えられた． ▶定義2 ❷ ❶ the right or ability to do or say what you want 自分の望む事をする，または言う権利または能力→**～の自由，～する自由，自由に～できること** ‖ *You have the freedom to come and go as you please.* 好きなときに自由に行き来して構いません． *freedom of speech* 言論の自由 *the rights and freedoms of the individual* 個人の権利と自由 ☞参 **liberty** ▶定義3 ❶ freedom from sth the state of not being affected by sth unpleasant 不快な～に影響されない状態→**～がないこと，解放，免除** ‖ *freedom from fear/hunger/pain* 恐怖・飢え・痛みがないこと ▶定義4 ❶ the freedom of sth the right to use sth without restriction 制限なしで～を使う権利→**特権，～の出入りの自由，通行の自由，自由使用権** ‖ *You can have the freedom of the ground floor, but please don't go upstairs.* 1階は自由に使って構いませんが，上の階には行かないでください．

**freedom fighter** 名 C ▶定義 a person who belongs to a group that uses violence to try to remove a government from power 暴力を行使して政府から権力を取り上げようとする集団に属する人→**自由の戦士**

**free enterprise** 名 ❶ ▶定義 the operation of trade and business without government control 政府の規制なしに貿易または事業を行うこと→**自由競争，自由企業制**

**freehand** /frí:hænd/ 形 副 ▶定義 (used about a drawing) done by hand, without the help of any instruments (かくことについて) 道具の助けを得ずに手でかかれた→**手でかいた，手だけで，フリーハンドの[で]** ‖ *a freehand sketch* フリーハンドのスケッチ *to draw freehand* フリーハンドでかく

**free kick** 名 C ▶定義 (in football or rugby) a situation in which a player of one team is allowed to kick the ball because a member of the other team has broken a rule (サッカーまたはラグビーで) 一方のチームの選手がルールを破ったため，他方のチームの選手がボールをけることが認められている状態→**フリーキック**

**freelance** /frí:là:ns; -læns/ 形 副 ▶定義 earning money by selling your services or work to different organizations rather than being employed by a single company 1つの会社に雇われるのではなく，サービスまたは労働をいろいろな組織に売って金を稼いでいる→**自由契約の[で]，フリーランスの[で]** ‖ *a freelance journalist* フリーのジャーナリスト *She works freelance.* 彼女はフリーランスで働いている．— **freelance** (または **freelancer**) 名 C →**自由契約で働く人，フリーランサー** — **freelance** 動 自 →**自由契約で働く，フリーランスで働く，フリーで働く** ‖ *I left my job because I can earn more by freelancing.* フリーランスで働く方が多く稼げるので，私は仕事を辞めた．

**freely** /frí:li/ 副 ▶定義1 in a way that is not controlled or limited 規制または制限されずに→**自由に，障害なしに，勝手に，邪魔されずに** ‖ *He is the country's first freely elected president for 40 years.* 彼はその国で40年振りに自由選挙で選ばれた大統領である． ▶定義2 without trying to avoid the truth even though it might be embarrassing; in an honest way たとえ当惑させるような事だとしても，真実を避けようとせずに；正直に→**進んで，率直に，正直に，素直に** ‖ *I freely admit that I made a mistake.* 私は誤りを犯したことを正直に認めます．

**Freemason** /frí:méɪs(ə)n, ˌ--/ (または **mason**) 名 C ▶定義 a man who belongs to an international secret society whose members help each other and who recognize each other by secret signs そのメンバーは互いに助け合い，秘密の暗号で互いを確認するような国際的な秘密結社に属する人で，通常は男性 →フリーメーソンの会員

**free-range** 形 ▶定義 (used about farm birds or their eggs) kept or produced in a place where birds can move around freely（農場の鳥またはその卵について）鳥が自由に動き回ることができる場所で飼育される，または産み落とされる →放し飼いの（鳥の）‖ *free-range hens/turkeys* 放し飼いの雌鶏（めんどり）・七面鳥 *free-range eggs* 放し飼いの鶏の卵 ☛参 battery

**free speech** 名 U ▶定義 the right to express any opinion in public どのような意見でも公に発表できる権利 →言論の自由

**freeway** /fríːweɪ/ 米 =MOTORWAY

*****freeze**¹ /fríːz/ 動 (過 **froze** /fróʊz/; 過分 **frozen** /fróʊzn/) ▶定義 1 自他 to become hard (and often change into ice) because of extreme cold; to make sth do this 極端な寒さのために固くなる（そしてしばしば氷に変化する）；〜にそのようにさせる →凍る，固化する，氷結する，凍結する，氷が張る；〜を凍らせる，冷凍する‖ *Water freezes at 0° Celsius.* 水は摂氏０度で凍る. *The ground was **frozen solid** for most of the winter.* 冬のほとんどの間，地面は固く凍っていた. *frozen peas/fish/food* 冷凍のグリーンピース・冷凍魚・冷凍食品 ▶定義 2 自 used with 'it' to describe extremely cold weather when water turns into ice it と共に用いられて，水が氷になるときの極端に寒い天候を表す →非常に寒い，凍るほど寒い，凍（い）てつく‖ *I think it's going to freeze tonight.* 今夜は凍てつくだろう. ▶定義 3 自他 to be very cold or to die from cold とても寒い，または寒さで死ぬ →凍るように寒く感じる，凍える，凍死する；〜を凍えさせる‖ *It was so cold on the mountain that we thought we would **freeze to death**.* 山の上はとても寒かったので，私たちは凍死するかと思った. *Turn the heater up a bit - I'm **frozen stiff**.* 暖房を少し強くしてください － 私は身動きできないほど寒いので. ▶定義 4 自 to stop moving suddenly and completely because you are frightened or in danger

おびえているまたは危険であるため，突然，完全に動くことをやめる →凍りつく，動けなくなる，身動きできなくなる，立ちすくむ，こわばる‖ *The terrible scream made her freeze with terror.* 恐ろしい悲鳴が聞こえて，彼女は恐怖で動けなくなった. *Suddenly the man pulled out a gun and shouted 'Freeze!'* 突然その男が銃を取り出し，「動くな」と叫んだ. ▶定義 5 他 to keep the money you earn, prices, etc at a fixed level for a certain period of time 稼ぐお金または価格などを一定の期間，固定された水準に保つ →〜を凍結する，固定する‖ *Spending on defence has been frozen for one year.* 防衛費は１年間凍結されている.

**freeze**² /fríːz/ 名 C ▶定義 1 a period of weather when the temperature stays below 0°C (**freezing point**) 気温が０℃（氷点）以下のままである天候の期間 →氷結期，厳寒期 ▶定義 2 the fixing of the money you earn, prices, etc at one level for a certain period of time ある期間，稼ぐお金または価格などをある水準に固定すること →凍結，据え置き

**freezer** /fríːzər/（または **deep freeze**）名 C ▶定義 a large box or cupboard in which you can store food for a long time at a temperature below 0° Celsius (**freezing point**) so that it stays frozen 食品を凍ったままにしておくために，長い間摂氏０度（氷点）より低い温度で保管することができる大型の箱または戸棚 →冷凍庫，冷凍器，冷凍室，フリーザー ☛参 fridge ☛ C7 ページのさし絵

**freezing**¹ /fríːzɪŋ/ 形 略式 ▶定義 very cold 非常に寒い →とても寒い，凍えるほど寒い，酷寒の，凍るような‖ *Can we turn the central heating on? I'm freezing.* セントラルヒーティングをつけませんか. 凍えそうです. *Put a coat on, it's absolutely freezing outside.* コートを着なさい. 外は絶対に凍えるほど寒いから.

**freezing**² /fríːzɪŋ/（または **freezing point**）名 U ▶定義 the temperature at which water freezes 水が凍る温度 →氷点，摂氏０度‖ *Last night the temperature fell to six degrees below freezing.* 昨夜は気温が零下６度まで下がった.

**freight** /freɪt/ 名 U ▶定義 goods that are carried from one place to another by ship, lorry, etc; the system for carrying goods in this way 船またはトラックなどである場所からほかの場

所へ運ばれる品物; そのようにして品物を運ぶシステム ➡ (運送・空輸)貨物, 積み荷, 船荷, 貨物運送, 普通貨物便 ‖ *Your order will be sent by air freight.* ご注文の品物は航空普通貨物便で届けられます. *a freight train* 貨物列車

**freighter** /fréɪtər/ 名 C ▶定義 a ship or an aircraft that carries only goods and not passengers 乗客ではなく貨物だけを運ぶ船または航空機 ➡ 貨物船, 貨物輸送機

**French window** (米 **French door**) 名 C
▶定義 one of a pair of glass doors that open onto a garden or balcony 庭またはバルコニーに向かって開く, 一組のガラス戸の1枚1枚 ➡ フランス窓

**frenzied** /frénzid/ 形 ▶定義 that is wild and out of control 狂気染みていて制御しきれない ➡ 凶暴な, 狂乱した, 熱狂した, 逆上した, 取り乱した ‖ *a frenzied attack* 怒とうの攻撃 *frenzied activity* 狂乱した行動

**frenzy** /frénzi/ 名 [単数扱い, U] ▶定義 a state of great emotion or activity that is not under control 制御されていない強い感情または行動の状態 ➡ 熱狂, 狂乱, 乱心, 取り乱すこと, 大慌て ‖ *There's no need to get **in a frenzy** - you've got until Friday to finish your essay.* 慌てる必要はありません-小論文は金曜日までに仕上げればいいのだから. *I could hear a frenzy of activity in the kitchen.* 台所で大騒ぎしているのが聞こえた.

**frequency** /frí:kwənsi/ 名 (複 **frequencies**)
▶定義1 U the number of times sth happens in a particular period ある特定の期間に~が起こる回数 ➡ 頻度, 度々, 回数 ‖ *Fatal accidents have decreased in frequency in recent years.* 近年, 死亡事故の発生頻度は減少している.
▶定義2 U the fact that sth happens often ~がしばしば起こること ➡ 頻繁, 頻発, よくあること, しばしば起こること ‖ *The frequency of child deaths from cancer near the nuclear power station is being investigated.* 原子力発電所の近くでがんによる子供の死亡が多いことについて調査が行われている.
▶定義3 C U the rate at which a sound wave or radio wave moves up and down (vibrates) 音波または電波が強くなったり弱くなったりする(振動する)割合 ➡ 周波数, 振動数 ‖ *high-frequency/low-frequency sounds* 高周波・低周波の音

*★**frequent**¹ /frí:kwənt/ 形 ▶定義 happening often しばしば起こっている ➡ 度々の, 頻繁な, よくある, 度々~する ‖ *His visits became less frequent.* 彼はあまり訪ねてこなくなった. ⇔ **infrequent** ― **frequently** 副 ➡ 度々, しばしば, しょっちゅう, 頻繁に

**frequent**² /fríkwént, frí:kwənt/ 動 他 正式 ▶定義 to go to a place often ある場所にしばしば行く ➡ ~によく行く, 常に出入りする, 頻繁に訪れる ‖ *He spent most of his evenings in Paris frequenting bars and clubs.* パリでは彼は大抵の晩をバーやクラブによく出掛けて過ごした.

*★**fresh** /freʃ/ 形 ▶定義1 (used especially about food) produced or picked very recently; not frozen or in a tin (特に食品について)ごく最近に作られた, またはとられた; 冷凍されていない, または缶詰に入っていない ➡ 新鮮な, 出来立ての, 生の, 冷凍したものでない ‖ *fresh bread/fruit/flowers* 焼き立てのパン・新鮮な果物・摘んだばかりの花 ☛参 **stale** ▶定義2 left somewhere or experienced recently 最近どこかに残された, または経験された ➡ 鮮やかな, 鮮明な, できたばかりの, 生々しい ‖ *fresh blood/footprints* 鮮血・付いたばかりの足跡 *Write a few notes while the lecture is still **fresh in your mind**.* その講義がまだ記憶に新しいうちに, メモを取っておきなさい. ▶定義3 new and different 新しくて異なる ➡ 新規の, 新たな, 斬新(ざんしん)な, 独創的な ‖ *They have decided to **make a fresh start** in a different town.* 彼らは別の町で再出発することを決心した. *I'm sure he'll have some fresh ideas on the subject.* 彼はきっとこの問題について何か斬新な考えを思い付くはずだ. ▶定義4 (used about water) without salt; not sea water (水について)塩を含まない; 海水でない ➡ 塩気のない, 塩分のない, 無塩の, 淡水の, 真水の ▶定義5 pleasantly clean or bright 心地良くきれいな, または明るい ➡ 清らかな, すがすがしい, さわやかな, 新鮮な ‖ *Open the window and let some **fresh air** in.* 窓を開けて新鮮な空気を入れてください. ▶定義6 not tired 疲れていない ➡ 元気な, 生き生きした, はつらつとした, 活発な ‖ *I'll think about the problem again in the morning when I'm fresh.* 元気である朝のうちに, その問題をもう一度考えてみよう. ▶定義7 **fresh from/out of sth** having

just finished sth ～を終えたばかりである➡～したばかりの, ～から出立ての ‖ *Life isn't easy for a young teacher fresh from university.* 大学を出たばかりの若い教師にとっては毎日が大変だ. ― **freshly** 副➡ 新しく, 新たに, 新鮮に, 生き生きと, はつらつと ‖ *freshly baked bread* 焼き立てのパン ― **freshness** 名 U➡ 新鮮さ, 新鮮味, 生々しさ, 生き生きしていること, さわやかさ

感句 **break fresh/new ground** ⇒ **GROUND**¹

**freshen** /fréʃ(ə)n/ 動 他 定義 **freshen sth (up)** to make sth cleaner or brighter ～をきれいに, または明るくする➡～を新鮮にする, 新しくする, 一新する ‖ *Some new curtains and wallpaper would freshen up this room.* カーテンと壁紙を新しくすれば, この部屋は見違えるようにきれいになるでしょう.

句動詞 **freshen up** 定義 to wash and make yourself clean and tidy 自分自身を洗い, 清潔にきちんとする➡さっぱりする, すっきりする

**fresher** /fréʃər/ 名 C 英 定義 a student who is in his/her first year at university, college, etc 総合大学または単科大学などの 1 年生である学生➡新入生, 1 年生

**freshman** /fréʃmən/ 名 C (複 **-men**/-mən/) 定義 a student who is in his/her first year at college, high school, university, etc 単科大学, 高校, 総合大学などの 1 年生である学生➡新入生, 1 年生

**fret**¹ /fret/ 動 自 (**fretting**; **fretted**) 定義 **fret (about/at/over sth)** to be worried and unhappy about sth ～について心配して不安である➡～のことでいらいらする, やきもきする, 心配する, 気に病む, 思い悩む ‖ *I was awake for hours fretting about my exams.* 私は試験のことが不安で, 何時間も眠れなかった.

**fret**² /fret/ 名 C 定義 one of the bars across the long thin part of a guitar, etc that show you where to put your fingers to produce a particular sound ある特定の音を出すために指を置く場所を示す, ギターなどの細長い部分と交差している棒の 1 つ 1 つ➡フレット ☞参 **music** のさし絵

**Fri** 略 Friday➡金曜日 ‖ *Fri 27 May* 5 月 27 日金曜日

**friction** /fríkʃ(ə)n/ 名 U 定義 **1** the rubbing of one surface or thing against another 1 つの面または物をほかの面または物とこすり合わせること➡摩擦, こすること ‖ *You have to put oil in the engine to reduce friction between the moving parts.* 可動部品の間の摩擦を減らすため, エンジンに油を差す必要がある. 定義 **2** **friction (between A and B)** disagreement between people or groups 人々または集団の間の意見の相違➡不和, いさかい, あつれき, 摩擦, 衝突 ‖ *There is a lot of friction between the older and younger members of staff.* スタッフの中の年長者と若手の間には多くのあつれきがある.

***Friday** /fráɪdeɪ, -di/ 名 C U (略 **Fri**) 定義 the day of the week after Thursday 木曜日の次の曜日➡金曜日

▶曜日は最初の文字を必ず大文字で書く. 文中での曜日の使い方の例については, **Monday** を参照.

***fridge** /frɪdʒ/ (または 正式 **refrigerator**, 米 **icebox**) 名 C 定義 a metal container with a door in which food, etc is kept cold (but not frozen) so that it stays fresh ドアの付いた金属の容器で, その中で食品などを新鮮なままにしておくために (凍らせずに) 低温に保っている➡冷蔵庫 ☞参 **freezer** ☞ C7 ページのさし絵

***friend** /frend/ 名 C 定義 **1** a person that you know and like (not a member of your family), and who likes you 自分が知っていて好ましく思っている人 (家族の一員ではない) で, 相手も自分を好ましく思ってくれている人➡友, 友達, 友人, 仲良し ‖ *Trevor and I are old friends. We were at school together.* トレヴァーと私は旧友だ. 私たちは同じ学校に通った. *We're only inviting close friends and relatives to the wedding.* 私たちは結婚式に親しい友人と親戚 (しんせき) だけを招待している. *Helen's my best friend.* ヘレンは私の親友だ. *A friend of mine told me about this restaurant.* 私の友達の 1 人がこのレストランのことを教えてくれた. *One of my friends told me about this restaurant.* 私の友達の 1 人がこのレストランのことを教えてくれた. ☞参 **boyfriend**, **girlfriend**, **penfriend** 定義 **2** **a friend of/to sth** a person who supports an organization, a charity, etc, especially by giving money; a person who supports a particular idea, etc ある組織または慈善事業などを, 特に金を出して, 支援する人; ある特定の考

えなどを支持する人→**支持者, 後援者, 共鳴者, 味方** ‖ *the Friends of the Churchill Hospital* チャーチル病院の後援者

**成句** **be/make friends (with sb)** to be/become a friend (of sb) （～の）友達である・友達になる→**～と親しい, 仲良くしている, 親しくなる, 友達を作る, 仲良くなる, 友人ができる** ‖ *Tony is rather shy and finds it hard to make friends.* トニーはかなり内気で, 友達を作るのが難しいと感じている.

**a false friend** ⇒ **FALSE**

*****friendly**¹ /fréndli/ 形 (**friendlier;friendliest**)
▶定義1 friendly (to/toward(s) sb) behaving in a kind and open way 親切で率直に振る舞っている→**好意的な, 親切な, 優しい** ‖ *Everyone here has been very friendly towards us.* ここの人たちは皆, 私たちにとても親切だった.
▶定義2 showing kindness in a way that makes people feel happy and relaxed 人に幸福でくつろいでいると感じさせるようにして, 親切さを示している→**人懐こい, 親しみのある, 居心地の良い, 歓迎する** ‖ *a friendly smile/atmosphere* 人懐こい笑み・居心地の良い雰囲気 ⇔ 定義1, 2 **unfriendly** ▶定義3 friendly with sb treating sb as a friend ～を友達として扱っている→**～と親しい, 仲が良い, 友好的な, 友人の** ‖ *Nick's become quite friendly with the boy next door.* ニックは隣の家の少年ととても仲良くなった. *Are you on friendly terms with your neighbours?* 近所とはうまくいっていますか.
▶定義4 （複合語で） helpful to sb/sth; not harmful to sth ～の助けとなる；～に害を与えない→**～に役立つ, 好都合な, 分かりやすい, 使いやすい, 優しい** ‖ *Our computer is extremely **user-friendly**.* 当社のコンピューターは, ユーザーにとって, とても使いやすい. *ozone-friendly sprays* オゾンを破壊しないスプレー ▶定義5 in which the people, teams, etc taking part are not competing seriously 参加している人々, チームなどが真剣に競争していないような→**友好的な, 親善の, 親睦（しんぼく）のための, 敵意のない** ‖ *a friendly argument* 友好的な議論 *I've organized a friendly match against my brother's team.* 私は兄のチームとの親善試合を計画した. ─ **friendliness** 名 **U**→**友情, 親切, 好意, 親善, 親睦**
**friendly**² /fréndli/ 名 **C** （複 **friendlies**） ▶定義 a sports match that is not part of a serious competition 真剣な競争の一部ではないスポーツの試合→**親善試合, 親睦（しんぼく）試合**

*****friendship** /fréndʃɪp/ 名 ▶定義1 **O** a friendship (with sb); a friendship (between A and B) a relationship between people who are friends 友人である人々の間の関係→**友人関係, 友達であること, 親交, 交際** ‖ *a close/lasting/lifelong friendship* 親しい・長続きする・生涯の友人関係 ▶定義2 **O** the state of being friends 友達である状態→**友情, 友愛, 親睦（しんぼく）** ‖ *Our relationship is based on friendship, not love.* 私たちの関係は恋愛ではなく友情に基づいている.

**fright** /fráɪt/ 名 **C U** ▶定義 a sudden feeling of fear or shock 突然の恐怖感またはショックの気持ち→**激しい恐怖, 驚き** ‖ *I hope I didn't give you a fright when I shouted.* 私が叫んだ時にあなたを驚かせたのでなければいいのですが. *The child cried out in fright.* 子供はぎょっとして叫んだ.

*****frighten** /fráɪtn/ 動 他 ▶定義 to make sb/sth afraid or shocked ～を怖がらせる, または衝撃を与える→**～をおびえさせる, びっくりさせる, ぞっとさせる, ぎょっとさせる** ‖ *That programme about crime really frightened me.* 犯罪についてのその番組を見て私は本当にぞっとした.
**句動詞** frighten sb/sth away/off ▶定義 to cause a person or animal to go away by frightening him/her/it 人または動物を怖がらせて立ち去らせる→**～を脅して追い払う, 驚かせて～を追い立てる** ‖ *Walk quietly so that you don't frighten the birds away.* 鳥たちが驚いて逃げないように静かに歩きなさい.

*****frightened** /fráɪtnd/ 形 ▶定義1 full of fear or worry 恐怖または不安で一杯の→**おびえた, ぎょっとした** ‖ *Frightened children were calling for their mothers.* おびえた子供たちが母親を呼んでいた. *I was frightened that they would think that I was rude.* 彼らが私のことを無礼だと思うのではないかと不安だった. ▶定義2 frightened of sb/sth afraid of a particular person, thing or situation ある特定の人, 物または状態を恐れる→**～を怖がって, ～が怖くて** ‖ *When I was young I was frightened of spiders.* 私は幼いころ, クモが怖かった. ☞参 **afraid** の注

***frightening** /fráɪtnɪŋ/ [形] ▸定義 making you feel afraid or shocked 怖がらせたり衝撃を与えている ➜**恐ろしい, ぞっとする, ぎょっとさせるような, 驚くべき** ‖ *a frightening experience* ぞっとするような経験 *It's frightening that time passes so quickly.* 時間がそんなに早くたつとは驚きだ.

**frightful** /fráɪtfʊl, -f(ə)l/ [形] (古) ▸定義1 very bad or unpleasant 非常に悪い, または不快な ➜**恐ろしい, ぞっとするような, ひどい, 全く不愉快な** ‖ *The weather this summer has been frightful.* この夏の天気は実にひどいものだった. ▸定義2 (used for emphasizing sth) very bad or great (〜を強調するために用いて) 非常に悪い, または際立った ➜**大変な, 非常な, ひどい, すごい** ‖ *We're in a frightful rush.* 私たちはものすごく急いでいる.

**frightfully** /fráɪtfʊli, -f(ə)li/ [副] (古) ▸定義 very 非常に ➜**とても, 大変, すごく, ひどく** ‖ *I'm frightfully sorry.* 本当にすみません.

**frill** /frɪl/ [名] [C] ▸定義1 a decoration for the edge of a dress, shirt, etc which is made by forming many folds in a narrow piece of cloth 細長い布に多くの折り目を付けて作られる, ワンピース, シャツなどの縁の飾り ➜**フリル, ひだ飾り, 縁飾り** ▸定義2 [通常は複数] something that is added for decoration that you feel is not necessary 飾りとして付け加えられているが必要ないと思われるもの ➜**余分なもの, 装飾的なもの, 無駄なもの, ごてごてした装飾** ‖ *We just want a plain simple meal - no frills.* 私たちはごく簡単な食事がしたいのです－ぜいたくな物は要りません. — **frilly** [形] ➜**フリルの付いた, 多くのひだ飾りの, 本質的でない, 重要でない** ‖ *a frilly dress* フリルの付いたドレス

**fringe**[1] /frɪndʒ/ [名] [C] ▸定義1 ([米] **bangs** [複数扱い]) the part of your hair that is cut so that it hangs over your forehead 額に垂れかかるように切られた髪の部分 ➜**前髪, 切下げ前髪** ‖ *Your hair looks better with a fringe.* あなたの髪は前髪を切った方が似合いますよ. ☛ **hair** のさし絵 ▸定義2 a border for decoration on a piece of clothing, etc that is made of lots of hanging threads 垂れ下がった多くの糸からできている, 布などの装飾用の縁 ➜**房べり, 房飾り, 縁飾り** ▸定義3 [英] the outer edge of an area or a group that is a long way from the centre or from what is usual 中心または通常のものからは遠く離れている, ある範囲または集団の外縁 ➜**縁, へり, 外辺, 周辺 (部), 二次的なもの, 非主流派** ‖ *Some people* ***on the fringes of*** *the socialist party are opposed to the policy on Europe.* 労働党の非主流派の中には欧州政策に反対している者もいる.

**fringe**[2] /frɪndʒ/ [動]
[成句] **be fringed with sth** ▸定義 to have sth as a border or around the edge 縁として, または縁の周りに〜がある ➜**〜を…で縁取る, 囲む** ‖ *The lake was fringed with pine trees.* その湖に沿って松の木が並んでいた.

**fringe benefit** [名] [C, 通常は複数] ▸定義 an extra thing that is given to an employee in addition to the money he/she earns 稼いだ金に加えて従業員に与えられる余分のもの ➜**付加給付** ‖ *The fringe benefits of this job include a car and free health insurance.* この仕事の付加給付には, 車と無料の健康保険が含まれます. ☛ perk の方がくだけた言い方である.

**frisk** /frɪsk/ [動] ▸定義1 [他] to pass your hands over sb's body in order to search for hidden weapons, drugs, etc 隠された武器または麻薬などを捜すために, 〜の体を触る ➜**〜の身体検査をする, 〜のボディーチェックをする** ▸定義2 [自] (used about an animal or child) to play and jump about happily and with a lot of energy (動物または子供について) うれしそうに元気一杯に遊び, 跳ね回る ➜**飛び回る, じゃれる, はしゃぐ, ふざける**

**frisky** /fríski/ [形] ▸定義 full of life and wanting to play 元気一杯で遊びたがっている ➜**活発な, 陽気な, はしゃいでいる, よくじゃれる**

**fritter** /frítər/ [動]
[句動詞] **fritter sth away (on sth)** ▸定義 to waste time or money on things that are not important 重要でないものに時間または金を浪費する ➜**〜をつまらぬ事に費やす, 浪費する, 無駄に使う**

**frivolity** /frɪvɑ́ləti/ [名] [U] ▸定義 silly behaviour (especially when you should be serious) (特にまじめにしているべきときの) 愚かな振る舞い ➜**軽薄, 浮薄, 浅薄, 軽率, 不まじめ**

**frivolous** /frív(ə)ləs/ [形] ▸定義 not serious; silly まじめではない; 愚かな ➜**軽薄な, 浅薄な, 浮つい**

た, 軽々しい

**frizzy** /frízi/ 形 ▶定義 (used about hair) with a lot of very small tight curls (髪について) 非常に小さなきつい巻き毛がたくさんある→細かく縮れている, 縮れ毛の

**fro** /fróu/ 副
成句 to and fro ⇒ **TO**

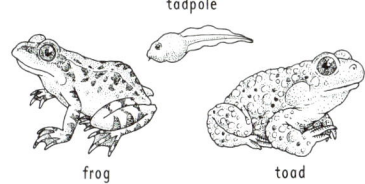

**frog** /fró(:)g, frág/ 名 ● ▶定義 a small animal with smooth skin and long back legs that it uses for jumping. Frogs live in or near water. 滑らかな皮膚と, 跳ねるために使う長い後ろ足を持った小動物. 水中または水の近くに生息する→カエル

**frogman** /frágmæn, -mən/ 名 ● (複) **-men** /-mèn, -mən/) ▶定義 a person whose job is to work under the surface of water wearing special rubber clothes and using breathing equipment 特別なゴムの服を着て呼吸装置を使い, 水面下で働くことを仕事とする人→潜水夫, 潜水工作員, 水中処理兵 ‖ *Police frogmen searched the river.* 警察の潜水夫たちがその川を捜索した.

\***from** /frəm, 強形 frɑm, frʌm/ 前 ▶定義 **1** showing the place, direction or time that sb/sth starts or started ~が出発する, または出発した場所, 方向, あるいは時間を示している→~から(ずっと), ~以来 ‖ *She comes home from work at 7 o'clock.* 彼女は7時に仕事を終えて家へ帰る. *a cold wind from the east* 東からの冷たい風 *Water was dripping from the tap.* 蛇口から水が滴っていた. *Peter's on holiday from next Friday.* ピーターは次の金曜日から休暇を取る. *The supermarket is open from 8am till 8pm every day.* そのスーパーマーケットは毎日午前8時から午後8時まで開いている. ▶定義 **2** showing the person who sent or gave sth ~を送った, または与えた人を示している→~から(の) ‖ *I borrowed this jacket from my sister.* 私はこの上着を妹から借りた. *a phone call from my father* 父からの電話 ▶定義 **3** showing the origin of sb/sth ~の起源を示している→~からの, ~出身の, ~産の, ~に由来する ‖ *'Where do you come from?' 'I'm from Australia.'* 「ご出身はどちらですか」「オーストラリアです」 *cheeses from France and Italy* フランス産とイタリア産のチーズ *quotations from Shakespeare* シェークスピアからの引用 ▶定義 **4** showing the material which is used to make sth ~を作るために使用された原料を示している→~から, ~で(でき た), ~製の ‖ *Paper is **made from** wood.* 紙は木から作られる. *This sauce is made from cream and wine.* このソースはクリームとワインから作られている.

➤ made of は, 材料その物自体で成り立っている, ということを表す: *a table made of wood* (木製のテーブル) *a house made of bricks* (レンガ作りの家)

▶定義 **5** showing the distance between two places 2つの場所の間の距離を示している→~から(離れて) ‖ *The house is five miles from the town centre.* その家は町の中心から5マイル離れている. *I work not far from here.* 私はここからそう遠くない所で働いている. ▶定義 **6** showing the point at which a series of prices, figures, etc. start 一連の価格, 数字などが始まる点を示している→~から ‖ *Our prices start from £2.50 a bottle.* 価格は1びん2.50ポンドからです. *Tickets cost from £3 to £11.* チケットの値段は3ポンドから11ポンドまでです. ▶定義 **7** showing the state of sb/sth before a change 変化の前の~の状態を示している→~から ‖ *The time of the meeting has been changed **from** 7 **to** 8 o'clock.* 会議の時間が7時から8時に変更になりました. *The article was translated **from** Russian **into** English.* その記事はロシア語から英語に翻訳された. *Things have gone **from bad to worse**.* 事態は悪化した. ▶定義 **8** showing that sb/sth is taken away, removed or separated from sb/sth else ~がほかの…から取り去られた, 取り除かれた, または分離されたことを示している→~から(取って), ~から離して ‖ *Children don't like being separated from their parents for a long period.* 子供たちは長期間, 両親から引き離されることを嫌がる. *(in mathematics) 8 from 12 leaves 4.* (数学で) 12から8

を引くと4になる. ▶定義9 showing sth that you want to avoid 避けたい〜を示している➔〜から(避けて), 〜から防いで, 〜しないように ‖ *There was no shelter from the wind.* 風を避けられる場所がなかった. *This game will stop you from getting bored.* このゲームなら退屈することはありません. ▶定義10 showing the cause of sth 〜の原因を示している➔〜から, 〜で, 〜によって, 〜のために ‖ *People in the camps are suffering from hunger and cold.* キャンプの人々は飢えと寒さに苦しんでいる. ▶定義11 showing the reason for making a judgement or forming an opinion 判断をする, または意見をまとめる理由を示している➔〜から, 〜によって, 〜に基づいて, 〜を根拠として ‖ *You can tell quite a lot from a person's handwriting.* 人の筆跡からかなり多くの事が分かる. ▶定義12 showing the difference between two people, places or things 2人, 2つの場所, または2つの物の違いを示している➔〜から, 〜と(違って) ‖ *Can you tell margarine from butter?* マーガリンとバターを区別できますか. *Is Portuguese very different from Spanish?* ポルトガル語はスペイン語とかなり違うのですか.

成句 from...on ▶定義 starting at a particular time and continuing for ever ある特定の時間に始まって永久に続いている➔〜以降, 〜から以後ずっと, これからずっと ‖ *She never spoke to him again from that day on.* 彼女はその日以降, 二度と彼に話し掛けなかった. ***From now on** you must earn your own living.* これからは自分で生活費を稼がなくてはなりません.

\***front**¹ /frʌnt/ 名 ▶定義1 **the front** [ C, 通常は単数] the side or surface of sth/sb that faces forward 〜の, 前を向いている側または面➔前(面), 正面, 表(面) ‖ *a dress with buttons down the front* 前面にボタンが縦に並んでいるワンピース *the front of a building* (= the front wall) 建物の正面(= 正面の壁) *a card with flowers **on the front*** 表に花の付いたカード *She slipped on the stairs and spilt coffee all down her front.* 彼女は階段で滑って, コーヒーを服の前面に掛けてしまった. ▶定義2 **the front** [ C, 通常は単数] the most forward part of sth; the area that is just outside of or before sb/sth 〜の最も前の部分; 〜のすぐ外側, または前の部分➔**最前部・列, 先頭, 前部・方** ‖ *Young children should not travel **in the front of** the car.* 幼い子供は車の前の席に乗るべきではない. *There is a small garden **at the front of** the house.* その家の前には小さな庭がある.

▶ **on the front of** は「〜の前面に」を意味する: *The number is shown on the front of the bus.* (番号はバスの前面に表示されています.) **in front (of sth)** は「ほかの人または物より前に; ほかの〜の前に」を意味する: *A car has stopped in front of the bus.* (バスの前に車が止まった.) *There were three people in front of me in the queue.* (その行列には私の前に3人の人がいた.) **at/in the front (of sth)** は「〜の内部の最も前の部分に」を意味する: *The driver sits at the front of the bus.* (運転手はバスの前の席に座る.) 以下の文も参照のこと: *The teacher usually stands in front of the class.* (教師は通常, 教室の前の方に立つ.) *The noisy children were asked to sit at the front of the class* (= in the front seats). (騒々しい子供たちは教室の前の方に(= 前の方の席に)座るように言われた.)

▶定義3 C a particular area of activity 行動のある特定の範囲➔**活動の場, 活動領域, 活動範囲, 分野, 方面** ‖ *Things are difficult **on the** domestic/political/economic **front** at the moment.* 現在は家庭・政治・経済面で困難な状況である. *Progress has been made **on all fronts**.* あらゆる局面で進歩した. ▶定義4 **the front** [単数扱い] the line or area where fighting takes place in a war 戦争で戦闘が起こる境界線または範囲➔**最前線, 戦線, 戦場, 戦地** ‖ *to be sent to the front* 戦地へ送られる ▶定義5 [単数扱い] a way of behaving that hides your true feelings 本当の感情を隠すような振る舞い方➔**見せ掛け, 素振り, 体裁, 外見上の態度** ‖ *His brave words were just a front. He was really feeling very nervous.* 彼の勇敢な言葉は単なる見せ掛けにすぎなかった. 彼は本当はとても神経質になっていたのだった. ▶定義6 C a line or area where warm air and cold air meet 暖かい空気と冷たい空気が出会う境界線または範囲➔**前線** ‖ *A cold front is moving in from the north.* 寒冷前線が北からやって来ている.

成句 back to front ⇒ **BACK**¹

in front ▶定義 further forward than sb/sth; ahead ～より前に; 先に➜**前(方)に, 前部に, 先(頭)に, リードして, 人目に付く所に** ‖ *Some of the children ran on in front.* 何人かの子供たちが前方へ走った. *After three laps the Kenyan runner was in front.* 3周した後, ケニアの走者が先頭に立った.

in front of sb/sth ▶定義 **1** in a position further forward than but close to sb/sth ～より前だが近い位置に➜**～の前に, ～の正面に** ‖ *The bus stops right in front of our house.* バスは私たちの家の真ん前に止まる. *Don't stand in front of the television.* テレビの前に立たないでください. *The book was open in front of her on the desk.* 机の上の彼女の真ん前に本が開いてあった. ☛ in front of は opposite と同じ意味ではない. ☛ **opposite** のさし絵 ▶定義 **2** if you do sth in front of sb, you do it when that person is there in the same room or place as you. ～の前で…をすると言う場合は, その～が自分と同じ部屋または場所にいるときにするということである➜**～の(面)前で, ～の眼前で, ～のいる所で** ‖ *I couldn't talk about that in front of my parents.* 私は両親の前ではそれについて話せなかった.

up front [略式] ▶定義 as payment before sth is done ～が行われる前の支払いとして➜**前金で, 前払いで** ‖ *I want half the money up front and half when the job is finished.* 半額を前金で, 残りの半額をその仕事が終わったときに支払ってもらいたい.

**front**[2] /frʌnt/ [形] (名詞の前だけ) ▶定義 of or at the front (1,2) (front[1](1,2) の意味の) 前の, または前にある➜**正面の, (最)前面の, 表の** ‖ *the front door/garden/room* 正面玄関・前庭・居間 *sit in the front row* 最前列に座る *front teeth* 前歯

**frontal** /frʌ́ntl/ [形] (名詞の前だけ) ▶定義 from the front 前からの➜**正面の, 前面の, 正面からの, 前面からの** ‖ *a frontal attack* 正面攻撃

**frontier** /frʌntíər, ⌐ ⌐/ [名] ▶定義 **1** [C] the frontier (between A and B) the line where one country joins another; border ある国がほかの国と接する線; 境界➜**国境** ‖ *The end of frontier controls in Europe.* ヨーロッパにおける国境での検問の終焉(しゅうえん) ☛参 **border** の注 ▶定義 **2** [複数扱い] **the frontiers** the limit between what we do and do not know 人が知っている事と知らない事の境界➜**限界, 最先端, 未開拓の領域, 未知の領域, 新分野** ‖ *Scientific research is constantly* ***pushing back the frontiers of*** *our knowledge about the world.* 科学研究は絶えず, 世界についての我々の知識の限界を押し広げている.

**front-page** [形] ▶定義 interesting or important enough to appear on the front page of a newspaper 新聞の第1面に載るほど十分に興味深い, または重要な➜**新聞の第1面向きの, 新聞の第1面にふさわしい, 重要な** ‖ *front-page news/headlines* トップニュース・新聞の第1面にふさわしい見出し

***frost**[1] /frɔ(:)st, frɑst/ [名] [C] [U] ▶定義 the weather condition when the temperature falls below 0° Celsius (freezing point) and a thin layer of ice forms on the ground and other surfaces, especially at night 気温が摂氏0度(氷点)以下に下がり, 特に夜に, 薄い氷が地面またはそのほかの表面に張るような天候状態➜**(降)霜, 寒気, 氷点下の冷え込み, 厳寒** ‖ *There was a* ***hard frost*** *last night.* 昨夜はひどく冷え込んだ. *It will be a chilly night with some* ***ground frost****.* 地面に霜が降りるような肌寒い夜になるだろう.

**frost**[2] /frɔ(:)st, frɑst/ [動] [他] 特に [米] = **ICE**[2]

[句動詞] frost over/up ▶定義 to become covered with a thin layer of ice 氷の薄い層で覆われる➜**霜で覆われる, 一面に霜が降りる** ‖ *The window has frosted over/up.* その窓は霜で覆われた. ☛参 **defrost**

**frostbite** /frɔ́(:)stbàɪt, frɑ́st-/ [名] [U] ▶定義 a serious medical condition of the fingers, toes, etc that is caused by very low temperatures 非常に低い温度によって引き起こされる, 手の指または足の指などの重い症状➜**霜焼け, 凍傷** ‖ *All the climbers were suffering from frostbite.* 登山者全員が凍傷になっていた.

**frosted** /frɔ́(:)stəd, frɑ́st-/ [形] ▶定義 (used about glass or a window) with a special surface so you cannot see through it (ガラスまたは窓について) 透けて見えないように特殊な表面をしている➜**つや消しの, すりガラスの**

**frosting** /frɔ́(:)stɪŋ, frɑ́st- / 特に [米] = **ICING**

**frosty** /frɔ́(:)sti, frɑ́st-/ [形] ▶定義 **1** very cold, with frost とても寒く, 霜の降りている➜**凍るように寒い, 霜の降るほど寒い, 霜で覆われた** ‖ *a cold*

F

and frosty morning 寒くて霜の降りた朝 ▶定義2 cold and unfriendly 冷たく, 友好的でない→冷たい, 冷ややかな, 冷淡な, よそよそしい ‖ a frosty welcome 冷たい歓迎

**froth**[1] /frɔ(ː)θ, frɑθ/ 名 ⓤ ▶定義 a mass of small white bubbles on the top of a liquid, etc 液体などの表面の小さな白い泡の塊→泡, あぶく — **frothy** 形→泡の多い, 泡立った, 泡だらけの, 泡のような ‖ frothy beer 泡立ったビール a frothy cappuccino 泡の多いカプチーノ

**froth**[2] /frɔ(ː)θ, frɑθ/ 動⾃ ▶定義 to have or produce a mass of white bubbles 白い泡の塊がある, または生じる→泡立つ, 泡を吹く ‖ The mad dog was frothing at the mouth. その狂犬は口から泡を吹いていた.

**frown** /fráun/ 動⾃ ▶定義 to show you are angry, serious, etc by making lines appear on your forehead above your nose 額の鼻の上にしわを寄せて, 怒っていることまたは真剣であることなどを示す→顔をしかめる, まゆをひそめる, しかめっ面をする, 難しい顔をする — **frown** 名 ⓒ→しかめっ面, 渋い顔, 真剣な顔付き, まゆをひそめること

句動詞 **frown on/upon sth** ▶定義 to disapprove of sth ~に不賛成である→~に賛成しない, 難色を示す, 嫌な顔をする, ~を認めない ‖ Smoking is very much frowned upon these days. 最近では喫煙が非常に嫌がられることが多い.

**froze** FREEZE[1] の過去形
**frozen**[1] FREEZE[1] の過去分詞形
**frozen**[2] /fróuzn/ 形 ▶定義1 (used about food) stored at a low temperature in order to keep it for a long time (食品について) 長く保存するために低温で保管されている→凍った, 冷凍の, 冷凍した ‖ frozen meat/vegetables 冷凍の肉・野菜 ▶定義2 略式 (used about people and parts of the body) very cold (人またはその体の部分について) 非常に寒い→凍えそうな, 凍死しそうな, 体が凍りそうな, 極寒の ‖ My feet are frozen! 足が凍えそうだ. I was frozen stiff. 私は寒さで体がこわばった. ⬅類 **freezing** ▶定義3 (used about water) with a layer of ice on the surface (水について) 表面に氷の層がある→凍った, 氷結した ‖ The pond is frozen. Let's go skating. 池が凍っている. スケートに行こう.

**\*fruit** /fruːt/ 名 ▶定義1 ⓒ ⓤ the part of a plant or tree that contains seeds and that we eat 植物または木の, 種を含み, 食用にする部分→果物, 果実 ‖ Try and eat more **fresh fruit** and vegetables. 新鮮な果物と野菜をもっとたくさん食べるようにしなさい. Marmalade is made with **citrus fruit** (= oranges, lemons, grapefruit, etc). マーマレードは, かんきつ類の果物 (= オレンジ, レモン, グレープフルーツなど) から作られる a **fruit juice** 果汁
▶ a fruit と言うときは, 「果物の種類」を意味する: Most big supermarkets sell all sorts of tropical fruits. (多くの大型スーパーマーケットでは, あらゆる種類のトロピカルフルーツを売っている.) 個々の果物について言う場合は, 通常その果物の名前を用いる: Would you like an apple? (リンゴはいかがですか.) または不可算形を用いる: Would you like some fruit? (何か果物はいかがですか.)

▶定義2 ⓒ the part of any plant in which the seed is formed 植物の, 種子が作られる部分→果実, 実 ▶定義3 [複数扱い] **the fruits (of sth)** a good result or success from work that you have done 自分がした仕事の良い結果または成功→成果, 結果, 産物, 所産 ‖ It will be years before we see the fruits of this research. この研究の成果が現れるまでには何年もかかるだろう.
成句 **bear fruit** ⇒ **BEAR**[2]

**fruitful** /frúːtfʊl, -f(ə)l/ 形 ▶定義 producing good results; useful 良い結果を生み出している; 有益な→実りの多い, 有益な, 良い結果を生む, 成果を上げた, 有利な, 成功した ‖ fruitful discussions 実りの多い議論

**fruition** /fruːíʃ(ə)n/ 名 ⓤ 正式 ▶定義 the time when a plan, etc starts to be successful 計画などが成功し始めるとき→達成, 実現, 成功, 成果 ‖ After months of hard work, our efforts were **coming to fruition**. 何か月もの熱心な研究の結果, 私たちの努力が実を結ぼうとしていた.

**fruitless** /frúːtləs/ 形 ▶定義 producing poor or no results; not successful 不十分な結果を生み出している, または何の結果も生み出していない; 成功していない→実を結ばない, 成果の上がらない, いい結果を生まない, 効果のない, 無益な, むなしい ‖ a fruitless search 成果の上がらない捜索

**frustrate** /frʌ̀stréit/ 動⾃ ▶定義1 to cause a

person to feel annoyed or impatient because he/she cannot do or achieve what he/she wants 人が自分の望む事をするまたは達成することができないため、その人を不愉快に感じさせるあるいはいらいらさせる→～に挫折(ざせつ)感を与える、～を失望させる、～に欲求不満を感じさせる‖ *It's the lack of money that really frustrates him.* 彼を本当にいら立たせているのは、お金がないことである. ▶定義2 正式 to prevent sb from doing sth or sth from happening ～が…をするのを防ぐ、または～が起こるのを妨げる→～を失敗させる、挫折させる、無効にする、駄目にする‖ *The rescue work has been frustrated by bad weather conditions.* 救助作業は悪天候に阻まれている. — **frustrated** 形→欲求不満の、フラストレーションのたまった、挫折した、くじけた、失意の、がっかりした‖ *He felt very frustrated at his lack of progress in learning Chinese.* 中国語の勉強が進まないので彼はとてもフラストレーションがたまっていた. — **frustrating** 形→いら立たしい、欲求不満に陥らせるような、挫折感を引き起こす

**frustration** /frʌstréɪʃ(ə)n/ 名 ⓒⓊ ▶定義 a feeling of anger because you cannot get what you want; sth that causes you to feel like this 望むものを得られないことによる怒りの感情; そのように感じさせる～→フラストレーション、いら立ち、欲求不満(の原因)‖ *He felt anger and frustration at no longer being able to see very well.* もう目があまりよく見えないことに、彼は怒りといら立ちを感じた. *Every job has its frustrations.* どのような仕事にも欲求不満の原因となるものはある.

\***fry**¹ /fráɪ/ 動⾃⽥ (現分 **frying**; 三単現 **fries**; 過、過分 **fried** /fráɪd/) ▶定義 to cook sth or to be cooked in hot fat or oil ～を熱した脂または油で調理する、またはそのように調理される→～を油でいためる、揚げる、焼く、フライにする、フライパンで温める‖ *to fry an egg* 目玉焼きを作る *a fried egg* 目玉焼き *I could smell bacon frying in the kitchen.* 台所でベーコンをいためているにおいがした. ☞参 **cook** の注

**fry**² /fráɪ/ ( 米 **French fry**) 名 ⓒ ( 複 **fries**) ▶定義 a long thin piece of potato fried in oil 油で揚げた細長いジャガイモ→フライドポテト

**frying pan** ( 米 **frypan**) 名 ⓒ ▶定義 a flat pan with a long handle that is used for frying food 食品を油でいためるために用いられる、長い柄の付いた平たいなべ→フライパン ☞ **pan** のさし絵

**ft** 略 foot, feet ▶定義 a measure of length, about 30.5 cm 長さの単位、約 30.5 cm→フィート‖ *a room 10 ft by 6 ft* 10 フィート×6 フィートの部屋

\***fuel**¹ /fjúː(ə)l/ 名 ▶定義1 ❶ material that is burned to produce heat or power 熱または動力を生み出すために燃やされる材料→燃料 ▶定義2 ❷ a type of fuel 燃料の種類→燃料‖ *I think gas is the best fuel for central heating.* ガスはセントラルヒーティングに最適の燃料だと思う.

**fuel**² /fjúː(ə)l/ 動⽥ ( **fuelling**; **fuelled**: 米 **fueling**; **fueled**) ▶定義 to make sb feel an emotion more strongly ～にある感情をより強く感じさせる→～を刺激する、活気づける、あおる、たき付ける‖ *Her interest in the Spanish language was fuelled by a visit to Spain.* スペインを訪ねたことで、彼女のスペイン語に対する興味は強まった.

**fugitive** /fjúːdʒətɪv/ 名 ⓒ ▶定義 a person who is running away or escaping (for example from the police) (例えば警察から)逃走している、または脱出している人→逃亡者、脱走者、避難民、亡命者 ☞参 **refugee**

**fulfil** ( 米 **fulfill**) /fʊlfíl/ 動⽥ ( **fulfilling**; **fulfilled**) ▶定義1 to make sth that you wish for happen; to achieve a goal 望む～を起こらせる; 目的を達成する→～を実現する、かなえる、果たす、全うする‖ *He finally fulfilled his childhood dream of becoming a doctor.* 彼は医師になるという子供のころからの夢をついに実現した. *to fulfil your ambition/potential* 夢をかなえる・能力を発揮する ▶定義2 to do or have everything that you should or that is necessary するべきまたは持つべきものすべてを、あるいは必要なもののすべてを、するまたは持つ→～を果たす、実行する、履行する、満たす‖ *to fulfil a duty/obligation/promise/need* 務めを果たす・義務[約束]を果たす・必要を満たす *The conditions of entry to university in this country are quite difficult to fulfil.* この国の大学入学の条件を満たすのは、かなり難しい. ▶定義3 to have a particular role or purpose ある特定の役割または目的を持つ→

## fulfilment

〜を担う, 務める, 果たす ‖ *Italy fulfils a very important role within the European Union.* イタリアは欧州連合の中で非常に重要な役割を担っている. ▶定義4 to make sb feel completely happy and satisfied 〜を完全に幸福で満足していると感じさせる➔**〜の資質を十分に発揮する, 〜を満たす, 充足する, 〜に充実感を感じさせる** ‖ *I need a job that really fulfils me.* 私は自分の能力を十分に発揮できる仕事を必要としている. — **fulfilled** 形➔満ち足りた, 満たされた ‖ *When I had my baby I felt totally fulfilled.* 子供が産まれた時, 私は充足感を感じた. — **fulfilling** 形➔満足のいく, 満足できる, 申し分のない ‖ *I found working abroad a very fulfilling experience.* 海外で働くことはとても充実した経験だと知った.

**fulfilment** /fʊlfɪlmənt/ (米 **fulfillment**) 名 U
▶定義 the act of achieving a goal; the feeling of satisfaction that you have when you have done sth 目的を達成すること; 〜をやり終えたときに感じる満足感➔**実現, 成就, 達成(感), 充実感** ‖ *the fulfilment of your dreams/hopes/ambitions* 夢・希望・大望の実現 *to find personal/emotional fulfilment* 個人的・感情的な達成感を見いだす

★**full**¹ /fʊl/ 形 ▶定義1 holding or containing as much or as many as possible 可能な限り多くの量または数を持っている, または含んでいる➔**一杯の, 満ちた, ぎっしり詰まった, あふれるほどの, 満員の** ‖ *The bin needs emptying. It's **full up** (= completely full).* ごみ箱を空にしなければならない. あふれているから (= 完全に一杯). *a full bottle* 中身が一杯に入ったびん *The bus was full so we had to wait for the next one.* そのバスは満員だったので, 私たちは次のバスを待たなければならなかった. (比喩) *We need a good night's sleep because we've got a full (= busy) day tomorrow.* 明日はする事が一杯ある (= 忙しい) ので, 私たちは夜にぐっすり眠る必要がある. ▶定義2 **full of sb/sth** containing a lot of sb/sth 多くの〜を含む➔**〜が多くて, たくさんある, 一杯の, 十分な, 豊かな** ‖ *The room was full of people.* その部屋は人が一杯だった. *His work was full of mistakes.* 彼の仕事は間違いだらけだった. *The children are full of energy.* 子供たちは元気一杯だ. ▶定義3 full (up) having had enough to eat and drink 十分に飲み食いした➔**満腹の, 腹一杯の, 満足した** ‖ *No more, thank you. I'm full (up).* もう結構です, ありがとう. おなかが一杯です. ▶定義4 (名詞の前だけ) complete; not leaving anything out 完全な; 何も抜けていない➔**全体の, 全部の, 省略しない, 正規の** ‖ *I should like **a full report** on the accident, please.* その事故について詳細な報告をしてください. ***Full details** of today's TV programmes are on page 20.* 今日のテレビ番組の詳細は20ページにあります. *He took **full responsibility** for what had happened.* 彼は起こった事の全責任を負った. *Please give your **full name and address**.* フルネームと住所をお願いします. ▶定義5 (名詞の前だけ) the highest or greatest possible 可能な限り最も高い, または最も大きい➔**最高(潮)の, 盛りの, 最大限の, 精一杯の** ‖ *She got **full marks** in her French exam.* 彼女はフランス語の試験で満点を取った. *The train was travelling **at full speed**.* 列車は全速力で走っていた. ▶定義6 **full of sb/sth/yourself** thinking or talking a lot about sb/sth/yourself 〜・自分自身についてたくさん考えている, または話している➔**〜のことばかり考えて, 〜のことで頭が一杯の, 〜のことしか話さない, 〜で心が一杯で** ‖ *When she got back from holiday she was full of everything they had seen.* 休暇から帰ると, 彼女は見てきたあらゆる事について話してばかりいた. *He's **full of himself** (= thinks that he is very important) since he got that new job.* 新しい仕事に就いてから, 彼は自分のことばかりだ (= 自分が非常に重要だと考えている). ▶定義7 round in shape 丸みのある形の➔**ふっくらした, 豊満な, まるまるとした, ぽっちゃりした** ‖ *She's got quite **a full figure**.* 彼女はかなりふっくらした体型だ. *He's quite **full in the face**.* 彼の顔はかなりぽっちゃりしている. ▶定義8 (used about clothes) made with plenty of material (衣服について) たっぷりの生地で作られた➔**ゆったりとした, ゆとりのある, 緩やかな, だぶだぶの** ‖ *a full skirt* ゆったりとしたスカート

成句 **at full stretch** ▶定義 working as hard as possible できる限り一生懸命に働いている➔**全力を尽くして, 全力で, 精一杯, 最大限に利用して** ‖ *When the factory is operating at full stretch, it employs 800 people.* 工場がフル稼働している

ときは，800人を雇用している．

**full of beans/life** ▶定義 with a lot of energy and enthusiasm 活力または熱意がたくさんある→元気一杯の，活力に満ちて，活気にあふれて，やる気満々で ‖ *They came back from holiday full of beans.* 彼らは元気一杯で休暇から帰ってきた．

**have your hands full** ⇒ **HAND**¹

**in full** ▶定義 with nothing missing; completely 欠けているものがない；完全に→全部，完全な形で，詳細に，省略せずに ‖ *Your money will be refunded in full (= you will get all your money back).* 金は全額返金されます(＝すべての金が戻ってくる)．*Please write your name in full.* フルネームを書いてください．

**in full swing** ▶定義 at the stage when there is the most activity 最も多くの活動が行われる段階→真っ最中で，最高潮で，たけなわで，山場で ‖ *When we arrived the party was already in full swing.* 私たちが着いた時は，パーティーは既にたけなわだった．

**in full view (of sb/sth)** ▶定義 in a place where you can easily be seen 簡単に見られる場所に→～からよく見える所に，すっかり見える所に，丸見えの所で，～の見ている前で ‖ *In full view of the guards, he tried to escape over the prison wall.* 看守からよく見える所で，彼は刑務所の壁を越えて逃げようとした．

**to the full** ▶定義 as much as possible 可能な限り→十分に，たっぷり，心行くまで ‖ *to enjoy life to the full* 人生を十分に楽しむ

**full²** /fʊl/ ▶定義 **full in/on (sth)** straight; directly まっすぐに；直接→まっすぐに，真っ正面から，まともに ‖ *John hit him full in the face.* ジョンは彼の顔をまともに殴った．*The two cars crashed full on.* 2台の車は正面衝突した．

**full-blown** 形 ▶定義 fully developed 完全に発達した→本格的な，全面的な，成熟しきった，必要なものすべてを備えた ‖ *to have full-blown Aids* 完全なエイズの症状が出ている

**full board** 名 Ⓤ ▶定義 (in a hotel, etc) including all meals (ホテルなどで)すべての食事を含んでいる→全食付きの宿泊 ☛参 **half board, bed and breakfast**

**full-length** 形 ▶定義 **1** (used about a picture, mirror, etc) showing a person from head to foot (絵，鏡などについて)人の頭から足までを見せている→全身の，全身を描いた，全身を映す，姿見の ▶定義 **2** not made shorter 短く作られていない→標準の長さの，省略なしの，原作のままの ‖ *a full-length film* カットなしの映画 ▶定義 **3** (used about a dress, skirt, etc) reaching the feet (ワンピースまたはスカートなどについて)足まで届いている→床まで届く，地面に届く

**full moon** 名 [単数扱い] ▶定義 the moon when it appears as a complete circle 完全な円に見えるときの月→満月

**full-scale** 形 (名詞の前だけ) ▶定義 **1** using every thing or person that is available 利用できるすべての物または人を使っている→総力挙げての，全面的な，本格的な，徹底的な ‖ *The police have started a full-scale murder investigation.* 警察は殺人事件の徹底的な捜査を開始した．
▶定義 **2** (used about a plan, drawing, etc) of the same size as the original object (設計図，図面などについて)原物と同じ大きさの→実物大の，原寸の ‖ *a full-scale plan/model* 実物大の設計図・模型

*****full stop** (特に 米 **period**) 名 Ⓒ ▶定義 a mark (.) that is used in writing to show the end of a sentence 文の終わりを示すために文章の中で用いられる記号(.)→ピリオド，終止符

**full-time** 形副 ▶定義 for a whole of the normal period of work 通常の勤務時間全部の[で]→全時間(勤務)の，常動の[で]，専任の[で]，フルタイムの[で] ‖ *He has a full-time job.* 彼は常勤の仕事に就いている．*He works full-time.* 彼はフルタイムで働いている．*We employ 800 full-time staff.* 私たちは800人の専任職員を雇用している． ☛参 **part-time**

*****fully** /fʊ(l)li/ 副 ▶定義 completely; to the highest possible degree 完全に；可能な限り最も高度に→十分に，すっかり，たっぷり，優に，まるまる ‖ *I'm fully aware of the problem.* 私はその問題を完全に承知している．*All our engineers are fully trained.* 当社の技術者は全員，十分に訓練を受けている．

**fully-fledged** (米 または **full-fledged**) 形 ▶定義 completely trained or completely developed; mature 完全に訓練された，または完全に発達した；成熟した→一人前の，資格十分な，十分に成長した，成熟した ‖ *Computer science is* *now a fully-fledged academic subject.* コンピューターサイエンスは現在ではれっきとした学問の分野である.

**fumble** /fˈʌmb(ə)l/ 動 自 ▶定義 to try to find or take hold of sth with your hands in a nervous or careless way 神経質に, または不注意に手で〜を見つけようとする, またはつかもうとする→**手探りする, 探る, 不器用にいじる, いじくり回す** ‖ *'It must be here somewhere', she said, fumbling in her pocket for her key.* 「どこかこの辺にあるはずです」と, 彼女はポケットの中のかぎを手探りで探しながら言った.

**fume** /fjuːm/ 動 自 ▶定義 to be very angry about sth 〜について激しく怒る→**いきり立つ, いら立つ, 腹を立てる, 息巻く, ぷりぷりする**

**fumes** /fjuːmz/ 名 [複数扱い] ▶定義 smoke or gases that smell unpleasant and that can be dangerous to breathe in 不快なにおいがして, 吸い込むと危険な場合もある煙または気体→**煙, ガス, 臭気, 煙霧** ‖ *diesel/petrol/exhaust fumes* ディーゼルエンジン・ガソリン・排気ガスの臭気

**★fun**[1] /fʌn/ 名 U ▶定義 pleasure and enjoyment; an activity or a person that gives you pleasure and enjoyment 喜びと楽しみ; 喜びと楽しみを与えてくれる活動または人→**楽しみ, 面白い事物・人, 気楽な事物, 娯楽** ‖ *We had a lot of fun at the party last night.* 昨夜のパーティーはとても楽しかった. *The party was great fun.* パーティーはとても楽しかった. *Have fun! (= enjoy yourself)* 行ってらっしゃい(= 楽しんできてね) *It's no fun having to get up at 4 o'clock every day.* 毎日4時に起きなければならないのは気楽な事ではない.

成句 **(just) for fun/for the fun of it** ▶定義 (just) for amusement or pleasure; not seriously (単に)楽しみと喜びのために; まじめにではなく→**娯楽のために, 楽しみで, 趣味で** ‖ *I don't need English for my work. I'm just learning it for fun.* 私の仕事には英語は必要ありません. 単に趣味で習っているのです.

**in fun** ▶定義 as a joke 冗談で→**面白半分に, 遊び半分で, 戯れに, ふざけて** ‖ *It was said in fun. They didn't mean to upset you.* 冗談で言ったのですよ. 彼らは, あなたを心配させるつもりではなかったのです.

**make fun of sb/sth** ▶定義 to laugh at sb/sth in an unkind way; to make other people do this 意地悪く〜を笑う; ほかの人にそのような事をさせる→**〜をからかう, あざける, 笑い者にする, 〜に…をからかわせる** ‖ *The older children are always making fun of him because of his accent.* 彼にはなまりがあるため, 年上の子供たちはいつも彼をからかっている.

**poke fun at sb/sth** ⇒ **POKE**

**★fun**[2] /fʌn/ 形 ▶定義 amusing or enjoyable 面白い, または楽しい→**面白い, 楽しい, 愉快な** ‖ *to have a fun time/day out* 楽しい時を過ごす・外出して楽しむ *Brett's a fun guy.* ブレットは面白い男だ.

▶ funny は, 笑わせるような, または風変わりなものまたは人について述べる場合に用いる. fun と同じではないので注意: *Jane is fun (= I enjoy being with her).* (ジェーンは楽しい (= 彼女と一緒にいると楽しい).) *Jane is funny (= she tells jokes and makes me laugh all the time/she is strange).* (ジェーンは面白い (= 彼女は冗談を言っていつも私を笑わせてくれる・彼女は変わっている).)

**★function**[1] /fˈʌŋ(k)ʃ(ə)n/ 名 C ▶定義 **1** the purpose or special duty of a person or thing 人または物の目的または特別な務め→**機能, 働き, 効用, 職務, 役割** ‖ *The function of the heart is to pump blood through the body.* 心臓の機能は血液を体に循環させることである. *to perform/fulfil a function* 職務を遂行する・役目を果たす ▶定義 **2** an important social event, ceremony, etc 重要な社会的催し, 儀式など→**祭典, 祝典, 儀式, 行事, 社交的会合** ‖ *The princess attends hundreds of official functions every year.* 王女は毎年何百という公式行事に参列する.

**function**[2] /fˈʌŋ(k)ʃ(ə)n/ 動 自 ▶定義 to work correctly; to be in action 正しく働く; 動いている→**働く, 機能を果たす, 作動する, 作用する, 機能している** ‖ *Only one engine was still functioning.* 1台のエンジンだけがまだ動いていた.

◆類 **operate**

**functional** /fˈʌŋ(k)ʃ(ə)n(ə)l/ 形 ▶定義 **1** practical and useful rather than attractive 魅力的であるよりはむしろ実用的で役立つ→**機能的な, 実用本位の, 便利な** ‖ *cheap functional furniture* 安価で機能的な家具 ▶定義 **2** working; being used 作

動している; 使用されている→**機能する, 作動できる, 正常に作動している, 使用中の** ‖ *The system is now fully functional.* そのシステムは現在, 完全に機能している.

**function key** 🔢 ❶ ▶定義 one of the buttons (**keys**) on a computer which are used to perform a particular operation ある特定の操作を行うために使われるコンピューターのボタン (キー) の1つ1つ→**機能キー, ファンクションキー**

*****fund**[1] /fʌnd/ 🔢 ▶定義 **1** ❶ a sum of money that is collected for a particular purpose ある特定の目的のために集められるお金の総額→**基金, 資金** ‖ *They contributed £30 to the disaster relief fund.* 彼らは災害救済基金に30ポンド寄付した. ▶定義 **2 funds** [複数扱い] money that is available and can be spent 入手可能で使うことのできる金→**財源, 所持金, 手元資金** ‖ *The hospital is trying to **raise funds** for a new kidney machine.* その病院は, 新しい人工腎臓 (じんぞう) のための資金を募ろうとしている.

**fund**[2] /fʌnd/ 🔢 ▶定義 to provide a project, school, charity etc with money プロジェクト, 学校, 慈善団体などに金を提供する→**～に資金を提供する, 資金援助する, 基金を出す** ‖ *The Channel Tunnel is not funded by government money.* 英仏海峡トンネルの資金は政府から提供されていない.

**fundamental** /fʌndəméntl/ 🔢 ▶定義 basic and important; from which everything else develops 基本的で重要な; そこからほかのすべてが発展する→**主要な, 根本的な, 基礎の, 土台となる** ‖ *There will be fundamental changes in the way the school is run.* 学校の運営方法は根本的に変わるだろう. *There is a fundamental difference between your opinion and mine.* あなたの意見と私の意見には根本的な違いがある. — **fundamentally** /-tli/ 🔢 →**基礎から, 根底から, 抜本的に, 全く** ‖ *The government's policy has changed fundamentally.* 政府の政策は抜本的に変わった.

**fundamentals** /fʌndəméntlz/ 🔢 [複数扱い] ▶定義 basic facts or principles 基本的な事実または原理→**基本, 根本, 基礎, 原理, 原則**

**fund-raiser** 🔢 ❶ ▶定義 a person whose job is to find ways of collecting money for a charity or an organization 慈善団体または組織のために金を集める方法を見つけることを仕事とする人→**資金調達者, 資金調達係** — **fund-raising** 🔢 ❶ →**資金調達** ‖ *fund-raising events* 資金調達のための催し

*****funeral** /fjúːn(ə)rəl/ 🔢 ❶ ▶定義 a ceremony (usually religious) for burying or burning a dead person 死んだ人を埋葬する, または火葬するための (通常は宗教的な) 儀式→**葬式, 葬儀, 告別式** ‖ *The funeral will be held next week.* 葬儀は来週行われます.

▶ 遺体は coffin (ひつぎ) に入れて運ばれ, その上には wreath (花輪) が載せられることが多い. ひつぎは grave (墓地) に埋葬されるか, cremated (火葬) される.

**funeral director** = **UNDERTAKER**
**funfair** /fʌnfeər/ = **FAIR**[2](1)
**fungus** /fʌ́ŋɡəs/ 🔢 ❶ ❶ (複 **fungi** /-dʒaɪ, -ɡaɪ/ または **funguses**) ▶定義 a plant that is not green and does not have leaves or flowers (for example a mushroom), or that is like a wet powder and grows on old wood or food, walls, etc. Some fungi can be harmful. 緑色ではなく葉または花のない植物 (例えばマッシュルーム), または湿った粉末のようで, 古い木材または食品, 壁などに生える植物. 中には有害なものもある→**菌類, キノコ, カビ** ☞参 **mould, toadstool** — **fungal** 🔢 →**菌類の, 菌による** ‖ *a fungal disease/infection/growth* 菌による病気・菌による感染・菌の増殖

**funnel** /fʌ́nl/ 🔢 ❶ ▶定義 **1** an object that is wide at the top and narrow at the bottom, used for pouring liquid, powder, etc into a small opening 液体, 粉末などを狭い口へつぐために用いられる, 上部が広く, 下部が狭くなっている物→**漏斗 (ろうと) (状の物)** ☞ **kitchen** のさし絵 ▶定義 **2** the metal chimney of a ship, engine, etc 船, 機関車などの金属製の煙突→**煙突**

**funnily** /fʌ́nili/ 🔢 ▶定義 in a strange or unusual way 奇妙に, または一風変わって→**妙に, 変に, こっけいに, 面白く** ‖ *She's walking very funnily.* 彼女はとても奇妙な歩き方をしている.

成句 **funnily enough** ▶定義 used for expressing surprise at sth strange that has happened 起こった奇妙な～に対する驚きを表すために用いられて→**奇妙なことには, 不思議なことに** ‖ *Funnily enough, my parents weren't at all cross about it.*

奇妙なことに、両親はそれについて全く腹を立てなかった.

**\*funny** /fÁni/ 形 (**funnier**; **funniest**) ▶定義 1 that makes you smile or laugh ほほえませる、または笑わせるような→**おかしい、こっけいな、面白い、愉快な** ‖ *a funny story* おかしな話 *He's an extremely funny person.* 彼はとても愉快な人だ. *That's the funniest thing I've heard in ages!* ここ何年もそんなおかしな話は聞いたことがなかった. ▶定義 2 strange or unusual; difficult to explain or understand 奇妙な、または普通ではない; 説明するまたは理解するのが難しい→**変な、不思議な、調子の良くない、疑わしい** ‖ *Oh dear, the engine is making a funny noise.* あら、エンジンが変な音を立てている. *It's funny that they didn't phone to let us know they couldn't come.* 彼らが電話で来られないと知らせてこなかったのは奇妙だ. ***That's funny*** - *he was here a moment ago and now he's gone.* おかしいぞ ― 彼はちょっと前までここにいたのにもういない. *Can I sit down for a minute? I feel a bit funny (= a bit ill).* ちょっと座ってもいいですか. 少し調子がおかしいのです (= 少し具合が悪い). ☛参 **fun²** の注

**\*fur** /fɚːr/ 名 ▶定義 ❶ the soft thick hair that covers the bodies of some animals ある動物の体を覆っている、柔らかく厚い毛→**柔らかい毛、にこ毛** ☛ C1 ページのさし絵 ▶定義 2 ❒ ❶ the skin and hair of an animal that is used for making clothes, etc; a piece of clothing that is made from this 衣服などを作るために用いられる動物の皮と毛; それから作られる衣類→**毛皮(製品), 毛皮服** ‖ *a fur coat* 毛皮のコート

**furious** /fjÚəriəs/ 形 ▶定義 1 **furious (with sb)**; **furious (at sth)** very angry 非常に怒っている→**怒り狂った、激怒した、ひどく腹を立てた** ‖ *He was furious with her for losing the car keys.* 彼女が車のキーをなくしたことで、彼はひどく腹を立てた. *He was furious at having to catch the train home.* 家に帰るためにその列車に間に合わせなければならないことに、彼はひどく腹を立てていた. ☛ 名 **fury** ▶定義 2 very strong; violent 非常に強い; 暴力的な→**荒れ狂う、猛烈な、激しい、すさまじい** ‖ *A furious row has broken out over the closing of the school.* その学校の閉鎖をめぐって激しい論争が起こっている.
― **furiously** 副→**激しく、荒れ狂って、猛烈に[と], 激怒して**

成句 **fast and furious** ⇒ **FAST¹**

**furnace** /fɚ́ːrnəs/ 名 ⓒ ▶定義 a large, very hot, enclosed fire that is used for melting metal, burning rubbish, etc 金属を溶かすまたはごみを燃やすなどのために用いられる、大型で非常に熱い、囲いの中の火→**(溶鉱)炉, 焼却炉, 暖房炉, かまど**

**furnish** /fɚ́ːrnɪʃ/ 動 ⓣ ▶定義 to put furniture in a room, house, etc 部屋または家などに家具を置く→**〜に家具を備える、家具を取り付ける** ‖ *The room was comfortably furnished.* その部屋にはよく家具がそろっていた. ― **furnished** 形→**家具を備えた、家具付きの** ‖ *She's renting a furnished room in Birmingham.* 彼女はバーミンガムで家具付きの部屋を借りている.

**furnishings** /fɚ́ːrnɪʃɪŋz/ 名 [複数扱い] ▶定義 the furniture, carpets, curtains, etc in a room, house, etc 部屋または家などの家具、じゅうたん、カーテンなど→**備え付け家具、備品、調度品**

**\*furniture** /fɚ́ːrnɪtʃər/ 名 Ⓤ ▶定義 the things that can be moved, for example tables, chairs, beds, etc in a room, house or office 例えば部屋、家、あるいは事務所のテーブル、いす、ベッドなどのように動かせる物→**家具, 備品, 調度品** ‖ *modern/antique/second-hand furniture* 今風の家具・時代物の家具・中古の家具 *garden/office furniture* 庭・事務所の備品

▶ furniture は不可算名詞であることに注意する: *They only got married recently and they haven't got much furniture.* (彼らは最近結婚したばかりで、あまり家具を持っていない.) 個々の家具について話している場合は、a piece of furniture と言わなければならない: *The only nice piece of furniture in the room was an antique desk.* (その部屋にある良い家具と言えば、時代物の机だけだった.)

**furrow** /fÁroʊ; fɚ́ː-/ 名 ⓒ ▶定義 1 a line in a field that is made for planting seeds in by a farming machine that turns the earth (**plough**) 地面を掘り起こす農機具 (すき) で、種子をまくために畑に作られた筋→**あぜ溝、うね、すじ** ▶定義 2 a deep line in the skin on a person's face, especially on the forehead 人の顔の皮膚にある、特に額の、深い筋→**深いしわ** ☛参 **wrinkle**

**furry** /fə́ːri/ 形 ▶定義 having fur 毛皮の付いている 毛皮の, 毛皮で覆われた, 毛皮を着た, 毛皮付きの ‖ *a small furry animal* 毛皮で覆われた小さな動物

\***further**¹ /fə́ːrðər/ 形副 ▶定義 **1** more; to a greater degree もっと; より大きな程度に→その上の, 一層の, さらに進んだ, もっと ‖ *Are there any further questions?* ほかに質問はありませんか. *Please let us know if you require any further information.* さらに情報が必要な場合は, お知らせください. *I have nothing further to say on the subject.* この話題についてはもうお話しする事はありません. *The museum is closed until further notice (= until another announcement is made).* 追ってお知らせするまで博物館は閉館します (= ほかの発表がなされるまで). *Can I have time to consider the matter further?* その事についてもう少し考える時間を頂けますか. ▶定義 **2** (far の比較級) at or to a greater distance in time or space 時間または空間が大きく隔たった所で, またはそのような所に→さらに遠い, もっと先の, さらに離れた, 遠い方の ‖ *It's not safe to go any further.* これ以上進むのは安全ではない. *I can't remember any further back than 1970.* 1970年よりさらにさかのぼっては思い出せない.
➤ further と farther は両方とも距離について話している場合に用いられる: *Bristol is further/farther from London than Oxford is.* (ブリストルは, オックスフォードからよりもロンドンからの方が遠い.) *I jumped further/farther than you did.* (私はあなたより遠くまでジャンプした.) そのほかの意味では, further のみを用いることができる: *We need a further week to finish the job.* (その仕事を終わらせるにはさらに1週間必要だ.)
成句 further afield ⇒ **FAR**²

**further**² /fə́ːrðər/ 動他 正式 ▶定義 to help sth to develop or be successful 〜が発達する, または成功することを助ける→〜を助成する, 進める, 促進する, 推進する ‖ *to further the cause of peace* 平和運動を推進する

**further education** 名 ❶ (略 **FE**) 英 ▶定義 education for people who have left school (but not at a university) 学校を卒業してしまった (が大学には行っていない) 人のための教育→生涯教育 ☛参 **higher education**

**furthermore** /fə́ːrðəːmɔ̀ːr/ 副 ▶定義 also; in addition 〜もまた; 〜に加えて→その上, なお, さらに, おまけに

\***furthest** /fə́ːrðəst/ **FAR** の最上級

**furtive** /fə́ːrtɪv/ 形 ▶定義 secret, acting as though you are trying to hide sth because you feel guilty 秘密の, 後ろめたく思っているため〜を隠そうとしているかのように振る舞っている→こそこそした, 人の目を盗んだ, 人目を気にした, 内密の ‖ *a furtive glance at the letter* 手紙の盗み見 ─ **furtively** 副 →こっそりと, 人の目を盗んで, ひそかに

**fury** /fjúəri/ 名 ❶ ▶定義 very great anger 非常に大きな怒り→激しい怒り, 激怒, 憤激 ‖ *She was speechless with fury.* 彼女は激しい怒りで言葉を失った. ☛形 **furious**

**fuse**¹ /fjuːz/ 名 ❻ ▶定義 **1** a small piece of wire in an electrical system, machine, etc that melts and breaks if there is too much power. This stops the flow of electricity and prevents fire or damage. 電力が大きすぎる場合に溶けて切れる, 電気系統, 機械などの小さな針金. これによって電気の流れを止めて, 火災または損傷を防ぐ→ヒューズ ‖ *A fuse has blown - that's why the house is in darkness.* ヒューズが飛んだ ─ だから家が真っ暗になったのだ. *That plug needs a 15 amp fuse.* そのプラグには15アンペアのヒューズが必要だ. ▶定義 **2** a piece of rope, string, etc or a device that is used to make a bomb, etc explode at a particular time 爆弾などを特定の時間に爆発させるために使われる綱, ひも, 装置など→導火線, 信管, 起爆装置

**fuse**² /fjuːz/ 動 自 他 ▶定義 **1** (used about two things) to join together to become one; to make two things do this (2つの物について) つながって1つになる; 2つのものをそのようにする→融合する・させる, 連合する・させる ‖ *As they heal, the bones will fuse together.* 治るにつれて, 骨がつながるでしょう. *The two companies have been fused into one large organization.* その2社は合併して1つの大会社になった. ▶定義 **2** to stop working because a fuse1(1) has melted; to make a piece of electrical equipment do this ヒューズ (fuse¹(1)) が溶けたため動作が止まる; 電気機器をそのようにする→ヒ

ューズが飛ぶ, ヒューズが飛んで消える, 〜のヒューズを飛ばす ‖ *The lights have fused.* ヒューズが飛んで照明が消えた. *I've fused the lights.* 私は照明のヒューズを飛ばした.

**fuselage** /fjúːsəlɑ̀ːʒ, -zə-, -lɪdʒ/ 名 ⓒ ▶定義 the main part of a plane (not the engines, wings or tail) 飛行機の主要部分（エンジン, 翼, 尾部以外）→ **胴体, 機体**

**fusion** /fjúːʒən/ 名 [Ⓤ, 単数扱い] ▶定義 the process or the result of joining different things together to form one 異なる物をつなげて1つにする過程, またはその結果 → **融合, 結合, 混合物, 連合体, 溶解物** ‖ *the fusion of two political systems* 2つの政治体制の融合

**fuss**[1] /fʌs/ 名 [単数扱い, Ⓤ] ▶定義 a time when people behave in an excited, a nervous or an angry way, especially about sth unimportant 特に重要でない〜に対して, 人々が興奮して, 神経質に, または怒って振る舞うようなとき → **空騒ぎ, 無用な大騒ぎ, 一騒動** ‖ *The waiter didn't make a fuss when I spilt my drink.* 私が飲み物をこぼした時, ウエーターは落ち着いていた. *What's all the fuss about?* 一体何を大騒ぎしているのですか.

成句 **make/kick up a fuss (about/over sth)** ▶定義 to complain strongly 強く不平を言う → **苦情を言う, 文句を言う, もめる**

**make a fuss of/over sb/sth** ▶定義 to pay a lot of attention to sb/sth 〜に多くの注意を払う → **〜をもてはやす, ちやほやする** ‖ *My grandmother used to make a big fuss of me when she visited.* 祖母は, 訪ねてくると, 私のことをとてもよく世話をしてくれたものだ.

**fuss**[2] /fʌs/ 動 ⓘ ▶定義 **1** to be worried or excited about small things ささいな事について心配または興奮する → **空騒ぎする, 気をもむ, 心配しすぎる, そわそわする** ‖ *Stop fussing. We're not going to be late.* そわそわしないで. 遅れることはありませんから. ▶定義 **2** fuss (over sb/sth) to pay too much attention to sb/sth 〜にあまりに多くの注意を払う → **やきもきする, もてはやす, ちやほやする, 〜の世話を焼く** ‖ *Stop fussing over all the details.* 細かい事ばかり気にするのはやめなさい.

成句 **not be fussed (about sb/sth)** 医 (口語) ▶定義 to not care very much あまり気に掛けない → **どうでもいい, 気にしない** ‖ *'Where do you want to go for lunch?' 'I'm not fussed.'*「どこで昼食を食べたいかな」「どこでもいいよ」

**fussy** /fʌsi/ 形 ▶定義 **1** fussy (about sth) (used about people) giving too much attention to small details and therefore difficult to please（人について）細かい事に注意を払いすぎるので喜ばせるのが難しい → **神経質な, 小うるさい, こだわる, 気難しい** ‖ *He is very fussy about food (= there are many things which he does not eat).* 彼は食べ物についてとてもうるさい (= 食べない物がたくさんある). ☛参 **particular, picky**
▶定義 **2** having too much detail or decoration 細かい部分または装飾が多すぎる → **細かすぎる, こまごました, 凝りすぎた, ごてごてした** ‖ *I don't like that pattern. It's too fussy.* その模様は好きではありません. ごてごてしすぎています.

**futile** /fjúːtaɪl; -tl/ 形 ▶定義 (used about an action) having no success; useless（行動について）成功していない; 役に立たない → **無駄な, 不首尾に終わった, 無益な** ‖ *They made a last futile attempt to make him change his mind.* 彼らは, 彼に考えを変えさせようと最後の努力をしたが無駄だった. — **futility** 名 Ⓤ → **無駄, 無益, 無用**

*****future** /fjúːtʃər/ 名 ▶定義 **1** the future [単数扱い] the time that will come after the present 現在の後に来る時 → **未来, 将来, 今後** ‖ *Who knows what will happen in the future?* 未来に何が起こるかだれにも分からない. *in the near/distant future (= soon/not soon)* 近い将来に・遠い将来に (= すぐに・すぐにではなく) ▶定義 **2** ⓒ what will happen to sb/sth in the time after the present 現在の後の時に〜に起こるであろう事 → **将来起ころうとする事, 行く末** ‖ *Our children's futures depend on a good education.* 子供たちの将来は良い教育に懸かっている. *The company's future does not look very hopeful.* その会社の前途はあまり有望ではないように見える.

▶定義 **3** Ⓤ the possibility of being successful 成功する可能性 → **うまくいく見込み, 将来性, 前途, 成算** ‖ *I could see no future in this country so I left to work abroad.* この国には将来性が見られなかったので, 海外に働きに出た.
▶定義 **4 the future (tense)** [単数扱い]（文法）the tense of a verb that expresses what will

happen after the present 現在の後に起こるであろう事を表す動詞の時制→**未来時制**
▶未来形についての説明は, 巻末の「文法早見表」を参照.
— future 形 (名詞の前だけ) →**未来の, 将来の, 今後の, 来世の** ‖ *She met her future husband when she was still at school.* 彼女はまだ学生のころに未来の夫に出会った. *You can keep that book for future reference (= to look at again later).* 後で参考にするために (= 後でまた見るために) その本を持っていても構いません.
成句 **in future** ▶定義 from now on これから→**今後は, 将来は, これからは** ‖ *Please try to be more careful in future.* 今後はもっと注意するようにしてください.

**fuzzy** /fʌzi/ 形 ▶定義 not clear はっきりしない→**あいまいな, はっきりしない, ぼやけた, 不明瞭 (めいりょう) な** ‖ *The photo was a bit fuzzy but I could just make out my mother on it.* その写真は少しぼやけていたが, 母が写っているのが何とか分かった.

# G g

**G, g**¹ /dʒiː/ 名 C (複 **G's**; **g's**) ▶定義 the seventh letter of the English alphabet 英語アルファベットの第7文字→**g(G)が表す音, g(G)の文字, g(G)の字形のもの** ‖ *'Girl' begins with (a) 'G'.* Girl は G で始まる.

**g**² 略 gram(s)→**グラム**

**gable** /ɡéɪb(ə)l/ 名 C ▶定義 the pointed part at the top of an outside wall of a house between two parts of the roof 屋根に左右から挟まれた家の外壁の頂点に当たるとがった部分→**切り妻, 破風 (はふ)**

**gadget** /ɡǽdʒət/ 名 C 略式 ▶定義 a small device, tool or machine that has a particular but usually unimportant purpose 小さな装置, 道具または機械で, 特定だが普通あまり重要でない用途を持つ→**ちょっとした装置・仕掛け, 気の利いた小道具** ‖ *This car has all the latest gadgets.* この車には最新装置がすべて付いている.

**Gaelic** /ɡéɪlɪk, ɡǽ-/ 形 U ▶定義 (of) the Celtic language and the culture of Ireland or Scotland アイルランドまたはスコットランドのゲール [ケルト] 語とその文化 (の) →**ゲール [ケルト] 語 (の), ゲール [ケルト] 人 (の)**

**gag**¹ /ɡæɡ/ 名 C ▶定義 **1** a piece of cloth, etc that is put in or over sb's mouth in order to stop him/her from talking 人を黙らせるため口の中に詰め込んだり, 口を覆ったりする布切れなど→**猿ぐつわ** ▶定義 **2** a joke 冗談→**ギャグ, だじゃれ, 冗談**

**gag**² /ɡæɡ/ 動 他 (**gagging**; **gagged**) ▶定義 to put a gag in or over sb's mouth 人の口の中や上に猿ぐつわを付ける→**～に猿ぐつわをはめる, ～の言論を抑圧する**

**gage** 米 = GAUGE¹

★**gain**¹ /ɡeɪn/ 動 ▶定義 **1** 他 to obtain or win sth, especially sth that you need or want 特に必要なまたは欲しい～を得る・勝ち取る→**～を得る, 手に入れる** ‖ *They managed to gain access to secret information.* 彼らは何とか秘密情報を入手した. *The country gained its independence ten years ago.* その国は10年前に独立を勝ち取った. ▶定義 **2** 他 to gradually get more of sth 次第により多くの～を得る→**～を増す, 加える** ‖ *The train was gaining speed.* その列車は速度を増していた. *to gain weight/confidence* 体重・信頼が増す ⇔ **lose** ▶定義 **3** 自 **gain (sth) (by/from sth/doing sth)** to get an advantage 有利性を得る→**(～で・～して) 利益を得る, 得をする** ‖ *I've got **nothing to gain** by staying in this job.* この仕事に就いていても, 何も得る事がない. ⇔ **lose**

成句 **gain ground** ▶定義 to make progress; to become stronger or more popular 進歩する; 強さまたは人気の度合いが増す→**進む, 力を増す, 広まる**

句動詞 **gain in sth** ▶定義 to gradually get more of sth 次第に多くの～を得る→**増大する, 増進する, 向上する** ‖ *He's gained in confidence in the past year.* この1年間で彼に対する信頼はますます厚くなった.

**gain on sb/sth** ▶定義 to get closer to sb/sth that you are trying to catch 捕らえようとしている～にさらに接近する→**～に迫る, 追い付く** ‖ *I saw the other runners were gaining on me so I increased my pace.* ほかの走者たちが追い付いてきたのに気付いて私はペースを上げた.

**gain**[2] /géɪn/ 名 C U ▶定義 an increase, improvement or advantage in sth 〜の増加, 改善または有利性→**得ること, 利益, もうけ, 増加, 増進** ‖ *We hope to make a gain (= more money) when we sell our house.* 我々は家を売却して利益(＝より多くのお金)を得たい. *a gain in weight* of one kilo　1キロの体重増加

**gait** /géɪt/ 名[単数扱い] ▶定義 the way that sb/sth walks 〜の歩き振り→**足取り, 足並み**

**gala** /gálə, géɪ-/ 名 C ▶定義 a special social or sporting occasion 特別な社交またはスポーツの機会→**お祭り, にぎやかな催し物,** 医 **スポーツ大会** ‖ *a swimming gala* 水泳大会

**galaxy** /gǽləksi/ 名 C (複 **galaxies**) ▶定義 a large group of stars and planets in space 宇宙の恒星や惑星の大きな集まり→**銀河, 星雲, 小宇宙**

**gale** /géɪl/ 名 C ▶定義 a very strong wind とても強い風→**強風, 疾風** ‖ *Several trees blew down in the gale.* 数本の木が強風に吹かれて倒れた. ☛参 **storm** の注

**gall** 略 gallon(s) →ガロン

**gallant** /gǽlənt/ 形 正式 ▶定義 **1** showing courage in a difficult situation 困難な状況下で勇気を示す→**勇敢な, 勇ましい** ‖ *gallant men/soldiers/heroes* 勇敢な男性・兵士・英雄 *He made a gallant attempt to speak French, but nobody could understand him.* 彼は果敢にもフランス語を話そうと試みたが, だれにも理解してもらえなかった. ☛類 **brave** ▶定義 **2** (used about men) polite to and showing respect for women(男性について)女性に対し親切で敬意を払う→**(女性に)親切な, いんぎんな**

**gallantry** /gǽləntri/ 名 C U (複 **gallantries**) ▶定義 **1** courage, especially in battle 特に戦いにおける勇気→**勇気, 勇敢な行為, 武勇** ▶定義 **2** polite behaviour towards women by men 男性の女性に対する親切な言動→**(女性に対する)いんぎんな言葉・行い, 女性への献身**

**gallery** /gǽlə(ə)ri/ 名 C (複 **galleries**) ▶定義 **1** a building or room where works of art are shown to the public 芸術作品が展示公開されている建物または部屋→**画廊, 美術館, 陳列室** ‖ *an art gallery* 画廊, 美術品展示室・館 ▶定義 **2** an upstairs area at the back or sides of a large hall or theatre where people can sit 大きなホールや劇場の後方または左右に人が座れるよう設けられた2階の部分→**天井桟敷**

**gallon** /gǽlən/ 名 C (略 **gall**) 医 ▶定義 a measure of liquid; 4.5 litres 液量の単位で4.5 リットルに当たる→**ガロン** ☛ 1ガロンは8パイント. ►米国の1ガロンは3.8リットルに相当する.

**gallop** /gǽləp/ 動 自 ▶定義 (used about a horse or a rider) to go at the fastest speed(馬や騎手について)全速力で進む→**(馬などが)ギャロップで駆ける, (人が)ギャロップで馬を走らせる** ☛参 **canter, trot** — **gallop** 名[単数扱い]→**ギャロップ**

**gallows** /gǽloʊz, -əz/ 名 C (複 **gallows**) ▶定義 a wooden frame used in the past for killing people by hanging 人をつるして殺すために昔使われていた木の枠→**絞首台**

**galore** /gəlɔ́ːr/ 副 (名詞の後だけ) ▶定義 in large numbers or amounts 数または量が多い→**たくさんの, 豊富な**

**gamble**[1] /gǽmb(ə)l/ 動 自 他 ▶定義 gamble (sth) (on sth) to bet money on the result of a card game, horse race, etc トランプ, 競馬などの結果にお金をかける→**かけ事をする; (金など)を(〜に)かける** ‖ *to gamble on horses* 競馬でかける *She gambled all her money on the last race.* 彼女は最終レースにありったけのお金をかけた. ☛類 **bet** — **gambler** 名 C →**とばく師, ばくち打ち, 投機家** ‖ *He's a compulsive gambler.* 彼はかけ事をせずにはいられない人だ. — **gambling** 名 U →**とばく, かけ事**

句動 **gamble on sth/on doing sth** ▶定義 to act in the hope that sth will happen although it may not 確実性がないのに〜が起こるのを当てにして行動する→**一か八かの冒険をする, 〜にかける, 〜を当てにして行動する** ‖ *I wouldn't gamble on the weather staying fine.* 私は, 天気が持つことはあまり当てにしていない.

**gamble**[2] /gǽmb(ə)l/ 名 C ▶定義 something you do that is a risk 行う事で危険を伴うもの→**危険なかけ, 一か八かの冒険, ばくち** ‖ *Setting up this business was a bit of a gamble, but it paid off (= was successful) in the end.* この商売を始めるのはちょっとした冒険だったが, 結局うまくいった(＝成功した).

**game**[1] /géɪm/ 名 ▶定義 **1** C **a game (of sth)** a

form of play or sport with rules; a time when you play it ルールのある遊びまたはスポーツの形式; またそれをする時間→(ルールのある)遊び, ゲーム, 試合, 勝負 ‖ *Shall we **play a game**?* ゲームをしましょうか. *Let's **have a game** of chess.* チェスの勝負をしよう. *a game of football/rugby/tennis* フットボール・ラグビー・テニスの試合 *'Monopoly' is a very popular **board game**.* 「モノポリー」はとても人気のあるボードゲームです. *Tonight's game is between Holland and Italy.* 今夜の試合はオランダ対イタリアだ. *The game ended in a draw.* その試合は引き分けに終わった. ▶定義2 ❻an activity that you do to have fun 楽しみでする活動→遊び, 遊戯, ゲーム ‖ *Some children were playing a game of cowboys and Indians.* 何人かの子供たちは西部劇ごっこをしていた. ▶定義3 ❻how well sb plays a sport 〜があるスポーツをどれだけうまくこなすか→試合振り, 試合運び, 勝負の形勢 ‖ *My new racket has really improved my game.* 新しいラケットのお陰で, 試合運びががくんと楽になった. ▶定義4 **games** [複数扱い]an important sports competition 重要なスポーツ競技会→競技会, 大会 ‖ *Where were the last Olympic Games held?* 前回のオリンピック大会の開催地はどこでした. ▶定義5 ❻略式 a secret plan or trick 秘密の計画またはたくらみ→やり口, 計略, 策略, たくらみ ‖ *Stop **playing games** with me and tell me where you've hidden my bag.* 私を担ぐのはもうやめにして, どこにバッグを隠したのか教えてよ. ▶定義6 ❿wild animals or birds that are killed for sport or food スポーツとしてまたは食用に仕留められる野生の動物・鳥→(猟の)獲物, 猟獣 ‖ *big game (= lions, tigers, etc)* 大きな獲物(= ライオン, トラなど), 大物

成句 **give the game away** ▶定義 to tell a person sth that you are trying to keep secret 秘密にしておくつもりの何かをだれかに教える→作戦[秘密の計画]を漏らす・明かす ‖ *It was the expression on her face that gave the game away.* 秘密が漏れたのは, 彼女の表情がそれを物語っていたからだ.

**game**² /ɡéɪm/ 形 ▶定義 (used about a person) ready to try sth new, unusual, difficult, etc (人について)新しい, 普段と違う, 難しい事などをやってみる準備がある→する勇気, 元気, 意志がある ‖ *I've never been sailing before but I'm game to try.* ヨットを走らせた経験は全くないが, 勇気を出してやってみたい.

**gamekeeper** /ɡéɪmkìːpər/ 名 ❻ ▶定義 a person who is responsible for private land where people hunt animals and birds 人が動物や鳥を狩猟する私有地の管理責任者→狩猟番人

**gander** /ɡǽndər/ 名 ❻ ▶定義 a male bird (goose) (ガチョウの)雄→雄のガチョウ

**gang**¹ /ɡǽŋ/ 名[❻, 単数または複数形の動詞と共に] ▶定義1 an organized group of criminals 組織化された犯罪者集団→一味, 暴力団, ギャング(の一団) ▶定義2 a group of young people who cause trouble, fight other groups, etc ほかのグループと争うなど, 問題を起こす若者の集まり→非行・不良グループ ‖ *The woman was robbed by a gang of youths.* その女性は不良グループから金品を奪われた. *gang warfare/violence* 不良グループの闘争・暴力行為 ▶定義3 略式 a group of friends who meet regularly 定期的に顔を合わせる友達の集まり→遊び仲間, 連中, やつら

**gang**² /ɡǽŋ/ 動

句動詞 **gang up on sb** 略式 ▶定義 to join together with other people in order to act against sb 〜に対抗するため他人と一致団結する→〜に団結して対抗する, 〜を集団で襲う, 〜を袋だたきにする ‖ *She's upset because she says the other kids are ganging up on her.* 彼女はほかの子供たちが寄ってたかって自分をいじめると言って取り乱している.

**gangrene** /ɡǽŋɡriːn/ 名 ❿ ▶定義 the death of a part of the body because the blood supply to it has been stopped as a result of disease or injury 病気やけがのため血流が遮られて身体の一部が死ぬこと→壊疽(えそ), 脱疽 ― **gangrenous** /ɡǽŋɡrɪnəs/ 形→壊疽の, 腐った

**gangster** /ɡǽŋstər/ 名 ❻ ▶定義 a member of a group of criminals 犯罪者集団の一員→ギャング(の一員), やくざ, 暴力団員

**gangway** /ɡǽŋwèɪ/ 名 ❻ ▶定義1 a passage between rows of seats in a cinema, an aircraft, etc 映画館, 飛行機内などの座席間通路→通路 ▶定義2 a bridge that people use for getting on or off a ship 人が船に乗り降りするのに用いられる橋→タラップ

**gaol, gaoler** 英 = JAIL, JAILER

*__gap__ /gæp/ 名 ● ▶定義1 a gap (in/between sth) an empty space in sth or between two things ～に空いた空白スペース→**すきま, 裂け目, 割れ目, 切れ目** ‖ *The sheep got out through a gap in the fence.* その羊は柵(さく)のすきまから外へ出た. ▶定義2 a period of time when sth stops, or between two events ～がとぎれた期間, または2つの出来事の間→**中断, 合間, 間隔** ‖ *I returned to teaching after a gap of about five years.* 私は約5年間の中断の後, 教職に復帰した. *a gap in the conversation* 会話のとぎれ ▶定義3 a difference between people or their ideas 人や考え方の相違→**相違, 不一致, 断絶** ‖ *The gap between the rich and the poor is getting wider.* 貧富の差が拡大しつつある. ▶定義4 a part of sth that is missing 欠落している～の一部分→**空白, 欠陥, 欠落** ‖ *In this exercise you have to fill (in) the gaps in the sentences.* この練習問題では文章中の空欄を埋める必要があります. *I think our new product should fill a gap in the market.* この製品は, 市場の空白(人が買いたい商品の欠如)を埋めるに違いないと思う.

成句 bridge a/the gap ⇒ **BRIDGE**²

**gape** /ɡeɪp/ 動 ⓔ ▶定義1 gape (at sb/sth) to stare at sb/sth with your mouth open ～を口を開けて見詰める→(驚きで口を開けて)～をぽかんとして見る ‖ *We gaped in astonishment when we saw what Amy was wearing.* エイミーが着ているものを見た時, 我々は驚きのあまり口をあんぐりと開けた. ▶定義2 gape (open) to be or become wide open→**大きく開いている・開く** ‖ *a gaping hole/wound* 大きく開いている穴・傷口

*__garage__ /ɡǽrɑːʒ, -rɪdʒ; ɡərάːʒ/ 名 ● ▶定義1 a small building where a car, etc is kept 車などを保管する小さな建物→**ガレージ, 車庫** ‖ *The house has a double garage (= with space for two cars).* その家はダブルガレージ付きだ(= 車2台分の駐車スペースがある). ▶定義2 a place where vehicles are repaired and/or petrol is sold 車を修理したり, またはガソリンを販売する所→**(自動車)修理[整備]工場, ガソリンスタンド** ‖ *a garage mechanic* 自動車修理工 ☞参 **petrol station**

**garbage** /ɡάːrbɪdʒ/ 特に 米 = RUBBISH

**garbage can** 米 = DUSTBIN

**garbled** /ɡάːrb(ə)ld/ 形 ▶定義 (used about a message, story, etc) difficult to understand because it is not clear (伝言, 話などについて)はっきりしないので理解しづらい→**不明瞭(めいりょう)な, 要領を得ない**

*__garden__¹ /ɡάːrdn/ 名 ● ▶定義1 (米 **yard**) a piece of land next to a house where flowers and veg-

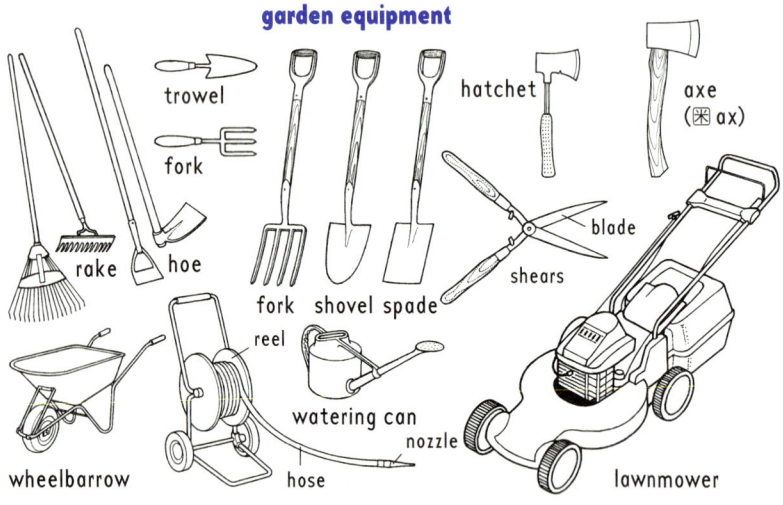

**garden equipment**

trowel, fork, rake, hoe, fork, shovel, spade, hatchet, axe (米 ax), blade, shears, wheelbarrow, reel, watering can, nozzle, hose, lawnmower

etables can be grown, usually with a piece of grass (lawn) 家に隣接する土地で, 花や野菜を栽培することができ, 普通草地(芝生)の一角を伴う→**庭, 庭園** ‖ *the back/front garden* 裏・前庭 *garden flowers* 庭園用の花 *garden chairs (= for using in the garden)* ガーデンチェア(=庭で用いるいす) ☛ C7ページのさし絵 ☛参 **yard**の注 ▶定義2 **gardens** [複数扱い] a public park→**公園**

**garden**² /gáːrdn/ 動⾃ ▶定義 to work in a garden 庭で仕事をする→**園芸をする, 庭いじりをする** ‖ *She's been gardening all afternoon.* 彼女は午後ずっと庭仕事をしている.

**garden centre** 名ⓒ ▶定義 a place where plants, seeds, garden equipment, etc are sold 植物, 種, 園芸用品などを売っている場所→**園芸用品販売所**

**gardener** /gáːrdnər/ 名ⓒ ▶定義 a person who works in a garden as a job or for pleasure 仕事として, または楽しみで庭園で働く人→**植木屋, 庭師, 庭いじりが好きな人**

**gardening** /gáːrdnɪŋ/ 名Ⓤ ▶定義 looking after a garden 庭の手入れ→**園芸・造園(術), ガーデニング, 庭師の仕事** ‖ *I'm going to do some gardening this afternoon.* 今日の午後は庭いじりでもするつもりだ. *gardening tools/gloves* 園芸用具・園芸用手袋

**garden party** 名ⓒ ▶定義 a formal social event that takes place outside usually in a large garden in summer 普通は夏に大きな庭園など, 屋外で行われる正式な社交の催し→**園遊会, ガーデンパーティー**

**gargle** /gáːrg(ə)l/ 動⾃ ▶定義 to wash your throat with a liquid (which you do not swallow) 液体でのどを洗浄する(その液体は飲み込まない)→**うがいをする**

**garish** /ɡéərɪʃ/ 形 ▶定義 very bright or decorated and therefore unpleasant とても派手な, または装飾が多いため心地良くない→**けばけばしい, 飾り立てた** ☛類 **gaudy**

**garlic** /gáːrlɪk/ 名Ⓤ ▶定義 a plant with a strong taste and smell that looks like a small onion and is used in cooking 風味と香りが強い植物で, 小さいタマネギに似ていて料理に使われる→**ニンニク(の球根)** ‖ *Chop two cloves of garlic and fry in oil.* ニンニク2かけを刻んで油でいためます. ☛ C3ページのさし絵

gas meter  693

**garment** /gáːmənt/ 名ⓒ正式 ▶定義 one piece of clothing 一着の衣服→**衣服(の一品), 着物** ☛参 **clothes**

**garnish** /gáːnɪʃ/ 動他 ▶定義 to decorate a dish of food with a small amount of another food 一皿の料理を少量の別の食べ物で飾る→**(料理)に~を添える, ~に装飾を添える** ‖ *Garnish the soup with a little parsley before serving.* スープにパセリ少々を添えてから出してください. — **garnish** 名Ⓤⓒ→**つま, 付け合わせ, 装飾**

**garrison** /ɡǽrəs(ə)n/ 名ⓒ ▶定義 a group of soldiers who are living in and guarding a town or building 町や建物の中に住みながら, その場を守っている兵士の一団→**守備隊, 駐屯軍**

★**gas**¹ /ɡǽs/ 名 (復 **gases**: 困 または **gasses**) ▶定義1 Ⓤⓒa substance like air that is not a solid or a liquid 固体でも液体でもない空気のような物質→**気体, ガス** ‖ *Hydrogen and oxygen are gases.* 水素と酸素は気体です. ▶定義2 Ⓤa particular type of gas or mixture of gases that is used for heating or cooking 暖房や料理に用いる特定の種類のガス, またはガスの混合物→**(灯用・燃料用の)ガス** ‖ *a gas cooker* ガスレンジ ▶定義3 Ⓤ 困 = PETROL

**gas**² /ɡǽs/ 動他 (**gassing; gassed**) ▶定義 to poison or kill sb with gas ガスを使って~を中毒させる・殺す→**~を毒ガスで攻撃する, ~をガス中毒させる**

**gas chamber** 名ⓒ ▶定義 a room that can be filled with poisonous gas in order to kill animals or people 動物や人間を殺すために毒ガスを充満できる部屋→**ガス室, ガス処刑室**

**gash** /ɡǽʃ/ 名ⓒ ▶定義 a long deep cut or wound 長く深い切り傷・負傷→**(長く深い)切り傷, ふかで** ‖ *He had a nasty gash in his arm.* 彼は腕にひどい切り傷を負った. — **gash** 動他 →**~を深く傷付ける, ~を深く裂く**

**gas mask** 名ⓒ ▶定義 an piece of equipment that is worn over the face to protect against poisonous gas 毒ガスから身を守るため顔を覆って装着する器具→**ガスマスク, 防毒マスク**

**gas meter** 名ⓒ ▶定義 an instrument that measures the amount of gas that you use in your home 家庭で使用するガスの計量器→**ガスメーター**

**gasoline** /gǽsəlìːn, ˌ-ˈ-/（または **gas**）⚑ = PETROL

**gasp** /gɑːsp; gæsp/ 動 ▶定義1 ⓐ gasp (at sth) to take a sudden loud breath with your mouth open, usually because you are surprised or in pain 普通は驚きや痛みが原因で、口を開けて突然大きく息を吸う →はっと息をのむ, 息が止まる ‖ *She gasped in surprise as she read the letter.* 彼女はその手紙を読んだ時、驚きで息が止まる思いがした. ▶定義2 ⓐ to have difficulty breathing 呼吸が困難になる →あえぐ, 息を切らす ‖ *I pulled the boy out of the pool and he lay there gasping for breath.* 私がその男の子をプールから引き上げると, 彼は苦しげな息をしてそこに横になった. — gasp 名 ⓒ (→驚きなどで)息が止まること, あえぎ, 息切れ ‖ *to give a gasp of surprise/pain/horror* 驚いて・痛くて・恐怖で息をのむ

**gas station** ⚑ = PETROL STATION

**gastronomic** /gæstrənɑ́mɪk/ 形 ▶定義 connected with good food おいしい食べ物と関連のある →美食の, 食い道楽の

★**gate** /géɪt/ 名 ⓒ ▶定義1 the part of a fence, wall, etc like a door that can be opened to let people or vehicles through 塀・壁などの一部分で, 人や車を通すために扉のように開けられるもの →門, 出入り口, 木戸, 城門 ‖ *Please keep the garden gate closed.* 庭門は閉めておいてください. ☛ C7ページのさし絵 ▶定義2（または **gateway**）the space in a wall, fence, etc where the gate is 壁・塀などの出入り口になる場所 →入り口, 通路 ‖ *Drive through the gates and you'll find the car park on the right.* 車で入り口を入ると, 右手に駐車場が見えます. ▶定義3 the place at an airport where you get on or off a plane 空港で機体に乗り降りする場所 →搭乗口 ‖ *Swissair Flight 139 to Geneva is now boarding at gate 16.* スイス航空ジュネーブ行き139便は, ただ今16番搭乗口から搭乗中です.

**gateau** /gɑːtóʊ; gǽtoʊ/ F gato/ 名 ⓒ (複 **gateaux**) ▶定義 a large cake that is usually decorated with cream, fruit, etc 普通, クリームや果物などで飾られた大きなケーキ →デコレーションケーキ, ガトー・菓子ケーキ ☛ C4 ページのさし絵

**gatecrash** /géɪtkræʃ/ 動 ⓐ ⓘ ▶定義 to go to a private party without being invited 招待されていない内輪の集まりに出掛ける →招待されないのに押し掛ける, 切符を持たないで入場する — **gatecrasher** 名 ⓒ ⓘ 押し掛け客, 切符を持たない入場者

**gateway** /géɪtweɪ/ 名 ⓒ ▶定義1 = GATE(2) ▶定義2 [単数扱い] the gateway to sth the place which you must go through in order to get to somewhere else どこか別の所へ行くのに通らねばならない場所 →関門, (比喩的に)〜への道・手段

★**gather** /gǽðər/ 動 ▶定義1 ⓐ ⓘ gather (round) (sb/sth); gather sb/sth (round) (sb/sth) (used about people) to come or be brought together in a group（人について）集団で来る・連れてこられる →寄り集まる, 蓄積する, たまる; 集める ‖ *A crowd soon gathered at the scene of the accident.* その事故現場にはすぐにたくさんの人が押し掛けた. *We all gathered round and listened to what the guide was saying.* 私たちは皆集まってガイドの話に耳を傾けた. ▶定義2 ⓐ gather sth (together/up) to bring many things together 多くのものを1つにまとめる →あちこちから(拾い)集める, 〜を集める ‖ *He gathered up all his papers and put them away.* 彼は自分の書類を全部集め, 片付けた. *They have gathered together a lot of information on the subject.* 彼らはその問題に関する情報を, あちこちからたくさん集めた. ▶定義3 ⓘ 正式 to pick wild flowers, fruit, etc from a wide area 野生の花・果物などを広い範囲から取る →〜を収穫・採取する, 摘む ‖ *to gather mushrooms* きのこ狩りをする ▶定義4 ⓘ to understand or find out sth (from sb/sth)（〜から）…を理解する・知る →〜を(…から)知る, 〜だと推測する ‖ *I gather from your letter that you have several years' experience of this kind of work.* お手紙によると, あなたはこの種のお仕事に数年の経験をお持ちのようですね. *'She's been very ill recently.' 'So I gather.'* 「彼女はこのところ容体がとても悪い」「察するところです」 ▶定義5 ⓐ ⓘ to gradually become greater; to increase 次第に大きくなる; 増加する →(次第に)増す; 〜を加える ‖ *I gathered speed as I cycled down the hill.* 坂を下ると, 私の自転車は速度を増した.

**gathering** /gǽðərɪŋ/ 名 ⓒ ▶定義 a time when people come together; a meeting 人々が一堂に集まる時間; 集会 →集まり, 会合 ‖ *a family gath-*

*ering* 家族の集い

**gaudy** /ɡɔ́ːdi/ 形 ▶定義 very bright or decorated and therefore unpleasant とても派手な，または装飾が多いため心地良くない→**けばけばしい，飾り立てた** ☛類 garish

**gauge**¹ (米 または **gage**) /ɡeɪdʒ/ 名 Ⓒ ▶定義 1 an instrument for measuring the amount of sth 〜の分量を計る器具→**計量器，計器** ‖ *a fuel/temperature/pressure gauge* 燃料・温度・圧力計 ▶定義 2 (専門用語) a measurement of the width of sth or of the distance between two things 〜の幅や2つの…の間隔→**(レールの)軌間，ゲージ** ‖ *a narrow-gauge railway* 狭軌鉄道 (標準軌間より狭い軌幅の鉄道) ▶定義 3 **a gauge (of sth)** a fact that you can use to judge a situation, sb's feelings, etc 状況や〜の気持ちなどを判断するのに役立つ事実 →**(評価・判断の)尺度，基準**

**gauge**² /ɡeɪdʒ/ 動 他 ▶定義 1 to make a judgement or to calculate sth by guessing 推測で，〜を判断または算出する→**〜を評価する，見積もる** ‖ *It was difficult to gauge the mood of the audience.* 聴衆の気持ちを推し量るのは難しかった． ▶定義 2 to measure sth accurately using a special instrument 特別な道具を使って〜を正確に計測する→**(計器で)〜を正確に計る，測定する**

**gaunt** /ɡɔːnt/ 形 ▶定義 (used about a person) very thin because of hunger, illness, etc (人について) 飢え・病気などでひどくやせた→**やせこけた，やせ衰えた**

**gauze** /ɡɔːz/ 名 Ⓤ ▶定義 a thin material like a net, that is used for covering an area of skin that you have hurt or cut 網目になった薄い生地で，痛みや切り傷のある皮膚を覆うために用いられる→**ガーゼ，包帯，(絹・綿などの)薄織**

**gave** GIVE¹ の過去形

**gawp** /ɡɔːp/ 動 自 略式 ▶定義 **gawp (at sb/sth)** to look or stare in a stupid way 愚かな様子で見る・見詰める→**ぽかんと見詰める** ‖ *Lots of drivers slowed down to gawp at the accident.* たくさんのドライバーが速度を落とし，その事故にあぜんと見とれた．

**gay**¹ /ɡeɪ/ 形 ▶定義 1 sexually attracted to people of the same sex; homosexual 同性に性的魅力を感じる；同性愛の→**ゲイの，ホモの，同性愛(者)の** ‖ *the gay community of New York* ニューヨークのゲイ共同体 *a gay bar/club (= for gay people)* ゲイバー・クラブ (= 同性愛者が集まる) ☛

名 gayness ☛参 lesbian ▶定義 2 (古) happy and full of fun 幸福で楽しくてたまらない→**陽気な，快活な，楽しい** ☛ 名 gaiety

**gay**² /ɡeɪ/ 名 Ⓒ ▶定義 a person, especially a man, who is sexually attracted to people of the same sex; a homosexual 特に男性で，同性に性的魅力を感じる人；同性愛者→**同性愛者，ホモ** ☛参 lesbian

**gaze** /ɡeɪz/ 動 自 ▶定義 to look steadily for a long time 長い時間じっと見詰める→**じっと見詰める，凝視する** ‖ *She sat at the window gazing dreamily into space.* 彼女は窓辺に腰掛け，宙を夢見るように見詰めていた．— gaze 名 [単数扱い]→**注視，凝視**

**GB** 略 Great Britain→**大ブリテン島，グレートブリテン**

**GCSE** /ˌdʒiː siː es iː/ 略 General Certificate of Secondary Education ▶定義 an examination that schoolchildren in England, Wales and Northern Ireland take when they are about sixteen. They often take GCSEs in five or more subjects. For Scottish examinations, look at SCE. イングランド，ウェールズおよび北アイルランドの学生が，およそ16歳で受ける試験．GCSE は5つ以上の教科で受験することが多い．スコットランドの試験については，SCE を参照→**一般中等教育修了試験** ▶ A level と比較．

★**gear**¹ /ɡɪər/ 名 ▶定義 1 Ⓒ the machinery in a vehicle that turns engine power into a movement forwards or backwards エンジンの力を前方または後方の動きに変える，車に装備された機器→**(車の)歯車，ギア** ‖ *Most cars have four or five forward gears and a reverse.* ほとんどの車には4段あるいは5段の前進ギアと，後進ギアが付いている． ▶定義 2 Ⓤ a particular position of the gears in a vehicle 車のギアの特定位置→**かみ合い位置** ‖ *first/second/top/reverse gear* ロー・セカンド・トップ・後進ギア *to change gear* 変速する ▶定義 3 Ⓤ equipment or clothing that you need for a particular activity, etc 特定の活動などをするのに必要な装備や衣服→**道具，用具一式，服装(品)** ‖ *camping/fishing/sports gear* キャンプ・釣り・スポーツ用品 ▶定義 4 [単数扱い] an instrument or part of a machine that is used for a particular purpose 特定の目的に使われる器機あるいは機械の一部➡装置, 仕掛け ‖ *the landing gear of an aeroplane* 航空機の着陸装置

**gear**² /gɪɔr/ **動**
**句動詞** **gear sth to/towards sb/sth** (しばしば受動態で) ▶定義 to make sth suitable for a particular purpose or person 〜を特定の目的または…に適合させる➡〜を(…に)適合させる ‖ *There is a special course geared towards the older learner.* 年配の学習者に適した特別コースがあります.

**gear up (for sb/sth); gear sb/sth up (for sb/sth)** ▶定義 to get ready or to make sb/sth ready 用意する, あるいは〜を準備する➡準備をする, 準備を整える

**gearbox** /gíɔrbɑ̀ks/ **名 C** ▶定義 the metal case that contains the gears¹(1) of a car, etc 車などに付いている金属の箱で, gear¹(1)が入っている➡ギアボックス, 歯車箱

**gear lever** (图 **gearshift**) **名 C** ▶定義 a stick that is used for changing gear¹(2) in a car, etc 車などに付いているレバーでgear¹(2)を変えるのに使う➡変速レバー ☞ S7ページのさし絵

**gee** /dʒiː/ **間 図** ▶定義 used for expressing surprise, pleasure, etc 驚き, 喜びなどの表現に用いて➡おやまあ, へえ, うわー

**geese** GOOSEの複数形

**gel** /dʒel/ **名 C U** (しばしば複合語で) ▶定義 a thick substance that is between a liquid and a solid 液体と固体の中間のようなどろっとした物質➡ゲル, ゼリー状物質, ジェル ‖ *hair gel* ゼリー状整髪料 *shower gel* 入浴用ジェル

**gelignite** /dʒélɪɡnàɪt/ **名 U** ▶定義 a substance that is used for making explosions 爆発を引き起こすため使われる物質➡ゼリグナイト(ニトログリセリンを含む爆薬の一種)

**gem** /dʒem/ **名 C** ▶定義**1** a jewel or precious stone 宝石または貴重な石➡宝石, 珠玉 ▶定義**2** a person or thing that is especially good 特に良い人や物➡美しくて貴重な人・物, 珠玉, 逸品

**Gemini** /dʒémənàɪ, -nìː/ **名 C U** ▶定義 the third sign of the zodiac, the Twins 黄道十二宮の第3番目である双子座➡双子座, 双子宮

**Gen** **略** General ▶定義 an officer in the British and US armies 英国および米国軍の将校➡大将, 将官, 軍司令官

**gender** /dʒéndər/ **名 C U** ▶定義**1** **正式** the fact of being male or female 男性または女性であること➡性 ☞ 類 sex ▶定義**2** (文法) (in some languages) the division of nouns, pronouns, etc into different classes (masculine, feminine and neuter); one of these three types (ある言語において) 名詞, 代名詞などの区分(男性・女性・中性); またその3つのうちの1つ➡(名詞・代名詞などの)性

**gene** /dʒiːn/ **名 C** ▶定義 a unit of information inside a cell which controls what a living thing will be like. Genes are passed from parents to children. 細胞内の情報の単位で, 生物がどのようであるかを支配している. それらは親から子供に引き継がれる➡遺伝子, ジーン ☞ 参 genetics

★**general**¹ /dʒén(ə)rəl/ **形** ▶定義**1** affecting all or most people, places, things, etc すべて, あるいはほとんどの人, 場所, 物などに影響を与える➡一般の, 世間一般の, 全般に共通な ‖ *Fridges were once a luxury, but now they are in general use.* 冷蔵庫はかつてぜいたく品だったが, 今は世間一般で使われている. *That is a matter of general interest.* それは世間一般の関心事です. *the general public* (= *most ordinary people*) 一般大衆(= ほとんどの普通の人々) ▶定義**2** (名詞の前だけ) referring to or describing the main part of sth, not the details 〜の詳細ではなく主要な部分を言及した, または説明した➡大体の, 総括的な ‖ *Your general health is very good.* あなたの健康状態は概して良好です. *The introduction gives you a general idea of what the book is about.* 導入部分を読めばその本の内容が大体分かります. *As a general rule, the most common verbs in English tend to be irregular.* 総則として, 英語で最も使用頻度の高い動詞の活用は, 不規則であることが多い. ▶定義**3** not limited to one subject or area of study; not specialized 1つの課題や研究領域に限らない; 特定でない➡(専門的でなく)一般的な, 雑多な ‖ *Children need a good general education.* 子供には良質な一般教育が必要だ. *The quiz tests your general knowledge.* そのクイズはあなたの一般知識を試すものです. *a general hospital* 総合病院 ▶定義**4** (しばしば複合語で) with responsibility for the whole of an organization ある組織の全体的責任を持つ→総～，～長官 ‖ *a general manager* 総支配人

**成句** in general ▶定義1 in most cases; usually ほとんどの場合；通常→**一般に，大抵** ‖ *In general, standards of hygiene are good.* 一般に衛生水準が高い. ▶定義2 as a whole 全体として→**全般に，全体に** ‖ *I'm interested in Spanish history in general, and the civil war in particular.* 私はスペインの歴史全般に，中でも特に内乱に興味を持っています．

**general**² /dʒén(ə)rəl/ 名 ⓒ (略 Gen) ▶定義 an army officer in a very high position 非常に地位の高い軍の司令官→**大将，将官，軍司令官**

**general election** 名 ⓒ ▶定義 an election in which all the people of a country vote to choose a government 統治者を選出するため，国中の人が投票する選挙→**総選挙，一般選挙**
☞参 by-election

**generalization** (または **-isation**) /dʒèn(ə)rəlaɪzéɪʃ(ə)n; -lə-/ 名 ⓒ Ⓤ ▶定義 a general statement that is based on only a few facts or examples; the act of making such a statement わずかな事実や事例だけに基づいた一般論；また，そういう事を述べる行為→**一般化，普遍化，総合** ‖ *You can't **make** sweeping **generalizations about** French people if you've only been there for a day!* フランスに1日しか滞在したことがないのに，フランス人について大雑把な一般論を述べるのはむちゃだよ．

**generalize** (または **-ise**) /dʒén(ə)rəlàɪz/ 動 ⓘ ▶定義 generalize (about sth) to form an opinion or make a statement using only a small amount of information instead of looking at the details 詳細を調べないで，わずかな情報だけを用いて評価する，または声明を出す→**一般法則化する，概括する，一般に走る** ‖ *You can't generalize about English food from only two meals.* 2度食事しただけで，イギリスの食べ物について一般論に走るのは無理だよ．

*****generally** /dʒén(ə)rəli/ 副 ▶定義1 by or to most people ほとんどの人によって・とって→**一般に，広く** ‖ *He is generally considered to be a good doctor.* 彼は一般に良い医者と見なされている．
▶定義2 usually 普通→**通例，通常** ‖ *She generally cycles to work.* 彼女は普段自転車で通勤している． ▶定義3 without discussing the details of sth ～の詳細を議論しないで→**概して，大体** ‖ *Generally speaking, houses in America are bigger than houses in this country.* 概して言えることだが，アメリカの家はこの国の家よりも大きい．

**generate** /dʒénərèɪt/ 動 ⓣ ▶定義 to produce or create sth ～を製造する・創造する→**～を起こす，生み出す** ‖ *to generate heat/power/electricity* 熱・力・電気を発する・起こす

*****generation** /dʒènəréɪʃ(ə)n/ 名 ▶定義1 ⓒ all the people in a family, group or country who were born at about the same time 家庭・グループ・国において，ほぼ同じ時に生まれたすべての人々→**同世代の人々，同時代の人々** ‖ *We should look after the planet for future generations.* 私たちは，次世代の人々のために地球を大切にしなければならない．*This photograph shows three generations of my family (= children, parents and grandparents).* この写真には，我が家の3代 (= 子供，親，祖父母) が写っている．

▶ generationは単数形で，単数形または複数形の動詞を伴って用いられる：*The younger generation only seem/seems to be interested in money.* (若い世代の人々は，お金にしか興味がないように見える．)

▶定義2 ⓒ the average time that children take to grow up and have children of their own, usually considered to be about 25-30 years 子供が成長して自分の子供を持つまでに要する平均的期間で，普通25～30年と考えられている→**1世代，1代** ‖ *A generation ago foreign travel was still only possible for a few people.* 1世代前までは，外国旅行はまだ少数の人だけに可能だった． ▶定義3 Ⓤ the production of sth, especially heat, power, etc ～，特に熱・力などを生じさせること→**(電気・熱・ガスなどの)発生**

**the generation gap** 名 [単数扱い] ▶定義 the difference in behaviour, and the lack of understanding, between young people and older people 若者と年配の人の間で，言動が異なったり理解できないこと→**世代間の断絶**

**generator** /dʒén(ə)rèɪtər/ 名 ⓒ ▶定義 a machine that produces electricity 電気を発生させる機械→**発電機，発生器**

**generosity** /dʒènərásəti/ 名 Ⓤ ▶定義 the quality of being generous 寛大な・気前の良い性質→**寛大さ, 気前の良さ**

\***generous** /dʒén(ə)rəs/ 形 ▶定義1 happy to give more money, help, etc than is usual or expected 通常より, または期待されるより多くのお金・助けなどを喜んで提供する→**気前の良い, 寛大な** ‖ *It was very generous of your parents to lend us all that money.* そのお金を全部私たちに貸してくださるとは, あなたのご両親はとても気前が良かった. ▶定義2 larger than usual 通常より大きい→**たくさんの, 豊富な** ‖ *a generous helping of pasta* 大盛りのパスタ ― generously 副→**たっぷりと, 気前良く, どっさり** ‖ *People gave very generously to our appeal for the homeless.* 私たちがホームレスのために呼び掛けると, 人々はとても気前良く寄付してくれた.

**genetic** /dʒənétɪk/ 形 ▶定義 connected with the units in the cells of living things (genes) that control what a person or plant is like, or with the study of genes (genetics) 生き物の細胞の中にある単位で, 人や植物がどうあるかを支配するもの(遺伝子)に関連して, あるいは遺伝子の研究(遺伝学)に関連して→**遺伝子の, 遺伝学に関する** ‖ *The disease is caused by a genetic defect.* その病気は遺伝子の欠陥により引き起こされる. ― genetically /-k(ə)li/ 副→**遺伝子(学)的に**

**genetically modified** 形 (略GM) ▶定義 (used about food, plants, etc) that has been grown from cells whose units of information (genes) have been changed artificially (食品, 植物などについて) 人工的に情報単位(遺伝子)を組み替えた細胞から発育した→**遺伝子組み換えの**

**genetic engineering** 名 U ▶定義 the science of changing the way a human, animal or plant develops by changing the information in its genes 遺伝子内の情報を組み替えることにより, 人・動物・植物の成長を変える科学→**遺伝子工学**

**genetics** /dʒənétɪks/ 名 U ▶定義 the scientific study of the way that the development of living things is controlled by qualities that have been passed on from parents to children 両親から子供へと受け継がれる資質によって, 生き物の成長がどのように支配されるかを, 科学的に研究する学問→**遺伝学** ☞参 gene

**genial** /dʒíːnjəl, -niəl/ 形 ▶定義 (used about a person) pleasant and friendly (人について) 楽しく友好的な→**にこにこと愛想の良い, 朗らかで付き合いやすい**

**genitals** /dʒénətlz/ (または **genitalia** /dʒènətéɪliə, -ljə/) 名 [複数扱い] 正式 ▶定義 the parts of a person's sex organs that are outside the body 体外にある人の生殖器の部分→**生殖器** ― genital /dʒénətl/ 形→**生殖器の**

**genius** /dʒíːnjəs, -niəs/ 名 ▶定義1 ❶ very great and unusual ability 非常に優れた, 普通でない能力→**才能, 天分, 非凡な才能** ‖ *Her idea was a stroke of genius.* 彼女のアイデアは, 才能のなせる業だった. ▶定義2 ❸ a person who has very great and unusual ability, especially in a particular subject 特定の分野において, 非常に優れた普通でない能力を持つ人→**天才** ‖ *Einstein was a mathematical genius.* アインシュタインは数学の天才だった. ☞参 prodigy ▶定義3 [単数扱い] a genius for (doing) sth a very good natural skill or ability 生まれ持った, 非常に優れた技能や能力→**天性, 素質, 生まれ持った資質**

**genocide** /dʒénəsàɪd/ 名 U ▶定義 the murder of all the people of a particular race, religion, etc 特定の人種・宗教などの人々を全員殺すこと→**計画的大量虐殺, 民族・種族根絶**

**gent** /dʒent/ 略式 = GENTLEMAN

**genteel** /dʒentíːl/ 形 ▶定義 behaving in a very polite and quiet way, often in order to make people think that you are from a high social class とても礼儀正しく物静かに振る舞う, 多くは社会的に高い階層の出身と人に思われようとそうする→**いやに上品振った, 気取った, 表面を取り繕った** ― gentility /dʒentíləti/ 名 U→**お上品振り, 上流気取り**

\***gentle** /dʒéntl/ 形 ▶定義1 (used about people) kind and calm; touching or treating people or things in a careful way so that they are not hurt (人について) 親切で穏やかな; 傷付けないように人や物を大切に扱ったり触れる→**優しい, 厳しくない, 親切な** ‖ *'I'll try and be as gentle as I can,' said the dentist.* 「できる限り痛くないようにやってみましょう」と歯科医が言った. ▶定義2 not strong, violent or extreme 強力・暴

力的・極端でない→**柔らかな, 静かな, 緩い** ‖ *gentle exercise* 軽い運動 *a gentle slope/curve* なだらかな坂・緩やかな曲線 — gentleness /dʒéntlnəs/ 名 ⓤ ▶定義 **親切, 優しさ, 穏やかさ** — gently /dʒéntli/ 副 ▶**親切に, 優しく**

**gentleman** /dʒéntlmən/ 名 ⓒ (複 **-men** /-mən/) ▶定義 1 a man who is polite and who behaves well towards other people 礼儀正しく, 他人に対して品行の良い男性→**紳士, まともな人** ‖ *Everyone likes and respects Joe because he's a real gentleman.* ジョーは真の紳士なので, だれからも好かれ尊敬されている. ▶定義 2 [正式] used when speaking to or about a man or men in a polite way 1人あるいは複数の男性に対して・関して, 丁寧に話すときに用いて→**男の方, 殿方, 諸君** ‖ *Ladies and gentlemen* (= at the beginning of a speech) 皆様 (= 演説の冒頭で) *Mrs Flinn, there is a gentleman here to see you.* フリンさん, 男の方がお見えになりましたよ. ▶定義 3 (古) a rich man with a high social position 社会的地位の高いお金持ちの男性→**家柄の良い人, 地位の高い人**

**the Gents** 名 [単数扱い] 英 略式 ▶定義 a public toilet for men 男性用の公衆トイレ→**男子用トイレ, 「殿方用」** ☞参 **toilet** の注

*****genuine** /dʒénjuən, -ɪn/ 形 ▶定義 1 real; true→**本物の, 真の** ‖ *He thought that he had bought a genuine Rolex watch but it was a cheap fake.* 彼は本物のロレックスの時計を買ったと思っていたが, 実は安いにせ物だった. ☞参 **imitation** ▶定義 2 sincere and honest; that can be trusted 誠実で正直な; 信用できる→**心からの, 見せ掛けでない, 誠実な** — genuinely 副 →**純粋に, 本当に, 心から**

**geographer** /dʒiágrəfər/ 名 ⓒ ▶定義 an expert in geography or a student of geography 地理学の専門家または学生→**地理学者**

*****geography** /dʒiágrəfi/ 名 ⓤ ▶定義 1 the study of the world's surface, physical qualities, climate, population, products, etc 世界の地表・物理的性質・気候・人口・産物に関する学問→**地理学** ‖ *human/physical/economic geography* 人文・自然・経済地理学 ▶定義 2 the physical arrangement of a place ある場所の実際の配置→**地理, 地形** ‖ *We're studying the geography of Asia.* 私たちはアジアの地理を学んでいます. — geographical /dʒì:əgræfɪk(ə)l/ 形 →**地理的な,**

### German measles 699

地理学 (上) の — geographically /-k(ə)li/ 副 →**地理的に**

**geologist** /dʒiálədʒɪst/ 名 ⓒ ▶定義 an expert in geology or a student of geology 地質学の専門家, またはその学生→**地質学者**

**geology** /dʒiálədʒi/ 名 ⓤ ▶定義 the study of rocks, and of the way they are formed 岩盤自身やそれがどのように形成されたかを研究する学問→**地質学** — geological /dʒì:əládʒɪk(ə)l/ 形 →**地質学的な, 地質学 (上) の**

**geometric** /dʒì:əmétrɪk/ (または **geometrical** /-ɪk(ə)l/) 形 ▶定義 1 of geometry→**幾何学 (上) の, 幾何学的図形の** ▶定義 2 consisting of regular shapes and lines 規則的な図形や線を入れる→**幾何学様式の** ‖ *a geometric design/pattern* 幾何学 (的) デザイン・模様 — geometrically /-k(ə)li/ 副 →**幾何学的に**

**geometry** /dʒiámətri/ 名 ⓤ ▶定義 the study in mathematics of lines, shapes, curves, etc 数学の分野で線・図形・曲線などに関する学問→**幾何学, 幾何学書**

**geothermal** /dʒì:ouθə́:rm(ə)l, dʒì:ə-/ 形 ▶定義 connected with the natural heat of rock deep in the ground 地中深い岩盤が自然に持つ熱に関連した→**地熱の** ‖ *geothermal energy* 地熱エネルギー

**geriatrics** /dʒèriætrɪks/ 名 ⓤ ▶定義 the medical care of old people 高齢者への医療→**老人学・科** — geriatric 形 →**老人病の, 老人の**

**germ** /dʒə:rm/ 名 ▶定義 1 ⓒ a very small living thing that causes disease 病気の原因となる非常に小さい生物→**病原菌, ばい菌, 細菌** ☞参 **bacteria**, **virus** ▶定義 2 [単数扱い] **the germ of sth** the beginning of sth that may develop 展開していくかもしれない事・物の始まり→**芽生え, 兆し** ‖ *the germ of an idea* アイデアの芽生え

**German measles** /dʒə́:rmən mí:z(ə)lz/ (または **rubella**) 名 ⓤ ▶定義 a mild disease that causes red spots all over the body. It may damage a baby if the mother catches it when she is pregnant. 体中に赤い斑点 (はんてん) ができる軽い疾病. 妊娠中に母親がかかると, 赤ちゃんに害が及ぶことがある→**風疹 (ふうしん), 三日麻疹 (はしか)**

**germinate** /dʒə́ːrmənèit/ 動自他 ▶定義 (used about a seed) to start growing; to cause a seed to do this (種について)発育を始める; 種を発育させる→(種が)芽を出す, 生長する; ～を発芽させる, ～を生じさせる ― **germination** /dʒə̀ːrmənéiʃ(ə)n/ 名 U→発芽, 発生; 発達

**gerund** /dʒérənd/ 名 C (文法) ▶定義 a noun, ending in -ing, that has been made from a verb 動詞から作られた名詞で, 語尾が -ing→動名詞 ‖ *In the sentence 'His hobby is collecting stamps', 'collecting' is a gerund.* His hobby is collecting stamps という文章において, collecting が動名詞である.

**gesticulate** /dʒestíkjəlèit/ 動自 ▶定義 to make movements with your hands and arms in order to express sth 手や腕を使って～を表現する→身振りたっぷりで話す

**gesture**¹ /dʒéstʃər/ 名 C ▶定義 1 a movement of the hand, head, etc that expresses sth ～を表現するための, 手・頭などの動作→身振り, 手まね, しぐさ ‖ *I saw the boy make a rude gesture at the policeman before running off.* 私は, その少年が警察官に対して無礼なしぐさをして逃げ去るのを見た. ▶定義 2 something that you do that shows other people what you think or feel 自分の考えや気持ちを他人に表現するためにすること→意思表示(の行為・言葉), 感情表現, 素振り

**gesture**² /dʒéstʃər/ 動自他 ▶定義 to point at sth, to make a sign to sb ～を指す, ～に合図を送る→～に・～を手振りで示す, 身振りをする ‖ *She asked them to leave and gestured towards the door.* 彼女は彼らに立ち去るように言って, ドアの方を指した.

★**get** /get/ 動 (現分 **getting**; 過 **got** /gɑt/; 過分 **got**; 米 **gotten** /gɑtn/) ▶定義 1 他 (受動態では使われない) to receive, obtain or buy sth ～を受け取る, 手に入れる, または買う→～を受け取る, ～を得る, ～を手に入れる ‖ *I got a letter from my sister.* 私は姉[妹]からの手紙を受け取った. *Did you get a present for your mother?* お母さんへのプレゼントを買いましたか. *Did you get your mother a present?* お母さんにプレゼントを買いましたか. *She got a job in a travel agency.* 彼女は旅行会社での職を得た. *Louise got 75 % in the maths exam.* ルイーズは数学の試験で75点を取った. *I'll come if I can get time off work.* もし仕事の休みが取れたら行きます. *How much did you get for your old car (= when you sold it)?* あなたは, 古い車でいくら手に入れたのですか(= それを売った時). *to get a shock/surprise* 衝撃を受ける・びっくりする ▶定義 2 他 *have/has got sth* to have sth ～がある→～する・～の事がある ‖ *I've got a lot to do today.* 私は今日やるべき事がたくさんある. *Lee's got blond hair.* リーの髪の色はブロンドだ. *Have you got a spare pen?* 余分にペンを持っていますか. ▶定義 3 他 (受動態では使われない) to go to a place and bring sth back; fetch ある場所へ行って～を持ち帰る; 取ってくる→～を持ってくる; 取ってくる ‖ *Go and get me a pen, please.* 私にペンを取ってきてちょうだい. *Sam's gone to get his mother from the station.* サムは, 母親を迎えに駅まで出掛けた. ▶定義 4 自 to become; to reach a particular state or condition; to make sb/sth be in a particular state or condition なる; 特定の状態や状況に至る; ～を特定の状態や状況に至らせる→するようになる, ～になる, される ‖ *It's getting dark.* 暗くなってきた. *to get angry/bored/hungry/fat* 怒る・退屈する・空腹になる・太る *I can't get used to my new bed.* 私は新しいベッドに慣れない. *to get dressed* 洋服を着る *When did you get married?* あなたはいつ結婚したのですか. *to get pregnant* 妊娠する *Just give me five minutes to get ready.* とにかく5分も待ってもらえれば, 準備ができます. *He's always getting into trouble with the police.* 彼はいつも警察ともめ事を起こしてばかりいる. *She's shy, but she's great fun once you get to know her.* 彼女は恥ずかしがり屋だが, いったん知り合いになればとても面白い人だ. ▶定義 5 自 to arrive at or reach a place ある場所に着く, または到達する→至る, たどり着く ‖ *We should get to London at about ten.* 我々は10時ころロンドンにたどり着くはずだ. *Can you tell me how to get to the hospital?* その病院へどうやって行けばよいか, 教えてくれますか. *What time do you usually get home?* 普段何時ころ帰宅しますか. *I got half way up the mountain then gave up.* 私はその山を半分までは何とか登ったが, そこで断念した. *How far have you got with* your book? あなたは本をどれくらい読み進みましたか. ☞参 get in, on など ▶定義6 🈓🈔 to move or go somewhere; to move or put sth somewhere 移動する, どこかへ行く；～をどこかへ移動する・置く→移動する, 行く, 運ぶ, 持っていく, 置く ‖ *I can't swim so I couldn't get across the river.* 私は泳げないので, 川を渡ることができなかった. *My grandmother's 92 and she doesn't get out of the house much.* 私の祖母は92歳で, あまり家の外には出掛けません. *We couldn't get the piano upstairs.* 私たちはピアノを2階に運ぶことができなかった. *My foot was swollen and I couldn't get my shoe off.* 片足がはれて, 靴を脱ぐことができませんでした.

▶定義7 🈓 used instead of 'be' in the passive 受動態で be に代わって用いられる→～になる ‖ *She got bitten by a dog.* 彼女は犬にかまれた. *Don't leave your wallet on the table or it'll get stolen.* テーブルの上に財布を置きっ放しにしないでください, さもないと盗まれますよ.

▶定義8 🈔 get sth done, mended etc to cause sth to be done, mended, etc ～を終わらせる, 修繕などをしてもらう→～をしてしまう, ～をしてもらう ‖ *Let's get this work done, then we can go out.* この仕事を終わらせましょう, そうすれば出掛けられます. *I'm going to get my hair cut.* 私は髪を切りに行くつもりだ.

▶定義9 🈔 get sb/sth to do sth to make or persuade sb/sth to do sth→(説得などして)～に…をさせる, してもらう ‖ *I got him to agree to the plan.* 私は彼を説得して計画に同意してもらった. *I can't get the television to work.* 私はそのテレビをうまく作動させることができない. ▶定義10 🈔 to catch or have an illness, pain, etc→(病気に)かかる, ～の目に遭う ‖ *I think I'm getting a cold.* 私は風邪にかかったようだ. *He gets really bad headaches.* 彼は本当にひどい頭痛に悩まされています. ▶定義11 🈔 to use a form of transport 交通手段を使う→乗る, 使う ‖ *Shall we walk or get the bus?* 歩きますか, それともバスに乗りますか. ▶定義12 🈓 to hit, hold or catch sb/sth→～の…をたたく・握る・つかむ ‖ *He got me by the throat and threatened to kill me.* 彼は私ののどをつかんで, 殺すぞと脅した. *A boy threw a stone at me but he didn't get me.* 男の子が私に向かって石を投げ付けたが, 当たらなかった. ▶定義13 🈔 to hear

get  701

or understand sth→～を聞き取る, 理解する ‖ *I'm sorry, I didn't get that. Could you repeat it?* すみません, おっしゃることが聞き取れません. もう1回言っていただけますか. *Did you get that joke that Karen told?* あなたは, カレンの言ったあのジョークが理解できましたか. ▶定義14 🈔 get (sb) sth; get sth (for sb) to prepare food 食べ物を用意する→～に…を準備する, 支度する ‖ *Can I get you anything to eat?* 何か食べる物を用意しましょうか. *Joe's in the kitchen getting breakfast for everyone.* ジョーは台所で, みんなの朝食の支度をしている.

▶定義15🈓 get to do sth to have the chance to do sth→する機会がある, チャンスがある ‖ *Did you get to try the new computer?* あなたは, 新しいコンピューターを試してみる機会がありましたか. ▶定義16🈓 (-ingの形で動詞と用いられて)to start doing sth→～を始める, かかる ‖ *We don't have much time so we'd better get working.* あまり時間がないから, 私たちは仕事に取り掛かった方がいい. *I got talking to a woman on the bus.* 私はバスで女の人と話し始めた. *We'd better get going if we don't want to be late.* 遅刻したくなかったら, 私たちはもう出発した方がいい.

▶語法

get on/off と get in/out

「電車・バスに乗る／から降りる」の場合は get on/off... で,「自家用車・タクシーに乗る／から降りる」場合には get in/out... を用います. この違いは乗り物をどのような空間として認識しているかの違いを反映しています. 電車・バスのような大きな乗り物の場合には「広い床面」を連想するので, 平面(二次元)との接触のイメージで on/off を用います. 一方, タクシーなどの比較的小さな乗り物の場合は「箱」のような空間(三次元)を連想するので, 出入りを表す in/out を使うのです.

成句 get somewhere/nowhere (with sb/sth)
▶定義 to make/not make progress→進歩する・進歩がない, 成功する・成功しない ‖ *I'm getting nowhere with my research.* 私の研究は進んでいません.

## 702　get

▶ getを含むこのほかの成句については，名詞，形容詞などの項を参照．例えばget rid ofはridの項にある．

**句動詞** get about/around ▶定義 to move or travel from place to place→(あちこち)動き回る，歩き回る，旅行する ‖ *My grandmother needs a stick to get around these days.* このごろ私の祖母は出歩くのにつえが必要だ．

get about/around/round ▶定義 (used about news, a story, etc) to become known by many people (ニュース・話などについて)大勢の人の知るところとなる→広まる，知れ渡る ‖ *The rumour got around that Freddie wore a wig.* フレディーはかつらをかぶっているといううわさが広まった．

get sth across (to sb) ▶定義 to succeed in making people understand sth 人々に〜をうまく理解させる→(話・意味などが)理解される，通じる ‖ *The party failed to get its policies across to the voters.* その政党は有権者に政策を理解してもらうことができなかった．

get ahead ▶定義 to progress and be successful in sth, especially a career 特に職において前進する・成功する→成功する，出世する，うまく進む

get along ▶定義 1 (口語)(通常は進行形で用いて) to leave a place ある場所を去る→立ち去る，帰る ‖ *I'd love to stay, but I should be getting along now.* ここにいたいのはやまやまですが，そろそろおいとましなければ．▶定義 2 ⇒ GET ON

get around ▶定義 1 ⇒ GET ABOUT/AROUND ▶定義 2 ⇒ GET ABOUT/AROUND/ROUND

get around sb ⇒ GET ROUND/AROUND SB

get around sth ⇒ GET ROUND/AROUND STH

get around to sth/doing sth ⇒ GET ROUND/AROUND TO STH/DOING STH

get at sb ▶定義 to criticize sb a lot 〜をひどく批判する→〜を攻撃する，〜に文句を言う ‖ *The teacher's always getting at me about my spelling.* 先生は私のつづり方にいつも文句を付けてばかりいる．

get at sb/sth ▶定義 to be able to reach sth; to have sth available for immediate use 〜に到達できる；〜をすぐ使えるように持っている→〜に届く，〜をつかむ，〜を手に入れる ‖ *The files are locked away and I can't get at them.* そのファイルにはかぎがかかっているので，私はそれを手にすることができない．

get at sth (進行形だけ) ▶定義 to try to say sth without saying it in a direct way; to suggest 〜を直接言わずに伝えようとする；暗示する→〜をほのめかす，暗示する ‖ *I'm not quite sure what you're getting at - am I doing something wrong?* あなたが私に何をおっしゃりたいのかよく分かりません ― 私が何か間違った事をしていますか．

get away (from...) ▶定義 to succeed in leaving or escaping from sb or a place 〜・場所から去る・脱出するのに成功する→去る，逃げる ‖ *He kept talking to me and I couldn't get away from him.* 彼は私にずっとしゃべり通しで，私はその場を立ち去ることができなかった．*The thieves got away in a stolen car.* 泥棒たちは盗難車で逃げ去った．

get away with sth/doing sth ▶定義 to do sth bad and not be punished for it 何か悪い事をして，その罰を受けない→(悪事などを罰せられずに)うまくやってのける，(軽い罪で)逃れる，済む ‖ *He lied but he got away with it.* 彼はうそをついたが，見つからないで済んだ．

get away with murder ⇒ MURDER

get back ▶定義 to return to the place where you live or work 自分の住むまたは働く場所に戻る→戻る，帰る ‖ *When did you get back from Italy?* いつイタリアから帰ったのですか．

get sth back ▶定義 to be given sth that you had lost or lent なくした・貸した物を返してもらう→〜を取り戻す，〜を取り返す ‖ *Can I borrow this book? You'll get it back next week, I promise.* この本借りてもいいですか．来週お返しすると約束しますよ．

get back to sb ▶定義 to speak to, write to or telephone sb later, especially in order to give an answer→後で返事をする，後日手紙を書く，折り返し電話する ‖ *I'll get back to you on prices when I've got some more information.* 価格に関しては，もっと情報を集めてからまたお返事します．

get back to sth ▶定義 to return to doing sth or talking about sth ～を再開する、または～について改めて話す➡**再度～をする、～の話に戻る** ‖ *I woke up early and couldn't get back to sleep.* 私は朝早く目覚めてしまい、再び眠りに就くことができなかった。*Let's get back to the point you raised earlier.* さっきあなたが提起したところまで、話を戻しましょう。

get behind (with sth) ▶定義 to fail to do, pay sth, etc on time, and so have more to do, pay, etc the next time ～を期限内に行う・支払うことなどができない、したがって、これから行う・支払うなどの必要がある➡**仕事が滞っている、滞納している** ‖ *to get behind with your work/rent* 仕事が滞っている・家賃を滞納している

get by (on/in/with sth) ▶定義 to manage to live or do sth with difficulty 何とか生活する、困難を伴いながら～を行う➡**何とか暮らす、どうにかうまくいく** ‖ *It's very hard to get by on such a low income.* こんな低所得では暮らしが非常に苦しい。*My Italian is good and I can get by in Spanish.* 私のイタリア語はなかなかのものだし、スペイン語も何とか使えます。

get sb down ▶定義 to make sb unhappy ～を不幸にする➡**がっかりさせる、失望させる**

get down to sth/doing sth ▶定義 to start working on sth➡**～に取り掛かる、本腰を入れて取り組む** ‖ *We'd better stop chatting and get down to work.* 我々もおしゃべりはやめて、仕事に取り掛かった方がいい。*I must get down to answering these letters.* 私はこれらの手紙に返事を書き始めなければなりません。

get in ▶定義 to reach a place ある場所に着く➡**到着する、入港する** ‖ *What time does your train get in?* あなたが乗る電車は何時に到着しますか。

get in; get into sth ▶定義1 to climb into a car 車に乗り込む➡**(中へ)入る、～に乗り込む** ‖ *We all got in and Tim drove off.* 私たちは全員車に乗り込み、ティムが運転した。▶定義2 to be elected to a political position 政治的役職に選出される➡**(議員などに)選ばれる、当選する、政権をとる**

get sb in ▶定義 to call sb to your house to do a job 家に人を呼んで仕事をしてもらう➡**家に呼び入れる、～を家に呼ぶ** ‖ *We had to get a plumber in to fix the pipes.* 私たちは配管工を呼んで、配管を修理してもらわねばならなかった。

get sth in ▶定義1 to collect or bring sth inside; to buy a supply of sth ～を中に集める・持ってくる；金を払って～の供給を受ける➡**取り入れる；仕入れる** ‖ *It's going to rain - I'd better get the washing in from outside.* 雨が降りそうだ － 洗濯物を取り込んだ方が良さそうです。▶定義2 to manage to find an opportunity to say or do sth 発言したり～をする機会を、何とか見つける➡**(言葉を)差し挟む** ‖ *He talked all the time and I couldn't get a word in.* 彼はずっと話し続けたので、私は口を挟むことができなかった。

get in on sth ▶定義 to become involved in an activity 活動に巻き込まれる➡**一枚加わる、～にありつく**

get into sb 略式 ▶定義 (used about a feeling or attitude) to start affecting sb strongly, causing him/her to behave in an unusual way (気持ちや態度について)～に強く影響を及ぼし始め、その人がいつもと違った振る舞いをする原因となる➡**人を(ある状態)に陥れる** ‖ *I wonder what's got into him - he isn't usually unfriendly.* 彼の様子は一体どうしたのだろう － いつもの彼は、もっと親しみやすいのに。

get into sth ▶定義1 to put on a piece of clothing with difficulty 苦労して洋服を身に着ける➡**～を身に着ける、着る、履く** ‖ *I've put on so much weight I can't get into my trousers.* 私は体重が大分増えてしまったので、ズボンがきつくて履けない。▶定義2 to start a particular activity; to become involved in sth➡**～の活動を始める；～の仲間に加わる** ‖ *How did you first get into the music business?* あなたは、最初にどのようにして音楽の業界に入ったのですか。*She has got into the habit of turning up late.* 彼女は遅れてやって来る癖がついた。*We got into an argument about politics.* 私たちは政治に関して議論になった。▶定義3 to become more interested in or familiar with sth ～にもっと興味を持つ、～をより深く知る➡**のめり込む、精通する** ‖ *I've been getting into yoga recently.* 私はこのところ、ヨガにのめり込んでいます。*It's taking me a while to get into my new job.* 私は新しい仕事に慣れるのに、しばらく時間がかか

っている.

**get off (sb/sth)** ▶定義 used especially to tell sb to stop touching you/sb/sth ～に, 自分や…に触るのをやめるよう言うのに, 特に用いて → **～から放れる, ～を放す** ‖ *Get off (me) or I'll call the police!* 放してください, さもないと警察を呼びますよ. *Get off that money, it's mine!* その金から離れろ, 私のものだぞ.

**get off (sth)** ▶定義 1 to leave a bus, train, etc; to climb down from a bicycle, horse, etc バス・電車などを降りる; 自転車・馬などから降りる → **～から降りる, 降車する** ▶定義 2 to leave work with permission at a particular time 許可を得て, ある時間に仕事から帰る → **(仕事から)帰る, (仕事を)終える** ‖ *I might be able to get off early today.* 今日は早く帰れるかもしれない.

**get off (with sth)** ▶定義 to be lucky to receive no serious injuries or punishment 運良く, ひどい傷も罰も受けない → **(事を)逃れる, うまく避ける** ‖ *to get off with just a warning* 警告だけで済む

**get on** ▶定義 1 to progress or become successful in life, in a career, etc 人生・職などにおいて出世・成功する → **成功する, 出世する, 昇進する** ▶定義 2 to be getting old 年を取ってくる → **(人が)年を取る** ‖ *He's getting on - he's over 70, I'm sure.* 彼も年を取ってきました - 確かもう 70 歳を超えています. ▶定義 3 to be getting late 遅くなりつつある → **(時が)たつ, 遅くなる** ‖ *Time's getting on - we don't want to be late.* どんどん時間がたっています - 私たちは遅刻するのは嫌です.

▶定義 2 と 3 の意味では, 進行形のみが用いられる.

**get on/along** ▶定義 to have a particular amount of success ある一定の成功を手にする → **うまくいく, 進行する** ‖ *How are you getting on in your course?* 教科の進度はいかがですか. *'How did you get on at your interview?' 'I got the job!'* 「面接はうまくいきましたか」「雇ってもらうことができました」

**get on/onto sth** ▶定義 to climb onto a bus, train, bicycle, horse, etc バス・電車・自転車・馬などに乗り込む → **(乗り物に)乗る** ‖ *I got on just as the train was about to leave.* 私はその電車の発車間際に乗り込んだ.

**get on for** (進行形だけ) ▶定義 to be getting near to a certain time or age ある時刻・年齢に近付いている → **(時間・年齢に)近付く** ‖ *I'm not sure how old he is but he must be getting on for 50.* 彼の年はよく分からないが, 50 歳近いのは間違いない.

**get on to sb (about sth)** ▶定義 to speak or write to sb about a particular matter ～に特定の事柄について話をする・手紙を書く → **(電話・手紙などで)～に関して連絡を取る**

**get on/along with sb; get on/along (together)** ▶定義 to have a friendly relationship with sb ～と友好的関係を持つ → **～と仲良くやる, 協調してやっていく** ‖ *Do you get on well with your colleagues?* 同僚とは仲良くやっていますか. *We're not close friends but we get on together quite well.* 私たちは親しい友人ではないが, とても良い関係を保っている.

**get on/along with sth** ▶定義 to make progress with sth that you are doing やっている事が進む → **はかどる, 進む** ‖ *How are you getting on with that essay?* そのエッセーのはかどり具合はいかがですか.

**get on with sth** ▶定義 to continue doing sth, especially after an interruption 特に中断の後, ～を継続して行う → **(仕事などを)(中断後)続ける** ‖ *Stop talking and get on with your work!* 話をするのはやめて, 仕事を続けなさい.

**get out** ▶定義 (used about a piece of information) to become known, after being secret until now (情報について) 今まで秘密だった事が知れ渡る → **(秘密などが)漏れる, 知られる**

**get sth out (of sth)** ▶定義 to take sth from its container ～を容器から取り出す → **取り出す, 引き抜く** ‖ *I got my keys out of my bag.* 私はバッグからかぎを取り出した.

**get out of sth/doing sth** ▶定義 to avoid a duty or doing sth that you have said you will do いったん自分がやると言った義務・～から逃れる → **(責任・義務など)を逃れる, 回避する**

**get sth out of sb** ▶定義 to persuade or force sb to give you sth ～を説得して・強制して…をもらう → **～から…を引き出す, 奪う** ‖ *His parents finally got the truth out of him.* 彼の両親は, 彼からやっと真実を聞き出した.

**get sth out of sb/sth** ▶定義 to gain sth from

sb/sth→(取り引きなど)から(利益など)を得る ‖ *I get a lot of pleasure out of music.* 私は音楽から多くの楽しみを得ている.

**get over sth** ▶定義1 to deal with a problem successfully 問題をうまく処理する→〜を乗り切る,克服する ‖ *We'll have to get over the problem of finding somewhere to live first.* 私たちは,まずどこか住む場所を見つけるという問題を解決せねばならないでしょう. ▶定義2 to feel normal again after being ill or having an unpleasant experience 病気・不愉快な経験の後,再び正常な状態になる→(病気)から回復する,(ショック・不幸)から立ち直る ‖ *He still hasn't got over his wife's death.* 彼はまだ奥さんの死から立ち直っていません.

**get sth over with** 略式 ▶定義 to do and complete sth unpleasant that has to be done しなければならない面倒な〜をやり遂げる→〜を済ませてしまう,終わりにする ‖ *I'll be glad to get my visit to the dentist's over with.* 歯医者通いが終わるとうれしいです.

**get round** ⇒ **GET ABOUT/AROUND/ROUND**

**get round/around sb** 略式 ▶定義 to persuade sb to do sth or agree with sth 〜を説得して…をしてもらう・〜に同意してもらう→〜をうまく説き伏せる,〜を言いくるめる ‖ *My father says he won't lend me the money but I think I can get round him.* 父は私にお金を貸さないと言っているが,私は父をうまく説き伏せることができると思う.

**get round/around sth** ▶定義 to find a way of avoiding or dealing with a problem 問題を避ける・解決する方法を見つける→(障害・困難など)を避ける,克服する,逃れる

**get round/around to sth/doing sth** ▶定義 to find the time to do sth, after a delay 遅れた後で〜をする時間を見つける→〜をする(時間的)余裕を見つける,〜に手が回る,〜するに至る ‖ *I've been meaning to reply to that letter for ages but I haven't got round to it yet.* 私はその手紙に返事を書こうと,随分前から思っているが,いまだに手を付けていない.

**get through sth** ▶定義 to use or complete a certain amount or number of sth ある量・数の〜を使う・終える→〜を終える,全部使う,平らげる ‖ *I got through a lot of money at the week-end.* 私は週末にお金をたくさん使ってしまった. *I got through an enormous amount of work today.* 今日私はばく大な量の仕事をこなした.

**get (sb) through (sth)** ▶定義 to manage to complete sth difficult or unpleasant; to help sb to do this 難しい・不愉快な〜を何とか終える;〜がそうするのを助ける→切り抜ける,〜に(窮地などを)切り抜けさせる ‖ *She got through her final exams easily.* 彼女は最終試験を楽に切り抜けた.

**get through (to sb)** ▶定義1 to succeed in making sb understand sth 〜に…をうまく理解させる→〜を…に分からせる,分かってもらう ‖ *They couldn't get through to him that he was completely wrong.* 彼らは,彼が完全に間違っていることを彼に分かってもらえなかった. ▶定義2 to succeed in speaking to sb on the telephone 〜と電話で話ができる→(電話などが)〜に通じる,〜に電話をつなぐ ‖ *I couldn't get through to them because their phone was engaged all day.* 彼らの電話は一日中ふさがっていて,私は彼らと電話で話ができなかった.

**get to sb** 略式 ▶定義 to affect sb in a bad way 〜に悪い影響を与える→〜を怒らせる,いらいらさせる ‖ *Public criticism is beginning to get to the team manager.* 大衆の批判が,チームマネージャーをいら立たせ始めている.

**get sb/sth together** ▶定義 to collect people or things in one place 人々または複数の物を,1箇所に集める→〜を集める,〜を寄せ集める ‖ *I'll just get my things together and then we'll go.* 私はちょっと自分の持ち物をまとめます.それから出発しましょう.

**get together (with sb)** ▶定義 to meet socially or in order to discuss or do sth 社交で会う,または議論などをするために会う→集まる,寄り合う ‖ *Let's get together and talk about it.* みんな集まって,その事について話しましょう.

**get up** ▶定義 to stand up→立ち上がる,起き上がる ‖ *He got up to let an elderly woman sit down.* 彼は年配の女性を座らせるために立ち上がった.

**get (sb) up** ▶定義 to get out of bed or make sb get out of bed ベッドから出る,〜をベッドから出させる→起床する,起きる,人を起こす ‖

## 706　getaway

*What time do you have to get up in the morning?* あなたは朝, 何時に起きなければなりませんか. *Could you get me up at 6 tomorrow?* 明日6時に私を起こしていただけますか.

**get up to sth** ▶定義1 to reach a particular point or stage in sth ～がある特定の地点・段階に到達する➡(ある所)まで達する, 進む ‖ *We've got up to the last section of our grammar book.* 私たちは文法の本の最終章まで進んだ. ▶定義2 to be busy with sth, especially sth secret or bad 特に秘密や悪い事をして忙しい➡(いたずらなど)をしでかす, やってくれる ‖ *I wonder what the children are getting up to?* 一体子供たちは, 何をしでかしているのだろう.

**getaway** /gétəwèɪ/ 名 C ▶定義 an escape (after a crime) (犯行後)逃げること➡逃走, 脱走 ‖ *to make a getaway* 逃走する *a getaway car/driver* 逃走した車・ドライバー

**get-together** 名 C 略式 ▶定義 an informal social meeting or party 略式の社交的会合・集まり➡(非公式な)集まり, 懇親会 ‖ *We're going to have a get-together on Saturday evening.* 私たちは土曜の夜, 集まりを開く予定です.

**ghastly** /gáːstli; gǽst-/ 形 ▶定義 extremely unpleasant or bad 極端に不愉快な, 悪い➡身の毛のよだつほど恐ろしい, ぞっとする, 醜悪な ‖ *a ghastly accident* 恐ろしい事故

**ghetto** /gétoʊ/ 名 C (複 **ghettoes**) ▶定義 a part of a town where many people of the same race, religion, etc live in poor conditions 同じ人種・宗教などの大勢の人々が貧しく暮らしている町の一角➡スラム街, 貧民地区, ユダヤ人(強制)居住地区

★**ghost** /góʊst/ 名 C ▶定義 the spirit of a dead person that is seen or heard by sb who is still living まだ生きている人に, 見えたり聞こえたりする死んだ人の魂➡幽霊, 亡霊, 死者の霊 ‖ *I don't believe in ghosts.* 私は幽霊を信じません. *a ghost story* 怪談　☛参 **spectre**

**ghostly** /góʊstli/ 形 ▶定義 looking or sounding like a ghost; full of ghosts 幽霊のように見え, 聞こえる; 霊に満ちた➡幽霊のような, ぼんやりとした, 影のような ‖ *ghostly noises* かすかな物音

**ghost town** 名 C ▶定義 a town whose inhabitants have all left 住民が皆去った町➡ゴーストタウン, 廃墟(はいきょ)の町

**ghostwriter** /góʊstraɪtər/ 名 C ▶定義 a person who writes a book, etc for a famous person (whose name appears as the author) 有名人(著者としては, その有名人の名前を使う)にかわって本などを書く人➡代作者, ゴーストライター

★**giant** /dʒáɪənt/ 名 C ▶定義1 an extremely large, strong person 極端に大きい・強い人➡巨人, 巨漢, 大男 ▶定義2 something that is very large とても大きい物➡巨大な動物・植物・企業・組織など ‖ *the multinational oil giants* (= very large companies) 多国籍石油企業 (= 非常に大きな複数から成る会社) ― **giant** ➡巨大な, 偉大な ‖ *a giant new shopping centre* 大規模な新しいショッピングセンター

**gibberish** /dʒíbərɪʃ, gíb-/ 名 U ▶定義 words that have no meaning or that are impossible to understand 意味のない, または理解できない言葉➡ちんぷんかんぷんの言葉・話・文章 ‖ *I was so nervous in my interview I just spoke gibberish.* 私は面接でとても上がってしまい, 訳の分からない事しか言えなかった.

**giddy** /gídi/ 形 ▶定義 having the feeling that everything is going round and that you are going to fall; dizzy すべてが回っていて, 自分が倒れそうな感じに; めまいがして➡めまいがする, めまいを起こさせるような ‖ *I feel giddy. I must sit down.* 私はめまいがしてきました. 座らなくては.

★**gift** /gɪft/ 名 C ▶定義1 something that you give to sb; a present ～にあげる物; 贈り物➡贈り物, 寄贈品, 土産物 ‖ *This watch was a gift from my mother.* この時計は母からの贈り物でした. *This week's magazine contains a **free gift** of some make-up.* その雑誌の今週号には, 化粧品のおまけが付いている. *The company **made a gift of** a computer to a local school.* その会社は, 地元の学校にコンピューターを寄贈した. ☛参 **present**の注　▶定義2 **a gift (for sth/doing sth)** natural ability 授かった能力➡天性, 才能

**gifted** /gíftəd/ 形 ▶定義 having natural ability or great intelligence 天性の能力・優れた知能を持った➡天賦の才能のある, 優れた才能・知能のある

**gig** /gɪg/ 名 C 略式 ▶定義 an event where a

**musician or band is paid to perform** 音楽家やバンドが、お金をもらって演奏する催し→ライブハウスでのコンサート、ギグ、演奏の仕事 ‖ *The band are doing gigs all around the country.* そのバンドはその国の至る所でライブをやっています.

**gigantic** /dʒaɪɡǽntɪk, dʒə-/ 形 ▶定義 extremely big 極端に大きい→巨大な、膨大な、巨人のような

**giggle** /ɡíɡ(ə)l/ 動 ⾃ ▶定義 to laugh in a silly way that you can't control, because you are amused or nervous おかしくて、または緊張して我慢ができずに思慮なく笑う→くすくす笑う、忍び笑いをする — **giggle** 名 ⃝ ▶くすくす笑い、忍び笑い ‖ *I've got the giggles (= I can't stop laughing).* くすくす笑いが止まらない (= 私は笑いをこらえきれない).

**gill** /ɡɪl/ 名 [⃝, 通常は複数] ▶定義 one of the parts on the side of a fish's head that it breathes through 魚の頭側にある呼吸をする器官の1つ→(魚などの)えら→C1ページのさし絵

**gilt** /ɡɪlt/ 名 ⓤ ▶定義 a thin covering of gold 金製の薄い膜→金ぱく、金粉、金色塗料

**gimmick** /ɡímɪk/ 名 ⃝ ▶定義 an idea for attracting customers or persuading people to buy sth 顧客を引き付けたり、人が~を買うよう促すための考案→(人目をひくための)余分な仕掛け、おまけ ‖ *New magazines often use free gifts or other gimmicks to get people to buy them.* 新刊雑誌は人々に購入を促すために、景品やそのほかのおまけをよく使う.

**gin** /dʒɪn/ 名 ⃝ⓤ ▶定義 a strong, colourless alcoholic drink 無色でアルコール度の強い飲料→ジン

**ginger** /dʒíndʒər/ 名 ⓤ形 ▶定義 **1** a root that tastes hot and is used in cooking 辛味があり、料理に使われる根→ショウガ、ショウガの根 ‖ *ground ginger* おろしショウガ *ginger biscuits* ショウガ入りビスケット ▶定義 **2** (of) a light brownish-orange colour 明るい茶色がかったオレンジ色(の)→ショウガ色、赤[黄]褐色、(頭髪の)赤毛色 ‖ *ginger hair* 赤毛色の髪

**ginger ale** 名 ⓤ ▶定義 a drink that does not contain alcohol and is flavoured with a spice (ginger) アルコール分を含まず、香辛料(ショウガ)で風味付けされた飲み物→ジンジャーエール
▶ ginger beer(ジンジャービア)は似ているが、少量のアルコール分を含む.

## girlhood 707

**gingerly** /dʒíndʒərli/ 副 ▶定義 very slowly and carefully so as not to cause harm, make a noise, etc 傷付けたり、音を立てないように、非常にゆっくり注意深く→非常に慎重に、極めて用心深く、恐る恐る ‖ *I removed the bandage very gingerly and looked at the cut.* 私は恐る恐る包帯を取って、切り傷を見てみた.

**gipsy** = GYPSY

**giraffe** /dʒərǽf, -rάːf/ 名 ⃝ (複 **giraffe**, **giraffes**) ▶定義 a large African animal with a very long neck and legs and big dark spots on its skin 大型でアフリカ産の動物、首や脚がとても長く、表皮に大きな濃い斑点(はんてん)がある→キリン、ジラフ

**girder** /ɡə́ːrdər/ 名 ⃝ ▶定義 a long, heavy piece of iron or steel that is used in the building of bridges, large buildings, etc 橋や大きな建物などの建造に用いられる、長く重い鉄・鋼鉄の塊→ガーダー、けた、大梁(おおばり)

★**girl** /ɡəːrl/ 名 ⃝ ▶定義 **1** a female child 女の子、少女 ‖ *Is the baby a boy or a girl?* その赤ちゃんは男の子ですか、それとも女の子ですか. *There are more boys than girls in the class.* そのクラスは、女の子より男の子の方が多い. ▶定義 **2** a daughter→娘 ‖ *They have two boys and a girl.* 彼らには息子2人と娘1人がいる. ▶定義 **3** a young woman→若い女性、女の子 ‖ *He was eighteen before he became interested in girls.* 彼は女の子に興味を持つようになる前に、18歳になっていた. *The girl at the cash desk was very helpful.* レジの女の子はとても親切だった. ▶定義 **4** **girls** [複数扱い] a woman's female friends of any age 年に関係なく女性の友達→女友達 ‖ *a night out with the girls* 女友達との夜のお出掛け

★**girlfriend** /ɡə́ːrlfrènd/ 名 ⃝ ▶定義 **1** a girl or woman with whom sb has a romantic and/or sexual relationship ~が恋愛感情と・または性的関係を持っている、女の子または女性→恋人、愛人 ‖ *Have you got a girlfriend?* 恋人はできましたか. ▶定義 **2** 特に 米 a girl or woman's female friend 女の子・女性の友達→女友達

**Girl Guide** (古) = **GUIDE¹(5)**

**girlhood** /ɡə́ːrlhùd/ 名 ⓤ ▶定義 the time when sb is a girl (1) ~が girl (1) である時期→少女時

### girlish

代, 少女であること

**girlish** /gə́ːrlɪʃ/ 形 ▶定義 looking, sounding or behaving like a girl 少女らしい外見・しゃべり方・振る舞い→**少女の, 少女時代の, 少女らしい** ‖ *a girlish figure/giggle* 少女らしい姿・くすくす笑い

**giro** /dʒáɪroʊ/ 名 (複 **giros**) 英 ▶定義1 ❶a system for moving money from one bank, etc to another お金を, ある銀行などから別の銀行などに移すシステム→**振替為替(制度), (ジャイロ)為替** ▶定義2 ❸a cheque that the government pays to people who are unemployed or cannot work 政府が失業者・働けない人に支払う小切手→**(ジャイロ)小切手**

**gist** /dʒɪst/ 名 the gist (of sth) [単数扱い] ▶定義 the general meaning of sth rather than all the details 〜の詳細にわたるというより, むしろ一般的な意味→**要点, 要旨, 主意** ‖ *I know a little Spanish so I was able to **get the gist** of what he said.* 私はスペイン語が少し分かるので, 彼が言った事の要旨は理解できた.

\*　**give**¹ /gɪv/ 動 (過 **gave** /géɪv/; 過分 **given** /gív(ə)n/) ▶定義1 ❶ give sb sth; give sth to sb to let sb have sth, especially sth that he/she wants or needs 〜に, 特にその人が欲しい・望む物を与える→**与える, 贈る, 渡す** ‖ *I gave Jackie a book for her birthday.* 私はジャッキーの誕生日に本を贈った. *Give me that book a minute - I just want to check something.* その本をほんの少しの間私に貸してください - ちょっと調べたい事がありますので. *I gave my bag to my friend to look after.* 私は友達にバッグを預けて見ていてもらった. *I'll give you my telephone number.* あなたに私の電話番号をお渡しします. *The doctor gave me this cream for my skin.* 医者はこのクリームを, 私の皮膚に塗るためにくれた. *He was thirsty so I gave him a drink.* 彼はのどが渇いていたので, 私は飲み物を上げた. *Just phone and I'll give you all the help you need.* お電話さえくだされば, 必要なときいつでも力になります. ▶定義2 ❸ give sb sth; give sth to sb to make sb have sth, especially sth he/she does not want 〜に特にその人が欲しくないものを与える→**(打撃・苦痛・罰などを)与える, 課す** ‖ *Mr Johns gives us too much homework.* ジョーンズ先生は私たちに多すぎるほどの宿題を出す. *Playing chess gives me a headache.* 私はチェスをすると頭が痛くなる. ▶定義3 ❸ to make sb have a particular feeling, idea, etc 〜にある特定の気持ち・思い付きなどを引き起こす→**感じさせる, 生じさせる** ‖ *Swimming always gives me a good appetite.* 水泳をすると, 私はいつも食欲がもりもりわく. *to give sb a surprise/shock/fright* 〜を驚かす・衝撃を与える・恐怖に陥れる *What gives you the idea that he was lying?* 彼がうそをついていたと, なぜ分かるのですか. ▶定義4 ❸ give (sb) sth; give sth to sb to let sb have your opinion, decision, judgement, etc 〜にあなたの意見・決定・判断などを伝える→**述べる, 伝える, 言い渡す** ‖ *Can you give me some advice?* 私に何か助言を頂けますか. *My boss has given me permission to leave early.* 上司は私に早退の許可をくれた. *The judge gave him five years in prison.* 裁判官は彼に5年の禁固を言い渡した. ▶定義5 ❸ give sb sth; give sth to sb to speak to people in a formal situation 公式の場で人々に演説する→**(演説・授業・講演など)を行う** ‖ *to give a speech/talk/lecture* 演説・講話・講演を行う *The officer was called to give evidence in court.* その警察官は証言を行うため法廷に呼ばれた. *Sarah's going to give me a cooking lesson.* サラは私にお料理を教えてくれることになっている. ▶定義6 ❸ give (sb) sth for sth; give (sb) sth (to do sth) to pay in order to have sth 〜をしてもらうのに支払う→**(代償として)支払う, 与える** ‖ *How much did you give him for fixing the car?* この車を修理してもらうのに, 彼にいくら支払いましたか. (比喩) *I'd give anything (= I would love) to be able to sing like that.* あんな風に歌えるためなら, どんな代償でも払う (= 喜んで代償を払う). ▶定義7 ❸ to spend time dealing with sb/sth 〜を扱うのに時間を費やす→**(時間を)〜に費やす, (精力を)〜に注ぐ** ‖ *We need to give some thought to this matter urgently.* 私たちは, この件に関して早急に, 何か考える必要がある. ▶定義8 ❸ give (sb/sth) sth to do sth to sb/sth; to make a particular sound or movement 〜に…をする; 特定の音を出す・動きをする→**(動作を)する, (音・声など)を出す・上げる** ‖ *to give sb a kiss/push/hug/bite*

〜にキスする・(一押し)押す・抱擁をする・かみ付く to give sth a clean/wash/polish 〜を掃除する・洗濯する・磨く **Give me a call when you get home.** 家に着いたら電話をして. **She opened the door and gave a shout of horror.** 彼女は扉を開けて, 恐怖の叫び声を上げた. ▶定義 **9** ⓔ to perform or organize sth for people 人々のために〜を実施する・組織する→**開く, 催す** ‖ **The company gave a party to celebrate its 50th anniversary.** その会社は50周年を祝ってパーティーを開いた. ▶定義 **10** ⓔ to bend or stretch under pressure 押されて曲がる・伸びる→**(力を受けて)へこむ, しなう** ‖ **The branch began to give under my weight.** その枝は私の体重でしなり始めた.

成句 not care/give a damn (about sb/sth) ⇒ **DAMN**³

give or take ▶定義 more or less the number mentioned 提示された数字に対し, 多かれ少なかれ→**(少しの出入りは)あるとして, (時間・量の)多少の増減を伴って** ‖ **It took us two hours to get here, give or take five minutes.** 私たちはここへ来るのに2時間かかりました, 5分くらい誤差があるかもしれませんが.

▶ giveを含むこのほかの成句については, 名詞, 形容詞などの項を参照. 例えばgive wayはwayの項にある.

句動詞 give sth away ▶定義 to give sth to sb without wanting money in return 〜に…を, お金の代償を求めずに与える→**〜に…を寄付する, ただでやる** ‖ **When she got older she gave all her toys away.** 彼女は成長した時, おもちゃをすべて寄付した. **We are giving away a free CD with this month's issue.** 今月号ではCDを無料で差し上げています.

give sth/sb away ▶定義 to show or tell the truth about sth/sb which was secret 秘密だった〜に関して, 真実を示す・語る→**(秘密など)をうっかり漏らす, ばらす, 正体を現す** ‖ **He smiled politely and didn't give away his real feelings.** 彼は礼儀正しくほほえんで, 本心を隠していた.

give (sth) back ▶定義 to return sth to the person that you took or borrowed it from 人からもらった・借りた〜をその人に返す→**〜を返却する, 返す** ‖ **I lent him some books months ago and he still hasn't given them back to me.** 私は数か月前に何冊かの本を彼に貸したが, いまだに返してくれない.

give sth in ▶定義 to give sth to the person who is collecting it 〜を(それを)集めている人に渡す→**〜を提出する, 手渡す** ‖ **I've got to give this essay in to my teacher by Friday.** 私はこの小論文を, 金曜日までに先生に提出しなければならない.

give in (to sb/sth) ▶定義 to stop fighting against sb/sth; to accept that you have been defeated 〜と争うことをやめる; 負けを認める→**〜に降参する, 屈服する**

give sth off ▶定義 to send sth (for example smoke, a smell, heat, etc) out into the air 〜(例えば煙・におい・熱など)を空気中に放つ→**〜を発する, 放出する** ‖ **Cars give off poisonous fumes.** 車は有毒ガスを排出する.

give out ▶定義 (used about a machine, etc) to stop working (機械などについて)動かなくなる→**故障で止まる, 駄目になる** ‖ **His heart gave out and he died.** 彼は心臓が停止して死亡した.

give sth out ▶定義 to give one of sth to each person 〜を1つずつ各人に渡す→**〜を配る, 配布する** ‖ **Could you give out these books to the class, please?** どうぞ, これらの本をクラスの皆に配ってもらえますか.

give up ▶定義 to stop trying to do sth; to accept that you cannot do sth 〜をする試みをやめる; 〜をすることができないと認める→**あきらめる, やめる, 降参する** ‖ **They gave up once the other team had scored their third goal.** 相手チームが3度目のゴールを決めた時, 彼らは試合をあきらめた. **I give up. What's the answer?** 降参です. 答えは何ですか.

give sb up; give up on sb ▶定義 to stop expecting sb to arrive, succeed, improve, etc 〜の到着・成功・改善などを期待しなくなる→**〜を捨てる, あきらめる, 見放す** ‖ **When he was four hours late, I gave him up.** 私は彼が4時間遅れた時点で, もう来ないものとあきらめた. **Her work was so poor that all her teachers gave up on her.** 彼女は勉強があまりにできなかったので, 全員の先生が彼女を見放した.

give sth up; give up doing sth ▶定義 to stop

doing or having sth that you did or had regularly before 以前は定期的にやっていた事をやめる,持っていた物を持たなくなる→**〜を断つ, (〜するの)をやめる** ‖ *I've tried many times to give up smoking.* 私は今まで何度もたばこをやめようとしました. *Don't give up hope. Things are bound to improve.* 望みを断ってはいけません.事態は必ず良い方向に向かいます.

give yourself/sb up (to sb) ▶定義 to go to the police when they are trying to catch you; to tell the police where sb is 警察が捕まえようとしている時,自分から出頭する;警察に〜の居どころを知らせる→**(警察に)自首する,引き渡す**

give sth up (to sb) ▶定義 to give sth to sb who needs or asks for it それを必要としている,または依頼した人に〜を与える→**譲る,明け渡す** ‖ *He gave up his seat on the bus to an elderly woman.* 彼はバスの中で年配の女性に席を譲った.

**give**² /gɪv/ 名 **U** ▶定義 the quality of being able to bend or stretch a little 少し曲がる・伸びることができる性質→**しなやかさ,弾性**

成句 **give and take** ▶定義 a situation in which two people, groups, etc, respect each others' rights and needs 2人・2つのグループなどが, 相互の権利や望んでいるものを尊重し合う状況→**対等・公平な交換,互譲,妥協** ‖ *There has to be some give and take for a marriage to succeed.* 結婚がうまくいくためには,いくらか妥協が必要です.

**giveaway** /ɡívəwèɪ/ 名 **C** 略式 ▶定義 1 a thing that is included free when you buy sth 〜を買ったとき,無料で含まれるもの→**景品,プレミアム** ‖ *There's usually some giveaway with that magazine.* あの雑誌には通常何かプレミアムが付いている. ▶定義 2 something that makes you guess the truth about sb/sth 〜に関する真実を推測させるもの→**(秘密などを)うっかり漏らすこと,明白な証拠** ‖ *She said she didn't know about the money but her face was **a dead giveaway**.* 彼女は,そのお金について何も知らないと言ったが,彼女の表情が(知っているという)動かぬ証拠だった.

**given**¹ /ɡív(ə)n/ 形 (名詞の前だけ) ▶定義 already stated or decided 既に述べられた・決められた→**与えられる,所定の,一定の** ‖ *At any given time, up to 200 people are using the library.* 所定の時間中はいつも,200名もの人々がその図書館を利用しています.

**given**² /ɡív(ə)n/ 前 ▶定義 considering sth→**〜を考慮すれば,〜と仮定すれば** ‖ *Given that you had very little help, I think you did very well.* ほとんど手伝ってもらわなかったということを考慮すれば,あなたはよくやったと私は思います.

**given name** 特に 米 = FIRST NAME ☞参 **name** の注

**glacier** /ɡlǽsiər, ɡléɪʃər/ 名 **C** ▶定義 a mass of ice that moves slowly down a valley 谷をゆっくりと下降する氷の塊→**氷河**

★**glad** /ɡlǽd/ 形 ▶定義 1 (名詞の前は不可) glad (about sth); glad to do sth/that... happy; pleased 幸せな,うれしい→**〜をうれしく思う, 喜んで〜する** ‖ *Are you glad about your new job?* 新しいお仕事は楽しいですか. *I'm glad to hear he's feeling better.* 彼の具合が良くなっていると聞いてうれしいです. *I'm glad (that) he's feeling better.* 彼の具合が良くなっていると聞いてうれしいです. *I'll be glad when these exams are over.* これらの試験が終わったらうれしいだろう.

▶ある特定の出来事や状況については,通常 glad または pleased を使う. happy は事態・状態などを説明するのに使われる.また happy は説明している名詞の前で用いることもできる: *This kind of music always makes me feel happy.* (私はこの種の音楽を聴くと,いつも幸せな気持ちになる.) *She's such a happy child - she's always laughing.* (彼女は何と幸せそうな子供だろう — いつでも笑っている.)

▶定義 2 glad (of sth); glad (if...) grateful for sth 〜を有り難く思う→**〜に感謝する,〜を光栄に思う** ‖ *If you are free, I'd be glad of some help.* もし手が空いていたら,ちょっと手伝っていただけると助かります. *I'd be glad if you could help me.* もしも手伝っていただけたら,とても有り難い. — **gladness** 名 **U** ▶うれしさ,喜び

**gladiator** /ɡlǽdièɪtər/ 名 **C** ▶定義 (in ancient Rome) a man who fought against another man or a wild animal in a public show (古代ローマで)大衆の見ている前で人や野生の動物と戦う男

の人→剣闘士，奴隷の剣士

**gladly** /ɡlǽdli/ 形 ▶定義 used for politely agreeing to a request or accepting an invitation 要請・招待を丁重に受けるときに用いて→**喜んで，(自ら)進んで** ‖ *'Could you help me carry these bags?' 'Gladly.'* 「これらのバッグを運ぶのを手伝っていただけますか」「ええ喜んで」 *She gladly accepted the invitation to stay the night.* 彼女はその晩泊まるよう誘われたので，喜んで受けた．

**glamorize**(または**-ise**) /ɡlǽməràɪz/ 動他 ▶定義 to make sth appear more attractive or exciting than it really is 〜が実際よりもっと魅力的に・面白く見えるようにする→**魅力的にする，美化する** ‖ *Television tends to glamorize violence.* テレビは暴力を美化する傾向がある．

**glamour**(米 または**glamor**) /ɡlǽmər/ 名 U ▶定義 the quality of seeming to be more exciting or attractive than ordinary things or people 普通の物や人々より面白く・魅力的に見える性質→**うっとりさせる美しさ，魅惑，あでやかさ** ‖ *Young people are often attracted by the glamour of city life.* 若者は往々にして都会生活の魅力にひかれるものだ．— **glamorous** /-mərəs/ 形→**魅惑的な，魅力に満ちた** ‖ *the glamorous world of show business* ショービジネスの魅惑的世界 — **glamorously** 副→**魅力的に**

**glance**¹ /ɡlɑːns; ɡlæns/ 動自 ▶定義 to look quickly at sb/sth 〜を急いで見る→**ちらっと見る，ざっと目を通す** ‖ *She glanced round the room to see if they were there.* 彼女は彼らがいるかどうか，その部屋をざっと見回した． *He glanced at her and smiled.* 彼は彼女をちらっと見てほほえんだ． *The receptionist glanced down the list of names.* 受付の人は名簿をちらっと見下ろした．

句動詞 **glance off (sth)** ▶定義 to hit sth at an angle and move off again in another direction 〜にある角度から当たり，今度は別の方向に戻ってくる→**(弾丸・打撃などが)斜めに当たってそれる・跳ね返る，かすめる** ‖ *The ball glanced off his knee and into the net.* 球は彼のひざをかすめてネットの中に入った．

**glance**² /ɡlɑːns; ɡlæns/ 名 C ▶定義 a quick look 素早く見ること→**ちらっと見ること，一瞥(べつ)，一見** ‖ *to take/have a glance at the newspaper headlines* 新聞の見出しにさっと目を通す

成句 **at a (single) glance** ▶定義 with one look→一目見て ‖ *I could tell at a glance that something was wrong.* 私は一目見て何かがおかしいと察知しました．

**at first glance/sight** ⇒ **FIRST**¹

**gland** /ɡlænd/ 名 C ▶定義 any of the small parts (**organs**) inside your body that produce chemical substances for your body to use 身体で使う化学物質を作り出す体内にある小さな器官→**腺(せん)** ‖ *sweat glands* 汗腺

**glare**¹ /ɡleər/ 動自 ▶定義 **1** glare (at sb/sth) to look at sb in a very angry way 〜を激怒して見る→**(怒って)にらみつける** ▶定義 **2** to shine with strong light that hurts your eyes 目にまぶしい強い光で光る→**ぎらぎら輝く，まぶしく光る**

**glare**² /ɡleər/ 名 ▶定義 **1** U strong light that hurts your eyes 目にまぶしい強い光→**まぶしい光，ぎらぎらする光** ‖ *the glare of the sun/a car's headlights* 太陽・車のヘッドライトのまぶしい光 ▶定義 **2** C a very angry look 激怒して見ること→**(怒って)にらみつけること**

**glaring** /ɡléərɪŋ/ 形 ▶定義 **1** very easy to see; shocking とても目立つ；衝撃的な→**紛れもない，歴然とした，明白な** ‖ *a glaring mistake/injustice* 明らかな誤り・不正 ▶定義 **2** (used about a light) too strong and bright (光について)強すぎる，明るすぎる→**ぎらぎら輝く，まぶしい** ▶定義 **3** angry→怒った ‖ *glaring eyes* にらみつけるような目 — **glaringly** 副→**ぎらぎらと，どぎつく，歴然と** ‖ *a glaringly obvious mistake* だれの目にも明らかな間違い

★**glass** /ɡlɑːs; ɡlæs/ 名 ▶定義 **1** U a hard substance that you can usually see through that is used for making windows, bottles, etc 通常は透かして見ることができる硬い物質で，窓・びんなどの材料に使われる→**ガラス，ガラス状の物** ‖ *He cut himself on broken glass.* 彼はガラスの破片で切り傷を負った． *a sheet/pane of glass* 1枚のガラス板・窓ガラス *a glass jar/dish/vase* ガラスのびん・皿・花びん ▶定義 **2** C a drinking container made of glass; the amount of liquid it contains ガラス製の飲み物の容器；それに入る液体の量→**コップ，グラス，杯** ‖ *a wine glass* ワイングラス *a brandy glass* ブランデーグラス *Could I have a glass of water, please?* すみませんがお水を1杯頂けますか． ☞**cup**のさし絵

**glasses**

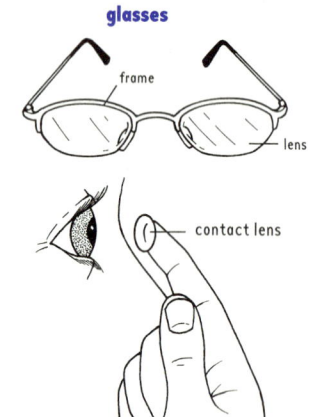

frame
lens
contact lens

\***glasses** /glǽsəz, -ɪz; glǽsəz, -ɪz/（または **spectacles**, **specs**; 困 または **eyeglasses**）图 [複数扱い] ▶定義 two pieces of glass or plastic (**lenses**) in a frame that a person wears in front of his/her eyes in order to be able to see better よく見えるように人が目の前に掛けて使うフレームに入った2枚のガラスまたはプラスチックの（レンズ）→眼鏡, 双眼鏡 ‖ *My sister has to wear glasses.* 私の姉[妹]は眼鏡を掛ける必要があります. *I need a new pair of glasses.* 私は新しい眼鏡が必要です. *I need some new glasses.* 私は新しい眼鏡が必要だ. *reading glasses* 読書用眼鏡 *dark glasses/sunglasses* 色付き眼鏡・サングラス

**glass fibre** = FIBERGLASS

**glasshouse** /glǽːshàʊs; glǽs-/ = GREENHOUSE

**glassy** /glǽsi; glǽsi/ 形 ▶定義1 looking like glass ガラスのように見える→ガラス質の, ガラスのような ▶定義2 (used about the eyes) showing no interest or expression（目について）興味を示さない, または無表情な→どんよりした, 生気のない, 無表情な

**glaze**¹ /gléɪz/ 動他 ▶定義1 to fit a sheet of glass into a window, etc ガラス板を窓などにはめ込む→（窓・ドアなど）にガラスをはめる, 〜にガラス窓を取り付ける ☞ **double-glazing**

▶定義2 **glaze sth (with sth)** to cover a pot, brick, pie, etc with a shiny transparent substance (before it is put into an oven)（オーブンに入れる前に）つぼ・れんが・パイなどを, つやのある透明な物質で覆う→〜にうわ薬・上塗りをかける, 〜につや出しをする

句動詞 **glaze over** ▶定義 (used about the eyes) to show no interest or expression（目について）興味を失う・表情をなくす→（目が）光を失う, どんよりする, かすむ

**glaze**² /gléɪz/ 图 ⓒⓊ ▶定義 (a substance that gives) a shiny transparent surface on a pot, brick, pie, etc つぼ・れんが・パイなどの, つやのある透明な表面（そのような表面を作り出す物質）→光沢のある表面, つや, うわ薬

**glazed** /gléɪzd/ 形 ▶定義 (used about the eyes, etc) showing no interest or expression（目などについて）興味を示さない, 表情のない→（目が）光を失った, どんよりした, 無表情な

**glazier** /gléɪziər, -ʒər/ 图 ⓒ ▶定義 a person whose job is to fit glass into windows, etc ガラスを窓などにはめ込む職人→ガラスはめ職人, ガラス工

**gleam** /gliːm/ 图 [ⓒ, 通常は単数] ▶定義1 a soft light that shines for a short time 短時間光る弱い光→かすかな光・きらめき・輝き ‖ *the gleam of moonlight on the water* 水に映るかすかな月の光 ▶定義2 a sudden expression of an emotion in sb's eyes 〜の目に映るとっさの感情表現→（感情・希望・機知などの）かすかな表れ, ひらめき ‖ *I saw a gleam of amusement in his eyes.* 私は彼の目がかすかに笑っているのが分かった. ▶定義3 a small amount of sth わずかな量の物→わずかな〜 ‖ *a faint gleam of hope* ほんのかすかな望み — **gleam** 動 自 →（かすかに・鋭く・白く）光る・輝く ‖ *gleaming white teeth* 輝く白い歯 *Their eyes gleamed with enthusiasm.* 彼らは夢中になって目を輝かせた.

**glee** /gliː/ 图 Ⓤ ▶定義 a feeling of happiness, usually because sth good has happened to you or sth bad has happened to sb else 幸福な気持ち（通常は良い〜が起こったため, またはだれか別の…に悪い事が起こったため）→大喜び, 歓喜, (他人の不幸などを見て)ほくそ笑むこと ‖ *She couldn't hide her glee when her rival came last in the race.* 彼女はライバルがレースで最下位になった時, 喜びを隠しきれなかった. — **gleeful** /-fʊl, -f(ə)l/ 形→大喜びの, 上機嫌の, 陽気

でにぎやかな — **gleefully** /-fʊli, -f(ə)li/ 副 ➔大喜びで,楽しそうに

**glen** /ɡlen/ 名 C ▶定義 a deep, narrow valley, especially in Scotland or Ireland 特にスコットランドまたはアイルランドの,深く細い谷➔峡谷,谷間

**glib** /ɡlɪb/ 形 ▶定義 using words in a way that is clever and quick, but not sincere 賢く迅速に,しかし心のこもっていない言葉を使う➔口の達者な,ぺらぺらよくしゃべる,上辺だけの ǁ *a glib salesman/politician* 口の達者なセールスマン・政治家 *a glib answer/excuse* 上辺だけの返事,達者な言い訳 — **glibly** 副➔(けなして)ぺらぺらと,上辺で — **glibness** 名 U➔(けなして)おしゃべり,口の達者な人

**glide** /ɡlaɪd/ 動 自 ▶定義1 to move smoothly without noise or effort 物音を立てずに,または力を使わず滑らかに動く➔滑る,滑るように進む ǁ *The dancers glided across the floor.* ダンサーたちは床を滑るように踊った. ▶定義2 to fly in a glider グライダーで飛ぶ➔グライダーで飛ぶ,滑空・滑降する ǁ *I've always wanted to go gliding.* 私はいつもグライダーで飛びたいと思っていた.

**glider** /ɡlaɪdər/ 名 C ▶定義 a light aircraft without an engine that flies using air currents エンジンを持たない軽量飛行機で,大気の流れを利用して飛ぶ➔グライダー,滑るもの ⚫参 **hang-glider** ☞ **parachute** のさし絵 — **gliding** 名 U➔グライダー飛行・競技 ǁ *to go gliding* グライダー飛行に出掛ける

**glimmer** /ɡlɪmər/ 名 C ▶定義1 a weak light that is not steady 安定していない弱い光➔かすかな光,微光,ちらちらする光 ǁ *I could see a faint glimmer of light in one of the windows.* 私は窓の1つに光がちらちらするのを見ることができた. ▶定義2 a small sign of sth 〜のわずかな兆候➔わずかな印,おぼろげな感知 ǁ *a glimmer of hope* わずかな希望の兆候 — **glimmer** 動 自➔ちらちら光る,ぼんやりと現れる

**glimpse** /ɡlɪm(p)s/ 名 C ▶定義1 a glimpse (at/of sth) a very quick and not complete view of sb/sth とても素早く,不完全に〜が見えること➔ちらりと見えること,一目,一見 ǁ *I just managed to **catch a glimpse** of the fox's tail as it ran down a hole.* 私には,穴の中へ駆け込むキツネのしっぽが,何とかちらっと見えただけです. ▶定義2 a glimpse (into/of sth) a short experience of sth that helps you understand it 〜の理解の助けとなるちょっとした経験➔〜をかいま見る ǁ *The programme gives us an interesting glimpse into the life of the cheetah.* その番組は興味深いことに,私たちにチーターの生活をかいま見せてくれる. — **glimpse** 動 他➔ちらっと見る,かすかに見る

**glint** /ɡlɪnt/ 動 自 ▶定義 to shine with small bright flashes of light 小さな明るい光を反射して輝く➔きらきらする,反射する,ぴかりとする ǁ *His eyes glinted at the thought of all that money.* 彼はそのすべてのお金に思いを巡らせて,目をきらりと光らせた. — **glint** 名 C➔閃光(せんこう),きらめき

**glisten** /ɡlɪs(ə)n/ 動 自 ▶定義 (used about wet surfaces) to shine (ぬれた表面について)輝く➔表面などがぴかぴかする,ちかちかする ǁ *Her eyes glistened with tears.* 彼女の目は涙できらきら光っていた. *Tears glistened in her eyes.* 涙が彼女の目の中できらきら光っていた.

**glitter** /ɡlɪtər/ 名 U ▶定義1 a shiny appearance consisting of many small flashes of light たくさんの小さなきらめきから構成された輝き➔きらめき,輝き,光 ǁ *the glitter of jewellery* 宝石の輝き ▶定義2 the exciting quality that sth appears to have 〜に備わっていると思われる刺激的な性質➔きらびやかさ,華やかさ,華麗 ǁ *the glitter of a career in show business* ショービジネスにおける華麗な経歴 ▶定義3 very small, shiny pieces of thin metal or paper, used as a decoration とても小さい,輝く薄い金属・紙片で装飾に用いる➔きらきら輝く小さな装飾(ラメなど) ǁ *The children decorated their pictures with glitter.* 子供たちは自分たちの絵に,きらきら輝く装飾を施した. — **glitter** 動 自➔きらめく,きらきら輝く,ぴかぴか光る

**glittering** /ɡlɪtərɪŋ/ 形 ▶定義1 very impressive or successful とても印象的な・成功した➔輝かしい,華麗な,きらびやかな ǁ *a glittering career/performance* 輝かしい経歴・実績 ▶定義2 shining brightly with many small flashes of light たくさんの小さな光を反射して明るく輝く➔きらめく,輝く

**gloat** /ɡloʊt/ 動 自 ▶定義 gloat (about/over

sth) to feel or express happiness in an unpleasant way because sth good has happened to you or sth bad has happened to sb else 良い〜が自分の身に起こった，あるいはだれか別の〜に悪い…が起こったことを，喜ばしく思う，またその喜びを不快な感じで表現する →いい気になる, ほくそ笑む

**global** /glóub(ə)l/ 形 ▶定義1 affecting the whole world 全世界に影響する →世界的な, 地球上の, 全世界の ‖ the global effects of pollution 汚染の世界的影響 ▶定義2 considering or including all parts すべての部分を考慮して, または包括して →全体的な, 包括的な ‖ We must take a global view of the problem. 私たちはその問題に対し, 包括的な視野を持たなければならない. — globally /-b(ə)li/ 副 →全世界から見て, 全体的に, 包括的に

**the global village** 名 [単数扱い] ▶定義 the world considered as a single community linked by computers, telephones, etc コンピューターや電話などで結ばれた1つの社会と見なすことができる世界 →地球村

**global warming** 名 [単数扱い] ▶定義 the increase in the temperature of the earth's atmosphere, caused by the increase of certain gases ある種のガスが増加することにより引き起こされる, 地球環境における気温の上昇 →地球温暖化 ⇒参 greenhouse effect

**globe** /glóub/ 名 ▶定義1 the globe [単数扱い] the earth →地球, 世界 ‖ to travel all over the globe 世界中を旅行する ▶定義2 ● a round object with a map of the world on it 世界地図がその上に載っている球体 →地球儀, 天体儀 ▶定義3 ● any object shaped like a ball 球のような形をしたすべての物体 →球, 球状の物

**globe artichoke** = ARTICHOKE

**globetrotter** /glóubtràtər/ 名 ● 略式 ▶定義 a person who travels to many countries 各国を旅行する人 →世界観光旅行者・漫遊者

**globule** /glábjuːl/ 名 ● ▶定義 a small drop or ball of a liquid 液体の小滴または小球体 →小滴, 小球体 ‖ There were globules of fat in the soup. そのスープには小さい脂肪の玉が浮いていた.

**gloom** /gluːm/ 名 ● ▶定義1 a feeling of being sad and without hope 悲しく希望のない気持ち →深い悲しみ, 陰気, 憂鬱(ゆううつ) ‖ The news brought deep gloom to the village. その知らせは村に深い悲しみをもたらした. ▶定義2 almost total darkness ほぼ全体的な暗闇(やみ) →薄暗がり, 薄暗闇, 薄暗い場所

**gloomy** /glúːmi/ 形 (**gloomier**; **gloomiest**) ▶定義1 dark in way that makes you feel sad 悲しい気持ちにさせるような暗い →憂鬱(ゆううつ)な, 陰気な ‖ This dark paint makes the room very gloomy. この暗い色の塗料が, 部屋を非常に陰気臭くしている. ▶定義2 sad and without much hope 悲しく, 望みもあまりない →悲観的な, 希望のない ‖ Don't be so gloomy - cheer up! そんなに悲観的にならないで ー 元気を出して. — **gloomily** 副 →陰気に, 悲観的に — **gloominess** 名 ● →陰気, 憂鬱, 悲観

**glorified** /glɔ́ːrəfàɪd/ 形 (名詞の前だけ) ▶定義 described in a way that makes sb/sth seem better, bigger, more important, etc than he/she/it really is 〜を実際より良く・大きく・重要などに見せるよう描写された →賞賛された, 美化された

**glorify** /glɔ́ːrəfàɪ/ 動 他 (現分 **glorifying**; 三単現 **glorifies**; 過, 過分 **glorified**) ▶定義 to make sb/sth appear better or more important than he/she/it really is 〜を実際よりも良く・重要に見えるようにする →褒め上げる, 美化する ‖ His biography does not attempt to glorify his early career. 彼の自叙伝は初期の経歴を美化しようとはしていない.

**glorious** /glɔ́ːriəs/ 形 ▶定義1 having or deserving fame or success 名声や成功を得る・に値する →光栄ある, 栄誉に満ちた ‖ a glorious victory 堂々たる勝利 ▶定義2 wonderful; splendid すばらしい; すてきな →すばらしく愉快な, 楽しい, すてきな ‖ a glorious day/view すばらしい1日・眺め — **gloriously** 副 →華々しく, すばらしく

**glory**¹ /glɔ́ːri/ 名 ● ▶定義1 fame or honour that you get for achieving sth 〜を達成したことで手にする名声・栄誉 →栄光, 誉れ ‖ The winning team was welcomed home **in a blaze of glory**. 勝ったチームはさん然たる栄光の中, 大歓迎を受け帰省した. ▶定義2 great beauty 偉大なる美しさ →荘厳, 壮観, 華々しさ

**glory**² /glɔ́ːri/ 動 (現分 **glorying**; 三単現 **glories**; 過, 過分 **gloried**)

**句動詞 glory in sth** ▶定義 to take (too much) pleasure or pride in sth 〜に(過剰な)楽しみ・誇りを感じる ➔〜を得意になって喜ぶ, 鼻に掛ける ‖ *He gloried in his sporting successes.* 彼はスポーツで得た勝利の数々を鼻に掛けていた.

**gloss**[1] /glɔ(ː)s, glɑs/ 名[Ⓤ, 単数扱い] ▶定義 (a substance that gives sth) a smooth, shiny surface (〜の)表面をつるつるにかがやかせる(物質) ➔ 光沢, つや ‖ *gloss paint* 光沢のある塗料 *gloss photographs* 光沢のある写真 ☞参 **matt**

**gloss**[2] /glɔ(ː)s, glɑs/ 動

**句動詞 gloss over sth** ▶定義 to avoid talking about a problem, mistake, etc in detail 問題・誤りなどについて詳細に語るのを避ける ➔〜の上辺を飾る, ぼろを隠す

**glossary** /glɔ́(ː)səri, glɑ́-/ 名 Ⓒ (複 **glossaries**) ▶定義 a list of special or unusual words and their meanings, usually at the end of a text or book 特別または通常と違う用語とそれらの意味の一覧で, 普通テキストや本の最後にある ➔ 語彙(ごい)・用語解説

**glossy** /glɔ́(ː)si, glɑ́si/ 形 (**glossier**; **glossiest**) ▶定義 smooth and shiny 滑らかで輝く ➔光沢のある, つやつやした ‖ *glossy hair* つやのある髪の毛 *a glossy magazine* (= printed on shiny paper) 光沢紙の雑誌 ( = 光沢紙に印刷された雑誌)

★**glove** /glʌv/ 名 Ⓒ ▶定義 a piece of clothing that covers your hand and has five separate parts for the fingers 手を覆う衣服で, 指が5本に分かれたもの ➔**手袋, グローブ** ‖ *I need a new pair of gloves for the winter.* 私は冬支度に新しい手袋が必要だ. *leather/woollen/rubber gloves* 皮製・毛糸の・ゴム手袋 ☞参 **mitten** ➔ C6 ページのさし絵

★**glow** /glóʊ/ 動 Ⓘ ▶定義 **1** to produce light and/or heat without smoke or flames 煙や炎を出さずに光や熱を発する ➔(火などが)白熱して輝く, (煙・炎を出さずに)真っ赤に燃える ‖ *A cigarette glowed in the dark.* 暗闇(やみ)でたばこの火が光を放った. ▶定義 **2 glow (with sth)** to be warm or red because of excitement, exercise, etc 興奮・運動などで暖かくなる, または赤くなる ➔(体などが)火照る, (ほおが)赤くなる ‖ *to glow with health/enthusiasm/pride* 健康で・夢中になって・誇りに思って体が火照る — **glow** 名[単数扱い] ➔白熱, 真っ赤な輝き, 火照り ‖ *the glow of the sky at sunset* 夕焼け空の真っ赤な輝き

**glower** /gláʊər/ 動 Ⓘ ▶定義 **glower (at sb/sth)** to look angrily (at sb/sth) 〜を怒って見る ➔(怒って)にらみつける, 〜に顔をしかめる

**glowing** /glóʊɪŋ/ 形 ▶定義 saying that sb/sth is very good 〜が非常に良いと言って ➔熱のこもった, 賞賛に満ちた ‖ *His teacher wrote a glowing report about his work.* 先生は, 彼の学業を絶賛する調査書を書いた. — **glowingly** 副 ➔熱烈に, 白熱して, 紅潮して

**glucose** /glúːkoʊs, -z/ 名 Ⓤ ▶定義 a type of sugar that is found in fruit 果実に含まれている種類の糖 ➔ブドウ糖, グルコース

★**glue**[1] /gluː/ 名 Ⓤ ▶定義 a thick sticky liquid that is used for joining things together 物と物を接着するために使われる, 粘りのあるべたべたした液体 ➔**にかわ, 接着剤, のり** ‖ *You can make glue from flour and water.* のりは小麦粉と水から作ることができます. *Stick the photo in with glue.* のりを使って, その写真をはめ込んでください.

**glue**[2] /gluː/ 動 Ⓣ (現分 **gluing**) ▶定義 **glue A (to/onto B); glue A and B (together)** to join a thing or things together with glue 1つまたは複数の物を, のりを使って接着する ➔(A)を接着剤で付ける, (AとB)をのり付けする ‖ *Do you think you can glue the handle back onto the teapot?* このきゅうすの取っ手を接着して直すができると思いますか.

**成句 glued to sth** 略式 ▶定義 giving all your attention to sth and not wanting to leave it 〜に全神経を集中させており, それから離れたくない ➔〜から離れない, 〜に注意を集中する ‖ *He just sits there every evening glued to the television.* 彼は, 毎晩そこに座ってテレビにくぎ付けになっています.

**glum** /glʌm/ 形 ▶定義 sad and quiet 寂しく静かな ➔つまらなそうな, 憂鬱(ゆううつ)な — **glumly** 副 ➔つまらなそうに, むっつりと

**glut** /glʌt/ 名 Ⓒ, 通常は単数] ▶定義 more of sth than is needed 必要とするより物が多くあること ➔**供給過剰, 飽満** ‖ *The glut of coffee has forced down the price.* コーヒーは供給過剰により, 価格の下落を余儀なくされた.

**glutton** /glʌ́tn/ 名 Ⓒ ▶定義 **1** a person who eats

**gluttony** 716

too much 食べすぎる人→**大食家,暴食する人**
▶定義2 [成句] **a glutton for sth** a person who enjoys having or doing sth difficult, unpleasant, etc 困難・不快(など)の事があっても,行っても,苦にならない人→**(苦難・不快に)じっと耐えられる人** || *She's a glutton for hard work - she never stops.* 彼女はつらい仕事も耐え抜く人だ － 彼女は決して休むことをしない.

**gluttony** /glʌ́tni/ [名] [U] ▶定義 the habit of eating and drinking too much 暴飲暴食の習慣→**暴飲暴食,大食**

**GM** /dʒì: ém/ [略] genetically modified→**遺伝子組み替えの**

**GMT** /dʒì: em tí:/ [略] Greenwich Mean Time
▶定義 the time system that is used in Britain during the winter and for calculating the time in other parts of the world 英国で冬用いられる標準時で,全世界どこの場所でも時刻を決める基準となる→**グリニッジ標準時**

**gnarled** /nɑ:rld/ [形] ▶定義 rough and having grown into a strange shape, because of old age or hard work 年を取って,または大変な仕事のためごつごつした, 奇妙な形になった→**節・こぶだらけの,ごつごつした** || *The old man had gnarled fingers.* その老人はごつごつした指をしていた. *a gnarled oak tree* 節のあるオークの木

**gnash** /næʃ/ [動]
[成句] **gnash your teeth** ▶定義 to feel very angry and upset about sth ～に関して大変な怒り・不愉快を感じる→**歯ぎしりする**

**gnat** /næt/ [名] [C] ▶定義 a type of very small fly that bites 非常に小さいハエ科の刺す昆虫→**カ,ブヨ** ☞類 **midge**

**gnaw** /nɔː/ [動] ▶定義1 [自][他] **gnaw (away) (at/on) sth** to bite a bone, etc many times with your back teeth 奥歯で何度も骨などをかむ→**かじる,絶え間なくかむ** ▶定義2 [自] **gnaw (away) at sb** to make sb feel worried or frightened over a long period of time ～が長い期間,心配な思いをさせる・脅かされる→**(人・良心などを)苦しめる,悩ます** || *Fear of the future gnawed away at her all the time.* 将来に対する不安がいつも彼女を悩ませた.

**gnome** /nóum/ [名] [C] ▶定義 (in children's stories, etc) a little old man with a beard and a pointed hat who lives under the ground (子供向けのお話などで)地下に住む小さなおじいさんで,口ひげを生やし,とんがり帽子をかぶっている→**地の精・神,ノーム,小鬼**

★**go**¹ /góu/ [動] [自] (現分 **going**; 三単現 **goes** /góuz/; 過 **went** /went/; 過分 **gone** /gɔ(ː)n, gɑn/)
▶定義1 to move or travel from one place to another ある場所から別の場所へ移動する・行く→**行く,向かう,出掛ける** || *She always goes home by bus.* 彼女はいつもバスで家に帰る. *We're going to London tomorrow.* 私たちは明日ロンドンに向かいます. *He went to the cinema yesterday.* 彼は昨日映画館に行った. *We've still got fifty miles to go.* 私たちはあと50マイルも進まなければならない. *How fast does this car go?* この車はどのくらい速く走ることができますか. *I threw the ball and the dog went running after it.* 私がボールを投げると,犬がそれを追い掛けた.

▶ been は人がある場所に出掛けて戻ってきた場合,go の過去分詞として使われる. gone は人がある場所に出掛けたが,まだ戻っていないことを意味する: *I've just been to Berlin. I got back this morning.* (私はベルリンに行ってきたところです.今朝戻ってきました.) *John's gone to Peru. He'll be back in two weeks.* (ジョンはペルーに行っています.2週間後に戻る予定です.)

▶定義2 to travel to a place to take part in an activity or do sth ある活動に参加したり～をするためにある場所に行く→**～しに行く,出掛ける** || *Are you going to Dave's party?* あなたはデーヴのパーティーに行きますか. *Shall we go swimming this afternoon?* 午後に泳ぎに行きませんか. *to go for a swim/drive/drink/walk/meal* 泳ぎ・ドライブ・飲み・散歩・食事に行く *We went on a school trip to a museum.* 私たちは遠足で博物館に行った. *They've gone on holiday.* 彼らは休暇に出掛けています. *We went to watch the match.* 私たちは試合を見に行った. *I'll go and make the tea.* 私が行ってお茶をいれましょう.

▶定義3 to belong to or stay in an institution ある組織に属している・とどまる→**通う,入っている** || *Which school do you go to?* あなたはどちらの学校に通っているのですか. *to go to hospital/prison/college/university* 病院に通っている・

刑務所に入っている・大学・総合大学に通っている ▶定義4 to leave a place ある場所を離れる→**去る, 出掛ける, 出発する** ‖ *I have to go now. It's nearly 4 o'clock.* 私はもう行かなくてはなりません. もうすぐ4時です. *What time does the train go?* その列車は何時に発車しますか. ▶定義5 to lead to or reach a place or time 場所に連れていく・至る, または時間に達する→**至る, 届く, 達する** ‖ *Where does this road go to?* この道はどこに通じていますか. ▶定義6 to be put or to fit in a particular place ある特定の場所に置かれる・はまる→**(ある場所に)置かれる, 納まる** ‖ *Where does this vase go?* この花びんはどこに置きましょうか. *My clothes won't all go in one suitcase.* 私の洋服全部は, 1個のスーツケースに納まらないだろう. ▶定義7 to happen in a particular way; to develop ある方法で起こる; 進展する→**(事が)進行する, 運ぶ** ‖ *How's the new job going?* 新しい仕事の調子はいかがですか. ▶定義8 to become; to reach a particular state なる; ある特定の状態に達する→**(〜の状態)になる** ‖ *Her hair is going grey.* 彼女の頭は白髪混じりになってきた. *to go blind/deaf/bald/senile/mad* 目が見えなく・耳が聞こえなく・髪の毛が薄く・老いぼれに・頭がおかしくなる *The baby has gone to sleep.* その赤ちゃんは眠りに就いた. ▶定義9 to stay in the state mentioned 述べられた状態のままである→**(〜の状態)である** ‖ *Many mistakes go unnoticed.* たくさんの間違いが気付かれないでいる. ▶定義10 to be removed, lost; used, etc; to disappear→**消え去る, なくなる; 使われる; 消滅する** ‖ *Has your headache gone yet?* 頭痛はもう収まりましたか. *I like the furniture, but that carpet will have to go.* 私は, その家具は気に入っているけど, あのカーペットは取らなくては. *About half my salary goes on rent.* 給料の半分は家賃でなくなる. *Jeans will never go out of fashion.* ジーンズは決してすたれることがないでしょう. ▶定義11 to work correctly 正常に働く→**(機械などが)動く, 作動する** ‖ *This clock doesn't go.* この時計は動いていない. *Is your car going at the moment?* ちょうど今, あなたの車は動いていますか. ▶定義12 to become worse or stop working correctly 悪化する, 正常に働かなくなる→**衰える, 弱る, 壊れる** ‖ *The brakes on the car have gone.* その車のブレーキは壊れてしまっ

---

## go 717

た. *His sight/voice/mind has gone.* 彼は視力が衰えた・声が出なくなった・精神がおかしくなった. ▶定義13 to go (with sth); go (together) to look or taste good with sth else 何か別の〜を伴うと似合う・おいしい→**似合う, 調和する, 相性が良い** ‖ *This sauce goes well with rice or pasta.* このソースはご飯にもパスタにも良く合います. *These two colours don't really go.* これら2つの色はあまりしっくりこない. ▶定義14 to have certain words or a certain tune ある言葉・メロディーを持つ→**(文句・歌詞などが)〜と言っている, (旋律・調子などが)〜となっている** ‖ *How does that song go?* その歌はどんな歌詞・節(ふし)ですか. ▶定義15 (used about time) to pass→**(時が)過ぎる, たつ** ‖ *The last hour went very slowly.* 最後の1時間はとてもゆっくりと過ぎた. ▶定義16 to start an activity→**(活動を)始める, 取り掛かる** ‖ *Everybody ready to sing? Let's go!* 皆さん歌う準備はいいですか. さあ始めましょう. ▶定義17 to make a sound 音を立てる→**(鐘・銃・時計などが)鳴る, 響く, (動物などが)鳴く** ‖ *The bell went early today.* 今日はベルが早く鳴った. *Cats go 'miaow'.* 猫は「ミャー」と鳴きます. ▶定義18 (口語) 略式 used in the present tense for saying what a person said 現在形で用いて, 人が言った事を述べる→**(人・話が)〜と言っている** ‖ *I said, 'How are you, Jim?' and he goes, 'It's none of your business!'* 私が「ジム, 元気かい」と言うと, 彼は「余計なお世話だ」と言った. ▶定義19 略式 (進行形だけ) to be available→**利用できる, 提供できる, 開いている** ‖ *Are there any jobs going in your department?* あなたの部署で, 提供できる仕事はありますか. ▶定義20 略式 used for saying that you do not want sb to do sth bad or stupid 〜が悪い・ばかな事をしてほしくないと, 言うときに用いて→**(悪い事を)しでかす** ‖ *You can borrow my bike again, but don't go breaking it this time!* 私の自転車をまた君に貸してあげてもいいが, 今度は壊さないでくれよ. *I hope John doesn't go and tell everyone about our plan.* ジョンがみんなに私たちの計画を話さなければいいが.

成句 as people, things, etc go ▶定義 compared to the average person or thing 平均的な人または物と比較して→**平均的に見て, 他**

## 718　go¹

**と比べてみて** ‖ *As Chinese restaurants go, it wasn't bad.* 中華レストランの中では、まあまあだった。

**be going to do sth** ▶定義1 used for showing what you plan to do in the future 将来やろうや計画している事を表すのに用いて ➡ **〜するつもりだ、しようと思っている** ‖ *We're going to sell our car.* 私たちは車を売るつもりです。▶定義2 used for saying that you think sth will happen 〜が起こるだろうと思う、と言うのに用いて ➡ **〜しようとしている、しそうである** ‖ *It's going to rain soon.* もうすぐ雨が降りそうです。*Oh no! He's going to fall!* 大変だ。彼は今にも落っこちそうだ。

**go all out for sth; go all out to do sth** ▶定義 to make a great effort to do sth 〜をするのに大変な苦労をする ➡ **全力を尽くして〜する**

**go for it** 略式 ▶定義 to do sth after not being sure about it 〜が確実でないと分かっていて、やってみる ➡ **ともかくやってみる、(とにかくにも)さあやるんだ** ‖ *'Do you think we should buy it?' 'Yeah, let's go for it!'* 「私たちはそれを買うべきだと思いますか」「そうだね、とにかく買ってみようよ」

**have a lot going for you** ▶定義 to have many advantages ➡ **たくさんの利点がある、多くのメリットがある**

**Here goes!** ▶定義 said just before you start to do sth difficult or exciting 何か難しい、またはどきどきする事を始める直前に言う ➡ **さあやるぞ、さあ頑張るぞ**

**to go** ▶定義 that is/are left before sth ends 〜が終了するまで残っている ➡ **残っている、あと〜だけある** ‖ *How long (is there) to go before the end of the lesson?* 授業が終わるのに、あとどれくらいかかりますか。

▶ goを含むこのほかの成句については、名詞、形容詞などの項を参照。例えばgo astrayはastrayの項にある。

**句動詞** **go about** ⇒ **GO ROUND/AROUND/ABOUT**

**go about sth/doing sth** ▶定義 to start trying to do sth difficult 難しい事をしようと取り掛かる ➡ **〜に取り掛かる、〜に精を出す** ‖ *I wouldn't have any idea how to go about building a house.* 私はどのように家の建築に取り掛かったらいいか、全然分からない。

**go about with sb** ⇒ **GO ROUND/AROUND/ABOUT WITH SB**

**go after sb/sth** ▶定義 to try to catch or get sb/sth 〜を捕まえよう・得ようとする ➡ **追い掛ける、追跡する、追い求める** ‖ *I went after the boy who stole my wallet but he was too fast for me.* 私は財布を盗んだ男の子を追跡しようとしたが、あまりに速くて駄目だった。

**go against sb** ▶定義 to not be in sb's favour or not be to sb's advantage 〜の望むように・または〜の利益になるようにしない ➡ **人に反対する、従わない、合わない** ‖ *The referee's decision went against him.* 審判は彼に不利な決定をした。

**go against sb/sth** ▶定義 to do sth that sb/sth says you should not do 〜にすべきではないと止められた…をする ➡ **〜に従わない、背く、〜の意に反する** ‖ *She went against her parents' wishes and married him.* 彼女は両親の意向に反して彼と結婚した。

**go ahead** ▶定義1 to take place after being delayed or in doubt 遅延または迷った後に行われる ➡ **(先へ)進める、進められる** ‖ *Although several members were missing, the meeting went ahead without them.* 数名来ていない人がいたが、その会合はそのまま進められた。▶定義2 to travel in front of other people in your group and arrive before them 自分のグループのほかの人々より先に進み、早く到着する ➡ **先行する、先に行く** ‖ *I'll go ahead and tell them you're coming.* 私が先に行って、あなた方はもうすぐ来ると彼らに伝えましょう。

**go ahead (with sth)** ▶定義 to do sth after not being sure that it was possible 可能かどうか分からない〜をやる ➡ **とにかくやってみる、決行する** ‖ *We decided to go ahead with the match in spite of the heavy rain.* 雨がひどく降っていたが、私たちは試合を決行することにした。*'Can I take this chair?' 'Sure, go ahead.'* 「このいすに座ってもよろしいですか」「もちろん、どうぞ」

**go along** ▶定義 to continue; to progress 継続する; 進行する ➡ **やっていく、進んでいく** ‖ *The course gets more difficult as you go along.* その講座は、進んでいくにつれてますます難しくなります。

**go along with sb/sth** ▶定義 to agree with

sb/sth; to do what sb else has decided ～に同意する; だれか別の～が決めた事を行う→～に賛成する,～に迎合する‖ *I'm happy to go along with whatever you suggest.* あなたが提案する事なら、私は何でも喜んで賛成します.

go around ⇒ **GO ROUND/AROUND/ABOUT**

go around with sb ⇒ **GO ROUND/AROUND/ABOUT WITH SB**

go away ▶定義1 to disappear or leave 消える, または立ち去る→なくなる,立ち去る‖ *I've got a headache that just won't go away.* 私は頭痛がしていて、ちょっと良くなりそうもないです. *Just go away and leave me alone!* とにかくここから立ち去って、私を1人にしてください. ▶定義2 to leave the place where you live for at least one night 生活している場所を少なくとも1晩以上空ける→旅行に出掛ける,(外泊を伴って)出掛ける‖ *We're going away to the coast this weekend.* 私たちは今週末、海岸へ旅行に出掛けるつもりです.

go back (to sth) ▶定義1 to return to a place ある場所に戻る→戻る,帰る‖ *It's a wonderful city and I'd like to go back there one day.* そこはすばらしい町なので、いつの日かまた戻りたい. ▶定義2 to return to an earlier matter or situation→(元・以前の場所・状態に)戻る,(話題などに)戻る‖ *Let's go back to the subject we were discussing a few minutes ago.* 2, 3分前に話し合っていた議題に戻りましょう. ▶定義3 to have its origins in an earlier period of time さかのぼった時期に起源を持つ→(過去に)さかのぼる,回顧する‖ *A lot of the buildings in the village go back to the fifteenth century.* その村にある多くの建物の起源は15世紀にまでさかのぼる.

go back on sth ▶定義 to break a promise, an agreement, etc 約束・合意などを破る→～を裏切る,(約束・取り決め)を破る‖ *I promised to help them and I can't go back on my word.* 私は彼らを助けると約束したので、その言葉を裏切ることはできません.

go back to sth/doing sth ▶定義 to start doing again sth that you had stopped doing 既にやめていた事を再びし始める→再開する‖ *When the children got a bit older she went back to full-time work.* 子供たちが少し大きくなると、彼女はフルタイムの仕事を再開した.

go by ▶定義1 (used about time) to pass→(時がたつ,経過する‖ *As time went by, her confidence grew.* 時がたつにつれて、彼女の信頼は増した. ▶定義2 to pass a place→(場所を)通り過ぎる‖ *She stood at the window watching people go by.* 彼女は窓辺に立って、過ぎ行く人々を見ていた.

go by sth ▶定義 to use particular information, rules, etc to help you decide your actions or opinions 行動または意見を決める助けにするために特定の情報・規則などを利用する→～によって行動・判断する,～に頼る‖ *You can't go by the railway timetables - the trains are very unreliable.* その時刻表を見て行動するのは無理です－その列車は、時間がとても不正確ですから.

go down ▶定義1 (used about a ship, etc) to sink→(船などが)沈む,沈没する ▶定義2 (used about the sun) to disappear from the sky (太陽について)空から消える→(太陽が)沈む ▶定義3 to become lower in price, level, etc; to fall→(価格・レベルが)下がる,低下する‖ *The number of people out of work went down last month.* 失業者の数が先月は減少した.

go down (with sb) (副詞, 特に well または badly と共に, または how で始まる疑問文で用いて) ▶定義 to be received in a particular way by sb ～に特定のやり方で迎えられる→(人に)受け入れられる,気に入られる,納得される‖ *The film went down well with the critics.* その映画は批評家に好意的に受け入れられた.

go down with sth ▶定義 to catch an illness; to become ill with sth→病気にかかる; ～で病気になる

go for sb ▶定義 to attack sb→～を攻撃する,襲う,批判する

go for sb/sth ▶定義1 to be true for a particular person or thing ある人または物にとって真実である→(事が)～に適用される,当てはまる‖ *We've got financial problems but I suppose the same goes for a great many people.* 私たちは財政問題を抱えていますが、非常に多くの人に同じ事が言えると思います. ▶定義2 to choose sb/sth→～を選ぶ,～を支持する‖ *I think I'll go for the roast chicken.* (私は)ローストチキンにします.

go in ▶定義 (used about the sun) to disappear behind a cloud (太陽について)雲に隠れて消える→(太陽などが)雲に隠れる

go in for sth ▶定義 to enter or take part in an exam or competition 試験を受ける、または競技に参加する→(試験など)を受ける、(競技など)に参加する

go in for sth/doing sth ▶定義 to do or have sth as a hobby or interest ～を趣味または興味があるものとしてする、または持つ→(趣味などとして)～を始める、する

go into sth ▶定義1 to hit sth while travelling in/on a vehicle 車で移動しているとき、～にぶつかる→～にぶつかる、衝突する ‖ I couldn't stop in time and went into the back of the car in front. 私は停止が間に合わず、前の車の後部に追突した. ▶定義2 to start working in a certain type of job ある種の仕事を始める→(職業など)に就く、～に入る ‖ When she left school she went into nursing. 彼女は学校を出ると、看護の仕事に就いた. ▶定義3 to look at or describe sth in detail ～を詳細に観察する、または説明する→～を(徹底的に)調べる、説明する ‖ I haven't got time to go into all the details now. 私は今、詳細にすべてを調べている時間がありません.

go off ▶定義1 to explode→爆発する、急に～する ‖ A bomb has gone off in the city centre. 町の中心で爆弾が爆発した. ▶定義2 to make a sudden loud noise 突然大きな音を立てる→(警報などが)鳴る、鳴り始める ‖ I woke up when my alarm clock went off. 目覚まし時計が鳴った時、私は目が覚めた. ▶定義3 (used about lights, heating, etc) to stop working (明かり・暖房などについて)作動しなくなる→(電灯・ガスなどが)止まる、消える ‖ There was a power cut and all the lights went off. 停電のため、すべての明かりが消えた. ▶定義4 (used about food and drink) to become too old to eat or drink; to go bad (食べ物・飲み物について)古くなりすぎて食べたり飲んだりできない; 悪くなる→(食料品などが)悪くなる、傷む、腐る ▶定義5 to become worse in quality 質が悪化する→(腕・質などが)衰える、鈍る、落ちる ‖ I used to like that band but they've gone off recently. 私はかつてそのバンドが好きだったが、このごろは落ちぶれてきている.

go off sb/sth ▶定義 to stop liking or being interested in sb/sth ～が嫌いになる、または興味を失う→～が嫌になる、～に飽きる ‖ I went off spicy food after I was ill last year. 私は去年病気をしてから、香辛料の効いた食べ物が嫌いになりました.

go off (with sb) ▶定義 to leave with sb ～と共に立ち去る→～と一緒にいなくなる、～と駆け落ちする ‖ I don't know where Sid is - he went off with some girls an hour ago. 私はシッドの行方を知らない － 彼は1時間前に、女の子たちと連れ立っていなくなった.

go off with sth ▶定義 to take sth that belongs to sb else だれかほかの人の物を取る→～を持ち去る、持ち逃げする

go on ▶定義1 (used about lights, heating, etc) to start working (明かり・暖房などについて)作動を始める→(電灯・暖房などについて)つく、出る ‖ I saw the lights go on in the house opposite. 私は、向かいの家に明かりがつくのを見た. ▶定義2 (used about time) to pass→(時間が)たつ、経過する ‖ As time went on, she became more and more successful. 時がたつにつれて、彼女はますます成功を収めた. ▶定義3 (特に進行形で用いて)to happen or take place→(事が)起こる、行われる ‖ Can anybody tell me what's going on here? ここで何が起こっているのか、だれか私に教えてくれますか. ▶定義4 (used about a situation) to continue without changing (状況について)変化することなく続く→(事が)続く、進み続ける ‖ This is a difficult period but it won't go on forever. 今は困難な時期ですが、この状態が永遠に続くわけではありません. ▶定義5 to continue speaking after stopping for a moment 少し中断した後、話を続ける→話を続ける、話に戻る ‖ Go on. What happened next? 話を続けてください. それからどうなりましたか. ▶定義6 used for encouraging sb to do sth ～に…をするようけしかけるのに用いて→どんどんやれ、さあ続けて ‖ Oh go on, let me borrow your car. I'll bring it back in an hour. ねえいいじゃないか、君の車を使わせてくれよ. 1時間もしたら返すから.

go on sth ▶定義 to use sth as information so that you can understand a situation 状況を理解するための情報として～を用いる→～に基づ

く，〜に頼る ‖ *There were no witnesses to the crime, so the police had very little to go on.* この犯罪の目撃者はいないので，警察はほとんど手掛かりがなかった．

**go on (about sb/sth)** ▶定義 to talk about sb/sth for a long time in a boring or annoying way 〜について，つまらない・気に障るやり方で長々と話す→延々と話す，しゃべり続ける，まくしたてる ‖ *She went on and on about the people she works with.* 彼女は一緒に仕事をしている人々のことを延々と話し続けた．

**go/be on (at sb) (about sth)** ▶定義 to keep complaining about sth 〜について不満を言い続ける→〜にがみがみ言う，〜をののしる ‖ *She's always (going) on at me to mend the roof.* 彼女はいつも私に屋根を直すよう，うるさく言っている．

**go on (doing sth)** ▶定義 to continue doing sth without stopping or changing やめたり変更したりせずに，〜をやり続ける→(事を)続ける，し続ける ‖ *We don't want to go on living here for the rest of our lives.* 私たちは余生をここで暮らし続けるのは嫌です．

**go on (with sth)** ▶定義 to continue doing sth, perhaps after a pause or break 〜をし続ける，ことによると，一時停止または小休止の後→(事を)再び続ける，また続ける ‖ *She ignored me and went on with her meal.* 彼女は私を無視して，また食事を続けた．

**go on to do sth** ▶定義 to do sth after completing sth else 何か別の〜を完了してから…をする→〜してから…をする，〜を終えてから…に取り掛かる

**go out** ▶定義1 to leave the place where you live or work for a short time, returning on the same day 住んでいる，または仕事をしている場所を短期間離れて，その日のうちに帰ってくる→(日帰りで)出ていく，外出する ‖ *Let's go out for a meal tonight (= to a restaurant).* 今晩外に(= レストランに)食事をしに行きましょう． *I'm just going out for a walk, I won't be long.* ちょっと散歩に出掛けてきますが，すぐ戻ります． ▶定義2 to stop shining or burning 光または火が消える→(電灯・火などが)消える ‖ *Suddenly all the lights went out.* 突然，すべての明かりが消えた． ▶定義3 to stop being fashionable or in use 流行遅れになる，または使われなくなる→すたれる，流行しなくなる ‖ *That kind of music went out in the seventies.* その種の音楽は70年代にすたれてしまった． ▶定義4 (used about the sea) to move away from the land (海について)陸から離れる→(潮が)引く ‖ *Is the tide coming in or going out?* 潮は満ちてきていますか，それとも引いていますか． ☛類 **ebb** ☛参 **tide**¹

**go out (with sb); go out (together)** ▶定義 to spend time regularly with sb, having a romantic and/or sexual relationship 恋愛または性的関係を伴って，定期的に〜と共に時間を過ごす→(異性と)(結婚を前提として)付き合う，交際する ‖ *Is Fiona going out with anyone?* フィオナはだれかと付き合っていますか． *They went out together for five years before they got married.* 彼らは結婚するまで5年間交際していました．

**go over sth** ▶定義 to look at, think about or discuss sth carefully from beginning to end 〜の一部始終を念入りに見る，考える，または議論する→〜をよく検討する，よく吟味する，討議を尽くす ‖ *Go over your work before you hand it in.* 自分の仕事をよく吟味してから提出してください．

**go over to sth** ▶定義 to change to a different side, system, habit, etc 異なった側・制度・習慣などに変わる→(ほかの党派・思想・好み・習慣・宗教などに)変わる，転向する，身を投じる

**go round** (特に enough の後に用いて) ▶定義 to be shared among all the people すべての人々に共有されて→みんなに行き渡る，皆の分がある ‖ *In this area, there aren't enough jobs to go round.* この地域には，皆の分の就職口がありません．

**go round/around/about** ▶定義 (used about a story, an illness, etc) to pass from person to person (話・病気などについて)人から人へ伝わる→(ニュース・うわさ・病気などが)広まる，伝わる，伝染する ‖ *There's a rumour going round that he's going to resign.* 彼が辞任するといううわさが広がっている． *There's a virus going round at work.* 仕事場でウイルスが広まっています．

**go round (to...)** ▶定義 to visit sb's home, usually a short distance away 通常近くにあるだれかの家を訪問する→(〜の家を)ちょっと訪れる ‖ *I'm going round to Jo's for dinner tonight.* 私

は今夜ジョーの家の夕食に呼ばれることになっています.

go round/around/about with sb ▶定義 to spend time and go to places regularly with sb 〜と定期的に時間を過ごしたり,いろいろな所に出掛けたりする➡(異性と)付き合う,交際する ‖ *Her parents don't like the people she has started going round with.* 彼女の両親は,彼女が付き合い始めた人々を好ましく思っていない.

go throuth ▶定義 to be completed successfully うまく完了する➡(取り引きが)まとまる,(法案などが)議会を通過する,(申請などが)承認される ‖ *The deal went through as agreed.* その取り引きは,合意通りにまとまった.

go through sth ▶定義1 to look in or at sth carefully, especially in order to find sth 〜を,特に…を見つけるために念入りに見る,または観察する➡〜をくまなく調べる,綿密に調べる ‖ *I went through all my pockets but I couldn't find my wallet.* 私はポケットを全部くまなく調べましたが,財布を見つけられませんでした. ▶定義2 to look at, think about or discuss sth carefully from beginning to end 〜の一部始終を念入りに見る,考える,または議論する➡よく検討する,よく吟味する,討議を尽くす ‖ *We'll start the lesson by going through your homework.* 授業を始めるに当たって,まず皆さんの宿題(の出来)から見ていきましょう. ▶定義3 to have an unpleasant experience 不愉快な経験をする➡(苦しみなど)を受ける,経験する,味わう ‖ *I'd hate to go through such a terrible ordeal again.* こんな厳しい試練はもう2度とごめんだ.

go throuth with sth ▶定義 to do sth unpleasant or difficult that you have decided, agreed or threatened to do 自分で決めたり合意したりまたは脅したりした,不愉快なまたは困難な事をする➡(しばしば困難を伴って)〜をやり通す,成し遂げる ‖ *Do you think she'll go through with her threat to leave him?* 別れるという彼への脅しを彼女がきっぱりとやり通すと思いますか.

go together (2つ以上のものについて) ▶定義1 to belong to the same set or group 同じ集団,またはグループに属する➡同行する,共存する ▶定義2 to look or taste good together 似合う,または味の相性がいい➡(色・味などが)よく調和する,釣り合う

go towards sth ▶定義 to be used as part of the payment for sth 〜の支払いの一部として使われる➡〜の支払いに充てる,支払いの一部である ‖ *The money I was given for my birthday went towards my new bike.* 誕生日にもらったお金は,新しいバイクの支払いの一部に充てた.

go under ▶定義1 to sink below the surface of some water 水面下に沈む➡(船などが)沈む,下に沈む ▶定義2 略式 (used about a company) to fail and close (会社について)失敗して閉鎖になる➡(事業・会社などが)失敗する,倒産・破産する ‖ *A lot of firms are going under in the recession.* この不景気で,たくさんの会社が倒産するでしょう.

go up ▶定義1 to become higher in price, level, amount, etc; to rise 価格・レベルなどが上がる,数量などが増える;上昇する➡(物価・温度などが)上がる,(質・価値などが)良くなる,上昇する ‖ *The birth rate has gone up by 10%.* 出生率は10パーセント上昇した. ▶定義2 to start burning suddenly and strongly 突然勢いよく燃え出す➡爆発する,(爆発で)炎上する ‖ *The car crashed into a wall and went up in flames.* 車が壁に激突して炎上した. ▶定義3 to be built➡(建物などが)建てられる,建つ

go with sth ▶定義1 to be included with sth; to happen as a result of sth 〜に含まれる;〜の結果として起こる➡〜に付属する,伴う ‖ *Pressure goes with the job.* 仕事に困難は付き物だ. ▶定義2 to look or taste good with sth else 何か別の物と似合う,または味の相性が良い➡〜と調和する,よく合う ‖ *What colour carpet would go with the walls?* その壁には何色のカーペットが合いますか.

go without (sth) ▶定義 to choose or be forced to not have sth 〜を持たないことに決める,またはそう強いられる➡(物・事を)なしで済ます,(我慢して)やっていく ‖ *They went without sleep night after night while the baby was ill.* 彼らは赤ちゃんが病気の間,いく夜も眠らずに過ごした.

**go**² /góu/ 名 (複) **goes** /góuz/ ▶定義1 ❶a turn to play in a game, etc ゲームなどでプレーする順番➡(ゲームなどの)順番 ‖ *Whose go is it?* 今度はだれの順番ですか. *Hurry up - it's your go.* 急

いで ― 君の番だよ. ☛類 **turn** ▶定義**2** [C][略式] a go (at sth/doing sth) an occasion when you try to do sth; an attempt 物を試してみる機会; 試み➜**機会, 試み, 試し** ‖ *Shall I **have a go** at fixing it for you?* 試しに私がそれを直してみましょうか. *I've never played this game before, but I'll **give it a go**.* このゲームを前にやったことはありませんが, 試しにやってみましょう. *Andrew passed his driving test **first go**.* アンドリューは運転試験に1回で合格した.

[成句] be on the go [略式] ▶定義 to be very active or busy とても活発な, または忙しい➜**絶えず活動して, (常に)忙しく働いて, じっとしていないで** ‖ *I'm exhausted. I've been on the go all day.* 私は疲れてくたくたです. 一日中働き詰めでした.

have a go at sb [略式] ▶定義 to criticize sb/sth ～を批判する➜**～に苦情·不平を言う, ～を批判する** ‖ *Dad's always having a go at me about my hair.* パパは私の髪のことで, いつも文句ばかり言っています.

make a go of sth [略式] ▶定義 to be successful at sth➜**～に成功する, ～がうまくいく**

**goad** /góʊd/ [動][他] ▶定義 goad sb/sth (into sth/doing sth) to cause sb to do sth by making him/her angry ～を怒らせて…をさせる➜**人を駆り立てる, 人を刺激·扇動して～させる**

**go-ahead**[1] [名] [単数扱い] ▶定義 the go-ahead (for sth) permission to do sth ～をする許可➜**進行許可·合図·命令, 青信号, ゴーサイン** ‖ *It looks like the council are going to **give** us **the go-ahead** for the new building.* 評議会は, 我々に新しい建築の許可を与えてくれるようだ.

**go-ahead**[2] [形] ▶定義 enthusiastic to try new ways of doing things 物事を行うのに, 新しい方法を試してみることに熱心な➜**進取的な, 野心的な, 積極的な**

***goal** /góʊl/ [名] [C] ▶定義**1** (in football, rugby, hockey, etc) the area between two posts into which the ball must be kicked, hit, etc for a point or points to be scored (サッカー, ラグビー, ホッケーなどで) 得点を上げるのに, ボールをけり入れる·打ち込むなどをする必要がある2本の柱に挟まれた領域➜**ゴール** ‖ *He crossed the ball in front of the goal.* 彼はゴール正面でボールをクロスパスした. ▶定義**2** a point that is scored when the ball goes into the goal ボールがゴールに入ったとき得点されるポイント➜**得点, ゴール** ‖ *Everton won by three goals to two.* エヴァートンが3対2で勝った. *to score a goal* 得点を上げる ▶定義**3** your purpose or aim 目的または目標➜**(野心·努力などの)目的, 目標** ‖ *This year I should **achieve** my **goal** of visiting all the capital cities of Europe.* 私は今年こそ, ヨーロッパのすべての首都を訪れるという目標を達成しなければ.

**goalkeeper** /góʊlkìːpər/ (または [略式] **goalie** /góʊli/ または **keeper**) [名] [C] ▶定義 (in football, hockey, etc) the player who stands in front of the goal(1) and tries to stop the other team from scoring (サッカー, ホッケーなどで) goal(1) の正面に立って, 相手チームが得点するのを阻止しようとする選手➜**ゴールキーパー** ‖ *The goalkeeper made a magnificent save.* ゴールキーパーがすばらしい守備をした.

**goalless** /góʊlləs/ [形] ▶定義 with no goals scored 得点が入らないで➜**無得点で** ‖ *a goalless draw* 無得点での引き分け *The match finished goalless.* その試合は無得点で終わった.

**goalpost** /góʊlpòʊst/ [名] [C] ▶定義 (in football, hockey, etc) one of the two posts that form the sides of a goal. They are joined together by a bar (the crossbar). (サッカー, ホッケーなどで) ゴールの両側に立っている2本の柱のうち1本. 柱は横棒 (ゴールの横木) で連結されている➜**ゴールポスト**

**goat** /góʊt/ [名] [C] ▶定義 a small animal with horns which lives in mountain areas or is kept

G

**goatee** /goutí:/ 名 C ▶定義 a small pointed beard on a man's chin 男性のあごに生えた、先のとがった小振りのひげ→ヤギひげ ☞ hairのさし絵

**gobble** /gάb(ə)l/ 動自他 略式 ▶定義 gobble sth (up/down) to eat quickly and noisily 素早く、音を立てて食べる→がつがつ食べる、むさぼり食う、うのみにする

**gobbledegook** (または **gobbledygook**) /gάb(ə)ldɪgùk, -gù:k/ 名 U 略式 ▶定義 complicated language that is hard to understand 理解し難い複雑な言葉→お役所言葉、堅苦しい言い回し

**go-between** 名 C ▶定義 a person who takes messages between two people or groups 2人の、またはグループ間の言づてを橋渡しする人→仲介者、仲立ちをする人、仲人、メッセンジャー

**goblin** /gάblən/ 名 C ▶定義 (in stories) a small ugly creature who tricks people (物語で)人にいたずらをする小さな醜い生き物→(人間にいたずらを働く)小人、子鬼、悪鬼、ゴブリン

**gobsmacked** /gάbsmækt/ 形 略式 ▶定義 so surprised that you cannot speak; speechless 驚きのあまり話もできずに；無言で→驚いて言葉を失って、びっくりして話もできずに

★**god** /gɔ(:)d, gɑd/ 名 ▶定義 **1** [単数扱い] **God**(theを伴わないで用いて) the being or spirit in Christianity, Islam and Judaism who people pray to and who people believe created the universe キリスト教、イスラム教、ユダヤ教における人々の祈りの対象であり、またこの宇宙を創造したと人々から信じられている存在または霊→神、創造主、万有の神、造物主 ‖ *Do you believe in God?* あなたは神を信じますか. *Muslims worship God in a mosque.* イスラム教徒はモスクで神を礼拝します. ▶定義 **2** (女性形 **goddess**) [単数扱い] a being or spirit that people believe has power over a particular part of nature or that represents a particular quality 自然界のある特定の分野に力を及ぼす、あるいはある特質を代表していると人々から信じられている存在または霊→(多神教で、特定の属性を持つ)神, (特にローマ神話の)男神 ‖ *Mars was the Roman god of war and Venus was the goddess of love.* マールスは古代ローマの戦争の神で、ビーナスは恋愛の女神でした.
▶ God は数々の表現に用いられる. 神の名を、そのように用いるのは間違っていると考える人もいる. *Oh my God!* は驚きやショックを表現する: *Oh my God! I've won the lottery!* (まあ大変. 宝くじに当たったよ.) thank god は何かに対してうれしく思い、ほっとしたとき使われる: *Thank God you've arrived − I was beginning to think you'd had an accident.* (よかった、あなたが到着して − 事故に遭ったのではと思い始めたところだったよ.) for God's sake はだれかに何かをしてほしいと、より緊急に聞こえるように頼むとき、またはだれかに腹を立てているときに使われる: *For God's sake, shut up!* (お願いだから黙ってくれ.)

**godchild** /gɔ́(:)dtʃàɪld, gάd-/ (または **goddaughter; godson**) 名 C ▶定義 a child who a chosen friend of the family (**godmother** or **godfather**) promises to help and to make sure is educated as a Christian 家族が選んだ友人(教父または教母)から、援助と、キリスト教の宗教教育を保証された子供→名付け子

**goddess** /gɔ́(:)dəs, gάd-, -ɪs/ 名 C ▶定義 a female god 女性の神→女神, 崇拝される女性, 絶世の美女

**godfather** /gɔ́(:)dfὰ:ðər, gάd-/ (または **godmother; godparent**) 名 C ▶定義 a person chosen by a child's family who promises to help the child and to make sure he/she is educated as a Christian 家族から選ばれ、その子を助け、またキリスト教の宗教教育を保証する人→名付け親、教父、代父、後見人

**godforsaken** /gɔ́(:)dfərsèɪk(ə)n, gάd-, ˌ--ˈ--/ 形 ▶定義 (used about a place) not interesting or attractive in any way (場所について)とにかく面白くない、または魅力がない→救いようのない、神に見捨てられた、惨めな

**godsend** /gɔ́(:)dsènd, gάd-/ 名 C ▶定義 something unexpected that is very useful because it comes just when it is needed 予期しなかったものがちょうど必要とする時にやって来たので、非常に役立つ→思わぬ幸運・幸福・出来事、天のたまもの、天の与え

**goggles** /gάg(ə)lz/ 名 [複数扱い] ▶定義

special glasses that you wear to protect your eyes from water, wind, dust, etc 目を水・風・ほこりなどから守るために身に着ける, 特別の眼鏡➔ゴーグル ☛参 mask ☛ ski のさし絵

**going**¹ /góuiŋ/ 名 ▶定義1 [単数扱い] 正式 the act of leaving a place; departure ある場所を去る行為; 出発➔行くこと, 去ること, 出発 ‖ *We were all saddened by his going.* 彼が行ってしまって我々は皆悲しんだ. ▶定義2 ❶ the rate or speed of travel, progress, etc 移動, 進行などの度合い, または速さ➔進み方, 進行速度, (事の)進行振り ‖ *Three children in four years? That's not bad going!* 4年間で3人ものお子さんを持たれたのですね. それは大したものです. ▶定義3 ❶ how difficult it is to make progress 進むのがどのくらい困難な状況なのか➔状態, 状況 ‖ *The path up the mountain was rough going.* その山を登る道のりは険しかった. *It'll be hard going if we need to finish this by Friday!* 私たちがこれを金曜日までに終わらせる必要があるのなら, 状況は厳しくなりそうです. 成句 get out, go, leave, etc while the going is good ▶定義 to leave a place or stop doing sth while it is still easy to do so まだ簡単なうちに, 場所を去る, または〜をするのをやめる➔状況が悪くならないうちに, 立ち去る・手を引く

**going**² /góuiŋ/ 形 成句 a going concern ▶定義 a successful business うまくいっている事業➔順調に動いている・繁盛している会社・事業

the going rate (for sth) ▶定義 the usual cost (of sth) (〜の) 通常のコスト➔現行利率・料金 ‖ *What's the going rate for an office cleaner?* 事務所の清掃にかかる現行の料金はいくらですか.

**going-over** 名 [単数扱い] 略式 ▶定義1 a very careful examination of sth 〜の非常に念入りな検査➔徹底的調査・試験 ‖ *Give the car a good going-over before deciding to buy it.* 車の購入を決める前に, 徹底した点検をしなさい. ▶定義2 a serious physical attack on sb 〜に対する激しい肉体的攻撃➔激しくむちで打つこと, 痛烈な叱責 (しっせき)

**goings-on** 名 [複数扱い] 略式 ▶定義 unusual things that are happening 現在起こっている普通でないこと➔出来事, 事件

**go-kart** /góukɑːrt/ 名 C ▶定義 a vehicle like a very small car with no roof or doors, used for racing 屋根もドアもなく, レースに使われるとても小さな車のような車両➔ゴーカート

**\*gold** /góuld/ 名 ▶定義1 ❶ (元素記号 Au) a precious yellow metal that is used for making coins, jewellery, etc 硬貨・宝石などを作るのに用いられる黄金色の貴金属➔金, 黄金 ‖ *Is your bracelet made of solid gold?* あなたのブレスレットは純金製ですか. *22 carat gold* 22カラット金 *a gold chain/ring/watch* 金の鎖・指輪・時計 ▶定義2 = GOLD MEDAL ― gold 形 ➔金(製)の, 金色の ‖ *The invitation was written in gold letters.* その招待状は金文字で書かれていました. ☛参 golden

成句 (as) good as gold ⇒ GOOD¹
have a heart of gold ⇒ HEART

**\*golden** /góuld(ə)n/ 形 ▶定義1 made of gold or bright yellow in colour like gold 金製の, または金のように明るい黄色の➔金(製)の, 金色の, 山吹色の ‖ *a golden crown* 金の王冠 *golden hair/sand* 金髪・金色の砂 ▶定義2 best, most important, favourite, etc 最高の, 最重要な, 一番のお気に入りの, など➔すばらしい, 見事な, 絶好の ‖ *The golden rule is 'Keep your eye on the ball'.* 黄金律は, 「ボールから目を離すな」 *a golden opportunity* 絶好の機会 ▶定義3 celebrating the 50th anniversary of sth➔〜の50周年(記念)の ‖ *The couple celebrated their golden wedding last year.* その夫婦は去年めでたく金婚式を迎えました. ☛参 silver, diamond

成句 the golden rule (of sth) ⇒ RULE¹(2)

**goldfish** /góuldfɪʃ/ 名 C (複 goldfish) ▶定義 a small orange fish, often kept as a pet in a bowl or a small pool in the garden (pond) 小さなオレンジ色の魚で, しばしばペットとして水槽, または庭の池で飼われる➔金魚

**gold medal** (または **gold**) 名 C ▶定義 the prize for first place in a sports competition スポーツ競技会で1位になった人のための賞➔金メダル ‖ *How many gold medals did we win in the 2000 Olympics?* 2000年のオリンピックで, 私たちは金メダルを何個獲得しましたか. ☛参 **silver medal**, **bronze medal**

**gold medalist** 名 C ▶定義 the winner of a gold medal 金メダル受賞者➔金メダリスト

**gold mine** 名 C ▶定義1 a place where gold is

taken from the ground 土壌から金が採取できる場所→**金鉱,金山** ▶定義2 **a gold mine (of sth)** a place, person or thing that provides a lot of sth たくさんの〜を供給する場所,人または物→**(〜の)宝庫** ‖ *This web site is a gold mine of information.* このウェブサイトは情報の宝庫だ.

**★golf** /gɔ(:)lf, gɑlf/ 名 U ▶定義 a game that is played outdoors on a large area of grass (**golf course**) and in which you use a stick (**golf club**) to hit a small hard ball (**golf ball**) into a series of holes (usually 18) 屋外の広大な芝地(ゴルフコース)で行われるゲームで,棒(ゴルフクラブ)を使って小さな硬球(ゴルフボール)を打ち,一連の穴(通常は18個ある)に入れる→**ゴルフ** ‖ *to play a round of golf* ゴルフを1ラウンドする

**golfer** /gɔ́(:)lfər, gɑ́lf-/ 名 C ▶定義 a person who plays golf ゴルフをする人→**ゴルファー**

**golly** /gɑ́li/ 間 略式 ▶定義 used for expressing surprise 驚きを表現するのに用いて→**おやまあ,えっ**

**gone**[1] **GO**[1]の過去分詞形

**gone**[2] /gɔ(:)n, gɑn/ 形 (名詞の前は不可) ▶定義 not present any longer; completely used or finished もう存在しない; 完全に消耗した,もう終わった→**去った,過ぎ去った,弱り切った,使い切った** ‖ *He stood at the door for a moment, and then he was gone.* 彼はドアの所にしばらく立っていて,それから立ち去った. *Can I have some more ice cream please or is it all gone?* アイスクリームをもう少しもらえますか,それとももう全部なくなりましたか.

▶「消えた」または「終わった」を意味する場合のgoneは,上の例のように,be動詞と共に用いられる. 何かが消えてしまった行く先を考えに入れているときには,haveを使う: *Nobody knows where John has gone.* (だれもジョンがどこに行ってしまったか知らない.)

**gone**[3] /gɔ(:)n, gɑn/ 前 ▶定義 later than よりも後の→**(時間・年齢が)〜を過ぎて,超えて** ‖ *Hurry up! It's gone six already!* 急いで. もう6時を過ぎていますよ.

**gonna** /gɔ́(:)nə, gənə/ 略式 ▶定義 a way of writing 'going to' to show that sb is speaking in an informal way going to を,〜がくだけて話しているこ とを示して表記された形

▶自分自身がgonnaと書くことは(だれかの口調をまねている場合を除き)避けないと,誤りとして採点されることがある. wanna (= want to) と gotta (= got to) も同様.

**goo** /gu:/ 名 U 略式 ▶定義 a sticky wet substance べたべたして湿った物質→**粘り着くもの,べたつくもの** — **gooey** /gú:i/ 形 →**ねばねばした,べたべたした**

**★good**[1] /gʊd/ 形 (**better** /bétər/, **best** /best/) ▶定義1 of a high quality or standard 高品質または高水準の→**(質・量・程度などの点で)良い,上等な,申し分ない,優れた** ‖ *a good book/film/actor* 優れた本・映画・俳優 *That's a really good idea!* それは本当に名案だ. *The hotel was quite/pretty good, but not fantastic.* そのホテルはかなり上等だったが,それほどすばらしくはなかった. ▶定義2 **good at sth; good with sb/sth** able to do sth or deal with sb/sth well 〜をうまくすることができる,または〜をうまく扱うことができる→**〜が上手な,うまい,巧みな,得意な,〜に熟達した** ‖ *Jane's really good at science subjects but she's **no good at** languages.* ジェーンは,理系科目には非常にたけていますが,言語は苦手です. *He's very good with children.* 彼は子供の扱いがとてもうまい. *Are you any good at drawing?* あなたは多少は絵がかけますか. ▶定義3 pleasant or enjoyable 楽しい,または楽しめる→**(物・事が)楽しい愉快な,目を楽しませる,快適な** ‖ *It's good to be home again.* また我が家に帰れてよかった. *good news/weather* 吉報・よく晴れた天気 **Have a good time** *at the party!* パーティーで楽しんでね. ▶定義4 morally right or well behaved 道徳的に正しい,または品行の良い→**(人・行為が)(道徳的に)立派な,公正な,行儀の良い,おとなしい** ‖ *She was a very good person - she spent her whole life trying to help other people.* 彼女はとても立派な人でした - 他人を助けることに一生を費やしました. *Were the children good while we were out?* 私たちが出掛けている間,子供たちはいい子にしていましたか. ▶定義5 **good (to sb); good of sb (to do sth)** kind; helpful 親切な; 助けになる→**(〜に)…が(〜するとは)親切な,心の優しい,寛大な** ‖ *They were good to me when I was ill.* 私が病気をした時,彼らはとても親切にしてくれた. *It* *was good of you to come.* 来てくださってどうもありがとう. ▶定義6 good (for sb/sth) having a positive effect on sb/sth's health or condition 〜の健康, または状態にとって良い効果がある→(健康に)良い, 適した, (薬が病気などに)効く‖ *Green vegetables are very good for you.* 緑の野菜は健康にとても良い. *This cream is good for burns.* このクリームはやけどに効き目があります. ▶定義7 good (for sb/sth) suitable or convenient 適している, または都合が良い→(〜に)適した, 望ましい, 好都合の, (〜するのに)ふさわしい‖ *This beach is very good for surfing.* このビーチはサーフィンに最適です. *I think Paul would be a good person for the job.* 私はポールがその仕事の適任者だと思います. *'When shall we meet?' 'Thursday would be a good day for me.'* 「いつ会いましょうか」「私は木曜日が都合が良いのですが」 ▶定義8 (used about a reason, etc) acceptable and easy to understand (理由などについて)受け入れられる, 好ましい, また理解しやすい→もっともな, 妥当な‖ *a good excuse/explanation/reason* もっともな言い訳・説明・理由 *She has good reason to be pleased - she's just been promoted.* 彼女が喜んでいるのはもっともです − 昇進したばかりなのですから. ▶定義9 good (for sth) that can be used or can provide sth 使用できる, または〜を供給できる→使用可能な, 通用する, 確かな‖ *I've only got one good pair of shoes.* 私はちゃんと履ける靴を1足しか持っていません. *This ticket's good for another three days.* この切符はあと3日間通用します. ▶定義10 a good... more, larger, etc than is usual or expected 通常または期待しているより多い, 大きいなど→十分な, たっぷりな, 相当の‖ *a good many/a good few people* (= a lot of people) かなりたくさんの・少なからざる人々 (= 大勢の人々) *a good distance* (= a long way) 相当な距離 (= 長い距離) *a good* (= at least) *ten minutes/a good three miles* たっぷり (= 少なくとも)10分・たっぷり3マイル *Take a good* (= long and careful) *look at this photograph.* この写真を十分(= 長時間念入りに)見てください. *What you need is a good rest.* あなたに必要なのは十分な休養です. *Give the fruit a good wash before you eat it.* その果物は食べる前によく洗ってください. ▶定義11 used when you are pleased about sth 〜についてうれしいときに用いて→よかった, すごい‖ *'Lisa's invited us to dinner next week.' 'Oh, good!'*「リーサが私たちを来週夕食に招待してくれたわ」「それはよかったね」

成句 a good/great many ⇒ **MANY**

as good as ▶定義 almost; virtually ほとんど; 実質→(ほとんど)〜も同様, 〜と同じ(ほど良い・良く)‖ *The project is as good as finished.* そのプロジェクトは終わったも同然です.

(as) good as gold ▶定義 very well-behaved とても行儀の良い→(子供などが)ほんとに良い, 行儀が良い

be in/for a good cause ⇒ **CAUSE**¹

in good faith ⇒ **FAITH**

good for you, him, her, etc 略式 ▶定義 used to show that you are pleased that sb has done sth clever 〜がうまく…をやり遂げたのを, 喜ぶ気持ちを表すのに用いて→でかした, うまいぞ‖ *'I passed my driving test!' 'Well done! Good for you!'*「私は車の試験に通りました」「よくやったね. でかした」

for good measure ⇒ **MEASURE**²

so far so good ⇒ **FAR**²

**good**² /gʊd/ 名 U ▶定義1 behaviour that is morally right or acceptable 道徳的に正しいまたは好ましい言動→善, 美徳, 良いところ‖ *the difference between good and evil* 善悪の区別 *I'm sure there's some good in everybody.* 私はだれにも必ず良いところがあると思います. ▶定義2 something that will help sb/sth; advantage 〜の助けとなる何か; 利益→役に立つ事, 価値(のある事), 利益, ため(になる事)‖ *She did it for the good of her country.* 彼女はそれを国益のため行いました. *I know you don't want to go into hospital, but it's for your own good.* あなたが入院したくないのは分かりますが, それがご自分のためです. ***What's the good of*** *learning French if you have no chance of using it?* あなたは使う機会もないのに, フランス語を習って何の役に立ちますか. ☞参 **goods**の項

成句 be no good (doing sth) ▶定義 to be of no use or value 使い道, または価値がない→役に立たない, 足しにならない, 無駄だ‖ *It's no good standing here in the cold. Let's go home.*

寒い中ここに立っていても仕方がありません．さあ，家に帰りましょう． *This sweater isn't any good. It's too small.* このセーターは役に立ちません．小さすぎます．

do you good ▶定義 to help or be useful to you 人の助けになる，または役に立つ→〜のためになる，〜に役立つ ‖ *It'll do you good to meet some new people.* 何人かの人々との新しい出会いが，あなたのためになるでしょう．

for good ▶定義 for ever 永遠に→**永久に，これを最後に，きっぱりと** ‖ *I hope they've gone for good this time!* これで永久に彼らがいなくなればいいのに．

not much good 略式 ▶定義 bad or not useful 悪い，または役に立たない→**ひどい，ぱっとしない，無益な** ‖ *'How was the party?' 'Not much good.'* 「パーティーはいかがでしたか」「ぱっとしませんでした」

a/the world of good ⇒ **WORLD**

*\***goodbye** /gʊ(d)báɪ/ 間 ▶定義 said when sb goes or you go だれかまたは自分が去るときに言う→**さようなら，じゃまたね** ‖ *We said goodbye to Steven at the airport.* 私たちは空港でスティーヴンにさようならを言った．— goodbye 名 C→**別れのあいさつ，いとまごい，告別** ‖ *We said our goodbyes and left.* 私たちは別れのあいさつをして立ち去った．

**Good Friday** 名 C ▶定義 the Friday before Easter when Christians remember the death of Christ 復活祭前の金曜日で，キリスト教徒がキリストの死を思い起こす日→**聖金曜日，受難日**

**good-humoured** 形 ▶定義 pleasant and friendly 楽しく親しみやすい→**上機嫌の，陽気な，気さくな**

**goodies** /gʊ́diz/ 名［複数扱い］略式 ▶定義 exciting things that are provided or given 供給された，または与えられたわくわくするもの→**魅力的なもの，特別いいもの，菓子，キャンデー，食べておいしい物** ‖ *There were lots of cakes and other goodies on the table.* テーブルの上にはたくさんのケーキとおいしそうな物が並んでいた．

**good-looking** 形 ▶定義 (usually used about a person) attractive (通常は人について) 魅力的な→**(人が)顔立ちの良い，美しい，(着物などが)よく似合う** ☛参 **beautiful** の注

**good-natured** 形 ▶定義 friendly or kind 親しみやすい，または親切な→**気さくな，気立ての良い，親切な**

**goodness** /gʊ́dnəs/ 名 U ▶定義 1 the quality of being good 良い性質→**(人柄の) 善良さ, 有徳, 親切(心)** ☛類 **virtue** ▶定義 2 the part of sth that has a good effect, especially on sb/sth's health 〜の一部で，特に…の健康にとって，良い影響を与える部分→**良いところ，美点，精髄，(食品の)滋養分** ‖ *Wholemeal bread has more goodness in it than white.* 全粒パンは白パンよりも滋養分が多い．

➤ Goodness は数多くの表現に用いられる．Goodness (me)! は驚きを表して「えっ，おや」，Thank goodness は喜びや安堵(あんど)を表し「有り難い，よかった」: *Thank goodness it's stopped raining!* (有り難い，雨がやんでくれた．) For goodness' sake はだれかに何かをするよう頼むのに，より緊急に聞こえるように，またはだれかに腹を立てているとき用いて「後生だから，一体全体」: *For goodness' sake, hurry up!* (お願いだから急いで．)

*\***goods** /gʊdz/ 名［複数扱い］▶定義 1 things that are for sale 売りに出されている物→**商品, 品物, 物資** ‖ *a wide range of consumer goods* 広い範囲の消費財 *electrical goods* 電化製品 *stolen goods* 盗難品 ▶定義 2 (特に 米 **freight**) things that are carried by train or lorry 鉄道または トラックで運ばれる物→**貨物** ‖ *a goods train* 貨物列車 *a heavy goods vehicle (= HGV)* 重量積載物車両 (= HGV)

成句 **come up with/deliver the goods** 略式 ▶定義 to do what you have promised to do 約束した事を行う→**実績を上げる，約束を果たす，期待通りにする**

**good sense** 名 U ▶定義 good judgement or intelligence 正しい判断または知性→**良識，分別** ‖ *He had the good sense to refuse the offer.* 彼は賢明にもその申し出を断った．

**goodwill** /gʊdwíl/ 名 U ▶定義 friendly, helpful feelings towards other people 他人に対する親愛の，また助けになりたい気持ち→**善意，好意，親善，友好** ‖ *The visit was designed to promote friendship and goodwill.* その訪問は友好と親善を深めるため計画されました．

**goody** (または **goodie**) /gʊ́di/ 名 C (複 **goodies**) 略式 ▶定義 a good person in a film, book, etc

映画・本などに出てくる良い人物➡(映画・劇・小説における)善人,善玉 ⇔ **baddy**

**goody-goody** 名 C ▶定義 a person who always behaves well so that other people have a good opinion of him/her 他人から良く思われたいため,いつも善人の振る舞いをしている人 ➡善良・信心家振った人,殊勝げな人 ☞ だれかを goody-goody と呼ぶとき,通常はその人を好ましく思っていないことを意味する.

**gooey** /gúːi/ 形略式 ▶定義 soft and sticky 柔らかくべとべとした➡ねばねばする,べとべとする ‖ *gooey cakes* べたべたするケーキ

**goof** /guːf/ 動自 特に困略式 ▶定義 to make a silly mistake 愚かな間違いをする➡しくじる,急ける,時間をつぶす

**goose** /guːs/ 名 C (複 **geese** /ɡiːs/) ▶定義 a large white bird that is like a duck, but bigger. Geese are kept on farms for their meat and eggs. アヒルに似ているがもっと大きな白い鳥. goose は肉や卵をとるため農場で飼育される➡(雌の)ガチョウ,(野生の)ガン

▶ goose の雄は gander, ひなは gosling と呼ばれる.

☞ **duck** のさし絵

**gooseberry** /ɡúzb(ə)ri; ɡúːsbèri, ɡúːz-/ 名 C (複 **gooseberries**) ▶定義 a small green fruit that is covered in small hairs and has a sour taste 短い毛に覆われた小さな緑の酸味がある果物➡グズベリー(の実),セイヨウスグリ ☞ C3 ページのさし絵

成句 **play gooseberry** ▶定義 to be present when two lovers want to be alone 恋人同士が2人きりになりたいときそこに居合わせる➡(恋人同士・若い夫婦などの)付き添い役をする,邪魔をする

**goose pimples** (または **goosebumps** /ɡúːsbʌmps/) 名[複数扱い] ▶定義 small points or lumps which appear on your skin because you are cold or frightened 寒気・恐怖を感じたとき皮膚に表れる小さなぼつぼつ,または突起➡鳥肌(が立つこと)

**gore**[1] /ɡɔːr/ 名 U ▶定義 thick blood that comes from a wound 外傷から出るどろどろした血液➡血のり,血の塊 ☞ 形 **gory**

**gore**[2] /ɡɔːr/ 動他 ▶定義 (used about an animal) to wound sb with a horn, etc(動物について)〜を角(つの)などで傷付ける➡(牛などが)〜を角・きばで突く・突き刺す,〜を(とがった物で)貫く・傷付ける ‖ *She was gored to death by a bull.* 彼女は雄牛の角で突かれて死んだ.

**gorge**[1] /ɡɔːrdʒ/ 名 C ▶定義 a narrow valley with steep sides and a river running through it 川が流れている両側が急勾配(こうばい)の峡谷➡(両側が絶壁の)峡谷,山峡

**gorge**[2] /ɡɔːrdʒ/ 動自他 ▶定義 **gorge (yourself) (on/with sth)** to eat a lot of food たくさんの食べ物を食べる➡(食べ物を)がつがつ腹一杯に詰め込む,むさぼり食う

**gorgeous** /ɡɔ́ːrdʒəs/ 形略式 ▶定義 extremely pleasant or attractive 極度に愉快または魅力的な➡豪華な,見事な,すばらしい ‖ *What gorgeous weather!* 何てすばらしい天気なのだろう. *You look gorgeous in that dress.* そのドレス見事に似合っていますよ. ― **gorgeously** 副 ➡豪華に,すばらしく

**gorilla** /ɡərílə/ 名 C ▶定義 a large black African animal like a monkey (**ape**) 猿(類人猿)に似ている大型で黒いアフリカ産の動物➡ゴリラ

**gory** /ɡɔ́ːri/ 形 ▶定義 full of violence and blood 暴力や血に満ちた➡流血の,血みどろの,残忍な ‖ *a gory film* 残虐映画

**gosh** /ɡɑʃ/ 間略式 ▶定義 used for expressing surprise, shock, etc 驚き,ショックなどを表現するのに用いて➡あれっ,おやっ,えっ

**gosling** /ɡɔ́(ː)slɪŋ, ɡɑ́z-/ 名 C ▶定義 a young bird (**goose**) (雌のガチョウの)ひな➡ガチョウのひな

**gospel** /ɡɑ́sp(ə)l/ 名 ▶定義 **1 Gospel**[単数扱い] one of the four books in the Bible that describe the life and teachings of Jesus Christ 聖書の中にあるイエス キリストの生涯と教えを説いている4書のうちの1つ➡福音書(新約聖書の最初の4書, Matthew, Mark, Luke, John のいずれか1つ) ‖ *St Matthew's/Mark's/Luke's/John's Gospel* (聖)マタイ・マルコ・ルカ・ヨハネによる福音書 ▶定義 **2** (または **gospel truth**) U the truth 真理➡絶対的真理,完全に本当の事 ‖ *You can't take what he says as gospel.* 彼の言っている事が絶対的真理だと思ってはいけないよ.

▶定義 **3** (または **gospel music**) U a style of religious music that is especially popular among black American Christians 特にアメリカの黒人

キリスト教徒の間で広まっている宗教音楽のスタイル→ゴスペル

**gossip** /gásəp/ 名 ▶定義1 ❶informal talk about other people and their private lives, that is often unkind or not true 他人やその私生活についてのくだけた話,多くは不親切であるか,また真実でない→(人の)うわさ話,陰口,(新聞・雑誌などの)ゴシップ(記事) ‖ *Matt phoned me up to tell me the latest gossip.* マットは私に電話をかけてきて,最新のうわさ話を教えてくれた.
▶定義2 ❷an informal conversation (including gossip) (gossipを含む)くだけた会話→打ち解け話,無駄話,世間話 ‖ *The two neighbours were having a good gossip over the fence.* 隣人2人が垣根越しに世間話の花を咲かせていた.
▶定義3 ❷a person who enjoys talking about other people's private lives 他人の私生活について話すのが好きな人→うわさ話の好きな人,おしゃべりな人 — gossip 動 ⾃ →うわさ話をする,無駄話・雑談をする

**gossip column** 名 ❷ ▶定義 a part of a newspaper or magazine where you can read about the private lives of famous people 有名人の私生活についての記事が読める新聞・雑誌の部分→(新聞・雑誌の)ゴシップ欄・記事

**got** GET の過去・過去分詞形

**gotta** /gátə/ 困 話 ▶定義 a way of writing 'got to' or 'got a' to show that sb is speaking in an informal way got to または got a の表記法で,～が略式に話していることを表す.
▶(だれかの口調をまねている場合を除き) gotta と書くことは避けないと,誤りとして採点されることがある. gonna と wanna も同様: *I gotta go (= I have got to go).*(おれ,行かなきゃ.) *Gotta (= have you got a) minute?*(ちょっと時間あるかい.)

**gotten** 困 GET の過去・過去分詞形

**gouge** /gáʊdʒ/ 動 他 ▶定義 to make a hole in a surface using a sharp object in a rough way 鋭利な物を使って手荒いやり方で表面に穴を開ける→～を(丸のみで)彫る,丸のみで穴を掘る・溝を作る

句動詞 **gouge sth out** ▶定義 to remove or form sth by digging into a surface 表面を掘ることにより～をえぐり出す,または形づくる→(目玉・石などを)えぐり出す

**gourmet** /gúəmèɪ/ 名 ❷ ▶定義 a person who enjoys food and knows a lot about it 食べ物を楽しみ,また食事について知識が豊富な人→食通,美食家,グルメ,ブドウ酒通

★**govern** /gávən/ 動 ▶定義1 ❷ ❶ to rule or control the public affairs of a country, city, etc 国・町などの公務を決定したり統制する→(国・国民などを)治める,統治する ‖ *Britain is governed by the Prime Minister and the Cabinet.* 英国は首相と内閣により統治されています.
▶定義2 ❷ (しばしば受動態で)to influence or control sb/sth ～に影響を与える,またはそれを支配する→～に影響する,(人・動機・結果など)を左右する,決定する ‖ *Our decision will be governed by the amount of money we have to spend.* われわれの決定は使えるお金がいくらあるかによって左右されるだろう.

★**government** /gávə(n)mənt/ 名 ▶定義1 ❷(しばしば **the Government**)the group of people who rule or control a country 国を統治または支配する人々の集まり→政府,統治機関,(英国などの)内閣 ‖ *He has resigned from the Government.* 彼は内閣を辞任しました. *The foreign governments involved are meeting in Geneva.* 関係国政府はジュネーブで会合する予定です. *government policy/money/ministers* 政策・財政・閣僚 ☛ 単数形の government の後は単数の動詞も複数の動詞も来る. government を単一の政体のまとまりとして考えている場合は,単数形の動詞を使う. *The Government welcomes the proposal.*(政府はその提案を歓迎しています.)政府を構成する個人すべてを考えている場合は,複数形の動詞を使う. *The Government are still discussing the problem.*(政府はまだその問題を討議中です.)
▶いろいろな種類の政府としては,communist(共産), conservative(保守), democratic(民主), liberal(自由), reactionary(反動), socialist(社会主義)などがある.国または州は,military(軍事), provisional(暫定), central(中央)または federal(連邦), coalition(連立)などの政府を持つこともある. local government, opposition を参照.
▶定義2 ❶the activity or method of controlling a country 国を支配する活動または手法→政治,行政,統治権,政体 ‖ *weak/strong/corrupt gov-*

ernment 弱い・強い・腐敗した行政 Which party is **in government**? どちらの政党が政権を握っていますか. — governmental /gÀvər(n)méntl; gÀv(ə)n-/ 形 →政府の, 政治(上)の, 国営の ‖ a governmental department 政府機関 different governmental systems 異なった政治体制

**governor** /gÁvərnər/ 名 C ▶定義1 a person who rules or controls a region or state (especially in the US) ある地域または州を統治するまたは支配する人(特に米国で)→(州)知事, (昔の植民地の)総督 ‖ the Governor of New York State ニューヨーク州知事 ▶定義2 the leader or member of a group of people who control an organization ある機関を支配する集団の指導者, またはその一員→支配・統治者, (官庁・学校・病院・銀行などの)長(官), 理事(長), 頭取, 総裁 ‖ the governor of the Bank of England イングランド銀行頭取 school governors 学校理事長

**gown** /gáon/ 名 C ▶定義1 a long formal dress for a special occasion 特別の機会に着る丈の長い正装用の服→ガウン ‖ a ball gown 夜会服 ▶定義2 a long loose piece of clothing that is worn by judges, doctors performing operations, etc 判事, 手術を行っている医者などが着用する丈の長いゆったりしたワンピース型の衣服→(職業・身分を示す)正服, 法服, 手術着, 白衣, 文官服

**GP** /dʒìː píː/ 略 general practitioner ▶定義 a doctor who treats all types of illnesses and works in a practice in a town or village, not in a hospital 病院勤めではなく, 町や村で開業しているどんな種類の病気でも診てくれる医者→一般開業医, 町医者

*****grab** /græb/ 動 (**grabbing**; **grabbed**) ▶定義1 他他 grab sth (from sb) to take sth with a sudden movement ～を突然の動作で取る→(人・物)を不意につかむ, 引っつかむ, 物を(人から)引ったくる ‖ Helen grabbed the toy car from her little brother. ヘレンは弟からおもちゃの車を引ったくった. **Grab hold of** his arm in case he tries to run! 彼が逃げようとしたら, 腕をつかんで捕まえなさい. Someone had arrived before us and grabbed all the seats. だれかが先に来て席を全部取ってしまった. (比喩)He grabbed the opportunity of a free trip to America. 彼はアメリカにただで行ける機会をうまくつかんだ. (比喩)I'll try to grab the waitress's attention. あの

---

**graceful** 731

ウエートレスに気が付いてもらえるようにやってみるよ. ☛参 **snatch** ▶定義2 自 grab at/for sth to try to get or catch sb/sth ～を得ようと, または捕まえようとする→(～を)つかもうとする, 捕まえようとする ‖ Jonathan grabbed at the ball but missed. ジョナサンはボールを捕らえようとしたが, 取り損なった. ▶定義3 他 to do sth quickly because you are in a hurry 急いでいるので～を素早くやる→～を素早く食べる・飲む, ～に素早く乗る ‖ I'll just grab something to eat and then we'll go. 私はとにかく何か食べてくるから, その後出発しましょう. — grab /græb/ 名 C→引っつかむこと, 引ったくり, 略奪 ‖ She made a grab for the boy but she couldn't stop him falling. 彼女はその男の子をとっさにつかもうとしたが, その子が落ちるのを助けることはできなかった.

**grace** /gréɪs/ 名 U ▶定義1 the ability to move in a smooth and controlled way 滑らかで抑制された動き方ができること→(形・動作などの)優美, 上品, しとやかさ ▶定義2 extra time that is allowed for sth ～に許された余分の時間 →(遅延・義務などに対する)猶予, 支払猶予(期間) ▶定義3 a short prayer of thanks to God before or after a meal 食前・食後の神に感謝する短いお祈り→(食前・食後の)感謝の祈り(「いただきます」「ごちそうさま」に当たる) ‖ to say grace 食前・食後のお祈りをする

成句 sb's fall from grace ▶定義 a situation in which sb loses the respect that people had for him/her by doing sth wrong or immoral 誤った, または非道徳的な事をしたことが原因で, 尊敬を受けていた人がそれを失ってしまう状況→～が好意・恩寵(おんちょう)などを失うこと, (他人の)機嫌を損ねること, 失墜, (道徳的)堕落

have the grace to do sth ▶定義 to be polite enough to do sth ～をするのに十分なほど礼儀正しい→～する礼儀をわきまえている, 潔く～する with good grace ▶定義 in a pleasant and reasonable way, without complaining 心地良く合理的なやり方で, 不平を言わないで→進んで, 快く, 潔く ‖ He accepted the refusal with good grace. 彼はその辞退を快諾してくれました.

**graceful** /gréɪsfʊl, -f(ə)l/ 形 ▶定義 having a smooth, attractive movement or form 滑らかで

## 732  graceless

魅力的な動作の,またはそういう形をした→(人・動作・形などが)優美な,上品な,優雅な ‖ *a graceful dancer* 優雅な踊り手 *graceful curves* 優美な曲線 ☞参 **gracious** は意味が異なる. — **gracefully** /-əfʊli, -f(ə)li/ 副 ▶優美に,上品に,しとやかに ‖ *The goalkeeper rose gracefully to catch the ball.* ゴールキーパーは優雅な身のこなしでボールを捕らえた. *She accepted the decision gracefully (= without showing her disappointment).* 彼女はその決定を潔く受け入れた(= 失望を表さないで). — **gracefulness** 名 U ▶優美さ,上品さ

**graceless** /gréɪsləs/ 形 ▶定義1 not knowing how to be polite to people 人に礼儀正しくする方法を知らずに→礼儀をわきまえない,無作法な,野卑な ▶定義2 (used about a movement or a shape) ugly and not elegant (動作または形について)醜く洗練されていない→優雅さのない,品のない,見苦しい — **gracelessly** 副 ▶下品に,見苦しく

**gracious** /gréɪʃəs/ 形 ▶定義1 (used about a person or his/her behaviour) kind, polite and generous(人またはその行動について)親切で,礼儀正しく,寛容な→優しい,恵み深い,情け深い ‖ *a gracious smile* 慈愛に満ちたほほえみ ▶定義2 (名詞の前だけ) showing the easy comfortable way of life that rich people can have 裕福な人々のゆったりした心地良い生活様式を表して→(生活などが)優雅な,ゆったりした ‖ *gracious living* 優雅な生活 ☞参 **graceful** は意味が異なる.

成句 **good gracious!** ▶定義 used for expressing surprise 驚きを表現するのに用いて→まあ,驚いた ‖ *Good gracious! Is that the time?* 驚いた.もう時間ですか. — **graciously** 副 ▶愛想良く,丁寧に,慈悲深く — **graciousness** 名 U ▶優しさ,優雅さ

**grade**¹ /gréɪd/ 名 C ▶定義1 the quality or the level of ability, importance, etc that sb/sth has ～の持つ能力・重要性などの質または水準→(価値・質などの)等級,(過程・進歩の)段階,程度,(軍などの)階級 ‖ *Which grade of petrol do you need?* どのグレードのガソリンにいたしましょうか. *We need to use high-grade materials for this job.* この仕事には高品質の材料を使う必要があります. ▶定義2 a mark that is given for school work, etc or in an exam 学校の勉強などや試験で与えられる成績→(生徒の)成績,評価,評定 ‖ *He got good/poor grades this term.* 彼は今学期は良い・悪い成績を取りました. *Very few students pass the exam with a grade A.* その試験にA評定で受かる生徒はほとんどいません. ▶定義3 米 a class or classes in a school in which all the children are the same age 学校で同年齢の子供たちを集めた1つまたは複数のクラス→(小・中・高校まで通しての)学年,年級 ‖ *My daughter is in the third grade.* 私の娘は小学3年生です.

| ▶社会・文化 |
|---|
| 成績の付け方 |
| 日本の学校では5段階で成績が付けられることが多いようですが,アメリカの学校でも5段階で付けられることがあります.表示は通例,A(Excellent), B(Good), C(Fair,Satisfactory), D(Passing), F(Failure)のようになっています.これらのうち,A〜D は合格ですが,F が付くと不合格ということです. |

成句 **make the grade** 略式 ▶定義 to reach the expected standard; to succeed 期待される水準に達する;成功する→規定の水準に達する,(障害を克服して)成功・合格する ‖ *She wanted to be a professional tennis player, but she didn't make the grade.* 彼女はプロのテニスプレーヤーになりたかったが,その水準に達しなかった.

**grade**² /gréɪd/ 動 他 (しばしば受動態で) ▶定義 to put things or people into groups according to their quality, ability, size, etc 物や人を質・能力・サイズなどに応じてグループ分けする→(～により・～で)等級に分ける,段階別にする,～を格付けする ‖ *I've graded their work from 1 to 10.* 私は彼らの作品を1から10までに格付けしました. *Eggs are graded by size.* 卵は大きさによって等級分けされます.

**gradient** /gréɪdiənt/ 名 C ▶定義 the degree at which a road, etc goes up or down 道などが上ったり下ったりする角度→(道路・鉄道などの)勾配(こうばい),傾斜(度) ‖ *The hill has a gradient of 1 in 4 (= 25%).* その丘の傾斜は1/4(= 25%)です. *a steep gradient* 急勾配

*★**gradual** /grǽdʒuəl, -dʒəl/ 形 ▶定義 happening

slowly or over a long period of time; not sudden ゆっくりと,または長い期間にわたって起こる;突然でない→**徐々の,漸進的な,緩やかな** ‖ *There has been a gradual increase in the number of people without jobs.* 働き口のない人の数が徐々に増加している. — gradually 副 →だんだんと,次第に,じわじわと ‖ *After the war life gradually got back to normal.* 戦争の後,生活は次第に普通に戻った.

**graduate**¹ /grǽdʒuət/ 名 C ▶定義1 a graduate (in sth) a person who has a first degree from a university, etc 大学などの学士号を持つ人→**(大学の)卒業生,学士,大学院学生** ‖ *a law graduate/a graduate in law* 法学部出身者・法学部の卒業生 *a graduate of London University/a London University graduate* ロンドン大学の出身・ロンドン大学卒業生 ☞参 **postgraduate, undergraduate, bachelor, student** ▶定義2 米a person who has completed a course at a school, college, etc 学校・大学などにおいて,ある学科を修了した人→**(学科の)卒業生,(各種学校の)卒業生** ‖ *a high-school graduate* 高卒者

**graduate**² /grǽdʒueɪt/ 動 自 ▶定義1 graduate (in sth) (from sth) to get a (first) degree from a university, etc→**大学を卒業して称号・学士号を受ける,(～学科を,大学などを)卒業する** ‖ *She graduated in History from Cambridge University.* 彼女はケンブリッジ大学の史学科を卒業しました. ▶定義2 米 graduate (from sth) to complete a course at a school, college, etc 各種学校,大学などの課程を終える→**(～を)卒業する** ▶定義3 graduate (from sth) to sth to change (from sth) to sth more difficult, important, expensive, etc ～より困難・重要・高価な…に変わる→**～を卒業して…になる,(ある段階から)(一段高い段階)へ進む,進級する,昇進する** ‖ *She's graduated from being a classroom assistant to teaching.* 彼女は教室の助手から教師に昇進した.

**graduation** /grǽdʒuéɪʃ(ə)n/ 名 ▶定義1 U the act of successfully completing a university degree or (in the US) studies at a high school 大学の学位を授与される,または(米国で)高校の課程を無事修了する行為→**(大学の)卒業,(小・中・高校の)卒業** ▶定義2 [単数扱い]a ceremony in which certificates are given to people who have graduated 卒業生に終了証書が授与される式→**学位授与式,卒業式**

**graffiti** /grəfíːti, græ-/ 名 [U,複数扱い] ▶定義 pictures or writing on a wall, etc in a public place 公共の壁などに書かれた絵や文字→**(壁・便所などの)落書き** ‖ *The wall was covered with graffiti.* その壁は落書きで一杯だった.

**graft** /grɑːft; græft/ 名 C ▶定義1 a piece of living plant that is fixed onto another plant so that it will grow 別の植物につぎ木され生長する植物→**つぎ穂・枝・芽,つぎ木(法)** ▶定義2 a piece of living skin, bone, etc that is fixed onto a damaged part of a body in an operation 身体の損傷を受けた部分に手術により移植される生きた皮膚,骨などの一片→**(皮膚・骨などの)移植組織,移植片** ‖ *a skin graf* 皮膚の移植片 — graft 動 他 graft sth onto sth →**～を(…に)移植する** ‖ *Skin from his leg was grafted onto the burnt area of his face.* 彼の顔のやけどを負った部分に,足の皮膚が移植された. ☞参 **transplant**

*****grain** /ɡreɪn/ 名 ▶定義1 U C the seeds of wheat, rice, etc 小麦・米などの種子→**(穀物の)粒,(集合的)穀物,穀類** ‖ *The US is a major producer of grain.* 合衆国は穀物の主要産出国です. *grain exports* 穀物の輸出 *a few grains of rice* 2～3粒の米 ▶定義2 C a grain of sth a very small piece of sth ほんの小さな1つの～→**(砂・塩・砂糖などの)1粒,ほんの少しの～,ごく微量,みじん** ‖ *a grain of sand/salt/sugar* 1粒の砂・塩・砂糖(比喩)*There isn't a grain of truth in the rumour.* そのうわさには真実のかけらもありません. ▶定義3 U the natural pattern of lines that can be seen or felt in wood, rock, stone, etc 木・岩・石などに見られる,または感じられる自然の線模様→**(木材・なめし皮・岩などの)きめ,はだ,木目(もくめ),石目** ‖ *to cut a piece of wood along/across the grain* 木目に沿って・反して木を切る

成句 (be/go) against the grain ▶定義 to be different from what is usual or natural 普通または自然なものと違って→**性分に合わない,不本意で**

*****gram** (または **gramme**) /græm/ 名 C (略 g) ▶定義 a measure of weight. There are 1000 grams in a kilogram. 重さの単位. 1キログラムは1000グラムに相当する→**グラム**

*****grammar** /grǽmər/ 名 ▶定義1 U the rules of

a language, for example for forming words or joining words together in sentences 言語の規則, 例えば単語の形成法や文における単語同士のつながり方の規則→**文法(学)・研究, 文法体系** ‖ *Russian grammar can be difficult for foreign learners.* ロシア語の文法は外国人学習者にとっては難しいことがある. ▶定義2 ❶the way in which sb uses the rules of a language 〜の言語規則の用い方→**(個人の)言葉遣い, 語法** ‖ *You have a good vocabulary, but your grammar needs improvement.* あなたはかなりの語彙(ごい)力がありますが, 文法はもっと努力が必要です. ▶定義3 ❷a book that describes and explains the rules of a language ある言語の規則を記述説明した本→**文法書, 文典** ‖ *a French grammar* フランス語の文法書

**grammar school** 名 ❷ (英国で, 特に昔) ▶定義 a type of secondary school for children from 11-18 who are good at academic subjects 学科目の成績が良い 11〜18歳の子供を対象とした一種の中等学校→**グラマースクール(パブリックスクールと並ぶ大学進学コースの公立中等学校), 古典文法学校(グラマースクールの前身)**

**grammatical** /grəmǽtɪk(ə)l/ 形 ▶定義1 connected with grammar 文法に関連した→**文法(上)の, 文法に関する** ‖ *the grammatical rules for forming plurals* 複数形を作る文法上の規則 ▶定義2 following the rules of a language 言語の規則に従った→**文法的に正しい** ‖ *The sentence is not grammatical.* この文章は文法的に正しくありません. — **grammatically** /-k(ə)li/ 副 →文法的に, 文法上正確に

**gramme** = GRAM

**gran** /grǽn/ 英 略式 = GRANDMOTHER

★**grand**¹ /grǽnd/ 形 ▶定義1 impressive and large or important (also used in names) 印象的で大きい, または重要な(名前にも用いられる)→**(大きさ・程度・範囲の点で)壮大な, 雄大な, 重要・主要な, (階級・称号について)最高の** ‖ *Our house isn't very grand, but it has a big garden.* 私たちの家はあまり豪華ではありませんが, 大きな庭園があります. *She thinks she's very grand because she drives a Porsche.* 彼女はポルシェを運転しているので, 自分が重要人物だと思っている. *the Grand Canyon* グランドキャニオン *the Grand Hotel* グランドホテル ☞ 名 grandeur ▶定義2 used before a noun to show a family relationship 名詞の前に用いて家族関係を表す→**(親族名の前で)さらに1親等隔てた, 1親等上・下の** ▶定義3 略式 very good or pleasant とても良いまたは愉快な→**すばらしい, 快適な, 楽しい** ‖ *You've done a grand job!* すばらしい出来栄えです. — **grandly** 副 →壮大に, 堂々と, 崇高に, もったい振って — **grandness** 名 ❶→壮大なこと, 偉業

**grand**² /grǽnd/ 名 ❷ ((複) **grand**) (俗語) ▶定義 1000 pounds or dollars 1000 ポンド・ドル→**1000 ポンド, 1000 ドル**

**grandad** /grǽndæd/ 英 略式 = GRANDFATHER

**grandchild** /grǽn(d)tʃaɪld/ (または **granddaughter**; **grandson**) 名 ❷ ▶定義 the daughter or son of your child 子供の娘または息子→**孫, 孫息子, 孫娘**

**grandeur** /grǽndʒər/ 名 ❶ 正式 ▶定義1 the quality of being large and impressive 大きくて印象的な性質→**壮大, 雄大, 偉観** ‖ *the grandeur of the Swiss Alps* スイスアルプスの雄大さ ▶定義2 the feeling of being important 重要であるという感じ→**偉大, 崇高, 威風, 威光**

**grandfather clock** 名 ❷ ▶定義 a clock that stands on the floor in a tall wooden case 背の高い木製のケースに入った床置き式の時計→**(人の背より高い振り子式の)大型箱時計**

**grandiose** /grǽndiòʊs/ 形 ▶定義 bigger or more complicated than necessary 必要以上に大きいまたは複雑な→**気負った, 誇大な, おおげさな**

**grandma** /grǽn(d)màː, grǽm-, -mɔ̀ː/ 略式 = GRANDMOTHER

**grandpa** /grǽn(d)pàː/ 略式 = GRANDFATHER

**grandparent** /grǽn(d)pèərənt/ (または **grandmother**; **grandfather**) 名 ❷ ▶定義 the mother or father of one of your parents 両親のうち一方の父または母→**祖父, 祖母** ‖ *This is a picture of two of my great-grandparents (= the parents of one of my grandparents).* これは私の曾(そう)祖父母(= 私の祖父母の両親)の写真です. ▶どの祖父母のことを話しているかはっきりさせる必要がある場合は, 次のように言える: *My maternal/paternal grandfather or my* *mother's/father's father.* (私の母方の・父方の祖父または, 母の・父の父)

**grand piano** 名 C ▶定義 a large flat piano (with horizontal strings) 大きくて平型のピアノ(水平なピアノ線を持つ)➡グランドピアノ, 平型ピアノ

**grand slam** 名 C ▶定義 winning all the important matches or competitions in a particular sport, for example tennis or rugby テニスやラグビーなど, ある特定のスポーツにおけるすべての重要な試合または競技で勝つこと➡(テニス・ゴルフの)グランドスラム(世界4大トーナメントの個人戦すべてに同一年度内に優勝すること), 大成功, 総なめ, 全勝

**grandstand** /grǽn(d)stænd/ 名 C ▶定義 rows of seats, usually covered by a roof, from which you get a good view of a sports competition, etc 通常屋根付きで, そこからスポーツ競技などの眺めが良い列になった座席➡(競技場などの)正面(特別)観覧席, 特別観覧席の観衆

**grand total** 名 C ▶定義 the amount that you get when you add several totals together 数個の合計を総計して得られる数量➡総計, 累計

**granite** /grǽnɪt/ 名 U ▶定義 a hard grey rock 硬くて灰色の岩➡花崗(こう)岩, 御影(みかげ)石

**granny** /grǽni/ (複 **grannies**) 略式 = GRANDMOTHER

**grant**¹ /grɑːnt; grænt/ 動 他 ▶定義 1 正式 to (officially) give sb what he/she has asked for ～が依頼したものを(公式に)与える➡～の(願い)をかなえてやる, (要求など)を聞き入れる, (請求にこたえて)(金品・権利など)を与える, 譲渡する ‖ *He was granted permission to leave early.* 彼は早速許可を与えられた. ▶定義 2 to agree (that sth is true) (～が真実である)と認める➡(議論・主張・真実性など)を承認する, 認容する, 真実を認める ‖ *I grant you that New York is an interesting place but I still wouldn't want to live there.* 私はニューヨークが面白い場所だと認めますが, それでもそこに住みたいと思いません.

成句 **take sb/sth for granted** ▶定義 to be so used to sb/sth that you forget his/her/its true value and are not grateful ～に慣れすぎて, その本当の価値を忘れてしまい有り難いと感じない➡～がいつでもいる[ある]ものと期待・当てにする, (長期にわたる所有・権利・存在など)を当然のこととしておろそかにする, ～に慣れすぎてしまいもはや重宝がらない ‖ *In developed countries we take running water for granted.* 先進国において私たちは水道の水を当たり前だと思っています.

**take sth for granted** ▶定義 to accept sth as being true ～が真実であると受け入れる➡～だということが真実・妥当・正常だと思う ‖ *We can take it for granted that the new students will have at least an elementary knowledge of English.* 新入生は少なくとも初歩的な英語の知識を持っていてしかるべきだと考えられます.

**grant**² /grɑːnt; grænt/ 名 C ▶定義 money that is given by the government, etc for a particular purpose ある特定の目的のため政府などから与えられるお金➡補助金, 助成金, 奨学金 ‖ *a student grant* (= *to help pay for university education*) 学生奨学金(= 大学教育にかかる支払いの援助) *to apply for/be awarded a grant* 奨学金を申請する・授与される

**granted** /grɑ́ːntəd; grǽnt-/ 副 ▶定義 used for saying that sth is true, before you make a comment about it ～について, コメントを述べるのに先立って, それが真実であると言うときに用いて➡仮に～としても, ～と認めても ‖ *'We've never had any problems before.' 'Granted, but this year there are 200 more people coming.'* 「私たちは今まで何1つ問題がありませんでした」「それは認めますが, 今年は来る人が200名も増えています」

**granule** /grǽnjuːl/ 名 C ▶定義 a small hard piece of sth 1つの小さな硬い～➡小粒, 細粒, 微粒 ‖ *instant coffee granules* 顆(か)粒状インスタントコーヒー

★**grape** /ɡreɪp/ 名 C ▶定義 a green or purple berry that grows in bunches on a climbing plant (a vine) and that is used for making wine 緑または紫のベリーで, つる植物(ブドウ)に房でなり, ワインの原料となる➡ブドウ(の実) ‖ *a bunch of grapes* 1房のブドウ ☛ C3ページのさし絵

▶通常緑色のブドウはwhite, 紫色のものはblackと呼ばれる. 乾燥させたブドウはraisins(レーズン), currants(カラント)またはsultanas(スルタナ)と呼ばれる.

成句 **sour grapes** ⇒ **SOUR**

**grapefruit** /gréɪpfruːt/ 名 ⓒ (複 **grapefruit** または **grapefruits**) ▶定義 a large round yellow fruit with a thick skin and a sour taste 皮が厚く酸味がある大きくて丸い黄色の果物 →グレープフルーツ, グレープフルーツの木

**the grapevine** /gréɪpvàɪn/ 名 [単数扱い] ▶定義 the way that news is passed from one person to another 人から人への情報の伝わり方 →(秘密)情報・うわさのルート, 情報の秘密伝達経路 ‖ I heard **on/through the grapevine** that you're moving. 私はあなたが引っ越すとうわさで聞きました.

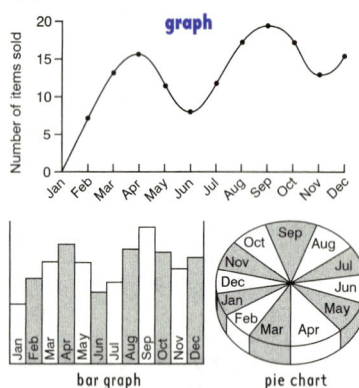

**graph** /grɑːf; græf/ 名 ⓒ ▶定義 a diagram in which a line or a curve shows the relationship between two quantities, measurements, etc 2つの数量, 寸法などの関係を線や曲線で表す図表 →図式, 表, グラフ ‖ a graph showing/to show the number of cars sold each month 車の月別販売数を表すグラフ

**graphic** /gréfɪk/ 形 ▶定義 1 (名詞の前だけ) connected with drawings, diagrams, etc 絵や図表などに関連した →図式・グラフによる, 図解の, 図示の ‖ graphic design グラフィックデザイン a graphic artist グラフィックアーティスト ▶定義 2 (used about descriptions) clear and giving a lot of detail, especially about sth unpleasant (描写について)特に不愉快な〜に関して, はっきりと細部をよく説明した →(言葉・書き方が)生き生きした, 絵のような, 写実的な ‖ She described the accident in graphic detail. 彼女はその事故について生々しい描写をした.
— **graphically** /-k(ə)li/ 副 →グラフで示して, 図解で, 絵を見るように, 生き生きと

**graphics** /gréfɪks/ 名 [複数扱い] ▶定義 the production of drawings, diagrams, etc デッサン, 図表などを作成すること →製図法, 図学, グラフィクス ‖ computer graphics コンピューターグラフィクス(電子計算機の出力をディスプレーに図形で表示する技術)

**grapple** /grép(ə)l/ 動 ⓘ ▶定義 grapple (with sb) to get hold of sb and fight with or try to control him/her 〜を手でつかみ戦いを挑む, または支配しようとする →つかむ, 握る, (人と)つかみ合う, 格闘する

★**grasp**¹ /grɑːsp; græsp/ 動 ⓣ ▶定義 1 to take hold of sb/sth suddenly and firmly 〜を突然, しっかりとつかむ →〜を(手でしっかりと)つかむ, 握る ‖ Lisa grasped the child firmly by the hand before crossing the road. リーサは子供の手をしっかり握ってから道路を横断した. (比喩) to grasp an opportunity/a chance 機会・チャンスをつかむ ▶定義 2 to understand sth completely 〜を完全に理解する →〜を掌握する, 〜がすっかり分かる ‖ I don't think you've grasped how serious the situation is. あなたには状況の深刻さがまだ分かっていないと思います.

句動詞 grasp at sth ▶定義 to try to take hold of sth 〜をつかもうとする →〜をつかもうとする, 捕らえようとする

**grasp**² /grɑːsp; græsp/ 名 [単数扱い, ⓤ] ▶定義 1 a firm hold of sb/sth 〜をしっかり握ること →握ること, つかむこと ‖ Get a good grasp on the rope before pulling yourself up. ロープをしっかりと握ってから体を引き上げてください. I grabbed the boy, but he slipped from my grasp. 私はその男の子を捕まえたが, 彼は私の手からするりと抜け出した. ▶定義 2 a person's understanding of a subject or of difficult facts 人が対象物または難しい事実を理解すること →理解(力), 把握, 会得 ‖ He has **a good grasp of** English grammar. 彼は英文法をよく理解している. ▶定義 3 the ability to get or achieve sth 〜を手に入れる, または達成する能力 →手の届く距離, 理解力の及ぶ範囲, 統御(力), 支配 ‖ Finally their dream was **within** their **grasp**. とうとう彼らは夢に手が届くところまで来た.

**grasping** /grάːspɪŋ; græsp-/ 形 ▶定義 wanting

very much to have a lot more money, power, etc より多くのお金, 権力などを強く望んで→**貪欲(どんよく)な, 欲深い, 強欲な**

**✱grass** /grɑːs; græs/ ▶定義1 ❶the common green plant with thin leaves which covers fields and parts of gardens. Cows, sheep, horses, etc eat grass. 野原や庭園の一部を覆う細い葉を持つありふれた緑の植物. 牛, 羊, 馬などはそれを食べる→**草, 牧草, 芝** ‖ *Don't walk on the grass.* 芝生の上を歩いてはいけない. *I must cut the grass at the weekend.* 私は週末芝生刈りをしなければなりません. *a blade (= one leaf) of grass* 草の葉1枚

▶庭園で草の生えた区域はlawn(芝生)と呼ばれる.

▶定義2 ❻one type of grass 1つの種類の草→**草, 草の葉・茎** ‖ *an arrangement of dried flowers and grasses* ドライフラワーと草のアレンジメント

**grasshopper** /ɡrɑ́ːsˌhɒpər; ɡrǽs-/ 名 ❻ ▶定義 an insect that lives in long grass or trees and that can jump high in the air. Grasshoppers make loud noises. 背の高い草や木に住む昆虫で, 空中を高く飛び, とても大きな音を立てる→**バッタ, イナゴ, キリギリス ☛ insect** のさし絵

**grass roots** 名 [複数扱い] ▶定義 the ordinary people in an organization, not those who make decisions 組織において決定権を持たない普通の人々→**一般大衆, 庶民,「草の根」**‖ *the grass roots of the party* その政党の(一般)党員

**grassy** /ɡrɑ́ːsi; ɡrǽsi/ 形 ▶定義 covered with grass→**草で覆われた, 草の多い**

**grate**¹ /ɡréɪt/ 動 ▶定義1 ⓑto rub food into small pieces using a metal tool (a grater) 金属の道具(おろし金)でこすって食べ物を細かくする→**(食物を)(おろし金で)おろす** ‖ *grated cheese/carrot* 擦りおろしたチーズ・ニンジン

▶定義2 ⓘ grate (on sb) to annoy or irritate うるさがらせる, またはいら立たせる→**(人を)いら立たせる, 怒らせる** ▶定義3 ⓘ grate (against/on sth) to make a sharp unpleasant sound (when two metal surfaces rub against each other) 鋭く不愉快な音を出す(2つの金属の表面をこすり合わせたときの音)→**(戸・車輪・ちょうつがいなどが)擦れ合う, きしむ, (キーキーという)音を立てる**

**grate**² /ɡréɪt/ 名 ❻ ▶定義 the metal frame that holds the wood, coal, etc in the space at the bottom of the chimney where you make a fire (fireplace) 煙突の一番下にある火を燃やす場所(暖炉)の, 木・炭などを入れておく金属の枠→**(暖炉の)火床(ひどこ), 火格子 ☛ fireplace** のさし絵

**✱grateful** /ɡréɪtfʊl, -f(ə)l/ 形 ▶定義 grateful (to sb)(for sth); grateful (that...) feeling or showing thanks (to sb) (~に)感謝して, または感謝を表して→**(行為など)に対して(人に)感謝する, (~して・~であることを)有り難く思う, うれしく思う** ‖ *We are very grateful to you for all the help you have given us.* 私たちにいろいろとお力添えを頂き, 大変感謝しています. *He was very grateful that you did as he asked.* お願いした通りにやっていただいて彼は大変喜んでいました. ⇔ **ungrateful ☛** 名 gratitude — **gratefully** /-fʊli, -f(ə)li/ 副 →**感謝して, 喜んで**

**grater** /ɡréɪtər/ 名 ❻ ▶定義 a kitchen tool that is used for cutting food (for example cheese) into small pieces by rubbing it across its rough surface ざらざらした表面で食べ物(例えばチーズ)をこすって小さくおろすのに使われる台所用具→**おろし金, 擦りおろし器 ☛ kitchen** のさし絵

**gratify** /ɡrǽtəfàɪ/ 動 ⓑ (現分 **gratifying**; 三単現 **gratifies**, 過, 過分 **gratified**) (通常は受動態で) 正式 ▶定義 to give sb pleasure and satisfaction ~に喜びや満足を与える→**人を喜ばせる, 満足させる** — **gratifying** 形 →**(精神的に)(~に)満足を与える, 愉快な**

**grating** /ɡréɪtɪŋ/ 名 ❻ ▶定義 a frame made of metal bars that is fixed over a hole in the road, a window, etc 道路・窓などの穴を覆うように取り付けられている金属棒でできた枠→**(排水口・窓などの)格子**

**gratitude** /ɡrǽtət(j)ùːd/ 名 ❶ ▶定義 gratitude (to sb)(for sth) the feeling of being grateful or of wanting to give your thanks to sb ~に対する感謝の, またはその思いを伝えたい気持ち→**感謝(の気持ち), 恩を知ること, 謝意** ⇔ **ingratitude**

**grave**¹ /ɡréɪv/ 名 ❻ ▶定義 the place where a dead body is buried 死体が埋葬される場所→**墓地, 墓穴, 墓所** ‖ *I put some flowers on my grandmother's grave.* 私は祖母の墓に花を供え

ました。☞参 tomb
**成句 have one foot in the grave** ⇒ **FOOT¹**

**grave²** /greɪv/ 形 正式 ▶定義 **1** bad or serious 悪いまたは容易ならない→(物事が)重大な,ゆゆしい,危険をはらんだ‖ *These events could have* **grave consequences** *for us all.* これらの出来事は私たち全員に重大な影響を及ぼす可能性があります. *The children were* **in grave danger**. その子供たちは重大な危機にあった. ▶定義 **2** (used about people) sad or serious (人々について)悲しそうな,または深刻な→厳粛な,重々しい,威厳のある ☞ 名 gravity ☞ どちらの意味においても serious の方がずっとより一般的. — gravely 副 →深刻に,重大に,厳粛に,重々しく‖ *gravely ill* 重病で

**gravel** /grǽv(ə)l/ 名 Ⓤ ▶定義 very small stones that are used for making roads, paths, etc 道路・歩道などを造るのに使われる非常に小さな石→砂利, バラス

**gravestone** /ɡréɪvstòun/ 名 Ⓒ ▶定義 a stone in the ground that shows the name, dates, etc of the dead person who is buried there そこに埋葬されている故人の名前・日付などを記している地面に埋め込まれた石→墓石, 墓碑 ☞参 **headstone, tombstone**

**graveyard** /ɡréɪvjɑ̀ːrd/ 名 Ⓒ ▶定義 an area of land next to a church where dead people are buried 故人が埋葬されている教会に隣接した土地→墓地 ☞参 **cemetery, churchyard**

**gravity** /ɡrǽvəti/ 名 Ⓤ ▶定義 **1** the natural force that makes things fall to the ground when you drop them 物を落とすと地面まで落下する現象を引き起こす自然の力→重力, 地球引力, 引力‖ *the force of gravity* 重力 ▶定義 **2** 正式 importance; seriousness 重要性;深刻さ→(事態の)重大さ,(病気・罪などの)重いこと,(態度・性格・振る舞い・話し方の)厳粛さ, まじめさ
➤ seriousness の方がより一般的な単語.
☞ 形 grave

**gravy** /ɡréɪvi/ 名 Ⓤ ▶定義 a thin sauce that is made from the juices that come out of meat while it is cooking 調理中に出た肉汁から作るさらっとしたソース→肉汁ソース, グレイビー, 肉汁 ☞参 **sauce**

**gray** 特に 米 = **GREY**

**graze¹** /ɡreɪz/ 動 ▶定義 **1** Ⓘ (used about cows, sheep, etc) to eat grass (that is growing in a field) (牛, 羊などについて)(牧草地に生えている)草を食べる→(家畜が)生草を食う,(牧草を)食う‖ *There were cows grazing by the river.* 川辺で草をはんでいた牛がいた. ▶定義 **2** Ⓣ to break the surface of your skin by rubbing it against sth rough ざらざらした~でこすって皮膚の表面を傷付ける→(皮膚などを)(~にこすって)擦りむく,触れて擦りむく‖ *The child fell and grazed her knee.* その子供は転んでひざを擦りむいた. ▶定義 **3** Ⓣ to pass sth and touch it lightly →~に軽く触れて通る, ~をかすめる, ~をかする‖ *The bullet grazed his shoulder.* その銃弾は彼の肩をかすめた.

**graze²** /ɡreɪz/ 名 Ⓒ ▶定義 a slight injury where the surface of the skin has been broken by rubbing it against sth rough ざらざらした~でこすって皮膚に負った軽い傷→擦りむき, かすり傷

**grease¹** /ɡriːs/ 名 Ⓤ ▶定義 **1** a thick substance containing oil used, for example, to make engines run smoothly 油を含んだどろどろした物質で, 例えばエンジンを滑らかに動かすのに使われる→(常温で固体の)油脂, 油(潤滑・頭髪用)‖ *engine grease* エンジン潤滑油 ▶定義 **2** animal fat that has been softened by cooking 料理で柔らかくなった動物の脂肪→(柔らかい)獣脂, グリース‖ *You'll need very hot water to get all the grease off those pans.* それらの平なべに付いた脂をきれいに落としたければ, 非常に熱いお湯が必要でしょう.

**grease²** /ɡriːz/ 動 Ⓣ ▶定義 to rub grease or fat on or in sth ~の表面または中に油, または油脂を塗る・差す→~に油を塗る,油を差す,(油を差して)~の動きを滑らかにする‖ *Grease the tin thoroughly to stop the cake from sticking.* ケーキがくっつかないように焼き型に満遍なく油を塗ります.

**greasy** /ɡríːsi/ 形 ▶定義 covered with or containing a lot of grease たくさんの油に覆われた, または油が入った→脂っこい, 脂ぎった‖ *greasy skin/hair* 脂ぎった肌・べとべとした髪 *greasy food* 脂っこい食べ物

★**great¹** /ɡreɪt/ 形 ▶定義 **1** large in amount, degree, size, etc; a lot of 量, 程度, サイズなどが大きい; たくさんの→(数量の)多い,(規模・形

の)とても大きな,(時間・距離の)長い ‖ *We had great difficulty in solving the problem.* 私たちはその問題を解決するのに大変苦労しました. *The party was a great success.* そのパーティーは大成功でした. ▶定義2 particularly important; of unusually high quality 特に重要な; 並外れて高品質の→**偉大な,卓越した,有名な** ‖ *Einstein was perhaps the greatest scientist of the century.* アインシュタインはおそらく今世紀の最も偉大な科学者でした. ☛参 **big** の注 ▶定義3 略式 good; wonderful→**とても良い,すばらしい** ‖ *We had a **great time** in Paris.* 私たちはパリですばらしい時を過ごしました. *It's **great** to see you again.* あなたにまたお会いできてよかった. ▶定義4 略式 (サイズ,数量などの形容詞を強調するために用いて) very; very good とても; 非常に良い→**(大きさ・数量・程度の)大きな,非常な** ‖ *There was a **great big dog** in the garden.* 庭にとてもでっかい犬がいた. *They were great friends.* 彼らはとても良い友達でした. ▶定義5 **great-** used before a noun to show a family relationship 名詞の前に用いて家族関係を表す→**(〜より)1親等を隔てた**

▶ great-は家族の一員を指す単語に付加して,さらに一代遠いことを表すこともできる: *your **great-aunt** (= the aunt of your mother or father)* (あなたの大おば(= あなたの父母どちらかのおば)) *your **great-grandchild** (= the son or daughter of one of your grandchildren)* (あなたのひ孫(= あなたの孫の息子か娘)) *your **great-grandparents** (= the parents of your grandparents)* (あなたの曾(そう)祖父母(= あなたの祖父母の両親)) *your **great-great-grandfather** (= the grandfather of one of your grandparents)* (あなたの曾曾祖父(= あなたの祖父母の祖父))

— greatness 名 U→偉大さ,卓越,大きいこと
成句 go to great lengths ⇒ LENGTH
a good/great deal ⇒ DEAL²
a good/great many ⇒ MANY

**great²** /greɪt/ 名 [C, 通常は複数] 略式 ▶定義 a person or thing of special ability or importance 特別な能力を持った,または重要な人・物→**要人,名工,大家,重要なもの,お偉方** ‖ *That film is one of the all-time greats.* この映画は不朽の名作の1つです.

**Great Britain** (または **Britain**) (略 **GB**)

---

green¹ 739

▶定義 England, Wales and Scotland イングランド,ウェールズおよびスコットランド→**大ブリテン島(イングランド,スコットランド,ウェールズのある英国の主島),グレートブリテン** ☛参 **United Kingdom** の注

**greatly** /ˈɡreɪtli/ 副 ▶定義 very much→**大いに,非常に**

*★**greed** /ɡriːd/ 名 U ▶定義 greed (for sth) a desire for more food, money, power, etc than you really need 本当に必要以上に多くの食べ物,お金,権力などを望むこと→**(食べ物・富・権力に対する)貪欲(どんよく),欲深さ**

**greedy** /ˈɡriːdi/ 形 (**greedier**; **greediest**) ▶定義 greedy (for sth) wanting more food, money, power, etc than you really need 本当に必要以上の多くの食べ物,お金,権力などを望んで→**食い意地の張った,貪欲(どんよく)である,欲深い** ‖ *Don't be so greedy - you've had three pieces of cake already.* そんなに食い意地を張ってはいけません — あなたはもうケーキを3つも平らげています. — greedily 副→**欲張って,貪欲に**
— greediness 名→**欲張り,貪欲**

*★**green¹** /ɡriːn/ 形 ▶定義1 having the colour of grass or leaves 草または葉の色をした→**緑(色)の,(植物・草で)覆われた,青々とした** ‖ *dark/light/pale green* 濃い・明るい・淡い緑(色)の ▶定義2 connected with protecting the environment or the natural world 環境保護や自然界の保護に関連した→**環境保護(主義)の,(製品が)環境に優しい・を損なわない** ‖ *the Green party* 緑の党(地球環境保護を目指す政党) *green products* (= that do not damage the environment) 環境に優しい製品(= 環境を損なわない) ▶定義3 略式 (used about a person) with little experience of life or a particular job (人について)人生またはある特定の職業において経験のない→**未経験の,未熟な,世間知らずの,不慣れで** ▶定義4 jealous (wanting to have what sb else has got) しっとして(だれか別の人の持っているものが欲しくて)→**(〜のことを)うらやんで,(しっとなどで)顔色が青ざめて** ‖ *He was **green with envy** when he saw his neighbour's new car.* 彼は隣人の新車を見て(顔色が青ざめるほど)しっとした. ▶定義5 (used about the skin) a strange, pale colour (because you feel sick) (皮

膚について)変に青ざめた色(気分が悪くて)→(病気などで)青ざめた, 血の気のうせた ‖ *At the sight of all the blood he* **turned green** *and fainted.* その血を見た途端, 彼は青ざめて失神した.

▶日本語 vs 英語

「青信号」の色

文化によって色の表現はさまざまです. 例えば, 信号の色を言うとき, 日本での「青」信号は, 英語では green を使います. blue ではないことに注意しましょう.

成句 **give sb/get the green light** 略式 ▶定義 to give sb/get permission to do sth ~に…をする許可を与える・~から…をする許可を得る→人に~をする許可[ゴーサイン]を与える, 人から~をする許可[ゴーサイン]をもらう

**have green fingers;** 米 **have a green thumb** 略式 ▶定義 to have the ability to make plants grow well 植物をうまく育てる能力を有している→園芸の才能がある, 草木・青物栽培がうまい

\***green**² /gríːn/ 名 ▶定義 **1** ⓒ ⓤ the colour of grass or leaves 草や葉の色→緑, 緑色, 青 ‖ *They were dressed in green.* 彼らは緑色の服を着ていました. *The room was decorated in greens and blues.* その部屋は緑と青を使った装飾がなされていました. ▶定義 **2** **greens** [複数扱い] green vegetables that are usually eaten cooked 通常は調理して食べる緑野菜→(食用になる)葉, 茎, 野菜, 青物 ‖ *To have a healthy complexion you should eat more greens.* 血色を良くするためにはもっと緑の野菜を食べなければなりません. ▶定義 **3** ⓒ 英 an area of grass in the centre of a village 村の中心にある芝地→(公有・共有の)芝地, 村の共有草地 ▶定義 **4** ⓒ a flat area of very short grass used in games such as golf ゴルフなどのゲームで使われる非常に短い芝の生えた平らな部分→ゴルフコース, グリーン ▶定義 **5** **Green** ⓒ a member of a green political party→環境保護(主義)政党の党員

**green belt** 名 ⓒ ⓤ 英 ▶定義 an area of open land around a city where building is not allowed 建築が許可されていない都市の周りの空き地区域→(都市周辺の)緑地帯, グリーンベルト

**green card** 名 ⓒ ▶定義 a document that allows sb from another country to live and work in the US 合衆国以外の出身の人が合衆国に住み働くことを許可した書類→(米国国民以外の人への)労働許可証, グリーンカード, 永住権

**greenery** /gríːn(ə)ri/ 名 ⓤ ▶定義 attractive green leaves and plants 目を楽しませる緑の葉や植物→青葉, 緑樹, (装飾用の)緑の枝葉

**greengrocer** /gríːnɡrəʊsər/ 名 ⓒ ▶定義 **1** ⓒ a person who has a shop that sells fruit and vegetables 果物や野菜を売る店の人→青物商(人), 八百屋 ☞参 **grocer** ▶定義 **2** **the greengrocer's** [単数扱い] a shop that sells fruit and vegetables 果物や野菜を売る店→八百屋, 青物屋

**greenhouse** /gríːnhaʊs/ (または **glasshouse**) 名 ⓒ ▶定義 a building made of glass in which plants are grown 中で植物を栽培するガラスでできた建物→温室 ☞ C7 ページのさし絵. **hothouse** を参照.

**the greenhouse effect** 名 [単数扱い] ▶定義 the warming of the earth's atmosphere as a result of harmful gases, etc in the air 空気中の有害ガスなどによる地球環境の温暖化→温室効果 ☞参 **global warming**

**greenish** /gríːnɪʃ/ 形 ▶定義 slightly green わずかに緑色の→緑がかった

**green pepper** 名 ⓒ ⇒ **PEPPER**¹(2) ☞ C3 ページのさし絵

**greet** /gríːt/ 動 他 ▶定義 **1** greet sb (with sth) to welcome sb when you meet him/her; to say hello to sb ~に会ったときに歓迎する; ~にあいさつをする→人を迎える, ~に(口頭・動作・書面で)あいさつをする ‖ *He greeted me with a friendly smile.* 彼は人懐こくほほえんで私を迎えてくれた. (比喩) *As we entered the house we were greeted by the smell of cooking.* 家に入ると料理の香りが私たちを迎えてくれた.
▶定義 **2** greet sb/sth (as/with) sth (通常は受動態で) to react to sb or receive sth in a particular way ある方法で~に対応したり, …を受け入れる→(人・物)を(~で)迎える, (人・提案など)に(~で)反応する, (態度・反応などが)~に対して起こる ‖ *The news was greeted with a loud cheer.* その知らせに割れるような喝さいが送られました.

**greeting** /gríːtɪŋ/ 名 ⓒ ▶定義 the first words you say when you meet sb or write to him/her ~に会ったとき, または手紙を書くときの最初

の言葉→あいさつ(の言葉・しぐさ), 会釈 ‖ *'Hello' and 'Hi' are informal greetings.* HelloとHiは略式のあいさつです.

**gregarious** /grɪgéəriəs/ 形 ▶定義 liking to be with other people; sociable 他人と一緒にいるのを好んで; 社交的な→集団の, 集団を好む, 社交的な

**grenade** /grənéɪd/ 名 C ▶定義 a small bomb that is thrown by hand or fired from a gun 手で投げられる, または発砲される小型の爆弾→手榴(しゅりゅう)弾, 手投げ弾

**grew** GROWの過去形

★**grey**¹ (特に 米 **gray**) /gréɪ/ 形 ▶定義1 having the colour between black and white 黒と白の中間色をした →灰色の, ネズミ色の, 鉛色の ‖ *dark/light/pale grey* 濃い・明るい・淡い灰色の *He was wearing a grey suit.* 彼は灰色のスーツを着ていました. ▶定義2 having grey hair→白髪(混じり)の, 銀髪の ‖ *He's going grey.* 彼は白髪が混じってきました. ▶定義3 (used about the weather) full of cloud; not bright (天候について)雲に覆われた; 明るくない→曇った, どんよりした, 薄暗い ‖ *grey skies* どんよりした空 *a grey day* 曇り日 ▶定義4 boring and sad; without interest or variety つまらなく悲しい; 興味も変化もない→陰気な, 憂鬱(ゆううつ)な, 活気のない

**grey**² (特に 米 **gray**) /gréɪ/ 名 C U ▶定義 the colour between black and white 黒と白の中間色→灰色, ネズミ色, 鉛色 ‖ *dressed in grey* 灰色の服を着た

**greyhound** /gréɪhaʊnd/ 名 C ▶定義 a large thin dog that can run very fast and that is used for racing 非常に速く走ることができ, レースに使われる大きなやせ型の犬→グレイハウンド ‖ *greyhound racing* グレイハウンドレース

**greyish** (特に 米 **grayish**) /gréɪɪʃ/ 形 ▶定義 slightly grey わずかに灰色の→灰色がかった, くすんだ

**grid** /grɪd/ 名 C ▶定義1 a pattern of straight lines that cross each other to form squares 互いに交差して正方形を形づくる直線の模様→格子(こうし), 碁盤目, 一覧表などの網目枠 ‖ *She drew a grid to show how the students had scored in each part of the test.* 彼女は生徒たちが試験の各分野でどのように得点したかを表すため(碁盤目の)一覧表を作成しました.

▶定義2 a frame of parallel metal or wooden bars, usually covering a hole in sth 金属または木製の棒を平行に並べた枠で, 通常何かの穴を覆っている→鉄格子 ▶定義3 a system of squares that are drawn on a map so that the position of any place can be described or found ある場所の位置を説明したり見つけるのに使われる地図上に書かれた碁盤目→(地図の上に引かれた検索用の)碁盤目, 方眼 ‖ *a grid reference* グリッド照合 ▶定義4 the system of electricity wires, etc taking power to all parts of a country 電線などの組織網で国中に電力を送る→配電網, 送電網, (電線・水道・ガスなどの)敷設網, (テレビ・ラジオの)放送網 ‖ *the National Grid* 全国高圧送電線網

**gridlock** /grídlɑ̀k/ 名 U C ▶定義 a situation in which there are so many cars in the streets of a town that the traffic cannot move at all 町の路上に車が多数ありすぎて交通渋滞で全く動けない状況→どこにも抜けられない交通渋滞, 全交通網渋滞 — **gridlocked** 形→どこにも抜けられない交通渋滞で, 全交通網渋滞で

**grief** /gri:f/ 名 U ▶定義 great sadness (especially because of the death of sb you love) 深い悲しみ(特に愛する人の死による)→深い悲しみ, 悲嘆

成句 **good grief** (口語) ▶定義 used for expressing surprise or shock 驚きまたは衝撃を表すのに用いて→おやまあ, やれやれ ‖ *Good grief! Whatever happened to you?* おやまあ. 一体全体どうしたの.

**grievance** /grí:v(ə)ns/ 名 C ▶定義 **a grievance (against sb)** something that you think is unfair and that you want to complain or protest about 不公平なので, それに対し不満を述べたり抗議したいと思う物事→(労働条件・不当な扱いなどに対する)不平, 苦情, 不満・抗議の原因(と考えられる状況)

**grieve** /gri:v/ 動 ▶定義1 自 **grieve (for sb)** to feel great sadness (especially about the death of sb you love) 深い悲しみを感じる(特に愛する〜の死に関して)→(死者・死などを)深く悲しむ, 悲嘆に暮れる, 心を痛める ▶定義2 他 正式 to cause unhappiness 不幸を引き起こす→(事が)人を深く悲しませる, 悲嘆に暮れさせる

★**grill**¹ /grɪl/ 名 C ▶定義 1 a part of a cooker where the food is cooked by heat from above オーブン(レンジ)の一部で食物を上から熱調理する場所→グリル(装置) ▶定義 2 a metal frame that you put food on to cook over an open fire 金属の枠組みで、その上に食物を置き火の上で調理する→焼き網, 鉄きゅう ▶定義 3 ⇒ GRILLE

★**grill**² /grɪl/ 動 ▶定義 1 (特に 米 broil) 他 自 to cook under a grill グリル装置に入れて調理する→(〜を)あぶる, 焼く・焼ける, 網焼きにする・される ‖ grilled steak/chicken/fish あぶり焼きのステーキ・鶏肉・魚 ▶定義 2 他 略式 grill sb (about sth) to question sb for a long time 〜に長時間かけて質問する→(警察などが)〜を厳しく(ぶっ通しで)尋問・詰問する

**grille** /grɪl/ (または grill) 名 C ▶定義 a metal frame that is placed over a window, a piece of machinery, etc 窓・機械などを覆って取り付ける金属製の枠組み→(門・窓の)格子(こうし), 鉄格子, 格子窓口, (自動車エンジンの)放熱格子

**grim** /grɪm/ 形 (grimmer; grimmest) ▶定義 1 (used about a person) very serious; not smiling (人について)非常にまじめな; 笑っていない→厳格な, 厳しい, (表情・態度が)険しい, いかめしい ▶定義 2 (used about a situation, news, etc) unpleasant or worrying (状況, 知らせなどについて)不愉快な, または心配な→(事実などが)不愉快な, 冷酷な, 妥協を許さない ‖ The news is grim, I'm afraid. 残酷な知らせです, 残念ですが. ▶定義 3 (used about a place) unpleasant to look at; not attractive (場所について)見ていて不愉快な; 魅力がない→不愉快な, 気味の悪い, ぞっとするような ‖ a grim block of flats 気味の悪いアパート ▶定義 4 英 略式 feeling ill→気分・具合が悪くて ‖ I was feeling grim yesterday but I managed to get to work. 私は昨日具合が悪かったが何とか仕事に行った. — **grimly** 副→厳格に, 冷酷に, 気味悪く

**grimace** /ɡrɪˈmeɪs, ɡrɪˈmeɪs/ 名 C ▶定義 an ugly expression on your face that shows that you are angry, disgusted or that sth is hurting you 怒っている, 嫌気が差している, または〜に痛められていることを示す醜い表情→(心配・苦痛による)しかめっ面, 顔をゆがめること ‖ a grimace of pain 苦痛にゆがんだ顔 — **grimace** 動 自 →しかめっ面をする, 顔をゆがめる ‖ She grimaced with pain. 彼女は苦痛に表情をゆがめた.

**grime** /ɡraɪm/ 名 U ▶定義 a thick layer of dirt 厚い汚れの層→汚れ, あか, ほこり, すす

**grimy** /ˈɡraɪmi/ 形 ▶定義 very dirty とても汚い→あかで汚れた, 汚い, すすけた

**grin** /ɡrɪn/ 動 自 (grinning; grinned) ▶定義 grin (at sb) to give a broad smile (so that you show your teeth) 大きく口を横に開いて笑う(歯を見せて)→(大きく口を開いて)歯を見せて笑う, にっこり笑う, にやりとする ‖ She grinned at me as she came into the room. 彼女は部屋に入ってくると私ににっこりと笑った. — **grin** 名 C →(歯を見せて)にっこり笑うこと, にたにた笑い

**grind**¹ /ɡraɪnd/ 動 他 (過, 過分 **ground** /ɡraʊnd/) ▶定義 1 grind sth (down/up); grind sth (to/into sth) to press and break sth into very small pieces or into a powder between two hard surfaces or in a special machine 表面が硬い2つの物に〜を挟んで, または特別の機械に〜を入れて圧力をかけて砕き, 非常に細かくする, または粉にする→(人・機具などが)(穀物など)を(粉・小片に)ひく, 砕く ‖ Wheat is ground into flour. 小麦をひいて小麦粉を作る. ground pepper/coffee ひいたコショウ・コーヒー ▶定義 2 to make sth sharp or smooth by rubbing it on a rough hard surface 〜をざらざらした硬い表面にこすり付けて鋭くする, または滑らかにする→(人などが)物を研ぐ, 磨いて(〜に)する, 削る ‖ to grind a knife on a stone ナイフを砥石(といし)で研ぐ ▶定義 3 grind sth in/into sth to press or rub sth into a surface→物を(〜に)押し付ける, こすり付ける, 〜を踏み付ける ‖ He ground his cigarette into the ashtray. 彼はたばこを灰皿に押し付けて消した. ▶定義 4 to rub sth together or make sth rub together, often producing an unpleasant noise 〜をこすり合わせる, または〜がこすれるようにして, 不愉快な音を出す→(歯などを)きしらせる, 〜をギシギシこすり合わせる, (物を)ギシギシ鳴らす ‖ Some people **grind** their **teeth** while they're asleep. 睡眠中に歯ぎしりをする人もいます. 成句 grind to a halt/standstill ▶定義 to stop slowly ゆっくりと止まる→(車などが)車輪をきしませて止まる, (抵抗に遭って)止まる, 頓挫(とんざ)する

**grind**[2] /gráɪnd/ 名 [単数扱い] 略式 ▶定義 an activity that is tiring and boring and that takes a lot of time 疲れて退屈で長時間かかる活動➡骨の折れる退屈な仕事・勉強, 長くつらいレース(マラソンなどの) ‖ the **daily grind** of working life 労働生活において毎日繰り返される退屈な仕事

**grinder** /gráɪndər/ 名 C ▶定義 a machine for grinding 粉砕する機械➡粉砕・研磨機 ‖ a coffee grinder コーヒー豆用ひき具

**grip**[1] /grɪp/ 動 他 (**gripping**; **gripped**) ▶定義 1 to hold sb/sth tightly ~をしっかり握る➡(人が)(人・体の部分・物を)(手・歯・器具などで)しっかりつかむ・握る・締める ‖ She gripped my arm in fear. 彼女は恐怖で私の腕をしっかりとつかんだ. ▶定義 2 to interest sb very much; to hold sb's attention ~に非常に興味を持たせる; ~の注意を引き付けておく➡(物・事が)(人・注意など)を引き付けてそらさない, ~の心をつかむ ‖ The book grips you from start to finish. その本は最初から最後まであなたを引き付けて離しません. ☛ 形 gripping

**grip**[2] /grɪp/ 名 ▶定義 1 [単数扱い] a grip (on sb/sth) a firm hold (on sb/sth) ➡~にしっかりつかまること・~を強く握ること ‖ I relaxed my grip and he ran away. 私がつかんだ手を緩めると, 彼は逃げ出した. The climber slipped and lost her grip. その登山者は足を滑らせつかまっていた手を離してしまった. (比喩)The teacher kept a firm grip on the class. 先生はクラスをしっかりと掌握していた. ▶定義 2 [単数扱い] a grip (on sth) an understanding of sth ~の理解➡(問題などに対する)理解力, 把握力, (仕事などの)処理能力 ▶定義 3 C the person whose job it is to move the cameras while a film is being made 映画製作中のカメラ移動を仕事とする人➡(カメラ班の)裏方, 道具方, (劇場)舞台係

成句 **come/get to grips with sth** ▶定義 to start to understand and deal with a problem 問題を理解し対処し始める➡(困難・問題などに)真剣に取り組む, (~を)理解し始める

**get/keep/take a grip/hold (on yourself)** 略式 ▶定義 to try to behave in a calmer or more sensible way; to control yourself より平静に, あるいはもっと賢明に振る舞おうとする; 自分自身を抑制する➡自分(の感情)を抑える, 気を引き締める

**in the grip of sth** ▶定義 experiencing sth unpleasant that cannot be stopped やめることのできない不愉快な~を経験して➡~から逃れられずに, ~から抜け出せないで ‖ a country in the grip of recession 不景気から抜け出せない国

**gripe** /graɪp/ 名 C ▶定義 a complaint about sb/sth ~に関する不満➡不平, 泣き言 — gripe 動 自 ▶定義 不平を言う, こぼす

**gripping** /grípɪŋ/ 形 ▶定義 exciting; holding your attention わくわくさせる; 注意を引き付けておく➡注意・興味をひく ‖ a gripping film/book 興味をひかれる映画・本

**grisly** /grízli/ 形 ▶定義 (used for describing sth that is concerned with death or violence) terrible; horrible(死または暴力に関係した~を描写するために用いて)ひどい; 恐ろしい➡ぞっとする, 気味悪い, ものすごい ‖ a grisly crime/death/murder 恐ろしい犯罪・死・殺人 ☛参 **gruesome** 意味は類似している.

**gristle** /grís(ə)l/ 名 U ▶定義 a hard substance in a piece of meat that is unpleasant to eat 肉片の中にある, 食べにくい硬い物質➡(食用肉中の)すじ, 軟骨 — gristly 形 ➡(食肉に)すじのある, 軟骨のある

**grit**[1] /grɪt/ 名 U ▶定義 1 small pieces of stone or sand 石または砂の小さな粒々➡砂, 荒砂, 小石, 砂利 ‖ I've got some grit/a piece of grit in my shoe. 私は片方の靴の中に小石がいくつか・1個入ってしまった. ▶定義 2 略式 courage; determination that makes it possible for sb to continue doing sth difficult or unpleasant 勇気; ~が困難な, またはやりたくない…をやり続ける決意➡(どんな苦難にも耐える)根性, 気骨, 肝っ玉

**grit**[2] /grɪt/ 動 他 (**gritting**; **gritted**) ▶定義 to spread small pieces of stone and sand on a road that is covered with ice 氷が張った道路に小石や砂をまく➡(道などに)荒砂をまく

成句 **grit your teeth** ▶定義 1 to bite your teeth tightly together 歯をぎゅっとかみ締める➡歯を食いしばる ‖ She gritted her teeth against the pain as the doctor examined her injured foot. 医者がけがをした足を診察する間, 彼女は歯を食いしばって痛みに耐えた. ▶定義 2 to use your courage or determination in a difficult situation 困難な状況下において勇気や決意を見せ

る→(決意を固めて)ぎゅっと歯をかみ締める, (怒り・恐れ・失望などを抑えて)歯を食いしばる

**groan** /gróun/ 動⾃ ▶定義 groan (at/with sth) to make a deep sad sound because you are in pain, or to show that you are unhappy about sth 痛みを訴えて, または~に関して不満を表して, 深い悲しみの声を上げる→(苦痛・悲嘆・失望などで)うめく, うなる, (不満・怒りなどで)ぶうぶう言う‖ *He groaned with pain.* 彼は苦痛のためにうめき声を上げた. *All the students were moaning and groaning (= complaining) about the amount of work they had to do.* 生徒たちは皆, 課せられた勉強量が不満でぶうぶう言っていた(= 不平を述べていた). — groan 名 C → うめき声, うなり声, 不満の声

**grocer** /gróusər/ 名 ▶定義 1 Ca person who has a shop that sells food and other things for the home 家庭向けに食物やそのほかの物を売る店の持ち主→食料雑貨店主, 食料品店主 ◆参 greengrocer ▶定義 2 **the grocer's** [単数扱い] a shop that sells food and other things for the home 家庭向けに食物やそのほかの物を売る店→食料雑貨店, 食料品店

**groceries** /gróus(ə)riz/ 名 [複数扱い] ▶定義 food, etc that is sold by a grocer or in a larger food shop (supermarket) 食料雑貨店またはもっと大規模な食料品店(スーパーマーケット)で売られる食物など→食料雑貨類, 食料品‖ *Can you help me unload the groceries from the car, please?* 車から食料品を積み降ろすのを手伝ってくれますか.

**groggy** /grági/ 形 略式 ▶定義 weak and unable to walk steadily because you feel ill, have not had enough sleep, etc 気分が悪い, 睡眠不足などの理由で力がなくしっかりと歩けない→足元がふらつく, 意識がもうろうとして, よろめく‖ *She felt a bit groggy when she came round from the operation.* 彼女は手術から意識を回復した時少し足元がふらついた.

**groin** /grɔ́ɪn/ 名 C ▶定義 the front part of your body where it joins your legs 両足の付け根のある身体の前の部分→鼠蹊(そけい), ももの付け根

**groom**¹ /gru:m, grum/ 名 C ▶定義 1 = BRIDEGROOM ▶定義 2 a person who looks after horses, especially by cleaning and brushing them 馬の面倒を見る人で, 特に洗ってやったりブラシをかけたりする→馬丁(ばてい), 別当, 下僕

**groom**² /gru:m, grum/ 動他 ▶定義 1 to clean or look after an animal by brushing, etc 動物にブラシをかけるなどきれいにしてやる, または世話をする→(馬・犬など)の手入れをする, ~をきれいにしてやる‖ *to groom a horse/dog/cat* 馬・犬・猫の手入れをする ▶定義 2 **groom sb (for/as sth)** (通常は受動態で) to choose and prepare sb for a particular career or job ある特定の職業または仕事のために~を選出し準備させる→人を(身分[地位]に就けるように・~として)準備させる, 仕込む, 教育する

**groove** /gru:v/ 名 C ▶定義 a long deep line that is cut in the surface of sth ~の表面に切り込まれた長く深い線→溝, わだち, 車の跡

**grope** /group/ 動⾃他 ▶定義 1 **grope (about/around) (for sth)** to search for sth or find your way using your hands because you cannot see 見えないので手探りで~を探したり前進する→手探りする, 模索する, 手探りで進む‖ *He groped around for the light switch.* 彼は電灯のスイッチを手探りで探し回った. ▶定義 2 略式 to touch sb sexually, especially when he/she does not want you to 特に相手がそれを望んでいないとき, ~を性的に触る→(人の)体をまさぐる

**gross** /grous/ 形 ▶定義 1 (名詞の前だけ) being the total amount before anything is taken away 何も差し引かれていない総量の→総計の, 全体の, 風袋(ふうたい)込みの‖ *gross income (= before tax, etc is taken away)* 総収入(= 税などを差し引く前の) ⇔ net ▶定義 2 正式 (名詞の前だけ) very great or serious とても甚だしくて容易ならない→ひどい, 甚だしい, 紛れもない‖ *gross indecency/negligence/misconduct* 甚だしい不作法・怠慢・違法行為 ▶定義 3 very rude and unpleasant ひどく粗野で不愉快な→粗野な, 荒い, 下品な ▶定義 4 very fat and ugly とても太って醜い→でぶの, 肥満体の

**grossly** /gróusli/ 副 ▶定義 very 非常に→大いに, ひどく‖ *That is grossly unfair.* それは不公平極まりない.

**grotesque** /groutésk/ 形 ▶定義 strange or ugly in a way that is not natural 不自然なほど奇妙または醜い→怪奇な, 異様な, 風変わりな

**grotty** /gráti/ 形 医 略式 ▶定義 unpleasant; of

poor quality 不愉快な; 質の悪い➜**汚い, 安っぽい, 不潔な, うんざりする** ‖ *She lives in a grotty flat.* 彼女は安っぽいアパートに住んでいます.

***ground**[1] /gráund/ [名] ▸定義 1 **the ground**[単数扱い]the solid surface of the earth 地球の表面の硬い部分➜**地面, 地表, 土, 土地** ‖ *We sat on the ground to eat our picnic.* 私たちはお弁当を食べるために地面に座りました. *He slipped off the ladder and fell to the ground.* 彼ははしごから滑って地面に落ちた. *waste ground (= that is not being used)* 荒野(= 使用されていない) ▸定義 2 [U] an area or type of soil 地域または土壌の種類➜**地域, 土壌** ‖ *solid/marshy/stony ground* 硬い·湿地帯の·石の多い土壌

➤ the Earth は私たちの住む惑星の名前. land は sea に対する反意語: *The sailors sighted land./The astronauts returned to Earth.* (船乗りたちは陸を見つけた·宇宙飛行士たちは地球に帰った.) land は売買することもできる: *The price of land in Tokyo is extremely high.* (東京の地価は高騰しています.) 屋外にいるときに足の下に感じる表面を ground と呼ぶ. 屋内にいるときはそれを floor と呼ぶ: *Don't sit on the ground. You'll get wet.* (地面に座らないでください. ぬれてしまいますよ.) *Don't sit on the floor. I'll get another chair.* (床に座らないでください. もう 1 ついすをお持ちしますから.) 植物は earth または soil に育つ.

▸定義 3 [C] a piece of land that is used for a particular purpose ある特定の目的に使われる土地➜**場所, 用地, 敷地** ‖ *a sports ground* スポーツ用グラウンド *a playground* (学校の) 運動場, 遊び場 ▸定義 4 **grounds** [複数扱い] land or gardens surrounding a large building 大きな建物を囲む土地または庭➜**(建物の周囲にある塀·生け垣に囲まれた) 構内, 敷地, 庭, 庭園** ‖ *the grounds of the palace* 宮殿の敷地 ▸定義 5 [U] an area of interest, study, discussion, etc 興味·研究·議論などの分野➜**領域, 分野, 話題** ‖ *The lecture went over **the same old ground**/covered a lot of **new ground**.* その講義はいつもの古い話題を繰り返していた·多くの新しい領域を取り扱っていた. *to be on dangerous ground (= saying sth likely to cause anger)* 危険な領域に触れる (= 怒りを買いそうな事に言及する) ▸定義 6 [[C], 通常は複数] **grounds (for sth/doing sth)** a reason for sth 〜の理由➜**(〜の) 根拠, 理由, 原因** ‖ *She retired **on** medical **grounds**.* 彼女は健康上の理由で退職しました. *grounds for divorce* 離婚の原因 ▸定義 7 [米] = **EARTH**[1](4)

[成句] **above/below ground** ▸定義 above/below the surface of the earth 地上に·地面の下に➜**地上に·生きて, 墓に埋められて·死んでいる**

**break fresh/new ground** ▸定義 to make a discovery or introduce a new method or activity 発見をする, または新しい方法や活動を紹介する➜**新発見をする, 新天地を開く, 新方面を開拓する**

**gain ground** ⇒ **GAIN**[1]

**get off the ground** ▸定義 (used about a business, project, etc) to make a successful start (事業, プロジェクトなどについて) うまいスタートを切る➜**(計画などが) うまくスタートする, 実行に移される**

**hold/keep/stand your ground** ▸定義 to refuse to change your opinion or to be influenced by pressure from other people 自分の意見を変えるのを拒む, または他人からの圧力に影響されるのを拒否する➜**自分の立場·主張·意見を固守する, 一歩も退かない, 初心を貫く**

**thin on the ground** ▸定義 difficult to find; not common 見つけるのが難しい; 一般的でない➜**数が少ない, まばらな** ‖ *Jobs for people with my skills are fairly thin on the ground these days.* 最近では私のような技能を持つ人向けの職は, 数がかなり少ない.

**ground**[2] /gráund/ [動] [他] ▸定義 1 (通常は受動態で) to force an aircraft, etc to stay on the ground 航空機などに地上にとどまることを強いる➜**(航空機·操縦士) を地上にとどまらせる, 強制着陸させる, (濃霧などが) 飛行·離陸を不可能にする** ‖ *to be grounded by fog* 濃霧により飛行·離陸不可能になっている ▸定義 2 (通常は受動態で) to punish a child by not allowing them to go out with their friends for a period of time 罰として子供に一定期間友人と外出するのを許可しない➜**(罰として) (子供の) 外出を禁止する** ▸定義 3 特に [米] = **EARTH**[2]

**ground**[3] **GRIND**[1] の過去·過去分詞形 ‖ *ground almonds* アーモンド粉

**ground beef** [米] = **MINCE**

G

## ground crew

**ground crew** (または **ground staff**) 名 ⓒ ⓤ
▶定義 the people in an airport whose job it is to look after an aircraft while it is on the ground 航空機が地上にいる間その手入れを仕事とする人々 → (飛行機の) 地上整備員

**ground floor** (米 **first floor**) 名 ⓒ ▶定義 the floor of a building that is at ground level 建物で地面の高さにある階 → 1階 ‖ *a ground-floor flat* 1階建てのアパート ☛参 floor の注

**grounding** /gráundɪŋ/ 名 [単数扱い] ▶定義 a grounding (in sth) the teaching of the basic facts or principles of a subject ある教科の基礎または基礎となる原理を教えること → (～の) 基礎, 基礎知識, 基礎作り, 手ほどき ‖ *This book provides a good grounding in grammar.* この本は文法の基礎がよく説明されています.

**groundless** /gráundləs/ 形 ▶定義 having no reason or cause 理由も原因もない → 理由のない, 根拠のない, 事実無根の ‖ *Our fears were groundless.* 私たちの恐怖は理由のないものでした.

**groundnut** = PEANUT

**groundwork** /gráundwə̀ːrk/ 名 ⓤ ▶定義 work that is done in preparation for further work or study 今からの仕事または勉強に備えてする仕事・勉強 → 基礎, 基礎作業, 土台, 第1段階

*__group__¹ /gruːp/ 名 ⓒ ▶定義1 [単数または複数形の動詞と共に] a number of people or things that are together in the same place or that are connected in some way 同じ場所に集まっている, または何らかの方法で結び付いている何人かの人々またはいくつかの物 → 集団, 集まり, 群れ, グループ, 団体 ‖ *Our discussion group is/are meeting this week.* 私たちの討議グループは今週集まる予定です. *A group of us are planning to meet for lunch.* 私たちグループは昼食の集いを予定しています. *Students were standing in groups waiting for their exam results.* 生徒たちが試験の結果待ちで, いくつかのグループに分かれて立っていました. *He is in the 40-50 age group.* 彼は40～50歳のグループに属しています. *people of many different social groups* 多種多様な社会集団の人々 *a pressure group* (= a political group that tries to influence the government) 圧力団体 (= 政府に影響を与えようとする政治団体) *Which blood group (for example A, O, etc) do you belong to?* あなたの血液型 (例えばA, Oなど) は何ですか. *Divide the class into groups.* クラスをグループ分けしてください. ☛ group は単数形で, 動詞は単・複数形どちらでも使える. グループのメンバーを, 一同に集まった数名の個人と見なす場合は, 複数形の動詞を使う方が一般的. ▶定義2 (used in business) a number of companies that are owned by the same person or organization (事業に用いて) 同一人物または組織に所有されたいくつかの会社 → ～グループ, 同系列の会社, 企業グループ ▶定義3 (古) a number of people who play music together 音楽を共に演奏する何人かの人々 → 小演奏家グループ ‖ *a pop group* ポップグループ ☛参 band

**group**² /gruːp/ 動 ⓘ ⓣ ▶定義 group (sb/sth) (around/round sb/sth); group (sb/sth) (together) to put sb/sth or to form into one or more groups ～を, 1つまたは複数のグループにまとめる, またはそういったグループにまとまる → (人・物を) 1箇所にまとめる・まとまる, ～を一団 [集団] にする, 群がる, ～を (…に) 分類する ‖ *Group these words according to their meaning.* これらの単語を意味によって分類しなさい.

**grouse** /graus/ 名 ⓒ (複 **grouse**) ▶定義 a fat brown bird with feathers on its legs that is shot for sport 足に羽毛が生えており, スポーツとして狩猟される太った茶色の鳥 → ライチョウ (の類)

**grovel** /gráv(ə)l, gráv-/ 動 ⓘ (**grovelling; grovelled**: 米 **groveling; groveled**) ▶定義1 grovel (to sb) (for sth) to try too hard to please sb who is more important than you or who can give you sth that you want 自分より地位の高い人, または欲しい～をくれる人を喜ばせるため必要以上に頑張る → (へりくだって, 恐れて) (～を得ようと) (人の前に・人の足元に) ひれ伏す, こびる, へつらう, ぺこぺこする ‖ *to grovel for forgiveness* 許しを求めてへつらう ▶定義2 grovel (around/about) (for sth) to move around on your hands and knees (usually when you are looking for sth) 四つんばいになって動き回る (通常は～を探すとき) → (～を探して) はいつくばう, 腹ばう — **grovelling** 形 → 平伏した, はいつくばう ‖ *I wrote a grovelling letter to my bank manager.* 私は銀行の支配人あてに平身低頭の

手紙を書いた.

**\*grow** /gróu/ 動 (過 **grew** /gru:/; 過分 **grown** /gróun/) ▶定義1 ❸ grow (in sth) to increase in size or number; to develop into an adult form 大きさまたは数が増える; 大人になる→**大きくなる, 増える, (〜に)成長する** ‖ *a growing child* 成長期の子供 *She's growing in confidence all the time.* 彼女は常に信頼を増しています. *You must invest if you want your business to grow.* 事業を大きくしたいなら投資をしなければなりません. *Plants grow from seeds.* 植物は種から成長します. *Kittens soon grow into cats.* 小猫はすぐに大きくなって親猫になります. ▶定義2 ❹ (used about plants) to exist and develop in a particular place; to make plants grow by giving them water, etc (植物について) ある特定の場所に存在し成長する; 水をやるなどして植物を栽培する→**育つ, 伸びる, 生える; 〜を栽培する, 育てる, 産出する** ‖ *Palm trees don't grow in cold climates.* やしの木は寒い気候では育ちません. *We grow vegetables in our garden.* 私たちは庭で野菜を栽培しています. ▶定義3 ❹ to allow your hair or nails to grow→**(髪・つめなど)を伸ばす, 生やす** ‖ *Claire's growing her hair long.* クレアは髪の毛を長く伸ばしています. *to grow a beard/moustache* あごひげ・口ひげを生やす ▶定義4 ❸ to gradually change from one state to another; to become ある状態から別の状態へ次第に変化する; 〜になる→**成長して(〜に)なる, (〜に)変化する, 〜になる** ‖ *It began to grow dark.* だんだん暗くなってきました. *to grow older/wiser/taller/bigger* だんだん年老いる・賢く・背が高く・大きくなる *The teacher was growing more and more impatient.* 先生はだんだん我慢できなくなってきた. ▶ get の方が略式.

句動詞 grow into sth ▶定義1 to gradually develop into a particular type of person 次第に成長してある特定の種類の人になる→**だんだんと〜になる, 大きくなって〜になる** ‖ *She has grown into a very attractive young woman.* 彼女は非常に魅力的で若々しい女性に成長しました. ▶定義2 to become big enough to fit into clothes, etc→**(服など)に合うほどに大きくなる・成長する** ‖ *The coat is too big for him, but he will soon grow into it.* そのコートは彼には大きすぎますが, 彼はすぐに大きくなってちょうど良くなるでしょう.

grow on sb ▶定義 to become more pleasing→**人の気に入るようになる, 心をひくようになる** ‖ *I didn't like ginger at first, but it's a taste that grows on you.* 私は初めショウガが好きではありませんでした. でもそれは慣れてくるとおいしく思いますよ.

grow out of sth ▶定義 to become too big or too old for sth 〜にとって大きく, または古くなりすぎる→**(人が)大きくなって(服が)着られなくなる, 〜しなくなる, (習慣など)を脱皮する** ‖ *She's grown out of that dress I made her last year.* 彼女は大きくなり私が去年作ってあげた服が着られなくなりました.

grow (sth) out ▶定義 (used about hairstyles, etc) to disappear gradually as your hair grows; to allow your hair to grow in order to change the style (髪型などについて) 髪の毛が伸びるにつれてだんだんと見えなくなる; 髪型を変えるために髪を伸ばす→**髪を伸ばしてスタイルを変える**

grow up ▶定義1 to develop into an adult; to mature 成長して成人になる; 成熟する→**成長する, 大人になる, 大きくなって〜になる** ‖ *What do you want to be when you grow up? (= what job do you want to do later?)* 大きくなったら何になりたいですか. (= 将来何の仕事をしたいですか). *She grew up (= spent her childhood) in Spain.* 彼女はスペインで育った (子供時代を過ごしました). ▶定義2 (used about a feeling, etc) to develop or become strong (気持ちなどについて) 発展するまたは強くなる→**(友情・気持ちなどが)強まる, 深まる** ‖ *A close friendship has grown up between them.* 彼らの間に深い友情が芽生えた.

**growing** /gróuɪŋ/ 形 ▶定義 increasing 増加する→**次第に大きくなる, 増大する** ‖ *A growing number of people are becoming vegetarian these days.* 最近では菜食主義者になる人が増えています.

**growl** /grául/ 動 ❸ ▶定義 growl (at sb/sth) (used about dogs and other animals) to make a low noise in the throat to show anger or to give a warning (犬やそのほかの動物について) 怒りを表す, または警告するためのどの奥で低

い声を上げる→(犬などが怒って)(〜に)(ウウッと)うなる,うなり声を上げる — **growl** 名 C→うなり声,ほえ声

**grown** /gróun/ 形 ▶定義 physically an adult 身体的に大人の→**大人の,成長した,成熟した** ‖ *a fully-grown elephant* 完全に成熟した象

**grown-up**¹ 形 ▶定義 physically or mentally adult; mature 身体的に,または精神的に大人になった; 成熟した→**成人した,大人らしい,成熟した** ‖ *She's very grown-up for her age.* 彼女は年の割に大人びています.

**grown-up**² 名 C ▶定義 an adult person→**成人,大人**

*__growth__ /gróuθ/ 名 ▶定義 1 Ⓤ the process of growing and developing 成長・発展する過程→**成長,発育,発達,発展** ‖ *A good diet is very important for children's growth.* 良い食生活は子供たちの発育にとって大変重要です. *a growth industry (= one that is growing)* 成長期にある産業(= 発展している産業) ▶定義 2 [Ⓤ, 単数扱い] an increase (in sth) 増加(〜における)→**増加,増大,伸び** ‖ *population growth* 人口増加[単数扱い] ▶定義 3 Ⓒ a lump caused by a disease that grows in a person's or an animal's body 人または動物の体で大きくなる病気によるこぶ→**腫瘍(しゅよう)** ‖ *a cancerous growth* 悪性腫瘍 ▶定義 4 Ⓤ something that has grown 生えているもの→**(草・木・髪・ひげ・つめなど)生えた・伸びたもの,茂み** ‖ *several days' growth of beard* 数日間伸ばしたあごひげ

**grub** /grʌb/ 名 ▶定義 1 Ⓒ the first form that an insect takes when it comes out of the egg. Grubs are short fat and white. 昆虫が卵からかえったときに最初になる姿.短く太くて白い→**幼虫,地虫** ☛ **insect**のさし絵 ▶定義 2 Ⓤ 略式 food→**食べ物**

**grubby** /grʌbi/ 形 (**grubbier**; **grubbiest**) 略式 ▶定義 dirty after being used and not washed 使用後洗っていないので汚い→**汚い,だらしない**

**grudge**¹ /grʌdʒ/ 名 Ⓒ ▶定義 *a grudge (against sb)* unfriendly feelings towards sb, because you are angry about what has happened in the past 過去に起こった事に腹を立てているため,〜に抱く敵対心→**悪意,敵意,恨み,遺恨** ‖ *to bear a grudge against sb* 〜に対して恨みを抱く

**grudge**² /grʌdʒ/ 動他 ▶定義 *grudge sb sth; grudge doing sth* to be unhappy that sb has sth or that you have to do sth 〜が…を所有していること,または〜をせねばならないのを不満に思う→**人の物・事をねたむ,ねたんで認めない,物を・〜することを惜しむ** ‖ *I don't grudge him his success - he deserves it.* 私は彼の成功をねたんではいません — 彼はそれに値しますから. *I grudge having to pay so much tax.* 私はこんなに多額のお金を税金に費やしたくない.
☛参 **begrudge**

**grudging** /grʌdʒɪŋ/ 形 ▶定義 given or done although you do not want to やりたくないが与えられた,または行った→**しぶしぶの,嫌々の** ‖ *grudging thanks* しぶしぶ礼を言うこと — **grudgingly** 副→**嫌々ながら,しぶしぶ**

**gruelling** (米**grueling**) /grúːəlɪŋ/ 形 ▶定義 very tiring and long とても疲れる,長い→**へとへとに疲れさせる,厳しい** ‖ *a gruelling nine-hour march* へとへとにくたびれる9時間の行進

**gruesome** /grúːsəm/ 形 ▶定義 (used about sth concerned with death or injury) very unpleasant or shocking (死または外傷に関する〜について)非常に不愉快な,または衝撃的な→**ぞっとするような,恐ろしい,気味な** ☛参 **grisly** 意味は類似している.

**gruff** /grʌf/ 形 ▶定義 (used about a person or a voice) rough and unfriendly (人や声について)粗っぽく不親切な→**荒々しい,無愛想な,しわがれた** — **gruffly** 副→**荒々しく,耳障り,無愛想に**

**grumble** /grʌmb(ə)l/ 動自 ▶定義 to complain in a bad-tempered way; to keep saying that you do not like sth 機嫌悪く不満を述べる; 〜が気に入らないと言い続ける→**(怒って)ぶつぶつ言う,不平を言う,不満・苦情を漏らす** ‖ *The students were always grumbling about the standard of the food.* 生徒たちはいつも食べ物の基準に不満があると漏らしていた.

▶何かが期待ほど良くないとき,通常**grumble**または**moan**(不平を言う,嘆く)と表現する.前向きな行動を取りたい場合は権限を持つだれかに**complain**(訴える,苦情を言う)と言う.

— **grumble** 名 C→**ぶつぶつ言うこと,不平,苦情**

**grumpy** /grʌmpi/ 形 略式 ▶定義 bad-tempered→**機嫌の悪い,気難しい,険しい** — **grumpily** 副→

むっつりと,不機嫌に

**grunt** /grʌnt/ 動自他 ▶定義 to make a short low sound in the throat. People grunt when they do not like sth or are not interested and do not want to talk. のどで短く低い音を出す.人は〜が好きでないときまたは興味がなく話をしたくないときに grunt する→(人が)ぶうぶう言う,不平を言う‖ *I tried to find out her opinion but she just grunted when I asked her.* 私は彼女の意見を聞こうとしたが尋ねてもただ不平を言うだけだった. ― grunt 名 ⓒ→ぶうぶう言う声,不平

★**guarantee**¹ /gæ̀r(ə)ntíː/ 名 ⓒⓊ ▶定義1 a firm promise that sth will be done or that sth will happen 〜がなされる,または起こるだろうという堅い約束→(品質・物事の)保証(となるもの),請け合い‖ *The refugees are demanding guarantees about their safety before they return home.* 亡命者たちは本国に帰る前に身の安全を保証するよう要求しています. ▶定義2 a written promise by a company that it will repair or replace a product if it breaks in a certain period of time 会社からの約束で,製品がある一定期間中に壊れたら修理または交換するという内容の書類→保証書,保証契約‖ *The watch comes with a year's guarantee.* その時計は1年間の保証付きです. *Is the computer still **under guarantee**?* このコンピュータはまだ保証期間中ですか. ☛参 **warranty** ▶定義3 something that makes sth else certain to happen ほかの物事が確実に起こるようにする何か→〜する…という保証‖ *Without a reservation there's no guarantee that you'll get a seat on the train.* 予約していないならその列車で席が見つかる保証はありません.

> ▶日本語 vs 英語
>
> 「ギャラ」の語源 guarantee
>
> 日本語では「ギャラ」だけが独り歩きし,「補償金」「契約金」「前もって契約された出演料」の意味で使われています.ギャラは英語では,advance (契約金,前金), performance fee (出演料)と言います.英語 guarantee「保証する」の関連語として, guarantor は「(身元)保証人」の意味に使われます.名詞 guarantee (保証)は guaranty とも言い, warranty と区別なく使われています.

---

guard¹    749

**guarantee**² /gæ̀r(ə)ntíː/ 動他 ▶定義1 to promise that sth will be done or will happen 〜がなされる,または起こるだろうと約束する→(〜すると)約束する,(〜に対する)保証をする‖ *They have guaranteed delivery within one week.* 彼らは1週間以内の搬入を保証しています. ▶定義2 to give a written promise to repair or replace a product if anything is wrong with it 製品に何か悪い所があったら修理または交換するという約束を書面で与える→(商品など)を保証する,〜に保証を与える‖ *This washing machine is guaranteed for three years.* この洗濯機は3年間の保証付きです. ▶定義3 to make sth certain to happen 〜が確実に起こるようにする→〜すると・〜であると保証する,〜を約束する,きっと〜する‖ *Tonight's win guarantees the team a place in the final.* 今夜の勝利でチームの決勝進出が確実となりました.

★**guard**¹ /gɑːrd/ 名 ▶定義1 ⓒa person who protects a place or people, or who stops prisoners from escaping 場所や人々を守る,または囚人の逃亡を阻止する人→護衛者,番人,守衛,ガードマン,看守‖ *a security guard* 警備員 ☛参 **warder, bodyguard** ▶定義2 Ⓤthe state of being ready to prevent attack or danger 攻撃または危険を防ぐ準備ができた状態→見張り,監視,警戒,用心‖ *Soldiers keep guard at the gate.* 兵士たちは門で番をしています. *Who is **on guard**?* だれが見張りについていますか. *The prisoner arrived **under** armed **guard**.* 囚人は武装監視体制の中到着した. *a guard dog* 番犬 ▶定義3 [単数扱い,単数または複数形の動詞と共に]a group of soldiers, police officers, etc who protect sb/sth 〜を守る一団の兵士,警官など→護衛兵・隊,守備隊,近衛隊‖ *The president always travels with an armed guard.* 大統領はいつも武装した護衛隊と共に移動します. ▶定義4 ⓒ(しばしば複合語で)something that covers sth dangerous or protects sth 危険な〜を覆うもの,または〜を保護するもの→保護・防護物,安全装置,防具,つば,すね当て‖ *a fireguard* 火よけ *a mudguard (= over the wheel of a bicycle)* 泥よけ(= 自転車の車輪をカバーする) ▶定義5 (米**conductor**) a person who is in charge of a train but does not drive it 列車の安

全を預かるが運転はしない人➜(列車の)車掌, ドア開閉係, 制動手 ▸定義6 [U]a position that you take to defend yourself, especially in sports such as boxing 特にボクシングのようなスポーツで, 自分を防御するために取る姿勢➜ガード, 防衛(姿勢)

[成句] off/on (your) guard ▸定義 not ready/ready for an attack, surprise, mistake, etc 攻撃, 驚き, 誤りなどに対し準備できていない·いる➜油断して·用心して ‖ *The question caught me off (my) guard and I didn't know what to say.* その質問に対し意表を突かれて, 何と答えていいか分からなかった.

***guard**[2] /gɑːrd/ [動][他] ▸定義1 to keep sb/sth safe from other people; protect ～を他人から安全に守る; 保護する➜～を(攻撃·危害·盗難などから)守る, 保護する ‖ *The building was guarded by men with dogs.* この建物は犬を従えた男たちで守られていた. (比喩) *a closely guarded secret* 固く閉ざされた秘密 ▸定義2 to be ready to stop prisoners from escaping 囚人の逃亡を防ぐ準備ができている➜(囚人)を監視する, (人·場所·動物)を見張る

[句動詞] guard against sth ▸定義 to try to prevent sth or stop sth happening ～を防ごうと, または～が起こるのを阻止しようとする➜～に用心する, 警戒する, ～が起こらないよう気を付ける, ～を監視する

**guarded** /gɑ́ːrdəd/ [形] ▸定義 (used about an answer, statement, etc) careful; not giving much information or showing what you feel (答え, 言明などについて)注意深い; あまり情報を与えない, または感じたことを表さない➜(人·言葉が)慎重な, 用心·注意深い, 言葉を選んだ ⇔ **unguarded** — guardedly [副]➜慎重に, 用心深く, 言葉を選んで

**guardian** /gɑ́ːrdiən/ [名][C] ▸定義1 a person or institution that guards or protects sth ～を守るまたは保護する人または組織➜保護者, 守護者, 保管者, 管理者 ‖ *The police are the guardians of law and order.* 警察は法と秩序の番人です. ▸定義2 a person who is legally responsible for the care of another person, especially of a child whose parents are dead 特に両親を亡くした子供について法的に人の面倒を見る責任を持つ人➜後見人, 保護者

**guerrilla**(または **guerilla**) /gərílə/ [名][C] ▸定義 a member of a small military group who are not part of an official army and who make surprise attacks on the enemy 公式の軍隊に属さず, 敵に奇襲をかける小さな軍事集団の一員➜ゲリラ兵, 遊撃兵, 不正規兵

***guess**[1] /ges/ [動] ▸定義1 [自][他] guess (at sth) to try and give an answer or make a judgement about sth without being sure of all the facts すべての事実を確信しているわけではないが, 答えを出そうと, または～について判断しようとする➜(～を)推測する, ～と·～であると推測する ‖ *I'd guess that he's about 45.* 彼は45歳くらいだと思います. *If you're not sure of an answer, guess.* 答えが分からなければ, 推測してごらんなさい. *We can only guess at her reasons for leaving.* 私たちは彼女が去った訳を推測するほかはありません. ▸定義2 [自][他] to give the correct answer when you are not sure about it; to guess correctly 答えに確信がないときに正解する; 正しく推測する➜～を解き当てる, ～の答えを言い当てる, (答えなど)を思い付く ‖ *Can you guess my age?* 私が何歳だか分かりますか. *You'll never guess what Adam just told me!* アダムが私になんて言ったか君には絶対に分からないよ. *Did I guess right?* 私の推測は当たっていますか. ▸定義3 [他] 特に [米][略式] to imagine that sth is probably true or likely; to suppose ～がおそらく正しい, またはそうらしいと想像する; 仮定する➜(根拠はないが何となく)(～だと)思う ‖ *I guess you're tired after your long journey.* 長旅でお疲れのことと思います. ▸定義4 [他] used to show that you are going to say sth surprising or exciting 驚く事·面白い事をこれから言うときに用いて➜想像してごらんよ, とんでもない事だけど ‖ *Guess what! I'm getting married!* びっくりする事があるよ. 結婚することになったんだ.

***guess**[2] /ges/ [名][C] ▸定義 an effort you make to imagine a possible answer or give an opinion when you cannot be sure if you are right 正しいかどうか自分で確信が持てないとき, 可能性のある答えを想像する, または意見を述べようとする努力➜推測, 推量, 憶測 ‖ *If you don't know the answer, then **have a guess**!* 答えが分からなければ, 推測してごらんなさい. *I don't* know how far it is, but **at a guess** I'd say about 50 miles. どれくらい遠いか分かりませんが,推測では50マイルくらいだと思います. I'd say it'll take about four hours, but that's just a **rough guess**. 大体4時間くらいはかかるでしょう,これもほんの見当にすぎませんが.

成句 **anybody's/anyone's guess** ▶定義 something that nobody can be certain about だれもそれについて確信が持てないもの→予測し難いこと, 断定できないこと ‖ What's going to happen next is **anybody's guess**. 次に何が起こるかはだれにも分からない.

**your guess is as good as mine** ▶定義 I don't know 私には分からない→あなたが分からないように私も分かりません ‖ 'Where's Ron?' '*Your guess is as good as mine.*'「ロンはどこですか」「私にも分かりません」

**guesswork** /ɡéswɚːrk/ 名 Ⓤ ▶定義 an act of guessing 推測する行為→当てずっぽう(の意見・判断), 当て推量 ‖ I arrived at the answer **by pure guesswork**. 私は全くの当てずっぽうで答えを得ました.

\***guest** /gest/ 名 Ⓒ ▶定義 **1** a person who is invited to a place or to a special event ある場所または特別の催しに招待されている人→(招待された)客, 賓客, 来賓, 特別出演者 ‖ *wedding guests* 結婚式の招待客 *Who is the guest speaker at the conference?* その会議で来賓演説するのはどなたですか. ▶定義 **2** a person who is staying at a hotel, etc ホテルなどに滞在している人→(ホテル・下宿などの)泊まり客, 宿泊客, 宿泊人 ‖ *This hotel has accommodation for 500 guests.* このホテルは500名の宿泊設備を備えている.

成句 **be my guest** 略式 ▶定義 used to give sb permission to do sth that he/she has asked to do ～から頼まれた…に対して, する許可を与えるのに用いて→どうぞご自由に, いいですとも, ご遠慮なく(お使い・お召し上がりください) ‖ '*Do you mind if I have a look at your newspaper?*' '*Be my guest!*'「あなたの新聞を見せていただいてもいいですか」「いいですとも」

**guest house** 名 Ⓒ ▶定義 a small hotel, sometimes in a private house 小さなホテル, 時に個人の家→客用の離れ, 迎賓館, 旅館, 民宿

**guidance** /ɡáɪdns/ 名 Ⓤ ▶定義 **guidance (on sth)** help or advice 助けまたは助言→案内指導, 手引き, 指図 ‖ *The centre offers guidance for unemployed people on how to find work.* そのセンター[総合施設]は非雇用者に対して仕事の見つけ方を指導しています.

\***guide**¹ /ɡáɪd/ 名 Ⓒ ▶定義 **1** a book, magazine, etc that gives information or help on a subject ある課題に対し情報を与える, または助けになる本, 雑誌など→案内書, 手引き書, 入門書 ‖ *Your Guide to Using the Internet* インターネット活用の手引き *Have we got a TV guide for this week?* 今週のテレビガイドは買ってあったかな. ▶定義 **2** (または **guidebook**) a book that gives information about a place for travellers and tourists 旅行者または観光客向けに, ある場所に関する情報を提供する本→ガイドブック, 旅行案内 ‖ *The guide says that it was built 500 years ago.* ガイドブックによればそれは500年前に建てられたようです. ▶定義 **3** a person who shows tourists or travellers where to go 観光客または旅行者がどこへ行けばいいか案内する人→(旅行・登山・狩猟などの)案内者, ガイド ‖ *She works as a tour guide in Venice.* 彼女はベニスで観光ガイドとして働いています.

▶定義 **4** something that helps you to judge or plan sth ～を判断または計画する助けとなるもの→指針, 基準, 道しるべ, 手本 ‖ *As a rough guide, use twice as much water as rice.* 大体の目安として, 米の倍量の水を使いましょう.

▶定義 **5 Guide** a member of an organization (**the Guides**) that teaches girls practical skills and organizes activities such as camping 少女たちに実践的技術を教え, キャンプなどの活動を企画する組織(ガイド)の一員→少女団員, ガールガイド

➤ 少年向けの同様の組織はthe Scouts.

\***guide**² /ɡáɪd/ 動 ⊕ ▶定義 **1** to help a person or a group of people to find the way to a place; to show sb a place that you know well ある場所に行く道が分かるよう人または一団の人々を助ける; ～に自分がよく知っている場所を示す→～を案内する, 道案内する ‖ *He guided us through the busy streets to our hotel.* 彼はにぎやかな通りを抜けて私たちをホテルまで案内してくれました. ☛参 **lead** の注 ▶定義 **2** to have an influence on sb/sth ～に影響を与える→～

を導く, 指導をする ‖ *I was guided by your advice.* 私はあなたの助言に導かれました. ▶定義2 to help sb deal with sth difficult or complicated ～が困難または複雑な…を扱うのを手伝う→人に(～を)切り抜けさせる, うまく処理させる ‖ *The manual will guide you through every step of the procedure.* この手引きがあれば各段階での手続きを切り抜けることができるでしょう. ▶定義4 to carefully move sb/sth or to help sb/sth to move in a particular direction ～を注意深く動かして, または…の移動を助けてある特定の方向に導く→～を誘導する, ～の方向を定める, ～の指針となる ‖ *A crane lifted the piano and two men carefully guided it through the window.* クレーンがピアノを持ち上げ, 2人の男が注意深く誘導してそのピアノを窓から中へ入れた.

**guided** /gáɪdəd/ 形 ▶定義 led by a guide 案内者に導かれた→案内者の付いた, 指導された, 誘導された ‖ *a guided tour/walk* ガイド付きの観光・散策

**guideline** /gáɪdlàɪn/ 名 **C** ▶定義1 [通常は複数] official advice or rules on how to do sth ～のやり方に関する公式の助言または規則→(政策・外交などの)ガイドライン, 指針, 誘導指標 ▶定義2 something that can be used to help you make a decision or form an opinion 決定, または意見形成の助けとして利用できるもの→指針, 指標 ‖ *These figures are a useful guideline when buying a house.* これらの数値は家を購入するときの指針として役立ちます.

**guillotine** /gíləti:n, --́/ 名 **C** ▶定義1 a machine used for cutting paper 紙を切るのに用いる機械→(紙などの)裁断機 ▶定義2 a machine that was used in France in the past for cutting people's heads off 昔フランスで人の首を切るのに用いられた機械→ギロチン, 断頭台 — guillotine 動他 (紙など)を裁断機で切る, 人をギロチンで斬首(ざんしゅ)する

★**guilt** /gɪlt/ 名 **U** ▶定義1 guilt (about/at sth) the bad feeling that you have when you know that you have done sth wrong 自分が悪い事をしたと分かっていて申し訳なく思う気持ち→罪悪感, 自責, 責任, 後ろめたさ ‖ *I sometimes feel guilt about not spending more time with my children.* 私は子供たちと十分な時間を過ごしていないことに罪悪感を持つときがあります. ▶定義2 the fact of having broken a law 法律を破った事実→罪, 犯罪(行為), 非行, 有罪 ‖ *We took his refusal to answer questions as an admission of guilt.* 私たちは, 彼が質問に答えるのを拒否したのを, 罪を認めたものと解釈しました. ⇔ **innocence** ▶定義3 the responsibility for doing sth wrong or for sth bad that has happened; the blame for sth 悪い事をしたこと, または悪い事が起こってしまったことへの責任; ～に対する責任→罪, 責任 ‖ *It's difficult to say whether the guilt lies with the parents or the children.* 両親か子供どちらに責任があるのかは言い難い.

**guilty** /gíltɪ/ 形 ▶定義1 guilty (of sth) having broken a law; being responsible for doing sth wrong 法律を犯した; 悪い事をした責任がある→有罪の, (～の)罪を犯した ‖ *She pleaded guilty/not guilty to the crime.* 彼女はその犯罪に対し有罪・無罪を申し立てた. *to be guilty of murder* 殺人罪を犯す *The jury found him guilty of fraud.* 陪審は彼が詐欺行為で有罪と評決しました. ⇔ **innocent** ▶定義2 guilty (about sth) having an unpleasant feeling because you have done sth bad 悪い事をしたので不愉快な気持ちになる→(～について)罪の意識がある, やましい, 後ろめたい ‖ *I feel really guilty about lying to Sam.* サムにうそをついた自分に後ろめたさを感じています. *It's hard to sleep with a guilty conscience.* 罪の意識があると眠れないものです. — **quiltily** 副→罪を犯して, やましい・後ろめたい気持ちで, ばつの悪い顔をして

**guinea pig** /gíni pìg/ 名 **C** ▶定義1 a small animal with no tail that is often kept as a pet 小動物でしっぽがなく, しばしばペットとして飼われる→テンジクネズミ, モルモット ▶定義2 a person who is used in an experiment 実験に使われる人→実験材料, 実験台となる人, 「モルモット」 ‖ *I volunteered to act as a guinea pig in their research into dreams.* 私は彼らが行う夢の研究の実験台になることを申し出ました.

**guise** /gáɪz/ 名 **C** ▶定義 a way in which sb/sth appears, which is often different from usual or hides the truth ～の表し方で, しばしば通常と異なっている, または真実を隠している有り様→(ごまかすため装った偽りの)外観, 見せ掛け,

振り ‖ *The President was at the meeting **in his guise as** chairman of the charity.* 大統領は会合に出席してその慈善行為の指導者を装いました. *His speech presented racist ideas **under the guise of** nationalism.* 彼の演説には国家主義を装った人種差別の考え方が表れていました.

*__guitar__ /gɪtάːr, gə-/ 图 C ▶定義 a type of musical instrument with strings that you play with your fingers or with a piece of plastic (*a plectrum*) 弦楽器の一種で, 指またはプラスチック製の物 (つめ) で演奏する→ギター ☞参 **piano** の注 ☞ **music** のさし絵

**guitarist** /gɪtάːrɪst, gə-/ 图 C ▶定義 a person who plays the guitar ギターを演奏する人→ギター奏者

**gulf** /gʌlf/ 图 ▶定義 1 C a part of the sea that is almost surrounded by land ほとんどを陸で囲まれている海の一部分→湾 ‖ *the Gulf of Mexico* メキシコ湾 ▶定義 2 **the Gulf** [単数扱い] the Persian Gulf→ペルシャ湾 ▶定義 3 C an important or serious difference between people in the way they live, think or feel 人の生活様式・考えかたまたは感じ方における重要な, または重大な違い→(意見・理解・気持ちなどの) 大きな隔たり, 越え難い溝・理解・気持ち ‖ *the gulf between rich and poor* 貧富の大きな隔たり

**gull** /gʌl/ (または **seagull**) 图 C ▶定義 a white or grey seabird that makes a loud noise 大きな声で鳴く白または灰色の海鳥→カモメ

**gullible** /gʌ́ləb(ə)l/ 形 ▶定義 (used about a person) believing and trusting people too easily, and therefore easily tricked (人について) 人を簡単に信じる, または信頼しすぎるため, だまされやすい→だまされやすい, お人よしの, 間抜けな

**gulp**¹ /gʌlp/ 動 ▶定義 1 ● @ gulp sth (down); gulp (for) sth to swallow large amounts of food, drink, etc quickly 多量の食物, 飲み物などを素早く飲み込む→(〜を) がつがつ・ごくごく飲み込む, がぶ飲みにする, 一飲みにする ‖ *He gulped down his breakfast and went out.* 彼は朝食を急いで飲み込んで出掛けていった. *She finally came to the surface, desperately gulping (for) air.* 彼女はやっと海面に上がってくると, あえぐようにして空気を吸い込んだ. ▶定義 2 @ to make a swallowing movement because you are afraid, surprised, etc 恐怖, 驚きなどのため飲み込む動作をする→はっと息をのむ, 言葉まる, あえぐ

**gulp**² /gʌlp/ 图 ▶定義 1 the action of breathing in or swallowing sth 何かを吸い込む, または飲み込む行為→ぐっと飲み込むこと ‖ *I drank my coffee in one gulp and ran out of the door.* 私はコーヒーを一飲みにして, ドアから走って出た. ▶定義 2 **a gulp (of sth)** the amount that you swallow when you gulp 一飲みするときに, 飲み込める量→ごくり・がぶりと飲める分量, 一口, 一息分

**gum** /gʌm/ 图 ▶定義 1 C either of the firm pink parts of your mouth that hold your teeth 口の中の硬いピンク色のどちらか一方で, 歯を支えている部分→歯茎, 歯肉 ☞ C5 ページのさし絵 ▶定義 2 U a substance that you use to stick things together (especially pieces of paper) 物 (特に紙) を付けるときに用いる物質→ゴムのり, アラビアのり ▶定義 3 = **CHEWING GUM** ☞参 **bubblegum**

*__gun__¹ /gʌn/ 图 C ▶定義 1 a weapon that is used for shooting 撃つのに用いる武器→銃, 鉄砲, ピストル, 大砲 ‖ *The robber held a gun to the bank manager's head.* 強盗は銀行支配人の頭に銃を突き付けた.

▶ gun と共にしばしば使われる動詞には load (弾丸を込める), unload (弾丸を抜き取る), point (向ける), aim (ねらう), fire (発砲する) がある. gun の異なる種類としては, machine gun (機関銃), pistol (ピストル), revolver (リボルバー, 回転式連発けん銃), rifle (ライフル銃), shot gun (ショットガン, 散弾銃) がある.

▶定義 2 a tool that uses pressure to send out a substance or an object ある物質または物体を圧力で押し出す道具→(銃の形をした) 注入器, 噴霧器, 吹き付け器 ‖ *a grease gun* グリース注入器 *a staple gun* ステープルガン (木やボードなどを留めるための大型ホチキスを打ち付ける道具)

成句 **jump the gun** ⇒ **JUMP**¹

**gun**² /gʌn/ 動 ⑲ (**gunning**; **gunned**)
句動詞 **gun sb down** 略式 ▶定義 to shoot and kill or seriously injure sb 〜を撃って殺す, または重傷を負わせる→〜を射殺する, 撃って重傷を

負わせる

**gunboat** /gʌ́nbòʊt/ 名 C 定義 a small ship used in war that carries heavy guns 戦争に用いられる小型の船で、重い銃を運ぶ → **小型砲艦**

**gunfire** /gʌ́nfàɪər/ 名 U 定義 the repeated firing of guns 繰り返される発砲 → **発砲,砲火,砲撃,銃撃** ‖ *We could hear gunfire.* 私たちは銃声が飛び交うのが聞こえました.

**gunman** /gʌ́nmən/ 名 C (複 **-men** /-mən/)
▶定義 a man who uses a gun to rob or kill people 強盗または殺人に銃を用いる人 → **殺し屋,無法者,ガンマン**

**gunpoint** /gʌ́npɔ̀ɪnt/ 名
成句 **at gunpoint** ▶定義 threatening to shoot sb ～を撃つと脅して → **銃を突き付けて・突き付けられて** ‖ *He held the hostages at gunpoint.* 彼は人質に銃を向けていた.

**gunpowder** /gʌ́npàʊdər/ 名 U 定義 an explosive powder that is used in guns, etc 銃などに使われる爆発性の粉 → **火薬**

**gunshot** /gʌ́nʃɑ̀t/ 名 C 定義 the firing of a gun or the sound that it makes 銃の発砲またはその時の音 → **発砲,砲撃,射撃,銃声**

**gurgle** /gə́ːrg(ə)l/ 動 自 定義1 to make a sound like water flowing quickly through a narrow space 水が細い空間を素早く流れるような音を立てる → **(水などが)ゴボゴボ・ドクドク流れる[音を立てる]** ‖ *a gurgling stream* ゴボゴボと音を立てる流れ ▶定義2 if a baby gurgles, it makes a noise in its throat because it is happy 赤ん坊の gurgle は, 喜んでのどを鳴らすこと → **(赤ん坊が)(喜んで)のどをゴロゴロ鳴らす** ― **gurgle** 名 C → **ゴボゴボいう音, (人が)のどを鳴らす音**

**guru** /gúːruː/ 名 C ▶定義1 a spiritual leader or teacher in the Hindu religion ヒンズー教における精神的指導者または教師 → **教師, 導師** ▶定義2 somebody whose opinions you admire and respect, and whose ideas you follow その持論が人から賞賛・尊敬され, その考えに人々が従う人物 → **指導者, 権威者, 専門家, リーダー** ‖ *a management/fashion guru* 経営の神様・ファッション界の指導者

**gush** /gʌ́ʃ/ 動 ▶定義1 ● **gush (out of/from/into sth)**; **gush out/in** (used about a liquid) to flow out suddenly and in great quantities (液体について)突然多量に流れ出る → **(水・涙・血などが)(～から)どくどく流れ出る・(～へ)流れ込む, ほとばしる, 噴き出る, わき出る** ‖ *Blood gushed from the wound.* 傷口から血が噴き出した. *I turned the tap on and water gushed out.* 私が蛇口を開けると水が噴き出した. ▶定義2 ⊕ (used about a container/vehicle, etc) to produce large amounts of a liquid (容器・乗り物などについて)多量の液体を流出する → **～を噴出させる, 勢いよく噴き出す** ‖ *The broken pipe was gushing water all over the road.* 壊れたパイプから道路一面に水が噴き出していた. ▶定義3 自 ⊕ to express pleasure or admiration too much so that it doesn't sound sincere 喜びや賞賛がすぎて本心には感じられないほど表現する → **感情的にしゃべりまくる, 感傷的・おおげさ・うれしそうにしゃべり立てる・書き立てる, とうとうしゃべる** ― **gush** 名 C → **ほとばしり, 噴出, おおげさな感情的おしゃべり** ‖ *a sudden gush of water* 突然の水の噴出

**gust** /gʌ́st/ 名 C 定義 a sudden strong wind 突然の強風 → **突風, 一陣の風** ― **gust** 動 自 → **(風が)急に吹く, 突風が吹く**

**gusto** /gʌ́stoʊ/ 名
成句 **with gusto** ▶定義 with great enthusiasm かなり熱中して → **うれしげに, 楽しそうに, 舌鼓を打って, 熱心に**

**gut¹** /gʌ́t/ 名 ▶定義1 ● the tube in your body that food passes through when it leaves your stomach 胃からの食物が体内で通る管 → **腸, 消化器官** ☞参 **intestine**. こちらの方がより専門的な用語. ▶定義2 **guts** [複数扱い] the organs in and around the stomach, especially of an animal 胃の中と回りにある器官で, 特に動物について用いて → **内臓, はらわた** ▶定義3 **guts** [複数扱い] 略式 courage and determination 勇気または決意 → **根性, 勇気, 決断力, ガッツ** ‖ *It takes guts to admit that you are wrong.* 自分の誤りを認めるには勇気が要ります. *I don't have the guts to tell my boss what he's doing wrong.* 上司に対して, やっている事が間違っていると言う勇気は私にはない. ▶定義4 ● a person's fat stomach 人の太ったおなか → **(突き出た)腹, おなか, 太鼓腹**

成句 **work/sweat your guts out** ▶定義 to work extremely hard 極端に激しく働く → **一心不乱に**

働く, 精根傾ける

**gut**[2] /gʌt/ 動 他 (**gutting**; **gutted**) ▶定義1 to remove the organs from inside an animal, fish, etc 動物, 魚などのはらわたを取り除く→～の内臓を取る, はらわたを抜く ▶定義2 to destroy the inside of a building 建物の中を破壊する→(建物・部屋など)の内部を全焼・全壊させる ‖ *The warehouse was gutted by fire.* その倉庫は火事で内部が全焼しました.

**gut**[3] /gʌt/ 形 (名詞の前だけ) ▶定義 based on emotion or feeling rather than on reason 理屈よりも感情または気持ちに基づいて→**本能的な, 切実な, 直感的な** ‖ *a gut feeling/reaction* 直感・本能的な反応

**gutter** /gʌ́tər/ 名 C ▶定義1 a long piece of metal or plastic with a curved bottom that is fixed to the edge of a roof to carry away the water when it rains 底が曲線になっており, 雨水を運び去るため屋根の端に固定されている細長い金属またはプラスチック→**雨どい, とい** ☞ C7ページのさし絵 ▶定義2 a lower part at the edge of a road along which the water flows away when it rains 道路わきの低くなった部分で, 雨水がそこを流れて運ばれる所→**(道路の) みぞ, 排水溝, 水路** ▶定義3 the very lowest level of society 社会におけるぎりぎりの最低水準→**貧民街, どん底の生活状態** ‖ *She rose from the gutter to become a great star.* 彼女はどん底の生活から身を起こして偉大なスターになりました.

**guy** /gáɪ/ 名 ▶定義1 C 略式 a man or a boy 男性または少年→**男, やつ** ‖ *He's a nice guy.* 彼はいいやつだ. ▶定義2 **guys** [複数扱い] 略式 used when speaking to a group of men and women 一団の男性または女性に話し掛けるときに用いて→**皆さん, 諸君** ‖ *What do you guys want to eat?* 君たち何が食べたい. ▶定義3 [単数扱い] 英 a model of a man that is burned on 5 November in memory of Guy Fawkes ガイ フォークスを記念して11月5日に焼かれる男性の模型→**ガイ(フォークスの)人形** ☞参 **Bonfire Night**

**guzzle** /gʌ́z(ə)l/ 動 自 他 略式 ▶定義 to eat or drink too fast and too much 急いでたくさん食べる, または飲む→**(～を)がつがつ食う, がぶがぶ飲む**

**gym** /dʒɪm/ 名 ▶定義1 (または 正式 **gymnasium**) C a large room or a building with equipment for doing physical exercise 体を動かすための設備を持った大きな部屋または建物→**体育館, 屋内体操場, ジム** ‖ *I work out at the gym twice a week.* 私は週2日ジムで運動しています. ▶定義2 U = **GYMNASTICS** ‖ *gym shoes* 運動靴

**gymnasium** /dʒɪmnéɪziəm/ 名 C (複 **gymnasiums** または **gymnasia** /-ziə/) = **GYM(1)**

**gymnast** /dʒɪ́mnæst, -nəst/ 名 C ▶定義 a person who does gymnastics 体操をする人→**体操選手, 体操教師**

**gymnastics** /dʒɪmnǽstɪks/ (または **gym**) 名 U ▶定義 physical exercises that are done indoors, often using special equipment such as bars and ropes しばしば棒やロープなどの特別の器具を使う室内で行う運動→**体操, 器械体操, 体育** ‖ *I did gymnastics at school.* 私は学校で体操競技をしました.

**gynaecology** (米 **gynecology**) /ɡàɪnəkɑ́lədʒi/ 名 U ▶定義 the study and treatment of the diseases and medical problems of women 女性の病気や医学的問題の研究および治療→**婦人科医学** ― **gynaecological** (米 **gyne-**) /ɡàɪnəkɑlɑ́dʒɪk(ə)l/ 形→**婦人科医学の** ― **gynecologist** (米 **gyne-**) /ɡàɪnəkɑ́lədʒɪst, dʒàɪ-, dʒìn-/ 名 C→**婦人科医**

**gypsy** (または **gipsy**) /dʒɪ́psi/ 名 C (複 **gypsies**) ▶定義 a member of a race of people who traditionally spend their lives travelling around from place to place, living in homes with wheels (**caravans**) 伝統的に場所を変えて移り住み, 車輪の付いた家(幌(ほろ)馬車)に生活する民族の一員→**ジプシー** ☞参 **traveller**

# H h

**H, h** /éɪtʃ/ 名 C (複 H's; h's) ▶定義 the eighth letter of the English alphabet 英語アルファベットの第8文字→h (H) が表す音, h (H) の文字, h (H) の字形のもの ‖ *'Hat' begins with (an) 'H'.* Hat は H で始まる.

**ha**[1] /hɑː/ 間 ▶定義 1 used for showing that you are surprised or pleased 驚いたり, または喜んだりすることを表すために用いて→**はあ, ほう, おや** ‖ *Ha! I knew he was hiding something!* ほう. 彼が何か隠していたのは知っていましたよ.
▶定義 2 **ha! ha!** used in written language to show that sb is laughing 書き言葉で〜が笑っていることを表して→**ハハ(と笑う声)**

**ha**[2] 略 hectare(s)→**ヘクタール**

*****habit** /hǽbət/ 名 ▶定義 1 **a/the habit (of doing sth)** something that you do often and almost without thinking, especially sth that is hard to stop doing ほとんど考えることなく, しばしば行う事で, 特にやめるのが難しい事→**習慣, 癖, 習癖** ‖ *I'm trying to **get into the habit** of hanging up my clothes every night.* 私は毎晩洋服をハンガーに掛ける習慣にしようとしています. *Once you start smoking it's hard to **break the habit**.* いったんたばこを吸い始めるとその習慣をやめるのは難しい. ☞ 形 habitual
▶ habit は通常個人によって行われる(ある)事. custom は団体, 地域社会または国によって行われる(ある)事: *the custom of giving presents at Christmas* (クリスマスに贈り物をする習慣)
▶定義 2 Ⓤ usual behaviour いつもの振る舞い→**常習(癖), 習性, 習慣** ‖ *I think I only smoke out of habit now - I don't really enjoy it.* 今はいつもの癖でたばこを吸っているだけだと思います − 心からおいしいとは思いません.
成句 **force of habit** ⇒ **FORCE**[1]
**kick the habit** ⇒ **KICK**[1]

**habitable** /hǽbətəb(ə)l/ 形 ▶定義 (used about buildings) suitable to be lived in (建物について) 住むのに適した→**住むのに適した, 住むことができる** ⇔ **uninhabitable**

**habitat** /hǽbətæt/ 名 C ▶定義 the natural home of a plant or an animal 動植物の自然の住みか→**生息地, 自生地, 産地, 本場** ‖ *I've seen wolves in the zoo, but not in their natural habitat.* 私はオオカミを動物園で見たことがありますが, 自然の中の生息地では見たことがありません.

**habitation** /hæbətéɪʃ(ə)n/ 名 Ⓤ 正式 ▶定義 living in a place ある場所に住んでいること→**居住, 住所, 住宅**

**habitual** /həbítʃuəl, -bítʃəl/ 形 ▶定義 1 doing sth very often 非常に頻繁に〜を行って→**習慣的な, 常習の, ひっきりなしの** ‖ *a habitual liar* 常習のうそつき ▶定義 2 which you always have or do; usual いつも持っている, またはする; 通常の→**平素の, いつもの, 例の** ‖ *He had his habitual cigarette after lunch.* 彼は昼食後にいつもの通りたばこを吸った. — **habitually** /-tʃuəli/ 副 →**習慣的に, いつも, 決まって**

**hack** /hǽk/ 動 自 他 ▶定義 1 **hack (away) (at) sth** to cut sth in a rough way with a tool such as a large knife 大きなナイフなどの道具を使って〜を荒々しいやり方で切る→**〜を(たたき)切る, 切り刻む, ずたずたに切る** ‖ *He hacked at the branch of the tree until it fell.* 彼はその木の枝が落ちるまでずたずたに切った. ▶定義 2 略式 **hack (into) (sth)** to use a computer to look at and/or change information that is stored on another computer without permission コンピューターを使い, ほかのコンピューターに蓄積された情報を許可なく見る, および・または変更する→**他人のコンピューターへ不法侵入する**

**hacker** /hǽkər/ 名 C 略式 ▶定義 a person who uses a computer to look at and/or change information on another computer without permission コンピューターを使い, ほかのコンピューターに蓄積された情報を許可なく見る, および・または変更する人→**コンピューター専門家・マニア, 他人のシステムへの不法侵入者**

**had**[1] /hǽd/ **HAVE** の過去・過去分詞形

**had**[2] /hǽd/ 形
成句 **be had** 略式 ▶定義 to be tricked→**だまされる, してやられる** ‖ *I've been had. This watch I bought doesn't work.* だまされた. 私が買ったこの時計は動かない.

**hadn't HAD NOT** の短縮形

**haemophilia** ( 米 **hemophilia**) /hìːmoʊfíliə, hèm-, -mə-/ 名 Ⓤ ▶定義 a disease that causes a person to bleed a lot even from very small injuries because the blood does not stop flowing (clot) 血液が止まら（凝固し）ないため, 非常に小さな傷からも多量に出血する病気→血友病

**haemophiliac**（米 **hemophiliac**）/hìːmoufíliæk, hèm-, -mə-/ 名 C ▶定義 a person who suffers from haemophilia 血友病を患う人→血友病患者

**haemorrhage**（米 **hemorrhage**）/hém(ə)ridʒ/ 名 C U ▶定義 a lot of bleeding inside the body 体内で多量に出血すること→大出血,（多量）出血
— haemorrhage 動 自 →大出血する, 多量に出血する

**haemorrhoids**（特に 米 **hemorrhoids**）/hém(ə)rɔidz/（または **piles**）名 ［複数扱い］▶定義 a medical condition in which the tubes that carry blood (veins) to the opening where waste food leaves the body (the anus) swell and become painful 不用な食物を体外に排せつする開口部（肛門）へ血液を運ぶ管（血管）がはれて痛くなる病状→痔（じ）

**haggard** /hǽgərd/ 形 ▶定義 (used about a person) looking tired or worried（人について）疲れた, または心配そうな様子の→目の落ちくぼんだ, やつれた, 憔悴（しょうすい）しきった

**haggle** /hǽg(ə)l/ 動 自 ▶定義 haggle (with sb) (over/about sth) to argue with sb until you reach an agreement, especially about the price of sth 特に～の価格について…と合意に至るまで口論する→（値段などを）値切る,（～のことで）言い争う, やり合う, 掛け合う ‖ In the market, some tourists were haggling over the price of a carpet. 市場では, 何人かの観光客がカーペットの価格を値切っていた.

**hail**¹ /héil/ 動 ▶定義 1 他 hail sb/sth as sth to say in public that sb/sth is very good or very special ～が大変良い, または他とは違うということを公に言う→（人が）人を（～として）迎える, 物・事を（～として）認める, 褒める ‖ The book was hailed as a masterpiece. その本は傑作として認められました. ▶定義 2 他 to call or wave to sb/sth ～に声を掛ける, または手を振る→～に合図する, 声を掛ける, ～を呼び止める ‖ to hail a taxi タクシーを呼び止める ▶定義 3 自 when it hails, small balls of ice fall from the sky like rain 空から小さな氷の粒が雨のように降る→あられ・ひょうが降る,（物・事が）あられのように降る・のしかかる ☞参 weather の注

**hail**² /héil/ 名 ▶定義 1 U small balls of ice (hail-stones) that fall from the sky like rain 雨のように空から降る小さな氷の粒（あられ・ひょう）→あられ, ひょう（の粒）▶定義 2 ［単数扱い］a hail of sth a large amount of sth that is aimed at sb in order to harm him/her ～を傷付けるためにその人に向けて投げられる多量の…→（～の）雨, 雨 あられのような～ ‖ a hail of bullets/stones/abuse 銃弾の雨・小石の雨・雨あられのような罵詈雑言（ばりぞうごん）

\***hair** /héər/ 名 ▶定義 1 U C the mass of long thin things that grow on the head and body of people and animals; one of these things 人や動物の頭や体に生えている長くて細い物の集まり; それらの1本→（人・動物の）毛, 体毛, 髪の毛, 頭髪,（1本の）毛 ‖ He has got short black hair. 彼の髪の毛は短くて黒い. Dave's losing his hair (= going bald). デーヴの頭髪は薄くなりかけている (= はげてきている). The dog left hairs all over the furniture. 家具という家具にその犬の毛が残っていました. ▶定義 2 **-haired** 形（複合語で用いて）having the type of hair mentioned 言及された種類の髪・毛をした→～の頭髪をした, ～な毛の ‖ a dark-haired woman 濃い色の髪をした女性 a long-haired dog 毛足の長い犬
▶毛の色を表す特別の単語は次の通り: auburn（赤［金］褐色の）, blond（金髪・ブロンドの）, fair（金色の）, ginger（赤味がかった茶色の）, red（赤毛の）. 髪の毛を手入れする, または髪を整えるには, brush（ブラシでとかす）, comb（くしでとかす）, wash（洗髪する）（または shampoo（シャンプーする））, そして blow-dry（ドライヤーでセットする）という方法がある. 髪の毛は真ん中または横で part（分ける）(a parting（分け目）を持つ) ことができる. hairdresser's（美容院）に行ったときは, 髪の毛を cut（カット）してもらう, または permed（パーマ）をかけてもらえる.

▶定義 3 a thing that looks like a very thin thread that grows on the surface of some plants ある種の植物の表面に生える, 非常に細い糸のように見えるもの→（葉・茎の表面の）毛, 毛状の物 ‖ The leaves and stem are covered in fine hairs. 葉と茎は細かい毛で覆われています.

成句 keep your hair on（口語）▶定義 (used to tell sb to stop shouting and become less angry)

758　hairbrush

### hair

straight hair　　wavy hair　　curly hair　　He is bald.
moustache

He has receding hair　　He has a bald patch　　He has long straight hair　　He has dreadlocks
goatee　　parting　　ponytail　　
　　beard　　bristles/stubble
　　　　　　dreadlocks

pigtails (⦅米⦆ braids)　　plait (⦅米⦆ braid)　　bunches　　bun
pigtail　　bunch　　fringe (⦅米⦆ bangs)

calm down (〜に大声を出すのをやめて怒りを静めるように言うために用いて) 気を静める➔落ち着いている, 怒らないでいる, 平静を保つ, 「さあさあ, 落ち着けよ」

let your hair down 略式 ▶定義 to relax and enjoy yourself after being formal かしこまった後でリラックスして楽しむ➔自然に振る舞う, リラックスする, くつろぐ, 打ち解けて話す

make sb's hair stand on end ▶定義 to frighten or shock sb 〜に恐怖または衝撃を与える➔ (恐怖で) 人をびっくり・ぎょっとさせる, 身の毛のだつ思いをさせる, 〜をぞっとさせる

not turn a hair ▶定義 to not show any reaction to sth that many people would find surprising or shocking 多くの人々が驚きまたは衝撃を覚える事に対し何の反応も示さない➔ (困ったときでも) 平然としている, 悩んだ様子を見せない

split hairs ⇒ **SPLIT**¹

**hairbrush** /héərbrʌʃ/ 名 ⓒ ▶定義 a brush that you use on your hair 髪の毛に使うブラシ➔ヘアブラシ ☛ **brush** のさし絵

**haircut** /héərkʌt/ 名 ⓒ ▶定義 1 the act of sb cutting your hair 〜に髪を切ってもらう行為➔散髪, (ヘア) カット ‖ *You need (to have) a haircut.* あなたは散髪してもらう必要があります.

▶定義 2 the style in which your hair has been cut 散髪された頭髪のスタイル➔ヘアスタイル, 髪型 ‖ *That haircut really suits you.* その髪型は本当によくお似合いです.

**hairdo** /héərdùː/ 略式 = **HAIRSTYLE**

**hairdresser** /héərdresər/ 名 ▶定義 1 ⓒ a person whose job is to cut, shape, colour, etc hair 髪を切る, 整える, 染めるなどを仕事とする人➔美容師, 理容師, 調髪師, 髪結い
　▶ **barber** は男性の理容師で男性の髪だけを散髪する.

▶定義 2 **the hairdresser's** [単数扱い] the place where you go to have your hair cut 髪を切って

もらうために行く場所→美容院

**hairdryer**(または **hairdrier**) /héədràiər/ 名 C
▶定義 a machine that dries hair by blowing hot air through it 温風を髪の間に吹き込むことによって髪を乾かす機械→ヘアドライヤー

**hairgrip** /héəɡrìp/ 名 C ▶定義 a U-shaped pin that is used for holding the hair in place U字型のピンで、髪の毛を適所に留めておくために使われる→平たいヘアピン, (U字型の)髪留め

**hairless** /héələs/ 形 ▶定義 without hair→毛のない, はげの ☞参 bald

**hairline**[1] /héəlàin/ 名 C ▶定義 the place on a person's forehead where his/her hair starts growing 人の額で、髪が生え始めている場所→(頭髪の)生え際

**hairline**[2] /héəlàin/ 形 ▶定義 (used about a crack in sth) very thin (〜の割れ目について)→非常に細い, 非常に狭い ‖ a hairline fracture of the leg 足の骨に入ったひび

**hairpin bend** /héəpìn bènd/ 名 C 英 ▶定義 a very sharp bend in a road, especially a mountain road 道路, 特に山道における非常に急なカーブ→U字型曲折路, ヘアピンカーブ

**hair-raising** 形 ▶定義 that makes you very frightened 非常に恐ろしくするような→身の毛のよだつ, ぞっとする, ぞくっとする ‖ a hair-raising experience 身の毛のよだつ体験

**hairspray** /héəsprèi/ 名 U C ▶定義 a substance you spray onto your hair to hold it in place 髪を固定しておくために頭髪に吹き付けるもの→ヘアスプレー ☞類 lacquer

**hairstyle** /héəstàil/ (または 略式 **hairdo**) 名 C ▶定義 the style in which your hair has been cut or arranged 髪をカットして、または整えてもらったその形→髪型, ヘアスタイル

**hairstylist** /héəstàilist/ (または **stylist**) 名 C ▶定義 a person whose job it is to cut and shape sb's hair 〜の髪を切ったり整えることを仕事にする人→ヘアスタイリスト, 美容師

**hairy** /héəri/ 形 (**hairier**; **hairiest**) ▶定義 1 having a lot of hair たくさんの毛の生えた→毛むくじゃらの, 毛深い, 毛だらけの ▶定義 2 (俗語) dangerous or worrying 危険な, または心配な→危険な, 困難な, 苦しい

**hajj** (または **haj**) /hædʒ/ 名 [単数扱い] ▶定義 the religious journey (**pilgrimage**) to Mecca that many Muslims make 多くのイスラム教徒が行うメッカを訪ねる宗教的な旅(巡礼)→(イスラム教徒の)メッカ巡礼

**halal** /həlá:l/ 形 (名詞の前だけ) ▶定義 (used about meat) from an animal that has been killed according to Muslim law (肉について)イスラム教の戒律にのっとって殺された動物からとった→イスラム教の戒律にのっとって屠殺(とさつ)した動物の

\***half**[1] /hɑːf; hæf/ 名 C (複 **halves** /hɑːvz; hævz/) ▶定義 one of two equal parts of sth 2等分された〜の1つ→半分, 2分の1, 半分にしたもの ‖ three and a half kilos of potatoes 3キロ半のジャガイモ Two halves make a whole. 半分のものが2つで全体になる. half an hour 半時間 an hour and a half 1時間半 The second half of the book is more exciting. その本の後半はもっと刺激的です. Giggs scored in the first half (= of a match). Giggs は前半(= 試合の)で得点しました. Half of this money is yours. このお金の半分はあなたのものです. Half the people in the office leave at 5. 事務所にいる人々の半数は5時に帰ります. ☞動 halve

成句 **break, cut, etc sth in half** ▶定義 to break, etc sth into two parts 〜を2つの部分に分けるなどする→〜を半分・2等分に分ける[切る・割る]

**go half and half/go halves with sb** 英 ▶定義 to share the cost of sth with sb 〜の費用を…と分担する→(〜の費用・支払いなど)を人と折半する

**do nothing/not do anything by halves** ▶定義 to do whatever you do completely and properly することのすべてを完全に, また正確に行う→何事も中途半端にしない, 物事をいいかげんにしない, 何事も身を入れてやる

\***half**[2] /hɑːf; hæf/ 副 ▶定義 not completely; to the extent of half 完全ではなく; 半分程度まで→不完全に, 不十分に, 半分(だけ), 半ば, いくぶん ‖ half full 半分入った The hotel was only half finished. そのホテルは半分までしか仕上がっていなかった. He's half German (= one of his parents is German). 彼はドイツ人のハーフです(= 両親のどちらかがドイツ人である).

成句 **half past...** ▶定義 (in time) thirty minutes past an hour (時間で)30分過ぎて→30分過ぎ, 半過ぎ ‖ half past six (= 6.30) 6時半(過

ぎ)(= 6時30分) ● イギリス英語の口語では, 6時30分のことを half six とも言う.

**not half as much, many, good, bad, etc** ▶定義 much less→(に比べて)全く~ない, 少しも~でない ‖ *This episode wasn't half as good as the last.* 今回の話は前回に比べて少しも良くなかった.

**half-baked** 形略式 ▶定義 not well-planned or considered よく計画されていない, または熟考されていない→未完成の, 不完全な, 検討が不十分な, 生半可な ‖ *a half-baked idea/scheme* 生半可な考え・不十分な計画

**half board** 名Ⓤ英 ▶定義 a price for a room in a hotel, etc, which includes breakfast and an evening meal 朝食と夕食を含むホテルなどの部屋の値段→2食付きの宿泊料, 1泊2食制 ●参 **full board**, **bed and breakfast**

**half-brother** 名Ⓒ ▶定義 a brother with whom you share one parent 片方の親を同じくする兄弟→異母兄弟・異父兄弟
▶ stepbrother と比較.

**half-hearted** 形 ▶定義 without interest or enthusiasm 興味または熱心さがない→熱が入らない, 気乗りのしない, いいかげんな ― **half-heartedly** 副→気・身を入れずに, 嫌々ながら, 不熱心に

**half-sister** 名Ⓒ ▶定義 a sister with whom you share one parent 片方の親を同じくする姉妹→異母姉妹・異父姉妹
▶ stepsister と比較.

**half-term** 名Ⓒ英 ▶定義 a holiday of one week in the middle of a three-month period of school (term) 学校において, 3か月(学期)の中間にある1週間の休み→学期間の中間休み, 学期途中の短い休暇

**half-time** 名Ⓤ ▶定義 (in sport) the period of time between the two halves of a match (スポーツで)試合の前半と後半の間の一定の時間→ハーフタイム, 中休み

**halfway** /hɑ́:fwèr; hæf-/ 形副 ▶定義 at an equal distance between two places; in the middle of a period of time 2つの地点から等距離にある; ある期間の中間の→中間の[で・まで], 中間にある, 途中の[で・まで] ‖ *They have a break halfway through the morning.* 彼らは午前の中間で休みを取っています. ●類 **midway**

***hall** /hɔ:l/ 名Ⓒ ▶定義1 (または **hallway**) a room or passage that is just inside the front entrance of a house or public building 家または公共建築の正面入り口のすぐの部屋または通路→玄関(の広間), 玄関ホール, ロビー, 廊下 ‖ *There is a public telephone in the entrance hall of this building.* この建物の玄関に公衆電話がある. ● C7ページのさし絵 ▶定義2 a building or large room in which meetings, concerts, dances, etc can be held 会合, コンサート, 舞踏会などを開催できる建物または大きな部屋→ホール, 集会所, 大広間, 娯楽場, 演芸場, 会館, 公会堂 ‖ *a concert hall* コンサートホール ●参 **town hall**

**hallmark** /hɔ́:lmɑ̀:rk/ 名Ⓒ ▶定義1 a characteristic that is typical of sb ~の典型的な特徴→際立った特徴, 特質, 目印 ‖ *The ability to motivate students is the hallmark of a good teacher.* 生徒にやる気を起こさせる能力は良い先生の特質です. ▶定義2 a mark that is put on objects made of valuable metals, giving information about the quality of the metal and when and where the object was made 貴金属で作られた物に付いている印で, その金属の質やそれがいつ, どこで作られたかに関する情報を提供するためのもの→(金・銀などの)純度検証極印; 品質(優良)証明, 太鼓判, 保証するもの

**hallo** = HELLO

**hall of residence** 名Ⓒ (複 **halls of residence**) (米 **dormitory**) ▶定義 (in colleges, universities, etc) a building where students live (カレッジ, 大学などで)学生の住む建物→学寮, 学生寮, 学生会館

**Hallowe'en** /hæ̀ləwí:n, hàl-; hæ̀ləlúːn/ 名[単数扱い] (または **Halloween**) ▶定義 the night of October 31st (before All Saints' Day) 10月31日の夜(万聖(ばんせい)節の前夜)→ハロウィーン

> ▶社会・文化
>
> ハロウィーン
>
> All Saints' Day(万聖節)の前夜(10月31日)の祭り. この日, 先祖の精霊が迷い出るとされ, 多くの人が墓参りをします. jack-o'-lantern と呼ばれるカボチャを顔の形にくり抜いた提灯(ちょうちん)を窓辺や玄関に飾ります. 子供たちは悪魔や妖怪(ようかい)などのふ

ん装をして近所や親戚(しんせき)の家を訪ね、玄関口で Trick or treat? (いたずらしようか、それともごちそうしてくれるかな)と言ってキャンデーやチョコレートなどをもらいます。パーティーや仮装パレードなどもよく行われ、子供たちには大変楽しみな一日です。

**hallucination** /həlùːs(ə)néɪʃ(ə)n/ 名 C U ▶定義 seeing or hearing sth that is not really there (because you are ill or have taken a drug) (病気のため、または薬を服用したため)実際にはそこに存在しない物を見たり、または聞いたりすること➡幻覚、幻想、妄想

**halo** /héɪloʊ/ 名 C (複 **halos** または **haloes**) ▶定義 the circle of light that is drawn around the head of an important religious person in a painting 絵画において宗教的に重要な人物の頭の回りに描かれる光の輪➡(聖者などの頭部の)後光、光背、光輪

**halt** /hɔːlt/ 名 [単数扱い] ▶定義 a stop (that does not last very long) (あまり長く続かない)停止➡停止、休止、中断 || *Work came to a halt when the machine broke down.* 機械が壊れた時、作業が中断されました。— halt 動 自 他 正式 ➡立ち止まる、停止する、休止する || *An accident halted the traffic in the town centre for half an hour.* 事故のために街の中心部で30分間交通が遮断されました。

成句 grind to a halt/standstill ⇒ **GRIND**[1]

**halve** /haːv; hæv/ 動 ▶定義 1 自 他 to reduce by a half; to make sth reduce by a half 半分に減らす; ~を半分に減らす➡(時間・費用・価格などを)半分にする || *Shares in the company have halved in value.* その会社の株価が半減しました。*We aim to halve the number of people on our waiting list in the next six months.* 私たちはこの先6か月以内にキャンセル待ちの人数を半分にすることを目指しています。▶定義 2 他 to divide sth into two equal parts ~を2つの等しい部分に分ける➡~を2等分する、2分の1にする、折半する、山分けする || *First halve the peach and then remove the stone.* まず桃を2等分して種を取り除きます。

**ham** /hæm/ 名 U ▶定義 meat from a pig's back leg that has been smoked, etc (cured) to keep it fresh 豚の後ろ足の肉を、新鮮さを保つため燻製(くんせい)などに(保存処理)したもの➡ハム、豚のもも肉の塩漬け ☞参 **bacon, pork** と **meat** の注

**hamburger** /hǽmbəːrɡər/ 名 ▶定義 1 (または **burger**) C meat that has been cut up small and pressed into a flat round shape. Hamburgers are often eaten in a bread roll. 細かく刻んだ肉を圧縮して平たく円い形にしたもの。ロールパンに挟んで食べることが多い➡ハンバーガー、ハンバーグステーキ ☞ C4 ページのさし絵 ☞参 **beefburger** ▶定義 2 U 米 = **MINCE**

**hamlet** /hǽmlət/ 名 C ▶定義 a very small village 非常に小さな村➡(教会・学校のない)小村、小集落、村

*****hammer**[1] /hǽmər/ 名 C ▶定義 a tool with a heavy metal head that is used for hitting nails, etc くぎなどを打つのに使われる重い金属製の頭を持った道具➡金づち、ハンマー ☞ **tool** のさし絵

**hammer**[2] /hǽmər/ 動 ▶定義 1 自 他 hammer sth (in/into/onto sth) to hit with a hammer➡金づちで打つ・たたく、(くぎなど)を(〜に)打ち込む、〜を打ち付ける、金づちで打って作る || *She hammered the nail into the wall.* 彼女はくぎを壁に打ち込んだ。▶定義 2 自 to hit sth several times, making a loud noise 〜を何度か打って大きな音を立てる➡どんどん・がんがんたたく、(曲を)(ピアノで)がんがん弾く || *He hammered on the door until somebody opened it.* 彼はだれかが開けてくれるまでドアをどんどんたたいた。

成句 hammer sth into sb ▶定義 to force sb to remember sth by repeating it many times 〜に…を、何回も繰り返して覚えさせる➡〜を人にたたき込む、教え込む

hammer sth out ▶定義 to succeed in making a plan or agreement after a lot of discussion 議論を重ねた後、うまく計画を立てたり合意に達する➡(結論・政策・解決案など)を徹底的に検討して出す、(意見の相違など)を徹底的に議論して取り除く

**hammering** /hǽmərɪŋ/ 名 ▶定義 1 U the noise that is made by sb using a hammer or by sb hitting sth many times 〜が金づちを使って出す音、または〜が…を何回も打って出す音➡ハンマーで打つこと・音 ▶定義 2 C 英 略式 a very bad defeat ひどく負けること➡打ちのめされる

## 762　hammock

こと、徹底的にやられること

**hammock** /hǽmək/ 名 C ▶定義 a bed, made of strong cloth (canvas) or rope, which is hung up between two trees or poles. 2本の木または棒の間につるした丈夫な布（キャンバス）やロープで作ったベッド➡ハンモック、つり床

**hamper**¹ /hǽmpər/ 動 他（通常は受動態で）▶定義 to make sth difficult ～を難しくする➡～の邪魔をする、～を妨害する、～の身動きを取れなくする ‖ *The building work was hampered by bad weather.* 悪天候が建築作業の障害となった．

**hamper**² /hǽmpər/ 名 C ▶定義 a large basket with a lid that is used for carrying food 食料品を運ぶのに用いるふた付きの大きなかご➡詰めかご、大型バスケット

**hamster** /hǽmstər/ 名 C ▶定義 a small animal that is kept as a pet. Hamsters are like small rats but are fatter and do not have a tail. They store food in the sides of their mouths. ペットとして飼われる小動物．小さなネズミのようだが、もっと太っていてしっぽがない．食べ物を口の両側に蓄える➡ハムスター、キヌゲネズミ

***hand**¹ /hǽnd/ 名 ▶定義 1 C the part of your body at the end of your arm which has five fingers 腕の先端にあり5本の指が生えている身体の一部➡手、（動物の）手、前足 ‖ *He took the child by the hand.* 彼は子供の手をとった．*She was on her hands and knees (= crawling on the floor) looking for an earring.* 彼女は四つんばいになって（＝床をはって）片方のイヤリングを捜していた．☛ C5ページのさし絵 ▶定義 2 **a hand**［単数扱い］略式 some help 何らかの助け➡（援助の）手、手助け ‖ *I'll give you a hand with the washing up.* 食器洗いをお手伝いしましょう．*Do you want/need a hand?* 手を貸しましょうか．▶定義 3 C the part of a clock or watch that points to the numbers 数字を指し示す時計または腕時計の部品➡（時計の）針 ‖ *the hour/minute/second hand* 時・分・秒針 ☛ **clock** のさし絵 ▶定義 4 C a person who does physical work on a farm, in a factory etc 農場、工場などで肉体労働をする人➡人手、働き手、労働者、職人 ‖ *farmhands* 農場労働者 ▶定義 5 C the set of playing cards that sb has been given in a game of cards トランプゲームで～に与えられた1そろいの札➡持ち札、手、手の内 ‖ *have a good/bad hand* (トランプで)手がいい・悪い ▶定義 6 **-handed** 形（複合語で用いて）having, using or made for the type of hand(s) mentioned 言及された種類の手をした・を用いた・で作られた➡～の手をした、～の人数である、～の手を使う ‖ *heavy-handed (= clumsy and careless)* 不器用な（＝下手で、そそっかしい）*right-handed/left-handed* 右利きの・左利きの

成句 **(close/near) at hand** 正式 ▶定義 near in space or time 位置的にまたは時間的に近い➡近くの［に］、近付いて、すぐ近くに ‖ *Help is close at hand.* 助けはもうすぐそこだ．

**be an old hand (at sth)** ⇒ **OLD**

**by hand** ▶定義 1 done by a person and not by machine 機械を使わず人の手で行われる➡（機械でなく）手で、手書きで ‖ *I had to do all the sewing by hand.* 私はその縫い物をすべて手縫いでしなければなりませんでした．▶定義 2 not by post 郵便を使わずに➡手渡しで、手ずから ‖ *The letter was delivered by hand.* その手紙は手渡しされた［人を遣って渡された］．

**catch sb red-handed** ⇒ **CATCH**¹

**change hands** ⇒ **CHANGE**¹

**a firm hand** ⇒ **FIRM**¹

**(at) first hand** ▶定義 (used about information that you have received) from sb who was closely involved (受け取った情報について)密接に関与した～からの➡直接に ‖ *Did you get this information first hand?* この情報は直接得たものですか．☛参 **second-hand**

**get, have, etc a free hand** ⇒ **FREE**¹

**get, etc the upper hand** ⇒ **UPPER**

**get/lay your hands on sb/sth** ▶定義 1 to find or obtain sth ～を見つける、または手に入れる➡～を探し出す、手に入れる、入手する ‖ *I need to get my hands on a good computer.* 私は良いコンピューターを手に入れる必要があります．▶定義 2 略式 to catch sb ～を捕まえる、(追い掛けて)捕らえる、引っ捕らえる ‖ *Just wait till I get my hands on that boy!* 私があの少年を引っ捕らえるまで、とにかく待ってくれ．

**give sb a big hand** ▶定義 to hit your hands together to show approval, enthusiasm, etc 賛成、熱狂などを表すため両手をたたく➡～に盛大

な拍手を送る ‖ *The audience gave the girl a big hand when she finished her song.* その少女が歌い終えると聴衆から盛大な拍手が送られた.

hand in hand ▶定義1 holding each other's hands→互いに手を取り合って, 手に手を取って ‖ *The couple walked hand in hand along the beach.* そのカップルは手を取り合って海辺を歩きました. ▶定義2 usually happening together; closely connected 通常同時に起こる; 密接に結び付いて→密接な関係を持って, (〜と)協力して ‖ *Drought and famine usually go hand in hand.* 干ばつと飢饉(ききん)は通常密接な関係にあります.

your hands are tied ▶定義 to not be in a position to do as you would like because of rules, promises, etc 規則や約束などのため, やりたい事ができない立場にある→手も足も出ない, 何もできない

hands off (sb/sth) 略式 ▶定義 used for ordering sb not to touch sth 〜に…を触らないよう命令するのに用いて→(〜に)触るべからず, 手を触れるな

hands up ▶定義1 used in a school, etc for asking people to lift one hand and give an answer 学校などで人々に片手を上げて答えるよう求めるのに用いて→手を上げてください, 挙手を願います ‖ *Hands up, who'd like to go on the trip this afternoon?* 今日の午後その旅行に行きたい人は手を上げてください. ▶定義2 used by a person with a gun to tell other people to put their hands in the air 銃を持った人がほかの人々に両手を宙に上げるよう言うのに用いて→手を上げろ

have a hand in sth ▶定義 to take part in or share sth 〜に参加する, または〜を分担する→〜に加わる, 手を染める, 関与している ‖ *Even members of staff had a hand in painting and decorating the new office.* 新しい事務所の塗装と装飾には職員たちまで参加しました.

have sb eating out of your hand ⇒ **EAT**

have your hands full ▶定義 to be very busy so that you cannot do anything else 非常に忙しくほかの事は何もできないで→(〜で)手がふさがっている, 手一杯だ, 多忙だ

a helping hand ⇒ **HELP¹**

hold sb's hand ▶定義 to give sb support in a difficult situation 〜が困難な状況にあるとき支えてやる→(精神的に)〜を支える, 励ます, 慰める, 〜の力になる ‖ *I'll come to the dentist's with you to hold your hand.* 困ったときのために歯医者まで一緒に行ってあげましょう.

hold hands (with sb) ▶定義 (used about two people) to hold each other's hands (2人の人について)互いに手を取る→手を取り合う, (男女が)仲むつまじくする

in hand ▶定義1 being dealt with at the moment; under control とりあえず対処中で; 支配下において→進行中で[の], 考慮中で[の], (動物・感情などを)支配下に[の], 管理・制御して[した] ‖ *The situation is in hand.* 対処可能な状況である. ⇔ **out of hand** ▶定義2 (used about money, etc) not yet used (お金などについて)まだ使っていない→手元に[の], 手持ちの, 用意して ‖ *If you have time in hand at the end of the exam, check what you have written.* 試験を終えてまだ時間があったら, 書いた事を見直しなさい.

in safe hands ⇒ **SAFE¹**

in your hands ▶定義 in your possession, control or care 人が所有・支配・または保護して→〜の手中に, 〜にゆだねられて ‖ *The matter is in the hands of a solicitor.* その件は弁護士の手にゆだねられています.

keep your hand in ▶定義 to do an activity from time to time so that you do not forget how to do it or lose the skill やり方を忘れないように, または腕が鈍らないように, ある活動を時々行う→(練習して)技・腕が衰えないようにする ‖ *I play tennis from time to time just to keep my hand in.* 私は腕前を落とさないように時々テニスをやります.

lend (sb) a hand/lend a hand (to sb) ⇒ **LEND**

off your hands ▶定義 not your responsibility any more もはや(人の)責任範囲外の→〜の責任・管理から離れて・離れた

on hand ▶定義 available to help or to be used 助けるまたは使うことができる→近くに居合わせて, 持ち合わせて ‖ *There is always an adult on hand to help when the children are playing outside.* 子供たちが外で遊ぶときは, いつも大人が1人は近くにいて助けられるようにしています.

on your hands ▶定義 being your responsibility 人の責任で→〜の責任・重荷となる(なって), 持

## 764 hand[2]

て余して ‖ *We seem to have a problem on our hands.* 私たちに責任のある問題があるようだ.

**on the one hand...on the other (hand)** ▶定義 used for showing opposite points of view 相反する見解を示すのに用いて→**一方では〜, 他方では, これに対して** ‖ *On the one hand, of course, cars are very useful. On the other hand, they cause a huge amount of pollution.* 一方で無論, 車はとても役立ちます. 他方でそれはばく大な汚染の原因となっています.

**(get/be) out of hand** ▶定義 not under control 統制が利かない→**手に負えなくなる, 手に余る, 手配・支配を離れる** ‖ *Violence at football matches is getting out of hand.* フットボールの試合における暴力はだんだん手に負えなくなっています. ⇔ **in hand**

**out of your hands** ▶定義 not in your control; not your responsibility 支配下にない; 責任外の→**手配・支配を離れた[離れて]** ‖ *I can't help you, I'm afraid. The matter is out of my hands.* 残念ですがお力になれません. この件は私にはどうにもなりません.

**shake sb's hand/shake hands (with sb)/shake sb by the hand** ⇒ **SHAKE**[1]

**to hand** ▶定義 near or close to you 人の近くにまたはそばに→**手近に, 手の届く所に, 所有して, 入手して** ‖ *I'm afraid I haven't got my diary to hand.* 残念ながら今日記が, 手元にありません.

**try your hand at sth** ⇒ **TRY**[1]

**turn your hand to sth** ▶定義 to have the ability to do sth→**〜をする能力がある, 〜をこなせる** ‖ *She can turn her hand to all sorts of jobs.* 彼女はどんな種類の仕事でもこなせます.

**wash your hands of sb/sth** ⇒ **WASH**[1]

**with your bare hands** ⇒ **BARE**

★**hand**[2] /hænd/ 動⊕ ▶定義 hand sb sth; hand sth to sb to give or pass sth to sb→**物を人に(手)渡す, 与える**

成句 **have (got) to hand it to sb** ▶定義 used to show admiration and approval of sb's work or efforts 〜の仕事または努力に賞賛や同意を示すのに用いて→**人にかぶとを脱ぐ, 〜の優越・正しさを認める必要がある** ‖ *You've got to hand it to Rita - she's a great cook.* あなたはリタにかぶとを脱がなければなりません − 彼女の料理の腕前は大したものです.

句動詞 **hand sth back (to sb)** ▶定義 to give or return sth to the person who owns it or to where it belongs 〜を持ち主に渡す・返す, またはそれが属する所に戻す→**物を(〜に)手渡して返す, 〜に返す**

**hand sth down (to sb)** ▶定義**1** to pass customs, traditions, etc from older people to younger ones 習慣, 伝統などを年配の者から若者に伝える→**(伝統など)を(子孫・後世に)伝える** ▶定義**2** to pass clothes, toys, etc from older children to younger ones in the family 家庭で衣服, 玩具などを大きい子から小さい子に回す→**(服・本・靴など)をお下がりにする**

**hand sth in (to sb)** ▶定義 to give sth to sb in authority 〜を, 権力を持つ…に与える→**(報告など)を(〜に)提出する, 差し出す** ‖ *I found a wallet and handed it in to the police.* 私は財布を見つけたので警察に提出しました.

**hand sth on (to sb)** ▶定義 to send or give sth to another person 〜を別の人に送る, または与える→**物を(次の人などに)手渡す, 回す, 回覧する** ‖ *When you have read the article, please hand it on to another student.* この記事を読んだら次の生徒に回してください.

**hand sth out (to sb)** ▶定義 to give sth to many people in a group 一団を成す大勢の人々に〜を与える→**(ビラ・印刷物など)を(〜に)配る, (施し物・給付として)分け与える, (忠告・お世辞・罰)をふんだんに与える** ‖ *Food was handed out to the starving people.* 飢えた人々に食べ物が分け与えられた.

**hand (sth) over (to sb)** ▶定義 to give sb else your position of power or the responsibility for sth 権力の座または〜の責任を別の…に与える→**(財産・権限などを)(〜に)譲り渡す, 譲渡する** ‖ *She resigned as chairperson and handed over to one of her younger colleagues.* 彼女は議長を辞任して, その座を若手同僚の1人に譲り渡した.

**hand (sb) over to sb** ▶定義 (used at a meeting or on the television, radio, telephone, etc) to let sb speak or listen to another person (会合で, またはテレビ, ラジオ, 電話などで用いて)〜に話をしてもらう, または別の人の話を聞いてもらう→**人に話してもらう, 人の話を聞く, 電話を替わってもらう**

**hand sb/sth over (to sb)** ▶定義 to give sb/sth (to sb) ～を(…に)与える→(人・物を)人に引き渡す, 手渡す ‖ *People were tricked into handing over large sums of money.* 人々はだまされて多額のお金を奪われました.

**hand sth round** ▶定義 to offer to pass sth, especially food and drinks, to all the people in a group ～, 特に食べ物や飲み物をグループの全員に振る舞う→～を順々に回す, みんなに配る

**handbag** /hǽndbæg/ (米 **purse**) 图 ⓒ ▶定義 a small bag in which women carry money, keys, etc 女性がお金, かぎなどを入れて持ち運ぶ小さなバッグ→ハンドバッグ, 手提げかばん ☛類 **shoulder bag** ☛ **bag** のさし絵

**handbook** /hǽndbʊk/ 图 ⓒ ▶定義 a small book that gives instructions on how to use sth or advice and information about a particular subject ～の使い方またはある特定の題目に関する助言や情報を提供する小型の本→入門書, 手引き, ハンドブック, ガイドブック, 便覧, 旅行・観光案内

**handbrake** /hǽndbreɪk/ (米 **emergency brake**; **parking brake**) 图 ⓒ ▶定義 a device that is operated by hand to stop a car from moving when it is parked 駐車中の車が動かないようにする手で操作する装置→ハンドブレーキ, 手動ブレーキ ☛ S7 ページのさし絵

**handcuffs** /hǽndkʌf/ (または **cuffs**) 图 [複数扱い] ▶定義 a pair of metal rings that are joined together by a chain and put around the wrists of prisoners 鎖でつながっており囚人の手首の回りに付ける, 金属でできた一対の輪→手錠, 手かせ

**handful** /hǽn(d)fʊl/ 图 ▶定義 1 ⓐ a handful (of sth) as much or as many of sth as you can hold in one hand 片手で持てるだけの量または数の～→一握りの量・数(の～), ひとつかみ, 手一杯(の量) ‖ *a handful of sand* 一握りの砂 ▶定義 2 [単数扱い] a small number (of sb/sth) →少数(の～), わずか ‖ *Only a handful of people came to the meeting.* 会合に来た人はほんの数えるほどだった. ▶定義 3 **a handful** [単数扱い] 略式 a person or an animal that is difficult to control 扱いにくい人・動物→問題児, 厄介もの ‖ *The little girl is quite a handful.* その小さな女の子はかなりの問題児です.

**handgun** /hǽndɡʌn/ 图 ⓒ ▶定義 a small gun that you can hold and fire with one hand 片手で持って発砲できる小型の銃→ピストル, けん銃

**handicap**¹ /hǽndikæp/ 图 ▶定義 1 ⓒ something that makes doing sth more difficult; a disadvantage ～を行うのをより困難にするもの; 不利な条件→不利な条件, ハンディキャップ, 不利益 ‖ *Not speaking French is going to be a bit of a handicap in my new job.* 私の新しい仕事ではフランス語を話さないと少しばかり不利でしょう. ▶定義 2 a disadvantage that is given to a strong competitor in a sports event, etc so that the other competitors have more chance ほかの競技者たちにより多くのチャンスを与えるように, スポーツ競技などで強い競技者に与えられる不利な条件→ハンディキャップ, ハンディ, ハンディキャップ付きの競技・競馬・競走 ▶定義 3 (古) = **DISABILITY** ☛ 今はこの単語を侮辱的と見なす人が多い.

**handicap**² /hǽndikæp/ 動 他 (**handicapping**; **handicapped**) (通常は受動態で) ▶定義 to give or be a disadvantage to sb ～に不利益を与える, または不利になる→人にハンディキャップを付ける, 人を不利な立場に置く ‖ *They were handicapped by their lack of education.* 彼らは教育を受けていないというハンディを負っています.

**handicapped** /hǽndikæpt/ 形 (古) = **DISABLED** ☛ 今はこの単語を侮辱的と見なす人が多い.

**handicraft** /hǽndikrɑːft; -kræft/ 图 ▶定義 1 ⓒ an activity that needs skill with the hands as well as artistic ability, for example sewing 芸術的能力と共に, 手を使う技術を必要とする活動, 例えば裁縫など→手芸, 手仕事, 手工芸 ▶定義 2 **handicrafts** [複数扱い] the objects that are produced by this activity その活動により生み出されたもの→手工芸品, 手細工品

**handiwork** /hǽndiwɜːrk/ 图 ⓤ ▶定義 1 a thing that you have made or done, especially using your artistic skill 特に芸術的手腕を用いて作った, または行ったもの→手仕事[細工]手作り品, 手細工[工芸]品 ‖ *She put the dress on and stood back to admire her handiwork.* 彼女はそのドレスを着て後ろに立ち, 自分の手仕事をほれぼれと眺めた. ▶定義 2 a thing done by a particular person or group, especially sth bad ある特定の人またはグループによってなされたもの, 特に悪い→**仕業, しでかした事**

**handkerchief** /hǽŋkətʃɪf, -tʃiːf/ 名 C (複) **handkerchiefs** または **handkerchieves** /-tʃiːvz/ ▶定義 a square piece of cloth or soft thin paper that you use for clearing your nose 正方形の布または柔らかく薄い紙で, 鼻をかむのに用いる→**(布・紙製の) ハンカチ** ☛より略式な単語は hanky または hankie. 柔らかく薄い紙でできたハンカチは paper handkerchief (ペーパーハンカチーフ) または tissue (ティッシュペーパー) とも呼ばれる.

\***handle**¹ /hǽndl/ 動 他 ▶定義 1 to touch or hold sth with your hand(s) ～を手で触るまたはつかむ→**(人が) 物に手を触れる, 物を手で持ち上げる・握る・動かす** ‖ *Wash your hands before you handle food.* 食べ物に手を触れる前に手を洗ってください. ▶定義 2 to deal with or to control sb/sth ～を扱うまたは支配する→**(人が)(問題など) を扱う, 論じる, 解決する, ～を処理する, (人・動物) を扱う, (道具など) を使う** ‖ *This port handles 100 million tons of cargo each year.* この港は毎年 1 億トンもの貨物を取り扱っています. *I have a problem at work and I don't really know how to handle it.* 私は仕事上問題を抱えており, どのようにして解決するべきか全く分かりません. — handler 名 C→**取り扱う人, (ボクシングの) トレーナー, 付き添い人, (警察犬などの) 調教師** ‖ *baggage/dog/food handlers* 手荷物係員・犬の調教師・食品取扱者

> ▶日本語 vs 英語
>
> handle と「ハンドル」
>
> 自動車の「ハンドル」は, 英語では a steering wheel と言います. なお, 自転車やオートバイのハンドルについては, handlebar という表現を使います.

\***handle**² /hǽndl/ 名 C ▶定義 a part of sth that is used for holding or opening it ～の一部でそれをつかんだり開けたりするのに使われる→**取っ手, ハンドル, 柄** ‖ *She turned the handle and opened the door.* 彼女は取っ手を回してドアを開けた.

成句 **fly off the handle** ⇒ **FLY**¹

**handlebar** /hǽndlbɑːr/ 名 [C, 通常は複数] ▶定義 the metal bar at the front of a bicycle that you hold when you are riding it 乗るときにつかまる, 自転車の前面に付いた金属の棒→**(自転車・オートバイなどの) ハンドル** ☛ S7 ページのさし絵

**hand luggage** (米 **carry-on bag**) 名 U ▶定義 a small bag, etc that you can keep with you on a plane 機内に持ち込める小さなバッグなど→**(旅行者の) 手荷物**

**handmade** /hæ̀ndméɪd/ 形 ▶定義 made by hand and of very good quality, not by machine 手作りで非常に高品質な, 機械を使わない→**(家具・衣服などが) 手製の, 手作りの**

**handout** /hǽndaʊt/ 名 C ▶定義 1 food, money, etc given to people who need it badly 食物, お金などでそれに窮している人々に与えられるもの→**施し, 恵み物, (政府の) 補助金** ▶定義 2 a free document that is given to a lot of people, to advertise sth or explain sth, for example in a class 大勢の人々に無料で配布される書類で、〜の宣伝または説明をするために教室などで配られる物→(講演などの)配布資料, ハンドアウト, プリント, 広告, 散らし, ビラ, (商品の)サンプル

**handpicked** /hǽndpíkt/ 形 ▶定義 chosen carefully or personally 入念にまたは個人的に選ばれた→**精選された, 粒よりの, えり分けた**

**handrail** /hǽndreɪl/ 名 C ▶定義 a long narrow wooden or metal bar at the side of some steps, a bath, etc that you hold for support or balance 人が体を支えたりバランスを取るのにつかまれるよう階段や浴室などの側に付いている, 木製または金属製の細長い棒→**手すり, 欄干(らんかん)**

**handset** = RECEIVER(1)

**handshake** /hǽndʃeɪk/ 名 C ▶定義 the action of shaking sb's right hand with your own when you meet him/her 〜に会ったとき, 右手で相手の右手を握る行為→**握手**

\***handsome** /hǽnsəm/ 形 ▶定義 1 (used about a man) attractive (男性について)魅力的な→**(男性が)ハンサムな, 美男子の, 端整な, 目鼻立ちの整った** ☞参 **beautiful** の注 ▶定義 2 (used about money, an offer, etc) large or generous (お金, 申し出などについて)多額のまたは相当の良い→**(金額等が)かなり大きな, 相当な, (行為が)寛大な, 気前の良い, 物惜しみしない** ‖ *a handsome profit* かなり大きな利益 — **handsomely** 副→**立派に, 見事に, 鷹揚(おうよう)に, 気前良く** ‖ *Her efforts were handsomely rewarded.* 彼女の努力は手厚く報われた.

**hands-on** /hǽndzɑ́n/ ▶定義 learnt by doing sth yourself, not watching sb else do it; practical ほかの人がするのを見てではなく自分でやって身に付けた; 実践的な→**実践で身に付けた, 実際に役に立つ, 実践的な** ‖ *She needs some hands-on computer experience.* 彼女には少しばかりコンピューターの実地訓練が必要だ.

**handwriting** /hǽndràɪtɪŋ/ 名 U ▶定義 a person's style of writing by hand 人が手で書いた特徴→**(ペン・鉛筆を用いた)手書き(の文字), 筆跡, 自筆, 書体**

**handwritten** /hǽndrìtn/ 形 ▶定義 written by hand, not typed or printed タイプや印刷ではなく, 手で書いた→**手書きの, 自筆の, 肉筆の**

**handy** /hǽndi/ 形 (**handier; handiest**) ▶定義 1 useful; easy to use 役に立つ; 使いやすい→**便利な, 手ごろな, 扱いやすい, 操縦しやすい** ‖ *a handy tip* 役立つヒント *a handy gadget* 便利な小物 ▶定義 2 **handy (for sth/doing sth)** within easy reach of sth; nearby 〜が届きやすい範囲にある; 近くの→**手近にある, すぐ手に入る, 利用できる, すぐに行ける** ‖ *Always keep a first-aid kit handy for emergencies.* 緊急に備えて, いつも救急箱を手近に保管しなさい. ▶定義 3 skilful in using your hands or tools to make or repair things 手または道具を使って物を作るまたは修理するのがうまい→**(〜の扱いが)上手な, 巧みな, 器用な, 手際良い** ‖ *James is very handy around the house.* ジェームズは家回りのことをするのは非常にうまい.

成句 **come in handy** ▶定義 to be useful at some time いつか役に立つ→**(いざというとき)役に立つ** ‖ *Don't throw that box away. It may come in handy.* その箱を捨てないで. いつか役に立つかもしれません.

**handyman** /hǽndimən, -mæn/ 名 [単数扱い] ▶定義 a person who is clever at making or repairing things, especially around the house 特に家回りの物を作るまたは修理するのがうまい人→**雑用をする男, 器用な男, 何でも屋**

\***hang**¹ /hǽŋ/ 動 (過, 過分 **hung** /hʌŋ/) ☞ 過去時制および過去分詞 hanged は定義2の意味においてのみ用いられる. ▶定義 1 ⑤ ⑪ to fasten sth or be fastened at the top so that the lower part is free or loose 一番上の部分で〜をしっかり留めるまたは留められることにより下の部分をそのままにまたは解き放たれた状態にする→**物が掛かる, (〜から・〜に)ぶら下がる, 垂れ下がる, 物を掛ける, ぶら下げる** ‖ *Hang your coat on the hook.* コートをフックに掛けておきなさい. *I left the washing hanging on the line all day.* 私は洗濯物を物干しひもに一日中つるしておきました. *A cigarette hung from his lips.* 彼はたばこをくわえていました. ▶定義 2 ⑪ to kill sb/yourself by putting a rope around the neck and allowing the body to drop downwards 首の回りにロープを掛けて身体をぶら下がらせて〜を殺す・または自殺する→**〜を首つりにする・して殺す, (犯罪のために)人を絞首刑にする, 首つり自殺する** ‖ *He was hanged for murder.* 彼は殺人罪で絞首刑になった. ▶定義 3 ⑤ **hang (above/over sb/sth)** to stay in the air in a way that is unpleasant or threatening 不快にまたは脅かすように宙に浮いている→宙に浮く, 漂う‖ *Smog hung in the air over the city.* 町中にスモッグが漂っていた.

> ►コミュニケーション
>
> 「頑張って」に当たる英語表現
>
> 日本では特に若い人たち同士, 別れ際のあいさつに「頑張って」とよく言います. 英米では, Take it easy, Don't work too hard, Have fun などと, むしろ頑張るなと言って別れる方が多いのです. とはいえ, 英語(特にアメリカ英語)にも「頑張れ」に似た意味の Hang in there! という表現があります. これは問題を抱えて頑張っている人に対する明るいくだけた声援と言えるでしょう.

**成句** be/get hung up (about/on sb/sth) ▶定義 to think about sb/sth all the time in a way that is not healthy or good 健康的でない, または好ましくないやり方で〜についていつも考える→(〜のことで)夢中になる, いらいらする‖ *She's really hung up about her parents' divorce.* 彼女は両親の離婚のことで本当にいらいらしている.

hang (on) in there (口語) ▶定義 to have courage and keep trying, even though a situation is difficult たとえ困難な状況でも勇気をもって試みを続ける→あきらめない, 頑張り通す‖ *The worst part is over now. Just hang on in there and be patient.* 最もつらい部分は今終わったところだ. 何とかあきらめないで辛抱しなさい.

**句動詞** hang about/around 略式 ▶定義 to stay in or near a place not doing very much あまり多くの事をしないで, ある場所にまたはその近くにとどまる→何するわけでもなく時を過ごす, ぶらつく, 近くにいる, 〜で待っている, ぐずぐずする, 人に付きまとう, (病気・悪天候などが)長引く

hang back ▶定義1 to not want to do or say sth, often because you are shy or not sure of yourself しばしば内気であるまたは自信がないため, 〜をするまたは言うのを嫌がる→しりごみする, (〜を)嫌がる, 躊躇(ちゅうちょ)する ▶定義2 to stay in a place after other people have left it ほかの人々が去った後もその場所にいる→遅れる, 人の後ろからのろのろと付いていく

hang on ▶定義1 to wait for a short time 短時間待つ(立ち止まって)待つ, 電話を切らずにおく‖ *Hang on a minute. I'm nearly ready.* ちょっと待って. すぐ準備ができるから. ▶定義2 to hold sth tightly 〜にしっかりつかまる→(〜に)つかまる, しがみ付く‖ *Hang on, don't let go!* しっかりつかまって, 放さないで.

hang on sth ▶定義 to depend on sth 〜に依存する→〜次第である, 〜に依存している

hang on to sth ▶定義1 略式 to keep sth 〜を取っておく→(〜を)売らず・捨てずに取っておく, 手放さない, 維持する, 続ける‖ *Let's hang on to the car for another year.* この車をもう1年取っておきましょう. ▶定義2 to hold sth tightly→〜をしっかり握る, 〜にしがみ付く‖ *He hung on to the child's hand as they crossed the street.* 彼は通りを横断する時, 子供の手をしっかりと握った.

hang sth out ▶定義 to put washing, etc on a clothes line so that it can dry 洗濯物などが乾くように物干しなどに掛ける→(洗濯物)を外に干す, (旗など)を揚げる

hang over sb ▶定義 to be present or about to happen in a way which is unpleasant or threatening 不快にまたは脅かすように存在する, または今にも起こりそうになる→〜の上に張り出す, 〜に差し迫る, 脅威となっている‖ *This essay has been hanging over me for days.* 私は何日もの間この随筆のことが気に掛かっています.

hang sth up ▶定義 to put sth on a nail, hook, etc 〜をくぎ, フックなどに掛ける→〜を(…に)掛ける, つるす‖ *Hang your coat up over there.* コートをあそこに掛けておきなさい.

hang up ▶定義 to end a telephone conversation and put the telephone down 電話で話を終えて受話器を置く→電話を切る, 受話器を置く

hang up on sb 略式 ▶定義 to end a telephone conversation without saying goodbye because you are angry 怒ってさよならを言わずに電話での会話を終わりにしてしまう→(人との)電話を(一方的に)切る

**hang**² /hæŋ/ 名
**成句** get the hang of (doing) sth 略式 ▶定義 to learn how to use or do sth 〜の使い方またはやり方を習う→〜の使い方・やり方が分かる, 意

味が分かる ‖ *It took me a long time to get the hang of my new computer.* 私は新しいコンピューターの使い方が分かるまで長い時間がかかりました.

**hangar** /hǽŋər/ 名 C ▶定義 a big building where planes are kept 飛行機を保管する大きな建物→(飛行機の)格納庫

**hanger** /hǽŋər/ (または **coat hanger**, **clothes-hanger**) 名 C ▶定義 a metal, plastic or wooden object with a hook that is used for hanging up clothes in a cupboard 戸棚に洋服を掛けるのに使う鉤(かぎ)の付いた金属, プラスチックまたは木製の物→(服などを)つるす物, 掛ける物, ハンガー, つり手 ☞ **hook** のさし絵

**hanger-on** /hæ̀ŋər ɑ́n/ 名 C (複 **hangers-on**) ▶定義 a person who tries to be friendly with sb who is rich or important 裕福な〜, または地位の高い〜に愛想良くしようとする人→ごますり, おべっか使い, 子分, 手下

**hang-glider** 名 C ▶定義 a type of frame covered with cloth, which a person holds and flies through the air with as a sport 布を張った骨組みの一種で, 人がつかまりスポーツとして空を飛ぶのに使うもの→ハンググライダー ☞参 **glider** ☞ **parachute** のさし絵 — **hang-gliding** 名 U → ハンググライダーで飛ぶこと

**hanging** /hǽŋɪŋ/ 名 C U ▶定義 death as a form of punishment for a crime, caused by putting rope around a person's neck and letting the body drop downwards 犯罪に対する罰として, 人の首の回りにロープを掛けて身体ごとぶら下げることでなされる死→絞首刑

**hangman** /hǽŋmən/ 名 [単数扱い] ▶定義 **1** a person whose job is to kill criminals as a form of punishment by hanging them with a rope 犯罪者を罰としてロープにつるして殺すことを仕事にする人→絞首刑執行人 ▶定義 **2** a word game where the aim is to guess all the letters of a word before a picture of a person hanging is completed 言葉遊びで, 首つりの人の絵が完成する前にすべての文字を当てようとするもの→(ゲーム)ハングマン

**hangover** /hǽŋòʊvər/ 名 C ▶定義 pain in your head and a sick feeling that you have if you have drunk too much alcohol the night before 前夜にアルコールを飲みすぎたとき感じる頭痛または気分の悪さ→二日酔い

# happen 769

**hang-up** 名 C (俗語) ▶定義 a hang-up (about sb/sth) an emotional problem about sth that makes you embarrassed or worried 恥ずかしく思ったり, 心配している物事についての感情的問題→(個人的・心理的な)厄介事, 悩み, 思い詰め, 心がかり, コンプレックス, こだわり ‖ *He has a real hang-up about his height.* 彼は身長のことを本気で悩んでいます.

**hanker** /hǽŋkər/ 動 自 ▶定義 hanker after/for sth to want sth very much (often sth that you cannot easily have) 〜(しばしば簡単には手に入らない〜)を非常に欲しいと思う→(〜に)あこがれる, (〜を)欲しいと思う, (〜)してみたいと思う

**hanky** (または **hankie**) /hǽŋki/ 名 C (複 **hankies**) 略式 ⇒ **HANDKERCHIEF**

**haphazard** /hæ̀phǽzərd/ 形 ▶定義 with no particular order or plan; badly organized 特に順序も計画もしていない; 準備の悪い→無計画な, でたらめな, 偶然の — **haphazardly** 副 →行き当たりばったりに, でたらめに, 偶然に

*__**happen**__ /hǽp(ə)n/ 動 自 ▶定義 **1** (of an event or situation) to take place, usually without being planned first (事件または状況が)通常は前もって計画されないで起こる→(計画されていない事が)(偶然に)起きる, 生じる ‖ *Can you describe to the police what happened after you left the party?* パーティーから帰った後に起こった事を警察で説明できますか. *How did the accident happen?* その事故はどんな風に起こったのか.

▶ happen と occur は通常計画されていない出来事に用いる. occur の方が happen よりも正式. take place は出来事が計画されていることを示唆する: *The wedding took place on Saturday June 13th.* (結婚式は6月13日土曜日に行われました.)

▶定義 **2** happen to sb/sth to be what sb/sth experiences 〜が経験する事である→〜が(人・物・事)に降り懸かる, 起こる ‖ *What do you think has happened to Julie? She should have been here an hour ago.* ジュリーの身に何があったと思いますか. 1時間前にはここに来ていなければならないのに. *What will happen to the business when your father retires?* あなたのお父様がご退任されたら事業はどうなるでしょう.

## 770　happening

▶定義3 **happen to do sth** to do sth by chance 偶然〜をする→**(人・物・事が)偶然〜する、たまたま〜する** ‖ *I happened to meet him in London yesterday.* 私は昨日ロンドンで偶然彼に会いました．

成句 **as it happens/happened** ▶定義 (used when you are adding to what you have said) actually (既に言ったことに付け加えるとき用いて) 実際→**実際、あいにく、(意外にも)実は、折良く** ‖ *As it happens, I did remember to bring the book you wanted.* 実は、あなたが欲しがっていた本をちゃんと忘れず持ってきました．

**it (just) so happens** ⇒ **SO**¹

**happening** /hǽp(ə)nɪŋ/ 名 [ **C**, 通常は複数]
▶定義 a thing that happens; an event (that is usually strange or difficult to explain) 起こること; (通常は奇妙なまたは説明するのが難しい) 出来事→**出来事、事件、(集会などでの)ハプニング、(劇などの)即興的な演技** ‖ *Strange happenings have been reported in that old hotel.* あの古いホテルで奇妙な出来事が報告されている．

▶ happening は通常偶然起こる物事. event は通常あらかじめ計画された、しばしば特別なまたは重要な物事.

**happily** /hǽpɪli/ 副 ▶定義1 in a happy way→**幸福に、楽しく、愉快に、喜んで、満足して** ‖ *I would happily give up my job if I didn't need the money.* お金を稼ぐ必要がなければ喜んで仕事をやめます． ▶定義2 it is lucky that; fortunately →**運良く、幸いにも** ‖ *The police found my handbag and, happily, nothing had been stolen.* 警察が私のハンドバッグを見つけました．幸い何も盗まれていませんでした．

\***happy** /hǽpi/ 形 (**happier**; **happiest**) ▶定義1 **happy (to do sth); happy for sb; happy that...** feeling or showing pleasure; pleased 喜びを感じてまたは表して; うれしくて →**喜んで〜する、(人が)(〜のことで)うれしい、(人は)〜して・するのがうれしい** ‖ *I was really happy to see Mark again yesterday.* 昨日はマークに再会できて本当にうれしかった． *You look very happy today.* 今日はとてもうれしそうですね． *Congratulations! I'm very happy for you.* おめでとう．私もとてもうれしいです． ⇔ **unhappy**, **sad** ☞参 **glad** の注 ▶定義2 giving or causing pleasure 喜びを与えるまたは感じさせる→**(人・行為などが)幸福な、幸せそうな、楽しい** ‖ *a happy marriage/memory/childhood* 幸せな結婚・思い出・幼少期 *The film is sad but it has a happy ending.* その映画は悲しい映画だけれども結末はハッピーエンドです． ▶定義3 **happy (with/about sb/sth)** satisfied that sth is good and right; not worried 〜が優れていて正しいのに満足して; 心配しないで→**(〜に)喜んで、うれしい、満足して、安心して、ほっとして、不満・不安・違和感などを持たず** ‖ *I'm not very happy with what you've done.* 私はあなたがした事に少し不満があります． *She doesn't feel happy about the salary she's been offered.* 彼女は提示された給料に対し不満を感じています．

▶定義4 (名詞の前は不可) **happy to do sth** ready to do sth; pleased 〜をする準備ができた; 満足した→**喜んで〜する、〜できてうれしい** ‖ *I'll be happy to see you any day next week.* 来週ならいつでもあなたに喜んでお会いします．

▶定義5 **Happy** used to wish sb an enjoyable time 〜が楽しく過ごすよう祈るのに用いて→**でたい、良い〜を、〜おめでとう** ‖ *Happy Birthday!* お誕生日おめでとう． ▶定義6 (名詞の前だけ) lucky; fortunate 運のいい; 幸運な→**ついている、幸運な** ‖ *a happy coincidence* 幸運な偶然 ⇔ **unhappy** — **happiness** 名 **U**→**幸福、幸せ、喜び、満足、幸運**

▶コミュニケーション

「よかったね」に当たる英語表現

喜ばしい事が起きた人への祝いの言葉として，Congratulations が一般的ですが，英語には I'm very (so) happy for you (あなたのことでほんとにうれしい) という個人的な喜びを表す表現もあります．これに当たる日本語は「ほんとによかった(ですね)」でしょう．日本語と比べてみると，英語が喜びの主体はだれで，その喜びの源は何かをはっきり表す言語であることがはっきりします．

**happy-go-lucky** 形 ▶定義 not caring or worried about life and the future 人生や未来について考えていない、または心配しない→**(人・行為が)のんきな、楽天的な、運任せの、日和見(ひよりみ)的な**

**happy hour** 名 **C** [通常は単数] ▶定義 a time,

usually in the evening, when a pub or bar sells alcoholic drinks at lower prices than usual 通常は夕方でパブやバーがアルコール飲料をいつもより安く販売する時間帯➡サービスタイム, ハッピーアワー

**harass** /hǽrəs, həræs/ 動 ⓤ ▶定義 to annoy or worry sb by doing unpleasant things to him/her, especially over a long time 特に長時間にわたって不愉快な事をして~を困らせるまたは心配させる➡人を (厄介な事・心配な事で)(絶えず)困らせる, 悩ます, ~に嫌がらせをする, 迷惑を掛ける ‖ *The court ordered him to stop harassing his ex-wife.* 法廷は彼に先妻への嫌がらせをやめるよう命じました. ― **harassment** 名 ⓤ ー悩ますこと・悩まされること, 悩み (の種), 嫌がらせ, 困らせること ‖ *She accused her boss of sexual harassment.* 彼女は上司をセクハラで訴えた.

**harassed** /hǽrəst, həræst/ 形 ▶定義 tired and worried because you have too much to do やるべき事が多すぎて, 疲れて心配になって➡(~で)疲れきった, いらいらした

**harbour**[1] (米 **harbor**) /háːrbər/ 名 ⓒ ⓤ ▶定義 a place on the coast where ships can be tied up (moored) and protected from the sea and bad weather 船をつなげ (停泊させ), 海や悪天候から守る海岸沿いの場所➡港 ☛ C8 ページのさし絵

**harbour**[2] (米 **harbor**) /háːrbər/ 動 ⓤ ▶定義 1 to keep feelings or thoughts secret in your mind for a long time 気持ちや考えを他人に言わず心の中に長いことしまっておく➡(悪意・疑いなど)を (心に) 抱く ‖ *She began to harbour doubts about the decision.* 彼女はその決定に対し疑いを抱き始めた. ▶定義 2 to hide or protect sb/sth that is bad 悪い~を隠すまたは守る➡~に隠れ場所を与える, ~をかくまう, 隠匿 (いんとく) する ‖ *They were accused of harbouring terrorists.* 彼らはテロリストたちをかくまった罪で訴えられた.

*****hard**[1] /háːrd/ 形 ▶定義 1 not soft to touch; not easy to break or bend 触って柔らかくない; 壊すまたは曲げるのが容易でない➡物が硬い, しっかりした ‖ *The bed was so hard that I couldn't sleep.* ベッドが硬すぎて眠れませんでした. *Diamonds are the hardest known mineral.* ダイヤモンドは私たちの知る最も硬い鉱物だ. ⇔

# hard[1]  771

**soft** ▶定義 2 hard (for sb) (to do sth) difficult to do or understand; not easy するのが難しい, または理解するのが難しい; 容易でない ➡(問題・仕事などが)(人に) 難しい, 困難な, 厄介な, (~するのが) 難しい ‖ *The first question in the exam was very hard.* 試験の最初の問題は非常に難しかった. *This book is hard to understand./It is a hard book to understand.* この本は分かりにくい・それは理解するのが難しい本です. *It's hard for young people to find good jobs nowadays.* 最近は若い人々が良い仕事を見つけるのが難しい. *I find his attitude very hard to take (= difficult to accept).* 私は彼の態度は非常に受け入れ難いと思います (= 容認するのは難しいと思います). ⇔ **easy** ▶定義 3 needing or using a lot of physical strength or mental effort 多くの肉体的な力または精神的な努力を必要とする, または使う➡(運動・動作が) 強力な, 激しい, (仕事などが) 力の要る, 骨の折れる, 熱心な, 勤勉な, 努力家の ‖ *It's a hard climb to the top of the hill.* あの丘の頂上まで上るのは大変です. ***Hard work** is said to be good for you.* 勤勉であることが自分のためだと言われています. *He's a hard worker.* 彼は勉強熱心です. ▶定義 4 (used about a person) not feeling or showing kindness or pity; not gentle (人について) 親切心または同情を感じないまたは示さない; 優しくない➡厳しい, 無情な, きつい ‖ *You have to be hard to succeed in business.* ビジネスで成功するには冷酷でないといけません. ⇔ **soft, lenient** ▶定義 5 (used about conditions) unpleasant or unhappy; full of difficulty (状況について) 不愉快なまたは満足のいかない; 困難に満ちた➡つらい, 耐え難い, 苦しい, 苦難の ‖ *He had a hard time when his parents died.* 彼は両親を亡くしつらい思いをしました. *to have a hard day/life/childhood* つらい1日・苦しい生活・つらい幼少期を送る ▶定義 6 (used about the weather) very cold (天候について) 大変寒い ➡(天候・季節などが) 厳しい, 激しい, ひどい ‖ *The forecast is for a hard winter/frost.* 予報によると厳冬・ひどい霜だそうです. ⇔ **mild** ▶定義 7 (used about water) containing particular minerals so that soap does not make many bubbles (水について) せっけんが泡立たない特定の鉱物を含んだ ➡(水が) 硬質の, 硬水の ‖ *We* *live in a **hard water** area.* 私たちの住む地域は水が硬質です. ⇔ **soft** — **hardness** 名 ❶ →硬いこと, 硬さ, 困難さ, 無情, 冷淡

成句 **a hard act to follow** ▶定義 a person or a thing that it is difficult to do better than その人・物より上手に行うのが難しい人または物→**まねのできないこと・行為, 打ち負かし難い人・物**

**be hard at it** ▶定義 to be working very hard doing sth ～をするのに非常に熱心に取り組んでいる→**一生懸命取り組んでいる, 専念する, 没頭する**

**be hard on sb/sth** ▶定義 **1** to treat sb/sth in a harsh way or to make things difficult ～につらく当たる, または事を難しくする→**～に厳しい, ～につらく当たる, ～を手荒に扱う** || *Don't be too hard on her - she's only a child.* 彼女にそんなにつらく当たってはいけません - まだ子供なんですから. ▶定義 **2** to be unfair to sb→**人にとって不公平・不利だ** || *Moving the office to the country is a bit hard on the people who haven't got a car.* 事務所を地方に移転すると車を持たない人にはちょっと不利になります.

**give sb a hard time** 略式 ▶定義 to make a situation unpleasant, embarrassing or difficult for sb ～を不愉快な, ばつの悪いまたは困難な状況に陥れる→**～をひどい目に遭わす, 困難を強いる**

**hard and fast** ▶定義 (used about rules, etc) that cannot be changed (規則などについて) 変更できない→**動かせない, 厳重な (規則・区別など), 変更が利かない** || *There are no hard and fast rules about this.* これに関してはどのようにも変更が利きます.

**hard facts** ▶定義 information that is true, not just people's opinions 単に人々の意見ではない真実の情報→**厳然とした事実, 動かし難い事実**

**hard luck** ⇒ **LUCK**

**hard of hearing** ▶定義 unable to hear well よく聞こえない→**(人が) 耳の遠い, 耳が不自由な, 耳の遠い人**

**hard to swallow** ▶定義 difficult to believe 信じ難い→**受け入れ難い, 信じられないような**

**have a hard job doing/to do sth; have a hard time doing sth** ▶定義 to do sth with great difficulty 大変な苦労をして～を行う→**とても苦労して～する, 大変な思いをして～する**

**learn the hard way** ⇒ **LEARN**

**no hard feelings** (口語) ▶定義 used to tell sb you do not feel angry after an argument, etc 口論などの後でもう怒っていないことを～に伝えるのに用いて→**もうわだかまりはない, もう怒っていない** || *'No hard feelings, I hope,' he said, offering me his hand.* 「もうわだかまりはないといいんだけど」と彼が手を差し出して言った.

**the hard way** ▶定義 through having unpleasant or difficult experiences, rather than learning from what you are told 人から教えられた事から学ばないで, むしろ不愉快なまたはつらい経験を通して→**つらい経験をして, 苦労して, こつこつと** || *She won't listen to my advice so she'll just have to learn the hard way.* 彼女は私の忠告に耳を貸さないので, 多分痛い目に遭って覚えることになるでしょう.

**take a hard line (on sth)** ▶定義 to deal with sth in a very serious way that you will not allow anyone to change ～をだれにも変えさせない非常に厳しいやり方で扱う→**(～に) 強硬路線で臨む, 非妥協的方針を取る** || *The government has taken a hard line on people who drink and drive.* 政府は飲酒運転をする人に対し強硬な姿勢を取っています.

\***hard**² /hɑːrd/ 副 ▶定義 **1** with great effort, energy or attention 大変な努力, 精力または注意を伴って→**一生懸命に, 骨を折って, 熱心に** || *He worked hard all his life.* 彼は一生, 勤勉に働いた. *You'll have to try a bit harder than that.* あなたは今よりもう少し身を入れてやってみる必要がありそうだ. ▶定義 **2** with great force; heavily 強い力で; 大量に→**激しく, 強く, ぐいっと** || *It was raining/snowing hard.* 雨・雪が激しく降っていました. *He hit her hard across the face.* 彼は彼女のほおを強くたたいた.

成句 **be hard up (for sth)** ▶定義 to have too few or too little of sth, especially money ～がほんの少数または少量しかない, 特にお金→**金に困っている, 文なしの, (時間・物などを) 欠いている**

**be hard pressed/pushed/put to do sth** ▶定義 to find sth very difficult to do ～をするのが非常に困難だと思う→**～するのにひどく困っている, ～できなくて困る, 進退窮まっている** || *He was hard pressed to explain his wife's sudden disappearance.* 彼は妻が突然失踪 (しっそう) した

ことの説明にひどく困っていた.

die hard ⇒ **DIE**

hard done by [英] ▶定義 not fairly treated➜**正当な扱いを受けない, 不公平に扱われる** ‖ *He felt very hard done by when he wasn't chosen for the team.* 彼はチーム選出から漏れた時, 非常に不公平な扱いを受けたと感じた.

**hardback** /hɑ́ːrdbæ̀k/ [名] [C] ▶定義 a book that has a hard rigid cover 堅くて曲がらない表紙の付いた本➜**本装訂の本, 堅表紙の本, ハードカバー** ‖ *This book is only available* ***in hardback.*** この本は本装訂版しか出ていません. ☛参 **paperback**

**hard-boiled** [形] ▶定義 (used about an egg) boiled until it is solid inside (卵について) 中が固まるまでゆでた➜**固ゆでの**

**hard core** [名] [単数扱い, 単数または複数形の動詞と共に] ▶定義 the members of a group who are the most active グループ内の最も活動的なメンバー➜**中核, 中心 (人物), 強硬派, 核心部**

**hard currency** [名] [U] ▶定義 money belonging to a particular country that is easy to exchange and not likely to fall in value ほかの通貨への両替が容易で, 価値が下がりそうにないある特定の国のお金➜**硬貨 (外貨と交換できる通貨)**

**hard disk** [名] [C] ▶定義 a piece of hard plastic that is fixed inside a computer and is used for storing data and programs permanently コンピューターに内蔵されており, データやプログラムを永久に記憶させるのに使われる1枚の硬いプラスチック➜**ハードディスク** ☛参 **floppy disk**

**hard drug** [名] [[C], 通常は複数] ▶定義 a powerful and illegal drug that some people take for pleasure and may become dependent on (addicted) 強力で非合法な薬で, 快楽を得るため服用し, それに依存性を持つようになる (中毒になる) 人もいる➜**習慣・依存性の強い麻薬** ‖ *Heroin and cocaine are hard drugs.* ヘロインとコカインは依存性の強い麻薬です.

➤ soft と比較.

**harden** /hɑ́ːrd(ə)n/ [動] ▶定義1 [自][他] to become or to make sth hard or less likely to change ～が硬くなる, ～を硬くする, または～が変わりそうにない➜**(物が) 硬くなる・物を硬くする, 固まって～になる・固める** ‖ *The concrete will harden in 24 hours.* そのコンクリートは24時間で固まるでしょう. *The firm has hardened its attitude on this question.* 会社はこの問題に関し態度を硬化した. ▶定義2 [他] (通常は受動態で) harden sb (to sth/doing sth) to make sb less kind or less easily shocked ～をより不親切にさせる, または衝撃を受けにくくさせる➜**(人・心など) を非情にする, 冷酷にする, (人が) (～に対して) 無感覚になる** ‖ *a hardened reporter/criminal* 非情な取材記者・犯罪者 [犯人] *Police officers get hardened to seeing dead bodies.* 警察官は死体を見ても何とも思わなくなるものだ. ▶定義3 [自] (used about a person's face, voice, etc) to become serious and unfriendly (人の顔, 声などについて) 深刻で不親切になる➜**こわばらせる, 無情になる**

**hard-headed** [形] ▶定義 determined and not allowing yourself to be influenced by emotions 決心が固く感情に左右されることを自分自身に許さない➜**冷徹な, 非業な, 現実主義の, 私情を挟まない** ‖ *a hard-headed businessman* 冷徹なビジネスマン

**hard-hearted** [形] ▶定義 not kind to other people and not considering their feelings 他人に不親切で, その気持ちを考えない➜**(人・態度などが) 無情な, 冷酷な, 無慈悲な** ⇔ **soft-hearted**

**hard-hitting** [形] ▶定義 that talks about or criticizes sb/sth in an honest and very direct way 包み隠さず, また非常に直接的に～について話すまたは批判する➜**歯に衣 (きぬ) を着せない, 率直な, はっきりとものを言う, パンチの効いた, 強力な, 精力的な** ‖ *a hard-hitting campaign/speech/report* 精力的な運動・痛烈な演説・歯に衣着せない報告

***hardly** /hɑ́ːrdli/ [副] ▶定義1 almost no; almost not; almost none➜**ほとんど～ない, ほとんどだれも～ない** ‖ *There's* ***hardly any*** *coffee left.* コーヒーはほとんど残っていません. *We* ***hardly ever*** *go out nowadays.* 私たちはこのごろ, ほとんど外出しません. *I hardly spoke any English when I first came here.* 最初ここに来たころは英語をほとんど話せませんでした. ☛参 **almost** ▶定義2 used especially after 'can' and 'could' and before the main verb to emphasize that sth is difficult to do 特に can や could の後, 本動詞

H

の前に用いて、〜をするのが困難であることを強調する→ほとんど〜できない、満足に〜ない、辛うじて、わずかに‖ *Speak up - I can hardly hear you.* もう少し大きい声で話してください - ほとんど聞こえません. ▶定義3 (used to say that sth has just begun, happened, etc) only just (〜が始まったばかり、起こって間もないなどと言うために用いて) ほんのちょっと→辛うじて、やっと、するかしないうちに‖ *She'd **hardly** gone to sleep **than** it was time to get up again.* 彼女がやっと眠るか眠らないかのうちに、また起きる時間になってしまった.

▶ hardly が文頭にある場合、動詞が直後に来ることに注意. この用法は正式な文章に見られる: *Hardly had she gone to sleep than it was time to get up again.* (彼女がやっと眠るか眠らないかのうちに、また起きる時間になってしまった.)

▶定義4 (used to suggest that sth is unlikely or unreasonable) not really (〜がありそうもない事だ、または不合理だとほのめかすために用いて) 本当に〜というわけではない→まず〜ない、〜そうにもない、とても〜ない、どうみても〜ない‖ *You can hardly expect me to believe that excuse!* 私がそんな言い訳を信じるとはまさか思っていないでしょうね. ☞参 **barely**, **scarcely**

**hard-nosed** 形 ▶定義 not affected by feelings or emotions when trying to get what you want 欲しいものを手に入れようとするとき、気持ちや感情に左右されない→情に流されない、不屈の、冷静な、実際的な‖ *hard-nosed journalists/politicians* 冷静な新聞記者・抜け目なく実際的な政治家

**hardship** /háːrdʃip/ 名 C U ▶定義 the fact of not having enough money, food, etc お金、食べ物などが十分にないこと→困窮、苦難、辛苦、困難‖ *This new tax is going to cause a lot of hardship.* この新税は多くの辛苦をもたらすだろう.

**hard shoulder** (困 **shoulder**) 名 C ▶定義 a narrow section of road at the side of a motorway where cars are allowed to stop in an emergency 緊急時に停車することが許されている、高速道路のわきの幅の狭い部分→硬路肩

**hardware** /háːrdwèər/ 名 U ▶定義1 the machinery of a computer, not the programmes written for it コンピューター用に書かれたプログラムではなく、コンピューターの機械装置・機器→ハードウェア ☞参 **software** ▶定義2 tools and equipment that are used in the house and garden 家や庭で使われる道具や設備→金物、鉄器類‖ *a hardware shop* 金物屋

**hard-wearing** 形 英 ▶定義 (used about materials, clothes, etc) strong and able to last for a long time (生地、衣類などについて) 丈夫で長持ちする→(布地などが) 持ちの良い、長持ちする

**hard-working** 形 ▶定義 working with effort and energy 努力して精力的に働く→勤勉な、よく働く、よく勉強する‖ *a hard-working man* 勤勉な男性

**hardy** /háːrdi/ 形 (**hardier**; **hardiest**) ▶定義 strong and able to survive difficult conditions and bad weather 強くて、苦しい条件や悪天候にも耐えられる→(人・動物・体格などが) 頑丈な、頑健な、我慢強い、(動植物が) 耐寒性の‖ *a hardy plant* 耐寒性植物

**hare** /heər/ 名 C ▶定義 an animal like a rabbit but bigger with longer ears and legs 家ウサギに似ているがもっと大きくて、耳や足も長い動物→野ウサギ ☞ **rabbit** のさし絵

**harem** /háːrim, héərəm/ 名 C ▶定義 a number of women living with one man, especially in Muslim societies. The part of the building the women live in is also called a harem. 特にイスラム社会において、1人の男性と暮らす何人かの女性. 建物の中でその女性たちが住んでいる部分も harem と呼ばれる→(1人の男性を囲む) 多数の女性、後宮の女たち、婦人部屋、後宮、ハレム

*****harm**[1] /haːrm/ 名 U ▶定義 damage or injury→損傷、損害、害、危害‖ *Peter ate some of those berries but they didn't **do** him any **harm**.* ピーターはこれらのベリーをいくらか食べましたが何の害もありませんでした. *Experienced staff watch over the children to make sure they don't **come to any harm**.* 経験豊富なスタッフが子供たちにいかなる危害も及ぶことがないよう見守っています.

成句 **no harm done** 略式 ▶定義 used to tell sb that he/she has not caused any damage or injury 〜が何の損傷も損害も引き起こさなかったと、その本人に言うのに用いて→いかなる不都合もない、無害だ、被害なし、全員異常なし‖

*'Sorry about what I said to you last night.' 'That's all right, Jack, no harm done!'* 「昨晩はあんな事を言ってごめんなさい」「いいんだよジャック，何の問題もないよ」
out of harm's way ▶定義 in a safe place ➜ **安全な所に，無事に** ‖ *Put the medicine out of harm's way where the children can't reach it.* この薬を子供たちの手が届かない安全な所に置きなさい.
there is no harm in doing sth; it does no harm (for sb) to do sth ▶定義 there's nothing wrong in doing sth (and sth good may result) ～をすることに何の問題もない（また結果として何か良い～があるかもしれない） ➜ **～して差し支えない，～していかなる不都合もない** ‖ *I'm sure he'll say no, but there's no harm in asking.* 彼はきっと嫌と言うでしょうが，聞いてみることには何の差し支えもありません.

**harm**[2] /hɑːrm/ [動][他] ▶定義 to cause injury or damage; hurt 損害または損傷を引き起こす; 痛める ➜ **～を害する，傷付ける，痛める** ‖ *Too much sunshine can harm your skin.* 太陽の光に当たりすぎると皮膚を害する可能性がある.

***harmful** /hɑ́ːrmfʊl, -f(ə)l/ [形] ▶定義 harmful (to sb/sth) causing harm ➜ **害を及ぼす，有害な** ‖ *Traffic fumes are harmful to the environment.* 排気ガスは環境に害を及ぼします.

***harmless** /hɑ́ːrmləs/ [形] ▶定義 1 not able or not likely to cause damage or injury; safe 損傷や損害を引き起こす可能性がない，または引き起こしそうにない; 安全な ➜ **（ほとんど）害のない，無害の，損害を受けない** ‖ *You needn't be frightened - these insects are completely harmless.* 怖がる必要はありません ー これらの虫たちは全く害がありません. ▶定義 2 not likely to upset people 人を動揺させそうにない ➜ **罪のない，悪意のない，悪気のない，無邪気な** ‖ *The children can watch that film - it's quite harmless.* 子供たちはその映画を見ても差し支えありません ー 全く無害な映画です. — harmlessly [副] ➜ **無害に，無邪気に**

**harmonica** /hɑːrmɑ́nɪkə/ （または **mouth organ**） [名] [C] ▶定義 a small musical instrument that you play by moving it across your lips while you are blowing 息を吹き込みながら唇を左右に移動して演奏する小さな楽器 ➜ **ハーモニカ** ☛ **music** のさし絵

**harmonious** /hɑːrmóʊniəs/ [形] ▶定義 1 friendly, peaceful and without disagreement 友好的で平和で，意見の相違がない ➜ **友好的な，仲の良い，むつまじい** ▶定義 2 (used about musical notes, colours, etc) producing a pleasant effect when heard or seen together （音楽の調子，色などについて）一緒に聞いてまたは見て，心地良い効果を生み出す ➜ **調和した，釣り合いの取れた，（旋律などが）耳に快い，調子の良い** — harmoniously [副] ➜ **仲むつまじく，調和して，釣り合いが取れて**

**harmonize** （または **-ise**） /hɑ́ːrmənàɪz/ [動][自] ▶定義 1 harmonize (with sth) (used about two or more things) to produce a pleasant effect when seen, heard, etc together （２つ以上のものについて）一緒に見たり聞いたりなどして心地良い効果を生み出す ➜ **（～と）調和する，和合する，（配色などが）よく映える** ▶定義 2 harmonize (with sb/sth) to sing or play music that sounds good combined with the main tune 主旋律と調子を合わせて歌う，または演奏する ➜ **（～に）調和して歌う・演奏する** — harmonization （または -isation） /hɑ̀ːrmənaɪzéɪʃ(ə)n; -nə-/ [名] [U] ➜ **調和する・されること，和合，一致**

**harmony** /hɑ́ːrməni/ [名] （[複] **harmonies**） ▶定義 1 [U] a state of agreement or of peaceful existence together 合意し，または平和的に共存している状態 ➜ **調和，和合，一致** ‖ *We need to live more **in harmony with** our environment.* 私たちはもっと環境と調和して生活する必要があります. ▶定義 2 [C][U] a pleasing combination of musical notes, colours, etc 音楽の調子，色などの心地良い組み合わせ ➜ **（音・色などの）ハーモニー，調和，（全体の中での）バランス，（協）和音，和声** ‖ *There are some beautiful harmonies in that music.* その音楽にはいくつかの美しいハーモニーが含まれている.

**harness**[1] /hɑ́ːrnəs/ [名] [C] ▶定義 1 a set of leather straps that is put around a horse's neck and body so that it can pull sth 馬の首と胴体の回りに付けて～を引っ張れるようにする一組の革ひも ➜ **馬具（一式），引き具（一式）** ▶定義 2 a set of straps for fastening sth to a person's body or for stopping sb from moving around, falling, etc 人の体に～をくくり付けたり，～が動き回らない，または落ちないようにするための一組の革

**harness²**

ひも➡(パラシュートの)背負い革, (子供を連れて歩くときの)皮帯, (犬の首輪の代わりに付ける)皮帯, (電話線作業員の)安全ベルト ‖ *a safety harness* 安全ベルト

**harness²** /háːrnəs/ 動 ▶定義1 harness sth (to sth) to put a harness on a horse, etc or to tie a horse, etc to sth using a harness ➡(馬など)に馬具を付ける・に引き具を付ける, 馬具を使って(馬など)を～につなぐ ‖ *Two ponies were harnessed to the cart.* 2頭のポニーが荷車につながれていました. ▶定義2 to control the energy of sth in order to produce power or to achieve sth 力を生み出す, または～を成し遂げるために, …のエネルギーを制御する➡(自然力)を制御・利用する ‖ *to harness the sun's rays as a source of energy* 太陽光線をエネルギー源として利用する

**harp** /hɑːrp/ 名 C ▶定義 a large musical instrument which has many strings stretching from the top to the bottom of a frame. You play the harp with your fingers. 枠組みの一番上から下まで, たくさんの弦が張られていて, 指を使って演奏する大型の楽器➡ハープ, たて琴 ● *music* のさし絵 — harpist 名 C➡ハープ奏者

**harpoon** /hɑːrpúːn/ 名 C ▶定義 a long thin weapon with a sharp pointed end and a rope tied to it that is used to catch large sea animals (whales) 大型の海の動物(鯨)を捕獲するために用いる, 先端が鋭くとがり, ロープが結び付けられた細長い武器➡(捕鯨用の)銛(もり) — harpoon 動 他 ➡～を銛で仕留める, ～に銛を打ち込む

**harrowing** /hærouɪŋ/ 形 ▶定義 making people feel very sad or upset 人々を非常に悲しませる, または動揺させる➡痛ましい, 悲惨な ‖ *The programme showed harrowing scenes of the victims of the war.* その番組は戦争の犠牲者の痛ましい映像を放映した.

**harsh** /hɑːrʃ/ 形 ▶定義1 very strict and unkind 非常に厳しく不親切な➡厳しい, 無情な, 残酷な, 辛辣(しんらつ)な ‖ *a harsh punishment/criticism* 厳しい罰・批判 *The judge had some harsh words for the journalist's behaviour.* 裁判官はその新聞記者の振る舞いに対し, 厳しい言葉を述べた. ▶定義2 unpleasant and difficult to live in, look at, listen to, etc 住む, 見る, 聞くなどに不快で耐え難い➡(気候・状況などが)厳しい, 過酷な, 不快な, 耳障りな, 目障りな ‖ *She grew up in the harsh environment of New York City.* 彼女はニューヨークシティーの過酷な環境で育ちました. *a harsh light/voice* どぎつい光・耳障りな声 ▶定義3 too strong or rough and likely to damage sth 強すぎる, または粗すぎて, ～に害を与えそうな➡きつすぎる, 粗い, ざらざらした, 荒っぽい ‖ *This soap is too harsh for a baby's skin.* このせっけんは赤ちゃんの肌には強すぎます. — harshly 副 ➡厳しく, 耳・目障りに, 荒く — harshness 名 U➡厳しさ, 粗さ

**harvest** /hɑːrvəst/ 名 ▶定義1 C U the time of year when the grain, fruit, etc is collected on a farm; the act of collecting the grain, fruit, etc 1年のうちの, 農園で穀物, 果実などが収穫される時期; 穀物, 果物などを収穫すること➡収穫期, 取り入れ期; 収穫, 取り入れ ‖ *Farmers always need extra help with the harvest.* 農民たちはいつも臨時に収穫の手伝いを必要とする. ▶定義2 C the amount of grain, fruit, etc that is collected 収穫される穀物, 果実などの総量➡収穫高, 収穫物 ‖ *This year's wheat harvest was very poor.* 今年は小麦の収穫量が大変乏しかった. — harvest 動 自 他 ➡(作物を)収穫する, 取り入れる ● 参 combine harvester

**has** /həz, əz 強形 hæz/ ⇒ HAVE

**has-been** 名 C 略式 ▶定義 a person or thing that is no longer as famous, successful or important as before 今は前ほど有名でない, 成功していない, 重要ではない人や物➡過去の人・物, 盛りを過ぎた人・物

**hash** /hæʃ/ 名 U ▶定義1 a hot dish of meat mixed together with potato and fried じゃがいもと一緒にいためた温かい肉料理➡こまぎれ肉料理, ハヤシ肉料理 ▶定義2 = HASHISH 成句 make a hash of sth 略式 ▶定義 to do sth badly ～を下手にやる➡(物・事)をめちゃめちゃにする, 台なしにする

**hashish** /hæʃiːʃ, -ɪʃ/ (または hash) 名 U ▶定義 a drug made from a plant (hemp) that some people smoke for pleasure and which is illegal in many countries ある植物(タイマ)から作られた薬で, 一部の人は快楽のためそれを吸うが, 多くの国では違法となっている➡大麻, ハッシシ

**hasn't** HAS NOT の短縮形

**hats**

- woolly hat (米 stocking cap)
- bowler hat — crown, brim
- top hat
- crash helmet — visor
- sun hat — ribbon
- hard hat
- beret
- cap
- baseball cap — peak (米 bill)

**hassle**[1] /hǽs(ə)l/ 名 略式 ▶定義1 ❻ ❶ a thing or situation that is annoying because it is complicated or involves a lot of effort 複雑なため，または多くの努力を伴うため，迷惑なもの，またはその状況→一苦労, 苦心, 厄介な事 ‖ *It's going to be a hassle having to change trains with all this luggage.* これだけの荷物をすべて持って列車を乗り換えねばならないのは，一苦労だろう.

▶定義2 ❶ disagreeing or arguing 意見の相違または口論→口論, 激論, 乱戦 ‖ *I've decided what to do - please don't give me any hassle about it.* もうどうするかは決めています － お願いだからもうその事で口論を持ちかけるのはやめてください.

**hassle**[2] /hǽs(ə)l/ 動 ❶ ▶定義 to annoy sb, especially by asking him/her to do sth many times 特にその人に～をしてほしいと何回も頼むことにより…を困らせる→いじめる, 苦しめる ‖ *I wish he'd stop hassling me about decorating the house.* 彼がもう家の装飾のことで私を苦しめないでくれるとよい.

**haste** /héɪst/ 名 ❶ ▶定義 speed in doing sth, especially because you do not have enough time 特に十分な時間がないため～をするのが速いこと→急ぐこと, 迅速, 急速 ‖ *It was obvious that the letter had been written **in haste**.* その手紙が急いで書かれたことは明白だった.

**hasten** /héɪsn/ 動 正式 ▶定義1 ❸ hasten to do sth to be quick to do or say sth→急いで～する・言う, 取り急ぎ～する ‖ *She hastened to apologize.* 彼女は急いで謝りました. ▶定義2 ❶ to make sth happen or be done earlier or more quickly より早くまたは素早く～が起こる，または行われるようにする→(人・事)を急がせる, せき立てる, ～(の時期・速度)を早める

**hasty** /héɪsti/ 形 ▶定義1 said or done too quickly 言う，または行うのを急ぎすぎた→(判断・決定などが)軽率な, 早まった, 急いだ, 迅速な, 慌ただしい, せわしい ‖ *He said a hasty 'goodbye' and left.* 彼は慌ただしく「さよなら」と言って立ち去った. ▶定義2 hasty (in doing sth/to do sth) (used about a person) acting or deciding sth too quickly or without enough thought (人について)急いで，または十分考えないで行動する，または～を決める→(人・性質などが)せっかちな ‖ *Maybe I was too hasty in rejecting her for the job.* 彼女にこの仕事をさせなかったのは，私の早まった判断だったかもしれません. ― hastily 副→急いで, 慌てて, 軽率に

**\*hat** /hæt/ 名 ❻ ▶定義 a covering that you wear on your head, usually when you are outside 普通, 外にいるときに頭の上にかぶる物→帽子 ‖ *to wear a hat* 帽子をかぶる

成句 at the drop of a hat ⇒ **DROP**[2]

**hatch**[1] /hætʃ/ 動 ▶定義1 ❸ hatch (out) (used about a baby bird, insect, fish, etc) to come out hatch² of an egg (生まれたばかりの鳥,昆虫,魚などについて)卵から出てくる→(ひな・卵が)かえる‖ *Ten chicks hatched (out) this morning.* 今朝10匹のひながかえった. ▶定義2 ⓗ to make a baby bird, etc come out of an egg→(卵から)(ひな)をかえす,(卵)をかえす,孵化(ふか)させる,(卵)を抱く ▶定義3 ⓗ **hatch sth (up)** to think of a plan (usually to do sth bad) ある計画 (通常は悪いこと)を思い付く→(陰謀・計画など)をこっそりたくらむ,もくろむ‖ *He hatched a plan to avoid paying any income tax.* 彼は所得税を全く支払わないで済む計画をもくろんだ.

**hatch²** /hætʃ/ 图 ⓒ ▶定義1 an opening in the floor of a ship (the deck) through which cargo is lowered 船荷が下ろされる船の床(甲板)に開いている穴→(船の)昇降口 ▶定義2 an opening in the wall between a kitchen and another room that is used for passing food through 食べ物を渡すのに使われる台所とほかの部屋の間にある壁に開いている穴→配ぜん窓 ▶定義3 the door in a plane or spacecraft 航空機や宇宙船の扉→(航空機の)ハッチ,ハッチのふた

**hatchback** /hætʃbæk/ 图 ⓒ ▶定義 a car with a large door at the back that opens upwards 後部に上向きに開く大きなドアが付いた車→ハッチバック ☛ **car** のさし絵

**hatchet** /hætʃɪt/ 图 ⓒ ▶定義 a tool with a short handle and a heavy metal head with a sharp edge used for cutting wood 短い取っ手および鋭い刃の付いた重い金属の頭が付いていて,まきを切るのに用いる道具→手おの,ちょうな,まさかり ☛ **garden** のさし絵

*****hate¹** /heɪt/ 動ⓗ ▶定義1 to have a very strong feeling of not liking sb/sth at all ～を全く好きになれないと非常に強く感じる→～をひどく嫌う,憎む,～が嫌いである,～することを嫌がる,嫌う‖ *I hate grapefruit.* 私はグレープフルーツが嫌いです. *I hate it when it's raining like this.* 私はこんな雨降りが大嫌いです. *I hate to see the countryside spoilt.* 田舎が破壊されていくのを見るのはいやなものです. *He hates driving at night.* 彼は夜間運転するのを嫌がります. ☛参 **detest, loathe**. これらの方がさらに強い気持ちを表す. ▶定義2 used as a polite way of introducing sth that you would prefer not to have to say できれば言いたくない～について,丁寧に切り出す方法として用いて→(人が)～するのを残念に思う,～するのに気が進まない‖ *I hate to bother you, but did you pick up my keys by mistake?* ご迷惑を掛けてすみませんが,私のキーを間違って受け取られたのではありませんか.

**hate²** /heɪt/ 图 ⓤ ▶定義1 a very strong feeling of not liking sb/sth at all; hatred ～が全く好きになれないという強い感情,憎しみ→憎悪,憎しみ(の念),嫌悪‖ *Do you feel any hate towards the kidnappers?* 子供を誘拐する人に対し憎悪を感じますか. ▶定義2 ⓒ a thing that you do not like at all 全く好きでないもの→嫌われる人・物・事‖ *Plastic flowers are one of my pet hates (= the things that I particularly dislike).* プラスチック製の造花は,私が大嫌いなもの(=私がとりわけ嫌っているもの)の1つです.

**hateful** /héɪtful, -f(ə)l/ 形 ▶定義 **hateful (to sb)** extremely unpleasant; horrible 極度に不快な,ひどい→ひどく嫌な,憎むべき,不愉快な‖ *It was a hateful thing to say.* それは口にするのもおぞましいことでした.

**hatred** /héɪtrəd/ 图 ⓤ ▶定義 **hatred (for/of sb/sth)** a very strong feeling of not liking sb/sth; hate ～を好きになれない非常に強い気持ち;憎しみ→憎しみ,憎悪,嫌悪

**hat-trick** 图 ⓒ ▶定義 three points, goals, etc scored by one player in the same game; three successes achieved by one person 1人の選手が同じ試合で得点する3つのポイント,ゴールなど;1人が成し遂げる3つの成功→ハットトリック,1人で1試合に3点得点すること,投手が3人連続で打者をアウトにすること,サイクルヒット‖ *to score a hat-trick* ハットトリックを決める

**haughty** /hɔ́ːti, hɑ́ː-/ 形 ▶定義 proud, and thinking that you are better than other people 高慢で,自分が他人よりも優れていると思っている→ごう慢な,横柄な,高慢な‖ *She gave me a haughty look and walked away.* 彼女は高慢な態度で私をちらっと見て,歩き去りました. — **haughtily** 副→高慢に,偉そうに

**haul¹** /hɔːl/ 動ⓗ ▶定義 to pull sth with a lot of effort or difficulty 大変な努力をして,または苦労して～を引っ張る→～をぐいと引っ張る,引きずる,(強く)引っ張る‖ *A lorry hauled the car out of the mud.* トラックがその車を沼から引き

上げた.

**haul**² /hɔːl/ 名 ▶定義1 [C, 通常は単数] a haul (of sth) a large amount of sth that has been stolen, caught, collected, etc 盗む, 捕まえる, 集めるなどされた多量の～→**稼ぎ, もうけ, 獲得, 入手, 獲物** ‖ *The fishermen came back with a good haul of fish.* その漁師たちは大漁の獲物を持って帰ってきた. ▶定義2 [単数扱い] a distance to be travelled 移動すべき距離→**運送・運搬距離** ‖ *It seemed a long haul back home at night.* 夜の家路は遠く感じられた.

**haulage** /ˈhɔːlɪdʒ/ 名 Ü 英 ▶定義 the transport of goods by road, rail, etc; the money charged for this 道路, 鉄道などによる品物の輸送; それにかかる料金→**運搬, 運搬業, 運賃, 貨車使用料**

**haunt**¹ /hɔːnt/ 動 ▶定義1 (しばしば受動態で) (used about a ghost of a dead person) to appear in a place regularly (死んだ人の幽霊について) ある場所に決まって現れる→**(場所)によく出る, 出没する** ‖ *The house is said to be haunted.* その家に幽霊が出るらしい. ▶定義2 (used about sth unpleasant or sad) to be always in your mind (不快または悲しい～について) いつも心の中にある→**(嫌な考え・思い出などが)に取り付く, ～の頭から離れない, ～に付きまとって悩ます** ‖ *His unhappy face has haunted me for years.* 彼の悲しそうな顔がもう何年も頭から離れません.

**haunt**² /hɔːnt/ 名 C ▶定義 a place that you visit regularly 定期的に訪れる場所→**人がよく行く場所, たまり場, 通い先** ‖ *This cafe has always been a favourite haunt of mine.* このカフェは私がよく行くお気に入りの店です.

**haunting** /ˈhɔːntɪŋ/ 形 ▶定義 having a quality that stays in your mind 心に残る性質の→**しばしば心に浮かぶ, 忘れられない** ‖ *a haunting song* いつまでも心に残る歌

*****have**¹ /həv 強形 hæv/ 動 ▶定義 used for forming the perfect tenses→**完了時制を形成する助動詞** ☛巻末の「文法早見表」を参照.

*****have**² /hæv/ 動 ⊕ ▶定義1 (英 または **have got**) (進行形は不可) to own or to hold sth; to possess→**物を持っている, (財産などを)所有する, ～がある, (友人・親類などを)持っている, (特徴・物など)を持っている** ‖ *I've got a new camera.* 私は新しいカメラを持っています. *The flat has two bedrooms.* そのアパートには寝室が2つあります. *He's got short dark hair.* 彼は短くて濃い色の髪をしています. *to have patience/enthusiasm/skill* 忍耐強い・熱心な・技術を身に付けた *Have you got any brothers and sisters?* 兄弟姉妹はいますか. *Do you have time to check my work?* 私の作品をチェックする時間がありますか. ▶定義2 used with many nouns to talk about doing sth 多くの名詞と共に用いて, ～を行うことを表す→**(ある行為・行動を)行う, する, 食べる, 飲む, とる** ‖ *What time do you have breakfast?* 何時に朝食を食べますか. *to have a drink/something to eat* 1杯飲む・何か食べ物を食べる *I'll just have a shower then we'll go.* ちょっとシャワーを浴びてきます, それから出発しましょう. *to have an argument/talk/chat* 口論・話・おしゃべりをする ▶定義3 to experience sth ～を経験する→**(困難・楽しみなど)を経験する, 被る, (楽しい・つらい目に)遭う, (感情・慈悲・疑い・考えなど)を持っている, 抱く** ‖ *to have fun* 楽しむ *to have problems/difficulties* 問題・困難にぶつかる *to have an idea/an impression/a feeling* ある考え・印象・感じを抱く *to have an accident* 事故に遭う *She had her bag stolen on the underground.* 彼女は地下鉄でバッグを盗まれました. ▶定義4 (または **have got**) (進行形は不可) to be ill with sth ～で調子が悪い[病気である]→**(病気)にかかっている, ～を患う** ‖ *She's got a bad cold.* 彼女はひどい風邪を引いています. *to have flu/a headache/cancer/Aids* 流感にかかる, 頭が痛い, がん・エイズにかかっている ▶定義5 **have sth done** to arrange for sb to do sth ～が…をするように手配する→**(人が)人に～させる, 人に～してもらう** ‖ *I have my hair cut every six weeks.* 私は6週間ごとに髪を切ってもらいます. *You should have your eyes tested.* あなたは目の検査をしてもらうべきです. ▶定義6 (または **have got**) to have a particular duty or plan ある特定の義務または計画がある→**(人が)～する(必要のある)人・物がある, ～しなければならない, することになっている** ‖ *Do you have any homework tonight?* あなたは今夜, 宿題がありますか. *I've got a few things to do this morning, but I'm free later.* 今朝は少しすることがありますが, その後は空いています. ▶定義7 (または **have got**) (進行形は

不可) to hold sb/sth; to keep sth in a particular place ～を保持する；～をある特定の場所に保管する➔～を持っている，物を置く，保管する ‖ *The dog had me by the leg.* その犬は私の足を離しませんでした． *We've got our TV up on a shelf.* 私たちはテレビを棚の上に置いています．

▶定義 **8** to cause sb/sth to do sth or to be in a particular state ～にある事をさせる，またはある特定の状態でいさせる➔(人・物)を～させる，保つ，～の状態にしておく ‖ *The music soon had everyone dancing.* その音楽を聞いてみんなはすぐ踊り出しました． *I'll have dinner ready when you get home.* あなたが帰宅するまでに夕食の用意をしておきましょう． ▶定義 **9** to look after or entertain sb ～の面倒を見る，または楽しませる➔(パーティーなど)を催す，(客などを)迎える，招待する ‖ *We're having some people to dinner tomorrow.* 私たちは明日の夕食に何人かの来客を予定しています．

成句 **have had it** ▶定義 used about things that are completely broken, or dead 完全に壊れた，または死んだものについて用いて➔もう駄目だ，後の祭りだ，助かる見込みがない，既に事切れている ‖ *This television has had it. We'll have to buy a new one.* このテレビはもう駄目だ．新しい物を買わなくては．

▶ have を含むこのほかの成句については，名詞，形容詞などの項を参照．例えば not have a clue は clue の項にある．

句動詞 **have sb on** ▶定義 to trick sb as a joke 冗談でからかって～をだます➔(だまして)人をからかう，担ぐ ‖ *Don't listen to what Jimmy says - he's only having you on.* ジミーの言うことを聞いちゃ駄目だよ — 彼はあなたをからかってるだけだから．

**have (got) sth on** ▶定義 **1** to be wearing sth➔(衣類など)を身に着けている，着て・履いて・かぶっている ‖ *She's got a green jumper on.* 彼女は緑色のプルオーバーを着ている． ▶定義 **2** 略式 to have an arrangement to do sth ～をする取り決めがある➔(会合・約束・仕事など)の予定がある ‖ *I've got a lot on this week (= I'm very busy).* 私は今週たくさんの予定があります (= 私は大変忙しい)．

**have sth out** ▶定義 to allow part of your body to be removed 人に任せて身体の一部を取り除く➔～を抜いてもらう，切ってもらう ‖ *to have a tooth/your appendix out* 歯を抜いてもらう・盲腸を切ってもらう

**haven** /héɪv(ə)n/ 名 C ▶定義 *a haven (of sth); a haven (for sb/sth)* a place where people or animals can be safe and rest 人々または動物が安全に休むことのできる場所➔避難所，安息の地，安全な場所 ‖ *The lake is a haven for water birds.* この湖は水鳥たちの安息の地です．

▶ *a tax haven* とは所得税の低い国のこと．「租税回避地，タックスヘイブン」

\***have to** /hǽv tə; hæf tə/ (または **have got to**) 法助動詞 ▶定義 used for saying that sb must do sth or that sth must happen ～が…をしなければならない，または～が起こるはずだと言うのに用いて➔～しなければならない，～に違いない ‖ *I usually have to work on Saturday mornings.* 私は通常土曜の午前中は働かなければなりません． *Do you have to have a visa to go to America?* アメリカに行くには査証が必要ですか． *She's got to go to the bank this afternoon.* 彼女は今日の午後銀行に行かなければならない． *We don't have to (= it's not necessary to) go to the party if you don't want to.* あなたが行きたくなければ，私たちはパーティーに行く必要はありません (= ～する必要がない)． *We had to do lots of boring exercises.* 私たちはうんざりするような練習をたくさんしなければならなかった．

▶ 法助動詞についての説明は，巻末の「文法早見表」を参照．

**havoc** /hǽvək, -ɪk/ 名 U ▶定義 a situation in which there is a lot of damage or confusion 多くの損害または混乱がある状況➔(地震・台風などによる)大破壊，大損害，大荒れ ‖ *The rail strikes will* **cause havoc** *all over the country.* の鉄道ストライキは国中に大混乱をもたらすでしょう．

**hawk** /hɔːk/ 名 C ▶定義 a type of large bird that catches and eats small animals and birds. Hawks can see very well. 小動物や小鳥を捕えて食べる大型の鳥の一種．hawks は非常に目がいい➔タカ(の類)

▶ hawks は *bird of prey*（猛禽（もうきん））の一種．

**hay** /heɪ/ 名 U ▶定義 grass that has been cut

and dried for use as animal food 動物のえさとして使う刈って乾燥させた草→干し草, まぐさ

**hay fever** 名 U ▶定義 an illness that affects the eyes, nose and throat and is caused by breathing in the powder (pollen) produced by some plants ある植物から出る粉（花粉）を吸い込むことが原因の目, 鼻, のどに症状が出る病気→枯草(こそう)熱, 花粉症

**haywire** /héɪwàɪər/ 形
成句 be/go haywire 略式 ▶定義 to be or become out of control 制御が利かない, または利かなくなる→(人が)発狂する,(機械が)故障する,(計画が)台なしになる ‖ I can't do any work because the computer's gone haywire. コンピューターが故障して, 全く仕事になりません.

**hazard**¹ /hǽzərd/ 名 C ▶定義 a danger or risk 危険またはおそれ→(偶然性の強い)危険, 冒険,(～への)危険要素 ‖ Smoking is a serious health hazard. 喫煙は健康上極めて有害です.

**hazard**² /hǽzərd/ 動 他 ▶定義 to make a guess or to suggest sth even though you know it may be wrong たとえ間違っている可能性があると分かっていても予測する, または～を提案する→(不確定要素の多い予想など)を思い切って言う・を運任せにやってみる ‖ I don't know what he paid for the house but I could **hazard a guess**. 彼がこの家にいくら支払ったのか知りませんが, 当て推量を言ってみることはできます.

**hazardous** /hǽzərdəs/ 形 ▶定義 dangerous; risky→危険な, 冒険的な

**haze** /héɪz/ 名 C U ▶定義 1 air that is difficult to see through because of heat, dust or smoke 熱, ほこりまたは煙が原因での見通しが悪い空気→もや, かすみ, 煙霧 ☞参 fog の注 ▶定義 2 a mental state in which you cannot think clearly はっきりと思考できない精神状態→(精神の)もうろうとした状態

**hazel**¹ /héɪz(ə)l/ 名 C ▶定義 a small tree or bush that produces nuts 木の実をつける小さな木または潅木(かんぼく)→ハシバミ, その実

**hazel**² /héɪz(ə)l/ 形 ▶定義 (used especially about eyes) light brown in colour (特に目に付いて) 薄い茶色の→ハシバミ色の, 薄茶色の

**hazelnut** /héɪz(ə)lnʌ̀t/ 名 C ▶定義 a small nut that we eat 食用にもなる小さな木の実→ハシバミの実 ☞ nut のさし絵

**hazy** /héɪzi/ 形 ▶定義 1 not clear, especially because of heat 特に熱気のため, 澄み切っていない→かすんだ, もやのかかった ‖ The fields were hazy in the early morning sun. 早朝の太陽の光が当たって, 野原はもやがかかっていました. ▶定義 2 difficult to remember or understand clearly 思い出しにくい, または分かりにくい→ぼんやりした, 不明確な, あいまいな ‖ a hazy memory ぼんやりした記憶 ▶定義 3 (used about a person) uncertain, not expressing things clearly (人について) はっきりしない, 物事を明確に表現しない→はっきりしない, あいまいな, 不明確な ‖ She's a bit hazy about the details of the trip. 彼女はその旅行の詳細についてちょっとあいまいです.

★**he**¹ /(h)i, hi:/ 代 (動詞の主語) ▶定義 the male person mentioned earlier 前述の男性を指す→彼は, 彼が, その男が, あいつが ‖ I spoke to John before he left. 私はジョンが行ってしまう前に話をしました. Look at that little boy - he's going to fall in! あの小さな男の子を見てください － 今にも落っこちそうです.

▶ 男性または女性どちらでもあり得る人に言及するには, いくつかの方法がある. he or she, him or her, また文字に表す場合には he/she または s/he などを用いることができる : If you are not sure, ask your doctor. He/she can give you further information. (もしはっきりと分からなければ, 医師に尋ねなさい. 彼・彼女がより詳しい情報を提供してくれるでしょう.) くだけた表現では, they, them または their を使うこともできる : Everybody knows what they want. (だれでも自分が何を望んでいるか分かっています.) When somebody asks me a question I always try to give them a quick answer. (だれかから質問を受けたら, いつも素早く返答するよう心掛けています.) あるいは, 複数形にして文章を作ってもよい : A baby cries when s/he is tired. (赤ちゃんは疲れると泣きます) は, Babies cry when they are tired. のように言える.

**he**² /hi:/ 名 [単数扱い] ▶定義 a male animal 動物の雄→男, 雄 ‖ Is your cat a he or a she? あなたの猫は雄ですか, それとも雌ですか.

★**head**¹ /hed/ 名 C ▶定義 1 the part of your body

# head¹

above your neck 首より上の体の部分→**頭, 首, 頭の丈** ‖ *She turned her head to look at him.* 彼女は振り向いて彼を見ました. ☞ C5 ページのさし絵 ▶定義2 **-headed**(複合形容詞を作るために用いて) having the type of head mentioned 言及した種類の頭をした→**頭が〜の** ‖ *a bald-headed man* 頭のはげた男性 ▶定義3 a person's mind, brain or mental ability 人の知能, 脳または知力→**頭脳, 理性, 分別, 才能, 能力** ‖ *Use your head! (= think!)* 頭を使え. (= 考えろ.) *A horrible thought entered my head.* 私の頭に恐ろしい考えが浮かんだ. ▶定義4 the top, front or most important part 頂上, 正面または最も重要な部分→**先端, (列などの) 先頭, 上部, (ページ・リストの) 上部, (道具・機械などの) 頭部, (テープレコーダーなどの) ヘッド, (谷・坂・崖 (がけ)・はしごなどの) 最上端, (川の注ぎ込む) 湖頭** ‖ *to sit at the head of the table* テーブルの上席に座る *the head of a nail* つめの先端 *the head of the queue* 列の先頭 ▶定義5 the person in charge of a group of people 一団の人々を仕切る人→**(部局・組織・集団などの) 長, 頭 (かしら), 指導的地位, (形容詞的に) 長の, 首位の** ‖ *the head of the family* 家長 *Several* **heads of state** *(= official leaders of countries) attended the funeral.* 数か国から指導的地位にある人々 (= 国々の公式の指導者たち) がその葬儀に参列しました. *the head waiter* ウエーター長 ▶定義6 (または **head teacher**) the teacher in charge of a school 学校を取り仕切る先生→**校長** ‖ *Who is going to be the new head?* だれが新しい校長先生になる予定ですか. ▶定義7 **heads** the side of a coin with the head of a person on it 人の顔が付いている側の, 硬貨の面→**(硬貨の) 表** ‖ *Heads or tails? Heads I go first, tails you do.* 表か裏か. 表なら私が先, 裏ならあなたから.

成句 **a/per head** ▶定義 for each person→**1人当たり, 1人に付き** ‖ *How much will the meal cost a head?* この食事は1人当たりいくらになるでしょうか.

**bite sb's head off** ⇒ **BITE¹**

**come to a head; bring sth to a head** ▶定義 if a situation comes to a head or if you bring it to a head, it suddenly becomes very bad and you have to deal with it immediately ある状況が come to a head または you bring 〜 to a head という場合, 状況が突然とても悪化し, 即座に対処しなくてはならない→**(事態が) 危機に陥る, (行動の機が) 熟する, 山場を迎える**

**do sb's head in** 英略式 ▶定義 to make sb upset and confused 〜を動転させ混乱させる→**人をうろたえさせる, かっとさせる, のぼせさせる**

**get sth into your head; put sth into sb's head** ▶定義 to start or to make sb start believing or thinking sth 〜を信じ始める, または考え始める, …に〜を信じさせる, または考えさせる→**(〜だと) 十分理解する, 気付く, 信じ始める, 〜に…を十分理解させる, 気付かせる** ‖ *Barry's got it into his head that glasses would make him more attractive.* バリーは眼鏡を掛けると自分が一層魅力的に見えることに気付いた.

**go to sb's head** ▶定義1 to make sb too proud 〜を得意にさせすぎる→**人を慢心させる, うぬぼれさせる, 有頂天にさせる** ‖ *If you keep telling him how clever he is, it will go to his head!* 彼に賢いといつも言っていると, うぬぼれてしまうわよ. ▶定義2 to make sb drunk 〜を酔わせる→**(酒が人を) 酔わせる** ‖ *Wine always goes straight to my head.* 私はいつもワインですぐ酔ってしまいます.

**have a head for sth** ▶定義 to be able to deal with sth easily 〜に容易に対処することができる→**〜しても平気な, 〜に強い, 通じている** ‖ *You need a good head for heights if you live on the top floor!* 最上階に住むのであれば高い所が平気でないと. *to have a head for business/figures* ビジネスに通じている・数字は得意だ

**head first** ▶定義1 with your head before the rest of your body 体のほかの部分より先に頭から→**頭から先に, 真っ逆さまに** ‖ *Don't go down the slide head first.* 頭から先に滑り台を滑ってはいけません. ▶定義2 too quickly or suddenly あまりに急いで, または突然→**向こう見ずに, 性急に, 慌てて** ‖ *Don't rush head first into a decision.* 向こう見ずに決断を急ぎすぎてはなりません.

**head over heels (in love)** ▶定義 loving sb very much; madly 〜を非常に愛して; 熱烈に→**深く, 完全に, すっかり, 真っ逆さまに** ‖ *Jane's fallen head over heels in love with her new boss.* ジェーンは新しい上司に熱烈に恋している.

hit the nail on the head ⇒ **HIT**¹
keep your head ▶定義 to stay calm→冷静さを保つ, 落ち着いている
keep your head above water ▶定義 to just manage to survive in a difficult situation, especially one in which you do not have enough money 困難な状況（特に十分なお金がないという状況）で何とかして持ちこたえる→借金せずにいる, 大過なく過ごす
keep your head down ▶定義 to try not to be noticed→気付かれないようにする, 身を隠す
laugh, scream, etc your head off ▶定義 to laugh, shout, etc very loudly and for a long time 非常に大声で長時間笑う, 叫ぶなどする→大笑いする, 声を限りに叫ぶ, 大騒ぎする
lose your head ⇒ **LOSE**
make head or tail of sth ▶定義 to understand sth→～を理解する, 分かる ‖ *I can't make head or tail of this exercise.* 私はこの練習問題が分からない.
off the top of your head ⇒ **TOP**¹
out of/off your head 略式 ▶定義 crazy, often because of the effects of drugs or alcohol しばしば薬物またはアルコールの影響により, 気が狂った→気がふれて, 精神錯乱して, ひどく興奮して
put/get your heads together ▶定義 to make a plan with sb ～と一緒に計画を立てる→(2人以上の人が)額を寄せて相談・密議する
a roof over your head ⇒ **ROOF**
shake your head ⇒ **SHAKE**¹
take it into your head to do sth ▶定義 to suddenly decide to do sth that other people consider strange ほかの人が奇妙だと思うような～をしようと突然決心する→～しようとふと思い付く, ～だと思い込む, 突然決心する ‖ *I don't know why Kevin took it into his head to enter that marathon!* ケヴィンがどうしてそのマラソンに出ようと思い立ったのか分からない.

*****head**² /hed/ 動 ▶定義 1 自 to move in the direction mentioned 言及した方向に移動する→(～に向かって)まっすぐ進む, 向かう, 進行する ‖ *The ship headed towards the harbour.* その船は港へ向かいました. *Where are you heading?* あなたはどこへ向かっているのですか. ▶定義 2 他 to be in charge of or to lead sth ～を取り仕切る, または率いる→～を率いる, ～の頭(かしら)・長である ▶定義 3 他 to be at the front of a line, top of a list, etc 列の先頭, リストの一番上などにいる→～の先頭に立つ, 名簿の筆頭となる ▶定義 4 他 (しばしば受動態で) to give a title at the top of a piece of writing 一編の書き物の冒頭に見出しを付ける→～に見出し・題名を付ける ‖ *The report was headed 'The State of the Market'.* その報告書の題名は「市場の状況」となっていました. ▶定義 5 他 (in football) to hit the ball with your head (フットボールで)ボールを頭で打つ→(ボール)をヘディングする

句動詞 **head for** ▶定義 to move towards a place ある場所に向かって移動する→～に向かって進む, ～に向かう ‖ *It's getting late - I think it's time to head for home.* 暗くなってきました — もう家へ向かう時間だと思います.

*****headache** /hédèɪk/ 名 C ▶定義 1 a pain in your head 頭の痛み→頭痛 ‖ *I've got a splitting (= very bad) headache.* 頭が割れるように(= 非常にひどく)痛い. ☛参 **ache** の注 ▶定義 2 a person or thing that causes worry or difficulty 心配または困難の原因となる人または物→困った問題, 悩みの種, 心配事 ‖ *Paying the bills is a constant headache.* 請求書の支払いをするのがいつも頭痛の種です.

**heading** /hédɪŋ/ 名 C ▶定義 the words written as a title at the top of a page or a piece of writing 1ページあるいは一編の書き物の冒頭に表題として書かれる言葉→表題, 見出し, 項目 ‖ *I've grouped our ideas under three main headings.* 私たちの考えを3つの主要項目にまとめました.

**headland** /hédlənd, -lænd/ 名 C ▶定義 a narrow piece of land that sticks out into the sea 海に突き出した幅の狭い陸地→岬, 突端

**headlight** /hédlàɪt/ (または **headlamp** /hédlæmp/) 名 C ▶定義 one of the two large bright lights at the front of a vehicle 車の前面にある2つの明るいライトのうちの1つ→(車などの)ヘッドライト

**headline** /hédlàɪn/ 名 ▶定義 1 C the title of a newspaper article printed in large letters above the story 大文字で記事の上に印刷されている新聞記事の見出し→(新聞・雑誌などの大文字の)見出し, 表題 ▶定義 2 **the headlines** [複数扱い] the main items of news read on television or radio テレビまたはラジオで読まれるニュースの主な項目→(ニュース放送の)主な項目(の要約・要点), ヘッドライン

**headlong** /hédlɔ(:)ŋ, -làŋ/ 副形 ▶定義1 with your head before the rest of your body 体のほかの部分よりも先に頭から→**頭から先に, 真っ逆さまに[の]** ‖ *I tripped and fell headlong into the road.* 私はつまずいて道路に真っ逆さまに落ちました. ▶定義2 too quickly; without enough thought あまりに即座に; 十分に考えないで→**まっしぐらに[の], 向こう見ずに[な], 軽率に[な]** ‖ *He rushed headlong into buying the business.* 彼は軽率にもその取り引きで買いを急ぎました.

**head-on** 形 ▶定義 with the front of one car, etc hitting the front of another 1台の車などの正面がもう1台の(車の)正面とぶつかって→**正面(から)の, 正面に** ‖ *a head-on crash* 車の正面衝突

**headphones** /hédfòʊnz/ 名 [複数扱い] ▶定義 a piece of equipment worn over the ears that makes it possible to listen to music, the radio, etc without other people hearing it 耳を覆って付ける1個の装置で, 他人に聞こえないように音楽, ラジオなどを聴くことができる→**ヘッドホン**

**headquarters** /hédkwɔ̀ːrtərz/ 名 [複数扱い, 単数または複数形の動詞と共に] (略 **HQ**) ▶定義 the place from where an organization is controlled; the people who work there ある組織が支配されている場所; そこで働く人々→**本部, 司令部, 本署, 本拠, 本社, (集合的に)本部員, 司令部員** ‖ *Where is/are the firm's headquarters?* この会社の本社はどこにありますか.

**headset** /hédsèt/ 名 C ▶定義 a piece of equipment that you wear on your head that includes a device for listening (headphones) and/or a device for speaking into (a microphone) 頭に付ける1個の装置で, 聞く装置(ヘッドホン)と・または話す装置(マイクロホン)を含む→**(マイク付きの)ヘッドホン** ‖ *The pilot was talking into his headset.* そのパイロットはヘッドセットのマイクロホンで話をしていた.

**head start** 名 [単数扱い] ▶定義 an advantage that you have from the beginning of a race or competition 競争または競技の初めに与えられている有利な条件→**(走者を有利にする)飛び出し, 先手, 有利なスタート**
➤ start²(4)と比較.

**headstone** /hédstòʊn/ 名 C ▶定義 a large stone with writing on, used to mark where a dead person is buried 死者が埋葬されている場所を示すのに用いる, 書き込みがされている大きな石→**墓石, (墓の)笠石(かさいし)** ☛参 **gravestone, tombstone**

**headstrong** /hédstrɔ̀(:)ŋ, -stràŋ/ 形 ▶定義 doing what you want, without listening to advice from other people 他人の忠告に耳を貸さないで, 自分のやりたいことをやる→**強情な, わがままな, 頑固な, 片意地な**

**head teacher** = HEAD¹(6)

**headway** /hédwèɪ/ 名

成句 **make headway** ▶定義 to go forward or make progress in a difficult situation 困難な状況下で前進する, または進歩する→**前進・進歩する, 進行する**

**heal** /hiːl/ 動 自 他 ▶定義 heal (over/up) to become healthy again; to make sth healthy again 再び健康になる; 〜を再び健康にする→**治る, いえる; (病気・傷・心の痛手など)を治す, いやす** ‖ *The cut will heal up in a few days.* この傷は2, 3日で治るでしょう. (比喩) *Nothing he said could heal the damage done to their relationship.* 彼が何を言っても, 彼らの関係を修復することはできませんでした.

\***health** /helθ/ 名 U ▶定義1 the condition of a person's body or mind 人の身体または心の状態→**(心身の健康)状態, 調子** ‖ *Fresh fruit and vegetables are good for your health.* 新鮮な果物と野菜は体のために良い. *in good /poor health* 健康である・でない (比喩) *the health of your marriage/finances* 結婚生活・財政の(健全な)状態 ▶定義2 the state of being well and free from illness 調子が良く, 病気でない状態→**(心身の)健康, 健康・健全であること** ‖ *As long as you have your health, nothing else matters.* 健康でありさえすれば, ほかの事は構わない. ▶定義3 the work of providing medical care 医療を提供する仕事→**保健, 衛生** ‖ *health and safety regulations* 保健安全規則

**health centre** 名 C ▶定義 a building where a group of doctors see their patients 一団の医師たちが患者を診る建物→**保健所, 医療センター**

**health food** 名 C U ▶定義 natural food that

many people think is especially good for your health because it has been made or grown without adding chemicals 化学薬品を加えずに作られた、または育てられたため多くの人が特に体に良いと考えている自然食品➡健康食品, 自然食品

**the health service** 名 C ▶定義 the organization of the medical services of a country ある国の医療サービスを行う組織➡公共医療サービス ☛参 the National Health Service

*healthy /hélθi/ 形 (healthier; healthiest) ▶定義1 not often ill; strong and well あまり病気をしない; 丈夫で健康な➡(人・動植物・心・体などが) 健康な、健全な、(経済・社会などが) 健全な ‖ a healthy child/animal/plant 健康な子供・動物・植物 ▶定義2 showing good health (of body or mind) (体または心の) 健康な状態を表して➡(態度・顔色・食欲などが) 健康そうな、はつらつとした ‖ healthy skin and hair 健康そうな皮膚と髪の毛 ▶定義3 helping to produce good health 健康増進を助ける➡(食物・場所などが) 健康に良い、健康を増進させる ‖ a healthy climate/diet/lifestyle 健康に良い気候・食事・生活様式 ▶定義4 normal and sensible 正常で分別のある➡健全な、健康的な ‖ There was plenty of healthy competition between the brothers. その兄弟間には健全な競争心が多く見られました. ⇔ すべての定義 unhealthy — healthily 副 ➡健康で, 健全に

**heap**¹ /hi:p/ 名 C ▶定義1 a heap (of sth) an untidy pile of sth 大量の取り散らかした~➡(寄せ集めて乱雑に重なった物の) 山, 塊, 堆積(たいせき) ‖ a heap of books/papers 本・書類の山 All his clothes are **in a heap** on the floor! 彼の洋服は皆床に山積みになっています. ☛参 pile の注 ▶定義2 略式 a heap (of sth); heaps (of sth) a large number or amount; plenty 多数、または多量; 豊富➡たくさんの~, 多数・多量の ‖ I've got a heap of work to do. 私はやらなきゃならない仕事がたくさんあるよ. There's heaps of time before the train leaves. 列車が発車するまでたっぷり時間があるよ.

成句 **heaps better, more, older, etc** 略式 ▶定義 much better, etc ずっと良く, など➡大層, 非常に, ずっと

**heap**² /hi:p/ 動 他 ▶定義1 heap sth (up) to put things in a pile➡物を積み上げる, 蓄積する ‖ I'm going to heap all the leaves up over there. 葉っぱはすべてあそこに積み上げておきましょう. Add six heaped tablespoons of flour (= in a recipe). テーブルスプーン山盛り6杯の小麦粉を加えます (料理のレシピで). ▶定義2 heap A on/onto B; heap B with A to put a large amount of sth on sth/sb ~の上に多量の…を置く➡物に物を山積みする, 人に物をたくさん与える ‖ He heaped food onto his plate. 彼はお皿に食べ物を山盛りにしました. The press heaped the team with praise. 報道陣はそのチームを褒めちぎった.

*hear /hiər/ 動 (過, 過分 heard /hə:rd/) ▶定義1 自他 (進行形は不可) to receive sounds with your ears 耳で音を聞く➡(音・声・人など) が聞こえる; ~を聞く ‖ Can you speak a little louder - I can't hear very well. もう少し大きな声で話してくれますか - あまりよく聞こえません. I didn't hear you go out this morning. 今朝あなたが出掛ける音に気付きませんでした. Did you hear what I said? 私の言った事が聞こえましたか.

▶ hear, listen と比較. 多くの場合, hear は必ずしも聞こうとしないで, ある音が耳に入ってくることを意味する. listen は意識的または積極的に努力をして何かを聞くこと: I always wake up when I hear the milkman come. (牛乳配達の音が聞こえると私はいつも目が覚めます.) I love listening to music in the evening. (私は夜, 音楽を聴くのが大好きです.) Listen - I've got something to tell you. (まあ聞いてください - あなたにお話したい事があります.) 時に, hear が listen to と類似した意味を持つこともある: We'd better hear what they have to say. (私たちは彼らの言い分も聞いた方がいい.)

▶定義2 他 (進行形は不可) to be told or informed about sth ~について教えられる, または知らされる➡(~ということ) を耳にする, (人から・~について) 聞いて知る, ~とうわさに聞いている, ~だそうだ ‖ I hear that you've been offered a job in Canada. カナダでの仕事を打診されているそうですね. 'I passed my test!' '**So I've heard** - well done!' 「テストに合格しました」「うわさでそう聞きましたよ - よくやりま

したね」 *I was sorry to hear about your mum's illness.* あなたのお母様がご病気と聞いて残念に思いました.

►この動詞は進行形では使われないが, 現在分詞(= -ing 形)ではよく見られる: *Not hearing what he'd said over the roar of the machines, she just nodded in reply.* (機械が大きな音を立てていて彼の言う事が聞こえなかったので, 彼女はただうなずいて返事をした.)

▶定義3 ⓤ (used about a judge, a court, etc) to listen to the evidence in a trial in order to make a decision about it (裁判官, 法廷などについて)裁判で証言を聞き, それについて判断を下す→ (事件など)を(公式に)聴く, (被告など)から証言を聴く, 〜の申し立てを聴く, 〜を審理する ∥ *Your case will be heard this afternoon.* あなたの事例は今日の午後審理される予定です.

▶語法

hear と listen の違い

hear は「(自然と)耳に入る」で, listenは「耳を傾ける」です. listen は必ずしも音が聞こえることを意味しません. 例えば, *I listened carefully, but I couldn't hear anything.* (注意深く耳を傾けたが何も聞こえなかった.)というようなことがあり得ます. また「聞き耳を立てる」というときには, *I listened for his footsteps.* のように for を用います.

成句 hear! hear! ▶定義 used for showing that you agree with what sb has just said, especially in a meeting 特に会合などにおいて, 人がたった今言った〜に同意することを表して→ 賛成, そうだそうだ, いいぞ

won't/wouldn't hear of sth ▶定義 to refuse to allow sth 〜を認めるのを拒否する→ 物を聞き入れない, いかなる〜も容赦しない, 〜を許さない ∥ *I wanted to go to art school but my parents wouldn't hear of it.* 私は美術学校に行きたかったが, 両親は聞き入れてくれなかった.

句動詞 hear from sb ▶定義 to receive a letter, telephone call, etc from sb 〜から手紙, 電話などをもらう→人から手紙・伝言・電話・返信をもらう, 便り・連絡がある

hear of sb/sth ▶定義 to know that sb/sth exists because you have heard him/her/it mentioned 話に聞いたことがあるので〜の存在を知っている→ (人・物・事)のこと・存在を耳にする, 〜のことをうわさに聞く ∥ *Have you heard of the Bermuda Triangle?* バミューダ トライアングルのことを耳にしたことがありますか.

**hearing** /híərɪŋ/ ⓑ 定義1 ⓤ the ability to hear 聞く能力→ 聴力, 聴覚, 聞き取り ∥ *Her hearing isn't very good so you need to speak louder.* 彼女は耳が少し遠いのでもっと大きな声で話す必要があります. ▶定義2 [単数扱い] a time when evidence is given to a judge in a court of law 法廷で裁判官に証言が行われる時間→ 証言聴取, 審問, 審査 ∥ *a court/disciplinary hearing* 法廷・懲戒審問 ▶定義3 [単数扱い] a chance to give your opinion or explain your position 自分の意見を述べる, または自分の立場を説明する機会→ 発言の機会, 聞いてもらう機会, 聞いてあげる機会 ∥ *to get/give sb a fair hearing* 自分の意見を公平に聞いてもらう・〜の言い分を公平に聞いてあげる

成句 hard of hearing ⇒ **HARD**¹

in/within sb's hearing ▶定義 near enough to sb so that he/she can hear what is being said 〜に十分近いので, その〜に言っている事が聞こえる→ 人に聞こえる所で

**hearing aid** ⓑ ⓒ ▶定義 a small device for people who cannot hear well that fits inside the ear and makes sounds louder 聴力があまりない人に音が大きく聞こえるようにするために, 耳の内側に付ける小さな装置→ 補聴器

**hearsay** /híərseɪ/ ⓑ ⓤ ▶定義 things you have heard another person or other people say, which may or may not be true ほかの人または人々が言っているのを聞いたことで, 本当かもしれないし, 本当でないかもしれない事柄→ うわさ, 風聞, 風評

**hearse** /hɜːs/ ⓑ ⓒ ▶定義 a large, black car used for carrying a dead person to his/her funeral 死んだ人を葬儀まで運ぶのに用いる大きな黒い車→ 霊柩(れいきゅう)車, 葬儀用自動車

*****heart** /hɑːt/ ⓑ ▶定義1 ⓒ the organ inside your chest that sends blood round your body 血液を体中に送るための胸の内部にある臓器→ 心臓, 胸部 ∥ *When you exercise your heart beats faster.* 運動をすると心臓の鼓動が速くなります. *heart disease/failure* 心臓病・心不全[心臓

まひ] ☛ C5 ページのさし絵 ▶定義2 ❻ the centre of a person's feelings and emotions 人の気持ちや感情の中心→(喜怒哀楽などの感情が宿る)心, 感情, 気持ち, 精神, 魂 ‖ *She has a kind heart (= she is kind and gentle).* 彼女は親切な心の持ち主です(= 彼女は親切で優しい). *They say she died of a broken heart (= unhappiness caused by sb he loved).* 彼は傷心のあまり死んだと言われている(= 愛した人から悲しい目に遭わされて). ▶定義3 **-hearted** (複合形容詞を作るために用いて) having the type of feelings or character mentioned 言及された種類の気持ちまたは性質を持った→〜の心を持った, 心が〜な ‖ *kind-hearted* 親切な心を持った *cold-hearted* 心が冷たい ▶定義4 [単数扱い] the heart (of sth) the most central or important part of sth; the middle 〜の一番中心または最重要部分; 真ん中→(物・事の)中心, 核心, 本質, (キャベツ・レタスなどの)芯(しん) ‖ *Rare plants can be found in the heart of the forest.* この森の奥地では珍しい植物を見つけることができます. *Let's get straight to the heart of the matter.* 直接, 問題の核心に触れてみよう.

▶定義5 ❻ a symbol that is shaped like a heart, often red or pink and used to show love 心臓のような形をした1つの象徴で, 多くは赤またはピンク色で愛を表すのに用いる→心臓状・ハート形の物, ハート ‖ *He sent her a card with a big red heart on it.* 彼は大きな赤いハートの付いたカードを彼女に贈りました. ▶定義6 **hearts** [複数扱い] the group (suit) of playing cards with red shapes like hearts (5) on them 赤いハート型の印の付いたカードの組(組札)→ハートの組札 ‖ *the queen of hearts* ハートのクイーン ☛参 **card** の注とさし絵 ▶定義7 ❻ one of the cards from this suit その組札の1枚→ハートの札 ‖ *Play a heart, if you've got one.* 持っていたらハートを出しなさい.

成句 **after your own heart** ▶定義 (used about people) similar to yourself or of the type you like best (人々について)自分自身に似ている, または一番好きな種類の→〜の(一番に)気に入った(ように), 心にかなった(ように), 思い通りの

**at heart** ▶定義 really; in fact→実際は, 本当は, 心の底では, 根(ね)は ‖ *My father seems strict but he's a very kind man at heart.* 私の父は厳しく見えますが, 本当はとても心の優しい人です.

**break sb's heart** ▶定義 to make sb very sad →人をひどく悲しませる, 悲嘆に暮れさせる

**by heart** ▶定義 by remembering exactly; from memory はっきりと覚えていて; 記憶から→そらで ‖ *Learning lists of words off by heart isn't a good way to increase your vocabulary.* 単語の一覧を丸暗記するのは語彙(ごい)を増やすのに良い方法ではありません.

**a change of heart** ⇒ **CHANGE**²

**close/dear/near to sb's heart** ▶定義 having a lot of importance and interest for sb 〜にとって大変重要で興味深い→(人が)〜にとって懐かしい, 最も親愛な, いとしい, (物が)〜にとって大事な, 最も大切な ‖ *a subject that is very dear to my heart* 私にとって大切な題目

**cross my heart** ⇒ **CROSS**²

**from the (bottom of your) heart** ▶定義 in a way that is true and sincere 真実で本心から→心(の底)から, 本心から, 誠実に ‖ *I mean what I said from the bottom of my heart.* 私は誠実に本心を申し上げています.

**have a heart of gold** ▶定義 to be a very kind person 非常に親切な人である→心が優しい, 思いやりがある

**have/with sb's (best) interests at heart** ⇒ **INTEREST**¹

**heart and soul** ▶定義 with a lot of energy and enthusiasm 大変な精力と熱意をもって→全身全霊を打ち込んで, 熱心に, 全く

**your heart is not in sth** ▶定義 used to say that you are not very interested in or enthusiastic about sth 〜にあまり関心がない, または熱意を感じないことを言うのに用いて→心ここにあらず, 〜に上の空で, 身が入らずに

**your heart sinks** ▶定義 to suddenly feel disappointed or sad 突然失望または悲しみを感じる→がっかりする, 落ち込む ‖ *When I saw the queues of people in front of me my heart sank.* 私は目の前に行列する人々を見てがっかりしました.

**in your heart (of hearts)** ▶定義 used to say that you know that sth is true although you do not want to admit or believe it 認めたくない, または信じたくないが〜が真実であると分かっていると言うのに用いて→心の中で, 心の奥底で,

ひそかに ‖ *She knew in her heart of hearts that she was making the wrong decision.* 彼女は自分が間違った決定をしていると心の奥底で気付いていた.

**lose heart** ⇒ **LOSE**

**not have the heart (to do sth)** ▶定義 to be unable to do sth unkind 不親切な事をすることができない→～する勇気がない, ～するに忍びない, ～する気になれない ‖ *I didn't have the heart to say no.* 断る勇気がなかった.

**pour your heart out (to sb)** ⇒ **POUR**

**set your heart on sth; have your heart set on sth** ▶定義 to decide you want sth very much; to be determined to do or have sth ～を非常に欲しいと決心する; ～をする, または所有すると強く決心する→～を熱望する, ～に熱中する, ～すると心に決める

**take heart (from sth)** ▶定義 to begin to feel positive and hopeful about sth ～について肯定的で望みがあると感じ始める→(物・事で)気を取り直す, 元気を出す, 活気を取り戻す, 勇気づけられる

**take sth to heart** ▶定義 to be deeply affected or upset by sth ～に強く影響を受ける, または気が動転する→～を肝に銘じる, 心に留める, (不幸・不運など)をひどく気にする, 深く悲しむ

**to your heart's content** ▶定義 as much as you want 望むだけたくさん→心行くまで, 存分に, 気の済むまで

**with all your heart; with your whole heart** ▶定義 completely 完全に→心から喜んで, 心を込めて, 全く ‖ *I hope with all my heart that things work out for you.* あなたにとって事がうまく運べばいいと心から思っています.

**young at heart** ⇒ **YOUNG**[1]

**heartache** /háːrtèɪk/ 名 Ｕ ▶定義 great sadness or worry 深刻な悲しみ, または心配→心痛, 悲嘆, 心の痛手, 煩悶(はんもん)

**heart attack** 名 Ｃ ▶定義 a sudden serious illness when the heart stops working correctly, sometimes causing death 心臓の正常な機能が停止し, 時に死に至る突然の重い病気→心臓発作, 心臓まひ ‖ *She's had a heart attack.* 彼女は心臓発作に見舞われた.

**heartbeat** /háːrtbìːt/ 名 Ｃ ▶定義 the regular movement or sound of the heart as it sends blood round the body 心臓が血液を体中に送るときの規則的な動きまたは音→心臓の鼓動, 動悸(どうき)

**heartbreak** /háːrtbrèɪk/ 名 Ｕ ▶定義 very great sadness 非常に深い悲しみ→悲痛, 悲嘆, 断腸の思い

**heartbreaking** /háːrtbrèɪkɪŋ/ 形 ▶定義 making you feel very sad 非常に悲しい気持ちにさせる→胸の張り裂けるような, 断腸の思いの

**heartbroken** /háːrtbròʊk(ə)n/ (または **broken-hearted**) 形 ▶定義 extremely sad because of sth that has happened ある出来事のために極度に悲しい→(～で)深く傷付いた, 悲嘆に暮れた, 悲しみに満ちた ‖ *Mary was heartbroken when John left her.* ジョンに見捨てられ, メアリーは深く傷付いた.

**hearten** /háːrt(ə)n/ 動 他 (通常は受動態で) ▶定義 to encourage sb; to make sb feel happier ～を元気づける; ～にもっと幸せを感じさせる→～を励ます, 元気・勇気づける, 激励する ⇔ **dishearten**

**heartening** /háːrt(ə)nɪŋ/ 形 ▶定義 making you feel more hopeful; encouraging もっと望みがあると感じさせる; 元気づけられる→元気づける, 励みになる, 頼もしい, うれしい ⇔ **disheartening**

**heartfelt** /háːrtfèlt/ 形 ▶定義 deeply felt; sincere 深く感じた; 本心からの→(同情などが)心からの, 深く感じた, 偽りのない ‖ *a heartfelt apology* 心からの謝罪

**hearth** /hɑːrθ/ 名 Ｃ ▶定義 the place where you have an open fire in the house or the area in front of it 家の中で火を燃やす場所またはその正面の空間→炉床, 暖炉の前, 炉辺 ☛ **fireplace** のさし絵

**heartily** /háːrtɪli/ 副 ▶定義 **1** with obvious enthusiasm and enjoyment はっきりと熱意を見せ, 楽しんで→思う存分, 心から, 熱心に, 元気良く ‖ *He joined in heartily with the singing.* 彼はその歌に加わって熱唱した. ▶定義 **2** very much; completely→非常に; 完全に, 全く

**heartland** /háːrtlænd, -lənd/ 名 Ｃ ▶定義 the most central or important part of a country, area, etc 国, 地域などの最も中心となる, または重要な部分→(政治・経済・戦略上の)中核地域, 心臓地帯; 中心地, 心臓部 ‖ *Germany's industrial* *heartland* ドイツの産業中核地域

**heartless** /háːrtləs/ 形 ▶定義 unkind; cruel →不親切な; 冷酷な — heartlessly 副 →無情に, 冷酷に — heartlessness 名 Ⓤ →無情, 薄情, 冷酷さ

**heart-rending** 形 ▶定義 making you feel very sad とても悲しい気持ちにさせる →胸を引き裂くような, 悲痛な ‖ *The mother of the missing boy made a heart-rending appeal on television.* 行方不明になった男の子の母親はテレビで胸の詰まるような訴え掛けをした.

**heart-to-heart** 名 Ⓒ ▶定義 a conversation in which you say exactly what you really feel or think 実際に感じている事, または思っている事をはっきりと言う会話 →腹を割った話し合い, 打ち解けた会話 ‖ *John's teacher had a heart-to-heart with him to find out what was worrying him.* 先生はジョンが何を悩んでいるかを理解するため, 彼と腹を割った話し合いを持った.

**hearty** /háːrti/ 形 ▶定義1 showing warm and friendly feelings 暖かく友好的な気持ちを表す →心の温かい, 心からの, 親切な ‖ *a hearty welcome* 心からの歓迎 ▶定義2 loud, happy and full of energy 大きな声で, 楽しく活力に満ちて →元気な, 達者な, 力強い, 盛んな, (笑い声などが) 腹の底からの, はしゃいだ ‖ *a hearty laugh* 腹の底からの笑い声 ▶定義3 large; making you feel full 多量の; 満腹にさせる →たっぷりある, (人が) 食欲旺盛 (おうせい) な, (食欲などが) 旺盛な ‖ *a hearty appetite* 旺盛な食欲 ▶定義4 showing that you feel strongly about sth ～を強く感じていることを表して →激しい, 強い, 心底からの ‖ *He nodded his head in hearty agreement.* 彼は全く同感だとうなずいた.

*****heat**¹ /hiːt/ 名 ▶定義1 Ⓤ the feeling of sth hot 熱い物の感触 →熱, 熱さ, 温度 ‖ *This fire doesn't give out much heat.* この火はあまり熱を放出していません. ▶定義2 [単数扱い] (しばしば the を伴って) hot weather 暑い気候 →暑さ, 高温, 暑い天気・気候・季節 ‖ *I like the English climate because I can't stand the heat.* 私は暑さに耐えられないのでイギリスの気候が気に入っています. ▶定義3 [単数扱い] a thing that produces heat 熱を発するもの →(エネルギーとしての) 熱(源) ‖ *Remove the pan from the heat (= the hot part of the cooker).* なべを熱源 (= 調理器の熱い部分) から離しなさい. ▶定義4 Ⓤ a state or time of anger or excitement 怒ったり興奮したりしている状態, またはそうしている時間 →(怒り・興奮などの) 熱烈さ, 興奮, 情熱, 激怒, (議論・論争などの) 最高潮 ‖ *In the heat of the moment, she threatened to resign.* かっとした弾みで, 彼女は辞めると言って脅かした. ▶定義5 Ⓒ one of the first parts of a race or competition. The winners of the heats compete against other winners until the final result is decided. 競争または競技の最初の部分の1つ. heats の勝者は, 最終結果が出るまでほかの勝者と競い合う →(競技の) 1回, 予選

成句 **be on heat** ▶定義 (used about some female animals) to be ready to have sex because it is the right time of the year (ある種の動物の雌について) 1年のうちのしかるべき時で, 交尾する準備のできた →盛りがついている, 発情期の

*****heat**² /hiːt/ 動 Ⓘ Ⓣ ▶定義 **heat (sth) (up)** to become or to make sth hot or warm 熱くまたは暖かくなる, または～を熱くするまたは暖める →(物が) 熱くなる, 暖まる; 物を熱する, 暖める ‖ *Wait for the oven to heat up before you put the pie in.* オーブンが熱くなるまで待ってパイを中に入れます. *The meal is already cooked but it will need heating up.* この食事は調理済みですが, 暖める必要があるでしょう.

**heated** /híːtəd/ 形 ▶定義 (used about a person or discussion) angry or excited (人または議論について) 怒ったまたは興奮した →激した, 興奮した, 高ぶった ‖ *a heated argument/debate* 白熱した議論・ディベート — heatedly 副 →激して, 興奮して, 高ぶって

**heater** /híːtər/ 名 Ⓒ ▶定義 a machine used for making water or the air in a room, car, etc hotter 部屋, 車などの水または空気を暖めるのに用いる器械 →暖房・加熱器具, ストーブ, (車の) ヒーター ‖ *an electric/gas heater* 電気・ガスストーブ *a water heater* 湯沸かし器

**heath** /hiːθ/ 名 Ⓒ ▶定義 an area of open land that is not used for farming and that is often covered with rough grass and other wild plants 耕作地として使われていない広々とした地域で, 多くは雑草とそのほかの野生の植物で覆われている →(ヒースの生い茂った) 荒れ野, 荒れ地

**heather** /héðər/ 名 Ⓤ ▶定義 a low wild plant

that grows especially on hills and land that is not farmed and has small purple, pink or white flowers 背の低い野生の植物で、丘や耕作されていない土地に自生し、紫、ピンク、または白い小さな花をつける➡ヘザー（各種ヒースの総称）、ギョリュウモドキ

**heating** /híːtɪŋ/ 名 Ｕ ▶定義 a system for making rooms and buildings warm 部屋や建物を暖かくする方式➡暖房装置、暖房（設備）‖ *Our heating goes off at 10 pm and comes on again in the morning.* うちの暖房は午後10時に消えて、朝になるとまたつきます．☞参 **central heating**

**heatwave** /híːtwèɪv/ 名 Ｃ ▶定義 a period of unusually hot weather 異常に暑い気候の時期➡酷暑、熱波

**heave**¹ /híːv/ 動 ▶定義 1 Ｃ Ｕ to lift, pull or throw sb/sth heavy with one big effort 重い〜を1度の多大な努力で持ち上げる、引っ張る、または投げる➡（重い物）を力を入れて持ち上げる、（石など）を持ち上げて（〜に）投げる‖ *Take hold of this rope and heave!* このロープをつかんで引っ張りなさい．*We heaved the cupboard up the stairs.* 私たちは戸棚を2階まで持ち上げました．▶定義 2 Ｃ heave (with sth) to move up and down or in and out in a heavy but regular way 激しいけれども規則的に上下に、または出たり入ったりの動きをする➡（波・地面などが）うねる、上下動を繰り返す、（胸などが）（激しい息遣いで）波打つ、あえぐ‖ *His chest was heaving with the effort of carrying the cooker.* 彼はそのレンジを懸命に運んだので、息遣いで胸が波打っていた． ▶定義 3 Ｃ to experience the tight feeling you get in your stomach when you are just about to vomit 今にもおう吐しそうなときに胃が締め付けられる感じを経験する➡むかつく、（胃が）むかむかする、吐き気を催す‖ *The sight of all that blood made her stomach heave.* 彼女は辺り一面の血を見て、吐き気を催した．

成句 **heave a sigh** ▶定義 to breathe out slowly and loudly ゆっくりと大きな音を立てて息を吐き出す➡胸をなで下ろす、大きなため息をつく‖ *He heaved a sigh of relief when he heard the good news.* 彼はその良い知らせを聞いてほっと胸をなで下ろしました．

**heave**² /híːv/ 名 Ｃ Ｕ ▶定義 a strong pull, push, throw, etc 強く引く、押す、投げるなどすること➡（力を入れて）持ち上げること、たぐり寄せること

**heaven** /hév(ə)n/ ▶定義 1 [単数扱い] the place where, in some religions, it is believed that God lives and where good people go when they die ある宗教において、神が住む所で善人が死んだときそこへ行くと信じられている場所➡天国、極楽‖ *to go to/be in heaven* 天国に行く・天国にいる ☞参 **hell**

▶ heaven はいくつかの表現において God の代わりに用いられるが、一部の人々はそれを無礼な表現と見なしている．God の注を参照．

▶定義 2 Ｕ Ｃ a place or a situation in which you are very happy 人がとても幸福である場所または状況➡天国のような所、楽園、極楽、至上の幸福‖ *It was heaven being away from work for a week.* 1週間仕事から離れるのは天国のようでした．▶定義 3 **the heavens** [複数扱い] (used in poetry and literature) the sky (詩や文学に用いて) 空➡天、（地球から見た）空

**heavenly** /hév(ə)nli/ 形 ▶定義 1 （名詞の前だけ）connected with heaven or the sky 天国または空に関連して➡天国の、天来の、えもいわれない、神聖な、神々（こうごう）しい、天の、天空の‖ *heavenly bodies* (= the sun, moon, stars, etc) 天体 (= 太陽、月、恒星など) ▶定義 2 略式 very pleasant; wonderful 非常に愉快な；すばらしい➡とても楽しい、すばらしい、とても美しい

＊**heavy** /hévi/ 形 (**heavier**; **heaviest**) ▶定義 1 weighing a lot; difficult to lift or move 重量が重い；持ち上げるまたは動かすのが難しい➡重い、重たい、比重の大きい‖ *This box is too heavy for me to carry.* この箱は重すぎて私には運べません．▶定義 2 used when asking or stating how much sb/sth weighs 〜がどれだけの重量か尋ねるまたは述べるのに用いて➡（特定の）重さのある‖ *How heavy is your suitcase?* あなたのスーツケースはどれくらいの重さですか．▶定義 3 larger, stronger or more than usual 普通よりも大きい、強いまたは多い➡（量・程度・力などが）大きい、すごい、たっぷりの、（風・雨などが）強い、（交通が）激しい、（眠りが）深い、（食事が）こってりとした、胃にもたれる‖ *heavy rain* 豪雨 *heavy traffic* 激しい交通量 *a heavy smoker/drinker* (=

*a person who smokes/drinks a lot)* ヘビースモーカー・大酒飲み (= たくさんたばこを吸う・飲む人) *The sound of his heavy (= loud and deep) breathing told her that he was asleep.* 深い (= 大きくて深い) 寝息を立てたので、彼女は彼が眠っていると分かりました. *a heavy sleeper (= sb who is difficult to wake)* 眠りの深い人 (= 目を覚ましにくい人) *a heavy meal* (胃に) もたれる食事 ▶定義 4 serious, difficult or boring 深刻な、難しい、またはつまらない→**物々しい、深刻な、難解な、読みづらい、退屈な、面白くない** ‖ *His latest novel makes **heavy reading**.* 彼の最新の小説は読みづらいです. *Things got a bit heavy when she started talking about her failed marriage.* 彼女が破局を迎えた結婚生活のことを話し始めると、少々重苦しい雰囲気になった. ▶定義 5 full of hard work; (too) busy きつい仕事がたくさんある; (あまりにも) 忙しい→**(時・時間表などに) 仕事がぎっしり詰まった、多忙な** ‖ *a heavy day/schedule/timetable* 多忙な1日、ぎっしり詰まったスケジュール・予定表 ▶定義 6 (used about a material or substance) solid or thick (素材または物質について) 頑丈なまたは厚い→**(霧などが) 濃い、(服などが) 厚手の、(土地が) ぬかるんだ、歩きにくい** ‖ *heavy soil* 粘土質の (粘つく) 土壌 *a heavy coat* 厚手のコート ⇔ すべての定義 light — **heavily** 副→**重く、重そうに、激しく、濃密に** — **heaviness** 名 U→**重いこと、重さ、無気力、重苦しさ**

成句 **make heavy weather of sth** ▶定義 to make sth seem more difficult than it really is 〜を実際よりも難しく見えるようにする→**〜の困難さを誇張する、〜をおおげさに考える**

**heavy-duty** 形 ▶定義 not easily damaged and therefore suitable for regular use or for hard physical work 容易には傷付かないので、定期的使用または激しい肉体労働に適している→**頑丈な、丈夫な、酷使に耐える** ‖ *a heavy-duty carpet/tyre* 耐久性のあるじゅうたん・タイヤ

**heavy-handed** 形 ▶定義 1 not showing much understanding of other people's feelings 他人の気持ちにあまり理解を示さない→**ぞんざいな、がさつな、荒っぽい、高圧的な** ‖ *a heavy-handed approach* 荒っぽいアプローチ ▶定義 2 using unnecessary force 必要以上に力を使った→**厳しい、容赦しない** ‖ *heavy-handed police methods* 警察の重圧的やり方

**heavy industry** 名 C U ▶定義 industry that uses large machinery to produce metal, coal, vehicles, etc 金属、石炭、車両などを生産するため大型の機械を使用する産業→**重工業**

**heavy metal** 名 U ▶定義 a style of very loud rock music that is played on electric instruments 電子式の楽器で演奏される、非常に大きい音を出すロック音楽の様式→**ヘビーメタル**

**heavyweight** /héviwèit/ 名 C ▶定義 a person who is in the heaviest weight group in certain fighting sports ある種の格闘技で最も重量の重いグループに属する人→**ヘビー級のボクサー、ヘビー級の重量挙げ・レスリング選手** ‖ *the world heavyweight boxing champion* ボクシングのヘビー級の世界チャンピオン

**heckle** /hék(ə)l/ 動 他 自 ▶定義 to interrupt a speaker at a public meeting with difficult questions or rude comments 公式の会合で演説している人を、難しい質問または失礼なコメントなどで遮る→**(演説者を) (しつこく) やじる、邪魔する、やり込める** — **heckler** 名 C→**(弁士などを) 質問攻めにする人、やじり倒す人**

**hectare** /héktèər/ 名 C (略 ha) ▶定義 a measurement of land; 10000 square metres 土地の大きさ; 1万平方メートル→**ヘクタール (面積の単位)**

**hectic** /héktɪk/ 形 ▶定義 very busy with a lot of things that you have to do quickly すぐにしなければならない事が多くあって忙しい→**大変忙しい、てんやわんやの、大騒ぎの** — **hectically** /-k(ə)li/ 副→**てんてこまいで、多忙で**

**he'd** /(h)id, hi:d/ HE HAD; HE WOULD の短縮形

*★**hedge**¹ /hedʒ/ 名 C ▶定義 a row of bushes or trees planted close together at the edge of a garden or field to separate one piece of land from another ある土地を別の土地と区分けしている、庭または畑の端に間を詰めて植えられている一列の低木または木→**生け垣、垣根** ☛ C7 ページのさし絵

**hedge**² /hedʒ/ 動 自 ▶定義 to avoid giving a direct answer to a question 質問に対し直接答えるのを避ける→**(〜について) 言葉を濁す、はぐらかす**

成句 **hedge your bets** ▶定義 to protect yourself

against losing or making a mistake by supporting more than one person or opinion 複数の人または意見を支持することにより、負けたり、間違うことから身を守る→かけ金を分散する, 危険を分散・回避する, 丸損を防ぐため両掛けする

**hedgehog** /hédʒhɒ(ː)g/ 名 C ▶定義 a small brown animal covered with sharp needles (prickles) 鋭い針（とげ）で覆われた小さな茶色の動物→ハリネズミ, ヤマアラシ

hedgehog
prickle

**hedgerow** /hédʒroʊ/ 名 C ▶定義 a row of bushes, etc especially at the side of a country road or around a field 特に田舎道の傍ら、または畑の回りに巡らしてある, 一列になった低木など→(田舎の)生け垣, (生け垣の)低木の列

**heed**[1] /hiːd/ 動他 正式 ▶定義 to pay attention to advice, a warning, etc 忠告, 警告などに注意を払う→(人・忠告など)に注意する, 〜を心に留める

**heed**[2] /hiːd/ 名 正式
成句 take heed (of sb/sth); pay heed (to sb/sth) ▶定義 to pay careful attention to what sb says 〜の言うことに入念な注意を払う→〜を心に留めておく, 〜に気を付ける, 十分注意を払う‖ *You should take heed of your doctor's advice.* 医者の忠告には十分注意を払うべきです.

*heel[1] /hiːl/ 名 C ▶定義 1 the back part of your foot 足の後ろの部分→(人の)かかと, (馬などの)後ろひづめ, (動物の)後ろ足 ☞ C5 ページのさし絵 ▶定義 2 the part of a sock, etc that covers your heel 靴下などのかかとを覆う部分→(靴・靴下の)かかと（部）▶定義 3 the higher part of a shoe under the heel of your foot 足のかかとの下に来る靴の高くなった部分→(靴の)かかと, ハイヒール‖ *High heels (= shoes with high heels) are not practical for long walks.* ハイヒール（＝かかとの高い靴）は長距離歩くのに向いていません. ☞ shoe のさし絵 ▶定義 4 -heeled having the type of heel mentioned 言及されたような種類のかかとを持った→〜ヒールの, かかとが〜の‖ *high-heeled/low-heeled shoes* かかとが高い・低い靴

成句 dig your heels in ⇒ **DIG**[1]

head over heels ⇒ **HEAD**[1]

**heel**[2] /hiːl/ 動他 ▶定義 to repair the heel of a shoe 靴のかかとを修理する→(靴など)にかかとを付ける, (靴)のかかとを直す

**hefty** /héfti/ 形 略式 ▶定義 big and strong or heavy 大きくて強いまたは重い→がっしりした, たくましい, ずっしりと重い‖ *a hefty young man* がっしりした若者

*height /haɪt/ 名 ▶定義 1 C U the measurement from the bottom to the top of a person or thing 人または物の一番下から最高点までの寸法→高さ, 身長‖ *The nurse is going to check your height and weight.* その看護婦があなたの身長と体重を調べることになっています. *We need a fence that's about two metres in height.* 私たちは高さ約2メートルのフェンスが必要だ. 形 **high** ☞参 **tall** の注 ☞ **length** のさし絵 ▶定義 2 U the fact that sb/sth is tall or high 〜が背丈が高いという事実→背丈が高いこと, 長身, 高いこと‖ *He looks older than he is because of his height.* 彼は背が高いので実際より年上に見えます. ▶定義 3 C U the distance that sth is above the ground 〜の地面からの距離→高度, 海抜, 標高‖ *We are now flying at a height of 10000 metres.* 現在高度1万メートルで飛行中です.
▶飛行機は高度を gain (上げる) または lose (下げる) と言う. 飛行機に関して話すとき, 高度を表す正式な語は altitude.

▶定義 4 [C, 通常は複数] a high place or area 高い場所または地域→高い所, 高地, 丘, 高台‖ *I can't go up there. I'm afraid of heights.* 私はそこへは上れません. 高所恐怖症です. ▶定義 5 U the strongest or most important part of sth 〜の最強または最重要な部分→絶頂, 極致, 最高潮, 最中‖ *the height of summer* 夏真っ盛り

**heighten** /háɪt(ə)n/ 動自他 ▶定義 to become or to make sth greater or stronger 大きくまたは強くなる; 〜を大きくまたは強くする→高まる, 増す, 強まる; 〜を高める, 増やす, 強める‖ *I'm using yellow paint to heighten the sunny effect of the room.* この部屋は日当たりの効果を高めるため黄色の塗料を使っています.

**heir** /eər/ 名 C ▶定義 heir (to sth) the person with the legal right to receive (inherit) money, property or a title when the owner dies 所有者が死んだときに, お金, 所有物, または称号を受

け取る(相続する)法的権利を持つ人➡(**遺産の**)**相続人, 跡取り,** (**王位・役職などの**) **継承者, 後継者** || *He's the heir to a large fortune.* 彼はばく大な財産の相続人です.

▶女性の相続人はしばしば heiress と呼ばれる.

**heirloom** /éərlùːm/ 名 C ▶定義 something valuable that has belonged to the same family for many years 同じ一族に長年属してきた価値のあるもの➡**先祖伝来の家財・家宝, 家の伝統**

**held** HOLD¹ の過去・過去分詞形

\***helicopter** /hélɪkɑ̀ptər, híː-/ (または 略式 **chopper**) 名 C ▶定義 a small aircraft that can go straight up into the air. Helicopters have long thin metal parts on top that go round. 直接空中に上がることができる小型の航空機. てっぺんに, 回転する長くて薄い金属の部品がある➡**ヘリコプター**

**he'll** /(h)ɪl, hiːl/ HE WILL の短縮形

**hell** /hel/ 名 ▶定義 **1** [単数扱い] the place where, in some religions, it is believed that the Devil lives and where bad people go to when they die ある宗教において, 悪魔が住む所で悪い人が死んだときそこに行くと信じられている場所➡**地獄, 冥土(めいど)** || *to go to/be in hell* 地獄に落ちる・いる ☞参 **heaven** ▶定義 **2** C U 略式 a situation or place that is very unpleasant or painful 非常に不快または苦痛の状況または場所➡**生き地獄, 地獄のような場所・状態, 逆境** || *He went through hell when his wife left him.* 彼は妻に出ていかれて, 地獄のような苦しみを味わった. ☞ 要注意. hell の以下の意味と成句を無礼と見なす人もいる. ▶定義 **3** U (俗語) used as a swear word to show anger 怒りを表して悪態をつく言葉として用いて➡**畜生, 断じて** || *Oh hell, I've forgotten my money!* 畜生, 金を忘れてきた. ▶定義 **4 the hell** (俗語) used as a swear word in questions to show anger or surprise 疑問文で, 怒りまたは驚きを表し, 悪態をつく言葉として用いて➡**一体全体, 〜なんてとんでもない** || *Why the hell didn't you tell me this before?* なんでまたそれを前もって話してくれなかったのですか.

成句 **a/one hell of a...** 略式 ▶定義 used to make an expression stronger or to mean 'very' 表現を強める, または「とても」を意味するのに用いて➡**どえらい〜, すごい〜, とんでもない〜** || *He got into a hell of a fight (= a terrible fight).* 彼はひどいけんか(= ものすごいけんか)に巻き込まれた.

**all hell broke loose** 略式 ▶定義 there was suddenly a lot of noise and confusion 突然たくさんの騒音と混乱に見舞われた➡**大変なことになった, 世の中がひっくり返った**

**(just) for the hell of it** 略式 ▶定義 for fun 楽しみで➡**ほんの冗談に, 面白半分に, 一時的に興奮して, 魔が差して**

**give sb hell** 略式 ▶定義 to speak to sb very angrily or to be very strict with sb とても怒って〜に話をする, または〜に非常に厳しくする➡**〜をしかりつける, 怒鳴りつける, ひどい目に遭わせる, 居たたまれないようにする**

**like hell** 略式 ▶定義 very much; with a lot of effort 非常にたくさん; とても努力して➡**猛烈に, 死ぬほど** || *I'm working like hell at the moment.* 私はただ今, 猛烈に働いて[勉強して]います.

**hellish** /hélɪʃ/ 形 ▶定義 terrible; awful ひどい; 恐ろしい➡**地獄のような, 大変困難な・不快な** || *a hellish experience* 地獄のような経験

\***hello** (英 または **hallo**) /həlóu, hélou/ 間 ▶定義 used when you meet sb, for attracting sb's attention or when you are using the telephone 〜に会ったとき, 〜の注意をひくために, または電話を使うときに用いて➡**やあ, こんにちは, あのう, ちょっと, おい, (電話で)もしもし**

**helm** /helm/ 名 C ▶定義 the part of a boat or ship that is used to guide it. The helm can be a handle or a wheel. ある方向に進めるのに使われるボートまたは船の一部分. 取っ手またはハンドルになっていることがある➡**かじ, 舵柄(だへい), 舵輪, 操舵装置**

成句 **at the helm** ▶定義 in charge of an organization, group of people, etc 組織, 人々の集団などを統制して➡**かじを取って, 支配的地位に, 実権を握って**

**helmet** /hélmət/ 名 C ▶定義 a type of hard hat that you wear to protect your head 硬い帽子の一種で, 頭を保護するためにかぶる➡**ヘルメット, (フェンシング)面, (フットボール)ヘルメット** || *a crash helmet* 安全ヘルメット(自動車レーサー・オートバイ乗りなどが用いる) ☞ S1 ページのさし絵

\***help¹** /help/ 動 ▶定義 **1** 自 他 help (sb) (with

## help²

sth); help (sb) (to) do sth; help sb (across, over, out of, into, etc) to do sth for sb in order to be useful or to make sth easier for him/her ～の役に立つように、または～にとって…が容易になるように、その～のために…をする➔**人を手伝う，手助けする，(人が)～するのを手伝う，助ける** ‖ *Can I help?* お手伝いしましょうか． *Could you help me with the cooking?* 料理を手伝ってくださいますか． *I helped her to organize the day.* 私は彼女が1日の計画を立てるのを手助けした． *My son's helping in our shop at the moment.* 今のところ息子はうちの店を手伝っています． *She helped her grandmother up the stairs (= supported her as she climbed the stairs).* 彼女は祖母が階段を上るのを助けた(＝祖母が階段を上る時支えてあげた)． ▶定義2 ⦿ to make sth better or easier ～をもっと良く，またはもっと楽にする➔**(苦痛・病気などを)和らげる，軽減する，楽にする，(欠陥などを)補う，救う** ‖ *If you apologize to him it might help.* あなたが彼に謝れば効果があるかもしれません． *This medicine should help your headache.* この薬で頭痛が和らぐはずです． ▶定義3 ⦿ help yourself (to sth) to take sth (especially food and drink) that is offered to you 出された物(特に食べ物や飲み物)を取る➔**(食べ物・飲み物などを)自分で取って食べる・飲む・吸う，自分で取って使う** ‖ *'Can I borrow your pen?' 'Yes, help yourself.'* 「ペンをお借りしてもよろしいですか」「ええ，どうぞ」 ▶定義4 ⦿ help yourself to sth to take sth without asking permission; to steal 許可を得ずに～を取る；盗む➔**物を失敬する，盗む，横領する** ▶定義5 ⦿ (口語) used to get sb's attention when you are in danger or difficulty 危険または困難な状況にあるときに～の注意をひくのに用いて➔**助けて，だれか** ‖ *Help! I'm going to fall!* 助けて．落っこちそうだ．

成句 **can/can't/couldn't help sth** ▶定義 be able/not be able to stop or avoid doing sth ～をするのをやめる，または避けることができる・できない➔**～せずにいる・せずにはいられない，～を避ける・するのは仕方ない，思わず～してしまう** ‖ *It was so funny I couldn't help laughing.* あまりおかしかったので笑わずにはいられませんでした． *I just couldn't help myself - I had to laugh.* どうにも我慢できなかった － 思わず笑い出してしまった．

**a helping hand** ▶定義 some help いくらかの助け➔**手伝い，援助(の手)** ‖ *My neighbour is always ready to give me a helping hand.* 近所の人はいつでも喜んで私を手伝ってくれます．

句動詞 **help (sb) out** ▶定義 to help sb in a difficult situation; to give money to help sb 困っている状況の～を助ける；金を与えて～を援助する➔**救出する，手を貸す，～を援助する，(人を)助けて切り抜けさせる**

*★**help²** /help/ 名 ▶定義1 ❶ help (with sth) the act of helping 助ける行為➔**助け，助力，救済** ‖ *Do you need any help with that?* その事で何か助けが必要ですか． *This map isn't much help.* この地図はあまり役に立ちません． *She stopped smoking with the help of her family and friends.* 彼女は家族と友達の助けを借りてたばこをやめました． *'Run and get help - my son's fallen in the river!'* 「走って助けを呼んで来てくれ － うちの息子が川に落ちてしまった」 ▶定義2 [単数扱い] **a help (to sb)** a person or thing that helps➔**助けになる人・物，役立つ人・物** ‖ *Your directions were a great help - we found the place easily.* あなたが行き方を教えてくれてとても助かりました － その場所は簡単に見つかりました．

**helper** /hélpər/ 名 ❻ ▶定義 a person who helps (especially with work) (特に仕事を)手伝ってくれる人➔**助ける人，救助者，助手，お手伝い，後援者，慰安者**

*★**helpful** /hélpfl, -f(ə)l/ 形 ▶定義 giving help **助けになる，役立つ，有益な，重宝な** ‖ *helpful advice* 役立つ忠告 ― **helpfully** 副 ➔**助けになって，役に立つように** ― **helpfulness** 名 ❿➔**助けになること，有用性**

**helping** /hélpɪŋ/ 名 ❻ ▶定義 the amount of food that is put on a plate at one time 一度にお皿の上に盛り付けられた食べ物の量➔**(食べ物の)1杯，一盛り** ‖ *After two helpings of pasta, I couldn't eat any more.* パスタを2皿も食べた後，それ以上食べられませんでした． ☛参**portion**

**helpless** /hélpləs/ 形 ▶定義 unable to take care of yourself or do things without the help of other people 自分の面倒を見ることができな

い、または他人の助けを借りずに物事をすることができない→(病人・赤ん坊などが)自分ではどうすることもできない,自分で用の足せない,無力な,手も足も出ない‖ *a helpless baby* 自分では何もできない赤ん坊 — **helplessly** 副 ▶どうしようもなく,力なく,頼るものなく,困惑して‖ *They watched helplessly as their house went up in flames.* 彼らは家が炎に包まれるのをなすすべもなく見ていた. — **helplessness** 名 Ⓤ →どうしようもないこと,無力

**hem**¹ /hem/ 名 Ⓒ ▶定義 the edge at the bottom of a piece of cloth (especially on a skirt, dress or trousers) that has been turned up and sewn 服地(特にスカート,ワンピース,またはズボン)のすそのへりで,折り返して縫ってあるもの→(布の)へり,(衣服の)ヘム,へり ☞ C6 ページのさし絵

**hem**² /hem/ 動 (**hemming**; **hemmed**) ▶定義 to turn up and sew the bottom of a piece of clothing or cloth 洋服または布のすそを折り返して縫う→(布・衣服の)へりを(折り返して)縫う,まつる,～の縁取りをする

句動詞 **hem sb in** ▶定義 to surround sb and prevent him/her from moving away ～を取り囲んでどこかへ行ってしまうのを防ぐ→～を囲む,取り巻く,閉じ込める,～を(精神的に)身動きできなくする,がんじがらめにする‖ *We were hemmed in by the crowd and could not leave.* 私たちは人込みに取り巻かれて身動きが取れませんでした.

**hemisphere** /héməsfɪər/ 名 Ⓒ ▶定義 1 one half of the earth 地球の半分→(地球・天球の)半球(の地図)‖ *the northern/southern/eastern/western hemisphere* 北・南・東・西半球 ☞ **earth** のさし絵 ▶定義 2 the shape of half a ball; half a sphere 半球の形;半球→半球(体),(大脳の)半球

**hemophilia, hemophiliac** 米 = **HAEMOPHILIA, HAEMOPHILIAC**

**hemorrhage** 米 = **HAEMORRHAGE**

**hemorrhoids** 米 = **HAEMORRHOIDS**

**hemp** /hemp/ 名 Ⓤ ▶定義 a plant that is used for making rope and rough cloth and for producing an illegal drug (cannabis) ロープや目の粗い布を作ったり,また不法な薬物(カンナビス)を製造するのに用いられる植物→アサ(麻),タイマ(大麻)

★**hen** /hen/ 名 Ⓒ ▶定義 1 a female bird that is kept for its eggs or its meat 卵または肉をとるため飼育される雌の鳥→雌鶏(めんどり),雌のひよこ,鶏 ☞参 **chicken** の注とさし絵 ▶定義 2 the female of any type of bird あらゆる種類の雌の鳥→(一般に)雌の鳥,(鳥が)雌の‖ *a hen pheasant* 雌のキジ

▶ 雄の鳥は **cock**.

**hence** /hens/ 副 正式 ▶定義 for this reason この理由により→それゆえに,したがって‖ *I've got some news to tell you - hence the letter.* あなたにお知らせする事があります－それでこの手紙を書いてきました.

**henceforth** /hénsfɔːrθ, -ˈ-/ (または **henceforward** /hénsfɔːrwərd/) 副 (文) ▶定義 from now on; in future 今から;将来→今後は,これからは

**henchman** /héntʃmən/ 名 Ⓒ (複 **-men** /-mən/) ▶定義 a person who is employed by sb to protect him/her and who may do things that are illegal or violent ～を守るためにその～から雇われており,違法または暴力的な事をすることがある人→(政界・暗黒街のボスの)取り巻き,子分,共犯者,信頼のおける部下,側近

**hen party** (または **hen night**) 名 [単数扱い] ▶定義 a party that a woman who is getting married soon has with her female friends 間もなく結婚する女性が女友達と開くパーティー→女性だけのパーティー ☞参 **stag night**

**henpecked** /hénpèkt/ 形 ▶定義 used to describe a husband who always does what his wife tells him to do いつも妻の指図に従っている夫を描写するのに用いて→女房のしりに敷かれた,恐妻家の

**hepatitis** /hèpətáɪtəs/ 名 Ⓤ ▶定義 a serious disease of one of the body's main organs (liver) 身体の主要な臓器の1つ(肝臓)の深刻な病気→肝炎

★**her**¹ /(h)ər, həːr/ 代 (動詞または前置詞の目的語) ▶定義 the female person that was mentioned earlier 前述された女の人→彼女を,彼女に‖ *He told Sue that he loved her.* 彼はスーに彼女(スー)を愛していると言った. *I've got a letter for your mother. Could you give it to her, please?* 私はあなたのお母様あての手紙を持っています. どうか彼女に渡していただけますか. ☞参 **she** と **he** の注

**her²** /(h)ər, hɜːr/ 代 ▶定義 of or belonging to the female person mentioned earlier 前述された女の人の、またはその人に属する→**彼女の** ‖ *That's her book. She left it there this morning.* それは彼女の本です。彼女が今朝そこへ置いていきました。*Fiona has broken her leg.* フィオナは足を骨折しています。 ☞参 **hers**

**herald** /hérəld/ 動他 (文) ▶定義 to be a sign that sb/sth is going to happen soon 〜が間もなく起こるであろう前触れとなる→**〜の先触れをする、〜を布告する、予告する** ‖ *The minister's speech heralded a change of policy.* その大臣の演説は政策の変更を予告していました。

**herb** /əːb, hɜːrb/ 名 C ▶定義 a plant whose leaves, seeds, etc are used in medicine or in cooking 葉や種などが薬や調理に用いられる植物→**ハーブ、香草、薬草** ‖ *Add some herbs, such as rosemary and thyme.* ローズマリーやタイムなどのハーブを加えます。 ☞参 **spice**

**herbal** /ɜ́ːrb(ə)l, hɜ́ːrb-/ 形 ▶定義 made of or using herbs ハーブで作った、またはハーブを使った→**ハーブの、香草の、薬草の** ‖ *herbal medicine/remedies* ハーブを使った薬・療法

**herd¹** /hɜːrd/ 名 C ▶定義 a large number of animals that live and feed together 一緒に生活してえさをとる多数の動物→**(動物の) 群れ** ‖ *a herd of cattle/deer/elephants* 牛・シカ・象の群れ ☞参 **flock**

**herd²** /hɜːrd/ 動他 ▶定義 to move people or animals somewhere together in a group 人々または動物を集団でまとめてどこかへ移動させる→**(人・家畜) を集める、駆り立てる、〜の群れを番する・導く、(人の集団) を目的地に導く** ‖ *The prisoners were herded onto the train.* 囚人たちはその列車へと駆り立てられた。

**here¹** /hɪər/ 副 ▶定義1 (動詞または前置詞の後で) in, at or to the place where you are or which you are pointing to 自分のいる、または指し示している場所に [で・へ]→**ここに、ここで、こちらへ** ‖ *Come (over) here.* さあ、こちらにこなさい。*The school is a mile from here.* 学校はここから1マイルです。*Please sign here.* ここに署名してください。 ▶定義2 used at the beginning of a sentence to introduce or draw attention to sb/sth 文頭に用いて、〜を導入する、またはそれらに注意を向ける働きをする→**ここで、こちらは、さあ、ほら、おい** ‖ *Here is the nine o'clock news.* ここで9時のニュースです。*Here comes the bus.* ほら、バスが来た。*Here we are (= we've arrived).* さあ着きました (= 到着しました)。
▶最後の例文の語順に注意。名詞の場合は *Here are the children.* (ここに子供がいます) と言うが代名詞になると、*Here they are.* (ほら、ここに彼らがいます) となる。*Here you are.* (はい、どうぞ) という表現にも注意。この表現は、だれかに何かを渡すときに用いられる: *Here you are - this is that book I was talking about.* (さあどうぞ — これがお話ししていた例の本です。)
▶定義3 (used for emphasizing a noun) (名詞を強調するために用いて)→**ここにある・いる** ‖ *I think you'll find this book here very useful.* ここにあるこの本はとても役に立つことがお分かりになると思いますよ。 ▶定義4 at this point in a discussion or a piece of writing 議論または一編の書き物の、この時点において→**ここで、この点で、この時に** ‖ *Here the speaker stopped and looked around the room.* ここで話し手は語るのをやめて部屋を見回した。

---

▶語法

*Here you are.* と *Here it is.* の違い

どちらも「はい、どうぞ」の意味になりますが、相手に差し出す物が異なります。*Here you are.* の場合には制限がありませんが、*Here it is.* の場合は既に話題になった特定の物に限ってのみ使用可能です。例えば、*Where is my eraser?* に対する応答は *Here you are. / Here it is.* (複数の場合は *Here they are.*) のどちらでも構いません。しかし、*Do you have an eraser?* に対する応答には *Here you are.* しか使えません。

---

成句 **here and there** ▶定義 in various places あらゆる場所で→**あちこちに [で]、ここかしこで**

**here goes** 略式 ▶定義 used to say that you are about to do sth exciting, dangerous, etc わくわくするような事や、危険な事などをこれからすると言うときに用いて→**さあやるぞ、それ** ‖ *I've never done a backward dive before, but here goes!* 後ろ向きの飛び込みはまだやったことがないのですが、さあやりますよ。

**here's to sb/sth** ▶定義 used for wishing for the health, success, etc of sb/sth while holding a drink 酒を手に持ちながら、〜の健康、成功などを祈るのに用いて→**〜のために乾杯、〜を祝して、願って** ‖ *Here's to a great holiday!* すばらしい休日に乾杯.

**neither here nor there** ▶定義 not important 重要でない→(物事が) **見当外れだ、問題外だ、取るに足らない、大したことではない** ‖ *My opinion is neither here nor there. If you like the dress then buy it.* 私の意見など大したことじゃないよ. そのドレスが気に入ったのならお買いなさい.

**here**² /hɪər/ 間 ▶定義 used for attracting sb's attention, when offering help or when giving sth to sb 〜に助けを申し出る、または〜に…を与えるとき、その〜の注意をひくのに用いて→**さあ、ほら、おい、はい、さあどうぞ** ‖ *Here, let me help!* さあ、手を貸しましょう.

**hereabouts** /híərəbàuts/ (困 **hereabout**) 副 ▶定義 around or near here→(どこか) **この辺で [に], この辺りに, (この) 近所に**

**hereafter** /hìərǽftər, -ráːf-/ 副 (文) ▶定義 (used in legal documents, etc) from now on (法的な書類などに用いて) この時点から→**今後は, 将来は**

**hereditary** /hərédət(ə)ri, -tèri/ 形 ▶定義 passed on from parent to child 親から子に受け継がれた→**世襲の, 相続権のある, 遺伝 (性) の, 代々の, 親譲りの, 伝統的な** ‖ *a hereditary disease* 遺伝性の病気

**heredity** /hərédəti/ 名 ● ▶定義 the process by which physical or mental qualities pass from parent to child 親から子へ身体的または精神的性質が受け継がれる過程→**遺伝 (形質), 遺伝傾向**

**heresy** /hérəsi/ 名 ● ● (複 **heresies**) ▶定義 a (religious) opinion or belief that is different from what is generally accepted to be true 一般的に真実だと受け入れられているものと異なった (宗教的) 意見または信念→**(キリスト教・定説などに対する) 異端, 異説, 異端信仰・行動**

**heretic** /hérətɪk/ 名 ● ▶定義 a person whose religious beliefs are believed to be wrong or evil 間違ったまたは邪悪な宗教的信念を持っていると信じられている人→(特にローマカトリック教会から見て) **異教徒, 異端者, 反対論者** — **heretical** /hərétɪk(ə)l/ 形 →**異教 (徒) の, 異端 (者) の, 正統でない**

# heroine 797

**heritage** /hérətɪdʒ/ 名 [ ●, 通常は単数] ▶定義 the traditions, qualities and culture of a country that have existed for a long time and that have great importance for the country ある国に長年存在してきて、その国にとって大変重要な伝統, 性質, 文化→**文化的遺産, 伝統**

**hermit** /háːmət/ 名 ● ▶定義 a person who prefers to live alone, without contact with other people 他人との接触をせずに、1人で生きることを好む人→**隠者, 世捨て人, 行者, 隠遁 (いんとん) 者, 独居者**

**hernia** /háːmɪə/ ( または **rupture**) 名 ● ● ▶定義 the medical condition in which an organ inside the body, for example the stomach, pushes through the wall of muscle which surrounds it 体内 (例えば腹部) の臓器がそれを取り囲んでいる筋肉の壁を押して出る病状→**ヘルニア, 脱腸**

*****hero** /híəroʊ, híː-/ 名 ● (複 **heroes**) ▶定義 **1** a person who is admired, especially for having done sth difficult or good 特に困難なまたは良い事を行ったために, 賞賛されている人→**英雄, 勇士, 偉人, 理想的人物** ‖ *The team were given a hero's welcome on their return home.* そのチームは故郷へ帰ると英雄的歓迎を受けた.

▶定義 **2** the most important male character in a book, play, film, etc 本, 劇, 映画などにおいて最も重要な男の登場人物→**(小説・劇・詩などの男の) 主人公** ‖ *The hero of the film is a little boy.* この映画の主人公は小さな男の子です. ☛参 **heroine, villain**

**heroic** /hɪróʊɪk/ 形 ▶定義 (used about people or their actions) having a lot of courage (人々またはその行為について) 多大な勇気がある→**英雄の, 英雄的な, 〜にふさわしい, 大胆な, とても勇敢な, 高潔な** ‖ *a heroic effort* 英雄的な努力 — **heroically** /-k(ə)li/ 副 →**英雄にふさわしく, 大胆に, とても勇敢に**

**heroin** /hérouən/ 名 ● ▶定義 a powerful illegal drug that some people take for pleasure and then cannot stop taking 快楽のため使用し, やめることができなくなる人がいる強力な違法薬物→**ヘロイン**

**heroine** /hérouɪn, hɪər-/ 名 ● ▶定義 **1** a woman who is admired, especially for having done sth difficult or good 特に困難なまたは良い事をしたために，賞賛されている女性→**英雄的女性，女傑，女丈夫（じょじょうふ）** ▶定義2 the most important female character in a book, play, film, etc 本，劇，映画などで最も重要な女の登場人物→**ヒロイン，（女の）主人公** ☞参 hero

**heroism** /héroʊìz(ə)m/ 名 Ⓤ ▶定義 great courage 多大な勇気→**英雄的行為，勇気，勇敢さ**

**herring** /hérɪŋ/ 名 Ⓒ Ⓤ (複 **herring** または **herrings**) ▶定義 a fish that swims in large groups (shoals) in cold seas and is used for food 冷たい海を大群（魚群）で泳ぎ，食用にされる魚→**ニシン，その肉**

成句 a red herring ⇒ RED

**hers** /hɚːrz/ 代 ▶定義 of or belonging to her→**彼女の，彼女のもの** ‖ I didn't have a pen but Helen lent me hers. 私はペンを持っていませんでしたが，ヘレンが彼女のを貸してくれました．

\***herself** /(h)ərsélf/ 代 ▶定義1 used when the female who does an action is also affected by it ある行動の主体である女性が自分の行動に影響を受けるときに用いて→**彼女自身を，彼女自身に** ‖ She hurt herself quite badly when she fell downstairs. 彼女は階段から落下した際，かなりひどいけがをした．Irene looked at herself in the mirror. アイリーンは鏡に映っている自分の姿を見ました．▶定義2 used to emphasize the female who did the action その行動をした女性を強調するのに用いて→**彼女自身** ‖ She told me the news herself. 彼女はその知らせを，自ら私に話してくれた．Has Rosy done this herself? (= or did sb else do it for her?) ロージーはこれを自分でやったのですか．(= それともだれか別の～が彼女の代わりにやりましたか．)

成句 (all) by herself ▶定義1 alone→**1人で，単独で，単身で** ‖ She lives by herself. 彼女は1人で住んでいます．☞参 alone の注 ▶定義2 without help 助けなしに→**自力で，独力で，自分で** ‖ I don't think she needs any help - she can change a tyre by herself. 彼女は助けを必要としていないと思います－自分でタイヤ交換をすることができますから．

(all) to herself ▶定義 without having to share 共有する必要がなくて→**自分だけのものに，独り占めして** ‖ Julie has the bedroom to herself now her sister's left home. 今や姉［妹］が家を出たので，ジュリーはその寝室を独り占めしています．

**he's** HE IS, HE HAS の短縮形

**hesitant** /hézɪt(ə)nt/ 形 ▶定義 hesitant (to do)/about doing sth) slow to speak or act because you are not sure if you should or not するべきか否かの自信がないので，話すまたは行動するのが遅い→**(～を・～するのを)(恐れたりして)躊躇（ちゅうちょ）する，ためらいがちの，煮え切らない，気乗りしない，口ごもる** ‖ I'm very hesitant about criticizing him too much. 彼を余り責め立てることに，私はかなり躊躇している．— **hesitancy** /-(ə)nsi/ 名 Ⓤ→**ためらい，躊躇，しりごみ，優柔不断，疑い** — **hesitantly** 副→**ためらって，躊躇して**

\***hesitate** /héz(ə)tèɪt/ 動 Ⓘ ▶定義1 hesitate (about/over sth) to pause before you do sth or before you take a decision, usually because you are uncertain or worried 通常，確信がないため，または心配なために，～をする前，または決断する前に一息つく→**(～のことで)ためらう，躊躇（ちゅうちょ）する，二の足を踏む，(～の)選択に迷う** ‖ He hesitated before going into the room. 彼はその部屋に入るのをためらった．She's still hesitating about whether to accept the job or not. 彼女はその仕事を引き受けるか否か，まだ選択に迷っている．▶定義2 hesitate (to do sth) to not want to do sth because you are not sure that it is right その事が正しいということに確信がないため，～をしたがらない→**(～するのを)ためらう，しりごみする，嫌がる** ‖ Don't hesitate to phone if you have any problems. 何か問題があったら遠慮なくお電話ください．— **hesitation** /hèzətéɪʃ(ə)n/ 名 Ⓒ Ⓤ→**ためらい，躊躇（ちゅうちょ），不決断，嫌気** ‖ She agreed without a moment's hesitation. 彼女は一瞬のためらいもなく同意した．

**heterosexual** /hètərovsékʃuəl, -rə-; -sjuəl/ 形 ▶定義 sexually attracted to a person of the opposite sex 異性に性的魅力を感じる→**異性愛の，(生物学)異性の** ☞参 bisexual, homosexual — **heterosexual** 名 Ⓒ→**異性愛の人**

**het up** /hèt ʌ́p/ 形略式 ▶定義 (名詞の前は不可) het up (about/over sth) worried or excited about sth ～に関して心配する，または興奮する→**興奮した，怒った**

**hexagon** /héksəgàn, -gən/ 名 Ⓒ ▶定義 a shape

with six sides 6つの辺を持つ形→六角形 — **hexagonal** /héksəgən(ə)l, -gən(ə)l/ 形 六角形の, 六方晶系の

**hey** /héɪ/ 間 略式 ▶定義 used to attract sb's attention or to show that you are surprised or interested 〜の注意を引き付ける, または驚いたり, 興味があることを示すのに用いて→おい, ちょっと, おや, ええ ‖ *Hey, what are you doing?* おい, 何してるんだい?

成句 **hey presto** ▶定義 people sometimes say 'hey presto' when they have done sth so quickly that it seems like magic あまりに素早く〜をしたので魔法のように思えるとき hey presto と言うときがある→(手品師などの掛け声で) はい, あら不思議

**heyday** /héɪdèɪ/ 名 [単数扱い] ▶定義 the period when sb/sth was most powerful, successful, rich, etc 〜が最も活力に満ち, 成功している, 裕福であるなどの期間→(若さ・元気・繁栄などの) 盛り, 絶頂, 全盛期

**HGV** /èɪtʃ dʒi: víː/ 略 医 ▶定義 heavy goods vehicle, such as a lorry トラックなどの重量積載物車両→重量積載物車両

**hi** /háɪ/ 間 略式 ▶定義 an informal word used when you meet sb you know well; hello よく知った人に会ったとき使われる略式の言葉; こんにちは→やあ, こんにちは, おい, ごきげんよう

**hibernate** /háɪbənèɪt/ 動 ▶定義 (used about animals) to spend the winter in a state like deep sleep (動物について) 深く眠ったような状態で冬を過ごす→(動物が) 冬眠する, 冬ごもりする, 越冬する — **hibernation** /háɪbənèɪʃ(ə)n/ 名 Ⓤ→冬眠, 避寒

**hiccup** (または **hiccough**) /híkəp/ 名 ▶定義 1 Ⓒ a sudden, usually repeated sound that is made in the throat and that you cannot control 自分では制御できない, のどから出る突然の, 通常は繰り返される音→しゃっくり ▶定義 2 **(the) hiccups** [複数扱い] a series of hiccups 一連のしゃっくり→しゃっくりの発作 ‖ *Don't eat so fast or you'll get hiccups!* そんなに急いで食べてはいけません, さもないとしゃっくりが出ますよ. *If you have the hiccups, try holding your breath.* しゃっくりが止まらない場合は, 息を止めてみなさい. ▶定義 3 Ⓒ small problem or difficulty 小さな問題または困難→(一時的な) 障害, 支障, 滞り ‖ *There's been a slight hiccup in our holi-day arrangements but I've got it sorted out now.* 私たちの休日の手はずにはちょっとした問題があったが, 今は私がそれを解決した. — **hiccup** (または **hiccough**) 動 自 →しゃっくりする

*****hide**[1] /háɪd/ 動 (過 **hid** /híd/; 過分 **hidden** /hídn/) ▶定義 1 Ⓣ to put or keep sb/sth in a place where he/she/it cannot be seen; to cover sth so that it cannot be seen 〜を見えない場所に置く, または保管する; …を覆って見えないようにする→(人・物) を (人から・場所に) 隠す, 覆い隠す, 見えないようにする ‖ *Where shall I hide the money?* お金をどこに隠しましょうか. *You couldn't see Bill in the photo - he was hidden behind John.* その写真にはビルが見当たらなかったでしょう - 彼はジョンの後ろに隠れていたから. ▶定義 2 自 to be or go in a place where you cannot be seen or found 見えないまたは見つからない場所にいる, または行く→(人・動物が) (〜から・〜の後ろに・場所に) 隠れる ‖ *Quick, run and hide!* 急いで, 走っていって隠れなさい. *The child was hiding under the bed.* その子供はベッドの下に隠れていた. ▶定義 3 Ⓣ **hide sth (from sb)** to keep sth secret, especially your feelings 〜 (特に自分の感情) を秘密にする→(人が) (情報・感情など) を包み隠す, (人に) 秘密にする ‖ *She tried to hide her disappointment from them.* 彼女は失望を彼らに悟られまいとしていた.

**hide**[2] /háɪd/ 名 ▶定義 1 Ⓒ Ⓤ the skin of an animal that will be used for making leather, etc なめし皮などを作るのに用いられる動物の皮膚→(獣の) 皮 ▶定義 2 Ⓒ a place from which people can watch wild animals, birds, etc without being seen 人々が動物, 鳥などを向こうからは見られずに観察することができる場所→(野生動物狩り・観察・写真撮影のための) 隠れ場所

**hide-and-seek** 名 Ⓤ ▶定義 a children's game in which one person hides and the others try to find him/her 1人が隠れてほかの子供たちがその子を捜そうとする子供の遊び→隠れん坊

**hideous** /hídiəs/ 形 ▶定義 very ugly or unpleasant 非常に醜い, または不快→恐ろしい, ぞっとする, ひどく醜い, (道徳的に) ひどく不愉快な, 忌まわしい ‖ *a hideous sight* 恐ろしい光景 *a hideous crime* 忌まわしい犯罪 — **hideously** 副

## hiding

→恐ろしく、ぞっとするほど

**hiding** /háɪdɪŋ/ 名 ▶定義1 ❶ the state of being hidden 隠された状態→隠すこと、隠れること、隠匿(いんとく)、隠遁(いんとん) ‖ *The escaped prisoners are believed to be in hiding somewhere in London.* 脱走した囚人たちはロンドンのどこかに潜伏していると信じられている. *to go into hiding* 身を隠す ▶定義2 [ C, 通常は単数] 略式 a punishment involving being hit hard many times 何回も強くたたかれることを含む罰→むち打ち、ひどく打つこと ‖ *You deserve a good hiding for what you've done.* 君は自分のやった事で、したたかに打たれて当然だ.

**hierarchy** /háɪərɑ̀ːrki/ 名 C (複 **hierarchies**) ▶定義 a system or organization that has many levels from the lowest to the highest 最低から最高まで多くの階級がある制度または組織→階層制度、階級組織、職階制、ヒエラルキー — **hierarchical** /hàɪərɑ́ːrkɪk(ə)l/ 形 →階級組織の、階層的な

**hieroglyphics** /hàɪərəɡlífɪks/ 名 [複数扱い] ▶定義 the system of writing that was used in ancient Egypt in which a small picture represents a word or sound 古代エジプトで使われていた表記法で、小さな絵が単語や音を表す→ヒエログリフ、象形文字、象形文字の書き物・表記法

**hi-fi** /háɪ fàɪ/ 名 C ▶定義 equipment for playing recorded music that produces high quality sound 録音された音楽を質の高い音で再生する機器→ハイファイ再生装置 — **hi-fi** 形 →ハイファイの ‖ *a hi-fi system* ハイファイ方式

**higgledy-piggledy** /hìɡ(ə)ldi píɡ(ə)ldi/ 副形 略式 ▶定義 not in any order; mixed up together 順序のない; 一緒くたになった→乱雑な[に]、めちゃくちゃな[に]

*★**high**¹ /háɪ/ 形 ▶定義1 (used about things) having a large distance between the bottom and the top (物について) 底と頂上の間に長い距離がある→高い、丈の高い ‖ *high cliffs* 高い崖(がけ) *What's the highest mountain in the world?* 世界で一番高い山は何ですか. *high heels* (= on shoes) ハイヒール (= 靴の) *The garden wall was so high that we couldn't see over it.* その庭の塀は高すぎて私たちは中を見ることができなかった. ⇔ **low** ☞ 名 **height** ☞参 **tall** の注 ▶定義2 having a particular height ある特定の高さのある→高さが〜の ‖ *The hedge is one metre high.* その生け垣の高さは1メートルです. *knee-high boots* ひざまでのブーツ ▶定義3 at a level which is a long way from the ground, or from sea level 地面または海面から長距離離れた高さの→高い所にある、高地にある、高い所の[からの] ‖ *a high shelf* 高い所にある棚 *The castle was built on high ground.* その城は高台に建てられました. ⇔ **low** ▶定義4 above the usual or normal level or amount 通常または正常な高さまたは量を上回る→(価格・給料・率などが)高い、(生活などが)ぜいたくな、(〜の)含有量が多い、高度の、激しい ‖ *high prices* 高い物価 *at high speed* 高速で *a high level of unemployment* 高失業率 *He's got a high temperature.* 彼は高熱を出している. *Oranges are high in vitamin C.* オレンジはビタミンCを多く含んでいる. ⇔ **low** ▶定義5 better than what is usual 通常よりも良い→(程度が)普通以上の、並でない、(評価が)高い、上等な、高級な、高性能の ‖ *high-quality goods* 高品質の品物 *Her work is of a very high standard.* 彼女の仕事は非常に水準が高い. *He has a high opinion of you.* 彼はあなたを高く買っています. ⇔ **low** ▶定義6 having an important position 重要な地位にある→(身分・地位などが)高い、高位の、主要な、重要な、重大な ‖ *Sam only joined the company three years ago, but she's already quite high up.* サムは3年前この会社に入ったばかりですが、既にかなり重要なポストに就いています. ▶定義7 morally good 道徳的に正しい→崇高な、高潔な、高尚な ‖ *high ideals* 崇高な理想 ▶定義8 (used about a sound or voice) not deep or low (音または声について) 深くない、または低くない→(声が)甲(かん)高い、(音が)高い、鋭い ‖ *Dogs can hear very high sounds.* 犬には非常に高い音が聞こえる. *Women usually have higher voices than men.* 女性は普通男性よりも高い声をしている. ⇔ **low** ▶定義9 略式 **high (on sth)** under the influence of drugs, alcohol, etc 薬物、アルコールなどの影響下で→(麻薬・酒などで)酔った、(〜で)ハイになって ▶定義10 (used about a gear in a car) that allows a faster speed (車のギアについて) より速い速度を可能にする→(車のギアが)ハイの ⇔ **low**

成句 **be left high and dry** ▶定義 to be left without help in a difficult situation 困難な状況で助け

もなく取り残される➡見放される, 干される, (船が) 砂上に乗り上げる

*high² /hái/ 副 ▶定義1 at or to a high position or level 高い位置または高度に[へ]➡(物理的に)高く, 高い所に[へ] ‖ *The sun was high in the sky.* 太陽が空高く上っていた. *I can't jump any higher.* 私はこれ以上高く跳ぶことができない. *The plane flew high overhead.* その飛行機は頭上高く飛んでいった. ☞ 名 height ▶定義2 (used about a sound) at a high level (音について) 高い音域の➡甲高く, 高い調子で ‖ *How high can you sing?* どのくらい高い音域で歌えますか. ⇔ low

成句 high and low ▶定義 everywhere どこでも➡至る所, 貴賤 (きせん) を問わず ‖ *We've searched high and low for the keys.* 私たちはかぎを至る所探し回りました.

run high ▶定義 (used about the feelings of a group of people) to be especially strong (一団の人々の気持ちについて) 特に強くなる➡(感情・言葉などが) 激する, 高ぶる ‖ *Emotions are running high in the neighbourhood where the murders took place.* その殺人事件のあった界隈 (かいわい) では, 人々の感情が高ぶっています.

*high³ /hái/ 名 ⓒ ▶定義1 a high level or point 高い水準または地点➡最高水準・価格・記録 ‖ *Profits reached an all-time high last year.* 去年は利益が過去最高に達しました. ▶定義2 an area of high air pressure 気圧が高い地域➡高気圧(圏) ▶定義3 略式 a feeling of great pleasure or happiness that sb gets from doing sth exciting or being successful 〜がわくわくするような… をしたり, または物事がうまくいくことにより得る大きな喜びの感情, または幸福な気持ち➡熱狂した気持ち, ご機嫌, 恍惚 (こうこつ) ‖ *He was on a high after passing all his exams.* 彼はすべての試験に合格してご機嫌だった. *She talked about the highs and lows of her career.* 彼女は自分の人生の浮き沈みについて語った.

▶定義4 略式 a feeling of great pleasure or happiness that may be caused by a drug, alcohol, etc 薬物, アルコールなどによりもたらされることのある, 大きな喜びの感情, または幸福感➡(麻薬・酒などに) 酔いしれた状態, 恍惚状態, 高揚, ハイの状態 ⇔ すべての定義 low

成句 on high 正式 ▶定義 (in) a high place, the sky or heaven 高い場所, 空または天 (に)➡高所

に, 天に ‖ *The order came from on high.* 天から命令が下りました.

**highbrow** /háibràu/ 形 ▶定義 interested in or concerned with matters that many people would find too serious to be interesting 内容が硬すぎて興味を持てないと多くの人が感じるであろう事に興味がある, またはかかわる➡知的な, 教養のある, 知識人 (向き) の, 学者振る, 小難しい ‖ *highbrow newspapers/television programmes* 知識人向きの新聞・テレビ番組

**high-class** 形 ▶定義 of especially good quality 特に高品質の➡高級な, 一流の ‖ *a high-class restaurant* 一流のレストラン

**High Court** 名 ⓒ ▶定義 the most important court of law in some countries ある国において最も重要な法廷➡最高裁判所, 高等法院, 上級裁判所, 高等裁判所

**higher education** 名 Ⓤ ▶定義 education and training at a college or university, especially to degree level カレッジまたは大学における, 特に学位レベルまでの教育または研修➡高等教育, 大学教育 ☞参 further education

**high jump** 名 [単数扱い] ▶定義 the sport in which people try to jump over a bar in order to find out who can jump the highest 人々がバーの跳び越しを試みて, だれが一番高く跳べるかを競うスポーツ➡(走り) 高跳び ☞参 long jump

**highland** /háilənd/ 形 ▶定義1 in or connected with an area of land that has mountains 山岳地域にある, またはそこに関連した➡高地の, 高原の, 台地の, 山地の, 山岳地方の ‖ *highland streams* 高原の小川 ☞参 lowland ▶定義2 [複数扱い] in or connected with the part of Scotland where there are mountains (the Highlands) スコットランドの山岳地方 (the Highlands) にある, またはそこに関連した➡スコットランド高地地方の, ハイランドの

**high-level** 形 ▶定義 involving important people 重要人物を含む➡上層の, 上級幹部の, 地位の高い ‖ *high-level talks* 上層部による話し合い

**highlight¹** /háilàit/ 動 ⓣ ▶定義1 to emphasize sth so that people give it special attention 人々が特別注意を払うように〜を強調する➡〜を目立たせる, 強調する ‖ *The report highlighted the need for improved safety at football grounds.* そ

の報告はフットボール場の安全性を向上させなければならないことを強調していました． ▶定義2 to mark part of a text with a different colour, etc so that people give it more attention 人々がより注意を払うように，本文の一部に違った色などで印を付ける→〜にマーカーで印を付ける，ラインマーカーをひく

**highlight**[2] /háɪlàɪt/ 名 ▶定義1 ⓒthe best or most interesting part of sth 〜の最も面白い，または最重要な部分→(事件・催し物などの)ハイライト，山場，最重要点，呼び物，目玉商品 ‖ *The highlights of the match will be shown on TV tonight.* その試合のハイライトは今夜テレビ放映される予定です． ▶定義2 **highlights** [複数扱い] areas of lighter colour that are put in a person's hair 人の髪でより明るい色が入った部分→髪を明るい色に染めた部分

\***highly** /háɪli/ 副 ▶定義1 to a high degree; very 高い程度まで；とても→非常に，大いに，高度に ‖ *highly trained/educated/developed* 高度に訓練された・高い教育を受けた・高度に発達した *a highly paid job* 給料の高い仕事 *It's highly unlikely that anyone will complain.* だれかが不平を言うことはまずないだろう． ▶定義2 with admiration 賞賛して→大いに褒めて，とても好意的に ‖ *I think very highly of your work.* 私はあなたの仕事をとても高く評価しています．

**highly strung** 形 ▶定義 nervous and easily upset 神経質で動揺しやすい→緊張した，非常に神経質な，興奮しやすい

**Highness** /háɪnəs/ 名 ⓒ ▶定義 **your/his/her Highness** a title used when speaking about or to a member of a royal family 王室の人に関して話すときに，またはそういう人に話し掛けるときに用いる称号→殿下，妃殿下(王族，皇族の敬称)

**high-powered** 形 ▶定義1 (used about things) having great power (物について)大きな力を持った→高出力の，高性能の ‖ *a high-powered engine* 高性能エンジン ▶定義2 (used about people) important and successful (人々について)有力で成功している→精力的な，活動的な，重い役目をこなす ‖ *high-powered executives* 精力的な経営者

**high-rise** 形 (名詞の前だけ) ▶定義 (used about a building) very tall and having a lot of floors (建物について)とても高く多数の階がある→高層の，高層建築の

**high school** 名 ⓒⓤ ▶定義 a school for children who are about 13-18 years old 13〜18歳くらいの子供を対象とした学校→高等学校，ハイスクール，米 (公立の)中等学校

**high street** 名 ⓒ 英 ▶定義 (often used in names) the main street of a town (しばしば名前で用いて)町の主要な通り→(町の)本通り ‖ *The Post Office is in the High Street.* 郵便局は本通りにあります．

**high-tech** (または **hi-tech**) /ˌhàɪ ték/ 形 ▶定義 using the most modern methods and machines, especially electronic ones 特に電子工学の，最新の方式または機械を使った→高度先端(科学)技術の，ハイテクの ‖ *high-tech industries/hospitals* ハイテク産業，高度先端技術の病院

**high tide** 名 ⓤ ▶定義 the time when the sea comes furthest onto the land 海が陸地に最も近付く時間→満潮(時)，高潮(時) ⇔ **low tide**

**highway** /háɪwèɪ/ 名 ⓒ 特に 米 ▶定義 a main road (between towns) (町と町を結ぶ)幹線道路→幹線道路，主要道路，公道，街道 ☞参 **road** の注

**hijack** /háɪdʒæk/ 動 他 ▶定義1 to take control of a plane, etc by force, usually for political reasons 通常は政治的理由で，飛行機などを力ずくで支配する→(飛行機など)を乗っ取る，ハイジャックする，略奪する ‖ *The plane was hijacked on its flight to Sydney.* その飛行機はシドニーへ飛行中，ハイジャックされました． ☞参 **kidnap** ▶定義2 to take control of a meeting, an event, etc in order to force people to pay attention to sth 人々を強制して〜に注意を払わせるため会合，催しなどを支配する→(組織)を乗っ取る，(人に)強要・強制する ‖ *The peace rally was hijacked by right-wing extremists.* その平和大集会は右翼過激派の乗っ取りに遭いました． — hijack 名 ⓒ→乗っ取り，ハイジャック ‖ *The hijack was ended by armed police.* そのハイジャックは武装した警察によって阻止されました．— hijacker 名 ⓒ→ハイジャック犯人 — hijacking 名 ⓒⓤ→飛行機乗っ取り，ハイジャック

**hike** /háɪk/ 名 ⓒ ▶定義 a long walk in the country 田舎を長い距離歩くこと→ハイキング，徒歩旅行 ‖ *We went on a ten-mile hike at the week-*

*end.* 私たちは週末に10マイルのハイキングに出掛けました. — **hike** 動自 ➔ハイキングする, 徒歩旅行する ☛ go hiking はハイキングして時間を過ごすことについて言うのに用いられる. *They went hiking in Wales for their holiday.* 彼らは休日ウェールズにハイキングに出掛けました. — **hiker** 名C ➔ハイカー, 徒歩旅行者 ☛ C8ページのさし絵

**hilarious** /hɪléəriəs/ 形 ▶定義 extremely funny 極めて面白い➔陽気な, 楽しい, 浮かれ騒ぐ, とても面白い — **hilariously** 副 ➔陽気に, 浮かれ騒いで

**hilarity** /hɪlérəti/ 名 U ▶定義 great amusement or loud laughter 大変に愉快なこと, または大きな笑い声➔陽気, 愉快, 浮かれ騒ぎ

***hill** /hɪl/ 名 C ▶定義 a high area of land that is not as high as a mountain 山ほどは高くないが, 土地が高くなった場所➔丘, 小山 ‖ *There was a wonderful view from the top of the hill.* 丘の頂上からはすばらしい眺めでした. ☛参 **uphill, downhill**

**hillside** /hílsàɪd/ 名 C ▶定義 the side of a hill 丘の側面➔丘の中腹, 丘の斜面

**hilltop** /hílt(ɔ)p/ 名 C ▶定義 the top of a hill ➔丘・小山の頂上

**hilly** /híli/ 形 ▶定義 having a lot of hills➔丘・小山の多い, 起伏の多い, 険しい ‖ *The country's very hilly around here.* この国ではこの辺りがとても丘が多い.

**hilt** /hɪlt/ 名 C ▶定義 the handle of a knife or a similar weapon (**sword**) ナイフまたはそれに類する武器 (剣) の取っ手➔ (刀剣の) 柄 (つか), (道具・武器の) 柄 (え)

成句 **to the hilt** ▶定義 to a high degree; completely 高い程度まで; 完全に➔つか元までも, 徹底的に ‖ *I'll defend you to the hilt.* あなたをとことん守ります.

*****him** /(h)ɪm, hɪm/ 代 (動詞または前置詞の目的語) ▶定義 the male person who was mentioned earlier 前述の男性➔彼を, 彼に ‖ *Helen told Ian that she loved him.* ヘレンはイアンに彼 (イアン) を愛していると言った. *I've got a letter for your father - can you give it to him, please?* 私はあなたのお父様あての手紙を持っています – お父様に渡していただけますか. ☛参 **he** の注

*****himself** /(h)ɪmsélf/ 代 ▶定義 **1** used when the male who does an action is also affected by it ある行動の主体である男性が, 自分もその行動の影響を受けるときに用いて➔彼自身を, 彼自身に ‖ *He cut himself when he was shaving.* 彼はひげをそっていて顔を切ってしまった. *John looked at himself in the mirror.* ジョンは鏡に映っている自分の姿を見た. ▶定義 **2** used to emphasize the male who did the action その行動をした男性を強調するのに用いて➔彼自身 ‖ *He told me the news himself.* 彼本人が私にそのニュースを知らせてくれた. *Did he write this himself? (= or did sb else do it for him?)* これは彼が自分で書いたのですか. (= それともだれか別の人が彼の代わりに書きましたか.)

成句 **(all) by himself** ▶定義 **1** alone➔1人で, 単独で, 単身で ‖ *He lives by himself.* 彼は1人で住んでいる. ☛参 **alone** の注 ▶定義 **2** without help 助けなしに➔自力で, 独力で, 自分で ‖ *He should be able to cook a meal by himself.* 彼は自分で食事が作れるようにならなければいけない.

**(all) to himself** ▶定義 without having to share 共有する必要がなくて➔自分だけのものに, 独り占めして ‖ *Charlie has the bedroom to himself now his brother's left home.* 今や兄 [弟] が家を出たので, チャーリーはその寝室を独り占めしている.

**hind** /haɪnd/ 形 ▶定義 (used about an animal's legs, etc) at the back (動物の足などについて)➔後ろの, 後部の, 後方の
▶ back legs とも言う. 前足は front legs または forelegs.
☛ C1ページのさし絵

**hinder** /híndər/ 動他 ▶定義 to make it more difficult for sb/sth to do sth ～が…を行うのをより困難にする➔ (人・物・事) が～を妨げる, 遅らせる, 人の (仕事など) を邪魔する, できないようにする ‖ *A lot of scientific work is hindered by lack of money.* 多くの科学的研究が資金不足によって困難になっている.

**hindrance** /híndrəns/ 名 C ▶定義 a person or thing that makes it difficult for you to do sth あなたがある～をするとき, それを困難にさせる原因となる人または物➔ (～の) 妨害, 邪魔, (～の) 邪魔になる物・人, 障害物

**hindsight** /háɪndsàɪt/ 名 U ▶定義 the understanding that you have of a situation only after it has happened 事が起きてから初めて状況が理

解できること→後知恵 ‖ *With hindsight, I wouldn't've lent him the money.* 今だから分かることだけど、私だったら彼にお金を貸さなかったと思う. ☛参 **foresight**

**Hindu** /híndu:/ 图 ❻ ▶定義 a person whose religion is Hinduism ヒンズー教を信仰する人→ヒンズー教徒 — Hindu 形→ヒンズー教の, ヒンズー人の, インド人の ‖ *Hindu beliefs* ヒンズー教信仰

**Hinduism** /híndu:ìz(ə)m/ 图 ❶ ▶定義 the main religion of India. Hindus believe in many gods and that, after death, people will return to life in a different form. インドの主信仰. ヒンズー教徒は多数の神を信仰し、死後人々は姿を変えて生き返ると信じている→ヒンズー教

hinge

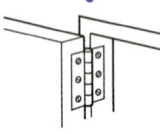

**hinge**¹ /híndʒ/ 图 ❻ ▶定義 a piece of metal that joins two sides of a box, door, etc together and allows it to be opened or closed 箱, ドアなどの両側を結合し, 開閉できるようにするための1片の金属→（開き戸などの）ちょうつがい, 関節

**hinge**² /híndʒ/ 動 句動詞 hinge on sth ▶定義 to depend on sth 〜に依存している→〜次第である, 〜に懸かっている ‖ *The future of the project hinges on the meeting today.* このプロジェクトの将来は今日の会議次第です.

**hint**¹ /hínt/ 图 ❻ ▶定義 1 something that you suggest in an indirect way 人が間接的にそれとなく示唆する物事→（〜に関する）ほのめかし, ヒント, 暗示, 手掛かり ‖ *If you keep mentioning parties, maybe they'll **take the hint** and invite you.* あなたがパーティーのことを話していれば、彼らはぴんと来てあなたを招待してくれるでしょう. ▶定義 2 sth that suggests what will happen in the future 将来何が起こるかを示唆する事→（〜の）兆候, 兆し, 〜しそうな気配 ‖ *The first half of the match **gave** no **hint** of the excitement to come.* その試合の前半では、そのあと続くはらはらする試合の兆候が全く見られなかった. ▶定義 3 a small amount of sth 少量の〜→微量, わずかな量, (〜の) かすかな兆候 ‖ *There was a hint of sadness in his voice.* 彼の声にはや

や悲しみが感じられた. ▶定義 4 a piece of advice or information 1つの忠告または情報→（〜のための・〜についての）手引き, 助言, 情報, 注意, 心得, 指示 ‖ *helpful hints* 役立つ忠告

**hint**² /hínt/ 動 自 他 ▶定義 hint (at sth); hint that... to suggest sth in an indirect way 間接的にそれとなく〜を言う→（〜を）ほのめかす, それとなく言う, 当てこする; (〜であることを) (人に) ほのめかす, 暗示する, 〜とそれとなく言う ‖ *They only hinted at their great disappointment.* 彼らはひどく失望したことをそれとなく言った.
*He hinted that he might be moving to Greece.* 彼はギリシャに引っ越すかもしれないとほのめかした.

*****hip**¹ /híp/ 图 ❻ ▶定義 the part of the side of your body above your legs and below your waist 身体の脚より上で腰より下の部分の片方→腰, しり ‖ *He stood there angrily with his hands on his hips.* 彼は両手を腰に当てて怒って立っていた. ☛ C5 ページのさし絵

**hip**² /híp/ 間
成句 hip, hip, hurray/hurrah ▶定義 shouted three times when a group wants to show that it is pleased with sb or with sth that has happened 〜または起こった…に対して、一団の人々が喜びを表現したいとき、3回叫ばれる→ヒップ, ヒップ, フレー.

**hippie** (または **hippy**) /hípi/ 图 ❻ (複 **hippies**) ▶定義 a person who rejects the usual values and way of life of western society. Especially in the 1960s, hippies showed that they were different by wearing colourful clothes, having long hair and taking drugs. 西洋社会の普通の価値観および生活様式を否定する人. 特に1960年代 hippies は色彩に富んだ洋服を着て、髪を伸ばし麻薬を服用して人との違いを表現した→ヒッピー(族)

**hippopotamus** /hìpəpátəməs/ 图 ❻ (複 **hippopotamuses** /-sɪz, əz/ または **hippopotami** /-maɪ, -mi/) (または 略式 **hippo** /hípou/) ▶定義 a large African animal with a large head and short legs that lives in or near rivers アフリカ産の大型動物で、大きな頭と短い足を持ち川の中またはその近辺で生活する→カバ

*****hire**¹ /háɪər/ 動 他 ▶定義 1 (冕 **rent**) hire sth (from sb) to have the use of sth for a short time by paying for it お金を支払って〜を短期間使用

する➡物を(人から)(一時的に・特定の目的で)賃借りする, ～を(損料を払って)借りる
▶イギリス英語では, 短期間何かを賃借りすることを hire と言う: *We hired a car for the day.* (私たちはその日車を借りました.) 期間がより長期にわたるときは何かを rent (賃借りする) と言う: *to rent a house/flat/television* (家・アパート・テレビを賃借りする). アメリカ英語ではどちらの状況でも rent が用いられる.

▶定義2 to give sb a job for a short time ～に短期間の仕事を与える➡人を雇う‖ *We'll have to hire somebody to mend the roof.* 私たちはだれかを雇って屋根を修理してもらう必要がある.
▶アメリカ英語では正式な雇用についても hire を用いる: *We just hired a new secretary.* (私たちは新しい秘書を雇ったばかりです.)

▶定義3 (困 **rent**) hire sth (out) (to sb) to allow sb to use sth for a short fixed period in exchange for money 一定の短期間, お金と引き換えに～に…を使うことを許可する➡物を(～に)賃貸しする, 貸し出す‖ *We hire (out) our vans by the day.* 私たちはバンを1日単位で貸し出している. ● イギリス英語では, 期間がより長期にわたる場合 rent または let が用いられる. *Mrs Higgs rents out rooms to students.* ヒッグス婦人は学生に部屋を賃貸ししている. *We let our house while we were in France for a year.* フランスにいた1年間, 私たちは家を賃貸した.

**hire**² /háɪər/ 名 ▶定義 the act of paying to use sth for a short time ～を短期間使うため支払いをする行為➡(物の)賃借り・貸し‖ *Car hire is expensive in this country.* この国では車を借りるのに高額の使用料がかかる. *Do you have bicycles for hire?* 貸し出し用自転車はありますか.

**hire purchase** 名 Ⓤ 医 (略 **HP**) ▶定義 a way of buying goods. You do not pay the full price immediately but make regular small payments (**instalments**) until the full amount is paid. 品物を購入する方法の1つ. 即座に全額支払わずに, 定期的な小額の支払い(分割払い)を全額に達するまで行う➡分割払い購入方式‖ *We're buying the video on hire purchase.* 私たちはそのビデオを分割払いで買います.

***his** /(h)ɪz, hɪz/ 代 ▶定義 of or belonging to the male person that was mentioned earlier 前述の男性の, またはその人に属する➡彼の, 彼のもの‖ *Matthew has hurt his shoulder.* マシューは肩にけがをした. *This is my book so that one must be his.* これは私の本ですから, あれが彼のに違いありません. ☞参 **he** の注

**hiss** /hɪs/ 動 ▶定義1 自 他 to make a sound like a very long 's' to show that you are angry or do not like sth 怒っていること, または～が好きでないことを表すため, とても長く伸ばしたSのような音を出す➡(人などが)(～に)シーッと言う, (非難・警告など)を(役者・演説者などに)シーッと言って表す‖ *The cat hissed at me.* その猫は私を見てシューとうなり声を上げた. *The speech was hissed and booed.* その演説は「シーッ」とか「ブー」と言う音でやじられた.

▶定義2 他 to say sth in an angry hissing voice 怒ってシーッというときの声で～を言う➡(怒って・あせって)～とささやく, (人など)をシーッと言ってしかる・制止する・けなす, (人・動物)をシッシッと言って追い払う・やじり倒す・引っ込ませる‖ *'Stay away from me!' She hissed.* 「私に近付かないで」と彼女は怒った声でささやいた.
— hiss 名 C➡(非難・不賛成・怒りなどの)シュー[シーッ]という声

**historian** /hɪstɔ́(:)riən/ 名 C ▶定義 a person who studies or who is an expert in history 歴史を研究する, または専門とする人➡歴史家, 歴史学者

**historic** /hɪstɔ́(:)rɪk, -stɑ́r-/ 形 ▶定義 famous or important in history 歴史上有名な, または重要な➡歴史上有名な, 歴史上重要な‖ *The ending of apartheid was a historic event.* アパルトヘイトの終局は歴史上重要な出来事です.

***historical** /hɪstɔ́(:)rɪk(ə)l, -stɑ́r-/ 形 ▶定義 that really lived or happened; connected with real people or events in the past 本当に生きていたまたは起こった; 過去の実在の人物または出来事に関連した➡歴史の, 歴史に関する, 歴史上の, 歴史上実在した, 史実に基づく‖ *historical events/records* 歴史上の事件(実際にあった事)・史料 *This house has great historical interest.* この家は歴史的に非常に興味深い. — historically /-k(ə)li/ 副➡歴史的に, 歴史上

***history** /hístə(r)i/ 名 ( 複 **histories** ) ▶定義1

## 806　hit¹

❶ all the events of the past 過去のあらゆる出来事→歴史 ‖ *an important moment in history* 歴史上重要な時期　☛参 **natural history** ▶定義2
[❻, 通常は単数] the series of events or facts that is connected with sb/sth ～に関連する一連の出来事または事実→(人の)履歴, 経歴, 前歴, 病歴, 由来, 沿革 ‖ *He has a history of violence.* 彼には暴力事件の前科がある. *a patient's medical history* 患者の病歴　▶定義3 ❶ the study of past events 過去の出来事の研究→(歴)史学 ‖ *She has a degree in history.* 彼女は歴史学の学位を持っている. *History was my favourite subject at school.* 歴史学は私の好きな教科でした.
▶定義4 ❻ a written description of past events 過去の出来事を描写した書物→(歴)史書 ‖ *a new history of Europe* ヨーロッパの新しい歴史書
▶ history は実際に起こった本当の事. story は起こったかもしれないし, 起こらなかったかもしれない一連の出来事の描写.

**成句 go down in/make history** ▶定義 to be or do sth so important that it will be recorded in history 歴史に記録されるであろうほど有名になる, または重要な～をする→歴史に記録されて伝えられる, 歴史に残るような重要な事をする ‖ *She made history by becoming the first woman President.* 彼女は初代女性大統領となり歴史に名を残した.

**the rest is history** ▶定義 used when you are telling a story to say that you are not going to tell the end of the story, because everyone knows it already 話をしている際に, 皆が既に知っているので結末は話さないと言うときに用いて→後はご存じの通りです

\*hit¹ /hɪt/ 動 ❻ (現分 **hitting**; 過, 過分 **hit**)
▶定義1 to make sudden, violent contact with sb/sth ～と突然, 乱暴に接触する→(人・物)を(～で)打つ, たたく, 殴る, (人・物)にぶつかる ‖ *The bus left the road and hit a tree.* そのバスは道路から外れて木にぶつかった. *to hit somebody in the eye/across the face/on the nose* 人の目・横面・鼻っ柱を殴る

▶ strike は hit よりも正式な語. beat は何回も hit することを意味する: *He was badly beaten in the attack.* (彼はその襲撃で袋だたきに遭った.)

▶定義2 **hit sth (on/against sth)** to knock a part of your body, etc against sth 体の一部などを～にぶつける→物を(～に)ぶつける ‖ *Peter hit his head on the low beam.* ピーターは低い梁(はり)に頭をぶつけた. ▶定義3 to have a bad or unpleasant effect on sb/sth ～に悪いまたは不愉快な影響を与える→(人など)に打撃・影響を与える, (人・場所など)を襲う, 攻撃する ‖ *Inner city areas have been badly hit by unemployment.* 都市の中心部は失業の深刻な打撃を受けている. *Her father's death has hit her very hard.* 彼女は父親の死にかなりの打撃を受けている. ▶定義4 to experience sth unpleasant or difficult 不愉快な, または困難な～を経験する→(障害・困難・問題など)に出くわす, 出会う ‖ *Things were going really well until we hit this problem.* この問題に出くわすまで物事は本当にうまくいっていた. ▶定義5 to reach a place or a level→(水準・程度など)に達する, (場所)に着く, 至る ‖ *If you follow this road you should hit the motorway in about ten minutes.* この道を進めば約10分で高速道路に至るはずです. *The price of oil hit a new high yesterday.* 昨日, 原油価格が最高値記録を更新した. ▶定義6 to suddenly come into sb's mind; to make sb realize or understand sth ～の心に突然浮かぶ; ～に…を悟らせる, または理解させる→(考えなどが)～に思い浮かぶ, (正しい道など)をうまく・偶然見つける ‖ *I thought I recognized the man's face and then it hit me – he was my old maths teacher!* 私はその男の人の顔に見覚えがある気がして, それから思い当たりました － 彼は昔, 私の数学の先生でした.

**成句 hit it off (with sb)** 略式 ▶定義 to like sb when you first meet him/her 初対面で～を好きになる→(～と)(すぐに)仲良くなる, 意気投合する ‖ *When I first met Tony's parents, we didn't really hit it off.* 初めてトニーの両親に会った時, 私たちはあまり仲良くなれなかった.

**hit the nail on the head** ▶定義 to say sth that is exactly right ぴったり正しい～を言う→うまく言い当てる, 図星を指す

**hit the jackpot** ▶定義 to win a lot of money or have a big success 多額のお金をもうける, または大成功する→賞金を手に入れる, 大当たりを取る, 大成功する

**句動詞 hit back (at sb/sth)** ▶定義 to attack

(with words) sb who has attacked you 攻撃してきた〜に (言葉で) 反撃する➡(人に) 仕返しをする, 反論する, (人に) 抵抗する ‖ *The Prime Minister hit back at his critics.* 首相は彼の批判者に対して反論した.

**hit on sth** ▶定義 to suddenly find sth by chance 〜を不意に, また偶然見つける➡〜を思い付く, 〜に出くわす ‖ *I finally hit on a solution to the problem.* 私はとうとうその問題の解決策を思い付きました.

**hit out (at sb/sth)** ▶定義 to attack sb/sth 〜を攻撃する➡(〜に) 殴り掛かる, (〜を) 激しく非難・攻撃する ‖ *The man hit out at the policeman.* その男性は警官に殴り掛かった.

*★**hit**² /hɪt/ 名 C ▶定義 1 the act of hitting sth 〜を打つ行為➡打撃, 衝突, (〜への) 命中 ‖ *The ship took a **direct hit** and sank.* その船は, 受けた攻撃が命中して沈没した. *She gave her brother a hard hit on the head.* 彼女は弟の頭をひどく殴り付けた. ☛参 **miss** ▶定義 2 a person or thing that is very popular or successful 非常に人気のある, または成功した人または物➡(興行などの) ヒット, 大成功, 幸運, ヒット曲, 人気者 ‖ *The record was a big hit.* そのレコードは大ヒットした. ▶定義 3 (computing) a result of a search on a computer, especially on the Internet (コンピューター) コンピューター, 特にインターネットによる検索結果➡**ヒット, 検索で目的とする情報を探し当てること**

成句 **make a hit (with sb)** 略式 ▶定義 to make a good impression on sb 〜に良い印象を与える➡〜に気に入られる, 〜に大当たりする ‖ *The new teacher seems to have made a hit with the girls.* その新しい先生は女生徒たちに気に入られたようだ.

**hit-and-miss** (または **hit-or-miss**) 形 略式 ▶定義 not well organized; careless よく組織されていない; 不注意な➡行き当たりばったりに, (のるかそるか) 運に任せた, 当てずっぽうな, いいかげんな ‖ *This method is a bit hit-or-miss, but it usually works.* このやり方はちょっと行き当たりばったりですが, 普通うまくいきます.

**hit-and-run** 形 ▶定義 (used about a road accident) caused by a driver who does not stop to help (交通事故について) 車を止めて助けようとしない運転者が引き起こした➡ひき逃げの, 当て逃げの

---

HIV 807

**hitch**¹ /hɪtʃ/ 動 ▶定義 1 自他 略式 to travel by waiting by the side of a road and holding out your hand or a sign until a driver stops and takes you in the direction you want to go 道路わきで手またはサインを出して運転者が止まるまで待ち, 行きたい方向へ連れていってもらって旅行する➡**ヒッチハイクする** ‖ *I managed to hitch to Paris in just six hours.* 私はうまくヒッチハイクして, パリまでたった6時間で行きました. *We missed the bus so we had to **hitch a lift**.* 私たちはバスに乗り遅れたのでヒッチハイクしなければならなかった. ☛参 **hitchhike** ▶定義 2 他 to fasten sth to sth else 〜を別の…に留める➡(かぎ・縄など) を引っ掛ける, (動物) を (〜に) つなぐ, (牛・馬など) を車につなぐ ‖ *to hitch a trailer to the back of a car* トレイラーを車の後ろにつなぐ

**hitch**² /hɪtʃ/ 名 C ▶定義 a small problem or difficulty 小さな問題または困難➡(計画などの) 延期, 障害, 中断 ‖ *a technical hitch* 技術的な難点

**hitchhike** /hítʃhaɪk/ (または 略式 **hitch**) 動 自 ▶定義 to travel by waiting by the side of a road and holding out your hand or a sign until a driver stops and takes you in the direction you want to go 道路わきで手またはサインを出して運転者が止まるまで待ち, 行きたい方向へ連れていってもらって旅行する➡**ヒッチハイクする** ‖ *He hitchhiked across Europe.* 彼はヨーロッパ中をヒッチハイクで旅行した.

▶ hitchhike は通常このように娯楽として長距離旅行をすることを言うのに使われる. hitch は同じ意味で用いることができるが, 例えば車が故障したり, あるいはバスに乗り遅れたなどの理由による短距離の移動を言うのにも使われる. また hitch は他動詞的に用いることもできる: *I hitched a lift/ride to the nearest petrol station.* (私は一番近いガソリンスタンドまでヒッチハイクした.) thumb a lift も同じ意味.

— **hitchhiker** 名 C ➡ ヒッチハイクする人, ヒッチハイカー

**hi-tech** = HIGH-TECH

**hitherto** /hídətù, -ˊ-/ 副 正式 ▶定義 until now➡今まで, 従来, 今のところ (まだ)

**HIV** /èɪtʃ aɪ víː/ 略 human immunodeficiency

### hive

virus ▶定義 the virus that is believed to cause AIDS AIDSの原因と信じられているウイルス→ヒト免疫不全ウイルス, エイズウイルス

**hive** /háɪv/ = BEEHIVE

**hiya** /háɪjə/ 間 略式 ▶定義 an informal word used when you meet sb you know well; hello よく知っている～に会ったとき, 使われるくだけた調子の言葉; こんにちは→やあ, おっす, よお

**HM** 略 His/Her Majesty's→陛下 ‖ *HMS* (= *Her Majesty's Ship*) *Invincible* 英国軍艦 (= 女王陛下の船)「無敵号」

**hm** /hʌm/ 間 ▶定義 (used when you are not sure or when you are thinking about sth) (確信がないときや, ～について考えているとき用いて) →フーム, ウーン

**hoard**[1] /hɔːrd/ 名 C ▶定義 a store (often secret) of money, food, etc お金, 食べ物などの (多くは秘密の) 備蓄→(金銭・財宝・食物などの) 貯蓄, 貯蔵・[退蔵] 物, 買いだめ

**hoard**[2] /hɔːrd/ 動 自他 ▶定義 hoard (sth) (up) to collect and store large quantities of sth (often secretly) (多くは秘密で) 大量の～を収集するまたは備蓄する→(ひそかに) 蓄える, (財宝・食糧など) を蓄える, 買いだめする

**hoarding** /hɔ́ːrdɪŋ/ 英 = BILLBOARD

**hoarse** /hɔːrs/ 形 ▶定義 (used about a person or his/her voice) sounding rough and quiet, especially because of a sore throat (人またはその声について) 特にのどが炎症を起こしたため, かすれておとなしい声の→(声が) しわがれた, かすれた, (人・動物などが) しわがれ声の, 耳障りな, ざわめく ‖ *a hoarse whisper* かすれ声のささやき — **hoarsely** 副→しわがれ声で, 耳障りに

**hoax** /hóʊks/ 名 C ▶定義 a trick to make people believe sth that is not true, especially sth unpleasant 本当でない, 特に不愉快な事を人々に信じさせる仕掛け→一杯食わせる, いたずら, 食わせ物, 作り事 ‖ *The fire brigade answered the call, but found that it was a hoax.* 消防隊員は電話に出たが, いたずらであることが分かった.

**hob** /hɒb/ (米 **stovetop**) 名 C ▶定義 the surface on the top of a cooker that is used for boiling, frying, etc 湯沸かし, いため物などに使われる調理器の最上部に来る面→ガス・電子レンジの (なべなどを載せる) トップ

**hobble** /hɒ́b(ə)l/ 動 自 ▶定義 to walk with difficulty because your feet or legs are hurt 足が痛むので歩きにくい→足を引きずって歩く ‖ *He hobbled home on his twisted ankle.* 彼は足首を捻挫 (ねんざ) して足を引きずって家まで帰りました.

***hobby** /hɒ́bi/ 名 C ( 複 **hobbies**) ▶定義 something that you do regularly for pleasure in your free time 自由時間に楽しみのため定期的にする事→(本業以外の) 趣味, 道楽 ‖ *Barry's hobbies are stamp-collecting and surfing the net.* バリーの趣味は切手収集とネットサーフィンです.
☛類 **pastime**

**hockey** /hɒ́ki/ 名 U ▶定義 **1** a game that is played on a field (**pitch**) by two teams of eleven players who try to hit a small hard ball into a goal with a curved wooden stick (**hockey stick**) フィールド (競技場) で11人の選手から成る2つのチームにより行われる競技で, 小さな硬球を曲がった木製のスティック (ホッケースティック) で打ってゴールに入れようとする→ホッケー

▶米国では, ホッケーを通常 **field hockey** (フィールドホッケー) と呼んで **ice hockey** (アイスホッケー) と区別する.

▶定義 **2** 米 = ICE HOCKEY

**hoe** /hóʊ/ 名 C ▶定義 a garden tool with a long handle that is used for turning the soil and for removing plants that you do not want 長い柄の付いた園芸用具で, 土地を耕したり不用な植物を取り除くのに用いられる→鍬 (くわ), (鍬形) 除草器 ☛ **garden** のさし絵

**hog**[1] /hɔ(ː)g/ 名 C ▶定義 a male pig that is kept for its meat 食肉用に飼育される雄豚→(食肉用に去勢した) 雄豚, 飼い豚

成句 **go the whole hog** 略式 ▶定義 to do sth as completely as possible ～をできるだけ完全にやる→徹底的にやる, とことんまでいく ‖ *Instead of getting a taxi, why not go the whole hog and hire a limousine for the evening?* タクシーを使う代わりに, この際徹底してリムジンを1晩貸ったらいかがですか.

**hog**[2] /hɔ(ː)g/ 動 他 (**hogging**; **hogged**) 略式 ▶定義 to take or keep too much or all of sth for yourself ～を自分のためにたくさん取りすぎる, または取り置きすぎる→～をむさぼる, 独り占めする, 分け前以上に取る ‖ *The red car was hog-*

*ging the middle of the road so no one could overtake.* その赤い車は道路の真ん中を独占していたので、だれも追い越すことができなかった。

**Hogmanay** /hɒ́ɡmənéɪ/ 名 C ▶定義 the Scottish name for New Year's Eve (31 December) and the celebrations that take place then 大みそか（12月31日）のスコットランド式名称、およびその時に行われるお祝い→（スコットランドで）大みそか（のお祝い・贈り物）

**hoist** /hɔ́ɪst/ 動他 ▶定義 to lift or pull sth up, often by using ropes, etc 多くはロープなどを使って～を持ち上げるまたは引き上げる→(旗・帆など)を揚げる、(船荷)を(クレーンなどで)巻き・つり上げる、～を高く揚げる、持ち上げる ‖ *to hoist a flag/sail* 旗・帆を揚げる

\***hold**¹ /hóʊld/ 動 (過, 過分 **held** /héld/)
▶定義 1 他 to take sb/sth and keep him/her/it in your hand, etc ～を取って、手などに持っている→物を持っている、握っている、つかんでいる、くわえている ‖ *He held a gun in his hand.* 彼は手に銃を持っていた。 *The woman was holding a baby in her arms.* その女性は赤ちゃんを腕に抱いていた。 *Hold my hand. This is a busy road.* 私の手につかまって。ここは交通量が多い通りだから。 ☛ S6 ページのさし絵 ▶定義 2 他 to keep sth in a certain position ～をある姿勢に保つ→～を…にしておく、～を（…に）固定する ‖ *Hold your head up straight.* 頭をまっすぐ上げていなさい。 *Hold the camera still or you'll spoil the picture.* カメラをしっかり固定しなさい、さもないと写真が台なしになってしまうでしょう。 *These two screws hold the shelf in place.* この2本のねじで棚は固定されている。 ▶定義 3 他 to take the weight of sb/sth ～の重さを支える→(屋根など)を支える、(重さなど)に耐える、持ちこたえる ‖ *Are you sure that branch is strong enough to hold you?* その枝があなたを支えられるだけの強度があるのは確かですか。
▶定義 4 他 to organize an event; to have a meeting, an election, a concert, etc 催しを企画する；会合、選挙、コンサートなどを開く・行う→(会・式など)を催す、開く、行う、開催する、(クリスマスなど)を祝う ‖ *They're holding a party for his fortieth birthday.* 彼の40歳の誕生パーティーを開く予定です。 *The Olympic Games are held every four years.* オリンピック競技会は4年ごとに開催されます。

▶定義 5 自 to stay the same 同じ状態でいる→～（の状態）のままである、持ちこたえる、耐える、持つ、(天候などが)続く、持続する、有効である ‖ *I hope this weather holds till the weekend.* この天候が週末まで続いてほしい。 *What I said still holds - nothing has changed.* 私が言った事はまだ有効です―何も変わっていません。

▶定義 6 他 to contain or have space for a particular amount ある一定量が入る、またはそれに対する場所が空いている→(容器・場所が)～を収納・収容できる、物を含んでいる、入れている ‖ *The car holds five people.* その車は5人乗りです。 *How much does this bottle hold?* このびんにはどれだけ入りますか。 ▶定義 7 他 to keep a person in a position or place by force 人を強制してある位置または場所にいさせる→人を拘束する、留置する ‖ *The terrorists are holding three men hostage.* テロリストたちは3人を人質として拘束している。 *A man is being held at the police station.* 1人の男性が警察署に留置されている。 ▶定義 8 他 to have sth, usually in an official way 通常、正式に～を所有している→物を所有する、保管する、(物・部屋など)を取っておく、(記録など)を保持する、(役職・地位など)に就く ‖ *Does she hold a British passport?* 彼女は英国のパスポートを所有していますか。 *She holds the world record in the 100 metres.* 彼女は100メートル走の世界記録保持者です。
▶定義 9 他 to have an opinion, etc 意見などを持つ→(考え・感情など)を心に抱く、人を(～だと)思う・考える、人を～と判決する ‖ *They hold the view that we shouldn't spend any more money.* 彼らは私たちがもうこれ以上お金を使うべきでないという見解を持っている。 ▶定義 10 他 to believe that sth is true about a person 人について～が本当であると思う→人を～だと思う、～だと考える ‖ *I hold the parents responsible for the child's behaviour.* 両親は子供の行動に責任があると思います。 ▶定義 11 自他 (used when you are telephoning) to wait until the person you are calling is ready (電話しているときに用いて) 呼び出している相手が電話に出られるまで待つ→(電話を)切らないでおく、そのまま待つ ‖ *I'm afraid his phone is engaged. Will you hold the line?* 残念ですが彼の電話は話し中で

す. このままお待ちになりますか. ▶定義 12 ⓘ to have a conversation 会話をする→(会話などを)続ける、やめない ∥ *It's impossible to **hold a conversation** with all this noise.* こんな騒音の中で会話を続けることは不可能です.

成句 **Hold it!** (口語) ▶定義 Stop! Don't move! → 止まれ. 動くな. 待て.

▶ hold を含むこのほかの成句については、名詞、形容詞などの項を参照. 例えば hold your own は own の項にある.

句動詞 **hold sth against sb** ▶定義 to not forgive sb because of sth he/she has done ～を、その～がした…のために許さない→～のことで人を責める、～を取り上げて人を非難する

**hold sb/sth back** ▶定義 1 to prevent sb from making progress →～の発展・進歩を妨げる[遅らせる] ▶定義 2 to prevent sb/sth from moving forward ～が前進するのを妨げる→～を押しとどめる、食い止める、引き止める ∥ *The police tried to hold the crowd back.* 警察は群衆を引き止めようとした.

**hold sth back** ▶定義 1 to refuse to give some of the information that you have 持っている情報のある部分を提供することを拒否する→(情報など)を出し渋る、秘密にしておく ∥ *The police are sure that she is holding something back. She knows much more than she is saying.* 警察は彼女が何かを隠していると確信している. 彼女は言っている事よりはるかに多くの事を知っている. ▶定義 2 to control an emotion and stop yourself from showing what you really feel 感情を抑制して本当の気持ちを表さないようにする→(感情・涙など)を抑える、控える ∥ *He fought to hold back tears of anger and frustration.* 彼は怒りと挫折 (ざせつ) の涙を懸命にこらえた.

**hold off (sth/doing sth)** ▶定義 to delay sth ～を遅らせる→(～を)延ばす、ためらう

**hold on** ▶定義 1 to wait or stop for a moment 一時的に待つ、または止める→待つ、(電話を)切らないで待つ ∥ *Hold on. I'll be with you in a minute.* そのままお待ちください. すぐに戻ります. ▶定義 2 to manage in a difficult or dangerous situation 困難または危険な状況においてどうにかやっていく→頑張る、持ちこたえる、耐える ∥ *They managed to hold on until a rescue party arrived.* 彼らは救助隊が到着するまで何とか持ちこたえた.

**hold onto sb/sth** ▶定義 to hold sb/sth tightly ～をしっかりと握る→～をつかんで離さない、～にしがみ付く、すがり付く ∥ *The child held on to his mother; he didn't want her to go.* その子供は母親にしがみ付いていた. 母親に行って欲しくなかったのだ.

**hold onto sth** ▶定義 to keep sth; to not give or sell sth ～を取っておく；～をやらない、または売らない→～を手離さない、～を売らない ∥ *They've offered me a lot of money for this painting, but I'm going to hold onto it.* 彼らはこの絵画に多額のお金を支払うと申し出ているが、私は手放すつもりはありません.

**hold out** ▶定義 to last (in a difficult situation) (困難な状況で)存続する→最後まで頑張る、最後まで持ちこたえる ∥ *How long will our supply of water hold out?* 私たちの水の供給はどれくらい持つでしょうか.

**hold sth out** ▶定義 to offer sth by moving it towards sb in your hand ～を手に持ち…の方に差し出す→(手で)物を差し出す、伸ばす ∥ *He held out a carrot to the horse.* 彼は馬にニンジンを差し出した.

**hold out for sth** 略式 ▶定義 to cause a delay while you continue to ask for sth ～を依頼し続けている間に遅れが生じる→(～が認められるまで)妥協しない、我慢して待つ ∥ *Union members are holding out for a better pay offer.* 組合員たちはより高い賃金の申し出があるまで妥協しません.

**hold sb/sth up** ▶定義 to make sb/sth late; to cause a delay ～を遅れさせる；遅れを生じさせる→(出発など)を遅らせる、停滞させる ∥ *We were held up by the traffic.* 私たちは交通渋滞に巻き込まれた.

**hold up sth** ▶定義 to rob a bank, shop, vehicle, etc using a gun 銃を使って銀行、商店、車などに強盗に入る→～に強盗に入る、(人・車など)を(強奪の目的で)止める

**hold**² /hóʊld/ 🔊 ▶定義 1 ⓒ the act or manner of having sb/sth in your hand(s) ～を手に持つ行為またはそのやり方→握ること、つかむこと ∥ *to have a firm hold on the rope* ロープにしっかりとつかまる *judo/wrestling holds* 柔道の固め技、レスリングのホールド ▶定義 2 [単数扱い] a

**hold (on/over sb/sth)** influence or control→（～に対する）影響力, 支配力,（～についての）把握力, 理解力 ‖ *The new government has strengthened its hold on the country.* 新政府は国に対する統率力を強化した. ▶定義3 ❻the part of a ship or an aircraft where cargo is carried 船または航空機の貨物を入れて運ぶ場所→船倉,（航空機の）貨物室

成句 **catch, get, grab, take, etc hold (of sb/sth)** ▶定義1 to take sb/sth in your hands ～を両手でつかむ→～をつかむ, 捕らえる, 捕まえる, 握る, 手に入れる ‖ *I managed to catch hold of the dog before it ran out into the road.* 私はその犬が走り出して道路に走っていく前に何とか捕まえた. ▶定義2 to take control of sb/sth; to start to have an effect on sb/sth ～を支配する; ～に影響を及ぼし始める→～に対して支配力・権力がある, ～を掌握する, 捕らえている ‖ *Mass hysteria seemed to have taken hold of the crowd.* 集団ヒステリーがその群衆を支配しているように見えた.

**get hold of sb** ▶定義 to find sb or make contact with sb ～を見つける, または～と接触する→～を捕まえる, 人と接触する, 連絡を取る ‖ *I've been trying to get hold of the complaints department all morning.* 私は午前中ずっと苦情係への連絡を試みているのですが.

**get hold of sth** ▶定義 to find sth that will be useful 役に立ちそうな～を見つける→～を見つけて・借りて使う, 手に入れる ‖ *I must try and get hold of a good second-hand bicycle.* 私は何とかして良い中古の自転車を見つけなければならない.

**holdall** /hóuldɔ̀ːl/ 图 ❻ ▶定義 a large bag that is used for carrying clothes, etc when you are traveling 旅行するときに洋服などを持ち運ぶのに使われる大きなバッグ→旅行者用衣類入れ・袋, 合切袋 ☞ **bag** のさし絵

**holder** /hóuldər/ 图 ❻（しばしば複合名詞で）▶定義1 a person who has or holds sth ～を持っているまたは握っている人→所有・保有・保持・所持者, ～を持っている人 ‖ *a season ticket holder* 定期乗車券所持者 *the world record holder in the 100 metres* 100メートル走の世界記録保持者 *holders of European passports* 欧州連合のパスポート所持者 ▶定義2 something that contains or holds sth ～を収容する, または入れておく物→入れ物, 容器, ～を入れる物 ‖ *a toothbrush holder* 歯ブラシ用容器

**hold-up** 图 ❻ ▶定義1 a delay 遅れ→停止, 中止, 休止, 延期, 妨害, 交通渋滞 ‖ *'What's the hold-up?' 'There's been an accident ahead of us.'* 「この交通渋滞は何事ですか」「前方で事故があったのです」 ▶定義2 the act of robbing a bank, etc using a gun 銃を使って銀行などを強奪する行為→強奪, 強盗 ‖ *The gang have carried out three hold-ups of high street banks.* その一味は目抜き通りにある3つの銀行で強盗を働いた.

\***hole** /hóul/ 图 ▶定義1 ❻an opening; an empty space in sth solid 開いている所; 固形の～に開いた何もない空間→穴, 破れ目, くぼみ ‖ *The pavement is full of holes.* その舗装道路は穴だらけです. *There are holes in my socks.* 靴下に穴が開いてしまった. *I've got a hole in my tooth.* 歯に穴が開いてしまった. ▶定義2 ❻the place where an animal lives in the ground or in a tree 地面または樹木にあり, 動物の住んでいる場所→(動物の)穴, 巣穴 ‖ *a mouse hole* ネズミの巣穴 ▶定義3 ❻(in golf) the hole in the ground that you must hit the ball into. Each section of the land where you play (golf course) is also called a hole. (ゴルフで)ボールを打ってその中に入れなければならない地面の穴. プレーするための土地(ゴルフコース)の各区画も hole と呼ばれる ‖ *an eighteen-hole golf course* 18 ホールのゴルフコース

\***holiday** /hɔ́lədèi, -di/ 图 ▶定義1 (米**vacation**) ❻ ❶a period of rest from work or school (often when you go and stay away from home) 仕事または学校の休みの期間(その時期は出掛けて家を離れることが多い)→休日, 休み, 休暇 ‖ *We're going to Italy **for our** summer **holidays** this year.* 私たちは今年の夏の休暇でイタリアに行く予定です. *How much holiday do you get a year in your new job?* 新しい仕事では1年にどれくらいの休日が取れますか. *Mr Philips isn't here this week. He's away **on holiday**.* フィリップ氏は今週不在です. 休暇に出掛けております. *I'm going to **take a** week's **holiday** in May and spend it at home.* 私は5月に1週間の休暇を取って家で過ごすつもりです. *the school/Christmas/Easter/summer holidays* 学校の・ク

# holiday camp

リスマス・イースター(復活祭)・夏季休暇
▶ leave は特別な理由で仕事に行かないときのこと: *sick leave* ((有給の) 病気休暇) *maternity leave* (= *when you are having a baby*) (産休 = 子供を産むむとき) *unpaid leave* (無給休暇)

▶定義2 ⓒa day of rest when people do not go to work, school, etc often for religious or national celebrations しばしば宗教的または国民的祝い事で、人々が仕事や学校などに行かない休みの日→**公休日, 祭日, 祝日** ‖ *Next Monday is a holiday.* 次の月曜日は祭日です. *New Year's Day is a bank/public holiday in Britain.* 元日は英国では一般公休日・公務休業日です.

▶この意味の holiday はイギリス英語とアメリカ英語の両方で使われる。自分で仕事に行かないと決めた日は day off とも呼ばれる: *I'm having two days off next week when we move house.* (私は来週引っ越しなので2日休む予定です.)

### ▶社会・文化

**英米の祝祭日**

1月1日 New Year's Day / 1月15日 Martin Luther King Day (米) / 2月14日 St. Valentine's Day / 2月22日 Washington's Birthday (米) / 3月 Easter / 5月1日 May Day / 5月30日 Memorial Day (米) / 6月10日 Queen's (Official) Birthday (英) / 7月4日 Independence Day (米) / Labor Day (米) / 10月12日 Columbus Day (米) / 10月31日 Halloween / 11月1日 All Saints' Day / 11月5日 Guy Fawkes Day (英) / 11月11日 Veterans' Day (米) / 11月第4木曜 Thanksgiving Day (米) / 12月25日 Christmas Day / 12月26日 Boxing Day

**holiday camp** 图 ⓒ 英 ▶定義 a place that provides a place to stay and organized entertainment for people on holiday 休暇中の人々の滞在場所と, 組織された娯楽を提供する場所→**休暇村, 行楽地**

**holidaymaker** /hálədeɪmèɪkər, -di-/ 图 ⓒ 英 ▶定義 a person who is away from home on holiday 休暇で家を離れている人→**休暇を取っている人, (休日の) 行楽客**

**\*hollow**¹ /hálou/ 形 ▶定義1 with a hole or empty space inside 内部に穴または空洞がある→**(物の中が) 空っぽの, うつろの, 空洞の** ‖ *a hollow tree* 中ががらんどうの木 ▶定義2 (used about parts of the face) sinking deep into the face (顔の部分について) 顔の奥深くに入り込んだ→**落ち込んだ, くぼんだ, へこんだ** ‖ *hollow cheeks* こけたほお *hollow-eyed* くぼんだ目をした ▶定義3 not sincere 誠実でない→**(言葉・感情などが) 上辺だけの, 内容のない, 不誠実な, (心が) むなしい** ‖ *a hollow laugh/voice* うつろな笑い・弱々しい声 *hollow promises/threats* 空約束・上辺だけの脅し ▶定義4 (used about a sound) seeming to come from a hollow place (音について) 空洞の場所から聞こえてくるような→**(音・声などが) こもった音で反響する, うつろに響く** ‖ *hollow footsteps* 低く反響する足音

**hollow**² /hálou/ 動
句動詞 **hollow sth out** ▶定義 to take out the inside part of sth ～の内側の部分を取り出す→**～をえぐり抜く, ～をくりぬく**

**hollow**³ /hálou/ 图 ⓒ ▶定義 an area that is lower than the land around it 周りよりも土地が低くなっている地域→**くぼみ, へこみ, 穴, くぼ地, 盆地, 谷間**

**holly** /háli/ 图 ⓒ ▶定義 a plant that has shiny dark green leaves with sharp points and red berries in the winter. It is often used as a Christmas decoration. 鋭い刺があり, つやのある濃い緑色をした葉をつけ, 冬に赤い実がなる植物. クリスマスの装飾用によく使われる→**セイヨウヒイラギ (の類), その赤い実のついた枝葉**

**holocaust** /hálǝkɔ̀:st, hóʊ-/ 图 ⓒ ▶定義 a situation where a great many things are destroyed and a great many people die 大量の物が破壊され大勢の人々が死ぬ状況→**(特に火による) 大虐殺, 大量焼殺, 大破壊, 全滅** ‖ *a nuclear holocaust* 核兵器による人類破滅

**hologram** /hóʊlougræ̀m, hálou-/ 图 ⓒ ▶定義 an image or picture which appears to stand out from the flat surface it is on when light falls on it 平らな表面に上から光が当たったとき, そこから浮き上がるように見える画像, または絵→**ホログラム (レーザー光線を利用した立体画像), レーザー写真**

**holster** /hóʊlstər/ 名 C ▶定義 a leather case for a gun that is fixed to a belt or worn under the arm ベルトに固定するか、または腕の下に装着する皮製の銃の入れ物 → (腰に下げる) ピストルの皮ケース

*****holy** /hóʊli/ 形 (**holier**; **holiest**) ▶定義 1 connected with God or with religion and therefore very special or important 神または宗教に関連した、したがって非常に特別なまたは重要な → 神聖な, 神聖にした, 神事のための ‖ *the Holy Bible* 聖書 *holy water* 聖水 *The Koran is the holy book of Islam.* コーランはイスラム教の聖典です.

▶定義 2 (used about a person) serving God; pure (人について) 神に仕える; 純粋な → 信心深い, 気高い, 高徳な, 清らかな, 聖人のような ― **holiness** 名 U → 神聖なこと, 聖性

**homage** /hάmɪdʒ/ 名 [ U C, 通常は単数 ] 正式 ▶定義 homage (to sb/sth) something that is said or done to show respect publicly for sb 〜に対する尊敬を公式に表すために言われる、またはなされる事 → 尊敬, 敬意, (封建時代の) 臣従の誓い, 忠誠の宣誓 ‖ *Thousands came to **pay/do homage** to the dead leader.* 亡くなったその指導者に敬意を表すため、何千人もの人がやって来た.

*****home¹** /hóʊm/ 名 ▶定義 1 C U the place where you live or where you feel that you belong 生活している、またはそこに属していると感じる場所 → 家庭, 家, 故郷 ‖ *She left home (= left her parents' house and began an independent life) at the age of 21.* 彼女は21歳で家を出ました (= 両親の家を出て自立した生活を始めました). *Children from **broken homes** (= whose parents are divorced) sometimes have learning difficulties.* 崩壊した家庭 (= 両親が離婚している) の子供たちは時に学習困難になる. *That old house would make an ideal **family home**.* あの古い家屋は家族向きの理想的な住まいになるでしょう. ☛参 **house** の注

▶ 要注意. home の前には前置詞 to を用いない: *It's time to **go home**.* (家へ帰る時間です.) *She's usually tired when she gets/arrives home.* (普通彼女は疲れて帰宅します.) だれか別の人の家を表したい場合は以下のように言う必要がある: *at Jane and Andy's* または *at Jane and Andy's place/house* (ジェーンとアンディーの家で)

▶定義 2 C a place that provides care for a particular type of person or for animals ある特定の種類の人または動物のために世話を提供する場所 → 療養所, 収容所, 宿泊所, 精神病院 ‖ *a children's home (= for children who have no parents to look after them)* 子供の家 (= 面倒を見てくれる両親がいない子供たちのため) *an old people's home* 養老院 ▶定義 3 [ 単数扱い ] **the home of sth** the place where sth began ある〜が始まった場所 → 発祥地, 本場, (物の) 原産地 ‖ *Greece is said to be the home of democracy.* ギリシャは民主主義発祥の地と言われている.

成句 **at home** ▶定義 1 in your house, flat, etc 自分の家、アパートなどで → 在宅して, 家で, 自宅で ‖ *Is anybody at home?* だれかご在宅ですか. *Tomorrow we're staying at home all day.* 明日私たちは一日中家にいます.

▶ アメリカ英語で home はしばしば前置詞 at を伴わずに使われる: *Is anybody home?* (だれかご在宅ですか.)

▶定義 2 comfortable, as if you were in your own home まるで自分の家にいるように心地良い → 気楽に, くつろいで ‖ *Please make yourself at home.* どうぞお楽にしてください. *I felt quite at home on the ship.* 私はその船でとてもくつろいでいた. ▶定義 3 (used in sport) played in the town to which the team belongs (スポーツで) チームが所属する町で行われて → 本拠地で (行われる) ‖ *Manchester City are playing at home on Saturday.* マンチェスターシティは土曜日にホームグラウンドで試合をすることになっている.

**romp home/to victory** ⇒ **ROMP**

*****home²** /hóʊm/ 形 (名詞の前だけ) ▶定義 1 connected with home 家に関連して → 家庭 (用) の, 自家製の, 自宅の, 故郷の ‖ *home cooking* 家庭料理 *your home address/town* 自宅住所・郷里 *a happy home life (= with your family)* 幸せな家庭生活 (= 家族との生活) ▶定義 2 特に 英 connected with your own country, not with a foreign country 外国ではなく母国に関連した → 本国の, 国内の ‖ *The **Home Secretary** is responsible for **home affairs**.* 内務大臣は内政に責任がある. ▶定義 3 (used in sport) connected with a team's own sports ground (スポーツで) チーム

自身のスポーツグラウンドに関連した➡地元の, 本拠地での ‖ *The home team has a lot of support.* その地元チームは多くの支援を受けている. *a home game* ホームグラウンドでの試合 ⇨ **away**

\***home**³ /hóʊm/ 副 ▶定義 at, in or to your home or home country 自分の家または国に[で・へ]➡我が家に[へ], 故郷に[へ], 自国に[へ] ‖ *We must be getting home soon.* 私たちはもうすぐ家に着くはずだ. *She'll be flying home for New Year.* 彼女は新年に飛行機で帰国するでしょう.

成句 **bring sth home to sb** ▶定義 to make sb understand sth fully ~に…を完全に理解させる➡人に~をはっきり悟らせる, 十分納得させる, 痛切に感じさせる

**drive sth home (to sb)** ⇒ **DRIVE**¹

**home**⁴ /hóʊm/ 動
句動詞 **home in on sb/sth** ▶定義 to move towards sb/sth ~に向かって移動する➡~に正確に向かう, 的を絞る, 焦点を合わせる ‖ *The police homed in on the house where the thieves were hiding.* 警察は泥棒たちが潜んでいる家に向かった.

**homecoming** /hóʊmkÀmɪŋ/ 名 C U ▶定義 the act of returning home, especially when you have been away for a long time 特に長期間家を離れていたときに家に帰る行為➡帰宅, 帰省, 帰郷, 帰国

**home-grown** 形 ▶定義 (used about fruit and vegetables) grown in your own garden (果物や野菜について) 自分の庭で栽培した➡自家栽培の

**homeland** /hóʊmlÆnd, -lənd/ 名 C ▶定義 the country where you were born or that your parents came from, or to which you feel you belong 自分が生まれた, または両親の出身地である, またはそこに属していると感じる国➡故国, 自国, 母国

**homeless** /hóʊmləs/ 形 ▶定義 **1** having no home 家を持たない➡家のない, 飼い主のいない ▶定義 **2 the homeless** 名 [複数扱い] people who have no home 家を持たない人々➡家のない人々, ホームレスの人たち — **homelessness** 名 U ▶定義 家がないこと, ホームレスであること

**homely** /hóʊmli/ 形 英 ▶定義 (used about a place) simple but also pleasant or welcoming (場所について) 簡素だが楽しい, または居心地の良い➡(雰囲気などが) 家庭的な, 気持ちが安らぐ, (食事などが) 質素な, 素朴な, 気取らない

**home-made** 形 ▶定義 made at home; not bought in a shop 家で作られた; 店で買った物ではない➡(飲食物などが) 自家製の, 手作りの ‖ *home-made cakes* 自家製ケーキ

**the Home Office** 名 [単数扱い] 英 ▶定義 the department of the British Government that is responsible for the law, police and prisons within Britain and for decisions about who can enter the country 英本国内の法律, 警察および刑務所を管轄し, 入国者の決定に責任を持つ英国政府の部門➡内務省

**homeopath** (または **homoeopath**) /hóʊmiəpà:θ/ 名 C ▶定義 a person who treats sick people using homoeopathy 同毒療法を使って病気の人を治療する人➡同毒療法医師

**homeopathy** (または **homoeopathy**) /hòʊmiɑ́pəθi/ 名 U ▶定義 the treatment of a disease by giving very small amounts of a drug that would cause the disease if given in large amounts 多量に投与すれば病気を引き起こす薬を, ごく少量投与することによってその病気を治療する方法 ➡同毒療法 — **homeopathic** (または **homoeopathic**) /hòʊmiəpǽθɪk/ 形 ▶定義 同毒療法の ‖ *homeopathic medicine* 同毒療法の薬

**home page** 名 C ▶定義 (computing) the first of a number of pages of information on the Internet that belongs to a person or an organization. A home page contains connections to other pages of information. (コンピューター) 人または組織に属するインターネット上の情報の何枚かあるページのうちの第1ページ. home page はほかのページの情報への接続を含んでいる➡ホームページ

**the Home Secretary** 名 C 英 ▶定義 a politician in the British Government (**minister**) who is in charge of the Home Office 内務省の仕事を担当している英国政府の政治家 (大臣) ➡内務大臣 ☞参 **the Foreign Secretary**

**homesick** /hóʊmsìk/ 形 ▶定義 **homesick (for sb/sth)** sad because you are away from home and you miss it 家から離れていて家を恋しく思うために寂しい➡ホームシックの, (~を) 恋しく思う, 故郷を懐かしむ ‖ *She was very homesick* *for Canada.* 彼女はカナダを非常に恋しく思いました. — **homesickness** 名 ❶ ➔ ホームシック, 郷愁

**homeward** /hóʊmwərd/ 形 副 ▶定義 going towards home 家に向かって行く➔家路へ向かう, 帰途の; 自宅・本国へ向かって ‖ *the homeward journey* 本国への旅 *to travel homeward* 帰途に就く

\***homework** /hóʊmwəːrk/ 名 ❶ ▶定義 the written work that teachers give to students to do away from school 生徒が学外で行うように, 先生が与える書く学習➔宿題 ‖ *Have we got any homework?* 何か宿題がありますか. *We've got a translation to do for homework.* 私たちは宿題で翻訳をしなければなりません.

▶ homework は数えられない. したがって複数形で用いることはできないことに注意する. 1つの単位を言いたい場合 (「1つの宿題」と言いたい場合) は, a piece of homework と言う必要がある.

☞参 **housework** の注

> ▶日本語 vs 英語
>
> homework と assignment
>
> 「ホームワーク」に当たる英語は homework ですが, homework は, classwork (授業中に行う活動) に対して, 家で行う課題や下準備を指します. 宿題は必ずしも家庭でするとは限りません. 図書館などで, 与えられた課題 (レポート提出などに) に取り組むことが少なくないので, assignment という表現の方が好まれます. なお assignment の名詞語尾を取り, 動詞として, I was assigned to read Chapter 5. (5章を読む課題が与えられた) のように表現することもあります.

**homicidal** /hòʊməsáɪdl, hàm-/ 形 ▶定義 likely to murder sb ～を殺しそうな➔殺人 (犯) の, 殺人の傾向のある ‖ *a homicidal maniac* 殺人傾向のある狂人

**homicide** /hóʊməsàɪd, hám-/ 名 ❻ ❶ 特に 困 ▶定義 the illegal killing of one person by another; murder 人を別の人が違法に殺すこと; 殺人➔殺人, 殺人行為

**homonym** /hóʊmənìm, há-/ 名 ❻ (文法) ▶定義 a word that is spelt and pronounced like another word but that has a different meaning つづりおよび発音はほかの単語と同じだが, 異なった意味を持つ単語➔同音異義語, 同綴 (どうてつ) 同音異義語, 同綴異義語, 同名異人・物

**homophone** /hóʊmoʊfòʊn, hɑm-, -mə-/ 名 ❻ (文法) ▶定義 a word that is pronounced the same as another word but that has a different spelling and meaning 発音はほかの単語と同じだが, つづりおよび意味が異なる単語➔同音字, (異綴 (いてつ)) 同音異義語 ‖ *'Flower' and 'flour' are homophones.* flower と flour は同音異義語です.

**homosexual** /hòʊmoʊsékʃuəl, hàm-, -mə-; -sjʊəl/ 形 ▶定義 sexually attracted to people of the same sex 同性の人々に性的魅力を感じる➔同性愛の, ホモの ☞参 **heterosexual, bisexual, gay, lesbian** — **homosexual** 名 ❻ ➔ 同性愛の人, ホモ — **homosexuality** /hòʊmoʊsəkʃuǽlət̬i, hàm-, -mə-; -sjʊ-/ 名 ❶ ➔ 同性愛, ホモ

**Hon** 名 ▶定義 1 Honorary; used to show that sb holds a position without being paid for it 給料を支払われずにある地位に就いている人を表すのに用いて➔肩書きだけの, 名誉職の, 無給の ‖ *Hon President* 名誉会長 ▶定義 2 Honourable; a title for Members of Parliament and some high officials 英国下院議員および一部の高官に対する敬称➔閣下

\***honest** /ánəst/ 形 ▶定義 1 (used about a person) telling the truth; not deceiving people or stealing (人について) 真実を話す; 人をだましたり盗んだりしない➔正直な, 誠実な, うそを言わない, 本当のことを言う, 尊敬に値する ‖ *Just be honest - do you like this skirt or not?* 正直に言ってください - このスカートが好きですか嫌いですか. *To be honest, I don't think that's a very good idea.* 本当の事を言うと, それはあまり名案ではないと思います. ▶定義 2 showing honest qualities 正直さが表れた➔実直そうな, (意見などが) 率直な, 偽りのない, ごまかしのない ‖ *an honest face* 実直そうな顔 *I'd like your honest opinion, please.* あなたの率直な意見を聞かせてください. ⇔ 両方の定義 **dishonest** — **honesty** 名 ❶ ➔ 正直, 誠実 ⇔ **dishonesty**

**honestly** /ánəstli/ 副 ▶定義 1 in an honest way 正直なやり方で➔正直に, 純粋に, 正当に, 公正に

‖ *He tried to answer the lawyer's questions honestly.* 彼は弁護士の質問に対し正直に答えようと努めました. ▶定義2 used for emphasizing that what you are saying is true 言っている事が真実だと強調するのに用いて→**正直に言って, 実際に, 本当に** ‖ *I honestly don't know where she has gone.* 彼女がどこへ行ったか本当に知りません. ▶定義3 used for expressing disapproval 非難を表すのに用いて→**いやはや, 全く** ‖ *Honestly! What a mess!* 全く. 何て散らかっているんだ.

**honey** /hʌ́ni/ 名 Ⓤ ▶定義 the sweet sticky substance that is made by bees and that people eat ミツバチにより作られ, 人の食用になる甘くて粘り気のある物質→**はちみつ** ☞ C4 ページのさし絵

▶ honey は darling (特に米国で用いられる) に代わる語でもある.

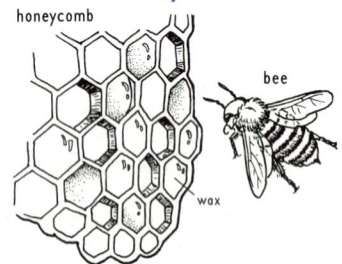
**honeycomb**

**honeycomb** /hʌ́nɪkòʊm/ 名 Ⓒ Ⓤ ▶定義 a structure of holes (cells) with six sides, in which bees keep their eggs and the substance they produce (honey) ミツバチが卵および自分たちが作った物質 (はちみつ) を保存する六角形の穴 (ハチの巣穴) から成る構造→**ミツバチの巣, ハチの巣, ハチの巣状のもの**

**honeymoon** /hʌ́nimùːn/ 名 Ⓒ ▶定義 a holiday that is taken by a man and a woman who have just got married 結婚したばかりの男女が取る休暇→**新婚旅行, 新婚休暇, 蜜月 (みつげつ)** ‖ *We had our first argument while we were on our honeymoon.* 私たちは新婚旅行中に初めて口論しました.

**honk** /hɑŋk/ 動 Ⓘ Ⓣ ▶定義 to sound the horn of a car; to make this sound 車の警笛を鳴らす; そういった音を鳴らす→**(〜に) 警笛を鳴らす, (警笛が) 鳴る; (警笛) を鳴らす**

**honorary** /ɑ́nr(ə)ri; ɑ́nərèri/ 形 ▶定義1 given as an honour (without the person needing the usual certificates, etc) (その人が通常の履修証明書などを必要とせずに) 名誉として与えられた→**(学位などが) 名誉として与えられる, 名誉 (上) の** ‖ *to be awarded an honorary degree* 名誉学位を与えられる ▶定義2 (しばしば **Honorary**) (略 **Hon**) not paid→**無給の, 肩書きだけの, 名誉職の** ‖ *He is the Honorary President.* 彼は名誉会長です.

**honour**¹ (米 **honor**) /ɑ́nər/ 名 ▶定義1 ❶ the respect from other people that a person, country, etc gets because of high standards of behaviour and moral character 行動規範および道徳的人格において優れているため, 人, 国などが他人から受ける尊敬→**名誉, 名声, 信用, 面目, 体面, 道義 [道徳] 心** ‖ *the guest of honour* (= *the most important one*) (晩餐 (ばんさん) 会などの) 主賓 (= 最重要来賓) ☞参 **dishonour** ▶定義2 [単数扱い] 正式 something that gives pride or pleasure 名誉または喜びを与えるもの→**(地位の高い人から好意を受ける) 光栄, 特権, 名誉となるもの, 誉れ** ‖ *It was a great honour to be asked to speak at the conference.* その会議で演説を依頼されたことは大変光栄でした. ▶定義3 ❶ the quality of doing what is morally right 道徳的に正しい事をする性質→**道義心, 自尊心, 体面** ‖ *I give you my word of honour.* 私の名誉にかけてあなたに約束します. ▶定義4 **Honours** [複数扱い] the four highest marks you can be given in Bachelor degrees 学士号において授与される4つの優等賞→**(大学の) 優等** 成句 **in honour of sb/sth; in sb/sth's honour** ▶定義 out of respect for sb/sth 〜に対する尊敬から→**〜に敬意を表して, 〜を祝・記念して** ‖ *A party was given in honour of the guests from Bonn.* ボンからの来賓に敬意を表してパーティーが開かれた.

**honour**² (米 **honor**) /ɑ́nər/ 動 Ⓣ ▶定義1 honour sb/sth (with sth) to show great (public) respect for sb/sth or to give sb pride or pleasure 〜に (公式に) 大変な敬意を表す, または〜に名誉または喜びを与える→**人に (〜の) 栄誉 [名誉・光栄] を授ける** ‖ *I am very honoured by the* confidence you have shown in me. あなたに信頼していただき、とても光栄です. ▶定義2 to do what you have agreed or promised 同意または約束した事を行う→(約束・協定など)を守る

**honourable** (米 **honorable**) /ˈɒn(ə)rəb(ə)l/ 形 ▶定義1 acting in a way that makes people respect you; having or showing honour 人から尊敬されるような行動を取る;敬意を持ったまたは表した→尊敬すべき、立派な、あっぱれな、高潔な ⇔ **dishonourable** ▶定義2 **the Honourable** (略 **the Hon**) a title that is given to some high officials and to Members of Parliament when they are speaking to each other 一部の高官および英国下院議員がお互いに話し掛けるときに使う敬称→閣下 ― **honourably** /-əb(ə)li/ 副 →立派に、尊敬されるように

**Hons** /ɒnz/ 略 Honours (in Bachelor degrees) (学士号で)→(大学の)優等 ‖ John North BSc (Hons) ジョン ノース理学士 (優等学位)

**hood** /hʊd/ 名 C ▶定義1 the part of a coat, etc that you pull up to cover your head and neck in bad weather 天候が悪いとき引き上げて頭および首を覆う外套 (がいとう) などの一部→(外套などの)フード、ずきん ▶定義2 特に 米 a soft cover for a car that has no roof, or a folding cover on transport for a baby (a pram) that can be folded down in good weather 屋根のない車のための柔らかい覆い、または赤ちゃんを運ぶ乗り物 (乳母車) に付いた折り畳み式覆いで、天候が良いときは折り畳んでおけるもの→自動車・乳母車の幌 (ほろ),フード・ずきん状の物 ▶定義3 米 = BONNET(1)

**hoof** /huːf, hʊf/ 名 C (複 **hoofs** または **hooves** /hʊvz, huːvz; huːvz/) ▶定義 the hard part of the foot of horses and some other animals 馬およびその他一部の動物にある足の硬い部分→(馬・牛・シカなどの)ひづめ、(馬・牛などのひづめのある)足 ☞参 paw と horse のさし絵

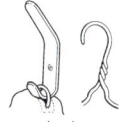
hooks

hanger

★**hook**¹ /hʊk/ 名 C ▶定義1 a curved piece of metal, plastic, etc that is used for hanging sth on or for catching fish ～を掛ける、または魚を捕まえるのに使われる曲がった金属、プラスチックなど→(物を掛ける・引っ掛けるための)かぎ、留め金、ホック、釣り針、わな ‖ Put your coat on the hook over there. コートをあちらの洋服掛けに掛けておきなさい. a fish-hook 魚の釣り針 ▶定義2 (used in boxing) a way of hitting sb that is done with the arm bent (ボクシングで用いて)ひじを曲げて～を打つやり方→フック ‖ a right hook (= with the right arm) 右フック (= 右腕で打った)

成句 **off the hook** ▶定義 (used about the top part of a telephone) not in position, so that telephone calls cannot be received (電話の受話器を置く部分について)受話器がきちんと置かれていないので、電話を受けることができない→(受話器が)外れて

**get/let sb off the hook** 略式 ▶定義 to free yourself or sb else from a difficult situation or punishment 自分またはほかの人を、困難な状況からまたは罰から解放する→窮地を脱する、解放される;解放してやる ‖ My father paid the money I owed and got me off the hook. 父は私の借金を支払って窮地から救ってくれた.

**hook**² /hʊk/ 動 ▶定義1 自他 to fasten or catch sth with a hook or sth in the shape of a hook; to be fastened in this way かぎ、またはかぎ型の～を使って…をしっかり留める、または捕まえる;そのような方法でしっかり留められている→物をかぎで引っ掛ける・留める、～をホックで留める、(魚など)を釣り上げる、かぎ針・釣り針に引っ掛ける;かぎ・ホックで留まる ‖ We hooked the trailer to the back of the car. 私たちはトレーラーを車の後ろにしっかりつないだ. The curtain simply hooks onto the rail. そのカーテンは簡単にレールに掛けられる. ▶定義2 他 to put sth through a hole in sth else ～を別の…の穴に通す→物をかぎ形に曲げて物と組む、～を曲げてつなぐ ‖ Hook the rope through your belt. そのロープをあなたのベルトに通しなさい.

句動詞 **hook (sth) up (to sth)** ▶定義 to connect sb/sth to a piece of electronic equipment or to a power supply ～を1個の電子機器または動力源に接続する→物を物につなぐ、接続する

**hook and eye** 名 C ▶定義 a thing that is used

for fastening clothes 洋服を留めるのに用いられる物→(服の)かぎホック ☞ button のさし絵

**hooked** /hokt/ 形 ▶定義1 shaped like a hook→かぎの形をした ‖ *a hooked nose* かぎ鼻 ▶定義2 (名詞の前は不可) 略式 hooked (on sth) dependent on sth bad, especially drugs 悪い〜, 特に薬物に依存した→常習して, 中毒になって ‖ *to be hooked on gambling* とばくがやめられない ☞類 **addicted** ▶定義3 (名詞の前は不可) 略式 hooked (on sth) enjoying sth very much, so that you want to do it, see it, etc as much as possible 〜をとても楽しんでいるので, できるだけたくさんやりたい, 見たいなど→夢中になっている, 病み付きになっている ‖ *Suzi is hooked on computer games.* スージーはコンピューターゲームに夢中になっている.

**hooligan** /húːlɪɡən/ 名 C ▶定義 a person who behaves in a violent and aggressive way in public places 公共の場において暴力的および攻撃的に振る舞う人→フーリガン(特にサッカー場など公共の場で暴れる若者), 熱狂的ファン ‖ *football hooligans* サッカーフーリガン ☞参 **lout, yob** — **hooliganism** /-ɪz(ə)m/ U → 乱暴, 無頼生活

**hoop** /huːp/ 名 C ▶定義 a large metal or plastic ring 金属またはプラスチック製の大きな輪→輪, 環帯, (たるの)たが, (一般に)輪状の物

**hooray** = HURRAY

**hoot**¹ /huːt/ 名 ▶定義1 C 特に 英 a short loud laugh or shout 大声の短い笑いまたは叫び→笑い, (不満・不賛成・軽べつの)叫び声, あざけり(の叫び声), ワーワーやじる声 ‖ *hoots of laughter* 叫ぶような笑い声 ▶定義2 [単数扱い] (口語) a situation or a person that is very funny 非常におかしい状況または人→笑いの原因, 底抜けに面白い事・物・人 ‖ *Bob is a real hoot!* ボブは本当におかしなやつだ. ▶定義3 C the loud sound that is made by the horn of a vehicle 乗り物の警笛が出す大きな音→(汽笛・警笛の)ブーブー, ポー(という音), 警笛, 汽笛 ▶定義4 C the cry of a particular bird (an owl) ある特定の鳥(フクロウ)の鳴き声→(フクロウの)ホーホーと鳴く声

**hoot**² /huːt/ 動 自 他 ▶定義 to sound the horn of a car or to make a loud noise 車の警笛を鳴らす, または大きな音を立てる→(車・運転手が)ブーブーと鳴らす, (汽車・サイレンなどが)ブーブーと鳴る, (軽べつの笑いなどで)はやし立てる, ワーワー言い立てる ‖ *The driver hooted (his horn) at the dog but it wouldn't move.* 運転手はその犬に警笛を鳴らしたが, 犬は動こうとしなかった. *They hooted with laughter at the suggestion.* 彼らはその提案に大笑いした.

**hoover** /húːvər/ 動 自 他 英 ▶定義 to clean a carpet, etc with a machine that sucks up the dirt 汚れを吸い込む機械を使ってじゅうたんなどを掃除する→(床・カーペットなど)に電気掃除機をかける ‖ *This carpet needs hoovering.* このカーペットは掃除機をかける必要があります. ☞類 **vacuum** — **Hoover**™ 名 C →フーバー電気掃除機 ☞類 **vacuum cleaner**

**hooves** /huːvz/ **HOOF** の複数形

### hop/jump/bounce

hopping　jumping　bouncing

**hop**¹ /hɑp/ 動 自 (**hopping**; **hopped**) ▶定義1 (used about a person) to jump on one leg (人について)片足で跳ぶ→(人が)(片足で)ぴょんぴょん跳ぶ, ひょい・ぴょんと跳ぶ ‖ *I had twisted my ankle so badly I had to hop all the way back to the car.* 私は大層ひどく足首を捻挫(ねんざ)したので, 車までずっと片足跳びで戻らねばならなかった. ▶定義2 (used about an animal or bird) to jump with both or all feet together (動物または鳥について)両足または全部の足をそろえて跳ぶ→(小鳥・カエルなどが)(足をそろえて)ぴょんぴょん跳ぶ ▶定義3 hop (from sth to sth) to change quickly from one activity or subject to another 1つの活動または対象から次のものへ素早く移る→(〜から…へと)あちこちに跳ぶ, 転々とする, ひょいひょいと移っていく

成句 **hop it!** (俗語) ▶定義 Go away! →あっちへ行け. 行っちまえ. うせろ.

句動詞 **hop in/into sth; hop out/out of sth**

略式 ▶定義 to get in or out of a car, etc (quickly) 車などに（急いで）乗る；車から（急いで）降りる→〜に飛び乗る，さっと・ひょいと乗る；〜から飛び降りる，さっと・ひょいと降りる

**hop on/onto sth; hop off sth** 略式 ▶定義 to get onto/off a bus, etc (quickly) バスなどに（急いで）乗る；バスから（急いで）降りる→〜に飛び乗る，さっと・ひょいと乗る；〜から飛び降りる，さっと・ひょいと降りる

**hop**² /hάp/ 图 ▶定義1 **C** a short jump by a person on one leg or by a bird or animal with its feet together 人が片足で，あるいは鳥または動物が足をそろえて短く跳ぶこと→（人の）片足跳び，跳躍，けんけん，（小鳥・カエルなどの）両足跳び，カエル跳び ▶定義2 **C** a tall climbing plant with flowers 花をつける丈の高いつる性の植物→ホップ ▶定義3 **hops**［複数扱い］the flowers of this plant that are used in making beer ビールを作るのに使われるこの植物の花→ホップ（の実）

★**hope**¹ /hóup/ 動 自他 ▶定義 hope that...; hope to do sth; hope (for sth) to want sth to happen or be true 〜が起きること，または本当であることを望む，〜であることを願う，〜したいと思う，〜することを望む，(〜を)望む，期待する‖ 'Is it raining?' '**I hope not**. I haven't got a coat with me.'「雨は降っていますか」「降っていなければいいのですが．私はコートを持ってきていないのです」'Are you coming to London with us?' 'I'm not sure yet but **I hope so**.'「ロンドンまで私たちと一緒にいらっしゃいますか」「まだはっきり分かりませんが，そうしたいと思っています」 I hope that you feel better soon. すぐに良くなるよう祈っています． Hoping to hear from you soon (= at the end of a letter). お返事をお待ちしています（= 手紙の末尾で）．

★**hope**² /hóup/ 图 ▶定義1 **C U** (a) hope (of/for sth); (a) hope of doing sth; (a) hope that... the feeling of wanting sth to happen and thinking that it will 〜が起こってほしいと望み，なおかつ起こるだろうと思う気持ち→（〜に対する）希望，望み，見込み，期待，可能性‖ What hope is there for the future? 将来にどんな希望がありますか． There is no hope of finding anybody else alive. ほかに生存者が見つかる見込みはありません． David has **high hopes** of becoming a jockey (= is very confident about it). デーヴィッ

### hopefully 819

ドは騎手になるという大望を抱いています（= その事に関してとても自信を持っている）． She never **gave up hope** that a cure for the disease would be found. 彼女はその病気の治療法が見つかるという望みを決して捨てなかった．

▶定義2［単数扱い］a person, a thing or a situation that will help you get what you want 自分が望むものを手に入れることの助けになりそうな人，物，または状況→希望を与える人・物，期待される人・物，頼み，ホープ‖ Please can you help me? You're my **last hope**. 力を貸してくださいますか．あなたが最後の頼みの綱なのです．

成句 **dash sb's hopes (of sth/of doing sth)** ⇒ **DASH**²

**in the hope of sth/that...** ▶定義 because you want sth to happen 〜が起こるよう望んでいるので→（〜することを・〜であることを）希望して‖ I came here in the hope that we could talk privately. あなたと個人的にお話できると期待してここに来ました．

**pin (all) your hopes on sb/sth** ⇒ **PIN**²
**a ray of hope** ⇒ **RAY**

**hopeful** /hóupful, -f(ə)l/ 形 ▶定義1 hopeful (about sth); hopeful that... believing that sth that you want will happen 望んでいる〜が確かに起こるだろうと思う→（人が）(〜に)望みを抱いている，(〜を・〜だと) 希望・期待している，希望に満ちた‖ He's very hopeful about the success of the business. 彼はその事業の成功にとても期待している． The ministers seem hopeful that an agreement will be reached. 大臣たちは協定が結ばれるだろうと楽観しているように見える． ▶定義2 making you think that sth good will happen 何か良い〜が起こるだろうと思わせる→（人・事が）有望な，見込みがある‖ a hopeful sign 有望な兆し

**hopefully** /hóupfəli, -f(ə)li/ 副 ▶定義1 略式 I/We hope; if everything happens as planned 願わくば；すべてが計画通りいけば→うまくいけば，できれば，願わくば‖ Hopefully, we'll be finished by six o'clock. うまくいけば6時までには終わるだろう． ▶定義2 hoping that what you want will happen 自分が望んでいることが起こるだろうと期待して→希望を持って，期待して‖ She smiled hopefully at me, waiting for my *answer.* 彼女は期待して私にほほえみかけ、私が答えるのを待っていた.

**hopeless** /hóʊpləs/ 形 ▶定義1 giving no hope that sth/sb will be successful or get better 〜がうまくいく望みがない、または良くなる望みがない→見込み・望みのない、絶望的な；望みを失った、絶望した‖ *It's hopeless. There is nothing we can do.* 絶望的です. 私たちにできることは何もありません. ▶定義2 略式 **hopeless (at sth)** 特に 英 (used about a person) often doing things wrong; very bad at doing sth（人について）しばしば間違った事をする；〜をするのがとても下手な→どうしようもない、(人が)(〜が)下手な、うまくない‖ *I'm absolutely hopeless at tennis.* 私はテニスは全然駄目です. — **hopelessly** 副 →望みを失って、絶望して；見込みなく、手が付けられないくらい‖ *They were hopelessly lost.* 彼らは完全に迷子になった. — **hopelessness** 名 ❶→絶望、絶望的な状態

**horde** /hɔːrd/ 名 a very large number of people 非常に大勢の人々→大群、群衆

**horizon** /həráɪz(ə)n/ 名 ▶定義1 [単数扱い] the line where the earth and sky appear to meet 大地と空が出会っているように見える線→地平線、水平線、地平‖ *The ship appeared on/disappeared over the horizon.* 船が水平線から現れた・水平線のかなたに消えた. ▶定義2 **horizons** [複数扱い] the limits of your knowledge or experience 知識または経験の限界→(知識・経験などの)限界、範囲、(思考などの)視野、展望‖ *Foreign travel is a good way of expanding your horizons.* 海外旅行は視野を広げるのに役立つ.

成句 **on the horizon** ▶定義 likely to happen soon 直に起こりそうな→兆しが見えて、起こりかかって、差し迫って‖ *There are further job cuts on the horizon.* さらに仕事が削減される兆しが現れている.

*★**horizontal** /hɔ̀(ː)rəzántl, hɑ̀r-/ 形 ▶定義 going from side to side, not up and down; flat or level 上から下ではなく端から端への；平らな、または水平の→水平の、横向きの、地平線(上)の、平面の、平らな‖ *The gymnasts were exercising on the horizontal bars.* その体操選手は鉄棒の練習をしていた.

➤ vertical, perpendicular と比較.
● **line** のさし絵 — **horizontally** /-tli/ 副 →水平に、横に、水平方向に

**hormone** /hɔ́ːrmoʊn/ 名 Ⓒ ▶定義 a substance in your body that influences growth and development 成長と発達に影響を与える体内の物質→ホルモン

*★**horn** /hɔːrn/ 名 Ⓒ ▶定義1 one of the hard pointed things that some animals have on their heads ある種の動物の頭にある硬くてとがった物の一方→角(つの) ☛ **cow** のさし絵 ☛ **goat** のさし絵 ▶定義2 the thing in a car, etc that gives a loud warning sound 車などに付いていて、大きな警告音を出す物→警笛、クラクション‖ *Don't sound your horn late at night.* 夜遅くクラクションを鳴らしてはいけません. ☛ S7ページのさし絵 ▶定義3 one of the family of metal musical instruments that you play by blowing into them 吹いて演奏する金管楽器の一種→ホルン、金管楽器、ラッパ、角笛‖ *the French horn* フレンチホルン ☛参 **piano** の注 ☛ **music** のさし絵

**horoscope** /hɔ́(ː)rəskoʊp, hɑ́r-/ 名 Ⓒ (または **stars** [複数扱い]) ▶定義 a statement about what is going to happen to a person in the future, based on the position of the stars and planets when he/she was born 人が誕生した時の星や惑星の位置に基づいて、将来その人に何が起こるかについて述べるもの→星占い、占星術、運勢‖ *What does my horoscope for next week say?* 星占いで来週の私の運勢はどうなっていますか. ☛参 **astrology, zodiac**

**horrendous** /hɔ(ː)réndəs, hɑr-, hə-/ 形 略式 ▶定義 very bad or unpleasant 大変ひどいまたは不愉快な→とても嫌な、ひどい、とても恐ろしい、ぞっとするような‖ *The queues were absolutely horrendous.* その行列は全くもってひどいものでした. — **horrendously** 副 →恐ろしく、ものすごく、ひどく

*★**horrible** /hɔ́(ː)rəb(ə)l, hɑ́r-/ 形 ▶定義1 略式 bad or unpleasant ひどいまたは不愉快な→ひどい、嫌な、不愉快、不親切な‖ *This coffee tastes horrible!* このコーヒーはとてもひどい味です. *Don't be so horrible! (= unkind)* そんなに冷たく(=不親切に)しないで. *I've got a horrible feeling that I've forgotten something.* 何か忘れ物をしたような嫌な予感がします. ☛類 hor-

**rid** ▶定義2 shocking and/or frightening 衝撃的な、および・またはぞっとするような➡恐ろしい、身の毛のよだつような、ものすごい ‖ *a horrible murder/death/nightmare* 身の毛もよだつ殺人・恐ろしい死に方・ぞっとするような悪夢 ― **horribly** /-əb(ə)li/ 副 ➡恐ろしく、ものすごく、ひどく

**horrid** /hɔ́(:)rəd, hár-/ 形略式 ▶定義 very unpleasant or unkind 非常に不愉快な、または不親切な ➡大変ひどい、不愉快な、不親切な ‖ *horrid weather* とてもひどい天気 *I'm sorry that I was so horrid last night.* 昨夜はあんなにひどいことをしてすみません。 ☛類 **horrible**

**horrific** /hɔ(:)rífɪk, hə-/ 形 ▶定義1 extremely bad and shocking or frightening 極めてひどく、衝撃的なまたはぞっとするような ➡恐ろしい、ものすごい、ぞっとするような ‖ *a horrific murder/accident/attack* ぞっとするような殺人・恐ろしい事故・猛攻撃 ▶定義2 略式 very bad or unpleasant とてもひどい、または不愉快な ➡ひどい、嫌な、ひどく不愉快な ― **horrifically** /-k(ə)li/ 副 ➡恐ろしく、ものすごく、ひどく ‖ *horrifically expensive* ひどく高価な

**horrify** /hɔ́(:)rəfàɪ, hár-/ 動他 (現分 **horrifying**; 三単現 **horrifies**; 過、過分 **horrified**) ▶定義 to make sb feel extremely shocked, disgusted or frightened 〜にものすごい衝撃・失望・恐怖を与える ➡人をぞっとさせる、怖がらせる、人にショックを与える ― **horrifying** 形 ➡恐ろしい、ぞっとするような

**horror** /hɔ́(:)rər, hár-/ 名 ▶定義1 [U、単数扱い] a feeling of great fear or shock 大変な恐怖または衝撃を感じること ➡恐怖、恐ろしさ ‖ *They watched in horror as the building collapsed.* 彼らは恐怖を感じながらその建物が崩壊するのを見守った。 ▶定義2 Ⓒsomething that makes you feel frightened or shocked 恐怖または衝撃を感じさせるもの ➡恐ろしい[ぞっとする]人・物、嫌な[ひどい]事・物 ‖ *a horror film/story* ホラー映画・スリラー小説

*****horse** /hɔ́:rs/ 名 ▶定義1 Ⓒa large animal that is used for riding on or for pulling or carrying heavy loads その上に乗ったり、重い荷物を引いたり運ぶのに使われる大型の動物 ➡馬
 ▶ 雄馬は **stallion**、雌馬は **mare**、子馬は **foal**.
▶定義2 **the horses** [複数扱い] 略式 ▶定義 horse racing 馬のレース ➡競馬

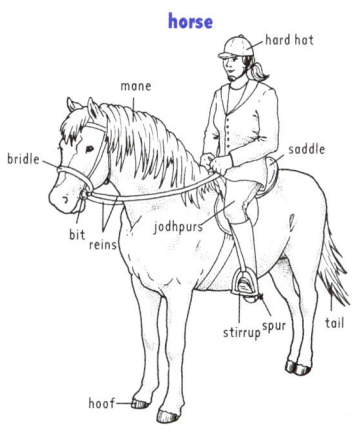

成句 **on horseback** ▶定義 sitting on a horse ➡馬に乗って
 ▶ 馬に乗った警察は **mounted police** (騎馬警察隊) と呼ばれる。

**horse chestnut** 名 Ⓒ ▶定義1 a large tree that has leaves divided into seven sections and pink or white flowers 7つに分かれた葉を持ち、ピンクまたは白い花をつける大きな木 ➡セイヨウトチノキ、マロニエ ▶定義2 (または 略式 **conker**) the nut from this tree その木になる実 ➡セイヨウトチノキの実

**horseman** /hɔ́:rsmən/ 名 Ⓒ (複 **-men** /-mən/) ▶定義 a man who rides a horse well 馬に乗るのが上手な男性 ➡騎手、騎兵、馬術士 ‖ *an experienced horseman* 経験豊富な騎手

**horsepower** /hɔ́:rspàʊər/ 名 Ⓒ (複 **horsepower**) (略 **hp**) ▶定義 a measurement of the power of an engine エンジンの出力の大きさ ➡馬力

**horse racing** (または **racing**) 名 Ⓤ ▶定義 the sport in which a person (**jockey**) rides a horse in a race to win money 人 (競馬騎手) が賞金獲得のため馬に乗って競い合うスポーツ ➡競馬
 ▶ horse racing (競馬) は **racecourse** (競馬場) で行われる。人々は競馬の結果に **bet** (お金をかける) ことが多い。

**horseshoe** /hɔ́:rsʃùː/ (または **shoe**) 名 Ⓒ

**horsewoman**

▶定義 a U-shaped piece of metal that is fixed to the bottom of a horse's foot (hoof). Some people believe that horseshoes bring good luck. 1個のU字型の金属で、馬の足（ひづめ）の底に付ける。それが幸運をもたらすと信じる人もいる→蹄鉄（ていてつ）

**horsewoman** /hɔ́ːrswùmən/ 名 C (複 -women /-wìmən/) ▶定義 a woman who rides a horse well 馬に乗るのが上手な女性→女性騎手, 女性馬術士

**horticulture** /hɔ́ːrtəkʌ̀ltʃər/ 名 U ▶定義 the study or practice of growing flowers, fruit and vegetables 花, 果物, 野菜などを育てる研究または実践→園芸（学・術）— **horticultural** /hɔ̀ːrtəkʌ́ltʃər(ə)l/ 形→園芸（学・術）の

**hose** /hóuz/（または **hosepipe** /hóuzpàɪp/）名 C U ▶定義 a long rubber or plastic tube that water can flow through 中を水が流れるゴムまたはプラスチック製の長い管→ホース ☞ garden のさし絵

**hospice** /háspəs/ 名 C ▶定義 a special hospital where people who are dying are cared for 死期が近い人々が世話をされる特別の病院→ホスピス

**hospitable** /háspɪtəb(ə)l, -́--́-/ 形 ▶定義 (used about a person) friendly and kind to visitors (人について)訪問者に対し友好的で親切な→(客を)親切に・手厚くもてなす, 歓待する ⇔ **inhospitable**

*****hospital** /háspɪtl/ 名 C ▶定義 a place where ill or injured people are treated 病気またはけがをした人々が治療を受ける場所→病院 ‖ *He was rushed to hospital in an ambulance.* 彼は救急車で病院へ担ぎ込まれた。*to be admitted to/discharged from hospital* 入院・退院する *a psychiatric/mental hospital* 精神病院

▶人が go to hospital（病院へ行く）または be in hospital（入院している）（the を伴わないで）の場合、その人はそこで治療を受けている患者である: *His mother's in hospital.*（彼の母親は入院している。）*She cut her hand and had to go to hospital.*（彼女は手を切ったので病院に行かねばならなかった。）the hospital はある特定の病院を表す、あるいはその人が病院の建物を一時的に訪問しているだけであることを表す: *He went to the hospital to visit Muriel.*（彼はミュリエルを見舞いにその病院に行った。）

病院で doctor（医師）または nureses（看護婦）の治療を受けている人は patient（患者）。事故に遭うと、最初に casualty department（救急病棟）（米 emergency room）に連れていかれる。

**hospitality** /hàspətǽləti/ 名 U ▶定義 looking after guests and being friendly and welcoming towards them 客のお世話をし, 温かく親切にもてなすこと→親切なもてなし, 歓待, 厚遇

*****host** /hóust/ 名 C ▶定義 1 a person who invites guests to his/her house, etc and provides them with food, drink, etc 客を自分の家などに招待して、食べ物、飲み物などでもてなす人→(客を接待する)主人(役), 主催者, ホスト ‖ *It's polite to write a thank-you letter to your host.* ホストにお礼状を書くのが礼儀です。☞参 **hostess**
▶定義 2 a person who introduces a television or radio show and talks to the guests テレビまたはラジオのショーを始め、またゲストと話をする人→(テレビ・ラジオ番組の)司会者
▶定義 3 **a host of sth** a large number of people or things 大勢の人または多数の物→～の大勢, 多数, 群れ — **host** 動 他 →(会など)を主催する, (テレビなどで)(番組)を司会する, (客)を接待する ‖ *The city is aiming to host the Olympic Games in ten years' time.* その町は10年後のオリンピック競技会の主催地となることを目指しています。

*****hostage** /hástɪdʒ/ 名 C ▶定義 a person who is caught and kept prisoner. A hostage may be killed or injured if the person or group who is holding him/her does not get what it is asking for. 捕まって監禁されている人。hostage を拘束している人または集団の要求が満たされない場合, 殺される, または負傷させられることがある→人質, 人質の状態 ‖ *The robbers tried to take the staff hostage.* その強盗たちは職員を人質にしようとした。*The hijackers say they will hold the passengers hostage until their demands are met.* ハイジャック犯人たちは要求が満たされるまで乗客を人質にすると言っている。☞参 **ransom**

**hostel** /hástl/ 名 C ▶定義 1 a place like a cheap hotel where people can stay when they are living away from home 安いホテルのような場所

で，人々が家を離れて生活しているとき滞在することができる→(青年旅行者用の)ホステル，(看護婦・学生の)寄宿寮‖ *a youth hostel* ユースホステル *a student hostel* 大学寄宿寮 ▶定義2 a building where people who have no home can stay for a short time 家のない人々が短期間滞在することのできる建物→簡易宿泊所，宿舎

**hostess** /hóustəs/ 名 C ▶定義1 a woman who invites guests to her house, etc and provides them with food, drink, etc 客を家などに招待して食べ物，飲み物などでもてなす女性→(家庭で客をもてなす)(女)主人(役) ☞参 host ▶定義2 a woman who introduces a television or radio show and talks to the guests テレビまたはラジオのショーを始めめ，またゲストと話をする女性→(テレビ・ラジオ番組の)(女性)司会者 ▶定義3 = AIR HOSTESS

**hostile** /hástaɪl/ 形 ▶定義 hostile (to/toward sb/sth) having very strong feelings against sb/sth 〜に対抗する非常に強い感情を持った→(〜に)敵意のある，反感を持った，非友好的な，冷淡な‖ *a hostile crowd* 反感を持った群衆 *They are very hostile to any change.* 彼らはいかなる変化にも断固反対している．

**hostility** /hɑstíləti/ 名 ▶定義1 Ⓤ hostility (to/toward sth) very strong feelings against sb/sth 〜に対抗する非常に強い気持ち→敵意，反感‖ *She didn't say anything but I could sense her hostility.* 彼女は何も言わなかったが，私には彼女の敵意を感じ取ることができた. ▶定義2 **hostilities** [複数扱い] fighting in a war 戦争で戦うこと→敵対行為，交戦状態，戦闘

\*hot¹ /hɑt/ 形 (**hotter**; **hottest**) ▶定義1 having a high temperature 高温の→暑い，熱い，熱帯(地方)の‖ *Can I open the window? I'm really hot.* 窓を開けてもいいですか．暑くてたまりません． *It was **boiling hot** on the beach.* ビーチはうだるような暑さでした． *a hot meal* 温かい食事 *Don't touch the plates - they're **red hot**!* そのお皿に触ってはいけません－とても熱いです.

▶物の温度は，freezing (cold) (凍るように冷たい・寒い)，cold (冷たい・寒い)，cool (気持ち良く冷たい・涼しい)，tepid (水について)(生ぬるい)，warm (温かい・暖かい，やや暑い)，hot (熱い・暑い)または boiling (hot) (猛烈に熱い・うだるように暑い)，というように描写できる．cold¹ の注も参照．

▶定義2 (used about food) causing a burning feeling in your mouth; spicy (食べ物について)口の中が燃えるような感じになる；薬味の利いた→辛い，ぴりっとする，ひりひりする‖ *hot curry* 辛いカレー ▶定義3 略式 difficult or dangerous to deal with 扱うのが困難な，または危険な→激しい，激烈な，物議をかもしている，(状況などが)危険な‖ *The defenders found the Italian strikers **too hot to handle**.* ディフェンダーたちはそのイタリア人ストライカーの激しさに対処できないと思った． ▶定義4 略式 exciting and popular 人をわくわくさせて人気のある→すばらしい，優れた，人気のある‖ *This band is **hot stuff**!* このバンドは最高です．

成句 **in hot pursuit** ▶定義 following sb who is moving fast 動きの速い〜を追い掛けて→(人を)激しく追跡・追撃して

> ▶日本語 vs 英語
>
> hot は「辛い」と「熱い」
>
> スパイスのよく効いた辛さを hot と言います．料理に用いられた場合は文字通り「熱い」という意味もあるので文脈から判断することが必要です．

**hot²** /hɑt/ 動 (**hotting**; **hotted**)
句動詞 **hot up** 英略式 ▶定義 to become more exciting 人をはらはらするような状況になる→(競り合いなどが)激しくなる，一段と熱気を帯びてくる‖ *The election campaign has really hotted up in the past few days.* 選挙運動はここ2〜3日本当に激しさを増している．

**hot-air balloon** = BALLOON(2)

**hot dog** 名 C ▶定義 a hot sausage in a soft bread roll 柔らかいロールパンの中に熱いソーセージを挟んだもの→ホットドッグ ☞ C4 ページのさし絵

\***hotel** /hoʊtél/ 名 ▶定義 a place where you pay to stay when you are on holiday or travelling 休暇中または旅行中にお金を払って滞在する場所→ホテル，旅館‖ *to stay in/at a hotel* ホテルに滞在する *I've booked a double room at the Grand Hotel.* グランドホテルに2人用の部屋を予約してある． *a two-star hotel* 2つ星のホテル

## 824　hotelier

➤ ホテルでは double（2人用の部屋），single（1人用の部屋）または twin-bedded（ツインベッドのある部屋）を予約する．到着するときは check in（チェックインする）または register（宿泊簿に記載する），またホテルを出るときは check out（チェックアウトする）必要がある．

**hotelier** /hoʊtéljər, ὸʊtljéɪ; (h)əʊtéliei/ 名 C
▶定義 a person who owns or manages a hotel ホテルを所有または経営する人→ホテル経営者，ホテル支配人

**hothouse** /hάtһὰʊs/ 名 C ▶定義 a heated glass building where plants are grown 植物を栽培する室温を高くしたガラスの建物で→(植物を育てる)温室 ☛参 greenhouse

**hotline** /hάtlὰɪn/ 名 C ▶定義 a direct telephone line to a business or organization 店・会社または組織へ直通の電話回線→緊急用直通電話(線)，ホットライン

**hotly** /hάtli/ 副 ▶定義 1 in an angry or excited way→怒って，興奮して，むきになって，激しく ‖ *They hotly denied the newspaper reports.* 彼らはその新聞報道を激しく否定した．▶定義 2 closely and with determination 一心に決意して → 熱心に，懸命に，猛烈に ‖ *The dog ran off, hotly pursued by its owner.* その犬が逃げ出すと，飼い主は懸命に追い掛けた．

**hot-water bottle** 名 C ▶定義 a rubber container that is filled with hot water and put in a bed to warm it ベッドを暖めるためその中に入れる，湯を入れたゴム製の容器→湯たんぽ

**hound**¹ /hάʊnd/ 名 C ▶定義 a type of dog that is used for hunting or racing 狩猟またはレースに使われる犬の一種 ‖ 猟犬 ‖ *a foxhound* フォックスハウンド(キツネ狩り用に改良された，足が速くて鼻が鋭敏な大型猟犬)

**hound**² /hάʊnd/ 動 他 ▶定義 to follow and disturb sb ～を追い掛けて悩ませる→人を追い詰める，しつこく悩ます，追い回す ‖ *Many famous people complain of being hounded by the press.* 有名人の多くが報道陣に追い回されて不平を言っている．

\***hour** /άʊər/ 名 ▶定義 1 C a period of 60 minutes 60分間→1時間，60分 ‖ *He studies for three hours most evenings.* 彼はほとんど毎晩3時間勉強します．*The programme lasts about half an hour.* その番組は約30分続きます．*I'm going shopping now. I'll be back in about an hour.* 今から買い物に行きます．1時間ほどで戻ります．*In two hours' time I'll be having lunch.* 2時間後には昼食を取っているでしょう．*a four-hour journey* 4時間の旅 *Japan is eight hours ahead of the UK.* 日本の時刻は英国よりも8時間進んでいます．*I get paid by the hour.* 私は時給制でお金をもらっている．*How much do you get paid per/an hour?* 時給はいくらもらっていますか．▶定義 2 C the distance that you can travel in about 60 minutes 約60分で移動できる距離→1時間で行ける距離・行程 ‖ *London is only two hours away.* ロンドンはここからたった2時間の所にあります．▶定義 3 **hours** [複数扱い] the period of time when sb is working or a shop, etc is open ～が働いている，または店などが開いている時間→(勤務・生活・営業などの)時間 ‖ *Employees are demanding shorter working hours.* 従業員たちは労働時間の短縮を要求している．▶定義 4 C a period of about an hour when sth particular happens ある特定の～が起きている約1時間→時刻，(ある一定の)時間，期間 ‖ *I'm going shopping in my lunch hour.* 私は昼食時間に買い物に行くつもりです．*The traffic is very bad in the rush hour.* ラッシュアワーはひどい交通渋滞になる．

▶定義 5 **the hour** [単数扱い] the time when a new hour starts (= 1 o'clock, 2 o'clock, etc) 新しい時間が始まるとき(= 1時，2時など)→正時(しょうじ)(分などの端数の付かない時刻) ‖ *Buses are on the hour and at twenty past the hour.* バスの時刻は正時および毎時20分です．

▶定義 6 **hours** [複数扱い] a long time→長時間，何時間も ‖ *He went on speaking for hours and hours.* 彼は何時間も話し続けた．

成句 **at/till all hours** ▶定義 at/until any time いつでも・いつまでも→いつでも，昼夜を問わず；いつまでも，遅くまで ‖ *She stays out till all hours* (= very late). 彼女は遅くまで(= 深夜遅くまで)帰宅しない．

**the early hours** ⇒ **EARLY**

**hourly** /άʊərli/ 形 副 ▶定義 1 done, happening, etc every hour 毎時行われる，起こるなどの→1時間ごとの，1時間に1度の，1時間当たりの ‖ *an hourly news bulletin* 1時間ごとのニュース速報

*Trains are hourly.* 列車は1時間に1本あります. ▶定義2 for one hour→ **1時間の** ‖ *What is your hourly rate of pay?* あなたの時給はいくらですか.

**\*house**¹ /háʊs/ 🔲 ⓒ ( 複 **houses** /háʊsəz/)
▶定義1 a building that is made for people to live in 人々が住むために造られた建物→**家, 家屋, 住宅, 人家** ‖ *Is yours a four-bedroomed or a three-bedroomed house?* あなたの家は寝室が4つですか, それとも3つですか. ☛参 **bungalow, cottage, flat.** home は生活している場所で, たとえ house でなくともよい. *Let's go home to my flat.* (私のアパートへ帰りましょう.) home はそこに属していると感じる場所でもある. house は単なる建物. *We've only just moved into our new house and it doesn't feel like home yet.* (私たちは新居に引っ越したばかりで, まだ我が家のような感じがしません.)
➤ house は build (建築する), do up (修理する), redecorate (改築する) または expand (増築する) ことができる. 人から house を rent (賃借りする), またはだれか別の人に house を let out (賃貸しする) こともある. move house (引っ越しをする) ときは, estate agent (不動産屋) に行く.

▶定義2 [通常は単数] all the people who live in one house 1つの家に生活しているすべての人々→**家族, 家庭, 一族** ‖ *Don't shout. You'll wake the whole house up.* 大声を出してはいけません. 家族みんなを起こしてしまいます.
▶定義3 a building that is used for a particular purpose 特定の目的に使われる建物→**(特定の目的のための) 建物, 〜小屋, 〜置き場** ‖ *a warehouse* 倉庫 ▶定義4 a large firm involved in a particular kind of business 特定の業務にかかわっている大きな会社→**〜会社, 商社, 商店** ‖ *a fashion/publishing house* ファッション商店・出版社 ▶定義5 a restaurant, usually that sells one particular type of food 通常は特定の食べ物を扱うレストラン→**〜店, 〜屋** ‖ *a curry/spaghetti house* カレー・スパゲッティ屋 *house wine (= the cheapest wine on a restaurant's menu)* ハウスワイン (= レストランのメニューにある廉価なワイン) ▶定義6 **House** a group of people who meet to make a country's laws ある国の法律を作るために一同に会する人々→**議員, 議会** ‖ *the House of Commons* 英国下院 *the*

*Houses of Parliament* 国会議事堂 ☛参 **Parliament** の注 ▶定義7 [通常は単数] the audience at a theatre or cinema, or the area where they sit 劇場または映画館の観衆, または観衆が座る区画→**観衆, 聴衆, 劇場, 演芸場** ‖ *There was a full house for the play this evening.* 今夜の芝居は大入りでした.

成句 move house ⇒ **MOVE**¹
on the house ▶定義 paid for by the pub, restaurant, etc you are visiting; free 訪れているパブ, レストランなどが勘定を支払う; 無料の→**(飲食物が) 経営者のおごりで, 無料で** ‖ *Your first drink is on the house.* 1杯目の飲み物は店のおごりです.
get on/along like a house on fire ▶定義 to immediately become good friends with sb 〜と即座に良い友達になる→**速やかに打ち解ける, (会ったばかりで) すぐ仲良くなる**

**house**² /háʊz/ 🔲 ⓒ ▶定義1 to provide sb with a place to live 〜に住む場所を提供する→**(人・建物が) 人を収容する, 泊める, 〜に住宅を与える** ‖ *The Council must house homeless families.* 評議会はホームレスの家族に住む場所を与えねばならない. ▶定義2 to contain or keep sth 〜を収納する, または保管する→**〜を格納する, 収納する, 貯蔵する** ‖ *Her office is housed in a separate building.* 彼女の事務所は別の建物の中にある.

**houseboat** /háʊsbòʊt/ 🔲 ⓒ ▶定義 a boat on a river, etc where sb lives and which usually stays in one place 川などに浮かぶボートで, 〜が住んでいて, 通常は1箇所に留まっている→**(住居用の) ハウスボート, 居住船, (宿泊設備付きの) ヨット**

**housebound** /háʊsbàʊnd/ 形 ▶定義 unable to leave your house because you are old or ill 高齢, または病気のため家の外へ出ることができない→**家の外へ出られない, 家に引きこもった**

**household** /háʊshòʊld/ 🔲 ⓒ ▶定義 all the people who live in one house and the work, money, organization, etc that is needed to look after them 1つの家に住むすべての人々, およびその人たちの面倒を見るのに必要な仕事, お金, 組織など→**(雇い人を含めて) 家中の者, 家族 (全員・全体), 世帯, 家庭** ‖ *household expenses* 家計費

**householder** /háʊshòʊldər/ 🔲 ⓒ ▶定義 a person who rents or owns a house 家を賃借りしている，または所有している人→世帯主, 家屋所有者, 戸主

**housekeeper** /háuskìːpər/ 名 C ▶定義 a person who is paid to look after sb else's house and organize the work in it 他人の家族の世話をし, 家事をするために雇われた人→（職業としての賃金を支払われる）家政婦, ハウスキーパー

**housekeeping** /háuskìːpɪŋ/ 名 U ▶定義 1 the work involved in looking after a house 家の世話に関連した仕事→家事, 家政 ▶定義 2 the money that you need to manage a house 家を切り盛りするのに必要なお金 → 家計費

**the House of Commons** 名 [単数扱い] ▶定義 the group of people (Members of Parliament) who are elected to make new laws in Britain 英国の新しい法律を作るため選挙により選ばれた一団の人々（国会議員）→英国下院

**the House of Lords** 名 [単数扱い] ▶定義 the group of people (who are not elected) who meet to discuss the laws that have been suggested by the House of Commons 会合を開いて, 英国下院によって提出された法案を議論する, (選挙で選ばれたのではない) 一団の人々 → 上院

**the House of Representatives** 名 [単数扱い] ▶定義 the group of people who are elected to make new laws in the US 米国で新しい法律を作るため選挙により選ばれた一団の人々→（米国議会の）下院 ☞参 **Congress, the Senate**

**house-proud** 形 ▶定義 paying great attention to the care, cleaning, etc of your house 家の管理, 掃除などに大変な注意を払って→家・家政自慢の

**house-to-house** 形 ▶定義 going to each house それぞれの家に行って→戸別（訪問）の, 軒並みの ‖ *The police are making house-to-house enquiries.* 警察は戸別に聴き込みをしている.

**house-warming** 名 C ▶定義 a party that you have when you have just moved into a new home 新居に引っ越したばかりの時に開くパーティー→新居開きの祝い

**housewife** /háuswàɪf/ 名 C (複 **housewives**) ▶定義 a woman who does not have a job outside the home and who spends her time cleaning the house, cooking, looking after her family, etc 家庭外に職業を持たずに, 家の掃除, 料理, 家族の世話などで時間を過ごす女性→（主に専業の）主婦
►このような事を行う男性は house husband （専業主夫）と呼ばれる.

\***housework** /háuswəˋːrk/ 名 U ▶定義 the work that is needed to keep a house clean and tidy 家を清潔にきちんと保つのに必要な仕事→家事
►要注意. 先生が生徒に課す課題で, 学課時間外に行うものを表す語は, homework.

**housing** /háuzɪŋ/ 名 U ▶定義 houses, flats, etc for people to live in 人が住むための家, アパートなど→住宅, 住宅供給, 家

**housing estate** 名 C ▶定義 an area where there are a large number of similar houses that were built at the same time 同時期に建てられた, 類似の家が多数ある地域→住宅団地

**hover** /hávər, hív-/ 動 自 ▶定義 1 (used about a bird, etc) to stay in the air in one place (鳥などについて) 空中のある1箇所にとどまる→(鳥・昆虫・ヘリコプターなどが) (〜の上で) 空中(の一点)に止まる ▶定義 2 (used about a person) to wait near sb/sth (人について) 〜の周辺で待つ→(〜のそばを)うろつく, (〜を)さまよう, 行きつ戻りつする ‖ *He hovered nervously outside the office.* 彼は事務所の外を神経質そうにうろついていた.

**hovercraft** /hávərkrɑ̀ːft, háv-; -kræft/ 名 C (複 **hovercraft**) ▶定義 a type of boat that moves over land or water on a cushion of air 陸上または水上を噴射空気で移動する種類のボート→ホバークラフト（水陸両用）

\***how** /háu/ 副 接 ▶定義 1 (often used in questions) in what way (しばしば質問で) どんな方法で→どのようにして, どんな方法で・具合に・風に ‖ *How do you spell your name?* あなたの名前はどのようにつづりますか. *Can you show me how to use this machine?* この機械をどうやって使うか見せていただけますか. *I can't remember how to get there.* どのようにしてそこまで行くか思い出せない. ▶定義 2 used when you are asking about sb's health or feelings 〜の健康または気持ちについて尋ねるときに用いて→（健康, 気持ちなどが）どんな状態・

合で ‖ 'How is your mother?' 'She's much better, thank you.' 「お母さんはいかがですか」「ありがとう,大分良くなりました」 How are you feeling today? 今日の調子はどうですか. How do you feel about your son joining the army? 息子さんが入隊されることについてどんなお気持ちですか.

▶ how を用いるのは人の健康について尋ねるときのみ. 人の性格または外見について尋ねるときは what... like? と言う: 'What is your mother like?' 'Well, she's much taller than me and she's got dark hair.' (「あなたのお母さんはどんな外見ですか」「そうですね,私よりずっと長身で,濃い色の髪をしています」)

▶定義3 used when you are asking about sb's opinion of a thing or a situation ある物または状況について~の意見を尋ねるのに用いて→(天候・状況などが)どんな状態・具合で ‖ How was the weather? お天気はどうでしたか. How is your meal? お食事はいかがでしたか. **How did the interview go?** 面接はどんな具合でしたか.

▶定義4 used in questions when you are asking about the degree, amount, age, etc of sb/sth ~の程度,量,年齢などを尋ねる問いで用いて→どれほど,どれくらい ‖ How old are you? (年齢は)おいくつですか. How much is that? それは(値段が)おいくらですか. ▶定義5 used for expressing surprise, pleasure, etc 驚き,喜びなどを表現するのに用いて→何と,いかに ‖ She's gone. How strange! 彼女はいなくなってしまった. 何と奇妙な事でしょう. I can't believe how expensive it is! 何とも信じられないほど高価だ.

感句 how/what about...? ⇒ **ABOUT**²
how come? ⇒ **COME**
how do you do? 正式 ▶定義 used when meeting sb for the first time ~に初対面のとき用いて→初めまして,こんにちは

▶要注意. How are you? と How do you do? に対する返答は異なる. How do you do? への返答は同じ表現の How do you do? が使われる. How are you? への返答はどのように感じているかによって異なる: 'I'm fine.'/'Very well.'/'Much better.' (「元気です」「とても元気です」「随分いいです」)

\*however /hauévər/ 副接 ▶定義1 正式 (used for adding a comment to what you have just said) although sth is true (言ったばかりの事にコメン

トを付け加えるために用いて)~は真実ではあるが→(先に述べられた事に対照させて)しかしながら,けれども,それにもかかわらず ‖ Sales are poor this month. There may, however, be an increase before Christmas. 今月の販売は振るわない. けれどもクリスマス前には販売が増加するかもしれない. ▶定義2 (used in questions for expressing surprise) in what way; how (質問で驚きを表すために用いて)どのような方法で;いかに→一体どのようにして ‖ However did you manage to find me here? 一体どのようにして私がここだと分かったのですか.

▶ このような質問で how だけを用いるとき,驚きの気持ちはさほど強くない.

▶定義3 in whatever way どんな方法でも→どんな方法で・どんな風に~(しよう)とも ‖ However I sat I couldn't get comfortable. どんな風にしても座り心地は良くならなかった. You can dress however you like. どんな服でも好きなものを着て構いません. ▶定義4 (形容詞または副詞の前で) to whatever degree いかなる程度でも→どんなに~(しよう)とも,どれほど~で(あって)も ‖ He won't wear a hat however cold it is. どんなに寒くても彼は帽子をかぶらないでしょう. You can't catch her however fast you run. あなたがどんなに速く走っても彼女を捕まえることはできない.

**howl** /háʊl/ 動自 ▶定義 to make a long loud sound 大きな,長く伸ばした音を出す→(犬・オオカミなどが)(~に)遠ぼえする,(風が)ヒューヒューうなる,(人が)(苦痛・悲しみなどで)うめく,うなる,わーわー泣く ‖ I couldn't sleep because there was a dog howling all night. 犬が一晩中遠ぼえしていたので眠れなかった. The wind howled around the house. 風が家の回りでヒューヒュー鳴っていました. —howl 名 C→(犬・オオカミの)遠ぼえ,(風の)うなり,(怒り・苦痛の)わめき声

**hp** /éɪtʃ píː/ ▶定義1 (used about an engine) (エンジンについて) horsepower→馬力
▶定義2 **HP** 英 hire purchase→分割払い購入方式
**HQ** /éɪtʃ kjúː/ 略 headquarters→本部,司令部
**hr** (複 **hrs**) 略 hour→1時間,60分間 ‖ 3 hrs 15 min 3時間15分
**hub** /hʌb/ 名 [通常は複数] ▶定義1 the hub (of

sth) the central and most important part of a place or an activity ある場所または活動の中心の最重要部分→**中心地・点, 中枢** ‖ *the commercial hub of the city* その都市の商業上の中心(地) ▶定義2 the central part of a wheel 車輪の中心部→**(車輪の) ハブ, こしき**

**hubbub** /hÁbʌb/ 名 [単数扱い, ❶] ▶定義1 the noise made by a lot of people talking at the same time 大勢の人が同時に話すことによって起こる騒音→**どよめき, ワイワイガヤガヤ** ‖ *I couldn't hear the announcement over the hubbub.* 人々のざわめきでそのアナウンスが聞こえなかった. ▶定義2 a situation in which there is a lot of noise, excitement and activity 騒音, 興奮および活動にあふれた状況→**混乱, 騒動, 騒ぎ** ‖ *the hubbub of city life* 都会生活の喧噪 (けんそう)

**huddle**¹ /hÁdl/ 動 ❶ huddle (up) (together) ▶定義1 to get close to other people because you are cold or frightened 寒いまたは恐ろしいために他人に寄り添う→**群がる, 身を寄せ合う, 密集する** ‖ *The campers huddled together around the fire.* キャンプをしていた人々は火の回りに寄り集まった. ▶定義2 to make your body as small as possible because you are cold or frightened 寒いまたは恐ろしいために体をできるだけ小さくする→**体を丸める, 縮こまる** ‖ *She huddled up in her sleeping bag and tried to get some sleep.* 彼女は寝袋の中で体を丸めて, いくらか睡眠を取ろうと努めた. ― **huddled** 形→**体を寄せ合った, 縮こまっている** ‖ *We found the children lying huddled together on the ground.* 私たちは子供たちが体を寄せ合って地面に横になっているのを見つけた.

**huddle**² /hÁdl/ 名 ❷ ▶定義 a small group of people or things that are close together 互いに寄り添った人または物の小さな集まり→**群衆, 寄せ集め, 一団** ‖ *They all stood in a huddle, laughing and chatting.* 彼らは皆体を寄せ合って, 笑ったりおしゃべりをしながら立っていた.

**huff** /hʌf/ 名 ❷
成句 **in a huff** 略式 ▶定義 in a bad mood because sb has annoyed or upset you 他人に悩まされまたは動揺させられて機嫌が悪い→**ぷんぷん怒って, むっとして** ‖ *Did you see Stan go off in a huff when he wasn't chosen for the team?* チームに選ばれなかった時, スタンがむっとして出ていくのを見ましたか.

**hug** /hʌg/ 動 ❹ (**hugging**; **hugged**) ▶定義1 to put your arms around sb, especially to show that you love him/her 特にその〜に対する愛情を示すために〜を両腕で抱く→**(人) を (両腕で) しっかりと抱き締める** ‖ *He hugged his mother and sisters and got on the train.* 彼は母と妹たちをしっかりと抱き締めて列車に乗った.

▶定義2 to hold sth close to your body 〜を身体にしっかりと抱き抱える→**(物) をしっかりと抱き抱える** ‖ *She hugged the parcel to her chest as she ran.* 彼女はその小包を胸に抱えて走った. ▶定義3 (used about a ship, car, road, etc) to stay close to sth (船, 車, 道路などについて) 〜の近くにとどまる→**〜のそばを離れない, 〜に沿って進む** ‖ *to hug the coast* 海岸沿いに進む ― **hug** 名 ❹→**(愛情・友情を表す) 抱擁** ‖ *Noel's crying - I'll go and give him a hug.* ノエルが泣いています ― 行って彼を抱き締めてあげましょう.

*****huge** /hjuːdʒ/ 形 ▶定義 very big 非常に大きい→**巨大な, ばく大な, 膨大な** ‖ *a huge amount/quantity/sum/number* 膨大な分量・数量・総数・数 *a huge building* 巨大な建物 *The film was a huge success.* その映画は大成功を収めた. ― **hugely** 副→**巨大に, 非常に** ‖ *hugely successful/popular/expensive* 非常に成功した・人気のある・高価な

**huh** /hʌ/ 間 略式 ▶定義 used for expressing anger, surprise, etc or for asking a question 怒り, 驚きなどを表現するのに, または質問するときに用いて→**(不賛成・驚きなどを表して) へー, ほー, (聞き返して) えっ, 何と言った, (念を押すように) どうなんだい, そうだろう** ‖ *They've gone away, huh? They didn't tell me.* 彼らは行ってしまったんだね. 私には何も言ってくれなかった.

**hull** /hʌl/ 名 ❷ ▶定義 the body of a ship→**船体, (飛行艇の) 艇体, (飛行船の) 船体**

**hullabaloo** /hÁləbəluː; ˌ--ˈ-/ 名 ❷ [単数扱い]
▶定義 a lot of loud noise, for example made by people shouting 例えば人々の叫び声などによる多数の大きな騒音→**大騒ぎ, 喧噪 (けんそう), ごった返し, がやがや**

**hum** /hʌm/ 動 (**humming**; **hummed**) ▶定義1 ❶ to make a continuous low noise 低く継続的な音を立てる→**(ハチ, 機械などが) ブンブン音を立てる, (〜で) (ブーンと) うなる, (聴衆などが) がや**

がや言う ‖ *The machine began to hum as I switched it on.* 私がスイッチを入れるとその機械はブーンと音を立て始めた. ▶定義2 📵🔟 to sing with your lips closed 唇を閉じて歌う➡ハミングする, 鼻歌を歌う, (歌など)をハミングする ‖ *You can hum the tune if you don't know the words.* 歌詞が分からなければ旋律をハミングしても構いません. ― hum 名 [単数扱い]➡ブンブン(いう音), ブーン, ざわめき, がやがや, 鼻歌 ‖ *the hum of machinery/distant traffic* 機械・遠くを往来する車がブーンとうなる音

\*human¹ /hjúːmən/ 形 ▶定義 connected with people, not with animals, machines or gods; typical of people 動物, 機械または神ではなく, 人間に関連した; 人間らしい➡人間の, 人間に関する, 人間が持っている, 人間らしい ‖ *the human body* 人体 *The disaster was caused by **human error**.* その大惨事は人災でした. ― humanly 副➡人間らしく, 人間的に, 人間の力で(は) ‖ *They did all that was humanly possible to rescue him (= everything that a human being could possibly do).* 彼らは彼を救出するために人間の力でできる(= 人間ができる限りの)すべての事をした.

**human²** /hjúːmən/ (または **human being**) 名 ⓒ ▶定義 a person 人➡人, 人間

**humane** /hjuːméɪn/ 形 ▶定義 having or showing kindness or understanding, especially to a person or animal that is suffering 特に苦しんでいる人または動物に対して親切な, または理解のある➡思いやりのある, 心の優しい, 慈悲深い, 人道的な ‖ *Zoo animals must be kept in humane conditions.* 動物園の動物は人道的な環境で飼育されるべきだ. ⇔ **inhumane** ― humanely 副➡思いやりを持って, 慈悲深く, 人道的に

**humanitarian** /hjuːmænətéəriən/ 形 ▶定義 concerned with trying to make people's lives better and reduce suffering 人々の生活を改善し, 苦しみを和らげようとすることに関心を持って➡人道・博愛主義の, 人道的な ‖ *Many countries have sent humanitarian aid to the earthquake victims.* その地震の犠牲者に対し, 多くの国が人道的援助を送った.

**humanity** /hjuːmænəti/ 名 🔘 ▶定義 **1** all the people in the world, thought of as a group 1つの集団と見なされる世界中すべての人々➡人類, 人間 ‖ *crimes against humanity* 人類に対する犯罪 ☛類 **the human race** ▶定義 **2** the quality of being kind and understanding 親切で理解のある性質➡慈悲, 人情, 人間味, 親切 ‖ *The prisoners were treated with humanity.* 囚人たちは人道的扱いを受けた. ⇔ **inhumanity**

**human nature** 名 🔘 ▶定義 feelings, behaviour, etc that all people have in common すべての人に共通する感情, 行動など➡人間性, 人間の本性, 人情

**the human race** 名 [単数扱い] all the people in the world, thought of as a group 1つの集団と見なされる世界中すべての人々➡人類 ☛類 **humanity**

**human rights** 名 [複数扱い] ▶定義 the basic freedoms that all people should have, for example the right to say what you think, to travel freely, etc すべての人が持つべき基本的な自由, 例えば考えている事を言う権利, 自由に移動する権利など➡(基本的)人権

**humble¹** /hʌ́mb(ə)l/ 形 ▶定義 **1** not thinking that you are better or more important than other people; not proud 他人よりも自分の方が優れている, または重要だと思わない; 高慢でない➡(人の行為が)(〜について)つつましやかな, 謙そんした, 謙虚な ‖ *He became very rich and famous but he always remained a very humble man.* 彼はとても金持ちで有名になったが, 相変わらずいつも大変謙虚だった. ☛ 名 **humility** ☛参 **modest** ▶定義 **2** not special or important 特別でも重要でもない➡質素な, 粗末な, つまらない, 重要でない, 卑しい, 地位・身分が低い ‖ *She comes from a humble background.* 彼女は卑しい素性の持ち主だ. ― humbly /hʌ́mbli/ 副➡謙そんして, 卑しく ‖ *He apologized very humbly for his behaviour.* 彼は自分の行いについて謙虚に謝った.

**humble²** /hʌ́mb(ə)l/ 動 🔟 ▶定義 to make sb feel that he/she is not as good or important as he/she thought 〜に自分が思うほど優れていない, または重要でないと感じさせる➡〜を謙虚にさせる, 〜のプライドを傷付ける, 〜の威信を落とす

**humid** /hjúːmɪd/ 形 ▶定義 (used about the air or climate) containing a lot of water; damp (空気または天候について) たくさんの水分を含んだ; 湿気のある➡(不快なほど)湿気の多い, (高温)多

湿の, 湿っぽい ‖ *Hong Kong is hot and humid in summer.* 香港の夏は高温多湿だ. — **humidity** 名 U → 湿気, 湿度

**humiliate** /hjuːmílièɪt/ 動他 ▶定義 to make sb feel very embarrassed 〜に非常に恥ずかしい思いをさせる→**人に(公衆の面前で)恥をかかせる, 屈辱を与える** ‖ *I felt humiliated when the teacher laughed at my work.* 先生が私の作品を見て笑った時, 恥ずかしい思いをした. — **humiliating** 形→屈辱的な, 不面目な ‖ *a humiliating defeat* 屈辱的敗退 — **humiliation** 名 C U →恥をかかせること, かかされること, 屈辱, 不面目

**humility** /hjuːmíləti/ 名 U ▶定義 the quality of not thinking that you are better than other people 自分が他人より優れていると思わない性質→**謙そん, 謙虚, 卑下** ☞ 形 **humble**

**humorous** /hjúːmərəs/ 形 ▶定義 amusing or funny 愉快なまたはおかしい→**(物事が)こっけいな, おどけた, ユーモアのある** — **humorously** 副→こっけいに

***humour**[1] ( 米 **humor**) /hjúːmər/ 名 U ▶定義 1 the funny or amusing qualities of sb/sth 〜のおかしいまたは愉快な性質→**ユーモア, こっけい, おかしみ** ‖ *It is sometimes hard to understand the humour (= the jokes) of another country.* 外国のユーモア(=ジョーク)を理解するのは難しいときがある. ▶定義 2 being able to see when sth is funny and to laugh at things 〜のおかしさを理解し, 物事を笑える能力→**ユーモアをよく解する・表現する力** ‖ *Rose has a good sense of humour.* ローズにはユーモアをよく解する心がある. ▶定義 3 **-humoured** ( 米 **-humored**) (複合形容詞を作るために用いて) having or showing a particular mood ある特定の気分でいる, または気分を表した→**機嫌が〜の** ‖ *good-humoured* 上機嫌の

**humour**[2] ( 米 **humor**) /hjúːmər/ 動他 ▶定義 to keep sb happy by doing what he/she wants 〜が望む事をすることによりその〜を喜ばせておく→**〜の機嫌を取る, 〜に調子を合わせる, 〜をなだめる, あやす**

**humourless** /hjúːmərləs/ ( 米 **humorless**) 形 ▶定義 having no sense of fun; serious 面白さを解する心を持たない; まじめな→**ユーモアのない, ユーモアを解さない**

**hump** /hʌmp/ 名 C ▶定義 a large round lump, for example on the back of an animal who lives in the desert (**camel**) 砂漠に住む動物(ラクダ)の背などにある大きくて丸いこぶ→**(人の背中の)こぶ, (ラクダの)背こぶ** ☞ **camel** のさし絵

**hunch**[1] /hʌntʃ/ 名 C 略式 ▶定義 a thought or an idea that is based on a feeling rather than on facts or information 事実または情報よりむしろ感情に基づいた考えまたは思い付き→**直感, 予感, 勘, 虫の知らせ** ‖ *I'm not sure, but I've got a hunch that she's got a new job.* 確信はないが, 彼女は新しい職を得たような気がする.

**hunch**[2] /hʌntʃ/ 動自他 ▶定義 to bend your back and shoulders forward into a round shape 背中と肩を前方に丸く曲げる→**背中を丸くする, 身をかがめる, (背など)を丸くする**

**hunchback** /hʌntʃbæk/ 名 C ▶定義 a person with a back that has a round lump on it 背中に丸いこぶがある人→**猫背の人**

*__hundred__ /hʌ́ndrəd/ 数 ▶定義 1 ( 複 **hundred**) 100 ‖ *two hundred* 200 *There were a/one hundred people in the room.* その部屋には100人の人がいた. *She's a hundred today.* 彼女は今日で100歳です.

▶ある数, 例えば1420と言うとき, hundred の後に and を用いることに注意する: *one thousand four hundred **and** twenty*.
文中での数詞の使い方については, six の項を参照.

▶定義 2 **hundreds** 略式 a lot; a large amount たくさん; 多量→**何百という, 非常に多数の** ‖ *I've got hundreds of things to do today.* 私は今日する事が山ほどある.

▶数についての説明は, 巻末の数についての特別項目を参照.

**hundredth**[1] /hʌ́ndrədθ, -drətθ/ 名 C ▶定義 the fraction 1/100; one of a hundred equal parts of sth 100分の1; 〜を100等分にしたうちの1つ→**100分の1**

**hundredth**[2] /hʌ́ndrədθ/ 代形副 ▶定義 100th→**100番目(の, に), 第100(の, に)** ☞参 **sixth**[1] の例

**hundredweight** /hʌ́ndrədwèɪt/ 名 C ( 略 **cwt**) ▶定義 a measurement of weight 重さの単位→**ハンドレッドウエート**

▶ weight についての説明は, 巻末の数についての特別項目を参照.

**hung** HANG¹ の過去・過去分詞形

**\*hunger¹** /hʌ́ŋɡər/ 名 ▶定義1 ❶the state of not having enough food to eat, especially when this causes illness or death 食べる物が十分になく，特に病気または死に至る状態→飢え，飢餓，飢饉（ききん）‖ *In the Third World many people die of hunger each year.* 第三世界においては毎年たくさんの人が餓死している. ☛参 **thirst**
▶定義2 ❶the feeling caused by a need to eat 食べる必要から起こる感覚→空腹（感），ひもじさ‖ *Hunger is one reason why babies cry.* 空腹は赤ちゃんが泣く理由の1つだ．
▶要注意．英語では I have hunger. とは言えない．I am hungry. と言わねばならない．
▶定義3 ［単数扱い］hunger (for sth) a strong desire for sth 〜に対する強い欲求→(〜に対する) 飢え，渇望‖ *a hunger for knowledge/fame/success* 知識欲・名誉欲・成功に対する渇望

**hunger²** /hʌ́ŋɡər/ 動 正式
句動詞 hunger for/after sth ▶定義 to have a strong desire for sth 〜を欲しいと強く思う→〜を切望する，〜することを切望する，渇望する

**hunger strike** 名 ❸ ❶ ▶定義 a time when sb (especially a prisoner) refuses to eat because he/she is protesting about sth 〜（特に囚人）が…について抗議しているという理由で，食べるのを拒否すること→ハンガーストライキ，ハンスト（抗議のための断食）‖ *to be/go on hunger strike* ハンストをしている・する

**\*hungry** /hʌ́ŋɡri/ 形.(**hungrier**; **hungriest**)
▶定義1 wanting to eat 食べたがって→(人・動物が) 空腹の，飢えた，ひもじそうな‖ *I'm hungry. Let's eat soon.* おなかがすいた．早く食べよう．*There were hungry children begging for food in the streets.* 通りには，腹をすかせた子供たちが食べ物を請うていた．☛参 **thirsty** ▶定義2 hungry for sth wanting sth very much 〜を非常に欲しがって→(〜を) 渇望して‖ *I'm hungry for some excitement tonight.* 今夜私は何かたまらなく刺激が欲しい．— hungrily 副→ひもじそうに，がつがつと，熱心に，むさぼるように

成句 go hungry ▶定義 to not have any food 食べる物が何もない→空腹のままでいる，食べないで暮らす，飢えている

**hunk** /hʌŋk/ 名 ❸ ▶定義1 a large piece of sth 一塊の大きな〜→(パン・チーズ・肉などの) 厚切れ，大きな塊‖ *a hunk of bread/cheese/meat* 大きな塊のパン・チーズ・肉 ▶定義2 略式 a man who is big, strong and attractive 大きく，強く魅力的な男性→体のがっちりした魅力的な男，たくましくていかす男

**\*hunt¹** /hʌnt/ 動 ❸ ❶ ▶定義1 to run after wild animals, etc in order to catch or kill them either for sport or for food 野生動物などをスポーツまたは食用として捕獲したり殺すために追い掛ける→狩りをする，狩猟する，(人・動物が) (鳥・獣など) を狩る，狩猟する‖ *Owls hunt at night.* フクロウは夜狩りをする．*Are tigers still hunted in India?* インドでは今もトラ狩りをしていますか．☛ 人が狩猟をして過ごすことを言うのに，しばしば go hunting という表現を用いる．
▶定義2 hunt (for) (sb/sth) to try to find sb/sth 〜を見つけようとする→(人が) (犯人・真相など) を追う，捜す，追跡する‖ *The police are still hunting the murderer.* 警察はその殺人犯をまだ追跡中です．

**hunt²** /hʌnt/ 名 ❸ ▶定義1 the act of hunting wild animals, etc 野生動物などを狩猟する行為→狩り，狩猟‖ *a fox-hunt* キツネ狩り ▶定義2 ［通常は単数］a hunt (for sb/sth) the act of looking for sb/sth that is difficult to find 見つけるのが困難な〜を捜す行為→(〜の) 探求，捜索，(〜を) 捜し求めること‖ *The police have launched a hunt for the missing child.* 警察は行方不明になった子供の捜索を開始した．

**hunter** /hʌ́ntər/ 名 ❸ ▶定義 a person that hunts wild animals for food or sport; an animal that hunts its food 野生動物をスポーツまたは食用として狩猟する人；食べるために狩りをする動物→狩りをする人，猟師，ハンター，(ほかの動物を捕食する) 猛獣

**hunting** /hʌ́ntɪŋ/ 名 ❸ ❶ ▶定義 the act of following and killing wild animals or birds as a sport or for food 野生動物または鳥をスポーツまたは食用として追い掛け殺す行為→狩猟，狩り ☛参 **shoot**

**hurdle¹** /hə́ːrdl/ 名 ▶定義1 ❸ a type of light fence that a person or a horse jumps over in a race 人や馬がレースで飛び越える軽い障害物の一種→(競技用の) ハードル，障害物‖ *to clear a hurdle (= to jump over it successfully)* ハードルを越える (= うまく飛び越える) ▶定義2

**hurdles** [複数扱い] a race in which runners or horses have to jump over hurdles 走者または馬がハードルを飛び越えるレース→ハードルレース, 障害物競走 ‖ *the 200 metres hurdles* 200メートルハードル走 ▶定義3 ⒸⒶ problem or difficulty that you must solve or deal with before you can achieve sth ~を達成するために解決または処理せねばならない問題や困難→(一般に)**障害, 困難**

**hurdle**² /hə́:rdl/ 動 ⒺⒾ ▶定義 hurdle (over sth) to jump over sth while you are running 走りながら~を飛び越える→ハードル競走をする, (人が)(障害・困難など)を飛び越す, 乗り越える

**hurl** /həːrl/ 動 Ⓘ ▶定義 to throw sth with great force ~を非常に強い力で投げる→物を(~に)**強くほうる, 投げ付ける**

**hurray** (または **hooray**) /hʊréɪ, hə-/ (または **hurrah** /hʊrɑ́ː, -rɔ́ː, hə-/) 間 ▶定義 used for expressing great pleasure, approval, etc 大喜び, 大賛成などを表すときに用いて→**万歳, フレー** ‖ *Hurray! We've won!* 万歳. 勝ったぞ.

成句 hip, hip, hurray/hurrah ⇒ **HIP**²

**hurricane** /hə́ːrəkèɪn, hə́rə-, hə́ːrɪkən, hə́rɪ-; hə́rɪkən, -kèɪn/ 名 Ⓒ ▶定義 a violent storm with very strong winds 非常に強い風を伴う激しいあらし→ハリケーン, 大暴風, あらし ☛参 **storm** の注

**hurried** /hə́rid/ hə́ːr-/ 形 ▶定義 done (too) quickly 急いで(急ぎすぎて)なされた→(人が)**せき立てられた, 急いでいる, 大急ぎの, 急いでなされた, 急いで作られた** ‖ *a hurried meal* 慌ただしい食事 — **hurriedly** 副 →**大急ぎで, 慌ただしく, せかせかと**

★**hurry**¹ /hə́ːri, hə́ri/ 名 Ⓤ ▶定義 the need or wish to do sth quickly ~を急いで行う必要性または願望→**急ぐ必要, 急ぐこと, 大慌て** ‖ *Take your time. There's no hurry.* ゆっくりやりなさい. 急ぐ必要はありません.

成句 in a hurry ▶定義 quickly →**急いで, 慌てて, 早まって** ‖ *She got up late and left in a hurry.* 彼女は遅く起きたので慌てて出掛けた.

in a hurry (to do sth) ▶定義 wanting to do sth soon; impatient ~をすぐにやりたい; 我慢できない →(~を)したがって, 待ちきれない ‖ *They are in a hurry to get the job done before the winter.* 彼らは冬になる前にその仕事を終わらせたがっている.

in no hurry (to do sth); not in any hurry (to do sth) ▶定義1 not needing or wishing to do sth quickly ~を急いでやる必要がない, または急いでやりたがらない→(~を・~するのを)**急がないで** ‖ *We weren't in any hurry so we stopped to admire the view.* 私たちは急いでいなかったので, 立ち止まってそのすばらしい景色を眺めた.

▶定義2 not wanting to do sth ~を(~を)したがらない ‖ *I am in no hurry to repeat that experience.* あんな経験はもう二度としたくありません.

★**hurry**² /hə́ːri, hə́ri/ 動 (現分 **hurrying**; 三単現 **hurries**; 過, 過分 **hurried**) ▶定義1 Ⓘ to move or do sth quickly because there is not much time あまり時間がないので急いで移動するまたは~を行う→(~へ)**急ぐ, 急いでする** ‖ *Don't hurry. There's plenty of time.* 急がなくても大丈夫. 時間はたっぷりあります. *They hurried back home after school.* 彼らは放課後急いで帰ってきた. *Several people hurried to help.* 数人が助けに駆け付けた. ▶定義2 Ⓣ hurry sb (into sth/doing sth) to cause sb/sth to do sth, or sth to happen more quickly ~に…をもっと急いでさせる, または~がもっと早く起こるようにする→(人が)(人・馬など)を**急がせる, せき立てる, 人をせかして~させる, (仕事など)を急いでする, (歩調など)を早める** ‖ *Don't hurry me. I'm going as fast as I can.* 私をせかさないでください. できる限り急いでつもりですから. *He was hurried into a decision.* 彼は決定を迫られた.

▶定義3 (通常は受動態で) to do sth too quickly→**早まって(~)する, あせって(~)する**

句動詞 hurry up (with sth) 略式 ▶定義 to move or do sth more quickly より急いで移動するまたは~を行う→(~へ)**急ぐ, (~を)急いでする** ‖ *Hurry up or we'll miss the train.* 早くしなさい, さもないと列車に乗り遅れますよ.

★**hurt**¹ /həːrt/ 動 (過, 過分 **hurt**) ▶定義1 ⒾⒾ to cause sb/yourself physical pain or injury ~・自分自身に身体的苦痛または損傷を生じさせる→**~を傷付ける, ~にけがをさせる, 傷付く, けがをする** ‖ *Did he hurt himself?* 彼はけがをしましたか. *I fell and hurt my arm.* 私は転んで腕にけがをした. *No one was seriously hurt in the accident.* その事故ではだれも重傷を負わなかった. *These shoes hurt; they're too tight.* この靴

は痛い, きつすぎる.

➤ hurt, injure, wound と比較. 普通は戦いの結果, 人はナイフ, 剣, 銃などにより be wounded (外傷を負う) ことがある: *a wounded soldier* (負傷兵). 人々は普通, 事故により be injured (けがをする): *Five people were killed in the crash and twelve others were injured.* (その衝突事故で, 5人が死亡, ほかの12人がけがをしました.) hurt と injured の意味は類似しているが, あまり重傷でない場合は hurt の方がより頻繁に使われる: *I hurt my leg when I fell off my bike.* (私は自転車から落ちて足をけがした.)

▶定義2 @ to feel painful 痛みを感じる ➤ (体の部分が) 痛む, (注射などが) 痛みを与える ‖ *My leg hurts.* 私は足が痛む. *It hurts when I lift my leg.* 私は足を持ち上げると痛い. *Where exactly does it hurt?* 正確にはどこが痛みますか.

▶定義3 @ to make sb unhappy; to upset sb 〜を嫌な気持ちにさせる; 〜を動揺させる ➤ 人の感情を害する, 〜の気に障る, (感情・評判など) を害する ‖ *His unkind remarks hurt her deeply.* 彼の心ない言葉が彼女を深く傷付けた. *I didn't want to hurt his feelings.* 私は彼の感情を害したくなかった.

感句 it won't/wouldn't hurt (sb/sth) (to do sth) 略式 ▶定義 used to say that sb should do sth 〜が…をするべきだと言うのに用いて ➤ (人・物が) 〜しても差し障りはない・問題はない・不都合はない ‖ *It wouldn't hurt you to help with the housework occasionally.* たまには家事を手伝ってくれても損はしないでしょうに.

*hurt² /həːrt/ 形 ▶定義1 injured physically 身体的損傷を受けて ➤ (人の体が) 傷付いた, けがをした ‖ *None of the passengers were badly/seriously hurt.* 乗客で重傷を負った人はだれもいなかった. ▶定義2 upset and offended by sth that sb has said or done 〜が言ったまたは行った事により動揺する, または感情を害する ➤ (〜で) 感情を害した ‖ *She was deeply hurt that she had not been invited to the party.* 彼女はパーティーに招待されなかったことに深く傷付いた.

hurt³ /həːrt/ 名 ❶ ▶定義 a feeling of unhappiness because sb has been unkind or unfair to you 〜が自分に不親切または不公平であることが原因の, 嫌な気持ち ➤ (精神的) 苦痛, 打撃 ‖ *There was hurt and real anger in her voice.* 彼女

の声から精神的打撃を受けていること, また本気で怒っていることが感じ取れた.

**hurtful** /hə́ːrtfʊl, f(ə)l/ 形 ❶ ▶定義 hurtful (to sb) unkind; making sb feel upset and offended 不親切な; 〜に動揺および精神的苦痛を与える ➤ 感情を傷付ける

**hurtle** /hə́ːrtl/ 動 @ ▶定義 to move with great speed, perhaps causing danger 危険をもたらすほどのすごい速さで動く ➤ (車などが) 突進する, 猛スピードで進む, (石・矢などが) 突き当たる ‖ *The lorry came hurtling towards us.* トラックが私たちに向かって突進してきた.

*husband /hʌ́zbənd/ 名 ❶ ▶定義 a man that a woman is married to ある女性が結婚している男性 ➤ 夫 ‖ *Her ex-husband sees the children once a month.* 彼女の元夫は月1回子供たちに会う.

hush¹ /hʌʃ/ 動 @ (口語) ▶定義 used to tell sb to be quiet, to stop talking or crying 〜に静かにする, 話すあるいは泣くのをやめるよう言うのに用いて ➤ 黙る, 静かになる ‖ *Hush now and try to sleep.* 今は静かにして眠ろうとしなさい.

句動詞 hush sth up ▶定義 to hide information to stop people knowing about sth; to keep sth secret 人々が〜について知るのを阻止するため情報を隠す; 〜を秘密にしておく ➤ (事実など) を口止めする, 秘密にしておく, もみ消す

hush² /hʌʃ/ 名 [単数扱い] ▶定義 silence ➤ 静けさ, 沈黙

**hush-hush** 形略式 ▶定義 very secret ➤ 極秘の, 内密の

**husky¹** /hʌ́ski/ 形 ▶定義 (used about a person's voice) sounding rough and quiet as if your throat were dry (人の声について) まるでのどが乾いているような粗く低い声の ➤ (声が) ハスキーな, しゃがれた, 低音でささやくような

**husky²** /hʌ́ski/ 名 ❶ ( 複 huskies) ▶定義 a strong dog with thick fur that is used in teams for pulling heavy loads over snow チームを組んで雪上の重い荷物を引くのに利用される, 厚い毛皮を持つ頑強な犬 ➤ ハスキー犬, エスキモー犬

**hustle** /hʌ́s(ə)l/ 動 @ ▶定義 to push or move sb in a way that is not gentle 〜を優しくないやり方で押すまたは動かす ➤ 〜を乱暴に押す・動かす, 押し込む・出す

**hut** /hʌt/ 名 C ▶定義 a small building with one room, usually made of wood or metal 通常は木造または金属製の、一部屋になっている小さな建物→小屋, 簡易住居, バンガロー ‖ *a wooden/mud hut* 木造バンガロー・泥小屋

**hutch** /hʌtʃ/ 名 C ▶定義 a wooden box with a front made of wire, that is used for keeping rabbits or other small animals ウサギまたはそのほかの小動物を飼うのに使われる、正面が針金でできた木箱→(小動物を飼う)おり, ウサギ小屋

**hydrant** /háɪdrənt/ 名 C ▶定義 a pipe in a street from which water can be taken for stopping fires, cleaning the streets, etc そこから水を引いて消火, 通りの清掃などを行うことができる, 通りにある管→(公共用の)給水栓, 消火栓

**hydraulic** /haɪdrɔ́(ː)lɪk, -drʌ́l-/ 形 ▶定義 operated by water or another liquid moving through pipes, etc under pressure 管などの中を, 圧力をかけられて動く水またはそのほかの液体の力で動く→水力(式)の, 水圧・油圧(式)の ‖ *hydraulic brakes* 水圧式ブレーキ

**hydroelectric** /ˌhaɪdroʊɪléktrɪk/ 形 ▶定義 using the power of water to produce electricity; produced by the power of water 電力を起こすのに水力を使った; 水力により生じた→水力発電の, 水力電気の ‖ *a hydroelectric dam* 水力発電ダム *hydroelectric power* 水力発電の電力

**hydrogen** /háɪdrədʒ(ə)n/ 名 U (元素記号 H) ▶定義 a light colourless gas. Hydrogen and another gas (oxygen) form water (H₂O). 比重の軽い無色の気体. hydrogen とほかの気体(酸素)で水(H₂O)ができる→水素

**hygiene** /háɪdʒiːn/ 名 U ▶定義 (the rules of) keeping yourself and things around you clean, in order to prevent disease 病気を防ぐために, 自分自身および身の回りの物を清潔に保つこと(またそのための規則)→衛生, 衛生学, 清潔, 健康法 ‖ *High standards of hygiene are essential when you are preparing food.* 食べ物を調理するときには衛生水準を高く保つことが不可欠です. *personal hygiene* 個人の身だしなみの清潔さ

**hygienic** /haɪdʒíːnɪk/ 形 ▶定義 clean, without the bacteria that cause disease 清潔な, 病原菌がない→衛生的な, 衛生(学)に関する ‖ *hygienic conditions* 衛生状態 — **hygienically** /-k(ə)li/ 副 → 衛生的に

**hymn** /hɪm/ 名 C ▶定義 a religious song that Christians sing together in church, etc キリスト教徒が教会などで合唱する宗教的な歌→賛美歌, 聖歌, 賛歌

**hype¹** /haɪp/ 名 U ▶定義 advertisements that tell you how good and important a new product, film, etc is 新しい製品, 映画などがいかに優れており, また重要であるかを説く宣伝→誇大宣伝, 過剰宣伝 ‖ *Don't believe all the hype - the book is rubbish!* 誇大宣伝をうのみにしてはいけない — その本は下らないものだ.

**hype²** /haɪp/ 動 他 ▶定義 hype sth (up) to exaggerate how good or important sth is ～がいかに優れているかまたは重要であるかを誇張する→～を誇大に宣伝する ‖ *His much-hyped new movie is released next week.* 彼の誇大宣伝された新作映画が来週封切りになる.

**hypermarket** /háɪpəmɑ̀ːrkət/ 名 C 英 ▶定義 a very large shop that is usually situated outside a town and sells a wide variety of goods 通常は郊外にあり, 広範囲の商品を扱う大変大型の店舗→大型スーパーマーケット

**hyphen** /háɪf(ə)n/ 名 C ▶定義 the mark (-) used for joining two words together (for example left-handed, red-hot) or to show that a word has been divided and continues on the next line (-) という印で, 2つの単語を連結するのに用いられる(left-handed, red-hot)か, またはある単語が分割され次の行に続くことを表す→ハイフン ☞参 dash

**hyphenate** /háɪf(ə)nèɪt/ 動 他 ▶定義 to join two words together with a hyphen 2つの単語をハイフンでつなぐ→～をハイフンでつなぐ — **hyphenation** /ˌhaɪf(ə)néɪʃ(ə)n/ 名 U →ハイフンでつなぐこと, ハイフンで分けること

**hypnosis** /hɪpnóʊsəs/ 名 U ▶定義 (the producing of) an unconscious state where sb's mind and actions can be controlled by another person 人の心および行動を別の人が支配することができる無意識の状態(を作ること)→催眠, 催眠状態・現象, 催眠術 ‖ *She was questioned under hypnosis.* 彼女は催眠状態で質問された.

**hypnotize** (または **-ise**) /hípnətàɪz/ 動 他 ▶定義 to put sb into an unconscious state where the person's mind and actions can be controlled 心および行動を別の人が支配するこ

とができるような無意識の状態に〜を至らせる ➡〜に催眠術をかける, 催眠術をかけて〜させる ― hypnotic /hɪpnάtɪk/ 形 ➡催眠(術)の, 催眠状態の ― hypnotism /hípnətìz(ə)m/ 名 ❶➡催眠術・法, 催眠状態 ― hypnotist /hípnətɪ̀st/ 名 ❻➡催眠術をかける人, 催眠術師

**hypochondriac** /hàɪpəkάndriæk/ 名 ❻ ▶定義 a person who is always worried about his/her health and believes he/she is ill, even when there is nothing wrong いつも健康を気に掛けていて, どこも悪くなくても自分が病気だと思う人➡心気症の患者

**hypocrisy** /hɪpάkrəsi/ 名 ❶ ▶定義 behaviour in which sb pretends to have moral standards or opinions that he/she does not really have 〜が実際は持っていない道徳の規範または意見を持っている振りをする行為➡偽善, 見せ掛け, 偽善的行為

**hypocrite** /hípəkrìt/ 名 ❻ ▶定義 a person who pretends to have moral standards or opinions which he/she does not really have. Hypocrites say one thing and do another. 実際には持っていない道徳の規範または意見を持っている振りをする人. hypocrites は言動が一致しない➡偽善者 ‖ What a hypocrite! She says she's against the hunting of animals but she's wearing a fur coat. 何という偽善者. 彼女は動物の狩猟に反対している一方で毛皮のコートを着ている. ― hypocritical /hìpəkrítɪk(ə)l/ 形➡見せ掛けの, 偽善(者)的な ― hypocritically /hìpəkrítɪk(ə)li/ 副➡偽善的に

**hypodermic** /hàɪpoʊdˈɚːmɪk, -pə-/ 形 ▶定義 a medical instrument with a long needle that is used for putting drugs under the skin (giving an injection) 皮下に薬を入れる(注射する)のに使われる, 長い針が付いた医療器機の1つ➡皮下注射の, 皮下の・にある ‖ a hypodermic needle/syringe (皮下)注射針・器

**hypothesis** /haɪpάθəsəs, hɪ-/ 名 ❻ (複) **hypotheses** /-sìːz/) ▶定義 an idea that is suggested as the possible explanation for sth but has not yet been found to be true or correct 〜に対し可能性のある解釈として提示されているが, 真実かまたは正しいかがまだ分からない考え方➡仮説, 前提, 仮定

**hypothetical** /hàɪpəθétɪk(ə)l/ 形 ▶定義 based on situations that have not yet happened, not on facts 事実にではなく, まだ起こったことがない状況に基づいた➡仮定・仮説(上)の, 仮想の ‖ That's a hypothetical question because we don't know what the situation will be next year. それは仮想の問題です, なぜなら来年の状況についてはまだ分からないからです. ― hypothetically /-k(ə)li/ 副➡仮に, 仮定的に, 仮説上に

**hysteria** /hɪstíəriə/ 名 ❶ ▶定義 a state in which a person or a group of people cannot control their emotions, for example cannot stop laughing, crying, shouting, etc 一個人または一団の人々が感情, 例えば笑う, 泣く, 大声を出すことなどを抑制できない状態➡ヒステリー, (一般に)病的興奮(状態), 狂乱 ‖ mass hysteria 集団ヒステリー・集団的躁状態

**hysterical** /hɪstérɪk(ə)l/ 形 ▶定義 1 very excited and unable to control your emotions 非常に興奮して自分の感情を抑制できない➡ヒステリー状態の, 狂乱状態の ‖ hysterical laughter ヒステリックな笑い She was hysterical with grief. 彼女は悲しみのあまり狂乱状態だった. ▶定義 2 略式 very funny とても面白い➡腹の皮がよじれるほどおかしい, 笑いの止まらない ― hysterically /-k(ə)li/ 副➡狂乱状態で, ヒステリックに, 笑いが止まらないほど

**hysterics** /hɪstérɪks/ 名 [複数扱い] ▶定義 1 an expression of extreme fear, excitement or anger that makes sb lose control of his/her emotions 〜から感情を抑制できなくなるほどの極度の恐怖, 興奮または怒りなどを表現すること➡ヒステリーの発作, 狂乱 ‖ She **went into hysterics** when they told her the news. 彼女はその知らせを聞いてヒステリー状態になった. 略式 My father would **have hysterics** (= be furious) if he knew I was going out with you. 私の父は私があなたと出掛けると知ったらヒステリーを起こす(= 激怒する)でしょう. ▶定義 2 略式 laughter that you cannot control 抑制できない笑い➡突然の笑い, 発作的笑い ‖ The comedian had the audience **in hysterics**. その喜劇役者は聴衆を腹の皮がよじれるほど笑わせた.

**Hz** /hɚːts/ 略 hertz ▶定義 (used in radio) a measure of frequency, one cycle per second (ラジオで用いて)周波数の単位, 毎秒1サイクル➡ヘルツ

# I i

**I, i¹** /áɪ/ 名 C (複 **I's; i's**) ▶定義 the ninth letter of the English alphabet 英語アルファベットの第9文字 → i(I)が表す音, i(I)の文字, i(I)の字形のもの ‖ *'Island' begins with (an) 'I'.* Island は I で始まる.

*__I²__ /áɪ, ə/ 代 (動詞の主語) ▶定義 the person who is speaking or writing 話し手または書き手→私は, 私が ‖ *I phoned and said that I was busy.* 私は電話をかけ, 忙しいと言った. *I'm not going to fall, am I?* 私は落ちぶれていってませんよね.

*__ice¹__ /áɪs/ 名 U ▶定義 water that has frozen and become solid 凍って固体状になった水→氷 ‖ *Do you want ice in your orange juice?* オレンジジュースに氷を入れますか. *I slipped on a patch of ice.* 私は氷片を踏んで滑って転んでしまった. *black ice (= ice on roads, that cannot be seen easily)* 黒氷(= 道路上の氷で, 路面の色と変わらなく見えるもの)

成句 **break the ice** ▶定義 to say or do sth that makes people feel more relaxed, especially at the beginning of a party or meeting (特にパーティーや会議の最初に)何かを話したり行ったりして人々の緊張をほぐす→座を打ち解けさせる, 話の口火を切る ‖ *She smiled to break the ice.* 彼女は笑顔で座を和ませた.

**cut no ice (with sb)** ▶定義 to have no influence or effect on sb ～に影響や効果がない→(人に)効果がない, 問題にされない ‖ *His excuses cut no ice with me.* 彼がいくら弁解しても私には効果がなかった.

**on ice** ▶定義 **1** (used about wine, etc) kept cold by being surrounded by ice (ワインなどについて)氷で囲まれて冷やされた → 氷で冷やされた[て] ▶定義 **2** (used about a plan, etc) waiting to be dealt with later; delayed (計画などについて)処理を保留して先に延ばす; 延期される→保留されて ‖ *We've had to put our plans to go to Australia on ice for the time being.* オーストラリア行きの計画は, 当分棚上げしなければならなかった.

**ice²** /áɪs/ (特に 米 **frost**) 動 他 ▶定義 to decorate a cake by covering it with a mixture of sugar, butter, chocolate, etc 砂糖, バター, チョコレートなどを混ぜ合わせた衣を塗ってケーキを飾る→(ケーキなど)に糖衣をかける, ～に砂糖の衣を付ける ☛参 **icing**

句動詞 **ice (sth) over/up** ▶定義 to cover sth or become covered with ice 氷で～を覆う, または～が氷で覆われる→～を凍らせる, 一面に凍る ‖ *The windscreen of the car had iced over in the night.* 車のフロントガラスは一晩で凍ってしまった.

**iceberg** /áɪsbɜːrɡ/ 名 C ▶定義 a very large block of ice that floats in the sea 海に浮かんでいる巨大な氷塊→氷山

成句 **the tip of the iceberg** ⇒ **TIP¹**

**icebox** /áɪsbɑ̀ks/ 米 = FRIDGE

**ice-cold** 形 ▶定義 very cold とても冷たい→氷のように冷たい ‖ *ice-cold beer* よく冷えたビール *Your hands are ice-cold.* あなたの手は氷のように冷えきっている.

**ice cream** 名 ▶定義 **1** U a frozen sweet food that is made from cream クリームで作られた氷菓子→アイスクリーム ☛ C4 ページのさし絵 ▶定義 **2** C an amount of ice cream that is served to sb, often in a special container (a cone) →アイスクリームを人に出す形にしたもので, 特別な入れ物(コーン = 円錐(えんすい)形のウエハース)に入っていることが多い ‖ *a strawberry ice cream* イチゴのアイスクリーム

**ice cube** 名 C ▶定義 a small block of ice that you put in a drink to make it cold 飲み物を冷やすために入れる小さな氷塊→(冷蔵庫で作る)角氷

**iced** /áɪst/ 形 ▶定義 (used about drinks) very cold (飲み物について)とても冷たい→(氷で)冷やした ‖ *iced tea* アイスティー

**ice hockey** (米 **hockey**) 名 U ▶定義 a game that is played on ice by two teams who try to hit a small flat rubber object (a puck) into a goal with long wooden sticks 氷上で2チームで争われる競技で, 小さなゴム製の円盤(パック)を長い木製のスティックで打ってゴールをねらうもの→アイスホッケー

**ice lolly** 名 C (複 **ice lollies**) (米 **Popsicle**) ▶定義 a piece of flavoured ice on a stick 風味を付けた氷を棒に刺したもの→アイスキャンデー ☛参 **lollipop**

**ice rink** = SKATING RINK

**ice-skate** = SKATE²

**ice skating** = SKATING(1)

**icicle** /áɪsɪk(ə)l/ 名 C ▶定義 a pointed piece of ice that is formed by water freezing as it falls or runs down from sth 先のとがった氷柱で, 水が物から滴り落ちたり流れ落ちる際に氷結したもの→つらら

**icing** /áɪsɪŋ/ (米 **frosting**) 名 U ▶定義 a sweet mixture of sugar and water, milk, butter, etc that is used for decorating cakes 砂糖, 水, 牛乳, バターなどを混ぜた甘い物で, ケーキの飾り付けに使われる→(ケーキなどに振り掛ける)砂糖衣, アイシング ☛ **cake** のさし絵

**icon** /áɪkàn/ 名 C ▶定義 1 (computing) a small picture or symbol on a computer screen that represents a program (コンピューター) コンピューターの画面上の小さな絵や記号で, プログラムを表すもの→アイコン ‖ *Click on the printer icon with the mouse.* マウスでプリンターのアイコンをクリックしてください. ☛ S5 ページのさし絵 ▶定義 2 a person or thing that is considered to be a symbol of sth 〜の象徴と見なされる人または物事→象徴, 偶像 ‖ *Madonna and other pop icons of the 1980s* マドンナその他, 1980 年代のポップスを象徴する人々 ▶定義 3 (または **ikon**) a picture or figure of an important religious person, used by some types of Christians 宗教上の重要人物の肖像画または像で, キリスト教の一部の宗派で使われるもの→**イコン, 聖画像, 聖像**

**icy** /áɪsi/ 形 ▶定義 1 very cold 非常に冷たい→氷のように冷たい, 氷のような ‖ *icy winds/water/weather* 刺すように冷たい風・氷のように冷たい水・とても寒い天気 ▶定義 2 covered with ice 氷で覆われた→氷の, 凍った ‖ *icy roads* 凍結した道路

**I'd** /áɪd/ **I HAD, I WOULD** の短縮形

**ID** /àɪ díː/ 略 略式 identification; identity→同一であることの証明, 身元 ‖ *an ID card* 身分証明書

**Id** = EID

*****idea** /aɪdíːə; -díːə/ 名 ▶定義 1 C an idea (for sth); an idea (of sth/of doing sth) a plan, thought or suggestion, especially about what to do in a particular situation 特に, 特定の状況の下で何をすべきかに関する計画, 考え, 提案→思い付き, 案, アイデア ‖ *That's a good idea!* それはいい考えですね. *He's got an idea for a new play.* 彼は新しい演劇の着想を得た. *I had the bright idea of getting Jane to help me with my homework.* 私はジェーンに宿題を手伝ってもらうという名案を思い付いた. *Has anyone got any ideas of how to tackle this problem?* だれかこの問題の解決方法について何か名案がありますか. *It was your idea to invite so many people to the party.* パーティーにそんなに大勢の人を招待したのは, あなたの提案でしたよ. ▶定義 2 [単数扱い] an idea of sth a picture or impression in your mind 心に浮かぶ像または考え→見当, 理解, 想像, 概念 ‖ *You have no idea (= you can't imagine) how difficult it was to find a time that suited everybody.* みんなに都合のいい時間を見つけるのがどんなに困難だったか, あなたには分からないでしょう (= 想像できないでしょう). *The programme gave a good idea of what life was like before the war.* その番組からは戦前の生活がありありと想像できた. *Staying in to watch the football on TV is not my idea of a good time.* 家にいてフットボールの試合をテレビで見るのは, 面白くないと思います.

▶定義 3 C an idea (about sth) an opinion or belief 意見, 見解→(〜についての)考え方, 信念 ‖ *She has her own ideas about how to bring up children.* 彼女は子供の育て方について自分なりの信念を持っています. ▶定義 4 the idea [単数扱い] the idea (of sth / of doing sth) the aim or purpose of sth 〜の目標, 目的→意図 ‖ *The idea of the course is to teach the basics of car maintenance.* このコースの目的は車の整備の基本を教えることです.

成句 get the idea ▶定義 to understand the aim or purpose of sth 〜のねらいや目的を理解する →やり方・意味が分かる ‖ *Right! I think I've got the idea now.* 分かりました. やっと理解できた気がします.

get the idea that... ▶定義 to get the feeling or impression that... 〜であるという感じ, または印象を持つ→(しばしば間違って)(〜と)思い込む ‖ *Where did you get the idea that I was paying for this meal?* 何でまた私がこの食事代を払うなんて思ったの.

have an idea that... ▶定義 to have a feeling or think that... 〜であるという気がする, 〜であると考える→〜のような感じ・予感がする ‖ *I'm not* sure but I have an idea that they've gone on holiday. 断定できないが，彼らは休暇で留守のような気がする.

**not have the faintest/foggiest (idea)** ⇒ **FAINT**¹

**\*ideal¹** /aɪdíəl; -díːəl/ 形 ▶定義 **ideal for sb/sth** the best possible; perfect→ ～として理想の; 完ぺきな ‖ *She's the ideal candidate for the job.* 彼女はその仕事の候補として申し分ない. ***In an ideal world*** *there would be no poverty.* 理想の世界では貧困がなくなるだろう. *It would be an **ideal opportunity** for you to practise your Spanish.* それはスペイン語の練習には絶好の機会だ.

**ideal²** /aɪdíəl; -díːəl/ 名 C ▶定義 1 an idea or principle that seems perfect to you and that you want to achieve 完ぺきであるように思え, 実現したいと思う考えまたは原理→ 理想, 究極的な目標, 極致 ‖ *She finds it hard to live up to her parents' high ideals.* 彼女は両親の高い理想にこたえるのは無理だと分かっている. *political/moral/social ideals* 政治的・道徳的・社会的理想 ▶定義 2 [通常は単数] **an ideal (of sth)** a perfect example of a person or thing 人または物の申し分のない例→ 理想的な人・物, 模範, かがみ ‖ *It's my ideal of what a family home should be.* これは, 家族で住む家はこうあるべきだという, 私の理想です.

**idealism** /aɪdíəlìz(ə)m; -díːəl-/ 名 U ▶定義 the belief that a perfect life, situation, etc can be achieved, even when this is not very likely たとえあまり実現可能ではないときであっても, 完ぺきな暮らしや状況などが実現され得るという信念→ 理想主義 ‖ *Young people are usually full of idealism.* 青年というのは普通, 理想主義にあふれているものだ. ☞参 **realism** — **idealist** 名 C → 理想主義者 ‖ *Most people are idealists when they are young.* ほとんどの人は, 若い時は理想主義者である. — **idealistic** /aɪdìːə(ə)lístɪk, àɪdɪ-/ 形 → 理想主義的な, 現実的でない

**idealize** (または **-ise**) /aɪdíəlàɪz; -díːəl-/ 動他 ▶定義 to imagine or show sb/sth as being better than he/she/it really is ～を実際よりも良く想像したり, そのように見せる→ ～を理想化する, ～を美化する ‖ *Old people often idealize the past.* 老人というものは過去をしばしば理想化するものだ.

**ideally** /aɪdíəli; -díːəli/ 副 ▶定義 1 perfectly 完ぺきに→ 理想的に, 申し分なく ‖ *They are ideally suited to each other.* 彼らは理想のカップルだ.
▶定義 2 in an ideal situation 理想的な状況では→ 理想的には, 理想を言えば ‖ *Ideally, no class should be larger than 25.* 理想的には, 学級の人数は25人以下にすべきである.

**identical** /aɪdéntɪk(ə)l/ 形 ▶定義 1 **identical (to/with sb/sth)** exactly the same as; similar in every detail ～と全く同じ; あらゆる点で同様の→ (～に)一致する, 全く同様の ‖ *I can't see any difference between these two pens - they look identical to me.* この2本のペンはどこが違うのか分かりません － 私には全く同じように見えます. *That watch is identical to the one I lost yesterday.* その時計は昨日なくしたのと全く同じものだ. ▶定義 2 **the identical** (名詞の前だけ) the same 同一の→ 全く同じ, 同じ ‖ *This is the identical room we stayed in last year.* これは私たちが去年泊まったのと同じ部屋だ. — **identically** /-k(ə)li/ 副 → 全く同じに, 同様に

**identical twin** 名 C ▶定義 one of two children born at the same time from the same mother, and who are of the same sex and look very similar. 同じ母親から同じ時間に生まれ, 性別が同じでうり二つの双子のうちの1人→ 一卵性双生児

**\*identification** /aɪdèntəfəkéɪʃ(ə)n, ə-/ 名 U C ▶定義 1 the process of showing, recognizing or giving proof of who or what sb/sth is ～がだれであるか・何であるかを明らかにし, 見分け, 証明をする過程→ 同一であることの証明, (身元などの)確認, 身分証明 ‖ *The identification of the bodies of those killed in the explosion was very difficult.* 爆発事故での死亡者の遺体確認は困難を極めた. ▶定義 2 (略 **ID**) ❶ an official paper, document, etc that is proof of who you are 身分を証明する正式な紙や書類など→ 身分を証明できるもの, 身分証明書 ‖ *Do you have any identification?* 身分を証明するものは何かお持ちですか. ▶定義 3 **identification (with sb/sth)** a strong feeling of understanding or sharing the same feelings as sb/sth ～を理解しているという強い気持ち, または相手と同じ気持ちを共有しているという強い感情→ (～と)同一であると

感じること，一体感，共感，感情移入 ‖ *children's identification with TV heroes* 子供たちがテレビの主人公になったような気分になること

***identify** /aɪdéntəfàɪ/ [動][他]（現分 **identifying**; 三単現 **identifies**; 過，過分 **identified**）▶定義 identify sb/sth (as sb/sth) to recognize or be able to say who or what sb/sth is ～がだれであるか・何であるかを明らかにする，またはそう断定することができる➜**その人・物であると見分ける，身元を確認する** ‖ *The police need someone to identify the body.* 警察はだれかに遺体の確認をしてもらう必要がある．*We must identify the cause of the problem before we look for solutions.* 私たちは解決策を探す前に問題の原因を明らかにしなければなりません．

[句動詞] identify sth with sth ▶定義 to think or say that sth is the same as sth else ある～をほかの別の…と同じであると思う，またはそう断言する➜**～を…と同一視する，同一であると見なす，結び付ける** ‖ *You can't identify nationalism with fascism.* ナショナリズムとファシズムを同一視することはできません．

identify with sb ▶定義 to feel that you understand and share what sb else is feeling 他人の感情が理解でき，共感していると感じる➜**～と同一視する，一体感を持つ，～に共鳴する** ‖ *I found it hard to identify with the woman in the film.* 映画に登場した女性の気持ちになるのは困難でした．

identify (yourself) with sb/sth ▶定義 to support or be closely connected with sb/sth ～を支持する，密接に結び付く➜**～に賛同する，共鳴する，～と行動を共にする，～の仲間になる** ‖ *She became identified with the new political party.* 彼女は新しい政党を支持した．

***identity** /aɪdéntəti/ [名][C][U]（[複] **identities**）▶定義 who or what a person or a thing is 人または物の本体がだれであるか，あるいは何であるかということ➜**身元，正体，主体性，アイデンティティー** ‖ *There are few clues to the identity of the killer.* 人殺しの身元を知る手掛かりはほとんどない．*The region has its own* ***cultural identity****.* その地域には独自の文化がある．*The arrest was a case of mistaken identity (= The wrong person was arrested).* その逮捕は人違いであった（= 間違った人物が逮捕された）．

**identity card**（または **ID card**）[名][C] ▶定義 a card with your name, photograph, etc that is proof of who you are 氏名，写真などが付いて，持ち主の身分を証明するカード➜**身分を証明できるもの，身分証明書**

**ideology** /àɪdiálədʒi, ìd-/ [名][C][U]（[複] **ideologies**）▶定義 a set of ideas which form the basis for a political or economic system 政治制度または経済制度の根本を成す思想体系➜**イデオロギー，空理，空論，観念学［論］，観念形態，思想傾向** ‖ *Marxist ideology* マルクス主義のイデオロギー — ideological /àɪdiəládʒɪk(ə)l, ìd-/ [形]➜**イデオロギー（上）の，（人が）観念的な**

**idiom** /ídiəm/ [名][C] ▶定義 an expression whose meaning is different from the meanings of the individual words in it その表現を構成する個々の単語の意味（の総和）とは異なる意味を持つ表現➜**慣用句，熟語，成句** ‖ *The idiom 'bring sth home to sb' means 'make sb understand sth'.* bring sth home to sb という熟語は，「～を人に痛感させる」ことを意味する．

**idiomatic** /ìdiəmǽtɪk/ [形] ▶定義1 using language that contains expressions that are natural to a native speaker 言語を，それを母国語とする人から見ても自然な表現を使って操る➜**慣用語法にかなった，いかにもその言語らしい** ‖ *He speaks good idiomatic English.* 彼はとても英語らしい英語を話す．▶定義2 containing an idiom 熟語を含んだ➜**慣用句の，慣用句を用いた** ‖ *an idiomatic expression* 熟語表現

**idiot** /ídiət/ [名][C][略式] ▶定義 a very stupid person とても愚かな人➜**ばか，間抜け，白痴** ‖ *I was an idiot to forget my passport.* パスポートを忘れるなんて，私は何てばかだったのだろう．— idiotic /ìdiátɪk/ [形]➜**ばかな，愚かな** — idiotically /-k(ə)li/ [副]➜**ばかげて，愚かにも**

**idle** /áɪdl/ [形] ▶定義1 not wanting to work hard; lazy まじめに働くのを嫌う；怠惰な➜**怠けている，怠け者で，のらくらしている** ‖ *He has the ability to succeed but he is just* ***bone*** *(= very)* ***idle****.* 彼は成功するだけの能力があるのに，根っからの（= とても）怠け者である．▶定義2 not doing anything; not being used 何もしていない；使用されていない➜**仕事のない，暇な，（機械・工場などが）動いていない** ‖ *She can't bear to be idle.* 彼女は無為な時を過ごすのに耐えら

I

れない. *The factory **stood idle** while the machines were being repaired.* その工場は機械を修理している間, 操業を停止した. ▶定義3 (名詞の前だけ) not to be taken seriously because it will not have any result 実質を伴わないのでまじめに受け止められない→**無駄な, 無意味な** ‖ *an idle promise/threat* 空約束・こけおどし *idle chatter/curiosity* 下らないおしゃべり・つまらぬ好奇心 — **idleness** 名 U⇒怠惰, 無為 — **idly** /áɪdli/ 副⇒怠けて, 無益に, ぼんやりと

**idol** /áɪdl/ 名 C ▶定義1 a person (such as a film star or pop musician) who is admired or loved (映画スターやポピュラー音楽家など) 崇拝され, 愛される人→**英雄的存在, アイドル, 崇拝の的** ‖ *a pop/football/teen/screen idol* アイドル歌手・フットボールの花形選手・ティーンエージャーのアイドル・映画の人気俳優 ▶定義2 a statue that people treat as a god 人々が神としてあがめる像→**偶像, 神像**

**idolize** (または **-ise**) /áɪdlàɪz/ 動 他 ▶定義 to love or admire sb very much or too much ～を非常に愛し, 賞賛する, またはその度が過ぎる→**～を偶像化する, ～を盲目的に崇拝する, ～に心酔する, 溺愛 (できあい) する** ‖ *He is an only child and his parents idolize him.* 彼は一人っ子で, 両親に溺愛されている.

**idyllic** /aɪdílɪk/ ▶定義 very pleasant and peaceful; perfect とても心地良く穏やかな; 申し分のない→**牧歌的な, のどかな** ‖ *an idyllic holiday* 穏やかな休日

**ie** /àɪ íː, ðæt ɪz/ 略 that is; in other words→**すなわち; 言い換えれば** ‖ *deciduous trees, ie those which lose their leaves in autumn* 落葉樹, すなわち秋になると葉が落ちる樹木

\***if** /ɪf, əf/ 接 ▶定義1 used in sentences in which one thing only happens or is true when another thing happens or is true ある物事が起きた・本当であったときにのみ, 別の物事が起きる・本当になる, という文章で用いて→**もし～ならば, ～とすれば** ‖ *If you see him, give him this letter.* 彼に会ったら, この手紙を渡してください. *We won't go to the beach if it rains.* 雨が降ったら海には行きません. *If I had more time, I would learn another language.* もっと時間があれば, ほかの言語も勉強するのだが. *I might see her tomorrow. If not, I'll see her at the weekend.* 彼女には明日会うかもしれない. そうでなければ, 週末に会う. ▶定義2 when; every time→**～するときには, ～するときはいつでも** ‖ *If I try to phone her she just hangs up.* 彼女に電話をしようとすると, 彼女は必ず電話を切るんだ. *If metal gets hot it expands.* 金属は熱くなると膨張する. ▶定義3 used after verbs such as 'ask', 'know', 'remember' ask, know, remember などの動詞の後で用いて→**～かどうか** ‖ *They asked if we would like to go too.* 彼らは我々に, 同じく一緒に行くかどうか尋ねた. *I can't remember if I posted the letter or not.* その手紙を投かんしたかどうか思い出せない. ☛参 **whether** の注 ▶定義4 used when you are asking sb to do sth or suggesting sth politely ～に…をしてくれと頼んだり, ～を提案する際の丁寧な言い方→**もし～ならば申しますが** ‖ *If you could just come this way, sir.* ちょっとこちらにいらしてくださいませんか. *If I might suggest something...* 提案させていただくならば

> ▶語法
>
> **if のイメージは二者択一**
>
> どうして, 条件の副詞節と間接疑問の名詞節に if を使うことができるのでしょう. それは共通のイメージがあるからです. それは「二者択一, 二またの分かれ道」です. 条件の if it is rainy の場合「雨か, 雨でないか」の二者択一ですし, I don't know if she is busy. の場合「忙しいか, 忙しくないか」の二者択一なのです. Yes/No 疑問文を間接疑問にすると if が必要になるのは, このような理由によります.

**成句** os if ⇒ **AS**
even if ⇒ **EVEN**²
**if I were you** ▶定義 used when you are giving sb advice ～に助言するときに用いて→**私があなたの立場なら** ‖ *If I were you, I'd leave now.* 私があなたなら, 今すぐに辞めます.
**if it wasn't/weren't for sb/sth** ▶定義 if a particular person or situation did not exist or was not there; without sb/sth 特定の人または状況が存在しなかったら, もしくは (い) なかったら; ～が (い) なければ→**もし～がいなければ, もし～がなければ** ‖ *If it wasn't for him, I wouldn't stay in this country.* もし彼がいなければ, 私はこの国に

は滞在していないだろう.

**if only** ▶定義 used for expressing a strong wish 強い願望を表すのに用いて→~でありさえすれば ‖ *If only I could drive!* 運転さえできればなあ. *If only he'd write!* 彼が書いてくれさえすればなあ.

**igloo** /íglu:/ 名 C ( 複 **igloos**) ▶定義 a small house that is built from blocks of hard snow 硬い雪の塊を積み上げて造った小さな家→イグルー(イヌイット族(エスキモー)の住む雪や氷で作ったドーム型の家)

**ignite** /ɪgnáɪt/ 動自他 正式 ▶定義 to start burning or to make sth start burning 燃え始める, または何かを燃やし始める→引火する, 火がつく; ~に点火する, ~に火をつける ‖ *A spark from the engine ignited the petrol.* エンジンから出た火花がガソリンに引火した.

**ignition** /ɪgníʃ(ə)n/ 名 ▶定義 1 C the electrical system that starts the engine of a car 車のエンジンをかけるための電気装置→(車のエンジンの)点火装置, イグニッション ‖ *to turn the ignition on/off* 点火装置を入れる・切る *First of all, put the key in the ignition.* まず, イグニッションにキーを差し込みます. ▶定義 2 U the action of starting to burn or making sth start to burn 発火する, または点火させること→発火, 点火, 燃焼

**ignominious** /ìgnəmíniəs/ 形 正式 ▶定義 making you feel embarrassed ばつの悪い思いをさせる→恥ずべき, 不名誉な, 屈辱的な ‖ *The team suffered an ignominious defeat.* そのチームは屈辱的な敗北を経験した. ― **ignominiously** 副 →不名誉にも, 屈辱的なことに

**ignorance** /íɡn(ə)rəns/ 名 U ▶定義 ignorance (of/about sth) a lack of information or knowledge 情報や知識が不足していること→(~についての)無知, (~を)知らないこと ‖ *The workers were in complete ignorance of the management's plans.* 従業員は経営計画について全く無知であった.

**ignorant** /íɡn(ə)rənt/ 形 ▶定義 1 ignorant (of/about sth) not knowing about sth ~について知らない→(~に)無知な, 意識しない ‖ *Many people are ignorant of their rights.* 人々の多くは自分たちの権利について無知である. ▶定義 2 略式 having or showing bad manners→礼儀知らずの, 無礼な ‖ *an ignorant person/remark* 無礼な人・無礼な発言

---

illegal　841

*****ignore** /ɪgnɔ́:r/ 動他 ▶定義 to pay no attention to sb/sth ~に対して全く注意を払わない→~を無視する, ~を見て見ぬ振りをする ‖ *I said hello to Debbie but she totally ignored me (= acted as though she hadn't seen me).* デビーにあいさつをしたが, 完全に無視された (= まるで私を見なかったかのように振る舞った). *Alison ignored her doctor's advice about drinking and smoking less.* アリソンは, 酒とたばこを減らすようにという医者の助言を無視した.

▶注意. ignore と be ignorant は意味が異なる.

**ikon** = ICON(3)

**I'll** /áɪl/ I WILL, I SHALL の短縮形

*****ill**[1] /ɪl/ 形 ▶定義 1 (困 **sick**) (名詞の前は不可) not in good health; not well 健康でない; 体の調子が悪い→病気で気分が悪い ‖ *I can't drink milk because it makes me feel ill.* 気持ちが悪くなるので, 牛乳は飲めない. *My mother was taken ill suddenly last week.* 母は先週急に病気になった. *My grandfather is seriously ill in hospital.* 祖父は重病で入院している. ☞参 **sick** の注 ▶定義 2 (名詞の前だけ) bad or harmful→悪い, 害のある ‖ *He resigned because of ill health.* 彼は健康を害したため辞職した. *I'm glad to say I suffered no ill effects from all that rich food.* あのこってりした食事を全部食べても体に何の悪影響もなくてよかった. ☞ 名 illness

**ill**[2] /ɪl/ 副 ▶定義 1 (しばしば複合語で) badly or wrongly 悪く, 不正に→意地悪く, 不親切に, 都合悪く ‖ *You would be ill-advised to drive until you have fully recovered.* 完全に回復するまでに, 運転をするなんて無分別だ. ▶定義 2 only with difficulty; not easily 辛うじて; 容易ではない→不十分に, 不満足に, ほとんど~ない ‖ *They could ill afford the extra money for better heating.* 彼らにはもっと良い暖房装置を買う余裕はほとんどなかった.

成句 augur well/ill for sb/sth ⇒ **AUGUR**
bode well/ill (for sb/sth) ⇒ **BODE**

*****illegal** /ɪlí:g(ə)l/ 形 ▶定義 not allowed by the law 法律で認められない→非合法の, 不法な, 違法な ‖ *It is illegal to own a gun without a special licence.* 特別な免許を持たずにけん銃を所持することは違法です. *illegal drugs/immigrants/*

activities 非合法ドラッグ・不法滞在の移民・非合法活動 ⇔ **legal** — illegally /-g(ə)li/ [副] ➜**不法に, 非合法に**

**illegible** /ɪlédʒəb(ə)l/ [形] ▶定義 difficult or impossible to read 読みにくい, 読むのが不可能な➜**判読し難い, 解読できない** ‖ *Your handwriting is quite illegible.* あなたの書く字は極めて読みにくい. ⇔**legible** — illegibly /-əb(ə)li/ [副] ➜**読みにくく, 判読しにくく**

**illegitimate** /ɪlədʒítəmət/ [形] ▶定義1 ([古]) (used about a child) born to parents who are not married to each other (子供について) 結婚していない両親の間に生まれた➜**非嫡出(ちゃくしゅつ)の, 庶出の** ▶定義2 not allowed by law; against the rules 法律で認められない; 規則違反の➜**違法の, 非合法の** ‖ *the illegitimate use of company money* 会社の金の不正使用 ⇔**legitimate** — illegitimacy /ɪlɪdʒítəməsi/ [名] [U]➜**非嫡出(ちゃくしゅつ), 庶出, 違法, 非合法**

**ill-fated** [形] ▶定義 not lucky 運が悪い➜**不運な, 不幸な, のろわれた** ‖ *the ill-fated ship, the Titanic* のろわれた船, タイタニック号

**illicit** /ɪlísət/ [形] ▶定義 (used about an activity or substance) not allowed by law or by the rules of society (行為または物について) 法律または社会の決まりで認められない➜**合法でない, 不法の, 社会常識に反した** ‖ *the illicit trade in ivory* 象牙(ぞうげ)の密貿易 *They were having an illicit affair.* 彼らは不義の関係にあった.

**illiterate** /ɪlít(ə)rət/ [形] ▶定義1 not able to read or write 読み書きができない➜**無学の, 無教育の, 文盲の** ⇔ **literate** ▶定義2 (used about a piece of writing) very badly written (文書について) 非常に拙劣に書かれていて➜**無教養さの表れた, 教養のない** ▶定義3 not knowing much about a particular subject ある特定の分野についてあまり知識がない➜**(特定の分野に) 無知な, (ある事柄の) 知識に乏しい, 素養がない** ‖ *computer illiterate* コンピューターの知識に乏しい — illiteracy /ɪlít(ə)rəsi/ [名] [U]➜**読み書きができないこと, 文盲, 無学** ‖ *adult illiteracy* 成人の非識字 ⇔ **literacy**

***illness** /ílnəs/ [名] ▶定義1 [U] the state of being physically or mentally ill 肉体的にまたは精神的に病気の状態➜**病気, 不健康** ‖ *He's missed a lot of school through illness.* 彼は病気のため, 大変よく学校を欠席した. *There is a history of mental illness in the family.* その家族には精神病の病歴がある. ▶定義2 [C] a type or period of physical or mental ill health 肉体的または精神的不健康の期間, もしくはそれをもたらした特定の病気➜**(特定の) 病気** ‖ *minor/serious/childhood illnesses* 軽い病気・重い病気・小児病 *My dad is just getting over his illness.* 父はちょうど病気が良くなりつつある. ☛ [形] ill ☛参 **disease** の注

**illogical** /ɪlάdʒɪk(ə)l/ [形] ▶定義 not sensible or reasonable 思慮分別がない, 筋が通らない➜**非論理的な, 不合理な** ‖ *It seems illogical to me to pay somebody to do work that you could do yourself.* 自分でできる事なのに, お金を払ってだれかにやってもらうのは不合理のように思える. ⇔ **logical** — illogicality /ɪlɑdʒɪkǽləti/ [名] [C] [U] ([複] illogicalities) ➜**不合理, 無分別** — illogically [副] ➜ **非論理的に, 不合理に**

**ill-treat** [動][他] ▶定義 to treat sb/sth badly or in an unkind way ～をひどく扱う, 思いやりなく扱う ➜**～を虐待する, ～を酷使する** ‖ *This cat has been ill-treated.* この猫は虐待されている. — ill-treatment [名] [U]➜**虐待, 酷使**

**illuminate** /ɪlúːmənèɪt/ [動][他][正式] ▶定義1 to shine light on sth or to decorate sth with lights ～を照らす, 明かりで～を装飾する ➜**～を照らす, ～を明るくする, ～にイルミネーションを施す** ‖ *The palace was illuminated by spotlights.* 宮殿はスポットライトで照らされていた. ▶定義2 to explain sth or make sth clear ～を説明する, ～を明らかにする➜**(難題などを) 分かりやすくする, 明確にする**

**illuminating** /ɪlúːmənèɪtɪŋ/ [形] ▶定義 helping to explain sth or make sth clear ～の説明を助ける, ～を明らかにする助けとなる➜**理解を助ける, 事態を明らかにする, 啓発的な** ‖ *an illuminating discussion* 事態を解明する討議

**illumination** /ɪlùːmənéɪʃ(ə)n/ [名] ▶定義1 [U][C] light or the place where a light comes from 光がそこから入ってくる (明かりがそこから照らし出される) 場所や照明➜**照明, 明かり** ‖ *These big windows give good illumination.* これらの大きな窓からたくさんの光が入ってきます. ▶定義2 **illuminations** [複数扱い] [英] bright colourful lights that are used for decorating a street, town, etc 街路や街などを装飾するため

の, 鮮やかな色とりどりの明かり→(街の)イルミネーション

**illusion** /ɪlúːʒ(ə)n/ 名 ▶定義1 ⓒ ⓤ a false idea, belief or impression 誤った考え, 信念, 印象→幻想, 誤解, 迷妄, 錯覚 ‖ *I have no illusions about the situation - I know it's serious.* 私はその事態について何も誤解しているところはない — 事態が深刻なことは分かっている. *I think Peter's **under the illusion** that he will be the new director.* ピーターは新しい重役になれると勘違いをしているのだと思います. ▶定義2 ⓒ something that your eyes tell you is there or is true but in fact is not 実際はそうではないのに(視覚によって)そこにあるように見えたり, 本当のように見えるもの→幻覚, 幻影, 錯覚 ‖ *That line looks longer, but in fact they're the same length. It's an **optical illusion**.* あちらの線の方が長く見えますが, 実際は同じ長さです. これは目の錯覚なのです.

**illusory** /ɪlúːs(ə)ri, -z(ə)-/ 形正式 ▶定義 not real, although seeming to be それらしく見えるが実在しない・本当でない→人を欺く, 錯覚に基づく, 架空の, 虚妄の ‖ *The profits they had hoped for proved to be illusory.* 期待した利益は, 結局, 幻だった.

*****illustrate** /íləstrèɪt/ 動中 ▶定義1 to explain or make sth clear by using examples, pictures or diagrams 例, 絵, 図などで~を説明し, 明らかにする→~を説明する, ~を例証する ‖ *These statistics **illustrate the point** that I was making very well.* これらの統計は私の主張をとても良く例証している. ▶定義2 to add pictures, diagrams, etc to a book or magazine 本や雑誌に絵, 図などを入れる→~のさし絵を入れる, (本など)に(図表・写真・絵などを)入れる ‖ *Most cookery books are illustrated.* 料理の本はほとんどがさし絵入りだ.

**illustration** /ìləstréɪʃ(ə)n/ 名 ▶定義1 ⓒa drawing, diagram or picture in a book or magazine 本や雑誌などのさし絵, 図, 写真→イラスト, 説明図 ‖ *colour illustrations* 色刷りのさし絵 ▶定義2 ⓤ the activity or art of illustrating 実例を挙げて説明をすること, またその方法→例証, 例解, 図解 ▶定義3 ⓒ an example that makes a point or an idea clear 要点や考えを明らかにする例→実例 ‖ *Can you give me an illustration of what you mean?* 実例を挙げて説明できますか.

**illustrious** /ɪlʌ́striəs/ 形正式 ▶定義 famous and successful 有名で成功した→(人が)著名な, (業績などが)輝かしい

**I'm** /áɪm/ I AM の短縮形

*****image** /ímɪdʒ/ 名 ⓒ ▶定義1 the general impression that a person or organization gives to the public 個人や団体が世間一般に与える全体的な印象→(人に与える)イメージ, 印象, 評判 ‖ *When you meet him, he's very different from his public image.* 彼に実際に会うと, 世間のイメージとは全く掛け離れている. ▶定義2 a mental picture or idea of sb/sth 頭の中に思い浮かべる~の像や概念→心像, 表象, 概念 ‖ *I have an image of my childhood as always sunny and happy.* 心に浮かぶ子供時代は, いつも明るくて幸せなものだ. ▶定義3 a picture or description that appears in a book, film or painting 本, 映画, 絵画に描かれた映像や描写→像, 画像, 絵姿 ‖ *horrific images of war* 恐ろしい戦争の描写 ▶定義4 a copy or picture of sb/sth seen in a mirror, through a camera, on television, computer, etc 鏡, カメラ, テレビ, コンピューターなどに映った~の映像や写し→(鏡やレンズの)映像, (テレビなどの)画像; 生き写し ‖ *A perfect image of the building was reflected in the lake.* そのビルが完全な姿で湖に映っていた. (比喩) *He's **the (spitting) image of** his father (= he looks exactly like him).* 彼は父親にそっくりだ (= 彼は父親と全くよく似ている).

**imagery** /ímɪdʒ(ə)ri/ 名 ⓤ ▶定義 language that produces pictures in the minds of the people reading or listening 読んだり聞いたりしている人々の心の中に像を描く言葉→心像, イメージ ‖ *poetic imagery* 詩的イメージ

**imaginable** /ɪmǽdʒ(ə)nəb(ə)l/ 形 ▶定義 that you can imagine 想像できる→考えられる, 考えられる限りの ‖ *Sophie made all the excuses imaginable when she was caught stealing.* 盗みで捕まった時, ソフィーは考えられるあらゆる言い訳をした. *His house was equipped with every imaginable luxury.* 彼の家には, ありとあらゆる考えられる限りのぜいたくな物がそろっていた.

*****imaginary** /ɪmǽdʒən(ə)ri; -nèri/ 形 ▶定義 existing only in the mind; not real 心の中にだけ

存在する; 現実ではない→想像(上)の, 架空の ‖ Many children have imaginary friends. 子供たちの多くには想像上の友達がいる.

**imagination** /mæd͡ʒənéɪʃ(ə)n/ 名 ▶定義1 ⓤ ⓒ the ability to create mental pictures or new ideas 頭の中に映像を思い浮かべたり, 新しい考えを創り出したりする能力→想像(力), 空想力, 創作力 ‖ He has a lively imagination. 彼には豊かな想像力がある. She's very clever but she doesn't **have** much **imagination**. 彼女はとても賢いが, あまり想像力はない.

➤ imagination とは, 人間の創造的な能力のことである. fantasy は現実とは関連のない考えや物語などのことを指す.

▶定義2 ⓒ the part of the mind that uses this ability 精神活動の中で, この能力(想像力)を働かせる部分→想像力 ‖ If you **use** your **imagination**, you should be able to guess the answer. 想像力を働かせれば, 答えを推測できるはずです. — imaginatively 副 →想像を働かせて, 想像力豊かに

**imaginative** /ɪmæd͡ʒ(ə)nətɪv/ 形 ▶定義 having or showing imagination 想像力を持つ, 示す→想像力に富む, 創造性のある, 想像力を働かせた ‖ She's always full of imaginative ideas. 彼女はいつも想像的なアイデアに満ちている.

*imagine /ɪmæd͡ʒən/ 動 他 ▶定義1 imagine that...; imagine sb/sth (doing/as sth) to form a picture or idea in your mind of what sth/sb might be like ~がどのようなものか, 心の中で描いたり考えたりする→~が…しているのを・・・なのを想像する, ~を思い描く ‖ Imagine that you're lying on a beach. 海辺で寝そべっていると想像してください. It's not easy to imagine your brother as a doctor. あなたのお兄さんが医者だとは想像し難い. I can't imagine myself cycling 20 miles a day. 1日に20マイルも自転車で走るなんて想像もできない.

▶定義2 to see, hear or think sth that is not true or does not exist 本当ではない~や存在しない…について, 見たり聞いたり考えたりする→(勝手に) ~を思い込む, ~を想像する ‖ She's always imagining that she's ill but she's fine really. 彼女は自分が病気だといつも思い込んでいるが, 実際は健康だ. I thought I heard someone downstairs, but I must have been **imagining** things. だれかが階下にいる物音がしたと思ったが, きっと気のせいだったのだろう. ▶定義3 to think that sth is probably true; to suppose ~が多分正しいであろうと考える; (多分) ~だと思う→~を…だと思う, ~を推測する ‖ I imagine he'll be coming by car. 彼は車で来ると思う.

**imbalance** /ɪmbǽləns/ 名 ⓒ ▶定義 an imbalance (between A and B); an imbalance (in/of sth) a difference; not being equal 相違; 等しくないこと→不均衡, アンバランス ‖ an imbalance in the numbers of men and women teachers 男性教諭と女性教諭の数の不均衡

**imbecile** /ímbəsìːl, -səl, -sàɪl/ 名 ⓒ ▶定義 a stupid person; an idiot 愚かな人; ばか→精神薄弱者, 痴愚

**IMF** /àɪ em éf/ 略 International Monetary Fund→国際通貨基金

**imitate** /ímətèɪt/ 動 他 ▶定義1 to copy the behaviour of sb/sth ~の振る舞いをまねする→~をまねる, ~を模倣する, ~を見習う ‖ Small children learn by imitating their parents. 幼児は両親のまねをして学んでいく. ▶定義2 to copy the speech or actions of sb/sth, often in order to make people laugh 普通, 人を笑わせるために~の話し方や動作をまねる→(ふざけて)(人や動物の声・身振りなどの)物まねをする ‖ She could imitate her mother perfectly. 彼女は母親そっくりに物まねができた.

**imitation** /ìmətéɪʃ(ə)n/ 名 ▶定義1 ⓒ a copy of sth real 実物を模倣したもの→模造品, にせ物 ‖ Some artificial flowers are good imitations of real ones. 造花には本物そっくりのものもある. ☞参 genuine ▶定義2 ⓤ the act of copying sb/sth ~をまねること→手本をまねること, 模倣 ‖ Good pronunciation of a language is best learnt **by imitation**. 言語の良い発音の習得には, まねることが一番です. ▶定義3 ⓒ the act of copying the way sb talks and behaves, especially in order to make people laugh 特に人を笑わせるために, ~の話し方や動作をまねること→まね, 物まね ‖ Can you **do** any **imitations** of politicians? 政治家の物まねは, 何かできますか.

**immaculate** /ɪmǽkjələt/ 形 ▶定義1 perfectly clean and tidy 完全に清潔できちんと片付いている→染み一つない, 少しも汚れていない ‖

*immaculate white shirts* 染み一つない白いシャツ ▶定義2 without any mistakes; perfect→誤りのない; 完ぺきな ‖ *His performance of 'Romeo' was immaculate.* 彼の「ロミオ」の演技は完ぺきだった. — **immaculately** 副 →染み一つなく, 完ぺきに

**immaterial** /ˌɪməˈtɪəriəl/ 形 ▶定義 **immaterial (to sb/sth)** not important→(〜にとって)重要でない, 取るに足りない ‖ *It's immaterial to me whether we go today or tomorrow.* 我々が今日行こうが明日行こうが, 私には重要ではない.

**immature** /ˌɪməˈtjʊər, -ˈtʃʊər/ 形 ▶定義1 not fully grown or developed; not mature 十分に成長または, 発達していない; 成熟していない→未成熟の, 未発達の ‖ *an immature body* 未熟な体 ▶定義2 (used about a person) behaving in a way that is not sensible and is typical of people who are much younger (人について) 思慮分別がなく, 実際の年齢よりもはるかに幼い振る舞いをする→(人が) 未熟な, 子供っぽい ‖ *I think he's too immature to take his work seriously.* 彼は未熟すぎて自分の仕事にまじめに取り組めないのだと思う. ⇨ **mature**

**immediacy** /ɪˈmiːdiəsi/ 名 ❶ ▶定義 the quality of being available or seeming to happen close to you and without delay 即座に利用できるという特性, 身近で即座に起きるように見えるという特性→**直接性, 緊急性, 即時性** ‖ *Letters do not have the same immediacy as e-mail.* 手紙には, 電子メールのような即時性がない.

\***immediate** /ɪˈmiːdiət/ 形 ▶定義1 happening or done without delay 即座に起きる, なされる→**すぐさまの, 即時の, 即刻の** ‖ *I'd like an immediate answer to my proposal.* 私の提案について即答してもらいたい. *The government responded with immediate action.* 政府はそれにこたえて, 即刻行動を起こした. ▶定義2 (名詞の前だけ) existing now and needing urgent attention 今現在存在しており, 緊急の対応を必要とする→**当面の, 目前の** ‖ *Tell me what your immediate needs are.* 当面必要な事は何か教えてください. ▶定義3 (名詞の前だけ) nearest in time, position or relationship 時間, 位置, 関係が最も近い→(関係, 位置などが) **近い, 近接した, 直接の** ‖ *They won't make any changes in **the immediate future**.* 彼らは近い将来には何も変更を加えない. *He has left most of his money to his immediate family (= parents, children, brothers and sisters).* 彼はお金の大部分を近親者 (= 両親, 子供, 兄弟, 姉妹) に残していた.

**immediately** /ɪˈmiːdiətli/ 副 接 ▶定義1 at once; without delay すぐに; 即座に→**直ちに, 早速** ‖ *Can you come home immediately after work?* 仕事が終わったらすぐに家に帰れますか. *I couldn't immediately see what he meant.* 彼の意図がすぐには分からなかった. ▶定義2 very closely; directly 非常に密接に; 直接に→**じかに** ‖ *He wasn't immediately involved in the crime.* 彼はその犯罪に直接はかかわっていなかった. ▶定義3 nearest in time or position 時間, 場所などが最も近く→**すぐ近くに, すぐ接して** ‖ *Who's the girl immediately in front of Simon?* サイモンのすぐ前の少女はだれですか. *What did you do immediately after the war?* 戦争が終わった直後に何をしましたか. ▶定義4 英 as soon as→**〜するとすぐ** ‖ *I opened the letter immediately I got home.* 家に着くと手紙を開けた.

**immense** /ɪˈmens/ 形 ▶定義 very big or great→**とても大きい, ばく大な** ‖ *immense difficulties/importance/power* 計り知れぬ困難・重要性・力 *She gets immense pleasure from her garden.* 彼女は自分の庭から計り知れぬ喜びを得ている.

**immensely** /ɪˈmensli/ 副 ▶定義 extremely; very much→**非常に, 大いに** ‖ *immensely enjoyable* 極めて楽しい *'Did you enjoy the party?' 'Yes, immensely.'* 「パーティーは楽しかったですか」「はい, とっても」

**immensity** /ɪˈmensəti/ 名 ❶ ▶定義 an extremely large size 極めて大きな規模→**ばく大さ, 広大さ** ‖ *the immensity of the universe* 宇宙の広大さ

**immerse** /ɪˈmɜːrs/ 動 他 ▶定義1 **immerse sth (in sth)** to put sth into a liquid so that it is covered 〜を液体に入れ, 浸す→**〜を (液体に) 浸す, 沈める, 漬ける** ‖ *Make sure the spaghetti is fully immersed in the boiling water.* スパゲッティが沸騰したお湯に完全に入っているか確認してください. ▶定義2 **immerse yourself (in sth)** to involve yourself completely in sth so that you give it all your attention 〜に完全に没頭し, その結果, 全神経を集中する→**〜に没頭する, ふける** ‖ *Rachel's usually immersed in a book.* レイチ

ェルは大抵本に没頭している.

**\*immigrant** /ímɪɡrənt/ 名 ❻ ▶定義 a person who has come into a foreign country to live there permanently 外国に来て, そのままその国に永住する人→移民, 入国者 ‖ *The government plans to tighten controls to prevent **illegal immigrants**.* 政府は不法移民を阻止するために, 管理を厳しくする計画だ. *London has a high immigrant population.* ロンドンでは人口に占める移民の割合が高い.
▶英国には移民のコミュニティーが多数あり, multicultural society (多種類の文化を持つ社会) を作っている. 共通の伝統文化を持つ移民やその子供たちの集団が, ethnic minority (少数民族集団) を形成している.

**\*immigration** /ìmɪɡréɪʃ(ə)n/ 名 ❶ ▶定義 1 the process of coming to live permanently in a country that is not your own; the number of people who do this 他国に永住するために入国してくること; 移民の数→(外国からの) 移住; 移民 ‖ *There are greater controls on immigration than there used to be.* 移民に対する管理は, 以前に比べて厳しくなっている. ▶定義 2 (または **immigration control**) the control point at an airport, port, etc where the official documents of people who want to come into a country are checked 空港, 港などにある管理機関で, 入国者の公文書が審査される→(空港・港の) 入国管理 (審査) 所 ‖ *When you leave the plane you have to go through customs and immigration.* 飛行機を降りたら, 税関と入国管理所を通らなければならない. ☛ immigrate という動詞もあるが, ほとんど使用されない. 通常は be an immigrant を使うか, または出身国に関連させて, emigrate という動詞を使用する. *My parents emigrated to this country from Jamaica.* 私の両親は, ジャマイカからこの国に移住した. ☛参 emigrate, emigrant, emigration

**imminent** /ímənənt/ 形 ▶定義 (usually used about sth unpleasant) almost certain to happen very soon (通常は良くない〜について) すぐに起こることがほぼ確実な→(良くない事が) 差し迫った, 切迫した, 今にも起こりそうな ‖ *Heavy rainfall means that flooding is imminent.* 豪雨になると洪水の危険が差し迫ってくる. — imminently 副→今にも起こりそうに, 切迫して

**immobile** /ɪmóʊbaɪl, -b(ə)l/ 形 ▶定義 not moving or not able to move 動かない, 動けない→静止した, 不動の, 固定された ‖ *The hunter stood immobile until the lion had passed.* 猟師は, ライオンが通り過ぎるまでじっとして動かなかった. ⇔ **mobile** — immobility /ìmoʊbíləti/ 名 ❶ →静止 (状態), 不動, 固定

**immobilize** (または **-ise**) /ɪmóʊbəlàɪz/ 動 他 ▶定義 to prevent sb/sth from moving or working normally 〜が正常に動く・働くことを妨げる→〜を動けなくする, 〜を停止させる ‖ *The railways have been completely immobilized by the strike.* 鉄道はストのために完全に停止した. *This device immobilizes the car to prevent it being stolen.* この装置は車を固定させて盗難を防ぎます. ⇔ **mobilize**

**immobilizer** (または **-iser**) /ɪmóʊbəlàɪzər/ ▶定義 a device in a vehicle that prevents thieves from starting the engine when the vehicle is parked 車に付いている装置で, 駐車中に泥棒がエンジンをスタートさせるのを防ぐもの→盗難防止装置

**immoral** /ɪmɔ́(ː)r(ə)l, -már-/ 形 ▶定義 (used about people or their behaviour) considered wrong or not honest by most people (人またはその行動について) ほとんどの人が, 悪い・正直ではないと見なすような→不道徳な, 不品行な ‖ *It's immoral to steal.* 物を盗むのは不道徳な事だ. ⇔ **moral**. **amoral** を参照. 意味が異なる.
— immorality /ìmərǽləti/ 名 ❶ →不道徳さ, 反倫理性 ⇔ **morality** — immorally /-r(ə)li/ 副 →道徳に反して, 不道徳に, ふしだらに

**immortal** /ɪmɔ́ːrtl/ 形 ▶定義 living or lasting for ever 永遠に生きる, 永続する→不死の, 不滅の, 不朽の ‖ *Nobody is immortal - we all have to die some time.* 不死身の人間はいない —皆いつかは死すべき運命だ. ⇔ **mortal** — immortality /ìmɔːrtǽləti/ 名 ❶ →不滅, 不死, 不朽の名声

**immortalize** (または **-ise**) /ɪmɔ́ːrtlàɪz/ 動 他 ▶定義 to give lasting fame to sb/sth 〜に不朽の名声を与える→〜を不滅にする, 〜を不朽にする ‖ *He immortalized their relationship in a poem.* 彼は詩の中で, 彼らの関係を永遠のものとした.

**immune** /ɪmjúːn/ 形 ▶定義 1 immune (to sth) having natural protection against a certain disease or illness 特定の病気・疾患に対して自然

の免疫を持つ➡**免疫(性)の, (〜に対して)免疫がある** ‖ *You should be immune to measles if you've had it already.* 麻疹(はしか)にかかったことがあるのなら, それに対して免疫があるはずだ. ▶定義2 immune (to sth) not affected by sth 〜に影響されない➡**(〜には)動じない, 慣れて, 免疫になって** ‖ *You can say what you like - I'm immune to criticism!* 何でも好きな事を言ってください — 私は批判には慣れていますから.
▶定義3 immune (from sth) protected from a danger or punishment 危険や罰から保護されて➡**(〜を)免除されて, 免れて** ‖ *Young children are immune from prosecution.* 青少年は処罰を免除される.

**immunity** /ɪmjúːnəti/ 名 U ▶定義 the ability to avoid or not be affected by disease, criticism, punishment by law, etc 病気, 批判, 法などによる処罰などから逃れたり, 影響を受けずに済む能力➡**免疫, 免除, 免責** ‖ *In many countries people have no immunity to diseases like measles.* 多くの国では, 国民は麻疹(はしか)などの病気に対する免疫がない. *Ambassadors to other countries receive diplomatic immunity (= protection from prosecution, etc).* 外国に駐在する大使には, 外交官免除特権(= 起訴などから保護される)がある.

**immunize**(または **-ise**) /ímjunàɪz/ 動他 ▶定義 to make sb immune to a disease, usually by putting a substance (vaccine) into his/her body 〜に病気に対する免疫を与える. 通常は物質(ワクチン)を体内に入れることで行われる➡**〜に免疫を与える, 〜に予防接種をする** ‖ *Before visiting certain countries you will need to be immunized against cholera.* 特定の国に行く場合は, 渡航前にコレラに対する予防接種を受ける必要がある. ☛ inoculate と vaccinate も同様の意味を持つ. — **immunization** (または **-isation**) /ɪmjənəzéɪʃ(ə)n; -naɪ-/ 名 C U ➡**免疫法, 予防接種**

**imp** /ɪmp/ 名 C ▶定義 (in stories) a small creature like a little devil (物語の中の)小悪魔などの小さな生き物➡**(おとぎばなしの)小鬼, 小悪魔**

*****impact** /ímpækt/ 名 ▶定義1 [C, 通常は単数] an impact (on/upon sb/sth) an effect or impression 影響, 印象➡**(〜への)(強い)影響(力), 衝撃** ‖ *I hope this anti-smoking campaign will make/have an impact on young people.* この反喫煙運動が若者に影響を与える・持つことを期待します. ▶定義2 ❶ the action or force of one object hitting another 2つの物がぶつかったための影響, またはそれによる力➡**衝突, ぶつかること, 衝撃(力)** ‖ *The impact of the crash threw the passengers out of their seats.* 衝突事故の衝撃で, 乗客は座席からほうり出された. *The bomb exploded on impact.* 爆弾は衝突の衝撃で爆発した.

**impair** /ɪmpéə<sup>r</sup>/ 動他 ▶定義 to damage sth or make it weaker 〜に損害を与える, 弱くする➡**〜を悪くする, 損なう, 弱める** ‖ *Ear infections can result in impaired hearing.* 耳に病原菌が入ると, 聴力を損なう場合もある.

**impale** /ɪmpéɪl/ 動他 ▶定義 impale sb/sth (on sth) to push a sharp pointed object through sb/sth 先が鋭くとがった物で〜を突き刺す➡**〜を(…に)突き刺す, 〜をくし刺しにする** ‖ *The boy fell out of the tree and impaled his leg on some railings.* 少年は木から落ちて, 足に柵(さく)が突き刺さった.

**impart** /ɪmpáː<sup>r</sup>t/ 動他 正式 ▶定義1 impart sth (to sb) to pass information, knowledge, etc to other people 人に情報や知識などを伝える➡**(秘密, 情報, 知識など)を(〜に)知らせる, 伝える** ‖ *He rushed home eager to impart the good news.* 彼は良い知らせを伝えようと, 家に大急ぎで帰った. ▶定義2 impart sth (to sth) to give a certain quality to sth 〜にある特性を与える➡**(性質など)を(〜に)分け与える, 〜を添える** ‖ *The low lighting imparted a romantic atmosphere to the room.* 照明を抑えると, 部屋にロマンチックな雰囲気が出た.

**impartial** /ɪmpáː<sup>r</sup>ʃ(ə)l/ 形 ▶定義 not supporting one person or group more than another; fair ある人や集団を, 他に比べてひいきしない; 公平な➡**中立の, 偏らない** ‖ *The referee must be impartial.* 審判は公平でなければならない. — **impartiality** /ɪmpɑː<sup>r</sup>ʃiæləti/ 名 U ➡**公平さ, 中立性** ⇔ **partiality** — **impartially** 副 ➡**公平に, 偏らずに**

**impassable** /ɪmpáːsəb(ə)l; -pǽs-/ 形 ▶定義 (used about a road, etc) impossible to travel on because it is blocked (道路などについて)ふさがれているためにそこを進むことができない➡**(道が)通り抜けできない, 通行不能の** ‖ *Flooding* *and fallen trees have made many roads impassable.* 洪水と倒木により、多くの道路が通行不能になっている。⇔ **passable**

**impassive** /ɪmpǽsɪv/ 形 ▶定義 (used about a person) showing no emotion or reaction (人などについて)感情や反応を見せない→無表情な、平然とした、冷静な — impassively 副 →平然と、無表情に

\***impatient** /ɪmpéɪʃ(ə)nt/ 形 ▶定義 1 impatient (at sth/with sb) not able to stay calm and wait for sb/sth; easily annoyed by sb/sth that seems slow ～を落ち着いて待っていられない；～が遅いように感じられてすぐにいらいらする→気短な、せっかちな、いらいらした ‖ *The passengers are getting impatient at the delay.* 乗客は遅延にいらいらしてきた。*It's no good being impatient with small children.* 小さな子供に対していら立つのは良くありません。⇔ **patient** ▶定義 2 impatient for/to do sth wanting sth to happen soon ～がすぐに起きることを望む→(～を・～することを)切望して、～したくてたまらない ‖ *By the time they are sixteen many young people are impatient to leave school.* 16歳になるころにはもう、学校を何とか早く卒業したくてじりじりしている若者が多い。— impatience 名 Ⓤ →じれったさ、いら立ち ‖ *He began to explain for the third time with growing impatience.* 彼はいら立ちを募らせながら、3度目の説明を始めた。— impatiently 副 →いらいらして、我慢できずに

**impeccable** /ɪmpékəb(ə)l/ 形 ▶定義 without any mistakes or faults; perfect 誤りや欠陥がない；完ぺきな→非の打ち所のない、完ぺきな ‖ *impeccable behaviour* 非の打ち所のない振る舞い *His accent is impeccable.* 彼のアクセントは完ぺきだ。— impeccably /-b(ə)li/ 副 →非の打ち所がないほどに、完ぺきに

**impede** /ɪmpíːd/ 動 他 正式 ▶定義 to make it difficult for sb/sth to move or go forward ～を動きづらくする、前進しづらくする→(進行、発展など)を妨げる、～を遅らせる ‖ *The completion of the new motorway has been impeded by bad weather conditions.* 新しい高速道路の完成は、悪天候により遅れている。

**impediment** /ɪmpédəmənt/ 名 Ⓒ 正式 ▶定義 1 an impediment (to sth) something that makes it difficult for a person or thing to move or progress 人・物事の動きや発展を困難にするもの→(～を)妨げるもの、障害 ‖ *The high rate of tax will be a major impediment to new businesses.* 税率の高さが、新しいビジネスにとって大きな障害となる。▶定義 2 something that makes speaking difficult 話すことの障害となるもの→言語障害 ‖ *a speech impediment* 発話障害

**impending** /ɪmpéndɪŋ/ 形 ▶定義 (名詞の前だけ) (usually used about sth bad) that will happen soon (通常は悪い事について)すぐに起こるであろう→差し迫った、今にも起こりそうな ‖ *There was a feeling of impending disaster in the air.* 災害が今にも起こりそうな気がした。

**impenetrable** /ɪmpénətrəb(ə)l/ 形 ▶定義 1 impossible to enter or go through→入り込めない、通り抜けられない、見通しの利かない ‖ *The jungle was impenetrable.* そのジャングルには入り込むこともできなかった。▶定義 2 impossible to understand 理解できない→不可解な、計り知れない ‖ *an impenetrable mystery* 不可解ななぞ

**imperative**[1] /ɪmpérətɪv/ 形 ▶定義 very important or urgent とても重要な、緊急の →急を要する、避けられない ‖ *It's imperative that you see a doctor immediately.* 直ちに医者に診てもらうことが絶対に必要だ。

**the imperative**[2] /ɪmpérətɪv/ 名 Ⓒ (文法) ▶定義 the form of the verb that is used for giving orders 命令に使われる動詞の形→命令法、命令文、命令形の動詞 ‖ *In 'Shut the door!' the verb is in the imperative.* Shut the door! の文中で、動詞は命令形です。

**imperceptible** /ɪmpərséptəb(ə)l/ 形 ▶定義 too small to be seen or noticed とても小さいので目に留まらない、気が付かない→(変化・動きなどが)気付かないほどの、わずかな ‖ *The difference between the original painting and the copy was almost imperceptible.* 原画と複製の違いは、ほとんど気が付かないほどだった。⇔ **perceptible** — imperceptibly /-əb(ə)li/ 副 →気付かないほどに、わずかに ‖ *Almost imperceptibly winter was turning into spring.* いつの間にか、冬から春へと季節が移っていた。

**imperfect**[1] /ɪmpə́ːrfɪkt/ 形 ▶定義 with mistakes

or faults 誤りや欠陥がある➡不完全な, 不十分な ‖ *This is a very imperfect system.* これは非常に欠点の多いシステムです. ⇔ **perfect** ― **imperfectly** 副 ➡不完全に, 不十分に

**the imperfect**[2] /ɪmpə́ːrfɪkt/ 名 ❶(文法) ▶定義 used for expressing action in the past that is not completed 過去に起こり, まだ完了していない行為の表現に用いて ➡未完了時制, 半過去, 未完了形の動詞 ‖ *In 'I was having a bath', the verb is in the imperfect.* I was having a bath. の文中で, 動詞は未完了形です.

　➤ この時制は, past continuous または past progressive (過去進行形) と呼ばれる方が一般的である.

**imperial** /ɪmpíəriəl/ 形 ▶定義 **1** connected with an empire or its ruler 帝国やその統治者に関連する ➡帝国の, 皇帝・天皇の ‖ *the imperial palace* 皇帝の宮殿 ▶定義 **2** belonging to a system of weighing and measuring that, in the past, was used for all goods in the United Kingdom and is still used for some 英国で過去においてあらゆる物に対して用いられ, 現在もなおその一部が使われている度量衡法による ➡ (英国の)度量衡法による, (度量衡が)英国法定標準による　☛参 **metric**; **inch**, **foot**, **yard**, **ounce**, **pond**, **pint**, **gallon**

**imperialism** /ɪmpíəriəlìz(ə)m/ 名 ❶ ▶定義 a political system in which a rich and powerful country controls other countries (colonies) which are not as rich and powerful as itself 富と力を持つ国が, それに劣る国々(植民地)を支配する, という政治制度 ➡帝国主義, 領土拡張 [侵略] 主義 ― **imperialist** 名 ❻ ➡帝国主義者, 帝政主義者

**impersonal** /ɪmpə́ːrs(ə)n(ə)l/ 形 ▶定義 **1** not showing friendly human feelings; cold in feeling or atmosphere 親しみのある人間的な感情を表さない; 印象・雰囲気が冷たい ➡非人間的な, 事務的な, よそよそしい ‖ *The hotel room was very impersonal.* ホテルの部屋はとても冷たい感じがした. ▶定義 **2** not referring to any particular person 特定のいかなる個人にも言及しない ➡私情を含まない, 客観的な ‖ *Can we try to keep the discussion as impersonal as possible, please?* この討論は, できるだけ私情を交えずにやりましょう.

**impersonate** /ɪmpə́ːrs(ə)nèɪt/ 動 他 ▶定義 to copy the behaviour and way of speaking of a person or to pretend to be a different person 人の動作や話し方をまねる, 他人にふんする ➡~の振りをする, ~を装う, ~の物まねをする ‖ *a comedian who impersonates politicians* 政治家の物まねをするコメディアン ― **impersonation** /ɪmpə̀ːrs(ə)néɪʃ(ə)n/ 名 ❻ ❶ ➡物まね, 装うこと ― **impersonator** 名 ❻ ➡物まね芸人, ふん装する人, 役者

**impertinent** /ɪmpə́ːrt(ə)nənt/ 形 正式 ▶定義 not showing respect; rude 敬意を示さない; 無礼な ➡生意気な, ぶしつけな ‖ *I do apologize. It was impertinent of my daughter to speak to you like that.* 心からおわび申し上げます. あのような話し方をするなんて, 娘は本当に無礼でした. ☛ 反対語は pertinent ではなく, polite または respectful. ― **impertinence** 名 ❶ ➡無礼, 生意気 ― **impertinently** 副 ➡無礼に, 生意気に

**imperturbable** /ɪ̀mpərtə́ːrbəb(ə)l/ 形 正式 ▶定義 not easily worried by a difficult situation 困難な状況にあっても容易に不安がらない ➡動揺しない, 冷静な, 落ち着いた

**impervious** /ɪmpə́ːrviəs/ 形 impervious (to sth) ▶定義 **1** not affected or influenced by sth ~に影響されない, 感化されない ➡ (人が)(~に)動じない, 影響されない ‖ *She was impervious to criticism.* 彼女は批判に動じなかった. ▶定義 **2** not allowing water, etc to pass through 水などを通さない ➡ (物が)(~を)通さない, 防~性の

**impetuous** /ɪmpétʃuəs/ 形 ▶定義 acting or done quickly and without thinking 即座に考えもなしに行動する, またはそのようになされた ➡性急な, 衝動的な, せっかちな ‖ *Her impetuous behaviour often got her into trouble.* 彼女は衝動的に行動したために面倒な事に巻き込まれることがよくあった. ☛ impulsive の方が一般的. ― **impetuously** 副 ➡性急に, 衝動的に, 猛烈に

**impetus** /ímpətəs/ 名 [ ❶, 単数扱い] ▶定義 (an) impetus (for sth); (an) impetus (to do sth) something that encourages sth else to happen 何か別の~が起こるのを刺激するもの ➡ (~への・~するための) 刺激, 推進力, 勢い, 弾み ‖ *This scandal provided the main impetus for changes in the rules.* この不祥事により, 規則の主だった改正が推し進められた. *I need fresh impetus to start working on this essay*

**impinge** /ɪmpíndʒ/ 動自 正式 ▶定義 impinge on/upon sth to have a noticeable effect on sth, especially a bad one ～に対して著しい影響, 特に悪影響を与える→(～に)影響を及ぼす, (～を)侵害する, 犯す ‖ *I'm not going to let my job impinge on my home life.* 私は仕事のせいで家庭生活に支障が出ないようにするつもりです.

**implant** /ɪmplɑ́ːnt; -plǽnt/ 名 C ▶定義 something that is put into a part of the body in a medical operation, often in order to make it bigger or a different shape 手術によって体の一部に埋め込まれたもの, 多くはその部分を大きくしたり異なった形状にするためになされる→移植された組織・臓器

**implausible** /ɪmplɔ́ːzəb(ə)l/ 形 ▶定義 not easy to believe 信じ難い→ありそうにない, 受け入れ難い ‖ *an implausible excuse* 信じ難い言い訳 ⇔ plausible

**implement**[1] /ímpləmənt/ 名 C ▶定義 a tool or instrument (especially for work outdoors) 道具, 器具 (特に野外の作業に使われるもの) →用具 ‖ *farm implements* 農具 ☞参 **tool** の注

**implement**[2] /ímpləmənt/ 動他 ▶定義 to start using a plan, system, etc 計画, 制度などを動かし始める→(政策, 計画など)を実行する, 履行する ‖ *Some teachers are finding it difficult to implement the government's educational reforms.* 教師たちの中には, 政府の教育改革を実行するのは難しいと悟り始めている者もいる. — implementation /ìmpləməntéɪʃ(ə)n/ 名 U→実行, 履行

**implicate** /ímpləkèɪt/ 動他 ▶定義 implicate sb (in sth) to show that sb is involved in sth unpleasant, especially a crime 人が不愉快な事, 特に犯罪に関係している事を示す→～を(犯罪などに)巻き込む, ～の(犯罪などへの)かかわりを示す ‖ *A well-known politician was implicated in the scandal.* 有名な政治家がその不祥事に関与していた.

**implication** /ìmpləkéɪʃ(ə)n/ 名 ▶定義 **1** [C, 通常は複数] implications (for/of sth) the effect that sth will have on sth else in the future ある物事がほかの物事に対して将来及ぼすであろう影響→(～に与える・～の)(将来的)影響, 結果 ‖ *The new law will have serious implications for our work.* 新しい法律は, 我々の仕事に多大な影響を及ぼすであろう. ▶定義**2** C U something that is suggested or said indirectly 間接的にほのめかされたり, 言われた事→言外の意味, ほのめかし, 含み ‖ *The implication of what she said was that we had made a bad mistake.* 彼女は, 我々がひどい過ちを犯したとほのめかした. ☞ 動 imply ▶定義**3** U implication (in sth) the fact of being involved, or of involving sb, in sth unpleasant, especially a crime 人を不愉快な事, 特に犯罪に巻き込む, または人が巻き込まれているという事実→(犯罪への) かかわり合い, 関与 ‖ *The player's implication in this scandal could affect his career.* このスキャンダルへの関与によって, その選手の経歴に傷が付くこともあり得る. ☞ 動 implicate

**implicit** /ɪmplísət/ 形 ▶定義 **1** not expressed in a direct way but understood by the people involved 直接表現はされないが, 関係する人々には了解されている→暗黙の, 遠回しの ‖ *We had an implicit agreement that we would support each other.* 私たちには, お互いに支援し合うという暗黙の了解があった. ☞参 explicit ▶定義**2** complete; total 完全な; 全くの→信じて疑わない, 盲目的な ‖ *I have implicit faith in your ability to do the job.* あなたがその仕事をすることができると絶対的に確信している. — implicitly 副 →暗に, 完全に

**implore** /ɪmplɔ́ːr/ 動他 正式 ▶定義 to ask sb with great emotion to do sth, because you are in a very serious situation 非常に重大な状況にあるので, ～に…をしてくれるように心底から頼む→～を嘆願する, ～を熱心に頼む ‖ *She implored him not to leave her alone.* 彼女は彼に, 1人にしないでくれと嘆願した. ☞類 beg

**imply** /ɪmplái/ 動他 (現分 **implying**; 三単現 **implies**; 過, 過分 **implied**) ▶定義 to suggest sth in an indirect way or without actually saying it 間接的に～をほのめかす, 実際には言葉にしないでほのめかす→～をほのめかす, ～を暗に示す, ～とにおわす ‖ *He didn't say so - but he implied that I was lying.* 彼ははっきりとは口では言わなかった － だが私がうそをついているとほのめかした. ☞ 名 implication

**impolite** /ìmpəláɪt/ 形 ▶定義 rude→無作法な,

失礼な‖ *I think it was impolite of him to ask you to leave.* あなたに出ていけと言ったなんて，彼は無礼だと思う． ⇔ **polite** — **impolitely** 副 → 無作法に，ぶしつけに

\***import**¹ /ímpɔːrt/ 名 ▶定義 1 [**C**, 通常は複数形] a product or service that is brought into one country from another 外国から買い入れる製品やサービス → 輸入品，導入されたもの‖ *What are your country's major imports?* あなたの国の主な輸入品は何ですか． ⇔ **export** ▶定義 2 **U** (または **importation**) the act of bringing goods or services into a country 製品やサービスを外国から買い入れる行為 → 輸入，輸入業‖ *new controls on the import of certain goods from abroad* 特定の製品の外国からの輸入に対する新たな取り締まり

\***import**² /ɪmpɔ́ːrt/ 動 ⊕ ⊕ ▶定義 1 import sth (from...) to buy goods, etc from a foreign country and bring them into your own country 外国から製品などを買い，自国に持ち込む → ～を(…から)輸入する，導入する，持ち込む‖ *imported goods* 輸入品 *Britain imports wine from France/Italy/Spain.* イギリスは，フランス・イタリア・スペインからワインを輸入する．(比喩) *We need to import some extra help from somewhere.* 我々は，どこかから追加援助が必要だ． ▶定義 2 (computing) to move information onto a program from another program (コンピューター) プログラム上の情報を，ほかのプログラムから移す → ～をインポートする(ファイルなどをコピーすること)，(データ)を移す — **importer** 名 **C** → 輸入業者，輸入国 ⇔ **exporter**

\***importance** /ɪmpɔ́ːrt(ə)ns/ 名 **U** ▶定義 the quality of being important 重要であるということ → 重要性，重大さ‖ *The decision was of great importance to the future of the business.* その決定は事業の将来にとって極めて重大なものだった．

\***important** /ɪmpɔ́ːrt(ə)nt/ 形 ▶定義 1 important (to sb); important (for sb/sth) (to do sth); important that... having great value or influence; very necessary 非常に価値がある，影響がある；とても必要な → (～にとって) 重要な，重大な，大切な‖ *an important meeting/decision/factor* 重要な会議・決定・要因 *This job is very important to me.* この仕事は私にとって非常に重要なものだ． *It's important not to be late.* 遅刻をしないことは大事なことだ． *It's important for people to see the results of what they do.* 自分が行った事の結果を見るのは重要な事だ． *It was important to me that you were there.* あなたがそこにいたことは私にとって重要な事だった． ▶定義 2 (used about a person) having great influence or authority (人について) 大きな影響力を持つ，権威を持つ → (人，地位などが) 有力な，影響力のある，偉い‖ *He was one of the most important writers of his time.* 彼はその時代では最も影響力のある作家の 1 人でした． — **importantly** 副 → 重大に，顕著に，偉そうに

**importation** /ìmpɔːrtéɪʃ(ə)n, -pər-/=**IMPORT**¹(2)

**impose** /ɪmpóʊz/ 動 ▶定義 1 ⊕ impose sth (on/upon sb/sth) to make a law, rule, opinion, etc be accepted by using your power or authority 権力や権限を使って，法律・規則・意見などに従わせる → (人に)(意見・権威など)を押し付ける，(税金・義務など)を課す‖ *A new tax will be imposed on cigarettes.* たばこに新たな税が課せられる． *Parents should try not to impose their own ideas on their children.* 親は子供に自分の意見を押し付けようとするべきではない． ▶定義 2 ⊜ impose (on/upon sb/sth) to ask or expect sb to do sth that may cause extra work or trouble 余分な仕事や迷惑を掛けるおそれのある事を～に頼んだり期待する → (人が)(人・親切などに) 付け込む，無理強いする‖ *I hate to impose on you but can you lend me some money?* ご迷惑を掛けたくはないのですが，いくらかお金を貸してもらえませんか． — **imposition** /ìmpəzíʃ(ə)n/ 名 **U C** → (負担などを) 課すこと，負わせること，賦課‖ *the imposition of military rule* 軍法を課すこと

**imposing** /ɪmpóʊzɪŋ/ 形 ▶定義 big and important; impressive 大きくて価値がある；強い印象を与える → 堂々とした，立派な，威厳のある‖ *They lived in a large, imposing house near the park.* 彼らは，公園のそばの大きくて立派な家に住んでいました．

\***impossible** /ɪmpɑ́səb(ə)l/ 形 ▶定義 1 not able to be done or to happen 行うことができない，起こり得ない → (計画・仕事などが) 不可能な，～できない‖ *It's impossible for me to be there before 12.* 12 時前にそこに行くのは無理だ． *I* *find it almost impossible to get up in the morning!* 朝起きるのはほとんど不可能だと悟った. *That's impossible! (= I don't believe it!)* そんなことはあり得ない (= 信じられない). ▶定義2 very difficult to deal with or control 対処するのがとても難しい, 管理するのが非常に困難な→(状況, 立場などが) 極めて困難な・不利な, どうしようもない, にっちもさっちもいかない ‖ *This is an impossible situation!* これは困難な状況だ. *He's always been an impossible child.* 彼はいつも扱いづらい子供だ. ⇔ **possible** — **the impossible** 名 [単数扱い]→不可能な事, 不可能に思える事 ‖ *Don't attempt the impossible!* 不可能な事を企てるな. — **impossibility** /ɪmpɑ̀sǝbíləti/ 名 ❶ ❶ (複 **impossibilities**)→不可能な事, あり得ない事 ‖ *What you are suggesting is a complete impossibility!* あなたの提案している事は全く不可能だ.

**impossibly** /ɪmpɑ́sǝbəli/ 副 ▶定義 extremely 極端に→不可能なほど, 考えられないほど, 途方もなく ‖ *impossibly complicated* 途方もなく複雑な

**impostor** /ɪmpɑ́stər/ 名 ❻ ▶定義 a person who pretends to be sb else in order to trick other people 人をだますために他人の振りをする人→他人の名をかたる詐欺師, ペテン師, 詐称者

**impotent** /ímpətənt/ 形 ▶定義1 without enough power to influence a situation or to change things 状況に影響を及ぼすほどの力がない, 物事を変えるだけの力がない→無力な, 力のない ▶定義2 (medical) (used about men) not capable of having sex (医学)(人について)性交をする能力がない→(男性が)性的不能の, インポテンツの — **impotence** 名 ❶→無力, 力のなさ; 性的不能, インポテンツ

**impoverish** /ɪmpʌ́v(ə)rɪʃ/ 動 ❻ 正式 ▶定義 to make sb/sth poor or lower in quality ～の質を貧しくする, 低下させる→(人を)貧しくする, 貧乏にする, ～の質を低下させる ⇔ **enrich**

**impractical** /ɪmprǽktɪk(ə)l/ 形 ▶定義1 not sensible or realistic 実用的でない, 現実的でない→実際的でない, 実際の役に立たない, 非現実的な, 常識のない ‖ *It would be impractical to take our bikes on the train.* 自転車を電車に乗せて運ぶのはできそうにない. ▶定義2 (used about a person) not good at doing ordinary things that involve using your hands; not good at organizing or planning things (人について) 手仕事を伴う日常的な作業が得意ではない; 物事を計画・準備するのが得意ではない→(人が) 実務に向いていない ‖ *He's clever but completely impractical.* 彼は頭はいいんだが, 全く実務能力がない. ⇔ **practical**

**imprecise** /ɪmprɪsáɪs/ 形 ▶定義 not clear or exact 明瞭(めいりょう)でない, 正確でない→不正確な, あいまいな ‖ *imprecise instructions* あいまいな説明書 ⇔ **precise**

*__impress__ /ɪmprés/ 動 ❻ ▶定義1 impress sb (with sth); impress sb that... to make sb feel admiration and respect ～に賞賛と敬意の気持ちを引き起こす→～に(…で)感銘を与える, ～を感動させる, ～に(…で・…という)印象を与える ‖ *She's always trying to impress people with her new clothes.* 彼女はいつも新しいドレスで人に印象づけようとするんだ. *It impressed me that he understood immediately what I meant.* 彼が私の言いたいことを即座に理解したのには感心した. ▶定義2 正式 impress sth on/upon sb to make the importance of sth very clear to sb ～の重要性を…に非常に明らかに理解させる→～を(人に)銘記させる, ～を(人・記憶に)とどめさせる ‖ *I wish you could impress on John that he must pass these exams.* あなたが, それらの試験に合格しなければならないということをジョンに理解させてくれるといいんだが.

*__impression__ /ɪmpréʃ(ə)n/ 名 ❻ ▶定義1 an idea, a feeling or an opinion that you get about sb/sth ～に対して抱く考え・感情・意見→印象, 感銘 ‖ *What's your **first impression** of the new director?* 新しい重役の第一印象はどうですか. *I'm not sure but I **have/get the impression** that Jane's rather unhappy.* 断定できないが, ジェーンはやや不幸せのような感じがする. *I was **under the impression** (= I believed, but I was wrong) that you were married.* あなたは結婚しているとばかり思っていました (= と思っていたが, 私の間違いだった). ▶定義2 the effect that a person or thing produces on sb else 人や物が他人に与える効果→(～という)感じ, 印象 ‖ *She **gives the impression** of being older than she really is.* 彼女は実際の年よりも老けて見える. *Do you think I **made a good impression** on your parents?* あなたのご両親に私が良い印

象を与えたと思いますか. ▶定義3 an amusing copy of the way a person acts or speaks; an imitation 人の動作や話し方の面白おかしいまね; 模倣→(有名人などの)まね, (芸人の)物まね ‖ *My brother can do a good impression of the Prime Minister.* 私の兄は総理大臣のまねがうまい.
▶定義4 a mark that is left when an object has been pressed hard into a surface 物の表面にしっかりと押されて付けられた印→(〜に)押印・刻印(すること), (押して作られた)痕跡(こんせき), 印

**impressionable** /ɪmpréʃ(ə)nəb(ə)l/ 形 ▶定義 easy to influence 影響されやすい→感じやすい, 感受性の強い, 感化されやすい ‖ *Sixteen is a very impressionable age.* 16歳というのは, 非常に感じやすい年ごろである.

*****impressive** /ɪmprésɪv/ 形 ▶定義 causing a feeling of admiration and respect because of the importance, size, quality, etc of sth そのものの重要性, 大きさ, 質などにより, 賞賛と敬意の感情を引き起こす→強い印象[感動]を与える, 深く心に感じる, すばらしい ‖ *an impressive building/speech* すばらしい建物・演説 *The way he handled the situation was most impressive.* 彼のその状況の処理の仕方は非常に見事だった.

**imprint** /ɪmprɪ́nt/ 名 C ▶定義 a mark made by pressing an object on a surface 物の表面に押してできる跡→(押して付けた)跡, 印 ‖ *the imprint of a foot in the sand* 砂に付いた足跡

**imprison** /ɪmprɪ́z(ə)n/ 動他 (しばしば受動態で) ▶定義 to put or keep in prison 刑務所に入れる, 刑務所に拘置する→〜を投獄する, 監禁する, 閉じ込める ‖ *He was imprisoned for armed robbery.* 彼は武装強盗の罪で刑務所に入れられた. — imprisonment 名 U→投獄, 拘置, 監禁, 懲役 ‖ *She was sentenced to five years' imprisonment.* 彼女は懲役5年の判決を受けた.

**improbable** /ɪmprɑ́bəb(ə)l/ 形 ▶定義 not likely to be true or to happen 本当らしくない, 起こりそうにない→ありそうもない, まず〜になりそうにない ‖ *an improbable explanation* 本当らしくない説明 *It is highly improbable that she will arrive tonight.* 彼女が今夜到着することはまずない. ☛類 **unlikely** ⇔ **probable** — improbability /ɪmprɑbəbɪ́ləti/ 名 U→ありそうもないこと, 本当らしくないこと — improbably /-əb(ə)li/ 副→何とも奇妙に, ありそうもなく

## improve 853

**impromptu** /ɪmprɑ́m(p)t(j)uː/ 形 ▶定義 (done) without being prepared or organized. 準備・計画なしで(なされた)→即席の, 即興の, 準備なしの, ぶっつけ本番の ‖ *an impromptu party* 即席のパーティー

**improper** /ɪmprɑ́pər/ 形 ▶定義1 illegal or dishonest→不法な, 不正の ‖ *It seems that she had been involved in improper business deals.* 彼女は不正な商取引に巻き込まれていたようだ.
▶定義2 not suitable for the situation; rude in a sexual way 状況にふさわしくない; 性的にみだらな→(場面・目的などに)不適当な, 無礼な; 卑わいな ‖ *It would be improper to say anything else at this stage.* この段階では, それ以外の事を口にするのは不適当であろう. *He lost his job for making improper suggestions to several of the women.* 彼は何人かの女性に下品な言葉を掛けたことにより, 職を失った. ⇔ **proper** — improperly 副→不適切に, 無作法に, 誤って ⇔ **properly**

**impropriety** /ɪ̀mprəpráɪəti/ 名 U C (複 **improprieties**) 正式 ▶定義 behaviour or actions that are morally wrong or not appropriate 道徳的に間違った, または適切でない態度や行為→不適切・無作法な言動, 不正行為 ‖ *She was unaware of the impropriety of her remark.* 彼女は自分の発言が不適切なものであったことに気付いていなかった.

*****improve** /ɪmprúːv/ 動自他 ▶定義 to become or to make sth better 〜が良くなる, 良くする→改良される, 改善される; 〜を改善する, (技術・能力など)を進歩させる, 〜を改良する ‖ *Your work has greatly improved.* あなたの作品は非常に良くなった. *I hope the weather will improve later on.* これから先は天候が回復するといいのですが. *Your vocabulary is excellent but you could improve your pronunciation.* あなたの語彙(ごい)力はすばらしいが, 発音には改善の余地があります.

句動詞 **improve on/upon sth** ▶定義 to produce sth that is better than sth else それ以外の物に比べて優れた物を作り出す→〜をより良いものにする, 〜に改良を加える ‖ *Nobody will be able to improve on that score (= nobody will be able to make a higher score).* この得点記録を超える者

はいないであろう (= だれもこの記録よりも高い得点を上げることはできないだろう).

**improvement** /ɪmprúːvmənt/ 名 C U ▶定義 (an) improvement (on/in sth) (a) change which makes the quality or condition of sb/sth better ～の質・状態をより良くするために加えられる変化 → (～の点で) 改善する・されること, 進歩, 上達 ‖ *Your written work is in need of some improvement.* あなたが書いた作品は, 改善の必要がある.

➤ improvement in はあるものが以前より良くなった場合に用いる: *There's been a considerable improvement in your mother's condition.* (あなたのお母さんの状態は, かなり回復しています.) improvement on は2つのものを比較して一方が他方より優れている場合に用いる: *These marks are an improvement on your previous ones.* (あなたの成績は, 以前よりも上がっています.)

**improvise** /ímprəvaɪz/ 動 自 他 ▶定義 1 to make, do, or manage sth without preparation, using what you have 準備なしで, 今あるものだけを使って～を作る・行う・何とかやり遂げる → ～を間に合わせに [有り合わせの物で] 作る, 即座に作る, 間に合わせる ‖ *If you're short of teachers today you'll just have to improvise (= manage somehow with the people that you've got).* 今日は教師の数が足りないのならば, それで間に合わせなければならない (= 何とかして確保した人だけでやり遂げる). ▶定義 2 to play music, speak or act using your imagination instead of written or remembered material 台本・楽譜などや記憶ではなく, 自分の想像力を使って, 演奏・演説・演技をする → (～を) 即席で行う・作る, (～を) 即興で演奏・演技する ‖ *It was obvious that the actor had forgotten his lines and was trying to improvise.* 俳優が台詞 (せりふ) を忘れて, 即興で演じようとしていたのは明らかだった. — improvisation /ˌɪmprəvaɪzéɪʃ(ə)n; ɪmˌprɑ̀vəzéɪʃ(ə)n, ˌɪmprə-/ 名 C U → 即席に行う・作ること, 即興, 即興演奏・演技

**impudent** /ímpjəd(ə)nt/ 形 正式 ▶定義 very rude; lacking respect and not polite 非常に無礼な; 敬意を欠き, 礼儀正しくない → 厚かましい, ずうずうしい, おくめんもない ☛ 略式語は cheeky. — impudently 副 → ずうずうしく, 生意気にも — impudence 名 U → 厚かましさ, ずうずうしさ

**impulse** /ímpʌls/ 名 C ▶定義 1 [通常は単数] an impulse (to do sth) a sudden desire to do sth without thinking about the results 結果を考えずに, ～を突然したくなること → (～したいという) 衝動, (心の) 弾み, 一時の感情 ‖ *She felt a terrible impulse to rush out of the house and never come back.* 彼女は, 家を飛び出して二度と帰りたくないという抑え難い衝動に駆られた. ▶定義 2 (専門用語) a force or movement of energy that causes a reaction 反応を引き起こすエネルギーの力や動き → 衝撃 (電流), 刺激, インパルス ‖ *nerve/electrical impulses* 神経衝撃・電気衝撃

成句 on (an) impulse ▶定義 without thinking or planning and not considering the results 考えや計画なしで, 結果もよく考えずに → 衝動的に, 衝動に駆られて, 出来心で ‖ *When I saw the child fall in the water, I just acted on impulse and jumped in after her.* 女の子が水中に落ちるのを見た時, 何も考えずにとっさにその子の後から飛び込んでいた.

**impulsive** /ɪmpʌ́lsɪv/ 形 ▶定義 likely to act suddenly and without thinking; done without careful thought よく考えないで突然に行動しがちな; 慎重に考えずになされた → (人・言動が) 衝動的な, 一時の感情に駆られた ‖ *an impulsive character* 衝動的な性格 — impulsively 副 → 衝動的に, 一時の感情に駆られて — impulsiveness 名 U → 衝動的に行動すること, 衝動に駆られること

**impure** /ɪmpjúər/ 形 ▶定義 1 not pure or clean; consisting of more than one substance mixed together (and therefore not of good quality) 純粋でない, 混ぜ物がある; 2種類以上の物質が混ざってできている (そのために品質が良くない) → 不純物の混じった, 不純な, 汚い, 不潔な ‖ *impure metals* 不純な金属 ▶定義 2 (古) (used about thoughts and actions connected with sex) not moral; bad (性に関する考えや行動について) 道徳的でない; 不品行な → (考え・行為などが) 不純な, 不道徳な, みだらな ⇔ pure

**impurity** /ɪmpjúərəti/ 名 (複 **impurities**) ▶定義 1 [C, 通常は複数] a substance that is present in small amounts in another substance, making it dirty or of poor quality ある物質の中

に少量存在する別の物質で,全体を汚染したり品質を悪くするもの➡**不純物,混ざり物** ‖ *People are being advised to boil their water because certain impurities have been found in it.* 不純物が混ざっているので,水は沸騰させてから使うように言われている. ▶定義2 Ⓤ (古) the state of being morally bad 道徳的に間違っている状態➡**不純,不潔,みだら,わいせつ** ☞参 **purity**

★**in**¹ /ɪn, ən/ 副前

▶ 名詞と結び付いた特別な用法(例 in time)が多くあり,それらについては名詞の項を参照のこと.また動詞と結び付いた特別な用法(例 give in)も多く,それらについては,動詞の項を参照のこと.

▶定義1 (used to show place) inside or to a position inside a particular area or object (場所を示すために用いて) 特定の地域・対象の中に,その中の場所に➡**(位置・場所)〜の中で[に・の],〜に,〜において** ‖ *a country in Africa* アフリカの国 *an island in the Pacific* 太平洋上の島 *in a box* 箱の中に *I read about it in the newspaper.* それについては新聞で読んだ. *He lay in bed.* 彼は床に就いていた. *She put the keys in her pocket.* 彼女はポケットにかぎをしまった. *His wife's in hospital.* 彼の妻は入院中だ. *She opened the door and went in.* 彼女はドアを開けて中に入った. *My suitcase is full. I can't get any more in.* 私のスーツケースは一杯だ. もう何も入らない. *When does the train get in (= to the station)?* 列車はいつ到着するのか(= 駅に). ▶定義2 at home or at work 在宅して,職場で➡**家に,家の中で,出勤して** ‖ *I phoned him last night but he wasn't in.* 昨夜彼に電話をしたが,家にいなかった. *She won't be in till late today.* 彼女は今日は遅くまで戻りません.

▶定義3 (showing time) during a period of time (時間を示して) ある一定の期間に➡**〜に,〜の間に** ‖ *My birthday is in August.* 私の誕生日は8月だ. *in spring/summer/autumn/winter* 春・夏・秋・冬に *He was born in 1980.* 彼は1980年に生まれた. *You could walk there in about an hour (= it would take that long to walk there).* 1時間ほど歩けばそこに着くだろう(= そこへ歩いていくにはそれだけの時間がかかる).

▶定義4 (showing time) after a period of time (時間を示して) ある期間の後に➡**〜のうちに,〜**もすれば,〜たてば ‖ *I'll be finished in ten minutes.* 10分で終わります. ▶定義5 wearing sth➡**〜を身に着けて,履いて** ‖ *They were all dressed in black for the funeral.* 彼らは皆,葬式のために黒い喪服を着ていた. *I've never seen you in a suit before.* あなたがスーツを着ているのを見たことがなかった. *a woman in a yellow dress* 黄色いドレスを着た女性 ▶定義6 showing the condition or state of sb/sth 〜の状況・状態を示す➡**〜の状態で,〜の状況で,〜の中で** ‖ *My father is in poor health.* 父は健康状態が思わしくない. *This room is in a mess!* この部屋はひどい散らかりようだ. *Richard's in love.* リチャードは恋をしている. *He's in his mid-thirties.* 彼は30代半ばだ. ▶定義7 showing sb's job or the activity sb is involved in 〜の職業を示して,〜が関係している活動を示して➡**(従事・所属・活動)〜に従事して,所属して,参加して** ‖ *He's got a good job in advertising.* 彼は広告関係の良い仕事に就いた. *All her family are in politics (= they are politicians).* 彼女の家族は全員が政治に携わっている(= 彼らは政治家だ). *He's in the army.* 彼は軍隊に所属している.

▶定義8 contained in; forming the whole or part of sth (あるものに) 含まれている;〜の全体・一部を形成する➡**(範囲・限定・包括)〜の範囲に,〜内に** ‖ *There are 31 days in January.* 1月は31日ある. *What's in this casserole?* このキャセロールには何が入っているのですか. ▶定義9 used for saying how things are arranged 物事がどのように整えられているかの説明に用いて➡**(配列・順序・形状)〜になって,〜を成して,〜の形で** ‖ *We sat in a circle.* 我々は輪になって座った. *She had her hair in plaits.* 彼女は髪を三つ編みにしていた. ▶定義10 used for saying how sth is written or expressed 〜がどのような方法で書かれているか・表現されているかの説明に用いて ➡**(手段・方法・材料)〜で,〜を使って** ‖ *Please write in pen.* ペンで書いてください. *They were talking in Italian/French/Polish.* 彼らはイタリア語・フランス語・ポーランド語で話していた. *to work in groups/teams* グループで・チームで働く ▶定義11 used with feelings 感情を表す語と用いて➡**〜の状態で,(〜の状態)の中で** ‖ *I watched in horror as the plane* *crashed to the ground.* 私は恐怖に駆られながら、飛行機が地面に墜落するのを見ていた。*He was in such a rage I didn't dare to go near him.* そばにも寄れないほど、彼は激怒していました。 ▶定義 **12** used for giving the rate of sth and for talking about numbers ～の割合を表すのに用いて、または数について用いて→(割合・比率)～に付き、～のうち ‖ *One family in ten owns a dishwasher.* 10世帯に1世帯の割合で、食器洗い機を持っている。 ▶定義 **13** received by sb official 公の～に受理される→(申込書などが)届いて、(手紙などが)到着して ‖ *Entries should be in by 20 March.* 参加作品は3月20日までに受理される必要があります。 *All applications must be in by Friday.* 願書はすべて金曜日までに到着しなければなりません。 ▶定義 **14** (used about the sea) at the highest point, when the water is closest to the land (海について) 干潮で、海水面が陸地に最も近い所に達して→(潮が)満ちて ‖ *The tide's coming in.* 潮が満ちてきた。

成句 **be in for it/sth** ▶定義 to be going to experience sth unpleasant 嫌な～を経験しそうだ→(嫌な事・悪天候などに)遭いそうである、悪い出来事に向かう ‖ *He'll be in for a shock when he gets the bill.* 請求書を見たら、彼はショックを受けるだろう。 *You'll be in for it when Mum sees what you've done.* あなたがした事をお母さんが見たら、あなたは罰を受けることになりますよ。

**be/get in on sth** ▶定義 to be included or involved in sth→(計画などに)参加している、関与している ‖ *I'd like to be in on the new project.* その新しいプロジェクトに参加したい。

**have (got) it in for sb** 略式 ▶定義 to be unpleasant to sb because he/she has done sth to upset you ～の行為で気分を害されたので、その～に対して不愉快な態度に出る→～に恨みを持っている、復讐(ふくしゅう)しようと思っている、悪意を持っている ‖ *The boss has had it in for me ever since I asked to be considered for the new post.* 新しいポストについて考慮してほしいと頼んで以来、上司は私を不愉快に思っている。

**in**² /ɪn/ 名

成句 **the ins and outs (of sth)** ▶定義 the details and difficulties (involved in sth) (～に関連した)詳細とさまざまな問題→(～の) 一部始終、詳細 ‖ *Will somebody explain the ins and outs of the situation to me?* だれか私に、この状況の一部始終を説明してくれますか。

**in**³ /ɪn/ 形 略式 ▶定義 fashionable at the moment →流行している、はやっている ‖ *the in place to go* 流行の場所 *The colour grey is very in this season.* グレーは今シーズン大流行の色です。

**in**⁴ 略 **inch(es)**→インチ

**inability** /ˌɪnəˈbɪləti/ 名 [単数扱い] ▶定義 **inability (to do sth)** lack of ability, power or skill 能力・力・技術不足→無能、無力、(～する)ことができないこと ‖ *He has a complete inability to listen to other people's opinions.* 彼は全く他人の意見を聞くことができない。 ☞ 形 **unable**

**inaccessible** /ˌɪnəkˈsesəbl/ 形 ▶定義 very difficult or impossible to reach or contact 到達できない・連絡できない、到達・連絡するのが非常に困難→近付きにくい、到達不可能な、入手し難い ‖ *That beach is inaccessible by car.* あの海岸は車では行けない。 ⇔ **accessible** — **inaccessibility** /ˌɪnɪkˌsesəˈbɪləti, ˌɪnæk-/ 名 Ⓤ→近付きにくいこと、入手[理解]し難いこと

**inaccurate** /ɪnˈækjərət/ 形 ▶定義 not correct or accurate; with mistakes→不正確な、不精密な、間違いのある ‖ *an inaccurate report/description/statement* 不正確なレポート・記述・声明 ⇔ **accurate** — **inaccuracy** /ɪnˈækjərəsi/ 名 Ⓒ Ⓤ (複 **inaccuracies**)→不正確(な点)、不精密、間違い ‖ *There are always some inaccuracies in newspaper reports.* 新聞の記事には、いつも何かしら誤りがあるものだ。 ⇔ **accuracy**

**inaction** /ɪnˈækʃ(ə)n/ 名 Ⓤ ▶定義 doing nothing; lack of action 何もしないこと；活動不足→無活動、無為、怠惰 ‖ *The crisis was blamed on the government's earlier inaction.* その危機では政府の初動対応の不足が非難された。 ⇔ **action**

**inactive** /ɪnˈæktɪv/ 形 ▶定義 doing nothing; not active 何もしない；活動的でない→活動・機能していない、不活発な ‖ *The virus remains inactive in the body.* ウイルスは体内で活動を停止している。 ⇔ **active** — **inactivity** /ˌɪnækˈtɪvəti/ 名 Ⓤ →無活動状態、不活動、怠惰 ⇔ **activity**

**inadequate** /ɪnˈædɪkwət/ 形 ▶定義 **1 inadequate (for sth/to do sth)** not enough; not good enough 十分ではない; ふさわしくない→**不十分な, 不適当な, 不備な点が多い, 不完全な** || *the problem of inadequate housing* 住宅不足の問題 ▶定義**2** (used about a person) not able to deal with a problem or situation; not confident (人について) 問題・状況に対処できない; 確信が持てない→**(人が) (〜に) 不適格な, (人が能力の点で) 太刀打ちできない** || *There was so much to learn in the new job that for a while I felt totally inadequate.* 新しい仕事について覚える事がとてもたくさんあったので, しばらくの間全く太刀打ちできなかった. ⇔ **adequate** — **inadequately** 副→**不十分に, 不適切に** — **inadequacy** /ɪnǽdɪkwəsi/ 名 ❻ ❶ (複 inadequacies)→**不十分さ, 不適切さ** || *his inadequacy as a parent* 親としての彼が不適切であること

**inadvertent** /ìnædvə́ːrt(ə)nt, -əd-/ 形 ▶定義 (used about actions) done without thinking, not on purpose (行為について) 故意にではなく, 何も考えないで行われた→**(行為などが) 不注意な, 慎重さを欠いた, 偶然の** ⇔ **intentional, deliberate** — **inadvertently** 副→**不注意に (も), うっかり, 偶然に** || *She had inadvertently left the letter where he could find it.* 彼女は彼に見つかりそうな場所に, 不注意にも手紙を置き忘れていた.

**inadvisable** /ìnədváɪzəb(ə)l, -æd-/ 形 ▶定義 not sensible; not showing good judgement 思慮分別のない; 適切な判断ではないことを示す→**勧められない, 賢明・得策ではない** || *It is inadvisable to go swimming when you have a cold.* 風邪を引いているときに水泳に行くのは勧められない. ⇔ **advisable**

**inane** /ɪnéɪn/ 形 ▶定義 without any meaning; silly→**無意味な; 下らない** || *an inane remark* 無意味な意見 — **inanely** 副→**意味もなく, ばかげた事に**

**inappropriate** /ìnəpróʊpriət/ 形 ▶定義 not suitable→**不適切な, 妥当でない, ふさわしくない** || *Isn't that dress rather inappropriate for the occasion?* そのドレスはその場にはふさわしくないのでは. ⇔ **appropriate**

**inarticulate** /ìnɑːrtíkjələt/ 形 ▶定義**1** (used about a person) not able to express ideas and feelings clearly (人について) 考えや感情をはっきりと表せない→**(人が) (考えを) はっきり言えない, 口下手な, はきはきしていない** ▶定義**2** (used about speech) not clear or well expressed (話し方について) はっきりとしていない, 上手に表現されていない→**(言葉などが) はっきりしない, 不明瞭 (めいりょう) な** ⇔ **articulate** — **inarticulately** 副→**不明瞭に**

**inasmuch as** /ìnəzmʌ́tʃ əz, -æz/ 接 正式 ▶定義 because of the fact that 〜という事実のために→**〜であるから, 〜なので, 〜である限り, 〜の点では** || *We felt sorry for the boys inasmuch as they had not realized that what they were doing was wrong.* 少年たちは自分たちの行為が悪い事だとは気付いておらず, その点が我々には残念だった.

**inattention** /ìnətén ʃ(ə)n/ 名 ❶ ▶定義 lack of attention 注意不足→**不注意, (〜への) 気配りのなさ** || *a moment of inattention* 不注意な時 ⇔ **attention**

**inattentive** /ìnəténtɪv/ 形 ▶定義 not paying attention 注意を払わない→**不注意な, 注意力の足りない, 散漫な** || *One inattentive student can disturb the whole class.* 注意力の散漫な生徒が１人いると, クラス全体の妨げになることがある. ⇔ **attentive**

**inaudible** /ɪnɔ́ːdəb(ə)l/ 形 ▶定義 not loud enough to be heard 聞き取るのに十分な音量でない→**(声などが) 聞こえない, 聞き取れない** ⇔ **audible** — **inaudibly** /-b(ə)li/ 副→**聞き取れないほど, 聞こえないほどに**

**inaugurate** /ɪnɔ́ːg(j)əreɪt; -gjʊ-/ 動 他 ▶定義**1** to introduce a new official, leader, etc at a special formal ceremony 特別な正式の式典で, 新しい政府高官や指導者などを紹介する→**〜を (ある地位に) 就任させる, 〜の就任式を行う** || *He will be inaugurated as President next month.* 彼は来月, 大統領に就任する. ▶定義**2** to start, introduce or open sth new (often at a special formal ceremony) 〜を新たに始める・紹介する・開く (しばしば特別な正式の式典で)→**(施設などを) 開く, 〜の開業 [落成] 式を行う** — **inaugural** /ɪnɔ́ːg(j)ər(ə)l; -gjʊ-/ 形 (名詞の前だけ)→**就任 (式) の, 開始の** || *the President's inaugural speech* 大統領の就任演説 — **inauguration** /ɪnɔ̀ːg(j)əréɪʃ(ə)n; -gjʊ-/ 名 ❻ ❶→**就任 (式), 開業 (式)**

**inauspicious** /ìnɔːspíʃəs/ 形 正式 ▶定義 showing signs that the future will not be good or successful 将来が良くない・成功しないという兆候を示して→**不吉な, 縁起の悪い, 先行きの危ぶまれる** ǁ *an inauspicious start* 不吉な始まり ⇔ **auspicious**

**Inc**(または **inc**) /ɪŋkɔːrp(ə)reɪtəd, ɪŋk/ 略 冠 Incorporated→**法人組織の, 株式[有限]会社の** ǁ *Manhattan Drugstores Inc* Manhattan Drugstores 社

**incalculable** /ɪnkǽlkjələb(ə)l/ 形 ▶定義 very great; too great to calculate とても大きい; 大きすぎて計算することができない→**計り知れない, 数えきれない, ばく大な** ǁ *an incalculable risk* 計り知れない危険

**incapable** /ɪnkéɪpəb(ə)l/ 形 ▶定義**1** incapable of sth/doing sth not able to do sth ~をすることができない→**(~の能力が) なくて, (~が) できなくて** ǁ *She is incapable of hard work/working hard.* 彼女はきつい仕事をすることができない. *He's quite incapable of unkindness (= too nice to be unkind).* 彼は完全に冷酷になりきることができない (= 良い人すぎて不親切になれない). ▶定義**2** not able to do, manage or organize anything well 何かを上手にすることができない・管理できない・取りまとめることができない→**無能な, 無力な, 役に立たない** ǁ *As a doctor, she's totally incapable.* 医者として, 彼女は全く能力がない. ⇔ **capable**

**incapacitate** /ɪnkəpǽsəteɪt/ 動他 ▶定義 to make sb unable to do sth ~が~をできないようにする→**~を無力化する, (事故・病気などが) (人から) 能力を奪う, ~を就労不能にする** ǁ *They were completely incapacitated by the heat in Spain.* 彼らはスペインで猛暑のために全く何もできなかった.

**incarnation** /ɪnkɑːrnéɪʃ(ə)n/ 名 Ⓒ ▶定義**1** a period of life on earth in a particular form 特定の姿形でこの世に生存している期間→**肉体を持って存在すること, 前世** ǁ *He believed he was a prince in a previous incarnation.* 彼は前世には王子だったと信じている. ▶定義**2** the incarnation of sth (a person that is) a perfect example of a particular quality ある特質を完全に具体化した例→**(~の) 化身, 権化** ǁ *She is the incarnation of goodness.* 彼女は善良を絵にかいたような人だ. ☛参 **reincarnation**

**incendiary** /ɪnséndɪəri; -dièri/ 形 ▶定義 that causes a fire 火災を引き起こす→**放火の, 焼夷(しょうい)性の** ǁ *an incendiary bomb/device* 焼夷弾・装置

**incense** /ínsens/ 名 Ⓤ ▶定義 a substance that produces a sweet smell when burnt, used especially in religious ceremonies 火で燃やすと芳しい香りがする物質, 特に宗教儀式で使われる→**香, 香煙**

**incensed** /ɪnsénst/ 形 ▶定義 incensed (by/at sth) very angry; furious→**(~に) 激怒した; 猛烈に腹を立てた**

**incentive** /ɪnséntɪv/ 名 Ⓒ Ⓤ ▶定義 (an) incentive (for/to sb/sth) (to do sth) something that encourages you (to do sth) 人が(~をすることを) 励ますもの→**(~する) 刺激, 誘引, 動機, 励み** ǁ *There's no incentive for young people to do well at school because there aren't any jobs when they leave.* 卒業しても職はないので, 若者にとって学校で良い成績を取ろうという励みがない.

**incessant** /ɪnsés(ə)nt/ 形 ▶定義 never stopping (and usually annoying) 決してやむことがない (そして通常は迷惑な)→**(不快な事が) 絶え間ない, ひっきりなしの** ǁ *incessant rain/noise/chatter* やむことのない雨・絶え間ない騒音・ひっきりなしのおしゃべり ☛参 **continual** — **incessantly** 副→**絶え間なく**

**incest** /ínsest/ 名 Ⓤ ▶定義 illegal sex between members of the same family, for example brother and sister 同じ家族内, 例えば兄と妹などの血縁同士の非合法な性交→**近親相姦(そうかん)**

**incestuous** /ɪnséstʃuəs/ 形 ▶定義**1** involving illegal sex between members of the same family 家庭内の血縁同士の非合法な性交に関する→**近親相姦(そうかん)の; 近親相姦を犯した** ǁ *an incestuous relationship* 近親相姦の関係 ▶定義**2** (used about a group of people and their relationships with each other) too close; not open to anyone outside the group (人々の集団およびその構成員同士の関係について) 密接すぎる; 集団の外に対して開かれていない→**(軽べつ的) (集団などが) 閉鎖的な, 排他的な** ǁ *Life in a small community can be very incestuous.* 小さな地域社会での生活は, 時に非常に閉鎖的になることがある.

**★inch**¹ /ɪntʃ/ 名 Ⓒ (略 **in**) ▶定義 a measure of

length; 2.54 centimetres. There are 12 inches in a foot. 長さの単位; 2.54cm. 1フィートは12インチ→インチ ‖ *He's 5 foot 10 inches tall.* 彼の身長は5フィート10インチだ. *Three inches of rain fell last night.* 昨夜は3インチの降雨量がありました.

**inch**² /ɪntʃ/ 動 自他 ▶定義 inch forward, past, through etc to move slowly and carefully in the direction mentioned 示された方向にゆっくりと注意深く動く ～を少しずつ動かす, 少しずつ(苦労しながら)動く・進む ‖ *He inched (his way) forward along the cliff edge.* 彼は崖(がけ)の端を少しずつ前進した.

**incidence** /ˈɪnsəd(ə)ns/ 名 [単数扱い] 正式 ▶定義 incidence of sth the number of times sth (usually unpleasant) happens; the rate of sth ～(通常は不愉快な事)が起きる回数; ～の率→(悪い事の)発生(率), 頻度 ‖ *a high incidence of crime/disease/unemployment* 高い犯罪発生率・病気の発生率・失業率

*__incident__ /ˈɪnsəd(ə)nt/ 名 C 正式 ▶定義 something that happens (especially sth unusual or unpleasant) (特に異常な, または不快な)出来事→(付随した)出来事, 事件, 小事件, (戦争などにつながる)事変, 紛争 ‖ *There were a number of incidents after the football match.* サッカーの試合の後で, たくさんの事件が発生した. *a diplomatic incident (= a dangerous or unpleasant situation between countries)* 外交的事件(= 2国間の危険な, または不快な状況)

**incidental** /ˌɪnsəˈdentl/ 形 ▶定義 incidental (to sth) happening as part of sth more important より重要な物事の一部として起こる→(～に)付随して起こる, 有りがちな ‖ *The book contains various themes that are incidental to the main plot.* この本には, 本筋に付随してさまざまなテーマが含まれている.

**incidentally** /ˌɪnsəˈdentli/ 副 ▶定義 used to introduce extra news, information, etc that the speaker has just thought of 話し手がちょうど思い付いた別のニュース・情報を伝えるのに用いて→ついでながら, ところで ‖ *Incidentally, that new restaurant you told me about is excellent.* ところで, あなたが話していた新しいレストランはすばらしい. ☛ incidentally の同意語は by the way.

**incinerate** /ɪnˈsɪnəreɪt/ 動 他 正式 ▶定義 to destroy sth completely by burning ～を完全に焼却する→～を焼却する, 焼いて灰にする, ～を焼死させる

**incinerator** /ɪnˈsɪnəreɪtər/ 名 C ▶定義 a container or machine for burning rubbish, etc ごみなどを焼却するための容器・機械→焼却炉

**incision** /ɪnˈsɪʒ(ə)n/ 名 C 正式 ▶定義 a cut carefully made into sth (especially into a person's body as part of a medical operation) ～に注意深く付けられた切り口(特に手術で人体に付けた切開部)→切り口[傷], 切開部

**incite** /ɪnˈsaɪt/ 動 他 ▶定義 incite sb (to sth) to encourage sb to do sth by making him/her very angry or excited ～を怒らせたり興奮させて, …を行うように扇動する→～を(…に)けしかける, ～を刺激する, 扇動する ‖ *He was accused of inciting the crowd to violence.* 彼は群集を扇動して暴力を振るわせたかどで告発された. ― incitement 名 C U (～への)扇動, 教唆 ‖ *He was guilty of incitement to violence.* 彼は暴行を扇動した罪で有罪となった.

**incl** 略 including; inclusive→～を含めて, すべて込みの ‖ *total £59.00 incl tax* 税込みで合計59.00ポンド

**inclination** /ˌɪnkləˈneɪʃ(ə)n/ 名 C U ▶定義 inclination (to do sth); inclination (towards/for sth) a feeling that makes sb want to behave in a particular way ～にある事を特定の方法でしたいという気を起こさせる感情→(～への)好み, (～したいという)気持ち, (～しがちな)傾向 ‖ *He did not show **the slightest inclination** to help.* 彼には助けようという気がみじんもなかった. *She had no inclination for a career in teaching.* 彼女には教職に就こうという気がなかった.

**incline**¹ /ɪnˈklaɪn/ 動 ▶定義 **1** 自 正式 incline to/toward sth to want to behave in a particular way or make a particular choice ある特定の行動を取りたい, ある特定の選択をしたいと思う→(人の)心が～へ傾く, (人が)(～に)気が向く, (～したい)気がする, (～への)傾向がある ‖ *I don't know what to choose, but I'm inclining towards the fish.* 何を選んだらよいのか分かりませんが, 魚にしたい気がします. ▶定義 **2** 他 正式 to bend (your head) forward (頭を)前に傾ける→(体, 頭など)をかがめる, 傾ける, 曲げる ‖ *They*

**incline**² /ɪnkláɪn/ ⓒ 正式 ▶定義 sat round the table, heads inclined, deep in discussion. 彼らはテーブルを囲んで座り，頭を前に寄せて討論に没頭した． ▶定義3 ⓑ incline toward sth to be at an angle in a particular direction ある方向に傾く → (物が)(〜に)傾く, 傾斜する ‖ The land inclines towards the shore. その土地は海岸に向かって傾いている．

**incline**² /ɪnkláɪn, -́ -/ ⓒ 正式 ▶定義 a slight hill; a slope → なだらかな坂; 傾斜 ‖ a steep/slight incline 急な・なだらかな斜面

**inclined** /ɪnkláɪnd/ 形 ▶定義1 inclined (to do sth) (名詞の前は不可) wanting to behave in a particular way ある特定の行動を取りたい → 〜する気である, したい ‖ I know Amir well so I'm inclined to believe what he says. アミールのことはよく知っているので，彼の言っている事を信じたい． ▶定義2 inclined to do sth likely to do sth 多分(〜)するだろう → 〜する傾向がある, 〜しがちだ ‖ She's inclined to change her mind very easily. 彼女はとても簡単に考えを変える傾向がある． ▶定義3 having a natural ability in the subject mentioned 言及された分野について生まれつき才能がある → 生まれつきの才能を持った, (才能が)(〜に)向いている, 才がある ‖ to be musically inclined 生まれつき音楽の才能を持っている

*__include__ /ɪnklúːd/ 動 他 (進行形は不可) ▶定義1 to have as one part; to contain (among other things) → 〜を(全体の一部として)含む, 包括する ‖ The price of the holiday includes the flight, the hotel and car-hire. 休暇の費用には, 飛行機・ホテル・レンタカー代が含まれます． The crew included one woman. 乗組員には女性が1名含まれていた． ☛参 **contain**の注 ⇔ **exclude** ▶定義2 include sb/sth (as/in/on sth) to make sb/sth part (of another group, etc) 〜を(グループなどに)含める → 〜を(…の中に)含める, 入れる ‖ The children immediately included the new girl in their games. 子供たちはすぐに新しい女の子をゲームに入れた． Everyone was disappointed, myself included. 私も含めて, 皆ががっかりした． — inclusion /ɪnklúːʒ(ə)n/ 名 ⓤ → 含むこと, 包含, 含有 ‖ The inclusion of all that violence in the film was unnecessary. その映画に含まれる暴力はすべて不要なものだった．

**including** /ɪnklúːdɪŋ/ 前 ▶定義 having as a part 一部として含んで → 〜を含めて, 〜を入れて ‖ It costs $17.99, including postage and packing. 送料と梱包(こんぽう)代を含めて17ドル99セントかかります． ⇔ **excluding**

**inclusive** /ɪnklúːsɪv/ 形 ▶定義1 inclusive (of sth) (used about a price, etc) including or containing everything; including the thing mentioned (値段などについて) すべて入っている, すべてを含んだ; 挙げた物は含んでいる → すべてを含んだ, すべて込みの, 包括的な ‖ Is that an inclusive price or are there some extras? それはすべて込みの値段ですか, それともいくらか別途料金がかかりますか． The rent is inclusive of electricity. 家賃には電気代が含まれる． ▶定義2 (名詞の後だけ) including the dates, numbers, etc mentioned 言及された日・番号などを含んだ → 両端を含んだ範囲の ‖ You are booked at the hotel from Monday to Friday inclusive (= including Monday and Friday). あなたは月曜日から金曜日までそのホテルを予約しています(= 月曜日と金曜日を含む)．
▶期間に関しては, アメリカ英語では inclusive よりも through の方がよく使われる: We'll be away from Friday through Sunday. (私たちは金曜日から日曜日まで留守にします．)

**incognito** /ɪnkágnətòʊ, ɪnkɑgníːtoʊ/ 副 ▶定義 hiding your real name and identity (especially if you are famous and do not want to be recognized) 本名と身分を隠して(特に有名人が気付かれないように) → 身元を隠して, 変名を使って, お忍びで ‖ to travel incognito お忍びで旅行をする

**incoherent** /ɪnkoʊhíərənt/ 形 ▶定義 not clear or easy to understand; not saying sth clearly 明瞭(めいりょう)でない, 分かりにくい; 〜をはっきりと言わない → (説明などが)つじつまの合わない, 支離滅裂な, (人が)しどろもどろの ⇔ **coherent** — incoherence 名 ⓤ → つじつまの合わないこと, 支離滅裂, しどろもどろ — incoherently 副 → 支離滅裂に, しどろもどろに

*__income__ /ɪnkʌm/ 名 ⓒ ⓤ ▶定義 the money you receive regularly as payment for your work or as interest on money you have saved, etc 仕事の報酬・預金の利子など, 定期的に受け取るお金 → 収入, 所得 ‖ It's often difficult for a family to live on one income. 家族が1人の収入で生計を立て

るのは，難しいことが多い．

▶ここでは monthly/annual income（月収・年収）について述べている．income（所得）は high（高く）なることも low（低く）なることもある．gross income とは税引き前の収入である．net income とは税引き後の所得である．pay² の注を参照．

**income tax** 名 Ｕ ▶定義 the amount of money you pay to the government according to how much you earn 所得に応じて政府に納めるお金の総額➡**所得税**

**incoming** /ínkʌmɪŋ/ 形（名詞の前だけ） ▶定義 1 arriving or being received 到着する，受け取られる➡**やって来る，入ってくる，(乗り物などが) 到着する** ‖ *incoming flights/passengers* 到着便・客 *incoming telephone calls* 外からかかってくる電話 ▶定義 2 new; recently elected 新しい；最近選ばれた➡**新任の，後任の，次期の** ‖ *the incoming government* 次期政府

**incomparable** /ɪnkɑ́mp(ə)rəb(ə)l/ 形 ▶定義 so good or great that it does not have an equal 非常にすばらしく偉大なので，肩を並べるものがない➡**比類のない，無類の，たぐいまれな，ずば抜けた** ‖ *incomparable beauty* 比類のない美しさ ☛ 動 compare

**incompatible** /ìnkəmpǽtəb(ə)l/ 形 ▶定義 incompatible with sb/sth very different and therefore not able to live or work happily with sb or exist with sth ～との違いが著しいので，一緒に楽しく暮らしたり仕事をしたりすることができない，共存することができない➡**(人が) (～と) うまが合わない，(物事が) (～と) 相いれない，相反する** ‖ *The working hours of the job are incompatible with family life.* その仕事の勤務時間は家庭生活とは相いれない． ⇔ **compatible** — incompatibility /ìnkəmpætəbíləti/ 名 Ｃ Ｕ （複 incompatibilities）➡**両立しないこと，矛盾すること；両立しない・相いれないもの**

**incompetent** /ɪnkɑ́mpət(ə)nt/ 形 ▶定義 lacking the necessary skill to do sth well ～をうまくやる技量が欠けている➡**無能な，役に立たない，不適格な** ‖ *He is completely incompetent at his job.* 彼は自分の仕事をこなす能力が全くない． *an incompetent teacher/manager* 無能な教師・経営者 ⇔ **competent** — incompetent 名 Ｃ➡**無能者，役立たず** ‖ *She's a total incompetent at basketball.* 彼女はバスケットボールが全くできない． — incompetence 名 Ｕ➡**無能力，不適格，無資格** — incompetently 副➡**無力にも，無能にも**

**incomplete** /ìnkəmplíːt/ 形 ▶定義 having a part or parts missing; not total 一部またはいくつかの部分が欠けている；完全ではない➡**不完全な，不十分な，不備な，未完成の** ‖ *Unfortunately the jigsaw puzzle was incomplete.* 残念ながら，そのジグソーパズルには不備があった． ⇔ **complete** — incompletely 副➡**不完全に，不十分に**

**incomprehensible** /ìnkɑ̀mprɪhénsəb(ə)l/ 形 ▶定義 impossible to understand 理解できない➡**分かりにくい，不可解な** ‖ *an incomprehensible explanation* 理解し難い説明 *Her attitude is incomprehensible to the rest of the committee.* 彼女の態度は，ほかの委員には不可解だ． ⇔ **comprehensible**, **understandable** — incomprehension /ìnkɑ̀mprɪhénʃ(ə)n/ 名 Ｕ➡**無理解，理解力のなさ**

**inconceivable** /ìnkənsíːvəb(ə)l/ 形 ▶定義 impossible or very difficult to believe or imagine 信じること・想像することが不可能な，または非常に困難な➡**想像を絶する，思いも寄らない，信じられない，あり得ない** ‖ *It's inconceivable that he would have stolen anything.* 彼が盗みを働いたなんて信じられない． ⇔ **conceivable**

**inconclusive** /ìnkənklúːsɪv/ 形 ▶定義 not leading to a definite decision or result 明確な決定・結果をもたらさない➡**結論の出ない，決着の付かない，(証拠・実験などが) 決定的でない，決め手に欠ける** ‖ *an inconclusive discussion* 結論の出ない討議 *inconclusive evidence* (= *that doesn't prove anything*) 決め手に欠ける (= 何も証明しない) 証拠 ⇔ **conclusive** — inconclusively 副➡**要領を得ないで，結論に達しないで，不十分に**

**incongruous** /ɪnkɑ́ŋgruəs/ 形 ▶定義 strange and out of place; not suitable in a particular situation 奇妙で場違いの；ある特定の状況にふさわしくない➡**不釣り合いな，ちぐはぐな，場違いの，似合わない** ‖ *That huge table looks rather incongruous in such a small room.* そのような狭い部屋には，大きなテーブルはややちぐはぐに見える． — incongruously 副➡**不釣り合いに，場違いに** — incongruity /ìnkɑŋgrúːəti, -kən-/ 名 Ｕ➡**不釣り合いなこと，場違いなこと**

**inconsiderate** /ìnkənsíd(ə)rət/ 形 ▶定義 (used

about a person) not thinking or caring about the feelings, or needs of other people (人について) ほかの人々の感情・要求を考えたり気に掛けたりしない→思いやりのない, 配慮のない, 身勝手な‖ *It was inconsiderate of you not to offer her a lift.* 彼女に車に乗せてあげようと申し出なかったとは、あなたも思いやりがない.
☛類 **thoughtless** ⇔ **considerate** — inconsiderately 副→思いやりなく、人の気持ちも考えないで — inconsiderateness 名 Ⓤ→思いやりのなさ

**inconsistent** /ˌɪnkənsíst(ə)nt/ 形 ▶定義 **1** inconsistent (with sth) (used about statements, facts, etc) not the same as sth else; not matching, so that one thing must be wrong or not true (陳述、事実などについて) ほかの〜と同じでない; 互いに合致しないので、一方が誤っているか、事実ではなくなる→(〜と) つじつまの合わない、食い違う、矛盾した、相いれない‖ *The witnesses' accounts of the event are inconsistent.* その事件に関する目撃者の説明は食い違う. *These new facts are inconsistent with the earlier information.* それらの新事実は、初期の情報とつじつまが合わない. ▶定義 **2** (used about a person) likely to change (in attitude, behaviour, etc) so that you cannot depend on him/her (人について) (態度、振る舞いなどが) 変わりやすいので、当てにできない→一貫性のない、むら気の‖ *She's so inconsistent - sometimes her work is good and sometimes it's really awful.* 彼女はとてもむらがある — 良い仕事をするときもあればとてもひどいときもある. ⇔ **consistent** — inconsistency /-ənsi/ 名 Ⓒ Ⓤ (複 inconsistencies) →つじつまが合わないこと、食い違い、矛盾‖ *There were a few inconsistencies in her argument.* 彼女の論拠には、いくつかの矛盾がある. ⇔ **consistency** — inconsistently 副→矛盾して、無節操に

**inconspicuous** /ˌɪnkənspíkjuəs/ 形 ▶定義 not easily noticed 容易には気付かれない→目立たない、人目に付かない、注意をひかない、地味な‖ *I tried to **make** myself as **inconspicuous** as possible so that no one would ask me a question.* だれからも質問されないように、できるだけ目立たないようにした. ⇔ **conspicuous** — inconspicuously 副→目立たずに、目立たないように

**incontinent** /ɪnkánt(ə)nənt/ 形 ▶定義 unable to control the passing of waste (urine and faeces) from the body 排せつ物 (小便と大便) が身体から流れ出るのを抑制できない→失禁する、排せつを抑制できない — incontinence 名 Ⓤ→失禁

**inconvenience** /ˌɪnkənvíːnjəns/ 名 Ⓤ Ⓒ ▶定義 trouble or difficulty, especially when it affects sth that you need to do; a person or thing that causes this 問題や困難で、特にする必要のある〜に影響を及ぼすもの; それを引き起こす人・事→不便、不自由、不都合、迷惑‖ *We apologize for any inconvenience caused by the delays.* 延期に伴うあらゆる不都合に対して、おわびいたします. — inconvenience 動 他 →〜に不便を掛ける、〜に迷惑を掛ける

**inconvenient** /ˌɪnkənvíːnjənt/ 形 ▶定義 causing trouble or difficulty, especially when it affects sth that you need to do 迷惑を掛けたり不都合を引き起こす、特にやらねばならない事に影響する場合→不便な、不自由な、都合の悪い、迷惑な‖ *It's a bit inconvenient at the moment - could you phone again later?* 今ちょっと都合が悪いです — 後でかけ直していただけますか. ⇔ **convenient** — inconveniently 副→不便に、都合の悪いことに

**incorporate** /ɪnkɔ́ːrpərèɪt/ 動 他 ▶定義 incorporate sth (in/into/within sth) to make sth a part of sth else; to have sth as a part 〜をほかの物の一部にする; 〜を一部としている→〜を (…に) 合体させる、組み入れる、取り入れる、合併させる‖ *I'd like you to incorporate this information into your report.* この情報を君の報告に組み入れてもらいたい. ☛類 **include** — incorporation /ɪnˌkɔːrpəréɪʃ(ə)n/ 名 Ⓤ→組み入れること、合併、合同、編入

**incorporated** /ɪnkɔ́ːrpərèɪtəd/ 形 (略 **Inc**) ▶定義 (following the name of a company) formed into a legal organization (corporation) (会社名の後に続く) 法律に基づいた団体 (法人) の形をとった→株式 [有限] 会社の、法人 [会社] 組織の

**incorrect** /ˌɪnkərékt/ 形 ▶定義 not right or true→不正確な、間違った‖ *Incorrect answers should be marked with a cross.* 間違った答えにはばつ印を付けてください. ⇔ **correct** — incorrectly

副 ➡不正確に, 間違って

**incorrigible** /ɪnkɔ́(ː)rədʒəb(ə)l, -kár-/ 形 ▶定義 (used about a person or his/her behaviour) very bad; too bad to be corrected or improved (人またはその行動について) とても悪い; 悪すぎて正したり, 改善したりすることができない**(人・欠点・癖などが) 矯正できない, 直しようがない, 手の施しようがない** || *an incorrigible liar* 手に負えないうそつき

\***increase**[1] /ɪnkríːs/ 動自他 ▶定義 increase (sth) (from A) (to B); increase (sth) (by sth) to become or to make sth larger in number or amount 〜の数・量が増える; 〜の数量を増やす**増える, 増加する; 〜を増やす, 増大させる** || *The rate of inflation has increased by 1% to 7%.* インフレ率は1パーセントから7パーセントに増加した. *My employer would like me to increase my hours of work from 25 to 30.* 雇用側は, 私の労働時間を25時間から30時間に増やしたがっている. *She increased her speed to overtake the lorry.* 彼女は速度を上げて, トラックを追い越した. ⇔ **decrease, reduce**

\***increase**[2] /ínkriːs, -́/ 名 C U ▶定義 (an) increase (in sth) a rise in the number, amount or level of sth 〜の数・量・水準の増加➡(〜の) **増加, 増大** || *There has been a sharp increase of nearly 50% on last year's figures.* 昨年の数値から約50パーセントも急増している. *Doctors expect some further increase in the spread of the disease.* 医者は, 病気がさらに蔓延 (まんえん) することを予測している. *They are demanding a large wage increase.* 彼らは大幅な賃金の増加を要求している. ⇔ **decrease, reduction**

成句 **on the increase** ▶定義 becoming larger or more frequent; increasing**大きくなる, 頻度が増す; 増加している** || *Attacks by dogs on children are on the increase.* 犬が子供を襲うことが増えている.

**increasingly** /ɪnkríːsɪŋli/ 副 ▶定義 more and more**だんだん** || *It's becoming increasingly difficult/important/dangerous to stay here.* ここに滞在するのはますます難しくなって・重要になって・危険になっている.

**incredible** /ɪnkrédəb(ə)l/ 形 ▶定義 1 impossible or very difficult to believe**信じられない, 信じることが非常に困難な** || *I found his account of the event incredible.* 彼の事件についての説明は信じられないことが分かった. ⇔ **credible**. unbelievableを参照. ▶定義 2 略式 extremely good or big 極めてすばらしい, または大きい➡(褒めて) **信じられないほどの, 途方もない, うそみたいな** || *He earns an incredible salary.* 彼は信じられないほどの給料を稼ぐ. —**incredibly** 副➡**信じられないほど, 非常に, 信じられないことに** || *We have had some incredibly strong winds recently.* 最近, 途方もない強風があった.

**incriminate** /ɪnkrímənɛɪt/ 動他 ▶定義 to provide evidence that sb is guilty of a crime 〜が罪を犯していることの証拠を示す➡**〜に罪を負わせる, 〜を有罪にする** || *The police searched the house but found nothing to incriminate the man.* 警察は家を捜索したが, 彼を有罪にする証拠は発見できなかった.

**incubate** /íŋkjəbèɪt/ 動 ▶定義 1 他 to keep an egg at the right temperature so that it can develop and produce a bird (**hatch**) 卵を適温に保ち, 発育してひなかがえるようにする (孵化 (ふか) する) ➡**(卵を) 抱く, 〜をかえす; 孵化する** ▶定義 2 自他 (used about a disease) to develop without showing signs; (used about a person or an animal) to carry a disease without showing signs (病気について) 兆候を見せずに進んでいく; (人・動物について) 兆候はないが, 病気に感染している➡**(病気が) 潜伏する; (病原菌) を体内に潜伏させる** || *Some viruses take weeks to incubate.* ウイルスの中には, 何週間も潜伏するものもある.

**incubation** /ìŋkjəbéɪʃ(ə)n/ 名 ▶定義 1 U the process of incubating eggs 卵が孵化 (ふか) する過程➡**孵化, 抱卵** ▶定義 2 C (または **incubation period**) the period between catching a disease and the time when signs of it (**symptoms**) appear 病気に感染してから, その兆候 (症状) が現れるまでの期間➡**(病気の) 潜伏期 (間)**

**incubator** /íŋkjəbèɪtər/ 名 C ▶定義 1 a heated machine used in hospitals for keeping small or weak babies alive 未熟・虚弱な赤ん坊を生かしておくために病院で使用する, 保温された器械➡**未熟児保育器, 人工保育器** ▶定義 2 a heated machine for keeping eggs warm until they break open (**hatch**) 卵がかえる (孵化 (ふか) す

る）まで暖めておく，保温器 ➜孵卵器

**incur** /ɪnkə́ːr/ [動][他] (**incurred**; **incurring**) [正式] ▶定義 to suffer the unpleasant results of a situation that you have caused 自分で引き起こした状況で不愉快な結果を被る ➜**（負債・損害など）を負う，被る，受ける，（危険・怒りなど）を招く** ‖ *to incur debts/sb's anger* 負債を負う・～の怒りを招く

**incurable** /ɪnkjʊ́ərəb(ə)l/ [形] ▶定義 that cannot be cured or made better 直すことができない，良くすることができない ➜**（病気などが）不治の，治せない，（習慣・性格などが）直すことのできない，手の施しようのない** ‖ *an incurable disease* 不治の病 ⇔ **curable** — incurably /-əbli/ [副] ➜**治療できないほど，手の施しようもなく** ‖ *incurably ill* 手の施しようもなく病気が重い

**indebted** /ɪndétəd/ [形] ▶定義 indebted (to sb) (for sth) very grateful to sb ～に非常に感謝して ➜**（～に）（…のことで）恩を受けている，有り難く思っている，負い目がある** ‖ *I am deeply indebted to my family and friends for all their help.* 私は家族や友人たちの手助けに深く感謝している．

**indecent** /ɪndíːs(ə)nt/ [形] ▶定義 shocking to many people in society, especially because sth involves sex or the body 特に性や体のことを含んでいるので，社会の多くの人々に衝撃を与える ➜**下品な，みだらな，卑わいな** ‖ *indecent photos/behaviour/language* 卑わいな写真・振る舞い・言葉 *You can't wear those tiny swimming trunks - they're indecent!* そんなに小さな水泳パンツを履いてはいけません － 下品です．⇔ **decent** — indecency /-nsi/ [名] [[U]，単数扱い] ➜**下品，卑わい** — indecently [副] ➜**下品に，みだらに**

**indecision** /ìndɪsíʒ(ə)n/（または **indecisiveness**）[名] [U] ▶定義 the state of being unable to decide 決断することができない状態 ➜**決断できないこと，優柔不断，躊躇（ちゅうちょ），ためらい** ‖ *This indecision about the future is really worrying me.* こんな風に将来について決断できないことにいら立つ．

**indecisive** /ìndɪsáɪsɪv/ [形] ▶定義 not able to make decisions easily すぐに決断することができない ➜**（人が）決断力のない，優柔不断の** ⇔ **decisive** — indecisively [副] ➜**決め手を欠いて，決定的でなく，ぐずぐずして，優柔不断に**

***indeed** /ɪndíːd/ [副] ▶定義1 (used for emphasizing a positive statement or answer) really; certainly（肯定的な意見や答えを強調するために用いて）➜**本当に，確かに** ‖ *'Have you had a good holiday?' 'We have indeed.'*「楽しい休暇でしたか」「ええ，とても楽しかったですよ」 ▶定義2 used after 'very' with an adjective or adverb to emphasize the quality mentioned very + 形容詞・副詞の後で用いて，その意味を強調する ➜**実に，全く** ‖ *Thank you very much indeed.* 本当にどうもありがとう．*She's very happy indeed.* 彼女はもう本当に幸せです． ▶定義3 (used for adding information to a statement) in fact（前言に情報を補足するために用いて）➜**実は，実のところ** ‖ *It's important that you come at once. Indeed, it's essential.* あなたがすぐに来ることが重要です．いや，もともと欠かせないことなのです． ▶定義4 used for showing interest, surprise, anger, etc 興味・驚き・怒りなどを表すのに用いて ➜**へぇー，まさか，まあ** ‖ *'They were talking about you last night.' 'Were they indeed!'*「昨夜，彼らは君のことを話していたよ」「へぇー，本当に」

**indefensible** /ìndɪfénsəb(ə)l/ [形] ▶定義 (used about behaviour, etc) completely wrong; that cannot be defended or excused（振る舞いなどについて）完全に間違っている；弁護・言い訳ができない ➜**弁解の余地のない，正当化できない**

**indefinable** /ìndɪfáɪnəb(ə)l/ [形] ▶定義 difficult or impossible to describe 説明が困難な・不可能な ➜**定義できない，漠然とした** ‖ *There was an indefinable atmosphere of hostility.* 漠然とした敵意の雰囲気があった．— indefinably /-əb(ə)li/ [副] ➜**何とも言いようがなく**

**indefinite** /ɪndéf(ə)nət/ [形] ▶定義 not fixed or clear 確定していない，明瞭（めいりょう）でない ➜**不明確な，あいまいな，漠然とした** ‖ *Our plans are still rather indefinite.* 我々の計画はまだかなりあいまいだ．⇔ **definite**

**the indefinite article** [名] [C]（文法）▶定義 the name used for the words a and an a および an に対して用いられる名称 ➜**不定冠詞** ☛参 **the definite article**

➤不定冠詞についての説明は，巻末の「文法早見表」を参照．

**indefinitely** /ɪndéf(ə)nətli/ 副 ▶定義 for a period of time that has no fixed end いつ終わるとも知れない期間に→**無期限に, いつまでも, 不明確に** ‖ *The meeting was postponed indefinitely.* その会議は無期限に延期された.

**indelible** /ɪndéləb(ə)l/ 形 ▶定義 that cannot be removed or washed out 取り除くことができない, 洗い落とすことができない→**(インクなどが) 消すことができない, (印象などが) 忘れられない** ‖ *indelible ink* 消すことができないインク (比喩) *The experience made an indelible impression on me.* その体験は, 私に忘れられない印象を残しました. — **indelibly** /-əb(ə)li/ 副 →**忘れられずに, 消さないように, 永遠に**

**indent** /ɪndént/ 動 自 他 ▶定義 to start a line of writing further from the left-hand side of the page than the other lines ほかの行よりも左側に余白を多く残して行を書き始める→**(行の頭を) 下げて書く; (新しい段落の行) をほかの行より引っ込めて書く, ~をインデントする**

\***independence** /ìndəpéndəns/ 名 Ｕ ▶定義 independence (from sb/sth) (used about a person, country, etc) the state of being free and not controlled by another person, country, etc (人・国などについて) 自由で, 他人・他国などに支配されていない状態→**独立, 自立** ‖ *In 1947 India achieved independence from Britain.* 1947年に, インドは英国からの独立を成し遂げた. *financial independence* 経済的な自立
▶ Independence Day (7月4日)「独立記念日」. アメリカでは, 自国が1776年に英国から独立を宣言したその日を祝う.

\***independent** /ìndəpéndənt/ 形 ▶定義 **1** independent (of/from sb/sth) free from and not controlled by another person, country, etc 他人・他国などから自由で支配されていない→**(~から) 独立した, 自治の, 自主の, (学校・組織などが) 民営の, 民間の, 私立の** ‖ *Many former colonies are now independent nations.* 旧植民地の多くは, 現在独立国である. *independent schools/television (= not supported by government money)* 私立学校・民間放送局 (= 政府の資金援助を受けていない) ▶定義 **2** independent (of/from sb/sth) not needing or wanting help 援助を必要としない, 援助を欲していない→**自活している, (~から) 独立した生活をしている** ‖ *I got a part-time job because I wanted to be financially independent from my parents.* 両親から経済的に独立したいので, パートタイムの仕事に就いた. ⇔ **dependent** ▶定義 **3** not influenced by or connected with sb/sth ~の影響を受けない, または関係していない→**独自の, (~とは) 無関係の, 別個の** ‖ *Complaints against the police should be investigated by an independent body.* 警察に対する苦情は, 独立した組織で調査されるべきだ. *Two independent opinion polls have obtained similar results.* ２つの別々の世論調査が, 同様の結果を得た. — **independently** 副 independently (of sb/sth)→**独立して, 自立して, (~とは) 無関係に** ‖ *Scientists working independently of each other have had very similar results in their experiments.* お互いに無関係に研究している科学者たちが, 極めて似通った実験結果を得た.

**indescribable** /ìndɪskráɪbəb(ə)l/ 形 ▶定義 too good or bad to be described すばらしすぎて, またはひどすぎて言葉で描写できない→**言葉では言い表せない, 筆舌に尽くし難い, 言語に絶する** ‖ *indescribable poverty/luxury/noise* 筆舌に尽くし難い貧困・ぜいたく, 言語に絶する騒音 — **indescribably** /-əb(ə)li/ 副 →**言葉では言い表せないほど, 言語に絶するほど**

**indestructible** /ìndɪstrʌ́ktəb(ə)l/ 形 ▶定義 that cannot be easily damaged or destroyed 容易には損害を与えることができない, 破壊することができない→**破壊できない, 不滅の**

\***index** /índeks/ 名 Ｃ (複 **indexes**) ▶定義 **1** a list in order from A to Z, usually at the end of a book, of the names or subjects that are referred to in the book アルファベット順の一覧表で, 通常は巻末に付き, その本で言及された名前や主題が載せてあるもの→**索引, 目録** ‖ *If you want to find all the references to London, look it up in the index.* ロンドンに言及した部分をすべて見つけたかったら, 索引を調べなさい. ▶定義 **2** (または **card index**) a list in order from A to Z of names, books, subjects, etc written on a series of cards (index cards) アルファベット順の一覧で, 氏名・書名・主題などが一連のカード (索引カード) に書かれているもの→**カード索引** ▶定義 **3** (複 **indexes** または **indices**) a way of showing how the price, value, rate, etc of sth has changed ～の値段・価値・割合などの変化を示す方法 → (物価などの)指数, (数学)指数;指標 ‖ *the cost-of-living index* 生活費指数 — **index** 動 → ～に索引を付ける, ～を索引に載せる ‖ *The books in the library are indexed by subject and title.* 図書館の本は, 主題および書名で索引が付けられている.

**index finger** 名 C ▶定義 the finger next to your thumb that you use for pointing 親指の隣にある指で, 指差す際に使う → 人差し指 ☞類 **forefinger**

*****Indian** /índiən/ 名 C 形 ▶定義 1 (a person) from the Republic of India → インドの, インド人(の), インド製の ‖ *Indian food is hot and spicy.* インド料理は辛くて香辛料が効いている.

▶定義 2 = **NATIVE AMERICAN** (先住アメリカ人, アメリカインディアン) ‖ *The Sioux were a famous Indian tribe.* スー族は, 有名な先住アメリカ人の部族だった. ☞参 **West Indian**

*****indicate** /índikèit/ 動 ▶定義 1 他 to show that sth is probably true or exists ～が多分本当である, または存在していることを示す → ～を指摘する, 明らかにする ‖ *Recent research indicates that children are getting too little exercise.* 最近の調査で, 子供たちがほとんど運動をしなくなってきていることが明らかになった.

▶定義 2 他 to say sth in an indirect way ～を間接的に言う → ～を(言葉・態度などで)示す, ～を(身振りなどで)ほのめかす, それとなく知らせる ‖ *The spokesman indicated that an agreement was likely soon.* 広報官は, 間もなく合意に至るであろうとほのめかした. ▶定義 3 他 to make sb notice sth, especially by pointing to it 特に指で差して～に…を気付かせる → ～を指し示す, 指差す ‖ *The receptionist indicated where I should sign.* 受付係は, どこに署名するかを指し示した. *The boy seemed to be indicating that I should follow him.* その少年は, 自分の後を付いてくるように指し示しているように見えた.

▶定義 4 自他 to signal that your car, etc is going to turn 車などが曲がることを合図する → (運転手・車などが)方向指示器で合図する, ウインカーを出す; (右折・左折)の合図をする ‖ *The lorry indicated left but turned right.* トラックは左にウインカーを出したが, 右折した.

**indication** /ìndəkéiʃ(ə)n/ 名 C U ▶定義 an indication (of sth/doing sth); an indication that... something that shows sth; a sign ～を示すもの; 兆候 (～の・～という)兆候, 印, 兆し ‖ *There was no indication of a struggle.* 戦いの兆しはなかった. *There is every indication that he will make a full recovery.* 彼が全快するという確かな兆候がある.

**indicative** /indíkətiv/ 形 正式 ▶定義 being or giving a sign of sth ～の兆候となる・兆候を示す → (～を・～ということを)表して, 示して, 示唆して ‖ *Is the unusual weather indicative of climatic changes?* この異常な天気は, 気候の変化の前触れなのだろうか.

**indicator** /índəkèitər/ 名 C ▶定義 1 something that gives information or shows sth; a sign 情報を与えてくれるもの, ～を示してくれるもの; 印 → 示すもの, 尺度; 計器, メーター ‖ *The indicator showed that we had plenty of petrol.* 表示器は, 十分な量の石油があることを示していた. *The unemployment rate is a reliable indicator of economic health.* 失業率は, 経済の健全度を示す信頼できる尺度だ. ▶定義 2 (米 **turn signal**) the flashing light on a car, etc that shows that it is going to turn right or left 右・左折を示す, 車などのフラッシュライト → (車の)方向指示器, ウインカー ☞ S7 ページのさし絵

**indices** /índəsiːz/ **INDEX**(3) の複数形

**indictment** /indáitmənt/ 名 C ▶定義 1 a written paper that officially accuses sb of a crime ～を罪により正式に告訴する書類 → 起訴状, 告発状 ▶定義 2 an indictment (of sth) something that shows how bad sth is ～がいかに悪いかを示すもの → (悪いことを)証明する物, 非難(の文書) ‖ *The fact that many children leave school with no qualifications is an indictment of our education system.* 多くの子供たちが技能・資格を取得することもなく学校を去っていくという事実は, 教育制度の不備を示している.

**indifference** /indíf(ə)rəns/ 名 U ▶定義 indifference (to sb/sth) a lack of interest or feeling towards sb/sth ～に対する興味・感情が欠けていること → (～に対する)無関心, 冷淡, むとんちゃく ‖ *He has always shown indifference to the needs of others.* 彼は他人の要求にはいつも無関心である.

**indifferent** /indíf(ə)rənt/ 形 ▶定義 1 indifferent (to sb/sth) not interested in or caring about sb/sth ～に興味がない, 気に掛けない→(～に) 無関心で, 冷淡で, むとんちゃくな ‖ *The manager of the shop seemed indifferent to our complaints.* その店の支配人は, 我々の苦情には無関心のように思われた. ▶定義2 not very good あまり良くない→平凡な; どうでもよい, 重要でない ‖ *The standard of football in the World Cup was rather indifferent.* ワールドカップでのサッカーの水準は, あまり良くなかった. ― **indifferently** 副→無関心に, 冷淡に, 良くも悪くもなく

**indigenous** /ɪndídʒənəs/ 形 ▶定義 (used about people, animals or plants) living or growing in the place where they are from originally (民族・動物・植物について) もともとの出身地で暮らす, 成長する→(動植物などが) (ある地域に) 固有の, 原産の, 土着の

**indigestible** /ìndaɪdʒéstəb(ə)l, ìndə-/ 形 ▶定義 (used about food) difficult or impossible for the stomach to deal with (食べ物について) 胃で消化するのが難しい・不可能な→(食べ物が) 消化しにくい, 消化に悪い

**indigestion** /ìndədʒéstʃ(ə)n, ìndaɪ-/ 名 ❶ ▶定義 pain in the stomach that is caused by difficulty in dealing with food 消化不良によって引き起こされる胃痛→消化不良(症), 胃弱 ‖ *Peppers give me indigestion.* コショウで消化不良になる.

**indignant** /ɪndígnənt/ 形 ▶定義 indignant (with sb) (about/at sth); indignant that... shocked or angry because sb has said or done sth that you do not like and do not agree with やって欲しくなく, 賛成できない～が…と言ったり行ったりしたために, ショックを受ける・怒る→(～に対して・～だと) 憤慨した, 怒った ‖ *They were indignant that they had to pay more for worse services.* 彼らは, ひどいサービスに対して余計にお金を払わなければならなかったので憤慨した. ― **indignantly** 副→憤慨して, 立腹して

**indignation** /ìndɪɡnéɪʃ(ə)n/ 名 ❶ ▶定義 indignation (at/about sth); indignation that... shock and anger ショックと怒り→(不正などに対する) 憤り, 怒り, 憤慨 ‖ *commuters' indignation at the rise in fares* 運賃の値上げに対する通勤客の怒り

**indirect** /ìndərékt, -daɪ-/ 形 ▶定義 1 not being the direct cause of sth; not having a direct connection with sth ～の直接の原因ではない; ～と直接の関係がない→間接的な, 二次的な ‖ *an indirect result* 間接的な結果 ▶定義2 that avoids saying sth in an obvious way ～をはっきり言わない→遠回しの, 率直でない ‖ *She gave only an indirect answer to my question.* 彼女は私の質問に対して遠回しに答えただけだった. ▶定義3 not going in a straight line or using the shortest route まっすぐに行かない, 最短の道筋を使わない→まっすぐでない, 遠回りの ‖ *We came the indirect route to avoid driving through London.* 我々は, ロンドンを車で通り抜けないで済むように遠回りをした. ⇔ **direct** ― **indirectly** 副→間接的に, 副次的に, 遠回しに ⇔ **directly** ― **indirectness** 名 ❶→間接的なこと, 遠回し(なこと)

**indirect object** 名 ❻ (文法) ▶定義 a person or thing that an action is done to or for 行為の対象 [目的] となる人・物→間接目的語 ‖ *In the sentence, 'I wrote him a letter', 'him' is the indirect object.* I wrote him a letter の文中で, him は間接目的語. ☞参 **direct object**
▶間接目的語についての説明は, 巻末の「文法早見表」を参照.

**indirect speech** (または **reported speech**) 名 ❶ (文法) ▶定義 reporting what sb has said, not using the actual words ～が話した事を, 実際に言った言葉を使わずに伝える→間接話法
▶ Hadi の言葉が *I'll phone again later.* (また後で電話します.) だった場合, 間接話法では次のような文になる: *Hadi said that he would phone again later.*
☞参 **direct speech**
▶間接話法についての説明は, 巻末の「文法早見表」を参照.

**indiscreet** /ìndɪskríːt/ 形 ▶定義 not careful or polite in what you say or do 話の内容や行動が, 注意深くない・礼儀正しくない→(言動などが) 軽率な, うかつな, 口の軽い ⇔ **discreet** ― **indiscreetly** 副→無分別に, 軽率に

**indiscretion** /ìndɪskréʃ(ə)n/ 名 ❻ ❶ ▶定義 behaviour that is not careful or polite, and that might cause embarrassment or offence 注意が足りず礼儀知らずな振る舞いで, 厄介事を引き

起こしたり人を不快にするおそれのあるもの→**無分別、無思慮、軽率**

**indiscriminate** /ɪndɪskríməneɪt/ 形 ▶定義 done or acting without making sensible judgement or caring about the possible harmful effects 思慮分別のある判断をせず、または危険な影響を及ぼす可能性について配慮せずになされた、そのように行動する→**無差別の、見境のない、手当たり次第の** ‖ He's indiscriminate in his choice of friends. 彼の友人選びは見境がない. — indiscriminately 副 →**無差別に、見境なく**

**indispensable** /ɪndɪspénsəb(ə)l/ 形 ▶定義 very important, so that it is not possible to be without it とても重要なので、それなしでは済まされない→(〜にとって・〜のために)**絶対必要な、欠くことのできない、(義務などが)避けられない** ‖ A car is indispensable nowadays if you live in the country. 近ごろでは、田舎に住むのに車は絶対必要だ. ☛類 essential ⇔ dispensable

**indisputable** /ɪndɪspjúːtəb(ə)l/ 形 ▶定義 definitely true; that cannot be shown to be wrong 明らかに正しい;それが間違っていると証明することができない→**議論の余地のない、明白な、確実な**

**indistinct** /ɪndɪstíŋ(k)t/ 形 ▶定義 not clear→**不明瞭(めいりょう)な、はっきりしない、ぼんやりした** ‖ indistinct figures/sounds/memories おぼろげな数字・かすかな物音・ぼんやりした記憶 ⇔ distinct — indistinctly 副 →**不明瞭に、ぼんやりと**

**indistinguishable** /ɪndɪstíŋ(g)wɪʃəb(ə)l/ 形 ▶定義 indistinguishable (from sth) appearing to be the same 同じように見える→(〜と)**区別できない、見分けの付かない** ‖ From a distance the two colours are indistinguishable. 遠くからだと、2つの色は見分けが付かない. ⇔ distinguishable

*****individual**[1] /ɪndəvídʒ(u)əl/ 形 ▶定義 1 (名詞の前だけ) considered separately rather than as part of a group 集団の一部としてではなく、それぞれ別個のものと見なされた→**個々の、個別の、それぞれの** ‖ Each individual animal is weighed and measured before being set free. それぞれの動物は、放される前に体長と体重を計られた. ▶定義 2 for or from one person 1人用の・1人からの→**個人の、個人的な、1人用(だけ)の** ‖ an individual portion of butter 1人分のバター Children need individual attention when they are learning to read. 子供たちが本を読み出す時は、個別に指導してやることが必要だ. ▶定義 3 typical of one person in a way that is different from other people 他人とは違っているために、ある人に特有な→**個性的な、独特の** ‖ I like her individual style of dressing. 私は彼女独特の着こなしが好きだ.

**individual**[2] /ɪndəvídʒ(u)əl/ 名 C ▶定義 1 one person, considered separately from others or a group ほかの人や集団からは区別してとらえられる一個人→(集団に対して)**個人、個、個体** ‖ Are the needs of society more important than the rights of the individual? 社会の要求は、個人の権利よりも大切なのだろうか. ▶定義 2 略式 a person of the type that is mentioned ある特定のタイプの人→**〜な人、人物** ‖ She's a strange individual. 彼女は変わった人だ.

**individuality** /ɪndəvɪdʒuæléləti/ 名 U ▶定義 the qualities that make sb/sth different from other people or things 〜を、ほかの人々や物事と違うものにする特質→**個性、特徴** ‖ Young people often try to express their individuality by the way they dress. 若者は服の着こなしで個性を表現しようとすることがよくある.

**individually** /ɪndəvídʒ(u)əli/ 副 ▶定義 separately; one by one 別々に;1つ[1人]ずつ→**個別に、個々に、それぞれは** ‖ The teacher talked to each member of the class individually. 教師はクラスの生徒1人1人と個別に話した.

**indivisible** /ɪndəvízəb(ə)l/ 形 ▶定義 that cannot be divided or split into smaller pieces 小さく分割できない、割ることができない→**分割できない、不可分の**

**indoctrinate** /ɪndɑ́ktrəneɪt/ 動 他 ▶定義 to force sb to accept particular beliefs without considering others 〜に、ほかの信条を考慮せず特定の信条を受け入れるように強制する→(人に)(思想などを)**教え込む、〜を洗脳する** ‖ For 20 years the people have been indoctrinated by the government. 20年の間、人民は政府に洗脳されていた. — indoctrination /ɪndɑ̀ktrənéɪʃ(ə)n/ 名 U →**教え込むこと、教化、洗脳**

*****indoor** /índɔːr/ 形 (名詞の前だけ) ▶定義 done or used inside a building 屋内で行われる、使わ

れる→屋内の, 室内の ‖ *indoor games* 室内ゲーム *an indoor swimming pool* 屋内プール ⇔ **outdoor**

**\*indoors** /ɪnˈdɔːrz/ 副 ▶定義 in or into a building→屋内に[で], 家の中に[で] ‖ *Let's go indoors.* 屋内に入ろう. *Oh dear! I've left my sunglasses indoors.* あら, サングラスを家の中に忘れてきたわ. ⇔ **outdoors, out of doors**

**induce** /ɪnˈd(j)uːs/ 動 中 正式 ▶定義 1 to make or persuade sb to do sth→(人を)～する気にさせる, (人を)誘って～させる, ～するよう誘導する ‖ *Nothing could induce him to change his mind.* 何事も彼の気を変えさせることはなかった.
▶定義 2 to cause or produce→～を引き起こす, 誘発する ‖ *drugs that induce sleep* 眠気を誘う薬

**inducement** /ɪnˈd(j)uːsmənt/ 名 ⓒ ⓤ ▶定義 something that is offered to sb to make him/her do sth ～に…をする気にさせるために提供されるもの→(～する)気にさせるもの, 誘引, 報酬 ‖ *The player was offered a car as an inducement to join the club.* その選手には, クラブに勧誘するために自動車が提供された.

**induction** /ɪnˈdʌkʃ(ə)n/ 名 ⓤ ⓒ ▶定義 the process of introducing sb to a new job, skill, organization, etc; an event at which this takes place ～を新しい仕事に就かせる・技能を手ほどきする・組織に入会させること; これが執り行われる行事→就任, 入会, 就任式, 入会式 ‖ *an induction day for new students* 新入生の初顔合わせの日

**indulge** /ɪnˈdʌldʒ/ 動 ▶定義 1 自 他 indulge (yourself) (in sth) to allow yourself to have or do sth for pleasure 楽しみのために, ～を手に入れる・行うことを自分に許す →(人が) (快楽などに)ふける, ～を欲しいままにする ‖ *I'm going to indulge myself and go shopping for some new clothes.* 私は自分の楽しみで, 新しい服の買い物に行きます. *Maria never indulges in gossip.* マリアは決してうわさ話にふけることはない. ▶定義 2 他 to give sb/sth what he/she/it wants or needs ～に対して, 欲しいもの・必要なものを与える→(人が) (子供などを)甘やかす, ～を思い通りにさせる ‖ *You shouldn't indulge that child. It will make him very selfish.* その子を甘やかしてはいけない. 自分勝手な子にしてしまうから. *At the weekends he indulges his passion for fishing.* 彼は週末になると心行くまで釣りをする.

**indulgence** /ɪnˈdʌldʒ(ə)ns/ 名 ▶定義 1 ⓤ the state of having or doing whatever you want 欲しい物は何でも手にすること, やりたい事は何でもすること→甘やかす[される]こと, 気まま, 放縦, (～への)甘やかし ‖ *to lead a life of indulgence* 気ままな生活を送る *Over-indulgence in chocolate makes you fat.* チョコレートを好きなだけ食べすぎると太る. ▶定義 2 ⓒ something that you have or do because it gives you pleasure 楽しみを与えてくれるために, 手に入れたり行ったりする事柄→楽しみ, 道楽, 耽溺(たんでき) ‖ *A cigar after dinner is my only indulgence.* 食後の一服が私の唯一のぜいたくです.

**indulgent** /ɪnˈdʌldʒ(ə)nt/ 形 ▶定義 allowing sb to have or do whatever he/she wants ～に好きな物を何でも手に入れさせる, 好きな事を何でもさせる→(～に)好きにさせる, 甘い, 寛大な ‖ *indulgent parents* 甘い両親 — **indulgently** 副→甘やかして, 寛大に

**\*industrial** /ɪnˈdʌstriəl/ 形 ▶定義 1 (名詞の前だけ) connected with industry 産業・工業に関係した→産業の, 工業の, 工業用の, 産業に従事する ‖ *industrial development* 産業の発達 *industrial workers* 産業労働者 ▶定義 2 having a lot of factories, etc 多くの工場などが立地する→産業が高度に発達した ‖ *an industrial region/country/town* 産業が発達した地域・国・町

**industrial action** 名 ⓤ ▶定義 action that workers take, especially stopping work, in order to protest about sth to their employers; a strike ～について雇用主に抗議するために労働者が取る行為で, 特に業務を停止すること; ストライキ→(ストライキなどの)労働者の示威運動, 争議行為 ‖ *to threaten (to take) industrial action* (ストライキ等の)示威行為に出ると脅す

**industrialist** /ɪnˈdʌstriəlɪst/ 名 ⓒ ▶定義 a person who owns or manages a large industrial company 大規模な製造企業を所有・経営する人→産業資本家, 企業経営者, 製造業者

**industrialize** (または **-ise**) /ɪnˈdʌstriəlaɪz/ 動 ⓤ ▶定義 to develop industries in a country 国の産業を発達させる→(国・地域などが[を])産業化・工業化する ‖ *Japan industrialized rapidly in the late nineteenth century.* 日本は19世紀後

半に急速に産業化した. —industrialization (または -isation) /-éɪʃ(ə)n/ 名 ❶→産業化, 工業化

**industrious** /ɪndʌ́striəs/ 形 ▶定義 always working hard いつも熱心に働く →勤勉な, よく働く

\***industry** /índəstri/ 名 (複 **industries**) ▶定義 1
❶ the production of goods in factories 工場で製品を生産すること→(工場での)生産・産業, (大規模な)工業, 製造業 ‖ *Is British industry being threatened by foreign imports?* イギリスの産業は, 海外からの輸入品に脅かされているのか. *heavy/light industry* 重・軽工業 ▶定義 2
❷ the people and activities involved in producing sth, providing a service, etc 〜の製造, サービスの提供などに関係する人・活動 →(産業部門の)〜業, 事業, 商売 ‖ *the tourist/catering/entertainment industry* 旅行・仕出し・娯楽業

**inedible** /ɪnédəb(ə)l/ 形 正式 ▶定義 not suitable to be eaten →食用に適さない ‖ *an inedible plant* 食用に適さない植物 ⇔ **edible**

**ineffective** /ìnɪféktɪv/ 形 ▶定義 not producing the effect or result that you want 望むような影響・結果を生じない →効果のない, 無駄な ⇔ **effective**

**inefficient** /ìnɪfíʃ(ə)nt/ 形 ▶定義 not working or producing results in the best way, so that time or money is wasted 最適な方法で働いたり結果を出したりしないので, 時間・お金を無駄にする →効率の悪い, 非能率な, (人が)役に立たない ‖ *Our heating system is very old and extremely inefficient.* 我々の暖房設備はとても古く, 非常に効率が悪い. *an inefficient secretary* 役に立たない秘書 ⇔ **efficient** — **inefficiency** /-(ə)nsi/ 名 ❶→非能率, 無能 — **inefficiently** 副 →非能率に

**ineligible** /ɪnélədʒəb(ə)l/ 形 ▶定義 ineligible (for/to do sth) without the necessary certificates, etc to do or get sth 〜を行う・手に入れるのに必要な免許状などを持たない →(〜の・〜する)資格がない, 不適格な ‖ *She was ineligible for the job because she wasn't a German citizen.* 彼女はドイツ国民ではないため, その仕事をする資格がなかった. ⇔ **eligible** — **ineligibility** /ɪnèlədʒəbíləti/ 名 ❶→不適格(であること), (選ばれる)資格のないこと

**inept** /ɪnépt/ 形 ▶定義 inept (at sth) not able to do sth well 〜をうまくやることができない→無能な, 下手な, 不適切な ‖ *She is totally inept at dealing with people.* 彼女は人の扱いが全く下手である. ⇔ **adept**

**inequality** /ìnɪkwáləti/ 名 ❷ ❶ (複 **inequalities**)
▶定義 (a) difference between groups in society because one has more money, advantages, etc than the other ある集団が他に比べて富裕である, 有利な立場にあるなどの理由で社会に存在する集団間の差異 →(富・地位などの)不平等, 不均衡, 不平等な事柄 ‖ *There will be problems as long as inequality between the races exists.* 人種間の不平等が存在する限りは, 問題はなくならないだろう. ⇔ **equality**

**inert** /ɪnə́ːrt/ 形 ▶定義 not able to move or act 動くことができない, 行動することができない→自力で動けない, 身動きできない

**inertia** /ɪnə́ːrʃ(i)ə/ 名 ❶ ▶定義 1 a lack of energy; an inability to move or change 活力不足; 動くことができないこと, 変わることができないこと→不活発, 無気力, 怠惰 ▶定義 2 the physical force that keeps things where they are or keeps them moving in the direction they are traveling 物体をそのままの位置に保ったり, 移動している方向そのままに動かしたりする物理的な力→慣性, 惰性

**inescapable** /ìnɪskéɪpəb(ə)l, -es-/ 形 正式
▶定義 that cannot be avoided 避けることができない→不可避の, 必然的な, 無視できない ‖ *an inescapable conclusion* 必然的な結論

**inevitable** /ɪnévətəb(ə)l/ 形 ▶定義 that cannot be avoided or prevented from happening 避けることができない, 発生を妨げることができない→避けられない, 必然的な, 当然の ‖ *With more cars on the road, traffic jams are inevitable.* 道路に自動車が増えては, 渋滞は避けられない. — the inevitable 名 [単数扱い] →避けられない物・事, 避けられない運命, 必然の運命 ‖ *They fought to save the firm from closure, but eventually had to accept the inevitable.* 彼らは会社を閉鎖から救おうと闘ったが, 結局避けられないものとして受け入れざるを得なかった. — **inevitability** /ɪnèvətəbíləti/ 名 ❶→不可避, 必然 — **inevitably** /-əbli/ 副 →必然的に, 必ず, 当然

**inexcusable** /ìnɪkskjúːzəb(ə)l/ 形 ▶定義 that cannot be allowed or forgiven 許されない, 勘弁されない→弁解の余地のない, 許し難い ‖ *Their* *behaviour was quite inexcusable.* 彼らの振る舞いは、全く許し難いものだった. ⇔ **excusable**

**inexhaustible** /ˌɪnɪɡzˈɔːstəb(ə)l/ 形 ▶定義 that cannot be finished or used up completely 使いきることができない，完全に使い果たすことができない→尽きない，無尽蔵の，枯渇することのない‖ *Our energy supplies are not inexhaustible.* エネルギーの供給は無尽蔵ではない.

**inexpensive** /ˌɪnɪkˈspensɪv/ 形 ▶定義 low in price→安価な，手ごろな値段の‖ *an inexpensive camping holiday* 手ごろな値段のキャンプで過ごす休暇 ☛類 **cheap** ⇔ **expensive** ─ inexpensively 副→安く，費用がかからずに

**inexperience** /ˌɪnɪkˈspɪəriəns/ 名 Ⓤ ▶定義 not knowing how to do sth because you have not done it before これまでに経験がないので，～をどのようにやったらよいのか分からない→経験のないこと，未熟，不慣れ‖ *The mistakes were all due to inexperience.* 間違いはすべて不慣れによるものだった. ⇔ **experience** ─ inexperienced 形→経験のない，未熟な，不慣れな‖ *He's too young and inexperienced to be given such responsibility.* 彼はそのような責任を与えるには、若くて経験がなさすぎる.

**inexplicable** /ˌɪnɪkˈsplɪkəb(ə)l, ɪnˈeksplɪkəb(ə)l/ 形 ▶定義 that cannot be explained 説明することができない→説明のつかない，不可解な‖ *Her sudden disappearance is quite inexplicable.* 彼女が急に姿を消したのは全く不可解だ. ⇔ **explicable** ─ inexplicably /-əb(ə)li/ 副→説明がつかないほどに，不可解なことに

**infallible** /ɪnˈfæləb(ə)l/ 形 ▶定義 **1** (used about a person) never making mistakes or being wrong (人について) 決して間違えることがない，または決して誤りを犯さない→(人・判断などが) 誤りを犯さない，間違いのない‖ *Even the most careful typist is not infallible.* 最も注意深いタイピストでも，間違えることもある.
 ▶定義 **2** always doing what you want it to do; never failing 常に思い通りに行ってくれる; 決して し損なうことがない→(方法などが) 絶対確実な，必ず効果のある‖ *No computer is infallible.* 絶対確実なコンピューターなどない. ⇔ **fallible** ─ infallibility /ɪnˌfæləˈbɪləti/ 名 Ⓤ→誤りを犯さないこと，絶対確実

**infamous** /ˈɪnfəməs/ 形 ▶定義 infamous (for sth) famous for being bad 悪いことで有名な→悪名高い，名うての，札付きの，不名誉な‖ *The area is infamous for drugs and crime.* その区域は，覚せい剤と犯罪で悪名高い. ☛類 **notorious** ☛参 **famous**

**infancy** /ˈɪnfənsi/ 名 Ⓤ ▶定義 the time when you are a baby or young child 赤ん坊の時代，幼年時代→幼時，幼年時代，初期段階‖ (比喩) *Research in this field is still in its infancy.* この分野の調査は、まだ始まったばかりだ.

**infant** /ˈɪnfənt/ 名 Ⓒ ▶定義 a baby or very young child 赤ん坊，幼児→幼児，小児，(4～7歳の) 児童‖ *There is a high rate of infant mortality (= many children die when they are still babies).* 幼児の死亡率は高い (= 多くの子供がまだ赤ん坊の時に死んでいる). *Mrs Davies teaches infants (= children aged between four and seven).* デーヴィス先生は児童 (4～7歳の子供) を教えている.

▶ baby, toddler, child の方が，口語・略式の英語では一般的.

**infantile** /ˈɪnfəntaɪl, -tl/ 形 ▶定義 (of behaviour) typical of, or connected with, a baby or very young child and therefore not appropriate for adults or older children (振る舞いが) 赤ん坊・幼児に特有なものであったり，それを連想させるものなので，大人や年齢の高い子供にはふさわしくない→幼児(期)の，子供っぽい，幼稚な‖ *infantile jokes* 子供染みた冗談

**infantry** /ˈɪnfəntri/ 名 [Ⓤ, 単数または複数形の動詞と共に] ▶定義 soldiers who fight on foot 徒歩で戦う兵士→歩兵隊‖ *The infantry was/were supported by heavy gunfire.* 歩兵隊は激しい砲撃に援護されていた.

**infant school** 名 Ⓒ ▶定義 a school for children between the ages of four and seven 4歳から7歳までの子供のための学校→匧 幼children学校

**infatuated** /ɪnˈfætʃueɪtɪd/ 形 ▶定義 infatuated (with sb/sth) having a very strong feeling of love or attraction for sb/sth that usually does not last long and makes you unable to think about anything else ～に対して一時的に非常に強く愛情を感じたり引き付けられたりして，ほかの事は何も考えられなくなる→(～に) 夢中になった，のぼせ上がった‖ *The young girl was infatuated with one of her teachers.* 若い女の子

は教師の1人に夢中になった. — infatuation /ɪnfætʃuéɪʃ(ə)n/ 名 ⓊⒸ (~に)夢中になること, うつつを抜かすこと, 心酔

\*infect /ɪnfékt/ 動他 ▶定義1 infect sb/sth (with sth) (通常は受動態で) to cause sb/sth to have a disease or illness ~が病気になる原因となる → (病気が)~に伝染する, (蚊, 人などが)~に病気を移す, ~を感染させる ‖ *We must clean the wound before it becomes infected.* 化膿(かのう)する前に傷を清潔にしなければならない. *Many thousands of people have been infected with the virus.* 何千もの多くの人々がウイルスに感染した. ▶定義2 to make people share a particular feeling or emotion 人々がある特定の感情や気持ちを分かち合うようにさせる → ~を感化する, ~に影響を及ぼす, ~を(思想などに)染まらせる ‖ *Paul's happiness infected the whole family.* ポールの幸せに, 家族全体が感化された.

\*infection /ɪnfékʃ(ə)n/ 名 ▶定義1 ❶ the act of becoming or making sb ill 病気になること, ~を病気にすること → (病気の)感染, 伝染, (空気や水による)感染 ‖ *A dirty water supply can be a source of infection.* 汚い水道水は, 感染原因になり得る. *There is a danger of infection.* 感染の危険がある. ▶定義2 ❷ a disease or illness that is caused by harmful bacteria, etc and affects one part of your body 有害なバクテリアなどが原因の病気で, 体の一部に影響を及ぼすもの → 伝染病 ‖ *She is suffering from a chest infection.* 彼女は胸部の伝染病にかかっている. *an ear infection* 耳の伝染病

▶ 伝染病は bacteria (バクテリア) や viruses (ウイルス) が原因になり得る. これらを指す略式な語は, germs (ばい菌)である.

\*infectious /ɪnfékʃəs/ 形 ▶定義 (used about a disease, illness, etc) that can be easily passed on to another person (病気・疾病などについて)他人に容易に移るもの → 伝染性の, 伝性病の, 伝染する ‖ *Flu is very infectious.* インフルエンザは非常に伝染しやすい. (比喩)*infectious laughter* 人に移る笑い

▶ infectious diseases は通常呼吸による空気感染である. contagious diseases は接触により感染する.

infer /ɪnfə́ːr/ 動他 (inferring; inferred) ▶定義 infer sth (from sth) to form an opinion or decide that sth is true from the information you 知り得た情報から考えをまとめたり, ~が本当であると判断する → ~を(…から)推論する, ~を判断する ‖ *I inferred from our conversation that he was unhappy with his job.* 我々が交わした会話から判断すると, 彼は仕事に不満なようだった. — inference 名 Ⓒ → 結論, 推定, 判断

inferior /ɪnfíəriər/ ▶定義 inferior (to sb/sth) low or lower in social position, importance, quality, etc 社会的な地位, 重要性, 質などにおいて低い, より低い → (~より)(質・価値などが)劣っている, 二流の ‖ *This material is obviously inferior to that one.* この素材は, 明らかにあちらの素材よりも質が悪い. *Don't let people make you feel inferior.* 自分の方が劣っていると他人に感じさせてはいけない. ⇔ **superior** — inferior 名 Ⓒ → 目下のもの, 後輩, 劣った人・物 ‖ *She always treats me as her intellectual inferior.* 彼女はいつも私を知的に劣っているように扱う. — inferiority /ɪnfìəriɔ́(ː)rəti, -ár-/ 名 Ⓤ → 劣っていること, 劣等, 下級

inferiority complex 名 Ⓒ ▶定義 the state of feeling less important, clever, successful, etc than other people ほかの人に比べて, 重要ではない・賢くない・成功していないなどと思う気持ち → 劣等感, コンプレックス

infertile /ɪnfə́ːrtaɪl; -tl/ 形 ▶定義1 (used about a person or animal) not able to have babies or produce young (人や動物について)子を産むことができない → 繁殖力のない, 生殖力のない, (卵が)無精の ▶定義2 (used about land) not able to grow strong healthy plants (土地について)強く健康な植物を生育することができない → (土地などが)肥沃(ひよく)でない, やせた, 不毛の ⇔ **fertile** — infertility /ɪnfərtíləti/ 名 Ⓤ → 繁殖力・生殖力のないこと, 不妊 ‖ *infertility treatment* 不妊治療 ⇔ **fertility**

infested /ɪnféstəd/ 形 ▶定義 infested (with sth) (used about a place) with large numbers of unpleasant animals or insects in it (場所について)嫌な動物・虫が多数いる → (~の)はびこる, 蔓延(まんえん)している ‖ *The warehouse was infested with rats.* 倉庫にはネズミがはびこっていた.

infidelity /ìnfədéləti, faɪ-/ 名 ⓊⒸ (複 infidelities) ▶定義 the act of not being faithful to your wife or husband by having a sexual relationship with sb else ほかのだれかと性的関係を持つことで, 妻・夫に対して誠実ではない行い➜**不義, 不貞** ☛ 略式な語は, unfaithfulness.

**infiltrate** /ínfıltrèıt/ [動][他] ▶定義 to enter an organization, etc secretly so that you can find out what it is doing 組織などに秘密裏に入り, その活動を知る➜**〜に潜入する, (人を) 〜に潜入させる** ‖ *The police managed to infiltrate the gang of terrorists.* 警察はテロリストの一味に何とか潜入できた. — infiltration /-éıʃ(ə)n/ [名] [C] [U] ➜ **潜入** — infiltrator [名] [C] ➜ **潜入者, 侵入者**

**infinite** /ínfənət/ [形] ▶定義1 very great 非常に大きい➜**無限の, 果てしない, 計り知れないほど大きい** ‖ *You need infinite patience for this job.* この仕事には, 相当の忍耐が要る. ▶定義2 without limits; that never ends 限界のない; 決して尽きることのない➜**無限の** ‖ *Supplies of oil are not infinite.* 石油の供給は無限ではない. ⇔ **finite**

**infinitely** /ínfənətli/ [副] ▶定義 very much 非常に ➜**大いに, はるかに, ずっと** ‖ *Compact discs sound infinitely better than audio cassettes.* コンパクトディスクは, 録音テープよりもはるかに音が良い.

**infinitive** /ınfínətıv/ [名] [C] (文法) ▶定義 the basic form of a verb 動詞の基本の形➜**不定詞**
➤英語では不定詞はその前に来るものによって to と共に使われる場合と, to なしで使われる場合がある: *He can sing.* (彼は歌うことができる.) *He wants to sing.* (彼は歌いたい.)

**infinity** /ınfínəti/ [名] ▶定義1 [U] space or time without end 終わりのない空間・時間➜**無限, 無限のかなた** ‖ (比喩) *The ocean seemed to stretch over the horizon into infinity.* 海は水平線のかなたに無限に広がっていくように見えた. ▶定義2 [U] [C] (記号 ∞) (in mathematics) the number that is larger than any other that you can think of (数学で) 考え得るどのような数よりも大きな数➜**無限大**

**infirmary** /ınfə́ːrm(ə)ri/ [名] [C] ([複] **infirmaries**) ▶定義 (used mainly in names) a hospital (主に名称に用いて) 病院➜**病院, (学校・工場・修道院・刑務所などの) 医務室, 保健室** ‖ *The Manchester Royal Infirmary* マンチェスター ロイヤル病院

**inflamed** /ınfléımd/ [形] ▶定義 (used about a part of the body) red and swollen or painful because of an infection or injury (体の一部について) 感染, または傷のために赤くはれ, 痛みがある➜**(身体の一部が) 赤くはれた, 炎症を起こした**

**inflammable** /ınflǽməb(ə)l/ [形] ▶定義 that burns easily 簡単に燃える➜**燃えやすい, 引火しやすい, 可燃性の** ‖ *Petrol is highly inflammable.* 石油は可燃性が高い. ☛参 **flammable**. 同義語であるが, 使用頻度は低い. ⇔ **non-flammable**

**inflammation** /ìnfləméıʃ(ə)n/ [名] [C] [U] ▶定義 a condition in which a part of the body becomes red, sore and swollen because of infection or injury 感染, または傷のために体の一部が赤くなり, ひりひりしてはれている状態➜**炎症**

**inflatable** /ınfléıtəb(ə)l/ [形] ▶定義 that can or must be filled with air 空気で満たすことができる, 満たさなくてはいけない➜**空気を入れて膨らませる, 膨らませて使う** ‖ *an inflatable dinghy/mattress* 空気で膨らませる救命ボート・マットレス

**inflate** /ınfléıt/ [動][自][他][正式] ▶定義 to fill sth with air; to become filled with air 〜を空気で満たす; 空気で一杯になる➜**(タイヤ・風船など) を (空気・ガスで) 膨らませる; 膨らむ** ☛ 略式な語は blow up. ⇔ **deflate**

***inflation** /ınfléıʃ(ə)n/ [名] [U] ▶定義 a general rise in prices; the rate at which prices rise 全般的に物価が上昇すること; 物価の上昇率➜**インフレーション, インフレ, 通貨膨張** ‖ *the inflation rate/rate of inflation* インフレ率 *Inflation now stands at 3%.* 現在のインフレ率は3パーセントである.

**inflection** (または **inflexion**) /ınflékʃ(ə)n/ [名] [C] [U] ▶定義1 (文法) a change in the form of a word, especially its ending, that changes its function in the grammar of the language, for example - ed, - est 言語の文法上の機能を変える語形変化で, 特に語尾の変化. 例: -ed, -est ➜ **屈折, 語形変化, 活用; 変化形, 屈折語尾** ▶定義2 the rise and fall of your voice when you are talking 話し声の上げ下げ➜**(声の) 抑揚, 音声の変化** ☛類 **intonation**

**inflexible** /ınfléksəb(ə)l/ [形] ▶定義1 that cannot be changed or made more suitable for a particular situation; rigid 変えられない, または特定の

## 874 inflict

状況に合わせてより適切なものにしていくことができない; 頑固な → (規則・決定などが) 曲げられない, (人・考え・意志などが) 確固とした, 不屈の, 融通の利かない ‖ *He has a very inflexible attitude to change.* 彼は変化に対して, 非常にかたくなな態度を取る. ▶定義2 (used about a material) not able to bend or be bent easily (材料について) 簡単には曲がらない, 曲げられない → **曲げられない, 堅い** ⇔ **flexible** — **inflexibly** /-əbli/ 副 不屈に, ひるまずに, 頑固に — **inflexibility** /ɪnfleksəbíləti/ 名 U 曲がらないこと, 不屈, 融通が利かないこと

**inflict** /ɪnflíkt/ 動他 ▶定義 inflict sth (on sb) to force sb to have sth unpleasant or that he/she does not want ~に不愉快な…・欲しない…を無理に押し付ける, 欲しくない~を無理に押し付ける → (~に) (苦痛・打撃・損害など) を与える, (世話など) を (人に) 押し付ける ‖ *Don't inflict your problems on me - I've got enough of my own.* 自分の問題を私に押し付けないでください — 私は自分の問題で手一杯なのです.

**in-flight** /ɪn fláɪt/ 形 (名詞の前だけ) ▶定義 happening or provided during a journey in a plane 飛行中に起きる, 飛行中に提供される → 飛行中の, 機内の ‖ *in-flight entertainment* 機内での娯楽

*__influence__*¹ /ínfluəns/ 名 ▶定義1 U C (an) influence (on/upon sb/sth) the power to affect, change or control sb/sth ~に影響を与える, 変える, 支配する力 → (~に対する) 影響, 作用 ‖ *Television can have a strong influence on children.* テレビは子供に強い影響を与え得る. *Nobody should drive while they are **under the influence of** alcohol.* お酒の影響がある間は運転すべきではない. ▶定義2 C **an influence (on sb/sth)** a person or thing that affects or changes sb/sth ~に影響を与えたり, 変える人または物 → (~に) 影響を及ぼすもの・人, 勢力者, 有力者 ‖ *His new girlfriend has been a good influence on him.* 彼の新しいガールフレンドは, 彼に良い影響を与えている. *cultural/environmental influences* 文化的・環境的影響

**influence**² /ínfluəns/ 動他 ▶定義 to have an effect on or power over sb/sth so that he/she/it changes ~に効果・支配力を及ぼし, その結果, …が変わる → ~に影響を及ぼす, ~を感化する ‖ *You must decide for yourself. Don't let anyone else influence you.* 自分自身で決めなくてはならない. 他人に左右されないようにしなさい. *Her style of painting has been influenced by Japanese art.* 彼女の画法は日本美術の影響を受けている.

▶ affect と influence は意味的に非常に似通っていることが多い. affect は通常, 物質的な変化について用いられ, 一方 influence は意見や態度の変化を表すのに多く用いられる: *Drinking alcohol can affect your ability to drive.* (飲酒が車の運転に影響を及ぼし得る.) *TV advertisements have influenced my attitude towards the homeless.* (テレビの広告は, ホームレスに対する私の態度に影響を与えた.)

**influential** /ɪnfluénʃ(ə)l/ 形 ▶定義 influential (in sth/in doing sth) having power or influence 力, または影響力がある → (~することに) 影響力を持った, 有力な, 勢力のある ‖ *an influential politician* 有力な政治家 *He was influential in getting the hostages set free.* 彼は人質の解放に重要な役割を果たした.

**influenza** /ɪnfluénzə/ 正式 = **FLU**

**influx** /ínflʌks/ 名 [C, 通常は単数] ▶定義 **an influx (of sb/sth) (into…)** large numbers of people or things arriving suddenly たくさんの人々・物事が突然やって来ること (人・物の) (~への) 流入, 殺到, 到来 ‖ *the summer influx of visitors from abroad* 夏になると海外から殺到する観光客

*__inform__* /ɪnfɔ́ːm/ 動他 ▶定義 inform sb (of/about sth) to give sb information (about sth), especially in an official way 特に公的な方法で, ~に (…に関する) 情報を与える → ~に (…を) 通知する, ~に知らせる, ~に伝える ‖ *You should inform the police of the accident.* その事故について警察に通報すべきだ. *Do **keep me informed** of any changes.* どのような変更も, 必ず私に知らせてください.

句動詞 **inform on sb** ▶定義 to give information to the police, etc about what sb has done wrong 警察などに, ~の悪事について情報を提供する → (人) について (警察などに) 密告する, 告げる ‖ *The wife of the killer informed on her husband.* 殺人者の妻は, 夫を密告した.

*__informal__* /ɪnfɔ́ːm(ə)l/ 形 ▶定義 relaxed and

friendly or suitable for a relaxed occasion くつろいでいて親しみのある，くつろいだ場にふさわしい→**非公式の，略式の，形式張らない，打ち解けた** ‖ *Don't get dressed up for the party - it'll be very informal.* パーティーには正装しないで来てください － とても略式のものですから．*The two leaders had informal discussions before the conference began.* 2人の指導者は，会議の前に非公式の話し合いを持った．⇔ **formal** ☛ この辞書の語・表現の中には，略式 と説明されているものがある．これらは，友人やよく知っている人と話す場合には用いることができるが，書物や公式な手紙などでは使うべきではない． ― **informality** /ˌɪnfɔːˈmæləti/ 名 Ｕ →**親しみやすさ，気安さ，気楽さ** ‖ *an atmosphere of informality* 打ち解けた雰囲気 ― **informally** 副 →**気安く，親しみやすく，非公式に** ‖ *I was told informally (= unofficially) that our plans had been accepted.* 我々の案が受け入れられたことを非公式に知らされた．

**informant** /ɪnˈfɔːmənt/ 名 Ｃ ▶定義 a person who gives secret knowledge or information about sb/sth to the police or a newspaper 〜についての秘密の知識や情報を，警察・新聞に提供する人→**情報提供者，内通者，密告者**‖ *The journalist refused to name his informant.* その新聞記者は，情報提供者の名を明かすことを拒んだ． ☛参 **informer**

\***information** /ˌɪnfəˈmeɪʃ(ə)n/ 名 Ｕ ▶定義 information (on/about sb/sth) knowledge or facts 知識，事実→**（〜に関する）情報，ニュース，消息，資料**‖ *For further information please send for our fact sheet.* さらに詳しい情報を知りたい方は，概況報告書をお取り寄せください．*Can you give me some information about evening classes in Italian, please?* イタリア語の夜間のクラスについて，何か情報を教えてくれませんか．

▶ information は不可算名詞なので，I need an information. と言うことはできない．しかし，a bit of information または a piece of information という使い方はできる．

▶語法

information は不可算名詞

informationは不可算(uncountable)名詞なので，*a lot of informations とは言えません．

あえて数える必要があるときは，piece を用います．同様に *a lot of advices も誤りです．furniture（家具）も不可算名詞なので，数えるときは a piece of furniture となります．

**information technology** 名 Ｕ （略 **IT**） ▶定義 (computing) the study or use of electronic equipment, especially computers, for collecting, storing and sending out information （コンピューター）電子機器，特にコンピューターを使った情報の収集・保存・発信に関する研究や実用→**情報工学**

**informative** /ɪnˈfɔːmətɪv/ 形 ▶定義 giving useful knowledge or information 役に立つ知識・情報を与える→**情報を提供する，有益な**

**informed** /ɪnˈfɔːmd/ 形 ▶定義 having knowledge or information about sth 〜に関する知識・情報を持っている→**知識のある，（〜に）詳しい，情報に通じている；情報に基づいた**‖ *Consumers cannot make informed choices unless they are told all the facts.* 消費者は，事実をすべて知らされていない限りは，情報に基づいた選択はできない．

**informer** /ɪnˈfɔːmə/ 名 Ｃ ▶定義 a criminal who gives the police information about other criminals ほかの犯罪者に関する情報を警察に提供する犯罪者→**密告者，内通者** ☛参 **informant**

**infrequent** /ɪnˈfriːkwənt/ 形 ▶定義 not happening often あまり度々は起こらない→**めったにない，たまの，まれな** ⇔ **frequent** ― **infrequently** 副 →**たまに，まれに，珍しく**

**infringe** /ɪnˈfrɪndʒ/ 動 正式 ▶定義 **1** 他 to break a rule, law, agreement, etc 規則，法律，契約などを破る→**(法律・規則など)を破る，犯す**‖ *The material can be copied without infringing copyright.* 著作権を侵害せずに，その資料をコピーできる．▶定義 **2** 自 infringe on/upon sth to reduce or limit sb's rights, freedom, etc 〜の権利・自由などを抑制する，制限する→**（権利などを）侵害する**‖ *She refused to answer questions that infringed on her private affairs.* 彼女は私事を侵害する質問には，返答を拒否した． ― **infringement** 名 Ｃ Ｕ →**(法律・規則などの)違反，(権利などの)侵害**

**infuriate** /ɪnˈfjʊərieɪt/ 動 他 ▶定義 to make sb

very angry ~を非常に怒らせる→~を激怒させる, 憤慨させる — infuriating 形→(人を)激怒させるような, 憤慨させるような ‖ *an infuriating habit* 人を怒らせる癖 — infuriatingly 副→激怒させるほど, 腹立たしいことに

**ingenious** /ɪnˈdʒiːnjəs/ 形 ▶定義1 (used about a thing or an idea) made or planned in a clever way (物・考えについて) 巧妙に作られて, 計画されて→(考え・装置などが) 巧妙な, 精巧な, 工夫に富む ‖ *an ingenious plan for making lots of money* 多額のお金をもうけるための巧妙な計画 *an ingenious device/experiment/invention* 精巧な装置・実験・発明品 ▶定義2 (used about a person) full of new ideas and clever at finding solutions to problems or at inventing things (人について) 新しい考えに満ちあふれていて, 問題の解決策を見つけるのがうまい, または物を発明することにたけている→(人が) 利口な, 器用な, 発明の才のある — ingeniously 副→巧妙に, 巧みに, 才気に富んで — ingenuity /ˌɪndʒəˈn(j)uːəti/ 名 Ｕ→発明の才, 創意, 独創性

**ingrained** /ɪnˈɡreɪnd/ 形 ▶定義 ingrained (in sb/sth) (used about a habit, an attitude, etc) that has existed for a long time and is therefore difficult to change (習慣・態度などについて) 長い間存在していて, それ故変えることが難しい→根強い, (~に) 深く染み込んだ, 容易に変わらない ‖ *ingrained prejudices/beliefs* 根強い偏見・信仰

**ingratiate** /ɪnˈɡreɪʃieɪt/ 動他 正式 ▶定義 ingratiate yourself (with sb) to make yourself liked by doing or saying things that will please people, especially people who might be useful to you 人, 特に自分にとって役に立つ人を喜ばせるような事を言ったり行ったりすることにより, その人に好かれようとする→~に取り入る, ~のご機嫌を取る ‖ *He was always trying to ingratiate himself with his teachers.* 彼はいつも教師に取り入ろうとしていた. — ingratiating 形→ご機嫌取りの, へつらいの, 愛想の良い ‖ *an ingratiating smile* 愛想笑い — ingratiatingly 副→ご機嫌を取るように, 取り入るように

**ingratitude** /ɪnˈɡrætət(j)uːd/ 名 Ｕ 正式 ▶定義 the state of not showing or feeling thanks for sth that has been done for you; not being grateful 自分のためになされた~に対して感謝の気持ちがない様子, 感謝を示さない様子; 感謝しないこと→感謝しないこと, 恩知らず ☞ 略式な語は ungratefulness. ⇔ **gratitude**

**ingredient** /ɪnˈɡriːdiənt/ 名 Ｃ ▶定義1 one of the items of food you need to make sth to eat 食べ物を作るのに必要な食材の1つ→(料理などの) 原料, 材料, 食材, 成分 ‖ *Mix all the ingredients together in a bowl.* 材料を全部, ボールで混ぜてください. ▶定義2 one of the qualities necessary to make sth successful ~を成功させるのに必要な特性の1つ→構成要素, 要因 ‖ *The film has all the ingredients of success.* その映画には, 成功する要因がすべて入っている.

***inhabit** /ɪnˈhæbət/ 動他 ▶定義 to live in a place ある場所に住む→(動物・人間が)(集団的に) ~に住む, 生息する ‖ *Are the Aran Islands still inhabited (= do people live there)?* アラン諸島にはまだ人が住んでいますか (= 人々がそこに住んでいますか).

**inhabitant** /ɪnˈhæbətənt/ 名 [Ｃ, 通常は複数] ▶定義 a person or animal that lives in a place ある場所に住む人・動物→住民, 定住者, 生息動物 ‖ *The local inhabitants protested at the plans for a new motorway.* 地元住民は, 新しい高速道路の計画に抗議した. ☞ ある特定の地域にどれくらいの人が住んでいるのか尋ねる場合は, 'What is the population of...?' (~の人口はどれくらいですか.) のように言い, 'How many inhabitants are there in...?' のようには言わない. しかし答えについては, 以下の2つの文を使うことができる. 'The population is 10000.' または 'It has 10000 inhabitants.' (人口は1万人です.)

**inhale** /ɪnˈheɪl/ 動自他 ▶定義 to breathe in→(息, 煙などを) 吸い込む, ~を吸入する ‖ *Be careful not to inhale the fumes from the paint.* ペンキのにおいを吸い込まないように注意してください. ⇔ **exhale**

**inherent** /ɪnˈhɪərənt/ 形 ▶定義 inherent (in sb/sth) that is a basic or permanent part of sb/sth and that cannot be removed ~に備わった基本的で不変な部分で, 取り除くことができない→(性質などが)(~に) 本来備わっている, 内在する, 固有の ‖ *The risk of collapse is inherent in any business.* どんな事業でも, 失敗する危険性はある. — inherently 副→本質的に, 生まれつき, 生来 ‖ *No matter how safe we make them, cars* *are inherently dangerous.* どんなに安全に作ろうとも、自動車は本質的に危険なものである.

**inherit** /ɪnhérət/ 動 他 inherit sth (from sb) ▶定義1 to receive property, money, etc from sb who has died 死亡した人から,財産・金銭などを受ける→(人から)(財産・地位などを)相続する,〜を受け継ぐ ‖ *I inherited quite a lot of money from my mother. She left me $12000 when she died.* 私は非常にばく大なお金を母から相続した. 母は亡くなった時に12000ドルを私に残した.

▶人から相続する人は,その人の heir (相続人) である.

▶定義2 to receive a quality, characteristic, etc from your parents or family 両親・家族から特質や性格などを受け継ぐ→(性格・体質など)を受け継ぐ; 受け継いだ性質, 遺伝 ‖ *She has inherited her father's gift for languages.* 彼女は父親の語学の才能を受け継いだ.

**inheritance** /ɪnhérətəns/ 名 C U ▶定義 the act of inheriting; the money, property, etc that you inherit 相続すること; 相続した金銭・財産など→相続, 相続財産, 遺産 ‖ *inheritance tax* 相続税

**inhibit** /ɪnhíbət/ 動 他 ▶定義1 to prevent sth or make sth happen more slowly 〜を妨げる,〜がもっとゆっくりと起きるようにする→〜を抑制する, 抑圧する, 妨げる ‖ *a drug to inhibit the growth of tumours* 腫瘍(しゅよう)の拡大を抑制する薬 ▶定義2 inhibit sb (from sth/from doing sth) to make sb nervous and embarrassed so that he/she is unable to do sth 〜を緊張させ, 当惑させることで, …をできなくする→(人に)(〜を)させない, (人が)(〜するのを)妨げる ‖ *The fact that her boss was there inhibited her from saying what she really felt.* 上司がそこにいたために,彼女は本音が言えなかった.

— inhibited 形→ 抑制された, 引っ込み思案な, 気後れした ‖ *The young man felt shy and inhibited in the roomful of women.* 若い男性は,部屋一杯の女性に恥ずかしくなり, 気後れしていた.

⇔ **uninhibited**

**inhibition** /ìn(h)əbíʃ(ə)n/ 名 C U ▶定義 a shy or nervous feeling that stops you from saying or doing what you really want 内気・緊張感で, 本当にしたい事をし, 言いたい事を言うことが妨げられること→抑制, 心理的抑圧, 気後れ, ためらい ‖ *After the first day of the course, people started to lose their inhibitions.* そのコースの初日が終わると,参加者は緊張感から解放され始めた.

**inhospitable** /ìnhɑ́spɪtəb(ə)l/ 形 ▶定義1 (used about a place) not pleasant to live in, especially because of the weather (場所について)(特に天候が理由で)住み心地の良くない→(土地などが)雨風を避ける所もない, 住みにくい, 荒れ果てた ‖ *the inhospitable Arctic regions* 吹きさらしの北極地方 ▶定義2 (used about a person) not friendly or welcoming to guests (人について)客に対して親しみがない, 歓迎しない→もてなしの悪い, 無愛想な, 不親切な ⇔ **hospitable**

**inhuman** /ɪnhjúːmən/ 形 ▶定義1 very cruel and without pity 非常に冷酷で, 同情のかけらもない→残忍な, 冷酷な, 非人間的な ‖ *inhuman treatment/conditions* 非人間的な扱い・状況 ▶定義2 not seeming to be human and therefore frightening 人間とは思えず, そのためにぎょっとさせるような→超人的な, 怪物的な ‖ *an inhuman noise* 人間のものとは思えない物音

**inhumane** /ìnhjuːméɪn/ 形 ▶定義 very cruel; not caring if people or animals suffer 非常に冷酷な; 人・動物が苦しんでも気にしない→非人道的な, 残酷な ‖ *the inhumane conditions in which animals are kept on some large farms* いくつかの大規模農場で動物が飼われている, 非人道的な状況 ⇔ **humane**

**inhumanity** /ìnhjuːmǽnəti/ 名 U ▶定義 very cruel behaviour とても冷酷な振る舞い→残忍さ, 非人間性 ‖ *The twentieth century is full of examples of man's inhumanity to man.* 20世紀は,人間が人間に対して与えた残忍さの実例に満ちている. ⇔ **humanity**

\*__initial__¹ /ɪníʃ(ə)l/ 形 (名詞の前だけ) ▶定義 happening at the beginning; first → 初めに起こった; 最初の ‖ *My initial reaction was to refuse, but I later changed my mind.* 私の最初の反応は拒否だったが, 後で考えを変えた. *the initial stages of our survey* 我々の調査の初期段階

\*__initial__² /ɪníʃ(ə)l/ 名 [C, 通常は複数] ▶定義 the first letter of a name 名前の最初の文字→(姓名・名称の)イニシャル・頭文字; (語頭の)頭文字 ‖ *Alison Elizabeth Waters' initials are A.E.W.* Alison Elizabeth Waters の頭文字は A.E.W.

です.

**initial**³ /ɪnɪ́ʃ(ə)l/ 動他 (**initialling**; **initialled**: 米 **initialing**; **initialed**) ▶定義 to mark or sign sth with your initials ～に頭文字で印を付ける・署名をする➔(承認などの印に)(公文書など)に頭文字で署名する, ～に頭文字を書く ‖ *Any changes made when writing a cheque should be initialled by you.* 小切手を書くときに変更がある場合は, どの変更箇所にもご本人が頭文字で署名をしなければなりません.

**initially** /ɪnɪ́ʃəli/ 副 ▶定義 at the beginning; at first ➔初めに; 最初は ‖ *I liked the job initially but it soon got quite boring.* 最初はその仕事が好きだったが, すぐにとても退屈になった.

**initiate** /ɪnɪ́ʃièɪt/ 動他 ▶定義1 正式 to start sth ～を始める ➔(計画・事業など)を開始する, ～に着手する ‖ *to initiate peace talks* 和平協議を開始する ▶定義2 initiate sb (into sth) to explain sth to sb or make him/her experience sth for the first time ～を…に説明する, 人に～を初めて経験させる ➔～に(秘伝・技術などの)手ほどきをする, ～に伝授する ‖ *I wasn't initiated into the joys of skiing until I was 30.* 私は30歳になるまで, スキーの楽しみについて手ほどきを受けたことがなかった. ▶定義3 initiate sb (into sth) to bring sb into a group by means of a special ceremony 特別な儀式をして, ～をグループに入れる➔～を(…に)入会させる, ～を加入させる ‖ *to initiate sb into a secret society* ～を秘密結社に入れる — **initiation** /-éɪʃ(ə)n/ 名 U ➔開始, 着手, 手ほどき, 伝授, 加入 ‖ *All the new students had to go through a strange initiation ceremony.* 新入生は全員, 奇妙な入会の儀式[入会式・通過儀礼]を経験しなければならなかった.

*****initiative** /ɪnɪ́ʃ(i)ətɪv/ 名 ▶定義1 C official action that is taken to solve a problem or improve a situation 問題解決や状況の改善のために取られる, 公の行動➔主導権, イニシアチブ ‖ *a new government initiative to help people start small businesses* 小企業の起業を援助する, 新政府のイニシアチブ ▶定義2 U the ability to see and do what is necessary without waiting for sb to tell you 人に言われなくても, 何が必要とされているのかを見極め実行する能力➔独創力, 実行力, 進取の精神, (判断・決定を下す)能力 ‖ *Don't keep asking me how to do it. Use your initiative.* どうしたらよいかをいちいち聞くな. 自分で判断しなさい. ▶定義3 **the initiative** [単数扱い] the stronger position because you have done sth first; the advantage ～を最初にやったことで得た, 他人より強い立場; 利点➔主導権, イニシアチブ ‖ *The enemy forces have lost the initiative.* 敵の軍隊は, 主導権を失った.

成句 **on your own initiative** ▶定義 without being told by sb else what to do ほかの人に何をするかを言われなくても➔自発的に, 率先して **take the initiative** ▶定義 to be first to act to influence a situation 最初に行動をして, 状況に影響を及ぼす➔(～を)先導する, 率先してやる, (～に)先手を打つ, イニシアチブを取る ‖ *Let's take the initiative and start organizing things now.* イニシアチブを取り, 今すぐに物事を取りまとめよう.

*****inject** /ɪndʒékt/ 動他 ▶定義1 to put a drug under the skin of person's or an animal's body with a needle (**syringe**) 針(注射器)で, 人・動物の身体の皮下に薬を注入する➔(薬などを)(人・身体の部分に)注射する, ～に注入する ▶定義2 inject sth (into sth) to add sth ～を追加する➔(金・設備)を(～に)つぎ込む, ～に投入する ‖ *They injected a lot of money into the business.* 彼らは事業に多額の金をつぎ込んだ.

*****injection** /ɪndʒékʃ(ə)n/ 名 ▶定義1 C U (an) injection (of sth) (into sb/sth) the act of putting a drug or substance under the skin of a person's or an animal's body with a needle (**syringe**) 針(注射器)で, 人・動物の身体の皮下に薬・物質を入れる行為➔注射, 浣腸(かんちょう) ‖ *to give sb an injection* ～に注射をする *a tetanus injection* 破傷風の注射 *An anaesthetic was administered by injection.* 麻酔薬は注射で入れられた. ◂類 **jab** ▶定義2 C a large amount of sth that is added to sth to help it ～を助けるために追加されるばく大な…➔(資本などの)投入, 導入 ‖ *The theatre needs a huge cash injection if it is to stay open.* 劇場の存続のためにはばく大な資金の投入が必要だ. ▶定義3 U C the act of forcing liquid into sth 液体を～に流し込む行為➔(～への)注入 ‖ *fuel injection* 燃料の注入

**injunction** /ɪndʒʌ́ŋ(k)ʃ(ə)n/ 名 C ▶定義 an

**injunction (against sb)** an official order from a court of law to do/not do sth ～をするように、またはしないようにという裁判所からの公式な命令→(公式的)命令,指令,(裁判所の)差止命令,履行命令 ‖ *A court injunction prevented the programme from being shown on TV.* 裁判所の差止命令により,その番組はテレビで放映されないことになった.

*★**injure** /índʒər/ 動他 ▶定義 to harm or hurt yourself or sb else physically, especially in an accident 自分自身、または他人を肉体的に害し傷付ける(特に事故で)→(人・身体・動物など)を傷付ける、～にけがをさせる、～を痛める ‖ *The goalkeeper seriously injured himself when he hit the goalpost.* ゴールキーパーは、ゴールポストにぶつかった際に重傷を負った. *She fell and injured her back.* 彼女は転倒して,背中を痛めた. ☞参 hurt の注

★**injured** /índʒərd/ 形 ▶定義 **1** physically or mentally hurt 肉体的、または精神的に傷付いた→負傷した, けがをした, (感情・名誉などが)傷付けられた ‖ *an injured arm/leg* 負傷した腕・足 *injured pride* 傷付けられた自尊心 ▶定義 **2 the injured** 名 [複数扱い] people who have been hurt 傷付いた人々→負傷者, けが人 ‖ *The injured were rushed to hospital.* 負傷者たちは,病院に急送された.

★**injury** /índʒ(ə)ri/ 名 Ⓒ Ⓤ (覆 **injuries**) ▶定義 **injury (to sb/sth)** harm done to a person's or an animal's body, especially in an accident 人・動物の身体に付けられた傷 (特に事故で)→(～への)負傷, 障害, 損害, 損傷 ‖ *They escaped from the accident with only **minor injuries**.* 彼らは軽傷を負っただけで,事故から逃れた. *Injury to the head can be extremely dangerous.* 頭部への損傷は,非常に危険だ.

**injury time** 名 Ⓤ 英 ▶定義 time that is added to the end of a rugby, football, etc match when there has been time lost because of injuries to players 選手のけがのために時間が使われた場合に、ラグビー・サッカーなどの試合の最後に追加される時間→(サッカー)ロスタイム, (ラグビー)インジャリータイム

**injustice** /ɪndʒʌ́stəs/ 名 Ⓤ Ⓒ ▶定義 the fact of a situation being unfair; an unfair act 状況が不公平だという事実; 不正な行為→不正, 不公平 ‖ *racial/social injustice* 人種的不公平・社会的不正 *People are protesting about the injustice of the new tax.* 人々は, 新しい税金が不公平であると抗議している.

成句 **do sb an injustice** ▶定義 to judge sb unfairly ～を不正に判断する→～を不当に扱う, ～を誤解する ‖ *I'm afraid I've done you both an injustice.* 君たちを2人とも誤解していたのではないかと思う.

★**ink** /ɪŋk/ 名 Ⓤ Ⓒ ▶定義 coloured liquid that is used for writing, drawing, etc 色付きの液体で, 字を書いたり絵をかいたりするときなどに使われる→インク ‖ *Please write **in ink**, not pencil.* 鉛筆ではなく、インクで書いてください.

**inkling** /íŋklɪŋ/ 名 [通常は単数] ▶定義 **an inkling (of sth/that…)** a slight feeling (about sth) (～に関する)かすかな感じ→(～を・～ということを)薄々感付いていること, おぼろげな見当 ‖ *I had an inkling that something was wrong.* 調子が悪いということは、薄々感付いていた.

**inky** /íŋki/ 形 ▶定義 made black with ink; very dark インクで黒くした; とても暗い→インクで染まった・汚れた, 真っ黒な, 真っ暗な ‖ *inky fingers* インクで汚れた指 *an inky night sky* 真っ暗な夜の空

**inland** /ínlænd, -lənd/ 形 副 ▶定義 away from the coast or borders of a country 沿岸・国境から離れて→沿岸・国境から離れた, 内陸・奥地の; 沿岸・国境から離れた所で[で], 内陸に[へ], 奥地に[へ] ‖ *The village lies twenty miles inland.* その村は、沿岸から20マイル離れた所にあります. *Goods are carried inland along narrow mountain roads.* 品物は狭い山道を通って、内陸に運ばれる.

**Inland Revenue** 名 [単数扱い] 英 ▶定義 the government department that collects taxes 税金を徴収する政府の部局→英国国税庁

**in-laws** 名 [複数扱い] 略式 ▶定義 your husband's or wife's mother and father or other relations 夫・妻の両親や親戚(しんせき)→義理の父母, 姻戚(いんせき) ‖ *My in-laws are coming to lunch on Sunday.* 義理の父母が日曜日の昼食に来る.

**inmate** /ínmeɪt/ 名 Ⓒ ▶定義 one of the people living in an institution such as a prison 刑務所などの施設に住んでいる人の1人→囚人, (精神病

院の)収容者, 入院患者

**inn** /ín/ 名 C 因 ▶定義 a small hotel or old pub usually in the country 大抵は田舎にある小さなホテル・古い居酒屋 → 宿屋, 小旅館, 居酒屋, 酒場

**innate** /ɪnéɪt, ‑/ 形 ▶定義 (used about an ability or quality) that you have when you are born (能力・性質などについて) 生まれつき持っている → (性格などが) 生まれつきの, 生来の, 天性の ‖ the innate ability to learn 生来の学習能力

\***inner** /ínər/ 形 (名詞の前だけ) ▶定義 1 (of the) inside; towards or close to the centre of a place 内側の; 場の中心に近い・向いている → 内部の, 内側の, 奥の ‖ The inner ear is very delicate. 内耳 (ないじ) はとても傷付きやすい. an inner courtyard 中庭 ⇔ outer ▶定義 2 (used about a feeling, etc) that you do not express or show to other people; private (感情などについて) 他人には表現しない・見せない; 秘密の → 内に秘めた, 内面の, 精神の ‖ Everyone has inner doubts. だれもが心の底では疑っている.

**inner city** 名 C ▶定義 the poor parts of a large city, near the centre, that often have a lot of social problems 大都市の中心近くにある貧困地域で, 多くの社会問題を抱えていることが多い → 都心 (部); (都市の) 過密地帯, スラム街 ― inner-city 形 (名詞の前だけ) → 都心 (部) の, スラム街の ‖ Inner-city schools often have difficulty in attracting good teachers. スラム街の学校では, 良い教師を集めるのに苦労することが多い.

**innermost** /ínərmòʊst/ 形 (名詞の前だけ) ▶定義 1 (used about a feeling or thought) most secret or private (感情・考えについて) 一番秘密にしている, 最も内密な → 心の奥底の, 心に秘めた ‖ She never told anyone her innermost thoughts. 彼女は心に秘めた思いについて, 決してだれにも話さなかった. ▶定義 2 nearest to the centre or inside of sth 中心に最も近い, ～の内側の → 最も内部の, 一番奥の ‖ the innermost shrine of the temple 神殿の一番奥の聖堂

**innings** /íniŋz/ 名 C ( 複 innings) ▶定義 a period of time in a game of cricket when it is the turn of one player or team to hit the ball (to bat) クリケットのゲームで, 1 人の選手や一方のチームがボールを打つ (打席に立つ) 順番・

回 → 攻撃回, (打者の) 打ち番, イニング

\***innocence** /ínəsns/ 名 U ▶定義 1 the fact of not being guilty of a crime, etc 罪を犯していないという事実 → 無罪の, 潔白な, (罪を) 犯していない ‖ The accused man **protested** his **innocence** throughout his trial. 被告人は裁判の間ずっと無実を訴えていた. ⇔ guilt ▶定義 2 lack of knowledge and experience of the world, especially of bad things 世間に対する, 特に悪い事に関する知識と経験がないこと → 無邪気, 天真爛漫 (らんまん), 無知 ‖ the innocence of childhood 無邪気な子供時代

\***innocent** /ínəsnt/ 形 ▶定義 1 innocent (of sth) not having done wrong 悪い事をしていない → 無罪の, 潔白な, (罪を) 犯していない ‖ An innocent man was arrested by mistake. 無実の男が誤って逮捕された. to be innocent of a crime ある罪を犯していない ● 類 blameless ⇔ guilty ▶定義 2 (名詞の前だけ) being hurt or killed in a crime, war, etc although not involved in it in any way 全く関係のない犯罪, 戦争などで傷付いたり殺された → (人が) 巻き添えを食った ‖ innocent victims of a bomb blast 爆弾の爆発の巻き添えになった犠牲者 an innocent bystander 事件とは何のかかわりもない見物人 ▶定義 3 not wanting to cause harm or upset sb, although it does そのつもりはないのだが, ～に害を与えたり不快な思いにさせる → 悪意のない, 悪気のない ‖ He got very aggressive when I asked an **innocent question** about his past life. 彼の過去について悪意のない質問をしたところ, 彼は非常に攻撃的になった. ▶定義 4 not knowing the bad things in life; believing everything you are told 人生の悪い面について何も知らない; 聞いた事はすべて信じてしまう → 無邪気な, 天真爛漫 (らんまん) な; 無知な, おめでたい ‖ She was so innocent as to believe that politicians never lie. 彼女はとても単純で, 政治家は決してうそをつかないと信じていた. ● 類 naive ― **innocently** 副 → 無邪気に, 何の悪気もなく, 何くわぬ顔で ‖ 'What are you doing here?' she asked innocently (= pretending she did not know the answer). 「ここで何をしているの」と, 彼女はとぼけて (= 答えが分からない振りをして) 尋ねた.

**innocuous** /ɪnɑ́kjuəs/ 形 正式 ▶定義 not meant to cause harm or upset sb ～に害を及ぼした

り，不愉快にさせるつもりのない➜(言動などが)当り障りのない，無難な，害のない ‖ *I made an **innocuous remark** about teachers and she got really angry.* 私は教師たちについて当り障りのない意見を言ったのだが，彼女は本当に怒ってしまった．☛類 **harmless** — **innocuously** [副] ➜無害に，(言動が)当り障りなく

**innovate** /ínəvèɪt/ [動][自] ▶定義 to create new things, ideas or ways of doing sth 新しい物・考え・～のやり方を創り出す➜刷新する，変革する，新しいものを導入する — **innovation** /ìnəvéɪʃ(ə)n/ [名] [C][U] (an) innovation (in sth)➜新しいものの導入，刷新，革新 ‖ *technological innovations in industry* 産業界における技術革新 — **innovative** /ínəvèɪtɪv/ [形] ➜独創的な，画期的な ‖ *innovative methods/designs/products* 独創的な方法・デザイン・製品 — **innovator** [名] [C]➜革新者，刷新者

**innuendo** /ìnjuéndoʊ/ [名] [C][U] ([複] **innuendoes** または **innuendos**) ▶定義 an indirect way of talking about sb/sth, usually suggesting sth bad or rude ～について間接的な表現で話すことで，通常は悪い事や無礼な事をそれとなくほのめかすこと➜ほのめかし，当てこすり，皮肉 ‖ *His speech was full of sexual innuendo.* 彼の話す事は，性的なほのめかしで一杯だった．

**innumerable** /ɪn(j)úːm(ə)rəb(ə)l/ [形] ▶定義 too many to be counted 多すぎて数えられない➜無数の，数えきれない

**inoculate** /ɪnákjəlèɪt/ [動][他] ▶定義 inoculate sb (against sth) to protect a person or animal from a disease by giving him/her/it a mild form of the disease with a needle which is put under the skin (an injection) 人・動物を病気から守るために，その病気を軽くしたものを針で皮下に入れる(注射する)➜～に(…の)予防接種(注射)をする ‖ *The children have been inoculated against tetanus.* 子供たちは破傷風の予防接種を受けている．☛ immunize と vaccinate は同様の意味を持つ． — **inoculation** /-éɪʃ(ə)n/ [名] [C][U]➜予防接種［注射］

**inoffensive** /ìnəfénsɪv/ [形] ▶定義 not likely to offend or upset sb; harmless ➜～の感情を害したり，不愉快にさせることがなさそうな；無害の ⇔ **offensive**

**inordinate** /ɪnɔ́ːrd(ə)nət/ [形][正式] ▶定義 much greater than usual or expected 通常の範囲や予想よりもはるかに大きく➜限度を超えた，過度の，法外な ‖ *They spent an **inordinate amount** of time and money on the production.* 彼らは生産に過度のお金と時間を費やしていた． — **inordinately** [副] ➜限度を超えて，過度に，法外に

**inorganic** /ìnɔːrgǽnɪk/ [形] ▶定義 not made of or coming from living things 生きているものから作られていない，生きているものからできたものではない➜無生物の，無機の ‖ *Rocks and metals are inorganic substances.* 石と金属は無機物である．⇔ **organic**

**input**[1] /ínpʊ̀t/ [名] ▶定義1 [C][U] input (of sth) (into/to sth) what you put into sth to make it successful 好結果を出すために，～に投入するもの➜(資金・情報・労働力などの)投入(量)，助力，援助 ‖ *We need some input from teachers into this book.* 我々はこの本について，教師からの援助を必要としている．▶定義2 [U] the act of putting information into a computer コンピューターに情報を入力する行為➜入力，インプット，入力情報 ‖ *The computer breakdown means we have lost the whole day's input.* コンピューターが壊れたということは，まる１日分の入力データをなくしたということだ．☛参 **output**

**input**[2] /ínpʊ̀t/ [動][他] (現分 **inputting**; 過，過分 **input** または **inputted**) to put information into a computer➜コンピューターに情報を入力する，インプットする

**inquest** /ínkwèst/ [名] [C] ▶定義 an official inquiry to find out how sb died ～がどのように死亡したかを明らかにするための，公式の調査➜(検死官の)死因審問，検死 ‖ *to hold an inquest* 検死を行う

**inquire** /ɪnkwáɪər/, **inquirer**, **inquiring**, **inquiry**/ɪŋkwaɪəri/＝ENQUIRE, ENQUIRER, ENQUIRING, ENQUIRY

**inquisitive** /ɪnkwízətɪv/ [形] ▶定義1 too interested in finding out about what other people are doing 他人のする事に興味を持ちすぎる➜しきりに知りたがる，詮索(せんさく)好きの，好奇心の強い ‖ *Don't be so inquisitive. It's none of your business.* そんなに詮索しないで．あなたには関係のないことです．▶定義2 interested in finding out about many different things 多くのいろいろな事柄を知ることに興味がある➜研究好きな，知識欲のある ‖ *You need an inquisitive*

I

mind to be a scientist. 科学者になるには、探究心を持つ必要がある. —inquisitively 副→しきりに知りたがって, 詮索(せんさく)するように, 根掘り葉掘り —inquisitiveness 名 ❶→しきりに知りたがること, 詮索好き

**insane** /ınséın/ 形 ▶定義1 crazy or mentally ill→ 正気でない, 狂気の ▶定義2 not showing sensible judgement 思慮分別のある判断ができない→気違い染みた, 非常識な, ばかげた ‖ You must be insane to leave your job before you've found another one. 新しい仕事を見つける前に仕事を辞めるなんて, あなたはどうかしているに違いない. ☛参 mad の注 — insanely 副→狂ったように, ひどく ‖ insanely jealous ひどくしっと深い — insanity /ınsǽnəti/ 名 ❶→狂気, 精神錯乱

**insanitary** /ınsǽnət(ə)ri; -tèri/ 形 正式 ▶定義 dirty and likely to cause disease 不潔で病気を引き起こすおそれのある→非衛生的な, 不潔な ‖ The restaurant was closed because of the insanitary conditions of the kitchen. そのレストランは, 調理場の状態が非衛生的であったために閉鎖された. ☛参 sanitary

**insatiable** /ınséıʃəb(ə)l/ 形 ▶定義 that cannot be satisfied; very great 満足させることができない; 非常に大きな→飽くことを知らない, 貪欲(どんよく)な, とめどのない ‖ an insatiable desire for knowledge 貪欲な知識欲 an insatiable appetite とめどない食欲

**inscribe** /ınskráıb/ 動 他 正式 ▶定義 inscribe A (on/in B); inscribe B (with A) to write or cut (carve) words on sth ~に文字を書く・刻む(彫る)→(名前・文字などを)(石碑・本などに)記す, ~を刻む, ~を彫る ‖ The names of all the previous champions are inscribed on the cup. 歴代の全優勝者の名前がカップに彫ってある. The book was inscribed with the author's name. その本には著者の名前が記されていた.

**inscription** /ınskrípʃ(ə)n/ 名 ❷ ▶定義 words that are written or cut on sth ~に書いてある言葉, 刻んである言葉→(石碑などの)銘, 碑文 ‖ There was a Latin inscription on the tombstone. 墓碑には, ラテン語の碑文が刻まれていた.

*****insect** /ínsekt/ 名 ❷ ▶定義 a small animal with six legs, two pairs of wings and a body which is divided into three parts 6本の足, 2対の羽, 3つの部分に分かれている胴体を持つ小さな生き物→昆虫, 虫 ‖ Ants, flies, beetles, butterflies and mosquitoes are all insects. アリ, ハエ, 甲虫, チョウ, 蚊はすべて昆虫だ. an insect bite/sting 虫に刺されること・刺し傷 ☛ C1 ページのさし絵
▶学問的には正しくないが, spider (クモ) のようなそのほかの小さな生き物も insect (昆虫) と呼ばれることがしばしばある.

**insecticide** /ınséktəsàıd/ 名 ❷ ❶ ▶定義 a substance that is used for killing insects 虫を殺すのに使われる物質→殺虫剤 ☛参 pesticide

**insecure** /ìnsıkjúər/ 形 ▶定義1 insecure (about sb/sth) not confident about yourself or your relationships with other people 自分に自信がない, 他人との関係に自信がない→自信のない, 不安な ‖ Many teenagers are insecure about their appearance. 容姿に自信がないティーンエージャーが多い. ▶定義2 not safe or protected 安全でない, 守られていない→不安定な, 危うい ‖ This ladder feels a bit insecure. このはしごは少し不安定だ. The future of the company looks very insecure. 会社の将来は非常に危うく見える. ⇔ secure — insecurely 副→不安定に, 危なっかしく, 自信なく — insecurity 名 ❶→自信のなさ, 不安 ‖ Their aggressive behaviour is really a sign of insecurity. 彼らの攻撃的な振る舞いは, 実は自信のなさの表れだ. ⇔ security

**insensitive** /ınséns(ə)tıv/ 形 insensitive (to sth) ▶定義1 not knowing or caring how another person feels and therefore likely to hurt or upset him/her 他人の気持ちが分からず, また気にしないので, 人を傷付け不愉快にさせることがあり得る→(~に対して)無神経な, 鈍感な, 冷淡な ‖ Some insensitive reporters tried to interview the families of the accident victims. 無神経なレポーターたちが, 事故の犠牲者の家族に取材をしようとした. an insensitive remark 無神経な言葉 ▶定義2 insensitive (to sth) not able to feel or react to sth ~に感じたり反応したりできない→(痛みなどに)無感覚の, 反応しない ‖ insensitive to pain/cold/criticism 痛み・寒さ・批判に無感覚の ⇔ sensitive — insensitively 副→無神経に, ずけずけと, 鈍感に —insensitivity /ınsèns(ə)tívəti/ 名 ❶→無神経, 鈍感

**inseparable** /ınsép(ə)rəb(ə)l/ 形 ▶定義 that

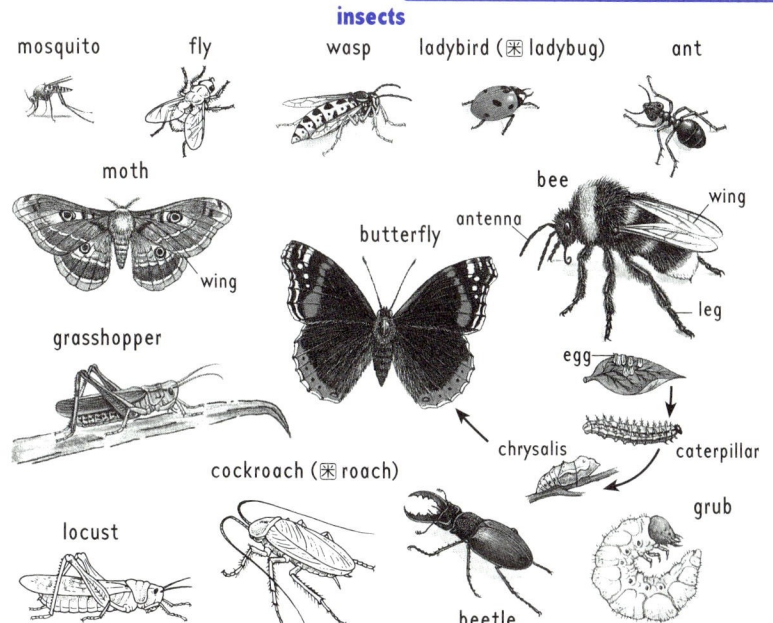

insects

mosquito, fly, wasp, ladybird (米 ladybug), ant, moth, bee (antenna, wing, leg), butterfly, grasshopper, egg, chrysalis, caterpillar, grub, locust, cockroach (米 roach), beetle

cannot be separated from sb/sth ～から引き離すことができない➔(～から)離れられない, 分離できない, 不可分の ‖ inseparable friends 無二の親友 ⇔ separable

**insert** /ɪnsə́ːrt/ 動他 正式 ▶定義 1 to put sth into sth or between two things ～を…の中, または2つのものの間に入れる➔～を(…に・…の間に)挿入する, ～を差し込む, ～を書き入れる ‖ I decided to insert an extra paragraph in the text. 本文に追加の段落を挿入することに決めた. — insertion 名 ⓒ ⓤ➔挿入, 差し込み

**inshore** /ɪnʃɔ́ːr/ 形副 ▶定義 in or towards the part of the sea that is close to the land 陸地近くの海で・に向かって➔岸に近い, 沿岸の, 近海の, 岸へ向かって, 岸の近くで ‖ inshore fishermen 沿岸漁業に携わる漁師 Sharks don't often come inshore. サメはあまり岸の近くには来ない.

*****inside**[1] /ɪnsáɪd, ínsàɪd/ 前 形 副 ▶定義 1 in, on or to the inner part or surface of sth➔～の内側・内部で[に・へ] ‖ Is there anything inside the box? 箱の中には何かあるのですか. It's safer to be inside the house in a thunderstorm. 激しい雷雨のときには家の中の方が安全だ. We'd better stay inside until the rain stops. 雨がやむまで屋内にいた方が良い. It's getting cold. Let's go inside. 寒くなってきた. 中に入ろう. the inside pages of a newspaper 新聞の内側のページ ▶定義 2 正式 (used about time) in less than; within (時間について) ～より短く; ～以内に➔(時間が)～以内に[で] ‖ Your photos will be ready inside an hour. 写真は1時間以内にできます. ▶定義 3 (used about information, etc) told secretly by sb who belongs to a group, organization, etc (情報などについて) 集団・組織などに属している～から秘密裏に話される➔(組織・集団の)内部の, 内輪の, 内幕の, 秘密の ‖ The robbers seemed to have had some inside information about the bank's security system. 強盗は銀行の警備システムについての内部情報を入手していたようだ. ▶定義 4 (俗語) in prison 刑務所に入って➔豚箱に入って, 獄中で

*inside² /ɪnsáɪd, ínsàɪd/ 名 ▶定義1 C the inner part or surface of sth→〜の内側, 内部 ‖ The door was locked from the inside. ドアは内側からかぎがかかっていた. There's a label somewhere on the inside. 内側のどこかにラベルがあります. ▶定義2 insides [複数扱い] 略式 the organs inside the body 体内の臓器→内臓, (特に)腹, 胃腸 ‖ The coffee warmed his insides. コーヒーで彼は腹の底から暖まった.

成句 inside out ▶定義1 with the inner surface on the outside 内側を外にして→表裏逆(で), 裏返しに ‖ You've got your jumper on inside out. セーターを裏返しに着ていますよ. ☞ back のさし絵 ▶定義2 very well, in great detail とてもよく, 大変詳しく→完全に, 徹底的に ‖ She knows these streets inside out. 彼女はこれらの通りを隅から隅まで知っている.

**insider** /ɪnsáɪdər, -́-/ 名 C ▶定義 a person who knows a lot about a group or an organization because he/she is a part of it そこに所属しているため, その集団・組織についてとてもよく知っている人→(集団の)内部の人, 内部情報に通じた人, インサイダー ‖ The book gives us an insider's view of how government works. その本は, 政府がいかに機能しているかについての内側から見た見解を教えてくれる.

**insight** /ínsaɪt/ 名 C U ▶定義 (an) insight (into sth) an understanding of what sb/sth is like 〜がどのようなものであるかを理解すること→(〜への)洞察(力), 眼識, 理解 ‖ The book gives a good insight into the lives of the poor. その本は貧しい人々の生活についての深い洞察を与えてくれる.

**insignificant** /ɪ̀nsɪɡnífɪkənt/ 形 ▶定義 of little value or importance ほとんど価値のない, 重要でない→取るに足りない, 無意味な, ささいな, 下らない ‖ an insignificant detail ささいな細かい点 Working in such a big company made her feel insignificant. そのような大企業で働くことで, 彼女は価値のない存在になったように感じられた. ─ insignificance 名 U →取るに足りないこと, 無意味 ─ insignificantly 副 →わずかに, 無意味に

**insincere** /ɪ̀nsɪnsíər/ 形 ▶定義 saying or doing sth that you do not really believe 本当に信じていない〜を言う・行う→不誠実な, 裏表のある, 上辺だけの ‖ His apology sounded insincere. 彼の謝罪は上辺だけのように聞こえる. an insincere smile 上辺だけのほほえみ ⇔ sincere ─ insincerely 副 →不誠実に, 不まじめに ─ insincerity /ɪ̀nsɪnsérəti, -síər-/ 名 U →不誠実さ ⇔ sincerity

**insinuate** /ɪnsínjuèɪt/ 動 他 ▶定義 to suggest sth unpleasant in an indirect way 不愉快な〜を間接的な言い方でほのめかす→(悪口など)を遠回しに言う, 当てこする ‖ She seemed to be insinuating that our work was below standard. 彼女は, 我々の仕事が水準以下であると遠回しに言っているようだった. ─ insinuation /ɪnsìnjuéɪʃ(ə)n/ 名 C U →ほのめかし, 遠回しに言うこと ‖ to make insinuations about sb's honesty 〜の誠実さについて遠回しに言う

**insipid** /ɪnsípəd/ 形 ▶定義 having too little taste, flavour or colour 味・風味・色がなさすぎる→(飲食物が)味のない, 風味のない

*insist /ɪnsíst/ 動 自 ▶定義1 insist (on sth/doing sth); insist that... to say strongly that you must have or do sth, or that sb else must do sth 自分が〜を持つ・…をすると言い張る, ほかの人が〜をすべきだと言い張る→(〜を)強く要求する; (自分が)〜すると言って聞かない, (人が)〜すべきだと言う ‖ He always insists on the best. 彼は常に最善を要求する. Dan insisted on coming too. ダンは自分も行くと言い張った. My parents insist that I come home by taxi. 両親は私にタクシーで帰るようにと言って聞かない. 'Have another drink.' 'Oh all right, if you insist.' 「もう1杯飲みなさい」「分かったよ, どうしてもと言うなら」 ▶定義2 insist (on sth); insist that... to say firmly that sth is true (when sb does not believe you) 〜が信じてくれない場合に, …が本当であると強く言う→(〜を)強く言い張る, (〜だと)主張する ‖ She insisted on her innocence. 彼女は無実を強く主張した. James insisted that the accident wasn't his fault. ジェームズは, 事故は自分の責任ではないと強く言い張った. ─ insistence 名 U →(〜の・〜という)頑固な主張[要求]

**insistent** /ɪnsíst(ə)nt/ 形 ▶定義1 insistent (on sth/doing sth); insistent that... saying strongly that you must have or do sth, or that sb else must do sth 自分が〜を持つ・…をする

と強く言う，ほかの~が…をすべきだと強く言う➡(~を・~すると・~だと)言い張って聞かない，力説する，譲らない，しつこい ‖ *Doctors are insistent on the need to do more exercise.* 医者は，もっと運動するように強く言う． *She was most insistent that we should all be there.* 彼女は，我々全員がそこにいるべきだと強く迫った．

▶定義2 continuing for a long time in a way that cannot be ignored 無視できないほど長く続く➡(音が)鳴りやまない，(色・音・程度などが)目立つ，強烈な ‖ *the insistent ringing of the telephone* 鳴りやまない電話 — **insistently** 副➡強情に，頑として，しつこく

**insolent** /íns(ə)lənt/ 形正式 ▶定義 lacking respect; rude 敬意が見られない；無礼な➡横柄な，無礼な ‖ *insolent behaviour* 横柄な振る舞い — **insolence** 名 Ⓤ➡横柄，尊大，ごう慢，無礼 — **insolently** 副➡横柄に，ごう慢に，無礼に

**insoluble** /ɪnsɑ́ljəb(ə)l/ 形 ▶定義1 that cannot be explained or solved➡説明できない，解決できない ‖ *We faced almost insoluble problems.* 我々はほとんど解決不可能な問題に直面した．

▶定義2 that cannot be dissolved in a liquid 液体に溶けない➡(物質が)非溶解性の ⇔ **soluble**

**insomnia** /ɪnsɑ́mniə/ 名 Ⓤ ▶定義 inability to sleep 眠ることができないこと➡不眠症 ‖ *Do you ever suffer from insomnia?* 不眠症にかかったことはありますか． ☞参 **sleepless**

**insomniac** /ɪnsɑ́mniæk/ 名 Ⓒ ▶定義 a person who cannot sleep 眠ることができない人➡不眠症の人，不眠症患者

\***inspect** /ɪnspékt/ 動他 ▶定義1 inspect sb/sth (for sth) to look at sth closely or in great detail ~を厳密に調べる，非常に詳細に調べる➡~を(欠陥などがないかと)詳しく調べる，検査する，点検する ‖ *The detective inspected the room for fingerprints.* 指紋を捜して，刑事は部屋を詳しく調べた． ▶定義2 to make an official visit to make sure that rules are being obeyed, work is being done properly, etc 公式に訪問し，規則が守られているか，仕事が適正に行われているかなどを確かめる➡~を視察する，検閲する ‖ *All food shops should be inspected regularly.* 食料品店はすべて，定期的に検査されなくてはならない． — **inspection** 名 Ⓒ Ⓤ➡詳しい調査，検査，点検 ‖ *The fire prevention service will carry out an inspection of the building next week.* 火

災予防局は，そのビルの検査を来週行います． ***On inspection**, the passport turned out to be false.* 調べてみると，パスポートはにせ物と判明した．

\***inspector** /ɪnspéktər/ 名 Ⓒ ▶定義1 an official who visits schools, factories, etc to make sure that rules are being obeyed, work is being done properly, etc 学校・工場などに行き，規則が守られているか，作業は適切に行われているかなどを確かめる公務員➡調査員，検査官，検閲者 ‖ *a health and safety inspector* 健康・安全審査官 ▶定義2 英 a police officer with quite an important position 非常に重要な地位にある警察官➡警部(補) ▶定義3 a person whose job is to check passengers' tickets on buses or trains バス・電車で乗客の切符を調べる仕事をする人➡(列車・バスなどの)検札係

**inspiration** /ɪ̀nspəréɪʃ(ə)n/ 名 ▶定義1 Ⓒ Ⓤ an inspiration (to/for sb); inspiration (to do/for sth) a feeling, person or thing that makes you want to do sth or gives you exciting new ideas 人に~をする気にさせる感情・人・事柄，わくわくするような新しい考えを与えてくれる感じ・人・事柄➡(~に対して)激励[鼓舞・感化・刺激](する人・物) ‖ *The beauty of the mountains was a great **source of inspiration** to the writer.* 山々の美しさは，作家に大きな刺激を与えてくれた． *What gave you the inspiration to become a dancer?* ダンサーになろうとしたきっかけは何ですか． ▶定義2 Ⓒ 略式 a sudden good idea 突然思い付いた良い考え➡(突然の)すばらしい思い付き，着想，名案 ‖ *I've had an inspiration - why don't we go to that new club?* 名案が浮かんだよ - その新しいクラブに行かないか．

**inspire** /ɪnspáɪər/ 動他 ▶定義1 inspire sth; inspire sb (to do sth) to make sb want to do or create sth ~に…をしたいまたは~を作成したいという気にさせる➡(人を)(~へ)奮い立たせる，~を奮起させる，~を激励する ‖ *Nelson Mandela's autobiography inspired her to go into politics.* ネルソン マンデラの自伝に奮起して，彼女は政治の道に入った． *The attack was inspired by racial hatred.* その襲撃は，人種間の憎悪によって引き起こされた． ▶定義2 inspire sb (with sth); inspire sth (in sb) to make sb feel, think, etc sth ～に…を感じさせる・考えさせるなど→～に(感情・考え・目標を)吹き込む, ～を抱かせる, ～の発生源になる ‖ *to be inspired with enthusiasm* 熱意がわく *The guide's nervous manner did not inspire much confidence in us.* ガイドの緊張した様子を見て, あまり信頼感がわかなかった. — inspiring 形→(人を)鼓舞する, 奮い立たせる ‖ *an inspiring speech* 人を鼓舞する演説

**inspired** /ɪnspáɪərd/ 形 ▶定義 influenced or helped by a particular feeling, thing or person 特定の感情・事柄・人に影響を受けた, 助けられた→(芸術家などが)霊感を受けた, インスピレーションを得た, (作品などが)すばらしい, 見事な ‖ *The pianist gave an inspired performance.* ピアニストは見事な演奏を披露した. *a politically inspired killing* 政治的な理由に触発された殺人

**instability** /ˌɪnstəbíləti/ 名 Ⓤ ▶定義 the state of being likely to change 変わるおそれのある状態→不安定(状態), (心の)不安定, 変わりやすさ ‖ *There are growing signs of political instability.* 政情不安の気配が濃厚になってきた. ☞ 形 unstable ⇔ stability

*__install__ (英 または install) /ɪnstɔ́ːl/ 動 他 ▶定義 1 to put a piece of equipment, etc in place so that it is ready to be used 装置の一部などを正しい位置に設置し, 使用できるように準備をする→(～に)(装置など)を取り付ける, 据え付ける ‖ *We are waiting to have our new washing machine installed.* 私たちは新しい洗濯機が据え付けられるのを待っている. *to install a computer system* コンピューターシステムをインストールする ☞類 put in ▶定義 2 install sb (as sth) to put sb/sth or yourself in a position or place ～または自身を, ある地位・場所に就ける→(人を)(～として)任命する, ～を就任させる ‖ *He was installed as President yesterday.* 彼は昨日, 大統領に就任した. — installation /ˌɪnstəléɪʃ(ə)n/ 名 Ⓒ Ⓤ→基地, 施設, (設備などの)取り付け, 就任, 任命 ‖ *a military/nuclear installation* 軍事・原子力施設 *the installation of a new chairman* 新しい議長の就任

**instalment** (米 installment) /ɪnstɔ́ːlmənt/ 名 Ⓒ ▶定義 1 one of the regular payments that you make for sth until you have paid the full amount 全額を払い終えるまで定期的に続く支払いの1回→分割払いの1回分 ‖ *to pay for sth in instalments* 分割払いで～の代金を払う ▶定義 2 one part of a story that is shown or published as a series 続き物で上映・出版されているものの1話→続き物の1回分 ‖ *Don't miss next week's exciting instalment.* 来週の面白い続きをお見逃しなく.

*__instance__ /ínstəns/ 名 Ⓒ ▶定義 an instance (of sth) an example or case (of sth) → (～の)例, 事例 ‖ *There have been several instances of racial attacks in the area.* その地域には, 人種間の襲撃の例がいくつかある. *In most instances the drug has no side effects.* ほとんどの場合, その薬に副作用はない.

成句 for instance ▶定義 for example→(文中・文頭・文尾で)例えば ‖ *There are several interesting places to visit around here - Warwick, for instance.* この辺りには, 訪ねるのに面白いところがいくつかあります ― 例えば, ウォーリックなどです.

*__instant__¹ /ínstənt/ 形 ▶定義 1 happening suddenly or immediately 突然に起こる, 即座に起こる→即時の, 即座の ‖ *The film was an instant success.* その映画はたちまち成功を収めた. ▶定義 2 (used about food) that can be prepared quickly and easily, usually by adding hot water (食品について)通常はお湯を注ぐだけで, すぐ簡単に用意ができる→(食品などが)即席の, インスタントの ‖ *instant coffee* インスタントコーヒー

**instant**² /ínstənt/ 名 [通常は単数] ▶定義 1 a very short period of time 非常に短い期間→瞬時, 瞬間 ‖ *Alex thought for an instant and then agreed.* アレックスは一瞬考えて賛成した. ▶定義 2 a particular point in time 特定の時→この・その瞬間, この・その場 ‖ *At that instant I realized I had been tricked.* その瞬間, 私はだまされていたことに気付いた. *Stop doing that this instant! (= now)* 即刻(= 今すぐに)それをやめなさい.

**instantaneous** /ˌɪnst(ə)ntéɪniəs/ 形 ▶定義 happening immediately or extremely quickly 即座に起こる, 非常に速く起こる→瞬間的な, 即席の — instantaneously 副→即刻, 一瞬にして

**instantly** /ínstəntli/ 副 ▶定義 without delay;

immediately 遅滞なく; 即座に→**直ちに, すぐに** ‖ *I asked him a question and he replied instantly.* 彼に質問すると, 即座に答えた.

**\*instead** /instéd/ 副前 ▶定義 instead (of sb/sth/doing sth) in the place of sb/sth 〜の代わりに→**その代わりに, 〜の・〜する代わりに, 〜しないで** ‖ *I couldn't go so my husband went instead.* 私は行けなかったので, 夫が代わりに行った. *You should play football instead of just watching it on TV.* テレビで見ているだけでなく, 実際にサッカーをやってみるべきだ. *Instead of 7.30 could I come at 8.00?* 7時半ではなくて, 8時に来てもいいですか.

**instigate** /ínstəgèɪt/ 動他 正式 ▶定義 to make sth start to happen 〜を開始させる→**(法的手続きなど)を起こす, 発動する, 開始する** — **instigation** /ìnstəgéɪʃ(ə)n/ 名 U→**開始, 扇動**

**instil** (米**instill**) /ɪnstíl/ 動他 (**instilling**; **instilled**) ▶定義 instil sth (in/into sb) to make sb think or feel sth 〜に…を感じさせる, 考えさせる→**(思想・感情など)を(人に)教え込む, 染み込ませる, 徐々に浸透させる** ‖ *Parents should try to instil a sense of responsibility into their children.* 両親は子供に責任感を教え込むようにすべきだ.

**instinct** /ínstɪŋ(k)t/ 名 C U ▶定義 the natural force that causes a person or animal to behave in a particular way without thinking or learning about it 人・動物に, 考えたり学習したりすることなく特定の行動を取らせる生まれつき備わった力→**本能** ‖ *Birds learn to fly by instinct.* 鳥は本能で飛び方を習得する. *In a situation like that you don't have time to think - you just act on instinct.* そのような状況では, 考える時間もない — ただ本能のままに行動するだけだ. — **instinctive** /ɪnstíŋ(k)tɪv/ 形→**本能の, 本能的な, 直観的な** ‖ *Your instinctive reaction is to run from danger.* あなたの本能的な反応は, 危険から逃れることだ. — **instinctively** 副→**本能的に, 直観的に**

**\*institute**[1] /ínstət(j)ùːt/ 名 C ▶定義 an organization that has a particular purpose; the building used by this organization 特定の目的を持った組織; この組織が使用する建物→**協会, 学会, 協会(学会)の建物, 会館** ‖ *the Institute of Science and Technology* 理工科大学 *institutes of higher education* 高等教育機関

**institute**[2] /ínstət(j)ùːt/ 動他 正式 ▶定義 to introduce a system, policy, etc, or start a process 制度, 政策などを取り入れる, 取り入れ始める→**〜を制定する, (制度など)を設ける, 開始する** ‖ *The government has instituted a new scheme for youth training.* 政府は青少年の訓練に新しい案を制定した.

**\*institution** /ìnstət(j)úːʃ(ə)n/ 名 ▶定義 **1** C a large, important organization that has a particular purpose, such as a bank, a university, etc 銀行, 大学などのような, 特定の目的を持った大規模で重要な組織→**(公共)施設, 機関, 協会, 組織, 学会** ‖ *the financial institutions in the City of London* ロンドンのシティにある金融機関 ▶定義 **2** C a building where certain people with special needs live and are looked after 特定の要求がある人々が住み, 介護されている施設の建物→**施設, 施設の建物** ‖ *a mental institution (= a hospital for the mentally ill)* 精神病院(=精神を病んだ人々の病院) *She's been in institutions all her life.* 彼女は一生を施設で送った. ▶定義 **3** C a social custom or habit that has existed for a long time 長い間存続している社会的慣習・習慣→**制度, 慣例, 慣習, 仕来り** ‖ *the institution of marriage* 結婚制度 ▶定義 **4** U the act of introducing a system, policy, etc, or of starting a process 制度・政策などを取り入れる行為, 取り入れ始める行為→**(〜の)制定, 設立, 開설, 創立** ‖ *the institution of new safety procedures* 新しい安全手順の制定

**institutional** /ìnstət(j)úːʃ(ə)n(ə)l/ 形 ▶定義 connected with an institution 施設・機関に関連した→**団体・機関による, 公共団体の, (福祉)施設の** ‖ *The old lady is in need of institutional care.* その老婦人は, 福祉施設の介護を必要としている.

**\*instruct** /ɪnstrʌ́kt/ 動他 ▶定義 **1** instruct sb (to do sth) to give an order to sb; to tell sb to do sth 〜に命令をする; 〜に…をするように言う→**(人に)〜するように指示する, 指図する** ‖ *The soldiers were instructed to shoot above the heads of the crowd.* 兵士たちは群集の頭上を撃つように指図された. ▶定義 **2** 正式 instruct sb (in sth) to teach sb sth→**人に(〜を)教える, 〜を(…の点で)指導する** ‖ *Children must be instructed in road safety before they are allowed to ride a bike on the road.* 子供たちは, 道路で自

転車に乗る許可を得る前に，交通安全についての指導を受けるべきだ．

**\*instruction** /ɪnstrʌ́kʃ(ə)n/ 名 ▶定義1 instructions [複数扱い] detailed information on how you should use sth, do sth, etc ～を使用すべきか，～をどのように行うべきか，などの詳細な情報→(器械・器具などの)使用説明，説明書 ‖ *Read the instructions on the back of the packet carefully.* 包みの裏にある使用説明をよく読んでください．*You should always **follow the instructions**.* 常に説明書に従ってください．▶定義2 **C** an instruction (to do sth) an order that tells you what to do or how to do sth 何をすべきか，～をどのようにすべきか，という命令→(～せよという)指図，指示，命令 ‖ *The guard was **under** strict **instructions** not to let anyone in or out.* 警備員は，だれも出入りさせぬように，という厳命を受けていた．▶定義3 **U** instruction (in sth) the act of teaching sth to sb ～に…を教える行為→(～の)指導 ‖ *The staff need instruction in the use of computers.* 職員には，コンピューターの使用方法についての指導が必要だ．

**instructive** /ɪnstrʌ́ktɪv/ 形 ▶定義 giving useful information 役立つ情報を提供する→ためになる，教育的な，教訓的な — **instructively** 副→教育的に，有益に

**instructor** /ɪnstrʌ́ktər/ 名 **C** ▶定義 a person whose job is to teach a practical skill or sport 実用的な技能・スポーツを教える仕事をする人→指導者，教授，教師 ‖ *a driving/fitness/golf instructor* 自動車教習所の指導員・フィットネスインストラクター・ゴルフの指導者

**\*instrument** /ɪ́nstrəmənt/ 名 **C** ▶定義1 a tool that is used for doing a particular job or task 特定の仕事・作業をするための道具→道具，器具，器械 ‖ *surgical/optical/precision instruments* 外科用器械・光学機器・精密器機 ☛参 **tool** の注 ▶定義2 something that is used for playing music 音楽演奏のために使われるもの→楽器 ‖ *'What instrument do you play?' 'The violin.'* 「何の楽器を演奏しますか」「バイオリンです」

▶ musical instruments (楽器)には，stringed (弦楽器: バイオリン，ギターなど)，brass (金管楽器: ホルン，トランペットなど)，wood wind (木管楽器: フルート，クラリネットなど)，keyboard (鍵盤楽器: ピアノ，オルガン，シンセサイザーなど)が含まれる．percussion instruments (打楽器)には，太鼓とシンバルが含まれる．

▶定義3 something that is used for measuring speed, distance, temperature, etc in a car, plane or ship 車・飛行機・船の中で速度・距離・温度などを計るのに使われるもの→計器 ‖ *the instrument panel of a plane* 飛行機の計器盤 ▶定義4 something that sb uses in order to achieve sth ～が…を成し遂げるために使用するもの→(人・組織などの)道具，手先，(～のための)手段，方法 ‖ *The press should be more than an instrument of the government.* 新聞は，政府の手先以上のものであるべきだ．

**\*instrumental** /ɪ̀nstrəméntl/ 形 ▶定義1 instrumental in doing sth helping to make sth happen ～を起こすのを助ける→(～に)役立つ，手助けとなる ‖ *She was instrumental in getting him the job.* 彼女は彼の就職の手助けをした．▶定義2 for musical instruments without voices 歌はなく楽器だけの→楽器の，楽器を用いる ‖ *instrumental music* 器楽曲

**insubordinate** /ɪ̀nsəbɔ́ːrd(ə)nət/ 形 正式 ▶定義 (used about a person or behaviour) not obeying rules or orders (人または行動について)規則・命令に従っていない→服従しない，反抗的な — **insubordination** /ɪ̀nsəbɔ̀ːrd(ə)néɪʃ(ə)n/ 名 **C U** →不従順，反抗 ‖ *He was dismissed from the army for insubordination.* 彼は反抗により，軍隊から除隊を命じられた．

**insubstantial** /ɪ̀nsəbstǽnʃ(ə)l/ 形 ▶定義 not large, solid or strong 大きくない，頑丈でない，強くない→内容のない，もろい，不十分な，弱い ‖ *a hut built of insubstantial materials* もろい材料で建てられた掘っ立て小屋 ⇔ **substantial**

**insufferable** /ɪnsʌ́f(ə)rəb(ə)l/ 形 正式 ▶定義 (used about a person or behaviour) extremely unpleasant or annoying (人または行動について) 非常に不愉快な，腹の立つ→耐え難い，鼻持ちならない，我慢できない

**insufficient** /ɪ̀nsəfíʃ(ə)nt/ 形 ▶定義 insufficient (for sth/to do sth) not enough 十分でない→(～に・～するのに)不十分な，足りない ‖ *The students complained that they were given insufficient time for the test.* 生徒たちは試

験の時間が足りなかったと不平を言った. ⇔ **sufficient** —insufficiently [副] ➜**不十分に, 不適当に**

**insular** /ɪ́ns(j)ələr; -sjʊ-/ [形] ▶定義 not interested in or able to accept new people or different ideas 新しい人々や異なる考えに興味を持たない, 受け付けない➜**島国根性の, 偏狭な** ☛類 **narrow-minded** —insularity /ɪ̀nsjʊlǽrəti/ [名] [U] ➜**島国根性, 狭量**

**insulate** /ɪ́nsəlèɪt; -sjʊ-/ [動][他] ▶定義 insulate sth (against/from sth) to protect sth with a material that prevents electricity, heat or sound from passing through 電気・熱・音を通さない物質で～を保護する➜**～を(…から)絶縁する, 断熱する, 防音する** ‖ *The walls are insulated against noise.* 壁は騒音に対して防音されている. (比喩) *This industry has been insulated from the effects of competition.* この産業は, 競争による影響から保護されている. —insulation /ɪ̀nsəléɪʃ(ə)n; -sjʊ-/ [名] [U] ➜**(外部の影響からの)保護, 絶縁, 断熱, 防音**

***insult**[1] /ɪnsʌ́lt/ [動][他] ▶定義 to speak or act rudely to sb ～に対して無作法に話す, 失礼な態度を取る➜**～を侮辱する, 辱める** ‖ *I felt very insulted when I didn't even get an answer to my letter.* 手紙に対する返事すら来ないので, 私はとても侮辱された感じがした. *He was thrown out of the hotel for insulting the manager.* 彼は支配人を侮辱したためにホテルから追い出された.

**insult**[2] /ɪ́nsʌlt/ [名] [C] ▶定義 a rude remark or action 無礼な言葉・行い➜**(～に対する)侮辱, 無礼, 無礼な言葉** ‖ *The drivers were standing in the road yelling insults at each other.* 運転手たちは互いに侮辱し合いながら道路に立ち止まっていた.

**insulting** /ɪnsʌ́ltɪŋ/ [形] ▶定義 insulting (to sb/sth) making sb feel offended ～の感情を害する➜**無礼な, 侮辱的な** ‖ *insulting behaviour/remarks* 無礼な振る舞い・言葉 *That poster is insulting to women.* そのポスターは女性に対して侮辱的だ.

**insuperable** /ɪnsjúːpərəb(ə)l; -s(j)úː-/ [形][正式] ▶定義 (used about a problem, etc) impossible to solve (問題などについて) 解決が不可能な➜**(障害・問題が)克服できない, 乗り越えられない**

***insurance** /ɪnʃɔ́ːrəns/ [名] ▶定義1 [U] insurance (against sth) an arrangement with a company in which you pay them regular amounts of money and they agree to pay the costs if, for example, you die or are ill, or if you lose or damage sth (保険) 会社との取り決めで, 会社に一定の金額を支払う代わりに, 支払った人の死亡・けが, ～の損害・紛失などの場合にかかった費用を会社が払うというもの➜**保険,保険契約, 保険料, 保険証書** ‖ *Builders should always have insurance against personal injury.* 建築業者は個人のけがに対して常に保険を掛けておくべきだ.
➤保険を掛けることを take out an insurance policy と言う. insurance premium (保険料) とは保険会社に支払う一定の金額のことである. life insurance (生命保険) ・ health insurance (健康保険) ・ car insurnance (自動車保険) ・ travel insurance (旅行保険) ・ household insurance (家族保険) などを掛けることができる.
▶定義2 [U] the business of providing insurance 保険を提供する事業➜**保険業** ‖ *He works in insurance.* 彼は保険の仕事をしている. ▶定義3 [[U], 単数扱い] (an) insurance (against sth) something you do to protect yourself (against sth unpleasant) 自分自身を (不愉快な～から) 守るために行うこと➜**(～に対する)予防手段, 用心** ‖ *Many people take vitamin pills as an insurance against illness.* 病気予防のためにビタミン剤を飲んでいる人は多い.

***insure** /ɪnʃɔ́ːr, -ʃʊ́ə/ [動][他] ▶定義1 insure yourself/sth (against/for sth) to buy or to provide insurance 保険に入る, 保険を提供する➜**(人・財産など)に(～に備えて・～の額の)保険を掛ける, (保険業者が)～の保険契約をする** ‖ *They insured the painting for £10000 against damage or theft.* 彼らは損害・盗難に備えてその絵に1万ポンドの保険を掛けた. ▶定義2 [米] = **ENSURE**

**insurmountable** /ɪ̀nsərmáʊntəb(ə)l/ [形][正式] ▶定義 (used about a problem, etc) impossible to solve (問題などについて) 解決することができない➜**(困難, 障害が)乗り越えられない, 克服できない** ☛参 **surmountable**

**insurrection** /ɪ̀nsərékʃ(ə)n/ [名] [C] [U] [正式] ▶定義 violent action against the rulers of a country or the government 国の支配者・政府に対する暴力

行為➜反乱, 暴動, 謀反

**intact** /ɪntǽkt/ [形] (名詞の前は不可) ▶定義 complete; not damaged 完全な; 損害を受けないで➜**無傷の, 損なわれないで, 元のままの** ‖ *Very few of the buildings* ***remain intact*** *following the earthquake.* 地震の後, 無傷の建物はほとんどない.

**intake** /ínteɪk/ [名] [[C], 通常は単数] ▶定義1 the amount of food, drink, etc that you take into your body 体内に摂取した食べ物・飲み物の総量➜**(食べ物などの) 摂取 (量), 取り入れること** ‖ *The doctor told me to cut down my alcohol intake.* 医者はお酒の量を減らすように言った. ▶定義2 the (number of) people who enter an organization or institution during a certain period ある特定の期間に組織・機関に入った人 (の数) ➜**(組織などの) 採用人数, 受け入れた人・物** ‖ *This year's intake of students is down 10%.* 今年の入学者数は, 10パーセントの減少です. ▶定義3 the act of taking sth into your body, especially breath ～を体内に取り入れる行為, 特に呼吸➜**(水・空気などの) 吸い込み, 取り入れ**

**intangible** /ɪntǽndʒəb(ə)l/ [形] ▶定義 difficult to describe, understand or measure 言葉で説明する・理解する・測るのが難しい➜**触れることのできない, 実体のない, 無形の; つかみどころのない, 漠とした** ‖ *The benefits of good customer relations are intangible.* 顧客との良好な関係から得られる利益は, 計り知れません. ⇔**tangible**

**integral** /íntɪgrəl/ [形] ▶定義1 integral (to sth) necessary in order to make sth complete ～を完全にするために必要な➜**(～にとって) 不可欠な, 必須 (ひっす) の** ‖ *Spending a year in France is* ***an integral part of*** *the university course.* 1年間のフランス滞在は, 大学の課程では必須だ. ▶定義2 including sth as a part ～を一部として含む➜**内蔵した, 組み込まれた** ‖ *The car has an integral CD player.* その車はCDプレーヤーを内蔵している.

**integrate** /íntɪgreɪt/ [動] ▶定義1 [他] integrate sth (into sth); integrate A and B/integrate A with B to join things so that they become one thing or work together 物事を合わせて1つのものにする・一緒に働かせる➜**～を (…に・…と) 統合する, ～をまとめる** ‖ *The two small schools were integrated into one large one.* 2つの小規模な学校は統合されて1つの大規模な学校となった. *These programs can be integrated with your existing software.* これらのプログラムは, 貴社の既存のソフトウェアに統合される. ▶定義2 [自][他] integrate (sb) (into/with sth) to join in and become part of a group or community, or to make sb do this 仲間に加わって, 集団・地域社会の一員となる, また人にそうさせる➜**(集団に) 溶け込む; ～を (集団に) 溶け込ませる** ‖ *It took Amir a while to integrate into his new school.* アミールが新しい学校に溶け込むのには, しばらく時間がかかった. ☛参 **segregate**
—integration /ìntəgréɪʃ(ə)n/ [名] [U] ➜**統合, 集大成, 融合** ‖ *racial integration* 人種の融合 ☛参 **segregation**

**integrity** /ɪntégrəti/ [名] [U] ▶定義 the quality of being honest and having strong moral principles 誠実で強い倫理観を備えた人柄➜**高潔, 実直, 誠実** ‖ *He's a person* ***of great integrity*** *who will say exactly what he thinks.* 彼は思ったままを口にする, 非常に実直な人だ.

**intellect** /ínt(ə)lèkt/ [名] ▶定義1 [U] the power of the mind to think and to learn 考えたり学んだりする知力➜**知性, 知力** ‖ *a woman of considerable intellect* かなりの知性がある女性 ▶定義2 [C] an extremely intelligent person 非常に知性のある人➜**知的な人, 知識人** ‖ *He was one of the most brilliant intellects of his time.* 彼はその時代の最も立派な知識人の1人だった.

***intellectual**[1] /ìnt(ə)léktʃuəl/ [形] ▶定義1 (名詞の前だけ) connected with a person's ability to think logically and to understand things 論理的に考え物事を理解する, という人の能力に関連した➜**知性の, 知的な, 知力を要する** ‖ *The boy's intellectual development was very advanced for his age.* その少年の知的な発達は, その年齢にしては非常に進んでいた. ▶定義2 (used about a person) enjoying activities in which you have to think deeply about sth (人について) ～について深く考えなければならない, 知的活動を楽しむ➜**(人が) 知性的な, 理知的な** —intellectually [副] ➜**知的に, 知性に関しては**

**intellectual**[2] /ìnt(ə)léktʃuəl/ [名] [C] ▶定義 a person who enjoys thinking deeply about things 物事について深く考えることを楽しむ人➜**知識人, インテリ**

**\*intelligence** /ɪntélədʒ(ə)ns/ 名 Ｕ ▶定義1 the ability to understand, learn and think 理解し, 学び, 考える能力 →知能, 理解力, 知恵 ‖ *a person of normal intelligence* 標準的な知能の人 *an intelligence test* 知能テスト ▶定義2 important information about an enemy country 敵国に関する重要な情報→(重要な)情報, 知識; 情報機関, 諜報(ちょうほう)部 ‖ *to receive intelligence about sb* ～に関する情報を受け取る

**\*intelligent** /ɪntélədʒ(ə)nt/ 形 ▶定義 having or showing the ability to understand, learn and think; clever 理解し, 学び, 考える能力を持っている, またはそういった能力を示す; 賢い→(人・動物の)知能が高い, 頭が良い, 理解力がある, 聡明(そうめい)な ‖ *All their children are very intelligent.* 彼らの子供は皆, 非常に頭が良い. *an intelligent question* 気の利いた質問 — **intelligently** 副 →知的に, 聡明に, 物分かり良く

**intelligible** /ɪntélədʒəb(ə)l/ 形 ▶定義 (used especially about speech or writing) possible or easy to understand (特に話し言葉・書き言葉について)→理解できる, 分かりやすい ⇔ **unintelligible**

**\*intend** /ɪnténd/ 動他 ▶定義1 intend to do sth/doing sth to plan or mean to do sth→～するつもりである, ～しようと決めている ‖ *I'm afraid I spent more money than I had intended.* 予定していたよりも多くのお金を使ってしまったのではないかと思う. *I certainly don't intend to wait here all day!* 私はここで一日中待つつもりは全くない. *They had intended staying in Wales for two weeks but the weather was so bad that they left after one.* 彼らはウェールズに２週間滞在するつもりであったが, 天候が非常に悪く１週間で切り上げた. ☛ 名 **intention** ▶定義2 intend sth for sb/sth; intend sb to do sth to plan, mean or make sth for a particular person or purpose →～を(特定の目的・用途として)意図[計画・予定]する ‖ *You shouldn't have read that letter - it wasn't intended for you.* その手紙を読んではいけなかったのよ － あなたにあてて書かれたものではなかったんだから. *I didn't intend you to have all the work.* あなたに全部の仕事をしてもらおうとは思っていませんでした.

**\*intense** /ɪnténs/ 形 ▶定義 very great, strong or serious 非常に大きい・強い・深刻な→(熱・痛みなどが)激しい, (色などが)濃い ‖ *intense heat/cold/pressure* 猛暑・厳寒・激しい圧力 *intense anger/interest/desire* 激怒・強い興味・激しい欲望 — **intensely** 副 →激しく, 熱烈に ‖ *They obviously dislike each other intensely.* 彼らは明らかにお互いを激しく嫌っていた. — **intensity** /-səti/ 名 Ｕ →(感情・気候などの)激しさ, 強烈さ ‖ *I wasn't prepared for the intensity of his reaction to the news.* 私は, 彼があのニュースにあんなに激しく反応するとは思ってもいなかった.

**intensify** /ɪnténsəfàɪ/ 動自他 (現分 **intensifying**; 三単現 **intensifies**; 過, 過分 **intensified**) ▶定義 to become or to make sth greater or stronger→～が大きくなる・強くなる; ～を大きくする・強くする ‖ *The government has intensified its anti-smoking campaign.* 政府は禁煙運動を強化している. *Fighting in the region has intensified.* その地域での戦闘は激しさを増してきた. — **intensification** /ɪntènsɪfɪkéɪʃ(ə)n/ 名 Ｕ →強化, 激化, 増大, 高まり

**intensive** /ɪnténsɪv/ 形 ▶定義1 involving a lot of work or care in a short period of time 短期間に多大な仕事・手当てがなされる→集中的な, 徹底的な ‖ *an intensive investigation/course* 徹底的な調査・集中講座 ▶定義2 (used about methods of farming) aimed at producing as much food as possible from the land or money available (農業の手法について) 利用可能な土地・資金からできるだけ多くの食料を生産しようとする→集約的な ‖ *intensive agriculture* 集約農業 — **intensively** 副 →集中的に, 徹底的に, 激しく

**intensive care** 名 Ｕ ▶定義 special care in hospital for patients who are very seriously ill or injured; the department that gives this care 病状・けがが非常に深刻な患者に対して病院でなされる特別な手当て; この治療が行われる部署→集中治療 ‖ *She was in intensive care for a week after the crash.* 彼女は衝突事故の後１週間集中治療を受けた.

**intent**¹ /ɪntént/ 形 ▶定義1 intent (on/upon sth) showing great attention 高い注意力を示す→(目・心などが)(～に)しっかりと向けられた, 集中した, 真剣な ‖ *She was so intent upon her* work that she didn't hear me come in. 彼女は非常に仕事に集中していたので、私が入ってきたのに気付かなかった. ▶定義2 intent on/upon sth/doing sth determined to do sth ～をすることを固く決心している →(人が)(～しようと) 熱心で, 没頭して ‖ *He's always been intent on making a lot of money.* 彼は常に大金を稼ぐことに没頭していた. ―intently 副 →集中して, 熱心に

**intent²** /ɪntént/ 名 ❶ 正式 ▶定義 what sb intends to do; intention ～がしようとすること; 意図 →(～する) 意図, 目的 ‖ *He was charged with possession of a gun with intent to commit a robbery.* 彼は強盗を働く意図を持ってけん銃を所持した罪に問われた. *to do sth with evil/good intent* 悪意で・善意で～を行う

成句 **to/for all intents and purposes** ▶定義 in effect, even if not completely true たとえすべてが本当ではないにしても事実上 →どの点から見ても, 実際上 ‖ *When they scored their fourth goal the match was, to all intents and purposes, over.* 4点目のゴールを上げた時点で、試合は実際には終わっていた.

*★**intention** /ɪnténʃ(ə)n/ 名 ❸ ❶ ▶定義 (an) intention (of doing sth/to do sth) what sb intends or means to do; a plan or purpose ～がしようとすること, 意図すること; 計画, 目的 →(～する) 意図, 目的, 意志 ‖ *Our intention was to leave early in the morning.* 我々の計画は、朝早く出発することだった. *I have no intention of staying indoors on a nice sunny day like this.* こんなすばらしく晴れた日に家の中にいるつもりはない. *I borrowed the money with the intention of paying it back the next day.* 私は翌日返すつもりでお金を借りた.

*★**intentional** /ɪnténʃ(ə)n(ə)l/ 形 ▶定義 done on purpose, not by chance 偶然ではなく, 意図的になされた→故意の, 意図的な, 計画的な ‖ *I'm sorry I took your jacket - it wasn't intentional!* あなたの上着を持っていってしまってすみません ― わざとではなかったのです. ☛類 **deliberate** ⇔ **unintentional, inadvertent** ―intentionally /-ʃ(ə)n(ə)li/ 副 →故意に, 意図的に, わざと ‖ *I can't believe the boys broke the window intentionally.* 少年たちがわざと窓を割ったなんて、信じられない.

**interact** /ɪ̀ntəækt/ 動 ❸ ▶定義1 interact (with sb) (used about people) to communicate or mix with sb, especially while you work, play or spend time together (人について) ～と情報を伝え合う, 付き合う. 特に一緒に働いたり遊んだりして時間を過ごしながら→(～と) 相互に作用する, 触れ合う, 影響を及ぼし合う ‖ *He is studying the way children interact with each other at different ages.* 彼は、子供たちが異なった年齢段階でどのように影響を及ぼし合うのかを研究している. ▶定義2 (of two things) to have an effect on each other →(2つのものが) 影響を及ぼし合う ― **interaction** 名 ❶ ❸ **interaction (between/with sb/sth)** →(～の・～との) 相互作用, 打ち解けること ‖ *There is a need for greater interaction between the two departments.* その2つの部署間の一層の相互作用が必要だ.

**interactive** /ɪ̀ntəæktɪv/ 形 ▶定義1 that involves people working together and having an influence on each other 人々が一緒に働き, お互いに影響を及ぼし合うことに関する→相互対話のある, 相互に作用[影響] し合う, 触れ合い, 協力し合った ‖ *interactive language-learning techniques* 相互対話方式の言語習得技術 ▶定義2 (computing) involving direct communication both ways, between the computer and the person using it (コンピューター) コンピューターとユーザー間の双方向の直接対話の→(コンピューターシステムが) 対話型の, (通信) 双方向の ‖ *interactive computer games* 対話型のコンピューターゲーム

**intercept** /ɪ̀ntəsépt/ 動 ❶ ▶定義 to stop or catch sb/sth that is moving from one place to another ある場所から別の場所に移動している～を止める・捕まえる→～を途中で押さえる・遮る, 横取りする, 迎撃する ‖ *Detectives intercepted him at the airport.* 刑事は彼を空港で押さえた. ― **interception** 名 ❶ ❸ →途中で押さえる・遮ること, 横取り, 迎撃, 傍受

**interchangeable** /ɪ̀ntətʃéɪndʒəb(ə)l/ 形 ▶定義 **interchangeable (with sth)** able to be used in place of each other without making any difference to the way sth works 作用など何も変えることなくお互いに相手の代わりができる→(～と) 置き換えられる, 交換できる, 互換性のある ‖

*Are these two words interchangeable (= do they have the same meaning)?* これらの2つの語は置き換えられますか (= これらは同じ意味ですか). — **interchangeably** /-əbli/ 副 →交換可能で, 互いに交換して

**intercom** /íntərkàm/ 名 ⓒ ▶定義 a system of communication by radio or telephone inside an office, plane, etc; the device you press or switch on to start using this system 事務所・飛行機内などで, 無線・電話で連絡を取る仕組み; この仕組みを使い始めるためにスイッチを入れるか, 押す装置→内部相互通信装置, インターホン

**interconnect** /ìntərkənékt/ 動 自他 ▶定義 interconnect (A) (with B); interconnect A and B to connect similar things; to be connected to similar things 同様なものを連結させる; 同様なものに連結される→(〜と)相互に連結[関連]し合う, (〜と)相互に連結[関連]させる ‖ *electronic networks which interconnect thousands of computers around the world* 世界中の何千というコンピューターを連結する電子ネットワーク

**intercontinental** /ìntərkɑnt(ə)néntl/ 形 ▶定義 between continents→大陸間の ‖ *intercontinental flights* 大陸間飛行

**intercourse** /íntərkɔːrs/ = **SEX**(3)

**interdependent** /ìntərdɪpénd(ə)nt/ 形 ▶定義 depending on each other お互いに依存している→相互依存の, 互いに頼り合う ‖ *Exercise and good health are generally interdependent.* 運動と健康は, 一般的に相互依存している. *interdependent economies/organizations* 相互依存経済・相互依存関係にある組織 ― **interdependence** 名 Ⓤ →相互依存

\***interest**[1] /ínt(ə)rəst, -t(ə)rèst/ 名 ▶定義1 [ Ⓤ, 単数扱い] an interest (in sb/sth) a desire to learn or hear more about sb/sth or to be involved with sb/sth 〜についてもっと知りたい・聞きたいという願望, 〜とかかわり合いたいという願望→(〜に対する)興味, 関心 ‖ *She's begun to **show** a great **interest** in politics.* 彼女は政治に大いに興味を示し始めた. *I wish he'd **take** more **interest** in his children.* 彼がもっと子供に関心を持ってくれたらよいのだが. *Don't **lose interest** now!* 今興味を失ってはいけない. ▶定義2 Ⓤ the quality that makes sth interesting 〜を興味深くしている特質→興味を引き付ける力, 面白み ‖ *I thought this article might **be of interest to** you.* この記事はあなたの興味をひくのではないかと思った. *Computers **hold no interest for** me.* 私はコンピューターには関心がない. *places of historical interest* 歴史的興味のある場所 ▶定義3 [ ⓒ, 通常は複数] something that you enjoy doing or learning about 楽しんで行うもの, 楽しんで学ぶもの→関心事, 興味の対象, 趣味 ‖ *What are your interests and hobbies?* あなたの関心事と趣味は何ですか. ▶定義4 Ⓤ interest (on sth) the money that you pay for borrowing money from a bank, etc or the money that you earn when you keep money in a bank, etc 銀行からの借金などに対して払うお金, 銀行に貯金をしたときに得るお金→(〜の)利子, 利息 ‖ *We pay 6% interest on our mortgage at the moment.* 私たちのローンの利率は当座は6パーセントだ. *The **interest rate** has never been so high/low.* 利率がこれほど高く・低くなったことはない. *Some companies offer **interest-free** loans.* 利息なしのローンを提供する会社もある.

成句 **have/with sb's interests at heart** ▶定義 to want sb to be happy and successful, even though your actions may not show it たとえ行動ではっきり示さなくても, 〜が幸せで成功してほしいと願う→〜のことを気に掛ける ‖ *Don't be angry with your father - you know he has your best interests at heart.* お父さんに腹を立てないで — お父さんがあなたのことを一番心配していることは分かっているでしょう.

**in sb's interest(s)** ▶定義 to sb's advantage→〜に有利に[で] ‖ *Using lead-free petrol is in the public interest.* 無鉛ガソリンを使うことは, 公共の利益になる.

**in the interest(s) of sth** ▶定義 in order to achieve or protect sth 〜を達成・保護するために→〜のため[利益]になる, 〜のために, 〜のことを考えて ‖ *In the interest(s) of safety, please fasten your seat belts.* 安全のために, シートベルトをお締めください.

\***interest**[2] /ínt(ə)rəst, -t(ə)rèst/ 動 他 ▶定義 to make sb want to learn or hear more about sth or to become involved in sth 〜に…についてよ

り学びたい・聞きたいと思わせる, …に関係したいと思わせる➔(人の)(〜に対する)関心[興味]をそそる, (〜が)(人)に(…に)興味を持たせる‖ *It might interest you to know that I didn't accept the job.* 私がその仕事を引き受けなかったことをお伝えします. *The subject of the talk was one that interests me greatly.* その話のテーマは私にとって大変興味のあるものだった.

句動詞 interest sb in sth ▶定義 to persuade sb to buy, have, do sth 〜に…を買う・持つ・するように説得する➔(人に)(〜を)買いたく[やりたく・食べたく]させる‖ *Can I interest you in our new brochure?* 新しいパンフレットはいかがですか.

\***interested** /íntə̀rəstəd; -t(ə)rèstəd/ 形 ▶定義 1 (名詞の前は不可) interested (in sth/sb); interested in doing sth; interested to do sth wanting to know or hear more about sth/sb; enjoying or liking sth/sb 〜についてもっと知りたい, 聞きたいと願う; 〜を楽しむ, 好む➔(〜に)興味を持った, 関心がある‖ *They weren't interested in my news at all!* 彼らは私の知らせに全く興味を持たなかった. *I'm really not interested in going to university.* 私は大学に行くことには全く関心がない. *I was interested to hear that you've got a new job. Where is it?* あなたが新しい仕事に就いたと聞いて興味を持ったよ. どこで働くの. ⇔ **uninterested**

▶自分のしている事が気に入っていたり, それについてもっと知ったり聞いたりしたい場合は, それについて interested (興味がある), ということになる. このような気にさせる人や物は, interesting (興味深い), ということになる.

▶定義 2 (名詞の前だけ) involved in or affected by sth; in a position to gain from sth 〜に関係している, 影響を受ける; 〜から利益を得る立場の➔利害関係がある, 私利私欲のある‖ *As an interested party (= a person directly involved), I was not allowed to vote.* 利害関係者(=直接の関係者)であるので, 私は投票できない. ⇔ **disinterested**

\***interesting** /íntə̀rəstɪŋ; -t(ə)rèst-/ 形 ▶定義 interesting (to do sth); interesting that… enjoyable and entertaining; holding your attention 楽しく面白い; 興味を引き付ける➔(〜するのは)面白い, 興味深い‖ *an interesting person/book/idea/job* 面白い人・本・考え・仕事 *It's always interesting to hear about the customs of other societies.* ほかの社会の慣習について聞くことは, いつも興味深いものだ. *It's interesting that Luisa chose Peru for a holiday.* ルイーザが休暇にペルーを選んだのは興味深い.

— interestingly 副 ➔興味深く, 面白いことに

\***interfere** /ɪ̀ntərfíər/ 動 自 ▶定義 1 interfere (in sth) to get involved in a situation which does not involve you and where you are not wanted 関係もなく, 望まれてもいない状況にかかわっていく➔(〜に)干渉する, 口出しする‖ *You shouldn't interfere in your children's lives - let them make their own decisions.* 子供の人生に干渉すべきではない — 子供自身に決めさせなさい. ▶定義 2 interfere (with sb/sth) to prevent sth from succeeding or to slow down the progress that sb/sth makes 〜がうまくいくことを妨げる, 〜の進行を遅くする➔(〜の)妨げとなる, 邪魔になる‖ *Every time the telephone rings it interferes with my work.* 電話がかかってくる度に, 仕事が邪魔される. *She never lets her private life interfere with her career.* 彼女は私生活を仕事の妨げにする事は決してしない.

▶定義 3 interfere (with sth) to touch or change sth without permission 許可なく〜に触る, 〜を変える➔(〜に)触る, ひっかき回す, 干渉する‖ *Many people feel that scientists shouldn't interfere with nature.* 多くの人々は, 科学者たちが自然を干渉すべきではないと感じている.

— interfering 形 ➔干渉する, お節介を焼く

**interference** /ɪ̀ntərfíər(ə)ns/ 名 U ▶定義 1 interference (in sth) the act of getting involved in a situation that does not involve you and where you are not wanted 自分が関係せず, 望まれてもいない状況にかかわりを持つための行為➔(〜への)妨害, 障害, 干渉, 邪魔‖ *I left home because I couldn't stand my parents' interference in my affairs.* 両親にいちいち干渉されることに我慢できなかったので, 家を出た.

▶定義 2 extra noise (because of other signals or bad weather) that prevents you from receiving radio, television or telephone signals clearly ラジオ・テレビ・電話の信号を鮮明に受信するのを妨げる, (ほかの信号や悪天候による)不用

な雑音→(音波・電波・光などの)干渉, (ラジオなどの)混信

**interim**¹ /íntərəm/ 形 (名詞の前だけ) ▶定義 not final or lasting; temporary until sb/sth more permanent is found 最終的ではない, 永続的ではない; より永続的な〜が見つかるまでの一時的な→当座の, 仮の, 暫時の ‖ *an interim arrangement* 仮協定 *The deputy head teacher took over in **the interim period** until a replacement could be found.* 代わりの人が見つかるまでしばらくの間, 代理の校長が引き継いだ.

**interim**² /íntərəm/ 名
成句 **in the interim** ▶定義 in the time between two things happening; until a particular event happens 2つの出来事が起こる間に; 特定の出来事が起きるまでに→その間, 当座の間

\*__interior__ /intíəriər/ 名 ▶定義 1 [ C, 通常は単数] the inside of sth 〜の内側→内部, 内側, 室内 ‖ *I'd love to see the interior of the castle.* お城の内部を見たいのです. *interior walls* 内壁 ⇔ **exterior** ▶定義 2 **the interior** [単数扱い] the central part of a country or continent that is a long way from the coast 海岸から遠く離れた, 国・大陸の中心部→内陸, 内地, 奥地 ▶定義 3 **the Interior** [単数扱い] a country's own news and affairs that do not involve other countries 国内のニュースや出来事で, 他国が関係しないもの→内政 ‖ *the Department of the Interior* 内務省

**interior design** 名 Ⓤ ▶定義 the art or job of choosing colours, furniture, carpets, etc to decorate the inside of a house 家の内装のために, 色・家具・じゅうたんなどを選ぶ技術・仕事→インテリアデザイン, 室内装飾 — **interior designer** 名 Ⓒ →インテリアデザイナー, 室内装飾家

**interjection** /ìntərdʒékʃ(ə)n/ 名 Ⓒ (文法) ▶定義 a word or phrase that is used to express surprise, pain, pleasure, etc (for example Oh!, Hurray! or Wow!) 驚き・痛み・喜びなどを表す語・句 (例 Oh!, Hurray!, Wow!) →間投詞, 感嘆詞 ☛類 **exclamation**

**interlude** /íntərlùːd/ 名 Ⓒ ▶定義 a period of time between two events or activities 2つの出来事・活動の間の期間→合間, 合間の出来事 ‖ *They finally met again after an interlude of 20 years.* 彼らは20年振りに, ついに再会した.

---

**intermittent** 895

☛参 **interval** の注

**intermarry** /ìntərmǽri/ 動 Ⓘ (現分 **intermarrying**; 三単現 **intermarries**; 過, 過分 **intermarried**) ▶定義 to marry sb from a different religion, culture, country, etc 異なった宗教・文化・国などの人と結婚する→(異なる民族・宗教・階級の人と)結婚する — **intermarriage** /ìntərmǽridʒ/ 名 Ⓤ →異なる民族・宗教・階級間の結婚

**intermediary** /ìntərmíːdièri, -dièri/ 名 Ⓒ (複 **intermediaries**) ▶定義 an intermediary (between A and B) a person or an organization that helps two people or groups to reach an agreement, by being a means of communication between them 両者間の意志伝達の中継ぎをすることによって, 2人の人・2つの集団が合意に至るのを助ける人・組織→仲介者, 媒介人, 調停者

\*__intermediate__ /ìntərmíːdiət/ 形 ▶定義 1 situated between two things in position, level, etc 位置・水準などにおいて, 2つのものの間にある→中間の, 間にある, 介在している, 中級の ‖ *an intermediate step/stage in a process* ある過程における中間段階 ▶定義 2 having more than a basic knowledge of sth but not yet advanced; suitable for sb who is at this level 〜に関して基礎レベル以上の知識はあるが, まだ上級には達していない; この水準の〜に適した→中級の ‖ *an intermediate student/book/level* 中級の生徒・本・レベル

**interminable** /ìntə́ːm(ə)nəb(ə)l/ 形 ▶定義 lasting for a very long time and therefore boring or annoying 非常に長時間続き, そのために退屈でいらいらさせる→いつ終わるとも知れない, 延々と続く, 切りのない ‖ *an interminable delay/wait/speech* 延々と続く遅れ・果てしなく待たされること・いつ終わるとも知れない演説 ☛類 **endless** — **interminably** /-əbli/ 副 →延々と, 果てしなく, 長々と

**intermission** /ìntərmíʃ(ə)n/ 名 Ⓒ 特に 米 ▶定義 a short period of time separating the parts of a film, play, etc 映画・演劇などで, 各部を分ける短い時間→(劇場などの)休憩時間, 幕間(まくあい) ☛参 **interval** の注

**intermittent** /ìntərmít(ə)nt/ 形 ▶定義 stopping

for a short time and then starting again several times 短時間停止してから再開することを数回繰り返す➡断続的な, 間隔をおいて起こる ‖ *There will be intermittent showers.* 時々にわか雨があるでしょう. — **intermittently** 副 ➡断続的に, 時々とぎれながら

**intern** /ɪntə́ːn/ 動 ⊕ 正式 ▶定義 intern sb (in sth) (通常は受動態で) to keep sb in prison for political reasons, especially during a war 特に戦争中に, ~を政治的な理由で獄中に置く➡(捕虜・外国人など)を抑留する, ~を(…に)強制収容する — **internment** 名 ⓤ ➡抑留, 拘留, 収容

*****internal** /ɪntə́ːnl/ 形 ▶定義1 (名詞の前だけ) of or on the inside (of a place, person or object) (場所・人・物の)内側の[に] ➡内部の, 内部にある, 体内の ‖ *He was rushed to hospital with internal injuries.* 彼は内傷で病院に急送された. ▶定義2 happening or existing inside a particular organization 特定の組織の内部で起こった, 内部に存在している➡組織内の ‖ *an internal exam* (= one arranged and marked inside a particular school or college) 内部試験 (= 特定の学校・大学内で準備され採点された試験) *an internal police inquiry* 警察の内部調査 ▶定義3 (used about political or economic affairs) inside a country; not abroad (政治・経済問題について)国内の; 海外ではない➡国内の, 内政の ‖ *a country's internal affairs/trade/markets* 一国の国内問題・貿易・市場 *an internal flight* 国内線 ⇔ **external** — **internally** /-n(ə)li/ 副 ➡内部に, 内面的に, 国内で ‖ *This medicine is not to be taken internally* (= not swallowed). この薬は内服薬ではない (= 飲まない).

*****international** /ɪntəːnǽʃ(ə)n(ə)l/ 形 ▶定義 involving two or more countries 2つ以上の国が関係して➡国際的な, 国家間の, 国際上の ‖ *an international agreement/flight/football match* 国際協定・国際線・サッカーの国際試合 *international trade/law/sport* 国際貿易・国際法・国際スポーツ ☞参 **local, national, regional** — **internationally** /-n(ə)li/ 副 ➡国際的に, 国際間で

*****the Internet** /ɪntənèt/ (または **the Net**) 名 [単数扱い] ▶定義 (computing) the international system of computers that makes it possible for you to see information from all around the world on your computer and to send information to other computers (コンピューター) 国際的なコンピューターシステムで, それにより世界中のコンピューターからの情報を自分のコンピューターで見ることができ, ほかのコンピューターに情報を送ることができる➡インターネット(世界規模のコンピューターネットワーク) ‖ *I read about it on the Internet.* それについては, インターネットで読んだ.
➤ **intranet** と比較.

*****interpret** /ɪntə́ːprət/ 動 ▶定義1 ⊕ interpret sth (as sth) to explain or understand the meaning of sth ~の意味を説明する, 理解する➡~を(…と)解釈する ‖ *Your silence could be interpreted as arrogance.* あなたの沈黙は, ごう慢さと見なされかねない. *How would you interpret this part of the poem?* 詩のこの部分をどのように解釈しますか. ⇔ **misinterpret** ▶定義2 ⊕ interpret (for sb) to translate what sb is saying into another language as you hear it ~が言っている事を聞きながら, ほかの言語に訳する➡(~のために)通訳する, (データを)翻訳する ‖ *He can't speak much English so he'll need somebody to interpret for him.* 彼はあまり英語が話せないので, だれか通訳をしてくれる人が必要だ.

**interpretation** /ɪntəːprətéɪʃ(ə)n/ 名 ⓒⓤ ▶定義1 an explanation or understanding of sth➡説明, 理解, 解釈 ‖ *What's your interpretation of these statistics?* これらの統計をどのように解釈しますか. *What he meant by that remark is* **open to interpretation** (= it can be explained in different ways). 彼の発言の意味するところは解釈次第だ (= さまざまに説明できる). ▶定義2 the way an actor or musician chooses to perform or understand a character or piece of music 役者が選択する演じ方や登場人物の理解の仕方, 音楽家が選択する演奏の仕方や曲に対する理解の仕方➡(自分の解釈・理解による)役作り, 演出, 演奏 ‖ *a modern interpretation of 'Hamlet'*「ハムレット」の現代的な演出

**interpreter** /ɪntə́ːprətər/ 名 ⓒ ▶定義 a person whose job is to translate what sb is saying immediately into another language ~の発言を直ちにほかの言語に通訳する仕事に就いている人➡通訳者 ‖ *The president spoke through an interpreter.* 大統領は通訳を介して話した.

☞参 translator

**interrelate** /ìntərɪléɪt/ 動自他（通常は受動態で）**正式** ▶定義 (used about two or more things) to connect or be connected very closely so that each has an effect on the other（2つ以上の事柄について）非常に密接に関係し，関連づけられているので，それぞれがほかのものに影響を及ぼす→（〜と）相互に関連する；〜を（…と）相互に関連させる ― interrelated 形→相互に関連する，相関する

**interrogate** /ɪntérəgèɪt/ 動他 ▶定義 interrogate sb (about sth) to ask sb a lot of questions over a long period of time, especially in an aggressive way 長時間にわたって〜にたくさんの質問をする．特に攻撃的な方法で行う→〜を（…について）尋問する，審問する，取り調べる ‖ *The prisoner was interrogated for six hours.* 囚人は6時間にわたって取り調べを受けた．― interrogator 名 C→尋問者，取り調べ官 ― interrogation /ɪntèrəgéɪʃ(ə)n/ 名 C U→尋問，審問，取り調べ ‖ *The prisoner broke down under interrogation and confessed.* 囚人は取り調べに屈し，自白した．

**interrogative**¹ /ìntərάgətɪv/ 形 ▶定義 1 **正式** asking a question; having the form of a question 質問をして，質問の形をとって→（口調・表情などが）問い掛けるような，物問いたげな ‖ *an interrogative tone/gesture/remark* 問い掛けるような口調・身振り・発言 ▶定義 2（文法）used in questions 疑問に使用される→疑問の ‖ *an interrogative sentence/pronoun/determiner/adverb* 疑問文・疑問代名詞・疑問限定詞・疑問副詞

**interrogative**² /ìntərάgətɪv/ 名 C（文法）▶定義 a question word 疑問を表す語→疑問詞，疑問文 ‖ *'Who', 'what' and 'where' are interrogatives.* who, what, where は疑問詞である．

*****interrupt** /ìntərʌ́pt/ 動 ▶定義 1 自他 interrupt (sb/sth) (with sth) to say or do sth that makes sb stop what he/she is saying or doing 〜を言ったり行ったりして，…が話している・行っていることをやめさせる→（〜の）邪魔をする，（〜を）（…で）妨害する，中断する ‖ *He kept interrupting me with silly questions.* 彼はばかげた質問をして私の邪魔をし続けた． ▶定義 2 他 to stop the progress of sth for a short time 〜の進行を短時間止める→（仕事など）を中断する，中止する，分断する ‖ *The programme was inter-rupted by an important news flash.* その番組は重要なニュース速報のために中断した．

**interruption** /ìntərʌ́pʃ(ə)n/ 名 U C ▶定義 the act of interrupting sb/sth; the person or thing that interrupts sb/sth 〜を邪魔する行為；〜を邪魔する人・事柄→邪魔，妨害，中断，休止 ‖ *I need to work for a few hours without interruption.* 私は数時間ぶっ通しで働かねばならない． *I've had so many interruptions this morning that I've done nothing!* 今朝は邪魔が多かったので何もできなかった．

**intersect** /ìntərsékt/ 動自他 ▶定義 (used about roads, lines, etc) to meet or cross each other（道路・線路などについて）お互いに接続する，交差する→〜を横切る，〜と交差する；交わる ‖ *The lines intersect at right angles.* 直線は直角に交わっている．

**intersection** /ìntərsékʃ(ə)n/ 名 C ▶定義 the place where two or more roads, lines, etc meet or cross each other 2つ以上の道路・線路などがお互いに接続・交差する場所→（道路の）交差点，交差，横断；（数学）交点

**intersperse** /ìntərspə́ːrs/ 動他（通常は受動態で）▶定義 to put things at various points in sth 〜の途中のいろいろな地点に，ものを差し挟む→〜を（…の間に・…の一帯に）散在させる，まき散らす，散りばめる ‖ *He interspersed his speech with jokes.* 彼は演説の所々に冗談を交えた．

**intertwine** /ìntərtwáɪn/ 動自他 ▶定義 if two things intertwine or if you intertwine them, they become very closely connected and difficult to separate 2つの事柄が絡み合う (intertwine) 場合，または絡み合わせる (intertwine them) 場合，それらは非常に密接に結び付き，離すのが難しくなる→（糸・指などが）絡み合う，より合わさる；（糸・指など）を（〜と）絡み合わせる ‖ *His interests in business and politics were closely intertwined.* 彼の事業と政治における利害関係は，密接に絡み合っていた．

*****interval** /ìntərv(ə)l/ 名 C ▶定義 1 a period of time between two events 2つの出来事の間→（時間・空間の）間隔，隔たり ‖ *There was a long interval between sending the letter and getting a reply.* 手紙を出してから返事を受け取るまでに

は長い間隔があった． ▶定義2 a short break separating the different parts of a play, film, concert, etc 芝居，映画，コンサートなどの部を分ける短い休憩→**(劇・コンサートなどの) 幕間 (まくあい), 休憩時間** ▶定義3 [通常は複数] a short period during which sth different happens from what is happening for the rest of the time それ以外の時間に起きている事とは異なった〜が起きている短い時間→**合間, 休止期間** ‖ *There'll be a few sunny intervals between the showers today.* 本日は，にわか雨の合間に少し晴れ間もあるでしょう．

➤ interval と同様の意味を持つ語としては，intermission, break, recess, interlude, pause がある．イギリス英語では，interval は幕間 (まくあい) の意味で使われる．この意味で使われるアメリカ英語は，intermission である．break は特に，仕事・勉強の休憩として使われる．例えば，事務所・工場・学校での a lunch/tea break (昼休み・休憩時間) などである: *The children play outside in the breaks at school.* (学校で子供たちは休み時間に外で遊ぶ．) *You've worked so hard you've earned a break.* (とても熱心に働いたのだから，一休みしてください．) アメリカ英語では，breaks at school (学校の休み時間) は (a) recess と言う．イギリス英語では，recess は仕事・事務が休みのもっと長い期間のことを指し，特に議会や法廷に使われる: *Parliament is in recess.* (議会は休会中だ．) *the summer recess* (夏の休会期). interlude は2つの出来事の間の短い期間のことで，その間に何か違った事が起きる: *a peaceful interlude in the fighting* (戦いの間の平和休暇). a pause は活動・演説の短い一時的な停止のことである: *After a moment's pause, she answered.* (一瞬の間をおいてから，彼女は答えた．)

**成句** **at intervals** ▶定義 with time or spaces between 時間・間隔をおいて→**時々, あちこちに, 所々に** ‖ *I write home at regular intervals.* 私は時々，家に手紙を書いた． *Plant the trees at two-metre intervals.* 2メートル間隔で木を植えなさい．

**intervene** /ɪntəvíːn/ 動⊜ ▶定義1 intervene (in sth) to act in a way that prevents sth happening or influences the result of sth 〜が起こるのを防ぐように行動する，〜の結果に影響を及ぼすように行動する→**(〜に) 介入する, 干渉する, 仲裁に入る** ‖ *She would have died if the neighbours hadn't intervened.* 隣の人が仲裁に入らなかったなら，彼女は死んでいたであろう． *to intervene in a dispute* 紛争の調停をする ▶定義2 to interrupt sb who is speaking in order to say sth 何か言う目的で，話している〜を遮る→**邪魔に入る** ▶定義3 (used about events, etc) to happen in a way that delays sth or stops it from happening (出来事などについて) 〜を遅らせる，〜が起きることを止める→**(不測の事態などが) 邪魔をする, 妨げる** ‖ *If no further problems intervene we should be able to finish in time.* もしその間にこれ以上問題が起きなければ，時間までに終わらせることができるだろう． — **intervention** /ɪntəvénʃ(ə)n/ 名 ⓤ ⓒ intervention (in sth) →**(〜への) 介入, 干渉, 仲裁** ‖ *military intervention in the crisis* 危機に対する軍事介入

**intervening** /ɪntəvíːnɪŋ/ 形 (名詞の前だけ) ▶定義 coming or existing between two events, dates, objects, etc 2つの出来事・日付・物などの間に来る，存在する→**(年月・距離が) 間に横たわる, 介在する** ‖ *the intervening years/days/months* その間の何年間・何日間・何か月間

*__interview__¹ /ɪ́ntəvjuː/ 名ⓒ ▶定義1 an interview (for sth) a meeting at which sb is asked questions to find out if he/she is suitable for a job, course of study, etc 〜が質問を受け，仕事・学習課程などに適しているかを調べられる場→**(就職などの) 面接, 面接試験, 面談** ‖ *to attend an interview* 面接に出席する ▶定義2 an interview (with sb) a meeting at which a journalist asks sb questions in order to find out his/her opinion, etc ジャーナリストが〜に質問をし，その意見などを知るための会見→**(〜の) インタビュー, 取材, 記者会見** ‖ *There was an interview with the Prime Minister on television last night.* 昨夜テレビで，首相の記者会見があった． *The actress refused to __give an interview__ (= answer questions).* 彼女の女優はインタビュー (= 質問に答えること) に応じなかった．

*__interview__² /ɪ́ntəvjuː/ 動⓽ ▶定義1 interview sb (for sth) to ask sb questions to find out if he/she is suitable for a job, course of study, etc 〜に質問をし, 仕事・学習課程などに適しているかを調べる➔〜に面接する, 面接試験をする ‖ *How many applicants did you interview for the job?* その仕事に対して何人の志願者に面接しましたか. ▶定義2 **interview sb (about sth)** to ask sb questions about his/her opinions, private life, etc especially on the radio or television or for a newspaper, magazine, etc 特に, ラジオ・テレビや新聞・雑誌で, 〜に意見・私生活などについて質問をする➔〜に(…について)インタビューする, 〜に会って取材する ▶定義3 **interview sb (about sth)** to ask sb questions at a private meeting 個人的に会って, 〜に質問をする➔〜を取材訪問する, 〜に聴き込み捜査をする, 面談する ‖ *The police are waiting to interview the injured girl.* 警察はけがをした少女に直接事情を聴くのを待ち望んでいる.

**interviewee** /ˌɪntərvjuːˈiː/ 名 C ▶定義 a person who is questioned in an interview インタビューで質問される人➔(求職などの)面接を受ける人, インタビューされる人

**interviewer** /ˈɪntərvjuːər/ 名 C ▶定義 a person who asks the questions in an interview インタビューで質問をする人➔面接をする人, インタビューする人, 聞き手

**intestine** /ɪnˈtɛstən/ 名 [C, 通常は複数] ▶定義 the tube in your body that carries food away from your stomach to the place where it leaves your body 体内の管状器官で, 食物を胃から運び, 体外に出ていく場所まで持っていく➔腸 ☛ gut は略式な語. ☛ C5 ページのさし絵 — **intestinal** /ɪnˈtɛstənəl/ 形 ➔腸の, 腸内の, 腸に発生する

**intimacy** /ˈɪntəməsi/ 名 U ▶定義 the state of having a close personal relationship with sb 〜と親密な個人的関係を結んだ状態➔(〜との・〜の間の)親密さ, 懇意 ‖ *Their intimacy grew over the years.* 彼らの親密さは, 何年もの間に深まってきたものだった.

**intimate** /ˈɪntəmət/ 形 ▶定義1 (used about people) having a very close relationship (人々について)非常に親密な関係を持つ➔(人と)親しい, 親密な, 懇意な ‖ *They're intimate friends.* 彼らは親友だ. ▶定義2 very private and personal 非常に私的で個人的な➔私的な, 個人的な, 私事の ‖ *They told each other their most intimate thoughts and secrets.* 彼らはお互いに, 最も個人的な考えや一身上の秘密を話した. ▶定義3 (used about a place, an atmosphere, etc) quiet and friendly (場所・雰囲気などについて)静かで親しみやすい➔(場所などが)くつろげる ‖ *I know an intimate little restaurant we could go to.* 私はこぢんまりと居心地の良い手ごろなレストランを知っています. ▶定義4 very detailed 非常に詳しい➔詳しい, 精通した ‖ *He's lived here all his life and has an intimate knowledge of the area.* 彼は生まれてからずっとここに住んでいるので, この辺りには精通している. — **intimately** 副 ➔親密に, 親しく, 詳細に

**intimidate** /ɪnˈtɪmədeɪt/ 動 他 ▶定義 **intimidate sb (into sth/doing sth)** to frighten or threaten sb, often in order to make him/her do sth 多くは〜に…をやらせるために〜を脅す, 脅迫する➔〜を脅迫する, 脅す, 〜を脅して…させる ‖ *She refused to be intimidated by their threats.* 彼女は彼らの脅しに頑として屈しなかった. — **intimidating** 形 ➔人を怖がらせる, 威嚇する ‖ *The teacher had rather an intimidating manner.* その教師はやや威嚇的な態度だった. — **intimidation** /ɪnˌtɪməˈdeɪʃ(ə)n/ 名 U ➔脅し, 脅迫 ‖ *The rebel troops controlled the area by intimidation.* 反乱軍は脅してその地域を制圧した.

*__**into**__ /ˈɪntə, 母音の前 ˈɪntu/ 前 ▶定義1 moving to a position inside or in sth 〜(の中)のある場所に移動する➔〜の中へ, 〜の中に ‖ *Come into the house.* 家に入りなさい. *I'm going into town.* 私は街に入るところです. ⇔ **out of**(1) ▶定義2 in the direction of sth➔〜の方向へ[に], 〜(の内部)に向かって ‖ *Please speak into the microphone.* マイクロホンに向かってしゃべってください. *At this point we were driving into the sun and had to shade our eyes.* この時点で我々は太陽の方に向かって運転しており, サングラスをする必要があった. ▶定義3 to a point at which you hit sth 〜のぶつけた所へ➔(接触・衝突)〜に(ぶつかって) ‖ *I backed the car into a wall.* 私は車をバックして壁にぶつけた. *She walked into a glass door.* 彼女は歩いてガラスのドアにぶつかった. ▶定義4 showing a change from one thing to another あるものからほかのものへの変化を示

## 900 intolerable

して→(ある状態への推移・変化・結果)～に(変わる), ～に(なる), ～の状態に(なる・する) || *We're turning the spare room into a study.* 我々は予備の部屋を勉強部屋に変える予定だ. *She changed into her jeans.* 彼女はジーンズに着替えた. *Translate the passage into German.* その一節をドイツ語に訳しなさい. ▶定義5 concerning or involving sth→～に関する, 関係する || *an inquiry into safety procedures* 安全手順に関する調査 ▶定義6 used when you are talking about dividing numbers 数を割るときに用いて→～を割って || *7 into 28 goes 4 times* 28を7で割ると4になる.

成句 **be into sth** (口語) ▶定義 to be very interested in sth, for example as a hobby 例えば趣味として, ～に非常に興味がある→～に熱中・没頭して, ～に夢中になって, ～にのめり込んで || *I'm really into canoeing.* 私はカヌー競技にとても熱中している.

**intolerable** /ɪntɑ́l(ə)rəb(ə)l/ 形 ▶定義 too bad, unpleasant or difficult to bear or accept あまりにもひどくて・不愉快で・厳しくて我慢できない, 受け入れ難い→耐えられない, 我慢できない || *The living conditions were intolerable.* 生活状況は耐え難いものだった. *intolerable pain* 耐えられない痛み ☛類 **unbearable** ⇔ **tolerable** ☛動 **tolerate** — **intolerably** /-əbli/ 副 →耐えられないほど, 我慢できないほど

**intolerant** /ɪntɑ́l(ə)rənt/ 形 ▶定義 **intolerant (of sb/sth)** not able to accept behaviour or opinions that are different from your own; finding sb/sth too unpleasant to bear 自分と異なる意見・行動を受け入れられない; ～が非常に不愉快で我慢できないと感じる→(異説・異民族などに対して)不寛容な, 狭量な, (～を)認めない || *She's very intolerant of young children.* 彼女は小さな子供に対して非常に不寛容だ. ⇔ **tolerant** — **intolerance** 名 U → (異説・異民族などに対する)不寛容, 狭量 ⇔ **tolerance** — **intolerantly** 副 →偏狭に, 我慢できないで

**intonation** /ɪ̀ntənéɪʃ(ə)n, -tou-/ 名 C U ▶定義 the rise and fall of your voice while you are speaking 話している間の声の上がり下がり→イントネーション, (声の)抑揚, 音調 ☛類 **inflection**

### ▶音声とつづり字

**John に呼び掛けるときの口調**

/ John? (= Are you John? ジョンかい?)
～John! (= John, don't do that. ジョン, 駄目だよ, そんな事しちゃ.)
∧John! (= You are John. Pleasant surprise! ジョンじゃないか! 会えるなんて!)
∨John? (= You are John, aren't you? ほんとにジョンかい?)
| Joh-| n! (= John. Where are you? ジョン, 一体どこにいるの?)

**intoxicated** /ɪntɑ́ksəkèɪtəd/ 形 正式 ▶定義1 having had too much alcohol to drink; drunk 酒を飲みすぎて; 酔っ払って→酒に酔った ▶定義2 very excited and happy 非常に興奮して楽しい→(～に)熱狂して, 夢中になって, 酔って || *She was intoxicated by her success.* 彼女は成功に酔いしれた. — **intoxication** /ɪntɑ̀ksəkéɪʃ(ə)n/ 名 U →(酒に)酔うこと, 熱狂, 興奮

**intranet** /ɪ́ntrənèt/ 名 C ▶定義 (computing) a system of computers inside an organization that makes it possible for people who work there to look at the same information and to send information to each other (コンピューター) 組織内のコンピューターシステムで, そこで働く人々が共通の情報を参照し, お互いに情報を送ることができる→イントラネット
▶ **Internet** と比較.

**intransitive** /ɪntrǽnsətɪv, -zə-/ 形 (文法) (動詞について) ▶定義 used without an object 目的語を伴わないで用いられる→自動詞 ⇔ **transitive**
▶ この辞書では, 自動詞は 自 で表示している. 自動詞についての説明は, 「文法早見表」を参照. — **intransitively** 副 →自動詞として

**intrepid** /ɪntrépəd/ 形 ▶定義 without any fear of danger 危険に対する恐怖心のない→恐れを知らない, 怖いもの知らずの, 大胆不敵な || *an intrepid climber* 怖いもの知らずの登山家

**intricacy** /ɪ́ntrɪkəsi/ 名 ▶定義1 **intricacies** [複数扱い] **the intricacies of sth** the complicated parts or details of sth ～の込み入った部分, 細部→込み入った事柄, 事情 || *It's difficult to understand all the intricacies of the situation.* その状況の込み入った事情をすべて理解するのは難し

い． ▶定義2 ❶the quality of having complicated parts, details or patterns 複雑な部分・細部・模様を持っていること→複雑さ，込み入っていること

**intricate** /ˈɪntrɪkət/ 形 ▶定義 having many small parts or details put together in a complicated way たくさんの細かい部分・細部が複雑に入り組んでいる→(話・絵柄・機械などが)複雑な，入り組んだ ‖ *an intricate pattern* 複雑な模様 *The story has an intricate plot.* その物語は筋が入り組んでいる． ― **intricately** 副 →複雑に，入り組んで

**intrigue**¹ /ɪnˈtriːɡ/ 動 ⊕ ▶定義 to make sb very interested and wanting to know more 〜の興味をひき，もっと知りたい気にさせる→〜の好奇心をそそる，興味をひく ‖ *I was intrigued by the way he seemed to know all about us already.* 彼が私たちについて既に何でも知っているような態度を取ることに興味をひかれた． ― **intriguing** 形 →好奇心をそそる，興味をひく，魅力的な ‖ *an intriguing story* 好奇心をそそる物語

**intrigue**² /ˈɪntriːɡ/ 名 ❷ ⊕ ▶定義 secret plans to do sth, especially sth bad 〜を行う秘密の計画で，特に悪いもの→陰謀，策略，たくらみ ‖ *The film is about political intrigues against the government.* この映画は政府に対する政治的陰謀についてのものです． *His new novel is full of intrigue and suspense.* 彼の新しい小説は，陰謀とサスペンスに満ちている．

**intrinsic** /ɪnˈtrɪnsɪk, -zɪk/ 形 (名詞の前だけ) ▶定義 belonging to sth as part of its nature; basic 〜に本質的に備わっている；根本的な→(価値・性質などが)(〜に)本来備わっている，本質的な，固有の ‖ *The object is of no intrinsic value (= the material it is made of is not worth anything).* そのものには本質的な価値はない (= それを作っている素材には価値がない)． ― **intrinsically** /-k(ə)li/ 副 →本質的に，本来

*****introduce** /ˌɪntrəˈd(j)uːs/ 動 ⊕ ▶定義1 introduce sth (in/into sth) to bring in sth new, use sth, or take sth to a place for the first time 初めて新しい〜を持ち込む，初めて〜を使う，初めて〜をある場所に持っていく→(〜に)(新しい事物)を取り入れる，導入する，(新製品など)を売り出す，発表する ‖ *The new law was introduced in 1991.* 新しい法律は1991年に導入された． *The company is introducing a new range of cars this summer.* その会社は新しい品ぞろえの車を今年の夏に発表する． *Goats were first introduced to the island in the 17th century.* ヤギは17世紀に初めてこの島に連れてこられた． ▶定義2 introduce sb (to sb) to tell two or more people who have not met before what each others' names are それまで会ったことのなかった2人以上の人に，お互いの名前などを教える→〜を(…に)紹介する ‖ *'Who's that girl over there?' 'Come with me and I'll introduce you to her.'* 「あそこの少女はだれ」「一緒に来て．あなたを彼女に紹介するから」 ▶定義3 introduce yourself (to sb) to tell sb you have met for the first time what your name is 初めて会った〜に自分の名前を伝える→(〜に)自己紹介する ‖ *He just walked over and introduced himself to me.* 彼はちょっとこちらに来て，私に自己紹介をした． ▶定義4 introduce sb to sth to make sb begin to learn about sth or do sth for the first time 〜に…を習い始めさせる，…を初めて経験させる→〜に(新しい事物)を経験させる，〜を…に触れさせる，手ほどきする ‖ *This pamphlet will introduce you to the basic aims of our society.* このパンフレットは，我々の協会の基本的な目的を知る手掛かりとなるでしょう． ▶定義5 to be the first or main speaker on a radio or television programme telling the audience who is going to speak, perform, etc ラジオ・テレビ番組で最初の，または主な話し手となり，聴衆にだれがこれから話をするか，演技するかなどを案内する→〜に(番組など)を紹介する，〜を案内する ‖ *May I introduce my first guest on the show tonight...* 今夜のショーの最初のゲストを紹介いたします．

▶英国では，人を紹介する方法がさまざまあり，場合によって使い分ける．正式な紹介では，人の称号と，それに続けて名字を使う．略式な場合や子供を紹介する場合は，名前を使う．正式な場合も略式な場合も，紹介する人に触れるときは this is を使い，he/she is は使わない： 略式 *'John, meet Mary.'* (「ジョン，メアリーを紹介するよ」) 略式 *'Mrs Smith, **this is** my daughter, Jane.'* (「スミスさん，これが私の娘のジェーンです」) 正式 *'May I introduce you. Dr Waters, **this is** Mr Jones. Mr Jones, Dr Waters.'*

## 902 introduction

(「ご紹介いたします．ウォーターズ博士，こちらがジョーンズさんです．ジョーンズさん，こちらがウォーターズ博士です」) 紹介に対する略式の返事は，Hello または Nice to meet you. である．正式な返事は，How do you do? で，紹介された方も How do you do? と答える．紹介されたときは，多くの場合握手をする．

**\*introduction** /ɪntrədʌkʃ(ə)n/ 名 ▶定義1 ❶ introduction of sth (into sth) the action of bringing in sth new; using sth or taking sth to a place for the first time 新しい〜を持ち込む行為，初めて〜を使用すること，初めて〜をある場所に持っていくこと→(〜の・〜への) **導入, 採用, 取り入れ, 伝来** ‖ *the introduction of computers into the classroom* 学校へのコンピューターの導入 ▶定義2 [❸, 通常は複数] the act of telling two or more people each others' names for the first time 2人以上の人に初めてお互いの名前を教える→(〜への) **紹介, 披露** ‖ *I think I'll get my husband to* **make/do the introductions** *- he's better at remembering names!* 夫に紹介をしてもらおうと思います — 彼の方が名前を覚えるのが得意なので．▶定義3 ❸ the first part of a book, a piece of written work or a talk which gives a general idea of what is going to follow 本・文書・話の最初の部分で，それに続く部分の概要を表したもの→(本・話・曲の) **導入部, 序論, 序文, 序表, 前奏** ▶定義4 ❸ an introduction (to sth) a book for people who are beginning to study a subject ある主題について勉強をし始めた人のための本→(〜への) **手引き(書), 入門(書), 概説** ‖ *'An Introduction to English Grammar'*『英文法入門』 ▶定義5 [単数扱い] an introduction to sth first experience of sth→**〜の初めての経験, 〜を初めて知ること** ‖ *My first job - in a factory - was not a pleasant introduction to work.* 私の初めての仕事は ー工場に入ったけど ー 愉快な仕事始めじゃなかった．

**introductory** /ɪntrədʌkt(ə)ri/ 形 ▶定義1 happening or said at the beginning in order to give a general idea of what will follow 初めの出来事・発言で，それに続くものの概要を示すためのもの→**導入の, 前置きの** ‖ *an introductory speech/chapter/remark* 紹介の話・序章・前置き ▶定義2 intended as an introduction to a subject or an activity ある主題や活動についての導入として考えられた→**入門の** ‖ *introductory courses* 入門コース

**introvert** /ˈɪntrəvɜːrt, -/ 名 ❸ ▶定義 a quiet, shy person who prefers to be alone than with other people 物静かで内気な性格で, 人の中にいるよりも1人でいることを好む人→**内向的な人, 内気な人** ⇔ **extrovert** — introverted 形→**内向性の, 内向的な, 内気な**

**intrude** /ɪntruːd/ 動 ❸ ▶定義 intrude on/upon sb/sth to enter a place or situation without permission or when you are not wanted 許可なく, あるいは望まれてもいないのに, ある場所に入り込む・状況に加わる→**〜に押し入る, 侵入する, 邪魔をする, 割り込む** ‖ *I'm sorry to intrude on your Sunday lunch but...* 日曜日の昼食のお邪魔をして申し訳ありませんが...

**intruder** /ɪntruːdər/ 名 ❸ ▶定義 a person who enters a place without permission and often secretly 許可なく, 多くはこっそりとある場所に入る人→**(盗みなどの目的での) 侵入者, 邪魔者, 出しゃばり**

**intrusion** /ɪntruːʒ(ə)n/ 名 ❸ ❹ ▶定義 (an) intrusion (on/upon/into sth) something that disturbs you or your life when you want to be private 私的な立場でいたいときに, その人・その生活を邪魔するもの→**(プライバシーなどの) 侵害, 邪魔, (〜に) みだりに立ち入ること** ‖ *This was another example of press intrusion into the affairs of the royals.* これは, またしても王室に対してのマスコミによるプライバシー侵害の一例だった． — intrusive /ɪntruːsɪv/ 形→**プライバシーを侵害する, 私生活に立ち入る**

**intuition** /ɪnt(j)uˈɪʃ(ə)n/ 名 ❸ ❹ ▶定義 the feeling or understanding that makes you believe or know sth is true without being able to explain why その理由は説明できないが〜が正しいと分かり, 信じる気にさせる感覚・認識力→**直観, 勘** ‖ *She knew, by intuition, about his illness although he never mentioned it.* 彼は決してそれには触れなかったが, 彼女には直感的に彼の病気が分かった． — intuitive /ɪnt(j)uːɪtɪv/ 形→**直観的な, 直観による, 直観力のある** — intuitively 副→**直観的に (言えば)** ‖ *Intuitively, she knew that he was lying.* 直観的に, 彼女は彼がうそをついていると分かった．

**Inuit** /ˈɪn(j)uət/ 名 ❸ (複 **Inuit** または **Inuits**)

▶定義 (a member of) the race of people from northern Canada and parts of Alaska, Greenland, and eastern Siberia カナダ北部とアラスカの一部, グリーンランド, 東シベリア出身の民族, またその民族の一員➜イヌイット族(の1人) — Inuit [形]➜イヌイットの, イヌイット語の

**inundate** /ínəndèɪt/ [動][他] (通常は受動態で) ▶定義1 inundate sb (with sth) to give or send sb so many things that he/she cannot deal with them all ～に非常にたくさんのものを送ったり, 与えて全部を処理しきれなくする➜**(場所・人)に(おびただしい数のものを) 殺到させる, ～に(…を) どっと押し寄せさせる** ‖ *We were inundated with applications for the job.* 我々の元には, 仕事への申し込みが殺到した. ☛類 **swamp** ▶定義2 [正式] to cover an area of land with water 水で陸地を覆う➜**(洪水・河川などが) ～を水浸しにする** ‖ *After the heavy rains the fields were inundated.* 豪雨の後, 畑は水浸しになった. ☛ 略式な語は flood.

**invade** /ɪnvéɪd/ [動] ▶定義1 [自][他] to enter a country with an army in order to attack and take control of it 攻撃して制圧するために, 軍隊を伴って国に入る➜**(～を) 侵略する, (～に) 侵入する, 侵攻する** ‖ *When did the Romans invade Britain?* ローマ人はいつ大ブリテン島に侵攻したのですか. ▶定義2 [他] to enter in large numbers, often where sb/sth is not wanted 多数で入り込む. 特にその～が望まれていない所であることが多い➜**～にどっと押し寄せる, 殺到する** ‖ *The whole area has been invaded by tourists.* その地域全体に, 観光客がどっと押し寄せた. ☛ [名] invasion — invader [名] [C]➜**侵略者, 侵略国**

**invalid¹** /ɪnvǽləd/ [形] ▶定義1 not legally or officially acceptable 法的・公的に受諾されない➜**(文書などが) (法的に) 無効の** ‖ *I'm afraid your passport is invalid.* 残念ながら, あなたのパスポートは無効です. ▶定義2 not correct according to reason; not based on all the facts 理屈上正しくない; すべての事実に基づいているわけではない➜**(議論・主張などが) 正当な根拠のない, 妥当性を欠いた, 説得力のない** ‖ *an invalid argument* 正当な根拠のない議論 ▶定義3 (computing) (used about an instruction, etc) of a type that the computer cannot recognize (コンピューター) (命令などについて) コンピューターが認識できない型の ➜**無効の, 不当な** ‖ *an invalid command* 無効なコマンド ⇔ **valid**

**invalid²** /ínvələd/ [名] [C] ▶定義 a person who has been very ill for a long time and needs to be looked after 長期間にわたって病気で, 介護を必要とする人➜**(介護が必要な) 病弱者, (長患いの) 病人, 身体障害者**

**invaluable** /ɪnvǽlj(u)əb(ə)l/ [形] ▶定義 invaluable (to/for sb/sth) extremely useful 非常に有用な➜**計り知れないほど価値のある, 非常に貴重な** ‖ *invaluable help/information/support* 大変貴重な手助け・情報・支援 ☛ 注意. invaluable は valuable の反意語ではない. valuable の反意語は valueless または worthless である.

**invariable** /ɪnvéəriəb(ə)l/ [形] ▶定義 not changing➜**変わらない, 不変の, 一定の**

**invariably** /ɪnvéəriəbli/ [副] ▶定義 almost always ほとんど常に➜**変わることなく, いつも, 決まって** ‖ *She invariably arrives late.* 彼女は決まって遅れて到着する.

***invasion** /ɪnvéɪʒ(ə)n/ [名] ▶定義1 [C] [U] the action of entering another country with your army in order to take control of it 制圧するために, 他国に軍隊を伴って入る行動➜**侵略, 侵入, 侵攻** ‖ *the threat of invasion* 侵略の脅威 ▶定義2 [C] the action of entering a place where you are not wanted and disturbing sb 望まれていない場所に入り, ～の邪魔をする行動➜**侵害** ‖ *Such questions are an* ***invasion of privacy****.* そのような質問は, プライバシーの侵害だ. ☛ [動] invade

***invent** /ɪnvént/ [動][他] ▶定義1 to think of or make sth for the first time ～を最初に思い付く, 最初に作る➜**～を発明する, 創り出す, 考案する** ‖ *When was the camera invented?* カメラが発明されたのはいつですか. ▶定義2 to say or describe sth that is not true 本当ではない～を言う・説明する➜**(うそ・言い訳を) でっち上げる, ～をねつ造する** ‖ *I realized that he had invented the whole story.* 彼がその話のすべてをでっち上げたことを私は悟った. — inventor [名] [C]➜**発明者, 発明家, 考案者**

***invention** /ɪnvénʃ(ə)n/ [名] ▶定義1 [C] a thing that has been made or designed by sb for the first time 初めて人によって作られた・設計されたもの➜**発明品, 考案品** ‖ *The microwave oven is a very useful invention.* 電子レンジは有用な発

明品だ. ▶定義2 ❶the action or process of making or designing sth for the first time 初めて〜を作る・設計する行為, 過程→**発明, 考案** ‖ *Books had to be written by hand before the invention of printing.* 印刷術の発明以前は, 本は手書きされなければならなかった. ▶定義3 **C** ❶telling a story or giving an excuse that is not true うその話をする, うその言い訳をする→(記事・話などの)ねつ造, でっち上げ, 作り話 ‖ *It was obvious that his story about being robbed was (an) invention.* 強盗に遭ったという彼の話はでっち上げであることは明らかだった.

**inventive** /ɪnvéntɪv/ 形 ▶定義 having clever and original ideas うまい独創的な着想を持っている→(人が)発明・工夫の才のある, 創作力に富んだ, (作品などが)創意に富む — **inventiveness** 名 **U**→**独創性**

**inventory** /ɪ́nvənt(ə)ri, -tɔ̀ːri/ 名 **C** (覆 **inventories**) ▶定義 a detailed list, for example of all the furniture in a house 詳細な一覧表, 例えば家にある家具全部の一覧表→(商品などの)**目録, 一覧表** ‖ *The landlord is coming to **make an inventory** of the contents of the flat.* 家主が, アパートの付帯設備の一覧表を作成するために来るところだ.

**invert** /ɪnvə́ːrt/ 動他 正式 ▶定義 to put sth in the opposite order or position to the way it usually is 〜を通常とは反対の順番・場所に置く→**〜を逆にする, ひっくり返す, 転倒させる** ‖ *What you see in a mirror is an inverted image of yourself.* 鏡に映る姿は, 実際の姿を逆にしたものだ.

**inverted commas** 英 = QUOTATION MARKS ‖ *to put sth **in inverted commas*** 〜を引用符で囲む

*****invest** /ɪnvést/ 動自他 **invest (sth) (in sth)** ▶定義1 to put money into a bank, business, property, etc in the hope that you will make a profit 利益を上げることを目的に, お金を銀行・事業・不動産などにつぎ込む→**(金を)(〜に)投資する, 支出・運用する** ‖ *Many firms have invested heavily in this project.* 多くの会社がこのプロジェクトにばく大な投資をしている. *I've invested all my money in the company.* 私は有り金を全部その会社に投資した. ▶定義2 to spend money, time or energy on sth that you think is good or useful 自分が良い・有用だと思う〜にお金・時間・精力を費やす→**(金・時間・精力など)を〜に使う, 〜に注ぐ** ‖ *I'm thinking of investing in a computer.* 私はコンピューターにお金をかけようかなと考えている. *You have to invest a lot of time if you really want to learn a language well.* 言葉を本当によく学習したいなら, 多くの時間を費やさなくてはなりません. — **investor** 名 **C**→**投資者, 出資者**

*****investigate** /ɪnvéstəgèɪt/ 動自他 ▶定義 to try to find out all the facts about sth 〜についての事実をすべて調べようとする→**(〜を)調査する, 研究する, 捜査する** ‖ *A murder was reported and the police were sent to investigate.* 殺人が報告され, 警察官が捜査のために派遣された. *A group of experts are investigating the cause of the crash.* 専門家集団が墜落事故の原因を調査中だ. — **investigator** 名 **C**→**調査員, 研究者, 捜査員**

*****investigation** /ɪnvèstəgéɪʃ(ə)n/ 名 **C U** ▶定義 **(an) investigation (into sth)** →**(〜への)調査, 研究, 捜査** ‖ *The airlines are going to **carry out an investigation** into security procedures at airports.* 航空会社は空港の安全手続きについての調査を実行する予定だ. *The matter is still **under investigation**.* その事件は依然調査中だ.

**investigative** /ɪnvéstəgèɪtɪv/ 形 ▶定義 trying to find out all the facts about sb/sth 〜についての事実をすべて調べようとする→**調査の, 研究の** ‖ *investigative journalism* (マスコミ独自の)調査報道

**investment** /ɪnvéstmənt/ 名 ▶定義1 **U C** (an) investment (in sth) the act of putting money in a bank, business, property, etc; the amount of money that you put in お金を銀行・事業・不動産などにつぎ込む行為; つぎ込んだお金の総額→**投資, 出資, 投資額, 出資金** ‖ *investment in local industry* 地場産業への投資 *The company will have to **make an** enormous **investment** to computerize production.* その会社は生産のコンピューター化のためにばく大な投資をしなければならない. ▶定義2 **C** 略式 a thing that you have bought 購入したもの→**投資物件, 投資の対象** ‖ *This coat has been a good investment - I've worn it for three years.* このコートは良い買い物だった - 3年も着たのだから.

**invigilate** /ɪnvídʒəleɪt/ 動自他 英 ▶定義 to

watch the people taking an exam to make sure that nobody is cheating 試験を受けている人を監視し,不正行為を行う人がいないことを確認する➔(〜の)試験監督をする — **invigilator** 图 ●➔試験監督者

**invigorate** /invígərèit/ 動 圁 他 ▶定義 to make sb feel healthy, fresh and full of energy 〜を,健康で生き生きとしている;活力に満ちあふれているように感じさせる➔〜に活力を与える,〜を元気づける ‖ *I felt invigorated after my run.* 走った後は爽快(そうかい)な気分になった. — **invigorating** 形 ➔(天候・運動などが)元気づけるような,活力を与える

**invincible** /invínsəb(ə)l/ 形 ▶定義 too strong or powerful to be defeated 非常にたくましく,あるいは強力で,負けることがない ➔(軍隊・チームなどが)無敵の,不敗の

**invisible** /invízəb(ə)l/ 形 ▶定義 invisible (to sb/sth) that cannot be seen➔目に見えない,肉眼では見えない,隠れた ‖ *bacteria that are invisible to the naked eye* 肉眼では見えない細菌 ⇔ **visible** — **invisibility** /invìzəbíləti/ 图 ❶➔目に見えないこと,不可視 — **invisibly** 副 ➔目に付かないほど,目に見えないように

**invitation** /ìnvətéiʃ(ə)n/ 图 ▶定義 1 ❶ the act of inviting sb or being invited 〜を招くこと,招かれること➔(〜への)招待,案内 ‖ *Entry is by invitation only.* 入場は招待客に限ります. *a letter of invitation* 招待状 ▶定義 2 ❷ an invitation to sb/sth (to sth/to do sth) a written or spoken request to go somewhere or do sth ある場所に来てください・〜をしてください,という文書・口頭による要請➔(〜への)招待状,案内状 ‖ *Did you get an invitation to the conference?* 会議の招待状を受け取りましたか. *a wedding invitation* 結婚式の招待状 ☛ 招待を accept (受ける)こともあれば,turn it down (断る)ことや decline (辞退する)こともある.

\***invite** /inváit/ 動 他 ▶定義 1 invite sb (to/for sth) to ask sb to come somewhere or to do sth 〜に,ある場所に来てください・・・をしてください,と頼む➔〜を(・・・に)招く,招待する,誘う ‖ *We invited all the family to the wedding.* 我々は家族全員を結婚式に招待した. *Successful applicants will be invited for interview next week.* 合格した応募者には,来週の面接の案内をします. ▶定義 2 to make sth unpleasant likely to happen 嫌な〜が起きるようにする➔(危険・非難など)をもたらす,招く,引き起こす ‖ *You're inviting trouble if you carry so much money around.* そんなに多額のお金をあちこち持ち歩くと,面倒な事を引き起こしますよ.

句動詞 invite sb back ▶定義 1 to ask sb to return with you to your home 〜に一緒に帰宅してくれるように頼む➔(一緒に帰る)人を自宅に誘う ‖ *Shall we invite the others back for coffee after the meeting?* 会議が終わったら,コーヒーを飲みにほかの連中を家に連れてこようか.

▶定義 2 to ask sb to come to your home a second time, or after you have been a guest at his/her home 〜にまた家に来てくれるように頼む,招待された後に,招いてくれた…自分の家に来てくれるように頼む➔〜をお返しに招く

invite sb in ▶定義 to ask sb to come into your home 〜に自分の家に来てくれと頼む➔〜を(家に)招き入れる

invite sb out ▶定義 to ask sb to go out somewhere with you 〜に一緒にどこかに行こうと頼む➔〜を(食事・ドライブなどに)誘い出す ‖ *We've been invited out to lunch by the neighbours.* 私たちはお隣に,外で一緒に昼食をしようと招かれた.

invite sb over/round 略式 ▶定義 to ask sb to come to your home 〜に家に来てくれと頼む➔〜を家に招待する ‖ *I've invited Mohamed and his family round for lunch on Sunday.* モハメド一家を日曜日の昼食に招待している.

▶ここに挙げたすべての意味で ask を invite の代わりに使うことができることに注意する.

**inviting** /inváitiŋ/ 形 ▶定義 attractive and pleasant 魅力的で好ましい➔人を引き付ける,魅力的な ‖ *The smell of cooking was very inviting.* 料理のにおいはとてもうまそうだった.

**invoice** /ínvɔis/ 图 ●▶定義 an official paper that lists goods or services that you have received and says how much you have to pay for them 受け取った品物・サービスの一覧とその値段が記されている公式の書類 ➔ 送り状,明細記入請求書,仕切り状,インボイス

**involuntary** /inválənt(ə)ri; -tèri/ 形 ▶定義 done without wanting or meaning to 望まないで・意図しないで行う➔(行為などが)無意識の,知らず

知らずの, 強制された ‖ *She gave an involuntary gasp of pain as the doctor inserted the needle.* 医者が針を刺し込んだ時, 彼女は思わず痛みであえいだ. ⇔ **voluntary, deliberate** —involuntarily /ɪnvɑ́ləntərɪli/ [副] ➜ **無意識に, 知らず知らず**

***involve** /ɪnvɑ́lv/ [動][他] ▶定義1 (進行形は不可) to make sth necessary ～を必要とする ➜ **～を(必ず)含む, 伴う** ‖ *The job involves a lot of travelling.* その仕事には多くの旅行が付き物だ. ▶定義2 (進行形は不可) if a situation, an event or an activity involves sb/sth, he/she/it takes part in it 状況・出来事・活動が～を involve であるなら, ～はその事に直接かかわっている [参加している] ということである ➜ **(人が) (けんか・犯罪などに, 人と) 関係する** ‖ *The story involves a woman who went on holiday with her child.* その話には, 子供を連れて休暇に出掛けた女の人がかかわっている. *More than 100 people were involved in the project.* その事業には, 100人以上の人が関係していた.

➤ この意味では進行形では使われないが, 現在分詞 (= -ing 形) では通常使用される: *There was a serious accident involving a stolen car.* (盗難車に関係した重大事故があった.)

▶定義3 involve sb/sth in (doing) sth to cause sb/sth to take part in or be concerned with sth ～を…に参加させる, 関係させる ➜ **～を(事件・犯罪など)に巻き込む, 巻き添えにする** ‖ *Please don't involve me in your family arguments.* あなたの家族のけんかに私を巻き込まないでください. — involvement [名][C][U] ➜ **(～に) 巻き込む [巻き込まれる] こと, (～との) かかわり合い** ‖ *The men deny any involvement in the robbery.* その男たちは強盗事件とのいかなるかかわり合いも否定した.

**involved** /ɪnvɑ́lvd/ [形] ▶定義1 difficult to understand; complicated 理解し難い; 複雑な ➜ **複雑な, 込み入った** ‖ *The book has a very involved plot.* この本は非常に込み入った筋だ. ▶定義2 (名詞の前は不可) involved (in sth) closely connected with sth; taking an active part in sth ～と密接に関係している; ～に積極的に参加している ➜ **～に関係している, かかわっている** ‖ *I'm very involved in local politics.* 私は地元の政治に深くかかわっている. ▶定義3 (名詞の前は不可) involved (with sb) having a sexual relationship with sb ～と性的関係を持つ ➜ **(遠回しに) (性的に) (～と) 関係がある** ‖ *She is involved with an older man.* 彼女は年上の男と関係がある.

**inward** /ínwərd/ [副][形] ▶定義1 (または **inwards**) towards the inside or centre 内側・中心に向かって ➜ **内部に [へ・の], 内側に [へ・の]** ‖ *Stand in a circle facing inwards.* 輪になって立ち, 中心を向きなさい. ▶定義2 inside your mind, not shown to other people 心の中で, 他人には見えない ➜ **内面に・へ (の)** ‖ *my inward feelings* 私の心の中の感情 ⇔ **outward**

**inwardly** /ínwərdli/ [副] ▶定義 in your mind; secretly 心の中で; こっそり ➜ **内心** ‖ *He was inwardly relieved that they could not come.* 彼らが来られないので, 彼は内心ほっとしていた.

**iodine** /áɪədàɪn, -diːn/ [名][U] ▶定義 a dark-coloured substance that is found in sea water. A purple liquid containing iodine is sometimes used to clean cuts in your skin. 海水に含まれる, 暗色の物質. これを含む赤紫色の液体が皮膚の傷口を消毒するのに使われることがある ➜ **ヨウ素, ヨード; ヨードチンキ**

**IOU** /àɪ oʊ júː/ [略] I owe you. ▶定義 a piece of paper that you sign showing that you owe sb some money 署名をした書面で, 人からお金を借りていることを証明するもの ➜ **借用証書**

**IPA** /àɪ piː éɪ/ [略] the International Phonetic Alphabet ➜ **国際音標文字**

**IQ** /àɪ kjúː/ [略] intelligence quotient ▶定義 a measure of how intelligent sb is ～がどのくらい知能があるかを示す尺度 ➜ **知能指数** ‖ *have a high/low IQ* IQ が高い・低い *an IQ of 120* 知能指数 120

**IRA** /áɪrə/ [略] the Irish Republican Army ➜ **アイルランド共和国軍**

**irate** /aɪréɪt, ⸗-/ [形][正式] ▶定義 very angry 非常に怒った ➜ **激怒した, 憤慨した**

**iris** /áɪərəs/ [名][C] ▶定義 the coloured part of your eye 目の色の付いた部分 ➜ **(眼球の) 虹彩 (こうさい)**

***Irish** /áɪərɪʃ/ [形] ▶定義 from Ireland アイルランド出身の ➜ **アイルランドの, アイルランド人の, アイルランド系の, アイルランド語の** ☛ 巻末の地名の項を参照.

***iron**[1] /áɪərn/ [名] ▶定義1 [U] (元素記号 **Fe**) a hard strong metal that is used for making steel and is found in small quantities in food and in blood 鋼鉄の原料になり, 食物・血中に少量含まれる, 硬くて強い金属➔**鉄, 鉄分** ‖ *an iron bar* 鉄棒 *iron ore* 鉄鉱石 *The doctor gave me iron tablets.* 医者は私に鉄分の錠剤を出した. (比喩) *The general has an iron (= very strong) will.* 将軍は鉄のような(= 非常に強い)意志を持っている.

▶**定義2** **C** an electrical instrument with a flat bottom that is heated and used to smooth clothes after you have washed and dried them 平らな底が熱くなり, 洗濯・乾燥後の衣類のしわを伸ばすために使われる電気器具➔**アイロン, こて** ‖ *a steam iron* スチームアイロン

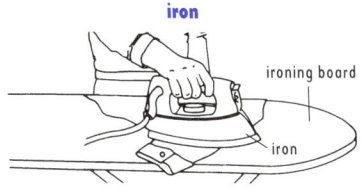

iron
ironing board
iron

\*iron² /áɪəm/ 動 自 他 ▶定義 to use an iron to make clothes, etc smooth アイロンを使って衣類などのしわを伸ばす➔**(人が)アイロンをかける; (衣類など)にアイロンをかける** ‖ *Could you iron this dress for me?* 私のためにこのドレスにアイロンをかけてくれますか. ☛ iron の代わりに do the ironing が使われることが多い. *I usually do the ironing on Sunday.* 私は普通, 日曜日にアイロンがけをします.

句動詞 **iron sth out** ▶定義 to get rid of any problems or difficulties that are affecting sth ~に影響を及ぼすあらゆる問題・困難を取り除く➔**(問題・困難など)を取り除く, 解決する**

**ironic** /aɪərɑ́nɪk/ (または **ironical** /aɪərɑ́nɪk(ə)l/) 形 ▶定義1 meaning the opposite of what you say 言葉とは反対の事を意味する➔**皮肉な, 反語的な** ‖ *Jeff sometimes offends people with his ironic sense of humour.* ジェフは, その皮肉なユーモアのセンスで人を不愉快な思いにさせることがある. ☛参 **sarcastic** ▶定義2 (used about a situation) strange or amusing because it is unusual or unexpected (状況について)めったにない思い掛けないことなので, 奇妙な・面白い➔**皮肉な** ‖ *It is ironic that the busiest people are often the most willing to help.* 最も忙しい人々が最も援助をいとわないことが多いのは, 皮肉にも. ―**ironically** /-k(ə)li/ 副 ➔**皮肉っぽく, 皮肉にも, 反語的に**

**ironing** /áɪəmɪŋ/ 名 U ▶定義 clothes, etc that need ironing or that have just been ironed アイロンがけが必要な衣服や, アイロンをかけたばかりの衣服など➔**アイロンをかける[かけた]衣類, アイロンがけ** ‖ *a large pile of ironing* 山と積まれたアイロン待ちの衣服 ☛参 **iron** の注

**ironing board** 名 **C** ▶定義 a special table that is used for putting clothes on when we are making them smooth with an iron アイロンをかけてしわを伸ばすときに使う, 衣服を置くための特別な台➔**アイロン台** ☛ **iron** のさし絵

**irony** /áɪərəni/ 名 (複 **ironies**) ▶定義1 **C U** an unusual or unexpected part of a situation, etc that seems strange or amusing 異常で思い掛けない状況などにおいて, 奇妙で面白く思えること➔**皮肉な結果・事態・事件, 皮肉な巡り合わせ** ‖ *The irony was that he was killed in a car accident soon after the end of the war.* 皮肉にも, 彼は戦争が終わってからすぐに自動車事故で死んでしまった. ▶定義2 **U** a way of speaking that shows you are joking or that you mean the opposite of what you say 冗談であったり, 言葉とは反対の事を意味したりしていることを示す話し方➔**皮肉, 当てこすり, 反語** ‖ *'The English are such good cooks',* he said with heavy irony. 「イギリス人は本当に料理が上手だ」と彼は辛辣(しんらつ)な皮肉を込めて言った.

**irrational** /ɪræʃnəl, ɪræʃənl/ 形 ▶定義 not based on reason or clear thought 理屈や明瞭(めいりょう)な考えに基づいていない➔**理性のない, 無分別な, 不合理な, ばかげた** ‖ *an irrational fear of spiders* クモに対するばかげた恐怖心 ―**irrationality** /ɪræʃənǽləti/ 名 U ➔**理性のないこと, 無分別, 不合理** ― **irrationally** /-nəli, -nli/ 副 ➔**無分別に, 不合理に**

**irreconcilable** /ɪrèkənsáɪləb(ə)l/ 形 正式 ▶定義 (used about people or their ideas and beliefs) so different that they cannot be made to agree (人々について, またはその考えと信念について)あまりにも掛け離れているので, 合意・合致することができない➔**(人が)(~と)和解[妥協]できない, 対立する, (思想・行動などが)矛盾する**

— irreconcilably /-əbli/ 副 →妥協せずに

***irregular** /ɪrégjələr/ 形 ▶定義 1 not having a shape or pattern that we recognize or can predict 認識でき, 予測が付く形や模様ではない→ふぞろいの, でこぼこした, むらのある ‖ *an irregular shape* ふぞろいの形 ▶定義 2 happening at times that you cannot predict 予測できないときに起きる→不規則な, 変則的な, 不定期の ‖ *His visits became more and more irregular.* 彼の訪問はますます不定期になってきた. ▶定義 3 not allowed according to the rules or social customs 規則・社会の慣習では許されない→無効の, 不法な, 不正な ‖ *It is highly irregular for a doctor to give information about patients without their permission.* 医師が本人の許可なく患者の情報を提供することは, 極めて不当な事だ. ▶定義 4 (文法) not following the usual rules of grammar 通常の文法規則に従っていない→不規則な, 不規則変化の ‖ *'Caught' is an irregular past tense form.* caught は不規則変化の過去形だ. ⇔ 定義 1, 2, 4 **regular** — **irregularity** /ɪregjəlǽrəti/ 名 **C U** ( 複 irregularities) →不規則, 変則, 不規則なもの — **irregularly** 副 →不規則に, ふぞろいに, 不正規に

**irrelevancy** /ɪréləvənsi/ 名 **C** ( 複 **irrelevancies**) ▶定義 something that is not important because it is not connected with sth else ほかの物事と関連がないので, 重要ではないもの→無関係な・見当違いの言動, 的外れの質問

**irrelevant** /ɪréləvənt/ 形 ▶定義 not connected with sth or important to it ～に関係ない, 重要ではない→(～に) 無関係な, 不適切な, 見当違いの, 的外れな ‖ *That's completely irrelevant to the subject under discussion.* それは, 議論している問題とは全く無関係だ. ⇔ **relevant** — **irrelevance** 名 **U C** →無関係, 不適当, 無関係な言動 — **irrelevantly** 副 →不適切に, 関係なく

**irreparable** /ɪrép(ə)rəb(ə)l/ 形 ▶定義 that cannot be repaired →修復 [回復] できない, 取り返しのつかない ‖ *Irreparable damage has been done to the forests of Eastern Europe.* 東ヨーロッパの森林は, 取り返しのつかないほど破壊されている. — **irreparably** 副 →修復 [回復] 不能なほど, 取り返しのつかないほど

**irreplaceable** /ɪrɪpléɪsəb(ə)l/ 形 ▶定義 (used about sth very valuable or special) that cannot be replaced (非常に貴重で特別な～について) それに取って代わるものがない→(貴重品などが) 取り替えの利かない, 掛け替えのない ⇔ **replaceable**

**irrepressible** /ɪrɪprésəb(ə)l/ 形 ▶定義 full of life and energy 活力と精力に満ちている→元気に満ちあふれた, 快活な; (感情などが) 抑えきれない ‖ *young people full of irrepressible good humour* あふれ出る快活な気分に満ちた若者たち — **irrepressibly** /-əbli/ 副 →抑えきれずに

**irresistible** /ɪrɪzístəb(ə)l/ 形 ▶定義 1 so strong that it cannot be stopped or prevented 非常に強力なので, 止めたり妨げることができない→(欲求・感情などが) 抑えられない, 抵抗できない, 打ち勝てない ‖ *an irresistible urge to laugh* 抑えきれない笑いの衝動 ▶定義 2 irresistible (to sb) very attractive 非常に魅力的な→(人・性格などが) (～にとって) たまらなく魅力的な, あらがえない ‖ *He seems to think he's irresistible to women.* 彼は, 自分が女性にとってたまらなく魅力があると思っているようだ. ☞ 動 **resist** — **irresistibly** /-əbli/ 副 →抵抗できないほど, 魅力的に

**irrespective of** /ɪrɪspéktɪv ə(v), -əv/ 前 ▶定義 not affected by ～に影響されることなく→～に関係なく, かかわりなく ‖ *Anybody can take part in the competition, irrespective of age.* この競技会には, 年齢に関係なくだれでも参加できる.

**irresponsible** /ɪrɪspɑ́nsəb(ə)l/ 形 ▶定義 not thinking about the effect your actions will have; not sensible 自分の行動が及ぼす影響について考えない; 思慮分別のない→無責任な, 責任感のない, いいかげんな ‖ *It is irresponsible to let small children go out alone.* 小さな子供を1人で外に出すのは無責任だ. ⇔ **responsible** — **irresponsibility** /ɪrɪspɑnsəbíləti/ 名 **U** →無責任, 責任感のないこと — **irresponsibly** /-əbli/ 副 →無責任に(も)

**irreverent** /ɪrév(ə)rənt/ 形 ▶定義 not feeling or showing respect 敬意を感じない, 敬意を示さない→無礼な, 不敬な, 不遜 (ふそん) な ‖ *This comedy takes an irreverent look at the world of politics.* この喜劇は, 政治の世界に対して無礼な見方をしている. — **irreverence** 名 **U** →不敬, 無礼 — **irreverently** 副 →不遜 (ふそん) にも, 不敬にも

**irreversible** /ˌɪriˈvɜːrsəb(ə)l/ 形 ▶定義 that cannot be stopped or changed 止めることができない，変えることができない→元に戻せないほどの，撤回できない，取り消せない ‖ *The disease can do irreversible damage to the body.* 病気のために体が回復できない痛手を受けることがある． — **irreversibly** 副 →元に戻せないほど，撤回できないほど

**irritable** /ˈɪrətəb(ə)l/ 形 ▶定義 becoming angry easily すぐに怒る→怒りっぽい，短気な，いらいらした ‖ *to be/feel/get irritable* 怒りっぽい・じれったく感じる・いらいらしてくる — **irritability** /ˌɪrətəˈbɪləti/ 名 ❶ →怒りっぽいこと，短気 — **irritably** /-əb(ə)li/ 副 →いらいらして，怒って

**irritate** /ˈɪrəteɪt/ 動 他 ▶定義 1 to make sb angry; to annoy→怒らせる，〜をいらいらさせる ‖ *It really irritates me the way he keeps repeating himself.* 彼が同じ事を繰返し言い続けるので，実にいらいらする． ▶定義 2 to cause a part of the body to be painful or sore 体の一部に痛み・炎症を起こさせる→〜を刺激する，ひりひりさせる，〜に炎症を起こさせる ‖ *I don't use soap because it irritates my skin.* 皮膚に炎症を起こすので，せっけんは使わない． — **irritation** /ˌɪrəˈteɪʃ(ə)n/ 名 ❸ ❶ →いら立ち，怒り，いら立たせるもの，炎症

**is** ⇒ BE

*★**Islam** /ɪzˈlɑːm, ɪs-, -læm/ 名 ❶ ▶定義 the religion of Muslim people. Islam teaches that there is only one God and that Muhammad is His Prophet. イスラム教徒が持つ宗教．イスラム教の教えは唯一神で，その預言者をムハンマドとする→イスラム教，回教，イスラム教徒(全体)，イスラム教世界 — **Islamic** 形 →イスラム教の，回教(徒)の ‖ *Islamic law* イスラム教の戒律

*★**island** /ˈaɪlənd/ 名 ❶ ▶定義 1 a piece of land that is surrounded by water 水に囲まれた土地→島 ‖ *the Greek islands* ギリシャの島々 ▶定義 2 = **TRAFFIC ISLAND**

**islander** /ˈaɪləndər/ 名 ❶ ▶定義 a person who lives on a small island 小さな島に住む人→島民，島の住人

**isle** /aɪl/ 名 ❶ ▶定義 an island→島，小島 ‖ *the Isle of Wight* ワイト島 *the British Isles* 英国諸島 ☛ **isle** は名称に多く使われる．

**isn't** IS NOT の短縮形

**isolate** /ˈaɪsəleɪt/ 動 他 ▶定義 **isolate** sb/sth (from sb/sth) to put or keep sb/sth separate from other people or things 〜をほかの人々や物から離す・離しておく→〜を(…から)孤立させる，〜を分離する，(患者など)を隔離する ‖ *Some farms were isolated by the heavy snowfalls.* 農場の中には，大雪のために孤立した所もあった． *We need to isolate all the animals with the disease so that the others don't catch it.* ほかの動物に移さないために，病気の動物はすべて隔離する必要がある．

**isolated** /ˈaɪsəleɪtəd/ 形 ▶定義 1 **isolated** (from sb/sth) alone or apart from other people or things ただ1人[1つ]の，ほかの人々・物から離れた→孤立した，遠く離れた ‖ *an isolated village deep in the countryside* 遠く田舎にぽつんと離れてある村 *I was kept isolated from the other patients.* 私はほかの患者から隔離されていた． ▶定義 2 not connected with others; happening once 他と結び付かない；一度だけしか起きない→ただ1つの，他に例のない，単発的な，まれな ‖ *Is this an isolated case or part of a general pattern?* これは単独の事例なのか，それとも一般的な傾向の一部なのか．

**isolation** /ˌaɪsəˈleɪʃ(ə)n/ 名 ❶ ▶定義 **isolation** (from sb/sth) the state of being separate and alone; the act of separating sb/sth 引き離されてただ1人[1つ]の状態；〜を引き離す行為→(〜からの)孤立，分離，隔離 ‖ *He lived in complete isolation from the outside world.* 彼は外の世界から完全に孤立して暮らしていた． *In isolation each problem does not seem bad, but together they are quite daunting.* 単独ではそれぞれの問題は悪くないように見えますが，一緒にすると非常に厳しいものです．

▶ loneliness, solitude と比較．

*★**issue**¹ /ˈɪsjuː, ˈɪʃuː/ 名 ▶定義 1 ❸ a problem or subject for discussion 議論の対象となる問題点・議題→問題(点)，争点，重要課題，論点 ‖ *I want to raise the issue of overtime pay at the meeting.* 私は会議で，超過勤務手当の問題を提起したい． *The government cannot avoid the issue of homelessness any longer.* 政府はホームレスの問題をもはや避けることはできない．

▶定義 2 ❸ one in a series of things that are published or produced 連続物の出版物・製品

の1つ→(新聞・雑誌などの)出版物, ～号, ～版, 発行物 ‖ *Do you have last week's issue of this magazine?* この雑誌の先週号はありますか.

▶定義3 ❶ the act of publishing or giving sth to people・～を人に出版する・与える行為→発行, 刊行; 支給, 配布 ‖ *the issue of blankets to the refugees* 難民への毛布の支給

成句 make an issue (out) of sth ▶定義 to give too much importance to a small problem 小さな問題を過度に重要視する→(小さな問題)をおおげさに扱う, ～で騒ぎ立てる ‖ *OK, we disagree on this but let's not make an issue of it.* 分かりました. それについての意見は異なりますが, その事は問題にしないでおきましょう

**issue**² /ˈɪsjuː, ˈɪʃuː/ 動 ▶定義1 ❶ to print and supply sth ～を印刷し提供する→(通貨・切手など)を発行する,(新聞・雑誌など)を発行[出版・刊行]する ‖ *to issue a magazine/newsletter* 雑誌・会報を発行する ▶定義2 ❶ to give or say sth to sb officially ～に…を公式に与える・言う→～を配布する, 支給する, 発給する;(宣言・命令など)を出す ‖ *The new employees were issued with uniforms.* 新しい従業員に制服が支給された. *to issue a visa* ビザを発行する *The police will issue a statement later today.* 警察は本日遅くに声明を発表します. ▶定義3 ⊜ 正式 to come or go out 出る, 出てくる→(液体・音・においなどが)(～から)発する, 流れ出る ‖ *An angry voice issued from the loudspeaker.* 拡声器から怒声が発せられた.

**IT** /ˌaɪ ˈtiː/ 略 (computing) Information Technology →(コンピューター)情報技術, 情報産業

*__it__ /ɪt, ət/ 代 ▶定義1 (動詞の主語・目的語として, または前置詞の後で用いて) the animal or thing mentioned earlier 前述された動物または物→(既述の語・句・節を受けて)それは[が], それを[に・と] ‖ *Look at that car. It's going much too fast.* あの車を見て. すごいスピードを出して走っているわ. *The children went up to the dog and patted it.* 子供たちは犬の所に近付いていって, それをなでた. ☛ 性別の分からない赤ん坊にも使うことができる. *Is it a boy or a girl?* 赤ちゃんは男の子ですか, 女の子ですか. ▶定義2 used for identifying a person 人を指す場合に用いる ‖ *It's your Mum on the phone.* お母さんら電話です. *'Who's that?' 'It's the postman.'* 「あれはだれ」「郵便配達だわ」 *It's me!* 私です. *It's him!* 彼よ. ▶定義3 used in the position of the subject or object of a verb when the real subject or object is at the end of the sentence 真の主語・目的語が文末にある場合に, 動詞の主語・目的語の位置に置かれる ‖ *It's hard for them to talk about their problems.* 彼らが問題点を話し合うのは難しい. *I think it doesn't really matter what time we arrive.* 何時に到着しようと全く構わないと思う. ▶定義4 used in the position of the subject of a verb when you are talking about time, the date, distance, the weather, etc 時間, 日付, 距離, 天候などを表す場合, 動詞の主語の位置に置かれる ‖ *It's nearly half past eight.* 8時半ごろだ. *It's Tuesday today.* 今日は火曜日です. *It's about 100 kilometres from London.* ロンドンから約100キロ離れている. *It was very cold at the weekend.* 週末はとても寒かった. *It's raining.* 雨が降っている.

▶定義5 used when you are talking about a situation 状況について話す場合に用いる ‖ *It gets very crowded here in the summer.* ここは, 夏は非常に混雑する. *I'll come at 7 o'clock if it's convenient.* 都合がよろしければ, 7時に行きます. *It's a pity they can't come to the party.* 彼らがパーティーに来られないのは残念です.

▶定義6 used for emphasizing a part of a sentence 文の一部を強調する場合に用いる→(強調構文)～なのは…だ ‖ *It was Jerry who said it, not me.* それを言ったのはジェリーで, 私ではない. *It's your health I'm worried about, not the cost.* 私が心配しているのはあなたの健康で, 費用のことではありません.

成句 that/this is it ▶定義1 that/this is the answer それ・これが答えだ→その通り, それだ ‖ *That's it! You've solved the puzzle!* その通り. なぞが解けましたね. ▶定義2 that/this is the end→これで終わりです, それまでだ ‖ *That's it, I've had enough! I'm going home!* もういい. もうたくさんだ. 家に帰る.

**italics** /ɪˈtælɪks/ 名 [複数扱い] ▶定義 a type of writing or printing in which the letters do not stand straight up 書体・活字の一種で, 文字が垂直ではないもの→**イタリック体, 斜字体** ‖ *All the example sentences in the dictionary are printed __in italics__.* 辞書の例文はすべてイタリッ

ク体で印刷されている． — **italic** 形 →（活字・書体が）イタリック体の，斜字体の

**itch** /ítʃ/ 名 C ▶定義 the feeling on your skin that makes you want to rub or scratch it こすったりかいたりしたくなるような皮膚の感覚→**かゆみ，かゆいこと** ‖ *I've got an itch on my back.* 背中がかゆい． — **itch** 動 →（人・体の部分が）かゆい，むずむずする ‖ *My nose is itching.* 鼻がかゆい． — **itchy** 形 →（からだが）かゆい，（セーターなどが）ちくちくする ‖ *This shirt is itchy.* このシャツはちくちくする． *My skin is all itchy.* 体中がかゆい．

**it'd** /ítəd/ **IT HAD**, **IT WOULD** の短縮形

\*__item__ /áɪtəm/ 名 C ▶定義 1 one single thing on a list or in a collection 一覧表・所蔵品の中の個々の物→**項目，品目，種目，箇条** ‖ *Some items arrived too late to be included in the catalogue.* 品目の中には到着するのが遅すぎてカタログに入れられない物もあった． *What is the first item on the agenda?* 最初の協議事項は何ですか．

▶定義 2 one single article or object 1つの品物・物 →**（〜の）1つ，1個** ‖ *Can I pay for each item separately?* 1個ずつ別々に払っていいかしら． *an item of clothing* 1着の衣類 ▶定義 3 a single piece of news 1つのニュース →**（新聞・雑誌などの）1つの記事，1項目** ‖ *There was an interesting item about Spain in yesterday's news.* 昨日のニュースで，スペインについて興味深い記事があった．

**itemize**（または **-ise**）/áɪtəmàɪz/ 動 ▶定義 to make a list of all the separate items in sth 〜の各項目をすべて網羅した一覧表を作成する→**〜のリストを作る，明細を記す，〜を箇条書きにする** ‖ *an itemized telephone bill* 明細が記された電話料金の請求書

**itinerant** /aɪtín(ə)r(ə)nt, ə-/（名詞の前だけ）▶定義 travelling from place to place ある場所から次の場所へと旅をする→**（商人・芸人などが）旅回りの，各地を巡回する** ‖ *an itinerant circus family* 旅回りのサーカス一家

**itinerary** /aɪtín(ə)ri, ə-; -rèri/ 名 C （複 **itineraries**）▶定義 a plan of a journey, including the route and the places that you will visit 旅の計画で，経路や訪れる場所を含む→**旅行計画，旅程**

**it'll** /ítl/ **IT WILL** の短縮形

**it's** /íts, əts/ **IT IS**, **IT HAS** の短縮形

▶注意. it's は it is または it has の短縮形．its は，それ (it) が所有している，という意味: *The bird has broken its wing.* （鳥は羽を痛めた．）

\*__its__ /íts, əts/ 代 ▶定義 of or belonging to a thing あるものの，あるものに属した 人称代名詞 it の所有格，（名詞の前だけ）**その，それの** ‖ *The club held its Annual General Meeting last night.* クラブは昨夜，年次総会を開いた． ☛参 **it's** の注

\*__itself__ /ɪtsélf/ 代 ▶定義 1 used when the animal or thing that does an action is also affected by it ある行動をしている動物，あるいは事柄自身が，またその行動に影響を受けている場合に使用する→**それ自身を [に]，それ自身の身体を [に]** ‖ *The cat was washing itself.* 猫は自分の体を洗っていた（自分の体をなめて毛繕いをしていた）． *The company has got itself into financial difficulties.* その会社は財政危機に陥った． ▶定義 2 used to emphasize sth 〜を強調するために使用する ‖ *The building itself is beautiful, but it's in a very ugly part of town.* その建物は，それ自体は美しいのだが，街の中のとても醜い一角にある．

成句 **(all) by itself** ▶定義 1 without being controlled by a person; automatically 人に制御されていない；自動的に→**ひとりでに，自動的に，自然に** ‖ *The central heating comes on by itself before we get up.* セントラルヒーティングは，私たちが起きる前に自動的に作動する． ▶定義 2 alone→**独りぼっちで** ‖ *The house stood all by itself on the hillside.* その家は丘の中腹にぽつんと1軒だけ建っていた． ☛参 **alone** の注

**ITV** /àɪ tíː víː/ 略 医 Independent Television ▶定義 the group of television companies that are paid for by advertising 広告によって収入を得ているテレビ局のグループ→**独立テレビ放送** ‖ *watch a film on ITV* 映画を ITV で見る

**I've** /áɪv/ **I HAVE** の短縮形

**ivory** /áɪv(ə)ri/ 名 U ▶定義 the hard white substance that the long teeth (tusks) of an elephant are made of 象の長い歯（きば）でできた固く白い物質→**象牙（ぞうげ）**

**ivy** /áɪvi/ 名 U ▶定義 a climbing plant that has dark leaves with three or five points 3または5裂の暗色の葉を持つ，つる性植物→**ツタ，つる植物の総称** ☛ C2 ページのさし絵

# J j

**J, j** /dʒéɪ/ 名 C (複 J's; j's) ▶定義 the tenth letter of the English alphabet 英語アルファベットの第10文字→j(J)が表す音,j(J)の文字,j(J)の字形のもの ‖ *'Jam' begins with (a) 'J'.* Jam は J で始まる.

**jab¹** /dʒæb/ 動 自 他 ▶定義 jab sb/sth (with sth); jab sth into sb/sth to push at sb/sth with a sudden, rough movement, usually with sth sharp 突然,荒っぽい動きで,通常鋭い物を使って〜を押す→(〜を)素早く突く,突き刺す,差し込む ‖ *She jabbed me in the ribs with her elbow.* 彼女は私のわき腹をひじで突いた. *The robber jabbed a gun into my back and ordered me to move.* 強盗が銃で私の背中を突き,動けと命令した.

**jab²** /dʒæb/ 名 C ▶定義 1 a sudden rough push with sth sharp 鋭い物で突然乱暴に押すこと→突き,不意打ち ‖ *He gave me a jab in the ribs with the stick.* 彼はつえで私のわき腹を突いた.
▶定義 2 略式 the action of putting a drug, etc under sb's skin with a needle 針を使って薬などを〜の皮下に注入する行為→注射,接種 ‖ *I'm going to the doctor's to have a flu jab today.* 私は今日インフルエンザの注射を受けに医者の所へ行くつもりだ. ☛類 injection

**jack¹** /dʒæk/ 名 C ▶定義 1 a piece of equipment for lifting a car, etc off the ground, for example in order to change its wheel 例えば車輪を換えるために,車などを地面から持ち上げるための道具→ジャッキ,押し上げ万力 ▶定義 2 the card between the ten and the queen in a pack of cards トランプの組で10とクイーンの間にあるカード→ジャック(の札) ☛参 card の注とさし絵

**jack²** /dʒæk/ 動
句動詞 jack sth in (俗語) ▶定義 to stop doing sth 〜をするのをやめる→やめる,放棄する ‖ *Jerry got fed up with his job and jacked it in.* ジェリーは仕事に嫌気が差して途中でほうり出した.
jack sth up ▶定義 to lift a car, etc using a jack ジャッキを使って車などを持ち上げる→〜をジャッキで上げる ‖ *We jacked the car up to change the wheel.* 私たちは車輪を換えるために車をジャッキで持ち上げた.

**\*jacket** /dʒækət/ 名 C ▶定義 1 a short coat with sleeves そでの付いた短いコート→上着,ジャケット,ジャンパー ‖ *Do you have to wear a jacket and tie to work?* あなたは仕事で上着とネクタイを着用しなければならないのですか. ☛ C6 ページのさし絵 ☛参 life jacket

**jacket potato** 名 C ▶定義 a potato that is cooked in the oven in its skin 皮のままオーブンで焼いたジャガイモ→皮ごと焼いたジャガイモ

**jackknife** /dʒæknaɪf/ 動 自 ▶定義 (used about a lorry that is in two parts) to go out of control and bend suddenly in a dangerous way (2つの部分から成るトラックについて)ハンドル操作が利かなくなり,突然危険な状態で曲がる→V字型に折れ曲がる,(トレーラートラックや車両が)90度以下の角度に折り曲げたようになる

**the jackpot** /dʒækpɑt/ 名 C ▶定義 the largest money prize that you can win in a game ゲームで勝ち取ることができる最高の賞金→多額の積み立て賞金
成句 hit the jackpot ⇒ HIT¹

**Jacuzzi**™ /dʒəkúːzi, dʒæ-/ 名 C ▶定義 a special bath in which powerful movements of air make bubbles in the water 空気の強力な噴流で水の中に泡を立てる特別なふろ→ジャクジ,気泡ぶろ

**jaded** /dʒéɪdəd/ 形 ▶定義 tired and bored after doing the same thing for a long time without a break 長い間休まずに同じ事をした後で疲れてうんざりする→疲れきった,飽き飽きした,へとへとになった

**jagged** /dʒægəd/ 形 ▶定義 rough with sharp points とがった先があり,でこぼこした→のこぎりの歯のような,ぎざぎざの ‖ *jagged rocks* のこぎりの歯のような岩

**jaguar** /dʒæg(jə)wɑːr, -gwər; -gjuər/ 名 C ▶定義 a large wild cat with black spots that comes from Central and South America 中央および南アメリカ原産の黒い斑点(はんてん)のある野生の大きなネコ科の動物→ジャガー,アメリカヒョウ ☛ lion のさし絵

**jail¹** /dʒéɪl/ 名 C U ▶定義 (a) prison 牢獄(ろうごく)→刑務所,監獄,牢獄 ‖ *She was sent to jail for ten years.* 彼女は10年間刑務所に入れられていた. ☛参 prison の注

**jail²** /dʒéɪl/ 動 他 ▶定義 to put sb in prison 〜を刑務所に入れる→投獄する ‖ *She was jailed for* ten years. 彼女は10年間投獄された.

**jailer** /dʒéɪlər/ 名 ⓒ(古) ▶定義 a person whose job is to guard prisoners 囚人を監視することを仕事にする人→看守

*****jam**¹ /dʒæm/ 名 ▶定義1 Ⓤ(特に 米 **jelly**) a sweet substance that you spread on bread, made by boiling fruit and sugar together 果物と砂糖を一緒に煮て作る, パンの上に塗る甘い物→ジャム ‖ *a jar of raspberry jam* キイチゴジャムのびん ☞ **container** のさし絵
► オレンジまたはレモンから作られるジャムは marmalade(マーマレード)と呼ばれることに注意.

▶定義2 ⓒ a situation in which you cannot move because there are too many people or vehicles 人または車が多すぎるために動くことができない状態→混雑, 雑踏 ‖ *a traffic jam* 交通渋滞 ▶定義3 ⓒ 略式 a difficult situation 難しい状況→困った立場, やばい立場 ‖ *We're in a bit of a jam without our passports or travel documents.* パスポートや旅行書類がなく, 私たちはいささか困ったことになった.

**jam**² /dʒæm/ 動 (**jamming**; **jammed**) ▶定義1 ⓣ jam sb/sth in, under, between, etc sth to push or force sb/sth into a place where there is not much room あまりスペースのない場所に〜を押し込むまたは無理やり詰め込む→〜を詰め込む, 押し込む ‖ *She managed to jam everything into her suitcase.* 彼女はすべての物をスーツケースに何とか詰め込んだ. ▶定義2 ⓘⓣ jam (sth) (up) to become or to make sth unable to move or work 動けなくなるまたは働けなくなる, または〜をそのようにさせる→動かなくなる; 〜を動かなくする, つかえる ‖ *Something is jamming (up) the machine.* 何かが機械につかえている. *The paper keeps jamming in the photocopier.* コピー機に紙が詰まって動かない. *I can't open the door. The lock has jammed.* ドアを開けられない. かぎがつかえている. ▶定義3 ⓣ jam sth (up) (with sb/sth) (通常は受動態で) to fill sth with too many people or things 〜をあまりにもたくさんの人または物で一杯にする→〜に詰め込む ‖ *The cupboard was **jammed full** of old newspapers and magazines.* 戸棚には古新聞や雑誌が詰め込まれていた. *The suitcase was **jam-packed with** (= completely full of)*

# January    913

*designer clothes.* スーツケースにはデザイナーブランドの服がぎゅうぎゅうに(=完全に一杯に)詰め込まれていた. *The switchboard was jammed with calls from unhappy customers.* 電話交換台はお客からの苦情電話でパンクした.
▶定義4 ⓣ to send out signals in order to stop radio programmes, etc from being received or heard clearly ラジオ番組などが受信されるまたは明瞭(めいりょう)に聞こえるのを止めるために信号を送信する→妨害する
句動詞 **jam on the brakes/jam the brakes on** ▶定義 to stop a car suddenly by pushing hard on the controls (**brakes**) with your feet 足で制御装置(ブレーキ)を強く踏むことによって, 車を突然止める→ブレーキをぐいと踏む, ブレーキをぐいと踏む

**Jan** 略 January→1月 ‖ *1 Jan 1993* 1993年1月1日

**jangle** /dʒǽŋg(ə)l/ 動 ⓘⓣ ▶定義 to make a noise like metal hitting against metal; to move sth so that it makes this noise 金属が互いにぶつかり合うような音を立てる; そのような音が鳴るように〜を動かす→じゃらじゃらいう・鳴る; 〜をじゃらじゃらいわせる・鳴らす ‖ *The baby smiles if you jangle your keys.* かぎをじゃらじゃらさせると, その赤ん坊は笑う. ─ **jangle** 名 Ⓤ じゃらじゃらいう音

**janitor** /dʒǽnətər/ 米 =**CARETAKER**

*****January** /dʒǽnjuə)ri; -èri/ 名 Ⓤ ⓒ (略 **Jan**)
▶定義 the first month of the year, coming after December 12月の次に来る, 1年の最初の月→1月 ‖ *We're going skiing **in January**.* 私たちは1月にスキーに行くつもりだ. *last/next January* この前の・来年の1月 *We first met **on January 31st, 1989**.* 私たちは1989年1月31日に初めて会った. *Christine's birthday is (on) January 17.* クリスティーンの誕生日は1月17日だ. *Our wedding anniversary is at the end of January.* 私たちの結婚記念日は1月末日だ. *January mornings can be very dark in Britain.* 英国では1月の朝は非常に暗いことがある. ☞「1月17日に」を on January the seventeenth または on the seventeenth of January と言う. さらにアメリカ英語では on January seventeenth と言う. イギリス英語, アメリカ英

語共に，1年の月名は capital letter（大文字）で始める．

**＊jar¹** /dʒɑːr/ 名 C ▶定義1 a container with a lid, usually made of glass and used for keeping food, etc in 通常ガラスでできていて，食べ物などを中に入れておくのに使われるふたの付いた容器→**びん，つぼ** ‖ *a jam jar* ジャムのびん ‖ *a large storage jar for flour* 小麦粉の大きな保存つぼ ▶定義2 the food that a jar contains びんに入った食べ物→**びん1杯の量，つぼ1杯の量** ‖ *a jar of honey/jam/coffee* びん1杯のはちみつ・ジャム・コーヒー

**jar²** /dʒɑːr/ 動 (**jarring**; **jarred**) ▶定義1 他 to hurt or damage sth as a result of a sharp knock 激しくぶつかった結果，〜を傷付けるまたは損壊する→**傷付ける** ‖ *He fell and jarred his back.* 彼は転んで背中を痛めた．▶定義2 自 **jar (on sb/sth)** to have an unpleasant or annoying effect 不快なまたは困った影響を受ける→**不快な感じを与える，神経に障る，いら立たせる** ‖ *The dripping tap jarred on my nerves.* 滴の落ちる音が私の神経に障った．

**jargon** /dʒɑ́ːrɡən/ 名 U ▶定義 special or technical words that are used by a particular group of people in a particular profession and that other people do not understand 特定の職業に就く特定の人々の集団によって使われ，ほかの人々は理解しない特別なまたは技術的な言葉→**特殊用語，隠語，専門語だらけの話** ‖ *medical/scientific/legal/computer jargon* 医療・科学・法律・コンピューターの特殊用語

**jaundice** /dʒɔ́ːndəs/ 名 U ▶定義 a disease that makes your skin and eyes yellow 人の皮膚や目を黄色くする病気→**黄疸（おうだん）**

**javelin** /dʒǽv(ə)lən/ 名 ▶定義1 C a long stick with a pointed end that is thrown in sports competitions 運動競技で投げられる，先のとがった長い棒 →**（やり投げ用の）やり** ▶定義2 **the javelin** ［単数扱い］the event or sport of throwing the javelin as far as possible やりをできる限り遠くまで投げる種目またはスポーツ→**やり投げ**

**jaw** /dʒɔː/ 名 ▶定義1 C either of the two bones in your face that contain your teeth 顔を構成する骨で歯を含む上下2つの部分のどちらか一方→**あご** ‖ *the lower/upper jaw* 下あご・上あご ☛ C5ページのさし絵 ▶定義2 **jaws** ［複数扱い］the mouth (especially of a wild animal) （特に野生動物の）口→**口部，あご部** ‖ *The lion came towards him with its jaws open.* ライオンは口を開けて彼に向かって来た．

**＊jazz¹** /dʒæz/ 名 U ▶定義 a style of music with a strong rhythm, originally of African American origin アフリカ系アメリカ人から生まれた，強いリズムの音楽の種類→**ジャズ** ‖ *modern/traditional jazz* モダン・伝統的ジャズ ☛参 **classical, pop, rock**

**jazz²** /dʒæz/ 動 句動詞 **jazz** sth **up** 略式 ▶定義 to make sth brighter, more interesting or exciting 〜をより明るく，面白く，または刺激的にする→**活気づける，面白くする，飾り立てる**

**＊jealous** /dʒéləs/ 形 ▶定義1 feeling upset or angry because you think that sb you like or love is showing interest in sb else 自分が好きな人または愛する人がほかの人に興味を示していると思い，動揺するまたは怒りを感じる→**しっと深い** ‖ *Tim seems to get jealous whenever Sue speaks to another boy!* ティムは，スーがほかの男の子に話し掛けるといつも焼きもちを焼いているみたいだね．▶定義2 **jealous (of sb/sth)** feeling angry or sad because you want to be like sb else or because you want what sb else has ほかの人のようになりたいためにまたはほかの人が持つ物が欲しいために，腹立たしさまたは悲しみを感じる→**ねたんでいる** ‖ *He's always been jealous of his older brother.* 彼はいつも兄をねたんでいた．*I'm very jealous of your new car - how much did it cost?* 君の新車がとてもうらやましい － いくらしたの．☛類 **envious**―**jealously** 副→**しっと深く，ねたんで**―**jealousy** 名 C U （複 **jealousies**）→**しっと，ねたみ**

**＊jeans** /dʒiːnz/ 名 ［複数扱い］▶定義 trousers made of strong, usually blue, cotton cloth (denim) 丈夫な，通常藍（あい）色の，木綿の布（デニム）でできたズボン→**ジーンズ，ジーパン** ‖ *These jeans are a bit too tight.* このジーンズは少しきつすぎる．*a pair of jeans* ジーンズ1着

**Jeep**™ /dʒiːp/ 名 C ▶定義 a small, strong vehicle suitable for travelling over rough ground でこぼこの地面を走るのに適した小型で丈夫な車→

ジープ

**jeer** /dʒɪər/ 動自他 ▶定義 jeer (at) sb/sth to laugh or shout rude comments at sb/sth to show your lack of respect for him/her/it ～を尊敬する気持ちがないことを示すために、その～を笑うまたは無礼な言葉を叫ぶ→(～を)やじる，あざける，ばかにする ‖ *The spectators booed and jeered at the losing team.* 観客たちは負けたチームにブーイングしたりやじを飛ばしたりした. — jeer 名［C, 通常は複数］→冷やかし ‖ *The Prime Minister was greeted with jeers in the House of Commons today.* 首相は今日下院でやじを浴びた.

**jelly** /dʒéli/ 名（複 **jellies**）（米 **Jell-O**™）
▶定義 1 C U a soft, solid brightly-coloured food that shakes when it is moved. Jelly is made from sugar and fruit juice and is eaten cold at the end of a meal, especially by children. 動かすと揺れる，柔らかい固形の鮮やかな色の食べ物. 砂糖と果汁から作られ，冷たくして食後に特に子供が食べる→ゼリー(菓子)
▶定義 2 U 特に 米 a type of jam that does not contain any solid pieces of fruit 果物の固形部分が入っていないジャムの一種→ジェリージャム
成句 be/feel like jelly ▶定義 (used especially about the legs or knees) to feel weak because you are nervous, afraid, etc (特に脚またはひざについて)おくびょうや恐怖などのために力が入らなくなる→震える ‖ *My legs felt like jelly before the exam.* 試験の前に脚が震えた.
turn to jelly ▶定義 (used about the legs and knees) to suddenly become weak because of fear (脚やひざについて)恐怖のために突然力が入らなくなる→すくむ

**jellyfish**

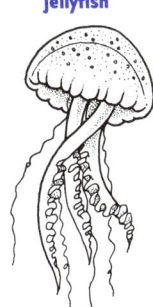

**jellyfish** /dʒélɪfɪʃ/ 名 C
（複 **jellyfish**）▶定義 a sea animal with a soft colourless body and long thin parts that can sting you. 柔らかい透明の体と，人を刺す細長い部分を持つ海の生物→くらげ

**jeopardize**（または **-ise**）/dʒépərdaɪz/ 動他 ▶定義 to do sth that may damage sth or put it at risk 何かに損害を与えるまたは危険な状態に置く可能性のある事をする→危うくする，危険にさらす ‖ *He would never do anything to jeopardize his career.* 彼は自分の経歴を危うくするような事は決してしないだろう.

**jeopardy** /dʒépərdi/ 名
成句 in jeopardy ▶定義 in a dangerous position and likely to be lost or harmed 危険な立場に置かれ，失われるまたは傷付けられそうな→危うくなっている ‖ *The future of the factory and 15,000 jobs are in jeopardy.* その工場の未来と15000人の職が存続の危機にさらされている.

**jerk**¹ /dʒɜːrk/ 動自他 ▶定義 to move or make sb/sth move with a sudden sharp movement 突然素早い動作で動く，または～を動かす→ぐいと引く，ぐいと押す，ひょいと投げる ‖ *She jerked the door open.* 彼女は扉をぐいと押し開けた. *His head jerked back as the car suddenly set off.* 車が突然発進したので，彼の頭が後ろへのけぞった. — jerky 形→がたがた動く，びくびく動く— jerkily 副→がたがたと，びくびくと，ぎくしゃくして

**jerk**² /dʒɜːrk/ 名 C ▶定義 1 a sudden sharp movement 突然の素早い動作→ぐいと引くこと，ぐいと押すこと ▶定義 2 特に 米 (俗語)a stupid or annoying person 愚鈍なまたはいらいらさせる人→ばか，間抜け

**jersey** /dʒɜ́ːrzi/ 名 ▶定義 1 C a piece of clothing made of wool that you wear over a shirt シャツの上に着る羊毛製の衣服→ジャージーのセーター，婦人用の毛編みジャケット ☛ jersey, jumper, pullover および sweater はいずれも同じような衣服を表す語. ▶定義 2 U a soft thin material made of cotton or wool that is used for making clothes 衣服を作るのに使われる，綿または羊毛でできた柔らかく薄い生地→ジャージー

**Jesus** /dʒíːzəs, -z/ = CHRIST

★**jet** /dʒet/ 名 C ▶定義 1 a fast modern aeroplane 最新式の高速飛行機→ジェット機 ▶定義 2 a fast, thin current of water, gas, etc coming out of a small hole 小さな穴から発射される水，ガスなどの速くて細い流れ→噴出，噴射

**jet-black** 形 ▶定義 very dark black in colour 非常に深い黒い色の→漆黒(しっこく)の，濡れ羽(ぬれば)色の

**jet engine** 定義 a powerful engine that makes planes fly by pushing out a current of hot air and gases at the back 高温の空気とガスの気流を後部から発射し, 飛行機を飛ばす強力なエンジン→ジェットエンジン

**jet lag** 定義 the tired feeling that people often have after a long journey in a plane to a place where the local time is different 飛行機で現地時間の異なる場所へ旅をした後に, 人々がしばしば受ける疲労感→時差ぼけ—**jet-lagged** 形→時差ぼけの

**the jet set** [単数扱い] 定義 the group of rich, successful and fashionable people (especially those who travel around the world a lot) 成功した金満家の上流社会の人々(特に世界中を何度も旅する人々)の集団→ジェット族, 金持ち族

**jetty** /dʒéti/ (複 **jetties**) (米 **dock**) 定義 a stone wall or wooden platform built out into the sea or a river where boats are tied and where people can get on and off them 海または川に突き出て建てられた石造りの岸壁または木造の台状のもので, 船がつながれ人々がそこで乗り降りする→突堤, 防波堤, 桟橋 類 **landing stage** ☛ C8 ページのさし絵

*****Jew** /dʒuː/ 定義 a person whose family was originally from the ancient land of Israel or whose religion is Judaism イスラエルの古代の地を故郷とする一族の人, またはユダヤ教を信仰する人→ユダヤ人—**Jewish** 形→ユダヤ人の

*****jewel** /dʒúːəl/ 定義 1 a valuable stone (for example a diamond) 高価な石(例えばダイヤモンド)→宝石 定義 2 [複数扱い] a piece of jewellery or an object that contains precious stones 宝石類の1つ, または高価な石を含む物→宝石入りの飾り, 宝石入りの装身具

**jeweller** (米 **jeweler**) /dʒúːələr/ 定義 1 a person whose job is to buy, sell, make or repair jewellery and watches 宝飾品や時計を買う, 売る, 作るまたは直すことを仕事とする人→宝石商, 宝石店店員, 宝石細工人, 宝石修理人 定義 2 **the jeweller's** [単数扱い] a shop where jewellery and watches are made, sold and repaired 宝飾品や時計が作られ, 売られ, 修理される店→宝石店

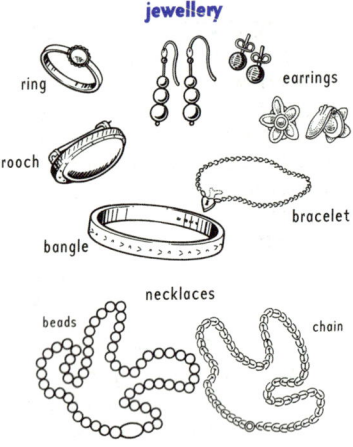
jewellery / ring / earrings / brooch / bangle / bracelet / necklaces / beads / chain

**jewellery** (米 **jewelry**) /dʒúːəlri/ 定義 objects such as rings, etc that are worn as personal decoration 個人の装飾として身に着けられる指輪などのような物→宝石類, 貴金属, 宝石装身具 ∥ *a piece of jewellery* 宝石1つ

**jig**¹ /dʒɪg/ 定義 a type of quick dance with jumping movements; the music for this dance 跳ねる動きをする, テンポの速い踊りの一種; その踊りのための音楽→ジグ

**jig**² /dʒɪg/ (**jigging; jigged**) 定義 **jig about/around** to move about in an excited or impatient way 興奮またはいらいらしたように動く→急激に前後または上下に動く, 急激に前後にまたは上下に動かす

**jiggle** /dʒɪ́g(ə)l/ 定義 to move sth quickly from side to side 〜を端から端まで速く動かす→軽く揺さぶる ∥ *She jiggled her car keys to try to distract the baby.* 彼女はその赤ん坊をあやそうとして, 車のかぎを振った.

**jigsaw** /dʒɪ́gsɔː/ (または **jigsaw puzzle**) 定義 a picture on cardboard or wood that is cut into small pieces and has to be fitted together again 厚紙または木にかかれた絵で, 細かい断片に切り分けられていて, 再び集めて組み合わされなければならないもの→ジグソーパズル ☛ S1 ページのさし絵

**jingle**¹ /dʒɪ́ŋg(ə)l/ 定義 1 [単数扱い] a ringing sound like small bells, made by metal objects gently hitting each other 金属が互いに

緩やかにぶつかり合って鳴る，小さなベルのように鳴り響く音→**ちりんちりんという音** ‖ *the jingle of coins* 硬貨がじゃらじゃらとぶつかり合う音 ▶定義2 ❸a short simple tune or song that is easy to remember and is used in advertising on television or radio 覚えやすい短い簡単な曲または歌で，テレビやラジオの宣伝に使われる→**調子良く響くコマーシャル，調子良く響く詩句**

**jingle**² /dʒíŋg(ə)l/ 動 圓 他 ▶定義 to make or cause sth to make a pleasant gentle sound like small bells ringing 小さなベルが鳴り響くような，心地良く優しい音を立てる；または〜にそのような音を立てさせる→**調子良く響く，ちりんちりんと鳴る；〜をちりんちりんと鳴らす** ‖ *She jingled the coins in her pocket.* 彼女はポケットの中で硬貨をちりんちりんと鳴らした．

**jinx** /dʒɪŋ(k)s/ 名 [ ❸, 通常は単数 ] 略式 ▶定義 bad luck; a person or thing that people believe brings bad luck to sb/sth 不運；〜に不運をもたらすと人々が信じている人または物→**縁起の悪い物・人，不運をもたらす物**—jinx 動 他 →**悪運をもたらす，けちを付ける**—jinxed 形 →**縁起の悪い，悪運をもたらす** ‖ *After my third accident in a month, I began to think I was jinxed.* 一月のうちで3回目の事故の後，私は悪運に取り付かれたと思い始めた．

**the jitters** /dʒítərz/ 名 [ 複数扱い ] 略式 ▶定義 feelings of fear or worry, especially before an important event or before having to do sth difficult 特に重要な行事の前，または難しい〜をしなければならない前に感じる恐れや心配→**不安感，神経過敏** ‖ *Just thinking about the exam gives me the jitters!* 試験のことを考えただけで，不安になってくる．

**jittery** /dʒítəri/ 形 略式 ▶定義 nervous or worried 神経質な，または心配している→**神経過敏な，びくびくしている，いらいらしている**

**Jnr**（または **Jr**）/dʒúːnjər/ 略 特に 米 Junior→**2世** ‖ *Samuel P Carson, Jnr* サムエル P カーソン2世

*★**job** /dʒɒb/ 名 ❸ ▶定義1 the work that you do regularly to earn money お金を稼ぐために定期的にする仕事→**勤め口，定職** ‖ *She took/got a job as a waitress.* 彼女はウエートレスの職に就いた．*A lot of people will lose their jobs if the factory closes.* その工場が閉鎖されると，多くの人々が職を失うことになる．

# job  917

▶ job（職）を look for（探す），apply for（志望する），find（得る）と言う．job（職）は，給料が well-paid/highly-paid（良い・高い），または給料が badly-paid/low-paid（悪い・低い）ことがある．job（職）は，full-time（常勤）と part-time（非常勤），permanent（終身雇用）と temporary（一時雇用）であることがある．非常勤で働きたい人々には job sharing（ジョブシェアリング）が人気になっている．

☛参 **work**¹ の注 ▶定義2 a task or a piece of work 一定期間にやるべき仕事または1つの作業→**仕事，賃仕事** ‖ *I always have a lot of jobs to do in the house at weekends.* 私はいつも週末に家でする仕事がたくさんある．*The garage has **done a good/bad job on** our car.* その自動車修理工場は，私たちの車の修理がうまかった・下手だった．▶定義3 [ 通常は単数 ] a duty or responsibility 義務または責任→**勤め，役目** ‖ *It's not his job to tell us what we can and can't do.* 私たちができる事とできない事を私たちに告げるのは彼の勤めではない．

成句 **do the job/trick** 略式 ▶定義 to get the result that is wanted 望まれている結果を得る→**目的にかなう，うまくいく** ‖ *This extra strong glue should do the job.* この超強力接着剤でうまくいくだろう．

**have a hard job to do sth/doing sth** ⇒ **HARD**¹

**it's a good job**（口語）▶定義 it is a good or lucky thing それは良いまたは幸運なことだ→**幸いだ，運が良い** ‖ *It's a good job you reminded me - I had completely forgotten!* あなたが私に思い出させくれて助かった - 私は完全に忘れていた．

**just the job/ticket** 略式 ▶定義 exactly what is needed in a particular situation 特定の状況でまさに必要とされているもの→**おあつらえ向きのもの，打って付けのもの** ‖ *This dress will be just the job for Helen's party.* このドレスは，ヘレンのパーティーに着ていくのにちょうど欲しかったものだわ．

**make a bad, good, etc job of sth** ▶定義 to do sth badly, well, etc 〜を下手に・上手にするなど→**下手にやる，立派にやってのける**

**make the best of a bad job** ⇒ **BEST**³

**out of a job** ▶定義 without paid work 給与をも

らえる仕事がない→失業して ☛ より正式な語は unemployed.

**jobless** /dʒáblǝs/ ▶定義1 形 (usually used about large numbers of people) without paid work (通常大勢の人々について) 給与をもらえる仕事がない→**仕事のない, 失業中の** ☛ 類 **unemployed** ▶定義2 the jobless 名 [複数扱い] people without paid work 給与をもらえる仕事のない人々→失業者 — **joblessness** 名 U →失業(状態) ☛ 類 **unemployment**

**jockey** /dʒáki/ 名 C ▶定義 a person who rides horses in races, especially as a profession 特に職業として, レースで馬に乗る人→**騎手** ☛ 参 **DJ**

**jodhpurs** /dʒádpǝrz/ 名 [複数扱い] ▶定義 special trousers that you wear for riding a horse 馬に乗るための特別なズボン→**乗馬ズボン** ☛ **horse** のさし絵

**jog**¹ /dʒɑg/ 動 (**jogging**; **jogged**) ▶定義1 自 to run slowly, especially as a form of exercise 特に運動の1つの形態として, ゆっくり走る→**ゆっくりと駆ける, ジョギングをする** ☛ 娯楽または運動として行うジョギングについて述べるときには, go jogging という表現の方がよく使われる. *I go jogging most evenings.* 私は大抵夕方にはジョギングに行く. ▶定義2 他 to push or knock sb/sth slightly 〜を軽く押すまたはたたく→**ちょっと突く, ちょっと押す** || *He jogged my arm and I spilled the milk.* 彼が私の腕にちょっとぶつかり, 私は牛乳をこぼした.

成句 **jog sb's memory** ▶定義 to say or do sth that makes sb remember sth 〜に…を思い出させるような〜を言うまたはする→**〜の記憶を呼び覚ます**

**jog**² /dʒɑg/ 名 [単数扱い] ▶定義1 a slow run as a form of exercise 運動の1つの形態としてゆっくり走ること→**ゆっくりとした駆け足** || *She goes for a jog before breakfast.* 彼女は朝食の前にジョギングに行く. ▶定義2 a slight push or knock 軽く押すことまたはたたくこと→**そっと押すこと, そっと突くこと**

**jogger** /dʒɑ́gǝr/ 名 C ▶定義 a person who goes jogging for exercise 運動のためにジョギングをする人→**ジョギングをする人, ジョギングをしている人**

\*join¹ /dʒɔɪn/ 動 ▶定義1 他 join A to B; join A and B (together) to fasten or connect one thing to another 1つのものをほかのものに固定するまたはつなぐ→**AとBを結合する, つなぐ, 連結する** || *The Channel Tunnel joins Britain to Europe.* 英仏海峡トンネルはイギリスをヨーロッパとつなぐ. *The two pieces of wood had been carefully joined together.* 2本の木材が丁寧に接合されていた. *We've knocked down the wall and joined the two rooms into one.* 私たちは壁を壊して, 2つの部屋を1つにつなげた. ▶定義2 自他 join (up) (with sb/sth) to meet or unite (with sb/sth) to form one thing or group 1つのものまたは集まりを形成する→**交わる, 一緒になる, 合流する** || *Do the two rivers join (up) at any point?* 2つの川はどこかで合流しますか. *Where does this road join the motorway?* この道路はどこで高速道路に合流しますか. *Would you like to join us for a drink?* よろしければ私たちと一緒に一杯やりませんか. ▶定義3 他 to become a member of a club or organization あるクラブまたは組織の一員となる→**〜に加わる, 加入する** || *I've joined an aerobics class.* 私はエアロビクスの教室に加入した. *He joined the company three months ago.* 彼は3か月前にその会社に入った. ▶定義4 他 to take your place in sth or to take part in sth 〜に自分の場所を取る, または〜に参加する→**〜に合流する, 参加する** || *We'd better go and join the queue if we want to see the film.* その映画を見たければ, 私たちは出掛けてその列に加わった方が良いだろう. *Come downstairs and join the party.* 下に下りてきてパーティーに参加しなさい. ▶定義5 自他 join (with) sb in sth/in doing sth/to do sth; join together in doing sth/to do sth to take part with sb (often in doing sth for sb else) (しばしばほかの〜のために…をして) 〜に組する→**一緒になる** || *Everybody here joins me in wishing you the best of luck in your new job.* ここにいる皆が私と共にあなたの新しい仕事でのご幸運を祈っております. *The whole school joined together to sing the school song.* 全校生徒が校歌を歌うために一堂に会した.

成句 join forces (with sb) ⇒ **FORCE**¹

句動詞 **join in** (**sth/doing sth**) ▶定義 to take part in an activity ある活動に参加する→**参加す**

る‖ *Everyone started singing but Frank refused to join in.* 皆が歌い始めたが,フランクは参加することを拒んだ.

**join up** ▶定義 to become a member of the army, navy or air force 陸軍,海軍または空軍の一員になる→**入隊する**

**join**² /dʒɔɪn/ **名 C** ▶定義 a place where two things are fixed or connected 2つの物が固定されているまたはつながれている箇所→**接合箇所,継ぎ目**‖ *He glued the handle back on so cleverly that you couldn't see the join.* 彼は継ぎ目が分からないほどとてもうまく取っ手を接着剤で付け直した.

**joiner** /dʒɔɪnər/ **名 C** ▶定義 a person who makes the wooden parts of a building 建物の木の部分を作る人→**指物師,建て具工**
☞参 **carpenter**

*****joint**¹ /dʒɔɪnt/ **名 C** ▶定義 **1** a part of the body where two bones fit together and are able to bend 体の部分で,2つの骨が連結し曲げることができる部分→**関節,節** ▶定義 **2** the place where two or more things are fastened or connected together, especially to form a corner 特に角を形づくるために,2つまたはそれ以上のものが一緒に固定されているまたは接続されている場所→**継ぎ目,継ぎ手** ▶定義 **3** a large piece of meat that you cook whole in the oven オーブンで全体を焼く肉の大きな切り身→**焼き肉,(骨の付いた)焼き肉用の肉,ロース**‖ *a joint of lamb* 子羊肉のロース

*****joint**² /dʒɔɪnt/ **形** (名詞の前だけ) ▶定義 shared or owned by two or more people 2人以上の人によって共有されるまたは所有される→**共同の,共有の,連帯の**‖ *Have you and your husband got a **joint account**? (=a shared bank account)* あなたとご主人は共同預金口座(=共有する銀行の預金口座)を持っていますか. *a joint decision* 共同決議—**jointly 副**→**共同で,連帯して,合弁で**

*****joke**¹ /dʒóʊk/ **名** ▶定義 **1** **C** something said or done to make you laugh, especially a funny story 人を笑わせるために言われるまたは行われること,特におかしな話→**冗談,ジョーク,しゃれ**‖ *to tell/crack jokes* 冗談を言う・飛ばす *a dirty joke (=about sex)* わい談(=セックスについて) *I'm sorry, I didn't **get the joke** (=understand it).* ごめんなさい,私はその冗談が分かりません(=理解しない).

➤ practical joke(悪ふざけ,いたずら)とは,人を愚かに見せるためにする行為で,口で言う冗談ではない.

▶定義 **2** 〔単数扱い〕a ridiculous person, thing or situation ばかげた人,物または状態→**笑い草,物笑いの種,取るに足らぬこと**‖ *The salary he was offered was a joke!* 彼が提示された給料は取るに足らぬ額だった.

**成句 play a joke/trick on sb** ▶定義 to trick sb in order to amuse yourself or other people 自分自身または他人を面白がらせるために〜に悪ふざけをする→**〜にいたずらする,〜をからかう**

**see the joke** ▶定義 to understand what is funny about a joke or trick 冗談または悪ふざけについて何がおかしいかを理解する→**冗談(の落ち)が分かる**

**take a joke** ▶定義 to be able to laugh at a joke against yourself 自分に対する冗談を笑うことができる→**冗談を平気で受け流す,冗談を言われて気にしない**‖ *The trouble with Pete is he can't take a joke.* ピートの欠点は冗談を受け流せないことだ.

**joke**² /dʒóʊk/ **動 自** ▶定義 **1 joke (with sb) (about sth)** to say sth to make people laugh; to tell a funny story 人々を笑わせる〜を言う;面白い話をする→**冗談を言う,しゃれを言う,からかう**‖ *She spent the evening laughing and joking with her old friends.* 彼女は旧友たちと笑って冗談を言いながらその晩を過ごした. ▶定義 **2** to say sth that is not true because you think it is funny それが面白いと思うので,事実ではない事を言う→**冗談を言う**‖ *I never joke about religion.* 私は宗教について決して冗談を言わない. *Don't get upset. I was **only joking**!* 怒らないで.冗談を言っただけだから.

**成句 you must be joking; you're joking**(口語) ▶定義 (used to express great surprise) you cannot be serious(非常な驚きを表現するために用いて)あなたは本気ではないだろう→**ご冗談でしょう**

**joker** /dʒóʊkər/ **名 C** ▶定義 **1** a person who likes to tell jokes or play tricks 冗談を言うまたはふざけるのが好きな人→**冗談を言う人,おどけ者** ▶定義 **2** an extra card which can be used instead of any other one in some card games トランプゲームによってほかのどのカードの代わりにも使うことができる余分なカード➔ジョーカー ☞ card のさし絵

**jolly** /dʒɑ́li/ 形 ▶定義 happy うれしい➔楽しい, 気持ちの良い

**jolt**[1] /dʒóʊlt/ 動 自 他 ▶定義 to move or make sb/sth move in a sudden rough way 突然荒っぽく動くまたは〜を動かす➔急に揺れる, 急に上下する, がたがた揺れる; がたがた揺する ‖ *The lorry jolted along the bumpy track.* トラックはでこぼこ道を揺れながら進んだ. *The crash jolted all the passengers forward.* その衝突で乗客全員が急に前へつんのめった.

**jolt**[2] /dʒóʊlt/ 名 [通常は単数] ▶定義 1 a sudden movement 突然の動き➔激しい揺れ ‖ *The train stopped with a jolt.* 列車は激しく揺れて止まった. ▶定義 2 a sudden surprise or shock 突然の驚きまたは衝撃➔ショック ‖ *His sudden anger gave her quite a jolt.* 彼の突然の怒りは彼女にかなりのショックを与えた.

**jostle** /dʒɑ́s(ə)l/ 動 自 他 ▶定義 to push hard against sb in a crowd 人込みの中で〜を激しく押す➔突き飛ばす, 押しのける

**jot** /dʒɑt/ 動 (**jotting**; **jotted**)
句動詞 **jot sth down** ▶定義 to make a quick short note of sth 〜についての急ぎの短いメモを書く➔〜をちょっと書き留める, メモをする ‖ *Let me jot down your address.* 君の住所をちょっと書き留めさせてください.

**journal** /dʒə́:ml/ 名 C ▶定義 1 a newspaper or a magazine, especially one in which all the articles are about a particular subject or profession 特にその中のすべての記事が特定の主題または職業に関するものである, 新聞または雑誌➔雑誌, 新聞, 機関誌 ‖ *a medical/scientific journal* 医学・科学雑誌 ▶定義 2 a written account of what you have done each day 自分がそれぞれの日に行ったことを書き留めた報告➔日記, 日誌 ‖ *Have you read his journal of the years he spent in India?* 彼がインドで過ごした数年間の日誌を読みましたか. ☞参 **diary**

**journalism** /dʒə́:rnlɪzəm/ 名 U ▶定義 the profession of collecting and writing about news in newspapers and magazines or talking about it on the television or radio 新聞や雑誌のニュースを集めて書いたり, テレビやラジオでそれについて話す職業➔ジャーナリズム, 新聞・雑誌界

*****journalist** /dʒə́:mlɪst/ 名 C ▶定義 a person whose job is to collect and write about news in newspapers and magazines or to talk about it on the television or radio 新聞や雑誌のニュースを集めて書いたり, テレビやラジオでそれについて話すことを仕事とする人➔ジャーナリスト, 新聞記者, 雑誌記者 ☞参 **reporter**

*****journey** /dʒə́:mi/ 名 C ▶定義 the act of travelling from one place to another, usually on land 通常陸上を, ある場所からほかの場所へと旅をする行為➔旅行, 旅 ‖ *Did you have a good journey?* 良い旅でしたか. *a two-hour journey* 2時間の旅 *The journey to work takes me forty-five minutes.* 私は通勤に45分かかる. *We'll have to break the journey (=stop for a rest).* 私たちは旅の途中で休憩しなければならない(=休むために止まる)だろう.

▶ journey は空と海の旅のいずれも表すことができるが, 特に空の旅について述べるときには **flight** と言い, 海の旅は **voyage** もしくはそれが遊覧の旅であれば **cruise** と言う.

☞参 **travel** の注

**jovial** /dʒóʊviəl, -vjəl/ 形 ▶定義 (used about a person) happy and friendly(人について)楽しい, そして友好的な➔陽気な, 楽しい

**joy** /dʒɔ́ɪ/ 名 ▶定義 1 ❶ a feeling of great happiness 非常に楽しい感情➔喜び, うれしさ ‖ *We'd like to wish you joy and success in your life together.* あなたたち2人の生活が喜びと成功にあふれることを祈ります. ▶定義 2 ❸ a person or thing that gives you great pleasure あなたに非常に楽しみを与える人または物➔喜びの種, うれしいこと ‖ *the joys of fatherhood* 父であることの喜び *That class is a joy to teach.* そのクラスで教えるのはうれしい. ▶定義 3 ❶ 英 略式 (疑問文や否定文で用いて) success or satisfaction➔成功, 満足, 幸運 ‖ '*I asked again if we could have seats with more legroom but got no joy from the check-in clerk.*' 「私はもっと脚を伸ばせる空間のある席はないかと再度尋ねたが, 受け付け係からは何も満足を得る回答はなかった」

成句 **jump for joy** ⇒ **JUMP**[1]
**sb's pride and joy** ⇒ **PRIDE**[1]

**joyful** /dʒɔ́ɪfʊl, -f(ə)l/ 形 ▶定義 very happy 非常にうれしい→喜ばしい, うれしい, 楽しい ‖ *a joyful occasion* 楽しい行事 ― **joyfully** /-fʊli, -f(ə)li/ 副 →楽しく, うれしそうに ― **joyfulness** 名 U →うれしさ, 喜ばしさ

**joyless** /dʒɔ́ɪləs/ 形 ▶定義 unhappy 不幸せな→楽しくない, 喜ばしくない, わびしい ‖ *a joyless marriage* 喜びのない結婚

**joyriding** /dʒɔ́ɪraɪdɪŋ/ 名 U ▶定義 the crime of stealing a car and driving it for pleasure, usually in a fast and dangerous way 車を盗み, 通常スピードを上げ危険な乗り方で, 運転して楽しむ犯罪→(盗難車での)暴走 ― **joyrider** 名 C →(盗難車を派手に乗り回す)暴走ドライバー ― **joyride** 名 C →(盗難車での)暴走, (面白半分の)危険なドライブ

**joystick** /dʒɔ́ɪstɪk/ 名 C ▶定義 a handle used for controlling movement on a computer, aircraft, etc コンピューター, 飛行機などの動きを制御するためのハンドル→操縦桿(かん), 操作レバー

**JP** /dʒèɪ píː/ 名 Justice of the Peace→治安判事

**Jr** 略 = JNR

**jubilant** /dʒúːbələnt/ 形 正式 ▶定義 extremely happy, especially because of a success 特に成功したために, 非常にうれしい→(歓声を上げて)喜ぶ ‖ *The football fans were jubilant at their team's victory in the cup.* サッカーファンたちは競技大会でのチームの優勝に歓声を上げて喜んだ.

**jubilation** /dʒùːbəléɪʃ(ə)n/ 名 U 正式 ▶定義 great happiness because of a success 成功による非常な喜び→歓喜, 歓呼

**jubilee** /dʒúːbəliː/ 名 C ▶定義 a special anniversary of an event that took place a certain number of years ago, and the celebrations that go with it ある特定の年数前に起きた出来事の特別な記念祭, およびそれと共に行われる祝典→記念祭, 祝典, 祝祭 ‖ *It's the company's **golden jubilee** this year (=it is fifty years since it was started).* 今年は会社の創立50周年だ (= 会社が創設されてから50年目だ).
▶ ほかに silver jubilee (25周年) と diamond jubilee (60周年) がある.

**Judaism** /dʒúːdeɪz(ə)m, -deɪ-/ 名 U ▶定義 the religion of the Jewish people ユダヤ人の宗教→ユダヤ教, ユダヤ主義

---

**judge**² 921

★**judge**¹ /dʒʌdʒ/ 名 C ▶定義 1 a person in a court of law whose job is to decide how criminals should be punished and to make legal decisions 犯罪者がどのように罰せられるべきかを決定し, 法的な裁決を下すことを仕事とする法廷にいる人→裁判官, 判事 ‖ *The judge sentenced the man to three years in prison.* 裁判官はその男に3年間の懲役を言い渡した. ▶定義 2 a person who decides who has won a competition 競技でだれが勝ったかを決定する人→審判員, 審査員 ‖ *a panel of judges* 審査員団 ▶定義 3 [通常は単数] **a judge of sth** a person who has the ability or knowledge to give an opinion about sth 〜について意見を述べる能力または知識を持つ人→鑑定家, 善しあしの分かる人 ‖ *You're a good judge of character - what do you think of him?* あなたは性格を見分けるのがうまいけど ― 彼をどう思いますか.

★**judge**² /dʒʌdʒ/ 動 ▶定義 1 自他 to form or give an opinion about sb/sth based on the information you have 自分が持っている情報に基づいて, 〜についての意見をまとめるまたは述べる→(〜を)判断する, 評価する ‖ ***Judging by/from** what he said, his work is going well.* 彼が言った事から判断すると, 彼の仕事はうまくいっている. *It's difficult to judge how long the project will take.* その計画にどのくらいの時間がかかるかを判断するのは難しい. *The party was judged a great success by everybody.* 皆からパーティーは非常に成功だったと評価された. ▶定義 2 他 to decide the result or winner of a competition 競技で結果または勝者を決定する→〜を審査する, 審判する ‖ *The head teacher will judge the competition.* 校長が競技を審査するだろう. ▶定義 3 他 to form an opinion about sb/sth, especially when you disapprove of him/her/it 特に〜に賛成しないときに, その〜について意見をまとめる→〜を判断する, 断定する ‖ *Don't judge him too harshly - he's had a difficult time.* 彼をあまり厳しく批評するな ― 彼はつらい目に遭ったのだ. ▶定義 4 他 to decide if sb is guilty or innocent in a court of law 法廷で〜が有罪か無罪かを決定する→裁く, 裁判する

**\*judgement**（または **judgment**）/dʒʌ́dʒmənt/ 名 ▶定義1 ❶the ability to form opinions or to make sensible decisions 意見をまとめたり賢明な判断をする能力→**判断力, 分別** ‖ *He always shows excellent judgement in his choice of staff.* 彼はいつも社員選びにおいて目が高い. *to have good/poor/sound judgement* 判断力がある・判断力が乏しい・分別がある ▶定義2 ❷❶an opinion formed after carefully considering the information you have 自分が持つ情報を慎重に考慮してまとめた意見→**判断, 見解, 意見** ‖ *What, in your judgement, would be the best course of action?* あなたの見解では, 最善策は何ですか.
▶定義3 judgment ❷an official decision made by a judge or a court of law 裁判官または法廷による公式な決定→**判決** ‖ *The man collapsed when the judgment was read out in court.* 法廷で判決が読み上げられた時, その男は倒れた.

**judicial** /dʒudíʃ(ə)l/ 形 ▶定義 connected with a court of law, a judge or a legal judgment 法廷, 裁判官, または判決に関連した→**裁判の, 司法の** ‖ *the judicial system* 司法制度

**judicious** /dʒudíʃəs/ 形 ▶定義 (used about a decision or an action) sensible and carefully considered; showing good judgement (決定または行動について) 賢明で慎重に考えられた; 良い判断を示す→**思慮分別のある, 賢明な**— judiciously 副 →**思慮深く, 賢明に**

**judo** /dʒúːdou/ 名 ❶ ▶定義 a sport from Asia in which two people fight and try to throw each other to the ground アジアで始まったスポーツで, 2人が対戦し相手を投げ倒そうと競う→**柔道** ☛参 **martial arts**

Jug
(米 pitcher)　pitcher　carafe

**jug** /dʒʌg/ (米 **pitcher**) 名 ❷ ▶定義 a container with a handle used for holding or pouring liquids 液体を入れたりつぐために使われる取っ手の付いた容器→**水差し, ジャグ** ‖ *a milk jug* ミルクジャグ *a jug of water* 水差し1杯分の水

**juggle** /dʒʌ́g(ə)l/ 動 自 他 ▶定義1 juggle (with sth) to keep three or more objects such as balls in the air at the same time by throwing them one at a time and catching them quickly 3つ以上のボールなどの物を, 次々に投げては素早く受け取ることにより, それらが同時に宙に舞っているように操作する→**空中に次々に投げて受け取る曲芸をする** ▶定義2 juggle sth (with sth) to try to deal with two or more important jobs or activities at the same time 同時に2つ以上の重要な仕事または活動を処理しようとする→**(～を)調整する, 都合をつける, 操作する**

**juggler** /dʒʌ́g(lə)r/ 名 ❷ ▶定義 a person who juggles to entertain people 人々を楽しませるために, 空中に投げて受け取る曲芸をする人→**(投げ物の)曲芸師, ジャグラー**

**\*juice** /dʒuːs/ 名 ❷ ❶ ▶定義1 the liquid that comes from fruit and vegetables 果物や野菜からとれる液体→**液, ジュース** ‖ *carrot/grapefruit/lemon juice* ニンジン・グレープフルーツ・レモンジュース *I'll have an orange juice, please.* 私にはオレンジジュースを下さい. ☛ C4ページのさし絵 ▶定義2 the liquid that comes from a piece of meat when it is cooked 肉を調理したときに出る液体→**肉汁** ‖ *You can use the juices of the meat to make gravy.* 肉汁を使ってグレービーソースを作ることができる. ▶定義3 the liquid in your stomach or another part of your body that deals with the food you eat 食べた食物を処理する, 胃または体のほかの部分にある液体→**体液, 分泌液** ‖ *gastric/digestive juices* 胃液・消化液

**juicy** /dʒúːsi/ 形 (**juicier**; **juiciest**) ▶定義1 containing a lot of juice 多くの汁を含む→**水分の多い, 汁の多い** ‖ *juicy oranges* 水分の多いオレンジ ▶定義2 略式 (used about information) interesting because it is shocking (情報について) びっくりするような事であるために興味深い→**(いかがわしくて)面白い, 興味をそそる** ‖ *juicy gossip* 面白いうわさ話

**jukebox** /dʒúːkbɑks/ 名 ❷ ▶定義 a machine in a cafe or bar, that plays music when money is put in お金を入れると音楽を演奏する, コーヒー店やバーにある機械→**ジュークボックス**

**Jul** 略 July→**7月** ‖ *4 Jul 1999* 1999年7月4日

**★July** /dʒuːláɪ/ 图 ❶ ❸ (略 **Jul**) ▶定義 the seventh month of the year, coming after June 6月の次に来る、1年の7番目の月→**7月**
▶文中での月の表し方については、January の例と注を参照.

**jumble**¹ /dʒʌmb(ə)l/ 動 ❸ (通常は受動態で)
▶定義 jumble sth (up/together) to mix things together in a confused and untidy way 混乱した乱雑な方法で物を混ぜ合わせる→**ごちゃ混ぜにする, 混乱させる** ‖ *I must sort my clothes out - they're all jumbled up in the drawer.* 私は服を整理しなければならない － 全部引き出しの中でごちゃ混ぜになっているのだ.

**jumble**² /dʒʌmb(ə)l/ 图 ▶定義 1 [単数扱い] an untidy group of things; a mess 物の乱雑な集まり; 混乱状態→**ごちゃ混ぜ, 寄せ集め, 混乱** ‖ *a jumble of papers/ideas* ごちゃ混ぜの書類・考え
▶定義 2 ❶ 英 a collection of old things for a jumble sale がらくた市用に集めた古い物→**がらくた, 不用品** ‖ *Have you got any jumble you don't want?* 要らなくなったがらくたがありますか.

**jumble sale** (米 **rummage sale**) 图 ❸ ▶定義 a sale of old things that people do not want any more. Clubs, churches, schools and other organizations hold jumble sales to get money. 人がもう要らないと思う古い物の販売. クラブ, 教会, 学校, そのほかの組織がお金を集めるために開く→**がらくた市**

**jumbo**¹ /dʒʌmboʊ/ 形 略式 (名詞の前だけ)
▶定義 very large 非常に大きな→**特大の, ジャンボな**

**jumbo**² /dʒʌmboʊ/ 图 ❸ (複 **jumbos**) (または **jumbo jet**) ▶定義 a very large aircraft that can carry several hundred passengers 数百人の乗客を運ぶことができる非常に大きな飛行機→**ジャンボ機, 超大型ジェット機**

**★jump**¹ /dʒʌmp/ 動 ▶定義 1 ❸ to move quickly into the air by pushing yourself up with your legs and feet, or by stepping off a high place 足で自分を上に押し上げたり, 高い場所から降りて, 素早く空中へと動く→**跳ぶ** ‖ *to jump into the air/off a bridge/onto a chair* 宙へ跳ぶ・橋から跳び降りる・いすに跳び乗る *How high can you jump?* あなたはどのくらい高く跳べるの. *Jump up and down to keep warm.* 暖まるために飛び跳ねなさい. ☞ **hop** のさし絵
▶定義 2 ❸ to move quickly and suddenly 素早く突然動く→**跳び上がる** ‖ *The telephone rang and she jumped up to answer it.* 電話が鳴り, 彼女は跳び上がって電話に出た. *A taxi stopped and we jumped in.* タクシーが止まると, 私たちは跳び乗った. ▶定義 3 ❸ to get over sth by jumping 跳ぶことによって~を越える→**~を跳び越える** ‖ *The dog jumped the fence and ran off down the road.* 犬が柵(さく)を跳び越えて, 道を駆け下りていった. ▶定義 4 ❸ to make a sudden movement because of surprise or fear 驚きまたは恐れのために突然動く→**びくりと動く, びくっとする, どきっとする** ‖ *'Oh, it's only you - you made me jump,' he said.* 「ああ, 君だったのか － びっくりした」と彼は言った.
▶定義 5 ❸ jump (from sth) to sth; jump (by) (sth) to increase suddenly by a very large amount 突然非常に大幅に増える→**急に高くなる, 急騰する** ‖ *His salary jumped from £20000 to £28000 last year.* 彼の給料は昨年2万ポンドから2万8千ポンドに跳ね上がった. *Prices jumped (by) 50% in the summer.* 価格は夏に50パーセント急騰した. ▶定義 6 ❸ jump (from sth) to sth to go suddenly from one point in a series, a story, etc to another ある連続もの, 物語などの1つの点から突然他へ移動する→**飛ぶ, 飛躍する, 急に変わる** ‖ *The book kept jumping from the present to the past.* その本は現在から過去へと話が飛び続けた.

成句 climb/jump on the bandwagon ⇒ **BANDWAGON**

jump for joy ▶定義 to be extremely happy about sth ~について非常に喜ぶ→**うれしくて飛び跳ねる**

jump the gun ▶定義 to do sth too soon, before the proper time 適切な時間より前に, ~を早くしすぎる→**物事を早まって始める, フライングする**

jump the queue ▶定義 to go to the front of a line of people (queue) without waiting for your turn 自分の順番を待たずに, 人々の列の前に出る→**列に割り込む**

jump to conclusions ▶定義 to decide that sth is true without thinking about it carefully enough 十分慎重に考えずに, ~が真実である

と決める→早合点をする, 軽々しく結論を出す
句動詞 jump at sth ▶定義 to accept an opportunity, offer, etc with enthusiasm 熱狂して, 機会, 申入れなどを受け入れる→~に飛び付く, 喜んで~に応じる ‖ *Of course I jumped at the chance to work in New York for a year.* もちろん私はニューヨークで1年間働くチャンスに飛び付きました.

★**jump²** /dʒʌmp/ 名 ● ▶定義 1 an act of jumping 跳ぶ行為→**跳躍, 一跳び, ジャンプ** ‖ *With a huge jump the horse cleared the hedge.* 大きなジャンプで馬は生け垣を跳び越えた. *to do a parachute jump* 落下傘降下をする ☞参 **high jump**, **long jump** ▶定義 2 a jump (in sth) a sudden increase in amount, price or value 数量, 価格または価値の突然の増加→**急騰, 急上昇** ▶定義 3 a thing to be jumped over 跳び越えられるもの→**ジャンプの障害物** ‖ *The horse fell at the first jump.* その馬は最初の障害物で倒れた.

**jumper** /dʒʌmpər/ 名 ● ▶定義 1 英 a piece of clothing with sleeves, usually made of wool, that you wear on the top part of your body 通常羊毛製の, 上半身に着るそでの付いた服→**セーター** ☞参 **sweater**の注 ▶定義 2 a person or animal that jumps 跳ぶ人または動物→**跳ぶ人, 跳躍選手, 障害レース用の馬**

**jumpy** /dʒʌmpi/ 形 略式 ▶定義 nervous or worried 神経質または心配している→**神経過敏な, びくびくした** ‖ *I always get a bit jumpy if I'm travelling by air.* 私は飛行機で旅行をすることになると, いつも少し神経過敏になる.

**Jun** 略 June→**6月** ‖ *10 Jun 1999* 1999年6月10日

**junction** /dʒʌŋ(k)ʃ(ə)n/ 名 ● ▶定義 a place where roads, railway lines, etc meet 道路, 鉄道線路などが合流する場所→**合流点, 接合点, 交差点**

★**June** /dʒuːn/ 名 ● ⓤ (略 **Jun**) ▶定義 the sixth month of the year, coming after May 5月の次に来る, 1年の6番目の月→**6月**

▶文中での月の表し方については, January の例と注を参照.

**jungle** /dʒʌŋɡ(ə)l/ 名 ● ⓤ ▶定義 a thick forest in a hot tropical country 暑い熱帯地域の国にある密集した森→**ジャングル, 密林(地帯)** ‖ *the jungles of Africa and South America* アフリカおよび南アメリカの密林地帯 ☞参 **forest**の注

**junior¹** /dʒúːnjər/ 形 ▶定義 1 junior (to sb) having a low or lower position (than sb) in an organization, etc 組織などで低いまたは(~よりも)さらに低い地位にある→**下の, 下級の, 後輩の** ‖ *a junior officer/doctor/employee* 下級の役人・医師・社員 *A lieutenant is junior to a captain in the army.* 陸軍で中尉は大尉より下級である. ▶定義 2 **Junior** (略 **Jnr**, **Jr**) 特に 米 used after the name of a son who has the same first name as his father 父親と同じファーストネームを持つ息子の名前の後に用いて→**2世** ‖ *Sammy Davis, Junior* サミー デービス2世 ▶定義 3 医 of or for children below a particular age 特定の年齢より下の子供たちの, または彼らのための→**年少組の, ジュニアの, 小学生の** ‖ *the junior athletics championships* ジュニア競技選手権大会 ☞参 **senior¹**

**junior²** /dʒúːnjər/ 名 ▶定義 1 ● a person who has a low position in an organization, etc 組織などで低い地位にある人→**下役** ▶定義 2 [単数扱い] (his, her, your などと用いて) a person who is younger than sb else by the number of years mentioned 言及された年数だけ, ほかの~よりも若い人→**後輩, 年下の者** ‖ *She's two years his junior/his junior by two years.* 彼女は彼よりも2つ年下だ. ▶定義 3 ● 医 a child who goes to junior school 小学校に通う子供→**小学生** ‖ *The juniors are having an outing to a museum today.* 小学生たちは今日博物館へ遠足に出ている. ☞参 **senior²**

**junior school** 名 ● ▶定義 a school for children aged between seven and eleven 7歳から11歳までの子供たちのための学校→**小学校**

**junk** /dʒʌŋk/ 名 ⓤ 略式 ▶定義 things that are old or useless or do not have much value 古かったり役に立たなかったりあまり価値がないもの→**がらくた, くず物, 古物, 中古品** ‖ *There's an awful lot of junk up in the attic.* 屋根裏部屋にすさまじくたくさんのがらくたがある.

**junk food** 名 ⓤ 略式 ▶定義 food that is not very good for you but that is ready to eat or quick to prepare 自分のためにはあまり良くないが, そのまま食べられるまたは手間がかからず準備できる食べ物→**ジャンクフード**

**junta** /dʒʌ́ntə, hón-/ 名 [●, 単数または複数形の動詞と共に] ▶定義 a group, especially of military officers, who rule a country by force 特に陸軍の将校の,力によって国を統治する集団 ➔(革命)軍事政権

**Jupiter** /dʒúːpətər/ 图 [単数扱い] ▶定義 the planet that is fifth in order from the sun 太陽から数えて5番目にある惑星➔木星

**jurisdiction** /dʒɜ̀ərəsdíkʃ(ə)n/ 图 ❶ ▶定義 legal power or authority; the area in which this power can be used 法的な力または権力;その力を用いることができる地域➔司法権,裁判権;司法権の及ぶ範囲,法域,管轄区域 ‖ *That question is outside the jurisdiction of this council.* その問題はこの議会の管轄外だ.

**juror** /dʒúərər/ 图 ❷ ▶定義 a member of a jury a jury の一員➔陪審員,審査員

\***jury** /dʒúəri/ 图 [❷,単数または複数形の動詞と共に] (覆 **juries**) ▶定義 **1** a group of members of the public in a court of law who listen to the facts about a crime and decide if sb is guilty or not guilty 法廷で犯罪について事実を聴き,~が有罪か有罪でないかを決める,一般人から選ばれた成員の集団➔陪審(団) ‖ *Has/have the jury reached a verdict?* 陪審団は評決に至りましたか. ▶定義 **2** a group of people who decide who is the winner in a competition 競技でだれが勝者かを決める人々の集団➔審査員団,審査委員会 ‖ *The jury is/are about to announce the winners.* 審査員団が優勝者を発表しようとしている.

\***just**¹ /dʒəst, dʒʌst/ 副 ▶定義 **1** a very short time before 非常に短時間前に➔ちょうど,まさに ‖ *She's just been to the shops.* 彼女はちょうど店に行ってきたところだ. *He'd just returned from France when I saw him.* 私が彼に会った時,彼はちょうどフランスから戻ってきたところだった. *They came here just before Easter.* 彼らは復活祭の直前にここに来た. ▶定義 **2** at exactly this/that moment, or immediately after まさにこの・その瞬間に,または直後に➔ちょうど今(~したばかり),たった今 ‖ *He was just about to break the window when he noticed a policeman.* 彼が警官に気付いた時,彼はちょうど窓を割ろうとしていたところだった. *I was just going to phone my mother when she arrived.* 母が到着した時,私はちょうど彼女に電話をしようとしていたところだった. *Just as I was beginning to enjoy myself, John said it was time to go.* ちょうど私が楽しみ始めたところで,ジョンは帰る時間だと言った. *Just then the door opened.* ちょうどその時扉が開いた. ▶定義 **3** exactly➔ちょうど,全く,まさに ‖ *It's just eight o'clock.* ちょうど8時だ. *That's just what I meant.* それはまさに私が言いたかった事だ. *You're just as clever as he is.* あなたは彼と全く同じくらい賢い. *The room was too hot before, but now it's just right.* その部屋は以前暑すぎたが,今はちょうど良い. *He looks just like his father.* 彼は彼の父親に全くそっくりだ. *My arm hurts just here.* 私の腕のちょうどここが痛い. ▶定義 **4** only➔ただ~だけ,ほんの~ ‖ *She's just a child.* 彼女はほんの子供だ. *Just a minute! I'm nearly ready.* ほんの少し待って.もう少しで準備ができる. ▶定義 **5** almost not; hardly およそ~ない;ほとんど~ない➔辛うじて,やっとのことで ‖ *I could only just hear what she was saying.* 彼女が言っている事が辛うじて聞こえた. *We got to the station just in time.* 私たちは辛うじて時間までに駅に着いた. ▶定義 **6** (しばしば命令形と共に) used for getting attention or to emphasize what you are saying 自分が言う事に注意をひくまたは強調するために用いて➔ちょっと,とにかく ‖ *Just let me speak for a moment, will you?* とにかく私に少し話しをさせてもらえますか. *I just don't want to go to the party.* 私はとにかくパーティーに行きたくない. ▶定義 **7** used with might, may or could to express a slight possibility わずかな可能性を表すために might, may または could と用いて➔ひょっとすると,もしかすると ‖ *This might just/just might be the most important decision of your life.* これはひょっとするとあなたの人生で最も重要な決断かもしれない. ▶定義 **8** really; absolutely➔本当に,全く ‖ *The whole day was just fantastic!* 本当にすばらしい1日だった.

成句 all/just the same ⇒ **SAME**

**it is just as well (that...)** ▶定義 it is a good thing➔~は良いことである,賢明である ‖ *It's just as well you remembered to bring your umbrella!* 忘れずに傘を持ってきたのは賢明だ.

☛参 **well** の **(just) as well (to do sth)**

**just about** ▶定義 almost or approximately➔ほ

## 926 just²

とんど, およそ, 大体 ‖ *I've just about finished.* 私は大体終わったところだ. *Karen's plane should be taking off just about now.* カレンの飛行機はまさに今飛び立とうとしているはずだ.

**just in case** ▶定義 in order to be completely prepared or safe 完全に準備ができているようにまたは安全のために ➡ 万一に備えて ‖ *It might be hot in France - take your shorts just in case.* フランスは暑いかもしれない — 念のためショートパンツを持っていきなさい.

**just now** ▶定義 1 at this exact moment or during this exact period ちょうどこの瞬間に, またはちょうどこの期間に ➡ ちょうど今, 今は ‖ *I can't come with you just now - can you wait 20 minutes?* 今すぐはあなたと一緒に出られません — 20分待ってもらえますか. ▶定義 2 a very short time ago 非常に短時間前に ➡ ちょっと前に, ついさっき ‖ *I saw Tony just now.* 私はついさっきトニーに会った.

**just so** ▶定義 exactly right 全く正しい ➡ 全くその通り

**not just yet** ▶定義 not now, but probably quite soon 今ではないが, おそらく間近に ➡ 今すぐには〜ない

**just²** /dʒʌst/ ▶定義 fair and right; reasonable 公正で正しい; 理にかなっている ➡ 公正な, 正当な, 正しい ‖ *I don't think that was a very just decision.* それは非常に公正な決定だったとは思わない. — **justly** 副 ➡ 当然のことながら, 正しく

*****justice** /ˈdʒʌstɪs/ 名 ▶定義 1 ❶ the fair treatment of people 人々の公正な扱い ➡ 公正, 公平, 正義 ‖ *a struggle for justice* 正義のための闘争 ▶定義 2 ❶ the quality of being fair or reasonable 公正または正当である性質 ➡ 正当性, 妥当性 ‖ *Everybody realized the justice of what he was saying.* 彼の言っていた事の正当性を皆が理解した. ▶定義 3 ❶ the law and the way it is used 法律および法律が行使される方法 ➡ 法務, 裁判, 処罰 ‖ *the criminal justice system* 刑事裁判の制度 ▶定義 4 ❸ 困 a judge in a court of law 法廷における裁判官 ➡ 裁判官, (最高裁判所の)判事

感句 **do justice to sb/sth; do sb/sth justice** ▶定義 to treat sb/sth fairly or to show the real quality of sb/sth 〜を公正に扱う, または〜の真の性質を示す ➡ 〜を公正に扱う, 正しく評価する ‖ *I don't like him, but to do him justice, he's a very clever man.* 私は彼を好きではないが, 正しく評価すれば彼は非常に賢い男だ. *The photograph doesn't do her justice - she's actually very pretty.* その写真は彼女の良さが十分に出ていない — 彼女は実際はとてもきれいだ.

**a miscarriage of justice** ➾ **MISCARRIAGE**

**Justice of the Peace**(略**JP**) 名 ❸ ▶定義 a person who judges less serious cases in a court of law in Britain 英国の法廷であまり重大ではない事件の審判をする人 ➡ 治安判事

**justifiable** /ˈdʒʌstəfaɪəb(ə)l, ˌ--ˈ--/ 形 ▶定義 that you can accept because there is a good reason for it 十分な理由があるために受け入れられるような ➡ 正当と認められる, 筋の通った ‖ *His action was entirely justifiable.* 彼の行動は全く正当であった. — **justifiably** /ˈdʒʌstəfaɪəb(ə)li, ˌdʒʌstəˈfaɪəb(ə)li/ 副 ➡ 正当に, 当然のこととして

**justification** /ˌdʒʌstɪfɪˈkeɪʃ(ə)n/ 名 ❸ ❶ ▶定義 **(a) justification (for sth/doing sth)** (a) good reason 十分な理由 ➡ 弁明, 正当化, 正当な理由 ‖ *I can't see any justification for cutting his salary.* 彼の給与を削減した正当な理由が分からない.

*****justify** /ˈdʒʌstəfaɪ/ 動 ❶ ▶定義 (現分 **justifying**; 三単現 **justifies**; 過, 過分 **justified**) to give or be a good reason for sth 〜についての正当な理由を与えるまたは正当な理由である ➡ 正しいとする, 正当化する ‖ *Can you justify your decision?* あなたは自分の決定を弁明できますか.

**jut** /dʒʌt/ 動 ⊜ (**jutting**; **jutted**) ▶定義 **jut (out) (from/into/over sth)** to stick out further than the surrounding surface, objects, etc 周囲の面, 物などよりも遠くに突き出す ➡ 突き出る, 張り出す, 飛び出る ‖ *rocks that jut out into the sea* 海に突き出している岩

**juvenile** /ˈdʒuːvənaɪl; -nàɪl, -nl/ 形 ▶定義 1 正式 of, for or involving young people who are not yet adults まだ大人ではない若い人々の[ための・にかかわる] ➡ 少年の, 少女の, 若い ‖ *juvenile crime* 少年犯罪 ▶定義 2 behaving like sb of a younger age; childish より若い年齢の〜のように振る舞う; 子供染みた ➡ 子供っぽい, 少年らしい, 少女らしい ‖ *He's twenty but he is still quite juvenile.* 彼は20歳だが, まだかなり子供っぽい. — **juvenile** 名 ❸ ➡ 未成年者, 少年少女

**juvenile delinquent** 名 ❸ ▶定義 a young

person who is guilty of committing a crime 犯罪を犯した有罪の若い人→非行少年, 少年犯罪者

**juxtapose** /dʒʌkstəpòʊz, ˌ-ˈ--/ 動 他 正式 ▶定義 to put two people, things, etc very close together, especially in order to show how they are different 特にその違いを示すために, 2人の人や2つの物などを非常に近くに一緒に置く→並列する, 並置する ‖ *The artist achieves a special effect by juxtaposing light and dark.* その芸術家は光と闇(やみ)を並置することによって特別な効果を生み出している. —*juxtaposition* /dʒʌkstəpəzíʃ(ə)n/ 名 U →並列, 並置

# K k

**K, k**¹ /kéɪ/ 名 C (複 **K's**; **k's**) ▶定義 the eleventh letter of the English alphabet 英語アルファベットの第11文字→k(K)が表す音, k(K)の文字, k(K)の字形のもの ‖ *'Kate' begins with (a) 'K'.* Kateは Kで始まる.

**K**² /kéɪ/ 略 略式 ▶定義 one thousand→千, 1000 ‖ *She earns 22K (= £22000) a year.* 彼女は年間2万2千(= 22000 ポンド)稼ぐ.

**kaleidoscope** /kəláɪdəskòʊp/ 名 C ▶定義 1 a large number of different things たくさんの異なるもの→多種多様なもの ▶定義 2 a toy that consists of a tube containing mirrors and small pieces of coloured glass. When you look into one end of the tube and turn it, you see changing patterns of colours. 鏡と色の付いた細かいガラス片が入った管からできたおもちゃ. 管の一方から中をのぞいてそれを回すと, 色の付いた模様が変化するのが見える→万華鏡, 百色眼鏡

**kangaroo**

**kangaroo** /kæ̀ŋɡərúː/ 名 C (複 **kangaroos**) ▶定義 an Australian animal that moves by jumping on its strong back legs and that carries its young in a pocket of skin (a pouch) on its stomach 強い後ろ足で立って跳ねて移動し, 子供をおなかにある皮のポケットの中に入れて運ぶオーストラリアの動物→カンガルー

**karaoke** /kæ̀rəóʊkeɪ, kæ̀rióʊki/ 名 U ▶定義 a type of entertainment in which a machine plays only the music of popular songs so that people can sing the words themselves 機械が流行の歌の伴奏だけを演奏し, 人々が歌詞を自分で歌うことができる娯楽の一種→カラオケ

**karat** 米 = CARAT

**karate** /kərɑ́ːti/ 名 U ▶定義 a style of fighting originally from Japan in which the hands and feet are used as weapons 手と足を武器として使う, 日本で始まった格闘の様式→空手 ☛参 **martial arts**

**kart** /kɑːrt/ = GO-KART

**kayak** /káɪæk/ 名 C ▶定義 a light narrow boat (a canoe) for one person, that you move using with a stick with a flat part at each end (a paddle) 先がそれぞれ平たくなった棒(かい)を使って動かす, 1人用の軽くて幅の狭い船(カヌー)→カヤック ☛ **boat** のさし絵

**kebab** /kəbáb/ 名 C ▶定義 small pieces of meat, vegetables, etc that are cooked on a stick (a skewer) 小さく切った肉, 野菜などを棒(くし)に刺して調理したもの→シシカバブ ☛ C4 ページのさし絵

**keel**¹ /kiːl/ 名 C ▶定義 a long piece of wood or metal on the bottom of a boat that stops it falling over sideways in the water 水の中で船が横転するのを止める, 船の底に付いた長い木または金属→キール, 竜骨

**keel**² /kiːl/ 動
句動詞 **keel over** ▶定義 to fall over→ひっくり返る, 横倒しになる

*****keen** /kiːn/ 形 ▶定義 **1** keen (to do sth/that…) very interested in sth; wanting to do sth ～に非常に興味のある; ～をしたがっている→(～に)熱心な, 熱望して, 切望して ‖ *They are both keen gardeners.* 彼らは2人とも園芸に熱心だ. *I failed the first time but I'm keen to try again.* 最初は失敗したが, 是非もう一度やってみたい. *She was keen that we should all be there.* 彼女は私たち皆がそこにいることを切望していた.
▶定義 **2** (used about one of the senses, a feeling, etc) good or strong (感覚, 感情などの1つについて) 良い, または強い→鋭い, 鋭敏な ‖ *Foxes have a keen sense of smell.* キツネは鋭

## 928　keep¹

い臭覚を持つ.

成句 **keen on sb/sth** ▶定義 very interested in or having a strong desire for sb/sth ～に非常に興味のある, または強い願望を持つ→**熱心な** ‖ *He's very keen on jazz.* 彼はジャズに夢中だ. ― **keenly** 副 →**熱心に, 鋭く** ― **keenness** 名 ① →**鋭さ, 敏感**

\***keep**¹ /kiːp/ 動 (過, 過分 **kept** /kept/) ▶定義1 ⊜ to continue to be in a particular state or position 特定の状態または位置にあり続ける→**ずっと～である, ～し続ける** ‖ *You must keep warm.* あなたは暖かくしていなければならない. *That child can't keep still.* その子供はじっとしていられない. *I still keep in touch with my old school friends.* 私は今でも古い学校時代の友人と連絡を取り合っている. ▶定義2 ⊕ to make sb/sth stay in a particular state, place or condition ～を特定の状態, 場所または状況にいさせる→**ずっと～にしておく, 保つ** ‖ *Please keep this door closed.* この扉を閉めたままにしておいてください. *He kept his hands in his pockets.* 彼はずっと手をポケットに入れていた. *I'm sorry to keep you waiting.* お待たせしてすみません. ▶定義3 ⊕ to continue to have sth; to save sth for sb ～を持ち続ける; ～のために…を取っておく→**～をずっと持っている, 保持する, 取っておく** ‖ *You can keep that book - I don't need it any more.* その本を持っていていいよ － 私はもう要らない. *Can I keep the car until next week?* その車を来週まで預かってもよいですか. *Can you keep my seat for me till I get back?* 私が戻るまで席を取っておいてくれませんか. ▶定義4 ⊕ to have sth in a particular place ～を特定の場所に置いておく→**～を保管する, 保存する** ‖ *Where do you keep the matches?* あなたはマッチをどこに保管していますか. *Keep your passport in a safe place.* パスポートを安全な場所に保管しなさい. ▶定義5 ⊕ **keep doing sth** to continue doing sth or to repeat an action many times ～をし続ける, またはある行動を何度も繰り返す→**～を続ける, 持続する** ‖ *Keep going until you get to the church and then turn left.* 教会までずっと行って, そこで左に曲がりなさい. *She keeps asking me silly questions.* 彼女は私にばかげた質問をし続けている. ▶定義6 ⊕ to do what you promised or arranged 自分が約束したまたは取り決めたことをする→**～を守る, 履行する** ‖ *Can you keep a promise?* あなたは約束を守れますか. *She didn't keep her appointment at the dentist's.* 彼女は歯医者の予約を守らなかった. *to keep a secret* (= *not tell it to anyone*) 秘密を守る(= それをだれにも話さない) ▶定義7 ⊕ to write down sth that you want to remember 覚えておきたい物事を書き留める→**(続けて)とる, つける** ‖ *Keep a record of how much you spend.* いくら使ったかをつけておきなさい. *to keep a diary* 日記をつける ▶定義8 ⊜ (used about food) to stay fresh (食べ物について)新鮮なままでいる→**持つ** ‖ *Drink up all the milk - it won't keep in this weather.* 牛乳を全部飲んでしまいなさい － この天気では持たないだろう. ▶定義9 ⊕ to support sb with your money 自分のお金で～を支える→**～を扶養する, 養う** ‖ *You can't keep a family on the money I earn.* 私が稼ぐお金で家族を養うことはできない. ▶定義10 ⊕ to have and look after animals 動物を飼って, 面倒を見る→**～を世話をする, 飼っている** ‖ *They keep ducks on their farm.* 彼らは農場でアヒルを飼っている. ▶定義11 ⊕ to delay sb/sth; to prevent sb from leaving ～を遅らせる; ～が去るのを妨げる→**～をぐずぐずさせる, 引き止めておく** ‖ *Where's the doctor? What's keeping him?* 医者はどこだい. 何をぐずぐずしているのだろう.

成句 **keep it up** ▶定義 to continue doing sth as well as you are doing it now ～を今しているのと同様にし続ける→**続ける, 持続する**

► keep を含むこのほかの表現については, 名詞, 形容詞などの項を参照. 例えば keep count は count の項にある.

句動詞 **keep at it/sth** ▶定義 to continue to work on/at sth→**～をやり続ける** ‖ *Keep at it - we should be finished soon.* それを続けてやりなさい － 間もなく終わるはずだ.

**keep away from sb/sth** ▶定義 to not go near sb/sth ～の近くに行かない→**～に近寄らない, 触れない** ‖ *Keep away from the town centre this weekend.* 今週末は町の中心に近寄るな.

**keep sb/sth back** ▶定義 to prevent sb/sth from moving forwards ～が前へ動くのを妨げる→**せき止める, 後ろにいさせる, 進歩を妨げる** ‖ *The police tried to keep the crowd back.* 警察は

群衆をせき止めておこうとした.

**keep sth back (from sb)** ▶定義 to refuse to tell sb sth ～に…を告げるのを拒む➡隠しておく ‖ *I know he's keeping something back; he knows much more than (what) he says.* 私は彼が何かを隠していることを知っていた. 彼は話している以上の事を知っている.

**keep sth down** ▶定義 to make sth stay at a low level, to stop sth increasing ～を低いレベルにしておく, ～が増えるのを止める➡下げている, 上げない, 抑えておく ‖ *Keep your voice down.* 声を低くしなさい.

**keep sb from sth/from doing sth** ▶定義 to prevent sb from doing sth ～が…をするのを妨げる➡～に…させない, ～が…しないようにする

**keep sth from sb** ▶定義 to refuse to tell sb sth ～に…を告げるのを拒む➡～に知らせないでおく

**keep your mouth shut** ⇒ **MOUTH**¹

**keep off sth** ▶定義 to not go near or on sth ～の近くまたはそこまで行かない➡近寄らない, 寄り付かない ‖ *Keep off the grass!* 芝生に入るな.

**keep sth off (sb/sth)** ▶定義 to stop sth touching or going on sb/sth ～が…に触るまたは行くのを止める➡～を近寄らせない ‖ *I'm trying to keep the flies off the food.* ハエを食べ物に近寄らせないようにしているところだ.

**keep on (doing sth)** ▶定義 to continue doing sth or to repeat an action many times, especially in an annoying way 特に迷惑な方法で, ～をし続けるまたはある行動を何度も繰り返す➡～し続ける, しきりに～する ‖ *He keeps on interrupting me.* 彼は私の邪魔をし続ける.

**keep on (at sb) (about sb/sth)** ▶定義 to continue talking to sb in an annoying or complaining way 迷惑な方法でまたは訴えるように, ～に話し掛け続ける➡～にやかましく言う, せがむ ‖ *She kept on at me about my homework until I did it.* 彼女は私が宿題をするまでやかましくその事を言った.

**keep (sb/sth) out (of sth)** ▶定義 to not enter sth; to stop sb/sth entering sth ～に入らない; ～が…に入るのを止める➡(～を)中に入れない, 締め出す ‖ *They put up a fence to keep people out of their garden.* 彼らは庭に人が入らないように柵(さく)を立てた.

**keep to sth** ▶定義 to not leave sth; to do sth in the usual, agreed or expected way ～を去ら

## keeping 929

ない; 通常の, 合意されたまたは期待される方法で～をする➡～から離れない, 堅く守る ‖ *Keep to the path!* 歩道を行きなさい. *He didn't keep to our agreement.* 彼は私たちの合意を守らなかった.

**keep sth to/at sth** ▶定義 to not allow sth to rise above a particular level ～が特定のレベルより上がるのを許さない➡引き止めておく, 抑える ‖ *We're trying to keep costs to a minimum.* 私たちは費用を最低限に抑えようとしている.

**keep sth up** ▶定義1 to prevent sth from falling down ～が下がるのを妨げる➡上げている, 落とさないようにしている ▶定義2 to make sth stay at a high level ～を高いレベルにとどめておく➡維持する, 保持する ‖ *We want to keep up standards of education.* 私たちは教育の水準を維持したい. ▶定義3 to continue doing sth➡～をし続ける

**keep up (with sb)** ▶定義 to move at the same speed as sb ～と同じ速度で動く➡～に遅れないで付いていく ‖ *Can't you walk a bit slower? I can't keep up.* もう少しゆっくり歩いていただけますか. 私は付いていくことができません.

**keep up (with sth)** ▶定義 to know about what is happening 起こっていることを知っている➡知っている, 遅れないように付いていく ‖ *You have to read the latest magazines if you want to keep up.* もし遅れないように付いていきたいならば, 最新の雑誌を読まなければならない.

**keep**² /kiːp/ 名 **U** ▶定義 food and other things that you need in your daily life 日常生活で自分が必要とする食べ物やそのほかのもの➡生活必需品

成句 **for keeps** 略式 ▶定義 for always➡いつまでも, 永久に ‖ *Take it. It's yours for keeps.* 持っていきなさい. それは永久にあなたのものだ.

**keeper** /kiːpər/ 名 **C** ▶定義1 a person who guards or looks after sth ～を保護し, 面倒を見る人➡飼い主, 飼育係, 守る人, 番人 ‖ *a zookeeper* 動物園の飼育係 ▶定義2 略式 = **GOAL-KEEPER**

**keeping** /kiːpɪŋ/ 名

成句 **in/out of keeping (with sth)** ▶定義1 that does/does not look good with sth ～に似合う・似合わない➡(～と)調和して・しないで ‖ *That* *modern table is out of keeping with the style of the room.* その現代的なテーブルは部屋の様式と調和しない. ▶定義2 in/not in agreement with a rule, belief, etc 規則, 信条などに合った・合わない→(~と)一致して・しない‖ *The Council's decision is in keeping with government policy.* 議会の決定は政府の政策と一致している.

**keg** /keg/ 名 © ▶定義 a round metal or wooden container, used especially for storing beer 特にビールを貯蔵するのに使われる, 金属または木製の丸い容器→たる

**kennel** /kénl/ 名 © ▶定義 a small house for a dog 犬用の小さな家→犬小屋

**kept** KEEP¹ の過去・過去分詞形

**kerb** (特に 米 **curb**) /kə:rb/ 名 © ▶定義 the edge of the path (the pavement) along the sides of a road 道路のわきに沿ってある, 小道(歩道)の端→縁石, へり石‖ *They stood on the kerb waiting to cross the road.* 彼らは道路を渡ろうと待ちながら縁石の上に立った.

**kerosene** /kérəsì:n, -̀-́-/ 米 = **PARAFFIN**

**ketchup** /kétʃəp, kǽtsəp/ 名 ∪ ▶定義 a cold sauce made from soft red fruit (**tomatoes**) that is eaten with hot or cold food 熱いまたは冷たい食べ物と一緒に食べる, 柔らかい赤い果実(トマト)から作られる冷たいソース→ケチャップ

**kettle** /kétl/ 名 © ▶定義 a container with a lid, used for boiling water 水を沸かすのに使う, ふたの付いた容器→やかん, 湯沸かし‖ *an electric kettle* 電気湯沸かし

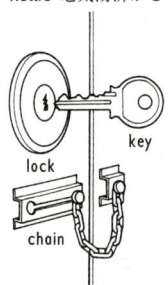

\***key**¹ /ki:/ 名 © ▶定義1 a metal object that is used for locking a door, starting a car, etc ドアにかぎをかける, 車を発進するなどのために使われる, 金属製の物→かぎ‖ *Have you seen my car keys anywhere?* どこかで私の車のかぎを見ましたか.

*We need a spare key to the front door.* 正面扉の予備のかぎが必要だ. *a bunch of keys* かぎの束 ▶定義2 [通常は単数] the key (to sth) something that helps you achieve or understand sth ~を達成するまたは理解するのに役立つ何か→かぎ, 手掛かり, 秘けつ‖ *A good education is the key to success.* 良い教育は成功のかぎだ. ▶定義3 one of the parts of a piano, computer, etc that you press with your fingers to make it work ピアノ, コンピューターなどの, それを動かすために指で押す部品の1つ→キー, 鍵(けん) **music**, S5 ページのさし絵 ▶定義4 a set of musical notes that is based on one particular note 特定の音調に基づいた一組の音符→調, 調性‖ *The concerto is in the key of A minor.* その協奏曲はイ短調だ. ▶定義5 a set of answers to exercises or problems 練習問題または問題への答え一式→解答集, 解答書‖ *an answer key* 解答集 ▶定義6 a list of the symbols and signs used in a map or book, showing what they mean 地図または本で用いられる印や記号についてその意味するものを示した一覧→解説, 記号表

成句 **under lock and key** ⇒ **LOCK**²

**key**² /ki:/ 動他 ▶定義 **key sth (in)** to put information into a computer or give it an instruction by typing タイプすることによって, コンピューターに情報を入れるまたは指示を与える→打ち込む‖ *Have you keyed that report yet?* あの報告書をもう打ち込みましたか. *First, key in your password.* まず, パスワードを打ち込みなさい.

**key**³ /ki:/ 形 (名詞の前だけ) ▶定義 very important 非常に重要な→重要な, 基本的な‖ *Tourism is a key industry in Spain.* 観光はスペインの重要な産業だ.

**keyboard** /kí:bɔ̀:rd/ 名 © ▶定義1 the set of keys on a piano, computer, etc ピアノ, コンピューターなどの鍵(けん)一式→鍵盤 ☞ S5 ページのさし絵 ▶定義2 an electrical musical instrument like a small piano 小さなピアノのような電動の楽器→キーボード ☞参 **piano** の注

**keyhole** /kí:hòul/ 名 © ▶定義 the hole in a lock where you put the key かぎを入れる錠前にある穴→かぎ穴

**keyring** /kí:rìŋ/ 名 © ▶定義 a ring on which you keep keys かぎをまとめておく輪→キーホルダー, かぎ輪

**keyword** /kí:wə̀:rd/ 名 © ▶定義1 a word that tells you about the main idea or subject of sth ~の主な思想または主題を人に告げる言葉→かぎとなる語, キーワード‖ *When you're studying a language, the keyword is patience.* あなたが言

語を勉強するとき、かぎとなる言葉は忍耐だ. ▶定義2 a word or phrase that is used to give an instruction to a computer コンピューターに指示を与えるのに使われる単語または語句→キーワード

**kg** 略 kilogram(s)→キログラム ‖ *weight 10kg* 重さ10キログラム

**khaki** /káːki, kǽki/ 形❻❶ ▶定義 (of) a pale brownish-yellow or brownish-green colour 淡い茶色がかった黄色、または茶色がかった緑色(の)→カーキ色(の) ‖ *The khaki uniforms of the desert soldiers.* 砂漠の兵士のカーキ色の軍服.

**kHz** /kíləhəːrts, -louˌ, kiːləˌ/ 略 kilohertz ▶定義 (used in radio) a measure of frequency (ラジオで用いて)周波数の単位→キロヘルツ

*kick¹ /kɪk/ 動 ▶定義1 ❶ to hit or move sb/sth with your foot 足で~を打つまたは動かす→~をける、け飛ばす ‖ *He kicked the ball wide of the net.* 彼はゴールを外してボールをけった. *The police kicked the door down.* 警官は扉をけり倒した. ▶定義2 ❶ to move your foot or feet 一方の足または両足を動かす→足をけり上げる ‖ *You must kick harder if you want to swim faster.* もっと速く泳ぎたければ、もっと強く足でけらなければならない.

成句 kick the habit ▶定義 to stop doing sth harmful that you have done for a long time 長い間してきた有害な事をするのをやめる→(悪習を)やめる

kick yourself ▶定義 to be annoyed with yourself because you have done sth stupid, missed an opportunity, etc ばかな事をした、機会を逸したなどのために、自分自身に腹を立てる→自分を責める、悔しがる

make, kick up, etc a fuss ⇒ **FUSS¹**

句動詞 kick off ▶定義 to start a game of football サッカーやラグビーの試合を始める→キックオフする、試合開始をする

kick sb out (of sth) 略式 ▶定義 to force sb to leave a place ~にある場所を去ることを強いる→~を(…から)追い出す ‖ *to be kicked out of university* 大学を辞めさせられる

*kick² /kɪk/ 名 ❻ ▶定義1 an act of kicking ける行為→けること、け飛ばすこと ‖ *She gave the door a kick and it closed.* 彼女は扉をけり、扉は閉まった. ▶定義2 略式 a feeling of great pleasure, excitement, etc 非常な喜び、興奮などの感情→

快感、スリル、興奮 ‖ *He seems to get a real kick out of driving fast.* 彼は高速でドライブすることで非常に快感を感じているようだ.

**kick-off** 名 ❻ ▶定義 the start of a game of football サッカーやラグビーの試合開始→キックオフ、始め ‖ *The kick-off is at 2.30.* キックオフは2時30分だ.

*kid¹ /kɪd/ 名 ▶定義1 ❻ 略式 a child or young person 子供、または若い人→子供、若者、青年 ‖ *How are your kids?* あなたの子供たちは元気ですか. ▶定義2 **kid brother/sister** ❻ 特に 米 略式 younger brother/sister→弟、妹 ▶定義3 ❻❶ a young animal (goat) or its skin 若い動物(ヤギ)またはその皮→子ヤギ、子ヤギの皮 ☛ **goat** のさし絵

**kid²** /kɪd/ 動 ❶❶ (kidding; kidded) 略式 ▶定義 to trick sb/yourself by saying sth that is not true; to make a joke about sth 事実ではない事を言って、他人や自分をだます; ~について冗談を言う→からかう、だます、担ぐ ‖ *I didn't mean it. I was only kidding.* 本気で言ったわけじゃなかった. からかっただけだ.

**kiddy** (または **kiddie**) /kídi/ 名 ❻ (複 **kiddies**) 略式 ▶定義 a child→子供

**kidnap** /kídnæp/ 動 ❶❶ (**kidnapping; kidnapped**) ▶定義 to take sb away by force and demand money for his/her safe return 力ずくで~を連れ去り、その~を無事に返すことに対してお金を要求する→~を誘拐する、さらう ‖ *The child was kidnapped and £50000 ransom was demanded for her release.* 子供が誘拐され、解放に5万ポンドの身の代金が要求された. ☛参 **hijack** — **kidnapper** 名 ❻→誘拐犯 ‖ *The kidnappers demanded £50000.* 誘拐犯は5万ポンドを要求した. —**kidnapping** 名 ❻❶→誘拐、人さらい

**kidney** /kídni/ 名 ▶定義1 ❻ one of the two parts of your body that separate waste liquid from your blood 血中から排出液を分ける体の2つの器官の1つ→腎臓(じんぞう) ☛ C5ページのさし絵 ▶定義2 ❶ ❻ the kidneys of an animal when they are cooked and eaten as food 調理して食品として食べられる動物の腎臓(じんぞう)→動物の腎臓 ‖ *steak and kidney pie* ステーキとキドニーパイ

*kill¹ /kɪl/ 動 ▶定義1 ❶❶ to make sb/sth die ~

## kill²

を死なせる➔**殺す, 枯らす** ‖ *Smoking kills.* 喫煙は命を奪う. *She was killed instantly in the crash.* 彼女はその衝突で即死した.

➤ murder は意図的に人を殺すことを意味する: *This was no accident. The old lady was murdered.* (これは事故ではなかった. 老婦人は殺害された.) assassinate は政治的な目的のために殺すことを意味する: *President Kennedy was assassinated.* (ケネディ大統領が暗殺された.) slaughter および massacre は大勢の人々を殺すことを意味する: *Hundreds of people were massacred when the army opened fire on the crowd.* (軍が群衆に向けて発砲し, 数百人が虐殺された.) slaughter は食べるために動物を殺すときにも用いられる.

▶定義**2** 略式 to cause sb pain; to hurt ～に痛みを起こさせる; 傷付ける➔**～をひどく苦しめる, 損なう** ‖ *My feet are killing me.* 足が死ぬほど痛む. ▶定義**3** ⓤ to cause sth to end or fail ～を終わらせる, または失敗させる➔**～を駄目にする** ‖ *The minister's opposition killed the idea stone dead.* 大臣の反対で, その案は完全に駄目になった. ▶定義**4** ⓤ (口語) to be very angry with sb ～に対して非常に怒る➔**～をひどく腹を立てる** ‖ *My mum will kill me when she sees this mess.* このごみの山を見たら, 母は僕にひどく腹を立てるだろう. ▶定義**5** ⓤ 略式 kill yourself/sb to make yourself/sb laugh a lot 自分や他人を大いに笑わせる➔**～を大いに笑わせる, 楽しませる** ‖ *We were killing ourselves laughing.* 私たちは腹の皮がよじれるほど笑った.

成句 **kill time, an hour, etc** ▶定義 to spend time doing sth that is not interesting or important while you are waiting for sth else to happen ほかの事が起きるのを待っている間に, 面白くないまたは重要でない事をして時を過ごす➔**暇をつぶす**

**kill two birds with one stone** ▶定義 to do one thing which will achieve two results 2つの結果を達成する1つの事をする➔**一石二鳥を得る, 一挙両得する**

句動詞 **kill sth off** ▶定義 to cause sth to die or to not exist any more ～を死なせるまたはもはや存在しないようにさせる➔**絶滅させる**

**kill²** /kɪl/ ⓒ [単数扱い] ▶定義**1** the act of killing 殺す行為➔**(獲物を)殺すこと** ‖ *Lions often make a kill in the evening.* ライオンはしばしば夕方に狩りをする. ▶定義**2** an animal or animals that have been killed 殺された1匹のまたは複数の動物➔**(狩りの)獲物** ‖ *The eagle took the kill back to its young.* ワシは獲物を子供の所へ持ち帰った.

**killer** /kílər/ ⓒ ▶定義 a person, animal or thing that kills 殺す人, 動物, または物➔**殺人者, 殺し屋** ‖ *a killer disease* 命取りとなる病気 *He's a dangerous killer who may strike again.* 彼は再び人を攻撃するかもしれない危険な殺人者だ.

**killing** /kílɪŋ/ ⓒ ▶定義 act of killing a person on purpose; a murder 意図的に人を殺す行為; 殺人➔**殺すこと, 殺害** ‖ *There have been a number of brutal killings in the area recently.* その地域では最近多くの残忍な殺人があった.

成句 **make a killing** ▶定義 to make a large profit quickly 大きな利益を手早く得る➔**大もうけをする**

*__kilo__ /kíːloʊ, kíl-/ (または **kilogram**; **kilogramme** /kíləgræm, -loʊ-, kiːlə-/ ⓒ (複 **kilos**) (略 **kg**) ▶定義 a measure of weight; 1000 grams 重さの単位; 1000グラム➔**キログラム**

*__kilometre__ (米 **kilometer**) /kíləmìːtər, kəlámə-/ ⓒ (略 **km**) ▶定義 a measure of length; 1000 metres 長さの単位; 1000メートル➔**キロメートル**

**kilt** /kɪlt/ ⓒ ▶定義 a skirt with many folds (**pleats**) that is worn by men as part of the national dress of Scotland スコットランドの民族衣装の一部として男性が着る, ひだ(プリーツ)のたくさん付いたスカート➔**キルト**

**kin** /kɪn/ ⇒ **NEXT OF KIN**

*__kind__¹ /káɪnd/ ⓒ ▶定義 a group whose members all have the same qualities 同じ性質を持つものばかりの集まり➔**部類, 種類, 種族** ‖ *The concert attracted people of all kinds.* そのコンサートはあらゆる人々を魅了した. *The concert attracted all kinds of people.* そのコンサートはあらゆる人々を魅了した. *What kind of car have you got?* どんな車を持っているの. *Many kinds of plant and animal are being lost every year.* 毎年多くの種類の植物や動物が滅びている. *In the evenings I listen to music, write letters, that kind of thing.* 夕方には, 私は音楽を聴いたり, 手紙を書いたり, そんな風な事をしてい

る. ☞類 **sort, type**
► kind は可算名詞であり次のような言い方はできない. *Those kind of dogs are really dangerous.* または *I like all kind of music.* 正しくは次のように言う: *That kind of dog is really dangerous./Those kinds of dogs are really dangerous.* (あの種の犬はとても危険だ.) *I like all kinds of music.* (私はあらゆる種類の音楽が好きだ.) kinds of には単数名詞または複数名詞が続く: *There are so many kinds of camera/cameras on the market that it's hard to know which is best.* (市場にはとても多くの種類のカメラがあり, どれが一番良いかを知るのは難しい.)

成句 a kind of 略式 ▶定義 used for describing sth in a way that is not very clear あまり明確ではない方法で～を説明するのに用いて→**一種の～, いわば～** ‖ *I had a kind of feeling that something would go wrong.* 私は何かが間違っていると漠然と感じた. *There's a funny kind of smell in here.* ここは何かおかしなにおいがする.

kind of 略式 ▶定義 slightly; a little bit→**わずかに; 少し** ‖ *I'm kind of worried about the interview.* その会見のことが多少心配だ.

of a kind ▶定義1 the same→**同じ種類の** ‖ *The friends were two of a kind - very similar in so many ways.* 友達は似た者同士だった - とても多くの点で非常に似ていた. ▶定義2 of poor quality 質の乏しい→**いいかげんな, 安物の**

\*kind² /káɪnd/ 形 kind (to sb); kind (of sb) (to do sth) ▶定義 caring about others; friendly and generous ほかの事を気遣う; 優しくて寛容な→**親切な, 心の優しい, 思いやりのある** ‖ *Everyone's been so kind to us since we came here!* 私たちがここに来て以来, 皆私たちにとても親切だった. *It was kind of you to offer, but I don't need any help.* お申し出は有り難いのですが, 手伝いは必要ありません. ⇔ **unkind**

**kindergarten** /kíndərgɑ̀:rtn/ 名 C ▶定義 a school for very young children, aged from about 3 to 5 3歳から5歳の非常に幼い子供のための学校→**幼稚園** ☞参 **nursery school**

**kind-hearted** 形 ▶定義 kind and generous 親切で寛容な→**心の優しい, 思いやりのある**

**kindly** /káɪndli/ 副形 ▶定義1 in a kind way 親切な方法で→**親切に, 優しく** ‖ *The nurse smiled kindly.* その看護婦は優しくほほえんだ. ▶定義2 (used for asking sb to do sth) please (～に…をすることを頼むために用いて)→**どうぞ(～してください)** ‖ *Would you kindly wait a moment?* すみませんが少しお待ちいただけますか. ▶定義3 kind and friendly→**優しい, 親切な**

**kindness** /káɪndnəs/ 名 C U ▶定義 the quality of being kind; a kind act 親切である性質; 親切な行為→**親切, 優しさ, 好意** ‖ *Thank you very much for all your kindness.* ご親切本当にありがとう.

\***king** /kɪŋ/ 名 C ▶定義1 (the title of) a man who rules a country. A king is usually the son or close relative of the former ruler. 国を統治する男性(の肩書き). 通常前の統治者の息子または近い親戚(しんせき)→**王, 国王** ‖ *The new king was crowned yesterday in Westminster Abbey.* 新国王は昨日ウエストミンスター寺院で戴冠(たいかん)した. *King Edward VII (= the seventh)* 国王エドワード7世(= VII は the seventh と読む)(比喩)*The lion is the king of the jungle.* ライオンはジャングルの王だ. ☞参 **queen, prince, princess** ▶定義2 one of the four playing cards in a pack with a picture of a king 王の絵の付いた, 一組のトランプに4枚あるカードの1枚→**キング(の札)** ‖ *the king of spades* スペードのキング ☞参 **card** の注とさし絵

**kingdom** /kíŋdəm/ 名 C ▶定義1 a country that is ruled by a king or queen 国王・女王によって統治される国→**王国** ‖ *the United Kingdom* 連合王国 ▶定義2 one of the parts of the natural world 自然界の一部→**～界** ‖ *the animal kingdom* 動物界

**king-size**(または **king-sized**) 形 ▶定義 bigger than usual 通常よりも大きい→**キングサイズの, 特大の** ‖ *a king-size bed* キングサイズのベッド

**kink** /kɪŋk/ 名 C ▶定義 a turn or bend in sth that should be straight まっすぐであるべき物のよじれ・曲がった状態→**よじれ, もつれ**

**kiosk** /kí:ɒsk/ 名 C ▶定義 a very small building in the street where newspapers, sweets, cigarettes, etc are sold 新聞, お菓子, たばこなどが売られている通りにある非常に小さな建物→**キオスク** ☞ C8ページのさし絵

**kip** /kɪp/ 動 自 (**kipping; kipped**) 英(俗語)

## kitchen utensils

rolling pin, sieve, colander, grater, peeler, whisk, funnel, tongs, knives, spoons, chopping board, spatula, ladle

▶定義 to sleep→眠る, 寝る ‖ *You could kip on the sofa if you like.* もしよければ、ソファーの上で寝るといいよ. — kip 名 [単数扱い, ⓤ]→(一)眠り ‖ *I'm going to have a kip.* 私は一眠りするところだ. *I didn't get much kip last night.* 昨夜はあまり眠れなかった.

**kipper** /kípər/ 名 © ▶定義 a type of fish that has been kept for a long time in salt, and then smoked 長い間塩の中に寝かせておいてから、燻製(くんせい)にした魚の一種→燻製・乾燥にしん

*****kiss** /kís/ 動 ⊜ ⊕ ▶定義 to touch sb with your lips to show love or friendship 愛情または友情を示すために、唇で～に触れる→キスする, 口ずけする ‖ *He kissed her on the cheek.* 彼は彼女のほおにキスをした. *They kissed each other goodbye.* 彼らは互いにお別れのキスをした. — kiss 名 ©→キス, 口づけ, 接吻(せっぷん) ‖ *a kiss on the lips/cheek* 唇・ほおへのキス

**kit**¹ /kít/ 名 ▶定義 **1** © ⓤ a set of tools, equipment or clothes that you need for a particular purpose, sport or activity 特定の目的, スポーツ・活動に必要な道具・器具・服一そろい→用具一そろい, 道具一式 ‖ *a tool kit* 道具一式 *a drum kit* ドラム一式 *football/gym kit* サッカー・体操用具一式 ▶定義 **2** © a set of parts that you buy and put together in order to make sth ～を作るために自分が買って組み立てる部品の一そろい→キット, 組み立て用部品一式 ‖ *a kit for a model aeroplane* 模型飛行機の組み立てキット

**kit**² /kít/ 動 (**kitting**; **kitted**)
句動詞 **kit sb/yourself out/up (in/with sth)**
▶定義 to give sb all the necessary clothes, equipment, tools, etc for sth ～に…のために必要なすべての服, 器具, 道具などを与える→装備させる, 用具[道具]をそろえてあげる

*****kitchen** /kítʃən/ 名 © ▶定義 a room where food is prepared and cooked 食べ物が準備・調理される部屋→台所, キッチン ‖ *We usually eat in the kitchen.* 私たちは通常キッチンで食べる.

**kite** /káɪt/ 名 © ▶定義 a toy which consists of a light frame covered with paper or cloth. Kites are flown in the wind on the end of a long piece of string. 軽い枠を紙・布で覆ったおもちゃ. 長い糸の先に付けて風の中を飛ばす→凧(たこ) ‖ *to fly a kite* 凧を飛ばす

**kitten** /kítn/ 名 © ▶定義 a young cat 若い猫→子猫

**kitty** /kíti/ 名 © ( 複 **kitties** ) ▶定義 **1** a sum of money that is collected from a group of people and used for a particular purpose 人々の集団から集められ特定の目的のために使われるお金の総額→共同の積立金 ‖ *All the students in the flat put £5 a week into the kitty.* そのアパートの学生は週11 5ポンドを積み立てている. ▶定義 **2** (口語) a way of calling or referring to a cat 猫を呼ぶ・猫について述べる言い方→子猫, 猫

**kiwi** /kíːwi/ 名 © ( 複 **kiwis** ) ▶定義 **1** a New Zealand bird with a long beak and short wings that cannot fly 長いくちばしと短い羽を持つ, 飛ぶことのできないニュージーランドの鳥→キーウィ ▶定義 **2** (または **kiwi fruit**) a fruit with brown skin that is green inside with black seeds 中身が緑色で黒い種のある, 茶色い皮の付いた果物→キーウィフルーツ ☞ C3 ページの

**km** 略 kilometre(s) → キロメートル

**knack** /næk/ 名 [単数扱い] 略式 ▶定義 **knack (of/for doing sth)** skill or ability to do sth (difficult) that you have naturally or you can learn 人が自然に持つ・学ぶ(難しい)～をする技能または能力→こつ,技巧 ‖ *Knitting isn't difficult once you've got the knack of it.* 一度こつをつかめば編み物は難しくない.

**knead** /niːd/ 動他 ▶定義 to press and squeeze a mixture of flour and water (**dough**) with your hands in order to make bread, etc パンなどを作るために,小麦粉と水を混ぜたもの(パン生地)を手で押してこねる→～をこねる,練る,こねて作る

*****knee** /niː/ 名 C ▶定義 **1** the place where your leg bends in the middle 脚の中程の曲がる部分→ひざ,ひざ頭 ‖ *Angie fell and grazed her knee.* アンジーは転んでひざ頭を擦りむいた. *She was on her hands and knees on the floor looking for her earrings.* 彼女はイヤリングを捜して床の上に四つんばいになっていた. *Come and sit on my knee.* こちらへ来て私のひざの上に座りなさい. ☞ C5ページのさし絵 ▶定義 **2** the part of a pair of trousers, etc that covers the knee ズボンなどのひざを覆う部分→ひざの部分 ‖ *There's a hole in the knee of those jeans.* このジーンズのひざの部分に穴がある.

**kneecap** /níːkæp/ 名 C ▶定義 the bone that covers the front of the knee ひざの前を覆う骨→ひざの皿,膝蓋(しつがい)骨 ☞ C5ページのさし絵

**knee-deep** 形副 ▶定義 up to your knees ひざの高さまで→ひざまでの深さの,ひざまで没して ‖ *The water was knee-deep in places.* 水は所々でひざまでの深さがあった.

*****kneel** /niːl/ 動自 (過, 過分 **knelt** /nelt/ または **kneeled**) ▶定義 **kneel (down)** to rest on one or both knees 片ひざ・両ひざを付けて身体を支える→ひざまずく ‖ *She knelt down to talk to the child.* 彼女はひざまずいて子供に話し掛けた.

**knew** **KNOW**¹ の過去形

**knickers** /níkərz/ (特に 米 **panties**) 名 [複数扱い] ▶定義 a piece of underwear for women that covers the area between the waist and the top of the legs 股間を覆う女性用の下着→女子用のパンツ ☞ *a pair of knickers* と言うことに注意.

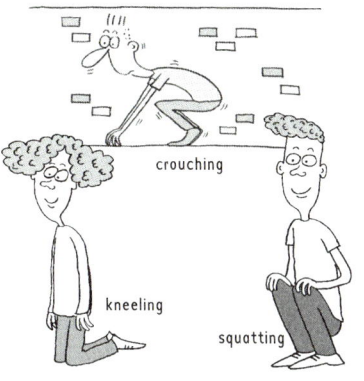

crouching
kneeling
squatting

*****knife**¹ /naɪf/ 名 C (複 **knives** /naɪvz/) ▶定義 a sharp flat piece of metal (**a blade**) with a handle. A knife is used for cutting things or as a weapon. 握り手の付いた鋭く平たい金属(刃). 物を切るのに,または武器として使われる→ナイフ,小刀,短剣 ‖ *The carving knife is very blunt/sharp.* その肉切り用ナイフは非常に切れ味が鈍い・鋭い. *a knife and fork* ナイフとフォーク *a penknife/pocket knife/flick knife* ペンナイフ・ポケットナイフ・飛び出しナイフ ☞ **kitchen** のさし絵

**knife**² /naɪf/ 動他 ▶定義 to deliberately injure sb with a knife ～をナイフで故意に傷付ける→～をナイフで刺す ☞類 **stab**

**knight** /naɪt/ 名 C ▶定義 **1** a man who has been given a title of honour by a king or queen for good work he has done and who can use Sir in front of his name 良い仕事をしたために,王・女王に位を与えられ,名前の前に卿(きょう)を付けることのできる男性→ナイト爵(しゃく),勲(くん)爵士 ▶定義 **2** a soldier of a high level who fought on a horse in the Middle Ages 中世に馬に乗って戦った位の高い兵士→騎士 — **knighthood** /náɪthʊd/ 名 C U →騎士の身分,勲爵士の称号,ナイトの称号

*****knit** /nɪt/ 動自他 (**knitting; knitted**) または (困 過, 過分 **knit**) ▶定義 **1** to make sth (for example an article of clothing) with wool using two long needles or a special machine 2本の長い編み物針・特別な機械を使って毛糸で～(例えば1着の

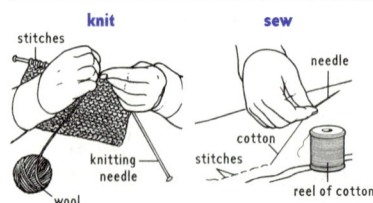

服)を作る→編む ‖ *I'm knitting a sweater for my nephew.* 私は甥(おい)のためにセーターを編んでいるところだ. ☞参 **crochet** ▶定義2 **knit**(この形でのみ用いる) joined closely together 密接につながれた→**くっつける, 結合する** ‖ *a closely/tightly knit village community* 密接に・堅く結び付いた村社会 ― **knitting** 名 U →編むこと, 編み物 ‖ *I usually do some knitting while I'm watching TV.* 私は通常テレビを見ながら編み物をする.

**knitting needle** = NEEDLE(2)

**knitwear** /nítwèər/ 名 U ▶定義 articles of clothing that have been knitted 編み上げられた衣類→**ニットウェア** ‖ *the knitwear department* ニットウェアの売り場

**knob** /nɑb/ 名 C ▶定義1 a round switch on a machine (for example a television) that you press or turn 機械(例えばテレビ)の押したり回したりするスイッチ→**つまみ** ‖ *the volume control knob* 音量調節つまみ ▶定義2 a round handle on a door, drawer, etc 扉, 引き出しなどに付いている丸い取っ手→**取っ手, 握り, ノブ** ☞ **handle** のさし絵

\***knock**¹ /nɑk/ 動 ▶定義1 自 knock (at/on sth) to make a noise by hitting sth firmly with your hand 手できつく〜をたたいて音を立てる→**ノックする, (こつこつと)たたく** ‖ *Someone is knocking at the door.* だれかが扉をノックしている. *I knocked on the window but she didn't hear me.* 私は窓をたたいたが, 彼女には聞こえなかった. ▶定義2 他 knock sth (on/against sth) to hit sb/sth hard, often by accident しばしば誤って, 〜に当たる→**〜に当たる, ぶつかって倒す, ぶつかって落とす** ‖ *He knocked the vase onto the floor.* 彼はぶつかって花びんを床に落とした. *Be careful not to knock your head on the shelf when you get up.* 立つときに棚に頭をぶつけないように気を付けなさい. *to knock sb unconscious* 無意識に〜にぶつかる ▶定義3 他 略式 to say bad things about sb/sth; to criticize sb/sth 〜について悪い事を言う; 〜を批判する→**〜をけなす, こき下ろす**

成句 knock on wood ⇒ **WOOD**

句動詞 **knock about/around** 略式 ▶定義 to be in a place; to travel and live in various places ある場所にいる・ある; 旅をしてさまざまな場所に暮らす→**ほったらかされている, 放浪する, (旅行して)あちこち回る** ‖ *Is last week's newspaper still knocking about?* 先週の新聞をまだほったらかしてあるの.

**knock sb down** ▶定義 to hit sb causing him/her to fall to the ground 〜にぶつかって転ばせる→**打ち(当たって)倒す** ‖ *The old lady was knocked down by a cyclist.* その老婦人は自転車に乗った人にぶつけられて倒れた.

**knock sth down** ▶定義 to destroy a building, etc 建物などを壊す→**取り壊す, 解体する** ‖ *They knocked down the old factory because it was unsafe.* 古い工場は危険だったので, 彼らはそれを取り壊した.

**knock off (sth)** (口語) ▶定義 to stop working 働くのをやめる→**中止する, やめる, 切り上げる** ‖ *What time do you knock off?* あなたは何時に切り上げるの.

**knock sth off** ▶定義1 略式 to reduce a price by a certain amount 価格をある金額下げる→**割り引く, 負ける** ‖ *He agreed to knock £10 off the price.* 彼は価格を10ポンド負けることに同意した. ▶定義2 (俗語) to steal sth 〜を盗む→**盗む, 強盗に入る**

**knock sb out** ▶定義1 to hit sb so that he/she becomes unconscious or cannot get up again for a while しばらく気絶する, または起き上がれないほど〜を殴る→**ノックアウトする, 殴って気絶させる** ‖ *The punch on the nose knocked him out.* 鼻にパンチを受けて彼は気絶した. ▶定義2 (used about a drug, alcohol, etc) to cause sb to sleep (薬, アルコールなどについて)〜を眠らせる→**意識を失わせる**

**knock sb out (of sth)** ▶定義 to beat a person or team in a competition so that they do not play any more games in it 競技で人・チームを打ち負かして, それ以上試合しないようにする→**(〜から)…を敗退させる, ノックアウトする** ‖

*Belgium was knocked out of the European Cup by France.* ベルギーはヨーロッパ杯でフランスに敗退した.

**knock sb/sth over** ▶定義 to cause sb/sth to fall over ～をひっくり返らせる→**当たってひっくり返す, 殴り倒す** || *Be careful not to knock over the drinks.* 飲み物に当たってひっくり返さないように気を付けなさい.

***knock**² /nɑk/ 名 C ▶定義 a sharp hit from sth hard or the sound it makes 硬い～が激しく当たること, またはその時の音→**たたくこと, ノック, たたく音** || *a nasty knock on the head* 頭をひどくたたくこと *I thought I heard a knock at the door.* 扉をノックする音が聞こえたと思った. (比喩)*She has suffered some hard knocks (= bad experiences) in her life.* 彼女は人生で何度かつらい目(= 悪い経験)に遭っている.

**knocker** /nɑ́kər/ 名 C ▶定義 a piece of metal fixed to the outside of a door that you hit against the door to attract attention 扉の外側に取り付けられた金属で, 注意をひくためにそれで扉をたたく→**ノッカー, たたき金**

**knock-on** 形 特に 英 ▶定義 causing other events to happen one after the other ほかの出来事を次から次へと起こさせる→**連鎖的な** || *An increase in the price of oil has **a knock-on effect** on other fuels.* 石油価格の値上げは, ほかの燃料に連鎖反応をもたらす.

**knockout** /nɑ́kàʊt/ 名 C ▶定義1 a hard hit that causes sb to become unconscious or to be unable to get up again for a while しばらく～を気絶させる, または起き上がれなくする強い打撃→**ノックアウト** ▶定義2 特に 英 (名詞の前だけ) a competition in which the winner of each game goes on to the next part but the person who loses plays no more games 各試合の勝者が次の試合へと進み, 敗者はそれ以上試合をしない競技会→**トーナメント, 勝ち抜き試合**

***knot**¹ /nɑt/ 名 C ▶定義1 a place where two ends or pieces of rope, string, etc have been tied together 縄・糸などの両端または複数の縄・糸の結び目→**結び目, 結び** || *to tie/untie a knot* 結び目を作る・ほどく ● loop のさし絵 ▶定義2 a measure of the speed of a ship; approximately 1.8 kilometres per hour 船の速度の単位; 時速約1.8キロメートル→**ノット**

**knot**² /nɑt/ 動 他 (**knotting**; **knotted**) ▶定義 to fasten sth together with a knot 結び付けて～を固定する→**～を結ぶ, 結び目を作る**

***know**¹ /nóʊ/ 動 (過 **knew** /n(j)uː/; 過分 **known** /nóʊn/) (進行形 は 不 可) ▶定義1 他 自 know (about sth); know that... to have knowledge or information in your mind 頭の中に知識・情報を持つ→**知っている, 分かっている** || *I don't know much about sport.* 私はスポーツをよく知らない. *Do you know where this bus stops?* このバスがどこで止まるか知っていますか. *Do you know their telephone number?* 彼らの電話番号を知っているかい. *'You've got a flat tyre.' 'I know.'* 「タイヤがパンクしているよ」「分かっているよ」 *Do you **know the way** to the restaurant?* レストランへの道順を知っていますか. *Knowing Katie, she'll be out with her friends.* ケイティのことだから, 友達と一緒に出掛けるだろう. ▶定義2 他 to be familiar with a person or a place; to have met sb or been somewhere before 人・場所に精通している; 以前～に会ったことがある, またはどこかへ行ったことがある→**～を精通している, 知り合いである, 知っている** || *We've known each other for years.* 私たちは数年来の知り合いだ. *I don't know this part of London well.* 私はロンドンのこの地域をよく知らない.

▶初めてだれかがあなたを人に紹介する, あるいは初めて人に会うまたは話す場合には, 動詞の meet を用いる: *Peter and I met at university in 1997.* (ピーターと私は1997年に大学で出会った.) 人に出会った後に次第に親しくなることを get to know sb と言う: *Kevin's wife seems very interesting. I'd like to get to know her better.* (ケヴィンの奥さんはとても面白そうな人だ. もっと親しくなりたい.) 初めて行く場所について述べるときには, see または visit を用いる: *I'd love to go to the States and see/visit San Francisco and New York.* (私は米国に行って, サンフランシスコとニューヨークを見たい・訪れたい.)

▶定義3 他 自 to feel certain; to be sure of sth 確かに感じる; ～を確信する→**承知している, 分かっている** || *I just know you'll pass the exam!* あなたは試験に絶対に合格すると私は確信している. *As far as I know (= I think it is true but I am not* absolutely sure), the meeting is next Monday afternoon. 私の承知している限り(= 真実だと思うが絶対的には確信していない), 打ち合わせは来週の月曜日の午後だ. ▶定義4 ⓟ (過去および完了形でのみ) to have seen, heard, or experienced sth ～を見た, 聞いた, または経験したことがある→～を(見聞きして)知っている, 見たことがある, 聞いたことがある, 経験している ‖ *I've known him go a whole day without eating.* 私は彼が一日中食べないでいたのを見たことがある. *It's been known to snow in June.* 6月に雪が降ったと聞いたことがある. ▶定義5 (しばしば受動態で) **know sb/sth as sth** to give sth a particular name; to recognize sb/sth as sth ～にある特定の名前を付ける; ～を…と認識する→～を区別する, 識別する, 認める ‖ *Istanbul was previously known as Constantinople.* イスタンブールはかつてコンスタンチノープルとして知られていた. ▶定義6 ⓟ **know how to do sth** to have learned sth and be able to do it ～を習得して, それをすることができる→～を知っている, 熟知している, 理解している ‖ *Do you know how to use a computer?* あなたはコンピュータの使い方を知っていますか.

▶動詞の前には how to を用いなければならないので注意. *I know use a computer* とは言わない.

▶定義7 ⓟ to have personal experience of sth ～について個人的な経験を持つ→(経験によって)知っている ‖ *Many people in western countries don't know what it's like to be hungry.* 西洋諸国の人々の多くは空腹がどんなものかを知らない.
▶この動詞は進行形では使われないが, 現在分詞(= -ing 形)は一般に用いられている: *Knowing how he'd react if he ever found out about it, she kept quiet.* (彼がそれを知ったらどんな反応をするか分かっていたので, 彼女は黙っていた.)

成句 **God/goodness/Heaven knows** ▶定義1 *I don't know* さあ→だれにも分からない. ‖ *They've ordered a new car but goodness knows how they're going to pay for it.* 彼らは新車を注文したが, どうやってその支払いをするつもりなのかはだれにも分からない. ▶定義2 used for emphasizing sth ～について強調するのに用いて→きっと, 確かに ‖ *I hope I get an answer soon. Goodness knows, I've waited long enough.* 間もなく答えをもらえるとよいのだが. 本当に私は十分に長く待った.

**know better (than that/than to do sth)** ▶定義 to have enough sense to realize that you should not do sth 自分が～をすべきではないということが分かるだけの十分な判断力を持つ→(～しないくらいの)分別はある, (～するほど)ばかではない ‖ *I thought you knew better than to go out in the rain with no coat on.* 雨の中コートを着ないで出掛けるほどあなたはばかではないと思った.

**know sth inside out/like the back of your hand** 略式 ▶定義 to be very familiar with sth ～に非常に精通している→よく知っている

**know what you are talking about** 略式 ▶定義 to have knowledge of sth from your own experience 自分の経験から～についての知識を持つ→経験からものを言う ‖ *I've lived in London so I know what I'm talking about.* 私はずっとロンドンに住んでいるので, その経験から言っているのだ.

**know what's what** 略式 ▶定義 to have all the important information about sth; to fully understand sth ～についての重要な情報をすべて持っている; ～を完全に理解している→物の道理を理解している, 違いが分かる

**let sb know** ▶定義 to tell sb; to inform sb about sth ～に告げる; ～について…に知らせる→知らせる ‖ *Could you let me know what time you're arriving?* 何時に到着するかを知らせていただけますか.

**you know** ▶定義 used when the speaker is thinking of what to say next, or to remind sb of sth 話している人が次に言おうとする事を考えているとき, または～に…を思い出させるときに用いて→あのー, えーと, ほら～だよ, ～だからね ‖ *Well, you know, it's rather difficult to explain.* ええと, あのー, それを説明するのは結構難しい. *I've just met Marta. You know - Jim's ex-wife.* ちょうどマルタに会ったところだ － ほら, ジムの前の奥さんだよ.

**you never know** (口語) ▶定義 you cannot be certain あなたは確信していないはずだ→さあどうだか, 先の事は分からない ‖ *Keep those empty boxes. You never know, they might come in* *handy one day.* 空き箱を取っておきなさい。どうだか分からないが、いつか役に立つかもしれない。 句動詞 **know of sb/sth** ▶定義 to have information about or experience of sb/sth ～についての情報または経験がある→～のことを知っている ‖ *Do you know of any pubs around here that serve food?* この辺りで食事ができるパブを知りませんか。

**know²** /nóu/ 名
成句 **in the know** 略式 ▶定義 having information that other people do not ほかの人々が知らない情報を持っている→事情に通じて，内情を知っていて

**know-all** (米 **know-it-all**) 名 C ▶定義 an annoying person who behaves as if he/she knows everything あたかもすべてを知っているかのように振る舞ううるさい人→何でも知ったか振りをする人

**know-how** 名 U 略式 ▶定義 practical knowledge of or skill in sth ～についての実践的知識または技能→ノウハウ，実際的知識，こつ，技術

**knowing** /nóuɪŋ/ 形 ▶定義 showing that you know about sth that is thought to be secret 特定の人しか知らないと考えられている～について知っていることを示すような→物知りの，抜け目のない ‖ *a knowing look* 心得顔

**knowingly** /nóuɪŋli/ 副 ▶定義 **1** on purpose; deliberately 故意に；わざと→承知の上で，故意に ‖ *I've never knowingly lied to you.* 私はあなたに故意にうそをついたことはない。 ▶定義 **2** in a way that shows that you know about sth that is thought to be secret 特定の人しか知らないと思われている～について自分が知っていることを示す方法で→心得顔に，知ったか振りをして ‖ *He smiled knowingly at her.* 彼は心得顔で彼女にほほえんだ。

*★**knowledge** /nálɪdʒ/ 名 ▶定義 **1** [ U，単数扱い] knowledge (of/about sth) information, understanding and skills that you have gained through learning or experience 学んだり経験したりして自分が得た情報・理解・技能→知識，理解，熟知 ‖ *I have **a working knowledge** of French (= enough to be able to make myself understood).* 私はフランス語についての実用的な知識を持っている(= 自分の言いたい事を伝えるのに十分な)。 ▶定義 **2** U the state of knowing about a particular fact or situation 特定の事実または状況について知っている状態→知っていること，知ること ‖ **To my knowledge** *(= from the information I have, although I may not know everything) they are still living there.* 私の知る限り(= 私はすべてを知らないかもしれないが，私の持っている情報からすると)，彼らはまだそこに住んでいる。 *She did it **without my knowledge** (= I did not know about it).* 彼女は私に無断でそれをした(= 私はそれについて知らなかった)。

成句 **be common/public knowledge** ▶定義 to be sth that everyone knows 皆が知っている～である→周知の事柄となる

**knowledgeable** /nálɪdʒəb(ə)l/ 形 ▶定義 having a lot of knowledge 多くの知識を持つ→知識のある，知力のある ‖ *She's very knowledgeable about history.* 彼女は歴史について非常に知識がある。 — **knowledgeably** /-əbli/ 副 →知識を発揮して

**knuckle** /nák(ə)l/ 名 C ▶定義 the bones where your fingers join the rest of your hand 指と手の甲をつなげる骨→指の付け根の関節 ☞ C5 ページのさし絵

**koala** /kouá:lə/ 名 C ▶定義 an Australian animal with thick grey fur that lives in trees and looks like a small bear 厚い灰色の毛皮を持つオーストラリアの動物，木に暮らしクマに似ている→コアラ

**the Koran** (または **Quran, Qur'an**) /kɔːrá:n, kɔːræn/ 名 [単数扱い] ▶定義 the most important book in the Islamic religion イスラム教で最も重要な本→コーラン

**kosher** /kóuʃər/ 形 ▶定義 (used about food) prepared according to the rules of Jewish law (食べ物について) ユダヤ人の慣例の規定に従って調理された→ユダヤ人のおきてにかなった

**kph** /kèɪ piː éɪtʃ/ 略 kilometres per hour→時速～キロメートル

**kung fu** /kàŋ fúː/ 名 U ▶定義 a Chinese style of fighting using the feet and hands as weapons 足と手を武器として使う中国式の武道→カンフー ☞参 **martial arts**

**kW** (または **kw**) /kíləwàt/ 略 kilowatt(s)→キロワット ‖ *a 2kw electric heater* 2キロワットの電気暖房器具

# Ll

**L, l**[1] /el/ 名 C (複 **L's; l's**) ▶定義 the twelfth letter of the English alphabet 英語アルファベットの第12文字→l(L)が表す音, l(L)の文字, l(L)の字形のもの ‖ *'Lake' begins with (an) 'L'.* Lake はLで始まる.

**l**[2] 略 ▶定義1 l litre(s)→1リットル ▶定義2 英 L (on a sign on a car) learner-driver→(車の表示) 仮免許運転者 ▶定義3 L large (size) 大きなサイズ→Lサイズ

**Lab** 略 (in British politics) (英 政治) Labour→(英国の政治で) 労働党

label / price tag / ticket
Oxford–London ADULT RETURN 0813 030400

*****label**[1] /ˈleɪb(ə)l/ 名 C ▶定義1 a piece of paper, etc that is fixed to sth and which gives information about it 〜に付ける紙片などで, その〜についての情報を示すもの→札, 荷札, レッテル, ラベル ‖ *There is a list of all the ingredients on the label.* ラベルにはすべての成分のリストが記載されている. ▶定義2 **record label** a company that produces and sells records, CDs, etc レコード, CD などを制作・販売する会社→(レコード) レーベル, 商標

**label**[2] /ˈleɪb(ə)l/ 動 他 (**labelling; labelled**: 米 **labeling; labeled**) ▶定義1 (通常は受動態で) to fix a label or write information on sth 〜にラベルを付けたり, 情報を書いたりする→〜にラベルをはる, 張り紙をする, 〜を分類する ▶定義2 **label sb/sth (as) sth** to describe sb/sth in a particular way, especially unfairly 〜について特定のやり方, 特に不当なやり方で述べる→〜を…と呼ぶ, 名付ける, 〜に…というレッテルをはる, 〜に…の烙印(らくいん)を押す

*****laboratory** /ləˈbɒrət(ə)ri; læb(ə)rəˌtɔːri/ 名 C (複 **laboratories**) (または略式 **lab**) ▶定義 a room or building that is used for scientific research, testing, experiments, etc or for teaching about science 科学研究・テスト・実験などのために, また は科学を教えるために使用する部屋または建物→実験室, 研究室, 研究所, 実習室 ‖ *The blood samples were sent to the laboratory for analysis.* 血液標本は分析のため研究所に送られた. *a physics laboratory* 物理学研究所 ☛参 **language laboratory**

**laborious** /ləˈbɔːriəs/ 形 ▶定義 needing a lot of time and effort 多くの時間と労力が必要な→骨の折れる, 面倒な, 困難な, つらい ‖ *a laborious task/process/job* 骨の折れる仕事・工程・作業 ― **laboriously** 副→骨折って, 苦労して

**labour**[1] (米 **labor**) /ˈleɪbər/ ▶定義1 **U** work, usually of a hard, physical kind 仕事, 通常きつい肉体労働→労働, 骨折り, 努力 ‖ *manual labour (= work using your hands)* 手仕事 (= 手を使う作業), 肉体労働, 力仕事 ▶定義2 **U** workers, when thought of as a group (集団としての) 労働者→労働者(階級), 被雇用者側, 肉体労働者たち ‖ *There is a shortage of skilled labour.* 熟練労働者が不足している. ▶定義3 [**U C**, 通常は単数] the process of giving birth to a baby 赤ん坊を出産する過程→分べん, 出産, 陣痛 ‖ *She went into labour in the early hours of this morning.* 彼女は今朝早く陣痛が始まった. *She was in labour for ten hours.* 彼女のお産は10時間かかった.

**labour**[2] (米 **labor**) /ˈleɪbər/ 動 自 ▶定義1 **labour (away)** to work hard at sth 〜に一生懸命取り組む→骨折る, (〜に) 精を出す, 取り組む, (しようと) 努力する ‖ *She laboured on her book for two years.* 彼女は2年がかりで苦心して本を書いた. ▶定義2 to move or do sth with difficulty and effort 苦労や努力をして進む, または何かをする→骨を折って進む, 難航する

**laboured** (米 **labored**) /ˈleɪbərd/ 形 ▶定義 done slowly or with difficulty ゆっくりと, または苦労してなされた→苦心した, ぎこちない, 苦しい ‖ *laboured breathing* 苦しそうな呼吸

**labourer** (米 **laborer**) /ˈleɪbərər/ 名 C ▶定義 a person whose job involves hard physical work きつい肉体労働を伴った仕事をする人→(肉体) 労働者 ‖ *unskilled/farm labourers* 不熟練・農場労働者

**the Labour Party** (または **Labour**) 名 [単数扱い, 単数または複数形の動詞と共に] ▶定義 one of the main political parties in Britain. The Labour Party supports the interests of working people. 英国の主要政党の1つ. 労働

党は労働者の利益を代表している→労働党 ‖ *He has always voted Labour.* 彼は常に労働党に投票してきた. *a Labour MP* 労働党議員 ☛参 **the Conservative Party, the Liberal Democrats**

**labour-saving** 形 ▶定義 reducing the amount of work needed to do sth 何かをするために必要な労力を削減する→労力節約の, 省力の ‖ *labour-saving devices such as washing machines and dishwashers* 洗濯機や皿洗い機のような, 労力を節約してくれる装置

**labyrinth** /lǽbərìnθ/ 名 C ▶定義 a complicated set of paths and passages, through which it is difficult to find your way 行き先を見つけることが難しい複雑な道や通路→迷路, 迷宮 ‖ *a labyrinth of corridors* 迷路のような回廊 ☛類 **maze**

lace
lace collar

**lace**¹ /léɪs/ 名 ▶定義 1 U cloth that is made of very thin threads sewn in patterns with small holes in between 非常に細い糸を細かい穴が開いた模様に縫い合わせて作られた布→レース, 透かし模様 ‖ *lace curtains* レースのカーテン *a collar made of lace* レースで作られたえり ☛ 形 **lacy** ▶定義 2 C a string that is used for tying a shoe 靴を履くのに使われるひも→靴ひも ‖ *Your shoelace is undone.* 靴ひもがほどけている. *Do up your laces or you'll trip over them.* 靴ひもを結ばないと, 靴ひもにつまずきますよ. ☛参 **shoe** のさし絵

**lace**² /léɪs/ 動 他 ▶定義 lace (sth) (up) to tie or fasten sth with a lace¹(2) ～をひも(靴ひも)で結ぶまたは締める→ひもで締める, ひもで結ぶ ‖ *She was sitting on the end of the bed lacing up her boots.* 彼女はベッドの端に座ってブーツのひもを結んでいた. — **lace-up** 形名 C ・編み上げの; 編み上げ靴 ‖ *lace-up boots/shoes* 編み上げブーツ・靴

**lack**¹ /lǽk/ 名 U ▶定義 lack (of sth) the state of not having sth or not having enough of sth ～を持っていない, または～が十分にない状態→不足していること, 欠乏, 欠如 ‖ *A lack of food forced many people to leave their homes.* 食料不足のため, 多くの人々が故郷を去らねばならなかった.

*****lack**² /lǽk/ 動 他 ▶定義 to have none or not enough of sth ～を全く, または十分に持っていない→～が不足している, 足りない, 欠けている ‖ *She seems to lack the will to succeed.* 彼女には成功しようという意思が欠けているようだ.

**lacking** /lǽkɪŋ/ 形 (名詞の前は不可) ▶定義 1 **lacking in sth** not having enough of sth ～が欠けている, ～を十分に持っていない→～に欠けて, 不足して, ～に乏しい ‖ *He's certainly not lacking in intelligence.* 確かに彼には知性が欠けていない. ▶定義 2 not present or available 存在しない, または手に入らない→(～が)ない, 持っていない ‖ *I feel there is something lacking in my life.* 私の人生には何かが欠けている気がする.

**lacklustre** /lǽklʌ̀stər/ 形 ▶定義 not interesting or exciting; dull 面白くない, 活気のない; どんよりした→退屈な, さえない ‖ *a lacklustre performance* 退屈な公演

**laconic** /ləkɑ́nɪk/ 形 正式 ▶定義 using only a few words to say sth 少ない言葉で何かを言う→簡潔な, ずばり言う, 無駄口をきかない — **laconically** /-k(ə)li/ 副 ▶簡潔に, ずばりと

**lacquer** /lǽkər/ 名 U ▶定義 1 a type of transparent paint that is put on wood, metal, etc to give it a hard, shiny surface 硬い光沢のある表面を得るために木材, 金属などに塗る透明な塗料→ラッカー, 漆 ▶定義 2 (古) a liquid that you put on your hair to keep it in place 頭髪を整えるために付ける液体→整髪料 ☛類 **hairspray**

**lacy** /léɪsi/ 形 ▶定義 made of or looking like material made of thin threads with small holes to form a pattern (**lace**) 細い糸で細かい穴がある模様を作った生地(レース)で作られた, またはこれと似ている→レースの, レースのような

**lad** /lǽd/ 名 C 略式 ▶定義 a boy or young man 少年または若い男→若者 ‖ *School has changed since I was a lad.* 私が少年だったころと比べると学校は変わった.

*****ladder** /lǽdər/ 名 C ▶定義 1 a piece of equipment that is used for climbing up sth. A ladder consists of two long pieces of metal, wood or rope with steps fixed between them. 何かに登るために使用する器具. 2本の長い金属, 木の棒, またはロープなどの間に段を取り付けたもの→はしご ‖ (比喩) *to climb the ladder of success* 成功のはしごを登る, 出世の階段を上

る ☞参 **stepladder** ▶定義2（困**run**) a long hole in the thin pieces of clothing that women wear to cover their legs (tights or stockings), where the threads have broken 女性が脚を覆うために身に着ける薄い衣類(タイツまたはストッキング)に開いた長い穴で,糸が切れた箇所→伝線 ‖ *Oh no! I've got a ladder in my tights.* 嫌だ,タイツが伝線しているわ.— **ladder** 動他→(靴下)を伝線させる

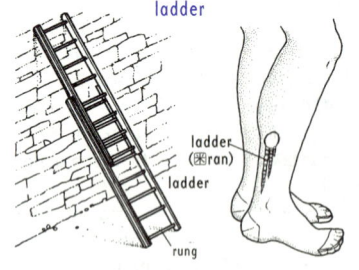

ladder
ladder (困ran)
rung

**laden** /léɪdn/ 形 **laden (with sth)**(名詞の前は不可) ▶定義 having or carrying a lot of sth ～をたくさん持っている,または携えている→荷を積んだ,～をたくさん積み込んだ ‖ *The travellers were laden down with luggage.* 旅行者たちは手荷物をたくさん持っていた. *The orange trees were laden with fruit.* オレンジの木には実がたくさんなっていた.

**the Ladies** 名 [単数扱い] 困略式 ▶定義 a public toilet for women 女性用の公共のトイレ→女性用トイレ ☞参 **toilet** の注

**ladle**¹ /léɪdl/ 名 C ▶定義 a large deep spoon with a long handle, used especially for serving soup 長い柄の付いた大きな深いスプーンで,特にスープをよそうのに使われる→ひしゃく,おたま ☞ **kitchen** のさし絵

**ladle**² /léɪdl/ 動他 ▶定義 to serve food with a ladle ひしゃく[おたま]で食物を配る→～をおたますくう[つぐ・よそう],ひしゃくでくむ

*★**lady** /léɪdi/ 名 C (複 **ladies**) ▶定義1 a polite way of saying 'woman', especially when you are referring to an older woman 女性に対する丁寧な語,特に年配の女性を言う場合の丁寧な語→ご婦人,女性(の方) ‖ *The old lady next door lives alone.* 隣の老婦人は一人暮らしだ.

▶定義2 正式 used when speaking to or about a woman or women in a polite way 女性に話し掛けるとき,または女性について述べるときに使う丁寧な言い方→奥さん,お嬢さん,女性 ‖ ***Ladies and gentlemen!*** (= at the beginning of a speech) 皆さん.(= スピーチの初めで) *Mrs Flinn, there's a lady here to see you.* フリンさん,あなたにお目に掛かりたいという女の方がいます. ▶定義3 a title that is used before the name of a woman who has a high social position 社会的地位の高い女性の名前の前に付ける敬称→～卿夫人,～令嬢,レディー ‖ *Lady Elizabeth Groves* エリザベス グローヴス卿夫人 ☞参 **Lord**

**ladybird** /léɪdibɜːrd/ (困**ladybug** /léɪdibʌg/) 名 C ▶定義 a small insect that is red or yellow with black spots 赤または黄に黒い斑点(はんてん)のある小さな昆虫→てんとう虫 ☞ **insect** のさし絵

**lag**¹ /læg/ 動自 (**lagging**; **lagged**) ▶定義 **lag (behind) (sb/sth)** to move or develop more slowly than sb/sth ～よりゆっくりと動く,または進展が遅い→(～に)遅れる,のろのろ歩く,ぐずぐずする ‖ *James has missed a lot of classes and is lagging behind the others at school.* ジェームズは多くの授業を欠席したので,学校のほかの者から遅れている.

**lag**² /læg/ (または **time lag**) 名 C ▶定義 a period of time between two events; a delay 2つの出来事の間の時間; 遅れ→遅れること,時間の隔たり ☞参 **jet lag**

**lager** /láːgər/ 名 C U 困 ▶定義 a type of light beer that is a gold colour 黄金色をした軽いビール→ラガー(ビール) ‖ *Three pints of lager, please.* ラガーを3パイント下さい.

**lagoon** /ləgúːn/ 名 C ▶定義 a lake of salt water that is separated from the sea by sand or rock 砂や岩で海から隔てられた塩水の湖沼→潟(かた),ラグーン,礁湖(しょうこ)

**laid** **LAY**¹ の過去・過去分詞形

**laid-back** /léɪdbǽk/ 形略式 ▶定義 calm and relaxed; seeming not to worry about anything 穏やかでくつろいだ; 心配事がないように見える→くつろいだ,のんびりした,気楽な

**lain** **LIE**² の過去分詞形

*★**lake** /léɪk/ 名 C ▶定義 a large area of water that is surrounded by land 陸地に囲まれた広い水域→湖,湖水 ‖ *They've gone sailing **on the lake**.*

彼らは湖へヨット遊びに行っている. *We all swam **in the lake**.* 私たちはみんな湖で泳いだ. *Lake Constance* コンスタンス湖
➤ pond は lake より小さい.
◉ C8 ページのさし絵

**lamb** /læm/ 名 ▶定義1 ❶a young sheep 若い羊→**子羊** ☞参 **sheep**の注 ☞参 **goat**のさし絵 ▶定義2 ❷the meat of a young sheep 子羊の肉→**ラム** ‖ *lamb chops* 子羊の厚切り肉 ☞参 **meat**の注

**lame** /léɪm/ 形 ▶定義1 (used mainly about animals) not able to walk properly because of an injury to the leg or foot (主に動物について)脚または足のけがのため正常に歩くことができない→**足が悪い,(足などが)不自由な** ‖ *The horse is lame and cannot work.* その馬は足が悪いので働けない.

➤ lame は現在では人に対してはあまり使われない. limp (動名) は人に対しては現在では lame よりよく使われる: *He's got a limp.* (彼は足が不自由だ.) *You're limping. Have you hurt your leg?* (足を引きずっていますね. 脚をけがしたのですか.)

▶定義2 (used about an excuse, argument, etc) not easily believed; weak (言い訳, 議論などについて)簡単には信じられない; 下手な→**(口実・話などが)下手な, 説得力のない**

**lament** /ləmént/ 名 ❸ 圉式 ▶定義 a song, poem or other expression of sadness for sb who has died or for sth that has ended 亡くなった人や終わった事に対する悲しみを表す歌, 詩, そのほかの表現方法→**悲嘆, 嘆き, 哀歌** — *lament* 動他 ～を嘆く, 悲しむ

**laminated** /læmənèɪtɪd/ 形 ▶定義1 (used about wood, plastic, etc) made by sticking several thin layers together (木, プラスチックなどについて)数枚の薄い層を張り合わせて作られた→**薄板状の, 薄層から成る, ラミネート加工した** ‖ *laminated glass* 合わせガラス ▶定義2 covered with thin transparent plastic for protection 保護のために薄い透明プラスチックで覆われた→**薄膜を持つ**

\***lamp** /læmp/ 名 ❸ ▶定義 a device that uses electricity, gas or oil to produce light 電気・ガス・石油を使用して光を発する装置→**ランプ, 電気スタンド, 明かり** ‖ *a street lamp* 街灯 *a table/desk/bicycle lamp* 卓上スタンド・電気スタンド・自転車のライト *a sunlamp* 太陽灯 ☞参 **light**, S7 ページのさし絵

**lamp post** 名 ❸ ▶定義 a tall pole at the side of the road with a light on the top 道路わきにある上部に電灯の付いた高い柱→**街灯の柱**

**lampshade** /læmpʃèɪd/ 名 ❸ ▶定義 a cover for a lamp that makes it look more attractive and makes the light softer ランプをより魅力的に見せ, 明かりを柔らかくするためのランプの覆い→**ランプのかさ, ランプシェード** ☞参 **light**のさし絵

\***land**¹ /lænd/ 名 ▶定義1 ❶the solid part of the surface of the earth (= not sea) 地表の硬い部分 (= 海でない部分)→**陸, 陸地** ‖ *Penguins can't move very fast on land.* ペンギンは陸上ではあまり速く動けない. ☞参 **ground**の注 ⇔ **sea** ▶定義2 ❷an area of ground 地面の範囲 →**土地, 地面** ‖ *The land rose to the east.* その土地は東に向かって高くなっていた. *She owns 500 acres of land in Scotland.* 彼女はスコットランドに500エーカーの土地を持っている.

▶定義3 ❷ground, soil or earth of a particular kind 特定の種類の土, 土壌または土地→**土地, 土壌, 耕地** ‖ *The land is rich and fertile.* その土壌は豊かで肥沃(ひよく)だ. *arid/barren land* 不毛の・やせた土地 *arable/ agricultural/industrial land* 耕地・農地・工業用地 ▶定義4 ❸(文) a country or region 国または地域→**領域, 世界** ‖ *She died far from her native land.* 彼女は生まれた国から遠い所で亡くなった. *to travel to distant lands* 遠い国へ旅する ☞参 **country**の注

\***land**² /lænd/ 動 ▶定義1 ❸ ❻ to come down from the air or to bring sth down to the ground 空から降りる, または～を地面に降ろす→**着陸する; 落ちる, 降りる, ～を着陸させる** ‖ *The bird landed on the roof.* 鳥が屋根に止まった. *He fell off the ladder and landed on his back.* 彼ははしごから落ち, 地面に背中を打ち付けた. *The pilot landed the aeroplane safely.* パイロットは飛行機を安全に着陸させた. *His flight is due to land at 3 o'clock.* 彼の乗った便は3時に着陸する予定だ. ☞ **take off**のさし絵 ▶定義2 ❸ ❻ to go onto land or put sth onto land from a ship 船から陸に上がる, または～を船から陸に揚げる→**上陸する; ～を上陸させる, 陸揚げする** ▶定義3 ❻ to succeed in getting sth, especially sth that

**a lot of people want** ～を, 特に多くの人が望む～を得ることに成功する➡～を獲得する, ものにする ‖ *The company has just landed a million-dollar contract.* その会社は100万ドルの契約を成立させたばかりだ.

**成句 fall/land on your feet** ⇒ **FOOT**¹

**句動詞 land up (in...)** 医略式 ▶定義 to finish in a certain position or situation ある地位や状況で結末を迎える➡(ある場所・困った状況に)立ち至る, 落ち着く ‖ *He landed up in a prison cell for the night.* 彼は一晩刑務所に入るはめになった.

**land sb with sb/sth** 略式 ▶定義 to give sb sth unpleasant to do, especially because no one else wants to do it 特にだれもやりたがらないという理由で～に不快な事をさせる➡～に(負担・問題など)を負わせる

**landfill** 名 ▶定義1 C U an area of land where large amounts of waste material are buried 大量の廃棄物が埋められる土地➡(ごみの)埋め立て地 ▶定義2 U waste material that will be buried; the burying of waste material 埋められる廃棄物; 廃棄物の埋め立て➡埋め立てごみ; 埋め立てによるごみ処理

*****landing** /ˈlændɪŋ/ 名 C ▶定義1 the action of coming down onto the ground (in an aircraft) 地面に降りること (航空機の場合)➡着陸, 着陸すること ‖ *The plane made an **emergency landing** in a field.* 飛行機は原野に緊急着陸した. *a crash landing* 不時着 *a safe landing* 安全な着陸 ⇔ **take-off** ▶定義2 the area at the top of a staircase in a house, or between one staircase and another in a large building 住宅の階段の最上部の四角い部分, または大きなビルの階段と階段の間の四角い部分➡踊り場 ☛ C7ページのさし絵

**landing card** 名 C ▶定義 a form on which you have to write details about yourself when flying to a foreign country 航空機で海外に行く際に自分についての詳細を書き込む用紙➡上陸証明書

**landing stage** (米 dock) 名 C ▶定義 a wooden platform built out into the sea or a river where boats are tied and where people can get on or off them 海または川に突き出して作られた木製の台で, 船をつないだり, 人々が船に乗り降りしたりする場所➡浮き桟橋, 突堤, 荷揚げ場 ☛類 jetty

**landing strip** = AIRSTRIP

**landlady** /ˈlændleɪdi/ 名 C (複 **landladies**) ▶定義1 a woman who rents a house or room to people for money 家や部屋を賃貸しする女性➡女家主, 大家, 女地主 ▶定義2 a woman who owns or manages a pub, small hotel, etc パブ, 小ホテルなどを所有または経営する女性➡女主人, 女将(おかみ)

**landlord** /ˈlændlɔːrd/ 名 C ▶定義1 a person who rents a house or room to people for money 家や部屋を賃貸しする人➡(男の)家主, 大家, 地主 ▶定義2 a person who owns or manages a pub, small hotel, etc パブ, 小ホテルなどを所有または経営する人➡主人, 亭主

**landmark** /ˈlændmɑːrk/ 名 C ▶定義1 an object (often a building) that can be seen easily from a distance and will help you to recognize where you are 遠くからでも容易に見える物(しばしば建物)で, 自分の位置を知る手掛かりになるもの➡陸標, 目印 ‖ *Big Ben is one of the landmarks on London's skyline.* ビッグベンはロンドンの地平線上にある目印の1つだ. ▶定義2 **a landmark (in sth)** an important stage or change in the development of sth ～の発展における重要な段階や変化➡(～における)画期的な事件, 歴史的建造物

**landscape**¹ /ˈlæn(d)skeɪp/ 名 ▶定義1 [C, 通常は単数] everything you can see when you look across a large area of land 広い範囲の土地を見渡したときに見えるすべてのもの➡景色, 風景, 景観 ‖ *an urban/industrial landscape* 都市景観・工業地帯の景観 ☛参 **scenery** の注 ▶定義2 C U a picture or a painting that shows a view of the countryside; this style of painting 田舎の風景の写真や絵画; そのような画法➡風景画; 風景画法

**landscape**² /ˈlæn(d)skeɪp/ 動 他 ▶定義 to improve the appearance of an area of land by changing its design and planting trees, flowers, etc 設計を変更し樹木や花などを植えて, 土地の景観を改良する➡～を美化する, 緑化する

**landslide** /ˈlændslaɪd/ 名 C ▶定義1 the sudden fall of a mass of earth, rocks, etc down the side of a mountain 突然大量の土砂, 岩などが山の斜面を落下すること➡地滑り, 山崩れ; 崩れた土砂 ‖ *Part of the railway line was buried beneath a* *landslide*. 鉄道の一部が崖（がけ）崩れで埋まった. ▶定義2 a great victory for one person or one political party in an election 選挙で1人または1つの政党が大勝利を収めること→**圧倒的勝利, 圧勝**

**lane** /léɪn/ 🔊 ⓒ ▶定義1 a narrow road in the country 田舎の細い道→**細道, 小道** ‖ *We found a route through country lanes to avoid the traffic jam on the main road.* 幹線道路の交通渋滞を避けるため, 田舎の細道を通るルートを見つけた. ▶定義2 used in the names of roads 道路の名前に用いて→**〜通り, 〜レーン** ‖ *Crossley Lane* クロスリー通り ▶定義3 a section of a wide road that is marked by painted white lines to keep lines of traffic separate 白線で示された広い道路の区分で, 交通の流れを分離するためのもの→**車線** ‖ *a four-lane motorway* 4車線の高速道路 *the inside/middle/fast/outside lane* 内側・中央・追い越し・外側車線 ▶定義4 a section of a sports track, swimming pool, etc for one person to go along 1人が進むための競技トラック, プールなどの区分→**コース** ‖ *The British athlete is in lane two.* 英国の選手は2コースだ. ▶定義5 a route or path that is regularly used by ships or aircraft 船舶や航空機が定期的に使用するルートまたは進路→**航路, 水路**

***language** /læŋgwɪdʒ/ 🔊 ▶定義1 ⓒ the system of communication in speech and writing that is used by people of a particular country 特定の国の人々が話すためと書くために使用する伝達の体系→**国語, 〜語** ‖ *How many languages can you speak?* あなたは何か国語が話せますか. *They fell in love in spite of the language barrier (= being unable to speak or understand each other's native language).* 言葉の障害にもかかわらず2人は恋に落ちた. (= お互いの母国語を話すことも理解することもできない). *What is your first language (= your mother tongue)?* あなたの第1言語 (= 母語) は何ですか. ▶定義2 Ⓤthe system of sounds and writing that human beings use to express their thoughts, ideas and feelings 人間が思想, 考え, 感情などを表現するために使う音声と記述の体系→**言語, 言葉** ‖ *written/spoken language* 書き言葉・話し言葉 ▶定義3 Ⓤwords of a particular type or words that are used by a particular person or group 特定の種類の言葉または特定の個人や集団が使う言葉→**言葉遣い, 言い回し, 用語, 術語, 文体** ‖ *bad (= rude) language* ひどい (= 下品な) 言葉遣い *legal language* 法律用語 *the language of Shakespeare* シェークスピアの文体 ▶定義4 Ⓤany system of signs, symbols, movements, etc that is used to express sth 何かを表すために使われる記号, 象徴, 動作などの体系→**(音声・文字を用いない) 伝達手段, 身振り言語, (動物の) 鳴き声** ‖ *sign language (= using your hands, not speaking)* 手話 (= 話す代わりに手を用いる) ☞参 **body language** ▶定義5 ⓒⓊ(computing) a system of symbols and rules that is used to operate a computer (コンピューター) コンピューターを操作するために使用される記号や規則の体系→**コンピューター言語**

**language laboratory** 🔊 ⓒ ▶定義 a room in a school or college that contains special equipment to help students to learn foreign languages by listening to tapes, watching videos, recording themselves, etc 学校や大学の特別な装置のある教室で, テープを聴いたり, ビデオを見たり, 自分の言葉を録音したりして, 学生の外国語学習を補助するための部屋→**語学練習室, LL教室**

**lanky** /læŋki/ 形 ▶定義 (used about a person) very tall and thin (人について) 非常に背が高くてやせている→**ひょろっとした**

**lantern** /læntən/ 🔊 ⓒ ▶定義 a type of light that can be carried with a metal frame, glass sides and a light or candle inside 金属枠にガラス板をはめ込み, 内部に電灯またはろうそくを入れた持ち運びできる明かり→**カンテラ, ランタン, 手提げランプ, 提灯 (ちょうちん)**

**lap**¹ /læp/ 🔊 ⓒ ▶定義1 the flat area that is formed by the upper part of your legs when you are sitting down 脚の上部の座ったときに平らになる部分→**ひざ** ‖ *The child sat quietly on his mother's lap.* その子供は母親のひざの上におとなしく座っていた. ▶定義2 one journey around a running track, etc 競技用トラックなどの1周→**1周, 1往復, ラップ** ‖ *There are three more laps to go in the race.* レースはあと3周だ. ▶定義3 one part of a long journey 長い旅の一部分→**一行程**

**lap²** /læp/ 動 (**lapping; lapped**) ▶定義 1 自 (used about water) to make gentle sounds as it moves against sth (水について) 〜に触れて動くときに小さな音を立てる →**ひたひたと打つ, (波などが)打ち寄せる** ‖ *The waves lapped against the side of the boat.* 波が船べりをひたひたと打った. ▶定義 2 他 (**lap sth (up)**) (usually used about an animal) to drink sth using the tongue (通常は動物について) 舌を使って〜を飲む →**〜をぺろぺろとなめる, ぴちゃぴちゃ飲む** ‖ *The cat lapped up the cream.* 猫はクリームをぺろぺろとなめた. ▶定義 3 他 to pass another competitor in a race who has been round the track fewer times than you 競技で自分より周回数の少ない別の選手を抜く →**〜を1周(以上)抜く, 周回遅れにする**

句動詞 **lap sth up** 略式 ▶定義 to accept sth with great enjoyment without stopping to think if it is good, true, etc 善悪や真偽などを考えずに〜を大喜びで受け入れる →**(お世辞・情報など)を真に受ける**

**lapel** /ləpél/ 名 C ▶定義 one of the two parts of the front of a coat or jacket that are folded back コートや上着の前身ごろの折り返す部分の片方 →**えりの折り返し, ラペル**

**lapse¹** /læps/ 名 C ▶定義 1 a short time when you cannot remember sth or you are not thinking about what you are doing 何かを思い出せない短い時間, 何をしていたか意識しない短い時間 →**一時, 空白** ‖ *a lapse of memory* ちょっとした物忘れ *The crash was the result of a temporary lapse in concentration.* ほんの一時の集中力のとぎれが衝突の原因だった. ▶定義 2 a period of time between two things that happen 2つの出来事の間の時間 →**(時の)経過, 期間, 中断** ‖ *She returned to work after a lapse of ten years bringing up her family.* 彼女は子育てのため10年間休職した後で仕事に戻った. ☛参 動 **elapse**

▶定義 3 a piece of bad behaviour from sb who usually behaves well 普段は行儀の良い人のちょっとした悪い振る舞い →**ちょっとした誤り, 失策, 失言**

**lapse²** /læps/ 動 自 ▶定義 1 (used about a contract, an agreement, etc) to finish or stop, often by accident (契約・協約などについて) しばしば偶発的原因によって, 終了または停止する →**消滅する, 失効する** ‖ *My membership has lapsed because I forgot to renew it.* 更新するのを忘れたので, 会員資格が消滅してしまった. ▶定義 2 to become weaker or stop for a short time 短い時間弱まる, または停止する →**とぎれる** ‖ *My concentration lapsed during the last part of the exam.* 試験の最後の部分で集中力がとぎれた.

句動詞 **lapse into sth** ▶定義 to gradually pass into a worse or less active state or condition; to start speaking or behaving in a less acceptable way 徐々により悪い, または活動的でない状態や状況になる; 好ましくない話し方や振る舞いをするようになる →**〜に下落する, 堕落する, (〜の状態)になる** ‖ *to lapse into silence/a coma* 黙りこくる・昏睡(こんすい)状態に陥る

**laptop** /léptɑp/ 名 C ▶定義 a small computer that is easy to carry and that can use batteries for power 簡単に持ち運べ, 電源にバッテリーを使用できる小型コンピューター →**ラップトップコンピューター** ☛参 **desktop**

**larder** /lɑ́ːrdər/ 名 C ▶定義 a large cupboard or small room that is used for storing food 食品を保管するための大きな戸棚や小部屋 →**食料品室, 食料置き場** ☛類 **pantry**

★**large** /lɑːrdʒ/ 形 ▶定義 greater in size, amount, etc than usual; big サイズ, 量などが通常より大きい; 大きい →**広い, 多い, 多数の, 多量の** ‖ *a large area/house/family/appetite* 広範囲・大きな家・大家族・旺盛(おうせい)な食欲 *a large number of people* 大勢の人々 *I'd like a large coffee, please.* コーヒーの大を下さい. *We have this shirt in small, medium or large.* このシャツにはS, M, Lサイズがございます. ☛参 **big** の注

成句 **at large** ▶定義 1 as a whole; in general 全体として; 一般に →**全般に, あまねく** ‖ *He is well known to scientists but not to the public at large.* 彼は科学者の間では有名だが, 一般には知られていない. ▶定義 2 (used about a criminal, animal, etc) not caught; free (犯罪者, 動物などについて) 捕まらないで; 自由で →**監禁されないで, 捕まらないで, 野放しで**

**by and large** ▶定義 mostly; in general 大部分, 一般に →**全体的に, 大体** ‖ *By and large the school is very efficient.* 全体的に見てその学校はとても能率が良い.

**largely** /láːrdʒli/ 副 ▶定義 mostly 大部分→大いに,主として ‖ *His success was largely due to hard work.* 彼の成功は主に努力によるものだった.

**large-scale** 形 ▶定義 happening over a large area or affecting a lot of people 広範囲で起こる,または大勢に影響する→**大規模な,大掛かりの** ‖ *large-scale production/unemployment* 大規模生産・大勢の失業者

**laryngitis** /lǽrəndʒáitəs/ 名 ⓤ ▶定義 a mild illness of the throat that makes it difficult to speak 声を出すのが困難になるのどの軽い病気→**喉頭(こうとう)炎**

**laser** /léizər/ 名 ⓒ ▶定義 a device that produces a controlled ray of very powerful light that can be used as a tool 工具として使用できる,制御された非常に強力な光線を発生する装置→**レーザー(装置)**

**lash**¹ /læʃ/ 動 ▶定義 1 自他 (used especially about wind, rain and storms) to hit sth with great force (特に風,雨,あらしについて)~を大きな力で打つ→**激しく打ち付ける,打ちかかる** ‖ *The rain lashed against the windows.* 雨が窓に激しく打ち付けた. ▶定義 2 他 to hit sb with a piece of rope, leather, etc; to move sth like a piece of rope, leather, etc violently ロープ,革ひもなどで~を打つ;~をロープ,革ひもなどのように激しく動かす→**~をむちで打つ,打ちのめす**
▶定義 3 他 *lash A to B; lash A and B together* to tie two thigs together firmly with rope, etc ロープなどで2つの物をしっかりと結ぶ→**~を…に・~と…を縛る,結び付ける** ‖ *The two boats were lashed together.* 2そうのボートは互いにしっかりとつながれた.

句動詞 **lash out (at/against sb/sth)** ▶定義 to suddenly attack sb/sth (with words or by hitting him/her/it) 突然~を攻撃する(言葉で,または人や動物を打って)→**(~に)非難を浴びせる,暴言を吐く,(~を)攻撃する,(~に)殴り掛かる** ‖ *The actor lashed out at a photographer outside his house.* その俳優は家の外にいたカメラマンにいきなり殴り掛かった.

**lash**² /læʃ/ 名 ⓒ ▶定義 1 = EYELASH ▶定義 2 a hit with a long piece of rope, leather, etc (*a whip*) 長いロープや革ひもなど(むち)で打つこと→**むちの一打ち,むち打つこと**

**lass** /læs/ (または **lassie** /lǽsi/) 名 ⓒ 略式 ▶定義 a girl or young woman 少女, 若い女性→**小娘, 若い娘, 娘っ子**

▶ lass は主にスコットランドと北イングランドで使われる.

**lasso** /læsúː; lǽsou/ 名 ⓒ (複 **lassos** または **lassoes**) ▶定義 a long rope tied in a circle at one end that is used for catching cows and horses 牛や馬を捕まえるために用いる一方の端を輪にした長いロープ→**投げ縄** — *lasso* 動 他 →**~を投げ縄で捕まえる**

*★**last**¹ /lɑːst; læst/ 形副名 ⓒ ▶定義 1 at the end; after all the others 最後の;あらゆるものの後の→**終わりの,最終の,ビリの** ‖ *December is the last month of the year.* 12月は1年の最後の月だ. *Would the last person to leave please turn off the lights?* 最後に出る人が明かりを消してくれませんか. *Our house is the last one on the left.* 私たちの家は左端です. *She lived alone for the last years of her life.* 彼女は晩年は一人暮らしだった. *The British athlete came in last.* 英国の選手が最下位だった. *Her name is last on the list.* 彼女の名前はリストの最後だ. *Alex was the last to arrive.* アレックスが1番最後に到着した.
▶定義 2 used about a time, period, event, etc in the past that is nearest to the present 現在に最も近い過去の時間,期間,出来事などに用いて→**この前(の), 昨~, 去る~, 先~** ‖ *last night/week/Saturday/ summer* 昨夜・先週・この前の土曜日・この前の夏 *We have been working on the book for the last six months.* 私たちはこの6か月ずっとこの本に取り組んでいる. ***The last time** I saw her was in London.* 最後に彼女を見たのはロンドンだった. *We'll win this time, because they beat us **last time**.* 今度は勝つぞ,この前は彼らに完敗したから. *When did you last have your eyes checked?* この前,目の検査をしたのはいつですか. *When I saw her last she seemed very happy.* この前彼女に会った時はとても幸福そうだった.

▶ the latest は「最新の」または「新しい」の意味. the last は現在のものより1つ前の意味: *His last novel was a huge success, but the latest one is much less popular.* (彼のこの前の小説は大成功だったが,最新作はそれほど人気がない.)

## 948 last²

▶定義3 final 最終的な→**最後の, 最終の** ‖ *This is my last chance to take the exam.* これが試験を受ける最後のチャンスだ. *Alison's retiring - tomorrow is her last day at work.* アリソンは退職する — 明日は彼女が出勤する最後の日だ. *We finished **the last of the** bread at breakfast so we'd better get some more.* 朝食の時, 最後に残ったパンを食べてしまったので買ってきた方がいい. ▶定義4 (名詞の前だけ) not expected or not suitable 予想できない, またはふさわしくない→**最も〜しそうにない, 最も不適切な** ‖ *He's the last person I thought would get the job.* 彼がその仕事に就けるとは夢にも思わなかった. —
**lastly** 副→**最後に, 終わりに, 結論として** ‖ *Lastly, I would like to thank the band who played this evening.* 最後に, 今夜演奏してくれたバンドの皆さんに感謝します. ☞類 **finally**

**成句 the last/next but one, two, etc** ▶定義 one, two, etc away from the last/next 最後・次から1つ, 2つ, …離れている→**最後から2番目, 3番目, …の・1つ, 2つ, …おいて次の** ‖ *I live in the next house but one on the right.* 私は右から1つおいて次の家に住んでいる. *X is the last letter but two of the alphabet* (= *the third letter from the end*). Xはアルファベットの最後から3番目の文字だ. (= 最後から数えて3番目の文字)

**at (long) last** ▶定義 in the end; finally 最後に; 最終的に→**やっと, ついに** ‖ *After months of separation they were together at last.* 何か月も離れ離れだったが, 彼らはついに一緒になった.

**first/last thing** ⇒ **THING**

**have the last laugh** ▶定義 to be the person, team, etc who is successful in the end 最後に成功する人, チームなどになる→**最後に勝つ, 最後に笑う**

**have, etc the last word** ▶定義 to be the person who makes the final decision or the final comment 最終決定を下す人や最後の一言を言う人になる→**決定的な発言をする, 最終的な意見を述べる**

**in the last resort; (as) a last resort** ▶定義 when everything else has failed; the person or thing that helps when everything else has failed ほかのすべてが失敗したときに; ほかのすべてが失敗したときに助けとなる人や物→**最後の手段(として), 結局** ‖ *In the last resort my grandad could play in the match.* 最後の手段として, おじいちゃんが試合に出ることもあり得る.

**last but not least** ▶定義 (used before the final item in a list) just as important as all the other items (一覧の最終項目の前に用いて) ほかの項目と同様に重要な→**大事な事を1つ言い残したが, (紹介の際に)最後になりましたが, 申し遅れましたが**

**a last-ditch attempt** ▶定義 a final effort to avoid sth unpleasant or dangerous 不快な事や危険な事を避ける最後の努力→**背水の陣**

**the last/final straw** ⇒ **STRAW**

**the last minute/moment** ▶定義 the final minute/moment before sth happens 何かが始まる前の最後の一瞬・瞬間→**ぎりぎりの瞬間(の), 土壇場(の)** ‖ *We arrived at the last minute to catch the train.* 私たちはぎりぎりで列車に間に合った. *a last-minute change of plan* 土壇場での計画変更

*★**last²** /lɑːst; læst/ 動 (進行形は不可) ▶定義1 自他 to continue for a period of time ある時間継続する→**続く, 持続する** ‖ *The exam lasts three hours.* 試験は3時間続く. *How long does a cricket match last?* クリケットの一試合はどのくらいかかりますか. *The flight seemed to last forever.* 空の旅は永遠に続くかと思われた.
▶定義2 自他 to continue to be good or to function 良好な状態が続く, 機能し続ける→**持ちこたえる, 長持ちする** ‖ *Do you think this weather will last till the weekend?* この天気が週末まで持つと思いますか. *It's only a cheap radio but it'll probably last a year or so.* それは安いラジオですが, 1年かそこらは持つでしょう. ▶定義3 自他 to be enough for what sb needs 〜が必要とするだけ十分にある→**足りる, 間に合う** ‖ *This money won't last me till the end of the month.* これだけのお金では月末まで持たない.

▶ この動詞は進行形では使用されないが, 現在分詞 (= -ing 形) で使用されることは多い: *An earthquake lasting approximately 20 seconds struck the city last night.* (約20秒続く地震が昨夜その都市を襲った.)

**lasting** /lɑːstɪŋ; læst-/ 形 ▶定義 continuing for a long time 長い間続く→**永続する, 永久の** ‖ *The* *museum left a lasting impression on me.* その博物館は長いこと忘れられない印象を私に残した.

**last name** = SURNAME ☞参 **name** の注

**latch**¹ /lætʃ/ 🔷 ⓒ ▶定義 1 a small metal bar that is used for fastening a door or a gate. You have to lift the latch in order to open the door. ドアや門を閉めるために使用する小さい金属の棒. ドアを開くためにはこれを上げなければならない→**掛け金, かんぬき** ▶定義 2 a type of lock for a door that you open with a key from the outside かぎで外から開けることのできるドアの錠→**錠(前), ラッチ**

**latch**² /lætʃ/ 🔶
句動詞 **latch on (to sth)** 略式 ▶定義 to understand sth 〜を理解する→**把握する, のみ込む** ‖ *It took them a while to latch on to what she was talking about.* 彼女が何を言っているかを彼らが把握するまでにしばらくかかった.

*****late** /leɪt/ 形副 ▶定義 1 near the end of a period of time 一定の時間の終わり近く→**遅い, 終わりごろの, 後期の, 後半の** ‖ *in the late afternoon/ summer/twentieth century* 午後遅く・夏の終わりに・20世紀後半に / *in the late morning* 昼近く / *His mother's in her late fifties (= between 55 and 60).* 彼の母親は50代後半だ(=55から60の間). / *in late May/late in May* 5月の後半に / *We got back home late in the evening.* 夜遅く家に戻った. ▶定義 2 after the usual or expected time 通常または予定の時刻より遅く→**遅れて, 遅刻して** ‖ *I'm sorry I'm late.* 遅れてすみません. / *She was ten minutes late for school.* 彼女は学校に10分遅刻した. / *The ambulance arrived too late to save him.* 救急車の到着が遅すぎて彼を救えなかった. / *to be late with the rent* 家賃の支払いが遅れる / *The buses are running late today.* 今日はバスが遅れている. / *to stay up late* 遅くまで起きている. ▶定義 3 near the end of the day 1日の終わり近くに→**(時刻が)遅い** ‖ *It's getting late - let's go home.* もう遅い — 家に帰りましょう. ▶定義 4 (名詞の前だけ) no longer alive; dead 亡くなった; 死んだ→**最近死んだ, 故〜** ‖ *his late wife* 彼の亡妻

成句 **an early/a late night** ⇒ NIGHT

**later on** ▶定義 at a later time→**後で** ‖ *Later on you'll probably wish that you'd worked harder at school.* 後になって, 学校でもっと良く勉強すればよかったと思うでしょう. / *Bye - I'll see you a bit later on.* じゃあ — 後ほどお会いしましょう.

**sooner or later** ⇒ SOON

**latecomer** /ˈleɪtkʌmər/ 🔷 ⓒ ▶定義 a person who arrives or starts sth late 遅く来る人, または何かを遅れて始める人→**遅刻者, 新参者**

*****lately** /ˈleɪtli/ 副 ▶定義 in the period of time up until now; recently 現在までの期間内に; 最近→**近ごろ, このごろ** ‖ *What have you been doing lately?* 最近はどうしているの. / *Hasn't the weather been dreadful lately?* このところひどい天気が続きますね.

*****latest** /ˈleɪtəst/ 形 ▶定義 very recent or new 非常に最近の, 非常に新しい→**最新の** ‖ *the latest fashions* 最新ファッション / *the latest news* 最新ニュース / *the terrorists' latest attack on the town* 最近テロリストが町を攻撃したこと ☞参 **last**¹ の注

**the latest** 🔷 [単数扱い] 略式 ▶定義 the most recent or the newest thing or piece of news 最も近い, または最も新しい出来事やニュース→**最新の物・事** ‖ *This is the very latest in computer technology.* これはコンピュータ技術の最新のものです. / *This is the latest in a series of attacks by this terrorist group.* これはこのテロリスト集団による一連の襲撃のうち最も新しいものです.

成句 **at the latest** ▶定義 no later than the time or the date mentioned 特定の時間または日に遅れない→**遅くとも** ‖ *You need to hand your projects in by Friday at the latest.* 遅くとも金曜日までにプロジェクトを提出しなければならない.

**lather** /ˈlæðər, ˈlɑː-/ 🔷 Ⓤ ▶定義 a white mass of bubbles that are produced when you mix soap with water せっけんを水と混ぜたときに発生する白い泡の塊→**せっけん[洗剤]の泡**

**Latin** /ˈlætɪn/ 🔷 Ⓤ ▶定義 the language that was used in ancient Rome 古代ローマで使われた言語→**ラテン語** — **Latin** 形→**ラテン語の, ラテン系の言語の, ラテン系の** ‖ *Latin poetry* ラテン語の詩 / *Spanish, Italian and other Latin languages (= that developed from Latin)* スペイン語, イタリア語, そのほかのラテン系言語 (= ラテン語から派生した言語)

**Latin American** 🔷 ⓒ形 ▶定義 (a person who

comes) from Latin America (the parts of Central and South America where Spanish or Portuguese is spoken) ラテンアメリカ(スペイン語やポルトガル語を話す中南米地域)出身の(人)→**ラテンアメリカの, ラテンアメリカ人(の), ラテン系民族(の)** ‖ *Latin American music* ラテンアメリカ音楽

**latitude** /lǽtət(j)ùːd/ 名 Ⓤ ▶定義 the distance of a place north or south of the line that we imagine around the middle of the earth (the equator) 地球の中央を巡る架空の線(赤道)から北または南に離れた距離→**緯度**

▶ latitude は度で表す. longitude を参照.

☞ earth のさし絵

**latter** /lǽtər/ 形 正式 (名詞の前だけ) ▶定義 nearer to the end of a period of time; later 一定の時間の終わり近く; 後の→**後半の, 終わりの** ‖ *Interest rates should fall in the latter half of the year.* 年の後半には金利は下がるはずだ. — **latterly** 副 →**後期に, 後に**

**the latter** 名 [単数扱い] ▶定義 the second (of two people or things that are mentioned) (前述の2人または2つのうちの)2番目→**後者** ‖ *The options were History and Geography. I chose the latter.* 選択科目は歴史と地理だった. 私は後者を選んだ.

▶ the former (前者)は前述の2人または2つのうちの1番目.

*****laugh**¹ /lɑːf; lǽf/ 動 自 ▶定義 to make the sounds that show you are happy or amused うれしさや面白さを表す声を立てる→**(声を立てて)笑う, 面白がる** ‖ *His jokes always make me laugh.* 彼のジョークにはいつも笑ってしまう. *to laugh out loud* 大声で笑う

成句 **die laughing** ⇒ **DIE**

句動詞 **laugh at sb/sth** ▶定義1 to show, by laughing, that you think sb/sth is funny 笑うことで〜がこっけいなことを示す→**〜を聞いて[見て]笑う** ‖ *The children laughed at the clown.* 子供たちは道化師を見て笑った. ▶定義2 to show that you think sb is ridiculous 〜がばかげていることを示す→**〜をあざける, あざ笑う, 嘲笑(ちょうしょう)する** ‖ *Don't laugh at him. He can't help the way he speaks.* 彼を笑ってはいけません. 彼はあのような話し方しかできないのです.

**laugh**² /lɑːf; lǽf/ 名 Ⓒ ▶定義1 the sound or act of laughing 笑い声, 笑うこと→**笑い, 笑い方** ‖ *Her jokes got a lot of laughs.* 彼女のジョークに大笑いした. *We all had a good laugh at what he'd written.* 彼の文章を読んで皆大笑いした. ▶定義2 略式 a person or thing that is amusing こっけいな人や物→**おかしな人, 面白いこと, 物笑いの種**

成句 **for a laugh** ▶定義 as a joke 冗談として→**冗談で, 面白半分に, 笑わせるために**

**have the last laugh** ⇒ **LAST**¹

**laughable** /lɑ́ːfəb(ə)l; lǽf-/ 形 ▶定義 deserving to be laughed at; of very poor quality; ridiculous 笑われるに値する; 非常に低級な; ばかげた→**ばかばかしい, 軽べつに値する, 愚かな**

**laughing stock** 名 Ⓒ ▶定義 a person or thing that other people laugh at or make fun of (in an unpleasant way) ほかの人々に笑われたりからかわれたりする人や物(不快なやり方で)→**嘲笑(ちょうしょう)の的, 笑い者**

**laughter** /lɑ́ːftər; lǽf-/ 名 Ⓤ ▶定義 the sound or act of laughing 笑い声, 笑うこと→**笑い** ‖ *Everyone roared with laughter.* 皆大笑いした.

**launch**¹ /lɔ́ːntʃ/ 動 他 ▶定義1 to send a ship into the water or a spacecraft into the sky 船を水面に下ろす, または宇宙船を発射する→**(船)を進水させる, (飛行機など)を飛び立たせる, (ロケット)を打ち上げる** ▶定義2 to start sth new or to show sth for the first time 新しい事を始める, または〜を初めて公開する→**〜を開始する, (新製品)を売り出す** ‖ *to launch a new product onto the market* 新製品を市場に出す

**launch**² /lɔ́ːntʃ/ 名 Ⓒ ▶定義1 [通常は単数] the act of launching a ship, spacecraft, new product, etc 船, 宇宙船, 新製品などを送り出すこと→**進水, 発射, (新製品を)売り出すこと** ▶定義2 a large motor boat 大型のモーターボート→**ランチ, 汽艇**

**launderette** /lɔ̀ːndərét/ (米 **Laundromat** /lɔ́ːndrəmæ̀t/) 名 Ⓒ ▶定義 a type of shop where you pay to wash and dry your clothes in machines 料金を払って機械で衣類を洗い乾燥させるための店→**コインランドリー**

**laundry** /lɔ́ːndri/ 名 (複 **laundries**) ▶定義1 Ⓤ clothes, etc that need washing or that are being washed 洗濯が必要な衣類など, または洗濯している衣類→**洗濯物** ‖ *dirty laundry* 汚れた洗濯物

➤洗濯する行為を言う場合は, (doing) the washing と言う方が the laundry より一般的.
▶定義2 ◉a business where you send sheets, clothes, etc to be washed and dried シーツ, 衣類などを洗濯・乾燥してもらうための店➔クリーニング店, 洗濯屋

**lava** /láːvə/ 名 Ս ▶定義 hot liquid rock that comes out of a mountain with an opening in the top (volcano) 頂上に開口(火口)のある山(火山)から出る熱い溶融(ようゆう)状態の岩➔溶岩, 火山岩 ☛ volcano のさし絵

**lavatory** /lǽvət(ə)ri; -tɔ̀ːri/ 名 ◉ (復 **lavatories**)
正式 ▶定義1 a toilet トイレット➔(水洗)便器
▶定義2 a room that contains a toilet, a place to wash your hands, etc トイレのある部屋, 手などを洗う場所➔洗面所, 手洗い, 便所, トイレ ‖ Where's the ladies' lavatory, please? 婦人用お手洗いはどこですか. ☛参 toilet の注

**lavender** /lǽvəndər/ 名 Ս ▶定義 a garden plant with purple flowers that smells very pleasant 良い香りのする紫の花をつける園芸植物➔ラベンダー

**lavish**¹ /lǽvɪʃ/ 形 ▶定義1 giving or spending a large amount of money 大金を与える, または浪費する➔気前の良い, 浪費癖のある, ぜいたくな ‖ She was always very lavish with her presents. 彼女はいつもとても気前良く贈り物をした.
▶定義2 large in amount or number 量や数が多い➔豊富な, 十分の, たっぷりの ‖ a lavish meal たっぷりの食事

**lavish**² /lǽvɪʃ/ 動
句動詞 lavish sth on sb/sth ▶定義 to give sth generously or in large quantities to sb 〜に…を気前良く, または大量に与える➔〜を惜しみなく与える, 無駄遣いする

*****law** /lɔː/ 名 ▶定義1 ◉an official rule of a country or state that says what people may or may not do してよい事とよくない事を述べた国や州の公式の規則➔法, 法律, 法規 ‖ There's a new law about wearing seat belts in the back of cars. 車の後部座席でもシートベルトを着用するという新しい法律がある. ▶定義2 **the law** Ս all the laws in a country or state 国または州の法律すべて➔法, 国法 ‖ Stealing is **against the law**. 窃盗は法に反する. to break the law 法を犯す to obey the law 法に従う ☛参 legal ▶定義3 Ս the law as a subject of study or as a profession 研究の対象としてのまたは職業としての法律➔法学, 法律学, 法律業, 法律界 ‖ She is studying law. 彼女は法律を学んでいる. My brother works for **a law firm** in Brighton. 兄[弟]はブライトンの法律事務所に勤めている. ☛参 legal
▶定義4 ◉(in science) a statement of what always happens in certain situations or conditions (科学で)特定の状況または条件下で何が起こるかを言い表したもの➔法則, 原理, 原則 ‖ the laws of mathematics/gravity 数学・重力の法則
成句 **law and order** ▶定義 order a situation in which the law is obeyed 法律が遵守されている状態➔法と秩序(が保たれていること)

**law-abiding** 形 ▶定義 (used about a person) obeying the law (人について) 法律に従う➔法律をよく守る ‖ law-abiding citizens 法を守る市民

**lawbreaker** /lɔ́ːbrèɪkər/ 名 ◉ ▶定義 a person who does not obey the law; a criminal 法律に従わない人; 犯罪者➔法律違反者, 罪人

**law court** (または **court of law**) 名 ◉ ▶定義 a place where legal cases are decided by a judge and often by twelve members of the public (a jury) 裁判官と, しばしば12人の市民(陪審)によって訴訟事件が裁かれる場所➔法廷
➤法廷は case (事件)を, try (審理する)場である. defence, prosecution, witness も参照.

**lawful** /lɔ́ːfʊl, -f(ə)l/ 形 ▶定義 allowed or recognized by law 法律によって許される, または認められる➔合法の, 適法の ‖ We shall use all lawful means to obtain our demands. 請求権を得るためにすべての法的手段を行使するつもりだ.
☛参 legal, legitimate

**lawless** /lɔ́ːləs/ 形 ▶定義 (used about a person or his/her actions) breaking the law (人, または人の行為について) 法律を破る➔非合法的な, 不法な — **lawlessness** 名 Ս ➔非合法的なこと, 不法行為

**lawn** /lɔːn/ 名 ◉ Ս ▶定義 an area of grass in a garden or park that is regularly cut 定期的に刈り込まれる庭や公園の草地➔芝生(の生えている場所), 芝地 ☛ C7 ページのさし絵

**lawnmower** /lɔ́ːnmòʊər/ 名 ◉ ▶定義 a machine that is used for cutting the grass in a garden 庭の草を刈るための機械➔芝刈り機 ☛ garden のさし絵

**lawsuit** /lɔ́ːs(j)ùːt; -sùːt/ 名 C ▶定義 a legal argument in a court of law that is between two people or groups and not between the police and a criminal 法廷で行われる法律上の議論で, 警察と犯罪者間で行われる2人の人または団体間で行われるもの→訴訟

\***lawyer** /lɔ́ːjər, lɔ́ɪər/ 名 C ▶定義 a person who has a certificate in law 法律に関する免許を持つ人→弁護士, 法律家 ‖ *to consult a lawyer* 弁護士に相談する

▶ solicitor(事務弁護士)は法律上の助言をし, 法律関係の書類を作成し, 不動産などの売買を手掛ける弁護士. barrister(法廷弁護士)は法廷で弁護を行う弁護士. アメリカ英語では, 一般に弁護士の意味では attorney を使う.

**lax** /læks/ 形 ▶定義 not having high standards; not strict 高水準でない; 厳格でない→緩い, 締まりのない, 怠慢な, だらしのない ‖ *Their security checks are rather lax.* 彼らの安全確認はかなり手ぬるい.

\***lay**¹ /léɪ/ 動 他 (過, 過分 **laid** /léɪd/) ▶定義 1 to put sb/sth carefully in a particular position or on a surface 〜を注意して特定の位置や面に置く→〜を横たえる, 置く, 敷く, 広げる ‖ *She laid a sheet over the dead body.* 彼女は死体をシーツで覆った. *He laid the child gently down on her bed.* 彼は子供をそっとベッドに寝かせた. *'Don't worry,' she said, laying her hand on my shoulder.* 彼女は私の肩に手を置いて「大丈夫よ」と言った. ▶定義 2 to put sth in the correct position for a particular purpose 〜を特定の目的で正しい場所に置く→〜を並べる, 積む, 据え付ける, 建設する ‖ *They're laying new electricity cables in our street.* この通りに新しい電線を敷設中だ.

▶定義 3 to prepare sth for use 〜を使う準備をする→(食事など)の用意をする, 支度をする, 〜を整える ‖ *The police have laid a trap for him and I think they'll catch him this time.* 警察はわなを仕掛けたので, 今度こそ彼を捕まえるだろう. *Can you lay the table please (= put the knives, forks, plates, etc on it)?* テーブルの準備をしてください. (= テーブルにナイフ, フォーク, 皿などを並べる) ▶定義 4 to produce eggs 卵を産む→〜を産む, 産卵する ‖ *Hens lay eggs.* 雌鶏(めんどり)は卵を産む. ▶定義 5 (used with some nouns to give a similar meaning to a verb) to put (一部の名詞と用いて動詞的な意味にする)置く→(ある状態に)置く, する, 〜を負わせる ‖ *They laid all the blame on him (= they blamed him).* 彼らは彼にすべての責任を負わせた. (= 彼のせいにした) *to lay emphasis on sth (= emphasize it)* 強調を置く (= 強調する)→〜を力説する, 際立たせる

**句動詞** **lay sth down** ▶定義 to give sth as a rule 規則として決める→〜を規定する, 定める ‖ *It's all laid down in the rules of the club.* それはすべてクラブの規則で決められている.

**lay off (sb)** 略式 ▶定義 to stop annoying sb 〜を煩わせるのをやめる→(不快な事・害になる事を)やめる ‖ *Can't you lay off me for a bit?* 少しほうっておいてくれ.

**lay sb off** ▶定義 to stop giving work to sb 〜に仕事を与えるのをやめる→〜を一時解雇する ‖ *They've laid off 500 workers at the car factory.* その自動車工場では500人の労働者が一時解雇された.

**lay sth on** 略式 ▶定義 to provide sth 〜を供給する→〜を与える, (パーティーなど)を催す, (電気・ガスなど)を引く, (ペンキ)を塗る ‖ *They're laying on a trip to London for everybody.* 皆にロンドン旅行が用意される.

**lay sth out** ▶定義 1 to spread out a number of things so that you can see them easily or so that they look nice 見やすいように, または見栄えが良いように多くの物を広げる→〜を並べる, レイアウトする ‖ *All the food was laid out on a table in the garden.* 食べ物はすべて庭のテーブルに並べられた. ▶定義 2 to arrange sth in a planned way 計画通りに手配する→〜を計画する, 〜の段取りを決める

**lay**² /léɪ/ 形 (名詞の前だけ) ▶定義 1 (used about a religious teacher) who has not been officially trained as a priest (宗教的指導者について)聖職者としての正式の教育を受けていない→平信徒の, 俗人の ‖ *a lay preacher* 俗人の伝道者 ▶定義 2 without special training in or knowledge of a particular subject 特定の対象についての特別の教育を受けていない, または特別の知識のない→素人の, 本職でない

\***lay**³ **LIE**² の過去形

**layabout** /léɪəbàʊt/ 名 C 英 略式 ▶定義 a person who is lazy and does not do much work 怠

惰であまり働かない人→浮浪者,怠け者

**lay-by** (米 **rest stop**) 名 C (複 **lay-bys**) ▶定義 an area at the side of a road where vehicles can stop for a short time 乗り物を短時間止めることのできる道路わきの場所→休憩所,(道路の)待避場所

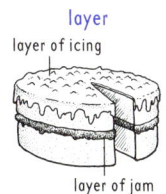
layer
layer of icing
layer of jam

***layer** /léɪər, léər/ 名 C ▶定義 a thickness or quantity of sth that is on sth else or between other things ほかの〜の上に重ねた,または間に挟まれた〜の厚さや量→層,重ね,(ペンキの)塗り ‖ *A thin layer of dust covered everything in the room.* 薄いほこりの層が部屋のすべての物を覆っていた. *It's very cold. You'll need several layers of clothing.* とても寒い.もっと重ね着した方がいいよ. *the top/bottom layer* 最上層・最下層 *the inner/outer layer* 内・外層

**layman** /léɪmən/ 名 C (複 -men /-men/) ▶定義 a person who does not have special training in or knowledge of a particular subject 特定の対象について特別の教育を受けていない,または特別の知識を持たない人→素人,門外漢 ‖ *a medical reference book for the layman* 一般の人のための医学参考書

**laze** /léɪz/ 動 自 ▶定義 laze (about/around) to do very little; to rest or relax ほんのわずかの事しかしない;休む,くつろぐ→怠ける,息抜きする,のんびりする

***lazy** /léɪzi/ 形 (**lazier**; **laziest**) ▶定義 1 (used about a person) not wanting to work (人について)働きたがらない→怠惰な,無精な ‖ *Don't be lazy. Come and give me a hand.* のらくらしていないで.手伝ってちょうだい. ▶定義 2 moving slowly or without much energy ゆっくりと,または活気なく動く様子→だるい,物憂げな ‖ *a lazy smile* 物憂げなほほえみ ▶定義 3 making you feel that you do not want to do very much あまり行動したくない気持ちにさせる→倦怠(けんたい)感を誘う,眠気を誘う ‖ *a lazy summer's afternoon* 気だるい夏の午後 — **lazily** 副 →怠惰に,気だるく — **laziness** 名 U →怠惰,だるさ,気だるさ

**lb** 略 pound(s) ▶定義 a measurement of weight 重さの単位→ポンド; 常衡16オンス(約454g), 金衡12オンス(約373g)

**lead**¹ /líːd/ 動 (過,過分 **led** /led/) ▶定義 1 他 to go with or in front of a person or animal to show the way or to make him/her/it go in the right direction 人や動物と一緒に,または先頭に立って進み,道を示す,または人・動物を正しい方向に導く→〜を導く,案内する,率いる ‖ *The teacher led the children out of the hall and back to the classroom.* 先生は子供たちを廊下から教室に連れ戻した. *She led the horse into its stable.* 彼女は馬を馬小屋に連れていった. *The receptionist **led the way** to the boardroom.* 受付係が会議室へ案内した. *to lead sb by the hand* 〜の手を引く

► guide は通常は旅行者や特に手助けが必要な人を案内すること: *to guide visitors around Oxford* (訪問者にオックスフォード近辺を案内する) *He guided the blind woman to her seat.* (彼は目の不自由な女性を席に案内した.) direct は道順などを言葉で説明すること: *Could you direct me to the nearest Post Office, please?* (一番近い郵便局までの道順を教えてください.)

▶定義 2 自 (used about a road or path) to go to a place (道路や通路について)ある場所へ行く→通じる,至る,つながる ‖ *I don't think this path leads anywhere.* この道は行き止まりのようだ. ▶定義 3 **lead to sth** to have sth as a result ある結果になる→〜を引き起こす,〜に結び付く,(ある結果)となる ‖ *Eating too much sugar can lead to all sorts of health problems.* 砂糖をとりすぎるとあらゆる健康障害が起こる可能性がある. ▶定義 4 **lead sb to do sth** to influence what sb does or thinks 〜の行動や考えに影響を与える→〜に…する気にさせる,〜に…するように仕向ける ‖ *He led me to believe he really meant what he said.* 彼は自分の言葉は本気だと私に信じさせた. ▶定義 5 他 to have a particular type of life ある特定の生活をする→過ごす,送る,暮らす ‖ *They lead a very busy life.* 彼らはとても忙しい暮らしをしている. *to lead a life of crime* 犯罪をなりわいとする ▶定義 6 自 他 to be winning or in first place in front of sb 勝者となる,または〜の前に立ち第1位となる→リードする,1番になる,他に勝る ‖ *Hingis is leading by* *two games to love.* ヒンギスが2対0でリードしている. *Hingis is leading Williams by two games to love.* ヒンギスが2対0でウィリアムズをリードしている. ▶定義7 🗐 ⓤ to be in control or the leader of sth 何かを支配する, または何かのリーダーとなる→(～を)指揮する, 先導する ‖ *Who is going to lead the discussion?* だれが議長を務めるのですか.

成句 **lead sb astray** ▶定義 to make sb start behaving or thinking in the wrong way 誤った行動を取らせたり, 誤った考えを持たせる→～を惑わす, 堕落させる, 邪道に導く

句動詞 **lead up to sth** ▶定義 to be an introduction to or cause of sth ～の導入部や原因となる→～につながる, ～に話を向ける, 結局は～ということになる

**lead**² /liːd/ 🗐 ▶定義1 **the lead** [単数扱い] the first place or position in front of other people or organizations ほかの人々や組織より前の第1位, または第1の地位→先頭, 先導, 優位 ‖ *The French athlete has gone **into the lead**.* フランス人の選手がトップになった. *Who is **in the lead**?* だれが先頭ですか. *Britain has **taken the lead** in developing computer software for that market.* その市場向けのコンピューターソフトウェア開発では英国が優位に立っている.

▶定義2 [単数扱い] the distance or amount by which sb/sth is in front of another person or thing ～がほかの人や物より先に立っている場合の距離や量→リード, 勝ち越し, 優勢 ‖ *The company has a lead of several years in the development of the new technology.* その会社は新技術の開発において数年進んでいる.

▶定義3 ⓒ the main part in a play, show or other situation 演劇, ショー, そのほかの主な役→主役, 主演俳優, 立役者 ‖ *Who's playing the lead in the new film?* 新しい映画の主演はだれ. *Jill played **a lead role** in getting the company back into profit.* ジルが会社を黒字に転換するための立役者だった. ▶定義4 ⓒ a piece of information that may help to give the answer to a problem 問題の答えのヒントとなる情報→手掛かり, 糸口, きっかけ ‖ *The police are following all possible **leads** to track down the killer.* 警察は殺人犯を捕まえるためあらゆる手掛かりを追っている. ▶定義5 ⓒ a long chain or piece of leather that is connected to the collar around a dog's neck and used for keeping the dog under control 犬の首輪につながれた長い鎖や革ひもで, 犬を制御しておくために使われる→引きひも ‖ *All dogs must be **kept on a lead**.* 犬はすべてつないでおかなければいけません.

▶定義6 ⓒ a piece of wire that carries electricity to a piece of equipment 装置に電気を伝える電線→導線, リード線 ☞ **cable** のさし絵

成句 **follow sb's example/lead** ⇒ **FOLLOW**

**lead**³ /led/ 🗐 ▶定義1 ⓤ (元素記号 Pb) a soft heavy grey metal. Lead is used in pipes, roofs, etc. 柔らかく重い灰色の金属. パイプ, 屋根などに使われる→鉛 ▶定義2 ⓒ ⓤ the black substance inside a pencil that makes a mark when you write 書くときに黒い跡を残す, 鉛筆の中にある黒い物質→(鉛筆の)黒鉛, 芯(しん)

***leader** /ˈliːdər/ 🗐 ⓒ ▶定義1 a person who is a manager or in charge of sth 管理者, 何かを統率する人→先導者, 指導者, リーダー, 統率者 ‖ *a weak/strong leader* 弱い・強いリーダー *She is a natural leader (= she knows how to tell other people what to do).* 彼女は生まれついての指導者だ (= 彼女はほかの人々に何をすべきか示す方法を知っている). ▶定義2 the person or thing that is best or in first place 最上, または第1位の～→首位・先頭の～ ‖ *The leader has just finished the third lap.* 先頭が3周目を終えたところだ. *The new shampoo soon became a market leader.* 新しいシャンプーはすぐに市場を先導する商品となった.

**leadership** /ˈliːdərʃɪp/ 🗐 ▶定義1 ⓤ the state or position of being a manager or the person in charge 管理者や責任者であること, またはその地位→指導, 指揮, 統率, リーダーシップ ‖ *Who will take over the leadership of the party?* だれがその政党の指導者の地位を引き継ぐのか.

▶定義2 ⓤ the qualities that a leader should have 指導者としての資質→指導力, 統率力 ‖ *She's got good leadership skills.* 彼女には優れた指導力がある. ▶定義3 [ⓒ, 単数または複数形の動詞と共に] the people who are in charge of a country, organization, etc 国, 組織などを統率する人々→指導部, 指導者たち, 首脳部

**leading** /ˈliːdɪŋ/ 🗐 ▶定義1 best or most important 最上の, 最も重要な→第一流の, 卓越した, 主

要な ‖ *He's one of the leading experts in this field.* 彼はこの分野の第一人者だ. *She played a leading role in getting the business started.* 彼女は業務の立ち上げにおいて中心的な役割を果たした. ▶定義2 that tries to make sb give a particular answer ～に特定の答えを与えさせるような→導く, 誘導的な ‖ *The lawyer was warned not to ask the witness leading questions.* 証人に誘導尋問をしないようにと弁護士は警告された.

**lead story** 名 ● ▶定義 the most important piece of news in a newspaper or on a news programme 新聞やニュース番組の最も重要なニュース→トップ記事, トップニュース

\***leaf**¹ /liːf/ 名 ● (覆 **leaves** /liːvz/) ▶定義 one of the thin, flat, usually green parts of a plant or tree 草や樹木の薄く平らで通常は緑色の部分→葉 ‖ *The trees lose their leaves in autumn.* 秋にはその木々は葉を落とす. ☞ C2, C3 ページのさし絵

**leaf**² /liːf/ 動
句動詞 **leaf through sth** ▶定義 to turn the pages of a book, etc quickly and without looking at them carefully 本などのページを素早くあまりよく見ずにめくる→(ページ)をさっとめくる, ～にざっと目を通す

\***leaflet** /ˈliːflət/ 名 ● ▶定義 a printed piece of paper that gives information about sth. Leaflets are usually given free of charge. ある事に関する情報が印刷された紙片. 通常無料で配布される→散らし, 折り込み印刷物, リーフレット ‖ *I picked up a leaflet advertising a new club.* 新しいクラブを宣伝する散らしをもらった.

**leafy** /ˈliːfi/ 形 ▶定義1 having many leaves 多くの葉をつけた→葉の多い, 葉の茂った ‖ *a leafy bush* 葉の茂った低木 ▶定義2 (used about a place) with many trees (場所について) 木が多い→緑の多い

**league** /liːɡ/ 名 ● ▶定義1 a group of sports clubs that compete with each other for a prize 賞を目指して競い合うスポーツクラブの集団→競技連盟, リーグ ‖ *the football league* サッカーリーグ *Which team is top of the league at the moment?* 今, リーグのトップのチームはどこですか. ☞参 **rugby league** ▶定義2 a group of people, countries, etc that join together for a particular purpose 特定の目的のために結び付いた人々

や国などの集団→同盟, 連盟, 盟約 ‖ *the League of Nations* 国際連盟 ▶定義3 a level of quality, ability, etc 品質, 能力などの水準→部類, 範疇(はんちゅう) ‖ *He is so much better than the others. They're just not in the same league.* 彼は皆よりはるかに優秀だ. 皆とは全く部類が違う.
成句 **in league (with sb)** ▶定義 having a secret agreement (with sb) ～とひそかに合意する→(～と)同盟して, 結託して, ぐるで

\***leak**¹ /liːk/ 動 ▶定義1 自 他 to allow liquid or gas to get through a hole or crack 穴や裂け目から液体や気体が通る→漏れる, 漏る; 少しずつ入ってくる, ～を漏らす ‖ *The boat was leaking badly.* ボートは浸水がひどかった. ▶定義2 自 (used about liquid or gas) to get out through a hole or crack (液体や気体について) 穴や裂け目から漏れる→漏れる, 漏れ出る ‖ *Water is leaking in through the roof.* 屋根から水が漏れている.
▶定義3 他 **leak sth (to sb)** to give secret information to sb ～に秘密の情報を与える→(人に)(秘密)を漏らす, (秘密・情報)を流す ‖ *The committee's findings were leaked to the press before the report was published.* 委員会の結論は報告書が発表される前に報道関係者に漏れた.
句動詞 **leak out** ▶定義 (used about secret information) to become known (極秘情報について) 知るところとなる→漏れる, ばれる, 漏洩(ろうえい)する

\***leak**² /liːk/ 名 ● ▶定義1 a small hole or crack which liquid or gas can get through 液体や気体が通ることのできる小さい穴や裂け目→漏れ口, 漏れ穴 ‖ *There's a leak in the pipe.* パイプに穴が開いている. *The roof has sprung a leak.* 屋根に穴が開いた. ▶定義2 the liquid or gas that gets through a hole 穴から出る液体や気体→漏れ, 漏出量 ‖ *a gas leak* ガス漏れ ▶定義3 the act of giving away information that should be kept secret 秘密にしておくべき情報を漏らすこと→漏洩(ろうえい), 漏洩の経路 ― **leaky** 形→穴の開いた, 漏れやすい

**leakage** /ˈliːkɪdʒ/ 名 ● ▶定義 the action of coming out of a hole or crack; the liquid or gas that comes out 穴や裂け目から漏れる様子; 漏れ出る液体や気体→漏れ, 漏出(量) ‖ *a leakage of dangerous chemicals* 危険な化学物質の漏出

956　lean¹

She is leaning against a tree.　He is leaning out of a window.

**\*lean**¹ /líːn/ 動(過, 過分 **leant** /lént/ または **leaned** /líːnd; lént/) ▶定義1 🅰 to move the top part of your body and head forwards, backwards or to the side 上半身と頭部を前方, 後方, または横に傾ける➡傾ける, 曲げる, かがむ ∥ *He leaned across the table to pick up the phone.* 彼はテーブルに身を乗り出して電話を取った. *She leaned out of the window and waved.* 彼女は窓から身を乗り出して手を振った. *Just lean back and relax.* さあ(体を後ろに傾けて), どうぞおくつろぎください. ▶定義2 🅰 to be in a position that is not straight or upright まっすぐや直立ではない状態➡傾いた, 傾斜している ∥ *That wardrobe leans to the right.* その洋服ダンスは右に傾いている. ▶定義3 🅰🅱 **lean (sth) against/on sth** to rest against sth so that it gives support; to put sth in this position 支えとして～に寄り掛かる; 物をそうした状態に置く➡～に寄り掛かる, もたれる, ～に(…を)もたせかける ∥ *She had to stop and lean on the gate.* 彼女は立ち止まって門に寄り掛からなければならなかった. *Please don't lean bicycles against this window.* この窓には自転車を立て掛けないでください.

**lean**² /líːn/ 形 ▶定義1 (used about a person or animal) thin and in good health (人や動物について)やせて健康状態がいいこと➡やせた, 身の締まった, 肉の落ちた ▶定義2 (used about meat) having little or no fat (肉について)ほとんど, または全く脂肪のない➡赤身の ▶定義3 not producing much 多くの収穫がない➡乏しい, (土地が)不毛の ∥ *a lean harvest* 凶作

**leap**¹ /líːp/ 動 🅰 (過, 過分 **leapt** /lépt, líːpt/ または **leaped** /líːp, lépt/) ▶定義1 to jump high or a long way 高く・遠く跳ぶ➡跳ぶ, 跳ねる, 躍る ∥ *The horse leapt over the wall.* 馬が塀を飛び越えた. *A fish suddenly leapt out of the water.* 突然水面に魚が飛び上がった. *We all leapt into the air when they scored the goal.* ゴールが決まると, みんなが躍り上がった. (比喩)*Share prices leapt to a record high yesterday.* 株価は昨日記録的に跳ね上がった. ▶定義2 to move quickly 素早く動く➡さっと動く, 急いで行く ∥ *I looked at the clock and leapt out of bed.* 私は時計を見てベッドから飛び起きた. *She leapt back when the pan caught fire.* なべが燃え上がったので, 彼女は後へ飛びのいた.

句動詞 **leap at sth** ▶定義 to accept a chance or offer with enthusiasm 喜んで機会や申し出を受け入れる➡～に飛び付く, 飛び付くように応じる ∥ *She leapt at the chance to work in television.* 彼女はテレビの仕事をするチャンスに飛び付いた.

**leap**² /líːp/ 名 🅲 ▶定義1 a big jump 大きな跳躍➡高く・遠く跳ぶこと ∥ *He took a flying leap at the wall but didn't get over it.* 彼は壁に向かって大きくジャンプしたが, 乗り越えられなかった. (比喩)*My heart gave a leap when I heard the news.* そのニュースを聞いて心臓が飛び上がった. ▶定義2 a sudden large change or increase in sth ～の急激で大きい変化・増加➡急変, 飛躍, 急増 ∥ *The development of penicillin was a great leap forward in the field of medicine.* ペニシリンの開発によって医学は大きく前進した.

**leapfrog** /líːpfrɔ(ː)g/ 名 🅄 ▶定義 a children's game in which one person bends over and another person jumps over his/her back 1人が前かがみになり, もう1人がその背中を飛び越す子供の遊び➡馬跳び

**leap year** 名 🅲 ▶定義 one year in every four, in which February has 29 days instead of 28 2月が28日ではなく29日ある4年に1度の年➡うるう年

**\*learn** /lə́ːm/ 動 (過, 過分 **learnt** /lə́ːmt/ または **learned** /-d, -t/) ▶定義1 🅰🅱 **learn (sth) (from sb/sth)** to get knowledge, a skill, etc (from sb/sth) ～から知識や技術などを得る➡(～を)(…から)学ぶ, 習う, 習得する, 覚える, 身に付ける ∥ *I'm not very good at driving yet - I'm still*

*learning.* まだ運転はあまりうまくありません－今も練習中です. *We're learning about China at school.* 学校で中国について学んでいる. *Debbie is learning to play the piano.* デビーはピアノを習っている. *to learn a foreign language/a musical instrument* 外国語・楽器を習う *Where did you learn how to swim?* どこで泳ぎを覚えたのですか. ▶定義2 ⓔ learn (of/about) sth to get some information about sth; to find out ～についての情報を得る; 知る → (～のことを・～について)耳にする, 聞く‖ *I was sorry to learn about your father's death.* お父さまがお亡くなりになったそうでお気の毒でした. ▶定義3 ⓑ to study sth so that you can repeat it from memory 記憶して繰り返せるように覚える→～を暗記する, 記憶する ▶定義4 ⓔ to understand or realize 理解する, 悟る→分かる, 気が付く‖ *We should have learned by now that we can't rely on her.* 彼女は当てにならないと早く気が付くべきだった. *It's important to learn from your mistakes.* 誤りから学ぶことが大切だ.
成句 **learn the hard way** ▶定義 to understand or realize sth by having an unpleasant experience rather than by being told 人から教えられるのではなくつらい経験を通して～を理解する・気付く→つらい思いをして知る, 痛い目に遭って覚える

**learn your lesson** ▶定義 to understand what you must do/not do in the future because you have had an unpleasant experience つらい経験から, これから先すべきこと・してはいけないことを理解する→経験で教えられる, 身をもって知る, いい教訓となる, 懲りる

**learned** /lə́ːmɪd/ 形 ▶定義 having a lot of knowledge from studying; for people who have a lot of knowledge 勉強の結果豊富な知識を持っている; 豊富な知識を持っている人向けの→学識のある, 学問のある, 博識な; 学問的な, 学術的な

**learner** /lə́ːmər/ 名 ⓒ ▶定義 a person who is learning 学習中の人→学習者, 初心者‖ *a learner driver* 仮免許運転者 *books for young learners* 若い学習者向けの本

**learning** /lə́ːmɪŋ/ 名 ⓤ ▶定義1 the process of learning sth ～を学ぶ過程→学ぶこと, 習うこと, 覚えること, 学習‖ *new methods of language learning* 新しい語学学習方法 ▶定義2 knowledge that you get from studying 学習して得られる知識→学問, 学識, (習得した)技能

**lease** /liːs/ 名 ⓒ ▶定義 a legal agreement that allows you to use a building or land for a fixed period of time in return for rent 賃料と引き換えに一定の期間, 建物や土地を使用できる法律上の取り決め→賃貸借契約, 借地(借家)契約, 賃貸制度‖ *The lease on the flat runs out/expires next year.* アパートの賃貸契約は来年切れる・終了する — **lease** 動→～を賃貸する, 借りる‖ *They lease the land from a local farmer.* 彼らは地元の農家から土地を借りている. *Part of the building is leased out to tenants.* そのビルの一部はテナントに賃貸されている.

***least** /liːst/ 形代副 ▶定義1 ( little の最上級) smallest in size, amount, degree, etc 大きさ, 量, 程度などが最も小さい→最小の(もの), 最も少ない, 最も少なく, 最も～でなく‖ *He's got the least experience of all of us.* 彼は我々の中で最も経験が浅い. *You've done the most work, and I'm afraid John has done the least.* あなたが一番たくさん働き, ジョンは一番働かなかったようだ. ▶定義2 less than anyone/anything else; less than at any other time ほかのどんな～より少ない; ほかのどんな時より少ない→最も～でない‖ *He's the person who needs help least.* 彼は最も助けを必要としない人だ. *I bought the least expensive tickets* 私は一番安いチケットを買った. *My uncle always appears when we're least expecting him.* おじはいつも意外なときに現れる. ⇔ most

成句 **at least** ▶定義1 not less than, and probably more ～より少なくない, おそらく～より多い→少なくとも, 内輪に見ても‖ *It'll take us at least two hours to get there.* そこに着くには少なくとも2時間はかかるだろう. *You could at least say you're sorry!* せめて謝ったらどうなの. ▶定義2 even if other things are wrong たとえほかのことが違っていても→(ほかのことは)ともかくも, いずれにせよ‖ *It may not be beautiful but at least it's cheap.* 美しくはないかもしれないが, ともかく安い. ▶定義3 used for correcting sth that you have just said 言ったばかりのことを訂正する場合に用いて→少なくとも, とにかく, おそらく‖ *I saw him - at least I think I saw him.* 彼を見掛けたよ － 少なくとも

見たような気がしたんだ.

at the (very) least ▶定義 not less and probably much more 少なくない, おそらくずっと多い→**少なくとも, 最低に見積もっても** ‖ It'll take six months to build at the very least. 建築には最低でも6か月かかるだろう.

least of all ▶定義 especially not とりわけ～でない→**最も～でない, とりわけ～ない** ‖ Nobody should be worried, least of all you. だれも, とりわけあなたが心配することはない.

not in the least (bit) ▶定義 not at all 全く～ない→**全然～ない, 少しも～ない** ‖ It doesn't matter in the least. そんな事は全くどうでもいいことだ. I'm not in the least bit worried. 私は全然心配していない.

last but not least ⇒ **LAST**¹

to say the least ▶定義 used to say that sth is in fact much worse, more serious, etc than you are saying ～が言葉よりも実際にははるかに悪い, または重大な場合に用いて→**控えめに言っても** ‖ Adam's going to be annoyed, to say the least, when he sees his car. 自分の車を見たら, アダムは不快に思うどころではないだろう.

***leather** /léðər/ 名 Ⓤ ▶定義 the skin of animals which has been specially treated. Leather is used to make shoes, bags, coats, etc. 特別な処理をした動物の皮. 靴, バッグ, コートなどに使用される→**なめし革, 皮革** ‖ a leather jacket 皮のジャケット

***leave**¹ /líːv/ 動 (過, 過分 **left** /léft/) ▶定義 1 圁 Ⓥ to go away from sb/sth ～から離れる→**(～を)去る, 離れる, 出発する** ‖ We should leave now if we're going to get there by eight o'clock. 8時までにそこに着くためにはもう出掛けなければならない. I felt sick in class so I left the room. 授業中気分が悪くなったので教室から出た. At what age do most people leave school in your country? あなたの国では普通何歳まで学校教育を受けますか. Barry left his wife for another woman. バリーは妻を捨て別の女性と一緒になった.

▶ leave sb/sth は永久に去る場合にも, 一時的な場合にも使われる: He leaves the house at 8.00 every morning. (彼は毎朝8時に家を出る.) He left New York and went to live in Canada. (彼はニューヨークを去ってカナダに移住した.) depart はより正式な語で, 船, 列車, 航空機などに用いる: The 6.15 train for Bath departs from Platform 3. (バース行きの6時15分の列車は3番線から発車します.)

▶定義 2 Ⓥ to cause or allow sb/sth to stay in a particular place or condition; to not deal with sth ～を特定の場所や状態に置いておく; ～に対処しない→**～を…のままにしておく, ～をほうっておく** ‖ Leave the door open, please. ドアは開けておいてください. Don't leave the iron on when you are not using it. 使わないときアイロンの電源をつけっ放しにしてはいけない. Why do you always leave your homework till the last minute? どうしていつもぎりぎりになるまで宿題をやらないの. ▶定義 3 Ⓥ **leave sth (behind)** to forget to bring sth with you ～を持っていくのを忘れる→**～を置き忘れる, 置いて立ち去る** ‖ I'm afraid I've left my homework at home. Can I give it to you tomorrow? 宿題を家に忘れてきてしまいました. 明日提出してもいいですか. I can't find my glasses. Maybe I left them behind at work. 眼鏡が見つからない. 仕事場に置き忘れたようだ. ▶定義 4 Ⓥ to make sth happen or stay as a result 結果として起こす, またはある状態にする→**(物・傷・印象など)を残す** ‖ Don't put that cup on the table. It'll leave a mark. カップをテーブルに置かないで. 跡が残るから. ▶定義 5 Ⓥ to not use sth ～を使わない→**～を取っておく, 残しておく** ‖ Leave some milk for me, please. ミルクをいくらか残しておいて. ▶定義 6 Ⓥ to put sth somewhere ～をどこかへ置く→**～を残す, 置いていく** ‖ Val left a message on her answerphone. ヴァルは留守番電話にメッセージを残した. I left him a note. 私は彼にメモを残した. ▶定義 7 Ⓥ to give sth to sb when you die 死ぬときに～に…を残す→**(財産など)を残して死ぬ** ‖ In his will he left everything to his three sons. 彼は遺言ですべてを3人の息子に残した. ▶定義 8 Ⓥ to give the care of or responsibility for sb/sth to another person ～に対する世話や責任を他人にゆだねる→**～を任せる, 預ける, 託す** ‖ I'll **leave it to you** to organize all the food. 食べ物の準備はあなたにお任せします.

成句 **leave sb/sth alone** ▶定義 to not touch, annoy or speak to sb/sth ～に触らない・煩わさ

ない・話し掛けない➡~をほうっておく,~に干渉しない

**leave go (of sth)** ▶定義 to stop touching or holding sth ~を触ったり,つかんだりするのをやめる➡(~を)放す,(~から)手を離す ‖ *Will you please leave go of my arm.* 腕を放してください.

**be left high and dry** ⇒ **HIGH**¹

**leave sb in the lurch** ▶定義 to leave sb without help in a difficult situation 難しい状況で~を助けずにほうっておく➡~を窮地に捨て置く,見殺しにする

**leave sth on one side** ⇒ **SIDE**¹

句動詞 **leave sb/sth out (of sth)** ▶定義 to not include sb/sth ~を含めない➡~を省く,除外する,無視する ‖ *This doesn't make sense. I think the typist has left out a line.* これでは意味が分からない.タイピストが1行抜かしたようだ.

**leave**² /liːv/ 名 **U** ▶定義 a period of time when you do not go to work 仕事に行かない期間➡休暇(期間),賜暇 ‖ *Diplomats working abroad usually get a month's home leave each year.* 海外に赴任する外交官は通常,年に1回自国で1か月の休暇を取る. *annual leave* 毎年の休暇 *sick leave* 病欠 *Molly's not working - she's **on maternity leave**.* モリーは勤務していません – 産休を取っています. ☛参 **holiday** の注

**leaves** **LEAF**¹ の複数形

**lecture** /léktʃər/ 名 **C** ▶定義 **1** a lecture (on/about sth) a talk that is given to a group of people to teach them about a particular subject, especially as part of a university course 人々に特定の対象について教えるために話すこと(特に大学課程として)➡(~についての)講演,講義 ‖ *The college has asked a journalist to come and **give a lecture** on the media.* その大学は,あるジャーナリストにメディアについての講義を頼んだ. *a course of lectures* 連続講義 ▶定義 **2** a serious talk to sb that explains what he/she has done wrong or how he/she should behave ~に誤った行いや取るべき行動について真剣に話すこと➡説教,叱責(しっせき) ‖ *We got a lecture from a policeman about playing near the railway.* 線路のそばで遊んでいて警察官からお説教された. ― **lecture** 動 ➡講義をする,説教をする ‖ *Alex lectures in European studies at London University.* アレックスはロンドン大学でヨーロッパ研究について講義をする. *The policeman lectured the boys about playing ball games in the road.* 警官は道路でボール遊びをすることについて少年たちに注意した.

**lecturer** /léktʃərər/ 名 **C** ▶定義 a person who gives talks to teach people about a subject, especially as a job in a university 人々にある学科について教えるために話す人(特に大学での仕事として)➡講演者,講師,(大学の)講師

**led** **LEAD**¹ の過去・過去分詞形

**ledge** /ledʒ/ 名 **C** ▶定義 a narrow shelf underneath a window, or a narrow piece of rock that sticks out on the side of a cliff or mountain 窓の下にある細長い棚,または崖(がけ)や山の斜面から突き出た細長い岩➡棚,岩棚,(棚状の)出っ張り

**leek** /liːk/ 名 **C** ▶定義 a long thin vegetable that is white at one end with thin green leaves 一方の端が白く,細い緑の葉のある細長い野菜➡リーキ,ニラネギ,ポロネギ,西洋ネギ ☛ C3 ページのさし絵

**left**¹ **LEAVE**¹ の過去・過去分詞形

*****left**² /left/ 形 ▶定義 **1** on the side where your heart is in the body 体の心臓がある側の➡左の,左側の,左方の ‖ *I've broken my left arm.* 左腕を骨折した. ⇔ **right** ▶定義 **2** still available after everything else has been taken or used すべてを取り上げたり使用した後でもなお利用可能な➡残った,残りの ‖ *Is there any bread **left**?* パンが残っていますか. *How much time do we have **left**?* あとどのくらい時間がありますか. *If there's any money **left over**, we'll have a cup of coffee.* お金が余っているなら,コーヒーを飲みましょう.

*****left**³ /left/ 副 ▶定義 to or towards the left 左へ向かって➡左へ,左側へ,左方へ ‖ *Turn left just past the Post Office.* 郵便局のすぐ先を左へ曲がってください. ⇔ **right**

*****left**⁴ /left/ 名 ▶定義 **1** **U** the left side 左側➡左,左側,左方 ‖ *In Britain we drive **on the left**.* 英国では車は左側通行だ. *Our house is just **to/on the left** of that tall building.* うちはあの高いビルのすぐ左です. *If you look **to** your **left** you'll see one of the city's most famous landmarks.* 左手にこの市の最も有名な建物が見えます. ⇔ **right** ▶定義 **2** **the Left** [単数または複数形の動詞と共に] political parties or groups that support a particular set of ideas and beliefs (socialism) 特定の思想と信念(社会主義)を持つ政党または政治的団体→**左翼,左派(勢力),革新派,急進派**

**left-hand** 形(名詞の前だけ) ▶定義 of or on the left 左の,左にある→**左側の,左手の** ‖ *the left-hand side of the road* 道路の左側 *a left-hand drive car* 左ハンドルの車

**left-handed** 形副 ▶定義1 using the left hand rather than the right hand 右手よりも左手を使う→**左利きの** ‖ *Are you left-handed?* あなたは左利きですか. *I write left-handed.* 私は左手で字を書く. ▶定義2 made for left-handed people to use 左利きの人々が使うために作られた→**左利き用の,左手用の** ‖ *left-handed scissors* 左利き用のはさみ

**left-luggage office** 英(困 **baggage room**) 名 C ▶定義 the place at a railway station, etc where you can leave your luggage for a short time 鉄道駅などで一時的に手荷物を預ける場所→**手荷物一時預かり所**

**leftovers** /léftòʊvərz/ 名[複数扱い] ▶定義 food that has not been eaten when a meal has finished 食事が終わっても食べていない食物→**食べ残し,残り物**

**left wing** 名[単数扱い] ▶定義1 [単数または複数形の動詞と共に] the members of a political party, group, etc that want more social change than the others in their party 政党または政治的団体などのメンバーで,同じ党のほかの人々よりもより多くの社会的変革を望む人々→**左翼,左派,急進派,革新派** ‖ *the left wing of the Labour Party* 労働党左派 ▶定義2 the left side of the field in some team sports ある種の団体スポーツ競技場の左側→**左翼** ‖ *He plays on the left wing for Ajax.* 彼はアヤックスの左ウイングだ. — **left-wing** 形→**左翼の** ⇔ **right-wing**

\***leg** /leg/ 名 C ▶定義1 one of the parts of the body on which a person or animal stands or walks 人や動物が立ったり歩くための体の部位→**脚,下肢** ‖ *A spider has eight legs.* クモには脚が8本ある. *She sat down and crossed her legs.* 彼女は座って脚を組んだ. ☛ **insect** のさし絵 ▶定義2 one of the parts of a chair, table etc on which it stands いす,テーブルなどを支える部分→**脚,脚部** ‖ *the leg of a chair/table* いす・テーブルの脚 *a chair/table leg* いす・テーブルの脚部 ▶定義3 the part of a pair of trousers, shorts, etc that covers the leg ズボン,ショートパンツなどの脚を覆う部分→**(衣服の)脚の部分** ‖ *There's a hole in the leg of my trousers/my trouser leg.* ズボンの脚の所に穴が開いている. ▶定義4 one part or section of a journey, competition, etc 旅,競争などの1部分・1区間→**1行程,1区間** ‖ *The band are in Germany on the first leg of their world tour.* そのバンドは世界ツアーの最初にドイツに来ている.
成句 **pull sb's leg** ⇒ **PULL**¹
**stretch your legs** ⇒ **STRETCH**¹

**legacy** /légəsi/ 名 C (複 **legacies**) ▶定義 money or property that is given to you after sb dies, because he/she wanted you to have it ~が死んだ後に,その人の望みによって残される金銭や財産→**遺産,遺贈財産** ‖ *He received a large legacy from his grandmother.* 彼は祖母から大きな遺産を受け継いだ.

\***legal** /líːg(ə)l/ 形 ▶定義1 (名詞の前だけ) using or connected with the law 法律を行使する,または法律に関連した→**法律の,法律に関する,法律上の** ‖ *legal advice* 法的助言 *to take legal action against sb* ~に対して法的手段をとる *the legal profession* 法律専門家 ▶定義2 allowed by law 法によって認められた→**合法の,適法の,正当な** ‖ *It is not legal to own a gun without a licence.* 許可証なしに銃を所有することは違法である. ⇔ **illegal** ☛参 **lawful, legitimate** — **legally** /líːg(ə)li/ 副→**法律上,合法的に** ‖ *Schools are legally responsible for the safety of their pupils.* 学校は生徒の安全に関して法律上の責任がある.

**legality** /liːgǽləti/ 名 U ▶定義 the state of being legal 合法であること→**適法,合法性**

**legalize** (または **-ise**) /líːg(ə)làɪz/ 動 他 ▶定義 to make sth legal 合法的にする→**~を法律上正当と認める,合法化する,公認する**

**legend** /lédʒənd/ 名 ▶定義1 C an old story that may or may not be true 真偽の定かでない古い物語→**伝説,言い伝え** ‖ *the legend of Robin Hood* ロビンフッドの伝説 ▶定義2 U such stories when they are grouped together そのような物語をまとめたもの→**伝説文学** ‖ *According to legend, Robin Hood lived in Sherwood Forest.* 伝説によると,ロビンフッドはシャーウ

ッドの森に住んでいた. ▶定義3 ❸ a famous person or event 有名な人・出来事➡伝説化した**話, 伝説的人物, 有名な出来事** ‖ *a movie/jazz/baseball legend* 映画・ジャズ・野球史上の伝説的人物 ― legendary /lédʒənd(ə)ri; -èri/ 形 ➡伝説の, 伝説的な ‖ *the legendary heroes of Greek myths* ギリシャ神話の伝説的英雄 *Michael Jordan, the legendary basketball star* 伝説的バスケットボールのスター, マイケル ジョーダン

**leggings** /légɪŋz/ 名 [複数扱い] ▶定義 a piece of women's clothing that fits tightly over both legs from the waist to the feet, like a very thin pair of trousers 腰から足までの両脚部をぴったりと覆う女性の衣類で, 非常に薄いズボンなど➡**スパッツ** ☛C 6 ページのさし絵

**legible** /lédʒəb(ə)l/ 形 ▶定義 that is clear enough to be read easily 鮮明で簡単に読み取れる➡**判読できる, 読みやすい** ‖ *His writing is so small that it's barely legible.* 彼の文字はとても小さいのでほとんど読み取れない. ⇔ illegible ☛参 readable ― legibility /lèdʒəbíləti/ 名 🇺 ➡判読できること, 読み取りやすいこと ― legibly /lédʒəbli/ 副 ➡読み取りやすく

**legislate** /lédʒəslèɪt/ 動 🇪 ▶定義 legislate(for/against sth) to make a law or laws 法律を制定する➡**(～を認める・～を禁止する)法律を制定する, 法的規制を設ける**

**legislation** /lèdʒəsléɪʃ(ə)n/ 名 🇺 ▶定義1 a group of laws 集合的に見た法律➡**法律** ‖ *The government is introducing new legislation to help small businesses.* 政府は中小企業を支援するための新法を提出する. ▶定義2 the process of making laws 法律を制定する過程➡**立法**

**legitimate** /lɪdʒítəmət/ 形 ▶定義1 reasonable or acceptable 道理にかなった, または受け入れられる➡**合理的な, 筋道の通った, 妥当な** ‖ *a legitimate excuse/question/concern* もっともな言い訳・質問・関心 ▶定義2 allowed by law 法律で認められた➡**適法の, 正当な** ‖ *Could he earn so much from legitimate business activities?* 彼は合法的な仕事でそんなにもうけられるものなのですか. ☛参 lawful, legal ▶定義3 (古) (used about a child) having parents who are married to each other (子供について)結婚している両親を持つ➡**嫡出の** ⇔ illegitimate ― legitimately 副 ➡妥当に, 合法に, 正式に

**leisure** /lí:ʒər, lí:ʒ-/ 名 🇺 ▶定義 the time when you do not have to work; spare time 働く必要のない時間; 余分な時間➡**暇, 余暇, 自由時間** ‖ *Shorter working hours mean that people have more leisure.* 労働時間の短縮は余暇の増加を意味する. *leisure activities* 余暇活動

成句 **at your leisure** 正式 ▶定義 when you have free time 自由時間があるときに➡**(～の)暇なときに, 都合の良いときに** ‖ *Look through the catalogue at your leisure and then order by telephone.* 都合の良いときにカタログを見て, 電話で注文してください.

**leisure centre** 名 ❸ ▶定義 a public building where you can do sports and other activities in your free time 自由時間にスポーツやほかの活動を行うための公共の建物➡**レジャーセンター**

**leisurely** /lí:ʒərli; lí:ʒ-/ 形 ▶定義 without hurry 急がずに➡**ゆっくり, 時間をかけた, ゆったりした** ‖ *a leisurely Sunday breakfast* 日曜日のゆったりした朝食 *I always cycle at a leisurely pace.* 私はいつもゆっくりしたペースで自転車を走らせる.

*__lemon__ /lémən/ 名 ❸ 🇺 ▶定義 a yellow fruit with sour juice that is used for giving flavour to food and drink 食べ物や飲み物に風味を添えるために使われる酸っぱい果汁の黄色い果実➡**レモン** ‖ *a slice of lemon* レモンの輪切り *Add the juice of 2 lemons.* レモン2個分の果汁を加えます. ☛C3 ページのさし絵

**lemonade** /lèmənéɪd/ 名 ❸ 🇺 ▶定義1 因 a colourless sweet drink with a lot of bubbles in it 多くの泡の出る透明な甘い飲み物➡**レモンソーダ** ▶定義2 a drink that is made from fresh lemon juice, sugar and water 生のレモン果汁, 砂糖, 水から作られた飲み物➡**レモネード**

*__lend__ /lend/ 動 🇹 (過, 過分 **lent** /lent/) ▶定義1 **lend sb sth; lend sth to sb** to allow sb to use sth for a short time or to give sb money that must be paid back after a certain period of time ～が…を短時間使用することを許可する, 一定の期間がたったら返さなくばならない金を～に与える➡**～に…を貸す, 貸し付ける** ‖ *Could you lend me £10 until Friday?* 金曜日まで10ポンド貸してくれませんか. *He lent me his bicycle.* 彼は私に自転車を貸してくれた. *He lent his bicycle to me.* 彼は自転車を私に貸してくれた.

## lender

⇔ **borrow** ☞ **borrow** のさし絵
▶銀行などから金を借りる場合は, 特定の期間後に追加の支払い額 (interest(利子)と呼ばれる)を加えて pay back(返す)・repay(返済する) 必要がある.

▶定義2 正式 **lend sth (to sth)** to give or add sth ~を与える, または加える→(比喩的に)~を貸す, 添える ‖ *to lend advice/support* 忠告・支援を与える *This evidence lends weight to our theory.* この証拠によって我々の理論が強化される.

成句 **lend (sb) a hand/lend a hand (to sb)** ▶定義 to help sb ~を助ける→~を手伝う, 手助けする

句動詞 **lend itself to sth** ▶定義 to be suitable for sth ~に適切な→~の役に立つ, ~に向いている

**lender** /léndər/ 名 C ▶定義 a person or organization that lends sth, especially money ~を, 特に金を貸す人や組織→貸す人, 貸し主, 金貸し

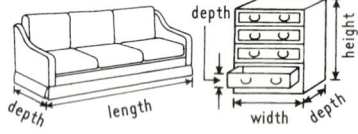

\*length /leŋ(k)θ/ 名 ▶定義1 U C the size of sth from one end to the other; how long sth is ~の端から端までの大きさ; ~の長さ→全長, 身長, 距離 ‖ *to measure the length of a room* 部屋の長さを測る *It took an hour to walk the length of Oxford Street.* オックスフォード通りを歩いて通り抜けるのに1時間かかった. *The tiny insect is only one millimetre* ***in length****.* その小さい昆虫の体長はわずか1ミリだ. *This snake can grow to a length of two metres.* この蛇は体長2メートルに成長することもある.
☞参 **width**, **breadth** ▶定義2 U the amount of time that sth lasts ~が持続する時間→(時間の)長さ, 全期間, 始めから終わりまで ‖ *Many people complained about the* ***length of time*** *they had to wait.* 大勢が待ち時間の長さに不平を言った. *the length of a class/speech/ film* 授業・スピーチ・映画の長さ ▶定義3 U the number of pages in a book, a letter, etc 本, 手紙などのページ数→(文などの)長さ・量 ▶定義4 C the distance from one end of a swimming pool to the other 水泳用プールの端から端までの距離→(泳いだ距離の単位としての)プールの長さ ‖ *I can swim a length in thirty seconds.* 私はこのプールを30秒で泳げる.
▶定義5 C a piece of sth long and thin 長く薄い~1つ→ある長さのもの ‖ *a length of material/rope/string* 1反の生地・1本のロープ・1本の糸

成句 **at length** ▶定義 for a long time or in great detail 長いこと, または大変詳しく→長々と, 詳細に, 徹底的に ‖ *We discussed the matter at great length.* 私たちはその問題について長時間議論した.

**go to great lengths** ▶定義 to make more effort than usual in order to achieve sth 何かを成し遂げるために通常よりも努力する→どんな事でもする, 徹底的にやる ‖ *I went to great lengths to find this book for you.* あらゆる手を尽くしてあなたのためにこの本を探しました.

**the length and breadth of sth** ▶定義 to or in all parts of sth ~のすべての部分の→~のあらゆる所, 隅々まで全部 ‖ *They travelled the length and breadth of India.* 彼らはインド全土をくまなく旅した.

**lengthen** /léŋ(k)θ(ə)n/ 動 自 他 ▶定義 to become longer or to make sth longer 長くなる, 長くする→伸びる; ~を伸ばす, 延長する

**lengthways** /léŋ(k)θwèɪz/ (または **lengthwise** /léŋ(k)θwàɪz/) 副 ▶定義 in a direction from one end to the other of sth ~の端から端までの方向に→縦に, 縦方向に, 長く ‖ *Fold the paper lengthwise.* 紙を縦に折りなさい.

**lengthy** /léŋ(k)θi/ 形 ▶定義 very long 非常に長い→長ったらしい, 冗長な

**lenient** /líːniənt/ 形 ▶定義 (used about a punishment or person who punishes) not as strict as expected (罰や罰を与える人について)求められるほど厳しくない→寛大な, 緩やかな, 手ぬるい, 甘い ― **lenience**(または **leniency** /-ənsi/) 名 U→寛大なこと, 緩やかなこと ― **leniently** 副→寛大に, 緩やかに, 甘く

**lens** /lenz/ 名 C (複 **lenses**) ▶定義1 a curved piece of glass that makes things look bigger, clearer, etc when you look through it 曲面になったガラスで, これを通して見ると物が大きく, 鮮明に見える→レンズ, 拡大鏡

➤ contact lenses(コンタクトレンズ)は視力を補うために使う人もいる. zoom/telephoto lens(ズーム・望遠レンズ)はカメラに使う.
☛**camera**のさし絵 ▶定義**2** ＝**CONTACT LENS** ☛**glasses**のさし絵

**lent**¹ **LEND**の過去・過去分詞形

**Lent**² /lént/ 名 ❶ ▶定義 a period of 40 days starting in February or March, when some christians stop doing or eating certain things for religious reasons 2月または3月に始まる40日の期間で,一部のキリスト教徒が宗教上の理由から特定の行為をやめたり,特定の物を食べなかったりする→**四旬節,受難節** ‖ *I'm giving up smoking for Lent.* 四旬節の間は禁煙するつもりだ.

**lentil** /lént(ə)l/ 名 ❻ ▶定義 a small brown, orange or green seed that can be dried and used in cooking 乾燥したり料理に使える茶,だいだい,または緑色の小さい種→**レンズ豆,ヒラ豆** ‖ *lentil soup/stew* レンズ豆のスープ・シチュー

**Leo** /líːoʊ/ 名 ❻ ❶ ▶定義 the fifth sign of the zodiac, the Lion 黄道十二宮の5番目である獅子(しし)座→**獅子座,獅子宮**

**leopard** /lépərd/ 名 ❻ ▶定義 a large wild animal of the cat family that has yellow fur with dark spots. Leopards live in Africa and Southern Asia. 暗色の斑点(はんてん)のある黄色い毛皮を持つネコ科の大型野生動物. アフリカと南アジアに生息する→**ヒョウ**

➤ leopardessは雌のヒョウ, cubはヒョウの子供.
☛**lion**のさし絵

**leotard** /líːətɑːrd/ 名 ❻ ▶定義 a piece of clothing that fits the body tightly from the neck down to the tops of the legs. Leotards are worn by dancers or women doing certain sports. 首から脚の付け根までの身体をぴったりと覆う衣類. ダンサーや特定のスポーツをする女性が身に着ける→**レオタード**

**leper** /lépər/ 名 ❻ ▶定義 a person who has leprosy ハンセン病の人→**ハンセン病患者**

**leprosy** /léprəsi/ 名 ❶ ▶定義 a serious infectious disease that affects the skin, nerves, etc and can cause parts of the body to fall off 皮膚,神経などを侵す伝染病で,身体の一部が脱落したりする→**ハンセン病**

**lesbian** /lézbiən/ 名 ❻ ▶定義 a woman who is

### lesser 963

sexually attracted to other women 女性に性的にひかれる女性→**レズビアン, 同性愛の女性, レズ** ― lesbian 形▶レズビアンの ‖ *a lesbian relationship* レズビアンの関係 ― lesbianism 名 ❶▶レズビアンであること, 女性間の同性愛
☛参 **gay, homosexual**

\***less**¹ /lés/ 形代副 ▶定義**1** (不可算名詞と共に用いて) a smaller amount (of) より少ない量(の)→**より少ない, より少ない量・程度・額** ‖ *It took less time than I thought.* 思っていたほど時間がかからなかった. *I'm too fat - I must try to eat less.* 私は太りすぎだ ― 食べる量を減らさなければ. *It's not far - it'll take less than an hour to get there.* 遠くはありません ― 1時間かからずにそこに着くでしょう.

➤ less cars のように, less が複数名詞に使われる場合もあるが, fewer cars のように, fewer の方が正しい形と見なされている.

▶定義**2** not so much (as) ほど~でなく→**より~でなく, より少なく** ‖ *He's less intelligent than his brother.* 彼は兄[弟]ほど聡明(そうめい)ではない. *It rains less in London than in Manchester.* ロンドンはマンチェスターより雨が少ない. *People work less well when they're tired.* 疲れていると十分に働けない. ⇔ **more**

成句 less and less ▶定義 becoming smaller and smaller in amount or degree 量や程度が次第に小さくなる→**だんだん少なく**

more or less ⇒ **MORE**²

**less**² /lés/ 前 ▶定義 taking a certain number or amount away; minus 一定の数や量を除く; マイナス→**~を減じた, ~を差し引いた, ~だけ足りない** ‖ *You'll earn £10 an hour, less tax.* 時給は税引きで10ポンドです.

**lessen** /lés(ə)n/ 動 ❶ ❶ ▶定義 to become less; to make sth less より少なくなる; より少なくする→**減る, ~を減らす**

**lesser** /lésər/ 形副 (名詞の前だけ) ▶定義 not as great/much as それほど重大でない, 多くない→**より劣る, つまらない, より少なく** ‖ *He is guilty and so, **to a lesser extent**, is his wife.* 彼は有罪であり, それほどではないが彼の妻も同様だ. *a lesser-known artist* あまり有名でない芸術家

成句 the lesser of two evils ▶定義 the better

of two bad things 2つの悪い事のうち良い方➔ ましな方

***lesson** /lés(ə)n/ 🔢 🅒 ▶定義1 a period of time when you learn or teach sth ～を学ぶ,または教える時間➔**学課,授業,稽古(けいこ),レッスン** ∥ *She gives piano lessons.* 彼女はピアノを教えている. / *I want to take extra lessons in English conversation.* 私は英会話の補習を受けたい. *a driving lesson* 自動車運転教習 ▶定義2 something that is intended to be or should be learnt 学ばせるつもりの,または学ばなければならないもの➔**教訓,みせしめ,訓戒** ∥ *I hope we can learn some lessons from this disaster.* この災害を教訓にしたいものだ.

成句 learn your lesson ⇒ **LEARN**
teach sb a lesson ⇒ **TEACH**

***let** /let/ 動 ⑭ (現分 **letting**; 過, 過分 **let**) ▶定義1 let sb/sth do sth to allow sb/sth to do sth; to make sb/sth able to do sth ～が何かをすることを許す;～が何かをできるようにする ➔**～に…させてやる,させておく,してもらう,することを許す** ∥ *My parents let me stay out till 11 o'clock.* 両親は私の外出を11時まで許可してくれる. / *I wanted to borrow Dave's bike but he wouldn't let me.* デーブの自転車を借りたかったのだが,彼は貸してくれなかった. *This ticket lets you travel anywhere in the city for a day.* この切符で1日,町中をどこでも見て回れる.

▶ let はこの意味では受動態は使えない. allow または permit と to 不定詞を使わねばならない: *They let him take the exam again.*(彼は追試を受けられた.) *He was allowed to take the exam again.*(彼は追試を受けることを許可された.) allow の注を参照.

▶定義2 to allow sth to happen ～が起こることを許す➔**～を…するままにしておく,うっかり～させる** ∥ *He's let the dinner burn again!* 彼はまた料理を焦がしたよ. *Don't let the fire go out.* 火が消えないようにして. ▶定義3 used for offering help to sb ～に手を貸す場合に用いて➔**～させる** ∥ *Let me help you carry your bags.* バッグをお持ちしましょう. ▶定義4 to allow sb/sth to go somewhere ～がどこかへ行くのを許す➔**～を…に行かせる,来させる,通す,入れる,～を…から出す** ∥ *Open the windows and let some fresh air in.* 窓を開けて新鮮な空気を入れなさい. *She was let out of prison yesterday.* 彼女は昨日釈放された. ▶定義5 used for making suggestions about what you and other people can do あなたとほかの人々ができることを提案する場合に用いて➔**～しよう,～しましょう** ∥ *'Let's go to the cinema tonight.' 'Yes, let's.'*「今夜,映画に行こう」ー「そうしよう」

▶ let's の否定形は let's not または(英のみで) don't let's: *Let's not/Don't let's go to that awful restaurant again.*(あのひどいレストランには二度と行かないことにしよう.)

▶定義6 let sth (out) (to sb) to allow sb to use a building, room, etc in return for rent 賃貸料と引き換えに～に建物,部屋などを使わせる ➔**～を(…に)貸す,賃貸する** ∥ *They let out two rooms to students.* 彼らは学生に2部屋貸している. *There's a flat to let in our block.* このブロックに賃貸用フラットがあります. ☛参 hire の注

成句 let alone ▶定義 and certainly not そしてもちろん～でない➔**～はもちろんとして,まして～はさらさらない** ∥ *We haven't decided where we're going yet, let alone booked the tickets.* まだどこに行くかも決めていないし,ましてや切符の予約なんて.

let sb/sth go; let go of sb/sth ▶定義 to stop holding sb/sth ～をつかむのをやめる➔**～から手を離す,～を放す** ∥ *Let me go. You're hurting me!* 離して.痛い. *Hold the rope and don't let go of it.* ロープをつかんで離さないで.

let sb know ▶定義 to give sb a piece of information; to tell sb ～に情報を与える;～に教える➔**～に知らせる,教える** ∥ *I'll phone you to let you know what time we'll be arriving.* 電話して,何時に着くかお知らせします.

let me see; let's see ▶定義 used when you are thinking or trying to remember sth 考えているときや何かを思い出そうとするときに用いて➔**ええと,はてな** ∥ *Where did I put the car keys? Let's see. I think I left them by the telephone.* 車のキーをどこへ置いたっけ.ええと.電話のそばに置いたと思うのだけど.

let sth slip ▶定義 to accidentally say sth that you should keep secret 秘密にしておくべき事を誤って言う➔**～について口を滑らす,～をうっかりしゃべる**

**let's say** ▶定義 for example 例えば→そうだな, まあ～くらい ‖ *You could work two mornings a week, let's say Tuesday and Friday.* 週に２回午前中に働けます, 例えば火曜日と金曜日に.

**let yourself go** ▶定義**1** to relax without worrying what other people think ほかの人々がどう思うかを気にせずにくつろぐ→**(いつもより)自由に振る舞う, 思い切り楽しむ, はめを外す** ‖ *After work I like to go out with friends and let myself go.* 仕事が終わったら, 友達と外出して思い切り楽しみたい. ▶定義**2** to allow yourself to become untidy, dirty, etc 無精・不潔にする→**(体などに)気を付けない, 身なりを構わない**

句動詞 **let sb down** ▶定義 to not do sth that you promised to do for sb; to disappoint sb ～にすると約束した事をしない;～を失望させる→**～をがっかりさせる, 裏切る** ‖ *Rob really let me down when he didn't finish the work on time.* 仕事を時間通りに終わらせないので, ロブには本当に失望した.

**let on (about sth) (to sb)** ▶定義 to tell sb a secret ～に秘密を話す→**白状する, 口外する** ‖ *He didn't let on how much he'd paid for the vase.* その花びんにいくら払ったのか, 彼は言わなかった.

**let sb off** ▶定義 to not punish sb, or to give sb a lesser punishment than expected ～を罰しない, または～に本来より軽い罰を与える→**～の罰を免除する, ～を(軽い刑などで)放免する** ‖ *He expected to go to prison but they let him off with a fine.* 彼は自分が実刑になると予想していたが, 罰金で許された.

**let sth out** ▶定義 to make a sound with your voice 声を出す→**(叫び声など)を出す, (秘密)を漏らす** ‖ *to let out a scream/sigh/groan/yell* 悲鳴を上げる・ため息をつく・うめき声を出す・わめく

**lethal** /líːθ(ə)l/ 形 ▶定義 that can cause death or great damage 死や大きな損害をもたらす→**致死の, 致命的な** ‖ *a lethal weapon/drug* 凶器・致死の薬物 — **lethally** /líːθ(ə)li/ 副 →**致命的に**

**lethargy** /léθərdʒi/ 名 U ▶定義 the feeling of being very tired and not having any energy 非常に疲れて全く活気がない感覚→**倦怠(けんたい), 脱力感, 無気力** — **lethargic** /ləθɑ́ːrdʒɪk, le-/ 形 →**気だるい, 無気力な**

## level¹ 965

\***letter** /létər/ 名 C ▶定義**1** a written or printed message that you send to sb ～に送る手書きや印刷の伝言→**手紙, 書簡** ‖ *I got a letter from Matthew this morning.* 今朝マシューから手紙が届いた. *I'm writing a thank-you letter to my uncle for the flowers he sent.* おじさんに花束の礼状を書いているところです.

▶手紙を書いたら, envelope (封筒)に入れる. あて名を書くことを address, 切手をはることを put/stick a stamp, 投かんすることを post (米 mail) と言う. 引っ越した人に手紙を forward (転送する) こともできる.

▶定義**2** a written or printed sign that represents a sound in a language ある言語の音を表す手書きや印刷された記号→**文字, 字** ‖ *'Z' is the last letter of the English alphabet.* Zは英語アルファベットの最後の文字です.

▶文字は capitals (大文字) でも small letters (小文字) でも書いたり印刷したりできる: *Is 'east' written with a capital or a small 'e'?* (east の e は大文字ですか, 小文字ですか.)

**letter box** 名 C ▶定義**1** a hole in a door or wall for putting letters, etc through 手紙などを入れるためのドアや壁の穴→**郵便受け** ▶定義**2** (米 **mailbox**) a small box near the main door of a building or by the road in which letters are left for the owner to collect 持ち主が受け取るために手紙が入れられる, 建物の玄関や道路の横にある小さな箱→**郵便箱** ▶定義**3** = **POSTBOX**

**lettuce** /létəs/ 名 C U ▶定義 a plant with large green leaves which are eaten cold in salads サラダにして冷たいままで食べる大きな緑の葉のある植物→**レタス, チシャ** ‖ *a lettuce leaf* レタスの葉 ☛ C3 ページのさし絵

**leukaemia** (米 **leukemia**) /luː(ː)kíːmiə/ 名 U ▶定義 a serious disease of the blood which often results in death 血液の重大な病気で, しばしば死に至る→**白血病**

\***level**¹ /lév(ə)l/ 名 C ▶定義**1** the amount, size or number of sth (compared to sth else) (ほかと比較した場合の)～の量, 大きさ, または数→**数値, 程度, 段階, レベル** ‖ *a low level of unemployment* 低い失業率 *high stress/pollution levels* 高い圧力・汚染レベル ▶定義**2** the height, position, standard, etc of sth ～の高さ, 位置, 標準など→

水準, 段階 ‖ *He used to play tennis at a high level.* 彼は高度なテニスをしたものだ. *an intermediate-level student* 中レベルの生徒 *top-level discussions* 高度な議論 ▶定義3 a way of considering sth ～を考えるやり方→面, 側面 ‖ *on a spiritual/personal/professional **level*** 精神的・個人的・プロ並みのレベルで ▶定義4 a flat surface or layer 平らな面, 層→平面, (建物などの)階 ‖ *a multi-level shopping centre* 階層構造のショッピングセンター

\***level**² /lév(ə)l/ 形 ▶定義1 with no part higher than any other; flat ほかより高い部分のない; 平らな→水平な, 平たんな ‖ *Make sure the shelves are level before you fix them in position.* 棚を取り付ける前に水平であることを確認しなさい. *Put the tent up on level ground.* 平らな地面にテントを張りなさい. *a level teaspoon of sugar* ティースプーンすり切り1杯の砂糖 ▶定義2 level (with sb/sth) at the same height, standard or position 同じ高さ, 水準, または位置の→(～と)同じ高さの, 同等の, 対等の ‖ *The boy's head was level with his father's shoulder.* 少年の頭は父親の肩の高さだった. *The teams are level on 34 points.* 両チームとも34点で互角だ.

成句 a level playing field ▶定義 a situation in which everyone has an equal chance of success 皆に等しく成功のチャンスがある状況→互角の立場, 同じ土俵

**level**³ /lév(ə)l/ 動 他 (**levelling**; **levelled**: 米 **leveling**; **leveled**) ▶定義 to make sth flat, equal or level ～を平らに, 同等に, または水平にする→～を水平にする, 平らにする, 平等にする, なぎ倒す, 一様にする ‖ *The ground needs levelling before we lay the patio.* スペイン風中庭を造る前に地面をならす必要がある. *Juventus levelled the score with a late goal.* ユベントスが後からゴールを決めて同得点になった. *Many buildings were levelled (= destroyed) in the earthquake.* 多くの建物が地震でなぎ倒された (= 破壊された).

句動詞 level sth at sb/sth ▶定義 to aim sth at sb/sth ～を…に向ける→(銃・視線・非難など)を～に向ける, ねらう, 構える ‖ *They levelled serious criticisms at the standard of teaching.* 彼らは授業の水準に対して厳しい非難を浴びせた.

level off/out ▶定義 to become flat, equal or level 平たんに, 同等に, または水平になる→平らになる, 同じになる

**level crossing** (米 **railroad crossing**) 名 C ▶定義 a place where a railway crosses the surface of a road 鉄道が道路面と交差する場所→踏切

**level-headed** 形 ▶定義 calm and sensible; able to make good decisions in a difficult situation 冷静で分別のある; 困難な状況で優れた判断ができる→穏健な, 理性的な, 冷静な, 分別のある

**lever** /lévər, líːvər/ 名 C ▶定義1 a handle that you pull or push in order to make a machine, etc work 機械などを作動させるために引いたり押したりするハンドル→レバー ‖ *Pull the lever towards you.* レバーを手前に引きなさい. *the gear lever in a car* 車の変速レバー ▶定義2 a bar or tool that is used to lift or open sth when you put pressure or force on one end 一方の端に圧力や力をかけて～を持ち上げたり開けたりするために使われる棒や道具→てこ, バール ‖ *You need to get the tyre off with a lever.* てこでタイヤを外す必要がある. — lever 動 他→～を (てこで) こじ開ける, レバーで動かす ‖ *The police had to lever the door open.* 警察はドアをこじ開けなければならなかった.

**leverage** /lév(ə)rɪdʒ/ 名 U ▶定義 the act of using a lever to lift or open sth; the force needed to do this ～を持ち上げたり開けるためにてこを使う動作; そのために必要な力→てこの作用, てこの力

**levy** /lévi/ 動 他 (現分 **levying**; 三単現 **levies**; 過, 過分 **levied**) (文) ▶定義 levy sth (on sb) to officially demand and collect money, etc 公式に金などを要求して取り立てる→(税金など)を (～に) 課す, 徴収する ‖ *to levy a tax/fine* 税・罰金を課す

**liability** /làɪəbíləti/ 名 (複 **liabilities**) ▶定義1 U liability (for sth) the state of being responsible for sth ～に対して責任があること→(～の) 責任 (を取ること), 責務, 義務 ‖ *The company cannot accept liability for damage to cars in this car park.* 当社はこの駐車場における車の損害に対しては責任を負いません. ▶定義2 C 略式 a person or thing that can cause a lot of problems, cost a lot of money, etc 多くの問題, 多額

の出費などをもたらす人や物➜厄介者, お荷物, 障害, 足手まといな人

**liable** /láɪəb(ə)l/ 形 (名詞の前は不可) ▶定義1 liable to do sth likely to do sth 〜をしそうな➜〜しがちである, しやすい ‖ *We're all liable to have accidents when we are very tired.* 非常に疲れているときはだれでも事故に遭いやすい. ▶定義2 liable to sth likely to have or suffer from sth 〜の被害を被りがちな➜〜にかかりやすい, 陥りやすい, 〜を免れない ‖ *The area is liable to floods.* この一帯は洪水が発生しやすい. ▶定義3 liable (for sth) (in law) responsible for sth (法律上) 〜に対して責任がある➜(〜に対して)法的責任がある

**liaise** /liéɪz/ 動 ⾃ ▶定義 liaise (with sb/sth) to work closely with a person, group, etc and give him/her/it regular information about what you are doing 人, グループなどと緊密に仕事をし, やっていることの情報をその人やグループに定期的に知らせる➜(〜と)連携する, 接触を保つ

**liaison** /líːəzɒn, liéɪzɒn/ 名 ▶定義1 (Ⓤ 単数扱い) liaison (between A and B) communication between two or more people or groups that work together 共に仕事をする複数の人々やグループ間の連絡 (〜間の) 連絡, 接触, 連携 ▶定義2 Ⓒ a secret sexual relationship 秘密の性的関係➜不倫, 密通, 私通

**liar** /láɪər/ 名 Ⓒ ▶定義 a person who does not tell the truth 真実を言わない人➜うそつき ‖ *She called me a liar.* 彼女は私をうそつきと呼んだ. ☛参 動 名 lie

**Lib Dem** /lɪb dém/ 名 (in British politics) Liberal Democrat (英国の政治で) 自由民主党

**libel** /láɪb(ə)l/ 名 Ⓒ Ⓤ ▶定義 the act of printing a statement about sb that is not true and would give people a bad opinion of him/her 〜について, 真実でなく悪い評判を与えるような陳述を印刷すること➜文書による名誉毀損(きそん)(罪), 中傷発言文 ‖ *The singer is suing the newspaper for libel.* その歌手は新聞を名誉毀損で訴えている. — libel 動 ⽤ (**libelling**; **libelled**: 米 **libeling**; **libeled**) ➜〜について名誉毀損文を公開する, 〜を中傷する ‖ *The actor claims he was libelled in the magazine article.* その俳優は雑誌記事で名誉を毀損されたと主張している.

**liberal** /líb(ə)rəl/ 形 ▶定義1 accepting different opinions or kinds of behaviour; tolerant 異なる意見や行動を受け入れる; 寛大な➜偏見のない, 進歩的な, 開放的な; 心の広い ‖ *He has very liberal parents.* 彼の両親はとても進歩的だ. ▶定義2 (in politics) believing in or based on principles of commercial freedom, freedom of choice, and avoiding extreme social and political change (政治で) 通商の自由, 選択の自由の原則を信じ, またはこれに基づき, 社会や政治の急激な変化を避ける➜自由主義の, 進歩的な ‖ *liberal policies/politicians* 自由主義政策・政治家 ▶定義3 not strictly limited in amount or variety 量や多様性が厳密に限られてはいない➜大まかな, 気前の良い, 物惜しみしない, たくさんの — liberal 名 Ⓒ➜自由主義者 ‖ *He's always considered himself a liberal.* 彼は常に自分を自由主義者だと考えてきた. — liberalism /líb(ə)rəlɪz(ə)m/ 名 Ⓤ➜自由主義

**the Liberal Democrats** 名 [複数扱い] ▶定義 a political party in Britain that represents views that are not extreme 過激でない意見を代表する英国の政党➜自由民主党

**liberally** /líb(ə)rəli/ 副 ▶定義 freely or in large amounts 自由に, 大量に➜気ままに, 気前良く

**liberate** /líbərèɪt/ 動 ⽤ ▶定義 liberate sb/sth (from sth) to allow sb/sth to be free 〜に自由を許す➜〜を(…から)解放する, 釈放する ‖ *France was liberated in 1945.* フランスは1945年に解放された. — liberation /lìbəréɪʃ(ə)n/ 名 Ⓤ➜解放すること, 解放運動

**liberated** /líbərèɪtɪd/ 形 ▶定義 free from the restrictions of traditional opinions or ways of behaving 伝統的意見や行動規範の束縛から自由な➜開放的な, 進歩的な

**liberty** /líbərti/ 名 Ⓒ Ⓤ (複 **liberties**) ▶定義 the freedom to go where you want, do what you want, etc 行きたい所へ行き, やりたい事をする自由➜(束縛・圧制などからの)自由, (思想・行動などの)自由 ‖ *We must defend our civil liberties at all costs.* 何をおいても市民としての自由を擁護しなければならない. ☛参 **freedom**

成句 **at liberty (to do sth)** ▶定義 free or allowed to do sth 自由にある事をしてよい, またはある事をすることを許されて➜自由に(〜して)よい, (〜することを)許されて ‖ *You are at liberty to leave when you wish.* いつでも好きな

ときに帰って構いません.

**Libra** /líːbrə, láɪbrə/ 图 ❻ ⓤ ▶定義 the seventh sign of the zodiac, the Scales 黄道十二宮の7番目である天秤(てんびん)座→**天秤座, 天秤宮**

**librarian** /laɪbréəriən/ 图 ❻ ▶定義 a person who works in or is in charge of a library 図書館で働く人, 図書館を管理する人→**司書, 図書館員**

*__library__ /láɪbrəri; -brèri/ 图 ❻ (複 **libraries**) ▶定義1 a room or building that contains a collection of books, etc that can be looked at or borrowed 参照したり借りたりすることのできる本などがそろった部屋や建物→**図書室, 図書館** ‖ *My library books are due back tomorrow.* 図書館から借りた本の返却期限は明日までだ. ☛参 **bookshop** ▶定義2 a private collection of books, etc 個人が集めた本など→**蔵書,(ビデオ・フィルム・レコードなどの)コレクション**

**lice** LOUSE の複数形

*__licence__ (米 **license**) /láɪs(ə)ns/ 图 ▶定義1 ❻a licence (for sth/to do sth) an official paper that shows you are allowed to do or have sth 何かをすることや所有することを許可されていることを示す公式の書類→**(~の・~する)許可証, 免許証, 鑑札** ‖ *Do you have a licence for this gun?* この銃の所有許可証をお持ちですか. *The shop has applied for a licence to sell alcoholic drinks.* その店はアルコール飲料を販売する免許を申請した. ☛参 **driving licence** ▶定義2 ⓤ 正式 licence (to do sth) permission or freedom to do sth 何かをする許可や自由→**(言動の)自由, 免許, 認可** ‖ *The soldiers were given licence to kill if they were attacked.* 兵士たちは攻撃された場合は相手を殺す権利を与えられた.

**licence plate**(米 **license plate**) = NUMBER PLATE

**license**[1] /láɪs(ə)ns/ 動他 ▶定義 to give official permission for sth ある物事に公式の許可を与える→**~に免許(証)を与える, ~を公式に許可する** ‖ *Is that gun licensed?* その銃は許可を受けたものですか.

**license**[2] 米 = LICENCE

**licensee** /làɪs(ə)nsíː/ 图 ❻ ▶定義 a person who has a licence to sell alcoholic drinks アルコール飲料を販売する許可証のある人→**酒類販売の許可を得た人**

**licensing laws** 图 [複数扱い] 英 ▶定義 the laws that control when and where alcoholic drinks can be sold いつどこでアルコール飲料を販売できるかを規制する法律→**事前許可制法**

### lick/bite/swallow

licking  biting  swallowing

*__lick__ /lɪk/ 動他 ▶定義 to move your tongue across sth ~に沿って舌を動かす→**~をなめる, なめて食べる** ‖ *The child licked the spoon clean.* 子供はスプーンをなめてきれいにした. *I licked the envelope and stuck it down.* 私は封筒をなめてくっつけた. — lick 图 ❻→**なめること**

**licorice** = LIQUORICE

**lid** /lɪd/ 图 ❻ ▶定義1 the top part of a box, pot, etc that can be lifted up or taken off 持ち上げたり取り外したりできる箱, なべなどの上部 →**ふた** ☛ **container, pan** のさし絵 ▶定義2 = EYELID

*__lie__[1] /laɪ/ 動他(現分 **lying**; 過, 過分 **lied**) ▶定義 lie (to sb) (about sth) to say or write sth that you know is not true 真実でないと知っている事を言ったり書いたりする→**(~に)(…について)うそをつく, だます** ‖ *He lied about his age in order to join the army.* 彼は軍隊に入るため年齢を偽った. *How could you lie to me?!* 一体どうして私にうそなどつけるのか. — lie 图 ❻→**うそ** ‖ *to tell a lie* うそをつく *That story about his mother being ill was just a pack of lies.* 彼の母が病気だという話は大うそだった.

➤ white lie は「悪意のないうそ」, 人の感情を傷付けないためのうそ. liar, fib を参照.

*__lie__[2] /laɪ/ 動自(現分 **lying**; 過 **lay** /léɪ/; 過分 **lain** /léɪn/) ▶定義1 to be in or move into in a flat or horizontal position (so that you are not standing or sitting) 平らな, または水平な姿勢でいる[になる](その結果立っていないし, 座っていない状態)→**横たわる, 横になる** ‖ *He lay on the sofa and went to sleep.* 彼はソファーに横たわって眠りに就いた. *to lie on your back/side/front*

あおむけ・横向き・うつぶせになる The book lay open in front of her. その本は彼女の前に開いたまま置いてあった.

➤ lie は目的語と共には使われないことに注意. 物を平らな状態に置く場合には, lay...down (lay down...) を使う.

▶定義2 to be or stay in a certain state or position ある状態や位置にある・とどまる➡位置する,置かれている,〜のままである‖ Snow lay thick on the ground. 雪が地面に厚く積もっていた. The hills lie to the north of the town. その丘は町の北側に連なっている. They are young and their whole lives **lie ahead** of them. 彼らは若く,人生のすべてが前途に待ち受けている. ▶定義3 lie (in sth) to exist or to be found somewhere ある場所に存在する・見つかる➡(〜に)ある,存在する,見いだされる‖ The problem lies in deciding when to stop. 問題はいつやめるか決めることにある.

成句 lie in wait (for sb) ▶定義 to hide somewhere waiting to attack, surprise or catch sb 〜を攻撃する・驚かす・捕まえるためにどこかに隠れる➡(〜を)待ち伏せする,待ち構える

lie low ▶定義 to try not to attract attention to yourself 自分に注意を引き付けないようにする➡隠れる,身を潜める,じっとしている

句動詞 lie about/around ▶定義 to relax and do nothing くつろいで何もしない➡ごろごろする,怠けている

lie back ▶定義 to relax and do nothing while sb else works, etc ほかの人が働いている間など,くつろいで何もしない➡休む,くつろぐ

lie behind sth ▶定義 to be the real hidden reason for sth 何かの隠れた本当の理由である➡〜の背後にある,隠れた原因[真意]である‖ We may never know what lay behind his decision to resign. 彼が辞任を決意した真の理由は決して分からないだろう.

lie down ▶定義 (used about a person) to be in or move into a flat or horizontal position so that you can rest (人について)休めるように平らな・水平な姿勢でいる[になる]➡横になる

➤ 関連した語法 have a lie-down にも注意.

lie in 略式 ▶定義 to stay in bed later than usual because you do not have to get up 起きる必要がないので,いつもより遅くまでベッドにいる➡朝寝坊する

# life 969

➤ 関連した語法 have a lie-in にも注意. oversleep と比較.

lie with sb 略式 ▶定義 to be sb's responsibility to do sth 人の責任・任務・義務である➡〜の責任・任務・義務である

**lie detector** 名 C ▶定義 a piece of equipment that can show if a person is telling the truth or not 人が真実を言っているかどうかを示すことのできる装置➡うそ発見機

**Lieut** (または **Lt**) 略 Lieutenant➡(陸軍) 中尉, (海軍) 大尉

**lieutenant** /lefténənt; lu:tén-/ 名 C ▶定義 an officer at a middle level in the army, navy or air force 陸軍, 海軍, 空軍の中位の士官➡(陸軍)中尉,(海軍)大尉

*****life** /láɪf/ 名 (複 **lives** /láɪvz/) ▶定義1 U the quality that people, animals or plants have when they are not dead 人,動物,植物が死んでいないときに持っている特質➡生命,命,生きていること‖ Do you believe in life after death? 死後の生命を信じますか. to bring sb/come back to life 〜の意識を取り戻させる・〜が意識を取り戻す ▶定義2 U living things 生きている物➡生き物,生物‖ Life on earth began in a very simple form. 地球の生物は非常に単純な形から始まった. No life was found on the moon. 月では生物は発見されなかった. There was no sign of life in the deserted house. その廃屋に生き物の気配はなかった. plant life 植物 ▶定義3 C U the state of being alive as a human being 人間として生きている状態➡命,人命‖ Would you **risk** your life to protect your property? 財産を守るために命を懸けますか. Doctors fought all night to **save** her life. 医師たちは彼女の命を救うため徹夜で闘った. ▶定義4 C U the period during which sb/sth is alive or exists 〜が生きている,または存在している期間➡一生,生涯,人生,寿命,耐用期間‖ I've lived in this town **all my life**. 私は生まれてからずっとこの町に住んでいる. I spent my early life in London. 私は若いころをロンドンで過ごした. to have a short/long/exciting life 短命である・長命である,刺激的な人生である ▶定義5 U the things that you may experience while you are alive 生きている間に体験する可能性のある事➡実生活,世

間, 人事 ‖ *Life can be hard for a single parent.* 片親にとっては生活は厳しいこともある. *I'm not happy with the situation, but I suppose that's life.* 状況に満足してはいないが, 人生とはこんなものだろう. (仕方がない) ▶定義6 ❶ a way of living 生き方 →**生活, 暮らし方** ‖ *They went to America to start a new life.* 彼らはアメリカに渡って新生活を始めた. *They lead a busy life.* 彼らは忙しい生活を送っている. *married life* 結婚生活 ▶定義7 ❶ energy; activity 活気; 活動 →**活力, 生気, 元気, 動き** ‖ *Young children are full of life.* 小さい子供は元気一杯だ. *These streets come to life in the evenings.* これらの通りは夕方になると活気づく. ▶定義8 ❶ something that really exists and is not just a story, a picture, etc 実際に存在していて, 単なる物語や絵などではないもの →**実物, 本物** ‖ *I wonder what that actor's like in real life.* 実生活ではあの俳優はどんな風なのだろう. *Do you draw people from life or from photographs?* 人物を描くには実物を基に描くのですか, それとも写真を基に描くのですか.

成句 a fact of life ⇒ **FACT**
the facts of life ⇒ **FACT**
full of beans/life ⇒ **FULL**[1]
get a life (口語) ▶定義 used to tell sb to stop being boring and do sth more interesting 〜に退屈な事をやめてもっと面白い事をするように言うときに用いて →**ちゃんとしろ, しっかりしろ, まともな生き方をしろ**
lose your life ⇒ **LOSE**
a matter of life and/or death ⇒ **MATTER**[1]
take your (own) life ▶定義 to kill yourself 自殺する →**自ら死を選ぶ**
a walk of life ⇒ **WALK**[2]
a/sb's way of life ⇒ **WAY**[1]
have the time of your life ⇒ **TIME**[1]

**life-and-death**(または **life-or-death**)形 (名詞の前だけ) ▶定義 very serious or dangerous 大変重大な, または危険な →**生死にかかわる, 極めて重大な** ‖ *a life-and-death struggle/matter/decision* 生死を懸けた闘争・死活問題・極めて重要な決定

**lifebelt** /láɪfbèlt/ (または **lifebuoy** /láɪfbɔ̀ɪ/) 名 ❸ 因 ▶定義 a ring that is made from light material which will float. A lifebelt is thrown to a person who has fallen into water to stop him/her from sinking. 水に浮く軽い材料で作った輪. 沈むのを防ぐため水に落ちた人に投げる →**救命帯, 救命ブイ**

**lifeboat** /láɪfbòʊt/ 名 ❸ ▶定義1 a small boat that is carried on a large ship and that is used to escape from the ship if it is in danger of sinking 大きな船に積まれた小さなボートで, 船が沈没する危険がある場合に脱出用に使用される →**救命艇, 救命ボート** ▶定義2 a special boat that is used for rescuing people who are in danger at sea 海上で危険に遭遇した人を救助するための特別な船舶 →**救助船, 救難船**

**life cycle** 名 ❸ ▶定義 the series of forms into which a living thing changes as it develops 生き物が発達するにつれて変化する一連の形 →**生活環, ライフサイクル, 生活周期**

**life expectancy** 名 ❸ ❶ (複 **life expectancies**) ▶定義 the number of years that a person is likely to live 人が生きる見込みのある年数 →**平均寿命, 平均余命, 予想される寿命**

**lifeguard** /láɪfɡɑ̀ːrd/ 名 ❸ ▶定義 a person at a beach or swimming pool whose job is to rescue people who are in difficulty in the water 海岸やプールで, 水の中で困難に遭遇した人々を救助することを仕事とする人 →**救助員, 監視員**

**life jacket** 名 ❸ ▶定義 a plastic or rubber jacket without sleeves that can be filled with air. A life jacket is used to make sb float if he/she falls into water. 空気を入れることのできるプラスチックやゴム製のそでなしの上着. 人が水に落ちた場合に浮かぶために使用される →**救命胴衣** ☛ **boat** のさし絵

**lifeless** /láɪfləs/ 形 ▶定義1 dead or appearing to be dead 死んだ, または死んでいるように見える →**生命のない, 生物の住んでいない, 気絶した** ▶定義2 without energy or interest; dull 活気や関心のない; 鈍い →**元気のない, 気の抜けた**

**lifelike** /láɪflàɪk/ 形 ▶定義 looking like a real person or thing 実際の人や物のように見える →**生きているような, 生き写しの, 真に迫った** ‖ *The flowers are made of silk but they are very lifelike.* その花は絹でできているが, 本物そっくりだ.

**lifeline** /láɪflàɪn/ 名 ❸ ▶定義 something that is very important for sb and that he/she depends on 〜にとって非常に重要で〜が頼りにしているもの→**命綱,(輸送・通信などの)生命線,頼みの綱** ‖ *For many old people their telephone is a lifeline.* 多くの老人にとって電話は命綱だ.

**lifelong** /láɪflɔ̀(ː)ŋ/ 形 ▶定義 for all of your life (名詞の前だけ)→**一生の, 生涯続く** ‖ *a lifelong friend* 生涯の友

**life-size(d)** 形 ▶定義 of the same size as the real person or thing 実際の人や物と同じ大きさの→**実物大の, 等身大の** ‖ *a life-sized statue* 等身大の彫像

**lifespan** /láɪfspæ̀n/ 名 C ▶定義 the length of time that sth is likely to live, work, last, etc 〜が生きる[作動する・持続する]見込みのある期間→**(生物, 機械などの)寿命** ‖ *A mosquito has a lifespan of only a few days.* 蚊の寿命はわずか数日である.

**life story** /láɪfstɔ́ːri/ 名 C ( 複 **life stories**) ▶定義 the story of sb's life 〜の人生の物語→**伝記**

**lifestyle** /láɪfstàɪl/ 名 C ▶定義 the way that you live 生き方→**生活様式, 暮らし振り, ライフスタイル**

**lifetime** /láɪftàɪm/ 名 C ▶定義 the period of time that sb is alive 〜が生きている時間→**一生, 生涯, 寿命**

*****lift**¹ /lɪft/ 動 ▶定義 **1** 他 lift sb/sth (up) to move sb/sth to a higher level or position 〜をより高いレベルや位置に移動する→**〜を持ち上げる, 引き上げる** ‖ *He lifted the child up onto his shoulders.* 彼は子供を肩車した. *Lift your arm very gently and see if it hurts.* 腕を静かに上げて痛むかどうか見てください. *It took two men to lift the piano.* そのピアノを持ち上げるのは2人がかりだった. ▶定義 **2** 他 to move sb/sth from one place or position to another 〜を1つの場所や位置から他へ移動する→**〜を動かす, 取る** ‖ *She lifted the suitcase down from the rack.* 彼女はスーツケースを棚から下ろした. ▶定義 **3** 他 to end or remove a rule, law, etc 規則, 法律などを終了する, または取り除く→**〜を解除する, 解く, 撤廃する** ‖ *The ban on public meetings has been lifted.* 集会の禁止は解除された. ▶定義 **4** 自 他 to become or make sb happier より幸福になる, 〜をより幸福にする→**高揚する; 〜を高揚させる, 活気づける** ‖ *The news lifted our spirits.* そのニュースを聞いて心が浮き立った. ▶定義 **5** 自 (used about clouds, fog, etc) to rise up or disappear (雲, 霧などについて)上昇する, または消える→**上がる, 晴れる, 消える** ‖ *The mist lifted towards the end of the morning.* 朝が終わるころには霧が晴れた ▶定義 **6** 他 略式 lift sth (from sb/sth) to steal or copy sth 〜を盗むために, 複製する→**〜を(…から)万引きする, 盗用する** ‖ *Most of his essay was lifted straight from the textbook.* 彼の作文の大部分は教科書から直接盗用したものだった. ☛参 **shoplifting**

句動詞 lift off ▶定義 (used about a spacecraft) to rise straight up from the ground (宇宙船について)地上からまっすぐに上昇する→**垂直離陸する, 打ち上げられる**

**lift**² /lɪft/ 名 ▶定義 **1** (米 **elevator**) C a machine in a large building that is used for carrying people or goods from one floor to another 人や品物を1つの階から別の階へ運ぶために使われる大きなビルにある機械→**エレベーター** ‖ *It's on the third floor so we'd better **take the lift**.* それは4階(英国式)にあるので, エレベーターに乗る方がいいでしょう. ▶定義 **2** C a free ride in a car, etc 車などにただで乗ること→**便乗, 同乗, (車に)乗せてあげる[もらう]こと** ‖ *Can you give me a lift to the station, please?* 駅まで乗せてくれませんか. *I got a lift from a passing car.* 通り掛かった車に乗せてもらった. ▶定義 **3** [単数扱い] 略式 a feeling of being happier or more confident than before 前より幸福な, またはより自信がある気持ち→**愉快な気持ち, 気持ちの高揚** ‖ *Her words of encouragement gave the whole team a lift.* 彼女の励ましの言葉にチーム全体の意気が上がった. ▶定義 **4** [単数扱い] the action of moving or being moved to a higher position より高い位置に移動すること, または移動されること→**持ち上げる[上がる]こと; 昇進, 昇級, 出世**

成句 thumb a lift ⇒ **THUMB**²

**lift-off** 名 C ▶定義 the start of the flight of a spacecraft when it leaves the ground 宇宙船が地上を離れて飛行を開始すること→**(ミサイル・ロケットなどの)発射**

**ligament** /lígəmənt/ 名 C ▶定義 a strong band in a person's or animal's body that holds the bones, etc together 骨などを結び付けるための人間や動物の体にある丈夫な帯→**靱帯(じんたい)**

## lights

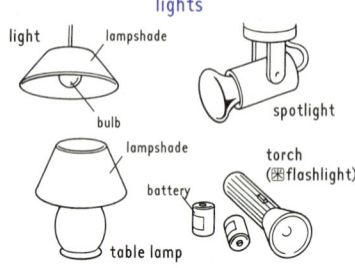

light, lampshade, bulb, spotlight, lampshade, torch (米flashlight), battery, table lamp

*light¹ /láɪt/ 名 ▶定義 1 ❶ ⓒ the energy from the sun, a lamp, etc that allows you to see things 太陽, 電灯などからのエネルギーで, これによって物を見ることができる➡光, 光線, 明かり ‖ *a beam/ray of light* 光線 *The light was too dim for us to read by.* 明かりが暗くて本を読めなかった. *Strong light is bad for the eyes.* 強い光線は目に悪い. *We could see strange lights in the sky.* 空に不思議な光が見えた.

▶ sunlight(太陽光線), moonlight(月光), firelight(火明かり), candlelight(ろうそくの明かり), lamplight(ランプの明かり)で物を見ることができる.

▶定義 2 ⓒ something that produces light, for example an electric lamp 例えば電灯のように光を発するもの➡明かり, 光源, 灯火, 照明 ‖ *Suddenly all the lights went out/came on.* 突然すべての照明が消えた・点灯した. *the lights of the city in the distance* 遠い街の明かり *If the lights (= traffic lights) are red, stop!* 信号(= 交通信号機)が赤なら, 止まりなさい. *That car hasn't got its lights on.* その車はライトをつけていない.

▶ 明かりは on(つける) off(消す)と言う: *put/switch/turn a light on/off/out.*(明かりをつける・消す) *Shall I put the light on? It's getting dark in here.*(明かりをつけてもいいですか. ここは暗くなってきたので.) *Please turn the lights out before you leave.*(帰る前に明かりを消してください.)

▶定義 3 ⓒ something, for example a match, that can be used to light a cigarette, start a fire, etc たばこに火をつけたり火をおこしたりするための, 例えばマッチのようなもの➡(ライター・マッチ・たばこなどの)火, 火花, 火をつけるもの ‖ *Have you got a light?* 火を貸してくれませんか.

成句 **bring sth/come to light** ▶定義 to make sth known or to become known 〜を知らせる・〜が知られる➡明るみに出す・出る, 世に出す・出る

**cast light on sth** ⇒ **CAST¹**

**give sb/get the green light** ⇒ **GREEN¹**

**in a good, bad, etc light** ▶定義 (used about the way that sth is seen or described by other people) well, badly, etc (〜がほかの人にどのように見えるか, どのように表されるかについて) 良く, 悪くなど➡良く・悪く見えるように, 良い・悪い点を強調して, 有利・不利になるように ‖ *The newspapers often portray his behaviour in a bad light.* 新聞はしばしば彼の行動を悪く書く.

**in the light of** ▶定義 because of; considering 〜のため; 〜を考慮して➡〜の観点から, 〜を考えて

**set light to sth** ▶定義 to cause sth to start burning 〜を燃やし始める➡〜に火をつける

**shed light on sth** ⇒ **SHED²**

*light² /láɪt/ 形 ▶定義 1 not of great weight 重量が大きくない➡軽い, 軽量の ‖ *Carry this bag - it's the lightest.* このバッグを持って — 一番軽いから. *I've lost weight - I'm five kilos lighter than I used to be.* 私はやせました — 前より5キロ体重が減りました. *light clothes (= for summer)* 薄い服(= 夏向きの) ⇔ **heavy** ▶定義 2 having a lot of light 光がたっぷりある➡明るい ‖ *In summer it's still light at 10 o'clock.* 夏は10時でもまだ明るい. *a light room* 明るい部屋 ⇔ **dark** ▶定義 3 (used about a colour) pale (色について)薄い➡淡い, (色が)明るい ‖ *a light-blue sweater* 水色のセーター ⇔ **dark** ▶定義 4 not great in amount, degree, etc 量や程度などが大きくない➡少ない, 小さい ‖ *Traffic in London is light on a Sunday.* ロンドンの交通量は日曜日には少ない. *a light prison sentence* 軽い実刑 *a light wind* そよ風 *a light breakfast* 軽い朝食 ▶定義 5 not using much force; gentle あまり力を使わない; 穏やかな➡軽い, 軽やかな ‖ *a light touch on the shoulder* 肩にそっと触れること ▶定義 6 not hard or tiring きつくない, 疲れない➡(仕事などが)軽い, 肩の凝らない, 気軽な, 楽な ‖ *light exercise* 軽い

運動 light entertainment/reading 肩の凝らない娯楽・読書 ▶定義7 (used about sleep) not deep (睡眠について)深くない→浅い ‖ *I'm a light sleeper, so the slightest noise wakes me.* 私は眠りが浅いので, ほんのちょっとした音でも目が覚めます. — **lightness** 名 U 軽いこと, 軽さ

\***light**³ /láɪt/ 動 (過, 過分 **lit** または **lighted**)
▶定義1 自他 to begin or to make sth begin to burn 燃え始める, 〜を燃やし始める→燃える, 火をつける; 〜に点火する ‖ *The gas cooker won't light.* ガスレンジに火がつかない. *to light a fire* 火をつける

➤ lighted は通常名詞の前で形容詞として用いる. lit は動詞の過去分詞として用いる: *Candles were lit in memory of the dead.* (死者を追悼してろうそくがともされた.) *The church was full of lighted candles.* (教会は灯をともしたろうそくで一杯だった.)

▶定義2 他 to give light to sth 〜に光を与える→〜を照らす, 明るくする, 〜に明かりつける ‖ *The street is well/badly lit at night.* その通りは夜は明るい・暗い. *We only had a small torch to light our way.* 道を照らすものは小さな懐中電灯だけだった.

句動詞 **light (sth) up** ▶定義1 to make sth bright with light 〜を光で明るくする→〜を照らし出す, 輝かせる ‖ *The fireworks lit up the whole sky.* 花火が空全体を照らし出した. ▶定義2 (used about sb's face, eyes, etc) to become bright with happiness or excitement (人の顔や目などについて)喜びや興奮で明るくなる→輝く, 生き生きする ▶定義3 to start smoking a cigarette たばこを吸い始める→たばこに火をつける

**light**⁴ /láɪt/ 形/ 副 ▶定義 without much luggage あまり荷物のない→軽装で, 軽い積み荷で ‖ *I always travel light.* 私はいつも軽装で旅行する.

**light bulb** = BULB(1)

**lighten** /láɪtn/ 動 自他 ▶定義1 to become lighter in weight or to make sth lighter 重さが軽くなる, 〜を軽くする→荷を少なくする, 軽減する
▶定義2 to become or to make sth brighter 明るくなる, または〜を明るくする→照らす

**lighter** /láɪtər/ = CIGARETTE LIGHTER

**light-headed** 形 ▶定義 feeling slightly ill and not in control of your thoughts and movements いくらか気分が悪く, 自分の考えや動作を抑制できない→くらくらする, もうろうとした

**light-hearted** 形 ▶定義1 intended to be funny and enjoyable こっけいで楽しそうに振る舞う→気楽な, 気軽な ▶定義2 happy and without problem 幸福で問題のない→陽気な, 快活な, 屈託のない, 楽天的な

**lighthouse** /láɪthàʊs/ 名 C ▶定義 a tall building with a light at the top to warn and guide ships near the coast 沿岸の船舶に警告したり案内するための最上部に光源のある高い建物→灯台

**lighting** /láɪtɪŋ/ 名 U ▶定義 the quality or type of lights used in a room, building, etc 部屋や建物などで使われる明かりの質や種類→照明, 照明装置, 照明方法

**lightly** /láɪtli/ 副 ▶定義1 gently; with very little force 穏やかに; 非常に小さい力で→軽く, そっと ‖ *He touched her lightly on the arm.* 彼は彼女の腕にそっと触れた. ▶定義2 only a little; not much 少しだけ; 多くない→少し, ちょっと ‖ *lightly cooked/spiced/whisked* 軽く火を通した・少々香辛料を入れた・軽く泡立てた
▶定義3 not seriously; without serious thought 本気にせずに; まじめに考えずに→軽んじて, 軽率に ‖ *We do not take our customers' complaints lightly.* 当店ではお客様の苦情を軽視したりいたしません.

成句 **get off/be let off lightly** ▶定義 to avoid serious punishment or trouble 厳しい罰や厄介な問題を避ける→軽い罰で済む・許される

**lightning**¹ /láɪtnɪŋ/ 名 U ▶定義 a bright flash of light that appears in the sky during a storm あらしの際に空に現れる明るい閃光(せんこう)→稲妻, 稲光 ‖ *The tree was struck by lightning and burst into flames.* 木が稲妻に打たれ燃え上がった. *a flash of lightning* 稲光

➤ 普通稲光の後には thunder (雷)と呼ばれる音が続く.

**lightning**² /láɪtnɪŋ/ 形 (名詞の前だけ) ▶定義 very quick or sudden 非常に早い, または突然の→電光石火の, 素早い, たちまちの ‖ *a lightning attack* 電撃攻撃

**lightweight** /láɪtwèɪt/ 名 C 形 ▶定義1 a person who is in one of the lightest weight groups in certain fighting sports 一部の格闘技で最も軽

い体重のグループの1つに属する人→(ボクシングなどの)ライト級の選手, ライト級の ‖ *a lightweight boxing champion* ボクシング級のライト級チャンピオン ▶定義2 (a thing) weighing less than usual 通常より軽い(物)→軽量の(物) ‖ *a lightweight suit for the summer* 夏向きの軽いスーツ

**likable** = LIKEABLE

**\*like**¹ /láɪk/ 動⓲ ▶定義1 like sb/sth; like doing sth; like to do sth; like sth about sb/sth to find sb/sth pleasant; to enjoy sth ～が好ましいと気付く; ～を楽しむ→～が好きである, ～を好む, ～を気に入る ‖ *He's nice. I like him a lot.* 彼はいい人よ. 私は大好き. *Do you like their new flat?* あなたは彼らの新しいフラットが気に入りましたか. *How do you like John's new girlfriend?* ジョンの新しいガールフレンドをどう思う. *I like my coffee strong.* 私はコーヒーは濃い方が良い. *I like playing tennis.* 私はテニスをするのが好きだ. *I like to go to the cinema on Thursdays.* 毎週木曜日は映画に行くことにしている. *What is it you like about Sarah so much?* サラのどこがそんなにいいの. *She didn't like it when I shouted at her.* 彼女は私にどなられるのを嫌がった. *I don't like him borrowing my things without asking.* 彼が私の物を黙って使うのが嫌だ. *The job seems strange at first, but you'll get to like it.* 最初はその仕事に慣れないかもしれないけれど, すぐに気に入りますよ. *I don't like the look/sound/idea/thought of that.* そんな様子・音・思い付き・考えは気に入らない. ⇔ dislike

▶「～の習慣がある」または「～するのは良い事だと思う」の意味で like を使う場合は後に不定詞がつく: *I like to get up early so that I can go for a run before breakfast.* (朝食の前に一走りできるように朝早く起きることにしている.)

▶定義2 to want 望む→～してほしいと思う, ～であるのを好む ‖ *Do what you like. I don't care.* 好きなようにしなさい. 気にしないから. *We can go whenever you like.* あなたの都合の良いときに行けます. *I didn't like to disturb you while you were eating.* 食事中にお邪魔したくなかったのです.

▶ would like は want の丁寧な言い方: *Would you like something to eat?* (何か召し上がりますか.) *I'd like to speak to the manager.* (支配人とお話ししたいのですが.) *We'd like you to come to dinner on Sunday.* (日曜日に食事にお招きしたいのですが.) *How would you like to come to Scotland with us?* (私たちと一緒にスコットランドにいらっしゃいませんか.) would like の後には必ず不定詞が付き, -ing 形は付かない.

> ▶音声とつづり字
>
> **I would like... の言い方**
>
> I would like は, 意味上は I want to と変わりませんが, 丁寧な表現として幅広く頻繁に使われます. 自分のしたい事, また相手にしてもらいたい事を表現できます. 発音上, d⌣like のつながり, like⌣to のつながりに注意する必要があります. d の発音のとき, 舌先を歯茎に付けたままにして l の発音に移行することが大事です. 舌先を付けたままなので, 舌の両側面で破裂音が生じることもあります. また k と t のつながりでは, k を完全に発音し終える前に t の発音に移行することが重要です.

成句 **if you like** ▶定義 used for agreeing with sb or suggesting sth in a polite way 丁寧に～に同意したり, ～を提案する場合に用いて→よろしければ ‖ *'Shall we stop for a rest?' 'Yes, if you like.'* 「一休みしませんか」「ええ, よろしければ」

**I like that!** 英略式 ▶定義 used for saying that sth is not true or not fair 何かが真実でない, または公正でないと言う場合に用いて→あきれた, ひどいじゃないか. (反語的に使って, 驚き・いら立ちなどを表す)

**like the look/sound of sb/sth** ▶定義 to have a good impression of sb/sth after seeing or hearing about him/her/it ～について見たり聞いたりした後で, 良い印象を持つ→気に入る

**\*like**² /láɪk/ 前接 ▶定義1 similar to sb/sth ～に似ている→～のような, ～に似た ‖ *You look very/just/exactly like your father.* あなたはお父さんにとても似ている・よく似ている・そっくりだ. *Those two singers sound like cats!* あの2人の歌手はまるで猫のような声だ. *Your house*

*is **nothing like** how I imagined it.* あなたの家は私が想像していたのと全く違う.

➤ **What's he/she/it like?**(何かについて説明してほしいときに使う): *Tell me about your town. What's it like?* (あなたの町について教えてください. どんな風ですか). *'What's your brother like?' 'He's tall and fair, and quite serious.'*(「お兄さんはどんな感じの人ですか」「背が高くて金髪で, とてもまじめです」) *What was it like being interviewed on TV?* (テレビのインタビューを受けるというのはどんな感じでしたか.)

▶定義2 (複合語で) in the manner of; similar to ～の様子で, ～に似た ➔ **～のような, ～風の** ‖ *childlike innocence/simplicity* 子供のような無邪気さ・単純さ *a very lifelike statue* まるで生きているような彫像 ▶定義3 in the same way as sb/sth ～と同じやり方で ➔ **～と同じように, 同じ方法で** ‖ *Stop behaving like children.* 子供のようなまねはやめなさい. *That's not right. Do it like this.* それは間違っている. こんな風にしなさい. *She can't draw like her sister can.* 彼女は姉[妹]のようには絵がかけない. ▶定義4 for example; such as 例えば; ～のような ➔ **～などの** ‖ *They enjoy most team games, like football and rugby.* 彼らはサッカーやラグビーのようなチームでやるほとんどのスポーツが好きだ. ▶定義5 typical of a particular person 特定の人に典型的な ➔ **～らしい, ～と同じ特質のある** ‖ *It was just like Maria to be late.* 遅れるのはいかにもマリアらしかった. ▶定義6 略式 as if まるで～かのように ➔ **～のように, ～と同じように** ‖ *She behaves like she owns the place.* 彼女はまるでその場所の所有者のように振る舞う. ▶定義7 (俗語) (used before saying what sb said, how sb felt, etc) (～が言った事や感じた事などを言う前に用いて) ➔ **まあ, 何となく, ～みたいな** ‖ *When I saw the colour of my hair I was like 'Wow, I can't believe it!'* 自分の髪の色を見たときは, なんて言うのか,「やだ, 信じられない」って感じだったわ.

成句 **like anything** (口語) ▶定義 very much, fast, hard, etc とても多く, 速く, 一生懸命になど ➔ **激しく, 猛烈に, どんどん** ‖ *We had to pedal like anything to get up the hill.* 丘を登るのに必死でペダルをこいだ.

**nothing like** ⇒ **NOTHING**

# likely 975

**something like** ▶定義 about; approximately 約; ほぼ ➔ **およそ, ～くらい** ‖ *The cathedral took something like 200 years to build.* その大聖堂は建設に200年ほどかかった.

**that's more like it** ▶定義1 (used to say that sth is better than before) (～が前よりいいことを言う場合に用いて) ➔ **今度の方がいい, そちらの方が良い** ‖ *The sun's coming out now - that's more like it!* もう太陽が昇る - よかった.

**like**³ /láɪk/ 名 ▶定義1 [単数扱い] a person or thing that is similar to sb/sth else ほかの～に似た人や物 ➔ **似た人・物, 同様な人・物, 匹敵する人・物** ‖ *I enjoy going round castles, old churches and the like.* 私は城や古い教会などを見て回るのが楽しみだ. *She was a great singer, and we may never see her like/the like of her again.* 彼女は偉大な歌手だったので, 彼女のような歌手はもう二度と現れないだろう. ▶定義2 **likes** [複数扱い] things that you like 好きなもの ➔ **好み, 嗜好(しこう)** ‖ *Tell me about some of your likes and dislikes.* 好きなものと嫌いなものを教えてください. — **like** 形 正式 ➔ **同じ, 似ている**

**likeable** (または **likable**) /láɪkəb(ə)l/ 形 ▶定義 (used about a person) easy to like; pleasant (人について) 容易に好きになれる; 気持ちの良い ➔ **好感の持てる, 魅力的な, 好ましい**

**likelihood** /láɪklihòd/ 名 Ⓤ ▶定義 the chance of sth happening; how likely sth is to happen ～が起こる可能性; ～がどの程度の可能性で起こるかということ ➔ **見込み, 公算** ‖ *There seems very little likelihood of success.* 成功の見込みはほとんどなさそうだ.

*★**likely** /láɪkli/ 形副 (**likelier; likeliest**) ▶定義1 **likely (to do sth)** probable or expected ありそうな, 予期される ➔ **～しそうな, おそらく～するだろう** ‖ *Do you think it's likely to rain?* 雨が降りそうだと思いますか. *The boss is not likely to agree.* 上司は同意しそうにない. *It's not likely that the boss will agree.* 上司が同意する見込みはないだろう. ▶定義2 probably suitable おそらく適切な ➔ **適当な, あつらえむきの, 有望な** ‖ *a likely candidate for the job* その仕事に打って付けの候補者 ⇨ **unlikely**

成句 **not likely!** 略式 ▶定義 certainly not もちろん違う ➔ **まさか, とんでもない**

**liken** /láikən/ 動他 正式 ▶定義 liken sb/sth to sb/sth to compare one person or thing with another 1人の人や1つの物を別の1つと比較する→～を…に例える, なぞらえる ‖ *This young artist has been likened to Picasso.* この若い芸術家はピカソに例えられてきた.

**likeness** /láiknəs/ 名 C U ▶定義 the fact of being similar in appearance; an example of this 外見が似ているということ; このような例→(よく)似ていること, 似せた物, 類似点 ‖ *The witness's drawing turned out to be **a good likeness of** the attacker.* 証人の絵は襲撃犯とよく似ていることが分かった.

**likewise** /láikwaɪz/ 副 正式 ▶定義 the same; in a similar way 同じ; 同じやり方で→同じように, 同様に, また ‖ *I intend to send a letter of apology and suggest that you do likewise.* 私は謝罪の手紙を送るつもりだが, 君も同じようにするべきだ.

**liking** /láikɪŋ/ 名 [単数扱い] ▶定義 a liking (for sb/sth) the feeling that you like sb/sth ～を好きだという感情→好み, 趣味, 嗜好(しこう) ‖ *I have a liking for spicy food.* 私は辛い食べ物が好きだ.

成句 **too...for your liking** ▶定義 that you do not like because he/she/it has too much of a particular quality 人や物が特定の資質をあまりに多く持っているので, 好きになれない→～すぎて好みに合わない・好きになれない ‖ *The music was a bit too loud for my liking.* その音楽はちょっとうるさすぎて私の好みではなかった.

**lilac** /láɪlək; -læk/ 名 C U 形 ▶定義 1 a tree or large bush that has large purple or white flowers in spring 春に紫や白の大輪の花をつける木または大型の低木→ライラック, リラ ▶定義 2 (of) a pale purple colour 薄い紫色(の)→ふじ色(の)

**lilo** (または **Li-lo**™) /láɪloʊ/ 名 C (複 **lilos**) 商 ▶定義 a plastic or rubber bed that you fill with air when you want to use it. A Lilo is used on the beach or for camping. 使用するときに空気を入れるプラスチックやゴム製のベッド. 海岸やキャンプで使う→ライロ(商標名), エアマットレス ☛ C8 ページのさし絵

**lily** /líli/ 名 C (複 **lilies**) ▶定義 a type of plant that has large white or coloured flowers in the shape of a bell 鐘形の白やさまざまな色の大輪の花をつける植物→ユリ, ユリの花 ☛ C2 ページのさし絵

**limb** /lím/ 名 C ▶定義 1 a leg or an arm of a person 人の脚または腕→肢, 手足 ▶定義 2 one of the main branches of a tree 樹木の主要な枝→大枝

成句 **out on a limb** ▶定義 without the support of other people ほかの人の支援なしで→困難な立場で, 不利で, 孤立した

**lime** /láim/ 名 ▶定義 1 C a fruit that looks like a small green lemon 緑色の小さなレモンのような果実→ライム ☛ C3 ページのさし絵 ▶定義 2 U (または **lime green**) a yellowish-green colour 黄色がかった緑色→ライムグリーン, 黄緑色 ▶定義 3 U a white substance that is used for making cement and also for adding to soil to improve its quality セメントの製造や土壌の改良のために土壌に加えるために使用される白色の物質→石灰

**the limelight** /láimlàit/ 名 U ▶定義 the centre of public attention 公衆の注目の的→脚光を浴びること, 目立つこと ‖ *to be in/out of the limelight* 注目の的になる・注目されない

★**limit**¹ /límət/ 名 C ▶定義 1 the greatest or smallest amount of sth that is allowed or possible 許容できる, または可能な～の最大・最小の量→制限, 限度, 限界 ‖ *a speed/age/time limit* 制限速度・年齢・時間 *He was fined for exceeding the speed limit.* 彼は制限速度オーバーで罰金を取られた. *There's a limit to the amount of time I'm prepared to spend on this.* この事に割ける時間には限りがある. ▶定義 2 the outside edge of a place or area 場所や範囲の外縁→境界(線), 範囲 ‖ *the city limits* 市の境界線 *Lorries are not allowed within a two-mile limit of the town centre.* トラックは町の中心から2マイル以内には入れない.

成句 **off limits** 米 = **OUT OF BOUNDS**

**within limits** ▶定義 only up to a reasonable point or amount 道理にかなった点・量まで→限度内で, 適度に

★**limit**² /límət/ 動他 ▶定義 limit sb/sth (to sth) to keep sb/sth within or below a certain amount, size, degree or area ～を特定の量, 大

きさ,程度,範囲内に制限する➡~に限る,限定する,制限する‖ *In China families are limited to just one child.* 中国では,家族は子供1人に制限されている.

**limitation** /lìmətéiʃ(ə)n/ ▶定義1 ❸ ❺(a) limitation (on sth) the act of limiting or controlling sth; a condition that puts a limit on sth ~を制限または制御すること; ~に制限を与える状況➡**制限,限定**‖ *There are no limitations on what we can do.* 私たちにできる事に限界はない. ▶定義2 [複数扱い] **limitations** things that you cannot do できないこと➡**(能力,行動などの)限界**‖ *It is important to know your own limitations.* 自分の限界を知ることは重要だ.

**limited** /límətəd/ 形 ▶定義 small or restricted in number, amount, etc 数や量が少ない,または限定された➡**わずかな,限られた,有限の**‖ *Book early because there are only a limited number of seats available.* 席には限りがあるので,お早めにご予約ください. ⇔ **unlimited**

**limited company** 名 ❸(略 **Ltd**) ▶定義 a company whose owners only have to pay a limited amount of its debts if it fails 破産した場合に所有者が支払う負債が有限である会社➡**有限責任会社,いわゆる有限会社,株式会社のこと**

**limousine** /límə zìːn, -ˊ-ˋ/ (または 略式 **limo** /líːmoʊ/) 名 ❸ ▶定義 a large expensive car that usually has a sheet of glass between the driver and the passengers in the back 通常,運転手と後部の乗客との間がガラス板で仕切られた高価な大型車➡**リムジン**

**limp**¹ /lɪmp/ 動 ❺ ▶定義 to walk with difficulty because you have hurt your leg or foot 脚や足を痛めたため苦労して歩く➡**足を引きずって歩く**‖ *The goalkeeper limped off the field with a twisted ankle.* ゴールキーパーは足首を捻挫(ねんざ)して,びっこを引きながらフィールドから出た. — **limp** 名[単数扱い]➡**足を引きずること,びっこ**‖ *to walk with a limp* 足を引きずって歩く

**limp**² /lɪmp/ 形 ▶定義 not firm or strong 堅固または強固でない➡**ぐにゃぐにゃした,弱々しい,元気のない; 柔軟な**‖ *You should put those flowers in water before they go limp.* 花がしおれる前に水につけた方がいい.

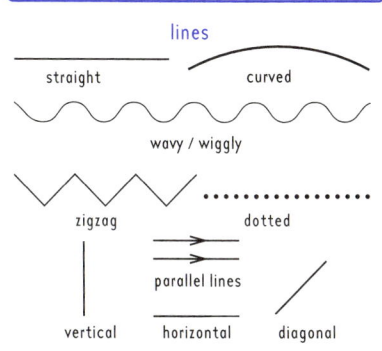

*line*¹ /laɪn/ 名 ▶定義1 ❸ a long thin mark on the surface of sth or on the ground ~の表面や地面の上の長く細い跡➡**線,筋,しわ,溝**‖ *to draw a line* 線を引く *a straight/wiggly/dotted line* 直線・波線・点線 *The old lady had lines on her forehead.* その老婦人は額にしわがあった. *The ball was definitely over the line.* ボールは絶対にラインの外に出ていた. *the finishing line of a race* レースのゴールライン ▶定義2 ❸ a row of people, things, words on a page, etc 人々,物,ページの単語などの列➡**行列,列,(文字の)行**‖ *There was a long line of people waiting at the Post Office.* 郵便局では人々が長い列を作って待っていた. *a five-line poem* 五行詩 *Start each paragraph on a new line.* 段落ごとに改行しなさい. ▶定義3 ❸ a border or limit between one place or thing and another 1つの場所や物と別の1つとの境界や限度➡**境界線,限界,限度**‖ *to cross state lines* 州境を越える. *There's a thin line between showing interest and being nosy.* 関心を持つこととお節介は違う. ▶定義4 [❸, 通常は単数] a direction or course of movement, thought or action 動き,思考,動作の方向や道筋➡**進行方向,進路,方針**‖ *He was so drunk he couldn't walk in a straight line.* 彼はひどく酔っていたのでまっすぐ歩けなかった. *The answer's not quite correct, but you're on the right lines.* 必ずしも正解とは言えないが,考え方は間違っていない. *The two countries' economies are developing along similar lines.* その2国の経済は同様の方向で発展しつつある. ▶定義5 ❸ a piece of rope or string ロープや糸➡**綱,ひも,針金**‖ *Hang out the* *clothes on the (washing) line, please.* 衣類を（物干し）綱に干してください. *a fishing line* 釣り糸 ▶定義6 ❻ a telephone or electricity wire or connection 電話や電気の線または接続 →**電話線, 電線, 通信線** ‖ *I'm sorry - the line is engaged. Can you try again later?* すみません — お話し中です. 後でかけ直してください. *I'll just check for you. Can you hold the line (= wait)?* 確認してみます. 電話を切らずにいて (= お待ち) ください.

▶定義7 ❻ a section of railway track 鉄道線路の区間 →**路線, 線路** ▶定義8 **lines** ［複数扱い］ the words that are spoken by an actor in a play, etc 俳優が劇中でしゃべる言葉など →**台詞（せりふ）** ▶定義9 ❻ a company that provides transport by air, ship, etc 空路, 海路などの交通手段を提供する会社 →**運輸会社, 定期航路（会社）** ‖ *an airline* 航空会社 ▶定義10 ［単数扱い］ one type of goods in a shop, etc 店の商品などの1種類 →**商品・製品の型** ▶定義11 ❻ the place where an army is fighting 軍隊が戦っている場所 →**戦線, 防御線** ‖ *There's renewed fighting on the front line.* 前線では新たに戦闘が始まった. ▶定義12 ❻ a series of people in a family, things or events that follow one another in time 時間経過に従って続いていく家族, 物, 出来事 →**家系, 血統, 歴代, 系列** ‖ *He comes from a long line of musicians.* 彼は長く続いた音楽家の家系の出身だ.

▶定義13 ❻ something that you do as a job, do well, or enjoy doing 仕事, 得意な事, 趣味としてするもの →**職業, 専門, 得手, 好み** ‖ *What line of business/work are you in?* お仕事は何ですか.

成句 draw the line at sth/doing sth ⇒ **DRAW**¹
drop sb a line ⇒ **DROP**¹

in line for sth ▶定義 likely to get sth 〜を得る見込みのある →**〜できそうな, 〜の候補で** ‖ *You could be in line for promotion if you keep working like this.* この調子で働けば, きっと昇進できるでしょう.

in line with sth ▶定義 similar to sth; in agreement with sth 〜と似ている; 〜に従って →**〜と一致して, 〜の趣旨に賛成して** ‖ *These changes will bring the industry in line with the new laws.* これらの変化によってその産業は新しい法律に沿ったものとなるだろう.

on line ▶定義 connected to or available on a computer system コンピューターシステムに接続した, または使用できる →**オンラインで**

somewhere along/down the line ▶定義 at some time; sooner or later いつか; 遅かれ早かれ →**そのうち, 早晩**

take a hard line (on sth) ⇒ **HARD**¹
toe the (party) line ⇒ **TOE**²

**line**² /láɪn/ 動 ⓣ ▶定義1 （しばしば受動態で）to cover the inside surface of sth with a different material 〜の内側を別の材料で覆う →**〜に裏を付ける, 裏打ちをする** ▶定義2 to form lines or rows along sth 〜に沿って縦列や横列を作る →**〜を一列に並べる, 〜に並ぶ** ‖ *Crowds lined the streets to watch the race.* レースを見るため群衆が通りに沿って並んだ.

句動詞 **line up (for sth)** 困 ▶定義 to form a line of people; to queue 人の列を作る; 列に加わる →**（〜を求めて）行列する, 整列する, 並ぶ, 並んで順番を待つ**

**line sth up** 略式 ▶定義 to arrange or organize sth 〜を配置する, または組織化する →**〜を一列にそろえる, 集める, 準備する, 手配する** ‖ *She lined the bottles up on the shelf.* 彼女はびんを棚にきちんと並べた.

**lined** /láɪnd/ 形 ▶定義1 covered in lines 線で覆われた →**線を引いた, 線のある** ‖ *a face lined with age* 年齢を表すしわのある顔 *lined paper* 罫（けい）線の引かれた紙 ▶定義2 -**lined**（複合語で用いて）having the object mentioned all along the side(s); having the inside surface covered with the material mentioned 〜がすべての側に沿っている; 〜で内側が覆われた →**〜で覆われた, 〜が多い, 〜で裏打ちされた** ‖ *a tree-lined avenue* 樹木が並ぶ大通り *fur-lined boots* 毛皮の裏が付いたブーツ

**linen** /línən/ 名 Ⓤ ▶定義1 a type of strong cloth that is made from a natural substance (**flax**) 天然素材（亜麻）から作られた丈夫な布 →**亜麻布, リンネル, リネン** ▶定義2 sheets and other cloth coverings used in the house on a bed, table, etc 家庭のベッドやテーブルなどに使われるシーツや布カバー →**リンネル製品** ‖ *bedlinen* シーツとまくらカバー

**liner** /láɪnər/ 名 ❻ ▶定義1 a large ship that carries people, etc long distances 人などを長距離運ぶ大型船 →**定期船, 大洋航路の豪華船** ▶定義2 something that is put inside sth else to keep it clean or protect it. A liner is usually thrown away after it has been used. ほかの〜を清潔に保つため、または保護するために内側に入れるもの. 普通は使用後に捨てられる→**裏当て, 裏打ち, ライナー** ‖ *a dustbin liner* ごみ入れの内袋

**linger** /líŋɡər/ 動 ▶定義 linger (on) to stay somewhere or do sth for longer than usual 通常より長くどこかにいる、または何かをする→**居残る, ぐずぐずする, 手間取る** ‖ *His eyes lingered on the money in her bag.* 彼の目は彼女のバッグの金から離れなかった.

**lingerie** /lǽnʒ(ə)ri; làːndʒəréi, -ríː/ 名 U ▶定義 (used in shops, etc) women's underwear (店などで用いて)女性の下着→**肌着類, ランジェリー**

**linguist** /líŋɡwɪst/ 名 C ▶定義 a person who is good at learning foreign languages; a person who studies or teaches language(s) 外国語の習得に優れた人; 言語を研究している人、または教えている人→**語学の才能のある人; 言語学者, 語学者**

**linguistic** /lɪŋɡwístɪk/ 形 ▶定義 connected with language or the study of language 言語または言語の研究と関連した→**言語の, 言語学(上)の**

**linguistics** /lɪŋɡwístɪks/ 名 U ▶定義 the scientific study of language 言語の科学的研究→**言語学**

**lining** /láɪnɪŋ/ 名 C U ▶定義 material that covers the inside surface of sth 〜の内側を覆うもの→**裏, 裏当て, 裏地** ‖ *I've torn the lining of my coat.* コートの裏地が裂けてしまった.
成句 every cloud has a silver lining ⇒ **CLOUD**¹

\***link**¹ /lɪŋk/ 名 C ▶定義 **1** a link (between A and B); a link (with sb/sth) a connection or relationship between two or more people or things 複数の人や物の間の結び付きや関係→**(〜の間の・〜との)つながり, きずな, 連結, 関連** ‖ *There is a strong link between smoking and heart disease.* 喫煙と心臓病には強い関連がある.
▶定義 **2** one ring of a chain 鎖の輪の1つ→**環, (鎖状ソーセージなどの)一節** ☞ **padlock** のさし絵 ▶定義 **3** a means of travelling or communicating between two places 2地点間の移動または通信の手段→**連絡線, 連絡道路, 接続路** ‖ *To visit similar web sites to this one, click on the links at the bottom of the page.* これと同様のウェブサイトを訪れるには、ページの下部のリンクをクリックしてください.

**link**² /lɪŋk/ 動 他 ▶定義 link A to/with B; link A

lion 979

and B (together) to make a connection between two or more people or things 複数の人や物の間を結ぶ→**〜を…に・〜と…を結び付ける, 連結する, つなぐ** ‖ *The new bridge will link the island to the mainland.* 新しい橋はその島を本土と結ぶことになる. *The computers are linked together in a network.* コンピューターはネットワークで接続されている.

何動詞 link up (with sb/sth) ▶定義 to join together (with sb/sth) (〜と)結び付ける→**〜を(…と)連結する, 同盟する, 仲間になる** ‖ *All our branches are linked up by computer.* 我が社の支社はすべてコンピューターで結ばれている.

**link-up** 名 C ▶定義 the joining together or connection of two or more things 複数の物を結び付けたり接続すること→**連結, 連合**

**linoleum** /lənóʊliəm, -ljəm/ (または 略式 **lino** /láɪnoʊ/) 名 U ▶定義 a type of plastic covering for floors ビニール製の床敷き →**リノリウム**

\***lion** /láɪən/ 名 C ▶定義 a large animal of the cat family that lives in Africa and parts of southern

Asia. Male lions have a large amount of hair around their head and neck (a mane). アフリカと南アジアの一部に住むネコ科の大型動物. 雄には頭部と首の回りに大量の毛(たてがみ)がある→ライオン, 獅子(しし)

▶ lioness は雌のライオン, cub は子供のライオン, roar はライオンが出す大きな声.

\*lip /lɪp/ 🔊 🄲 ▶定義1 either of the two soft edges at the opening of your mouth 口の開口部にある2つの柔らかい縁の一方→唇 ‖ *to kiss sb on the lips* ～の唇にキスする ☞ C5 ページのさし絵

▶ top/upper lip(上唇), bottom/lower lip(下唇).

▶定義2 **-lipped**(複合形容詞を作るために用いて) having the type of lips mentioned ～のような唇を持つ→～な唇の ‖ *thin-lipped* 薄い唇の ▶定義3 the edge of a cup or sth that is shaped like a cup カップなどの椀(わん)状のものの縁→唇状のもの, 注ぎ口, へり

> ▶日本語 vs 英語
>
> lip と「口」
>
> 英語の lip は, 日本語の唇より広い範囲(鼻の下を含む口の周り全体)を指します. ですから,「口を閉じなさい」は close your lips となります. mouth ではなく lip を使うことに注意しましょう.

成句 purse your lips ⇒ **PURSE**²

**lip-read** 動自他 (過, 過分 **lip-read** /-led/) ▶定義 to understand what sb is saying by looking at the movements of his/her lips ～の言っている事を唇の動きを見て理解する→ (～を)読唇術で理解する

**lipstick** /lípstɪ̀k/ 🔊 🄲 🅄 ▶定義 a substance that is used for giving colour to your lips 唇に色を付けるために使われるもの→口紅 ‖ *to put on some lipstick* 口紅を付ける *a new lipstick* 新しい口紅

**liqueur** /lɪkjʊ́ər, -kə́ːr/ 🔊 🅄 🄲 ▶定義 a strong sweet alcoholic drink that is often drunk in small quantities after a meal 強くて甘いアルコール飲料で, 食後に少量を飲むことが多い→リキュール

\***liquid** /líkwəd/ 🔊 🄲 🅄 ▶定義 a substance, for example water, that is not solid or a gas and that can flow or be poured 例えば水のように, 固体や気体ではなく流したり注いだりできる物質→液体, 流動体 — liquid 形→液体の, 液状の

**liquidate** /líkwədèɪt/ 動他 ▶定義1 to close a business because it has no money left 資金が尽きたために事業を畳む→～を清算する, (会社など)を整理・解散する ▶定義2 to destroy or remove sb/sth that causes problems 問題の原因となる～を破壊したり取り除く→～を一掃する, 廃止する, 粛清する — liquidation /lìkwədéɪʃ(ə)n/ 名 🅄→清算, 一掃, 廃止 ‖ *If the company doesn't receive a big order soon, it will have to go into liquidation.* すぐに大型の受注がない限り, 会社は破産せざるを得ないだろう.

**liquidize** (または **-ise**) /líkwədàɪz/ 動他 ▶定義 to cause sth to become liquid ～を液体にする→～を液化する, (食品)をミキサーにかける — liquidizer (または liquidiser) = **BLENDER**

**liquor** /líkər/ 🔊 🅄 🇺🇸 ▶定義 strong alcoholic drinks; spirits 強いアルコール飲料; 酒類→強い酒, 蒸留酒

**liquorice** ( 🇺🇸 **licorice**) /lík(ə)rɪʃ, -k(ə)rəs/ 🔊 🅄 ▶定義 a black substance, made from a plant, that is used in some sweets 植物から作る黒い物質で, 菓子などに使われる→カンゾウ, 甘草(かんぞう), 甘草入りのキャンデー

**lisp** /lɪsp/ 🔊 🄲 ▶定義 a speech fault in which 's' is pronounced as 'th' 話し方の誤りで s が th で発音される→舌をもつれさせて発音すること ‖ *He speaks with a slight lisp.* 彼の話し方はいくらか不明瞭(めいりょう)だ. — lisp 動 自他→舌をもつれさせて発音する

\***list** /lɪst/ 🔊 🄲 ▶定義 a series of names, figures, items, etc that are written, printed or said one after another 連続して書かれたり, 印刷されたり述べられたりする一続きの名前, 数字, 項目など→一覧, 一覧表, リスト ‖ *a checklist of everything that needs to be done* やるべき事すべてのチェックリスト *a waiting list* 空きを待つ人のリスト *Your name is third on the list.* あなたの名前はリストの3番目にあります. — list 動他→～を一覧にする, 一覧に載せる, リストにする ‖ *to list items in alphabetical order* アルファベット順に項目をリストにする

\***listen** /lís(ə)n/ 🔊 動自 ▶定義1 **listen (to sb/sth)** to pay attention to sb/sth in order to hear him/her/it 聞こえるように～に注意を払う➜(～を)**聴く,耳を傾ける** ‖ *Now please listen carefully to what I have to say.* では,私の言う事をよく聞いてください. *to listen to music/the radio* 音楽・ラジオを聴く ☛参 **hear** の注 ▶定義2 listen to sb/sth to take notice of or believe what sb says ～の言う事に注意を払う,または信じる➜**～に耳を貸す,従う** ‖ *You should listen to your parents' advice.* 両親の忠告には耳を貸すべきだ. — listen [名] [単数扱い] [略式] ➜**聴くこと** ‖ ***Have a listen*** *and see if you can hear anything.* 何か聞こえるかどうか耳を澄まして.

[句動詞] listen (out) for sth ▶定義 to wait to hear sth 何かが聞こえるのを待つ➜**聞こえないかと～に耳を澄ます** ‖ *to listen (out) for a knock on the door* ノックが聞こえないかと耳を澄ます

listen in (on/to sth) ▶定義 to listen to sb else's private conversation 他人の私的な会話を聞く➜**～を盗み聴きする,盗聴する** ‖ *Have you been listening in on my phone calls?* 私の電話を盗み聴きしていたのですか.

**listener** /lís(ə)nər/ [名] [C] ▶定義 a person who listens 聴く人➜**聞き手,ラジオ番組の聴取者** ‖ *When I'm unhappy I always phone Charlie - he's such a good listener.* 嫌な事があるといつもチャーリーに電話する — 彼は本当に聞き上手なんだ. *The new radio show has attracted a record number of listeners.* 新しいラジオ番組の聴取者数は記録的な数に達している.

**listless** /lístləs/ [形] ▶定義 tired and without energy 疲れて活気のない➜**元気のない,ぼんやりした** — listlessly [副] ➜**元気なく,ぼんやりと**

**lit** LIGHT[3] の過去・過去分詞形

**liter** [米] = LITRE

**literacy** /lít(ə)rəsi/ [名] [U] ▶定義 the ability to read and write 読み書きの能力➜**読み書きできること,識字,教育があること** ⇔ **illiteracy**

**literal** /lít(ə)rəl/ [形] ▶定義1 (used about the meaning of a word or phrase) original or basic (語や句の意味について)元来の,基本的な➜**文字通りの,事実そのままの,誇張なしの** ‖ *The adjective 'big-headed' is hardly ever used in its literal sense.* big-headed という形容詞が文字通りの意味で使われることはほとんどない. ☛参 **figurative**, **metaphor** ▶定義2 (used when translating, etc) dealing with each word separately without looking at the general meaning (翻訳などに用いて)全体の意味を考えずに単語を個々に扱って➜**逐語訳の,直訳の**

**literally** /lít(ə)rəli/ [副] ▶定義1 according to the basic or original meaning of the word, etc 語などの基本的,または元の意味の通りに➜**文字通りに,直訳的に** ‖ *You can't translate these idioms literally.* これらの成句を文字通りに訳すことはできない. ▶定義2 [略式] used for emphasizing sth ～を強調するために用いて➜**本当に,全く,まさに** ‖ *We were literally frozen to death (= we were very cold).* 私たちは文字通り凍死しそうだった(= とても寒かった).

**literary** /lít(ə)r(ə)ri; lítərèri/ [形] ▶定義 of or concerned with literature 文学の,文学に関する➜**文学上の,文芸の** ‖ *literary criticism* 文学評論 *a literary journal* 文学的日記

**literate** /lít(ə)rət/ [形] ▶定義1 able to read and write 読み書きのできる➜**文字が分かる** ⇔ **illiterate** ☛ [名] literacy ☛参 **numerate** ▶定義2 well-educated 教育のある➜**学問のある**

*__literature__ /lít(ə)rətʃər/ [名] [U] ▶定義1 writing that is considered to be a work of art. Literature includes novels, plays and poetry. 芸術作品と見なされる文章. 小説,演劇,詩が含まれる➜**文学,文学作品** ‖ *French literature* フランス文学 ▶定義2 literature (on sth) printed material about a particular subject 特定の対象についての印刷物 ➜**調査報告書,論文,文献**

*__litre__ ([米] **liter**) /lí:tər/ [名] [C] ([略] **l**) ▶定義 a measure of liquid 液体を計る単位➜**リットル** ‖ *ten litres of petrol* 10リットルのガソリン *a litre bottle of wine* 1リットルびん入りのワイン

**litter** /lítər/ [名] ▶定義1 [U] pieces of paper, rubbish, etc that are left in a public place 公共の場所に放置された紙切れやごみなど➜**散らかった物,くず,がらくた** ☛ **bin** のさし絵 ▶定義2 [C] all the young animals that are born to one mother at the same time 同じ母親から一度に生まれた動物の子➜**一腹の子** ‖ *a litter of six puppies* 一度に生まれた6匹の子犬 — litter [動] [他] ➜**～を散らかす,(ごみなどで)汚す** ‖ *The streets were lit-*

L

tered with rubbish. 通りにはごみが散らかっていた.

**litter bin** 名 C ▶定義 a container to put rubbish in, in the street or a public building 通りや公共の建物にある,ごみを入れるための容器→ごみ箱,くずかご ● bin のさし絵

**★little**¹ /lítl/ 形 ▶定義1 not big; small 大きくない;小さい→**小型の,少ない,わずかの** || *a little bag of sweets* お菓子の小袋 *Do you want the big one or the little one?* 大きい方と小さい方のどちらが欲しいですか. *a little mistake/problem* ちょっとした間違い・問題

▶ little はほかの形容詞と共に用いられることが多い: *a little old lady* (かわいいおばあさん) *a cute little kitten* (かわいらしい子猫) *What a funny little shop!* (何ておかしな小さなお店でしょう.) ☞ small の注

▶定義2 (used about distance or time) short (距離や時間について) 短い→**わずかな,ちょっと** || *Do you mind waiting a little while?* ちょっとお待ちいただけますか. *We only live a little way from here.* 私たちはこのすぐ先に住んでいます. *It's only a little further.* もうすぐ先です.

▶定義3 young 若い→**年少の,幼い** || *a little girl/boy* 幼い少女・少年 *my little brother* 私の弟 *I was very naughty when I was little.* 私は小さいころとても腕白だった.

**little**² /lítl/ 副 代 ▶定義1 (または the の後について名詞として) not much or not enough 多くない,十分でない→**ほとんど～ない,ほとんどないもの (金,時間など),ほとんどない～** || *I slept very little last night.* 昨夜はほとんど眠れなかった. *a little-known author* 無名の作家 *They have very little money.* 彼らにはほとんど金がない. *There is little hope that she will recover.* 彼女が回復できる望みはほとんどない. ☞ less, least ▶定義2 **a little** a small amount of sth ～の少量→**少し,わずか** || *I like a little sugar in my tea.* 紅茶に少し砂糖を入れるのが好きだ. *Could I have a little help, please?* ちょっと手伝っていただけますか.

成句 **little by little** ▶定義 slowly ゆっくりと→**少しずつ,徐々に** || *After the accident her strength returned little by little.* 事故の後,彼女の体力は徐々に戻った.

**a little** /ə lítl/ 副 代 ▶定義1 rather; to a small degree いくぶん; わずかな程度まで→**少し,少しは,わずかに** || *This skirt is a little too tight.* このスカートは少しきつすぎる.

▶ a little bit または a bit は a little の代わりによく用いられる: *I was feeling a little bit tired so I decided not to go out.* (少し疲れていたので,外出するのはやめた.)

▶定義2 a small amount 少量→**少しのもの,わずかしかないもの** || '*Is there any butter left?*' '*Yes, just a little*' 「バターが残っていますか」「はい,少しだけ」

**★live**¹ /lív/ 動 ▶定義1 自 to have your home in a particular place 特定の場所に自分の家を持つ→**住む,居住する** || *Where do you live?* どこにお住まいですか. *He still lives with his parents.* 彼はまだ両親と同居している. ▶定義2 自 to be or stay alive 生きている,生き長らえている→**生きる,生存する** || *She hasn't got long to live.* 彼女は先が長くない. *to live to a great age* 非常に長生きする ▶定義3 自 他 to pass or spend your life in a certain way 特定のやり方で人生を過ごす→**暮らす,生活する** || *to live a quiet life* 静かな暮らしをする *to live in comfort/poverty* 安楽に暮らす・暮らしが貧しい ▶定義4 to enjoy all the opportunities of life fully 人生の機会をすべて十分に楽しむ→**人生を楽しむ,面白く暮らす** || *I want to live a bit before settling down and getting married.* 身を固めて結婚する前にもう少し楽しみたい.

成句 **live/sleep rough** ⇒ **ROUGH**³
句動詞 **live by sth** ▶定義 to follow a particular belief or set of principles 特定の信念や原則に従う→**～を生活の指針とする,～に従って暮らす**
**live by doing sth** ▶定義 to get the money, food, etc you need by doing a particular activity 特定の活動によって必要な金や食物などを得る→**～を生活の糧とする,～から収入を得て暮らす,～で暮らす** || *They live by hunting and fishing.* 狩猟と釣りによって暮らしている.

**live for sb/sth** ▶定義 to consider sb/sth to be the most important thing in your life ～を人生で最も大切なものであると見なす→**～を生きがいにする,～に専念する** || *He felt he had nothing to live for after his wife died.* 妻が死んだ後は,彼は生きがいが何もないと感じた.

**not live sth down** ▶定義 to be unable to make

people forget sth bad or embarrassing that you have done ～に対して自分がした悪い事や恥ずかしい事を忘れさせることができない➔(過去, 恥, 失敗, 犯罪など)を償えない, 時と共に忘れさせることができない

**live it up** ▶定義 to enjoy yourself in an exciting way, usually spending a lot of money 普通は大金を使ってわくわくする方法で楽しむ➔楽しい時を過ごす, 大いに騒ぐ, ぜいたくに遊び暮らす, 豪遊する

**live off sb/sth** ▶定義 to depend on sb/sth in order to live 生きるために～に頼る➔～の世話になって暮らす, ～をよりどころに暮らす ‖ *Barry lives off tinned food.* バリーは缶詰ばかり食べて暮らしている. *She could easily get a job but she still lives off her parents.* 簡単に仕事に就けるはずなのに, 彼女はまだ両親の世話になって暮らしている.

**live on** ▶定義 to continue to live or exist 生き続ける, 存在し続ける➔(名声などが)残る ‖ *Mozart is dead but his music lives on.* モーツァルトは死んだが, 彼の音楽は生き続けている.

**live on sth** ▶定義 1 to have sth as your only food ～を唯一の食物とする➔～を常食とする, ～だけを食べて生きる ‖ *to live on bread and water* パンと水だけで生きる ▶定義 2 to manage to buy what you need to live 生活に必要な物を何とか買うことができる➔～に頼って暮らす, ～で暮らす ‖ *I don't know how they live on so little money!* 彼らがあんなにわずかの金でどうやって暮らせるのか分からない.

**live out sth** ▶定義 1 to actually do sth that you only imagined doing before 以前には空想していただけの事を実際にやる➔～を実現する, 現実のものとする ‖ *to live out your dreams/fantasies* 夢・空想を実現する ▶定義 2 to spend the rest of your life in a particular way 特定のやり方で残りの人生を過ごす➔～の終わりまで生きる, 切り抜ける

**live through sth** ▶定義 to survive an unpleasant experience つらい経験を生き延びる➔～を持ちこたえる, 乗り越える ‖ *She lived through two wars.* 彼女は2つの戦争を生き延びた.

**live together** ▶定義 to live in the same house, etc as sb and have a sexual relationship with him/her ～と同じ家などに住み, 性的な関係を持つ➔同居する, 同棲(どうせい)する

# lively 983

**live up to sth** ▶定義 to be as good as expected 予想した通りに良い➔(評判・期待)を裏切らない, ～にかなう, (約束)を果たす ‖ *Children sometimes find it hard to live up to their parents' expectations.* 子供たちは時には両親の期待にこたえるのが難しいと感じる.

**live with sb** = **LIVE TOGETHER**

**live with sth** ▶定義 to accept sth unpleasant that you cannot change 変えることのできない不快な～を受け入れる➔(現状など)を受け入れる, 我慢する, 耐える ‖ *It can be hard to live with the fact that you are getting older.* 年老いていくという事実を受け入れて生きていくのがつらいこともある.

***live**² /láɪv/ 形副 ▶定義 1 having life; not dead 生命のある; 死んでいない➔生きている, 生きた, 本物の ‖ *Have you ever touched a real live snake?* 生きた本物の蛇を触ったことがありますか. ▶定義 2 (used about a radio or television programme) seen or heard as it is happening (ラジオやテレビ番組について)起こっているのと同時に見る, 聴く➔生放送の, 生中継の, 実況の ‖ *live coverage of the Olympic Games* オリンピックの生中継 *This programme is coming live from Wembley Stadium.* この放送はウェンブリー競技場からの実況中継でお送りしています. *to go out live on TV* テレビに生出演する ▶定義 3 performed or performing for an audience 聴衆のために演じられる, 演じている➔実演の, ライブの ‖ *That pub has live music on Saturdays.* そのパブでは毎週土曜日に生演奏が聴ける. ▶定義 4 (used about a bomb, bullet, etc) that has not yet exploded (爆弾, 弾丸などについて)まだ爆発していない➔実弾の, 実爆弾の ▶定義 5 (used about a wire, etc) carrying electricity (電線などについて)電流が流れている➔電流の通じた, 作動中の

**livelihood** /láɪvlihʊd/ 名 [ Ⓒ, 通常は単数 ] ▶定義 the way that you earn money 金を稼ぐ方法➔生計の手段 ‖ *to lose your livelihood* 生活費を得る手段を失う

***lively** /láɪvli/ 形 (**livelier**; **liveliest**) ▶定義 full of energy, interest, excitement, etc 活気, 興味, 興奮などで一杯の➔活気のある, 元気な, 活発な, 生き生きとした, はつらつとした ‖ *lively children* 元

気な子供たち The town is quite lively at night. その町は夜はかなり活気がある.

**liven** /láɪv(ə)n/ 動
句動詞 liven (sb/sth) up ▶定義 to become or make sb/sth become more interesting and exciting ～がより面白く刺激的になる・する→活気づく, ～を活気づける, 精彩を帯びる, 陽気にする || Once the band began to play the party livened up. バンドが演奏を始めた途端, パーティーは盛り上がった.

**liver** /lívər/ 名 ▶定義1 ⓒthe part of your body that cleans your blood 血液を浄化する身体の器官→肝臓→C5 ページのさし絵 ▶定義2 Ⓤthe liver of an animal when it is cooked and eaten as food 調理して食用にする場合の動物の肝臓→レバー || fried liver and onions いためたレバーとタマネギ

**lives** LIFE の複数形

**livestock** /láɪvstɒk/ 名 Ⓤ ▶定義 animals that are kept on a farm, such as cows, pigs, sheep, etc 牛, 豚, 羊などのように農場で飼育される動物→家畜

**living**¹ /lívɪŋ/ 形 ▶定義1 alive now 今生きている→生命のある, 死んでいない || He has no living relatives. 彼には生存している肉親はいない. ☞参 alive の注 ▶定義2 still used or practised now 今でも使われている, 実施されている→現存の || living languages/traditions 現在も使用されている言語・現在も生きている伝統 ⇔ dead

**living**² /lívɪŋ/ 名 ▶定義1 [ⓒ, 通常は単数] money to buy things that you need in life 生活に必要なものを買うための金→生計, 生活の資, 収入 || What do you do *for a living*? 仕事は何ですか. ▶定義2 Ⓤyour way or quality of life 生活の仕方や質→暮らし方, 暮らし向き || The *cost of living* has risen in recent years. ここ数年生活費が上がっている. The *standard of living* is very high in that country. その国は生活水準が非常に高い.

**living room** (特に 英 **sitting room**) 名 ⓒ ▶定義 the room in a house where people sit, relax, watch TV, etc together 住宅にある部屋で, 人々が一緒に座り, くつろぎ, テレビを見たりする場所→居間

lizard

**lizard** /lízərd/ 名 ⓒ ▶定義 a small animal with four legs, dry skin and a long tail 4本の足と乾燥した皮膚, 長い尾を持つ小さな動物→トカゲ

**load**¹ /lóʊd/ 名 ⓒ ▶定義1 something (heavy) that is being or is waiting to be carried 運ばれている, またはこれから運ばれる(重い)物→(大量の)積み荷, 荷 || a truck carrying a load of sand 砂を積んだトラック ▶定義2 (しばしば複合語で) the quantity of sth that can be carried 運ぶことのできる～の量→(乗り物の)積載量 || bus loads of tourists バス一杯の旅行者 ▶定義3 **loads (of sth)** [複数扱い] 略式 a lot (of sth) 多くの(～)→多量, 多数 || There are loads of things to do in London in the evenings. ロンドンの夜にはやる事が山ほどある.

成句 **a load of rubbish, etc** 略式 ▶定義 nonsense 無意味→ばかげた事・行為, 下らない事

**load**² /lóʊd/ 動 ▶定義1 圓他 load (sth/sb) (up) (with sth); load (sth/sb) (into/onto sth) to put a large quantity of sth into or onto sb/sth 大量の～を…に入れる・負わせる→(～を)(…に)一杯に詰め込む, 載せる || They loaded the plane (up) with supplies. 彼らは飛行機に供給品を積み込んだ. Load the washing into the machine. 洗濯物を洗濯機に入れなさい. ▶定義2 圓to receive a load→荷を受け入れる || The ship is still loading. まだ船に荷物を積み込んでいる. ▶定義3 他to put a program or disk into a computer コンピューターにプログラムやディスクを入れる→(プログラム)を読み込む, (ディスクなど)を挿入する || First, switch on the machine and load the disk. まず, 機器の電源を入れディスクを挿入してください. ▶定義4 他to put sth into a machine, a weapon, etc so that it can be used ～を機械や武器などに入れて, 使用できるようにする→～を装着する, 装填(そうてん)する || to load film into a camera カメラにフィルムを装填する to load a gun 銃に弾を込める ⇔ **unload**

**loaded** /lóʊdəd/ 形 ▶定義1 **loaded (with sth)** carrying a load; full and heavy 荷を積んでいる; 一杯で重い→(～を)積んだ; 満載の, (～で)満員の

▶定義2 (used especially about a gun or a camera) containing a bullet, a film, etc(特に銃やカメラについて)弾丸, フィルムなどを入れた→装填(そうてん)された ▶定義3 giving an advantage 有利にする→一方に偏った, 含みのある, 誘導的な ‖ *The system is loaded in their favour.* その制度は彼らに有利にできている. ▶定義4 略式(名詞の前は不可) having a lot of money; rich 多くの金を持っている; 裕福な→うんと金がある, 金持ちの

**loaf** /lóuf/ 名 C (複 **loaves** /lóuvz/) ▶定義 bread baked in one piece 焼いた一塊のパン→パン1個, 一焼きのパン ‖ *a loaf of bread* パン1個 ☞ **bread** のさし絵

**loan** /lóun/ 名 ▶定義1 C money, etc that sb/sth lends you 〜が貸す金など→貸し付け, 貸し出し, ローン, 借金 ‖ *to take out a bank loan* 銀行ローンを組む *to pay off a loan* 借金を返済する ▶定義2 U the act of lending sth or the state of being lent 〜を貸すこと, または借りている状態→貸し付けること, 借りること ‖ *The books are on loan from the library.* それらの本は図書館から借りた物だ. ― loan 動他 正式 loan sth (to sb)→(〜に)物を貸す, (利子をとって)金を貸す

▶アメリカ英語では, loan はそれほど正式な語ではなく一般的に使われる.

**loathe** /lóuð/ 動他(進行形は不可) ▶定義 to hate sb/sth 〜を憎む→〜をひどく嫌う, ひどく嫌がる, 〜にむかつく, へどが出る

▶この動詞は進行形では使われないが, 現在分詞(= -ing 形)で使われることは多い. *Loathing the thought of having to apologize, she knocked on his door.* (謝らなければならないことがとても嫌だったが, 彼女は彼のドアをノックした.)

― **loathsome** /lóuðsəm/ 形→ひどく嫌な, いまわしい ― **loathing** 名 U→ひどく嫌うこと, 嫌悪, 大嫌い

**loaves** LOAF の複数形

**lob** /láb/ 動自他 (**lobbing**; **lobbed**) ▶定義 (sport) to hit, kick or throw a ball high into the air, so that it lands behind your opponent(スポーツ)相手の後ろに落ちるように, ボールを空中に高く打ったり, けったり, 投げる→ロブを打つ, 高く球を打つ ― **lob** 名 C→ロブ, (球を)高く打つこと, 高く打った球

**lobby**¹ /lábi/ 名 C (複 **lobbies**) ▶定義1 the area that is just inside a large building, where people can meet and wait 大きな建物の入ってすぐの場所で, 人々が待ち合わせできる→ロビー, ホール, 広間 ‖ *a hotel lobby* ホテルのロビー ▶定義2 [単数または複数形の動詞と共に] a group of people who try to influence politicians to do or not do sth 政治家に何かをするように, またはしないように影響を及ぼそうとする人々の団体→院外団, 圧力団体, 運動団体 ‖ *the anti-smoking lobby* 禁煙運動家

**lobby**² /lábi/ 動自他 (現分 **lobbying**; 三単現 **lobbies**; 過, 過分 **lobbied**) ▶定義 to try to influence a politician or the government to do or not do sth 政治家や政府に何かをするように, またはしないように影響を及ぼそうとする→(議員に)働き掛ける, 陳情運動をする

**lobe** /lóub/ 名 C ▶定義1 = EAR LOBE ▶定義2 one part of an organ of the body, especially the brain or lungs 体の器官, 特に脳や肺の一部→葉(よう)

**lobster** /lábstər/ 名 ▶定義1 C a large shellfish that has eight legs. A lobster is bluish-black but it turns red when it is cooked. 8本の足がある大型の甲殻類. 青みがかった黒色だが, 調理すると赤くなる→ウミザリガニ, ロブスター, イセエビ ☞ **shellfish** のさし絵 ▶定義2 U a cooked lobster eaten as food 食用の調理されたロブスター→ロブスターの肉

\***local**¹ /lóuk(ə)l/ ▶定義 of a particular place (near you) (近くの)特定の場所の→その土地の, その場所の, 地元の ‖ *local newspapers/radio* 地方新聞・ローカルラジオ *the local doctor/policeman/butcher* 地元の医者・警官・肉屋 ☞ 参 **international**, **national**, **regional** ― **locally** 副→その土地で, 地元で ‖ *I do most of my shopping locally.* 私は買い物の大部分を地元でする.

**local**² /lóuk(ə)l/ 名 C ▶定義1 [通常は複数] a person who lives in a particular place 特定の場所に住む人→地元の人々, 地元民 ‖ *The locals seem very friendly.* その土地の人々はとても親切なようだ. ▶定義2 英 略式 a pub that is near your home where you often go to drink よく飲みに行く家の近くのパブ→行き付けのパブ, 近所のパブ

**localize** (または **-ise**) /lóuk(ə)làiz/ 動他 ▶定義

to limit sth to a particular place or area ～を特定の場所や範囲に制限する→～を局地化する, 特定の地域に集中する

**local time** 名 ❶ ▶定義 the time at a particular place in the world 世界の特定地域の時間→地方時, 現地時間 ‖ *We arrive in Singapore at 2 o'clock in the afternoon, local time.* 私たちは現地時間の午後2時にシンガポールに着く.

**locate** /lóukéɪt; ←/ 動 ❶ ▶定義1 to find the exact position of sb/sth ～の正確な位置を見つける→～を突き止める, 探し出す ‖ *The damaged ship has been located two miles off the coast.* 損害を受けた船は海岸から2マイルの地点で見つかっている. ▶定義2 to put or build sth in a particular place 特定の場所に～を置く, または建設する→～を…に置く, 設ける, 定める ― **located** 形 →～に位置する, ～にある ‖ *Where exactly is your office located?* あなたの事務所は正確にはどこにあるのですか.

**location** /loʊkéɪ(ə)n/ 名 ▶定義1 ❻ a place or position 場所または位置→所在, 敷地, 立地 ‖ *Several locations have been suggested for the new office block.* 新しいオフィスビル用にいくつかの場所が提案されている. ▶定義2 ❶ the action of finding where sb/sth is ～の場所を見つけること→所在の探索, 位置測定

成句 **on location** ▶定義 (used about a film, television programme, etc) made in a suitable place outside the building where films, etc are usually made (a studio) (映画やテレビ番組などについて) 映画などが通常制作される建物 (スタジオ) の外の適切な場所で作られた→ロケで, 野外撮影で ‖ *The series was filmed on location in Thailand.* そのシリーズ物はタイのロケで撮影された.

**loch** /lɑk, lɑx/ 名 ❻ ▶定義 the Scottish word for a lake 湖のスコットランド語→湖, (細長い) 入り江 ‖ *the Loch Ness monster* ネス湖の怪物

★**lock**¹ /lɑk/ 動 ▶定義1 ❶ ❶ to close or fasten (sth) so that it can only be opened with a key ～を閉じたり締めたりして, かぎでのみ開けられるようにする→かぎがかかる; ～にかぎをかける, 錠を下ろす ‖ *Have you locked the car?* 車にかぎをかけましたか. *The door won't lock.* ドアにどうしてもかぎがかからない. ⇔ **unlock**

▶定義2 ❶ to put sb/sth in a safe place and lock it ～を安全な場所に入れてかぎをかける→～を(…に)閉じ込める, しまい込む ‖ *Lock your passport in a safe place.* パスポートは安全な場所にしまっておいてください. ▶定義3 ❶ **be locked in sth** to be involved in an angry argument, etc with sth, or to be holding sb very tightly ～についての険悪な口論などに巻き込まれる, または～を強く抱き締める→～を組み合わせて動けなくする, 捕まえる, 抱き締める ‖ *The two sides were locked in a bitter dispute.* 2組は痛烈な口論になり抜け出せなかった. *They were locked in a passionate embrace.* 彼らは情熱的に抱き合った.

句動詞 **lock sth away** ▶定義 to keep sth in a safe or secret place that is locked ～をかぎのかかる金庫や秘密の場所にしまう→～をしまい込む, (安全に)保管する

**lock sb in/out** ▶定義 to lock a door so that a person cannot get in/out ドアにかぎをかけて～が出入りできないようにする→閉じ込める, 閉め出す ‖ *I locked myself out of the house and had to climb in through the window.* 私はかぎを忘れて[なくして]家に入れなかったので, 窓からよじ登って入らなければならなかった.

**lock (sth) up** ▶定義 to lock all the doors, windows, etc of a building 建物のすべてのドアや窓などにかぎをかける→～の戸締まりをする ‖ *Make sure that you lock up before you leave.* 出掛ける前に戸締まりを確認しなさい.

**lock sb up** ▶定義 to put sb in prison ～を刑務所に入れる→～を収監する, 監禁する

★**lock**² /lɑk/ 名 ❻ ▶定義1 something that is used for fastening a door, lid, etc so that you need a key to open it again 再び開けるにはかぎを必要とするように, ドアやふたなどを閉めるのに使われるもの→錠, 錠前, ロック ‖ *to turn the key in the lock* 錠にかぎ差し込んで回す ☛参 **padlock** ☛ **key** のさし絵 ▶定義2 a part of a river or a canal where the level of water changes. Locks have gates at each end and are used to allow boats to move to a higher or lower part of the canal or river. 水位が変化する川や運河の部分. 両端に門があり小型船が運河や川の高い部分や低い部分に移動できる→水門

成句 **pick a lock** ⇒ **PICK**¹

**under lock and key** ▶定義 in a locked place 錠

が下ろされた場所で→かぎをかけられて，厳重に保管されて，安全に投獄されて

**locker** /lákər/ 名 C 定義 a small cupboard that can be locked in a school or sports centre, where you can leave your clothes, books, etc 学校やスポーツセンターにあるかぎのかかる小型の戸棚で，衣服や本などを入れる→ロッカー

**locket** /lákət/ 名 C 定義 a piece of jewellery that you wear on a chain around your neck and which opens so that you can put a picture, etc inside チェーンで首に下げる装身具で，開いて中に写真などを入れられる→ロケット

**locksmith** /láksmìθ/ 名 C 定義 a person who makes and repairs locks 錠を作ったり修理する人→錠前師

**locomotive** /lòʊkəmóʊtɪv/ = ENGINE(2)

**locust** /lóʊkəst/ 名 C 定義 a flying insect from Africa and Asia that moves in very large groups, eating and destroying large quantities of plants アフリカやアジア原産の飛ぶ昆虫で大群で移動し大量の植物を食べて全滅させる→イナゴ，バッタ ☞ **insect** のさし絵

**lodge**¹ /lɑdʒ/ 動 定義 1 自 to pay to live in sb's house with him/her 金を払って～の家にその～と一緒に住む→下宿する，(短期間)泊まる ‖ *He lodged with a family for his first term at university.* 彼は大学の1学期にある家族の家に下宿した. 定義 2 自他 to become firmly fixed or to make sth do this しっかりと固定される，または～をしっかりと固定する→(弾などが)入って止まる，～を打ち込む，(矢が)突き刺さる，～を突き刺す 定義 3 他 正式 to make an official statement complaining about sth ～についての苦情を公式に述べる→～を申し立てる，(苦情，反対など)を提出する，持ち出す

**lodge**² /lɑdʒ/ 名 C 定義 1 a room at the entrance to a large building such as a college or factory 大学や工場などの大きな建物の入り口にある部屋→番小屋，守衛室，管理人室 定義 2 a small house in the country 田舎の小さな家→小屋，山小屋，ロッジ

**lodger** /lɑ́dʒər/ 名 C 定義 a person who pays rent to live in a house as a member of the family 金を払って家族の一員として家に住む人→下宿人，同居人，間借り人 ☞参 **boarder**

**lodging** /lɑ́dʒɪŋ/ 名 定義 1 C U a place where you can stay 滞在することのできる場所→宿，下宿 ‖ *The family offered full board and lodging (= a room and all meals) in exchange for English lessons.* その一家は英語のレッスンと引き換えに，完全な賄い付きの下宿を提供した(= 部屋と3度の食事). 定義 2 (古) **lodgings** [複数扱い] a room or rooms in sb's house where you can pay to stay 人の家で，金を払って滞在できる1部屋または複数の部屋→貸間，下宿

**loft** /lɔ(:)ft, lɑft/ 名 C 定義 the room or space under the roof of a house or other building 家やそのほかの建物にある，屋根の下の部屋や空間→屋根裏(部屋)，ギャラリー，桟敷，ロフト ☞参 **attic**

**log**¹ /lɔ(:)g, lɑg/ 名 C 定義 1 a thick piece of wood that has fallen or been cut from a tree 樹木から落ちた，または切り落とした太い木材→丸太，丸木，まき 定義 2 (または **logbook**) the official written record of a ship's or an aircraft's journey 船舶や航空機の行程の正式な書面による記録→航海日誌，航空記録・日誌 ‖ *to keep a log* 航海日誌をつける

**log**² /lɔ(:)g, lɑg/ 動 他 (**logging**; **logged**) 定義 to keep an official written record of sth ～の正式な書面による記録をつける→～を航海日誌・航空日誌，走行記録などに記入する

句動詞 **log in/on** 定義 to perform the actions that allow you to start using a computer system コンピューターシステムの使用を開始できる動作を行う→ログイン・ログオンする ‖ *You need to key in your password to log on.* ログオンするにはパスワードを入力する必要があります．

**log off/out** 定義 to perform the actions that allow you to finish using a computer system コンピューターシステムの使用を終了できる動作を行う→ログオフ・ログアウトする

**logarithm** /lɔ́(:)gərìð(ə)m, lág-/ (または 略式 **log**) 名 C 定義 one of a series of numbers arranged in lists (**tables**) that allow you to solve problems in mathematics by adding or subtracting numbers instead of multiplying or dividing 一覧(表)に配列された，乗算や除算の代わりに加算や減算で数学の問題を解くことができる一連の数→対数，対数表

**loggerheads** /lɔ́(:)gərhèdz, lág-/ 名

成句 **at loggerheads (with sb)** ▶定義 strongly disagreeing (with sb) 強固に(〜に)反対する→(〜と)論争して, 言い争って

**logic** /ládʒɪk/ 图 ❶ ▶定義 1 a sensible reason or way of thinking 道理にかなった理屈, または考え方→**論理, 良識** ‖ *There is no logic in your argument.* 君の議論は全く筋が通っていない. ▶定義 2 the science of using reason 理性を使うことに関する科学→**論理学**

**logical** /ládʒɪk(ə)l/ 形 ▶定義 1 seeming natural, reasonable or sensible 自然に, 道理にかなった, 分別のあるように見える→**論理的な, 筋が通った, 必然の** ‖ *As I see it, there is only one logical conclusion.* 私の見るところ, 論理的な結論は1つしかない. ⇔ **illogical** ▶定義 2 thinking in a sensible way 分別のあるやり方で考える→**分析的な, 論理的に考える** ‖ *a logical mind* 論理的な精神 — **logically** /-kli/ 副 →**論理的に, 必然に**

**logo** /lóʊɡoʊ/ 图 ❻ (複 **logos**) ▶定義 a printed symbol or design that a company or an organization uses as its special sign 会社や組織が特別の印として使う印刷されたシンボルや図案→**シンボルマーク, ロゴ** ‖ *the company/ brand logo* 会社・商標のロゴ

**loiter** /lɔ́ɪtər/ 動 ❺ ▶定義 to stand or walk around somewhere for no obvious reason はっきりした理由もなくどこかに立ったり, 歩き回ったりする→**たたずむ, ふらふらする, ぶらぶら歩く**

**lollipop** /lάlipɑp/ (または **lolly**) 图 ❻ ▶定義 a sweet on a stick 棒に付いた甘い菓子→**棒付きキャンデー, ぺろぺろキャンデー** ☛参 **ice lolly**

**lone** /lóʊn/ 形 (名詞の前だけ) ▶定義 1 without any other people; alone ほかの人々なしで; 単独で→**ただ1人の, 連れのない, 孤立した, ただ1つの** ‖ *a lone swimmer* ただ1人の泳者 ☛類 **solitary** ▶定義 2 (used about a parent) single; without a partner (親について) 単独の; 配偶者のいない→**片親の, 未婚の** ‖ *a support group for lone parents* 片親に対する支援者グループ

✱**lonely** /lóʊnli/ 形 (**lonelier**; **loneliest**) ▶定義 1 unhappy because you are not with other people ほかの人々と一緒ではないので不幸な→**寂しい, 孤独で寂しい** ‖ *to feel sad and lonely* 悲しくて孤独に感じる ▶定義 2 (used about a situation or a period of time) sad and spent alone (状況または時間について) 悲しく1人で過ごされた→**独りぼっちの, 孤独な** ▶定義 3 (名詞の前だけ) far from other people and places where people live ほかの人々と, 人々が住む場所から遠く離れた→**人里離れた, 孤立した, 人気のない** ☛参 **alone** の注 — **loneliness** 图 ❶ →**寂しさ, 孤独**

▶ solitude, isolation と比較.

**loner** /lóʊnər/ 图 ❻ ▶略式 ▶定義 a person who prefers being alone to being with other people ほかの人と一緒にいるよりも1人を好む人→**単独で行動する人, 一匹狼(おおかみ), 孤高の人**

**lonesome** /lóʊnsəm/ 形 米 ▶定義 lonely or making you feel lonely 孤独な, または孤独な気持ちにさせる→**(人が)寂しい, 心細い, (場所が)孤独で寂しい** ☛参 **alone** の注

✱**long**¹ /lɔ(ː)ŋ, lάŋ/ 形 (**longer** /lɔ(ː)ŋɡər/, **longest** /lɔ(ː)ŋɡəst/) ▶定義 measuring a large amount in distance or time 距離や時間の量が大きい→**長い, 遠い, 長時間の** ‖ *She has lovely long hair.* 彼女の髪は長くて美しい. *We had to wait a long time.* 私たちは長いこと待たなければならなかった. *a very long journey/book/corridor* とても長い旅・本・廊下 *I walked a long way today.* 今日は長い距離を歩いた. *Nurses work very long hours.* 看護婦は非常に長時間働く. ☛图 **length**

▶ long は物の長さや距離, 時間がどのくらいあるか尋ねるときや教えるときにも用いる: *How long is the film?* (その映画はどのくらいの長さですか.) *The insect was only 2 millimetres long.* (その昆虫は体長わずか2ミリだった.) *a five-mile-long traffic jam* (5マイルの交通渋滞)

⇔ **short** — **long** 图 ❶ →**長い間, 長期** ‖ *I'm sorry I haven't written to you for so long.* 長いことお手紙を差し上げなくてすみません. *This shouldn't take long.* これは長くはかかりません.

成句 **a long shot** ▶定義 a person or thing that probably will not succeed, win, etc 成功, 勝利などを収める見込みのない人や物→**成功する望みの薄い企て, 勝ち目のない競技者**

**at (long) last** ⇒ **LAST**¹

**at the longest** ▶定義 not longer than the stated time 述べられた時間より長くない→**長くても, せいぜい** ‖ *It will take a week at the longest.* 長くても1週間だろう.

**go a long way** ▶定義 (used about money,

food, etc) to be used for buying a lot of things, feeding a lot of people, etc (金, 食べ物などについて) 多くの物を買ったり, または大勢の人を養うために使われる➡長く持つ, 食べでがある, (金が) 価値が大きい, 使いでがある

**have a long way to go** ▶定義 to need to make a lot more progress before sth can be achieved ある事を成し遂げるためにもっと多く進歩する必要がある➡多くの努力を要する, 困難な

**in the long run** ▶定義 after a long time; in the end 長い時間の後で; 結局➡長い目で見れば, 結局は

**in the long/short term** ⇒ **TERM**¹

*★**long**² /lɔ(ː)ŋ, lɑŋ/ 副 (**longer** /lɔ́(ː)ŋɡnər/, **longest** /lɔ́(ː)ŋɡəst/) ▶定義**1** for a long time 長い時間➡長く, 長いこと, 久しく ‖ *She didn't stay long.* 彼女は長くはとどまらなかった. *You shouldn't have to wait long.* 長く待つ必要はありません. *I hope we don't have to wait much longer.* これ以上待たずに済めばよいのだが. *They won't be gone for long.* 彼らはすぐに戻るでしょう. *Just wait here - I won't be long.* ここでお待ちください — すぐ戻ります. *'How long will it take to get there?' 'Not long.'* 「そこに着くまでにどのくらいかかりますか」「すぐです」

➤ long と long time は共に時間を表すために用いる. 肯定文では普通 a long time が使われる: *They stood there for a long time.* (彼らは長いことそこに立っていた.) long が肯定文で使われるのは, 例えば too, enough, ago などの副詞と共に用いる場合のみ: *We lived here long ago.* (私たちはずっと前にここに住んでいた.) *I've put up with this noise long enough. I'm going to make a complaint.* (私はこの騒音をずっと我慢してきた. これから苦情を言うつもりだ.) long と a long time は両方とも疑問文に使用できる: *Were you away long/a long time?* (長いこと出掛けていたのですか.) 否定文では場合によっては long と long time の意味が異なる: *I haven't been here long (= I arrived only a short time ago).* (ここに来てそれほどたっていない (= ちょっと前に着いたばかりだ).) *I haven't been here for a long time (= it is a long time since I was last here).* (私は長いことここに来なかった (= 最後にここに来てから長い時間がたった).)

▶定義**2** a long time before or after a particular time or event 特定の時刻や出来事の前または後までの時間が長く➡ずっと前に, ずっと後に ‖ *We got married long before we moved here.* 私たちはここに引っ越すずっと前に結婚した. *Don't worry - they'll be here before long.* 心配しないで — 彼らはすぐ来るよ. *All that happened long ago.* それはすべてずっと昔に起こった. ▶定義**3** for the whole of the time that is mentioned 言及されている間中ずっと➡ずっと, 〜通し ‖ *The baby cried all night long.* 赤ん坊は夜通し泣き続けた.

**成句 as/so long as** ▶定義 on condition that; provided (that) 〜という条件で; もし〜なら➡〜する限りは, 〜さえすれば ‖ *As long as no problems arise we should get the job finished by Friday.* 問題が何も起こらなければ, 金曜日までにその仕事を完了しなければならない.

**no/not any longer** ▶定義 not any more もはや〜ない➡もう〜しない, もう〜でない ‖ *They no longer live here.* 彼らはもうここには住んでいない. *They don't live here any longer.* 彼らはもうここには住んでいない.

**long**³ /lɔ(ː)ŋ, lɑŋ/ 動 ⓘ ▶定義 **long for sth; long (for sb) to do sth** to want sth very much, especially sth that is not likely 〜を, 特にありそうもない〜をとても強く望む➡〜を思いこがれる, あこがれる, 切望する, 〜したいと強く願う ‖ *She longed to return to Greece.* 彼女はギリシャに戻りたいと強く願っていた. — **longing** 名 ⒸⓊ ➡思いこがれること, 切望すること ‖ *a longing for peace* 平和を待ちこがれること — **longingly** 副➡思いこがれて, 強く願って

**long-distance** 形 副 ▶定義 (used about travel or communication) between places that are far from each other (旅行や通信について) 互いに遠く離れた場所の間の [で]➡長距離の, 長距離で ‖ *to phone long-distance* 長距離電話をかける

**long-haul** 形 ▶定義 (名詞の前だけ) connected with the transport of people or goods over long distances 長距離の人や品物の輸送に関連した➡長距離輸送の, 長距離の ‖ *a long-haul flight* 長距離飛行

**longitude** /lándʒət(j)ùːd/ 名 Ⓤ ▶定義 the distance of a place east or west of a line from the North Pole to the South Pole that passes through Greenwich in London. Longitude is measured in degrees. ロンドンのグリニッジを通る北極と南極を結ぶ線の東または西に離れた距離.度で測る→**経度** ☛参 **latitude** ☛ **earth** のさし絵

**long jump** 名 [単数扱い] ▶定義 the sport in which people try to jump as far as possible できる限り遠く跳ぶスポーツ→**幅跳び** ☛参 **high jump**

**long-life** 形 ▶定義 made to last for a long time 長期間持つように作られた→**長持ちする,耐久性のある** || *a long-life battery* 長持ちする電池 *long-life milk* 日持ちする牛乳

**long-lived** 形 ▶定義 that has lived or lasted for a long time 長期間生きる,持続する→**長命の,永続する** || *a long-lived dispute* 長く続く論争

**long-range** 形 ▶定義1 of or for a long period of time starting from the present 現在から始まる長期間の→**長期の,遠大な** || *the long-range weather forecast* 長期天気予報 ▶定義2 that can go or be sent over long distances 長距離を行くことのできる,または送ることのできる→**長距離に達する** || *long-range nuclear missiles* 長距離核ミサイル

**long-sighted** (米 **far-sighted**) 形 ▶定義 able to see things clearly only when they are quite far away 非常に遠くにある物だけをはっきりと見ることができる→**遠視の,遠目の利く** ⇔ **short-sighted** (米 **near-sighted**)

**long-standing** 形 ▶定義 that has lasted for a long time 長期間持続した→**長年にわたる,積年の** || *a long-standing arrangement* 長年にわたる協定

**long-suffering** 形 ▶定義 (used about a person) having a lot of troubles but not complaining (人について)大きな困難があるが不平を言わない→**辛抱強い,忍苦の**

**long-term** 形 ▶定義 of or for a long period of time 長い期間の→**長期の** || *long-term planning* 長期計画

**long-winded** 形 ▶定義 (used about sth that is written or spoken) boring because it is too long (書かれた物や話された事について)長すぎて退屈な→**長たらしい,くどい**

**loo** /luː/ 名 C (複 **loos**) 英 略式 ▶定義 toilet トイレ→**便所** ☛参 **toilet** の注

\***look**¹ /lʊk/ 動 ▶定義1 自 **look (at sth)** to turn your eyes in a particular direction (in order to pay attention to sb/sth) (~に注意を払うために)特定の方向に目を向ける→**(~を)見る,注視する,注目する** || *Sorry, I wasn't looking. Can you show me again?* すみません、見ていませんでした.もう一度見せてくれますか. *Look carefully at this picture.* この絵をよく見てください. *to look out of the window* 窓から外を見る *She blushed and looked away.* 彼女は赤くなって目をそらした. *Look who's come to see us.* だれが訪ねてきたのか見てごらん. *Look where you're going!* 行く手に気を付けて.

➤ see は注意を払わずに物を見る:*I saw a girl riding past on a horse.* (ある少女が馬に乗って通り過ぎるのが見えた.) look は注意して物を見る: *Look carefully. Can you see anything strange?* (よく見て.何かおかしなところが見えますか.)

▶定義2 自 **look (for sb/sth)** to try to find (sb/sth) ~を見つけようとする→**(~を)探す,求める** || *We've been looking for you everywhere. Where have you been?* あなたのことをあちこち捜していました.どこに行っていたのですか. *to look for work* 仕事を探す *'I can't find my shoes.' 'Have you looked under the bed?'* 「靴が見つからない」「ベッドの下を捜したかい」

▶定義3 自 **look (like sb/sth) (to sb); look (to sb) as if.../as though...** to seem or appear ~のように思える,見える→**~に似ている,~しそうだ,~らしい** || *You look very smart in that shirt.* そのシャツを着るととてもスマートに見えるよ. *to look tired/ill/sad/well/happy* 疲れているような・病気のような・悲しそうな・元気そうな・楽しそうな *The boy looks like his father.* その少年は父親に似ている. *That film looks good - I might go and see it.* その映画は良さそうだ - 見に行ってみようかな. *You look (to me) as if/as though you need some sleep.* あなたは一眠りした方がいいように私には見えます. ▶定義4 自 used for asking sb to listen to what you are saying ~に自分の言っている事を聞いてほしいときに用いて→**ほら,ちょっと,いい**

かい‖ *Look, Will, I know you are busy but could you give me a hand?* ちょっとウィル，忙しいのは分かるけど手伝ってくれない． ▶定義 5 ⃝自 to face a particular direction 特定の方向を向く→~に面している，~向き‖ *This room looks south so it gets the sun.* この部屋は南向きなので日当たりがいい． ▶定義 6 ⃝自 look to do sth to aim to do sth ある事をするつもりでいる→~することを期待する，当てにする‖ *We are looking to double our profits over the next five years.* 今後5年間で収益を2倍にするつもりだ．

> ▶語法
>
> look at と look on
>
> lookの意味は「視線を向ける」です．視線を向ける対象を1点に絞り込むときには「ねらい・焦点」を表す at を用います．一方，黒板・スクリーンのような広い面に目を向ける場合には on を用います．また，look はしばしば名詞としても使われ，Take a look at/on...（~を見なさい）のような表現にもなります．

成句 look bad; not look good ▶定義 to be considered bad manners 無礼だと見なされる→失礼な，不適当な‖ *It'll look bad if we get there an hour late.* 1時間遅れでそこに着くのはまずいだろう．

look good ▶定義 to seem to be encouraging 有望だ→励みになる，期待の持てる‖ *This year's sales figures are looking good.* 今年の販売高は有望だ．

look sb in the eye ▶定義 to look straight at sb without feeling embarrassed or afraid 照れたり恐れたりせずに~をまっすぐに見る→~をじっと見る，~の目をじっと見詰める

(not) look yourself ▶定義 to (not) look as well or healthy as usual いつものように元気そうに・健康そうに見える[見えない]→元気そうな・元気そうでない，具合が良さそう・悪そうな

look on the bright side (of sth) ▶定義 to think only about the good side of a bad situation and be happy and hopeful 悪い状況の良い面だけを考えて，幸福になり期待を持つ→楽観する，楽天的に考える

never/not look back ▶定義 to become and continue being successful 成功し，成功を持続する→中断されることなく先に進む，発展する，ためらわない

句動詞 look after sb/sth/yourself ▶定義 to be responsible for or take care of sb/sth/yourself ~や自分自身に責任を持つ，面倒を見る→~の世話をする，~に注意する，気に掛ける‖ *I want to go back to work if I can find somebody to look after the children.* 子供の面倒を見る人が見つかったら，仕事に戻りたい． *The old lady's son looked after all her financial affairs.* その老婦人の息子が彼女の財政上の面倒をすべて見ていた．

look ahead ▶定義 to think about or plan for the future 将来について考える，計画を立てる→先を見越す，備える

look at sth ▶定義 1 to examine or study sth ~を調べる，調査する→検査する，判断する，考察する‖ *My tooth aches. I think a dentist should look at it.* 歯が痛い．歯医者に診てもらおう． *The government is looking at ways of reducing unemployment.* 政府は失業者を減らす方法を考えている． ▶定義 2 to read sth ~を読む→目を通す，読み取る‖ *Could I look at the newspaper when you've finished with it?* 読み終わったら，新聞を見せていただけませんか． ▶定義 3 to consider sth ~を見なす，考える→~と見る，~の見方をする‖ *Different races and nationalities look at life differently.* 人種や国籍が違えば生活に対する考え方も異なる．

look back (on sth) ▶定義 to think about sth in your past 過去の~について考える→(~を)振り返る，回想する

look down on sb/sth ▶定義 to think that you are better than sb/sth ~より自分の方が優れていると考える→~を見下す，軽く見る，軽べつする

look forward to sth/doing sth ▶定義 to wait with pleasure for sth to happen ~が起こるのを楽しみに思って待つ→~を期待する，当てにする‖ *I'm really looking forward to the weekend.* 週末を心待ちにしています．

look into sth ▶定義 to study or try to find out sth ~を調べる，~を発見しようとする→~を研究する，調査する‖ *A committee was set up to look into the causes of the accident.* 事故原因を究明するため委員会が設立された．

**look on** ▶定義 to watch sth happening without taking any action 〜が起こるのを何の行動も取らずに見ている➡傍観する, 見物する ‖ *All we could do was look on as the house burned.* 私たちにできたのは家が燃えるのをなすすべもなく見詰めることだけだった.

**look on sb/sth as sth; look on sb with sth** ▶定義 to think of sb/sth in a particular way 〜を特定の方法で考える➡〜を…と見なす, 〜と考える ‖ *They seem to look on me as someone who can advise them.* 彼らは私が彼らに忠告できる人間だと考えているようだ.

**look out** ▶定義 to be careful or to pay attention to sth dangerous 危険な〜に気を付ける, または注意を払う➡用心する, 見張っている ‖ *Look out! There's a bike coming.* 気を付けて. 自転車が来るよ.

**look out (for sb/sth)** ▶定義 to pay attention in order to see, find or avoid sb/sth 〜を見る・見つける・避けるために注意を払う➡(〜に)用心する, 警戒する ‖ *Look out for thieves!* 泥棒に用心して.

**look round** ▶定義1 to turn your head in order to see sth 〜を見るために顔を向ける➡見回す, 振り向く ▶定義2 to look at many things (before buying sth) (物を買う前に)多くの物を見る➡見て回る ‖ *She looked round but couldn't find anything she liked.* 彼女はいろいろ見て回ったが, 気に入った物が見つからなかった.

**look round sth** ▶定義 to walk around a place looking at things 物を見ながら場所を歩き回る➡〜を見物して回る, 見て回る ‖ *to look round a town/shop/museum* 町・店・博物館を見て回る

**look through sth** ▶定義 to read sth quickly 〜を素早く読み取る➡〜に目を通す, 〜をざっと読む

**look to sb for sth; look to sb to do sth** ▶定義 to expect sb to do or to provide sth 〜が…をする, または…を与えてくれることを期待する➡〜に…を・〜が…してくれるのを当てにする, 待望する ‖ *He always looked to his father for advice.* 彼はいつも父のアドバイスを当てにしていた.

**look up** ▶定義1 to move your eyes upwards to look at sb/sth 〜を見るために目を上に向ける➡見上げる, 上を見る ‖ *She looked up and smiled.* 彼女は顔を上げてほほえんだ. ▶定義2 略式 to improve 改良する➡良くなる, 上向く ‖ *Business is looking up.* 事業が上向きになっている.

**look sth up** ▶定義 to search for information in a book で本で情報を探す➡〜を調べる ‖ *to look up a word in a dictionary* 辞書で単語を引く

**look up to sb** ▶定義 to respect and admire sb 〜を尊敬し賞賛する➡〜を敬う, 仰ぎ見る

★**look**² /lʊk/ 名 ▶定義1 ❸the act of looking 見る動作➡見ること, 見詰めること, 一見, 一目 ‖ *Have a look at this article.* この記事をちょっと見て. *Take a close look at the contract before you sign it.* 署名する前に契約書をよく読みなさい. ▶定義2 [❸, 通常は単数] a look (for sb/sth) a search 探すこと➡捜索, 探索, 調査 ‖ *I'll have a good look for that book later.* 後でその本をよく捜してみます. ▶定義3 ❸ the expression on sb's face 〜の顔の表情➡目付き, 顔付き, 表情 ‖ *He had a worried look on his face.* 彼は心配そうな顔をしていた. ▶定義4 **looks** [複数扱い] a person's appearance 人の外見➡容貌(ようぼう), 風采(ふうさい), 様子 ‖ *He's lucky - he's got good looks and intelligence.* 彼は幸運だ — 端正な容貌と知性を持っている. ▶定義5 ❸a fashion or style 流行やスタイル➡ファッション, はやりの型, 〜ルック, 装い, 外観, 様子 ‖ *The shop has a new look to appeal to younger customers.* その店は若い客を引き付ける目新しい外観をしている.

成句 **by/from the look of sb/sth** ▶定義 judging by the appearance of sb/sth 〜の外見から判断する➡〜の外観・様子から判断して, 〜を見たところでは ‖ *It's going to be a fine day by the look of it.* 空模様からすると良い天気になりそうだ.

**like the look/sound of sb/sth** ⇒ **LIKE**¹

**look-in** 名

成句 **(not) give sb a look-in; (not) get/have a look-in** 略式 ▶定義 to (not) give sb, or to (not) have a chance to do sth 〜に…をする機会を与える・与えない, 〜をする機会がある・ない➡加わる・加わらない, 参加する・しない, 成功の見込みがある・ない

**-looking** (複合形容詞を作って) ▶定義 having the appearance mentioned 述べられたような

外見である➡~に見える,~のような,~に似た ‖ *an odd-looking building* 奇妙な建物 *He's very good-looking.* 彼はとてもハンサムだ.

**lookout** /lúkaut/ 名 C ▶定義 (a person who has) the responsibility of watching to see if danger is coming; the place this person watches from 危険が近付いているかどうか見張る責任(のある人);そういった人が見張りをする場所➡見張り人,監視人;見張り所,監視所 ‖ *One of the gang acted as lookout.* ギャングの1人が見張りをした.

成句 be on the lookout for sb/sth; keep a lookout for sb/sth ▶定義 to pay attention in order to see, find or avoid sb/sth ~を見る,見つける,または避けるために注意を払う➡~を見張る,警戒する,監視する

**loom**[1] /lu:m/ 名 C ▶定義 a machine that is used for making cloth (weaving) by passing pieces of thread across and under other pieces 糸をほかの糸と交差させて下を通して布を作る(織る)ための機械➡織機,機織り機

**loom**[2] /lu:m/ 動 自 ▶定義 loom (up) to appear as a shape that is not clear and in a way that seems frightening はっきりしない形で,恐ろしそうな様子で現れる➡ぼうっと現れる,ぼんやりと見える ‖ *The mountain loomed (up) in the distance.* その山が遠くにぼんやりと見えた.

**loony** /lú:ni/ 名 C (複 **loonies**)(俗語) ▶定義 a person who is crazy 狂気染みた人➡狂人,間抜けな人,ばかな人 — **loony** 形 ➡狂気の,間抜けな,ばかな ‖ *I'm tired of listening to his loony plans.* 彼のばかげた計画を聞くのはうんざりだ.

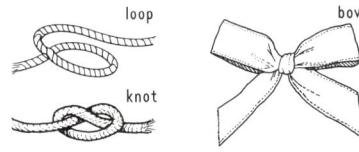

**loop** /lu:p/ 名 C ▶定義 a curved or round shape made by a line curving round and joining or crossing itself 曲線状または円の形.この形は線が曲がったり,結びあったり交差するときにできる➡輪,環,環状のもの ‖ *a loop in a rope* ロープの輪 *The road goes around the lake in a loop.* 道路は湖の回りを環状に巡っている. ☞ **coil** の

さし絵 — loop 動 自 他 ➡~を輪にする,輪で囲む,輪で結ぶ ‖ *He was trying to loop a rope over the horse's head.* 彼は馬の首にロープを巻き付けようとしていた.

**loophole** /lú:phòul/ 名 C ▶定義 a way of avoiding sth because the words of a rule or law are badly chosen 規則や法律の句を不適切に選択することによって~を避ける方法➡(法律などの)抜け穴,盲点,逃げ道

*★**loose**[1] /lu:s/ 形 ▶定義 1 not tied up or shut in sth; free 結ばれていない,または~に閉じ込められていない;自由な➡結んでいない,束ねていない,解き放たれた,逃れた ‖ *The horse managed to get loose and escape.* 馬は何とか束縛から逃れて逃げ出した. *I take the dog to the woods and let him loose.* 私は犬を森に連れていって放す. *She wore her long hair loose.* 彼女は長い髪を束ねていなかった. ▶定義 2 not firmly fixed しっかりと固定されていない➡緩んだ,がたがたした ‖ *a loose tooth* ぐらぐらしている歯 *The saucepan handle is a bit loose so be careful.* シチューなべの取っ手ががたついているので,注意して. ▶定義 3 not contained in sth or joined together ~に入っていない,または1つに結合していない;包装していない,ばらの ‖ *loose change (= coins)* 小銭(= 硬貨) *some loose sheets of paper* ばらばらの紙 ▶定義 4 not fitting closely; not tight ぴったりと合わない;窮屈でない➡だぶだぶの,緩い;ゆったりとした ‖ *These trousers don't fit. They're much too loose round the waist.* このズボンは合わない.ウエストがだぶついている. ⇔ **tight** ▶定義 5 not completely accurate or the same as sth 完全には正確でない,またはあるものと完全に同じではない➡不正確な,不明瞭(めいりょう)な,いいかげんな,散漫な ‖ *a loose translation* ずさんな訳 — **loosely** 副 ➡緩く,緩んで,大雑把に,いいかげんに ‖ *The film is loosely based on the life of Beethoven.* その映画はベートーベンの生涯にあまり正確に基づいてはいない.

成句 all hell broke loose ⇒ **HELL**

at a loose end ▶定義 having nothing to do and feeling bored 何もする事がなく退屈で➡ぶらぶらして,当てもなく

**loose**[2] /lu:s/ 名

## 994　loose-leaf

**成句** on the loose ▶定義 escaped and dangerous 逃げ出して危険な→**逃亡中で, 野放しで** ‖ *a lion on the loose from a zoo* 動物園から逃げ出したライオン

**loose-leaf** 形 ▶定義 (used about a book, file, etc) with pages that can be removed or added separately (本やファイルなどについて)ページを個別に取り外したり追加したりできる→**ルーズリーフ式の**

**loosen** /lúːs(ə)n/ 動 自他 ▶定義 to become or make sth less tight 〜がよりきつくなくなる, きつくなくする→**緩む；〜を緩める, ほどく** ‖ *to loosen your tie/belt* ネクタイ・ベルトを緩める. *Don't loosen your grip on the rope or you'll fall.* ロープをしっかり握って, さもないと落ちるぞ.

**句動詞** loosen (sb/sth) up ▶定義 to relax or move more easily くつろぐ, よりたやすく動く→**〜を楽にする, 筋肉をほぐす** ‖ *These exercises will help you to loosen up.* これらの運動によって筋肉をほぐすことができます.

**loot** /luːt/ 動 自他 ▶定義 to steal things during a war or period of fighting 戦争や戦闘中に物を盗む→**〜を略奪する, 強奪する**

**lop** /lɑp/ 動 他 (**lopping**；**lopped**) ▶定義 to cut branches off a tree 樹木の枝を切り落とす→**切る, 枝を下ろす, 刈り込む**

**句動詞** lop sth off/away ▶定義 to cut sth off/away 〜を切り落とす・切り離す→**切る, (首, 手足などを)はねる**

**lopsided** /lɑ̀psáɪdəd, -́-/ 形 ▶定義 with one side lower or smaller than the other 一方が他方より低い, 小さい→**釣り合っていない, 不均衡の, 偏った** ‖ *a lopsided smile* ゆがんだ笑み

**lord** /lɔːrd/ 名 C ▶定義 1 a man with a very high position in society 社会的地位が非常に高い男性→**支配者, 首長, 君主** ‖ *the Lord Mayor of London* ロンドン市長 *Lord and Lady Derby* ダービー卿(きょう)夫妻 ▶定義 2 **the Lord** [単数扱い] God; christ 神；キリスト→**主, イエス** ▶定義 3 **the Lords** [単数または複数形の動詞と共に] 英 (members of) the House of Lords 上院(議員)→**上院議員たち, 上院** ‖ *The Lords has/have voted against the bill.* 上院はその法案に反対票を投じた.

*****lorry** /lɔ́(ː)ri/ 英 名 C (複 **lorries**) (特に米 **truck**) ▶定義 a large strong motor vehicle that is used for carrying goods by road 道路を使って物品を運ぶための大型で強力な自動車→**トラック, 貨物自動車** ☞ **vehicle** のさし絵

*****lose** /luːz/ 動 (過, 過分 **lost** /lɔ(ː)st, lɑst/) ▶定義 1 他 to become unable to find sth 〜を見つけられなくなる→**〜をなくす, 失う, 置き忘れる** ‖ *I've lost my purse. I can't find it anywhere.* 私は財布をなくしてしまった. どこにも見つからない. ▶定義 2 他 to no longer have sb/sth 〜がもういない・〜をもう持っていない→**〜を失う, 〜と死別する** ‖ *She lost a leg in the accident.* 彼女は事故で片足を失った. *He lost his wife last year (= she died).* 彼は去年妻をなくした(= 彼女は死んだ). *to lose your job* 失業する ▶定義 3 他 to have less of sth より少なく〜を持つ→**〜を減らす, なくす** ‖ *to lose weight/interest/patience* 体重を減らす・興味をなくす・我慢できなくなる *The company is losing money all the time.* その会社は常に損失を出している. ⇔ **gain** ▶定義 4 自他 to not win; to be defeated 勝たない；負かされる→**負ける, 敗北する** ‖ *We played well but we lost 2-1.* よく戦ったが私たちは2対1で負けた. *to lose a court case/an argument* 敗訴する・議論に負ける *Parma lost to Milan in the final.* パルマは決勝でミランに負けた. ▶定義 5 他 to waste time, a chance, etc 時間, 機会などを浪費する→**無駄にする** ‖ *Hurry up! There's **no time to lose**.* 急いで. もう時間がない. ▶定義 6 自他 to become poorer (as a result of sth) 乏しくなる(何かの結果として)→**なくなる, 減る；〜をなくす, 〜を減らす** ‖ *The company lost on the deal.* その会社は取り引きに失敗した. ▶定義 7 他 略式 to cause sb not to understand sth 〜に…を理解できなくさせる→**〜を混乱させる, 戸惑わせる** ‖ *You've totally lost me! Please explain again.* あなたの言っている事がさっぱり分かりません. もう一度説明してください.

**成句** keep/lose your cool ⇒ **COOL**³
keep/lose count (of sth) ⇒ **COUNT**²
keep/lose your temper ⇒ **TEMPER**
keep/lose track of sb/sth ⇒ **TRACK**¹
lose your bearings ▶定義 to become confused about where you are どこにいるか混乱する→**方角が分からなくなる, 立場が分からなくなる**

**lose face** ▶定義 to lose the respect of other people ほかの人々の敬意を失う➔**面目を失う, メンツを失う**

**lose it** (口語) ▶定義 to go crazy or suddenly become unable to control your emotions 狂ったようになる, 突然感情を制御できなくなる➔**熱狂する, 夢中になる, 取り付かれたようになる**

**lose your head** ▶定義 to become confused or very excited 混乱する, 非常に興奮する➔**慌てる, 取り乱す, 夢中になる**

**lose heart** ▶定義 to stop believing that you will be successful in sth you are trying to do やろうとしている～で成功できると信じるのをやめる➔**自信を失う, 元気を失う, 意気消沈する**

**lose your life** ▶定義 to be killed 死ぬ➔**死ぬ, 命を失う, 亡くなる**

**lose sight of sb/sth** ▶定義 to no longer be able to see sb/sth ～をもう見ることができない➔**～を見失う, 忘れる, ～がいなくなる** ‖ *We eventually lost sight of the animal in some trees.* ついに一部の木々の動物がいなくなってしまった. (比喩) *We mustn't lose sight of our original aim.* 当初の目的を忘れてはいけない.

**lose your touch** ▶定義 to lose a special skill or ability 特別の技術や能力を失う➔**技量・腕が落ちる, 上手でなくなる**

**lose touch (with sb/sth)** ▶定義 to no longer have contact (with sb/sth) (～と)もう接触がない➔**(～と)連絡を失う, (時代など)に後れる** ‖ *I've lost touch with a lot of my old school friends.* 学生時代の古い友人たちの多くと連絡が取れなくなっている.

**a losing battle** ▶定義 a competition, fight, etc in which it seems that you will fail to be successful 成功できそうにない競争や戦いなど➔**見込みのない努力, 負け戦**

**win/lose the toss** ⇒ **TOSS**

[句動詞] **lose out (on sth/to sb)** [略式] ▶定義 to be at a disadvantage 不利になる➔**(惜しくも)負ける, やられる, 損をする** ‖ *If a teacher pays too much attention to the bright students, the others lose out.* 教師が頭のいい生徒ばかりに注意を払えば, ほかの生徒は不利になる.

**loser** /lúːzər/ 名 C ▶定義1 a person who is defeated 負けた人➔**敗者, 負けた方** ‖ *He is a bad loser. He always gets angry if I beat him.* 彼は負け際が悪い. 私が彼を負かすといつも怒り出す. ▶定義2 a person who is never successful 決して成功しない人➔**負け癖のついた人, 失敗者, 負け犬** ▶定義3 a person who suffers because of a particular situation, decision, etc 特定の状況や決定などによって被害を受ける人➔**損をする人**

★**loss** /lɔ(ː)s, lɑs/ 名 ▶定義1 C U (a) loss (of sth) the state of no longer having sth or not having as much as before; the act of losing sth ～をもう持っていない, または前ほど持っていない状態; ～を失うこと➔**(～を)失うこと, 喪失, 紛失, 減少** ‖ *loss of blood/sleep* 出血・不眠 *weight/hair loss* 体重・髪が減る *Have you reported the loss of your wallet?* 札入れをなくしたことを報告しましたか. *The plane crashed with great loss of life.* 飛行機が墜落して多くの生命が失われた. ▶定義2 C a loss (of sth) the amount of money which is lost by a business 事業によって失われる金額➔**損失額, 損害額** ‖ *The firm made a loss of £5 million.* その会社は500万ポンドの損失を出した. ☛参 **profit** ▶定義3 C a loss (to sb) the disadvantage that is caused when sb/sth leaves or is taken away; the person or thing that causes this disadvantage ～がいなくなることや持ち去られることが原因で発生する不利益; こうした不利益をもたらす人や物➔**損失, 不利, 損害** ‖ *If she leaves, it/she will be a big loss to the school.* 彼女がいなくなることは, 学校にとって大きな損失だ.

[成句] **at a loss** ▶定義 not knowing what to do or say 何をすべきか, 言うべきか分からずに➔**途方に暮れて, 困惑して, 困って**

**cut your losses** ▶定義 to stop wasting time or money on sth that is not successful うまくいかない～に時間や金を浪費するのをやめる➔**損失を減らす, (損になる)事業・取り引きをやめる**

**lost**[1] **LOSE** の過去・過去分詞形

★**lost**[2] /lɔ(ː)st, lɑst/ 形 ▶定義1 unable to find your way; not knowing where you are 道が見つからない; 自分がどこにいるか分からない➔**道に迷った, 迷子になった** ‖ *This isn't the right road - we're completely lost!* 道が間違っている — 私たちは完全に道に迷ってしまった. *If you get lost, stop and ask someone the way.* もし迷子

になったら, 立ち止まってだれかに道を聞きなさい. ▶定義2 that cannot be found or that no longer exists 見つからない, またはもう存在しない→**紛失した, 行方不明の, 消え去った, 失われた** ‖ *The letter must have **got lost** in the post.* その手紙は郵便配達の過程で紛失したに違いない. ▶定義3 unable to deal with a situation or to understand sth 状況に対処できない, または〜を理解できない→**途方に暮れて, 当惑して** ‖ *Sorry, I'm lost. Could you explain the last part again?* すみませんが, よく分かりません. 最後の部分をもう一度説明してくれませんか.

▶定義4 **lost on sb** not noticed or understood by sb 〜に気付かれない, 理解されない→**〜に通じない, 効き目がない, 無駄な** ‖ *The humour of the situation was completely lost on Joe.* その状況のおかしさがジョーには全く通じなかった.

成句 **get lost**(俗語) ▶定義 used to rudely tell sb to go away 〜に無礼なやり方で去るように言うときに用いて→**出ていけ, うせろ**

**a lost cause** ▶定義 a goal or an aim that cannot be achieved 達成することのできない目標や目的→**失敗に終わった・見込みのない運動・主義, 見込みのないこと**

**lost for words** ▶定義 not knowing what to say 言うべき事が分からずに→**言葉を失って, 絶句して**

**lost property** 名 🇺 ▶定義 things that people have lost or left in a public place and that are kept in a special office for the owners to collect 人が公共の場所で紛失したり忘れたりした物で, 所有者が取りに来るように特別な事務所に保管されている→**遺失物**

*__lot__¹ /lɑt/ 名 ▶定義1 ⓐ **a lot (of sth); lots (of sth)** a large amount or number of things or people 大量のまたは多数の物や人々→**たくさん(の〜), 多数, 大勢** ‖ *Sit here - there's lots of room.* ここに座りなさい - 場所は十分あります. *There seem to be **quite a lot** of new shops opening.* 非常に多くの新しい店が開店するようだ. ***An awful lot** of (= very many) people will be disappointed if the concert is cancelled.* コンサートが中止になったら, すごく大勢(= とても大勢)の人ががっかりするだろう. *I've got a lot to do today.* 今日はやる事がたくさんある.

▶否定文と疑問文では much, many をよく用いる: *A lot of girls go to dancing classes, but not many boys.* (大勢の女の子がダンス教室に行くが, 男の子たちはあまり行かない.) *'How much would a car like that cost?' 'A lot!'* 「ああいう車はいくらくらいするの」「とても高いよ」

▶定義2 [単数扱い, 単数または複数形の動詞と共に] 略式 all of sth; the whole of a group of things or people 〜のすべて; 物や人の集まり全体→**全部, 全体, 何もかも** ‖ *When we opened the bag of potatoes **the whole lot** was/were bad.* ジャガイモの袋を開けたら, 全部腐っていた. *The manager has just sacked **the lot of them**!* 支配人は彼ら全員をくびにしたところだ. *Just one more suitcase and **that's the lot!*** スーツケースあと1つで荷物は全部だ. *'How many of these books shall we take?' '**The lot**.'* 「この本を何冊持っていきましょうか」「全部だ」 *You count those kids and I'll count **this lot**.* 君はあの子供たちを数えてくれ, 私はこちらのグループを数える.

成句 **draw lots** ⇒ **DRAW**¹

*__lot__² /lɑt/ 副 略式 ▶定義1 **a lot; lots** (形容詞と副詞の前に用いて) very much 非常に→**とても, 大変, ずっと** ‖ *a lot bigger/better/faster* ずっと大きい・良い・速い ‖ *They see lots more of each other than before.* 彼らは前よりずっと頻繁に会っている. ▶定義2 **a lot** very much or often 非常に多く, しばしば→**とても, しょっちゅう** ‖ *Thanks a lot - that's very kind.* どうもありがとう - ご親切に. *It generally rains a lot at this time of year.* 1年のこの時期には普通は雨が多い.

**a lot of** /ə lɑ́t ə(v)/ (または 略式 **lots of** /lɑ́ts ə(v)/) 形 ▶定義 a large amount or number of (sb/sth) (〜が)大量の, またはたくさんの→**たくさんの, 多数の, 大量の, 大勢の** ‖ *There's been a lot of rain this year.* 今年は雨が多い. *Lots of love, Billy (= an informal ending for a letter).* 愛を込めて, ビリーより(= 手紙の略式の結語) *There were a lot of people at the meeting.* その会合には大勢の人が出ていた.

**lotion** /lóʊʃ(ə)n/ 名 🇨 🇺 ▶定義 liquid that you use on your hair or skin 髪や肌に付ける液体→**ローション, 化粧水** ‖ *suntan lotion* 日焼け用化粧水

**lottery** /lɑ́t(ə)ri/ 名 🇨 (複 **lotteries**) ▶定義 a

way of making money for the government, for charity, etc by selling tickets with numbers on them and giving prizes to the people who have bought certain numbers which are chosen by chance 番号の付いた券を売って，偶然選ばれた特定の番号を買った人に賞を与える方法→宝くじ，富くじ，抽選，くじ引き

***loud** /láυd/ 形副 ▶定義1 making a lot of noise; not quiet 多くの騒音を出す; 静かでない→(声・音が)大きい、うるさい‖ *Can you turn the television down, it's too loud.* テレビの音を小さくして，うるさいから. *Could you speak a bit louder - the people at the back can't hear.* もう少し大きな声で話していただけませんか — 後ろの人が聞き取れません. ⇔ **quiet, soft**

▶ loud は主に音そのものや音を出す物を言う場合に用いる: *a loud noise/bang* (騒々しい音・大きなバンという音) *loud music* (大音響の音楽) noisy は主に非常に音・声が大きい，または大きすぎる人，動物，場所，出来事などを言う場合に用いる: *a noisy road/party/engine/child* (騒々しい道路・パーティー・エンジン・子供)

▶定義2 (used about clothes or colours) too bright (衣服や色について) 鮮やかすぎる→派手な，けばけばしい‖ *a loud shirt* 派手なシャツ — **loudly** 副→うるさく，派手で — **loudness** 名 ❶音の強さ，騒々しさ，派手さ

成句 **out loud** ▶定義 so that people can hear it 人々が聞こえるように→(はっきりと)声に出して‖ *Shall I read this bit out loud to you?* この短文を声に出して読んで差し上げましょうか.

**loudspeaker** /láυdspìːkər/ 名 ❷ ▶定義1 (または **speaker**) the part of a radio, CD player, etc which the sound comes out of ラジオ，CDプレーヤーなどの音が出る部品→スピーカー ▶定義2 a piece of electrical equipment for speaking, playing music, etc to a lot of people 大勢の人々に向かって話したり，音楽を演奏するための電気機器→拡声器，スピーカー

**lounge**¹ /láυndʒ/ 名 ❷ ▶定義1 a comfortable room in a house or hotel where you can sit and relax 家やホテルなどの座ってくつろぐのできる快適な部屋→居間，休憩室，ロビー ☛ C7ページのさし絵 ▶定義2 the part of an airport where passengers wait 空港の乗客が待つ場所→ロビー‖ *the departure lounge* 出発ロビー

**lounge**² /láυndʒ/ 動❸ ▶定義 lounge (about/around) to sit, stand or lie in a lazy way ゆったりと座る，立つ，横になる→もたれ掛かる，ゆったり横になる

**louse** /láυs/ 名 ❷ (複 **lice**) ▶定義 a small insect that lives on the bodies of animals and people 動物や人の体に住む小さな虫→シラミ，寄生虫

**lousy** /láυzi/ 形略式 ▶定義 very bad 非常に悪い→汚い，卑劣な，けがらわしい，ひどい，不愉快な‖ *We had lousy weather on holiday.* 休日はひどい天気だった.

**lout** /láυt/ 名 ❷ ▶定義 a young man who behaves in a rude, rough or stupid way 無礼な，粗野な，ばかげた振る舞いをする若い男→**無骨者，乱暴者** ☛参 **hooligan, yob**

**lovable** (または **loveable**) /lʌ́v(ə)l/ 形 ▶定義 having a personality or appearance that is easy to love 愛されやすい人柄または外見の→愛らしい，愛すべき‖ *a lovable little boy* 愛らしい小さな男の子

*__love__¹ /lʌ́v/ 名 ▶定義1 ❶a strong feeling that you have when you like sb/sth very much ～を非常に好きになったときに抱く強い感情→愛，愛情，愛着‖ *a mother's love for her children* 母親の子供への愛情 **to fall in love with sb** ～と恋に落ちる‖ *It was love at first sight. They got married two months after they met!* それは一目ぼれだった. 2人は出会ってから2か月で結婚したのだ. *He's madly in love with her.* 彼は彼女に熱狂的に恋している. *a love song/story* 恋の歌・恋愛物語 ▶定義2 [ ❶, または単数扱い] a strong feeling of interest in or enjoyment of sth ～に対する強い興味や喜びの感情→愛好，好み，趣味‖ *a love of adventure/nature/sport* 冒険好き・自然愛好・スポーツ好き ▶定義3 ❷ a person, a thing or an activity that you like very much 非常に好きな人，物，活動→大好きな人・物，愛好していること，趣味‖ *His great love was always music.* 彼はいつも音楽を愛していた. *Who was your first love?* あなたの初恋の人はだれ. ▶定義4 ❷英略式 used as a friendly way of speaking to sb, often sb you do not know ～に，しばしば知らない～に親しく話し掛けるときに用いて→あなた，ねえ，ちょっと‖ *'Hello, love.*

love²

*What can I do for you?* 「いらっしゃい.何になさいますか」
➤しばしば luv とつづられる.
▶定義5 Ⓤ (used in tennis) a score of zero (テニスで用いて) 零点のスコア→ゼロ,ラブ ‖ *The score is forty-love.* 得点は40対0だ.

感句 give/send sb your love ▶定義 to give/send sb a friendly message ～に親しい伝言をする・伝える→よろしく,よろしくお伝えください ‖ *Give Maria my love when you next see her.* 次に会ったときにマリアに私からよろしくと伝えてください.

(lots of) love (from) ▶定義 used at the end of a letter to a friend or a member of your family 友達や家族への手紙の最後に用いて→さようなら,ではまた ‖ *See you soon. Love, Jim* また会いましょう.それでは,ジム

make love (to sb) ▶定義 to have sex 性交をする→(～と)寝る,愛撫(ぶ)する

*love² /lʌv/ 動他 ▶定義1 to like sb/sth in the strongest possible way できる限り強く～を好む→～を愛する,愛好する,～が大好きである ‖ *I split up from my girlfriend last year, but I still love her.* 去年ガールフレンドと別れたが,まだ彼女が好きだ. *She loves her children.* 彼女は自分の子供たちを愛している. ▶定義2 to like or enjoy sth very much ～をとても好む,楽しむ→～を愛好する,～が大好きである ‖ *I love the summer!* 私は夏が大好きだ. *I really love swimming in the sea.* 私は海で泳ぐのが本当に好きだ. *'What do you think of this music?' 'I love it!'* 「この音楽をどう思う」「とても気に入った」 ▶定義3 would love sth/to do sth used to say that you would very much like sth/to do sth ～を非常に欲しい,または非常にしたい場合に用いて→～が欲しい,～がしたい ‖ *'Would you like to come?' 'I'd love to.'* 「一緒に来ますか」「喜んで」 *'What about a drink?' 'I'd love one.'* 「飲み物はいかがですか」「頂くわ」 *We'd love you to come and stay with us.* 是非うちに来てお泊まりください.

love affair 名 C ▶定義1 a usually sexual relationship between two people who love each other but are not married 通常は,愛し合っているが結婚していない2人の性的関係→不倫,情事 ‖ *She had a love affair with her tennis coach.* 彼女はテニスのコーチと浮気していた. ▶定義2 a great enthusiasm for sth ～に対する強い熱狂→熱中,夢中になること

*lovely /lʌ́vli/ 形 (lovelier; loveliest) ▶定義1 beautiful or attractive 美しい,魅力的な→愛らしい,すてきな,心ひかれる ‖ *a lovely room/voice/expression* すてきな部屋・美しい声・魅力的な表情 *You look lovely with your hair short.* 短い髪が似合うよ. ▶定義2 enjoyable or pleasant; very nice 楽しい,快い; とても良い→愉快な,気持ちの良い; すばらしい ‖ *We had a lovely holiday.* すばらしい休暇を過ごした. ― loveliness 名 Ⓤ→愛らしさ,美しさ,すばらしさ

感句 lovely and warm, peaceful, fresh, etc ▶定義 used for emphasizing how good sth is because of the quality mentioned 述べられた特質のために,～がいかに良くできているかを強調するために用いて→とても～,すごく～,心地良く～だ ‖ *These blankets are lovely and soft.* これらの毛布は柔らかくて心地良い.

*lover /lʌ́vər/ 名 C ▶定義1 a partner in a sexual relationship with sb who he/she is not married to 結婚していない～との性的関係におけるパートナー→愛人,恋人 ‖ *He discovered that his wife had a lover.* 彼は妻に愛人がいることを知った. *The park was full of young lovers holding hands.* 公園は手をつないだ若い恋人たちで一杯だった. ▶定義2 a person who likes or enjoys the thing mentioned 言及された事柄をするのを好む,または楽しむ人→～愛好者,～好きな人 ‖ *a music lover* 音楽好き *an animal lover* 動物好き

loving /lʌ́viŋ/ 形 ▶定義1 feeling or showing love or care 愛や関心を持つ,示す→愛情に満ちた,(～を)大事に思う ‖ *She's very loving towards her brother.* 彼女は弟[兄]をとても大切に思っている. ▶定義2 (複合形容詞として) -loving loving the thing or activity mentioned ～を好む→～愛好者の,～好きな ‖ *a fun-loving girl* 楽しい事が大好きな少女 ― lovingly 副→愛情に満ちて,愛情を込めて

*low¹ /lóu/ 形副 ▶定義1 close to the ground or to the bottom of sth 地面や～の底に近い→低い,低く,低い所へ ‖ *Hang that picture a bit higher, it's much too low!* その絵はもう少し高い所に掛けてください,それでは低すぎます. *That plane is flying very low.* あの飛行機はとても低い所を飛

んでいる. ▶定義2 below the usual or normal level or amount 通常のレベルや量よりも低い→**低い**[く], **少ない**[く], **安い**[く] ‖ *Temperatures were very low last winter.* この前の冬は気温が非常に低かった. *The price of fruit is lower in the summer.* 果物の値段は夏には安くなる. **low wages** 低賃金 **low-fat yoghurt** 低脂肪ヨーグルト ▶定義3 below what is normal or acceptable in quality, importance or development 品質, 重要度, 発展が正常または許容範囲より低い→**低い**[く], **安い**[く], **遅れた**[て] ‖ *a low standard of living* 低い生活水準 **low status** 低い地位 ▶定義4 (used about a sound or voice) deep or quiet (音や声について) 深い, 静かな→**低音の**[で], **小声の**[で] ‖ *His voice is already lower than his father's.* 彼の声は既に父親より低い. *A group of people in the library were speaking in low voices.* 図書館で一塊の人々が小声で話していた. ▶定義5 not happy and lacking energy 幸福でなく元気のない→**弱った**[て], **意気消沈した**[て], **落ち込んだ**[て] ‖ *He's been **feeling** a bit **low** since his illness.* 彼は病気になってから少し元気がない. ▶定義6 (used about a light, an oven, etc) made to produce only a little light or heat (光, オーブンなどについて) 少しの光や熱しか発生しないような→**弱い**[く], **低い**[く] ‖ *Cook the rice on a low heat for 20 minutes.* 米を弱火で20分加熱します. *The low lighting adds to the restaurant's atmosphere.* 照明が暗めなのでそのレストランは雰囲気が良い. ▶定義7 (used about a gear in a car) that allows a slower speed (車のギアについて) 低速で→**ローギアの, ゆっくりと** ⇔ すべての定義 **high**

成句 high and low ⇒ **HIGH**²
lie low ⇒ **LIE**²
run low (on sth) ▶定義 to start to have less of sth than you need; to start to be less than is needed 必要なよりも少なくなり始める, 必要なより少ない状態になり始める→**欠乏する, 不足する, (〜を)不足させる** ‖ *We're running low on coffee - shall I go and buy some?* コーヒーがなくなりそうだ - 私が買ってきましょうか.
**low**² /lóʊ/ 名 ● ▶定義 a low point, level, figure, etc 低い点, レベル, 数字など→**最低地点, 最低値, 底値** ‖ *Unemployment has fallen to a new low.* 失業者は記録的に低い数になった. ⇔ **high**

**low-down** 名 [単数扱い] 略式
成句 give sb/get the low-down (on sb/sth) ▶定義 to tell sb/be told the true facts or secret information (about sb/sth) 〜に (…についての) 本当の事実や秘密の情報を教える・教えられる→**真相を知らせる, 知る; 内幕を知らせる, 知る**
**lower**¹ /lóʊər/ 形 ▶定義 below sth or at the bottom of sth 〜の下の, 〜の底の→**〜より低い, 下部の, 下方の** ‖ *She bit her lower lip.* 彼女は下唇をかんだ. *the lower deck of a ship* 船の下甲板 ⇔ **upper**
***lower**² /lóʊər/ 動 他 ▶定義1 to make or let sb/sth go down 〜を降ろす→**〜を下げる, 低くする, 落とす** ‖ *They lowered the boat into the water.* 彼らはボートを水に降ろした. *to lower your head/eyes* 顔を伏せる・視線を落とす
▶定義2 to make sth less in amount, quality, etc 〜の量や質などを低くする→**〜を下げる, 減らす, 弱める, 低下させる** ‖ *The virus lowers resistance to other diseases.* そのウイルスはほかの病気に対する抵抗力を弱める. *Could you **lower** your **voice** slightly? I'm trying to sleep.* もう少し声を小さくしてください. 眠りたいのです. ⇔ **raise**
**lower case** 名 ● ▶定義 letters that are written or printed in their small form; not in capital letters 小さい形で書かれたり印刷された文字; 大文字でない→**小文字** ‖ *The text is all in lower case.* 原文はすべて小文字で書かれている. *lower-case letters* 小文字 ⇔ **upper case**
**low-key** 形 ▶定義 quiet and not wanting to attract a lot of attention 静かであまり注目をひきたがらない→**控えめな, (強さ, 感情などを) 抑えた** ‖ *The wedding will be very low-key. We're only inviting ten people.* 結婚式はとても質素にするつもりです. 招待客は10人だけにします.
**lowland** /lóʊlənd, -lænd/ 名 [ ●, 通常は複数 ] ▶定義 a flat area of land at about sea level 海水面とほぼ同じ高さの平らな土地→**低地, 低地地方, 平野部** ‖ *the lowlands near the coast* 海岸近くの平地 *lowland areas* 低地地帯
**low-lying** 形 ▶定義 (used about land) near to sea level; not high (土地について) 海水面に近い; 高くない→**低い, 低地の**
**low tide** 名 ● ▶定義 the time when the sea is at its lowest level 海が最低水位になるとき→

1000 **loyal**

引き潮,引き潮時刻,低潮 || *At low tide you can walk out to the island.* 引き潮のときには島まで歩いて渡れる. ⇔ **high tide**

**loyal** /lɔ́ɪ(ə)l/ 形 ▶定義 (used about a person) not changing in your friendship or beliefs (人について)友情や信念を変えない ➔ **忠実な,誠実な** || *a loyal friend/supporter* 誠実な友・支援者 ➡類 **faithful** ⇔ **disloyal** — **loyally** 副 ➔ **忠実に,誠実に** — **loyalty** /lɔ́ɪ(ə)lti/ 名 **C U** (複 **loyalties**) ➔ **忠誠(心),誠実,誠実さ**

**lozenge** /lάz(ə)ndʒ/ 名 **C** ▶定義 a sweet that you suck if you have a cough or a sore throat せきやのどの痛みの際になめるキャンデー ➔ **せき止めドロップ,トローチ剤**

**L-plate** /él plèɪt/ 名 **C** ▶定義 a sign with a large red letter L (for 'learner') on it, that you fix to a car to show that the driver is learning to drive 大きな赤いL (learner) の字が書かれた表示で,車に付けて運転者が運転教習中であることを示す ➔ **仮免許運転中の表示板,L字のプレート**

**Ltd** /límətəd/ 略 医 ▶定義 (used about private companies) Limited (私会社について)有限責任の ➔ **有限(責任)会社** || *Pierce and Co Ltd* ピアス有限会社・株式会社

**lubricant** /lúːbrɪkənt/ 名 **C U** ▶定義 a substance, for example oil, that makes the parts of a machine work easily and smoothly 例えば油などのような,機械部品を容易に滑らかに動くようにするための物質 ➔ **潤滑油,潤滑剤**

**lubricate** /lúːbrɪkèɪt/ 動 他 ▶定義 to put oil, etc onto or into sth so that it works smoothly 滑らかに動くように〜に油などを塗る,差す ➔ **〜に油を差す,〜を滑らかにする** — **lubrication** /lùːbrɪkéɪ(ə)n/ 名 **U** ➔ **油を差すこと**

**lucid** /lúːsəd/ 形 正式 ▶定義**1** (used about sth that is said or written) clear and easy to understand (話されたり書かれたりした〜について)明確で理解しやすい ➔ **明快な,分かりやすい** || *a lucid style/description* 明快な文体・記述 ▶定義**2** (used about a person's mind) not confused; clear and normal (人の精神について)混乱していない;明せきで正常な ➔ **平静な,頭脳明せきな; 正気の** — **lucidly** 副 ➔ **明快に,分かりやすく** — **lucidity** /luːsídəti/ 名 **U** ➔ **明快さ,分かりやすさ,洞察力,頭のさえ**

*****luck** /lʌk/ 名 **U** ▶定義**1** success or good things that happen by chance 偶然に起こる成功や良い事 ➔ **幸運,つき,まぐれ当たり** || *We'd like to wish you lots of luck in your new career.* 新しいお仕事がうまくいくことを祈っています. *He says this necklace will bring you luck.* このネックレスは幸運を呼ぶと彼は言う. *I could hardly believe my luck when they offered me the job.* その仕事を与えられたとき,自分の幸運がほとんど信じられなかった. *With a bit of luck, we'll finish this job today.* ちょっと運が良ければ,この仕事を今日中に終えられるだろう. ▶定義**2** chance; the force that people believe makes things happen 偶然; 人々が,ものが起こる原因と信じる力 ➔ **チャンス; 運,巡り合わせ** || *There's no skill in this game - it's all luck.* このゲームには技術は要らない — 運がすべてだ. *to have good/bad luck* 運がいい・悪い

成句 **bad luck!; hard luck!** ▶定義 used to show pity for sb 〜に同情するときに用いて ➔ **お気の毒に,ついていませんね,おあいにくさま** || *'Bad luck. Maybe you'll win next time.'* 「残念だったね. 次はきっと勝てるよ」

**be in/out of luck** ▶定義 to be lucky/to not be lucky 幸運な・不運な ➔ **ついている・ついていない** || *I was in luck - they had one ticket left!* 私は運が良かった — チケットが1枚残っていたんだ.

**good luck (to sb)** ▶定義 used to wish that sb is successful 〜が成功するように祈るときに用いて ➔ **うまくいきますように,頑張ってください** || *Good luck! I'm sure you'll get the job.* 幸運を祈ります. きっとその仕事に就けますよ.

**worse luck** ⇒ **WORSE**

*****lucky** /lʌ́ki/ 形 (**luckier**; **luckiest**) ▶定義**1** (used about a person) having good luck (人について)運が良い ➔ **幸運である,ついている** || *He's lucky to be alive after an accident like that.* あんな事故に遭っても生きているなんて彼は運がいい. *With so much unemployment, I count myself lucky that I've got a job.* こんなに失業率が高いのに,仕事があるなんて私は運がいいと思う. *'I'm off on holiday next week.' 'Lucky you!'* 「来週は休暇で休みなんだ」「うらやましいね」 ▶定義**2** (used about a situation, event, etc) having a good result (状況,出来事などについて)良い結果になる ➔ **成功の,幸運をもたらす** || *It's lucky I got here before the rain started.* 雨が

降り出す前にここに着けて運が良かった. *a lucky escape* 幸運にも免れること ▶定義3 (used about a thing) bringing success or good luck (物について)成功や幸運をもたらす→縁起の良い, お守りの ‖ *a lucky number* 幸運な数 *It was not my lucky day.* その日はついてなかった. ⇔ **unlucky** — **luckily** 副 ▶運良く, 幸運にも ‖ *Luckily, I remembered to bring some money.* 幸運にも, 忘れずにいくらかお金を持っていった. 成句 **you'll be lucky** ▶定義 used to tell sb that sth they are expecting will probably not happen 期待している〜がおそらく起こらないだろうと…に言う場合に用いて→おあいにくさま, 残念ですね ‖ *You're looking for a good English restaurant? You'll be lucky!* おいしいイギリスのレストランを探しているんですか. それはおあいにくさま.

**lucrative** /lúːkrətɪv/ 形 正式 ▶定義 allowing sb to earn a lot of money 〜に大金をもうけさせる→得だ, もうかる ‖ *a lucrative contract/business* もうかる契約・事業

**ludicrous** /lúːdəkrəs/ 形 ▶定義 very silly; ridiculous 非常に愚かな; ばかげた→こっけいな, ばかばかしい ‖ *What a ludicrous idea!* 何てばかげた考えだろう. — **ludicrously** 副 →こっけいで, ばかげて

**lug** /lʌɡ/ 動 他 (**lugging**; **lugged**) 略式 ▶定義 to carry or pull sth very heavy with great difficulty 非常に重い〜を苦労して運ぶ, 引っ張る→〜をやっとのことで運ぶ, 力任せに引く

*****luggage** /lʌ́ɡɪdʒ/ 名 U ▶定義 bags, suitcases, etc used for carrying a person's clothes and things on a journey 旅行で衣服や物を運ぶためのバッグ, スーツケースなど→かばん類, 手荷物 ‖ *'How much luggage are you taking with you?' 'Only one suitcase.'* 「手荷物をいくつ持っていくんですか」「スーツケース1つだけです」 *You're only allowed one piece of **hand luggage** (= a bag that you carry with you on the plane).* 持ち込めるのは手荷物1つだけです(= 機内に持ち込めるかばん). ☛類 **baggage**

**luggage rack** 名 C ▶定義 a shelf above the seats in a train or bus for putting your bags, etc on かばんなどを載せるための列車やバスの座席の上にある棚→網棚, 荷物棚

**lukewarm** /lúːkwɔ̀ːrm/ 形 ▶定義1 (used about liquids) only slightly warm (液体について)わずかだけ暖かい→ぬるい, 生ぬるい ▶定義2 **lukewarm (about sb/sth)** not showing much interest; not keen あまり興味を示さない; 熱心でない→(〜に対して)いいかげんな, 気のない, 無関心な

**lull**¹ /lʌl/ 名 C, 通常は単数 ▶定義 **a lull (in sth)** a short period of quiet between times of activity 活動期間の間の平穏な短い期間→(〜の)小康, とぎれ, なぎ, こやみ

**lull**² /lʌl/ 動 他 ▶定義1 to make sb relaxed and calm 〜をくつろがせて平穏にする→〜を静める, なだめる, あやす ‖ *She sang a song to lull the children to sleep.* 彼女は子供たちをあやして寝かし付けるために歌を歌った. ▶定義2 **lull sb into sth** to make sb feel safe, and not expecting anything bad to happen 〜を安全な気持ちにし, 何も悪い事が起こることはないと思わせる→〜を安心させて…にする ‖ *Our first success lulled us into a false sense of security.* 最初の成功で安心して, 大丈夫だと思い込んだ.

**lullaby** /lʌ́ləbàɪ/ 名 C ( 複 **lullabies**) ▶定義 a gentle song that you sing to help a child to go to sleep 子供を寝かせるために歌う静かな歌→子守歌

**lumber**¹ /lʌ́mbər/ 特に 米 = **TIMBER(1)**

**lumber**² /lʌ́mbər/ 動 ▶定義1 自 to move in a slow, heavy way ゆっくりと重い足取りで動く→ドシンドシンと歩く, 重そうに動く ‖ *A family of elephants lumbered past.* 象の一家が重々しい足取りで通り過ぎた. ▶定義2 他 略式 **lumber sb (with sb/sth)** (通常は受動態で) to give sb a responsibility or job that he/she does not want 〜に望まない責任や仕事を与える→〜に(…を)押し付ける, 負わせる

**luminous** /lúːmənəs/ 形 ▶定義 that shines in the dark 暗い所で輝く→光を発する, 光る, 明るい ‖ *a luminous watch* 夜光塗料を使った時計

*****lump**¹ /lʌmp/ 名 C ▶定義1 a piece of sth solid of any size or shape 任意の大きさや形をした硬い〜の一片→塊, 一まとめ ‖ *a lump of coal/cheese/wood* 石炭・チーズ・まき一塊 *The sauce was full of lumps.* ソースにはだまがたくさんあった. ▶定義2 a swelling under the skin 皮膚の下のはれ→こぶ, はれ, しこり ‖ *You'll have a bit of a lump on your head where you banged it.* 頭

## 1002 lump[2]

のぶつけた所がちょっとこぶになるでしょう. ☞ **bump** のさし絵

**成句 have/feel a lump in your throat** ▶定義 to feel pressure in your throat because you are about to cry 今にも泣き出しそうでのどに圧迫を感じる→(感動・悲しみなどで)のどが締め付けられる, 胸が一杯になる

**lump**[2] /lʌmp/ 動他 ▶定義 lump A and B together; lump A (in) with B to put or consider different people or things together in the same group 異なる人々や物を同じグループに入れたり, 同じグループだと見なす→〜を…と十把一からげにする, 引っくるめる

**成句 lump it 略式** ▶定義 to accept sth unpleasant because you have no choice ほかに選択肢がないため不快な〜を受け入れる→我慢する, こらえる ‖ *That's the deal - like it or lump it.* それで決まりだ — 好むと好まざるとにかかわらず.

**lump sum** 名 C ▶定義 an amount of money paid all at once rather than in several smaller amounts 数回に少額に分けてではなく一度に支払われる金額→総額, 一括払い(の金額)

**lumpy** /lʌmpi/ 形 ▶定義 full of or covered with lumps 隆起物が多い, または隆起物で覆われた→塊の多い, (表面が)でこぼこの, ごつごつした ‖ *This bed is very lumpy.* このベッドはでこぼこだ. ⇔ **smooth**

**lunacy** /lúːnəsi/ 名 U ▶定義 very stupid behaviour; madness 非常に愚かな振る舞い; 狂気→愚行, 狂気のさた ‖ *It was lunacy to drive so fast in that terrible weather.* あのひどい天気にそんなに車を飛ばすなんて狂気のさただった.

**lunar** /lúːnər/ 形 (通常は名詞の前で) ▶定義 connected with the moon 月と関連した→月の, 月面の ‖ *a lunar spacecraft/eclipse/landscape* 月宇宙船・月食・月面の風景

**lunatic**[1] /lúːnətɪk/ 名 C 略式 ▶定義 a person who behaves in a stupid way doing crazy and often dangerous things 狂気染みた, しばしば危険な事をして愚かな振る舞いをする人→精神異常者, 狂人, 常軌を逸した人, ばかげた事をする人, 変人 ☞ 類 **madman**

**lunatic**[2] /lúːnətɪk/ 形 ▶定義 stupid; crazy 愚かな; 狂気の→精神異常の, 常軌を逸した ‖ *a lunatic idea* ばかげたアイデア

\***lunch** /lʌntʃ/ 名 C U ▶定義 a meal that you have in the middle of the day 昼に食べる食事→昼食, 弁当 ‖ *Hot and cold lunches are served between 12 and 2.* 12時から2時まで温かい食事と冷たい食事が用意されている. *What would you like for lunch?* 昼食は何にしますか.
▶ packed lunch(お弁当), picnic lunch(ピクニックの弁当)は外に出掛ける日持っていく. business lunch(商談しながらの昼食)または working lunch(仕事をしながらの昼食)は働いている場合(= 昼食を取りながら同時に仕事をする). school dinner(給食)は学校に通っている子供の場合.

— lunch 動自 正式 ▶昼食を取る

**lunch hour** 名 [C, 通常は単数] ▶定義 the time around the middle of the day when you stop work or school to have lunch 仕事や授業を中断して昼食を取る昼ごろの時間→昼食時間, お昼 ‖ *I went to the shops in my lunch hour.* 昼食時間に店に行った.

**lunchtime** /lʌntʃtaɪm/ 名 C U ▶定義 the time around the middle of the day when lunch is eaten 昼食を取る昼ごろの時間→昼食時(間), お昼 ‖ *I'll meet you at lunchtime.* 昼食時に会いましょう.

\***lung** /lʌŋ/ 名 C ▶定義 one of the two organs of your body that are inside your chest and are used for breathing 呼吸するために使われる胸の内部の器官→肺, 肺臓 ☞ C5ページのさし絵

**lunge** /lʌndʒ/ 名 [C, 通常は単数] a lunge (at sb); a lunge (for sb/sth) ▶定義 a sudden powerful forward movement of the body, especially when trying to attack sb/sth 特に〜を襲おうとするときの, 急激で勢いのある前方への体の動き→(〜への)突っ込み, 突進, 突き ‖ *She made a lunge for the ball.* 彼女はボールに飛び付いた.

— lunge 動自 ▶突進する, 突く ‖ *He lunged towards me with a knife.* 彼はナイフを持って私に襲い掛かった.

**lurch** /lɜːrtʃ/ 名 [C, 通常は単数] ▶定義 a sudden movement forward or to one side 前や横への突然の動き→急に傾くこと, よろめき — lurch 動自 ▶急に傾く, よろめく

**成句 leave sb in the lurch** ⇒ **LEAVE**[1]

**lure**[1] /lʊər/ 動他 ▶定義 to persuade or trick sb to go somewhere or do sth, usually by offering him/her sth nice 通常良い～を申し出て, …を説得したりだましたりしてどこかに行かせたり何かをさせる➔**～を誘惑する, 誘い込む, おびき出す** ‖ *Young people are lured to the city by the prospect of a job and money.* 仕事と金を期待して若者は都会に引き寄せられる.

**lure**[2] /lʊər/ 名 C ▶定義 the attractive qualities of sth ～の魅力的な質➔**引き付けるもの, 魅力, 誘惑** ‖ *the lure of money/fame/adventure* 金・名声・冒険の誘惑

**lurid** /lʊ́ərɪd/ 形 ▶定義 **1** having colours that are too bright, in a way that is not attractive 魅力的でないほど, 派手すぎる色をした➔**けばけばしい, 毒々しい** ‖ *a lurid purple and orange dress* けばけばしい紫とオレンジ色のドレス ▶定義 **2** (used about a story or a piece of writing) deliberately shocking, especially because of violent or unpleasant detail (物語や書き物について) 特に暴力的または不快な詳細のため, 故意に衝撃的な➔**不気味な, ぞっとする, 恐ろしい** — **luridly** 副 ➔けばけばしく, ぞっとするように

**lurk** /lɜːrk/ 動 自 ▶定義 to wait somewhere secretly especially in order to do sth bad or illegal 特に悪い事や不正な事をするためにどこかでひそかに待つ➔**潜む, 待ち伏せする, 潜伏する** ‖ *I thought I saw somebody lurking among the trees.* だれかが木々の間に隠れているのが見えたような気がした.

**luscious** /lʌ́ʃəs/ 形 ▶定義 (used about food) tasting very good (食べ物について) とてもおいしい➔**非常に風味の良い, 甘美な** ‖ *luscious fruit* とてもおいしい果物

**lush** /lʌʃ/ 形 ▶定義 (used about plants or gardens) growing very thickly and well (植物や庭について) こんもりと元気に生長している➔**青々とした, みずみずしく茂った**

**lust**[1] /lʌst/ 名 ▶定義 **1** U lust (for sb) strong sexual desire 強い性的欲望➔**肉欲, 色情** ▶定義 **2** C U (a) lust (for sth) (a) very strong desire to have or get sth ～を所有したり得たいという非常に強い欲望➔**切望, 渇望** ‖ *a lust for power* 権力欲 *(a) lust for life (= enjoyment of life)* 生への渇望 (= 人生の楽しみ)

**lust**[2] /lʌst/ 動 自 ▶定義 lust (after sb); lust (after/for sth) to feel a very strong desire for sb/sth ～に対して非常に強い欲望を感じる➔**渇望する, どん欲に求める** ‖ *to lust for power/suc-cess/fame* 権力・成功・名声を強く求める

**lustful** /lʌ́stfʊl, -f(ə)l/ 形 ▶定義 full of sexual desire 性的欲望で一杯の➔**好色の, みだらな** ‖ *lustful thoughts* みだらな考え — **lustfully** /-fʊli, -f(ə)li/ 副 ➔みだらに

**luxurious** /lʌgʒʊ́əriəs, lʌkʃʊ́ər-/ 形 ▶定義 very comfortable; full of expensive and beautiful things 非常に快適な; 高価で美しい物で一杯の➔**ぜいたくな, 豪華な** ‖ *a luxurious hotel* 豪華ホテル — **luxuriously** 副 ➔ぜいたくに, 豪華に

**luxury** /lʌ́kʃ(ə)ri/ 名 ( 複 **luxuries**) ▶定義 **1** U the enjoyment of expensive and beautiful things; great comfort and pleasure 高価で美しい物の楽しみ; 非常な快適さと満足➔**ぜいたく, 豪華; 享楽** ‖ *They are said to be **living in luxury** in Barbados.* 彼らはバルバドスでぜいたくざんまいに暮らしているそうだ. *to lead **a life of luxury*** ぜいたくな暮らしをする *a luxury hotel/car/yacht* 豪華ホテル・高級車・豪華ヨット ▶定義 **2** C something that is enjoyable and expensive that you do not really need 実際には必要ないが, 楽しくて高価な物➔**ぜいたく品, 豪華な物** ‖ *luxury goods, such as wine and chocolates* ワインやチョコレートなどの高価な嗜好 (しこう) 品 ▶定義 **3** U [単数扱い] a pleasure which you do not often have めったに味わえない楽しみ➔**ぜいたく, 満足, 享楽** ‖ *It was (an) absolute luxury to do nothing all weekend.* 週末ずっと何もしないのは本当のぜいたくだった.

**lynch** /lɪntʃ/ 動 他 ▶定義 (used about a crowd of people) to kill sb, usually by hanging, who is thought to be guilty of a crime without a legal trial in a court of law (群衆について) 有罪だと考えられる～を法廷での裁判なしに, 通常は縛り首で殺す➔**～を私刑によって殺す, リンチで殺す**

**lyric** /lɪ́rɪk/ 形 ▶定義 (used about poetry) expressing personal feelings and thoughts (詩について) 個人的な感情や考えを表現する➔**叙情的な, 感情を強く出した** ‖ *lyric poems* 叙情詩

**lyrical** /lɪ́rɪk(ə)l/ 形 ▶定義 like a song or a poem, expressing strong personal feelings 歌や詩のように, 強い個人的感情を表現した➔**熱情的な, 熱烈な, 叙情詩的な**

**lyrics** /lɪ́rɪks/ 名 [複数扱い] ▶定義 the words of a song 歌の言葉➔**歌詞**

# M m

**M, m¹** /em/ 名 C (複 **M's; m's**) ▶定義 the thirteenth letter of the English alphabet 英語アルファベットの第13文字→m(M)が表す音, m(M)の文字, m(M)の字形のもの ‖ *'Miranda' begins with (an) 'M'.* Miranda は M で始まる.

**M²** 略 ▶定義 **1** (または **med**) medium (size)→中間(の大きさ), M サイズ ▶定義 **2** 英 motorway→高速自動車道路 ‖ *heavy traffic on the M25* 高速自動車道路25号線の交通量の多さ ▶定義 **3** m metre(s)→メートル ‖ *a 500m race* 500メートル競争 ▶定義 **4** m million(s)→百万 ‖ *population 10m* 人口1千万人

**MA** /èm éɪ/ 略 Master of Arts ▶定義 a second degree that you receive when you complete a more advanced course or piece of research in an arts subject at university or college 大学の人文科学でさらに上級の講座を修了したときまたは研究を完了したときに受ける2番目の学位→文学修士(号) ☞参 **BA, MSc**

**mac** /mæk/ (または **mackintosh** /mǽkəntɑ̀ʃ/) 名 C 特に 英 ▶定義 a coat that is made to keep out the rain 雨を防ぐように作られたコート→レインコート

**macabre** /məkɑ́:brə, -bər/ 形 ▶定義 unpleasant and frightening because it is connected with death 死と結び付けられるために不快で怖い→死を暗示するような, 気味の悪い, 恐ろしい ‖ *a macabre tale/joke/ritual* 気味の悪い話・冗談・儀式

**macaroni** /mǽkəróʊni/ 名 U ▶定義 a type of Italian food made from dried flour and water (*pasta*) in the shape of short tubes 乾燥した小麦粉と水から作られる短い管の形をしたイタリアの食べ物(パスタ)の一種→マカロニ

*__machine__ /məʃíːn/ 名 C (しばしば複合語で) ▶定義 a piece of equipment with moving parts that is designed to do a particular job. A machine usually needs electricity, gas, steam, etc in order to work. 特定の仕事をするために設計された, 動く部品が付いている装置. 通常作動するために電気, ガス, 蒸気などを必要とする→機械 ‖ *a washing/sewing/knitting machine* 洗濯機・ミシン・編み機 *a machine for making pasta* パスタ製造機 ☞参 **tool** の注

**machine-gun** 名 C ▶定義 a gun that fires bullets very quickly and continuously 弾丸を非常に速く連続して発射する銃→機関銃

**machinery** /məʃíːnəri/ 名 U ▶定義 machines in general, especially large ones; the moving parts of a machine 機械の総称, 特に大きなもの; 機械の動く部分→**機械類, 装置, 部品** ‖ *farm/agricultural/industrial machinery* 農耕機具・農機具・工業機械

**macho** /mɑ́:tʃoʊ/ 形 略式 ▶定義 (used about a man or his behaviour) having typically male qualities like strength and courage, but using them in an aggressive way (男性または男性の振る舞いについて) 強さや勇気のような典型的な男性の性質を持ち, それらを攻撃的に使っている→男っぽい, やたらと男らしさを売り物にする ‖ *He's too macho to ever admit he was wrong and apologize.* 彼はやたらと男らしさを売り物にしていて, 自分の非を認めて謝ったことなどない.

**mackintosh** /mǽkɪntɑʃ/ =**MAC**

*__mad__ /mæd/ 形 ▶定義 **1** having a mind that does not work normally; mentally ill 正常に働かない心を持つ; 精神的に病んだ→気が狂った, 狂気の ▶精神的に正常でない人を言い表すとき, 現在では通常 mad や insane は用いない. mentally ill という表現を用いる.

▶定義 **2** 英 not at all sensible; crazy 良識が全くない; 狂った→狂ったような, ばかげた, 無謀な ‖ *You must be mad to drive in this weather.* この天気の中をドライブするなど無謀だ. ▶定義 **3** (名詞の前は不可) **mad (at/with sb) (about sth)** very angry 非常に怒った→腹を立てた, 怒った, 頭にきた ‖ *His laziness drives me mad!* 彼の怠慢には頭にくる. 特に 米 *Don't get/go mad at him. He didn't mean to do it.* 彼に腹を立てるな. 彼はそのようなつもりではなかったのだ.

▶定義 **4** 略式 **mad about/on sb/sth** liking sb/sth very much ～が非常に好きな→夢中になって ‖ *He's mad on computer games at the moment.* 彼は今コンピューターゲームに夢中になっている. *Steve's mad about Jane.* スティーヴはジェーンに夢中だ. ▶定義 **5** not controlled; wild or very excited 制御できない; 野性的なまたは非常に興奮した→(気が狂うほどに)興奮した ‖ *The audience was cheering and clapping like* *mad (= very hard).* 聴衆は気も狂わんばかりに (=非常に激しく)歓呼し拍手喝さいした. *When DiCaprio appeared on the hotel balcony his fans went mad.* ディカプリオがホテルのバルコニーに現れると、彼のファンは熱狂した.

**madam** /mǽdəm/ 名[単数扱い] ▶定義1 正式 used as a polite way of speaking to a woman, especially to a customer in a shop or restaurant 丁重に女性に話し掛けるときに用いる、特に店やレストランで客に対して→奥様, お嬢様 ‖ *Can I help you, madam?* 奥様、何にいたしますか. ☞参 **sir** ▶定義2 **Madam** used for beginning a formal letter to a woman when you do not know her name 名前を知らない女性にあてる正式な手紙の書き出しに用いて→拝啓 ‖ *Dear Madam, I am writing in reply...* 拝啓 . . .につきましてご返答申し上げます.

**mad cow disease** =**BSE**

**maddening** /mǽdnɪŋ/ 形 ▶定義 that makes you very angry or annoyed 非常に怒らせるまたは困らせるような→気を狂わすような, 腹立たしい ‖ *She has some really maddening habits.* 彼女は実に腹立たしい癖がいくつかある. — **maddeningly** 副→気を狂わすほどに, 腹立たしく

**made MAKE**¹ の過去・過去分詞形
成句 **made to measure** ⇒ **MEASURE**²

**madly** /mǽdli/ 副 ▶定義1 in a wild or crazy way 野性的なまたは正気でない方法で→気が狂ったように ‖ *They were rushing about madly.* 彼らは狂ったように走り回った. ▶定義2 非正式 very; extremely 非常に; 極度に→猛烈に, 必死に, 激しく ‖ *They're madly in love.* 彼らは激しい恋をしている.

**madman** /mǽdmæn, -mən/ 名 C (複 **madmen** /-men, -mən/) ▶定義 a person who behaves in a wild or crazy way 狂気染みたまたは正気でない振る舞いをする人→狂人, ばかな人 ☞類 **lunatic**

**madness** /mǽdnəs/ 名 U ▶定義 crazy or stupid behaviour that could be dangerous 危険なくらいの、正気でないまたはばかげた振る舞い→狂気, 精神錯乱, 狂気のさた ‖ *It would be madness to take a boat out in such rough weather.* このような荒れた天候の中で出航するのは狂気のさただ.

*****magazine** /mǽgəzìːn, -́-́/ (または 略式 **mag** /mǽg/) 名 C ▶定義 a type of large thin book with a paper cover that you can buy every week or month containing articles, photographs, etc often on a particular topic 毎週または毎月購入できる表紙の付いた大きな薄い本の一種で、多くの場合特定の話題についての記事、写真などが載っている→雑誌 ‖ *a woman's/computer/gardening magazine* 女性・コンピューター・園芸雑誌

**maggot** /mǽgət/ 名 C ▶定義 a young insect before it grows wings and legs and becomes a fly 羽と足が生えてハエになる前の幼虫→うじ虫, うじ ☞ **worm** のさし絵

*****magic**¹ /mǽdʒɪk/ 名 U ▶定義1 a secret power that some people believe can make strange or impossible things happen by saying special words or doing special things 特別な言葉を唱えたり、特別な事を行うことによって、不思議なまたは不可能な事を起こすことができると人々が信じる秘密の力→魔法 ☞参 **black magic** ▶定義2 the art of doing tricks that seem impossible in order to entertain people 人々を楽しませるために不可能に見える芸当を行う技→マジック, 手品, 奇術 ▶定義3 a special quality that makes sth seem wonderful ～をすばらしいと思わせる特別な性質→不思議な力, 魅力, すばらしい物・事 ‖ *I'll never forget the magic of that moment.* その瞬間のすばらしさを私は決して忘れないだろう.

**magic**² /mǽdʒɪk/ 形 ▶定義1 used in or using magic 魔法で使われる、または魔法を使う→魔法の, 魔法のような ‖ *a magic spell/potion/charm/trick* 魔法の呪文(じゅもん)・薬・おまじない・手品 *There is no magic formula for passing exams - just hard work.* 試験に合格する魔法の方法などない - ただよく勉強することだ. ▶定義2 having a special quality that makes sth seem wonderful ～をすばらしく見せる特別な性質を持つ→すばらしい, 不思議な魅力のある ‖ *Respect is the magic ingredient in our relationship.* 私たちの間柄では尊重する気持ちがすばらしいきずなとなっている. — **magically** /-k(ə)li/ 副→魔法のように, 不思議なほど, 神秘的に

**magical** /mǽdʒɪk(ə)l/ 形 ▶定義1 that seems to use magic 魔法を使うように見える→魔術的な, 不思議な ‖ *a herb with magical powers to heal* 治癒する魔法のような効果のあるハーブ ▶定義2 wonderful and exciting すばらしく、興

奮するような→魅力的な‖ *Our holiday was absolutely magical.* 休日は実にすばらしかった.

**magician** /mədʒíʃ(ə)n/ 图 ⓒ ▶定義1 a person who performs magic tricks to entertain people 人々を楽しませるために手品を行う人→奇術師, 手品師 ☛参 **conjuror** ▶定義2 (in stories) a man who has magic powers (お話の中で)魔力を持つ男性→魔術師, 魔法使い ☛参 **wizard**

**magistrate** /mǽdʒəstrèɪt, -trət/ 图 ⓒ ▶定義 an official who acts as a judge in cases involving less serious crimes それほど重くない犯罪にかかわる事件で判事を務める役人→治安判事

**magnanimous** /mæɡnǽnəməs/ 形 ▶定義 kind, generous and forgiving (especially towards an enemy or a competitor that you have beaten) (特に自分が打ち負かした敵または競争相手に対して)親切で, 気前が良く, そして寛大な→度量の大きい, 寛大な

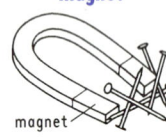

magnet

**magnet** /mǽɡnət/ ⓒ ▶定義 a piece of iron, steel, etc that can attract and pick up other metal objects ほかの金属を引き付けて持ち上げる鉄, 鋼などの一片→磁石

**magnetic** /mæɡnétɪk/ 形 ▶定義1 having the ability to attract metal objects 金属を引き付ける性能を持つ→磁石の, 磁気の‖ *magnetic fields* 磁場 *a magnetic tape/disk* (= containing electronic information which can be read by a computer or other machine) 磁気テープ・ディスク (= コンピューターまたはほかの機械で読み取ることのできる電子情報を含んでいる) ▶定義2 having a quality that strongly attracts people 人々を強く引き付ける性質を持っている→人を引き付ける, 魅力のある‖ *a magnetic personality* 魅力のある人柄 — **magnetism** /mǽɡnətìz(ə)m/ 图 ⓤ →磁性, 磁気, 人を引き付ける力, 魅力‖ *Nobody could resist his magnetism.* 彼の魅力にはだれも逆らえなかった.

**magnificent** /mæɡnífəs(ə)nt/ 形 ▶定義 extremely impressive and attractive 非常に印象的で魅力的な→見事な, すばらしい, 壮大な‖ *What a magnificent castle!* 何とすばらしい城

だ. — **magnificently** 副 →堂々と, 立派に — **magnificence** 图 ⓤ →壮大さ, 荘厳

magnify

magnifying glass

**magnify** /mǽɡnəfàɪ/ 動 ⓣ (現分 **magnifying**; 三単現 **magnifies**; 過, 過分 **magnified**) ▶定義1 to make sth look bigger than it is, usually using a special piece of equipment 通常特別な装置を使って, ～をそれ自体よりも大きく見せる→～を拡大する‖ *to magnify sth under a microscope* ～を顕微鏡で拡大する ▶定義2 to make sth seem more important than it really is ～を実際よりも重要に思わせる→～を誇張する‖ *to magnify a problem* 問題を誇張する — **magnification** /mæɡnəfəkéɪ(ə)n, məɡnɪf-/ 图 ⓤ →拡大, 誇張

**magnifying glass** 图 ⓒ ▶定義 a round piece of glass, usually with a handle, that is used for making things look bigger than they are 通常丸いガラスに取っ手が付いていて, 物をそれ自体よりも大きく見せるために使われる→拡大鏡, 虫眼鏡 ☛ **magnify** のさし絵

**magnitude** /mǽɡnət(j)ùːd/ 图 ⓤ ▶定義 the great size or importance of sth ～の大きさ, または重要性→大きさ, 重要さ

**mahogany** /məhágəni/ 图 ⓤ ▶定義 hard dark reddish-brown wood (from a tropical tree) that is used for making furniture 家具を作るために使われる, 堅くて, 濃い赤茶色の木(熱帯地方の木からとれる)→マホガニー

**maid** /méɪd/ 图 ⓒ ▶定義 a woman whose job is to clean in a hotel or large house ホテルまたは大きな家で掃除をすることを仕事にする女性 →お手伝い, メイド ☛参 **chambermaid**

**maiden name** 图 ⓒ ▶定義 a woman's family name before marriage 結婚前の女性の姓→旧姓 ☛参 **nee**

**maiden voyage** 图 ⓒ ▶定義 the first journey of a new ship 新しい船の最初の旅→処女航海

\***mail** /méɪl/ ( 粵 または **post**) 图 ⓤ ▶定義1 the system for collecting and sending letters and packages 手紙と小包を集めて送る仕組み→郵便, 郵便制度‖ *to send a parcel by airmail/sur-*

face mail 小包を航空便・陸便で送る ▶定義2 the letters, etc that you receive 受け取る手紙など→郵便物 ‖ junk mail (= letters, usually advertising sth, that are sent to people although they have not asked for them) ダイレクトメール (= 通常～の宣伝をするために,請求していないにもかかわらず人々に送られてくる手紙) ☞参 post の注 ▶定義3 特に 米 =E-MAIL — mail 動他 特に 米 →郵便で出す,郵送する,投かんする

**mailbox** /méɪlbɑ̀ks/ 名 ⓒ ▶定義1 米 =LETTER BOX(2) ▶定義2 米 =POSTBOX ▶定義3 a computer program that receives and stores electronic messages (e-mail) 電子メッセージ (e-mail) を受け取り,格納するコンピューターのプログラム→メールソフト

**mailing list** 名 ⓒ ▶定義 a list of the names and addresses of people to whom advertising material or information is regularly sent by a business or an organization 企業または団体により宣伝物や情報が定期的に送られてくる人たちの名前と住所の一覧表→郵送先名簿

**mailman** /méɪlmæn/ (複 **-men** /mèn/) 米 =POSTMAN

**mail order** 名 Ⓤ ▶定義 a method of shopping. You choose what you want from a special book (a catalogue) and the goods are then sent to you by post. 買い物の1つの方法.特別な本 (カタログ) から欲しい物を選び,その商品が郵送されてくる→通信販売

**maim** /méɪm/ 動他 ▶定義 to hurt sb so badly that part of his/her body can no longer be used ～をひどく傷付け,その～の体の部分がもはや使えないようにする→～を障害者にする,不具になる

★**main**¹ /méɪn/ 形 (名詞の前だけ) ▶定義 most important; chief 最も重要な;主な→主な,主要な ‖ My main reason for wanting to learn English is to get a better job. 私が英語を学びたい主な理由はもっと良い仕事を得るためです. a busy main road にぎやかな大通り He doesn't earn very much but he's happy, and that's **the main thing**. 彼はあまり多くは稼いでいないが,幸せであり,それが最も重要な事だ.

成句 **in the main** 正式 ▶定義 generally; mostly 一般的に;ほとんど→概して,大部分は ‖ We found English people very friendly in the main. 概して英国人は非常に親切だと私たちは思った.

**main**² /méɪn/ 名 ▶定義1 ⓒ a large pipe or wire that carries water, gas or electricity between buildings 建物間で,水,ガス,または電気を運ぶ大きな管や金属の線→本管,本線 ‖ The water main has burst. 水道の本管が破裂した.
▶定義2 **the mains** [複数扱い] 英 the place where the supply of gas, water or electricity to a building starts; the system of providing these services to a building 建物へのガス,水または電気の供給の始点;これらのサービスを建物に供給する仕組み→主管,コンセント,元栓 ‖ Turn the water off at the mains. 水道の元栓を締めなさい. mains gas/water/electricity ガスの元栓・水道の元栓・電気のコンセント

**mainland** /méɪnlænd, -lənd/ 名 [単数扱い] ▶定義 the main part of a country or continent, not including the islands around it 国または大陸の主要な部分.周囲にある島は含まない→本土 ‖ mainland Greece ギリシャ本土

**mainly** /méɪnli/ 副 ▶定義 mostly ほとんど→主に ‖ The students here are mainly from Japan. ここの学生は主に日本から来ている.

**mainstay** /méɪnstèɪ/ 名 ⓒ ▶定義 a person or thing that is the most important part of sth, which makes it possible for it to exist or to be successful ～の最も重要な部分である人また物で,その～が存在することまたは成功することを可能にしている→頼みの綱,大黒柱,主な生業 ‖ Cocoa is the mainstay of the country's economy. ココアは国の経済を支えている.

**mainstream** /méɪnstrìːm/ 名 [単数扱い] ▶定義 the ideas and opinions that are considered normal because they are shared by most people; the people who hold these opinions and beliefs 大部分の人々により共有されているため,標準と考えられている考えや意見;そのような意見や信条を持つ人々→主流,主潮 ‖ The Green Party is not **in the mainstream** of British politics. 緑の党は英国政界の主流ではない.

★**maintain** /meɪntéɪn, mən-/ 動他 ▶定義1 to make sth continue at the same level, standard, etc ～を同じ水準,基準などで継続させる→～を維持する,持続する,保持する ‖ We need to maintain the quality of our goods but not increase the price. 我々は製品の性能を維持することは必

要だが,価格を上げる必要はない. *to maintain law and order* 法と秩序を維持する ▶定義2 to keep sth in good condition by checking and repairing it regularly 定期的に点検し修理することによって～を良い状態に保つ→**～を整備する, 保全する, 管理する** ∥ *to maintain a road/building/machine* 道路・建物・機械を保全する *The house is large and expensive to maintain.* その家は大きくて管理するのに費用がかかる. ▶定義3 to keep saying that sth is true even when others disagree or do not believe it たとえ他人が異議を唱えたり信じなくても,その～が事実だと言い続ける→**～を主張する, 言い張る** ∥ *I still maintain that I was right to sack him.* 私は今でも彼を解雇したのは正しかったと主張する. *She has always maintained her innocence.* 彼女はずっと自らの無実を主張している. ▶定義4 to support sb with your own money ～を自分のお金で支える→**～を扶養する, 養う** ∥ *He has to maintain two children from his previous marriage.* 彼は前の結婚でもうけた2人の子供たちを養わなければならない.

**maintenance** /méɪnt(ə)nəns/ 名 U ▶定義1 keeping sth in good condition ～を良い状態で保つこと→**維持, 保全, 整備, メンテナンス** ∥ *This house needs a lot of maintenance.* この家はかなりの手入れが必要だ. *car maintenance* 自動車の整備 ▶定義2 因 money that sb must pay regularly to a former wife, husband or partner especially when they have had children together 特に共にもうけた子供がいるときに,～が先妻, 先夫または前の連れ合いに定期的に支払わなければならない費用→**養育費, 扶助料** ∥ *He has to pay maintenance to his ex-wife.* 彼は先妻に養育費を支払わなければならない.

**maisonette** /mèɪzə(ə)nét, -s(ə)n-/ 名 C 因 ▶定義 a flat/apartment on two floors that is part of a larger building 大きな建物の一部にある, 2つの階続きのアパート→**貸し室, メゾネット**

**maize** /méɪz/ (因 **corn**) 名 U ▶定義 a tall plant that produces yellow grains in a large mass (*a cob*) 多数の黄色い粒が一塊になったもの(トウモロコシの穂軸)がなる背の高い植物→**トウモロコシ**
▶野菜として食べる, トウモロコシからとれる黄色い穀粒はsweet corn (スイートコーン)と呼ばれている.
☛ **cereal** のさし絵

**majestic** /mədʒéstɪk/ 形 ▶定義 impressive because of its size or beauty その大きさまたは美しさのために印象的な→**荘厳な, 堂々とした** ∥ *a majestic mountain landscape* 雄大な山の景観 ― **majestically** /-k(ə)li/ 副 →荘厳に, 堂々と

**majesty** /mǽdʒəsti/ 名 (榎 **majesties**) ▶定義1 ❶ the impressive and attractive quality that sth has ～が持つ印象的で魅力的な性質→**荘厳, 威厳, 尊厳** ∥ *the splendour and majesty of the palace and its gardens* その宮殿と庭園の華麗さと荘厳さ ▶定義2 **His/Her/Your Majesty** C 正式 used when speaking to or about a royal person 王室の人に話し掛けるとき, または王室の人について話すときに用いて→**陛下** ∥ *Her Majesty the Queen* 女王陛下

★**major**¹ /méɪdʒər/ 形 ▶定義1 (名詞の前だけ) very large, important or serious 非常に大きな, 重要な, または深刻な→**大きな, 重要な, 主要な** ∥ *The patient needs major heart surgery.* その患者は心臓の大手術を必要としている. *There haven't been any major problems.* 何も大きな問題はなかった. ⇔ **minor** ▶定義2 of one of the two types of key¹(4) in which music is usually written 通常曲が書かれる2種類の調性のうちの1つの→**長調の, 長音階の** ∥ *the key of D major* ニ長調 ☛参 **minor**

**major**² /méɪdʒər/ 名 ▶定義1 (略 **Maj**) C an officer of a middle level in the army or the US air force 陸軍または米空軍で中間階級の将校→**陸軍[空軍]少佐** ▶定義2 C 米 the main subject or course of a student at college or university; the student who studies it 大学生の主要な科目または講座; それを学ぶ学生→**専攻科目, 専門課程, 専攻学生** ∥ *Her major is French.* 彼女の専門課程はフランス語だ. ▶定義3 U (used in music) a type of key¹(4) or scale (音楽で)調性または音階の一種→**長調, 長音階** ∥ *a change from major to minor* 長調から短調への転調

**major**³ /méɪdʒər/ 動 米
句動詞 **major in sth** ▶定義 to study sth as your main subject at college or university 大学で～を自分の主要な科目として勉強する→**～を専攻する**

**major general** 名 C ▶定義 an officer of a

high level in the army 陸軍の高い位の将校→**英陸軍・米陸[空]軍少将**

***majority*** /mədʒɔ́(ː)rəti, -dʒár-/ 名(複 **majorities**) ▶定義1 [単数扱い, 単数または複数形の動詞と共に] majority (of sb/sth) the largest number or part of a group of people or things 人々または物の集まりで最大の数または部分→**大多数, 大部分** ‖ *The majority of students in the class come/comes from Japan.* そのクラスの生徒の大多数は日本から来ている. *This treatment is not available in* **the vast majority** *of hospitals.* この治療法は大多数の病院で行われていない. ⇔ **minority** ▶定義2 [**C**, 通常は単数] majority (over sb) (in an election) the difference in the number of votes for the person/party who came first and the person/party who came second (選挙で)一番になった人・党と2番になった人・党の得票数の差→**得票差** ‖ *He was elected by/with a majority of almost 5000 votes.* 彼は5000票近くの得票差で選ばれた.

➤ have an overall majority は, ほかの人・党の得票数の合計よりも多くの票を得ることを表す.

成句 be in the/a majority ▶定義 to form the largest number or part of sth 〜の最大の数または部分を形成する→**過半数を占める** ‖ *Women are in the majority in the teaching profession.* 教職では女性が大半を占める.

*****make*****¹ /méɪk/ 動⓫ (過, 過分 **made** /méɪd/)
▶定義1 to produce or create sth 〜を作るまたは創造する→**〜を作る, 製作する** ‖ *to make bread* パンを作る *This model is **made of** steel, and that one is **made out of** used matches.* この模型は鋼鉄でできていて, あちらは使用済みのマッチでできている. *Cheese is **made from** milk.* チーズは牛乳から作られる. *Those cars are **made in** Slovakia.* あれらの車はスロバキア製だ. *Shall I make you a sandwich/make a sandwich for you?* サンドイッチを作りましょうか. *to make a hole in sth* 〜に穴を開ける *to make a law/rule* 法律・規則を制定する *to make a movie* 映画を制作する ▶定義2 (名詞と用いて)to perform a certain action 特定の行動を行う→**〜をする, 行う** ‖ *to make a mistake/noise* 誤りを犯す・物音を立てる *to make a guess/comment/statement/suggestion* 推測する・意見を言う・陳述をする・提案をする *to make progress* 進展する *I've made an appointment to see the doctor.* 私は医者に診てもらうために予約をした.

➤ しばしば似た形の動詞がある. 例えば decide = make a decision (決定をする). make + 名詞を用いる場合, 形容詞を共に用いることができる: *He made the right decision.* (彼は正しい決断をした.) *They made a generous offer.* (彼らは寛容な申し出をした.)

▶定義3 to cause a particular effect, feeling, situation, etc 特定の効果, 感情, 状況などを引き起こす→**〜を生じさせる, 作り出す, 引き起こす** ‖ *The film made me cry.* その映画に私は泣いた. *Flying makes him nervous.* 飛行機に乗ると彼は緊張する. *Her remarks made the situation worse.* 彼女の発言が事態を悪くさせた. *I'll **make it clear** to him that we won't pay.* 私たちは支払わないことを私が彼にはっきりさせます. ***Make sure*** *you lock the car.* 車のかぎをかけたことを確かめなさい. *You don't need to know much of a language to **make yourself understood**.* 自分の考えを人に伝えるためには, それほどたくさんの言葉を知る必要はない. *to make trouble/a mess/a noise* 問題を起こす・へまをする・物音を立てる ▶定義4 to force sb/sth to do sth 〜に…をすることを強いる→**〜させる** ‖ *You can't make her come with us if she doesn't want to.* 彼女がそうしたくないなら, あなたが彼女に私たちと一緒に来させることはできない. *They made him wait at the police station all day.* 彼らは彼を一日中交番で待たせた.

➤ 受身形ではtoを用いなければならない: *He was made to wait at the police station.* (彼は交番で待たされた.)

▶定義5 used with money, numbers and time お金, 数, 時間と用いて→**〜を得る, 手に入れる** ‖ *How much do you think he makes (= earns) a month?* 彼は月にいくら得ている(=稼ぐ)と思いますか. *to make a lot of money* 大金を稼ぐ *5 and 7 make 12.* 5たす7は12. *'What's the time?' 'I make it 6.45.'* 「タイムはどのくらいだい」「6時45だ」 ▶定義6 to make sb/sth become sth; to have the right qualities to become sth 〜を…にならせる; 〜になるのが当然な特質を持つ→**〜にする, 選ぶ, 任命する** ‖ *She was made (= given the job of) President.* 彼女は社長に選ばれた(=

## 1010 make¹

の職を与えられた）. *You can borrow some money this time, but don't **make a habit of** it.* 君は今回はいくらかお金を借りられるが、いつもそうしては駄目だよ. *Karen explains things very clearly - she'd make a good teacher.* カレンは物事を非常に分かりやすく説明する ー 彼女は良い先生になるだろう. ▶定義**7** to become sth; to achieve sth ～になる; ～を達成する➔**～になる, ～を成功させる** ‖ *I'm hoping to make head of the department by the time I'm thirty.* 私は30歳になるまでに部長になりたい. ▶定義**8** to manage to reach a place or go somewhere どうにかしてある場所に到達する, またはどこかへ行く➔**～に到着する, ～をする, 行う** ‖ *We should make Bristol by about 10.* 私たちは10時ころまでにブリストルに到着しなくてはならない. *I can't make the meeting next week.* 私は来週打ち合わせをすることができない.

成句 **make do with sth** ▶定義 to use sth that is not good enough because nothing better is available それより良いものが手に入らないために, 不十分な～を使う➔**～で間に合わせる, 済ます** ‖ *If we can't get limes, we'll have to make do with lemons.* ライムが手に入らなければ, レモンで間に合わせなければならないだろう.

**make it** ▶定義 to manage to do sth; to succeed どうにかして～をする; 成功する➔**うまくいく, 成功する, 間に合う** ‖ *She'll never make it as an actress.* 彼女は決して女優として成功しないだろう. *He's badly injured - it looks like he might not make it (= survive).* 彼はひどいけがをしている ー 持ちこたえる（= 生き抜く）ことができないかもしれない.

**make the most of sth** ▶定義 to get as much pleasure, profit, etc as possible from sth ～からできる限りの喜び, 利益などを得る➔**～を最大限に利用する, できる限り利用する** ‖ *You won't get another chance - make the most of it!* 別の機会はないだろう ー それを最大限に利用しなさい.

▶ make を含むそのほかの表現については, 名詞, 形容詞などの項を参照. 例えば make amends は amends の項にある.

句動詞 **make for sb/sth** ▶定義 to move towards sb/sth ～に向けて動く➔**～の方へ進む, ～に向かう**

**make for sth** ▶定義 to help or allow sth to happen ～が起こるのを助ける, または許す➔**～に役立つ, 寄与する** ‖ *Arguing all the time doesn't make for a happy marriage.* いつも言い争ってばかりいると幸せな結婚生活を送れない.

**be made for sb/each other** ▶定義 to be well suited to sb/each other ～・お互いにうまく合う➔**～向きにできている, ～に向いている** ‖ *Jim and Alice seem made for each other.* ジムとアリスはお似合いのカップルに見える.

**make sb/sth into sb/sth** ▶定義 to change sb/sth into sb/sth ～を…に変える➔**～を…にする** ‖ *She made her spare room into an office.* 彼女は空いている部屋を事務所にした.

**make sth of sb/sth** ▶定義 to understand the meaning or nature of sb/sth ～の意味または本質を理解する➔**～を…と思う** ‖ *What do you make of Colin's letter?* コリンの手紙をどう思いますか.

**make off (with sth)** 略式 ▶定義 to leave or escape in a hurry, for example after stealing sth 急いで去るまたは逃げる, 例えば～を盗んだ後に➔**急いで去る, 逃げ去る** ‖ *Someone's made off with my wallet!* だれかが私の財布を持って逃げた.

**make sb/sth out** ▶定義**1** to understand sb/sth ～を理解する➔**～を理解する, ～が分かる** ‖ *I just can't make him out.* 私は彼のことを全く理解できない. ▶定義**2** to be able to see or hear sb/sth; to manage to read sth ～を見るまたは聞くことができる; どうにかして～を読む➔**判読する, 見分ける, 分かる** ‖ *I could just make out her signature.* 私は辛うじて彼女の署名を判読することができた.

**make out that...; make yourself out to be sth** ▶定義 to say that sth is true and try to make people believe it ～が真実だと言い, 人々にそれを信じさせようとする➔**～と主張する, 見せ掛ける** ‖ *He made out that he was a millionaire.* 彼は自分を億万長者に見せ掛けた. *She's not as clever as she makes herself out to be.* 彼女は自分で言うほど賢くはない.

**make (yourself/sb) up** ▶定義 to put powder, colour, etc on your/sb's face to make it look attractive 粉, 色などを自分・～の顔に付けて魅力的に見せる➔**化粧をする, ふん装させる**

**make sth up** ▶定義**1** to form sth ～を形成す

る→**構成する, 編成する** ‖ *the different groups that make up our society* 私たちの社会を構成しているさまざまな集団 ▶定義**2** to invent sth, often sth that is not true しばしば真実ではない~について, ~を創作する→**作り上げる, でっち上げる** ‖ *to make up an excuse* 言い訳を考え出す ▶定義**3** to make a number or an amount complete; to replace sth that has been lost ある数または量を完全にする; 失われた~の代わりとなる→**完全にする, 埋め合わせる, 補う** ‖ *We need one more person to make up our team.* チームを補充するのにもう 1 人必要だ.

make up for sth ▶定義 to do sth that corrects a bad situation 悪い状態を直す~をする→**~の埋め合わせをする, ~を補う・償う** ‖ *Her enthusiasm makes up for her lack of experience.* 彼女の熱心さが経験不足を補う.

make it up to sb 略式 ▶定義 to do sth that shows that you are sorry for what you have done to sb or that you are grateful for what he/she has done for you あなたが~にした事について申し訳なく思っていることを, または彼・彼女があなたのためにしてくれた事に感謝していることを, ~に示す…をする→**~に対して埋め合わせ[償い]をする** ‖ *You've done me a big favour. How can I make it up to you?* あなたは私に非常に親切にしてくれました. どうやってお返しをしたらよいのでしょうか.

make (it) up (with sb) ▶定義 to become friends again after an argument 口論した後に再び友達になる→**仲直りをする** ‖ *Has she made it up with him yet?* 彼女はもう彼と仲直りしたの.

\*make² /méɪk/ 名 ⓒ ▶定義 the name of the company that produces sth ~を生産する会社の名前→**銘柄, 製造元** ‖ *'What make is your television?' 'It's a Sony.'* 「あなたのテレビの製造元はどこ」「ソニーだよ」

成句 on the make ▶定義 always trying to make money for yourself, especially in a dishonest way いつも自分のために金をもうけようとしている, 特に不正な方法で→**自分の利益[金もうけ]を求めて** ‖ *The country is being ruined by politicians on the make.* その国は己の利益を求める政治屋たちによって駄目になっている.

**make-believe** 名 Ⓤ ▶定義 things that sb imagines or invents that are not real ~が想像するまたはでっち上げる真実ではない物→**見せ掛**

け, 振り, 架空

\*maker /méɪkər/ 名 ⓒ ▶定義 a person, company or machine that makes sth ~を作る人, 会社または機械→**製作者, 作る人, 製造元, メーカー** ‖ *a film-maker* 映画の制作者 *If it doesn't work, send it back to the maker.* もしそれが動かなければ, 製造元に送り返しなさい. *an ice cream maker* アイスクリームのメーカー

**makeshift** /méɪkʃɪft/ 形 ▶定義 made to be used for only a short time until there is sth better より良い~があるまでの短期間だけに使うために作られた→**間に合わせの, 一時しのぎの** ‖ *makeshift shelters out of old cardboard boxes* 古いボール箱でできた間に合わせの避難所

**make-up** 名 ▶定義**1** Ⓤ powder, cream, etc that you put on your face to make yourself more attractive. Actors use make-up to change their appearance when they are acting. より魅力的にするために自分の顔に塗る粉, クリームなど. 俳優は演技をするときに, これを使って自らの外見を変える→**メーキャップ, ふん装, 化粧(品)** ‖ *to put on/take off make-up* 化粧をする・とる ☞参 cosmetic¹ ☞ 動 make (yourself/sb) up ▶定義**2** [単数扱い] a person's character 人の性格→**性質, 体質** ‖ *He can't help his temper. It's part of his make-up.* 彼はかんしゃくを抑えられない. それは彼の性質の一部なのだ.

**making** /méɪkɪŋ/ 名 [単数扱い] ▶定義 the act of doing or producing sth; the process of being made ~をするまたは作る行為; 作られる過程→**作ること, 製造** ‖ *breadmaking* パン作り *This movie has been three years in the making.* この映画は制作に 3 年かかった.

成句 be the making of sb ▶定義 to be the reason that sb is successful ~が成功する理由になる→**成功の原因[手段]となる** ‖ *University was the making of Gina.* 大学はジーナの成功の手段だった.

have the makings of sth ▶定義 to have the necessary qualities for sth ~に必要な性質を持つ→**素質・適性がある** ‖ *The book has the makings of a good film.* その本は良い映画になるすべての要素を備えている.

**maladjusted** /mæləʤʌstəd/ 形 ▶定義 (used about a person) not able to behave well with other people(人について)ほかの人々とうまく付き合えない→環境に不適応の

**malaria** /məléəriə/ 名 U ▶定義 a serious disease in hot countries that you get from the bite of a small flying insect (a mosquito) 小さな飛ぶ虫(蚊)に刺されることによって感染する,暑い国の重い病気→マラリア

★**male** /méɪl/ 形 ▶定義 belonging to the sex that does not give birth to babies or produce eggs 赤ん坊を産まないまたは卵子を作らない性に属する→男の,雄の ‖ *a male goat* 雄ヤギ *a male model/nurse* 男性のモデル・看護士 ☛参 **masculine** と **female** の 注 ― **male** 名 C ▶定義 a male person or animal 男の人,または雄の動物→男(性),雄

**malice** /mǽləs/ 名 U ▶定義 a wish to hurt other people ほかの人々を傷付けたいという願い→敵意,悪意 ― **malicious** /məlíʃəs/ 形 →悪意のある, 意地の悪い ― **maliciously** 副 →敵意を持って,意地悪く

**malignant** /məlígnənt/ 形 ▶定義 (used about a disease (cancer) that spreads in the body, or a growing mass (a tumour) caused by disease) likely to cause death if not controlled (体内で広がる病気(がん),または病気によって増殖する塊(腫瘍(しゅよう))について)もし抑えられなければ死に至るような→悪性の ‖ *He has a malignant brain tumour.* 彼には悪性の脳腫瘍がある. ⇔**benign**

**mall** /mɔːl/ =SHOPPING CENTRE

**mallet** /mǽlət/ 名 C ▶定義 a heavy wooden hammer 重い木製のハンマー→木づち,打球づち ☛ **tool** のさし絵

**malnutrition** /mæln(j)uːtríʃ(ə)n/ 名 U ▶定義 bad health that is the result of not having enough food or enough of the right kind of food 十分な食べ物または適切な種類の食べ物を十分にとっていないことに起因する悪い健康状態→栄養不足,栄養失調 ― **malnourished** 形 →栄養不良[失調]の ‖ *The children were badly malnourished.* 子供たちはひどい栄養失調だった.

**malt** /mɔːlt/ 名 U ▶定義 grain that is used for making beer and a strong alcoholic drink (whisky) ビールや強いアルコール飲料(ウイスキー)を作るために用いられる穀粒→モルト, 麦芽

**maltreat** /mæltríːt/ 動 他 正式 ▶定義 to treat a person or animal in a cruel or unkind way 人または動物を残酷なまたは思いやりのない方法で扱う→虐待する,酷使する ― **maltreatment** 名 U →虐待,酷使

**mammal** /mǽm(ə)l/ 名 C ▶定義 an animal of the type that gives birth to live babies, not eggs, and feeds its young on milk from its own body 卵ではなく赤ん坊を産み,子に自分の体から出す乳を与える種類の動物→ほ乳類,ほ乳動物 ‖ *Whales, dogs and humans are mammals.* 鯨, 犬,そしてヒトはほ乳類だ.

**mammoth** /mǽməθ/ 形 ▶定義 very big 非常に大きい→巨大な

★**man**¹ /mǽn/ 名 (複 **men** /men/) ▶定義 **1** C an adult male person 成人した男の人→男性,男 ▶定義 **2** C a person of either sex, male or female 男性または女性のどちらかの性の人→人 ‖ *All men are equal.* すべての人は平等だ. *No man could survive long in such conditions.* そのような状態でだれも長くは生きられなかった. ▶定義 **3** U the human race; human beings →人類,人間 ‖ *Early man lived by hunting.* 原始人は狩りをして暮らしていた. *the damage man has caused to the environment* 人類が環境に及ぼした損害 ▶定義 **4** C (しばしば複合語で)a man who comes from a particular place; a man who has a particular job or interest 特定の場所から来る人;特定の仕事または興味を持つ人→〜の人,〜者・家 ‖ *a Frenchman* フランス人 *a businessman* 実業家 *sportsmen and women* スポーツマンとスポーツウーマン

成句 the man in the street 英 ▶定義 an ordinary man or woman 普通の男性や女性→普通の人,一般市民,素人

the odd man/one out ⇒ **ODD**

**man**² /mǽn/ 動 他 (**manning**; **manned**) ▶定義 to operate sth or to provide people to operate sth 〜を動かす,または〜を動かすために人員を供給する→〜の部署[任務]に就く,〜に人を配置する ‖ *The telephones are manned 24 hours a day.* その電話は1日24時間対応している.

★**manage** /mǽnɪdʒ/ 動 ▶定義 **1** 自 他 (しばしば **can** または **could** と)to succeed in doing or dealing with sth difficult; to be able to do sth 難しい〜をするまたは扱うことに成功する;〜を

することができる➡**何とかやり遂げる, うまく〜する** ‖ *However did you manage to find us here?* 一体どうして私たちがここにいることが分かったの. *I can't manage this suitcase. It's too heavy.* 私にはこのスーツケースをうまく扱えない. 重すぎる. *Paula can't manage next Tuesday (= she can't come then) so we'll meet another day.* ポーラは今度の火曜日には都合がつかない (= 彼女はその時来ることができない) ので, 私たちは別の日に会うことにする. ▶定義2 ⓣto be in charge or control of sth 〜に責任のある, または〜を管理する➡**経営する, 管理する, 支配する** ‖ *She manages a small advertising business.* 彼女は小さい広告会社を経営している. *You need to manage your time more efficiently.* あなたはもっと効率的に自分の時間を管理することが必要です. ▶定義3 ⓘmanage (without/with sb/sth); manage (on sth) to deal with a difficult situation; to continue in spite of difficulties 難しい情勢に対処する; 難しいけれども継続する➡**どうにかやっていく, やりくりする** ‖ *My grandmother couldn't manage without her neighbours.* 私の祖母は近所の人々がいなければ暮らしていけない. *Can you manage with just one assistant?* たった1人の助手でやっていけますか. *It's hard for a family to manage on just one income.* 家族が, 1人の収入だけで暮らしていくことは難しい.

**manageable** /mǽnɪdʒəb(ə)l/ 形 ▶定義 not too big or too difficult to deal with 扱うのに大きすぎるまたは難しすぎることがない➡**扱いやすい, 御しやすい, 意のままになる**

\***management** /mǽnɪdʒmənt/ 名 ▶定義1 Ⓤthe control or organization of sth 〜の制御または組織➡**経営, 管理** ‖ *Good classroom management is vital with large groups of children.* 子供たちの大集団には, 上手な教室の監督が不可欠だ. ▶定義2 ⒸⓊthe people who control a business or company 店や会社を管理する人々➡**経営者側, 経営陣** ‖ *The hotel is now under new management.* そのホテルは現在新しい経営陣の下にある.

▶単数形の management は単数・複数形の動詞と共に用いることができる: *The management is/are considering making some workers redundant.* (経営陣は何人かの労働者を解雇することを検討している.)

mane 1013

\***manager** /mǽnɪdʒər/ 名 Ⓒ ▶定義1 a man or woman who controls an organization or part of an organization 組織または組織の一部を管理する男性または女性➡**経営者, 支配人, 幹事** ‖ *a bank manager* 銀行の支店長 ▶定義2 a person who looks after the business affairs of a singer, actor, etc 歌手, 俳優などの仕事の面倒を見る人➡**マネージャー** ▶定義3 a person who is in charge of a sports team スポーツのチームの責任者➡**監督** ‖ *the England manager* イングランドの監督

**manageress** /ˌmænɪdʒərés, -´-̀-/ 名 Ⓒ ▶定義 the woman who is in charge of a shop or restaurant 店またはレストランを管理する女性➡**女性経営者**

**managerial** /ˌmænədʒíəriəl/ 形 ▶定義 connected with the work of a manager 管理者の仕事に関連した➡**経営者の, 支配人の** ‖ *Do you have any managerial experience?* あなたは管理者としての経験がありますか.

**managing director** 名 Ⓒ ▶定義 a person who controls a business or company 店または会社を管理する人➡**専務取締役, 社長**

**mandarin** /mǽnd(ə)rən/ 名 Ⓒ ▶定義 a type of small orange 小さいオレンジの一種➡**マンダリン, ミカン**

**mandate** /mǽndèɪt/ 名 [通常は単数] ▶定義 the power that is officially given to a group of people to do sth, especially after they have won an election ある人々の集団に特に選挙の勝利後に正式に与えられた権限➡**権限** ‖ *The union leaders had a clear mandate from their members to call a strike.* 組合の委員たちは, ストライキを指令する明確な権限を組合員から与えられていた.

**mandatory** /mǽndət(ə)ri; -tɔ̀ːri/ 形 正式 ▶定義 that you must do, have, obey, etc 行う, 持つ, 従うなどしなければならない➡**強制的な, 必須(ひっす)の** ‖ *The crime carries a mandatory life sentence.* その犯罪は終身刑に処せられる.
☛類 **obligatory** ⇔ **optional**

**mane** /méɪn/ 名 Ⓒ ▶定義 the long hair on the neck of a horse or male lion 馬または雄のライオンの首に付いている長い髪➡**たてがみ** ☛ **horse**, **lion** のさし絵

**maneuver** /mən(j)úːvər/ 米 = **MANOEUVRE**

**mangle** /mǽŋɡ(ə)l/ 動他 (通常は受動態で)
▶定義 to damage sth so badly that it is difficult to see what it looked like originally 本来どのような形だったかが分からなくなるほど〜をひどく損傷する→〜をめった切りにする, つぶす, 台なしにする ‖ *The motorway was covered with the mangled wreckage of cars.* 高速自動車道路は無残な車の残骸(ざんがい)で埋め尽くされていた.

**mango** /mǽŋɡoʊ/ 名 C (複 **mangoes** または **mangos**) ▶定義 a tropical fruit that has a yellow and red skin and is yellow inside 黄色と赤色の皮が付いていて, 中が黄色い熱帯の果物→マンゴー ☛ C3 ページのさし絵

**manhole** /mǽnhòʊl/ 名 C ▶定義 a hole in the street with a lid over it through which sb can go to look at the pipes, wires, etc that are underground 路上にあるふたの付いた穴で, 〜がこれを通って地下にある管, 電線などを調べに行くことができる→マンホール

**manhood** /mǽnhʊ̀d/ 名 U ▶定義 the state of being a man rather than a boy 少年というよりも成人男子になった状態→**成人時代, 成年期, 壮年期**

**mania** /méɪniə, -njə/ ▶定義1 名略式 a great enthusiasm for sth 〜に対する強い情熱→**熱狂, 〜熱** ‖ *World Cup mania is sweeping the country.* ワールドカップ熱が国中に広がっている.
▶定義2 U a serious mental illness that may cause sb to be very excited or violent 〜が非常に興奮したり暴力的になったりすることがある深刻な精神病→**躁病**

**maniac** /méɪniæ̀k/ 名 C ▶定義1 a person who behaves in a wild and stupid way 荒々しくばかげたやり方で振る舞う人→**無謀な人, 狂人** ‖ *to drive like a maniac* 無謀な運転をする ▶定義2 a person who has a stronger love of sth than is normal 〜について普通よりも強い愛を抱く人→**熱狂的愛好者, 〜マニア** ‖ *a football/sex maniac* フットボールマニア, セックスマニア

**manic** /mǽnɪk, méɪnɪk/ 形 ▶定義1 full of nervous energy or excited activity 神経質なエネルギーまたは興奮した行動で一杯の→**興奮した, 熱狂的な** ‖ *His behaviour became more manic as he began to feel stressed.* ストレスを感じ始めると彼の行動はさらに熱狂的になってきた.
▶定義2 (medical) connected with mania(2) (医学) 躁病に関連した→**躁病の**

**manicure** /mǽnəkjʊ̀ər/ 名 C U ▶定義 treatment to make your hands and fingernails look attractive 手と指のつめを魅力的に見せるための処置→**手やつめの手入れ, マニキュア**

**manifest** /mǽnəfèst/ 動 自 他 正式 ▶定義 manifest (sth/itself) (in/as sth) to show sth or to be shown clearly はっきりと〜を示すまたは示される→**明らかにする, 表に出す, 証明する** ‖ *Mental illness can manifest itself in many forms.* 精神病は多くの形で表れます. ― manifest 形→**明白な, はっきりした** ‖ *manifest failure/anger* 明白な失敗・はっきりした怒り

**manifestation** /mæ̀nəfestéɪʃ(ə)n, -fəs-/ 名 C U 正式 ▶定義 a sign that sth is happening 〜が起きているという印→**表れ, 表面化, 出現**

**manifesto** /mæ̀nəféstoʊ/ 名 C (複 **manifestos**) ▶定義 a written statement by a political party that explains what it hopes to do if it becomes the government in the future 政党が将来政権を握った場合に行いたい事を宣言する文書→**声明(文), 宣言**

**manipulate** /mənípjəlèɪt/ 動他 ▶定義1 to influence sb so that he/she does or thinks what you want あなたが欲するものを〜がする・考えるように, その〜を感化する→**巧みに扱う, 操作する** ‖ *Clever politicians know how to manipulate public opinion.* 賢い政治家は世論を操作するすべを知っている. ▶定義2 to use, move or control sth with skill 技を用いて〜を使う, 動かす, または操作する→**巧みに扱う, 操縦する, 手際良く操作する** ‖ *The doctor manipulated the bone back into place.* 医者は手で(脱臼(だっきゅう)した)骨を元の位置に戻した. ― manipulation /mənìpjəléɪʃ(ə)n/ 名 C U→**巧みな扱い, 操作, 小細工**

**mankind** /mæ̀nkáɪnd, ´−`/ 名 U ▶定義 all the people in the world 世界中のすべての人々→**人類, 人間** ‖ *A nuclear war would be a threat to all mankind.* 核戦争はすべての人類への脅威になるだろう. ☛参 **man**の注

**manly** /mǽnli/ 形 ▶定義 typical of or suitable for a man 男性に典型的なまたは適した→**男らしい, 男性的な, 雄々しい** ‖ *a deep manly voice* 男らしい太い声 ― **manliness** 名 U→**男らしさ**

**man-made** ▶定義 made by people, not formed in a natural way; artificial 自然に形成されたのではなく,人によって作られた;人工的な→**人造の,人工の,合成の** ‖ *man-made fabrics such as nylon and polyester* ナイロンやポリエステルのような合成繊維

★**manner** /mǽnər/ 名 ▶定義**1** [単数扱い] the way that you do sth or that sth happens ～を行うまたは～が起こる方法→**方法,やり方** ‖ *Stop arguing! Let's try to act in a civilized manner.* 口論はやめろ.礼儀正しいやり方で行動しよう. ▶定義**2** [単数扱い] the way that sb behaves towards other people ～のほかの人々に対する振る舞い方→**態度,様子** ‖ *to have an aggressive/a relaxed/a professional manner* 積極的な・落ち着いた・プロの態度を取る ▶定義**3** **manners** [複数扱い] a way of behaving that is considered acceptable in your country or culture 国または文化で受け入れられると考えられるような振る舞い方→**行儀,(礼儀)作法** ‖ *In some countries it is bad manners to show the soles of your feet.* 国によっては,足裏を見せることは行儀が悪いとされている. *Their children have no manners.* 彼らの子供たちは行儀が悪い.

成句 **all manner of...** ▶定義 every kind of... すべての種類の...→**あらゆる種類の** ‖ *You meet all manner of people in my job.* 私の仕事ではあらゆる種類の人々に会う.

**mannerism** /mǽnərɪz(ə)m/ 名 C ▶定義 sb's particular way of speaking or a particular movement he/she often does ～の特定の話し方,またはしばしば行う特定の動き→**奇妙な癖,マンネリ(ズム)**

**manoeuvre**[1] (米**maneuver**) /mən(j)úːvər/ 名 ▶定義**1** C a movement that needs care or skill 注意または技能が必要な動き→**巧妙な動作,操作** ‖ *Parking the car in such a small space would be a tricky manoeuvre.* このような狭い場所に駐車するのは巧みな操作だ. ▶定義**2** C U something clever that you do in order to win sth, trick sb, etc ～を勝ち取る,～をだますなどのために行う巧妙なこと→**策略,策謀** ‖ *political manoeuvre(s)* 政治的策略 ▶定義**3** **manoeuvres** [複数扱い] a way of training soldiers when large numbers of them practise fighting in battles たくさんの兵士が戦場で戦う練習をする,兵士の訓練方法の1つ→**大演習,機動演習**

# manual[1] 1015

**manoeuvre**[2] (米**maneuver**) /mən(j)úːvər/ 動 自 他 ▶定義 to move (sth) to a different position using skill 技量を用いてほかの位置へ動く(～を動かす)→**巧みに動く[動かす],位置を変える** ‖ *The driver was manoeuvring his lorry into a narrow gateway.* 運転手はトラックを狭い入り口の中へ巧みに動かしていた.

**manor** /mǽnər/ (または **manor house**) 名 C ▶定義 a large house in the country that has land around it 田園にある,所有地に囲まれた大きな家→**大邸宅,やかた,豪邸**

**manpower** /mǽnpàʊər/ 名 U ▶定義 the people that you need to do a particular job 特定の仕事をするために必要とする人々→**人力,人的資源** ‖ *There is a shortage of skilled manpower in the computer industry.* コンピューター産業では技能を持った人材が不足している.

**mansion** /mǽnʃ(ə)n/ 名 C ▶定義 a very large house 非常に大きな家→**大邸宅,やかた,豪邸**

> ▶日本語 vs 英語
>
> mansion と「マンション」
>
> mansionは,英語では「大邸宅」を指します.日本語で言う「マンション」は,英語では flat [米 an apartment house] か condominium が相当します.

**manslaughter** /mǽnslɔ̀ːtər/ 名 U ▶定義 the crime of killing sb without intending to do so 意図せずに～を殺す犯罪→**過失致死** ☞参 **murder**

**mantelpiece** /mǽntlpìːs/ 名 C ▶定義 a narrow shelf above the space in a room where a fire goes 室内の,火が置かれている空間の上にある狭い棚→**マントルピース,炉棚** ☞ **fireplace** のさし絵

**manual**[1] /mǽnjuəl/ 形 ▶定義 using your hands; operated by hand 手を使う;手で操作される→**手で行う,肉体の,手動の** ‖ *Office work can sometimes be more tiring than manual work.* 事務仕事は時に肉体労働よりも疲れる. *a skilled manual worker* 熟練した職人 *Does your car have a manual or an automatic gearbox?* あなたの車には手動式と自動式のどちらの変速装置が付いていますか. ― **manually** 副 →**手で,手動で,手細工で**

**manual²** /mænjuəl/ 名 C ▶定義 a book that explains how to do or operate sth 〜を行うまたは操作する方法を説明した本→**説明書, マニュアル, 手引き** ‖ *a training manual* トレーニングの手引き書 *a car manual* 自動車の説明書

★**manufacture** /mæn(j)əfǽktʃərər/ 動 他 ▶定義 to make sth in large quantities using machines 機械を使って〜を大量に作る→**製造する, 製作する** ‖ *a local factory that manufactures furniture* 家具を製造する地元の工場 *manufacturing industries* 製造業 ☛類 **produce** ― **manufacture** 名 U →**製造, 製作** ‖ *The manufacture of chemical weapons should be illegal.* 化学兵器の製造は認められていないはずだ.

**manufacturer** /mæn(j)əfǽktʃərər/ 名 C ▶定義 a person or company that makes sth 〜を作る人または会社→**製造業者, メーカー** ‖ *a car manufacturer* 自動車メーカー

**manure** /mənʊ́ər/ 名 U ▶定義 the waste matter from animals that is put on the ground in order to make plants grow better 植物をよく成長させるために地面にまく, 動物から出る排出物→**肥やし, 肥料** ☛参 **fertilizer**

**manuscript** /mǽnjəskrɪpt/ 名 C ▶定義1 a copy of a book, piece of music, etc before it has been printed 印刷される前の本, 曲など→**原稿, 手書きのもの** ▶定義2 a very old book or document that was written by hand 手で書かれた非常に古い本や文書→**写本**

★**many** /méni/ 形 代 (複数名詞または動詞と用いて) ▶定義1 a large number of people or things たくさんの人々または物→**たくさんの, 多数(の), 多数の物・人** ‖ *Have you made many friends at school yet?* もう学校で友達がたくさんできましたか. *Not many of my friends smoke.* 私の友達でたばこを吸う人は多くない. *Many of the mistakes were just careless.* 誤りの多くは単なる不注意なものだった. *There are too many mistakes in this essay.* この小論には間違いが多すぎる.

▶肯定文中のmanyはかなり格式張って聞こえる: *Many schools teach computing nowadays.* (今日では多数の学校がコンピューターの操作を教える.) 略式で話す・書くときには通常 a lot of を用いる: *A lot of schools teach computing nowadays.* (今日ではコンピューターの操作を教える学校はたくさんある.) しかし, 否定文と疑問文においては, many は格式張って聞こえず, いつでも用いることができる: *I don't know many cheap places to eat.* (私は安く食べられる場所をたくさんは知らない.) *Are there many hotels in this town?* (この町にはホテルがたくさんありますか.)

▶定義2 used to ask about the number of people or things, or to refer to a known number 人や物の数を尋ねるため, または, 知られている数を引き合いに出すために用いて→**たくさんの, 多くの** ‖ *How many children have you got?* あなたには子供が何人いるの. *How many came to the meeting?* 打ち合わせには何人来ましたか. *I don't work as many hours as you.* 私はあなたほど長時間は働かない. *There are half/twice as many boys as girls in the class.* クラスには女子の半数・2倍の男子がいる. ▶定義3 (複合形容詞を作るために用いて) having a lot of the thing mentioned 述べられた物をたくさん持っている→**多数の, たくさんの** ‖ *a many-sided shape* 多面体 ▶定義4 **many a** (単数名詞や動詞と用いて) a large number of 多数の→**多数の, たくさんの** ‖ *I've heard him say that many a time.* 私は彼がそれを言うのを何度も聞いたことがある.

成句 **a good/great many** ▶定義 very many 非常に多くの→**(とても)多くの**

**Maori** /máʊ(ə)ri/ 名 C (複 **Maori** または **Maoris**) ▶定義 a member of the race of people who were the original inhabitants of New Zealand ニュージーランドの原住民だった種族の人→**マオリ人** ― **Maori** 形 →**マオリ人の, マオリの**

★**map** /mæp/ 名 C ▶定義 a drawing or plan of (part of) the surface of the earth that shows countries, rivers, mountains, roads, etc 国, 川, 山, 道などを示す地球の表面(の一部)の図または図面→**地図** ‖ *a map of the world* 世界地図 *a road/street map* 道路地図・街路図 *I can't find Cambridge on the map.* 地図でケンブリッジが見つからない. *to read a map* 地図を読む

▶地図帳はatlasと言う.

― **map** 動 他 (**mapping**; **mapped**)→**〜の地図を作る, 地図で表す** ‖ *The region is so remote it has not yet been mapped.* その地域はかなりへき地なのでまだ地図が作られてない.

**maple** /méɪp(ə)l/ 名 C ▶定義 a tree that has leaves with five points and that produces a very sweet liquid that you can eat 5つのとがった先のある葉を持ち、食べることができる非常に甘い液体を作り出す木→カエデ、もみじ‖ *maple syrup* カエデ糖みつ、メープルシロップ

**Mar** 略 March→3月‖ *17 March 1956* 1956年3月17日

**marathon** /mǽrəθɑ̀n; -θ(ə)n/ 名 C 定義1 a long-distance running race, in which people run about 42 kilometres or 26 miles 約42キロメートルまたは26マイルを走る長距離走の競技→マラソン競走 定義2 an activity that lasts much longer than expected 予期したよりもずっと長く続く活動→忍耐力が必要な競走、延々と続くもの‖ *The interview was a real marathon.* その記者会見は実に延々と続いた.

**marble** /mɑ́ːrb(ə)l/ 名 定義1 ❶ a hard attractive stone that is used to make statues and parts of buildings 彫像や建物の一部を作るために使われる硬い魅力的な石→大理石‖ *a marble statue* 大理石の彫像 定義2 ❷ a small ball of coloured glass that children play with 子供たちの遊び道具で、色の付いたガラス製の小さな玉→ビー玉 定義3 **marbles**[複数扱い] the children's game that you play by rolling marbles along the ground trying to hit other marbles 地面の上でビー玉を転がしてほかのビー玉にぶつける子供たちの遊び→ビー玉遊び

★**March**¹ /mɑːrtʃ/ 名 U C (略Mar) 定義 the third month of the year, coming after February 2月の次に来る、1年の3番目の月→3月

▶文中での月の表し方については、January の例と注を参照.

★**march**² /mɑːrtʃ/ 動 定義1 ❸ to walk with regular steps (like a soldier) 規則正しい歩調で(兵士のように)歩く→行進する、練り歩く‖ *The President saluted as the troops marched past.* 行進していく軍隊に、大統領は敬礼をした. 定義2 ❸ to walk in a determined way 堅く決心したように歩く→堂々と歩く、ずんずん歩く‖ *She marched up to the manager and demanded an apology.* 彼女は部長の所へずんずん歩いていき謝罪を要求した. 定義3 ❸ to make sb walk or march somewhere ~をどこかへ歩かせるまたは行進させる→~を行進させる、行軍させる‖ *The prisoner was marched away.* 囚人は無理に歩かせられていった. 定義4 ❸ to walk in a large group to protest about sth ~について抗議するために大勢で歩く→デモ行進をする‖ *The demonstrators marched through the centre of town.* デモ隊は町の中心を行進した.

★**march**³ /mɑːrtʃ/ 名 C 定義1 an organized walk by a large group of people who are protesting about sth ~について抗議する大勢の人々が組織的に歩くこと→デモ行進‖ *a peace march* 平和のデモ行進 ☞参 **demonstration** 定義2 a journey made by marching 行進による旅→行進、行軍‖ *The soldiers were tired after their long march.* 兵士たちは長い行軍の後で疲れていた.

**mare** /meər/ 名 C 定義 a female horse 雌の馬→雌馬 ☞参 **horse** の注

**margarine** /mɑ́ːrdʒ(ə)rən, -dʒəːrn; mɑ̀ːdʒərǐːn/ 名 U 定義 a food that is similar to butter, made of animal or vegetable fats バターに似た食べ物で、動物または植物性脂肪で作られる→マーガリン C4 ページのさし絵

**margin** /mɑ́ːrdʒən/ 名 定義1 ❸ the empty space at the side of a page in a book, etc 本などのページの端にある空白→余白、欄外 定義2 ❸ the amount of space, time, votes, etc by which you win sth それによって~を勝ち取るような空間、時間、票などの量→差、開き‖ *He won by a wide/narrow/comfortable margin.* 彼は大差で・小差で・楽に勝った. 定義3 ❸ the amount of profit that a company makes on sth 会社が~で得る利益の量→利ざや、マージン 定義4 ❸ the area around the edge of sth ~の端の辺りの部分→縁、へり、端‖ *the margins of the Pacific Ocean* 太平洋岸 定義5 ❶ an amount of space, time, etc that is more than you need 必要とする以上の空間、時間などの量→余裕、余地、ゆとり‖ *It is a complex operation with little **margin for error**.* それは間違いがほとんど許されない複雑な操作だ.

**marginal** /mɑ́ːrdʒən(ə)l/ 形 定義 small in size or importance 大きさまたは重要性が小さい→わずかな、重要でない‖ *The differences are marginal.* 差はわずかだ. —**marginally** 副→わずかに‖ *In most cases costs will increase only marginally.* 大抵の場合、費用はごくわずかしか増えないだろう.

**marijuana** /mæ̀rə(h)wɑ́ːnə/ 名 U 定義 a drug

that is smoked and is illegal in many countries 煙で吸われる麻薬, 多くの国で不法とされている →マリファナ, インド大麻

**marina** /mərí:nə/ 名 ▶定義 a small area of water (a harbour) designed for pleasure boats レジャー用の船のために作られた小さな水域(港) → マリーナ

**marine**¹ /mərí:n/ 形 ▶定義 1 connected with the sea 海に関連した→**海の, 海に住む** ‖ *the study of marine life* 海洋生物の研究 ▶定義 2 connected with ships or sailing 船または航海に関連した→**船舶の, 海運業の** ‖ *marine insurance* 海上保険

**marine**² /mərí:n/ 名 C ▶定義 a soldier who has been trained to fight on land or at sea 地上または海で戦う訓練を受けた兵士 →**海兵隊員**

**marital** /mǽrətl/ 形 (名詞の前だけ) ▶定義 connected with marriage 結婚に関連した→**婚姻の, 夫婦の** ‖ *marital problems* 夫婦間の問題

**marital status** 名 U (文) ▶定義 (used on official documents) if you are married, single, divorced, etc (公式の文書で用いられて) 結婚しているか, 独身か, 離婚したかなど→**婚姻関係の有無**

**maritime** /mǽrətàim/ 形 ▶定義 connected with the sea or ships 海または船に関連した→**海の, 海上の, 海運の**

★**mark**¹ /mɑːrk/ 名 C ▶定義 1 a spot or line that spoils the appearance of sth 〜の外見を台なしにする点や線→**染み, 傷, 汚れ, 斑点(はんてん)** ‖ *There's a dirty mark on the front of your shirt.* あなたのシャツの胸のところに汚い染みがある. *If you put a hot cup down on the table it will leave a mark.* 熱い茶わんをテーブルの上に置くと跡ができる. ← 参 birthmark ● blob のさし絵 ▶定義 2 something that shows who or what sb/sth is, especially by making him/her/it different from others 特に〜を他と違えることで, その〜がだれ・何であるかを示すもの→**目印, マーク** ‖ *My horse is the one with the white mark on its face.* 顔に白い印があるのが私の馬だ. ▶定義 3 a written or printed symbol that is a sign of sth 〜の印を表す, 書かれたまたは印刷された記号→**記号, 符号, 印** ‖ *a question/punctuation/exclamation mark* 疑問符·句読点·感嘆符 ▶定義 4 a sign of a quality or feeling 品質または感情の表れ→**表れ, 印, 跡** ‖ *They stood in silence for two minutes as a mark of respect.* 彼らは尊敬の意を表して2分間黙って起立した. ▶定義 5 a number or letter you get for school work that tells you how good your work was 学校の成績について与えられる数または文字で, 勉強がどの程度良くできたかを知らせる→**評点, 点数** ‖ *She got very good marks in the exam.* 彼女は試験で非常に良い点数を取った. *The pass mark is 60 out of 100.* 合格点は100点中60点だ. *to get full marks* (= everything correct) 満点を取る (=すべて正しい) ▶定義 6 the level or point that sth/sb has reached 〜が到達したレベルまたは点→**地点** ‖ *The race is almost at the half-way mark.* レースはほぼ中間地点だ. ▶定義 7 an effect that people notice and will remember 人々が気付いて覚えているような結果→**印象, 影響** ‖ *The time he spent in prison left its mark on him.* 牢獄(ろうごく)で過ごした時間が彼に影響を与えた. *He was only eighteen when he first made his mark in politics.* 政治活動で初めて名を上げた時, 彼はまだ18歳だった. ▶定義 8 a particular model or type of sth 〜の特定の型または種類→**型, 型式記号** ‖ *the new SL 53 Mark III* 新しい SL 53 III 型 ● 製品そのものまたはそれを作る会社について述べるときには mark は使えないので注意. その場合には brand または make を用いる. *What make is your car?* あなたの車のメーカーはどこですか. *What brand of coffee do you buy?* あなたはどの銘柄のコーヒーを買いますか. ▶定義 9 正式 a person or an object towards which sth is directed; a target 〜が向けられる人または物; 目標→**目標, ねらい, 的** ‖ *the arrow hit/missed its mark* 矢は的に当たった·を外れた *His judgement of the situation is wide of the mark* (= wrong). 彼の状況判断は見当違いだ (=間違っている). ▶定義 10 the unit of money in Germany ドイツの通貨単位→マルク 成句 **on your marks, get set, go!** ▶定義 used at the start of a sports race スポーツのレースの開始時に用いて→**位置について, 用意, ドン.** **quick, slow, etc off the mark** ▶定義 quick, slow, etc in reacting to a situation →ある状況に反応するのが早い, 遅いなど

★**mark**² /mɑːrk/ 動 他 ▶定義 1 to put a sign on sth 〜に印を付ける→**〜に印を付ける, スタンプを押す** ‖ *We marked the price on all items in the sale.* 私たちは特売中のすべての品物に価格を付けた. *I'll mark all the boxes I want you to move.*

動かしてほしい箱にすべて印を付けておきます. ▶定義2 to spoil the appearance of sth by making a mark on it 印を付けることによって〜の外観を台なしにする➜〜に跡を付ける,跡を残す‖ *The white walls were dirty and marked.* 白壁は汚れて跡が付いていた. ▶定義3 to show where sth is or where sth happened 〜がある場所または〜が起きた場所を示す➜〜に印を付けて示す‖ *The route is marked in red.* 道順は赤で示してあります. *Flowers mark the spot where he died.* 彼が死んだ場所には花を置いてある. ▶定義4 to celebrate or officially remember an important event 重要な行事を祝う,または正式に記念して後世に伝える➜〜を記念する‖ *The ceremony marked the fiftieth anniversary of the opening of the school.* その式典は学校の創立50周年を祝うものであった. ▶定義5 to be a sign that sth new is going to happen 新しい〜が起きようとしている印である➜示す,運命づける‖ *This decision marks a change in government policy.* この決定は政府の政策の変更を表明するものだ. ▶定義6 to look at sb's school, etc work, show where there are mistakes and give it a number or letter to show how good it is 〜の学校での勉強などを調べて,間違っている箇所を示し,どの程度良くできているかを示す数または文字を与える➜〜を採点する‖ *Why did you mark that answer wrong?* なぜあの答えを間違いと採点したの. *He has 100 exam papers to mark.* 彼には採点すべき試験用紙が100枚ある.

▶定義7 (in sport) to stay close to a player of the opposite team so that he/she cannot play easily (スポーツで)相手側チームのある選手に離れず付いていて,その選手が容易に行動できないようにする➜〜をマークする

句動詞 mark sb/sth down as/for sth ▶定義 to decide that sb/sth is of a particular type or suitable for a particular use 〜が特定の種類であるまたは特定の用途に適していることを決める➜〜を…と見なす・記す‖ *From the first day of school, the teachers marked Fred down as a troublemaker.* 登校した初日から,教師たちはフレッドを問題児と見なした.

mark sth out ▶定義 to draw lines to show the position of sth 〜の位置を示すために線をひく➜区切る,区画する‖ *Spaces for each car were marked out in the car park.* 駐車場では,そ

れぞれの車の場所が区切られていた.

mark sth up/down ▶定義 to increase/decrease the price of sth that you are selling 売っている〜の価格を上げる・下げる➜〜を値上げする,値下げする‖ *All goods have been marked down by 15%.* すべての商品は15パーセント値引きしてある.

**marked** /máːrkt/ 形 ▶定義 clear; noticeable 明らかな,顕著な➜著しい,目立った‖ *There has been a marked increase in vandalism in recent years.* 近年公共物への心ない破壊が著しく増えている.

**marker** /máːrkər/ 名 C ▶定義 something that shows the position of sth 〜の位置を示すもの➜印を付ける人・道具,マーカー‖ *I've highlighted the important sentences with a marker pen.* 私は重要な文をマーカーで強調してきた.

★**market**¹ /máːrkɪt/ 名 ▶定義1 C a place where people go to buy and sell things 人々が物を売買しに行く場所➜市場(いちば),市,食料品店‖ *a market stall/trader/town* 市場の売り場・商人・市が立つ町 *a cattle/fish/meat market* 家畜・魚・精肉市場 ☛ C8ページのさし絵 ☛参 **flea market, hypermarket, supermarket** ▶定義2 C business or commercial activity; the amount of trade in a particular type of goods 事業または商業活動; 特定種類の製品の取引高➜売買,取り引き,市場(しじょう)‖ *The company currently has a 10% share of the market.* その会社は現在市場の10パーセントのシェアを占めている. *the property/job market* 不動産・雇用市場 ▶定義3 C U a country, an area or a group of people that buys sth; the number of people who buy sth 〜を買う人々の国,地域または集団; 〜を買う人々の数➜市場(しじょう),需要‖ *The company is hoping to expand into the European Market.* 会社は欧州市場への進出を望んでいる. *There's no market for very large cars when petrol is so expensive.* ガソリンがとても高いときは超大型車への需要はない. ☛参 **black market, stock market**

成句 **on the market** ▶定義 available to buy 買うことができる➜売りに出ている‖ *This is one of the best cameras on the market.* このカメラは市場に出ている物の中で最高級品の1つだ.

**market²** /máːrkət/ 動他 ▶定義 to sell sth with the help of advertising 広告の助けで〜を売る→〜を売り込む

**marketable** /máːrkətəb(ə)l/ 形 ▶定義 that can be sold easily because people want it 人々がそれを欲しがるために簡単に売れるような→売れ口の良い、市場向きの

**marketing** /máːrkətɪŋ/ 名Ⓤ ▶定義 the activity of showing and advertising a company's products in the best possible way 会社の製品を可能な限り最善の方法で見せて宣伝する活動→マーケティング ‖ *Effective marketing will lead to increased sales.* 効果的なマーケティングは販売増加につながるだろう. *the marketing department* マーケティング部

**market place** ▶定義1 the market place [単数扱い] the activity of competing with other companies to buy and sell goods, services, etc 製品、サービスなどの売買を他社と競う活動→市場(しじょう)、商業界 ▶定義2 Ⓒ the place in a town where a market is held 町の中の市場(いちば)が開かれる場所→市の開かれる広場・建物、市場(いちば)

**market research** 名Ⓤ ▶定義 the study of what people want to buy and why 人々が何を買いたいかおよびその理由の研究→市場調査 ‖ *to carry out/do market research* 市場調査を実施する

**marking** /máːrkɪŋ/ 名 [Ⓒ, 通常は複数] ▶定義 shapes, lines and patterns of colour on an animal or a bird, or painted on a road, vehicle, etc 動物や鳥の表面に色で表れる、または道路や乗り物などに塗装された形、線、模様→斑紋(はんもん), 模様, しま, マーク

**marksman** /máːrksmən/ 名Ⓒ (複 -men /-men/) ▶定義 a person who can shoot very well with a gun 銃で撃つのが上手な人→射撃の名人, 狙撃(そげき)兵

**marmalade** /máːməleɪd, ‿‿‿/ 名Ⓤ ▶定義 a type of jam that is made from oranges or lemons オレンジまたはレモンから作られるジャムの一種→マーマレード ☞ C4ページのさし絵

**maroon** /mərúːn/ 形名Ⓤ ▶定義 (of) a dark brownish-red colour 濃い赤茶色(の)→えび茶色, クリ色

**marooned** /mərúːnd/ 形 ▶定義 in a place that you cannot leave 脱出できない場所にいる→置き去りにされた ‖ *The sailors were marooned on a desert island.* 船員たちは無人島に置き去りにされた.

**marquee** /mɑːkíː/ 名Ⓒ ▶定義 a very large tent that is used for parties, shows, etc パーティーや見せ物などで使われる非常に大きなテント→大テント

*****marriage** /mǽrɪdʒ/ 名 ▶定義1 ⒸⓊ the state of being husband and wife 夫と妻である状態→結婚, 婚姻, 結婚生活 ‖ *They are getting divorced after five years of marriage.* 彼らは結婚5年で離婚しようとしている. *a happy marriage* 幸せな結婚生活 ▶定義2 Ⓒ a wedding ceremony 結婚式→結婚式, 婚礼 ‖ *The marriage took place at a registry office in Birmingham.* 婚姻はバーミンガムの登記所で行われた. ☞参 **wedding** の注 ☞ 動 get married (to sb) または marry (sb)

*****married** /mǽrɪd/ 形 ▶定義1 married (to sb) having a husband or wife 夫または妻を持つ→結婚している, 既婚の, 夫[妻]のある ‖ *a married man/woman/couple* 結婚している男性・女性・夫婦 *Sasha's married to Mark.* サーシャはマークと結婚している. *They're planning to **get married** in summer.* 彼らは夏に結婚する予定だ. ⇔ **unmarried**, **single** ▶定義2 (名詞の前だけ) connected with marriage 結婚に関連した→結婚の, 結婚生活の ‖ *How do you like married life?* 結婚生活はどうですか.

**marrow** /mǽrəʊ/ 名 ▶定義1 ⒸⓊ a large vegetable with green skin that is white inside 中が白く, 緑色の皮が付いた大きな野菜→西洋カボチャ ☞ C3ページのさし絵 ▶定義2 =**BONE MARROW**

*****marry** /mǽri/ 動 (現分 **marrying**; 三単現 **marries**; 過, 過分 **married**) ▶定義1 自他 to take sb as your husband or wife 〜を自分の夫または妻とする→結婚する ‖ *They married when they were very young.* 彼らは非常に若いときに結婚した. *When did Rick ask you to marry him?* リックはいつあなたに結婚を申し込んだの.

▶ get married (to sb) は marry よりも一般的に用いられる: *When are Sue and Ian getting married?* (スーとイアンはいつ結婚するのだろう.) *They got married in 1997.* (彼らは1997年に結婚した.)

**▶定義2** ⓤ to join two people together as husband and wife 2人の人を夫と妻として一緒にする→~を結婚させる ‖ *We asked the local vicar to marry us.* 私たちは地元の教区主管者代理に結婚式を執り行ってくれるように頼んだ.
☞ 参 **marriage**

**Mars** /mɑːrz/ 名 [単数扱い] ▶定義 the red planet, that is fourth in order from the sun 太陽から4番目にある赤い惑星→火星 ☞ 参 **Martian**

**marsh** /mɑːrʃ/ 名 ⓒ ⓤ ▶定義 an area of soft wet land 柔らかく湿った地面の部分→沼地, 湿地 ─ marshy 形→沼地の, 湿地の

**marshal** /mɑːrʃ(ə)l/ 名 ⓒ ▶定義1 a person who helps to organize or control a large public event 大きな公式行事の準備または管理を手伝う人→儀式係, 接待係, 進行係 ‖ *Marshals are directing traffic in the car park.* 進行係が駐車場で交通整理をしている. ▶定義2 米 an officer of a high level in the police or fire department or in a court of law 警察, 消防署, または裁判所の高官→**警察[消防]署長, 連邦保安官, 連邦裁判所の裁判官**

**martial** /mɑːrʃ(ə)l/ 形 正式 ▶定義 connected with war 戦争に関連した→戦争の, 軍事の

**martial arts** /mɑːrʃ(ə)l/ [複数扱い] ▶定義 fighting sports such as karate or judo, in which you use your hands and feet as weapons 空手, 柔道のような, 手足を武器として戦うスポーツ→格闘技

**Martian** /mɑːrʃ(ə)n/ 名 ⓒ ▶定義 (in stories) a creature that comes from the planet Mars (物語で)火星から来た生物→火星人

**martyr** /mɑːrtər/ 名 ⓒ ▶定義1 a person who is killed because of what he/she believes 信じる事のために殺された人→殉教者, 殉じた人, 受難者 ▶定義2 a person who tries to make people feel sorry for him/her 人々を同情させようとする人→犠牲者振る人 ‖ *Don't be such a martyr! You don't have to do all the housework.* そんなに犠牲者振るな. 君がすべての家事をする必要はない. ─ martyrdom /mɑːrtərdəm/ 名 ⓤ→殉教, 殉死, 受難

**marvel** /mɑːrv(ə)l/ 名 ⓒ ▶定義 a person or thing that is wonderful or that surprises you すばらしい, あるいは驚かされる人または物→すばらしい事, 不思議な事, 驚異 ‖ *the marvels of modern technology* 現代技術のすばらしさ ─ marvel 動 ⓘ ( marvelling; marvelled: 米 marveling; marveled) 正式 marvel (at sth)→すばらしいと思う, 驚く ‖ *We marvelled at how much they had managed to do.* 私たちは彼らが成し遂げた事の大きさに驚いた.

**marvellous** /mɑːrv(ə)ləs/ (米 **marvelous**) 形 ▶定義 very good; wonderful 非常に良い; すばらしい→すばらしい, 驚くべき ‖ *a marvellous opportunity* すばらしい機会 ─ marvellously (米 marvelously) 副→すばらしく, 不思議なほど

**Marxism** /mɑːrksìz(ə)m/ 名 ⓤ ▶定義 the political and economic thought of Karl Marx カール マルクスの政治および経済の思想→マルクス主義 ☞ 参 **communism, socialism, capitalism** ─ Marxist 名 ⓒ 形→マルクス主義者(の) ‖ *Marxist ideology* マルクス主義のイデオロギー

**marzipan** /mɑːrtsəpæːn, -pæn; mɑːzɪpæn/ 名 ⓤ ▶定義 a food that is made of sugar, egg and nuts (almonds). Marzipan is used to make sweets or to put on cakes. 砂糖, 卵, 堅果(アーモンド)から作られる食べ物. お菓子を作ったり, ケーキに乗せたりして使う→マジパン

**masc** 略 masculine→男らしい, 男性の

**mascara** /mæskɑːrə; -kɑ́-/ 名 ⓤ ▶定義 a beauty product that is used to make the hairs around your eyes (eyelashes) dark and attractive 目の回りの毛(まつげ)を黒っぽく魅力的にするために使われる化粧品→マスカラ

**mascot** /mæskɒt, -kət/ 名 ⓒ ▶定義 a person, animal or thing that is thought to bring good luck 幸運をもたらすと考えられている人, 動物, または物→マスコット, 縁起の良い人[動物・物]

**masculine** /mǽskjələn/ 形 ▶定義 with the qualities that people think are typical of men 人々が男性的だと典型的に考えるような性質の→男性の, 男の, 男らしい ‖ *a deep, masculine voice* 太く, 男らしい声 *Her short hair makes her look quite masculine.* 短い髪のせいで彼女はとても男っぽく見える. ☞ 参 **male, manly, feminine** と **female** の注

▶英文法では masculine words (男性形) は男[雄]の人・動物を示す: '*He*' *is a masculine pronoun.* (he は男性代名詞だ.) ほかの言語では, すべての名詞に masculine (男性), feminine (女性), neuter (中性) の性別があるものもある.

─ masculinity /mæskjəlínəti/ 名 ⓤ→男性である

ること、男らしさ

**mash** /mæʃ/ 動他 ▶定義 to mix or crush sth until it is soft 柔らかくなるまで〜を混ぜるまたは押しつぶす→〜をつぶす‖ mashed potatoes マッシュポテト

**mask**[1] /mɑːsk; mæsk/ 名 C ▶定義 something that you wear that covers your face or part of your face. People wear masks in order to hide or protect their faces or to make themselves look different. 顔または顔の一部を覆うために身に着けるもの。顔を隠すためや守るため、または外見を異なるようにするために身に着ける→マスク, 面, 仮面 ☞参 gas mask, goggles

**mask**[2] /mɑːsk; mæsk/ 動他 ▶定義1 to cover or hide your face with a mask マスクで顔を覆うまたは隠す→マスク・仮面を付ける, 仮面で覆う‖ a masked gunman 仮面を付けた殺し屋 ▶定義2 to hide a feeling, smell, fact, etc 感情, におい, 事実などを隠す→〜を隠す‖ He masked his anger with a smile. 彼は怒りをほほえみで隠した.

**masochism** /mǽsəkɪz(ə)m/ 名 U ▶定義 the enjoyment of pain, or of what most people would find unpleasant 痛みまたは多くの人が不愉快と感じるような事を楽しむこと→マゾヒズム, 被虐性愛‖ He swims in the sea even in winter - that's sheer masochism! 彼は冬でも海で泳ぐ — 全くのマゾヒズムだ. ☞参 sadism — masochist /-kɪst/ 名 C→マゾヒスト, 被虐性愛者 — masochistic /mæsəkɪztɪk/ 形→マゾヒズム[マゾヒスト]的な, 被虐性愛の

**mason** /méɪs(ə)n/ 名 C ▶定義1 a person who makes things from stone 石から物を作る人→石工, 石屋 ▶定義2 =FREEMASON

**masonry** /méɪs(ə)nri/ 名 U ▶定義 the parts of a building that are made of stone 石でできた建物の部分→石造[れんが造り]建築

**masquerade** /mæskəréɪd, mɑː-/ 名 C ▶定義 a way of behaving that hides the truth or sb's true feelings 事実または〜の真実の感情を隠す振る舞い方→見せ掛け, 振り — masquerade 動自 masquerade as sth→〜の振りをする, 仮装する‖ Two people, masquerading as doctors, knocked at the door and asked to see the child. 医者の振りをした２人組が扉をたたき, その子供に面会を求めた.

**\*mass**[1] /mæs/ 名 ▶定義1 C a mass (of sth) a large amount or number of sth 大量または多数の〜→大きな塊, 一団, 大集団‖ a dense mass of smoke 大量の煙 略式 There were masses of people at the market today. 今日市場にはたくさんの人がいた. ▶定義2 the masses [複数扱い] ordinary people when considered as a political group 市民の集団として考えられている一般の人々→大衆, 庶民 ▶定義3 U (in physics) the quantity of material that sth contains (物理で)〜が含む成分の量→質量 ▶定義4 Mass C U the ceremony in some Christian churches when people eat bread and drink wine in order to remember the last meal that Christ had before he died キリストが死ぬ前にとった最後の食事を思い出すために、パンを食べてワインを飲む, いくつかのキリスト教会で行われる儀式→ミサ‖ to go to Mass ミサに行く

**mass**[2] /mæs/ 形 (名詞の前だけ) ▶定義 involving a large number of people or things 多数の人々または物を巻き込んで→多数の, 大量の‖ a mass murderer 大量殺人

**mass**[3] /mæs/ 動自他 ▶定義 to come together or bring people or things together in large numbers たくさんの人や物が集まる, または, それらを集める→一塊にする・なる, 一団に集める, 集合する‖ The students massed in the square. 生徒たちは広場に集合した.

**massacre** /mǽsɪkər/ 名 C ▶定義 the killing of a large number of people or animals 多数の人々・動物の殺戮(さつりく)→大虐殺 — massacre 動他 →〜を虐殺する, 皆殺しにする ☞参 kill の注

**massage** /məsɑ́ːʒ; məsɑ́ːʒ/ 名 C U ▶定義 the act of rubbing and pressing sb's body in order to reduce pain or to help him/her relax 〜の痛みを和らげるまたは〜をくつろがせるために, その〜の体をもんだり押す行為→マッサージ‖ to give sb a massage 〜にマッサージをする — massage 動他 →〜にマッサージをする

**massive** /mǽsɪv/ 形 ▶定義 very big; huge 非常に大きな; 巨大な→大きい, どっしりした‖ a massive increase in prices 大幅な値上げ

**mass media** 名 [複数扱い] ▶定義 newspapers, television and radio that reach a large number of people 多くの人々に届く新聞, テレビ, ラジオ→マスメディア, 大量伝達媒体, マスコミの媒体

**mass-produce** 動他 ▶定義 to make large numbers of similar things by machine in a factory 工場で機械を使って類似の物を大量に作る→**大量生産する** ‖ *mass-produced goods* 大量生産された製品 — *mass production* 名 Ⓤ →**大量生産**

**mast** /mɑːst; mæst/ 名 Ⓒ ▶定義1 a tall wooden or metal pole for a flag, a ship's sails, etc 旗や船の帆などを上げるための、背の高い木製または金属製の柱 →**マスト、帆柱** ▶定義2 a tall pole that is used for sending out radio or television signals ラジオやテレビの信号を送信するために使われる背の高い柱 →**鉄塔**

**master**¹ /mɑ́ːstər, mǽs-/ 名 Ⓒ ▶定義1 a person who has great skill at doing sth 〜をする非常に高い技能を持つ人 →**名人、達人** ‖ *a master builder* 棟梁(とうりょう) *an exhibition of work by French masters (= painters)* フランスの巨匠たち(=画家たち)による作品の展覧会 ▶定義2 (古) a male teacher (usually in a private school) (通常私立の学校の)男性教師 →**(男性の)教師** ‖ *the chemistry master* 化学の教師 ▶定義3 a film or tape from which copies can be made 複製を作ることができる元のフィルムまたはテープ →**親[マスター]盤**

**master**² /mɑ́ːstər, mǽs-/ 動他 ▶定義1 to learn how to do sth well 〜を上手に行う方法を学ぶ →**〜を修得する、熟練する** ‖ *It takes a long time to master a foreign language.* 外国語を修得するためには長い時間がかかる. ▶定義2 to control sth 〜を支配する →**〜を支配する、征服する、抑える** ‖ *to master a situation* 状況を掌握する

**mastermind** /mɑ́ːstərmàind, mǽs-/ 名 Ⓒ ▶定義 a very clever person who has planned or organized sth 〜を計画したまたは組織した非常に賢い人 →**優れた知能の持ち主、立案者** ‖ *The mastermind behind the robbery was never caught.* 強盗事件の黒幕は決して捕まらなかった. — *mastermind* 動他 →**〜を周到に計画する、陰で糸を引く** ‖ *The police failed to catch the man who masterminded the robbery.* 警察は強盗事件を背後から操っていた男の逮捕に失敗した.

**masterpiece** /mɑ́ːstərpìːs, mǽs-/ 名 Ⓒ ▶定義 a work of art, music, literature, etc that is of the highest quality 最高の質の芸術、音楽、文学などの作品 →**傑作、名作**

**Master's degree** (または **Master's**) 名 Ⓒ

# match¹ 1023

▶定義 a second or higher university degree. You usually get a Master's degree by studying for one or two years after your first degree. 高度の学位. 通常最初の学位を得た後に1年または2年学ぶことによって得られる学位 →**修士(号)** ‖ *Master of Arts (MA)* 文学修士(号) *Master of Science (MSc)* 理学修士(号) ☛参 **Bachelor's degree**

**mastery** /mɑ́ːst(ə)ri; mǽs-/ 名 Ⓤ ▶定義1 *mastery (of sth)* great skill at doing sth 〜をする高い技能 →**熟達、精通** ‖ *His mastery of the violin was quite exceptional for a child.* 彼のバイオリンの演奏技術は子供としては並外れていた.
▶定義2 *mastery (of/over sb/sth)* control over sb/sth 〜の支配 →**支配、制御** ‖ *The battle was fought for mastery of the seas.* その戦闘は海の支配権をめぐって戦われた.

**masturbate** /mǽstərbèrt; mǽs-/ 動他自 ▶定義 to make yourself or sb else feel sexually excited by touching and rubbing the sex organs 性器に触れるまたはつかむことによって、自分またはほかの〜に性的興奮を感じさせる →**オナニー・自慰をする** — *masturbation* /mæ̀stərbéɪʃən/ 名 Ⓤ →**オナニー、自慰、マスターベーション**

**mat** /mæt/ 名 Ⓒ ▶定義1 a piece of carpet or other thick material that you put on the floor 床の上に置く敷物またはほかの厚手の物 →**マット** ‖ *a doormat* 靴ふき ☛参 **rug** ▶定義2 a small piece of material that you put under sth on a table テーブルの上で、〜の下に敷く小さな物 →**敷物、下敷き** ‖ *a table mat* テーブルクロス *a beer mat* ビールマット、ビール用コースター *a mouse mat* マウスパッド ☛ S5ページのさし絵

*****match**¹ /mætʃ/ 名 ▶定義1 Ⓒ a small stick of wood, cardboard, etc that you use for starting a fire, lighting a cigarette, etc 火をおこすため、たばこに火をつけるためなどに使われる、木や厚紙などでできた小さな棒 →**マッチ** ‖ *to light/strike a match* マッチを擦る *a box of matches* マッチ箱
▶定義2 Ⓒ an organized game or sports event 組まれた試合またはスポーツの行事 →**試合競技、勝負** ‖ *a tennis/football match* テニス・サッカーの試合 ▶定義3 [単数扱い] *a match for sb; sb's match* a person or thing that is as good as or better than sb/sth else ほかの〜と同じくらいまたはそれよりも優れた人や物 →**競争相手、好敵手**

## 1024 match²

‖ *Charo is no match for her mother when it comes to cooking (= she doesn't cook as well as her mother).* 料理に関してはシャロは母親に太刀打ちできない(= 彼女は母親ほど上手に料理をできない). *I think you've met your match in Dave - you won't beat him.* あなたはデーヴという好敵手に出会ったのだ － あなたは彼を打ち負かせないだろう. ▶定義4 [単数扱い] a match (for sb/sth) something that looks good with sth else ほかの～と一緒で好ましく見えるもの➔似合いの人・物, 似合いの一対 ‖ *Those shoes aren't a very good match with your dress.* あの靴は君のドレスにあまり合わない.

\***match²** /mætʃ/ 動 ▶定義1 ⊜⊕ to have the same colour or pattern as sth else; to look good with sth else ほかの～と同じ色または模様を持つ; ほかの～と合わせるとよく見える➔調和する, 釣り合う, 似合う ‖ *That shirt doesn't match your jacket.* あのシャツは君の上着に似合わない. *Your shirt and jacket don't match.* 君のシャツと上着は釣り合っていない. ▶定義2 ⊕ to find sb/sth that is like or suitable for sb/sth else ほかの～に似たまたは適した…を見つける➔～と似合うものを見つける ‖ *The agency tries to match single people with suitable partners.* その代理店は独身者たちをふさわしい相手に会わせてくれる. ▶定義3 ⊕ to be as good as or better than sb/sth else ほかの～と同じくらいまたはそれよりも良い➔同等である, 匹敵する, 互角である ‖ *The two teams are very evenly matched.* ２つのチームは全く互角だ. *Taiwan produces the goods at a price that Europe cannot match.* 台湾は欧州が太刀打ちできない価格で製品を作る.

句動詞 **match up** ▶定義 to be the same 同じになる➔一致する, つじつまが合う ‖ *The statements of the two witnesses don't match up.* ２人の目撃者の証言は一致しない.

**match sth up (with sth)** ▶定義 to fit or put sth together (with sth else) ～を(ほかの…と)合わせるまたは置く➔調和させる, 適合させる, 組ませる ‖ *What you have to do is match up each star with his or her pet.* あなたがしなければならない事は, それぞれのスターと各自のペットを組み合わせることだ.

**match up to sb/sth** ▶定義 to be as good as sb/sth ～と同じくらい良い➔～に匹敵する ‖ *The film didn't match up to my expectations.* その映画は私の期待に沿わなかった.

**matchbox** /mætʃbɒks/ 名 ⊙ ▶定義 a small box for matches マッチ用の小さな箱➔マッチ箱 ☜ container のさし絵

**matchstick** /mætʃstɪk/ 名 ⊙ ▶定義 the thin wooden part of a match マッチの細い木の部分➔マッチ棒

**mate¹** /meɪt/ 名 ⊙ ▶定義1 略式 a friend or sb you live, work or do an activity with 共に生活する, 働く, または活動する友達➔仲間, 相棒 ‖ *He's an old mate of mine.* 彼は私の旧友だ. *a flatmate/classmate/team-mate/playmate* アパートの同居人・同級生・チーム仲間・遊び仲間 ▶定義2 英(俗語) used when speaking to a man 男性に話し掛けるときに用いる➔兄弟, 相棒 ‖ *Can you give me a hand, mate?* 手伝ってくれるかい, 兄弟. ▶定義3 one of a male and female pair of animals, birds, etc 動物, 鳥などの雄と雌の組み合わせの一方➔つがいの片方, 連れ合い, 一方 ‖ *The female sits on the eggs while her mate hunts for food.* つがいの片方(雄)がえさを探す間, 雌は卵を守る. ▶定義4 an officer on a ship 船の高級船員➔航海士

**mate²** /meɪt/ 動 ▶定義1 ⊜ (used about animals and birds) to have sex and produce young (動物と鳥について)性交を行い子供を作る➔つがう ‖ *Pandas rarely mate in zoos.* パンダはめったに動物園でつがいにならない. ▶定義2 ⊕ to bring two animals together so that they can mate ２匹の動物を一緒にしてつがいにする➔つがわせる ☜ 類 breed

\***material¹** /məˈtɪəriəl/ 名 ▶定義1 ⊙⊕ a substance that can be used for making or doing sth ～を作るまたはするために用いられる物質➔原料, 材料 ‖ *raw materials* 原料 *writing/teaching/building materials* 筆記用具・教材・建築材料 *This new material is strong but it is also very light.* この新素材は丈夫だが非常に軽い. ▶定義2 ⊙⊕ (for making clothes, etc) cloth (衣服などを作るための)布➔生地, 素材 ‖ *Is there enough material for a dress?* 生地は１着分のドレスに十分でしょうか. ▶定義3 ⊕ facts or information that you collect before you write a book, article, etc 本, 記事などを書く前に収集

する事実や情報→**資料, 題材**

**material**[2] /mətíəriəl/ 形 ▶定義1 connected with real or physical things rather than the spirit or emotions 精神的・感情的なものよりも事実や物理的なものに関する→**物質の, 物質的な, 肉体的な** ‖ *We should not value material comforts too highly.* 私たちは生活を快適にする物質的なものを高く評価しすぎるべきではない. ☛参 **spiritual** ▶定義2 important and needing to be considered 重要で考慮される必要がある→**重要な, 大切な** ‖ *material evidence* 決め手になる証拠 ☛ 一般的な語ではないが **immaterial** を参照. —materially 副→**物質的に, 実質的に**

**materialism** /mətíəriəlìz(ə)m/ 名 Ⓤ ▶定義 the belief that money and possessions are the most important things in life 金銭と財産が人生で最も重要なものとする考え方→**物質主義, 実利主義**— materialist /-lɪst/ 名 Ⓒ→**物質[実利]主義者**— materialistic /mətìəriəlístɪk/ 形→**物質[実利]主義的な**

**materialize**（または **-ise**）/mətíəriəlàɪz/ 動 Ⓘ ▶定義 to become real; to happen 事実になる; 起こる→**具体化する, 実現する** ‖ *The pay rise that they had promised never materialized.* 彼らが約束した賃金値上げは決して実現されたことはなかった.

**maternal** /mətə́:rnl/ 形 ▶定義1 behaving as a mother would behave; connected with being a mother 母親のように振る舞う; 母親であることに関した→**母の, 母らしい** ‖ *maternal love/instincts* 母性愛・本能 ▶定義2（名詞の前だけ）related through your mother's side of the family 家族の中で母親側の親類の→**母方の** ‖ *your maternal grandfather* 母方の祖父 ☛参 **paternal**

**maternity** /mətə́:rnəti/ 形 ▶定義 connected with women who are going to have or have just had a baby 赤ん坊をこれから持つ, または持つたばかりの女性に関した→**妊婦[出産用]の** ‖ *maternity clothes* 妊婦服 *the hospital's maternity ward* 病院の産科病棟 ☛参 **paternity**

**mathematician** /mæ̀θ(ə)mətíʃ(ə)n/ 名 Ⓒ ▶定義 a person who studies or is an expert in mathematics 数学を研究する人・専門とする人→**数学者, 数学の得意な人**

\***mathematics** /mæ̀θ(ə)mǽtɪks/ 名 Ⓤ ▶定義 the science or study of numbers, quantities or shapes 数, 量, または形の科学や研究→**数学**

▶英での省略形は maths, 米では math: *Maths is my favourite subject.*（数学は私の得意科目だ.）
☛参 **arithmetic, algebra, geometry** — mathematical /mæ̀θ(ə)mǽtɪk(ə)l/ 形→**数学の, 数理的な** ‖ *mathematical calculations* 数理的計算 — mathematically /-k(ə)li/ 副→**数学的に, 非常に正確に**

**matinee** /mǽtɪneɪ; mætnéɪ/ 名 Ⓒ ▶定義 an afternoon performance of a play, film, etc 演劇, 映画などの午後の上演→**昼間興行, マチネー**

**matrimony** /mǽtrəməni; -mòuni/ 名 Ⓤ 正式 ▶定義 the state of being married 結婚している状態→**結婚, 婚姻** —matrimonial /mæ̀trəmóuniəl/ 形→**結婚の, 夫婦間の**

**matron** /méɪtrən/ 名 Ⓒ ▶定義1（古）a nurse who is in charge of the other nurses in a hospital 病院でほかの看護婦の監督をする看護婦→**看護婦長** ☛ 現在では通常 senior nursing officer と言う. ▶定義2 a woman who works as a nurse in a school 学校で看護婦として働く女性→**学校看護婦**

**matt**（英 または **matte**）/mæt/ 形 ▶定義 not shiny 輝かない→**つや消しの, 光沢のない** ‖ *This paint gives a matt finish.* この塗料はつや消し仕上げになる. ☛参 **gloss**

**matted** /mǽtəd/ 形 ▶定義 (used especially about hair) forming a thick mass, especially because it is wet and/or dirty（特に髪について）特にぬれている, 汚れているために, 絡まって塊を作っている→**もつれた**

\***matter**[1] /mǽtər/ 名 ▶定義1 Ⓒ a subject or situation that you must think about and give your attention to よく考えて注意を払わなければならないような事柄や事態→**事件, 事柄, 事態** ‖ *It's a personal matter and I don't want to discuss it with you.* 私的な事柄なので, それについてあなたと話し合いたくありません. *Finding a job will be no easy matter.* 仕事を見つけるのは簡単なことではないだろう. *to simplify/complicate matters* 事態を単純・複雑にする ▶定義2 [単数扱い] **the matter (with sb/sth)** the reason sb/sth has a problem or is not good ～が問題を抱えている原因・良くない原因→**困ったこと, 問題, 事情** ‖ *She looks sad. What's the matter with her?* 彼女は悲しそうだ. どうしたのだろう. *There*

## matter²

seems to be **something the matter** with the car. その車には何か故障があるようだ. *Eat that food! There's **nothing the matter** with it.* その食物を食べなさい. 何も問題はない. ▶定義3 ❶ all physical substances; a substance of a particular kind すべての物理的な物質; 特定の種類の物質→**物質** ‖ *reading matter* 読み物 ▶定義4 ❶ the contents of a book, film, etc 本, 映画などの内容→**内容** ‖ *I don't think the **subject matter** of this programme is suitable for children.* この番組の内容が子供にふさわしいとは思わない.

成句 **a matter of hours, miles, etc** ▶定義 used to say that sth is not very long, far, expensive, etc 〜があまり長くない, 遠くない, 高くないなどと言うときに用いて→**わずか[せいぜい]〜だ** ‖ *The fight lasted a matter of seconds.* けんかはほんの数秒続いただけだ.

**a matter of life and/or death** ▶定義 extremely urgent and important 極めて緊急で重要な→**死活問題**

**another/a different matter** ▶定義 something much more serious, difficult, etc はるかに深刻なもの, 難しいものなど→**別問題** ‖ *I can speak a little Japanese, but reading it is quite another matter.* 私は少し日本語を話せるが, 読むのは全く別問題だ.

**as a matter of fact** ▶定義 to tell the truth; in reality 真実を述べると; 実際には→**実際は, 実を言うと** ‖ *I like him very much, as a matter of fact.* 実を言うと, 私はとても彼が好きだ.

**for that matter** ▶定義 in addition; now that I think about it さらに; 今それについて考えると→**そう言えばまた, それを言うならまた** ‖ *Mick is really fed up with his course. I am too, for that matter.* ミックは自分の進路に全くうんざりしている. それを言うなら私もだ.

**to make matters/things worse** ⇒ **WORSE**

**a matter of course** ▶定義 something that you always do; the usual thing to do いつも行うこと; 通常行うべきこと→**当然のこと** ‖ *Goods leaving the factory are checked as a matter of course.* 工場を出る製品は当然のことながら検査される.

**a matter of opinion** ▶定義 a subject on which people do not agree 人々が合意しないような主題→**見解の分かれる問題** ‖ *'I think the government is doing a good job.' 'That's a matter of opinion.'* 「私は政府はよくやっていると思う」「それは見解の分かれるところだ」

**(be) a matter of sth/doing sth** ▶定義 a situation in which sth is needed 〜が必要とされる状況→**〜の問題** ‖ *Learning a language is largely a matter of practice.* 言語を習得することは主に練習の問題だ.

**no matter who, what, where, etc** ▶定義 whoever, whatever, wherever, etc だれでも, 何でも, どこでもなど→**たとえだれ[何・どこ]〜でも** ‖ *They never listen no matter what you say.* あなたがたとえ何を言っても彼らは聞かない.

\***matter²** /mǽtər/ 動 ⾃ ▶定義 **matter (to sb)** (進行形は不可) to be important 重要である→**重要である, 重大である** ‖ *It doesn't really matter how much it costs.* それにいくらかかろうが全く問題ではない. *Nobody's hurt, and **that's all that matters**.* だれもけがをしなかった, それだけが重要である. *Some things matter more than others.* 他よりも重要な事がいくつかある. *It doesn't matter to me what he does in his free time.* 彼が自由時間に何をしようと私には関係がない.

**matter-of-fact** 形 ▶定義 said or done without showing any emotion, especially when it would seem more normal to express your feelings 特に感情を表現することが当然だと思われるときに, 感情を示さずに述べられたまたは行われた→**事務的な, 実際的な, 割り切った** ‖ *He was very matter-of-fact about his illness.* 彼は自分の病気について非常に冷静だった.

**mattress** /mǽtrəs/ 名 C ▶定義 a large soft thing that you lie on to sleep, usually put on a bed 大きな柔らかいもので, 通常ベッドの上に置き眠るときにその上で横になる→**マットレス** ☛ **bed** のさし絵

**mature** /mət(j)úər, -tʃúər/ 形 ▶定義 **1** fully grown or fully developed 完全に成熟した, または完全に発達した→**成熟した, 熟した, 熟成した** ‖ *a mature tree/bird/animal* 成熟した木・鳥・動物 ▶定義 **2** behaving in a sensible adult way 分別のある大人らしく振る舞う→**慎重な, 十分考慮した** ‖ *Is she mature enough for such responsibility?* 彼女はそのような責任を取る分別があるのだろうか. ⇔ **immature** — **mature** 動 ⾃ →**成熟する, 円熟する** ‖ *He matured a lot during his two* years at college. 彼は大学での2年間で非常に成長した. — **maturity** /mət(j)úərəti, -tʃúər-/ 名 ❶ →成熟, 円熟

**maul** /mɔ́ːl/ 動 他 ▶定義 (usually used about a wild animal) to attack and injure sb (通常野生の動物について) ~を攻撃し傷付ける → ~をひっかいて傷付ける, ずたずたに切り裂く

**mauve** /móuv, mɔ́ːv/ 形 名 ❶ ▶定義 (of) a pale purple colour 淡い紫色(の) → ふじ色(の)

**max** /mæks/ 略 maximum → 最大の, 最高の, 最大限 ‖ *max temp 21℃* 最高気温摂氏21度

**maxim** /mǽksəm/ 名 ⓒ ▶定義 a few words that express a rule for good or sensible behaviour 善いまたは分別のある行いの基準を短く表した言葉 → 格言, 金言 ‖ *Our maxim is: 'If a job's worth doing, it's worth doing well.'* 私たちの金言は「する価値のある仕事は, きちんとする価値がある」だ.

**maximize** (または **-ise**) /mǽksəmàɪz/ 動 他 ▶定義 to increase sth as much as possible ~をできる限り増やす → ~を最大・最高にする, 極限まで広げる ‖ *to maximize profits* 利益を最大にする ⇔ **minimize**

\***maximum** /mǽksəməm/ 名 [単数扱い] (略 **max**) ▶定義 the greatest amount or level of sth that is possible, allowed, etc 可能な, 許容されるなど, (~の)最大の量またはレベル → 最大限, 最大量 ‖ *The bus can carry a maximum of 40 people.* そのバスは最大40名を乗せられる. *That is the maximum we can afford.* それは私たちが用意できる最大限の金額だ. ⇔ **minimum** — **maximum** 形 (名詞の前だけ) → 最大(限度)の, 最高(限度)の ‖ *a maximum speed of 120 miles per hour* 最高時速120マイル

\***May**¹ /méɪ/ 名 ❶ ⓒ ▶定義 the fifth month of the year, coming after April 4月の次に来る, 1年の5番目の月 → 5月

▶文中での月の表し方については, January の例と注を参照.

\***may**² /méɪ/ 法助動詞 (否定形 **may not**) ▶定義 **1** used for saying that sth is possible ~の可能性があることを述べるときに用いて → かもしれない, することがある ‖ *'Where's Sue?' 'She may be in the garden.'* 「スーはどこだね」「庭にいるかもしれない」 *You may be right.* 君は正しいかもしれない. *I may be going to China next year.* 私は来年中国へ行くかもしれない. *They may have forgotten the meeting.* 彼らは会合を忘れたのかもしれない. ▶定義 **2** used as a polite way of asking for and giving permission 許可を求めるまたは与える丁寧な表現として用いて → してもよい, しても差し支えない ‖ *May I use your phone?* 電話を使ってもよいですか. *You may not take photographs in the museum.* 美術館で写真を撮ってはいけません. ▶定義 **3** used for contrasting two facts 2つの事実を対照させるために用いて → かもしれないが, たとえ~であっても ‖ *He may be very clever but he can't do anything practical.* 彼は非常に賢いかもしれないが, 実用的な事は何もできない. ▶定義 **4** 正式 used for expressing wishes and hopes 願望や要望を表現するために用いて → 願わくは~ならんことを ‖ *May you both be very happy.* どうかお2人ともお幸せに.

▶法助動詞についての説明は, 巻末の「文法早見表」を参照.

成句 may/might as well (do sth) ⇒ **WELL**¹

\***maybe** /méɪbi/ 副 ▶定義 perhaps; possibly 多分; かもしれない → もしかしたら, ことによると, あるいは ‖ *'Are you going to come?' 'Maybe.'* 「君も来るかい」「多分ね」 *There were three, maybe four armed men.* 武装した男が3人, あるいは4人いた. *Maybe I'll accept the invitation and maybe I won't.* 私はその招待を受けるかもしれないし, 受けないかもしれない. ☞参 **perhaps** の注

**May Day** 名 ⓒ ▶定義 1st May 5月1日 → メーデー, 労働祭

▶ May Day (メーデー) は, 伝統的な春の祭りとして祝われ, また働く人々の祭日とする国もある.

**mayonnaise** /mèɪənéɪz, ⌣́⌣̀/ 名 ❶ ▶定義 a cold thick pale yellow sauce made with eggs and oil 卵と油を使って作られる, どろっとした淡い黄色の冷たいソース → マヨネーズ

**mayor** /méɪər, (特に人名の前で) mɔːr/ 名 ⓒ ▶定義 a person who is elected to be the leader of the group of people (**a council**) who manage the affairs of a town or city 町や市の行政を管理する人々の集団(地方自治体の議会)の長として選出された人 → 市長, 町長

**mayoress** /méɪərəs, -ɪs, (特に人名の前で) mɔːrəs,

-ɪs/ 图 ● ▶定義 a woman mayor, or a woman who is married to or helps a mayor 女性の市長[町長], 市長[町長]と結婚しているまたは彼を助ける女性→**女性の市長[町長], 市長[町長]夫人**

**maze** /méɪz/ 图 ● ▶定義 a system of paths which is designed to confuse you so that it is difficult to find your way out 道の入り組んだ仕組みで, 出口を見つけられないように人を混乱させるために設計されている→**迷路, 迷宮** ‖ (比喩)*a maze of winding streets* 曲がりくねった街路の迷路 ☛類 **labyrinth**

**MBA** /èm biː éɪ/ 略 Master of Business Administration ▶定義 an advanced university degree in business ビジネスに関する高い学位→**経営(管理)学修士**

**MD** /èm díː/ 略 Doctor of Medicine→**医学博士**

★**me** /miː; mi, mɪ/ 代 ▶定義 (目的語として用いて) the person who is speaking or writing 話しているまたは書いているその人→**私に, 私を** ‖ *He telephoned me yesterday.* 彼は昨日私に電話をくれた. *She wrote to me last week.* 彼女は先週私に手紙をくれた. *Hello, is that Frank? It's me, Sadiq.* もしもし, フランクですか. 私です, サディックです.

**meadow** /médoʊ/ 图 ● ▶定義 a field of grass 牧草の生えた野原→**草地, 牧草地**

**meagre** (米 **meager**) /míːɡər/ 形 ▶定義 too small in amount 量の非常に少ない→**乏しい, わずかな, 貧弱な** ‖ *a meagre salary* わずかな給料

★**meal** /míːl/ 图 ● ▶定義 the time when you eat or the food that is eaten at that time 食べる時間, またはその時間に食べられる食べ物→**食事, 食事時間** ‖ *Shall we go out for a meal on Friday?* 金曜日に食事に出掛けましょうか. *a heavy/light meal* 十分な・軽い食事

▶1日の主な食事には breakfast (朝食), lunch (昼食) そして dinner (夕食) がある. tea (午後のお茶) と supper (夜食) は通常軽い食事 (ただし dinner の注を参照). 食事の合間に食べる軽いものは snack (軽食) と言う.

成句 **a square meal** ⇒ **SQUARE**²

**mealtime** /míːltàɪm/ 图 ● ▶定義 the time at which a meal is usually eaten 通常食事を取る時間→**食事時間**

★**mean**¹ /míːn/ 動 ● (過, 過分 **meant** /ment/)

▶定義 1 (進行形は不可) to express, show or have as a meaning 意味を表す, 示す, または持つ→**～を意味する** ‖ *What does this word mean?* この単語の意味は何ですか. *The bell means that the lesson has ended.* あのベルは授業が終わったことを意味します. *Does the name 'Michael Potter' mean anything to you?* 「マイケル・ポッター」という名前はあなたにとって何か意味があるのですか

▶この動詞は進行形では用いられないが, 現在分詞形 (=-ing 形) は一般的: *The weather during filming was terrible, meaning that several scenes had to be reshot later.* (撮影中の天気がひどかったので, いくつかの場面を後で取り直さねばならなかった.)

▶定義 2 to want or intend to say sth; to refer to sb/sth ～を言いたい, または言うつもりである; ～に言及する→**～を意図する, ～のつもりで言う, ～のことを指して言う** ‖ *Well, she said 'yes' but I think she really meant 'no'.* なるほど彼女は「はい」と言ったが, 実は「いいえ」のつもりだったのだと僕は思う. *What do you mean by 'a lot of money'?* 「大金」とは何の事だい. *I only meant that I couldn't come tomorrow - any other day would be fine.* 私はただ明日は来られないと言ったのだ - ほかの日は大丈夫だ. *I see what you mean, but I'm afraid it's not possible.* 君の意図するところは分かるが, 無理だと思うよ.

▶mean は「～という意見を持つ」という意味では使えないので注意. それについては I think that... (...と思う) または In my opinion... (私の意見では...) と言う: *I think that she'd be silly to buy that car.* (あの車を買うなんて彼女はばかだと思う.)

▶会話で述べたばかりの事について説明したり, 情報を追加したいときに, I mean がしばしば用いられる: *What a terrible summer - I mean it's rained almost all the time.* (何てひどい夏だ - だって, ずっと雨が降ってばかりいる.) I mean は自分が述べたばかりの事を訂正するときにも用いられる: *We went there on Tuesday, I mean Thursday.* (私たちは火曜日に, いや, 木曜日にそこへ行った.)

▶定義 3 (しばしば受動態で) **mean (sb) to do sth; mean sth (as/for sth/sb); mean sb/sth to be sth** to intend sth; to be supposed to be/do sth ～を意図して…になる; ～になる・をすると考えられている→～(する)ことになっている、～を意図している、～だと思われている ‖ *I'm sure she didn't mean to upset you.* 彼女は君の気を動転させるつもりはなかったはずだ. *She meant the present to be for both of us.* 彼女はその贈り物を私たち２人にくれたつもりだ. *I didn't mean you to cook the whole meal!* すべての食事をあなたに作ってもらおうとは考えていなかった. *It was only meant as a joke.* それはただの冗談のつもりだった. *What's this picture meant to be?* この絵の意味するところは何ですか. ▶定義4 to make sth likely; to cause ～をありそうにさせる; 原因となる→～の前兆[印]である、～を暗示する、引き起こす ‖ *The shortage of teachers means that classes are larger.* 教師が不足すればクラスが大きくなることになる. ▶定義5 mean sth (to sb) to be important to sb ～にとって重要である→(～に)重大な意味を持つ、重要である ‖ *This job means a lot to me.* この仕事は私にとってとても大事なのです. *Money means nothing to her.* お金は彼女にとって何の意味も持たない. ▶定義6 to be serious or sincere about sth ～について真剣または誠実である→本気で(～する)つもりでいる ‖ *He said he loved me but I don't think he meant it!* 彼は私を愛していると言ったが, 私は彼が本気で言っているとは思わない.

成句 be meant to be sth ▶定義 to be considered or said to be sth ～になると考えられるまたは言われる→～だと思われている、～ことになっている ‖ *That restaurant is meant to be excellent.* あのレストランは一流と言われている.

mean well ▶定義 to want to be kind and helpful but usually without success 親切に助けたいと思っているが, 通常うまくいかない→よかれと思ってする、悪気はない ‖ *My mother means well but I wish she'd stop treating me like a child.* 母はよかれと思ってするのだが, 子供扱いするのはやめてほしい.

\***mean**² /miːn/ 形 ▶定義1 mean (with sth) wanting to keep money, etc for yourself rather than let other people have it お金などをほかの人々に持たせるよりも自分のために取っておきたい→けちな、出し惜しみをする ‖ *It's no good asking him for any money - he's much too mean.* 彼にお金を無心しても無駄だ － 彼は非常にけちなのだ. *They're mean with the food in the canteen.* 社員食堂の食事はお粗末だ. ▶定義2 mean (to sb) (used about people or their behaviour) unkind (人またはその行動について)不親切な→意地の悪い、不親切な ‖ *It was mean of him not to invite you too.* あなたも招待しなかったとは彼も意地が悪い. ▶定義3 (名詞の前だけ) average 平均の→平均の、中間の ‖ *What is the mean annual temperature in California?* カリフォルニアの年間平均気温は何度ですか. ―meanness 名 Ⓤ→卑しいこと、けち、意地悪

**meander** /miˈændər/ 動 自 ▶定義1 (used about a river, road, etc) to have a lot of curves and bends (川, 道路などについて)湾曲や屈曲がたくさんある→曲がりくねって流れる、蛇行する ▶定義2 (used about a person or animal) to walk or travel slowly or without any definite direction (人または動物について)ゆっくりと, またははっきりした当てもなく歩くまたは旅をする→当てもなくさまよう、ぶらぶら歩く

\***meaning** /ˈmiːnɪŋ/ 名 ▶定義1 Ⓒ Ⓤ the thing or idea that sth represents; what sb is trying to communicate ～が表すものまたは考え; ～が伝えようとするもの→意味、伝えたい事、真意 ‖ *This word has two different meanings in English.* この単語には英語で２つの異なる意味がある. *What do you think the meaning is of the last line of the poem?* その詩の最後の行は何を意味していると思いますか. ▶定義2 Ⓤ the purpose or importance of an experience ある経験の成果または重要性→意義、価値、重要性 ‖ *With his child dead there seemed to be no meaning in life.* 彼の子供の死によって人生には何の価値もないように思えた.

**meaningful** /ˈmiːnɪŋfəl/ 形 ▶定義1 useful, important or interesting 有用な、重要な、または興味深い→意味のある、有意義な ‖ *Most people need a meaningful relationship with another person.* ほとんどの人は他者との意味のある関係を必要とする. ▶定義2 (used about a look, expression, etc) trying to express a certain feeling or idea (外見, 表情などについて)ある感情または考えを表現しようとしている→意味ありげな、意味深長な ‖ *They kept giving each other meaningful glances across the table.* 彼らはテ

—ブル越しに意味ありげな視線を交わし合っていた. — **meaningfully** /-fəli/ 副 ▶定義 **意味ありげに, 意味深長に**

**meaningless** /míːnɪŋləs/ 形 ▶定義 without meaning, reason or sense 意義, 理由, または意味のない→**意味のない, 無意味な, 目的のない** || *The figures are meaningless if we have nothing to compare them with.* 比較するものがなければ, それらの数字は意味のないものです.

\***means** /míːnz/ 名 ▶定義1 ⓒ (複) **means**) a means (of doing sth) a method of doing sth 〜をする方法→**手段, 方法** || *Do you have any means of transport (= a car, bicycle, etc)?* 輸送手段 (=車, 自転車など) は何かありますか. *Is there any means of contacting your husband?* あなたのご主人に何か連絡を取る方法はありますか. ▶定義2 [複数扱い] 正式 all the money that sb has 〜が持つすべてのお金→**財産, 資力** || *This car is beyond the means of most people.* この車はほとんどの人には手が届かない.

成句 **by all means** ▶定義 used to say that you are happy for sb to have or do sth 〜が…を持つまたは行うことについてあなたが満足していることを述べるときに用いて→**よろしいですとも, 是非どうぞ** || *'Can I borrow your newspaper?' 'By all means.'*「新聞を借りてもよいですか」「どうぞどうぞ」

**by means of** ▶定義 by using 使うことによって→**〜によって, 〜を用いて** || *We got out of the hotel by means of the fire escape.* 私たちは非常口を使ってホテルから脱出した.

**by no means; not by any means** ▶定義 (used to emphasize sth) not at all (〜を強調するために用いて) 全く〜でない→**決して〜でない, どんな事があっても〜しない** || *I'm by no means sure that this is the right thing to do.* これをすることが正しいとは私にはどうしても確信できない.

**a means to an end** ▶定義 an action or thing that is not important in itself but is a way of achieving sth else それ自体は重要ではないが, ほかの〜を達成する方法としての行動あるいは手段→**目的達成のための1つの手段** || *I don't enjoy my job, but it's a means to an end.* 仕事は楽しくないが, 目的達成のための1つの手段だ.

**meant** **MEAN**¹ の過去・過去分詞形

**meantime** /míːntaɪm/ 名

成句 **in the meantime** ▶定義 in the time between two things happening 2つの事が起きる間の間に→**その間に, とかくするうちに** || *Our house isn't finished so in the meantime we're living with my mother.* 私たちの家は完成していないので, その間私たちは私の母と一緒に住んでいる.

\***meanwhile** /míːn(h)waɪl/ 副 ▶定義 during the same time or during the time between two things happening 同時に, 2つの事が起きる間に→**その間に** || *Peter was at home studying. Omar, meanwhile, was out with his friends.* ピーターは家で勉強していた. オマールはその間友達と出掛けていた.

**measles** /míːz(ə)lz/ 名 Ⓤ ▶定義 a common infectious disease, especially among children, in which your body feels hot and your skin is covered in small red spots 特に子供たちがかかる, 一般的な伝染性の病気. 体が熱っぽく感じて皮膚が小さな赤い斑点 (はんてん) で覆われる→**はしか, 麻疹**

▶ measles は複数名詞のように見えるが, 単数形の動詞を伴う: *In many countries measles is a very dangerous disease.* (多くの国では, 麻疹は非常に危険な病気だ.)

**measly** /míːz(ə)li/ 形 略式 ▶定義 much too small in size, amount or value 大きさ, 量, 価値があまりにも小さすぎる→**貧弱な, わずかな, ちっぽけな** || *All that work for this measly amount of money!* あの仕事を全部して, このわずかなお金とは.

\***measure**¹ /méʒər/ 動 ▶定義1 🔵 to find the size, weight, quantity, etc of sb/sth in standard units by using an instrument 基準となる単位で表す〜の大きさ, 重さ, 量などを, 器具を使って確かめる→**(〜を) 測る, 測定する** || *to measure the height/width/length/depth of sth* 〜の高さ・幅・長さ・深さを測る *Could you measure the table to see if it will fit into our room?* テーブルの寸法を測って, 私たちの部屋に合うかどうかを見てもらえますか. ▶定義2 🔵 to be a certain height, width, length, etc ある高さ, 幅, 長さである→**(〜だけ) ある** || *The room measures five metres across.* その部屋は幅が5メートルある. ▶定義3 🔵 **measure sth (against sth)** to judge the value or effect of sth 〜の価値または効果を判断する→

(～を)評価する,判断する ‖ *Our sales do not look good when measured against those of our competitors.* 我々の売り上げは競合先の売り上げに比べるとあまりよくは見えない.

**句動詞** measure up (to sth) ▶定義 to be as good as you need to be or as sb expects you to be あなたが必要とするくらい,または～があなたに期待するのと同じくらい良い→…にかなう,達する ‖ *Did the holiday measure up to your expectations?* 休日はあなたの期待通りでしたか.

★**measure**² /méʒər/ 名 ▶定義1 [C,通常は複数] an action that is done for a special reason 特別な理由のために行われる行動→対策,処置 ‖ *The government is to take new measures to reduce inflation.* 政府はインフレを抑えるために新しい政策を講じる予定だ. *As a temporary measure, the road will have to be closed.* 一時的な措置として,道路は閉鎖されなければならないだろう. ▶定義2 [単数扱い] **正式** a/some measure of sth a certain amount of sth; some ある量の～;いくらかの→程度,適度,限度 ‖ *The play achieved a measure of success.* 芝居はある程度の成功を収めた. ▶定義3 [単数扱い] a way of understanding or judging sth ～を理解するまたは判断する方法→基準,尺度 ‖ *The school's popularity is a measure of the teachers' success.* 学校の評判は教師の成功の尺度である. ▶定義4 C a way of describing the size, amount, etc of sth ～の大きさ,量などを表す方法→単位,計算単位 ‖ *A metre is a measure of length.* メートルは長さの単位である. ☞ **tape measure**

**成句** for good measure ▶定義 in addition to sth, especially to make sure that there is enough 特に十分なものがあることを確実にするために,～に加えて→おまけに,余分として ‖ *He made a few extra sandwiches for good measure.* 彼はサンドイッチを余分に作っておいた.

made to measure ▶定義 specially made or perfectly suitable for a particular person, use, etc 特定の人,用途などのために特別に作られた,または完全に適した→合わせて作った,オーダーメード ‖ *I'm getting a suit made to measure for the wedding.* 私は結婚式のためにオーダーメードのスーツをあつらえる予定です.

**measurement** /méʒərmənt/ 名 ▶定義1 C a size, amount, etc that is found by measuring 測定することによって分かった大きさ,量など→量,寸法,大きさ ‖ *What are the exact measurements of the room? (= how wide, long, etc is it?)* その部屋の正確な寸法はいくつですか.(= どのくらい広い,長いなどですか.) ▶定義2 U the act or process of measuring sth ～を測る行為または過程→測定,測量

★**meat** /miːt/ 名 U ▶定義 the parts of animals or birds that people eat 食用にする動物または鳥の身体部位→肉 ‖ *She doesn't eat meat - she's a vegetarian.* 彼女は肉を食べない － 菜食主義者なのだ. *meat-eating animals* 肉食獣

▶その肉がとられた動物の種類によって,異なる名称で呼ばれる肉もある. pork(豚肉), ham(ハム), bacon(ベーコン)は豚から, beef(牛肉)は牛から, veal(子牛肉)は子牛からとれたもの. mutton(羊肉)は羊から, lamb(子羊肉)は子羊からとれたもの. 鳥や魚の肉には別の単語はない. しばしば牛肉,羊肉,子羊肉を red meat(赤肉)と呼ぶ. 鳥からとれた肉は white meat(白肉)と呼ばれる. 肉は, fry(揚げる), grill(焼き網で焼く), roast(直火で焼く), stew(とろ火で煮込む)などして食べることができる. joint of meat(大きな肉片)切り分けることを carve と言う. 肉は, tough(堅い), tender(柔らかい), lean(脂身がない), または fatty(脂身が多い)と表現できる. 料理していない肉を raw(生)と言う.

**meaty** /míːti/ 形 ▶定義1 like meat, or containing a lot of meat 肉のような,または多くの肉を含んだ→肉の(多い) ‖ *meaty sausages* 肉がたっぷり入ったソーセージ ▶定義2 large and fat 大きくて太った→肉づきの良い ‖ *meaty tomatoes* 肉づきの良いトマト ▶定義3 containing a lot of important or good ideas 重要なまたは良い考えを多く含んだ→内容の充実した,中身の濃い ‖ *a meaty topic for discussion* 充実した議題

**Mecca** /méka/ 名 ▶定義1 [単数扱い] the city in Saudi Arabia where Muhammad was born, which is the centre of Islam マホメットが生まれたサウジアラビアの町で,イスラム教の中心地である→メッカ ▶定義2 **mecca** [C,通常は単数] a place that many people wish to visit because of a particular interest 特定の興味のために,多くの人々が訪れたいと思う場所→あこがれの場所,発祥地 ‖ *Italy is a mecca for art lovers.* イタリアは

芸術を愛する人々のあこがれの地だ.

**mechanic** /mɪkǽnɪk/ 图 ▶定義1 ❻ a person whose job is to repair and work with machines 機械を修理し動かすことを仕事とする人→**機械工, 修理工** ‖ *a car mechanic* 自動車修理工 ▶定義2 **mechanics** ❶ the science of how machines work 機械がどのように作動するかについての科学→**機械学, 力学** ▶定義3 **the mechanics** [複数扱い] the way in which sth works or is done 〜が動くまたは行われる方法→**機構, 仕組み, 構造** ‖ *Don't ask me - I don't understand the mechanics of the legal system.* 私に聞かないで－法律の仕組みは私には分からない.

*****mechanical** /mɪkǽnɪk(ə)l/ 形 ▶定義1 connected with or produced by machines 機械に関連した, または機械で作られる→**機械の, 機械製の** ‖ *a mechanical pump* 機械式ポンプ *mechanical engineering* 機械工学 *mechanical problems* 機械にかかわる問題 ▶定義2 (used about a person's behaviour) done like a machine as if you are not thinking about what you are doing (人の行動について) あたかも自分がしていることについて何も考えていないかのように, 機械のように行われる→**機械的な, 無意識の** ‖ *He played the piano in a dull and mechanical way.* 彼は物憂げにそして機械的にピアノを弾いた. —**mechanically** /-k(ə)li/ 副→**機械的に**

**mechanism** /mékənìz(ə)m/ 图 ❻ ▶定義1 a set of moving parts in a machine that does a certain task ある作業を行う機械の中の作動する一連の部分→**(機械)装置, 機械部分** ‖ *Our car has an automatic locking mechanism.* 私たちの車には自動ロック装置が付いている. ▶定義2 the way in which sth works or is done 〜が動くまたは行われる方法→**仕組み, 機構** ‖ *I'm afraid there is no mechanism for dealing with your complaint.* 残念ながらあなたの不満に対処する仕組みはないと思う.

**mechanize** (または **-ise**) /mékənaɪz/ 動 ❶ ▶定義 to use machines instead of people to do work 仕事を行うために, 人の代わりに機械を使う→**〜を機械化する** ‖ *We have mechanized the entire production process.* 我が社は全生産工程を機械化した. —**mechanization** (または **-isation**) /mèkənaɪzéɪʃ(ə)n/ 图 ❶→**機械化**

**the Med** 略式 =THE MEDITERRANEAN

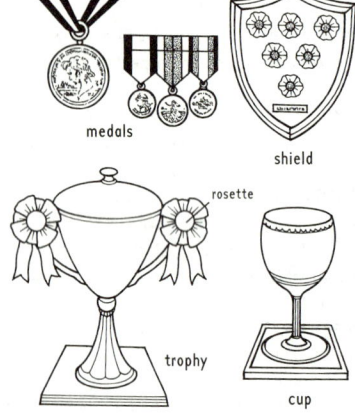

medals

shield

rosette

trophy

cup

**medal** /médl/ 图 ❻ ▶定義 a small flat piece of metal, usually with a design and words on it, which is given to sb who has shown courage or as a prize in a sporting event 通常図柄や言葉が書かれている小さな平たい金属で, 勇気を示した〜またはスポーツ種目での賞として与えられる→**メダル** ‖ *to win a gold/silver/bronze medal in the Olympics* オリンピックで金・銀・銅メダルを取る

**medallion** /mədǽljən/ 图 ❻ ▶定義 a small round piece of metal on a chain which is worn as jewellery around the neck 装身具として首に付ける鎖の付いた小さな円い金属→**大メダル, メダリオン**

**medallist** (米**medalist**) /médlɪst/ 图 ❻ ▶定義 a person who has won a medal, especially in sport 特にスポーツで, メダルを獲得した人→**メダリスト, メダル受領[獲得]者** ‖ *an Olympic gold medallist* オリンピック金メダル獲得者

**meddle** /médl/ 動 ❷ ▶定義 meddle (in/with sth) to take too much interest in sb's private affairs or to touch sth that does not belong to you 〜の個人的な事柄に過度に興味を持つ, または, 自分の所有するものではない〜に触れる→**干渉する, お節介を焼く, いじくる** ‖ *She criticized her mother for meddling in her private life.* 個人的な生活へ干渉していると彼女は母親を非難した.

**media** /míːdiə/ 名[複数扱い] ▶定義 television, radio and newspapers used as a means of communication 伝達の手段として使われるテレビ, ラジオ, 新聞→**大衆伝達の手段, マスメディア, マスコミ機関** ‖ *The reports in the media have been greatly exaggerated.* マスメディアでの報道は非常に誇張されていた. ☛参 **mass media**, **the press**

▶ media は複数名詞だが, 単数形の動詞と共に用いられることがある: *The media always take/takes a great interest in the Royal family.* (マスメディアはいつでも王室に非常に関心を持っている.)

**mediaeval** =MEDIEVAL

**mediate** /míːdièɪt/ 動自他 ▶定義 mediate (in sth) (between A and B) to try to end a disagreement between two or more people or groups 2人[つ]以上の人々[集団]の間での論争を終わらせようと努める→**調停する, 和解させる, 仲介をする** ‖ *As a supervisor she had to mediate between her colleagues and the management.* 管理者として, 彼女は同僚と経営者側の仲介をしなければならなかった. — mediation /mìːdiéɪʃ(ə)n/ 名 Ⓤ→**調停, 仲裁** — mediatorm Ⓒ→**調停者**

**\*medical**¹ /médɪk(ə)l/ 形 ▶定義 connected with medicine and the treatment of illness 薬および病気の治療に関連した→**医学の, 医療の, 医薬の** ‖ *medical treatment/care* 治療 *the medical profession* 医者仲間

**medical**² /médɪk(ə)l/ 名 Ⓒ ▶定義 an examination of your body by a doctor to check your state of health 健康状態を調べるための医師による体の検査→**診察** ‖ *to have a medical* 診察を受ける

**medication** /mèdəkéɪʃ(ə)n/ 名 Ⓒ Ⓤ 特に 米 ▶定義 medicine that a doctor has given to you 医師が与えた薬→**薬剤, 投薬** ‖ *Are you on any medication?* あなたは薬物治療を受けていますか.

**medicinal** /mədísɪnəl/ 形 ▶定義 useful for curing illness or infection 病気や伝染病を治すために役に立つ→**薬効のある, 薬用の** ‖ *medicinal plants* 薬草

**\*medicine** /médsn, médəsən/ 名 ▶定義 1 Ⓤ the science of preventing and treating illness 病気を防ぎ治す科学→**医学, 医療** ‖ *to study medi-* cine 医学を学ぶ ▶定義 2 Ⓒ Ⓤ a substance, especially a liquid, that you take in order to cure an illness 病気を治すために摂取する物, 特に液体→**薬, 内服薬, 水薬** ‖ *Take this medicine three times a day.* この薬を1日3回飲みなさい. *cough medicine* せき止め ☛ **bandage** のさし絵

> ▶語法
>
> drink medicine と言わない理由
>
> drinkの意味は「(液体を)飲む」です. しかし, 薬はliquid(水薬)に限りません. その他のpowder(粉薬), tablet(錠剤), pill(丸薬)は, 液体ではないので drink することはできません. したがって, 薬の形状を問わず用いることができる take(摂取する)を用いて, take medicine と言うのです.

**medieval** (または **mediaeval**) /mìːdíːv(ə)l, mèd-; mèd-/ 形 ▶定義 connected with the period in history between about 1100 and 1500 AD (**the Middle Ages**) 歴史上の紀元後1100年から1500年の間の期間(中世)に関連した→**中世の**

**mediocre** /mìːdióʊkər/ 形 ▶定義 of not very high quality 質が非常に高くはない→**並の, 平凡な** ‖ *a mediocre performance* 平凡な出来栄え — mediocrity /mìːdiákrəti/ 名 Ⓤ→**平凡, 並み, 凡庸**

**meditate** /médətèɪt/ 動自 ▶定義 meditate (on/upon sth) to think carefully and deeply, especially for religious reasons or to make your mind calm 特に宗教的な理由でまたは心を静めるために, 慎重に深く考える→**深く考える, 瞑想(めいそう)にふける** ‖ *I've been meditating on what you said last week.* 私は先週あなたが言った事についてじっくり考えている. — meditation /mèdətéɪʃ(ə)n/ 名 Ⓤ→**瞑想, 熟考**

**the Mediterranean** /mèdətəréɪniən, -njən/ (または 略式 **the Med**) 名[単数扱い]形 ▶定義 (of) the Mediterranean Sea or the countries around it 地中海またはその周りの国々(の)→**地中海(の), 地中海沿岸諸国(の)** ‖ *Mediterranean cookery* 地中海料理

**\*medium**¹ /míːdiəm/ 形 ▶定義 1 in the middle between two sizes, lengths, temperatures, etc; average 2つの大きさ, 長さ, 温度などの中間の;

**1034　medium²**

平均の→**中くらいの, 中間の, 並みの** ‖ *She was of medium height.* 彼女は中背だった. *Would you like the small, medium or large packet?* 小さい包み, 中くらいの包み, 大きい包みのどれがお好みですか. *a medium-sized car/town/dog* 中型車・の町・犬 ▶定義2 (used about meat) cooked until it is brown all the way through (肉について)中もすべて茶色くなるまで調理した→**中くらいに火を通した, ミディアムの**
▶ rare, well done と比較.

**medium²** /míːdiəm/ 名 ▶定義1 ❻ (複 **media** または **mediums**) a means you can use to express or communicate sth ～を表現するまたは伝えるために用いる手段→**手段, 媒体** ‖ *English is the medium of instruction in the school.* その学校では英語が教授手段です. ⬅参 **media**, **mass media** ▶定義2 ❻Ⓤ medium size 中くらいの大きさ→**中間, 中くらい** ‖ *Have you got this shirt in (a) medium?* このシャツの中間サイズはありますか. ▶定義3 ❻ (複 **mediums**) a person who says that he/she can speak to the spirits of dead people 死んだ人々の魂と話すことができると言う人→**巫女(みこ), 霊媒**

**medley** /médli/ 名 ❻ ▶定義1 a piece of music consisting of several tunes or songs played one after the other without a break いくつかの旋律または歌がとぎれずに次々と1つの曲として演奏される→**メドレー, 接続曲** ▶定義2 a mixture of different things 異なるものが混ざり合ったもの→**寄せ集め** ‖ *a medley of styles/flavours* いくつかの様式の寄せ集め・風味のごたまぜ

**meek** /miːk/ 形 ▶定義 (used about people) quiet, and doing what other people say without asking questions (人について)静かで, 質問をせずにほかの人々が言う事をするような→**おとなしい, 従順な** ―**meekly** 副→**おとなしく, 素直に**― **meekness** 名Ⓤ→**おとなしさ**

*****meet** /miːt/ 動 (過, 過分 **met** /met/) ▶定義1 ❸Ⓘ to come together by chance or because you have arranged it 偶然にまたは約束して, 1箇所に来る→**会う, 出会う** ‖ *I just met Kareem on the train.* 私はたった今電車の中でカリームに会った. *What time shall we meet for lunch?* 昼食は何時に会いましょうか. ▶定義2 ❸Ⓘ to see and know sb for the first time ～を初めて会って知り合う→**知り合いになる** ‖ *Where did you first meet your husband?* ご主人とは最初にどこで知り合われたのですか. *Have you two met before?* あなたたち2人は以前から知り合いなの. ▶定義3 Ⓘ to go to a place and wait for sb/sth to arrive ある場所に行き, ～が到着するのを待つ→**～を出迎える** ‖ *I'll come and meet you at the station.* 私が駅まで行ってあなたを出迎えます. ▶定義4 ❸Ⓘ to play, fight, etc together as opponents in a sports competition スポーツ競技で敵として一緒に試合をする, 戦うなど→**対戦する, 競争する** ‖ *These two teams met in last year's final.* これらの2つのチームは昨年の決勝戦で対戦した. *Yamada will meet Suzuki in the second round.* 山田は第2試合で鈴木と対戦するだろう. ▶定義5 Ⓘ to experience sth, often sth unpleasant しばしば不愉快な～について, 経験する→**～に遭遇する, 経験する** ‖ *We will never know how he met his death.* 彼がどうして死んだのか決して分からないだろう. ▶定義6 ❸Ⓘ to touch, join or make contact with 触れる, つながる, または接触する→**触れる, 接触する, 合流する** ‖ *The two roads meet not far from here.* その2つの道はここから遠くない所で交わる. *His eyes met hers.* 彼の目が彼女の目と合った. ▶定義7 Ⓘ to be enough for sth; to be able to deal with sth ～にとって十分である; ～に対応できる→**～を満たす, ～にこたえる** ‖ *The money that I earn is enough to meet our basic needs.* 私が稼ぐお金で基本的に必要なものは支払える. *to meet a challenge* 難問に対処する

成句 **make ends meet** ⇒ **END¹**
**there is more to sb/sth than meets the eye** ▶定義 sb/sth is more interesting or complicated than he/she/it seems ～が見えるよりももっと面白いまたは複雑である→**見える[聞こえる]以上のものである, もっと深い訳がある** ‖ *Do you think there's more to their relationship than meets the eye?* 彼らの関係にはもっと深い訳があると思いますか.

句動詞 **meet up (with sb)** ▶定義 to meet sb, especially after a period of being apart 特にある期間離れていた後に, ～に会う→**落ち合う** ‖ *I have a few things I need to do now, but let's meet up later.* 今はしなくてはならない事が2, 3あるので, 後で落ち合いましょう.

**meet with sb** 特に 困 ▶定義 to meet sb, especially for discussion 特に話し合いのために，〜に会う➡〜と会う，会見する ‖ *The President met with his advisers early this morning.* 大統領は今朝早く顧問たちと会議した．

**meet with sth** ▶定義 to get a particular answer, reaction or result 特定の答え，反応または結果を得る➡〜を受ける，〜に遭遇する ‖ *to meet with success/failure/opposition* 成功を収める・失敗に遭う・反対に遭う

\***meeting** /míːtɪŋ/ 名 ▶定義 1 ❻ an organized occasion when a number of people come together in order to discuss or decide sth 〜を討議するまたは決定するために，たくさんの人々が集まる計画された催し➡集会，大会，会 ‖ *The group hold regular meetings all year.* そのグループは1年を通じて定期的に集会を開く．*We need to have a meeting to discuss these matters.* これらの件について話し合う会議を開く必要がある．

  ▶会を call(召集する)，arrange(準備する)，または organize(主催する)と言う．会を cancel(中止する)または postpone(延期する)とも言う．

▶定義 2 [単数扱い] the people at a meeting 会にいる人々➡集まった人たち，会衆 ‖ *The meeting was in favour of the new proposals.* 集まった人たちは新しい提案に賛成した．▶定義 3 ❻ the coming together of two or more people 2人以上の人々が1箇所に集まること➡会うこと，出会い，遭遇 ‖ *Christmas is a time of family meetings and reunions.* クリスマスは家族が集まり，再会する時だ．

**megaphone** /mégəfòʊn/ 名 ❻ ▶定義 a piece of equipment that you speak through to make your voice sound louder when speaking to a crowd 群衆に向かって話すときに，自分の声が大きく聞こえるようにするために，それを通して話す道具➡メガホン，ハンドマイク

**melancholy** /mélənkəli; -kɑ̀li/ 名 ❿ 正式 ▶定義 a feeling of sadness which lasts for a long time 長い間続く悲しみの感情➡憂鬱(ゆううつ)，ふさぎ込み — melancholy 形 ➡憂鬱な，物悲しい

**mellow** /méloʊ/ 形 ▶定義 1 (used about colours or sounds) soft and pleasant (色または音について) 柔らかくて感じの良い➡柔らかで美しい，快い ▶定義 2 (used about people) calm and relaxed (人について) 穏やかでほっとする➡円熟した，円満な，穏健な ‖ *My dad's grown mellower as he's got older.* 私の父は年を取るにつれて穏やかになった．—mellow 動 自 他 ➡円熟させる[する]，丸くなる ‖ *Experience had mellowed her views about many things.* 経験によって多くの事柄について彼女の考え方は円熟した．

**melodrama** /mélədrɑ̀ːmə/ 名 ❻ ❿ ▶定義 a story, play or film in which a lot of exciting things happen and in which people's emotions are stronger than in real life 感動的な事がたくさん起こり，現実世界よりも感情的に激しい人物たちが登場するような物語，劇，または映画➡メロドラマ

**melodramatic** /mèlədrəmǽtɪk/ 形 ▶定義 (used about a person's behaviour) making things seem more exciting or serious than they really are (人の行動について) 実際よりも物事をより感動的または深刻に見せるような➡メロドラマ風の，芝居がかった，感傷的でおおげさな ‖ *Don't be so melodramatic, Simon - of course you're not going to die!* そんなにひどく感傷的になるなよ，サイモン—もちろん君が死ぬわけではない．

**melody** /mélədi/ 名 ❻ (複 **melodies**) ▶定義 a song or tune; the main tune of a piece of music 歌または旋律；曲の主な節➡(主)旋律，メロディー

**melon** /mélən/ 名 ❻ ❿ ▶定義 a large roundish fruit with a thick yellow or green skin and a lot of seeds 濃い黄色または緑色の皮が付いている，種がたくさん入った大きな丸みを帯びた果物➡メロン ☛ C3ページのさし絵

\***melt** /melt/ 動 ▶定義 1 自 他 to change or make sth change from a solid to a liquid by means of heat 熱によって固体から液体に変わる，または〜を変える➡溶ける[かす]，解ける[かす]，溶解する ‖ *When we got up in the morning the snow had melted.* 朝起きた時，雪は解けていた．*First melt the butter in a saucepan.* まずシチューなべでバターを溶かしなさい．☛参 thaw ▶定義 2 自 (used about sb's feelings, etc) to become softer or less strong (〜の感情などについて) 柔らかくなる，または激しさがなくなる➡和らぐ，優しくなる ‖ *My heart melted when I saw the baby.* 赤ん坊を見た時，私の心は和らいだ．

句動詞 **melt away** ▶定義 to disappear 消える➡消えてなくなる，溶けて消える ‖ *The crowd slowly* melted away when the speaker had finished. 演説が終わると, 群衆は次第に消えていった.

**melt sth down** ▶定義 to heat a metal or glass object until it becomes liquid 金属またはガラス物体を液体になるまで熱する➡~を溶かす, 鋳潰(つぶ)す

**melting pot** 名 C ▶定義 a place where a lot of different cultures, ideas, etc come together 多くの異なる文化, 思想などが1箇所に集まる場所➡多様な人種や階層の入り交じった国・都市, るつぼ ‖ *New York is a melting pot of different cultures.* ニューヨークはさまざまな文化のるつぼだ.

***member** /mémbər/ 名 C ▶定義 a person, animal or thing that belongs to a group, club, organization, etc ある集団, クラブ, 組織などに属する人, 動物, または物➡一員, メンバー ‖ *All the members of the family were there.* 家族の全員がそこにいた. *to become a member of a club* クラブの一員になる *a member of staff* 職員の一員

**Member of Parliament** 名 C (略 MP) ▶定義 a person who has been elected to represent people from a particular area in Parliament 議会での人々の代表として特定の地域から選出された人➡国会議員, 下院議員 ‖ *the MP for Oxford East* オックスフォード東部選出の下院議員

**membership** /mémbərʃɪp/ 名 ▶定義 1 ❶ the state of being a member of a group, organization, etc ある集団, 組織などの一員である状態➡ **会員であること, 会員の地位** ‖ *To apply for membership, please fill in the enclosed form.* 会員の申し込みをするには, 同封した用紙に記入してください. *a membership card/fee* 会員証・会費 ▶定義 2 C U the people who belong to a group, organization, etc ある集団, 組織などに属する人々➡**会員, 成員** ‖ *Membership has fallen in the past year (= the number of members).* この1年で会員(= 会員の数)が減った.

**membrane** /mémbreɪn/ 名 C ▶定義 a thin skin which covers certain parts of a person's or an animal's body 人または動物の体の特定の部分を覆う薄い皮➡膜

**memento** /məméntoʊ/ 名 C (複 **mementoes**; **mementos**) ▶定義 something that you keep to remind you of sb/sth ~のことを覚えておくために取っておくもの➡思い出になるもの, 記念品, 形見

**memo** /mémoʊ/ 名 C (複 **memos**) (または 正式 **memorandum**) a note sent from one person or office to another within an organization 組織で, 1人の人またはある事務所からほかへ送られる短い手紙➡メモ, 覚え書き ☞ S4ページのさし絵

**memoirs** /mémwɑːrz/ 名 [複数扱い] ▶定義 a person's written account of his/her own life and experiences; autobiography ある人の人生や経験についての記述; 自伝➡伝記, 体験記, 回顧録, 自伝

**memorabilia** /mèm(ə)rəbíliə, -bíːliə, -ljə/ 名 U ▶定義 things that people buy because they are connected with a famous person, event, etc 有名な人, 出来事などに関係があるために人々が買うもの➡記念品[物], 遺産 ‖ *Beatles/Titanic/war memorabilia* ビートルズ・タイタニック号・戦争にゆかりのある品

**memorable** /mém(ə)rəb(ə)l/ 形 ▶定義 worth remembering or easy to remember 覚えておく価値のある, または覚えておくのが容易な➡記憶すべき, 覚えやすい ‖ *The concert was a memorable experience.* そのコンサートは忘れ難い体験だった. — **memorably** 副 ➡記憶に残るように, はっきりと

**memorandum** /mèməréndəm/ (複 **memoranda** /mèməréndə/) 正式 = MEMO

**memorial** /məmɔ́ːriəl/ 名 C ▶定義 **a memorial (to sb/sth)** something that is built or done to remind people of an event or a person 人々にある出来事またはある人のことを思い出させるために建てられるまたは行われるもの➡記念物, 記念碑[館], 記念行事[祭] ‖ *a memorial to the victims of the bombing* 爆撃の犠牲者の慰霊碑 *a war memorial* 戦争記念碑 *a memorial service* 追悼式

**memorize** (または **-ise**) /méməraɪz/ 動 他 ▶定義 to learn sth so that you can remember it exactly 正確に覚えておけるように~について覚える➡~を記憶する, 暗記する ‖ *Actors have to memorize their lines.* 俳優たちは自分の台詞(せりふ)を覚えなければならない.

***memory** /mém(ə)ri/ 名 (複 **memories**) ▶定義 1 C a person's ability to remember things ものを覚えておく人の能力➡記憶力, 覚えていること ‖ *to have a good/bad memory* 記憶力が良い・悪い *The drug can affect your short-term memory.* そ

の薬は短期記憶に影響することがある. ▶定義2 ❻ ❶the part of your mind in which you store things that you remember 覚えている事を保存しておく頭の部分→記憶‖ *That day remained firmly in my memory for the rest of my life.* その日のことは生涯はっきりと記憶の中にあった. *Are you going to do your speech from memory, or are you going to use notes?* あなたは暗記して演説を行うつもりですか, それともメモを使いますか. ▶定義3 ❻something that you remember 覚えている事柄→思い出, 追憶‖ *That is one of my happiest memories.* それは私の最も幸せな思い出の1つだ. *childhood memories* 子供時代の思い出 ▶定義4 ❻ ❶the part of a computer where information is stored 情報が格納されているコンピューターの部分→記憶容量‖ *This computer has a 640k memory/640k of memory.* このコンピューターには640キロの記憶容量がある. 成句 in memory of sb ▶定義 in order to remind people of sb who has died 人々に死んだ〜を思い出させるために→〜を記念して, しのんで‖ *A service was held in memory of the dead.* 死者をしのんで礼拝が行われた.

jog sb's memory ⇒ **JOG**¹
refresh your memory ⇒ **REFRESH**

**men** **MAN**¹ の複数形

**menace** /ménəs/ ▶定義1 ❻ a menace (to sb/sth) a danger or threat 危険または脅かすもの→脅威‖ *The new road is a menace to everyone's safety.* 新しい道路は皆の安全を脅かしている. ▶定義2 ❶ a quality, feeling, etc that is threatening or frightening 脅かすまたは怖がらせるような性質, 感情など→脅迫, 脅し‖ *He spoke with menace in his voice.* 彼は脅かすような口調で話した. ▶定義3 ❻ a person or thing that causes trouble 問題を引き起こす人またはもの→厄介者・事 — menace 動 ⊕ →脅す, 脅迫する — menacing 形 →脅かすような, 脅迫的な, 荒れ模様の

★**mend**¹ /mend/ 動 ⊕ ▶定義 to repair sth that is damaged or broken 傷んだまたは壊れた〜を修理する→直す, 修繕する, 繕う‖ *Can you mend the hole in this jumper for me?* 私のためにこのセーターの穴を繕ってもらえませんか. ☛類 **repair**

**mend**² /mend/
成句 be on the mend 略式 ▶定義 to be getting better after an illness or injury 病気がけがの後で良くなっている→良くなってくる‖ *She's been in bed for a week but she's on the mend now.* 彼女は1週間床に就いていたが, 今良くなってきている.

**menial** /míːniəl/ 形 ▶定義 (used about work) not skilled or important (仕事について) 技能のない, または重要でない→熟練の要らない, つまらない‖ *a menial job* つまらない仕事

**meningitis** /mènəndʒáitəs/ 名 ❶ ▶定義 a dangerous illness which affects the brain and the inside of the bones in your back (the spinal cord) 脳や背中の骨の内側 (脊髄) を侵す危険な病気→髄[脳]膜炎

**the menopause** /ménəpɔːz, míː-/ 名 [単数扱い] ▶定義 the time when a woman stops losing blood once a month (menstruating) and can no longer have children. This usually happens around the age of 50. 女性の月に1度の出血がなくなり, もう子供を産めなくなるとき. 通常50歳前後で起こる→更年期, 閉経期

**menstruate** /ménstruèit/ 動 ⊜ 正式 ▶定義 (used about women) to lose blood once a month from the part of the body where a baby would develop (the womb) (女性について) 赤ん坊が発育する体の部分 (子宮) から月に1度出血する→生理・月経がある ☛ これよりも略式の表現に have a period がある. — menstruation /mènstruéiʃ(ə)n/ 名 ❶ →生理 (期間), 月経 (期間)

★**mental** /méntl/ 形 (名詞の前だけ) ▶定義1 of or in the mind; involving the process of thinking 心の, または心で; 考える過程に関する→心の, 精神の‖ *It's fascinating to watch a child's mental development.* 子供の心の発達を見るのはすばらしい. *mental arithmetic (= calculations done in your head)* 暗算 (= 頭の中で行う計算) ▶定義2 connected with illness of the mind 心の病気に関連した→精神病の, 精神を扱う‖ *a mental illness/hospital* 精神病・病院 — **mentally** /méntli/ 副 →精神的に‖ *She's mentally ill.* 彼女は精神的に病んでいる.

**mentality** /mentǽləti/ 名 ❻ ( 複 **mentalities**) ▶定義 a type of mind or way of thinking 精神の類型, または考え方→精神性, 心理状態, 考え方‖ *I just can't understand his mentality!* 私には彼の

考え方が全く理解できない. *the criminal mentality* 犯罪心理

\***mention** /ménʃ(ə)n/ 動他 ▶定義 to say or write sth about sb/sth without giving much information 多くの情報を与えることなく〜について…を言うまたは書く→〜に言及する,話に出す,〜の名を挙げる ‖ *He mentioned (to me) that he might be late.* 彼は遅れるかもしれないと(私に)言った. *Did she mention what time the film starts?* 彼女は,映画が何時に始まるか言っていましたか.

成句 don't mention it ▶定義 used as a polite reply when sb thanks you for sth 〜から…についてお礼を言われたときの丁寧な答え方→どういたしまして ‖ *'Thank you for all your help.' 'Don't mention it.'* 「いろいろと手伝ってくれてありがとう」「どういたしまして」

not to mention ▶定義 (used to emphasize sth) and also; as well as (〜を強調するために用いて) そしてまた; 〜も同様に→〜はさておき,〜は言うまでもなく ‖ *This is a great habitat for birds, not to mention other wildlife.* ほかの野生生物は言うまでもなく,ここは広大な鳥の生息地だ. ― mention 名 C U →言及,話に出すこと,表彰 ‖ *It was odd that there wasn't even a mention of the riots in the newspaper.* 暴動について新聞で触れられてさえいなかったのは奇妙だった.

\***menu** /ménjuː/ 名 C ▶定義 **1** a list of the food that you can choose at a restaurant レストランで選べる食べ物の一覧→メニュー,献立表,料理 ‖ *I hope there's soup on the menu.* メニューにスープがあると良いと思う. *They do a special lunchtime menu here.* ここには昼食時の特別料理がある. ▶定義 **2** a list of choices in a computer program which is shown on the screen 画面上に表示されるコンピュータープログラムの選択肢の一覧→メニュー ‖ *a pull-down menu* プルダウンメニュー ☞ S5 ページのさし絵

**MEP** /èm iː píː/ 略 Member of the European parliament→欧州議会議員

**mercenary**¹ /mə́ːrs(ə)n(ə)ri; -nèri/ 形 ▶定義 interested only in making money お金を稼ぐことだけに興味のある→欲得ずくの,報酬目当ての ‖ *His motives are entirely mercenary.* 彼の動機は完全に報酬目当てだ.

**mercenary**² /mə́ːrs(ə)n(ə)ri; -nèri/ 名 C (複 **mercenaries**) ▶定義 a soldier who fights for any group or country that will pay him/her お金を支払ってくれる集団または国のために戦う兵士→傭(よう)兵,雇い兵

**merchandise** /mə́ːrtʃ(ə)ndàɪz, -s/ 名 U 正式 ▶定義 goods that are for sale 販売されている製品→商品

**merchant** /mə́ːrtʃ(ə)nt/ 名 C ▶定義 a person whose job is to buy and sell goods, usually of one particular type, in large amounts 通常ある特定の種類の商品を大量に売買することを仕事にする人→商人

**the merchant navy** 名 [C, 単数または複数形の動詞と共に] ▶定義 a country's commercial ships and the people who work on them 国の商船およびその船上で働く人々→(国の)全商船,商船の船員(全体)

**merciful** /mə́ːrsɪf(ə)l/ 形 ▶定義 feeling or showing mercy 慈悲を感じることまたは示すこと→慈悲深い,情け深い ‖ *His death was a merciful release from pain.* 彼の死は神のおぼしめしによる痛みからの解放だった. ― **mercifully** 副 →慈悲深く,情け深く

**merciless** /mə́ːrsɪləs/ 形 ▶定義 showing no mercy 慈悲を示さないような→無慈悲な,無情な ― **mercilessly** 副 →無慈悲に,冷酷に

**Mercury**¹ /mə́ːrkjəri/ 名 [単数扱い] ▶定義 the planet that is nearest to the sun 太陽に最も近い惑星→水星

**mercury**² /mə́ːrkjəri/ 名 U (元素記号 **Hg**) ▶定義 a heavy silver-coloured metal that is usually in liquid form. Mercury is used in instruments that measure temperature (**thermometers**). 通常液状で銀色をした重金属. 温度を計る器具(温度計)に使われている→水銀

\***mercy** /mə́ːrsi/ 名 U ▶定義 kindness shown by sb/sth who has the power to make sb suffer 〜に刑罰を与える権力を持つ…によって示される親切心→慈悲,哀れみ ‖ *The rebels were shown no mercy. They were taken out and shot.* 反逆者たちには何の慈悲もかけられなかった. 彼らは連行され,射殺された.

成句 at the mercy of sb/sth ▶定義 having no power against sb/sth that is strong 強い〜に対して何の力も持たないで→〜のなすがままに(なって),〜に支配されて ‖ *The climbers spent the night on the mountain at the mercy of the wind and rain.* 登山者たちは風と雨のため山で夜を過ごすことを余儀なくされた.

**\*mere** /míər/ 形 (名詞の前だけ) ▶定義1 (used for emphasizing how small or unimportant sth is) nothing more than (〜がいかに小さいかまたはつまらない事かを強調するために用いて) 〜にすぎない→**ほんの, ただの, 全く〜にすぎない** ‖ *90% of the country's land is owned by a mere 2% of the population.* 国土の90パーセントが人口のわずか2パーセントによって所有されている. ▶定義2 used to say that just the fact that sb/sth is present in a situation is enough to have an influence ある状況に〜があるという事実だけで十分に影響力を持つと述べるのに用いて→**〜だけで** ‖ *The mere thought of giving a speech in public makes me feel sick.* 人前でスピーチをすると考えただけで, 私は気分が悪くなる.

成句 the merest ▶定義 even a very small amount of sth 非常に少量の〜でも→**ほんのささいな** ‖ *The merest smell of the fish market made her feel ill.* かすかに魚市場のにおいがしただけで彼女は気分が悪くなった.

**merely** /míərli/ 副 正式 ▶定義 only; just ただの; 〜だけ→**単に〜だけ, わずかに〜しか** ‖ *I don't want to place an order. I am merely making an enquiry.* 私は注文をしたいのではありません. 問い合わせをしているだけです.

**merge** /mɚːdʒ/ 動 ▶定義1 ⓘmerge (with/into sth); merge (together) to become part of sth larger より大きな〜の一部になる→**合併する, 合流する, 合わさる** ‖ *Three small companies merged into one large one.* 3つの小さな会社が合併して1つの大きな会社になった. *This stream merges with the river a few miles downstream.* 数マイル下流で, この流れはその川に合流する. ▶定義2 ⓗto join things together so that they become one 複数のものをまとめて1つにする→**〜を併合する, 合併する** ‖ *We have merged the two classes into one.* 私たちは2つの学級を併合して1つにした.

**merger** /mɚːdʒɚ/ 名 ⓒⓤ ▶定義 a merger (with sb/sth); a merger (between/of A and B) the act of joining two or more companies together 2つ以上の会社を1つにする行為→**合併, 合同**

**meridian** /mərídiən/ 名 ⓒ ▶定義 a line that we imagine on the surface of the earth that joins the North Pole to the South Pole and passes through a particular place 北極と南極を結んで特定の場所を通過するような地球の表面に引いた仮想の線→**経線, 子午線** ‖ *the Greenwich meridian* グリニッジ子午線 ☞参 longitude

**meringue** /məræŋ/ 名 ⓒⓤ ▶定義 a mixture of sugar and egg whites that is cooked in the oven; a cake made from this 砂糖と卵の白みを混ぜてオーブンで焼いた物; これから作られるケーキ→**メレンゲ, メレンゲ菓子**

**merit**¹ /mérət/ 名 ▶定義1 ⓤ the quality of being good 良い性質→**長所, 取り柄, 価値** ‖ *There is a lot of merit in her ideas.* 彼女の案には多くの長所がある. *He got the job on merit, not because he's the manager's son.* 彼は自分の実力でその仕事を得たのだ, 彼が部長の息子だからではない. ▶定義2 [ⓒ, 通常は複数]an advantage or a good quality of sb/sth 〜の利点または良い性質→**真価, 功績** ‖ *Each case must be judged separately on its own merits (= not according to general principles).* 各問題は別々にそれぞれの真価によって(=一般的な原則に従ってではなく)判断されなければならない.

**merit**² /mérət/ 動 ⓗ 正式 ▶定義 to be good enough for sth; to deserve 〜に十分良い; 値する→**〜に値する** ‖ *This suggestion merits further discussion.* この提案はさらに話し合いをする価値がある.

**mermaid** /mɚːmèɪd/ 名 ⓒ ▶定義 (in stories) a woman who has the tail of a fish instead of legs and who lives in the sea(物語で) 足の代わりにしっぽがあり, 海の中に住む女性→**人魚**

**merriment** /mérimənt/ 名 ⓤ ▶定義 laughter and enjoyment 笑い声および楽しむこと→**笑い(声), 楽しさ, 陽気な騒ぎ**

**merry** /méri/ 形 (**merrier**; **merriest**) ▶定義1 happy 幸せな→**陽気な, うきうきした** ‖ *merry laughter* 陽気な笑い声 *Merry Christmas (= used to say you hope sb has a happy holiday)* メリークリスマス(=〜が楽しいクリスマス休日を過ごすようにと願うときに用いる) ▶定義2 略式 slightly drunk わずかに酔った→**ほろ酔い(気分)で** —**merrily** 副→**陽気に, 楽しく, 愉快に**

**merry-go-round** (英 **roundabout** 米 **carousel**) 名 C ▶定義 a big round platform that turns round and round and has model animals, etc on it for children to ride on ぐるぐると回る大きな円い舞台で、その上に子供たちが乗る動物などの模型が置かれている→回転木馬, メリーゴーラウンド

**mesh** /meʃ/ 名 C U ▶定義 material that is like a net (= made of plastic, wire or rope threads with holes in between) 網のような素材(= ビニール, 針金, または縄糸を材料に, 間に穴をあけて作った物)→網(状の物) ‖ *a fence made of wire mesh* 金網でできた囲い

**mesmerize** /mézmərὰɪz/(または **-ise**) 動 他 ▶定義 to hold sb's attention completely ～の注意を完全にひく→～の目を奪う, ～を魅了する ‖ *The audience seemed to be mesmerized by the speaker's voice.* 聴衆は演説者の声に魅了されたようだった.

*****mess**¹ /mes/ 名 ▶定義 1 [ C, 通常は単数] the state of being dirty or untidy; a person or thing that is dirty or untidy 汚れているまたはだらしない状態; 汚れているまたはだらしない人や物→取り散らかした状態・物, 乱雑, だらしない人 ‖ *The kitchen's in a terrible mess!* 台所がひどく散らかっている. *My hair is a mess.* 私の髪はぼさぼさだ. *You can paint the door, but don't make a mess!* 扉にペンキを塗ってもいいけど, 失敗しないでよ. ▶定義 2 [単数扱い]the state of having problems or troubles 問題または困難を抱えている状態→困難, 困窮, 困った立場 ‖ *The company is in a financial mess.* その会社は財政が悪化している. *to make a mess of your life* 一生を台なしにする

**mess**² /mes/ 動 他 米略式 ▶定義 to make sth dirty or untidy ～を汚すまたはだらしなくする→～を汚す, 散らかす ‖ *Don't mess your hands.* 手を汚すな.

句動詞 mess about/around ▶定義 1 to behave in a silly and annoying way ばかげたあるいは迷惑な行動を取る→ばかげた事をする ▶定義 2 to spend your time in a relaxed way without any real purpose これといった目的もなく, くつろいで時間を過ごす→ぶらぶら暮らす, うろうろする ‖ *We spent Sunday just messing around at home.* 私たちは日曜日にはただ家でぶらぶらして過ごした.

mess sb about/around ▶定義 to treat sb in a way that is not fair or reasonable, for example by changing your plans without telling him/her 不公平なやり方あるいは筋の通ってない方法で～を扱う, 例えばその～に告げずに計画を変更するなど→～を乱暴に扱う, ～をいいかげんに扱う, ひどい目に遭わせる

mess about/around with sth ▶定義 to touch or use sth in a careless way 不注意に～に触れるまたは～を使う→いじくり回す ‖ *It is dangerous to mess about with fireworks.* 花火をいじくり回すのは危険だ.

mess sth up ▶定義 1 to make sth dirty or untidy ～を汚すまたは乱雑にする→取り散らかす, 汚す ▶定義 2 to do sth badly or spoil sth ～を駄目にするまたは台なしにする→台なしにする ‖ *I really messed up the last question in the exam.* 私は試験の最後の問題で全くへまをしてしまった.

mess with sb/sth ▶定義 to deal or behave with sb/sth in a way that you should not すべきではない方法で, ～を扱うまたは～に対して振る舞う→～に手を出す, 首を突っ込む ‖ *You shouldn't mess with people's feelings.* あなたは人の考えに干渉すべきではない.

*****message** /mésɪdʒ/ 名 ▶定義 1 C a written or spoken piece of information that you send to or leave for a person when you cannot speak to him/her 人と直接話ができないときにその人に送るまたは残す, 書面でまたは口頭での情報→伝言, 言付け, 言づて ‖ *Mr Khan is not here at the moment. Can I take a message?* カーン氏は今ここにはいません. 伝言を承りましょうか. *Could you give a message to Jake, please?* ジェークに伝言をしていただけないでしょうか. *If he's not in I'll leave a message on his answering machine.* 彼がいない場合は, 留守番電話に伝言を残します. ▶定義 2 [単数扱い]an important idea that a book, speech, etc is trying to communicate 本, 演説などが伝えようとしている重要な考え→主張, ねらい, 訴え ‖ *It was a funny film but it also had a serious message.* それはこっけいな映画だったが, 真剣な意図を伝えていた. *The advertising campaign is trying to get the message across that smoking kills.* その広告キャンペーンは喫煙による死を広く訴え

ようとしている.

**成句 get the message** 略式 ▶定義 to understand what sb means even if it is not clearly stated はっきりと述べられていなくても〜が意味するところを理解する→意をくみ取る, 本音を知る ‖ *He finally got the message and went home.* 彼はやっと意をくみ取って, 家に帰った.

**messenger** /més(ə)ndʒər/ 名 C ▶定義 a person who carries a message 伝言を運ぶ人→使者, 使いの者

**Messiah**（または **messiah**）/məsáɪə/ 名 C ▶定義 a person, for example Jesus Christ, who is expected to come and save the world 世界を救うために現れると待望されている人, 例えばイエスキリスト→救世主, メシア

**messy** /mési/ 形 (**messier**; **messiest**) ▶定義 1 dirty or untidy 汚れた, またはだらしない→取り散らかした, むさ苦しい ‖ *a messy room* 散らかった部屋 ▶定義 2 that makes sb/sth dirty 〜を汚すような→手の汚れる, 汚い ‖ *Painting the ceiling is a messy job.* 天井の塗装は手の汚れる仕事だ. ▶定義 3 having or causing problems or trouble 問題または困難を抱えた, または引き起こすような→厄介な ‖ *a messy divorce* 面倒な離婚

**met** MEET の過去形

\***metal** /métl/ 名 C U ▶定義 a type of solid substance that is usually hard and shiny and that heat and electricity can travel through 通常固く光沢があり, 硬質の物質の一種類で, 熱や電気を伝えることができる→金属 ‖ *metals such as tin, iron, gold and steel* スズ, 鉄, 金, 鋼鉄のような金属 *to recycle scrap metal* 鉄くずを再利用する *a metal bar/pipe* 金属の棒・パイプ

**metallic** /mətǽlɪk/ 形 ▶定義 looking like metal or making a noise like one piece of metal hitting another 金属のように見える, または1つの金属片が別の金属にぶつかるときのような音を立てる→金属の, 金属的な ‖ *a metallic blue car* メタリックブルーの車 *harsh metallic sounds* 耳障りな金属音

**metamorphosis** /mètəmɔ́ːrfəsəs/ 名 C (複)
**metamorphoses** /-sìːz/ 正式 ▶定義 a complete change of form (as part of natural development) （自然な発育の一部として）形が完全に変化すること→変態 ‖ *the metamorphosis of a tadpole into a frog* オタマジャクシのカエルへの変態

**metaphor** /métəfər, -fɔːr/ 名 C U ▶定義 a word or phrase that is used in an imaginative way to show that sb/sth has the same qualities as another thing. 'Her words were a knife in her heart' is a metaphor. 〜がほかのものと同じ本質を持つことを, 想像力を働かせて表すときに用いる言葉や語句.「彼女の言葉は, 彼の心をナイフのように突き刺した」は比喩→比喩 ☞参 figurative, literal ― **metaphorical** /mètəfɔ́(ː)rɪk(ə)l/ 形→比喩的な, 隠喩的な ― **metaphorically** /-k(ə)li/ 副→比喩的に, 隠喩で

**meteor** /míːtɪər, -ɔːr/ 名 C ▶定義 a small piece of rock, etc in space. When a meteor enters the earth's atmosphere it makes a bright line in the night sky. 宇宙の岩の小さなかけらなど. 地球の大気圏に突入する際に夜空に明るい線を描く→いん石, 流星

**meteoric** /mìːtiɔ́(ː)rɪk, -ár-/ 形 ▶定義 very fast or successful 非常に速いまたは成功した→流星のような, (一時的に)華々しい, 急速の ‖ *a meteoric rise to fame* 華々しく出世して名声を得ること

**meteorologist** /mìːtiərálədʒɪst/ 名 C ▶定義 a person who studies the weather 天気について研究する人→気象学者

**meteorology** /mìːtiərálədʒi/ 名 U ▶定義 the study of the weather and climate 気象と気候の研究→気象学 ― **meteorological** 形→気象(学上)の

**meter** /míːtər/ 名 C ▶定義 1 a piece of equipment that measures the amount of gas, water, electricity, etc you have used 使用したガス, 水, 電気などの量を計る器具→メーター, 計量器 ‖ *a parking meter* 駐車メーター ▶定義 2 米 =METRE ― **meter** 動 他→メーターで計る ‖ *Is your water metered?* あなたの水道使用量の検針は行われましたか.

\***method** /méθəd/ 名 C ▶定義 a way of doing sth 〜を行う方法→方法, 方式 ‖ *What method of payment do you prefer? Cash, cheque or credit card?* お支払い方法は何がご希望でしょうか. 現金, 小切手, それともカードになさいますか. *modern teaching methods* 現代の教授法

**methodical** /məθádɪk(ə)l/ 形 ▶定義 having or using a well-organized and careful way of doing sth 〜をするのに, 十分な段取りをして慎

重な方法で行う, またはそのような方法を用いる→**整然とした, 組織的な, きちょうめんな** ‖ *Paul is a very methodical worker.* ポールは非常にきちょうめんな仕事をする. — methodically /-k(ə)li/ 副 →**整然と, 組織的に**

**methodology** /mèθədálədʒi/ (複**methodologies**) 名 ● ▶定義 a way of doing sth based on particular principles and methods 特定の原則や方法にのっとって〜を行うやり方→**方法論, 方式, 方法** ‖ *language teaching methodologies* 言語教授の方法 — methodological /mèθədəláːdʒɪk(ə)l/ 形→**方法論的な**

**meticulous** /mətíkjələs/ 形 ▶定義 giving or showing great attention to detail; very careful 細かいところまで細心の注意を払うまたは示すような; 非常に注意深い→**細かい事に気を遣う, きちょうめんな** — meticulously 副→**細心に, こせこせと**

*****metre** (米**meter**) /míːtər/ 名 ● (略**m**) ▶定義 a measure of length; 100 centimetres 長さの単位; 100センチメートル→**メートル** ‖ *a two-metre high wall* 高さ2メートルの塀 *Who won the 100 metres?* だれが100メートル走で勝ったの.

**metric** /métrɪk/ ▶定義 using the system of measurement that is based on metres, grams, litres, etc (**the metric system**) メートル, グラム, リットルなどに基づいた測定方式(メートル法)を用いた→**メートル法の** ☞参 **imperial**

**metropolis** /mətrɑ́p(ə)ləs/ 名 ● ▶定義 a very large city 非常に大きな都市→**大都市, 首都** — metropolitan /mètrəpɑ́lət(ə)n/ 形→**大都市の, 首都の**

**mg** 略 milligram(s) →**ミリグラム**

**MHz** /méɡəhə̀ːrts/ 略 megahertz ▶定義 (used in radio) a measure of frequency (無線で使用して)周波数の単位→**メガヘルツ**

**miaow** /miáu/ 名 ● ▶定義 the sound that a cat makes 猫が出す声→**にゃあ** — miaow 動 ●→**にゃあと鳴く** ☞参 **purr**

**mice** MOUSE の複数形

**microchip** /máɪkroʊtʃɪp, máɪkrə-/ (または **chip**) 名 ● ▶定義 a very small piece of a special material (silicon) that is used inside a computer, etc to make it work コンピューターなどの内部で作動させるために使われている特別な素材(シリコン)でできた非常に小さな物→**マイクロチップ**

**microcosm** /máɪkrəkɑ̀z(ə)m/ 名 ● ▶定義 a microcosm (of sth) something that is a small example of sth larger 大きな〜の縮小版→**縮図, 小宇宙** ‖ *Our little village is a microcosm of society as a whole.* 私たちの小さな村は社会全体の縮図である.

**microphone** /máɪkrəfòʊn/ (または 略式 **mike**) 名 ● ▶定義 a piece of electrical equipment that is used for making sounds louder or for recording them 音を大きくするためまたは録音するために用いられる電気装置→**マイク, マイクロホン**

**microscope** /máɪkrəskòʊp/ 名 ● ▶定義 a piece of equipment that makes very small objects look big enough for you to be able to see them 非常に小さな対象物を調べることができるまで十分に大きく見せる装置→**顕微鏡** ‖ *to examine sth under a microscope* 〜を顕微鏡で検査する

**microscopic** /màɪkrəskɑ́pɪk/ 形 ▶定義 too small to be seen without a microscope 顕微鏡なしで見るには小さすぎる→**顕微鏡でしか見えない, 微小の**

**microwave** /màɪkrəwéɪv/ 名 ● ▶定義 **1** a short electric wave that is used for sending radio messages and for cooking food 無線通信を送ったり食べ物を調理したりするのに使われる短い電波→**極超短波, マイクロ波** ▶定義 **2** (または **microwave oven**) a type of oven that cooks or heats food very quickly using microwaves マイクロ波を用いて食べ物を非常に素早く調理したり温めたりするオーブンの一種→**電子レンジ**

**mid** /mɪd/ 形 (名詞の前だけ) ▶定義 **1** the middle of 〜の真ん中の→**中央の, 中間の** ‖ *I'm away from mid June.* 私は6月中旬から留守をします. *the mid 1990s* 1990年代半ば ▶定義 **2** **mid-** (複合形容詞を作るために用いて) in the middle of 〜の真ん中の→**中央の, 中間の** ‖ *a mid-air collision* 空中衝突

*****midday** /míddèɪ/ 名 ● ▶定義 at or around twelve o'clock in the middle of the day; noon 1日の真ん中の12時前後; 真昼→**正午, 真昼** ‖ *We arranged to meet at midday.* 私たちは正午に会う約束をした. *the heat of the midday sun* 真昼の太陽の熱 ☞参 **midnight**

*****middle**¹ /mídl/ 名 ▶定義 **1** [単数扱い] **the middle (of sth)** the part, point or position that is at about the same distance from the two ends or sides of sth ～の両端または両側からほぼ同じ距離にある部分, 点, または位置→**真ん中, 中央, 中間** ‖ the white line **in the middle of** the road 道路中央の白線 Here's a photo of me with my two brothers. I'm the one **in the middle**. これは私と私の2人の兄弟が写っている写真です. 真ん中にいるのが私です.

➤ centreとmiddleは非常に似ている意味で使われることが多いが, centreは何かの正確な中心を意味するときに用いられる: *How do you find the centre of a circle?* (円の中心をどのようにして見つけますか.) *There was a large table in the middle of the room.* (部屋の真ん中に大きなテーブルがあった.) *The bee stung me **right in the middle** of my back.* (ハチは私の背中のちょうど真ん中を刺した.) ある期間に関して述べるときにはmiddleだけが用いられる: *in the middle of the night* (真夜中) *the middle of July* (7月中旬)

▶定義2 ●略式 your waist ウエスト→**胴, ウエスト** ‖ *I want to lose weight around my middle*. 私はウエスト回りを細くしたい.

成句 **be in the middle of sth/doing sth**
▶定義 to be busy doing sth ～をするのに忙しい→**～の最中に, している最中に** ‖ *Can you call back in five minutes? - I'm in the middle of feeding the baby.* 5分後に電話をかけ直してもらえますか — 赤ん坊に授乳中なので.

**in the middle of nowhere** ▶定義 a long way from any town どの町からも遠い→**どこからも遠い所に, 何もない所に**

**middle²** /mídl/ 形(名詞の前だけ) ▶定義 in the middle 真ん中の→**真ん中の, 中央の, 中間の** ‖ *I wear my ring on my middle finger.* 私は中指に指輪をしている.

**middle age** 名 Ｕ ▶定義 the time when you are about 40 to 60 years old およそ40歳から60歳の年齢層→**中年, 初老** ‖ *in late middle age* 中老の — **middle-aged** 形→**中年の** ‖ *a middle-aged man* 中年の男性

**the Middle Ages** 名[複数扱い] ▶定義 the period of European history from about 1100 to 1500 AD 紀元後約1100年から1500年ころのヨーロッパ史の期間→**中世**

**the Middle East** 名[単数扱い] ▶定義 the part of the world between Egypt and Pakistan エジプトとパキスタンの間の地域→**中東, 中近東**

**middleman** /mídlmæn/ 名 Ｃ (複 **-men** /-men/)
▶定義1 a person or company who buys goods from the company that makes them and then sells them to sb else 製品を製造する会社から買ってほかの～に売る人または会社→**仲買人, 中間商人** ▶定義2 a person who helps to arrange things between two people who do not want to meet each other 互いに会いたくないと思っている2人の間で, 物事の調整の手助けをする人→**仲介者, 仲裁者**

**middle school** 名 Ｃ 米 ▶定義 a school for children aged between nine and thirteen 9歳から13歳の子供たちの学校→**中等学校, 中間学校, ミドルスクール**

**midge** /mɪdʒ/ 名 Ｃ ▶定義 a very small flying insect that can bite people 人を刺すことがある非常に小さな飛ぶ虫→**小昆虫(蚊・ブヨなど)**
☛類 gnat

**midget** /mídʒət/ 名 Ｃ ▶定義 a very small person 非常に小柄な人→**小人** ● 侮辱的な言葉として取られることがあるので注意すること.

**the Midlands** /mídləndz, -lændz/ 名[単数扱い, 単数または複数形の動詞と共に] ▶定義 the central part of England around Birmingham and Nottingham イングランドの中部でバーミンガムおよびノッティンガム辺り→**イングランドの中部地方**

\***midnight** /mídnaɪt/ 名 Ｕ ▶定義 twelve o'clock at night 夜の12時→**午前0時** ‖ *They left the party at midnight.* 彼らは午前0時にパーティーを後にした. *The clock struck midnight.* 時計が午前0時を打った. ☛参 midday

**midriff** /mídrɪf/ 名 Ｃ ▶定義 the part of your body between your chest and your waist 体で胸と胴の間の部分→**胴の中央部, 横隔膜**

**midst** /mɪdst, mɪtst/ 名 Ｕ ▶定義 the middle of sth; among a group of people or things ～の真ん中; 人や物の集まりの間→**真ん中, 中央** ‖ *The country is **in the midst of** a recession.* その国は景気後退のさなかにある. *They realized with a shock that there was an enemy **in their midst**.* 彼らは自分たちの内部に敵がいることに気付いて驚いた.

**midway** /mídweɪ, ⌵/ 形副 ▶定義 in the middle

of a period of time or between two places ある期間の，または2つの場所の真ん中の [に] →**中ほどの，中ほどに** ‖ *The village lies midway between two large towns.* その村は2つの大きな町の中間に位置する． ☛類 **halfway**

**midweek** /mídwìːk/ 名 Ü ▶定義 the middle of the week (=Tuesday, Wednesday and Thursday) 週の真ん中 (＝火曜日，水曜日，そして木曜日) →**週の半ば**— **midweek** 副 →**週半ばに** ‖ *If you travel midweek it will be less crowded.* 週の半ばに旅行をすれば，あまり混まないだろう．

**the Midwest** /mìdwést/ 名 [単数扱い] ▶定義 the northern central part of the US 米国中部の北方→**中西部**

**midwife** /mídwàɪf/ 名 C (複 **midwives**/-wàɪvz/) ▶定義 a person who has been trained to help women give birth to babies 女性が子供を産むのを手伝う訓練を受けた人→**助産婦，産婆**

\***might**¹ /máɪt/ 法助動詞(否定形 **might not**; 短縮形 **mightn't** /máɪtnt/) ▶定義 **1** used for saying that sth is possible 〜が可能であることを述べるために用いて→**〜かもしれない，多分〜だろう** ‖ *'Where's Vinay?' 'He might be upstairs.'*「ビネイはどこ」「上の階にいるかもしれない」 *I think I might have forgotten the tickets.* チケットを忘れたかもしれない． *She might not come if she's very busy.* 彼女は非常に忙しければ，多分来ないだろう． ▶定義 **2** 英 正式 used to ask for sth or suggest sth very politely 非常に丁寧に〜を求めるまたは〜を提案するときに用いて→**〜しても差し支えない，〜してもよい** ‖ *I wonder if I might go home half an hour early today?* 今日は30分早く家に帰ってもよろしいでしょうか．
▶定義 **3** used as the form of 'may' when you report what sb has said 〜が述べたことをあなたが報告するときに may の変化形として用いて→**〜かもしれない** ‖ *He said he might be late (= his words were, 'I may be late').* 彼は遅れるかもしれないと言っていた．(＝彼の述べた言葉は「僕は遅れるかもしれない」だった．)

▶法助動詞についての説明は，巻末の「文法早見表」を参照．

成句 **may/might as well (do sth)** ⇒ **WELL**¹
**you, etc might do sth** ▶定義 used when you are angry to say what sb could or should have done 〜ができたはずの，またはすべきだったことを怒って述べるときに用いて→**（〜してくれるつもりか）できるのに，〜してくれてもよいのに** ‖ *They might at least have phoned if they're not coming.* もし来ないのならば，電話くらいしてくれてもよいのに．

**I might have known** ▶定義 used for saying that you are not surprised that sth has happened 〜が起こったことに驚いていないことを述べるときに用いて→**〜だろうとは思っていた** ‖ *I might have known he wouldn't help.* 彼が助けてくれないことは分かっていた．

**might**² /máɪt/ 名 Ü 正式 ▶定義 great strength or power 大きな力または権力→**(大きな)力，権力，腕力** ‖ *I pushed **with all** my might, but the rock did not move.* 私は力一杯押したが，岩は動かなかった．

**mighty**¹ /máɪti/ 形 (**mightier**; **mightiest**) ▶定義 very strong or powerful 非常に強いまたは強力な→**力強い，強力な，強大な**

**mighty**² /máɪti/ 副 米 略式 ▶定義 very 非常に→**すごく，とても** ‖ *That's mighty kind of you.* それはご親切にどうもありがとう．

**migraine** /míːgreɪn; máɪ-/ 名 C Ü ▶定義 very bad pain in your head that makes you feel sick; a severe headache 気分が悪くなるほどのとてもひどい頭痛，激しい頭痛→**偏頭痛**

**migrant** /máɪgrənt/ 名 C ▶定義 a person who goes from place to place looking for work 仕事を探してあちこちに行く人→**移動労働者，季節労働者，移住者**

**migrate** /maɪgréɪt, ́-/ 動 Ï ▶定義 **1** (used about animals and birds) to travel from one part of the world to another at the same time every year (動物と鳥について)毎年同じ時期に，地球のある部分からほかへと移動する→**渡る，定期的に移動する** ▶定義 **2** (used about a large number of people) to go and live and work in another place (大勢の人について)ほかの場所へ行き，暮らし，働く→**移住する，転住する** ‖ *Many country people were forced to migrate to the cities to look for work.* 多くの地方の人々は仕事を求めて都市に移住しなければならなかった． ☛参 **emigrate**— **migration** /maɪgréɪʃ(ə)n/ 名 C Ü →**移住，移動，渡り**

**mike** /máɪk/ 略式 ＝**MICROPHONE**
**milage**＝**MILEAGE**

**\*mild** /máɪld/ 形 ▶定義1 not strong; not very bad 強くない; それほど悪くない→**強くない, 緩い, 軽い** ‖ *a mild soap* 刺激性の少ないせっけん *a mild winter* 穏やかな冬 *a mild punishment* 軽い罰 ▶定義2 (used about food) not having a strong taste (食べ物について) 味が強くない→**甘口の, まろやかな** ‖ *mild cheese* まろやかなチーズ ▶定義3 kind and gentle 親切で優しい→**温厚な, 優しい, おとなしい** ‖ *He's a very mild man - you never see him get angry.* 彼は非常に温厚な男だ — 彼が怒るのをだれも見たことはない. ⇔ **hard** — **mildness** 名 Ｕ→温和, 温厚, 穏やかさ

**mildly** /máɪldli/ 副 ▶定義1 not very; slightly あまり～でない; わずかに→**少し** ‖ *mildly surprised* 少し驚いた ▶定義2 in a gentle way 優しく→**優しく, 控えめに**

**\*mile** /máɪl/ 名 ▶定義1 Ｃa measure of length; 1.6 kilometres. There are 1760 yards in a mile. 長さの単位; 1.6キロメートル. 1マイルは1760ヤード→**マイル** ‖ *The nearest beach is seven miles away.* 最も近い海岸は7マイル離れている. *It's a seven-mile drive to the beach.* 海岸までは7マイルの道のりだ. ▶定義2 Ｃa lot たくさん→**何マイルも, かなりの程度** ‖ *He missed the target by a mile.* 彼は目標を大きく外した. *I'm feeling miles better this morning.* 今朝は気分がかなり良い. ▶定義3 **miles** [複数扱い] a long way 長い道→**かなりの距離** ‖ *How much further is it? We've walked miles already.* それはあとのどのくらい遠いの. 私たちはもうかなりの距離を歩いてきたよ. *From the top of the hill you can see* **for miles**. 丘の頂上からははるかなたまで見渡せる.

成句 **see, hear, tell, spot, etc sb/sth a mile off** 略式 ▶定義 used to say that sb/sth is very obvious ～が非常に明白であることを述べるときに用いて→**簡単に分かる, すぐ分かる** ‖ *He's lying - you can tell that a mile off.* 彼はうそをついている — それは簡単に分かるよ.

**mileage** (または **milage**) /máɪlɪdʒ/ 名 ▶定義1 Ｃ Ｕ the distance that has been travelled, measured in miles マイルで測った, 移動した距離→**総マイル数, 走行距離** ‖ *The car is five years old but it has a low mileage.* その車は5年目だが走行距離は少ない. ▶定義2 Ｕ 略式 the amount of use that you get from sth ～から得る利益の量→**利益, 有用性** ‖ *The newspapers got a lot of mileage out of the scandal.* 新聞はそのスキャンダルで多くの利益を得た.

**milestone** /máɪlstòʊn/ 名 Ｃ ▶定義 a very important event 非常に重要な出来事→**画期的事件** ‖ *The concert was a milestone in the band's history.* そのコンサートはそのバンドの結成以来画期的な出来事だった.

**militant** /mílət(ə)nt/ 形 ▶定義 ready to use force or strong pressure to get what you want 欲しいものを手に入れるために力または強い圧力を今にも使おうとする→**好戦的な, 闘争的な** ‖ *The workers were in a very militant mood.* 労働者たちは非常に闘争的な雰囲気にあった. — **militant** 名 Ｃ→好戦的な人, 闘士 — **militancy** /-(ə)nsi/ 名 Ｕ→好戦的なこと, 交戦状態, 闘士

**\*military** /mílət(ə)ri, -tèri/ 形 (名詞の前だけ) ▶定義 connected with soldiers or the army, navy, etc 兵士, または陸軍, 海軍などに関連した→**軍人の, 軍の, 軍事的な** ‖ *All men in that country have to do two years' **military service**.* その国のすべての男性は2年間の兵役に就かねばならない. *to take military action* 軍事行動を取る

**militia** /məlíʃə/ 名 [Ｃ, 単数または複数形の動詞と共に] ▶定義 a group of people who are not professional soldiers but who have had military training プロの兵士ではないが, 軍事訓練を受けた人々の集団→**市民軍, 国民軍, 義勇軍, 民兵**

**\*milk**¹ /mɪlk/ 名 Ｕ ▶定義1 a white liquid that is produced by women and female animals to feed their babies. People drink the milk of some animals and use it to make butter and cheese. 赤ん坊に授乳するために, 女性や雌の動物から出る白い液体. 人は数種類の動物のミルクを飲む. また, それを使ってバターやチーズを作る→**ミルク, 乳, 牛乳** ‖ *skimmed/long-life/low-fat milk* 脱脂乳・長期保存可能牛乳・低脂肪乳 *a bottle/carton of milk* 牛乳1本・1パック ▶定義2 the juice of some plants or trees that looks like milk ある種の植物または木の樹液でミルクのように見える→**樹乳, 乳状の液** ‖ *coconut milk* ヤシの実の乳液

**milk**² /mɪlk/ 動 他 ▶定義1 to take milk from a cow, goat, etc 牛, ヤギなどからミルクをとる→**（乳）をしぼる** ▶定義2 to get as much money, advantage, etc for yourself from sb/sth as you can, without caring about others ほかの人のことを気にせず〜からできる限りのお金,利益などを得る→**〜を搾取する,引き出す,しぼり取る**

**milkman** /mílkmən/ 名 C (複 **-men** /mən/) ▶定義 a person who takes milk to people's houses every day 人々の家に毎日ミルクを届ける人→**牛乳配達人,牛乳屋**

**milk shake** /mílkʃèik/ 名 C U ▶定義 a drink made of milk with an added flavour of fruit or chocolate ミルクから作られる,果物やチョコレートの風味を加えた飲み物→**ミルクセーキ,シェーク** ← C4ページのさし絵

**milky** /mílki/ 形 ▶定義 like milk, or made with milk ミルクのような,またはミルクで作られた→**乳のような,乳白色の,乳で作った,乳を含んだ,ミルクを含んだ** ‖ *milky white skin* 乳白色の肌 *milky coffee* ミルクコーヒー

**mill**¹ /míl/ 名 C ▶定義 1 a factory that is used for making certain kinds of material 特定の種類の材料を作るために使われる工場→**製造工場,製造所** ‖ *a cotton/paper/steel mill* 紡績・製紙・製鉄工場 ▶定義 2 a building that contains a large machine that was used in the past for making grain into flour 従来穀粒を粉にするために使われた大きな機械が入っている建物→**製粉所,製粉工場** ‖ *a windmill* 風車 ▶定義 3 a kitchen tool that is used for making sth into powder 〜を粉にするために使われる台所用具→**ミル,ひき割り器,製粉機** ‖ *a pepper mill* コショウひき器

**mill**² /míl/ 動 他 ▶定義 to produce sth in a mill 〜をミルで作る→**ひく,製粉する**

句動詞　**mill about/around** 略式 ▶定義 (used about a large number of people or animals) to move around in a place with no real purpose (たくさんの人々または動物について)本当の目的を持たずにある場所を動き回る→**うろうろする**

**millennium** /məléniəm/ 名 C (複 **millennia** /-niə/ または **milleniums**) ▶定義 a period of 1000 years 1000年の期間→**千年間,千年紀** ‖ *We are at the start of the new millennium.* 私たちは新しい千年紀の開始点にいる.

**millet** /mílət/ 名 U ▶定義 a plant with a lot of small seeds that are used as food for people and birds たくさんの小さな実をつける植物で,その実は人々や鳥の食べ物として利用される→

きび(の実) ← **cereal** のさし絵

**milligram** (または **milligramme**) /míləgræm/ 名 C (略 **mg**) ▶定義 a measure of weight. There are 1000 milligrams in a gram. 重さの単位. 1 グラムは1000ミリグラム→**ミリグラム**

**millilitre** (米 **milliliter**) /míləlìːtər/ 名 C (略 **ml**) ▶定義 a measure of liquid. There are 1000 millilitres in a litre. 液体を計る単位. 1 リットルは1000ミリリットル→**ミリリットル**

**millimetre** (米 **millimeter**) /míləmìːtər/ 名 C (略 **mm**) ▶定義 a measure of length. There are 1000 millimetres in a metre. 長さの単位. 1 メートルは1000ミリメートル→**ミリメートル**

▶語法

millimetre, million と mile の関係

milli- は「1000分の1」を表し,1mm (millimetre)は「1000分の1メートル」です.これは距離の単位 mile とも関係があります. mile は語源的には「1000歩分」の意味です. 1mile ＝ 1.6kmとなるのは,歩いて距離を測る際に2歩を1単位として数えたためです. millionは本来は「大きな千」の意味ですが,英語では「thousandの1000倍＝百万」の意味で用いられます.

**millinery** /mílən(ə)ri; -nèri/ 名 U ▶定義 the business of making or selling women's hats 女性の帽子を作るまたは売る仕事→**婦人用帽子製造業,婦人用帽子販売業**

＊**million** /míljən/ 数 ▶定義 1 1000000 ‖ *Nearly 60 million people live in Britain.* 英国には6000万人近い人々が暮らしている. *Millions of people are at risk from the disease.* 数百万の人々が病気の危険にさらされている.

▶100万以上について述べるときには,sなしで millionを用いるので注意: *six million people* (600万人).文中での数詞の使い方については,sixの項を参照.

▶定義 2 **a million; millions (of)** 略式 a very large amount 非常に大きな量→**何百万,多数(の),無数(の)** ‖ *I still have a million things to do.* 私にはまだしなければならない事が無数にある. *There are millions of reasons why you shouldn't go.* あなたが行くべきでない理由はたくさんある.

▶数についての説明は,巻末の数についての特別項目を参照.

**millionaire** /mìljənéər, ⌢/ 图 ● ▶定義 a person who has a million pounds, dollars, etc; very rich person 100万ポンド,ドルなどを所有している人;非常に金持ちな人→百万長者,大金持ち

**millionth**¹ /míljənθ/ 代形 ▶定義 1000000th→100万番目(の,に),第100万(の,に)

**millionth**² /míljənθ/ 图 ● ▶定義 one of a million equal parts of sth ～の100万等分したものの1つ→100万分の1 ‖ *a millionth of a second* 100万分の1秒

**mime** /máɪm/ (困**pantomime**) 图 ● ● ▶定義 the use of movements of your hands and body and the expression on your face to tell a story or to act sth without speaking; a performance using this method of acting 口をきかずに物語を伝えるために,または～を演じるために,手と体の動きそして顔の表情を使うこと;このような演技方法で行うパフォーマンス→身振り,手振り,パントマイム ‖ *The performance consisted of dance, music and mime.* その興行は,ダンス,音楽,そしてパントマイムから成っていた.— **mime** 動自他→身振りで表す,道化芝居をする

**mimic**¹ /mímɪk/ 動他 (現分 **mimicking**; 過,過分 **mimicked**) ▶定義 to copy sb's behaviour, movements, voice, etc in an amusing way ～のしぐさ,動き,声などを面白おかしくまねる→まねをする ‖ *She's always mimicking the teachers.* 彼女はいつも先生たちの物まねをしている.

**mimic**² /mímɪk/ 图 ● ▶定義 a person who can copy sb's behaviour, movements, voice, etc in an amusing way ～のしぐさ,動き,声などを面白おかしくまねることができる人→物まねをする人・役者,物まねのうまい人—**mimicry** /mímɪkri/ 图 ●→物まね,擬態

**min** 略 ▶定義 **1** minimum→最小の(量),最低(限度)(の) ‖ *min temp tomorrow 2°* 明日の最低気温は2度. ▶定義 **2** minute(s)→分 ‖ *fastest time: 6 min* 最速タイム:6分

**mince** /mɪns/ 医 (困**ground beef; hamburger**) 图 ● ▶定義 meat that has been cut into very small pieces with a special machine 特別な機械で非常に細かく刻まれた肉→細かく切った肉,ひき肉 — **mince** 動他→細かく切り刻む

**mince pie** 图 ● ▶定義 a small round cake with a mixture of dried fruit, sugar, etc (**mincemeat**) inside, traditionally eaten in Britain at Christmas time 英国でクリスマスの時に伝統的に食べられる,乾果,砂糖などを混ぜた物(ミンスミート)が中に入った小さな円いケーキ→ミンスパイ

---

mind¹ 1047

\***mind**¹ /máɪnd/ 图 ● ● ▶定義 the part of your brain that thinks and remembers; your thoughts, feelings and intelligence 考えたり,覚えたりする脳の部分;思考感情そして知性→**頭脳,心,精神,考え,知性** ‖ *He has a brilliant mind.* 彼は頭脳明せきだ. *Not everybody has the right sort of mind for this work.* この仕事に適したタイプの思考力をだれでも持っているわけではない.

成句 at/in the back of your mind ⇒ **BACK**¹

be in two minds (about sth/doing sth) ▶定義 to not feel sure of sth ～に確信が感じられない→～について心がぐらついている,迷っている ‖ *I'm in two minds about leaving Will alone in the house while we're away.* 私たちが出掛ける間ウィルを家に独りにしてしておくかどうか迷っている.

be/go out of your mind 略式 ▶定義 to be or become crazy or very worried 狂っている,狂う,または非常に心配する→気が狂う,(心配で)気違いのようになる ‖ *I was going out of my mind when Tina didn't come home on time.* ティナが時間通りに帰宅しなかった時,私は非常に心配した.

bear in mind (that); bear/keep sb/sth in mind ▶定義 to remember or consider (that); to remember sb/sth(～だと)覚えている;～を覚えている→**～を覚えている,心に留めている** ‖ *We'll bear/keep your suggestion in mind for the future.* あなたの提案を私たちはこれから先も心に留めておきます.

bring/call sb/sth to mind ▶定義 to be reminded of sb/sth; to remember sb/sth ～を思い出す;～を思い出させる→**思い出す,思い出させる**

cast your mind back ⇒ **CAST**¹
change your mind ⇒ **CHANGE**¹
come/spring to mind ▶定義 if sth comes/springs to mind, you suddenly remember or think of it. ～が comes/springs to mind と言えば,突然それを思い出すまたはその事を考えることを表す→**思い浮かぶ**

cross your mind ⇒ **CROSS**²
ease sb's mind ⇒ **EASE**²
frame of mind ⇒ **FRAME**¹

# mind²

**give sb a piece of your mind** ⇒ **PIECE¹**
**go clean out of your mind** ⇒ **CLEAN³**
**have/keep an open mind** ⇒ **OPEN¹**
**have sb/sth in mind (for sth)** ▶定義 to be considering sb/sth as suitable for sth; to have a plan ～が…に適していると考えている; 計画を持つ→～のことを考えている，～をもくろんでいる‖ *Who do you have in mind for the job?* その仕事にはだれがよいと考えていますか．

**keep your mind on sth** ▶定義 to continue to pay attention to sth ～に注意を払い続ける→～に関心を向けている，～のことを考えている，～に専念する‖ *Keep your mind on the road while you're driving!* 運転している間は道路に注意を向けていなさい．

**make up your mind** ▶定義 to decide 決意する→決心する，結論を出す‖ *I can't make up my mind which sweater to buy.* どちらのセーターを買おうか決められない．

**on your mind** ▶定義 worrying you 心配させている→気に掛かっている，気にしている‖ *Don't bother her with that. She's got enough on her mind already.* その事で彼女に心配させないで．彼女は既に十分気に掛けているから．

**prey on sb's mind** ⇒ **PREY²**
**put/set sb's mind at rest** ▶定義 to make sb stop worrying ～が心配するのをやめさせる→～を安心させる，～の不安を取り除く‖ *The results of the blood test set his mind at rest.* 血液検査の結果を見て彼は安心した．

**slip your mind** ⇒ **SLIP¹**
**speak your mind** ⇒ **SPEAK**
**state of mind** ⇒ **STATE¹**
**take sb's mind off sth** ▶定義 to help sb not to think or worry about sth ～が…について考えないようにまたは心配しないように手助けする→～から注意をそらせる，～に忘れさせる

**to my mind** ▶定義 in my opinion 私の意見では→私の考えでは‖ *To my mind, this is a complete waste of time!* 私の考えでは，これは全くの時間の無駄だ．

\*mind² /máɪnd/ 動 ▶定義 1 自他（特に疑問，応答，否定文で）to feel annoyed, upset or uncomfortable about sth/sb ～についていら立ちを感じる，気が動転する，または不愉快に感じる→嫌がる，迷惑に思う，気にする‖ *I'm sure Simon won't mind if you don't invite him.* もしあなたがサイモンを招待しなくても，彼は気にしないよ．*I don't mind what you do - it's your decision.* あなたが何をしても私は構いません－それはあなたが決める事ですから．*Do you mind having to travel so far to work every day?* 毎日そんなに遠くに通勤しなければならないことが嫌ではありませんか．*Are you sure your parents won't mind me coming?* 私が伺ってもあなたのご両親は気になさらないと本当に思いますか．*'Would you like tea or coffee?' 'I don't mind.'* (= I'm happy to have either)「紅茶とコーヒーどちらがよいですか」「どちらでも」(= どちらでもうれしいです．) *I wouldn't mind a break right now* (= I would like one). 今すぐ一休みしても構わないよ(= 一休みしたい)．▶定義 2 他（～に…をしてくれるように頼む，または～をすることの許可を求めるときの丁寧な言い方として疑問文で用いて）could you...?; may I...? ...していただけますか．; ...してもよいですか．→～を嫌に思う‖ *Would you mind closing the window for me?* 窓を閉めていただけますか．*Do you mind driving? I'm feeling rather tired.* 運転していただけませんか．私は少し疲れています．▶定義 3 他 used to tell sb to be careful of sth or to pay attention to sb/sth ～に気を付けるように，または～に注意を払うように…に言うときに用いて→注意する，用心する，気を付ける‖ *It's a very low doorway so mind your head.* 戸口がとても低いので頭に気を付けて．*Mind that step!* その階段に気を付けて．*Don't mind me! I won't disturb you.* 私のことなどどうぞ気にしないで．あなたのお邪魔はしません．▶定義 4 他 特に 英 to look after or watch sb/sth for a short time 短い間～の面倒を見る，または見ている→～の世話をする，番をする‖ *Could you mind my bag while I go and get us some drinks?* 私が飲み物を取ってくる間，私のバッグを見ていていただけますか．

---

### ▶語法

**動名詞をとる動詞は megafeps**

　動名詞だけを目的語にとる(不定詞は目的語にとらない)動詞の代表例の頭文字を並べたものです．このタイプの動詞を覚えるときの呪文(じゅもん)が megafeps (メガフェプス)です．M(mind, miss)，e(enjoy)，g(give up)，a(avoid, admit), f (finish), e (escape), p (practice, put s (stop)

成句 **mind you** ▶定義 used for attracting attention to a point you are making or for giving more information 主張している点に注意を引き付けるために，またはさらに詳しい情報を提供するのに用いて→**いいですか，よく聞いてよ，実は** ‖ *Paul seems very tired. Mind you, he has been working very hard recently.* ポールは非常に疲れているようだ．実は，彼は最近非常に忙しく働いている．

**mind your own business** ▶定義 to pay attention to your own affairs, not other people's 他人のではなく，自分自身のことに注意を払う→**自分自身のことをきちんとしなさい，要らぬお世話だ** ‖ *Stop asking me personal questions and mind your own business!* 個人的な質問を私にするのはやめなさい，要らぬお世話だ．

**never mind** ▶定義 don't worry; it doesn't matter 心配するな；構わない→**気にするな，しなくていい** ‖ *'I forgot to post your letter.' 'Never mind, I'll do it later.'* 「あなたの手紙を投かんするのを忘れた」「気にしないで．後で自分でするから」

句動詞 **mind out** 略式 ▶定義 Get out of the way! 道を空けろ→**道を空ける，気を付ける** ‖ *Mind out! There's a car coming.* 道を空けろ．車が来るぞ．

**mind-boggling** 形略式 ▶定義 difficult to imagine, understand or believe 想像する，理解する，または信じるのが難しい→**信じられない，うそみたいな** ‖ *Mind-boggling amounts of money were being discussed.* 信じられないほどの金額についての話し合いが行われていた．

**-minded** /máɪndəd/ 形 (複合形容詞を作るために用いて) ▶定義 1 having the type of mind mentioned ～の心を持つ→**～の心を持った** ‖ *a strong-minded/open-minded/narrow-minded person* 気性の強い・心の広い・心の狭い人 ▶定義 2 interested in the thing mentioned 言及されたものに興味を持つ→**～に関心の強い，～(的に)考える** ‖ *money-minded* お金に関心の強い

**minder** /máɪndər/ 名 ⓒ ▶定義 a person whose job is to look after and protect sb/sth ～の面倒を見て守ることを仕事にする人→**番人，用心棒，ボディーガード** ‖ *My son goes to a childminder so that I can work part-time.* 息子はベビーシッターの所へ行くので，私はパートタイムの仕事ができる．

**mindless** /máɪndləs/ 形 ▶定義 1 done or acting without thought and for no particular reason 考えなしに特別な理由もなく行われたまたは行動された→**思慮のない，愚かな，不注意で** ‖ *mindless violence* 非情な暴力 ▶定義 2 not needing thought or intelligence 思考または知性を必要としないような→**思考力を必要としない，思考力を持たない** ‖ *a mindless and repetitive task* 頭を使わない繰り返しの仕事

★**mine**¹ /máɪn/ 代 ▶定義 of or belonging to me 私のまたは私に属するもの→**私のもの** ‖ *'Whose is this jacket?' 'It's mine.'* 「この上着はだれのですか」「私のだ」 *Don't take your car - you can come in mine.* 車で来ないで － 私の車に乗れるから． *May I introduce a friend of mine (= one of my friends)?* 私の友達（＝私の友達の１人）を紹介してよいですか． ☛参 my

★**mine**² /máɪn/ 名 ⓒ ▶定義 1 a deep hole, or a system of passages under the ground where minerals such as coal, tin, gold, etc are dug 石炭，スズ，金などの鉱物が採掘される深い穴または地下の坑道→**鉱山，鉱坑** ‖ *a coal/salt/gold mine* 炭鉱・岩塩坑・金鉱 ☛参 quarry ▶定義 2 a bomb that is hidden under the ground or under water and explodes when sb/sth touches it 地面の下あるいは水中に隠されている爆弾で～がそれに触れると爆発する→**地雷，機雷** ‖ *The car went over a mine and blew up.* 車は地雷の上を通り，爆発した．

**mine**³ /máɪn/ 動 ▶定義 1 Ⓣ Ⓘ to dig in the ground for minerals such as coal, tin, gold, etc 石炭，スズ，金などの鉱物を地中から掘る→**採掘する，坑道を掘る** ‖ *Diamonds are mined in South Africa.* ダイヤモンドは南アフリカで採掘される． ☛参 mining ▶定義 2 Ⓣ to put mines²(2) in an area of land or sea 陸または海のある地域にmines²(2)を置く→**地雷・機雷を敷設する**

**minefield** /máɪnfiːld/ 名 ⓒ ▶定義 1 an area of land or sea where mines²(2) have been hidden mines²(2)が隠された陸または海の地域→**地雷原，機雷原** ▶定義 2 a situation that is full of hidden dangers or difficulties 隠れた危険または困難が多数ある状況→**危険をはらんだもの，難解なもの，難問** ‖ *a political minefield* 政治的な難問

**miner** /máɪnər/ 名 C ▶定義 a person whose job is to work in a mine²(1) to get coal, salt, tin, etc mine²(1) で働いて石炭, 塩, スズなどを得ることを仕事にする人→坑夫, 炭坑夫

**mineral** /mín(ə)rəl/ 名 C ▶定義 a natural substance such as coal, salt, oil, etc, especially one that is found in the ground. Some minerals are also present in food and drink and are very important for good health. 石炭, 塩, 石油などの自然物質, 特に地中で見つかる物. 食べ物や飲み物の中に含まれ健康のために非常に重要な物もある→鉱物, 無機物, ミネラル ‖ *a country rich in minerals* 鉱物に富んだ国 *the recommended daily intake of vitamins and minerals* ビタミンとミネラルの好ましい毎日の摂取

**mineral water** 名 U ▶定義 water that comes straight from a place in the ground (a spring), which contains minerals or gases and is thought to be good for your health 地面のある場所(泉)からわいてくる水で, 無機物またはガスを含み健康のために良いと考えられている→炭酸水, ミネラルウォーター ☛ C4 ページのさし絵

**mingle** /míŋg(ə)l/ 動自他 ▶定義 mingle A and B (together); mingle (A) (with B) to mix with other things or people ほかの物または人と混ぜる→混ぜる, 一緒にする, 交流する ‖ *The colours slowly mingled together to make a muddy brown.* 数色が次第に混ざり合いくすんだ茶色になった. *His excitement was mingled with fear.* 彼は興奮を感じていたが恐怖も入り交じっていた. *to mingle with the rich and famous* 金持ちや有名人と交際する

**mini-** /míni/ ▶定義 (複合名詞を作るために用いて) very small 非常に小さな→小の, 小型の ‖ *a miniskirt* ミニスカート *minigolf* ミニゴルフ

**miniature** /mínətʃər, -tʃʊər/ 名 C ▶定義 a small copy of sth which is much larger ずっと大きな〜の小さな模型→ミニチュア, 小型の模型, 小型(の) ‖ *a miniature camera* 小型カメラ

成句 **in miniature** ▶定義 exactly the same as sb/sth else but in a very small form ほかの〜と全く同じだが, 非常に小さい →(そっくりそのまま)縮めた, 縮めて, 縮小した, ミニチュアの

**minibus** /mínibʌs/ 名 C 特に 英 ▶定義 a small bus, usually for no more than 12 people 通常12人以下用の小さなバス→マイクロバス, ミニバス, 小型バス

**minimal** /mínəm(ə)l/ 形 ▶定義 very small in amount, size or level; as little as possible 量, 大きさ, または程度が非常に小さい; できる限り小さい→最低の, 最小(限)の ‖ *The project must be carried out at minimal cost.* その計画は最小限の費用で達成されなければならない.

**minimize** (または **-ise**) /mínəmàɪz/ 動他 ▶定義 1 to make sth as small as possible (in amount or level) 〜(の量または程度を)できる限り小さくする→〜を最小にする, 最低にする ‖ *We shall try to minimize the risks to the public.* 私たちは一般大衆への危険を最小限にするよう努力をするつもりです. ▶定義 2 to try to make sth seem less important than it really is 〜を実際よりも重要でないように見せようとする→〜を小さく見せる, 軽く扱う ▶定義 3 (computing) to make sth small on a computer screen (コンピューター) コンピューターの画面上で〜を小さくする→〜を最小化する⇔**maximize**

**minimum**¹ /mínəməm/ 名 [単数扱い] ▶定義 the smallest amount or level that is possible or allowed 可能なまたは許された範囲で最も少ない量または低い程度→最小限, 最少量 ‖ *I need a minimum of seven hours' sleep.* 私には最低7時間の睡眠が必要です. *We will try and keep the cost of the tickets to a minimum.* 私たちはチケットの値段を最低限に保つよう努めます. ⇔**maximum**

**minimum**² /mínəməm/ 形 (名詞の前だけ) ▶定義 the smallest possible or allowed; extremely small 可能な限りまたは許された中で最小の; 非常に小さい→最小の, 最低限度の ‖ *to introduce a national **minimum wage** (= the lowest wage that an employer is legally allowed to pay)* 国の最低賃金(= 雇用者が支払う法的に許された最低限度の賃金)を導入する⇔**maximum**—**minimum** 副 →最小で, 最低で ‖ *We'll need £200 minimum for expenses.* 私たちは最低で200ポンドの経費が必要だろう.

**mining** /máɪnɪŋ/ 名 U ▶定義 (しばしば複合名詞を作るために用いて) the process or industry of getting minerals, metals, etc out of the ground by digging 地中を掘って鉱物, 金属などを採る過程または産業→採鉱, 鉱業 ‖ *coal/tin/gold mining* 石炭・スズ・金の採鉱

**minister** /mínəstər/ 名 C ▶定義1 Minister (英 **Secretary**) a member of the government, often the head of a government department 政府の一員，しばしば政府の省の長→**大臣** ‖ *the Minister for Trade and Industry* 通産大臣 ☞参 **Prime Minister**, **Cabinet Minister** ▶定義2 a priest in some Protestant churches プロテスタント教会のある派の牧師→**牧師** ☞参 **vicar**

**ministerial** /ˌmìnəstíəriəl/ 形 ▶定義 connected with a government minister or department 政府の大臣または省に関連した→**大臣の, 政府の**

*__ministry__ /mínəstri/ 名 C (複 **ministries**) (または **department**) ▶定義 a government department that has a particular area of responsibility 特定の分野で責任を持つ政府の部署→**省** ‖ *the Ministry of Defence* 防衛庁 ☞ department はアメリカ英語でのみ使われる語．

**mink** /míŋk/ 名 C ▶定義 a small wild animal that is kept for its thick brown fur which is used to make expensive coats 厚く茶色い毛皮が高価なコートを作るのに使用されるため，飼育されている小型の野性の動物→**ミンク**

*__minor__¹ /máɪnər/ 形 ▶定義1 not very big, serious or important (when compared with others) (他と比べて)あまり大きくはない，深刻でない，または重要でない→**小さい方の** ‖ *It's only a minor problem. Don't worry.* それは小さな問題にすぎない．心配するな．*She's gone into hospital for a minor operation.* 彼女はちょっとした手術のために病院に入院した．⇔ **major** ▶定義2 of one of the two types of key¹(4) in which music is usually written 2種類の key¹(4) の調の1つで，通常音楽が書かれる→**短調の, 短音階の** ‖ *a symphony in F minor* へ短調の交響曲 ☞参 **major**

**minor**² /máɪnər/ 名 C ▶定義 (used in law) a person who is not legally an adult (法律で用いて)法的に大人ではない人→**未成年者, 成年に達しない者**

▶英国では come of age (成年に達する) 18歳になるまでは未成年者．

*__minority__ /maɪnɔ́(ː)rəti, -nár-/ 名 C (複 **minorities**) ▶定義1 [通常は単数，単数または複数形の動詞と共に] the smaller number or part of a group; less than half ある集団で小さい方の数または部分; 半分よりも少ないもの→**少数, 少数派** ‖ *Only a minority of teenagers become/becomes involved in crime.* ティーンエージャーの少数だ

けが犯罪にかかわるようになる．⇔ **majority** ▶定義2 a small group of people who are of a different race or religion to most of the people in the community or country where they live 社会または国の中で，大半の人々とは異なる人種または宗教の人々の小さな集団→**少数民族, 少数集団** ‖ *Schools in Britain need to do more to help children of ethnic/racial minorities.* 英国の学校は少数民族・人種の子供たちを助けるためにもっと尽力する必要がある．

成句 be in a/the minority ▶定義 to be the smaller of two groups 2つの集団で小さい方である→**少数派である** ‖ *Men are in the minority in the teaching profession.* 教職において男性は少数派だ．☞参 **in a/the majority**

**mint** /mɪnt/ 名 ▶定義1 ❶a type of plant (a herb) whose leaves are used to give flavour to food, drinks, toothpaste, etc 植物(ハーブ)の一種で，葉が食べ物，飲み物，歯磨き粉などに香りを与えるのに使われる→**ハッカ, ミント** ‖ *lamb with mint sauce* ミントソースの掛かった子羊肉 ▶定義2 ❷a type of sweet with a strong fresh flavour 強くさわやかな風味を持つ甘味の一種→**ハッカ入りキャンデー** ▶定義3 [単数扱い] the place where money in the form of coins and notes is made by the government 政府によって，硬貨や紙幣の形に貨幣が作られる場所→**造幣局** ― **mint** 動 他 →**鋳造する** ‖ *freshly minted coins* 新たに鋳造された硬貨

**minus**¹ /máɪnəs/ 前 ▶定義1 (used in sums) less; subtract; take away (計算で用いて)を差し引いた; 引く; 取り去る→**〜を引いた** ‖ *Six minus two is four (6 - 2 = 4).* 6引く2は4(6－2＝4)．⇔ **plus** ▶定義2 (used about a number) below zero (数について)ゼロ以下に→**マイナスの, 氷点下, 零下** ‖ *The temperature will fall to minus 10.* 気温は零下10度まで下がるでしょう．▶定義3 略式 without sth that was there before 以前そこにあった〜なしで→**〜がなく, 〜なしに** ‖ *We're going to be minus a car for a while.* しばらくの間，私たちは車なしで済ませるつもりだ．

**minus**² /máɪnəs/ 名 C ▶定義1 (または **minus sign**) (記号 －) the symbol which is used in mathematics to show that a number is below zero or that you should subtract the second number from the first 数がゼロ以下であることまたは最初の数から2番目の数を引くことを示す,数学で使われる記号➔**マイナス記号,減法記号,負符号** ▶定義**2** (または **minus point**) 略式 a negative quality; a disadvantage 否定的な性質;不利➔**欠点,不利なこと** ‖ *Let's consider the pluses and minuses of moving out of the city.* 町を出ることの有利な点と不利な点を検討しましょう. ⇨ **plus**

**minus**³ /máɪnəs/ 形 ▶定義**1** (used in mathematics) lower than zero (数学で用いて) ゼロよりも小さい➔**マイナスの,負の** ‖ *a minus figure* 負数 ▶定義**2** (used in a system of grades given for school work) slightly lower than (学校の勉強に対して与えられる評価方式で用いられて)〜よりもわずかに低い➔**マイナスの,〜の下(げ)** ‖ *I got A minus (A-) for my essay.* 小論で A の下をもらった. ⇨ **plus**

**minuscule** /mínəskjùːl/ 形 ▶定義 extremely small 極度に小さい➔**非常に小さい**

\***minute**¹ /mínət/ 名 ▶定義**1** C (略式 **min**) one of the 60 parts that make up one hour; 60 seconds 1時間を構成している60の部分の1つ; 60秒➔**分** ‖ *It's twelve minutes to nine.* 9時12分前だ. *He telephoned ten minutes ago.* 彼は10分前に電話をした. *The programme lasts for about fifty minutes.* その番組は約50分続く. ▶定義**2** [単数扱い] (口語) a very short time; a moment 非常に短い時間; 一瞬➔**瞬間,ちょっとの間** ‖ *Just/Wait a minute (= wait)! You've forgotten your notes.* ちょっと待って(=待って). メモを忘れているよ. *Have you got a minute? - I'd like to talk to you.* ちょっと時間をもらえますか―あなたと話したいのです. ▶定義**3 the minutes** [複数扱い] a written record of what is said and decided at a meeting 会議で述べられたまたは決定された事の書面による記録➔**議事録,会議録**

成句 **(at) any minute/moment (now)** 略式 ▶定義 very soon まさにすぐにも➔**今すぐにも,今か今かと** ‖ *The plane should be landing any minute now.* 飛行機は今すぐにも着陸するはずだ.
**in a minute** ▶定義 very soon まさにすぐにも➔**すぐに** ‖ *I'll be with you in a minute.* すぐに参ります.
**the last minute/moment** ⇒ **LAST**¹**(1)**
**the minute/moment (that)** ▶定義 as soon as 〜するや否や➔**〜するとすぐ,〜するや否や** ‖ *I'll tell him you rang the minute (that) he gets here.* 彼がここに着いたらすぐにあなたが電話をくれたと伝えます.
**this minute** ▶定義 immediately; now 直ちに; 今➔**今すぐ** ‖ *I don't know what I'm going to do yet - I've just this minute found out.* 私はこれから何をしていいのかまだ分からない - 今知ったばかりなのだ.
**up to the minute** 略式 ▶定義 having the most recent information 最も新しい情報を持っている➔**最新(流行)の** ‖ *For up to the minute information on flight times, phone this number...* フライト時間についての最新情報はこの番号...におかけください.

**minute**² /maɪn(j)úːt, mə-/ 形 (最上級 **minutest**) (比較級はなし) ▶定義**1** very small 非常に小さい➔**極めて小さい,微小の** ‖ *I couldn't read his writing. It was minute!* 彼の書いたものは読めなかった. とても小さい字だった. ▶定義**2** very exact or accurate 非常に正確なまたは精密な➔**綿密な,精密な** ‖ *She was able to describe the man in minute/the minutest detail.* 彼女は詳細にその男を描写することができた.

**miracle** /mírək(ə)l/ 名 ▶定義**1** C a wonderful event that seems impossible and that is believed to be caused by God or a god 不可能に思える,神によって起こされたと考えられるようなすばらしい出来事➔**奇跡,神技,不思議な出来事** ▶定義**2** [単数扱い] a lucky thing that happens that you did not expect or think was possible 期待しなかった事,または可能だと思わなかったような事が起きる幸運なこと➔**奇跡,驚くべきこと** ‖ *It's a miracle (that) nobody was killed in the crash.* その衝突でだれも死ななかったのは奇跡だ.

成句 **work/perform miracles** ▶定義 to achieve very good results 非常に良い結果を達成する➔**奇跡を起こす** ‖ *The new diet and exercise programme have worked miracles for her.* 新しい食事制限と運動のプログラムが彼女に奇跡を起こした.

**miraculous** /mərǽkjələs/ 形 ▶定義 completely unexpected and very lucky 全く予期していな

く,非常に幸運な→奇跡的な,不思議な,驚くべき ‖ *She's made a miraculous recovery.* 彼女は奇跡的な回復をした. — **miraculously** 副 →奇跡的に,不思議に

**mirage** /mírɑːʒ; məráːʒ/ 名 C ▶定義 something that you think you see in very hot weather, for example water in a desert, but which does not really exist 例えば砂漠での水など,非常に暑い天候の中で本当は存在しないのに見えたように思うもの→蜃気楼(しんきろう)

\*__mirror__ /mírər/ 名 C ▶定義 a piece of special flat glass that you can look into in order to see yourself or what is behind you 自分自身または自分の後ろにある物を見るためにのぞき込む特別な平らなガラス→鏡 ‖ *to look **in the mirror*** 鏡を見る *a **rear-view mirror*** (= in a car, so that the driver can see what is behind) バックミラー(= 車の中で,運転手が後ろにある物を見ることができるようにするもの)

➤鏡が画像を映すことを reflect と言う.鏡の中には reflection(映った像)が見える.

☞ **motorbike**, S7ページのさし絵 — **mirror** 動他 →映す,反射する ‖ *The trees were mirrored in the lake.* 木々が湖面に映っていた.

**mirth** /məːθ/ 名 U (文) ▶定義 amusement or laughter 楽しんでいる状態,笑い→陽気な騒ぎ,楽しい笑い

**misapprehension** /mìsæprɪhénʃ(ə)n/ 名 C U 正式 ▶定義 to have the wrong idea about sth or to believe sth is true when it is not ~について間違った考えを持つ,またはそうではないのに~が真実だと信じる→思い違い,誤解 ‖ *I was **under the misapprehension** that this course was for beginners.* 私はこの講座が初心者向けだと思い違いをしていた.

**misbehave** /mìsbɪhéɪv/ 動自 ▶定義 to behave badly 下手に振る舞う→不作法に振る舞う,不品行である,不正を働く⇔**behave** — **misbehaviour** (米 **misbehavior**) /mìsbɪhéɪvjər/ 名 U →不作法,不品行,不正行為

**misc** /mɪsk/ 略 miscellaneous→種々雑多な,いろいろな

**miscalculate** /mìskǽlkjəlèɪt/ 動自他 ▶定義 to make a mistake in calculating or judging a situation, an amount, etc 計算で間違いをする,または状況,量などの判断において間違いをする→計算を誤る,誤算する,判断を誤る ‖ *The driver totally miscalculated the speed at which the other car was travelling.* 運転手はもう一方の車が走行している速度について完全に判断を誤った. — **miscalculation** /mìskælkjəléɪʃ(ə)n/ 名 C U →計算違い,誤算

**miscarriage** /mìskǽrɪdʒ/ 名 C U ▶定義 (medical) giving birth to a baby a long time before it is ready to be born, with the result that it cannot live (医学)赤ん坊がまだ未熟なのに産まれてしまい,結果として赤ん坊が生きられないこと→流産

➤ abortion と比較.

成句 *a **miscarriage of justice*** ▶定義 an occasion when sb is punished for a crime that he/she did not do ~が犯していない犯罪について罰せられてしまう場合→誤審

**miscarry** /mìskǽri/ 動自 (現分 **miscarrying**; 三単現 **miscarries**; 過, 過分 **miscarried**) ▶定義 to give birth to a baby before it is ready to be born, with the result that it cannot live 赤ん坊がまだ未熟なのに産まれてしまい,その結果として赤ん坊が生きられない→流産する

**miscellaneous** /mìsəléɪniəs, -njəs/ 形 (略 **misc**) ▶定義 consisting of many different types or things 多くの異なる種類やもので構成される→種々雑多な,いろいろな ‖ *a box of miscellaneous items for sale* 売りに出されたいろいろな品物の入った箱

**mischief** /místʃəf/ 名 U ▶定義 bad behaviour (usually of children) that is not very serious あまり深刻でない(通常子供の)悪い行為→いたずら,わるさ ‖ *The children in Class 9 are always **getting into mischief**.* 9組の子供たちはいつもいたずらを始める.

**mischievous** /místʃəvəs/ 形 ▶定義 (usually used about children) liking to behave badly and embarrassing or annoying people (通常子供たちについて)行儀悪くするのが好きで,人々を当惑させるまたは困らせる→いたずら好きな,ちゃめっ気のある — **mischievously** 副 →いたずらに,ちゃめっ気で

**misconception** /mìskənsépʃ(ə)n/ 名 C ▶定義 a wrong idea or understanding of sth ~についての間違った考えまたは理解→思い違い,誤解 ‖ *It is a popular misconception (= many people* wrongly believe) that people need meat to be healthy. 人が健康でいるために肉が必要だというのは一般的な誤解だ(= 多くの人々は誤って信じている).

**misconduct** /mìskándʌkt/ ❷ ❶ 正式 ▶定義 unacceptable behaviour, especially by a professional person 特に専門職の人による,受け入れられない行為→**違法行為,非行,誤った処置** ‖ *The doctor was dismissed for **gross** (= very serious) **misconduct***. その医師はひどい(= 非常に深刻な)違法行為のために解雇された.

**misconstrue** /mìskənstrúː/ ❶ ❷ 正式 ▶定義 misconstrue sth (as sth) to understand sb's words or actions wrongly ～の言葉または行動を間違って理解する→**意味を取り違える,誤解する** ☛参 construe

**misdemeanour**(米 **misdemeanor**) /mìsdɪmíːnər/ ❷ ❸ ▶定義 something slightly bad or wrong that a person does; a crime that is not very serious 人が行う多少悪いまたは間違ったこと;深刻ではない犯罪→**非行,不品行,軽罪**

**miser** /máɪzər/ ❷ ❸ ▶定義 a person who loves having a lot of money but hates spending it お金をたくさん持つことが好きだが,それを使うことは嫌いな人→**けちんぼう,守銭奴,しみったれ** — **miserly** 形 →けちな,わずかな

★**miserable** /míz(ə)rəb(ə)l/ 形 ▶定義 **1** very unhappy 非常に不幸せな→**惨めな,不幸な,哀れな** ‖ *Oh dear, you look miserable. What's wrong?* あら,惨めそうな顔をしているわね.何があったの. ▶定義 **2** unpleasant; making you feel unhappy 不愉快な;不幸に感じさせる→**ひどい,惨めな気持ちにさせる** ‖ *What miserable weather!* (= *grey, cold and wet*) 何てひどい天気だ.(= どんよりとして肌寒い雨降りの) ☛類 dismal ▶定義 **3** too small or of bad quality 小さすぎる,または質の悪い→**貧弱な,みすぼらしい,お粗末な** ‖ *I was offered a miserable salary so I didn't take the job.* わずかな給与を提示されたので,その仕事を引き受けなかった. — **miserably** /-əb(ə)li/ 副 →**惨めに,情けないほどに** ‖ *I stared miserably out of the window.* 私は惨めな気分で窓の外を見つめた. *He **failed miserably** as an actor.* 彼は俳優として惨めに失敗した.

★**misery** /míz(ə)ri/ ❷ ❶ ❸ (複 **miseries**) ▶定義 great unhappiness or suffering とてつもない不幸せまたは苦しみ→**惨めさ,悲惨さ,窮状** ‖ *I couldn't bear to see him in such misery.* そのような窮状にある彼を見ることに私は耐えられなかった. *the miseries of war* 戦争の悲惨さ

成句 **put sb out of his/her misery** 略式 ▶定義 to stop sb worrying about sth by telling the person what he/she wants to know ～が知りたいことを話してあげることで,その～が…について心配するのをやめる→**真実を話して楽にしてやる** ‖ *Put me out of my misery - did I pass or not?* 真実を話して私を楽にさせてくれ — 私は合格したのか,それともしなかったのか.

**put sth out of its misery** ▶定義 to kill an animal because it has an illness or injury that cannot be treated 不治の病気またはけがを抱えている動物を殺す→**安楽死させる**

**misfire** /mìsfáɪər/ ❶ ❷ ▶定義 to fail to have the intended result or effect 意図した結果または効果を得られない→**不発になる,失敗する** ‖ *The plan misfired.* その計画は失敗した.

**misfit** /mísfɪt/ ✂ ❷ ❸ ▶定義 a person who not is accepted by other people, especially because his/her behaviour or ideas are very different 特にその人の行動または考えが非常に異なるために,ほかの人々に受け入れられない人→**順応できない人,不適格者,はみ出し者**

**misfortune** /mɪsfɔ́ːrtʃ(ə)n/ ❷ ❸ ❶ 正式 ▶定義 (an event, accident, etc that brings) bad luck or disaster 不運または災害(をもたらす出来事,事故など)→**不運(な出来事),不幸(な出来事),災難** ‖ *I hope I don't ever **have the misfortune to** meet him again.* 彼と再会するという不運が二度とないように願っている.

**misgiving** /mɪsgívɪŋ/ ❷ ❸ ❶ ▶定義 a feeling of doubt, worry or suspicion 疑問,心配,または疑いの感情→**不安,心配,疑い** ‖ *I had serious **misgivings** about leaving him on his own.* 彼を独りで残しておくことには非常に不安だった.

**misguided** /mɪsgáɪdəd/ 形 ▶定義 wrong because you have understood or judged a situation badly 状況を間違って理解したまたは判断したために,間違った→**心得違いの,見当違いの** ‖ *She only moved the victim in a misguided effort to help.* 彼女は助けようとしたが状況判断を誤り,犠牲者を動かしただけだった.

**mishap** /míshæp/ ✂ ❷ ❸ ❶ ▶定義 a small accident or piece of bad luck that does not have serious results 深刻な結果をもたらさない、小さな事故または不運**不幸な出来事, 事故, 不運** ‖ *to have a slight mishap* ちょっとした不運な出来事に出会う

**misinform** /mìsɪnfɔ́ːrm/ 動他 正式 ▶定義 to give sb the wrong information ～に間違った情報を与える➔**誤解させる, 誤った事柄を伝える** ‖ *I think you've been misinformed - no one is going to lose their job.* あなたは誤った情報を教えられたのだと思う － だれも首にならないよ.

**misinterpret** /mìsɪntə́ːrprət/ 動他 ▶定義 misinterpret sth (as sth) to understand sth wrongly ～を間違って理解する➔**誤解する, 誤って解釈する** ‖ *His comments were misinterpreted as a criticism of the project.* 彼の意見は、その計画への批判と誤解された. ⇔**interpret** — misinterpretation /mìsɪntə̀ːrprətéɪʃ(ə)n/ 名 C U ➔**誤解, 誤った解釈** ‖ *Parts of the speech were open to misinterpretation* (= easy to understand wrongly). その演説は部分的に誤解を受ける余地があった(= 間違って理解されやすい).

**misjudge** /mìsdʒʌ́dʒ/ 動他 ▶定義 **1** to form a wrong opinion of sb/sth, usually in a way which is unfair to him/her/it 通常不公平な方法で、～についての間違った意見をまとめる➔**～を誤審する, 見くびる** ▶定義 **2** to guess time, distance, etc wrongly 時間, 距離などを間違って推定する➔**見当を誤る, 判断を誤る** ‖ *He completely misjudged the speed of the other car and almost crashed.* 彼はもう1台の車の速度を完全に誤って判断し、衝突しそうになった. — misjudgement(または misjudgment) 名 C U ➔**誤審, 誤った判断, 見当違い**

**mislay** /mìsléɪ/ 動他 (現分 **mislaying**; 三単現 **mislays**; 過, 過分 **mislaid** /mìsléɪd/) ▶定義 to lose sth, usually for a short time, because you cannot remember where you put it どこに置いたか忘れたために、通常短い間～をなくす➔**～を置き忘れる, 見失う**

**mislead** /mìslíːd/ 動他 (過, 過分 **misled** /-léd/) ▶定義 to make sb have the wrong idea or opinion about sb/sth ～に…についての誤った考えまたは意見を持たせる➔**～を誤った方向に導く, 誤解させる, 惑わす** — misleading 形 ➔**人を誤らせるような, 誤解のおそれのある, 紛らわしい** ‖ *a misleading advertisement* 紛らわしい広告

Miss¹ 1055

**mismanage** /mìsmǽnɪdʒ/ 動他 ▶定義 to manage or organize sth badly ～を間違って管理するまたは組織する➔**～の管理を誤る, ～の経営を誤る** — mismanagement 名 U ➔**誤った管理, 誤った処理, 放漫経営**

**misplaced** /mìspléɪst/ 形 ▶定義 given to sb/sth that is not suitable or good enough to have it それを持つのに適さないまたは価値のない～に与えられた➔**見当違いの, お門違いの** ‖ *misplaced loyalty* 誤った忠誠

**misprint** /mísprɪ̀nt, ´-´/ 名 C ▶定義 a mistake in printing or typing 印刷またはタイプの間違い➔**ミスプリント, 誤植**

**mispronounce** /mìsprənáʊns/ 動他 ▶定義 to say a word or letter wrongly 言葉または文字を間違って言う➔**～を誤って発音する** ‖ *People always mispronounce my surname.* 人々はいつも私の名字を間違えて発音する. — mispronunciation /mìsprənʌ̀nsiéɪʃ(ə)n/ 名 C U ➔**誤った発音**

**misread** /mìsríːd/ 動他 (過, 過分 **misread** /mìsréd/) ▶定義 misread sth (as sth) to read or understand sth wrongly ～を間違って読むまたは理解する➔**～を読み違える, 誤解する** ‖ *He misread my silence as a refusal.* 彼は私の沈黙を拒絶と誤解した.

**misrepresent** /mìsreprɪzént/ 動他 (通常は受動態で) ▶定義 to give a wrong description of sb/sth ～を間違って説明する➔**～を誤って伝える, 間違って説明する** ‖ *In the newspaper article they were misrepresented as uncaring parents.* 新聞記事で彼らは面倒を見ない両親として誤って伝えられた. — misrepresentation /mìsrèprɪzentéɪʃ(ə)n, -z(ə)n-/ 名 C U ➔**誤伝, 間違った説明**

***Miss***¹ /mís/ ▶定義 used as a title before the family name of a young woman or a woman who is not married 若い女性または結婚していない女性の名字の前に敬称として用いて➔**～さん, ～嬢, ～様** ▶ Miss, Mrs, Ms および Mr はいずれも人の姓の前に付ける敬称. 姓なしの名の前には用いない: *Is there a Miss (Tamsin) Hudson here?* ((タムシン)ハドソンさんはこちらにいますか.) Miss Tamsin とはしない. *'Dear Miss Harris,' the letter began.* (「親愛なるハリスさん」とその手紙は始まった.)

**miss**² /mɪs/ 動 ▶定義1 自他 to fail to hit, catch, etc sth ～を打つ, 捕まえるなどで失敗する→**打ち損なう, 取り逃がす** ‖ *She tried to catch the ball but she missed.* 彼女はボールを取ろうとしたが, 失敗した. *The bullet narrowly missed his heart.* 銃弾は間一髪で彼の心臓を外した. ▶定義2 他 to not see, hear, understand, etc sb/sth ～を見ない, 聞かない, 理解しないなど→**見落とす, 聞き損なう, 理解し損なう** ‖ *The house is on the corner so **you can't miss it**.* その家は角にあるので見逃すことはないよ. *They completely **missed the point** of what I was saying.* 彼らは私が述べていた事の要点を全く理解していなかった. *My Mum will know there's something wrong. She **doesn't miss much**.* 母は何かおかしいと気付くでしょう. 彼女はささいな事も見逃しません. ▶定義3 他 to arrive too late for sth or to fail to go to or do sth ～にあまりにも遅く到着する, ～へ行くまたは～をすることに失敗する→**機会を逃す, 乗り損なう** ‖ *Hurry up or you'll miss the plane!* 急ぎなさい, さもないと飛行機に乗り損なうよ. *Of course I'm coming to your wedding. **I wouldn't miss it for the world** (= used to emphasize that you really want to do sth).* もちろん私はあなたの結婚式に行きます. 絶対に逃さないよ(= 本当に～をしたい事を強調するのに用いる). ▶定義4 他 to feel sad because sb is not with you any more, or because you have not got or cannot do sth that you once had or did ～がもうあなたと一緒にいないために, またはあなたがかつて持っていた・行った～を持てない・できないために, 悲しく感じる→**～がいない, またはないので寂しく思う, ～がいない, またはないのを惜しむ** ‖ *I'll miss you terribly when you go away.* あなたが行ってしまうと, とても寂しくなる. *What did you miss most when you lived abroad?* 外国で暮らしているときに何がないのが一番困りましたか. ▶定義5 他 to notice that sb/sth is not where he/she/it should be ～がいるべき場所にいない, またはあるべき場所にないことに気付く→**～がいないのに気付く, ～がないのに気付く** ‖ *When did you first miss your handbag?* あなたが最初にハンドバッグがないのに気付いたのはいつですか. ▶定義6 他 to avoid sth unpleasant 嫌な～を避ける→**～を避ける, 逃れる, 免れる** ‖ *If we leave now, we'll miss the rush-hour traffic.* 今出発すれば交通渋滞を避けることができるだろう.

句動詞 miss sb/sth out ▶定義 to not include sb/sth ～を含まない→**～を抜かす, 省く, 落とす** ‖ *You've missed out several important points in your report.* あなたは報告書でいくつかの重要な点を落としている.

miss out (on sth) ▶定義 to not have a chance to have or do sth ～を持つ・する機会がない→**もらい損なう, ありつけない, 楽しめない** ‖ *You'll miss out on all the fun if you stay at home.* 家にこもっていたら, あらゆる楽しみを逃してしまうよ.

**miss**³ /mɪs/ 名 C ▶定義 a failure to hit, catch or reach sth ～を打つ・捕らえる・～に届くことの失敗→**打ち損ない, 取り逃がし, 外れ** ‖ *After several misses he finally managed to hit the target.* 数回外した後, 彼はついに何とか的に当てた.

成句 give sth a miss 特に 英 略式 ▶定義 to decide not to do or have sth ～をしないまたは持たないことを決心する→**やめておく, 抜かす, 欠席する** ‖ *I think I'll give aerobics a miss tonight.* 私は今晩エアロビクスを休みます.

a near miss ⇒ **NEAR**¹

**missile** /ˈmɪsaɪl; ˈmɪs(ə)l/ 名 C ▶定義1 a powerful exploding weapon that can be sent long distances through the air 空中を遠くまで送れる強力な爆発する武器→**ミサイル, 誘導弾** ‖ *nuclear missiles* 核ミサイル ▶定義2 an object or weapon that is fired from a gun or thrown in order to hurt sb or damage sth ～を傷付けたり～を損壊させるために, 銃から発射されるまたは投じられる物体または武器→**飛び道具** ‖ *The rioters threw missiles such as bottles and stones.* 暴徒たちはびんや石などの物を投げ付けた.

**missing** /ˈmɪsɪŋ/ 形 ▶定義1 lost, or not in the right or usual place 失われた, 正しいまたは通常の場所にない→**行方不明の, 見当たらない, 紛失した** ‖ *a missing person* 行方不明者 *Two files have **gone missing** from my office.* 2つのファイルが事務所からなくなった. ▶定義2 (used about a person) not present after a battle, an accident, etc but not known to have been killed (人について)戦闘, 事故などの後にいないことが分かったが死亡したかが判明しない→**行方不明の** ‖ *Many soldiers were listed as **missing in action**.* 多くの兵士が戦闘中の行方不明として

記載された. ▶定義3 not included, often when it should have been しばしばあるべきときに, 含まれていない→**欠けている** ‖ *Fill in the missing words in the text.* 本文で欠けている単語を補いなさい.

**mission** /míʃ(ə)n/ 名 ⓒ ▶定義1 an important official job that sb is sent somewhere to do, especially to another country 〜がそれを行うためにどこかへ, 特にほかの国へ, 送られる重要な公式の仕事→**任務, 使命** ‖ *Your mission is to send back information about the enemy's movements.* あなたの使命は敵の動向についての情報を送り返すことだ. ▶定義2 a group of people who are sent to a foreign country to perform a special task 特別な仕事を遂行するために外国へ送られる人々の集団→**使節, 使節団, 派遣団** ‖ *a British trade mission to China* 対中国英国通商使節団 ▶定義3 a special journey made by a spacecraft or military aircraft 宇宙船または空軍機による特別な飛行→**飛行(任務), 特別任務** ‖ *a mission to the moon* 月への特別任務 ▶定義4 a place where people are taught about the Christian religion, given medical help, etc by people who are sent from another country to do this (missionaries) ほかの国からそれ(使命)を行うために派遣された人々によって, 人々がキリスト教の教えを受けたり, 治療を受けたりなどする場所→**教会, 伝道所** ▶定義5 a particular task which you feel it is your duty to do するのが自分の義務だと感じるような特別な仕事→**天職, 使命** ‖ *Her work with the poor was more than just a job - it was her **mission in life**.* 貧しい人々との仕事は彼女にとって単なる仕事以上のものだった－それは彼女の人生の使命だった.

**missionary** /míʃ(ə)n(ə)ri; -nèri/ 名 ⓒ (複 **missionaries**) ▶定義 a person who is sent to a foreign country to teach about the Christian religion キリスト教について教えるために外国に送られる人→**宣教師, 伝道者**

**misspell** /mì(s)spél/ 動 ⓣ (過, 過分 **misspelled** または **misspelt** /-spélt/) ▶定義 to spell sth wrongly 〜を間違ってつづる→**〜のつづりを間違える**

\***mist**¹ /mɪst/ 名 ⓒ ⓤ ▶定義 a cloud made of very small drops of water in the air just above the ground, that makes it difficult to see 地面のすぐ上の空気中に現れ視界を悪くする, 非常に小さな水滴でできた雲→**かすみ, もや** ‖ *The fields were covered in mist.* 野原はもやで覆われていた. ☞参 **fog, weather** の注—**misty** 形→**もやのかかった, ぼんやりとした** ‖ *a misty morning* もやのかかった朝 ☞参 **foggy**

**mist**² /mɪst/ 動

句動詞 **mist (sth) up/over** ▶定義 to cover or be covered with very small drops of water that make it difficult to see 視界を悪くする非常に小さな水滴で覆う, または覆われた→**もやがかかる, もやでかすませる** ‖ *My glasses keep misting up.* 私の眼鏡は曇ったままだ.

\***mistake**¹ /mɪstéɪk/ 名 ⓒ ▶定義 something that you think or do that is wrong 間違っている事を考えるまたは行うこと→**誤り, 間違い** ‖ *Try not to **make** any **mistakes** in your essays.* 論文で間違いのないようにしなさい. *a spelling mistake* つづり間違い *It was a big mistake to trust her.* 彼女を信じたのが大きな誤りだった. *I made the mistake of giving him my address.* 私は彼に住所を教えるという誤りを犯した.

成句 **by mistake** ▶定義 as a result of being careless 不注意の結果として→**誤って** ‖ *The terrorists shot the wrong man by mistake.* テロリストたちは誤って別の男性を撃った.

▶ error の方が mistake よりも正式: *a computing error* (コンピューター操作のエラー). fault は悪い事がだれの責任であるかを指摘する: *The accident wasn't my fault. The other driver pulled out in front of me.* (その事故は私の過失ではなかった. 相手側の運転手が私の前に出てきたのだ.) fault は〜が持つ問題または弱点を表現するときにも用いられる: *a technical fault* (技術的ミス)

\***mistake**² /mɪstéɪk/ 動 ⓣ (過 **mistook** /məstúk/; 過分 **mistaken** /məstéɪk(ə)n/) ▶定義1 **mistake A for B** to think wrongly that sb/sth is sb/sth else 間違って〜がほかの…だと思う→**〜を…と間違える** ‖ *I'm sorry, I mistook you for a friend of mine.* ごめんなさい, あなたを私の友達と間違えました. ▶定義2 to be wrong about sth 〜について間違っている→**間違う, 誤解する** ‖ *I think you've mistaken my meaning.* あなたは私の趣旨を誤解していると思う.

**mistaken** /mɪstéɪk(ə)n/ 形 ▶定義 wrong; not

correct 間違った; 正しくない→**間違った, 誤った** ‖ *a case of mistaken identity* 人違いのケース *a mistaken belief/idea* 誤った信念・考え ― **mistakenly** 副 →**間違って, 誤って**

**mister** ⇒ **MR**

**mistletoe** /mís(ə)ltòu/ 名 Ｕ ▶定義 a plant with white berries and green leaves. Mistletoe grows on trees. 白い漿果(しょうか)と緑の葉を持つ植物. 木で育つ→**やどりぎ**
▶英国ではクリスマスの時にやどりぎを家の中に飾る. under the mistletoe(「やどりぎの下で」)人々にキスをする伝統がある.

**mistook** **MISTAKE**² の過去形

**mistreat** /mɪstríːt/ 動 他 ▶定義 to be cruel to a person or animal 人または動物に残酷にする→**～を虐待する, 酷使する, 乱暴に扱う** ‖ *The owner of the zoo was accused of mistreating the animals.* 動物園の所有者が動物虐待で告発された. ― **mistreatment** 名 Ｕ →**虐待, 不当な扱い, 乱暴な扱い**

**mistress** /místrəs/ 名 Ｃ (古) ▶定義 a married man's secret lover 既婚男性の秘密の愛人→**女性の愛人, めかけ**

**mistrust** /mɪstrʌ́st/ 動 他 ▶定義 to have no confidence in sb/sth because you think he/she/it may be harmful ～が害を及ぼすのではと思うために, その～を信頼しない→**～を信用しない, 疑う** ‖ *I always mistrust politicians who smile too much.* 私はにこにこしすぎる政治家を信用しない. ― **mistrust** 名 [Ｕ, 単数扱い] →**不信感, 疑惑** ‖ *She has a deep mistrust of strangers.* 彼女は知らない人に対して根深い不信感を持っている. ☛参 **distrust**

**misty** /místi/ ⇒ **MIST**¹

**misunderstand** /mìsʌndərstǽnd/ 動 自 他 (過, 過分 **misunderstood** /mìsʌndərstúd/) ▶定義 to understand sb/sth wrongly ～を間違って理解する→**誤解する, 考え違いをする** ‖ *I misunderstood the instructions and answered too many questions.* 私は指示を誤解して, 多くの質問に答えすぎた.

**misunderstanding** /mìsʌndərstǽndɪŋ/ 名 ▶定義 **1** Ｃ Ｕ a situation in which sb/sth is not understood correctly ～が正しく理解されていない状態→**誤解, 考え違い** ‖ *The contract is written in both languages to avoid any misunderstanding.* 誤解が一切ないように, 契約書は両方の言語で書かれている. ▶定義 **2** Ｃ a disagreement or an argument 意見の不一致, または口論→**意見の相違, いざこざ**

**misuse** /mɪsjúːz/ 動 他 ▶定義 to use sth in the wrong way or for the wrong purpose ～を間違った方法で, または間違った目的のために使う→**～を誤用する, 悪用する** ‖ *These chemicals can be dangerous if misused.* これらの化学薬品は誤用すると危険になり得る. ― **misuse** /mɪsjúːs/ 名 Ｃ Ｕ →**誤用, 悪用, 濫用**

**mitigate** /mítəgeɪt/ 動 他 正式 ▶定義 to make sth less serious, painful, unpleasant, etc ～の深刻さ, 痛さ, 不快さなどを少なくする→**～を和らげる, 静める, 軽くする** ― **mitigating** 形 →**軽くする, 酌量すべき** ‖ *Because of the mitigating circumstances (= that made the crime seem less bad) the judge gave her a lighter sentence.* 酌量すべき情状(= 犯罪をより悪くなく思えるようにした)のために, 裁判官は彼女により軽い判決を下した.

**mitten** /mítn/ 名 Ｃ ▶定義 a type of glove that has one part for the thumb and another part for all four fingers 手袋の一種で, 親指を入れる部分と残りの4本の指を一緒に入れる部分に分かれている→**ミトン** ☛ C6ページのさし絵 ☛参 **glove**

\***mix**¹ /mɪks/ 動 ▶定義 **1** 自 他 mix (A) (with B), mix (A and B) (together) if two or more substances mix or if you mix them, they combine to form a new substance 2つ以上の物質が混ざると, またはそれらを混ぜると, それらは一緒になって新しい物質を作る→**混合する, 混ぜる, 混ざる, 調合する** ‖ *Oil and water don't mix.* 油と水は混ざらない. *Mix all the ingredients together in a bowl.* すべての材料をボールの中で混ぜなさい. *to mix cement (= to make cement by mixing other substances)* セメントを調合する(= ほかの物質を混ぜてセメントを作る) ▶定義 **2** 自 mix (with sb) to be with and talk to other people ほかの人々と一緒にいて話す→**交わる, 親しく付き合う** ‖ *He mixes with all types of people at work.* 彼は仕事であらゆる種類の人々と付き合う.

成句 **be/get mixed up in sth** 略式 ▶定義 to be/become involved in sth bad or unpleasant 悪いまたは嫌な～にかかわっている, かかわるこ

とになる→関係する,巻き込まれる,掛かり合いになる

句動詞 **mix sth up** ▶定義 to put something in the wrong order 何かを間違った順序で置く→**ごちゃ混ぜにする** ‖ *He was so nervous that he dropped his speech and got the pages all mixed up.* 彼は緊張のあまりスピーチ原稿を落とし,ページをごちゃ混ぜにしてしまった.

**mix sb/sth up (with sb/sth)** ▶定義 to confuse sb/sth with sb/sth else 〜をほかの…と混同する→**混同する,訳が分からなくする** ‖ *I always get him mixed up with his brother.* 私はいつも彼と彼の弟を混同する.

**mix**² /mɪks/ 名 ▶定義 **1** [ C, 通常は単数]a group of different types of people or things 異なる種類の人々または物の集まり→**混合** ‖ *We need a good racial mix in the police force.* 警察ではいろいろな人種をうまく混成させる必要がある. ▶定義 **2** C U a special powder that contains all the substances needed to make sth. You add water or another liquid to this powder. 〜を作るのに必要なすべての材料が調合されている特別な粉で,水またはほかの液体を加えて使う→**ミックス** ‖ *cake mix* ケーキミックス

\***mixed** /mɪkst/ 形 ▶定義 **1** being both good and bad 良くもあり悪くもある→**複合した,混合した** ‖ *I have mixed feelings about leaving my job.* 退職については複雑な気持ちだ. ▶定義 **2** made or consisting of different types of person or thing 異なる種類の人々または物から出来ている,または成り立っている→**男女混合の,共学の,種々雑多な** ‖ *Was your school mixed or single-sex?* あなたの学校は共学,それとも男女別学でしたか. *a mixed salad* ミックスサラダ

**mixed marriage** 名 C ▶定義 a marriage between people of different races or religions 人種または宗教の異なる人との間の結婚→**異民族間の結婚**

**mixed-up** 形 略式 ▶定義 confused because of emotional problems 情緒的な問題のために混乱した→**精神錯乱の,頭が混乱した** ‖ *He has been very mixed-up since his parents' divorce.* 彼は両親が離婚して以来,非常に心が乱れている.

**mixer** /ˈmɪksər/ 名 C ▶定義 a machine that is used for mixing sth 〜を混ぜるために用いる機械→**ミキサー,攪拌(かくはん)器** ‖ *a food/cement mixer* フード・セメントミキサー

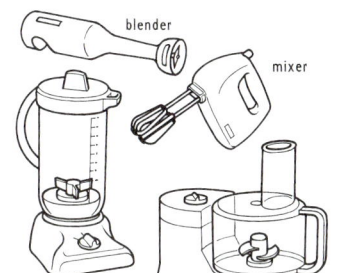

blender
mixer
blender (医または liquidizer)
food processor

\***mixture** /ˈmɪkstʃər/ 名 ▶定義 **1** [単数扱い]a combination of different things 異なるものが組み合わさったもの→**混合,混ぜ合わせること** ‖ *Monkeys eat a mixture of leaves and fruit.* 猿は葉と果物を混合で食べる. ▶定義 **2** C U a substance that is made by mixing other substances together ほかの物質を混ぜ合わせることによって作られる物質→**混合物,混合した物,混合薬** ‖ *cake mixture* ケーキミックス *a mixture of eggs, flour and milk* 卵と小麦粉と牛乳を混ぜた物

**mix-up** 名 C 略式 ▶定義 a mistake in the planning or organization of sth 〜の計画または手配上の間違い→**ごたごた,混乱** ‖ *There was a mix-up and we were given the wrong ticket.* 混乱があり,私たちは間違ったチケットを渡された.

**ml** 略 millilitre(s)→**ミリリットル** ‖ *contents 75ml* 内容量75ミリリットル

**mm** 略 millimetre(s)→**ミリメートル** ‖ *a 35mm camera* 35ミリフィルムのカメラ

**moan** /moʊn/ 動 自 ▶定義 **1** to make a low sound because you are in pain, very sad, etc 痛い,非常に悲しいなどのため,低い声を出す→**うめく,うなる** ‖ *to moan with pain* 痛みでうめく ▶定義 **2** 略式 to keep saying what is wrong about sth; to complain 〜についてどこが悪いか言い続ける;文句を言う→**不平を言う,不満を言う** ‖ *The English are always moaning about the weather.* 英国人はいつも天気について不満を言っている.—**moan** 名 C ▶**うめき,不平,不満**

**mob**¹ /mɑb/ 名 [ C, 単数または複数形の動詞と共に] ▶定義 a large crowd of people that may become violent or cause trouble 暴力的になる

1060　mob²

または問題を起こすかもしれない人々の大群衆→暴徒, やじ馬連, 群衆

**mob**² /mɑb/ 動他 (**mobbing**; **mobbed**) ▶定義 to form a large crowd around sb, for example in order to see or touch him/her 例えば～を見るまたは触るために, その～の周りに大きな群衆ができる→～を寄ってたかってもみくちゃにする ‖ *The band was mobbed by fans as they left the hotel.* そのバンドがホテルを出てきた時ファンによってもみくちゃにされた.

**mobile**¹ /móʊbaɪl, -bɪːl, -b(ə)l/ 形 ▶定義 able to move or be moved easily 簡単に動くまたは動かされることができる→動きやすい, 動かしやすい ‖ *My daughter is much more mobile now she has her own car.* 娘は今自分の車を持っているので, 以前よりはるかに動きやすい. ⇔ **immobile** — **mobility** /moʊbíləti/ 名 Ⓤ →可動性, 流動性, 機動力

**mobile**² /móʊbaɪl, -bɪːl, -b(ə)l/ 名 Ⓒ ▶定義 1 a decoration that you hang from the ceiling and that moves when the air around it moves 天井からつり下げられて, 周囲の空気が流れると動く飾り→モビール ▶定義 2 = MOBILE PHONE

**mobile phone** (または **mobile**; **cellphone**) 名 Ⓒ ▶定義 a telephone that you can carry around with you 持ち歩くことができる電話→携帯電話 ☞ **telephone** のさし絵

**mobilize** (または **-ise**) /móʊbəlaɪz/ 動 ▶定義 1 他 to organize people or things to do sth ～をする人々または物を編成する→～をかき集める, 駆り集める ‖ *They mobilized the local residents to oppose the new development.* 彼らは新しい開発に反対するために地域住民を駆り集めた. ▶定義 2 自他 (used about the army, navy, etc) to get ready for war (陸軍, 海軍などについて) 戦争の準備をする→動員する, 動員される ⇔ **immobilize**

**mock**¹ /mɑk/ 動自他 正式 ▶定義 to laugh at sb/sth in an unkind way or to make other people laugh at him/her/it ～を意地悪く笑う, またはほかの人々に～を笑わせる→あざける, あざ笑う, からかう, まねをする

▶ laugh at, make fun of は mock ほど正式ではなくより一般的.

**mock**² /mɑk/ 形 (名詞の前だけ) ▶定義 not real or genuine 真実または純粋でない→偽りの, まがいの, 模擬の ‖ *He held up his hands in mock surprise.* 彼は驚いた振りをして両手を上げた. *a mock (= practice) exam* 模擬 (=練習) 試験

**mock**³ /mɑk/ 名 [通常は複数] ▶定義 (in Britain) a practice exam that you do before the official one (英国で) 正式な試験の前に行う練習の試験→模擬試験

**mock-up** 名 Ⓒ ▶定義 a model of sth that shows what it will look like or how it will work それがどう見えるかまたはどのように働くかを示す～の見本→実物大の模型, レイアウト, 割り符

**modal** /móʊdl/ (または **modal verb**) 名 Ⓒ (文法) ▶定義 a verb, for example 'might', 'can' or 'must' that is used with another verb for expressing possibility, permission, intention, etc 可能性, 許可, 意図などを表現するためにほかの動詞と共に用いられる動詞. 例えば might, can または must→法助動詞

▶ 法助動詞についての説明は, 巻末の「文法早見表」を参照.

**mode** /móʊd/ 名 Ⓒ ▶定義 1 a type of sth or way of doing sth ～の種類, または～をする方法→様式, 方法, やり方 ‖ *a mode of transport/life* 輸送手段・生活様式 ▶定義 2 one of the ways in which a machine can work 機械が作動できる方法の1つ→モード ‖ *Switch the camera to automatic mode.* カメラを自動モードに切り替えなさい.

***model** /mɑ́dl/ 名 Ⓒ ▶定義 1 a copy of sth that is usually smaller than the real thing 実際の物よりも通常小さい, ～を模倣した物→模型, ひな型 ‖ *a model aeroplane* 飛行機の模型 ▶定義 2 one of the machines, vehicles, etc that is made by a particular company 特定の会社によって作られる機械, 乗り物などの1つ→型, 様式 ‖ *The latest models are on display at the show.* 最新型が展示会で展示されている. ▶定義 3 a person or thing that is a good example to copy まねるべき良い例である人または物→模範, 手本 ‖ *a model student* 模範的な生徒 *Children often use older brothers or sisters as **role models** (= copy the way they behave).* 子供たちはしばしば兄または姉を手本とする (= 彼らの行いをまねる). ▶定義 4 a person who is employed to wear clothes at a fashion show or for magazine photographs ファッションショーでまたは雑誌の写真用に服を着るために雇われる人→ファッショ

ンモデル ▶定義5 a person who is painted, drawn or photographed by an artist 芸術家によって絵にかかれる，デッサンされる，または写真を撮られる人→モデル

**\*model**² /mάdl/ 動 (**modelling; modelled**: 米 **modeling; modeled**) ▶定義1 **model sth/yourself on sb/sth** to make sth/yourself similar to sth/sb else 〜・自分自身をほかの…と似せる→〜を手本にする，倣う ‖ *The house is modelled on a Roman villa.* その家はローマの別荘に倣って作っている． ▶定義2 to wear and show clothes at a fashion show or for photographs ファッションショーでまたは写真のために服を着て見せる→モデルとなる，モデルを務める ‖ *to model swimsuits* 水着のモデルを務める ▶定義3 to make a model of sth 〜の模型を作る→模型を作る，モデルを作る，作る ‖ *This clay is difficult to model.* この粘土で模型を作るのは難しい．

**modelling** (米**modeling**) /mάdlɪŋ/ ▶定義 the work of a fashion model ファッションモデルの仕事→モデル業

**modem** /móʊdem, -dəm/ ▶定義 a piece of equipment that connects two or more computers together by means of a telephone line so that information can go from one to the other 2 台以上のコンピューターを電話回線でつなぎ，情報をやり取りできるようにする機器→モデム

**\*moderate**¹ /mάd(ə)rət/ ▶定義1 being, having, using, etc neither too much nor too little of sth 多すぎもせず少なすぎもしない〜である，〜を持つ，〜を使うなどの→適度の，程よい，ほどほどの ‖ *a moderate speed* 適度な速度 *We've had a moderate amount of success.* 私たちはほどほどに成功した． ▶定義2 having or showing opinions, especially about politics, that are not extreme 極端ではない意見を，特に政治について，持っているまたは示す→穏健な，極端に走らない ‖ *moderate policies/views* 穏健な政策・見方 ☞参 **extreme, radical** — **moderately**副 →適度に，程よく，控えめに ‖ *His career has been moderately successful.* 彼の経歴は程よく成功を収めてきている．

**moderate**² /mάd(ə)rət/ 動 ▶定義 to become or to make sth less strong or extreme 強くなくなるまたは極端でなくなる，または〜をそのようにさせる→和らげる，軽減する，和らぐ ‖ *The union moderated its original demands.* 組合は当初の要求を軟化させた．

**moderate**³ /mάd(ə)rət/ ▶定義 a person whose opinions, especially about politics, are not extreme 特に政治について，極端でない意見を持つ人→穏健派の人，穏健な人 ☞参 **extremist**

**moderation** /mὰd(ə)réɪʃ(ə)n/ ▶定義 the quality of being reasonable and not being extreme 理にかなっていて極端でない性質→穏健，中庸，適度 ‖ *Alcohol can harm unborn babies even if it's taken **in moderation**.* アルコールはたとえ適度に摂取しても胎児に害を及ぼすことがある．

**\*modern** /mάdəm/ 形 ▶定義1 of the present or recent times 現在のまたは最近の時代の→現代の，近代の ‖ *Pollution is one of the major problems in the modern world.* 汚染は現代世界における重大な問題の1つだ． ▶定義2 (used about styles of art, music, etc) new and different from traditional styles（芸術，音楽などの様式について）新しくて伝統的な様式とは異なる→現代的な，当世風の，モダンな ‖ *modern jazz/architecture* モダンジャズ・現代建築 ▶定義3 with all the newest methods, equipment, designs, etc; up-to-date すべての最新の方法，機器，デザインなどで；最新の→近代的な，最新の ‖ *It is one of the most modern hospitals in the country.* それはその国で最も近代的な病院の1つだ． ☞参 **old-fashioned**

**modernize** (または **-ise**) /mάdəmaɪz/ 動 ▶定義 to make sth suitable for use today using new methods, styles, etc 新しい方法，様式などを用いて〜を今日利用できるようにする→〜を近代化する，現代化する — **modernization** (または **-isation**) /mὰdəmɪzéɪʃ(ə)n/ →近代化，現代化 ‖ *The house is large but is in need of modernization.* その家は大きいが近代化が必要だ．

**modern languages** [複数扱い] ▶定義 languages that are spoken now 今話されている言語→現代語

**modest** /mάdəst/ 形 ▶定義1 not talking too much about your own abilities, good qualities, etc 自分自身の能力，優れた性質などについて語りすぎない→謙虚な，慎み深い，謙そんした ‖ *She got the best results in the exam but she was too*

**modest** to tell anyone. 彼女は試験で最高の成績を収めたが,非常に謙虚なのでだれにも話さなかった. ☛参 **humble, proud** ▶定義2 not very large あまり大きくない→適度の,穏当な ‖ a modest pay increase ささやかな賃金アップ ▶定義3 (used about a woman's clothes) not showing much of the body (女性の服について)体を見せすぎない→控えめな,地味な— **modesty** 名 Ⓤ→謙そん,謙虚— **modestly** 副→謙そんして,謙虚に

**modify** /mάdəfàɪ/ 動他 (現分 **modifying**; 三単現 **modifies**; 過,過分 **modified**) ▶定義 to change sth slightly 〜をわずかに変える→修正する,(少し)変更する ‖ We shall need to modify the existing plan. 既存の計画を修正する必要があるだろう. — **modification** /mὰdəfəkéɪʃ(ə)n/ 名 ⒸⓊ→修正,(部分的な)変更

**module** /mάdjul; mɔ́dʒul/ 名 Ⓒ ▶定義 a unit that forms part of sth bigger より大きな〜の部分を形成する部分→構成部分,ユニット,モジュール,履修単位 ‖ You must complete three modules (= courses that you study) in your first year. あなたは1年目に3つの履修単位(= 学ぶ講座)を終えなければならない.

**mohair** /móʊheər/ 名 Ⓤ ▶定義 very soft wool that comes from a certain type of animal (a goat) ある種の動物(ヤギ)から取れる非常に柔らかい羊毛→モヘア

**moist** /mɔ́ɪst/ 形 ▶定義 slightly wet; damp わずかにぬれた; 湿っぽい→湿った,ぬれた,しっとりした ‖ Her eyes were moist with tears. 彼女の目は涙で潤んでいた. Keep the soil moist or the plant will die. 土の湿り気をいつも保っておきなさい,さもないと植物は枯れるでしょう. ☛参 **wet** の注— **moisten** /mɔ́ɪsn/ 動自他→湿らせる,潤す

**moisture** /mɔ́ɪstʃər/ 名 Ⓤ ▶定義 water in small drops on a surface, in the air, etc 表面,空中などの細かな水滴→湿気,湿り気,水分

**molar** /móʊlər/ 名 Ⓒ ▶定義 one of the large teeth at the back of your mouth 口の後方にある大きな歯の1つ→臼歯(きゅうし),奥歯

**molasses** /məlǽsəz/ 米 =TREACLE
**mold** 米 =MOULD
**moldy** 米 =MOULDY

**mole** /móʊl/ 名 Ⓒ ▶定義1 a small dark spot on a person's skin that never goes away 決して消えない,人の皮膚上にある小さな黒っぽい点→ほくろ,あざ ☛参 **freckle** ▶定義2 a small animal with dark fur that lives underground and is almost blind 地面の下に生息する,ほぼ盲目の黒っぽい毛皮を持つ小さな動物→もぐら ▶定義3 略式 a person who works in one organization and gives secret information to another organization; a spy ある組織の中で働き,機密をほかの組織に流す人; スパイ→スパイ

**molecule** /mάləkjùːl/ 名 Ⓒ ▶定義 the smallest unit into which a substance can be divided without changing its chemical nature 物質が持つ化学的特質を変えずにそれを分割できる最小の単位→分子 ☛参 **atom**

**molest** /məlést/ 動他 ▶定義 to attack sb, especially a child, in a sexual way 〜を,特に子供を,性的に攻撃する→〜に性的な乱暴をする,性的ないたずらをする,危害を加える

**molt** 米 =MOULT

**molten** /móʊltn/ 形 ▶定義 (used about metal or rock) made liquid by very great heat (金属または岩について)非常に強い熱によって液化した→溶解した,溶解して作った

**mom** 米 =MUM

*__moment__ /móʊmənt/ 名 ▶定義1 Ⓒa very short period of time 非常に短い時間→瞬間,ちょっとの時間 ‖ One moment, please (= please wait). ちょっと待ってください(= お待ちください). Joe left just a few moments ago. ジョーはほんの少し前に発った. ▶定義2 [単数扱い]a particular point in time 特定の時点→時,時機 ‖ Just at that moment my mother arrived. ちょうどその時に私の母が到着した. the moment of birth/death 誕生・死の瞬間

成句 (at) any minute/moment (now)⇒ **MINUTE**¹

at the moment ▶定義 now 今→ちょうど今,ちょうどその時 ‖ I'm afraid she's busy at the moment. Can I take a message? 彼女は今ちょうど忙しいと思います.伝言をお伝えしましょうか.

for the moment/present ▶定義 for a short time; for now 短い間; 今のところ→差し当たり,当座は ‖ I'm not very happy at work but I'll stay there for the moment. 仕事はあまり楽しくないが,当面そこにいます.

**in a moment** ▶定義 very soon 非常にすぐに→瞬時に, あっと言う間に ‖ *Just wait here. I'll be back in a moment.* ちょっとここで待っていなさい. すぐに戻るから.
**the last minute/moment**⇒**LAST¹**
**the minute/moment (that)**⇒**MINUTE¹**
**on the spur of the moment**⇒**SPUR¹**

**momentary** /móʊmənt(ə)ri, -tèri/ 形 ▶定義 lasting for a very short time 非常に短い間続く→瞬間の, つかの間の, 一時的な ‖ *a momentary lack of concentration* 集中力の一時的な欠如 ─ **momentarily** /mòʊməntérəli, móʊmənt(ə)rɪli/ 副 →ちょっとの間, 一時的に

**momentous** /moʊméntəs, mə-/ 形 ▶定義 very important 非常に重要な→重大な, 重要な ‖ *a momentous decision/event/change* 重大な決定・出来事・変化

**momentum** /moʊméntəm, mə-/ 名 Ⓤ ▶定義 the ability to keep increasing or developing; the force that makes sth move faster and faster 増加または発達し続ける能力; ～をどんどん速く動かす力→勢い, 弾み ‖ *The environmental movement is **gathering momentum**.* 環境運動に弾みが付いている.

**mommy** 米=**MUMMY(1)**

**Mon** 略 Monday→月曜日 ‖ *Mon 6 June* 6月6日月曜日

**monarch** /mánərk, -ùːrk/ 名 Ⓒ ▶定義 a king or queen 王または女王→君主, 王者

**monarchy** /mánərki, -ùːr-/ 名 (複 **monarchies**) ▶定義 1 [単数扱い, Ⓤ] the system of government or rule by a king or queen 王または女王による政府または統治の制度→君主政治, 君主制度 ▶定義 2 Ⓒ a country that is governed by a king or queen 王または女王によって統治される国→君主国 ☛参 **republic**

**monastery** /mánəst(ə)ri, -tèri/ 名 Ⓒ (複 **monasteries**) ▶定義 a place where men (**monks**) live in a religious community 男性 (僧) が宗教的な共同体で暮らす場所→修道院, 僧院 ☛参 **convent**

*****Monday** /mándeɪ, -di/ 名 Ⓒ Ⓤ (略式 **Mon**) ▶定義 the day of the week after Sunday 日曜日の次の曜日→月曜日 ‖ *I'm going to see her on Monday.* 私は月曜日に彼女に会うつもりだ. 略式 *I'll see you Monday.* 月曜日に会いましょう. *I finish work a bit later on Mondays/on a Monday.* 月曜日には私は少し遅くまで仕事をする. *Monday morning/afternoon/evening/night* 月曜日の午前・午後・夕方・夜 *last/next Monday* この前の・次の月曜日 *a week on Monday/Monday week* (= not next Monday, but the Monday after that) その次の週の月曜日 (= 次の月曜日ではなく, さらにその次の月曜日) *The museum is open Monday to Friday, 10 till 4.30.* 美術館は月曜から金曜の10時から4時半まで開いている. *Did you see that article about Italy in Monday's paper?* 月曜の新聞のイタリアについての記事を見ましたか.

▶曜日は常に大文字で始める.

**monetary** /mánɪt(ə)ri; mánətèri/ 形 ▶定義 connected with money お金に関連した→通貨の, 貨幣の, 金銭の ‖ *the government's monetary policy* 政府の通貨政策

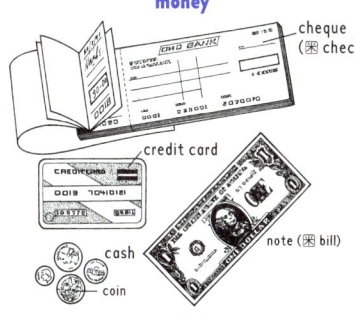
money

*****money** /máni/ 名 Ⓤ ▶定義 the means of paying for sth or buying sth (= coins or notes) ～の支払いをするまたは～を買う手段 (= 硬貨または紙幣)→金 (かね), 金銭 ‖ *Will you **earn** more money in your new job?* 新しい仕事ではもっとお金が稼げるのですか. *The new road will **cost** a lot of money.* 新しい道路には多くのお金がかかるだろう. *If we do the work ourselves we will **save** money.* その仕事を自分たちですれば, お金を節約できるだろう. *The government **make** a huge amount of money out of tobacco tax.* 政府はたばこ税でばく大な税収を得る.
☛参 **pocket money**
成句 **be rolling in money/in it**⇒**ROLL²**
**get your money's worth** ▶定義 to get full value for the money you have spent 費やしたお金に

対して十分な価値を得る→払った金[努力]に見合うだけのものを得る・楽しむ

**mongrel** /mʌ́ŋgr(ə)l/ 名 C ▶定義 a dog that has parents of different types (breeds) 異なる種類(品種)の両親を持つ犬→雑種,雑種犬 ☛参 pedigree

**monitor**¹ /mɑ́nətər/ 名 C ▶定義 1 a machine that shows information or pictures on a screen like a television テレビのように画面上に情報または画像を見せる機械→モニター ☛ S5 ページのさし絵 ▶定義 2 a machine that records or checks sth 〜を記録または検査する機械→チェック装置,監視装置 ‖ A monitor checks the baby's heartbeat. モニターが赤ん坊の心拍を確認します.

**monitor**² /mɑ́nətər/ 動他 ▶定義 to check, record or test sth regularly for a period of time 一定期間,定期的に〜を検査,記録または試験する→〜を監視する,チェックする,モニターで監視する ‖ Pollution levels in the lake are closely monitored. 湖の汚染レベルは厳密に監視されている.

**monk** /mʌŋk/ 名 C ▶定義 a member of a religious group of men who live in a special building (monastery) and do not get married or have possessions 特別な建物(修道院)に暮らし,結婚しないまたは財産を持たない男性の宗教的集団の一員→修道士 ☛参 nun

★**monkey** /mʌ́ŋki/ 名 C ▶定義 an animal with a long tail that lives in hot countries and can climb trees 長いしっぽを持つ動物で,暑い国に生息し木登りができる→猿 ☛参 ape. chimpanzee (チンパンジー) と gorilla (ゴリラ) は ape (類人猿) だが,monkey (猿) と呼ばれることもある.

成句 **monkey business** ▶定義 silly or dishonest behaviour ばかげたまたは不正直な行為→いんちき,ごまかし

**mono** /mɑ́nou/ 形 ▶定義 (used about recorded music or a system for playing it) having the sound coming from one direction only (録音された音楽またはそれを演奏する仕組みについて) 一方向からのみの音が出る→モノラルの ☛参 stereo

**monolingual** /mὰnoulíŋgwəl/ 形 ▶定義 using only one language 1つの言語だけを使う→1つの言語(だけ)を話す,または用いた ‖ This is a monolingual dictionary. これは国語辞典だ. ☛参 bilingual

**monologue** (米 または **monolog**) /mɑ́nəlɔ̀(ː)g, -lɑ̀g/ 名 C ▶定義 a long speech by one person, for example in a play 例えば演劇での,1 人の人による台詞(せりふ)→独白,長話

**monopolize** (または **-ise**) /mənɑ́pəlàɪz/ 動他 ▶定義 to control sth so that other people cannot share it ほかの人々がこれを共有できないように〜を支配する→〜の独占権を得る,〜の専売権を得る,独り占めする ‖ She completely monopolized the conversation. I couldn't get a word in. 彼女は完全に会話を独占した.私は一言も口を挟めなかった.

**monopoly** /mənɑ́pəli/ 名 C (複 **monopolies**) a monopoly (on/in sth) ▶定義 1 the control of an industry or service by only one company; a type of goods or a service that is controlled in this way 1 社のみによる,ある産業・サービスの支配;そのように支配されている商品・サービスの種類→独占業,専売品,専売業 ‖ The company has a monopoly on broadcasting international football. その会社は国際サッカーの放送を独占している. ▶定義 2 the complete control, possession or use of sth; something that belongs to only one person or group and is not shared 〜の完全な支配,所有または使用;1 人または 1 つの集団に属し,共有されないもの→独占,独り占め(にすること),独占品

**monorail** /mɑ́nərèɪl/ 名 C ▶定義 a railway in which the train runs on a single track, usually high above the ground 通常地面より高い所にあり,1 本の線路の上を列車が走る鉄道→モノレール,単軌鉄道

**monosyllable** /mɑ̀nəsíləb(ə)l/ 名 C ▶定義 a short word, such as 'leg', that has only one syllable leg などの音節が 1 つだけある短い単語→単音節語,1 音節語

**monotonous** /mənɑ́t(ə)nəs/ 形 ▶定義 never changing and therefore boring 決して変わらず,したがって退屈な→単調な,変化のない,退屈な ‖ monotonous work 単調な仕事 a monotonous voice 一本調子の声—**monotonously** 副→単調に,一本調子に

**monotony** /mənɑ́t(ə)ni/ 名 U ▶定義 the state of being always the same and therefore boring 常

に同じで,そのために退屈な状態→**単調さ,退屈,一本調子** || *the monotony of working on a production line* 流れ作業の仕事の単調さ

**monsoon** /mɑnsúːn/ 名 C ▶定義 the season when it rains a lot in Southern Asia; the rain that falls during this period 南アジアの雨がたくさん降る季節;その期間に降る雨→**雨期,モンスーン,豪雨**

**monster** /mɑ́nstər/ 名 C ▶定義 (in stories) a creature that is large, ugly and frightening(物語で)大きく,醜く,怖い生物→**怪物,化け物** || (比喩)*The murderer was described as a dangerous monster.* その殺人者は危険な化け物と呼ばれた.

**monstrosity** /mɑnstrɑ́səti/ 名 C (複 **monstrosities**) ▶定義 something that is very large and ugly, especially a building 非常に大きくて醜いもの,特に建物→**巨大な物,怪物**

**monstrous** /mɑ́nstrəs/ 形 ▶定義 1 that people think is shocking and unacceptable because it is morally wrong or unfair 道徳的に間違っているまたは不公平であるために,人々があきれて受け入れられないと思うような→**ひどい,恥ずべき,不公平な** || *It's monstrous that she earns less than he does for the same job!* 同じ仕事をして彼女が彼より給料が少ないというのはひどい. ▶定義 2 very large (and often ugly or frightening) 非常に大きな(そしてしばしば醜いまたは怖い)→**巨大な** || *a monstrous spider/wave* 化け物蜘蛛(ぐも)・波

★**month** /mʌnθ/ 名 C ▶定義 1 one of the twelve periods of time into which the year is divided 年を12の期間に分けたうちの1つ→**月** || *They are starting work next month.* 彼らは来月仕事を始めるところだ. *Have you seen this month's 'Vogue'?* 今月のVogueを見ましたか. ▶定義 2 the period of about four weeks from a certain date in one month to the same date in the next, for example 13 May to 13 June; a calendar month ある日から翌月の同じ日付までの約4週間の期間.例えば5月13日から6月13日まで;1つの暦月→**1か月(間)** || *'How long will you be away?' 'For about a month.'*「どのくらいの間留守にするの」「約1か月だ」*a six-month course* 6か月間の講座

**monthly**¹ /mʌ́nθli/ 形副 ▶定義 (happening or produced) once every month(発生するまたは生産される)毎月1度(の)→**毎月(の),月1回(の)** || *a monthly meeting/magazine/visit* 月例会議・月刊誌・月例訪問 *Are you paid weekly or monthly?* あなたの給与は週給ですか,それとも月給ですか.

**monthly**² /mʌ́nθli/ 名 C (複 **monthlies**) ▶定義 a magazine that is published once a month 月に1回発行される雑誌→**月刊誌**

**monument** /mɑ́njəmənt/ 名 C *a monument (to sb/sth)* ▶定義 1 a building or statue that is built to remind people of a famous person or event 人々に有名な人または出来事を思い出させるために建てられた建物または像→**記念碑,記念像,記念建築** ☛ **column** のさし絵 ▶定義 2 an old building or other place that is of historical importance 歴史的に重要な古い建物またはほかの場所→**遺跡,史跡**

**monumental** /mɑ̀njəméntl/ 形 (名詞の前だけ) ▶定義 very great, large or important 非常に偉大な,大きな,または重要な→**記念の,記念となる,とてつもない** || *a monumental success/task/achievement* 記念となる成功・仕事・偉業

**moo** /muː/ 名 C ▶定義 the sound that a cow makes 牛が出す声→**もー** ― moo 動 自 →**もーと鳴く**

★**mood** /muːd/ 名 ▶定義 1 C U the way that you are feeling at a particular time 特定の時に感じている状態→**気分,気持ち** || *to be in a bad/good mood (= to feel angry/happy)* 気分が悪い・良い(=怒り・喜びを感じる)*Turn that music down a bit - I'm not **in the mood for** it.* 音楽の音を少し小さくしてくれ ― そういう気分ではないのだ. ▶定義 2 C a time when you are angry or bad-tempered 怒っているまたは機嫌が悪いとき→**不機嫌,むっつり** || *Debby's in one of her moods again.* デビーは例によってご機嫌斜めだ. ☛類 **temper** ▶定義 3 [単数扱い]the way that a group of people feel about sth 人々の集団が〜について感じる状態→**雰囲気,感じ** || *The mood of the crowd suddenly changed and violence broke out.* 群衆の雰囲気が突然変わり,暴力行為が突発した.

**moody** /múːdi/ 形 ▶定義 1 often changing moods in a way that people cannot predict 人々が予測できないくらいにしばしば気分を変え

## moon

る→**むら気な, 気分屋の** || *You never know where you are with Andy because he's so moody.* アンディーはとても気分屋で捕らえ所がない.

▶定義2 bad-tempered or unhappy, often for no particular reason しばしば特別な理由もなく, 機嫌が悪いまたは不幸せな→**不機嫌な, むっつりした**—**moodily** 副→むら気に, 不機嫌に—**moodiness** 名 Ⓤ→むら気, 不機嫌

> ▶日本語 vs 英語
>
> moody と「ムーディー」
>
> 「ムーディー」という言葉は, 日本語では「ムードたっぷりの」という良い意味で用いられることが多いようですが, 英語の moody は,「むっつりして不機嫌な様子」という逆の意味を表すので注意が必要です.

\***moon** /múːn/ 名 ▶定義1 **the moon**［単数扱い］ the object that shines in the sky at night and that moves round the earth once every 28 days 夜空に輝く天体で, 28日間に地球の周りを一周する→**月**

> ▶月は異なる段階の見え方によって, new moon（新月）, full moon（満月）, half-moon（半月）, crescent moon（三日月）と呼ばれる.

☞ 形**lunar** ▶定義2 Ⓒ an object like the moon that moves around another planet 月のようにほかの惑星の周りを動く天体→**衛星** || *How many moons does Neptune have?* 海王星には衛星がいくつありますか.

成句 **once in a blue moon** ⇒ **ONCE**

**over the moon** 特に 英 略式 ▶定義 extremely happy and excited about sth 〜について非常に幸せで興奮した→**とても幸福で**

**moonlight** /múːnlàit/ 名 Ⓤ ▶定義 light that comes from the moon 月から来る光→**月光, 月の光** || *The lake looked beautiful in the moonlight.* 湖は月明かりの中で美しく見えた.

**moonlit** /múːnlìt/ 形 ▶定義 lit by the moon 月によって照らされた→**月の光に照らされた, 月明かりの**

**moor**¹ /mɔːr, muər/（または **moorland** /mɔ́ːrlənd, múər-/）名 Ⓒ Ⓤ ▶定義 a wild open area of high land that is covered with grass and other low plants (heather) 草やほかの丈の低い植物（ヒース）で覆われた荒れた高原地帯→**荒れ野, 荒れ地** || *We walked across the moors.* 私たちは荒れ野を徒歩で横断した. ☞ 参 **heath**

**moor**² /mɔːr, muər/ 動 他 ▶定義 **moor (sth to sth)** to fasten a boat to the land or to an object in the water with a rope or chain 陸または水中にある物に, ボートをロープや鎖でつなぐ→**停泊させる, 停泊する**

**mooring** 名［Ⓒ, 通常は複数］ ▶定義 a place where a boat is tied; the ropes, chains, etc used to fasten a boat ボートがつながれている場所; ボートをつなぐのに使われるロープ, 鎖など→**停泊地, 係船設備**

**moose** /muːs/ 名 特に 米 =**ELK**

**mop**¹ /mɑp/ 名 Ⓒ ▶定義 a tool for washing floors that consists of a long stick with thick strings, pieces of cloth or a sponge on the end 太いひも, 布きれ, またはスポンジが先端に付いた長い棒でできた床を掃除する道具→**モップ** ☞ **bucket** のさし絵

**mop**² /mɑp/ 動 他 (**mopping; mopped**) ▶定義1 to clean a floor with water and a mop 水とモップで床を掃除する→**〜を（モップで）ふく** ▶定義2 to remove liquid from sth using a dry cloth 乾いた布を使って〜から液体を取り去る→**ぬぐい取る,（涙・汗など）をぬぐう** || *to mop your forehead with a handkerchief* ハンカチで額をぬぐう

句動詞 **mop sth up** ▶定義 to get rid of liquid from a surface with a mop or dry cloth モップまたは乾いた布で, 表面から液体を取り去る→**ぬぐい取る, 片付ける** || *Mop up that tea you've spilt or it'll leave a stain!* こぼした紅茶をふき取りなさい, さもないと染みになってしまう.

**mope** /móup/ 動 自 ▶定義 **mope (about/around)** to spend your time doing nothing and feeling sorry for yourself because you are unhappy 不幸せであるために何もせずに自分のことを哀れに感じて時を過ごす→**意気消沈する, ふさぎ込む** || *Moping around the house all day won't make the situation any better.* 一日中家でふさぎ込んでいても状況は何も良くならない.

**moped** /móupèd/ 名 Ⓒ ▶定義 a type of small, not very powerful motorbike 小さく, あまり馬力のないオートバイの一種→**モペット** ☞ **motorbike** のさし絵

\***moral**¹ /mɔ́(ː)r(ə)l, mɑ́r-/ 形 ▶定義1（名詞の前だ

け) concerned with what is right and wrong 善悪に関連した→道徳(上)の, 倫理的な ‖ *Some people refuse to eat meat **on moral grounds** (= because they believe it to be wrong).* 道義上の理由で(= それが悪い事だと信じるために)肉を食べることを拒む人々もいる. *a moral dilemma/issue/question* 道義的なジレンマ・問題・争点 ▶定義 **2** having a high standard of behaviour that is considered good and right by most people ほとんどの人々に善いまたは正しいと考えられているような高い行動基準を持つ→道徳的な, 道義をわきまえた ‖ *She has always led a very moral life.* 彼女は常にとても道義をわきまえた生き方をした.

▶反対語はimmoralである. 異なる意味を持つ amoral と比較.

成句 moral support ▶定義 help or encouragement that you give to sb who is nervous or worried 不安なまたは心配している〜への援助または励まし→精神的な援助 ‖ *I went to the dentist's with him just to give him some moral support.* 彼を励ますために私は彼と一緒に歯医者に行った.

*****moral**[2] /mɔ́(:)r(ə)l, már-/ 名 ▶定義 **1 morals**[複数扱い] standards of good behaviour 善い行いの基準→道徳, モラル ‖ *These people appear to have no morals.* これらの人々にはモラルがないようだ. ▶定義 **2** ⓒ a lesson in the right way to behave that can be learnt from a story or an experience 話または経験から学ぶことができる正しい行いについての教え→教訓, 寓意(ぐうい) ‖ *The moral of the play is that friendship is more important than money.* その芝居の教訓は, 友情はお金よりも重要だということだ.

**morale** /mərá:l; -rǽl/ 名 Ⓤ ▶定義 how happy, sad, confident, etc that a group of people feels at a particular time 人々の集団が特定の時にどのくらい幸せ, 悲しみ, 自信など感じるか→士気, 勤労意欲 ‖ *The team's morale was low/high before the match (= they felt worried/confident).* 試合前のチームの士気は低かった・高かった(= 彼らは不安だった・自信があった). *to boost/raise/improve morale* 士気を高める・向上させる

*****morality** /mərǽləti/ 名 Ⓤ ▶定義 principles concerning what is good and bad or right and wrong behaviour 善悪または正しいまたは間違った行為に関する原則→道徳, 道義 ‖ *a debate about the morality of abortion* 中絶の道義についての議論⇨**immorality**

**moralize**(または **-ise**) /mɔ́(:)r(ə)làɪz, már-/ 動 ⓘ ▶定義 **moralize** (**about/on** sth) to tell other people what the right or wrong way to behave is 何が正しいまたは間違った行いかをほかの人々に述べる→道徳を説く, 説教する

**morally** /mɔ́(:)r(ə)li, már-/ ▶定義 connected with standards of what is right or wrong 正しいまたは間違った事の基準に関連して→道徳的に, 道徳上は

**morbid** /mɔ́:rbəd/ 形 ▶定義 showing interest in unpleasant things, for example disease and death 例えば病気と死など, 不快なものに興味を示す→病的な, 不健全な

*****more**[1] /mɔ́:r/ 形代 ▶定義 a larger number or amount of people or things; sth extra as well as what you have より多くの人または物; 持っているものだけでなく余分なもの→より多くの(人・物・事), これ以上の(もの), それ以上の(もの) ‖ *There were **more** people **than** I expected.* 予期していたよりも多くの人がいた. *We had more time than we thought.* 思ったよりも時間があった. *There's room for three more people.* さらに3名分の空きがある. *I couldn't eat any more.* 私はこれ以上食べられない. *I can't stand much more of this.* これ以上はあまりこれについて我慢できない. *Tell me more about your job.* あなたの仕事についてもっと話してください.⇨**less, fewer**

成句 more and more ▶定義 an increasing amount or number 量または数が増えていく→ますます多くの ‖ *There are more and more cars on the road.* 道路にはますます車が増える.

what's more ▶定義 (used for adding another fact) also; in addition(ほかの事実を付け加えるために用いて)〜もまた; さらに→その上, おまけに ‖ *The hotel was awful and what's more it was miles from the beach.* ひどいホテルで, その上海岸から何マイルも離れていた.

*****more**[2] /mɔ́:r/ 副 ▶定義 **1** (多くの形容詞・副詞の比較級を作るために用いて)→もっと, さらに ‖ *She was **far/much more** intelligent **than** her sister.* 彼女は妹よりもずっと聡明(そうめい)だった. *a course for more advanced students* さ

らに上級の生徒のための講座 *Please write more carefully.* もっと慎重に書いてください. ⇨ **less** ▶定義2 to a greater degree than usual or than sth else 通常またはほかの〜よりも程度が上で→**さらに一層, ずっと** ‖ *I like him far/much more than his wife.* 私は彼の奥さんよりも彼の方がずっと好きだ. ⇨ **less**

成句 **not any more** ▶定義 not any longer もはや〜でない→**もう〜でない, それ以上〜でない** ‖ *She doesn't live here any more.* 彼女はもうここに住んでいない.

**more or less** ▶定義 approximately; almost およそ; ほとんど→**大体, およそ** ‖ *We are more or less the same age.* 私たちは大体同じ年齢だ.

**moreover** /mɔːróuvər/ 副 (文) ▶定義 (used for adding another fact) also; in addition (ほかの事実を付け加えるために用いて) 〜もまた; さらに→**その上, さらに** ‖ *This firm did the work very well. Moreover, the cost was not too high.* この会社は非常に良い仕事をした. その上費用もあまり高くなかった.

**morgue** /mɔːrɡ/ 名 C ▶定義 a building where dead bodies are kept until they are buried or burned 死体が埋葬されるまたは火葬されるまで保管される建物→**遺体安置所, 死体公示所** ☞参 **mortuary**

\***morning** /mɔ́ːnɪŋ/ 名 C U ▶定義1 the early part of the day between the time when the sun rises and midday 太陽が昇ってから正午までの間の, 1日の初めの部分→**朝, 午前(中)** ‖ *Pat's going to London tomorrow morning.* パットは明日の朝ロンドンへ行く. *Bye, see you in the morning (= tomorrow morning).* さようなら, 朝 (= 明日の朝) に会いましょう. *I've been studying hard all morning.* 私は午前中ずっと勉強に励んでいた. *Dave makes breakfast every morning.* デーヴは毎朝朝食を作る. *She only works in the mornings.* 彼女は午前中だけ働く.

▶定義2 the part of the night that is after midnight 夜の12時以降の時間→**午前** ‖ *I was woken by a strange noise in the early hours of the morning.* 私は午前の早い時刻に奇妙な物音で起こされた. *He didn't come home until three in the morning.* 彼は午前3時まで帰宅しなかった.

➤ morning, afternoon または evening の前に形容詞の early または late を用いるときには, 前置詞は in を用いる: *The accident happened in the early morning.* (その事故は早朝に起こった.) *We arrived in the late afternoon.* (私たちは午後遅くに到着した.) ほかの形容詞の場合には on を用いる: *School starts on Monday morning.* (学校は月曜日の朝に始まる.) *They set out on a cold, windy afternoon.* (彼らは寒く, 風の強い午後に出発した.) this, tomorrow, yesterday の前では前置詞は用いない: *Let's go swimming this morning.* (今日の午前中に泳ぎに行きましょう.) *I'll phone Liz tomorrow evening.* (私は明日の夕方リズに電話をします.) *What did you do yesterday afternoon?* (昨日の午後は何をしましたか.)

成句 **Good morning** 正式 ▶定義 used when you see sb for the first time in the morning 〜に朝初めて会ったときに用いて→**おはよう(ございます)** ☞ より正式でない場では Morning とだけ言う. *Morning Kay, how are you today?* おはよう, ケイ, 今日はご機嫌いかが.

**moron** /mɔ́ːrɑn/ 名 C 略式 ▶定義 a rude way of referring to sb who you think is very stupid 非常にばかだと思う〜に対しての無礼な呼び方→**うすのろ, 間抜け** ‖ *Stop treating me like a moron!* 僕をうすのろ扱いするのはやめろ. — **moronic** /mərɑ́nɪk/ 形 →**精神薄弱の, 低能の**

**morose** /mərɔ́ʊs/ 形 ▶定義 bad-tempered, and not saying much to other people 機嫌が悪く, 他人にあまり話をしない→**気難しい, むっつりした**

**morphine** /mɔ́ːrfiːn/ 名 U ▶定義 a powerful drug that is used for reducing pain 痛みを減らすために用いられる強い薬→**モルヒネ**

**morsel** /mɔ́ːrs(ə)l/ 名 C ▶定義 a very small piece of sth, usually food 〜の非常に小さなかけら, 通常食べ物→**一口**

**mortal**[1] /mɔ́ːrtl/ 形 ▶定義1 that cannot live for ever and must die 永遠に生きることはできず死ななければならない→**死ぬことになっている, 死を免れない** ‖ *We are all mortal.* 私たちは皆死を免れない. ⇨ **immortal** ▶定義2 (文) that will result in death 死に至る→**命取りとなる, 致命的な** ‖ *a mortal wound/blow* 致命傷・致命的な一撃 *to be in mortal danger* 生命の危険にひんしている ☞参 **fatal**. これは同様の意味を持つ.

▶定義3 very great or extreme 非常に大きなま

たは極度の➡**非常な,ひどい** ‖ *They were in mortal fear of the enemy.* 彼らは敵をひどく恐れていた. ― **mortally** /-tli/ 副 ➡**死ぬほどに,致命的に,非常に**

**mortal²** /mɔ́ːrtl/ 名 C 正式 ▶定義 a human being 人➡**人間**

**mortality** /mɔːrtǽləti/ 名 U ▶定義 **1** the number of deaths in one period of time or in one place 一定期間のまたはある場所での死者数➡**死亡者数** ‖ *Infant mortality is high in the region.* その地域では幼児の死亡率が高い. ▶定義 **2** the fact that nobody can live forever だれも永遠には生きられないという事実➡**死ぬべき運命** ‖ *He didn't like to think about his own mortality.* 彼は自らの死ぬべき運命について考えたくなかった.

**mortar** /mɔ́ːrtər/ 名 ▶定義 **1** ❶a mixture of cement, sand and water used in building for holding bricks and stones together 建物でれんがや石をつなげ固定するために使われるセメント, 砂, 水を混ぜた物➡**モルタル, しっくい** ▶定義 **2** ❷a type of heavy gun that fires a type of bomb high into the air 爆弾の一種を空中へ高く発射する重砲の一種➡**迫撃砲, 臼砲(きゅうほう)** ▶定義 **3** ❷a small heavy bowl used for crushing some foods into powder using a special object (a pestle) 特別な物(すりこぎ)を使って食べ物を砕いて粉にするために使われる小さな重い鉢➡**乳鉢**

**mortgage** /mɔ́ːrɡɪdʒ/ 名 C ▶定義 money that you borrow in order to buy a house or flat 家または アパートを買うために借りるお金➡**抵当住宅ローン** ‖ *We took out a £40000 mortgage.* 私たちは4万ポンドの住宅ローンを組んだ.

▶通常お金は bank(銀行)または building society(住宅金融組合)から借り, これらの組織が loan(借入金)に対して支払われる rate of interest(利率)を決定する.

**mortician** /mɔːrtíʃ(ə)n/ 米 = **UNDERTAKER**

**mortuary** /mɔ́ːrtʃueri; mɔ́ːrtʃuəri/ 名 C (複 **mortuaries**) ▶定義 a room, usually in a hospital, where dead bodies are kept before they are buried or burned 通常病院にある, 死体を埋葬または火葬するまで保管しておく部屋➡**遺体安置所** ☛参 **morgue**

**mosaic** /moʊzéɪɪk/ 名 C U ▶定義 a picture or pattern that is made by placing together small coloured stones, pieces of glass, etc 小さな色付きの石, ガラス片などを並べて作られる絵や模様➡**モザイク(画, 模様)**

**Moslem** /mázləm/ = **MUSLIM**

**mosque** /mask/ 名 C ▶定義 a building where Muslims meet and pray イスラム教徒が集まり祈る建物➡**モスク, イスラム教寺院**

**mosquito** /məskíːtoʊ/ 名 C (複 **mosquitoes**) ▶定義 a small flying insect that lives in hot countries and bites people or animals to drink their blood. Some types of mosquito spread a very serious disease (malaria). 暑い国々に生息し, 人や動物を刺して血を吸う小さな飛ぶ虫. 非常に深刻な病気(マラリア)を広げる種類もいる➡**蚊** ☛ **insect**のさし絵

**moss** /mɔ(ː)s, mɑs/ 名 C U ▶定義 a small soft green plant, with no flowers, that grows in wet places, especially on rocks or trees 花をつけず, 特に岩や木の湿っぽい場所に生育する小さな柔らかい緑色の植物➡**こけ** ☛ C2 ページのさし絵 ― **mossy** 形 ➡**こけで覆われた, こけのような**

*★**most¹** /moʊst/ 形代 ▶定義 **1** (many および much の最上級として用いる) greatest in number or amount 数または量が最大の➡**最も多くの, 一番たくさんの** ‖ *Who got the most points?* だれが最も点を取りましたか. *The children had the most fun.* 子供たちが一番楽しんだ. *We all worked hard but I did the most.* 私たちは皆よく働いたが, 私が一番働いた. ⇔ **least, fewest** ▶定義 **2** nearly all of a group of people or things 人または物の集団のほとんどすべての➡**大抵の, 大部分の, ほとんど** ‖ *Most people in this country have a television.* この国のほとんどの人はテレビを持っている. *I like most Italian food.* 私は大抵のイタリア料理は好きだ.

▶ most の後に the, this, my などに続く名詞が来るときには, most of を用いなければならない: *Most of my friends were able to come to the wedding.*(私の友達のほとんどが結婚式に来ることができた.) *It rained most of the time we were in Ireland.*(私たちがアイルランドにいた間, ほとんどずっと雨が降っていた.)

成句 **at (the) most** ▶定義 not more than a certain number, and probably less ある数よりも多くない, おそらく少ない➡**せいぜい, 多くて** ‖ *There were 20 people there, at the most.* そこに

いたのはせいぜい20人だった.
make the most of sth ⇒ **MAKE**¹

\***most**² /móust/ 副 ▶定義 1 (多くの形容詞および副詞の最上級を作るために用いて)→最も ‖ *It's the most beautiful house I've ever seen.* それは私がこれまでに見た中で最も美しい家だ. *I work most efficiently in the morning.* 私は午前中最も効率的に仕事をする. ⇔ **least** ▶定義 2 more than anybody/anything else ほかのだれ・何よりも→一番 ‖ *What do you miss most when you're abroad?* 外国にいるときに何がないのが一番困りますか. ⇔ **least** ▶定義 3 正式 very 非常に→大変, 非常に, とても ‖ *We heard a most interesting talk about Japan.* 私たちは日本について大変興味深い話を聞いた.

**mostly** /móustli/ 副 ▶定義 in almost every case; almost all the time ほとんどすべての場合に; ほとんどずっと→大部分は, 大体, 大抵 ‖ *Our students come mostly from Japan.* 私たちの生徒の大部分は日本からです.

**MOT** /ém ou tí:/ 略 (または **MOT test**) ▶定義 a test to make sure that vehicles over a certain age are safe to drive 特定の使用年数を超えた車が運転しても安全だということを確かめる検査→車検 ‖ *My car failed its MOT.* 私の車は車検に落ちた.

**motel** /moutél/ 名 C ▶定義 a hotel near a main road for people who are travelling by car 車で旅をする人々のための主要な道路の近くにあるホテル→モーテル

**moth** /mɔ(:)θ, maθ/ 名 C ▶定義 an insect with a hairy body that usually flies at night. Some moths eat cloth and leave small holes in your clothes. 通常夜に飛ぶ体に毛の生えた虫. 衣服を食べて小さな穴を開けるものもいる→蛾, 衣蛾 ☛ **insect** のさし絵

**mothball** /mɔ́(:)θbɔ:l, máθ-/ 名 C ▶定義 a small ball made of a chemical substance that protects clothes in cupboards from moths 戸棚の中の衣服を虫から守る化学物質でできた小さな玉→防虫剤, モスボール

\***mother**¹ /mʌ́ðər/ 名 C ▶定義 the female parent of a person or an animal 人または動物の女性の親→母, 母親 ☛ **mum, mummy, stepmother**

**mother**² /mʌ́ðər/ 動 他 ▶定義 to look after sb as a mother does 母親がするように~の面倒を見る→~の母となる, 母のように世話をする ‖ *Stop mothering me - I can look after myself!* 母親のように私の世話をするのはやめてくれ - 自分のことは自分でできる.

**motherhood** /mʌ́ðərhùd/ 名 U ▶定義 the state of being a mother 母親である状態→母であること, 母性

**mother-in-law** 名 C (複 **mothers-in-law**) ▶定義 the mother of your husband or wife 自分の夫または妻の母→義理の母, 義母

**motherland** /mʌ́ðərlænd/ 名 C 正式 ▶定義 the country where you or your family were born and which you feel a strong emotional connection with 自分または自分の家族が生まれた, 強い感情的なつながりを感じる国→母国, 故国

**motherly** /mʌ́ðərli/ 形 ▶定義 having the qualities of a good mother 良い母親の性質を持つ→母親のような, 母としての ‖ *motherly love/instincts/advice* 母性愛・母性本能・母親のような忠告

**mother tongue** 名 C ▶定義 the first language that you learned to speak as a child 子供のとき話せるようになった最初の言語→母語, 母国語

**motif** /moutí:f/ 名 C ▶定義 a picture or pattern on sth ~の絵または模様→中心となる模様・デザイン, モチーフ

**motion**¹ /móuʃ(ə)n/ 名 ▶定義 1 U movement or a way of moving 動きまたは動き方→動き, 運動, 動作 ‖ *The motion of the ship made us all feel sick.* 船の揺れで私たちは皆酔った. *Pull the lever to set the machine in motion (= make it start moving).* 機械を作動させる(=動き始めさせる)ためにレバーを引きなさい. ☛参 **slow motion** ▶定義 2 C a formal suggestion at a meeting that you discuss and vote on 会議での正式な提案で, それについて議論して票を投じる→動議, 発議, 提案 ‖ *The motion was carried/rejected by a majority of eight votes.* 動議は8票差で可決・否決された.

**motion**² /móuʃ(ə)n/ 動 自 他 ▶定義 motion to sb (to do sth); motion (for) sb (to do sth) to make a movement, usually with your hand, that tells sb what to do 通常は手によって, ~にすべきことを伝えるための動きをする→身振りで示す, 合図する ‖ *I motioned to the waiter.* 私はウエ

ーターに合図した. *The manager motioned for me to sit down.* 部長は私に座るように身振りで示した.

**motionless** /móuʃ(ə)nləs/ 形 ▶定義 not moving 動いていない→**動かない, 静止した**

**motivate** /móutəvèit/ 動他 ▶定義1 (通常は受動態で) to cause sb to act in a particular way 〜にある特定の方法で行動させる→**〜に動機を与える, 刺激する** ‖ *Her reaction was motivated by fear.* 彼女の反応は恐れによって引き起こされた. ▶定義2 to make sb want to do sth, especially sth that involves hard work and effort 〜が…を, 特に熱心な勉強または努力を必要とする…をしたくなるようにさせる→**学習意欲をそそる, やる気を与える** ‖ *Our new teacher certainly knows how to motivate his classes.* 私たちの新しい先生はクラスの学習意欲を高める方法を確かに知っている. *I just can't motivate myself to do anything this morning.* 今朝私は, 全く何もする気になれない. —motivated 形→**動機づけられた, やる気のある** ‖ *highly motivated students* 非常にやる気のある生徒たち —motivation /mòutəvéiʃ(ə)n/ 名 C U→**動機づけ, 刺激, やる気** ‖ *He's clever enough, but he lacks motivation.* 彼は十分に賢いが, やる気に欠けている.

**motive** /móutiv/ 名 C U ▶定義 (a) motive (for sth/doing sth) a reason for doing sth, often sth bad しばしば悪い〜について, その〜をする理由→**動機, 真意** ‖ *The police couldn't discover a motive for the murder.* 警察はその殺人の動機を見つけられなかった.

\***motor**[1] /móutər/ 名 C ▶定義 a device that uses petrol, gas, electricity, etc to produce movement and makes a machine, etc work 作動させるために石油, ガス, 電気などを使い, 機械などに仕事をさせるための装置→**モーター, 発動機, エンジン** ‖ *The washing machine doesn't work. I think something is wrong with the motor.* 洗濯機が動かない. モーターの調子が悪いのだと思う.

▶ motor(モーター)ではなくengine(エンジン)は, 通常車やオートバイに関して使われる. 実際には車は, 時々正式にmotor carと呼ばれることがある.

**motor**[2] /móutər/ 形 ▶定義1 (名詞の前だけ) having or using the power of an engine or a motor エンジンまたはモーターの力を持っているまたは使っている→**モーターで動く, エンジンで動く** ‖ *a motor vehicle* 動力車(自動車) ▶定義2 特に 医 connected with vehicles that have engines, especially cars エンジンを持つ乗り物, 特に車に関連した→**自動車の, 自動車用の** ‖ *the motor industry* 自動車産業 *motor racing* 自動車レース

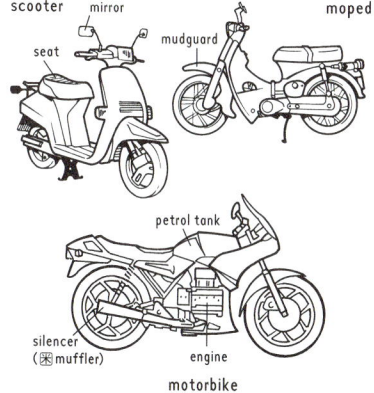

motorbike

**motorbike** /móutərbàik/ (または 正式 **motorcycle**) 名 C ▶定義 a vehicle that has two wheels and an engine 2つの車輪とエンジンを持つ乗り物→**オートバイ, 単車**

**motor boat** 名 C ▶定義 a small fast boat that has a motor モーターを持つ小さな速いボート→**モーターボート, 高速エンジン艇**

**motor car** 医 正式 = CAR(1)

**motorcycle** /móutərsàik(ə)l/ 正式 =MOTORBIKE

**motorcyclist** /móutərsàik(ə)list/ 名 C ▶定義 a person who rides a motorbike オートバイに乗る人→**オートバイ乗り, ライダー**

**motoring** /móutəriŋ/ 名 U ▶定義 driving in a car 自動車を運転すること→**自動車運転** ‖ *a motoring holiday* 自動車旅行の休日

**motorist** /móutərist/ 名 C ▶定義 a person who drives a car 車を運転する人→**自動車の運転者, ドライバー** ☞参 pedestrian

**motorized** (または **-ised**) /móutəràizd/ 形 (名詞の前だけ) ▶定義 that has an engine エンジンを持つ→**モーター式の, 動力式の** ‖ *a motorized wheelchair* 動力式の車いす

**motorway** /móutərwèi/ (医 **expressway; free-**

**way** 名 C ▶定義 a wide road connecting cities that is specially built for fast traffic 速く通行するために特別に建設された都市を結ぶ広い道路➡**高速自動車道路**

**motto** /mátou/ 名 C (複 **mottoes** または **mottos**) ▶定義 a short sentence or phrase that expresses the aims and beliefs of a person, a group, an organization, etc 人, グループ, 組織などの目的や信条を表現する短い文章または言葉➡**モットー, 標語** ‖ *'Live and let live' that's my motto.*「あなたはあなた, 私は私」というのが私のモットーだ.

**mould**¹ (米 **mold**) /móuld/ 名 ▶定義1 Ca container that you pour a liquid or substance into. The liquid then becomes solid (sets) in the same shape as the container, for example after it has cooled or cooked. 液体または物質を中に流し入れる容器. その液体は, 例えば冷やしたり火を加えたりすると, その容器と同じ形の固体になる(固まる)➡**鋳型, 流し型** ▶定義2 [C, 通常は単数] a particular type ある特定の種類➡**型** ‖ *She doesn't fit into the usual mould of sales directors.* 彼女は通常の営業部長の型にははまらない. ▶定義3 Ua soft green or black substance like fur (fungus) that grows in wet places or on old food 湿った場所または古い食べ物で生育する柔らかい緑色または黒色の柔毛状の付着物(菌類)のような物質➡**かび**―**mouldy** (米 **moldy**) 形➡**かびた, かびのような** ‖ *The cheese had gone mouldy.* そのチーズはかびてしまっていた.

**mould**² (米 **mold**) /móuld/ 動他 ▶定義 mould A (into B); mould B (from/out of A) to make sth into a particular shape or form by pressing it or by putting it into a mould¹(1) ～を押し付けるまたは mould¹(1) (型)にはめ込むことによって, 特定の形または形状にする➡**かたどる, 型に入れて作る, 形づくる** ‖ *First mould the dough into a ball.* まずパン生地を丸いボール状にしてください. *a bowl moulded from clay* 粘土で形づくられた鉢

**moult** (米 **molt**) /móult/ 動自 ▶定義 (used about an animal or a bird) to lose hairs or feathers before growing new ones (動物または鳥について)新しい物が生えてくる前に毛または羽を失う➡**生え変わる, 抜け変わる**

**mound** /máund/ 名 C ▶定義1 a large pile of earth or stones; a small hill 土または石の大きな山; 小さな丘➡**土手, 堤, 小丘** ▶定義2 (口語) a mound (of sth) a pile or a large amount of sth ～の山または～の大量➡**(山ほどの)多数, 大量** ‖ *I've got a mound of work to do.* する仕事が山ほどある.

*****mount**¹ /máunt/ 動 ▶定義1 他 to organize sth ～の準備をする➡**～を準備する, 始める** ‖ *to mount a protest/a campaign/an exhibition/an attack* 抗議を始める・キャンペーンを準備する・展示会を準備する・攻撃を仕掛ける ▶定義2 自 to increase gradually in level or amount 程度または量が次第に増える➡**上がる, かさむ, 増大する** ‖ *The tension mounted as the end of the match approached.* 試合が終わりに近付くにつれて, 緊張が高まった. ▶定義3 他(文) to go up sth or up on to sth ～を上がっていくまたは～の上に上がる➡**～を登る, 上がる** ‖ *He mounted the platform and began to speak.* 彼は演壇に上がり, 話し始めた. ▶定義4 自他 to get on a horse or bicycle 馬または自転車に乗る➡**乗る**⇔**dismount** ▶定義5 他 mount sth (on/onto/in sth) to fix sth firmly on sth else ～をほかの…の上に固定する➡**～を据え付ける, 乗せる, 張る** ‖ *The gas boiler was mounted on the wall.* ガス湯沸かし器が壁に取り付けられた.

句動詞 **mount up** ▶定義 to increase (often more than you want) (しばしば望んでいる以上に)増える➡**かさむ, 増大する** ‖ *When you're buying food for six people the cost soon mounts up.* 6人分の食料を買っていると, 費用はすぐにかさんでしまう.

**mount**² /máunt/ 名 C (略 **Mt**) ▶定義 (used in names) a mountain (名前に用いて)山➡**～山** ‖ *Mt Everest/Vesuvius/Fuji* エベレスト・ベスビオス・富士山

*****mountain** /máunt(ə)n/ 名 C ▶定義1 a very high hill 非常に高い丘➡**山, 山岳** ‖ *Which is the highest mountain in the world?* 世界で最も高い山はどれですか. *mountain roads/scenery/villages* 山道・山の景色・山村 *a mountain range* 山脈 ☞ C8 ページのさし絵 ▶定義2 a mountain (of sth) a large amount of sth 大量の～➡**(山ほど)多数, 大量** ‖ *I've got a mountain of work to do.* しなければならない仕事が山ほどある.

**mountain bike** 名 C ▶定義 a bicycle with a strong frame, wide tyres and many different speeds (gears) designed for riding on rough ground でこぼこ道で乗るために設計された，丈夫な構造，幅の広いタイヤ，何段もの変速装置（ギア）を持つ自転車→**マウンテンバイク** ☞ マウンテンバイクに乗って遊ぶことを，通常 go mountain biking と言う．

**mountaineering** /màunt(ə)níərɪŋ/ 名 U ▶定義 the sport of climbing mountains 山を登るスポーツ→**登山** ― mountaineer/-níər/ 名 C→登山者，登山家，山の住人

**mountainous** /máunt(ə)nəs/ 形 ▶定義 **1** having many mountains 多くの山がある→**山の多い，山地の** ‖ *a mountainous region* 山岳地帯 ▶定義 **2** very large in size or amount 大きさまたは量が非常に大きい→**山のような，巨大な** ‖ *The mountainous waves made sailing impossible.* 巨大な大波が航海を不可能にした．

**mountainside** /máunt(ə)nsàɪd/ 名 C ▶定義 the land on the side of a mountain 山の斜面にある土地→**山腹**

**mounted** /máuntəd/ 形 ▶定義 riding a horse→**馬に乗った** ‖ *mounted police* 騎馬警官隊

**mounting** /máuntɪŋ/ 形 (名詞の前だけ) ▶定義 increasing 増えている→**高まり行く** ‖ *mounting unemployment/tension* 高まる失業・緊張

**mourn** /mɔːrn/ 動 自 他 ▶定義 mourn (for/over) sb/sth to feel and show great sadness, especially because sb has died 特に～が亡くなったために，大きな悲しみを感じて示す→**～のために嘆き悲しむ，～のことを嘆き悲しむ，嘆く，喪に服する** ‖ *She is still mourning (for) her child.* 彼女は今もなお子供のことを嘆いている．― mourning 名 U→嘆き悲しむこと，悲嘆，哀悼 ‖ *He wore a black armband to show he was **in mourning**.* 彼は喪に服していることを示すために黒い喪章を付けた．

**mourner** /mɔːrnər/ 名 C ▶定義 a person who goes to a funeral as a friend or relative of the person who has died 亡くなった人の友人または親戚（しんせき）として葬式に行く人→**会葬者，弔問客**

**mournful** /mɔːrnfʊl,-f(ə)l/ 形 (文) ▶定義 very sad 非常に悲しい→**悲しみに沈んだ，悲しげな** ‖ *a mournful song* 悲しげな歌 ― mournfully /-fʊli, -f(ə)li/ 副→悲しみに沈んで

---

mouth² 1073

*****mouse** /máus/ 名 C (複 **mice** /máɪs/) ▶定義 **1** a very small animal with fur and a long thin tail 毛皮と細長いしっぽを持つ非常に小さな動物→**ネズミ，家ネズミ，ハツカネズミ**

▶ rat (ドブネズミ), hamster (ハムスター) などの mice (ネズミ) は，rodent (げっ歯類) に属する．

▶定義 **2** a piece of equipment, connected to a computer, for moving around the screen and entering commands without touching the keys コンピューターに接続された，画面上のポインターを動かしてキーに触れずにコマンドを入力するための器具→**マウス** ‖ *Use the mouse to drag the icon to a new position.* マウスを使ってアイコンを新しい位置にドラッグしなさい．☞ S5ページのさし絵

*****moustache** /məstǽʃ, məstǽʃ; místæʃ/ (困 **mustache**) 名 C ▶定義 hair that grows on a man's top lip, between the mouth and nose 男性の唇の上の，口と鼻の間に生える毛→**口ひげ** ☞ **hair** のさし絵

*****mouth¹** /máuθ/ 名 C (複 **mouths** /máuðz/)
▶定義 **1** the part of your face that you use for eating and speaking 食べるまたは話すために使う顔の部分→**口** ‖ *to open/close your mouth* 口を開ける・閉じる ☞ C5ページのさし絵
▶定義 **2** **-mouthed** /máuðd, -θt/ (複合形容詞を作るために用いて) having a particular type of mouth or a particular way of speaking 特定の種類の口を持つまたは話し方をする→**～な口をした，～な話し方をする** ‖ *We stared open-mouthed in surprise.* 私たちは驚いて口を開けたまま見詰めた．*He's a loud-mouthed bully.* 彼はやかましいごろつきだ．▶定義 **3** the place where a river enters the sea 川が海に流れ込む場所→**河口**

成句 keep your mouth shut 略式 ▶定義 to not say sth to sb because it is a secret or because it will upset or annoy him/her 秘密であるために，または人の気を動転させる・悩ませる事なので，～を…に言わない→**黙っている，秘密を守る**

**mouth²** /máuθ/ 動 自 他 ▶定義 to move your mouth as if you were speaking but without making any sound あたかも話しているかのように，しかし声を出さずに口を動かす→**声に出さずに**

## 1074　mouthful

口の動きで言う ‖ *Vinay was outside the window, mouthing something to us.* ビネイは窓の外にいて、口の動きで何かを私たちに言っていた．

**mouthful** /máυθfυl, -f(ə)l/ 名 ▶定義1 ❻ the amount of food or drink that you can put in your mouth at one time 一度に口の中に入れられる食べ物または飲み物の量 ➔ 一口分, 口一杯分 ▶定義2 ［単数扱い］a word or phrase that is long or difficult to say 長くて言うのが難しい単語または語句 ➔ 発音しにくい語(句) ‖ *Her name is a bit of a mouthful.* 彼女の名前は少し発音しにくい．

**mouth organ** = HARMONICA

**mouthpiece** /máυθpìːs/ 名 ❻ ▶定義1 the part of a telephone, musical instrument, etc that you put in or near your mouth 口に入れるまたは口のそばで使う、電話、楽器などの部分 ➔ 歌口, 吸い口, 送話口 ▶定義2 a person, newspaper, etc that a particular group uses to express its opinions 特定の集団が意見を述べるために使う人や新聞など ➔ 他人の意見の代弁者 ‖ *Pravda was the mouthpiece of the Soviet government.* プラウダはソビエト政府の代弁者だった．

**mouth-watering** 形 ▶定義 (used about food) that looks or smells very good (食べ物について) 非常においしそうに見える・良いにおいがする ➔ よだれの出そうな、うまそうな

**movable** /múːvəb(ə)l/ 形 ▶定義 that can be moved 動かすことができる ➔ 動かせる, 移動できる, 動産の ⇔ fixed ☞参 portable, mobile

\***move**¹ /muːv/ 動 ▶定義1 圁 ⓗ to change position or to put sth in a different position 位置を変えるまたは~を別の位置に置く ➔ 動かす, 動く ‖ *Please move your car. It's blocking the road.* 車を移動してください．道をふさいでいます．*The station is so crowded you* ***can hardly move****.* 駅は非常に混んでいてほとんど身動きも取れない．*The meeting has been moved to Thursday.* 会合は変更されて木曜になった．▶定義2 圁 ⓗ **move along, down, over, up, etc** to move (sth) further in a particular direction in order to make space for sb/sth else ほかの~のための場所を空けるために特定の方向へ動く、または~を動かす ➔ 動く, 動かす, 詰める ‖ *If we move up a bit, Rob can sit here too.* 私たちが少し詰めれば、ロブもここに座れる. *Move your head down - I can't see the screen.* 頭を下げてくれ ー スクリーンが見えない. ▶定義3 ⓗ to change the place where you live, work, study, etc 住む、働く、学ぶなどの場所を変える ➔ 引っ越す, 移転する, 転校する, 転職する ‖ *Our neighbours are moving to York next week.* 私たちの近所の人たちは来週ヨークに引っ越す. **to move house** 引っ越しをする *Yuka's moved down to the beginners' class.* ユカは初心者クラスに格下げされた. ▶定義4 圁 **move (on/ahead)** to make progress 進展する ➔ (先へ)進む, 進行する ‖ *When the new team of builders arrived things started moving very quickly.* 新しい建設業者チームが到着すると、事は非常に速く進み始めた. ▶定義5 圁 to take action 行動を取る ➔ 行動を起こす, 処置を講ずる ‖ *Unless we move quickly lives will be lost.* 私たちが素早く処置を講じなければ、生命が失われるだろう. ▶定義6 ⓗ to cause sb to have strong feelings, especially of sadness ~に強い感情, 特に悲しみを, 引き起こす ➔ 起こさせる, 感動させる, ~する気を起こさせる ‖ *Many people were* ***moved to tears*** *by reports of the massacre.* 多くの人々がその大量殺戮（さつりく）の知らせに涙を流した.

成句 get moving ▶定義 to go, leave or do sth quickly 速く行く、たつ、または~をする ➔ すぐに始める, すぐに出発する

get sth moving ▶定義 to cause sth to make progress ~を進展させる ➔ ~をどんどん進める

句動詞 move in (with sb) ▶定義 to start living in a new house (with sb) 新しい家で(~と)暮らし始める ➔ (~の所に)引っ越し住む

move on (to sth) ▶定義 to start doing or discussing sth new 新しい~をし始める、または議論し始める ➔ どんどん先へ進める, 進む

move off ▶定義 (used about a vehicle) to start a journey; to leave (乗り物について)旅を始める; 発つ ➔ 出発する, 立ち去る

move out ▶定義 to leave your old home 古い家を去る ➔ 引っ越して出ていく

\***move**² /muːv/ 名 ❻ ▶定義1 a change of place or position 場所または姿勢の変更 ➔ 動き, 行動 ‖ *She was watching every move I made.* 彼女は私の動きをすべて見ていた. ▶定義2 a change in the place where you live or work 住むまたは働く場所の変更 ➔ 転居, 移動 ‖ *a move to a bigger* *house* より大きな家への転居 ▶定義3 action that you take because you want to achieve a particular result 特定の結果を達成したいために取る行動→**処置, 措置** ‖ *Both sides want to negotiate but neither is prepared to **make the first move***. 双方とも交渉をしたがっているが, どちらも最初の手を打つ用意はない. *Asking him to help me was a good move.* 彼に私を手伝ってくれるよう頼んだのは良い措置だった. ▶定義4 (in chess and other games) a change in the position of a piece (チェスなどのゲームで) 駒 (こま) 位置の変更→**一手, 駒を指すこと** ‖ *It's your move.* あなたが駒を指す番だ.

成句 **be on the move** ▶定義 to be going somewhere どこかへ行っている→**移動中だ, 進行している** ‖ *We've been on the move for four hours so we should stop for a rest.* 私たちは4時間も移動していたので, 止まって休むべきだ.

**get a move on** 略式 ▶定義 to hurry→**急ぐ** ‖ *I'm late. I'll have to get a move on.* 私は遅れている. 急がなければならないだろう.

**make a move** ▶定義 to start to go somewhere どこかへ行くために出発する→**動く, 移動する** ‖ *It's time to go home. Let's make a move.* 家へ帰る時間だ. 移動しよう.

\***movement** /múːvmənt/ 名 ▶定義1 ⓒⓊ an act of moving 動く行為→**動き, 運動** ‖ *The dancer's movements were smooth and controlled.* ダンサーの動きは滑らかで統制が取れていた. *The seat belt doesn't allow much freedom of movement.* シートベルトであまり自由に動けない. *I could see some movement (= sb/sth moving) in the trees.* 木々の中に何かが動くの (= 動く〜) が見えた. ▶定義2 ⓒⓊ an act of moving or being moved from one place to another ある場所から他へと動く行為, 動かされること→**移動, 運行** ‖ *the slow movement of the clouds across the sky* 雲が空をゆっくりと移動すること ▶定義3 [ⓒ, 通常は単数] a movement (away from/towards sth) a general change in the way people think or behave 人々の考え方または振る舞い方の一般的な変化→**動向, 潮流, 傾向** ‖ *There's been a movement away from the materialism of the 1980s.* 1980年代の物質主義から離れる傾向がある. ▶定義4 **movements** [複数扱い] a person's actions or plans during a period of time 一定期間内の人の行動または計画→**行動, 活動, 動静** ‖ *Detectives have been watching the man's movements for several weeks.* 刑事たちはその男の行動を数週間にわたって監視している. ▶定義5 ⓒ a group of people who have the same aims or ideas 同じ目的または考えを持つ人々の集団→**運動団体, 運動** ‖ *I support the Animal Rights movement.* 私は動物の権利を守る運動を支持する. ▶定義6 ⓒ one of the main parts of a long piece of music 長い曲の主要部分の1つ→**楽章**

\***movie** /múːvi/ 名 特に 米 ▶定義1 = FILM¹(1) ‖ *Shall we go and **see a movie**?* 映画を見に行きましょうか. *a science fiction/horror movie* SF・恐怖映画 *a movie director/star* 映画監督・スター *a movie theater (= cinema)* 映画館 (= 映画館) ▶定義2 **the movies** [複数扱い] = CINEMA ‖ *Let's go to the movies.* 映画を見に行きましょう.

**moving** /múːvɪŋ/ 形 ▶定義1 causing strong feelings, especially of sadness 強い感情, 特に悲しみを引き起こす→**人を感動させる, 哀れな** ‖ *a deeply moving speech/story* 深く人の心を打つ演説・物語 ▶定義2 that moves 動くような→**動く, 移動する** ‖ *It's a computerized machine with few moving parts.* それは動く部品はほとんどない, コンピューター化された機械だ.

**mow** /móʊ, máʊ/ 動 ⓘⓉ (過 **mowed**) 過分 **mown** /móʊn/ または **mowed**) ▶定義 to cut grass using a machine (a mower) 機械 (草刈り機) を使って草を刈る→**刈る, 刈り取る** ‖ *to mow the lawn* 芝生を刈る

句動詞 **mow sb down** ▶定義 to kill sb with a gun or a car 銃または車で〜を殺す→**なぎ倒す, 殺す**

**mower** /móʊər, máʊ-/ 名 ⓒ ▶定義 a machine for cutting grass 草を刈る機械→**草刈り機** ‖ *a lawn-mower* 芝刈り機 *an electric mower* 電気草刈り機

**MP** /èmpíː/ 略 特に 英 Member of Parliament→**国会議員**

**mpg** /èm piː dʒíː/ 略 miles per gallon→**1ガロンに付き〜マイル** ‖ *This car does 40 mpg (= you can drive 40 miles on one gallon of petrol).* この車は1ガロンに付き40マイル走る (= ガソリン1ガロンで40マイル走行できる).

**mph** /èm piː éɪtʃ/ 略 miles per hour→**時速** ‖ *a 70 mph speed limit* 時速70マイルの速度制限

***Mr** /místər/ ▶定義 used as a title before the name of a man 男性の名前の前で敬称として用いて→〜さん,様,氏 ‖ *Mr (Matthew) Botham*(マシュー)ボザム様 ☛参 **Miss** の注

***Mrs** /mísəz/ ▶定義 used as a title before the name of a married woman 結婚した女性の名前の前で敬称として用いて→〜さん,様,夫人 ‖ *Mrs (Sylvia) Allen*(シルビア)アレン様 ☛参 **Miss** の注

**MS** /émés/ 略 multiple sclerosis→多発性硬化症

***Ms** /mɪz/ ▶定義 used as a title before the family name of a woman who may or may not be married 結婚しているまたはしていない女性の姓の前で敬称として用いて→〜さん,様 ‖ *Ms (Donna) Hackett*(ドナ)ハケット様

➤ Mrs または Miss よりも Ms を好む女性もいる. 女性が結婚しているかどうか分からない場合には Ms を使うことができる. Miss の注を参照.

**MSc** /èm es síː/ 略 Master of Science ▶定義 a second degree that you receive when you complete a more advanced course or piece of research in a science subject at university or college 大学で科学に関するより高度な課程または研究を修了したときに受ける学士の次の学位→理学修士(号) ☛参 **BSc, MA**

**Mt** 略 Mount→山 ‖ *Mt Everest* エベレスト山

**mth** (困 mo) (略 mths; 困 mos) 略 month→月 ‖ *6 mths old* 6か月

***much** /mʌtʃ/ 形代副 ▶定義 **1** (主に否定文や疑問文,または as, how, so, too の後で,不可算名詞と用いて) a large amount of sth 大量の〜→多くの(もの),多量(の),たくさん(のもの) ‖ *I haven't got much money.* あまりたくさんのお金は持っていない. *Did she say much?* 彼女はたくさん話しましたか. *You've given me **too much** food.* あなたは私にたくさん食べ物をくれすぎた. ***How much** time have you got?* どのくらい時間があるの. *I can't carry **that much**!* 私はそんなにたくさん持てない. *Eat **as much as** you can.* 食べられるだけ食べなさい.

➤意見を述べるときには通常 much ではなく a lot of を用いる: *I've got a lot of experience.* (私には多くの経験がある.)

▶定義 **2** to a great degree より強い度合いに→大変に,非常に ‖ *I don't like her very much.* 私は彼女をあまり好きではない. *Do you see Sashi much? (= very often)* あなたはサシによく(= 非常にしばしば)会いますか. *Do you see much of Sashi?* あなたはサシによく会いますか. *much taller/prettier/harder* ずっと背の高い・きれいな・困難な *much more interesting/unusual* ずっと興味深い・珍しい *much more quickly/happily* はるかに速く・楽しそうに *You ate **much more** than me.* あなたは私よりもずっとたくさん食べた.

▶定義 **3** (形容詞として用いられる過去分詞と共に) very 非常に→大いに,非常に ‖ *She was much loved by all her friends.* 彼女はすべての友達から非常に愛されていた.

➤ *She was very popular.* (彼女は非常に人気があった.) と比較.

成句 **much the same** ▶定義 very similar 非常に似た→ほぼ同じ,大体同じ ‖ *Softball is much the same as baseball.* ソフトボールは野球と大体同じだ.

**nothing much** ⇒ **NOTHING**

**not much good (at sth)** ▶定義 not skilled (at sth) (〜が)上手でない→あまり得意でない ‖ *I'm not much good at singing.* 私は歌があまり得意ではない.

**not much of a...** ▶定義 not a good... 良い...でない→大した...ではない ‖ *She's not much of a cook.* 彼女は大した料理人ではない.

**not up to much** ⇒ **UP**

**muck**¹ /mʌk/ 名 ❶ ▶定義 **1** the waste from farm animals, used to make plants grow better 植物の生育を促すのに使われる,農場の動物から出る排出物→牛馬糞(ふん),肥やし ☛ より一般的な単語に manure がある. ▶定義 **2** 略式 dirt or mud 汚物または泥→汚物,黒泥土

**muck**² /mʌk/ 動略式

句動詞 **muck about/around** ▶定義 to behave in a silly way or to waste time ばかげた方法で振る舞う,または時間を無駄にする→ぶらぶらする,だらだらする ‖ *Stop mucking around and come and help me!* だらだらするのはやめて,こちらへ来て手伝いなさい.

**muck sth up** ▶定義 to do sth badly; to spoil sth 〜を下手にする; 〜を台なしにする→台なしにする,しくじる ‖ *I was so nervous that I completely mucked up my interview.* 私はとても緊張してインタビューを完全にしくじってしまった.

**mucus** /mjúːkəs/ 名 ❶ 正式 ▶定義 a sticky substance that is produced in some parts of the body, especially the nose 体のある部分, 特に鼻で作られる粘々した→**粘液, 鼻汁**

\***mud** /mʌd/ 名 Ｕ ▶定義 soft, wet earth 柔らかい, ぬれた土壌→**泥, 泥んこ, ぬかるみ** ‖ *He came home from the football match **covered in mud**.* 彼はラグビーの試合から泥だらけになって帰宅した.

**muddle** /mʌ́dl/ 動他 ▶定義 1 muddle sth (up) to put things in the wrong place or order or to make them untidy 物を間違った場所にまたは順番で置く, または物を散らかす→**～をごちゃごちゃにする** ‖ *Try not to **get** those papers **muddled up**.* 書類をごちゃごちゃにしないようにしなさい. ▶定義 2 muddle sb (up) to confuse sb ～を混乱させる→**～を混乱させる, まごつかす** ‖ *I do my homework and schoolwork in separate books so that I don't **get muddled up**.* 私は宿題と授業内容を別々のノートに書くので, 混乱することはない. ―muddle 名 Ｃ Ｕ →**混乱, めちゃめちゃ, ごちゃごちゃ** ‖ *If you **get in a muddle**, I'll help you.* 君がもし混乱したら, 私が助けるよ. ―muddled 形 →**混乱した**

**muddy** /mʌ́di/ 形 ▶定義 full of or covered in mud 泥が一杯の, または泥で覆われた→**泥だらけの, ぬかるみの** ‖ *muddy boots* 泥だらけの長靴 *It's very muddy down by the river.* 川のそばは, ひどいぬかるみになっている.

**mudguard** /mʌ́dgɑːrd/ 名 Ｃ ▶定義 a curved cover over the wheel of a bicycle or motorbike 自転車またはオートバイの車輪の回りの曲線状の覆い→**泥よけ ☛ motorbike**, S7ページのさし絵

**muesli** /mjúːsli, mjúːz-/ 名 Ｕ ▶定義 food made of grains, nuts, dried fruit, etc that you eat with milk for breakfast 朝食として牛乳を加えて食べる, 穀粒, 木の実, 乾果などでできた食べ物→**ミューズリー**

**muffin** /mʌ́fən/ 名 Ｃ ▶定義 1 (米 **English muffin**) a type of bread roll often eaten hot with butter しばしば温めてバターを付けて食べる, 丸いパンの一種→**イングリッシュマフィン** ▶定義 2 a type of small cake 小さなケーキの一種→**マフィン ☛ cake** のさし絵

**muffle** /mʌ́f(ə)l/ 動他 ▶定義 to make a sound quieter and more difficult to hear 音をより静かにして, 聞くのをさらに難しくする→**～を消す, (音を立てないように)包む** ‖ *He put his hand over his mouth to muffle his laughter.* 彼は笑い声を出さないように口を手で覆った. ―muffled 形 →**こもった, 押し殺した** ‖ *I heard muffled voices outside.* 押し殺したような声が外で聞こえた.

**mug**¹ /mʌg/ 名 Ｃ ▶定義 1 a large cup with straight sides and a handle まっすぐな側面に取っ手の付いた大きなカップ→**マグ, マグ1杯分** ‖ *a coffee mug* コーヒーマグ *a mug of tea* マグ1杯分の紅茶 ☛ **cup** のさし絵 ▶定義 2 略式 a person who seems stupid ばかに見える人→**ばか, お人よし**

**mug**² /mʌg/ 動他 (**mugging**; **mugged**) ▶定義 to attack and rob sb in the street 通りで～を襲って奪う→**襲って金を奪う** ‖ *Keep your wallet out of sight or you'll **get mugged**.* 財布を見えないようにしておきなさい. さもないと取られるよ. ―mugger 名 Ｃ →**(辻(つじ))強盗 ☛参 thief** の注 ―mugging 名 Ｃ Ｕ →**(辻)強盗** ‖ *The mugging took place around midnight.* 辻強盗が深夜に起きた.

**muggy** /mʌ́gi/ 形 ▶定義 (used about the weather) warm and slightly wet in an unpleasant way (**humid**) (天気について) 気温が高く, 不快に暑くてややじめじめしている(湿気が多い)→**蒸し暑い, 暑苦しい**

**mule** /mjuːl/ 名 Ｃ ▶定義 an animal that is used for carrying heavy loads and whose parents are a horse and another animal (**a donkey**) 重い荷物を運ぶのに使われる, 馬とほかの動物(ロバ)を両親とする動物→**ラバ**

**mull** /mʌl/ 動

句動詞 mull sth over ▶定義 to think about sth carefully and for a long time ～について慎重に長い時間考える→**あれこれと考える** ‖ *Don't ask me for a decision right now. I'll have to mull it over.* 私に今すぐ決めるように求めるな. あれこれ考えなければならないのだ.

**multicultural** /mʌ̀ltɪkʌ́ltʃ(ə)rəl, mʌ̀ltaɪ-/ 形 ▶定義 for or including people of many different races, languages, religions and traditions 多くの異なる人種, 言語, 宗教および伝統を持つ人々のための, またはそのような人々を含む→**多様な文化から成る, 多文化の** ‖ *a multicultural society* 多様な文化から成る社会

**multilateral** /mʌ̀ltɪlǽt(ə)r(ə)l, mʌ̀ltaɪ-/ 形 ▶定義 involving more than two groups of people, countries, etc 人々, 国々などの2つ以上の集団

にかかわる➡**多面的な, 多国間の, 多者間の** ‖ *a multilateral agreement* 多国間合意 ☛参 **unilateral**

**multimedia** /mʌltɪmíːdiə, mʌltər-/ 形(名詞の前だけ) ▶定義 (computing) using sound, pictures and film in addition to text on a screen (コンピューター)画面上で文字以外に音, 絵, 映像などを使う➡**マルチメディアの** ‖ *multimedia systems/products* マルチメディアシステム・製品

**multinational** /mʌltɪnǽʃ(ə)n(ə)l, mʌltər-/ 形 ▶定義 existing in or involving many countries 多くの国々に存在する, またはかかわる➡**多国家の, 多国籍の** ‖ *multinational companies* 多国籍企業 ― multinational 名 C ➡**多国籍企業** ‖ *The company is owned by Ford, the US multinational.* その会社は, 米国の多国籍企業フォードが所有している.

**multiple**¹ /mʌltəp(ə)l/ 形 ▶定義 involving many people or things or having many parts 多くの人々または物にかかわる, または多くの部分を持つ➡**多様な, 多くの部分から成る** ‖ *Three drivers died in a multiple pile-up on the motorway.* 自動車道路の多重衝突で運転手3人が死んだ.

**multiple**² /mʌltəp(ə)l/ 名 C ▶定義 a number that contains another number an exact number of times ほかの数のちょうど数倍の数➡**倍数** ‖ *12, 18 and 24 are multiples of 6.* 12, 18, および24は6の倍数である.

**multiple-choice** 形 ▶定義 (used about exam questions) showing several different answers from which you have to choose the right one (試験の問題について)異なる数個の答えから正答を選ぶ形式の➡**多肢選択の**

**multiple sclerosis** /mʌltəp(ə)l skləróʊsəs, skliə-/ 名 U (略 **MS**) ▶定義 a serious disease which causes you to slowly lose control of your body and become less able to move 次第に体を動かせなくなり, 動きにくくなる深刻な病気➡**多発性硬化症**

\***multiply** /mʌltəplaɪ/ 動(現分 **multiplying**; 三単現 **multiplies**; 過, 過分 **multiplied**) ▶定義 **1** 自他 multiply A by B to increase a number by the number of times mentioned ある数(A)を述べられた倍数(B)分だけ大きくする➡**掛ける, ～倍にする** ‖ *2 multiplied by 4 makes 8 (2 × 4 = 8)* 2掛ける4は8 (2×4=8) ⇔ **divide** ▶定義 **2** 自他 to increase or make sth increase by a very large amount 非常に大量に増えるまたは～を増やす➡**増やす, 増える** ‖ *We've multiplied our profits over the last two years.* 私たちはこの2年にわたって収益を増やした. ― **multiplication** /mʌltəplɪkéɪʃ(ə)n/ 名 U ➡**掛け算, 乗法** ☛参 **division, addition, subtraction**

**multi-purpose** 形 ▶定義 that can be used for several different purposes 異なるいくつかの目的に用いることができる➡**多目的の, いろいろな目的に使う, 多用途の** ‖ *a multi-purpose tool/machine* 多目的の道具・機械

**multitude** /mʌltət(j)uːd/ 名 C 正式 ▶定義 a very large number of people or things 非常に多数の人または物➡**多数, 大勢**

**mum** /mʌm/ (米 **mom** /mɑm, mʌm/) 名 C 略式 ▶定義 mother 母親➡**お母さん, ママ** ‖ *Is that your mum?* あれは君のママかい. *Can I have a drink, Mum?* 飲み物をもらえるかな, お母さん. ☛参 **mummy**

**mumble** /mʌmb(ə)l/ 動 自他 ▶定義 to speak quietly without opening your mouth properly, so that people cannot hear the words 人々が言葉を聞き取れないくらい, きちんと口を開けずに小声で話す➡**もぐもぐ言う, ぶつぶつ言う** ‖ *I can't hear if you mumble.* ぶつぶつ言ったら聞こえないよ. ☛参 **mutter**

\***mummy** /mʌmi/ 名 C (複 **mummies**) ▶定義 **1** (米 **mommy** /mɑmi/) 略式 (used by or to children) mother (子供が, または子供に用いる)母親➡**お母さん, ママ** ‖ *Here comes your mummy now.* ほら, あなたのママが今来たよ. ▶定義 **2** the dead body of a person or animal which has been kept by rubbing it with special oils and covering it in cloth 特別な油を塗り布で包むことによって保存された人または動物の死体➡**ミイラ**

**mumps** /mʌmps/ 名 U ▶定義 an infectious disease, especially of children, that causes the neck to swell 特に子供がかかる, 首がはれる伝染性の病気➡**お多福風邪, 流行性耳下腺炎** ‖ *to have/catch (the) mumps* お多福風邪にかかる

**munch** /mʌntʃ/ 動 自他 ▶定義 munch (on sth) to bite and eat sth noisily ～にかみ付いて騒がしく食べる➡**むしゃむしゃ食べる, ぽりぽり食べる** ‖ *He sat there munching (on) an apple.* 彼はリンゴをむしゃむしゃ食べながらそこに座っていた.

**mundane** /mʌndéɪn, ˆ/ 形 ▶定義 ordinary; not interesting or exciting 普通の; 面白くない、または刺激的でない➔**日常の, ありきたりの** ‖ *a mundane job* ありきたりの仕事

**municipal** /mjuːnís(ə)p(ə)l/ 形 ▶定義 connected with a town or city that has its own local government 地方自治制を敷く町・市に関連した➔**市の, 町の, 自治都市の, 地方自治の** ‖ *municipal buildings (= the town hall, public library, etc)* 市の建物 (= 市役所, 公共の図書館など)

**munitions** /mjʊníʃ(ə)nz/ 名 [複数扱い] ▶定義 military supplies, especially bombs and guns 軍の補給品, 特に爆弾や銃➔**軍需品**

**mural** /mjúər(ə)l/ 名 C ▶定義 a large picture painted on a wall 壁にかかれた大きな絵➔**壁画**

*****murder** /mə́ːrdər/ 名 ▶定義 **1** C U the crime of killing a person illegally and on purpose 違法に故意に人を殺す犯罪➔**殺人, 虐殺** ‖ *to commit murder* 殺人を犯す *a vicious murder* 悪意のある殺人 *the murder victim/weapon* 殺人の犠牲者・凶器 ☛参 **manslaughter** ▶定義 **2** U 略式 a very difficult or unpleasant experience 非常に難しいまたはつらい経験➔**とても難しい事・物, とてもつらい事・物** ‖ *It's murder trying to work when it's as hot as this.* このように暑いときに働こうというのはとても難しい.

成句 **get away with murder** ▶定義 to do whatever you want without being stopped or punished 止められるまたは罰せられることなしに何でもしたい事をする➔**好き勝手に振る舞う, ひどい事をしても非難を免れる** ‖ *He lets his students get away with murder.* 彼は生徒たちを好き勝手にさせる. —**murder** 動 自 他 ➔殺害する, 殺す, 殺人を犯す ☛参 **kill** の注 —**murderer** 名 C ➔殺人犯, 殺人者

**murderous** /mə́ːrdərəs/ 形 ▶定義 intending or likely to murder 殺す意図のあるまたは殺しそうな➔**殺意のある, 残忍な, 殺人的な**

**murky** /mə́ːrki/ 形 ▶定義 dark and unpleasant or dirty 暗くて, 嫌なまたは汚い➔**暗くて陰気な, 汚い, 濁った** ‖ *The water in the river looked very murky.* 川の水は非常に濁って見えた. (比喩) *According to rumours, the new boss had a murky past.* うわさによると, 新しい上司には暗い過去があった.

**murmur** /mə́ːrmər/ 動 自 他 ▶定義 to say sth in a low quiet voice 低い静かな声で〜を言う➔**つぶやく, ささやく** ‖ *He murmured a name in his sleep.* 彼は寝言である名前をつぶやいた. —**murmur** 名 C ➔つぶやき, ささやき

*****muscle** /mʌ́s(ə)l/ 名 C U ▶定義 one of the parts inside your body that you can make tight or relax in order to produce movement 体の内側にある, 引き締めたり緩めたりして動かすことができる部分の1つ➔**筋肉** ‖ *Riding a bicycle is good for developing the leg muscles.* 自転車に乗るのは, 足の筋肉を付けるのに良い. *Lifting weights builds muscle.* ウエートリフティングは筋肉を作る.

**muscular** /mʌ́skjələr/ 形 ▶定義 **1** connected with the muscles 筋肉に関連した➔**筋肉の** ‖ *muscular pain/tissue* 筋肉痛・組織 ▶定義 **2** having large strong muscles 大きな強い筋肉を持つ➔**筋肉の発達した, 筋骨たくましい** ‖ *a muscular body* 筋肉の発達した体

*****museum** /mjuːzíːəm/ 名 C ▶定義 a building where collections of valuable and interesting objects are kept and shown to the public 価値のある興味深い収集品が保管され, 一般の人々に公開されている建物➔**博物館, 美術館, 展示館** ‖ *Have you been to the Science Museum in London?* ロンドンの科学博物館に行ったことがありますか. ☛C8 ページのさし絵

**mushroom** /mʌ́ʃruːm, -rʊm/ 名 C ▶定義 a type of plant which grows very quickly, has a flat or rounded top and can be eaten as a vegetable 非常に生長が早い, 平らなまたは丸い上部を持つ, 野菜として食べられる植物の一種➔**キノコ, マッシュルーム**

▶キノコは fungus (複 fungi) (菌類)の一種. すべてではないが, 食べられる物がある. toadstool (毒キノコ) は毒のあるいくつかの種類のキノコの名称.

*****music** /mjúːzɪk/ 名 U ▶定義 **1** an arrangement of sounds in patterns to be sung or played on instruments パターンになった音を組み合わせたもので, 歌われたり楽器で演奏されたりする➔**音楽, 楽曲, 曲** ‖ *What sort of music do you like?* どんな種類の音楽が好きですか. *classical/folk/pop/rock/world music* クラシック・民族・ポピュラー・ロック・ワールドミュージック *to write/*

*compose music* 作曲する *a music lesson/teacher* 音楽の授業・先生 ☛次のページのさし絵 ▶定義2 the written signs that represent the sounds of music 音楽の音を表すために書かれた記号→**楽譜** ‖ *Can you read music?* あなたは楽譜が読めますか.

★**musical¹** /mjúːzɪk(ə)l/ 形 ▶定義1 connected with music 音楽に関連した→**音楽の, 音楽を伴う, 音楽的な** ‖ *Can you play a musical instrument (= the piano, the violin, the trumpet, etc)?* あなたは楽器(= ピアノ・バイオリン・トランペットなど)を演奏できますか. ▶定義2 interested in or good at music 音楽に興味がある・得意な→**音楽の好きな, 音楽の上手な** ‖ *He's very musical.* 彼は非常に音楽のセンスがある. ▶定義3 having a pleasant sound like music 音楽のような心地良い音を持つ→**音楽のような, 耳に快い** ‖ *a musical voice* 耳に快い声 — **musically** /-k(ə)li/ 副→**音楽的に, 音楽のように**

**musical²** /mjúːzɪk(ə)l/ 名 C ▶定義 a play or film which has singing and dancing in it 中に歌と踊りのある劇または映画→**ミュージカル(映画)**

★**musician** /mjuːzíʃ(ə)n/ 名 C ▶定義 a person who plays a musical instrument or writes music, especially as a job 特に仕事として, 楽器を演奏するまたは作曲する人→**音楽家, ミュージシャン**

★**Muslim** /mázləm, múz-, mús-/ (または **Moslem** /mázləm/) 名 C ▶定義 a person whose religion is Islam イスラム教を宗教とする人→**イスラム教徒** — **Muslim**(または **Moslem**) 形→**イスラム教(徒)の** ‖ *Muslim traditions/beliefs* イスラム教の伝統・教義

**mussel** /más(ə)l/ 名 C ▶定義 a type of small sea animal (*a shellfish*) that can be eaten, with a black shell in two parts 2つに分かれた黒っぽい殻を持つ, 食べられる小さな海の動物(甲殻類動物)の一種→**紫貽貝(むらさきいがい), ムール貝** ☛ **shellfish** のさし絵

★**must¹** /məs(t), 強形 mʌst/ 法助動詞 (否定 **must not**; 省略形 **mustn't** /mʌsnt/) ▶定義1 used for saying that it is necessary that sth happens 〜が起きることが必要だと述べるのに用いて→**〜しなければならない, 〜でなければならない, 〜すべきである, 〜する必要がある** ‖ *I must remember to go to the bank today.* 私は今日忘れずに銀行に行かなければならない. *You mustn't take photographs in here. It's forbidden.* ここで写真を撮ってはいけません. それは禁止されています. ▶定義2 used for saying that you feel sure that sth is true 〜が真実であると確信していることを述べるのに用いて→**〜に違いない, 〜のはずだ, 絶対〜だ** ‖ *Have something to eat. You must be hungry.* 何か食べなさい. あなたはおなかがすいているはずだ. *I can't find my cheque book. I must have left it at home.* 小切手帳が見つからない. 家に置いてきたに違いない. ▶定義3 used for giving sb advice 〜に忠告をするのに用いて→**是非〜してください** ‖ *You really must see that film. It's wonderful.* あの映画は本当に是非見るべきです. すばらしいです.

▶法助動詞についての説明は, 巻末の「文法早見表」を参照.

> ▶語法
>
> イメージは「絶対…しろ」または「絶対…だ」
>
> 　助動詞 must は命令「…しなさい」と断定「…に違いない」の2つの意味があるように思われていますが, 共通のイメージが元になっています. それは「絶対…」です. したがって *You must eat it.* は「絶対に食べなさい」, *He must be lying.* は「彼は絶対うそをついている」となるのです.

**must²** /məs(t), 強形 mʌst/ 名 C ▶定義 a thing that you strongly recommend あなたが強く勧めること→**是非しなければならない事または物, 絶対必要な事または物** ‖ *This book is a must for all science fiction fans.* この本はすべての空想科学小説ファンの必読書だ.

**mustache** /məstáːʃ, mʌ́stæʃ/ 米 = **MOUSTACHE**

**mustard** /mʌ́stərd/ 名 U ▶定義 a cold yellow or brown sauce that tastes hot and is eaten in small amounts with meat 辛くて少量を肉と一緒に食べる, 黄色または茶色の冷たいソース→**からし, マスタード**

**musty** /másti/ 形 ▶定義 having an unpleasant old or wet smell because of a lack of fresh air 新鮮な空気がないために, 古い・湿った嫌なにおいのする→**かび臭い** ‖ *The rooms in the old house were dark and musty.* その古家の部屋は

## musical instruments

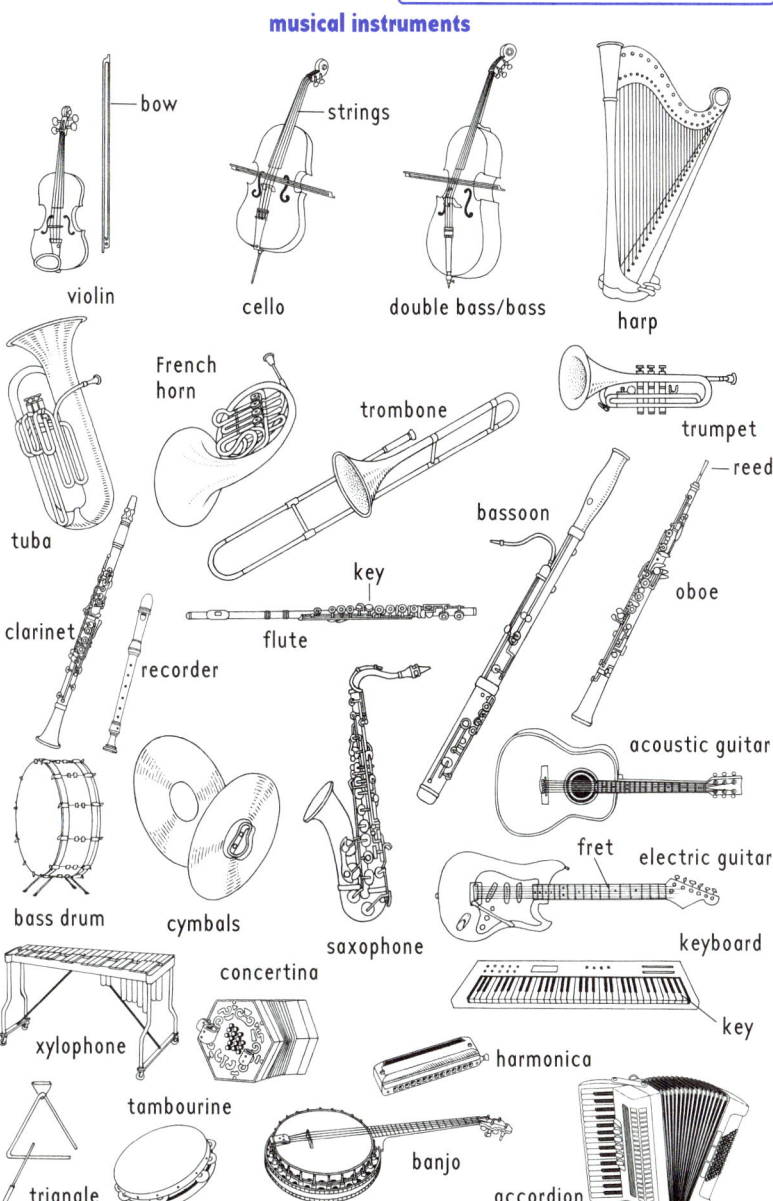

暗くてかび臭かった.

**mutant** /mjúːtnt/ 名 C ▶定義 a living thing that is different from other living things of the same type because of a change in its basic (genetic) structure 基本的(遺伝子の)構造が変わったために,同じ種類のほかの生物とは異なる生物→**突然変異体, 変種, ミュータント**

**mutation** /mjuːtéɪʃ(ə)n/ 名 C U ▶定義 a change in the basic (genetic) structure of a living or developing thing; an example of such a change 生きているまたは発達している物の基本的(遺伝子の)構造の変化; そのような変化の一例→**突然変異(体)** ‖ *mutations caused by radiation* 放射線による突然変異

**muted** /mjúːtəd/ 形 ▶定義1 (used about colours or sounds) not bright or loud; soft (色または音について)明るくない, または響かない; 柔らかい→**弱められた, 柔らかい, 弱音器の付いた** ▶定義2 (used about a feeling or reaction) not strongly expressed (感情または反応について)強く表現されない→**抑制された** ‖ *muted criticism* 抑えられた批判 *a muted response* 抑えた反応

**mutilate** /mjúːt(ə)leɪt/ 動他 (通常は受動態で) ▶定義 to damage sb's body very badly, often by cutting off parts しばしば部分を切り離すことによって, ~の体を非常にひどく傷付ける→**~を切断する, 重症を負わせる, 傷付ける, 切り刻む** — mutilation /mjùːt(ə)léɪʃ(ə)n/ 名 C U →**切断, 切除**

**mutiny** /mjúːt(ə)ni/ 名 C U (複 mutinies) ▶定義 an act of a group of people, especially sailors or soldiers, refusing to obey the person who is in command 人々の集団, 特に船員または軍人が, 指揮を取る人に従うことを拒む行為→**上官に対する反抗, 反乱** ‖ *There'll be a mutiny if conditions don't improve.* 状況が改善されなければ反乱が起きるだろう. — mutiny 動自 →**反乱を起こす, 反抗する**

**mutter** /mʌ́tər/ 動自他 ▶定義 to speak in a low, quiet and often angry voice that is difficult to hear 低い, 静かな, そしてしばしば怒ったような, 聞こえにくい声で話す→**つぶやく, ぶつぶつ言う** ‖ *He muttered something about being late and left the room.* 彼は遅れたことについて何かぶつぶつ言って, 部屋を出た. ☛参 **mumble**

**mutton** /mʌ́tn/ 名 U ▶定義 the meat from an adult sheep 大人の羊の肉→**羊の肉** ☛参 **meat** の注

**mutual** /mjúːtʃuəl, -tʃəl/ 形 ▶定義1 (used about a feeling or an action) felt or done equally by both people involved (感情または行為について)関係する両方の人によって平等に感じられるまたは行われる→**お互いの, 相互の** ‖ *We have a mutual agreement (= we both agree) to help each other out when necessary.* 私たちは必要があれば助け合うということに相互に合意している (= 2人とも同意している). *I just can't stand her and I'm sure the feeling is mutual (= she doesn't like me either).* 私は本当に彼女には我慢ができない. そして, この感情は相互のものだと私は確信している (= 彼女も私を好きではない). ▶定義2 shared by two or more people 2人以上によって共有される→**共通の, 共同の** ‖ *mutual interests* 共通の利害 *It seems that Jane is a mutual friend of ours.* ジェーンは私たちの共通の友達のようだ. — mutually /-li/ 副 →**相互に, 互いに**

**muzzle** /mʌ́z(ə)l/ 名 C ▶定義1 the nose and mouth of an animal (for example a dog or fox) 動物(例えば犬またはキツネ)の鼻と口→**鼻, 鼻面** ☛ C1 ページのさし絵 ▶定義2 a cover made of leather or wire that is put over an animal's nose and mouth so that it cannot bite 皮または針金でできた, 動物の鼻と口の上に付けて, それがかみ付けないようにする覆い→**口輪** ▶定義3 the open end of a gun where the bullets come out 銃弾が飛び出す銃の開いた先の部分→**銃口, 砲口** — muzzle 動他 (通常は受動態で) →**口輪をかける, 口止めする** ‖ *Dogs must be kept muzzled.* 犬には口輪をはめておかなければならない.

**\*my** /maɪ, mə/ 代 ▶定義 of or belonging to me 私に関する, または私の所有する→**私の** ‖ *This is my husband, Jim.* こちらは私の夫, ジムです. *My favourite colour is blue.* 私の好きな色は青だ. ☛参 **mine**[1]

**\*myself** /maɪsélf, mə-/ 代 ▶定義1 used when the person who does an action is also affected by it ある行為をする人とそれによって影響を受ける人が, 同じであるときに用いて→**私自身を, 私自身に** ‖ *I saw myself in the mirror.* 私は鏡で自分を見た. *I felt rather pleased with myself.* 私は, 自分自身に対していささか満足していた. ▶定義2 used to emphasize the person who does the action 行為をした本人を強調するのに用いて→

自分で, 私本人を, 私本人に ‖ *I'll speak to her myself.* 彼女には私が自分で話すよ. *I'll do it myself (= if you don't want to do it for me).* 私はそれを自分でする (= あなたが私のためにそれをしたくないならば).

成句 **(all) by myself** ▶定義 1 alone ➔独りで ‖ *I live by myself.* 私は独りで暮らしている. ☞参 **alone** の注 ▶定義 2 without help 助けなしに➔独力で, 私自身で ‖ *I painted the house all by myself.* 私はすべて独力で家にペンキを塗った.

*__mysterious__ /mɪstíəriəs/ 形 ▶定義 1 that you do not understand or cannot explain; strange 分からない・説明できないような; 奇妙な➔なぞの, 不思議な, 不可解な ‖ *Several people reported seeing mysterious lights in the sky.* 何人かの人が空に不思議な光を見たと報告した. ▶定義 2 (used about a person) keeping sth secret or refusing to explain sth (人について) ~を秘密にしておく, または~を説明するのを拒む➔秘密にしたがる, 話したがらない, 教えたがらない ‖ *They're being very mysterious about where they're going this evening.* 彼らは今晩どこに行くのか全く話したがらない. — **mysteriously** 副 ➔なぞのように, 不思議なことに

*__mystery__ /míst(ə)ri/ 名 (複 **mysteries**) ▶定義 1 ⓒ a thing that you cannot understand or explain 理解・説明できない事 ➔不可解な事, 不思議な事 ‖ *The cause of the accident is a complete mystery.* その事故の原因は全く不可解だ. *It's a mystery to me what my daughter sees in her boyfriend.* 娘がボーイフレンドの何を見ているのか私には不可解だ. ▶定義 2 Ⓤ the quality of being strange and secret and full of things that are difficult to explain 奇妙で秘密の, そして説明するのが難しい事で一杯のもの ➔神秘, なぞ ‖ *There's a lot of mystery surrounding this case.* この事件にはたくさんのなぞがある. ▶定義 3 ⓒ a story, film or play in which crimes or strange events are only explained at the end 犯罪または奇妙な出来事が最後に説明される物語, 映画, または劇➔推理もの, 怪奇もの, ミステリー

**mystic** /místɪk/ 名 ⓒ ▶定義 a person who spends his/her life developing his/her spirit and communicating with God or a god 霊能力を発達させ神の意志を理解することに人生をかける人➔神秘論者, 神秘主義者

**mystical** /místɪk(ə)l/ (または **mystic** /místɪk/)

# mythology 1083

形 ▶定義 connected with the spirit; strange and wonderful 霊魂に関連した; 不思議なそしてすばらしい➔神秘主義的な, 霊感による, 秘法の ‖ *Watching the sun set over the island was an almost mystical experience.* 島越しに日没を見るのは神秘的とも言える経験だった.

**mysticism** /místəsìz(ə)m/ 名 Ⓤ ▶定義 the belief that you can reach complete truth and knowledge of God or gods by prayer, thought and development of the spirit 祈り, 瞑想 (めいそう), 霊能力の発達によって完ぺきな真実や神の理解を達成できるという考え➔神秘説, 神秘主義 ‖ *Eastern mysticism* 東洋神秘主義

**mystify** /místəfàɪ/ 動 ⓗ (現分 **mystifying**; 三単現 **mystifies**; 過, 過分 **mystified**) ▶定義 to make sb confused because he/she cannot understand sth ~が…を理解できないことによって混乱するように仕向ける➔迷わす, 惑わす, 煙に巻く ‖ *I was mystified by the strange note he'd left behind.* 私は彼が残した奇妙なメモによって惑わされた.

**myth** /mɪθ/ 名 ⓒ ▶定義 1 a story from past times, especially one about gods and men of courage. Myths often explain natural or historical events. 過去からの物語, 特に神と勇気ある男性についてのもの. しばしば自然の出来事や歴史的な出来事を説明している➔神話 ▶定義 2 an idea or story which many people believe but that does not exist or is false 多くの人々が信じるかもしれないが, 存在しないまたは誤っている考えまたは話 ➔根拠のない考え, 根拠のない意見, 迷信 ‖ *The idea that money makes you happy is a myth.* お金があなたを幸せにするという考えは迷信だ.

**mythical** /míθɪk(ə)l/ 形 ▶定義 1 existing only in myths(1) myths(1) にのみ存在する➔神話の ‖ *mythical beasts/heroes* 神話上の動物・英雄 ▶定義 2 not real or true; existing only in the imagination 本物または真実でない; 想像上でだけ存在する➔作り話の, 架空の

**mythology** /mɪθάlədʒi/ 名 Ⓤ ▶定義 very old stories and the beliefs contained in them 非常に古い物語, およびその中にある考え➔神話, 神話学 ‖ *Greek and Roman mythology* ギリシャとローマの神話

# N n

**N, n**¹ /en/ 名 ⓒ (復 **N's;n's**) ▶定義 the fourteenth letter of the English alphabet 英語アルファベットの第14文字 →n(N)が表す音,n(N)の文字,n(N)の字形のもの ‖ *'Nicholas' begins with (an) 'N'.* Nicholas は N で始まる.

**N²** (困 **No**) 名 north(ern)北(の), 北方 ‖ *N Yorkshire* ノースヨークシャー州

**nag** /næg/ 動 (**nagging; nagged**) ▶定義 1 自他 **nag (at) sb** to continuously complain to sb about his/her behaviour or to ask him/her to do sth many times ～の振る舞いについて絶えず不平を言う, ～に何かをしてほしいと何回も頼む→(～に)うるさく文句を言う, (～に)(…するように)うるさくせがむ ‖ *My parents are always nagging (at) me to work harder.* 両親はもっとしっかり働くようにといつもうるさく小言を言う. ▶定義 2 他 to worry or irritate sb continuously ～を絶えず心配させる, いらいらさせる→(疑惑・不安などが)(～を)しつこく悩ます, ～を苦しめる ‖ *a nagging doubt/headache* いつまでも晴れない疑惑・しつこい頭痛

★**nail** /neɪl/ 名 ⓒ ▶定義 1 the thin hard layer that covers the ends of your fingers and toes 手の指先・足の指先を覆っている, 薄くて硬い角質層→(人間の手・足の)つめ ‖ *fingernails/toenails* 手のつめ・足のつめ ☛ C5 ページのさし絵 ▶定義 2 a small thin piece of metal that is used for holding pieces of wood together, hanging pictures on, etc 小さくて細い金属製のもので, 材木を継ぎ合わせたり, 絵を掛けるときなどに使う→くぎ, びょう ‖ *to hammer in a nail* くぎを打ち込む ☛ **bolt**, **tool** の挿し絵 — **nail** 動 →～をくぎで打ち付ける, ～をびょうで留める

成句 **hit the nail on the head** ⇒ **HIT**¹

句動詞 **nail sb down (to sth)** ▶定義 to make a person say clearly what he/she wants or intends to do したい事や意図している事を人にはっきりと言わせる→(～に)考えをはっきり言わせる ‖ *She says she'll visit us in the summer but I can't nail her down to a definite date.* 彼女は夏に我々の所に来てくれると言うが, はっきりとした日にちは分からない.

**nail brush** 名 ⓒ ▶定義 a small brush for cleaning your fingernails 手のつめをきれいにするための小さなブラシ→つめブラシ ☛ **brush** のさし絵

**nail file** 名 ⓒ ▶定義 a small metal tool with a rough surface that you use for shaping your nails つめの形を整えるために使う表面がざらざらした小さな金属製の道具 →つめやすり

**nail polish** (英 **nail varnish**) 名 ⓤ ▶定義 a liquid that people paint on their nails to give them colour つめに色を付けるために塗る液体 →マニキュア液

**naive** (または **naïve**) /naɪˈiːv; nɑːˈiːv/ 形 ▶定義 without enough experience of life and too ready to believe or trust other people 人生経験が十分ではなく, 他人を信じたり当てにしすぎる → 世間知らずな, だまされやすい ‖ *I was too naive to realize what was happening.* 私はあまりにも世間知らずで, 何が起きたのか分からなかった. *a naive remark/question/view* 素朴な感想・質問・見解 →類 **innocent** — **naively** (または **naïvely**) 副 →単純に, 愚直に, ばか正直に ‖ *She naively accepted the first price he offered.* 彼女はばか正直に, 彼が最初に示した値段を了承してしまった. — **naivety** (または **naïvety**) /nɑːˈiːv(ə)ti; naɪ-/ 名 ⓤ →世間知らず, お人よし

★**naked** /ˈneɪkəd,/ 形 ▶定義 1 not wearing any clothes 服を何も着ていない→裸の, 全裸の ‖ *He came to the door naked except for a towel.* 彼はタオルのほかは何も身にまとわず, 戸口に出てきた. *naked shoulders/arms* むき出しの肩・腕 ☛参 **bare**, **nude** ▶定義 2 (名詞の前だけ) (used about sth that is usually covered) not covered (通常覆われている物について) 覆われていない→むき出しの ‖ *a naked flame/bulb/light* 裸火・裸電球・裸電灯 ▶定義 3 (名詞の前だけ) clearly shown or expressed in a way that is often shocking 時として衝撃的な形で明らかにされる・表現される→あからさまな, 露骨な ‖ *naked aggression/ambition/fear* あからさまな敵対心・野心・恐れ

成句 **the naked eye** ▶定義 the normal power of your eyes without the help of glasses, a machine, etc 眼鏡・機具などの助けを借りない自然な状態での視力→肉眼, 裸眼 ‖ *Bacteria are too small to be seen with the naked eye.* バクテリアは非常に小さいので, 肉眼では見えない.

★**name**¹ /neɪm/ 名 ▶定義 1 ⓒ a word or words by which sb/sth is known ～が識別されるために使われる単語, 言葉→名, 名前, 名称 ‖ *What's your* *name, please?* あなたのお名前は. *Do you know the name of this flower?* この花の名前を知っていますか. ▶定義2 [単数扱い] an opinion that people have of a person or thing 人・事柄についての世間一般の意見 → (～という)**評判, 世評** ‖ *That area of London has rather a bad name.* ロンドンのその地域は, かなり評判が悪い. ☞類 **reputation** ▶定義3 ⓒ a famous person 有名な人 → **著名人, 名士** ‖ *All the big names in show business were invited to the party.* 芸能界の大物は皆, そのパーティーに招かれていた.

成句 by name ▶定義 using the name of sb/sth ～の名前を使って → **～の名前で, 名指しで** ‖ *It's a big school but the head teacher knows all the children by name.* 大きな学校なのですが, 校長は生徒全員を名前で知っている.

call sb names ⇒ **CALL**¹

in the name of sb; in sb's name ▶定義 for sb/sth; officially belonging to sb ～の代わりに; 公式に～のもので → **～に代わって, ～の名義で** ‖ *The contract is in my name.* その契約は私の名義だ.

in the name of sth ▶定義 used to give a reason or excuse for an action, even when what you are doing might be wrong 行っている事が間違っていても, それについて弁解や言い訳を言うときに用いて → **～の名において, ～の権威において** ‖ *They acted in the name of democracy.* 彼らは民主主義の名の下に行動した.

make a name for yourself; make your name ▶定義 to become well known and respected 有名になり, 評価されるようになる → **有名になる, 名を上げる** ‖ *She made a name for herself as a journalist.* 彼女はジャーナリストとして有名になった.

▶ first name (米 しばしば given name)（名前）とは, 出生時に両親が付けるものであり, キリスト教の国では Christian name (洗礼名) と呼ばれることもある. 両親はこの名前の後にもう1つ名前を付けることもあり, これは middle name (ミドルネーム) と呼ばれる. 正式な公文書ではこれら2つの名前を合わせて forename (名) とするが, それ以外でミドルネームはあまり使われない. surname (姓) とは通常, 生まれ持った family name (名字) を表す語である. 女性が結婚した場合, 姓が変わって夫と同じ姓になることもある. この場合, 結婚前の姓は maiden name (旧姓) と呼ばれる.

# name² 1085

### ▶音声とつづり字

name の発音は e の規則による

name を [néɪm] のように発音するのは「発音しない文字の e があると, その前の母音文字はアルファベット文字の呼び名で発音する」という規則によります. もし, e がなく, 子音で終わっていればその前の母音文字は, アルファベット母音文字の基本音で発音します.

A [éɪ] rate bake hate lake
　[æ] rat back hat lack

ただし, have, glove などは例外です.

**name**² /néɪm/ 動 他 ▶定義1 name sb/sth (after sb) to give sb/sth a name ～に名前を付ける → **～を命名する** ‖ *Columbia was named after Christopher Columbus.* コロンビアは, クリストファー コロンブスにちなんで名付けられた.

▶ 名前を知っている人を話題とする場合は, be called を用いる: *Their youngest is called Mark.* (彼らの一番下の子はマークという名前だ.)

▶定義2 to say what the name of sb/sth is ～の名前を言う → **～の名前を上げる** ‖ *The journalist refused to name the person who had given her the information.* ジャーナリストは情報提供者の名を明かすことを拒否した. *Can you name all the planets?* 惑星の名前をすべて言えますか.

▶定義3 to state sth exactly ～を明確に述べる → **(値段・日取りなど)を指定する, 提示する** ‖ *Name your price - we'll pay it!* いくら欲しいか言いなさい - 払いますから.

### ▶社会・文化

人名と呼び名の一覧表

【女性名】Alice → Ally, Allie, Elsie / Catharine → Kate, Katrine / Charlotte → Lola, Loleta / Dorothy → Dolly, Dora / Eleanor → Nora(h), Nelly / Elizabeth → Bess, Betsy, Betty / Juliana → Gill, Jill / Margaret → Maggie, Meg, Peggy / Martha, Patricia → Pat, Pattie / Rebecca → Beck, Becky / Susan, Susanna → Sue, Susie / Victoria → Vicky

【男性名】Augustus → Gus / Bartholomew → Bart / Benjamin → Ben / Daniel → Dan /

David → Davy / Edward → Eddie, Ted / Francis → Frank / Frederick → Fred / James → Jim, Jimmy / Michael → Mike / Nicholas → Nick / Richard → Dick, Rick / Robert → Bob, Rob, Robin / William → Bill, Will / Samuel → Sam, Sammy / Thomas → Tom, Tommy

**nameless** /néɪmləs/ 形 ▶定義1 without a name or with a name that you do not know 名前がない, 名前はあるが知らない→**名付けられていない, 無名の** ▶定義2 whose name is kept a secret 名前を秘密にしておく→**匿名で, 名前を出さないで** ‖ *a well-known public figure who shall remain nameless* 名前は伏せておくが或る有名人

**namely** /néɪmli/ 副 ▶定義 (used for giving more detail about what you are saying) that is to say (話の内容の詳細を述べるために用いて) すなわち→**換言すると, 詳しく言えば** ‖ *There is only one person who can overrule the death sentence, namely the President.* 死刑判決をくつがえせる人は1人しかいない, すなわち大統領である.

**namesake** /néɪmseɪk/ 名 C ▶定義 a person who has the same name as another 他人と同じ名前の人→**同名の人, (ある人に)ちなんで名付けられた人**

**nanny** /nǽni/ 名 C (複 **nannies**) 英 ▶定義 a woman whose job is to look after a family's children and who usually lives in the family home ある家族の子供の世話をする女性で, 通常はその家族の家に住み込む→**乳母, ばあや, ナニー**

**nap** /nǽp/ 名 C ▶定義 a short sleep that you have during the day 日中に取る短い睡眠→**昼寝, うたた寝** ●参 **snooze**— nap 動 自 (**napping; napped**)→昼寝する, うたた寝をする

**nape** /néɪp/ 名 [単数扱い] ▶定義 the back part of your neck 首の後ろの部分→**うなじ, えり首**

**napkin** /nǽpkən/ 名 C ▶定義 a piece of cloth or paper that you use when you are eating to protect your clothes or for cleaning your hands and mouth 食事中に服を汚さないため, または手や口をふくために用いる布または紙→**(食卓用)ナプキン** ‖ *a paper napkin* 紙ナプキン ●類 **serviette**

**nappy** /nǽpi/ 名 C (複 **nappies**) (米 **diaper**) ▶定義 a piece of soft thick cloth or paper that a baby or very young child wears around its bottom and between its legs 赤ん坊や幼児が腰回りから両足間に着ける柔らかい厚布, 厚紙→**おむつ** ‖ *Does his nappy need changing?* 坊やのおむつを変える必要がありますか. *disposable nappies* (= *that you throw away when they have been used*) 使い捨ての(= 使用後は捨てる)おむつ

**narcotic** /nɑːrkάtɪk/ 名 C ▶定義1 a powerful illegal drug that affects your mind in a harmful way 精神に悪影響を及ぼす, 強力で違法な薬→**麻薬** ▶定義2 a substance or drug that relaxes you, stops pain, or makes you sleep 緊張を和らげたり, 痛みを抑えたり, 眠らせるための物質・薬→**麻酔薬, 催眠薬** — **narcotic** 形 →**麻酔(性)の, 催眠(性)の, 麻薬の**

**narrate** /nəréɪt, nǽreɪt/ 動 他 正式 ▶定義 to tell a story 物語を語る→**(話など)を語る, ～を述べる, ～を物語る** — **narration** /nǽreɪʃ(ə)n, nə-; nə-, næ-/ 名 C U →語り, 叙述, ナレーション

**narrative** /nǽrətɪv/ 名 正式 ▶定義1 C the description of events in a story 物語中の出来事の描写→**物語, 話** ▶定義2 U the process or skill of telling a story 物語を話すこと, 話し方の技量→**語ること, 話術**

**narrator** /nəréɪtər, nǽreɪtər/ 名 C ▶定義 the person who tells a story or explains what is happening in a play, film, etc 演劇・映画などで, 物語を話したり, 場面で起きている事を説明したりする人→**語り手, ナレーター**

*****narrow** /nǽrou/ 形 ▶定義1 having only a short distance from side to side 左右の間の距離が極めて短い→**幅の狭い, 細い** ‖ *The bridge is too narrow for two cars to pass.* その橋はとても幅が狭いので, 2台の車が擦れ違うことができない. ⇔ **wide, broad** ▶定義2 not large 広くない→**(目的・範囲・解釈などが)限られた, 狭い** ‖ *a narrow circle of friends* 限られた友人仲間 ▶定義3 by a small amount 少しだけの→**辛うじての, ぎりぎりの, 間一髪の** ‖ *That was a very narrow escape. You were lucky.* それは本当に危機一髪でした. あなたは運が良かった. *a narrow defeat/victory* 惜敗・辛勝— **narrow** 動 自 他 →**狭くなる, 狭まる, 狭める** ‖ *The road narrows in 50 metres.* 道幅は50メートルに狭まる.— **narrowness** 名 U →

狭いこと，狭さ

句動詞 **narrow sth down** ▶定義 to make a list of things smaller 事物の一覧を絞り込む→(範囲・論点などを)絞り込む ‖ *The police have narrowed down their list of suspects to three.* 警察は容疑者を3人に絞り込んでいる．

**narrowly** /nǽrouli/ 副 ▶定義 only by a small amount ほんの少しだけ → 辛うじて，やっと，危うく

**narrow-minded** 形 ▶定義 not wanting to accept new ideas or the opinions of other people if they are not the same as your own 新しい考えや自分と異なる他人の意見を受け入れたくない→心の狭い，狭量な，不寛容な ☛類 **insular** ⇔ **broad-minded**

**nasal** /néɪz(ə)l/ 形 ▶定義 1 of or for the nose → 鼻の，鼻に関する ▶定義 2 produced partly through the nose 鼻の一部から生じる→鼻声の，鼻にかかった ‖ *a nasal voice* 鼻声

\***nasty** /nάːsti; nǽs-/ 形 (**nastier**; **nastiest**) ▶定義 very bad or unpleasant 非常にひどい，非常に不快な→嫌な，不快な，汚い，不潔な ‖ *a nasty accident* 大事故 *I had a nasty feeling he would follow me.* 彼が付いてくるという嫌な予感がした．*When she was asked to leave she got/turned nasty.* 立ち去るようにと言われて，彼女は不愉快になった．*a nasty bend in the road* 道路の危険なカーブ *What's that nasty smell in this cupboard?* この食器棚の嫌なにおいはなんですか．— **nastily** 副 →意地悪く，卑劣に— **nastiness** 名 ❶ →不快さ，悪意，卑劣

**nation** /néɪʃ(ə)n/ 名 ❻ ▶定義 a country or all the people in a country 国，一国の国民全体→国，国家，国民，民族 ‖ *a summit of the leaders of seven nations* 7か国首脳会議

\***national**¹ /nǽʃ(ə)n(ə)l/ 形 ▶定義 connected with all of a country; typical of a particular country 一国のすべてに関する；ある国に特有な→国家の，国民の，国立の，全国的な ‖ *Here is today's national and international news.* 本日の国内・海外のニュースです．*a national newspaper* 全国紙 ☛参 **international**, **regional**, **local** — **nationally** 副 →全国的に，国民的に

**national**² /nǽʃ(ə)n(ə)l/ 名 [❻，通常は複数] 正式 ▶定義 a citizen of a particular country 特定の国の一市民→(ある国の)一国民，同胞

**national anthem** 名 ❻ ▶定義 the official song of a country that is played at public events 公式行事で演奏される，国の公式な歌→国歌

**the National Health Service** 名 [単数扱い] (略 **NHS**) 英 ▶定義 the system that provides free or cheap medical care for everyone in Britain and that is paid for by taxes 全国民に無料あるいは低料金で医療を提供し，税金で賄う英国の制度→(英国の)国民健康保険制度 ☛参 **health service**

**National Insurance** 名 ❶ (略 **NI**) 英 ▶定義 the system of payments that have to be made by employers and employees to the government to help people who are ill, unemployed, old, etc 雇用主と従業員が政府に拠出(きょしゅつ)し，病気，失業，老齢などの人々の援助に支払われる制度→(英国の)国民保険制度(失業者・退職者・病人が対象) ‖ *to pay National Insurance contributions* 国民保険の負担分を支払う

**nationalism** /nǽʃ(ə)n(ə)lɪz(ə)m/ 名 ❶ ▶定義 1 the desire of a group of people who share the same race, culture, language, etc to form an independent country 同じ民族・文化・言語などを共有する集団が独立国を形成したいとする願望→民族(独立)主義，ナショナリズム ▶定義 2 a feeling of love or pride for your own country; a feeling that your country is better than any other 自国に対する愛や誇りの感情；自国がほかのどんな国よりも優れていると思う感情→(しばしば軽べつ的)国家主義，愛国心，国粋主義

**nationalist** /nǽʃ(ə)n(ə)lɪst/ 名 ❻ ▶定義 a person who wants his/her country or region to become independent 自国・地域の独立を願う人→民族(独立)主義者，国家主義者 ‖ *a Welsh nationalist* ウェールズ分離独立主義者

**nationalistic** /nǽʃ(ə)n(ə)lístɪk/ 形 ▶定義 having strong feelings of love or pride in your own country so that you think it is better than any other 自国に対する愛国心や誇りが非常に強いので，ほかのいかなる国よりも優れていると思う→(しばしば軽べつ的)国家主義の，国粋主義の ☛nationalistic は通常批判的な意味で使われ，誇りに思う気持ちが強すぎることを意味する．

\***nationality** /nǽʃ(ə)nǽləti/ 名 ❻❶ (複 **nationalities**) ▶定義 the state of being legally a citizen of a particular nation or country 法律的

にある国家・国の国民である状態→**国籍** ‖ *to have French nationality* フランス国籍を持つ *students of many nationalities* さまざまな国籍の学生たち *to have **dual nationality** (= of two countries)* 2つの国籍(= 2国の国籍)を持つ

**nationalize** (または **-ise**) /nǽʃ(ə)n(ə)làɪz/ 動 ⦿ ▶定義 to put a company or organization under the control of the government 会社・団体を政府の支配下に置く→**(企業・事業など)を国有化する, 国営にする** ⇔ **privatize** ― nationalization (または nationalisation) /nǽʃ(ə)n(ə)laɪzéɪʃ(ə)n; -lə-/ 名 Ⓤ→**国有化, 国営化**

**national park** 名 ⦿ ▶定義 a large area of beautiful land that is protected by the government so that the public can enjoy it 一般の人々が楽しめるようにと政府によって保護されている広大な美しい地帯→**国立公園**

**nationwide** /nèɪʃ(ə)nwáɪd, ˋ--ˊ/ 形副 ▶定義 over the whole of a country 国全体にわたって→**全国的な[に], 全国的規模の[で]** ‖ *The police launched a nationwide hunt for the killer.* 警察は全国規模で殺人犯の捜索を開始した.

**native**¹ /néɪtɪv/ 形 ▶定義1 (名詞の前だけ) connected with the place where you were born or where you have always lived 出生地・居住地に関連した→**出生地の, 故郷の** ‖ *your native language/country/city* 母語・母国・生まれ故郷 *native Londoners* 生っ粋のロンドンっ子 ▶定義2 (名詞の前だけ) connected with the people who originally lived in a country before other people, especially white people, came to live there ほかの民族, 特に白人が来る前にその国にもともと住んでいた人々に関連した→**(〜に)土着の, (白人に対して)原住[土着]民の** ‖ *native art/dance* 先住民の芸術・舞踊 ☞ 注意. この意味での native は侮辱的に取られる場合がある. ▶定義3 native (to...) (used about an animal or plant) living or growing naturally in a particular place (動物・植物について) 特定の場所に自然生息している, 自生する→**(動物・植物・産物などが)(ある場所)特有の, 原産の** ‖ *This plant is native to South America.* この植物は南アメリカ原産だ. *a native species/habitat* 原産種・自生地

**native**² /néɪtɪv/ 名 ⦿ ▶定義1 a person who was born in a particular place ある特定の場所に生まれた人→**(〜の)生まれの人, その土地の人** ‖ *a native of New York* ニューヨーク出身者 ▶定義2 [通常は複数](古) the people who were living in Africa, America, etc originally, before the Europeans arrived there ヨーロッパ人が来る前にアフリカ・アメリカ大陸にもともと住んでいた人々→**先住民, 原住民** ☞ 注意. この意味での native は現在, 侮辱的に取られる.

**Native American** (または **American Indian**) 形名 ⦿ ▶定義 (of) a member of the race of people who were the original inhabitants of America アメリカ大陸に先住していた民族に属する人(の)→**アメリカ先住民(の), アメリカンインディアン(の)**

**native speaker** 名 ⦿ ▶定義 a person who speaks a language as his/her first language and has not learned it as a foreign language ある言語を母語として話し, それを外国語として学習したことがない人→**ネイティブスピーカー, (ある言語を)母語とする人** ‖ *All our Spanish teachers are native speakers.* スペイン語の先生は全員, ネイティブスピーカーだ.

**NATO** (または **Nato**) /néɪtoʊ/ 略 National Atlantic Treaty Organization ▶定義 a group of European countries, Canada and the US, who agree to give each other military help if necessary ヨーロッパ諸国, カナダ, 米国が加盟し, 必要に応じて相互に軍事援助を行う約を締結している機構→**北大西洋条約機構**

★**natural** /nǽtʃ(ə)rəl/ 形 ▶定義1 (名詞の前だけ) existing in nature; not made or caused by human beings 自然界に存在する;人間が作ったり引き起こしたものではない→**自然の;天然の, 自然のままの** ‖ *I prefer to see animals in their natural habitat rather than in zoos.* 動物は動物園よりも自然の生息地で見る方が好きだ. *Britain's natural resources include coal, oil and gas.* 英国の天然資源には, 石炭・石油・ガスが含まれる. *She died of natural causes (= of old age or illness).* 彼女は自然死(= 老齢・病気で)だった. ⇔ **man-made** ▶定義2 usual or normal 普通の, 正常な→**当然の, 当たり前の** ‖ *It's natural to feel nervous before an interview.* 面接の前に緊張するのは当たり前だ. ⇔ **unnatural** ▶定義3 that you had from birth or that was easy for you to learn 生まれつき持っている, 容易に習得できる→**(能力などが)天性の, 生来の** ‖ *a natural gift for lan-*

*guages* 言語に対する生まれながらの才能 ▶定義4 (名詞の前だけ) (used about parents or their children) related by blood (両親・その子供について) 血がつながっている→(子供・親の)血のつながった, 実の ‖ *She's his stepmother not his natural mother.* 彼女は彼のまま母で, 実母ではない.

**natural history** 名 U ▶定義 the study of plants and animals 植物と動物の研究→博物学 (動物学・植物学・鉱物学などの昔の総称)

**naturalist** /nǽtʃ(ə)rəlɪst/ 名 C ▶定義 a person who studies plants and animals 植物と動物の研究をする人→自然研究者, 動植物研究者, 博物学者

**naturalize** (または **-ise**) /nǽtʃ(ə)rəlaɪz/ 動 (通常は受動態で) ▶定義 to make sb a citizen of a country where he/she was not born ～を出生地ではない国の国民にする →(外国人を)帰化させる, ～に市民権(国籍)を与える ― **naturalization** (または **-isation**) /nǽtʃ(ə)rəlaɪzéɪ(ə)n; -lə-/ 名 U →(外国人の)帰化

**naturally** /nǽtʃ(ə)rəli/ 副 ▶定義1 of course; as you would expect もちろん; 予想通りに→当然, もちろん, 予想通り(に) ‖ *The team was naturally upset about its defeat.* 当然, チームは敗北にうろたえた. ▶定義2 in a natural way; not forced or made artificially 自然に; 強制されたり人工的に作られたのではなく→生まれつき, 生来 ‖ *naturally wavy hair* 天然ウエーブの髪 *Vera is naturally a very cheerful person.* ベラは生来, とても陽気な人だ. ▶定義3 in a way that is relaxed and normal くつろいでいて, 普通通りに→自然に, 楽に, 気負わずに ‖ *Don't try to impress people. Just* **act naturally**. 人を感動させようとするな. 自然に演じなさい.

\***nature** /néɪtʃər/ 名 ▶定義1 ❶all the plants, animals in the universe and all the things that happen in it that are not made or caused by people 宇宙にあるすべての植物・動物など, およびそこで人の手によらずに起きるすべての事象→自然, 物質界, 万物, 自然現象 ‖ *the forces of nature (for example volcanoes, hurricanes, etc)* 自然の脅威(例えば火山, ハリケーンなど) *the wonders/beauties of nature* 自然の驚異・美しさ ▶定義2 ❷U the qualities or character of a person or thing 人・物の特質, 性質→特質, 性質, 本質, 性格 ‖ *He's basically honest by nature.* 彼は根本的には生まれついての正直者だ. *It's not in his nature to be unkind.* 不親切にするのは彼の性に合わない. *It's human nature never to be completely satisfied.* 完全に満足することがないのは, 人間の本質だ. ▶定義3 (単数扱い) a type or sort of sth ～の型, 種類→種類 ‖ *I'm not very interested in things of that nature.* 私はその種の事にはあまり興味がない. *books of a scientific nature* 科学的な本 ▶定義4 **-natured** (複合形容詞を作るために用いて) having a particular quality or type of character ～の性質・個性を持った→性質が～の ‖ *a kind-natured man* 親切な男性

成句 **second nature** ⇒ **SECOND**¹

**naughty** /nɔ́ːti/ 形 特に 英 ▶定義 (used when you are talking to or about a child) badly-behaved; not obeying (子供に対して, または子供について話すために用いて) 行儀が悪い; 従順でない→(子供などが)いたずらな; 言うことを聞かない ‖ *It was very naughty of you to wander off on your own.* 1人で道に迷うなんて, あなたは腕白な子だった. ― **naughtily** 副 →行儀悪く, 腕白に ― **naughtiness** 名 U →いたずら好き, 腕白

**nausea** /nɔ́ːziə, -siə/ 名 U ▶定義 the feeling that you are going to vomit (= bring up food from your stomach) 吐いてしまいそう (= 食べた物を胃から吐く) な感じ → 吐き気, むかつき ☞参 sick(2)

**nauseate** /nɔ́ːzièɪt, -ʒi-, -ʃi-, -si-/ 動 ▶定義 to cause sb to feel sick or disgusted ～に吐き気を催させる, むかむかさせる→(人に)吐き気を起こさせる, 嫌悪を感じさせる ― **nauseating** 形 →吐き気を起こさせるような, ぞっとするような

**nautical** /nɔ́ːtɪk(ə)l, nɑ́ː-/ 形 ▶定義 connected with ships, sailors or sailing 船・船員・航海に関連した→航海の, 船舶の, 船員の

**naval** /néɪv(ə)l/ 形 ▶定義 connected with the navy 海軍に関連した→海軍の, 軍艦の ‖ *a naval base/officer/battle* 海軍基地・海軍士官・海戦

**navel** /néɪv(ə)l/ (または 略式 **belly button**) 名 C ▶定義 the small hole or lump in the middle of your stomach 腹部の真ん中の小さなへこみ・突起→へそ

**navigable** /nǽvɪgəb(ə)l/ 形 ▶定義 (used about a river or narrow area of sea) that boats can sail along (川・海の狭い区域について) 船が航行できる

## navigate

→(川・海などが)(水深・川幅が十分で)航行できる

**navigate** /nǽvəgèɪt/ 動 ▶定義1 ❶ to use a map, etc to find your way to somewhere 地図などを使って、ある場所までの道順を見つける → (運転手・操縦手に)方向を指示する, 誘導する, (自動車の)ナビゲートを務める ‖ *If you drive, I'll navigate.* あなたが運転するのなら, 私が道順を指示します. ▶定義2 ❶ (文) to sail a boat along a river or across a sea 川・海で船が航行する → (川・海)を航行する — **navigator** 名 ❻ → 航海士, 航行者 — **navigation** /nævəgéɪʃ(ə)n/ 名 ❶ → 航行, 航海, 航空

★**navy** /néɪvi/ 名 ❻ (種 **navies**) ▶定義 the part of a country's armed forces that fights at sea in times of war 国軍の一部で, 戦時に海で戦闘する → 海軍 ‖ *to join the navy* 海軍に入隊する *Their son is in the Navy.* 彼らの息子は海軍にいる. ☛ 単数形で用いられる場合, 単数・複数のどちらの動詞をとることもできる. *The Navy is/are introducing a new warship this year.* 海軍は今年新しい軍艦を導入する予定だ. **army, air force, merchant navy** を参照 ☛ 形 **naval**

**navy blue** (または **navy**) 形名 ❶ ▶定義 (of) a very dark blue colour とても濃い青色(の) → 濃紺, ネービーブルー

**NB** (または **nb**) /èn bíː, nóʊtə bíːni, -béni/ 略 ▶定義 (used before a written note) take special notice of (注意書きの前に用いて) 特に注意しなさい → 注意せよ ‖ *NB There is an extra charge for reservations* 注意. 予約には割り増し料金がかかります.

**NE** 略 north-east → 北東, 北東部, 北東地方 ‖ *NE Scotland* 北東スコットランド

★**near**¹ /nɪər/ 形副前 ▶定義1 not far away in time or distance; close 時間・距離があまり離れていない; 近い → (距離的・時間的)(〜の)近くに[へ・で], (〜に)近い, 近くの ‖ *Let's walk to the library. It's quite near.* 図書館に歩いていこう. すぐそこだ. *We're hoping to move to Wales in the near future (= very soon).* 近い将来(= ごく近いうちに)ウェールズに引っ越したいと思っている. *Where's the nearest Post Office?* ここから一番近い郵便局はどこですか. *The day of the interview was getting nearer.* 面接の日が近付いてきた.

▶ close と near は意味としては同じことが多いが, 慣用的な言い回しの中にはどちらか一方だけしか使えないものもある: *a close friend/relative* (親友・近親者) *the near future* (近い将来) *a close contest* (接戦). next の注を参照.

▶定義2 **near-** (複合形容詞を作るために用いて) almost → ほぼ ‖ *a near-perfect performance* ほぼ完ぺきな演技

成句 **close/dear/near to sb's heart** ⇒ **HEART**

**or near(est) offer; ono** ▶定義 (used when you are selling sth) or an amount that is less than but near the amount that you have asked for (〜を売るときに用いて) または要求額に近いがそれよりも低い価格で / または(それに)近い値段で ‖ *Motorbike for sale. £750 ono.* オートバイ売ります. 750ポンドまたはそれに近い値段で.

**a near miss** ▶定義 a situation where sth nearly hits you or where sth bad nearly happens 〜が危うく衝突しそうになること, 悪い〜が危うく起きそうになること → 異常接近, もう一歩のところ ‖ *The bullet flew past his ear. It was a very near miss.* 銃弾が彼の耳をかすめて飛び去った. 非常に危ういところだった.

**nowhere near** ▶定義 far from 〜するどころではない → 全く〜でない, 〜に程遠い ‖ *We've sold nowhere near enough tickets to make a profit.* 我々はチケットを売ったが, 利益を出すには程遠かった.

**near**² /nɪər/ 動 ❶ ▶定義 to get closer to sth in time or distance 時間・距離的に〜に近付く → (〜に)近付く ‖ *At last we were nearing the end of the project.* ついにそのプロジェクトは終わりに近付いた.

**nearby** /nìərbáɪ, ≠/ 形副 ▶定義 not far away in distance 距離があまり離れていない → すぐ近くの, すぐ近くに ‖ *A new restaurant has opened nearby.* 新しいレストランがすぐ近くに開店した. *We went out to a nearby restaurant.* 私たちはすぐ近くのレストランに行った.

▶注意. 形容詞としての nearby は名詞の前だけで使われる. near はこのように名詞の前では使われない: *We went out to a nearby restaurant.* (彼はすぐ近くのレストランに行った.) *The restaurant we went to is quite near.* (私たちが行ったレストランはすぐ近くだ.)

★**nearly** /níərli/ 副 ▶定義 almost; not completely

or exactly ほとんど；完全には〜になっていない，正確には〜になっていない→もう少しで，すんでのことで〜するところ ‖ *It's nearly five years since I've seen him.* 彼に会ってから5年近くになる． *Linda was so badly hurt she very nearly died.* リンダは重傷を負ったので，危うく死ぬところだった． *It's not far now. We're nearly there.* もうそんなに遠くはない．もう少しでそこに着く． 成句 **not nearly** ▶定義 much less than; not at all 決して〜ではない，全然〜でない→到底〜ではない，決して〜でない ‖ *It's not nearly as warm as it was yesterday.* 決して昨日ほど暖かくはない．

**near-sighted** 困 =SHORT-SIGHTED(1)

**neat** /niːt/ 形 ▶定義 1 arranged or done carefully; tidy and in order 念入りに整えられた，念入りになされた；きちんと片付いて整然とした→きちんとした，こぎれいな ‖ *Please keep your room neat and tidy.* 部屋をきれいに整とんしておいてください． *neat rows of figures* きちんと並べられた数字 ▶定義 2 (used about a person) liking to keep things tidy and in order (人について)物事をきちんと秩序正しくしておくのが好きな→きれい好きな ‖ *The new secretary was very neat and efficient.* 新しい秘書は非常にきれい好きで有能であった． ▶定義 3 simple but clever 簡単だが巧みな→適切な，手際の良い，気の利いた ‖ *a neat solution/explanation/idea/trick* 適切な解決策・適切な説明・気の利いたアイデア・鮮やかな手品 ▶定義 4 困 (口語) good; nice 良い，すてきな→すばらしい，すてきな ‖ *That's a really neat car!* あれは本当にすてきな車だ． ▶定義 5 困 **straight**) (used about an alcoholic drink) on its own, without ice, water or any other liquid (アルコール飲料について)アルコールのみの，氷・水・そのほかの液体が入っていない→(酒が)生の，ストレートの ‖ *a neat whisky* ストレートのウイスキー — **neatly** 副 →きちんと，こぎれいに，適切に ‖ *neatly folded clothes* きちんと畳まれた服 — **neatness** 名 ❶→きちんとしていること，整然，適切さ

\***necessarily** /nésəs(ə)r(ə)li; nèsəsérəli/ 副 ▶定義 used to say that sth cannot be avoided or has to happen 避けることができず，必ず起きる〜を表す場合に用いて→必然的に，どうしても ‖ *The number of tickets available is necessarily limited.* 入手できるチケットの枚数は，当然ながら限られている．

---

neck 1091

成句 **not necessarily** ▶定義 used to say that sth might be true but is not definitely or always true 〜が本当かもしれないが，確かに常にそうであるとは限らない場合に用いて→必ずしも〜でない，必ず〜とは決まっていない

\***necessary** /nésəs(ə)ri; nésəsèri/ 形 ▶定義 **necessary (for sb/sth) (to do sth)** that is needed for a purpose or a reason ある目的・理由のために必要な→(〜にとって)必要な，なくてはならない ‖ *A good diet is necessary for a healthy life.* 良い食事は，健康的な生活を送るのに欠かせない． *It's not necessary for you all to come.* 君たち全員が来る必要はない． *If necessary I can take you to work that day.* 必要でしたら，その日あなたを職場まで連れていけます． ⇨ **unnecessary**

**necessitate** /nɪsésətèɪt/ 動 他 正式 ▶定義 to make sth necessary 〜を必要とする→〜を余儀なくさせる

**necessity** /nɪsés(ə)ti/ 名 (複 **necessities**) ▶定義 1 ❶ **necessity (for sth/to do sth)** the need for sth; the fact that sth must be done or must happen 〜の必要性；〜をする必要があるという事実，〜が必ず起こるという事実→(〜の・〜する)必要, 必要性 ‖ *Is there any necessity for change?* 何か変更する必要はありますか． *There's no necessity to write every single name down.* 1つ1つの名前を全部書き留める必要はない． *They sold the car out of necessity* (= because they had to). 彼らは必要に迫られて(=そうしなければならなくて)車を売った． ▶定義 2 ❷ something that you must have なければならないもの→(〜に)必要なもの，必需品 ‖ *Clean water is an absolute necessity.* 清潔な水は絶対に必要なものだ．

\***neck** /nek/ 名 ▶定義 1 ❶ the part of your body that joins your head to your shoulders 頭と肩をつなぐ体の部分→首，首の骨 ‖ *She wrapped a scarf around her neck.* 彼女はスカーフを首に巻いていた． *Giraffes have long necks.* キリンの首は長い． ☜C5 ページのさし絵 ▶定義 2 ❷ the part of a piece of clothing that goes round your neck 首の回りに来る服の部分→(衣服の)えり，ネック ‖ *a polo-neck/V-neck sweater* タートルネック・Vネックのセーター *The neck on this shirt is* *too tight.* このシャツはえりがきつすぎる. ☛C6ページのさし絵 ◗定義3 [C]the long narrow part of sth ～の長くて幅の狭い部分➜**首状の部分, (びん·つぼなどの)首** ‖ *the neck of a bottle* びんの首 ◗定義4 **-necked**(複合形容詞を作るために用いて) having the type of neck mentioned 首·えりの種類が～のような➜**～首の, 首が～の, ～えりの** ‖ *a round-necked sweater* 丸えりのセーター

[成句] by the scruff (of the/your neck) ⇒ **SCRUFF**

neck and neck (with sb/sth) ◗定義 equal or level with sb in a race or competition 競争·競走で～と互角に, 五分五分に➜**(選挙などで)肩を並べて, 互角に, (競走·競馬で)～と並んだ**

up to your neck in sth ◗定義 having a lot of sth to deal with 処理する～をたくさん抱えている➜**(～で)身動きが取れない, ひどく忙しい** ‖ *We're up to our necks in work at the moment.* ちょうど今, 仕事でひどく忙しい.

**necklace** /nékləs/ [名] [C] ◗定義 a piece of jewellery that you wear around your neck 首の回りに着ける装身具類➜**ネックレス, 首飾り** ☛ **jewellery** のさし絵

**necktie** /néktàɪ/ [米] = **TIE**[1](1)

**née** /néɪ/ [形] ◗定義 used in front of the family name that a woman had before she got married 女性が結婚する以前の姓の前に付けて用いる➜**旧姓は** ‖ *Louise Mitchell, née Greenan* ルイーズ ミッチェル夫人, 旧姓グリーナン ☛参 **maiden name**

***need**[1] /niːd/ [動][他](通常は進行形は不可)

◗定義1 need sb/sth (for sth/to do sth) if you need sth, you want it or must have it 「you need sth」ということは, そのものが欲しいかまたはなければならない, ということ➜**～を必要とする, ～が必要である** ‖ *All living things need water.* 生き物はすべて水を必要とする. *I need a new film for my camera.* カメラに新しいフィルムが必要だ. *Does Roshni need any help?* ローシュニは助けを必要としているのですか. *I need to find a doctor.* 医者を見つけなければならない. *I need you to go to the shop for me.* あなたにその店に行ってもらう必要がある. ◗定義2 to have to; to be obliged to しなければならない; やむを得ず～する➜**～する必要がある** ‖ *Do we need to buy the tickets in advance?* あらかじめチケットを買う必要がありますか. *I need to ask some advice.* 助言をしてもらう必要があります. *You didn't need to bring any food but it was very kind of you.* 食べ物を持ってきてくださらなくてもよかったのに.でもありがとうございます.

➤主動詞としての need の疑問形は do I need? などで, 過去形は needed(疑問形は did you need? など, 否定形は didn't need) であることに注意.

◗定義3 need (sth) doing if sth needs doing, it is necessary or must be done sth needs doing ということは, それが必要であるか, なされなければならない, ということである➜**～を…してもらう必要がある, (～が)…される必要がある** ‖ *This jumper needs washing.* このセーターは洗濯してもらう必要がある. *He needed his eyes testing.* 彼は目の検査をしてもらう必要があった.

➤動詞の need は通常, 進行形としては使われないが, 現在分詞(= -ing 形)としてはよくある: *Patients needing emergency treatment will go to the top of the waiting list.* (緊急処置が必要な患者は, 順番待ちリストの一番上に来る.)

***need**[2] /niːd/ 法助動詞

➤現在時制は人称にかかわりなく need, 否定形は need not (needn't) で, 疑問形は need I? など.

(進行形は不可; 主に疑問文·否定文で使われ, if や whether の後, または hardly, only, never などと共に使われる) ◗定義 to have to; to be obliged to しなければならない; やむを得ず～する➜**～する必要がある** ‖ *Need we pay the whole amount now?* 今全額を払う必要がありますか. *You needn't come to the meeting if you're too busy.* 忙しかったら, 会議に来なくてもいいです. ***I hardly need*** *remind you (= you already know) that this is very serious.* これが非常に重大であることをあなたに言う必要はあるまい(= あなたは既に分かっている).

➤過去の事柄について述べる場合は, needn't have + 過去分詞を使い, 「過去にある事を行ったが, 後になってそれが不必要であったと気が付いた」という意味を表す: *I needn't have gone to the hospital (= I went but it wasn't necessary).* (病院に行く必要はなかったのに

(= 病院に行ったが，その必要はなかった).) didn't need to + 不定詞は通常，「不必要であると既に知っていたので，〜を行わなかった」ことを意味する: *I didn't need to go to the hospital (= I didn't go because it wasn't necessary).* (病院に行く必要はなかった (= 必要なかったので行かなかった).) 法助動詞についての説明は，巻末の「文法早見表」を参照．

**need**³ /níːd/ 名 ▶定義1 [◐, 単数扱い] need (for sth); need (for sb/sth) to do sth a situation in which you must have or do sth 〜を所有している必要がある，または〜をする必要がある→(〜の・〜する)必要(性)，需要，義務 ‖ *We are all in need of a rest.* 我々は全員，休憩する必要がある． *There is a growing need for new books in schools.* 学校では新しい本の要求が高まっている． *There's no need for you to come if you don't want to.* 来たくなければ来る必要はない． *Do phone me if you feel the need to talk to someone.* だれかと話す必要があると思ったら，私に是非電話してください．▶定義2 [◐, 通常は複数] the things that you must have 必要とするもの→必要なもの，入用なもの ‖ *He doesn't earn enough to pay for his basic needs.* 彼は生活必需品を買うのに十分な稼ぎがない． *Parents must consider their children's emotional as well as their physical needs.* 両親は子供が物理的に必要としているものだけでなく，感情面で必要としているものについても考慮することが必要だ． ▶定義3 ❶ the state of not having enough food, money or support 十分な食糧・お金・援助がない状態→困っていること，困窮，貧困 ‖ *a campaign to help families in need* 困っている家族を助ける活動

\***needle** /níːdl/ 名 ◐ ▶定義1 a small thin piece of metal with a point at one end and a hole (an eye) at the other that is used for sewing 小さくて細い金属でできており，片方の先端は鋭くとがっていてもう片方には孔(めど)が開いており，裁縫に使われる→(裁縫用の)針，縫い針 ‖ *to thread a needle with cotton* 針に綿糸を通す ☞参 pins and needles ▶定義2 (または **knitting needle**) one of two long thin pieces of metal or plastic with a point at one end that are used for knitting 編み物に使う先端がとがった細長い金属製またはプラスチック製の一組の針のうちの1本→編み針，編み物針 ☞knitのさし絵 ▶定義3 the sharp metal part of a device (a syringe) that is used for putting drugs into sb's body and for taking blood out 器具(注射器)の鋭くとがった金属の部分で，薬を〜の体内に注入したり，採血をするときに使われる→注射針 ▶定義4 a thin metal part on a scientific instrument that moves to point to the correct measurement or direction 科学器具の細い金属の部分で，正確な測定値や方向を指し示すために動く→(磁石・羅針盤・計測器などの)針 ▶定義5 the thin, hard pointed leaf of certain trees that stay green all year 特定の常緑樹の葉で，細くて先が鋭くとがっている→針葉，針状葉 ‖ *pine needles* 松葉 ☞C2ページのさし絵

**needless** /níːdləs/ 形 ▶定義 that is not necessary and that you can easily avoid 必要でなく，簡単に避けることができる→不必要な ☞参 **unnecessary**(無駄な，無用の，余計な)とは意味が異なる．— **needlessly** 副→不必要に，用もないのに

**needlework** /níːdlwɜːrk/ 名 ❶ ▶定義 sth that you sew by hand, especially for decoration 手縫いの〜で，特に装飾用のもの→針仕事，裁縫，刺繡(ししゅう)

**needy** /níːdi/ 形 ▶定義1 not having enough money, food, clothes, etc 金銭・食べ物・衣類などが十分にない→貧乏な，貧困の，困窮した ▶定義2 **the needy** 名 [複数扱い] people who do not have enough money, food, clothes, etc 十分な金銭・食べ物・衣服などがない人々→貧しい人々

**neg** 略 negative → 否定の，負の

\***negative**¹ /néɡətɪv/ 形 ▶定義1 bad or harmful 悪い，有害な→(結果などが)思わしくない，(影響などが)不利に働く，マイナスの ‖ *The effects of the new rule have been rather negative.* 新しい規則はかなり良くない影響を及ぼしている． ▶定義2 only thinking about the bad qualities of sb/sth 〜の悪い面だけを考える→控えめな，悲観的な ‖ *I'm feeling very negative about my job — in fact I'm thinking about leaving.* 自分の仕事にとても気乗りがしない — 実のところ，辞めることを考えている． *If you go into the match with a negative attitude, you'll never win.* 試合に消極的な態度で臨むのなら，決して勝つことはない． ▶定義3 (used about a word, phrase or sentence) meaning 'no' or 'not' (語・句・文につい

て) 否定を表す語である no, not と同じ意味を持つ→否定の, 打ち消しの, 拒否の, 反対の ‖ *a negative sentence* 否定文 *His reply was negative/He gave a negative reply (= he said 'no').* 彼の返事は否定的なものであった・彼は断りの返事をよこした (=「ノー」と言った). ⇔ **affirmative** ▶定義4 (used about a medical or scientific test) showing that sth has not happened or has not been found (医療・科学的検査について) 〜が起きていないことを示す, 見つからなかったことを示す→(医学)検査結果が陰性の, (電気)負の, 陰の ‖ *The results of the pregnancy test were negative.* 妊娠検査の結果は陰性だった.
▶定義5 (used about a number) less than zero (数について) ゼロより小さい→(数学)負の, マイナスの ⇔ 定義1, 2, 4, 5 **positive** — **negatively** 副 →否定的に, 消極的に, (電気)負に

**negative**² /néɡətɪv/ 名 **C** ▶定義1 a word, phrase or sentence that says or means 'no' or 'not' 否定を表す語である no, not と同じ発音・意味の語・句・文→否定, 拒否, 否定の答え ‖ *Aisha answered in the negative (= she said no).* アイーシャは否定的な答えをした (「ノー」と言った). *'Never', 'neither' and 'nobody' are all negatives.* never, neither, nobody はすべて, 否定語だ. ⇔ **affirmative** ▶定義2 a piece of film from which we can make a photograph. The light areas of a negative are dark on the final photograph and the dark areas are light. 写真を作成する元のフィルム (= ネガ). ネガで明るい部分は実際の写真では暗く, 暗い部分は明るくなる→(写真)ネガ

**neglect** /nɪɡlékt/ 動 **他** ▶定義1 to give too little or no attention or care to sb/sth 〜に対してほとんど (全く) 注意を払ったり世話をしたりしない→(〜が) (怠慢・不注意から)…に十分な注意 [世話] をしない, 〜をほうっておく ‖ *Don't neglect your health.* 自分の健康を無視しては駄目だ. *The old house had stood neglected for years.* その古い家は何年もほったらかしにされていた. ▶定義2 **neglect to do sth** to fail or forget to do sth 〜をしない, し忘れる→〜するのをおこたる, 〜をしない ‖ *He neglected to mention that he had spent time in prison.* 彼は, 刑務所に入っていたことを言わなかった. — **neglect** 名 **U** →怠慢, ほうっておく [おかれる] こと, 無視 ‖ *The garden was like a jungle after years of neglect.* 長年ほったらかしにされて, 庭はジャングルのようだった. — **neglected** 形 →無視された, ほうっておかれた, ないがしろにされた ‖ *neglected children* ほったらかされた子供たち

**negligence** /néɡlɪdʒ(ə)ns/ 名 **U** ▶定義 not being careful enough; lack of care 注意が十分でない; 注意が足りない→怠慢, 不注意, 過失 ‖ *The accident was a result of negligence.* 事故は不注意によるものだった. — **negligent** /néɡlɪdʒ(ə)nt/ 形 →怠慢な, 不注意な — **negligently** 副 →怠慢で, 不注意に, むとんちゃくに

**negligible** /néɡlɪdʒəb(ə)l/ 形 ▶定義 very small and therefore not important 非常にわずかなのであまり重要でない→無視してよい, 取るに足りない, つまらない

**negotiable** /nɪɡóʊʃ(i)əb(ə)l/ 形 ▶定義 that can be decided or changed by discussion 討議により決定できる, 変更可能な→交渉できる, 交渉の余地のある ‖ *The price is not negotiable/non-negotiable.* 価格は相談に応じられない・相談不可.

**negotiate** /nɪɡóʊʃieɪt/ 動 ▶定義1 **自 negotiate (with sb) (for/about sth)** to talk to sb in order to decide or agree about sth 〜について決めるため, 合意するために…と話し合う→(〜と・〜について) 交渉する, 協議する ‖ *The unions are still negotiating with management about this year's pay claim.* 組合は今年の賃上げ要求について, まだ経営側と交渉中だ. ▶定義2 **他** to decide or agree sth by talking about it 話し合いにより, 〜について決定する, 合意に至る→(〜と)…を協定する, …を取り決める ‖ *to negotiate an agreement/a deal/a settlement* 契約・取り引き・和解を協定する ▶定義3 **他** to get over, past or through sth difficult 困難な〜を乗り越える, 通り抜ける, うまく成し遂げる→(障害・困難などを) うまく切り抜ける, 〜を乗り越える ‖ *To escape, prisoners would have to negotiate a five-metre wall.* 脱獄するには, 囚人は5メートルの塀を乗り越えなければならないだろう. — **negotiator** 名 **C** → 交渉 (担当) 者, 協議する人

**negotiation** /nɪɡòʊʃieɪʃ(ə)n/ 名 [複数扱い, **U**]
▶定義 discussions at which people try to decide or agree sth 参加者が〜を決めたり合意に至ろうと努力する討議 → 交渉, 折衝 ‖ *to enter into/break off negotiations* 交渉を開始する・打ち

切る *The pay rise is **still under negotiation**.* 賃上げはまだ交渉中だ.

**neigh** /néɪ/ 名 C ▶定義 the long high sound that a horse makes 馬が発する，長くて高い鳴き声 →**馬のいななき，ヒヒーン** ― neigh 動 自 →(馬が)いななく，(人が)大声を出す

*****neighbour** (米 **neighbor**) /néɪbər/ 名 C
▶定義 1 a person who lives near you 近所に住む人→**隣人，近所の人** ‖ *My neighbours are very friendly.* 私の近所の人たちはとても親切だ. *our next-door neighbours* 隣に住んでいる人たち
▶定義 2 a person or thing that is near or next to another 近くまたは隣の人・事物→**隣にあるもの，近くにあるもの** ‖ *Britain's nearest neighbour is France.* 英国に一番近い隣国はフランスだ. *Try not to look at what your neighbour is writing.* 隣の席の人が何を書いているか見ないようにしなさい.

**neighbourhood** (米 **neighborhood**) /néɪbərhʊd/ 名 C ▶定義 a particular part of a town and the people who live there 町の特定の地域と，そこに住む人々→**(町の特定の)地域，地区，地域の住民** ‖ *a friendly neighbourhood* 気さくな近所の人たち

**neighbouring** (米 **neighboring**) /néɪbərɪŋ/ 形 (名詞の前だけ) ▶定義 near or next to 近くの，隣の→**近くの，近隣の，隣接する** ‖ *Farmers from neighbouring villages come into town each week for the market.* 近隣の村から農民が市場を求めて，毎週町にやって来る.

**neighbourly** (米 **neighborly**) /néɪbərli/ 形 ▶定義 friendly and helpful 親切で助けになる→**隣人らしい，親切な，近所付き合いの良い**

*****neither** /náɪðər, níː-/ 形 代 副 ▶定義 1 (used about two people or things) not one and not the other (2人の人または2つの事物について)一方は〜でなく，もう1人[1つ]の方も〜でない→**(2つのうちの)どちらも〜(で)ない，どちらの〜も…でない** ‖ *Neither team played very well.* どちらのチームもあまり上手ではなかった. *Neither of the teams played very well.* 2つのチームのどちらもあまり上手ではなかった. *'Would you like tea or juice?' 'Neither, thank you. I'm not thirsty.'* 「紅茶かジュースはいかがですか」「どちらも結構です. のどが渇いていないので」

▶ neither の後には単数の名詞と動詞が続くことに注意: *Neither day was suitable.* (どちらの日も都合が悪い.) neither of の後に続く名詞・代名詞は複数形だが，動詞は単数でも複数でもよい: *Neither of the days is/are suitable.* (どちらの日も都合が悪い.)

▶定義 2 also not; not either→**〜もまた…ない; どちらも〜ない** ‖ *I don't eat meat and neither does Carlos.* 私は肉を食べないし，カルロスもまた肉を食べない. *'I don't like fish.' 'Neither do I.'* 「私は魚が好きではありません」「私もです」 略式 *'I don't like fish.' 'Me neither.'* 「私は魚が嫌いだ」「私も」

▶ この意味については，nor が同様に使える: *'I don't like fish.' 'Nor do I.'* (「私は魚が好きではありません」「私もです」)not... either を使う場合は語順が異なるので注意: *I don't eat meat and Carlos doesn't either.* (私は肉を食べないし，カルロスもまた肉を食べない.) *'I haven't seen that film.' 'I haven't either.'* (「その映画を見たことがない」「私もありません」)

▶定義 3 **neither... nor** not... and not 〜でなく，…でもない→**〜でもなく…でもない，どちらも〜でない・しない** ‖ *Neither Carlos nor I eat meat.* カルロスも私も肉を食べない.

▶ neither... nor は，単数・複数のどちらの動詞とも使うことができる: *Neither Stella nor Meena was/were at the meeting.* (ステラもミーナも会議に出ていなかった.)

**neon** /níːɒn/ 名 U (元素記号 Ne) ▶定義 a type of gas that is used for making bright lights and signs 気体の一種で，明るい光を放つ照明灯と，広告看板を作るために使用される→**ネオン(気体元素)**

*****nephew** /néfjuː, névjuː/ 名 C ▶定義 the son of your brother or sister, or the son of your husband's or wife's brother or sister 兄弟姉妹の息子，妻・夫の兄弟姉妹の息子→**甥(おい)** ☞参 niece

**Neptune** /népt(j)uːn/ 名 [単数扱い] ▶定義 the planet that is eighth in order from the sun 太陽から第8番目の惑星 → **海王星**

**nerd** /nɜːrd/ 名 C ▶定義 a person who is not fashionable and has a boring hobby あか抜けておらず，退屈な趣味を持つ人→**野暮ったい人，さえない人** ― nerdy 形 →**野暮ったい，ダサい**

*****nerve** /nɜːrv/ 名 ▶定義 1 C one of the long thin threads in your body that carry feelings or other messages to and from your brain 体内にある細長い糸状のもので,感情そのほかの情報を脳に伝達し,また脳から身体に伝達する→**神経,神経繊維** ▶定義2 **nerves** [複数扱い] worried, nervous feelings 心配で神経質になっている気持ち→**神経過敏,神経質であること** ‖ *Breathing deeply should help to **calm/steady your nerves**.* 深呼吸は,神経を鎮め,安定させるのに役立つはずだ. *I was **a bag of nerves** before my interview.* 私は面接の前にぴりぴりしていた. ▶定義3 **U** the courage that you need to do sth difficult or dangerous 困難や危険を伴う~を行う場合に必要な勇気→**勇気,度胸** ‖ *Racing drivers need a lot of nerve.* レーシングドライバーには相当な勇気が必要だ. *He didn't **have the nerve** to ask Maria to go out with him.* 彼にはマリアをデートに誘う度胸がなかった. *Some pilots **lose their nerve** and can't fly any more.* 勇気をなくして,もう飛行できなくなるパイロットもいる. ▶定義4 [単数扱い] a way of behaving that people think is not acceptable 人が好ましくないと思うような振る舞い→**厚かましさ,図太さ,無礼** ‖ *You've got a nerve, calling me lazy!* 私のことを怠け者と言うなんて,無礼なやつだ.

成句 **get on sb's nerves** 略式 ▶定義 to annoy sb or make sb angry ~をいらいらさせる,~を怒らせる→**(人の)神経に障る,(人を)いらいらさせる**

**nerve-racking** 形 ▶定義 making you very nervous or worried 非常に神経質にさせる,とても心配させる→**緊張を強いる**

*****nervous** /nə́ːrvəs/ 形 ▶定義1 nervous (about/ of sth/ doing sth) worried or afraid 心配な,不安な→**緊張して,(~について)心配な,不安な** ‖ *I'm a bit nervous about travelling on my own.* 私は一人旅が少々不安だ. *I always **get nervous** just before a match.* 私は試合の直前になるといつも緊張する. *a nervous laugh/smile/voice* 神経質な笑い・不安そうな微笑・不安そうな声 *She was nervous of giving the wrong answer.* 彼女は答えを間違えてしまうことを恐れていた. ▶定義2 connected with the nerves of the body 身体の神経に関連した→**神経の,神経に関する** ‖ *a nervous disorder* 神経障害— **nervously** 副 →**神経質に,いらいらして,緊張して**— **nervousness** 名 **U**→神経質,いらいら,緊張

**nervous breakdown** (または **breakdown**) 名 **C** ▶定義 a time when sb suddenly becomes so unhappy that he/she cannot continue living and working normally 突然不安になり,正常に生活や仕事を続けられなくなるとき → **神経衰弱,ノイローゼ** ‖ *to have a nervous breakdown* 神経衰弱になる

**the nervous system** 名 **C** ▶定義 your brain and all the nerves in your body 脳,および体内に分布するすべての神経→**神経系(統)**

*****nest** /nest/ 名 **C** ▶定義1 a structure that a bird builds to keep its eggs and babies in 中に卵とひなを入れておくために,鳥が作る物→**巣** ☞C1 ページのさし絵 ▶定義2 the home of certain animals or insects 特定の動物・昆虫の住みか→**(小動物・昆虫の)巣,巣穴** ‖ *a wasps' nest* スズメバチの巣— **nest** 動 **自** →**巣を作る,巣ごもる**

**nestle** /nésəl/ 動 **自他** ▶定義 to be or go into a position where you are comfortable, protected or hidden 心地良く,保護されていて,身を隠せるような場所にいる・行く→**心地良く身を落ち着ける,寄り添う,(頭・肩など)を擦り寄せる,~を抱く** ‖ *The baby nestled her head on her mother's shoulder.* 赤ん坊はお母さんの肩に頭を擦り寄せた.

*****net**[1] /net/ 名 ▶定義1 **U** material that has large, often square, spaces between the threads 糸で編まれており,その糸と糸の間に大きなすきま(通常は四角)がある→**網,ネット** ▶定義2 **C** a piece of net that is used for a particular purpose 特定の目的に使われるネット→**網,ネット** ‖ *a tennis/fishing/mosquito net* テニスのネット・魚網・かや ☞参 **safety net** ▶定義3 **the net** [単数扱い] =THE INTERNET

成句 **surf the net** ⇒ **SURF**[2]

**net**[2] /net/ 動 **他** (**netting; netted**) ▶定義1 to catch sth with a net ~を網を使って捕まえる → **~を網を使って捕らえる,~を網を張って捕まえる** ‖ *to kick a ball into a net* ボールをネットにけり込む ▶定義2 to gain sth as a profit ~を利益として得る→**(ある額)の純益を上げる**

**net**[3] (または **nett**) /net/ 形 ▶定義 net (of sth) (used about a number or amount) from which nothing more needs to be taken away (数・量について)そこからもう何も引く必要がない→**正味の,差引勘定後の** ‖ *I earn about £15000 net (= after tax, etc has been paid).* 私は手取りで

15000ポンド(= 税金などを差し引いた後)稼いでいる. *The net weight of the jam is 350g (= not including the jar).* ジャムの重さは正味350グラム(= びんの重さを含まない)だ. *a net profit* 純益 ⇨ **gross**

**netball** /nétbɔ̀ːl/ 名 Ｕ ▶定義 a game that is played by two teams of seven players, usually women. Players score by throwing the ball through a high net hanging from a ring. 通常は女性の7人の選手で構成される2組のチームで争われる競技. 選手が, 高い所から輪につるされたネットにボールを投げて通すことで得点を上げる→ネットボール

**netting** /nétɪŋ/ 名 Ｕ ▶定義 material that is made of long pieces of string, thread, wire, etc that are tied together with spaces between them 長いひも・糸・針金などでできた素材を, すきまを空けながら結び付けて作ったもの→網, 網細工, 網製品

**nettle** /nétl/ 名 Ｃ ▶定義 a wild plant with hairy leaves. Some nettles make your skin red and painful if you touch them. 野生の植物で, 葉に細いとげがある. 触ると皮膚が赤くなり, 痛くなるものがある→イラクサ

*****network** /nétwə̀ːrk/ 名 Ｃ ▶定義 **1** a system of roads, railway lines, nerves, etc that are connected to each other 互いに結合した道路・鉄道線路・神経などの系統→(鉄道・道路・血管などの)網状組織, 網状のもの ‖ *an underground railway network* 地下鉄網 ▶定義 **2** a group of people or companies that work closely together 人や会社が集まって密接に働くグループ→チェーン, (同一目的を持つ)関連組織 ‖ *We have a network of agents who sell our goods all over the country.* 我が社には, 製品を全国的に販売する代理店網がある. ▶定義 **3** a number of computers that are connected together so that information can be shared 情報が共有化できるようにと接続した一連のコンピューター→(コンピューターの)通信網, ネットワーク ▶定義 **4** a group of television or radio companies that are connected and that send out the same programmes at the same time in different parts of a country 複数のテレビ・ラジオ放送会社が提携し, 同一番組を同じ時間に異なった地域で放送するグループ→(テレビ・ラジオの)放送網, ネットワーク

**neurosis** /n(j)ʊəróʊsəs/ 名 Ｃ (複 **neuroses** /-sìːz/) ▶定義 (medical) a mental illness that causes strong feelings of fear and worry (医学)強い不安や心配を引き起こす, 精神的な病→神経症, ノイローゼ

**neurotic** /n(j)ʊərɑ́tɪk/ 形 ▶定義 **1** worried about things in a way that is not normal 物事の心配の仕方が普通ではない→神経過敏な, 過度に心配をする ▶定義 **2** (medical) suffering from a neurosis (医学)神経症を患う→神経症の, ノイローゼの

**neuter**¹ /n(j)úːtər/ 形 ▶定義 (used about a word in some languages) not masculine or feminine according to the rules of grammar (ある言語の語について)文法の規則により, 男性でも女性でもない→中性の

**neuter**² /n(j)úːtər/ 動 他 ▶定義 to remove the sexual parts of an animal 動物の生殖器を取る→(動物)を去勢する ☞参 **castrate**

**neutral**¹ /n(j)úːtrəl/ 形 ▶定義 **1** not supporting or belonging to either side in an argument, war, etc 議論・戦争などで, どちらの側も支持しない, どちらの側にも属さない→(人・国が)中立の, 中立的な ‖ *I don't take sides when my brothers argue - I remain neutral.* 私は, 兄弟が議論をしてもどちら側の味方もしない － 中立の立場を取る. *The two sides agreed to meet on neutral ground.* 両者は中立地域で会うことに合意した. ▶定義 **2** having or showing no strong qualities, emotions or colour 目立った特徴・感情・色を持たない, 見せない→はっきりとした特徴のない, あいまいな, 中間色の ‖ *neutral colours* 中間色 *a neutral tone of voice* 特徴のない声色

**neutral**² /n(j)úːtrəl/ 名 Ｕ ▶定義 the position of part of a vehicle (the gears), when no power is sent from the engine to the wheels エンジンから車輪に動力が送られていないときの, 車の部分(ギア)の位置→(自動車などのギアの)ニュートラル, 中立位置

**neutrality** /n(j)uːtrǽləti/ 名 Ｕ ▶定義 the state of not supporting either side in an argument, war, etc 議論・論争などでどちらの側も支持しない状態→中立, 中立の状態・立場

**neutralize** (または **-ise**) /n(j)úːtrəlàɪz/ 動 他 ▶定義 to take away the effect of sth ～の効果を減じる→～を無効・無力にする, ～を帳消しにする

## never

‖ to neutralize a threat 脅威を弱める

**never** /névər/ 副 ▶定義1 at no time; not ever → 一度も～ない、いまだかつて～ない ‖ *I've never been to Portugal.* まだポルトガルに行ったことがありません. *He never ever eats meat.* 彼は決して肉を食べない. 正式 *Never before has such a high standard been achieved.* いまだかつてこのような高い水準に達したことはなかった. ▶定義2 used for emphasizing a negative statement 否定文の強調に用いて →決して～でない、少しも～でない ‖ *I never realized she was so unhappy.* 彼女がそんなに不幸だなんて、全く気付かなかった. *Roy never so much as looked at us (= he didn't even look at us).* ロイは私たちを見ることすらしなかった(= 決して私たちを見なかった). *'I got the job!' 'Never!' (= expressing surprise)'* 「仕事が見つかったよ」「まさか(= 驚きの表現)」

成句 never mind ⇒ MIND²
you never know ⇒ KNOW¹

**nevertheless** /nèvərðəlés/ 副 接 正式 ▶定義 in spite of that それにもかかわらず →それにもかかわらず、それでもやはり ‖ *It was a cold, rainy day. Nevertheless, more people came than we had expected.* その日は寒く、雨も降っていた. それにもかかわらず、予想したよりも多くの人が来た. ☛類 **nonetheless**

**new** /n(j)uː/ 形 ▶定義1 that has recently been built, made, discovered, etc. 最近建てられた・作られた・発見されたなどのもの→新しい、新たに発見された・作られた ‖ *a new design/film/hospital* 新デザイン・新作映画・新しい病院 *a new method of treating mental illness* 精神病の新たな治療方法 *new evidence* 新たに見つかった証拠 ⇔ **old**
▶定義2 different or changed from what was before 以前とは違う、変更された→新たな、改まった ‖ *I've just started reading a new book.* ちょうど新しい本を読み始めたところだ. *to make new friends* 新しい友達ができる ⇔ **old**
▶定義3 new (to sb) that you have not seen, learnt, etc before 今まで見たこともないもの、知らなかったもの→(仕事などに)不慣れの、経験のない、(人に)よく知られていない ‖ *This type of machine is new to me.* 私はこの型の機械には慣れていない. *to learn a new language* 知らない言語を習う ▶定義4 new (to sth) having just started being or doing sth ある～になったばかりの、ある～を始めたばかりの→今度の、新任の、新入りの ‖ *a new parent* なり立ての親 *She's new to the job and needs a lot of help.* 彼女はその仕事に就いたばかりで、多くの手助けを必要としている. *a new member of the club* クラブの新入部員 —**newness** 名 ❶ →新しさ、新しいこと、不慣れ

成句 break fresh/new ground ⇒ **GROUND**¹

**New Age** 形 ▶定義 connected with a way of life that rejects modern Western values and is based on spiritual ideas and beliefs 近代の西洋的価値観を否定し、神秘的思想・信仰に基づいた生き方に関連して→ニューエイジ、新時代運動 ‖ *a New Age festival* ニューエイジ祭 ***New Age travellers*** *(= people in Britain who reject the values of modern society and travel from place to place living in their vehicles)* ニューエイジの旅人(= 近代社会の価値観を否定し、車で生活をしながらあちらこちらへ旅をするイギリスの人々)

**newborn** /n(j)ùːbɔ́ːm/ 形 ▶定義 (used about a baby) that has been born very recently (赤ん坊について)ごく最近生まれたばかりの→生まれたばかりの

**newcomer** /n(j)úːkÀmər/ 名 ● ▶定義 a person who has just arrived in a place ある場所に着いたばかりの人→(～へ)新しく来た人、(～の)新任者

**newfangled** /n(j)ùːfǽŋɡld, ´--/ 形 ▶定義 new or modern in a way that the speaker does not like 新しい・現代風だが、話し手・書き手は好ましく思わない様子→目新しいだけの、奇をてらった

**newly** /n(j)úːli/ 副 (通常過去分詞の前で) ▶定義 recently 最近→最近、近ごろ、新たに ‖ *the newly appointed Minister of Health* 新たに任命された保健大臣

**newly-wed** 名 [●、通常は複数] ▶定義 a person who has recently got married 最近結婚したばかりの人→結婚したばかりの人、新婚ほやほやの人

**news** /n(j)uːz/ 名 ▶定義1 ❶ information about sth that has happened recently 最近起きた～についての情報→(～に関する・～という)ニュース、報道、(～の・～という)知らせ、便り、消息 ‖ *Write and tell me all your news.* あなたに関して変った事があったらすべて書いて知らせなさい.

*Have you had any news from Nadia recently?* 最近ナディアから何か便りはありましたか. *That's news to me (= I didn't know that).* それは初耳だ (= それは知らなかった). *News is coming in of a plane crash in Thailand.* タイで飛行機が墜落したというニュースが入ってきている.

➤ news は不可算名詞である. 個々のニュースについて述べる場合は, a piece of news としなければならない: *We had two pieces of good news yesterday.* (昨日は良いニュースが2つあった.)

▶定義2 **the news** [単数扱い] a regular programme giving the latest news on the radio or television ラジオ・テレビで最新ニュースを報道する定期的な番組➡(テレビ・ラジオの)ニュース番組 ‖ *We always watch the nine o'clock news on television.* 私たちはいつも, 9時のニュース番組をテレビで見る. *I heard about the accident on the news.* その事故について, ニュース番組で聞いた.

成句 break the news (to sb) ▶定義 to be the first to tell sb about sth important that has happened 〜に持ち上がった重要な…について初めて話す➡(人に)悪い知らせを最初に伝える, 打ち明ける

**newsagent** /n(j)úːzèɪdʒ(ə)nt/ ( 米 **newsdealer**) 名 ▶定義1 ❻a person who owns or works in a shop that sells newspapers and magazines, etc 新聞・雑誌などの販売店の所有者, 従業員➡**新聞雑誌販売業者, 新聞雑誌販売人** ▶定義2 **the newsagent's** [単数扱い] a shop that sells newspapers, magazines, etc 新聞・雑誌などを販売する店➡**新聞雑誌販売店**

**newsletter** /n(j)úːzlètər/ 名 ❻ ▶定義 a printed report about a club or organization that is sent regularly to members and other people who may be interested クラブ・団体についての印刷した報告書で, 会員やその他興味のある人に定期的に送付される➡(会員に定期的に郵送される) **通信, 会報, ニューズレター**

★**newspaper** /n(j)úːzpèɪpər, -s-/ 名 ▶定義1 (または **paper**) ❻large folded pieces of paper printed with news, advertisements and articles on various subjects. Newspapers are printed and sold either every day or every week. 大きな折り畳まれた複数枚の紙で, ニュース・広告・さまざまな主題に関する記事が印刷されている. 毎日印刷・販売されるものと, 毎週のものがある➡**新聞** ‖ *a daily/weekly/Sunday newspaper* 日刊・週刊・日曜新聞 *a newspaper article* 新聞記事 *I read about it in the newspaper.* それについて新聞で読んだ.

▶定義2 (または **paper**) ❻an organization that produces a newspaper 新聞を発行する組織➡**新聞社** ‖ *Which newspaper does he work for?* 彼はどの新聞社に勤めているのですか. ▶定義3 ❶the paper on which newspapers are printed 新聞が印刷してある紙➡**新聞紙** ‖ *We wrapped the plates in newspaper so they would not get damaged.* 割れないように, 私たちはお皿を新聞紙で包んだ.

➤ journalists/reporters (新聞記者)は新聞のニュースを集める. editor (エディター)はどのニュースを活字にするかを決める. quality newspapers (高級紙)はニュースをまじめに扱う. tabloids (タブロイド判新聞)は大衆紙で紙面の大きさが小さく, 有名人に関する写真や記事が多い.

**newsreader** /n(j)úːzriːdər/ (または **newscaster** /n(j)úːzkàːstər, -kæ̀stər/) 名 ❻ ▶定義 a person who reads the news on the radio or television ラジオ・テレビでニュースを読む人➡**ニュースキャスター, ニュース放送(解説)者**

**news-stand** 米 = BOOKSTALL

**new year** (または **New Year**) 名 [単数扱い] ▶定義 the first few days of January 1月の初めの数日間➡**正月, 新年(年始の数日間)** ‖ *Happy New Year!* 新年おめでとう *We will get in touch in the new year.* 私たちはお正月に連絡を取ります. *New Year's Eve (= 31 December)* 大みそか (= 12月31日) *New Year's Day (= 1 January)* 元日 (= 1月1日)

★**next** /nekst/ 形副 ▶定義1 (通常 the を伴って) coming immediately after sth in order, space or time; closest 順番・場所・時間が〜のすぐ後に来る; 最も近い➡(時間・順序が)次の, 今度の, 翌〜, 来〜 ‖ *The next bus leaves in twenty minutes.* 次のバスは20分後に出発する. *The next name on the list is Paulo.* 表に載っている次の名前はパウロだ.

➤ nearest, next. next は一連の出来事・場所について「次に来る」を意味する: *When is your next appointment?* (あなたの次の予約はいつですか.) *Turn left at the next traffic lights.* (次の信号を左に曲がりなさい.) the nearest は時

## 1100 next door

間・場所において「最も近い」を意味する: *Where's the nearest supermarket?* (一番近いスーパーはどこですか.)

▶定義2 (週・月・季節・年などの時の前に the を付けずに用いる)the one immediately following the present one 現在の週・月・季節・年などすぐ次に来る→(時間的に)次の,すぐ後の,来~‖ *See you again next Monday.* また次の月曜日に会いましょう. *Let's go camping next weekend.* 来週末にキャンプに行きましょう. *next summer/next year/next Christmas* 次の夏・来年・次のクリスマス

▶定義3 after this or after that; then この後,その後; それから→次に,今度は‖ *I wonder what will happen next.* 次は何が起きるのだろうか. *I know Joe arrived first but who came next?* ジョーが最初に着いたことは知っているが,次に着いたのはだれだろう. *It was ten years until I next saw her.* 次に彼女に会ったのは,10年後だった.

▶定義4 **the next** 图[単数扱い]the person or thing that is next 次の人,次の事→次の人,次の物‖ *If we miss this train we'll have to wait two hours for the next.* この電車に乗り遅れたら,次の電車まで2時間待たなければならない.

成句 last/next but one, two, etc ⇒ **LAST¹**

### next door 形副 ▶定義 in or into the next house or building 隣の家・建物の,隣の家・建物に住む→隣(家)の[に住む]‖ *our next-door neighbours* 隣家の人たち *Who lives next door?* お隣にはだれが住んでいるのですか. *The school is next door to an old people's home.* 学校は老人ホームの隣にある.

### next of kin 图 ⓒ (複 next of kin) ▶定義 your closest living relative or relatives 生きている,最も近い親戚(しんせき)(たち)→近親者,最も近い親戚‖ *My husband is my next of kin.* 夫が私の近親者です.

### *next to 前 ▶定義1 at the side of sb/sth; beside ~の横に; ~のそばに→~の隣に[の],~の次に‖ *He sat down next to Gita.* 彼はギータの隣に座った. *There's a public telephone next to the bus stop.* バス停のそばに公衆電話がある. ▶定義2 in a position after sth 位置が~の次にある→~の次に,~に次いで‖ *Next to English my favourite subject is Maths.* 英語の次に好きな学科は数学です.

成句 **next to nothing** ▶定義 almost nothing → ほとんどない‖ *We took plenty of money but we've got next to nothing left.* 私たちは多額のお金を手に入れたが,ほとんど残っていない.

### NHS /èn eɪtʃ és/ 略 英 National Health Service → (英国の)国民健康保険制度

### nibble /níb(ə)l/ 動 @ 他 ▶定義 to eat sth by taking small bites ~を少しずつかじりながら食べる→(人・動物が)(~を)少しずつかじって食べる, (~を)そっとかむ‖ *The bread had been nibbled by mice.* パンはネズミに少しずつかじられていた. — **nibble** 图 ⓒ→少しずつかじること,一かじり

### *nice /náɪs/ 形 ▶定義1 pleasant, enjoyable or attractive →楽しい,愉快な,魅力的な‖ *a nice place/feeling/smile* 心地良い場所・愉快な気持ち・すてきなほほえみ *I'm not eating this - it doesn't taste very nice.* これは食べません — あまりおいしくないので. *It would be nice to spend more time at home.* 家で過ごす時間が増えたなら,とても楽しいでしょうに. *'Hi, I'm Tony.' 'I'm Ray - nice to meet you.'* 「どうも,トニーです」「レイです — はじめまして」▶定義2 **nice (to sb); nice (of sb) (to do sth); nice (about sth)** kind; friendly 親切な; 好意的な→(~に対して)親切な,優しい,思いやりがある‖ *What a nice girl!* 何て優しい女の子なのだろう. *Everyone was very nice to me when I felt ill.* 具合が悪かった時,皆がとても親切にしてくれた. *It was really nice of Donna to help us.* ドナはとても親切にも,私たちを助けてくれた. ▶定義3 略式 used before adjectives and adverbs to emphasize how pleasant or suitable sth is 形容詞・副詞の前に付けて,~がいかに心地良く,適切なものであるかを強調する→十分に,申し分なく,とても‖ *It's nice and warm by the fire.* 火のそばはとても暖かくて気持ちがいい. *a nice long chat* 楽しいおしゃべり — **nicely** 副→うまく,良く,きちんと — **niceness** 图 ⓤ→親切,優しさ,立派さ

> ▶音声とつづり字

### nice の c 規則と語法

一般に c の後に i, e, y があると[s]と発音し,それ以外は[k]と発音します(例: cinema, cent, bicycle). nice は日常会話でよく用いられる語です. 初対面の人には,(It's) nice to meet you. (お会いできてうれしいです.)の

ように言います.日本語と異なるのは英語では強弱を付けて言うことです.

```
(−)    ○   −   ◎   −         リズム
(It's)  nice to  meet  you.          つづり字
[ɪts   naɪs tə míːt   juː]           発音記号
「ｴｨｯﾂ ﾅｲｽ ﾀ ﾐｰ ﾁｭ」         近似カナ表記
```

**niche** /nɪtʃ, niːʃ/ 名 C ▶定義 1 a job, position, etc that is suitable for you 人にふさわしい仕事・地位など→(人に)最もふさわしい職業・居場所,適所 ‖ *to find your niche in life* 人生における適所を得る ▶定義 2 (in business) an opportunity to sell a particular product to a particular group of people (ビジネスで)特定の製品を,求めている人々に売る好機→(市場の)すきま,ニッチ ▶定義 3 a place in a wall that is further back, where a statue, etc can be put 壁面のくぼみで,像などが置ける場所→ニッチ,壁がん

**nick**¹ /nɪk/ 名 C ▶定義 a small cut in sth 〜に付いた小さな切り傷→ひっかき傷,擦り傷
成句 **in good/bad nick** 英 (俗語) ▶定義 in a good/bad state or condition 良い・悪い状態,良い・悪い調子→調子が良い・悪い
**in the nick of time** ▶定義 only just in time 辛うじて間に合って→ぎりぎり間に合って,間一髪のところで

**nick**² /nɪk/ 動 ▶定義 1 to make a very small cut in sb/sth 〜に小さな切り傷を付ける→〜に擦り傷を作る・負わせる,〜に刻み目を作る ▶定義 2 英 (俗語) to arrest sb 〜を逮捕する→〜を逮捕する,〜を連行する ▶定義 3 英 (俗語) to steal sth 〜を盗む→〜を盗む,〜をかっ払う

**nickel** /níkəl/ 名 ▶定義 1 U (元素記号 Ni) a hard silver-white metal that is often mixed with other metals 硬い銀白色の金属で,しばしばほかの金属と合金される→ニッケル ▶定義 2 C an American or Canadian coin that is worth five cents→アメリカ・カナダの5セント硬貨

**nickname** /níknèɪm/ 名 C ▶定義 an informal name that is used instead of your real name, usually by your family or friends 本名の代わりに使われる略式の名前で,普通は家族や友人により呼ばれる→愛称,あだ名,ニックネーム—
*nickname* 動 ▶定義 〜に…というあだ名を付ける,〜を愛称で呼ぶ

**nicotine** /níkətìːn/ 名 U ▶定義 the poisonous chemical substance in tobacco たばこに含まれる有毒な化学物質→ニコチン

★**niece** /niːs/ 名 C ▶定義 the daughter of your brother or sister; the daughter of your husband's or wife's brother or sister 兄弟姉妹の娘;夫・妻の兄弟姉妹の娘→姪(めい) ☞参 **nephew**

**niggle** /nígəl/ 動 ▶定義 1 他 **niggle (at) sb** to annoy or worry sb 〜をいらいらさせる,〜を悩ませる→(人を)悩ます,(人の)心に引っ掛かる ‖ *His untidy habits really niggled her.* 彼のだらしない癖は,彼女を本当に悩ませた. ▶定義 2 自 **niggle (about/over sth)** to complain or argue about things that are not important 重要ではない事に不平を言う,どうでもいい事を主張する→(つまらない事に)こだわる,(〜について)難癖を付ける

**niggling** /nígəlɪŋ/ 形 ▶定義 not very serious (but that does not go away) あまり重大ではない(が,心から消えない)→(ささいだが)いつまでも気に掛かる,心を悩ます ‖ *niggling doubts* いつまでも気に掛かる疑念 *a niggling injury* ささいな傷

★**night** /naɪt/ 名 C U ▶定義 1 the part of the day when it is dark and when most people sleep 1日のうちで,暗くてほとんどの人が眠る時間→夜,晩 ‖ *I had a strange dream last night.* 昨晩不思議な夢を見た. *The baby cried **all night**.* 赤ん坊は一晩中泣き続けた. *It's a long way home. Why don't you **stay the night**?* 家までは長い道のりだ. 今晩は泊まっていったらどうですか. *We will be away for a few nights.* 私たちは何日か留守にする. ▶定義 2 the time between late afternoon and when you go to bed 午後遅くから寝るまでの間→晩,夜 ‖ *Let's go out on Saturday night.* 土曜の晩に出掛けよう. *He doesn't get home until 8 o'clock **at night**.* 彼は夜8時までは家に帰らない. *I went out with Kate **the other night** (= a few nights ago).* 数日前の夜(= 数晩前),ケートとデートをした.

▶注意. night の前にはさまざまな前置詞が使われる. at は最も一般的である: *I'm not allowed out after 11 o'clock at night.* (私は夜 11 時以降の外出を禁じられている.) by は通常夜間に行うものについて用いられる: *These animals sleep by day and hunt by night.* (これらの動物は昼間眠り,夜間に獲物を探す.) in/during は通

常, ちょうど過ぎ去った夜について使われる: *I woke up twice in the night.* (夜中に2回も目が覚めた.) on はある特定の夜について述べる場合に用いる: *On the night of Saturday 30 June* (6月30日土曜日の夜に). tonight は今日の夕方・夜を意味する: *Where are you staying tonight?* (今夜はどこに泊まるのですか.)

成句 an early/a late night ▶定義 an evening when you go to bed earlier/later than usual 普段よりも早く・遅く寝る夜→早く寝る・遅くまで起きている夜

a night out ▶定義 an evening that you spend out of the house enjoying yourself 家の外で楽しく時を過ごす夜→外で楽しく過ごす一夜

in the/at dead of night ⇒ DEAD²

good night ▶定義 said late in the evening, before you go home or before you go to sleep 夜遅く, 家に帰る前や就寝前に言うあいさつ→おやすみなさい

**nightclub** /náɪtklʌ̀b/ 名 C ⇒ CLUB¹(2)

**nightdress** /náɪtdrès/ (または 略式 **nightie** /náɪti/) 名 C ▶定義 a loose dress that a girl or woman wears in bed 少女・女性が就寝時に着るゆったりとした衣服→(女性・子供用の丈の長い)寝巻き, ネグリジェ

**nightingale** /náɪtŋgèɪl, -tɪŋ-/ 名 C ▶定義 a small brown bird that has a beautiful song 小さな茶色の鳥で, 美しくさえずる→ナイチンゲール, サヨナキドリ

**nightlife** /náɪtlàɪf/ 名 U ▶定義 the entertainment that is available in the evenings in a particular place 特定の場所で夜間に利用できる娯楽→夜の歓楽, 夜遊び ‖ *It's a small town with very little nightlife.* そこは, 夜の娯楽がほとんどない小さな町だ.

**nightly** /náɪtli/ 形 副 ▶定義 happening every night 毎晩行われる→毎晩(の), 夜ごと(の) ‖ *a nightly news bulletin* 毎晩のニュース速報

**nightmare** /náɪtmèər/ 名 C ▶定義 1 a frightening or unpleasant dream 恐ろしい夢, 嫌な夢→悪夢, うなされること ‖ *I had a terrible nightmare about being stuck in a lift last night.* 昨夜, エレベーターの中に閉じ込められるという恐ろしい悪夢を見た. ▶定義 2 略式 an experience that is very unpleasant or frightening とても嫌な経験, とても恐ろしい経験→悪夢のような経験, 恐ろしい・不快な経験 ‖ *Travelling in the rush hour can be a real nightmare.* ラッシュアワーに移動することは本当に恐ろしいことになり得る.

**night-time** 名 U ▶定義 the time when it is dark 暗くなっている時間→夜, 夜間

**nightwatchman** /náɪtwɔ̀tʃmən/ C (複 **nightwatchmen** /-mæn/) ▶定義 a person who guards a building at night 夜間に建物の警備をする人→夜間警備員, 夜警

**nil** /nɪl/ 名 U ▶定義 the number 0 (especially as the score in some games) 数の0 (特に競技の得点)→無, (特にスポーツの得点の)ゼロ ‖ *We won two-nil/by two goals to nil.* 我々は2対0で勝った. ☛参 **zero** の注

**nimble** /nímb(ə)l/ 形 ▶定義 able to move quickly and lightly 素早くかつ身軽に動くことができる→(人・動作が)素早い, 身軽な, 軽快な — **nimbly** /nímb(ə)li/ 副 →素早く, 敏捷(びんしょう)に, 軽快に

*****nine** /náɪn/ 数 ▶定義 9

▶文中での数詞の使い方については, **six** の項を参照.

成句 nine to five ▶定義 the hours that you work in most offices 大多数の職場の勤務時間→(午前9時から午後5時までの)通常勤務時間 ‖ *a nine-to-five job* 9時〜5時の仕事

*****nineteen** /nàɪntí:n, ˵/ 数 ▶定義 19

▶文中での数詞の使い方については, **six** の項を参照.

**nineteenth** /nàɪntí:nθ, ˵/ 代形副 ▶定義 19th→19番目(の, に), 第19(の, に) ☛参 **sixth** の例

**ninetieth** /náɪntiəθ/ ▶定義 1 代形副 90th→90番目(の, に), 第90(の, に) ☛参 **sixth** の例 ▶定義 2 代名 C one of ninety equal parts of sth 〜を90等分したうちの1つ→90分の1

*****ninety** /náɪnti/ 数 ▶定義 90

▶文中での数詞の使い方については, **sixty** の項を参照.

**ninth¹** /náɪnθ/ 名 C ▶定義 the fraction 1/9; one of nine equal parts of sth 分数1/9; 〜を9等分したうちの1つ→9分の1 ☛参 **sixth** の例

**ninth²** /náɪnθ/ 代形副 ▶定義 9th→9番目(の, に), 第9(の, に) ☛参 **sixth** の例

**nip** /nɪp/ 動 (**nipping**; **nipped**) ▶定義 1 自 他 to give sb/sth a quick bite or to quickly squeeze a piece of sb's skin between your thumb and finger ~を素早くかむ. 親指と人差し指で~の皮膚を素早くぎゅっとつまむ→(~を)かむ,(~を)挟む,(~を)つねる ‖ *She nipped him on the arm.* 彼女は彼の腕をつねった. ▶定義2 自医(口語) to go somewhere quickly and/or for a short time (~に)素早く短い時間で行く→急く,素早く動く~ nip 名 C

慣用 nip sth in the bud ▶定義 to stop sth bad before it develops or gets worse 悪い~が進展する前にやめさせる, もっと悪くなる前にやめさせる→~を早いうちにやめさせる,(危険など)を未然に防ぐ

**nipple** /níp(ə)l/ 名 C ▶定義 either of the two small dark circles on either side of your chest. A baby can suck milk from his/her mother's breast through the nipples. 胸の左右部分のそれぞれにある, 色が濃くて小さな丸い形をしたもの. 赤ん坊はお母さんの胸の乳首から母乳を吸うことができる→乳首

**nit** /nít/ 名 C ▶定義 the egg of a small insect that lives in the hair of people or animals 人・動物の毛に住む小さな虫の卵→(シラミなどの)寄生虫の卵

**nit-picking** 形名 U ▶定義 the habit of finding small mistakes in sb's work or paying too much attention to small, unimportant details ~のすることに対してささいな間違いを見つけ出す癖, ささいな取るに足りない細かい事に注意を向けすぎること→あら捜し, 揚げ足取り

**nitrogen** /náɪtrədʒən/ 名 U (元素記号 N) ▶定義 a gas that has no colour, taste or smell. Nitrogen forms about 80% of the air around the earth. 無色・無味・無臭の気体. 窒素は地球周辺の大気の80パーセントを成している→窒素

**the nitty-gritty** /nìti grítɪ/ 名[単数扱い](口語) ▶定義 the most important facts, not the small or unimportant details ささいでどうでもいい枝葉の部分ではなく, 最も重要な事実→(物事の)核心, 本質

★**no**[1] /nóu/ 形副 ▶定義1 not any; not a →どの~も…ない; 1つも[1人も]~でない ‖ *I have no time to talk now.* 今は話す時間がない. *No visitors may enter without a ticket.* 切符をお持ちでない方はどなたも入れません. *He's no friend of mine.* 彼は友達などではない. *Alice is feeling no better this morning.* アリスは今朝は少しも気分が優れない. ▶定義2 used for saying that sth is not allowed ~が許されていないことを示す場合に使われて→(掲示・スローガンなどに用いて)~禁止 ‖ *No smoking.* 禁煙. *No flash photography.* フラッシュ撮影禁止. *No parking.* 駐車禁止.

> ▶語法
>
> no more/less は「差がゼロ」
>
> no+比較級+than... の no は I have no money.(金が全然ない)と同様に, 「…との差がゼロ」であることを表しています. much bigger > a little bigger > no bigger の順で差が小さくなり, 結局「差がない=同じ」に至ります. したがって, *A car seen from far away looks no bigger than a toy seen near.*(車は遠くから見ると, 近くにあるおもちゃと同じ大きさに見える)となります. 「同じくらい小さく見える」というのは常識などによる含意(implication)が加わった解釈です.

★**no**[2] /nóu/ 間 ▶定義1 used for giving a negative reply 否定の返事をする場合に用いて→いいえ, いや, 違います ‖ *'Are you ready?' 'No, I'm not.'* 「準備はできましたか」「いいえ,できていません」 *'Would you like something to eat?' 'No, thank you.'* 「何か召し上がりますか」「いいえ,結構です」⇔ **Yes, please**. *'Can I borrow the car?' 'No, you can't.'* 「車を借りることができますか」「いいえ, 駄目です」

▶否定文に同意する場合も no を使う: *'This programme's not very good.' 'No, you're right. It isn't.'*(「この番組はあまり良くないね」「ああ, その通りだ. 良くないよ」)

⇔ **yes** ▶定義2 used for expressing surprise or shock 驚き・衝撃を表すのに用いて→まさか, なんだって, そんなばかな ‖ *'Mike's had an accident.' 'Oh, no!'*「マイクが事故に遭った」「え, まさか」

**No**[3] (または **no**; 英 記号 #)(複 **Nos; nos**) 略 number→数 ‖ *No 10 Downing Street* ダウニング街 10 番地 *tel no 512364* 電話番号 512364

**nobility** /noʊbíləti/ 名 ▶定義1 **the nobility** [単数扱い, 単数または複数形の動詞と共に]the group of people who belong to the highest social class and have special titles such as (Duke) or (Duchess) 社会の最も上流の階級に属し, 公爵・公爵婦人などの肩書きを持つ人々→貴

族(階級), 高貴な人々 ☛類 aristocracy ▶定義2 ❶正式 the quality of having courage and honour 勇気と名誉を持ち合わせている性質→気高さ, 高貴さ

**noble**[1] /nóub(ə)l/ 形 ▶定義1 honest; full of courage and care for others 誠実な; 勇気に満ち, 他者に配慮する→気高い, 崇高な, 高潔な ‖ *a noble leader* すばらしい指導者 *noble ideas/actions* 崇高な考え・高潔な行動 ▶定義2 belonging to the highest social class 社会の最も上流の階級に属している→貴族の, 身分の高い, 高貴な ‖ *a man of noble birth* 高貴な生まれの男性— **nobly** /nóubli/ 副→気高く, 高潔に, 高い身分で

**noble**[2] /nóub(ə)l/ 名 C ▶定義 (in past times) a person who belonged to the highest social class and had a special title (昔に)最も上流の階級に属し, 特別の肩書を持っていた人→**貴族** ☛現在の一般的な語は peer.

★**nobody**[1] /nóubàdi, -bədi/ (または **no one** /nóu wʌn/) 代 ▶定義 no person; not anyone→だれも~でない, 1人も~でない ‖ *He screamed but nobody came to help him.* 彼は悲鳴を上げたが, だれも助けに来なかった. *No one else was around.* 辺りにはほかにだれもいなかった. *There was nobody at home.* 家にはだれもいなかった.

▶ none of は nobody と異なり, 必ず the, his, her, those などの語または代名詞の前に使う: *None of my friends remembered my birthday.* (友達はだれも私の誕生日を覚えていなかった.) *I've asked all my classmates but none of them are free.* (クラス全員に聞いてみたが, 手が空いている人はだれもいない.)

**nobody**[2] /nóubàdi, -bədi/ 名 C (複 **nobodies**) ▶定義 a person who is not important or famous 要人ではない人, 無名の人→**名もない人, 取るに足りない人** ‖ *She rose from being a nobody to a superstar.* 彼女は無名からのし上がってスーパースターになった.

**nocturnal** /nɑktə́ːml/ 形 ▶定義1 (used about animals and birds) awake and active at night and asleep during the day (動物・鳥について) 夜間起きて活動し, 昼間は寝ている→**夜行性の** ‖ *Owls are nocturnal birds.* フクロウは夜行性の鳥だ. ▶定義2 (文) happening in the night 夜に起こる→**夜の, 夜間の** ‖ *a nocturnal adventure* 夜の冒険

★**nod** /nɑd/ 動 自 他 (**nodding**; **nodded**) ▶定義 to move your head up and down as a way of saying 'yes' or as a sign to sb to do sth 首を縦に振って同意を表したり, 人に何かをすることを身振りで示す→(同意・合図・命令などを表して)うなずく, 首を縦に振る ‖ *Everybody at the meeting nodded in agreement.* 会議の参加者は全員, 賛成してうなずいた. *Nod your head if you understand what I'm saying and shake it if you don't.* 私の言うことが分かったら首を縦に振り, そうでなかったら横に振りなさい. ☛S6 ページのさし絵 — **nod** 名 C→**うなずき, 会釈**

句動詞 **nod off** 略式 ▶定義 to fall asleep for a short time 短時間眠る→**居眠りする, こっくりする**

**no-go area** 名 [単数扱い] ▶定義 a place, especially part of a city, where it is very dangerous to go because there is a lot of violence or crime 暴力行為や犯罪が多発しているため立ち入るには極めて危険な区域で, 特に都市にある→**立ち入り禁止区域**

★**noise** /nɔɪz/ 名 C U ▶定義 a sound, especially one that is loud or unpleasant 音, 特に大きくて不快な音→**音, 物音, 騒音** ‖ *Did you hear a noise downstairs?* 階下の物音を聞きましたか. *Try not to **make a noise** if you come home late.* 遅く帰宅したときは, 物音を立てないようにしてください. *What an awful noise!* 何てひどい騒音なの. *Why is the engine making so much noise?* どうしてそのエンジンがそんなに大きな音を立てるのかしら.

**noiseless** /nɔ́ɪzləs/ 形 ▶定義 making no sound 音を立てない→**音を立てない, 静かな**— **noiselessly** 副→**音を立てずに, 静かに**

★**noisy** /nɔ́ɪzi/ 形 (**noisier**; **noisiest**) ▶定義 making a lot of or too much noise; full of noise 大きな, または大きすぎる音を立てる; 騒音に満ちている→**やかましい, 騒がしい, 騒々しい** ‖ *The clock was so noisy that it kept me awake.* 時計がとてもうるさかったので, 眠れなかった. *noisy children/traffic/crowds* うるさい子供たち・騒々しい車の往来・騒がしい群集 *The classroom was very noisy.* 教室はとても騒々しかった. ☛参 **loud** の注— **noisily** 副→**やかましく, 騒々しく**

**nomad** /nóumæd/ 名 C ▶定義 a member of a group of people (a tribe) that moves with its animals from place to place 家畜と共に, ある場所から次の場所へと移動する人々の集団(部族)の１人→遊牧民― **nomadic** 形→遊牧(民族)の, 放浪する

**no-man's-land** 名 [ⓤ, 単数扱い] ▶定義 an area of land between the borders of two countries or between two armies during a war and which is not controlled by either ２国の国境間または戦時下に２つの軍隊の間の地帯で, いずれの側にも支配されていない→緩衝地帯, 中間[無人]地帯

**nominal** /nάmənl, nάmnəl/ 形 ▶定義 **1** being sth in name only but not in reality ～が名目上だけで, 実際にはそうではない→**名目上の, 名ばかりの** ‖ *the nominal leader of the country* (= *sb else is really in control*) 名目だけの国の指導者(= ほかの人が実際には統治している) ▶定義 **2** (used about a price, sum of money, etc) very small; much less than normal (価格・金額などについて)非常にわずかな; 普通よりずっと少ない→**(金額が)わずかな, 申し訳程度の** ‖ *Because we are friends he only charges me **a nominal rent**.* 彼とは友達なので, 申し訳程度の家賃しか請求してこない.

**nominate** /nάmənèɪt/ 動他 ▶定義 nominate sb/sth (for/as sth) to formally suggest that sb/sth should be given a job, role, prize, etc ～に職務・役割・賞などを与えるべきだと正式に提案する→**～を(…の候補として)指名する, (作品)を(…の)候補に** ‖ *I would like to nominate Bob Turner as chairman.* ボブ ターナーを議長に任命したい. *The novel has been nominated for the Booker prize.* その小説は, ブッカー賞の候補になった. *You may nominate a representative to speak for you.* あなたの代弁をする代理人を指名してよいです. ― **nomination** /nὰmənéɪʃ(ə)n/ 名 ⓒⓤ **▶指名, 任命, 推薦**

**nominee** /nὰməníː/ 名 ⓒ ▶定義 a person who is suggested for an important job, role, prize, etc 重要な職務・役割・賞などの候補になった人→**指名(任命, 推薦, ノミネート)された人**

**non-** /nɑn/ (複合語を作るために用いて) ▶定義 not ～ではない→名詞・形容詞について「非～, 不～, 無～」の意の語を作る ‖ *non-biodegradable* 生物分解性のない *non-flammable* 不燃性の

**non-academic** 形 ▶定義 connected with technical or practical subjects rather than subjects of interest to the mind 知的興味よりも, 技術的・実用的な事に関連して→**実用的な**

**non-alcoholic** 形 ▶定義 (used about drinks) not containing any alcohol (飲料について)アルコールを一切含んでいない→**アルコールを含まない, 非アルコール性の** ‖ *non-alcoholic drinks* 非アルコール性飲料

**nonchalant** /nὰnʃəláːnt, ´̀–, -lənt/ 形 ▶定義 not feeling or showing interest or excitement about sth ～に興味・興奮を感じない, 示さない→**むとんちゃくな, 無関心な, のんきな**― **nonchalance** 名 ⓤ→**むとんちゃく, 無関心, のんき**― **nonchalantly** 副→**むとんちゃくに, 無関心に, のんきに**

**noncommittal** /nὰnkəmít(ə)l/ 形 ▶定義 not saying or showing exactly what your opinion is or which side of an argument you agree with 意見をはっきりと言わない[示さない], 議論のどちら側に賛成するのかをはっきりと言わない[示さない]→**当たり障りのない, どっちつかずの, あいまいな**

**nonconformist** /nὰnkənfɔ́ːrmɪst/ 名 ⓒ ▶定義 a person who behaves or thinks differently from most other people in society 社会の大多数の人とは違った考えや行動をする人→**(慣習・体制などに)従わない人, 非同調者**⇔**conformist**― **nonconformist** 形→**慣習に逆らう, 反体制の**

**nondescript** /nὰndɪskrípt/ ´̀–/ 形 ▶定義 not having any interesting or unusual qualities 興味をそそるまたは目立つ特質を持たない→**特徴のない, ありふれた, ぱっとしない**

*__none__¹ /nʌn/ 代 ▶定義 none (of sb/sth) not any, not one (of a group of three or more) だれも～ない, (3人以上の集団の)１人も～ない→**～のだれも…(で)ない, ～のだれも…(で)ない** ‖ *They gave me a lot of information but none of it was very helpful.* 彼らは多くの情報を寄せてくれたが, どれもあまり役に立たなかった. *I've got four brothers but none of them live/lives nearby.* ４人兄弟がいるが, だれもそばに住んでいない. *'Have you brought any books to read?' 'No, none.'* 「何か読む本を持ってきましたか」「いいえ, 何も持ってきていません」 *I went to several shops but none had what I was looking for.* 何軒かお店に行ってみたが, どの店にも探しているものはなかった.

## none²

► none of を複数名詞と共に使う場合,動詞は文意によって単数にも複数にもなり得る.「~の1つも~ない」という意味の場合は,単数の動詞を使ってこれを強調する: *None of these trains goes to Birmingham.* (これらの列車はいずれもバーミンガムに行かない.)「~のどれも~ない」という意味の場合は,複数の動詞を使う: *None of the children like spinach.* (どの子もホウレンソウが好きではない.) 2人の人々,または2つの事について述べる場合は,none ではなく neither を使う: *Neither of my brothers lives nearby.* (私の兄弟は2人とも近くに住んでいない.) none と no の違いに注意する. no は必ず名詞の前に来るが,none は名詞を置き換える: *I told him that I had **no** money left.* (お金は残っていないと彼に言った.) *When he asked me how much money I had left, I told him that I had **none**.* (お金がいくら残っているか彼が聞いたとき,全く残っていないと答えた.)

**none²** /nʌn/ 副

成句 **none the wiser/worse** ▶定義 knowing no more than before; no worse than before 以前に比べてより知っているわけではない; 以前より悪くなったわけではない→だからといって少しも~ではない ‖ *We talked for a long time but I'm still **none the wiser**.* 我々は長い間話したが, 私は依然としてあまり分かっていない.

**none too happy, clean, pleased, etc** 略式 ▶定義 not very happy, clean, pleased, etc →あまり幸せで・清潔で・楽しくない, など

**nonetheless** /nʌnðəlés/ 副 (文) ▶定義 in spite of this fact この事実にもかかわらず→それにもかかわらず, それでもなお ‖ *It won't be easy but they're going to try **nonetheless**.* 容易ではなさそうだが, それでも彼らは試すつもりだ.
☛類 **nevertheless**

**non-existent** 形 ▶定義 not existing or not available 存在していない, 入手できない→存在しない, 実存しない

**non-fiction** /nʌnfíkʃ(ə)n/ 名 Ⓤ ▶定義 writing that is about real people, events and facts 実在の人々・出来事・事実に関して書かれたもの→ノンフィクション(事実に基づいた散文文学; 伝記・歴史文学など) ‖ *You'll find biographies in the non-fiction section of the library.* 図書館のノンフィクション部門に, 伝記があります. ⇨ **fiction**

**nonplussed** /nʌnplʌ́st, -/ 形 ▶定義 confused; not able to understand 困惑した; 理解できない→困惑した, 途方に暮れた

**non-renewable** /nʌnrɪn(j)úːəbl/ 形 ▶定義 (used about natural sources of energy such as gas or oil) that cannot be replaced after use (ガス・石油などの天然のエネルギー資源について) 使用後に戻せない→**(資源・エネルギーが)再生不可能な**

*★**nonsense** /nάnsèns, -s(ə)ns/ 名 Ⓤ ▶定義 1 ideas, statements or beliefs that you think are ridiculous or not true ばかげていると思える, あるいは本当ではないと思える発想, 主張, 信念→**無意味な言葉, たわ言, ナンセンス, ばかな考え・行為** ‖ *Don't talk **nonsense**!* ばかな事を言うな. *It's nonsense to say you aren't good enough to go to university!* あなたが大学に行くだけの学力がないと言うのはばかげている. ▶定義 2 silly or unacceptable behaviour ばかげた振る舞い, 容認できない振る舞い→**ばかげた行為** ‖ *The head teacher won't stand for any **nonsense**.* 校長先生は悪ふざけやいたずらにはとても厳しい.

**nonsensical** /nɑnsénsɪk(ə)l/ 形 ▶定義 ridiculous; without meaning ばかげた; 意味がない→**無意味な, 意味を成さない, ばかげた**

**non-smoker** /nʌnsmóʊkər/ 名 Ⓒ ▶定義 a person who does not smoke cigarettes or cigars たばこ・葉巻を吸わない人→たばこを吸わない人 ⇔ **smoker** — **non-smoking** 形 →禁煙の ‖ *Would you like a table in the smoking or the non-smoking section?* お食事の席は禁煙席と喫煙席のどちらがよろしいでしょうか.

**non-starter** /nʌnstάːrtər/ 名 Ⓒ ▶定義 a person, plan or idea that has no chance of success 成功する可能性がない人・計画・案→**(成功の)見込みのない人・物, 下らない[現実味のない]考え**

**non-stick** /nʌnstík/ 形 ▶定義 (used about a pan, etc) covered with a substance that prevents food from sticking to it (なべなどについて) 料理のこびりつきを防ぐための物質で表面が加工してある→**(フライパンなどが)焦げ付かない, 焦げ付き防止加工した**

**non-stop** /nʌnstάp/ 形副 ▶定義 without a stop or a rest 中断・休憩なしで→**直行の, ノンストップの** ‖ *a non-stop flight to Bombay* ボンベイまでの直行便 *He talked non-stop for two hours* *about his holiday.* 彼は休暇について, 休みなく2時間しゃべり続けた.

**non-violence** /nɑ̀nváɪələns/ 名 U ▶定義 fighting for political or social change without using force, for example by not obeying laws 暴力を用いることなく, 政治・社会変革のために闘うことで, 例えば法律に従わないなどの方法を採る→非暴力, 非暴力主義—**non-violent** 形→非暴力の, 非暴力主義の

**noodle** /núːdl/ 名 [C, 通常は複数] ▶定義 long thin pieces of food made of flour, egg and water that are cooked in boiling water or used in soups 小麦粉・卵・水で作られた細長い食品で, 沸騰したお湯でゆでて調理され, またはスープに使われる→ヌードル(小麦と卵で作るめん類), (中国や日本の)めん

**nook** /nʊk/ 名 C ▶定義 a small quiet place or corner (in a house, garden, etc)(家の中, 庭などの)小さくて静かな場所・隅→(部屋などの)隅, 角, (奥まった)片隅

成句 every nook and cranny 略式 ▶定義 every part of a place 場所のあらゆる所→隅から隅まで, ありとあらゆる所に

★**noon** /nuːn/ 名 U ▶定義 12 o'clock in the middle of the day; midday 昼間の12時; 正午 →正午, 真昼 ‖ *At noon* the sun is at its highest point in the sky. 正午には, 太陽は上空の一番高い所にある.
☛参 midnight

**no one**=NOBODY¹

**noose** /nuːs/ 名 C ▶定義 a circle that is tied in the end of the rope and that gets smaller as one end of the rope is pulled ロープの一方の端を結んで輪にして, もう一方の端を引くとその輪が小さくなる→輪縄, 引き結び

★**nor** /nɔːr, nər/ 接 副 ▶定義1 neither... nor... and not →〜でもなく…でもない, 〜も…もしない ‖ *I have neither the time nor the inclination to listen to his complaints again.* 私には, 彼の不満をもう一度聞く時間も気もない. ▶定義2 (肯定の動詞の前に用いて, 直前に述べられた否定の〜に同意する) also not; neither →〜もまた…ない, 〜もまた…しない ‖ *'I don't like football.' 'Nor do I.'* 「私はフットボールが好きではない」「私も」 *'We haven't been to America.' 'Nor have we.'* 「私たちは米国に行ったことがない」「私たちも」
☛ この用法では, neither も同様に使える. *'I won't be here tomorrow.' 'Nor/Neither will I.'* 「私

は明日はここに来ません」「私も」 ▶定義3 (否定文の後に用いて, さらに情報を追加する) also not →〜もまた…ない ‖ *Michael never forgot her birthday. Nor their wedding anniversary for that matter.* マイケルは彼女の誕生日を決して忘れたことはない. さらに言えば, 結婚記念日も忘れたことはない.

**norm** /nɔːm/ 名 C (しばしば the を伴って) ▶定義 a situation or way of behaving that is usual or expected 通常の状況・振る舞い方, 予測された状況・振る舞い方→典型, 標準, 規範

★**normal**¹ /nɔ́ːm(ə)l/ 形 ▶定義 typical, usual or ordinary; what you expect 典型的な, いつもの, 通常の; 予想通りの→標準の, 正常な, 通常の ‖ *I'll meet you at the normal time.* いつもの時間に会いましょう. *It's quite normal to feel angry in a situation like this.* このような状況で怒りを覚えるのは正常なことだ. ⇔**abnormal**

★**normal**² /nɔ́ːm(ə)l/ 名 U ▶定義 the usual or average state, level or standard 普通の, または平均的な状態・水準・基準→標準, 常態, 平均 ‖ *temperatures above/below normal* 平均以上・以下の気温 *Things are* **back to normal** *at work now.* 現在, 職場は平常に戻った.

**normality** /nɔːrmǽləti/ (米 **normalcy** /nɔ́ːm(ə)lsi/) 名 U ▶定義 the state of being normal 正常な状態→正常, 常態

**normalize** (または **-ise**) /nɔ́ːm(ə)laɪz/ 動 自 他 (文) ▶定義 to become or make sth become normal again or return to how it was before 〜が再び正常な状態になる, 以前と同じに戻る, そのようにする→(〜を)正常化する, (〜を)常態にする ‖ *The two countries agreed to normalize relations (= return to a normal, friendly relationship, for example after a disagreement or a war).* 2国は関係を正常化することに合意した (= 例えば意見の対立・戦争などの後に, 正常で友好的な関係に戻る).

★**normally** /nɔ́ːm(ə)li/ 副 ▶定義1 usually 普通は→通常は, 普通は ‖ *I normally leave the house at 8 o'clock.* 私はいつもは8時に家を出る. *Normally he takes the bus.* 通常, 彼はバスを利用する. ▶定義2 in the usual or ordinary way 普通の状態で, 正常な状態で→正常に, 正規に, 標準的に

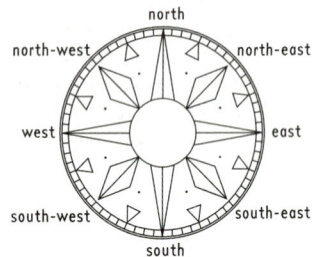

**\*north¹** /nɔːθ/ 名 [単数扱い] (略 **N**) (または **the north**) ▶定義 **1** the direction that is on your left when you watch the sun rise; one of the four main directions that we give names to (the points of the compass) 日の出の方向に向かって左手の方角;東西南北とした4つの主な方角 (羅針盤の方位)の1つ→北,北方 ‖ *cold winds from the north* 北からの冷たい風 *Which way is north?* どちらの方向が北ですか. *I live* **to the north of** (= further north than) *Belfast.* 私はベルファストから北の所に(= さらに北方に)住んでいる. ▶定義 **2 the North** the northern part of any country, city, region or the world あらゆる国・都市・地域・世界の北部→北部,北部地方 ‖ *Houses are less expensive in the North of England than in the South.* 住宅はイギリスの南部より北部の方が安い. *I live in the north of Athens.* 私はアテネの北部に住んでいる. ⇨参 **south**, **east**, **west**

**\*north²** /nɔːθ/ 形副 ▶定義 **1** (または **North**) (名詞の前だけ) in the north 北の[に]→北の[に],北部の[に],北向きの[に] ‖ *The new offices will be in North London.* 新しい職場はノース(北部)ロンドンになるだろう. *The north wing of the hospital was destroyed in a fire.* 病院の北ウイングは火災で焼け落ちた. ▶定義 **2** to or towards the north 北へ,北に向かって→北へ,北向きの ‖ *We got onto the motorway going north instead of south.* 我々は南ではなく北方面に向かう高速道路に乗った. *The house faces north.* その家は北に面している. *Is Leeds north of Manchester?* リーズはマンチェスターの北ですか. ▶定義 **3** (used about a wind) coming from the north (風について)北から来る→北からの

**northbound** /nɔːθbàʊnd/ 形 ▶定義 travelling or leading towards the north 北に向かって移動する,北に向けて行く→北へ向かう,北行きの ‖ *northbound traffic* 北へ向かう車の流れ

**\*north-east¹** 名 [単数扱い] (略 **NE**) (または **the North-East**) ▶定義 the direction or a region halfway between north and east 北と東の中間の方角,地域→北東,北東部,北東地方 ➡**north**のさし絵

**\*north-east²** 形副 ▶定義 in, from or to the north-east of a place or country ある場所・国の北東で,北東から,北東に→北東の[へ],北東部の,北東への,北東からの ‖ *the north-east coast of Australia* オーストラリア北東部の海岸 *If you look north-east you can see the sea.* 北東の方角を見ると,海が見えます.

**north-easterly** 形 ▶定義 **1** towards the north-east 北東に向かって→北東の,北東へ向かう ‖ *in a north-easterly direction* 北東の方向に ▶定義 **2** (used about a wind) coming from the north-east (風について)北東から来る→北東からの

**north-eastern** 形 (名詞の前だけ) ▶定義 connected with the north-east of a place or country ある場所・国の北東に関する→北東の,北東からの,北東への

**north-eastward(s)** 副 ▶定義 towards the north-east 北東に向かって→北東へ ‖ *Follow the A619 north-eastward.* 国道A619を北東へ進みなさい.

**northerly** /nɔːðəli/ 形 ▶定義 **1** to, towards or in the north 北へ,北に向かって,北に→北の,北へ向かう ‖ *Keep going in a northerly direction.* 北の方角にずっと行きなさい. ▶定義 **2** (used about a wind) coming from the north (風について)北から来る→北からの

**\*northern** (または **Northern**) /nɔːðəm/ 形 ▶定義 of, in or from the north of a place ある場所の北の,北に,北から→北の,北からの,北方の ‖ *She has a northern accent.* 彼女には北部のなまりがある. *in northern Australia* オーストラリア北部に

**northerner** (または **Northerner**) /nɔːðəmər/ 名 C ▶定義 a person who was born in or who lives in the northern part of a country 国の北部出身の人,国の北部に住んでいる人→北部出身者,北部地方の人,北国の人⇔**southerner**

**northernmost** /nɔːðəmmòʊst/ 形 ▶定義 furthest north 最も北に位置する→**最北の, 極北の** ‖ the northernmost island of Japan 日本最北の島

**the North Pole** 名[単数扱い] ▶定義 the point on the Earth's surface which is furthest north 地球上の最北端に位置する地点→**北極** ☞**earth** のさし絵

**northward** /nɔ́ːrθwərd/ (または **northwards**) 副形 ▶定義 towards the north 北へ向かって→**北へ向かう[向かって], 北向き[の], 北へ[の]** ‖ Continue northwards out of the city for about five miles. 町から北へ向かってそのまま5マイル進みなさい. in a northward direction 北の方向に

*★**north-west**[1] 形副 ▶定義 in, from or to the north-west of a place or country ある場所・国の北西に, 北西から, 北西へ→**北西の, 北西へ** ‖ the north-west coast of Scotland スコットランド北西部の海岸 Our house faces north-west. 私たちの家は北西に面している.

★**north-west**[2] 名[単数扱い](略 **NW**)(または **the North-West**) ▶定義 the direction or region halfway between north and west 北と西の中間の方角, 地域→**北西, 北西部, 北西地方** ☞**north** のさし絵

**north-westerly** 形 ▶定義1 towards the north-west 北西に向かって→**北西の, 北西へ向かう** ‖ in a north-westerly direction 北西の方向に ▶定義2 (used about a wind) coming from the north-west (風について)北西から来る→**北西からの**

**north-western** 形(名詞の前だけ) ▶定義 connected with the north-west of a place or country ある場所・国の北西に関する→**北西の, 北西への**

**north-westward(s)** 副 ▶定義 towards the north-west 北西に向かって→**北西の, 北西への, 北西へ向かう** ‖ Follow the A40 north-westward for ten miles. 国道A40を北西に10マイル行きなさい.

★**nose**[1] /nóuz/ 名 C ▶定義1 the part of your face, above your mouth, that is used for breathing and smelling 顔の中で口の上に位置する部分で, 呼吸したりにおいをかいだりするのに使う→**鼻** ☞C5ページのさし絵 ▶定義2 **-nosed** (複合形容詞を作るために用いて) having the type of nose mentioned 〜の特徴の鼻を持つ→**〜の鼻の, 〜鼻をした** ‖ red-nosed 赤鼻の big-nosed 大きな鼻をした ▶定義3 the front part of a plane, spacecraft, etc 飛行機・宇宙船などの正面の部分→**(鼻のような)突出部, 船首, 機首**

成句 blow your nose ⇒ **BLOW**[1]
follow your nose ⇒ **FOLLOW**
look down your nose at sb/sth 特に 英 略式 ▶定義 to think that you are better than sb else; to think that sth is not good enough for you 自分がほかの人よりも優れていると思う; 〜が自分にふさわしくないと思う→**〜を見下す, 軽べつする**
poke/stick your nose into sth (口語) ▶定義 to be interested in or try to become involved in sth which does not concern you 自分に関係ない〜に興味を示す, 自分に無関係な〜に首を突っ込もうとする→**(他人のことに)干渉する, 〜を詮索(せんさく)する**
turn your nose up at sth 略式 ▶定義 to refuse sth because you do not think it is good enough for you 〜が自分にふさわしくないと思い, 拒絶する→**〜をばかにする, 鼻であしらう, 軽べつする**

**nose**[2] /nóuz/ 動 自 ▶定義 (used about a vehicle) to move forward slowly and carefully (乗り物について) ゆっくりと注意深く前進する→**(車などが) ゆっくり[慎重に] 進む, (用心しつつ) 進む**
句動詞 nose about/around 略式 ▶定義 to look for sth, especially private information about sb 〜, 特に…のプライバシーに関する事を探る→**かぎ回る, 詮索(せんさく)する**

**nosebleed** /nóuzblìːd/ 名 C ▶定義 a sudden flow of blood that comes from your nose 鼻から突然血が流れ出ること→**鼻血が出ること, 鼻血**

**nosedive** /nóuzdàɪv/ 名 C ▶定義 a sudden sharp fall or drop 突然急降下・急落すること→**(飛行機の)急降下, (価格・人気などの)急落** ‖ Oil prices **took a nosedive** in the crisis. 危機により, 石油価格が急落した. — nosedive 動 自 →**(飛行機が) 急降下する, (価格・人気などが) 暴落・急落する**

**nostalgia** /nɑstǽldʒ(i)ə/ 名 U ▶定義 a feeling of pleasure, mixed with sadness, when you think of happy times in the past 過去の幸せな時を思い出して感じる, 楽しさと悲しみが入り交じった気持ち→**郷愁, ノスタルジア** ‖ She was suddenly filled with **nostalgia for** her university days. 彼女は急に, 大学時代の懐かしい思いで一杯になった. — nostalgic /-dʒɪk/ 形 →**郷愁の, 郷**

愁にふける、郷愁をかき立てる—nostalgically /-dʒɪk(ə)li/ 副 →郷愁にふけって、懐かしそうに

**nostril** /nástr(ə)l/ 名 C ▶定義 one of the two openings at the end of your nose that you breathe through 鼻の先端に開いた２つの穴の１つで、そこから呼吸をする → 鼻の穴、鼻孔 ☞C5ページのさし絵

**nosy** (または **nosey**) /nóuzi/ 形 ▶定義 too interested in other people's personal affairs 他人の私事に興味を持ちすぎる → 詮索(せんさく)好きな、お節介な ‖ a nosy neighbour 詮索好きな隣人

★**not** /nɑt; (助動詞の後ではまた) n(t)/ 副 ▶定義 1 used to form the negative with the verbs be, do and have (auxiliary verbs) and with verbs such as can, must, will, etc (modal verbs). Not is often pronounced or written n't in informal situations. 助動詞 be, do, have および法助動詞 can, must, will などと用いて否定文を作る。略式ではしばしば n't と発音されたり書かれたりする → (否定文) ～でない、～(し)ない ‖ It's not/it isn't raining now. 今は雨が降っていない。 I cannot/can't see from here. ここからは見えない。 He didn't invite me. 彼は私を招待しなかった。 Don't you like spaghetti? スパゲッティを好きではないのですか。 I hope she will not/won't be late. 彼女が遅れないことを願う。 You're German, aren't you? あなたはドイツ人でしょう。 ▶定義 2 used to give the following word or phrase a negative meaning 後に続く語・句に否定の意味を持たせる → (特定の語句の否定) ～でなく ‖ He told me not to telephone. 彼は私に、電話をしないように言った。 She accused me of not telling the truth. 彼女は私が真実を言わなかったことを責めた。 Not one person replied to my advertisement. だれ１人として私の広告に応じてこなかった。 It's not easy. それは容易ではない。 He's not very tall. 彼はあまり背が高くない。 ▶定義 3 used to give a short negative reply 否定の意味の短い返答に用いて → 否定を含む節の代用、not による節・文の代用 ‖ 'Do you think they'll get divorced?' 'I hope not.' (= I hope that they will not.) 「彼らは離婚すると思いますか」「そうでなければいいのですが(= 彼らがそうしないことを願います)」 'Can I borrow £20?' '**Certainly not!**' 「20 ポンド借用できますか」「とんでもない、駄目です」 'Whose turn is it to do the shopping?' 'Not mine.' 「だれが買い物をする番ですか」「私ではありません」 ▶定義 4 used with or to give a negative possibility or と用いて、否定の可能性を持たせる → 否定を含む節の代用 ‖ Shall we tell her or not? 彼女に話しましょうか、それとも話さないでおきましょうか。 I don't know if/whether he's telling the truth or not. 彼が本当の事を言っているのかどうか分からない。

成句 **not at all** ▶定義 1 used as a way of replying when sb has thanked you 〜からお礼を言われたときの返事に用いて → どういたしまして、とんでもない ‖ 'Thanks for the present.' 'Not at all, don't mention it.' 「贈り物をありがとう」「とんでもない、どういたしまして」 ▶定義 2 used as a way of saying 'no' or 'definitely not' 否定または明確な否定を表す場合に用いて → 少しも(～でない)、全然(～でない) ‖ 'Do you mind if I come too?' 'Not at all.' 「私も行って構いませんか」「ええ、どうぞ」 The instructions are not at all clear. その使用説明書は全く明確ではない。

**not only... (but) also** ▶定義 used for emphasizing the fact that there is something more to add そのほかにも追加するものがある、という事実を強調する場合に用いて → ～だけでなく…もまた、～ばかりでなく…も ‖ They not only have two houses in London, they also have one in France. 彼らはロンドンに２軒の家を持っているだけでなく、フランスにも１軒持っている。

> ▶語法
>
> 部分否定の意味
>
> 　部分否定(partial negation)は「100％ではない」ということを意味しているにすぎません。したがって数学の問題を10題与えられて I couldn't solve all of the problems. と言った場合「10題完答でない」と言っているだけで多様な解釈が可能です。通例は I was able to solve some problems. と解釈されますが、状況や前提によっては「8割方答えた」とも解釈されます。

**notable** /nóutəb(ə)l/ 形 ▶定義 **notable (for sth)** interesting or important enough to receive attention 注目をひくに値するほど興味深い・重要な → 注目に値する、目立つ、傑出した ‖ The area is notable for its wildlife. その地域はそこに生息する野生動物で有名だ。

**notably** /nóʊtəb(ə)li/ 副 ▶定義 used for giving an especially important example of what you are talking about 取り上げている話題について, 特に重要な例を挙げる場合に用いて→**特に, とりわけ** ∥ *Several politicians, most notably the Prime Minister and the Home Secretary, have given the proposal their full support.* 数人の政治家, とりわけ首相および内務大臣が, その提案を全面的に支持している.

**notch**¹ /nɑtʃ/ 名 C ▶定義 **1** a level on a scale of quality 品質基準の段階→**程度, 段階** ∥ *This meal is certainly a notch above the last one we had here.* この食事は, この前ここで食べた物より確かに一段優れている. ▶定義 **2** a cut in an edge or surface in the shape of a V or a circle, sometimes used to help you count sth 物の端や表面にV字型・円形に入れた切込みで, 〜を数えるために付ける場合もある→**(V字型の)刻み目, 印** ☞ **blob**のさし絵

**notch**² /nɑtʃ/ 動
句動詞 notch sth up ▶定義 to score or achieve sth 〜を数える, 〜を勝ち取る→**(得点など)を記録する, (勝利)を得る** ∥ *Lewis notched up his best ever time in the 100 metres.* ルイスは100メートルで自己最高記録を達成した.

***note**¹ /noʊt/ 名 ▶定義 **1** C some words that you write down quickly to help you remember sth 〜を覚えておくために素早く書き留める語など→**覚え書き, メモ, (簡単な)記録** ∥ *I'd better make a note of your name and address.* あなたの名前と住所をメモしておいた方がいいわね. *Keep a note of who has paid and who hasn't.* だれが払っていて, だれが払っていないかを書き留めておきなさい. *The lecturer advised the students to take notes while he was speaking.* 講師は学生に, 講義中にノートにとるように勧めた. ▶定義 **2** C a short letter 短い手紙→**短信** ∥ *This is just a note to thank you for having us to dinner.* これは, 私たちにごちそうをしてくださったことに対する, お礼の手紙です. *If Mark's not at home we'll leave a note for him.* マークが家にいなかったら, 置手紙を残していこう. *a sick note from your doctor* 主治医からの病欠証明書 ▶定義 **3** C a short explanation or extra piece of information that is given at the back of a book, etc or at the bottom or side of a page 巻末など, またはページの下や横に書かれた短い説明や追加情報→**注, 注釈, 注解** ∥ *See note 5, page 340.* 340ページの注5を参照. ☞参 **footnote** ▶定義 **4** C (または **banknote**; 困 **bill**) a piece of paper money 紙幣→**紙幣, 札** ∥ *I'd like the money in £10 notes, please.* 10ポンド紙幣でお願いします. ☞ **money**のさし絵 ▶定義 **5** C a single musical sound made by a voice or an instrument; a written sign that represents a musical sound 声・楽器で奏でられた音楽の1音; 音を示す記号→**音, 調子, 音符** ∥ *I can only remember the first few notes of the song.* 私はその歌の出だししか思い出せない. ▶定義 **6** [単数扱い] something that shows a certain quality or feeling ある特質や感じを示すもの→**気配, 様子, 特徴** ∥ *The meeting ended on a rather unpleasant note.* 会議はかなり嫌な雰囲気で終了した.
成句 compare notes (with sb) ⇒ **COMPARE**
take note (of sth) ▶定義 to pay attention to sth and be sure to remember it 〜に注意を払い, 覚えておくようにする→**〜に注目する, 注意する**

**note**² /noʊt/ 動 他 ▶定義 **1** to notice or pay careful attention to sth 〜に気が付く, 〜に十分注意する→**〜に注意を向ける, 〜に気付く** ∥ *He noted a slight change in her attitude towards him.* 彼は, 自分に対する彼女の態度のわずかな変化に気付いた. *Please note that this office is closed on Tuesdays.* この事務所は火曜日は休みですので, ご注意ください. ▶定義 **2** to mention sth 〜を述べる→**〜に言及する, 〜に触れる, 〜のことを述べる** ∥ *I'd like to note that the project has so far been extremely successful.* この事業は今のところ非常に順調に進んでいることを述べておきたい.
句動詞 note sth down ▶定義 to write sth down so that you remember it 覚えておくために〜を書き留める→**〜を書き留める, 〜をメモする**

***notebook** /nóʊtbʊk/ 名 C ▶定義 a small book in which you write things that you want to remember 小さな本のようにとじたもので, 覚えておきたい事を書いておくもの→**ノート, 手帳**

**noted** /nóʊtɪd/ 形 正式 ▶定義 noted (for/as sth) well-known; famous よく知られた; 有名な→**(〜で・〜として)有名な, 著名な** ∥ *The hotel is noted for its food.* そのホテルは料理で有名だ.

**notepad** /nóʊtpæd/ 名 C ▶定義 some sheets of paper in a block that are used for writing things on 紙を一まとめにしたもので,物事を書き留めるのに用いる➔メモ帳,レポート用紙 ☞S4ページのさし絵

**notepaper** /nóʊtpèɪpər/ 名 Ⓤ ▶定義 paper that you write letters on 手紙を書くための用紙➔便せん, メモ用紙

**noteworthy** /nóʊtwɜːrði/ 形 ▶定義 interesting or important; that is worth noticing 興味深い, 重要な; 注目に値する➔目立った, 顕著な, 注目に値する

★**nothing** /nʌ́θɪŋ/ 代 ▶定義 not anything; no thing ➔何も〜ない, 少しも〜ない ‖ *There's nothing in this suitcase.* このスーツケースの中には何もない. *I'm bored - there's **nothing to do** here.* 退屈だ ー ここでは何もする事がない. *There was **nothing else** to say.* ほかに何も言う事はなかった. *'What's the matter?' 'Oh, nothing.'*「どうしたの」「いや,何でもないよ」*'Thank you so much for all your help.' 'It was nothing.'*「助けてくれて本当にありがとう」「いや,大したことないよ」 *The doctor said there's nothing wrong with me.* 医者は, 私には悪い所はどこもないと言った. ☞参 **zero** の注

成句 **be/have nothing to do with sb/sth** ▶定義 to have no connection with sb/sth 〜と関係がない〜と全く関係がない, 何の関係もない ‖ *That question has nothing to do with what we're discussing.* その質問は我々が今討論している事とは何の関係もない. *Put my diary down - it's nothing to do with you.* 私の日記を置きなさいーあなたには何の関係もないものです.

**come to nothing** ⇒ **COME**

**for nothing** ▶定義 1 for no good reason or with no good result 何らちゃんとした理由もなく, 何らきちんとした結果が残らない➔無駄に, 何の理由もなく ‖ *His hard work was all for nothing.* 彼の懸命な努力も, すべて無駄だった. ▶定義 2 for no payment; free 何も支払わずに; 無料の➔ただで, 無料で ‖ *Children under four are allowed in for nothing.* 4歳未満の子供は入場無料です.

**nothing but** ▶定義 only ただ〜だけ➔ただ〜だけ, 〜にすぎない ‖ *He does nothing but sit around watching TV all day.* 彼は何もせずただ座って一日中テレビを見ているだけだ.

**nothing like** ▶定義 1 not at all like ➔〜に少しも似ていない ‖ *She looks nothing like either of her parents.* 彼女は両親のどちらにも少しも似ていない. ▶定義 2 not at all; not nearly 少しも〜ない; 到底〜でない➔ 〜に程遠い, 〜どころではない ‖ *There's nothing like enough food for all of us.* 我々全員に行き渡るだけの食料はない.

**nothing much** ▶定義 not a lot of sth; nothing of importance 〜があまりたくさんはない; 重要でない➔大したことない量, ごくわずか, 大したことのない物・事 ‖ *It's a nice town but there's nothing much to do in the evenings.* すてきな町だけれど, 夜は大してする事がない. *'What did you do at the weekend?' 'Nothing much.'*「週末は何をしたの」「大したことはしていません」

**(there's) nothing to it** ▶定義 (it's) very easy ➔(それは)とても簡単な事だ ‖ *You'll soon learn - there's nothing to it really.* あなたはすぐに覚えますよ ー 本当に簡単な事ですから.

**there is/was nothing (else) for it (but to do sth)** ▶定義 there is/was no other action possible ほかにとり得る行動がない・なかった➔〜するよりほかに仕方がない ‖ *There was nothing for it but to resign.* 辞職するよりほかに仕方がなかった.

★**notice**¹ /nóʊtɪs/ 名 ▶定義 1 Ⓤ the act of paying attention to sth or knowing about sth 〜に注意を向ける行為, 〜について知る行為➔注目, 注意, 観察 ‖ *The protests are finally making the government **take notice**.* その抗議は, ようやく政府の注意をひきつつある. ***Take no notice of** what he said - he was just being silly.* 彼が言った事に気を留めるな ー ばかげた事を言っていただけだ. *Some people don't take any notice of (= choose to ignore) speed limits.* 制限速度に全く注意を払わない (= 無視することに決める) 人たちもいる. *It has **come to** my **notice** that you have missed a lot of classes.* あなたが多くの授業に欠席していることを知りました. ▶定義 2 Ⓒ a piece of paper or a sign giving information, a warning, etc that is put where everyone can read it 情報や警告などを伝える1枚の紙または標識で, だれもが読めるところに掲示されている➔掲示(板), 告示, 公告, 看板 ‖ *There's a notice on the board saying that the meeting has been cancelled.* 会議が中止になったと掲示板に出ている. *The notice said 'No dogs allowed'.* 掲示には「犬お断り」と書かれていた. ▶定義 3 Ⓤ a warning that sth is going to happen 〜がこれか

ら起こるという注意➔**通知, 通達, 警告, 予告** ‖ *I can't produce a meal **at such short notice**!* そんなに急に言われても食事の支度はできない. *I wish you'd **give** me more **notice** when you're going to be off work.* あなたがいつ休暇を取るつもりか, 前もって知らせていただければと思います. *The swimming pool is closed **until further notice** (= until we are told that it will open again).* 水泳プールは, 追って通知があるまでは(= 再開を知らされるまでは)閉鎖される.

\***notice**² /nóʊtəs/ 動 自 他 (通常は進行形は不可) ▶定義 to see and become conscious of sth ~を見分け, 気が付く➔**(〜に)気が付く, (〜に)注意する** ‖ *'What kind of car was the man driving?' 'I'm afraid I didn't notice.'* 「その男はどんな車を運転していましたか」「残念ながら, 気が付きませんでした」 *I noticed (that) he was carrying a black briefcase.* 彼が黒い書類かばんを持っていたことに気が付いた. *Did you notice which direction she went in?* 彼女がどの方向に行ったのか, 分かりますか. *We didn't notice him leave/him leaving.* 私たちは彼が立ち去るのに気付かなかった.

**noticeable** /nóʊtəsəb(ə)l/ 形 ▶定義 easy to see or notice 容易に分かる, 容易に気が付く➔**人目をひく, 目立つ** ‖ *The scar from the accident was hardly noticeable.* 事故による傷跡は, ほとんど目立たなかった. —**noticeably** /-əb(ə)li/ 副➔**目立って, 著しく**

**noticeboard** /nóʊtəsbɔ̀ːrd/ (米 **bulletin board**) 名 C ▶定義 a board on a wall for putting written information where everyone can read it 書面で情報を掲示するために壁に設置された板で, だれもが見られる場所に置かれる➔**掲示板** ☛ S4ページのさし絵

**notify** /nóʊtəfàɪ/ 動 他 (現分 **notifying**; 三単現 **notifies**; 過, 過分 **notified**) ▶定義 notify sb (of sth) to inform sb about sth officially 〜について…に公式に知らせる➔**(人が)〜に通知する, 〜に通告する, 〜を発表・公示・掲示する** —**notification** /nòʊtəfəkéɪʃ(ə)n/ 名 C U➔**通知, 届け, 公告文**

**notion** /nóʊʃ(ə)n/ 名 C ▶定義 a notion (that.../ of sth) something that you have in your mind; an idea 心に抱いているもの; 考え➔**(〜についての・〜という)概念, 考え, 観念** ‖ *I had a vague notion that I had seen her before.* はっきりしないが, 彼女を以前見たような気がした.

**notional** /nóʊʃ(ə)n(ə)l/ 形 ▶定義 existing only in the mind; not based on facts or reality 心の中だけに存在する; 事実・現実に基づいていない➔**(知識などが)観念的な, 概念上の, (実験によらない)純理論的な**

**notoriety** /nòʊtəráɪəti/ 名 U ▶定義 the state of being well-known for sth bad 〜が悪いことで知られている状態➔**悪名, 悪評**

**notorious** /noʊtɔ́ːriəs, nə-/ 形 ▶定義 notorious (for/as sth) well-known for sth bad 〜が悪いことで知られている➔**(通常けなして)よく知られた, 悪名高い, 悪評の高い** ‖ *a notorious drug dealer* 悪名高い麻薬の売人 *This road is notorious for the number of accidents on it.* この道路は事故の件数で知られている. ☛類 **infamous** —**notoriously** 副➔**悪名高く, 周知のこととして**

**notwithstanding** /nɑ̀twɪðstǽndɪŋ, -wɪθ-/ 前 副 (文) ▶定義 in spite of sth 〜にもかかわらず➔**〜にもかかわらず, それにもかかわらず**

\***nought** /nɔːt/ (特に 米 **zero**) 名 C ▶定義 the figure 0 数字の 0➔**(数字の)0, ゼロ** ‖ *A million is written with six noughts.* 百万は, ゼロが 6 つ付く. *We say 0.1 'nought point one'.* 0.1 のことは, 「ゼロポイントワン」と読む.

**noughts and crosses**

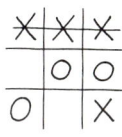

成句 **noughts and crosses** ▶定義 a game for two players in which each person tries to win by writing three 0s or three Xs in a line. 2人で行うゲームで, それぞれが○または×を3つ並ぶように書いていくことで勝ち負けを競う➔**○×遊び, 三目並べ**

\***noun** /naʊn/ 名 C (文法) ▶定義 a word that is the name of a thing, an idea, a place or a person 物, 概念, 場所, 人の名前を表す語➔**名詞** ‖ *'James', 'water', 'happiness' and 'France' are all nouns.* 「ジェームズ」, 「水」, 「幸福」, 「フランス」はすべて名詞です. ☛参 **countable, uncountable**

**nourish** /nə́ːrɪʃ, nʌ́r-/ 動 他 ▶定義 **1** to give sb/sth the right kind of food so that he/she/it can grow and be healthy 〜に適切な食物を与え, 成長させて健康な状態にする➔**(食物・栄養分を与えて)〜を養う, 〜を育てる** ▶定義 **2** 正式 to allow a feeling, an idea, etc to grow stronger 感情や考えがさらに強くなっていくに任せる→(感情・希望などを)抱く, はぐくむ— **nourishment** 名 ⓒ→食物, 栄養, 滋養

**Nov** 略 November→**11月** ‖ *17 Nov 2001* 2001年11月17日

★**novel**¹ /nάv(ə)l/ 名 ⓒ ▶定義 a book that tells a story about people and events that are not real 人や出来事についての本当の事ではない物語を語る本→(長編)小説 ‖ *a romantic/historical/detective novel* 恋愛・歴史・推理小説

**novel**² /nάv(ə)l/ 形 ▶定義 new and different 新しく独特な→目新しい, 新奇な, 斬新(ざんしん)な ‖ *That's a novel idea! Let's try it.* それは斬新なアイデアだ. やってみよう.

**novelist** /nάv(ə)list/ 名 ⓒ ▶定義 a person who writes novels 小説を書く人→小説家

**novelty** /nάv(ə)ləti/ 名 ( 複 **novelties**) ▶定義 **1** ⓤ the quality of being new and different 新しく独特なこと→目新しいこと, 斬新(ざんしん)さ, 新奇さ ‖ *The novelty of her new job soon wore off.* 彼女の新しい仕事の新鮮味はすぐに薄れてしまった. ▶定義 **2** ⓒ something new and unusual 新しく珍しいもの→新しいもの, 珍しい経験 ‖ *It was quite a novelty not to have to get up early.* 早起きをする必要がないというのは, 全く新しい経験だった. ▶定義 **3** ⓒ a small, cheap object that is sold as a toy or decoration おもちゃや装飾物として売られている, 小さくて安価なもの→(プレゼントとしての安い・珍しい)商品, 新案の商品

★**November** /noυvémbər, nə-/ 名 ⓤ ⓒ ( 略 **Nov**) ▶定義 the eleventh month of the year, coming after October 10月の次に来る1年の11番目の月→**11月**

▶ 文中での月の表し方については, January の例と注を参照.

**novice** /nάvəs/ 名 ⓒ ▶定義 a person who is new and without experience in a certain job, situation, etc; a beginner ある仕事・状況などに初めてで経験のない人; 初心者→初心者, 駆け出し, 新人

★**now** /nάυ/ 副 接 ▶定義 **1** (at) the present time 現在(は)→今, 現在(では) ‖ *We can't go for a walk now - it's raining.* 私たちは今散歩に行けません－雨が降っています. *Where are you living now?* 現在はどこに住んでいるのですか. *From now on I'm going to work harder.* これからはもっと一生懸命働きます. *Up till now we haven't been able to afford a house of our own.* 今までは自分の家を買う余裕がなかった. *He will be on his way home by now.* 彼は, 今ごろはもう帰宅途中だろう. *I can manage for now but I might need some help later.* 差し当たってはどうにかやっていけるが, 後で助けが必要になるかもしれない. ▶定義 **2** immediately すぐに→今すぐ, 直ちに ‖ *Go now before anyone sees you.* だれかに見られる前に, すぐに立ち去りなさい. *You must go to the doctor right now.* 直ちに医者に行く必要がある. ▶定義 **3** used to introduce or to emphasize what you are saying, or while pausing to think 話題になる事の前置きとして, またはそれを強調するために用いて, または考えるために少し間をおく場合に用いて→さて, ところで, さあ ‖ *Now listen to what he's saying.* さあ, 彼の発言を聞きましょう. *What does he want now?* 彼は今何が欲しいのかな. *Now, let me think.* えーと, 考えさせて.

➤ **now then** もまた用いられる: *Now then, what was I saying?* (さて, 私は何を言っていたのでしたっけ.)

▶定義 **4** now (that)... because of the fact that ～の理由で→今はもう～だから, ～する今となっては, ～するからには ‖ *Now (that) the children have left home we can move to a smaller house.* 今はもう子供たちも家を離れたので, もっと小さい家に移れます.

成句 any moment/second/minute/day (now) ⇒ **ANY**

(every) now and again/then ▶定義 from time to time; occasionally →時々, 時折 ‖ *We see each other now and then, but not very often.* 我々はお互いに時々会うが, あまり頻繁ではない.

just now ⇒ **JUST**¹

right now ⇒ **RIGHT**²

**nowadays** /nάυ(ə)dèiz/ 副 ▶定義 at the present time (when compared with the past) 現在は(過去と比較して)→今日では, 近ごろは ‖ *I don't go to London much nowadays (= but I did in the past).* 近ごろはあまりロンドンには行かない(＝しかし, 過去はよく行っていた). ☛類 **today**

★**nowhere** /nάυ(h)wèər/ 副 ▶定義 not in or to any place; not anywhere →どこにも～ない, どこへも～ない; どこにもない ‖ *I'm afraid there's nowhere to stay in this village.* この村には, どこ

にも宿泊できる所がないのではと思う. *I don't like it here, but there's **nowhere else** for us to sit.* ここは嫌だけれど, ほかに座る所はない.
成句 **get nowhere (with sth)** ▶定義 to not make any progress with sth ～に進展がない→うまくいかない, 成功しない
**in the middle of nowhere** ⇒ **MIDDLE**¹
**nowhere near** ⇒ **NEAR**¹

**noxious** /nákʃəs/ 形正式 ▶定義 harmful or poisonous 有害な, 有毒な→有害な, 有毒の ‖ *noxious gases* 有毒ガス

**nozzle** /názəl/ 名 C ▶定義 a narrow tube that is put on the end of a pipe to control the liquid or gas coming out 管の先端に付ける細いチューブで, 液体やガスの出を抑える→(ホースなどの)ノズル, 噴射口

**nr** 略 (used in addresses) (住所表記に用いられる) near→(手紙のあて名などに用いて)近く ‖ *Masham, nr Ripon* マシャム, リペン近く

**nuance** /n(j)úːɑːns, n(j)uɑ́ːns/ 名 C ▶定義 a very small difference in meaning, feeling, sound, etc 意味・感情・音などのかすかな違い→(意味・色・感情・音などの)微妙な違い, ニュアンス, 陰影

*****nuclear** /n(j)úːkliər/ 形 ▶定義 **1** using, producing or resulting from the energy that is produced when the central part (nucleus) of an atom is split 原子の中心部分(原子核)が分裂する際に生じるエネルギーを用いる・を作り出す・の結果の→**原子核の, 核による, 原子力の, 核エネルギーの** ‖ *nuclear energy* 原子力 *a nuclear power station* 原子力発電所 *nuclear war/weapons* 核戦争・核兵器 ☞参 **atomic** ▶定義 **2** connected with the nucleus of an atom 原子核に関する→核の, 原子核の ‖ *nuclear physics* 原子物理学

**nuclear reactor**(または **reactor**)名 C ▶定義 a very large machine that produces nuclear energy 原子力を作り出す, 非常に大型の機械→原子炉

**nucleus** /n(j)úːkliəs/ 名 C (複 **nuclei** /-kliàɪ/) ▶定義 **1** the central part of an atom or of certain cells 原子の中心部分, 特定の細胞の中心部分→原子核, 細胞核 ▶定義 **2** the central or most important part of sth ～の中心部分, 最重要部分→中核, 中心, 核心

**nude**¹ /n(j)uːd/ 形 ▶定義 not wearing any clothes 何も衣服を身に着けていない→裸の, 裸体の, ヌードの ☞参 **bare**, **naked** — **nudity** /n(j)úːdəti/

# number¹ 1115

名 U →裸, 裸であること ‖ *This film contains scenes of nudity.* この映画には裸の場面があります.

**nude**² /n(j)uːd/ 名 C ▶定義 a picture or photograph of a person who is not wearing any clothes 何も衣服を身に着けていない人の絵, 写真→(絵画・写真などの)裸体像, 裸体画, ヌード写真
成句 **in the nude** ▶定義 not wearing any clothes 何も衣服を身に着けていない→裸体の, 裸体で

**nudge** /nʌdʒ/ 動 他 ▶定義 to touch or push sb/sth with your elbow ～をひじで軽く打つ, 押す→(注意をひくために)人をひじで軽くつつく, 人を(ひじで)押しのける ☜ S6 ページのさし絵 — **nudge** 名 C →ひじで軽くつつくこと, 軽い一突き ‖ *to give sb a nudge* ～をひじで軽くつつく

**nuisance** /n(j)úːsəns/ 名 C ▶定義 a person, thing or situation that annoys you or causes you trouble いら立たせる, または迷惑を掛ける人・物事・状況→迷惑な人・物, 厄介な人・物 ‖ *It's a nuisance having to queue for everything.* あらゆる事に列を作らなければならないなんて面倒だ.

**numb** /nʌm/ 形 ▶定義 not able to feel anything; not able to move 感覚がない; 動かせない→(～で)まひした, しびれた ‖ *My fingers were numb with cold.* 寒さで指がかじかんでいた. *I'll give you an injection and the tooth will **go numb**.* 注射をしてあげましょう, そうすれば歯の感覚がなくなるでしょう. — **numb** 動 他 →～をまひさせる, ～をしびれさせる, ～をぼう然とさせる ‖ *We were numbed by the dreadful news.* 私たちはその恐ろしいニュースにぼう然となった. — **numbness** 名 U →無感覚, まひ, しびれ

*****number**¹ /nʌ́mbər/ 名 C ▶定義 **1** ⓐ a word or symbol that indicates a quantity 数量を表す語・記号→**数, 数字, 数詞** ‖ *Choose a number between ten and twenty.* 10と20の間から数を選びなさい. *2, 4, 6, etc are **even numbers** and 1, 3, 5, etc are **odd numbers**.* 2, 4, 6などは偶数で, 1, 3, 5などは奇数だ. *a three-figure number (= from 100 to 999)* 3けたの数字(=100から999まで) ▶定義 **2** ⓐ a group of numbers that is used to identify sb/sth ～を識別するために使われる, 一連の数字→(電話・部屋・家の)番号 ‖ *a telephone number* 電話番号 *a code number* コ

## 1116　number²

ード番号　▶定義3 ◉ ⓤ a number (of sth) a quantity of people or things 人・物の数量→(〜の)数量,総数 ‖ *a large number of visitors* 大勢の観光客 *We must reduce the number of accidents on the roads.* 交通事故の件数を減らさなくてはならない. *Pupils in the school have doubled* **in number** *in recent years.* ここ数年で,その学校の生徒数は倍増した. *There are* ***a number of*** *(= several) things I don't understand.* 私には理解できない事がいくつかある. ▶定義4 ◉ (略 **No; no**) used before a number to show the position of sth in a series 一連の中での位置を示す番号の前に用いて→〜番 ‖ *We live in Hazel Road, at number 21.* 私たちは,ヘイゼル ロード21番に住んでいる. *room No 347* 347号室 ▶定義5 ◉ a copy of a magazine, newspaper, etc 雑誌・新聞などの一冊→(雑誌などの)号数,〜号 ‖ *Back numbers of 'New Scientist' are available from the publishers.* 『ニューサイエンティスト』のバックナンバーは,出版社で入手できる. ▶定義6 ◉略式 a song or dance 歌, 踊り→曲目, 出し物

慣句 **any number of** ▶定義 very many 非常に多くの→たくさんの〜, (〜は)いくつでも ‖ *There could be any number of reasons why she hasn't arrived yet.* 彼女がまだ到着していない理由は, いくらでもあり得ます.

**in round fingers/numbers** ⇒ **ROUND¹**
**opposite number** ⇒ **OPPOSITE**

**number²** /ˈnʌmbər/ 動 他 ▶定義1 to give a number to sth →〜に番号を付ける ‖ *The houses are numbered from 1 to 52.* 家には1番から52番までの番号が付けられている. ▶定義2 used for saying how many people or things there are 何人の人がいるかを表す場合や, 何個のものがあるかを表す場合に用いて→〜の数に達する, 総計〜になる ‖ *Our forces number 40000.* 我々の部隊は, 総勢4万人に達する.

**number plate** (米 **license plate**) 名 ◉ ▶定義 the sign on the front and back of a vehicle that shows a particular combination of numbers and letters (**the registration number**) 自動車の前後に付いている標識で, 数字と文字の特定の組み合わせ(自動車登録番号)を表示する→(自動車の)ナンバープレート

**numeral** /ˈn(j)uːm(ə)rəl/ 名 ◉ ▶定義 a sign or symbol that represents a quantity 数量を表す記号・符号→**数字, 数詞** ‖ *Roman numerals (= I, II, III, IV, etc)* ローマ数字(= Ⅰ, Ⅱ, Ⅲ, Ⅳ, など)

**numerate** /ˈn(j)uːm(ə)rèɪt/ 形 ▶定義 having a good basic knowledge of mathematics 数学の基本知識に秀でている→**数学の基礎知識がある, 算数ができる** ☞参 **literate**

**numerical** /n(j)uˈmerɪk(ə)l/ 形 ▶定義 of or shown by numbers 数字の, 数字で表した→**数の, 数字で表した** ‖ *to put sth* ***in numerical order*** 〜を番号順に置く

**numerous** /ˈn(j)uːm(ə)rəs/ 形 正式 ▶定義 existing in large numbers; many 多数存在する; 多くの→**多数の, たくさんの, 非常に多い**

**nun** /nʌn/ 名 ◉ ▶定義 a member of a religious group of women who live together in a special building (**a convent**) away from other people 女性だけの宗教団体の一員で, ほかの人々から離れて特別な建物(女子修道院)で共同生活を行う人→**修道女, 尼僧** ☞参 **monk**

★**nurse¹** /nəːrs/ 名 ◉ ▶定義 a person who is trained to look after sick or injured people 病人やけが人の看護をするための訓練を受けた人→**看護婦, 看護する人** ‖ *a male nurse* 看護士 *a psychiatric nurse* 精神科の看護婦

▶ community/district nurse (地区担当訪問看護婦)は, 在宅の病人を訪問し必要な看護を行う. health visitor (訪問保健婦)は, 赤ん坊や幼い子供のいる両親に援助と助言を与える看護婦である. midwife (助産婦)は女性の出産を助ける.

**nurse²** /nəːrs/ 動 ▶定義1 他 to take care of sb who is sick or injured; to take care of an injury 病気や負傷した〜の看護をする; けがの手当てをする→(病人・けが人を)**看護する, (病気・けがなど)の治療に努める** ‖ *She nursed her mother back to health.* 彼女は母親が健康を回復するまで看病した. *Ahmed is still nursing a back injury.* アーメッドはまだ背中のけがの治療中だ. ▶定義2 他 to hold sb/sth in a loving way 愛情一杯に〜を抱く→(愛情を込めて)〜を抱き締める, 〜をかわいがる ‖ *He nursed the child in his arms.* 彼は子供を腕に抱き締めた. ▶定義3 他 正式 to have a strong feeling or idea in your mind for a long time 長い間強い感情や考えを心に抱く→(計画・悪意など)を心に抱く, 〜をはぐ

くむ ‖ *Tim had long nursed the hope that Sharon would marry him.* ティムは,シャロンが結婚してくれるという希望を長い間心に抱いていた. ▶定義4 ⓔto feed a baby or young animal with milk from the breast; to drink milk from the mother's breast 人間・動物の赤ん坊にお乳を上げる; 母乳を飲む→(赤ん坊に)乳をやる,授乳する; 乳を飲む

**nursery** /nə́ːrs(ə)ri/ 图 ⓒ (複 **nurseries**) ▶定義1 a place where small children and babies are looked after so that their parents can go to work 両親が仕事に行けるように,赤ん坊や幼い子供の面倒を見る所→保育所,託児所 ☞参 **creche** ▶定義2 a place where young plants are grown and sold 植物の苗を育て,販売する所→苗床,養樹園,(種苗・苗木を育てて売る)園芸店

**nursery rhyme** 图 ⓒ ▶定義 a traditional poem or song for young children 幼い子供たちのための,伝承の詩や歌→(伝承の)童謡,童歌

**nursery school** (または **playground**; **playschool**) 图 ⓒ ▶定義 a school for children aged from three to five 3歳から5歳の子供たちのための学校→(5歳以下の幼児の)保育所[園] ☞参 **kindergarten**

**nursing** /nə́ːrsiŋ/ 图 ⓤ ▶定義 the job of being a nurse 看護婦としての仕事→看護,介護

**nursing home** 图 ⓒ ▶定義 a small private hospital, often for old people 小さな私立病院で,老人のためのものが多い→(私立の)養護施設,老人ホーム

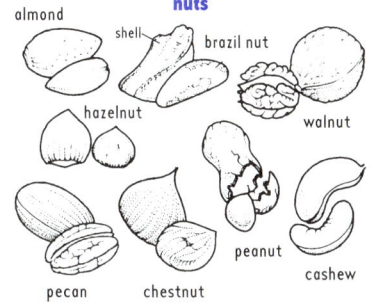

**nuts**
almond, shell, brazil nut, hazelnut, walnut, pecan, peanut, chestnut, cashew

***nut** /nʌt/ 图 ⓒ ▶定義1 a dry fruit that consists of a hard shell with a seed inside. Many types of nut can be eaten. 堅い殻に覆われていて中に種子がある乾果. 木の実の多くの種類は食べられる→木の実,堅果,ナッツ ▶定義2 a small piece of metal with a round hole in the middle through which you screw a long round piece of metal (a bolt) to fasten things together 小さな金属製のもので真ん中に穴が開いており,そこに長い円筒形の金属(ボルト)を通してねじで留め,物を固定する→ナット,留めねじ ☞**bolt**のさし絵

**nutcrackers** /nʌ́tkrækərz/ [複数扱い] ▶定義 a tool that you use for breaking open the shell of a nut 木の実の殻を割って開けるために用いる道具→くるみ割り器

**nutmeg** /nʌ́tmèg/ 图 ⓒ ⓤ ▶定義 a type of hard seed that is often made into powder and used as a spice in cooking 堅い実の一種で,よく粉末にして料理の香辛料として用いられる→ナツメグ,ニクズク(の種子)

**nutrition** /n(j)uːtríʃ(ə)n/ 图 ⓤ ▶定義 the food that you eat and the way that it affects your health 摂取する食物とそれが健康に与える影響→栄養の摂取,栄養学 ‖ *Good nutrition is essential for children's growth.* 適切な栄養の摂取は,子供の発育に不可欠である.—**nutritional** 形→栄養の,栄養上の,栄養に関する

**nutritious** /n(j)uːtríʃəs/ 形 ▶定義 (used about a food) very good for you (食べ物について)非常に健康に良い→栄養のある,滋養に富んだ

**nutshell** /nʌ́tʃèl/ 图
成句 **in a nutshell** ▶定義 using few words ほんのわずかの言葉を用いて→一言で言えば,要するに

**nutty** /nʌ́ti/ 形 ▶定義 containing or tasting of nuts 木の実が含まれている,木の実の味がする→木の実の味のする,木の実入りの

**nuzzle** /nʌ́z(ə)l/ 動 ⓗ ⓘ ▶定義 to press or rub sb/sth gently with the nose 〜に鼻を優しく押し付ける,鼻で優しくこする→(犬・馬などが)〜に鼻を擦り寄せる,押し付ける

**NW** 略 north-west(ern)→北西,北西部,北西地方 ‖ *NW Australia* オーストラリア北西部

**nylon** /náilɑn, -lən/ 图 ⓤ ▶定義 a very strong man-made material that is used for making clothes, rope, brushes, etc 非常に強固な合成素材で,布・縄・ブラシなどを作るのに用いる→ナイロン

# O o

**0, o** /óʊ/ 名 C (複 **0's; o's**) ▶定義1 the fifteenth letter of the English alphabet 英語アルファベットの第15文字→o(O)が表す音, o(O)の文字, o(O)の字形のもの ‖ *'Orange' begins with (an) 'O'.* Orange は O で始まる. ▶定義2 (used when you are speaking) zero (話しているときに用いて)(アラビア数字の)零→ゼロ, オー, マル ‖ *My number is five O nine double four (=50944).* 私の番号はファイブ オー ナイン ダブルフォー (=50944)です. ☞参 **zero** の注

**oak** /óʊk/ ▶定義1 (または **oak tree**) C a type of large tree with hard wood that is common in many northern parts of the world 世界の北部地方で見られる堅い大木の一種→ブナ科ナラ属の木の総称, オーク(の木) ▶定義2 U the wood from the oak tree オークの木からとった材木→オーク材 ‖ *a solid oak table* 堅いオーク材製の机 ▶オークの実は acorn (どんぐり).

**OAP** /óʊ eɪ píː/ 略 医 old-age pensioner→老齢年金受給者

**oar** /ɔ́ːr/ 名 C ▶定義 a long pole that is flat and wide at one end and that you use for moving a small boat through water (rowing) 先が平たい長い棒状の道具で, 手に持って水をかいて船を動かす(こぐ)→オール ☞参 **paddle**

**oasis** /oʊéɪsəs/ 名 C (複 **oases** / -sìːz/) ▶定義 a place in the desert where there is water and where plants grow 砂漠の中で水がわき出ている緑地→オアシス

**oath** /óʊθ/ 名 C ▶定義1 a formal promise 公式の約束→誓約 ‖ *They have to swear/take an oath of loyalty.* 彼らは忠誠を誓わなくてはならない. ▶定義2 (古) = **SWEAR WORD**
成句 **be on/under oath** ▶定義 to have made a formal promise to tell the truth in a court of law 法廷において真実を述べることを公式に約束する→宣誓する

**oats** /óʊts/ 名 [複数扱い] ▶定義 a type of grain that is used as food for people and animals 人や動物の食糧として用いられる穀物の一種→カラスムギ, オートムギ ☞ **cereal** のさし絵

**obedient** /oʊbíːdiənt, ə-/ 形 ▶定義 obedient (to sb/sth) doing what you are told to do 〜に言われた事に従う→従順な, 素直な ‖ *As a child he was always obedient to his parents.* 小さいころ, 彼は両親の言うことをよく聞く子供だった. ⇔ **disobedient** — **obedience** 名 U→従順, 服従 — **obediently** 副→従順に, 素直に

**obese** /oʊbíːs/ 形 ▶定義 (used about people) very fat, in a way that is not healthy (人について)不健康にとても太った→肥満した, 太りすぎの — **obesity** /oʊbíːsəti/ 名 U→肥満

*\***obey** /oʊbéɪ, ə-/ 動 自他 ▶定義 to do what you are told to do 言い付けに従う→〜に服従する, 従う ‖ *Soldiers are trained to obey orders.* 兵士は命令に従うように訓練される. ⇔ **disobey**

**obituary** /əbítʃuəri, oʊ-, -tʃəri; -tʃuèri/ 名 C (複 **obituaries**) ▶定義 a piece of writing about a person's life that is printed in a newspaper soon after he/she has died 新聞に印刷される死者に関する記事→死亡記事

*\***object**¹ /ábdʒɪkt/ 名 C ▶定義1 a thing that can be seen and touched, but is not alive 見たり触ったりできるが生きていない物体→物, 物体 ‖ *The shelves were filled with objects of all shapes and sizes.* その棚はあらゆる形と大きさの物で一杯だった. *everyday/household objects* 日常生活用品・家庭用品 ▶定義2 an aim or purpose 目的や目標→目的, 目標 ‖ *Making money is his sole object in life.* お金をもうけることが彼の人生の唯一の目的である. ▶定義3 **the object of sth** a person or thing that causes a feeling, interest, thought, etc 感情, 興味, 思考などを引き起こす対象物となる人または物→対象, 的 ‖ *the object of his desire/affections/interest* 彼の願望・愛情・興味の対象 ▶定義4 (文法) the noun or phrase describing the person or thing that is affected by the action of a verb 動詞の表す動作によって作用される人・物を説明する名詞・句→目的語

▶ *I sent a letter to Meera/I sent Meera a letter* (私はメーラに手紙を送った)という文において, a letter (手紙) は動詞の direct object (直接目的語) に, Meera (メーラ) は indirect object (間接目的語) なる.
☞参 **subject**

成句 **money, etc is no object** ▶定義 money, etc is not important or is no problem お金などは重要でない, 問題ではない→お金などは問題ではない ‖ *They always want the best. Expense is* *no object.* 彼らはいつも最高のものを求めている. 費用は問わない.

**object**[2] /əbdʒékt, ɑb-/ 動 ▶定義 **1** ⓑ object (to sb/sth); object (to doing sth/to sb doing sth) to not like or to be against sb/sth ～に反対する;(～をする・～が…をするのに)反対する; ～に反感を持つ, 反対する→**反対する, 反感を持つ** ‖ *Many people object to the new tax.* 多くの人々が新しい税金に反対している. *I object to companies trying to sell me things over the phone.* 私は電話で物を売り付けようとする会社は嫌いだ. ▶定義 **2** ⓑ to say a reason why you think sth is wrong ～がどうして悪いと考えるかの反対理由を述べる→**～に異議を唱える, 抗議する** ‖ *'I think that's unfair,' he objected.* 「それは不公平だと思う」と彼は異議を唱えた. ― objector 名 ⓒ →**反対者**

**objection** /əbdʒékʃ(ə)n/ 名 ⓒ ▶定義 an objection (to sb/sth); an objection (to doing sth/to sb doing sth) a reason why you do not like or are against sb/sth ～への反対;(～をする・～に…をすることへの)反対, ～に対して好きでないあるいは反対する理由→**反対, 異議, 嫌気** ‖ *We listed our objections to the proposed new road.* 我々は新しく提案された道路に対する反対理由を列記した. *I have no objection to you using my desk while I'm away.* 私がいない間, あなたが私の机を使うことに何の異論もありません.

**objectionable** /əbdʒékʃ(ə)nəb(ə)l/ 形 ▶定義 very unpleasant とても不愉快な, 反対すべき→**気に入らない, 不愉快な, 異議のある**

**objective**[1] /əbdʒéktɪv, ɑb-/ 名 ⓒ ▶定義 something that you are trying to achieve; an aim 自分の達成しようとする事柄; 目標→**目標; 目的** ‖ *Our objective is to finish by the end of the year.* 我々の目標は年末までに終わることだ. *to achieve your objective* あなたの目標を達成する

**objective**[2] /əbdʒéktɪv, ɑb-/ 形 ▶定義 not influenced by your own personal feelings; considering only facts 自分の個人的な感情に影響されない;事実のみを考慮して→**客観的な, 事実に基づく** ‖ *Please try and give an objective report of what happened.* 何が起こったか, 先入観のない報告をお願いします. *It's hard to be objective about your own family.* 自分の家族に関しては客観的になるのが難しい. ⇔ **subjective** ― objectively 副 →**客観的に, 客観的に言って** ‖ *He is too* upset to see things objectively. 彼は非常に怒っていて物事を客観的に見ることができない. ― objectivity /ὰbdʒèktívəti/ 名 ⓤ →**客観性, 客観的実在, 客観主義**

**obligation** /ὰbləgéɪʃ(ə)n/ 名 ⓒⓤ ▶定義 (an) obligation (to sb) (to do sth) the state of having to do sth because it is a law or duty, or because you have promised ～への…をする義務, 法律または義務によって, または自分が約束したことによって, 何かをしなくてはならない状態→**義務, 責任** ‖ *Unfortunately the shop is* ***under*** *no* ***obligation*** *to give you your money back.* 残念ですが, その店はあなたに返金する義務はないのです. *We* ***have an obligation*** *to help people who are in need.* 我々は助けが必要な人を助ける義務があります. *By refusing to examine the animal, the vet failed to fulfil his professional obligations.* 獣医は動物の診察を拒否し, 自分の職業を全うする義務をおこたった.

**obligatory** /əblígət(ə)ri, ɑb-; əblígətɔ̀:ri/ 形 正式 ▶定義 that you must do しなければならない→**義務的な, 強制的な** ‖ *It is obligatory to get insurance before you drive a car.* 車を運転する前に保険に入るのは義務です. ⇔ **optional**

**obliterate** /əblítərèɪt/ 動 ⓑ 正式 ▶定義 (しばしば 受 動 態 で) to remove all signs of sth by destroying or covering it completely 完全に破壊または隠すことによって～のすべての形跡を取り除く→**(～の)痕跡(こんせき)を消す, ～を抹殺する, 消滅させる**

**oblivion** /əblíviən/ 名 ⓤ ▶定義 **1** a state in which you do not realize what is happening around you, usually because you are unconscious or asleep 無意識でいるかまたは眠っているために, 自分の周りで何が起こっているか理解できない状態→**無意識状態, 人事不省** ‖ *I was in a state of complete oblivion.* 私は全く何も分からない状態でした. ▶定義 **2** the state in which sb/sth has been forgotten and is no longer famous or important ～が忘れられてしまい, もう有名でもあるいは重要でもない状態→**忘れられること, 忘却** ‖ *His work faded into oblivion after his death.* 彼の作品は彼の死後忘れ去られてしまった.

**oblivious** /əblíviəs/ 形 ▶定義 oblivious (to/of

sb/sth) not noticing or realizing what is happening around you 自分の周りで(〜に)何が起こっているか気付かない、または理解できない→気が付かないで,念頭にない,忘れっぽい ‖ *She was completely oblivious of all the trouble she had caused.* 彼女は自分の引き起こしたもめ事など全く念頭になかった.

**oblong** /άblɔ(:)ŋ, -lὰŋ/ 形名 ⓒ ▶定義 (of) a shape with two long sides and two short sides and four angles of 90˚ (right angles) 2つの長い辺と2つの短い辺から成り,4つの角度がそれぞれ直角の形(の) → 長方形(の) ☞類 **rectangle**

**obnoxious** /əbnάkʃəs, ab-/ 形 ▶定義 extremely unpleasant, especially in a way that offends people 特に人が腹を立てるほど,非常に不愉快な →嫌な,不快な,気に障る,嫌われている,悪評の

**oboe** /óubou/ 名 ⓒ ▶定義 a musical instrument made of wood that you play by blowing through it 息を吹いて音を出す木製の楽器→オーボエ ☞参 **piano** の注 ☞**music** のさし絵

**obscene** /əbsíːn, ab-/ 形 ▶定義 1 connected with sex in a way that most people find disgusting and which causes offence 性に関連して、ほとんどの人が嫌悪感・不快感を催すような→わいせつな,卑わいな ‖ *obscene books/gestures/language* わいせつな本・身振り・言葉 ▶定義 2 very large in size or amount in a way that some people find unacceptable 人がうんざりするほど大きなまたは多くの→いまいましいほどの ‖ *He earns an obscene amount of money.* 彼はいまいましいほどお金を稼ぐ.

**obscenity** /əbsénəti, -síː-, ab-/ 名 (複 **obscenities**) ▶定義 1 ⓒ sexual words or acts that shock people and cause offence 人にショックを与え感情を害させる具体的な性的言葉・行為→卑わいな言葉,わいせつ行為 ‖ *He shouted a string of obscenities out of the car window.* 彼は車の窓から卑わいな言葉を続けて叫んだ. ▶定義 2 Ⓤ sexual language or behaviour, especially in books, plays, etc which shocks people and causes offence 特に本,演劇などの性的言葉や行為で人にショックを与え感情を害させるもの→卑わいさ,わいせつ

**obscure**[1] /əbskjúər, ab-/ 形 ▶定義 1 not well-known よく知られていない→世に知られていない,無名の ‖ *an obscure Spanish poet* あまり知られていないスペインの詩人 ▶定義 2 not easy to see or understand 見づらい,理解しづらい→不明瞭(めいりょう)な,あいまいな,分かりにくい ‖ *For some obscure reason, he decided to give up his well-paid job, to become a writer.* はっきりしない理由で,彼は給料のいい仕事をやめて作家になることに決めた. — **obscurity** /əbskjúərəti, ab-/ 名 Ⓤ→不明瞭,あいまい,無名

**obscure**[2] /əbskjúər, ab-/ 動 他 ▶定義 to make sth difficult to see or understand 〜を見たり理解することを難しくする→〜を不明瞭(めいりょう)にする,分かりにくくする ‖ *A high fence obscured our view.* 高いフェンスで視界が遮られた.

**observance** /əbzə́ːrv(ə)ns/ 名 [Ⓤ, 単数扱い] ▶定義 observance (of sth) the practice of obeying or following a law, custom, etc 法律,習慣などに従うあるいは守ること→遵守

**observant** /əbzə́ːrv(ə)nt/ 形 ▶定義 good at noticing things around you 自分の周りの事をよく注意することに得意で→観察の鋭い,注意深い,よく気が付く ‖ *An observant passer-by gave the police a full description of the men.* 観察力のある通行人が警察にその男たちの様子を詳しく話した.

**observation** /ὰbzərvéiʃ(ə)n, -sər-/ 名 ▶定義 1 Ⓤ the act of watching sb/sth carefully, especially to learn sth 特に〜を学ぶのに,…を注意深く見る行為→観察,観測 ‖ *My research involves the observation of animals in their natural surroundings.* 私の研究は自然のままの動物の観察に関するものだ. *The patient is being kept under observation.* 患者は監視下に置かれている. ▶定義 2 Ⓤ the ability to notice things 物事に気付く能力→観察力 ‖ *Scientists need good powers of observation.* 科学者たちは鋭い観察力を必要とする. ▶定義 3 ⓒ an observation (about/on sth) something that you say or write about sth 〜について自分が言ったり書いたりするもの→観察報告,資料,記録 ‖ *He began by making a few general observations about the sales figures.* 彼は売り上げ数字についての総括的報告を書くところから始めた. ☞参 **remark, comment**. これらの単語はより一般的.

**observatory** /əbzə́ːrvət(ə)ri; -tə̀ːri/ 名 ⓒ (複 **observatories**) ▶定義 a building from which scientists can watch the stars, the weather, etc 科学者が星や天気を観察する建物➡観測所, 天文台, 気象台

\***observe** /əbzə́ːrv/ 動他 ▶定義1 to watch sb/sth carefully, especially to learn more about him/her/it ～を注意深く見る, 特に対象についてさらに学ぶために➡～を観察する, 監視する ‖ *We observed the birds throughout the breeding season.* 私たちは繁殖期間中ずっとその鳥を観察した. ▶定義2 正式 to see or notice sb/sth ～を見るまたは気付く➡(観察などによって)～を見て取る, 気付く ‖ *A man and a woman were observed leaving by the back door.* 男と女は後ろのドアから出ていくのを監視されていた.

▶定義3 正式 to make a comment 見解を述べる➡所見を述べる, 論評する ‖ *'We're late,' she observed.*「私たちは遅刻しました」と彼女は言った. ▶定義4 正式 to obey a law, rule, etc 法律, 規則などに従う➡～を守る, 遵守する ‖ *to observe the speed limit* 制限速度を守る

**observer** /əbzə́ːrvər/ 名 C ▶定義1 a person who watches sb/sth ～を見ている人➡観察者, 観測者, 監視者 ‖ *According to observers, the plane exploded shortly after take-off.* 見ていた人によれば, その飛行機は離陸直後に爆発した. ▶定義2 a person who attends a meeting, lesson, etc to watch and listen but who does not take part 会合, 練習などに参加している人だが, ただ見たり聞いたりするだけで何の役割も担わない人➡オブザーバー, 立ち会い, 傍観者

**obsess** /əbsés, ɑb-/ 動他 (通常は受動態で) ▶定義 **be obsessed (about/with sb/sth)** to completely fill your mind so that you cannot think of anything else ほかの事が考えられないほど完全に心が取り付かれている➡～を絶えず考える, ～に取り付かれている ‖ *He became obsessed with getting his revenge.* 彼は復讐(ふくしゅう)することに取り付かれた.

**obsession** /əbséʃ(ə)n, ɑb-/ 名 **obsession (with sb/sth)** ▶定義1 U the state in which you can only think about one person or thing so that you cannot think of anything else 1人または1つの物についてしか考えられず, ほかの事は何も考えられない状態➡取り付かれること, 妄執, 執着 ‖ *the tabloid press's obsession with the sordid details of the affair* タブロイド新聞の卑しい事柄に対する執着 ▶定義2 C a person or thing that you think about too much 考えすぎてしまう対象➡取り付いて悩ます人や物, 強迫観念

**obsessive** /əbsésɪv/ 形 ▶定義 thinking too much about one particular person or thing; behaving in a way that shows this 特定の個人または物について考えすぎている; そのように見えるような行動をしている➡取り付かれたような, 脅迫観念を起こさせるような, 異常なまでの ‖ *He's obsessive about not being late.* 彼は異常なまでに遅刻しないよう気を付けている. *obsessive cleanliness* 異常なまでの清潔さ

**obsolete** /ɑ̀bsəlíːt, ́ːː/ ▶定義 no longer useful because sth better has been invented さらにより良い～が発明されたのでもはや廃用になった➡すたれた, 時代後れの

**obstacle** /ɑ́bstɪk(ə)l/ 名 C ▶定義 **an obstacle (to sth/doing sth)** something that makes it difficult for you to do sth or go somewhere ～をしたりどこかへ行ったりすることを困難にする物➡障害(物), 邪魔 ‖ *Not speaking a foreign language was a major obstacle to her career.* 外国語を話せないのは彼女のキャリアにとって大きな障害だった.

**obstetrician** /ɑ̀bstətríʃ(ə)n/ 名 C ▶定義 a hospital doctor who looks after women who are pregnant 妊娠している女性を診る病院の医者➡産婦人科医

**obstinate** /ɑ́bstənət/ 形 ▶定義 refusing to change your opinions, way of behaving, etc when other people try to persuade you to ほかの人が説得しているのに自分の意見や行動方法などを変えることを拒んでいる➡頑固な, 強情な ‖ *an obstinate refusal to apologize* 謝罪することへの頑固な拒絶 ☛類 **stubborn** — **obstinacy** /ɑ́bstənəsi/ 名 U ➡強情, 頑固 — **obstinately** 副➡頑固に, 強情に

**obstruct** /əbstrʌ́kt/ 動他 ▶定義 to stop sb/sth from happening or moving either by accident or deliberately ～が起こったり動いたりすることを偶然または故意に止める➡～を妨害する, 邪魔する ‖ *Could you move on, please? You're obstructing the traffic if you park there.* そこに車を止めると交通の邪魔になりますから, 動いていただけますか.

**obstruction** /əbstrʌ́kʃ(ə)n/ 名 ▶定義1 U the act

## 1122 obstructive

of stopping sth from happening or moving ～が起こったり動いたりすることを止める行為➡妨害, 障害 ▶定義2 ❻a thing that stops sb/sth from moving or doing sth ～が動く, あるいは…をすることを止めるもの➡障害物, 妨害物‖ *This car is **causing an obstruction**.* この車は障害になっている.

**obstructive** /əbstrʌ́ktɪv/ 形 ▶定義 trying to stop sb/sth from moving or doing sth ～が動いたり, …をすることを止めている➡妨げとなる, 障害となる

\***obtain** /əbtéɪn/ 動 他 正式 ▶定義 to get sth ～を得る➡～を手に入れる, 獲得する‖ *to obtain advice/information/permission* 助言・情報・許可を得る

**obtainable** /əbtéɪnəb(ə)l/ 形 ▶定義 that you can get 得ることができる➡得られる, 手に入る‖ *That make of vacuum cleaner is no longer obtainable.* あの型の掃除機はもう手に入らない.

\***obvious** /ɑ́bviəs/ 形 ▶定義 obvious (to sb) easily seen or understood; clear 容易に見えるまたは理解できる; 明白な➡明らかな, 明瞭(めいりょう)な, 見え透いた‖ ***For obvious reasons,*** *I'd prefer not to give my name.* 理由は分かりきった事だが, 私は自分の名前は明かしたくない. *His disappointment was obvious to everyone.* 彼の落胆はだれの目から見ても明かなものだった. ― **obviously** 副 ➡明白に, 明らかに‖ *There has obviously been a mistake.* 明らかにミスがあった.

\***occasion** /əkéɪʒ(ə)n/ 名 ▶定義1 ❻a particular time when sth happens ～が起こる特定の時➡機会, 時, 場合‖ *I have met Bill on two occasions.* 私は2度ビルに会った. ▶定義2 ❻ a special event, ceremony, etc 特別な出来事, 式典など➡祝典, 大切な時, お祝い‖ *Their wedding was a memorable occasion.* 彼らの結婚式は記念すべき出来事だった. ▶定義3 [単数扱い] the suitable or right time (for sth) ～にとって適したまたは適切な時➡好機, チャンス‖ *I shall tell her what I think if the occasion arises (=if I get the chance).* 時が来たら(＝もし機会があれば)私の考えている事を彼女に言うことにする.

▶ occasion はその時が何かにふさわしい, または適しているという意味で使用する: *I saw them at the funeral, but it was not a suitable occasion for discussing holiday plans.* (私はお葬式で彼らと会ったが, 休みの計画について相談するべき時ではなかった.) opportunity, chance は何かをする可能性があるという意味で使用される: *I was only in Paris for one day and I didn't get the opportunity/chance to visit the Louvre.* (1日しかパリにいなかったので, ルーブル美術館を訪れる機会がなかった.)

成句 **on occasion(s)** ▶定義 sometimes but not often それほど頻繁ではないか時々➡時折, たまに

\***occasional** /əkéɪʒ(ə)n(ə)l/ 形 ▶定義 done or happening from time to time but not very often 時々行われたり起こったりするが頻繁ではない➡時々の, 時折の‖ *We have the occasional argument but most of the time we get on.* 私たちはたまに口げんかをするが, ほとんどの場合はうまくやっている. ― **occasionally** /-n(ə)li/ 副 ➡時々, 時折, たまに‖ *We see each other occasionally.* 私たちは時折会う.

**occult** /əkʌ́lt/ 形 ▶定義1 (名詞の前だけ) connected with magic powers and things that cannot be explained by reason or science 理性や科学では説明できない魔力の力や物に結び付いている➡神秘的な, 超自然的な, 魔術的な, オカルトの ▶定義2 **the occult** 名 [単数扱い] magic powers, ceremonies, etc 魔力の力, 儀式など➡秘学, 神秘

**occupant** /ɑ́kjəpənt/ 名 ❻ ▶定義 a person who is in a building, car, etc at a particular time ある特定の時間に建物や車などにいる人➡占有者, 居住者, 乗客

\***occupation** /ɑ̀kjəpéɪʃ(ə)n/ 名 ▶定義1 ❻(文) a job or profession; the way in which you spend your time 仕事や職業; 自分の時間の過ごし方➡職業, 仕事; 自分の時間を費やす方法‖ *Please state your occupation on the form.* 書類にご職業を記入してください. ☛参 **work**¹の注 ▶定義2 ❶ the act of the army of one country taking control of another country; the period of time that this situation lasts ある国の軍隊が他国を支配する行為; またはその状態が続く期間➡占領, 占領期間‖ *the Roman occupation of Britain* ローマ軍のイギリス占領 ▶定義3 ❶the act of living in or using a room, building, etc 部屋や建物等に住んだり使用する行為➡占有, 居住

**occupational** /ɑ̀kjəpéɪʃ(ə)n(ə)l/ 形 ▶定義 (名詞

の前だけ) connected with your work 仕事に関連した→**職業の，職業上の** ‖ *Accidents are an **occupational hazard** (=a risk connected with a particular job) on building sites.* 建設現場の事故は職業に伴う危険(＝特定の仕事に関連した危険)である．

**occupied** /ákjəpàɪd/ 形 ▶定義1 (名詞の前は不可) being used by sb 〜によって使用されている→**ふさがっている** ‖ *Is this seat occupied?* だれかこの席を使用していますか．(この席，空いてますか．) ▶定義2 busy doing sth 〜をするのに忙しい→**忙しい，多忙な** ‖ *Looking after the children keeps me fully occupied.* 私は子供の世話をするのに忙殺されている．☞参 preoccupied ▶定義3 (used about a country or a piece of land) under the control of another country (国や土地について)他国の支配下にある→**占領された，占拠された**

**occupier** /ákjəpàɪər/ 名 ❻(文) ▶定義 a person who owns, lives in or uses a house, piece of land, etc 家や土地などを所有，居住，使用する人→**占有者，居住人**

*****occupy** /ákjəpàɪ/ 動 ❽ (現分 **occupying**; 三単現 **occupies**; 過，過分 **occupied**) ▶定義1 to fill a space or period of time 空間または一定の時間を埋める→**〜を占める，要する** ‖ *The large table occupied most of the room.* その大きいテーブルが部屋の大半を占めていた．☞類 take up ▶定義2 正式 to live in or use a house, piece of land, etc 家，土地などに住む，または使用する→**居住する，使用する** ▶定義3 to take control of a building, country, etc by force 建物，国などを力によって支配下に置く→**〜を占拠する，占領する** ▶定義4 occupy sb/yourself to keep sb/yourself busy 〜・自分自身を忙しくする→**〜に従事する，〜に忙殺される**

*****occur** /əkɚ́ːr/ 動 ❾ (**occurring**; **occurred**) ▶定義1 正式 to happen, especially in a way that has not been planned 特に予定していなかった形で起こる→**起こる，生じる** ‖ *The accident occurred late last night.* その事故は昨夜遅くに起こった．☞参 happen の注 ▶定義2 to exist or be found somewhere 存在する，またはどこかで見受けられる→**存在する，見受けられる，出てくる** ‖ *The virus occurs more frequently in children.* そのウイルスはより頻繁に子供に見受けられる．▶定義3 occur to sb (used about an idea or a thought) to come into your mind (アイデアや着想について)〜に生じる，心にひらめく→**浮かぶ，生まれる** ‖ *It never occurred to John that his wife might be unhappy.* 妻が不幸かもしれないなどとジョンは思ってもみなかった．

**occurrence** /əkɚ́ːrəns, əkʌ́r-/ 名 ❻ ▶定義 something that happens or exists 起こったり存在したりすること→**事件，出来事**

*****ocean** /óʊʃ(ə)n/ 名 ▶定義1 ❿ 特に 困 the mass of salt water that covers most of the surface of the earth 地球の大半を覆っている大量の塩水→**海，大洋，海洋** ‖ *Two thirds of the earth's surface is covered by ocean.* 地球表面の3分の2は海洋で覆われている．▶定義2 ❻ (または **Ocean**) one of the five main areas into which the water is divided 5つに分かれた主要海域の1つ→**〜洋** ‖ *the Atlantic/Indian/Pacific Ocean* 大西・インド・太平洋 ☞参 sea

成句 **a drop in the ocean** ⇒ **DROP**²

*****o'clock** /əklɑ́k/ 副 ▶定義 used after the numbers one to twelve for saying what the time is 何時かを表すのに1から12の数字の後に使われる→**〜時** ‖ *Lunch is at twelve o'clock.* 昼食は12時です．

▶注意．o'clock は正時のときしか使用しない: *We arranged to meet at 5 o'clock.* (私たちは5時に会うことにした．) *It's 5.30 already and he's still not here.* (もう5時30分だというのに彼はまだここにいません．)

**Oct** 略 October→**10月** ‖ *13 Oct 1999* 1999年10月13日

**octagon** /áktəgɑ̀n; -gən/ 名 ❻ ▶定義 a shape that has eight straight sides 8つの辺から成る図形→**八角形**— **octagonal** /ɑktǽgənl/ 形→**八角形の**

**octave** /ɑ́ktɪv, -tèɪv/ 名 ❻ ▶定義 the set of eight musical notes that western music is based on 西洋音楽が基礎とする8つの音程のセット→**オクターブ**

*****October** /ɑktóʊbər/ 名 ❿ ❻ (略 **Oct**) ▶定義 the tenth month of the year, coming after September 9月の次に来る，1年の10番目の月→**10月**

▶文中での月の表し方については，January の例と注を参照．

**octopus** /ɑ́ktəpəs/ 名 C ( 複 **octopuses** ) ▶定義 a sea animal with a soft body and eight long arms (tentacles) 軟体で8本の長い脚(触手)を持つ海の生物➔タコ

★**odd** /ɑd/ 形 ▶定義 **1** strange; unusual 変わっている, 普通でない➔**風変わりな, 妙な** ‖ *There's something odd about him.* 彼は何か変だ. *It's a bit odd that she didn't phone to say she couldn't come.* 彼女が来られないと電話をくれなかったのは何かおかしい. ➠類 **peculiar**
▶定義 **2** odd- (複合形容詞を作るために用いて) strange or unusual in the way mentioned 〜が異常な, 変わった➔**風変わりな, 変な** ‖ *an odd-sounding name* 変わった響きを持つ名前
▶定義 **3** (名詞の前だけ) not regular or fixed; happening sometimes 規則的, 固定的ではない; 時折起こる➔**時折の, 臨時の, 偶然の** ‖ *He makes the odd mistake, but nothing very serious.* 彼は時折ミスをするが大したことではない. ▶定義 **4** (名詞の前だけ) that is left after other similar things have been used 同様のほかの物が使用された後に残ったもの➔**半端物の, 余りの** ‖ *He made the bookshelves out of a few odd bits of wood.* 彼は木材の切れ端を使って本棚を作った. ▶定義 **5** not with the pair or set it belongs to; not matching 一組または1セットにならない; 組み合わない➔**片方だけの, 一方だけの, 半端な** ‖ *You're wearing odd socks.* あなたはちぐはぐな靴下を履いていますよ. ▶定義 **6** (used about a number) that cannot be divided by two (数字について)2で割り切れない数字➔**奇数** ‖ *One, three, five and seven are all odd numbers.* 1, 3, 5, 7はすべて奇数です. ⇔ **even**
▶定義 **7** (usually used after a number) a little more than (通常は数字の後に用いて) もう少し多くの➔**〜といくらかの, 〜余り** ‖ *'How old do you think he is?' 'Well, he must be thirty-odd, I suppose.'*「彼は何歳だと思うかい」「そうだな, 彼は30ちょっとに違いないよ」— **oddly** 副 ➔奇妙に, 不思議にも ‖ *Oddly enough, the most expensive tickets sold fastest.* 不思議なことに, 最も高いチケットが一番早く売れた. — **oddness** 名 U ➔奇妙なこと, 半端

成句 **the odd man/one out** ▶定義 one that is different from all the others in a group グループの中で1人だけほかの人と異なる人➔**仲間外れ** ‖ *Her brothers and sisters were much older than she was. She was always the odd one out.* 彼女の兄弟姉妹は彼女よりはるかに年を取っていたので, 彼女はいつも仲間外れだった.

**oddity** /ɑ́dəti/ 名 ( 複 **oddities** ) C ▶定義 a person or thing that is unusual 普通でない奇妙な人や物➔**奇人, 変人, 奇妙な物**

**odd jobs** 名 [複数扱い] ▶定義 small jobs or tasks of various types 多種の細かな仕事や作業➔**臨時仕事, 片手間仕事**

**oddment** /ɑ́dmənt/ 名 [ C, 通常は複数] 特に 英 ▶定義 a small piece of material, wood, etc that is left after the rest has been used 使用された後に残った原料, 材木などの小さなかけら➔**残り物, 半端物, がらくた**

**odds** /ɑdz/ 名 [複数扱い] ▶定義 **the odds (on/against sth/sb)** the degree to which sth is likely to happen; the probability of sth happening 〜が起こりそうな度合い; 〜が起こる可能性➔**確率, 見込み, 可能性** ‖ *The odds on him surviving are very slim (=he will probably die).* 彼が助かる見込みはほとんどない(=彼は多分死ぬだろう). *The odds are against you (=you are not likely to succeed).* 君に勝つ目はない(=君は成功しそうにない). *The odds are in your favour (=you are likely to succeed).* 君には勝つ見込みがある(=君は成功するだろう).

成句 **against (all) the odds** ▶定義 happening although it seemed impossible 不可能に思えたのに実際に起こる➔**ものすごい困難にもかかわらず**

**be at odds (with sb) (over sth)** ▶定義 to disagree with sb about sth 〜や…について意見が合わない➔**不和で, 争って**

**be at odds (with sth)** ▶定義 to be different from sth, when the two things should be the same 2つのものが同じであるべきときに異なる➔**合致しない, ちぐはぐで**

**odds and ends** 英略式 ▶定義 small things of little value or importance 価値のないあるいは重要でない小さいもの➡がらくた,残り物,寄せ集め
**odometer** /oudάmətər/ 名 =**MILOMETER**
**odour** (米**odor**) /óudər/ 名 ●正式 ▶定義 a smell (often an unpleasant one) におい(しばしば不快なもの)➡ におい,香り
**odourless** (米**odorless**) /óudərləs/ 形 ▶定義 without a smell においのない➡無臭の
★**of** /ə(v), 強形 αv/ 前 ▶定義 **1** belonging to, connected with, or part of sth/sb ～に属している,～に関連している,あるいは～の一部にある➡～の,～に属する ‖ *the roof of the house* その家の屋根 *the result of the exam* その試験の結果 *the back of the book* その本の裏表紙 *the leader of the party* その政党の党首 *a friend of mine* (=one of my friends) 私の友達(=私の友達の1人)
▶定義 **2** made, done or produced by sb ～によって作られた,なされた,生産された➡～の,～による ‖ *the poems of Milton* ミルトンの詩
▶定義 **3** used for saying what sb/sth is or what a thing contains or is made of ～が何であるか,または物に何が含まれているか,何で作られているかを述べるのに用いて➡～から・～で・～を使って ‖ *a woman of intelligence* 知的な女性 *the city of Paris* パリ市 *a glass of milk* グラス1杯の牛乳 *a crowd of people* 群集 *It's made of silver.* それは銀でできています. *a feeling of anger* 怒りの感情
▶定義 **4** showing sb/sth ～を示して➡～についての ‖ *a map of York* ヨークの地図 *a photograph of my parents* 両親の写真 ▶定義 **5** showing that sb/sth is part of a larger group ～が大きなグループの一部だということを示して➡～の中での,～の ‖ *some of the people* その人々のうちのいくか *three of the houses* その家々の中の3軒
▶定義 **6** with measurements, directions and expressions of time and age 寸法,方向,時間と年齢を表現して➡～の,～から ‖ *a litre of milk* 1リットルの牛乳 *the fourth of July* 7月4日 *a girl of 12* 12歳の少女 *an increase of 2.5%* 2.5パーセントの増加 *five miles north of Leeds* リーズから5マイル北 ▶定義 **7** indicating the reason for or cause of sth ～の理由または原因を示して➡～のために,～で ‖ *He died of pneumonia.* 彼は肺炎で死亡した. ▶定義 **8** with some adjectives 形容詞を伴って➡～の点では ‖ *I'm proud of you.* 私はあなたを誇りに思っています. *She's jealous of her.*

彼女は彼女にしっとしている. ▶定義 **9** with some verbs 動詞を伴って➡～に関して,～についての ‖ *This perfume smells of roses.* この香水はバラの香りがする. *Think of a number.* 数を考えなさい. *It reminds me of you.* それがあなたのことを思い出させます. ▶定義 **10** used after a noun describing an action to show either who did the action or who it happened to 名詞の後に用いて,その行為をだれが行った(主語)か,またはだれに対して起こったのか(目的語)を示す➡～についての,～に関して ‖ *the arrival of the president* (=he arrives) 大統領の到着(=大統領が到着する). *the murder of the president* (=he is murdered) 大統領の殺人(=大統領が殺される).

★**off**¹ /ɔ(:)f, αf/ 副 前
➤例えば go off のような慣用表現は,それぞれの動詞の項を参照のこと.

▶定義 **1** down or away from a place or a position on sth ～の場所や位置から落ちてまたは離れて➡～から離れて,隔たって,落ちて ‖ *to fall off a ladder/motorbike/wall* はしご・バイク・塀から落ちる *We got off the bus.* 私たちはバスを降りた. *I shouted to him but he just walked off.* 私は彼に向かって叫んだが,彼はそのまま立ち去った. *I **must be off** (=I must leave here). It's getting late.* 私は離れなくてはならない(=私はここから去らなければならない). もう夜も更けてきた. *When are you off to Spain?* いつスペインへ行くのですか. (比喩) *We've got off the subject.* 我々はその主題からそれた. ▶定義 **2** used with verbs that mean 'remove' or 'separate' 「除去・分離」を意味する動詞と共に用いて➡別れて,分離して,取れて,はがれて ‖ *She took her coat off.* 彼女はコートを脱いだ. *He shook the rain off his umbrella.* 彼は傘に付いた雨を振り落とした. ⇨ **on**
▶定義 **3** joined to and leading away from (道で)つながった場所から他へ導いて➡向こうの方へ ‖ *My road is off the Cowley Road.* 私の家がある通りはコウレー通りを入った所です. ▶定義 **4** at some distance from sth ～からある程度離れて➡～から,～離れて,～の沖に ‖ *The Isle of Wight is just off the south coast of England.* ワイト島はイングランド南海岸沖すぐの所にあります. *Christmas is still a long way off* (=it is a long time till then). クリスマスはまだずっと先だ(=そ

## 1126 off²

れまでまだ時間がある). ▶定義5 (used about a machine, a light, etc) not connected, working or being used (機械,電気などについて)接続されていない,動いていない,使用されていない→**切れて,止まって,閉じて** ‖ *Please make sure the TV/light/heating is off.* テレビ・電気・暖房が切れているか確認してください. ▶定義6 not present at work, school, etc 職場や学校などに出席していない→**非番の,休みの,休暇の** ‖ *She's off work/off sick with a cold.* 彼女は仕事を休んでいる・彼女は風邪で病欠している. *I'm having a day off (=a day's holiday) next week.* 私は来週1日休みを取る(=1日の休暇) ▶定義7 (used about a plan or arrangement) not going to happen; cancelled (計画や準備について)起こらない;キャンセルされた→**中止になって,流れて** ‖ *The meeting/wedding/trip is off.* 会合・結婚式・旅行は中止である. ⇔on ▶定義8 cheaper; less by a certain amount 安い,ある一定量少ない→**～から差し引いて,～から割り引いて** ‖ *cars with £400 off* 400ポンド値引きされた車 *£400 off the price of a car* 車の値段から400ポンド割引 ▶定義9 not eating or using sth ～を食べたり,使用したりしない→**差し控えて,やめて** ‖ *The baby's off his food.* その赤ちゃんは食欲がない.

成句 **off and on; on and off** ▶定義 sometimes; starting and stopping 時折,始まったり止まったり→**時々,断続的に** ‖ *It rained on and off all day.* 一日中雨が降ったりやんだりした.

**off limits** 米 ▶定義 forbidden; not to be entered by sb 禁止されている,～が立ち入ることのできない→**立ち入り禁止の**

**off the top of your head** ⇒ **TOP¹**

**well/badly off** ▶定義 having/not having a lot of money 大金を持っている・いない→**裕福な・貧困の**

**off²** /ɔ(:)f, ɑ́f/ 形 (名詞の前は不可) ▶定義1 (used about food or drink) no longer fresh enough to eat or drink (食べ物や飲み物について)飲食するにはもはや新鮮ではない→**傷んでいる,鮮度が落ちた** ‖ *The milk's off.* この牛乳は傷んでいる. ▶定義2 (口語) unfriendly→**不親切な,友好的でない,冷たい,よそよそしい** ‖ *My neighbour was rather off with me today.* 今日,近所の人たちは私にかなり冷たかった.

**offal** /ɔ́(:)f(ə)l, ɑ́f-/ 名 Ⓤ ▶定義 the heart and other organs of an animal, used as food 食べ物として使用される動物の心臓やそのほかの内臓→**もつ,あら,くず肉など,一般的な食肉ではない部分**

**off chance** 名 [単数扱い] ▶定義 a slight possibility かすかな可能性→**めったにありそうもない,万が一** ‖ *She popped round on the off chance of finding him at home.* 彼女はひょっとすると彼が家にいるかもしれないと期待して,ちょっと立ち寄った.

**off-day** 名 Ⓒ 略式 ▶定義 a day when things go badly or you do not work well 物事が悪く転ぶ,あるいは仕事などがうまくいかない日→**ついてない日** ‖ *Even the best players have off-days occasionally.* たとえ優れた演奏家でも,時にはうまく演奏できない日があります.

*****offence** (米 **offense**) /əféns/ 名 ▶定義1 Ⓒ 正式 **an offence (against sth)** a crime; an illegal action 犯罪,違法な行為→**違反,反則,罪** ‖ *to commit an offence* 違反する *a criminal/minor/serious/sexual offence* 刑事・軽・重大・性的犯罪 ▶定義2 Ⓤ **offence (to sb/sth)** the act of upsetting or insulting sb ～を怒らせたり侮辱する行為→**人の感情を傷付けること,無礼,侮辱** ‖ *I didn't mean to cause you any offence.* あなたを怒らせるつもりはありませんでした.

成句 **take offense (at sth)** ▶定義 to feel upset or hurt by sb/sth ～によって,怒りを感じたり感情を傷付けられる→**怒る,腹を立てる**

*****offend** /əfénd/ 動 ▶定義1 Ⓣ (しばしば受動態で) to hurt sb's feelings; to upset sb 人の感情を傷付ける;人を怒らせる→**～を怒らせる,傷付ける,機嫌を損ねる** ‖ *I hope they won't be offended if I don't come.* もし私が行かなくても,彼らの機嫌を損ねないといいのですが. *He felt offended that she hadn't written for so long.* 彼女がとても長い間手紙を書かなかったので,彼は傷付いていた. ▶定義2 Ⓘ 正式 to do sth illegal; to commit a crime ～を違法に行う; 犯罪を犯す→**罪を犯す**

**offender** /əféndər/ 名 Ⓒ ▶定義1 正式 a person who breaks the law or commits a crime 法律を破る,あるいは罪を犯す人→**違反者,犯罪者** ‖ *Young offenders should not be sent to adult prisons.* 若年犯罪者は一般の刑務所に送るべきではない. *a first offender (=sb who has committed a crime for the first time)* 初犯者(=初めて罪を犯した人) ▶定義2 a person or thing that does sth wrong 悪い事を行う人または物➡元凶, 不快な人や物, 無礼な人

**offensive**[1] /əfénsɪv/ 形 ▶定義 1 offensive (to sb) unpleasant; insulting➡不快な, 侮辱的な ‖ *offensive behaviour/language/remarks* 侮辱的な振る舞い・言葉遣い・見解⇔**inoffensive**
▶定義 2 正式 (名詞の前だけ) used for or connected with attacking 攻撃するために, あるいは攻撃することに関連して用いて➡攻撃的な, 攻撃用の ‖ *offensive weapons* 攻撃用の武器⇔**defensive**—**offensively** 副 ➡無礼に, 攻勢的に

**offensive**[2] /əfénsɪv/ 名 ⓒ ▶定義 a military attack 軍隊による攻撃➡攻勢, 攻撃
成句 **be on the offensive** ▶定義 to be the first to attack, rather than waiting for others to attack you 他人が攻撃してくるのを待つよりは, 先に攻撃する➡攻撃中である

★**offer**[1] /ɔ́(:)fər, áf-/ 動 ▶定義 1 他 offer sth (to sb) (for sth); offer (sb) sth to ask if sb would like sth or to give sb the chance to have sth ～が…を欲しいか尋ねる, ～が…を持つ機会を与える➡～を提供する, 差し出す, 提案する ‖ *He offered his seat on the bus to an old lady.* 彼はバスの中で老女に自分の席を譲った. *I've been offered a job in London.* 私はずっとロンドンで仕事を提供されている. *He offered (me) £2000 for the car and I accepted.* 彼はその車の代金として2000ポンドを申し出て, 私は了承した.
▶定義 2 自 offer (to do sth) to say or show that you will do sth for sb if he/she wants もし人が望んでいるなら, その～のために…をするということを言う・示す➡しようと申し出る, しようと言う ‖ *I don't want to do it but I suppose I'll have to offer.* そうしたくはないが, 申し出なければならないようだ. *My brother's offered to help me paint the house.* 私の兄[弟]は家のペンキ塗りの手伝いをしようと言ってくれた.
▶定義 3 他 to make sth available or to provide the opportunity for sth ～を可能にする, または～の機会を提供する➡～を引き起こす, 生じる ‖ *The job offers plenty of opportunity for travel.* その仕事は旅行する機会が多い.

★**offer**[2] /ɔ́(:)fər, áf-/ 名 ⓒ ▶定義 1 an offer (of sth); an offer (to do sth) a statement offering to do sth or give sth to sb ～をする, あるいは～を…に与えるという申し出➡提供, 申し出, 提案 ‖ *She accepted my offer of help.* 彼女は私の援助

の申し出を受け入れてくれた. *Thank you for your kind offer to help.* ご親切に援助を申し出てくださってありがとう.
► 申し入れを make(する), accept(受け入れる), refuse(拒絶する), turn down(断る), または withdraw(取り消す)ことができる.

▶定義 2 an offer (of sth) (for sth) an amount of money that you say you will give for sth ～のために自分が出すと言った金額➡申し込み値段, 付け値 ‖ *They've made an offer for the house.* 彼らはその家を買いたいと言ってきた. *We've turned down (=refused) an offer of £90000.* 私たちは9万ポンドで買いたいと言ってきたのを断った(=拒絶した). ▶定義 3 a low price for sth in a shop, usually for a short time 店の～に付けた安い値段, 普通短い期間だけのもの➡バーゲン価格, 値引き値段 ‖ *See below for details of our special holiday offer.* 休日特別価格につきましては, 下記の詳細をご覧ください.

成句 **on offer** ▶定義 1 for sale or available 売りに出した, 利用できる➡提供されている ‖ *The college has a wide range of courses on offer.* その大学は幅広い分野の課程を用意している.
▶定義 2 特に 英 for sale at a lower price than usual for a certain time ある一定期間通常よりも安い値段で売りに出ている➡セール中の ‖ *This cheese is on offer until next week.* このチーズは来週までお安くなっています.

**or nearest offer; ono** ⇒**NEAR**[1]

**offering** /ɔ́(:)fərɪŋ, áf-/ 名 ⓒ ▶定義 something that is given or produced for other people to watch, enjoy, etc ほかの人々が見たり楽しんだりするために与えられる, 作られるもの➡供物, 献金, 贈り物, 寄付, 申し出, 提供

**offhand**[1] /ɔ́(:)fhǽnd, áf-/ 形 ▶定義 (used about behaviour) not showing any interest in sb/sth in a way that seems rude (振る舞いについて)失礼に見えるマナーで, ～に何の関心も示さない➡無造作な, ぶっきらぼうな, ぞんざいな ‖ *an offhand manner/voice* ぶっきらぼうなマナー・声

**offhand**[2] /ɔ́(:)fhǽnd, áf-/ 副 ▶定義 without having time to think; immediately 考える暇がなく; すぐに➡即座に, 即席に, 用意のない ‖ *I can't tell you what it's worth offhand.* それに何の価値があるのか, すぐには答えられないよ.

## office

**★office** /ɔ́(ː)fəs, ɑ́f-/ 名 ▶定義1 ❷ a room, set of rooms or a building where people work, usually sitting at desks 通常は机に座って人々が働く部屋, 複数の部屋, あるいは建物→**事務室, 事務所, オフィス, 職場** ‖ *I usually get to the office at about 9 o'clock.* 私は大抵9時ころ出社します. *The firm's **head office** (=the main branch of the company) is in Glasgow.* その会社の本社(=会社の本店)はグラスゴーにあります. *Please phone again during **office hours**.* 営業時間内にもう一度お電話ください.

▶米国では医者と歯医者は offices(診療所)を持っている. 英国では surgeries(診察室・医院)を持っている.

▶定義2 ❷ (しばしば複合名詞を作るために用いて) a room or building that is used for a particular purpose, especially for providing a service 特定の目的, 特にサービスを提供するために使用される部屋や建物→**会社, 営業所** ‖ *the tax/ticket/tourist office* 税務署・キップ売り場・観光会社 ☞参 booking office, box office, post office ▶定義3 ❽ office [単数扱い] a government department, including the people who work there and the work they do 政府の部署, そこで働く人々, および彼らのする仕事も含む→**(官庁の)〜局, 〜部, 〜省** ‖ *the Foreign/Home Office* 外務・内務省 ▶定義4 ❶ an official position, often as part of a government or other organization 公的地位, しばしば政府またはほかの機関の一部としての→**官職, 公職** ‖ *The Labour party has been **in office** since 1997.* 労働党は1997年から政権を握っている.

**office block** 名 ❷ ▶定義 a large building that contains offices, usually belonging to more than one company オフィスが入っている大きな建物, 大抵は複数の会社が入っている→**事務所ビル, オフィスビル**

**★officer** /ɔ́(ː)fəsər, ɑ́f-/ 名 ❷ ▶定義1 a person who is in a position of authority in the armed forces 軍隊において権限ある地位にいる人→**将校, 士官** ‖ *an army/air-force officer* 陸軍・空軍士官 ▶定義2 a person who is in a position of authority in the government or a large organization 政府または大きな機関において権限ある地位にいる人→**役人, 官僚, 公務員, 役員** ‖ *a prison/customs/welfare officer* 刑務所・税関・福祉職員 ▶定義3 =POLICE OFFICER ☞参 official² の注

**★official¹** /əfíʃ(ə)l/ 形 ▶定義1 (名詞の前だけで) connected with the position of sb in authority 権限のある〜の地位に関連して→**職務上の, 公務上の** ‖ *official duties/responsibilities* 公的義務・責任 ▶定義2 accepted and approved by the government or some other authority 政府またはほかの機関によって受け入れられ承認された→**公認の, 公式の, 正式の** ‖ *The scheme has not yet received official approval.* その計画はまだ正式な承認を受けていない. *The country's official language is Spanish.* その国の公用語はスペイン語です. ▶定義3 that is told to the public, but which may or may not be true 国民に対して述べられたが, 本当かどうかはっきりしない→**公式の, 表向きの, 一般に知られた** ‖ *The official reason for his resignation was that he wanted to spend more time with his family.* 彼が辞任する表向きの理由は, 家族ともっと時間を過ごしたいというものだった. ⇔ unofficial

**official²** /əfíʃ(ə)l/ 名 ❷ ▶定義 a person who has a position of authority 権威ある立場にいる人→**(高級な)公務員, 役人, (幹部)職員, 役員** ‖ *The reception was attended by MPs and high-ranking officials.* レセプションには下院議員と高級官僚が出席した.

▶ office worker はオフィスにおいて机に向かって仕事をする人のこと. official は機関, しばしば政府(機関)において責任ある地位にある人のこと: *senior government officials* (政府幹部役員) officer は軍隊または警察内において命令を下す人. しかし時折 official のように使用される: *She's a tax officer in the Civil Service.* (彼女は役所の税金担当者である.)

**officialdom** /əfíʃ(ə)ldəm/ 名 ❶ ▶定義 groups of people in positions of authority in large organizations who seem more interested in following the rules than in being helpful 大きな機関における権限のある地位にいる人々のグループのことで, 人々の役に立つことよりも規則に従う方に関心があるように見える→**役人, 官僚**

**officially** /əfíʃ(ə)li/ 副 ▶定義1 that is done publicly and by sb in a position of authority 権限のある地位の〜によって公的に行われる→**公式に, 正式に** ‖ *The new school was officially opened* *last week.* その新しい学校は先週正式に開校した. ▶定義2 according to a particular set of laws, rules, etc 特定の法律, 規則などに従って→**公式には, 正式には, 表向きは** ‖ *Officially we don't accept children under six, but we'll make an exception in this case.* 正式には6歳以下の子供は受け付けませんが, この場合は例外とします.

**officious** /əfíʃəs/ 形 ▶定義 too ready to tell other people what to do and use the power you have to give orders ほかの人にあれこれしろと言いすぎる, また命令する権力を使いすぎる→**お節介な, 差し出がましい, あれこれ指図する**

**offing** /ɔ́(:)fɪŋ, ɑ́f-/ 名

成句 **in the offing** 略式 ▶定義 likely to appear or happen soon すぐにも現れそう, あるいは起こりそう→**やがて起こりそうな**

**off-licence** 名 C ( 米 **liquor store**) ▶定義 a shop which sells alcoholic drinks in bottles and cans びん入り, 缶入りのアルコール飲料を売る店→**酒屋, 酒類販売許可店**

**offload** /ɔ̀(:)flóud, ɑ̀f-/ 動 他 略式 ▶定義 offload sth (on/onto sb) to give away sth that you do not want to sb else 自分が欲しくない〜をほかの…に渡す→**〜を引き渡す, 任せる, 処分する** ‖ *It's nice to have someone you can offload your problems onto.* 自分の厄介事を任せてしまえる人がいるのは良い事だ.

**off-peak** 形副 ▶定義 (名詞の前だけ) available, used or done at a less popular or busy time それほど人気がないか, あるいは忙しくない時間に利用できる, 使用できる, あるいはすることができる→**ピークを過ぎた, 閑散期の** ‖ *an off-peak train ticket/bus-pass/phone call* 閑散時の電車の切符・バスのパス・電話 *It's cheaper to travel off-peak.* 閑散期に旅行すると安い. ● 参 **peak**

**off-putting** 形 特に 英 ▶定義 unpleasant in a way that stops you from liking sb/sth 〜を嫌いになるほど不快な→**がっかりさせる, 不愉快な, 当惑させる, 反感を覚えさせる**

**offset** /ɔ̀(:)fsèt, ɑ́f-/ 動 他 ( **offsetting**, 過, 過分 **offset**) ▶定義 to make the effect of sth less strong or noticeable 〜の効果をより弱くする, あるいは目立たなくする→**〜を相殺する, 差し引きして埋め合わせする** ‖ *The disadvantages of the scheme are more than offset by the advantages.* その計画の不利な点は利点と相殺しても大きい.

**offshoot** /ɔ́(:)fʃùːt, ɑ́f-/ 名 C ▶定義 a thing that develops from sth else, especially a small organization that develops from a larger one 何か別の物から発達したもの, 特に大きな機関から展開した小さな機関→**(組織の)支流, 分派, (氏族の)分家, (幹から出た)横枝**

**offshore** /ɔ̀(:)fʃɔ́ːr, ɑ̀f-/ 形 ▶定義 in the sea but not very far from the land 海中だがそれほど陸地から離れていない→**沖合いの** ‖ *an offshore oil rig* 沖合いの石油掘削装置

**offside** 形 ▶定義1 /ɔ̀(:)fsáɪd, ɑ̀f-/ (used about a player in football) in a position that is not allowed by the rules of the game (競技中のサッカー選手について) ゲームの規則によって許されない位置にいて→**オフサイドの, 反則の位置の** ▶定義2 /ɔ̀(ə)fsaɪd, ɑ́f-/ 英 (used about a part of a vehicle) on the side that is furthest away from the edge of the road (車の一部について) 道路の端から一番遠い側の→**道路の中央側の**

**offspring** /ɔ́(:)fsprìŋ, ɑ́f-/ 名 C ( 複 **offspring**) 正式 ▶定義 a child or children; the young of an animal 子供(たち), 動物の子→**〜の子, 子孫, 末裔(まつえい), 子** ‖ *to produce/raise offspring* 子孫を産む・育てる

**off-white** 形 ▶定義 not pure white 純白ではない白の→**灰色[黄味]がかった白の, オフホワイトの**

*****often** /ɔ́(:)f(ə)n, ɑ́f-, -t(ə)n/ 副 ▶定義1 many times; frequently→**何度も, よく, 度々, しばしば** ‖ *We often go swimming at the weekend.* 私たちはよく週末に泳ぎに行く. *I'm sorry I didn't write very often.* ごめんなさいね, あまりお手紙を出さなくて. *How often should you go to the dentist?* どのくらいの頻度で歯医者に行かなくてはならないのですか. ▶定義2 in many cases; commonly→**多くの場合; 通常** ‖ *Old houses are often damp.* 古い家はジメジメしていることが多い.

成句 **every so often** ▶定義 sometimes; from time to time→**時々; 時折**

**more often than not** ▶定義 usually→**普段, よく**

**ogre** /óugər/ 名 C ▶定義1 (in children's stories) a very large, cruel and frightening creature that eats people (子供の話の中で) とても大きく残酷で怖い, 人食い生物→**人食い鬼** ▶定義2 a person who is unpleasant and frightening 不快感と恐怖を与える人→**鬼のような恐ろしい人**

## Oh

**\*Oh** /óʊ/ (または **o**) 圕 ▶定義 used for reacting to sth that sb has said, for emphasizing what you are saying, or when you are thinking of what to say next ～が言った…に反応するために使用され, 自分の言っている事を強調したり, 次に言う事を考えているときに使う→**おお, おや, あ, ああ** ‖ *'I'm a teacher.' 'Oh? Where?'*「私は教師です」「あら, どちらの」*'Oh no!' she cried as she began to read the letter.*「ああ, そんな」と, 彼女はその手紙を読み始めた途端に叫んだ.

**\*oil** /ɔɪl/ 图 Ⓤ ▶定義 **1** a thick dark liquid that comes from under the ground and is used as a fuel or to make machines work smoothly 地中から産出される濃い黒い液体で, 燃料として, あるいは機械を滑らかに動かすために使われる→**石油, 原油** ▶定義 **2** a thick liquid that comes from animals or plants and is used in cooking 動物または植物からとれる濃い液体で, 料理に使われる→**油** ‖ *cooking/vegetable/sunflower/olive oil* 料理用・植物性・ヒマワリ・オリーブオイル—**oil** 動他→～**に油を塗る, 油を差す**

**oilfield** /ɔ́ɪlfìːld/ 图 Ⓒ ▶定義 an area where there is oil under the ground or under the sea 地中または海底で石油がある場所→**油田**

**oil painting** 图 Ⓒ ▶定義 a picture that has been painted using paint made with oil 油を使った画材を使ってかかれた絵→**油絵**

**oil rig** (または **rig**) 图 Ⓒ ▶定義 a large platform in the sea with equipment for getting oil out from under the sea 海底から石油を掘り出す装置の付いた大きなプラットフォーム→**海上採油基地, 石油掘削装置**

**oil slick** (または **slick**) 图 Ⓒ ▶定義 an area of oil that floats on the sea, usually after a ship carrying oil has crashed 石油を積んだ船が衝突した後に通常見られる, 海面に浮いた石油の広がり→**水面に流出した油**

**oil well** (または **well**) 图 Ⓒ ▶定義 a hole that is made deep in the ground or under the sea in order to obtain oil 石油を得るために地中または海底深く作られた穴→**油田, 油井**

**oily** /ɔ́ɪli/ 形 ▶定義 covered with oil or like oil 油で覆われた, または油のような→**油を塗った, 油状の, 油のような** ‖ *oily food* 油っこい食べ物 *Mechanics always have oily hands.* 修理工はいつも油にまみれた手をしている.

**ointment** /ɔ́ɪntmənt/ 图 Ⓒ Ⓤ ▶定義 a smooth substance that you put on sore skin or on an injury to help it get better 滑らかな物質で, 荒れた肌やけがした部分に塗って早く治るようにするもの→**軟こう** ☛ **bandage** のさし絵

**\*OK¹** (または **okay**) /òʊkéɪ/ 形 副 間 略式 ▶定義 **1** all right; good or well enough よろしい; 十分に良い→**うまい[く], 順調な[に], 立派な[に]** ‖ *'Did you have a nice day?' 'Well, it was OK, I suppose.'*「楽しい1日でしたか」「ええ, そうだったと思います」 *Is it okay if I come at about 7?*「7時ころ伺ってもいいですか」 ▶定義 **2** yes; all right はい, 結構だ→**オーケー, よし, 承知した** ‖ *'Do you want to come with us?' 'OK.'*「君も私たちと一緒に来ますか」「分かりました」

**OK²** (または **okay**) /òʊkéɪ/ 图 [単数扱い] ▶定義 agreement or permission 同意, 許可→**同意, 許可, 承認** ‖ *As soon as my parents give me the OK, I'll come and stay with you.* 両親が許可したらすぐに, あなたの所へ行って一緒に住みます. —**OK** (または **okay**) (三単現 **OK's**; 現分 **OK'ing**, 過, 過分 **OK'd**) 動他 **OK sth (with sb)**→～**を…に承認する, オーケーする, 承知する** ‖ *If you need time off, you have to OK it with your boss.* もしお休みが欲しいのなら, 上司の許可が必要ですよ.

**\*old** /óʊld/ 形 ▶定義 **1** that has existed for a long time; connected with past times 長い間存在している; 過去とつながりのある→**古い, 昔の, 以前の** ‖ *This house is quite old.* この家はかなり古い. *old ideas/traditions* 古い考え・伝統 *In the old days, people generally had larger families than nowadays.* 昔は, 一般的に今より大家族だった. ⇔ **new, modern** ▶定義 **2** (used about people and animals) having lived a long time (人や動物について) 長い間生きている→**年を取った, 老いた** ‖ *My mother wasn't very old when she died.* 亡くなった時, 母はそれほど老齢ではなかった. *He's 50 but he looks older.* 彼はまだ50歳だが, もっと老けて見える. *to get/grow old* 年を取る ⇔ **young** ▶定義 **3** (used with a period of time or with how) of a particular age (期間を示す語または how と共に用いて) 特定の年齢の→**～歳になる, (物の寿命や物事の経過が)～年になる** ‖ *That building is 500 years old.* その建物は建ってから500年たっている. *The book is aimed at eight- to ten-year-olds.* その本は8歳から10歳の子供向けだ. *How*

old are you? おいくつですか. ☛参 **age¹** の注
➤ older と oldest は old の比較級,最上級: *My father's older than my mother.*(私の父は母より年上だ.)*I'm the oldest in the class.*(クラスの中で私が一番年上だ.) elder と eldest は人々の年齢,特に家族内で年齢を比較する際に使用することができるが, than と一緒には使えない.

▶定義4 **the old** 名[複数扱い] old people 老いた人々→老人,年寄り ☛参 **the elderly, the aged** ▶定義5 having been used a lot たくさん使われてきた→使い古した,古くなった ‖ *I got rid of all my old clothes.* 私は自分の古い服を全部処分した. ⇔ **new** ☛参 **second-hand** ▶定義6 (名詞の前だけ) former; previous →前の,以前の ‖ *I earn more now than I did in my old job.* 以前の仕事の時より,今の方が稼ぎが良い. ▶定義7 (名詞の前だけ) known for a long time 長い間知っている→古くからの,年来の,昔なじみの ‖ *She's a very old friend of mine. We knew each other at school.* 彼女は昔からの友人です. 学校で知り合いました. ▶定義8 (名詞の前だけ) 略式 used for emphasizing that sth has little importance or value ～が重要でない,価値がないことを強調するために用いて→いつもの,変り映えしない,月並みな ‖ *I write any old rubbish in my diary.* 私は日記帳に下らないことを書く.

成句 **be an old hand (at sth)** ▶定義 to be good at sth because you have done it often before 昔しばしばやっていたので～が得意である→得意である,熟練している

**old age** 名 Ⓤ ▶定義 the part of your life when you are old 人生の年老いた時期→老年 ‖ *He's enjoying life in his old age.* 彼は老年期を楽しんでいる. ☛参 **youth**

**old-age pension** 名 Ⓤ ▶定義 money paid by the state to people above a certain age 政府からある一定の年齢以上の人々に支払われるお金→老齢年金 — **old-age pensioner**(または **pensioner**) 名 Ⓒ (略式 **OAP**) → 老齢年金受給者 ☛ 今日では senior citizen (お年寄り,老齢市民) という表現の方が一般的で,受け入れられやすい.

**old-fashioned** 形 ▶定義1 usual in the past but not now 過去には普通だったが今は違う→旧式の,時代後れの,流行後れの ‖ *old-fashioned clothes/ideas* 時代後れの服・考え *That word sounds a bit old-fashioned.* その単語は少し古めかしく響く. ▶定義2 (used about people) believing in old ideas, customs, etc (人々について) 古い考えや習慣などを信じている→旧式な考えを持つ,保守的な,昔気質(かたぎ)の ‖ *My parents are quite old-fashioned about some things.* 私の両親はいくつかの事柄に関しては極めて保守的である. ☛参 **modern, unfashionable**

**the Old Testament** 名[単数扱い] ▶定義 the first part of the Bible that tells the history of the Jewish people. ユダヤ人の歴史を述べている,聖書の最初の部分→旧約聖書

**olive** /ɑ́lɪv/ 名 ▶定義1 Ⓒ a small green or black fruit with a bitter taste, used for food and oil 苦い味のする小さな緑または黒の果物で,食べ物として,また油として使用される→オリーブ ‖ *Fry the onions in a little olive oil.* タマネギを少量のオリーブオイルでいためます. ☛C3 ページのさし絵 ▶定義2 (または **olive green**) Ⓤ 形 (of) a colour between yellow and green 黄色と緑の中間の色(の) → 黄緑色(の),オリーブ色(の)

**the Olympic Games**(または **the Olympics**) /əlímpɪks, oʊ-/ 名[複数扱い] ▶定義 an international sports competition which is organized every four years in a different country 4年ごとに異なった国で開かれる国際スポーツ競技大会→オリンピック ‖ *to win a medal at/in the Olympics* オリンピックでメダルを獲得する *the Winter/Summer Olympics* 冬季・夏季オリンピック大会 — **Olympic** 形 (名詞の前だけ) → オリンピック競技の,オリンピックの ‖ *Who holds the Olympic record for the 1500 metres?* だれが1500メートルのオリンピック記録を持っているのですか.

**ombudsman** /ɑ́mbʊ̀dzmən, ɔ́(ː)m-, -bədz-, -mæ̀n/ 名 [単数扱い] ▶定義 a government official who deals with complaints made by ordinary people against public organizations 公共機関に対する一般人からの苦情を処理する政府の役人→オンブズマン,行政監察官,苦情調査官

**omelette**(または **omelet**) /ɑ́m(ə)lət/ 名 Ⓒ ▶定義 a dish made of eggs that have been mixed together very fast (beaten) and fried 卵を手早く混ぜ合わせて(かき混ぜて)焼いた料理→オムレツ ☛C4 ページのさし絵

**omen** /óʊmən/ 名 Ⓒ ▶定義 a sign of sth that will happen in the future 未来に起こる～の印→前

## 1132　ominous

兆, 予兆, 兆し, 前触れ || *a good/bad omen for the future* 未来の良い・悪い兆し

**ominous** /ámənəs/ 形 ▶定義 suggesting that sth bad is going to happen 悪い〜が起こると示唆している→**不吉な, 縁起の悪い, 不気味な** || *Those black clouds look ominous.* あそこの黒い雲が不吉に見える.

**omission** /oʊmíʃ(ə)n, ə-/ 名 C U ▶定義 something that has not been included; the act of not including sb/sth 含まれていなかったもの; 〜を含まないこと→**省くこと, 省略, 漏れ, 脱落** || *There were several omissions on the list of names.* その名簿にはいくつかの漏れがあった.

**omit** /oʊmít, ə-/ 動 他 (**omitting**; **omitted**)
▶定義 1 to not include sth; to leave sth out 〜を含まない; 〜を抜かす→**〜を省略する, 省く** || *Several verses of the song can be omitted.* その歌のいくつかの節は省略できる. ▶定義 2 正式 **omit to do sth** to forget or choose not to do sth 〜し忘れる, あるいは〜をしないことを選択する→**(うっかりして)〜し忘れる, (わざと〜することを)おこたる**

**on** /ɑn/ 副 前
▶例えば get on, on holiday など多種の動詞や名詞と使用する慣用表現の場合は, それぞれの動詞あるいは名詞の見出し語を参照.

▶定義 1 (または 正式 **upon**) supported by, fixed to or touching sth, especially a surface 〜に支えられて, 特にその表面に付着して, あるいは接触して→**〜の上に, 〜に接して** || *on the table/ceiling/wall* テーブル・天井・壁に *We sat on the beach/grass/floor.* 私たちは砂浜・芝生・床に座った. *She was carrying the baby on her back.* 彼女は背中に赤ちゃんを背負っていた. *Write it down on a piece of paper.* 紙に書いてください. *The ball hit me on the head.* 私の頭にボールが当たった. ▶定義 2 in a place or position ある場所, あるいは位置にあって→**〜に, 〜の近くに, 〜に接して, 〜に面して, 〜に沿って** || *on a farm/housing estate/campsite* 農場・団地・キャンプ場に *a house on the river/seafront/border* 川のほとりの家・海岸通りに面した家・国境付近の家 *I live on the other side of town.* 私は町の反対側に住んでいる. ▶定義 3 showing direction 方向を示して→**〜に向かって, 〜の方へ** || *on the right/left* 右・左に *on the way to school* 学校へ行く途中 ▶定義 4 used with ways of travelling and types of travel 移動の手段, あるいは移動の種類を表す言葉と一緒に用いて→**〜で** || *on the bus/train/plane* バス・電車・飛行機で *We came on foot* (=we walked). 私たちは徒歩で来た (=歩いてきた). *Eddie went past on his bike.* エディーは自転車で通り過ぎた. *to go on a trip/journey/excursion* (短い)旅行・旅行・遠足に出掛ける▶乗用車のときは **in the car** となることに注意.

▶定義 5 with expressions of time 時間の表現を伴って→**〜に** || *on August 19th* 8月19日に *on Monday* 月曜日に *on Christmas Day* クリスマスの日に *on your birthday* あなたの誕生日に▶定義 6 working; being used 作動している; 使用されている→**(機械などが)作動して, (電気・ガス・水道などが)通じて, 出て, ついて** || *All the lights were on.* すべての明かりはついていた. *Switch the television on.* テレビをつけてください. ▶定義 7 wearing sth; carrying sth in your pocket or bag 〜を着ている; 〜をポケットまたはバッグの中に入れて持ち歩いている→**身に着けて・着て・履いて・かぶって・携帯して** || *What did she have on?* 彼女は何を着ていたの. *to put your shoes/coat/hat/make-up on* 靴を履く・コートを着る・帽子をかぶる・化粧をする *I've got no money on me.* 今お金を持っていません. *You should carry ID on you at all times.* 身分証明書はいつも身に付けているべきです. ▶定義 8 about sth 〜について→**〜ついて, 〜に関して** || *We've got a test on irregular verbs tomorrow.* 明日, 不規則動詞のテストがある. *a talk/a book/an article on Japan* 日本についての話・本・記事▶定義 9 happening or arranged to happen 起こっている, あるいは起こるように手配されている→**(催し・活動などが)行われて, 進行中で** || *What's on at the cinema?* その映画館では何を上映してますか. *Is the meeting still on, or has it been cancelled?* 会議はまだ続いていますか, それとも中止されましたか. ▶定義 10 using sth; by means of sth 〜を使用していて; 〜を用いて→**〜で** || *I was (talking) on the phone to Laura.* 私はローラと電話でしゃべっていた. *I saw it on television.* 私はそれをテレビで見た. *I cut my hand on some glass.* 私はガラスで手を切った. *Dave spends most evenings on the Internet.*

ほとんど毎日,デーヴは夕方になるとインターネットをして過ごす. ▶定義 11 showing the thing or person that is affected by an action or is the object of an action 行為によって影響される物または人,その行為の対象を示す➔**〜に対して,〜に向かって** ‖ *Divorce can have a bad effect on children.* 離婚は子供に悪影響を与えかねない. *He spends a lot on clothes.* 彼は服にお金をたくさん使う. *Don't waste your time on that.* そんな事に時間を浪費するな. ▶定義 12 using drugs or medicine; using a particular kind of food or fuel 麻薬や薬を使っている;特定の種類の食物や燃料を使っている➔**〜中毒で,〜を常用して,〜を常食して** ‖ *to be on medication/antibiotics/heroin* 薬物・抗生物質・ヘロインを常用する *Gorillas live on leaves and fruit.* ゴリラは葉と果物が主食である. *Does this car run on petrol or diesel?* この車はガソリン車ですか,ディーゼル車ですか. ▶定義 13 receiving a certain amount of money 一定金額を受け取っている➔**(いくらの金額)で** ‖ *What will you be on (=how much will you earn) in your new job?* 新しい仕事でどのくらいもらえますか(=どのくらい稼ぎますか). *He's been (living) on unemployment benefit since he lost his job.* 彼は仕事をなくしてから失業保険で暮らしている. ▶定義 14 showing that sth continues 〜が続くことを示して➔**(ある行為を)続けて,ずっと,どんどん** ‖ *The man shouted at us but we walked on.* その男は私たちに向かって叫んだが,私たちは歩き続けた. *The speeches went **on and on** until everyone was bored.* その演説はみんなが飽きるまでずっと続いた. ▶定義 15 showing the reason for or basis for sth 〜の理由,あるいは根拠を示して➔**〜に基づいて,〜の理由で** ‖ *She doesn't eat meat **on principle**.* 彼女は主義として肉を食べない. *The film is **based on** a true story.* その映画は実際の話に基づいている. ▶定義 16 compared to 〜と比較して➔**〜に比べて** ‖ *Sales are up 10% on last year.* 売り上げは,昨年に比べて10パーセント上昇した. ▶定義 17 immediately; soon after すぐに;すぐ後に➔**〜するとすぐ,〜のすぐ後で** ‖ *He telephoned her on his return from New York.* 彼はニューヨークから帰るとすぐ彼女に電話した. ▶定義 18 paid for by sb 〜によって支払われた➔**〜の費用で,〜のおごりで,〜持ちで** ‖ *The drinks are on me!* 飲み物は私のおごりだ.

once 1133

**▶語法**

on は「接している」

「接している」が基本的な意味にあり,常に上にあるとは限らないので「壁に掛かった」状態でも on the wall と表すことができます.また,いくら「上に」存在しても接した場所にない場合は above や over などを用います.

成句 **from now/then on** ▶定義 starting from this/that time and continuing 今から始まり続いている・あの時から始まり続いている➔**今後,今から,それ以来,その時から** ‖ *From then on she never smoked another cigarette.* それ以降彼女はたばこを1本も吸わなかった.

**not on** ▶定義 not acceptable 受け入れられない➔**良くない,許されない,好ましくない** ‖ *No, you can't stay out that late. It's just not on.* ダメ,そんなに遅くまで外で遊んでいてはいけません.許しませんよ.

**off and on; on and off** ⇒ **OFF¹**
**be/go on at sb** ⇒ **GO¹**

\*once /wʌns/ 副接 ▶定義 1 one time only; on one occasion 1度だけ;1回の機会➔**1度,1回** ‖ *I've only been to France once.* 1度だけフランスに行ったことがある. *once a week/month/year* 1週間・1月・1年に1度 *I visit them about once every six months.* 私はほぼ6か月に1度,彼らを訪ねる. ▶定義 2 at some time in the past; formerly 過去のある時期に,以前に➔**かつて,以前,昔** ‖ *This house was once the village school.* この家はかつては村の学校だった. ▶定義 3 as soon as; when すぐに;〜の時➔**するや否や,いったん〜すると,1度〜すると** ‖ *Once you've practised a bit you'll find that it's quite easy.* 少し練習するとすぐに,とても簡単だということが分かるでしょう.

成句 **all at once** ▶定義 all at the same time or suddenly すべてが同時に,突然に➔**同時に,一斉に,不意に** ‖ *People began talking all at once.* 人々は同時に話し始めた. *All at once she got up and left the room.* 突然彼女は立ち上がって,部屋を出ていった.

**at once** ▶定義 1 immediately; now➔**すぐに;今**

‖ *Come here at once!* すぐここに来て.
▶定義2 at the same time→**同時に** ‖ *I can't understand if you all speak at once.* あなたたちが皆同時にしゃべったら,私には理解できない.

**just this once; (just) for once** ▶定義 on this occasion only この機会に限って→**今度だけは,その時限り** ‖ *Just this once, I'll help you with your homework.* 今度だけあなたの宿題を手伝ってあげます.

**once again/more** ▶定義 again, as before→**再び,以前と同様に** ‖ *Spring will soon be here once again.* すぐにまた春が巡ってきます.

**once and for all** ▶定義 now and for the last time 今,これが最後で→**ただ1度だけ,今回限り** ‖ *You've got to make a decision once and for all.* 今度ばかりは,あなたは決心しなくてはなりません.

**once in a blue moon** 略式 ▶定義 very rarely; almost never→**ごくまれに,稀有(けう)に**

**once in a while** ▶定義 sometimes but not often 時々,ただしあまり頻繁ではない→**時々,たまに**

**once more** ▶定義 one more time→**もう一度** ‖ *Let's listen to that cassette once more, shall we?* もう一度あのカセットを聴きませんか.

**once upon a time** ▶定義 (used at the beginning of a children's story) a long time ago; in the past (童話の始まりに用いて)→**昔々; 過去に** ‖ *Once upon a time there was a beautiful princess...* 昔々美しいお姫様がおりました...

**oncoming** /ɑ́nkʌ̀mɪŋ/ 形(名詞の前だけ)
▶定義 coming towards you 自分の方に向かってきている→**近付いてくる** ‖ *oncoming traffic* 対向車の流れ

*__one__¹ /wʌn/ 代形名 C ▶定義1 1→**(数としての)1,1つ** ‖ *There's only one biscuit left.* ビスケットが1枚しか残っていない. *The journey takes one hour.* その旅行は1時間かかる. *If you take one from ten it leaves nine.* 10から1を引くと9である. ☞参 **first**

▶文中での数詞の使い方については, **six** の項を参照.

▶定義2 (used when you are talking about a time in the past or future without actually saying when) a certain (特に具体的にいつということを言わないで,過去あるいは未来の時間について話すときに用いて)→**ある~** ‖ *He came to see me one evening last week.* 先週のある日の夕方,彼が私に会いに来ました. *We must go and visit them one day.* いつか彼らに会いに行かなければならない. ▶定義3 used with the other, another or other(s) to make a contrast 対照させるために the other, another, other(s) と一緒に用いて→**一方(のもの)** ‖ *The twins are so alike that it's hard to tell one from the other.* その双子はとてもよく似ているので,見分けが付かない.

▶定義4 **the one** used for emphasizing that there is only one of sth ~が1つしかないことを強調するために用いて→**ただ1つの** ‖ *She's the one person I trust.* 彼女は私が信頼するただ1人の人だ. *We can't all get in the one car.* その車1台に全員は乗れない.

成句 **(all) in one** ▶定義 all together or combined すべて一緒に,あるいはすべてが結合されて→**1つで全部を兼ねて** ‖ *It's a phone and fax machine all in one.* これは電話とファックスを兼ねています.

**one after another/the other** ▶定義 first one, then the next, etc 最初のもの,それから次のもの,など→**次々に,次から次へと** ‖ *One after another the winners went up to get their prizes.* 勝者が次々に賞品を受け取りに行った.

**one at a time** ▶定義 separately; individually 別々に,個々に→**1つずつ, 1人ずつ** ‖ *I'll deal with the problems one at a time.* 私は,1つずつ問題を処理していきます.

**one by one** ▶定義 separately; individually 別々に,個々に→**1つずつ, 1人ずつ** ‖ *One by one, people began to arrive at the meeting.* 1人,また1人と会議場に到着し始めた.

**one or two** ▶定義 a few→**少数の,数個の** ‖ *I've borrowed one or two new books from the library.* 私は図書館から新刊を少し借りてきた.

*__one__² /wʌn/ 代名 C ▶定義1 used instead of repeating a noun (同じ)名詞を繰り返す代わりに用いて→**それ, (同じ種類の)1つのもの** ‖ *I think I'll have an apple. Would you like one?* 私はリンゴを食べようと思っている.あなたもいかがですか.

▶定義2 **one of** a member (of a certain group) (あるグループの)メンバーの1人→**~の1人** ‖ *He's staying with one of his friends.* 彼は彼の友達の1人の家に滞在している. *One of the children is crying.* 子供のうちの1人が泣いている.

► one of の後には,名詞の複数形が続く.主語が one なので,動詞は単数形: *One of our assistants is ill.*(店員の1人が病気です.)*One of the buses was late.*(バスの1台が遅れた.)
▶定義3 used after this, that, which or after an adjective instead of a noun this, that, which の後,あるいは名詞の代わりに形容詞の後に用いて→(前に出た名詞と)同類のもの,(〜な)人,物 ∥ *'Which dress do you like?' 'This one.'*「どっちのドレスが好きですか」「これです」 *'Can I borrow some books of yours?' 'Yes. Which ones?'*「あなたの本を何冊かお借りしてもいいですか」「はい.どれですか」*This coat's a bit small. You need a bigger one.*「このコートは少し小さい.あなたにはもう少し大きいのが必要です」*That idea is a very good one.* あのアイデアはとてもいいものだ. ▶定義4 **the one/the ones** used before a group of words that show which person or thing you are talking about 話題となっている人・物を示す語句の前に用いて→(〜な)人,物 ∥ *My house is the one after the post office.* 私の家は郵便局の後ろです. *If you find some questions difficult, leave out the ones you don't understand.* もし問題の中に難しいものがあったら,分からないものはそのままにしておきなさい. ▶定義5 正式 used for referring to people in general, including the speaker or writer 一般論として,その話し手や書き手自身をも含む人々について述べるために用いて→人,私たち,だれでも ∥ *One must be sure of one's facts before criticizing other people.* 他人を非難する以前に,人は自分の現実に自信を持っていなければならない. ☛このように one を使用することは,非常に格式張っている.日常会話では you を使用するのが普通.

**one another** 代 ▶定義 each other→互い ∥ *We exchanged news with one another.* 私たちは互いに便りを交わした.

**one-off** 名 C 形 略式 ▶定義 something that is made or that happens only once 1度だけ作られる,あるいは起こるもの→ただ1回限りの(もの) ∥ *a one-off payment/opportunity* 1回限りの支払い・機会

\***oneself** /wʌnsélf/ 代 ▶定義1 used when the person who does an action is also affected by it ある行為をする人が,同時にその行為によって影響されるときに用いて→自分自身を,自分自身に ∥ *One can teach oneself to play the piano but it is easier to have lessons.* 人は独力でもピアノを学べる,しかしレッスンを受ける方がもっと楽である. ▶定義2 used for emphasis 強調に用いて→自分自身,自ら ∥ *One could easily arrange it all oneself.* (やろうと思えば) 1人で楽に準備することができるだろう.

成句 **(all) by oneself** ▶定義1 alone 1人で→独りぼっちで ☛参 **alone** の注 ▶定義2 without help 助けなしで→1人で,独力で

**one-sided** 形 ▶定義1 (used about an opinion, an argument, etc) showing only one point of view; not balanced (意見,議論などについて) 1つの見解しか示さない; バランスが取れていない→一方に偏った,不公平な ∥ *Some newspapers give a very one-sided view of politics.* 新聞の中には政治的に偏った見方をしているものがある. ▶定義2 (used about a relationship or a competition) not equal (関係や競争などについて) 平等でない→不釣り合いの,一方的な ∥ *The match was very one-sided - we lost 12-1.* その試合は一方的なものだった - 我々は12対1で負けた.

**one-to-one** (または **one-on-one**) 形 副 ▶定義 between only two people 2人だけの間で→1対1の,相手が1人の,2人だけの,マンツーマンの ∥ *one-to-one English lessons (=one teacher to one student)* 1対1の英語授業 (= 先生1人と生徒1人)

**one-way** 副 形 ▶定義1 (used about roads) that you can only drive along in one direction (道路について) 一方向にしか運転できない→一方通行の ∥ *a one-way street* 一方通行の道 ▶定義2 (used about a ticket) that you can use to travel somewhere but not back again (切符について) ある所まで行くことはできるが,再び戻ってはこられない→(切符が)片道の ∥ *a one-way ticket* 片道切符 ☛類 **single** ⇔ **return**

**ongoing** /ɒ́ŋɡòʊɪŋ/ 形 (名詞の前だけ) ▶定義 continuing to exist now 今も存在し続けている→継続・進行している ∥ *It's an ongoing problem.* それは,今でもある問題だ.

\***onion** /ʌ́njən/ 名 C U ▶定義 a white or red vegetable with many layers. Onions are often used in cooking and have a strong smell that makes some people cry. いくえもの層になっている白

色, 赤色の野菜. よく料理に使われ, 強いにおいがあり, そのために人が涙を流すこともある→タマネギ ‖ *a kilo of onions* タマネギ1キロ *onion soup* オニオンスープ ◯C3ページのさし絵

**online** /ònláın/ 形副 ▶定義 controlled by or connected to a computer or to the Internet コンピューターまたはインターネットに制御されている, 接続されている→オンラインの, オンラインで, ネットで ‖ *an online ticket booking system* オンラインのチケット予約システム *I'm studying French online.* 私はフランス語をネットで勉強しています.

**onlooker** /ánlùkər/ 名 C ▶定義 a person who watches sth happening without taking part in it 参加せずに~が起こるのを見ている人→傍観者, 見物人

★**only** /óʊnli/ 形副 {名詞の前だけ} ▶定義 1 with no others existing or present ほかに存在していない, あるいは居合わせていない→唯一の, ほかにない ‖ *I was the only woman in the room.* 私がその部屋でただ1人の女性だった. *This is the only dress we have in your size.* あなたのサイズでは, これが当店にあるただ1着のドレスです.

▶定義 2 and no one or nothing else; no more than ほかにだれもいない, あるいはほかに何もない; ~だけ→ただ~だけの ‖ *She only likes pop music.* 彼女はポップミュージックだけが好きです. *I've only asked a few friends to the party.* 私は数人の友達をパーティーに誘っただけだ. *It's only one o'clock.* まだたった1時だ. ▶定義 3 the most suitable or the best→最適の, 最良の ‖ *It's so cold that the only thing to do is to sit by the fire.* とても寒いので, 火のそばに座るに限る.

▶書き言葉では, only は普通強調する単語の前に置かれる. 話し言葉では, 強勢を使うことで, 強調する単語を示すことができるので, only は位置を変えなくてもよい: *I only kissed 'Jane* (=I kissed Jane and no one else). (私はジェーンにキスしただけだ(=私はジェーンにキスしたのであって, ほかの人ではない). (Janeにストレスが置かれている)) *I only 'kissed Jane* (=I kissed Jane but I didn't do anything else). (私はジェーンにキスしただけだ(=私はジェーンにキスしたが, ほかの事は何もしなかった). (kissed にストレスが置かれている))

▶定義 4 略式 except that; but ~を除いては; しかし→~ということさえなければ, ただし, だがしかし ‖ *The film was very good, only it was a bit too long.* その映画はとても良かった, だがしかしちょっと長すぎた.

成句 **if only** ⇒ **IF**

**not only... but also** ▶定義 both...and 両方とも→~のみならず…も, (ただ)~だけでなく…も(また) ‖ *He not only did the shopping but he also cooked the meal.* 彼は買い物をしただけなく, その食事の調理もした.

**only just** ▶定義 1 not long ago そんなに前ではない→たった今からしたばかり ‖ *I've only just started this job.* ちょうどこの仕事を始めたばかりだ. ▶定義 2 almost not; hardly ほとんどない, ほとんど~しない→辛うじて, やっと, ほとんど~しない ‖ *We only just had enough money to pay for the meal.* 辛うじて食事代を払うだけのお金しかなかった.

**only child** 名 C ▶定義 a child who has no brothers or sisters 兄弟姉妹がいない子供→一人っ子

**onset** /ánsèt/ 名 [単数扱い] ▶定義 the onset (of sth) the beginning (often of sth unpleasant) 始まり(しばしば不快な~の始まり)→始まり, (病気などの)発病 ‖ *the onset of winter/a headache* 冬の・頭痛の始まり

**onslaught** /ánslɔ̀ːt/ 名 C ▶定義 an onslaught (on/against sb/sth) a violent or strong attack 暴力的な, 激しい攻撃→猛攻撃, 猛襲 ‖ *an onslaught on government policy* 政府の政策への猛反対

★**onto** (または **on to**) /ántə, 母音の前 ántu/ 前 ▶定義 to a position on sth ~に接触する位置へ→~の上へ, ~へ, ~の方へ ‖ *The cat jumped onto the sofa.* 猫はソファーの上に飛び乗った. *The bottle fell off the table onto the floor.* テーブルの上のびんが床に落ちた. *The crowd ran onto the pitch.* 群集は(サッカー等の)フィールドへ向かって走った.

成句 **be onto sb** 略式 ▶定義 to have found out about sth illegal that sb is doing ~がしている違法なことについて事実をつかんでいる→(たくらみなどに)気付いている ‖ *The police were onto the car thieves.* 警察は車泥棒の一団に気付いていた.

**be onto sth** ▶定義 to have some information, etc that could lead to an important discovery 重要な発見につながる情報などを得る➔～について分かっている、～に気付いている

**onwards** /ˈɒnwədz/ (または **onward** /ˈɒnwəd/) 副 ▶定義1 from...onwards continuing from a particular time 特定の時間から継続している➔(時間的に)先へずっと ‖ *From September onwards it usually begins to get colder.* 一般に9月からずっと、寒さが増していきます. ▶定義2 正式 forward 前へ➔前へ、先へ、進んで ‖ *The road stretched onwards into the distance.* 道ははるかなたまで続いていた.

**ooze** /uːz/ 動 ▶定義 **ooze from/out of sth**; **ooze (with) sth** 自他 to flow slowly out or to allow sth to flow slowly out ゆっくり流れ出る、あるいは～をゆっくり流出させる➔染み出る、にじみ出る、流れ出る ‖ *Blood was oozing from a cut on his head.* 彼の頭の切り傷から血がにじみ出ていた. *The fruit was oozing with juice.* そのフルーツから果汁が染み出ていた.

**op** /ɒp/ (口語) =**OPERATION**(1)

**opaque** /əʊˈpeɪk/ 形 ▶定義1 that you cannot see through 通して見ることができない➔不透明な ‖ *opaque glass in the door* ドアにはまっているくもりガラス ▶定義2 正式 difficult to understand; not clear 理解するのが難しい; 明白ではない➔はっきりしない、不明瞭(めいりょう)な、分かりにくい⇔**transparent**

**OPEC** /ˈəʊpek/ 略 Organization of Petroleum Exporting Countries➔オペック、石油輸出国機構

★**open**¹ /ˈəʊp(ə)n/ 形 ▶定義1 not closed or covered 閉まっていない、あるいは覆われていない➔開いている、開いた、覆い・屋根のない、(衣服が)ボタン・ジッパーなどのない、開襟の ‖ *Don't leave the door open.* ドアを開けっ放しにしないでください. *an open window* 開いている窓 *I can't get this bottle of wine open.* 私はこのワインボトルが開けられない. *She stared at me with her eyes wide open.* 彼女は目を大きく見開いて私をじっと見詰めた. *The diary was lying open on her desk.* その日記は彼女の机の上に広げられたまま置かれていた. *The curtains were open so that we could see into the room.* カーテンが開いていたので、私たちは部屋の中を見ることができた. *His shirt was open at the neck.* 彼のシャツは首の所が開いていた. ▶定義2 **open (to sb/sth)**;

**open** 1137

**open (for sth)** available for people to enter, visit, use, etc; not closed to the public 人が入る、訪問する、使用するなどのことができる; 一般の人々に閉ざされていない➔(店などが)開いている・営業中の、出入り自由の、利用可能な、すぐ使える、公開の、一般参加できる ‖ *The bank isn't open till 9.30.* その銀行は9時半まで開きません. *The new shopping centre will soon be open.* 新しいショッピングセンターがそろそろオープンします. *The hotel damaged by the bomb is now open for business again.* 爆弾で被害を受けたあのホテルは、今また営業しています. *The competition is open to everyone.* その競技会にはだれもが参加できます. *The gardens are open to the public in the summer.* その庭園は夏の間一般公開されます. ⇔**closed**, **shut** ▶定義3 not keeping feelings and thoughts hidden 感情や思考を隠しておかない➔率直な、開けっ広げな、隠し立てのない ‖ *Elena doesn't mind talking about her feelings - she's a very open person.* エレナは自分の感情を語ることを気にしていない － 彼女はとても率直な人だ. *He looked at him with open dislike.* 彼はあからさまな嫌悪の目で彼を見た. ▶定義4 (名詞の前だけ) (used about an area of land) away from towns and buildings; (used about an area of sea) at a distance from the land (土地について)町や建物から離れて; (海域について)陸地から離れて➔広々とした、遮る物のない ‖ *open country* 広々とした田舎 ▶定義5 (名詞の前は不可) not finally decided; still being considered 最終的には決まっていない; まだ考えられている➔(問題などが)未解決の ‖ *Let's leave the details open.* 詳細については決めないでおこう.

成句 **have/keep an open mind (about/on sth)** ▶定義 to be ready to listen to or consider new ideas and suggestions 新しい考えや提案を聞く、あるいは考慮するための心の準備ができている➔柔軟な、開いた心を保つ

**in the open air** ▶定義 outside➔野外で ‖ *Somehow, food eaten in the open air tastes much better.* どういう訳か、野外で食べる食事はいつもよりずっとおいしい.

**keep an eye open/out (for sb/sth)** ⇒ **EYE**¹

**open to sth** ▶定義 willing to receive sth いとわ

## 1138　open²

ずに〜を受け取る→(提案・申し出などを)すぐに受け入れる ‖ *I'm always open to suggestions.* 私はいつでも提案を聞く.

with your eyes open ⇒ **EYE²**

with open arms ▶定義 in a friendly way that shows that you are pleased to see sb or have sth 〜に会ったり、…をもらってうれしいことを示す友好的な様子で→**両手を広げて、心から歓迎して** ‖ *The unions welcomed the government's decision with open arms.* 労働組合は政府の決定を心から歓迎した.

★**open²** /óʊp(ə)n/ 動 ▶定義1 自他 to move sth or part of sth so that it is no longer closed; to move so as to be no longer closed 〜(の一部を)動かし、閉じていない状態にする;閉じていない状態にするために動かす→**(閉じているものを)開ける、開く、開け放つ** ‖ *This window won't open - it's stuck.* この窓は開かない－動かない. *The parachute failed to open and he was killed.* パラシュートが開かなかったので、彼は死んだ. *The book opened at the very page I needed.* 本を開いたらちょうど私が必要としていたページだった. *Open the curtains, will you?* カーテンを開けてもらえますか. *to open your eyes/hand/mouth* 目を開ける・手を開く・口を開ける *to open a bag/letter/box* バッグを開ける・手紙を開封する・箱を開ける ⇔ **close, shut**

▶定義2 自他 to make it possible for people to enter a place 人々がある場所へ入ることを可能にさせる→**(店などを)開ける、公開する、開放する** ‖ *Does that shop open on Sundays?* あの店は日曜日に開いていますか. *The museum opens at 10.* その博物館は10時に開館します. *The company are opening two new branches soon.* その会社は直に新しい支店を2店舗開きます. *Police finally opened the road six hours after the accident.* 事故の6時間後、警察はようやくその道路を開通させた. ⇔ **close, shut** ▶定義3 自他 to start 始まる→**始まる;〜を開始する** ‖ *The chairman opened the meeting by welcoming everybody.* 議長は皆を歓迎して会議を始めた. *I'd like to open a bank account.* 銀行口座を開設したいのですが. ⇔ **close** ▶定義4 他 (computing) to start a program or file so that you can use it on the screen (コンピューター)ディスプレー上で使用できるようにプログラムを起動する、ファイルを開く→**(プログラムやファイル)を起動させる**

成句 open fire (at/on sb/sth) ▶定義 to start shooting 砲撃を開始する→**火ぶたを切る** ‖ *He ordered his men to open fire.* 彼は部下に攻撃開始を命令した.

句動詞 open into/onto sth ▶定義 to lead to another room, area or place 別の部屋、地域、場所へ通じている→**〜の方へ開く、〜の中へ通じる(into)、〜の方へ通じる(onto)** ‖ *This door opens onto the garden.* このドアは庭へ通じている.

open out ▶定義 to become wider 幅を広げる→**(地図などを)広げる、(包みなどを)開く**

open up ▶定義1 to talk about what you feel and think 自分が感じたり考えている事を話す→**打ち解ける、遠慮なく話す、ざっくばらんにしゃべる** ▶定義2 to open a door→**ドアを開ける**

open (sth) up ▶定義1 to become available or to make sth available 利用できるようになる、あるいは〜を利用できるようにする→**(機会などを)開く、利用できるようにする** ‖ *When I left school all sorts of opportunities opened up for me.* 学校を辞めた時、あらゆる好機が私に開かれていた. ▶定義2 to start business 事業を始める→**(店・商売などを)始める** ‖ *The restaurant opened up last year.* そのレストランは去年開店しました.

**the open³** /óʊp(ə)n/ 名 [単数扱い] ▶定義 outside or in the countryside 屋外あるいは郊外→**外、野外、郊外** ‖ *After working in an office I like to be out in the open at weekends.* 会社で働いた後、週末は郊外で過ごしたい.

成句 bring sth out into the open; come out into the open ▶定義 to make sth known publicly; to be known publicly 〜を公式に知らせる;公然と知られている→**〜を明るみに出す;明るみに出る** ‖ *I'm glad our secret has come out into the open at last.* ついに私たちの秘密が知られてしまって、私はうれしい.

**open-air** 形 ▶定義 not inside a building 建物の中ではない→**屋外で、野外で** ‖ *an open-air swimming pool* 屋外プール

**open day** 名 C ▶定義 a day when the public can visit a place that they cannot usually go into 通常は入れない場所に一般人が訪問できる日→**(学校・寮・クラブなどの)一般公開日** ‖ *The hospital is having an open day next month.* その

病院は来月が一般公開日です.

**opener** /óυp(ə)nər/ 名 C(複合名詞で) ▶定義 a thing that takes the lid, etc off sth ～からふたなどを取るもの→開ける道具 ‖ *a tin-opener* 缶切り *a bottle-opener* 栓抜き

**opening** /óυp(ə)nɪŋ/ 名 C ▶定義1 a space or hole that sb/sth can go through ～が通り抜けることのできる空間や穴→すきま, 穴, 裂け目 ‖ *We were able to get through an opening in the hedge.* 私たちは生け垣のすきまから通り抜けることができた. ☞ *tent²* のさし絵 ▶定義2 the beginning or first part of sth ～の始まり, あるいは最初の部分→開始, 始まり, 冒頭, オープニング ‖ *The film is famous for its dramatic opening.* その映画はドラマチックなオープニングで有名だ. ▶定義3 a ceremony to celebrate the first time a public building, road, etc is used 公共の建物や道路などが初めて使われるときを祝う儀式→開会式, 開通式 ‖ *the opening of the new hospital* 新しい病院の開院祝い ▶定義4 a job which is available 応募可能な勤め口→(地位・職などの)空き, 空席, 欠員 ‖ *We have an opening for a sales manager at the moment.* 現段階でセールスマネージャーに欠員があります. ▶定義5 a good opportunity 良い機会→好機, チャンス ‖ *I'm sure she'll be a great journalist - all she needs is an opening.* 彼女はすばらしいジャーナリストになると確信しています — 彼女に必要なのはチャンスなのです. ― **opening** 形(名詞の前だけで) ▶最初の, 開始の ‖ *the opening chapter of a book* 本の第1章 *the opening ceremony of the Olympic Games* オリンピックの開会式

**openly** /óυp(ə)nli/ 副 ▶定義 honestly; not keeping anything secret 正直に; 何事も秘密にしておかないで→公然と, おおっぴらに, 包み隠さず, 率直に, 遠慮なく ‖ *I think you should discuss your feelings openly with each other.* あなたの思っている事を率直に皆と話すべきだと思う.

**open-minded** 形 ▶定義 ready to consider new ideas and opinions 新しい考えや意見を考慮するための心の準備ができている→心の広い, 偏見のない

**openness** /óυp(ə)nnəs/ 名 U ▶定義 the quality of being honest and ready to talk about your feelings 正直に自分の考えを話せる資質→率直さ

**open-plan** 形 ▶定義 (used about a large area indoors) not divided into separate rooms (広い面積の室内について) 別々の部屋に分かれていない→(部屋が)オープンプランの, 間仕切りしていない, 細かく仕切っていない ‖ *an open-plan office* 間仕切りしていないオフィス

**the Open University** 名 [単数扱い] 英 ▶定義 a university whose students study mainly at home. Their work is sent to them by post and there are special television and radio programmes for them. 学生が主に自宅で学習する大学のこと. 課題は家へ郵送され, テレビやラジオで特別な番組が用意されている→通信制大学, 放送大学

**opera** /ɑ́p(ə)rə/ 名 C U ▶定義 a play in which the actors (*opera singers*) sing the words to music; works of this kind performed as entertainment 俳優(オペラ歌手)が音楽に乗せて台詞(せりふ)を歌う演劇; 娯楽として演じられるこの種の作品→オペラ, 歌劇 ‖ *an opera by Wagner* ワーグナー作曲のオペラ *Do you like opera?* オペラはお好きですか. *a comic opera* 喜歌劇 ☞参 **soap opera**

**opera house** 名 C ▶定義 a theatre where operas are performed オペラが上演される劇場→歌劇場, オペラ劇場

★**operate** /ɑ́p(ə)rèɪt/ 動 ▶定義1 自他 to work, or to make sth work 作動する, ～を作動させる→(機械などを)動かす, 運転する, 作動させる, 操作する ‖ *I don't understand how this machine operates.* この機械がどういう仕組みで動いているのか私には分からない. *These switches here operate the central heating.* ここにあるスイッチで中央暖房装置を操作する. ☞類 **function** ▶定義2 自他 to do business; to manage sth 経営する, ～を運営する→(～を) 運営・経営する, 操業する ‖ *The firm operates from its central office in Bristol.* その商社はブリストルの本社によって運営されている. ▶定義3 自 to act or to have an effect 作用する, あるいは効果がある→作用する, 影響する, 効く, 効果がある ‖ *Several factors were operating to our advantage.* いくつかの要因が私たちに有利に働いていた. ▶定義4 自 **operate (on sb/sth) (for sth)** to cut open a person's body in hospital in order to deal with a part that is damaged, infected, etc 病院で, 人の損傷を受けたり病気に侵されたりしている部分

を処置するために、その人の体を切り開く→**手術をする、手術を施す** || *The surgeon is going to operate on her in the morning.* その外科医は午前中に彼女を手術する. *He was operated on for appendicitis.* 彼は盲腸の手術を受けた.

**operatic** /ɑ̀pərǽtɪk/ 形 ▶定義 connected with opera オペラに関連した→**歌劇の、オペラの** || *operatic music* オペラ音楽

**operating system** 名 C ▶定義 a computer program that organizes a number of other programs at the same time 同時にほかの多数のプログラムを取りまとめるコンピュータープログラム→**(コンピューターの)総合管理プログラム、オペレーティングシステム、OS**

**operating theater** (または **theatre**) 名 C ▶定義 a room in a hospital where operations are performed 病院で手術が行われる部屋→**手術室**

★**operation** /ɑ̀pəréɪʃ(ə)n/ 名 ▶定義1 C (または口語では **op**) the process of cutting open a patient's body in order to deal with a part inside 患者の体内を処置するために、その体を切り開く過程→**手術** || *He had an operation to remove his appendix.* 彼は盲腸を取る手術を受けた. ▶定義2 C an organized activity that involves many people doing different things 異なった仕事をしている多くの人々がかかわっている組織的活動→**活動、作戦、事業活動、軍事行動** || *A rescue operation was mounted to find the missing children.* 行方不明の子供たちを捜索するための救援活動が開始された. ▶定義3 C a business or company involving many parts 多方面にわたる商売や会社→**(特にどのような商業活動を行っているのかを示したいときに用いて)事業活動、事業展開** ▶定義4 C an act performed by a machine, especially a computer 機械、特にコンピューターによって行われる行為→**オペレーション、演算** ▶定義5 U the way in which you make sth work 〜を働かせる方法→**(機械などの)操作、運転** || *The operation of these machines is extremely simple.* これらの機械の操作は極めて単純です.

成句 **be in operation; come into operation** ▶定義 to be/start working or having an effect 働いている・働き始める、あるいは実施されている・実施される→**(機械などが)運転中である・運転を始める、(法律などが)施行されている・施行され** る || *The new tax system will come into operation in the spring.* この春から新しい税制が実施されます.

**operational** /ɑ̀pəréɪʃ(ə)n(ə)l/ 形 ▶定義1 (通常は名詞の前だけ) connected with the way a business, machine, system, etc works ビジネス、機械、システムなどが働く方法に関連して→**運営上の、経営上の、操作上の** ▶定義2 (通常は名詞の前は不可) ready for use 使用できる→**使用可能な、運転可能な、機能を果たせる** || *The new factory is now fully operational.* 新しい工場は現在、完全に操業可能です. ▶定義3 (名詞の前だけ) connected with military operations 軍事行動に関連した→**作戦上の、戦闘中の**

**operative** /ɑ́p(ə)rətɪv, -rèɪ-/ 形 正式 ▶定義1 working, able to be used; in use 働いている、使用することができる、使用されて→**(機械などが)運転している、作用する、(薬などが)効き目のある、(法律などが)施行されている** || *The new law will be operative from 1 May.* 新しい法律は5月1日から施行されます. ▶定義2 connected with a medical operation 医療手術に関連して→**手術の**

★**operator** /ɑ́p(ə)rèɪtər/ 名 C ▶定義1 a person whose job is to connect telephone calls, for the public or in a particular building 国民のために、または特定の建物内で電話をつなぐ仕事をしている人→**電話交換手、オペレーター** || *Dial 100 for the operator.* オペレーターにつなぐには100をダイヤルしてください. *a switchboard operator* 電話交換手 ▶定義2 a person whose job is to work a particular machine or piece of equipment 特定の機械や機器を動かす仕事をしている人→**(機械の)操作者、運転者** || *a computer operator* コンピューターのオペレーター ▶定義3 a person or company that does certain types of business ある種のビジネスを行っている人、あるいは会社→**(しばしば軽べつ的)小規模の会社あるいはその経営者** || *a tour operator* ツアーオペレーター

★**opinion** /əpínjən/ 名 ▶定義1 C an opinion (of sb/sth); an opinion (on/about sth) what you think about sb/sth 〜について考えていること→**意見、見解** || *She asked me for my opinion of her new hairstyle and I told her.* 彼女が自分の新しい髪型について私に意見を求めたので、私は答えた. *He has very strong opinions on almost everything.* 彼はほとんどすべての事に対して強固な意見を持っている. *In my opinion, you're making* *a terrible mistake.* 私の見解では、あなたは重大なミスを犯しています. ▶定義2 ❶what people in general think about sth ～について人々が一般的に考えていること➡(一般の人々の)意見・評価, 世論 ‖ *Public opinion is in favour of a change in the law.* 世論は法律改正を支持している.

成句 be of the opinion that... 正式 ▶定義 to think or believe that... ～と考える, あるいは信じる➡～という意見を持っている

have a good/high opinion of sb/sth; have a bad/low/poor opinion of sb/sth ▶定義 to think that sb/sth is good/bad ～が良いと考える; ～が悪いと考える➡～を良く思う, 高く評価する; ～を悪く思う, 低く評価する

a matter of opinion ⇒ MATTER¹

opinion poll = POLL¹(1)

**opium** /óupiəm/ 名 ❶ ▶定義 a powerful drug that is made from the seeds of a flower (poppy) 花(けし)の種から作られる強い麻薬➡アヘン, 麻薬

**opp** 略 opposite➡向こう側に, 反対の位置に

*****opponent** /əpóunənt/ 名 ❻ ▶定義1 (in sport or competitions) a person who plays against sb (スポーツや競技で)～に対抗して運動する人➡敵, 相手, 対抗者 ‖ *They are the toughest opponents we've played against.* 彼らは我々が戦った中で最も手ごわい相手だ. ▶定義2 an opponent (of sth) a person who disagrees with sb's actions, plans or beliefs and tries to stop or change them ～の行動, 計画, 信念などに反対して, それを中止, あるいは変更しようと試みる人➡反対者 ‖ *the President's political opponents* 大統領の政敵

*****opportunity** /ὰpərt(j)úːnəti/ 名 ❻❶ (複 opportunities) ▶定義 an opportunity (for sth/to do sth) a chance to do sth that you would like to do; a situation or a time in which it is possible to do sth that you would like to do 自分のしたい～をする機会; 自分のしたい～をすることのできる状況や時➡機会, 好機 ‖ *There will be plenty of opportunity for asking questions later.* 後で質問をする機会はたっぷりあります. *I have a golden opportunity to go to America now that my sister lives there.* 姉[妹]が住んでいるので私にとってアメリカに行くには今が絶好の機会です. *When we're finally alone, I'll take the opportunity to ask him a few personal questions.* ついに私たちだけになったら、私はその好機を捕らえて彼にいくつか個人的な質問をします. *I'll give Steve your message if I get the opportunity.* 機会があったらスティーヴにあなたのメッセージを渡します. ☛参 occasion の注

**oppose** /əpóuz/ 動 ⓣ ▶定義 to disagree with sb's beliefs, actions or plans and to try to change or stop them ～の信念, 行動, 計画に反対して, それを変更したり止めようと試みる➡～に反対する, 対抗する ‖ *They opposed the plan to build a new road.* 彼らは新しい道路建設の計画に反対した.

**opposed** /əpóuzd/ 形 ▶定義 opposed to sth disagreeing with a plan, action, etc; believing that sth is wrong 計画, 行動などに反対している; ～が悪いと信じている➡～に対立して, ～に反対して ‖ *She has always been strongly opposed to experiments on animals.* 彼女は常に動物実験に強く反対し続けている.

成句 as opposed to ▶定義 (used to emphasize the difference between two things) rather than; and not (2つの物事の違いを強調するために用いて)～よりむしろ; ～ではなく➡～とは対照的に ‖ *Your work will be judged by quality, as opposed to quantity.* あなたの仕事は量ではなく、質で判断されるでしょう.

opposite

in front of

*****opposite** /ápəzət/ 形副前 ▶定義1 in a position on the other side of sb/sth; facing ～の反対側の位置にある; 向かい合っている➡(～の)向こう側に[の], 向かい合う位置に[の], 反対の位置・方向に[の] ‖ *The old town and the new town are on opposite sides of the river.* 旧市街と新市街は川を挟んで向かい合っている. *You sit there and I'll sit opposite.* あなたはそちらに座ってください. 私は反対側に座ります.

▶時折 opposite は名詞の後に使用される: *Write your answer in the space opposite.* (反対側の空欄に答えを記入しなさい.)

## opposition

▶定義2 completely different 全く異なった→全く逆の,正反対の ‖ *I can't walk with you because I'm going in the opposite direction.* 私は反対方向へ行くので,あなたと一緒には行けません. *the opposite sex (=the other sex)* 異性(=もう片方の性)—opposite 名 C→正反対の物・人・事,逆 ‖ *'Hot' is the opposite of 'cold'.* hot は cold の反対語です.

成句 your opposite number ▶定義 a person who does the same job or has the same position as you in a different company, organization, team, etc ほかの会社,機関,チームなどで,自分と同じ仕事をしている,あるいは自分と同じ地位にいる人→別の組織で~と対等の立場・地位にある人 ‖ *The Prime Minister met his Italian opposite number.* 首相はイタリアの首相に会った.

★**opposition** /ɑ̀pəzíʃ(ə)n/ 名 U ▶定義1 opposition (to sb/sth) the feeling of disagreeing with sth and the action of trying to change it ~に同意していない感情,~を変更しようとする行為→反対,対抗,妨害 ‖ *He expressed strong opposition to the plan.* 彼はその計画に強い反対を示した. ▶定義2 the opposition [単数扱い] the person or team who you compete against in sport, business, etc スポーツ,仕事などで自分が対抗して争う人またはチーム→対抗者,敵対者,ライバル,相手 ‖ *We need to find out what the opposition is doing.* 相手が何をしているか突き止める必要があります. ▶定義3 the Opposition [単数扱い] the politicians or the political parties that are in Parliament but not in the government 政府側でない議会における政治家または政治団体→野党,反対党 ‖ *the leader of the Opposition* 野党の党首 *Opposition MPs* 野党の下院議員たち ☛定義2と3で,opposition は動詞の単数形,複数形のどちらとでも一緒に使用できる.

**oppress** /əprés/ 動 他 (通常は受動態で) ▶定義 to treat a group of people in a cruel and unfair way by not allowing them the same freedom and rights as others ほかの人々と同じ自由と権利を与えないことによって,ある集団の人々を残酷かつ不公平に扱う→~を圧迫する,抑圧する,虐げる —oppressed 形→圧迫された,抑圧された,虐げられた ‖ *an oppressed minority* 虐げられた少数派 —oppression 名 U→抑圧,圧迫,圧制 ‖ *a struggle against oppression* 圧制に対するあがき

**oppressive** /əprésɪv/ 形 ▶定義1 allowing no freedom; controlling by force 自由を許さない;力ずくで支配している→抑圧的な,重圧的な,暴虐な,圧制的な ▶定義2 (used especially about heat or the atmosphere) causing you to feel very uncomfortable (特に熱気や雰囲気について)不快にさせる→(精神的に)重苦しい,気をめいらせる,(天候が)うっとうしい

**opt** /ɑ́pt/ 動 自 ▶定義 opt to do sth/for sth to choose or decide to do or have sth after thinking about it よく考えて~をする,持つことを選ぶ,決める→選ぶ,選択する

句動詞 opt out (of sth) ▶定義 to choose not to take part in sth; to decide to stop being involved in sth ~に加わらないことを選択する;~にかかわっていることをやめる決心をする→(~に)参加しないことにする,(~から)身を引くことにする,抜ける,脱退する

**optical** /ɑ́ptɪk(ə)l/ 形 ▶定義 connected with the sense of sight 視覚に関連した→視覚の,目の,視力の,光学の ‖ *optical instruments* 光学器械

**optical illusion** 名 C ▶定義 an image that tricks the eye and makes you think you can see sth that you cannot 視覚をだまして,見えない~を見えると思わせる幻影→目の錯覚,幻覚

**optician** /ɑptíʃ(ə)n/ 名 C ▶定義 a person whose job is to test eyes, sell glasses, etc 視力を検査したり,メガネを販売したりする人→眼鏡技師,検眼士 ‖ *I have to go to the optician's (=the shop) for an eye test.* 私は視力検査のために検眼士の所(=その店)に行かなくてはなりません.

**optimism** /ɑ́ptəmìz(ə)m/ 名 U ▶定義 the feeling that the future will be good or successful 未来は良い,または見通しが明るいという感情→楽観,楽天主義 ‖ *There is considerable optimism that the economy will improve.* 経済が上向きになるとのかなり楽観的な見解がある. ⇨ pessimism — optimist 名 C→楽天家,楽天主義者 ⇨ pessimist

**optimistic** /ɑ̀ptəmístɪk/ 形 ▶定義 optimistic (about sth/that ...) expecting good things to happen or sth to be successful; showing this feeling 良い事が起こるまたは成功するのを期待している;この気持ちを表している→楽観的な,楽天的な ‖ *I've applied for the job but I'm not very optimistic that I'll get it.* その仕事に応募し

たが、受かるという楽観視はあまりしていない. ⇔**pessimistic** — **optimistically** /-k(ə)li/ 副 →楽観的に、楽天的に⇔**pessimistically**

★**option** /άpʃ(ə)n/ 名 ❶ ❻ ▶定義 something that you can choose to do; the freedom to choose することを自分が選択できるもの; 選択する自由→選択するもの・されるもの, 選択肢; 選択の自由, 選択権 ‖ *She looked carefully at all the options before deciding on a career.* 職業を決める前に、彼女はすべての選択肢を注意深く検討した. *Students have the option of studying part-time or full-time.* 学生は全日制か定時制かを選択する自由があります. *If you're late again, you will give us no option but to dismiss you.* もしまた遅刻したら、私たちはあなたを解雇するほかない. ☛類 **choice**

**optional** /άpʃ(ə)n(ə)l/ 形 ▶定義 that you can choose or not choose 選んでも選ばなくてもよい→任意の, 随意の, 自由に選べる ‖ *an optional subject at school* 学校での選択科目⇔**compulsory, obligatory**

★**or** /ɔːr, ər/ 接 ▶定義 **1** used in a list of possibilities or choices 可能性や選択肢のリストにおいて使用される→～かあるいは、～かまたは ‖ *Would you like to sit here or next to the window?* 座席はここがよろしいですか、それとも窓際がよろしいですか. *Are you interested or not?* 興味がありますか、それともありませんか. *For the main course, you can have lamb, beef or fish.* メインコースとして、子羊, 牛肉, または魚を食べることができます. ☛参 **either...or** ▶定義 **2** if not; otherwise もしそうでなければ、でないと→さもないと、そうでないと ‖ *Don't drive so fast or you'll have an accident!* そんなにスピードを出さないで、そうでないと事故を起こしますよ. ☛ **or else** と **otherwise** はこの意味で用いることができる. ▶定義 **3** (否定形の後で) and neither; and not→～もまた…しない; ～もまた…でない ‖ *She hasn't phoned or written to me for weeks.* 彼女は何週間も私に電話も手紙もよこさなかった. *I've never been either to Italy or Spain.* 私はイタリアにもスペインにも行ったことがない. ☛参 **neither...nor** ▶定義 **4** used between two numbers to show approximately how many およそどのくらいなのかを示すために、2つの数の間で用いて→～か…か ‖ *I've been there five or six times.* そこへは5, 6回行ったことがあります. ▶定義 **5** used before a word or phrase that explains or comments on what has been said before 単語や句の前に用いて、前に言ったものを説明する, あるいはコメントを加える→つまり, すなわち, 言い換えると ‖ *20% of the population, or one in five* 人口の20パーセント、すなわち5人に1人

成句 **or else** ⇒ **ELSE**

**or so** ▶定義 about およそ～→～かそこら ‖ *You should feel better in three days or so.* 3日かそこらで気分が良くなるよ.

**or something/somewhere** (口語) ▶定義 used for showing that you are not sure, cannot remember or do not know which thing or place 物や場所について自信がない, 思い出せない, あるいは知らないということを示すために用いて→～か何か; ~かどこか ‖ *She's a computer programmer or something.* 彼女はコンピュータープログラマーか何かだよ.

▶確信のないことを示すほかの成句としては *...or other* がある: *He muttered something or other about having no time and disappeared.*（彼は時間がないとか何とかつぶやいて、いなくなった.）

★**oral**¹ /ɔ́ːr(ə)l, άr-/ 形 ▶定義 **1** spoken, not written 話された, 書かれていない→口頭の, 口述の ‖ *an oral test* 口頭試験 ▶定義 **2** concerning or using the mouth 口にかかわって, 口を使って→口の ‖ *oral hygiene* 口腔（こうくう）衛生学 ☛参 **aural** — **orally** 副 →口頭で, 口を通して ‖ *You can ask the questions orally or in writing.* 口頭もしくは文書で質問することができます. *This medicine is taken orally (=is swallowed).* この薬は経口摂取用です (=は飲み下されます)（この薬は内服薬です）.

**oral**² /ɔ́ːr(ə)l, άr-/ 名 ❻ ▶定義 a spoken exam 口頭の試験→口述試験, 面接試験 ‖ *I've got my German oral next week.* 来週ドイツ語の口頭試験がある.

★**orange**¹ /άrɪndʒ, ɔ́ːr(ə)ndʒ/ 名 ▶定義 **1** ❻ ❶ 英 a round fruit with a thick skin that is divided into sections (**segments**) inside and is a colour between red and yellow 赤と黄色の中間の色をした厚い皮の丸い果物, 中は複数の片（部分）に分かれている→オレンジ ‖ *orange juice/peel* オレンジジュース・オレンジの皮 *an orange tree* オ

# 1144　orange²

レンジの木　➡C3ページのさし絵　▶定義2
❶ⓊⒸ a drink made from oranges or with the taste of oranges; a glass of this drink オレンジから作られた飲み物,またはオレンジの味がする飲み物;この飲み物をグラス1杯➡オレンジジュース　▶定義3　ⓊⒸ the colour of this fruit, between red and yellow この果物の色,赤と黄色の中間色➡オレンジ色,だいだい色

**orange²** /árɪndʒ, ɑ́r(ə)ndʒ/ 形　▶定義 of the colour orange➡オレンジ色の,だいだい色の ‖ *orange paint* オレンジ色のペンキ

**orange squash** 名ⒸⓊ 英　▶定義 a drink made by adding water to an orange-flavoured liquid オレンジ味の液体に水を加えて作られた飲み物➡オレンジスカッシュ

**orator** /ɔ́(ː)rətər, ɑ́r-/ 名Ⓒ正式　▶定義 a person who is good at making public speechs 人前で演説をするのが得意な人➡雄弁家,弁士,講演家

**orbit** /ɔ́ːrbət/ 名ⒸⓊ　▶定義 a curved path taken by a planet or another object as it moves around another planet, star, moon, etc 惑星やそのほかの物体が,ほかの惑星,星,月などを周回するときにとる曲線を描く軌道➡(星や人工衛星などの)軌道 — orbit 動自他➡(衛星が)軌道に乗る,軌道を描いて〜を回る,(衛星を)軌道に乗せる

**orbital** /ɔ́ːrbət(ə)l/ 形　▶定義1 (used about a road) built around the outside of a city or town to reduce the amount of traffic travelling through the centre (道路について)市や町の中心を通り抜ける交通量を減少させるために,その外側にぐるりと周って建設された➡(道路が)環状の　▶定義2 connected with the orbit of a planet or another object in space 宇宙の惑星やそのほかの物体の軌道に関連して➡軌道の — orbital 名[Ⓒ,通常は単数]➡(都市郊外の)環状道路

**orchard** /ɔ́ːrtʃərd/ 名Ⓒ　▶定義 a piece of land on which fruit trees are grown 果物の木々が栽培されている土地➡果樹園 ‖ *a cherry orchard* サクランボ畑

**orchestra** /ɔ́ːrkəstrə/ 名Ⓒ　▶定義 a large group of musicians who play different musical instruments together, led by one person (a conductor) 1人の人(指揮者)に統率された,異なる楽器を一緒に演奏する音楽家たちの大きな集団➡オーケストラ,管弦楽団 ‖ *a symphony orchestra* 交響楽団

➤ orchestra(オーケストラ)は通常クラシック音楽を演奏する. group, band (グループ・バンド)はポップミュージック,ジャズなどを演奏する.

— orchestral /ɔːrkéstr(ə)l/ 形➡オーケストラの,オーケストラによる,オーケストラ用の

**orchid** /ɔ́ːrkəd/ 名Ⓒ　▶定義 a beautiful and sometimes rare type of plant that has flowers of unusual shapes and bright colours 美しく,時にはまれな植物の種,珍しい形の鮮やかな色の花をつける➡らん,らんの花➡C2ページのさし絵

**ordeal** /ɔːrdíːl, ´-/ 名[Ⓒ,通常は単数]　▶定義 a very unpleasant or difficult experience とても不快なまたは困難な経験➡(精神的に)苦しい体験,試練,困苦,苦難

**order¹** /ɔ́ːrdər/ 名　▶定義1 [Ⓤ,単数扱い] the way in which people or things are arranged in relation to each other 人や物が互いとの関係できちんと並べられる方法➡(前後の)順,順序,順番 ‖ *a list of names in **alphabetical order*** アルファベット順の名前のリスト *Try to put the things you have to do **in order of importance**.* 自分がしなくてはならない事を重要度の高い順に並べてみなさい. *What's the order of events today?* 今日の催しの順番はどうなっているのか. ▶定義2 Ⓤ an organized state, where everything is in its right place すべてが正しい場所に収まって,きちんと整理された状態➡整とん(された状態),整列 ‖ *I really must **put** my notes **in order**, because I can never find what I'm looking for.* 自分のメモを本当に整理しなければならない,捜しているものを見つけられないので. ⇔ **disorder** ▶定義3 Ⓒ **an order (for sb) (to do sth)** sth that you are told to do by sb in a position of authority 権威のある地位の〜によってそのように言われた…➡命令,指示,指図 ‖ *In the army, you have to **obey orders** at all times.* 軍隊ではいかなる時でも命令に従わなくてはならない. *She **gave the order** for the work to be started.* 彼女は仕事を始めるよう指示を出した. ▶定義4 Ⓤ the situation in which laws, rules, authority, etc are obeyed 法律,規則,権威などに人々が従っている状況➡(社会などの)秩序,治安 ‖ *Following last week's riots, order has now been restored.* 先週の暴動の後,今では秩序が取り戻されている. ☜参 **disorder** ▶定義5 ⒸⓊ

an order (for sth) a request asking for sth to be made, supplied or sent 〜が作られる,供給される,送られるように求める依頼➡注文,注文書,注文商品 ‖ *The company has just received a major export order.* その会社はちょうど大口の輸出の注文を受けたところだ. *The book I need is on order* (=they are waiting for it to arrive). 私の必要としている本は取り寄せ中だ(= 彼ら(本屋)は本が届くのを待っている). ▶定義 6 ●a request for food or drinks in a hotel, restaurant, etc; the food or drinks you asked for ホテル,レストランなどでの料理や飲み物の注文;自分が頼んだ料理や飲み物➡飲食物の注文;飲食物の注文(品),オーダー ‖ *Can I take your order now, sir?* ご注文をお伺いしてもよろしいですか.

成句 in order to do sth ▶定義 with the purpose or intention of doing sth; so that sth can be done 〜をする目的または意図を持って;〜がなされるように➡〜する目的で,〜するために,〜するつもりで ‖ *We left early in order to avoid the traffic.* 我々は交通渋滞を避けるために早く出発した.

in/into reverse order ⇒ **REVERSE**³

in working order ▶定義 (used about machines, etc) working properly, not broken (機械などについて)適切に動く,壊れていない➡調子良く動いて,故障なく

law and order ⇒ **LAW**

out of order ▶定義 1 (used about a machine, etc) not working properly or not working at all (機械などについて)適切に動かない,あるいは少しも動かない➡調子が悪くて,故障して ‖ *I had to walk up to the tenth floor because the lift was out of order.* エレベーターが故障していたので11階まで歩いて上がらなくてはならなかった.

▶定義 2 略式 (used about a person's behaviour) unacceptable, because it is rude, etc (人の行動について)無作法などの理由で受け入れられない➡ふさわしくない,適当でない ‖ *That comment was completely out of order!* あの論評は全く不適切だった.

★**order**² /ˈɔːrdər/ 動 ▶定義 1 ⓣ order sb (to do sth) to use your position of authority to tell sb to do sth or to say that sth must happen 自分の権威ある地位を用いて〜に…をするように言う,あるいは〜が起こるべきであると言う➡〜に命令する,指図する ‖ *I'm not asking you to do your homework, I'm ordering you!* あなたに宿題をするように頼んでいるのではない,私はあなたに命令しているのだ. *The company was ordered to pay compensation to its former employees.* その会社は元社員に補償金を支払うよう命じられた. ▶定義 2 ⓣ to ask for sth to be made, supplied or sent somewhere 〜が作られたり,供給されたり,どこかへ送られるように依頼する➡〜を注文する,〜を発注する ‖ *The shop didn't have the book I wanted so I ordered it.* お店には私が欲しかった本がなかったので注文した.

▶定義 3 order (sb) (sth); order (sth) (for sb) ⓘⓣ to ask for food or drinks in a restaurant, hotel, etc レストランやホテルなどで料理や飲み物を頼む➡(〜を)注文する,オーダーする ‖ *Are you ready to order yet, madam?* 奥様,ご注文をお伺いしてもよろしいですか. *Can you order me a sandwich while I make a phone call?* 私が電話をしている間に,私のサンドイッチを注文してくれるね. *Could you order a sandwich for me?* 私のためにサンドイッチを注文していただけますか.

句動詞 order sb about/around ▶定義 to keep telling sb what to do and how to do it 〜に何をどのようにしろと言い続ける➡人にあれこれ命令する,人をこき使う ‖ *Stop ordering me about! You're not my father.* 私にあれこれ命令するのはやめて.あなたは私の父親ではないのだから.

**orderly**¹ /ˈɔːrdərli/ 形 ▶定義 1 arranged or organized in a tidy way 整然とした形に整理して,あるいは組織して➡(物や場所が)順序正しい,整とんされた,きちんとした ‖ *an orderly office/desk* 整とんされたオフィス・机 ▶定義 2 well-behaved; peaceful よくしつけられた;穏やかな➡従順な,穏やかな⇔**disorderly**

**orderly**² /ˈɔːrdərli/ 名 ⓒ (複 **orderlies**) ▶定義 a worker in a hospital, usually doing jobs that do not need special training 病院で働いている人で,普通は特別な訓練を必要としない仕事をしている人➡(病院の)付き添い,介護員,用務員

**ordinal** /ˈɔːrdn(ə)l, -dnl/ (または **ordinal number**) 名 ⓒ ▶定義 a number that shows the order or position of sth in a series 一連のものの中で〜の順序や位置を示す数➡序数,序数詞 ‖ *'First', 'second', and 'third' are ordinals.* first, second, third は序数です. ☛参 **cardinal**

**ordinarily** /ˈɔːdn(ə)rəli, ˌɔːrdnˈérəli/ 副 ▶定義 usually; generally→大抵；一般的に‖ *Ordinarily, I don't work as late as this.* 通常私はこんな遅くまで働きません．

*__ordinary__ /ˈɔːdn(ə)ri; ˈɔːrdnèri/ 形 ▶定義 normal; not unusual or different from others 普通の；珍しくはない，あるいはほかと違わない→**普通の，通常の，並みの，平凡な**‖ *It's interesting to see how ordinary people live in other countries.* ほかの国の普通の人々がどのように暮らしているのかを知ることは，興味深い．

成句 **out of the ordinary** ▶定義 unusual; different from normal 珍しい；普通と違っている→**例外的な，異常な，並外れた**

**ore** /ɔːr/ 名 C U ▶定義 rock or earth from which metal can be taken 金属がとれる岩または大地→**鉱石，原鉱**‖ *iron ore* 鉄鉱石

*__organ__ /ˈɔːrɡən/ 名 C ▶定義 **1** one of the parts inside your body that have a particular function 体内の一部で特定の機能を備えている部分→**内臓，臓器，器官**‖ *vital organs* (=those such as the heart and liver which help to keep you alive) 生命の維持に必要な臓器(＝例えば心臓や肝臓などの臓器で，私たちが生き続けていくことに役立つもの) *sexual/reproductive organs* 性器・生殖器 ▶定義 **2** a large musical instrument like a piano with pipes through which air is forced. Organs are often found in churches. ピアノのように大きな楽器で，空気を通り抜けさせるパイプの付いたもの．オルガンは，よく教会で見受けられる→**オルガン，パイプオルガン**‖ *organ music* オルガン音楽 ●参 **piano** の注― **organist** 名 C ―（教会などの）パイプオルガン奏者

**organic** /ɔːrˈɡænɪk/ 形 ▶定義 **1** (used about food or farming methods) produced by or using natural materials, without artificial chemicals (食品や農業方式について) 人工の薬品などは使わないで，自然の材料で作られた，あるいは自然の材料を使っている→**(食品が)有機肥料・飼料を用いた，化学肥料・飼料・薬品を用いない**‖ *organic vegetables* 有機野菜 *organic farming* 有機農法 ▶定義 **2** produced by or existing in living things 生きている物によって作られた，あるいは生きている物に存在している→**有機の，有機物の**‖ *organic compounds/molecules* 有機化合物・分子 ⇔ **inorganic** ― **organically** /-k(ə)li/ 副 →**有機的に，有機肥料を用いて**‖ *organically grown/produced* 有機的に育てられた・作られた

**organism** /ˈɔːrɡənɪz(ə)m/ 名 C ▶定義 a living thing, especially one that is so small that you can only see it with a special instrument (a **microscope**) 生き物，特に特別の装置(顕微鏡)を使ってみることができるほど，とても小さい生命体→**有機体，微生物**

*__organization__ (または **-isation**) /ˌɔːrɡ(ə)nàɪzéɪʃ(ə)n; -nə-/ 名 ▶定義 **1** ❶ a group of people who form a business, club, etc together in order to achieve a particular aim 会社，クラブなどを一緒に形成して特定の目的を達成しようとする人々の集団→**(ある目的を持つ)団体，組織体，協会**‖ *She works for a voluntary organization helping homeless people.* 彼女はホームレスを援助するボランティア組織で働いている．
▶定義 **2** ❶ the activity of making preparations or arrangements for sth ～のために準備したり，あるいは手配する活動→**取りまとめ，計画，準備**‖ *An enormous amount of organization went into the festival.* とても多くの準備がそのフェスティバルに費やされた． ▶定義 **3** ❶ the way in which sth is organized, arranged or prepared ～が組織される，手配される，あるいは準備される方法→**組織化，編成，構成** ⇔ **disorganization** ― **organizational** (または **-isational**) /-ʃ(ə)n(ə)l/ 形 →**団体の，組織の**‖ *The job requires a high level of organizational ability.* その仕事は高度の組織力を要求する．

*__organize__ (または **-ise**) /ˈɔːrɡənaɪz/ 動 ▶定義 ❶ to plan or arrange an event, activity, etc イベント，活動などを計画，手配する→**～を計画する，催す**‖ *The school organizes trips to various places of interest.* 学校はいろいろな興味深い場所への小旅行を催します． ▶定義 **2** ❶ to put or arrange things into a system or logical order 物事を体系的に，あるいは論理にかなった順番に置く，あるいは整理する→**(～を)系統立てる，体系づける，整理する，(考えなどを)まとめる**‖ *Can you decide what needs doing? I'm hopeless at organizing.* 何をする必要があるか決めてもらえますか．私は系統立てることが苦手なのです． *You need to organize your work more carefully.* あなたは自分の仕事をもっと注意深く組織化する必要があります．― **organizer** (または **-iser**)

图 ⓒ →組織者, 主催者, まとめ役 ‖ *The organizers of the concert said that it had been a great success.* そのコンサートの主催者は, コンサートは大成功だったと言った.

**organized** (または **-ised**) /ɔ́ːrgənàɪzd/ 形 ▶定義 1 arranged or planned in the way mentioned ～のように手配された, 計画された→組織された, 編成された ‖ *a carefully/badly/well organized trip* 慎重に·不適切に·よく計画された旅行 ▶定義 2 (used about a person) able to plan your work, life, etc well (人について) 自分の仕事, 人生などをうまく計画できる→能率の良い, きちんと仕事をする, うまくやれる ‖ *I wish I were as organized as you!* あなたのように私もうまくやれたらなぁ. ⇔定義 1, 2 **disorganized** ▶定義 3 (名詞の前だけ) involving a large number of people working together to do sth in a way that has been carefully planned 慎重に計画された方法で～をするために一緒に働こうと, 多数の人々がかかわっている→組織された, 編成された ‖ *an organized campaign against cruelty to animals* 動物虐待に反対する組織的キャンペーン *organized crime* (=done by a large group of professional criminals) 組織犯罪(= 大きなプロの犯罪者グループによって行われる)

**orgasm** /ɔ́ːrgæz(ə)m/ 图 Ⓤ Ⓒ ▶定義 the point of greatest sexual pleasure 性的快感の頂点→快感の絶頂, オルガスム ‖ *to have an orgasm* オルガスムを得る

**orgy** /ɔ́ːrdʒi/ 图 ⓒ (複 **orgies**) ▶定義 1 a party, involving a lot of eating, drinking and sexual activity たくさんの飲食, 性的行為が行われる宴会→飲めや歌えやの大騒ぎ, 乱交パーティー ▶定義 2 **an orgy (of sth)** a period of doing sth in a wild way, without control 何の制御もなく, 狂気染みたやり方で～をしている期間→過度の熱中, やりすぎ ‖ *an orgy of destruction* 破壊の限りを尽くすこと

**orient** /ɔ́ːriənt/ (医 または **orientate** /ɔ́ːriəntèɪt, -ən-/) 動 ⓘ ▶定義 **orient yourself** to find out where you are; to become familiar with a place 自分がどこにいるかを知る; 場所になじんでくる→(自分の位置·立場)を見定める, (環境)に順応する ☛参 **disorientate**

**the Orient** /ɔ́ːriənt/ [単数扱い] 正式 ▶定義 the eastern part of the world, especially China and Japan 世界の東側部分, 特に中国と日本→東洋

**oriental** /ɔ̀ːriéntl/ 形 ▶定義 **Oriental**(古) coming from or belonging to the East or Far East 東洋または極東から来た, あるいは東洋または極東に属している→東洋の, 東洋風の ‖ *oriental languages* 東洋の言語 ☛注意. 多くの人々が現在ではこの言葉が侮辱的であると考えている. Asian を使用する方が良い.

**oriented** /ɔ́ːriəntɪd/ (または **orientated** /ɔ́ːriəntèɪtɪd/) 形 ▶定義 for or interested in a particular type of person or thing 特定のタイプの人間または物のための, あるいはそれに興味のある→～傾向の, ～志向の, ～に方向づけられた ‖ *Our products are male-oriented.* 私たちの商品は男性向けです. *She's very career orientated.* 彼女はとてもキャリア志向です.

**orienteering** /ɔ̀ːriəntíərɪŋ/ 图 Ⓤ ▶定義 a sport in which you find your way across country on foot, using a map and an instrument that shows direction (a compass) 地図と方角を示す道具(方位磁石)を使って, ある地域を歩いて自分の行くべき道を探すスポーツ→オリエンテーリング

**origin** /ɔ́ː(ː)rədʒən/ 图 ⓒ Ⓤ ▶定義 1 (しばしば複数形で用いて) the point from which sth starts; the cause of sth ～が始まる地点; ～の原因→起源, 起こり, 始まり, 発端 ‖ *This particular tradition has its origins in Wales.* この特有の伝統はウェールズにその起源を持つ. *Many English words are of Latin origin.* 多くの英語の単語はラテン語が起源です. ▶定義 2 (しばしば複数形で用いて) the country, race, culture, etc that a person comes from ある個人が生まれた国, 人種, 文化など→生まれ, 素性, 血統 ‖ *people of African origin* アフリカ系の人々

★**original**¹ /ərídʒənl/ 形 ▶定義 1 (名詞の前だけ) first; earliest (before any changes or developments) 最初の; 一番早い(どんな変化, 発達よりも前)→最初の, 本来の, 原始の ‖ *The original meaning of this word is different from the meaning it has nowadays.* この単語の本来の意味は今日のものとは異なります. ▶定義 2 new and interesting; different from others of its type 新しくて面白い; ほかのそのたぐいのものとは違っている→独創的な, 新奇な ‖ *There are no original ideas in his work.* 彼の作品には独創性がない.

▶定義3 made or created first, before copies 写す前の, 最初に作られた, あるいは創造された→原型の, 原文の, 原本の ‖ 'Is that the original painting?' 'No, it's a copy.'「これは原画ですか」「いいえ, これは模写です」

**original**² /ərídʒənl/ 图 ❻ ▶定義 the first document, painting, etc that was made; not a copy 最初に作られた文書, 絵画など; 写しではないもの→原物, 原本, 原画, 原文 ‖ Could you make a photocopy of my birth certificate and give the original back to me? 私の出生証明書をコピーして, 原本を私に戻していただけますか.

**originality** /ərìdʒənǽləti/ 图 ❶ ▶定義 the quality of being new and interesting 新しく面白いという特性→独創性・力, 創造力, 創意

**originally** /ərídʒənli/ 副 ▶定義1 in the beginning, before any changes or developments 始めに, あらゆる変化または発展の前に→元来(は), 初めは ‖ I'm from London originally, but I left there when I was very young. 私はもともとはロンドン出身ですが, 赤ん坊のころ離れてしまいました.
▶定義2 in a way or style that is new and different from any others 新しくほかとは異なる方法または様式で→独創的に, 奇抜に ‖ She has a talent for expressing simple ideas originally. 彼女は単純なアイデアを独創的に表現する才能を持っている.

**originate** /ərídʒənèɪt/ 動 ❶ 正式 ▶定義 to happen or appear for the first time in a particular place or situation 特定の場所や状況において初めて起きる, あるいは姿を現す→発生する, 起こる, (〜に)源を発する, (物事が人から)始まる, 〜の考案になる

**ornament** /ɔ́ːrnəmənt/ 图 ❻ ▶定義 an object that you have because it is attractive, not because it is useful. Ornaments are used to decorate rooms, etc. 利用価値があるからではなく, 魅力的だから持っているもの. 部屋などを飾るために使用される→装飾品, 飾り

**ornamental** /ɔ̀ːrnəméntl/ 形 ▶定義 made or put somewhere in order to look attractive, not for any practical use 実用ではなく, ある場所が魅力的に見えるように作られた, あるいは置かれた→装飾用の, 飾りの

**ornate** /ɔːnéɪt/ 形 ▶定義 covered with a lot of small complicated designs as decoration 飾りとして, たくさんの小さな複雑な模様で覆われている→飾り立てた, 華麗な, 華やかな

**ornithology** /ɔ̀ːnəθɑ́lədʒi/ 图 ❶ ▶定義 the study of birds 鳥についての学問→鳥類学 — **ornithologist** /-ɪst/ 图 ❻ →鳥類学者

**orphan** /ɔ́ːrf(ə)n/ 图 ❻ ▶定義 a child whose parents are dead 両親が死んでしまった子供→孤児 — **orphan** 動他 (通常は受動態で)→ 〜を孤児にする ‖ She was orphaned when she was three and went to live with her grandparents. 彼女は3歳の時に孤児になり, 祖父母と暮らし始めた.

**orphanage** /ɔ́ːrf(ə)nɪdʒ/ 图 ❻ ▶定義 a home for children whose parents are dead 両親の死んでしまった子供のための家→孤児院, 養護施設 ⟶ より一般的な語は children's home (子供の家).

**orthodox** /ɔ́ːrθədɑ̀ks/ 形 ▶定義1 that most people believe, do or accept; usual ほとんどの人々が信じ, 行い, あるいは受け入れている; 普通の→正統的な, 伝統的な, 世間一般で認められている, ありふれた ‖ orthodox opinions/methods 正統的な意見・方法 ⇔ **unorthodox** ▶定義2 (in certain religions) closely following the old, traditional beliefs, ceremonies, etc (ある宗教において) 古くからの伝統的信仰や儀式などに厳密に従って→正統派の, 正統的な ‖ an orthodox Jew 正統派ユダヤ教徒 the Greek Orthodox Church ギリシャ正教会

**ostentatious** /ɑ̀stəntéɪʃəs/ 形 ▶定義1 expensive or noticeable in a way that is intended to impress other people ほかの人々に印象を与えるように意図されたやり方で, 高価なまたは人目をひく→派手な, けばけばしい ‖ ostentatious gold jewellery 派手な金の宝飾品 ▶定義2 behaving in a way that is intended to impress people with how rich or important you are いかに金持ちであるか, あるいは重要人物であるかを人々に印象づけるように意図して振る舞う→見えを張る, これ見よがしの — **ostentatiously** 副 →これ見よがしに, けばけばしく

**ostracize** (または **-ise**) /ɑ́strəsàɪz/ 動他 正式 ▶定義 to refuse to allow sb to be a member of a social group; to refuse to meet or talk to sb 〜を社会的なグループの一員でいさせることを断る; 〜と会う, あるいは話すことを断る→〜を追放する, 排斥する, 村八分にする

**ostrich** /ɔ́(ː)strɪtʃ, ás-/ 图 ❻ ▶定義 a very large African bird with a long neck and long legs, which can run very fast but which cannot fly とても大きなアフリカの鳥で, 長い首と長い足を持ち, とても早く走れるが飛べない→ダチョウ

\***other** /ʌ́ðər/ 形代 ▶定義 1 in addition to or different from the one or ones that have already been mentioned 既に述べたものに加えて, あるいは既に述べたものとは異なる→ほかの, 別の, 異なった ‖ *I hadn't got any other plans that evening so I accepted their invitation.* その晩はほかにすべき事もなかったので, 彼らの招待を受けた. *If you're busy now, I'll come back some other time.* もし今忙しいのなら, 別のときに出直します. *I like this jumper but not the colour. Have you got any others?* このセーターが好きなのだけど, 色が嫌だ. ほかに何かありますか. *Some of my friends went to university, others didn't.* 何人かの友達は大学へ進学したが, ほかの友達は行かなかった. *She doesn't care what other people think.* 他人がどう考えているか彼女は気にしていない.

➤ other は an の後には使用できない. another を参照.

▶定義 2 (単数名詞を伴う the, my, your, his, her などの後に) the second of two people or things, when the first has already been mentioned 2人または2つの物のうちの一方について既に述べられた後の2つ目の (2つのうちの)もう1つの, もう片方の ‖ *I can only find one sock. Have you seen the other one?* 靴下が1つしか見つからない. あなた, もう片方を見掛けましたか. ▶定義 3 (複数名詞を伴う the, my, your, his, her などの後に) the rest of a group or number of people or things あるグループ, 複数の人や物の残り→(3つ以上のうちの)残り全部の, ほかの, 後の ‖ *Their youngest son still lives with them but their other children have left home.* 彼らの一番下の息子はまだ一緒に住んでいるが, ほかの子供たちは家を出てしまっている. *I'll have to wear this shirt because all my others are dirty.* ほかの服は全部汚れているので, このシャツを着なければなりません. *Mick and I got a taxi there, the others walked.* ミックと私はそこからタクシーに乗ったが, ほかの人たちは歩いていった.

成句 every other ⇒ **EVERY**
in other words ▶定義 used for saying sth in a different way 別の方法で~を言うために用いて→言い換えれば, つまり ‖ *My boss said she would have to let me go. In other words, she sacked me.* 上司は私を自由にしなければならないと言ったが, 言い換えれば彼女は私を解雇したのだ.
one after another/the other ⇒ **ONE**[1]
other than (通常は否定形の後で) ▶定義 apart from; except (for) ~を除けば; ~以外では→~のほかに, ~を除いて ‖ *The plane was a little late, but other than that the journey was fine.* 飛行機は多少遅れたが, それを除けば旅行は快適だった.
the other day/morning/week ▶定義 recently, not long ago 最近, それほど前ではない→先日; 先日の朝; 2, 3週間前 ‖ *An old friend rang me the other day.* 先日, 古い友人が私に電話をかけてきた.
the other way round ⇒ **ROUND**[2]
sb/sth/somewhere or other ⇒ **OR**

\***otherwise** /ʌ́ðərwàɪz/ 副接 ▶定義 1 (used for stating what would happen if you do not do sth or if sth does not happen) if not (~をしなかったり, ~が起きなかったときに, 何が起こるかを述べるときに用いて) もしそうでなかったら→そうでなければ, さもないと ‖ *You have to press the red button, otherwise it won't work.* 赤いボタンを押さないといけません, そうでないとそれは動きません. ▶定義 2 apart from that あれを別として→そのほかの点では ‖ *I'm a bit tired but otherwise I feel fine.* ちょっと疲れているが, そのほかの点では元気です. ▶定義 3 in a different way to the way mentioned; differently 述べた事とは異なった方法で; 違ったように→別な方法では, ほかのやり方では

**otter** /ɑ́tər/ 名 Ｃ ▶定義 a river animal with brown fur that eats fish 茶色の毛で覆われていて魚を食べる川の動物→カワウソ

**ouch** /áʊtʃ/ (または **ow** /áʊ, úə/) 間 ▶定義 used

when reacting to a sudden feeling of pain 突然の痛みに反応するときに用いて➔あっ痛い

**★ought to** /ɔ́ːt tə/ 助 (否定形 **ought not to**; 短縮形 **oughtn't to** /ɔ́ːtnt tə/) ▶定義1 used to say what sb should do ～が何をすべきか言うのに用いて➔～すべきである, ～するのが当然だ ‖ *You ought to visit your parents more often.* もっと頻繁にご両親を訪ねるべきです. *She oughtn't to make private phone calls in work time.* 彼女は勤務時間に私用電話をかけるべきではない. *He oughtn't to have been driving so fast.* 彼はそんなに速く運転するべきではなかった. ▶定義2 used to say what should happen or what you expect 何が当然起こるか, あるいは何を予期しているかを述べるときに用いて➔～のはずだ, おそらく～だ ‖ *She ought to pass her test.* 彼女は試験に合格するに決まっている. *They ought to be here by now. They left at six.* 彼らはもうここに来るはずだ. 彼らは6時に出発した(のだから). *There ought to be more buses in the rush hour.* ラッシュアワー時にはもっとバスがあってもいいはずだ. ▶定義3 used for asking for and giving advice about what to do 何をするかについて, 助言を求めたり与えたりするために用いて➔～した方が良い, ～する必要がある ‖ *You ought to read this book. It's really interesting.* あなたはこの本を読んだ方が良い. これはとても興味深い.

▶法助動詞についての説明は, 巻末の「文法早見表」を参照.

**ounce** /áʊns/ 名 ▶定義1 ⒸⓁ (略 **oz**) a measure of weight; 28.35 grams. There are 16 ounces in a pound. 重さの単位; 28.35グラム. 1ポンドは16オンス➔オンス ‖ *For this recipe you need four ounces of flour.* このレシピでは, 小麦粉が4オンス必要です. ▶定義2 [単数扱い] **an ounce of sth** (通常は否定文で) a very small amount of sth とても少量の～➔少量 ‖ *He hasn't got an ounce of imagination.* 彼はほんの少しの想像力も持っていなかった.

**★our** /áʊər, ɑːr/ 代 ▶定義 of or belonging to us 私たちの, あるいは私たちに属する➔私たちの, 我々の ‖ *Our house is at the bottom of the road.* 私たちの家は道の突き当たりにあります. *This is our first visit to Britain.* これが私たちにとって最初のイギリス訪問です.

**★ours** /áʊərz, ɑːrz/ 代 ▶定義 the one or ones belonging to us 私たちに属するもの➔私たちのもの, 我々のもの ‖ *Their garden is quite nice but I prefer ours.* 彼らの庭はとても良いが, 私たちのもののほうが気に入っている.

**★ourselves** /àʊərsélvz/ 代 ▶定義1 used when the people who do an action are also affected by it ある行動を起こす人々が, 同時にそのことによって影響を受けるときに用いて➔自分自身に, 自分自身を ‖ *Let's forget all about work and just enjoy ourselves.* 仕事のことはすべて忘れて, ただ楽しく過ごそうじゃないか. *They asked us to wait so we sat down and made ourselves comfortable.* 彼らは私たちにしばらく待つように言った, そこで私たちは座ってくつろいだ. ▶定義2 used for emphasis 強調に用いて➔(私たち)が自分たちで, (我々)が自分自身で ‖ *Do you think we should paint the flat ourselves? (=or should we ask sb else to do it for us?)* 私たちが自分たちでアパートのペンキ塗りをすべきだと思いますか(=または私たちの代わりに, ほかの人にそれをやるように頼むべきですか). 成句 **(all) by ourselves** ▶定義1 alone ～だけで➔私たちだけで ‖ *Now that we're by ourselves, could I ask you a personal question?* 今はもう私たちだけになったので, 個人的な質問をしていいですか. ☛参 **alone** の注 ▶定義2 without help 助けなしで➔自分たちの力だけで ‖ *We managed to move all our furniture into the new flat by ourselves.* 私たちは, 自分たちだけですべての家具を新しいアパートへ何とか移動させた.

**★out** /áʊt/ 形副

▶例えば **look out** などのように, 多くの動詞と共に用いられる慣用表現は, それぞれの動詞の記載を参照.

▶定義1 away from the inside of a place 場所の内部から離れて➔外へ, 外に, 外部へ ‖ *He opened the drawer and took a fork out.* 彼は引き出しを開けてフォークを取り出した. *She opened the window and put her head out.* 彼女は窓を開けて頭を外に出した. *Can you show me the way out?* 外への出方を教えてもらえますか. ▶定義2 not at home or in your place of work 自宅にいない, あるいは仕事場にいない➔外出して, 不在で ‖ *My manager was out when she called.* 彼女が電話をした時, 私の上司は外

出していた. *I'd love a night out - I'm bored with staying at home.* 私は夜外出したい － 家にいるのに飽きた. ▶定義3 a long distance away from a place, for example from land or your country ある場所, 例えば陸地や自分の国から遠く離れて→**遠く離れて** ‖ *The current is quite strong so don't swim too far out.* 潮の流れがとても強い, だから岸からあまり離れては泳ぐな. ▶定義4 (used about the sea) when the water is furthest away from the shore (海について) 水が海岸から最も離れているとき→**干潮** ‖ *Don't swim when the tide is on the way out.* 潮が引いている時は泳がないように. ▶定義5 used for showing that sth is no longer hidden 〜がもはや隠れていないことを示すのに用いて→**現れて** ‖ *I love the spring when all the flowers are out.* 私はすべての花の咲く春が大好きだ. *The secret's out now. There's no point pretending any more.* 今, その秘密は皆に知られてしまった. これ以上, 知らない振りをしても無意味だ. ▶定義6 made available to the public; published 一般の人が入手可能となった; 出版された→**公になって, 発表されて, 出版されて, 世に出て** ‖ *There'll be a lot of controversy when her book comes out next year.* 彼女の本が来年出版されると, 数々の議論を生むだろう. ▶定義7 in a loud voice; clearly 大きな声で; はっきりと→**大声で, はっきりと, 率直に** ‖ *She cried out in pain.* 彼女は痛みに大声で叫んだ. ▶定義8 not in fashion 流行していない→**(服装などが)流行しなくなって, すたれて** ‖ *Short skirts are out this season.* 短いスカートは今シーズンははやっていない. ▶定義9 (口語) not possible or acceptable 可能ではない, 受け入れられない→**(物事が)不可能で, 問題外で** ‖ *I'm afraid Friday is out. I've got a meeting that day.* 残念なことに金曜日は不可能です. その日は会議があります. ▶定義10 (used about a player in a game or sport) not allowed to continue playing (競技やスポーツの選手について) プレーを続けることが許されない→**アウトで** ‖ *If you get three answers wrong, you're out.* もし答えを3つ間違えたら, あなたは退場です. ▶定義11 (used about a ball, etc in a game or sport) not inside the playing area and therefore not allowed (競技やスポーツなどで, ボールなどについて) 競技エリア内ではないので許されない→**(ボールなどが)アウトになって** ▶定義12 (used

# outbound motor 1151

when you are calculating sth) making or containing a mistake; wrong (〜を計算しているときに用いて) ミスをする, あるいはミスを含んでいる; 間違っている→**間違って** ‖ *My guess was only out by a few centimetres.* 私の推測はわずかに数センチ間違っていた. ▶定義13 (used about a light or a fire) not on; not burning (照明や火について) スイッチが入っていない, 燃えていない→**(照明・火が)消えて** ‖ *The lights are out. They must be in bed.* 明かりが消えています. 彼らは寝ているに違いない. *Once the fire was completely out, experts were sent in to inspect the damage.* 火が完全に消えるやいなや, 損害を調べるために専門家が中に送り込まれた.

成句 **be out for sth; be out to do sth** ▶定義 to try hard to get or do sth 〜を手に入れる, するために一生懸命に頑張る→**(懸命に)〜を得ようとしている; 〜しようと努めている, 〜しようと決意している** ‖ *I'm not out for revenge.* 私は復讐 (ふくしゅう) しようとしているのではない.

**be/come out** ▶定義 to tell family, friends, etc that you are a homosexual→**家族, 友達などに自分がホモであると告げる**

**out-and-out** ▶定義 complete 完全な→**全く, 純然たる, 徹底的な** ‖ *It was out-and-out war between us.* 私たちの間は完全な戦争状態だった.

**out loud**=ALOUD

**out**² /áut/ 動他 ▶定義 to say publicly that sb is a homosexual, especially when he/she would rather keep it a secret 特に〜がホモセクシュアルであることをどちらかというと秘密にしている場合, その人がホモであると公表する→**(有名人など)がホモまたはレズであることをばらす** ‖ *The politician was eventually outed by a tabloid newspaper.* その政治家は最終的にはタブロイド新聞にホモだとすっぱ抜かれた.

**the outback** /áutbæk/ 名 [単数扱い] ▶定義 the part of a country (especially Australia) which is a long way from the coast and towns, where few people live 国 (特にオーストラリア) の一部で, 海岸や町から遠く離れていて人はほとんど住んでいない地域→**オーストラリアの内陸部**

**outbound motor** /áutbàund móutər/ 名 C ▶定義 an engine that can be fixed to a boat ボートに取り付けることのできるエンジン→モー

## 1152　outbreak

ターボートの)船外エンジン

**outbreak** /áʊtbrèɪk/ 名 C ▶定義 the sudden start of sth unpleasant (especially a disease or violence) 不快な～(特に病気または暴力)の突然の始まり→(火事・戦争・暴動などの)発生，勃発(ぼっぱつ)，突発，(怒りなどの)激発 ‖ *an outbreak of cholera/fighting* コレラの発生・闘争の勃発

**outburst** /áʊtbə̀ːrst/ 名 C ▶定義 a sudden expression of a strong feeling, especially anger 強烈な感情，特に怒りの突然の表現→(怒り・笑いなどの)爆発，激発 ‖ *Afterwards, she apologized for her outburst.* 後で，彼女は感情を爆発させたことを謝った．

**outcast** /áʊtkæ̀st; -kὰːst/ 名 C ▶定義 a person who is no longer accepted by society or by a group of people 社会，あるいはある集団の人々にもはや受け入れてもらえない人→(社会などから)追放された人，(家族などから)見捨てられた人 ‖ *a social outcast* 社会的追放者，浮浪者

**outclass** /àʊtklǽs; -klὰːs/ 動 他 (しばしば受動態で) ▶定義 to be much better than sb/sth, especially in a game or competition 特に試合や競争において，～よりはるかに優れている→～に断然勝る，～より格段優れている

**outcome** /áʊtkʌ̀m/ 名 C ▶定義 the result or effect of an action or an event 行為や出来事の結果または影響→結果，成果

**outcry** /áʊtkràɪ/ 名 [C，通常は単数] (複 **outcries**) ▶定義 a strong protest by a large number of people because they disagree with sth ～に反対している大勢の人々による強い抗議→(～に対する)激しい抗議 ‖ *The public outcry forced the government to change its mind about the new tax.* 国民の激しい抗議は政府に新しい税金についての考えを変えさせた．

**outdated** /àʊtdéɪtəd/ 形 ▶定義 not useful or common any more; old-fashioned 役に立たない，もはや一般的ではない；旧式の→時代後れの ‖ *A lot of the computer equipment is getting outdated.* 多くのコンピューター設備が時代後れになりつつある．

**outdo** /àʊtdúː/ 動 他 (現分 **outdoing**; 三単現 **outdoes** /-dʌ́z/，過 **outdid** /-díd/，過分 **outdone** /-dʌ́n/) ▶定義 to do sth better than another person; to be more successful than sb else ～を別の人よりうまくする；ほかの～より成功している→～に勝る，～をしのぐ ‖ *Not to be outdone* (=not wanting anyone else to do better), *she tried again.* 人に負けまいと(＝ほかのだれかがもっと上手にすることを望まない)，彼女は再び努力した．

＊**outdoor** /áʊtdɔ̀ːr/ 形 (名詞の前だけ) ▶定義 happening, done, or used outside, not in a building 建物の中ではなく，外で起こる・なされる，あるいは使われる→屋外の，野外の ‖ *an outdoor swimming pool* 屋外プール *outdoor clothing/activities* 野外服・野外活動⇔**indoor**

＊**outdoors** /àʊtdɔ́ːrz/ 副 ▶定義 outside a building 建物の外→屋外で，野外で ‖ *It's a very warm evening so why don't we eat outdoors?* 今晩はとても暖かいので，屋外で食事しませんか．
☛類 out of doors⇔indoors ☛参 outside

＊**outer** /áʊtər/ 形 (名詞の前だけ) ▶定義 **1** on the outside of sth ～の外側の→外側の，外部の ‖ *the outer layer of skin on an onion* タマネギの外側の層 ▶定義 **2** far from the inside or the centre of sth ～の内側・中心から遠い→中心から離れた ‖ *the outer suburbs of a city* 市から遠く離れた郊外⇔**inner**

**outermost** /áʊtəmóʊst/ 形 (名詞の前だけ) ▶定義 furthest from the inside or centre; most distant 内側・中心から最も遠くに；最も離れている→最も外部の，最も遠くの⇔**innermost**

**outer space** =SPACE¹(2)

**outfit** /áʊtfɪt/ 名 C ▶定義 a set of clothes that are worn together for a particular occasion or purpose 特定の機会や目的のために，すべて一緒に身に着ける洋服一そろい→身支度一式，衣装一式，装備一式 ‖ *I'm going to buy a whole new outfit for the party.* 私はそのパーティーのために，新しい衣装を一そろい購入します．

**outgoing** /áʊtɡòʊɪŋ/ 形 ▶定義 **1** friendly and interested in other people and new experiences 気さくで，ほかの人々や新しい経験に興味を持っている→社交性に富んだ，外向性の ▶定義 **2** (名詞の前だけ) leaving a job or a place 勤め口または場所から離れる→出ていく，去っていく，(職などを)辞めることになっている，引退する ‖ *the outgoing president/government* 辞任する大統領・政府 *Put all the outgoing mail in a pile on that table.* これから出すすべての郵便物をあのテーブルの上に積み重ねてください．⇔**incom-**

**outgoings** /áʊtgòʊɪŋz/ 名[複数扱い] 囲 ▶定義 an amount of money that you spend regularly for example every week or month 自分が規則的に,例えば1週間ごとまたは1か月ごとに使っているお金の額→**出費,支出**⇔**income**

**outgrow** /àʊtgróʊ/ 動他(過 **outgrew** /-grúː/; 過分 **outgrown** /-gróʊn/) ▶定義 to become too old or too big for sth 〜にとって古くなりすぎる,あるいは大きくなりすぎる→**大きくなりすぎて〜に合わない,年を取って〜から抜け出す**

**outing** /áʊtɪŋ/ 名 ⓒ ▶定義 a short trip for pleasure 楽しむための短い旅行→**遠足,ピクニック** ‖ *to go on an outing* to the zoo 動物園へ遠足に行く

**outlandish** /àʊtlændɪʃ/ 形 ▶定義 very strange or unusual とても変わっている,または普通でない→**異様な,風変わりな** ‖ *outlandish clothes* 風変わりな服装

**outlast** /àʊtlǽːst; -lǽst/ 動他 ▶定義 to continue to exist or to do sth for a longer time than sb/sth 〜より長い時間,存在し続ける,あるいは〜をし続ける→**〜より長持ちする,〜より長く続く,〜より長生きする**

**outlaw**¹ /áʊtlɔ̀ː/ 動他 ▶定義 to make sth illegal 〜を違法にする→**〜を法律の保護の外に置く,非合法化する**

**outlaw**² /áʊtlɔ̀ː/ 名 ⓒ (古) (過去形で用いて) ▶定義 a person who has done sth illegal and is hiding to avoid being caught 〜を非合法に行い,捕まるのを避けるために隠れている人→**常習的犯罪者,無法者**

**outlay** /áʊtlèɪ/ 名 [ⓒ, 通常は単数] ▶定義 *outlay (on sth)* money that is spent, especially in order to start a business or project 特に事業やプロジェクトを始めるために使われるお金→**投資,支出,出費,経費**

**outlet** /áʊtlèt, -lət/ 名 ⓒ *an outlet (for sth)* ▶定義 **1** a way of expressing and making good use of strong feelings, ideas or energy 強い感情,考え,エネルギーを表現したり,うまく使う方法→**(感情などの)はけ口** ‖ *Gary found an outlet for his aggression in boxing.* ゲーリーはボクシングに自分の攻撃性のはけ口を見つけた. ▶定義 **2** a shop, business, etc that sells goods made by a particular company or of a particular type 特定の会社によって作られた品物,あるいは特定の種類の品物を売る店や商売など→**特約店,(系列下の)直売店,アウトレット,アウトレットショップ** ‖ *fast food/retail outlets* 系列のファーストフード店・小売店 ▶定義 **3** a pipe through which a gas or liquid can escape そこを通るガスや液体が逃げられるパイプ→**(ガス・液体などの)出口,コンセント**

\***outline**¹ /áʊtlàɪn/ 名 ⓒ ▶定義 **1** a description of the most important facts or ideas about sth 〜についての最も重要な事実または考えの叙述→**概略,概要,あらまし** ‖ *a brief outline of Indian history* インド史の簡単な概要 ▶定義 **2** a line that shows the shape or outside edge of sb/sth 〜の形や外側の縁を表す線→**輪郭,外形線,形** ‖ *She could see the outline of a person through the mist.* 彼女は霧を通して人の輪郭を見ることができた.

**outline**² /áʊtlàɪn/ 動他 ▶定義 *outline sth (to sb)* to tell sb or give the most important facts or ideas about sth 〜についての最も重要な事実,または考えを〜に告げる,あるいは与える→**〜の概略,あらましを述べる**

**outlive** /àʊtlív/ 動他 ▶定義 to live or exist longer than sb/sth 〜より長く生きるまたは存在する→**〜より長生きする,〜より生き残る**

**outlook** /áʊtlʊ̀k/ 名 ⓒ ▶定義 **1** *an outlook (on sth)* your attitude to or feeling about life and the world 人生や世界に対する自分の態度や考え→**見解,〜観** ‖ *an optimistic outlook on life* 人生に対する楽観的な見解 ▶定義 **2** *outlook (for sth)* what will probably happen 多分起こる物事→**(将来の)見通し,展望** ‖ *The outlook for the economy is not good.* 経済の見通しは良くない.

**outlying** /áʊtlàɪɪŋ/ 形 (名詞の前だけ) ▶定義 far from the centre of a town or city 町や市の中心から離れた→**中心から離れた,遠い** ‖ *The bus service to the outlying villages is very poor.* 町から遠く離れた村へのバスの便はとても少ない.

**outmoded** /àʊtmóʊdəd/ 形 (名詞の前だけ) ▶定義 no longer common or fashionable もはや一般的ではない,あるいは流行でない→**流行後れの,旧式の**

**outnumber** /àʊtnʌ́mbər/ 動他 (しばしば受動態で) ▶定義 to be greater in number than an enemy, another team, etc 敵やほかのチームよ

## 1154 out of

りも数において勝っている→〜より数で勝る‖ *The enemy troops outnumbered us by three to one.* 敵軍は我々の3倍の人数だった.

**out of** 前 ▶定義1 (used with verbs expressing movement) away from the inside of sth (動きを表す動詞と共に用いて)〜の内側から離れて→(〜の中から)外へ‖ *She took her purse out of her bag.* 彼女はバッグからお財布を取り出した. *to get out of bed* ベッドから起き出す ⇔ **into** ▶定義2 away from or no longer in a place or situation 場所または状況から離れて, あるいはもはやいなくて→(ある状態を)離れて, 脱して‖ *He's out of the country on business.* 彼は商用で国を離れている. *The doctors say she's out of danger.* 医者たちは彼女が危険な状態を脱したと言っている. ▶定義3 at a distance from a place 場所からある距離を置いて→〜を離れて, 〜の外に‖ *We live a long way out of London.* 私たちはロンドンからかなり離れた所に住んでいます. ▶定義4 used for saying which feeling causes you to do sth どんな感情が人に〜をさせる原因となったのかを言うために用いて→〜から, 〜のために‖ *I was only asking out of curiosity.* 私はただ単に好奇心から尋ねたのです. ▶定義5 used for saying what you use to make sth else 〜を作るために何を使うかを言うために用いて→〜から, 〜で, 〜を素材として‖ *What is this knife made out of?* このナイフは何でできているのですか. *to be made out of wood/metal/plastic/gold* 木・金属・プラスチック・金で作られている ▶定義6 from among a number or set 数または集合の中から→(いくつかある)〜のうちから, (何人かの)中で‖ *Nine out of ten people prefer this model.* 10人中9人がこのモデルを好んでいる. ▶定義7 from; having sth as its source 〜から; 〜をその源として→〜から, 〜の出で‖ *I copied the recipe out of a book.* 本からその調理法を写した. *I paid for it out of the money I won on the lottery.* 宝くじで当てたお金でそれを支払った. ▶定義8 used for saying that you no longer have sth もはや〜を持っていないことを言うために用いて→〜がなくて, 〜が切れて, 〜を失って‖ *to be out of milk/sugar/tea* 牛乳・砂糖・紅茶を切らしている *He's been out of work for months.* 彼はもう何か月も仕事がない. ▶定義9 used for saying that sth is not as it should be そうあるべき姿に〜がなっていないと言うために用いて→〜がなくなって, 〜が切れて‖ *My notes are all out of order and I can't find the right page.* 私のメモは全部順番が狂ってしまっている. 正しいページを見つけられない.

感句 **be/feel out of it** ▶定義 to be/feel lonely and unhappy because you are not included in sth 〜に含まれていないので, 孤独で不幸せである; そう感じる→仲間外れでいる; 仲間外れでいると感じる‖ *I don't speak French so I felt rather out of it at the meeting.* 私はフランス語が話せないので, 会合のときはかなり孤立していると感じた.

out of bounds ⇒ **BOUNDS**
out of order ⇒ **ORDER**¹

**out-of-work** 形 ▶定義 unable to find a job; unemployed 仕事を見つけることができない; 失業した→失業中の, 働いていない‖ *an out-of-work actor* 仕事のない俳優

**outpatient** /áʊtpèɪʃ(ə)nt/ 名 ❻ ▶定義 a person who goes to a hospital for treatment but who does not stay there during the night 病院に治療のために行くが, 夜間そこに滞在しない人→外来患者

**output** /áʊtpʊ̀t/ 名 ❻❻ ▶定義1 the amount that a person or machine produces 人や機械が生産する量→生産高, 産出量, (文学などの)作品数 ▶定義2 the information that a computer produces コンピューターが生み出す情報→出力, アウトプット ☛参 input

**outrage** /áʊtreɪdʒ/ 名 ▶定義1 ❻ something that is very bad or wrong and that causes you to feel great anger とても悪いまたは間違っていて, それが自分に強い怒りを引き起こす事・物→乱暴, 暴行, 不法行為, 非道な行い, 憤慨させる行為, 侮辱‖ *It's an outrage that such poverty should exist in the 21st century.* 21世紀にそのような貧困が存在するなんておかしい. ▶定義2 ❶ great anger すさまじい怒り→激怒, 憤慨‖ *a feeling of outrage* 激怒の感情 ― outrage 動 他 ▶〜を激怒させる, 〜に暴力を振るう, (法律・道徳など)を破る

**outrageous** /aʊtréɪdʒəs/ 形 ▶定義 that makes you very angry or shocked 人を怒らせるまたはショックに陥れる→非常に乱暴な, 極悪の, 著しく常軌を逸脱した, けしからぬ, 途方もない, あきれるほどの‖ *outrageous behaviour/prices* とんでもない行動・法外な高値 ― outrageously 副 →乱

暴にも,非道にも,途方もなく

**outright** /áʊtràɪt, ´-´/ 形副 ▶定義1 open and direct; openly and directly 率直でしかも直接の; 率直にしかも直接に→**あからさまの, 率直な; あからさまに, 率直に** ‖ *She told them outright what she thought about it.* 彼女はそれについてどう考えているか彼らに率直に述べた.

▶定義2 complete and clear; completely and clearly 完全なしかも明白な; 完全にしかも明白に→**完全な, 徹底的な; 完全に, 徹底的に** ‖ *an outright victory* 完全な勝利 *to win outright* 完全に勝つ ▶定義3 not gradually; immediately だんだんとではなく, すぐに→**直ちに, すぐに** ‖ *They were able to buy the house outright.* 彼らは即座に家を買えた.

**outset** /áʊtsèt/ 名

成句 **at/from the outset (of sth)** ▶定義 at/from the beginning (of sth) (〜の)最初に・最初から→**初めに・初めから**

*★**outside**¹ /àʊtsáɪd, ´-´/ 副前 ▶定義1 in, at or to a place that is not in a room or not in a building 部屋の中でも建物の中でもない場所に[で・へ]→**外に, 外で, 外へ** ‖ *Please wait outside for a few minutes.* ちょっと外で待っていてください. *Leave your muddy boots outside the door.* 泥の付いたブーツはドアの外に置いてください.

☛参 **outdoors**, **out of doors** (**door** の項)

▶定義2 (米 または **outside of**) not in 中ではない→**〜の範囲外で, 〜の及ばないところで** ‖ *You may do as you wish outside office hours.* 勤務時間外は好きな事をして構いません. *a small village just outside Stratford* ストラットフォードをちょっと外れた小さな村

*★**outside**² /áʊtsàɪd/ 形 (名詞の前だけ) ▶定義1 of or on the outer side or surface of sth 〜の外側または表面の, あるいは上に→**外側の, 外部の** ‖ *the outside walls of a building* 建物の外壁

▶定義2 not part of the main building 主な建物の一部ではない→**外側の, 離れの** ‖ *an outside toilet* 離れのトイレ ▶定義3 not connected with or belonging to a particular group or organization 特定の団体や機関に関係していない, あるいは属していない→**部外の, 外部からの, よそからの** ‖ *We can't do all the work by ourselves. We'll need outside help.* 私たちだけですべての仕事はできない. 外部からの応援が必要だ. ▶定義4 (used about a chance or possibility) very small (機会や可能性について)とても小さい, 少ない→**ごくわずかな**

成句 **the outside world** ▶定義 people, places, activities, etc that are away from the area where you live and your own experience of life 人々, 場所, 行為などが自分の住んでいる地域, あるいは自分の人生経験から離れていて遠い→**別世界の**

*★**outside**³ /àʊtsáɪd, ´-´/ 名 ▶定義1 [ C, 通常は単数] the outer side or surface of sth 〜の外側または表面→**外側, 外面** ‖ *There is a list of all the ingredients on the outside of the packet.* その包みの表面にすべての原材料の一覧表がある.

▶定義2 [単数扱い] the area that is near or round a building, etc 建物などの近くまたは周りの区域→**近く, 周囲** ‖ *We've only seen the church from the outside.* 私たちはその教会を近くから見ただけだ. ▶定義3 [単数扱い] the part of a road, a track, etc that is away from the side that you usually drive on, run on, etc 道路やトラックで通常運転したり走ったりする所から離れた側→**(道路, 競争用トラックなどの)外側走路, 外側車線 (追い越し車線)** ‖ *The other runners all overtook him on the outside.* ほかの走者はすっかり彼を外側走路で追い越した. ⇔すべての定義 **inside**

成句 **at the outside** ▶定義 at the most 多くても→**せいぜい, たかだか** ‖ *It will take us 3 days at the outside.* かかってもせいぜい3日だろう.

**outsider** /àʊtsáɪdər, ´-´-/ 名 C ▶定義1 a person who is not accepted as a member of a particular group 特定のグループのメンバーとして受け入れられていない人→**部外者, よそ者, 第三者** ▶定義2 a person or animal in a race or competition that is not expected to win レースや競技で勝つとは期待されていない人や動物→**勝ち目のない人・動物** ⇔ **favourite**

**outsize** /áʊtsàɪz/ 形 ▶定義 (often used about clothes) larger than usual (しばしば衣服について) 通常より大きい→**特大の**

**outskirts** /áʊtskə̀ːrts/ 名 [複数扱い] ▶定義 the parts of a town or city that are furthest from the centre 町や市の一部で, その中心から一番離れている場所→**郊外, 町外れ** ‖ *They live on the outskirts of Athens.* 彼らはアテネ市郊外に住んでいる.

**outspoken** /àʊtspóʊk(ə)n/ 形 ▶定義 saying exactly what you think or feel although you may shock or upset other people ほかの人々を驚かせたり怒らせたりするかもしれないが，考えていたり感じている事を有りのまま言う→**遠慮なく言う，ずけずけ言う** ‖ *Linda is very outspoken in her criticism.* リンダは遠慮なく批判を言う．

**outstanding** /àʊtstǽndɪŋ/ ▶定義 **1** extremely good; excellent 極めて良い，すばらしい→**目立つ，傑出した，群を抜いた** ‖ *The results in the exams were outstanding.* 試験の結果は大変すばらしかった． ▶定義 **2** not yet paid, done or dealt with まだ払われていない，なされていない，あるいは処理されていない→**未払いの，未解決の，まだ終わっていない** ‖ *Some of the work is still outstanding.* 仕事のいくぶんかはまだ終わっていません． *outstanding debts/issues* 未払いの借金・未解決の問題

**outstandingly** /àʊtstǽndɪŋli/ 副 ▶定義 extremely; very well 極めて；とても良く→**目立って，傑出して，群を抜いて** ‖ *outstandingly good/successful* 極めて良い・極めて成功している

**outstretched** /àʊtstrétʃt/ 形 ▶定義 reaching as far as possible 可能な限り遠くまで(手を)伸ばしている→**(手・足などが)一杯に広げた，差し伸べた** ‖ *He came towards her with his arms outstretched.* 彼は両手を一杯に広げて彼女の方へ近付いてきた．

**outward** /áʊtwərd/ 形 (名詞の前だけ) ▶定義 **1** on the outside 外側の→**表面的な，外面的な** ‖ *Despite her cheerful outward appearance, she was in fact very unhappy.* 彼女の陽気な外見にもかかわらず，彼女は本当はとても不幸だった． ▶定義 **2** (used about a journey) going away from the place that you will return to later (旅について)後で戻ってくる場所から離れていく→**往路の**⇔**return** ▶定義 **3** away from the centre or from a particular point 中心から離れて，あるいは特定の地点から離れて→**外へ向かう，外向きの** ‖ *outward movement/pressure* 外へ向かう動き・圧力⇔**inward** — outwardly 副 →**見上は，表面上は，外の方へ** ‖ *He remained outwardly calm so as not to frighten the children.* 彼は子供たちを怖がらせないために，表面上は落ち着いたままだった．

**outwards** /áʊtwərdz/ (特に 米**outward**) 副 ▶定義 towards the outside or away from the place where you are 外へ向かって，あるいは今いる場所から離れて→**外へ向かって，国外へ** ‖ *This door opens outwards.* このドアは外へ向かって開きます．

**outweigh** /àʊtwéɪ/ 動 他 ▶定義 to be more in amount or importance than sth 〜より量の多い，〜より重要な→**〜より重い，〜より価値がある，〜より重要な，〜に勝る** ‖ *The advantages outweigh the disadvantages.* 利点は欠点に勝る．

**outwit** /àʊtwít/ 動 他 (**outwitting**; **outwitted**) ▶定義 to gain an advantage over sb by doing sth clever 賢く〜を行うことによって…より多く利点を得る→**〜を出し抜く，〜の裏をかく**

*★**oval** /óʊv(ə)l/ 形 名 © ▶定義 shaped like an egg; a shape like that of an egg 卵に似た形をした；卵のような形→**卵形の，楕円形の；卵形のもの，楕円形** ☛ **shape** のさし絵

**ovary** /óʊv(ə)ri/ 名 © (覆 **ovaries**) ▶定義 one of the two parts of the female body that produce eggs 女性の体内にある2つの部分のうちの1つで卵子を生み出す→**卵巣**

**ovation** /oʊvéɪʃ(ə)n/ 名 © ▶定義 an enthusiastic reaction given by an audience when it likes sb/sth very much. The people in the audience make a noise with their hands (**clap**) and shout (**cheer**) and often stand up. 〜をとても気に入った観客によって与えられる熱狂的な反応．観客は手で音を立て(拍手し)，叫び(歓声を上げ)，またしばしば立ち上がる→**大喝さい，熱烈な歓迎** ‖ *The dancers got a standing ovation at the end of the performance.* ダンサーたちは公演の最後に観客総立ちの大喝さいを受けた．

*★**oven** /ʌ́v(ə)n/ 名 © ▶定義 the part of a cooker that has a door. You put things inside an oven to cook them. 扉のある調理器．加熱するために，その中に物を入れる→**オーブン，天火** ‖ *Cook in a hot oven for 50 minutes.* 暖めたオーブンに入れて50分間火を通します． *a microwave oven* 電子レンジ

▶オーブンは食べ物を roast (蒸し焼きする)，あるいは bake (焼く)のに用いられる．

*★**over**¹ /óʊvər/ 副 前

▶例えば get over sth のように，いろいろな動詞と一緒に用いる特別な使い方については，それぞれの動詞の項を参照．

▶定義 1 straight above sth, but not touching it ～のまっすぐ上だが，それに触れていない→～の上に，～の上方に ‖ *There's a painting over the bookcase.* 本棚の上に絵が掛かっている. *We watched the plane fly over.* 私たちは頭上を飛行機が飛んでいくのを見た. ☞参 **above**
▶定義 2 covering sth ～を覆って→～を覆って，～かぶさって ‖ *He was holding a towel over the cut.* 彼は切り傷を覆ったタオルを押さえていた. *She hung her coat over the back of the chair.* 彼女は自分のコートをいすの背に掛けた.
▶定義 3 across to the other side of sth ～の反対側に渡って→～を越えて，渡って ‖ *The horse jumped over the fence.* その馬は柵(さく)を飛び越えた. *a bridge over the river* 川に架かる橋
▶定義 4 on or to the other side もう一方の側に→～の向こう側へ ‖ *The student turned the paper over and read the first question.* その学生は紙をめくって最初の問題を読んだ.
▶定義 5 down or sideways from an upright position まっすぐな姿勢から下の方へ，あるいははすかいに→かがんで，倒れて，横向きに上体を曲げて ‖ *He leaned over to speak to the woman next to him.* 彼は隣にいる女性に話し掛けようと，横向きに上体を曲げた. *I fell over in the street this morning.* 私は今朝通りで転んだ.
▶定義 6 above or more than a number, price, etc ある数，値段などより上，または超えて→～より多く，～を超えて ‖ *She lived in Athens for over ten years.* 彼女は10年以上アテネに住んだ. *suitable for children aged 10 and over* 10歳以上の子供向きの
▶定義 7 used for expressing distance 距離を表現するために用いて→(越えて)向こう側へ，こちらへ ‖ *He's over in America at the moment.* 彼は今のところアメリカに(渡って)いる. *Sit down **over there**.* あちらに座ってください. *Come **over** here, please.* こちらへいらしてください.
▶定義 8 not used; still remaining 使われていない；まだ残っている→余って，余分に ‖ *There are a lot of cakes **left over** from the party.* パーティーのケーキがまだたくさん残っています.
▶定義 9 (all と共に用いて) everywhere どこでも→～一面に，～の至る所に ‖ *There was blood **all over the place**.* 血が至る所にあった. *I can't find my glasses. I've looked all over for them.* 私の眼鏡が見つかりません. どこもかしこも捜したのに.
▶定義 10 used for saying that sth is repeated ～が繰り返されることを言うときに用いて→繰り返して，もう一度 ‖ *You'll have to start **all over again** (=from the beginning).* もう一度始めなくてはいけません(=最初から). *She kept saying the same thing **over and over again**.* 彼女は同じ事を何度も何度も言い続けた.
▶定義 11 about; on the subject of ～について；～に関して→～のことで，～に関して ‖ *We quarrelled over money.* 私たちはお金のことで口論した.
▶定義 12 during ～の間→～中ずっと，～の終わりまで ‖ *We met several times over the Christmas holiday.* 私たちはクリスマス休暇中に数回会った.

**over**² /óʊvər/ 形 ▶定義 1 finished 終わって→終わって，済んで ‖ *The exams are all over now.* 今，試験がすべて終わった. ▶定義 2 (複合動詞，複合名詞，複合形容詞，複合副詞を作るために用いて) too; too much あまりに；多すぎる→過度に，あまりに多く ‖ *overexcited/overworked* 興奮しすぎ・働きすぎ *to overeat/overreact* 食べすぎる・過剰反応する

> ▶語法
>
> 多義語 over の意味の展開
>
> over の原義は①She jumped over the fence. にある「～を越えて」です. この動きの前半に焦点を当てると②The milk is boiling over. (ミルクが吹きこぼれるよ) となり，後半に焦点を当てると③The tree is falling over. (木が倒れてくるよ) となります. 動きを延長して1周して視点に戻ると④Let's start over. (再出発しよう) や，over and over (何度も繰り返して) に発展します.
>
>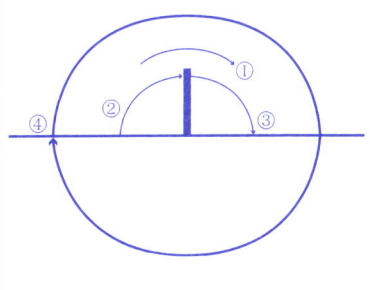

**overall**¹ /óʊvərɔ́ːl, ˼-˼/ 副形 ▶定義 1 including

**overall²**

everything; total すべてを含んでいる; 全体の→全部で,何から何まで入れて,全体にわたる,全体の‖ *What will the overall cost of the work be?* この仕事の全費用はどのくらいになりますか. ▶定義2 generally; when you consider everything 一般に; すべての事を考慮するとき→全体的に,全体として言えば‖ *Overall, I can say that we are pleased with the year's work.* 全体的に言って,私たちはこの1年の仕事を気に入っていると言える.

overall

aprons

overalls
(米 coveralls)

**overall²** /óʊvərɔ̀ːl/ 名 ▶定義1 ⓒ a piece of clothing like a coat that you wear over your clothes to keep them clean when you are working コートのような衣服の一種で,働いているとき自分の衣服をきれいに保つために衣服の上から着るもの→(作業用)上っ張り,スモック ▶定義2 **overalls** (米 **coveralls**) [複数扱い] a piece of clothing that covers your legs and body (and sometimes your arms) that you wear over your clothes to keep them clean when you are working 自分の足や体(時には腕も)を覆う1枚の衣服で,服の上から着用し,働いているとき自分の衣服をきれいに保つために衣服の上から着るもの→作業用胸当てズボン,オーバーオール

**overawe** /òʊvərɔ́ː/ 動他 (通常は受動態で) ▶定義 to impress sb so much that he/she feels nervous or frightened ～がびくびくしたり,またはおびえたりするほどの印象を与える→～をかしこまらせる,威圧する

**overbalance** /òʊvərbǽləns/ 動自 ▶定義 to lose your balance and fall 釣り合いを失って倒れる→平衡を失う,平均を失って倒れる

**overboard** /óʊvərbɔ̀ːrd/ 副 ▶定義 over the side of a boat or ship into the water ボートまたは船の側面を越えて水中へ→船外に,(船から)水中へ

成句 **go overboard (on/about/for sb/sth)** ▶定義 to be too excited or enthusiastic about sb/sth ～に興奮しすぎる, あるいは熱中しすぎる→夢中になる

**overcast** /òʊvərkǽst; -kɑ́ːst, ´-/ 形 ▶定義 (used about the sky) covered with cloud (空について)雲で覆われている→どんよりしている,曇った

**overcharge** /òʊvərtʃɑ́ːrdʒ/ 動他自 ▶定義 to ask sb to pay too much money for sth ～のために,…に多すぎる金を払うように頼む→(～に)不当な値段・掛け値を要求する,実際より高く(～に)請求する‖ *The taxi driver overcharged me.* そのタクシー運転手は実際より高く私に請求した.
☞参 charge

**overcoat** /óʊvərkòʊt/ 名 ⓒ ▶定義 a long thick coat that you wear in cold weather 寒い冬に着る,長い厚手のコート→オーバー, 外套(がいとう)

**overcome** /òʊvərkʌ́m/ 動他 (過 **overcame** /-kéɪm/; 過分 **overcome**) ▶定義1 to manage to control or defeat sb/sth ～をどうにか制御する,あるいは打ち負かす→(困難など)に打ち勝つ,～を克服する,～を負かす‖ *She tried hard to overcome her fear of flying.* 彼女は飛ぶことへの恐怖を克服しようと一生懸命努力した. ▶定義2 (通常は受動態で) to be extremely strongly affected by sth ～に極めて強く影響されている→～を参らせる

**overcrowded** /òʊvərkráʊdəd/ 形 ▶定義 (used about a place) with too many people inside (場所について)中に多すぎる人々がいて→超満員の,大変混雑した‖ *The trains are overcrowded on Friday evenings.* 金曜日の夜はいつも電車は超満員だ.

**overdo** /òʊvərdúː/ 動他 (過 **overdid** /-díd/; 過分 **overdone** /-dʌ́n/) ▶定義1 to use or do too much of sth ～をたくさん使いすぎる,あるいは行いすぎる→～を使いすぎる,入れすぎる,やりすぎる ▶定義2 to cook sth too long ～を長く加熱調理しすぎる→～を焼きすぎる,煮すぎる‖ *The meat was overdone.* その肉は焼きすぎだった.

成句 **overdo it/things** ▶定義 to work, etc too hard 度を越して仕事などをやりすぎる→働きすぎる,度がすぎる‖ *Exercise is fine but don't overdo it.* 運動はすばらしい, しかしやりすぎないように.

**overdose** /óʊvərdòʊs/ 名 ⓒ ▶定義 an amount of a drug or medicine that is too large and so is not safe 多すぎるために安全ではない薬の量→

(薬の)与えすぎ,過剰投与 ‖ to take an overdose 薬を飲みすぎる ☛参 dose

**overdraft** /óʊvərdræft; -drɑ̀ːft/ 名 ● ▶定義 an amount of money that you have spent that is greater than the amount you have in your bank account; an arrangement that allows you to do this 自分の銀行口座に入っている金額よりもはるかに多く使ってしまった金額;人にそうすることを許す取り決め→当座貸越高,(手形の)過振(かぶり)

**overdrawn** /òʊvərdrɔ́ːn/ 形 ▶定義 having spent more money than you have in your bank account 銀行口座に持っている金額より多くのお金を使っている→(口座が)借り越しの ‖ I checked my balance and discovered I was overdrawn. 私の預金残高を調べたら,借り越していたことを知った.

**overdue** /òʊvərd(j)úː/ 形 ▶定義 late in arriving, happening, being paid, returned, etc 時間に遅れて到着する,起こる,払われる,あるいは返却される→延着した,遅れた,(実現などを)ずっと待っている,支払期限の過ぎた,返却期限の過ぎた ‖ an overdue library book 返却期限の過ぎた図書館の本 Her baby is a week overdue. 彼女の赤ちゃんは出産予定日を1週間過ぎている.

**overestimate** /òʊvəréstəmeɪt/ 動他 ▶定義 to guess that sb/sth is bigger, better, more important, etc than he/she/it really is 〜が実際より,もっと大きい,良い,重要であるなどと推測する→〜を過大に評価する,〜を過大に見積もる,買いかぶる ‖ I overestimated how much we could paint in a day. 私は,私たちが1日にペンキを塗れる量を過大に見積もっていた. ⇔ **underestimate**

'Oh no! The bath's overflowing!'

**overflow** /òʊvərflóʊ/ 動 ▶定義1 自他 overflow (with sth) to be so full that there is no more space 一杯でもう余地がない→(〜で)一杯である,(〜が)有り余る(ほどである) ‖ The tap was left on and the bath overflowed. 蛇口が開いたままになっていたので,お風呂があふれた. The roads are overflowing with cars. 道は車でごった返している. ▶定義2 自 overflow (into sth) to be forced out of a place or a container that is too full 一杯すぎて,場所または容器の外に追いやられる→(川などが)氾濫(はんらん)する,あふれる,こぼれる ‖ The crowd overflowed into the street. 群衆は通りにあふれ出た.

**overgrown** /òʊvərgróʊn/ 形 ▶定義 covered with plants that have grown too big and untidy 大きくなりすぎて伸び放題の植物で覆われている→(土地が)草が生えるに任された,草ぼうぼうの

**overhang** /òʊvərhǽŋ/ 動自他 (過,過分 **overhung**) ▶定義 to stick out above sth else 何か別のものが〜の上に突き出る→(〜に)突き出る,張り出す,(〜の上に)差し掛かる ‖ The overhanging trees kept the sun off us. 張り出している木々が私たちから太陽を遮っていた.

**overhaul** /òʊvərhɔ́ːl/ 動他 ▶定義 to look at sth carefully and change or repair it if necessary 〜を注意深く見て,必要なら取り替えたり修理する→〜を分解検査する,〜を分解修理する,オーバーホールする ‖ to overhaul an engine エンジンを分解検査する ― overhaul /óʊvərhɔ̀ːl/ 名 ● →分解検査,分解修理,オーバーホール

**overhead** /òʊvərhèd/ 形副 ▶定義 above your head 頭の上の,頭の上に→頭上の,高架の,頭上に,高く ‖ overhead electricity cables 頭上の電線 A helicopter flew overhead. ヘリコプターが頭上を飛んだ.

**overheads** /óʊvərhèdz/ 名[複数扱い] ▶定義 money that a company must spend on things like heat, light, rent, etc 会社が光熱費,賃貸料などのものに費やさなければならない金→間接経費,一般経費

**overhear** /òʊvərhíər/ 動他 (過,過分 **overheard** /-hə́ːrd/) ▶定義 to hear what sb is saying by accident, when he/she is speaking to sb else and not to you 〜が,あなたにではなくほかの…に話している内容をたまたま聞く→〜をふと耳にする,偶然立ち聞きする

**overjoyed** /òʊvərdʒɔ́ɪd/ 形 (名詞の前は不可) ▶定義 overjoyed (at sth/to do sth) very happy とても幸せな→大喜びの,狂喜した

**overland** /óʊvərlænd/ 形 ▶定義 not by sea or by air 船でなく,あるいは飛行機でなく→陸上の,陸

路の ‖ *an overland journey* 陸路の旅 — **overland** 副 →陸上を, 陸路を

overlapping tiles

**overlap** /òuvərǽp/ 動 自 他 (**overlapping**; **overlapped**) ▶定義 1 when two things overlap, part of one covers part of the other 2つのものが重なるとき, 1つのものの一部分がもう1つの一部分を覆う→(部分的に)重なる, 重複する ‖ *Make sure that the two pieces of material overlap.* 2つの材料が部分的に重なっているかきちんと確認してください. ▶定義 2 to be partly the same as sth 〜と部分的に同じ→一部重なり合う, 重複する ‖ *Our jobs overlap to some extent.* 私たちの仕事はある程度重なるところがある. — **overlap** /óuvərlæp/ 名 C U →重複(すること), 重複する部分

**overleaf** /òuvərlíːf/ 副 ▶定義 on the other side of the page ページの裏側に→裏面に ‖ *Full details are given overleaf.* 完全な詳細は裏ページに載っています.

**overload** /òuvərlóud/ 動 他 ▶定義 1 (しばしば受動態で) to put too many people or things into or onto sth 多すぎる人々や物を〜の中, あるいは上に乗せる→荷を積みすぎる, 人を乗せすぎる ‖ *an overloaded vehicle* 荷物を積みすぎた(人を乗せすぎた)車 ▶定義 2 **overload sb (with sth)** to give sb too much of sth 〜に多すぎる…を与える→〜に負担をかけすぎる ‖ *to be overloaded with work/information* 仕事・情報の負担がかかりすぎている ▶定義 3 to put too much electricity through sth 〜に多すぎる電気を流す→〜に電荷・負荷をかけすぎる ‖ *If you use too many electrical appliances at one time you may overload the system.* 一度にたくさんの電気機器を使用すると, システムに負荷をかけすぎるかもしれない.

**overlook** /òuvərlúk/ 動 他 ▶定義 1 to fail to see or notice sth 〜を見忘れたり気付かなかったりする→〜を見落とす, 見逃す, 無視する ‖ *to overlook a spelling mistake* 語のスペリングの間違いを見逃す *She felt that her opinion had been completely overlooked.* 彼女は自分の意見が完全に無視されていたと感じた. ▶定義 2 to see sth wrong but decide to forget it 間違っている〜に気付くが, それを忘れようと決心する→〜を大目に見る, 見逃す ‖ *I will overlook your behaviour this time but don't let it happen again.* 今回はあなたの態度を大目に見ますが, 二度とこのような事のないように. ▶定義 3 to have a view over sth 〜を見渡す→〜を見渡す, 見下ろす ‖ *My room overlooks the sea.* 私の部屋からは海が見渡せる.

**overnight** /òuvərmáit, ˈ-ˌ-/ 形 副 ▶定義 1 for one night 一晩のための[に]→一泊の, 小旅行用の ‖ *an overnight bag* 小旅行用かばん *We stayed overnight in Hamburg.* 私たちはハンブルグに一泊した. ▶定義 2 (happening) very suddenly 突然急に(起こる)→一夜のうちに, 突然, たちまち, あっと言う間の ‖ *She became a star overnight.* 彼女は一夜にしてスターになった.

**overpass** /óuvərpɑ́ːs; -pǽs/ 英 =**FLYOVER**

**overpay** /òuvərpéi/ 動 他 (過, 過分 **overpaid**) (通常は受動態で) ▶定義 to pay sb too much; to pay sb more than his/her job is worth 〜に多すぎるほど払う; その〜の仕事に見合う以上に払う→〜に給料・賃金を払いすぎる, 余分に払う ⇔ **underpay**

**overpower** /òuvərpáuər/ 動 他 ▶定義 to be too strong for sb 〜に対して強くありすぎる→〜に打ち勝つ, 負かす, 圧倒する ‖ *The fireman was overpowered by the heat and smoke.* 消防士は熱と煙に圧倒されていた. — **overpowering** 形 圧倒的な, 強烈な ‖ *an overpowering smell* 強烈なにおい

**overrate** /òuvərréit/ 動 他 (しばしば受動態で) ▶定義 to think that sth/sb is better than he/she/it really is 〜がその実際よりもいいと思う→過大評価する, 買いかぶる ⇔ **underrate**

**override** /òuvərráid/ 動 他 (過 **overrode** /-róud/; 過分 **overridden** /-rídn/) ▶定義 1 to use your authority to reject sb's decision, order, etc 〜の決定, 命令などを拒絶するために, 自分の権威を使う→(命令, 要求など)を無視する, 拒否する ‖ *They overrode my protest and continued with the meeting.* 彼らは私の抗議を無視してその会議を続けた. ▶定義 2 to be more important than sth 〜よりもっと大切である→〜に優先する, 〜より大事である, 〜より先である

**overriding** /òuvərráidɪŋ/ 形 (名詞の前だけ) ▶定義 more important than anything else ほかの何よりも重要な→最優先の, 最も重要な ‖ *Our overriding concern is safety.* 私たちの最優先事項は安全性です.

**overrule** /òυvərúːl/ 動 ⦿ ▶定義 to use your authority to change what sb else has already decided or done ほかの~が既に決めた、あるいは行ったことを変えるために、自分の権威を使う→**~を権力ずくで取り消す, 覆す, 無効にする** ‖ *The Appeal Court overruled the judge's decision.* 控訴院はその裁判官の決定を取り消した.

**overrun** /òυvərʌ́n/ 動 (過 **overran** /-rǽn/; 過分 **overrun**) ▶定義 **1** ⦿ (しばしば受動態で) to spread all over an area in great numbers ある地域全体にものすごい数で広がる→**(害虫などが)~に群がる, (雑草などが)はびこる** ‖ *The city was overrun by rats.* その市の至る所にネズミが群がっていた. ▶定義 **2** ⊜⦿ to use more time or money than expected 予期した以上に時間または金を使う→**(範囲を)超える, ~を超過する** ‖ *The meeting overran by 30 minutes.* 会議は30分長引いた.

**overseas** /óυvərsíːz/ 形 (名詞の前だけで) 副 ▶定義 in, to or from another country that you have to cross the sea to get to 海を渡って別の国に, [へ・から]→**海外から, 海外の, 海外で** ‖ *overseas students studying in Britain* イギリスで勉強している外国から来ている学生 *Frank has gone to live overseas.* フランクは外国に住むために行ってしまった.

**oversee** /òυvərsíː/ 動⦿(過 **oversaw** /-sɔ́ː/; 過分 **overseen** /-síːn/) ▶定義 to watch sth to make sure that it is done properly 適切に行われていることを確認するために, ~をじっと見る→**(仕事・労働者など)を監督する, 監視する**

**overshadow** /òυvərʃǽdoυ/ 動⦿ ▶定義 **1** to cause sb/sth to seem less important or successful **~をより重要でない, あるいはより成功していないように見せる→~を見劣りさせる** ‖ *Connor always seemed to be overshadowed by his sister.* コナーはいつも彼の姉[妹]に比べて見劣りするように見えた. ▶定義 **2** to cause sth to be less enjoyable ~が面白くなさそうに見せる→**~の輝きを奪う, 影を薄くする**

**oversight** /óυvərsàιt/ 名 ⊜⓪ ▶定義 something that you do not notice or do (that you should have noticed or done) (気付くべきなのに)気付かないまたはしない事・物→**見落とし, 手落ち**

**oversimplify** /òυvərsímpləfaι/ 動⊜⦿ (現分 **oversimplifying**; 三単現 **oversimplifies**; 過, 過分 **oversimplified**) ▶定義 to explain sth in such a simple way that its real meaning is lost 実際の意味が見失われるほど簡単な方法で~を説明する→**(~を)単純化しすぎる, 簡素化しすぎる**

**oversleep** /òυvərslíːp/ 動⊜ (過, 過分 **overslept** /-slépt/) ▶定義 to sleep longer than you should have done 自分が寝るべき時間より長く寝る→**寝過ごす, 寝坊する** ‖ *I overslept and was late for school.* 私は寝坊して学校に遅刻した.
▶ lie in, sleep in と比較.

**overstate** /òυvərstéιt/ 動⦿ ▶定義 to say sth in a way that makes it seem more important than it really is ~が実際よりももっと重要に見えるように言う→**~を誇張して話す, おおげさに言う**⇔ **understate**

★**overtake** /òυvərtéιk/ 動⊜⦿ (過 **overtook** /-túk/; 過分 **overtaken** /-téιk(ə)n/) ▶定義 to go past another person, car, etc because you are moving faster 自分の方が速く移動しているので, ほかの人や車などを追い越す→**(~を)追い抜く, 追い越す** ‖ *The lorry overtook me on the bend.* トラックがカーブで私を追い越した.

**overthrow** /òυvərθróυ/ 動⦿ (過 **overthrew** /-θrúː/; 過分 **overthrown** /-θróυn/) ▶定義 to remove a leader or government from power, by using force 力を使って指導者または政府を権力から退かせる→**(政権など)を倒す, 打倒する, 覆す, ~をひっくり返す**— overthrow /óυvərθròυ/ 名 [単数扱い]→**(政権などの)転覆, 打倒すること, 打倒されること**

**overtime** /óυvərtàιm/ 名 ⓤ ▶定義 time that you spend at work after your usual working hours; the money that you are paid for this 通常の業務時間の後に仕事に費やす時間; そのために支払われる金→**規定外労働時間, 残業, 超過勤務; 超過勤務手当, 残業手当** ‖ *Betty did ten hours' overtime last week.* ベティは先週10時間残業をした. — overtime 副→**規定時間外に, 超過勤務で** ‖ *I have been working overtime for weeks.* ここ何週間もずっと残業している.

**overtone** /óυvərtòυn/ 名 [⦿, 通常は複数] ▶定義 something that is suggested but not expressed in an obvious way 示唆されているが, 明白には表現されていないもの→**含み, 含蓄, ニュアンス** ‖ *Some people claimed there were racist overtones in the advertisement.* その広告には人種差別がほのめかされていると主張する

人々がいた.

**overture** /óʊvərtʃər, -tʃʊər, -t(j)ʊər/ 名 ▶定義1 ⓒ a piece of music that is the introduction to a musical play (such as an opera or a ballet) (オペラやバレエの) 演奏への導入部分 → 序曲 ▶定義2 [ⓒ, 通常は複数] 正式 an act of being friendly towards sb, especially because you want to be friends, to start a business relationship, etc ～への気さくな行動, 特に友達になりたい, あるいは仕事上の関係を始めたいなどの理由があるとき → (協定などの) 提案, 申し入れ, 予備交渉

**overturn** /òʊvərtə́:rn/ 動 ▶定義1 自他 to turn over so that the top is at the bottom ひっくり返る, そのために上が下になる → ひっくり返る, 横転する ‖ *The car overturned but the driver escaped unhurt.* 車はひっくり返ったが, 運転手は無傷で脱出した. ▶定義2 他 to officially decide that a decision is wrong and change it 決定が間違っているのでそれを変えると公式に決定する → (政府など) を倒す, 打倒する

**overweight** /òʊvərwéɪt/ 形 ▶定義 too heavy or fat 重すぎる, または太りすぎている → 重量超過の, 太りすぎの ‖ *I'm a bit overweight - I think I might go on a diet.* 私は少し太りぎみだ — ダイエットしようかなと思っている. ☛参 fatの注 ⇨ underweight

**overwhelm** /òʊvər(h)wélm/ 動 他 (通常は受動態) ▶定義1 to cause sb to feel such a strong emotion that he/she does not know how to react どう反応していいか分からないほどの強い感情を～に引き起こす → (精神的に) ～を圧倒する, 押しつぶす, 気持ちを打ちひしぐ ‖ *The new world champion was overwhelmed by all the publicity.* 新しい世界チャンピオンはマスコミに圧倒されていた. ▶定義2 to be so powerful, big, etc, that sb cannot deal with it あまりに力強い, 大きいなどのために, ～はそれを扱えない → (数・勢力で) ～を圧倒する ‖ *He overwhelmed his opponent with his superb technique.* 彼はその卓越した技術で敵を圧倒した. *The television company were overwhelmed by complaints.* テレビ会社は苦情にすっかり参ってしまった.

**overwhelming** /òʊvər(h)wélmɪŋ/ 形 ▶定義 extremely great or strong 極めてすばらしい, また力強い → 圧倒的な, 抵抗できないほどの, 大変感動的な ‖ *Anna had an overwhelming desire to return home.* アンナはどうしても家に帰りたかった. — **overwhelmingly** 副 → 圧倒的に, 抵抗できないほど

**overwork** /òʊvərwə́:rk/ 動 他 ▶定義 to make sb work too hard ～を過度に働かせる → ～を働かせすぎる, 使いすぎる, 過労にさせる ‖ *They are overworked and underpaid.* 彼らは酷使されているのに, 十分な給料は支払われていない. — **overwork** /òʊvərwə́:rk/ 名 Ⓤ → 過労, 過度の労働・仕事・勉強

*****owe** /óʊ/ 動 他 ▶定義1 owe sth (to sb); owe sb for sth to have to pay money to sb for sth that he/she has done or given ～が行った, または与えた～のためにその人に金を支払わなくてはならない → ～に借りがある, 支払う義務がある ‖ *I owe Katrina a lot of money.* 私はカトリーナにたくさん借金をしています. *I owe a lot of money to Katrina.* 私はカトリーナにたくさん借金をしています. *I still owe you for that bread you bought yesterday.* 私はまだ昨日あなたが買ったパンの代金を借りている.

▶お金など借りているものはすべて debt と言う.

▶定義2 to feel that you should do sth for sb or give sth to sb, especially because he/she has done sth for you ～のために…をすべきである, あるいは～を…に与えるべきだと感じている, 特にその人が自分のために～をしてくれたため → ～を当然尽くすべきである, ～(の義務)を負っている ‖ *Claudia owes me an explanation.* クローディアは私に説明する義務があります. *I owe you an apology.* 私はあなたに謝らなければなりません. ▶定義3 owe sth (to sb/sth) to have sth (for the reason given) (～を持っている (与えられた理由によって) → ～から恩恵を受けている ‖ *She said she owes her success to hard work and determination.* 彼女は自分の成功は勤勉と決意によるものであると言った.

**owing** /óʊɪŋ/ 形 (名詞の前は不可) ▶定義 owing (to sb) not yet paid まだ払っていない → 借りになっている, 未払いのまま, 支払うべき

**owing to** 前 ▶定義 because of ～のために → ～が原因で, ～がもとで, ～のために ‖ *The match was cancelled owing to bad weather.* 悪天候のために試合は中止になった.

**owl** /áʊl/ 名 C ▶定義 a bird with large eyes that hunts small animals at night 夜間小さな動物を捕まえる,大きな目を持つ鳥→フクロウ

\***own**¹ /óʊn/ 形代 ▶定義 1 used to emphasize that sth belongs to a particular person 〜が特定の人に属していることを強調するのに用いて→自分・その人自身の,自身の ‖ *I saw him do it with my own eyes.* 私は彼がそれをするのを自分自身の目で見た. *This is **his own** house.* これは彼自身の家です. *This house is his own.* この家は彼自身のです. *Rachel would like her own room/a room **of her own**.* レイチェルは自分の部屋が欲しい. ▶定義 2 used to show that sth is done or made without help from another person 〜がほかの人からの助けなしに行われた,あるいは作られたことを示すのに用いて→自力で,人の手を借りないで ‖ *The children are old enough to get their own breakfast.* 子供たちはもう自分の朝食を作れるほど十分大きい.
成句 come into your own ▶定義 to have the opportunity to show your special qualities 自分の特性を示す機会を持つ→自分の本領を発揮する
hold your own (against sd/sth) ▶定義 to be as strong, good, etc as sb/sth else ほかの〜に劣らないほど強い,または良いなど→自分の立場を守り抜く,(競争などに)負けない,引けを取らない
(all) on your, etc own ▶定義 1 alone→自分で,独力で ‖ *John lives all on his own.* ジョンは自力で生活している. ☞参 **alone** の注 ▶定義 2 without help→助けなしに ‖ *I managed to repair the car all on my own.* 私は自分1人で車を何とか修理した.
get/have your own back (on sb) 略式 ▶定義 to hurt sb who has hurt you 自分を害した〜を害する→仕返しをする,敵(かたき)をとる

\***own**² /óʊn/ 動 他 ▶定義 to have sth belonging to you; possess 自分に属している〜を持つ;所有する→〜を持っている,所有する ‖ *We don't own the house. We just rent it.* 私たちはこの家を所有していない.私たちは借りているだけです. *a privately owned company* 個人所有の会社
句動 own up (to sth) 略式 ▶定義 to tell sb that you have done sth wrong 間違った〜を行ってしまったことを…に告げる→すっかり白状する,洗いざらい認める ‖ *None of the children owned up to breaking the window.* 子供たちのだれも窓ガラスを割ったことを白状しなかった.
☞参 **confess**. この方がさらに正式である.

\***owner** /óʊnər/ 名 C ▶定義 a person who owns sth 〜を所有している人→所有者,持ち主,オーナー ‖ *a house/dog owner* 家の持ち主・犬の飼い主

**ownership** /óʊnərʃɪp/ 名 U ▶定義 the state of owning sth 〜を所有している状態→所有権,所有者であること ‖ *in private/public ownership* 私有権・公的所有権

**ox** /áks/ 名 C (複 **oxen** /áks(ə)n/) ▶定義 a male cow that cannot produce young. Oxen were used in past times for pulling or carrying heavy loads. 子供を作れない雄の牛.昔は重たい荷物を引いて進んだり,背に乗せて運んだりすることに使われていた→(去勢された)雄牛 ☞参 **bull** ☞ **plough** のさし絵

\***oxygen** /áksɪdʒ(ə)n/ 名 U (元素記号 O) ▶定義 a gas that you cannot see, taste or smell. Plants and animals cannot live without oxygen. 見ることも,味わうことも,においをかぐこともできない気体.植物も動物もこれがないと生きていけない→酸素

**oyster** /ɔ́ɪstər/ 名 C ▶定義 a shellfish that we eat. Some oysters produce precious jewels (**pearls**). 食べられる貝.貴重な宝石(真珠)を生み出す貝もある→牡蠣(かき),カキ ☞ **shellfish** のさし絵

**oz** 略 ounce(s)=オンス ‖ *Add 4oz flour.* 4オンスの小麦粉を加えなさい.

**ozone** /óʊzðʊn/ 名 U ▶定義 a poisonous gas which is a form of another gas (**oxygen**) ほかの気体(酸素)の形をとっている有毒な気体→オゾン

**ozone-friendly** 形 ▶定義 (used about cleaning products, etc) not containing chemicals that could harm the atmosphere (**the ozone layer**) (製品などの洗浄について)大気(オゾン層)を破壊する化学物質を含んでいない→オゾン層に優しい,オゾン層を破壊しない

**the ozone layer** 名 [単数扱い] ▶定義 the layer of the gas (**ozone**) high up in the atmosphere that helps to protect the earth from the dangerous rays of the sun 気体(オゾン)の層で大気中の高い所にあり,地球を太陽の有害な光線から守っている→オゾン層 ‖ *a hole in the ozone layer* オゾン層の穴(オゾンホール) ☞参 **CFC**

# P p

**P, p**¹ /piː/ 图 ⓒ (複 **P's; p's**) ▶定義 the sixteenth letter of the English alphabet 英語アルファベットの第 16 文字→p(P)が表す音, p(P)の文字, p(P)の字形のもの ‖ *'Pencil' begins with (a) 'P'*. PencilはPで始まる.

**p**² 略 ▶定義1 (複 **pp**) page→ページ ‖ *See p94*. 94ページを参照しなさい. *pp 63-96* 63ページから96ページ ▶定義2 英略式 penny, pence →ペニー, ペンス ‖ *a 27p stamp* 27ペンス切手 ▶定義3 **P** (on a road sign) parking (道路標識で)→駐車(場)

**PA**¹ /ˌpiː ˈeɪ/ 略图 ⓒ 特に 英 personal assistant ▶定義 a person whose job is to type letters, answer the telephone, etc (a secretary) for just one manager 1人の上司のためだけに,手紙をタイプしたり,電話対応をすることが仕事の人(秘書)→個人秘書

**pa**² /pər ǽnəm/ 略 per annum ▶定義 in or for a year 1年に, または1年の間に→1年ごとに, 1年に付き ‖ *salary £15000 pa* 年給15000ポンド

\***pace**¹ /peɪs/ 图 ▶定義1 [Ⓤ, 単数扱い] **pace (of sth)** the speed at which you walk, run, etc or at which sth happens 人が歩く,走るなどの,または〜が起こる速さ→歩く・走る速さ,(進歩などの)速さ,ペース ‖ *to run at a steady/gentle pace* 一定の・緩やかな速さで走る *I can't stand the pace of life in London.* 私はロンドンでの生活の速さに我慢できない. *Students are encouraged to work at their own pace (= as fast or as slowly as they like).* 学生たちは自分のペースで(= 自分の好きな程度に速くまたはゆっくりと)勉強するよう奨励されている. ▶定義2 ⓒ the distance that you move when you take one step 1歩進むときに自分が動く距離→1歩, 歩幅 ‖ *Take two paces forward and then stop.* 前に2歩進んで止まりなさい.

成句 **keep pace (with sb/sth)** ▶定義 to move or do sth at the same speed as sb/sth else; to change as quickly as sth else is changing ほかの〜と同じ速度で動く, または…をする; ほかの〜が変わっている速さで変わる→(〜と)同じ速さで行く,(〜に)遅れないように付いていく, ペースを合わせる ‖ *Wages are not keeping pace with inflation.* 賃金はインフレと同じようには上がっていかないものだ.

**set the pace** ▶定義 to move or do sth at the speed that others must follow ほかの人たちが従わなければならない速度で動くまたは〜をする→歩調を示す, 模範を示す ‖ *Pinto set the pace for the first three miles.* 最初の3マイル, ピントは先頭に立ってペースを作った.

**pace**² /peɪs/ 動 ⾃ ⾃ ▶定義 to walk up and down in the same area many times, especially because you are nervous or angry 特に神経質になっているまたは怒っているために,同じ所を何度も行ったり来たりする→(行ったり来たりして)歩く;(行ったり来たりして)〜を歩く, 〜を歩いて測る

**pacemaker** /ˈpeɪsmeɪkər/ 图 ⓒ ▶定義1 a machine that helps to make a person's heart beat regularly or more strongly 人の心臓を定期的にまたは強く鼓動させることを手伝う機械→脈拍調整器, ペースメーカー ▶定義2 a person in a race who sets the speed that the others must follow 競走でほかの人たちが従わなければならない速度を設定する人→(先頭に立ち)ペースを作る走者, ペースメーカー

**pacifier** /ˈpæsəfaɪər/ 米 = DUMMY(3)

**pacifism** /ˈpæsəfɪz(ə)m/ 图 Ⓤ ▶定義 the belief that all wars are wrong and that you should not fight in them すべての戦争は間違っており, 戦争で戦うべきではないという信念→平和主義, 戦争反対, 参戦拒否 — **pacifist** /-ɪst/ 图 ⓒ →平和主義者, 不戦主義者

**pacify** /ˈpæsəfaɪ/ 動 ⾃ (現分 **pacifying**; 三単現 **pacifies**, 過, 過分 **pacified**) ▶定義 to make sb who is angry or upset be calm or quiet 怒っているまたは気が動転している〜を, 落ち着かせるまたは静かにさせる→〜をなだめる, 静める

\***pack**¹ /pæk/ 图 ⓒ ▶定義1 a set of things that are supplied together for a particular purpose 特定の目的のために, 一緒に供給される一組のもの→(小さな)包み, (食品などを一定量包装した)箱, パッケージ ‖ *an information pack* 一そろいの情報 *These batteries are sold in packs of four.* これらの電池は4つ1パックで売られています.(比喩) *Everything she told me was a pack of lies.* 彼女が私に語ったすべてが, うそ八百だった.

☛ **package**, **packet**, **parcel** の項を参照.

▶定義2 困=PACKET(1) ▶定義3 a bag that you carry on your back 背中に背負うバッグ➔リュックサック ☛類 rucksack, backpack ▶定義4 [単数または複数形の動詞と共に]a group of wild animals that hunt together 一緒に狩りをする野性動物の集団➔群れ ‖ *a pack of dogs/wolves* 犬・オオカミの群れ ▶定義5 a large group of similar people or things, especially one that you do not like or approve of 特に自分が好きではないまたは良いとは認められない、互いに似た人々または物の大きな集団➔一団,一味,一隊 ‖ *a pack of journalists* ジャーナリストの一団 ▶定義6 (困 **deck**) a complete set of playing cards トランプの完全な1そろい➔トランプの一組 ☛参 **card** の注とさし絵

\***pack**² /pæk/ 動 ▶定義1 自他 to put your things into a suitcase, etc before you go away or go on holiday 出掛けるまたは休暇になる前に、スーツケースなどに自分の物を入れる➔荷造りする,物を詰める; ~を荷造りする, ~に詰める ‖ *I'll have to pack my suitcase in the morning.* 午前中に、スーツケースに物を詰めなければならない. *Have you packed your toothbrush?* 歯ブラシは入れましたか.

➤ do your packing という表現は、同じ意味である.

⇔ **unpack** ▶定義2 自他 to put things into containers so they can be stored, transported or sold 貯蔵できる、移送できる、または売れるように、物を容器に入れる➔梱包(こんぽう)する; ~に詰める, ~を包装する ‖ *I packed all my books into boxes.* 私は自分の本をすべて箱に詰めた.

⇔ **unpack** ▶定義3 他 (しばしば受動態で) 略式 to fill with people or things until crowded or full 込み合うまたは一杯になるまで、人々または物で一杯にする➔~を詰め込む, ぎっしり入れる ‖ *The train was absolutely packed.* その電車はぎゅうぎゅう詰めだった. *The book is **packed** with useful information.* その本には有益な情報がぎっしり詰まっている. *People packed the pavements, waiting for the president to arrive.* 大統領が到着するのを待ちながら、人々は歩道に詰め掛けていた.

句動詞 pack sth in 略式 ▶定義 to stop doing sth ~をするのをやめる➔(仕事・習慣など)をやめる ‖ *I've packed in my job.* 私は仕事を辞めた. *I've had enough of you boys arguing - just pack it in, will you!* こら君たち、君たちの口げんかにはもううんざりだ - やめなさい、いいね.

pack sth in/into sth ▶定義 to do a lot in a short time 短い間にたくさんの事をする➔~を(限られた時間)に詰め込む, (短期間)で(多くの事)をする ‖ *They packed a lot into their three days in Rome.* 彼らはローマでの3日間で多くの事をした.

pack sth out (通常は受動態で) ▶定義 to fill sth with people ~を人々で一杯にする➔~を満員にする ‖ *The bars **are packed out** every night.* そのバーは毎夜満員だ.

pack up 略式 ▶定義1 to finish working or doing sth 働くことまたは~をすることを終える➔~を終える, (~することを)やめる ‖ *There was nothing else to do so we packed up and went home.* ほかにする事がなかったので、私たちは終わりにして家に帰った. ▶定義2 (used about a machine, engine, etc) to stop working (機械、エンジンなどについて)動くことをやめる➔止まる, 故障する ‖ *My old car packed up last week so now I cycle to work.* 私の古い車が先週故障してしまったので、今私は自転車で職場に通っている.

\***package** /ˈpækɪdʒ/ 名 C ▶定義1 英 something, or a number of things, covered in paper or in a box 紙に包まれているまたは箱に入った、物または複数の物➔包み, 小包, 小荷物 ‖ *There's a large package on the table for you.* テーブルの上にあなたへの大きな包みがあります. ☛ **pack, packet, parcel** の項を参照. ▶定義2 a number of things that must be bought or accepted together 一緒に買うまたは受け入れなければならない複数のもの➔セット販売, 一まとまりのもの, パッケージソフト ‖ *a word-processing package* ワープロ用パッケージソフト *a financial aid package* 包括的な財政援助 ▶定義3 米 = PARCEL, PACKET(1) ー package 動他➔~を包装する, 荷造りする, 一括する ‖ *Goods that are attractively packaged sell more quickly.* 魅力的に包装された品物はより速く売れる.

**package holiday** ( 米 **package tour**) 名 C ▶定義 a holiday that is organized by a company for a fixed price that includes the cost of travel, hotels, etc 移動費, ホテル代などを含む固定価格で, ある会社によって組織される休暇 →パック旅行, パッケージツアー

**packaging** /pǽkɪdʒɪŋ/ 名 U ▶定義 all the materials (boxes, bags, paper, etc) that are used to cover or protect goods before they are sold 売られる前に, 商品を包むまたは保護するために使用される, すべての素材(箱, 袋, 紙など) →包装・梱包(こんぽう)材料

**packed lunch** 名 C ▶定義 food that you prepare at home and take with you to eat at work or school 職場または学校で食べるために, 家で調理して持っていく食べ物→弁当

**packer** /pǽkər/ 名 C ▶定義 a person, company or machine that puts goods, especially food, into boxes, plastic, paper, etc to be sold 売るために, 商品, 特に食べ物を箱, ビニール袋, 紙袋などに入れる人, 会社, または機械→(容器に)詰める人, 缶詰業者, 荷造り業者, 荷造り・包装機

\***packet** /pǽkət/ 名 ▶定義1 (米 pack; package) ◎ a small box, bag, etc in which things are packed to be sold in a shop 店内にある, 売られるために物が詰められた小さな箱, 袋など→小さな包み, 小さな束, (たばこなどの)1箱 ‖ *a packet of sweets/biscuits/crisps* お菓子・ビスケット・ポテトチップの小袋 *a cigarette packet* たばこの1箱 ☞ **pack, package, parcel**の項を参照. ☞ **container**のさし絵 ▶定義2 [単数扱い](口語) a large amount of money→多額の金, 大金 ‖ *That new kitchen must have cost them a packet.* 彼らは, あの新しいキッチンに大金をかけたに違いない.

**packing** /pǽkɪŋ/ 名 U ▶定義1 the act of putting your clothes, possessions, etc into boxes or cases in order to take or send them somewhere どこかへ持っていくまたは送るために, 衣服や所有物などを箱または入れ物の中に入れる行為→荷造り, 包装, 梱包(こんぽう) ‖ *We're going on holiday tomorrow so I'll do my packing tonight.* 明日から休暇旅行に出掛けるので, 今夜荷造りします. ▶定義2 医 soft material that you use to stop things from being damaged or broken when you are sending them somewhere どこかへ物を送るときに, 物が損なわれるまたは壊れることを止めるために使う柔らかい素材→詰め物, パッキング, 包装用品 ‖ *The price of the book includes postage and packing.* その本の値段には郵便料金と包装代金が含まれています.

**pact** /pækt/ 名 C ▶定義 a formal agreement between two or more people, groups or countries 2つまたは2つ以上の人々, 集団, または国々の間での公式な同意→(国家間の)協定, 条約, (個人・団体間の)約束, 契約

\***pad**¹ /pæd/ 名 C ▶定義1 a thick piece of soft material, used for cleaning or protecting sth or to make sth a different shape 〜をきれいにするまたは保護する, あるいは〜を異なった形にするために使われる, 柔らかい素材の厚い一片→脱脂綿などの小片, 詰め物, 当て物, クッション ‖ *Remove eye make-up with cleanser and a cotton-wool pad.* 目の周りの化粧はクレンジングと脱脂綿を使ってふき取ります. *a jacket with shoulder pads* 肩パッドの付いているジャケット ▶定義2 a number of pieces of paper that are fastened together at one end 片端で, 一緒に留められているたくさんの紙→はぎ取り式ノート, 用紙つづり, 便せん ‖ *a notepad* 1冊のはぎ取り式ノート ▶定義3 the place where a spacecraft takes off 宇宙ロケットが飛び立つ場所→発射台 ‖ *a launch pad* 発射台 ▶定義4 the soft part on the bottom of the feet of some animals, for example dogs and cats ある種の動物, 例えば犬や猫, の足の裏の柔らかい部分→肉球, 肉趾(にくし) ☞ C1ページのさし絵

**pad**² /pæd/ 動 (**padding; padded**) ▶定義1 pad sth (with sth) (通常は受動態で) to fill or cover sth with soft material in order to protect it, make it larger or more comfortable, etc 保護する, あるいはより大きくまたは快適にするために, 〜を柔らかい素材で満たすまたは覆う→〜に詰め物・当て物をする ‖ *I sent the photograph frame in a padded envelope.* 私は詰め物のされている封筒で写真立てを送った. ▶定義2 自 pad about, along, around, etc to walk quietly, especially because you are not wearing shoes 特に靴を履いていないために, 静かに歩く→そっと歩く, ぶらぶら・てくてく歩く ‖ *He got up and padded into the bathroom.* 彼は起き上がり, そっと歩いてトイレへ行った.

句動詞 **pad sth out** ▶定義 to make a book, speech, etc longer by adding things that are not necessary 必要ではない事を加えて、本や演説などを長くする→~を引き延ばす,長引かせる

**padding** /pǽdɪŋ/ 名 ⓤ ▶定義 soft material that is put inside sth to protect it or to make it larger, more comfortable, etc 保護する,あるいはより大きくする,より快適にするなどのために,~の内側に入れられる柔らかい素材→詰め物,当て物

**paddle**¹ /pǽdl/ 名 ⓒ ▶定義 a short pole that is flat and wide at one or both ends and that you use for moving a small boat through water 片方または両方の端が平らで広く,小さいボートを水を縫って動かすために使う短い棒→かい,パドル ☛参 oar ☛ boat のさし絵

**paddle**² /pǽdl/ 動 ▶定義 **1** 📖 to move a small boat through water using a short pole that is flat and wide at one or both ends 片方または両方の端が平らで広い短い棒を使って,小さいボートを水を縫って動かす→かいでこぐ; ~を(かいで)こぐ ‖ *We paddled down the river.* 私たちはその川をこいで下った. ☛参 row ▶定義 **2** 📖 to walk in water that is not very deep それほど深くない水の中を歩く→浅瀬をぱちゃぱちゃ歩く ‖ *We paddled in the stream.* 私たちは小川をぱちゃぱちゃ歩いた. ☛ C8 ページのさし絵

**paddock** /pǽdək/ 名 ⓒ ▶定義 a small field where horses are kept 馬が飼われている小さな牧草地→小牧場,牧草地

**padlock** /pǽdlɑ̀k/ 名 ⓒ ▶定義 a type of lock that you can use for fastening gates, bicycles, etc 門や自転車などを固定するために使う錠の一種→南京(なんきん)錠 — padlock 動 ⓗ padlock sth (to sth)→~に南京錠を掛ける ‖ *I padlocked my bicycle to a post.* 私は自分の自転車と柱にチェーンを掛けて南京錠をした.

**paediatrician**(米**pediatrician**)/pìːdiətríʃ(ə)n/ 名 ⓒ ▶定義 a doctor who deals with the diseases of children 子供の病気に取り組んでいる医者→小児科医

**paediatrics**(米**pediatrics**)/pìːdiǽtrɪks/ 名 ⓤ ▶定義 the area of medicine connected with the diseases of children 子供の病気に関連した医療分野→小児科(学) — paediatric (米pediatric)形→小児科の

**paella** /paɪélə; pɑːjelə/ 名 ⓤ ⓒ ▶定義 a Spanish dish made with rice, meat, fish and vegetables 米と肉,魚,野菜を使って調理されたスペイン料理→パエリア(スペイン風炊き込みご飯)

**pagan** /péɪgən/ 形 ▶定義 having religious beliefs that do not belong to any of the main religions 主要な宗教のどれにも属していない宗教を信仰している→異教の,多神教の — pagan 名 ⓒ→異教徒,多神教信者,不信心者

★**page**¹ /péɪdʒ/ 名 ⓒ(略 p) ▶定義 one or both sides of a piece of paper in a book, magazine, etc 本,雑誌などの1枚の紙の片面または両面→ページ,(印刷物の)1枚 ‖ *The letter was three pages long.* その手紙は3枚の長さだった. *Turn over the page.* ページをめくってください. *Turn to page 12 of your book.* 本の12ページを開きなさい. *the front page of a newspaper* 新聞の第1面

**page**² /péɪdʒ/ 動 ⓗ ▶定義 to call somebody by sending a message to a small machine (a pager) that they carry, or by calling their name publicly through a device fixed to the wall (a loudspeaker) 人々が持ち歩く小さな器械(ポケットベル)にメッセージを送って,または壁に固定されている装置(スピーカー)を通して皆に聞こえるように名前を呼んで,人を呼び出す→(ポケットベルなどで)~を呼び出す,(デパート・駅・劇場などで)~を呼び出す

**pageant** /pǽdʒənt/ 名 ⓒ ▶定義 **1** a type of public entertainment at which people dress in clothes from past times and give outdoor performances of scenes from history 昔の衣装を着て,歴史的な出来事を野外で演じる,大衆娯楽の一種→野外劇,ページェント ▶定義 **2** 米 a beauty competition for young women 若い女性のための美のコンテスト→美人コンテスト

**pager** /péɪdʒər/ 名 ⓒ ▶定義 a small machine that you carry, that makes a sound when somebody sends you a message だれかが自分にメッセージを送ると音を鳴らす,人が持ち歩く小さな器械→ポケットベル ☛類 beeper

**paid** PAY² の過去・過去分詞形

**paid-up** 形(名詞の前だけ) ▶定義 having paid all the money that you owe, for example to become a member of a club 例えばクラブのメンバーになるために,支払う義務のあるすべての

お金を支払ってしまっている➜(会費などを)完納した, 納入済みの ‖ *He's a fully paid-up member of Friends of the Earth.* 彼は Friends of the Earth の会費を完納した会員である.

***pain**[1] /péɪn/ [名] [定義1] [C][U] the unpleasant feeling that you have when a part of your body has been hurt or when you are ill 体の一部をけがしたとき, または病気のときに持つ不快な感情➜**苦痛, 痛み** ‖ *to **be in pain*** 痛みがある *He screamed with pain.* 彼は苦痛に叫んだ. *chest pains* 胸の痛み

> ➤ ache は長く続く痛みに対して使い, pain は突然の短い鋭い痛みに対して使う. それで普通, *I've got earache/backache/toothache/a headache.* (私は耳·腰·歯·頭が痛い.) と言うときは ache を用いる. しかし, *He was admitted to hospital with pains in his chest.* (彼は胸の痛みで病院に入院した) と言うときは pain を用いる. ache に伴う a, an の使い方については, ache の注を参照.

[定義2] [U] sadness that you feel because sth bad has happened 悪い事が起きてしまったために人が感じる悲しみ➜**苦痛, 心痛, 苦悩** ‖ *the pain of losing a parent* 親を亡くした悲しみ

[成句] **be a pain (in the neck)** (口語) [定義] a person, thing or situation that makes you angry or annoyed あなたを怒らせる, またはうんざりさせる, 人, 物, または状況➜**嫌な物である, 嫌なやつだ, 頭痛の種である**

**pain**[2] /péɪn/ [動][他][正式] [定義] to make sb feel sad or upset ～を悲しませる, または困惑させる➜**～の心を痛める** ‖ ***It pains me** to think how much money we've wasted.* 私たちがどれほどお金を浪費したかを考えると苦痛だ.

**pained** /péɪnd/ [形] [定義] showing that you are sad or upset 悲しがっている, または怒っていることを示している➜**不機嫌な, 感情を害した, (～に)腹を立てた** ‖ *a pained expression* 不機嫌な表情

***painful** /péɪnfʊl, -f(ə)l/ [形] **painful (for sb) (to do sth)** [定義1] that causes pain or hurts 痛みまたは傷の原因となる➜**痛い, 苦痛を与える, 痛みを伴う** ‖ *A wasp sting can be very painful.* ジガバチに刺されるととても痛い. [定義2] making you feel upset or embarrassed 人を悩ませる, またはきまりの悪い思いをさせる➜**つらい, 苦しい, 骨の折れる** ‖ *The break-up of their marriage was very painful for the children.* 彼らの離婚は子供たちにとってとてもつらいものだった. — **painfully** /-fʊli/ [副] ➜**痛んで, つらく, 苦しく**

**painkiller** /péɪnkìlər/ [名] [C] [定義] a drug that is used for reducing pain 痛みを和らげるために使われる薬➜**痛み止め, 鎮痛剤**

**painless** /péɪnləs/ [形] [定義] that does not cause pain 痛みを引き起こさない➜**痛みのない, 苦しまない** ‖ *The animals' death is quick and painless.* 動物は速やかに死に, 苦しまない. — **painlessly** [副] ➜**痛みなく, 苦しまず, たやすく**

**pains** /péɪnz/ [名]

[成句] **be at/take (great) pains to do sth; take (great) pains (with/over sth)** [定義] to make a special effort to do sth well ～をうまく行うために, 特別な努力をする➜**(非常に)骨を折る, 苦労する, 努力する** ‖ *He was at pains to hide his true feelings.* 自分の本当の感情を隠すために, 彼は骨を折った.

**painstaking** /péɪnztèɪkɪŋ/ [形] [定義] very careful and taking a long time とても注意深くて, 長く時間をかける➜**骨身を惜しまない, 勤勉な, 丹精込めた** ‖ *The painstaking search of the wreckage gave us clues as to the cause of the crash.* 骨身を惜しまずに難破船の残骸を調べた結果, 私たちはその衝突を引き起こした原因への手掛かりを得た. — **painstakingly** [副] ➜**骨身を惜しまずに, 丹精込めて**

***paint**[1] /péɪnt/ [名] [定義1] [U] coloured liquid that you put onto a surface to decorate or protect it 装飾するまたは保護するために, 表面に塗る色の付いた液体➜**ペンキ, 塗料** ‖ *green/orange/yellow paint* 緑·オレンジ·黄色のペンキ *The door will need another **coat of paint**.* そのドアはもう1回ペンキを塗る必要があります. [定義2] [U] coloured liquid that you can use to make a picture 絵をかくために使う色の付いた液体➜**絵の具** ‖ *oil paint* 油絵の具 *watercolour paint* 水彩絵の具 [定義3] **paints** [複数扱い] a collection of tubes or blocks of paint that an artist uses for painting pictures 芸術家が絵をかくために使う, チューブまたは塊の絵の具一式➜**一そろいの絵の具**

***paint**[2] /péɪnt/ [動][自][他] [定義1] to put paint onto a surface or an object 表面または物にペンキを

P

塗る→ペンキを塗る; ～にペンキを塗る ‖ *We painted the fence.* 私たちは柵(さく)にペンキを塗った. *The walls were painted pink.* その壁はピンクに塗られた. ▶定義2 to make a picture of sb/sth using paints 絵の具を使って～の絵をかく→絵をかく;(絵)をかく ‖ *We painted some animals on the wall.* 私たちはその壁に何匹かの動物をかいた.

**paintbox** /péɪntbɑ̀ks/ 名 C ▶定義 a box that contains blocks or tubes of paint of many colours たくさんの色の絵の具の塊またはチューブが入っている箱→絵の具箱

**paintbrush** /péɪntbrʌ̀ʃ/ 名 C ▶定義 a brush that you use for painting with 塗るために使うブラシ, かくために使う筆→ペンキ用のはけ, 絵筆
☛ brush のさし絵

★**painter** /péɪntər/ 名 C ▶定義1 a person whose job is to paint buildings, walls, etc 建物や壁などを塗ることを仕事とする人→ペンキ屋, 塗装工 ▶定義2 a person who paints pictures 絵を描く人→画家

★**painting** /péɪntɪŋ/ 名 ▶定義1 C a picture that sb has painted ～が描いた絵→(絵の具の)絵 ‖ *a famous painting by Van Gogh* ヴァン ゴッホがかいた有名な絵
➤ drawing は painting に似ているが, 絵の具の代わりに鉛筆, ペン, またはクレヨンを使ってかかれたものである.
▶定義2 U the act of painting pictures or buildings 絵をかく, または建物にペンキを塗る行為→絵をかくこと, 画法, ペンキ塗装 ‖ *She studies Indian painting.* 彼女はインドの画法を勉強している.

**paintwork** /péɪntwɜ̀ːrk/ 名 U ▶定義 a painted surface, especially on a vehicle 特に乗り物の, 塗装された表面→塗装, 塗装部

★**pair¹** /peər/ 名 ▶定義1 C two things of the same type that are used or worn together 一緒に使用される, または身に着けられる同じ型の2つの物→(2個から成る)一組, 一対 ‖ *a pair of shoes/gloves/earrings* 靴1足・手袋の一組・イヤリングの一組 ▶定義2 C a thing that consists of two parts that are joined together 共につながっている2つの部分から成る物→(2つの部分から成る)1つ, 1個 ‖ *a pair of scissors/glasses/trousers* はさみ1丁・眼鏡1つ・ズボン1着 ▶定義3 [C, 複数形の動詞と共に] two people or animals that are doing sth together 一緒に～を行っている2人または2匹の動物→2人組, ペア, つがい ‖ *These boxers have fought several times, and tonight the pair meet again.* この2人のボクサーは何度も戦い, そして今夜その2人組がまた出会うのです.

➤ couple は, 結婚しているまたは恋愛関係にある2人について述べるために使われる.

成句 **in pairs** ▶定義 two at a time 同時に2つ→2つ・2人一組で ‖ *These earrings are only sold in pairs.* これらのイヤリングは2つ一組でのみ売られる. *The students were working in pairs.* 学生たちは2人一組になって勉強していた.

**pair²** /peər/ 動
句動詞 **pair (sb/sth) off (with sb)** ▶定義 to come together, especially to form a romantic relationship; to bring two people together for this purpose 特に恋愛関係を結ぶために, 会う; この目的のために, 2人を会わせる→恋人同士・夫婦・ペアになる; ～を(ペアとして)組ませる, 恋人同士・夫婦にする ‖ *She's always trying to pair me off with her brother.* 彼女は, いつも私と彼女のお兄さんを組ませようとする.

**pair up (with sb)** ▶定義 to join together with another person or group to work, play a game, etc 働く, ゲームをするなどのために, ほかの人または集団と一緒になる→ペアを組む; ～を(ペアとして)組ませる, ～を2人ずつ組にする ‖ *I paired up with another student and we did the project together.* 私はほかの学生とペアを組み, 私たちは一緒に課題に取り組んだ.

**pajamas** 米 = PYJAMAS

★**palace** /pǽləs/ 名 C ▶定義 a large house that is or was the home of a king or queen 王または女王の家である, または家だった大きな住宅→宮殿, 大邸宅, ご殿

**palate** /pǽlət/ 名 C ▶定義 the top part of the inside of your mouth 口の内側の上の部分→口蓋(こうがい)

★**pale²** /peɪl/ 形 ▶定義1 (used about a person or his/her face) having skin that is light in colour, often because of fear or illness (人または人の顔について)しばしば恐怖または病気が理由で, 色の薄い肌をしている→血の気がない, 血色が悪い, 青ざめた ‖ *She has a pale complexion.* 彼女の

顔が青白い. *I felt myself go/turn pale with fear.* 私は自分が恐怖で青ざめていくのを感じた. ☞ 名 pallor. pallidと比較. ▶定義2 not bright or strong in colour 色が明るくないまたは強くない→薄い,淡い,鈍い‖ *a pale yellow dress* 淡い黄色のドレス ⇔ **dark** — **pale** 動⾃→(顔色が)青ざめる,(色が)薄くなる,(光が)弱まる

**pall** /pɔːl/ 動⾃ ▶定義 to become less interesting or important 興味または重要性がより少なくなる→つまらなくなる,興味がなくなる‖ *After a few months, the excitement of his new job began to pall.* 2,3か月たつと,彼をわくわくさせていた新しい仕事はつまらなくなり始めた.

**pallid** /pǽləd/ 形 ▶定義 (used about a person or his/her face) light in colour, especially because of illness (人または人の顔について)特に病気で,色が薄い→青ざめた,青白い‖ *His pallid complexion made him look unhealthy.* 彼は青白い顔色をしていたので不健康に見えた.
▶ paleと比較.

**pallor** /pǽlər/ 名 Ⓤ ▶定義 pale colouring of the face, especially because of illness or fear 特に病気または恐怖のために,顔色が青白いこと→青白さ,蒼白(そうはく)

**palm**¹ /pɑːm/ 名 Ⓒ ▶定義1 the flat, inner surface of your hand 人の手の,平らな,内側の表面→てのひら,掌(たなごころ)‖ *She held the coins tightly in the palm of her hand.* 彼女はてのひらにコインをしっかりと握っていた. ☞ C5ページのさし絵 ▶定義2 (または **palm tree**) a tall straight type of tree that grows in hot countries. Palms have a lot of large leaves at the top but no branches. 熱帯の国々に育つ,高いまっすぐな木の一種.木の上の辺りにはたくさんの大きな葉が生えているが,枝はない→ヤシ,シュロ ☞ C2ページのさし絵

**palm**² /pɑːm/ 動
句動詞 **palm sb off (with sth)** 略式 ▶定義 to persuade sb to believe sth that is not true in order to stop him/her asking questions or complaining 人が質問するまたは不平を言うことをやめさせるために,事実ではない〜を…が信じるように説き伏せる→(〜で)ごまかす

**palm sth off (on sb)** ▶定義 to persuade sb to accept sth that he/she does not want 欲しがっていない〜を…が受け入れるように説き伏せる→〜をだましてつかませる,押し付ける,だまして売り付ける‖ *She's always palming off the worst jobs on her assistant.* 彼女はいつも最悪の仕事を自分の部下に押し付ける.

**paltry** /pɔ́ːltri/ 形 ▶定義 too small to be considered important or useful 重要であるまたは役に立つと見なされるには小さすぎる→(金額などが)わずかな,取るに足りない,たったの‖ *a paltry sum of money* はした金

**pamper** /pǽmpər/ 動⾃ ▶定義 to take care of sb very well and make him/her feel as comfortable as possible 〜の面倒をよく見て,できるだけ心地良くさせる→(子供など)を甘やかす,過保護にする,増長させる

**pamphlet** /pǽmflət/ 名 Ⓒ ▶定義 a very thin book with a paper cover containing information about a particular subject 特定のテーマについての情報が書かれた,紙の表紙の付いたとても薄い本→パンフレット,小冊子,(時事問題などの)論説

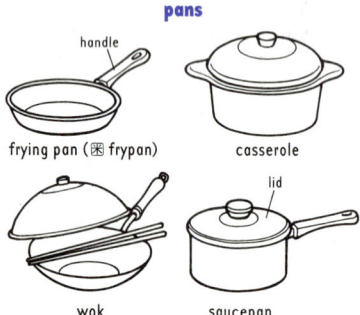

pans — handle — frying pan (英 frypan) — casserole — lid — wok — saucepan

★**pan** /pǽn/ 名 Ⓒ ▶定義 a metal container with a handle or handles that is used for cooking food in; the contents of a pan 中に食べ物を入れて調理するために使われる,1つまたは複数の取っ手の付いた金属製の容器;平なべの中身→平なべ,フライパン;平なべ1杯(分)‖ *Cook the spaghetti in a large pan of boiling water.* 大きな平なべの沸騰したお湯にスパゲッティを入れてゆでてください.

**pancake** /pǽnkèɪk/ 名 Ⓒ ▶定義 a type of very thin round cake that is made by frying a mixture of flour, milk and eggs (**batter**) 小麦粉,牛乳,卵を混ぜた物(ケーキのたね)を,薄く油をひいて焼いて

## Pancake Day (または Shrove Tuesday)
▶定義 a Tuesday in February when people in Britain traditionally eat pancakes. Pancake Day is the day before the period of Lent begins. 英国の人々が伝統的にパンケーキを食べる2月のある火曜日.この日は四旬節の始まる前日である➡懺悔(ざんげ)火曜日

## panda /pǽndə/ 图 ⓒ
▶定義 a large black and white bear that comes from China 中国原産の,大きな白黒の熊➡(ジャイアント)パンダ

## pandemonium /pæ̀ndəmóuniəm/ 图 Ⓤ ▶定義
a state of great noise and confusion ものすごい騒音と混乱の状態➡大混乱,大騒ぎ,修羅場

## pander /pǽndər/ 動
句動詞 pander to sb/sth ▶定義 to do or say exactly what sb wants especially when this is not reasonable 特にこれが道理に合っていないとき,〜が望んでいる通りの事を行うまたは言う➡(人に)おもねる,迎合する ‖ *He refuses to pander to his boss's demands.* 彼は上司の要求に迎合することを拒む.

## p and p 略 英 postage and packing➡郵送料と包装料 ‖ *price: £29 incl p and p* 価格: 郵送料と包装料込みで29ポンド

## pane /péin/ 图 ⓒ ▶定義 a piece of glass in a window, etc 窓などのガラスの1枚➡窓ガラス ‖ *a windowpane* 窓ガラス ☞ C7ページのさし絵

## panel /pǽnl/ 图 ⓒ ▶定義 1 a square or rectangular piece of wood, metal or glass that forms part of a door or wall ドアまたは壁の部分を形づくる,木,金属,またはガラスの,正方形または長方形の1枚➡羽目板,鏡板,パネル ▶定義 2 [単数または複数形の動詞と共に] a group of people who give their advice or opinions about sth; a group of people who discuss topics of interest on television or radio 〜について助言をする,または意見を述べる人々の集団;テレビまたはラジオで興味深い話題を討論する人々の集団➡(専門家の)委員会;(討論者・解答者・審査員などの)一団,グループ ‖ *a panel of judges (= in a competition)* 審査員団 (= コンテストにおいて) *a panel game (= a TV game show with two teams)* パネルゲーム (= 2チームで行うテレビの娯楽番組) ▶定義 3 a flat surface that contains the equipment for controlling a vehicle, machine, etc 乗り物,機械などを制御するための装置が収納された,平らな表面➡計器盤,配電盤,制御盤 ‖ *a control/display panel* 制御盤・表示盤

## panellist (米 panelist) /pǽnlɪst/ ⓒ ▶定義 a member of a panel(2) panel(2)の一員➡パネルディスカッションの討論者,パネリスト,クイズ番組の解答者

## pang /pǽŋ/ 图 [ⓒ, 通常は複数] ▶定義 a sudden strong feeling of emotional or physical pain 突然の鋭い感情的または肉体的痛み➡心痛,苦悩,激痛 ‖ *a pang of jealousy* しっとの苦悩 *hunger pangs* 空腹の苦痛

## *panic /pǽnɪk/ 图 ⓒ Ⓤ ▶定義 a sudden feeling of fear that cannot be controlled and stops you from thinking clearly 自制できなくて,明瞭(めいりょう)に考えることを妨げる突然の恐怖の感情➡恐怖,恐慌,パニック ‖ *People fled in panic as the fire spread.* 火事が拡大した時,人々は慌てふためいて逃げた. *There was a mad panic when the alarm went off.* 警報が鳴り響いた時,狂ったようなパニックが起こった. ― panic 動 ⓘ (panicking; panicked)➡うろたえる,慌てふためく ‖ *Stay calm and don't panic.* 落ち着きなさい,そしてうろたえないようにしなさい.

## panic-stricken 形 ▶定義 very frightened in a way that stops you from thinking clearly 明瞭(めいりょう)に考えることを妨げられた様子で,とてもおびえた➡恐怖を来した,狼狽(ろうばい)した

## panorama /pæ̀nərάːmə, -rǽmə/ 图 ⓒ ▶定義 a view over a wide area of land 土地の広範囲にわたる眺め➡パノラマ,全景 ― panoramic /pæ̀nərǽmɪk/ 形➡全景の

## pant /pǽnt/ 動 ⓘ ▶定義 to breathe quickly, for example after running or because it is very hot 例えば走った後,またはとても暑いので,素早く呼吸する➡荒い息をする,息を切らす,あえぐ ― pant 图 ⓒ➡あえぎ,息切れ

## panther /pǽnθər/ 图 ⓒ ▶定義 a large wild ani-

mal of the cat family with black fur 黒い毛皮で覆われている、ネコ科の大きな野生動物→クロヒョウ ☛ **lion** のさし絵

**panties** /pǽntiz/ 特に 米 = **KNICKERS**

**pantomime** /pǽntəmàim/ 名 C U ▶定義1 （または 略式 **panto** /pǽntou, -tə/） 英 a type of play for children, with music, dancing and jokes, that is usually performed at Christmas. Pantomimes are based on traditional children's stories (*fairy stories*). 通常クリスマスに演じられる、音楽、踊り、ジョークを伴う子供向けの芝居の一種. 伝統的な童話（妖精（ようせい）の話）に基づいている→おとぎ芝居 ▶定義2 米 = **MIME**

**pantry** /pǽntri/ 名 C （複 **pantries**） ▶定義 a small room where food is kept 食べ物が保存されている小さな部屋→食料品貯蔵室, 食器室 ☛類 **larder**

\***pants** /pǽnts/ 名 [複数扱い] ▶定義1 英 = **UNDERPANTS** ▶定義2 米 = **TROUSERS**

**pantyhose** /pǽntihòuz/ 米 = **TIGHTS**

**paparazzi** /pàːpərάːtsi/ 名 [複数扱い] ▶定義 photographers who follow famous people around in order to get pictures of them to sell to a newspaper or magazine 新聞または雑誌に売ろうとして有名人の写真を撮るために、有名人を追い回すカメラマン→芸能記者・カメラマン, パパラッチ

**papaya** /pəpάːjə, -páɪə/（または **pawpaw** /pɔ́ːpɔː, pəpɔ́ː/）名 C ▶定義 a large tropical fruit which is sweet and orange inside and has small black seeds 甘く、オレンジ色の果肉と小さな黒い種のある、大きな熱帯の果物→パパイヤ（の木・果実） ☛ C3 ページのさし絵

\***paper** /péɪpər/ 名 ▶定義1 U a material made in thin sheets that you use for writing or drawing on, covering things, etc その上に書くまたは描く, 物を包むなどに使う、薄いシート状に作られた素材→紙 ‖ *a piece/sheet of paper* 1枚の紙 *a paper handkerchief* 紙ナプキン

▶紙の種類には, filter paper（ろ過紙）, tissue paper（ティッシュペーパー）, toilet paper（トイレットペーパー）と writing paper（便せん）が含まれる.

▶定義2 = **NEWSPAPER(1)** ‖ *Where's today's paper?* 今日の新聞はどこですか.

➤新聞は, paper shop（新聞販売店）または newsagent's（新聞雑誌販売店）で買う.

▶定義3 **papers** [複数扱い] important letters or pieces of paper that have information written on them 重要な手紙、または情報が書かれている複数の紙→文書, 書類, 証明書 ‖ *The document you want is somewhere in the pile of papers on her desk.* あなたが捜している文書は、彼女の机の上の書類の山のどこかにありますよ. ▶定義4 C the written questions or the written answers in an exam 試験で、書かれた問題または書かれた答え→試験問題(用紙), 答案(用紙) ‖ *The history exam is divided into three papers.* その歴史の試験は、試験問題用紙3枚に分かれている.

▶定義5 C a piece of writing on a particular subject that is written for specialists 専門家を対象に書かれた、特定の課題についての論文の1つ→論文, レポート ‖ *At the conference, the Professor presented a paper on Sri Lankan poetry.* その会議で、教授はスリランカの詩についての論文を発表した.

成句 **on paper** ▶定義1 in writing 書面で, 文書に書いて→紙面で[の], 文書で[の] ‖ *I've had nothing on paper to say that I've been accepted.* 私が採用されたという文書での通知は受けていません.（電話で連絡はあったが）▶定義2 as an idea, but not in a real situation; in theory 実際の状況ではなく、考えとして; 理論的には→紙上では, 理論上は ‖ *The scheme seems fine on paper, but would it work in practice?* その計画は理論的にはすばらしく見えますが、実際にうまくいくのですか.

**paperback** /péɪpərbæ̀k/ 名 C U ▶定義 a book that has a paper cover 紙の表紙の本→柔らかい紙表紙の本, ペーパーバック ‖ *The novel is available in paperback.* その小説には、ペーパーバック版もあります. ☛参 **hardback**

**paper boy** 名 C ▶定義 a boy who takes newspapers to people's houses 新聞を人々の家へ持っていく少年→新聞配達の少年, 新聞売りの少年

**paper clip** 名 C ▶定義 a small piece of bent wire that is used for holding pieces of paper together 複数枚の紙を一緒に留めておくために使われる、小さな曲げられた針金→クリップ ☛ S4 ページのさし絵

**paper girl** 名 C ▶定義 a girl who takes newspapers to people's houses 新聞を人々の家へ持

っていく少女→新聞配達の少女, 新聞売りの少女

**paperwork** /péɪpərwɚːrk/ 名 U ▶定義1 the written work that is part of a job, such as writing letters and reports and filling in forms, etc 仕事の一部としての書く作業, 例えば手紙や報告書を書いたり書類に書き込む作業など→(書類作成などの)一般事務, 文書業務 ‖ *I hate doing paperwork.* 私は一般事務をすることは大嫌いです.
▶定義2 documents that need to be prepared, collected, etc in order for a piece of business to be completed 1つの仕事を仕上げるために, 準備され, 集められる必要のある書類→事務書類 ‖ *Some of the paperwork is missing from this file.* いくつかの事務書類がこのファイルからなくなっている.

**paprika** /pæpríːkə, pə-, pǽprəkə/ 名 U ▶定義 a red powder made from a sweet red pepper that you can use in cooking 料理に使う, 赤のアマトウガラシから作られる赤い粉→パプリカ(赤色の香辛料)

**par**¹ /pɑːr/ 名 U ▶定義 (in golf) the standard number of times a player should hit the ball in order to complete a particular hole or series of holes (ゴルフで)特定のホールまたは一連のホールを終えるために, 競技者がボールを打つべき基準の回数→パー, 基準打数
成句 below par 略式 ▶定義 not as good or as well as usual いつもと同じほど良くない, 元気でない→調子・具合が悪い・悪く, 水準以下で
on a par with sb/sth ▶定義 of an equal level, standard, etc to sb/sth else ほかの〜と同じ水準, 基準などの→〜と同等・同程度で, 肩を並べる ‖ *Is a teacher's salary on a par with a doctor's?* 教師の給料は医者と同じくらいですか.

**par**² /pɑːr/ (または **para**) 略 paragraph→段落, パラグラフ

**parable** /pǽrəb(ə)l/ 名 C ▶定義 a short story that teaches a lesson, especially one told by Jesus in the Bible 教訓を説く短い話, 特に聖書の中のキリストによって語られたもの→寓話(ぐうわ), 例え話

**parabola** /pərǽbələ/ 名 C ▶定義 a curve like the path of an object that is thrown through the air and falls back to earth 物体が空中に投げられてから地上に戻ってくるまでの軌跡のような曲線→放物線

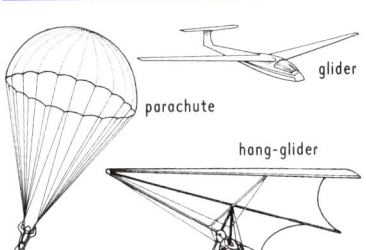

**parachute** /pǽrəʃùːt/ 名 C ▶定義 a piece of equipment that opens and lets the person fall to the ground slowly when he/she jumps from a plane 人が飛行機から飛び降りたとき, その人が地面にゆっくり落ちていくようにするために開く, 装備→パラシュート, 落下傘 ― parachute 動 自→パラシュートで降りる

**parade** /pəréɪd/ 名 C ▶定義 an occasion when a group of people stand or walk in a line so that people can look at them 人々の集団が列になって立つまたは歩くことでその集団を見ることのできる機会→行列, 行進, パレード ‖ *a military parade* 観兵式 *a fashion parade* ファッションショー

**paradise** /pǽrədàɪs, -z/ 名 ▶定義1 **Paradise** [単数扱い] (不定冠詞も定冠詞もなしで) the place where some people think that good people go after they die; heaven 善良な人々が死後行くと考えられている場所; 天国→天国, 極楽
▶定義2 C a perfect place 完ぺきな場所→楽園, 絶好の場所 ‖ *This beach is a paradise for windsurfers.* この海岸はウインドサーフィンをする人にとって絶好の場所です.

**paradox** /pǽrədɑ̀ks/ 名 C ▶定義 a situation or statement with two or more parts that seem strange or impossible together 同時には奇妙にまたは不可能に見える部分が2つまたはそれより多くある状況または陳述→逆説, 矛盾, つじつまの合わない言葉・行為・状況 ‖ *It's a paradox that some countries produce too much food while in other countries people are starving.* 多すぎるほど食べ物を生産する国々がある一方で, 人々が飢えている国々があるのはつじつまが合わない. ― paradoxical /pǽrədɑ́ksɪk(ə)l/ 形→矛盾する,

逆説的な, 逆説の

**paraffin** /pǽrəfən/ (米**kerosene**) 名 U ▶定義
a type of oil that is burned to produce heat or light 熱または光を生み出すために燃やされる, 油の一種 → 灯油

★**paragraph** /pǽrəgrὰːf, -grǽf/ 名 C ▶定義 a part of a piece of writing that consists of one or more sentences. A paragraph always starts on a new line. 1 つまたはそれより多い文章から成る文書の一部分. 段落は, 常に改行して始まる → 段落, パラグラフ

★**parallel**¹ /pǽrəlèl/ 形副 ▶定義 1 parallel (to sth) (used about two lines, etc) with the same distance between them for all their length (2 つの線などについて) それら自体の長さ全体で, お互いの距離が同じで → 平行の, 平行した; 平行して ‖ parallel lines 平行線 The railway runs parallel to the road. その鉄道は道路と平行に走っている. ☞ **line** のさし絵 ▶定義 2 similar and happening at the same time 似通った, そして同時に起こる → 同方向・傾向の, 対応・相応する, 類似した; 同方向へ ‖ The two brothers followed parallel careers in different companies. その 2 人の兄弟は, 違う会社でよく似た経歴をたどった.

**parallel**² /pǽrəlèl/ 名 C U ▶定義 a person, thing or situation that is similar to another one in a different situation, place or time 違う状況, 場所または時間にありながら, ほかのものと似通った人, 物または状況 → 匹敵・相当する物, 対等の物・人 ‖ The government's huge election victory is **without parallel** this century. 政府が大々的に選挙に勝ったが, これは今世紀比べるものがないほどの勝利である.

**paralyse** (米**paralyze**) /pǽrəlàɪz/ 動他 ▶定義 1 to make a person unable to move his/her body or a part of it 人の体またはその一部分を動けなくさせる → 〜をまひさせる, しびれさせる ‖ Miriam is paralysed from the waist down. ミリアムは腰から下がまひしている. ▶定義 2 to make sb/sth unable to work in a normal way 〜を通常のようには働けなくさせる → 〜を無力にする, 無効にする, (機能などを)まひさせる ― **paralysis** /pərǽləsəs/ 名 ▶まひ, まひ状態, 無力力 ‖ The disease can cause paralysis or even death. その病気はまひの, あるいは死の原因にすらなり得る.

There has been complete paralysis of the railway system. 鉄道は完全にまひ状態になっている.

**paramedic** /pærəmédɪk/ 名 C ▶定義 a person who has had special training in treating people who are hurt or ill, but who is not a doctor or nurse けがをしている, または病気の人々を手当てするよう特別の訓練受けた人であるが, 医者でも看護婦でもない → 医療補助員 (救護員・X 線技師・薬剤師など)

**paramilitary** /pærəmílət(ə)ri, -tèri/ 形 ▶定義 organized in the same way as, but not belonging to, an official army 正式な軍隊に属しているのではないが, 同じように組織されている → (主に非合法組織・活動が)準軍事的な, 軍補助の ‖ a paramilitary group 準軍事的集団

**paramount** /pǽrəmàʊnt/ 形 正式 ▶定義 most important 最も重要な → 最高の, 最も重要な ‖ Safety is paramount in car design. 安全性は車のデザインにおいて最も重要な事である.

**paranoia** /pærənɔ́ɪə/ 名 U ▶定義 1 a type of mental illness in which you wrongly believe that other people want to harm you ほかの人々が自分を傷付けたがっていると, 間違って信じる精神的な病気の一種 → 妄想症, パラノイア ▶定義 2 略式 a feeling of fear and suspicion of other people ほかの人々への恐怖と疑いの感情 → 被害妄想

**paranoid** /pǽrənɔ̀ɪd/ 形 ▶定義 wrongly believing that other people are trying to harm you or are saying bad things about you ほかの人々が自分を傷付けようとしている, または自分の悪口を言っていると, 間違って信じている → 被害妄想の, 妄想症・パラノイアの

**paraphernalia** /pærəfəméɪljə/ 名 U ▶定義 a large number of different objects that you need for a particular purpose 特定の目的に必要な, 数多くの異なったもの → 身の回りの品, 諸道具, 面倒な事・手続き

**paraphrase** /pǽrəfrèɪz/ 動他 ▶定義 to express sth again using different words so that it is easier to understand より理解しやすいように, 違う言葉を使って〜を表現し直す → 〜を易しく言い換える, 意訳する ― paraphrase 名 C → 別の・易しい言い方による言い換え

**parasite** /pǽrəsàɪt/ 名 C ▶定義 a plant or an animal that lives in or on another plant or animal and gets its food from it ほかの植物や動物

の中に、またはくっついて生きていて、そこから食物を得る植物または動物→寄生虫、寄生植物

**parasol** /pǽrəsɔ̀(ː)l, -sɔ̀l/ 图 ❸ ▶定義 an umbrella that you use to protect yourself from the sun 自分自身を日光から守るために使う傘→日傘、パラソル ☞ C8 ページのさし絵

**paratroops** /pǽrətrùːps/ 图 [複数扱い] ▶定義 soldiers who are trained to jump from a plane with a piece of equipment on their backs that opens to help them fall slowly (a parachute) 開いてゆっくり落ちるようにする装備 (パラシュート) を背中に背負って飛行機から飛び降りることを訓練された兵士たち→落下傘部隊

★**parcel** /pɑ́ːrs(ə)l/ (困 または **package**) 图 ❸ ▶定義 something that is covered in brown paper and sent to sb 茶色の紙に包まれて〜に送られる物→小包、包み、小荷物 ☞参 pack, package, packet の項を参照.

**parched** /pɑːrtʃt/ 形 ▶定義 very hot and dry, or very thirsty とても暑くて乾燥している、またはとてものどが渇いている→(土地などが) からからの、干からびた、のどがからからの ‖ Can I have a drink? I'm parched! 飲んでもいいですか。のどがからからなんだ。

★**pardon**¹ /pɑ́ːrdn/ 图 ❸ ❶ ▶定義 an official decision not to punish sb for a crime 〜を罪のために罰しないという公式の決定→許し、許すこと、容赦
▶ I beg your pardon は sorry の正式な言い方である: Oh, I do beg your pardon. I had no idea this was your seat. (あっ、失礼しました。あなたの席だとは知りませんでした。) また自分が理解できなかったため、言った事を繰り返すように人に頼みたいときにも用いられる.

> ▶コミュニケーション ♥
>
> 会話で「繰り返して」と頼むとき
>
> 相手の言った事がよく聞き取れないとき、What did you say? とストレートに聞き返すこともできますが、I beg your pardon? と言った方が丁寧に聞こえます。Pardon me? または Pardon? と短く省略することも可能です。いずれの場合も、必ず上昇調のイントネーションを使います。下降調は、「ごめんなさい」「失礼しました」といったわび、「もしもし、失礼ですが」と人の注意をひく場合などに使われます。

— pardon 動 ⓣ pardon sb (for sth/doing sth) →〜を許す、大目に見る

**pardon**² /pɑ́ːrdn/ (または **pardon me**) 間 ▶定義 1 used for asking sb to repeat what he/she has just said because you did not hear or understand it 聞こえなかった、または理解できなかったので、たった今言った事を繰り返すように〜に頼むために用いて→すみませんがもう一度おっしゃっていただけますか ▶定義 2 used by some people to mean sorry or excuse me 「ごめんなさい」または「失礼ですが」の意味で用いて→ごめんなさい、失礼ですが

★**parent** /pé(ə)rənt/ 图 ❸ ▶定義 1 a person's mother or father 人の母親または父親→親
▶ single parent は、自分の子供を二親ではなく独りで育てている母親または父親である。foster-parent は、法的には自分の子供ではない子供の世話をしている人である。

▶定義 2 a company that owns smaller companies of the same type 同種のさらに小さな会社を所有している会社→親会社 ‖ a parent company 親会社

**parental** /pəréntl/ 形 (名詞の前だけ) ▶定義 of a parent or parents 親の、または両親の→親の、親としての、親らしい ‖ parental support/advice 親としての援助・忠告

**parentheses** /pərénθəsìːz/ 特に 困 = BRACKET¹(1)

**parenthood** /pé(ə)rənthùd/ 图 ❶ ▶定義 the state of being a parent 親である状態→親であること

**parish** /pǽrɪʃ/ 图 ❸ ▶定義 an area or district which has its own church; the people who live in this area 教会のある地域または区域; この地域に住んでいる人々→教区、教区の住民 ‖ the parish church 教区教会 — **parishioner** /pərɪ́ʃ(ə)nər/ 图 ❸ →教区民

★**park**¹ /pɑːrk/ 图 ❸ ▶定義 1 an open area in a town, often with grass or trees, where people can go to walk, play, etc しばしば芝生または木々が植えられていて、人々が歩いたり遊んだりできる、街にある開放された地域→公園 ‖ Let's go for a walk in the park. 公園を散歩しよう。

▶定義 2 (複合語で) a large area of land that is used for a special purpose 特別の目的のために使われる、広い土地→公園、遊園地、〜場 ‖ a national park 国立公園 a business park ビジネス街 a theme park テーマ遊園地

**park²** /pɑːrk/ 動 📘 ▶定義 to leave the vehicle that you are driving somewhere for a period of time 運転している乗り物をしばらくどこかに置いたままにしておく→駐車する，止めておく ‖ *You can't park in the centre of town.* 街の中心には駐車できませんよ. *Somebody's parked their car in front of the exit.* だれかが車を出口の前に止めている.

**parking** /pάːrkɪŋ/ 名 ▶定義 the action of leaving a car, lorry, etc somewhere for a time 車，トラックなどをしばらくどこかに置いたままにしておく行為→駐車 ‖ *The sign said 'No Parking'.* 標識に「駐車禁止」と書かれていた.

▶たくさんの車を駐車しておける場所は，car park と言われる．1台の車を駐車しておける場所は，parking space と言われる．

**parking lot** 米 = CAR PARK

**parking meter** 名 C ▶定義 a metal post that you put coins into to pay for parking a car in the space beside it for a period of time しばらくその横の空間に車を駐車させるために，支払いにコインを入れる金属の柱→パーキングメーター

**parking ticket** 名 C ▶定義 a piece of paper that orders you to pay money (a fine) for parking your car where it is not allowed 駐車禁止の場所に駐車したために，お金（罰金）を払うよう命令する文書→駐車違反の切符

**parliament** /pάːrləmənt/ 名 C ▶定義 **1** the group of people who are elected to make and change the laws of a country 国の法律を作りまた変更するために選ばれた人々の集団→議会，国会 ☞ 単数の場合，単数形または複数形動詞のどちらかと共に使える. ▶定義 **2 Parliament** [単数扱い] the parliament of the United Kingdom→英国の議会 ‖ *a Member of Parliament (MP)* 下院議員（MPと略す）

▶英国の議会は，議員が選挙ではなく指名される the House of Lords（上院）と，議員が民衆によってその地域（constituencies（選挙区）と言われる）を代表するよう選出される the House of Commons（下院）によって構成される.

▶社会・文化

**英米の議会**

アメリカ議会は Congress, イギリス議会は Parliament と呼ばれます．両者とも上院（the Upper house）と下院（the Lower house）がありますが，アメリカの上院は the Senate, 下院は the House of Representatives, イギリスの上院・下院はそれぞれ the House of Lords, the House of Commons と呼ばれます．

なお，日本の国会は the Diet, 上院の参議院は the House of Councilors, 下院である衆議院は the House of Representatives と言います．

**parliamentary** /pὰːrləmént(ə)ri/ 形（名詞の前だけ）▶定義 connected with parliament 議会に関連した→議会の，議会で制定した

**parody** /pǽrədi/ 名 C U (複 **parodies**) ▶定義 a piece of writing, speech or music that copies the style of sb/sth in a funny way 面白いやり方で，～の表現方法をまねして書かれた作品，演説，または音楽→パロディー，もじり文 ‖ *a parody of a spy novel* スパイ小説のパロディー ― **parody** 動 他（現分 **parodying**; 三単現 **parodies**; 過，過分 **parodied**）▶～をもじる，パロディー化する

**parole** /pəróʊl/ 名 U ▶定義 permission that is given to a prisoner to leave prison early on the condition that he/she behaves well 行いが良いという条件で，囚人に与えられる，予定より早く刑務所を出る許可→仮出所（許可）‖ *He's going to be released on parole.* 彼は仮出所する．

**parrot** /pǽrət/ 名 C ▶定義 a type of tropical bird with a curved beak and usually with very bright feathers. Parrots that are kept as pets can be trained to copy what people say. 曲がったくちばしと，通常とても鮮やかな色の羽の，熱帯の鳥の一種．ペットとして飼われているこの鳥は，人々の言う事をまねるように訓練できる→おうむ

**parrot-fashion** 副 ▶定義 without understanding the meaning of sth ～の意味を理解していなくて→おうむ返しに，棒暗記に ‖ *to learn sth parrot-fashion* ～を丸暗記する

**parsley** /pάːrsli/ 名 U ▶定義 a plant (herb) with very small leaves that are used for adding taste to or decorating food 食べ物に風味を加えるま

たは飾るために使われる, とても小さな葉の植物(ハーブ)→パセリ

**parsnip** /pάːrsnəp/ 名 C ▶定義 a long thin white vegetable, that grows under the ground 地中で育つ, 長く薄くて白い野菜→アメリカほうふう(根が食用) ☞ C3ページのさし絵

★**part**¹ /pάːrt/ 名 ▶定義1 C U (a) part (of sth) one of the pieces, areas, periods, things, etc that together with others forms the whole of sth; some, but not all of sth ほかのものと一緒になって～の全体を形づくる, 複数の部品, 地域, 期間, 物などの1つ; ～の全体ではないいくらかのもの→～の一部(分), ～の一員; 部分 ‖ *Which part of Spain do you come from?* スペインのどちらのご出身ですか. *The film is good **in parts**.* その映画は部分的には良い. ***spare parts*** *for a car* 車の予備部品 *a part of the body* 体の一部分 *Part of the problem is lack of information.* 問題の1つは, 情報が欠如しているということだ. *I enjoy being part of a team.* 私はチームの一員であることを喜んでいます. ▶定義2 C a role or character in a play, film, etc 芝居, 映画などの中での役や登場人物→役 ‖ *He played the part of Macbeth.* 彼はマクベスの役を演じた. *I had a small part in the school play.* 私は学校劇で端役を演じた. ▶定義3 **parts**[複数扱い]a region or area→地方, 地域 ‖ *Are you from these parts?* あなたはこの辺りの地方のご出身ですか. ▶定義4 C a section of a book, television series, etc 本, テレビシリーズなどの部分→(第～)部, 編, 巻 ‖ *You can see part two of this programme at the same time next week.* 来週, 同じ時間にこの番組の第2部が見られる. ▶定義5 C an amount or quantity (of a liquid or substance)(液体または物質の)量→(全体をいくつかに)等分した部分, ～分の… ‖ *Use one part cleaning fluid to ten parts water.* 水10に対して洗剤液1を用います.

成句 **the best/better part of sth** ▶定義 most of sth; more than half of sth, especially a period of time ～のほとんど; 特に時間について, ～の半分より多く→～の大部分, ～の大半 ‖ *They've lived here for the best part of forty years.* 彼らは40年の大半をここで過ごした.

**for the most part** ▶定義 usually or mostly 通常または大部分は→大抵は, いつもは, 大部分は

**for my, his, their, etc part** ▶定義 speaking for myself, etc; personally 自分自身の意見を述べると; 自分個人としては→～としては

**have/play a part (in sth)** ▶定義 to be involved in sth ～に巻き込まれている→役目を果たす, 役割を遂行する, かかわる

**in part** ▶定義 not completely 完全にではない→一部分は, いくらか ‖ *The accident was, in part, the fault of the driver.* その事故は, 運転手にもある程度の責任があった.

**on the part of sb/on sb's part** ▶定義 made, done or felt by sb ～によって作られた, 行われたまたは感じられた→～の方で[の], ～の側では[の] ‖ *There is concern on the part of the teachers that class sizes will increase.* 教師側は, 1クラスの人数が増えることを心配している. *I'm sorry. It was a mistake on my part.* ごめんなさい, 私の方のミスでした.

**take part (in sth)** ▶定義 to join with other people in an activity ある活動にほかの人々と参加する→(～に)加わる, 参加する ‖ *Everybody took part in the discussion.* だれでも皆その討論に加わった.

**part**² /pάːrt/ 動 ▶定義1 自他 正式 **part (sb) (from sb)** to leave or go away from sb; to separate people or things ～から離れるまたは立ち去る; 人々または物を引き離す→別れる; ～を引き離す, 別々にする ‖ *We exchanged telephone numbers when we parted.* 私たちは別れる時に電話番号を教え合った. *He hates being parted from his children for long.* 彼は長い間子供と離れていることが嫌いだ. ▶定義2 自他 to move apart; to make things or people move apart 離れる; 物または人々を動かして離す→分かれる, 離れる; ～を分ける, 分割する ‖ *Her lips were slightly parted.* 彼女の唇はわずかに開いていた. ▶定義3 他 to separate the hair on the head with a comb so as to make a clear line はっきりと分け目を付けるために, くしで髪を分ける→(髪)を分ける ‖ *She parts her hair in the middle.* 彼女は髪を真ん中で分けている.

☞参 parting

成句 **part company (with sb/sth)** ▶定義 to go different ways or to separate after being together 一緒にいた後, 違う方向に向かうまたは分かれる→(～と)別れる, 絶交する, 意見を異に

する

**句動詞** part with sth ▶定義 to give or sell sth to sb ～を…に与えるまたは売る→～を手放す, ～を譲り・売り渡す ‖ *When we went to live in Italy, we had to part with our horses.* イタリアに引っ越す時, 私たちは馬を手放さなくてはならなかった.

**part³** /pɑːrt/ 副 ▶定義 not completely one thing and not completely another 完全に1つのものではなく, 完全にほかのものでもない→一部分は, いくぶん ‖ *She's part Russian and part Chinese.* 彼女はロシア人の血も中国人の血も引いている.

**part exchange** 名 U ▶定義 a way of buying sth, such as a car, in which you give your old one as some of the payment for a more expensive one もっと高い物の代金の一部として自分の古い物を渡す, ～を, 例えば車を買う方法→下取り

**partial** /pɑ́ːrʃ(ə)l/ 形 ▶定義 1 not complete 完全ではない→一部分の, 部分的な, 不完全な ‖ *The project was only a partial success.* その計画は部分的な成功にすぎなかった. ▶定義 2 （古） partial to sb/sth liking sth very much ～をとても好きでいる→（～が）好きで, お気に入りで ‖ *He's very partial to ice cream.* 彼はとてもアイスクリームが好きだ. — **partially** 副 →部分的に, 不完全に

**partiality** /pɑ̀ːrʃiǽləti/ 名 U 正式 ▶定義 the unfair support of one person, team, etc above another 他よりも優先して, 1人の人, チームなどへの不公平な支持→不公平, えこひいき, 偏愛 ‖ *The referee was accused of partiality towards the home team.* その審判は地元チームへのえこひいきを非難された. ⇔ **impartiality** ☞参 **impartial**

**participant** /pɑːrtísəpənt/ 名 C ▶定義 a person who takes part in sth ～に参加する人→参加者, 関係者

**participate** /pɑːrtísəpèɪt/ 動 自 ▶定義 participate (in sth) to take part or become involved in sth ～に参加するまたは関係するようになる→参加する, 加入する ‖ *Students are encouraged to participate in sporting activities.* 生徒たちはスポーツ活動に参加するよう奨励されている. —

**participation** /pɑːrtìsəpéɪʃ(ə)n/ 名 U →参加, 加入

**participle** /pɑ́ːrtɪsɪp(ə)l/ 名 C （文法） ▶定義 a word that is formed from a verb and that ends in -ing (present participle) or -ed, -en, etc (past participle). Participles are used to form tenses of the verb, or as adjectives. 動詞から作られる語で最後が -ing 形（現在分詞）または -ed, -en 形など（過去分詞）. participles は動詞の時制を作るために, あるいは形容詞として使用される→分詞 ‖ *'Hurrying' and 'hurried' are the present and past participles of 'hurry'.* hurrying と hurried は, hurry の現在分詞と過去分詞です.

**particle** /pɑ́ːrtɪk(ə)l/ 名 C ▶定義 1 a very small piece; a bit とても小さな一片; 小片→小さな粒, 微粒子, 小片 ‖ *dust particles* 粉じん ▶定義 2 （文法）a small word that is not as important as a noun, verb or adjective 名詞, 動詞, または形容詞と同じほどには重要ではない, ささいな単語→不変化詞, 接頭辞, 接尾辞 ‖ *In the phrasal verb 'break down', 'down' is an adverbial particle.* 句動詞 break down の down は副詞的不変化詞です.

***particular** /pərtíkjələr/ 形 ▶定義 1 （名詞の前だけ） used to emphasize that you are talking about one person, thing, time, etc and not about others ほかのものについてではなく, ある個人, 物, 時間などについて話していることを強調するために用いて→特定の, 個々の ‖ *Is there any particular dish you enjoy making?* あなたにとって作るのが楽しい料理がありますか. ▶定義 2 （名詞の前だけ）greater than usual; special 通常よりすごい; 特別な→ことさらの, 特別な ‖ *This article is of particular interest to me.* この記事はことさら私の興味をひきます. ▶定義 3 connected with one person or thing and not with others 他にではなく, ある個人, または物に関連した→特有の, 固有の ‖ *Everybody has their own particular problems.* だれでもその人固有の問題を抱えている. ▶定義 4 particular (about/over sth)（名詞の前は不可）difficult to please 喜ばせることが難しい→好みがやかましい, 気難しい ‖ *Some people are extremely particular about what they eat.* 自分の食べる物の好みがとてもやかましい人がいる. ☞参 **fussy**

**成句** in particular ▶定義 especially 特に→特に, とりわけ ‖ *Is there **anything in particular***

*you'd like to do this weekend?* この週末何か特にしたい事がありますか.

**\*particularly** /pərtíkjələrli/ 副 ▶定義 especially; more than usual or more than others 特に; 通常よりさらに, またはほかのものよりさらに→**特に, とりわけ; 大変** ‖ *I'm particularly interested in Indian history.* 私はインドの歴史にとても興味があります. *The match was excellent, particularly the second half.* その試合はすばらしく, 特に後半が良かった.

**particulars** /pərtíkjələrz/ 名 [複数扱い] 正式 ▶定義 facts or details about sb/sth 〜についての事実または詳細→**詳しい事実・点, 詳細** ‖ *The police took down all the particulars about the missing child.* 警察はその行方不明の子供についてのすべての詳細を記録した.

**parting** /páːrtɪŋ/ 名 ▶定義 1 ❶⓾saying goodbye to, or being separated from, another person (usually for quite a long time) ほかの人にさよならを言う, または(通常はかなり長い間)ほかの人から離されている→**別れること, 別離, 分離** ▶定義 2 ❷the line in a person's hair where it is divided in two with a comb くしで2つに分けられた髪の線→**(髪の)分け目** ‖ *a side/centre parting* 横分け・真ん中分け ☛参 **part** ☛ **hair** のさし絵

**partition** /pɑːrtíʃ(ə)n, pər-/ 名 ▶定義 1 ❷something that divides a room, office etc into two or more parts, especially a thin or temporary wall 部屋, オフィスなどを2つ, またはそれより多い部分に分ける物, 特に薄い, または一時的な壁→**仕切り, パーティション** ☛ S4 ページのさし絵 ▶定義 2 ⓾the division of a country into two or more countries 国を2つ, またはそれより多い国々に分けること→**分割** ― **partition** 動⓽→(部屋など)を仕切る, (土地など)を分割する, 区分する

**partly** /páːrtli/ 副 ▶定義 not completely 完全ではなく→**少しは, 部分的に, ある程度** ‖ *She was only partly responsible for the mistake.* 彼女はその間違いに対してほんの部分的に責任があるだけだった.

**\*partner** /páːrtnər/ 名 ❷ ▶定義 1 the person that you are married to or live with as if you are married 自分が結婚している, または結婚しているかのように一緒に住んでいる相手→**配偶者, 同棲(どうせい)相手** ▶定義 2 one of the people who owns a business 会社を所有している人々の1人→**(共同事業などの)仲間, 共同経営者, 共同出資者** ‖ *business partners* 事業の仲間 ▶定義 3 a person that you are doing an activity with as a team, for example dancing or playing a game 例えばダンスまたは競技などで, チームとして一緒に活動をしている人→**パートナー, 組む相手** ▶定義 4 a country or organization that has an agreement with another 他と協定を結んでいる国または組織→**(同盟関係などにある)国, 組織** ― **partner** 動⓾→〜と組む ‖ *Hales partnered his brother in the doubles, and they won the gold medal.* ヘイルズはダブルスで自分の兄と組み, 金メダルを獲得した.

**partnership** /páːrtnərʃɪp/ 名 ▶定義 1 ⓾the state of being a partner in business 仕事でパートナーでいる状態→**協力, 提携, 共同(経営)** ‖ *Simona went into partnership with her sister and opened a shop in Rome.* シモーナは自分の姉と共同で, ローマに店を開いた. ▶定義 2 ❷a relationship between two people, organizations, etc 2人の人, 2つの組織などの関係→**共同経営, 共同事業** ‖ *Marriage is a partnership for life.* 結婚は人生の共同事業である. ▶定義 3 ❷a business owned by two or more people 2人, またはそれより多い人々で所有されている会社→**合資会社, 合名会社**

**part of speech** 名 ❷(文法) ▶定義 one of the groups that words are divided into, for example noun, verb, adjective, etc 単語が分けられるグループの1つ, 例えば名詞, 動詞, 形容詞など→**品詞**

**part-time** 形副 ▶定義 for only a part of the working day or week 仕事をする日または週の一部分だけの→**パートタイム, 非常勤** ‖ *She's got a part-time job.* 彼女はパートタイムの仕事をしている. ☛参 **full-time**

**\*party** /páːrti/ 名 ❷( 複 **parties**) ▶定義 1 a social occasion to which people are invited in order to eat, drink and enjoy themselves 食べて飲んで楽しむために, 人々が招待される社交的機会→**集まり, 会, パーティー** ‖ *When we've moved into our new house we're going to have a party.* 新しい家に引っ越したら, 私たちはパーティーをすることにしている. *a birthday/*

dinner party お誕生日会・晩餐（ばんさん）会 ▶定義2 (または **Party**) a group of people who have the same political aims and ideas and who are trying to win elections to parliament, etc 同じ政治的目標と考えを持ち、議会などの選挙に勝とうとする人々の集団→政党, 党, 党派

▶英国での２大政党は, Labour Party (left-wing)（労働党（左翼））と Conservative (Tory) Party (right-wing)（保守党（右翼））である．その中立の立場として Liberal Democrats（自由民主党）といくつかの小さな政党がある．米国における２大政党は, Republicans（共和党）と Democrats（民主党）である．

▶定義3（しばしば複合語として）a group of people who are working, travelling, etc together 一緒に働く、または旅行などをする、人々の集団→一団, 一行 ‖ a party of tourists 旅行者の一団

▶定義4 正式 one of the people or groups of people involved in a legal case 法的訴訟に関係している人々の１人、または集団→当事者, 関係者, 相手方 ‖ the guilty/innocent party 有罪・無罪の人 ☞参 third party

*__pass__¹ /pɑːs; pæs/ 動 ▶定義1 自 他 to move past or to the other side of sb/sth ～のそばを通り過ぎる、または反対側へ動く→通り過ぎる, 進む, 追い越す ‖ The street was crowded and the two buses couldn't pass. その通りは混んでいて、２台のバスが擦れ違うことができなかった. I passed him in the street but he didn't say hello. 私は彼と通りで擦れ違ったが、彼はあいさつもしなかった. The number of children at the school has passed 500. その学校の生徒数は、500人を超えた.

▶passの過去形は、形容詞または前置詞のpastではなく、passedである: The summer months passed slowly.（夏の月は、ゆっくりと過ぎた.）The past week was very hot.（この１週間はとても暑かった.）Our house is just past the church.（私たちの家はちょうど教会を通り過ぎた所です.）

▶定義2 自 他 pass (sth) along, down, through, etc (sth) to go or move, or make sth move, in the direction mentioned 言及された方向へ行くまたは動く、あるいは～を動かす→通る, 通り過ぎる; ～を動かす ‖ A plane passed overhead. 飛行機が上空を通り過ぎた. We'll have to pass the wire through the window. 私たちは窓を貫いて針金を通さなければならない. ▶定義3 他 pass sth (to sb) to give sth to sb ～を…に与える→～を手渡す, 回す, ～を配る ‖ Could you pass (me) the salt, please? 塩を取ってくださいますか. ▶定義4 自 他 pass (sth) (to sb) (in some sports) to kick, hit or throw the ball to sb on your own team（いくつかのスポーツにおいて）自分のチームの～へ、ボールをける、打つ、または投げる→(ボール)を渡す, パスする ▶定義5 自 (used about time) to go by（時間について）たつ→たつ, 経過する ‖ At least a year has passed since I last saw them. 最後に彼らと会ってから、少なくとも１年はたった. It was a long journey but the time passed very quickly. それは長い旅だったが、時間はあっと言う間に過ぎてしまった. ▶定義6 他 to spend time, especially when you are bored or waiting for sth 時を過ごす、特に退屈なときまたは～を待っているとき→～を過ごす, 送る ‖ I'll have to think of something to do to **pass the time** in hospital. 私は、病院で過ごすために何かする事を考えなければならない. ▶定義7 自 他 to achieve the necessary standard in an exam, test, etc 試験などで必要な基準を達成する→合格する, 受かる ‖ Good luck in the exam! I'm sure you'll pass. 試験頑張って．絶対、合格するわよ. ⇔ fail ▶定義8 他 to test sb/sth and say that he/she/it is good enough ～をテストして、その人・それが十分に良いと言う→～を合格させる, 認可する ‖ The examiner passed most of the students. 試験官はほとんどの生徒を合格させた. ▶定義9 他 to officially approve a law, etc by voting 投票によって、公式に法律などを認める→(議案など)を可決する, (議案などが議会など)を通過する ‖ One of the functions of Parliament is to **pass new laws**. 議会の機能の１つは、新しい法律を可決することである. ▶定義10 他 pass sth (on sb/sth) to give an opinion, judgement, etc 意見または判断などを与える→(判決・決断など)を下す, (意見)を述べる ‖ The judge passed sentence on the young man (= said what his punishment would be). 裁判官はその若者に判決を下した(=彼への罰が何であるかを言った). ▶定義11 自 to be allowed or accepted 許される、または受け入れられる→大目に見られる, 見逃される ‖ I didn't *like what they were saying but I **let** it **pass**.* 私は彼らの言っている事が気に入らなかったが、大目に見た.

成句 **pass the buck (to sb)** ▶定義 to make sb else responsible for a difficult situation 難しい状況はほかの~に責任があるとする→**(~に)責任を転嫁する**

**pass water** 正式 ▶定義 to get rid of waste liquid from your body 身体から不用の液体を取り除く→**小便をする**

句動詞 **pass away** ▶定義 used as a polite way of saying 'die'「死ぬ」の礼儀正しい言い方として用いて→**亡くなる、息を引き取る**

**pass by (sb/sth)** ▶定義 to go past 通り過ぎる→**(時が)過ぎ去る、(そばを)通り過ぎる** ∥ *I pass by your house on the way to work.* 私は職場に行く途中、あなたの家のそばを通ります.

**pass sth down** ▶定義 to give or teach sth to people who will live after you have died 自分が死んだ後も生きる人々に~を与えるまたは教える→**~を(次の人へ)渡す、伝える**

**pass for sb/sth** ▶定義 to be accepted as sb/sth that he/she/it is not 実際は違うが、~として受け入れられている→**~として通る** ∥ *His mother looks so young she'd pass for his sister.* 彼のお母さんはとても若く見えるので、彼のお姉さんとして通るでしょう.

**pass sb/sth off (as sb/sth)** ▶定義 to say that a person or a thing is sth that he/she/it is not 人または物が、実際はそうでない~であると言う→**(偽って)~を(…として)通す** ∥ *He tried to pass the work off as his own.* 彼は仕事を自分のものとして通そうとした.

**pass sth on (to sb/sth)** ▶定義 to give sth to sb else, especially after you have been given it or used it yourself 特にもらったまたは自分が使った後、~をほかの…に与える→**~を与える、(知らせなど)を伝える、(伝染病など)を移す** ∥ *Could you pass the message on to Mr Roberts?* このメッセージをロバーツさんに伝えていただけますか.

**pass out** ▶定義 to become unconscious; to faint 意識を失う;気絶する→**意識を失う、気絶する、酔いつぶれる** ⇔ **come round/to**

★**pass**² /pɑːs; pæs/ 名 C ▶定義 1 a successful result in an exam 試験で成功した結果→**合格** ∥ *The pass mark is 50%.* 合格ラインは、100点満点の50点です. *Grades A, B and C are passes.* 評価のA, B, Cが合格です. ⇔ **fail** ▶定義 2 an official piece of paper that gives you permission to enter or leave a building, travel on a bus or train, etc 建物に入るまたは出る、あるいはバスや電車などに乗る許可を、あなたに与える公式の文書→**入場・通行・外出許可証、定期(乗車)券、無料入場券** ∥ *Show your student pass when you buy a ticket.* チケットを買うとき、学生証を見せなさい. ▶定義 3 the act of kicking, hitting or throwing the ball to sb on your own team in some sports ある種のスポーツで、自分のチームの~に向かってボールをける、打つまたは投げる行為→**パス、送球** ▶定義 4 a road or way over or through mountains 山を越えるまたは通り抜ける道または道筋→**山道、峠** ∥ *a mountain pass* 山道

**passable** /pάːsəb(ə)l; pǽs-/ 形 ▶定義 1 good enough but not very good 必要な程度には良いが、とても良いのではない→**まずまずの、一応の、悪くはない** ∥ *My French is not brilliant but it's passable.* 私のフランス語はすばらしくはないが、悪くはない. ▶定義 2 (名詞の前は不可) (used about roads, rivers, etc) possible to use or cross; not blocked (道や川などについて)利用できるまたは横断できる;ふさがれていない→**通行できる、渡れる** ⇔ **impassable**

★**passage** /pǽsɪdʒ/ 名 ▶定義 1 C (または **passageway**) a long, narrow way with walls on either side that connects one place with another ある場所を別の場所とつなぐ、両側に壁のある長く細い通路→**通路、廊下** ∥ *a secret underground passage* 秘密の地下通 ▶定義 2 C a tube in your body which air, liquid, etc can pass through 空気、液体などが通り抜けられる、体の中の管→**管、導管** ∥ *the nasal passages* 鼻腔(こう) ▶定義 3 C a short part of a book, a speech or a piece of music 本、演説、または楽曲などの短い一部分→**一節、引用部分** ∥ *The students were given a passage from the novel to study.* 生徒たちは、その小説の一節を勉強するように与えられた. ▶定義 4 [単数扱い] the process of passing 通り過ぎる過程→**(時の)流れ、経過** ∥ *His painful memories faded with **the passage of time**.* 彼の苦い思い出は時の流れと共に消えていった.

**passenger** /pǽs(ə)ndʒər/ 名 C ▶定義 a person who is travelling in a car, bus, train, plane, etc but who is not driving it or working on it 車, バス, 電車, 飛行機などで移動しているが, それを運転している, またはそこで働いているのではない人▶乗客, 旅客

**passer-by** /ˌpɑ́ːsər bɑ́ɪ/ 名 C (複 **passers-by**) ▶定義 a person who is walking past sb/sth ～を歩いて通り過ぎている人▶通り合わせた人, 通行人

**passing**¹ /pάːsɪŋ; pǽs-/ 形 (名詞の前だけ) ▶定義 1 lasting for only a short time; brief ほんの少しの間続いている; 短時間の→一時の, つかの間の, ちょっとの間だけの ‖ *a passing phase/thought/interest* つかの間の局面・考え・興味 ▶定義 2 going past 通り過ぎていっている→通り掛かりの, 通過する, (時が)過ぎ行く ‖ *I stopped a passing car and asked for help.* 私は通り掛かりの車を止めて助けを求めた.

**passing**² /pάːsɪŋ; pǽs-/ 名 U ▶定義 the process of going by 通り過ぎる過程→(時の)流れ, 経過 ‖ *the passing of time* 時の経過

成句 **in passing** ▶定義 done or said quickly, while you are thinking or talking about sth else ほかの～について考えているまたは話している間に, 素早く行われたまたは言われた→ついでに(言えば), そう言えば ‖ *He mentioned the house in passing but he didn't give any details.* 彼はついでにその家について触れたが, 詳細は述べなかった.

**passion** /pǽʃ(ə)n/ 名 ▶定義 1 C U (a) very strong feeling, especially of love, hate or anger 特に愛, 憎悪, または怒りの, とても強い感情→熱情, 激情, 激怒 ‖ *He was a violent man, controlled by his passions.* 彼は激情に駆られて暴力を振るう男だった. ▶定義 2 [単数扱い] *a passion (for sb)* very strong sexual love or attraction とても強い性的な愛または魅力→熱愛, 情欲, 色情 ‖ *His longed to tell Sashi of his passion for her.* 彼はサシに彼女への熱愛を伝えたいと思い焦がれていた. ▶定義 3 [単数扱い] *a passion for sth* a very strong liking for or interest in sth ～へのとても強い好意, または興味→熱中, 愛着, 熱中するもの ‖ *He has a passion for history.* 彼は歴史に熱中している.

**passionate** /pǽʃ(ə)nət/ 形 ▶定義 1 showing or caused by very strong feelings とても強い感情を示して, またはとても強い感情によって引き起こされた→情熱的な, 熱烈な, 激しい ‖ *The President gave a passionate speech about crime.* 大統領は犯罪について情熱的な演説を行った. ▶定義 2 showing or feeling very strong love or sexual attraction とても強い愛, または性的な魅力を示して, または感じて→熱愛の, 情欲の ‖ *a passionate kiss* 熱烈なキス — **passionately** 副→情熱的に, 熱烈に, 激しく ‖ *He believes passionately in democracy.* 彼は民主主義を熱烈に信じている.

**passive** /pǽsɪv/ 形 ▶定義 1 showing no reaction, feeling or interest; not active 反応, 感情, または興味を示さない; 行動的でない→受け身の, 活気のない, 消極的な ‖ *Some people prefer to play a passive role in meetings.* 会議中に聞き役でいる方を好む人がいる. ▶定義 2 used about the form of a verb or a sentence when the subject of the sentence is affected by the action of the verb 文章の主語が動詞の作用に影響されるとき, 動詞または文章の形式について→受動態の, 受け身の ‖ *In the sentence 'He was bitten by a dog', the verb is passive.* He was bitten by a dog (彼は犬にかまれた) の文中で, その動詞は受動態です. ☛ または the verb is in the passive とも言える. **active** を参照. — **passively** 副→受け身に, 不活発に, 消極的に, 無抵抗に

**Passover** /pάːsòʊvər, pǽs-/ 名 [単数扱い] ▶定義 the most important Jewish festival, which takes place in spring and lasts seven or eight days 春に行われ, 7日ないし8日続く, ユダヤ教で最も重要な祝祭→過ぎ越しの祭り

**passport** /pάːspɔːrt; pǽs-/ 名 C ▶定義 1 an official document that identifies you as a citizen of a particular country and that you have to show when you enter or leave a country 自分を特定の国の国民として証明し, 入国するまたは出国する際に提示しなければならない公式の書類→パスポート, 旅券, 通行証

▶自分のパスポートを apply for (申請する), または renew (更新する) のは passport office (旅券課) である. 新しいパスポートを issue (発行する) のがこの課である.

▶定義 2 *a passport to sth* a thing that makes it possible to achieve sth ～を達成することを可能にさせるもの→(ある目的のための)手段, 方法

‖ *a passport to success* 成功へのかぎ

**password** /pá:swə:rd; pǽs-/ 名 ⓒ ▶定義1 a secret word or phrase that you need to know in order to be allowed into a place ある場所へ入ることを許されるために知らなくてはならない, 秘密の言葉または句→**合い言葉** ▶定義2 a series of letters or numbers that you must type into a computer or computer system in order to be able to use it コンピューターまたはコンピューターシステムを使えるようにするために, 打ち込まなくてはならない一連の文字または数字→**パスワード, 暗証番号** ‖ *Please enter your password*. パスワードを入力してください.

***past**¹ /pɑ:st; pæst/ 形 ▶定義1 already gone; belonging to a time before the present 既に過ぎた; 現在より前の時に属している→**過去の, 過ぎ去った** ‖ *in past centuries/times* 過去の世紀に・過去の時代に *I'd rather forget some of my past mistakes.* 私はむしろ過去の失敗を忘れたいと思う. ▶定義2 (名詞の前だけ) just finished; last ちょうど終了した; この前の→**過ぎたばかりの, 過去〜, この〜** ‖ *He's had to work very hard during the past year.* 彼は去年一生懸命働かなくてはならなかった.

***past**² /pɑ:st; pæst/ 前副 ▶定義1 (used when telling the time) after; later than (時間を述べるときに) 以後に; 〜より遅く→**過ぎて; 〜を過ぎて, 〜時(…分)過ぎで** ‖ *It's ten (minutes) past three.* 今3時10分です. *It was past midnight when we got home.* 私たちが帰宅したのは真夜中を過ぎていた. ▶定義2 from one side to the other of sb/sth; further than or on the other side of sb/sth 〜の片方からもう片方へ; 〜より遠くに, または〜の反対側に→**〜を通り過ぎて, 〜と擦れ違って; 〜を過ぎた所に** ‖ *He walked straight past me.* 彼は私を通り過ぎてまっすぐ歩いていった. *She looked right past me without realizing who I was.* 彼女の視線は私だと気付かずに通り過ぎた. ▶定義3 above or further than a certain point, limit or age ある点, 制限, または年齢より上またはそれ以上の→**〜の及ばぬ所に, 〜の限界を超えて, 〜の年齢を超えて** ‖ *Unemployment is now past the 2 million mark.* 失業者は今や200万の大台を超えている. *I'm so tired that I'm past caring* (= *I don't care any more*) *what we eat.* 私は疲れていて私たちが何を食べるか気にする限度を超えている (= もう気にしない).

成句 **not put it past sb (to do sth)** (would と用いて) ▶定義 to think sb is capable of doing sth bad 〜は悪い…を行うことができると考える→**〜は…をやりかねないと思う** ‖ *I wouldn't put it past him to do a thing like that.* 彼ならそのような事をやりかねないと思う.

**past it** 略式 ▶定義 too old 古すぎる→**年を取りすぎて, 昔のようにはいかなくなって**

***past**³ /pɑ:st; pæst/ 名 ▶定義1 **the past** [単数扱い] the time that has gone by; the things that happened before now 過ぎ去った時間; 前に起こった物事→**過去, 過去の事** ‖ *in the recent/distant past* 近い過去・遠い過去に *The art of writing letters seems to be a thing of the past.* 手紙を書く技術は, 過去のもののように思える. ▶定義2 ⓒ a person's life and career before now 以前の, 人の人生または職業→**経歴** ‖ *We know nothing about his past.* 私たちは彼の経歴について何も知らない. ▶定義3 **the past** (または **past tense**) [単数扱い] (文法) a form of a verb used to describe actions in the past 過去の行為を述べるために用いられる動詞の形→**過去形, 過去時制** ‖ *The past (tense) of the verb 'come' is 'came'.* 動詞 come の過去形(時制)は came です.

▶過去時制についての説明は, 巻末の「文法早見表」を参照.

**pasta** /pá:stə, pǽstə/ 名 ⓤ ▶定義 an Italian food made from flour, eggs and water, formed into different shapes, cooked, and usually served with a sauce 小麦粉, 卵と水から作られるイタリアの食べ物でいろいろな形に作られ, 料理され, 通常ソースと一緒に出される→**パスタ(スパゲッティ, マカロニなど)**

**paste**¹ /péɪst/ 名 ▶定義1 ⓒⓤ a soft, wet mixture, usually made of a powder and a liquid and sometimes used for sticking things 普通は粉と液体から作られ, 時には物を張り付けるために利用される, 柔らかい湿った混ぜ物→**練り物, ペースト状の物, のり** ‖ *wallpaper paste* 壁紙用ののり *Mix the flour and milk into a paste.* ペースト状になるまで, 小麦粉と牛乳を混ぜてください.

▶定義2 ⓤ (通常複合名詞として用いて) a soft mixture of food that you can spread onto bread, etc パンなどの上に塗られる, 食物を柔ら

かく混ぜ合わせた物→ペースト ‖ *fish/chicken paste* 魚のペースト・チキンペースト

**paste**² /péɪst/ 動他 ▶定義1 to stick sth to sth else using paste or a similar substance (glue) のりまたは似た物質(接着剤)を使って, ～をほかの…にくっつける→～をのりではる ‖ *He pasted the picture into his book.* 彼は自分の本にその写真をのりではった. ▶定義2 (computing) to copy or move text into a document from somewhere else (コンピューター)別の場所から文字データをある文書へ複写するまたは移動させる→～を張り付ける, ペーストする ‖ *This function allows you to **cut and paste** text.* この機能を使って, 文字データの切り取りと張り付けができます.

**pastel** /pǽst(ə)l, pæstél/ 形 ▶定義 (used about colours) pale; not strong (色について)淡い; 強くない→パステル調の, 淡い

**pasteurized** (または **-ised**) /páːstʃəràɪz, -stə-; pǽstə-, pǽs-/ 形 ▶定義 (used about milk or cream) free from bacteria because it has been heated and then cooled (牛乳またはクリームについて)熱せられてから冷却されたので, バクテリアのいない→低温殺菌された

**pastime** /páːstàɪm; pǽs-/ 名 C ▶定義 something that you enjoy doing when you are not working 働いていないときに, 楽しんで行う物事→気晴らし, 娯楽, 慰み ☛類 **hobby**

**pastoral** /páːst(ə)rəl; pǽs-/ 形 ▶定義1 (connected with the work of a priest or a teacher) giving help and advice on personal matters rather than on matters of religion or education (聖職者または教師の仕事に関連して)宗教上または教育的な事柄よりむしろ個人的な事柄について, 手助けをし, 忠告する→(精神的)指導の, (生徒の)生活相談の ▶定義2 connected with pleasant country life 心地良い田園生活に関連して→田園生活の, 牧歌的な

**past participle** ⇒ **PARTICIPLE**

**past perfect** (または **pluperfect**) 名 [単数扱い] (文法) ▶定義 the tense of a verb that describes an action that was finished before another event happened 別の事柄が起こったよりも前に終わってしまった行為を述べる, 動詞の時制→過去完了(形)

▶過去完了(形)についての説明は, 巻末の「文法早見表」を参照.

**pastry** /péɪstri/ 名 (複 **pastries**) ▶定義1 ❶ a mixture of flour, fat and water that is rolled out flat and cooked as a base or covering for pies, etc 小麦粉と油脂, 水が混ぜ合わされた物で, 平らに伸ばされて, パイなどの底または包む物として焼かれる→練り粉 ▶定義2 ❷ a small cake made with pastry 練り粉で作られた小さなケーキ→ペストリー(パイやタルトなど)

**pasture** /páːstʃər, pǽs-/ 名 C U ▶定義 a field or land covered with grass, where cows, etc can feed 牛などが食べられる草で覆われた土地→牧草地, (放牧用の)牧場

**pasty** /péɪsti/ 名 C (複 **pasties**) 英 ▶定義 a small pie containing meat and/or vegetables 肉か野菜または両方が入っている小さなパイ→パスティー

pat

**pat**¹ /pǽt/ 動他 (**patting**; **patted**) ▶定義 to touch sb/sth gently with a flat hand, especially as a sign of friendship, care, etc 特に友情, 心配などの合図として, てのひらで～を優しく触る→～を軽く打つ, 軽くたたく

---

**▶コミュニケーション**

「自画自賛」の身振り

**pat oneself on the back**: 片方の手で反対側の肩の下辺りをポンポンと軽くたたくしぐさ. 自画自賛を表します. 英米では, 何かをよくやり遂げた人に対する賞賛, 祝意, ねぎらいを, その人の背を軽くたたいて (pat someone on the back) 表すところから, 我ながらよくやったことを比喩的に pat oneself on the back と言います. この比喩表現をもとにしてできたのがこのしぐさです.

---

**pat**² /pǽt/ 名 C ▶定義 a gentle friendly touch with a flat hand てのひらで優しく好意的に触れること→軽く打つこと, 軽くたたくこと ‖ *He gave her knee an affectionate pat.* 彼は慈しみを込めて, 彼女のひざを軽くたたいた.

成句 **a pat on the back** (for sth/doing sth)

▶定義 approval for sth good that a person has done 人が行った良い〜を是認すること →〜の背中をぽんとたたくこと(賛成・賞賛・激励・慰めのしぐさ) ‖ *She deserves a pat on the back for all her hard work.* 彼女の熱心な仕事振りは、賞賛に値する.

**pat**³ /pæt/ 形副(名詞の前だけ) ▶定義 (used about an answer, comment, etc) said in a quick or simple way that does not sound natural or realistic(回答、コメントなどについて)自然にまたは現実的には思えない速さ、または簡潔さで言った→(言葉などが)滑らかすぎる、うますぎる;(あらかじめ用意していたかのように)すらすらと

**patch**¹ /pætʃ/ 名 ⓒ ▶定義 1 **a patch (of sth)** a part of a surface that is different in some way from the area around it 周りの地域とはある点で違っている表面の部分→斑点(はんてん)、まだら、(ほかと異なっている)部分 ‖ *Drive carefully. There are patches of ice on the roads.* 気を付けて運転しなさい.道路は所々氷が張っています.
*a bald patch* はげた部分 ▶定義 2 a piece of material that you use to cover a hole in clothes, etc 衣服などの穴をふさぐために使う素材の1枚→継ぎ当て、当て布 ‖ *I sewed patches on the knees of my jeans.* 私は自分のジーンズのひざに当て布を縫い付けた. ▶定義 3 a small piece of material that you wear over one eye, usually because the eye is damaged 通常目が傷んでいるので、その目を覆うように着ける小さな素材の1つ→眼帯 ▶定義 4 a small piece of land, especially for growing vegetables or fruit 特に野菜または果実を育てるための、狭い土地→(耕作した)小地面、畑 ‖ *a vegetable patch* 野菜畑
成句 **go through a bad patch** 特に 英 略式 ▶定義 to experience a difficult or unhappy period of time 困難なまたは不幸な時期を経験する→ひどい目に遭う
**not a patch on sb/sth** 特に 英 略式 ▶定義 not nearly as good as sb/sth 到底〜ほど良くない→〜とは比べ物にならない(ほど劣る) ‖ *Her new book isn't a patch on her others.* 彼女の新しい本は、これまでの作品とは比べ物にならないほど劣っている.

**patch**² /pætʃ/ 動 他 ▶定義 to cover a hole in clothes, etc with a piece of material in order to repair it 繕うために、素材の1枚で衣服などの穴をふさぐ→〜に継ぎを当てる ‖ *patched jeans* 継

# patent leather 1185

ぎの当たったジーンズ
句動詞 **patch sth up** ▶定義 1 to repair sth, especially in a temporary way by adding a new piece of material 特に新しい素材の1枚を加えて一時的に〜を繕う→〜に応急の処置を施す、応急の修理をする、継ぎを当てる ▶定義 2 to stop arguing with sb and to be friends again 〜との口論をやめて、また友達でいる→〜と仲直りする ‖ *Have you tried to* **patch things up** *with her?* 彼女と仲直りするよう努力しましたか.

**patchwork** /pætʃwɜːrk/ 名 Ⓤ ▶定義 a type of sewing in which small pieces of cloth of different colours and patterns are sewn together いろいろな色と模様の小さな布切れが一緒に縫われている、裁縫の一種→パッチワーク

**patchy** /pætʃi/ 形 ▶定義 1 existing or happening in some places but not others いくつかの場所で存在している、または起きているが、ほかの所にはない→所々の、まだらの、切れ切れの ‖ *patchy fog/clouds/rain* とぎれとぎれの霧・雲・雨 ▶定義 2 not complete; good in some parts but not in others 完全ではない;いくつかの部分では良いが、ほかでは良くない→不完全な、不備な; むらのある ‖ *My knowledge of German is rather patchy.* 私のドイツ語の知識にはとてもむらがある.

**pâté** /pɑːteɪ, pæ-; pǽteɪ; F pate/ 名 Ⓤ ▶定義 food that is made by making meat, fish or vegetables into a smooth, thick mixture that is served cold and spread on bread, etc 冷たくしてパンなどに塗る、肉、魚、または野菜などを滑らかで濃いペースト状にすることで作られた食べ物→パテ ‖ *liver pâté* レバーのパテ

**patent**¹ /pǽtnt, péɪ-/ 形 正式 ▶定義 clear; obvious→明白な; 明らかな ‖ *a patent lie* 明らかなうそ — **patently** 副 →明らかに、はっきりと

**patent**² /pǽtnt, péɪ-/ 名 ⓒ Ⓤ ▶定義 the official right to be the only person to make, use or sell a product or an invention; the document that proves this 製品または発明品を作る、使う、または売ることができるただ1人の人である公的権利; これを証明する文書→特許、特許権; 特許状 — **patent** 動 他 →〜の(専売)特許を取る、〜の特許権を与える

**patent leather** 名 Ⓤ ▶定義 a type of leather

with a hard, shiny surface, used especially for making shoes and bags 特に靴やバッグを作るために用いられる，硬く，光沢のある表面の革の一種→(黒の)エナメル革

**paternal** /pətə́:ml/ 形 (名詞の前だけ) ▶定義1 behaving as a father would behave; connected with being a father 父親ならするように振る舞っている；父親であることに関連した→父の，父らしい ▶定義2 related through the father's side of the family 一族の父親側を経て親類の→父方の ‖ *my paternal grandparents* 父方の祖父母 ☞参 **maternal**

**paternity** /pətə́:məti/ 名 Ⓤ ▶定義 the fact of being the father of a child 子供の父親であるという事実→父であること ‖ *paternity leave (= time that the father of a new baby is allowed to have away from work)* 父親の育児休暇(= 新生児の父親が仕事を休むことが許される時) ☞参 **maternity**

*__path__ /pɑː θ; pæθ/ 名 Ⓒ ▶定義1 a way across a piece of land that is made by or used by people walking 人々によって作られた，または使われた，ある土地を横切っている通り道→小道，細道，歩道 ‖ *the garden path* 庭の小道 ☞ C7ページのさし絵

▶ pathway も意味的に似ている: *There was a narrow pathway leading down the cliff.* (崖(がけ)を降りる細い小道があった.) footpath も参照.

▶定義2 the line along which sb/sth moves; the space in front of sb/sth as he/she/it moves 〜の動きに沿う線；〜が動くとき，その前の場所→軌道；進路，(〜への)道 ‖ *the flight path of an aeroplane* 飛行機の空路

**pathetic** /pəθétɪk/ 形 ▶定義1 causing you to feel pity or sadness 哀れみまたは悲しみを感じさせる→哀れを誘う，悲しい，感傷的な ‖ *the pathetic cries of the hungry children* 飢えている子供たちの哀れを誘う叫び ▶定義2 略式 very bad, weak or useless とても悪い，弱い，または役に立たない→とても下手な，まるで不十分な，ひどい ‖ *What a pathetic performance! The team deserved to lose.* 何て下手な演技なのだろう．チームが負けるのも当然だった．— **pathetically** /-k(ə)li/ 副 →哀れっぽく，悲しそうに，情けなく

らい(下手に)

**pathological** /pæ̀θəlɑ́dʒɪk(ə)l/ 形 ▶定義1 caused by feelings that you cannot control; not reasonable or sensible 制御できない感情によって引き起こされた；理にかなっていない，または分別がない→病的な，異常な(ほどの) ‖ *He's a pathological liar (= he cannot stop lying).* 彼は病的なうそつきだ(= 彼はうそをつかずにはいられない). *pathological fear/ hatred/violence* 異常なほどの恐怖・嫌悪・暴力 ▶定義2 caused by or connected with disease or illness 病気または精神的な病気によって起こるまたは関連している→(精神の)病気の，病気による ‖ *pathological depression* 病気による憂鬱(ゆううつ) ▶定義3 (medical) connected with pathology(医学)病理学に関連した→病理学(上)の — **pathologically** /-k(ə)li/ 副 →病的なほど，病気によって

**pathologist** /pəθɑ́lədʒɪst/ 名 Ⓒ ▶定義 a doctor who is an expert in pathology, and examines dead bodies to find out why a person has died 病理学の専門家で，人がなぜ亡くなったのかを見つけ出すために死体を調べる医者→病理学者

**pathology** /pəθɑ́lədʒi/ 名 Ⓤ ▶定義 (medical) the scientific study of diseases of the body (医学) 体の病気についての科学的学問→病理学

*__patience__ /péɪʃ(ə)ns/ 名 Ⓤ ▶定義1 patience (with sb/sth) the quality of being able to stay calm and not get angry, especially when there is a difficulty or you have to wait a long time 特に困難な事がある，あるいは長い間待たなくてはならないときに，平静で怒らずにいられる性質→忍耐(力)，我慢・辛抱強さ ‖ *I've got no patience with people who don't even try.* やろうともしない人々に対して，私は我慢できない. *to lose patience with sb* 〜に対して堪忍袋の緒が切れる ⇔ **impatience** ▶定義2 (米 **solitaire**) a card game for only one player 1人用のトランプゲーム→ソリテア

*__patient__¹ /péɪʃ(ə)nt/ 形 ▶定義 patient (with sb/sth) able to stay calm and not get angry, especially when there is a difficulty or you have to wait a long time 特に困難な事がある，あるいは長い間待たなくてはならないときに，平静で怒らずにいられる→我慢強い，辛抱強い ‖ *She's very patient with young children.* 彼女は幼い子供相手でもとても我慢強い． ⇔ **impatient** —

patiently 副 →我慢強く, 根気良く, 気長に ‖ to wait patiently 忍耐強く待つ

\*patient² /péɪʃ(ə)nt/ 名 ❹ ▶定義 a person who is receiving medical treatment 医学的治療を受けている人→患者, 病人 ‖ a hospital patient 入院患者 He's one of Dr Waters' patients. 彼はウォーターズ先生の患者の1人です.

patio /pǽtiòu, páː-/ 名 ❹ (  patios /-óuz/) ▶定義 a flat, hard area, usually behind a house, where people can sit, eat, etc outside 戸外で人々が座ったり, 食べたりできる, 通常家の裏にある, 平らで堅い場所→パティオ ☛参 balcony, verandah, terrace ☛ C7 ページのさし絵

patriot /péɪtriət, pǽtriət/ 名 ❹ ▶定義 a person who loves his/her country and is ready to defend it against an enemy 自分の国を愛していて, 敵から守る覚悟ができている人→愛国者 — patriotism /-ùz(ə)m/ 名 ❶→愛国心

patriotic /pèɪtriátɪk; pǽt-/ 形 ▶定義 having or showing great love for your country 自分の国に対しての深い愛情を持っているまたは示している→愛国心の強い, 愛国的な — patriotically /-k(ə)li/ 副→愛国心を持って

patrol¹ /pətróul/ 動 ❹ ❶ (patrolling; patrolled) ▶定義 to go round an area, building, etc at regular times to make sure that it is safe and that nothing is wrong 安全であり, 何も悪くないことを確認するために定期的に, ある地域, 建物などを回る→巡回する, パトロールする; ~を巡回する

patrol² /pətróul/ 名 ▶定義 1 ❹ ❶ the act of going round an area, building, etc at regular times to make sure that it is safe and that nothing is wrong 安全であり, 何も悪くないことを確認するために定期的に, ある地域, 建物などを回る行為→巡回, パトロール ‖ a police car on patrol in the area その地域を巡回しているパトカー ▶定義2 ❹ a group of soldiers, vehicles, etc that patrol sth ~を巡回する兵士, 乗り物などの集団→偵察隊, パトロール隊 ‖ a naval/police patrol 海軍の・警察の偵察隊 a patrol car/boat 巡回車・巡視船

patron /péɪtr(ə)n/ 名 ❹ ▶定義1 a person who gives money and support to artists, writers and musicians 芸術家や作家, 音楽家などにお金を与えて支援する人→後援者, パトロン ‖ a patron of the arts 芸術の後援者 ▶定義2 a famous person who supports an organization such as a charity and whose name is used in advertising よい組織, 例えば慈善団体を支援し, 名前がその組織の広告に使われる有名人→広告塔 ☛参 sponsor ▶定義3 正式 a person who uses a particular shop, theatre, restaurant, etc 特定の店, 劇場, レストランなどを使う人→顧客, お得意, ひいき客, 常連 ‖ This car park is for patrons only. この駐車場はお得意さま専用です.

patronize (または -ise) /péɪtr(ə)nàɪz, pǽtrə-/ 動 ❶ ▶定義1 to treat sb in a way that shows that you think you are better, more intelligent, experienced, etc than he/she is 自分は~より良い, 聡明(そうめい)である, 経験抱負であるなどと考えていることを示す方法で~を扱う→~に目上のような態度を取る, 先輩振る ▶定義2 正式 to be a regular customer of a shop, restaurant, etc 店, レストランなどの常連客でいる→~をひいきにする, 後援する — patronizing (または -ising) 形→目上のような態度の, 先輩振った, 横柄な ‖ I really hate that patronizing smile of hers. 私は彼女の横柄な笑顔が大嫌いだ. — patronizingly (または -isingly) 副→先輩振って, 横柄に

patron saint 名 ❹ ▶定義 a religious being who is believed by Christians to protect a particular place or people doing a particular activity 特別な場所または特定の活動をしている人々を守る, キリスト教信者によって信じられている宗教的な存在→守護聖者, 守護神, 守り神

patter /pǽtər/ 名 [単数扱い] ▶定義 the sound of many quick light steps or knocks on a surface 表面をたたく, たくさんの素早く軽い足音またはノックの音→ぱらぱら・ぱたぱたという音 ‖ the patter of the children's feet on the stairs 階段での子供たちのぱたぱたいう足音 — patter 動 ❶→ぱたぱたと音を立てる, 音を立てて歩く, (雨などが)ぱらぱらと音を立てる

\*pattern /pǽtərn/ 名 ❹ ▶定義1 the way in which sth happens, develops, or is done ~が起こる, 発展するまたは行われる方法→型, 様式, パターン ‖ Her days all seemed to follow the same pattern. 彼女の日々はすべて同じパターンに従っているように見えた. changing patterns of behaviour/work/weather 行動・仕事・天

# 1188 patterned

気のパターンの変化 ▶定義2 an arrangement of lines, shapes, colours, etc as a design デザインとしての線, 形, 色などの配列→**模様, 柄** ‖ *a shirt with a floral pattern on it* 花柄のシャツ ☛類 **design** ▶定義3 a design, a set of instructions or a shape to cut around that you use in order to make sth ～を作るために使う, 設計図, 一連の指示, または周囲を切り取った形→**原型, 型紙, 鋳型**

**patterned** /pǽtəmd/ 形 ▶定義 decorated with a pattern(2) pattern(2) で飾られている→**模様・柄の付いた**

*****pause**[1] /pɔːz/ 名 ▶定義1 ⓒ a pause (in sth) a short period of time during which sb stops talking or stops what he/she is doing ～が話していることをやめる, または行っていることをやめる間の短い時間→**とぎれ, 間, 休み** ‖ *He continued playing for twenty minutes without a pause.* 彼は休みなしに20分間弾き続けた. ☛参 **interval** の注 ▶定義2 (または **pause button**) ⓤ a control on a video player, etc that allows you to stop playing or recording for a short time 短い間再生または録画を止める, ビデオ装置などの調整つまみ→**一時停止ボタン, ポーズボタン** ‖ *Can you press pause to stop the tape while I go and make a cup of tea?* 私が紅茶をいれに行っている間, 一時停止ボタンを押してテープを止めてもらえますか.

**pause**[2] /pɔːz/ 動自 ▶定義 pause (for sth) to stop talking or doing sth for a short time before continuing 次を続けるまで, しばらくの間話すことまたは～を行うことをやめる→**中断する, 少し休む, 間を空ける**

**pave** /peɪv/ 動他 ▶定義 pave sth (with sth) (しばしば受動態で) to cover an area of ground with flat stones (**paving stones**) or bricks 平らな石 (敷石) またはれんがで地面を覆う→**～を舗装する**

**pavement** /péɪvmənt/ (米 **sidewalk**) 名 ⓒ ▶定義 a hard flat area at the side of a road for people to walk on 人々が歩くための, 道路のわきにある硬い平らな場所→**歩道** ☛ **roundabout** のさし絵

**pavilion** /pəvíljən/ 名 ⓒ 英 ▶定義 a building at a sports ground where players can change their clothes 選手たちが服を着替えられる, スポーツ競技場の建物→**(クリケット競技場などの)付属建物**

**paving stone** 名 ⓒ ▶定義 a flat piece of stone that is used for covering the ground 地面を覆うために使われる平らな石→**敷石** ☛ C7 ページのさし絵

*****paw**[1] /pɔː/ 名 ⓒ ▶定義 the foot of animals such as dogs, cats, bears, etc 動物, 例えば犬, 猫, クマなどの足→**足** ☛ C1 ページのさし絵

**paw**[2] /pɔː/ 動自他 ▶定義 paw (at) sth (used about an animal) to touch or scratch sb/sth several times with a paw (動物について) 足で何度も～に触る, またはひっかく→**前足 (など) で (～を) ひっかく, 地面をける** ‖ *The dog pawed at my sleeve.* その犬は私のそでをひっかいた.

**pawn**[1] /pɔːn/ 名 ⓒ ▶定義1 (in the game of chess) one of the eight pieces that are of least value and importance (チェスゲームにおいて) 価値と重要性が一番低い8個の駒 (こま) の1つ→**ポーン, 歩 (ふ)** ▶定義2 a person who is used or controlled by other more powerful people ほかのもっと力のある人々に使われている, または支配されている人→**手先**

**pawn**[2] /pɔːn/ 動他 ▶定義 to leave a valuable object with a person who lends money, (a **pawnbroker**) in return for money. If you cannot pay back the money after a certain period, the object can be sold or kept. お金を貸す人 (質屋) の所に, お金の見返りとして, 自分の価値ある物を預けていく. ある期間の後にお金を返すことができなければ, その物は売られる, またはそのままになる→**～を質に入れる**

**pawnbroker** /pɔ́ːnbròukər/ 名 ⓒ ▶定義 a person who lends money to people when they leave sth of value with him/her 人々が自分の価値ある～を預けていくとき, その人にお金を貸す人→**質屋 (の主人)**

*****pay**[1] /peɪ/ 動 (過, 過分 **paid**) ▶定義1 自他 pay (sb) (for sth); pay (sb) sth (for sth) to give sb money for work, goods, services, etc ～に仕事, 品物, サービスなどに対してお金を与える→**代金を払う; ～を支払う, 払う** ‖ *She is very well paid.* 彼女は給料をたくさんもらっている. *The work's finished but we haven't paid for it yet.* その仕事は終わったが, 私たちはまだお金を支払っていない. *We paid the dealer £3000* for the car. 私たちはディーラーに車の代金として 3000 ポンド払った. ▶定義 2 🔟 **pay sth (to sb)** to give the money that you owe for sth 〜のために支払う義務のあるお金を与える→**〜を支払う, 〜に返済する** ‖ *Have you paid her the rent yet?* もう彼女に家賃を払いましたか. *to pay a bill/fine* 勘定・罰金を支払う ▶定義 3 🔟 🔟 to make a profit; to be worth doing 利益を得る; する価値がある→**(〜にとって) 利益になる, 引き合う, 価値がある** ‖ *It would pay you to get professional advice before making a decision.* 決める前に専門家の意見を聞く価値はあるでしょう. ▶定義 4 🔟 **pay (for sth)** to suffer or be punished because of your beliefs or actions 自分の信念または行為によって災いを被るまたは罰せられる→**罰を受ける, 償いをする** ‖ *You'll pay for that remark!* あなたは, あの発言で報いを受けるでしょう.

成句 be paid in arrears ⇒ **ARREARS**

**pay attention (to sb/sth)** ▶定義 to listen carefully to or to take notice of sb/sth 〜を注意して聞く, または〜に注意する→**〜に注意を払う, 留意する, 注目する**

**pay sb a compliment; pay a compliment to sb** ▶定義 to say that you like sth about sb 〜について…が好きであるという→**〜を褒める, 〜にお世辞を言う**

**pay your respects (to sb)** 正式 ▶定義 to visit sb as a sign of respect 尊敬の表れとして〜を訪問する→**〜を公式に訪問する, 〜にあいさつする** ‖ *Hundreds came to pay their last respects to her (= to go to sb's funeral).* 何百人もの人が彼女に最後のあいさつをしに来た (= 〜の葬式に行く).

**pay tribute to sb/sth** ▶定義 to say good things about sb/sth and show your respect for sb/sth 〜について良い事を言って, 〜への自分の尊敬の念を表す→**〜に敬意を表する, 〜を褒めたたえる**

**put paid to sth** ▶定義 to destroy or finish sth 〜を破壊するまたは終わらせる→**(計画・希望など)を駄目にする, ぶち壊す, (事件など)を解決する** ‖ *The bad weather put paid to our picnic.* 天気が悪くて, ピクニックが台なしだった.

句動詞 **pay sth back (to sb)** ▶定義 to give money back to sb that you borrowed from him/her 〜から借りたお金をその人に返す→**〜**

## payable 1189

**を返す, 〜に金を返す** ‖ *Can you lend me £5? I'll pay you back/I'll pay it back to you on Friday.* 5ポンドを貸してもらえるかい. 金曜日には返すよ.

**pay sb back (for sth)** ▶定義 to punish sb for making you or sb else suffer 自分またはほかの〜が損害を受けるようにした…を罰する→**〜に仕返しをする, 腹いせをする** ‖ *What a mean trick! I'll pay you back one day.* 何て卑劣な策略だ. いつか仕返ししてやる.

**pay off** 略式 ▶定義 to be successful 成功する→**もうかる, 利益をもたらす, (失敗しそうな計画などが) うまくいく** ‖ *All her hard work has paid off! She passed her exam.* これまで彼女が熱心に勉強してきたことが報われた. 彼女は試験に合格した.

**pay sth off** ▶定義 to pay all the money that you owe for sth 〜に対して支払う義務のあるすべてのお金を支払う→**〜をすっかり返す, 完済する** ‖ *to pay off a debt/mortgage* 借金・ローンを完済する

**pay up** 略式 ▶定義 to pay the money that you owe 支払う義務のあるお金を支払う→**〜をすっかり払う, 完納・完済する** ‖ *If you don't pay up, we'll take you to court.* もし完納しなければ, 裁判にかけます.

★**pay**² /péɪ/ 🔟 🔟 ▶定義 money that you get regularly for work that you have done 自分がした仕事に対して定期的に得るお金→**給料, 報酬, 手当**
▶ pay は自分がした仕事に対して定期的に得るお金の一般的な語である. wages は週単位または日払いで現金で支払われるお金である. salary は毎月, 直接銀行口座に支払われる. fee は知的職業の貢献, 例えば医者, 弁護士などへ払うお金である. payment は 1 回の仕事, 定期的ではない仕事に対してのお金である. income は自分がした仕事に対してと, 貯金しているお金の利子としての, 共に定期的に自分が得ている全部のお金である.

**payable** /péɪəb(ə)l/ 形 ▶定義 that should or must be paid 払われるべき, または払わなければならない→**支払うべき, 支払うことのできる** ‖ *A 10% deposit is payable in advance.* あらかじめ10パーセントの保証金をお支払いください. *Make the cheque payable to Pauline Nolan.*

小切手はポーリン ノランあてでお願いします．

**payee** /peíː/ 名（文）▶定義 a person that money, especially a cheque, is paid to お金，特に小切手が支払われる相手→(手形・小切手の)受取人，被支払人

\***payment** /péɪmənt/ 名 **payment (for sth)** ▶定義1 ❶the act of paying sb or of being paid 〜に支払う，または支払われる行為→支払い，(支払い金を)納めること，払い込み ‖ *I did the work last month but I haven't had any payment for it yet.* 私は先月働いたが，まだその分を支払ってもらっていない．● 参 **pay**² の注 ▶定義2 ❷an amount of money that you must pay 自分が支払わなくてはならない金額→支払い金(額) ‖ *They asked for a payment of £100 as a deposit.* 彼らは予約金として100ポンドの支払い金額を要求した．

**PC** /piː síː/ 名 ❷ ▶定義1 (computing) personal computer; a computer that is designed for one person to use at work or at home (コンピューター) personal computer の略；職場または家で1人の人が使うように設計されたコンピューター→パソコン，パーソナルコンピューター ▶定義2 =POLICE CONSTABLE ▶定義3 略=POLITICALLY CORRECT

**PE** /piː íː/ 略 physical education→(学校の)体育 ‖ *a PE lesson* 体育の授業

**pea** /piː/ 名 ❷ ▶定義 a small round green seed that is eaten as a vegetable. A number of peas grow together in a long thin case (*a pod*). 野菜として食べる，小さな丸い緑の種．長く薄い入れ物（さや）の中で，たくさんの pea が一緒に育つ→えんどう豆，ひよこ豆，えんどう豆に似た豆 ● C3 ページのさし絵

\***peace** /piːs/ 名 ❶ ▶定義1 a situation or a period of time in which there is no war or violence in a country or area 国または地域内に戦争または暴力がない状況または期間→平和，和平，停戦 ‖ *The two communities now manage to live in peace together.* その2つの共同体は，今，何とか平和に共存している． *A UN force has been sent in to keep the peace.* 国連軍が平和維持のために派遣された． ▶定義2 the state of being calm or quiet 平穏なまたは静かな状態→平穏，安らぎ，静寂 ‖ *He longed to escape from the city to the peace and quiet of the countryside.* 彼は街から平穏でのんびりした田舎へ逃げ出したいと思い焦がれていた．

\***peaceful** /piːsfʊl, -f(ə)l/ 形 ▶定義1 not wanting or involving war, violence or argument 戦争，暴力，または口論を欲していない，または伴わない→平和的な，平和を愛する ‖ *a peaceful protest/demonstration/solution* 平和的な抗議・デモ・解決 ▶定義2 calm and quiet 平穏で静かな→静かな，平穏な，安らかな ‖ *a peaceful village* のんびりした村 ― **peacefully** /-fʊli/ 副→平和に，穏やかに，静かに ‖ *The siege ended peacefully.* その包囲期間は武力を行使せずに終わった．― **peacefulness** 名 ❶→穏やかさ，平穏

**peacetime** /píːstàɪm/ 名 ❶ ▶定義 a period when a country is not at war 国が戦争状態でない期間→平和な時，平時

**peach** /piːtʃ/ 名 ▶定義1 ❷a soft round fruit with orange-red skin. A peach is soft inside and has a large stone in its centre. オレンジのような赤色の皮の，柔らかくて丸い果実．その内側は柔らかくて真ん中に大きな種がある→桃，桃の実 ● C3 ページのさし絵 ▶定義2 ❶a pinkish-orange colour ピンクのようなオレンジ色→桃色

**peacock** /píːkɒk/ 名 ❷ ▶定義 a large bird with beautiful long blue and green tail feathers that it can lift up and spread out 持ち上げて広げられる美しい長い青と緑の尾羽を持った大きな鳥→雄の孔雀，孔雀

**peak**¹ /piːk/ 名 ❷ ▶定義1 the point at which sth is the highest, best, strongest, etc 〜が最も高い，良い，強いなどの点→(特に変動する量・過程などの)最高地点，絶頂，ピーク(時) ‖ *a man at the peak of his career* 仕事の絶頂期にいる男 ▶定義2 the pointed top of a mountain 山のとがっている頂→山頂，峰 ‖ *snow-covered peaks* 雪で覆われた山頂 ● C8 ページのさし絵 ▶定義3 the rigid front part of a cap that sticks out above your eyes 人の目より上に突き出る，帽子の堅い前の部分→ひさし，つば ● **hat** のさし絵

**peak**² /piːk/ 形 (名詞の前だけ) ▶定義 used to describe the highest level of sth, or a time when the greatest number of people are doing or using sth 〜の最高水準を，あるいは多くの人々が〜を行っている，または使っているときの様子を述べるために用いて→最高の，絶頂の，ピーク

(時)の ‖ *Summer is the peak period for most hotels.* 夏はほとんどのホテルにとって最も忙しい時期だ. *The athletes are all in peak condition.* スポーツ選手たちは皆最高のコンディションである. ☛参 **off-peak**

**peak**² /piːk/ 動倉 ▶定義 to reach the highest point or value 最も高い地点または価値に到達する→(売り上げ・需要などが)頂点・ピークに達する ‖ *Sales peak just before Christmas.* 売り上げはクリスマス直前にピークに達する.

**peal** /piːl/ 名C ▶定義 the loud ringing of a bell or bells 1つまたは複数の鐘の鳴る大きな音→鐘の響き ‖ (比喩) *peals of laughter* どっとわき起こる笑い声 — peal 動倉→(鐘が)鳴り響く, (雷が)とどろく

**peanut** /píːnʌt/ (または **groundnut** /ɡráʊndnʌt/) 名 ▶定義 1 Ca nut that grows under the ground that we eat 私たちが食べる, 地中で育つ堅果→落花生, 落花生の実, ピーナッツ ☛ **nut** のさし絵 ▶定義 2 **peanuts** [複数扱い] 略式 a very small amount of money とても小額のお金→わずかな金額, はした金 ‖ *We get paid peanuts for doing this job.* 私たちはこの仕事をしてわずかなはした金をもらう.

**pear** /peər/ 名C ▶定義 a fruit that has a yellow or green skin and is white inside. Pears are thinner at the top than at the bottom. 黄色または緑の皮で中身は白い果物. 底が上の方が細い→西洋なし ☛ C3ページのさし絵

\***pearl** /pɜːrl/ 名C ▶定義 a small, hard, round, white object that grows inside the shell of a type of shellfish (an oyster). Pearls are used to make jewellery. ある種の貝(カキ)の貝殻の中で育つ, 小さい堅い丸い白い物. 装身具を作るために使われる→真珠 ‖ *pearl earrings* 真珠のイヤリング

\***peasant** /péz(ə)nt/ 名C ▶定義 (used especially in past times) a person who owns or rents a small piece of land on which he/she grows food and keeps animals in order to feed his/her family (特に過ぎ去った時代に用いて)自分の家族を養うために, 食用の植物を栽培し動物を飼う小さな土地を所有しているまたは借りている人→小農, 小作農民, 農夫
➤ peasant は現在では無礼だとされている.

**peat** /piːt/ 名U ▶定義 a soft black or brown natural substance that is formed from dead plants just under the surface of the ground in cool, wet places. It can be burned as a fuel or put on the garden to make plants grow better. 地表のすぐ下の冷たくしけった場所に, 枯れた植物で構成される, 柔らかい黒または茶色の自然の物質. 燃料として燃やす, または植物がよく育つように庭にまくことができる→泥炭, ピート, 泥炭塊

**pebble** /péb(ə)l/ 名C ▶定義 a smooth round stone that is found in or near water 水の中または近くに見られる, 滑らかな丸い石→(川岸・海岸の)小石

**pecan** /píːkən, pɪkǽn, -káːn, píːkæn/ 名C ▶定義 a type of nut that we eat 私たちが食べる, ナッツの一種→ペカン ☛ **nut** のさし絵

**peck** /pek/ 動倉他 ▶定義 1 peck (at) sth (used about a bird) to eat or bite sth with its beak (鳥について)そのくちばしで~を食べるまたはかじる→くちばしでつつく, ついばむ ▶定義 2 略式 to kiss sb quickly and lightly ~に素早く軽くキスする→(お義理で)~に軽くキスをする ‖ *She pecked him on the cheek and then left.* 彼女は彼のほおに軽くキスし, そして去った. — peck 名C→(くちばしなどで)つつくこと, (お義理の)軽いキス

**peckish** /pékɪʃ/ 形略式 ▶定義 hungry 空腹な→少しおなかがすいて

**peculiar** /pɪkjúːljər/ 形 ▶定義 1 unusual or strange 通常でない, または変な→妙な, 変な, 一風変わった ‖ *There's a very peculiar smell in here.* ここでとても変なにおいがする. ☛類 **odd** ▶定義 2 **peculiar to sb/sth** only belonging to one person or found in one place 1人の人にしか属さない, または1箇所でしか見つからない→独特の, 固有の, (~に)特有である ‖ *a species of bird peculiar to South East Asia* 東南アジア特有の鳥の一種

**peculiarity** /pɪkjùːliǽrəti/ 名 (複 **peculiarities**) ▶定義 1 Ca strange or unusual characteristic, quality or habit 変わったまたは珍しい性格, 性質, または癖→風変わりな点, 妙な癖 ‖ *There are some peculiarities in her behaviour.* 彼女の行動には, いくつか風変わりな点がある. ▶定義 2 C a characteristic or a quality that only belongs to one particular person, thing or place 特定の人, 物, または場所にしか属さない性格または性質→

特色, 特性 ‖ *the cultural peculiarities of the English* イングランド人の文化的特性 ▶定義3
❶the quality of being strange or unusual 変わったまたは珍しい特性→奇癖, 奇習

**peculiarly** /pɪkjúːljərli/ 副 ▶定義1 in a strange and unusual way 変わった珍しい方法で→妙に, 変に ‖ *Luke is behaving very peculiarly.* ルークはとても妙に振る舞っている. ▶定義2 especially; very 特に; とても→特別に, とりわけ ‖ *Lilian's laugh can be peculiarly annoying.* リリアンの笑いにはとりわけいらいらさせられる. ▶定義3 in a way that is especially typical of one person, thing or place 特にある人, 物, または場所の典型的な方法で→固有に, 特有に ‖ *a peculiarly French custom* フランス特有の習慣

**pedagogical** /pèdəgádʒɪk(ə)l, -góu-/ 形 ▶定義 connected with ways of teaching 教え方に関連した→教育学の, 教育的な

**pedal** /pédl/ 名 C ▶定義 the part of a bicycle or other machine that you push with your foot in order to make it move or work 動かすまたは働かせるように, 自分の足で押す自転車またはほかの機械の一部→ペダル, 踏み板 ☞ S7ページのさし絵 — **pedal** 動 自 他 (*pedalling*; *pedalled*: 米 *pedaling*; *pedaled*) ペダルを踏む; ～のペダルを踏んで動かす ‖ *She had to pedal hard to get up the hill.* 彼女は丘を上がるために一生懸命ペダルをこがなくてはならなかった.

**pedantic** /pɪdǽntɪk/ 形 ▶定義 too worried about rules or details 規則または詳細についてこだわりすぎる→学者振った, 物知り顔の, 石頭の — **pedantically** /-k(ə)li/ 副 →学者振って, 物知り顔で

**pedestal** /pédəstl/ 名 C ▶定義 the base on which a column, statue, etc stands 円柱, 彫像などが立っている基礎→台

**pedestrian** /pədéstriən/ 名 C ▶定義 a person who is walking in the street (not travelling in a vehicle) 道を歩いている人(車で移動しているのではない)→歩行者 ☞参 **motorist**

**pedestrian crossing** (米 **crosswalk**) 名 C ▶定義 a place for pedestrians to cross the road 歩行者が道を横切るための場所→横断歩道 ☞参 **zebra crossing** ☞ **roundabout** のさし絵

**pediatrician** 米 = **PAEDIATRICIAN**

**pedigree**[1] /pédəgriː/ 名 C ▶定義1 an official record of the parents, grandfather, grandmother, etc from which an animal has been bred その動物が生まれた, 両親, 祖父, 祖母などの公式記録→血統 ☞参 **mongrel** ▶定義2 a person's family history, especially when this is impressive 特に強い印象を与える, 人の一族の歴史→家系, 立派な家柄, 名門

**pedigree**[2] /pédəgriː/ 形 (名詞の前だけ) ▶定義 (used about an animal) of high quality because the parents, grandfather, grandmother, etc are all of the same breed and specially chosen (動物について)両親, 祖母, 祖父などが皆同じ品種であり, しかも特に選ばれているので高品質の→血統の良い

**pee** /piː/ 動 自 略式 ▶定義 to get rid of waste water from your body; urinate 身体から不用の液体を取り除く; 排尿する→おしっこをする ― **pee** 名 [単数扱い]→おしっこ

**peek** /piːk/ 動 自 略式 ▶定義 **peek (at sth)** to look at sth quickly and secretly because you should not be looking at it 見てはいけないので, ～を素早く秘密裏に見る→ちらっとのぞく ‖ *No peeking at your presents before your birthday!* 誕生日前にプレゼントをのぞき見してはいけません. ― **peek** 名 [単数扱い] →のぞき見 ‖ *to have a quick peek* ちらっと素早くのぞく

**peel**[1] /piːl/ ▶定義1 他 to take the skin off a fruit or vegetable 果実または野菜の皮をむく→～の皮をむく ‖ *Could you peel the potatoes, please?* ポテトの皮をむいてもらえますか. ▶定義2 自 他 **peel (sth) (off/away/back)** to come off or to take sth off a surface in one piece or in small pieces 表面から, 1つまたはいくつかの小さな片になって～が取れる, または～を取り除く→(皮が)むける, (ペンキなどが)はげ落ちる; (皮など)をはぐ, むく ‖ *I peeled off the price label before handing her the book.* 彼女にその本を渡す前に, 私は値札をはがした.

成句 **keep your eyes peeled/skinned (for sb/sth)** ⇒ **EYE**[1]

**peel**[2] /piːl/ 名 U ▶定義 the skin of a fruit or vegetable 果実または野菜の皮→皮 ‖ *apple/potato peel* リンゴ・ポテトの皮 ☞ C3ページのさし絵 ☞参 **rind, skin**

**peeler** /píːlər/ 名 C ▶定義 a special knife for taking the skin off fruit and vegetables 果実と野

菜の皮をむくための特別なナイフ→皮むき器 ‖ *a potato peeler* ジャガイモ皮むき器 ☛ **kitchen** のさし絵

**peep¹** /píːp/ 動 ▶定義1 peep (at sth) to look at sth quickly and secretly, especially through a small opening 特に小さい開口部から、〜を素早くひそかに見る→のぞき見する、こっそりと見る ▶定義2 to be in a position where a small part of sb/sth can be seen 〜の小さな部分が見える場所にいる→見え始める、ちらっと見える、顔を出す ‖ *The moon is peeping out from behind the clouds.* 月は雲のすきまから顔をのぞかせている.

**peep²** /píːp/ 名 [単数扱い] 略式 ▶定義1 a quick look 素早く見ること→のぞき見、こっそりと見ること ‖ *Have a peep in the bedroom and see if the baby is asleep.* 寝室をこっそりと見て、赤ちゃんが寝ているかどうか様子を見なさい. ▶定義2 a sound 音→音, (小さな)話し声, 一言 ‖ *There hasn't been a peep out of the children for hours.* もう何時間も子供たちは音一つ立てていない.

**peer¹** /píər/ 名 ⓒ ▶定義1 a person who is of the same age or position in society as you 自分と同じ年齢または社会的地位の人→仲間, 同輩, 同僚 ‖ *Children hate to look stupid in front of their peers.* 子供たちは自分の仲間の前でばかに見えることを嫌う. ▶定義2 医 a member of the top level of society (the nobility) 社会の最上位階層の人(貴族)→貴族(の一員)

**peer²** /píər/ 動 自 ▶定義 peer (at sb/sth) to look closely or carefully at sb/sth, for example because you cannot see very well 例えばよく見えないので、〜を念入りにまたは注意深く見る→じっと見る, 凝視する ‖ *He peered at the photo, but it was blurred.* 彼は写真をじっと見たが、それはぼやけていた.

**peerage** /píərɪdʒ/ 名 ▶定義1 [単数または複数形の動詞と共に] all the peers'(2) as a group 集団としてのすべての peer¹(2)→貴族 ▶定義2 ⓒ the social position (rank) of a peer¹(2) peer¹(2) の社会的地位(階級)→貴族階級

**peer group** 名 ⓒ ▶定義 a group of people who are all of the same age and social position 年齢と社会的地位が全員同じ人々の集団→同輩の集団、仲間集団

**peeved** /píːvd/ 形 略式 ▶定義 quite angry or annoyed とても怒っているまたはいらいらして

いる→怒った、いらいらした

**peg¹** /péɡ/ 名 ⓒ ▶定義1 a piece of wood, metal, etc on a wall or door that you hang your coat on 人がそのコートを掛ける, 壁またはドアにある木、金属などの小片→掛けくぎ、〜掛け ▶定義2 (または **tent peg**) a piece of metal that you push into the ground to keep one of the ropes of a tent in place 正しい位置にテントのロープの1本を保つために、地面に突き刺す金属の小片→くい、留めくぎ ☛ **tent** のさし絵 ▶定義3 (または **clothes peg**, 米 **clothes pin**) a type of small wooden or plastic object used for fastening wet clothes to a clothes line 物干し用のロープにぬれた衣類を留めるために使われる、小さな木製またはプラスチック製の物の一種→洗濯ばさみ、干し物留め

**peg²** /péɡ/ 動 他 (**pegging; pegged**) ▶定義1 peg sth (out) to fix sth with a peg くいで〜を固定する→〜をくい・くぎで留める、〜にくい・くぎを打つ ▶定義2 peg sth (at/to sth) to fix or keep sth at a certain level 〜を一定のレベルで固定するまたは維持する→〜をくぎ付けにする, 固定する, 凍結する ‖ *Wage increases were pegged at 5%.* 賃金の増加は5パーセントに固定されていた.

**pelican** /pélɪkən/ 名 ⓒ ▶定義 a large bird that lives near water in warm countries. A pelican has a large beak that it uses for catching and holding fish. 温暖な国々の水辺に生息している大きな鳥. 魚を捕まえて放さない大きなくちばしがある→ペリカン

**pellet** /pélət/ 名 ⓒ ▶定義1 a small hard ball of any substance, often of soft material that has become hard あらゆる素材の小さい堅い玉で, しばしば柔らかい素材が堅くなったもの→(紙・パン・ろうなどを指で丸めた)小球, 玉 ▶定義2 a very small metal ball that is fired from a gun 銃から発射される、とても小さな金属の弾→小弾丸, 散弾 ‖ *shotgun pellets* ショットガンの散弾

**pelt** /pélt/ 動 ▶定義1 他 to attack sb/sth by throwing things 物を投げて〜を攻撃する→(石などを続けて)〜に[を]投げ付ける ▶定義2 自 pelt (down) (used about rain) to fall very heavily (雨について) とても激しく降る→激しく降る、激しく打ち付ける ‖ *It's absolutely pelting*

*down.* 雨がとても激しく降っている. ▶定義3
目睛式 to run very fast とても速く走る→**全速力で走る** ‖ *Some kids pelted past us.* 何人かの子供たちが私たちを全速力で追い越していった.

**pelvis** /pélvəs/ 名 C (複 **pelvises**) ▶定義 the set of wide bones at the bottom of your back, to which your leg bones are joined 背中の下にある一組の広い骨で,脚の骨がつながっている→**骨盤** ☞ C5 ページのさし絵 — **pelvic** /pélvɪk/ 形 →骨盤の

\***pen** /pen/ 名 C ▶定義1 an object that you use for writing in ink インクで物を書くときに使う物 →**ペン** ‖ *a ballpoint/felt-tip/marker/fountain pen* ボールペン・フェルトペン・マーカー・万年筆 ▶定義2 a small piece of ground with a fence around it that is used for keeping animals in 動物を入れておくために使われる,その周りを柵(さく)で囲んだ狭い地面→**おり,囲い**

**penal** /píːnl/ 形 (名詞の前だけ) ▶定義 connected with punishment by law 法律による処罰に関連する→**刑罰の,刑事・刑法上の,刑事罰を受ける** ‖ *the penal system* 行刑制度

**penalize** (または -**ise**) /píːnəlaɪz/ 動他 ▶定義1 to punish sb for breaking a law or rule 法律または規則を破ったために~を罰する→**~に刑を科す,~を処罰する,~に罰則を適用する** ▶定義2 to cause sb to have a disadvantage ~に不利益をもたらす→**~を不利な立場に置く・追いやる** ‖ *Children should not be penalized because their parents cannot afford to pay.* 両親に支払う余裕がないからといって,子供たちを不利な立場に立たせるべきではありません.

**penalty** /pénlti/ 名 C (複 **penalties**) ▶定義1 a punishment for breaking a law, rule or contract 法律,規則,または契約を破ったことによる処罰→**刑罰,罰** ‖ *the death penalty* 死刑 *What's the maximum penalty for smuggling drugs?* 麻薬の密輸に対する最高刑は何ですか. ▶定義2 a disadvantage or sth unpleasant that happens as the result of sth ~の結果として起こる不利益または不快な事→**報い,天罰** ‖ *I didn't work hard enough and I paid the penalty. I failed all my exams.* 私は一生懸命勉強しなかったので,すべての試験に落ちるという報いを受けた. ▶定義3 (in sport) a punishment for one team and an advantage for the other team because a rule has been broken (スポーツで) 規則が破られたので,あるチームへの罰ともう一方のチームへの利益→**ペナルティー** ‖ *The referee awarded a penalty to the home team.* 審判は地元チームにペナルティーを与えた.

**the penalty area** 名 C ▶定義 the marked area in front of the goal in football サッカーにおいて,ゴールの前の印が付いた部分→**ペナルティーエリア(ここで守備側が反則すると相手側にペナルティーキックが与えられる)**

**penance** /pénəns/ 名 C U ▶定義 a punishment that you give yourself to show you are sorry for doing sth wrong 悪い~をしたことを申し訳なく思っていることを示すために自分自身に与える罰→**悔い改め,罪の償い,罪滅ぼし**

\***pence** PENNY の複数形

\***pencil**[1] /péns(ə)l/ 名 C U ▶定義 an object that you use for writing or drawing. Pencils are usually made of wood and contain a thin stick of a black or coloured substance. 書くまたは描くために使う物.通常は木製で,細い棒状の黒または色付いた物質が入っている→**鉛筆** ‖ *Bring a pencil and paper with you.* 鉛筆と紙を持参してください. *Write in pencil, not ink.* ペンではなく,鉛筆で書いてください.

**pencil**[2] /péns(ə)l/ 動他 ( **pencilling; pencilled**: 米 **penciling; penciled**) ▶定義 to write or draw with a pencil 鉛筆で書くまたは描く→**~を鉛筆で書く・描く**

句動詞 **pencil sth/sb in** ▶定義 to write down the details of an arrangement that might have to be changed later 後で変わらなくてはならないかもしれない予定の詳細を書き留める→**~を予定として一応入れておく** ‖ *Shall we pencil the next meeting in for the fourteenth?* 次の会合は,とりあえず14日にしておきましょうか.

**pencil case** 名 C ▶定義 a small bag or box that you use to keep pens, pencils, etc in ペン,鉛筆などを入れて置く,小さなバッグまたは箱→**筆箱,鉛筆入れ**

**pencil sharpener** 名 C ▶定義 an instrument that you use for making pencils sharp 鉛筆を鋭くするために使う道具→**鉛筆削り** ☞ S4 ページのさし絵

**pendant** /péndənt/ 名 C ▶定義 a small attractive object that you wear on a chain around

your neck 首の回りに着ける鎖に付いた小さな魅力的な物→ペンダント

**pending** /péndɪŋ/ 形前 正式 ▶定義1 waiting to be done or decided なされるまたは決定されるのを待っている→未決定の, 懸案中の, 審理中の ‖ *The judge's decision is still pending.* 裁判官の裁決はまだ審理中である. ▶定義2 until sth happens 〜が起こるまで→〜まで, 〜を待つ間 ‖ *He took over the leadership pending the elections.* 選挙まで彼が主導権を取った.

**pendulum** /péndʒələm; -djʊ-/ 名 ❻ ▶定義1 a chain or stick with a heavy weight at the bottom that moves regularly from side to side to work a clock 時計を動かすために規則的に左右に動く, 一番下に重いおもりの付いた鎖または棒→振り子 ▶定義2 a way of describing a situation that changes from one thing to its opposite ある事からその反対へ変わる状況を述べる方法→(世論・流行などの)変動, 揺れ動き, 揺り戻し ‖ *Since last year's election, the pendulum of public opinion has swung against the government.* 去年の選挙以来, 世論は政府に反対の動きを示している.

**penetrate** /pénətreɪt/ 動 自 他 ▶定義1 to go through or into sth, especially when this is difficult 〜を通り抜けるまたは〜の中に入る, 特にこれが困難なとき→(におい・液体などが)染み通る, (音が)遠くまで伝わる; 〜に突き通る, 〜を貫く ‖ *The knife penetrated ten centimetres into his chest.* 彼の胸にナイフが10センチ突き刺さった. ▶定義2 to manage to understand sth difficult 難しい〜を何とか理解する→〜を解き明かす, 理解する, (人の心・意図など)を見抜く ‖ *Scientists have still not penetrated the workings of the brain.* 科学者たちはいまだに脳の働きを解明していない. ▶定義3 to be understood or realized 理解される, または認識される→(真意などが)理解される, 意味が通じる ‖ *I was back at home when the meaning of her words finally penetrated.* 家に帰り着いた時やっと彼女の言葉の意味を理解した. — penetration /pènətréɪʃ(ə)n/ 名 ❶ /浸透, 貫通, 見抜く力, 洞察力

**penetrating** /pénətreɪtɪŋ/ 形 ▶定義1 (used about sb's eyes or of a way of looking) making you feel uncomfortable because it seems sb knows what you are thinking (〜の目または見方について) 〜が自分の考えている事を知っていそうで, 居心地悪くさせる→鋭い, うがった, 心を見透かすような ‖ *a penetrating look/stare/gaze* うがった目付き・心を見透かすようにじっと見ること・鋭い凝視 *penetrating blue eyes* 心を見透かすような青い目 ▶定義2 showing that you have understood sth completely and quickly 〜を完全に素早く理解したことを示している→鋭い見抜く力がある, 洞察力がある ‖ *a penetrating question/comment* 鋭い質問・意見 ▶定義3 that can be heard, felt, smelled, etc a long way away 遠くで, 聞こえる, 感じられる, においがするなどの→(四方に)広がった, 浸透する

**penfriend** /pénfrènd/ (特に 米 **pen pal**) 名 ❻ ▶定義 a person that you become friendly with by exchanging letters, often a person who you have never met 手紙を交換して親しくなる人, 大抵は会ったことのない人→ペンフレンド, 文通友達

penguin

**penguin** /péŋgwən/ 名 ❻ ▶定義 a black and white seabird that cannot fly and that lives in the Antarctic 南極に生息する, 飛べない, 黒と白の海鳥→ペンギン

**penicillin** /pènəsílən/ 名 ❶ ▶定義 a substance that is used as a medicine (an antibiotic) for preventing and treating diseases and infections caused by bacteria 細菌が原因の病気と伝染病を防止し治療する, 薬(抗生物質)として用いられる物質→ペニシリン

**peninsula** /pənínsjələ/ 名 ❻ ▶定義 an area of land that is almost surrounded by water ほとんどを海に囲まれた地域→半島

**penis** /píːnəs/ 名 ❻ ▶定義 the male sex organ that is used for getting rid of waste liquid and having sex 尿を排せつし, また性行為をするために使う, 雄の性器→ペニス, 陰茎(男性器)

**penitent** /pénət(ə)nt/ 形 正式 ▶定義 sorry for having done sth wrong 悪い〜をしてしまったことを申し訳なく思って→後悔している, 悔い改めた

**penitentiary** /pènəténʃ(ə)ri/ 名 ❻ (複 **penitentiaries**) 米 ▶定義 a prison→刑務所

penknife

**penknife** /pénnàɪf/ 名 C ( 複 **penknives**) ▶定義 a small knife with parts used for cutting (blades), opening bottles, etc that fold safely away when not being used 切ったり(刃), びんのふたなどを開けたりするために使われる部品を備えた小さいナイフで, 使用されないときは安全に折り畳めるもの→ポケットナイフ

**penniless** /pénɪləs/ 形 ▶定義 having no money; poor お金がない; 貧乏な→無一文の; 非常に貧しい

\***penny** /péni/ 名 C ( 複 **pence** /péns/ または **pennies**) ▶定義 1 (略 p) a small brown British coin. There are a hundred pence in a pound. 小さな茶色の英国の硬貨. 1 ポンドは, 100 ペンスである→ペンス, ペニー, ペニー貨 ‖ *a fifty-pence piece/coin* 50 ペンス硬貨 ▶定義 2 米 a cent 1 セント→1 セント貨

\***pension** /pénʃ(ə)n/ 名 C ▶定義 money that is paid regularly by a government or company to sb who has stopped working (retired) because of old age or who cannot work because he/she is ill 政府または会社から, 老齢で働くことをやめた(退職した)または病気で働けない〜へ定期的に支払われるお金→公的扶助, 年金, 恩給 ─ **pensioner** = **OLD-AGE PENSIONER**

**pentagon** /péntəgàn/ 名 ▶定義 1 ❶a shape that has five straight and equal sides 5つのまっすぐで同じ長さの辺を持つ形→五角形 ▶定義 2 **the Pentagon** [単数扱い] a large government building near Washington DC in the US that contains the main offices of the US military forces; the military officials who work there 米国のワシントンD.C.の近くにある, 米国の軍隊の主要な事務所が入っている, 大きな政府の建物; そこで働く軍隊の幹部職員→米国国防総省, 米国国防総省指導部

**pentathlon** /pentǽθlən, -làn/ 名 C ▶定義 a sports competition in which you have to take part in five different events 5つの異なる種目に参加しなければならないスポーツ競技→五種競技

**penthouse** /pénthàʊs/ 名 C ▶定義 an expensive flat at the top of a tall building 高い建物の一番上にある, 費用のかかるアパート→ビルの屋上に作ったアパート式住宅, (マンションの)最上階の部屋

**pent-up** /pèntʌ́p/ 形 (名詞の前だけ) ▶定義 (used about feelings) that you hold inside and do not express (感情について) 自分の心に持っているだけで, 表に出さない→閉じ込められた, 鬱積(うっせき)した ‖ *pent-up anger* 鬱積した怒り

**penultimate** /pɪnʌ́ltəmət/ 形 ▶定義 (in a series) the one before the last one (連続のもので) 最後の前のもの→最後から2番目の ‖ *'Y' is the penultimate letter of the alphabet.* Yはアルファベットの最後から2番目の文字です.

\***people** /píːp(ə)l/ 名 ▶定義 1 [複数扱い] more than one person 1人より多い人→人々, 人たち ‖ *How many people are coming to the party?* そのパーティーに何人来ますか.

▶注意. peopleはほとんど常に複数形の persons の代わりに用いられる. persons はとても正式で, 通常法律的な文中で用いられる: *Persons under the age of sixteen are not permitted to buy cigarettes.* (16歳未満の人々がたばこを買うことは許されていません.)

▶定義 2 C ( 複 **peoples**) 正式 all the men, women and children who belong to a particular place or race 特定の場所や人種に属している, すべての男女および子供→国民, 民族 ‖ *The President addressed the American people.* 大統領はアメリカ国民に話し掛けた. *the French-speaking peoples of the world* 世界中のフランス語を話す諸国民 ▶定義 3 [複数扱い] men and women who work in a particular activity 特定の活動をしている男女→(ある職業, 階級の)人々, 人たち ‖ *business/sports people* 実業家たち・運動選手たち ▶定義 4 **the people** [複数扱い] the ordinary citizens of a country 国の一般の市民→国民, 民衆, 庶民 ‖ *The President is popular because he listens to the people.* その大統領は民衆の声を聞くので, 人気がある.

**pepper**¹ /pépɚ/ ▶定義 1 ❶a black or white powder with a hot taste that is used for flavouring food 食品に風味を添えるために使われる, 辛い味の黒いまたは白い粉→コショウ ‖ *salt and pepper* 塩コショウ ▶定義 2 ❸a green, red or yellow vegetable that is almost empty inside 内

側がほとんど空洞な, 緑, 赤, または黄色の野菜➔ピーマン, トウガラシ(の総称) ☛ C3ページのさし絵

**pepper**² /pépər/ 動⊕ pepper sb/sth with sth (通常は受動態で) ▶定義 to hit sb/sth with a series of small objects, especially bullets 小さな物, 特に弾丸を連続して〜に当てる➔(弾丸・質問などを)〜に浴びせ掛ける‖ *The wall had been peppered with bullets.* その壁に弾丸が浴びせ掛けられていた.

**peppermint** /pépəmìnt/ 图 ▶定義 1 ❶ a natural substance with a strong fresh flavour that is used in sweets and medicines お菓子や薬に用いられる, 強いさわやかな風味の自然の物質➔ペパーミント, 西洋ハッカ ▶定義 2 ❷ (または **mint**) a sweet with a peppermint flavour ペパーミント風味のお菓子➔ハッカ入り菓子 ☛参 spearmint

**pep talk** /péptɔ̀ːk/ 图 ❷略式 ▶定義 a speech that is given to encourage people or to make them work harder 人々を勇気づける, または熱心に働くようにさせるための談話➔激励, 発破

*****per** /pər, pəːr/ 前 ▶定義 for each それぞれに➔(一定の時間や数量)に付き, 〜ごとに‖ *The speed limit is 110 kilometres per hour.* 制限速度は時速110キロです. *Rooms cost 60 dollars per person per night.* 部屋は1泊1人に付き60ドルかかります.

**perceive** /pəsíːv/ 動⊕正式 ▶定義 1 to notice or realize sth 〜に気が付く, または理解する➔〜に気付く, 〜を知覚する, 認める‖ *Scientists failed to perceive how dangerous the level of pollution had become.* 科学者たちは汚染の度合いがいかに危険になっていたか気付かなかった. ▶定義 2 to understand or think of sth in a particular way 特定の方法で, 〜を理解する, または考える➔〜が…と分かる, 了解する, 〜を…と受け取る‖ *I perceived his comments as a criticism.* 私は彼の意見を非難として受け取った. ☛ 图 perception

*****per cent** (米 **percent**) 形副图 [❷, 単数または複数形の動詞と共に] (複 **per cent**) (記号 %) ▶定義 in or of each hundred; one part in every hundred 100ごとに, または100ごとの; すべての100の中の1つの部分➔パーセント, 100分の1, 100に付き‖ *You get 10% off if you pay cash.* もし現金でお支払いなら, 10パーセントの割引になります. *90% of the population owns a television.* 人口の90パーセントがテレビを持っている. *The price of bread has gone up by 50 per cent in two years.* パンの値段はこの2年で50パーセントも値上がりした.

**percentage** /pəséntɪdʒ/ 图 [❷, 単数形または複数形の動詞と共に] ▶定義 the number, amount, rate, etc of sth, expressed as if it is part of a total which is a hundred; a part or share of a whole 合計を100とし, その合計に対する部分であるかのように表現された, 〜の数, 量, 率など; 全体の一部分または占有部分➔百分率, 比率; 割合, 部分‖ *What percentage of people voted in the last election?* 前回の選挙で投票した人々の割合は, どれくらいでしたか.

**perceptible** /pəséptəb(ə)l/ 形正式 ▶定義 that can be seen or felt 見られる, または感じられる➔知覚・認識できる, 気付くことができるほどの, 目立つ‖ *a barely perceptible change in colour* 色のほとんど目立たない違い ⇔ **imperceptible** — perceptibly /-əb(ə)li/ 副➔感知できるほど, 目立って

**perception** /pəsépʃ(ə)n/ 图 ▶定義 1 ❶ the ability to notice or understand sth 〜に気付くまたは理解する能力➔知覚(作用), 知覚力, 認知 ▶定義 2 ❷ a particular way of looking at or understanding sth; an opinion 〜を見るまたは理解する特定の方法; 意見➔理解, 認識‖ *What is your perception of the situation?* この状況をあなたはどう認識していますか. ☛ 動 perceive

**perceptive** /pəséptɪv/ 形正式 ▶定義 quick to notice or understand things 物事に気付くまたは理解することが速い➔知覚の鋭い, 鋭敏な — perceptively 副➔鋭く(知覚・洞察して), 鋭敏に

**perch**¹ /pəːrtʃ/ 動 ▶定義 1 ❸ (used about a bird) to sit on a branch, etc (鳥について)枝などに止まる➔止まる ▶定義 2 ❸⊕ to sit or be put on the edge of sth 〜の端に座るまたは置かれる➔(人が高い所などに)ちょこんと座る, (物・町などが〜に)ある; 〜を(高い所などに)置く‖ *The house was perched on the edge of a cliff.* その家は崖(がけ)っぷちにあった.

**perch**² /pəːrtʃ/ 图 ❷ ▶定義 a branch (or a bar in a cage) where a bird sits 鳥が止まる枝(または鳥かごの中の棒)➔鳥の止まる所(木の枝など),

(鳥かごの)止まり木

**percussion** /pərkʌ́ʃ(ə)n/ 名 Ｕ ▶定義 drums and other instruments that you play by hitting them たたいて演奏する, 太鼓などの楽器→**打楽器, パーカッション**

**perennial** /pərénɪəl/ 形 ▶定義 that happens often or that lasts for a long time しばしば起こるまたは長い間続く→**絶え間のない, 長続きする** ‖ *a perennial problem* 長引く問題

*****perfect**¹ /pə́ːrfɪkt/ 形 ▶定義 **1** completely good; without faults or weaknesses 完全に良い; 欠点または弱点のない→**完全な, 完ぺきな, 欠点・欠陥のない** ‖ *The car is two years old but it is still in perfect condition.* その車は製造されてから2年たつが, 今でも完ぺきな状態だ. ⇔ **imperfect**
▶定義 **2** perfect (for sb/sth) exactly suitable or right まさに適した, ちょうど良い→**最適の, 申し分のない, 打って付けの** ‖ *Ken would be perfect for the job.* ケンはその仕事に打って付けだろう. ▶定義 **3** (名詞の前だけ) complete; total 完全な, 全くの→**全くの, 純然たる** ‖ *What he was saying made perfect sense to me.* 彼が言っていた事は全く道理にかなっていると, 私は思った. *a perfect stranger* 全く知らない人 ▶定義 **4** used to describe the tense of a verb that is formed with has/have/had and the past participle has, have, had と過去分詞で作られる, 動詞の時制を述べるために用いて→**完了の, 完了形の** ― **perfectly** 副 →**完全に, 完ぺきに, 全く, すっかり** ‖ *He played the piece of music perfectly.* 彼はその楽曲を完ぺきに演奏した.

**perfect**² /pərfékt/ 動 他 ▶定義 to make sth perfect ～を完ぺきにする→**～を完成する, 仕上げる** ‖ *Vinay is spending a year in France to perfect his French.* ビネイは自分のフランス語を完ぺきにするために, フランスで1年間過ごしている.

**perfection** /pərfékʃ(ə)n/ 名 Ｕ ▶定義 the state of being perfect or without fault 完全である, または欠点のない状態→**完全(なこと), 完ぺき, 申し分のないこと** ‖ *The steak was cooked to perfection.* そのステーキは申し分なく焼かれていた.

**perfectionist** /pərfékʃ(ə)nst/ 名 Ｃ ▶定義 a person who always does things as well as he/she possibly can and who expects others to do the same いつもできるだけ良く物事を行い, ほかの人々にも同じように行うことを期待する人→**完全主義者, 凝り性の人**

**the perfect tense** (または **the perfect**) 名 [単数扱い](文法) ▶定義 the tense of a verb that is formed with has/have/had and the past participle has, have, had と過去分詞で作られる動詞の時制→**完了時制** ‖ *'I've finished' is in the present perfect tense.* I've finished は現在完了時制です.

▶完了時制についての説明は, 巻末の「文法早見表」を参照.

**perforate** /pə́ːrfərèɪt/ 動 他 ▶定義 to make a hole or holes in sth ～に1つまたは複数の穴を開ける→**～に穴を開ける, (紙)にミシン目を入れる, 目打ちする**

**perforation** /pə̀ːrfəréɪʃ(ə)n/ 名 ▶定義 **1** Ｃ a series of small holes in paper, etc that make it easy for you to tear 紙などにある連続した小さな穴で切るのを楽にしてくれるもの→**ミシン目, 目打ち, 切り取り線** ▶定義 **2** Ｕ the action of making a hole or holes in sth ～に1つまたは複数の穴を開ける行為→**穴を開けること, 貫通**

*****perform** /pərfɔ́ːrm/ 動 ▶定義 **1** 他 正式 to do a piece of work or sth that you have been ordered to do するように言われていた仕事または～を行う→**～を実行する, 果たす** ‖ *to perform an operation/an experiment/a task* 手術をする・実験をする・職務を果たす ▶定義 **2** 自他 to take part in a play or to sing, dance, etc in front of an audience 観衆の前で芝居に出演する, 歌う, 踊る, など→**演じる, 演奏する** ‖ *She is currently performing at the National Theatre.* 彼女は今のところ国立劇場で公演している. ▶定義 **3** 自 perform (well/badly/poorly) to work or function well or badly うまくまたはまずく働くまたは機能する→**(機械などが)(うまく・まずく)働く, 作動する, (人が)(うまく・まずく)成し遂げる, 行う** ‖ *The company has not been performing well recently.* その会社は最近うまくいっていない.
成句 work/perform miracles ⇒ **MIRACLE**

*****performance** /pərfɔ́ːrm(ə)ns/ 名 ▶定義 **1** Ｃ the act of performing sth in front of an audience; something that you perform 観衆の前で～を演じる行為; 演じるもの→**公演, 上演** ‖ *What time does the performance start?* 公演は何時から始まりますか. ▶定義 **2** Ｃ the way a person performs in a play, concert, etc 人が芝居, コ

ンサートなどで演じる方法→**演技, 演奏** ‖ *His moving performance in the film won him an Oscar.* その映画での彼の演技が感動的だったため, 彼はオスカー賞を勝ち取った. ▶定義3 **C** the way in which you do sth, especially how successful you are 人が〜をするやり方, 特にどの程度うまくいったか→**作業能力, 出来栄え, 成績** ‖ *The company's performance was disappointing last year.* その会社の去年の業績は期待外れだった. ▶定義4 **U** (used about a machine, etc) the ability to work well(機械などについて)うまく働く能力→**性能** ‖ *This car has a high performance engine.* この車には高性能エンジンが搭載されている. ▶定義5 [単数扱い] 正式 the act or process of doing a task, an action, etc 職務や行動などをする行為または過程→**実行, 履行** ‖ *the performance of your duties* 自分の義務の履行

**performer** /pərfɔ́ːrmər/ 名 **C** ▶定義1 a person who performs for an audience 観衆のために演じる人→**演技者, 演奏者, 歌手** ▶定義2 a person or thing that behaves or works in the way mentioned 言及されたように振る舞うまたは働く人または物→**(〜を)行う者, 行為者** ‖ *Diana is a poor performer in exams.* ダイアナは試験では全く駄目だ.

*__perfume__ /pə́ːrfjùːm/ 名 **C U** ▶定義1 (医 または **scent**) a liquid with a sweet smell that you put on your body to make yourself smell nice 自分自身が良い香りを放つように体に付ける甘い香りのする液体→**香水, 香料** ‖ *Are you wearing perfume?* あなたは香水を付けていますか. ▶定義2 a pleasant, often sweet, smell 気持ちの良い, しばしば甘い香り→**芳香**

*__perhaps__ /pərhǽps, (口語) præps/ 副 ▶定義 (used when you are not sure about sth) possibly; maybe (〜について確信がないときに)ことによると; もしかしたら→**もしかしたら, ひょっとすると, 多分** ‖ *Perhaps he's forgotten.* もしかしたら, 彼は忘れているのかもしれない. *She was, perhaps, one of the most famous writers of the time.* 彼女はおそらく, その時代の最も著名な作家の1人だった.

▶ perhapsとmaybeの意味は類似している. この2語は, より礼儀正しい言い方をするためにしばしば用いられる: *Perhaps I could borrow your book, if you're not using it?* (もし使っていないなら, あなたの本をお借りしてもよろしいですか.) *Maybe I'd better explain...* (もしかすると, 私が説明した方がいいかもしれません.)

**peril** /pérəl/ 名 (文) ▶定義1 **U** great danger 大変な危険→**危険** ‖ *A lack of trained nurses is putting patients' lives **in peril**.* 熟練した看護婦たちの不足は, 患者たちの生命を危険な状態に陥れている. ▶定義2 **C** sth that is very dangerous とても危険な〜→**危険な事・物** ‖ *the perils of drug abuse* 麻薬中毒の危険性 ― **perilous** /pérələs/ 形→**危険な, 冒険的な** ☞ danger と dangerous の方がより一般的な語である.

**perimeter** /pərímətər/ 名 **C** ▶定義 the outside edge or limit of an area of land ある区域の外側のへりまたは限界→(飛行場・軍事施設などの)**周囲, 周辺, 境界線** ‖ *the perimeter fence of the army camp* 軍駐屯地の境界線の柵(さく)

*__period__ /píəriəd/ 名 **C** ▶定義1 a length of time 時間の長さ→**期間, 時期** ‖ *The scheme will be introduced for a six-month trial period.* その計画は, 6か月の試行期間に導入される. *Her son is going through a difficult period at the moment.* 彼女の息子は今難しい時期に来ている. *What period of history are you most interested in?* どの時代の歴史に最も興味がありますか. ▶定義2 a lesson in school 学校の授業→**時限, こま, 授業時間** ‖ *We have five periods of English a week.* 私たちは1週間に5こま英語の授業がある. ▶定義3 the time every month when a woman loses blood from her body 女性の体から血液が排出される毎月の時→**生理, 月経** ▶定義4 特に 米 = **FULL STOP**

**periodic** /pìəriɑ́dɪk/ (または **periodical** /-k(ə)l/) 形 ▶定義 happening fairly regularly かなり定期的に起こる→**定期的な, 周期的な** ‖ *We have periodic meetings to check on progress.* 進展をチェックするために, 私たちは定期的な会議を持っている. ― **periodically** /-k(ə)li/ 副→**定期的に, 周期的に** ‖ *All machines need to be checked periodically.* すべての機械は定期的に検査する必要があります.

**periodical** /pìəriɑ́dɪk(ə)l/ 名 **C** 正式 ▶定義 a magazine that is produced regularly 定期的に発行される雑誌→(日刊以外の)**定期刊行物, 月刊・**

季刊雑誌

**perish** /périʃ/ 動自 (文) ▶定義 to die or be destroyed 死ぬまたは破壊される→(飢え・悪天候・事故などで)死ぬ, 滅びる ‖ *Thousands perished in the war.* 多くの人々がその戦争で死んだ.

**perishable** /périʃəb(ə)l/ 形 ▶定義 (used about food) that will go bad quickly (食べ物について)すぐに悪くなる→腐りやすい⇔**non-perishable**

**perjury** /pə́ːdʒ(ə)ri/ 名 U 正式 ▶定義 the act of telling a lie in a court of law 法廷でうそをつく行為→偽証(罪) — **perjure** /pə́ːrdʒər/ 動他 **perjure yourself**→(宣誓後に)偽証する ‖ *She admitted that she had perjured herself while giving evidence.* 証言中に偽証したことを, 彼女は認めた.

**perk**¹ /pəːrk/ 動
句動詞 **perk (sb/sth) up** ▶定義 to become or make sb become happier and have more energy もっと陽気に元気良くなる, または~をそうさせる→元気になる; 元気づける, ~の見栄えを良くする

**perk**² /pəːrk/ 名 C 略式 ▶定義 something extra that you get from your employer in addition to money お金に加えて雇い主からもらうもの→(給料以外の)臨時収入, (仕事に伴う)特典, 恩恵 ‖ *Travelling abroad is one of the perks of the job.* 海外旅行はその仕事の恩恵の1つだ.

**perm** /pəːm/ 名 C ▶定義 the treatment of hair with special chemicals in order to make it curly カールさせるために, 特別な薬品で髪を処理すること→パーマ ☛参 **wave** — **perm** 動他→~にパーマをかける ‖ *She has had her hair permed.* 彼女は髪にパーマをかけた.

*****permanent** /pə́ːmən(ə)nt/ 形 ▶定義 lasting for a long time or for ever; that will not change 長い間, または永遠に続く; 変わらない→永久的な, いつまでも続く, 終身の ‖ *The accident left him with a permanent scar.* 彼は, その事故で一生消えない傷を負った. *Are you looking for a permanent or a temporary job?* 終身雇用の仕事, それとも一時的な仕事を探しているのですか. — **permanence** 名 U→永久, 不変, 永続性 — **permanently** 副→永久に, いつまでも ‖ *Has she left permanently?* 彼女は永久に去っていったのですか.

**permissible** /pəmísəb(ə)l/ 形 正式 ▶定義 **permissible (for sb) (to so sth)** that is allowed by law or by a set of rules 法律, 規則によって許されている→(~にとって)許される, 差し支えない ‖ *They have been exposed to radiation above the permissible level.* 彼らは許容限度を超える放射能を浴びてしまった.

*****permission** /pəmíʃ(ə)n/ 名 U ▶定義 **permission (for sth); permission (for sb) (to do sth)** the act of allowing sb to do sth, especially when this is done by sb in a position of authority ~に…をすることを許す行為, 特に権威ある~によって行われるとき→許可, 許し, 認可 ‖ *I'm afraid you can't leave **without permission**.* 申し訳ありませんが, 許可なしで出掛けることはできませんが. *to **ask/give permission** for sth* ~に対する許可を申請する・与える

▶注意. permissionは数えられない. 人が何かすることを許可されると伝える文書は, permitである.

**permissive** /pəmísiv/ 形 ▶定義 having, allowing or showing a lot of freedom that many people do not approve of, especially in sexual matters 多くの人々が承認しないような自由をたくさん持っている, 許している, または示している (特に性的な事柄において)→(道徳や性に対して) 寛大な, 緩やかな, 甘い

*****permit**¹ /pəmít/ 動 (**permitting**; **permitted**)
▶定義 **1** 正式 to allow sb to do sth or to allow sth to happen ~に…をすることを許す, または~が起こることを許す→許可する, 許す, ~に(…を)させておく ‖ *You are not permitted to smoke in the hospital.* 病院内での喫煙は認められていません. *His visa does not permit him to work.* 彼のビザでは, 働くことを許されない. ☛参 **allow**の注 ▶定義 **2** 他 to make sth possible ~を可能にさせる→(物事を)可能にする, (事情が)~するのを許す, 人が~できるようにする ‖ *Let's have a barbecue at the weekend, **weather permitting**.* 天気が良ければ, 週末外でバーベキューをしましょう.

**permit**² /pə́ːmɪt/ 名 C ▶定義 an official document that says you are allowed to do sth, especially for a limited period of time 特に限定された期間, ~をしてもよいと伝える公式文書→許可証(書) ‖ *Next month I'll have to apply for a new **work permit**.* 来月, 新しい労働許可証を申請しなくてはならない.

**perpendicular** /pə̀ːrpəndíkjələr/ 形 ▶定義1 at an angle of 90° to sth ～に対して90度の角度で→垂直の, (線や面に対して)直角を成す ‖ *Are the lines perpendicular to each other?* それらの直線は互いに直角になっていますか.

▶ horizontal, vertical と比較.

▶定義2 pointing straight up; upright まっすぐ上を指している; まっすぐに立っている→直立した, (崖(がけ)などが)切り立った ‖ *The path was almost perpendicular (= it was very steep).* その小道はほとんど垂直だった(= それはとても急勾配(こうばい)だった).

**perpetual** /pərpétʃuəl/ 形 ▶定義1 continuing for a long period of time without stopping 長い間止まらずに続ける→永続的な, いつまでも続く, 変わらない ‖ *They lived in perpetual fear of losing their jobs.* 彼らは, 仕事を失うのではないかと恐れながらずっと生きていた. ▶定義2 frequently repeated in a way which is annoying いらいらさせる方法でしばしば繰り返される→絶え間のない, ひっきりなしの, のべつ幕なしの ‖ *How can I work with these perpetual interruptions?* こうひっきりなしに邪魔されて, どうすれば仕事ができるのでしょうか. — perpetually /-tʃuəli/ 副 →永続的に, 絶え間なく, ひっきりなしに

**perpetuate** /pərpétʃuèɪt/ 動⊕正式 ▶定義 to cause sth to continue for a long time 長い間～を続けさせる→～を永続化させる, いつまでも継続させる, 不滅にする ‖ *to perpetuate an argument* 議論をずっと続けさせる

**perplexed** /pərplékst/ 形 ▶定義 not understanding sth; confused ～を理解していない; 混乱した→まごついている, 戸惑っている; 複雑な, 面倒な

**persecute** /pə́ːrsɪkjùːt/ 動⊕ ▶定義1 persecute sb (for sth) (しばしば受動態で) to treat sb in a cruel and unfair way, especially because of race, religion or political beliefs 残酷で不公平なやり方で～を扱う, 特に人種, 宗教, または政治的信条の理由から→～を迫害する ▶定義2 to deliberately annoy sb and make his/her life unpleasant わざと～をいらいらさせて, その生活を不快にする→～をうるさく悩ませる, 苦しめる — persecution /pə̀ːrsɪkjúːʃ(ə)n/ 名 ⊝⓪→迫害, 虐待 ‖ *the persecution of minorities* 少数民族への迫害 — persecutor /pə́ːrsɪkjùːtər/ 名 ⊝→迫害者, 虐待者

person 1201

**persevere** /pə̀ːrsəvíər/ 動⊜ ▶定義 persevere (at/in/with sth) to continue trying to do or achieve sth that is difficult 難しい～をしたり達成したりする試みを続ける→根気強くやり通す, へこたれないで続ける, 頑張る ‖ *The treatment is painful but I'm going to persevere with it.* 治療は痛いけれど, 根気強くやり通します. — perseverance 名 ⓤ→根気, 頑張り, 不屈の精神

**persist** /pərsíst/ 動⊜ ▶定義1 persist (in sth/doing sth) to continue doing sth even though other people say that you are wrong or that you cannot do it あなたは間違っているまたはあなたにはできないと, たとえほかの人々が言っているとしても, ～を行い続ける→(自分の考えなどを)あくまで通す, 強く主張する, 固執する ‖ *If you persist in making so much noise, I shall call the police.* もしあなたがこんなにうるさくし続けるのなら, 私は警察を呼びます. ▶定義2 to continue to exist 存在し続ける→(嫌な事が)続く, 持つ ‖ *If your symptoms persist you should consult your doctor.* もしその症状が続くのなら, 医者に診てもらった方がいいですよ. — persistence 名 ⓤ→頑固, 頑張り, 粘り ‖ *Finally her persistence was rewarded and she got what she wanted.* ついに頑張ったかいがあって, 彼女は欲しがっていたものを手に入れた.

**persistent** /pərsíst(ə)nt/ 形 ▶定義1 determined to continue doing sth even though people say that you are wrong or that you cannot do it あなたは間違っているまたはあなたにはできないとたとえ人々が言っているとしても, ～を行い続けると決心している→(自分の考えに)固執する, 頑固な, しつこい ‖ *Some salesmen can be very persistent.* 営業マンの中にはとてもしつこい人がいる. ▶定義2 lasting for a long time or happening often 長い間続く, またはしばしば起こる→(嫌な事が)いつまでも続く, 持続する, 頻発する ‖ *a persistent cough* ひっきりなしに出るせき — persistently 副 →頑固に, しつこく, 粘り強く

\***person** /pə́ːrs(ə)n/ 名 © (複 **people**) ▶定義1 a man or woman; a human being 男, または女; 人間→人, 人間, 個人 ‖ *I would like to speak to the person in charge.* ご担当の方とお話したいのですが.

## 1202 personal

▶とても正式な場合には、personの複合形はpersonsとなることもある。peopleの注を参照。

▶定義2 -person(複合名詞を作るために用いて) a person doing the job mentioned 言及された仕事をしている人→〜に従事・関係する人 ‖ *a salesperson/spokesperson* 店員・スポークスマン ▶定義3 (文法) one of the three types of pronoun in grammar. I/we are the first person, you is the second person and he/she/it/they are the third person. 文法において、代名詞の3種類のうちの1つ。Iとweは一人称、youは二人称、he, she, it, theyは三人称である→人称

成句 **in person** ▶定義 seeing or speaking to sb face to face (not speaking on the telephone or writing a letter) (電話で話す、または手紙を書くのではなく)面と向かって〜と会っているまたは話している→自分で、本人が(出向いて)

★**personal** /pə́ːrs(ə)n(ə)l/ 形 ▶定義1 (名詞の前だけ) of or belonging to one particular person 特定の個人の、または特定の個人に属する→個人の、個人的な ‖ *personal belongings* 個人の所持品 *Judges should not let their **personal feelings** influence their decisions.* 裁判官は判決に個人的な感情を影響させてはいけない。

▶定義2 concerning your feelings, health or relationships with other people 自分の感情、健康、またはほかの人々との人間関係に関する→個人の(内面)に関する、私事に立ち入る、ぶしつけな ‖ *I should like to speak to you in private. I have something personal to discuss.* あなたと2人だけで話したいのですが。個人的な事を話し合いたいのです。*Do you mind if I ask you a **personal question**?* 個人的な質問をしてもいいですか。▶定義3 not connected with a person's job or official position その人の仕事、または公的な立場に関連していない→私的な ‖ *Please keep personal phone calls to a minimum.* 私用電話は最低限に控えてください。*I try not to let work interfere with my **personal life**.* 私は仕事が私的な生活を妨げることがないようにしている。▶定義4 (名詞の前だけ) done by a particular person rather than by sb who is acting for him/her 特定の人のために行動している〜によって、というよりむしろその特定の人によって行われた→自分自身で、直々に、本人が直接行う ‖ *The Prime Minister made a personal visit to the victims in hospital.* 首相が直々に犠牲者たちを病院に見舞った。▶定義5 (名詞の前だけ) made or done for one particular person rather than for a large group of people or people in general 人々の大きな集団または一般的な人々よりむしろ1人の特定の人のために、作られたまたは行われた→個人・自分に向けられた ‖ *We offer a personal service to all our customers.* 私どもはすべてのお客様、お一人お一人にサービスをご提供いたします。▶定義6 speaking about sb's appearance or character in an unpleasant or unfriendly way 感じの悪いまたは敵意を持った様子で、〜の身なりまたは性格について話している→個人に向けられた、個人攻撃の ‖ *It started as a general discussion but then people started to **get personal** and an argument began.* 一般的な討論として始まったが、人々が個人攻撃を始め、口論となった。▶定義7 (名詞の前だけ) connected with the body 身体に関する→身体の、身なりの ‖ *personal hygiene* 身体を衛生的に保つこと *She's always worrying about her personal appearance.* 彼女はいつも自分の容姿を気にしている。

**personal assistant** = PA¹
**personal computer** = PC(1)
**personality** /pə̀ːrs(ə)nǽləti/ 名 (複 **personalities**)
▶定義1 **C U** the different qualities of a person's character that make him/her different from other people ほかの人々と異なるような、人の性格の異なる資質→個性、性格、人柄 ‖ *Joe has a kind personality.* ジョーは優しい性格だ。
▶定義2 **U** the quality of having a strong, interesting and attractive character 強い、面白い、して魅力的な性格を持っているという資質→人間的魅力 ‖ *A good entertainer needs a lot of personality.* すばらしいエンターテイナーには多くの人間的魅力が必要だ。▶定義3 **C** a famous person (especially in sport, on television, etc) 有名な人(特にスポーツ、テレビなどで)→名士、有名人、タレント ‖ *a television personality* テレビタレント

**personalize** (または **-ise**) /pə́ːrs(ə)n(ə)làɪz/ 動 ▶定義 to mark sth with the first letters of your name (your initials), etc to show that it belongs to you それが自分のものだと示すために、自分の名前の最初の文字(自分のイニシャル)

などで~に印を付ける➡~に個人名・イニシャルを入れる ‖ *a car with a personalized number plate* 自分のイニシャルが入ったナンバープレートの車

**personally** /pə́ːrs(ə)n(ə)li/ 副 ▶定義1 used to show that you are expressing your own opinion 自分自身の意見を表明していることを示すために用いて➡自分・個人としては, 個人的な意見では ‖ *Personally, I think that nurses deserve more money.* 私としては, 看護婦たちはもっと給料が高くてもいいと思います. ▶定義2 done by you yourself, not by sb else acting for you 自分の代わりにほかの~が行ったのではなく, 自分自身で行った➡直接自分で ‖ *I will deal with this matter personally.* この件に関しては, 私が直接自分で処理します. ▶定義3 in a way that is connected with one particular person rather than a group of people 人々の集団としてよりむしろ1人の特定の個人に関係したやり方で➡(一個の)人間として(は), 一個人として ‖ *I wasn't talking about you personally - I meant all teachers.* 私はあなたについて一個人として話していたのではありません－教師たち全員のことを話したのです. ▶定義4 in a way that is intended to offend 怒らせようと意図するやり方で➡個人に向けられたものとして, 自分への当て付け・攻撃として ‖ *Please don't **take it personally**, but I would just rather be alone this evening.* どうか気を悪くしないでください, 今夜はむしろ1人でいたいのです. ▶定義5 in a way that is connected with sb's private life, rather than his/her job ~の仕事というよりもむしろ~の個人的生活に関連した➡私的に, 個人的に

**personal pronoun** 名 ⓒ (文法) ▶定義 any of the pronouns I, me, she, her, he, him, we, us, you, they, them 代名詞I, me, she, her, he, him, we, us, you, they, themのどれでも➡人称代名詞

**personal stereo** 名 ⓒ ▶定義 a small machine that plays CDs or cassettes that you can carry round with you and listen to through a wire which goes in each ear (headphones) 持ち運びができ, 両耳につながったコード (ヘッドホン) を通して聞く, CDまたはカセットを再生する小さな機械➡携帯用のステレオカセットプレーヤー, ウォークマン

**personify** /pərsánəfàɪ/ 動 ⓣ (現分 **personifying**; 三 単 現 **personifies**; 過, 過分 **personified**) ▶定義1 to be an example in human form of a particular quality 特定の資質を形成する人間の例えとする➡~を体現する, ~を具現する, 象徴する, ~の典型である ‖ *She is kindness personified.* 彼女は優しさそのものだ. ▶定義2 to describe an object or a feeling as if it were a person, for example in a poem 例えば詩の中で, 物または感情を人間のように描写する➡~を擬人化する, 人間のように扱う — personification /pərsànəfəkéɪʃ(ə)n/ 名 ⓒ ⓤ ➡~の化身, 権化, 擬人化

**personnel** /pə̀ːrs(ə)nél/ 名 ▶定義1 [複数扱い] the people who work for a large organization or one of the armed forces 大きな組織または軍隊のために働く人々➡職員, 人員, 隊員 ‖ *sales/medical/technical personnel* 販売部員・医療職員・技術職員 ▶定義2 (または **personnel department**) [ⓤ, 単数または複数形の動詞と共に] the department of a large company or organization that deals with employing and training people 雇用や人々の訓練を担当する, 大きな会社または組織の部署➡人事部・課 ‖ *Personnel is/are currently reviewing pay scales.* 現在, 人事部は給与表を再検討している.

**perspective** /pərspéktɪv/ 名 ▶定義1 ⓤ the ability to think about problems and decisions in a reasonable way without exaggerating them 問題や決定について, 誇張しないで, 理にかなった方法で考えられる能力➡釣り合いの取れた見方, 大局的な観点, 相関関係 ‖ *Hearing about others' experiences often helps to **put** your own problems **into perspective** (= makes them seem less important then you thought).* ほかの人の経験を聞くことによって, しばしば自分の抱えている問題を大局的な観点から見られるようになる (= 自分が考えていたよりも, 問題が重要なものではないと思わせる). *Try to **keep** these issues **in perspective** (= do not exaggerate them).* これらの問題点の重要性を正しく判断するように努めてください (= 誇張しないように).

▶定義2 ⓒ your opinion or attitude towards sth ~に対する自分の意見または態度➡見方, 観点 ‖ *Try and look at this from my perspective.* 私の観点からこれを見るようにしてください. ▶定義3

❶ the art of drawing on a flat surface so that some objects appear to be farther away than others いくつかの物がほかの物よりもはるか遠くにあると見えるように，平面にかく技法→遠近画法，透視画法

**perspire** /pərspáɪər/ 動自 正式 ▶定義 to lose liquid through your skin when you are hot; to sweat 人が暑いとき，皮膚を通して液体を失う；汗をかく→汗をかく，汗ばむ — **perspiration** /pə̀ːrspəréɪʃ(ə)n/ 名 Ⓤ→発汗(作用)，汗 ☞ sweat の方がより一般的な語である．

＊**persuade** /pərswéɪd/ 動他 ▶定義 **1** persuade sb (to do sth); persuade sb (into sth/doing sth) to make sb do sth by giving him/her good reasons もっともな理由を与えて，〜に…をさせる→〜を説得して…させる，説き伏せる，勧めて〜させる ‖ *It was difficult to persuade Louise to change her mind.* 彼女の決心を変えるよう，ルイーズを説き伏せることは難しかった．*We eventually persuaded Sanjay into coming with us.* 私たちは最終的にサンジェイを説得して一緒に来させた．⇔ dissuade ▶定義 **2** 正式 persuade sb that...; persuade sb (of sth) to make sb believe sth 〜に…を信じさせる→〜と信じさせる，〜に納得させる ‖ *She had persuaded herself that she was going to fail.* 彼女は自分が失敗すると信じていた．*The jury was not persuaded of her innocence.* 陪審員は彼女の無実を信じなかった．☞参 **convince**

**persuasion** /pərswéɪʒ(ə)n/ 名 ▶定義 **1** ❶ the act of persuading sb to do sth or to believe sth 〜に…を行うまたは…を信じるように説得する行為→説得，説得すること ‖ *It took a lot of persuasion to get Alan to agree.* アランから同意を得るためには，長時間の説得が必要だった．▶定義 **2** Ⓒ 正式 a religious or political belief 宗教的または政治的信念→信仰，信条，宗派，党派 ‖ *politicians of all persuasions* すべての党派の政治家

**persuasive** /pərswéɪsɪv/ 形 ▶定義 able to persuade sb to do or believe sth 〜が…を行うまたは信じるように説き伏せられる→説得力のある，なるほどと思わせる ‖ *the persuasive power of advertising* 広告が持つ説得力 — **persuasively** 副→説得力を持って，言葉巧みに — **persuasiveness** 名 Ⓤ→説得力のあること

**pertinent** /pə́ːrt(ə)nənt/ 形 正式 ▶定義 closely connected with the subject being discussed 討論されているテーマと密接に関連した→適切な，妥当な，(〜に)関連する ‖ *to ask a pertinent question* 適切な質問をする

**perturb** /pərtə́ːrb/ 動他 正式 ▶定義 to make sb worried or upset 〜を心配させる，または悩ませる→〜を動揺させる，気をもませる，不安にする — **perturbed** 形→動揺した，気をもんだ

**pervade** /pərvéɪd/ 動他 正式 ▶定義 to spread through and be noticeable in every part of sth あちこちに広がり，〜のどの部分でも気付くようになる→(においなどが)〜に広がる，(思想などが)〜に普及する，浸透する ‖ *A sadness pervades most of her novels.* ほとんどの彼女の小説は，悲しみに満ちている．

**pervasive** /pərvéɪsɪv/ 形 ▶定義 that is present in all parts of sth 〜のすべての部分に存在する→広がった，充満した，行き渡っている ‖ *a pervasive mood of pessimism* 辺りを覆う悲観的な雰囲気

**perverse** /pərvə́ːrs/ 形 正式 ▶定義 liking to behave in a way that is not acceptable or reasonable or that most people think is wrong 受け入れられない，ふさわしくない，あるいはほとんどの人々が間違っていると考えるようなやり方で振る舞うことを好んでいる→つむじ曲がりの，ひねくれた，片意地な ‖ *Derek gets perverse pleasure from shocking his parents.* デリクは，両親をびっくりさせることを，ひねくれた喜としている．— **perversely** 副→片意地を張って，ひねくれて — **perversity** 名 Ⓤ→つむじ曲がり，強情，倒錯

**perversion** /pərvə́ːrʒ(ə)n, -ʃ(ə)n/ 名 Ⓤ Ⓒ ▶定義 **1** sexual behaviour that is not considered normal or acceptable by most people ほとんどの人々が，正常でないまたは受け入れられないと見なす性的行動→異常，性的倒錯 ▶定義 **2** the action of changing sth from right to wrong or from good to bad 〜を正しいものから悪いものへ，または良いものから悪いものへ変化させる行為→曲解，こじつけ，悪用 ‖ *That statement is a perversion of the truth.* その供述は事実を曲解したものだ．

**pervert**[1] /pərvə́ːrt/ 動他 ▶定義 **1** to change a system, process, etc in a bad way 方式，過程な

どを悪い方向へ変える→〜を悪用する, ゆがめる, 歪曲(わいきょく)する ‖ *to pervert the course of justice* (= *to deliberately prevent the police from finding out the truth about a crime*) 裁判の経過をゆがめる(=警察が犯罪についての事実を見つけ出すことを故意に妨げる) ▶定義2 to cause sb to think or behave in a way that is not moral or acceptable 道徳的でない, または受け入れられないやり方で, 〜が考えるまたは行動するようにさせる→〜を堕落させる, 邪道に導く

**pervert²** /pɚːrvɚːrt/ 名 C ▶定義 a person whose sexual behaviour is not thought to be natural or normal by most people ほとんどの人々が自然であるまたは正常であるとは考えない性的な振る舞いをする人→性的倒錯者, 変質者

**pessimism** /pésəmìz(ə)m/ 名 U ▶定義 pessimism (about/over sth) the state of expecting or believing that bad things will happen and that sth will not be successful 悪い事が起こり, 〜が成功しないと予期しているまたは信じている状態→悲観主義, 厭世(えんせい)主義 ⇔ optimism — pessimistic /pèsəmístɪk/ 形 →悲観的な, 厭世的な ⇔ optimistic — pessimistically /-k(ə)li/ 副 →悲観的に, 厭世的に ⇔ optimistically

**pessimist** /pésəmɪst/ 名 C ▶定義 a person who always thinks that bad things will happen or that sth will be not be successful 悪い事が起こるまたは〜が成功しないと, いつも考えている人→悲観論者, 厭世家 ⇔ optimist

**pest** /pést/ 名 C ▶定義1 an insect or animal that destroys plants, food, etc 植物, 食物などを駄目にする虫または動物→害虫, 有害な小動物 ▶定義2 略式 a person or thing that annoys you あなたをいらいらさせる人または物→手に負えない人・子供, 厄介物, 嫌な物 ‖ *That child is such a pest!* あの子は何て手に負えない子供だろう.

**pester** /péstɚr/ 動 他 ▶定義 pester sb (for sth); pester sb (to do sth) to annoy sb, for example by asking him/her sth many times 例えば何度も〜をせがんで, …をいらいらさせる→〜を困らせる, せがむ ‖ *to pester sb for money* 〜にお金をせがむ *The kids kept pestering me to take them to the park.* 子供たちは私に公園へ連れていってくれとせがんで, 私を困らせ続けた.

**pesticide** /péstəsàɪd/ 名 C U ▶定義 a chemical substance that is used for killing animals, especially insects, that eat food crops 動物, 特に農作物を食べる虫を殺すために使われる化学物質→殺虫剤 ☞参 insecticide

*__pet__ /pét/ 名 C ▶定義1 an animal or bird that you keep in your home for pleasure rather than for food or work 食用または仕事のためでなくむしろ楽しみのために, 自宅で飼っている動物または鳥→ペット, かわいがっている動物 ‖ *a pet dog/cat/hamster* ペットの犬・猫・ハムスター *a pet shop* (= *where pets are sold*) ペットショップ(=ペットが売られている店) ▶定義2 a person who is treated as a favourite お気に入りとして扱われている人→かわいがられている人, お気に入り ‖ *teacher's pet* 先生のお気に入り

**petal** /pétl/ 名 C ▶定義 one of the thin soft coloured parts of a flower 花の薄く柔らかい色の付いた部分の1枚→花びら, 花弁 ☞ C2 ページのさし絵

**peter** /píːtɚr/ 動
句動詞 peter out ▶定義 to slowly become smaller, quieter, etc and then stop ゆっくりとより小さく, より静かに, などとなってそして止まる→次第に消える, 尽きていく, 徐々に終わる

**pet hate** 名 C ▶定義 sth that you particularly do not like 中でも好きでない〜→(〜の)大嫌いなもの, しゃくの種 ‖ *Filling in forms is one of my pet hates.* 書類に記入することは, 私の大嫌いな事の1つだ.

**petition** /pətíʃ(ə)n/ 名 C ▶定義 a written document, signed by many people, that asks a government, etc to do or change sth 政府などに〜を行うようにまたは変えるように要求する, 多くの人々が署名した文書→請願・陳情・嘆願書 ‖ *More than 50000 people signed the petition protesting about the new road.* 5万人以上もの人々が, 新道路建設反対の嘆願書に署名した. — petition 動 自 他 →請願する, 陳情する

**petrified** /pétrəfàɪd/ 形 ▶定義 very frightened とてもおびえた→(〜に)すくみ上がった, おびえた

*__petrol__ /pétr(ə)l/ (米 **gas**; **gasoline**) 名 U ▶定義 the liquid that is used as fuel for vehicles such as cars and motorbikes 乗り物, 例えば車やバイクの燃料として使われる液体→ガソリン

## petroleum 1206

⇨参 diesel

**petroleum** /pətróuliəm/ 名 Ü ▶定義 mineral oil that is found under the ground or sea and is used to make petrol, plastic and other types of chemical substances 地中または海底で発見され、ガソリン、プラスチック、そのほかの種類の化学物質を製造するために使われる、鉱油→**石油, 鉱油**

**petrol station** (米**gas station**) 名 C ▶定義 a place where you can buy petrol and other things for your car ガソリンとそのほかの車用品が買える場所→**ガソリンスタンド, 給油所**
⇨参 garage

**petty** /péti/ 形 ▶定義 1 small and unimportant 小さくて重要でない→**取るに足らない、ささいな、つまらない** ‖ He didn't want to get involved with the petty details. 彼はそんなささいな事にかかわりたくなかった. petty crime/theft (= that is not very serious) 軽犯罪・ささいな窃盗(= あまり重大ではない) ▶定義 2 unkind or unpleasant to other people (for a reason that does not seem very important)(非常に重要であるとは思えない理由で)ほかの人々に対して不親切な、または不快→**心の狭い、狭量な** ‖ petty jealousy/revenge 心の狭さから起こるしっと・仕返し

**PG** /píː dʒíː/ 略 医 ▶定義 (used about films in which there are scenes that are unsuitable for children) parental guidance (子供たちにふさわしくない場面がある映画について)親の指導→**父母同伴(親の同伴で入場可能)**

**phantom** /fǽntəm/ 名 C ▶定義 1 (文) the spirit of a dead person that is seen or heard by sb who is still living まだ生きている人によって見られるまたは聞かれる、死んだ人の精神→**幽霊** ‖ ghost の方がより一般的な語である. ▶定義 2 something that you think exists, but that is not real 存在していると思うが、現実ではないもの→**幻、幻影、妄想**

**pharmaceutical** /fàːməs(j)úːtɪk(ə)l; -s(j)úː-/ 形 ▶定義 connected with the production of medicines and drugs 薬の製造に関する→**製薬の、薬剤の、薬学の** ‖ pharmaceutical companies 製薬会社

**pharmacist** /fáːməsɪst/ 名 = **CHEMIST**(1)

**pharmacy** /fáːməsi/ 名 ( 複 **pharmacies**)
▶定義 1 C a shop or part of a shop where medicines and drugs are prepared and sold 薬が調合されて売られる、店または店の一部→**薬屋、(ドラッグストアなどの)薬局**
▶薬を売る店は、英国では chemist's (shop)、また米国では drugstore とも呼ばれる.
▶定義 2 Ü the preparation of medicines and drugs 薬と薬剤の調合→**調剤、薬学**

★**phase**¹ /féɪz/ 名 C ▶定義 a stage in the development of sth ～の発達の段階→**段階、局面** ‖ Julie went through a difficult phase when she started school. ジュリーは学校に通い始めたころに、難しい段階を経験した.

**phase**² /féɪz/ 動
句動詞 **phase sth in** ▶定義 to introduce or start using sth gradually in stages over a period of time 時間をかけて段階的に、～をだんだんと導入するまたは使い始める→**～を段階的に導入する** ‖ The metric system was phased in over several years. メートル法は数年間かけて段階的に導入された.

**phase sth out** ▶定義 to stop using sth gradually in stages over a period of time 時間をかけて段階的に、～の使用をだんだんとやめる→**～を段階的に廃止する** ‖ The older machines are gradually being phased out and replaced by new ones. 古い機械はだんだんと段階的に廃止され、新しい物に置き換えられている.

**PhD** /píː eɪtʃ díː/ 略 Doctor of Philosophy
▶定義 an advanced university degree that you receive when you complete a piece of research into a special subject 特別なテーマの学術研究を完成させたときに、その人が得る大学の高い学位→**博士号** ‖ She has a PhD in History. 彼女は史学の博士号を持っている.

**pheasant** /féz(ə)nt/ 名 C ( 複 **pheasants** または **pheasant**) ▶定義 a type of bird with a long tail. The males have brightly coloured feathers. Pheasants are often shot for sport and eaten. 長い尾羽を持つ鳥の一種. 雄は明るい色の羽毛を持つ. しばしば狩猟のために撃たれて食べられる→**キジ**

**phenomenal** /fɪnάmənl/ 形 ▶定義 very great or impressive とてもすばらしいまたは感銘を与える→**並外れた、驚異的な、たぐいまれな** ‖ phenomenal success 驚異的な成功 — **phenomenally**

/-nli/ 副 ➔驚異的に,並外れて

**phenomenon** /fɪnάmənàn, -nən/ 名 ❻ (複 **phenomena** /-ənə, -ənὰː/) ▶定義 a fact or an event in nature or society, especially one that is not fully understood 自然界または社会での,事実または出来事で,特に十分理解されていないもの➔**現象,事象** ‖ *Acid rain is not a natural phenomenon. It is caused by pollution.* 酸性雨は自然現象ではありません.汚染が引き起こしているものです.

**phew** /fju:/ 間 ▶定義 a sound which you make to show that you are hot, tired or happy that sth bad did not happen or has finished 暑い,疲れた,あるいは悪い事が起こらなかったまたは悪い事が終わったので幸福だ,ということを示すために出す声➔**ふう,ひゃあ,ちえっ,やれやれ** ‖ *Phew, it's hot!* ひゃあ,暑い. *Phew, I'm glad that interview's over!* ふう,面接が終わってうれしいよ.

**philanthropist** /fəlǽnθrəpɪst/ 名 ❻ ▶定義 a rich person who helps the poor and those in need, especially by giving money 特にお金を与えるという方法で,貧しい人,困っている人を助ける金持ち➔**慈善家,篤志家,社会奉仕家**

**philosopher** /fəlάsəfər/ 名 ❻ ▶定義 a person who has developed a set of ideas and beliefs about the meaning of life 人生の意義についての思想と信条を発展させてきた人➔**哲学者,悟りを開いた人,達観した人**

**philosophical** /fìləsάfɪk(ə)l/ (または **philosophic**) 形 ▶定義 1 of or concerning philosophy 哲学の,または哲学に関する➔**哲学の,哲学に関する,哲学に通じている** ‖ *a philosophical debate* 哲学的な討論 ▶定義 2 philisophical (about sth) staying calm and not getting upset or worried about sth bad that happens 落ち着いていて,悪い事が起こることについてうろたえないまたは心配しない➔**達観した,淡々とした,あきらめのよい** ‖ *He is quite philosophical about failing the exam and says he will try again next year.* 彼は試験に落ちたことについてとても淡々としていて,また来年受けると言う. ― philosophically /-k(ə)li/ 副 ➔哲学的に,達観して,冷静に,あきらめよく

*****philosophy** /fəlάsəfi/ 名 (複 **philosophies**) ▶定義 1 ❶the study of ideas and beliefs about the meaning of life 人生の意義についての思想と信条の学問➔**哲学** ▶定義 2 ❻a set of beliefs that tries to explain the meaning of life or give rules about how to behave 人生の意義を説明しようとする,またはどのように振る舞うかについての規則を与えようとする信条➔**人生観,主義,持論** ‖ *Her philosophy is 'If a job's worth doing, it's worth doing well'.* 彼女の持論は「もし,することに価値のある仕事なら,それはうまくやるだけの価値がある」だ.

**phlegm** /flem/ 名 ❶ ▶定義 the thick substance that is produced in your nose and throat when you have a cold 風邪を引いたとき,鼻やのどで作られる濃い物質➔**たん**

**phlegmatic** /flegmǽtɪk/ 形 正式 ▶定義 not easily made angry or upset; calm 簡単には怒らない,または慌てない;落ち着いた➔**落ち着いた,冷静な**

**phobia** /fóʊbiə/ 名 ❻ (しばしば複合語で) ▶定義 a very strong fear or hatred that you cannot explain 説明できない,とても強い恐怖または嫌悪➔**病的恐怖,恐怖症** ‖ *arachnophobia (= fear of spiders)* クモ恐怖症(= クモへの恐怖)

*****phone** /fóʊn/ 名 略式 ▶定義 1 ❶ = TELE-PHONE(1) ‖ *a phone conversation* 電話での会話 *You can book the tickets **over the/by phone**.* 電話でチケットが予約できます. ▶定義 2 ❻=TELEPHONE(2) ‖ *The phone is ringing - could you answer it?* 電話が鳴っています ― 出ていただけますか. ― phone 動 ⾃ ⽤ ➔電話をかける,電話で話す;~に電話する ‖ *Did anybody phone while I was out?* 私がいない間,だれか電話してきましたか. *Could you phone the restaurant and book a table?* レストランに電話して,席を予約していただけますか.

◆類 **ring, call**

成句 **on the phone/telephone** ▶定義 1 using the telephone 電話を使っている➔**電話に出ている,電話で話している** ▶定義 2 having a telephone in your home 自宅に電話を持っている➔**電話を引いている** ‖ *I'll have to write to her because she's not on the phone.* 彼女の家には電話がないので,私は手紙を書かなくてはならない.

**phone book**=TELEPHONE DIRECTORY
**phone box** = TELEPHONE BOX
**phonecard** /fóʊnkὰːrd/ 名 ❻ ▶定義 a small plastic card that you can use to pay for calls in

a public telephone box 公衆電話で電話代を払うために使う, 小さなプラスチックのカード→テレホンカード ☛ telephone のさし絵

**phone-in** 名 C ▶定義 a radio or television programme during which you can ask a question or give your opinion by telephone 電話で質問するまたは意見を言うことのできる, ラジオやテレビの番組→視聴者参加番組

**phonetic** /fənétɪk/ 形 ▶定義 **1** connected with the sounds of human speech; using special symbols to represent these sounds 人間が話す音声に関連した; これらの音声を表現するために, 特別な記号を使っている→音声の, 音声学の ‖ the phonetic alphabet 音標文字 ▶定義 **2** (used about spelling) having a close relationship with the sounds represented (つづりについて) 表現された音と近い関係を持つ→音声・発音を表す ‖ Spanish spelling is phonetic, unlike English spelling. 英語のつづりとは違って, スペイン語のつづりは発音を表している. — phonetically /-k(ə)li/ 副 →音声学的に, 発音通りに

**phonetics** /fənétɪks/ 名 U ▶定義 the study of the sounds of human speech 人間が話す音声の学問→音声学

**phoney** (困 **phony**) /fóʊni/ 形 ▶定義 not real; false 本当でない; 間違った→にせの, いんちきな, 偽りの ‖ She spoke with a phoney Russian accent. 彼女はにせのロシアなまりで話した. — phoney (困 phony) 名 C →にせ物, 詐欺師, ペテン師

*****photo** /fóʊtoʊ/ 名 C ( 複 **photos** /-toʊz/) 略式 =PHOTOGRAPH

**photocopier** /fóʊtoʊkɑ̀piər/ 名 C ▶定義 a machine that makes copies of documents by photographing them 文書を写真に撮って, その写しを作る機械→コピー機, 写真複写機

**photocopy** /fóʊtoʊkɑ̀pi/ 名 ( 複 **photocopies**) ▶定義 a copy of a document, a page in a book, etc that is made by a special machine (a photocopier) 特別な機械 (コピー機) で作られた, 文書の 1 冊, 本の 1 ページなど→コピー, 複写 ☛類 Xerox ☛参 copy — photocopy 動 自他 (現分 photocopying; 三単現 photocopies; 過, 過分 photocopied) →コピーを取る, 複写する

*****photograph** /fóʊtoʊgrɑ̀ːf; -græ̀f/ (または **photo**) 名 C ▶定義 a picture that is taken with a camera カメラで撮られた写真→写真 ‖ to take a photograph 写真を撮る She looks younger in real life than she did in the photograph. 彼女は, 写真で見たときより実際の方が若く見える. ☛参 **negative, slide** — photograph 動他 →〜の写真を撮る

**photographer** /fətɑ́grəfər/ 名 C ▶定義 a person who takes photographs 写真を撮る人→カメラマン, 写真を撮る人, 写真家 ☛参 **cameraman**

**photographic** /fòʊtəgrǽfɪk/ 形 ▶定義 connected with photographs or photography 写真または写真撮影に関連した→写真の, 写真撮影 (用) の

**photography** /fətɑ́grəfi/ 名 U ▶定義 the skill or process of taking photographs 写真を撮る技術または過程→写真術, 写真撮影 (業)

**phrasal verb** /frèɪz(ə)l vɜ́ːrb/ 名 C ( 文 法 ) ▶定義 a verb that is combined with an adverb or a preposition to give a new meaning, such as 'look after' or 'put sb off' 副詞または前置詞と結合して新しい意味を持つ動詞, 例えば look after または put sb off→句動詞 ☛参 **verb**

*****phrase**¹ /fréɪz/ 名 C ( 文法 ) ▶定義 a group of words that are used together. A phrase does not contain a full verb. 一緒に使われる言葉のまとまり. 動詞は含まれない→句 ‖ 'First of all' and 'a bar of chocolate' are phrases. first of all と a bar of chocolate は句です. ☛参 **sentence**

**phrase**² /fréɪz/ 動他 ▶定義 to express sth in a particular way 特定の方法で〜を表現する→〜を言葉で表す, 〜を表現する ‖ The statement was phrased so that it would offend no one. その陳述はだれにも不快な感じを与えないようになされた.

**phrase book** 名 C ▶定義 a book that gives common words and useful phrases in a foreign language. People often use phrase books when they travel to another country whose language they do not know. 外国語の一般的な言葉と役に立つフレーズを載せた本. 言葉の分からない国を旅するとき, 人々はこの種の本をしばしば使う→(外国語の) 基本会話集, 慣用表現集

**\*physical** /fízɪk(ə)l/ 形 ▶定義1 connected with your body rather than your mind 心よりも体に関係した→**身体の, 肉体の** ‖ *physical fitness/strength/disabilities* 健康状態・体力・身体の障害 ▶定義2 (名詞の前だけ) connected with real things that you can touch, or with the laws of nature 自分が触れることのできる実在の物, あるいは自然の法則に関係した→**物質的な, 自然界の, 有形な** ‖ *physical geography (= the natural features on the face of the earth)* 自然地理学 (=地球の表面の自然の特徴) ▶定義3 (名詞の前だけ) connected with the study of natural forces (physics) and things that are not alive 自然の力の学問 (物理学) と生きていない物に関連した→**物理学 (上) の, 物理的な** ― physically /-k(ə)li/ 副→身体上, 物理的に, 実際に ‖ *to be physically fit* 体調が良い *It will be physically impossible to get to London before ten.* 10時までにロンドンに着くのは物理的に不可能です.

**physician** /fəzíʃ(ə)n/ 米 正式 = DOCTOR¹(1)

**physicist** /fíz(ə)sɪst/ 名 C ▶定義 a person who studies or is an expert in physics 物理学を勉強する, または物理学を専門とする人→**物理学者**

**\*physics** /fízɪks/ 名 U ▶定義 the scientific study of natural forces such as light, sound, heat, electricity, pressure, etc 自然の力, 例えば光, 音, 熱, 電気, 圧力などを研究する, 科学的な学問→**物理学**

**physiotherapist** /fìziouθérəpɪst/ 名 C ▶定義 a person who is trained to use physiotherapy 物理療法を使う訓練を受けた人→**物理療法医**

**physiotherapy** /fìziouθérəpi/ (米 **physical therapy**) 名 U ▶定義 the treatment of disease or injury by exercise, light, heat, rubbing the muscles (massage), etc 運動, 光, 熱, 筋肉をさすること (マッサージ) などによって, 病気またはけがを治療すること→**物理療法**

**physique** /fəzíːk/ 名 C ▶定義 the size and shape of a person's body 人の身体の大きさと体形→**(特に男性の) 体格, 体付き** ‖ *a strong muscular physique* 筋肉質の体格

**pianist** /piǽnɪst, píːə-; píːənɪst/ 名 C ▶定義 a person who plays the piano ピアノを弾く人→**ピアニスト, ピアノ演奏者**

**\*piano** /piǽnou, pjǽn-/ 名 C (複 **pianos** /-nouz/) ▶定義 a large musical instrument that you play by pressing down black and white keys 黒と白の鍵盤 (けんばん) を指で押して演奏する, 大きな楽器→**ピアノ** ‖ *an upright piano* アップライトピアノ *a grand piano* グランドピアノ
▶通常 play the piano, the violin, the guitar, etc と言うことに注意: *I've been learning the piano for four years.* (私はピアノを4年間習っています.) 現代音楽, 例えばジャズやロックなど, について話しているときは, play drums, guitar, etc と, the を付けないのが通常である: *He plays bass in a band.* (彼はバンドでベースを弾いている.) *This recording features Miles Davis on trumpet.* (このCDは, トランペットのマイルス デイビスを特集している.)

**\*pick¹** /pɪk/ 動 他 ▶定義1 to choose sb/sth from a group of people or things 人々または物の集団の中から~を選ぶ→**~を選ぶ, 選び取る, 選んで~させる** ‖ *I was upset not to be picked for the team.* チームの一員に選ばれなかったので, 私はおろおろしてしまった. *Have I picked a bad time to visit?* お訪ねするには時期が悪かったかしら. ▶定義2 to take a flower, fruit or vegetable from the place where it is growing 育っている場所から, 花, 果物, または野菜を取る→**~を摘む, 摘み取る, もぐ** ‖ *to pick flowers/grapes/cotton* 花を摘む・ぶどうをもぐ・綿を摘む ▶定義3 to remove a small piece or pieces of sth with your fingers ~の小さな1つの, または複数の片を指で取り除く→**~を抜き取る, 抜く, ~をむしり取る** ‖ *Don't pick your nose!* 鼻をほじらないで! *She picked a hair off her jacket.* 彼女はジャケットに付いた髪の毛を取った. ▶定義4 **pick your way across, over, through, etc sth** to walk carefully, choosing the best places to put your feet 足を置く一番良い場所を選びながら, 注意深く歩く→**道を選びながら進む, 道を拾っていく**

> ▶日本語 vs 英語
>
> 「ピックアップする」は pick out
>
> 「要点をピックアップする」は pick out main points であり pick up は用いません. 要点を「抽出する」ので out を用います. 一方, pick up はドにある物を「つまむ/拾い上げる」の意味に限られます. ここから発展して「車で拾う (=人を乗せる)」の意味で pick up を

## 1210　pick²

用います. Can you pick me up at the station?(駅で拾ってください.)反対の表現はI'll drop you off at the post office.(郵便局の所で降ろしてあげよう.)になります.

**成句** have a bone to pick with sb ⇒ **BONE**¹
**pick a fight (with sb)** ▶定義 to start a fight with sb deliberately わざと～と争いを始める→～にけんかを売る
**pick a lock** ▶定義 to open a lock without using a key かぎを使わないで,錠を開ける→錠前をこじ開ける
**pick and choose** ▶定義 to choose only the things that you like or want very much とても好きなもの,または欲しいものだけを選ぶ→念入りに選ぶ,より好みする
**pick sb's pocket** ▶定義 to steal money, etc from sb's pocket or bag ～のポケットまたはバッグから,お金などを盗む→～のふところをする,～にすりを働く
**句動詞** **pick at sth** ▶定義 1 to eat only small amounts of food because you are not hungry おなかがすいていないので,ほんの少量の食べ物を食べる→～をつつく,ついばむ,ちょっとだけ食べる ▶定義 2 to touch sth many times with your fingers 指で,～に何回も触れる→～をいじくる,つまむ,ひっぱる
**pick on sb** ▶定義 to behave unfairly or in a cruel way towards sb ～に対して不公平なまたはひどい態度を取る→～のあら捜しをする,～がみがみしかる,いじめる
**pick sb/sth out** ▶定義 to choose or recognize sb/sth from a number of people or things; identify 多数の人々または物から,～を選ぶまたは認識する;見分ける→～を見分ける,見つけ出す ‖ I immediately picked Jean out in the photo. 私はすぐに写真の中のジーンを見つけ出した.
**pick up** ▶定義 to become better; to improve 良くなる;進歩する→(元気・健康が)回復する,(景気・天候などが)良くなる
**pick sb up** ▶定義 to collect sb, in a car, etc 車などに乗って,～を迎えに行く→～を迎えに行く・来る ‖ We've ordered a taxi to pick us up at ten. 私たちは10時に迎えに来るようにタクシーを頼んだ.

**pick sb/sth up** ▶定義 1 to take hold of and lift sb/sth ～をつかんで持ち上げる→～を拾い上げる,拾う,取り上げる ‖ Lucy picked up the child and gave him a cuddle. ルーシーはその子供を抱き上げて抱き締めた. ▶定義 2 to receive an electronic signal, sound or picture 電気的な信号,音声,または画像を受け取る→～を受信・傍受する ‖ In the north of France you can pick up English television programmes. フランス北部では,イギリスのテレビ番組を受信できます.
**pick sth up** ▶定義 1 to learn sth without formal lessons 正式に勉強したわけでなく,～を習得する→(外国語など)を聞き覚える,身に付ける,(知識・情報など)を得る ‖ Joe picked up a few words of Spanish on holiday. ジョーは休暇中に2,3語のスペイン語を聞き覚えた. ▶定義 2 to get or find sth ～を得るまたは見つける→～を手に入れる,見つける,買う ‖ I picked up this book at the market. 私は市場でこの本を買った. ▶定義 3 to go and get sth; to collect sth 行って～を得る;集める→物を取りに行く・来る,取ってくる ‖ I have to pick up my jacket from the cleaner's. 私はクリーニング屋からジャケットを取ってこないといけない.

**pick²** /pɪk/ 名 ▶定義 1 [単数扱い]the one that you choose; your choice あなたが選ぶもの;選択→選ばれた人・物;選択(権),選ぶこと ‖ You can have whichever cake you like. **Take your pick.** どれでもお好きなケーキをどうぞ.ご自由に選んでください. ▶定義 2 [単数扱い]the best of a group ある集合体の中で最高のもの→えり抜き,最上のもの ‖ You can see **the pick of** the new films at this year's festival. 今年のフェスティバルで,最高の新作映画を見られます. ▶定義 3 (または **pickaxe** 米 **pickax** /píkæks/ ) ⓒ a tool that consists of a curved iron bar with sharp points at both ends, fixed onto a wooden handle. Picks are used for breaking stones or hard ground. 木の柄に固定された,鋭くとがった両端を持つ曲がった鉄の棒から成る道具.石または硬い地面を打ち砕くために使われる→つるはし

**picket** /píkət/ 名 ⓒ ▶定義 a worker or group of workers who stand outside the entrance to a building to protest about sth, especially in order to stop people entering a factory, etc during a strike ストライキの間, ～に抗議するため, 特に人々を工場などに入れないように, 建物の入り口の外に立つ, 労働者または労働者の集団→**ストライキの裏切り者・スト破りの監視員, ピケ, 見張り** — picket 動自他 ▶見張りをする;(スト中に)～の監視をする, ～にピケを張る

**pickle** /pík(ə)l/ 名 C U ▶定義 food such as fruit or vegetables that is put in salt water or another liquid (vinegar) so that it can be kept for a long time 長持ちするように, 塩水または別の液体(酢)に漬けられた食べ物, 例えば果物または野菜→**ピクルス, 漬物** — pickle 動他 ▶～を漬物にする ‖ pickled onions 漬物のタマネギ

**pickpocket** /píkpàkət/ 名 C ▶定義 a person who steals things from other people's pockets or bags in public places 公共の場所で他人のポケットまたはバッグから物を盗む人→**すり**

**pickup** /píkʌp/(または **pickup truck**) 名 C ▶定義 a type of vehicle that has an open part with low sides at the back 後部の側面が低く, 覆われていない, 乗り物の一種→**小型無蓋(むがい)トラック** ☞ vehicle のさし絵

**picky** /píki/ 形 略式 ▶定義 (used about a person) liking only certain things and difficult to please (人について)特定のものだけが好きで, 喜ばせることが難しい→**えり好みする, 好みがうるさい, 気難しい** ☞参 fussy

*__picnic__ /píknɪk/ 名 C ▶定義 a meal that you take with you to eat outdoors 戸外で食べようと持っていく食事→**野外での食事・会食** ‖ We had a picnic on the beach. 私たちは海辺でピクニックをした. — picnic 動自(現分 picnicking; 過, 過分 picnicked)→**野外で食事を楽しむ, ピクニックに行く**

**pictorial** /pɪktɔ́:riəl/ 形 ▶定義 expressed in pictures 絵に表されている→**絵の, 絵・写真で表した** ‖ pictorial representations of objects 物体の図解

*__picture__¹ /píktʃər/ 名 C ▶定義 1 a painting, drawing or photograph 絵の具でかかれた絵, 鉛筆などでかかれた絵, または写真→**絵, 写真** ‖ Who painted the picture in the hall? ホールにある絵はだれがかいたのですか. The teacher asked us to **draw a picture** of our families. 先生は私たちに家族の絵をかきなさいと言った. ▶定義 2 an image on a television screen テレビ画面の画像→**画像, 映像, 画面** ‖ They showed pictures of the crash on the news. ニュースで, その衝突の

**piece**¹  1211

映像を放送した. ▶定義 3 a description of sth that gives you a good idea of what it is like それがどんな風であるか, 人に正しい観念を与える, ～の描写→**生き生きとした描写, (心に描く)像, 観念** ‖ The police are trying to build up a picture of exactly what happened. 警察は, 正確には何が起こったのか, 考えを組み立てようとしている.

▶語法

a picture of my father playing golf

「父がゴルフをしている写真」はこのように, a picture of ＋名詞＋動詞のパターンで表し, *a picture that my father is playing golf のように接続詞 that を使って表現することはできません. したがって「ハイジャックされた飛行機がビルに突っ込む写真」は a picture of hijacked airplanes crashing into buildings のように表現します.

**picture**² /píktʃər/ 動他 ▶定義 1 picture sb/sth (as sth) to imagine sth in your mind ～を心の中で想像する→**～を心に描く, 想像する** ‖ I can't picture Ivan as a father. アイヴァンがお父さんだなんて想像できません. ▶定義 2 to make a picture of sb/sth ～の絵を作る→**～を絵にかく, 描写する** ‖ She is pictured here with her parents. 彼女は両親と一緒にここに描かれている.

**picturesque** /pìktʃərésk/ 形 ▶定義 (usually used about an old building or place) attractive (通常古い建物または場所について)魅力的な→**絵のように美しい** ‖ a picturesque fishing village 絵のように美しい漁村

*__pie__ /páɪ/ 名 C U ▶定義 a type of food consisting of fruit, meat or vegetables inside a pastry case 果実, 肉, または野菜を練り粉の包みの中に入れた, 食べ物の一種→**パイ** ‖ apple pie アップルパイ meat pie ミートパイ ☞ C4 ページのさし絵

*__piece__¹ /pí:s/ 名 C ▶定義 1 an amount or example of sth ～の量または例→**1つ, 1個, 1枚, 1切れ** ‖ a piece of paper 1枚の紙 a piece of furniture 1つの家具 a good piece of work 良い作品 a piece of advice/information/news あるアドバイス・情報・ニュース ▶定義 2 one of the parts that sth is made of ～が作られた, 部分の1つ→**一部分, 一片, 一部, 部品** ‖ We'll have to **take the** engine **to pieces** to find the problem. どこが悪いのか見つけるために、私たちはそのエンジンをばらばらに分解しなければならないでしょう．▶定義**3** one of the parts into which sth breaks ～が壊れてばらばらになった、その１つ→**一片、断片** ‖ The plate fell to the floor and smashed **to pieces**. お皿が床に落ちて粉々になった．The vase lay **in pieces** on the floor. 花びんが粉々になって床にあった．▶定義**4** a piece (on/about sb/sth) an article in a newspaper or magazine 新聞または雑誌の記事→**記事** ‖ There's a good piece on China in today's paper. 今日の新聞に中国についてのいい記事が載っている．▶定義**5** a single work of art, music, etc 芸術、音楽などの１つの作品→**芸術作品，小品** ‖ He played a piece by Chopin. 彼はショパンの作品を１曲演奏した．▶定義**6** one of the small objects that you use when you are playing games such as chess ゲーム、例えばチェスで、遊んでいるときに使う、小さな物の１つ→**(チェスなどの)駒(こま)** ▶定義**7** a coin of the value mentioned 言及された価値の硬貨→**貨幣，硬貨** ‖ a fifty-pence piece 50ペンス硬貨

成句 bits and pieces ⇒ **BIT**¹

give sb a piece of your mind ▶定義 to speak to sb angrily because of sth he/she has done ある人が行った事が原因で、その人に怒って言う→**～にずけずけと文句を言う，～をしかりつける**

go to pieces ▶定義 to be no longer able to work or behave normally because of a difficult situation 難しい状況が原因で、もはや正常に働けない、または振る舞えない→**ばらばらになる，(人が肉体的・精神的に)参ってしまう** ‖ When his wife died he seemed to go to pieces. 彼の妻が死んだ時、彼は参ってしまったようだった．

in one piece ▶定義 not broken or injured 壊れていない、または傷付いていない→**(物が)壊れないで，(人が)無事に** ‖ I've only been on a motorbike once, and I was just glad to get home in one piece. 一度だけオートバイに乗ったことがあります．無事に家に着いてうれしかったです．

a piece of cake 略式 ▶定義 something that is very easy とても簡単な事→**楽々とできる事**

**piece**² /piːs/ 動

句動詞 piece sth together ▶定義**1** to discover the truth about sth from different pieces of information いくつかの違った情報から、～についての事実を発見する→**(話など)をまとめ上げる，総合する** ‖ Detectives are trying to piece together the last few days of the man's life. 刑事たちはその男の人生の最後の数日間をまとめ上げようとしている．▶定義**2** to put sth together from several pieces いくつかの断片から～を組み立てる→**～をつなぎ合わせる，つなぎ合わせて作る**

**piecemeal** /ˈpiːsmiːl/ 形圖 ▶定義 done or happening a little at a time 一度に少し行われる、または起きている→**少しずつの，断片的な；少しずつ，断片的に**

**pie chart** 名 C ▶定義 a diagram consisting of a circle divided into parts to show the size of particular parts in relation to the whole 全体に対する特定の部分の大きさを示すために、複数の部分に分けられた円で構成される図表→**円グラフ** ● graph のさし絵

**pier** /pɪər/ 名 C ▶定義**1** a large wooden or metal structure that is built out into the sea from the shore. Boats can stop at piers so that people or goods can be taken on or off. 岸から海にせり出して建てられている、大きな木製または金属製の構造物．人々または品物が運び込まれるまたは運び出せるように、船がそこに停泊する→**埠頭(ふとう)，船着き場** ▶定義**2** (in Britain) a large wooden or metal structure that is built out into the sea in holiday towns, where people can walk (英国で)休暇村の海に建造された、人々が歩くことのできる、大きな木製または金属製の構造物→**桟橋** ☞ C8 ページのさし絵

**pierce** /pɪərs/ 動 ▶定義**1** 他 to make a hole in sth with a sharp point 鋭い先で～に穴を開ける→**～に穴を開ける，～を突き抜く，貫く** ‖ I'm going to **have** my ears **pierced**. 私は耳にピアスの穴を開けることにします．▶定義**2** 自他 pierce (through/into) sth to manage to go through or into sth 何とか～を通り抜けたり、～の中に入る→**(音や光が)入り込む；(光が暗闇(やみ)に)差し込む，(声などが静けさ)を破る** ‖ A scream pierced the air. 空気を裂いて悲鳴が聞こえた．

**piercing** /ˈpɪərsɪŋ/ 形 ▶定義**1** (used about the wind, pain, a loud noise, etc) strong and unpleasant (風、痛み、騒音などについて)強くて不快な→**身を切るような，刺すような，耳をつん**

ざくような ▶定義2 (used about sb's eyes or a look) seeming to know what you are thinking (〜の目付きまたは表情について) 人が何を考えているか知っているようで→(物事を)見通すような

**piety** /páɪəti/ 名 U ▶定義 a way of behaving that shows a deep respect for God and religion 神と宗教への深い尊敬を示す振る舞い方→敬虔(けいけん)さ, 信心深さ, 信仰心 ☛ 形 **pious**

★**pig**¹ /pɪɡ/ 名 C ▶定義1 a fat pinkish animal with short legs and a short tail that is kept on farms for its meat (pork) その肉(ポーク)のために農場で飼われている, 短い脚と短いしっぽを持つ, 太ったピンク色の動物→豚

▶雄の豚はboar, 雌の豚はsow, 子豚はpigletである. 音を立てることを, 豚はgrunt(ぶうぶう鳴く)と言い, 子豚はsqueal(キーキー鳴く)と言う. meatの注を参照.

▶定義2 略式 an unpleasant person or a person who eats too much 不快な人または食べすぎる人→意地汚い人, 薄い人, 欲深な人

**pig**² /pɪɡ/ 動自 (**pigging**; **pigged**) (俗語) ▶定義 pig yourself to eat too much 食べすぎる→大食いする

句動詞 pig out (on sth) (俗語) ▶定義 to eat too much of sth 〜を食べすぎる→〜をがつがつ大食いする

**pigeon** /píʤən/ 名 C ▶定義 a fat grey bird that often lives in towns しばしば街に生息する, 太った灰色の鳥→ハト

**pigeon-hole** 名 C ▶定義 one of a set of small open boxes that are used for putting papers or letters in 書類または手紙を入れておくために使われる, 一組の小さなふたのない箱の1つ→区分け棚, 整理棚

**piggyback** /pígibæk/ 名 C ▶定義 the way of carrying sb, especially a child, on your back 〜を, 特に子供を, 背負って運ぶ方法→肩車, おんぶ ‖ to give sb a piggyback 〜を肩車する

**piggy bank** 名 C ▶定義 a small box, often shaped like a pig, that children save money in 子供がお金をその中にためる, しばしば豚のような形をした, 小さな箱→子豚の形の貯金箱, 貯金箱

**pig-headed** 形 略式 ▶定義 not prepared to change your mind or say that you are wrong 自分の考えを変える, または自分が悪かったと言う覚悟ができていない→頑固な, 強情な, つむじ曲がりの ☛ 参 **stubborn**, **obstinate**

**piglet** /pígləf/ 名 C ▶定義 a young pig→子豚

**pigment** /pígmənt/ 名 C U ▶定義 a substance that gives colour to things 物に色を与える物質→絵の具, 顔料, 色素 ‖ The colour of your skin depends on the amount of pigment in it. 肌の色はその中にある色素の量によります.

**pigsty** /pígstaɪ/ (または **sty** 米 **pigpen**) 名 C (複 **pigsties**) ▶定義 a small building where pigs are kept 豚が飼われている, 小さな建物→豚小屋

**pigtail** /pígteɪl/ (米 **braid**) 名 C ▶定義 hair that is tied together in one or two thick pieces made by putting (plaiting) three pieces of hair in and out of each other 3つの髪の束を交互に中に入れたり出したりして(編むこと), 1つまたは2つの太い束にまとめて結んだ, 髪の毛→三つ編み, お下げ髪 ☛ **hair** のさし絵

★**pile**¹ /paɪl/ 名 C ▶定義1 a number of things lying on top of one another, or an amount of sth lying in a mass 同じ種類の別の物の上に置いてあるかなりの物, またはごちゃごちゃになって置いてある〜の量→積み重ね, 〜の山 ‖ a pile of books/sand 本・砂の山 He put the coins *in* neat *piles*. 彼は硬貨をきちんと積み重ねた. She threw the clothes *in a pile* on the floor. 彼女は衣服を床の衣服の山に投げ付けた.

▶pileは整とんされているかもしれないし, あるいは乱雑かもしれない. heapは乱雑である.

▶定義2 (通常は複数) 略式 piles of sth a lot of sth たくさんの〜 →山積み ‖ I've got *piles of* work to do this evening. 今夜しなくてはならない仕事が山積みだ. ▶定義3 piles = **HAEMORRHOIDS**

**pile**² /paɪl/ 動他 ▶定義1 pile sth (up) to put things one on top of the other to form a pile 山を作るために, ほかの物の上に物を置く→〜を積み重ねる, 山と積む ‖ We piled the boxes in the corner. 私たちは隅に箱を積み重ねた. ▶定義2 pile A on(to) B; pile B with A to put a lot of sth on top of sth 〜の上にたくさんの…を置く→AをBに積み上げる ‖ She piled the papers on the desk. 彼女は書類を机の上に積み上げた. *The desk was piled with papers.* 机の上には書類が積み上げられていた.

## 1214 pile-up

**句動詞** pile into, out of, off, etc sth **略式** ▶定義 to go into, out of, off, etc sth quickly and all at the same time 素早く，みんなが同時に～の中に入る，～から出る，～から立ち去るなど→どやどやと入る・出る・立ち去る・移動する ‖ *The children piled onto the bus.* 子供たちがどやどやとバスに乗った．

pile up ▶定義 (used about sth bad) to increase in quantity (悪い物事について) 多量に増える→(難問・赤字などが) 累積する ‖ *Our problems are really piling up.* 私たちの問題は本当に山積みになっている．

**pile-up** 名 C ▶定義 a crash that involves several cars, etc 数台の車などを巻き込む衝突→玉突き衝突

**pilgrim** /pílgrəm/ 名 C ▶定義 a person who travels a long way to visit a religious place 宗教的な場所を訪れるために，長い道のりを旅する人→巡礼者

**pilgrimage** /pílgrəmɪdʒ/ 名 C U ▶定義 a long journey that a person makes to visit a religious place 宗教的な場所を訪れるために，人がする長い旅→巡礼，聖地巡り

**pill** /pɪl/ 名 ▶定義 **1** C a small round piece of medicine that you swallow 人が飲み込む，小さな丸い薬→丸薬，錠剤 ‖ *Take one pill, three times a day after meals.* 1日3回食後に1錠飲みなさい．*a sleeping pill* 睡眠薬 ☛参 **tablet** ☛ **bandage** のさし絵 ▶定義 **2 the pill** [単数扱い] a pill that some women take regularly so that they do not become pregnant 妊娠しないように，一部の女性たちが定期的に飲む薬→経口避妊薬，ピル ‖ *She is on the pill.* 彼女はピルを常用している．

**pillar** /pílər/ 名 C ▶定義 **1** a column of stone, wood or metal that is used for supporting part of a building 建物の一部を支えるために使われる，石，木，または金属の柱→柱，支柱 ▶定義 **2** a person who has a strong character and is important to sb/sth 強い性格を持ち，～にとって重要な人→中心人物，大黒柱 ‖ *Dave was a pillar of strength to his sister when she was ill.* デーブの妹が病気になった時，デーブは妹にとって頼りになる人だった．

**pillar box** 名 C ▶定義 (in Britain) a tall round red box in a public place into which you can post letters, which are then collected by sb from the post office (英国で) そこに手紙を投かんし，後で郵便局から来た～によって集められる，公共の場所にある高い丸い赤い箱→(柱状の) 郵便ポスト ☛参 **postbox, letter box**

**pillion** /píljən/ 名 C ▶定義 a seat for a passenger behind the driver on a motorbike オートバイの運転者の後ろの乗客用の席→後部座席 ― **pillion** 副→後部に，後部座席に ‖ *to ride pillion on a motorbike* バイクの後ろに相乗りする

*****pillow** /píloʊ/ 名 C ▶定義 a large cushion that you put under your head when you are in bed ベッドに寝ているとき頭の下に置く，大きなクッション→まくら ☛ **bed** のさし絵

**pillowcase** /píloʊkeɪs/ 名 C ▶定義 a thin soft cover for a pillow まくら用の薄い柔らかいカバー→まくらカバー

*****pilot**¹ /páɪlət/ 名 C ▶定義 a person who flies an aircraft 飛行機を飛ばす人→パイロット，操縦士 ‖ *an airline pilot* 飛行機の操縦士

**pilot**² /páɪlət/ 動 他 ▶定義 **1** to operate the controls of a vehicle, especially an aircraft or a boat 乗り物，特に飛行機または船の操縦装置を操作する→～を操縦する，～のパイロットを務める ‖ *to pilot a ship* 船を操縦する ▶定義 **2** to lead sb/sth through a difficult situation ～を困難な状況の初めから終わりまで導く→～の水先案内をする，案内する，指導する ‖ *The booklet pilots you through the process of starting your own business.* その小冊子は自分で商売を始める過程の初めから終わりまでを紹介しています．

▶定義 **3** to be the first to test sth that will be used by everyone 将来みんなに使われる～を試す1回目である→～を試験的に行う ‖ *The new exam is being piloted in schools in Italy.* その新しい試験はイタリアの学校で試験的に行われています．

**pilot**³ /páɪlət/ 形 (名詞の前だけ) ▶定義 done as an experiment or to test sth that will be used by everyone 将来みんなに使われる～を，実験としてまたは試すために行われた→試験的な，実験的な，予備的な ‖ *The pilot scheme will run for six months.* その試験的な計画は6か月行われる．

**pimple** /pímp(ə)l/ 名 C ▶定義 a small spot on your skin 肌の小さな出来物→にきび，吹き出物

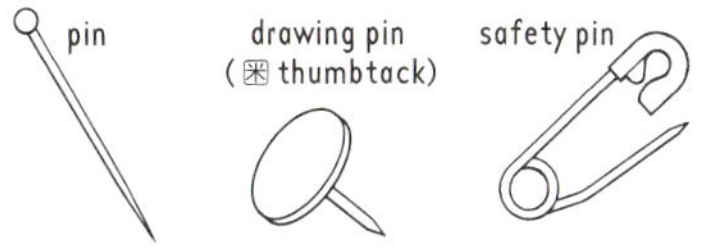


***pin**[1] /pɪn/ [名] [C] ▶定義1 a short thin piece of metal with a round head at one end and a sharp point at the other. Pins are used for fastening together pieces of cloth, paper, etc. 一方の端に丸い頭が, 他方の端に鋭い先が付いた短くて細い金属. 衣服, 紙などを一まとめにするために使われる ➜**ピン, 留め針** ▶定義2 a thin piece of wood or metal that is used for a particular purpose 特定の目的に使われる, 細い木片または金属片 ➜**飾りピン, 留め具·くぎ, 洗濯ばさみ** ‖ *a hairpin* ヘアピン *a two-pin plug* ピンが2本付いたプラグ ☛ **plug** のさし絵

**pin**[2] /pɪn/ [動] [他] (**pinning**; **pinned**) ▶定義1 **pin sth to/on sth**; **pin sth together** to fasten sth with a pin or pins 1本または複数のピンで～を留める ➜**ピンで留める, 画びょうで留める** ‖ *Could you pin this notice on the board, please?* このお知らせを掲示板に画びょうで留めていただけますか. ▶定義2 **pin sb/sth against, to, under, etc sth** to make sb/sth unable to move by holding or pressing down on him/her/it ～を抱えるまたは押し倒すことで, それを動けなくさせる ➜**動かないようにする, 押さえ付ける** ‖ *He caught his brother and pinned him to the floor.* 彼は弟を捕まえ, 床に押さえ付けた. *He was pinned under the fallen tree.* 彼は倒れた木の下敷きになって動けなかった.

[成句] **pin (all) your hopes on sb/sth** ▶定義 to believe completely that sb/sth will help you or will succeed ～が自分を助けてくれる, または～が成功すると完全に信じている ➜**～に運命を託す, 望みをかける**

[句動詞] **pin sb down** ▶定義1 to hold sb so he/she cannot move ～が動けないように抱える ➜**動かないようにする, くぎ付けにする** ▶定義2 to force sb to decide sth or to say exactly what he/she is going to do ～に…を決定させる, または何をしようとしているのか正確に言わせる ➜**～をのっ引きならないところへ追い込む, 考えをはっきり言わせる** ‖ *Can you pin her down to what time she'll be coming?* 何時に来るのか, 彼女にはっきりした返事をさせてもらえますか.

**pin sth down** ▶定義 to describe or explain exactly what sth is ～が何であるか正確に描写するまたは説明する ➜**～の正体を突き止める, はっきりさせる, 明言する**

**PIN**[3] /pɪn/ (または **PIN number**) [名] [[C], 通常は単数] ▶定義 personal identification number; a number given to you by your bank so that you can use a plastic card to take out money from a cash machine personal identification number のこと; 現金支払機からお金を引き出すためのプラスチックのカードを人が使えるように, 銀行から人に与えられる番号 ➜**暗証番号**

**pincer** /pínsər/ [名] ▶定義1 **pincers** [複数扱い] a tool made of two crossed pieces of metal that is used for holding things, pulling nails out of wood, etc 物をつかむ, 木材からくぎを抜く, などに使われる, 2つの交差する金属で作られた道具 ➜**やっとこ, くぎ抜き** ▶定義2 [C] one of the two sharp, curved front legs of some shellfish that are used for holding things 物をつかむために使われる, ある種の甲殻類の2本の鋭い, 曲がった前足の1本 ➜**はさみ** ☛ **shellfish** のさし絵

**pinch**[1] /pɪntʃ/ [動] ▶定義1 [他] to hold a piece of sb's skin tightly between your thumb and first finger, especially in order to hurt him/her 特に人に痛みを与えようとして, 親指と人差し指の間に～の皮膚をしっかりとつかむ ➜**～をつねる, 挟む** ‖ *Paul pinched his brother and made him cry.* ポールは自分の弟をつねって泣かせた. ☛ S6ページのさし絵 ▶定義2 [自] [他] to hold sth too tight, often causing pain きつすぎるほどに, しばしば傷みを伴うほどに, ～をつかむ ➜**～を締め付ける** ‖ *I've got a pinched nerve in my neck.* 私の首の神経が締め付けられている. ▶定義3 [他] [略式] to steal 盗む ➜**～を盗む, くすねる** ‖ *Who's pinched my pen?* 私のペンをくすねたのはだれ.

**pinch**[2] /pɪntʃ/ [名] [C] ▶定義1 the holding of sb's skin tightly between your finger and thumb 指と親指の間に～の皮膚をしっかりとつかむこと ➜**つねること, 挟むこと** ‖ *She gave him a little pinch on the arm.* 彼女は彼の腕を軽くつねった. ▶定義2 the amount of sth that you can pick

P

up with your thumb and first finger 親指と人差し指で拾い上げられる〜の量→一つまみ,少量 ‖ *a pinch of salt* 塩を一つまみ

**成句** **at a pinch** ▶定義 used to say that sth can be done if it is really necessary 本当に必要なら,〜は行われることができると言うために用いて→いざというときには,差し迫ったときには ‖ *We really need three cars but we could manage with two at a pinch.* 実際は3台の車が必要ですが,いざというときには2台で何とかできるでしょう.

**take sth with a pinch of salt** ▶定義 to think that sth is probably not true or accurate 〜が多分,事実または正確ではないと考える→話半分に聞く,(話を)割り引いて聞く

**pinched** /pɪntʃt/ 形 ▶定義 (used about sb's face) thin and pale because of illness or cold (〜の顔について)病気または寒さのため,やせて青白い→やつれた,青白い

**pine**¹ /páɪn/ 名 ▶定義 **1** C (または **pine tree**) a tall tree that has thin sharp leaves (needles) 高い木で細くとがった葉(針葉)をつける,高い木→マツ,松の木

▶ 冬に葉が落ちない,マツのような樹木は, evergreen(常緑樹)と言われる.

▶定義 **2** U the wood from pine trees (which is often used for making furniture) 松の木から取れる木材(しばしば家具を作るために用いられる)→松材 ‖ *a pine table* 松材のテーブル

**pine**² /páɪn/ 動 自 ▶定義 **pine (for sb/sth)** to be very unhappy because sb has died or gone away 〜が死んでしまった,または立ち去ってしまったので,とても不幸である→思いこがれる,(〜を)切望する ‖ *The dog sat outside, pining for its owner.* 飼い主を思いこがれながら,その犬は外に座っていた.

**pineapple** /páɪnæp(ə)l/ 名 C U ▶定義 a large sweet fruit that is yellow inside and has a thick brown skin with sharp points. Pineapples grow in hot countries. 内側は黄色く,鋭い先がいくつもある厚い茶色の皮で覆われた,大きな甘い果物.熱帯の国々で育つ→パイナップル ☞ C3ページのさし絵

**ping** /pɪŋ/ 名 C ▶定義 a short high noise that is made by a small bell or by a metal object hitting against sth 小さな鐘または金属の物が〜と当たって鳴る,短くて高い音→ピシッ,ピューンという音 ‖ *The lift went ping and the doors opened.* そのエレベーターはピューンという音がしてドアが開いた. ― **ping** 動 自 →ピシッ・ピューンという音を立てる

**ping-pong** 略式 = **TABLE TENNIS**

*****pink** /pɪŋk/ 形 名 U ▶定義 (of) a pale red colour 薄い赤い色(の)→ピンクの,桃色の,薄赤色の; ピンク,桃色,薄赤色

**pinnacle** /pínək(ə)l/ 名 C ▶定義 **1** the most important or successful part of sth 〜の最も重要なまたは成功している部分→頂点,絶頂 ‖ *Celia is at the pinnacle of her career.* シーリアは自分の経歴の頂点にいる. ▶定義 **2** a high pointed rock on a mountain 山の上の先のとがった高い岩→頂上,峰

**pinpoint** /pínpɔɪnt/ 動 他 ▶定義 **1** to find the exact position of sth 〜の正確な位置を見つける→〜の位置・本質を正確に指摘・記述する,突き止める ‖ *to pinpoint a place on the map* 地図上に場所を突き止める ▶定義 **2** to describe or explain exactly what sth is 〜が何であるか正確に描写するまたは説明する→正確に指摘する ‖ *First we have to pinpoint the cause of the failure.* まず,私たちは失敗の原因を正確に指摘しなければなりません.

**pins and needles** 名 [複数扱い] ▶定義 a strange, sometimes painful feeling that you get in a part of your body after it has been in one position for too long and when the blood is returning to it 身体の一部を長すぎる間同じ姿勢にしていた後,血液がそこへ戻っているときに感じる,変な,時々痛い感じ→ぴりぴり・ちくちくする感じ

*****pint** /páɪnt/ 名 C ▶定義 **1** (略 **pt**) a measure of liquid; 0.57 of a litre. There are 8 pints in a gallon. 液体の測定単位.0.57リットル.1ガロンは8パイント→パイント ‖ *a pint of milk* 1パイントの牛乳 ☞ 米国では1パイントは0.47リットルである. ▶定義 **2** 英略式 a pint of beer ビール1パイント→1パイントのビール

**pin-up** 名 C 略式 ▶定義 a picture of an attractive person, made to be put on a wall; a person who appears in these pictures 壁に張るように作られた,魅力的な人の写真; これらの写真に写っている人→ピンナップ; ピンナップのモデル,ピ

**pioneer** /pàiəníər/ 名 ● ▶定義1 a pioneer (in/of sth) a person who is one of the first to develop an area of human knowledge, culture, etc 人間の知識, 文化などの領域を開拓した最初の人々の1人→**先駆者, 創始者, 草分け** ‖ *Yuri Gagarin was one of the pioneers of space exploration.* ユーリー ガガーリンは宇宙探検の先駆者たちの1人だった. ▶定義2 a person who is one of the first to go and live in a particular area 特定の地域に行って住んだ最初の人々の1人→**開拓者** ‖ *the pioneers of the American West* アメリカ西部の開拓者たち — pioneer 動 ⾃他 ⽤ →**開拓者となる, 率先する; ～を開拓する** ‖ *a technique pioneered in the US* アメリカで開拓された技術

**pious** /páiəs/ 形 ▶定義 having or showing a deep belief in religion 宗教への深い信仰を持っている, または表している→**信心深い, 敬虔(けいけん)な** — piously 副 →**信心深く, 敬虔に** ☞ 名 piety

**pip** /pɪp/ 名 ● 英 ▶定義 the small seed of an apple, a lemon, an orange, etc リンゴ, レモン, オレンジなどの小さな種→**種** ☞ C3 ページのさし絵

*__pipe__*¹ /páip/ 名 ● ▶定義1 a tube that carries gas or liquid 気体または液体を送る管→**管, パイプ** ‖ *Waste water is carried away down the drainpipe.* 汚水は排水管を通って運び去られる.
▶定義2 a tube with a small bowl at one end that is used for smoking tobacco たばこを吸うために使われる, 片方の端に小さな火皿が付いている管→**パイプ** ‖ *to smoke a pipe* 一服吸う
▶定義3 a simple musical instrument that consists of a tube with holes in it. You blow into it to play it. 穴の開いた管で成り立っている, 構造が簡単な楽器. 演奏するために, 人はそれに息を吹き込む→**笛, 管楽器**

**pipe**² /páip/ 動 他 ▶定義 to carry liquid or gas in pipes 管の中の液体または気体を送る→**～を管・パイプで送る, 管・パイプで運ぶ** ‖ *Water is piped to all the houses in the village.* 水はその村のすべての家へパイプで送られています.

句動詞 pipe up ▶定義 to suddenly say sth 突然～を言う→**急に話し・歌い出す** ‖ *Suddenly Shirin piped up with a question.* 突然シリンが質問し始めた.

**pipeline** /páiplàin/ 名 ● ▶定義 a line of pipes that are used for carrying liquid or gas over a long distance 液体または気体を長い距離にわたって送るために使われる, 管の列→**輸送管, パイプライン**

成句 in the pipeline ▶定義 being planned or prepared 計画されている, または準備されている→**輸送中で, (法律・改革などが) 準備・進行中で**

**piper** /páipər/ 名 ● ▶定義 a person who plays music on a pipe, or who plays a musical instrument that is typical in Scotland (the bagpipes) 笛で音楽を演奏する, またはスコットランドの典型的な楽器 (バグパイプ) を演奏する人→**笛吹き, バグパイプ奏者**

**piracy** /páiərəsi/ 名 ⓤ ▶定義1 the crime of attacking ships in order to steal from them 盗むために船を攻撃する犯罪→**海賊行為** ▶定義2 the illegal copying of books, video tapes, etc 本, ビデオテープなどを不法にコピーすること→**著作権・特許権侵害, 違法コピー**

**pirate**¹ /páiərət/ 名 ● ▶定義1 (usually in the past or in stories) a criminal who attacks ships in order to steal from them (通常は過去, または物語において) 盗むために船を攻撃する犯罪者→**海賊, 略奪者** ▶定義2 a person who copies books, video tapes, computer programs, etc in order to sell them illegally 不法に販売するために, 本, ビデオテープ, コンピューターのプログラムなどをコピーする人→**著作権・特許権侵害者**

**pirate**² /páiərət/ 動 他 ▶定義 to make an illegal copy of a book, video tape, etc in order to sell it 販売するために, 本, ビデオテープなどの不法なコピーを作る→**～の著作権を侵害する, 海賊版を作る**

**Pisces** /páisiːz, písiːz, pískèis/ 名 ● ⓤ ▶定義 the twelfth sign of the zodiac, the Fishes 黄道十二宮の12番目である魚座→**魚座, 双魚宮**

**pistol** /pístl/ 名 ● ▶定義 a small gun that you hold in one hand 片手で握れる小型の銃→**ピストル** ☞ 参 gun の注

**piston** /pístən/ 名 ● ▶定義 a piece of metal in an engine, etc that fits tightly inside a tube (shaft). The piston is moved up and down inside the tube and causes other parts of the engine to move. 管 (シャフト) の内部にぴった

り収まる,エンジンなどの中の金属の小片.管の中を上下に動いて,エンジンのほかの部分を動かす→ピストン

**pit**¹ /pɪt/ 名 ▶定義1 ❻a large hole that is made in the ground 地面に作られた大きな穴→穴,くぼみ ‖ *They dug a large pit to bury the dead animals.* 死んだ動物を埋めるために,彼らは大きな穴を掘った. ▶定義2 = COAL MINE ▶定義3 **the pits**[複数扱い] the place on a motor racing track where cars stop for fuel, new tyres, etc during a race 競技中に車が燃料,新しいタイヤなどのために止まる,自動車競技場にある場所→修理場,ピット

成句 **be the pits**(俗語) ▶定義 to be very bad とても悪い→最低・最悪である ‖ *The food in that restaurant is the pits!* そのレストランの食事は最悪だ.

**pit**² /pɪt/ 動 ⊕ (**pitting**; **pitted**) ▶定義 to make small holes in the surface of sth 〜の表面に小さな,複数の穴を作る→〜に穴を開ける,〜をあばたにする ‖ *The front of the building was pitted with bullet marks.* 建物の正面は弾痕で穴だらけだった.

句動詞 **pit A against B** ▶定義 to test one person or thing against another in a fight or competition 争いまたは試合で,1人または1つの物が別のものと張り合う→AをBと戦わせる・対抗させる,BとAを争う ‖ *The two strongest teams were pitted against each other in the final.* 最強の2チームは決勝戦で互いに戦った.

**pitch**¹ /pɪtʃ/ 名 ▶定義1 ❻医 a special area of ground where you play certain sports ある決まったスポーツを競技する,特定の地面の区域→競技場 ‖ *a football/hockey/cricket pitch* サッカー競技場・ホッケー競技場・クリケット競技場 ▶court, field と比較.

▶定義2 [単数扱い] the strength or level of feelings, activity, etc 感情,活動などの強さ,または水準→程度,調子 ‖ *The children's excitement almost reached fever pitch.* 子供たちの興奮はほとんど熱狂的な程度に達していた. ▶定義3 ❻ how high or low a sound is, especially a musical note どの程度音,特に楽音,が高いまたは低いか→高さ,調子 ▶定義4 ❻ talk or arguments used by sb who is trying to sell sth or persuade sb to do sth 〜を売ろうと,または〜を説得させて…をさせようとしている〜によって使われる話または主張→(商品の)強引な売り込み(口上),宣伝文句 ‖ *a sales pitch* 売り込み口調 *to make a pitch for sth* 〜を強引に売り込む

**pitch**² /pɪtʃ/ 動 ▶定義1 ⊕ to set sth at a particular level 特定の水準に〜を定める→(音・曲など)をある高さに決める,(話・声などの)調子・レベルを決める ‖ *The talk was pitched at people with far more experience than me.* その談話は私よりもさらに経験ある人たちのレベルに合わせてあった. *a high-pitched voice* 甲高い声 ▶定義2 ⊜ ⊕ to throw sth/sb; to be thrown 〜を投げる;投げられる→投げる,投球する;〜を投げる,投げ入れる[込む] ‖ *Doug pitched his can into the bushes.* ダグはやぶの中に缶をほうり投げた. ▶定義3 ⊕ to put up a tent or tents 1つまたは複数のテントを張る→〜を張る,設営する,(くいなど)を立てる ‖ *They pitched their tents in the valley.* 彼らはテントを谷に張った. ▶定義4 **pitch sth (at sb)** to try to sell a product to a particular group of people or in a particular way 特定の人々の集団に,または特定の方法で商品を売ろうとする→(表現など)を(相手に合わせて)調節・加減する,〜の調子・レベルを合わせる ‖ *This new breakfast cereal is being pitched at kids.* この新しい朝食用シリアルは子供の味覚に合わせてある.

句動詞 **pitch in** 略式 ▶定義 to join in and work together with other people ほかの人々に加わって一緒に働く→援助する,協力する ‖ *Everybody pitched in to clear up the flood damage.* 洪水の被害を片付けるために,すべての人が協力した.

**pitch-black** 形 ▶定義 completely dark; with no light at all 真っ暗闇(やみ);全く光がない→真っ暗闇の,真っ黒の

**pitcher** /ˈpɪtʃər/ 名 ❻ ▶定義1 a large container for holding and pouring liquids 液体を入れてつぐための大きな容器→水差し ☛ **jug** のさし絵 ▶定義2 (in baseball) the player who throws (**pitches**) the ball to a player from the other team, who tries to hit it (野球で)ボールを打とうとする相手チームの選手に向かって,ボールを投げる(投球する)選手→投手,ピッチャー

**piteous** /ˈpɪtiəs/ 形 正式 ▶定義 that makes you feel pity or sadness 哀れに,または悲しく感じさせる→哀れな,痛ましい,悲しげな — **piteously**

副 ➡哀れに, 悲惨な様子で

**pitfall** /pítfɔːl/ 名 C ▶定義 a danger or difficulty, especially one that is hidden or not obvious 特に隠れているまたは明らかでない, 危険または困難➡落とし穴, 隠れた危険, 陥りやすい誤り

**pith** /píθ/ 名 U ▶定義 the white substance inside the skin of an orange, lemon, etc オレンジ, レモンなどの皮の内側の白い物➡中果皮

**pithy** /píθi/ 形 ▶定義 expressed in a clear, direct way 明白で直接的に表現された➡きびきびした, 簡にして要を得た, 核心を突いた ‖ *a pithy comment* 核心を突いた意見

**pitiful** /pítɪfəl/ 形 ▶定義 causing you to feel pity or sadness 哀れに, または悲しく感じさせる➡哀れな, かわいそうな, 惨めな ‖ *the pitiful groans of the wounded soldiers* 傷付いた兵士たちの哀れなうめき声 ― pitifully /-fəli/ 副 ➡哀れなほど, 惨めに

**pitiless** /pítɪləs/ 形 ▶定義 having or showing no pity for other people's suffering ほかの人々の苦しみに同情しないまたは同情を示さない➡無情な, 冷酷な, 容赦のない ― pitilessly 副 ➡無情に, 冷酷に

\***pity**¹ /píti/ 名 ▶定義 **1** Ⓤ a feeling of sadness that you have for sb/sth that is suffering or in trouble 苦しんでいるまたは困っている〜への悲しみの感情➡哀れみ, 同情 ‖ *The situation is his fault so I don't feel any pity for him.* そうなったのは彼が悪いので, 私は彼に同情しない.
▶定義 **2** [単数扱い] something that makes you feel a little sad or disappointed ちょっと悲しませる, または落胆させるもの➡残念な事, 気の毒な・惜しい事 ‖ *You're too late. Emily left five minutes ago.' 'Oh, what a pity!'* 「遅すぎたね. エミリーは5分も前に行ってしまいましたよ」「ああ, 残念だ」 *It's a pity that Bina couldn't come.* ビナが来られなかったとは残念だ.

成句 **take pity on sb** ▶定義 to help sb who is suffering or in trouble because you feel sorry for him/her 気の毒に思うので, 苦しんでいるまたは困っている〜を助ける➡〜を気の毒・かわいそうに思って手を貸す, 助ける

**pity**² /píti/ 動 他 (現分 **pitying**; 三単現 **pities**; 過, 過分 **pitied**) ▶定義 to feel pity or sadness for sb who is suffering or in trouble 苦しんでいるまたは困っている〜に哀れまたは悲しみを感じる➡〜をかわいそうに思う, 気の毒に思う, 〜に同情する ‖ *We shouldn't just pity these people; we must help them.* 私たちはこの人たちを気の毒に思うだけではいけません. 私たちは彼らを助けなければなりません.

**pivot**¹ /pívət/ 名 C ▶定義 **1** the central point on which sth turns or balances 〜が回転するまたは釣り合いを保つ, 中心点➡回転軸, ピボット
▶定義 **2** the central or most important person or thing 中心または最も重要な人または物➡中心となる人・物, (議論などの)中心点, 要点 ‖ *West Africa was the pivot of the cocoa trade.* 西アフリカはココア貿易の中心地だった.

**pivot**² /pívət/ 動 自 ▶定義 to turn or balance on a central point 中心点を軸に回る, または釣り合いを保つ➡(〜を軸にして)回転する, 釣り合う

**pixie** /píksi/ 名 C ▶定義 (in children's stories) a creature like a small person with pointed ears that has magic powers (童話の中で)とがった耳をして, 魔法が使える, 小さな人間のような生き物➡(いたずら好きな)小妖精(ようせい)

**pizza** /píːtsə/ 名 C U ▶定義 an Italian dish consisting of a flat round bread base with vegetables, cheese, meat, etc on top, which is cooked in an oven オーブンで焼かれ, 平らで円形のパンの上に乗せられた野菜, チーズ, 肉などから成るイタリア料理➡ピザ, ピッツア

**pkt** 略 packet➡束, 一包み

**pl** 略 (文法) plural➡複数の

**placard** /plǽkɑːrd/ 名 C ▶定義 a large written or printed notice that is put in a public place or carried on a stick in a protest march 公共の場所に置かれる, または棒に付けて抗議デモに持ち歩かれる, 大きな手書きまたは印刷された掲示物➡プラカード, 張り紙, 掲示, ポスター

**placate** /pləkéɪt; pléɪkèɪt, plǽk-/ 動 他

## 1220 place¹

▶定義 to make sb feel less angry about sth ～についての…の怒りを和らげる→～をなだめる，慰める，鎮める

**★place¹** /pleɪs/ 🔤 ⓒ ▶定義1 a particular position or area 特定の位置または区域→**場所，所** ‖ *Show me the exact place where it happened.* それが起こった正確な場所を教えてください．*This would be a good place to sit down and have a rest.* 座って休むために，ここはちょうどいい場所だろう．*The wall was damaged in several places.* その壁は何箇所か壊れていた．▶定義2 a particular village, town, country, etc 特定の村，町，国など→**地域，地方，市町村** ‖ *Which places did you go to in Italy?* イタリアではどの地域に行きましたか．*Vienna is a very beautiful place.* ウィーンはとても美しい町です．▶定義3 a building or area that is used for a particular purpose 特定の目的に使われる建物または区域→**土地，場所，建物** ‖ *The square is a popular **meeting place** for young people.* その広場は若者に人気の集合場所だ．*The town is full of inexpensive eating places.* その町には安い食堂がたくさんある．▶定義4 a seat or position that can be used by sb/sth ～によって使われることができる席または位置→**席，(定められた)位置** ‖ *They went into the classroom and sat down in their places.* 彼らは教室に入って，自分の席に座った．*Go on ahead and **save me a place in the queue**.* 先に行って，列に並んで私の順番を確保してください．

▶ a placeは～の席または定められた位置である．自動車を駐車できる場所は，a spaceとも言われる．空いている場所について話しているとき，spaceとroomを使える: *This piano **takes up** too much **space**.* (このピアノは場所を取りすぎる．) *There is enough **room for** three people in the back of the car.* (その車の後ろには3人に十分な空間があります．)

▶定義5 your position in society; your role 社会での自分の位置; 自分の役割→**地位，立場，身分，仕事; 役目** ‖ *I feel **it is not my place** to criticize my boss.* 私は上司を批判する立場ではないと思います．▶定義6 an opportunity to study at a college, play for a team, etc 単科大学で学ぶ，またはチームのために試合する機会→(学校・大学の)入学資格, (運動チームの)一員・選手としての資格 ‖ *Abina has got a place to study law at Hull.* アビナはハルで法律を勉強する入学資格を得た．*Laila is now sure of a place on the team.* ライラは今，そのチームの一員としての資格があると確信している．▶定義7 the usual or correct position or occasion for sth ～にとって，通常のまたは正しい位置または機会→**ふさわしい場所・機会，当然あるべき場所** ‖ *The room was tidy. Everything had been put away **in its place**.* 部屋は整とんされていた．すべての物が，適切な場所にしまい込まれていた．*A funeral is not the place to discuss business.* 葬式は，仕事の話をするのにふさわしい場ではない．▶定義8 the position of a number after the decimal point 小数点の後の数字の位置→**けた，位** ‖ *Your answer should be correct to three decimal places.* あなたの答えは，小数点3けたまで正しくなくてはなりません．▶定義9 [単数扱い] (口語) a person's home 個人の家庭→**うち，住居，部屋** ‖ *Her parents have got a place on the coast.* 彼女の両親の住居は海岸にある．▶定義10 the position that you have at the end of a race, competition, etc 競争, 試合の最後に自分が保持している位置→**順位，順番** ‖ *Cara finished **in second place**.* キャラは2位でゴールインした．

成句 **all over the place** ▶定義 everywhere 至る所で→**至る所に，どこでも，ごちゃごちゃと**

**change/swap places (with sb)** ▶定義 to take sb's seat, position, etc and let him/her have yours ～の席または位置などを取り，その人に自分の席または位置などに着かせる→(～と)席・場所を交換する・変わる，立場を変える ‖ *Let's change places so that you can look out of the window.* あなたが窓の外を見られるように，席を交換しましょう．

**fall/slot into place** ▶定義 (used about sth that is complicated or difficult to understand) to become organized or clear in your mind (複雑なまたは理解するのが困難な～について)自分の考えがうまくまとまってくる，または明確になる→(事情・事態などが)はっきりしてくる，つじつまが合う，(様子が)見えてくる ‖ *After two weeks in my new job, everything suddenly started to fall into place.* 新しい仕事に就いて2週間後に，突然すべてがはっきりし始めた．

**in my, your, etc place/shoes** ▶定義 in my,

your, etc situation or position 私·あなたなどの状況または立場に➜**～の立場にいて** ‖ *If I were in your place I would wait a year before getting married.* もし私があなたの立場なら, 結婚するまでに１年待つだろう.

in place ▶定義 1 in the correct or usual position 正しい, またはいつもの位置に➜**正しい位置に [の], いつもの所に, きちんとして** ‖ *Use tape to hold the picture in place.* 絵を正しい位置に保つためにテープを使いなさい. ▶定義 2 (used about plans or preparations) finished and ready to be used (計画または準備について) 済ませてしまっていて, 使う用意ができた➜**適切に, 当を得た** ‖ *All the preparations for the trip are now in place.* 今, 旅行の準備はすべて整った.

in place of sb/sth; in sb/sth's place ▶定義 instead of sb/sth ～の代わりに➜**～の代わりに, ～に代わって**

in the first, second, etc place [略式] ▶定義 used when you are giving a list of reasons for sth or explaining sth; firstly, secondly, etc ～に対する理由をいろいろ挙げているとき, または～を説明しているときに用いて; まず最初に, 第２に, など➜**まず第１に, 第２に, など**

out of place ▶定義 1 not suitable for a particular situation 特定の状況に適していない➜**不適当な [に], 場違いの [で]** ‖ *I felt very out of place among all those clever people.* それらすべての才気ある人々に囲まれて, 自分をとても場違いに感じていた. ▶定義 2 not in the correct or usual place 正しいまたはいつもの場所でなく➜**本来·元の場所から外れて, 間違った場所の [に]**

put sb in his/her place ▶定義 to show that sb is not as clever, important, etc as he/she believes ～は, 本人が信じているほどには賢くない, または重要ではないことを示す➜**～に身の程を知らせる·わきまえさせる, ～の高慢をたしなめる** ‖ *It really put her in her place when she failed to qualify for the race.* その競技の予選に落ちた時, 彼女はしみじみと身の程を思い知らされた.

put yourself in sb's place ▶定義 to imagine that you are in the same situation as sb else 自分がほかの～の状況と同じ状況にいると想像する➜**～の身になってみる** ‖ *Put yourself in Steve's place and you will realize how worried he must be.* スティーヴの身になってみなさい, そうすればどれだけ彼が心配しているに違いないかが分かるでしょう.

take place ▶定義 (used about a meeting, an event, etc) to happen (会議, 出来事などについて) 起こる➜**起こる, 行われる** ‖ *The ceremony took place in glorious sunshine.* その儀式はすばらしい晴天の下で行われた.

***place**[2] /pléɪs/ [動][他] ▶定義 1 [正式] to put sth carefully or deliberately in a particular position 特定の場所に注意深くまたはわざと～を置く➜**～を置く, 据える, 設置する** ‖ *The chairs had all been placed in neat rows.* いすは全部, 整然と列を作って置かれていた. *The poster was placed where everyone could see it.* そのポスターは皆が見られる所にあった. ▶定義 2 to put sb in a particular position or situation 特定の場所または状況に～を置く➜**～を配置する, 任命する** ‖ *His behaviour placed me in a difficult situation.* 彼の行動によって, 私は難しい状況に置かれた. *to place sb in charge* ～を責任者に任命する *Rhoda was placed third in the competition.* ローダはその試合で３位だった. ▶定義 3 used to express the attitude that sb has to sb/sth ～が…へ持つ態度を表現するために用いて➜**(信用など) を置く, (期待など) をかける** ‖ *We placed our trust in you and you failed us.* 私たちはあなたを信用していたが, あなたは私たちを失望させた. *The blame for the disaster was placed firmly on the company.* その災害を引き起こした責任は, その会社に厳しく負わされた. ▶定義 4 (通常は否定文の中で) to recognize sb/sth and be able to identify him/her/it ～を見分けて, それがだれ·何であるか分かる➜**～がだれ·何であるか思い出す, ～を確認する, 突き止める** ‖ *Her face is familiar but I just can't place her.* 彼女の顔は知っているが, 名前が思い出せない. ▶定義 5 to give instructions about sth or to ask for sth to happen ～についての指示を与える, または～が起こるように頼む➜**(注文·広告など) を出す, (電話) を入れる** ‖ *to place a bet on sth* ～へのかけ金を出す *to place an order for sth* ～を注文する

**place name** [名] [C] ▶定義 the name of a city, town, etc 市, 町などの名前➜**地名**

**placid** /plǽsəd/ [形] ▶定義 (used about a person or an animal) calm and not easily excited (人や動物について) 穏やかで, 簡単には興奮しない➜**穏**

P

やかな, 物静かな, 落ち着いた — **placidly** 副 →穏やかに, 平静に, 落ち着いて

**plague**¹ /pléɪɡ/ 名 ▶定義 1 C U any infectious disease that spreads quickly and kills many people 素早く広まって多くの人々を殺す伝染病 →**疫病, 伝染病** ▶定義 2 **the plague** U an infectious disease spread by rats that causes swellings on the body, a very high temperature and often results in death 身体中にはれもの, 高熱を引き起こし, しばしば死に至る, ネズミによって広まる伝染病 →**ペスト, 黒死病** ▶定義 3 C **a plague of sth** a large number of unpleasant animals or insects that come into an area at one time 一度にある地域へ入ってくる不快な動物または虫の大群 →**(害虫などの)突然の侵入, 異常発生, はびこり** ‖ *a plague of ants/locusts* アリの大発生・イナゴの異常発生

**plague**² /pléɪɡ/ 動 他 ▶定義 to cause sb/sth a lot of trouble 〜に多くの心配事をもたらす →**〜を絶えず悩ませる, 〜にしつこくせがむ・言う** ‖ *The project was plagued by a series of disasters.* その計画は次々に起こる災難にしつこく見舞われた.

**plaice** /pléɪs/ 名 C U (複 **plaice**) ▶定義 a type of flat sea fish that we eat 私たちが食べる, 平らな海の魚の一種 →**カレイ, ヒラメ**

★**plain**¹ /pléɪn/ 形 ▶定義 1 easy to see, hear or understand; clear 見る, 聞く, または理解することが簡単な; はっきりした →**明白な, 分かりやすい, はっきりした** ‖ *It was plain that he didn't want to talk about it.* 彼がその事について話したくないのは明らかだった. *She made it plain that she didn't want to see me again.* もう二度と私に会いたくないことを, 彼女は明らかにした. ▶定義 2 (used about people, thoughts, actions, etc) saying what you think; direct and honest (人々, 考え, 行動について)考えている事を言う; 率直で正直な →**飾り気のない, 率直な, あからさまな** ‖ *I'll be plain with you. I don't like the idea.* 率直に言って, 私はその考えが好きではない. ▶定義 3 simple in style; not decorated or complicated 様式が簡素な; 飾られていない, または複雑でない →**簡素な, 質素な, (食べ物が)あっさりした, (衣服などが)地味な** ‖ *My father likes plain English cooking.* 私の父はあっさりしたイギリス料理が好きです. ▶定義 4 (名詞の前だけ) all one colour; without a pattern on it すべてが1色で; そこに模様がなくて →**(生地が)無地の, (物が)飾りのない, (紙が)無罫(けい)の** ‖ *a plain blue jumper* 青無地のセーター ▶定義 5 (used especially about a woman or girl) not beautiful or attractive (特に女性や少女について)美しくない, または魅力的でない →**平凡な, 並みの, 不器量な** ‖ *She's a rather plain child.* 彼女はかなり不器量な子供だ.

**plain**² /pléɪn/ 名 C ▶定義 a large area of flat land with few trees 木々がほとんどない, 平らな土地の広い区域 →**平原, 平野, 大草原**

**plain**³ /pléɪn/ 副 (口語) ▶定義 completely 完全に →**全く** ‖ *That's plain silly.* あれは全くばかばかしい.

**plain clothes** 形 ▶定義 (used about a police officer) in ordinary clothes; not uniform (警官について)普通の衣服で; 制服ではない →**私服の** ‖ *a plain-clothes detective* 私服の刑事

**plain flour** 名 U ▶定義 flour that does not contain a powder (baking powder) which makes cakes, etc rise ケーキなどを膨らませる粉(ベーキングパウダー)を入れてない小麦粉 →**普通の小麦粉** ☛参 **self-raising flour**

**plainly** /pléɪnli/ 副 ▶定義 1 clearly はっきりと →**はっきりと, 分かりやすく, 明白に** ‖ *He was plainly very upset.* 彼は明らかにひどく動揺した. ▶定義 2 using simple words to say sth in a direct and honest way 率直で正直に〜を言うために, 飾らない言葉を使っている →**飾り気なく, 率直に, 有りのままに** ‖ *She told him plainly that he was not doing his job properly.* 彼が仕事をきちんとやっていないと, 彼女は彼に率直に言った. ▶定義 3 in a simple way, without decoration 装飾なしに簡素なやり方で →**質素に, 地味に, 飾らずに** ‖ *She was plainly dressed and wore no make-up.* 彼女は地味に装い, 化粧もしていなかった.

**plaintiff** /pléɪntɪf/ 名 C ▶定義 a person who starts a legal action against sb in a court of law 裁判所で〜を告訴する人 →**原告, 提訴人, 起訴人** ☛参 **defendant**

**plaintive** /pléɪntɪv/ 形 ▶定義 sounding sad, especially in a weak complaining way 特に弱々しく訴える様子で, 悲しく聞こえている →**悲しそうな, 哀れな, 切々とした** — **plaintively** 副 →悲し

げに, 哀れに

**plait** /plæt/ (困 **braid**) 動 他 ▶定義 to cross three or more long pieces of hair, rope, etc over and under each other to make one thick piece 太い1本を作るために, 3つまたはそれより多い本数の長い髪の毛, ロープなどを互いの上や下に交差させる→〜を編む, お下げに結う ☞ hair のさし絵 ─ plait 名 ⓒ→編んだ物, 三つ編み, お下げ髪

*★**plan**¹* /plæn/ 名 ▶定義1 ⓒ **a plan (for sth/to do sth)** an idea or arrangement for doing or achieving sth in the future 将来, 〜をするまたは達成するための, 考えまたは準備→**計画, 案, 予定** ‖ *We usually **make** our holiday **plans** in January.* 普通私たちは1月に休暇の計画を立てる. *The firm has no plans to employ more people.* その会社ではこれ以上人を雇う予定はない. *There has been **a change of plan** - we're meeting at the restaurant.* 計画が変更になりました － 私たちはレストランで会うことになります. *If everything **goes according to plan** (= happens as we planned) we should be home by midnight.* もしすべてが計画通りにいけば(= 私たちが計画したように起こる), 真夜中には家に着いているでしょう. ▶定義2 ⓒ a detailed map of a building, town, etc 建物, 町などの詳細な地図→**地図, 見取り図, 平面図** ‖ *a street plan of Berlin* ベルリンの街の地図 ▶定義3 **plans** [複数扱い] detailed drawings of a building, machine, road, etc that show its size, shape and measurements その大きさ, 形状および寸法が示されている, 建物, 機械, 道路などの詳細な図→**設計図, 配線図, 図面** ‖ *We're getting an architect to **draw up** some **plans** for a new kitchen.* 建築家に新しいキッチンの設計図を何枚かかいてもらおうとしているところです. ▶定義4 ⓒ a diagram that shows how sth is to be organized or arranged どのように〜が組織されるか, または準備されるかを示す図表→**概要, 大要, 概略** ‖ *Before you start writing an essay, it's a good idea to make a brief plan.* 論文を書き始める前に, 概略を作ることは良い考えだと思う.

**plan**² /plæn/ 動 (**planning**; **planned**) ▶定義1 自他 **plan (sth) (for sth)** to decide, organize or prepare for sth you want to do in the future 将来自分がしたい〜を決定する, きちんと取りまとめる, または準備する→**〜を計画する, 企画する** ‖ *to plan for the future* 将来の計画を立てる *You need to plan your work more carefully.* あなたはもっと注意深く自分の仕事を計画する必要があります. ▶定義2 自他 **plan (on sth/doing sth)** to intend or expect to do sth 〜をするつもりである, またはするだろうと期待する→**〜するつもりである, 〜する予定である** ‖ *I'm planning on having a holiday in July.* 私は7月に休暇を取るつもりだ. *We plan to arrive at about 4 o'clock.* 私たちは4時ころ到着する予定だ. ▶定義3 他 to make a diagram or a design of sth 〜の図面または設計図を書く→**〜の図面を書く, 〜を設計する** ‖ *The new shopping centre is very badly planned.* 新しいショッピングセンターは非常に下手な設計だ. ─ planning 名 Ⓤ→計画(すること), 立案, 都市計画 ‖ *The project requires careful planning.* その企画には, 綿密な計画が必要である.

*★**plane**¹* /pleɪn/ 名 ⓒ ▶定義1 = AEROPLANE ‖ *Has her plane landed yet?* 彼女が乗っている飛行機はもう着陸しましたか. ▶定義2 a tool used for making the surface of wood smooth by taking very thin pieces off it 表面をとても薄く削り取って, 木材の表面を滑らかにする道具→**かんな** ☞ tool のさし絵 ▶定義3 (専門用語)a flat surface 平らな表面→**平面, 水平面**

**plane**² /pleɪn/ 動 他 ▶定義 to make the surface of a piece of wood flat and smooth using a plane¹(2) plane¹(2)を使って, 木材の表面を平らで滑らかにする→**〜にかんなをかける, 〜を平ら・水平にする**

*★**planet**¹* /ˈplænət/ 名 ▶定義1 ⓒ a very large round object in space that moves around the sun or another star 太陽やほかの星の周りを回っている, 宇宙のとても大きな丸い物体→**惑星** ‖ *the planets of our solar system* 私たちの太陽系の惑星 ▶定義2 **the planet** [単数扱い]the world we live in; the Earth, especially when talking about the environment 私たちが住んでいる世界; 地球, 特に環境について話しているとき→**地球**

**planetarium** /ˌplænəˈteəriəm/ 名 ⓒ ▶定義 a building with a curved ceiling that represents the sky at night. It is used for showing the positions and movements of the planets and stars for education and entertainment. 夜空を表現する, 曲線を描く天井の建物. ここでは, 教育と娯楽を目的として, 惑星と星の位置と運行を示すために用いられる➡️プラネタリウム, 天文館

**plank** /plæŋk/ 名 C ▶定義 a long flat thin piece of wood that is used for building or making things 物を建てるまたは作るために使われる, 長く平らで薄い木材の1枚➡️板材, 厚板(通例, 厚さ5〜15センチ)

*__plant__¹ /plɑːnt; plænt/ 名 ▶定義 1 C a living thing that grows in the ground and usually has leaves, a long thin green central part (a stem) and roots 通常は葉, 細長い緑色の中心部(茎), および根を持つ, 地中に育つ生きている物➡️(動物に対して)植物, (樹木に対して)草, 苗 ‖ *a tomato plant* トマトの苗 *a plant pot (= a container for plants)* 植木鉢(= 植物用の容器) ☞ C2 ページのさし絵 ▶定義 2 C a very large factory とても大きな工場➡️工場, 製造工場 ‖ *a car plant* 乗用車製造工場 *a nuclear reprocessing plant* 核再処理工場

*__plant__² /plɑːnt; plænt/ 動 他 ▶定義 1 to put plants, seeds, etc in the ground to grow 育つように, 植物, 種などを地面に置く→〜を植える, まく ‖ *Bulbs should be planted in the autumn.* 球根は秋に植えるべきです. ▶定義 2 **plant sth (with sth)** to cover or supply a garden, area of land, etc with plants 庭, 地面などを植物で覆う, または植物を補充する→〜に(植物を)植える ‖ *The field's been planted with wheat this year.* 今年, その畑には小麦が植えられている. ▶定義 3 to put yourself/sth firmly in a particular place or position 特定の場所または位置に, 自分または〜をしっかりと置く→〜をしっかりと据える, 配置する ‖ *He planted himself in the best seat.* 彼は一番良い席に陣取った. ▶定義 4 **plant sth (on sb)** to hide sth, especially sth illegal, in sb's clothing, property, etc in order to make him/her seem guilty of a crime 人が犯罪を犯しているように見えるようにするために, 〜の衣服, 所有などの中に, …を, 特に不法な…を隠す→(人を陥れるために盗品など)を人の持ち物に紛れ込ませる, 〜を(…に)仕掛ける ‖ *The police think that terrorists may have __planted__ the bomb.* テロリストたちがあの爆弾を仕掛けたかもしれないと, 警察は考えている. *The women claimed that the drugs had been planted on them.* だれかが麻薬を自分たちの持ち物の中に入れたと, その女たちは主張した.

**plantation** /plænˈteɪʃ(ə)n/ 名 C ▶定義 1 a large area of land, especially in a hot country, where tea, cotton, tobacco, etc are grown 紅茶, 綿花, たばこなどが栽培されている, 特に熱帯の国の, 広大な土地の区域➡️プランテーション, 大農園 ‖ *a coffee plantation* コーヒー農園 ▶定義 2 an area of land where trees are grown to produce wood 木材を生産するために木々が栽培されている土地の区域➡️植林地, 造林地

**plaque** /plɑːk; plæk/ 名 ▶定義 1 C a flat piece of stone or metal, usually with names and dates on it, that is fixed on a wall in memory of a famous person or event 有名な人または出来事を記念して壁に固定された, 通常名前と日付が彫り込まれてある平らな石または金属➡️飾り板, 銘板, 額 ☞ **column** のさし絵 ▶定義 2 U a harmful substance that forms on your teeth 歯に形成される有害な物質➡️歯石, 歯垢(しこう)

**plaster**¹ /ˈplɑːstər, ˈplæs-/ 名 ▶定義 1 U a mixture of a special powder and water that becomes hard when it is dry. Plaster is put on walls and ceilings to form a smooth surface. 乾くと固くなる, 特別な粉と水の混ぜ物. 滑らかな表面を作るために, 壁と天井に塗られる➡️しっくい, 壁土, プラスター ▶定義 2 (または **sticking plaster**) C a small piece of sticky material that is used to cover a cut, etc on the body 体の傷口などを覆うために使われる, 粘り気のある物質の小さな1枚➡️ばんそうこう ▶定義 3 U a white powder that is mixed with water and becomes hard when dry. It is used for putting round broken bones, etc until they get better. 水と混ぜられて乾くと固くなる, 白い粉. 折れた骨などが良くなるまで, その周りを塗り固めるために用いられる➡️石こう ‖ *When Alan broke his leg it was __in plaster__ for six weeks.* アランが足を折った時, 6週間ギプスをした. ☞ **bandage** のさし絵

**plaster**² /ˈplɑːstər, ˈplæs-/ 動 他 ▶定義 1 to cover a wall, etc with plaster¹(1) to make the surface smooth 表面を滑らかにするために, 壁などを plaster¹(1) で覆う→〜にしっくいを塗る ▶定義 2 **plaster sb/sth (in/with sth)** to cover sb/sth with a large amount of sth 〜を大量の…

で覆う→(〜に)…をべたべた塗る・張り付ける ‖ *He plastered his walls with posters.* 彼は、自分の部屋の壁にポスターをべたべた張り付けた.

**plastic**¹ /plǽstɪk/ 名 C U ▶定義 a light, strong material that is made with chemicals and is used for making many different sorts of objects 化学物質から作られて、多くの異なる種類の物を作るために使われる、軽くて強い物質→プラスチック, ビニール, 合成樹脂

> ▶日本語 vs 英語
>
> プラスチック？ビニール？
>
> 日本語では、「プラスチック」は硬いもので「ビニール」は柔らかいものという区別をしますが、英語では硬くても柔らかくてもplastic という語を用います. したがって「ビニール袋」は plastic bag です. vinyl という語は化学用語で、一般にはあまり使われません.

**plastic**² /plǽstɪk/ 形 ▶定義 made of plastic 合成樹脂で作られた→**プラスチック製の, ビニール(製)の, 合成樹脂の** ‖ *plastic cups* プラスチックのコップ *a plastic bag* ビニール袋

**plastic surgery** 名 U ▶定義 a medical operation to repair or replace damaged skin or to improve the appearance of a person's face or body 損傷した皮膚を修復するまたは取り替える、あるいは人の顔または体の外見を良くするための、医療手術→**整形手術, 形成外科** ☛参 **facelift, surgery**

**plate** /pléɪt/ 名 ▶定義 1 C a flat, usually round, dish for eating or serving food from そこから料理を食べるまたは料理を出すための、平らな、通常円形の皿→**取り皿, 平皿** ‖ *a plastic/paper/china plate* プラスチックの皿・紙皿・磁器の皿 *a plate of food* 料理1皿

▶ 人は、主な料理を dinner plate (ディナー皿) から食べる. パンなどはディナー皿の右側に置かれる side plate (小皿) に置くこともある. コーンフレークまたはプリンは bowl (小鉢) から食べる.

▶定義 2 C a thin flat piece of metal or glass 1枚の薄くて平らな金属またはガラス→**金属板, ガラス板, めっき板** ‖ *a steel/metal plate* 鋼板・板金 ▶定義 3 C a flat piece of metal with sth written on it そこから〜が書かれている、1枚の平らな金属→**(医者・弁護士などの)表札, 名札** ‖ *The brass plate beside the door said 'Dr Waters'.* ドアの横の真鍮(しんちゅう)の名札には、「医師 ウォーターズ」と書かれていた.

▶定義 4 U metal that has a thin covering of gold or silver 金または銀の薄い皮膜のある金属→**(金・銀の、またはめっきされた)食器類** ‖ *gold/silver plate* 金・銀製の食器類

**plateau** /plǽtoʊ, -'-/ 名 C ( 複 **plateaus** /-tóʊz/ または **plateaux** /-tóʊ/ ) ▶定義 1 a large high area of flat land 平らな土地の、広く高い区域→**高原, 台地** ▶定義 2 a state where there is little development or change ほとんど発展または変化のない状態→**(成長・学習・事業などの)停滞期, (価格などの高値)安定期** ‖ *House prices seem to have reached a plateau.* 家の価格は今, 安定期に入ったようだ.

**plateful** /pléɪtfʊl, -f(ə)l/ 名 C ▶定義 the amount of food that a plate(1) can hold plate(1)に盛られる料理の量→**1皿分(の料理)**

**platform** /plǽtfɔːrm/ 名 C ▶定義 1 the place where you get on or off trains at a railway station 鉄道の駅で列車に乗るまたは降りる場所→**プラットホーム** ‖ *Which platform does the train to York leave from?* ヨーク行きの電車はどのプラットホームから出発しますか. ▶定義 2 a flat surface, higher than the level of the floor or ground, on which public speakers or performers stand so that the audience can see them 聴衆が見られるように、演説する人々または演奏者たちがその上に立つ、床または地面の水平面より高い平らな表面→**壇, 演壇, 教壇** ▶定義 3 [通常は単数] the ideas and aims of a political party who want to be elected 当選したいと願っている政党の考えと目的→**綱領, 政綱, 公約** ‖ *They fought the election on a platform of low taxes.* 彼らは低税率という公約で選挙を戦った.

**platinum** /plǽt(ə)nəm/ 名 U ( 元素記号 Pt) ▶定義 a silver-grey metal that is often used for making expensive jewellery しばしば高価な装身具を作るために用いられる、銀灰色の金属→**プラチナ, しろがね** ‖ *a platinum wedding ring* プラチナの結婚指輪

**platonic** /plətɑ́nɪk, pleɪ-/ 形 ▶定義 (used about a relationship between two people) friendly but not sexual (2人の人間の関係について) 親しい

が, 性的関係はない➜**純粋に精神的な, プラトニックな**

**platoon** /plətúːn/ [名] [C] ▶定義 a small group of soldiers 兵士たちの小さな集団➜**小隊**

**plausible** /plɔ́ːzəb(ə)l/ [形] ▶定義 that you can believe; reasonable 信じられる; 道理に合った➜**(言っている事が)本当と思える, もっともらしい, まことしやかな** ‖ *a plausible excuse* もっともらしい言い訳 ⇔ **implausible**

***play**[1] /pléɪ/ [動] ▶定義1 [自] play (with sb/sth) to do sth to enjoy yourself; to have fun 愉快に過ごすために～をする; 面白く遊ぶ➜**遊ぶ, 戯れる** ‖ *The children have been playing on the beach all day.* 子供たちは一日中浜辺で遊んでいる. *Emma's found a new friend to play with.* エマは一緒に遊ぶ新しい友達を見つけた. ▶定義2 [自][他] to take part in a game or sport ゲームまたはスポーツに参加する➜**競技・試合をする, 競技・試合に出る** ‖ *to play football/tennis/hockey* サッカー・テニス・ホッケーをする *I usually play against Bill.* 普通, 私はビルと対戦する. *She played him at table tennis and won.* 彼女は彼と卓球をして勝った. *Do you know how to play chess?* チェスの仕方を知っていますか. *Who's Brazil playing next in the World Cup?* 次のワールドカップではブラジルはどこと対戦するのか. ▶定義3 [自][他] play (sth) (on sth) to make music with a musical instrument 楽器で音楽をする➜**演奏する, 弾く** ‖ *to play the piano/guitar/trumpet* ピアノを弾く・ギターを弾く・トランペットを吹く *My son's learning the piano. He plays very well.* 私の息子はピアノを習っています, 彼はとても上手に演奏します. *She played a few notes on the violin.* 彼女はバイオリンを弾いて, 2, 3の音を鳴らした. ☛参 **piano** の注 ▶定義4 [他] to turn on a video, tape, etc so that it produces sound ビデオテープ, テープなどが音を生じるように, かける➜**～をかける** ‖ *Shall I play the CD for you again?* もう一度, そのCDをかけましょうか. ▶定義5 [自][他] to act in a play, film, TV programme, etc; to act the role of sb 芝居, 映画, テレビ番組などで演じる; ～の役を演じる➜**演じる, ～にふんする** ‖ *Richard is going to play Romeo.* リチャードはロミオを演じます.

➤ play a part, role, etc はしばしば比喩的に使われる: *Britain has played an active part in the recent discussions.* (英国は最近の討議で積極的な役割を果たした.) *John played a key role in organizing the protest.* (抗議集会の計画で, ジョンは重要な役割を務めた.)

▶定義6 [自][正式] to move quickly and lightly 素早く軽く動く➜**(水, 光などを)浴びせる, 放射する** ‖ *Sunlight played on the surface of the sea.* 太陽の光が海面を照らしていた.

➤ play を含む成句については, 名詞, 形容詞などの項を参照. 例えば play it by ear は ear の項にある.

**➤語法**

試合は game, match, bout

アメリカ英語では baseball のように -ball が付く球技には play を用い, それ以外の競技 (tennis, golf など) には match を用います. イギリス英語では, それ以上に match を使う傾向が強いようです. 一方, play を用いない競技 (格闘技) の試合には bout を用います. boxing, wrestling, fencing などは動詞の box, wrestle, fence に由来しますから, play を使わずに Let's wrestle after school. (放課後レスリングをしよう) のように表現します.

[句動詞] **play at sth/being sth** ▶定義 to do sth with little interest or effort ほとんど興味または努力なしに, ～を行う➜**～を遊び半分にやる, いいかげんにする** ‖ *He's only playing at studying. He'd prefer to get a job now.* 彼は遊び半分に勉強しているだけだ. 彼は今仕事を得たいと思っている. *What is that driver playing at (= doing)?* あの運転手は何をしているのだ.

**play sth back (to sb)** ▶定義 to turn on and watch or listen to a film, tape, etc that you have recorded 自分が録画したフィルム, テープなどをかけて見るまたは聴く➜**～を再生する, プレーバックする** ‖ *Play that last scene back to me again.* もう一度あの最後の場面を再生してください.

**play sth down** ▶定義 to make sth seem less important than it really is 実際よりも～が重要でないように見せる➜**～を重要でないように見せる, (新聞などが記事)を小さく扱う, 軽くあしらう** ‖ *to play down a crisis* 危機を重要でないよう

に見せる

**play A off against B** ▶定義 to make people compete or argue with each other, especially for your own advantage 特に自分自身の利益のために,人々を互いに競争させる,または口論させる→**AとBを張り合わせる,対抗させる** ‖ *I think she enjoys playing one friend off against another.* 彼女は友達同士を張り合わせて楽しんでいるように思う.

**play on sth** ▶定義 to use and take advantage of sb's fears or weaknesses ~の恐怖または弱点を利用して,そこに付け込む→**~に付け込む, ~を利用する** ‖ *This advertising campaign plays on people's fears of illness.* この広告キャンペーンは,人々の病気への恐れに付け込んでいる.

**play (sb) up** 略式 ▶定義 to cause sb trouble or pain ~に心配事や痛みをもたらす→**~を困らせる, 悩ます** ‖ *The car always plays up in wet weather.* 雨の日にはいつも,この車に悩まされる.

★**play**² /pléɪ/ ▶定義 **1** ●a piece of writing performed by actors in the theatre, or on television or radio 劇場,テレビ,またはラジオで俳優たちによって演じられる,一編の作品→**劇,芝居,戯曲, 脚本** ‖ *Would you like to see a play while you're in London?* ロンドンにいる間に芝居を見たいですか. *a radio/television play* ラジオ・テレビドラマ ▶俳優たちと女優たちが芝居を rehearse (稽古(けいこ)する) と言う. 劇場付きの一座, 劇団が芝居を produce (製作する) と言う. 芝居は通常 stage (舞台) で行われる.

▶定義 **2** ❶the playing of a game or sport ゲームまたはスポーツをすること→**競技・試合をすること, 勝負事** ‖ *Bad weather stopped play yesterday.* 昨日は天気が悪くて試合は中止となった. ▶テニス, サッカーなどをするという意味で動詞の play を使うが, テニスの試合については, a play of tennis とは言わずに a game of tennis と言う.

▶定義 **3** ❶activity done for enjoyment only, especially by children 特に子供たちによって, 楽しみのためだけに行われる活動→**遊び, 遊戯, 気晴らし** ‖ *Young children learn through play.* 幼い子供たちは遊びを通して学ぶ. *the happy sound of children at play* 遊んでいる子供たちの幸せそうな声 ▶定義 **4** ❶a control on a video or cassette player, etc that you press to start the tape running テープが動き始めるように人が押

す, ビデオまたはカセットプレーヤーの調整装置→**再生ボタン** ‖ *Put the video into the machine then press play.* ビデオを機械に入れ, そして再生ボタンを押してください.

成句 fair play ⇒ **FAIR**¹

**playboy** /pléɪbɔ̀ɪ/ 名 ● ▶定義 a rich man who spends his time enjoying himself 自分の時間を愉快に過ごすことに使う, 金持ちの男→**道楽者, プレーボーイ, 遊び人**

★**player** /pléɪər/ 名 ● ▶定義 **1** a person who plays a game or sport ゲームまたはスポーツをする人→**ゲームをする人, 競技者** ‖ *a game for four players* 4人でするゲーム *She's an excellent tennis player.* 彼女はすばらしいテニス選手だ. ▶定義 **2** (複合名詞を作るために用いて) a machine on which you can listen to sound that has been recorded on CD, tape, etc CD, テープなどに録音されている音を人が聞ける, 機械→**プレーヤー, 演奏装置** ‖ *a CD/cassette player* CD・カセットプレーヤー ▶定義 **3** a person who plays a musical instrument 楽器を演奏する人→**演奏者** ‖ *a piano player* ピアノ奏者

**playful** /pléɪfʊl, -f(ə)l/ 形 ▶定義 **1** done or said in fun; not serious ふざけて行った, または言った; まじめではなく→**ふざけている, まじめでない** ‖ *a playful remark* ふざけた感想 ▶定義 **2** full of fun; wanting to play 楽しさばかりで; 遊びたがっている→**陽気な, 元気で楽しそうな** ‖ *a playful puppy* 元気で楽しそうな子犬

**playground** /pléɪgràʊnd/ 名 ● ▶定義 an area of land where children can play 子供たちが遊べる土地の区域→**遊び場, 運動場** ‖ *the school playground* 学校の運動場

**playgroup** /pléɪgrùːp/ (または **playschool** /pléɪskùːl/) 英 =**NURSERY SCHOOL**

**playhouse** /pléɪhàʊs/ 名 ▶定義 **1** [単数扱い] used in the name of some theatres ある劇場の名前として用いて→**~劇場** ‖ *the Liverpool Playhouse* リバプール劇場 ▶定義 **2** ●a model of a house for children to play in 子供たちがその中で遊ぶ, 模型の家→**子供が入って遊ぶ小屋, おもちゃの家**

**playing card** = **CARD(4)**

**playing field** 名 ● ▶定義 a large field used for sports such as cricket and football スポー

ツ，例えばクリケットとサッカー，のために使われる，広い競技場→**運動場，競技場**
成句 a level playing field ⇒ **LEVEL**²

**play-off** 名 C 定義 a match between two teams or players who have equal scores to decide the winner 勝者を決めるための，同じ得点を持っている2つのチームまたは2人の選手の間の試合→**決勝試合，プレーオフ** ‖ *They lost to Chicago in the play-offs.* 彼らはシカゴに決勝試合で負けた．

**plaything** /pléɪθɪŋ/ 名 C 正式 定義 a toy→**おもちゃ**

**playtime** /pléɪtàɪm/ 名 C U 定義 a period of time between lessons when children at school can go outside to play 学校で子供たちが外に遊びに行ける，授業の合間の時間→**休み時間**

**playwright** /pléɪràɪt/ 名 C 定義 a person who writes plays for the theatre, television or radio 劇場，テレビ，またはラジオのために脚本を書く人→**脚本家，劇作家**

**PLC**（または **plc**）/ˌpì: el sí:/ 略 英 Public Limited Company→**公開有限（責任）会社**

**plea** /pli:/ 名 C 定義1 正式 a plea (for sth) an important and emotional request 重要で感情に訴える要求→**嘆願，請願** ‖ *a plea for help* 救援の嘆願 定義2 a plea of sth a statement made by or for sb in a court of law 法廷で，〜によって，または〜のために行われた供述→**抗弁，申し立て** ‖ *a plea of guilty/not guilty* 有罪の・無罪の申し立て

**plead** /pli:d/ 動 定義1 自 plead (with sth) (to do/for sth) to ask sb for sth in a very strong and serious way とてもきついまじめな様子で〜に…を頼む→**嘆願する，懇願する** ‖ *She pleaded with him not to leave her.* 彼女は彼に自分と別れないように懇願した．*He pleaded for mercy.* 彼は慈悲を懇願した．定義2 他 to state in a court of law that you did or did not do a crime あなたが罪を犯した，または犯していないことを法廷で述べる→**〜を弁護する，〜を抗弁として主張する** ‖ *The defendant pleaded not guilty to the charge of theft.* 被告は窃盗の罪に対して無実を主張した．定義3 自他 plead (sth) (for sb/sth) (used especially about a lawyer in a court of law) to support sb's case（特に法廷内の弁護士について）〜の訴訟事件を立証する→**弁護する，申し開きをする** ‖ *He needs the very best lawyer to plead (his case) for him.* 彼のために（彼の訴訟事件を）弁護する，最高の弁護士が，彼には必要だ．定義4 他 to give sth as an excuse or explanation for sth 〜のための言い訳または説明として，…を与える→**言い訳として〜と言う，〜を申し立てる** ‖ *He pleaded family problems as the reason for his lack of concentration.* 自分に集中力が欠けているのは，家族に問題があるからだ，と彼は弁解した．

*****pleasant** /pléz(ə)nt/ 形 定義 nice, enjoyable or friendly 良い，楽しい，または親しみやすい **気持ちの良い，快適な，感じの良い，愛想の良い** ‖ *a pleasant evening/climate/place/view* 快適な夜・天候・場所・眺め *a pleasant smile/voice/manner* 感じの良い笑顔・声・行儀 ⇔ **unpleasant** — **pleasantly** 副→**心地良く，快適に，感じ良く**

*****please**¹ /pli:z/ 副 定義 used as a polite way of asking for sth or telling sb to do sth 〜を頼む，または〜に…をするように言う，礼儀正しい言い方として用いて→**どうぞ，すみませんが，どうか** ‖ *Come in, please.* 入ってください，どうぞ．*Please don't spend too much money.* どうかそんなにお金を使わないでください．*Sit down, please.* どうぞ，お掛けください．*Two cups of coffee, please.* コーヒー2つ，お願いします．
成句 **yes, please** 定義 used when you are accepting an offer of sth politely 〜の申し出を礼儀正しく受け入れるときに用いて→**はい，お願いします** ‖ *'Sugar?' 'Yes, please.'*「お砂糖入れますか」「はい，お願いします」⇔ **No, thank you.**

*****please**² /pli:z/ 動 定義1 自他 to make sb happy; to satisfy 〜を喜ばせる；満足させる→**気に入る，好む；〜を喜ばせる，満足させる** ‖ *There's just no pleasing some people (= some people are impossible to please).* ある人々を満足させることはできない（= ある人々が満足することは不可能だ）．定義2 自（文中で主な動詞としてではなく用いて；as, what, whatever, anything などのような単語の後に用いて）to want; to choose 欲しい；選ぶ→**したいと思う** ‖ *You can't always do as you please.* いつも自分の好きなようにできるわけではありません．*She has so much money she can buy anything she pleases.* 彼女は大金を持っているので，欲しい

ものは何でも買える. **成句 please yourself** ▶定義 to be able to do whatever you want あなたのしたい事は何でもできる→自分の好きなようにする, 勝手に・気ままに行動する ‖ *Without anyone else to cook for I, can please myself what I eat.* 料理してあげる人がほかにだれもいないので, 自分が食べたい物を食べられる.

**pleased** /pliːzd/ 形（名詞の前は不可）▶定義 pleased (with sb/sth); pleased to do sth; pleased that... happy or satisfied about sth ～について幸福な, または満足している→喜んだ, 満足した, うれしい ‖ *John seems very pleased with his new car.* ジョンは新しい車にとても満足しているようだ. *Aren't you pleased to see me?* 私に会えてうれしくないの. *We're **only too pleased** (= very happy) to help.* 私たちは手助けできて, とても満足している（= とてもうれしい）. *I'm so pleased that you've decided to stay another week.* あなたがもう1週間滞在すると決心してくれて, 私はとてもうれしい. ☛参 glad の注 ⇔ **displeased**

**pleasing** /pliːzɪŋ/ 形 ▶定義 giving you pleasure and satisfaction 喜びと満足を与える→愉快な, 心地良い, 満足のいく ‖ *The exam results are very pleasing this year.* 今年の試験結果はとても満足のいくものだ. ⇔ **displeasing**

**pleasurable** /pléʒ(ə)rəb(ə)l/ 形正式 ▶定義 enjoyable 楽しい→愉快な, 楽しい, 心地良い ‖ *a pleasurable experience* 愉快な経験

**pleasure** /pléʒər/ 名 ▶定義 1 ❶the feeling of being happy or satisfied 幸福である, または満足している, という感情→楽しみ, 喜び, 満足 ‖ *Parents **get** a lot of **pleasure out of** watching their children grow up.* 子供たちが成長していく姿を見ることは, 親たちにとても多くの喜びをもたらす. *It **gives** me great **pleasure** to introduce our next speaker.* 次の話し手をご紹介します. ▶定義 2 ❶enjoyment (rather than work) （仕事ではなく）楽しみ→楽しみ ‖ *What brings you to Paris - business or pleasure?* なぜパリへお越しですか - 仕事それとも遊び. ▶定義 3 ❻ an event or activity, that you enjoy or that makes you happy 楽しんでいる, または自分を幸せにしてくれる活動または出来事→楽しい事, 娯楽 ‖ *It's been a pleasure to work with you.* あなたとご一緒に仕事ができてとても楽しかった

です. *'Thanks for your help.' **'It's a pleasure.'*** 「助けてくれてありがとう」「どういたしまして」

> ▶コミュニケーション
>
> 「いいですとも」に当たる快諾表現
>
> 人にものを頼まれたとき, 「いいですとも」と快く承諾するには With pleasure がよく使われます. 「喜んでする」に当たる英語は be willing to *do* だと機械的に覚えて, "Will you help me?" に, "Yes. I'm willing to help you." とやったのでは, 快諾にはなりません. この表現は「～しても構わない」(do not mind *doing*, have no objection to *doing*) を意味します.

**成句 take (no) pleasure in sth/doing sth** ▶定義 to enjoy/not enjoy (doing) sth (～をすること)を楽しむ・楽しまない→～を楽しむ・楽しまない, 喜んで～する・しない

**with pleasure** ▶定義 used as a polite way of saying that you are happy to do sth 喜んで～をすることを言う, 礼儀正しい言い方として用いて→喜んで, よろしいですとも ‖ *'Could you give me a lift into town?' 'Yes, with pleasure.'* 「街まで乗せていってもらえますか」「ええ, 喜んで」

**pleat** /pliːt/ 名 ❻ ▶定義 a permanent fold that is sewn or pressed into a piece of cloth 布地に縫い付けられている, または型押しされている, 耐久性のあるひだ→(スカートなどの)プリーツ, ひだ ‖ *a skirt with pleats at the front* 前にプリーツの入ったスカート

**pledge** /pledʒ/ 名 ❻ ▶定義 a pledge (to do sth) a formal promise or agreement 正式な約束または同意→誓い, 誓約, 約束 — pledge 動他 pledge (sth) (to sb/sth) ▶～を誓約・保証・約束する ‖ *The Government has pledged £250000 to help the victims of the crash.* 政府はその衝突の被害者の救済に25万ポンドを約束した.

**plentiful** /pléntɪfəl, -f(ə)l/ 形 ▶定義 available in large amounts or numbers 大量, または多数を入手できる→(あり余るほど)たっぷりある, 十分な, 豊富な ‖ *Fruit is plentiful at this time of year.* この時期, フルーツは豊富です. ⇔ **scarce**

**plenty** /plénti/ 代副 ▶定義 1 plenty (of sb/sth)

## pliable

as much or as many of sth as you need 人が必要なだけの量または数の〜→**たっぷり, 十分, 豊富** ‖ *'Shall I get some more coffee?' 'No, we've still got plenty.'*「コーヒーのお代わりをお持ちしましょうか」「いえ、まだ十分あります」 *There's still plenty of time to get there.* そこに着くにはまだたっぷり時間がかかる. *Have you brought plenty to drink?* 飲み物を十分持ってきましたか. ▶定義**2** (more の前で) a lot たくさん→**たっぷり, 十分に** ‖ *There's plenty more ice cream.* まだたっぷりアイスクリームがある. ▶定義**3** 略式 (enough が後に続く, big, long, tall などと共に用いて) easily 確かに→**とても, 非常に** ‖ *'This shirt's too small.' 'Well, it looks plenty big enough to me.'*「このシャツは小さすぎる」「そうかな、私にはとても大きく見えるけど」

**pliable** /plάɪəb(ə)l/ (または **pliant** /plάɪənt/) 形 ▶定義**1** easy to bend or shape 曲げるまたは形づくることが簡単な→**曲げやすい, 柔軟な** ▶定義**2** (used about a person) easy to influence (人について) 影響することが簡単な (〜に) 影響されやすい, (〜の) 言いなりになる

**pliers** /plάɪɚz/ 名 [複数扱い] ▶定義 a tool made of two crossed pieces of metal with handles, that is used for holding things firmly and for cutting wire 物をしっかりつかんだり針金を切るために使われる, 取っ手のある, 2枚の交差した金属片で作られている道具→**ペンチ, プライヤー** ‖ *a pair of pliers* ペンチ1丁 ☞ tool のさし絵

**plight** /plάɪt/ 名 [単数扱い] 正式 ▶定義 a bad or difficult state or situation 悪いまたは難しい状態または状況→**苦しい状態, 苦境, 窮状**

**plimsoll** /plíms(ə)l, -sɔ̀(ː)l, -sɑ̀l/ (または **pump** 英 **sneaker**) 名 **⊙** ▶定義 a light shoe made of strong material (canvas) that is especially used for sports, etc 特に運動などに使われる, 強い素材 (キャンバス布) でできた軽い靴→**スニーカー, 運動靴** ‖ *a pair of plimsolls* スニーカー1足 ☞参 trainer

**plod** /plɑd/ 動 **(plodding; plodded)** plod **(along/on)** ▶定義**1** to walk slowly and in a heavy or tired way ゆっくりと重そうに, または疲れたように歩く→**とぼとぼ歩く, 重い足取りで進む** ‖ *We plodded on through the rain for nearly an hour.* 私たちは雨の中を1時間近くとぼとぼ歩いた. ▶定義**2** to make slow progress, especially with difficult or boring work 特に困難なまたは退屈な仕事で, ゆっくりと進展する→**こつこつ働く・勉強する** ‖ *I just plod on with my work and never seem to get anywhere.* 私はただこつこつ勉強しているが, 成果が上がらないように思える.

**plonk**¹ /plɔ(ː)ŋk, plɑŋk/ 動 英 (口語) ▶定義**1** **plonk sth (down)** to put sth down on sth, especially noisily or carelessly 特に騒々しく, またはむとんちゃくに〜を…に置く→**〜をドサッと置く, 無造作にほうり出す** ‖ *Just plonk your bag down anywhere.* その辺にかばんを置いてください. ▶定義**2** **plonk (yourself) (down)** to sit down heavily and carelessly どっかとむとんちゃくに座る→**〜に身を投げ出す, どすんと倒れる・座る** ‖ *He just plonked himself down in front of the TV.* 彼はテレビの前にどすんと座った.

**plonk**² /plɔ(ː)ŋk, plɑŋk/ 名 **⓿** 英 略式 ▶定義 cheap wine 安いワイン→**安物のワイン** ‖ *Let's open a bottle of plonk!* 安物のワインを開けよう.

**plop**¹ /plɑp/ 名 [通常は単数] ▶定義 a sound like that of a small object dropping into water ぽちゃんという音を立てて落ちる→**ぽちゃん, どぶん**

**plop**² /plɑp/ 動 **(plopping; plopped)** ▶定義 to fall making a plopping noise ぽちゃんという音を立てて落ちる→**ぽちゃんと音がする, どぶんと落ちる** ‖ *The frog plopped back into the water.* カエルが水の中にぽちゃんと戻った.

★**plot**¹ /plɑt/ 名 **⊙** ▶定義**1** the series of events which form the story of a novel, film, etc 小説, 映画などの話を形づくる, 一連の出来事→**筋, 構想** ‖ *The play had a very weak plot.* その芝居の構想はとても劣っていた. *I can't follow the plot of this novel.* 私はこの小説の筋に付いていけない. ▶定義**2** **a plot (to do sth)** a secret plan made by several people to do sth wrong or illegal 悪いまたは不法な〜をするためにいく人かによってなされる, 秘密の計画→**陰謀, (秘密の) 計画** ‖ *a plot to kill the president* 大統領殺害の陰謀 ▶定義**3** a small piece of land, used for a special purpose 特定の目的に使用される, 狭い土地→**(小区画の) 土地** ‖ *a plot of land* 小区画の土地

**plot**² /plɑt/ 動 **(plotting; plotted)** ▶定義**1**

自他 plot (with sb) (against sb) to make a secret plan to do something wrong or illegal 悪いまたは不法な物事をするために,秘密の計画を立てる→陰謀をたくらむ;～をたくらむ,企てる‖ *They were accused of plotting against the government.* 彼らは,政府に反対して陰謀をたくらんだと告発された. *The terrorists had been plotting this campaign for years.* テロリストたちはこのテロ行為を長い間たくらんでいた. ▶定義2 他 to mark sth on a map, diagram, etc 地図,図表などの上に～を示す→～の図表・地図・グラフなどを書く‖ *to plot the figures on a graph* グラフに数字を記入する

plough

plough (米 plow) /pláu/ 名 C ▶定義 a large farm tool which is pulled by a vehicle (a tractor) or by an animal. A plough turns the soil over ready for seeds to be planted. 乗り物(トラクター)または動物によってけん引される,大きな農耕用の道具. plough は,土を掘り返して種が植えられるようにする→すき ● 参 snowplough — plough 動自他 (比喩)→骨を折って進む,(仕事を)こつこつする,(本を)こつこつ読む‖ *The book was long and boring but I managed to plough through it (= read it with difficulty).* その本は長くてつまらなかったが,私は何とかこつこつと読み通した(やっとのことで読んだ).

ploy /plɔ́ɪ/ 名 C ▶定義 a ploy (to do sth) something that you say or do in order to get what you want or to persuade sb to do sth 自分の欲しいものを得る,または～に…をするように説得するために言う,またはすること→うまい手,策略,術策

pluck¹ /plʌk/ 動他 ▶定義1 pluck sth/sb (from sth/out) to remove or take sth/sb from a place ある場所から～を取り除く→～を引き抜く,引っ張る,ひょいと取る‖ *He plucked the letter from my hands.* 彼は私の手から手紙をひょいと取った. ▶定義2 to pull the feathers out of a bird in order to prepare it for cooking 料理の準備をするために,鳥の羽を引き抜く→～をむしり取る ▶定義3 to make the strings of a musical instrument play notes by moving your fingers across them 指を楽器の弦を横切って動かして,音を出す→～をかき鳴らす

成句 pluck up courage ▶定義 to try to get enough courage to do sth ～をするために十分な勇気を得ようとする→勇気を奮い起こす

句動詞 pluck at sth ▶定義 to pull sth gently several times 穏やかに数回,～を引く→ぐいと引く・引っ張る

pluck² /plʌk/ 名 U 略式 ▶定義 courage and determination 勇気と決断→勇気,決断 — plucky 形→勇気のある,元気な

plugs

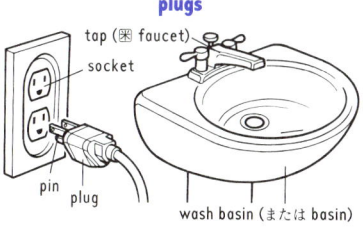

plug¹ /plʌg/ 名 C ▶定義1 a plastic or rubber object with two or three metal pins, which connects a piece of electrical equipment to the electricity supply 電気器具を電源とつなぐ,2つまたは3つの金属のピンが付いている,プラスチックまたはゴムの物→差し込み,プラグ ▶定義2 a round piece of rubber or plastic that you use to block the hole in a sink, bath, etc 洗面台,風呂などの穴をふさぐために使う,円形のゴムまたはプラスチック→栓 ▶定義3 a mention that sb makes of a new book, film, etc in order to encourage people to buy or see it 人々がそれを買うまたは見ることを促進させるために,～が新しい本,映画などについて取り立てて言うこと→推薦の言葉,宣伝,売り込み

plug² /plʌg/ 動他 (plugging; plugged) ▶定義1 to fill or block a hole with sth that fits tightly into it それにきつくぴったり合った～で,穴を埋めるまたはふさぐ→～に栓をする,ふさぐ,～を詰める‖ *He managed to plug the leak in the pipe.* 彼はパイプの漏れを何とかふさいだ. ▶定義2 略式 to say good things about a new book, film, etc in order to make people buy or see it 人々にそれを買わせるまたは見させるために、新しい本、映画などについて良い事を言う→～を盛んに宣伝する ‖ *They're really plugging that song on the radio at the moment.* 今のところラジオではあの音楽を本当に盛んに宣伝している．

句動詞 **plug sth in** ▶定義 to connect a piece of electrical equipment to the electricity supply or to another piece of equipment 電気器具を電源または別の器具とつなぐ→～のプラグをコンセントに差し込む，(ほかの電気器具に)接続する ‖ *Is the microphone plugged in?* そのマイクは接続されてますか． ⇨ **unplug**

**plughole** /plʌ́ghòʊl/ 名 英 ▶定義 a hole in a bath, etc where the water flows away 水が流れ出す，風呂などの穴→排水口

**plum** /plʌm/ 名 C ▶定義 a soft, round fruit with red or yellow skin and a stone in the middle 赤または黄色の皮と真ん中に種のある、柔らかくて丸い果物→西洋スモモ、プラム ☛ C3 ページのさし絵

**plumber** /plʌ́mər/ 名 C ▶定義 a person whose job is to put in or repair water pipes, baths, toilets, etc 送水管、お風呂、トイレなどを取り付けるまたは修理することが仕事の人→配管工

**plumbing** /plʌ́mɪŋ/ 名 U ▶定義 1 all the pipes, taps, etc in a building 建物の中のすべての管、栓など→配管(設備)、下水(設備) ▶定義 2 the work of a person who puts in and repairs water pipes, taps, etc 送水管、栓などを取り付けて修理する人の仕事→配管工事、衛生工事

**plume** /pluːm/ 名 C ▶定義 1 a quantity of smoke that rises in the air 空気中に立ち昇る、多量の煙→煙の柱 ▶定義 2 a large feather or group of feathers, often worn as a decoration しばしば飾りとして着けられる、大きな羽、または羽の集まり→羽、羽飾り

**plump**¹ /plʌmp/ 形 ▶定義 (used about a person or an animal) pleasantly fat (人または動物について)感じ良く太っている→ぽっちゃりした、ふっくらした ‖ *the baby's plump cheeks* 赤ちゃんのぽっちゃりしたほお

**plump**² /plʌmp/ 動

句動詞 **plump (yourself/sb/sth) down** ▶定義 to sit down or to put sb/sth down heavily 重そうに座る、または～を置く→どすんと座る；～をどさっと置く、無造作に置く ‖ *She plumped herself down by the fire.* 火のそばに彼女はどすんと座った．

**plump for sb/sth** 英 略式 ▶定義 to choose or decide to have sb/sth ～を持つことを選ぶまたは決定する→～を(迷った挙げ句)選ぶ、～を絶対に支持する ‖ *I think I'll plump for the roast chicken, after all.* 何だかんだ言っても、結局は私はローストチキンを選ぶだろうな．

**plunder** /plʌ́ndər/ 名 U ▶定義 the action of stealing from people or places, especially during war or fighting; the goods that are stolen 特に戦争中またはけんかの間に、人々または当然あるべき場所から盗む行為；盗まれた品物→略奪(行為)、略奪品、盗品 — **plunder** 動 自 他→略奪する、盗む；～を略奪する、分捕る

**plunge**¹ /plʌndʒ/ 動 ▶定義 1 自 plunge (into sth/in) to jump, drop or fall suddenly and with force 突然に勢いで、跳ぶ、落とす、または落ちる→飛び込む、潜る、つんのめる ‖ *He ran to the river and plunged in.* 彼は川まで走り、飛び込んだ．(比喩) *Share prices plunged overnight.* 一晩で株価が急落した． ▶定義 2 他 plunge sth in/into sth to push sth suddenly and with force into sth 突然に勢いで、～を…に押し入れる→～を(急に)入れる、突っ込む、つんのめらす ‖ *He plunged the knife into the table in anger.* 彼は怒りでナイフをテーブルに突き立てた． ▶定義 3 他 to cause sb/sth to suddenly be in the state mentioned ～を突然に言及された状態にさせる→～を(急に)…の状態にする、～に陥れる ‖ *The country has been plunged into chaos by the floods.* その国は洪水によって大混乱となっている． ▶定義 4 自 plunge into sth to start doing sth with energy and enthusiasm 気力と熱意を持って～をすることを始める→(急に)～し始める、～の状態になる・突入する ‖ *Think carefully before you plunge into buying a house.* 家を買う前に、慎重に考えなさい．

**plunge**² /plʌndʒ/ 名 C ▶定義 a sudden jump, drop or fall 突然の跳躍、落下または転倒→飛び込むこと、突入、降下 ‖ *I slipped and took a plunge in the river.* 私は滑って川に落ちた．*the plunge in house prices* 住宅価格の急落

成句 **take the plunge** ▶定義 to decide to do

sth difficult after thinking about it for quite a long time かなり長い間考えた後,難しい〜をすると決定する➔思い切ってやってみる,(思い切って)結婚する ‖ *After going out together for five years, they took the plunge and got married.* 5年間付き合った後,彼らは思い切って結婚した.

**pluperfect** /pluːpə́ːrfɪkt/ = **PAST PERFECT**

★**plural** /plúərəl/ 名 (文法) ▶定義 the form of a noun, verb, etc which refers to more than one person or thing 2人以上の人,2つ以上の物に言及する名詞,動詞などの形➔複数形 ‖ *The plural of 'boat' is 'boats'.* boat の複数形はboats です. *The verb should be in the plural.* その動詞は複数形でなければなりません.— plural 形➔複数の〜参 singular

★**plus**¹ /plʌs/ 前 ▶定義 **1** and; added to と;〜を加えた➔〜を加えて,プラスして ‖ *Two plus two is four (2 + 2 = 4).* 2足す2は4です(2 + 2 = 4). ⇔ **minus** ▶定義 **2** in addition to; and also 〜に加えて;〜もまた➔〜に加えて,〜のほかに,その上に ‖ *You have to work five days a week plus every other weekend.* あなたは週5日,それに加えて隔週末に働かなくてはなりません.

**plus**² /plʌs/ 名 C ▶定義 **1** the sign (+) + の記号➔プラス記号,正符号 ⇔ **minus** ▶定義 **2** an advantage of a situation 状況の利点➔有利な点,利益

**plus**³ /plʌs/ 形 (名詞の後だけ) ▶定義 **1** or more またはより多く➔〜以上 ‖ *I'd say there were 30000 plus at the match.* 多分,その試合には3万人以上がいた. ▶定義 **2** (used for marking work done by students) slightly above (生徒がした勉強を評価するために)わずかに上の➔〜の上,プラスの ‖ *I got a B plus (= B+) for my homework.* 私は宿題でBの上 (= B+)をもらった. ⇔ **minus**

**plush** /plʌʃ/ 形 ▶定義 comfortable and expensive 快適で高価な➔すばらしい,豪華な ‖ *a plush hotel* 豪華なホテル

**Pluto** /plúːtoʊ/ 名 [単数扱い] ▶定義 the planet that is furthest from the sun 太陽から一番遠い惑星➔冥王星(めいおうせい)

**ply** /plaɪ/ 動 (現分 **plying**;三単現 **plies**;過,過分 **plied**) 自他 ▶定義 to try to sell services or goods to people, especially on the street 特に路上で,人々にサービスまたは品物を売ろうとする➔〜に精を出す,〜にしつこく勧める ‖ *Boat owners were **plying** their **trade** to passing tourists.* 船の所有者たちは,通り掛かりの旅行者たちに自分の船に乗らないかとしつこく勧めていた. *to ply for business* 商売に精を出す

句動詞 ply sb with sth ▶定義 to keep giving sb food and drink, or asking sb questions 〜に食べ物と飲み物を与え続ける,または〜に質問し続ける➔〜にしつこく勧める,〜を悩ます,質問攻めにする ‖ *They plied us with food from the moment we arrived.* 私たちが到着してから ずっと,彼らは私たちに食べ物をしつこく勧めた.

**plywood** /pláɪwòd/ 名 U ▶定義 board made by sticking several thin layers of wood together いく枚かの薄い木材を層のように重ねて一緒に張り合わせて作られる板➔合板,ベニヤ板

★**pm** (困 **PM**) /pìː ém, ≈/ 副 ▶定義 after midday 正午の後➔午後の ‖ *2 pm (= 2 o'clock in the afternoon)* 2 pm (= 午後2時) *11.30 pm (= 11.30 in the evening)* 11:30 pm (= 晩の11時30分)

**pneumonia** /n(j)uːmóʊnjə/ 名 U ▶定義 a serious illness of the lungs which makes breathing difficult 呼吸することを困難にさせる,肺の重い病気➔肺炎

**PO** /pìː óʊ, ≈/ 略 (複合名詞で用いて) Post Office➔郵便局 ‖ *a PO box* 私書箱

**poach** /poʊtʃ/ 動 他 ▶定義 **1** to cook food (especially fish or eggs) gently in a small amount of liquid 少量の液体の中で,食べ物(特に魚または卵)を穏やかに調理する➔〜を熱湯の中に落としてゆでる ‖ *poached eggs* 落とし卵 ▶定義 **2** to hunt animals illegally on sb else's land ほかの〜の土地で動物を不法に狩る➔〜を密猟・密漁する ‖ *The men were caught poaching elephants.* その男たちは象を密猟していて捕まった. ▶定義 **3** to take an idea from sb else and use it as though it is your own ほかの〜の考えを盗んで,あたかも自分の考えであるかのように使う➔〜を横取りする ▶定義 **4** to take members of staff from another company in an unfair way 不正な方法で,別の会社から従業員を連れてくる➔〜を引き抜く

**poacher** /póʊtʃər/ 名 C ▶定義 a person who hunts animals illegally on sb else's land ほかの〜の土地で不法に動物を狩る人➔密猟者,密漁者

**PO box** /pìː oʊ báks/ 名 C ▶定義 a place in a

post office where letters, packages, etc are kept until they are collected by the person they were sent to 送られた人に回収されるまで手紙、小包などが保管される、郵便局内の場所→私書箱 ‖ *The address is PO Box 4287, Nairobi, Kenya.* 住所はケニアのナイロビ、私書箱4287だ.

★**pocket**¹ /pákət/ 名 C ▶定義 **1** a piece of material like a small bag that is sewn inside or on a piece of clothing and is used for carrying things in 衣服の内側または外側に縫い付けられ、その中に物を入れて運ぶために使われる、小さなかばんのような物→ポケット ‖ *He always walks with his hands in his trouser pockets.* 彼はいつもズボンのポケットに手を入れて歩く. *a pocket dictionary/calculator (= one small enough to fit in your pocket)* 小型辞書・携帯用計算機 (= ポケットに収まるほど小さい物) ← C6 ページのさし絵 ▶定義 **2** a small bag or container that is fixed to the inside of a car door, suitcase, etc and used for putting things in 車のドア、スーツケースなどの内側に固定されていて、物を中に入れるために使われる、小さな袋または入れ物→ポケット状の物 ‖ *There are safety instructions in the pocket of the seat in front of you.* あなたの前の座席のポケットに安全指示書が入っています. ■ **bag** のさし絵 ▶定義 **3** used to talk about the amount of money that you have to spend 自分が使わなければならない金額について話すために用いて→(懐中の)金、所持金、資力 ‖ *They sell cars to suit every pocket.* 彼らはそれぞれの所持金に見合った車を売る. *The school couldn't afford a CD player, so the teacher bought one **out of** his **own pocket**.* その学校はCDプレーヤーを買う余裕がなかったので、その先生が自腹を切って1台買った. ▶定義 **4** a small area or group that is different from its surroundings 周りとは異なる地域または集団→(周囲から)孤立した地域・集団 ‖ *a pocket of warm air* そこだけ温かい雰囲気

成句 pick sb's pocket ⇒ **PICK**¹

**pocket**² /pákət/ 動 他 ▶定義 **1** to put sth in your pocket ～を自分のポケットに入れる→～をポケットに入れる・しまう ‖ *He took the letter and pocketed it quickly.* 彼は手紙を取って素早くポケットにしまった. ▶定義 **2** to steal or win money お金を盗む、または獲得する→～を横領・着服する

**pocket money** 名 U (米 **allowance**) ▶定義 an amount of money that parents give a child to spend, usually every week 通常毎週、親が子供に使うように与える金額→小遣い、小遣い銭

**pod** /pɑd/ 名 C ▶定義 the long, green part of some plants, such as peas and beans, that contains the seeds 種を含んでいる、ある植物 (例えばえんどう豆とそら豆のような) の長い緑の部分→さや ← C3 ページのさし絵

**podiatrist** /poʊdáɪətrɪst, pə-/ 米 = **CHIROPODIST**

**podium** /póʊdiəm/ 名 C ▶定義 a small platform for a speaker, a performer, etc to stand on 話し手、演奏者などが立つための小さな壇→(オーケストラの) 指揮台、演壇

★**poem** /póʊəm/ 名 C ▶定義 a piece of writing arranged in short lines. Poems try to express thoughts and feelings with the help of sound and rhythm. 短い行に整えられた、書かれた作品. 音やリズムの助けを借りて、思考と感情を表現しようとする→詩、韻文

★**poet** /póʊət/ 名 C ▶定義 sb who writes poems 詩を書く～→詩人、詩的才能のある人

**poetic** /poʊétɪk/ (または **poetical** /-ɪk(ə)l/) 形 ▶定義 connected with poets or like a poem 詩人または詩のようなものに関連している→詩の、詩的な、詩のような ― **poetically** /-k(ə)li/ 副 →詩的に

★**poetry** /póʊətri/ 名 U ▶定義 a collection of poems; poems in general 詩集; 一般的な詩→詩、詩文、詩歌 ‖ *Shakespeare's poetry and plays* シェークスピアの詩と劇 *Do you like poetry?* あなたは詩が好きですか.

▶ **prose** と比較.

**poignant** /pɔ́ɪnjənt, -nənt/ 形 ▶定義 causing sadness or pity 悲しみまたは哀れを誘うような→痛ましい、痛切な、痛烈な ‖ *a poignant memory* 胸が痛む思い出 ― **poignancy** /-jənsi/ 名 U →鋭さ、激しさ、辛辣 (しんらつ) ― **poignantly** 副 →痛ましく

★**point**¹ /pɔɪnt/ 名 ▶定義 **1** C a particular fact, idea or opinion that sb expresses ～が表現する特定の事実、考えまたは意見→事項、問題、(考える)点 ‖ *You **make** some interesting **points** in your essay.* あなたは、小論文の中で興味深い指

摘をいくつかされています. *I see your point but I don't agree with you.* あなたの考えは分かるが、私は同意できない.

➤ a point（問題）には bring up（持ち出す）, raise（提出する）, make（指摘する）, argue（議論する）, emphasize（強調する）, そして illustrate（説明する）という表現がある.

▶定義2 **the point**[単数扱い] the most important part of what is being said; the main piece of information 言われた事の最も重要な部分; 重要な情報 → **要点, 眼目, 触り** ‖ *It makes no difference how much it costs - **the point is** we don't have any money!* それがいくらだろうと構わない — 要は私たちにお金がないということだ. *She always talks and talks and takes ages to **get to the point**.* 彼女はいつもああだ, こうだと話して, 要点を話すまでにえらく長い時間がかかる. ▶定義3 ❹an important idea or thought that needs to be considered 考慮される必要のある重要な着想, または考え → **論点, 問題, 事柄** ‖ *'Have you checked what time the last bus back is?' 'That's a point - no I haven't.'*「帰りの最終バスが何時か確認しましたか」「それは問題ですね — いえ, まだしていません」▶定義4 ❹a detail, characteristic or quality of sb/sth 〜の詳細, 特色, または性質 →**（特徴, 特質, 特色のある）点** ‖ *Make a list of your **strong points** and your **weak points** (= good and bad qualities).* あなたの長所と短所（= 良い性質と悪い性質）を表にしなさい. ▶定義5 [単数扱い] **the point (of/in sth/doing sth)** the meaning, reason or purpose of sth 〜の意味, 理由または目的 → **効果, 意味, 目的** ‖ *She's said no, so **what's the point** of telephoning her again?* 彼女は駄目だと言った, だからまた彼女に電話をかけて何になるんだ. *There's no point in talking to my parents - they never listen.* 私の両親に話しても無駄ですよ — 彼らは決して耳を貸さないんです. ▶定義6 ❹（しばしば複合語で）a particular place, position or moment 特定の場所, 位置または時 →**（空間や時間の）点, 地点, 時点,（目盛りの）度** ‖ *The library is a good **starting point** for that sort of information.* 図書館はその種の情報を調べ始めるにはもってこいの場所です. *He has reached the **high point** of his career.* 彼は自分の職業の絶頂にたどり着いた. *the boiling/freezing point of water* 水の沸点・氷点 *He waved to the crowd and it was **at that point** that the shot was fired.* 彼は群集に手を振った, そして彼が撃たれたのは, その時だった. ***At one point** I thought I was going to laugh.* ある時点で, 私は笑い出してしまうと思った. ▶定義7 ❹the thin sharp end of sth 〜の薄い鋭い端 → **先端, 先** ‖ *the point of a pin/needle/pencil* ピンの先・針先・鉛筆の先 ▶定義8 ❹a small round dot used when writing parts of numbers 数字の部分を書いているときに使用される, 小さな円形の点 → **小数点** ‖ *She ran the race in 11.2 (eleven point two) seconds.* 彼女は11.2秒でレースを走った. ▶定義9 ❹a single mark in some games, sports, etc that you add to others to get the score ある種のゲーム, スポーツなどで, 得点とするためにこれまでのものに加える, 1点 → **点数, 得点** ‖ *to score a point* 得点する *Rios needs two more points to win the match.* ライオスはその試合に勝つためにあと2点必要である. ▶定義10 ❹a unit of measurement for certain things あるものの測定の単位 → **（活字・相場の）ポイント** ‖ *The value of the dollar has fallen by a few points.* ドルの価値は数ポイント下落した.

成句 **be on the point of doing sth** ▶定義 just going to do sth ちょうど今〜をしようと → **まさに〜しようとしている, 〜するところである** ‖ *I was on the point of going out when the phone rang.* 電話が鳴った時, 私は出掛けるところだった.

**beside the point** ⇒ **BESIDE**

**have your, etc (good) points** ▶定義 to have some good qualities いくつか良い質を持っている → **(それなりに) 良いところがある** ‖ *Bill has his good points, but he's very unreliable.* ビルにも良いところはあるが, 頼りにならない.

**make a point of doing sth** ▶定義 to make sure you do sth because it is important or necessary それが重要または必要であるので, 必ず〜するようにする → **必ず〜することにしている, 努めて〜することにしている** ‖ *I made a point of locking all the doors and windows before leaving the house.* 私は家を出る前に, 必ずすべてのドアと窓のかぎをかけることにした.

**point of view** ▶定義 a way of looking at a situation; an opinion 状況の見方; 意見 → **観点, 見地, 意見** ‖ *From my point of view it would be better* *to wait a little longer.* 私の意見では、もうしばらく待った方がいいでしょう. ☛類 **viewpoint, standpoint**

▶ from my point of view と in my opinion を混同しないように. 最初のものは「私の生活の立場からすれば」(= 女性, 社会人, 教師などとして) を意味する. 2番目のものは「私が思うに」を意味する: *From an advertiser's point of view, television is a wonderful medium.*(広告者側の観点では、テレビはすばらしい媒体だ.) *In my opinion people watch too much television.*(私が思うに、人々はテレビを見すぎている.)

**prove your/the case/point** ⇒ **PROVE**
**a sore point** ⇒ **SORE**¹
**sb's strong point** ⇒ **STRONG**
**take sb's point** ▶定義 to understand and accept what sb is saying 〜の言っている事を理解して受け入れる→(人の意見など)を正しいものと見なす

**to the point** ▶定義 connected with what is being discussed; relevant 議論されていることに関連して; 関連した→要領を得た, 適切な ∥ *His speech was short and to the point.* 彼のスピーチは短くて要領を得ていた.

**up to a point** ▶定義 partly→部分的に ∥ *I agree with you up to a point.* 部分的にはあなたに同意します.

*★**point**² /pɔ́int/ 動 ▶定義1 ⊜ point （at/to sb/sth） to show where sth is or to draw attention to sth using your finger, a stick, etc 〜がある所を示す, または指, 棒などを使って〜へ注意を引く→指差す, 指示する ∥ *'I'll have that one,' she said, pointing to a chocolate cake.*「あれにするわ」と, チョコレートケーキを指差しながら, 彼女は言った. ▶定義2 ⊜⊕ point （sth） （at/towards sb/sth） to aim (sth) in the direction of sb/sth 〜の方向に（…を）向ける→(〜の方を)向いている; 〜を向ける ∥ *She pointed the gun at the target and fired.* 彼女は銃を標的に向けて撃った. ▶定義3 ⊜ to face in a particular direction or to show that sth is in a particular direction 特定の方向に向く, または〜が特定の方向あることを示す→(〜の方向に)向く,（〜に）面している, 指し示す ∥ *The sign pointed towards the motorway.* その標識は高速道路の方向を指し示していた. *Turn round until you're pointing north.* 北に向くまで回ってください. ▶定義4 ⊜ point to sth to show that sth is likely to exist, happen or be true 〜が存在するような, 起こりそうな, または事実でありそうなことを示す→（方向・傾向を）示す, 暗示する ∥ *Research points to a connection between diet and cancer.* 研究は食餌（しょくじ）療法とがんの関係を示している.

▶コミュニケーション

「自分を指す」動作の日英比較

point one's finger at one's chest: 日本人は, 自分のことを指すのに, 主として人差し指で鼻を指しますが, 英米人が鼻を指すことはありません.「だれのこと, 私のこと？」(Do you mean me?)「私にご用？」(Do you want me?) などと尋ねるときは, 英米人は人差し指で胸の辺りを指すのが普通です.

句動詞 **point sth out (to sb)** ▶定義 to make sb look at sth; to make sth clear to sb 〜に…をよく見させる; 〜に…をはっきりさせる→〜を指し示す, 指差す; 〜を指摘する ∥ *The guide pointed out all the places of interest to us on the way.* そのガイドは私たちに道すがら面白そうな場所すべてを指し示した. *I'd like to point out that we haven't got much time left.* はっきりさせておきたいんだけど, 私たちにはそんなに時間が残っていないよ.

**point-blank** 形副 ▶定義1 (used about a shot) from a very close position (射撃について) とても近い位置から→至近距離から射った・ねらった, 直射の; 至近距離で, 直射で ∥ *He was shot in the leg at point-blank range.* 彼は至近距離から足を撃たれた. ▶定義2 (used about sth that is said) very direct and not polite; not allowing any discussion (言われている〜について) とても直接的で礼儀正しくない; どんな議論も許されない→単刀直入の, あからさまの, きっぱりした; 単刀直入に, あからさまに, きっぱりと ∥ *He told her point-blank to get out of the house and never come back.* 彼は彼女に, 家から出ていって二度と戻ってくるなと単刀直入に言った.

**pointed** /pɔ́intəd/ 形 ▶定義1 having a sharp end 鋭い端を持っている→(先の)とがった, 鋭い ∥ *a pointed stick/nose* 先のとがったつえ・鼻

▶定義2 (used about sth that is said) critical of sb in an indirect way（言われる～について）間接的に…に批判的な**➔辛辣(しんらつ)な,批判的な,当て付けた** ‖ *She made a pointed comment about people who are always late.* いつも遅刻する人々について,彼女は批判的な意見を言った. ― **pointedly** 副 ➔**辛辣に,当て付けて**

**pointer** /pɔ́ɪntər/ 名 **C** ▶定義1 a piece of helpful advice or information 役に立つ情報または助言➔**助言,ヒント,指針** ‖ *Could you give me some pointers on how best to tackle the problem?* どうやったら一番よくその問題に取り組めるか助言を頂けますか. ▶定義2 a small arrow on a computer screen that you move by moving the mouse 人がマウスを動かすことで動かせる,コンピューター画面上の小さな矢➔**矢印,ポインター** ☞ S5 ページのさし絵 ▶定義3 a stick that is used to point to things on a map, etc 地図上の物を指すときに使われる棒➔**棒,ポインター**

**pointless** /pɔ́ɪntləs/ 形 ▶定義 without any use or purpose 全く使えないまたは何の目的もない➔**要領を得ない,無益な,無意味な** ‖ *It's pointless to try and make him agree.* 彼を同意させるのは無意味だ. ― **pointlessly** 副 ➔**無意味に** ― **pointlessness** 名 **U** ➔**無意味**

**poise** /pɔ́ɪz/ 名 **U** ▶定義 a calm, confident way of behaving 落ち着いて確信に満ちた態度➔**平静,落ち着き,自信**

**poised** /pɔ́ɪzd/ 形 ▶定義1 not moving but ready to move 動いていないが,動く準備のできた➔**～しようと身構えた** ‖ *'Shall I call the doctor or not ?' he asked, his hand poised above the telephone.* すぐにも電話しようと手を電話にかざして「医者を呼びますか」と彼は尋ねた. ▶定義2 poised (to do sth) ready to act; about to do sth 行動する準備のできた; まさに～をしようとしている➔**いつでも～できる,体勢が整った** ‖ *The government is poised to take action if the crisis continues.* もしもこの危機が続くようなら,政府は行動を起こす体勢が整っている. ▶定義3 calm and confident 落ち着いて確信に満ちた➔**落ち着いた,自信のある**

\***poison**¹ /pɔ́ɪz(ə)n/ 名 **C U** ▶定義 a substance that kills or harms you if you eat or drink it もし人が食べるまたは飲むと,人を殺すまたは害する物質➔**毒,毒薬** ‖ *rat poison* 殺鼠(さっそ)剤 *poi-son gas* 毒ガス

**poison**² /pɔ́ɪz(ə)n/ 動 他 ▶定義1 to kill, harm or damage sb/sth with poison 毒によって～を殺す,害する,または傷付ける➔**～を毒殺する,人に毒を盛る** ▶定義2 to put poison in sth➔**～に毒を入れる** ‖ *The cup of coffee had been poisoned.* そのコーヒーには毒が入っていました. ▶定義3 to spoil or ruin sth ～を腐らせる,駄目にする➔**～を汚染する,害する,毒する** ‖ *The quarrel had poisoned their relationship.* そのけんかで彼らの関係が駄目になった. ― **poisoned** 形 ➔**毒入りの,毒を塗った** ‖ *a poisoned drink* 毒入りの飲み物

**poisoning** /pɔ́ɪz(ə)nɪŋ/ 名 **U** ▶定義 the giving or taking of poison or a dangerous substance 毒または危険な物質を与えているまたは取っていること➔**中毒,毒物混入** ‖ *He got food poisoning from eating fish that wasn't fresh.* 彼は新鮮でない魚を食べて食中毒になった.

**poisonous** /pɔ́ɪz(ə)nəs/ 形 ▶定義1 causing death or illness if you eat or drink it もし食べるまたは飲むと,病気または死の原因となる➔**有毒な,有害な** ▶定義2 (used about animals, etc) producing and using poison to attack its enemies（動物などについて）敵を攻撃するために,毒を作っているまたは使っている➔**有害な,有毒な** ‖ *He was bitten by a poisonous snake.* 彼は毒蛇にかまれた. ▶定義3 very unpleasant and intended to upset sb とても不愉快で～を怒らせようと計画された➔**悪意に満ちた,ひどく不快な** ‖ *She wrote him a poisonous letter criticizing his behaviour.* 彼女は彼の行動を批判した悪意に満ちた手紙を書いた.

**poke** /póʊk/ 動 ▶定義1 ⊕ to push sb/sth with a finger, stick or other long, thin object 指,棒,またはほかの細長い物で,～を押す➔**～をつつく,押す,突く** ‖ *Be careful you don't poke yourself in the eye with that stick!* そのつえで自分の目をつつかないように気を付けなさい.
▶定義2 ⊜⊕ poke (sth) into, through, out of, down, etc sth to push sth quickly into sth or in a certain direction ～にまたはある方向に…を素早く押す➔**(～に)…を突っ込む,押し込む,(～から)…を突き出す** ‖ *He poked the stick down the hole to see how deep it was.* その穴が

## 1238 poker

どれだけ深いか見ようとして,彼は穴に棒切れを突っ込んだ. *A child's head poked up from behind the wall.* 子供の頭が塀の裏から突き出ていた. ☛ S6 ページのさし絵 ― poke 名 C →突くこと,つつくこと

成句 **poke fun at sb/sth** ▶定義 to make jokes about sb/sth, often in an unkind way しばしば思いやりのないやり方で,〜について冗談を言う → ～をからかう

**poke/stick your nose into sth** ⇒ **NOSE**¹

**poker** /póʊkər/ 名 ▶定義 1 ❶ a type of card game usually played to win money 普通お金をかけてするトランプゲームの一種 → ポーカー
▶定義 2 ❸ a metal stick for moving the coal or wood in a fire 火中の石炭または木材を動かすための金属の棒 → 火かき棒 ☛ fireplace のさし絵

**poky** /póʊki/ 形 略式 ▶定義 (used about a house, room, etc) too small (家,部屋などについて)小さすぎる → 狭い,狭苦しい ‖ *a poky little office* 狭苦しい小さな事務所

**polar** /póʊlər/ 形 (名詞の前だけ) ▶定義 of or near the North or South Pole 北極または南極の,または北極または南極に近い → 北極の,南極の,極地に近い ‖ *the polar regions* 極地帯

**polar bear** 名 ❸ ▶定義 a large white bear that lives in the area near the North Pole 北極に近い地域に生息する,大きなシロクマ → 北極グマ,シロクマ

★**pole** /póʊl/ 名 ❸ ▶定義 1 a long, thin piece of wood or metal, used especially to hold sth up 特に～を支えるために使われる,長くて細い木材または金属 → 棒,さお,柱 ‖ *a flagpole* 旗ざお *a tent pole* テントの支柱 ☛ ski のさし絵
▶定義 2 either of the two points at the exact top and bottom of the earth 地球のまさに最上部と最下部にある 2 地点のどちらか一方 → 極,極地 ‖ *the North/South Pole* 北極・南極 ☛ **earth** のさし絵

**the pole vault** 名 ❸ ▶定義 the sport of jumping over a high bar with the help of a long pole 長い棒の助けを借りて,高い横木を飛び越す競技 → 棒高跳び

★**police**¹ /pəlíːs/ 名 [複数扱い] ▶定義 the official organization whose job is to make sure that people obey the law, and to prevent and solve crime 人々が法律に従っているか確認することと,犯罪を防ぎまた解決することが仕事である,公的な組織 → **警察** ‖ *Dial 999 if you need to call the police.* もし警察に電話する必要があるなら,999にかけなさい. *a police car* パトカー *Kamal wants to join the police force when he finishes school.* カマルは学校を卒業したら,警察に入りたいと思っている. *the local police station* 地元の警察署

▶ police は複数名詞で,常に複数動詞が使われる. 1 人の男または女の意味で a police とは言えない. 組織について話しているときは,常に the を使う: *There were over 100 police on duty.* (100 人を超える警官が任務に就いていた.) *The police are investigating the murder.* (警察はその殺人を捜査している.)

**police**² /pəlíːs/ 動 他 ▶定義 to keep control in a place by using the police or a similar official group 警察または類似の公的な集団を使って,ある場所を監督する → ～を警備する,取り締まる,～の治安を保つ ‖ *The cost of policing football games is extremely high.* サッカー競技を警備する費用はとても高い.

**police constable** (または **constable**) 名 ❸ 英 (略 **PC**) ▶定義 a police officer of the lowest rank 一番低い階級の警察官 → 巡査

**police officer** (または **officer**) 名 ❸ ▶定義 a member of the police 警察の一員 → 警察官,警官,巡査

★**policy** /páləsi/ 名 ❸ U (複 **policies**) ▶定義 1 **policy** (on sth) a plan of action agreed or chosen by a government, a company, etc 政府,会社などによって同意,または選択された行動計画 → 政策,方針 ‖ *Labour has a new set of policies on health.* 労働党は健康に関する新しい政策を持っている. *It is company policy not to allow smoking in meetings.* 会議中の禁煙は,会社の方針だ. ▶定義 2 a way of behaving that you think is best in a particular situation 特定の状況において最善であると自分が考える振る舞い方 → やり方,手段,方策 ‖ *It's my policy only to do business with people I like.* 自分の好む人々とだけ仕事をすることが私のやり方だ. ▶定義 3 a document that shows an agreement that you have made with an insurance company 保険会社と結んだ契約を示す書類 → 保険証券・証書 ‖ *an insurance policy* 保険証書

**polio** /póuliòu/ 名 U ▶定義 a serious disease which can cause you to lose the power in certain muscles 筋肉の力を衰えさせる深刻な病気→小児まひ, ポリオ

**polish**¹ /pɑ́lɪʃ/ 動 他 ▶定義 to make sth shine by rubbing it and often by putting a special cream or liquid on it しばしば特別なクリームまたは液体を付けて, ~をこすって輝かせる→~を磨く, ~のつやを出す ‖ *to polish your shoes/a table* 靴・テーブルを磨く

句動詞 **polish sth off** 略式 ▶定義 to finish sth quickly ~を素早く終わらせる→~を素早く仕上げる, 手早く処理する, さっさと食べてしまう ‖ *The two of them polished off a whole chicken for dinner!* 彼らのうちの2人が夕食用のチキンを丸ごと平らげてしまった.

**polish**² /pɑ́lɪʃ/ 名 ▶定義 1 ❶ a cream, liquid, etc that you put on sth to clean it and make it shine 清潔にするまたは輝かせるために, ~に付けるクリーム, 液体など→つやを出す物, 磨き粉, 光沢剤 ‖ *a tin of shoe polish* 靴磨きの缶 ☞ **bucket** のさし絵 ▶定義 2 [単数扱い] the action of polishing sth ~を磨く行為→磨きをかけること, 磨くこと ‖ *I'll give the glasses a polish before the guests arrive.* お客様が到着する前に, グラスに磨きをかけておきます.

**polished** /pɑ́lɪʃt/ 形 ▶定義 1 shiny because of polishing 磨かれているから輝いている→光沢のある, 磨き上げた ‖ *polished wood floors* 光沢のある木の床 ▶定義 2 (used about a performance, etc) of a high standard (演技などについて) 高い水準の→洗練された, 上品な, 巧みな ‖ *Most of the actors gave a polished performance.* 俳優たちの多くが巧みな演技を行った.

*****polite** /pəláɪt/ 形 ▶定義 having good manners and showing respect for others 良いマナーを持ち, ほかの人に対して尊敬の念を表している→礼儀正しい, 丁寧な, 行儀の良い ‖ *The assistants in that shop are always very helpful and polite.* あの店の店員たちはいつも親切で礼儀正しい. *He gave me a polite smile.* 彼は私に行儀良くほほえんだ. ⇔ **impolite, impertinent** — **politely** 副→礼儀正しく, 行儀良く, 丁寧に — **politeness** 名 U→礼儀正しさ, 丁寧, 礼儀正しい行為

*****political** /pəlítɪk(ə)l/ 形 ▶定義 1 connected with politics and government 政治と政府にかかわった→政治の, 政治に関する, 政治上の ‖ *a political leader/debate/party* 政治上の指導者・政治に関する論争・政党 *She has very strong political opinions.* 彼女はとても強い政治上の意見を持っている. ▶定義 2 (used about people) interested in politics (人々について) 政治に興味のある→政治に関心のある, 政治活動をする ▶定義 3 concerned with the competition for power inside an organization 組織内での権力争いに関連する→政略上の, 政略的な, 政治的な ‖ *I suspect he was dismissed for political reasons.* 彼は政略的な理由で解雇されたのではないかと思う. — **politically** 副→政治的に, 政略上 ‖ *Politically he's fairly right wing.* 政治的には, 彼はかなり右翼である.

**political asylum** 名 U ▶定義 protection given by a state to a person who has left his/her own country for political reasons 政治的理由によって自分の国を去った人に, 国家から与えられる保護→政治的亡命者の保護

**politically correct** 形 (略 PC) ▶定義 used to describe language or behaviour that carefully avoids offending particular groups of people 特定の人々の集団に不快感を与えることを注意深く避ける言葉または行動について述べるために用いて→(人種・性別などの差別をせず)政治的に正当・妥当な, 反差別の立場を取った — **political correctness** 名 U →政治的妥当さ, 反差別

---

▶社会・文化

**差別を避ける言い方**

メディアは社会的弱者とされる人々に対する配慮として, 差別的表現を避けることがあります. 例えば housewife, stewardess, policeman などは女性蔑視(べっし)につながるとして, それぞれ domestic engineer, flight attendant, law enforcement officer などと言い換えます. また, deaf「聾唖(ろうあ)者」や handicapped「身体障害者」は, visually oriented, physically challenged と, 前向きな言い方をします. ただし, cheating「カンニング」を academic dishonesty, trees「木」を oxygen exchange units とされると, 何かの冗談かと思うでしょう.

---

*****politician** /pɑ̀lətíʃ(ə)n/ 名 C ▶定義 a person

whose job is in politics, especially one who is a member of parliament or of the government その仕事が政治にかかわっている人, 特に議会の, または政府の一員→**政治家, 政治屋** ‖ *Politicians of all parties supported the war.* すべての政党の政治家がその戦争を支持した.

*__politics__ /pálətɪks/ 名 ▶定義1 [**U**, 単数または複数形の動詞と共に] the work and ideas that are connected with governing a country, a town, etc 国, 町などを治めることに関連した仕事と考え→**政治** ‖ *to go into politics* 政治の世界に入る *Politics has/have never been of great interest to me.* 私は政治には全く興味を持ったことがない. ▶定義2 [複数扱い] a person's political opinions and beliefs 人の政治的意見と信念→**政見, 政治についての意見** ‖ *His politics are extreme.* 彼の政治についての意見は極端すぎる. ▶定義3 [**U**, 単数または複数形の動詞と共に] matters concerned with competition for power between people in an organization 組織内の人々の権力争いに関する事柄→**政争, 駆け引き, 政略** ‖ *I never get involved in office politics.* 私は決して社内の権力争いにかかわらない. ▶定義4 (略 **Political Science**) **1** the scientific study of government 政治についての科学的学問→**政治学** ‖ *a degree in Politics* 政治学の学位

__poll__¹ /póʊl/ 名 **C** ▶定義1 (または **opinion poll**) a way of finding out public opinion by asking a number of people their views on sth 多くの人に～についての意見を聞くことによって, 世論を突き止める方法→**世論調査, 世論調査の結果** ‖ *This was voted best drama series in a viewers' poll.* これは視聴者投票でベストドラマシリーズと認められた. ▶定義2 the process of voting in a political election; the number of votes given 政治の選挙において投票する過程; 獲得された投票数→**投票, 選挙, 投票数, 得票数** ‖ *The country will go to the polls* (= vote) *in June.* その国では6月に投票が行われる.

__poll__² /póʊl/ 動他 ▶定義1 to receive a certain number of votes in an election 選挙において, ある程度の数の投票を受ける→**～を得る, 獲得する** ‖ *The Liberal Democrat candidate polled over 3000 votes.* 自由民主党の候補は3000を超える票を獲得した. ▶定義2 to ask members of the public their opinion on a subject 一般の人々に, あるテーマについての意見を聞く→**(地域・集団)の世論を調査する** ‖ *Of those polled, only 20 per cent were in favour of changing the law.* 世論調査した中の20パーセントだけが, 法改正に賛成だった.

__pollen__ /pálən/ 名 **U** ▶定義 a fine, usually yellow, powder which is formed in flowers. It makes other flowers of the same type produce seeds when it is carried to them by the wind, insects, etc. 花の中で作られる細かい, 通常は黄色の粉. 風, 虫などによってほかの同種の花へ運ばれると, そこに種ができる→**花粉** ☛ C2ページのさし絵

__polling__ /póʊlɪŋ/ 名 **U** ▶定義 the process of voting in an election 選挙で投票をする過程→**投票**

__pollutant__ /pəlúːt(ə)nt/ 名 **C** ▶定義 a substance that pollutes air, rivers, etc 空気, 川などを汚染する物質→**汚染物質**

*__pollute__ /pəlúːt/ 動他 ▶定義 to make air, rivers, etc dirty and dangerous 空気, 川などを汚して危険にする→**～を汚染する, 汚す** ‖ *Traffic fumes are polluting our cities.* 排気ガスが私たちの町を汚染している. *The beach has been polluted with oil.* その浜辺は石油で汚染されてしまった.

*__pollution__ /pəlúːʃ(ə)n/ 名 **U** ▶定義1 the action of making the air, water, etc dirty and dangerous 空気, 水などを汚して危険にする行為→**汚すこと, 汚染, 公害** ‖ *Major steps are being taken to control the pollution of beaches.* 浜辺の汚染を管理するために, 大々的な方策が取られています. ▶定義2 substances that pollute 汚染する物質→**汚染物質** ‖ *The rivers are full of pollution.* それらの河川は汚染しつくされている.

__polo__ /póʊloʊ/ 名 **U** ▶定義 a game for two teams of horses and riders. The players try to score goals by hitting a ball with long wooden hammers. 複数の馬と騎手たちから成る2チームで行うゲーム. 選手たちは長い木づちでボールを打って得点しようと努める→**ポロ**

__polo neck__ 名 **C** ▶定義 a high collar on a piece of clothing that is rolled over and that covers most of your neck; a piece of clothing with this type of collar 折り返されて首のほとんどを被う, 衣類に付いた高いえり; この種類のえりを持つ衣類→**タートルネック; タートルネックの衣類** ☛ C6ページのさし絵

**polyester** /pάlièstər/ 名 U ▶定義 an artificial material that is used for making clothes, etc 衣服などを作るために使われる人工的な素材→ポリエステル

**polystyrene** /pὰlistάiəri:n/ 名 U ▶定義 a light firm plastic substance that is used for packing things so that they do not get broken 物が壊れないように包装するために使われる、軽くて堅い合成樹脂の物質→ポリスチレン

**polythene** /pάləθi:n/ (米 **polyethylene** /pὰliéθəli:n/) 名 U ▶定義 a type of very thin plastic material often used to make bags for food, etc or to keep things dry 食物などの袋を作るために、あるいは物を乾燥した状態に保つためにしばしば使われる、とても薄い合成樹脂の素材の一種→ポリエチレン

**pomp** /pɑmp/ 名 U ▶定義 the impressive nature of a large official occasion or ceremony 盛大な公式の行事または儀式での感動を与える特性→華やかさ, 壮観

**pompous** /pάmpəs/ 形 ▶定義 showing that you think you are more important than other people, for example by using long words that sound impressive 例えば感慨深く聞こえる長い言い回しを使って、ほかの人々よりも自分がより重要だと考えていることを示している→もったい振った, 尊大な, おおげさな ☞ この単語は批判的に使われる.

**pond** /pɑnd/ 名 C ▶定義 an area of water that is smaller than a lake 湖よりも小さい水域→池 ☞ C7 ページのさし絵
► lake は通常船が航行するのに十分な大きさがある: *Lake Como* (コモ湖). pond は動物がそこから水を飲むのに十分な大きさの、または庭にあるとても小さい水域くらいであろう: *We have a fish pond in our garden.* (うちの庭には魚のいる池がある.) pool はさらに小さい水域である: *When the tide went out, pools of water were left among the rocks.* (引き潮の後に、岩の間に潮だまりがあった.) しかし、人工的な pool はもっと大きいこともある: *a swimming pool* (スイミングプール). puddle は雨によってできる小さい水たまりである.

**ponder** /pάndər/ 動 自他 ▶定義 ponder (on/over sth) to think about sth carefully or for a long time 〜について注意深く、または長い時間考える→〜をじっくりと考える, 熟考する ∥ *The teacher gave us a question to ponder over before the next class.* 先生は次の授業までにじっくりと考えるべき問題を出した.

**pong** /pɑŋ/ 名 C 英 (俗語) ▶定義 a strong unpleasant smell 強い不快なにおい→悪臭, 嫌なにおい — pong 動 自 →悪臭を放つ, におう

**pony** /póʊni/ 名 C (複 **ponies**) ▶定義 a small horse 小さな馬→ポニー(小型種の馬), 小馬

**ponytail** /póʊnitèil/ 名 C ▶定義 long hair that is tied at the back of the head and that hangs down in one piece 頭の後ろで1つに束ねて垂れ下がっている長い髪→ポニーテール ☞ **hair** のさし絵

**pony-trekking** (英 **trail riding**) 名 U ▶定義 the activity of riding horses for pleasure in the country 田舎で楽しみのために馬に乗ること→(ポニーに乗っての) 小旅行

**poodle** /pú:dl/ 名 C ▶定義 a type of dog with thick curly fur that is sometimes cut into a special pattern 密集した巻き毛を時折特殊なスタイルにカットしている, 犬の一種→プードル

**pooh** /pu:/ 間 英 略式 ▶定義 said when you smell sth unpleasant 不快な〜のにおいをかいだときに言う→うっ臭い, あー臭い

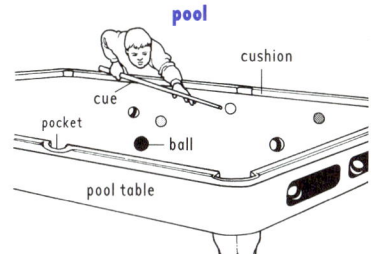
pool

*****pool**¹ /pu:l/ 名 ▶定義 1 C a pool (of sth) a small amount of liquid lying on a surface 表面にある少量の液体→(液体などの)たまったもの, 水たまり, (小さな)池 ∥ *There's a huge pool of water on the kitchen floor.* キッチンの床がびしょぬれだ. ☞参 **pond** の注 ▶定義 2 C a small area of light 光の当たっている小さな場所→陽だまり ∥ *a pool of light* 陽だまり ▶定義 3 C = SWIMMING POOL ∥ *He swam ten lengths of the pool.* 彼はプールで5往復泳いだ. ▶定義 4 C a quantity of money, goods, etc that is shared between a group of people 人々の間で共同で使われる, 一定量のお金, 品物など ➜**共同資金, 共同利用施設** ‖ *There is a pool of cars that anyone in the company can use.* 会社の人ならだれでも使える社用の車がある. ▶定義5 [U]a game that is played on a table with 16 coloured and numbered balls. Two players try to hit these balls into holes in the table (pockets) with long thin sticks (cues). 16 の色と番号の付いた球を使って, テーブルの上で競技するゲーム. 2人の競技者はこれらの球を, 長く細い棒(キュー)でテーブルの中の穴(ポケット)に打ち込もうとする ➜**玉突き, ビリヤード** ☛参 **billiards, snooker** ▶定義6 **the pools**[複数扱い] = **FOOTBALL POOLS**

**pool**[2] /puːl/ [動][他] ▶定義 to collect money, ideas, etc together from a number of people お金, 考えなどを多数の人々から一斉に集める ➜**〜を持ち寄る, 出し合う, 共同出資する** ‖ *If we pool our ideas we should come up with a good plan.* もし考えを出し合えば, 良い計画を思い付くでしょう.

P

***poor** /pʊər, pɔːr/ [形] ▶定義1 not having enough money to have a comfortable life 快適な生活をするための十分なお金を持っていない ➜**貧しい, 貧乏な** ‖ *The family was too poor to buy new clothes.* その家族は貧しすぎて新しい衣服が買えなかった. *Richer countries could do more to help poorer countries.* 比較的裕福な国々はより貧しい国々をもっと援助することができるはずだ. ⇔ **rich** ▶定義2 **the poor** [名][複数扱い]people who do not have enough money to have a comfortable life 快適な生活を送るための十分なお金を持っていない人々 ➜**貧しい人々** ▶定義3 of low quality or in a bad condition 低い品質の, または悪い状態の ➜**質の悪い・劣った, 粗悪な, 粗末な** ‖ *Paul is in very poor health.* ポールはひどく健康を害している. *The industry has a poor safety record.* その業界は安全について粗末な記録を残している. ▶定義4 used when you are showing that you feel sorry for somebody ある人を気の毒だと感じていることを表しているときに用いて ➜**哀れな, 気の毒な, かわいそうな** ‖ *Poor Dan! He's very upset!* かわいそうなダン. 彼はひどく動転しているのね.

**poorly**[1] /pʊ́ərli, pɔ́ːr-/ [副] ▶定義 not well; badly 良くはない; 悪く ➜**貧しく, 乏しく, 不十分に** ‖ *a poorly paid job* 給料の良くない仕事

**poorly**[2] /pʊ́ərli, pɔ́ːr-/ [形] [英] [略式] ▶定義 not well; ill 健康でない; 病気の ➜**気分・健康が優れない** ‖ *I'm feeling a bit poorly.* 私は少し気分が優れない.

**pop**[1] /pɑp/ [動] (**popping**; **popped**) ▶定義1 [自][他] to make a short sudden sound like a small explosion; to cause sth to do this 小さい爆発のような, 短い突然の音を出す; 〜にこうすることを引き起こす ➜**ポンという音を出す, ポンとはじける; (栓)をポンと抜く, パーンと破裂させる** ‖ *The balloon popped.* 風船が破裂した. *He popped the balloon.* 彼は風船を破裂させた. ▶定義2 [自] pop across, down, out, etc to come or go somewhere quickly or suddenly 素早くまたは突然, どこからか来る, あるいはどこかへ行く ➜**ひょいと入る・出る, 急に動く・行く・来る, ひょっこり現れる** ‖ *I'm just popping out to the shops.* ちょうど店へ行くところです. ▶定義3 [他] pop sth in, into, etc sth to put or take sth somewhere quickly or suddenly 素早くまたは突然に〜をどこかへ置く, またはどこかに持っていく ➜**〜を急に・ひょいと動かす・入れる・出す** ‖ *She popped the note into her bag.* 彼女はバッグにそのメモをひょいと入れた.

[句動詞] pop in ▶定義 to make a quick visit ちょっと立ち寄る ➜**ちょっと訪ねる, (立ち)寄る** ‖ *Why don't you pop in for a cup of tea?* ちょっと寄ってお茶でも飲んでいかない.

pop out ▶定義 to come out (of sth) suddenly or quickly 突然にまたは素早く(〜から)出てくる ➜**急に外へ出る, 急に現れる, (驚いて目玉が)飛び出る** ‖ *Her eyes nearly popped out of her head in surprise.* 驚きのあまり, 彼女の目は飛び出さんばかりだった.

pop up [略式] ▶定義 to appear or happen when you are not expecting it 自分がそれを期待していないときに現れるまたは起こる ➜**突然起こる, 急に起こる, 不意に現れる**

***pop**[2] /pɑp/ [名] ▶定義1 [U]( または **pop music**) modern music that is most popular among young people 若者の間で最も人気のある現代音楽 ➜**ポピュラー音楽, ポップス** ‖ *a pop group* ポピュラー音楽のバンド ☛参 **jazz, rock, clas-**

**sical** ▶定義2 ⓒa short sudden sound like a small explosion 小さい爆発のような短い突然の音→ポンという音 ‖ *There was a loud pop as the champagne cork came out of the bottle.* シャンパンのコルクがびんから抜ける時に,ポンと大きな音がした.

**pop**³ 略 population→人口 ‖ *pop 12m* 人口1200万人

**popcorn** /pápkɔːm/ 名 Ⓤ ▶定義 a type of corn that is heated until it bursts and forms light whitish balls that are eaten with salt or sugar on them 破裂するまで加熱されて,塩または砂糖を付けて食べられる,軽い白っぽい玉となる,トウモロコシの一種→ポップコーン

*__pope__ /póʊp/ 名 Ⓒ ▶定義 the head of the Roman Catholic Church ローマカトリック教会の最高位→ローマ法王, ローマ教皇

**popper** /pápər/ (または **press stud**; 米 **snap**) 名 Ⓒ ▶定義 two round pieces of metal or plastic that you press together in order to fasten a piece of clothing 衣服をしっかり留めるために一緒に押し付ける,2つの円形の金属またはプラスチック→スナップ ☛ **button**のさし絵

**poppy** /pápi/ 名 Ⓒ (複 **poppies**) ▶定義 a bright red wild flower that has small black seeds 小さい黒い種を持つ,鮮やかな赤い野生の花→けし, ポピー ☛ C2ページのさし絵

**Popsicle**™ /pápsìk(ə)l/ 名 Ⓒ 米 =**ICE LOLLY**

*__popular__ /pápjələr/ 形 ▶定義1 popular (with sb) liked by many people or by most people in a group 多くの人から,または集団内のほとんどの人から好まれている→人気のある,評判の良い,流行した ‖ *a popular holiday resort* 人気のあるリゾート地 *He's always been very popular with his pupils.* 彼はいつでも生徒たちに大人気だ.⇔ **unpopular** ▶定義2 made for the tastes and knowledge of ordinary people 一般の人々の好みと知識に向けて作られた→大衆向きの,通俗的な, ポピュラーな ‖ *The popular newspapers seem more interested in scandal than news.* 大衆紙はニュースよりもゴシップ記事により興味があるようだ. ▶定義3 (名詞の前だけで) of or for a lot of people 多くの人々の,または多くの人々のための→民衆の,庶民の,人民の ‖ *The programme is being repeated by popular demand.* その番組は一般大衆の要求により再放送されている.

# porch 1243

**popularity** /pàpjəlǽrəti/ 名 Ⓤ ▶定義 the quality or state of being liked by many people 多くの人々から好まれていることまたは状態→人気, 評判, 流行 ‖ *The band's popularity is growing.* そのバンドの人気が高まっている.

**popularize** (または **-ise**) /pápjələràɪz/ 動 他 ▶定義 to make a lot of or most people like sth 多くのまたはほとんどの人々が〜を好むようにさせる→〜を大衆化する,普及させる,〜の人気を高める ‖ *The film did a lot to popularize her novels.* その映画は,彼女の小説の人気を高めるために多大な貢献をした.

**popularly** /pápjələrli/ 副 ▶定義 by many people; generally 多くの人々によって; 一般的に→俗に, 一般的に ‖ *The Conservatives are popularly known as the Tories.* 保守派は一般的にトーリー党として知られている.

**populate** /pápjəlèɪt/ 動 他 (通常は受動態で) ▶定義 to fill a particular area with people 特定の地域を人々で一杯にする→〜に人を住まわせる, 植民する ‖ *Parts of the country are very thinly populated.* その国のいくつかの地方は,とても人口が少ない.

*__population__ /pàpjəléɪʃ(ə)n/ 名 ▶定義1 Ⓒ Ⓤ the number of people who live in a particular area, city or country 特定の地域,町,または国に住んでいる人々の数→人口 ‖ *What is the population of your country?* あなたの国の人口はどれくらいですか. *an increase/a fall in population* 人口の増加・減少 ▶定義2 Ⓒ all the people who live in a particular place or all the people or animals of a particular type that live somewhere 特定の場所に住んでいるすべての人々, あるいはどこかに住んでいる特定の種類の人々または動物の全部→(ある地域の)住民, (共通の特徴を持った)人々・動物 ‖ *the local population* 地域住民 *the male/female population* 男・女の住民 *The prison population has increased in recent years.* 最近, 囚人の数が増加している.

**porcelain** /pɔ́ːrs(ə)lən, -lèɪn/ 名 Ⓤ ▶定義 a hard white substance that is used for making expensive cups, plates, etc 高価なカップ, 皿などを作るために使われる硬い白い物質→磁器

**porch** /pɔ́ːrtʃ/ 名 Ⓒ ▶定義1 英 a small covered area at the entrance to a house or church 家ま

たは教会への入り口の,覆いのある小さな場所➔**ポーチ(玄関前の屋根の張り出した部分)** ▶定義2 米 = VERANDA

**pore**¹ /pɔːr/ 名 C ▶定義 one of the small holes in your skin through which sweat can pass 汗が通って出てくる,皮膚にある小さな穴の1つ➔**毛穴**

**pore**² /pɔːr/ 動 句動詞 pore over sth ▶定義 to study or read sth very carefully ~をとても注意深く勉強するまたは読む➔**~を研究する,熟読する**

**pork** /pɔːrk/ 名 U ▶定義 meat from a pig 豚の肉➔**豚肉** ▶参 bacon, ham と meat の注

**pornography** /pɔːrˈnɑɡrəfi/ (または 略式 **porn** /pɔːrn/) 名 U ▶定義 books, magazines, films, etc that describe or show sexual acts in order to cause sexual excitement 性的快感を引き起こすために性的行動を描写する,または見せる本,雑誌,映画など➔**好色文学作品,ポルノ,ポルノ写真・映画** — **pornographic** /pɔːrnəˈɡræfɪk/ 形 ➔**好色文学の,ポルノ(写真)の**

**porpoise** /ˈpɔːrpəs/ 名 C ▶定義 a sea animal with a pointed nose that lives in groups. Porpoises are similar to another sea animal (a dolphin). 群れを成して暮らす,鼻先のとがった海の動物. ほかの海の動物(イルカ)に似ている➔**ネズミイルカ**

**porridge** /ˈpɔː(ː)rɪdʒ, ˈpɑːr-/ 名 U ▶定義 a soft, thick white food that is made from a type of grain (oats) boiled with milk or water and eaten hot 牛乳または水で煮立てた穀類の一種(カラスムギ)から作られ,温かいうちに食べられる,柔らかいどろっとした白い食べ物➔**かゆ,ポリッジ**

***port** /pɔːrt/ 名 ▶定義1 C U an area where ships stop to let goods and passengers on and off 商品と乗客を乗せてまた降ろすために,船が停泊する場所➔**港,海港** ‖ *a fishing port* 漁港 *The damaged ship reached port safely.* 破損した船は無事に港に着いた. ▶定義2 C a town or city that has a large area of water where ships load cargo, etc 船が積み荷などを積む,広い水域のある町または市➔**港町,港湾都市** ‖ *Hamburg is a major port.* ハンブルクは主要な港湾都市です. ▶定義3 U a strong sweet red wine 強くて甘い赤ワイン➔**ポートワイン(ポルトガル原産)** ▶定義4 U the side of a ship that is on your left when you are facing towards the front of the ship 人が船首に向いているとき,その人の左側にある船の側➔**左舷(さげん)** ⇔ **starboard**

**portable** /ˈpɔːrtəb(ə)l/ 形 ▶定義 that can be moved or carried easily 簡単に移動させられる,または持ち運ばれる➔**携帯用の,持ち運びしやすい,ポータブルの** ‖ *a portable television* 携帯用テレビ ▶参 **movable, mobile**

**porter** /ˈpɔːrtər/ 名 ▶定義1 a person whose job is to carry suitcases, etc at a railway station, airport, etc 鉄道の駅,空港などでスーツケースなどを運ぶことを仕事とする人➔**ポーター,赤帽** ▶定義2 a person whose job is to be in charge of the entrance of a hotel or other large building ホテルまたはほかの大きな建物の玄関を担当することを仕事とする人➔**玄関番,守衛,門番**

**porthole** /ˈpɔːrthoʊl/ 名 C ▶定義 a small round window in a ship 船の小さな円形の窓➔**舷窓(げんまど),丸窓**

**portion** /ˈpɔːrʃ(ə)n/ 名 C a portion (of sth) ▶定義1 a part or share of sth ~の一部または共有部分➔**部分,一部** ‖ *What portion of your salary goes on tax?* 給料のどのくらいが税金に取られるのですか. *We must both accept a portion of the blame.* 私たちは2人ともその責任の一部を負わなければならない. ▶定義2 an amount of food for one person (especially in a restaurant) (特にレストランにおいて)1人に対する食べ物の量➔**一人前,盛り** ‖ *Could we have two extra portions of chips, please?* ポテトをあと2人分頂けますか. ▶参 **helping**

**portrait** /ˈpɔːrtrət, -treɪt/ 名 C ▶定義1 a picture, painting or photograph of a person 人物の絵または写真による肖像➔**肖像画,似顔絵,肖像写真** ‖ *to paint sb's portrait* ~の肖像画をかく ▶定義2 a description of sb/sth in words 言葉による~の描写➔**描写,叙述**

**portray** /pɔːrˈtreɪ/ 動 他 ▶定義1 to show sb/sth in a picture; to describe sb/sth in a piece of writing 絵の中に~を表す; ~を著述の中で描写する➔**~を描写する,~の肖像をかく,(言葉で)~を生き生きと表現する** ‖ *Zola portrayed life in 19th-century France.* ゾラは19世紀のフランスの生活を生き生きと表現した. ▶定義2 portray sb/sth as sth to describe sb/sth in a particular way ~を特定の方法で描写する➔**~を…であると描写する,~を言葉で描く** ‖ *In many of his nov-*

els life is portrayed as being hard. 彼の多くの小説の中で,人生とはつらいものであると描かれている. ▶定義3 to act the part of sb in a play or film 芝居または映画で,〜の役を演じる➡〜の役を演じる ‖ *In this film she portrays a very old woman.* この映画で彼女は老婆を演じている.— portrayal /pɔːrtréɪ(ə)l/ 名 ⓒ➡描写,記述,(〜の役を)演じること

**pose**¹ /póʊz/ 動 ▶定義1 ⓔ to create or give sb sth that he/she has to deal with 処理しなければならない〜を引き起こすまたは与える➡(問題・危険など)を引き起こす,(疑問)を提出する ‖ *to pose a problem/threat/challenge/risk* 問題・恐怖・挑戦・危険を引き起こす *to pose (= ask) a question* 質問をする ▶定義2 ⓘ to sit or stand in a particular position for a painting, photograph, etc 絵,写真などのために,特定の姿勢で座るまたは立つ➡ポーズをとる ‖ *After the wedding we all posed for photographs.* 結婚式の後,写真を撮るためにみんなでポーズをとった. ▶定義3 ⓘ pose as sb/sth to pretend to be sb/sth 〜である振りをする➡〜の振りをする,〜の態度を示す ‖ *The robbers got into the house by posing as telephone engineers.* 泥棒たちは電話工事人の振りをして,家の中に入った. ▶定義4 ⓘ to behave in a way that is intended to impress people who see you 自分を見ている人々に感銘を与えるやり方で振る舞う➡気取った態度を取る,装って見せる ‖ *They hardly swam at all. They just sat posing at the side of the pool.* ともかく彼らはほとんど泳がなかった.プールサイドに座って格好をつけているだけだった.

**pose**² /póʊz/ 名 ⓒ ▶定義1 a position in which sb stands, sits, etc especially in order to be painted or photographed 特に絵にかかれるまたは写真に撮られるために,立っている,座っているなどの姿勢➡姿勢,様子,ポーズ ▶定義2 a way of behaving that is intended to impress people who see you 自分を見ている人々に感銘を与えるように振る舞う方法➡気取った態度,気取った行動,見せ掛け

**posh** /pɑʃ/ 形 略式 ▶定義1 fashionable and expensive 高級で高価な➡ぜいたくな,すばらしい,豪華な ‖ *We went for a meal in a really posh hotel.* 私たちは実に豪華なホテルへ食事に出掛けた. ▶定義2 英 (used about people) belonging to or typical of a high social class (人々について)上流階級に属する,または上流階級に典型的な➡上品な,上流の

**★position**¹ /pəzíʃ(ə)n/ 名 ▶定義1 ⓒ ⓤ the place where sb/sth is or should be 〜がいる・ある,またはいる・あるべき場所➡位置,所在地 ‖ *Are you happy with the position of the chairs?* いすの配置はこれで良いですか. *All the dancers were in position waiting for the music to begin.* すべてのダンサーは位置について音楽が始まるのを待っていた. ▶定義2 ⓒ ⓤ the way in which sb/sth sits or stands, or the direction that sth is pointing in 〜が座っているまたは立っている様子,あるいは〜が向いている方向➡姿勢,構え,様子 ‖ *My leg hurts when I change position.* 姿勢を変えると足が痛みます. *Turn the switch to the off position.* スイッチをオフの位置に回してください. ▶定義3 [ⓒ,通常は単数] the state or situation that sb/sth is in 〜がいる状態または状況➡境遇,立場,状態 ‖ *I'm in a very difficult position.* 私は非常に難しい立場にいます. *I'm sorry, I'm not in a position to help you financially.* ごめんなさい,私はあなたを経済的に助けられる状況にはないのです. ▶定義4 ⓒ a position (on sth) what you think about sth; your opinion 〜について自分が考えている事;自分の意見➡(〜に対する)考え方,意見,(心の)態度 ‖ *What is your position on smoking?* 喫煙に対してどう思いますか. ▶定義5 ⓒ ⓤ the place or level of a person, company, team, etc compared to others ほかと比べて人,会社,チームなどの位置または水準➡地位,身分,順位 ‖ *the position of women in society* 社会での女性の地位 *Max finished the race in second position.* マックスはその競走で2位だった. *Wealth and position are very important to some people.* ある人々にとって,富と地位はとても大切である. ▶定義6 ⓒ a job 仕事➡勤め口,職 ‖ *There have been over a hundred applications for the position of Sales Manager.* 営業部長の職に100を超える応募があった. ☛類 post ▶定義7 ⓒ the part you play in a team game チームで行うゲームにおいて,自分がする役割➡守備,ポジション ‖ *Danny can play any position except goalkeeper.* ダニーはゴールキーパー以外ならどのポジションでも

## 1246 position²

**position²** /pəzíʃ(ə)n/ 動他 ▶定義 to put sb/sth in a particular place or position ～を特定の場所または位置に置く → (～を適当な場所に)置く, ～の位置を定める ‖ *Mary positioned herself near the door so she could get out quickly.* メアリーは素早く外に出られるようにドアの近くにいた.

***positive** /pázətɪv/ 形 ▶定義1 thinking or talking mainly about the good things in a situation, in a way that makes you or sb else feel hopeful and confident 自分またはほかの～に希望または確信を持たせるような方法で, 主にその状況での良い物事について考えているまたは話している → 積極的な, 建設的な, 前向きな ‖ *Their reaction to my idea was generally positive.* 私の考えに対する彼らの反応は, おおむね肯定的だった. *I feel very positive about our team's chances this season.* 今シーズンの我がチームにはかなり勝ち目があると思う. *Positive thinking will help you to succeed.* 建設的な考え方をすれば, あなたは成功するでしょう. ⇔ **negative**
▶定義2 positive (about sth/that...) certain; sure 確信して; 確実な → 確信した, 自信のある ‖ *Are you positive that this is the woman you saw?* この人があなたの見た女性だと確信しますか.
▶定義3 clear; definite はっきりした; 明確な → 明白な, 明確な ‖ *There is no positive evidence that he is guilty.* 彼が有罪であるという明白な証拠はない. *to take positive action* はっきりした態度を取る ▶定義4 (used about a medical or scientific test) showing that sth has happened or is present (医療上のまたは科学上の検査について)～が起こったまたは存在していることを表している → 陽性の, プラスの, 正の ‖ *The result of the pregnancy test was positive.* 妊娠検査の結果は陽性だった. *Two athletes tested positive for steroids.* 2人のスポーツ選手がステロイド剤のテストで陽性反応だった. ⇔ **negative**
▶定義5 (used about a number) more than zero (数について)ゼロより多い → 正の, プラスの ⇔ **negative**

**positively** /pázətɪvli/ 副 ▶定義1 with no doubt; firmly 疑いなく; 断固として → 確かに, 断固として, きっぱりと ‖ *I was positively convinced that I was doing the right thing.* 私は自分が正しい事をしていると断固確信していた. ▶定義2 in a way that shows you are thinking about the good things in a situation, not the bad ある状況での良い物事(悪い物事ではなく)について考えていることを示すやり方で → 肯定的に, 積極的に, 前向きに ‖ *Thinking positively helps many people deal with stress.* 前向きに考えることによって, 多くの人々はストレスに対処していくことができる. ▶定義3 (used about a person's way of speaking or acting) in a confident and hopeful way (人が話すまたは行動する方法について)確信と希望に満ちたやり方で → 肯定的に, 積極的に, 前向きに ‖ *The team played cautiously for the first ten minutes, then continued more positively.* そのチームは最初の10分間は注意深く競技し, それからより積極的に競技し続けた.
▶定義4 略式 (used for emphasizing sth) really; extremely (～を強調するために用いて)本当に; 極めて → 本当に, 全くその通り, もちろん ‖ *He wasn't just annoyed - he was positively furious!* 彼はただむっとしたのではなかった - 彼は本当に怒り狂っていたのだ.

***possess** /pəzés/ 動他 (進行形は不可)
▶定義1 正式 to have or own sth ～を持つ, または所有する → ～を所有する, 所持する, 持つ ‖ *They lost everything they possessed in the fire.* 彼らは火事によって所有していたすべての物を失った. *Paola possesses a natural ability to make people laugh.* パオラには人々を笑わせる生まれつきの才能がある. ▶定義2 to influence sb or to make sb do sth ～に影響する, または～に…をさせる → (考えなどが)～に取り付く, ～を支配する, ～の心を奪う ‖ *What possessed you to say a thing like that!* そんな事を言うなんてあなたはどうかしてる.

▶ この動詞は進行形では使用されないが, 現在分詞(= -ing形)はよく見受けられる: *Any student possessing the necessary qualifications will be considered for the course.* (必要な資格を持っている学生ならだれでも, その課程を受講させる考慮の対象になります.)

***possession** /pəzéʃ(ə)n/ 名 ▶定義1 ❶ the state of having or owning sth ～を持っている, または所有している状態 → 所有, 占有, 占拠 ‖ *The gang were caught in possession of stolen goods.* その一味は盗品を所有していて逮捕された. *Enemy forces managed to take possession of* *the town.* 敵の軍隊はその街をどうにか占拠した. ▶定義**2** [ **⊙**, 通常は複数] something that you have or own 自分が持っているまたは所有している物→**所有物,財産,領土** ‖ *Bud packed all his possessions and left.* バッドは自分の持ち物をすべて荷造りして, 出ていった.

**possessive** /pəzésɪv/ **形** ▶定義**1** possessive (of/about sb/sth) not wanting to share sb/sth 〜を共有することを望まない→**所有欲・独占欲・支配欲の強い** ‖ *Dan is so possessive with his toys - he won't let other children play with them.* ダンは自分のおもちゃへの独占欲がとても強い － 自分のおもちゃをほかの子供たちに使わせない. ▶定義**2**（文法）used to describe words that show who or what a person or thing belongs to 人または物がだれにまたは何に属するかを示す言葉を表すために用いて→**所有格の, 所有の** ‖ *'My', 'your' and 'his' are possessive adjectives.* my, your と his は所有形容詞です. *'Mine', 'yours' and 'his' are possessive pronouns.* mine, yours と his は所有代名詞です.

**possessor** /pəzésər/ **名 ⊙** ▶定義 a person who has or owns sth 〜を持っている, または所有している人→**所有者, 持ち主**

*★**possibility** /pɑ̀səbíləti/ **名**（複 **possibilities**) ▶定義**1 ⓤ⊙**(a) possibility (of sth/doing sth); (a) possibility that... the fact that sth might exist or happen, but is not likely to おそらくはないであろうが, 〜が存在するまたは起こるかもしれない事実→**可能性, 実現性** ‖ *There's not much possibility of the letter reaching you before Saturday.* その手紙が土曜日より前にあなたへ届く可能性は少ない. *There is **a strong possibility** that the fire was started deliberately.* その火事が放火であった可能性は高い.

▶定義**2 ⊙**one of the different things that you can do in a particular situation or in order to achieve sth 特定の状況においてまたは〜を達成するために, 人がすることができるさまざまな物事の1つ→**将来性, 見込み, 発展・改良の可能性** ‖ *There is a wide range of possibilities open to us.* 私たちには広い範囲への可能性が開かれている.

*★**possible** /pɑ́səb(ə)l/ **形** ▶定義**1** that can happen or be done 起こり得る, またはなされ得る→**起こり得る, あり得る, できる限りの** ‖ *I'll phone you back **as soon as possible**.* できるだ

## post¹ 1247

け早くこちらからお電話します. *Could you give me your answer today, **if possible**?* できれば今日ご返事を頂けますか. *The doctors did **everything possible** to save his life.* その医者は彼の命を救うあらゆる限りの事をした. *You were warned of all the possible dangers.* 起こり得るすべての危険について警告された. ⇔ **impossible** ▶定義**2** that may be suitable or acceptable 適している, または受け入れられるかもしれない→**まずまずの, 満足・我慢できる** ‖ *There are four possible candidates for the job.* その仕事にはまずまずの4人の候補者がいる. ☛参 **probable** ▶定義**3** used after adjectives to emphasize that sth is the best, worst, etc of its type 〜がその種類の中で最高, 最低などであると強調するために, 形容詞の後に用いて→**可能な限りの, できる限りの, できるだけ〜で** ‖ *Alone and with no job or money, I was in the worst possible situation.* たった1人で仕事も金もなく, 最悪の状況にあった.

**possibly** /pɑ́səb(ə)li/ **副** ▶定義**1** perhaps; maybe →**ことによると, もしかすると** ‖ *'Will you be free on Sunday?' 'Possibly.'*「日曜日, 暇ですか」「多分ね」 ▶定義**2** (used for emphasizing sth) according to what is possible（〜を強調するために用いて）起こり得ること次第で→**何とかして, できる限り** ‖ *I will leave as soon as I possibly can.* できるだけ早く出発します.

*★**post**¹ /póust/ **名** ▶定義**1** (特に **米 mail**) **ⓤ** the system or organization for collecting and dealing with letters, packages, etc 手紙, 小包などを集めて処理するための制度または組織→**郵便, 郵便制度** ‖ *The document is too valuable to send **by post**.* その書類はとても重要なものなので郵便では送れません. *If you hurry you might **catch the post** (= post it before everything is collected).* 急げば, 集配に間に合う(= すべてが収集される前に, それを投かんできる)かもしれませんよ. ▶定義**2**（米 **mail**) **ⓤ**letters, packages, etc that are collected or brought to your house 集められるまたは家に届けられる, 手紙, 小包など→**郵便物** ‖ *Has the post come yet this morning?* 今朝, 郵便物はもう届きましたか. *There wasn't any post for you.* あなたあての郵便物はありませんでした. ▶定義**3 ⊙**a job 仕

事➡職, 勤め口, 地位 ‖ *The post was advertised in the local newspaper.* その職は地方紙に公示されていた. ☞類 **position** ▶定義4 ⓒa place where sb is on duty or is guarding sth ～が勤務している, または…を監視している場所**持場, 任務の場所, 部署** ‖ *The soldiers had to remain at their posts all night.* 兵士たちは一晩中自分の持ち場に居続けなければならなかった. ▶定義5 ⓒan upright piece of metal or wood that is put in the ground to mark a position or to support sth 位置を示す, または～を支えるために地面に突き立てられている, 縦型の金属または木材の一片**柱, 支柱** ‖ *a goal post* ゴールポスト *Can you see a signpost anywhere?* どこかに道路標識が見えますか.

成句 **by return (of post)** ⇒ **RETURN**²

\***post**² /póʊst/ 動他 ▶定義1 (特に 米 **mail**) to send a letter, package, etc by post 手紙, 小包などを郵便で送る➡**～を郵送する, 郵便で出す, 投かんする** ‖ *This letter was posted in Edinburgh yesterday.* この手紙は昨日エディンバラで投かんされました.

▶ post (名詞と動詞) はイギリス英語でより一般的に使われ, mail はアメリカ英語で使われる. しかし, イギリス英語では名詞の mail もまた, しばしば使う. 郵政組織の正式名称は the Royal Mail である. airmail と surface mail の語句にも注意. 手紙で品物を注文するときは, mail-order service を利用する.

▶定義2 to send sb to go and work somewhere ～をどこかに行かせて仕事をさせる➡**～を勤務に就かせる, 配属する** ‖ *After two years in London, Rosa was posted to the Tokyo office.* ロンドンでの2年間の後, ローザは東京の支店に配属された. ▶定義3 to put sb on guard or on duty in a particular place 特定の場所に～を, 当番または勤務に就かせる➡**～を配置する, 持ち場に就かせる** ‖ *Policemen were posted outside the building.* 警察官たちが建物の外に配置された. ▶定義4 正式 (しばしば受動態で) to put a notice where everyone can see it だれもが見られる場所へ告示を置く➡**～を張る, 掲示する** ‖ *The exam results will be posted on the main noticeboard.* 試験の結果は大掲示板に張り出される.

**postage** /póʊstɪdʒ/ 名 Ⓤ ▶定義 the amount that you must pay to send a letter, package etc 手紙, 小包などを送るために支払わなくてはならない金額➡**郵便料金**

**postage stamp** = **STAMP**¹(1)

\***postal** /póʊst(ə)l/ 形 ▶定義 connected with the sending and collecting of letters, packages, etc 手紙, 小包などを送ることと集めることに関連した➡**郵便の, 郵便による**

**postal order** 名 Ⓒ ▶定義 a piece of paper that you can buy at a post office that represents a certain amount of money. A postal order is a safe way of sending money by post. 郵便局で買える, ある金額に相当する1枚の書類. postal order は郵便でお金を送る安全な方法である➡**郵便為替**

**postbox** /póʊstbɑ̀ks/ (または **letter box**, 米 **mail box**) 名 Ⓒ ▶定義 a box in a public place where you put letters, etc that you want to send 送りたい手紙などを入れる, 公共の場所にある箱➡**ポスト, 郵便ポスト** ☞参 **pillar box**

**postcard** /póʊstkɑ̀ːrd/ 名 Ⓒ ▶定義 a card that you write a message on and send to sb. Postcards have a picture on one side and are usually sent without an envelope. メッセージを書いて～に送るカード. postcard は片面に絵があり, 通常は封筒に入れないで送られる➡**はがき, 絵はがき**

**postcode** /póʊstkòʊd/ (米 **ZIP code**) 名 Ⓒ ▶定義 a group of letters and/or numbers that you put at the end of an address 住所の最後に付ける, 文字あるいは番号の1つのまとまり➡**郵便番号**

\***poster** /póʊstər/ 名 Ⓒ ▶定義1 a large printed picture or a notice in a public place, often used to advertise sth しばしば～を広告するために使用される, 公共の場所にある大きな印刷された写真または掲示➡**ポスター, 広告ビラ** ▶定義2 a large picture printed on paper that is put on a wall for decoration 装飾として壁に張られる, 紙に印刷された大きな写真➡**ポスター**

**posterity** /pɑstérəti/ 名 Ⓤ ▶定義 the future and the people who will be alive then 未来と未来に生きている人々➡**後世, 後の世の人々, 子孫** ‖ *We should look after our environment for the sake of posterity.* 後の世の人々のために, 私たちは現在の環境に気を配らなければならない.

**postgraduate** /pòʊstgrǽdʒuət/ 名 C ▶定義 a person who is doing further studies at a university after taking his/her first degree 総合大学で最初の学位を取った後,さらに勉強をしている人→大学院生 ☛参 **graduate**, **undergraduate**

**posthumous** /pástʃəməs/ 形 ▶定義 given or happening after sb has died ～が死んだ後に与えられる,または起こる,(賞が)死後に与えられた,(作品が)著者の死後に出版される,死後に起こる ‖ *a posthumous medal for bravery* 勇敢ある行為をたたえて死後に与えられる勲章 — **posthumously** 副→死後に

**posting** /póʊstɪŋ/ 名 C ▶定義 a job in another country that you are sent to do by your employer 雇い主によって,それをするために人が派遣された他国での仕事→(特に軍隊の)任命,配属

**postman** /póʊs(t)mən, -mæ̀n/ ( 困 **mailman**) 名 C ( 複 **-men** /-mən, -mèn/) ▶定義 a person whose job is to collect letters, packages, etc and take them to people's houses 手紙,小包などを集めることと,それらを人の住居へ持っていくのを仕事とする人→郵便集配人

**postmark** /póʊstmɑ̀ːrk/ 名 C ▶定義 an official mark over a stamp on a letter, package, etc that says when and where it was posted いつどこで投かんされたかを示す,手紙,小包などにはられた切手の上の公式の印→消印

**post-mortem** /pòʊs(t) mɔ́ːrtəm/ 名 C ▶定義 a medical examination of a dead body to find out how the person died その人がどのように死んだかを解明するための,死体の医学的な検査→検死(解剖)

**post-natal** /pòʊst néɪtl/ 形 (名詞の前だけ) ▶定義 connected with the period after the birth of a baby 赤ちゃんの生後の期間に関連した→出生後の,産後の ⇔ **antenatal**

**post office** 名 C ▶定義 1 a place where you can buy stamps, post packages, etc 切手を買ったり小包を郵送したりできる場所→郵便局 ▶定義 2 **the Post Office** the national organization that is responsible for collecting and dealing with letters, packages, etc 手紙,小包などを集めることと処理することに責任がある国の組織→郵政省

**postpone** /pòʊs(t)póʊn, pəs-/ 動 他 ▶定義 to arrange that sth will happen at a later time than the time you had planned; to delay 計画した時間より遅く～が起こるように手はずを整える; 延期する→～を遅らせる,延期する ‖ *The match was postponed because of water on the pitch.* 競技場が水浸しのため,その試合は延期された. ☛参 **cancel** — **postponement** 名 C U →延期,後回し

**postscript** /póʊs(t)skrɪ̀pt/ 名 C ▶定義 an extra message or extra information that is added at the end of a letter, note, etc 手紙,メモなどの末尾に追加される,余分の言づてまたは余分の情報→追伸,追記,後書き ☛参 **PS**

**posture** /pástʃər/ 名 C U ▶定義 the way that a person sits, stands, walks, etc 人が座る,立つ,歩くなどのやり方→姿勢,ポーズ ‖ *Poor posture can lead to backache.* 悪い姿勢をしていると,腰痛になることがある.

**postwar** /pòʊstwɔ́ːr/ 形 ▶定義 existing or happening in the period after the end of a war, especially the Second World War 戦争,特に第2次世界大戦の後の期間に存在している,または起こっている→戦後の,戦後に

\***pot**¹ /pɑt/ 名 C ▶定義 1 a round container that is used for cooking food in 食べ物を入れて料理するために使われる,円形の入れ物→丸い入れ物,なべ,ポット ▶定義 2 a container that you use for a particular purpose 特定の目的に使う入れ物→花びん,つぼ,鉢,かめ ‖ *a flowerpot* 植木鉢 *a pot of paint* ペンキの缶 ▶定義 3 the amount that a pot contains 1つのポットに入る量→ポット1杯分 ‖ *We drank two pots of tea.* 私たちは紅茶をポット2杯分飲んだ.

**pot**² /pɑt/ 動 他 (**potting**; **potted**) ▶定義 1 to put a plant into a pot filled with soil 土を入れた鉢に植物を入れる→～を鉢に植える ▶定義 2 to hit a ball into one of the pockets in the table in the game of (pool, billiards or snooker)(賭(かけ)玉突き,ビリヤード,スヌーカー)のゲームで,球を当てて台のポケットの1つに入れる→(球)をポケットに入れる ‖ *He potted the black ball into the corner pocket.* 彼は角のポケットに黒い球を入れた.

\***potato** /pətéɪtoʊ/ 名 C U ( 複 **potatoes**) ▶定義 a round vegetable that grows under the ground with a brown, yellow or red skin. Potatoes are white or yellow inside. 茶色,黄色または赤い皮

を持ち,土中で育つ,丸い野菜.内側は白または黄色い→**ジャガイモ, ポテト** ‖ *mashed potato* マッシュポテト *to peel potatoes* ジャガイモの皮をむく ● C3ページのさし絵

**potato crisp** (圏 **potato chip**) = **CRISP²**

**potent** /póutnt/ 形 ▶定義 strong or powerful 強いまたは強力な→**(薬・酒などが)よく効く, 効能のある, 強力な, 勢力のある** ‖ *a potent drug/drink* 良く効く薬・強い酒 — **potency** /-nsi/ 名 ❶→(薬の)効能, 権力, 潜在力

*****potential¹** /pəténʃ(ə)l/ 形(名詞の前だけ) ▶定義 that may possibly become sth, happen, be used, etc もしかすると～になる, 起こる, 使用されるなどがあるかもしれない→**可能性のある, (～になる)見込みのある, 潜在的な** ‖ *Wind power is a potential source of energy.* 風力はエネルギー資源としての可能性がある. *potential customers* 見込み客 — **potentially** /-ʃ(ə)li/ 副→**潜在的に, 可能性を持って**

**potential²** /pəténʃ(ə)l/ 名 ❶ ▶定義 the qualities or abilities that sb/sth has but that may not be fully developed yet 持っていても, まだ十分に発達していないかもしれない性質または能力→**可能性, 潜在力, 素質** ‖ *That boy has great potential as an athlete.* あの男の子は運動選手としてのすばらしい素質を持っている.

**pothole** /pάthòul/ 名 ❸ ▶定義 1 a hole in the surface of a road that is formed by traffic and bad weather 交通と悪天候によって形成された, 道の表面の穴→**穴ぼこ, くぼみ** ▶定義 2 a deep hole in rock that is formed by water over thousands of years and often leads to underground rooms (caves) 何千年以上もかけて水によって形成され, しばしば地下の空洞(洞窟(どうくつ))につながっている, 岩にある深い穴→**深い岩穴, 甌穴(おうけつ)**

**potholing** /pάthòulɪŋ/ 名 ❶ ▶定義 the sport of climbing down inside potholes(2), walking through underground tunnels, etc 地下のトンネルを歩いて通り抜けながら, pothole(2)の中を降りていくスポーツ→**洞窟(どうくつ)探検** ‖ *to go potholing* 洞窟探検に行く

**pot plant** 名 ❸ 医 ▶定義 a plant that you keep indoors 室内で育てている植物→**鉢植え植物**

**potter¹** /pάtər/ (圏 **putter** /pάtər/) 動 ❸ ▶定義 **potter (about/around)** to spend your time doing small jobs or things that you enjoy without hurrying 急がずに自分が楽しむためのささやかな仕事または物事に自分の時間を費やす→**ぶらつく, ゆっくり行く, だらだら働く** ‖ *Grandpa spends most of the day pottering in the garden.* 祖父は1日の大半を庭でぶらぶらして過ごす.

**potter²** /pάtər/ 名 ❸ ▶定義 a person who makes pots, dishes, etc (pottery) from baked clay 土を焼いてポット, 皿など(陶器)を作る人→**焼き物師, 陶工, 陶芸家**

**pottery** /pάtəri/ 名 (複 **potteries**) ▶定義 1 ❶ pots, dishes, etc that are made from baked clay 焼かれた土から作られるつぼ, 皿など→**陶器類** ▶定義 2 ❶ the activity or skill of making dishes, etc from clay 土から皿などを作る活動または技術→**陶器製造法・業, 陶芸** ‖ *a pottery class* 陶芸の授業 ▶定義 3 ❸ a place where clay pots and dishes are made 土製のつぼと皿が作られる場所→**陶器製作所, 陶器産地**

**potty¹** /pάti/ 形 英略式 ▶定義 1 crazy or silly 狂っているまたはばかな→**ばかな, ばかげた, 常軌を逸した** ▶定義 2 **potty about sb/sth** liking sb/sth very much ～がとても好きな→**～に夢中になって, のぼせて** ‖ *Penny's potty about Mark.* ペニーはマークに夢中になっている.

**potty²** /pάti/ 名 ❸ (複 **potties**) ▶定義 a plastic bowl that young children use when they are too small to use a toilet 幼い子供たちが幼すぎてトイレが使えないとき, 彼らが使うプラスチックの鉢→**おまる, 幼児用便器**

**pouch** /páutʃ/ 名 ❸ ▶定義 1 a small leather bag 小さな皮の袋→**(ポケットなどに入れておく)小袋, ポーチ** ▶定義 2 a pocket of skin on the stomach of some female animals, for example kangaroos, in which they carry their babies ある種の動物の雌, 例えばカンガルー, が中に子供を入れて運ぶ, おなかにある皮膚の袋→**育児嚢(のう)**

**poultry** /póultri/ 名 ▶定義 1 [複数扱い]birds, for example chickens, ducks, etc that are kept for their eggs or their meat その卵または肉のために飼われている鳥, 例えば鶏, アヒルなど→**家禽(かきん)類** ▶定義 2 ❶ the meat from these birds それら鳥の肉→**家禽類の肉, 鳥肉** ‖ *Eat plenty of fish and poultry.* 魚と鳥肉をたくさん食べなさい.

**pounce** /páuns/ 動 ❸ ▶定義 pounce (on

sb/sth) to attack sb/sth by jumping suddenly on him/her/it 突然〜に飛び掛かって攻撃する➡️**急に飛び掛かる,突然襲う,(人の誤りや失態を)逃さず攻撃・非難する** ‖ (比喻) *He was quick to pounce on any mistakes I made.* 彼は私の犯したミスを逃さず非難した.

\***pound**¹ /páʊnd/ 图 ▶定義1 ●(または **pound sterling**) (記号£) the unit of money in Britain; one hundred pence (100p) 英国のお金の単位; 100ペンス➡️**ポンド** ‖ *Melissa earns £16000 a year.* メリッサは年に16000ポンド稼ぐ. *Can you change a ten-pound note?* 10ポンド紙幣を崩してもらえますか. *a pound coin* 1ポンド硬貨 ▶定義2 [単数扱い] **the pound** the value of the British pound on international money markets 国際通貨市場での英国ポンドの価値➡️**ポンド相場** ‖ *The pound has fallen against the dollar.* ドルに対してポンド安になった. *How many yen are there* **to the pound**? 1ポンドは円にするといくらですか. ▶定義3 ●(略 **lb**) a measurement of weight; equal to 0.454 of a kilogram 重さの単位; 0.454キロと等しい➡️**ポンド** ‖ *The carrots cost 30p a pound.* ニンジンは1ポンド30ペンスである. *Half a pound of mushrooms, please.* マッシュルームを半ポンド下さい.

▶重量単位についての説明は,巻末の数についての特別項目を参照.

### ▶社会・文化

**ポンド**

ポンドは通貨単位であり,重さの単位でもあります.

ポンドはイギリスの通貨です.1 pound (£1) = 100 pence (ペンス)であり,1 ポンドのレートは2001年10月12日現在で179.7円でした.

一方,重さの単位のポンドはイギリスに限らず英語圏ではまだ広く使われています. 1 pound (1 lb.) = 16 ounces (オンス)で,約453.6 grams (グラム)に当たります. ですから体重が45キロの人はおよそ100 pounds (100 lbs.) と言えるのです.

**pound**² /páʊnd/ 動 ▶定義1 ⓐ pound (at/against/on sth) to hit sth hard many times making a lot of noise 大きな騒音を出しながら,〜を何回も強くたたく➡️**強く何回も打つ,連打する** ‖ *She pounded on the door with her fists.* 彼女はこぶしで強く何回もドアをたたいた. ▶定義2 ⓐ **pound along, down, up, etc** to walk with heavy, noisy steps in a particular direction 特定の方向へ,重たげなうるさい足取りで歩く➡️**ずしずし・どすんどすんと歩く,どたばた走る** ‖ *Jason went pounding up the stairs three at a time.* ジェーソンは2段飛ばしで,階段をどすんどすんと上がっていった. ▶定義3 ⓐ (used about your heart, blood, etc) to beat quickly and loudly (心臓,血液などについて)速く大きく鼓動する➡️**激しく鼓動する** ‖ *Her heart was pounding with fear.* 彼女の心臓は恐怖で激しく鼓動していた. ▶定義4 to hit sth many times to break it into smaller pieces より小さな片に砕くために〜を何回もたたく➡️**〜をすりつぶす,砕いて粉々にする**

\***pour** /pɔːr/ 動 ▶定義1 ⓑ to make a liquid or other substance flow steadily out of or into a container 液体またはほかの物体をしっかりと入れ物から流れ出させる,または入れ物に流れ込ませる➡️**〜を注ぐ,つぐ,流れ出させる** ‖ *Pour the sugar into a bowl.* その砂糖をボールに入れなさい. ▶定義2 ⓐ (used about a liquid, smoke, light, etc) to flow out of or into sth quickly and steadily, and in large quantities (液体,煙,光などについて)素早く着実に,そして大量に〜から流れ出す,または〜に流れ込む➡️**流れる,流れ出る,つぐ** ‖ *Tears were pouring down her cheeks.* 涙が彼女のほおを流れ落ちていた. *She opened the curtains and sunlight poured into the room.* 彼女がカーテンを開けると,太陽の光が部屋に降り注いだ. ▶定義3 ⓑ **pour sth (out)** to serve a drink to sb by letting it flow from a container into a cup or glass 容器からカップまたはグラスに注いで,〜に飲み物を給仕する➡️**〜をついでやる,つぐ** ‖ *Have you poured out the tea?* 紅茶をつぎましたか. ▶定義4 ⓐ **pour (down) (with rain)** to rain heavily 激しく雨が降る➡️**激しく降る** ‖ *The rain poured down all day long.* 日中土砂降りの雨だった. *I'm not going out. It's pouring with rain.* 雨がひどく降っているので,私は出掛けません. ▶定義5 ⓐ to come or go somewhere continuously in large numbers 大勢で次々とどこからか来る,またはどこかへ行く➡️**殺到す**

## 1252 pout

る, どっと押し寄せる ‖ *People were pouring out of the station.* 人々が駅の外にどっと出て行った.
**成句 pour your heart out (to sb)** ▶定義 to tell sb all your personal problems, feelings, etc ~に自分の個人的な問題, 感情などをすべて告げる→(悩みなど)をぶちまける, 吐露する
**句動詞 pour sth out** ▶定義 to speak freely about what you think or feel about sth that has happened to you 自分に起こった~について考えるまたは感じる事を遠慮なく話す→~をとめどなくしゃべる, 吐露する ‖ *to pour out all your troubles* 自分の心配事を全部吐露する

**pout** /páʊt/ **動自** ▶定義 to push your lips, or your bottom lip, forward to show that you are annoyed about sth or to look sexually attractive ~にいら立っていることを示す, または性的に魅力的に見せるために, 唇または下唇を前に押し出す→口をとがらす, ふくれる, 唇を突き出す ― **pout 名 C**→口をとがらすこと, ふくれっ面, 不機嫌

\***poverty** /pávɚti/ **名 U** ▶定義 the state of being poor 貧しい状態→貧乏, 貧しさ, 貧困 ‖ *There are millions of people in this country who are living **in poverty**.* この国には貧しい暮らしをしている人々が何百万人もいる.

**poverty-stricken** /pávɚti strìk(ə)n/ **形** ▶定義 very poor とても貧しい→非常に貧しい, 貧困にあえぐ

\***powder** /páʊdɚ/ **名 U C** ▶定義 a dry substance that is in the form of very small grains とても細かな粒子状の乾いた物質→粉, 粉末 ‖ *washing powder* 粉せっけん *Grind the spices into a fine powder.* スパイスを粉末にすりつぶしなさい. ― **powder 動他** ~に粉を塗る, 粉を振り掛ける, おしろいを付ける

**powdered** /páʊdɚd/ **形** ▶定義 (used about a substance that is usually liquid) dried and made into powder(通常は液体の物質について)乾いていて粉になった→粉末の, 粉状の, 粉に覆われた ‖ *powdered milk/soup* 粉末ミルク・スープ

\***power**¹ /páʊɚ/ **名** ▶定義 1 **U** power (over sb/sth); power (to do sth) the ability to control people or things or to do sth 人々または物事を管理する, あるいは~を行う能力→力, 能力, 力強さ ‖ *The aim is to give people more power over their own lives.* その目的は, 人々に自分の人生をコントロールできるより一層の能力を与えることです. *to have sb **in your power*** ~を支配する *It's not in my power (= I am unable) to help you.* あなたを助けることは, 私にできることではありません(= 私にはできない).
▶定義 2 **U** political control of a country or area 国または地域での政治的支配→権力, 政権, 軍事力 ‖ *When did this government **come to power?*** いつこの政府が権力を握ったのですか. *to take/seize power* 権力を握る・奪う
▶定義 3 **C the power (to do sth)** the right or authority to do sth ~をする権利または権限→権限, 法的能力 ‖ *Do the police have the power to stop cars without good reason?* 警察には正当な理由なしに車を止める権限があるのですか.
▶定義 4 **C** a country with a lot of influence in world affairs or that has great military strength 世界情勢に多大な影響力がある, または強大な軍事力を持つ国→強国, 大国 ‖ *Britain is no longer **a world power**.* もはやイギリスは世界の大国ではない. *a military/economic power* 軍事国家・経済大国 ▶定義 5 **powers**[複数扱い] a particular ability of the body or mind 体または心の特定の能力→体力, 知力, 才能 ‖ *He has great powers of observation.* 彼は鋭い観察眼を持っている. *She had to use all her powers of persuasion on him.* 彼女は彼を説き伏せるために, 全身全霊を傾けなければならなかった.
▶定義 6 **U** the energy or strength that sb/ sth has ~が持っているエネルギーまたは強さ→力, 力強さ, 迫力 ‖ *The ship was helpless against the power of the storm.* この船はあらしの猛威にどうすることもできなかった. *I've lost all power in my right arm.* 私の右腕は全く力を失った.
▶定義 7 **U** energy that can be collected and used for operating machines, making electricity, etc 機械を動かす, 電力を作るなどのために集められて使われるエネルギー→力, 動力, 電力 ‖ *nuclear/wind/ solar power* 原子力・風力・太陽熱 *This car has power steering.* この車はパワーステアリングです.

**power**² /páʊɚ/ **動他** ▶定義 to supply energy to sth to make it work 動かすために, ~にエネルギーを供給する→~に動力を供給する, ~を動力で動かす, ~にエネルギーを供給する ‖ *What powers the motor in this machine?* この機械のモーターは何で動いているのですか. ― **powered 形**

→〜の動力を備えた, エンジンの付いた ‖ *a solar-powered calculator* 太陽電池の計算機 *a high-powered engine* 高性能エンジン

**power cut** 名 C 定義 a time when the supply of electricity stops, for example during a storm 電気の供給が止まるとき, 例えばあらしの間→停電, 送電停止

***powerful** /páʊərfʊl, -f(ə)l/ 形 定義 1 having a lot of control or influence over other people ほかの人々に対して強い支配力または影響力を持っている→支配力のある, 影響力のある, 有力な ‖ *a powerful nation* 影響力のある国 *He's one of the most powerful directors in Hollywood.* 彼はハリウッドでも最も影響力のある監督の1人だ. 定義 2 having great strength or force 優れた体力または腕力を持っている→強力な, 力強い, たくましい ‖ *a powerful car/engine/telescope* 馬力のある車・馬力のあるエンジン・良く見える望遠鏡 *a powerful swimmer* たくましい水泳選手 定義 3 having a strong effect on your mind or body 自分の心や体に強い影響力を持っている→説得力のある, 効能のある, 効果的な ‖ *The Prime Minister made a powerful speech.* 首相は力強い演説を行った. *a powerful drug* 良く効く薬 — powerfully /-fʊli, -f(ə)li/ 副 →力強く, 強力に, 激しく

**powerless** /páʊərləs/ 形 定義 1 without strength, influence or control 力, 影響力または統率力なしに→権力のない, 無力な 定義 2 powerless to do sth completely unable to do sth 全く〜ができない/→〜することができない, 〜する力のない ‖ *I stood and watched him struggle, powerless to help.* 私は助けることもできないで, 彼がもがいているのを立って見ていた.

**power point** 英 = SOCKET(1)

**power station** (困 **power plant**) 名 C 定義 a place where electricity is made (generated) 電力が作られる(発生させられる)場所→発電所

**pp** 略 定義 1 pages→ページ 定義 2 (署名の前で) on behalf of 〜の代わりに→代理で ‖ *pp J Symonds* (= signed, for example, by a secretary in sb's absence) J Symondsの代理 (= 例えば〜の不在時に秘書によって署名される)

**PR** /ˌpiː ˈɑːr/ 略 定義 1 public relations→広報活動 定義 2 proportional representation→比例代表制

**practicable** /præktɪkəb(ə)l/ 形 定義 (used about an idea, a plan or a suggestion) able to be done successfully (考え, 計画または提案について) 首尾良く行われる→実行可能な, 実施できる ‖ *The scheme is just not practicable.* その計画は全く実行可能ではない. ⇔ **impracticable**

***practical¹** /præktɪk(ə)l/ 形 定義 1 concerned with actually doing sth rather than with ideas or thought 意図または考えよりもむしろ実際に〜を行うことに関連した→実際的な, 現実的な, 実行可能の ‖ *Have you got any practical experience of working on a farm?* 農場で実際に働いた経験がありますか. ☛参 **theoretical** 定義 2 that is likely to succeed; right or sensible 成功しそうな; 適切なまたは実用本位の→現実的な, 実際的な, 実務に適した ‖ *We need to find a practical solution to the problem.* その問題に対する現実的な解決法を見つける必要がある. 定義 3 very suitable for a particular purpose; useful ある特定の目的にとても適している; 役に立つ→実用的な, (実際の)役に立つ, 効果的な ‖ *a practical little car, ideal for the city* その街には理想的な, 実用的な小型車 定義 4 (used about people) making sensible decisions and good at dealing with problems (人々について) 分別のある決定をして問題をうまく取り扱う→分別のある, 現実的に振る舞う ‖ *We must be practical. It's no good buying a house we cannot afford.* 現実的になりましょう. 私たちに払う余裕がないのに家を買うなんて良くない. ⇔ 定義 2, 3, 4 **impractical** 定義 5 (used about a person) good at making and repairing things (人について) 物を作ったり修理することが上手で→実地経験のある, 老練な ‖ *Brett's very practical and has made a lot of improvements to their new house.* ブレットはかなりの実地経験があり, 彼らの新しい家をあちこち改善している.

**practical²** /præktɪk(ə)l/ 名 C 英 定義 a lesson or exam where you do or make sth rather than just writing ただ書くだけではなく, 〜を行うまたは作るレッスンまたは試験→実習, 実技・実地試験 ‖ *He passed the theory paper but failed the practical.* 彼は論文は合格したが, 実技試験で落ちた.

**practicality** /ˌpræktɪkǽləti/ ( 複 **practicalities**) 名 定義 1 ❶ the quality of being suitable and realistic, or likely to succeed 適していて現実的な、または成功しそうな素質→**実際・実用的であること, 実用性** ‖ *I am not convinced of the practicality of the scheme.* 私は、その計画が実際的であるとは納得できない. ▶定義2 **practicalities** [複数扱い] the real facts rather than ideas or thoughts 意図または考えよりもむしろ現実に起こった事→**実際・実用的なもの, 現実的な問題・面** ‖ *Let's look at the practicalities of the situation.* その状況の現実的な側面について見ましょう.

**practical joke** 名 C ▶定義 a trick that you play on sb that makes him/her look silly and makes other people laugh いたずらされた人が困っているところを周りの人に見せて笑わせるたくらみ→**悪ふざけ, いたずら**

**practically** /præktɪk(ə)li/ 副 ▶定義1 (口語) almost; very nearly→**ほとんど; ほぼ** ‖ *My essay is practically finished now.* 今, 私の論文はほぼ仕上がっている. ▶定義2 in a realistic or sensible way 現実的に, または分別のある方法で→**現実的に, 実際・実用に基づいて**

\***practice** /præktəs/ 名 ▶定義1 ❶ action rather than ideas or thought 意図または考えではなく行動→**実行, 実施, 実際** ‖ *Your suggestion sounds fine in theory, but would it work **in practice**?* あなたの提案は理論的には良さそうですが、実際に機能するのでしょうか. *I can't wait to **put** what I've learnt **into practice**.* 私は習った事を実行するのが待ちきれない. ▶定義2 C U 正式 the usual or expected way of doing sth in a particular organization or situation; a habit or custom 特定の組織または状況で, 通常のまたは予期された〜をする方法→**習慣, 慣例, 慣行** ‖ *It is standard practice not to pay bills until the end of the month.* 月末まで勘定を支払わないことが標準的な習慣です. ▶定義3 C U (a period of) doing an activity many times or training regularly so that you become good at it 上手になるために何度も活動を行うこと, または規則的に練習すること, その期間→**練習, 稽古(けいこ), 練習期間** ‖ *piano/football practice* ピアノ・サッカーの練習 *His accent should improve **with practice**.* 彼のなまりは練習で改善するはずだ.

▶定義4 ❶ the work of a doctor or lawyer 医者または弁護士の仕事→**業務, 仕事** ‖ *Dr Roberts doesn't work in a hospital. He's in **general practice** (= he's a family doctor).* ロバーツ医師は病院で働いていない. 彼は一般開業医です(=彼は家庭医です). ▶定義5 ❷ the business of a doctor, dentist or lawyer 医者, 歯医者, 弁護士の仕事→**業務, 仕事, (医者・歯医者の)患者(全体), (弁護士の)依頼人(全体)** ‖ *a successful medical/dental practice* 成功した医者・歯医者

成句 be/get **out of practice** ▶定義 to find it difficult to do sth because you have not done it for a long time 自分が長い間やっていなかったため, 〜をするのが難しいと分かる→**練習をおこたっている, 腕が鈍っている** ‖ *I'm not playing very well at the moment. I'm really out of practice.* 本当に練習をおこたっているので, 今は上手に弾けません.

**in practice** ▶定義 in reality 実際は→**実際には, 事実上は**

\***practise** (米 **practice**) /præktəs/ 動 自 他 ▶定義1 to do an activity or train regularly so that you become very good at sth 〜が上手になるように活動または訓練を定期的に行う→**練習する, 稽古(けいこ)する** ‖ *If you want to play a musical instrument well, you must practise every day.* 楽器をうまく演奏したいのなら, 毎日練習しなければならない. *He always wants to **practise** his English **on** me.* 彼はいつも私を相手に英語の練習をしたがる. ▶定義2 to do sth or take part in sth regularly or publicly 定期的または公的に, 〜をするまたは〜に参加する→**〜を実行する, (習慣的に)行う, (信仰・理念などを)実践する** ‖ *a practising Catholic/Jew/Muslim* カトリック教・ユダヤ教・イスラム教を実践する ▶定義3 **practise (sth/as sth)** to work as a doctor or lawyer 医者または弁護士として働く→**〜を開業する・している** ‖ *She's practising as a barrister in Leeds.* 彼女はリーズで法廷弁護士をしている. *He was banned from practising medicine.* 彼は医者としての開業を禁じられた.

**practised** (米 **practiced**) /præktəst/ 形 ▶定義 **practised (in sth)** very good at sth, because you have done it a lot or often たくさんまたはしばしばやったので, 〜が得意な→**熟達した, 習熟した, 経験を積んだ** ‖ *He was practised in the art of inventing excuses.* 彼は言い訳を作り出す技術に習熟していた.

**practitioner** /præktíʃ(ə)nər/ 名 C 正式 ▶定義 a person who works as a doctor, dentist or lawyer 医者, 歯医者または弁護士として働く人 →開業医, 弁護士 ☞参 GP

**pragmatic** /prægmǽtɪk/ 形 ▶定義 dealing with problems in a practical way rather than by following ideas or principles 考えまたは原理に基づくのではなく, むしろ現実的な方法で問題を取り扱う →実際的な, 実用的な

**prairie** /préəri/ 名 C ▶定義 a very large area of flat land covered in grass with few trees (especially in North America) (特に北米で) 木はほとんどなく草で覆われた, とても広い平地 →大草原, プレーリー

★**praise**¹ /préɪz/ 動他 ▶定義 praise sb/sth (for sth) to say that sb/sth is good and should be admired 〜が良く, 賞賛されるべきだと言う →〜を賞賛する, 褒める, たたえる ‖ *The fireman was praised for his courage.* 消防士はその勇気を褒めたたえられた.

★**praise**² /préɪz/ 名 U ▶定義 what you say when you are expressing admiration for sb/sth 〜への賞賛を表しているときに言うこと →賞賛, 賛美, 褒めること ‖ *The survivors were full of praise for the paramedics.* 生存者たちは救急隊員たちへの賞賛で胸が一杯だった.

**praiseworthy** /préɪzwɜːrði/ 形 ▶定義 that should be admired and recognized as good 賞賛され, 良いとして認識されるべき →賞賛に値する, 感心な, 立派な

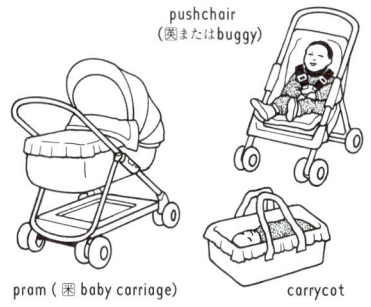

pushchair (英またはbuggy)

pram (米 baby carriage)    carrycot

**pram** /præm/ (米 **baby carriage**) 名 C ▶定義 a small vehicle on four wheels for a young baby, pushed by a person on foot 人が歩いて押す, 乳児のための4輪の小さな乗り物 →乳母車, ベビーカー

**prance** /prɑːns; præns/ 動 自 ▶定義 to move about with quick, high steps, often because you feel proud or pleased with yourself しばしば自分を誇りに思うまたは満足しているので, 速く, 陽気な足取りで動き回る →意気揚々と進む, 陽気に・誇らしげに歩く, 跳ね回る

**prat** /præt/ 名 C 英 (俗語) ▶定義 a stupid person ばかな人 →役立たず, 間抜け ‖ *What a prat!* 何て役立たずなの.

**prawn** /prɔːn/ (米 shrimp) 名 C ▶定義 a small shellfish that we eat and that becomes pink when cooked 調理するとピンク色になる食用の小さい甲殻類 →クルマエビ類 ☞参 **shrimp** ☞ **shellfish**のさし絵

★**pray** /préɪ/ 動 自 他 ▶定義 pray (to sb) (for sb/sth) to speak to God or a god in order to give thanks or to ask for help 感謝する, または助けを求めるために, 一神教のまたは多神教の神へ話す →祈る, 祈願する ‖ *They knelt down and prayed for peace.* 彼らはひざまずいて平和を祈った.

★**prayer** /préər/ 名 ▶定義 1 C a prayer (for sb/sth) the words that you use when you speak to God or a god 一神教, または多神教の神へ話すときに使う言葉 →祈りの言葉, 祈り ‖ *Let's **say a prayer** for all the people who are ill.* すべての病気の人たちのために祈りましょう. *a prayer book* 祈祷 (きとう) 書 ▶定義 2 U the act of speaking to God or a god 一神教のまたは多神教の神へ話す行為 →祈り, 礼拝 ‖ *to kneel **in prayer*** ひざまずいて祈る

**preach** /priːtʃ/ 動 ▶定義 1 自 他 to give a talk (a sermon) on a religious subject, especially in a church 特に教会で, 宗教的なテーマについての話 (説教) を与える →説教する, 説く ▶定義 2 他 to say that sth is good and persuade other people to accept it 〜が良いと言って, ほかの人々がそれを受け入れるように説得する →(真理・主義など)を説く, 説き進める ‖ *I always preach caution in situations like this.* 私は常に, このような状況での警告を説いている. ▶定義 3 自 to give sb advice on morals and how to behave in a way which he/she finds boring or annoying 聞いている人が退屈またはいら立つようなやり方で, 〜に道徳についてまたどのように振る舞うかを忠

告する→**小言を言う, お説教をする** ‖ *I'm sorry, I didn't mean to preach.* ごめんなさい, 小言を言うつもりはなかったのです.

**preacher** /príːtʃər/ 名 ❶ ▶定義 a person who gives religious talks (sermons), for example in a church 例えば教会で, 宗教の話(説教)をする人→**牧師, 伝道者, 説教者**

**precarious** /prɪkéəriəs/ 形 ▶定義 not safe or certain; dangerous 安全でない, または確かでない; 危険な→**不安定な, 当てにならない, 成り行き任せの, (足場が)危うい** ‖ *Working on the roof of that building looks very precarious.* あの建物の屋根で働くことはとても危険に見える. ― precariously 副 →**不安定に, 頼りにならない状態で**

**precaution** /prɪkɔ́ːʃ(ə)n/ 名 ❶ ▶定義 a precaution (against sth) something that you do now in order to avoid danger or problems in the future 未来の危険または問題を避けるために, 今, 人がすること→**用心, 警戒, 予防策** ‖ *You should always take the precaution of locking your valuables in the hotel safe.* 常に用心して, 貴重品はホテルの金庫に預けた方が良い. *precautions against fire/theft* 火事・盗難に対する予防策 ― precautionary /prɪkɔ́ːn(ə)n(ə)ri/ 形 →**用心の, 警戒の, 予防の**

**precede** /prɪsíːd/ 動 ⊜ ⊕ (文) ▶定義 to happen, come or go before sb/sth 〜の前に起こる, 来る, または行く→**〜に先行する, 〜より先に起こる, 〜の前に述べる** ‖ *Look at the table on the preceding page.* 前のページの表を見てください.

**precedence** /présəd(ə)ns, prɪsíː-/ 名 ❶ ▶定義 precedence (over sb/sth) the right that sb/sth has to come before sb/sth else because he/she/it is more important 〜の方がより重要なので, 〜がほかの…より先に来るべき権利→**優先, 優先されること** ‖ *In business, making a profit seems to take precedence over everything else.* 商売では, 利益を上げることがほかの何よりも優先するように思われる.

**precedent** /présəd(ə)nt, prɪsíː-/ 名 ❶ ❶ ▶定義 an official action or decision that has happened in the past and that is considered as an example or rule to follow in the same situation later 過去に起こり, 後に同じ状況下で従うために, 実例または規則として見なされる公的な行動または決定→**先例, 前例, 判例** ‖ *We don't want to set a precedent by allowing one person to come in late or they'll all want to do it.* 1人の遅刻した人を許すことで, 先例を作りたくない. さもないと皆がそうしたがるようになる. *Such protests are without precedent in recent history.* 最近ではそのような抗議は前例がない.
☞参 **unprecedented**

**precinct** /príːsɪŋ(k)t/ 名 ❶ ▶定義1 ❶ 英 a special area of shops in a town where cars are not allowed 車の通行が許されない, 町の中の特別な商店街→**(特定の)地区, 区域(歩行者天国・ショッピングセンターなど)** ‖ *a shopping precinct* 商店街
▶定義2 ❶ 米 a part of a town that has its own police station その地区の警察署がある, 町の一部分→**行政区域, 警察管区** ▶定義3 precincts [複数扱い] 正式 the area near or around a building 建物の周りまたは近くの地域→**(教会などの)境内, 構内** ‖ *the hospital and its precincts* 病院とその構内

*★**precious** /préʃəs/ 形 ▶定義1 of great value (usually because it is rare or difficult to find) (通常, 見つけることがまれで, または難しいので) 大変な価値のある→**貴重な, 高価な, 掛け替えのない** ‖ *In overcrowded Hong Kong, every small piece of land is precious.* 人口過密の香港では, どんな狭い土地も貴重だ. ▶定義2 loved very much とても愛されている→**いとしい, かわいい, 大切な, 最愛の** ‖ *The painting was very precious to her.* その絵は彼女にとってとても大切なものだった.

**precious metal** 名 ❶ ▶定義 a metal which is very rare and valuable and often used in jewellery とてもまれで価値があり, しばしば装飾品に使われる金属→**貴金属** ‖ *Gold and silver are precious metals.* 金と銀は貴金属です.

**precious stone** (または **stone**) 名 ❶ ▶定義 a stone which is very rare and valuable and often used in jewellery とてもまれで価値があり, しばしば装飾品に使われる石→**宝石** ‖ *diamonds and other precious stones* ダイヤモンドとそのほかの宝石

**precipice** /présəpəs/ 名 ❶ ▶定義 a very steep side of a high mountain or cliff 高い山または崖(がけ)のとても急な斜面→**絶壁, 断崖(だんがい), 崖** ☞比 **cliff**

**précis** /preɪsíː, préɪsi/ 名 ❶ ❶ ( 複 **précis**

/preɪsíːz, préɪsiz/) ▶定義 a short version of a speech or written text that contains only the most important points 最も重要な事項だけを含んだ，演説または著作物の短縮版➡**大要，要約** ‖ *Jim gave us a précis of the main points.* ジムは私たちに主要な箇所の要約をくれた． ☛類 **summary**

**\*precise** /prɪsáɪs/ 形 ▶定義 **1** clear and accurate 明確で正確な➡**正確な，精密な** ‖ *precise details/instructions/measurements* 正確な詳細・指示・測定 *He's in his forties - well, forty-four, to be precise.* 彼は40代です － ええ，正確には44歳です． *She couldn't be very precise about what her attacker was wearing.* 襲撃者が何を着ていたかを，彼女はあまり正確に言えなかった． ⇔ **imprecise** ▶定義 **2** (名詞の前だけ) exact; particular ➡**まさにその；特定の** ‖ *I'm sorry. I can't come just at this precise moment.* すみません．私はその時間ちょうどには行けません． ▶定義 **3** (used about a person) taking care to get small details right (人について) 取るに足りない細部を正しくするために気を遣う➡**きちょうめんな，やかましい，堅苦しい** ‖ *He's very precise about his work.* 彼は自分の仕事についてとてもきちょうめんだ．

**\*precisely** /prɪsáɪsli/ 副 ▶定義 **1** exactly 正確に➡**正確に，ちょうど，まさに** ‖ *The time is 10.03 precisely.* 時間は正確には10時3分です． ☛類 **exactly** ▶定義 **2** used to emphasize that sth is very true or obvious ～が確かに事実，または明らかであることを強調するために用いて➡**まさに，まさしく** ‖ *It's precisely because I care about you that I got so angry when you stayed out late.* あなたが遅くまで外出しているのを怒るのは，まさにあなたを心配しているからですよ． ▶定義 **3** (口語) (used for agreeing with a statement) yes, that is right (言われた事に同意するために用いて) はい，それは正しいです➡**まさにその通り** ‖ *'So, if we don't book now, we probably won't get a flight?' 'Precisely.'* 「ということは，もし予約しないと，私たちは多分飛行機の席が取れないのですか」「まさにその通りです」

**precision** /prɪsíʒ(ə)n/ 名 Ⓤ ▶定義 the quality of being clear or exact 明確または正確である特質➡**正確さ，精密さ，明確さ** ‖ *The plans were drawn with great precision.* その計画はとても綿密に立てられた．

**precocious** /prɪkóʊʃəs/ 形 ▶定義 (used about children) having developed certain abilities and ways of behaving at a much younger age than usual (子供について) 通常の年齢よりもはるかに幼い段階において，ある種の能力と動き方が発達している➡**早熟の，発達の早い，ませた** ‖ *a precocious child who started her acting career at the age of 5* 5歳で芸能活動を始めた早熟な子供 ☛ この単語はしばしば批判的に使われる．

**preconceived** /prìːkənsíːvd/ 形 (名詞の前だけ) ▶定義 (used about an idea or opinion) formed before you have enough information or experience (考えまたは意見について) 十分な情報または経験を持つ前に抱いた➡**前もって考えた，予想した**

**preconception** /prìːkənsépʃ(ə)n/ 名 Ⓒ ▶定義 an idea or opinion that you have formed about sb/sth before you have enough information or experience 十分な情報または経験を持つ前に，～について出来上がった自分の考えまたは意見➡**予想，予断，先入観**

**predator** /prédətər/ 名 Ⓒ ▶定義 an animal that kills and eats other animals ほかの動物を殺して食べる動物➡**肉食動物，捕食動物**

**predecessor** /príːdəsesər, préd-, ˌ--´-/ 名 Ⓒ ▶定義 **1** the person who was in the job or position before the person who is in it now 今いる人の前にその人の仕事をしたりまたはその地位にいた人➡**前任者** ‖ *The new head teacher is much better than her predecessor.* 新しい校長先生は前任の校長先生よりはるかにいい． ▶定義 **2** a thing such as a machine, that has been followed or replaced by sth else 例えば機械のようなものが，ほかの物に差し替えられたりあるいは取って代わられてしまった➡**前の型，前に存在していた物，前の物** ‖ *This computer has a larger memory than its predecessors.* このコンピューターは前の型よりもメモリ容量が大きい． ☛参 **successor**

**predicament** /prɪdíkəmənt/ 名 Ⓒ ▶定義 an unpleasant and difficult situation that is hard to get out of 抜け出すことが難しい，不快で困難な状況➡**苦しい立場，苦境，窮地**

**predicative** /prɪdíkətɪv; prédɪkətɪv, -dəkèɪ-/ 形 (文法) (形容詞について) ▶定義 not used before a noun 名詞の前では使用されない➡**述語的な，**

## predict

叙述的な ‖ You cannot say 'an asleep child' because 'asleep' is a predicative adjective. an asleep childとは言えないのはasleepが叙述形容詞だから. ☞ 名詞の前で使われる形容詞はattributive（限定形容詞）と呼ばれる. 多くの形容詞, 例えばbigは叙述的または限定的のどちらにもなり得る. *The house is big.* その家は大きい. *It's a big house.* それは大きな家だ. — **predicatively** 副 → 述語的に, 叙述的に

**★predict** /prɪdíkt/ 動他 ▶定義 to say that sth will happen in the future ～が未来に起こると言う → ～を予言する, 予測する, 予報する ‖ *Scientists still cannot predict exactly when earthquakes will happen.* 科学者たちは地震が起こる時を, まだ正確には予測できない.

**predictable** /prɪdíktəb(ə)l/ 形 ▶定義 **1** that was or could be expected to happen 起こると予期された, または予期し得る → 予言・予想できる, 予測の付く ‖ *The match had a predictable result.* その試合の結果は予測通りだった. ▶定義 **2** (used about a person) always behaving in a way that you would expect and therefore rather boring (人について) いつも人が予測通りに行動するのでかなり退屈である → 決まりきった, 意外性のない, あらかじめ分かっている ‖ *I knew you were going to say that - you're so predictable.* そう言うと思っていました — あなたはとても型通りな人ですね. — **predictably** 副 → 予想通り, 案の定

**prediction** /prɪdíkʃ(ə)n/ 名 C U ▶定義 saying what will happen; what sb thinks will happen これから起こる事を言うこと; ～が起こるだろうと考えている事 → 予言, 予測, 予報 ‖ *The exam results confirmed my predictions.* 試験の結果は予測通りだった.

**predominance** /prɪdámənəns/ 名 [単数扱い] ▶定義 the state of being more important or greater in number than other people or things ほかの～よりもっと重要な, または数が多い状態 → (力・数が) 勝っていること, 優勢 ‖ *There is a predominance of Japanese tourists in Hawaii.* ハワイには日本人旅行客が圧倒的に多い.

**predominant** /prɪdámənənt/ 形 ▶定義 most noticeable, powerful or important 最も顕著な, 力強い, または重要な → 優勢な, 有力な, 目立った ‖ *The predominant colour was blue.* 最も目立つ色は青だった.

**predominantly** /prɪdámənəntli/ 副 ▶定義 mostly; mainly ほとんど; 主に → 他に勝って, 優勢に, 圧倒的に ‖ *The population of the island is predominantly Spanish.* 島の人口は圧倒的にスペイン人が占めている.

**predominate** /prɪdámənèɪt/ 動自 正式 ▶定義 predominate (over sb/sth) to be most important or greatest in number 最も重要な, または数において最も多い → 影響力を持つ, 支配する, 優勢である ‖ *Private interest was not allowed to predominate over public good.* 個人的な利益が社会一般の利益に勝ることは許されなかった.

**preface** /préfəs/ 名 C ▶定義 a written introduction to a book that explains what it is about or why it was written 何について, またはどうして書かれたかを説明する, 本の序文 → 序文, 端書き

**prefect** /príːfekt/ 名 C 英 ▶定義 an older girl or boy in a school who has special duties and responsibilities. Prefects often help to make sure that the younger schoolchildren behave properly. 特別な義務と責任のある, 学校の年上の少年または少女. しばしば下級生が適切に行動しているかを確認する手伝いをする → 学級委員, 風紀委員, 監督生 (規律面で権限と責任を与えられた上級生)

**★prefer** /prɪfə́ːr/ 動他 (**preferring**; **preferred**) ▶定義 prefer sth (to sth); prefer to do sth; prefer doing sth (進行形は不可) to choose sth rather than sth else; to like sth better ほかよりむしろこちらのものを選ぶ; ～をより好む → むしろ～の方を好む, ～を選ぶ ‖ *Would you prefer tea or coffee?* 紅茶とコーヒーとどちらがお好きですか. *Marianne prefers not to walk home on her own at night.* マリアンは, 夜1人で歩いて家に帰ることを好まない. *My parents would prefer me to study law at university.* 私の両親は, 私が法律の勉強をすることを望んでいる.

▶ prefer の異なる使い方に注意: *Helen **prefers going** by train to flying* (= generally or usually). (ヘレンは飛行機よりも電車で行くのが好きです (= 一般的にまたは通常).) *Helen **would prefer to go** by train rather than (to) fly* (= on this occasion). (ヘレンは飛行機よりも電車で行きたいのです (= この場合では).)

☞ prefer は一般的にかなり堅い感じの語であ

る. *Would you prefer tea or coffee?* (紅茶とコーヒーとどちらがお好きですか.)の代わりに, *Would you rather have tea or coffee?* と言える. *I prefer skating to skiing.* (私はスキーよりスケートの方が好きだ.)の代わりに, *I like skating better than skiing.* と言える.

▶この動詞は進行形では使われないが,現在分詞形(= -ing形)で見ることは一般的である: *Their elder son had gone to work in London, preferring not to join the family firm.* (家族経営の会社に参加したくないため, 彼らの上の息子はロンドンに働きにいってしまっていた.)

**preferable** /préf(ə)rəb(ə)l/ 形 ▶定義 preferable (to sth/doing sth) better or more suitable より良い, またはもっと適している→(〜よりも)好ましい, 望ましい, (〜の方を)選ぶべき ‖ *Going anywhere is preferable to staying at home for the weekend.* 週末には家にいるよりどこかへ行く方が好ましい.

**preferably** /préf(ə)rəb(ə)li/ 副 ▶定義 used to show which person or thing would be better or preferred, if you are given a choice もし選択権が与えられたなら, どの人または物がより良い, あるいは好まれているかを表すために用いて→(もし)できれば, なるべく, むしろ ‖ *Give me a ring tonight - preferably after 7 o'clock.* 今夜電話をください - できれば7時以降に.

**preference** /préf(ə)rəns/ 名 ▶定義 **1** C U (a) preference (for sth) an interest in or desire for one thing more than another ほかの物より, ある1つの物事への興味または欲望→〜を好むこと, 好み, (好みによる)選択 ‖ *What you wear is entirely a matter of **personal preference**.* あなたが何を着るかは全く個人的な好みの問題だ. *Please list your choices **in order of preference** (= put the things you want most first on the list).* お好みの順に選択して, 表にしてください(= 最も欲しいものを一覧表の1番目に置く).
▶定義 **2** U special treatment that you give to one person or group rather than to others ほかよりはむしろ1人または1つの集団に与える特別な取り扱い→優先(権), 特典, (貿易上の)特恵 ‖ *When allocating accommodation, we will **give preference to** families with young children.* 宿泊先を割り当てるとき, 幼い子供のいる家族を優先します.

**preferential** /prèfərénʃ(ə)l/ 形 (名詞の前だけ) ▶定義 giving or showing special treatment to one person or group rather than to others 特別な取り扱いを, ほかよりはむしろ1人または1つの集団に与えている, または示している→優先の, 優先権のある, (貿易上の)特恵のある ‖ *I don't see why he should get **preferential treatment** - I've worked here just as long as he has!* どうして彼が優遇されるのか分からない - 私だってここで彼と同じくらいの間働いてきたのに.

**prefix** /príːfɪks/ 名 C (文法) ▶定義 a letter or group of letters that you put at the beginning of a word to change its meaning 意味を変えるために単語の最初に付ける, 文字または文字群→接頭辞 ☞参 suffix

**pregnancy** /prégnənsi/ 名 (複 **pregnancies**) C U ▶定義 the state of being pregnant 妊娠している状態→妊娠

\***pregnant** /prégnənt/ 形 ▶定義 (used about a woman or female animal) having a baby developing in her body (女性または雌の動物について)体の中に成長している赤ちゃんを持っている→妊娠している ‖ *Liz is five months pregnant.* リズは妊娠5か月だ. *to get pregnant* 妊娠する ☞ この文は, *Liz is expecting a baby.* または *Liz is going to have a baby.* (リズは妊娠している.)と言うことも可能である.

**prehistoric** /prìːhɪstɔ́(ː)rɪk, -stár-/ 形 ▶定義 from the time in history before events were written down 出来事が記録される以前の歴史上の時代から→有史以前の, 先史時代の

\***prejudice**¹ /prédʒədəs/ 名 C U ▶定義 prejudice (against sb/sth) a strong unreasonable feeling of not liking or trusting sb/sth, especially when it is based on his/her/its race, religion or sex 特に〜の人種, 宗教, 性別に基づく場合, 〜への好きではないまたは信用できないという, 強くて道理に合わない感情→偏見, 先入観, 悪感情 ‖ *a victim of **racial prejudice*** 人種偏見の犠牲者

**prejudice**² /prédʒədəs/ 動 他 ▶定義 **1** prejudice sb (against sb/sth) to influence sb so that he/she has an unreasonable or unfair opinion about sb/sth 〜に影響を与えて, …についての道理に合わないまたは不公平な見解を〜が持つようにする→〜に偏見を持たせる, 好意・反感を持

たせる, 先入観を持たせる ‖ *The newspaper stories had prejudiced the jury against him.* 新聞の記事は, 陪審員に彼への反感を抱かせるものだった. ▶定義2 to have a harmful effect on sb/sth ～を傷付ける効果を持つ➡～の権利を侵害する, ～を害する, 損なう ‖ *Continuing to live with her violent father may prejudice the child's welfare.* 暴力的な父親との生活を続けることは, その少女の幸福を損なうかもしれない.

**prejudiced** /prédʒədəst/ 形 ▶定義 not liking or trusting sb/sth for no other reason than his/her/its race, religion or sex ～の人種, 宗教, または性別が理由で, その～を好きでないまたは信用していない➡偏見のある, 先入観を持った, 公平でない

**preliminary**¹ /prɪlímən(ə)ri; -nèri/ 形 ▶定義 coming or happening before sth else that is more important もっと重要なほかの～の前に来る, または起こる➡予備的な, 準備の, 前置きの ‖ *After a few preliminary remarks the discussions began.* 少し前置きがあって, 討論は始まった.

**preliminary**² /prɪlímən(ə)ri; -nèri/ 名 [ ●, 通常は複数 ] ( 棚 **preliminaries**) ▶定義 an action or event that is done before and in preparation for another event ほかの出来事の前にそれに備えて行われる, 行動または出来事➡予備行為, 予備段階, 下ごしらえ ‖ *Once the preliminaries are over, we can get down to business.* 予備段階が終わったら, 私たちは職務に本腰を入れて取り組めます.

**prelude** /prél(j)uːd/ 名 ● ▶定義1 a short piece of music, especially an introduction to a longer piece 短い楽曲, 特に後に続くより長い楽曲への導入部➡前奏曲, プレリュード ▶定義2 (文) prelude (to sth) an action or event that happens before sth else or that forms an introduction to sth ほかの～の前に起こる, または～への導入部を形づくる, 行動または出来事➡序幕, 序文, 前口上, 前兆

**premature** /prìːmət(j)úər, -tʃúər/ 形 ▶定義1 happening before the normal or expected time 標準のまたは予期された時より前に起こる➡(普通・予想より)早い, 年齢の割には早い, 早産の ‖ *Her baby was premature (= born before the expected time).* 彼女の赤ちゃんは早産で生まれた(= 予定日の前に生まれた). ▶定義2 acting or happening too soon 早すぎる行動または出来事➡早まった, 時期尚早の ‖ *I think our decision was premature. We should have thought about it for longer.* 私たちの決断は時期尚早だったと思う. もっとじっくり考えるべきでした. ― **prematurely** 副 ➡(普通・予想より)早く, 早産で, 早まって

**premeditated** /prɪmédətèɪtəd/ 形 ▶定義 (used about a crime) planned in advance (犯罪について)前もって計画された➡あらかじめ計画された, 計画的な

**premier**¹ /prémɪər, prɪmíːər/ 形 (名詞の前だけ) ▶定義 most important; best 最も重要な; 最高の➡首位の, 最も重要な; 最高の ‖ *a premier chef* 最高の料理長 *the Premier Division* (= *in football*) プレミアリーグ(= サッカーで)(野球の大リーグに相当する, サッカーチームが属する最高位の集団)

**premier**² /prémɪər, prɪmíːər/ 名 ● ▶定義 (used especially in newspapers) the leader of the government of a country (**prime minister**) (特に新聞で用いて) 一国の政府の指導者(総理大臣)➡首相, 総理大臣

**première** /prémieər, -mɪər/ 名 ● ▶定義 the first public performance of a play, film, etc 演劇, 映画などの最初の公演➡初日, 初演, 封切り

**premises** /prémɪsɪz/ 名 [複数扱い] ▶定義 the building and the land that around it that a business owns or uses 会社が所有するまたは使用する, 建物とその周辺の土地➡(土地・建物を含む)構内, 敷地, 家屋敷 ‖ *Smoking is not allowed on the premises.* この敷地内は禁煙です.

**premium** /príːmiəm/ 名 ● ▶定義1 an amount of money that you pay regularly to a company for insurance against accidents, damage, etc 事故, 損害などの保険のために定期的にある会社に払う, 金額➡保険料 ‖ *a monthly premium of £25* 月額25ポンドの保険料 ▶定義2 an extra payment 余分な支払い➡割り増し額, プレミアム ‖ *You must pay a premium for express delivery.* 速達には割り増し料金を払わなければいけない.

**premonition** /prìːmənɪ́ʃ(ə)n, prèm-/ 名 ● ▶定義 *a premonition (of sth)* a feeling that sth unpleasant is going to happen in the future 不快な～が将来起こるという感情➡悪い予感, 虫の知らせ, 前兆 ‖ *a premonition of disaster* 大災

害の前兆

**preoccupation** /priàkjəpéiʃ(ə)n/ 名 ❶ ❸ ▶定義
preoccupation (with sth) the state of thinking and/or worrying continuously about sth 〜について ずっと考えている, そして・あるいは, 心配している状態 → (〜への)没頭, 執心, 関心事, 夢中になっている問題 ‖ *She was irritated by his preoccupation with money.* 彼がお金に執着していることに, 彼女はいらいらした.

**preoccupied** /priákjəpàid/ 形 ▶定義 preoccupied (with sth) not paying attention to sb/sth because you are thinking or worrying about sb/sth else 何かほかのことについて考えている, または心配しているので, 〜に注意を払わない → (〜に)夢中の, 心を奪われた, 上の空の ‖ *Sarah is very preoccupied with her work at present.* 今, サラは仕事にすごく没頭している. ☞参 occupied

**preoccupy** /priákjəpài/ 動 他 (現分 **preoccupying**; 三単現 **preoccupies** 過, 過分 **preoccupied**) ▶定義 to fill sb's mind so that he/she does not think about anything else; to worry ほかのことを考えないほど, 〜の心を一杯にする; 心配する → 〜の心を奪う, 夢中にさせる

\***preparation** /prèpəréiʃ(ə)n/ 名 ▶定義 1 ❶getting sb/sth ready 〜の準備をすること → 準備, 用意すること, 支度ができていること ‖ *The team has been training hard **in preparation for** the big game.* そのチームは, 大きな試合へ向けて熱心に訓練している. *exam preparation* 試験の準備 ▶定義 2 [❶, 通常は複数] preparation (for sth/to do sth) something that you do to get ready for sth 〜の準備をするために人が行う物事 → (具体的な)準備, 用意, 支度 ‖ *We started to **make preparations** for the wedding six months ago.* 私たちは6か月前から結婚式の準備を始めた.

**preparatory** /pripǽrət(ə)ri; -pǽrətòːri/ 形 ▶定義 done in order to get ready for sth 〜の準備をするために行った → 準備の, 予備の

**preparatory school**(または **prep school**) 名 ❸ ▶定義 1 英 a private school for children aged between seven and thirteen 7歳から13歳までの子供のための私立学校 → (パブリックスクールへの進学希望者の)私立小学校 ▶定義 2 米 a private school that prepares students for college or university 学生たちに単科大学または総合大学への準備をさせる私立学校 → (大学進学希望者のための)私立高校

\***prepare** /pripéər/ 動 自 他 ▶定義 prepare (sb/sth) (for sb/sth) to get ready or to make sb/sth ready 準備する, または〜に準備させる → 準備・用意・支度する; 〜の準備・用意・支度をする, 〜に準備させる ‖ *Bo helped me prepare for the exam.* ボウは試験の準備を手伝ってくれた. *The course prepares foreign students for studying at university.* その課程は, 留学生たちが大学で勉強するための準備をさせる. *to prepare a meal* 食事を用意する

成句 be prepared for sth ▶定義 to be ready for sth difficult or unpleasant 困難な, または不快な〜に対する準備ができている → 〜の用意・覚悟ができている, 〜に備えている

be prepared to do sth ▶定義 to be ready and happy to do sth 〜をするための準備ができていて, 楽しい → 〜する用意・覚悟ができている, 喜んで〜する ‖ *I am not prepared to stay here and be insulted.* 私は, ここにとどまって侮辱されたいとは思いません.

**preposition** /prèpəzíʃ(ə)n/ 名 ❸ ▶定義 a word or phrase that is used before a noun or pronoun to show place, time, direction, etc 場所, 時間, 方向などを表すために, 名詞または代名詞の前に使われる単語または句 → 前置詞 ‖ *'In', 'for', 'to' and 'out of' are all prepositions.* in, for, to, out ofは, すべて前置詞である.

**preposterous** /pripást(ə)rəs/ 形 ▶定義 silly; ridiculous; not to be taken seriously ばかな; ばかげた; 真剣には受け取られない → 非常識な, 不合理な, ばかげた

**prerequisite** /priːrékwəzət/ 名 ❸ ▶定義 a prerequisite (for/of sth) something that is necessary for sth to happen or exist 〜が起こる, または存在するために必要な事 → あらかじめ必要なもの, 必須(ひっす)・必要条件 ‖ *Is a good education a prerequisite of success?* 良い教育は成功への必須条件ですか.

**prerogative** /prirágətiv/ 名 ❸ ▶定義 a special right that sb/sth has 〜が持っている特別な権利 → (役職上の)特権, 特典 ‖ *It is the Prime Minister's prerogative to fix the date of the election.* 選挙の日程を決めることは総理大臣の特

権だ.

**Pres** 略 President→大統領

**prescribe** /prɪskráɪb/ 動他 ▶定義1 to say what medicine or treatment sb should have どの薬をまたは治療法を〜が受けるべきかを言う→〜を処方する,指示する ‖ Can you prescribe something for my cough please, doctor? 先生, 私のせきのために何か処方してもらえますか.

▶定義2 正式 (used about a person or an organization with authority) to say that sth must be done (権威ある人または組織について) 〜が行わなければならないと言う→〜を規定する,指示する,指図する ‖ The law prescribes that the document must be signed in the presence of two witnesses. その文書は2人の証人の立ち会いの下で署名されなければならない, と法律は規定しています.

**prescription** /prɪskrípʃ(ə)n/ 名CU ▶定義 a paper on which a doctor has written the name of the medicine that you need. You take your prescription to a shop (the chemist's) and get the medicine there. 医者が必要な薬の名前を書いた用紙. 受け取った人は自分の prescription を店(薬局)に持っていき, そこで薬を買う→処方せん ‖ a prescription for sleeping pills 睡眠薬の処方せん Some medicines are only available **on prescription** (= with a prescription from a doctor). 薬によっては処方せんがないと買えないものもあります (= 医者からの処方せんで).

**presence** /préz(ə)ns/ 名 ▶定義1 ❶the fact of being in a particular place 特定の場所にいるという事実→いること, あること, 存在 ‖ He apologized to her **in the presence of** the whole family. 家族全員のいる前で, 彼は彼女に謝った. an experiment to test for the presence of oxygen 酸素の存在を検査する実験⇔absence ▶定義2 [単数扱い] a number of soldiers or police officers who are in a place for a special reason 特別な理由である場所にいる, 多数の兵士または警察官→駐留, 滞在 ‖ There was a huge police presence at the demonstration. そのデモの場にはばく大な数の警察官がいた.

*****present**¹ /préz(ə)nt/ 形 ▶定義1 (名詞の前だけ) existing or happening now 今, 存在しているまたは起こっている→現在の, 今の ‖ We hope to overcome our present difficulties very soon. 私たちはすぐにも, 現在直面している難局を克服したいと思う. ▶定義2 (名詞の前は不可) being in a particular place 特定の場所にいる→出席している, 居合わせている ‖ There were 200 people present at the meeting. その集会に200人が出席した. ⇔absent

成句 the present day ▶定義 modern times 現代→現代, 現在 ‖ In some countries traditional methods of farming have survived to the present day. いくつかの国では, 伝統的な農業のやり方が現代まで続いている.

*****present**² /préz(ə)nt/ 名 ▶定義1 ❶something that you give to sb or receive from sb; a gift 〜に上げる, または〜からもらう物→贈り物, プレゼント ‖ a birthday/wedding/leaving/Christmas present 誕生日・結婚・お別れ・クリスマスのプレゼント

▶ gift はもっと正式で, しばしば店, カタログなどで使用される.

▶定義2 (通常 the present) [単数扱い] the time now 今の時間→今, 現在 ‖ We live in the present but we must learn from the past. 私たちは現在に生きているが, 過去から学ばなければならない. I'm rather busy **at present**. Can I call you back later? 私は今かなり忙しい. 後でこちらから電話をかけ直していいですか. ▶定義3 the present [単数扱い] = THE PRESENT TENSE

成句 for the moment/present ⇒ MOMENT

**present**³ /prɪzént/ 動他 ▶定義1 present sb with sth; present sth (to sb) to give sth to sb, especially at a formal ceremony 特に正式な式典で, 〜を…に与える→〜を贈呈する, 贈与する ‖ All the dancers were presented with flowers. すべてのダンサーが花を贈呈された. Flowers were presented to all the dancers. 花がすべてのダンサーに贈呈された. ▶定義2 present sth (to sb) to show sth that you have prepared to people 準備した〜を人々に見せる→〜を提示する, 見せる ‖ Good teachers try to present their material in an interesting way. 良い教師たちは興味深い方法で教材を提示しようとする.

▶定義3 present sb with sth; present sth (to sb) to give sb sth that has to be dealt with 〜に, 対処しなければならない…を与える→〜をもたらす, 差し出す, 提出する ‖ Learning English presented no problem to him. 英語を学ぶことは, 彼にとってやさしいことだった. *The manager presented us with a bill for the broken chair.* 支配人は私たちに壊したいすの請求書を差し出した. ▶定義4 to introduce a television or radio programme テレビまたはラジオの番組の司会を務める→**〜の司会をする** ▶定義5 to show a play, etc to the public 一般大衆に芝居などを上演する→**〜を上演する** || *The Theatre Royal is presenting a new production of 'Ghosts'.* ロイヤル劇場は新作「ゴースト」を上演している. ▶定義6 **present sb (to sb)** to introduce sb to a person in a formal ceremony 〜を人に正式な式典で紹介する→**〜を紹介する, 披露する** || *The teams were presented to the President before the game.* 試合の前に, それらのチームが大統領に紹介された.

**presentable** /prɪzéntəb(ə)l/ 形 ▶定義 good enough to be seen by people you do not know well よく知らない人々に見られてもよい→**人前に出せる, 見苦しくない, 体裁の良い**

**presentation** /prèz(ə)ntéɪʃ(ə)n/ 名 ▶定義1 C U the act of giving or showing sth to sb 〜を…に見せる, または与える行為→**提示, 贈呈, 授与式** || *The head will now **make a presentation** to the winners of the competition.* これから会長によるコンテストの優勝者たちへの授与式を執り行います. ▶定義2 U the way in which sth is shown, explained, offered, etc to people 〜が人々に示される, 説明される, 差し出される, などの方法→**(案などの)提示, 披露, 紹介** || *Untidy presentation of your work may lose you marks.* あなたの仕事をきちんと発表できないと, あなたの評価が落ちるかもしれない. ▶定義3 C a meeting at which sth is shown or explained to a group of people 〜が人々の1集団に示される, または説明される集会→**公開, 発表** || *Each student has to **give a** short **presentation** on a subject of his/her choice.* 生徒たちはそれぞれ, 自分が選択したテーマについての短い発表を行わなければならない. ▶定義4 C a formal ceremony at which a prize, etc is given to sb 賞などが〜に与えられる正式な式典→**贈呈式, 授与式**

**presenter** /prɪzéntər/ 名 C ▶定義 a person who introduces a television or radio programme テレビまたはラジオの番組で紹介する人→**番組司会者, (ニュース)キャスター**

preserve 1263

**presently** /préz(ə)ntli/ 副 ▶定義1 soon; shortly **すぐに; 間もなく** || *I'll be finished presently.* 間もなく終わります. ▶定義2 (文) after a short time 短時間の後→**やがて** || *Presently I heard the car door shut.* やがて, 私は車のドアが閉まる音を聞いた. ▶定義3 特に 米 now; currently 今; 今のところ→**現在(は), 目下** || *The management are presently discussing the matter.* 現在, 経営陣はその事柄について討論している.

▶ presentlyがsoonを意味するときは, 普通は文の最後に来て, after a short timeを意味するときには, 普通は文の最初に来ることに注意. presentlyがnowを意味するときは, 動詞に付随して用いられる.

**present participle** 名 C (文法) ▶定義 the form of the verb that ends in -ing -ingで終わる, 動詞の形→**現在分詞**

**the present perfect** 名 [単数扱い] (文法) ▶定義 the form of a verb that expresses an action done in a time period from the past to the present, formed with the present tense of have and the past participle of the verb 過去から現在までの間に行われた行為を表現し, haveの現在形と動詞の過去分詞で作られる, 動詞の形→**現在完了形** || *'I've finished', 'She hasn't arrived' and 'I've been studying' are all **in the present perfect**.* I've finished, She hasn't arrived, I've been studyingはすべて現在完了形である.

▶ 時制の使用についての説明は, 巻末の「文法早見表」を参照.

**the present tense** (または **the present**) 名 C (文法) ▶定義 the tense of the verb that you use when you are talking about what is happening or what exists now 今起きている, または存在する物事について話しているときに使う動詞の時制→**現在形**

**preservative** /prɪzə́ːrvətɪv/ 名 C U ▶定義 a substance that is used for keeping food, etc in good condition 食物などを良い状態に保つために使われる物質→**防腐剤, 予防薬**

*****preserve** /prɪzə́ːrv/ 動 他 ▶定義 to keep sth safe or in good condition 〜を安全に, または良い状態に保つ→**〜を保存する, (自然・環境など)を保護する** || *They've managed to preserve most of the* wall paintings in the caves. 洞窟(どうくつ)内のほとんどの壁画は首尾良く保存されている. — preservation /ˌprezərˈveɪʃ(ə)n/ 名 ❶ ➡保存, 貯蔵, (自然・環境などの)保護

**preside** /prɪˈzaɪd/ 動 ❶ ▶定義 to be in charge of a discussion, meeting, etc 討論, 会議などの責任を持っている➡議長・座長となる, 司会を務める, 統括・主催する

句動詞 preside over sth ▶定義 to be in control of or responsible for sth ~を管理している, または~に対して責任がある➡~を管理する, 統括する, 取り仕切る

**presidency** /ˈprezɪd(ə)nsi/ 名 ( 複 **presidencies**)
▶定義1 the presidency [単数扱い] the position of being president presidentであることの地位➡大統領・社長・会長・学長の地位 ▶定義2 ❶ the period of time that sb is president presidentである期間➡大統領・社長・会長・学長の任期

*president /ˈprezɪd(ə)nt/ 名 ❶ ▶定義1 (または **President**) the leader of a republic 共和国の指導者➡大統領 ‖ the President of France フランス大統領 the US President アメリカ大統領 ▶定義2 the person with the highest position in some organizations いくつかの組織の中で一番高い地位にいる人➡社長, 会長, 学長 — presidential /ˌprezɪˈdenʃ(ə)l/ 形 ➡大統領の, 大統領に関する, 社長・会長・学長の ‖ presidential elections 大統領選挙

*press¹ /pres/ 名 ▶定義1 (通常は **the press**) [単数扱い, 単数または複数形の動詞と共に]newspapers and the journalists who work for them 新聞と新聞のために働くジャーナリストたち➡新聞, 新聞界, 報道陣 ‖ The story has been reported on TV and **in the press**. その話はテレビと新聞で報道された. the local/national press 地方・全国紙 The press support/supports government policy. 新聞は政府の政策を支持している. ▶定義2 [単数扱い, ❶] what or the amount that is written about sb/sth in newspapers ~について新聞に書かれた事柄または量➡論評, 批評 ‖ This company has had **a bad press** recently. 最近この会社は紙上で酷評された. The strike got very little press. そのストライキはほとんど記事にならなかった. ▶定義3 ❶❶ a machine for printing books, newspapers, etc; the process of printing them 本, 新聞などを印刷する機械; それらを印刷する工程➡印刷機, 印刷すること ‖ All details were correct at the time of going to press. すべての詳細事項は印刷機に送られる時点で修正されていた. ▶定義4 ❶ a business that prints books, etc 本などを出版する商売➡発行所, 出版部, 出版局 ‖ Oxford University Press オックスフォード大学出版局 ▶定義5 ❶ an act of pushing sth firmly ~をしっかりと押す行為➡押すこと ‖ Give that button **a press** and see what happens. あのボタンを押して, 何が起こるか見なさい.

*press² /pres/ 動 ▶定義1 ❶❶ to push sth firmly ~をしっかりと押す➡押す, 押し付ける ‖ Just press that button and the door will open. あのボタンを押しなさい, するとドアが開きます. He pressed the lid firmly shut. 彼はふたを押してしっかりと閉めた. ▶定義2 ❶ to put weight onto sth, for example in order to get juice out of it 例えばそれから果汁を得るために, ~に圧力を加える➡~を押しつぶす, しぼる, 圧搾する ‖ to press grapes ぶどうをしぼる ☛ **squeeze** のさし絵 ▶定義3 ❶ to make a piece of clothing smooth by using an iron アイロンをかけて衣服を滑らかにする➡~にアイロンをかける ‖ This shirt needs pressing. このシャツにはアイロンをかける必要がある. ▶定義4 ❶ to hold sb/sth firmly in a loving way 愛情に満ちたやり方で, ~をしっかりと抱える➡~を握りしめる, 抱き締める ‖ She pressed the photo to her chest. 彼女はその写真を自分の胸に抱き締めた. ▶定義5 ❶ **press across, against, around, etc (sth)** (used about people) to move in a particular direction by pushing (人々について)押して特定の方向へ動く➡押し寄せる, どっと群がる ‖ The crowd pressed against the wall of policemen. 群集が警察官たちの壁に向かって押し寄せた.

▶定義6 ❶❶ **press (sb) (for sth/to do sth)** to try to persuade or force sb to do sth ~に…をするように説き伏せようと, または強いようとする➡~に無理に…させる, ~をせき立てる, ~にせがむ ‖ I pressed them to stay for dinner. 私は彼らに夕飯を食べていくよう引き止めた. to press sb for an answer ~に答えをしつこくせがむ

▶定義7 ❶ to express or repeat sth in an urgent way 切迫した様子で~を表現する, または繰り返す➡~を強調・力説・主張する, 強いる ‖

don't want to press the point, but you still owe me money. せき立てるつもりはないけれど、あなたはまだ私からお金を借りていますよね.
成句 be hard pressed/pushed/put to do sth ⇒ HARD²
be pressed for sth ▶定義 to not have enough of sth 十分な～を持っていない→～のために苦しんでいる・悩んでいる ‖ I must hurry. I'm really pressed for time. 急がなくては。本当に時間がなくて困っている.
bring/press charges (against sb) ⇒ CHARGE¹
句動詞 press ahead/forward/on (with sth) ▶定義 to continue doing sth even though it is difficult or hard work たとえ困難な, またはつらい仕事でも～をすることを続ける→(仕事・行動など)をどんどん進める ‖ They pressed on with the building work in spite of the bad weather. 悪天候にもかかわらず, 彼らは建設作業をどんどん進めた.

**press conference** 名 C ▶定義 a meeting when a famous or important person answers questions from newspaper and television journalists 有名な, または重要な人が新聞とテレビの報道陣からの質問に答える会合→記者会見 ‖ to hold a press conference 記者会見を開く

**pressing** /présɪŋ/ 形 ▶定義 that must be dealt with immediately; urgent すぐに処理されなければならない～; 緊急の→差し迫った, 急を要する; 緊急の

**press stud** 名 C = POPPER

**press-up** (米 **push-up**) 名 C ▶定義 a type of exercise in which you lie on your front on the floor and push your body up with your arms 床にうつぶせになって両腕で自分の体を持ち上げる, 運動の一種→腕立て伏せ ‖ I do 50 press-ups every morning. 私は毎朝腕立て伏せを50回する. ☛ S1 ページのさし絵

*****pressure** /préʃər/ 名 ▶定義 1 ❶ the force that is produced when you press on or against sth ～を強く押す, または～に押しつけるときに発生する力→圧力 ‖ Apply pressure to the cut and it will stop bleeding. 傷口を押さえなさい, それで出血が止まるでしょう. The pressure of the water caused the dam to crack. 水圧でダムが決壊した. ▶定義 2 C U the force that a gas or liquid has when it is contained inside sth 物質の内部に含まれている気体, または液体が持っている

力→圧力, 気圧, 血圧 ‖ high/low blood pressure 高・低血圧 You should check your tyre pressures regularly. 定期的にタイヤの空気圧を点検した方がいいですよ. ▶定義 3 C U worries or difficulties that you have because you have too much to deal with; stress 処理する事が多すぎることから来る心配事または苦境; ストレス→困難, 窮乏, 苦悩 ‖ financial pressures 財政難 I find it difficult to cope with pressure at work. 職場でストレスをうまく処理することは難しいと思う.
成句 put pressure on sb (to do sth) ▶定義 to force sb to do sth ～に…をするよう強制する→～に圧力をかける, 強制する ‖ The press is putting pressure on him to resign. 新聞は彼に辞任するよう圧力をかけている.
under pressure ▶定義 1 being forced to do sth ～をするよう強いられている→強制されて, 圧力を加えられて ‖ Anna was under pressure from her parents to leave school and get a job. アンナは両親から学校を辞めて働くように強制されていた. ▶定義 2 worried or in difficulty because you have too much to deal with 処理する事が多すぎて, 心配な, または困って→プレッシャーを感じて, ストレスがたまって, 切迫して ‖ I perform poorly under pressure, so I hate exams. プレッシャーを感じるといつもうまく対処できないので, 試験は嫌いだ. ▶定義 3 (used about liquid or gas) contained inside sth or sent somewhere using force (液体または気体について)～の内部に含まれていて, または力を使ってどこかへ送られて→加圧されて, 圧力をかけられて ‖ Water is forced out through the hose under pressure. 水は加圧されてホースから流れ出る. — pressure 動 他 = PRESSURIZE

**pressure group** 名 C, 単数または複数形の動詞と共に] ▶定義 a group of people who are trying to influence what a government or other organization does 政府またはほかの機関が行う事に影響を及ぼそうとする人々の集団→圧力団体

**pressurize** (または **-ise**) /préʃəraɪz/ (または **pressure**) 動 他 ▶定義 pressurize sb (into sth/doing sth) to use force or influence to make sb do sth ～に…をさせるために, 実力または影響力を使う→～に圧力をかける, 強制する ‖ Some workers were pressurized into taking *early retirement.* 何人かの従業員は早期退職をするよう圧力をかけられた.

**pressurized** (または **-ised**) /préʃəràɪzd/ 形 ▶定義 (used about air in an aircraft) kept at the pressure at which people can breathe (飛行機内の空気について) 人々が呼吸できる気圧に保たれた→**気圧調整された, 一定の気圧に保たれた**

**prestige** /prestíːʒ, -dʒ, préstɪdʒ/ 名 ❶ ▶定義 the respect and admiration that people feel for a person because he/she has a high social position or has been very successful 高い地位にあるまたはとても成功しているので, その人に対して人々が感じる尊敬と感嘆→**名声, 信望, 威信** ‖ *Nursing isn't a high prestige job.* 看護は高い名声を伴う職業ではない. — **prestigious** /prestídʒ(i)əs, -tíːdʒ(i)əs/ 形→**名声のある, 一流の, 名門の** ‖ *a prestigious prize/school/job* 一流の賞・名門校・社会的地位の高い仕事

**presumably** /prɪz(j)úːməb(ə)li/ 副 ▶定義 I imagine; I suppose 私が想像する; 私が思う→**多分, おそらく, 推定するところ** ‖ *Presumably this rain means the match will be cancelled?* この雨でおそらく試合は中止になるでしょうね.

**presume** /prɪz(j)úːm/ 動⑭ ▶定義 to think that sth is true even if you do not know for sure; to suppose たとえはっきりとわからなくても, 〜は事実であると考える; 想定する→**〜を推定する, 想像する, 〜と考える** ‖ *The house looks empty so I presume they are away on holiday.* 家にはだれもいないようなので, 彼らは休暇で出掛けているのだと思う. — **presumption** /prɪzʌ́m(p)ʃ(ə)n/ 名 ❷→**推定, 仮定, 憶測**

**presumptuous** /prɪzʌ́m(p)tʃuəs/ 形 ▶定義 confident that sth will happen or that sb will do sth without making sure first, in a way that annoys people, 人々をいらいらさせてる様子で, 最初に確かめないで〜が起こるまたは〜が…をすることに自信を持っている→**出しゃばりな, おこがましい, 生意気な** ‖ *It was very presumptuous of him to say that I would help without asking me first.* 最初に私に頼みもしないで私が手伝うだろうと言うなんて, 彼はとてもずうずうしい人だった.

**pretence** (米 **pretense**) /prɪténs/ 名 [ ❶, 単数扱い] ▶定義 an action that makes people believe sth that is not true 事実でない〜を人々に信じさせる行為→**見せ掛け, (〜の)振り** ‖ *She was unable to keep up the pretence that she loved him.* 彼女は, 彼を愛しているという振りを続けられなかった.

成句 **on/under false pretences** ⇒ **FALSE**

★**pretend** /prɪténd/ 動⑬⑭ ▶定義 **1** to behave in a particular way in order to make other people believe sth that is not true 事実でない〜をほかの人々に信じさせるために, ある特定のやり方で振る舞う→**〜の振りをする, 〜に見せ掛ける** ‖ *You can't just pretend that the problem doesn't exist.* その問題が存在しない振りはできませんよ. *Paul's not really asleep. He's just pretending.* ポールは本当は寝ていません. 狸(たぬき)寝入りしているのです. ▶定義 **2** (used especially about children) to imagine that sth is true as part of a game (特に子供について) 遊びの一部として, 〜が事実であると想像する→**まねをして遊ぶ, 〜ごっこをする** ‖ *The kids were under the bed pretending to be snakes.* 子供たちはベッドの下で, 蛇のまねをして遊んでいた.

**pretentious** /prɪténʃəs/ 形 ▶定義 trying to appear more serious or important than you really are 実際の自分よりもっと重要に, または偉く見えるように努めている→**気取った, うぬぼれた, きざな** ‖ *I think it sounds pretentious to use a lot of foreign words.* 外国の言葉をたくさん使うと, きざに聞こえると思う.

**pretext** /príːtèkst/ 名 ❸ ▶定義 a reason that you give for doing sth that is not the real reason 〜をするために与える, 実際の理由ではない理由→**口実, 弁解** ‖ *Tariq left **on the pretext of** having an appointment at the dentist's.* 歯医者に予約していることを口実にして, タリクは去った.

★**pretty**¹ /príti/ 形 (**prettier**; **prettiest**) ▶定義 attractive and pleasant to look at or hear 見る, または聞くのに魅力的で好ましい→**かわいらしい, きれいな** ‖ *a pretty girl/smile/dress/garden/name* かわいい少女・あどけない笑顔・きれいなドレス・すてきな庭・かわいい名前
▶ prettyは通常男性または少年を描写するためには使われない. good-lookingはすべての人々に用いられることができ, handsomeは通常男性に使われる. beautifulの注も参照.
— **prettily** 副→**きれいに, かわいらしく, 行儀良く** ‖ *The room is prettily decorated.* その部屋は

きれいに飾られている. — prettiness 名 U→きれいさ,かわいらしさ,こぎれいさ

**\*pretty**² /príti/ 副 略式 ▶定義 quite; fairly かなり; 随分→**かなり,相当,とても** ‖ *The film was pretty good but not fantastic.* 映画はかなり良かったが,とてもすばらしいというほどではなかった. *I'm pretty certain that Alex will agree.* アレックスが同意するだろうと,私はほとんど確信している. ☛参 **rather**の注

成句 pretty much/nearly/well ▶定義 almost; very nearly ほとんど; 本当にもう少しで→**ほとんど,大体** ‖ *I won't be long. I've pretty well finished.* そんなに長くかかりません.ほとんど終わりましたから.

**prevail** /prɪvéɪl/ 動 自 ▶定義 **1** to exist or be common in a particular place or at a particular time 特定の場所または特定の時間で存在する,または一般的である→**広く行われている,普及している,流行している** ‖ *In some remote areas traditional methods of farming still prevail.* いくつかのへき地では,いまだに伝統的な農耕が広く行われている. ▶定義 **2** 正式 prevail (against/over sb/sth) to win or be accepted, especially after a fight or discussion 特に試合や討論の後で,勝つまたは受け入れられる→**打ち勝つ,克服する,うまくいく** ‖ *In the end justice prevailed and the men were set free.* 最後には正義が勝ち,男たちは自由の身になった.

**prevailing** /prɪvéɪlɪŋ/ 形 (名詞の前だけ) ▶定義 **1** existing or most common at a particular time 特定の時間に存在している,または最も一般的である→**広く行われている,(最も)普通の,(最も)優勢な** ‖ *the prevailing climate of opinion* 一般的な意見の傾向 ▶定義 **2** (used about the wind) most common in a particular area (風について)特定の地域で最も一般的な→**最も頻繁に吹く** ‖ *The prevailing wind is from the south-west.* 最も頻繁に吹く風は南西方向からです.

**prevalent** /prév(ə)lənt/ 形 正式 ▶定義 most common in a particular place at a particular time 特定の場所で特定の時間に最も一般的な→**広く行き渡っている,流行・普及している,(病気などが)蔓延(まんえん)している** ‖ *The prevalent atmosphere was one of fear.* 辺りを満たしている空気は恐怖の空気だった.

**\*prevent** /prɪvént/ 動 他 ▶定義 prevent sb/sth (from) (doing sth) to stop sth happening or to stop sb doing sth ～が起きることを止める,または～が…をすることを妨げる→**～を防ぐ,防止する,予防する** ‖ *This accident could have been prevented.* この事故は防ぐことができただろうに. *Her parents tried to prevent her from going to live with her boyfriend.* 彼女の両親は,彼女が恋人と一緒に住もうとするのをやめさせようとした. ☛ preventは stopよりも正式である. — prevention 名 U→**止めること,防止,予防** ‖ *accident/crime prevention* 事故・犯罪の防止

**preventable** /privéntəb(ə)l/ 形 ▶定義 that can be prevented 防ぐことができる→**予防できる,防止できる** ‖ *Many accidents are preventable.* 多くの事故は防止できるものだ.

**preventive** /privéntiv/ (または **preventative** /privéntətiv/) 形 ▶定義 intended to stop or prevent sth from happening 起こらないように,～を止めるまたは予防することを意図して→**予防の,予防・防止に役立つ** ‖ *preventative medicine* 予防医学

**preview** /príːvjuː/ 名 C ▶定義 a chance to see a play, film, etc before it is shown to the general public 一般大衆に公開する前に,劇,映画などを見る機会→**試写会,試演,内覧**

**\*previous** /príːviəs/ 形 ▶定義 coming or happening before or earlier 前に,または早く来ている,または起きている→**先の,前の** ‖ *Do you have previous experience of this type of work?* この種の仕事を前にやった経験がありますか. — previously 副 →**以前に,前に,前もって** ‖ *Before I moved to Spain I had previously worked in Italy.* スペインに引っ越す以前はイタリアで働いていました.

**prey**¹ /préɪ/ 名 U ▶定義 an animal or bird that is killed and eaten by another animal or bird ほかの動物または鳥に殺されて食べられてしまう動物または鳥→**えじき,獲物** ‖ *The eagle is a bird of prey (= it kills and eats other birds or small animals).* タカは猛禽(もうきん)です(= ほかの鳥または小動物を殺して食べる).

**prey**² /préɪ/ 動

成句 prey on sb's mind ▶定義 to cause sb to worry or think about sth ～に…について心配させる,または考えさせる→**～を苦しめる,悩ます** ‖ *The thought that he was responsible for the* *accident preyed on the train driver's mind.* 事故の責任に対する思いが、その列車の運転手の心を苦しめた．

句動詞 **prey on sth** ▶定義 (used about an animal or bird) to kill and eat other animals or birds (鳥または動物について) ほかの動物または鳥を殺して食べる →~を捕食する ‖ *Owls prey on mice and other small animals.* フクロウはネズミとほかの小動物を捕食する．

★**price**[1] /práɪs/ 名 ▶定義 **1** ❻ the amount of money that you must pay in order to buy sth ~を買うために支払わなければならない金額 →値段，価格 ‖ *What's the price of petrol now?* 今、ガソリンの値段はいくらですか．*We can't afford to buy the car at that price.* 私たちには、あの値段でこの車を買う余裕はない．*There's no price on (= written on) this jar of coffee.* このコーヒーポットには値段が付いていない (= 書かれていない)．

▶ charge は何かを使うために支払わなければならない金額である: *Is there a charge for parking here?* (ここに駐車するのに料金がかかりますか．) admission charges (入学金)．サービスに対する支払いについて、または実際の金額に触れないで一般の値段について話しているときは、cost が用いられる: *The cost of electricity is going up.* (電気代が高くなっている．) the cost of living (生活費)．物の price は、それを買うために支払わなければならない金額である．

店はその価格を raise, increase (上げる・増額する), reduce, bring down (減額する・下げる) または freeze (凍結する) と言う．価格は rise, go up (上昇する・上がる) または fall, go down (下降する・下がる) と言う．

▶定義 **2** [単数扱い] unpleasant things that you have to experience in order to achieve sth or as a result of sth ~を成し遂げるためにまたは~の結果として，体験しなければならない不快なこと →代償，代価，犠牲 ‖ *Sleepless nights are a small price to pay for having a baby.* 眠れない夜は、子供を持ったことのささやかな代価である．

成句 **at a price** ▶定義 costing a lot of money or involving sth unpleasant 多額のお金がかかる、または不快な~がかかわっている →かなりの値段で，高い値で，かなりの代価・犠牲を払って ‖ *He'll help you get a job - at a price.* 彼はあなたが仕事を得られるように手伝ってくれますよ — 高額でね．

**at any price** ▶定義 even if the cost is very high or if it will have unpleasant results たとえ対価がとても高くても、またはたとえ嫌な結果になろうとも →どんな犠牲を払っても ‖ *Richard was determined to succeed at any price.* リチャードはどんな犠牲を払っても成功しようと決意した．

**not at any price** ▶定義 never; under no circumstances 決して~ない；どんな事情があっても~しない →どうしても~しない，どんな条件でも，どうあっても

**price**[2] /práɪs/ 動 ⓣ ▶定義 to fix the price of sth or to write the price on sth ~の値段を決定する，または~に値段を書く →~に値段・定価を付ける，~に値段を表示する ‖ *The books were all priced at between £5 and £10.* それらの本には、すべて5ポンドから10ポンドの間の値が付いていた．

**priceless** /práɪsləs/ 形 ▶定義 of very great value とてもすごい価値の →(値段を付けられないくらい) 非常に価値のある，金で買えない，掛け替えのない ‖ *priceless jewels and antiques* 非常に価値のある宝石と骨董 (こっとう) 品 ☛参 **worthless, valuable, invaluable**

**price list** 名 ❻ ▶定義 a list of the prices of the goods that are on sale 売られている品物の値段の一覧表 →価格表，定価表

**pricey** /práɪsi/ 形格式 ▶定義 expensive 高価な →値段が高い，高価な

**prick**[1] /prɪk/ 動 ⓣ ▶定義 to make a small hole in sth or to cause sb pain with a sharp point ~に小さな穴を開ける、または~に鋭い痛みを起こさせる →~をちくりと刺す，~に刺し傷を付ける，刺して (穴を) 開ける ‖ *She pricked her finger on a needle.* 彼女は針で自分の指を刺した．

成句 **prick up your ears** ▶定義 (used about an animal) to hold up the ears in order to listen carefully to sth (動物について) ~を注意して聞くために、耳を立てる →耳を立てる，耳をそばだてる ‖ (比喩) *Mike pricked up his ears when he heard Emma's name mentioned.* エマの名前が聞こえたとき、マイクは耳をそばだてた．

**prick**[2] /prɪk/ 名 ❻ ▶定義 the sudden pain that you feel when sth sharp goes into your skin 鋭

い物が肌に刺さったときに感じる,突然の痛み→**痛み,うずき**

**prickle**¹ /prík(ə)l/ 名 ● ▶定義 one of the sharp points on some plants and animals ある種の植物と動物にある鋭い先端の1つ→**とげ,針** ‖ *Hedgehogs are covered in prickles.* ハリネズミは針で覆われている. ☞参 **spine** ☞ **hedgehog** のさし絵

**prickle**² /prík(ə)l/ 動 ● ▶定義 to have or make sb/sth have an uncomfortable feeling on the skin 肌に不快な感じがある,または〜にそのように感じさせる→**ちくちくする,うずく,総毛立つ** ‖ *I don't like that shirt - it prickles.* 私はあのシャツが嫌いです — ちくちくするので. *His skin prickled with fear.* 彼の肌は恐怖で総毛立った.

**prickly** /prík(ə)li/ 形 ▶定義 1 covered with sharp points 鋭い先端で覆われている→**とげだらけの,針のある** ‖ *a prickly bush* とげだらけの茂み ▶定義 2 causing an uncomfortable feeling on the skin 肌に不快な感じを引き起こす→**ちくちくする,刺すような** ‖ *That T-shirt makes my skin go all prickly.* あのTシャツは着るとちくちくする. ▶定義 3 略式 (used about a person) easily made angry (人について)怒りやすい→**怒りっぽい,扱いにくい,厄介な** ‖ *Don't mention his accident - he's a bit prickly about it.* 彼の事故については言わないでください — その事について彼はちょっと怒りっぽくなっているから.

★**pride**¹ /práɪd/ 名 ▶定義 1 [ U,単数扱い] pride (in sth/doing sth) the feeling of pleasure that you have when you or people who are close to you do sth good or own sth good 自分または自分に近い人々が良い〜をする,または良い〜を所有するときに,感じる喜びの感情→**誇り,自慢,得意(な気持ち),満足(感)** ‖ *I take a great pride in my work.* 私は,自分の仕事をとても誇りにしている. *Her parents watched with pride as Milena went up to collect her prize.* ミレナが賞をもらいに壇上に上がるのを,彼女の両親は満足げに見ていた. *You should feel pride in your achievement.* 自分の成し遂げたことに満足感を持つべきです. ☞ **proud** ▶定義 2 ❶the respect that you have for yourself 自分自身への尊敬→**自尊心,プライド** ‖ *You'll hurt his pride if you refuse to accept the present.* その贈り物を受け取らないと,彼の自尊心を傷付けることになりますよ. ▶定義 3 ❶the feeling that you are

**primary**¹ 1269

better than other people 自分はほかの人々より優れているという感情→**うぬぼれ,思い上がり,高慢** ▶定義 4 [単数扱い] the pride of sth/sb a person or thing that is very important or of great value to sth/sb 〜にとってとても重要な,または価値のある人または物→**自慢の種** ‖ *The new stadium was the pride of the whole town.* その新しい競技場は街中の自慢の種だった.

成句 sb's pride and joy ▶定義 a thing or person that gives sb great pleasure or satisfaction 〜にすばらしい喜び,または満足感を与える物事または人→**〜の大変な自慢の種**

**pride**² /práɪd/ 動

句動詞 pride yourself on sth/doing sth ▶定義 to feel pleased about sth good or clever that you can do 自分ができる良いまたは気の利いた〜について喜びを感じる→**〜を誇る,自慢する** ‖ *Fabio prides himself on his ability to cook.* ファビオは自分の料理の腕前を誇っている.

★**priest** /priːst/ 名 ● ▶定義 a person who performs religious ceremonies in some religions いくつかの宗教で,宗教的儀式を行う人→**司祭,聖職者,僧**

▶いくつかの宗教で,女性の priest は priestess と呼ばれる.

**prim** /prɪm/ 形 ▶定義 (used about a person) always behaving in a careful or formal way and easily shocked by anything that is rude (人について)常に慎重なまたは格式張った方法で振る舞い,失礼な物事からは簡単に衝撃を受ける→**きちょうめんな,しかつめらしい,堅苦しい** — **primly** 副 →**きちょうめんに,しかつめらしく,堅苦しく**

**primarily** /práɪmərɪli; praɪmérə-/ 副 ▶定義 more than anything else; mainly ほかのものよりもっと;主に→**主として,主に** ‖ *The course is aimed primarily at beginners.* その講座は主に初心者を対象としている.

★**primary**¹ /práɪm(ə)ri; -mèri/ 形 ▶定義 1 most important; main 最も重要な;主な→**第1(番)の,第1位・次の,最も重要な** ‖ *Smoking is one of the primary causes of lung cancer.* 喫煙は,肺がんの第1位の原因の1つだ. ▶定義 2 connected with the education of children between about five and eleven years old 5歳から11歳までの

子供たちの教育に関連した→**初級の, 初等の** ‖ *Their children are at primary school.* 彼らの子供たちは小学校に通っている.

**primary**² /práim(ə)ri; -mèri/(または **primary election**) 名 C (複 **primaries**) 米 ▶定義 an election in which a political party chooses the person who will represent the party (the candidate) in a later important election, such as for president 政党が後にある重要な選挙, 例えば大統領のための選挙, で党を代表する人(候補者)を選ぶ選挙→**予備選挙**

**primary colour** 名 C ▶定義 any of the colours red, yellow or blue. You can make any other colour by mixing primary colours in different ways. 赤, 黄, または青のいずれかの色. ほかのどんな色でも primary colour を異なる組み合わせで混ぜて作ることができる→**原色**

**prime**¹ /práim/ 形 (名詞の前だけ) ▶定義 1 main; the first example of sth that sb would think of or choose 主な; 〜が思いつく, または選ぶ〜の最初の例→**最も重要な, 第1の, 主な** ‖ *She is a prime candidate as the next team captain.* 彼女は次のチームキャプテンの第1候補だ. ▶定義 2 of very good quality; best とても良い品質の; 最も良い→**最優秀の, 第1級の, 特上の** ‖ *prime pieces of beef* 特上の牛肉 ▶定義 3 having all the typical qualities すべての典型的な質を持っている→**典型的な** ‖ *That's a prime example of what I was talking about.* それが, 私が話していた事の典型的な例です.

**prime**² /práim/ 名 [単数扱い] ▶定義 the time when sb is strongest, most beautiful, most successful, etc 〜が最も強く, 最も美しく, 最も成功している, などの時期→**全盛期, 最良の時** ‖ *Several of the team are past their prime.* そのチームのいく人かは全盛期を過ぎている. *In his prime, he was a fine actor.* 全盛期には彼はいい役者だった. *to be in the prime of life* 人生の最良の時にいる

**prime**³ /práim/ 動 他 ▶定義 prime sb (for/with sth) to give sb information in order to prepare him/her for sth 〜への準備をさせるために, …に情報を与える→**〜に入れ知恵をする, 前もって教えておく** ‖ *The politician had been well primed with all the facts before the interview.* インタビューの前に, その政治家はあらかじめすべての事実を十分に知らされていた.

**prime minister** 名 C (略 PM) ▶定義 the leader of the government in some countries, for example Britain いくつかの国々, 例えばイギリス, の政府の指導者→**総理大臣** ☞参 minister

**primitive** /prímətiv/ 形 ▶定義 1 very simple and not developed とても単純で発達していない→**素朴な, 幼稚な, 旧式で不便な** ‖ *The washing facilities in the camp were very primitive.* そのキャンプ場の洗濯設備はとても旧式で不便だった. ▶定義 2 (名詞の前だけ) connected with a very early stage in the development of humans or animals 人間または動物の発達のとても早い段階と関連した→**原始の, 原始時代の, 太古の** ‖ *Primitive man lived in caves and hunted wild animals.* 原始人は洞窟(どうくつ)に住んで, 野生の動物を狩っていた.

**primrose** /prímròuz/ 名 C ▶定義 a yellow spring flower 黄色い春の花→**桜草** ☞ C2 ページのさし絵

*__**prince**__ /prins/ 名 C ▶定義 1 a son or other close male relative of a king or queen 王または女王の息子, またはほかの近親の男→**王子, 親王** ▶定義 2 the male ruler of a small country 小国の男性の統治者→**小国の王, 君主**

**princess** /prinsés; prínsəs, -sès/ 名 C ▶定義 1 a daughter or other close female relative of a king or queen 王または女王の娘, またはほかの近親の女→**王女, 内親王** ▶定義 2 the wife of a prince 王子の妻→**親王妃, (小国の)王妃**

*__**principal**__¹ /prínsəp(ə)l, -s(ə)pəl/ 形 (名詞の前だけ) ▶定義 most important; main 最も重要な; 主な→**最も重要な, 主な, 主要な** ‖ *the principal characters in a play* 劇の主要な登場人物たち — principally /-p(ə)li, -pəli/ 副 →**主として, 主に** ‖ *Our products are designed principally for the European market.* 当社の製品は主にヨーロッパ市場に向けてデザインされている.

**principal**² /prínsəp(ə)l, -s(ə)pəl/ 名 C ▶定義 the head of some schools, colleges, etc いくつかの学校, 単科大学などの長→**校長, 学長**

*__**principle**__ /prínsəp(ə)l, -s(ə)pəl/ 名 ▶定義 1 C U a rule for good behaviour, based on what a person believes is right 人が正しいと信じる物事に基づいた, 良い振る舞いのための規則→

主義,信条,方針 ‖ He doesn't eat meat **on principle**. 主義として彼は肉を食べない. She refuses to wear fur. It's **a matter of principle** with her. 彼女は毛皮を着ることを拒んでいる. それは彼女の主義にかかわる問題だ. ▶定義2 ●a basic general law, rule or idea 基本的で一般的な法則,規則,または考え→**原理,原則,(機械などが動く)原理,仕組み** ‖ The system works **on the principle that** heat rises. そのシステムは,熱が上昇する仕組みで動く. The course teaches the basic principles of car maintenance. その講座では,自動車整備の基礎的な原則を教えています.

成句 **in principle** ▶定義 in general, but possibly not in detail 一般には,もしかすると詳細では違う→**原則的には** ‖ His proposal sounds fine in principle, but there are a few points I'm not happy about. 原則的には彼の提案は良いようだが,納得のいかない部分が何点かある.

\***print**¹ /prínt/ 動 ▶定義1 ●to put words, pictures, etc onto paper by using a special machine 特別な機械を使って,言葉,絵などを紙に書き付ける→**~を印刷する** ‖ How much did it cost to print the posters? そのポスターを印刷するために,どのくらいお金がかかりましたか. ▶定義2 ●to produce books, newspapers, etc in this way 本,新聞などをこの方法で生産する→**出版する; ~を出版・刊行・発行する** ‖ 50000 copies of the textbook were printed. その教科書は5万部発行された. ▶定義3 ●to include sth in a book, newspaper, etc 本,新聞などの中に~を含む→**活字にして・印刷して~を公表する** ‖ The newspaper should not have printed the photographs of the crash. その新聞社は,事故の写真を印刷して公表するべきではなかった. ▶定義4 ●to make a photograph from a piece of negative film ネガから写真を作る→**~を焼き付ける,プリントする** ▶定義5 ●to write with letters that are not joined together 互いにつながっていない文字で書く→**活字体で書く;~を活字体で書く** ‖ Please print your name clearly at the top of the paper. 書類の上部にお名前を活字体ではっきり書いてください. ▶定義6 ●to put a pattern onto cloth, paper, etc 布,紙などに模様をかき付ける→**(判などを)押す,~に捺染(なっせん)する,プリントする**

句動詞 **print (sth) out** ▶定義 to print information from a computer onto paper コンピューターからの情報を紙に印刷する→**~を打ち出す,印字する** ‖ I'll just print out this file. ちょうどこのファイルを印字するところです. — **printing** 名 ●→**印刷,焼き付け,活字体で書いた文字**

\***print**² /prínt/ 名 ▶定義1 ●the letters, words, etc in a book, newspaper, etc 本,新聞などの中の文字または言葉など→**印刷(物),印刷された文字・言葉** ‖ The print is too small for me to read without my glasses. 印刷の文字が小さすぎて眼鏡がないと読めない. ▶定義2 ●used to refer to the business of producing newspapers, books, etc 新聞,本などを印刷する商売を言及するために用いて→**印刷業者,印刷所** ‖ the print unions/workers 印刷業組合・印刷工 ▶定義3 ●a mark that is made by sth pressing onto sth else ほかの~に…を押し付けてできる印→**跡,痕跡(こんせき),指紋** ‖ The police are searching the room for fingerprints. 警察はその部屋で指紋を捜している. footprints in the snow 雪の上の足跡 ▶定義4 ●a picture that was made by printing 印刷されてできた絵→**版画,複製画** ▶定義5 ●a photograph (when it has been printed from a negative) 写真(ネガから焼き付けされたとき)→**印画,陽画** ‖ I ordered an extra set of prints for my friends. 私は友人たちのために余分に焼き増しを頼んだ.

> ▶**日本語 vs 英語**
>
> **print と handout の違い**
>
> 「プリント」と言うと学校でもらう配布物を思い浮かべる人が多いでしょう.しかし英語で print と言うとそういう意味にはなりません.学校でもらう「プリント」は handout と言います.また授業中に書き込んだりするような練習用のプリントは worksheet とも呼ばれます.

成句 **in print** ▶定義1 (used about a book) still available from the company that published it (本について)それを発行した会社から,いまでも入手可能な→**入手可能な,絶版でない** ▶定義2 (used about a person's work) published in a book, newspaper, etc (人の仕事について)本,新

聞などに出版された→**出版物で, 本で**

**out of print** ▶定義 (used about a book) no longer available from the company that published it; not being printed any more (本について)それを発行した会社から, もはや入手不可能な; もはや印刷されてない→**絶版になって**

**printer** /príntər/ 名 ● ▶定義 **1** a person or company that prints books, newspapers, etc 本, 新聞などを印刷する人または会社→**印刷工, 印刷業者, 印刷所** ▶定義 **2** a machine that prints out information from a computer onto paper コンピューターからの情報を紙に印刷する機械→**印刷機, プリンター** ‖ *a laser printer* レーザープリンター ☞ S5ページのさし絵

**printing press**(または **press**) 名 ● ▶定義 a machine that is used for printing books, newspapers, etc 本, 新聞などを印刷するために使われる機械→**印刷機**

**printout** /príntàut/ 名 ● ● ▶定義 information from a computer that is printed onto paper 紙に印刷された, コンピューターからの情報→**プリントアウト**

**prior** /práiər/ 形 (名詞の前だけ) ▶定義 coming before or earlier 前に, または早く来ている→**前の, 先の**

\*__priority__ /praió(:)rəti, -ár-/ 名 ( 複 **priorities**) ▶定義 **1** ● priority (over sb/sth) the state of being more important than sb/sth or of coming before sb/sth else 〜よりもっと重要な, またはほかの〜の前に来ている状態→**優先, 先行(する・させること)** ‖ *We give priority to families with small children.* 私たちは幼い子供のいる家族を優先させる. *Emergency cases take priority over other patients in hospital.* 緊急医療患者はほかの入院患者より優先される. ▶定義 **2** ● something that is most important or that you must do before anything else 最も重要な, またはほかの〜の前にしなければならない物事→**優先事項, 優先する・させる物事** ‖ *Our top priority is to get food and water to the refugee camps.* 私たちの最優先事項は, 避難民キャンプへの食糧と水を調達することだ. *I'll make it my priority to sort out your problem.* あなたの問題を解決することを, 優先させましょう.

**prior to** 前 正式 ▶定義 before 〜の前に→**〜より**前に, 〜より優先的に ‖ *Passengers are asked to report to the check-in desk prior to departure.* 乗客は出発前にチェックインカウンターに出向くように言われている.

**prise** /práiz/ (特に 米 **prize**, **pry**) 動 他 ▶定義 **prise sth off, apart, open, etc** to use force to open sth, remove a lid, etc 〜を開ける, ふたを取り除く, などのために力を使う→**〜をこじ開ける, てこで動かす** ‖ *He prised the door open with an iron bar.* 彼は鉄の棒でドアをこじ開けた.

\*__prison__ /prízən/ (または **jail**) 名 ● ● ▶定義 a building where criminals are kept as a punishment 刑罰として, 犯罪者が収容される建物→**刑務所, 監獄, 拘置所** ‖ *The terrorists were **sent to prison** for twenty-five years.* そのテロリストたちは25年の刑で刑務所へ送られた. *He will be **released from prison** next month.* 彼は来月刑務所から出所する. ☞参 **imprison**, **jail**

▶もし人が, go to prison または be in prison (the なし)なら, その人は受刑者としてそこに滞在しなければならない: *He was sent to prison for two years.*(彼は2年の刑で刑務所に送られた.)the prison は特定の刑務所を指すか, または人が一時的にその建物をただ訪れているだけであることを示唆している: *The politician visited the prison and said that conditions were poor.*(その政治家は刑務所を訪れ, 管理状態が良くないと言った.)

\*__prisoner__ /prízənər/ 名 ● ▶定義 a person who is being kept in prison 刑務所に収容されている人→**囚人, 刑事被告人** ‖ *a political prisoner* 政治犯

**prisoner of war** 名 ● ▶定義 a soldier, etc who is caught by the enemy during a war and who is kept in prison until the end of the war 戦争中に敵に捕まり, 戦争が終わるまで刑務所に収容されている, 兵士など→**捕虜**

**privacy** /prívəsi; práiv-/ 名 ● ▶定義 **1** the state of being alone and not watched or disturbed by other people 1人でいて, ほかの人々に見られないまたは邪魔されない状態→**プライバシー, 個人の自由な生活, 他人から干渉されないこと** ‖ *There is not much privacy in large hospital wards.* 大きな病棟には, ほとんど個人の自由な生活がない. ▶定義 **2** the state of being free from the attention of the public 社会一般の注目から自由な状態→**プライバシー, 私生活** ‖ *The* *actress claimed that the photographs were an **invasion of privacy**.* それらの写真はプライバシーの侵害だと,その女優は主張した.

**＊private¹** /práɪvət/ 形 ▶定義1 belonging to or intended for one particular person or group and not to be shared by others ほかの人々とは共有されないで,ある特定の人または集団に属している,またはある特定の人または集団のための➡個人の,私有の,私用の ‖ *This is private property. You may not park here.* ここは私有地です.駐車しないでください. *a private letter/conversation* 私用の手紙・会話 ▶定義2 not connected with work or business 仕事または商売に関連していない➡私的な,個人的な ‖ *He never discusses his **private life** with his colleagues at work.* 彼は仕事場の同僚とは決して私生活について話さない. ▶定義3 owned, done or organized by a person or company, and not by the government 政府によってではなく,人または会社によって所有された,なされた,または組織された➡私立の,私営の,民営の ‖ *a private hospital/school (= you pay to go there)* 私立病院・学校(= そこへ通うためには,費用がかかる) *a private detective (= one who is not in the police)* 私立探偵(= 警察官ではない) ☛参 **public** ▶定義4 with no one else present ほかにだれもいない➡非公開の,秘密の,内密の ‖ *I would like a private interview with the personnel manager.* 私は人事課長と内密に話がしたい. ▶定義5 not wanting to share thoughts and feelings with other people ほかの人々と考えおよび感情を共有したくない➡社交的でない,人と交わらない,引っ込み思案の ‖ *He's a very private person.* 彼はとても引っ込み思案だ. ▶定義6 (used about classes, lessons, etc) given by a teacher to one student or a small group for payment (講習,授業などについて) 有料で,1人の先生によって1人の生徒または少人数に対して行われる➡私的な,個人的な ‖ *Claire gives private English lessons at her house.* クレアは自宅で英語の個人指導を行っている. — privately 副 ➡個人的に,内緒で,秘密に

**private²** /práɪvət/ 名 ●▶定義 a soldier of the lowest level 最も低い身分の兵士➡兵卒,兵士
成句 **in private** ▶定義 with no one else present ほかにだれもいない➡非公式に,内緒で,人のいないところで ‖ *May I speak to you in private?* 人のいないところでお話してもいいですか.

**privatize** (または **-ise**) /práɪvətaɪz/ 動他 ▶定義 to sell a business or an industry that was owned by the government to a private company 政府が所有していた事業または産業を民営の会社に売る➡～を民営化する ‖ *The water industry has been privatized.* 水道事業が民営化された. ⇔ **nationalize** — privatization (または -isation) /praɪvətaɪzéɪʃ(ə)n/ 名 Ｕ➡民営化

**＊privilege** /prív(ə)lɪdʒ/ 名 ▶定義1 ＣＵa special right or advantage that only one person or group has 1人または1集団のみが持つ,特別な権利または利益➡特権,特典,特別扱い ‖ *Prisoners who behave well **enjoy** special privileges.* 行いの良い囚人たちは特別扱いされる. ▶定義2 [単数扱い] a special advantage or opportunity that gives you great pleasure 喜びをもたらす特別な利益または機会➡恩典,光栄,特別な名誉 ‖ *It was a great privilege to hear her sing.* 彼女が歌うのを聴けるなんて,光栄なことだった.

**privileged** /prív(ə)lɪdʒd/ 形 ▶定義 having an advantage or opportunity that most people do not have ほとんどの人が持たない利益または機会を持っている➡特典を与えられた,特権のある,光栄な ‖ *Only **a privileged few** are allowed to enter this room.* 特権のある数人だけがこの部屋に入ることを許されている. *I feel very privileged to be playing for the national team.* ナショナルチームで競技できるなんて光栄だ. ⇔ **underprivileged**

**＊prize¹** /práɪz/ 名 ●▶定義 something of value that is given to sb who is successful in a race, competition, game, etc 競走,試合,競技などで成功した～に与えられる価値あるもの➡賞,賞品,賞金 ‖ *She won **first prize** in the competition.* 彼女はその試合で1等賞を獲得した. *a prize-winning novel* 入賞した小説

**prize²** /práɪz/ 形 (名詞の前だけ) ▶定義 winning, or good enough to win, a prize 賞を獲得している,または獲得するために十分良い➡入賞した,受賞に値する ‖ *a prize flower display* 入賞した花の飾り付け

**prize³** /práɪz/ 動他 ▶定義 to consider sth to be very valuable ～をとても価値のあるものと考え

る➡～を大切にする,重んじる,高く評価する ‖ *This picture is one of my most prized possessions.* この絵は,私が最も大切にしている財産の1つです.

**prize**[4] /práɪz/ 特に 米 = PRISE

**pro** /próu/ 图 ⓒ ( 複 **pros**) 略式 ▶定義1 a person who plays or teaches a sport for money お金のためにスポーツをする,または教える人➡プロスポーツ選手,プロ ‖ *a golf pro* プロゴルファー ▶定義2 a person who has a lot of skill and experience 高い技能と多くの経験がある人➡本職,専門家,プロ ☞類 professional

成句 **the pros and cons** ▶定義 the reasons for and against doing sth ～をすることへの賛成と反対の理由➡賛成反対の両意見,賛否両論 ‖ *We should consider all the pros and cons before reaching a decision.* 結論に達する前に,私たちは賛成反対の両意見のすべてをじっくり考えなければならない.

**probability** /pràbəbíləti/ 图 ( 複 **probabilities**) ▶定義1 [ⓤ,単数扱い] how likely sth is to happen ～がどれだけ起こりやすいか➡起こりそう・ありそうなこと,見込み,公算 ‖ *At that time there seemed little probability of success.* その時点では成功の見込みはほとんどないように思えた.

▶定義2 ⓒ something that is likely to happen 起こりそうな物事➡起こりそう・ありそうな事柄,生じそうな結果 ‖ *Closure of the factory now seems a probability.* 現時点での工場閉鎖はありそうだ.

*__probable__ /prábəb(ə)l/ 形 ▶定義 that you expect to happen or to be true; likely 起こることを,または事実であることを期待する;ありそうな➡ありそうな,(起こる)見込みのある,多分そうなりそうな・しそうな

▶ probable と likely は同じ事を意味するが,異なった使われ方をすることに注意: *It's probable that he will be late.* (彼が遅れることはありそうなことだ.) *He is likely to be late.* (彼は多分遅れるだろう.)

⇔ **improbable** ☞参 **possible**

**probably** /prábəbli/ 副 ▶定義 almost certainly ほとんど確かに➡**多分,おそらく** ‖ *I will phone next week, probably on Wednesday.* 来週電話します,多分水曜日にでも.

**probation** /prouбéɪʃ(ə)n/ 图 ⓤ ▶定義1 a system that allows sb who has committed a crime not to go to prison if he/she goes to see to an official (**a probation officer**) regularly for a fixed period of time 犯罪を犯した～が決められた期間,定期的に役人(保護観察官)に会うなら刑務所に入らないことを許す制度➡保護観察,執行猶予 ‖ *Jamie is on probation for two years.* ジェーミーは2年間の執行猶予中である.

▶定義2 a period of time at the start of a new job when you are tested to see if you are suitable 人が適正かどうかを知るために試される,新しい仕事に就いたばかりの期間➡見習い・実習期間,仮及第,仮採用 ‖ *a three-month probation period* 3か月の仮採用期間

**probe**[1] /próub/ 動 圓 ⑪ ▶定義1 **probe (into sth)** to ask questions in order to find out secret or hidden information 秘密または隠された情報を突き止めるために質問をする➡突き止める,探る;～を徹底的に調査する,探り立てる ‖ *The newspapers are now probing into the President's past.* 新聞は大統領の過去を徹底的に調査している. ▶定義2 to examine or look for sth, especially with a long thin instrument 特に細長い器具で,～を検査するまたは探す➡～を探り針で探る,(指や棒などで)探る ‖ *The doctor probed the cut for pieces of broken glass.* 医者は傷口に探り針を入れてガラスの破片がないか探った. — **probing** 形 ➡探りを入れる,徹底的な,鋭い ‖ *to ask probing questions* 鋭い質問をする

**probe**[2] /próub/ 图 ⓒ ▶定義1 the process of asking questions, collecting facts, etc in order to find out hidden information about sth ～についての隠された情報を突き止めるために,質問をする,事実を集める,などの過程➡徹底的な調査 ‖ *a police probe into illegal financial dealing* 違法な金融取引への警察の徹底的な調査 ▶定義2 a long thin tool that you use for examining sth that is difficult to reach, especially a part of the body 届きにくい～,特に体の一部,を検査するために使う細長い道具➡探り針

*__problem__ /prábləm/ 图 ⓒ ▶定義1 a thing that is difficult to deal with or to understand 取り扱う,または理解することが難しい物事➡**問題,課題,難題** ‖ *social/family/financial/technical problems* 社会的な・家族の・経済的な・技術的な問題 *You won't **solve the problem** if you ignore it.* も

しそれを無視するなら、その問題は解けません よ. *The company will **face problems** from unions if it sacks workers.* もし会社が労働者たちを解雇するなら、会社は労働組合の問題に直面することになる. *It's going to **cause problems** if Donna brings her husband.* もしドナが彼女の夫を連れてくるなら、問題が起きるだろう. *I can't play because **I've got a problem with** my knee.* ひざが故障しているので、競技できません. *'Can you fix this for me?' '**No problem**.'*「これを直してもらえる」「いいよ」 *It's a great painting - **the problem is** I've got nowhere to put it.* それはすばらしい絵です － 問題はそれを飾る場所がないことです. ▶定義**2** a question that you have to solve by thinking about it それについて考えて解決しなければならない疑問→**問題, 課題** ‖ *a maths/logic problem* 数学・論理の問題

> ►コミュニケーション
>
> 相手の気持ちを楽にする応答
>
> 問題, 難問を意味する problem に no が付いた no problem は, 何か頼まれたときのOKの返事に使われます. 例:Could you help me change the tires?(タイヤ交換手伝ってくれる？)Yes. No problem. 同じく快諾表現 Yes, I'd be happy to. などよりくだけた表現です. No problem は感謝や謝罪に対する応答にも使われます. 例:Thank you so much for your help.(助けていただいてほんとにありがとう)Oh, no problem.

\***procedure** /prəsíːdʒər/ 名 🅒 🅤 ▶定義 the usual or correct way for doing sth ～をするための通常の、または正しい方法→**手続き, 手順, 方法** ‖ *What's the procedure for making a complaint?* 訴えるための手続きはどのようになっていますか.

\***proceed** /prəsíːd, proʊ-/ 動 🅐 ▶定義**1** 正式 to continue doing sth; to continue being done ～をすることを続ける; され続ける→**(中断した話・仕事などを)続ける, 進行する, 続けて～する** ‖ *The building work was proceeding according to schedule.* その建設作業は計画に従って進行していた. ▶定義**2** 正式 proceed (with sth/to do sth) to start doing the next thing after finishing the last one 最後の1つが終わった後に, 次の事

process² 1275

を始める→**進む, 向かう** ‖ *Once he had calmed down he proceeded to tell us what had happened.* ひとたび落ち着くと、彼は何が起こったのか私たちに語り始めた.

**proceedings** /prəsíːdɪŋz, proʊ-/ 名 [複数扱い] ▶定義**1** proceedings (against sb/for sth) legal action 法的な行動→**訴訟手続き** ‖ *to start divorce proceedings* 離婚訴訟の手続きを取る ▶定義**2** events that happen, especially at a formal meeting, ceremony, etc 特に正式な会合, 儀式などにおいて起きる出来事→**(一連の)出来事, (議事・儀式などの)進行, 式次第** ‖ *The proceedings were interrupted by demonstrators.* その式次第はデモによって中断された.

**proceeds** /próʊsìːdz/ 名 [複数扱い] ▶定義 proceeds (of/from sth) money that you get when you sell sth ～を売ったときに得るお金→**収益, 収入** ‖ *The proceeds from the sale will go to charity.* この販売の収益金は慈善団体へ送られます.

\***process**¹ /próʊses, prá-/ 名 🅒 ▶定義**1** a series of actions that you do for a particular purpose 特定の目的のために人が行う, 一連の行動→**過程, 経過, 進行, (～の)最中** ‖ *We've just begun the complicated process of selling the house.* 私たちは, 家を売るための複雑な作業を始めたばかりだ. ▶定義**2** a series of changes that happen naturally 自然に起こる, 一連の変化→**過程, 経過, (自然の)作用** ‖ *Mistakes are part of the learning process.* 学んでいる過程での誤りは付き物だ.

成句 in the process ▶定義 while you are doing sth else 人がほかの～をしている間→**その過程において, (それと)同時に** ‖ *We washed the dog yesterday - and we all got very wet in the process.* 昨日私たちは犬を洗った － そして同時に私たちも全員ひどくぬれてしまった.

in the process of sth/doing sth ▶定義 in the middle of doing sth ～をしている最中に→**～が進行中で, ～しているところで, ～中で** ‖ *They are in the process of moving house.* 彼らは引っ越しの最中である.

**process**² /próʊses, prá-/ 動 🅑 ▶定義**1** to treat sth, for example with chemicals, in order to keep it, change it, etc 保存する, 変化させる, などのために, 例えば化学薬品で～を処理する→

～を加工する, (化学的に)処理する, 現像・焼き付けする ‖ *Cheese is processed so that it lasts longer.* 長持ちするように, チーズは加工されている. / *I sent two rolls of film away to be processed.* 私は現像してもらうためにフィルムを2本送った. ▶定義2 to deal with information, for example on a computer 例えばコンピュータ上の, 情報を扱う→**～を処理する** ‖ *It will take about ten days to process your application.* あなたの願書を処理するためには, およそ10日かかるでしょう.

**procession** /prəséʃ(ə)n/ 名 C U ▶定義 a number of people, vehicles, etc that move slowly in a line, especially as part of a ceremony 特に儀式の一部として, 一列に並んでゆっくり進む多くの人々, 乗り物など→**行列, 列, 行進** ‖ *to walk in procession* 列になって歩く / *a funeral procession* 葬列

**processor** /próusesər, prá-/ 名 C ▶定義 a machine that changes food or information into a suitable form 食物または情報を適切な形に変える機械→**(食品)加工機, (中央)処理装置, (言語)処理プログラム** ‖ *Mix the ingredients in a food processor.* フードプロセッサーに材料を入れて混ぜなさい. / *a word processor* ワープロ

**proclaim** /prouklém, prə-/ 動他 (文) ▶定義 to make sth known officially or publicly ～を正式に, または公に知られるようにする→**～を宣言する, 布告する, 発表・声明・公表する** ‖ *The day was proclaimed a national holiday.* その日を国の休日にすると発表された. — proclamation /pràkləméɪʃ(ə)n/ 名 C U →**宣言, 布告, 声明, 発表** ‖ *to make a proclamation of war* 宣戦布告する

**procure** /prəkjúər, prou-/ 動他 (文) ▶定義 procure sth (for sb) to obtain sth, especially with difficulty 特にやっとのことで, ～を手に入れる→**(苦労・努力して)～を手に入れる, 入手する, 獲得する** ‖ *I managed to procure two tickets for the match.* その試合のチケットを2枚, 辛うじて手に入れた.

**prod** /prɑd/ 動自他 (**prodding**; **prodded**) ▶定義 to push or press sb/sth with your finger or a pointed object 人の指または先がとがった物で, ～を押すまたは押し付ける→**～を突く, 刺す, 促す, 励ます** ‖ (比喩) *Ruth works quite hard but she does need prodding occasionally.* ルースはとても熱心に働いているが, それでもたまには彼女をせかさないと駄目だ. ☞ S6ページのさし絵 — prod 名 C →**突くこと, 促すこと, 刺激** ‖ *to give the fire a prod with a stick* 棒でつついて火を大きくする — prodding 名 U →**駆り立てること, 励まし**

**prodigious** /prədídʒəs/ 形 ▶定義 very large or powerful and surprising とても大きなまたは力強くて驚くべき→**巨大な, 驚異的な, ばく大な** ‖ *He seemed to have a prodigious amount of energy.* 彼は驚異的なエネルギーを持っているようだった.

**prodigy** /prάdədʒi/ 名 C (複 **prodigies**) ▶定義 a child who is unusually good at sth 異常に～が得意な子供→**驚異的な才能を持つ人, 天才** ‖ *Mozart was a child prodigy.* モーツァルトは神童だった. ☞参 genius

*★**produce**¹ /prəd(j)úːs, prou-/ 動他 ▶定義1 to make sth to be sold, especially in large quantities 特に大量に, 売られる～を作る→**～を作り出す, (大量に)生産する, 製造する** ‖ *The factory produces 20000 cars a year.* その工場では, 毎年2万台の車が生産されている. ☞類 manufacture ▶定義2 to grow or make sth by a natural process 自然の経過で, ～を育てるまたは作る→**～を生ずる, 産出する, ～を輩出する** ‖ *This region produces most of the country's wheat.* この地域では, その国の小麦のほとんどを生産している. / (比喩) *He's the greatest athlete this country has produced.* 彼は, この国が生み出した最もすばらしい運動選手だ. ▶定義3 to create sth using skill 技術を使って～を作り出す→**(食事・芸術作品など)を作る, 創作する** ‖ *The children have produced some beautiful pictures for the exhibition.* 子供たちは, 展覧会のために美しい絵を何枚かかいた. ▶定義4 to cause a particular effect or result 特定の効果または結果を引き起こす→**～を招く, 引き起こす** ‖ *Her remarks produced roars of laughter.* 彼女のコメントは笑いの渦を巻き起こした. ▶定義5 to show sth so that sb else can look at or examine it ほかの～がそれを見られる, または調べられるように, …を見せる→**(見えるように)取り出す, (証拠など)を提示する** ‖ *to produce evidence in court* 法廷で証拠を提示する ▶定義6 to be in charge of preparing a film, play, etc so that it can be shown to the

public 一般大衆に見せられるように, 映画, 劇などの準備を担当している➡️**制作する, プロデュースする** ‖ *She is producing 'Romeo and Juliet' at the local theatre.* 彼女は, その地元の劇場で「ロミオとジュリエット」をプロデュースしている.

**produce**² /prədjúːs; próuduːs/ 名 ❶ ▶定義 food, etc that is grown on a farm and sold 農場で育ち売られる, 食物など➡️**生産物, 農産物, 製品** ‖ *fresh farm produce* 新鮮な農作物 ☞参 **production** の注

**producer** /prəd(j)úːsər, prou-/ 名 ❻ ▶定義 1 a person, company or country that makes or grows sth ～を作るまたは育てる人, 会社, または国➡️**生産者, 製造者, 産出国** ‖ *Brazil is a major producer of coffee.* ブラジルはコーヒー豆の主要な産出国です. ▶定義 2 a person who deals with the business side of organizing a play, film, etc 劇, 映画などを企画・準備する実務面を扱う人➡️**プロデューサー, 制作者** ▶定義 3 a person who arranges for sb to make a programme for TV or radio, or a record ～がテレビまたはラジオ番組, またはレコードを製作できるように手配する人➡️**ディレクター, 演出家**

★**product** /prάdəkt/ 名 ❻ ▶定義 1 something that is made in a factory or that is formed naturally 工場で作られる, または自然に形成される物➡️**(人工の)製品, (天然の)産物** ‖ *dairy/meat/pharmaceutical/software products* 乳製品・肉製品・薬品・ソフトウエア製品 *Carbon dioxide is one of the waste products of this process.* 二酸化炭素は, この過程で生じる廃棄物の1つである. ☞参 **production** の注 ▶定義 2 **product of sth** the result of sth ～の結果➡️**結果, 成果, 産物** ‖ *The industry's problems are the product of government policy.* 政府の政策がその産業問題を引き起こした.

★**production** /prədʌ́kʃ(ə)n/ 名 ▶定義 1 ❶ the making or growing of sth, especially in large quantities 特に大量に, ～を作るまたは育てること➡️**(大量の)生産, 産出, 製造** ‖ *The latest model will be* ***in production*** *from April.* 最新型はこの4月から製造開始となる. *This farm specializes in the production of organic vegetables.* この農場は有機野菜の生産を専門にしている. *mass production* 大量生産 ▶定義 2 ❶ the amount of sth that is made or grown 作られたまたは育てられた～の量➡️**生産高, 生産量** ‖ *a rise/fall in*

# profess 1277

*production* 生産高の上昇・下降 *a high level of production* 生産量の高い水準 ▶定義 3 ❻ a play, film or programme that has been made for the public 一般大衆のために作られた劇, 映画または番組➡️**制作, 創作, 演出**

▶ produce (名詞) は農場で産出される食べ物などを意味し, product は工場で作られた物を意味することに注意. production は劇, 映画などである: *The label on the bottle says 'Produce of Italy'.*（びんのラベルに「イタリア産」と書いてある.）*The company's main products are plastic toys.*（その会社の主な製品はプラスチック製のおもちゃだ.）*the Bolshoi Ballet's production of Swan Lake*（ボリショイバレエ団制作の白鳥の湖）

成句 **on production of sth** ▶定義 when you show sth 人が～を見せるとき➡️**～を提示して** ‖ *You can get a ten per cent discount on production of your membership card.* メンバーカードを提示すると10パーセントの割引になります.

**productive** /prədʌ́ktɪv/ 形 ▶定義 1 that makes or grows sth, especially in large quantities 特に大量に, ～を作るまたは育てる➡️**生産力のある, 実りの多い, 肥沃(ひよく)な** ‖ *The company wants to sell off its less productive factories.* その会社は, 生産力の低いいくつかの工場を売り払いたいと思っている. ▶定義 2 useful (because results come from it) 役に立つ（なぜなら結果がそこから生じるから）➡️**(議論などが)実り多い, 建設的な, 生産的な** ‖ *a productive discussion* 実りのある討論 — **productivity** /prὰdəktívəti; pròu-/ 名 ❶➡️**生産力(があること), 生産性**

**profess** /prəfés/ 動 他 正式 ▶定義 1 to say that sth is true or correct, even when it is not たとえそうでないときでも, ～が事実であるまたは正しいと言う➡️**～する・できる振りをする, ～を装う, (知識など)を持っていると称する** ‖ *Marianne professed to know nothing at all about it, but I did not believe her.* マリアンはそれについて全く何も知らないように装っていたが, 私は彼女を信じていなかった. ▶定義 2 to state honestly that you have a particular belief, feeling, etc 自分が特定の信念, 感情などを持っていることを, 正直に述べる➡️**～をはっきりと言う, 公言・明言する** ‖ *He professed his hatred of war.* 彼は戦争が

大嫌いであるとはっきりと言った.

**profession** /prəféʃ(ə)n/ 名 C ▶定義 1 a job that needs a high level of training and/or education 高い水準の訓練および・または教育を必要とする仕事→(知的な)職業, 専門職 ‖ *the medical/legal/teaching profession* 医療に携わる職業・法律関係の職業・教職 *She's thinking of entering the nursing profession.* 彼女は看護婦の道に進むことを考えている. ☞参 work¹ の注 ▶定義 2 *the...profession* [単数または複数形の動詞と共に] all the people who work in a particular profession 特定の職業で働くすべての人々→同業者たち, 同業者仲間 ‖ *The legal profession is/are trying to resist the reforms.* 法律に携わる同業者たちはその改正に反対しようと努めている.

成句 *by profession* ▶定義 as your job 自分の仕事として→職業は(〜である) ‖ *George is an accountant by profession.* ジョージの職業は会計士である.

**professional**¹ /prəféʃ(ə)n(ə)l/ 形 ▶定義 1 (名詞の前だけ) connected with a job that needs a high level of training and/or education 高い水準の訓練および・または教育を必要とする仕事に関連した→(専門的な)職業の, 専門職の, 職業上の ‖ *Get professional advice from your lawyer before you take any action.* 何らかの行動を起こす前に, 自分の弁護士から専門的な助言を得なさい. ▶定義 2 doing sth in a way that shows skill, training or care 技能, 訓練または配慮を示す方法で, 〜を行っている→本職の, プロの, 職業的な ‖ *The police are trained to deal with every situation in a calm and professional manner.* 警察官は, 冷静でしかも職業的な態度ですべての状況に対処するように訓練されている. *Her application was neatly typed and looked very professional.* 彼女の願書はきちんとタイプされて, プロの仕事のようだった. ⇔ **unprofessional** ▶定義 3 doing a sport, etc as a job or for money; (used about a sport, etc) done by people who are paid 仕事として, またはお金のために, スポーツなどを行う;(スポーツなどについて)金が支払われる人々によって行われた→本職のプロの ‖ *He's planning to turn professional* ^he Olympics. オリンピックの後, 彼はプロに転向しようと計画している. *professional football* プロサッカー ⇔ **amateur**

**professional**² /prəféʃ(ə)n(ə)l/ 名 C ▶定義 1 a person who works in a job that needs a high level of training and/or education 高い水準の訓練および・または教育を必要とする職について働いている人→専門家, 本職の人 ▶定義 2 (または 略式 *pro*) a person who plays or teaches a sport, etc for money お金のためにスポーツなどをする, または教える人→職業選手, プロ ▶定義 3 (または 略式 *pro*) a person who has a lot of skill and experience 豊かな技量と経験を持つ人→玄人

**professionalism** /prəféʃ(ə)n(ə)lìz(ə)m/ 名 U ▶定義 a way of doing a job that shows great skill and experience すばらしい技能と経験を示す, 仕事のやり方→専門家・プロの技術, 専門家・プロ気質(かたぎ) ‖ *We were impressed by the professionalism of the staff.* 私たちはスタッフのプロ気質に感服した.

**professionally** /prəféʃ(ə)n(ə)li/ 副 ▶定義 1 in a way that shows great skill and experience すばらしい技能と経験を示すやり方で→専門的に, プロにふさわしく ▶定義 2 for money; by a professional person お金のために;プロの人によって→本職として, プロとして ‖ *Rob plays the saxophone professionally.* ロブはプロとしてサックスを演奏する.

**professor** /prəfésər/ 名 C (略 **Prof**) ▶定義 1 a university teacher of the highest level 最も高い地位の総合大学の教師→教授 ‖ *She's professor of English at Bristol University.* 彼女はブリストル総合大学の英語の教授です. ▶定義 2 米 a teacher at a college or university 単科大学または大学の教師→(一般的に)大学教授・教官

**proficient** /prəfíʃənt/ 形 ▶定義 *proficient (in/at sth/doing sth)* able to do a particular thing well; skilled ある特定の事がうまくできる;熟練した→熟達・熟練した, たんのうな, 上手な ‖ *We are looking for someone who is proficient in French.* 私たちはフランス語にたんのうな人を探している. — **proficiency** 名 U **proficiency (in sth/doing sth)**→熟達, 熟練, たんのう ‖ *a certificate of proficiency in English* 英語の実力の証明書

**profile** /próufaɪl/ 名 C ▶定義 1 a person's face or head seen from the side, not the front 正面

らではなく，横から見られた人の顔または頭→**横顔，プロフィール，(彫像の)側面** ‖ *I did a sketch of him **in profile**.* 私は彼の横顔をスケッチした．

▶定義**2** a short description of sb/sth that gives useful information 有益な情報を与える，〜の短評→**(簡単な)人物紹介，プロフィール** ‖ *We're building up a profile of our average customer.* 私たちは平均的な顧客のプロフィールを作成している．

成句 **a high/low profile** ▶定義 a way of behaving that does/does not attract other people's attention ほかの人々の関心を引き付ける・引き付けない振る舞い方→**高姿勢，目立つ; 低姿勢，目立たない** ‖ *I don't know much about the subject - I'm going to keep a **low profile** at the meeting tomorrow.* そのテーマについて私はあまり知りません － 明日の会合では目立たないようにします．

★**profit**¹ /práfət/ 图 ❻ Ⓤ ▶定義 the money that you make when you sell sth for more than it cost you かかった費用より高く〜を売ったとき，生じるお金→**もうけ，利益** ‖ *Did you **make a profit on** your house when you sold it?* あなたの家を売ったとき，利益が出ましたか．*I'm hoping to sell my shares **at a profit**.* もうかるように，株を売りたいものです．☞参 **loss**

**profit**² /práfət/ 動 ⾃ ⾃他 正式 ▶定義 profit (from/by sth) to get an advantage from sth; to give sb an advantage 〜から利益を得る; 〜に利益を与える→**利益を得る，恩恵を受ける; 〜の利益になる** ‖ *Who will profit most from the tax reforms?* 税改革で，最も恩恵を受けるのはだれですか．

**profitable** /práfətəb(ə)l/ 形 ▶定義**1** that makes money お金を作る→**もうけになる，有利な** ‖ *a profitable business* もうかる商売 ▶定義**2** helpful or useful 助けになる，または役に立つ→**ためになる，有益な** ‖ *We had a very profitable discussion yesterday.* 昨日の話し合いはとても有益だった．— **profitably** 副 →**有利に，有益に，もうかって** ‖ *to spend your time profitably* 時間を有益に使う — **profitability** /práfətəbìləti/ 图 Ⓤ →**収益性，もうけ，利益率**

**profound** /prəfáund/ 形 ▶定義**1** very great; that you feel very strongly とても大きい; とても強く感じる→**心の底からの，深い，強い** ‖ *The experience had a profound influence on her.* その経験は彼女に深い影響を与えた．▶定義**2** needing or showing a lot of knowledge or thought 多くの知識または考えを必要としている，または表している→**深遠な，深い，難解な** ‖ *He's always making profound statements about the meaning of life.* 彼はいつも，人生の意義について難解な事を言う．— **profoundly** 副 →**深く，心から，激しく** ‖ *I was profoundly relieved to hear the news.* 私はそのニュースを聞いて心から安心した．

**profuse** /prəfjúːs/ 形 正式 ▶定義**1** given or produced in great quantity 大量に与えられた，または作り出された→**豊富な，おびただしい，十分な** ‖ *profuse apologies* 十分な謝罪 — **profusely** 副 →**豊富に，おびただしく，気前良く** ‖ *She apologized profusely for being late.* 彼女は遅刻したことを何度も謝った．

★**program**¹ /próugræm/ 图 ❻ ▶定義**1** a set of instructions that you give to a computer so that it will do a particular task コンピューターが特定の仕事をするように，与える一連の指示→**プログラム** ‖ *to write a program* プログラムを書く

▶コンピューターについて話しているとき，アメリカ英語とイギリス英語のつづりは共に program である．ほかの意味のためには，イギリス英語のつづりは programme，アメリカ英語のつづりは program である．

▶定義**2** 米=**PROGRAMME**¹

★**program**² /próugræm/ 動 他 (**programming**; **programmed**) ▶定義 to give a set of instructions to a computer コンピューターに一連の指示を与える→**プログラムを組み込む・入れる**

★**programme**¹ (米 **program**) /próugræm/ 图 ❻ ▶定義**1** a show or other item that is sent out on the radio or television ラジオまたはテレビで放送されるショーまたはほかの番組→**番組，プログラム** ‖ *a TV/radio programme* テレビ・ラジオ番組 *We've just missed an interesting programme on elephants.* 私たちはちょうど今，象についての興味深い番組を見逃してしまった．▶定義**2** a plan of things to do; a scheme 物事をする予定; 計画→**計画，予定** ‖ *What's (on) your programme today? (= what are you going to do today?)* 今日のあなたの予定はどうなっていますか．(＝今日，あなたは何をするのですか．) *The leaflet out-*

lines the government's programme of educational reforms. その小冊子には,政府の教育改革計画の概要が書かれている. ▶定義3 a little book or piece of paper which you get at a concert, a sports event, etc that gives you information about what you are going to see コンサート,スポーツ観戦などで人が手に入れる,これから見るものについての情報を人に与える,薄い本,または1枚の紙→プログラム,パンフレット

**programme**² /próʊɡræm/ (米 **program**) 動他 (**programming; programmed**: 米 または **programing; programed**) ▶定義1 to plan for sth to happen at a particular time 特定の時に,~が起こるよう計画する→~の計画を立てる ‖ The road is programmed for completion next May. その道路は今度の5月に完成する計画です. ▶定義2 to make sb/sth work or act automatically in a particular way 特定の方法で,~を自動的に働かせる,または動かす→(~するように)セットする,組み込む ‖ The lights are programmed to come on as soon as it gets dark. それらの明かりは,暗くなるとすぐに点灯するようにセットされている.

**programmer** /próʊɡræmər/ 名 C ▶定義 a person whose job is to write programs for a computer コンピューターのためのプログラムを書くことが仕事である人→プログラマー

★**progress**¹ /próʊɡres, práɡ-/ 名 U ▶定義1 movement forwards or towards achieving sth 前向きの,または~を達成することに向かっての動き→進歩,向上,上達 ‖ Anna's **making progress** at school. アンナは学校での勉強が上達している. to make slow/steady/rapid/good progress ゆっくりとした・着実な・速い・順調な進歩をする ▶定義2 change or improvement in society 社会における変化または進歩→進歩,向上,発展 ‖ scientific progress 科学の進歩

成句 in progress ▶定義 happening now 現在起きている→進行中で[の] ‖ Silence! Examination in progress. 静かに.試験中です.

**progress**² /prəɡrés/ 動自 ▶定義1 to become better; to develop (well) より良くなる;(良く)発展する→進歩する,上達する,快方に向かう ‖ Medical knowledge has progressed rapidly in the last twenty years. この20年間で医学的知識は急速に進歩した. ▶定義2 to move forward; to continue 前に進む;続く→前進する,進展する,進行する ‖ I got more and more tired as the evening progressed. 夜が更けるにつれて,私はますます疲れ果てた.

**progression** /prəɡréʃ(ə)n/ 名 C U ▶定義 (a) progression (from sth) (to sth) movement forward or a development from one stage to another 前向きの動き,またはある段階から次の段階への発展→前進,進歩,推移 ‖ You've made the progression from beginner to intermediate level. あなたは初級から中級レベルに進歩しました.

**progressive** /prəɡrésɪv/ 形 ▶定義1 using modern methods and ideas 現代的な方法と考え方を使っている→進歩的な,革新的な ‖ a progressive school 進歩的な学校 ▶定義2 happening or developing steadily 着実に起きている,または発展している→(絶えず)前進する,進行している,漸進的な ‖ a progressive reduction in the number of staff 漸進的なスタッフの削減

**progressively** /prəɡrésɪvli/ 副 ▶定義 steadily; a little at a time 着実に;1度に少し→次第に,だんだんと,累進的に ‖ The situation became progressively worse. 状況は次第に悪くなっていった.

**the progressive tense** 名 [単数扱い](文法) =THE CONTINUOUS TENSE

**prohibit** /proʊhíbət/ 動他 正式 ▶定義 prohibit sb/sth (from doing sth) to say that sth is not allowed by law; to forbid ~が法律によって許可されていないと言う;禁じる→~を禁止する,~に禁じる ‖ English law prohibits children under 16 from buying cigarettes. 英国の法律は,16歳未満の子供がたばこを買うことを禁じている.

**prohibition** /proʊ(h)əbíʃ(ə)n/ 名 ▶定義1 C 正式 a prohibition (on/against sth) a law or rule that forbids sth ~を禁止する法律または規則→禁止命令,禁止令 ‖ There is a prohibition on the carrying of knives. 刃物携行禁止令がある. ▶定義2 U the action of stopping sth being done or used, especially by law 特に法律によって,~が行われるまたは使用されることをやめる行為→(規則・法律などで)禁止する・されること,禁止 ‖ the prohibition of alcohol in the 1920s 1920年代の禁酒

**prohibitive** /proʊhíbətɪv/ 形 ▶定義 (used about

a price or cost) so high that it prevents people from buying sth or doing sth (価格または費用について)とても高いので,人が〜を買うまたは〜を行うことを妨げる➡手が出ないほどに高い,法外な ‖ *The price of houses in the centre of town is prohibitive.* 町の中心地にある家々の値段は法外だ. — prohibitively 副 ➡手が出ないほど高く,法外に

\*project¹ /prɑ́dʒèkt/ 图 ⓒ ▶定義1 a piece of work, often involving many people, that is planned and organized carefully 慎重に計画され組織される,しばしば多くの人がかかわる,1つの仕事➡計画,企画 ‖ *a major project to reduce pollution in our rivers* 河川の汚染を減らすための大計画 ▶定義2 a piece of school work in which the student has to collect information about a certain subject and then write about it 生徒たちがあるテーマについての情報を集めてから,それについて書かなければならない,学校の授業の1つ➡研究課題,学習課題 ‖ *Our group chose to do a project on rainforests.* 私たちのグループは,熱帯雨林を研究課題にしようと選んだ.

project² /prədʒékt/ 動 ▶定義1 ⓗ (通常は受動態で) to plan sth that will happen in the future 未来に起こる〜を計画する➡〜を計画する,企てる,企画する ‖ *the band's projected world tour* バンドが企画したワールドツアー ▶定義2 ⓗ (通常は受動態で) to guess or calculate the size, cost or amount of sth 〜の大きさ,費用または量を推測する,または計算する➡〜を予想する,予測する ‖ *a projected increase of 10%* 10パーセントの増加予測 ▶定義3 ⓗ project sth (on/onto sth) to make light, a picture from a film, etc appear on a flat surface or screen 平らな表面またはスクリーンに,光,フィルムからの絵などを出現させる➡〜を投影する,映写する,映し出す ▶定義4 ⓗ to show or represent sb/sth/yourself in a certain way 〜をある方法で見せる,または表現する➡(感情・性質など)を表に出す,(態度で)示す,〜を(…として)印象づける ‖ *The government is trying to project a more caring image.* 政府はもっと思いやりのあるイメージを印象づけようと努めている. ▶定義5 圁 正式 to stick out➡突き出る ‖ *The balcony projects one metre out from the wall.* そのバルコニーは,壁から1メートル突き出ている. ▶定義6 ⓗ to send or throw sth upwards or away from you 〜を上

向きに,または自分より向こうに送るまたは投げる➡〜を投げ出す,放出する,(声)を出す ‖ *Actors have to learn to project their voice.* 俳優は,通るように声を出すことを学ばなくてはならない.

projection /prədʒékʃ(ə)n/ 图 ▶定義1 ⓒ a guess about a future amount, situation, etc based on the present situation 現在の状況に基づいた,未来の量,状況などについての推測➡見積もり,推定,予測 ‖ *sales projections for the next five years* 次の5年間の販売予測 ▶定義2 ⓤ the act of making light, a picture from a film, etc apper on a surface ある表面に,光,フィルムからの絵などを出現させる行為➡投影,映写

projector /prədʒéktər/ 图 ⓒ ▶定義 a piece of equipment that projects pictures or films onto a screen or wall スクリーンまたは壁に,写真またはフィルムを投影する1台の装置➡映写機,プロジェクター ‖ *a film/slide/overhead projector* フィルム・スライド・オーバーヘッドプロジェクター

proliferate /prəlíf(ə)rèɪt/ 動 圁 正式 ▶定義 to increase quickly in number 数が急速に増える➡急増する,激増する,(細胞などが)増殖する — proliferation /prəlìf(ə)rèɪʃ(ə)n/ 图 ⓤ ➡激増,拡散,(細胞などの)増殖

prolific /prəlífɪk/ 形 ▶定義 (used especially about a writer, artist, etc) producing a lot (特に著述家,芸術家などについて)たくさん作り出している➡多作の,創造力に富む,(スポーツ選手が)勝ち・得点の多い ‖ *a prolific goal scorer* 得点の多い選手

prologue /próʊlɔ(ː)g, -lɑ̀g/ 图 ⓒ ▶定義 a piece of writing or a speech that introduces a play, poem, etc 劇,詩などを始める文章または台詞(せりふ)➡序詞,序幕,プロローグ ☛参 epilogue

prolong /prəlɔ́(ː)ŋ, -lɑ́ŋ/ 動 ⓗ ▶定義 to make sth last longer 〜をより長く続くようにする➡延長する,長引かせる

prolonged /prəlɔ́(ː)ŋd, -lɑ́ŋd/ 形 ▶定義 continuing for a long time 長く続いている➡〜を延長した,長引いた,(非常に)長い ‖ *There was a prolonged silence before anybody spoke.* だれかが話すまで長く沈黙が続いた.

prom /prɑm/ 图 ⓒ ▶定義1 =PROMENADE ▶定義2 米 a formal dance that is held by a high school class at the end of a school year 学校の年度末に, 高校のクラスによって開かれる, 正式なダンス➜**ダンスパーティー**

**promenade** /pràmənάːd; -néɪd/ (または **prom**) [名] [C] ▶定義 a wide path where people walk beside the sea in a town on the coast 海岸にある街の海沿いを人々が歩く, 広い道➜**散歩道, 遊歩道, プロムナード** ☛ C8 ページのさし絵

**prominent** /prάm(ə)nənt/ [形] ▶定義1 important or famous 重要なまたは有名な➜**著名な, 傑出した, 卓越した** ‖ *a prominent political figure* 著名な大政治家 ▶定義2 noticeable; easy to see 目立った; 見ることが簡単な➜**人目に付く, ほかよりも目立つ** ‖ *The church is the most prominent feature of the village.* その教会は, その村で最も目立つ特徴である. — prominence [名] [U] ➜**ほかよりも目立っていること, 卓越, 著名** ‖ *The newspaper gave the affair great prominence.* 新聞はその事件をとても大きく扱った. — prominently [副] ➜**目立って, 顕著に**

**promiscuous** /prəmískjuəs/ [形] ▶定義 having sexual relations with many people 多くの人と性的関係を持っている➜**相手を選ばない, 乱交の** — promiscuity /prὰməskjuːəti, pròʊ-/ [名] [U] ➜**(セックスで)相手を選ばないこと, 乱交**

P

***promise**[1] /prάməs/ [動] ▶定義1 [自][他] promise (to do sth); promise (sb) that... to say definitely that you will do or not do sth or that sth will happen ～をするまたはしない, あるいは～が起きることを, はっきり言う➜**約束する; ～を約束する, 断言する** ‖ *She promised (me) that she would write every week.* 彼女は毎週手紙を書くと(私に)約束した. *She promised not to forget to write.* 彼女は手紙を書くのを忘れないと約束した. ▶定義2 [他] promise sth (to sb); promise sb sth to say definitely that you will give sth to sb ～を…に与えるとはっきり言う➜**～と請け合う, (～する)と約束する** ‖ *Can you promise your support?* あなたは援助すると約束できますか. *My dad has promised me a bicycle.* 私に自転車を買ってくれると, 父は請け合った. *You have to give him the money if you promised it to him.* 彼に約束したのなら, あなたは彼にお金を与えなければならない. ▶定義3 [他] to show signs of sth, that you expect it to happen ～の兆候を示して, それが起こることを予期する➜**～の見込みがある, ～を期待させる, ～のおそれがある** ‖ *It promises to be an exciting occasion.* 楽しくなりそうだ.

***promise**[2] /prάməs/ [名] ▶定義1 [C] a promise (to do sth/that...) a written or spoken statement or agreement that you will or will not do sth ～をするまたはしないと書かれた, または口頭での申し立てあるいは契約➜**約束, 契約** ‖ *I want you to* ***make a promise*** *that you won't do that again.* あなたがもう二度とそれをしないという約束をしていただきたい. *Make sure you* ***keep your promise*** *to always do your homework.* いつも宿題をするという約束を, 確実に守りなさい. *You should never* ***break a promise.*** 約束を決して破ってはいけません. *I* ***give*** *you my* ***promise*** *that I won't tell anyone.* だれにも言わないことを約束します. ▶定義2 [U] signs that you will be able to do sth well or be successful 将来～が上手にできる, または成功するという兆候➜**見込み, 有望なこと, 将来性** ‖ *He* ***showed*** *great* ***promise*** *as a musician.* 音楽家として彼はとても有望だった.

**promising** /prάməsɪŋ/ [形] ▶定義 showing signs of being very good or successful とても良いまたは成功するという兆候を表している➜**前途有望な, 末頼もしい, 見通しが明るい** ‖ *a promising young writer* 前途有望な若い作家

**promote** /prəmóʊt/ [動][他] ▶定義1 to encourage sth; to help sth to happen or develop ～を促進する; ～が起きる, または発展するために手助けする➜**～を促進する, 助長する, 奨励する** ‖ *to promote good relations between countries* 国々の良い関係を促進する ▶定義2 promote sth (as sth) to advertise sth in order to increase its sales or make it popular 売り上げを増やすまたは人気を高めるために, ～を宣伝する➜**宣伝で～の販売を促進する, 販売促進をする** ‖ *The new face cream is being promoted as a miracle cure for wrinkles.* 新発売のフェースクリームは, 奇跡のようなしわ取り効果をうたい文句にして販売を促進している. ▶定義3 promote sb (from sth) (to sth) (しばしば受動態で) to give sb a higher position or more important job ～により高い地位またはより重要な仕事を与える➜**～を昇進させる, 昇格させる** ‖ *He's been promoted from assistant manager to manager.* 彼は, 副支

配人から支配人に昇格した.

**promoter** /prəmóutər/ 名 C ▶定義 a person who organizes or provides the money for an event 催し物を企画・準備し、そのために必要なお金を提供する人→**主催者,推進者,(会社などの)設立人・発起人**

***promotion** /prəmóuʃ(ə)n/ 名 ▶定義1 promotion (to sth) C U a move to a higher position or more important job より高い地位、またはより重要な仕事への移動→**昇進,昇格,進級** || *The new job is a promotion for her.* その新しい仕事は彼女にとって昇進だ. ▶定義2 U C things that you do in order to advertise a product and increase its sales 製品を宣伝して売り上げを伸ばすために,人が行う物事→**販売促進活動** || *It's all part of a special promotion of the new book.* それはすべて,その新刊書の特別販売促進活動の一部です. ▶定義3 U 正式 promotion (of sth) the activity of trying to make sth develop or become accepted by people ～を発展させる,または人々に受け入れられるために努める活動→**促進,助長,奨励** || *We need to work on the promotion of health, not the treatment of disease.* 私たちは病気の治療ではなく、健康の促進に取り組む必要がある.

***prompt**¹ /prɑm(p)t/ 形 ▶定義1 immediate; done without delay すぐに; 遅れないで行われる→**迅速な,素早い** || *We need a prompt decision on this matter.* 私たちはこの件を迅速に決断する必要がある. ▶定義2 prompt (in doing sth/to do sth)(名詞の前は不可) (used about a person) quick; acting without delay (人について) 素早い; 遅れないで行動している→**すぐさま～する,時間を守る** || *We are always prompt in paying our bills.* 私たちはいつも期日を守って請求書の支払いをする. *She was prompt to point out my mistake.* 彼女はすぐさま私の間違いを指摘した.

**prompt**² /prɑm(p)t/ 動 ▶定義1 他 to cause sth to happen; to make sb decide to do sth ～が起きる原因となる; ～に…をすることを決心させる→**～を促す,刺激する,促して・刺激して～させる** || *What prompted you to give up your job?* なぜあなたは仕事を辞めたの. ▶定義2 自 他 to encourage sb to speak by asking questions or to remind an actor of his/her words in a play 質問することで～に話すことを促す,または劇の台詞(せりふ)を俳優に思い出させる→**人を促して**話を続けさせる,(俳優)に台詞を付ける・教える || *The speaker had to be prompted several times.* その話し手は、何度か促されて何とか話を続けた. ― prompting 名 U ▶促すこと,刺激,檄(げき) || *He apologized without any prompting.* 彼は人に言われるまでもなく自分から謝罪した.

**prompt**³ /prɑm(p)t/ 名 C ▶定義1 a word or words said to an actor to remind him/her of what to say next 俳優に次に何を言うか思い出させるために言われた、1つまたは複数の言葉→**教えられた・促された台詞(せりふ)** || *When she forgot her lines I had to give her a prompt.* 彼女が台詞を忘れた時,私が台詞を付けなければならなかった. ▶定義2 (computing) a sign on a computer screen that shows that the computer has finished what it was doing and is ready for more instructions (コンピューター) コンピューターがしていた事を終了して,次の指示を待っていることを示す,コンピューターの画面上の印→**プロンプト** || *Wait for the prompt to come up then type in your password.* プロンプトが表示されてからパスワードをタイプしてください.

**promptly** /prɑ́m(p)tli/ 副 ▶定義1 immediately; without delay すぐに; 遅れないで→**敏速に,素早く,即座に** || *I invited her to dinner and she promptly accepted.* 私が彼女を夕食に招待すると,素早く出席の答えが返ってきた. ▶定義2 (または **prompt**) at exactly the time that you have arranged; punctually 人が取り決めた、まさにその時間に; 時間通りに→**きっかり,ちょうど(～に)** || *We arrived promptly at 12 o'clock.* 私たちは、きっかり12時に到着した. *I'll pick you up at 7 o'clock prompt.* 7時ちょうどに車で迎えに来ます.

**prone** /próun/ 形 ▶定義 prone to sth/to do sth likely to suffer from sth or to do sth bad ～を患いがちな,または悪い～を行うことがありそうな→**～の・する傾向がある,～にかかりやすい,～しがちな** || *prone to infection/injury/heart attacks* 感染しやすい・けがしやすい・心臓発作を起こしやすい *Working without a break makes you more prone to error.* 休みなしで働くと,もっと間違いを起こしやすくなりますよ. *to be accident-prone* (= to have a lot of accidents) 事故がちである (= 何度も事故を起こしている)

**prong** /prɔ(ː)ŋ, prɑŋ/ 名 C ▶定義1 each of the two or more long pointed parts of a fork フォークの，2つまたはそれより多い長い先端部分のそれぞれ→また，先のとがった部分 ▶定義2 each of the separate parts of an attack, argument, etc that sb uses to achieve sth ～を達成するために…が使う，攻撃，口論などに含まれている1つ1つの部分→点, 要点, 論点 ▶定義3

**-pronged** (複合形容詞を作るために用いて) having the number or type of prongs mentioned 言及された数の，または種類のprongを持っている→～方面・方向の，～のまたの ‖ *a three-pronged attack* 3方向からの攻撃

**pronoun** /próʊnàʊn/ 名 C (文法) ▶定義 a word that is used in place of a noun or a phrase that contains a noun 名詞または名詞を含む句に代わって用いられる単語→代名詞 ‖ *'He', 'it', 'hers', 'me', 'them', etc are all pronouns.* he, it, hers, me, themなどはすべて代名詞だ．☛参 **personal pronoun**

*****pronounce** /prənáʊns/ 動 ▶定義1 他 to make the sound of a word or letter in a particular way 単語または文字を特定の方法で音にする→～を発音する, 言う ‖ *You don't pronounce the 'b' at the end of 'comb'.* combの最後のbは発音しない．*How do you pronounce your surname?* あなたの姓はどう読むのですか．☛名 **pronunciation** ▶定義2 正式 to say or give sth formally, officially or publicly ～を正式に，公式にまたは公然と言うまたは与える→～が…であると宣言する, 公言する, (判決など)を宣告する ‖ *The judge will pronounce sentence today.* 今日, 裁判官は判決を下す．▶定義3 自 他 正式 **pronounce (on sth)** to give your opinion on sth, especially formally 特に正式に，～について の自分の意見を述べる→(～について)意見を述べる ‖ *The play was pronounced 'brilliant' by all the critics.* その劇はすべての批評家たちから「すばらしい」と評価された．

**pronounced** /prənáʊnst/ 形 ▶定義 very noticeable; obvious とても目立った; 明らかな→明白な, 著しい, 目立った ‖ *His English is excellent although he speaks with a pronounced French accent.* 彼の英語はフランス語なまりが顕著ではあるが，すばらしい．

*****pronunciation** /prənʌ̀nsiéɪʃ(ə)n/ 名 ▶定義1 U C the way in which a language or a particular word or sound is said 言語, 特定の言葉または音が言われる方法→発音, 発音法 ‖ *American pronunciation* アメリカ人の発音 ☛動 **pronounce** ▶定義2 U a person's way of speaking a language 個人の言語の話し方→発音の仕方 ‖ *His grammar is good but his pronunciation is awful!* 彼の文法は問題ないが, その発音はひどい．

*****proof** /pruːf/ 名 ▶定義1 U **proof (of sth); proof that...** information, documents, etc which show that sth is true ～が事実であることを示す, 情報, 文書など→証拠, 証明, 証拠となるもの ‖ *'We need some proof of identity,' the shop assistant said.*「身分を証明するものが必要です」と店員は言った．*You've got no proof that John took the money.* ジョンがそのお金を取ったという証拠はどこにもない．☛動 **prove** ▶定義2 [ C, 通常は複数 ] (専門用語) a first copy of printed material that is produced so that mistakes can be corrected 誤りを修正するために刷られる, 印刷物の最初の刷り→校正刷り(の段階)

**-proof** /pruːf/ 形 (複合形容詞を作るために用いて) ▶定義 able to protect against the thing mentioned 言及された物事から守ることができる→～を防ぐ, 防～の ‖ *a soundproof room* 防音室 *a waterproof/windproof jacket* 防水・防風ジャケット *bulletproof glass* 防弾ガラス

**prop¹** /prɑp/ 動 他 (**propping; propped**) ▶定義 to support sb/sth or keep sb/sth in position by putting him/her/it against or on sth ～に対してまたは～に，…を置くことによって，～を支えるまたは適した位置に～を保つ→～につっかえ棒をする, (つっかえ棒として)～を置く・支える・留める, 立て掛ける ‖ *I'll use this book to prop the window open.* 窓を開けたままにするために，この本を使おう．*He propped his bicycle against the wall.* 彼は自分の自転車を壁に立て掛けた．句動詞 **prop sth up** ▶定義 to support sth that would otherwise fall そうしなければ落ちてしまうに違いない～を支える→～をつっかえ棒で支える, 補強する, ～を(経済的に)支える, 支援する

**prop²** /prɑp/ 名 C ▶定義1 a stick or other object that you use to support sth or to keep sth in position ～を支える, または適した位置に～を保つために, 人が使う棒またはほかの物→支え, つ

つかえ棒 ‖ *Rescuers used props to stop the roof of the tunnel collapsing.* 救助隊は，トンネルの天井が崩れるのを止めるために，支え棒を使った. ▶定義2 [通常は複数] an object that is used in a play, film, etc 劇，映画などで使われる物→**小道具** ‖ *He's responsible for all the stage props, machinery and lighting.* 彼は，すべての舞台小道具，舞台装置，照明を担当している.

**propaganda** /prɒpəɡǽndə/ 名 Ⓤ ▶定義 information and ideas that may be false or exaggerated, which are used to gain support for a political leader, party, etc 政治的指導者，政党などに支持を得るために使われる，間違っているまたは誇張されているかもしれない情報と考え→**(主義・主張の)宣伝，プロパガンダ** ‖ *political propaganda* 政治的宣伝

**propel** /prəpél/ 動 Ⓣ (**propelling; propelled**) ▶定義 to move, drive or push sb/sth forward or in a particular direction ～を前へまたは特定の方向へ動かす，駆り立てる，または押す→**～を推進する，駆り立てる**

**propeller** /prəpélər/ 名 Ⓒ ▶定義 a device with several flat metal parts (**blades**) which turn round very fast in order to make a ship or a plane move 船または飛行機を動かすためにとても速く回転する，いく枚かの平らな金属部分(羽)を持つ装置→**スクリュー，プロペラ**

★**proper** /prɒ́pər/ 形 ▶定義1 特に 英 (名詞の前だけ) right, suitable or correct 適切な，適したまたは正しい→**適切な，ぴったり合う** ‖ *If you're going skiing you must have the proper clothes.* もしスキーに行くなら，適切な服を持たなくてはならない. *I've got to get these pieces of paper in the proper order.* これらの紙を適切な順序にしなければならない. ▶定義2 (名詞の前だけ) that you consider to be real or good enough 十分に本物である，または良いと人が見なしている→**妥当な，ふさわしい** ‖ *I didn't see much of the flat yesterday. I'm going to go today and have a proper look.* 昨日はアパートをゆっくり見てこなかった．今日また行って，きちんと見てくる. ▶定義3 正式 socially and morally acceptable 社会的および道徳的に受け入れられる→**礼儀正しい，作法にかなった** ‖ *I think it would be only proper for you to apologize.* あなたが謝罪することが唯一礼儀にかなうことだと思いますよ. ⇔ **improper** ▶定義4 (名詞の後だけ) real or main 現実のまたは主要な→**本来の，～本体，厳密な意味での** ‖ *We travelled through miles of suburbs before we got to the city proper.* 中心の市街地に着く前に，私たちは何マイルも郊外を通り抜けた.

**properly** /prɒ́pərli/ 副 ▶定義1 特に 英 correctly; in an acceptable way 正しく；受け入れられる方法で→**正しく，適切に，適当に** ‖ *The teacher said I hadn't done my homework properly.* 先生は私が宿題をきちんとしなかったと言った. *These shoes don't fit properly.* この靴はサイズが合わない. ▶定義2 in a way that is socially and morally acceptable; politely 社会的および道徳的に受け入れられる方法で；丁寧に→**礼儀正しく，作法にかなって** ‖ *If you two children can't behave properly then we'll have to go home.* もし2人ともお行儀良くできないなら，私たちは家に帰らなければなりませんよ. ⇔ **improperly**

**proper name** (または **proper noun**) 名 Ⓒ (文法) ▶定義 a word which is the name of a particular person or place and begins with a large letter (**a capital letter**) 特定の人または場所の名前で大きな文字(大文字)で始まる単語→**固有名詞** ‖ *'Mary' and 'Rome' are proper names.* Mary と Rome は固有名詞である.

★**property** /prɒ́pərti/ 名 ( 複 **properties**) ▶定義1 Ⓤ a thing or things that belong to sb ～に属している，1つまたは複数の物→**財産，資産，所有物** ‖ *The sack contained stolen property.* その袋には盗難品が入っていた. *Is this bag your property?* このバッグはあなたのものですか. *This file is government property.* このファイルは政府の所有物です. ☞参 **lost property** ▶定義2 Ⓤ land and buildings 土地と建物→**不動産** ‖ *Property prices vary enormously from area to area.* 不動産の価格は，場所によって非常にさまざまである. ▶定義3 Ⓒ one building and the land around it 建物とその周囲の土地→**地所，所有地** ‖ *There are a lot of empty properties in the area.* この地域には，使われていない地所がたくさんある. ▶定義4 [Ⓒ, 通常は複数] 正式 a special quality or characteristic that a substance, etc has 物質などが持つ，特別な質または特性→**特性，属性** ‖ *Some plants have healing properties.* ある種の植物は，いやし効果を持

**prophecy** /práfəsi/ 图 ❶ ( 複 **prophecies**) ▶定義 a statement about what is going to happen in the future 将来、起きることについての申し立て→**予言** ‖ *to fulfil a prophecy (= to make it come true)* 予言を果たす(= それを現実にする)

**prophesy** /práfəsàɪ/ 動 ⓘ (現分 **prophesying**; 三単現 **prophesies**; 過, 過分 **prophesied**) ▶定義 to say what you think will happen in the future 将来、起こると思う事を言う→**～を予言する、～だと予言する** ‖ *to prophesy disaster/war* 災害・戦争を予言する

**prophet** /práfət/ 图 ❶ ▶定義 1 (または **Prophet**) (in the Christian, Jewish and Muslim religions) a person who is sent by God to teach the people and give them messages from God(キリスト教、ユダヤ教、イスラム教において)人々を教え諭し、唯一神からのメッセージを彼らに伝えるために、唯一神によって遣わされた人→**預言者、マホメット** ▶定義 2 a person who tells what will happen in the future 将来、起こる事を告げる人→**予言者** ― **prophetic** 形 /prəfétɪk/→**預言者の, 予言者の, 予言的な**

**＊proportion** /prəpɔ́ːrʃ(ə)n/ 图 ▶定義 1 ❶a part or share of a whole 全体の一部または分け前→**部分, 分け前** ‖ *A large proportion of the earth's surface is covered by sea.* 地球の表面の大部分は海で覆われている. ▶定義 2 ⓤ **proportion (of sth to sth)** the relationship between the size or amount of two things 2つのものの大きさまたは量の関係→**割合, 比率** ‖ *The proportion of men and women in the college has changed dramatically over the years.* 単科大学での男女の比率は、数年で急激に変化した. ▶定義 3 **proportions** [複数扱い] the size or shape of sth ～の大きさまたは形→**大きさ, 広さ** ‖ *a room of odd proportions* 変わった形の部屋 *Political unrest is reaching alarming proportions.* 政治的不安が急を告げる状況になり始めている.

成句 **in proportion** ▶定義 the right size in relation to other things ほかのものとの関係で適切な大きさ→**釣り合って, 均整が取れて, 分別があって** ‖ *to draw sth in proportion* 釣り合いを取って～をかく *She's so upset that it's hard for her to keep the problem in proportion (= to her it seems more important or serious than it really is).* 彼女はとてもうろたえているので、その問題について分別ある状態を保つことが難しい(= 彼女には、その問題が実際よりも重要または深刻に思える).

**in proportion to sth** ▶定義 1 by the same amount or number as sth else; relative to ほかの～と同じ量または数によって; ～に比べて→**～に比例して** ‖ *Salaries have not risen in proportion to inflation.* 給料はインフレに比例して上がらなかった. ▶定義 2 compared with ～と比較すると→**～の割には、～と比べると** ‖ *In proportion to the number of students as a whole, there are very few women.* 全体の生徒数の割には、女子生徒はとても少ししかいない.

**out of proportion (to sth)** ▶定義 1 too big, small, etc in relation to other things ほかのものとの関係で、大きすぎる、小さすぎるなど→**釣り合いを失って** ▶定義 2 too great, serious, important, etc in relation to sth ～との関係で、すばらしすぎる、真剣すぎる、重要すぎるなど→**不釣り合いに大きく、おおげさで** ‖ *His reaction was completely out of proportion to the situation.* 彼の反応は状況に比べて全くおおげさだった.

**proportional** /prəpɔ́ːrʃ(ə)n(ə)l/ 形 ▶定義 **proportional (to sth)** of the right size, amount or degree compared with sth else ほかの～と比べて、適切な大きさ、量または程度の→**比例した, 釣り合った, 均整の取れた** ‖ *Salary is proportional to years of experience.* 給料は経験年数に比例する.

**proportional representation** 图 ⓤ (略 **PR**) ▶定義 a system that gives each political party in an election a number of representatives in parliament in direct relation to the number of votes its candidates receive 選挙で政党の候補者の得票数に基づいて、各政党に議会での議席数を与える制度→**比例代表制** ☞参 **representation**

**＊proposal** /prəpóʊz(ə)l/ 图 ❶ ▶定義 1 a **proposal (for/to do sth); a proposal that...** a plan that is formally suggested 正式に提案されている計画→**提案, (提案された)計画** ‖ *a new proposal for raising money* 賃上げの新提案 *a proposal to build more student accommodation* 学生寮をさらに建築する計画 *May I make a* *proposal* that we all give an equal amount? 私たち皆が同じ量を与えることを提案してもよろしいですか. ▶定義2 an act of formally asking sb to marry you 自分と結婚してくださいと, 〜に正式に言う行為→**結婚の申し込み, プロポーズ**

**＊propose** /prəpóuz/ 動 ▶定義1 to formally suggest sth as a possible plan or action 可能な計画または行為として, 〜を正式に提案する→**〜を提案する, 提唱する, 申し出る** ‖ *At the meeting a new advertising campaign was proposed.* 会議で新しい広告キャンペーンが提案された.

▶定義2 to intend to do sth; to have sth as a plan 〜をしようと思う; 計画として〜を持つ→**〜を計画する, 企てる, 〜するつもりである** ‖ *What do you propose to do now?* 今何をしたいですか. ▶定義3 propose (to sb) to ask sb to marry you 自分と結婚してくださいと, 〜に言う→**結婚を申し込む; (結婚)を申し込む** ‖ *to propose marriage* 結婚を申し込む ▶定義4 propose sb for/as sth to suggest sb for an official position 〜に公務上の地位を提案する→**〜を推薦する, 指名する** ‖ *I'd like to propose Anna Marsland as Chairperson.* アンナ マースランドを議長に推薦いたします.

**proposition** /prὰpəzíʃ(ə)n/ 名 C ▶定義1 an idea, a plan or an offer, especially in business; a suggestion 特に商売上の, 考え, 計画または申し出; 提案→**計画, 提案, 申し出** ‖ *A month's holiday in Spain is an attractive proposition.* スペインでの1か月の休暇は魅力的な企画だ.

▶定義2 an idea or opinion that sb expresses about sth 〜が…について表明する考えまたは意見→**(〜という)陳述, 主張, 説** ‖ *That's a very interesting proposition. But can you prove it?* それはとても面白い説だ. しかし, あなたはそれを証明できますか.

**proprietor** /prəpráiətər/ 名 C (女性形 **proprietress** /prəpráiətrəs/) ▶定義 the owner of a business, a hotel, etc 事業またはホテルなどの所有者→**持ち主, 所有者, 事業主**

**prose** /próuz/ 名 U ▶定義 written or spoken language that is not poetry 詩ではない, 書かれたまたは話された言葉→**散文** ‖ *to write in prose* 散文で書く

▶ poetryと比較.

**prosecute** /prάsıkjù:t/ 動 ▶定義 prosecute sb (for sth) to officially charge sb with a crime and try to show that he/she is guilty, in a court of law 正式に〜を犯罪で告発して, 法廷でその人が有罪であることを示そうと努める→**検察官・訴追者を務める; 〜を起訴する, 告発する** ‖ *the prosecuting counsel/lawyer/attorney* 法廷弁護団・法廷弁護士・(下級裁判所中心の)事務弁護士, あるいは 米 検事 *He was prosecuted for theft.* 彼は窃盗の罪で起訴された. ☞参 **defend**

**prosecution** /prὰsıkjú:ʃ(ə)n/ 名 ▶定義1 U C the process of officially charging sb with a crime and of trying to show that he/she is guilty, in a court of law 正式に〜を犯罪で告発して, 法廷でその人が有罪であることを示そうと努める過程→**起訴, 告発** ‖ *to bring a prosecution against sb* 〜を告発する *Failure to pay your parking fine will result in prosecution.* 駐車違反の罰金を払わないと起訴されますよ.

▶定義2 **the prosecution** [単数扱い, 単数または複数形の動詞と共に] a person or group of people who try to show that sb is guilty of a crime in a court of law 法廷において〜が有罪であることを示そうと努める人または人々の集団→**検察側** ‖ *The prosecution claim/claims that Lloyd was driving at 100 miles per hour.* 検察側は, ロイドが時速100マイルで走っていたと主張している. ☞参 **defence**

**prospect** /prάspèkt/ 名 ▶定義1 [U, 単数扱い] prospect (of sth/of doing sth) the possibility that sth will happen 〜が起きる可能性→**可能性, ありそうなこと, 見込み** ‖ *There's little prospect of better weather before next week.* 来週までは天気が良くなる見込みはない. ▶定義2 [単数扱い] prospect (of sth/of doing sth) a thought about what may or will happen in the future 将来, 起こるかもしれない, または起こる事についての考え→**期待, 予想, 見通し** ‖ *The prospect of becoming a father filled James with horror.* 父親になることを予想すると, ジェームズは恐怖に包まれた. ▶定義3 **prospects** [複数扱い] chances of being successful in the future 将来, 成功する見込み→**(成功・利益などの)見込み, (人・会社などの)将来性** ‖ *good job/career/promotion prospects* 良い仕事・職業・昇進の見込み

**prospective** /prəspéktıv/ 形 ▶定義 likely to be or to happen; possible ありそうな, または起こ

りそうな；～になりそうな→**予想される, 将来～となると思われる, 見込みのある** ‖ prospective changes in the law 予想される法改正

**prospectus** /prəspéktəs/ 名 ⓒ ▶定義 a small book which gives information about a school or college in order to advertise it 単科大学を宣伝するために, それについての情報を与える本→**案内書**

**prosper** /práspər/ 動 ⓘ ▶定義 to develop in a successful way; to be successful, especially with money 成功するやり方で発展する; 特に金銭面で, 成功する→**繁栄する, 繁盛する, 成功する**

**prosperity** /prɑspérəti/ 名 ⓤ ▶定義 the state of being successful, especially with money 特に金銭面で, 成功している状態→**繁栄, 繁盛** ‖ Tourism has brought prosperity to many parts of Spain. スペインの多くの地域は観光によって繁栄をもたらされている.

**prosperous** /práspərəs/ 形 ▶定義 rich and successful 金持ちで成功している→**裕福な, 成功している, 繁栄している**

**prostitute** /prástət(j)ùːt/ 名 ⓒ ▶定義 a person, especially a woman, who earns money by having sex with people 人々と性交渉をしてお金を稼ぐ人, 特に女性→**売春婦**

**prostitution** /prɑ̀stət(j)úːʃ(ə)n/ 名 ⓤ ▶定義 working as a prostitute 売春婦としての労働→**売春**

**prostrate** /prástrèɪt/ 形 ▶定義 lying flat on the ground, facing downwards 顔を下に向けて, 地面に平らに横たわっている→**うつぶせになった, ひれ伏して**

*****protect** /prətékt/ 動 ⓗ ▶定義 protect sb/sth (against/from sth) to keep sb/sth safe; to defend sb/sth ～を安全に保つ; ～を守る→**～を保護する, 守る, 防ぐ** ‖ Parents try to protect their children from danger as far as possible. 親は自分の子供をできる限り危険から守ろうとするものだ. Bats are a **protected species** (= they must not be killed). コウモリは保護種である(=殺してはいけない).

*****protection** /prətékʃ(ə)n/ 名 ⓤ ▶定義 protection (against/from sth) the act of keeping sb/sth safe so that he/she/it is not harmed or damaged ～が傷付かない, または損害を受けないように, その安全を保つ行為→**保護, 庇護(ひご), 擁護** ‖ Vaccination gives protection against diseases. ワクチンは病気を防ぐ. After the attack he was put **under police protection**. その襲撃の後, 彼は警察の保護下に置かれた.

**protective** /prətéktɪv/ 形 ▶定義 **1** (名詞の前だけ) that prevents sb/sth from being damaged or harmed ～を損害を受ける, または傷付くことから守る→**保護する, 守る, 保護・安全のための** ‖ In certain jobs workers need to wear protective clothing. ある種の仕事では, 労働者は安全服を着用する必要がある. ▶定義 **2** protective (of/towards sb/sth) wanting to keep sb/sth safe ～を安全に保ちたいと思っている→**保護的な, かばう** ‖ Female animals are very protective of their young. 動物の雌は, 自分の幼い子供を保護する気持ちが非常に強い.

**protector** /prətéktər/ 名 ⓒ ▶定義 a person who protects sb/sth ～を保護する人→**保護する人, 保護者, 擁護者**

**protein** /próʊtiːn/ 名 ⓒ ⓤ ▶定義 a substance found in food such as meat, fish, eggs and beans. It is important for helping people and animals to grow and be healthy. 例えば肉, 魚, 卵, 豆のような食品に存在する物質. それは人間と動物が成長し, 健康であるために重要である→**たんぱく質**

*****protest**¹ /próʊtest/ 名 ⓤ ⓒ ▶定義 protest (against sth) a statement or action that shows that you do not like or approve of sth 自分が～を好まない, または承認しないことを示す, 申し立てまたは行為→**抗議, 異議(の申し立て), 抗議文** ‖ He resigned **in protest** against the decision. 彼はその決定に抗議して辞任した. The union organized a protest against the redundancies. 労働組合は, 余剰人員の削減に対する抗議集会を主催した.

成句 under protest ▶定義 not happily and after expressing disagreement 喜んでではなく, 意見の相違を表したあとで→**ぶつぶつ言いながら, しぶしぶ** ‖ Fiona agreed to pay in the end but only under protest. 最後にはフィオナも払うことに同意したが, しぶしぶだった.

*****protest**² /prətést/ 動 ▶定義 **1** ⓘ ⓗ protest (about/against/at sth) to say or show that you do not approve of or agree with sth, especially publicly 特に公的に, 〜を承認しない, または同意しないことを言うまたは示す →**抗議する, 異議を唱える, 反対する** ‖ *Students have been protesting against the government's decision.* 学生たちは政府の決定にずっと抗議している.

▶アメリカ英語では protest は前置詞なしで使われる: *They protested the government's handling of the situation.* (彼らはその状況への対応に抗議した.)

▶定義2 ⑭ to say sth firmly, especially when others do not believe you 特にほかの人たちが自分を信じていないときに, 断固として〜を言う →**〜を主張する, 〜と断言する** ‖ *She has always protested her innocence.* 彼女はいつも自分の無実を主張してきた. ☞ protest はとても激しいので, 通常は complain よりももっと深刻な物事について使われる. 正しくない, または不公平だと感じた物事について, 人は protest し, 物の品質について, またはそれほど深刻でない行為について, 人は complain する. *to protest about a new tax* 新しい税金について抗議する *to complain about the poor weather* 良くない天気に不平を言う ― protester 図 ⑥→**抗議する人, 異議を唱える人, 主張者** ‖ *Protesters blocked the road outside the factory.* 抗議者たちは, 工場の外の道路を封鎖した.

\***Protestant** /prάtəst(ə)nt/ 図 ⑥ ▶定義 a member of the Christian church that separated from the Catholic church in the 16th century 16世紀にカトリック教会から分かれたキリスト教会の会員→**プロテスタント, 新教徒** ― Protestant 形 →**プロテスタント(教会)の, 新教の** ‖ *a Protestant church* プロテスタント教会 ☞参 Roman Catholic

> ▶社会・文化
>
> Protestant と Catholic の違い
>
> プロテスタントの名称はカトリック教会に対する「protestation(抗議)」に由来します. カトリックと異なる点は, およそ(1)神による救済は, 信仰のみによってなされる「信仰義認」, (2)聖書のみを権威とする「聖書原理」, (3)信者各人が直接神の前に立つ「万人司祭主義」の3点と言えます. したがって, 礼拝は説教を中心とし, 典礼は極めて簡素化され, サクラメントは洗礼と聖餐(せいさん)に限

られます. カトリック教会のように教皇を頂点とする世界規模の統一的な体制はありません.

**prototype** /próutətàip/ 図 ⑥ ▶定義 the first model or design of sth from which other forms will be developed そこからほかの形態が発展する, 〜の最初の型式またはデザイン→**原型, プロトタイプ, ひな型**

**protrude** /proutrúːd, prə-/ 動 ⓐ ▶定義 protrude (from sth) to stick out from a place or surface ある場所または表面から突き出ている→**突き出る** ‖ *protruding eyes/teeth* 出目・出っ歯

\***proud** /práud/ 形 ▶定義1 proud (of sb/sth); proud to do sth/that... feeling pleased and satisfied about sth that you own or have done 自分が所有している, または自分のした〜について喜びを感じ満足している→**誇りに思う, 自慢している, 〜で得意になって** ‖ *They are very proud of their new house.* 彼らは自分たちの新しい家にとても誇りを持っている. *I feel very proud to be part of such a successful organization.* このような成功している団体の一員であることを, 私はとても誇りに思っています. *You should feel very proud that you have been chosen.* あなたは自分が選ばれたことを誇りに思うべきだ. ▶定義2 feeling that you are better and more important than other people ほかの人々より自分の方がもっと良くて重要だと感じている→**うぬぼれた, 尊大な, 思い上がった** ‖ *Now she's at university she'll be much too proud to talk to us!* 彼女は今や大学生だから思い上がっていて, 私たちとは話しもしないでしょうね. ▶定義3 having respect for yourself and not wanting to lose the respect of others 自分自身を尊敬していて, ほかの人々からの尊敬も失いたくない→**自尊心のある, プライドがある, 誇り高い** ‖ *He was too proud to ask for help.* 彼はプライドが高すぎて手助けを頼めなかった. ☞ 図 pride ― proudly 副 →**誇らしげに, 自慢して, うぬぼれて** ‖ *'I did all the work myself,' he said proudly.*「この仕事を全部, 自分でやったんだ」と彼は誇らしげに言った.

\***prove** /pruːv/ 動 (過分 **proved**; 困 **proven**) ▶定義1 ⑭ prove sth (to sb) to use facts and evidence to show that sth is true 〜が真実であることを示すために，事実と証拠を使う→〜を証明する，立証する，証拠立てる ‖ *It will be difficult to prove that she was lying.* 彼女がうそをついていたと立証することは難しいでしょう. *She tried to prove her innocence to the court.* 彼女は裁判所で自分の潔白を証明しようとした. *He felt he needed **to prove a point** (= show other people that he was right).* 彼は主張の正しさを証明する必要を感じた(= ほかの人々に彼が正しいと示す). ☞ **proof**　▶定義2 ⓔ to show a particular quality over a period of time ある期間ずっと，ある特性を示す→〜であることが分かる，〜と判断する，(結果として)〜となる・である ‖ *The job proved more difficult than we'd expected.* その仕事は，私たちが予想していたよりも難しかったことが分かった. ▶定義3 ⓘ **prove yourself (to sb)** to show other people how good you are at doing sth and/or that you are capable of doing sth 自分は〜をすることにどれほど優れているかを，そして・または自分は〜をする能力があることを，ほかの人たちに示す→自分の価値・能力を立証する，自分が〜であると証明する，自分が〜であることを示す ‖ *He constantly feels that he has to prove himself to others.* ほかの人たちに自分の価値を立証しなければならないと，彼は常に感じている.

**proven** /prúːv(ə)n/ 形 ▶定義 that has been shown to be true 真実であると示された→立証済みの，試験済みの，保証付きの ‖ *a proven fact* 立証済みの事実

**proverb** /prɔ́vəːrb/ 名 ⓒ ▶定義 a short well-known sentence or phrase that gives advice or says that sth is generally true in life 忠告を与える，または人生において〜が一般に真実だと言う，短いよく知られた文または節→ことわざ，格言 ‖ *'Too many cooks spoil the broth,' is a proverb.* 「料理人が多すぎるとスープがまずくなる(船頭多くして船山に登る)」はことわざです. ☞参 **saying**

★**provide** /prəváɪd/ 動 ⓣ ▶定義 **provide sb (with sth); provide sth (for sb)** to give sth to sb or make sth available for sb to use; to supply sth 〜を…に与えるまたは〜が…を使えるようにする；〜を供給する→〜を供給する，支給する，提供する ‖ *This book will provide you with all the information you need.* この本にはあなたが必要としている情報がすべて載っています. *We are able to provide accommodation for two students.* 私たちは，2 人の学生を宿泊させられる. ☞ 名 **provision**

句動詞 **provide for sb** ▶定義 to give sb all that he/she needs to live, for example food and clothing 生きるために必要なすべて，例えば食物と衣服を〜に与える→〜に必要なものを与える，(家族など)を扶養する，(必要など)を満たす ‖ *Robin has four children to provide for.* ロビンには養っている子供が 4 人いる.

**provide for sth** ▶定義 to make preparations to deal with sth that might happen in the future 将来起こるかもしれない〜に対処するための準備をする→〜のために手を打つ，〜(のこと)を考えておく ‖ *We did not provide for such a large increase in prices.* 私たちは，このような物価の高騰を考えておかなかった.

★**provided** /prəváɪdɪd/(または **providing**) 接 ▶定義 **provided/providing (that)** only if; on condition that 〜する場合にだけ；〜という条件で→仮に〜とすれば，〜という条件で ‖ *She agreed to go and work abroad provided (that) her family could go with her.* 彼女は，家族も一緒に行くという条件で外国で働くことに同意した.

★**province** /prɔ́vəns/ 名 ▶定義1 ⓒ one of the main parts into which some countries are divided with its own local government いくつかの国々では，その地方の行政を持つ主な区域に分かれていて，その区域の 1 つ→州，(中国の)省 ‖ *Canada has ten provinces.* カナダには，10 の州がある.

➤ county, state と比較.

▶定義2 **the provinces** [複数扱い] 英 the part of a country that is outside the most important city (**the capital**) 最も重要な都市(首都)の外側にある，田舎の部分→田舎，地方

**provincial** /prəvínʃ(ə)l/ 形 ▶定義1 (名詞の前だけ) connected with one of the large areas that some countries are divided into いくつかの国々で分かれている，広い地域の 1 つに関連した→州の，(中国の)省の ‖ *provincial governments/elections* 州政府・州選挙 ▶定義2 connected with the parts of a country that do not include its most important city 最も重要な都市を含まな

い, 田舎の部分に関連した➜**田舎の, 地方の** ‖ *a provincial town/newspaper* 田舎の町·地方新聞 ▸定義3 (used about a person or his/her ideas) not wanting to consider new or different ideas or fashions (人, または人の考えについて) 新しいまたは異なった考え, あるいは流行しているものを考えたくないと思っている➜**偏狭な, 視野の狭い, 頭の古い** ‖ *provincial attitudes* 偏狭な態度

***provision** /prəvíʒ(ə)n/ [名] ▸定義1 [U] the giving or supplying of sth to sb or making sth available for sb to use ～に…を与えることまたは供給すること, あるいは～が…を使えるようにすること➜**供給, 支給** ‖ *The council is responsible for the provision of education and social services.* 議会は, 教育と社会福祉を提供する責任がある. ▸定義2 [U] provision for sb/sth preparations that you make to deal with sth that might happen in the future 将来起こるかもしれない～に対処するために, 行う準備➜**用意, 準備, 備え** ‖ *She **made provision for** (= planned for the financial future of) the children in the event of her death.* 彼女は自分が死んだ場合の備えを子供たちのためにした (= 彼らの経済的な将来を計画した). ▸定義3 **provisions** [複数扱い] [正式] supplies of food and drink, especially for a long journey 特に長期旅行のための, 食べ物と飲み物の蓄え➜**食糧, 貯蔵品** ☛ [動] provide

**provisional** /prəvíʒ(ə)n(ə)l/ [形] ▸定義 only for the present time, that is likely to be changed in the future 現在のためだけの, 将来には変えられそうである➜**仮の, 暫定的な, 臨時の** ‖ *The provisional date for the next meeting is 18 November.* 次回の会合は, とりあえず11月18日ということにしておきましょう. *a **provisional driving licence** (= that you use when you are learning to drive)* 仮運転免許 (= 運転を習っているときだけに使う) — provisionally /-n(ə)li/ [副] ➜**仮に, 暫定的に** ‖ *I've only repaired the bike provisionally - we'll have to do it properly later.* 私はその自転車をざっと修理しただけだ – 後できちんと修理しなければいけないよ.

**provocation** /pràvəkéɪʃ(ə)n/ [名] [U] [C] ▸定義 doing or saying sth deliberately to try to make sb angry or upset; sth that is said or done to cause this ～を怒らせる, または狼狽(ろうばい)させるために, 故意に…をするまたは言うこと; これを引き起こそうとして言われたまたは行われた～➜**挑発, じらすこと, 怒らすこと** ‖ *You should never hit children, even **under** extreme **provocation**.* どんなにひどく憤慨しても, 決して子供たちを殴ってはならない. ☛ [動] provoke

**provocative** /prəvάkətɪv/ [形] ▸定義1 intended to make sb angry or upset or to cause an argument ～を怒らせる, または狼狽(ろうばい)させる, あるいは口論を引き起こすことを意図している➜**刺激する, 怒らせる, 挑発的な** ‖ *He made a provocative remark about a woman's place being in the home.* 彼は, 女性の居場所は家庭であるという, 挑発的な発言をした. ▸定義2 intended to cause sexual excitement 性的興奮を引き起こそうとする➜**挑発的な, なまめかしい** — provocatively [副] ➜**挑発的に, なまめかしく**

**provoke** /prəvóʊk/ [動][他] ▸定義1 to cause a particular feeling or reaction 特定の感情または反応を引き起こす➜**(怒り·笑いなど)を起こす, 誘う, (事件)を引き起こす** ‖ *an article intended to provoke discussion* 議論を引き起こそうと意図された記事 ▸定義2 provoke sb (into sth/into doing sth) to say or do sth that you know will make a person angry or upset 人を怒らせる, または狼狽(ろうばい)させると分かっている～を言うまたはする➜**～を怒らせる, いら立たせる, 刺激する** ‖ *The lawyer claimed his client was provoked into acts of violence.* 自分の依頼者は挑発されて暴力行為に走ったと, その弁護士は主張した. ☛ [名] provocation

**prow** /práʊ/ [名] [C] ▸定義 the front part of a ship or boat 船またはボートの前の部分➜**船首, へさき** ☛ 船の後ろは, stern (船尾, とも) である.

**prowess** /práʊəs/ [名] [U] [正式] ▸定義 great skill at doing sth ～を行うことのすばらしい技量➜**(際立って優れた)腕前, 技量** ‖ *academic/sporting prowess* 優れた学習能力·優れた運動神経

**prowl** /práʊl/ [動][自][他] ▸定義 prowl(about/around) (used about an animal that is hunting or a person who is waiting for a chance to steal sth or do sth bad) to move around an area quietly so that you are not seen or heard (狩りをしている動物, あるいは～を盗むまたは悪い事をしようと機会を待っている人について) 見られない, または聞かれないように, ある区域を静かに動き回る➜**足音を忍ばせて歩き回る, うろうろす**

P

る, ぶらつく ‖ *I could hear someone prowling around outside so I called the police.* だれかが家の外をうろついているのが聞こえたので, 私は警察を呼んだ. ☛ うろついている人または動物は, on the prowl(うろついている)と言う. — **prowler** 名 C →うろつく人・動物, 空き巣ねらい ‖ *The police arrested a prowler outside the hospital.* 警察は病院の外でうろついていた人を逮捕した.

**proximity** /prɒksíməti/ 名 U 正式 ▶定義 **proximity (of sb/sth) (to sb/sth)** the state of being near to sb/sth in distance or time 距離的または時間的に～の近くにいる状態→近いこと, 接近 ‖ *An advantage is the proximity of the new offices to the airport.* 利点は新しい事務所が空港に近いことだ.

**proxy** /prɒksi/ 名 U ▶定義 the authority that you give to sb to act for you if you cannot do sth yourself ～を自分でできない場合, 自分の代わりに行動してもらうために…に与える自分の権限→委任, 代理 ‖ *to vote by proxy* 委任投票する

**prude** /pruːd/ 名 C ▶定義 a person who is easily shocked by anything connected with sex 性に関することなら何にでも簡単に憤慨する人 →上品振る人, 淑女振る人 — **prudish** 形 →淑女振る, 上品振った, 取り澄ました

**prudent** /prúːd(ə)nt/ 形 正式 ▶定義 sensible and careful when making judgements and decisions; avoiding unnecessary risks 判断して決意するとき, 分別があって注意深い; 不必要な危険を避けている→慎重な, 用心深い, 分別のある ‖ *It would be prudent to get some more advice before you invest your money.* お金を投資する前に, もう少し忠告を得て慎重を期した方がいいでしょう. ⇔ **imprudent** — **prudence** 名 U →慎重さ, 用心深さ, 分別 — **prudently** 副 →慎重に, 用心深く, 分別を働かせて

**prune**¹ /pruːn/ 名 C ▶定義 a dried fruit (plum) 乾燥された果物(スモモ) →プルーン, 干しスモモ

**prune**² /pruːn/ 動 他 ▶定義 to cut branches or parts of branches off a tree or bush in order to make it a better shape より良い形にするために, 木または茂みの枝または枝の一部を切り落とす→～を刈り込む, 剪定(せんてい)する, (枝)を下ろす

**pry** /praɪ/ 動 (現分 **prying**; 三単現 **pries**; 過, 過分 **pried**) ▶定義 1 自 **pry (into sth)** to try to find out about other people's private affairs ほかの人々の私的な事柄を見つけ出そうとする→(好奇心で)のぞく, (こっそり)様子をうかがう, 詮索(せんさく)する ‖ *I'm sick of you prying into my personal life.* 私の個人的な生活を詮索されて, あなたにうんざりだ. ▶定義 2 他 特に 米 = **PRISE**

**PS** (または **ps**) /piː és/ 略 ▶定義 (used for adding sth to the end of a letter) postscript(手紙の最後に～を加えるために用いて) →追伸 ‖ *Love Tessa. PS I'll bring the car.* テッサより愛を込めて. 追伸 私が車を運びます.

**pseudonym** /sjúːd(ə)nɪm; súː-/ 名 C ▶定義 a name used by sb, especially a writer, instead of his/her real name ～, 特に作家, によって本名の代わりに用いられる名前→ペンネーム, 筆名, 雅号

**psych** /saɪk/ 動

句動詞 **psych yourself up** 略式 ▶定義 to prepare yourself in your mind for sth difficult 心の中で困難な～への覚悟をする→心の準備をする, 心構えをする, 覚悟をする ‖ *I've got to psych myself up for this interview.* 私はこの面接に備えて心の準備をしなくてはならない.

**psyche** /sáɪki/ 名 C 正式 ▶定義 the mind; your deepest feelings and attitudes 心; 人の最も深い感情と心構え →魂, 精神 ‖ *the human/female/national psyche* 人間・女性・国の精神

**psychedelic** /saɪkədélɪk/ 形 ▶定義 (used about art, music, clothes, etc) having bright colours or patterns or strange sounds(芸術, 音楽, 衣服などについて)鮮やかな色または模様, あるいは奇妙な音の→サイケ調の, サイケデリックな

**psychiatrist** /saɪkáɪətrɪst, sə-/ 名 C ▶定義 a doctor who is trained to treat people with mental illness 精神が病気の人々を治療する訓練を受けた医者→精神病医, 精神科医, 精神医学者

**psychiatry** /saɪkáɪətri, sə-/ 名 U ▶定義 the study and treatment of mental illness 精神の病気の研究と治療→精神医学, 精神治療法
▶ **psychology** と比較.
— **psychiatric** /saɪkiætrɪk/ 形 →精神医学の, 精神病治療の ‖ *a psychiatric hospital/unit/nurse* 精神病院・精神病棟・精神科の看護婦

**psychic** /sáɪkɪk/ 形 ▶定義 (used about a person or his/her mind) having unusual powers that cannot be explained, for example knowing what sb else is thinking or being able to see

**psychoanalysis** /sàɪkoʊənǽləsɪs, -kə-/ (または **analysis**) 名 U ▶定義 a method of treating sb with a mental illness by asking about his/her past experiences, feelings, dreams, etc in order to find out what is making him/her ill 人を病気にしている原因を見つけ出すために, 過去の経験, 感情, 夢などを尋ねて, 精神の病気の〜を治療する方法 → **精神分析, 精神分析療法** — psychoanalyse (英 -lyze) /sàɪkoʊǽn(ə)laɪz, -kə-/ 動他 →〜の精神分析をする, 〜に精神分析療法を施す

**psychoanalyst** /sàɪkoʊǽn(ə)ləst, -kə-/ 名 C ▶定義 a person who treats sb with a mental illness by using psychoanalysis 精神分析療法を用いて, 精神の病気の〜を治療する人 → **精神分析医, 精神分析学者**

**psychological** /sàɪkəládʒɪk(ə)l/ 形 ▶定義1 connected with the mind or the way that it works 精神または精神の働き方に関連した → **心理的な, 精神的な** ‖ *Has her ordeal caused her long-term psychological damage?* 彼女の過酷な体験が, 長期の心理的な障害を引き起こしたのでしょうか. ▶定義2 connected with the study of the mind and the way people behave (psychology) 精神と人々の振る舞い方の研究 (心理学) に関連した → **心理学上の, 心理学的な** — psychologically /-k(ə)li/ 副 → **心理学的に, 心理的に, 精神的に** ‖ *Psychologically, it was a bad time to be starting a new job.* 精神的には, 新しい仕事を始めるには悪い時期だった.

**psychologist** /saɪkálədʒɪst/ 名 C ▶定義 a scientist who studies the mind and the way that people behave 精神と人々の振る舞い方を研究している科学者 → **心理学者**

**psychology** /saɪkálədʒi/ 名 ▶定義1 U the scientific study of the mind and the way that people behave 精神と人々の振る舞い方についての科学的な研究 → **心理学** ‖ *child psychology* 児童心理学
➤ psychiatryと比較.
▶定義2 [単数扱い] the type of mind that a person or group of people has 個人または人々の集団が持つ精神の型 → **心理 (状態), 精神状態, 気持ち** ‖ *If we understood the psychology of the killer we would have a better chance of catching him.* もし殺人者の心理状態が理解できるなら, 我々がやつを捕まえる機会が増えるだろうに.

**psychopath** /sáɪkəpæθ/ (または 口語 **psycho**) 名 C ▶定義 a person who has a serious mental illness that may cause him/her to hurt or kill other people ほかの人々を傷付けるまたは殺す原因になるかもしれない, 深刻な精神の病気にかかっている人 → **精神異常者, 精神病質者**

**psychosis** /saɪkóʊsɪs/ 名 C U (複 **psychoses**) ▶定義 a very serious mental illness that affects your whole personality 人格の全体に影響を与える, とても深刻な精神の病気 → **精神病, 精神異常** — psychotic /saɪkátɪk/ 形名 C → **精神病の, 精神異常の; 精神異常者** ‖ *a psychotic patient/individual* 精神病患者・精神異常者

**psychotherapy** /sàɪkoʊθérəpi, -kə-/ 名 U ▶定義 the treatment of mental illness by discussing sb's problems rather than by giving him/her drugs 薬を与えることよりむしろ〜の問題を話し合って行う, 精神の病気の治療 → **精神療法**

**pt** (複 **pts**) 略 ▶定義1 pint → **パイント (量の単位)** ‖ *2 pts milk* 2パイントの牛乳 ▶定義2 (in a game or competition) point (ゲームまたは試合において) → **ポイント, 得点** ‖ *Laura 5pts, Arthur 4pts* ローラは5ポイント, アーサーは4ポイント

**PTO** (または **pto**) /pì: ti: óʊ/ 略 ▶定義 (at the bottom of a page) please turn over (ページの最後で) → **裏へ続く, 裏面をご覧ください**

*★**pub** /pʌb/ (または 正式 **public house**) 名 C 英 ▶定義 a place where people go to buy and drink alcohol and that also often serves food 人々がお酒を買って飲み, またしばしば食べ物も出る場所 → **パブ, 酒場**

**puberty** /pjú:bərti/ 名 U ▶定義 the time when a child's body is changing and becoming physically like that of an adult 子供の体が変化して, 身体的に大人のようになる時期 → **思春期, 年ごろ** ‖ *to reach puberty* 思春期になる

**pubic** /pjú:bɪk/ 形 ▶定義 of the area around the sexual organs 性器の周辺の → **陰部の, 恥骨の** ‖ *pubic hair* 陰毛

**public¹** /pʌblɪk/ 形 ▶定義1 (名詞の前だけ) connected with ordinary people in general, not those who have an important position in society 社会において重要な地位にいる人々ではなく, 一般の普通の人々に関連した→**社会一般の, 一般大衆の, 公衆の** ‖ *Public opinion was in favour of the war.* 世論は戦争を支持した. *How much public support is there for the government's policy?* その政府の政策をどれほどの一般大衆が支持しているのか. ▶定義2 provided for the use of people in general; not private 一般の人々が使うために提供された; 私用ではなく→**公共の, 公立の, 公の** ‖ *a public library/telephone* 公共図書館・公衆電話 *public spending (= money that the government spends on education, health care, etc)* 公共のための支出 (= 政府が教育, 公共医療などに費やすお金) ▶定義3 known by many people 多くの人に知られている→**だれでも知っている, 周知の, 公開の** ‖ *We're going to **make** the news **public** soon.* すぐにそのニュースを公開します. ☛参 private
— **publicly** /-kli/ 副 →**公然と, おおっぴらに** ‖ *The company refused to admit publicly that it had acted wrongly.* その会社は, 不適切に行動してしまったことを公式に認めることを拒否した.

成句 **be common/public knowledge** ⇒ **KNOWLEDGE**

**go public** ▶定義1 to tell people about sth that is a secret 秘密である〜について人々に話す→**公表する** ‖ *The sacked employee went public with his stories of corruption inside the company.* 解雇された従業員は, その会社内部の腐敗を公表した. ▶定義2 (used about a company) to start selling shares to the public (会社について) 社会一般に株式を売り始める→**株式を公開する**

**in the public eye** ▶定義 often appearing on television, in magazines, etc しばしばテレビ, 雑誌などに登場している→**世間の注目を浴びている, マスコミで報道されている**

**★public²** /pʌblɪk/ 名 [単数扱い, 単数または複数形の動詞と共に] ▶定義1 **the public** people in general 一般の人々→**民衆, 世間** ‖ *The university swimming pool is **open to the public** in the evenings.* その大学のプールは夜, 一般に開放されている. *The police have asked for help from members of the public.* 警察は, 一般の人々の協力を求めた. *The public is/are generally in favour of the new law.* 世間は一般的に新しい法律を支持している. ▶定義2 a group of people who are all interested in sth or who have sth in common 全員が〜に興味がある, または共通の〜を持つ人々の集団→**(趣味などを共有する)仲間, 〜愛好家, 〜層** ‖ *the travelling public* 旅行愛好家

成句 **in public** ▶定義 when other people are present ほかの人々がいるとき→**公然と, 人前で** ‖ *This is the first time that Miss Potter has spoken about her experience in public.* ポッターさんが人前でご自分の体験を話されたのは, これが初めてです.

**publican** /pʌblɪkən/ 名 C ▶定義 a person who owns or manages a pub パブを所有する, または経営する人→**パブの主人**

**★publication** /pʌblɪkeɪʃ(ə)n/ 名 ▶定義1 U the act of printing a book, magazine, etc and making it available to the public 本, 雑誌などを印刷して, 一般大衆が入手できるようにする行為→**出版, 発行, 刊行** ‖ *His latest book has just been accepted for publication.* 彼の最新の本が出版されることになった. ▶定義2 C a book, magazine, etc that has been published 出版された本, 雑誌など→**出版物, 刊行物** ▶定義3 U the action of making sth known to the public 一般大衆が〜を知るようにさせる行為→**発表, 公表, 公布** ‖ *the publication of exam results* 試験結果の公表

**public company** (または **public limited company**) 名 C 英 (略 **plc**) ▶定義 a large company that sells shares in itself to the public 自社の株を一般大衆に売る, 大きな会社→**株式公開会社**

**public convenience** 名 C 英 ▶定義 a toilet in a public place that anyone can use だれでも使える, 公共の場にあるトイレ→**公衆便所**

**public house** 正式 =**PUB**

**publicity** /pʌblɪsəti/ 名 U ▶定義1 notice or attention from the newspapers, television, etc 新聞, テレビなどからの告示または注目→**知れ渡ること, 世間の注目, 評判** ‖ *to seek/avoid publicity* 世間の注目を得ようと努める・避ける ▶定義2 the business of attracting people's attention to sth/sb; advertising 人々の注目を〜へ引き付ける商売; 宣伝→**宣伝, 広告, 広報** ‖ *There has been a lot of publicity for this film.* こ

の映画はよく宣伝されてきた.

**publicize**(または **-ise**)/pʌ́bləsàɪz/ 動他 ▶定義
to attract people's attention to sth 人々の注意を〜に引き付ける→〜を広告する, 宣伝する ‖ *The event has been well publicized and should attract a lot of people.* その催しは十分に宣伝されていて多くの人々を引き付けるだろう.

**public relations** 名(略**PR**) ▶定義1 [複数扱い] the state of the relationship between an organization and the public ある組織と一般の人々との関係の状態→対社会関係, (世間に対する)受け ‖ *Giving money to local charities is good for public relations.* 地元の慈善団体にお金を寄付することは, 地域社会との関係の上で良い事だ. ▶定義2 ❶ the job of making a company, organization, etc popular with the public 会社, 組織などを一般大衆に人気があるようにする仕事→宣伝, 広報活動, 渉外(事務) ‖ *a Public Relations Officer* 広報官

**public school** 名 ❻ ▶定義1 (in Britain, especially in England) a private school for children aged between 13 and 18. Parents have to pay to send their children to one of these schools. Many of the children at public schools live (board) there while they are studying. (英国, 特にイングランドで) 13から18歳の子供たちのための私立学校. これらの学校に子供を通わせるために, 両親はお金を払わなければならない. public school で学んでいる間, 多くの子供たちはそこに住む→パブリックスクール(全寮制の男子私立学校) ▶定義2 (in the US, Australia, Scotland and other countries) a local school that any child can go to that provides free education (米国, オーストラリア, スコットランドとほかの国々で) どの子供でも通える, 無料で教育を提供する, 地元の学校→公立学校

**public-spirited** 形 ▶定義 always ready to help other people and the public in general 常にほかの人々と一般大衆を助ける準備ができている→公共心・ボランティア精神のある

**public transport** 名 ❶ ▶定義 (the system of) buses, trains, etc that run according to a series of planned times and that anyone can use 一連の計画された時間に従って走り, だれでも利用できる, バス, 電車など(の網)→公共輸送機関 ‖ *to travel by/on public transport* 公共輸送機関で旅する

puff 1295

***publish** /pʌ́blɪʃ/ 動 ▶定義1 ❶他 to prepare and print a book, magazine, etc and make it available to the public 本, 雑誌などを準備し印刷して, 一般大衆がそれを入手できるようにする→〜を出版する, 発行する, 刊行する ‖ *This dictionary was published by Oxford University Press.* この辞書はオックスフォード大学出版局から出版された. ▶定義2 ❹ (used about a writer, etc) to have your work put in a book, magazine, etc (作家などについて) 自分の作品を本, 雑誌などに出してもらう→〜を発表する, (本など)を出す ‖ *Dr Wreth has published several articles on the subject.* レス博士は, そのテーマでいくつか記事を発表したことがある. ▶定義3 ❹ to make sth known to the public 一般大衆が〜を知るようにさせる→〜を(新聞・雑誌などで)発表する, 公表する ‖ *Large companies must publish their accounts every year.* 毎年, 大企業は会計を公表しなければならない.

**publisher** /pʌ́blɪʃər/ 名 ▶定義 a person or company that publishes books, magazines, etc 本雑誌などを出版する人または会社→出版業者, 出版社, 発行人

**publishing** /pʌ́blɪʃɪŋ/ 名 ❶ ▶定義 the business of preparing books, magazines, etc to be printed and sold 本, 雑誌などを印刷して売る準備をする商売→出版業 ‖ *She's aiming for a career in publishing.* 彼女は出版業界で働くことを目指している.

***pudding** /pʊ́dɪŋ/ 名 ❻ ❶ 医 ▶定義1 any sweet food that is eaten at the end of a meal 食事の後に食べられる, 甘い食べ物の1つ→デザート ‖ *What's for pudding today?* 今日のデザートは何ですか. ☛ dessert はより正式である. ☛参 **sweet** ▶定義2 a type of sweet food that is made from bread, flour or rice with eggs, milk, etc 卵, 牛乳などとパン, 小麦粉, または米で作られる, 甘い食べ物の一種→プディング ‖ *rice pudding* ライスプディング

**puddle** /pʌ́dl/ 名 ❻ ▶定義 a small pool of water or other liquid, especially rain, that has formed on the ground 地面にできる, 水またはほかの液体, 特に雨の, 小さなたまり→水たまり, たまり ☛参 **pond** の注

**puff**¹ /pʌf/ 動 ▶定義1 ❶他 (used about air,

smoke, wind, etc) to blow or come out in clouds (空気, 煙, 風などについて)雲となって吹くまたは出てくる➡ぷっと吹き出す, ぱっぱっと出る; 〜をぱっぱっと吐く・出す ‖ *Smoke was puffing out of the chimney.* 煙が煙突からぱっぱっと出ていた. ▶定義2 ⊜⊕ to smoke a cigarette, pipe etc たばこ, パイプなどを吸う➡(ぷかぷか)吹かす; 〜を(ぷかぷか)吹かす ‖ *to puff on a cigarette* たばこをぷかぷか吹かす ▶定義3 ⊜ to breathe loudly or quickly, for example when you are running 例えば走っているとき, 騒々しくまたは慌ただしく呼吸する➡荒い息遣いをする, ぜいぜいと息を切らす, あえぐ ‖ *He was puffing hard as he ran up the hill.* 彼は丘を駆け上がりながら, ぜいぜいと息を切らしていた.
▶定義4 ⊜ puff along, in, out, up, etc to move in a particular direction with loud breaths or small clouds of smoke 騒々しい息遣い, または小さな煙の雲を伴って, 特定の方向へ動く➡(蒸気・煙などを)ぱっぱっと出しながら動く・進む, あえぎながら進む ‖ *The train puffed into the station.* 汽車は煙をぱっぱっと出しながら駅に入ってきた.

句動詞 puff sth out/up ▶定義 to cause sth to become larger by filling it with air 空気をそれに満たすことで, 〜が大きくなる原因となる➡〜を(空気で)膨らませる ‖ *The trumpet player was puffing out his cheeks.* そのトランペット奏者はほおを膨らませていた.

puff up ▶定義 (used about part of the body) to become swollen (体の一部について)はれてくる➡はれる, 膨らむ ‖ *Her arm puffed up when she was stung by a wasp.* ジガバチに刺された時, 彼女の腕ははれた.

**puff**² /pʌf/ 名 Ⓒ ▶定義1 a small amount of air, smoke, wind, etc that is blown or sent out 吹かれたまたは外へ出された, 少量の空気, 煙, 風など➡一吹き, ぷっと・さあっと吹くこと ‖ *a puff of smoke* 煙の一吹き ▶定義2 one breath that you take when you are smoking a cigarette or pipe たばこまたはパイプを吸っているとき, 人が呼吸する一息➡(たばこの)一服 ‖ *to take/ have a puff on a cigarette* たばこを一服する

**puffed** /pʌft/ (または **puffed out**) 形 ▶定義 finding it difficult to breathe, for example because you have been running 例えばずっと走っているので, 呼吸することが困難であると分かっている➡あえいで, 息切れして

**puffin** /ˈpʌfɪn/ 名 Ⓒ ▶定義 a North Atlantic seabird with a large brightly-coloured beak 大きくて鮮やかな色のくちばしを持つ, 北大西洋の海鳥➡ニシツノメドリ

**puffy** /ˈpʌfi/ 形 ▶定義 (used about a part of a person's body) looking soft and swollen (人の体の一部について)柔らかく, はれているように見えている➡丸く膨れている, 膨れ上がった, 柔らかくて軽い ‖ *Your eyes look a bit puffy. Have you been crying?* あなたの目は少しはれていますね. 泣いていたのですか.

**puke** /pjuːk/ 動 ⊜⊕ (俗語) ▶定義 to be sick; to vomit 吐く ➡〜を吐く, 吐き出す, ゲロする — puke 名 Ⓤ ➡ヘド, ゲロ, 吐き出した物

### pull/push/drag

pull

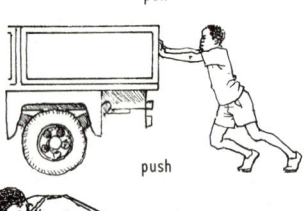

push

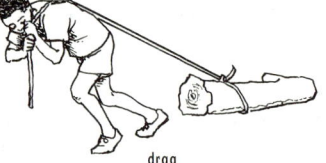

drag

*****pull**¹ /pʊl/ 動 ▶定義1 ⊜⊕ to use force to move sb/sth towards yourself 〜を自分の方へ動かすために力を使う➡引っ張る, 引く ‖ *I pulled on the rope to make sure that it was secure.* それが安全かどうか確かめるために, 私はロープを引っ張った. *to pull the trigger of a gun* 銃の引き金を引く *I felt someone pull at my sleeve and turned round.* だれかが私のそでを引くのを感じ

て, 振り返った. *They managed to pull the child out of the water just in time.* 彼らはぎりぎり間に合って, その子供を水から首尾良く引き上げた.
▶定義2 ⓖ **pull sth on, out, up, down, etc** to move sth in the direction that is described 言及された方向へ~を動かす→**~を引き寄せる, (車など)を寄せる** ∥ *She pulled her sweater on/She pulled on her sweater.* 彼女はセーターを素早く着た. *He pulled up his trousers/He pulled his trousers up.* 彼はズボンをさっと履いた. *I switched off the TV and pulled out the plug.* 私はテレビを消して, コンセントを抜いた.
▶定義3 ⓖ to hold or be fastened to sth and move it along behind you in the direction that you are going ~につかまったり, しっかりくくりつけた状態にして, 自分の進行方向に自分の背後で移動させていく→**~を (引くようにして) 動かす, ~を引っ張って…にする** ∥ *That cart is too heavy for one horse to pull.* あの荷馬車は一頭の馬で引くには重すぎる. ▶定義4 ⓔ ⓖ to move your body or a part of your body away with force 力で自分の体または体の一部をどける→**動かして~ (の状態) にする** ∥ *She pulled away as he tried to kiss her.* 彼がキスしようとしたので, 彼女は身を振り離した. *I pulled back my fingers just as the door slammed.* ドアがバタンと閉まると同時に, 私は指を引っこめた.
▶定義5 ⓖ to damage a muscle, etc by using too much force 力の使いすぎで, 筋肉などに損害を受ける→**痛める, 違える** ∥ *I've pulled a muscle in my thigh.* 私は太ももの筋肉を痛めてしまった.
成句 **make/pull faces/a face (at sb)** ⇒ **FACE**¹

**pull sb's leg** 略式 ▶定義 to play a joke on sb by trying to make him/her believe sth that is not true 本当でない~を人に信じさせて, からかう→**~を担ぐ, からかう**

**pull out all the stops** 略式 ▶定義 to make the greatest possible effort to achieve sth ~を達成するために, できる限りの努力をする→**最大限の努力をする, 全力を傾ける**

**pull your punches** 略式 (通常は否定文で用いて) ▶定義 to be careful what you say or do in order not to shock or upset anyone だれにもショックを与えない, またはうろたえさせないために, 自分が言うまたは行う事に気を付ける→**手加減する, 手心を加える** ∥ *The film pulls no punches in its portrayal of urban violence.* その映画は, 都会の暴力を手心を加えないで描写している.

**pull strings** ▶定義 to use your influence to gain an advantage 利益を得るために, 自分の影響力を使う→**(黒幕となって) 陰で操る, 裏面工作をする, コネを使う**

**pull your weight** ▶定義 to do your fair share of the work 自分の正当な分担分の仕事をする→**自分の役割・職分を果たす**

句動詞 **pull away (from sb/sth)** ▶定義 to start moving forward, leaving sb/sth behind ~を残して先へ動き始める→**出ていく, 発車する; ~を引き離す, もぎ取る** ∥ *We waved as the bus pulled away.* バスが発車した時, 私たちは手を振った.

**pull sth down** ▶定義 to destroy a building 建物を壊す→**~を取り壊す**

**pull in (to sth); pull into sth** ▶定義1 (used about a train) to enter a station (列車について) 駅に入る→**到着する, 駅に入る** ▶定義2 (used about a car, etc) to move to the side of the road and stop (車などについて) 道の端へ動いて止まる→**寄って止まる, (運転手が) 車を寄せる・入れる**

**pull sth off** 略式 ▶定義 to succeed in sth ~で成功する→**~をうまくやり遂げる, やってのける** ∥ *to pull off a business deal* 商取引をうまくやり遂げる

**pull out** ▶定義 (used about a car, etc) to move away to the side of the road (車などについて) 道の端から離れる→**道路に出る, 出発する** ∥ *I braked as a car suddenly pulled out in front of me.* 急に私の前に車が出てきたので, ブレーキをかけた.

**pull out (of sth)** ▶定義 (used about a train) to leave a station (列車について) 駅を去る→**駅を出る, 出発する**

**pull (sb/sth) out (of sth)** ▶定義 (to cause sb/sth) to leave sth (~が)…をやめる (原因となる)→**手を引く; ~に (仕事などから) 手を引かせる, 撤退させる** ∥ *The Americans have pulled their forces out of the area.* アメリカ軍はその地域から彼らの軍隊を撤退させた. *We've pulled out of the deal.* 私たちはその取り引きから手を引いた.

pull sth out ▶定義 to take sth out of a place suddenly or with force 突然にまたは力ずくで，〜を場所から取り出す➔〜を抜く，引き・取り出す，取り外す ‖ She walked into the bank and pulled out a gun. 彼女は銀行に入って，銃を抜いた．

pull over ▶定義 (used about a vehicle or its driver) to slow down and move to the side of the road(乗り物またはその運転者について)速度を落として道の端へ動く➔(車などが)わきに寄る，(運転者が)車を道路際に寄せる；〜を片側に寄せる ‖ I pulled over to let the ambulance past. 私は車を道端に寄せて救急車を通した．

pull through (sth) ▶定義 to survive a dangerous illness or a difficult time 危険な病気，または困難な時を切り抜けて生き残る➔切り抜ける，元気・意識を回復する；〜を切り抜ける

pull together ▶定義 to do sth or work together with other people in an organized way and without fighting 組織された方法で争うこともなく，ほかの人々と一緒に〜を行うまたは働く➔協力して働く，協力してやっていく

pull yourself together ▶定義 to control your feelings and behave in a calm way 自分の感情を制御して，穏やかな様子で振る舞う➔気を静める，しっかりする，元気を取り戻す ‖ Pull yourself together and stop crying. 落ち着いて，泣くのはやめなさい．

pull up ▶定義 (to cause a car, etc) to stop (車などが)止まる(原因となる)➔止まる；〜を止める

**pull**² /pʊl/ 名 ▶定義 1 ❶a pull (at/on sth) the action of moving sb/sth towards you using force 力を使って，〜を自分の方へ動かす行為➔引くこと，引っ張ること，引っ張り ‖ I gave a pull on the rope to check it was secure. それが安全であることを確かめるために，私はそのロープを引っ張った．▶定義 2 [単数扱い]a physical force or an attraction that makes sb/sth move in a particular direction 〜を特定の方向へ動かす，物理的な力または魅力➔引く力，引力，人を引き付ける力，魅力 ‖ the earth's gravitational pull 地球の引力 He couldn't resist the pull of the city. 彼はその町の魅力に引き付けられた．▶定義 3 [単数扱い]the act of taking a breath of smoke from a cigarette たばこを一服する行為➔(たばこの)一服

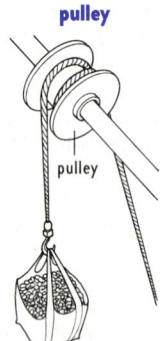
pulley

**pulley** /pʊ́li/ 名 ⓒ ▶定義 a piece of equipment, consisting of a wheel and a rope, that is used for lifting heavy things 重い物を持ち上げるために使われる，輪と縄から成る一組の装置➔滑車，ベルト車

**pullover** /pʊ́loʊvər/ 名 ⓒ ▶定義 a knitted woollen piece of clothing for the upper part of the body, with long sleeves and no buttons 体の上の部位のための，長そででボタンのない，毛糸で編まれた1着の衣服➔頭から被って着るセーター・シャツ，プルオーバー ☞参 sweater の注

**pulp** /pʌlp/ 名 ▶定義 1 [単数扱い, Ⓤ]a soft substance that is made especially by crushing sth 特に〜を押しつぶして，作られる柔らかい物質➔つぶした物，おろした物，ピューレ ‖ Mash the beans to a pulp. 豆をつぶしてピューレにしなさい．▶定義 2 Ⓤthe soft inner part of some fruits or vegetables ある種の果物または野菜の内側の柔らかい部分➔果肉，髄

**pulsate** /pʌ́lsèit, -́-/ 動⊜ ▶定義 to move or shake with strong regular movements 強い規則的な動きで動く，または振動する➔(脈などが)打つ，正しく鼓動する，振動する ‖ a pulsating rhythm 正しく鼓動している調子

**pulse**¹ /pʌls/ 名 ▶定義 1 [ⓒ, 通常は単数]the regular beating in your body as blood is pushed around it by your heart. You can feel your pulse at your wrist, neck, etc. 心臓によって血液が体のあちこちへ押し進められるときの，体の規則正しい振動．人は，自分の pulse を手首，首などで感じ取れる➔脈拍，鼓動 ‖ Your pulse rate increases after exercise. 運動の後，人の脈拍は速くなる．to feel/take sb's pulse (= to count how many times it beats in one minute) 〜の脈を取る(= 1分間に何回脈打つか数える) ▶定義 2 pulses[複数扱い] The seeds of some plants such as beans and peas that are cooked and eaten as food 食物として料理されて食べられる，例えばそら豆とえんどう豆のような，ある種の植物の種➔豆類

**pulse**[2] /pʌls/ [動][自] ▶定義 to move with strong regular movements 強い規則的な動きで動く➜**鼓動する, 脈打つ**

***pump**[1] /pʌmp/ [動] ▶定義1 [他] to force a gas or liquid to go in a particular direction 気体または液体を特定の方向に行くように強いる➜**〜をポンプで押し出す･くみ上げる･吸い出す** ‖ *Your heart pumps blood around your body.* 人の心臓は体中に血液を押し出している. ▶定義2 [自] (used about a liquid) to flow in a particular direction as if forced by a pump (液体について)ポンプの力によって強いられているかのように, 特定の方向に流れる➜**噴出する** ‖ *Blood was pumping out of the wound.* 血液が傷口から噴き出ていた. ▶定義3 [自][他] to be moved or to move sth very quickly up and down or in and out 上下に, または内外にとても素早く〜が動かされるまたは〜を動かす➜**上下に動く; 〜を上下に動かす** ‖ *He pumped his arms up and down to keep warm.* 体を暖かく保つために, 彼は腕を上下に動かした.

[句動詞] pump sth into sth/sb ▶定義 to put a lot of sth into sth/sb 多くの〜を…に入れる➜**〜をつぎ込む, 浴びせる, 〜につぎ込む** ‖ *He pumped all his savings into the business.* 彼はすべての貯金をその商売につぎ込んだ.

pump sth up ▶定義 to fill sth with air, for example by using a pump 例えばポンプを使って, 〜を空気で満たす➜**〜にポンプで空気を入れる** ‖ *to pump up a car tyre* 車のタイヤにポンプで空気を入れる

**pump**[2] /pʌmp/ [名] [C] ▶定義1 a machine that is used for forcing a gas or liquid in a particular direction 気体または液体を特定の方向へ強引に進ませるために使われる機械➜**ポンプ** ‖ *Have you got a bicycle pump?* 自転車の空気入れを持っていますか. *a petrol pump* 給油ポンプ ☛ S7 ページのさし絵 ▶定義2 [通常は複数] a flat woman's shoe with no fastening 留め具の付いていない, 平らな女性の靴➜**パンプス** ‖ *ballet pumps* ダンス用パンプス

**pumpkin** /pʌ́m(p)kən/ [名] [C] [U] ▶定義 a very large round fruit with thick orange-coloured skin that is cooked and eaten as a vegetable 野菜として調理され食べられる, 厚いオレンジ色の皮の, とても大きな丸い果物➜**カボチャ** ☛ C3 ページのさし絵

**pun** /pʌn/ [名] [C] ▶定義 an amusing use of a word that can have two meanings or of different words that sound the same 2つの意味を持つ単語の, または同じ発音をする異なる単語の, 面白い使い方➜**だじゃれ, ごろ合わせ**

**punch**[1] /pʌntʃ/ [動][他] ▶定義1 punch sb (in/on sth) to hit sb/sth hard with your closed hand (fist) 閉じられた手(こぶし)で〜を激しくたたく➜**〜にパンチ･げんこつを食らわす, 〜をこぶしで殴る** ‖ *to punch sb on the nose* 〜の鼻にパンチを食らわす *He punched the air when he heard the good news.* 良い知らせを聞いた時, 彼はげんこつで宙をたたいた. ☛ S6 ページのさし絵 ▶定義2 to make a hole in sth with a special tool (a punch) 特別な道具(穴開けばさみ)で〜に穴を開ける➜**〜に穴を開ける, パンチを入れる** ‖ *He punched a hole in the ticket.* 彼は切符に穴を開けた.

**punch**[2] /pʌntʃ/ [名] ▶定義1 [C] a hard hit with your closed hand (fist) 閉じられた手(こぶし)での強打➜**パンチ, (こぶしの)一発･一撃, 強打** ▶定義2 [C] a machine or tool that you use for making holes in sth 〜に穴を開けるために使う機械または道具➜**穴開けばさみ, 穴開け機, 穿孔(せんこう)機** ‖ *a ticket punch* 切符切りばさみ *a hole punch* 穴開け機 ☛ S4 ページのさし絵 ▶定義3 [U] a drink made from wine, fruit juice and sugar ワイン, 果汁と砂糖から作られた飲み物➜**ポンチ, パンチ**

[成句] pull your punches ⇒ **PULL**[1]

**punchline** /pʌ́ntʃlàɪn/ [名] [C] ▶定義 the last and most important words of a joke or story 冗談または話の, 最後で最も重要な言葉➜**落ち, 聞かせどころ**

**punch-up** [名] [C] [英][略式] ▶定義 a fight in which people hit each other 人々が互いにたたき合うけんか➜**殴り合い**

***punctual** /pʌ́ŋktʃuəl/ [形] ▶定義 doing sth or happening at the right time; not late 正しい時間に〜を行っている, または〜が起きている; 遅れていない➜**時間･期日厳守の, 時間･期日を守る** ‖ *It is important to be punctual for your classes.* 授業の時間を守ることは重要です.

➤電車, バスなどについては, on time (時間通り)を使い, punctual は使わない.

P

| 1300 | punctuate |

— **punctuality** /pʌŋktʃuǽləti/ 名 ⓤ ▶時間・期日厳守, きちんと〜すること, きちょうめんさ ‖ *Japanese trains are famous for their punctuality.* 日本の電車は時間厳守で有名です. — **punctually** 副 ▶時間通りに, きちんと

**punctuate** /pʌ́ŋktʃueɪt/ 動 ▶定義1 ⑯ punctuate sth (with sth) to interrupt sth many times 何度も〜の邪魔をする ➡〜を何度も中断させる・破る・遮る ‖ *Her speech was punctuated with bursts of applause.* 彼女のスピーチは拍手のあらしで何度も中断した. ▶定義2 ⒠⑯ to divide writing into sentences and phrases by adding full stops, question marks, etc ピリオド, 疑問符などを加えて, 文章を文と節に分ける ➡句読点を付ける; 〜に句読点を付ける, 〜を句読点で区切る

**punctuation** /pʌŋktʃuéɪʃ(ə)n/ 名 ⓤ ▶定義 the marks used for dividing writing into sentences and phrases 文章を文と節に分けるために使われる印 ▶句読点 ‖ *Punctuation marks include full stops, commas and question marks.* 句読点にはピリオド, コンマや疑問符が含まれる.

**puncture** /pʌ́ŋktʃər/ 名 ⓒ ▶定義 a small hole made by a sharp point, especially in a bicycle or car tyre 特に自転車または車のタイヤの, 鋭い先で作られた小さな穴 ➡パンクの穴, パンク — **puncture** 動 ⒠⑯ ➡パンクする, 穴が開く; 〜をパンク・破裂させる, 〜に穴を開ける

**pungent** /pʌ́ndʒ(ə)nt/ 形 ▶定義 (used about a smell) very strong (においについて) とても強い ➡刺激する, ぴりっとする

★**punish** /pʌ́nɪʃ/ 動 ⑯ ▶定義 punish sb (for sth/for doing sth) to make sb suffer because he/she has done sth bad or wrong 〜が悪いまたは間違った…をしたので, 〜に罰を受けさせる ➡〜を罰する, 処罰する, 懲らしめる ‖ *The children were severely punished for telling lies.* その子供たちは, うそをついたことでひどい罰を受けた.

**punishable** /pʌ́nɪʃəb(ə)l/ 形 ▶定義 punishable (by sth) (used about a crime, etc) that you can be punished for doing (犯罪行為について) 行ったために罰せられ得る ➡罰することができる, 罰すべき ‖ *a punishable offence* 罰すべき過失 *In some countries drug smuggling is punishable by death.* いくつかの国々では, 麻薬の密輸は死刑となる.

**punishing** /pʌ́nɪʃɪŋ/ 形 ▶定義 that makes you very tired or weak 人をとても疲れさせる, または弱らせる ➡へとへとに疲れさせる, 過酷な ‖ *The Prime Minister had a punishing schedule, visiting five countries in five days.* 首相は, 5日間で5か国を訪問するという, とても過酷なスケジュールだった.

★**punishment** /pʌ́nɪʃm(ə)nt/ 名 ⓒⓤ ▶定義 the action or way of punishing sb 〜を罰する行為または方法 ➡処罰, 刑罰, 懲罰 ‖ *He was excluded from school for a week as a punishment.* 罰として, 彼は1週間の自宅謹慎となった. *capital punishment* (= punishment by death) 死刑 (= 死による刑罰)

**punitive** /pjúːnətɪv/ 形 正式 ▶定義1 intended as a punishment 処罰として意図された ➡罰の, 刑罰の, 懲罰の ‖ *to take punitive measures against sb* 〜を処罰する ▶定義2 very harsh and that people find difficult to pay とても過酷で人々は支払うことが難しいと悟っている ➡(税金などが) 過酷な, 厳しい ‖ *punitive taxation* 過酷な税金

**punk** /pʌŋk/ 名 ▶定義1 ⓤ a type of loud music that was popular in Britain in the late 1970s and early 1980s. Punk deliberately tried to offend people with traditional views and behaviour. 1970年代後期から1980年代初期にイギリスではやった, 騒々しい音楽の一種. punk は伝統的な見方と振る舞いをする人々を故意に攻撃しようとした ➡パンクロック ▶定義2 ⓒ a person who likes punk music and often has brightly-coloured hair and unusual clothes punk の音楽が好きで, しばしば鮮やかな色の髪で, 異常な服装をした人 ➡パンクロックファッション愛好者, 不良, チンピラ

**puny** /pjúːni/ 形 ▶定義 very small and weak とても小さくて弱い ➡ちっぽけな, 取るに足りない, 虚弱な

**pup** /pʌp/ 名 ⓒ ▶定義1 =PUPPY ▶定義2 the young of some animals, for example seals いくつかの種の動物, 例えばアザラシの子供 ➡(キツネ・オオカミ・アザラシ・鯨などの) 子

★**pupil** /pjúːp(ə)l/ 名 ⓒ ▶定義1 a child in school 学校に通う子供 ➡生徒 ‖ *There are 28 pupils in my class.* 私のクラスには28人の生徒がいる. ▶定義2 a person who is taught artistic, musical, etc skills by an expert 芸術的, 音楽的などの技能を専門家から教わっている人 ➡弟子, 教え子

‖ *He was a pupil of Liszt.* 彼はリストの弟子だった.

➤student と比較.

▶定義3 the round black hole in the middle of your eye 目の中央にある円く黒い穴→**ひとみ, 瞳孔**

**puppet** /pʌ́pət/ 图 ⓒ ▶定義1 a model of a person or animal that you can move by pulling the strings which are tied to it or by putting your hand inside it and moving your fingers それと結ばれているひもを引っ張る,またはその内側に手を入れて指を動かすことで,動かせる人または動物の模型→**操り人形** ▶定義2 a person or organization that is controlled by sb else ほかの～に支配されている人または組織→**人の手先, 傀儡（かいらい）**‖ *The occupying forces set up a puppet government.* 占領軍は傀儡政権を据えた.

**puppy** /pʌ́pi/ (または **pup**) 图 ⓒ ( 複 **puppies**) ▶定義 a young dog 幼い犬→**子犬**

**purchase** /pə́ːrtʃəs/ 图 正式 ▶定義1 ❶the action of buying sth ～を買う行為→**購入, 買うこと**‖ *to take out a loan for the purchase of a car* 車を購入するためにローンを組む. ▶定義2 ⓒ something that you buy 人が買うもの→**購入品, 買ったもの, 買い物**‖ *These shoes were a poor purchase - they're falling apart already.* この靴は高い買い物になった － 既に壊れている. *to make a purchase* 買い物をする ― purchase 動 他 →**～を購入する, 買う**‖ *Many employees have the opportunity to purchase shares in the company they work for.* 多くの従業員は,自分たちが働いている会社の株を買うことができる.

**purchaser** /pə́ːrtʃəsər/ 图 ⓒ 正式 ▶定義 a person who buys sth ～を買う人→**購入者, 買い手**‖ *The purchaser of the house agrees to pay a deposit of 10%.* その家の購入者は,10パーセントの手付け金を払うことに同意する. ☛参 **vendor**

*★**pure** /pjʊər/ 形 ▶定義1 not mixed with anything else ほかの物が混ぜられていない→**混じり気のない, 純粋な**‖ *pure orange juice/silk/alcohol* 果汁100パーセントのオレンジジュース・絹100パーセント・アルコール100パーセント ▶定義2 clean and not containing any harmful substances 清潔でどんな害になる物質も含まれていない→**清潔な, 汚れていない, きれいな**‖ *pure air/water* きれいな空気・水 ⇔ **impure** ▶定義3 (名詞の前だけ) complete and total 完全な→**全**

## puritan 1301

**くの, 単なる**‖ *We met by pure chance.* 私たちは全く偶然に出会った. ▶定義4 (used about a sound, colour or light) very clear; perfect (音, 色, 光について) とてもきれいな; 完ぺきな→**澄んだ, 濁りのない**‖ *She was dressed in pure white.* 彼女は純白の服を着ていた. ▶定義5 (名詞の前だけ) (used about an area of learning) concerned only with increasing your knowledge rather than having practical uses (学問の領域について) 実用的な用途があるというよりも,むしろ自分の知識を増やすことのみに関心を持っている→**理論的な, 純粋の**‖ *pure mathematics* 理論数学 ⇔ **applied** ▶定義6 not doing or knowing anything evil or anything that is connected with sex 邪悪な事または性に関する事を,何もしないまたは知らない→**汚れのない, 純潔な, 高潔な**‖ *a young girl still pure in mind and body* 心も体もまだ純潔な幼い少女 ⇔ **impure**

**purée** /pjúːərei, pjɔ́ː; pjuːréi/ 图 ⓒ ⓤ ▶定義 a food that you make by cooking a fruit or vegetable and then pressing and mixing it until it is smooth and liquid フルーツまたは野菜に火を通し,それから滑らかな液体になるまでそれを押しつぶして混ぜて作られる食品→**ピューレ**‖ *apple/ tomato purée* リンゴ・トマトピューレ

**purely** /pjʊ́ərli/ 副 ▶定義 only or completely それだけまたは完全に→**全く, 単に, ただ**‖ *It's not purely a question of money.* それは単にお金の問題ではない.

**purge** /pəːrdʒ/ 動 他 ▶定義 purge sth (of sth); purge sb (from sth) to remove people that you do not want from a political party or other organization 政党またはほかの組織から,自分が不要だと思う人々を立ち退かせる→**～から一掃・粛清する, ～を追放・弾圧する** ― purge 图 ⓒ →**粛清, 追放**‖ *The General carried out a purge of his political enemies.* 将軍は,政敵の追放を実行した.

**purify** /pjʊ́ərəfài/ 動 他 (現分 **purifying**; 三単現 **purifies**; 過, 過分 **purified**) ▶定義 to remove dirty or harmful substances from sth ～から汚いまたは有害な物質を取り除く→**清める, 清潔にする, 浄化する**‖ *purified water* 浄化された水

**puritan** /pjʊ́ərət(ə)n/ 图 ⓒ ▶定義 a person who thinks that it is wrong to enjoy yourself 楽しい思いをすることは間違っていると考える人→**厳格**

な人, 禁欲的な人 — **puritan**(または **puritanical** /pjùərətǽnɪk(ə)l/) 形→禁欲的な, 厳格な, 狭量な ‖ *a puritan attitude to life* 人生への禁欲的な姿勢

**purity** /pjúərəti/ 名 Ⓤ ▶定義 the state of being pure 純粋である状態→**純粋さ, 汚れのなさ, 清浄** ‖ *to test the purity of the air* 空気の汚れを検査する ☛参 **impurity**

\***purple** /pə́ːrp(ə)l/ 形 Ⓤ ▶定義 (of) a reddish-blue colour 赤みがかった青色(の)→**紫色(の)** ‖ *His face was purple with rage.* 彼の顔は激怒で紫だった.

\***purpose** /pə́ːrpəs/ 名 ▶定義 1 Ⓒ the aim or intention of sth 〜の目的または意図→**目的, 意図, 用途** ‖ *The main purpose of this meeting is to decide what we should do next.* この会合の主な目的は, 私たちが次にすべき事を決めることです. *You may only use the telephone for business purposes.* 電話は仕事のためだけに使ってください. ▶定義 2 **purposes**[複数扱い] what is needed in a particular situation 特定の状況で必要とされるもの→**目的** ‖ *For the purposes of this demonstration, I will use model cars.* この実物宣伝をするために, 複数の模型の車を使います. ▶定義 3 Ⓤ a meaning or reason that is important to you 人にとって重要な意味または理由→**目的, 目標** ‖ *A good leader inspires people with a **sense of purpose**.* 良い指導者は人々に目的意識を抱かせる. ▶定義 4 Ⓤ the ability to plan sth and work hard to achieve it 〜を計画し, それを達成するために熱心に働く能力→**決心, 決意** ‖ *I was impressed by his **strength of purpose**.* 私は, 彼の強い決意に感服した.

成句 **to/for all intents and purposes** ⇒ **INTENT**²

**on purpose** ▶定義 not by accident; with a particular intention 偶然ではなく; 特定の意図を持って→**故意に, わざと** ‖ *'You've torn a page out of my book!' 'I'm sorry, I didn't do it on purpose.'* 「私の本から1ページ引きちぎったね」「ごめんなさい. わざとじゃなかったのです」 ☛類 **deliberately**

**purposeful** /pə́ːrpəsfʊl, -f(ə)l/ 形 ▶定義 having a definite aim or plan 明確な目的または計画を持っている→**明確な目的・意図のある, 断固とした, 決然とした** ‖ *Greg strode off down the street looking purposeful.* グレッグは明確な目的があるように, 通りを大またに歩き去った. — **purposefully** /-fʊli, -f(ə)li/ 副→**断固・決然として, 意図的に**

**purposely** /pə́ːrpəsli/ 副 ▶定義 with a particular intention 特定の意図で→**故意に, わざと, わざわざ** ‖ *I purposely waited till everyone had gone so that I could speak to you in private.* あなたと内緒で話ができるように, 皆がいなくなるまでわざわざ待っていました. ☛類 **deliberately**

**purr** /pəːr/ 動 ⓘ ▶定義 (used about a cat) to make a continuous low sound that shows pleasure (猫について)喜びを表す連続的な低い音を出す→**ゴロゴロ言う, のどを鳴らす** ☛参 **miaow**

\***purse**¹ /pəːrs/ 名 Ⓒ ▶定義 1 a small bag made of leather, etc, for carrying coins and often also paper money, used especially by women 特に女性に使用される, 硬貨としばしば紙幣をも持ち運ぶための, 皮などでできた小さい袋→**小銭入れ, がま口, 財布** ☛参 **wallet** ▶定義 2 米 = **HANDBAG** ☛ **bag** のさし絵

**purse**² /pəːrs/ 動

成句 **purse your lips** ▶定義 to press your lips together to show that you do not like sth 〜を好きではないことを表すために, 上下の唇を押し付けあう→**唇をすぼめる, 口をぎゅっと結ぶ, 口を真一文字に結ぶ**

\***pursue** /pərsjúː, -súː/ 動 他 正式 ▶定義 1 to follow sb/sth in order to catch him/her/it 捕まえるために, 〜の後に付いていく→**〜の後を追う, 〜を追跡する** ‖ *The robber ran off pursued by two policemen.* その泥棒は2人の警察官の追跡を振り切って逃げた. ☛ pursue は chase よりも正式である. ▶定義 2 to try to achieve sth or to continue to do sth over a period of time 〜を達成しようと, またはある期間にわたって〜を行い続けようと努める→**〜を追い求める, 探求する, 続行する, 〜に従事する** ‖ *to pursue a career in banking* 銀行業に従事する *She didn't seem to want to pursue the discussion so I changed the subject.* 彼女に議論を続ける気がないようだったので, 私は話を変えた.

**pursuer** /pərsjúːər, -súːər/ 名 Ⓒ ▶定義 a person who is following and trying to catch sb/sth 〜を捕まえようと後を追っている人→**追跡する人, (知識・快楽などを)追い求める人, 研究者**

**pursuit** /pərsjúːt, -súːt/ 名 ▶定義 1 Ⓤ the action of trying to achieve or get sth 〜を達成する, ま

たは得るために努める行動→**追求, 遂行, 続行** ‖ *the pursuit of pleasure* 楽しみの追求 ▶定義**2** ❹an activity that you do either for work or for pleasure 仕事または楽しみのために行う活動→**(継続する)仕事, 研究, 趣味, 娯楽** ‖ *outdoor/leisure pursuits* 戸外での・余暇のための娯楽
成句 in hot pursuit ⇒ **HOT**¹
in pursuit (of sb/sth) ▶定義 trying to catch or get sb/sth ～を捕らえる, または得るために努めている→**～を(全力で)求めて, (必死で)追って, 追求して** ‖ *He neglected his family in pursuit of his own personal ambitions.* 彼は自分自身の個人的な野心を追求して, 家族をないがしろにした.

**pus** /pʌs/ 名 ❶ ▶定義 a thick yellowish liquid that may form in a part of your body that has been hurt 人の体の傷付いた部分で作られることがある, どろっとした黄みがかった液体→**膿(うみ)**

\***push**¹ /pʊʃ/ 動 ▶定義 **1** 自他 to use force to move sb/sth forward or away from you ～を前へまたは自分から離すように動かすために, 力を使う→**～を押す, 押しやる, 押して動かす** ‖ *She pushed him into the water.* 彼女は彼を水の中に突き落とした. *to push a pram* 乳母車を押す *She pushed the door shut with her foot.* 彼女は足で扉を押して閉めた. ☛ **pull** のさし絵 ▶定義**2** 自他 to move forward by pushing sb/sth ～を押して前へ動かす→**押し進む, 突き進む** ‖ *John pushed his way through the crowd.* ジョンは群集の中を突き進んだ. *to push past sb* ～を押しのけて通る *People were **pushing and shoving** to try to get to the front.* 人々は前へ出ようとして, 押し合いへし合いしていた. ▶定義**3** 自他 to press a switch, button, etc, for example in order to start a machine 例えば機械を始動させるために, スイッチ, ボタンなどを押す→**押す; ～を押す** ‖ *Push the red button if you want the bus to stop.* もしバスを止めたければ, 赤いボタンを押してください. ▶定義**4** 他 push sb (to do sth/into doing sth); push sb (for sth) to try to make sb do sth that he/she does not want to do ～がしたいと思っていない…をその人にさせようとする→**～に強要する, 強いる, ～をせき立てて…させる** ‖ *My friend pushed me into entering the competition.* 私の友人は, 私をせき立てて試合に参加させた. *Ella will not work hard unless you push her.* あなたがせき立てない限り, エラは熱心には仕事し

ませんよ. ▶定義**5** 他 略式 to try to make sth seem attractive, for example so that people will buy it 例えば人々がそれを買うように, ～を魅力的に見せる→**～を売り込む** ‖ *They are launching a major publicity campaign to push their new product.* 彼らは新製品を売り込むために, 大々的な宣伝キャンペーンを始めている.
成句 be hard pressed/pushed/put to do sth ⇒ **HARD**²
be pushed for sth 略式 ▶定義 to not have enough of sth 十分な～を持っていない→**～が足りなくて困っている, ～が(十分に)ない** ‖ *Hurry up. We're really **pushed for time**.* 急いでください. 本当に時間が足りなくて困っているのです.
句動詞 push sb about/around ▶定義 to give orders to sb in a rude and unpleasant way 失礼で不愉快なやり方で～に命令を与える→**～をいじめる, こき使う** ‖ *Don't let your boss push you around.* 上司にこき使われないようにしなさい.
push ahead/forward (with sth) ▶定義 to continue with sth ～を続ける→**(計画などを)どんどん進める, 推進する; (困難に負けず)突き進む**
push for sth ▶定義 to try hard to get sth ～を得るために熱心に努める→**～を得ようと努める, 強く要求する** ‖ *Jim is pushing for a pay rise.* ジムは昇給を強く要求している.
push in ▶定義 to join a line of people waiting for sth by standing in front of others who were there before you 自分より早くからそこにいたほかの人々の前に立って, ～を待っている人々の列に加わる→**～が押し入る, 列に割り込む**
push on ▶定義 to continue a journey 旅行を続ける→**どんどん進む, 急ぐ, 続ける** ‖ *Although it was getting dark, we decided to push on.* 暗くなってきたが, 私たちは先を進むことに決めた.
push sb/sth over ▶定義 to make sb/sth fall down by pushing him/her/it ～を押して, 倒す→**～を押し倒す, ひっくり返す**

\***push**² /pʊʃ/ 名 ❻ ▶定義 an act of pushing 押す行為→**押すこと, 押し, 突き** ‖ *Can you help me **give** the car **a push** to get it started?* 車のエンジンをかけたいので, 車を押してもらえますか. *The car windows opened at the push of a button.* ボタンを押すと, その車の窓は開いた.
成句 at a push 略式 ▶定義 if it is really neces-

sary (but only with difficulty) もしそれが本当に必要なら(ただしやっとのことだが)→**うまくいけば,いざというときには,辛うじて** ‖ *We can get ten people round the table at a push.* うまくいけばそのテーブルに10人座れる.

**give sb the push** ▶定義 to tell sb you no longer want him/her in a relationship, or in a job 自分は友好関係においてまたは仕事において,もはや～は要らないと,その～に告げる→**～を解雇する,首にする,縁を切る**

**push-button** 形 (名詞の前だけ) ▶定義 (used about a machine, etc) that you work by pressing a button (機械などについて)ボタンを押して操作する→**押しボタン式の,(自動のため)人手の要らない,遠隔操作による** ‖ *a radio with push-button controls* 押しボタン式のラジオ

**pushchair** /pʊ́ʃtʃeər/ (囲 または **buggy**) 名 C ▶定義 a chair on wheels that you use for pushing a young child in 幼い子供を乗せて押すために使う,車輪の付いたいす→ベビーカー← **pram** のさし絵

**pusher** /pʊ́ʃər/ 名 C ▶定義 a person who sells illegal drugs 違法な麻薬を売る人→**麻薬の密売人**

**pushover** /pʊ́ʃoʊvər/ 名 C 略式 ▶定義1 something that is easy to do or win 行う,または勝つことが簡単な物事→**たやすいこと,朝飯前**
▶定義2 a person who is easy to persuade to do sth ～をするよう説き伏せることが簡単な人→**簡単に屈服する人,楽な相手**

**push-up** 米 =PRESS-UP

**pushy** /pʊ́ʃi/ 形 略式 ▶定義 (used about a person) trying hard to get what you want, in a way that seems rude (人について)欲しいものを得るために,無作法に見える方法で熱心に努めている→**押しの強い,強引な,出しゃばりの** ‖ *You need to be pushy to be successful in show business.* 芸能界で成功するためには,強引でなければならない.

*****put** /pʊt/ 動 他 (現分 **putting**; 過, 過分 **put**)
▶定義1 to move sb/sth into a particular place or position ～を特定の場所または位置へ動かす→**～を置く,据える,入れる** ‖ *She put the book on the table.* 彼女はその本をテーブルに置いた. *Did you put sugar in my tea?* 私の紅茶に砂糖を入れましたか. *When do you put the children to bed?* いつ子供たちを寝かせるのですか.
▶定義2 to fix sth to or in sth else ～をほかの…に,または…の中に固定する→**～を入れる,付ける,置く** ‖ *Can you put (= sew) a button on this shirt?* このシャツにボタンを付け(= 縫い付け)られますか. *We're going to put a picture on this wall.* 私たちは,この壁に写真を飾るつもりです.
▶定義3 to write sth ～に書く→**～を書き付ける,記入する,記す** ‖ *12.30 on Friday? I'll put it in my diary.* 金曜日の12時半ですか. 予定表に書いておきます. *What did you put for question 2?* 問題2に何と記入しましたか. ▶定義4 **put sb/sth in/into sth** to bring sb/sth into the state or condition mentioned ～を言及された状態または状況に持ってくる→**(ある状態・変化など)を(～に)もたらす,～を(仕事・行動などに)就かせる** ‖ *This sort of weather always puts me in a bad mood.* このような天気の日には,いつも私は嫌な気分になる. *I was put in charge of the project.* 私はその企画の担当を任された. *It was time to put our ideas into practice.* 私たちの考えをもう実行に移す時だった. ▶定義5 to make sb/sth feel sth or be affected by sth ～に…を感じさせる,または…によって影響を受けさせる→**(活気・考えなど)をつぎ込む,注入する,(責任・不都合など)を(～の)せいにする** ‖ *This will put pressure on them to finish the job quickly.* これは仕事を急いで終わらせるように,彼らを強いることになる. *Don't put the blame on me!* 私を責めないでください. *The new teacher soon put a stop to cheating in tests.* 新しい先生はすぐにテストでのカンニングをやめさせた. ▶定義6 to give or fix a particular value or importance to sb/sth 特定の価値または重要性を～に与える,または決定する→**～を(…と)評価する,見積もる,考える** ‖ *We'll have to put a limit on how much we spend.* 私たちが使う金額の限度を考えなければならないだろう. *I'd put him in my top five favourite writers.* 彼は私の好きな作家上位5位までに入っています. ▶定義7 to say or express sth ～を言う,または表現する→**～を言い表す,言う,述べる** ‖ *I don't know exactly how to put this, but...* 正確にはどう言ったらよいのか分かりませんが,でも... *To put it another way, you're sacked.* 言い換えると,あなたは解雇されたのです. *Put simply, he just wasn't good enough.* 簡

単に言えば、彼はそれほど良くなかったのです. 成句 **put it to sb that...** 正式 ▶定義 to suggest to sb that sth is true 〜が本当であると…に言い出す→〜に…という事実を提起する, 〜ではないかと…にただす ‖ *I put it to you that this man is innocent.* この男は潔白ではないかと, あなたにただします.

**put together**(人々または物の集団を言及する, 1つまたは複数の名詞の後で) ▶定義 combined; in total 組み合わさった; 全部で→〜を合わせる, 一緒にする ‖ *You got more presents than the rest of the family put together.* あなたは, あなた以外の家族の分を合わせたよりもたくさんプレゼントをもらいましたね.

➤ putを含むこのほかの成句については, 名詞, 形容詞などの項を参照. 例えばput an end to sthはendの項にある.

句動詞 **put sth/yourself across/over** ▶定義 to say what you want to say clearly, so that people can understand it はっきりと自分の言いたい事を言う, それで人々はそれを理解できる→〜を理解させる, 分からせる, 伝える ‖ *He didn't put his ideas across very well at the meeting.* 彼はその会合で自分の考えをきちんと伝えなかった.

**put sth aside** ▶定義 1 to save sth, especially money, to use later 〜を, 特にお金を後で使うために蓄える→〜を取っておく, 蓄える ▶定義 2 to ignore or forget sth 〜を無視するまたは忘れる→(不和・憎しみなど)を忘れる, 無視する, (事実や問題など)を一応手付かずにしておく ‖ *We agreed to put aside our differences and work together.* 私たちは意見の相違を無視して, 一緒に働くことに同意した.

**put sb away** 略式 ▶定義 to send sb to prison →〜を刑務所に入れる

**put sth away** ▶定義 1 to put sth where you usually keep it because you have finished using it 〜を使い終わったので, 普段それを保管しているところに置く→〜をしまう, 片付ける ‖ *Put the tools away if you've finished with them.* 使い終わったら, 道具を片付けなさい. ▶定義 2 to save money to spend later 後で使うために蓄える→〜を蓄える, 貯金する, 取っておく

**put sth back** ▶定義 1 to return sth to its place 〜をその場所へ返す→〜を返す, 戻す ‖ *to put books back on the shelf* 本を棚に戻す ▶定義 2 to move sth to a later time より遅い時へ〜を動かす→〜を延期する ‖ *The meeting's been put back until next week.* その会合は来週に延期された. ⇨ **bring sth forward** ▶定義 3 to change the time shown on a clock to an earlier time 時計に示されている時間を, より早い時間に変える→(時計)の針を戻す ‖ *We have to put the clocks back tonight.* 今夜, 時計の針を戻さなければならない. ⇨ **put sth forward**

**put sb/sth before/above sb/sth** ▶定義 to treat sb/sth as more important than sb/sth else 〜をほかの…より重要に扱う→〜を…より優先させる ‖ *He puts his children before anything else.* 彼には, 自分の子供たちが一番大切だ.

**put sth by** ▶定義 to save money to use later 後で使うために金を蓄える→〜を蓄える, ためておく ‖ *Her grandparents had put some money by for her wedding.* 彼女の祖父母は, 彼女の結婚式のためにお金をためていた.

**put sb down** ▶定義 1 略式 to say things to make sb seem stupid or foolish 〜がばかか間抜けに見えるようにすることを言う→〜をけなす, こき下ろす, やり込める ‖ *He's always putting his wife down.* 彼はいつも自分の妻をこき下ろしている. ▶定義 2 to put a baby to bed 赤ちゃんをベッドに置く→赤ちゃんを寝かし付ける

**put sth down** ▶定義 1 to stop holding sth and put it on the floor, a table, etc 〜を抱えているのをやめて, 床, テーブルなどに置く→〜を(下に)置く, 下ろす ‖ *The policeman persuaded him to put the gun down.* 警察官は, 彼に銃を下へ置くよう説得した. ▶定義 2 to write sth 〜を書く→〜を書き記す, 記入する ‖ *I'll put that down in my diary.* 日記にそれを書いておきます. ▶定義 3 to pay part of the cost of sth 〜の代金の一部を払う→頭金・内金として(ある金額)を払う ‖ *We put down a 10% deposit on a car.* 私たちは車の頭金として代金の10パーセントを払った. ▶定義 4 (used about a government, an army or the police) to stop sth by force (政府, 軍隊または警察について)強制的に〜を止める→(反乱など)を鎮める, (犯罪など)を取り締まる, 抑える ‖ *to put down a rebellion* 反乱を鎮圧する ▶定義 5 to kill an animal because it is old, sick or dangerous 年老いている, 病気で, または危険なので, 動物を殺す→〜を殺す, 安楽死させる ‖ *The dog was put*

## 1306　put

*down after it attacked a child.* その犬は，子供を襲ったのでその後，殺された．

put sth down to sth ▶定義 to believe that sth is caused by sth ～は…によって引き起こされたと信じる➔～を…のせいにする，～の原因・理由は…にあるとみる ‖ *I put his bad exam results down to laziness rather than a lack of ability.* 私は，彼のテストの出来の悪さは能力の欠如であるよりはむしろ怠惰にあると考える．

put yourself/sb forward ▶定義 to suggest that you or another person should be considered for a job, etc 自分または別の人がある役目などに考慮されるべきであると提案する➔(候補者などとして)～を推薦する，(人の名)を挙げる ‖ *His name was put forward for the position of chairman.* 議長として彼の名が挙がった．

put sth forward ▶定義1 to change the time shown on a clock to a later time 時計に示された時間を後の時間に変える➔(時計の)針を進ませる ‖ *We put the clocks forward in spring.* 私たちは春になると時計の針を進ませる．⇨ put sth back ▶定義2 to suggest sth ～を提案する➔(考え・案など)を提出する，提案する ‖ *She put forward a plan to help the homeless.* 彼女は，ホームレスを助ける計画を提案した．

put sth in ▶定義1 to fix equipment or furniture in position so that it can be used 使うことができるように，器具または家具を位置に固定する➔～を入れる，差し込む，取り付ける ‖ *We're having a shower put in.* 私たちはシャワーを取り付けてもらっている．☛類 install ▶定義2 to include a piece of information, etc in sth that you write 自分の書く～に情報などを含める➔(言葉)を差し挟む，付け加える ‖ *In your letter, you forgot to put in the time your plane would arrive.* 手紙の中で，あなたは飛行機の到着時間を付け加えるのを忘れましたね．▶定義3 to ask for sth officially 正式に～を頼む➔(書類・要求など)を提出する，申し立てる ‖ *to put in an invoice/request* 送り状を提出する・要求を申し立てる

put sth in; put sth into sth/into doing sth ▶定義 to spend time, etc on sth ～に時間などを費やす➔(一定の時間・労力)を費やす，注ぐ，(仕事)を行う ‖ *She puts all her time and energy into her business.* 彼女はすべての時間と労力を自分の商売に注いでいる．

put sb off (sb/sth/doing sth) ▶定義1 to make sb not like sb/sth or not want to do sth ～に…を嫌いに，または…をしたくなくさせる➔～に…への意欲・興味・集中力・食欲を失わせる，～に…する気をなくさせる ‖ *The accident put me off driving for a long time.* その事故で私は長い間，車を運転する気がなくなった．▶定義2 to say to a person that you can no longer do what you had agreed 同意した事をこれ以上はできないと，人に言う➔～を取りやめる ‖ *They were coming to stay last weekend but I had to put them off at the last moment.* 先週末，彼らは泊まりに来ることになっていたが，私は土壇場になって取りやめなければならなかった．▶定義3 to make sb unable to give his/her attention to sth ～の注意を…に向けられないようにする➔～の邪魔をして…から気をそらす，～の気を散らす，～をはぐらかす ‖ *Don't stare at me - you're putting me off!* 私をじろじろ見るな － 気が散る．

put sth off ▶定義 to turn or switch a light off 明かりを消す，または明かりのスイッチを切る➔～のスイッチを切る，消す ‖ *She put off the light and went to sleep.* 彼女は明かりを消して寝た．

put sth off; put off doing sth ▶定義 to move sth to a later time; to delay doing sth ～を後の時間へ移動させる；～を行うことを延ばす➔～を延期する，遅らせる ‖ *She put off writing her essay until the last minute.* 彼女は土壇場まで論文の執筆を延期した．

put sth on ▶定義1 to dress yourself in sth ～を着る➔～を身に着ける，着る，履く，かぶる ‖ *Put on your coat!* コートを着なさい．*I'll have to put my glasses on.* 私は眼鏡を掛けなければならない．▶定義2 to cover an area of your skin with sth ～で自分の肌を覆う➔(化粧など)をする ‖ *You'd better put some sun cream on.* 日焼け止めクリームを塗った方がいいですよ．▶定義3 to switch on a piece of electrical equipment 電気機器のスイッチを入れる➔(ラジオ・電灯など)をつける ‖ *It's too early to put the lights on yet.* まだ電灯をつけるには早すぎる．▶定義4 to make a tape, a CD, etc begin to play テープ，CDなどに演奏を始めさせる➔～をかける ‖ *Let's put some music on.* 何か音楽をかけましょう．▶定義5 to become fatter or heavier より太る，または重くなる➔(体重など)を増す ‖ *I put on weight very easily.* いとも簡単に体重が増えちゃった. ⇔ **lose** ▶定義 **6** to organize or prepare sth for people to see or use 人々が見るまたは使うために, ～を組織するまたは準備する➔**～を上演する, 催す,(列車など)を増発・増便する** ‖ *The school is putting on 'Macbeth'.* その学校は「マクベス」を上演している. *They put on extra trains in the summer.* 夏には臨時列車が増発される. ▶定義 **7** to pretend to be feeling sth; to pretend to have sth ～を感じている振りをする;～を持っている振りをする➔**～の振りをする,(～の態度)を取る** ‖ *He's not angry with you really. He's just putting it on.* 彼は本当にはあなたを怒っていませんよ. ただ振りをしているだけです.

**put sth on sth** ▶定義 **1** to add an amount of money, etc to the cost or value of sth ～の値段または価値にお金などの量を追加する➔**～に(税など)を課す, 加える** ‖ *The government want to put more tax on the price of a packet of cigarettes.* 政府はたばこ1箱の価格にもっと税金を課したいと考えている. ▶定義 **2** to bet money on sth➔**～に金をかける** ‖ *He put all his money on a horse.* 彼は有り金すべてを馬にかけた. ☛類 **bet**

**put sb out** ▶定義 **1** to give sb trouble or extra work ～に困難または余分な仕事を与える➔**～に迷惑・面倒を掛ける** ‖ *He put his hosts out by arriving very late.* 彼はひどい遅刻をして, 主催者に迷惑を掛けた. ▶定義 **2** to make sb upset or angry ～をうろたえさせるまたは怒らせる➔**～を悩ます, 怒らせる, 困らせる** ‖ *I was quite put out by their selfish behaviour.* 私は, 彼らの自分勝手な行動にとても腹が立った.

**put sth out** ▶定義 **1** to make sth stop burning ～が燃えているのを止める➔**～を消す** ‖ *to put out a fire* 火を消す ☛類 **extinguish** ▶定義 **2** to switch off a piece of electrical equipment 電気機器のスイッチを切る➔**～を消す, ～のスイッチを切る** ‖ *They put out the lights and locked the door.* 彼らは明かりを全部消してドアを施錠した. ▶定義 **3** to take sth out of your house and leave it 自分の家から～を出して, そのままにしておく➔**～を外に出す, 追い出す** ‖ *to put the rubbish out* ごみを外に出す ▶定義 **4** to give or tell the public sth, often on the television or radio or in newspapers しばしばテレビまたはラジオ, あるいは新聞で, 一般大衆に～を与えるまたは伝

**put** 1307

える➔**～を公にする, 出版する, 放送する** ‖ *The police put out a warning about the escaped prisoner.* 警察は, その脱獄囚についての警告を発表した.

**put yourself out** 略式 ▶定義 to do sth for sb, even though it brings you trouble or extra work 自分に迷惑または余分な仕事がもたらされるとしても, ～のために…をする➔**(人のために)骨を折る, 尽くす** ‖ *'I'll give you a lift home.' 'I don't want you to put yourself out. I'll take a taxi.'* 「家まで送りますよ」「お構いなく, タクシーを拾いますから」

**put sth/yourself over** ⇒ **PUT STH/YOURSELF ACROSS/OVER**

**put sb through sth** ▶定義 to make sb experience sth unpleasant ～に不愉快な…を経験させる➔**～に(苦しみなど)を経験させる**

**put sb/sth through** ▶定義 to make a telephone connection that allows sb to speak to sb ～が話し合えるように電話の接続をする➔**(～に)…の電話をつなぐ,(電話)をする** ‖ *Could you put me through to Jeanne, please?* ジーンにつないでもらえますか.

**put sth to sb** ▶定義 to suggest sth to sb; to ask sb sth ～に…を提案する;～に…を尋ねる➔**(質問・申し込み)を～にする,(問題・案など)を～に提出する** ‖ *I put the question to her.* 私は彼女に質問をした.

**put sth together** ▶定義 to build or repair sth by joining its parts together 部品を結合して～を作る, または修理する➔**～を組み立てる** ‖ *The furniture comes with instructions on how to put it together.* その家具には, 組み立て方が載った手引を付けてございます.

**put sth towards sth** ▶定義 to give money to pay part of the cost of sth ～の費用の一部を払うためのお金を与える➔**(お金)を～(の費用)に充てるために蓄える** ‖ *We all put a pound towards a leaving present for Joe.* 私たち全員が1ポンドずつをジョーへのお別れの贈り物に充てるために出した.

**put sb up** ▶定義 to give sb food and a place to stay ～に食物と滞在する場所を与える➔**～を泊まらせる, 宿泊させる** ‖ *She had missed the last train home, so I offered to put her up for the* night. 彼女は最終電車を逃してしまったので、その夜うちに泊まるように提案した.

**put sth up** ▶定義1 to lift or hold sth up 〜を持ち上げる、または掲げる→〜を上げる、(髪)を結い上げる、(掲示など)を掲げる ‖ *Put your hand up if you know the answer.* 答えが分かる人は手を上げなさい. ▶定義2 to build sth 〜を建てる→(家など)を建てる、(像など)を立てる、(テント)を張る ‖ *to put up a fence/tent* 柵(さく)を設ける・テントを張る ▶定義3 to fix sth to a wall, etc so that everyone can see it だれもがそれを見られるように、〜を壁などに固定する→(掲示物などを)張る、掛ける ‖ *to put up a notice* お知らせを張り出す ▶定義4 to increase sth 〜を増やす→(価格など)を上げる ‖ *Some shops put up their prices just before Christmas.* クリスマス直前に価格を上げる店もある.

**put up sth** ▶定義 to try to stop sb attacking you 自分を攻撃している〜を止める→(抵抗・戦いなど)を行う、続ける ‖ *The old lady put up a struggle against her attacker.* その老女は襲撃者を相手に必死に抵抗した.

**put up with sb/sth** ▶定義 to suffer sb/sth unpleasant and not complain about it 不快な〜に耐えて、不平を言わない→〜を我慢する、耐える ‖ *I don't know how they put up with this noise.* どうやって彼らがこの騒音に耐えているのか、私には分からない.

**putt** /pʌt/ 動 他 ▶定義 (used in golf) to hit the ball gently when it is near the hole (ゴルフで)ボールがホールに近いとき、そのボールを緩やかに打つ→パットを打つ、パットを決める；〜をパットする

**putty** /pʌ́ti/ 名 U ▶定義 a soft substance that is used for fixing glass into windows that becomes hard when dry 窓にガラスを固定するために使われる、乾くと硬くなる、柔らかい物質→パテ、充填(じゅうてん)剤

**puzzle**¹ /pʌ́z(ə)l/ 名 C ▶定義1 [通常は単数] something that is difficult to understand or explain; a mystery 理解するまたは説明することが難しい物事；なぞ→難問、なぞ ‖ *The reasons for his actions have remained a puzzle to historians.* 彼の行動の理由が、歴史家たちにはなぞのままになっている. ▶定義2 a game or toy that makes you think a lot 人をじっくり考えさせるゲームまたはおもちゃ→パズル、クイズ ‖ *a crossword/jigsaw puzzle* クロスワード・ジグソーパズル *I like to do puzzles.* 私はパズルをするのが好きだ.

**puzzle**² /pʌ́z(ə)l/ 動 ▶定義1 他 to make sb feel confused because he/she does not understand sth 〜が…を理解できないので、その〜を混乱させる→〜を困らせる、途方に暮れさせる ‖ *Her strange illness puzzled all the experts.* 彼女の奇病に、すべての専門家は途方に暮れた. ▶定義2 自 **puzzle over sth** to think hard about sth in order to understand or explain it 〜を理解するまたは説明するために、〜について熱心に考える→頭を悩ます、知恵を絞る ‖ *to puzzle over a mathematical problem* 数学の問題を熱心に考える

句動詞 **puzzle sth out** ▶定義 to find the answer to sth by thinking hard 熱心に考えて〜の答えを見つける→〜をじっくり考え出す、〜の解決策を考え出す、〜を解き明かす ‖ *The letter was in Italian and it took us an hour to puzzle out what it said.* その手紙はイタリア語だったので、私たちは書かれている事を解き明かすのに1時間かかった.

**puzzled** /pʌ́z(ə)ld/ 形 ▶定義 not able to understand or explain sth 〜を理解するまたは説明することができない→困惑した、途方に暮れた ‖ *a puzzled expression* 当惑した表情

★**pyjamas**(困**pajamas**) /pədʒáːməz; -dʒǽm-/ 名 [複数扱い] ▶定義 loose trousers and a loose jacket or T-shirt that you wear in bed 寝るときに着る、ゆったりしたズボンとゆったりしたジャケットまたはTシャツ→パジャマ ☞ pyjama(s なし)はほかの名詞の前で使われることに注意. *pyjama trousers* パジャマのズボン

**pylon** /páɪlən, -lən/ 名 C ▶定義 a tall metal tower that supports heavy electrical wires 重い電線を支える、高い金属の塔→(高圧線用の)鉄塔

**pyramid** /pírəmɪd/ 名 C ▶定義 a shape with a flat base and three or four sides in the shape of triangles 平らな底と、3つまたは4つの三角の形をした側面を持つ形→角錐(かくすい)、ピラミッド ☞ cube のさし絵

**python** /páɪθən, -θən/ 名 C ▶定義 a large snake that kills animals by squeezing them very hard 動物に強く巻き付いて絞め殺す、大きな蛇→ニシキヘビ

# Q q

**Q, q¹** /kjuː/ 名 C (複 **Q's**; **q's** /kjuːz/) ▶定義 the seventeenth letter of the English alphabet 英語アルファベットの第17文字→q(Q)が表す音, q(Q)の文字, q(Q)の字形のもの ‖ *'Queen' begins with (a) 'Q'.* Queen は Q で始まる.

**Q²** 略 question→質問, 問い ‖ *Qs 1-5 are compulsory.* 問いの1~5は必ず答えてください.

**qt** 略 quart(s)→クオート

**quack** /kwæk/ 名 C ▶定義 the sound that a duck makes アヒルが出す声→ガーガー, ペちゃくちゃ, がやがや — **quack** 動 自 →(アヒルなどが) ガーガー鳴く, (人が) 大声でがやがや・ペちゃくちゃしゃべる

**quadrangle** /kwάdræŋ(ə)l/ (または **quad**) 名 C ▶定義 a square open area with buildings round it in a school, college, etc 学校, 大学などの構内で建物に囲まれた四角形の空き地→中庭, **中庭を囲む建物**

**quadruple** /kwάdrʊpl, kwɑdrúːp(ə)l/ 動 自 他 ▶定義 to multiply or be multiplied by four 4倍にする, または4倍にされる→~を4倍にする, ~が4倍になる

**quaint** /kwéɪnt/ 形 ▶定義 attractive or unusual because it seems to belong to the past 過去のものと思えるために, 魅力的なまたは珍しい→**古風で趣のある, (古風・風変わりで) 面白い**

**quake** /kwéɪk/ 動 自 ▶定義 (used about a person) to shake (人について) 震える→(人が)(恐怖・寒さなどで)震える, おののく, (~に)身震いする ‖ *to quake with fear* 恐怖に震える — **quake** 名 C 略式 = EARTHQUAKE

*****qualification** /kwὰləfəkéɪʃ(ə)n/ 名 ▶定義**1** C an exam that you have passed or a course of study that you have completed 合格した試験または終了した課程→資格証明書, 免許状 ‖ *to have a teaching/nursing qualification* 教職免許・看護資格を取る *She left school at 16 with no formal qualifications.* 彼女は正式な資格証明書を取らずに16歳で学校を辞めた. ▶定義**2** C a skill or quality that you need to do a particular job 特定の仕事をするのに必要な技術または資質→(~の・~する) 資格, 技能, 適正, 条件 ‖ *Is there a height qualification for the police force?* 警官隊になるのに身長制限はありますか. ▶定義**3** C U something that limits the meaning of a general statement or makes it weaker 一般に言われている意味を制限する, またはその意味を弱めるもの→(前言などの) 修正, 緩和, 制限 ‖ *I can recommend him for the job without qualification.* 彼を無条件でその仕事に推薦します. *She accepted the proposal with only a few qualifications.* 彼女は2, 3の条件を付けただけでその提案を受け入れた. ▶定義**4** U the fact of doing what is necessary in order to be able to do a job, play in a competition, etc ある仕事をする, 競技へ出場するなどのことができるために, 必要な事をしたという事実→(職などに就くための) 資格・免許を持っていること, 出場資格を満たしていること

**qualified** /kwάləfaɪd/ 形 ▶定義**1** qualified (for sth/to do sth) having passed an exam or having the knowledge, experience, etc in order to be able to do sth ~を行うことができるために, 試験に合格している, または知識, 経験などを身に付けている→(~に・~するのに) 資格・免許を有する, 有能な, 適任の ‖ *Edward is well qualified for this job.* エドワードはまさにこの仕事にぴったりだ. *a fully qualified doctor* 十分な医師の資格を持つ医者 *I don't feel qualified to comment - I know nothing about the subject.* 私には意見を述べる資格がないと思いますーその議題に関して何も知りませんので. ▶定義**2** not complete; limited 完全ではない; 制限された→限定・修正された, 条件付きの ‖ *My boss gave only qualified approval to the plan.* 私の上司はその提案を条件付きでしか承認してくれなかった. ⇔ **unqualified**

*****qualify** /kwάləfaɪ/ 動 (現分 **qualifying**; 三単現 **qualifies**; 過, 過分 **qualified**) ▶定義**1** 自 qualify (as sth) to pass the examination that is necessary to do a particular job; to have the qualities that are necessary for sth 特定の仕事をするのに必要な試験に合格する; ~に必要な資質を持っている→(人が)(~の・~する) 資格がある, 適任である ‖ *It takes five years to qualify as a vet.* 獣医としての資格取得には5年かかります. *A cup of coffee and a sandwich doesn't really qualify as a meal.* 1杯のコーヒーとサンド

イッチ1切れでは実際には食事とは言えない. ▶定義2 🔵🔴 qualify (sb) (for sth/to do sth) to have or give sb the right to have or do sth ～を持つまたは行う権利を, 持つまたは…に与える→(～の)**資格を得る**; …に(～の, ～する, ～としての)**資格を与える, ～を適任とする** ‖ *How many years must you work to qualify for a pension?* 年金受給の資格を得るには, あなたは何年働く必要がありますか. *This exam will qualify me to teach music.* 私はこの試験に合格すれば音楽教師の資格を取れます. ▶定義3 🔵 qualify (for sth) to win the right to enter a competition or continue to the next part 競技への出場権を, または次の段階へ続く権利を勝ち取る→**予選を通過する, 勝ち抜く** ‖ *Our team has qualified for the final.* 私たちのチームは決勝戦まで勝ち残っている. ▶定義4 🔴 to limit the meaning of a general statement or make it weaker 一般に言われている意味を制限する, またはその意味を弱める→**～を(…で)修正する, 弱める, 和らげる, 制限する**

★**quality** /kwάləti/ 🔵(🔴 **qualities**) ▶定義1 [🔵, 単数扱い] how good or bad sth is ～がどのくらい良いかまたは悪いか→**質, 性質** ‖ *This paper isn't very good quality.* この紙はあまり良い質ではない. **to be of good/poor/top quality** 良い・悪い・最高級の品質である *goods of a high quality* 高品質の商品 *high-quality goods* 高品質の商品 *the **quality of life** in our cities* 私たちの都市の生活環境基準 ▶定義2 🔴a high standard or level 高い水準または程度→**良質, 上質** ‖ *Aim for quality rather than quantity in your writing.* 書く量よりもむしろ質を追求しなさい.

▶定義3 🔵something that is typical of a person or thing 人または物に特有なもの→(物・人がその物・人たるための)**特性, 本質, 属性** ‖ *Vicky has all the qualities of a good manager.* ヴィッキーは優れた経営者の特質をすべて備えた人だ.

**qualm** /kwά:m, kwɔ́:m/ 🔵[🔵, 通常は複数] ▶定義 a feeling of doubt or worry that what you are doing may not be morally right 自分のしている事が道徳的に正しくないかもしれないという疑いまたは心配の気持ち→(～についての・～の点での)**良心の呵責(かしゃく), 気のとがめ, 心配, 疑惑** ‖ *I don't have any **qualms** about asking them to lend us some money.* 私たちにいくらかお金を貸してほしいと彼らに頼むことに, 私は少しの後ろめたさも持っていない.

**quandary** /kwάnd(ə)ri/ 🔵[🔵, 通常は単数] ▶定義 a state of not being able to decide what to do; a difficult situation 何をすべきかを決めることができないでいる状態; 困難な状況→(～についての)**困惑, 当惑, 板挟み, 窮地** ‖ *I'm in a **quandary** - should I ask her or not?* 私は途方に暮れている－彼女に尋ねるべきかそれともやめるべきか.

★**quantity** /kwάntəti/ 🔵(🔴 **quantities**) 🔵🔴 ▶定義1 a number or an amount of sth ～の数または量→(～の)**分量, 数量** ‖ *Add a small quantity of salt.* 少量の塩を加えなさい. *It's cheaper to buy goods **in large quantities**.* 多量に商品を購入した方が廉価です. ▶定義2 a large number or amount of sth 多数または多量の～→**多量, 多数** ‖ *It's cheaper to buy goods **in quantity**.* 多量に商品を購入した方が廉価です. 成句 an unknown quantity ⇒ **UNKNOWN**¹

**quarantine** /kwɔ́(:)r(ə)nti:n/ 🔵🔴 ▶定義 a period of time when a person or animal that has or may have an infectious disease must be kept away from other people or animals 伝染性の病気を持つ, またはその可能性のある人または動物がほかの人または動物から隔離されなければならない期間→(伝染病予防のための)**隔離期間**

★**quarrel**¹ /kwɔ́(:)r(ə)l, kwάr-/ 🔵🔵 ▶定義1 a quarrel (about/over sth) an angry argument or disagreement 怒って口論すること, または意見が食い違うこと→(～に関する)**口論, 口げんか, 反目, 不和, 仲たがい** ‖ *We sometimes **have a quarrel** about who should do the washing-up.* 私たちはどちらが食器洗いをすべきかについて時々口論になります. 参 **argument**, **fight**²(3) ▶定義2 a quarrel with sb/sth a reason for complaining about or disagreeing with sb/sth ～について不平を言うまたは反対する理由→(～に対する)**けんか・口論の原因, 苦情** ‖ *I have no quarrel with what has just been said.* 今言われた事について何の文句もない.

★**quarrel**² /kwɔ́(:)r(ə)l, kwάr-/ 🔵(🔵 **quarrelling**; **quarrelled**: 米 **quarreling**; **quarreled**) ▶定義1 quarrel (with sb) (about/over sth) to have an angry argument or disagreement 怒って口論する, または意見が食い違う→(人と・

～のことで)口論する,けんかする,言い争う,不和になる ‖ *The children are always quarrelling!* その子供たちはいつもけんかをしている. *I don't want to quarrel with you about it.* その事についてあなたと言い争うつもりはない. ☛参 **argue**, **fight**'(4) ▶定義**2** quarrel with sth to disagree with sth ～と意見が合わない (～に対して)苦情・小言・不平・文句を言う, (～を)非難する, とがめる

**quarry**¹ /kwɔ́(ː)ri, kwɑ́ri/ 名 (複 **quarries**) ▶定義**1** ⓒa place where sand, stone, etc is dug out of the ground 地面から砂,石などが掘り出される場所→(通常,露天の)石切り場,砕石場 ☛参 **mine** ▶定義**2** [単数扱い]a person or animal that is being hunted 追われている人または狩り立てられている動物→追跡されている人,(狩りの)獲物

**quarry**² /kwɔ́(ː)ri, kwɑ́ri/ 動自他 ( 現 分 **quarrying**; 三単現 **quarries**; 過,過分 **quarried**) ▶定義 to dig, stone, sand, etc out of the ground 地面から石,砂などを掘り出す→(石を)切り出す,砕石する ‖ *to quarry for marble* 大理石を切り出す

**quart** /kwɔːrt/ 名 ⓒ (略 **qt**) ▶定義 a measure of liquid; 1.14 litres. There are 2 pints in a quart. 液体の重量の単位; 1.14リットル. 1クォートは2パイント→**クォート**

➤アメリカのクォートは0.94リットル.

\***quarter** /kwɔ́ːrtər/ 名 ▶定義**1** ⓒone of four equal parts of sth ～の4等分の1つ→**4分の1,4等分したものの1つ** ‖ *The programme lasts for three quarters of an hour.* その番組は45分間続く. *a mile and a quarter* 1と4分の1マイル *to cut an apple into quarters* リンゴを4等分に切る ▶定義**2** [単数扱い]fifteen minutes before or after every hour 毎正時15分前または後→(**毎正時前・後)15分** ‖ *I'll meet you at (a) quarter past six.* 6時15分に会いましょう. *It's (a) quarter to three.* 3時15分前です.

➤アメリカ英語では (a) quarter after および (a) quarter of と言う: *I'll meet you at (a) quarter after six.* (6時15分に会いましょう.) *It's a quarter of three.* (3時15分前です.)

▶定義**3** ⓒa period of three months 3か月の期間→**四半期,(支払等で1年を4等分した)1期,3か月** ‖ *You get a gas bill every quarter.* ガスの請求書は3か月ごとに来ます. ▶定義**4** ⓒa part of a town, especially a part where a particular group of people live 街の一部,特に特定の人々が集団で住む場所→(**都市内で特定の人々の住む)地域,～街** ‖ *the Chinese quarter of the city* その都市の中国人街 ▶定義**5** ⓒa person or group of people who may give help or information or who have certain opinions 援助または情報を提供してくれるかもしれない,またはある意見を持つ,人または集団の人々→(**援助者または情報源などを明示しないで)ある方面の人(々),その筋** ▶定義**6** ⓒ(in the US or Canada) a coin that is worth 25 cents (1/4 dollar) (米国またはカナダで)25セント硬貨 (1/4ドル)→**25セント貨,25セント** ▶定義**7** **quarters**[複数扱い]a place that is provided for people, especially soldiers, to live in 人々,特に軍人などが住むために提供された場所→**宿所,住居,宿舎,兵舎** ▶定義**8** ⓒfour ounces of sth; 1/4 of a pound 4オンスの～; 1/4ポンド→**4オンス,4分の1ポンド** ‖ *a quarter of mushrooms* 4分の1ポンドのマッシュルーム 成句 **at close quarters** ⇒ **CLOSE**³

**quarter-final** 名 ⓒ ▶定義 one of the four matches between the eight players or teams left in a competition 競技で勝ち残った8選手または8チームにより戦われる4試合のうちの1つ→**準々決勝** ☛参 **semi-final**

**quarterly** /kwɔ́ːrtərli/ 形副 ▶定義 (produced or happening)once every three months 3か月に1度(作られるまたは起こる)→**年4回(の),3か月に1度(の)** ‖ *a quarterly magazine* 季刊雑誌

**quartet** /kwɔːrtét/ 名 ⓒ ▶定義**1** four people who sing or play music together 一緒に歌うまたは音楽を演奏する4人→**カルテット(四重唱・奏団)** ▶定義**2** a piece of music for four people to sing or play together 4人が一緒に歌うまたは演奏するための曲→**四重唱・奏曲**

**quartz** /kwɔːrts/ 名 Ⓤ ▶定義 a type of hard rock that is used in making very accurate clocks or watches 非常に正確な時計または腕時計を作るのに用いられる硬質な石の一種→**石英**

**quash** /kwɒʃ, kwɔːʃ/ 動他 正式 ▶定義**1** to say that an official decision is no longer true or legal 公式な決議を,もはや真実ではないまたは

合法ではないと言う→**(判決など)を破棄・廃棄する, 無効にする** ▶定義2 to stop or defeat sth by force 〜を力ずくでやめさせる, または負かす→**(反乱など)を鎮圧する, 鎮める** ‖ *to quash a rebellion* 反乱を鎮める

**quay** /kiː, k(w)éɪ/ 名 C ▶定義 a platform where goods and passengers are loaded on and off boats 品物および乗客をボートに載せ[乗せ]たり降ろしたりするデッキ→**波止場, 埠頭(ふとう)**

**quayside** /kíːsàɪd, k(w)éɪ-/ 名 [単数扱い] ▶定義 the area of land that is near a quay 波止場に近い地域→**波止場・埠頭(ふとう)付近**

*__queen__ /kwíːn/ 名 C ▶定義1 (または **Queen**) the female ruler of a country 女性の国家元首→**女王** ‖ *Queen Elizabeth II (= the second)* 女王エリザベス2世 (= II は the second と読む) ☛参 king, prince, princess ▶定義2 (または **Queen**) the wife of a king 国王の妻→**王妃, 皇后** ▶定義3 the largest and most important female in a group of insects 昆虫の1つの群において最大で最も重要な雌→**女王バチ・アリ** ‖ *the queen bee* 女王バチ ▶定義4 one of the four playing cards in a pack with a picture of a queen 女王の絵がかいてある, 4枚一組になったカードの1枚→**(トランプ)クイーンの札** ‖ *queen of hearts* ハートのクイーン ☛参 **card** の注とさし絵 ▶定義5 (in chess) the most powerful piece, that can move any distance and in all directions (チェスで)最も強い駒(こま)で, いくつでもまたどの方向にでも移動できる→**(チェス)クイーン**

**quell** /kwel/ 動 他 正式 ▶定義 to end sth 〜を終らせる →**(反乱など)を鎮圧する, (恐怖・感情など)を抑える, 和らげる**

**quench** /kwentʃ/ 動 他 ▶定義 to satisfy your feeling of thirst by drinking liquid 液体を飲んでのどの渇きをいやす→**(渇き)を(〜で)いやす** ‖ *He drank some juice to quench his thirst.* 彼はのどの渇きをいやすためにジュースをいくらか飲んだ.

**query** /kwíəri/ 名 C (複 **queries**) ▶定義 a question, especially one asking for information or expressing a doubt about sth 質問, 特に〜についての情報を求めるものまたは疑問を表現するもの→**質問, 疑問** ‖ *Does anyone have any queries?* だれか質問のある人はいますか. ― **query** 動 他 (現分 querying; 三単現 queries; 過, 過分 queried)→**〜を尋ねる, 質問する, 疑う** ‖ *We queried the bill but were told it was correct.* 私たちはその請求書を疑ったが, 正しいと言われた.

**quest** /kwest/ 名 C 正式 ▶定義 a long search for sth that is difficult to find 見つけるのが難しい〜を長い間探し求めること→**(〜の)探求, 探索, 追求** ‖ *the quest for happiness/knowledge/truth* 幸福・知識・真実の追求

*__question__¹ /kwéstʃ(ə)n/ 名 ▶定義1 C a question (about/on sth) a sentence or phrase that asks for an answer 答えを求める文章または句→**質問, 問い** ‖ *Put up your hand if you want to ask a question.* 質問をしたいなら手を上げなさい. *In the examination, you must answer five questions in one hour.* 試験では1時間で5つの問いに答えなければならない. *What's the answer to Question 5?* 問い5の答えは何ですか. ▶定義2 C a problem or difficulty that needs to be discussed or dealt with 議論または処理されねばならない問題または困難→**(〜の・〜かという)(解決すべき)問題, 論点** ‖ *The resignations raise the question of who will take over.* 辞任には後継者問題が必ず起きる. *The question is, how are we going to raise the money?* 問題はいかに資金を集めるかということだ. ▶定義3 U doubt or uncertainty 疑いまたは不確実性→**(〜についての・〜という)疑問, 疑い, 疑義, (〜の)可能性** ‖ *There is no question about Brenda's enthusiasm for the job.* ブレンダがその仕事に情熱を持っていることは疑う余地がない. *His honesty is beyond question.* 彼の正直さは疑問の余地がない. *The results of the report were accepted without question.* その報告結果は異議なく認められた.

成句 **(be) a question of sth/of doing sth** ▶定義 a situation in which sth is needed 〜が必要とされる状況→**(〜の)問題, 事柄** ‖ *It's not difficult - it's just a question of finding the time to do it.* それは難しくはない―ただそれを行う時間を見つけるのが問題なだけだ.

**in question** ▶定義 that is being considered or talked about それについて検討されている, または話されている→**問題の, 当の, 論争・審議中の** ‖ *The lawyer asked where she was on the* night in question. 弁護士は、問題の夜に彼女がどこにいたのかと尋ねた.

no question of ▶定義 no possibility of 〜の可能性がない→〜のようなことはない,論外である ‖ There is no question of him leaving hospital yet. 彼が退院するようなことはまだないはずだ.

out of question ▶定義 impossible 不可能な→問題にならない,全く不可能だ ‖ A new car is out of the question. It's just too expensive. 新車は問題になりません.とにかく高価すぎます.

★**question**[2] /kwéstʃ(ə)n/ 動他 ▶定義 **1** question sb (about/on sth) to ask sb a question or questions 〜に1つまたはいくつかの質問をする→〜に(…について)質問する,問う,(証人など)を尋問する ‖ The police questioned him for several hours. 警察は数時間にわたり彼を尋問した. ▶定義 **2** to express or feel doubt about sth 〜について疑問を示す,または疑問を感じる→〜を疑う,〜に質疑を差し挟む,〜に異議を唱える,(〜かどうか)を疑う ‖ She told me she was from the council so I didn't question her right to be there. 彼女が私に評議会のものだと言ったので,彼女がそこにいる権利について私は疑問を持たなかった. to question sb's sincerity/honesty 〜の誠実さ・正直さを疑う

**questionable** /kwéstʃ(ə)nəb(ə)l/ 形 ▶定義 **1** that you have doubts about; not certain 〜について疑問を持っている;不確実な→**疑わしい,疑問の余地のある,不確かな** ‖ It's questionable whether we'll be able to finish in time. 私たちが時間内に終えることができるかどうかは疑問です. ▶定義 **2** likely to be dishonest or morally wrong 不正直である,または道徳的に間違っていると思われる→**いかがわしい,不審な,信用のおけない** ‖ questionable motives いかがわしい動機 ⇔ unquestionable

**question mark** 名 C ▶定義 the sign (?) that you use when you write a question 疑問文を書く時に使う,「?」のマーク→**疑問符**

**questionnaire** /kwèstʃənéər/ 名 C ▶定義 a list of questions that are answered by many people. A questionnaire is used to collect information about a particular subject. 多くの人々によって回答される,質問のリスト.ある特定の議題に関する情報を収集するのに用いられる→**アンケート,アンケート用紙,質問票** ‖ to complete/fill in a questionnaire アンケートに答える・記入する

**question tag** (または **tag**) 名 C ▶定義 a short phrase such as 'isn't it?' or 'did you?' at the end of a sentence that changes it into a question and is often used to ask sb to agree with you 文末にある isn't it? または did you? のような短い句で,その文章を疑問文に変え,そしてしばしば〜に同意を求めるために使われる→**付加疑問**

★**queue** /kju:/ (米 **line**) 名 C ▶定義 a line of people, cars, etc that are waiting for sth or to do sth 〜が変わるのを,または〜をするために待っている,一列になった人々,車など→**(順番を待つ人・車などの)列** ‖ We had to **wait in a queue** for hours to get tickets. 私たちはチケットを手に入れるため,何時間も並んで待たなければならなかった. to **join** the end of **a queue** 列の最後尾に付く We were told to **form a queue** outside the doors. 私たちはドアの外に一列に並ぶように言われた. ―queue 動 自 queue (up) (for sth)→**(〜を求めて・〜するために)列を作る,列に並ぶ** ‖ to queue for a bus 並んでバスを待つ

成句 jump the queue ⇒ **JUMP**[1]

**quiche** /ki:ʃ/ 名 C U ▶定義 a type of food made of pastry filled with a mixture of eggs and milk with cheese, onion, etc and cooked in the oven. You can eat quiche hot or cold. ペーストリーの生地で作られた食べ物の一種で,中にチーズ,タマネギなどの入った,卵と牛乳を混ぜたものを入れてオーブンで焼いたもの.温かいうちでもまた冷めても食べられる→**キッシュ** ☛ C4 ページのさし絵

★**quick**[1] /kwɪk/ 形 ▶定義 **1** done with speed; taking or lasting a short time 速く行われる;短時間でできる,または短時間継続する→**(動作・行動などが)速い,素早い,迅速な,機敏な** ‖ May I make a quick telephone call? ちょっと電話をかけてもよろしいですか. This dish is quick and easy to make. この料理は手早く簡単に作れます. His quick thinking saved her life. 彼の素早い判断が彼女の命を救った. We need to make a quick decision. 私たちは迅速な決定をする必要がある. ▶定義 **2** quick (to do sth)

## quick²

doing sth at speed or in a short time ～を早くまたは短時間でする→(～するのが)早くて[速くて], 早く[速く]～する ‖ *It's quicker to travel by train.* 列車で旅行する方が早い. *Nicola is a quick worker.* ニコラは仕事をするのが速い. *She was quick to point out all the mistakes I had made.* 彼女は, 私がした間違いをすべて素早く指摘した.

▶かなりの速さで動くまたは動ける人または物を表現するのには fast がより頻繁に使われる: *a fast horse/car/runner* (駿足(しゅんそく)の馬・高速で走る車・駿足の走者(ランナー)). 短時間でなされる事を表すには quick がより頻繁に使われる: *a quick decision/visit* (素早い決定・短時間の訪問)

▶定義3 used to form compound adjectives 複合形容詞を作るために用いて→速い～‖ *quick-thinking* 素早い思考 *quick-drying paint* 速乾性の塗料

成句 **(as) quick as a flash** ▶定義 very quickly 非常に早く→あっと言う間に, 電光石火のように ‖ *Quick as a flash, he grabbed my money and ran.* あっと言う間に, 彼は私のお金をつかんで走り去った.

**quick/slow on the uptake** ⇒ **UPTAKE**

**quick²** /kwɪk/ 副 略式 ▶定義 quickly 素早く→速く, 素早く, 迅速に ‖ *Come over here quick!* 速くここに来なさい.

*★**quickly*** /kwíkli/ 副 ▶定義 fast; in a short time 速く; 短時間で→速く, 急いで, すぐに, 敏速に ‖ *He quickly undressed and got into bed.* 彼は急いで服を脱いでベッドに入った. *I'd like you to get here as quickly as possible.* あなたに一刻も早くここに来てほしい.

**quid** /kwɪd/ 名 C (複 quid) 英 略式 ▶定義 a pound (in money); £1 (お金で)→1ポンド ‖ *Can you lend me a couple of quid until tomorrow?* 明日まで私に2, 3ポンド貸してくれないか.

*★**quiet¹*** /kwáɪət/ 形 ▶定義1 with very little or no noise ほとんどまたは全く騒音がない→(動き・音がなく)静かな, 音を立てない ‖ *Be quiet!* 静かになさい. *His voice was quiet but firm.* 彼の声は静かだがしっかりしていた. *Go into the library if you want to work. It's much quieter in there.* 勉強したいなら図書館に行きなさい. あそこならずっと静かですよ. ⇔ **loud** ▶定義2 without much activity or many people あまり活気がない, またはあまり大勢の人がいない→ひっそりした, 穏やかな, じっとしている, 閑静な ‖ *The streets are very quiet on Sundays.* その通りは日曜日にはとてもひっそりしている. *Business is quiet at this time of year.* 1年のこの時期は商売に活気がない. *a quiet country village* 閑静な田舎町 *We lead a quiet life.* 私たちは静かな生活を送っている. ▶定義3 (used about a person) not talking very much (人について)あまり多くを話さない→(人・態度・言葉などが)控えめな, 物静かな, おとなしい, 無口な ‖ *You're very quiet today. Is anything wrong?* 今日は随分おとなしいですね. どこか具合が悪いのですか. *He's very quiet and shy.* 彼は非常に無口で恥ずかしがりやだ.
— **quietly** 副 →静かに, そっと ‖ *Try and shut the door quietly!* 扉を静かに閉めるようになさい. — **quietness** 名 U →静けさ, 静寂, 落ち着き, 平穏

成句 **keep quiet about sth; keep sth quiet** ▶定義 to say nothing about sth ～について何も言わない→(物事を)内緒にしておく ‖ *Would you keep quiet about me leaving until I've told the boss?* 私から上司に話をするまでは, 私が辞めることを内密にしておいてくださいね.

**quiet²** /kwáɪət/ 名 U ▶定義 the state of being calm and without much noise or activity 静かで, あまり物音や活動がない状態→静けさ, 静寂, 閑静, (心の)平静, 安らか ‖ *the peace and quiet of the countryside* 田舎の平和と静けさ

成句 **on the quiet** ▶定義 secretly 秘密にして→ひそかに, こっそりと, 内密に ‖ *She's given up smoking but she still has an occasional cigarette on the quiet.* 彼女は喫煙をやめたが, まだこっそりと時々たばこを吸うことがある.

**quieten** /kwáɪət(ə)n/ 動 他 ▶定義 to make sb/sth quiet ～を静かにさせる→～を静める

句動詞 **quieten (sb/sth) down** ▶定義 to become quiet or to make sb/sth quiet 静かになる, または～を静かにさせる→静まる, ～を静める ‖ *When you've quietened down, I'll tell you what happened.* あなたが落ち着いたら, 起こった事をお話しましょう.

**quilt** /kwɪlt/ 名 C ▶定義 a cover for a bed that has a thick warm material, for example feathers, inside it 例えば羽毛などが中に入った，厚く暖かな生地でできたベッドカバー→（一般に厚手の）ベッドカバー，キルト，キルト風に仕上げたもの ☞ duvet

**quintet** /kwɪntét/ 名 ⓒ ▶定義1 a group of five people who sing or play music together 一緒に歌うまたは演奏する5人の人々の集まり→五重唱・五重奏団 ▶定義2 a piece of music for five people to sing or play together 5人の人々が一緒に歌うまたは演奏するための曲→五重唱・五重奏曲

**quirk** /kwə:rk/ 名 ⓒ ▶定義1 an aspect of sb's character or behaviour that is strange 〜の性格または行動の奇妙な面→奇行，気まぐれ，癖 ‖ You'll soon get used to the boss's little quirks. 上司のちょっとした癖にはすぐ慣れるでしょう. ▶定義2 a strange thing that happens by chance たまたま起きる不思議なこと→（運命などの）急転，急変，巡り合わせ ‖ By a strange **quirk of fate** they met again several years later. 運命の不思議な巡り合わせで彼らは数年後に再会した. — quirky 形→気まぐれな，奇妙な，風変わりな ‖ Some people don't like his quirky sense of humour. 彼の風変わりなユーモアのセンスを好ましく思っていない人がいる.

**quit** /kwɪt/ 動 (現分 **quitting**; 過，過分 **quit**) ▶定義1 自他 **quit (as sth)** to leave a job, etc or to go away from a place 仕事などを辞める，またはある場所から立ち去る→辞職する，立ち退く；（仕事など）を辞める，（人・場所）を去る ‖ She quit as manager of the volleyball team. 彼女はバレーボールチームのマネージャーを辞めた. ▶定義2 他 特に 困略式 to stop doing sth 〜をするのをやめる→〜することをやめる，中止する ‖ to quit smoking 禁煙する ▶定義3 自他 (computing) to close a computer program （コンピューター）→（コンピューターの）プログラムを閉じる

*****quite** /kwáɪt/ 副 ▶定義1 not very; to a certain degree; rather あまり〜ない；ある程度まで；むしろ→かなり，なかなか，まあまあ，ほどほどに，多少 ‖ The film's quite good. その映画はなかなか良い. It's quite a good film. それはなかなか良い映画です. I quite enjoy cooking. 私はほどほどに料理を楽しんでいる. They had to wait quite a long time. 彼らはかなり長時間待たなければならなかった. It's quite cold today. 今日はかなり寒い. We still meet up quite often. 私たちは今でもかなり頻繁に会っています. ☞参 **rather** の注 ▶定義2 (used for emphasizing sth) completely; very (〜を強調するために用いて) 完全に；とても→全く，完全に，すっかり ‖ Are you quite sure you don't mind? 本当に構わないのですか. I quite agree - you're quite right. 全く同感です — あなたのおっしゃる通りです. To my surprise, the room was quite empty. 驚いたことに，その部屋は全くもぬけの殻だった. ▶定義3 used for showing that you agree with or understand sth 〜に同意する，または〜を理解することを示すのに用いて→全くその通り

成句 **not quite** ▶定義 used for showing that there is almost enough of sth, or that it is almost suitable 〜がほぼ十分にある，またはほぼ適していることを示すのに用いて→それほどでもない，必ずしも〜というわけではない，完全には〜ではない ‖ There's not quite enough bread for breakfast. 朝食に十分なほどのパンはない. These shoes don't quite fit. この靴は完全にぴったりだというわけではない.

**quite a** ▶定義 used for showing that sth is unusual 〜が普通でないことを示すのに用いて→実際に(良い)〜，本当に(すばらしい)〜，並外れて〜 ‖ It's quite a climb to the top of the hill. 丘の頂上まではかなりの登り坂です.

**quite a few; quite a lot (of)** ▶定義 a fairly large amount or number かなり多量のまたは多数の→かなり多量(の〜)，かなり多数(の〜) ‖ We've received quite a few enquiries. 私たちはかなりたくさんの引き合いを受けた.

**quite enough** ▶定義 used for emphasizing that no more of sth is wanted or needed 〜をもうこれ以上欲しくない，または必要ないと強調するのに用いて→十分すぎるほど(ある) ‖ I've had quite enough of listening to you two arguing! 私はあなた方2人の口論をもう聞き飽きた. That's quite enough wine, thanks. もう十分にワインを頂きました.

> ▶語法
>
> quite, rather, pretty などの違い
>
> 　意味の強さは，rather/pretty > quite > fairly の順です．また rather は It's rather cold.

(結構寒いね)のように、どちらかというと否定的な語と共に使ったり、This book is rather interesting.(この本、割と面白いよ)のように「期待以上に」の含みを持つことがあります。

**quits** /kwɪts/ 形
成句 **be quits (with sb)** 略式 ▶定義 if two people are quits, it means that neither of them owes the other anything 2人の人がbe quitsならば、どちらもお互いに貸し借りなしということを意味する → (返済・仕返しなどによって)五分五分で、あいこで ‖ *You buy me a drink and then we're quits.* 君が私に飲み物を1杯おごってくれれば、おあいこだ.

**quiver** /kwívər/ 動自 ▶定義 to shake slightly; tremble わずかに揺れる; 振動する → (人・葉・翼・声・光などが)(〜で・〜などに)ぶるぶる震える, 揺れる ‖ *to quiver with rage/excitement/fear* 怒り・興奮・恐怖に震える

**quiz**¹ /kwɪz/ 名 C (複 **quizzes**) ▶定義 a game or competition in which you have to answer questions 質問に答えなければならないゲームまたは競技→簡単な口頭・筆記のテスト・試問, (ラジオ・テレビの)クイズ ‖ *a quiz programme on TV* テレビのクイズ番組 *a general knowledge quiz* 一般教養クイズ

**quiz**² /kwɪz/ (三単現 **quizzes**; 現分 **quizzing**; 過 **quizzed**) 動他 ▶定義 to ask sb a lot of questions in order to get information 情報を得るために〜にたくさんの質問をする→〜に(…について)(繰り返し)質問・尋問する

**quizzical** /kwízɪk(ə)l/ 形 ▶定義 (used about a look, smile, etc) seeming to ask a question (様子, 笑いなどについて)質問をするように見える→(表情・笑いが)尋ねるような, いぶかしげな, まごついた, からかうような — **quizzically** /-k(ə)li/ 副→いぶかしげに, からかうように

**quorum** /kwɔ́ːrəm/ 名 [単数扱い] ▶定義 the smallest number of people that must be at a meeting before it can make official decisions 公式決定を行う前に、会議に出席していなければならない最低限の人数→(議決のために必要な)定足数, 定員

**quota** /kwóʊtə/ 名 C ▶定義 the number or amount of sth that is allowed or that you must do 許可される, または行わねばならない〜の数または量 → (生産・販売・輸出入などの)割り当て(量), (入学・移民などの)割り当て(人)数 ‖ *We have a fixed quota of work to get through each day.* 私たちは毎日こなさねばならない仕事の一定の割り当てがあります.

**quotation** /kwoʊtéɪʃ(ə)n/ ( または 略式 **quote**) 名 C ▶定義1 a phrase from a book, speech, play, etc, that sb repeats because it is interesting or useful 興味深いまたは役に立つという理由で〜が繰り返し言う, 本, 演説, 演劇などからの句→引用, 引用文, 引用句 ‖ *a quotation from Shakespeare* シェークスピアからの引用句 ▶定義2 a statement that says how much a piece of work will probably cost 1つの仕事にどのくらいの費用がかかるかを述べた計算書→見積額, 見積書, 価格表 ‖ *You should get quotations from three different builders.* 3つの異なる建築業者から見積もりを取るべきです.
☛参 **estimate**

**quotation marks** ( または 略式 **quotes** 英 または **inverted commas**) 名 [複数扱い] ▶定義 the signs ('...') or ("...") that you put around a word, a sentence, etc to show that it is what sb said or wrote, that it is a title or that you are using it in a special way '...' または "..." の記号で語句, 文章などを囲んで付けることにより, それを〜が言ったものまたは書いたものである, それが題名である, または特別な方法で用いている, ということを示す→引用符

**quote** /kwóʊt/ 動 ▶定義1 自他 **quote (sth) (from sb/sth)** to repeat exactly sth that sb else has said or written before ほかの〜が以前言ったまたは書いた…をそっくり繰り返す → (人が)(人の言葉・文章)を(〜から)引用する, 引き合いに出す, 人の言葉・文句を(〜から)引用する ‖ *The minister asked the newspaper not to quote him.* 大臣は, その新聞社に彼のことを引き合いに出さないよう依頼した. ▶定義2 他 to give sth as an example to support what you are saying 自分が言っている事を裏付けるために, 〜を例として挙げる→(実例・典拠など)を示す, 持ち出す ▶定義3 他 to say what the cost of a piece of work, etc will probably be 1つの仕事などの費用がいくらくらいかかるかを言う→(値段)を言う, (商品など)に(値段)を付ける

# R r

**R, r**¹ /ɑːr/ 名 C (複 **R's; r's**) ▶定義 the eighteenth letter of the English alphabet 英語アルファベットの第18文字→r(R)が表す音, r(R)の文字, r(R)の字形のもの ‖ *'Rabbit' begins with an 'R'.* RabbitはRで始まる.

**R**² 略 river→川, 〜川 ‖ *R Thames* テムズ川

**rabbi** /rǽbaɪ/ 名 C (複 **rabbis**) ▶定義 a Jewish religious leader and teacher of Jewish law ユダヤ教の宗教的指導者およびユダヤ律法の教師→**ラビ, ユダヤ教牧師, 律法博士, 先生**

hare / rabbit

*****rabbit** /rǽbət/ 名 C ▶定義 a small animal with long ears 長い耳を持つ小さな動物→**飼いウサギ, (一般的に)ウサギ** ‖ *a wild rabbit* 野生のウサギ / *a rabbit hutch* (= *a cage for rabbits*) ウサギ小屋 (= ウサギを飼う囲い)
▶ rabbit の幼児語は bunny (うさぎちゃん).

**rabble** /rǽb(ə)l/ 名 C ▶定義 a noisy crowd of people who are or may become violent 暴徒化した, または暴徒化しそうな, 騒いでいる大勢の人々→**やじ馬, 暴徒, 暴民**

**rabies** /réɪbiːz/ 名 U ▶定義 a very dangerous disease that a person can get if he/she is bitten by an animal that has the disease その病気にかかった動物にかまれると, かまれた人もかかることがある, 非常に危険な病気→**狂犬病, 恐水病**

**RAC** /ɑ̀ːr eɪ síː/ 略 英 the Royal Automobile Club ▶定義 an organization for motorists. If you are a member of the RAC and your car breaks down, you can phone them and they will send sb to help you. 自動車の運転者のための組織. RAC の会員の車が故障した場合は, 電話で連絡すると救援の人を派遣してくれる→**英国自動車クラブ**

*****race**¹ /réɪs/ 名 ▶定義1 C a race (against/with sb/sth); a race for sth/to do sth a competition between people, animals, cars etc to see which is the fastest or to see which can achieve sth first どれが一番速いか, またはどれが〜を最初に成し遂げることができるかを見るための, 人, 動物, 車などの競走→**(〜との・〜間の)競走, レース, (〜のための・〜との)競争, 争い** ‖ *to run/win/lose a race* 競走する・競走に勝つ・競走に負ける / *to come first/second/last in a race* レースで1着・2着・最下位になる / *the race for the presidency* 大統領選挙戦 / *the race to find a cure for Aids* エイズの治療法を見つける競争 / *Rescuing victims of the earthquake is now **a race against time**.* その地震の犠牲者の救助は今や時間との戦いです. ▶定義2 **the races** [複数扱い] 英 an occasion when a number of horse races are held in one place 1箇所で競馬がいくつも実施される催し→**競馬, 競馬の開催**
▶ 英国では, 競馬やドッグレースに出掛けるのがとても一般的である. そこでは bookie (私設馬券屋)を使ってレースの結果に bet (かける)ことが多い.

▶定義3 C U one of the groups into which people can be divided according to the colour of their skin, their hair type, the shape of their face, etc 皮膚の色, 毛髪の種類, 顔の形などによって分類された人の集団→**人種** ☞参 human race ▶定義4 C a group of people who have the same language, customs, history, etc 同じ言語, 慣習, 歴史などを持つ人々の集団→**民族**

成句 the rat race ⇒ **RAT**

*****race**² /réɪs/ 動 ▶定義1 C U race (against/with) (sb/sth) to have a competition with sb/sth to find out who is the fastest or to see who can do sth first だれが一番速いか, またはだれが〜を最初に行うことができるかを見るために, …と競争する→**〜と競走する, 競争する** ‖ *I'll race you home.* 家まで競走しよう. ▶定義2 C U to go very fast or to move sb/sth very fast 大急ぎで行く, または〜を非常に速く動かす→**速く走る, 全速力で行く, 疾走する; 〜を大急ぎで運ぶ, 急がせる** ‖ *We raced up the stairs.* 私たちは階段を駆け上がった. *The child had to be raced to hospital.* その子は大急ぎで病院に運ぶ必要があった. ▶定義3 U to make an animal or a vehicle take part in a race 動物または乗り物をレースに

出場させる→～を…と競走させる，～に出す，出走させる

**racecourse** /réɪskɔ̀ːrs/ ( 米 **racetrack**) 名 C
▶定義 a place where horse races take place 競馬が開催される場所→**競馬場，競走場**

**racehorse** /réɪshɔ̀ːrs/ 名 C ▶定義 a horse that is trained to run in races レースで走るよう訓練された馬→**(競馬の)競走馬**

**race relations** 名 [複数扱い] ▶定義 the relations between people of different races who live in the same town, area, etc 同じ町，地域などに住む，異なる人種の人々との関係→**人種関係，人種間関係，異民族関係**

**racial** /réɪʃ(ə)l/ 形 ▶定義 connected with people's race; happening between people of different races 人種に関連した; 異なる人種の人々の間に起こっている→**人種の，人種的な，民族の，種族の** ‖ *racial tension/discrimination* 人種間の緊張・人種差別 — **racially** /-ʃ(ə)li/ 副 ▶**人種上，人種的に見て，民族的に見て** ‖ *a racially mixed school* さまざまな人種の生徒から成る学校

\***racing** /réɪsɪŋ/ 名 U ▶定義1 = HORSE RACING ▶定義2 the sport of taking part in races レースを行うスポーツ→**競走，競漕（きょうそう）** ‖ *motor racing* 自動車レース *a racing driver/car* レーシングドライバー・レーシングカー

**racism** /réɪsɪz(ə)m/ 名 U ▶定義 the belief that some races of people are better than others; unfair ways of treating people that show this belief ある人種がほかの人種よりも優れているという信念; この信念を表すような，人々に対する不公平な扱い方→**人種主義，民族主義，人種差別，人種的偏見** ‖ *to take measures to combat racism* 人種差別をなくすための施策をとる — **racist** /réɪsɪst/ 名 C ▶**人種差別主義者，民族主義者** — **racist** /réɪsɪst/ 形 ▶**人種差別的な，人種的偏見に基づく，人種差別主義者の，民族主義者の** ‖ *He's a racist.* 彼は人種差別主義者だ．*racist beliefs/views/remarks* 人種差別的な信念・見解・意見

**rack**[1] /ræk/ 名 C (しばしば複合語で) ▶定義 a piece of equipment, usually made of bars, that you can put things in or on 中や上に物を入れたり載せたりできる設備→**～掛け，ラック，置き棚，～棚** ‖ *I got on the train and put my bags up in the luggage*

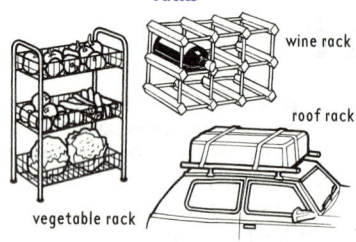

**racks**
wine rack
roof rack
vegetable rack

*rack.* 私は列車に乗り，バッグを荷物棚に載せた．*We need a roof rack on the car for all this luggage.* これだけの荷物を全部積むには，車にルーフラックが必要です．

成句 **go to rack and ruin** ▶定義 to be in or get into a bad state because of a lack of care 手入れを欠いたために悪い状態にある，または陥る→**荒廃する，破滅する，荒れ果てる，悪くなる**

**rack**[2] /ræk/ 動

成句 **rack your brains** ▶定義 to try hard to think of sth or remember sth ～について考えようと，または思い出そうと懸命に努力する→**知恵を絞る，懸命に思い出そうとする，腐心する，考え抜く**

**racket** /rǽkɪt/ 名 ▶定義1 [単数扱い] 略式 a loud noise 大きな騒音→**(迷惑なほどの)大騒ぎ，騒音** ‖ *Stop making that terrible racket!* そんなにひどい大騒ぎをするのはやめてくれ．▶定義2 C an illegal way of making money 違法な金もうけ→**不正な金もうけ，ゆすり，詐欺，横領，脅迫** ‖ *a drugs racket* 麻薬の密売 ▶定義3 (または **racquet**) C a piece of sports equipment that you use to hit the ball with in sports such as tennis and badminton テニスやバドミントンなどのスポーツで，ボールを打つ運動用具→**(テニス・バドミントン・卓球などの)ラケット**

▶ racket（ラケット）は strings（ガット）が張ってある点で，bats（バット）とは異なる．

☛ S1ページのさし絵

**radar** /réɪdɑ̀ːr, -dər/ 名 U ▶定義 a system that uses radio waves for finding the position of moving objects, for example ships and planes 船や飛行機のような動いている物体の位置を知るために，電波を用いるシステム→**レーダー，電波探知法，レーダー装置，電波探知機** ‖ *This plane is hard to detect by radar.* この飛行機はレーダーで探知されにくい．

**radiant** /réɪdi(ə)nt/ 形 ▶定義1 showing great

happiness 大きな喜びを表している➜(人·表情が) (〜で) 晴れやかな, うれしそうな, 輝いた, にこやかな ‖ *a radiant smile* 晴れやかな笑顔 ▶定義2 sending out light or heat 光または熱を放っている➜光を放つ, 熱を放つ, きらきらと輝く, 放射する ‖ *the radiant heat/energy of the sun* 太陽の輻射 (ふくしゃ) 熱·太陽の放射エネルギー

**radiate** /réɪdièɪt/ [動] ▶定義1 [他] (used about people) to clearly show a particular quality or emotion in your appearance or behaviour (人々について) 外見または振る舞いに特定の性質または感情をはっきりと表す➜(喜びなど)をまき散らす, 発散させる, (主義など)を広める, (影響など)を広く及ぼす ‖ *She radiated self-confidence in the interview.* 彼女はインタビューにおいて自信に満ちあふれていた. ▶定義2 [他] to send out light or heat 光または熱を放つ➜(光·熱など)を放射する, 放出する, 発する, 照らす ▶定義3 [自] to go out in all directions from a central point 中心点から全方向に向かって出ていく➜(中心から)放射状に延びる, 四方に広がる ‖ *Narrow streets radiate from the village square.* その村の広場から細い通りが四方に延びている.

**radiation** /rèɪdiéɪʃ(ə)n/ [名] [U] ▶定義1 powerful and very dangerous rays that are sent out from certain substances. You cannot see or feel radiation but it can cause serious illness or death. ある特定の物質から放出される, 強力で非常に危険な放射線. 目で見たり感じたりすることはできないが, 重病または死亡の原因となることがある➜放射線 ☛参 **radioactive** ▶定義2 heat, light or energy that is sent out from sth 〜から放出される熱, 光, またはエネルギー➜(光·熱などの)放射, 発光, 放熱, 発散 ‖ *ultraviolet radiation* 紫外線放射

**radiator** /réɪdièɪtər/ [名] [C] ▶定義1 a piece of equipment that is usually fixed to the wall and is used for heating a room. Radiators are made of metal and filled with hot water. 通常は壁に固定され, 部屋を暖めるために使用される機器. 金属製で, 中には湯が一杯に入っている➜ラジエーター, 暖房器, 放熱器 ☛ C7 ページのさし絵 ▶定義2 a piece of equipment that is used for keeping a car engine cool 車のエンジンを冷却するために用いられる機器➜ラジエーター, エンジンの冷却装置

**radical**[1] /rǽdɪk(ə)l/ [形] ▶定義1 (used about changes in sth) very great; complete (〜の変更について) とても大掛かりな; 完全な➜根本的な, 基本的な, 徹底的な, 完全な ‖ *The tax system needs radical reform.* その税制は根本的な改革が必要です. *radical change* 抜本的な変更 ▶定義2 wanting great social or political change 社会的または政治的に大きな変革を求めている➜過激な, 急進的な, 急進派の ‖ *to have radical views* 過激な意見を持つ ☛参 **moderate**[1]**(2)**, **extreme**[2] — **radically** /-k(ə)li/ [副] ➜根本的に, 徹底的に, 急進的に ‖ *The First World War radically altered the political map of Europe.* 第1次世界大戦によりヨーロッパの政治地図は完全に塗り替えられた.

**radical**[2] /rǽdɪk(ə)l/ [名] [C] ▶定義 a person who wants great social or political change 社会的または政治的に大きな変革を求める人➜急進論者, 急進党員, 過激派 ☛参 **moderate**[3], **extremist**

***radio** /réɪdiòʊ/ [名] ([複] **radios**) ▶定義1 (しばしば **the radio**) [[U], 単数扱い] the activity of sending out programmes for people to listen to on their radios 人がラジオで聴く番組を電波で流す行為➜ラジオ, ラジオ放送 ‖ *I always* ***listen to the radio*** *in the car.* 私はいつも車の中でラジオを聴く. *I heard an interesting report* ***on the radio*** *this morning.* 私は今朝, ラジオで興味深い報道を耳にした. *a radio station/programme* ラジオ放送局·ラジオ番組 *national/local radio* 国営·地方ラジオ放送 ▶定義2 [C] a piece of equipment that is used for receiving and/or sending radio messages or programmes (on a ship, plane, etc or in your house) (船上, 機上など, または自宅で) 無線通信あるいは番組を受信したり送信したりするために用いられる機器➜ラジオ, ラジオ受信機, 無線電信機

➤ラジオの電源は put/switch/turn on/off (入れる.切る) と言う. 音を大きく, または小さくすることには, turn up/down (音量を上げる.下げる) と言う.

☛ S7 ページのさし絵 ▶定義3 [U] the sending or receiving of messages through the air by electrical signals 電気信号により空気中を通して通信を送る, または受けること➜無電, 無線電信, 無線電話 ‖ *to keep in radio contact* 無電連絡を保つ *radio signals/waves* 無線信号·電波 — **radio**

R

オ放送する(過,過分 radioed)→(～に) 無電を打つ, 無線連絡をする,(通信などを) 無電で送る, ラジ

**radioactive** /rèɪdioʊǽktɪv/ ▶定義 sending out powerful and very dangerous rays that are produced when atoms are broken up. These rays cannot be seen or felt but can cause serious illness or death. 原子が破壊されたときに生じる,強力で非常に危険な放射線を放出している.これらの放射線は目で見たり感じたりすることができないが,重病または死亡の原因となることがある→放射性の,放射能を持つ ‖ *the problem of the disposal of* **radioactive** *waste from power stations* 原子力発電所から出る放射性廃棄物の問題 ☛参 radiation — **radioactivity** /rèɪdioʊæktɪvəti/ 名 Ⓤ→放射能,放射性

**radiographer** /rèɪdiɑ́grəfər/ 名 Ⓒ ▶定義 a person who is trained to take pictures of your bones, etc (X-rays) in a hospital or to use them for the treatment of certain illnesses 病院で骨などの写真(X線)を撮る,またはそれをある種の病気の治療に利用する訓練を受けた人→放射線技師,レントゲン技師,X線技師

**radish** /rǽdɪʃ/ 名 Ⓒ ▶定義 a small red vegetable that is white inside with a strong taste. You eat radishes in salads. 辛い味のする,内側の白い,小さな赤色の野菜.サラダにして食べる→ハツカダイコン,ラディッシュ ☛ C3 ページのさし絵

**radius** /réɪdiəs/ 名 Ⓒ (複 **radii** /-diàɪ/) ▶定義 1 the distance from the centre of a circle to the outside edge 円の中心から円周までの距離→半径 ☛参 diameter, circumference ☛ circle のさし絵 ▶定義 2 a circular area that is measured from a point in its centre 中心にある点を基準とした,その周辺の領域→(活動・行動・影響・能力などの)範囲,圏 ‖ *The wreckage of the plane was scattered over a* **radius** *of several miles.* 機体の残骸(ざんがい)は数マイルの範囲にわたって散らばった.

**RAF** /ræf/ 略 奥the Royal Air Force→英国空軍

**raffle** /rǽf(ə)l/ 名 Ⓒ ▶定義 a way of making money for a charity or a project by selling tickets with numbers on them. Later some numbers are chosen and the tickets with these numbers on them win prizes. 番号の入ったチケットを販売して,慈善またはある計画のために金を稼ぐ方法.後日いくつかの番号が選ばれ,その番号のチケットには賞品が付く→ラッフル,富くじ(販売),当て物販売,くじ引き販売

**raft** /rɑːft; ræft/ 名 Ⓒ ▶定義 a flat structure made of pieces of wood tied together and used as a boat or a floating platform 木を結び合わせて作られ,ボートまたは浮かんだ台として使用される平たい構造物→いかだ(船),救命ボート,(水泳者用)浮き台,浮き桟橋

**rafter** /rɑ́ːftər, rǽftər/ 名 Ⓒ ▶定義 one of the long pieces of wood that support a roof 屋根を支える長い材木の1つ→たるき

**rag** /ræg/ 名 ▶定義 1 Ⓒ Ⓤ a small piece of old cloth that you use for cleaning 掃除のために使う小さな古い布切れ→ぼろ切れ,ぼろ,ぼろ布 ▶定義 2 **rags** [複数扱い] clothes that are very old and torn とても古く,擦り切れた衣服→ぼろ服,古着

**rage**¹ /reɪdʒ/ 名 Ⓒ Ⓤ ▶定義 a feeling of violent anger that is difficult to control 抑制するのが困難な,激しい怒りの気持ち→激怒,憤慨,憤怒 ‖ *He was trembling with* **rage**. 彼は怒りに身を震わせていた. *to fly into a* **rage** かっとなる

**rage**² /reɪdʒ/ 動 ⾃ ▶定義 1 **rage** (**at/against/about sb/sth**) to show great anger about sth, especially by shouting 特に大声を出して,～に対する大きな怒りを表す→(～に対して・～のことで)激怒する,暴れる,しかりとばす,怒り狂う ‖ *He raged against the injustice of it all.* 彼はそれが全く の不公平であることに激怒した. ▶定義 2 (used about a battle, disease, storm, etc) to continue with great force (戦い,病気,あらしなどについて) 猛烈で続く→荒れ狂う,猛威を振るう ‖ *The battle raged for several days.* その激戦は数日間にわたり続いた. — **raging** 形 (名詞の前だけ)→ 強烈な,激怒した,荒れ狂う,猛威を振るう ‖ *a raging headache* 激しい頭痛

**ragged** /rǽgəd/ 形 ▶定義 1 (used about clothes) old and torn (衣服について) 古く擦り切れた→ぼろぼろの,ほつれた,着古した,破れた ▶定義 2 not straight; untidy もつれた; 取り散らかした→ごつごつの,ぎざぎざの,ざらざらの,荒れ放題の ‖ *a ragged edge/coastline* ぎざぎざの刃・海岸線

**raid** /reɪd/ 名 Ⓒ **a raid (on sth)** ▶定義 1 a short surprise attack on an enemy by soldiers, ships or aircraft 兵士,船舶,または航空機による,敵へ

の短時間の急襲➜(～への)襲撃, 急襲, 奇襲 ‖ *an air raid* 空襲 ▶定義2 a surprise visit by the police looking for criminals or illegal goods 犯人または違法な物を捜している警察による, 不意の訪問➜(～への)手入れ, 踏み込み ▶定義3 a surprise attack on a building in order to steal sth ～を盗むために建物を不意に襲撃すること➜(～への)侵入, 侵略 ‖ *a bank raid* 銀行強盗 — **raid** [動][他] ➜～を急襲する, 襲撃する, ～に侵入する, (警察が)～を手入れする ‖ *Police raided the club at dawn this morning.* 警察は今日の明け方, そのクラブを手入れした.

***rail** /réɪl/ [名] ▶定義1 [C]a wooden or metal bar fixed to a wall, which you can hang things on 壁に固定された木製または金属製の棒で, その上に物を掛けることができる➜**レール·横木状のもの, 横棒** ‖ *a towel/curtain/picture rail* タオル掛け·カーテンレール·額長押(なげし)☛ C7 ページのさし絵 ▶定義2 [C]a bar which you can hold to stop you from falling (on stairs, from a building, etc) (階段, 建造物などから)落ちないようにつかまることができる棒➜**横木, 手すり, 横棒, 欄干** ▶定義3 [[C], 通常は複数] each of the two metal bars that form the track that trains run on 列車が走る鉄道に敷かれた2本の金属製の棒のそれぞれ➜**レール, 線路, 軌条** ▶定義4 [U]the railway system; trains as a means of transport 鉄道便; 輸送手段としての列車➜**鉄道** ‖ *rail travel/services/fares* 鉄道旅行·鉄道事業·鉄道料金

**railcard** /réɪlkɑ̀ːrd/ [名][C][英] ▶定義 a special card that allows you to buy train tickets at a lower price if you are an old person, student, etc 高齢者, 学生などであれば低料金で列車の切符を購入できる特別のカード➜**鉄道運賃割引身分証明書, レールカード**

**railing** /réɪlɪŋ/ [名][[C], 通常は複数] ▶定義 a fence (around a park, garden, etc) that is made of metal bars 金属製の棒でできた, (公園, 庭などの回りの)柵(さく)➜ **柵, 手すり, 垣, レール**

***railway** /réɪlwèɪ/ ([米] **railroad**) [名][C] ▶定義1 ([英] **railway line**) the metal lines on which trains travel between one place and another 金属製の線状のもので, その上をある場所から別の場所へ列車が移動する➜**鉄道線路** ▶定義2 the whole system of tracks, the trains and the organization and people needed to operate them 鉄道線路, 列車, およびそれらを運営する組織と人々から成る全体的な体制➜**鉄道, 鉄道会社** ‖ *He works on the railways.* 彼は鉄道会社で働いています. *a railway engine/company* 機関車·鉄道会社

**railway station** = STATION[1](1)

***rain**[1] /réɪn/ [名] ▶定義1 [U]the water that falls from the sky 空から降ってくる水➜**雨, 雨水** ‖ *Take your umbrella, **it looks like rain** (= as if it is going to rain).* 傘を持っていきなさい. 雨が降りそうです(= もうすぐ雨になりそうです). ***It's pouring with rain** (= the rain is very heavy).* 土砂降りです(= 雨がとても激しい). ☛参 **shower(3)**, **acid rain** と **weather** の注 ▶定義2 **rains**[複数扱い] (in tropical countries) the time of the year when there is a lot of rain (熱帯の国々で) 1年のうちで多量の雨が降る時期➜**雨季**
[成句] (as) right as rain ⇒ **RIGHT**[1]

***rain**[2] /réɪn/ [動] ▶定義1 [自] (it と用いて) to fall as rain 雨として降る➜**雨が降る** ‖ *Oh no! **It's raining** again!* ああ大変だ. また雨が降っている. *Is it **raining hard**?* 雨はひどく降っていますか. *We'll go out when it stops raining.* 雨がやんだら出掛けましょう. ▶定義2 [自][他] **rain (sth) (down) (on sb/sth)** to fall or make sth fall on sb/sth in large quantities ～の上に大量に降る, または～を降らせる➜(～に)**雨のように降る, 落ちる, ～を雨と降らす, 浴びせる** ‖ *Bombs rained down on the city.* その都市に爆弾が雨のごとく降ってきた.
[句動詞] **be rained off** ▶定義 to be cancelled or to have to stop because it is raining 雨が降っているので中止される, または中止しなければならない➜(試合などが)**雨で中止·順延になる** ‖ *The tennis was rained off.* テニスの試合は雨で中止になりました.

**rainbow** /réɪnbòʊ/ [名][C] ▶定義 an arch of many colours that sometimes appears in the sky when the sun shines through rain 太陽の光がさすと空中の雨を通して空に現れることがある, 多くの色の付いた弓形のもの➜**にじ**

**rain check** [名] 特に[米]
[成句] **take a rain check on sth** (口語) ▶定義 to refuse an invitation or offer but say that you might accept it later 招待または申し出を断るが, 後日なら受け付け可能と言う➜**また次の機会に受けると約束する, 今は断るが次の機会に受ける**

R

**raincoat** /réɪnkòʊt/ 图 ❼ ▶定義 a long light coat which keeps you dry in the rain 雨でも人がぬれないようにする, 丈が長く軽い上着→レインコート

**raindrop** /réɪndràp/ 图 ❼ ▶定義 a single drop of rain 1滴の雨水→雨滴, 雨垂れ, 雨の滴, 雨粒

**rainfall** /réɪnfɔ̀:l/ 图 [❶, 単数扱い] ▶定義 the total amount of rain that falls in a particular place during a month, year, etc 1か月, 1年などの間に特定の場所に降る雨の総量→雨量, 降雨量, 降水量

**rainforest** /réɪnfɔ̀(:)rest, -fàr-/ 图 ❼ ▶定義 a thick forest in tropical parts of the world that have a lot of rain 地球上の熱帯地域にある, 雨の多い密林→熱帯雨林, 熱帯多雨林 ‖ *the Amazon rainforest* アマゾンの熱帯雨林

**rainy** /réɪni/ 形 ▶定義 having or bringing a lot of rain 多量の雨が降っている, またはもたらしている→雨の多い, 雨降りの, 雨がちの, 雨をもたらす ‖ *a rainy day* 雨の日 *the rainy season* 雨季, 梅雨

成句 **keep/save sth for a rainy day** ▶定義 to save sth, especially money, for a time when you really need it 特に金を本当に必要とするきのために取っておく→まさかのときに備えて貯金する, 蓄えておく

*★**raise** /réɪz/ 動 ⓘ ▶定義1 to lift sth up 〜を持ち上げる→〜を上げる, 持ち上げる, 揚げる, 起こす ‖ *If you want to leave the room raise your hand.* 部屋から出たい場合は手を上げなさい. *He raised himself up on one elbow.* 彼は片ひじをついて起き上がった. ▶定義2 **raise sth (to sth)** to increase the level of sth or to make sth better or stronger 〜の程度を上げる, または〜を改善するまたは強くめる→〜を(…まで)上げる, 増す, 高くする, 高める ‖ *to raise taxes/salaries/prices* 増税する・昇給する・値上げする *The hotel needs to raise its standards.* そのホテルは水準を上げる必要がある. *There's no need to raise your voice (= speak loudly or angrily).* 声を張り上げる(=大声で, または怒って話す)必要は全くありません. ⇔定義1, 2 **lower** ▶定義3 to get money from people for a particular purpose 特定の目的のために人々からお金を募る→〜を集める, 調達する, 工面する ‖ *We are doing a sponsored walk to raise money for charity.* 私たちは慈善事業にお金を集めるために, 慈善ウォークを行っている. *a fund-raising event* 募金のための催し ▶定義4 to introduce a subject that needs to be talked about or dealt with 話される, または処理される必要のある問題を持ち出す→〜を提起する, 提出する, 話題に乗せる, 持ち出す ‖ *I would like to raise the subject of money.* お金のことを話したいと思います. *This raises the question of why nothing was done before.* これにより, 以前に何もなされなかったのはなぜかという疑問が生じる. ▶定義5 to cause a particular reaction or emotion 特定の反応または感情を引き起こす→〜を起こす, 起こさせる, 引き起こす, 催させる ‖ *The neighbours raised the alarm (= told everybody there was a fire/an emergency) when they saw smoke coming out of the window.* 窓から煙が出ているのを見て, 近所の人々は警報を発した(= 皆に火事・緊急事態だと伝えた). *to raise hopes/fears/suspicions in people's minds* 人の心に希望をもたらす・恐怖心を起こす・疑念を起こさせる ▶定義6 to look after a child or an animal until he/she is an adult 大人になるまで子供または動物の面倒を見る→〜を育てる, 養う ‖ *You can't raise a family on what I earn.* 私の稼ぎでは家族を養うことはできません. ☛参 **bring sb up** ▶定義7 to breed animals or grow a particular plant for a specific purpose 特定の目的のために動物を飼育する, または植物を育てる→〜を飼育する, 栽培する

成句 **raise your eyebrows** ▶定義 to show that you are surprised or that you do not approve of sth 驚いていること, または〜を承認しないことを表す→まゆを上げる, まゆをひそめる

> ▶コミュニケーション
>
> 「上げたまゆ」は「あきれた」ときの表情
>
> **raise an eyebrow**: 片方のまゆを上げて, あきれた, まさか, など驚きと非難の入り交じった気持ちを表すしぐさ. 両方のまゆを上げて同じ意味を表すこともあります. このしぐさを表す **raise an eyebrow, raise one's eyebrows** は, 「驚く」「あきれる」を意味する比喩表現としても使われます. 例: *If my mother found out about this, she might raise an eyebrow.*(母がこの事を知ったらあきれるかもしれない)

**raisin** /réɪz(ə)n/ 名 C ▶定義 a dried grape, used in cakes, etc 乾燥したブドウで、ケーキなどに入れて使われる→干しブドウ、レーズン ☛参 **sultana**

**rake** /réɪk/ 名 C ▶定義 a garden tool with a long handle and a row of metal teeth, used for collecting leaves or making the earth smooth 長い柄と列になった金属製の刃が付いており、葉を集めるまたは地面をならすために使われる園芸用具→くま手、馬ぐわ、レーキ、草かき ☛ **garden** のさし絵 ― rake 動→～を(くま手で)集める、かき集める、かきならす、掃く ‖ *to rake up the leaves* 枯れ葉をくま手でかき集める

句動詞 rake sth in 略式 ▶定義 to earn a lot of money, especially when it is done easily 特に簡単に多額のお金を稼ぐ→～を(くま手でかき寄せるように)もうける、かき入れる、うんと稼ぐ、さっとかき集める ‖ *She's been raking it in since she got promoted.* 彼女は昇進してからというもの大いに稼いでいる.

rake sth up ▶定義 to start talking about sth that it would be better to forget 忘れた方がいい～について話し始める→～を思い出させる、蒸し返す、～を暴き立てる ‖ *Don't rake up all those old stories again.* そんな昔の話ばかり、今更また蒸し返すな.

**rally**¹ /ræli/ 名 C (複 **rallies**) ▶定義 1 a large public meeting, especially one held to support a political idea 大規模な公開の会合で、特に特定の政治思想を支援するために開催されるもの→集会、大会 ‖ *a peace rally* 平和集会 ▶定義 2 医 a race for cars or motorbikes on public roads 公道で行われる車またはオートバイのレース→ラリー、長距離レース ▶定義 3 (used in tennis and similar sports) a series of hits of the ball before a point is won (テニスまたは同じようなスポーツで用いて) 点数が入るまでの連続した球の打ち合い→ラリー

**rally**² /ræli/ 動 (現分 **rallying**; 三単現 **rallies**); 過、過分 **rallied**) ▶定義 1 動 自 rally (sb/sth) (around/behind/to sb) to come together or to bring people together in order to help or support sb/sth ～を助けるまたは支援するために集まる、あるいは人々を集める→一致結束する、(～の回りに・～に)援助に集まる、結集する；～を一致結束させる、(人の回りに・一緒に)呼び集める ‖ *The cabinet rallied behind the Prime Minister.* 内閣は首相の後ろ盾として一致結束した. ▶定義 2 自 to get stronger, healthier, etc after an illness or a period of weakness 病後または虚弱である期間の後、丈夫に健康的になる→(～から)回復する、良くなる、立ち直る、元気を取り戻す ‖ *He never really rallied after the operation.* 彼は手術後、完全には回復しなかった.

句動詞 rally round ▶定義 to come together to help sb ～を助けるために集まる→援助に集まる、助けに駆け付ける、はせ参じる ‖ *When I was in trouble my family all rallied round.* 私が困っていた時、家族全員が助けに駆け付けてくれた.

**ram**¹ /ræm/ 名 C ▶定義 a male sheep 雄の羊→雄羊 ☛参 **sheep** の注 ☛ **goat** のさし絵

**ram**² /ræm/ 動 他 (**ramming**; **rammed**) ▶定義 to crash into sth or push sth with great force ～にぶつかる、または～を強い力で押す→～に衝突する、ぶつかる、～を打ち込む、押し込む

**Ramadan** /rǽmədæn, rà:-, ræmədæn/ 名 C U ▶定義 a period of a month when, for religious reasons, Muslims do not eat anything from early morning until the sun goes down in the evening 宗教的理由で、イスラム教徒が早朝から夕方太陽が沈むまで何も食べない1か月の期間→ラマダーン ☛参 **Eid**

**ramble**¹ /rǽmb(ə)l/ 動 自 ▶定義 1 to walk in the countryside for pleasure 田舎を楽しみのために散策する→ぶらつく、散策する、散歩する、そぞろ歩く ‖ *to go rambling* 散策に出掛ける ▶定義 2 ramble (on) (about sth) to talk for a long time in a confused way 長時間、すっきりしない話をする→～のことを取り留めなく話す、漫然と話す、だらだら書く ‖ *Halfway through his speech he began to ramble.* 演説が半分を過ぎた辺りから、彼の話は取り留めがなくなった.

**ramble**² /rǽmb(ə)l/ 名 C ▶定義 a long, organized walk in the country for pleasure 田舎を楽しみのために、長い距離を計画を立てて歩くこと→(田舎道・森などの)散歩、漫歩、そぞろ歩き

**rambling** /rǽmb(ə)lɪŋ/ 形 ▶定義 1 (used about speech or writing) very long and confused (演説または文章について) とても長く、混乱している→取り留めのない、漫然とした、まとまりのない、ばらばらの ▶定義 2 (used about a building) spreading in many directions (建物に

1324 ramp

ついて) 多くの方向に広がっている→だだっ広い, まとまりなく広い, 四方八方に広がった ‖ *a rambling old house in the country* 田舎のだだっ広い古い家

**ramp** /rǽmp/ 名 C ▶定義 a path going up or down which you can use instead of steps or stairs to get from one place to a higher or lower place ある場所からより高いまたは低い場所へ行くために, 屋外や屋内の階段の代わりに使用することができる, 上りまたは下りの小道→(段違いの道路・建物のフロアなどを結ぶ)傾斜路, スロープ, (高速道路の)ランプ, (飛行機用の)タラップ ‖ *There are ramps at both entrances for wheelchair access.* 両方の入り口に車いす用のスロープがあります.

**rampage**¹ /ræmpèɪdʒ/ 動 自 ▶定義 to move through a place in a violent group, usually breaking things and attacking people 通常物を壊し人々を襲いながら, 暴力的な集団になってある場所を動き回る→〜を暴れ回る, 走り回る ‖ *The football fans rampaged through the town.* サッカーファンは街中を暴れ回った.

**rampage**² /ræmpèɪdʒ/ 名
成句 **be/go on the rampage** ▶定義 to move through a place in a violent group, usually breaking things and attacking people 通常物を壊し人々を襲いながら, 暴力的な集団としてある場所を動き回る→暴れ回る

**rampant** /rǽmpənt/ 形 ▶定義 (used about sth bad) existing or spreading everywhere in a way that is very difficult to control (悪い〜について) 統制するのが非常に難しい方法で, あらゆる所に存在しているまたは広がっている→〜にはびこっている, 蔓延(まんえん)した, (病気・悪業が)〜で猛威を振るう ‖ *Car theft is rampant in this town.* この街では自動車泥棒がはびこっている.

**ramshackle** /rǽmʃæk(ə)l/ 形 ▶定義 (usually used about a building) old and needing repair (通常は建物について) 古くなって, 修理を必要としている→今にも崩れそうな, がたがたの, 倒れそうな, ぐらぐらする

**ran** RUN¹の過去形

**ranch** /rɑːntʃ, ræntʃ/ 名 C ▶定義 a large farm, especially in the US or Australia, where cows, horses, sheep, etc are kept 特に米国やオーストラリアの牛, 馬, 羊などが飼育されている大規模な農園→牧場, 放牧場, 〜園, 農場, 農園, 飼育場

**random** /rǽndəm/ 形 ▶定義 chosen by chance たまたま選ばれた→無作為の, 任意の, (無差別・無目的で)でたらめの, 手当たり次第の ‖ *For the opinion poll they interviewed a random selection of people in the street.* 世論調査のため, 街で無作為に抽出された人々に対して取材が行われた. — randomly 副 →無作為に, 任意に, 手当たり次第に, ふと

成句 **at random** ▶定義 without thinking or deciding in advance what is going to happen 何が起こるか前もって考えないで, または決めないで→でたらめに, 任意に, 無作為に, 手当たり次第に ‖ *The competitors were chosen at random from the audience.* 出場者は観客の中から無作為に選ばれた.

**randy** /rǽndi/ 形 英略式 ▶定義 sexually excited 性的に興奮した→好色な, 性欲を感じている, 欲情した

**rang** RING²の過去形

★**range**¹ /réɪndʒ/ 名 ▶定義 1 [ C, 通常は単数 ] a range (of sth) a variety of things that belong to the same group 同じグループに属するさまざまな物→(同種の物の)集まり, 一式, 連続, 組 ‖ *The course will cover a whole range of topics.* その講座ではあらゆる話題を取り扱います. *This shop has a very wide range of clothes.* この店は洋服の品数が大変多い. ▶定義 2 C the limits between which sth can vary 〜が変動し得る範囲→(変動可能な)幅, 範囲, 限度, 限界 ‖ *That car is outside my price range.* その車は私の手の届かない価格だ. *I don't think this game is suitable for all age ranges.* 私はこのゲームがすべての年齢層に適しているとは思いません. ▶定義 3 C U the distance that it is possible for sb/sth to travel, see, hear, etc 〜が移動できる, 見える, 聞ける距離→範囲, 限界, 視界, 音域, 射程距離 ‖ *Keep out of range of the guns.* 銃の射程距離に入ってはいけません. *The gunman shot the policeman at close range.* 殺し屋は警官を至近距離から撃った. *They can pick up signals at a range of 400 metres.* 彼らは400メートルの範囲での信号を受信することができる. ▶定義 4 C a line of mountains or hills 連なった山または丘陵→山脈, 連山, 山並み, 連なり

**range**² /réɪndʒ/ 動 自 ▶定義 1 range between A

and B; **range from A to B** to vary between two amounts, sizes, etc, including all those between them 2つの量、大きさなどで上限と下限の間にあるものすべてを含んでいて、さまざまに及んでいる→(年齢・範囲・程度などが)〜から…へ及んでいる、またがる ‖ *The ages of the students range from 15 to 50.* 学生の年齢層は15歳から50歳にまで及んでいる. ▶定義2 **range (from A to B)** to include a variety of things in addition to those mentioned 言及されたものに加え、いろいろなものを含む→(活動・話題などが)〜の範囲にわたる、〜に及ぶ、広がる

*****rank**¹ /ræŋk/ 名 ▶定義1 ᴄᴜ the position, especially a high position, that sb has in an organization such as the army, or in society 軍隊のような組織または社会において、〜が持っている地位、特に高い地位→階級、等級、地位、身分、順位 ‖ *General is one of the highest ranks in the army.* 大将は軍隊で最も高い地位の1つである. *She's much higher in rank than I am.* 彼女は私よりずっと高い地位にある. ▶定義2 ᴄ a group or line of things or people 物または人の集まりまたは列→列、並び ‖ *a taxi rank* タクシーを待つ行列 ▶定義3 **the ranks**[複数扱い] the ordinary soldiers in the army; the members of any large group 軍隊の中での並みの兵士; 大きな集団の一員→下士官兵、兵卒、庶民、一般会員、社員 ‖ *At the age of 43, he was forced to **join the ranks of** the unemployed.* 彼は43歳の時、失業者の仲間入りをした.

成句 **the rank and file** ▶定義 the ordinary soldiers in the army; the ordinary members of an organization 軍隊の中での並みの兵士; 組織の中の平凡な一員→兵卒たち、一般大衆、平社員たち、一般社員

**rank**² /ræŋk/ 動 自 他 ▶定義 **rank (sb/sth) (as sth)**(進行形不可) to give sb/sth a particular position on a scale according to importance, quality, success, etc; to have a position of this kind 重要性、質、成功などに応じて、〜に程度の面から特定の等級を与える; そのような種類の地位を持つ→(〜を…に)位置付ける、〜という等級を付ける、格付けする、〜に位置する、占める ‖ *She's ranked as one of the world's top players.* 彼女は世界のトッププレーヤーの1人として位置付けられている. *a high-ranking police officer* 警察の高官

**ransom** /ˈrænsəm/ 名 ᴄᴜ ▶定義 the money that you must pay to free sb who has been captured illegally and who is being kept as a prisoner 非合法的に捕らえられた人や捕虜として捕らえられている人を解放するために支払わなければならない金→身の代金、賠償金 ‖ *The kidnappers demanded a ransom of $500000 for the boy's release.* 誘拐犯はその男の子の解放と引き換えに50万ドルの身の代金を要求した.

成句 **hold sb to ransom** ▶定義 to keep sb as a prisoner and say that you will not free him/her until you have received a certain amount of money 〜を捕虜に取り、ある金額の金を受け取るまではその〜を解放しないと言う→〜を監禁して身の代金を要求する、身の代金目当てに拘禁する ☛参 **hostage**

**rap**¹ /ræp/ 名 ▶定義1 ᴄ a quick, sharp hit or knock on a door, window, etc ドア、窓などを速く鋭い音を立ててたたく、またはノックすること→(〜を)軽くたたくこと・音、コツンコツン・トントンとたたくこと ‖ *There was a sharp rap on the door.* ドアをトントンとたたく音がした. ▶定義2 ᴄᴜ a style or a piece of music with a fast strong rhythm, in which the words are spoken fast, not sung 速く強いリズムを持つ音楽のスタイルまたは作品で、歌詞が歌われるのではなく、早口で話される→ラップ、ラップミュージック

**rap**² /ræp/ 動 (**rapping; rapped**) ▶定義1 自他 to hit a hard object or surface several times quickly and lightly, making a noise 硬い物または表面を数回、素早く軽く、音を立ててたたく→〜をコツンとたたく、〜をトントンとたたく ‖ *She rapped angrily on/at the door.* 彼女は怒ってドアをトントンとたたいた. ▶定義2 他 略式 (used mainly in newspaper headlines) to criticize sb strongly (主に新聞の見出しで)〜を強く非難する→〜を(厳しく)非難する、酷評する ‖ *Minister raps police over rise in crime.* 大臣は犯罪の増加について警察を厳しく非難した. ▶定義3 自 to speak the words of a song (*a rap*) that has music with a very fast strong rhythm 大変速く強いリズムを持つ曲の付いた歌(ラップ)の歌詞を言う→ラップを歌う、ラップミュージックのビートに合わせてリズミカルにしゃべる

## 1326 rape¹

### ▶コミュニケーション

「けんか」を表す身振りの日英比較

rap one's fists together: 左右のこぶしの甲を外側にして,指の関節部分 (knuckles) を打ち合わせるしぐさ. 力と力の衝突,争いを意味する当て振りです. 日本では人差し指を刀に見立て,これを交互に掛け合わせてけんかを合図します. これは,日本特有の「チャンバラ」あっての当て振りでしょう.

**rape¹** /réɪp/ 動他 ▶定義 to force a person to have sex when he/she does not want to, using threats or violence 脅しまたは暴力を使って,人にその人の望まない性行為を強いる→～を犯す,強姦(ごうかん)する,レイプする

**rape²** /réɪp/ 名 ▶定義1 ❶❸the crime of forcing sb to have sex when he/she does not want to ～にその人の望まない性行為を強いる犯罪→強姦(ごうかん),レイプ ‖ to commit rape 強姦の罪を犯す ▶定義2 [単数扱い](文) the rape (of sth) the destruction of sth beautiful 美しい～の破壊→(土地・環境の)破壊,略奪,侵犯

**rapid** /rǽpəd/ 形 ▶定義 happening very quickly or moving with great speed 非常に速く起こっている,または相当な速度で動いている→速い,急速な,素早い,迅速な ‖ She made rapid progress and was soon the best in the class. 彼女は急に上達し,間もなくクラスで1番になった. ― rapidity 名 正式 →急速,敏捷(びんしょう),速度,素早さ ‖ The rapidity of change has astonished most people. その急速な変化は多くの人々を驚かせた. ― rapidly 副 →速く,急速に,迅速に,素早く

**rapids** /rǽpədz/ 名 ❸ ▶定義 a part of a river where the water flows very fast over rocks 水が岩の上を非常に早く流れる,川の一部分→急流,早瀬

**rapist** /réɪpɪst/ 名 [複数扱い] ▶定義 a person who forces sb to have sex when he/she does not want to ～にその人の望まない性行為を強要する人→強姦(ごうかん)犯,強姦者

**rapture** /rǽptʃər/ 名 ❶ ▶定義 a feeling of extreme happiness 極度の幸福感→有頂天,歓喜,狂喜,恍惚(こうこつ)

成句 **go into raptures (about/over sb/sth)** ▶定義 to feel and show that you think that sb/sth is very good ～が大変優れていると感じて,そう思っていることを表現する→～に有頂天になっている・なる,～でほくほくしている・する,～にうっとりする ‖ I didn't like the film much but my boyfriend went into raptures about it. 私はその映画があまり気に入らなかったが,私のボーイフレンドは夢中になっていた.

★**rare** /réər/ 形 ▶定義1 rare (for sb/sth to do sth); rare (to do sth) not done, seen, happening, etc very often あまり頻繁に行われない,見られない,起こらないなど→まれな,珍しい,めったにない ‖ a rare bird/flower/plant 珍しい鳥・花・植物 ▶定義2 (used about meat) not cooked for very long so that the inside is still red (肉について)長時間焼いてないので内側はまだ赤い→レアの,生焼けの ‖ a rare steak レアのステーキ ▶ medium, well done と比較.
― **rarely** 副 →めったに～ない,まれに,珍しいほど ‖ People rarely live to be over 100 years old. 100歳以上生きる人はめったにいません.

**raring** /réərɪŋ/ 形 ▶定義 raring to do sth wanting to start doing sth very much ～をやり始めたいと非常に強く望んでいる→しきりに～したがって,～しようとうずうずして,～したくてたまらない ‖ They were raring to try out the new computer. 彼らは新しいコンピューターを試したくてうずうずしていた.

**rarity** /réərəti/ 名 (複 **rarities**) ▶定義1 ❸a thing or a person that is unusual and is therefore often valuable or interesting 普通でないためにしばしば価値がある,または興味深い物事や人→まれな物・事・人,珍品,希少価値のある物 ‖ Women lorry drivers are still quite a rarity. 女性のトラック運転手はまだ極めて珍しい. ▶定義2 ❶the quality of being rare めったにないということ→まれなこと,珍奇,珍しさ ‖ The rarity of this stamp increases its value a lot. この切手は希少なので,価値がかなり上がっている.

**rash¹** /rǽʃ/ 名 ▶定義1 [❸, 通常は単数] an area of small red spots that appear on your skin when you are ill or have a reaction to sth 病気のときまたは～に反応したときに,皮膚に現れる赤い小さな斑点(はんてん)→発疹(はっしん),吹き出物 ‖ He came out in a rash where the plant had touched him. 彼はその植物が触れた

所に発疹が出た. ▶定義2 [単数扱い] a rash (of sth) a series of unpleasant events of the same kind happening close together 間隔を空けずに起こる, 同じ種類の連続した不快な出来事→**多発, 続発, 頻発**

**rash**² /ræʃ/ 形 ▶定義 (used about people) doing things that might be dangerous or bad without thinking about the possible results first; (used about actions) done in this way (人々について) 起こり得る結果についてあらかじめ考えることなく, 危険なまたは悪い行為かもしれない事をしている; (行動について) そのようなやり方で行われた→**(人が) 無鉄砲な, 思慮のない, 無分別な, 軽率な** ‖ *a rash decision/promise* 軽はずみな決定・約束 ― **rashly** 副→**無鉄砲に, 軽率に, 向こう見ずに**

**rasher** /ræʃər/ 名 C 医 ▶定義 a slice of meat (bacon) from a pig 薄い1切れの豚肉(ベーコン)→**ベーコン・ハムの薄切り, スライス**

**raspberry** /rá:zb(ə)ri; ræzbèri/ 名 C (複 **raspberries**) ▶定義 a small, soft, red fruit which grows on bushes 灌木(かんぼく)で, 小さくて柔らかい赤色の実→**キイチゴ(の実), ラズベリー** ‖ *raspberry jam* ラズベリーのジャム ☞ C3 ページのさし絵

★**rat**¹ /ræt/ 名 C ▶定義 an animal like a large mouse 大きなハツカネズミのような動物→**ネズミ, ドブネズミ**

▶ rats は, rodents (げっ歯類) と呼ばれる動物の科に属する.

成句 **rat race** ▶定義 the way of life in which everyone is only interested in being better or more successful than everyone else だれもが他人より秀でるまたは成功することにだけ興味を持っているような生活の仕方→**人生の厳しい生存競争, 出世競争, 激しい無意味な競争**

★**rate**¹ /réɪt/ 名 C ▶定義1 a measurement of the speed at which sth happens or the number of times sth happens or exists during a particular period ある特定の期間に〜が起こる速さの度合い, または〜が起こるあるいは現れる回数→**速度, ペース, 進度, 割合, (比)率, レート** ‖ *The birth rate (= the number of children born each year) is falling.* 出生率(= 1年に生まれる子供の数)は低下している. *The population is increasing at the rate of less than 0.5% a year.* 人口は1年に0.5パーセントを下回る割合で増加している.

---

rather 1327

*an exchange rate of one pound to ten francs* 1ポンドに対し10フランの交換レート ▶定義2 a fixed amount of money that sth costs or that sb is paid 〜にかかるまたは〜に対して支払われる, 固定の金額→**(主にサービスの)料金, 値段, 相場, レート** ‖ *The basic rate of pay is £10 an hour.* 基本賃金は1時間当たり10ポンドです. *We offer special reduced rates for students.* 私たちは学生向けに特別割引料金を設けている.

☛参 **first-rate**, **second-rate**

成句 **at any rate** (口語) ▶定義1 used when you are giving more exact information about sth 〜に関する, より正確な情報を提供する際に用いて→**少なくとも, もっと正確に言えば** ‖ *He said that they would be here by ten. At any rate, I think that's what he said.* 彼は彼らが10時までにここに来るだろうと言いました. 少なくとも, 彼はそう言っていたと思います. ▶定義2 whatever else might happen ほかのどんな事が起ころうとも→**(前に述べた事はさておき) とにかく, いずれにしても, どんな事が起こっても, 何があっても** ‖ *Well, that's one good piece of news at any rate.* なるほど, いずれにしてもそれはいい知らせです.

**the going rate (for sth)**⇒**GOING**²

**rate**² /réɪt/ 動 他 (進行形は不可) ▶定義1 (通常は受動態で) to say how good you think sb/sth is 〜がどれくらい優れていると思うかを述べる→**〜を…と見なす, 思う, 評価する, 見積もる** ‖ *She's rated among the best tennis players of all time.* 彼女は古今を通じて最も優れたテニスプレーヤーの1人と見なされている. ▶定義2 to be good, important, etc enough to be treated in a particular way 特別に扱われるほど十分に優れている, 重要であるなど→**〜に値する, 〜の価値がある** ‖ *The accident wasn't very serious - it didn't rate a mention in the local newspaper.* その事故はそれほど深刻ではなかった ― 地方紙に載るほどのことではなかった.

★**rather** /rá:ðər; ræðər/ 副 ▶定義 quite; to some extent かなり; ある程度→**やや, 多少** ‖ *It was a rather nice day.* かなり天気の良い1日でした. *It was rather a nice day.* 天気のかなり良い1日でした. *It cost rather a lot of money.* それにはかなり多額のお金がかかる. *I was rather hoping that* *you'd be free on Friday.* 私はあなたが金曜日は空いているだろうとかなり期待していました.

▶ fairly, quite, rather, pretty はどれも not very (あまり～ない) を意味することがある. fairly が最も意味が弱い. rather と pretty 略式 が最も意味が強い. fairly と quite はほとんどの場合, 肯定的な語と共に用いられる: *The room was fairly tidy.* (その部屋はよく片付いている.) rather は～を批判しているときに用いられる: *This room's rather untidy.* (この部屋はあまり片付いていない.) rather を肯定的な語と共に用いると, 驚いたり喜んでいるように聞こえる: *The new teacher is actually rather nice, though he doesn't look very friendly.* (新しい先生はあまり親しみやすく見えませんが, 実はなかなかいい先生です.)

成句 **or rather** ▶定義 used as a way of correcting sth you have said, or making it more exact 自分が言った～を訂正する, またはそれをより明確にする方法として用いて→いやそうでなくて, ～と言うよりは, 正しくは, もっと正確に言えば ‖ *She lives in London, or rather she lives in a suburb of London.* 彼女はロンドンに, もっと正確に言えばロンドン郊外に住んでいます.

**rather than** ▶定義 instead of; in place of ～しないで; ～に代わって→～するよりもむしろ, どちらかといえば ‖ *I think I'll just have a sandwich rather than a full meal.* 私はちゃんとした食事を取るよりも, サンドイッチでもつまもうと思っています.

**would rather... (than)** ▶定義 would prefer to ～することを好む→(～するよりも)むしろ…したい, …する方が良い ‖ *I'd rather go to the cinema than watch television.* 私はテレビを見るよりむしろ映画を見に行きたい.

**rating** /réɪtɪŋ/ 名 **C** ▶定義 **1** a measurement of how popular, important, good, etc sth is ～がいかに人気があるか, 重要か, 優れているかなどについての測定→人気度, 売れ行き, 格付け, 重要度, ランキング, 評価 ▶定義 **2** (通常は **the ratings**) a set of figures showing the number of people who watch a particular television programme, etc, used to show how popular the programme is 特定のテレビ番組などを見ている人の数を表す一連の数値で, その番組の人気の度合いを示すために使われる→視聴率

**ratio** /réɪʃoʊ, -ʃiòʊ/ 名 **C** ▶定義 **ratio (of A to B)** the relation between two numbers which shows how much bigger one quantity is than another 一方がもう一方よりどれだけ大きいかを表す, 2つの数字の間の関係→(AのBに対する)比, 比率, 歩合, 割合 ‖ *The ratio of boys to girls in this class is three to one* (= *there are three times as many boys as girls*). このクラスの男女比は3対1です (= 女子の3倍の人数の男子がいる).

**ration** /ræʃ(ə)n, réɪ-/ 名 **C** ▶定義 a limited amount of food, petrol, etc that you are allowed to have when there is not enough for everyone to have as much as he/she wants 全員が手に入れたいだけの量がないときに, 各自が得ることを許された食べ物, 石油などの限られた量→(兵士・水夫の) 1回分の食糧, (食糧不足時の) 割り当て量, 配給量, 定量 ── **ration** 動 他 →～を (一定量に) 制限する, ～を…に配給する, 供給する, 支給する ‖ *In the desert water is strictly rationed.* 砂漠では水の消費が厳しく制限されています. ── **rationing** 名 **U** →配給制度

**rational** /ræʃnəl, ræʃənl/ 形 ▶定義 **1** (used about a person) able to use logical thought to make decisions rather than emotions (人について) 物事を決める際に, 感情よりむしろ論理的な思考を用いることができる→(感情に走らず) 理性のある, 理性的な, 分別のある, 道理をわきまえた⇔ **irrational** ▶定義 **2** based on reason; sensible or logical 理性に基づいた; 賢明な, または論理的な→(言動・考えなどが) 合理的な, 理にかなった, 論理的な ‖ *There must be a rational explanation for why he's behaving like this.* 彼がなぜこのような振る舞いをしているのかについて論理的な説明ができるはずです. ── **rationally** 副 →理性的に, 合理的に

**rationalize** (または **-ise**) /ræʃnəlàɪz, ræʃənlàɪz/ 動 ▶定義 **1** 自 他 to find reasons that explain why you have done sth (perhaps because you do not like the real reason) (おそらく本当の理由が気に入らないために) なぜ～を行ったかを説明する理屈を見いだす→～を合理的・論理的に説明する, 理屈づける, 正当化する ▶定義 **2** 他 to make a business or a system better organized 事業または制度の組織化を進める→～を合理化する, 再組織する ── **rationalization** (または **rationalisation**) /ræʃnəlaɪzéɪʃ(ə)n; -lə-/ 名 **C U**

→理屈づけ, 正当化, 合理化

**rattle**¹ /rǽtl/ 動 ▶定義1 ⾃⽥ to make a noise like hard things hitting each other or to shake sth so that it makes this noise 硬い物がぶつかり合うような音を立てる, またはそのような音がするように〜を振り動かす➡ガタガタいう, ガラガラ鳴る; 〜をガタガタいわせる, カチャカチャいわせる ‖ *The windows were rattling all night in the wind.* 窓が風で一晩中ガタガタ音を立てていた. *He rattled the money in the tin.* 彼は缶に入ったお金をガチャガチャいわせた. ▶定義2 ⽥ 略式 to make sb suddenly become worried 〜を突如, 不安にさせる➡〜を混乱させる, どぎまぎさせる, 動揺させる, 狼狽(ろうばい)させる ‖ *The news of his arrival really rattled her.* 彼が到着したという知らせに彼女は本当に動揺した.

句動 **rattle sth off** ▶定義 to say a list of things you have learned very quickly 覚えた物事を1つ1つ非常に早口で言う➡〜を早口で読む・言う, ぺらぺらしゃべり立てる, すらすら唱える ‖ *She rattled off the names of every player in the team.* 彼女はそのチームの選手1人1人の名前をすらすらと言った.

**rattle**² /rǽtl/ 名 ⒞ ▶定義1 a toy that a baby can shake to make a noise 赤ん坊が振って音を出すことができるおもちゃ➡ガラガラ鳴るおもちゃ, ガラガラ ▶定義2 a noise made by hard things hitting each other 硬い物がぶつかり合って生じる音➡ガチャガチャ・ガラガラいう音

**raucous** /rɔ́ːkəs/ 形 ▶定義 (used about people's voices) loud and unpleasant (人々の声について)大きくて不快な➡耳障りな, 騒々しい, しわがれ声の ‖ *raucous laughter* 騒々しい笑い声

**ravage** /rǽvɪdʒ/ 動 ⽥ ▶定義 to damage sth very badly; to destroy sth 〜にかなりひどい損傷を与える; 〜を破壊する➡〜を荒らす, 破壊する, 荒廃させる, 損なう ‖ *The forests were ravaged by the winter storms.* その森林は冬のあらしによって破壊された.

**rave**¹ /réɪv/ 動 ⾃ ▶定義1 略式 rave (about sb/sth) to say very good things about sb/sth 〜について非常に好意的な事を言う➡〜を激賞する, 褒める, 絶賛する, 褒めちぎる ‖ *Everyone's raving about her latest record!* 皆が彼女の最新記録のことを熱狂的に語っています. ▶定義2 to speak angrily or wildly 怒って, または荒々しく話す➡(〜に・〜のことで)どなり散らす, わめく

**rave**² /réɪv/ 名 ⒞ 英 ▶定義 a large party held outside or in an empty building, at which people dance to electronic music 屋外またはだれも住んでいない建物の中で開かれる大きなパーティーで, 人々は電子音による音楽に合わせて踊る➡乱ちきパーティー, どんちゃん騒ぎ

**raven** /réɪv(ə)n/ 名 ⒞ ▶定義 a large black bird that has an unpleasant voice 不快な声をした, 大きな黒い鳥➡ワタリガラス, 大ガラス

**ravenous** /rǽv(ə)nəs/ 形 ▶定義 very hungry 非常に空腹の➡腹ぺこの, ひどく空腹の, 飢え切った ― **ravenously** 副 ➡腹ぺこで, ひどく空腹で, 飢え死にしそうに

**rave review** 名 ⒞ ▶定義 an article in a newspaper, etc that says very good things about a new book, film, play, etc 新しい本, 映画, 演劇などに関して非常に好意的に述べている新聞などの記事➡べた褒めの評, 絶賛の評

**ravine** /rəvíːn/ 名 ⒞ ▶定義 a narrow deep valley with steep sides 険しい斜面に挟まれた細長く深い谷➡峡谷, 谷間, 山峡

**raving** /réɪvɪŋ/ 形 副 略式 ▶定義 used to emphasize a particular state or quality 特定の状況または性質を強調するために用いて➡非常な, すばらしい, 完全に, すさまじく ‖ *Have you gone raving mad?* 全く頭がどうかしてしまったのですか.

*★**raw** /rɔ́ː/ 形 ▶定義1 not cooked 調理されていない➡(食物が)生の, 加熱されていない, 料理していない ‖ *Raw vegetables are good for your teeth.* 生野菜は歯に良い. ▶定義2 in the natural state; not yet made into anything 自然な状態で; まだ何にも加工されていない➡原料のままの, 加工していない, 処理されていない ‖ *raw materials* (= that are used to make things in factories, etc) 原料 (= 工場などで物を作るために使われる) ▶定義3 used about an injury where the skin has come off from being rubbed 皮膚がこすれてできた傷について用いて➡皮の擦りむけた, ひりひり痛む

**ray** /réɪ/ 名 ⒞ ▶定義 a line of light, heat or energy 光, 熱, またはエネルギーの放射➡光線, 熱線, 放射線 ‖ *the sun's rays* 太陽光線 *ultraviolet rays* 紫外線 ☛参 **X-ray**

成句 **a ray of hope** ▶定義 a small chance that things will get better 事態が改善するわずかな可

1330　razor

能性→わずかな希望, 希望の光, いちるの望み

*__razor__ /réizər/ 名 C ▶定義 a sharp instrument which people use to cut off the hair from their skin (shave) 人が肌から毛を切り落とす(そる)ために用いる鋭利な器具→**かみそり, ひげそり** ‖ *an electric razor* 電気かみそり　*a disposable razor* 使い捨てかみそり

__razor blade__ 名 C ▶定義 the thin sharp piece of metal that you put in a razor かみそりにはめ込む, 薄く鋭利な金属→**かみそりの刃**

__Rd__ 略 road→**道, 道路** ‖ *21 Hazel Rd* ヘーゼル通り21番地

*__reach__[1] /ríːtʃ/ 動 ▶定義1 to arrive at a place or condition that you have been going towards 自分が目指してきた場所または状態に到達する→**～に着く, 到着する, 達する, ～を達成する** ‖ *We won't reach Dover before 12.* ドーバーに12時前には到着しないでしょう. *The two sides hope to __reach an agreement__ sometime today.* 双方が今日中に合意に達することを望んでいる. *Sometimes the temperature reaches 45℃.* 気温が摂氏45度に達することもある. *The team reached the semi-final last year.* そのチームは去年, 準決勝まで進んだ. *to reach a decision/conclusion/compromise* 決定・結論・妥協案に至る

▶定義2 自 他 reach (out) (for sb/sth); reach (sth) (down) to stretch out your arm to try and touch or get sth ～に触れるようにまたは～が取れるように, 腕を伸ばす→**伸びる; ～を差し出す, 差し伸べる, 伸ばす** ‖ *The child reached out for her mother.* その子供は母親の方に手を伸ばした. *She reached into her bag for her purse.* 彼女は財布を取ろうとバッグに手を入れた.

▶定義3 自 他 to be able to touch sth ～に触れることができる→**～に手が届く, ～を取ることができる** ‖ *Can you get me that book off the top shelf? I can't reach.* 一番上の棚からあの本を取ってくれませんか. 私には手が届かないので. *He couldn't reach the light switch.* 彼は電灯のスイッチに手が届かなかった. *I need a longer ladder. This one won't reach.* もっと長いはしごが必要です. これでは届かないでしょう.

▶定義4 他 to communicate with sb, especially by telephone; contact 特に電話で, ～と連絡を取る; 接触する→**～と連絡を取る, 連絡が取れる** ‖ *You can reach me at this number.* この電話番号にかければ私と連絡が取れます.

__reach__[2] /ríːtʃ/ 名 U ▶定義 the distance that you can stretch your arm 自分が腕を伸ばして届く距離→**手の届く範囲, 届く距離, 腕の長さ, リーチ**

成句 __beyond/out of (sb's) reach__ ▶定義1 outside the distance that you can stretch your arm 腕を伸ばして届く距離を超えている→**～の手の届かない所に, 手の届く範囲にない** ‖ *Keep this medicine out of the reach of children.* この薬は子供の手の届かない所に保管してください. ▶定義2 not able to be got or done by sb ～によって得られる, または行われることができない→**～の力の及ばない, 能力を超えた** ‖ *A job like that is completely beyond his reach.* そのような仕事は完全に彼の能力を超えています.

__within (sb's) reach__ ▶定義1 inside the distance that you can stretch your arm 腕を伸ばして届く距離にある→**～の手の届く所に, 手の届く範囲の** ▶定義2 able to be achieved by sb ～によって成し遂げられる→**～の力の及ぶところに** ‖ *We were one goal ahead with ten minutes left and so could sense that victory was within our reach.* 私たちは残り時間10分で1点リードしていたので, 勝利に手が届きそうだと感じた.

__within (easy) reach of sth__ ▶定義 not far from sth →**～から遠くもない**→**～の(容易に)手の届く[達する]ところに**

*__react__ /riǽkt/ 動 自 ▶定義1 react (to sth) (by doing sth) to do or say sth because of sth that has happened or been said 起こったまたは言われた～が原因で, …を行う, あるいは言う→**(刺激などに)反応する, 対応する, 反応を示す** ‖ *He reacted to the news by jumping up and down and shouting.* 彼はその知らせに, 飛び跳ねて大声を上げた. *The players reacted angrily to the decision.* 選手たちはその決定に怒りの反応を示した. ▶定義2 react (to sth) to become ill after eating, breathing, etc a particular substance 特定の物質を食べる, 吸い込むなどした後, 具合が悪くなる→**(～に)悪い反応を示す, 反応する** ▶定義3 react (with sth/together) (used about a chemical substance) to change after coming into contact with another substance (化学物質について) ほかの物質と接触した後で変化する→**(～に･～と)反応する**

句動詞 __react against sb/sth__ ▶定義 to behave

or talk in a way that shows that you do not like the influence of sb/sth (for example authority, your family, etc)(例えば権威, 家族など)～からの影響を好まないことを示すように振る舞う, またはしゃべる➡～に反発する, 反抗する

**\*reaction** /riǽkʃ(ə)n/ 名 ▶定義1 ⓒⓤ(a) reaction (to sb/sth) something that you do or say because of sth that has happened 起こったか原因で行う, または言う事柄➡～に対する反応, ～への反響, 跳ね返り ‖ *Could we have your reaction to the latest news, Prime Minister?* 最新ニュースに対する反応をお聞かせ願います, 首相. *I shook him to try and wake him up but there was no reaction.* 私は彼を揺さぶって目を覚まさせようと試みたが, 何の反応もなかった. ▶定義2 ⓒⓤ (a) reaction (against sb/sth) behaviour that shows that you do not like the influence of sb/sth (for example authority, your family, etc)(例えば権威, 家族など)～からの影響を好まないことを示す振る舞い➡～への反発, 反動, 反抗 ▶定義3 ⓒ a reaction (to sth) a bad effect that your body experiences because of sth that you have eaten, touched or breathed 食べた, 触った, または吸い込んだ～が原因で, 身体が受ける悪い影響➡～に対する悪い反応 ‖ *She had an **allergic reaction** to something in the food.* 彼女は食べ物に含まれている何かにアレルギー反応を起こした. ▶定義4 [ⓒ, 通常は複数] the physical ability to act quickly when sth happens ～が起きたときに素早く反応できる身体的な能力➡反射能力 ‖ *If the other driver's reactions hadn't been so good, there would have been an accident.* 相手の運転手の反射能力があれほど良くなかったとしたら, 事故になっていたでしょう. ▶定義5 ⓒⓤ (専門用語) a chemical change produced by two or more substances coming into contact with each other 2つ以上の物質が互いに接触することによって生じる化学変化➡反応

**reactionary** /riǽkʃ(ə)n(ə)ri/ 名 ⓒ (複 **reactionaries**) ▶定義 a person who tries to prevent political or social change 政治的または社会的な変化を避けようとする人➡反動主義者, 保守的な人 ― **reactionary** 形➡反動的な, 保守的な ‖ *reactionary views/politics/groups* 保守的な見解・政治・集団

**reactor** /riǽktər/ = **NUCLEAR REACTOR**

read¹ 1331

**\*read**¹ /ri:d/ 動 (過, 過分 **read** /red/) ▶定義1 自他 to look at words or symbols and understand them 言葉や記号を見て理解する➡読書する, 読める, 読んで知る; ～を読む, 読んで理解する ‖ *He never learnt to read and write.* 彼は読み書きができるようにならなかった. *Have you read any good books lately?* 最近何か良い本を読みましたか. *Can you read music?* 楽譜が読めますか. ▶定義2 自他 read (sb) (sth); read sth (to sb) to say written words to sb 書かれた言葉を口に出して～に言う➡(～を)声に出して読む, 音読する, 朗読する, 読んで聞かせる ‖ *My father used to read me stories when I was a child.* 私が子供のころ, 父は物語を読んで聞かせてくれたものです. *I hate reading out loud.* 私は大きな声で読み上げるのが嫌いだ. ▶定義3 他 to be able to understand sth from what you can see 目に見えるものから～が理解できる➡～を読み取る, 解釈する, (人の心・考えなど)を読む, 見抜く ‖ *A man came to read the gas meter.* 男の人がガスメーターを読み取りに来た. *Profoundly deaf people train to **read** lips.* 全く耳の聞こえない人は唇を読む訓練をする. *I've no idea what he'll say - I can't **read** his mind!* 私には彼が何と言うか見当も付かない―彼の心を読むことはできませんか. ▶定義4 他 to show words or a sign of sth ～を意味する言葉または記号を表示する➡(文字・数・記号などで)～と示している, 書いてある, ～を指す, 表示する ‖ *The sign read 'Keep Left'.* その標識は「左側通行」と書いてあった. ▶定義5 他 正式 to study a subject at university ある科目を大学で勉強する➡～を専攻する, 研究する, 勉強する ‖ *She read Modern Languages at Cambridge.* 彼女はケンブリッジ大学で現代語学を専攻した.

句動詞 read sth into sth ▶定義 to think that there is a meaning in sth that may not really be there 実際にはそこにないかもしれない～の中に, 何か意味があると考える➡～の中に考えなどを読み取る, ～の中に…が意図されていると考える, ～に勝手な意味・考えを読み込む

read on ▶定義 to continue reading; to read the next part of sth 読むことを続ける; ～の次の部分を読む➡続けて読む, (中断して)再び読み続ける

## 1332 read²

**read sth out** ▶定義 to read sth to other people ～をほかの人々に読んで聞かせる ➔ ～を読み上げる, 音読する, 朗読する

**read sth through** ▶定義 to read sth to check details or to look for mistakes 詳細を確認するまたは誤りがないかどうかを見るために, ～を読む ➔ ～を通読する, 最後まで読み通す ‖ *I read my essay through a few times before handing it in.* 私は自分の書いた小論を提出する前に2, 3回通読した.

**read up on sth** ▶定義 to find out everything you can about a subject ある題目について, できる限り何でも調べる ➔ ～をよく調べる, 研究する

**read²** /riːd/ 名 [単数扱い] 略式 ▶定義 a period or the action of reading 読んでいる時間, または読むという行為 ➔ 読書時間, 読書 ‖ *Her detective novels are usually a good read.* 彼女の推理小説はいつも読みごたえがある.

**readable** /ríːdəb(ə)l/ 形 ▶定義1 able to be read 読むことができる ➔ 読むことができる, 判読できる, 読みやすい ‖ *machine-readable data* 機械で読み取り可能なデータ ☛参 **legible** ▶定義2 easy or interesting to read 読みやすい, または読んで面白い ➔ 分かりやすい, 読んで面白い, 面白く読める

***reader** /ríːdər/ 名 C ▶定義1 a person who reads sth (a particular newspaper, magazine, type of book, etc) (ある特定の新聞, 雑誌, 特別な種類の本など) ～を読む人 ➔ 読者, 読む人, 読書家 ‖ *She's an avid reader of science fiction.* 彼女はSFの愛読者だ. ▶定義2 (形容詞と共に) a person who reads in a particular way あるやり方で読む人 ➔ 読むのが～な人 ‖ *a fast/slow reader* 読むのが速い・遅い人 ▶定義3 a book for practising reading 読む練習をするための本 ➔ (初級の) 読本, リーダー, 教科書

**readership** /ríːdərʃɪp/ 名 [単数扱い] ▶定義 the number of people who regularly read a particular newspaper, magazine, etc ある特定の新聞, 雑誌などをいつも読んでいる人々の数 ➔ 読者数, 購読者数 ‖ *The newspaper has a readership of 200000.* その新聞の読者数は20万人である.

**readily** /rédəli; rédɪ-/ 副 ▶定義1 easily, without difficulty 簡単に, 困難を伴わないで ➔ 容易に, 難なく, たやすく, 簡単に ‖ *Most vegetables are readily available at this time of year.* 1年のうち今の時期は, ほとんどの野菜が容易に手に入る. ▶定義2 without pausing; without being forced ためらわずに; 強制されることなく ➔ 快く, 喜んで, 進んで, すぐに ‖ *He readily admitted that he was wrong.* 彼は自分が間違っていたことをあっさりと認めた.

**readiness** /rédinəs/ 名 U ▶定義1 readiness (for sth) the state of being ready or prepared 用意ができている, または準備されている状態 ➔ 準備・用意のできていること, 支度 ▶定義2 readiness (to do sth) the state of being prepared to do sth without arguing or complaining 口論したり不満を述べたりすることなく, ～を行う準備ができている状態 ➔ 喜んで・進んですること, 快諾, 意向, 意欲 ‖ *The bank have indicated their readiness to lend him the money.* 銀行は彼にその金を貸す意向を示した.

***reading** /ríːdɪŋ/ 名 ▶定義1 U what you do when you read 読むときにすること ➔ 読書, 読むこと ‖ *I haven't had time to do much reading lately.* 最近はあまり読書をする時間がなかった. *Her hobbies include painting and reading.* 彼女の趣味には絵をかくことと読書がある. ▶定義2 U books, articles, etc that are intended to be read 読まれることが意図された本, 記事など ➔ 読み物, 読本, 記事, 選集 ‖ *The information office gave me a pile of reading matter to take away.* その案内所は, 持ち帰って読む物を山ほどくれた. ▶定義3 C the particular way in which sb understands sth ～が…を理解する特定の方法 ➔ (～の) 解釈, 見解, 見方, 判断 ‖ *What's your reading of the situation?* この状況をあなたはどのように見ますか. ▶定義4 C the number or measurement that is shown on an instrument 器具に示された数値または目盛り ➔ (晴雨計・温度計などの) 示度, 示数, 度数, 表示 ‖ *a reading of 20°* 20度の表示

**readjust** /riːədʒʌ́st, rɪ̀-/ 動 ▶定義1 I readjust (to sth) to get used to a different or new situation 異なるまたは新しい状況に慣れる ➔ (～に) 再び順応する, 再び適応する ‖ *After her divorce, it took her a long time to readjust to being single again.* 彼女は離婚後, 再び1人の生活に順応するのに長い時間がかかった. ▶定義2 T to change or move sth slightly ～をわずかに変更する, または動かす ➔ ～を調整し直す, 再調整する

る,修正する — readjustment 名 C U →再調整,再整理,修正

*ready /rédi/ 形 ▶定義1 ready (for sb/sth); ready (to do sth) prepared and able to do sth or to be used 準備されていて、〜をすることができるまたは〜を使用することができる→(〜する・〜の)用意ができた、準備ができた、支度ができた ‖ *The car will be ready for you to collect on Friday.* その車は金曜日に引き取ることができるでしょう. *He isn't ready to take his driving test - he hasn't had enough lessons.* 彼は運転免許試験を受ける準備ができていない − まだ必要なだけの講習を受けていないので. *I'm meeting him at 7, so I don't have long to **get ready**.* 私は彼に7時に会う予定なので用意する時間があまりない. *I'll go and **get** the dinner **ready**.* 私が行って夕食の準備をしましょう. ***Have** your money **ready** before you get on the bus.* バスに乗る前にお金を用意しておきなさい. ▶定義2 ready to do sth; ready (with/for sth) prepared and happy to do sth 〜を行う準備ができていて喜んでいる→いつでも〜する,喜んで〜する,進んで〜する,〜したがる ‖ *You know me - I'm always ready to help.* あなたは私のことをよくご存じでしょう − 私はいつでも喜んで援助しますよ. *Charlie's always ready with advice.* チャーリーはいつも忠告をしたがる. *The men were angry and ready for a fight.* その男たちは怒っていて、今にもけんかをしそうだった. *I know it's early, but I'm **ready for bed**.* まだ早いのは分かっていますが、私はもう寝られます. ▶定義3 副 (複合形容詞を作るために用いて) that has already been made or done; not done especially for you 既に作られた、または行われた; 特にその人のために行われたのではない→前もって、あらかじめ ‖ *ready-cooked food* 調理済みの食品 *There are no **ready-made** answers to this problem - we'll have to find our own solution.* この問題に決まった答えは存在しません − 私たちが自分で解決策を見つけなければならないでしょう.

*real¹ /ríəl, rí:(ə)l/ 形 ▶定義1 actually existing, not imagined 実際に存在している、想像されたのではない→(想像でなく)現実の、実際の、実在する ‖ *The film is based on real life.* この映画は実生活に基づいている. *This isn't a real word, I made it up.* これは実在する言葉ではなく、私が

real estate 1333

作り上げたものです. *We have a real chance of winning.* 私たちには実際に勝てるチャンスがある. *Closure of the factory is a very real danger.* 工場の閉鎖はまさしく現実の危機である. ▶定義2 actually true; not only what people think is true 実際に本当の; 人々が正しいと思っているだけではない→本当の、正確な ‖ *The name he gave to the police wasn't his real name.* 彼が警察に語った名前は実名ではなかった. ▶定義3 (名詞の前だけ) having all, not just some, of the qualities necessary to really be sth 本当に〜であるために必要な性質のうち、一部だけではなくすべてを備えている→真の、真正の、本物の ‖ *She was my first real girlfriend.* 彼女は私にとって初めての真のガールフレンドだった. ▶定義4 natural, not false or artificial 自然の、にせ物や人造ではない→(まがい物ではない)本物の、天然の ‖ *This shirt is real silk.* このシャツは本物の絹です. ▶定義5 (名詞の前だけ) (used to emphasize a state, feeling or quality) strong or big (状態、気持ち、または性質を強調するために用いて)強い、または大きな→全くの、大変な ‖ *Money is a real problem for us at the moment.* お金は私たちにとって当面の大問題です. *He made a real effort to be polite.* 彼は礼儀正しくしようと大変な努力をした.

成句 **for real** ▶定義 genuine or serious 正真正銘の、または真剣な→本物の、真正の、本気の ‖ *Her tears weren't for real.* 彼女の涙は本物ではなかった. *Was he for real when he offered you the job?* 彼はあなたにその仕事を申し出たとき、本気だったのですか.

**the real thing** ▶定義 something genuine, not a copy 写しではなく本物→本物、本場物 ‖ *This painting is just a copy. The real thing is in a gallery.* この絵はただの複製です. 本物は美術館にあります. *She's had boyfriends before but this time she says it's the real thing (= real love).* 彼女には以前ボーイフレンドがいたが、今度こそは本命(=本当の恋人)だと言っている.

**real²** /ríəl, rí:(ə)l/ 副 困 略式 ▶定義 very; really→非常に; 本当に

**real estate** 名 U ▶定義 property in the form of land and buildings 土地または建物の形をとる財産→不動産、土地家屋、(売買される)家

**real estate agent** 英 = ESTATE AGENT

**realism** /ríəlìz(ə)m, ríː(ə)lìz(ə)m/ 名 U ▶定義1 behaviour that shows that you accept the facts of a situation and are not influenced by your feelings ある状況の事実を受け入れ，感情に左右されていないことを表すような振る舞い→現実主義 ☞参 idealism ▶定義2 (in art, literature, etc) showing things as they really are (芸術, 文学などで) 物事を有りのままに表現している→写実主義, リアリズム

**realist** /ríəlɪst, ríː(ə)lɪst/ 名 C ▶定義1 a person who accepts the facts of a situation, and does not try to pretend that it is different ある状況の事実を受け入れ，それを異なっているように見せ掛けようとしない人→現実主義者, 実際家 ‖ *I'm a realist - I don't expect the impossible.* 私は現実主義者です—不可能な事は期待しません. ▶定義2 an artist or writer who shows things as they really are 物事を有りのままに表現する芸術家または作家→写実主義者, リアリスト

**realistic** /ríəlístɪk, ríːə-/ 形 ▶定義1 sensible and understanding what it is possible to achieve in a particular situation ある状況において達成可能なものに気付いている，また理解している→現実的な, 実際的な ‖ *We have to be realistic about our chances of winning.* 私たちは勝てる見込みについて現実的に考える必要があります. ▶定義2 showing things as they really are 物事を有りのままに表現している→写実主義の, 写実的な, 写実派の ‖ *a realistic drawing/description* 写実的なスケッチ・描写 ▶定義3 not real but appearing to be real 本物ではないが本物らしく見えている→リアルな, 真に迫った ‖ *The monsters in the film were very realistic.* 映画に出てくる怪獣たちはとてもリアルだった. — **realistically** /ríəlístɪk(ə)li, ríːə-/ →現実的に, 現実主義的に, 写実的に, リアルに

**\*reality** /riǽləti/ 名 (複 **realities**) ▶定義1 ❶ the way life really is, not the way it may appear to be or how you would like it to be そのように見えるまたはそうあってほしいと望むような在り方ではなく，実際の生活の在り方→現実(のもの), 実体, 実態, 実情 ‖ *I enjoyed my holiday, but now it's back to reality.* 私は休暇を楽しんだが，今度は現実の生活に戻らなければならない. *We have to face reality and accept that we've failed.* 私たちは現実と向き合い，失敗を認める必要がある. ▶定義2 ❷ a thing that is actually experienced, not just imagined 単に想像されたのではなく，実際に経験された物事→事実・真実であること, 実在, 実質 ‖ *Films portray war as heroic and exciting, but the reality is very different.* 映画では戦争を英雄的に，また刺激的に描いているが，事実とは非常に異なる.

成句 **in reality** ▶定義 in fact, really (not the way sth appears or has been described) 事実, 本当に (〜がどのように見えるか，または描かれたかではない)→実は, 実際は ‖ *People say this is an exciting city but in reality it's rather boring.* ここは刺激的な都市だと言われていますが，実際はかなり退屈です.

**\*realize** (または **-ise**) /ríəlàɪz, ríːə-/ 動 他 ▶定義1 to know and understand that sth is true or that sth has happened 〜が本当であることを，または〜が起こったことを知る, あるいは理解する→〜を悟る, 認識する, 〜だとはっきり理解する, (実感として)〜がよく分かる ‖ *I'm sorry I mentioned it, I didn't realize how much it upset you.* その事を口にしてしまい，申し訳ありません. あなたをどれほど動揺させてしまうか分かっていませんでした. *Didn't you realize (that) you needed to bring money?* お金を持ってくる必要があることを承知していなかったのですか. ▶定義2 to become conscious of sth or that sth has happened, usually some time later 〜に，または〜が起きたことに，通常はしばらくしてから気付く→〜を自覚する, 〜に気付く ‖ *When I got home, I realized that I had left my keys at the office.* 私は家に着いた時に，事務所にかぎを置き忘れたことに気付いた. ▶定義3 to make sth that you imagined become reality 想像していた〜を現実のものとする→〜を実現する, 達成する, (事が) 現実化する, 起こる ‖ *His worst fears were realized when he saw the damage caused by the fire.* その火事による被害を目にした時，彼が最も恐れていた事が現実となった. — **realization** (または **-isation**) /ríːəlaɪzéɪʃ(ə)n, ríːə-; -lə-/ 名 U →悟ること, 感得, 実感, 実現, 現実化

**\*really** /ríː(ə)li, ríː(ə)li/ 副 ▶定義1 actually; in fact 実際に; 事実→実際は, 本当は, 実を言うと, 真に ‖ *I couldn't believe it was really happening.* それが実際に起こっていたとは信じられなかった.

*He said he was sorry but I don't think he really meant it.* 彼は申し訳ないと言ったが、私には本心からそう言ったとは思えない. *She wasn't really angry, she was only pretending.* 彼女は実は怒っていなかった、そう見せ掛けていただけだった. *Is it really true?* それは本当に事実なのですか. ▶定義2 very; very much 大いに; 非常にたくさん→**全く、実に、本当に、確かに** ‖ *I'm really tired.* 私は実に疲れた. *Are you really sure?* 本当に確かですか. *I really hope you enjoy yourself.* あなたが楽しく過ごされることを心から願っています. *I really tried but I couldn't do it.* 私は非常に努力したのだが、それをすることはできなかった. ▶定義3 used as a question for expressing surprise, interest, doubt, etc 驚き、興味、疑いなどを表す問いとして用いて→**えっ、ほんと、おや、へえ、まさか** ‖ *'She's left her husband.' 'Really? When did that happen?'*「彼女はご主人と別れました」「まさか. それはいつのことですか」▶定義4 used in negative sentences to make what you are saying less strong 否定文において、言っている内容を和らげるために用いて→**それほど～ない、～というわけではない** ‖ *I don't really agree with that.* 私はその事にあまり賛成しません. ▶定義5 used in questions when you are expecting sb to answer 'No' 疑問文において、～が No と答えることを期待しているときに用いて→**まさか** ‖ *You don't really expect me to believe that, do you?* まさか私がそれを信じるとは思っていないでしょうね.

**Realtor**™ /ríəltər, -tɔːr, ríː(ə)l-/ 米 = **ESTATE AGENT**

**reap** /ríːp/ 動 他 ▶定義 to cut and collect a crop (corn, wheat, etc) 穀物（トウモロコシ、小麦など）を刈り取って集める→**～を収穫する、刈る、刈り取る、刈り入れる** ‖ （比喩）*Work hard now and you'll reap the benefits later on.* 今、しっかり働いておきなさい、そうすれば後で報われるでしょう.

**reappear** /rìːəpíər/ 動 自 ▶定義 to appear again or be seen again 再び現れる、または見られる→**再び現れる、再現する、再発する** — reappearance /-rəns/ 名 C U →再び現れること、再現、再発

**reappraisal** /rìːəpréiz(ə)l/ 名 C U ▶定義 the new examination of a situation, way of doing sth, etc in order to decide if any changes are necessary 何らかの変更が必要かどうかを判断するために、状況、～のやり方などを新たに検討すること→**再評価、再検討、再考、見直し**

★**rear**¹ /ríər/ 名 [単数扱い] ▶定義1 the rear the back part 後ろの部分→**後部、後ろ、後方、背後** ‖ *Smoking is only permitted at the rear of the bus.* 喫煙はバスの後部でのみ許可されている. ▶定義2 the part of your body that you sit on; bottom 座るとき下になる身体の部分; しり→**しり** — rear 形 →**後部の、背後の、後ろの、後方の** ‖ *the rear window/lights of a car* 車の後部の窓・ライト

成句 **bring up the rear** ▶定義 to be the last one in a race, a line of people, etc 競走、人の列などで最後である→**（競技などで）最下位になる、（行列などの）最後尾を行く、しんがりを務める**

**rear**² /ríər/ 動 ▶定義1 他 to look after and educate children 子供を世話し、教育する→**～を（成人するまで）育てる、養育する、しつける** ‖ *This generation of children will be reared without fear of war.* 今の世代の子供たちは戦争の恐ろしさを知らずに育てられるでしょう. ▶定義2 他 to breed and look after animals on a farm, etc 農場などで動物を育て、世話をする→**～を飼育する** ‖ *to rear cattle/poultry* 畜牛・鳥（類）を飼育する ▶定義3 自 rear (up) (used about horses) to stand only on the back legs （馬について）後ろ足のみで立つ→**後ろ足で立つ**

**rearrange** /rìːəréindʒ/ 動 他 ▶定義1 to change the position or order of things 物の位置または順序を変える→**～を配置・配列し直す、配置・配列を変える、並べ換える、再整理する** ‖ *We've rearranged the living room to make more space.* 私たちは空間をもっと広くとるために、居間の配置替えをした. ▶定義2 to change a plan, meeting, etc that has been fixed 決まっていた計画、会合などを変更する→**（場所・日程など）を変更する、再調整する、再指定する** ‖ *The match has been rearranged for next Wednesday.* その試合は来週の水曜日に日程が変更になった.

★**reason**¹ /ríːzn/ 名 ▶定義1 C a reason (for sth/for doing sth); a reason why.../that... a cause or an explanation for sth that has happened or for sth that sb has done 起こった～の、または～が行った…の原因あるいは説明→**（～の・～する・～に反対する・～の背後の）理由、訳、**

## 1336 reason[2]

動機 ‖ *What's your reason for being so late?* こんなに遅くなった理由は何ですか. *Is there any reason why you couldn't tell me this before?* この事を前に私に話せなかったのには何か訳があるのですか. *He said he couldn't come but he didn't **give a reason**.* 彼は来られないと言ったが、理由は言わなかった. *The reason (that) I'm phoning you is to ask a favour.* 私があなたに電話をしているのは、お願いがあってのことです.
***For some reason** they can't give us an answer until next week.* 訳があって、彼らは来週まで私たちに返答ができない. *She left the job for personal reasons.* 彼女は個人的な理由でその仕事を辞めた. ▶定義2 ⒞ ⓤ (a) reason (to do sth); (a) reason (for sth/for doing sth) something that shows that it is right or fair to do sth ～を行うのが正しい、または公正であることを示すもの→根拠, 理屈 ‖ *I **have reason** to believe that you've been lying.* あなたがうそをついていたと私が思うのには根拠があります. *I think we have reason for complaint.* 私たちが文句を言うのはもっともなことだと思う. *You **have every reason** (= you are completely right) to be angry, considering how badly you've been treated.* どれほどひどい扱いを受けたかを考えると、あなたが腹を立てるのも無理はない(= あなたが全面的に正しい). ▶定義3 ⓤ the ability to think and to make sensible decisions 考えて、分別のある判断ができる能力→理性, 思考力, 判断力, 思慮, 分別 ‖ *Only human beings are capable of reason.* 人間だけが理性を備えている. ▶定義4 ⓤ what is right or acceptable 正しい、または受け入れられていること→道理, 理屈, 良識, 筋道 ‖ *I tried to persuade him not to drive but he just wouldn't **listen to reason**.* 私は彼に運転しないよう説得したが、彼は聞き入れようとしなかった. *I'll pay anything **within reason** for a ticket.* 私はそのチケットのためなら常識の範囲内でいくらでも支払います.
成句 **it stands to reason** 略式 ▶定義 it is obvious if you think about it 考えてみれば明白である→(～は)当然である, 理にかなう

**reason**[2] /ríːzn/ 動 ⓘ ⓣ ▶定義 to form a judgement or opinion, after thinking about sth in a logical way ～を論理的に考えてから判断する、または意見をまとめる→(論理的に)思考する; ～から推論する, 推理する, 判断する
句動詞 **reason with sb** ▶定義 to talk to sb in order to persuade him/her to behave or think in a more reasonable way もっと理性的に行動する、または考えるよう説得するために～に話をする→(論じて)～に理を説く, 説得する, 説き伏せる

★**reasonable** /ríːznəbl/ 形 ▶定義1 fair, practical and sensible 公平で実際的で分別のある→(人・行為などが)道理をわきまえた, 分別のある, (人が)理性的な, 思慮分別のある ‖ *I think it's reasonable to expect people to keep their promises.* 人に約束を守ることを期待するのは理にかなっていると思う. *I tried to be reasonable even though I was very angry.* 私はとても腹が立っていたが理性的になろうと努めた. ▶定義2 acceptable and appropriate in a particular situation ある特定の状況において受け入れられ, 適切である→もっともな, 妥当な, 適当な, 程よい, ほどほどの ‖ *It was a lovely meal and the bill was very reasonable!* 楽しい食事でしたし、金額もとても手ごろでした. ⇔ **unreasonable** ▶定義3 quite good, high, big, etc but not very かなり良い, 高い, 大きいなど, しかし非常にというわけではない→まずまずの, まあまあの, ほどほどの ‖ *His work is of a reasonable standard.* 彼の作品はまずまずの水準にある.

**reasonably** /ríːznəb(ə)li/ 副 ▶定義1 fairly or quite (but not very) かなり, またはなかなか(しかし非常にというわけではない)→適当に, 程よく, かなり, 相当に ‖ *The weather was reasonably good but not brilliant.* 天気はまあまあ良かったが, すばらしい晴天というわけではなかった. ▶定義2 in a sensible and fair way 分別ある公平なやり方で→分別よく, 賢明に, 理性的に, 正当に

**reasoning** /ríːznɪŋ/ 名 ⓤ ▶定義 the process of thinking about sth and making a judgement or decision ～について考え, 判断や決定をする過程→推理, 推論, 論法, 議論の筋道 ‖ *What's the reasoning behind his sudden decision to leave?* 彼が突然去ることを決めた裏にはどんな理由があるのだろう.

**reassure** /rìːəʃúər/ 動 ⓣ ▶定義 to say or do sth in order to stop sb worrying or being afraid ～が心配すること, または恐れることをやめさせるために, ～を言うあるいは行う→～を(…に関し

て)安心させる, 自信・元気を回復させる ‖ *The mechanic reassured her that the engine was fine.* その整備工はエンジンは大丈夫であると彼女を安心させた. — **reassurance** /rɪˈʃʊər(ə)ns, rɪ-/ 名 ❶ ❻ ▶定義 advice or help that you give to sb to stop him/her worrying or being afraid 〜が心配すること, または恐れることをやめさせるために, その〜に与える助言または援助➡️**安心させるもの, 元気づけ(の言葉など), 新たな自信** ‖ *I need some reassurance that I'm doing things the right way.* 私は物事を正しく行っているという新たな自信を必要としている. — **reassuring** 形➡️安心させる, 心強い, 元気づけてくれる — **reassuringly** 副➡️安心して, 自信を持って, 元気づけるように

**rebate** /ˈriːbeɪt, rɪˈbeɪt/ 名 ❻ ▶定義 a sum of money that is given back to you because you have paid too much 過剰に支払ったために返却される金額➡️**払い戻し, 割り戻し** ‖ *to get a tax rebate* 税金の払い戻しを受ける

**rebel**¹ /ˈrɛb(ə)l/ 名 ❻ ▶定義 **1** a person who fights against his/her country's government because he/she wants things to change 事態が変わることを望んでいるため, 自国の政府と戦う➡️**反逆者, 謀反人, 反乱軍兵士** ▶定義 **2** a person who refuses to obey people in authority or to accept rules 権威のある人に従うことや規則を受け入れることを拒否する人➡️**反逆者, 反抗者, 謀反人** ‖ *At school he had a reputation as a rebel.* 彼は学校で反逆児という評判を取っていた.

**rebel**² /rɪˈbɛl/ 動 ❶ (**rebelling**; **rebelled**) ▶定義 **rebel (against sb/sth)** to fight against authority, society, a law, etc 権威, 社会, 法律などに反対して戦う➡️**(〜に)謀反を起こす, 反乱を起こす, 反抗する, 抵抗する** ‖ *She rebelled against her parents by marrying a man she knew they didn't approve of.* 彼女は認めてくれないと分かっている人と結婚して, 両親に反発した.

**rebellion** /rɪˈbɛljən/ 名 ❻❿ ▶定義 **1** an occasion when some of the people in a country try to change the government, using violence 国の一部の人が暴力に訴えて政府を変えようとする機会➡️**(〜に対する)反乱, (不成功に終わった)謀反, 暴動** ▶定義 **2** the action of fighting against authority or refusing to accept rules 権威に対して戦う行為, または規則を受け入れることを拒否する行為➡️**反抗, 背反, 造反, 抵抗** ‖ *Voting against the leader of the party was an act of open rebellion.* その政党の指導者に反対票を投じることは, 公然の造反行為だった.

**rebellious** /rɪˈbɛljəs/ 形 ▶定義 not doing what authority, society, etc wants you to do 権威, 社会などが人にしてほしいと望む事をしていない➡️**反抗的な, 言うことを聞かない, 挑戦的な** ‖ *rebellious teenagers* 反抗的な10代の若者

**reboot** /ˌriːˈbuːt, rɪ-/ 動 ❶ ❿ ▶定義 (computing) if you reboot a computer or if it reboots, you turn it off and then turn it on again immediately (コンピューター)コンピューターの操作で, またはコンピューター自体の動作で, 電源を切ってからすぐに入れ直す➡️**プログラムを再起動する; させる**

**rebound** /rɪˈbaʊnd/ 動 ❶ ▶定義 **rebound (from/off sth)** to hit sth/sb and then go in a different direction 〜にぶつかってから別の方向に行く➡️**(〜から)跳ね返る, (音が)反響する** ‖ *The ball rebounded off a defender and went into the goal.* そのボールは守備の選手に跳ね返ってゴールに入った. — **rebound** /ˈriːbaʊnd, rɪˈbaʊnd/ 名 ❻➡️跳ね返り, 反響, リバウンドボール(を取ること)

**rebuff** /rɪˈbʌf/ 名 ❻ ▶定義 an unkind refusal of an offer or suggestion 申し出または提案に対する冷酷な拒絶➡️**すげない拒絶, 阻止, (計画などの)挫折(ざせつ)** — **rebuff** 動 ❿➡️拒絶する

**rebuild** /ˌriːˈbɪld/ 動 ❿ (過, 過分 **rebuilt** /ˌriːˈbɪlt/) ▶定義 to build sth again 〜を再び建てる➡️**〜を改築する, 再建する, 建て直す, 組み立て直す** ‖ *Following the storm, a great many houses will have to be rebuilt.* あらしの後, 非常に多くの家を建て直す必要があるでしょう.

**rebuke** /rɪˈbjuːk/ 動 ❿ 正式 ▶定義 to speak angrily to sb because he/she has done sth wrong 〜が悪い事をしたので, その〜に怒って話す➡️**〜を強く非難する, 厳しくしかる, 叱責(しっせき)する** — **rebuke** 名 ❻➡️非難, 叱責

**recall** /rɪˈkɔːl/ 動 ❿ ▶定義 **1** to remember sth (a fact, event, action, etc) from the past 過去の〜(事実, 出来事, 行動など)を思い出す➡️**(意識的に努力して)〜を思い出す, 思い起こす, 思い出を語る** ‖ *I don't recall exactly when I first met her.* 彼女に初めて会ったのがいつだったか正確に思い出せない. *She couldn't recall meeting him before.*

## 1338 recap

彼女は以前彼に会ったことがあるのを思い出せなかった. ▶定義2 to order sb to return; to ask for sth to be returned 〜に戻るよう命令する;〜が戻されるように頼む→**〜を(…から…へ)呼び戻す,召還する,〜を回収する,元へ戻す** ‖ *The company has recalled all the fridges that have this fault.* その会社はこのような欠陥がある冷蔵庫をすべて回収した.

**recap** /ríːkæp/ (口語) (または (文) **recapitulate** /rìːkəpítʃlèɪt/) 動自他 (**recapping**; **recapped**) ▶定義 to repeat or look again at the main points of sth to make sure that they have been understood 〜の要点を, 確実に理解されるようにするために繰り返す, またはもう一度見る→**〜を要約する, 〜の要点を繰り返す** ‖ *Let's quickly recap what we've done in today's lesson, before we finish.* 終わる前に, 今日の授業でやった事をさっとまとめてみましょう.

**recapture** /rìːkǽptʃər/ 動他 ▶定義1 to win back sth that was taken from you by an enemy or a competitor 敵または競争相手に奪われた〜を取り戻す→**〜を取り戻す, 奪い返す, 奪還する** ‖ *Government troops have recaptured the city.* 政府軍はその都市を奪回した. ▶定義2 to catch a person or animal that has escaped 逃げ出した〜または動物を捕まえる→**〜を再び捕らえる** ▶定義3 to create or experience again sth from the past 過去の〜を再び作り出す, または経験する→**〜を再現する, 再び経験する, よみがえらせる** ‖ *The film brilliantly recaptures life in the 1930s.* その映画は1930年代の生活を鮮やかに描き出している.

**recede** /rɪsíːd/ 動自 ▶定義1 to move away and begin to disappear 離れていき, 消え始める→**(〜から)(徐々に)退く, 後退する, 遠ざかる, 消えていく** ‖ *The coast began to recede into the distance.* 海岸がかなたに消え始めた. ▶定義2 (used about a hope, fear, chance, etc) to become smaller or less strong (希望, 恐怖, 機会などについて)小さくなる, または弱くなる→**減ずる, 薄れる, 低下する, 弱まる** ▶定義3 (used about a man's hair) to fall out and stop growing at the front of the head (人の髪について)前頭部の髪が抜け落ちて, 生えるのが止まる→**(生え際が)後退する, 薄くなる** ‖ *He's got a receding hairline.* 彼は髪の生え際が後退している.
☞ **hair** のさし絵

*****receipt** /rɪsíːt/ 名 ▶定義1 ❻ **a receipt (for sth)** a piece of paper that is given to show that you have paid for sth 〜に対して支払ったことを示すために渡される1枚の紙→**領収証, 受領書, 受け取り, レシート** ‖ *Keep the receipt in case you want to exchange the shirt.* そのシャツを交換する場合のために領収書を保管しておきなさい.
▶定義2 ❶正式 **receipt (of sth)** the receiving of sth 〜を受領すること→**受領すること, 受領されること**

*****receive** /rɪsíːv/ 動他 ▶定義1 **receive sth (from sb/sth)** to get or accept sth that sb sends or gives to you 〜が送ってくれた, または渡してくれた〜を受け取る, あるいは受領する→**〜を(…から)受け取る, 受領する, もらう, 受ける** ‖ *I received a letter from an old friend last week.* 私は先週, 昔の友達から手紙を受け取った. *to receive a phone call/a prize* 電話を受ける・賞をもらう ▶定義2 to experience a particular kind of treatment or injury ある特定の種類の扱いを経験する, または傷を負う→**〜を(受動的に)受ける, 経験する, 被る, 負わされる** ‖ *We received a warm welcome from our hosts.* 私たちは主催者から温かいもてなしを受けました. *He received several cuts and bruises in the accident.* 彼はその事故で数箇所に切り傷と打撲傷を負った.
▶定義3 (しばしば受動態で) to react to sth new in a particular way 新しい〜に対し, ある特定のやり方で反応する→**〜を受け入れる, 〜を(…と)見なす, 認める, 理解する** ‖ *The film has been well received by the critics.* その映画は批評家たちに好意的に受け入れられた.

**receiver** /rɪsíːvər/ 名 ❻ ▶定義1 (または **handset**) the part of a telephone that is used for listening and speaking 聞いたり話したりするために使われる電話の部分→**受話器**
▶電話に出たりかけたりするには, 受話器を pick up(取る)または lift(上げる)と言う. 電話を終えるには, 受話器を put down(置く), replace(戻す), または hang up(電話を切る)と言う.

▶定義2 a piece of television or radio equipment that changes electronic signals into sounds or pictures 電子信号を音声または画像に変換する, テレビまたはラジオの機器→**受信**

機, 受像機

\*recent /ríːsnt/ 形 ▶定義 that happened or began only a short time ago ほんの少し前に起こった，または始まった→最近の，近ごろの，(同じ日で)いましがた起きたばかりの，さっきの，ごく新しい，近代の ‖ *In recent years there have been many changes.* ここ数年でさまざまな変化があった. *This is a recent photograph of my daughter.* これは私の娘の最近の写真です.

\*recently /ríːsntli/ 副 ▶定義 not long ago あまり昔ではなく→(近い過去のある時を指して)ついこの間，先ごろ，つい最近，近来 ‖ *She worked here until quite recently.* 彼女はつい最近までここで働いていた. *Have you seen Paul recently?* 最近ポールに会いましたか.

▶ recently は，ある時点とある期間のどちらも指すことができる. 現在形には用いない. ある時点を指す場合は，単純過去時制を使う：*He got married recently.*(彼は最近結婚した.) ある期間を指す場合は，現在完了形または現在完了進行形を使う：*I haven't done anything interesting recently.*(私は最近，面白い事を何もやっていない.) *She's been working hard recently.*(彼女は最近，一生懸命働いている.) lately は，ある期間のみを指す. 現在完了形または現在完了進行形でしか用いられない：*I've seen a lot of films lately.*(私は最近たくさんの映画を見た.) *I've been spending too much money lately.*(私は近ごろ，お金を使いすぎている.)

**receptacle** /rɪséptək(ə)l/ 名 正式 ▶定義 a container 容器→容器, 入れ物

\***reception** /rɪsépʃ(ə)n/ 名 ▶定義 1 Ⓤ the place inside the entrance of a hotel or office building where guests or visitors go when they first arrive 来客または訪問者が到着したときに最初に行く，ホテルまたはオフィスビルの玄関の内側にある場所→(ホテルの)フロント，(会社などの)受付 ‖ *Leave your key at/in reception if you go out, please.* 出掛けるときはかぎをフロントにお預けください. *the reception desk* (ホテル・会社などの)フロント・受付 ▶定義 2 Ⓒ a formal party to celebrate sth or to welcome an important person ～を祝う，または重要な人物を歓迎するための正式なパーティー→宴会, レセプション, 歓迎会 ‖ *Their wedding reception was held at a local hotel.* 彼らの結婚披露宴は地元のホテルで開かれた. *There will be an official reception at the embassy for the visiting ambassador.* 訪問中の大使のために大使館で公式のレセプションが催されるでしょう. ▶定義 3 [単数扱い] the way people react to sth 人の～に対する反応の仕方→受け止め方, 反応, 反響, 評判 ‖ *The play got a mixed reception (= some people liked it, some people didn't).* その演劇は賛否両論の評価を受けた(= ある人には好評で, ある人には不評だった). ▶定義 4 Ⓤ the quality of radio or television signals ラジオまたはテレビの信号の質→(ラジオ・テレビなどの)受信能力, 受信状態 ‖ *TV reception is very poor where we live.* 私たちの住んでいる所はテレビの映りが非常に悪い.

**receptionist** /rɪsépʃ(ə)nɪst/ 名 Ⓒ ▶定義 a person who works in a hotel, office, etc answering the telephone and dealing with visitors and guests when they arrive ホテル，事務所などで，電話に応答したり，到着する訪問者や来客に応対する仕事をする人→(ホテル・会社などの)応接係, 受付係 ‖ *a hotel receptionist* ホテルの受付係

**receptive** /rɪséptɪv/ 形 ▶定義 receptive (to sth) ready to listen to new ideas, suggestions, etc 新しい考え，提案などに耳を傾ける用意のある→～に受容力がある, 理解力がある, ～をよく受け入れる

**recess** /ríːses, rɪsés/ 名 ▶定義 1 Ⓒ Ⓤ a period of time when Parliament, committees, etc do not meet (英国の)国会，委員会などが開かれない期間→(議会などの)休会期間 ▶定義 2 Ⓤ 米 a short break during a trial in a court of law 法廷で裁判の途中の短い休み時間→休廷 ☛参 **interval** の注 ▶定義 3 Ⓒ part of a wall that is further back than the rest, forming a space ほかの部分よりもさらに後ろに下がり，空間を作っている壁→(部屋などの)凹所, くぼんだ部分, 引っ込んだ部分 ▶定義 4 Ⓒ a part of a room that receives very little light 光をほとんど受けていない部屋の部分→奥まった所, 隅, 奥

**recession** /rɪséʃ(ə)n/ 名 Ⓒ Ⓤ ▶定義 a period when the business and industry of a country is not successful 国の景気および産業がうまくいっていない時期→一時的不景気, 景気後退 ‖ *The country is now in recession.* その国は現在，景気が後退している. *How long will the recession* *last?* 不景気はいつまで続くでしょうか.

**recharge** /riːtʃɑːrdʒ/ 動自他 ▶定義 to fill a battery with electrical power; to fill up with electrical power バッテリーに電力を満たす; 電力で一杯にする→(〜を)充電する‖ *He plugged the drill in to recharge it.* 彼はドリルを充電するため, プラグをコンセントに差し込んだ. ☞参 **charge** — **rechargeable** 形 ▶充電が可能な‖ *rechargeable batteries* 蓄電池

***recipe** /résəpiː, -pi/ 名 C ▶定義1 a recipe (for sth) the instructions for cooking or preparing sth to eat. A recipe tells you what to use (the ingredients) and what to do. 食べる〜を料理または準備するための説明書. 何を使うか(材料)と何をしたらよいかが書いてある→調理法, レシピ‖ *a recipe for chocolate cake* チョコレートケーキのレシピ ▶定義2 a recipe for sth the way to get or produce sth 〜を手に入れる, または作り出す方法→〜の秘けつ, 方法, こつ‖ *Putting Dave in charge of the project is a recipe for disaster.* デーヴにそのプロジェクトを任せると大失敗に終わるだろう.

**recipient** /rɪsípiənt/ 名 C 正式 ▶定義 a person who receives sth 〜を受け取る人→受取人, 受領者, 受納者, 受賞者

**reciprocal** /rɪsíprək(ə)l/ 形 ▶定義 involving two or more people or groups who agree to help each other or to behave in the same way towards one another 互いに助け合うこと, または互いに利益を与えるように同じように行動することに同意している, 2人以上の人またはグループを含んでいる→相互の, 互いの, 互恵的な, 相補的な‖ *The arrangement is reciprocal. They help us and we help them.* その取り決めは相互的です. 彼らは私たちを助け, 私たちは彼らを助けます.

**recital** /rɪsáɪtl/ 名 C ▶定義 a formal public performance of music or poetry 音楽または詩の正式な公演→独奏会, 独唱会, リサイタル, 朗読会‖ *a piano recital* ピアノのリサイタル ☞参 **concert**

**recite** /rɪsáɪt/ 動自他 ▶定義 to say aloud a piece of writing, especially a poem or a list, from memory 書かれたもの, 特に詩または一覧表を, そらで声に出して言う→(聴衆などに向かって〜を)暗唱する, 朗読する, 列挙する, 読み上げる

**reckless** /réklǝs/ 形 ▶定義 not thinking about possible bad or dangerous results that could come from your actions 自分の行動に起因して起こり得る悪い, または危険な結果について考えていない→(人・行為が)向こう見ずな, 無謀な, 〜を気に掛けない, 意に介さない‖ *reckless driving* 無謀運転 — **recklessly** 副 ▶無鉄砲に, 無謀に, 向こう見ずに

**reckon** /rék(ə)n/ 動自他 略式 ▶定義1 to think; to have an opinion about sth 考える; 〜について意見を持つ→〜を…だと考える, 〜と(勝手に)思う, 憶測する‖ *She's very late now. I reckon (that) she isn't coming.* 彼女は大幅に遅刻している. もう来ないと私は思います. *I think she's forgotten. What do you reckon?* 私は彼女が忘れたのだと思います. あなたはどう思いますか. ▶定義2 to calculate sth approximately 〜を大まかに計算する→(費用・利益などを)ざっと数える, 計算する, 合計する‖ *I reckon the journey will take about half an hour.* 私はその行程はおよそ30分かかると見積もっている.

句動 **reckon on sth** ▶定義 to expect sth to happen and therefore to base a plan or action on it 〜が起きると期待し, それゆえに計画または行動の基礎をその〜に置く→〜を(…するものと)当て込む, 想定する, 〜するつもりである‖ *I didn't book in advance because I wasn't reckoning on tickets being so scarce.* 私はチケットがそんなに不足するとは思っていなかったので, 前もって予約をしなかった.

**reckon (sth) up** ▶定義 to calculate the total amount or number of sth 〜の総額または総数を計算する→合算する, 総計する

**reckon with sb/sth** ▶定義 to think about sb/sth as a possible problem 〜を起こり得る問題として考える→〜を(無視できない敵・危険などとして)考慮に入れる, 予期する, 覚悟する

**reclaim** /rɪkléɪm/ 動他 ▶定義1 **reclaim sth (from sb/sth)** to get back sth that has been lost or taken away 失われた, または奪われた〜を取り戻す→(〜から)…の返還を要求する, 〜を取り戻す, 回収する‖ *Reclaim your luggage after you have been through passport control.* パスポートの照合検査が終わった後で荷物を引き取りなさい. ▶定義2 to get back useful materials from waste products 不用になった製品から有用な物質を回収する→〜を再利用する, (再生)利

用のために回収する, 再生する, リサイクルする ▶定義3 to make wet land suitable for use 湿地を利用に適するものにする➜(沼地・海などから)(土地)を干拓する, (沼地・海など)を埋め立てる

**recline** /rɪkláɪn/ [動][自] ▶定義 to sit or lie back in a relaxed and comfortable way くつろいで心地良く寄り掛かかって座る, または横になる➜(~に)もたれる, 寄り掛かる, 横たわる — reclining [形]➜リクライニング式の, 背もたれを倒すことができる ‖ *The car has **reclining seats** at the front.* その車には前部にリクライニング式の座席が付いている.

**recognition** /rèkəgníʃ(ə)n/ [名] ▶定義1 [U] the fact that you can identify sb/sth that you see 見えている~を認識することができるということ➜それと分かること, 見分けが付くこと, 認識, 認知 ‖ *When I arrived no sign of recognition showed on her face at all.* 私が到着した時, 彼女は私を全く覚えていない面持ちだった. ▶定義2 [[U], 単数扱い] the act of accepting that sth exists, is true or is official ~が存在する, 正しい, または公式であることを受け入れること➜承認, 認可, 認知, 認識, 評価 ▶定義3 [U] a public show of respect for sb's work or actions ~の仕事または行動に対し, 公式に敬意を表すること➜表彰, お礼 ‖ *She has **received** public **recognition** for her services to charity.* 彼女は慈善事業において公に認められた. *Please accept this gift **in recognition of** the work you have done.* あなたが行った仕事をたたえてこれを贈ります, どうかお受け取りください.

**recognizable** (または **recognisable**) /rékəgnàɪzəb(ə)l/ [形] ▶定義 recognizable (as sb/sth) that can be identified as sb/sth ~として認識できるような➜(~として)見分けが付く, それと分かる, 認識できる ‖ *He was barely recognizable with his new short haircut.* ショートカットの髪型に変えたせいで, 彼であるとはほとんど分からなかった. — recognizably /-əb(ə)li/ [副]➜見分けが付くほど, それと分かるほどに

***recognize** (または**-ise**) /rékəgnàɪz/ [動][他] ▶定義1 to know again sb/sth that you have seen or heard before 以前に見た, または聞いたことがある~が再度分かる➜~に覚えがある, ~を…で識別する, ~がだれ・何であるか分かる, ~の見分けが付く ‖ *I recognized him but I couldn't remember his name.* 私は彼に見覚えがあったが, 名前を思い出すことができなかった. ▶定義2 to accept that sth is true ~が真実であると受け入れる➜~を認める, 認識する, 受け入れる ▶定義3 to accept sth officially ~を公式に受け入れる➜~を認可する, 承認する, 公認する ‖ *My qualifications are not recognized in other countries.* 私の資格はほかの国では認められていない. ▶定義4 to show officially that you think sth that sb has done is good ~が行った…が良いと思っていることを公式に示す➜~を表彰する, 評価する, 認める

**recoil** /rɪkɔ́ɪl/ [動][自] ▶定義 to quickly move away from sb/sth unpleasant 不愉快な~から素早く離れる➜~から(恐怖・嫌悪を感じて)後ずさりする, しりごみする, 後退する, 飛びのく ‖ *She recoiled in horror at the sight of the corpse.* 彼女は死体を見て, 怖くなって後ずさりした.

**recollect** /rèkəlékt/ [動][自][他] ▶定義 to remember sth, especially by making an effort 特に努力して~を思い出す➜~を思い出す, 回想する, 想起する ‖ *I don't recollect exactly when it happened.* それがいつ起こったのか正確には思い出せない.

**recollection** /rèkəlékʃ(ə)n/ [名] ▶定義1 [U] recollection (of sth/doing sth) the ability to remember 思い出せる能力➜(~を)(詳しく)思い出すこと, 記憶, 記憶力 ‖ *I have no recollection of promising to lend you money.* 私はあなたにお金を貸すと約束した覚えがない. ▶定義2 [[C], 通常は複数] something that you remember 覚えているもの➜思い出, (~という)記憶, 追憶 ‖ *I have only vague recollections of the town where I spent my early years.* 私は幼少期を過ごした町について, ぼんやりした記憶しかない.

***recommend** /rèkəménd/ [動][他] ▶定義1 recommend sb/sth (to sb) (for/as sth) to say that sb/sth is good and that sb should try or use him/her/it ~が優れており, ~がその…を試すべきまたは使うべきだと言う➜~を(…として…に適していると)推奨する, 推薦する, 勧める ‖ *Which film would you recommend?* どの映画があなたのお薦めですか. *Could you recommend me a good hotel?* 私にいいホテルを推薦していただけますか. *We hope that you'll recommend this restaurant to all your friends.* あなたがこの

R

## 1342 recommendation

レストランをお友達全員に薦めてくださることを願っています。*Doctors don't always recommend drugs as the best treatment for every illness.* 医者はどの病気の場合でも最適な治療法として必ずしも薬を薦めるとは限らない. ▶定義2 to tell sb what you strongly believe he/she should do 〜がするべきだと自分が強く思うことを, その〜に言う→〜することを勧める, 奨励する, 勧告する, 促す ‖ *I recommend that you get some legal advice.* あなたが何らかの法的な助言を受けることをお勧めします. *I wouldn't recommend (your) travelling on your own. It could be dangerous.* 一人旅はお勧めしたくありません. 危ない場合がありますから. ☛参 suggest

**recommendation** /rèkəməndéɪʃ(ə)n, -mèn-/ 名 ▶定義1 ●Ⓤ saying that sth is good and should be tried or used 〜が優れており, 試されるべきあるいは使われるべきだと言うこと→推薦(すること), 推奨, 推奨, 勧める行為 ‖ *I visited Seville on a friend's recommendation and I really enjoyed it.* 私は友達の勧めでセビリアを訪問して, 本当に楽しく過ごした. ▶定義2 ●a statement about what should be done in a particular situation ある状況で行われるべき事に関する陳述→勧告, 忠告 ‖ *In their report on the crash, the committee make several recommendations on how safety could be improved.* その衝突に関する報告の中で, 委員会は安全性を向上させる方法についていくつかの勧告を行っている.

**recompense** /rékəmpèns/ 動 ⓗ 正式 ▶定義 response sb (for sth) to give money, etc to sb for special efforts or work or because you are responsible for a loss he/she has suffered 特別な努力または仕事に対し, あるいは〜が被った損害に責任があるため, その〜に金などを渡す→〜に(…で)報いる, 〜に…の償いをする, 弁償をする, 賠償をする ‖ *The airline has agreed to recompense us for the damage to our luggage.* その航空会社は私たちの荷物の損害賠償をすることに同意した. —recompense 名 [単数扱い, Ⓤ]→(〜に対する)償い, 補償, 弁償, 賠償, 返礼 ‖ *Please accept this cheque in recompense for our poor service.* 私たちのサービスが至らなかったおわびとして, この小切手をお受け取りください.

**reconcile** /rékənsàɪl/ 動ⓗ ▶定義1 reconcile sth (with sth) to find a way of dealing with two ideas, situations, statements, etc that seem to be opposite to each other 互いに相反すると思われる2つの考え, 状態, 陳述などに対処する方法を見つける→〜を(…)と調和させる, 一致させる ‖ *She finds it difficult to reconcile her career ambitions with her responsibilities to her children.* 彼女は自分の職業上の野心と子供に対する責任といった相反するものを調和させるのは難しいと感じている. ▶定義2 (しばしば受動態で) reconcile sb (with sb) to make people become friends again after an argument 論争の後, 人々を仲直りさせる→〜を和解させる, 仲直りさせる, 〜を仲裁する, 調停する ‖ *After years of not speaking to each other, she and her parents were eventually reconciled.* 互いに何年も口をきかなかった期間を経て, 彼女と両親はやっと和解した. ▶定義3 reconcile yourself to sth to accept an unpleasant situation because there is nothing you can do about to change it それを変えるためにできることが何もないので, 不愉快な状況を受け入れる→〜に甘んじる, 満足する, 〜をあきらめる —reconciliation /rèkənsɪ̀liéɪʃ(ə)n/ 名 [単数扱い, Ⓤ]→和解・調和すること, 和解・調和させること, 調停, あきらめ ‖ *The negotiators are hoping to bring about a reconciliation between the two sides.* 交渉者たちは両者を和解させたいと願っている.

**reconnaissance** /rɪkɑ́nəzəns, -səns; -s(ə)ns/ 名 ●Ⓤ ▶定義 the study of a place or area for military reasons 軍事的な理由による, ある場所または地域の調査→偵察 ‖ *The plane was shot down while on a reconnaissance mission over enemy territory.* その飛行機は, 敵の領土を偵察中に撃ち落とされた.

**reconsider** /rìːkənsídər, rì-/ 動ⓑⓗ ▶定義 to think again about sth, especially because you may want to change your mind 特に気が変わるかもしれないので, 〜についてもう一度考える→(〜を)再考する, 考え直す, 再審議する ‖ *Public protests have forced the government to reconsider their policy.* 民衆の抗議により, 政府はその政策の再考を強いられた.

**reconstruct** /rìːkənstrʌ́kt, rì-/ 動ⓗ ▶定義1 to

build again sth that has been destroyed or damaged 破壊された、または損害を受けた〜を再び建てる➔〜を再建する, 改築する, 復興する, 建て直す ▶定義2 to get a full description or picture of sth using the facts that are known 知られている事実を用いて、〜に関する詳細な状況またはイメージをつかむ➔〜の全体を(断片的な資料から)推測する, 再現する, 復元する, 再構成する ‖ *The police are trying to reconstruct the victim's movements on the day of the murder.* 警察は殺人のあった日の被害者の行動を再現しようとしている. — reconstruction /ˌriːkənˈstrʌkʃ(ə)n, ˌrɪ-/ 名 ❻❿➔再建, 改築, 復興, 推測, 再現 ‖ *a reconstruction of the crime using actors* 関係者を使った犯罪の再現

*★**record**¹* /ˈrekɔːd/ 名 ▶定義1 ❻ a record (of sth) a written account of what has happened, been done, etc 起こった事, 行われた事などについての記述➔記録, 登録, 記録文書, 議事録 ‖ *The teachers* **keep records** *of the children's progress.* 教師たちは子供たちの発達を記録に残している. *medical records* カルテ *It's **on record** that he was out of the country at the time of the murder.* 殺人があった時、彼は国外にいたことが記録されている. ▶定義2 [単数扱い] the facts, events, etc that are known (and sometimes written down) about sb/sth 〜に関して知られている(そして時には書き記されている)事実, 出来事など➔〜に関する記録, 経歴, 前科, 業績 ‖ *The police said that the man had **a criminal record** (= he had been found guilty of crimes in the past).* 警察は、その男には前科がある(= 過去に有罪となったことがあった)と言った. *This airline has a bad safety record.* この航空会社の安全性に関する実績は悪い. ▶定義3 ❻(または **album**) a thin, round piece of plastic which can store music so that you can play it when you want 音楽を収録できるので好きなときにかけることができるような, 1枚の薄くて円いプラスチック➔レコード(盤) ▶定義4 ❻ the best performance or the highest or lowest level, etc ever reached in sth, especially in sport 〜, 特にスポーツにおいて, 今までに達成された最高の成績, または最高あるいは最低の水準など➔最高記録, レコード, 最低記録 ‖ *Who* **holds** *the* **world record for** *high jump?* 走り高跳びの世界記録保持者はだれですか. *She's hoping to **break the record** for the 100 metres.* 彼女は100メートルで記録を破りたいと願っている. *He did it **in record time** (= very fast).* 彼はそれを記録的な速さで(= 非常に速く)行った.

**成句 off the record** ▶定義 (used about sth sb says) not to be treated as official; not intended to be made public (〜が言う…について)公式のものであるとして扱われない; 公表されるつもりでない➔非公式に, オフレコで ‖ *She told me off the record that she was going to resign.* 彼女はここだけの話として、退職するつもりであることを私に教えてくれた.

**put/set the record straight** ▶定義 to correct a mistake by telling sb the true facts 〜に真実を話すことにより, 間違いを正す➔これまでの記録・報道・資料の誤りを訂正する, 正確な説明をする, 誤解を正す

*★**record**²* /rɪˈkɔːd/ 動 ▶定義1 ❿ to write down or film facts or events so that they can be referred to later and will not be forgotten 後で参照できるようにそして忘れないように, 事実または出来事を書き記すまたは撮影する➔〜を記録する, 記録に残す, 書き留める, 登録する ‖ *He recorded everything in his diary.* 彼は日記に何でも記録していた. *At the inquest the coroner **recorded a verdict** of accidental death.* 検死の結果, 検死官は事故死という判断を記載した. ▶定義2 ❽❿ to put music, a film, a programme, etc onto a CD or cassette so that it can be listened to or watched again later 後で再び聞けるように, または見られるように, 音楽, 映画, 番組などをCDやカセットに収録する➔(〜を)録音する, 録画する ‖ *Quiet, please! We're recording.* 静かにしてください. 録音中です. *The band has recently recorded a new album.* そのバンドは最近新しいアルバムを収録した. *There's a concert I would like to record from the radio this evening.* 今夜, ラジオから録音したいと思っているコンサートがある.

**record-breaking** 形 (名詞の前だけ) ▶定義 the best, fastest, highest, etc ever 今までで最も良い, 最も速い, 最も高いなど➔記録破りの, 空前の, 記録的な ‖ *We did the journey in record-breaking time.* 私たちは記録的な時間でその行程をこなした.

## recorder

**recorder** /rɪkɔ́ːrdər/ 名 C ▶定義1 a machine for recording sound and/or pictures 音声や画像を記録するための機器→録音機器, 録画機器, テープレコーダー ‖ *a tape/cassette/video recorder* テープレコーダー・カセットレコーダー・ビデオテープレコーダー ▶定義2 a type of musical instrument that is often played by children. You play it by blowing through it and covering the holes in it with your fingers. 子供によってよく演奏される楽器の一種. 息を吹き込み, 指で楽器にある穴をふさぐことによって演奏する→リコーダー, 縦笛 ☞参 piano の注 ☞ music のさし絵

**recording** /rɪkɔ́ːrdɪŋ/ 名 ▶定義1 C sound or pictures that have been put onto a cassette, CD, film, etc カセット, CD, 映画などに収録される音声または画像→録音テープ, レコード, CD, 録音・録画されたもの ‖ *the Berlin Philharmonic's recording of Mahler's Sixth symphony* ベルリンフィルによるマーラーの交響曲第6番の録音 ▶定義2 U the process of making a cassette, record, film, etc カセット, レコード, 映画などを作成する過程→録音・録画すること, 吹き込み, レコーディング ‖ *a recording session/studio* レコーディングセッション・レコーディングスタジオ

**record player** 名 C ▶定義 a machine that you use for playing records レコードをかけるために使う機器→レコードプレーヤー

**recount** /rɪkáʊnt/ 動 他 正式 ▶定義 to tell a story or describe an event 話を聞かせる, または出来事を説明する→〜を(…に)詳しく話す, 物語る

**recourse** /ríːkɔːrs, rɪkɔ́ːrs/ 名 C 正式 ▶定義 having to use sth or ask sb for help in a difficult situation 困難な状況において〜を使わねばならない, または〜に助けを求めねばならないこと→〜に頼ること, 助け, 依頼 ‖ *She made a complete recovery **without recourse to** surgery.* 彼女は手術に頼らずに完全に回復した.

*****recover** /rɪkʌ́vər/ 動 ▶定義1 自 recover (from sth) to become well again after you have been ill 病気だった後に再び元気になる→(〜から)回復する, 治る ‖ *It took him two months to recover from the operation.* 彼は手術から回復するのに2か月かかった. ▶定義2 自 recover (from sth) to get back to normal again after a bad experience, etc 悪い経験などの後に再び通常の状態に戻る→(〜から)元通りになる, 復旧する, 立ち直る, 取り戻す ‖ *The old lady never really recovered from the shock of being mugged.* その年配の女性は, 襲われたショックから完全には立ち直ることができなかった. ▶定義3 他 recover sth (from sb/sth) to find or get back sth that was lost or stolen 失われたまたは盗まれた〜を見つける, あるいは取り戻す→〜を(…から)取り戻す, 奪回する, 回復する, 取る ‖ *Police recovered the stolen goods from a warehouse in South London.* 警察は, 南部ロンドンの倉庫から盗難品を取り戻した. ▶定義4 他 to get back the use of your senses, control of your emotions, etc 感覚, 感情の制御などを取り戻す→〜を取り戻す, 回復する, 正気に返る, 落ち着く

*****recovery** /rɪkʌ́vəri/ 名 ▶定義1 [通常は単数, U] recovery (from sth) a return to good health after an illness or to a normal state after a difficult period of time 病気の後に健康な状態に戻ること, または困難な時期の後に通常の状態に戻ること→(〜からの)回復, 復旧 ‖ *to make a good/quick/speedy/slow recovery* 順調に・急速に・速やかに・ゆっくりと回復する *She's on the road to recovery (= getting better all the time) now.* 彼女は現在, 回復しつつある (= 刻々と良くなっている). *the prospects of economic recovery* 経済復興の見通し ▶定義2 U recovery (of sth/sb) getting back sth that was lost, stolen or missing 失われた, 盗まれた, または行方の分からない〜を取り戻すこと→取り戻すこと, (〜の)回復, 回収

**recreation** /rèkriéɪʃ(ə)n/ 名 [U, 単数扱い] ▶定義 enjoying yourself and relaxing when you are not working; a way of doing this 働いていないときに, 楽しく過ごしてくつろぐこと; そのようにする方法→休養, 気晴らし, レクリエーション, 娯楽 ‖ *recreation activities such as swimming or reading* 水泳や読書のような気晴らしの活動

**recrimination** /rɪkrìmənéɪʃ(ə)n/ 名 [C, 通常は複数, U] ▶定義 an angry statement accusing sb of sth, especially in answer to a similar statement from him/her 特に〜からの同じような陳述に応じて, …の事でその〜を非難する怒りの陳述→非難し返すこと, 責め合うこと, 非難の応酬, 逆襲 ‖ *bitter recriminations* 激しい逆襲

**recruit**[1] /rɪkrúːt/ 名 C ▶定義 a person who has just joined the army or another organization 軍

隊やそのほかの組織に入ったばかりの人→新兵,最下級兵,新入生,新入社員,初心者

**recruit**[2] /rɪkrúːt/ 動⓸⓱ ▶定義 to find new people to join a company, an organization, the armed forces, etc 会社,組織,軍隊などに新しく入る人を探す→(〜を)新しく入れる,勧誘する,募集する,補充する ‖ *to recruit young people to the teaching profession* 教職に就く若者を募集する — **recruitment** 名 ⓤ→新兵・新会員の募集,新人募集,補充,人員補充

**rectangle** /réktæ̀ŋ(ə)l/ 名 ⓒ ▶定義 a shape with four straight sides and four angles of 90 degrees (right angles). Two of the sides are longer than the other two. 4本の直線の辺と4つの90度の角(直角)を持つ図形,辺のうち2辺は残りの2辺よりも長い→長方形 ☞類 **oblong** ☞ **shape** のさし絵 — **rectangular** /rektǽŋɡjələr/ 形→長方形の,直角の,直角を成す

**rectify** /réktəfàɪ/ 動他 (現分 **rectifying**; 三単現 **rectifies**; 過,過分 **rectified**) 正式 ▶定義 to correct sth that is wrong 間違っている〜を正す→〜を正す,改正する,訂正する,修正する

**recuperate** /rɪk(j)úːpərèɪt/ 動⓸正式 ▶定義 **recuperate (from sth)** to get well again after an illness or injury 病気またはけがの後に再び元気になる→〜から回復する,健康を取り戻す — **recuperation** /rɪk(j)ùːpəréɪʃ(ə)n/ 名 ⓤ→回復,立ち直り

**recur** /rɪkə́ːr/ 動⓸ (**recurring**; **recurred**) ▶定義 to happen again or many times 再び,または何回も起こる→再発する,繰り返される,回帰する ‖ *a recurring problem/illness/nightmare* 繰り返し発生する問題・再発する病気・繰り返される悪夢 — **recurrence** /rɪkə́r(ə)ns/, -kə́ːr-/ 名 ⓒⓤ→再発,再現,再起,回帰,繰り返し — **recurrent** /rɪkə́r(ə)nt/, -kə́ːr-/ 形→頻発する,再発する,周期的に起こる,繰り返される

**recycle** /rìːsáɪk(ə)l, rɪ-/ 動⓱ ▶定義 1 to put used objects and materials through a process so that they can be used again 再び利用できるように,使用済みの物や物質をある工程にかける→〜を再生する,循環処理する ‖ *recycled paper* 再生紙 *Aluminium cans can be recycled.* アルミ缶は再生利用できる. ▶定義 2 to keep used objects and materials and use them again 使用済みの物や物質を取っておいて再び使う→〜を再利用する,再使用する,リサイクルする ‖

---

**red card** 1345

*Don't throw away your plastic carrier bags - recycle them!* プラスチック製の袋を捨ててはいけません−再利用しなさい. — **recyclable** 形→再利用可能な,再生使用できる ‖ *Most plastics are recyclable.* ほとんどのプラスチックは再生利用できる.

**★red** /red/ 名 ⓒⓤ 形 (**redder**; **reddest**) ▶定義 1 (of) the colour of blood 血の色(の)→赤,赤色,赤い,赤色の ‖ *red wine* 赤ワイン *She was dressed in red.* 彼女は赤い服を着ていた.

 ▶赤の濃淡の違いを描写するには,**crimson** (深紅色),**maroon** (クリ色),**scarlet** (緋(ひ)色) を用いる.

▶定義 2 a colour that some people's faces become when they are embarrassed, angry, shy, etc 人によっては恥ずかしいとき,怒ったとき,はにかんだときなどになる顔→真っ赤になった,赤面した ‖ *He went bright red when she spoke to him.* 彼女が彼に話し掛けると,彼は真っ赤になった. *to turn/be/go red in the face* 顔が赤くなる・赤い・赤くなる ▶定義 3 (used about a person's hair or an animal's fur) (of) a colour between red, orange and brown (人の髪または動物の毛について)赤,オレンジおよび茶の中間の色(の)→明るい茶色がかった,赤銅色の,赤毛の ‖ *She's got red hair and freckles.* 彼女は赤毛でそばかすがある.

成句 **be in the red** ▶定義 to have spent more money than you have in the bank, etc 銀行などに持っている額より多くのお金を使った→赤字である ‖ *I'm £500 in the red at the moment.* 私は現在,500ポンド赤字です. ⇨ **be in the black** **catch sb red-handed** ⇨ **CATCH**[1]

**a red herring** ▶定義 an idea or subject which takes people's attention away from what is really important 本当に重要な事から人々の注意をそらすような考え,または話題→人の注意をほかにそらすもの

**see red** 略式 ▶定義 to become very angry 非常に怒る→激怒する,かっとなる,ひどく怒り出す

**red card** 名 ⓒ ▶定義 (in football) a card that is shown to a player who is being sent off the field for doing sth wrong (サッカーで)悪い〜をしたのでフィールドから退場させられる選手に示されるカード→レッドカード ☞参 **yellow card**

## 1346 the red carpet

**the red carpet** 名[単数扱い] ▶定義 a piece of red carpet that is put outside to receive an important visitor; a special welcome for an important visitor 重要な訪問者を迎えるために外に敷かれた赤いじゅうたん; 重要な訪問者に対する特別な歓迎→赤じゅうたん, 丁重な歓待, 丁重なもてなし, 歓迎 ‖ *I didn't expect to be given the red carpet treatment!* 私は丁重なもてなしを受けるなんて思ってもいなかった.

**redcurrant** /rédkʌ́rənt, -kə́ːr-/ 名 C ▶定義 a small red berry that you can eat 食べられる小さくて赤いベリー→カーラント ‖ *redcurrant jelly* カーラントのゼリー

**redden** /réd(ə)n/ 動 自 他 ▶定義 to become red or to make sth red 赤くなる, または〜を赤くする→赤くなる, 赤面する, 顔を赤らめる; 〜を赤くする
▶ go red または blush の方が一般的である.

**reddish** /rédɪʃ/ 形 ▶定義 fairly red in colour 色がいくぶん赤い→赤味がかった, 赤味を帯びた, 赤らんだ

**redeem** /rɪdíːm/ 動 他 ▶定義 1 to prevent sth from being completely bad 〜が完全に悪くなるのを妨げる→〜を補う, 埋め合わせる, 救う ‖ *The redeeming feature of the job is the good salary.* その仕事で救われる点は給料が良い事だ. ▶定義 2 **redeem yourself** to do sth to improve people's opinion of you, especially after you have done sth bad 特に悪い〜をした後で, 自分についての人々の評価を良くする→〜を(努力して)回復する, 取り戻す, 取り返す

**redemption** /rɪdém(p)ʃ(ə)n/ 名 U ▶定義 (according to the Christian religion) the action of being saved from evil (キリスト教によれば)悪から救われる行為→(キリスト教による)罪のあがない, 救い, しょく罪

成句 **beyond redemption** ▶定義 too bad to be saved or improved 悪すぎて, 救うまたは改善することができない→救いようのない, 済度し難い, 回復する見込みのない

**redevelop** /rìːdɪvéləp/ 動 他 ▶定義 to build or arrange an area, a town, a building, etc in a different and more modern way 地域, 町, 建物などを, 今までとは異なった, より近代的方法で建設するまたは整備する→〜を再開発する, 再興する, 再建する, 建て直す ‖ *They're redeveloping the city centre.* 彼らはその町の中心部を再開発している. —**redevelopment** 名 U →再開発, 再興, 再建

**redhead** /rédhèd/ 名 C ▶定義 a person, usually a woman, who has red hair 赤毛の人で, 通常は女性→赤毛の人

**red hot** 形 ▶定義 (used about a metal) so hot that it turns red (金属について)赤くなるほど非常に熱い→真っ赤に熱せられた

**redial** /rɪdáɪ(ə)l/ 動 自 他 ▶定義 to call the same number on a telephone that you have just called かけたばかりの番号と同じ番号に電話をかける→リダイヤルする, リダイヤルで電話をかける

**redistribute** /rìːdɪstríbjuːt, -bjət, -dístrɪbjùːt, rì-/ 動 他 ▶定義 to share sth out among people in a different way from before 以前と異なったやり方で人々に〜を分配する→〜を再分配する, 分配し直す, 再区分する, 再区画する — **redistribution** /rìːdɪstrəbjúːʃ(ə)n, rɪ-/ 名 U →再分配, 再配分, 再区分, 再区画

**red-light district** 名 C ▶定義 a part of a town where there are a lot of people, especially women, who earn money by having sex with people 性行為をすることによって金を稼ぐ多くの人々, 特に女性がいるような町の中の地域→赤線地区, 赤線地帯, 紅灯のちまた

**red pepper** 名 C = PEPPER¹(2) ☞C3 ページのさし絵

**red tape** 名 U ▶定義 official rules that must be followed and papers that must be filled in, which seem unnecessary and often cause delay and difficulty in achieving sth 不必要に見え, しばしば〜の達成する上で後れや困難の原因となるような, 従わなければならない公務上の規則および記入しなければならない書類→お役所的取り扱い, お役所仕事, 官僚的形式主義, (形式にとらわれた)非効率的な事務

\***reduce** /rɪd(j)úːs/ 動 他 ▶定義 1 **reduce sth (from sth) (to sth); reduce sth (by sth)** to make sth less or smaller in quantity, price, size, etc 〜の数量, 価格, 大きさなどを少なく, または小さくする→〜を(…から…へ)減少させる, 減らす, 縮小する, 下げる, 低減する ‖ *The sign said 'Reduce speed now'.* その標識には「ここで減速せよ」と書いてあった. ⇔ **increase** ▶定義 2

**reduce sb/sth (from sth) to sth**(しばしば受動態で) to force sb/sth into a particular state or condition, usually a bad one 〜をある特定の状態または状況、通常は悪い状態や状況に、追いやる→〜を…に(無理に)変える、変化させる、無理やりさせる、陥れる ‖ *One of the older boys **reduced** the small child **to tears**.* 年長の男の子たちの1人が小さい子を泣かせた.

**★reduction** /rɪdʌkʃ(ə)n/ 名 ▶定義1 ❻ Ⓤ reduction (in sth) that action of making sth or of becoming less or smaller 〜を少なくまたは小さくすること、あるいはそのようになること→少なく・小さくすること、減少、縮小 ‖ *a sharp reduction in the number of students* 生徒数の急減 ▶定義2 ❻ the amount by which sth is made smaller, especially in price 特に価格において、〜が少なくされる量→削減量、割引(高)、値下げ、値引き ‖ *There were massive reductions in the June sales.* 6月の売り上げは大幅に減少した.

**redundant** /rɪdʌndənt/ 形 ▶定義1 (used about employees) no longer needed for a job and therefore out of work (従業員について)もはや仕事で必要とされていないので職がない→過剰な、余剰な、不要になった ‖ *When the factory closed 800 people were made redundant.* その工場が閉鎖された時、800名の余剰人員が出た. ▶定義2 not necessary or wanted 必要ではない、または望まれていない→不要な、余分な、冗長な ― **redundancy** /-dənsi/ 名 ❻ Ⓤ (複 **redundancies**) →余剰労働者、余分、余剰、過剰 ‖ *redundancy pay* (余剰従業員に支払われる)解雇手当、退職手当

**reed** /riːd/ 名 ❻ ▶定義1 a tall plant, like grass, that grows in or near water 水中または水際に生える、草のような背の高い植物→アシ、ヨシ ☛ C2ページのさし絵 ▶定義2 a thin piece of wood at the end of some musical instruments which produces a sound when you blow through it 息を吹き込むと音が出る、一部の楽器の先端にある薄い木片→舌、リード ☛ *music*のさし絵

**reef** /riːf/ 名 ❻ ▶定義 a long line of rocks, plants, etc just below or above the surface of the sea 海面より少し下または上にある、岩、植物などの長い列→岩礁、暗礁、砂州、リーフ ‖ *a coral reef* さんご礁

**reek** /riːk/ 動 ⓐ ▶定義 reek (of sth) to smell strongly of sth unpleasant 不快な〜の強烈なにおいがする→(〜の)悪臭を放つ、強いにおいを放つ ‖ *His breath reeked of tobacco.* 彼の息はたばこ臭かった. ― **reek** 名 [単数扱い] →(不快な)におい、悪臭

**reel**¹ /riːl/ 名 ❻ ▶定義 a round object that thread, wire, film for cameras, etc is put around 糸、ワイヤー、カメラ用フィルムなどが巻き付けられている丸い物→巻き枠、リール、糸巻き、糸車 ‖ *a cotton reel* カタン糸の糸巻き *a reel of film* フィルム1巻 ☛参 **spool** ☛ *garden*, *knit*のさし絵

**reel**² /riːl/ 動 ⓐ ▶定義1 to walk without being able to control your legs, for example because you are drunk or you have been hit 例えば酒に酔っている、または殴られたために、足を制御できずに歩く→よろよろ歩く、千鳥足で歩く、よろめく、ぐらつく ▶定義2 to feel very shocked or upset about sth 〜について大変な衝撃を受ける、または狼狽(ろうばい)する→頭が混乱する、動揺する、くらくらする ‖ *His mind was still reeling from the shock of seeing her again.* 彼の頭は、彼女に再会したショックでまだ混乱していた.

[句動詞] **reel sth off** ▶定義 to say or repeat sth from memory quickly and without having to think about it 記憶している〜を早く、考える必要もなく言う→〜を立て板に水のように言う、すらすら言う、よどみなく話す、ぺらぺらしゃべる ‖ *She reeled off a long list of names.* 彼女は列記された名前をすらすらと言った.

**ref** 略 reference→参照 ‖ *ref no 3456* 参照番号3456

**★refer** /rɪfɜːr/ 動 (**referring**; **referred**) ▶定義1 ⓐ **refer to sb/sth (as sth)** to mention or talk about sb/sth 〜について述べる、または話す→〜に(直接・はっきりと)言及する、口に出す、触れる、〜を…と言う ‖ *When he said 'some students', do you think he was referring to us?* 彼が「一部の生徒たち」と言った時、私たちのことに触れていたのだと思いますか. *She always referred to Ben as 'that nice man'.* 彼女はベンのことをいつも「あの親切な人」と言っていた. ▶定義2 **refer to sb/sth** to describe or be connected with sb/sth 〜を記述する、またはそれらに関連している→〜に関係する、当てはまる、関連している、適用される ‖ *The term 'adolescent' refers to young people between the ages of 12 and 17.* 「青年」という言葉は、12〜17歳の若者に当て

はまる. ▶定義3 🇪 refer to sb/sth to find out information by asking sb or by looking in a book, etc ～に尋ねて,または本などを調べて情報を探し出す➡～に問い合わせる,照会する,～を参照する,参考にする ‖ *If you don't understand a word you may refer to your dictionaries.* 単語の意味が理解できない場合は,辞書を参照しなさい. ▶定義4 🇪 refer sb/sth to sb/sth to send sb/sth to sb/sth else for help or to be dealt with 助けを求めて,または対処されるように,～を別の…の所に送る➡～を…に差し向ける,引き合わせる,照会させる,委託する ‖ *The doctor has referred me to a specialist.* その医者は私に専門医を紹介してくれた.

**referee** /rèfərí:/ 名(または 略式 ref) 🇨 ▶定義1 the official person in sports such as football who controls the match and prevents players from breaking the rules サッカーのようなスポーツで,試合を管理し選手たちがルールを破らないようにする,公式な立場の人➡審判員,レフェリー ☛テニスのようなスポーツで,同様の競技役員は umpire と呼ばれる. ▶定義2 因 a person who gives information about your character and ability, usually in a letter, for example when you are hoping to be chosen for a job 例えばある職に選ばれることを望んでいるときなどに,通常は手紙で,その人の性格や能力に関する情報を提供する人➡身元保証人,身元照会先 ‖ *Her teacher agreed to act as her referee.* 先生は彼女の身元保証人を引き受けてくれた. — referee 動自他 ➡～のレフェリーを務める,審判をする,仲裁をする

*****reference** /réf(ə)rəns/ 名 ▶定義1 🇨 🇺 (ɑ)reference (to sb/sth) a written or spoken comment that mentions sb/sth ～について言及している書面または口頭での論評➡(～への)言及,論及,言及した事柄 ‖ *The article made a direct reference to a certain member of the royal family.* その記事は王家のある一員について直接言及していた. ▶定義2 🇺 looking at sth for information 情報を求めて～を見ること➡(～の)参照,参考 ‖ *The guidebook might be useful for future reference.* その手引き書は今後の参考として役立つかもしれない. ▶定義3 🇨 a note, especially in a book, that tells you where certain information came from or can be found ある情報について出所はどこか,またはどこで見つけることができるかを示す,特に本の中の,注釈➡出典,参考文献,参考資料,典拠,参考事項 ▶定義4 🇨 (略 ref) (used on business letters, etc) a special number that identifies a letter, etc (ビジネスレターなどで)手紙などを区別するための固有の番号➡照会番号,整理番号 ‖ *Please quote our reference when replying.* 返信の際にはこの照会番号を付けてください. ▶定義5 🇨 a statement or letter describing a person's character and ability that is given to a possible future employer 将来雇用主になる可能性がある人に渡される,ある人の性格や能力などを説明している陳述または手紙➡推薦状,人物証明書 ‖ *My boss gave me a good reference.* 上司は私に立派な推薦状を書いてくれた.

成句 **with reference to sb/sth** 正式 ▶定義 about or concerning sb/sth ～について,または関連して➡～について,～に関して ‖ *I am writing with reference to your letter of 10 April...* あなたからの4月10日付けの手紙について返事を書いています.

**reference book** 名 🇨 ▶定義 a book that you use to find a piece of information ある情報を探すために使う本➡参考図書 ‖ *dictionaries, encyclopedias and other reference books* 辞書,百科事典,そのほかの参考図書

**referendum** /rèfəréndəm/ 名 🇨 🇺 (複 **referendums** または **referenda** /-də/) ▶定義 an occasion when all the people of a country can vote on a particular political question すべての国民が特定の政治問題について投票できる制度➡国民投票,住民投票,レファレンダム ‖ *to hold a referendum* 国民投票を行う

**refill** /rɪfíl, rì:-/ 動他 ▶定義 to fill sth again ～を再び満たす➡～を再び満たす,詰め替える,補充する ‖ *Can I refill your glass?* グラスについてでもいいですか. — refill /rí:fɪl, rí-/ 名 🇨 ➡詰め替え品,補品,スペア,2杯目 ‖ *a refill for a pen* ペンの替え芯(しん)

**refine** /rɪfáɪn/ 動他 ▶定義1 to make a substance pure and free from other substances ある物質を純粋にしてほかの物質をなくする➡～を精製する,精錬する,純化する ‖ *to refine sugar/oil* 砂糖・石油を精製する ▶定義2 to improve sth by changing little details 細部を変

更して〜を改善する➡〜を磨く, 能率化する, 洗練する, 上品にする ‖ to refine a theory 理論を精密にする

**refined** /rɪfáɪnd/ 形 ▶定義1 (used about a substance) that has been made pure by having other substances taken out of it (物質について) ほかの物質が取り除かれたことにより純粋にされた➡精製された, 精錬された ‖ refined sugar/oil/flour 精糖・精油・精製した小麦粉 ▶定義2 (used about a person) polite; having very good manners (人について) 礼儀正しい; 非常に良い作法を身に付けている➡上品な, 洗練された, 優雅な, あか抜けした ⇔ 定義1, 2 **unrefined** ▶定義3 improved and therefore producing a better result 改善され, その結果もっと良い結果を生んでいる➡精密な, 精巧な, 厳密な, 正確な

**refinement** /rɪfáɪnmənt/ 名 ▶定義1 ●a small change that improves sth 〜を改善するような小さな変更➡凝った工夫, 改良(点), 改善(点) ‖ The new model has electric windows and other refinements. その新しいモデルには電動で開閉する窓などの改良がなされている. ▶定義2 ❶ good manners and polite behaviour 良い作法および礼儀正しい振る舞い➡上品, 優雅, 洗練

**refinery** /rɪfáɪn(ə)ri/ 名 ● ( 複 **refineries** ) ▶定義 a factory where a substance is made pure by having other substances taken out of it ほかの物質を取り除くことにより, ある物質が純粋にされる工場➡精製所, 精錬所 ‖ an oil/sugar refinery 精油所・精糖工場

*__reflect__ /rɪflékt/ 動 ▶定義1 ❶ to send back light, heat or sound from a surface 光, 熱, または音を表面から跳ね返す➡〜を反射させる, 反響する, 反射する ‖ The windows reflected the bright morning sunlight. 窓が朝の明るい太陽の光を反射していた. ▶定義2 ❶ reflect sb/sth (in sth) (通常は受動態で) to show an image of sb/sth on the surface of sth such as a mirror, water or glass 鏡, 水, ガラスなどのような〜の表面に, …の像を表す➡〜を (…に) 映す, 映し出す ‖ She caught sight of herself reflected in the shop window. 彼女はショーウインドウに映る自分の姿に気付いた. ▶定義3 ❶ to show or express sth 〜を示す, または表現する➡〜を映す, 反映する, 表す, 示す ‖ His music reflects his interest in African culture. 彼の音楽にはアフリカ文化への興味が反映されている. ▶定義4 ❶ reflect (on/upon sth) to think, especially deeply and carefully, about sth 〜について, 特に深く入念に, 考える➡ (〜を) 熟考する, 回想する, よく考える, 思案する

句動詞 reflect (well, badly, etc) on sb/sth ▶定義 to give a particular impression of sb/sth 〜についてある印象を与える➡(良い・悪い)印象を与える, (良く・悪く)見せる, (名誉・不名誉などを)〜にもたらす, 〜の名誉・不名誉になる ‖ It reflects badly on the whole school if some of its pupils misbehave in public. 一部の生徒が公の場でおかしな振る舞いをすれば, 学校全体の印象が悪くなります.

*__reflection__ (医 または **reflexion**) /rɪflékʃ(ə)n/ 名 ▶定義1 ● an image that you see in a mirror, in water or on a shiny surface 鏡, 水, または輝く面に見える像➡映像, 映った影 ‖ He admired his reflection in the mirror. 彼は鏡に映った自分の姿に見とれた. ▶定義2 ❶ the sending back of light, heat or sound from a surface 光, 熱, または音を表面から跳ね返すこと➡反射, 反響, 反映 ▶定義3 ● a thing that shows what sb/sth is like 〜がどのようなものであるかを表すもの➡反映, 現れ ‖ Your clothes are a reflection of your personality. あなたの服装には個性が現れています. ▶定義4 [単数扱い] a reflection on/upon sb/sth something that causes people to form a good or bad opinion about sb/sth 〜について人々が良く, または悪く思う原因となるもの➡反映, 投影, 影響 ‖ Parents often feel that their children's behaviour is a reflection on themselves. 親は, 子供の言動は自分たちを反映していると感じることが多い. ▶定義5 ❶ ● careful thought about sth 〜について入念に考えること➡熟考, 熟慮, (熟考して得た) 考え, 意見 ‖ a book of his **reflections on** fatherhood 彼が父親たることについての考えを記した本

成句 on reflection ▶定義 after thinking again 再考した後に➡よく考えた末に, よく考えてみると, 熟考した上で ‖ I think, on reflection, that we were wrong. よく考えてみると, 私は自分たちが間違っていたと思う.

**reflective** /rɪfléktɪv/ 形 ▶定義1 (文) (used about a person, mood, etc) thinking deeply about things (人, 気分などについて) 物事につい

て深く考えている→**思慮深い, 考え込んだ, 熟考する, 内省的な** ‖ *A reflective expression* 思慮深い表現 ▶定義2 (used about a surface) sending back light or heat (面について) 光または熱を跳ね返している→**反射する, 反照する, 反射される** ‖ *Wear reflective strips when you're cycling at night.* 夜, 自転車に乗るときは, 反射テープを付けなさい.

▶定義3 reflective (of sth) showing what sth is like ～がどのようものであるかを示している→**反映した, 映し出した**

**reflector** /rɪfléktər/ **名 C** ▶定義1 a surface that sends back (reflects) light, heat or sound that hits it それに当たった光, 熱, または音を跳ね返す(反射する)面→**反射面, 反射物** ▶定義2 a small piece of glass or plastic on a bicycle or on clothing that can be seen at night when light shines on it 光が当たると夜でも見えるような, 自転車または衣服に付けるガラスまたはプラスチックの小片→**(夜間)反射鏡, 反射板**

**reflex** /ríːfleks/ **名** ▶定義1 **C** (または **reflex action**) a sudden movement or action that you make without thinking 考えずに行う突然の動きまたは動作→**反射, 反射作用, 反射行動, 反射的行動** ‖ *She put her hands out as a reflex to stop her fall.* 彼女は倒れるのを食い止めようと反射的に両手を出した. ▶定義2 **reflexes** [複数扱い] the ability to act quickly when necessary 必要なときに素早く行動できる能力→**反射能力, 反射神経, 速やかに反応する能力** ‖ *A good tennis player needs to have excellent reflexes.* 優れたテニスプレーヤーは卓越した反射神経を持っていることが必要である.

**reflection** 英=REFLECTION

**reflexive** /rɪfléksɪv/ **形名 C** (文法) (単語または動詞形) ▶定義 showing that the person who performs an action is also affected by it 行動する人がその行動に影響を受けることを表している→**再帰の, 再帰用法の, 再帰代名詞, 再帰動詞** ‖ *In 'He cut himself', 'cut' is a **reflexive verb** and 'himself' is a **reflexive pronoun**.* He cut himselfの中で, cutは再帰動詞, himselfは再帰代名詞である.

*__reform__ /rɪfɔ́ːm/ **動** ▶定義1 **他** to change a system, the law, etc in order to make it better 制度, 法律などをより良くするため変更する→**～を改**善する, 改革する, 改正する, 刷新する ‖ *to reform the examination system* 試験制度を改革する ▶定義2 **自他** to improve your behaviour; to make sb do this 行動を改善する; ～にそのようにさせる→**改心する; ～を改心させる, 矯正する** ‖ *Our prisons aim to reform criminals, not simply to punish them.* この刑務所は単に犯罪者を罰するだけではなく, 改心させることを目的としている. ─**reform** **名 C U** →**改善, 改革, 改革運動, 改心**

**reformer** /rɪfɔ́ːmər/ **名 C** ▶定義 a person who tries to change society and make it better 社会を変えてより良くしようと努める人→**改良者, 改革者, 改革支持者**

**refrain**¹ /rɪfréɪn/ **動 自 正式** ▶定義 refrain (from sth/doing sth) to stop yourself doing sth; to not do sth ～を行うのを差し控える; ～をしない→**(～を)差し控える, 慎む, こらえる, 断つ, 我慢する** ‖ *Please refrain from smoking in the hospital.* 病院内での喫煙はご遠慮ください.

**refrain**² /rɪfréɪn/ **名 C 正式** ▶定義 a part of a song which is repeated, usually at the end of each verse 通常は各節の最後にある, 繰り返される歌の一部分→**折り返し(句), リフレイン** ☞類 **chorus**

**refresh** /rɪfréʃ/ **動他** ▶定義 to make sb/sth feel less tired or less hot and full of energy again ～の疲れや暑さを和らげ, 再び元気一杯にする→**～の気分をさわやかにする, ～を元気づける, ～に元の勢いを取り戻させる** ‖ *He looked refreshed after a good night's sleep.* 彼は夜ぐっすり眠って元気を回復したようだった.

**成句** refresh your memory (about sb/sth) ▶定義 to remind yourself about sb/sth ～について思い出す→**～についての記憶を新たにする, よみがえらせる, 呼び起こす** ‖ *Could you refresh my memory about what we said on this point last week?* この点について先週私たちが何を言ったのか, 思い出させてくれませんか.

**refreshing** /rɪfréʃɪŋ/ **形** ▶定義1 pleasantly new or different 心地良く新しい, または心地良く変化している→**すがすがしい, 清新で感じの良い・面白い, 新鮮な, 胸のすくような** ‖ *It makes a **refreshing change** to meet somebody who is so enthusiastic.* これほど熱心な人に会うとすがすがしい気分になります. ▶定義2 making you feel less tired or hot 疲れまたは暑さを和らげてくれている→**心身をさわやかにする, 元気づける,**

すっきりさせる ‖ *a refreshing swim/shower/drink* 気分をさわやかにする水泳・さっぱりさせるシャワー・清涼飲料

**refreshment** /rɪfréʃmənt/ 名 ▶定義1 **refreshments**[複数扱い] light food and drinks that are available at a cinema, theatre or other public place 映画館、劇場、またはそのほかの公共の場で販売される軽い食事と飲み物 → 軽食 ▶定義2 Ⓤ 正式 the fact of making sb feel stronger and less tired or hot; food or drink that helps to do this 〜をより元気にして、疲れや暑さが和らいで感じられるようにすること; そうすることを助ける食べ物または飲み物 → 気分一新, 気分爽快(そうかい), 元気を回復させるもの, 清涼剤

**refrigerate** /rɪfrídʒərèɪt/ 動他 ▶定義 to make food, etc cold in order to keep it fresh 食べ物などを新鮮に保つために冷やす → 〜を冷やす, 冷凍する, 冷却する, 冷蔵する — refrigerator 正式 = FRIDGE

**refuge** /réfjuːdʒ/ 名 Ⓒ Ⓤ ▶定義 refuge (from sb/sth) protection from danger, trouble, etc; a place that is safe 危険, 問題などから身を守ること; 安全な場所 → 避難, 保護, 避難所, 隠れ家 ‖ *We had to **take refuge** under a tree while it rained.* 私たちは雨が降っている間、木の下で雨宿りしなければならなかった. *a refuge for the homeless* ホームレスの人を保護する施設

★**refugee** /rèfjʊdʒíː/ 名 Ⓒ ▶定義 a person who has been forced to leave his/her country for political or religious reasons, or because there is a war, not enough food, etc 政治的または宗教的理由で, あるいは戦争がある, 食糧が十分にないなどのために, 自分の国を離れることを強いられた人 → 亡命者, 避難民, 難民 ‖ *a refugee camp* 難民キャンプ ☛参 **fugitive**, **exile**

**refund** /ríːfʌnd/ 名 Ⓒ ▶定義 a sum of money that is paid back to you, especially because you have paid too much or you are not happy with sth you have bought 特に多く支払いすぎたため、または購入した〜に満足できないため、払い戻される金 → 払い戻し, 返済, 返金, 払い戻し金 ‖ *to claim/demand/get a refund* 払い戻しを要求する・要求する・受ける — refund /rɪfʌnd/ 動他 → 〜に…を払い戻す, 返済する, 返還する — refundable 形 → 払い戻しの利く, 返済可能な, 返還される ‖ *The deposit is not refundable.* この手付け金は払い戻しできません.

★**refusal** /rɪfjúːz(ə)l/ 名 Ⓤ Ⓒ ▶定義 (a) refusal (of sth); (a) refusal (to do sth) saying or showing that you will not do, give or accept sth 〜を行う, 与える, または受け入れるつもりがないと言うこと, あるいは示すこと → (〜することの)拒絶, 拒否, 辞退 ‖ *I can't understand her refusal to see me.* 彼女が私に会うのを拒否したのは不可解だ.

★**refuse**¹ /rɪfjúːz/ 動自他 ▶定義 to say or show that you do not want to do, give, or accept sth 〜を行う, 与えるまたは受け入れることを望まないと言う, あるいは示す → 〜を拒む, 断る, 拒絶する, 辞退する ‖ *He refused to listen to what I was saying.* 彼は私が言っている事にどうしても耳を傾けようとしなかった. *My application for a grant has been refused.* 奨学金の申し込みは断られた ⇨ **agree**

**refuse**² /réfjuːs, -z/ 名 Ⓤ 正式 ▶定義 things that you throw away; rubbish 捨てるもの; ごみ → くず, ごみ, がらくた, 廃棄物 ‖ *the refuse collection (= when dustbins are emptied)* ごみの収集(= ごみ容器が空にされるとき)

**regain** /rɪɡéɪn/ 動他 ▶定義 to get sth back that you had lost 失った〜を取り戻す → 〜を取り戻す, 取り返す, 回復する ‖ *to regain consciousness* 意識を回復する

**regal** /ríːɡ(ə)l/ 形 ▶定義 very impressive; typical of or suitable for a king or queen 非常に印象的な; 王や王妃に特有な, またはふさわしい → 威厳ある, 堂々たる, 豪華な, 壮麗な, 王・女王にふさわしい

★**regard**¹ /rɪɡɑ́ːd/ 動他 ▶定義1 regard sb/sth as sth; regard sb/sth (with sth) to think of sb/sth (in the way mentioned) 〜について(言及された方法で)考える → 〜を(外見から)…と見なす, 考える, 〜を評価する ‖ *Do you regard this issue as important?* この問題が重要だと思いますか. *Her work is highly regarded (= people have a high opinion of it).* 彼女の仕事は高い評価を受けている(= 人々が彼女の仕事を並みでないと思っている). *In some villages newcomers are regarded with suspicion.* 村によっては新参者がいぶかしい目で見られることがある.

▶定義2 正式 to look at sb/sth for a while 〜をし

## 1352 regard²

しばらくの間,見る→~をじっと見る,見詰める,注視する,注目する

成句 **as regards sb/sth** 正式 ▶定義 in connection with sb/sth ~に関連して→~に関しては,~について言うと,~の点では ‖ *What are your views as regards this proposal?* この提案について,あなたはどのような見解をお持ちですか.

**regard²** /rɪɡɑ́ːrd/ 名 ▶定義 **1** ❶ **regard to/for sb/sth** attention to or care for sb/sth ~への注意または配慮→~への注意,心配,配慮,心遣い,思いやり ‖ *He shows little regard for other people's feelings.* 彼には他人の気持ちに対する配慮がほとんどない. ▶定義 **2** [ ❶, 単数扱い] **(a) regard (for sb/sth)** a feeling of admiration for sb/sth; respect ~に対する賞賛の気持ち;尊敬→(~への)尊敬,敬意,評価,好感 ‖ *She obviously has great regard for your ability.* 彼女は明らかにあなたの能力を高く評価しています.

▶定義 **3 regards** [複数扱い] (used especially to end a letter politely) kind thoughts; best wishes (特に手紙を丁寧に締めくくるために用いて)思いやり;ご多幸→**よろしくというあいさつ** ‖ *Please give my regards to your parents.* ご両親にどうぞよろしくお伝えください.

成句 **in/with regard to sb/sth; in this/that/one regard** 正式 ▶定義 about sb/sth; connected with sb/sth ~について;~に関連して→~について,~に関して(は),この・あの点に関して(は) ‖ *With regard to the details – these will be finalized later.* 細かい所に関しては – 後日,完成されるでしょう.

**regarding** /rɪɡɑ́ːrdɪŋ/ 前 正式 ▶定義 about or in connection with ~について,または~に関して→~について,~に関して,~の点では ‖ *Please write if you require further information regarding this matter.* この件に関してさらに情報が必要になりましたら,お手紙をください.

**regardless** /rɪɡɑ́ːrdləs/ 副 前 ▶定義 **regardless (of sb/sth)** paying no attention to sb/sth; treating problems and difficulties as unimportant ~に全く注意を払っていない;問題や困難を重要でないと見なしている→(~に)むとんちゃくな,注意しない,不注意な,(~を)気に掛けない ‖ *I suggested she should stop but she carried on regardless.* 私は彼女にやめるべきだと提案したが,彼女は構わずに続行した. *Everybody will receive the same, regardless of how long they've worked here.* ここでの勤続期間に関係なく,全員が同じだけもらえるでしょう.

**regatta** /rɪɡǽtə, -ɡɑ́ːtə/ 名 ❸ ▶定義 an event at which there are boat races ボートレースのある催し→**ボートレース,ヨットレース,レガッタ**

**reggae** /réɡeɪ/ 名 ❶ ▶定義 a type of West Indian music with a strong rhythm 力強いリズムを持つ,西インド諸島の音楽の一種→**レゲエ**

*__regime__ /reɪʒíːm/ 名 ❸ ▶定義 a method or system of government, especially one that has not been elected in a fair way 政府,特に公正な選挙で選ばれなかった政府の体制→**政治制度,政治形態,政権,政府,管理体制** ‖ *a military/fascist regime* 軍事政権・ファシスト政府

**regiment** /rédʒ(ə)mənt/ [❸, 単数または複数形の動詞と共に] ▶定義 a group of soldiers in the army who are commanded by a particular officer **(a colonel)** 特定の将校(大佐)に指揮される,軍隊の兵士の一団→**連隊** — **regimental** /rèdʒəméntl/ 形 →**連隊の,連隊付きの**

**regimented** /rédʒəmèntəd/ 形 正式 ▶定義 (too) strictly controlled (過度に)厳しく統制された→**厳しく・画一的に管理された,厳しく統制された**

*__region__ /ríːdʒ(ə)n/ 名 ❸ ▶定義 **1** part of the country or the world; a large area of land 国または世界のある地域;広い範囲にわたる土地→**(広大な)地域,地方,地帯,地区** ‖ *desert/tropical/polar regions* 砂漠地帯・熱帯地方・極地帯 *This region of France is very mountainous.* フランスのこの地域はとても山が多い. ☞参 **district** の注 ▶定義 **2** an area of your body 体の部分→**部位,部分**

成句 **in the region of sth** ▶定義 about or approximately およそ,または大体→**~の近くで,近くに,およそ,ほぼ~で** ‖ *There were somewhere in the region of 30000 people at the rally.* その集会にはおよそ3万人近くの人々が集まった.

**regional** /ríːdʒ(ə)n(ə)l/ 形 ▶定義 connected with a particular region ある特定の地域に関連している→**特定の地域の,地方の,局地的な,地方特有の** ‖ *regional accents* お国なまり ☞参 **local, international, national**

*__register__¹ /rédʒəstər/ 動 ▶定義 **1** 自他 to put a name on an official list 公式のリストに名前を載

せる➜(～に)登録する,記名する,登記する,記録する ‖ *You should register with a doctor nearby.* あなたは近所に主治医を持つべきです. *All births, deaths and marriages must be registered.* すべての出生,死亡,および婚姻は届け出が必要です. ▶定義2 [自][他] to show sth or to be shown on a measuring instrument 計器に～を示す,または～が示される➜～を自動的に記録する,表示する,示す,指す ‖ *The thermometer registered 32°C.* 温度計は32度を示していた. *The earthquake registered 6.4 on the Richter scale.* その地震はリヒタースケールで6.4を記録した. ▶定義3 [他] to show feelings, opinions, etc 感情,意見などを表す➜～を表す,示す,～の表情をする ‖ *Her face registered intense dislike.* 彼の顔には激しい嫌悪が表れていた. ▶定義4 [自][他] (しばしば否定文で用いて) to notice sth and remember it; to be noticed and remembered ～に気付き,覚えている; 気付かれ,覚えられている➜～の記憶に残る,～に印象づける; 心に銘記される,記憶にとどめる ‖ *He told me his name but it didn't register.* 彼は私に名前を教えてくれたが,記憶に残らなかった. ▶定義5 [他] to send a letter or package by special (registered) post 特別な(書留)郵便で手紙または小包を送る➜～を書留にする

***register**[2] /rédʒəstər/ [名] ▶定義1 [C] an official list of names, etc or a book that contains this kind of list 名前などが載った公的なリスト,またはこの種のリストを含む本➜記録表,登録表,名簿,記録簿,登録簿 ‖ *The teacher calls the register first thing in the morning.* 先生は朝一番に出席を取る. *the electoral register (= of people who are able to vote in an election)* 選挙人名簿(= 選挙で投票することができる人々の) ▶定義2 [C][U] the type of language (formal or informal) that is used in a piece of writing 一編の書き物に使われている言語の種類(正式か略式か)➜(語・文法などの)使用域,(特定の状況での)言語形態

**registered post** [名] [U] [英] ▶定義 a postal service that you pay extra for. If your letter or parcel is lost the post office will make a payment to you. 余分に支払う郵便サービス.手紙または小包が紛失した場合は郵便局が支払いをする➜書留郵便

**register office** = REGISTRY OFFICE

**registrar** /rédʒəstrɑːr, ˌ--ˈ-/ [名] [C] ▶定義1 a person whose job is to keep official lists, especially of births, marriages and deaths 特に出生,婚姻,および死亡などに関する,公的なリストの管理を仕事とする人➜登録官,記録係,戸籍係 ▶定義2 a person who is responsible for keeping information about the students at a college or university 単科大学や総合大学で学生に関する情報を管理することに責任がある人➜総務係,学籍係,教務係

**registration** /rèdʒəstréɪʃ(ə)n/ [名] [U] ▶定義 putting sb/sth's name on an official list ～の名前を公的なリストに載せること➜登録,登記,記録 ‖ *Registration for evening classes will take place on 8 September.* 夜間の授業の履修登録は9月8日に行われます.

**registration number** [名] [C] ▶定義 the numbers and letters on the front and back of a vehicle that are used to identify it 識別するために使われる,車の前と後ろに付いた番号と文字➜登録番号,プレート番号

**registry** /rédʒəstri/ [名] [C] ([複] **registries**) ▶定義 a place where official lists are kept 公的なリストが保管されている場所➜登記所,登録所

**registry office** (または **register office**) [名] [C] ▶定義 an office where a marriage can take place and where births, marriages and deaths are officially written down 結婚が成立する,また出生,婚姻,および死亡が公式に記録されている事務所➜戸籍登記所,戸籍役場 ☛参 **wedding** の注

***regret**[1] /rɪɡrét/ [動][他] (**regretting**; **regretted**) ▶定義1 to feel sorry that you did sth or that you did not do sth ～を行ったこと,または～を行わなかったことを残念に思う➜～を後悔する,悔いる,～したことを残念に思う ‖ *I hope you won't regret your decision later.* あなたが自分の決断を後で悔やまなければいいと思います. *Do you regret not taking the job?* その仕事に就かなかったことを後悔していますか. ▶定義2 [正式] used as a way of saying that you are sorry for sth ～を気の毒に思う言い方として用いて➜残念ながら～する,～であることを残念に思う,気の毒に思う,遺憾に思う ‖ *I regret to inform you that your application has been unsuccessful.* 残念ながらあなたの申請は受理されませんでした.

R

## regret²

**\*regret²** /rɪgrét/ 名 ⓒ ⓤ ▶定義 a feeling of sadness about sth that cannot now be changed 今となっては変えられない~への悲しみの気持ち→遺憾, 残念, 後悔, 悲しみ, 失望 ‖ *Do you have any regrets that you didn't go to university?* あなたは大学に行かなかったことを悔やんでいますか. — regretful /-fʊl, -f(ə)l/ 形 →後悔している, 残念がっている, 遺憾の意を表す ‖ *a regretful look/smile* 残念そうな様子·笑み — regretfully /-fʊli, -f(ə)li/ 副 →後悔して, 悔やまれる, 残念そうに, 悲しんで

**regrettable** /rɪgrétəb(ə)l/ 形 ▶定義 that you should feel sorry or sad about 残念がってしかるべき, または悲しむべきであるような→後悔させる, 残念な, 悔やまれる, 悲しむべき ‖ *It is regrettable that the police were not informed sooner.* 警察にもっと早く知らされなかったのが残念だ. — regrettably 副 →遺憾ながら, 残念なことには

**\*regular¹** /régjələr/ 形 ▶定義 1 having the same amount of space or time between each thing or part それぞれの物や部分の間に同じだけの空間または時間がある→定期的な, 定例の, 規則正しい, 規則的な ‖ *a regular heartbeat* 心臓の規則正しい鼓動 *Nurses checked her blood pressure **at regular intervals**.* 看護婦は彼女の血圧を規則的な間隔をおいて計った. *The fire alarms are tested **on a regular basis**.* その火災警報機は定期的にテストを受けている. *We have regular meetings every Thursday.* 私たちは毎週木曜日に定例会を開いている. ⇔ **irregular** ▶定義 2 done or happening often 頻繁に行われる, または起こっている→いつもの, 通常の, 通例の, 常の ‖ *The doctor advised me to take regular exercise.* その医者は私に通常通りの運動をするよう助言した. *Accidents are **a regular occurrence** on this road.* この道路では事故がいつも起きている. ▶定義 3 going somewhere or doing sth often しばしばある場所へ行っている, または~をしている→行き付けの, いつもの, お決まりの ‖ *a regular customer* 常連 *We're regular visitors to Britain.* 私たちはよく英国を訪れます. ▶定義 4 normal or usual 普通の, または通常の→**普通の, 通常の, 正式の, 正規の** ‖ *Who is your regular dentist?* 掛かり付けの歯医者はだれですか. ▶定義 5 not having any individual part that is different from the rest ほかの部分と異なる独特の部分を持っていない→**均整の取れた, 調和の取れた, 整った, 整然とした** ‖ *regular teeth/features* きれいにそろった歯·整った顔立ち *a regular pattern* 整然とした模様 ⇔ **irregular** ▶定義 6 fixed or permanent 安定した, または半永久的な→一定の, 決まった, 不変の, 常の, 正規の ‖ *a regular income/job* 定収入·定職 *a regular soldier/army* 正規兵·正規軍 ▶定義 7 特に 米 standard, average or normal 標準の, 平均的な, または普通の→普通の, 標準の ‖ *Regular or large fries?* ポテトのサイズはレギュラーとラージのどちらにしますか. ▶定義 8 (文法)(名詞, 動詞などについて) having the usual or expected plural, verb form, etc 規則的または予測される複数形, 動詞形などを持っている→規則変化の, 規則的な ‖ *'Walk' is a regular verb.* Walk は規則動詞である. ⇔ **irregular** — regularly 副 →規則正しく, 規則的に, 整然と, 定期的に, 必ず ‖ *to have a car serviced regularly* 車の定期サービスを受ける — regularity /règjəlǽrəti/ 名 ⓤ ⓒ →規則正しさ, 規則性, 整然, 正規 ‖ *My car breaks down with increasing regularity.* 私の車は故障する頻度が増している.

**regular²** /régjələr/ 名 ⓒ ▶定義 1 略式 a person who goes to a particular shop, bar, restaurant, etc very often 特定の店, バー, レストランなどに非常に頻繁に行く人→常客, 常連, お得意さま ▶定義 2 a person who usually does a particular activity or sport いつもある活動またはスポーツをする人→常雇い, 正職員, 正社員, レギュラーの選手 ▶定義 3 a permanent member of the army, navy, etc 陸軍, 海軍などの正式な一員→正規兵

**regulate** /régjəlèɪt/ 動 他 ▶定義 1 to control sth by using laws or rules 法律または規則によって~を統制する→~を規制する, 規定する, 統制する, 取り締まる ▶定義 2 to control a machine, piece of equipment, etc 機械, 設備などを制御する→~を調整する, 調節する ‖ *You can regulate the temperature in the car with this dial.* 車内の温度はこのつまみを使って調節できる.

**\*regulation** /règjəléɪʃ(ə)n/ 名 ▶定義 1 [ⓒ, 通常は複数] an official rule that controls how sth is done ~がどのように行われるかを規定する公の規則→規則, 規定, 規約, 法規 ‖ *to observe/obey the safety regulations* 安全規則を遵守する·安全規則に従う *The plans must comply with EU reg-*

**rehabilitate** /ˌriː(h)əbíləteɪt/ 動他 ▶定義 to help sb to live a normal life again after an illness, being in prison, etc 〜が病気, 服役などの後で再び普通の生活に戻るのを助ける→〜の機能回復訓練をする, 〜を社会復帰させる, 更生させる ― **rehabilitation** /ˌriː(h)əbɪləteɪʃ(ə)n/ 名 ❶→リハビリテーション, 社会復帰訓練, 更生 ‖ *a rehabilitation centre for drug addicts* 麻薬中毒者のためのリハビリテーションセンター

**rehearsal** /rɪhɜ́ːrs(ə)l/ 名 ❻ ❶ ▶定義 the time when you practise a play, dance, piece of music, etc before you perform it to other people 演劇, ダンス, 音楽などを他人に対して演ずる前に練習するとき→リハーサル, 下稽古 (げいこ), 試演 (会), 予行演習 ‖ *a dress rehearsal (= when all the actors wear their stage clothes)* 本稽古 (= すべての俳優がステージ衣装を着ける) ― **rehearse** /rɪhɜ́ːrs/ 動 自他 **rehearse (for sth)**→(〜を) 下稽古する, 試演する, 予行演習する, (〜の) リハーサルをする

**reign** /réɪn/ 動 自 ▶定義1 **reign (over sb/sth)** (used about a king or queen) to rule a country (王または女王について) 国を治める→(〜に) 君臨する, (〜を) 統治する, 支配する, 〜の主権を握る ‖ (比喩) *the reigning world champion* 現世界チャンピオン ▶定義2 **reign (over sb/sth)** to be in charge of a business or organization 事業または組織に対して責任がある→支配する ▶定義3 to be present as the most important quality of a particular situation ある状況において最も影響力を持つものとして存在する→勢力を振るう, 羽振りを利かす, 支配する, 広く行き渡る ‖ *Chaos reigned after the first snow of the winter.* その冬の初雪の後に大混乱になった. ― **reign** 名 ❻→君臨, 統治, 支配, 勢力, 権勢

**reimburse** /ˌriːəmbɜ́ːrs/ 動 他 正式 ▶定義 to pay money back to sb 〜にお金を払い戻す→〜を返済する, 弁済する, 補償金・報酬を払う, 払い戻す ‖ *The company will reimburse you in full for your travelling expenses.* 会社はあなたの旅費を全額返済するでしょう.

**rein** /réɪn/ 名 [ ❻, 通常は複数] ▶定義 a long thin piece of leather that is held by the rider and used to control a horse's movements 馬の乗り手によって握られ, 馬の動きを制御するために用いられる, 細長い皮ひも→手綱 ☛ **horse** のさし絵

**reincarnation** /ˌriːənkɑːrnéɪʃ(ə)n, ˌriːɪnkɑːr-/ 名 ▶定義1 ❶ the belief that people who have died can live again in a different body 死んだ人がほかの肉体で再び生きることができるという信仰→再生, 転生, 霊魂の生まれ変わり, 霊魂転生説 ‖ *Do you believe in reincarnation?* あなたは霊魂の生まれ変わりを信じますか. ▶定義2 ❻ a person or animal whose body is believed to contain the soul of a dead person その肉体に死者の魂を含んでいると信じられている人または動物→化身, 生まれ変わり, 再生 ‖ *He believes he is the reincarnation of an Egyptian princess.* 彼は自分がエジプト王女の生まれ変わりだと信じている. ☛ 参 **incarnation**

**reindeer** /réɪndɪər/ 名 ❻ (複 **reindeer**) ▶定義 a type of large brownish wild animal that eats grass and lives in Arctic regions 草食で北極地方に生息する, 大型で茶色の野生動物の一種→トナカイ

**reinforce** /ˌriːənfɔ́ːrs/ 動 他 ▶定義 to make sth stronger 〜をより強くする→〜を補強する, より効果的にする, 強固にする, 増強する ‖ *Concrete can be reinforced with steel bars.* コンクリートは鋼鉄の棒で補強できる.

**reinforcement** /ˌriːənfɔ́ːrsmənt/ 名 ▶定義1 ❶ making sth stronger 〜をより強くすること→補強, 強化 ‖ *The sea wall is weak in places and needs reinforcement.* その防波堤は所々もろくなっているので, 補強が必要である. ▶定義2 **reinforcements** [複数扱い] extra people who are sent to make an army, navy, etc stronger 陸軍, 海軍などをより強くするために, 追加して送られた人々→援軍, 増援

**reinstate** /ˌriːɪnstéɪt, ˌriː-/ 動 他 ▶定義1 **reinstate sb (in/as sth)** to give back a job or position that was taken from sb 〜から取り上げられた職または地位を返す→〜を…に復帰させる, 復職させる, 復位させる, 復権させる ‖ *He was cleared of the charge of theft and reinstated as Head of Security.* 彼は窃盗の容疑が晴らされ, 警備局長

として復職した. ▶定義2 to return sth to its former position or role ～をその前の地位または役割に戻す→～を元通りにする, 復活させる — reinstatement 名 Ⓤ →復帰, 復職, 復権, 復活

\*reject¹ /rɪdʒékt/ 動 ▶定義 to refuse to accept sb/sth ～を受け入れることを拒否する→～を拒絶する, 断る, 受け入れない, 否認する ‖ *The plan was rejected as being impractical.* その計画は実行不可能として却下された. — rejection 名 Ⓒ Ⓤ →拒絶, 拒否, 却下, 否決, 否認 ‖ *Gargi got a rejection from Leeds University.* ガーギはリーズ大学に受け入れられなかった. *There has been total rejection of the new policy.* 新しい政策は完全に否決された.

reject² /rídʒekt/ 名 Ⓒ ▶定義 a person or thing that is not accepted because he/she/it is not good enough 十分に良い状態ではないため受け入れられない人または物→拒絶された人, 徴兵不合格者, 不良品 ‖ *Rejects are sold at half price.* 不良品は半額で販売される.

rejoice /rɪdʒɔ́ɪs/ 動 自 正式 ▶定義 rejoice (at/over sth) to feel or show great happiness 大きな喜びを感じる, または表す→(～を大いに)喜ぶ, うれしく思う, うれしがる — rejoicing 名 Ⓤ →(特に大勢で分かち合う)喜び, 歓喜 ‖ *There were scenes of rejoicing when the war ended.* 戦争が終わると喜びを分かち合う光景が見られた.

rejuvenate /rɪdʒúːvənèɪt/ 動 他 (しばしば受動態で) ▶定義 to make sb/sth feel or look younger ～を若々しく感じさせる, または見せる→～を若返らせる, 若返った気分にさせる, 活気を与える, ～に元気を回復させる — rejuvenation /rɪdʒùːvənéɪʃ(ə)n/ 名 Ⓤ →若返り, 元気回復, 活性化

relapse /rɪlǽps/ 動 自 ▶定義 to become worse again after an improvement 改善の後, 再び悪くなる→再び陥る, 再び戻る, 再発する, ぶり返す ‖ *to relapse into bad habits* 悪い習慣に逆戻りする — relapse /rɪlǽps/ 名 Ⓒ →再発, ぶり返し, 逆戻り, 再転落 ‖ *The patient had a relapse and then died.* その患者は病気が再発して亡くなった.

\*relate /rɪléɪt/ 動 他 ▶定義1 relate A to/with B to show or make a connection between two or more things 2つ以上の物事の関連を示す, またはそれらを関連づける→～を関係づける, 関連させる ‖ *The report relates heart disease to high levels of stress.* その報告では心臓病を強度のストレスに関連づけている. ▶定義2 正式 relate sth (to sb) to tell a story to sb ～に話をする→(～に)(順序立てて)話す, 述べる, 物語る ‖ *He related his side of the story to a journalist.* 彼はある記者に自分の立場から話をした.

句動詞 relate to sb/sth ▶定義1 to be concerned or involved with sth ～に関連している, またはかかわり合っている→～に関係がある, 関連する, かかわる ▶定義2 to be able to understand how sb feels ～がどのように感じているか理解できる→～の気持ちが分かる, 心が通う ‖ *Some teenagers find it hard to relate to their parents.* ティーンエージャーの中には, 親とうまくやっていくのが難しいと感じている者もいる.

related /rɪléɪtɪd/ 形 related (to sb/sth) ▶定義1 connected with sb/sth ～に関連している→～に関係のある, 関連のある, 相関している ‖ *The rise in the cost of living is directly related to the price of oil.* 生活費の上昇は石油の価格と直接関連している. ▶定義2 of the same family 同じ家族の→～と親戚(しんせき), 親類の, 血縁の, 同じ家族の ‖ *We are related by marriage.* 結婚によって私たちは親戚になった.

\*relation /rɪléɪʃ(ə)n/ 名 ▶定義1 relations [複数扱い] relations (with sb); relations (between A and B) the way that people, groups, countries, etc feel about or behave towards each other 人々, 集団, 国々などが互いについてどのように感じているかということ, または互いに対する行動の仕方→関係, 交渉, 人間関係, 利害関係, 国際関係 ‖ *The police officer stressed that good relations with the community were essential.* その警官は地域社会との良好な関係が欠かせないと強調した. ▶定義2 Ⓤ relation (between sth and sth); relation (to sth) the connection between two or more things 2つ以上の物事の関連→関係, 関連 ‖ *There seems to be little relation between the cost of the houses and their size.* 家の価格と大きさにはほとんど関連がないように思われる. *Their salaries **bear no relation** to the number of hours they work.* 彼らの給料は働いた時間数とは関係がない. ▶定義3 Ⓒ a member of your family 家族の一員→親戚(しんせき), 親族, 親類 ‖ *a close/distant relation* 近親

者・遠い親戚 ☛類 **relative**

▶次のような表現に注意する: *'What relation are you to each other?'*（「あなたたちはお互いにどのような関係なのですか」）と *'Are you any relation to each other?'*（「あなたたちはお互いに何か関係があるのですか」）

**成句 in/with relation to sb/sth** ▶定義1 concerning sb/sth 〜に関して→**〜に関して, 〜について** ‖ *Many questions were asked, particularly in relation to the cost of the new buildings.* 特に新しい建物にかかる費用に関して多くの質問がなされた. ▶定義2 compared with 〜と比較されて→**〜と比較して, 〜との関係で** ‖ *Prices are low in relation to those in other parts of Europe.* 物価はヨーロッパのほかの地域に比べると安い.

\***relationship** /rɪléɪʃ(ə)nʃɪp/ 名 C ▶定義1 a relationship (with sb/sth); a relationship (between A and B) the way that people, groups, countries, etc feel about or behave towards each other 人々, 集団, 国々などが互いについてどのように感じているかということ, または互いに対する行動の仕方→**(〜の間の・〜との)関係** ‖ *The relationship between the parents and the school has improved greatly.* 親と学校の関係は大きく改善した. ▶定義2 a relationship (with sb); a relationship (between A and B) a friendly or loving connection between people 人と人との間の友情ある, または愛情に満ちた関係→**結び付き, 親交, 交際, 恋愛関係** ‖ *to have a relationship with sb* 〜と親交がある *He'd never been in a serious relationship before he got married.* 彼は結婚するまで一度も真剣な交際をしたことがなかった. *The film describes the relationship between a young man and an older woman.* その映画は若い男性と年上の女性の恋愛関係を描いている. *Do you have a close relationship with your brother?* お兄さんとは仲が良いですか. ▶定義3 a relationship (to sth); a relationship (between A and B) the way in which two or more things are connected 2つ以上の物事の関係の仕方→**関連** ‖ *Is there a relationship between violence on TV and the increase in crime?* テレビに出てくる暴力と犯罪の増加には関連がありますか. ▶定義4 a relationship (to sb); a relationship (between A and B) a family connection 家族の関係→**親戚（しんせき）関係, 血縁関係, 親類関係** ‖ *'What is your relationship to Bruce?' 'He's married to my cousin.'* 「あなたとブルースはどのような関係ですか」「彼は私のいとこと結婚しました」

\***relative**¹ /rélətɪv/ 形 ▶定義1 relative (to sth) when compared with sb/sth else ほかの〜と比べられた場合→**比較上の, 比較的な, 相対的な** ‖ *the position of the earth relative to the sun* 太陽を基準にした地球の相対的な位置 *They live in relative luxury.* 彼らは比較的ぜいたくな暮らしをしている. ▶定義2（文法）referring to an earlier noun, phrase or sentence その前の名詞, 節, または文に関連している→**関係を表す, 関係節を導く** ‖ *In the phrase 'the lady who lives next door', 'who' is a relative pronoun.* the lady who lives next door という節の中で, who は関係代名詞である.

▶関係代名詞および関係節の詳細については, 巻末の「文法早見表」を参照.

\***relative**² /rélətɪv/ 名 C ▶定義 a member of your family 家族の一員→**親族, 親戚（しんせき）, 親類, 身内** ‖ *a close/distant relative* 近い・遠い親類 ☛類 **relation**

**relatively** /rélətɪvli/ 副 ▶定義 to quite a large degree, especially when compared to others 特にほかと比較されたときに, かなりの程度で→**比較的, 相対的に, かなり, 比較して言えば** ‖ *Spanish is a relatively easy language to learn.* スペイン語は比較的の習得しやすい言語である.

\***relax** /rɪlǽks/ 動 ▶定義1 自 to rest while you are doing sth enjoyable, especially after work or effort 特に仕事または努力をした後で, 楽しめる〜をしながら休息する→**くつろぐ, リラックスする, 骨を休める** ‖ *This holiday will give you a chance to relax.* この休日は骨休めをする機会になるでしょう. *They spent the evening relaxing in front of the television.* その晩, 彼らはテレビの前でくつろいで過ごした. ▶定義2 自 to become calmer and less worried 落ち着きが増し, 不安が和らぐ→**和らぐ, ほぐれる, 緩む** ‖ *Relax - everything's going to be OK!* 気持ちを楽にして — すべてうまくいきますよ. ▶定義3 自他 to become or make sb/sth become less hard or tight 〜の厳しさまたは困難が和らぐ, またはそれらを和らげる→**和らぐ, 緩む, ほぐれる; 〜を和らげる, 緩める** ‖ *A hot bath will relax you after a*

## 1358 relaxation

hard day's work 1日の厳しい仕事の後に熱いふろに入ると,くつろげるでしょう. *Don't relax your grip on the rope!* ロープを握る手を緩めるな. ▶定義4 ⓤ to make rules or laws less strict 規則または法律の厳しさを緩和する➡～を緩める,緩和する,軽減する

**＊relaxation** /ˌriːlækˈseɪʃ(ə)n, rɪ-/ 名 ▶定義1 ⓒⓤ something that you do in order to rest, especially after work or effort 特に仕事または努力をした後に,休息するためにすること➡くつろぎ,息抜き,休養,気晴らし,娯楽‖ *Everyone needs time for rest and relaxation.* だれもが休息とくつろぎの時間を必要としている. ▶定義2 ⓤ making sth less strict, tight or strong ～の厳しさ,きつさ,または強さを和らげること➡緩み,緩和,軽減

**＊relaxed** /rɪˈlækst/ 形 ▶定義 not worried or tense 心配していない,または緊張しない➡くつろいだ,リラックスした,くだけた,打ち解けた‖ *The relaxed atmosphere made everyone feel at ease.* その場の打ち解けた雰囲気にだれもがくつろげた.

**relaxing** /rɪˈlæksɪŋ/ 形 ▶定義 pleasant, helping you to rest and become less worried 快適で,休息することや不安を和らげることに役立っている➡くつろがせる,リラックスさせる,くつろいだ気分にさせる‖ *a quiet relaxing holiday* 静かなくつろげる休日

**relay**¹ /ˈriːleɪ, rɪˈleɪ/ 動他 ( 過, 過 分 **relayed**) ▶定義1 to receive and then pass on a signal or message 信号またはメッセージを受け取って渡す➡～を中継する,中継して伝える,取り次ぐ‖ *Instructions were relayed to us by phone.* 指示は電話で私たちに伝えられた. ▶定義2 医 to put a programme on the radio or television 番組をラジオまたはテレビに流す➡～を中継する,中継放送する

**relay**² /ˈriːleɪ/ ( または **relay race** ) 名 ⓒ ▶定義 a race in which each member of a team runs, swims, etc one part of the race チームの各メンバーが競技の一部分を走る,泳ぐなどするレース➡リレー,リレー競走,リレー競泳

**＊release**¹ /rɪˈliːs/ 動他 ▶定義1 release sb/sth (from sth) to allow sb/sth to be free ～を自由にさせる➡～を(…から)解き放つ,解放する,釈放する,自由にする‖ *He's been released from prison.* 彼は刑務所から釈放された. (比喩) *His firm released him for two days a week to go on a training course.* 会社は彼が研修に行くために週2日,仕事を免除してくれた. ▶定義2 to stop holding sth so that it can move, fly, fall, etc freely ～が自由に動く,飛ぶ,落ちるなどできるように,つかんでいるのをやめる➡～を放つ,離す,外す,投下する‖ *1000 balloons were released at the ceremony.* その式典では1000個の風船が飛ばされた. (比喩) *Crying is a good way to release pent-up emotions.* 泣くことは鬱積(うっせき)した感情を解き放つのに良い方法である. ▶定義3 to move sth from a fixed position ～を固定した位置から動かす➡～を放す,外す,解く,緩める‖ *He released the handbrake and drove off.* 彼は車のハンドブレーキを外して走り去った. ▶定義4 to allow sth to be known by the public ～が一般に知られることを許可する➡～の公開・公表・販売を正式に許可する,～を公開する,公表する‖ *The identity of the victim has not been released.* 被害者の身元は公開されていない. ▶定義5 to make a film, record, etc available so the public can see or hear it 一般の人が見る,または聞くことができるように,映画,レコードなどを入手できるようにする➡～を公開する,封切る,発売する,発表する‖ *Their new single is due to be released next week.* 彼らのニューシングルは来週発売される予定です.

**＊release**² /rɪˈliːs/ 名 ⓒⓤ ▶定義1 (a) release (of sth) (from sth) the freeing of sth or the state of being freed ～を自由にすること,または自由になった状態➡解放,釈放,放免,救出,解除‖ *The release of the hostages took place this morning.* 人質は今朝,解放された. *I had a great feeling of release when my exams were finished.* 私は試験が終わった時,大きな解放感を味わった. ▶定義2 a book, film, record, piece of news, etc that has been made available to the public; the act of making sth available to the public 一般に入手できるようにされた本,映画,レコード,ニュースなど;～を一般に公開する行為➡新発売の本,封切り映画,新譜,発売,一般公開‖ *a press release* 新聞発表 *The band played their latest release.* そのバンドは最新の曲を演奏した. *The film won't be/go on release until March.* その映画は3月まで一般公開されないでしょう.

**relegate** /réləgèɪt/ [動][他] ▶定義 to put sb/sth into a lower level or position ～をより低い水準または位置に置く ➜**～を格下げする, 落とす, 降格させる, 左遷する** ‖ *The team finished bottom and were relegated to the second division.* そのチームは最下位に終わり, 2部に格下げされた. — relegation /rèləgéɪʃ(ə)n/ [名] [U] ➜**格下げ, 降格, 左遷, 追放**

**relent** /rɪlént/ [動][自] ▶定義1 to finally agree to sth that you had refused 拒否した～を最終的に認める ➜**態度を軟化する, 寛容になる, 折れる** ‖ *Her parents finally relented and allowed her to go to the concert.* 彼女の両親は最終的に折れて, 彼女がコンサートに行くことを許した. ▶定義2 to become less determined, strong, etc 決意が鈍くなる, 弱くなるなど ➜**和らぐ, 弱まる, 優しくなる, 同情的になる** ‖ *The heavy rain finally relented and we went out.* 激しい雨がやっと弱まったので, 私たちは外出した.

**relentless** /rɪléntləs/ [形] ▶定義 not stopping or changing 止まっていない, または変わっていない ➜**絶え間のない, 間断ない, 執拗(しつよう)な** ‖ *the relentless fight against crime* 犯罪に対抗する絶え間ない戦い — relentlessly [副] ➜**絶え間なく, 間断なく, 執拗に** ‖ *The sun beat down relentlessly.* 太陽が容赦なく照りつけた.

***relevant** /réləvənt/ [形] relevant (to sb/sth) ▶定義1 connected with what is happening or being talked about 起こっている, または話題に上っていることに関連した ➜**～と関係がある, 関連する, 意味のある** ‖ *Much of what was said was not directly relevant to my case.* 言われた事の多くは私の場合には直接関係なかった. ▶定義2 important and useful 重要で役立つ ➜**適切な, 妥当な** ‖ *Many people feel that poetry is no longer relevant in today's world.* 韻文はもはや今の時世に合っていないと多くの人が感じている. ⇔ **irrelevant** — relevance [名] [U] ➜**関連, 関連性, 重要性, 適合性, 妥当性** ‖ *I honestly can't see the relevance of what he said.* 正直なところ, 私には彼が言った事が適切であるとは思えない.

***reliable** /rɪláɪəb(ə)l/ [形] ▶定義 that you can trust 信頼することができるような ➜**信頼できる, 頼りになる, 頼もしい, 当てにできる** ‖ *Japanese cars are usually very reliable.* 日本車は大抵非常に信頼できる. *Is he a reliable witness?* 彼は信頼できる証人ですか. ⇔ **unreliable** ☛[動] rely — reliability /rɪlàɪəbíləti/ [名] [U] ➜**当てになること, 信頼性, 確実性, 信憑(しんぴょう)性** — reliably /-əb(ə)li/ [副] ➜**頼もしく, 信頼すべき筋から** ‖ *I have been reliably informed that there will be no trains tomorrow.* 信頼すべき筋から得た情報によると明日は電車が動かないそうです.

**reliance** /rɪláɪəns/ [名] [U] reliance on sb/sth ▶定義1 being able to trust sb/sth ～を信頼することができること ➜**信頼, 信用, 信任, 頼り** ‖ *Don't **place** too much **reliance** on her promises.* 彼女の約束をあまり当てにしてはいけません. ▶定義2 not being able to live or work without sb/sth; being dependent on sb/sth ～がなければ生活または仕事をすることができないこと; ～に依存すること ➜**頼ること, 依存** ☛[動] rely

**reliant** /rɪláɪ(ə)nt/ [形] ▶定義 reliant on sb/sth not being able to live or work without sb/sth ～がなければ生活または仕事をすることができない ➜**～に頼っている, ～依存している, ～を当てにしている** ‖ *They are totally reliant on the state for financial support.* 彼らは国の財政援助に頼り切っている. ☛[動] rely ☛参 **self-reliant**

**relic** /rélɪk/ [名] [C] ▶定義 an object, tradition, etc from the past that still survives today 現在もまだ残っている, 過去の物, 伝統など ➜**遺物, 遺跡, 名残, 記念品, 形見**

***relief** /rɪlíːf/ [名] ▶定義1 [[U], 単数扱い] relief (from sth) the feeling that you have when sth unpleasant stops or becomes less strong 不快な～がやむ, または和らいだときに抱く気持ち ➜**安堵(あんど), 安心, ほっとすること** ‖ ***What a relief!*** *That awful noise has stopped.* ほっとした. あのひどい騒音がやんだ. *It was a great relief to know they were safe.* 彼らが無事だと分かって本当に安心した. *to breathe **a sigh of relief*** ほっと安堵のため息をつく ***To my relief,*** *he didn't argue with my suggestion at all.* ほっとしたことに, 彼は私の提案に全く反論しなかった. ▶定義2 [U] the removal or reduction of pain, worry, etc 痛み, 心配などを取り除く, または軽減すること ➜**除去, 軽減, 緩和, 和らげること** ‖ *These tablets provide pain relief for up to four hours.* これらの錠剤を服用すると鎮痛効果が4時間持続する. ▶定義3 [U] money or food that is

## relieve

given to help people who are in trouble or difficulty 困っている，または困難な状況にある人々を助けるために与えられる金や食べ物→**福祉手当, 福祉金, 救援金, 救援物資** ‖ *disaster relief for the flood victims* 洪水の被害者への災害救援物資 ▶定義4 ❶a reduction in the amount of tax you have to pay 支払わなければならない税金の額の軽減→**控除**

**relieve** /rɪlíːv/ 動他 ▶定義 to make an unpleasant feeling or situation stop or get better 不快な気持ちや状態をやめさせる，または良くする→**~を取り除く, 和らげる, 軽減する, ほっとさせる** ‖ *This injection should relieve the pain.* この注射はおそらく痛みを和らげるでしょう. *We played cards to relieve the boredom.* 私たちは退屈しのぎにトランプをした.

句動詞 relieve sb of sth 正式 ▶定義 to take sth away from sb ~を…から取り除く→**~を…から解放する, 解雇する, 解任する** ‖ *to relieve sb of responsibility* ~を責任から解放する

*relieved /rɪlíːvd/ 形 ▶定義 pleased because your fear or worry has been taken away 不安または心配が取り除かれたのでうれしい→**安心した, ほっとした** ‖ *I was very relieved to hear that you weren't seriously hurt.* あなたのけがが大したことはなかったと聞いてとても安心しました.

*religion /rɪlídʒ(ə)n/ 名 ▶定義1 ❶the belief in a god or gods and the activities connected with this 神または神々の存在を信じること，およびそれに関連した活動→**宗教, 信仰, 信仰生活** ▶定義2 ❸one of the systems of beliefs that is based on a belief in a god or gods 神または神々の存在を信じることに基づいた信仰体系の1つ→**宗派, 宗旨, ~教** ‖ *the Christian/Hindu/Muslim/Sikh religion* キリスト教・ヒンズー教・イスラム教・シーク教

*religious /rɪlídʒəs/ 形 ▶定義1 connected with religion 宗教に関連した→**宗教の, 宗教に関する, 宗教上の, 宗教的な** ‖ *religious faith* 信仰心 ▶定義2 having a strong belief in a religion ある宗教に強い信仰心を持っている→**信心深い, 敬虔(けいけん)な, 信仰心の厚い** ‖ *a deeply religious person* 大変信心深い人

**religiously** /rɪlídʒəsli/ 副 ▶定義1 very carefully or regularly 大変入念に，または規則正しく→**誠実に, 細心に, 規則正しく, きちんと** ‖ *She stuck to the diet religiously.* 彼女は食事制限をきちんと守った. ▶定義2 in a religious way 宗教的に→**宗教的に, 宗教上, 信心深く, 宗教に関して**

**relinquish** /rɪlíŋkwɪʃ/ 動他 正式 ▶定義 to stop having or doing sth ~を持つこと，または行うことをやめる→**~を捨てる, 断念する, やめる, 放棄する, 手放す** ☛ give up の方が一般的である.

**relish**¹ /rélɪʃ/ 動他 ▶定義 to enjoy sth or to look forward to sth very much ~を楽しむ，または~を大変楽しみにする→**~を楽しむ, 賞味する, うれしく思う, わくわくする** ‖ *I don't relish the prospect of getting up early tomorrow.* 私は明朝早起きをすると思うと気が重い.

**relish**² /rélɪʃ/ 名 ▶定義1 ❶(文)great enjoyment 大きな楽しみ→**喜び, 楽しい味わい, 楽しい興奮, 大満足** ‖ *She accepted the award with obvious relish.* 彼女は見るからにうれしそうに賞を受け取った. ▶定義2 ❶❸a thick, cold sauce made from fruit and vegetables 果物と野菜から作られた，どろっとした冷たいソース→**付け合わせのソース, 薬味のソース**

**relive** /riːlív, rɪ-/ 動他 ▶定義 to remember sth and imagine that it is happening again ~を思い出し，それが再び起こっていることを想像する→**~を回想する, 思い起こす, 再び体験する, 追体験する**

**reload** /riːlóud, rɪ-/ 動自他 ▶定義 to put sth into a machine again ~を再び機器の中に入れる→**銃に弾丸を込め直す, 荷を積み直す, フィルムを入れ直す, 再ロードする** ‖ *to reload a gun* 銃に弾丸を込め直す *to reload a disk into a computer* コンピューターにディスクを再ロードする

**reluctant** /rɪlʌ́ktənt/ 形 ▶定義 reluctant (to do sth) not wanting to do sth because you are not sure it is the right thing to do 行うのが正しいことであるという確信がないので，~をしたがっていない→**~したくない, することに気が進まない, 渋る, 乗り気でない** — reluctance 名 ❶❶→**気が進まないこと, 嫌がること, 渋ること, 不本意** ‖ *Tony left with obvious reluctance.* トニーは見るからにしぶしぶ立ち去った. — reluctantly 副 →**嫌々ながら, しぶしぶ, 不本意ながら, 気が進まないで**

*rely /rɪláɪ/ 動自 (現分 relying; 三単現 relies; 過, 過分 relied) rely on/upon sb/sth (to do sth) ▶定義1 to need sb/sth and not be able to live or work properly without him/her/it ~を必

要とし,それがなくてはきちんと生活すること,または働くことができない→~に頼る‖ *The old lady had to rely on other people to do her shopping for her.* その年配の女性は,自分の買い物をするのに他人に頼らなければならなかった. ▶定義2 to trust sb/sth to work or behave well ~がよく働く,または動くと信じる→~を当てにする,信頼する‖ *Can I rely on you to keep a secret?* あなたが秘密を守ってくれると信じていいですか. ● 名 reliance ●参 reliable, reliant

\*remain /rɪméɪn/ 動⾃ ▶定義1 to stay or continue in the same place or condition 同じ場所または状態でとどまる,あるいは続く→とどまる,居残る,滞在する,依然として~のままである‖ *to remain silent/standing/seated* 黙った・立った・座ったままでいる *Josef went to live in America but his family remained behind in Europe.* ジョセフはアメリカに渡って生活したが,家族はヨーロッパに残っていた. ▶定義2 to be left after other people or things have gone ほかの人や物が去った後に残される→残っている,残されている,残存する,取り残される‖ *They spent the two remaining days of their holidays buying presents to take home.* 彼らは休日の残り2日を,家に持ち帰るお土産を買うことに費やした. ▶定義3 to still need to be done, said or dealt with まだ行われる,言われる,または処理される必要がある→これから~されねばならない,まだ~されないでいる,~する事が残っている‖ *It remains to be seen (= we do not know yet) whether we've made the right decision.* 私たちが正しい決断をしたかどうかは,後になってみないと分からない(= 私たちにはまだ分からない). *Although he seems very pleasant, the fact remains that I don't trust him.* 彼はとても感じが良さそうに見えるが,私が彼を信用していないということは否定できない.

**remainder** /rɪméɪndər/ 名 (通常は **the remainder**) [単数扱い,単数または複数形の動詞と共に] ▶定義 the people, things, etc that are left after the others have gone away or been dealt with; the rest ほかの人や物が去ったまたは処理された後に残された人々,物など;残り→残り,残りの人々,残り物,残余

**remains** /rɪméɪnz/ 名 [複数扱い] ▶定義1 what is left behind after other parts have been used or taken away ほかの部分が使われた,または取り除かれた後に残されたもの→残り,残り物,遺物,遺跡‖ *The builders found the remains of a Roman mosaic floor.* 建築業者たちは,ローマ時代のモザイク式の床の跡を発見した. ▶定義2 正式 a dead body (sometimes one that has been found somewhere a long time after death) 遺体(死後長い時間がたってから,どこかで発見されたものを指すこともある)→遺体,死体,なきがら,遺骨‖ *Human remains were discovered in the wood.* その森で遺体が発見された.

**remand** /rɪmǽnd; -mánd/ 名 ⓤ 医 ▶定義 the time before a prisoner's trial takes place 囚人の裁判が行われるまでの期間→再留置,再拘留‖ *a remand prisoner* 再拘留された囚人 ― **remand** 動⽋ →~を再拘留する,再留置する‖ *The man was remanded in custody (= sent to prison until the trial).* その男は再拘留された(= 裁判まで刑務所に送られた).

成句 **on remand** ▶定義 (used about a prisoner) waiting for the trial to take place(囚人について)裁判が行われるのを待っている→再拘留中の,再拘留されて

\*remark /rɪmɑ́ːrk/ 動⾃他 ▶定義 **remark (on/upon sb/sth)** to say or write sth; to comment ~を言う,または書く;批評する→~と言う,述べる,書く,一言する‖ *A lot of people have remarked on the similarity between them.* 多くの人らが類似していると言った. ●参 **observation**, **comment** ― **remark** 名 ⓒ →所見,意見,感想,見解

**remarkable** /rɪmɑ́ːrkəb(ə)l/ 形 ▶定義 unusual and surprising in a way that people notice 人が気付くほど普通とは違う,また驚かせるような→注目すべき,際立った,例外的な,目立った,顕著な‖ *That is a remarkable achievement for someone so young.* そんなに若い人がそれを成し遂げたとは驚きだ. ― **remarkably** /-əb(ə)li/ 副 →目立って,際立って,著しく,異常に,驚くほど

**remedial** /rɪmíːdiəl/ 形 ▶定義1 aimed at improving or correcting a situation ある状態を改善すること,または修正することを目的とした →治療のための,矯正の,改善のための ▶定義2 helping people who are slow at learning sth ~の学習に時間がかかる人を助けてい

る→補習の, 学業の後れを取り戻すための‖ *remedial English classes* 英語の補習授業

**remedy**¹ /rémədi/ 名 ❻ (複 **remedies**) a remedy (for sth) ▶定義1 something that makes you better when you are ill or in pain 病気または痛むときに, 良くなるようにするもの→治療, 治療法, 治療薬, 医薬品 ‖ *Hot lemon with honey is a good remedy for colds.* はちみつ入りのホットレモンは風邪によく効く. ▶定義2 a way of solving a problem 問題を解決する方法→解決策, 矯正法, 救済策, 改善法 ‖ *There is no easy remedy for unemployment.* 失業を容易に解決する方法はない.

**remedy**² /rémədi/ 動 ⓣ (現分 **remedying**; 三単現 **remedies**; 過, 過分 **remedied**) ▶定義 to change or improve sth that is wrong or bad 間違っている, または悪い〜を変える, あるいは改善する→〜を矯正する, 改善する, 治す, 治療する‖ *to remedy an injustice* 不公平を正す

*__remember__ /rɪmémbər/ 動 ⓘ ⓣ ▶定義1 remember (sb/sth); remember (doing sth); remember that... to have sb/sth in your mind or to bring sb/sth back into your mind 〜を心にとどめている, または〜を心に思い出させる→(〜を)覚えている, 記憶している, 忘れずにいる, 思い出す‖ *We arranged to go out tonight - remember?* 今晩は出掛けることになっています — 覚えていましたか. *As far as I can remember, I haven't seen him before.* 私が思い出せる限り, 以前彼に会ったことはない. *I'm sorry. I don't remember your name.* ごめんなさい. あなたのお名前が思い出せません. *Do you remember the night we first met?* 私たちが初めて会った夜の事を覚えていますか. *Remember that we're having visitors tonight.* 今夜, 来客があることを忘れないように. *Can you remember when we bought the stereo?* このステレオをいつ買ったか思い出せますか. ▶定義2 remember (sth/to do sth) to not forget to do what you have to do しなければならない事をするのを忘れない→忘れないで〜する, 〜するのを忘れない, 忘れないように注意する‖ *I remembered to buy the coffee.* 私はコーヒーを買うのを忘れないよう注意した. *Remember to turn the lights off before you leave.* 出掛ける前に忘れずに電灯を消しなさい.

▶ You remember to do something と言うと, ある事をするのを忘れていないという意味を表すことに注意する. You remember doing something と言うと, ある事をしたイメージまたは記憶の中にあるという意味を表す: *I remember leaving my keys on the table last night.* (私は昨晩, かぎをテーブルの上に置いたのを覚えている.) *Remember to take your keys when you go out.* (出掛けるときには, かぎを忘れずに持っていきなさい.)

成句 **remember me to sb** ▶定義 used when you want to send good wishes to a person you have not seen for a long time 長い間会っていない人によろしく伝えたいときに用いて→〜によろしくと伝える‖ *Please remember me to your wife.* 奥様にどうぞよろしくお伝えください.

☞参 **remind** の注

> ▶語法
>
> remember...ing と remember that SV
>
> remember *doing* (〜したのを覚えている) は, remember to *do* (忘れずに〜する) との対比だけが強調されがちですが, 次のように remember that SVの表現もよく用いられます. *I remember seeing him.* (彼に会ったのを覚えている)= I remember (that) I have seen him.
> 反意語の forget も同様の用法が可能です. *I will never forget visiting here.* (ここに来たことは決して忘れない)= I will never forget (that) I have visited here.

**remembrance** /rɪmémbr(ə)ns/ 名 ⓤ 正式 ▶定義 thinking about and showing respect for sb who is dead 亡くなった〜のことを思い, 敬意を表すること→思い出, 思い出すこと, 回想, 追想‖ *a service in remembrance of those killed in the war* 戦争で亡くなった人々を追悼する礼拝

*__remind__ /rɪmáɪnd/ 動 ⓣ ▶定義1 remind sb (about/of sth); remind sb (to do sth/that...) to help sb to remember sth, especially sth important that he/she has to do 〜を, 特に〜がしなければならない重要な…を, その〜が思い出す助けとなる→〜に気付かせる, 〜を思い起こさせる, 思い出させる‖ *Can you remind me of your address?* あなたの住所はどちらでしたでしょうか. *He reminded the children to wash* their hands. 彼は子供たちに手を洗うよう注意した. *Remind me what we're supposed to be doing tomorrow.* 私たちは明日何をする予定になっているのか, 念のため私に教えてください. ▶定義2 remind sb of sb/sth to cause sb to remember sb/sth 〜に…を思い出させる→〜に…を思い出させる, 連想させる ‖ *That smell reminds me of school.* そのにおいは学校を思い出させる. *You remind me of your father.* あなたはお父さん似だと思います.

► rememberは, 自分から何かを思い出すことである. remindは, だれか, または何かがある事を思い起こさせると, その人・物・事がある事を思い出す原因となる, ということである: *Did you remember to phone Ali last night?* (昨夜, 忘れずにアリに電話しましたか.) *Remind me to phone Ali later.* (後でアリに電話するのを忘れていたら教えてください.)

▶語法

remind someone that SV も忘れずに

*This photo reminds me of my trip to France.* (この写真を見るとフランス旅行を思い出す)のように「remind + 人 + of + 物事」のパターンで用いられますが, of 以下は *She reminded me that smoking was prohibited there.* (彼女はその場所が禁煙であることを思い出させてくれた)のように that SV でも表現できます. これは inform や afraid の場合と同様です.

**reminder** /rɪmáɪndər/ 名 ● ▶定義 something that makes you remember sth 〜を思い出させるもの→思い出させる物・人, 気付かせる物・人, 注意, 催促状 ‖ *We received a reminder that we hadn't paid the electricity bill.* 私たちは電気料金を納めていないという催促状を受け取った.

**reminisce** /rèmənís/ 動 ❸ ▶定義 reminisce (about sb/sth) to talk about pleasant things that happened in the past 過去に起こった楽しい事について話す→思い出話をして楽しむ, 懐かしむ, 回顧する

**reminiscent** /rèmənísənt/ 形 (名詞の前は不可) ▶定義 that makes you remember sb/sth; similar to 〜を思い出させるような; 〜によく似た→〜を思い出させる, 想起させる, しのばせる ‖ *His suit was reminiscent of an old army uniform.* 彼のスーツは昔の軍服を思わせた.

**remote control** 1363

**remnant** /rémnənt/ 名 ❸ ▶定義 a piece of sth that is left after the rest has gone ほかの部分がなくなった後に残っている物→残り, 残余, 遺物, 名残 ‖ *These few trees are the remnants of a huge forest.* これらのわずかな木々は巨大な森林の名残である.

**remorse** /rɪmɔ́ːrs/ 名 ❶ ▶定義 remorse (for sth/doing sth) a feeling of sadness because you have done sth wrong 悪い〜をしたための悲しみの気持ち→激しい後悔, 痛悔, 深い悔恨, 自責の念 ‖ *She was filled with remorse for what she had done.* 彼女は自分のした事に対し後悔の気持ちで一杯だった. ●参 guilt — remorseful /-fʊl, -f(ə)l/ 形→悔恨の, 深く後悔した, 自責の念に駆られている, 良心の呵責(かしゃく)に耐えない

**remorseless** /rɪmɔ́ːrsləs/ 形 ▶定義1 showing no pity 哀れみを全く示していない→情け容赦ない, 無慈悲な, 無情な, 冷酷な ▶定義2 not stopping or becoming less strong やむことのない, または和らぐことのない→容赦なく続く, 執拗(しつよう)な ‖ *a remorseless attack on sb* 〜への執拗な攻撃 — remorselessly 副→情け容赦なく, 無慈悲に, 冷酷に

**remote** /rɪmóʊt/ 形 ▶定義1 remote (from sth) far away from where other people live ほかの人々が住む場所から遠く離れた→遠く離れた, 辺鄙(へんぴ)な, 都会から離れた, 人里離れた ‖ *a remote island in the Pacific* 太平洋上ははるかかなたの孤島 ▶定義2 far away in time 時間的に遠い→遠く隔たった, 遠い ‖ *the remote past/future* はるか昔・遠い未来 ▶定義3 not very great あまり大きくない→かすかな, わずかな, ありそうにない, 微々たる ‖ *I haven't **the remotest** idea who could have done such a thing.* こんな事をだれができたのか全く見当が付かない. *a remote possibility* およそありそうもないこと ▶定義4 not very friendly or interested in other people あまり友好的ではない, または他人に興味がない→よそよそしい, 素っ気ない, 無関心な ‖ *He seemed rather remote.* 彼はかなりよそよそしく見えた. — remoteness 名 ❶→遠く離れていること, 遠隔, 掛け離れていること, 疎遠

**remote control** 名 ▶定義1 ❶a system for

## remotely

controlling sth from a distance ～を遠くから制御する方式➡**遠隔操作, 遠隔制御, リモートコントロール, リモコン** || *The doors can be opened by remote control.* そのドアはリモコンで開けることができる. ▶定義2 (または **remote**) ❸ a piece of equipment for controlling sth from a distance ～を遠くから制御するための機器➡**遠隔操作装置, 遠隔制御装置, リモートコントローラー, リモコン装置**

**remotely** /rɪmóʊtli/ 副 (否定文で用いて) ▶定義 to a very small degree; at all ほんのわずかな程度に; 全然➡**ほんのわずか(も), ほんの少しも, 全く** || *I'm not remotely interested in your problems.* 私はあなたの問題に全く関心がありません.

**removal** /rɪmúːv(ə)l/ 名 ▶定義1 ❶the action of taking sb/sth away ～を取り除く行為➡**解雇, 解任, 除去, 取り外し, 撤去** || *the removal of restrictions/regulations/rights* 制限の撤廃・規制の撤廃・権利の廃止 ▶定義2 ❸❶the activity of moving from one house to live in another ある家から別の家に移る行為➡**移動, 移転, 転居, 引っ越し** || *a removal van* 引っ越し用トラック

*__remove__ /rɪmúːv/ 動他 正式 ▶定義1 remove sb/sth (from sth) to take sb/sth off or away ～を取り去る, または取り除く➡**～を連れ去る, 取り去る, 取り除く, 移動させる** || *Remove the saucepan from the heat.* シチューなべを火から下ろします. *This washing powder will remove most stains.* この洗剤でほとんどの染みが落ちるでしょう. *to remove doubts/fears/problems* 疑念を振り払う・恐怖を取り払う・問題を一掃する *I would like you to remove my name from your mailing list.* あなた方の郵送先名簿から私の名前を削除してほしいのですが. *He had an operation to remove the tumour.* 彼は腫瘍(しゅよう)を切除する手術を受けた. ☞ take off, take out などは, くだけた言い方である. ▶定義2 remove sb (from sth) to make sb leave his/her job or position ～に仕事または地位を辞めさせる➡**～を解任する, 免職する, 解雇する**

**removed** /rɪmúːvd/ 形 (名詞の前は不可) ▶定義 far or different from sth➡**～と離れた, 異なった** || *Hospitals today are far removed from what they were fifty years ago.* 今日の病院は50年前の姿とは大きく変わっている.

**remover** /rɪmúːvər/ 名 ❸❶ ▶定義 a substance that cleans off paint, dirty marks, etc ペンキ, 汚れの跡などを消し去る物質➡**除去剤, 剥離(はくり)剤** || *make-up remover* 化粧落とし

**render** /réndər/ 動他 (文) ▶定義1 to cause sb/sth to be in a certain condition ～をある状態にする➡**～を…にする, させる, 変える** || *She was rendered speechless by the attack.* 彼女は責められて何も言えなくなった. ▶定義2 to give help, etc to sb ～に助けなどを与える➡**～を与える, する, 示す, 払う** || *to render sb a service/render a service to sb* ～に尽くす

**rendezvous** /rɑ́ːndɪvùː, -deɪ-/ 名 ❸ (複) **rendezvous** /-vuːz/) ▶定義1 a rendezvous (with sb) a meeting that you have arranged with sb ～と取り決めてある会合➡**会う約束, 会合, 待ち合わせ, ランデブー** || *He had a secret rendezvous with Daniela.* 彼はダニエラとこっそり会った. ▶定義2 a place where people often meet 人々が頻繁に会う場所➡**たまり場, よく待ち合わせる所, 会合に好んで利用される場所** || *The cafe is a popular rendezvous for students.* そのカフェは学生に人気のあるたまり場である.

**renew** /rɪn(j)úː/ 動他 ▶定義1 to start sth again ～を再び始める➡**～を再び始める, 再開する, 繰り返す** || *renewed outbreaks of violence* 暴力の再発 *to renew a friendship* 旧交を温める ▶定義2 to give sb new strength or energy ～に新たな力またはエネルギーを与える➡**～を取り戻す, 回復する, 新たにする** || *After a break he set to work with renewed enthusiasm.* 休憩の後, 彼は熱意を新たに仕事に取り組んだ. ▶定義3 to make sth valid for a further period of time ～をさらに長い期間, 有効にする➡**～を更新する, 継続する, 延長する, 書き換える** || *to renew a contract/passport/library book* 契約・パスポート・図書館の本を更新する — **renewal** /-n(j)úː(ə)l/ 名 ❸❶➡**新しくすること, 更新, 再開, 書き換え** || *When is your passport due for renewal?* あなたのパスポートの更新期限はいつですか.

**renewable** /rɪn(j)úːəb(ə)l/ 形 ▶定義1 (used about sources of energy) that will always exist (エネルギー源について) 常に存在し続けるような➡**無尽蔵な, 供給に限りがない, 再生可能な** || *renewable resources such as wind and solar power* 風力または太陽熱などの無尽蔵な資源 ⇔

**non-renewable** ▶定義2 that can be continued or replaced with a new one for another period of time 追加の期間に継続される,または新しいものと交換されることができるような→**継続できる,更新可能な,延長可能な**

**renounce** /rɪnáʊns/ 動他 正式 ▶定義 to say formally that you no longer want to have sth or to be connected with sth もはや〜を持つこと,または〜と関係があることを望まないと正式に言う→**〜を断念する,放棄する,〜との関係を断つ,縁を切る** ☛ 名 renunciation

**renovate** /rénəvèɪt/ 動他 ▶定義 to repair an old building and put it back into good condition 古い建物を修理して良い状態に戻す→**〜を修理する,復元する,修復する,改修する** ― renovation /rènəvéɪʃən/ 名 C U →修理,修復,改修,修繕 ‖ *The house is in need of complete renovation.* その家は全部修理する必要がある.

**renown** /rɪnáʊn/ 名 U 正式 ▶定義 fame and respect that you get for doing sth especially well 特別にうまく〜を行ったために獲得する名声と尊敬 →**名声,有名,誉れ** ― renowned 形 **renowned (for/as sth)**→(〜で・〜として)有名な,高名な,名高い,名をはせている ‖ *The region is renowned for its food.* その地域はおいしい食べ物で有名である.

*__rent__¹ /rent/ 名 U C ▶定義 money that you pay regularly for the use of land, a house or a building 土地,家,または建物を使用するため定期的に支払う金→**使用料,地代,賃貸料,家賃** ‖ *a high/low rent* 高い・安い賃貸料 *She was allowed to live there rent-free until she found a job.* 彼女は仕事が見つかるまで,家賃なしでそこに住むことを許された. *Is this house for rent (= available to rent)?* この家は賃貸ですか(= 賃借りできますか).

*__rent__² /rent/ 動他 ▶定義1 **rent sth (from sb)** to pay money for the use of land, a building, a machine, etc 土地,建物,機械などを使用するために金を支払う →**〜を(…から)賃借りする,借りる** ‖ *Do you own or rent your television?* あなたはテレビを所有していますか,それとも借りていますか. *to rent a flat* アパートを借りる ☛参 hire¹(1)の注 ▶定義2 **rent sth (out) (to sb)** to allow sb to use land, a building, a machine, etc for money 金を得るために〜に土地,建物,機械などを使用することを許可する→

〜を(…に)賃貸しする,貸し出す ‖ *We could rent out the small bedroom to a student.* 私たちは小さな寝室を学生に貸すことができた. ☛参 hire¹(3) ▶定義3 英 =HIRE¹(1) ▶定義4 米 = HIRE¹(3)

**rental** /rént(ə)l/ 名 C U ▶定義 money that you pay when you rent a telephone, television, etc 電話,テレビなどを借りるときに支払う金→**賃貸料,賃借料,レンタル料金**

**renunciation** /rɪnʌ̀nsiéɪ(ə)n/ 名 U 正式 ▶定義 saying that you no longer want sth or believe in sth もはや〜を望まない,または〜を信じないと言うこと→**断念,放棄,棄権,否認,拒絶** ☛ 動 renounce

**reorganize** (または **-ise**) /riːɔ́ːrɡənàɪz, rɪ-/ 動 自他 ▶定義 to organize sth again or in a new way 〜を再び,または新しい方法で組織する→**〜を再編成する,再組織する,改組する** ― reorganization (または -isation) /riːɔ̀ːrɡənaɪzéɪ(ə)n, rɪ-/ 名 C U →再組織,再編成,改組,立て直し

**Rep** 略 (in US politics) (米国の政治で) ▶定義1 Representative (in Congress)→(議会で)下院議員 ▶定義2 Republican (Party)→共和党

**rep** /rep/ 略式 (または **representative**) 名 C ▶定義 a person whose job is to travel round a particular area and visit companies, etc, to sell the products of the firm for which he/she works 自分が働いている会社の製品を販売するために特定の地域を回り,企業などを訪問することを仕事とする人→**販売代理人,販売外交員,販売員,セールスマン** ‖ *a sales rep* 販売外交員

*__repair__¹ /rɪpéər/ 動他 ▶定義 to put sth old or damaged back into good condition 古い,または破損した〜を良い状態に戻す→**〜を修理する,修繕する** ‖ *These cars can be expensive to repair.* これらの車の修理は高くつくかもしれない. *How much will it cost to have the TV repaired?* このテレビを修理してもらうといくらかかりますか. ☛類 fix, mend ☛参 irreparable

**repair**² /rɪpéər/ 名 C U ▶定義 something that you do to mend sth that is damaged 破損した〜を直すために行うこと→**修理,修繕,手入れ,修復** ‖ *The school is closed for repairs to the roof.* その学校は屋根の修理のため閉鎖されている. *The road is in need of repair.* その道路は補修

## 1366 repatriate

が必要である. *The bridge is **under repair**.* その橋は修理中です. *The bike was damaged **beyond repair** so I threw it away.* その自転車は修理できないほど破損したので廃却した.

**成句** in good, bad, etc repair ▶定義 in a good, bad, etc condition 良い, 悪いなどの状態で→良好な状態で・悪い状態で, 手入れが行き届いて・手入れが行き届かないで

**repatriate** /ri:pǽtrièit, -pæt-/ 動他 ▶定義 to send sb back to his/her own country ～をその～自身の国に送り返す→～を本国へ送還する — repatriation /rì:pætriéiʃ(ə)n, -pæt-/ 名 C U →本国への送還

**repay** /ripéi/ 動他 (過, 過分 **repaid** /ripéid/) ▶定義 1 repay sth (to sb); repay (sb) sth to pay back money that you owe to sb ～に借りている金を返す→（～に）…を払い戻す, 返す, 返金する, 返済する ‖ *to repay a debt/loan* 負債・ローンを返済する *When will you repay the money to them?* あなたはそのお金をいつ彼らに返済するつもりですか. *When will you repay them the money?* あなたはそのお金をいつ彼らに返済するつもりですか. ▶定義 2 repay sb (for sth) to give sth to sb in return for help, kindness, etc 援助, 親切などに対する返礼として, ～に…を与える→～に報いる, 恩返しをする, 返報する, お返しをする ‖ *How can I ever repay you for all you have done for me?* あなたが私にしてくださったすべての事に対し, どうやって恩返しをしたらいいでしょう.

**repayable** /ripéiəb(ə)l/ 形 ▶定義 that you can or must pay back 返金できる, または返金しなければならないような→払い戻しできる, 返済できる, 払い戻すべき, 返済しなければならない ‖ *The loan is repayable over three years.* そのローンの返済期間は3年です.

**repayment** /ripéimənt/ 名 ▶定義 1 U paying sth back ～を払い戻すこと→払い戻し, 返済, 報酬 ‖ *the repayment of a loan* ローンの返済 ▶定義 2 C money that you must pay back to sb/sth regularly ～に定期的に返済しなければならない金→返済金 ‖ *I make monthly repayments on my loan.* 私は毎月ローンの返済金を支払っています.

**repeal** /ripí:l/ 動他 正式 ▶定義 to officially make a law no longer valid 公式に法律をもはや有効ではないようにする→～を廃止する, 撤回する, 撤廃する, 破棄する, 無効にする

***repeat**¹ /ripí:t/ 動 ▶定義 1 自他 repeat (sth/yourself) to say, write or do sth again or more than once ～を再度または2回以上言う, 書く, あるいは行う→～を繰り返して言う, 繰り返し行う, 反復する ‖ *Don't repeat the same mistake again.* 同じ間違いを繰り返してはいけません. *Could you repeat what you just said?* 今おっしゃった事をもう一度言っていただけませんか. *The essay is quite good, but you repeat yourself several times.* その小論はかなり良くできているが, 同じ事を何度も繰り返し述べている. *Raise and lower your left leg ten times, then repeat with the right.* 左足を10回上げたり下げたりします. 次に右足も同じように繰り返します. ▶定義 2 他 repeat sth (to sb) to say or write sth that sb else has said or written or that you have learnt ほかの人が言った, または書いた～, あるいは自分が覚えた～を言う, または書く→～を人に知らせる, 口外する, 他言する, 復唱する ‖ *Please don't repeat what you've heard here to anyone.* あなたがここで聞いた事はだれにも教えないでください. *Repeat each sentence after me.* それぞれの文を私の後に付いて言いなさい. ☞ 名 repetition

**repeat**² /ripí:t/ 名 C ▶定義 something that is done, shown, given, etc again 再び行われる, 示される, 与えられるなどするもの→繰り返されるもの, 再演, 再放送 ‖ *I think I've seen this programme before - it must be a repeat.* 私はこの番組を以前見たことがあると思う — これは再放送に違いない.

**repeated** /ripí:təd/ 形 (名詞の前だけ) ▶定義 done or happening many times 何回も行われた, または起こっている→繰り返して行われる, 度々の, 再三再四の, 度重なる ‖ *There have been repeated accidents on this stretch of road.* 道路のこの辺りでは事故が度々発生している. — repeatedly 副→しばしば, 繰り返して, 何度も, 度々 ‖ *I've asked him repeatedly not to leave his bicycle there.* 私は彼に自転車をそこに置かないよう何度も言っている.

**repel** /ripél/ 動他 (**repelling**; **repelled**) ▶定義 1 to send or push sb/sth back or away ～を送り返す, 押し返す, または追い払う, 押しのける→～

を追い払う,退ける,拒絶する,受け入れない ▶定義2 to make sb feel disgusted 〜をうんざりした気持ちにさせる➔〜を不快な気持ちにする,嫌悪感を与える,不快にする ‖ *The dirt and smell repelled her.* その汚れとにおいに彼女はむかむかした. ☛ repulsion

**repellent**¹ /rɪpél(ə)nt/ 名 ❻ ❶ ▶定義 a chemical substance that is used to keep insects, etc away 虫などを寄せ付けないために使われる化学物質➔**防虫剤** ‖ *a mosquito repellent* 蚊よけの防虫剤

**repellent**² /rɪpél(ə)nt/ 形 ▶定義 causing a strong feeling of disgust 強い嫌悪感を引き起こしている➔**嫌な,不快な,虫の好かない** ‖ *a repellent smell* むかむかするにおい

**repent** /rɪpént/ 動 自 他 正式 ▶定義 repent (of) (sth) to feel and show that you are sorry about sth bad that you have done 自分がした悪い〜について悪いと感じ,それを表す➔**〜を後悔する,悔やむ,悔い改める,残念に思う** ‖ *to repent of your sins* 自分の罪を悔やむ *He repented his hasty decision.* 彼は自分の早まった決断を後悔した. ― repentance /rɪpént(ə)ns/ 名 ❶➔**後悔,悔い,悔恨,悔い改め** ― repentant /rɪpént(ə)nt/ 形➔**後悔している,悔いている,後悔の気持ちを表している**

**repercussion** /rìːpərkʌ́ʃ(ə)n/ 名 [❻, 通常は複数] ▶定義 an unpleasant effect or result of sth you do 自分が行う〜の好ましくない影響または結果➔**影響,波紋,反動,反響** ‖ *His resignation will have serious repercussions.* 彼の辞職により深刻な影響が出るでしょう.

**repertoire** /répərtwàːr/ 名 ❻ ▶定義1 all the plays or music that an actor or a musician knows and can perform ある俳優または音楽家が知っている,または演ずることができる,すべての劇あるいは楽曲➔**レパートリー,上演目録,演奏曲目,持ち歌** ‖ *He must have sung every song in his repertoire last night.* 彼は昨晩,持ち歌をすべて歌ったに違いない. ▶定義2 all the things that a person is able to do ある人が行うことができるすべての事➔**全技術,できる事のすべて,能力の範囲,レパートリー**

**repetition** /rèpətíʃ(ə)n/ 名 ❻ ❶ ▶定義 doing sth again; sth that you do or that happens again 〜を再度行うこと; 再度行う,または起こる事➔**繰り返すこと,繰り返されること,反復,復**

## replacement 1367

唱 ‖ *to learn by repetition* 反復学習する *Let's try to avoid a repetition of what happened last Friday.* この前の金曜日に起こった事を繰り返さないよう努めましょう. ☛ 動 repeat

**repetitive** /rɪpétətɪv/ (または **repetitious** /rèpətíʃəs/) 形 ▶定義 not interesting because the same thing is repeated many times 同じ事が何度も繰り返されるので面白味がない➔**繰り返しの多い,くどい**

***replace** /rɪpléɪs/ 動 他 ▶定義1 replace sb/sth (as/with sb/sth) to take the place of sb/sth; to use sb/sth in place of another person or thing 〜に取って代わる;ほかの人または物の代わりに〜を使う➔**〜に取って代わる,代わりをする,〜の後継者となる,後任になる** ‖ *Teachers will never be replaced by computers in the classroom.* 教室において教師がコンピュータに取って代わられることは決してないでしょう. ▶定義2 replace sb/sth (with sb/sth) to exchange sb/sth for sb/sth that is better or newer 〜をより優れた,または新しい〜と交換する➔**〜を(…と)取り替える,〜の代わりを見つける,交換する** ‖ *We will replace any goods that are damaged.* 破損している品物はすべてお取り替えします. ▶定義3 to put sth back in the place where it was before 〜を元あった場所に戻す➔**〜を戻す,返す** ‖ *Please replace the books on the shelves when you have finished with them.* 本を読み終えたら元の棚に戻してください. ☛ put back の方が一般的でくだけた言い方である.

**replaceable** /rɪpléɪsəb(ə)l/ 形 ▶定義 that can be replaced 取り替えられるような➔**取り替えられる,代わりのある,代用できる,代わりが利く**⇔ **irreplaceable**

**replacement** /rɪpléɪsmənt/ 名 ▶定義1 ❶ exchanging sb/sth for sb/sth that is better or newer 〜を,より優れたまたは新しい…と交換すること➔**取り替え,置き換え,交換,交替** ‖ *The carpets are in need of replacement.* そのカーペットは取り替える必要があります. ▶定義2 ❻ a person or thing that will take the place of sb/sth 〜に取って代わる人または物➔**交替者,代理人,交換品,代用品** ‖ *Mary is leaving next month so we must advertise for a replacement for her.* メ

## 1368　replay

アリーは来月からいなくなるので、彼女の後任の募集広告を出さなければならない.

**replay**¹ /ríːpleɪ, rɪ-/ 名 C ▶定義1 競 a sports match that is played again because neither team won the first time 1度目のときにどちらのチームも勝たなかったために再度行われるスポーツの試合 → **再試合, やり直しの試合** ▶定義2 something on the television, on a film or a cassette tape that you watch or listen to again 再び見る、または聴く、テレビ、映画、カセットテープのもの → **再演, 再上映, 再生** ‖ *Now let's see **an action replay** of that tremendous goal!* あのすばらしいゴールの場面を今すぐ再生して見てみましょう.

**replay**² /riːpléɪ, rɪ-/ 動 他 ▶定義1 to play a sports match, etc again because neither team won the first time 1度目のときにどちらのチームも勝たなかったため、スポーツの試合などを再度行う → **～を再び行う, やり直す** ▶定義2 to play again sth that you have recorded 録音・録画した～を再生する → **～を再生する** ‖ *They kept replaying the goal over and over again.* 彼らはそのゴールの場面を何回も繰り返し再生した.

**replica** /réplɪkə/ 名 C ▶定義 **a replica of (sth)** an exact copy of sth ～の正確な写し → **複写, 複製品, レプリカ, 正確な模写**

★**reply**¹ /rɪpláɪ/ 動 自 他 (現分 **replying**; 三単現 **replies**; 過, 過分 **replied**) ▶定義 **reply (to sb/sth) (with sth)** to say, write or do sth as an answer to sb/sth ～に対する答えとして…を言う、書くまたは行う → **(～に・～で)返事をする, 答える, 回答する, 応じる** ‖ *I wrote to Sue but she hasn't replied.* 私はスーに手紙を書いたが、彼女はまだ返事をくれない. *'Yes, I will,' she replied.* 「はい、やります」と彼女は答えた. *to reply to a question* 質問に答える ☛参 **answer**¹の注 ― reply 名 C U (複 **replies**) → **返事, 回答, 応答, 応酬** ‖ *Al nodded **in reply to** my question.* アルは私の問いへの答えとしてうなずいた.

★**report**¹ /rɪpɔ́ːt/ 動 他 ▶定義1 他 **report (on sb/sth) (to sb/sth); report sth (to sb)** to give people information about what you have seen, heard, done, etc 見る、聞く、行うなどしたことについて人に情報を与える → **(～を…に)報告する, 知らせる, 伝達する, 通報する** ‖ *Several people reported seeing/having seen the boy.* 数人がその男の子を見たと報告した. *Several people reported that they had seen the boy.* 数人がその男の子を目撃したと報告した. *The company reported huge profits last year.* その会社は去年、ばく大な利益を報告した. *Call me if you have anything new to report.* 何か新しい知らせがあれば私に電話をください. ▶定義2 自 他 **report (on) sth** (in a newspaper or on the television or radio) to write or speak about sth that has happened (新聞、テレビ、またはラジオで)起こった物事について書く、または話す → **～を報道する, 伝える, 報じる, 記事の取材をする** ‖ *The paper sent a journalist to report on the events.* その新聞は事件を報道するために記者を派遣した. ▶定義3 他 **report sb (to sb) (for sth)** to tell a person in authority about an accident, a crime, etc or about sth wrong that sb has done 事故、犯罪などについて、または～がした悪い…について、権威ある人に知らせる → **～に報告する, ～を告げ口する, 言い付ける, 訴える** ‖ *All accidents must be reported to the police.* すべての事故は警察に報告する義務がある. *The boy was reported missing early this morning.* その男の子は今日の早朝から行方不明であると報告されている. ▶定義4 自 **report (to sb/sth) for sth** to tell sb that you have arrived ～に到着したことを告げる → **(～で・～に)所在を報告する, 出頭する** ‖ *On your arrival, please report to the reception desk.* 到着されたら受付まで来てください. ▶定義5 他 正式 **be reported to be/as sth** used to say that you have heard sth said, but you are not sure if it is true 言われた～を聞いたことがあるが、それが本当かどうかは確かではないと言うために用いて → **～が…だと報じられている, 伝えられている, ～という話・評判である** ‖ *The 70-year-old actor is reported to be/as being comfortable in hospital.* その70歳の俳優は入院中だが病状は安定しているという話だ.

句動詞 **report back (on sth) (to sb)** ▶定義 to give information to sb about sth he/she has asked you to find out about ～が自分に調べるように頼んだ…についての情報を、その～に与える → **～に帰って報告する, 折り返し報告する** ‖ *One person in each group will then report back on what you've decided to the class.* 各グループの1人がクラスに戻ってあなたが決めた事を

報告するでしょう.

**report to sb**(進行形は不可) ▶定義 to have sb as your manager in the company or organization that you work for 勤務している会社または組織で, ~を自分の管理者として持つ→~の監督下にある, ~に直属している

▶この動詞は進行形では使われないが, 現在分詞(= -ing 形)はよく見掛けられる: *A new team was put together for the project, reporting to Michael Nolan.*(そのプロジェクトのために, マイケル ノラン氏の率いる新しいチームが結成された.)

**★report²** /rɪpɔ́ːrt/ 名 C ▶定義1 a report (on/of sth) a written or spoken description of what you have seen, heard, done, studied, etc 見る, 聞く, 行う, 学ぶなどしたものについての, 書かれた, または口頭での説明→(~に関する)報告, 報告書, レポート, 記事 ‖ *newspaper reports* 新聞記事 *a report on the company's finances* 会社の財務報告 *a first-hand report (= from the person who saw what happened)* 直接得た報告(= 起こった事を見た人からの報告) ▶定義2 a written statement about the work of a student at school, college, etc 学校, 大学などの学生の学習について書かれたもの→成績報告書, 成績表, 通信簿 ‖ *to get a good/bad report* 良い・悪い成績を取る

**reported speech** = **INDIRECT SPEECH**

▶巻末の「文法早見表」を参照.

**reporter** /rɪpɔ́ːrtər/ 名 C ▶定義 a person who writes about the news in a newspaper or speaks about it on the television or radio ニュースについて新聞に書く, またはテレビやラジオで話す人→報道記者, 放送記者, 通信員, レポーター ☞参 **journalist**

**★represent** /rèprɪzént/ 動他 ▶定義1 to act or speak in the place of sb else; to be the representative of a group or country ほかの~に代わって行動する, または話す; ある集団または国を代表している→~を代表する, ~の代理をする, 代表として出席している ‖ *You will need a lawyer to represent you in court.* あなたには法廷で代理を務めてもらう弁護士が必要になるでしょう. *It's an honour for an athlete to represent his or her country.* スポーツ選手にとって自国の代表になるのは名誉なことである. ▶定義2 to be equal to sth; to be sth ~と同等になる; ~である→~を意味する, ~の意義がある, ~であると示す, ~に相当する ‖ *These results represent a major breakthrough in our understanding of cancer.* これらの成果は, 私たちががんを理解する上で大きな突破口になる. ▶定義3 to be a picture, sign, example, etc of sb/sth ~の絵, 記号, 例である→~を示す, 象徴する, 意味する, ~の記号・印である ‖ *The yellow lines on the map represent minor roads.* その地図では, 黄色い線は幹線以外の道路を表している. ▶定義4 to describe sb/sth in a particular way ~をある方法で説明する→~を説明する, はっきり述べる, 指摘する, 表明する

**★representation** /rèprɪzèntéɪʃ(ə)n, -z(ə)n-/ 名 ▶定義1 ❶ C the way that sb/sth is shown or described; something that shows or describes sth ~が表現される, または説明される方法; ~を表現する, または説明すること→表現, 表示, 描写, 描出 ‖ *The article complains about the representation of women in advertising.* その記事は広告における女性の描写の仕方に不満を述べている. ☞参 **proportional representation** ▶定義2 ❶ 正式 having sb to speak for you 自分の代わりに話す~を持つこと→代表, 代理, 代行

**representative¹** /rèprɪzéntətɪv/ 形 ▶定義 representative (of sb/sth) typical of a larger group to which sb/sth belongs ~が属する大きな集団を代表している→(~を)代表する, 代理の, 代表的な ‖ *Tonight's audience is not representative of national opinion.* 今夜の聴衆は世論を代表しているわけではありません.

**representative²** /rèprɪzéntətɪv/ 名 C ▶定義1 a person who has been chosen to act or speak for sb else or for a group ほかの~や集団に代わって, 行動するためまたは話すために選ばれた人→代表者, 代理人, 代議士, 国会議員 ▶定義2 正式 = **REP**

**repress** /rɪprés/ 動他 ▶定義1 to control an emotion or to try to prevent it from being shown or felt 感情を抑制する, あるいは感情が表に出るまたはそれに気付かれるのを防ごうと努める→~を抑える, こらえる, 抑制する, 押し殺す ‖ *She tried to repress her anger.* 彼女は怒りを抑えようと努めた. ▶定義2 to limit the freedom of a group of people ある集団の人々の自由を制限する→~を制止する, 制圧する, 抑圧する, 弾圧す

る — **repression** /rɪpréʃ(ə)n/ 名 ◎ →抑制, 抑圧, 鎮圧, 弾圧 ‖ *protests against government repression* 政府による弾圧への抗議

**repressed** /rɪprést/ 形 ▶定義1 (used about a person) having emotions and desires that he/she does not show or express（人について）見せないまたは表さない感情や欲望を持っている→抑圧された, 抑圧に悩む, 鬱屈(うっくつ)した ▶定義2 (used about an emotion) that you do not show（感情について）見せない→抑圧された ‖ *repressed anger/desire* 抑圧された怒り・欲望

**repressive** /rɪprésɪv/ 形 ▶定義 that limits people's freedom 人々の自由を制限するような→抑圧的な, 鎮圧の ‖ *a repressive government* 弾圧的な政府

**reprieve** /rɪpríːv/ 動 ◎ ▶定義 to stop or delay the punishment of a prisoner who was going to be punished by death 死刑によって罰せられることになっている囚人の処罰をやめる, または遅らせる→～の死刑執行を中止する, 猶予する, 延期する — **reprieve** 名 ◎ →死刑執行中止・猶予・延期 ‖ *The judge granted him a last-minute reprieve.* 裁判官は彼に死刑執行間際で猶予を認めた.

**reprimand** /réprəmàːnd, -mænd/ 動 ◎ ▶定義 *reprimand sb (for sth)* to tell sb officially that he/she has done sth wrong ～が間違った…をしたと公式にその～に言う→～を叱責(しっせき)する, 懲戒する — **reprimand** 名 ◎ →叱責, 懲戒, 非難 ‖ *a severe reprimand* 厳しい叱責

**reprisal** /rɪpráɪz(ə)l/ 名 ◎ ◎ ▶定義 punishment, especially by military force, for harm that one group of people does to another ある集団の人々がほかの集団の人々に及ぼした損害に対する, 特に軍事力による, 処罰→仕返し, 報復, 返報

**reproach** /rɪpróʊtʃ/ 動 ◎ ▶定義 *reproach sb (for/with sth)* to tell sb that he/she has done sth wrong; to blame sb ～が間違った…をした場合, その～に言う; ～を責める→～を(…の理由で)非難する, とがめる, 責める, 叱責(しっせき)する ‖ *You've nothing to reproach yourself for. It wasn't your fault.* あなたが自分を責める理由は何もありません. あなたに非はなかったのですから. — **reproach** 名 ◎ ◎ →非難, とがめ, 叱責 ‖ *His behaviour is **beyond reproach** (= cannot be criticized).* 彼の行動は非の打ちどころがない (= 批判を受ける余地がない). *Alison felt his reproaches were unjustified.* アリソンは自分に対する叱責を不当だと感じた. — **reproachful** /-fʊl, -f(ə)l/ 形 →非難する, 非難がましい, とがめるような, 責めるような ‖ *a reproachful look* とがめるような顔付き — **reproachfully** /-fʊli, -f(ə)li/ 副 →非難して, とがめるように

\***reproduce** /ìːprəd(j)úːs, -proʊ-, rì-/ 動 ▶定義1 ◎ to produce a copy of sth ～の写しを作る→～を再生する, 再現する, 複写する, 複製する ‖ *It is very hard to reproduce a natural environment in the laboratory.* 実験室で自然環境を再現するのは非常に難しい. ▶定義2 ◎ (used about people, animals and plants) to produce young（人, 動物, および植物について）子を産む→繁殖する, 増える

\***reproduction** /ìːprədʌ́kʃ(ə)n, rì-/ 名 ▶定義1 ◎ the process of producing babies or young 赤ん坊または子を産む過程→生殖, 繁殖 ‖ *sexual reproduction* 有性生殖 ▶定義2 ◎ the production of copies of sth ～の写しを作ること→再生, 再現 ‖ *Digital recording gives excellent sound reproduction.* デジタル式の録音により高音質な音声が再生できる. ▶定義3 ◎ a copy of a painting, etc 絵画などの模写→複製, 複写, 模造品

**reproductive** /ìːprədʌ́ktɪv, rì-/ 形 ▶定義 connected with the production of young animals, plants, etc 動物の子が生まれたり, 植物が新たに生えてくることに関連した→生殖の, 繁殖の ‖ *the male reproductive organs* 男性生殖器

**reproof** /rɪprúːf/ 名 ◎ ◎ 正式 ▶定義 something that you say to sb when you do not approve of what he/she has done ～が行った事に同意しないとき, その～に言うこと→叱責(しっせき), 非難, 意見, 小言

**reptile** /réptàɪl/ 名 ◎ ▶定義 an animal that has cold blood and a skin covered in scales, and whose young come out of eggs, for example crocodiles and snakes 例えばワニや蛇のように, 冷血でうろこに覆われた皮を持ち, 子は卵から生まれる動物→は虫類の動物
▶ *amphibian*と比較.

\***republic** /rɪpʌ́blɪk/ 名 ◎ ▶定義 a country that has an elected government and an elected leader (president) 選出された政府と選出された指導者（大統領）を持つ国→共和国, 共和政体, 共和制国家 ‖ *the Republic of Ireland* アイルラン

ド共和国 ☛参 monarchy

**republican** /rɪpʌ́blɪkən/ 名 C ▶定義 1 a person who supports the system of an elected government and leader 選出された政府と指導者から成る制度を支持する人→**共和主義者, 共和制支持者** ▶定義 2 **Republican** a member of the Republican Party 共和党の一員→**共和党員** ☛参 Democrat — republican 形→共和国の, 共和制の, 共和政体の, 共和主義の

**the Republican Party** 名 [単数扱い] ▶定義 one of the two main political parties of the US 米国の2大政党のうちの1つ→**共和党** もう1つは the Democratic Party (民主党) で, 党員は Democrat (民主党員).

**repudiate** /rɪpjúːdièɪt/ 動 他 ▶定義 to say that you refuse to accept or believe sth ~を受け入れることを, または信じることを, 拒むと言う→**~を拒絶する, 拒否する, 否認する** ‖ to repudiate a suggestion/an accusation/responsibility 提案・告訴・責任を拒絶する

**repulsive** /rɪpʌ́lsɪv/ 形 ▶定義 that causes a strong feeling of disgust 強い嫌悪感を引き起こすような→**大変嫌な, 不快な, おぞましい** ☛動 repel — repulsion 名 U→大嫌い, 嫌悪, 不快感

**reputable** /répjətəb(ə)l/ 形 ▶定義 that is known to be good 優れていることで知られているような→**尊敬すべき, 立派な, 評判の良い, 信頼のおける** ⇔ disreputable

*****reputation** /rèpjətéɪʃ(ə)n/ 名 C ▶定義 a reputation (for/as sth) the opinion that people in general have about what sb/sth is like ~がどのようなものであるかについて一般の人々が抱いている意見→**評判, 世評, 風評, うわさ** ‖ to have a good/bad reputation 評判が良い・悪い Adam has a reputation for being late. アダムはよく遅刻するという評判だ. ☛類 name

**reputed** /rɪpjúːtəd/ 形 ▶定義 generally said to be sth, although it is not certain 確かではないが, 一般に~であると言われている→**~と一般に称せられる, ~という評判の, うわさの** ‖ He's reputed to be the highest-paid sportsman in the world. 彼は世界一高給取りの運動選手だと言われている. — reputedly 副→評判によれば, うわさでは

*****request**¹ /rɪkwést/ 名 C U ▶定義 request (for sth/that...) an act of asking for sth ~を頼む行為→**頼むこと, 要請, 要望, 依頼** ‖ a request for help 援助の要請 I'm going to **make a request** for a larger desk. 私はもっと大きい机を頼むつもりです. to grant/turn down a request 要求を認める・却下する Single rooms are available **on request**. ご要望であればシングルルームがご利用できます.

**request**² /rɪkwést/ 動 他 正式 ▶定義 request sth (from/of sb) to ask for sth ~を頼む→**~を頼む, 要請する, 要望する, 依頼する** ‖ Passengers are requested not to smoke on this bus. このバスの中では喫煙をご遠慮願います. to request a loan from the bank 銀行にローンを頼む ☛ request は ask よりも改まった語.

*****require** /rɪkwáɪər/ 動 他 ▶定義 1 to need sth ~を必要とする→**~を必要とする, 要する, ~が欠かせない** ‖ a situation that requires tact and diplomacy 機転と駆け引きを必要とする状況 ☛ require は need よりも改まった語. ▶定義 2 (しばしば受動態で) to officially demand or order sth ~を公式に要求する, または命令する→**~を要求する, 命ずる** ‖ Passengers are required by law to wear seat belts. 乗客は法律によりシートベルトの着用が義務付けられている.

**requirement** /rɪkwáɪərmənt/ 名 C ▶定義 something that you need or that you must do or have 必要とする [しなければならない・持たなければならない] もの→**必需品, 要求されるもの, 必要条件** ‖ university entrance requirements 大学入学資格

*****rescue** /réskjuː/ 動 他 ▶定義 rescue sb/sth (from sb/sth) to save sb/sth from a situation that is dangerous or unpleasant ~を危険なまたは不快な状況から救う→**~を(…から)救う, 救助する, 救出する** ‖ He rescued a child from drowning. 彼はおぼれかかっていた子供を救助した. — rescue 名 C U→救助, 救出, 救援 ‖ Ten fishermen were saved in a daring sea rescue. 10人の漁師たちは勇敢な海難救助活動によって救出された. Blow the whistle if you're in danger, and someone should **come to** your **rescue**. 身の危険に遭遇した場合, その笛を吹きなさい. そうすればだれかが助けに来るはずです. rescue workers/boats/helicopters 救助隊員・救命ボート・救援用ヘリコプター — rescuer 名 C→救助者, 救出者

**research** /rɪsə́ːrtʃ, ríːsəːrtʃ/ 名 U ▶定義 research (into/on sth) a detailed and careful study of sth to find out more information about it ～についてもっと情報を得るために, 詳細にまた入念に調べること→研究, 学術研究, 探求, 調査, リサーチ ‖ to do research into sth ～について研究する scientific/medical/historical research 科学的研究・医学的研究・歴史学的研究 We are carrying out **market research** to find out who our typical customer is. 私たちはどのような人が典型的な顧客であるかを把握するため, 市場調査を行っている. — research 動他自 research (into/in/on) (sth)→～を研究する, 調査する ‖ They're researching ways of reducing traffic in the city centre. 彼らは都心の交通量を減らす方法を研究している.

**researcher** /rɪsə́ːrtʃər, ríːsəːrtʃər/ 名 C ▶定義 a person who does research 研究をする人→研究者, 研究員, 調査員, 調査する人

**resemble** /rɪzémb(ə)l/ 動他 ▶定義 to be or look like sb/sth else ほかの～に似ている, またはそのように見える→～に似ている, 類似している ‖ Laura resembles her brother. ローラはお兄さんに似ている. — resemblance /rɪzémbləns/ 名 C U (a) resemblance (between A and B); (a) resemblance (to sb/sth)→(～の間で・～と)似ていること, (～の間の・～との)類似点, 似ている点 ‖ a family resemblance 家族の類似点 The boys bear no **resemblance** to their father. その男の子たちは父親に全く似ていない.

**resent** /rɪzént/ 動他 ▶定義 to feel angry about sth because you think it is unfair ～が不公平であると思うため, その～に対して怒りを感じる→～に憤慨する, 腹を立てる, 怒る, 憤る ‖ I resent his criticism. 私は彼の批判に憤慨している. Louise bitterly resented being treated differently from the men. ルイーズは男性と違った扱いを受けてひどく腹を立てた. — resentful /-fʊl, -f(ə)l/ 形→憤慨している, 腹を立てている, 怒りっぽい — resentment 名 [単数扱い, U]→憤り, 憤慨, 怒り ‖ to feel resentment towards sb/sth ～に対して憤りを感じる

**reservation** /rèzərvéɪʃ(ə)n/ 名 ▶定義1 C a seat, table, room, etc that you have booked 予約しておいた座席, テーブル, 部屋など→予約, 指定, 予約席, 指定席 ‖ We have reservations in the name of Petrovic. 私たちはペトロヴィックの名前で予約している. I'll phone the restaurant to **make a reservation**. 私がレストランに電話して予約しましょう. ▶定義2 C U a feeling of doubt about sth (such as a plan or an idea) ～(計画や考えなど)についての疑いの気持ち→疑い, 不安, 懸念, 危惧(きぐ)の念 ‖ I have some **reservations** about letting Julie go out alone. ジュリーを1人で外出させることに少々不安を感じる.

**reserve**¹ /rɪzə́ːrv/ 動他 ▶reserve sth (for sb/sth) ▶定義1 to keep sth for a special reason or to use at a later time 特別の理由で, または後で使うために～を取っておく→～を取っておく, 使わずに残しておく, 備えておく ‖ The car park is reserved for hotel guests only. この駐車場はホテルのお客様専用です. ▶定義2 to ask for a seat, table, room, etc to be available at a future time; to book 座席, テーブル, 部屋などを将来使えるように依頼する; 予約する→～を取っておく, 予約する, 指定する, 確保しておく ‖ to reserve theatre tickets 劇場の切符を予約する

**reserve**² /rɪzə́ːrv/ 名 ▶定義1 [C, 通常は複数] something that you keep for a special reason or to use at a later date 特別な理由で, または後日使用するために取っておくもの→蓄え, 備え, 予備, 蓄積, 予備品 ‖ The US has huge oil reserves. 米国はばく大な量の石油を備蓄している. ▶定義2 C an area of land where the plants, animals, etc are protected by law 植物, 動物などが法律によって保護されている地域→保留地, 指定地, 指定保護区 ‖ a nature reserve 自然保護地 He works as a warden on a **game reserve** in Kenya. 彼はケニアの禁猟地域で監視員として働いている. ▶定義3 U the quality of being shy or keeping your feelings hidden 人見知りする, または自分の感情を隠す性質→遠慮, 慎み, 控えめ, よそよそしさ ‖ It took a long time to break down her reserve and get her to relax. 彼女に打ち解けてくつろいでもらうには長い時間がかかった. ▶定義4 C (in sport) a person who will play in a game if one of the usual members of the team cannot play (スポーツで)チームのレギュラー選手の1人がプレーできなくなった際にプレーする人→補欠選手, 二軍選手, 控え選手 成句 **in reserve** ▶定義 that you keep and do not use unless you need to 必要としないときは，使わない→取ってある，備えてある，予備の[に] ‖ *Keep some money in reserve for emergencies.* 緊急時に備えてお金をいくらか蓄えておきなさい．

**reserved** /rɪzə́ːrvd/ 形 ▶定義 shy and keeping your feelings hidden 人見知りして，自分の感情を隠している →控えめな，遠慮がちな，打ち解けない，内気な ⇔ **unreserved**

**reservoir** /rézərvwὰːr/ 名 C ▶定義 a large lake where water is stored to be used by a particular area, city, etc ある地域，都市などで使用するために水が蓄えられている大きな池 →貯水池，ため池，給水所，貯水槽

**reside** /rɪzáɪd/ 動 自 正式 ▶定義 reside (in/at…) to have your home in or at a particular place ある場所に家を持つ →(〜に)住む，居住する

**residence** /rézəd(ə)ns/ 名 ▶定義 1 ❶ the state of having your home in a particular place ある場所に家を持っている状態 →居住，在住，居留，駐在 ‖ *The family applied for permanent residence in the United States.* その家族は米国での永住権を申請した． *a hall of residence* for college students 大学生のための学生寮 *Some birds have taken up residence in our roof.* 私たちの家の屋根に鳥が巣を作ってしまった．▶定義 2 ❷ 正式 a house, especially an impressive or important one 一家，特に堂々とした，または重要な家 →住宅，住居，家，邸宅，官邸

***resident** /rézəd(ə)nt/ 名 C ▶定義 1 a person who lives in a place ある場所に住んでいる人 →居住者，在住者 ‖ *local residents* 地元在住者 ▶定義 2 a person who is staying in a hotel ホテルに滞在している人 →泊まり客，滞在客，宿泊客 ‖ *The hotel bar is open only to residents.* そのホテルバーは宿泊客専用です． — resident 形 →住んでいる，住み込みの，居住・在住している，専属の

**residential** /rèzədén(ʃ)əl/ 形 ▶定義 1 (used about a place or an area) that has houses rather than offices, large shops or factories (場所または地域について) 事務所，大型店舗，工場などよりもむしろ住宅があるような →住宅の，住宅向きの，住宅に適した，住宅用の ‖ *They live in a quiet residential area.* 彼らは閑静な住宅街に住んでいる． ▶定義 2 that provides a place for sb to live 〜が生活できる場所を提供するような →居住の，居住に関する，宿泊設備のある ‖ *This home provides residential care for the elderly.* このホームは高齢者のための養護施設です．

**residue** /rézɪd(j)ùː/ 名 [ C，通常は単数] 正式 ▶定義 what is left after the main part of sth is taken or used 〜の主要な部分が取られたり使われたりした後に残ったもの →残り，残余財産，残留物 ‖ *The washing powder left a white residue on the clothes.* 余分な粉せっけんが服地に白く残った．

**resign** /rɪzáɪn/ 動 ▶定義 1 自他 resign (from/as) (sth) to leave your job or position 仕事または地位を離れる →(〜を)辞職する，辞任する，辞める，退く ‖ *He's resigned as chairman of the committee.* 彼は委員長の職を退いた． ▶定義 2 他 resign yourself to sth/doing sth to accept sth that is unpleasant but that you cannot change 好ましいものではないが自分では変えることのできない〜を受け入れる →〜に身を任せる，甘んじて従う，あきらめて従う ‖ *Jamie resigned himself to the fact that she was not coming back to him.* ジェーミーは彼女がもう自分の元に戻らないものとあきらめた．

**resignation** /rèzɪɡnéɪ(ʃ)ən/ 名 ▶定義 1 C U resignation (from sth) a letter or statement that says you want to leave your job or position 仕事または地位を辞めたいと述べた手紙または声明 →辞表，辞職願 ‖ *to hand in your resignation* 辞表を出す ‖ *a letter of resignation* 辞表 ▶定義 2 ❶ the state of accepting sth unpleasant that you cannot change 自分では変えることのできない不快な〜を受け入れた状態 →忍従，服従，放棄，断念

**resigned** /rɪzáɪnd/ 形 ▶定義 resigned (to sth/doing sth) accepting sth that is unpleasant but that you cannot change 自分では変えることのできない不快な〜を受け入れている →あきらめた，観念した，〜にあきらめて従う，〜を甘受する ‖ *Ben was resigned to the fact that he would never be an athlete.* ベンは自分が陸上選手になれないという事実を甘受していた．

**resilient** /rɪzíli(ə)nt/ 形 ▶定義 strong enough to deal with illness, a shock, change, etc 病気，衝撃，変化などに対応できるほど十分強い →立ち直りの早い，回復の早い，回復力のある — resilience 名 U →回復力，立ち直りの早さ，快活さ，跳ね返り

## 1374　resist

**resist** /rɪzíst/ 動 ▶定義1 自他 to try to stop sth happening or to stop sb from doing sth; to fight back against sth/sb 〜が起こるのを止めようとする、または〜が…を行うのをやめさせようとする；〜に反撃する→〜に抵抗する，反抗する，敵対する，〜を阻止する，妨害する‖ *The government are resisting pressure to change the law.* 政府は法律を改正させようとする圧力に対抗している．*to resist arrest* 逮捕されまいと抵抗する ▶定義2 他 to stop yourself from having or doing sth that you want to have or do 欲しい〜を持つことを，またはやりたい〜をすることを抑える→〜を我慢する，こらえる，抑える，控える‖ *I couldn't resist telling Nadia what we'd bought for her.* 私は，私たちがナディアのために何を買ったかを彼女に話さずにはいられなかった．

**resistance** /rɪzíst(ə)ns/ 名 U ▶定義1 resistance (to sb/sth) trying to stop sth from happening or to stop sb from doing sth; fighting back against sb/sth 〜が起こるのを止めようとすること，または〜が…を行うのをやめさせようとすること；〜に対抗して戦うこと→(〜に対する)抵抗，妨害，阻止，反抗，敵対‖ *The government troops overcame the resistance of the rebel army.* 政府軍は反乱軍の抵抗に打ち勝った．
▶定義2 resistance (to sth) the power in a person's body not to be affected by disease 病気に侵されないようにする人体に備わった力→(〜に対する)抵抗力

**resistant** /rɪzíst(ə)nt/ 形 resistant (to sth) ▶定義1 not wanting sth and trying to prevent sth happening 〜を望まず，〜が起こるのを妨げようとする→(〜に)抵抗する，反抗する，抵抗力を示す，抵抗力のある‖ *resistant to change* 変化に抵抗する ▶定義2 not harmed or affected by sth 〜によって傷付かない，または影響されない→〜を通さない，〜を防ぐ，不浸透の，耐〜の‖ *This watch is water-resistant.* この時計は耐水性があります．

**resolute** /rézəlùːt/ 形 ▶定義 having or showing great determination 強い決意を持っている，または示している→決心の堅い，意志の堅い，断固とした，確固とした‖ *a resolute refusal to change* 変化に対する断固とした拒否 ☛ determined の方が一般的である．— **resolutely** 副 →堅く決心して，断固として，意志強固に，決然と

**resolution** /rèzəlúːʃ(ə)n/ 名 ▶定義1 U the quality of being firm and determined 堅実で決然としている性質→断固としていること，堅忍不抜，不屈 ▶定義2 U solving or settling a problem, dispute, etc 問題，論争などを解決する，または決着を付けること → 解決，解答，解明，解消 ▶定義3 C a formal decision that is taken after a vote by a group of people 集団の人々によって投票後に下された正式な決定→決議，決定‖ *The UN resolution condemned the invasion.* 国連の決議はその侵略を非難した．▶定義4 C a firm decision to do or not to do sth 〜を行う，または行わないという堅い決心→決意，決心，決断

**resolve** /rɪzálv/ 動 正式 ▶定義1 他 to find a answer to a problem 問題に対する答えを見付ける→〜を解決する，解く，説明する，解明する‖ *Most of the difficulties have been resolved.* ほぼ問題点は解決された．▶定義2 自他 to decide sth and be determined not to change your mind 〜を決め，その考えを変えまいと決意する→(〜を)決心する，決意する‖ *He resolved never to repeat the experience.* 彼はその経験を二度と繰り返すまいと心に決めた．

**resort¹** /rɪzɔ́ːrt/ 名 C ▶定義 a place where a lot of people go to on holiday 多くの人が休暇に出掛ける場所→行楽地，保養地，リゾート‖ *a seaside/ski resort* 海辺の保養地・宿泊施設のあるスキー場
成句 in the last resort; (as) a last resort ⇒ **LAST¹**

**resort²** /rɪzɔ́ːrt/ 動 ▶定義 resort to sth/doing sth to do or use sth bad or unpleasant because you feel you have no choice 選択の余地がないと感じて，悪いまたは好ましくない〜を行う，あるいは使う→〜に訴える，頼る，助けを求める‖ *After not sleeping for three nights I finally resorted to sleeping pills.* 3日間眠れない夜が続き，とうとう私は睡眠薬に頼った．

**resounding** /rɪzáʊndɪŋ/ 形 (名詞の前だけ)
▶定義1 very loud 音がとても大きい→鳴り響く，響き渡る，反響する，こだまする‖ *resounding cheers* とどろく声援 ▶定義2 very great 非常に偉大な→目覚ましい，華々しい‖ *a resounding victory/win/defeat/success* 華々しい勝利・大勝利・完敗・目覚ましい成功

**resource** /ríːsɔːrs, -zɔːrs/ 名 [ C ，通常は複数]

[定義] a supply of sth, a piece of equipment, etc that is available for sb to use ～が使用できるように用意されている～の在庫,装備品など➜**資源,物資,財源,資金,資産** ‖ *Russia is rich in* ***natural resources*** *such as oil and minerals.* ロシアは石油や鉱物などの天然資源が豊富です.

**resourceful** /ríːsɔ̀ːrsfʊl, -f(ə)l/ [形] [定義] good at finding ways of doing things 物事をする方法を見つけるのがうまい➜**機知·工夫に富んだ,臨機の才のある,やりくり上手の**

***respect**[1] /rɪspékt/ [名] [定義]**1** [U] respect (for sb/sth) the feeling that you have when you admire or have a high opinion of sb/sth ～を賞賛する,または～を良く思うときに抱く気持ち➜**(～に対する)尊敬,敬意** ‖ ***I have*** *little* ***respect*** *for people who are arrogant.* 私がごう慢な人々を尊敬することはまずない. *to win/lose sb's respect* ～からの尊敬を得る·失う ☛参 **self-respect** [定義]**2** [U] respect (for sb/sth) polite behaviour or care towards sb/sth that you think is important 大切であると思う～に対する礼儀正しい振る舞いまたは思いやり➜**尊重,重視,顧慮,配慮,注意** ‖ *We should all treat older people with more respect.* 私たちは皆,目上の人をもっと尊重すべきだ. ⇔ **disrespect** [定義]**3** [C] a detail or point 細かい点,またはある点➜**細目,事項,点,箇所** ‖ ***In what respects*** *do you think things have changed in the last ten years?* この10年間にどのような点で状況が変わってきたと思いますか. *Her performance was brilliant* ***in every respect.*** 彼女の演技はあらゆる点において申し分なかった.

[成句] with respect to sth [正式] [定義] about or concerning ～について,または関して➜**～については,～に関して,～の件について**

pay your respects ⇒ **PAY**[1]

***respect**[2] /rɪspékt/ [動][他] [定義]**1** respect sb/sth (for sth) to admire or have a high opinion of sb/sth ～を賞賛する,または良く思う➜**～を(…に対して)尊敬する,敬う,～に敬意を表す** ‖ *I respect him for his honesty.* 私は彼の誠実さを尊敬している. [定義]**2** to show care for or pay attention to sb/sth ～に配慮する,または注意を払う➜**～を尊重する,大切にする,～に注意する,留意する** ‖ *We should respect other people's cultures and values.* 私たちは他民族の文化と価値観を尊重するべきである. — respectful [形] respectful (to/towards sb)➜**礼儀正しい,丁寧な,恭しい,(～に)敬意を表する** ‖ *The crowd listened in respectful silence.* 群衆は礼儀正しく静粛に耳を傾けた. ⇔ **disrespectful** — respectfully /-fʊli, -f(ə)li/ [副]➜**恭しく,謹んで,丁重に**

**respectable** /rɪspéktəb(ə)l/ [形] [定義]**1** considered by society to be good, proper or correct 社会から良い,適している,または正しいと見なされている➜**立派な,ちゃんとした,まともな,恥ずかしくない** ‖ *a respectable family* ちゃんとした家庭 *He combed his hair and tried to look respectable for the interview.* 彼は髪をくしでとかし,面接で恥ずかしくないようにしようとした. [定義]**2** quite good or large かなり良い,または大きい➜**かなりの,相当な,なかなかの,まずまずの** ‖ *a respectable salary* かなりの給料 — respectability /rɪspèktəbíləti/ [名] [U]➜**社会的にちゃんとしていること,尊敬に値すること,立派な態度**

**respective** /rɪspéktɪv/ [形](名詞の前だけ) [定義] belonging separately to each of the people who have been mentioned 言及された人間の1人1人に個別に属している➜**それぞれの,各自の,銘々の,各々の**

**respectively** /rɪspéktɪvli/ [副] [定義] in the same order as sb/sth that was mentioned 言及された～と同じ順序で➜**(述べられた順に)それぞれ,銘々に,各々**

**respiration** /rèspəréɪʃ(ə)n/ [名] [U][正式] [定義] breathing 呼吸➜**呼吸(作用)**

**respite** /réspaɪt/ [名] [単数扱い, [U]] [定義] respite (from sth) a short period of rest from sth that is difficult or unpleasant 困難な,または不愉快な～をしばらく休むこと➜**一時的中断,小休止,休息,中休み** ‖ *There was a brief respite from the fighting.* その戦いには短い休戦期間があった.

***respond** /rɪspɑ́nd/ [動][自] [定義]**1** [正式] respond (to sb/sth) (with/by sth) to say or do sth as an answer or reaction to sth ～に対する答えまたは反応として…を言う,または行う➜**(～に)答える,応答する,反応する,応ずる** ‖ *He responded to my question with a nod.* 彼は私の質問にうなずいて答えた. *Owen responded to the manager's criticism by scoring two goals.*

R

## 1376 response

オーエンは監督の批判に対し，2ゴールを決めてこたえた．☞ respond は answer や reply よりも改まった言い方．▶定義2 respond (to sb/sth) to have or show a good or quick reaction to sb/sth ～に対して適切に，または素早く作用する，またはそのような反応を示す→(～に対して)好反応を示す，(～の)効果を現す ‖ *The patient did not respond well to the new treatment.* その患者には新しい治療法の効果があまり現れなかった．

\***response** /rɪspάns/ 名 **C U** ▶定義 (a) response (to sb/sth) an answer or reaction to sb/sth ～に対する答えまたは反応→～への返答，応答，反響，感応 ‖ *I've sent out 20 letters of enquiry but I've had no responses yet.* 私は問い合わせの手紙を20通出したが，まだ何の返答ももらっていない．*The government acted **in response to** economic pressure.* 政府は経済的圧力に応じて行動した．

\***responsibility** /rɪspὰnsəbíləti/ 名 (複 **reponsibilities**) ▶定義1 **U C** responsibility (for sb/sth); responsibility (to do sth) a duty to deal with sth so that it is your fault if sth goes wrong ～がうまくいかない場合は自分の責任と覚悟を決めて，その～に向かう義務感→(～に対する)責任，責務 ‖ *I refuse to **take responsibility** if anything goes wrong.* 何か問題があっても私は一切の責任を負うこと拒否します．*It is John's responsibility to make sure the orders are sent out on time.* 注文品が時間通りに発送されたことを確認するのは，ジョンの責任である．*I feel that I **have a responsibility** to help them - after all, they did help me.* 私には彼らを助ける責任があると思います－何しろ彼らは私を助けてくれたのですから．*Who **has responsibility** for the new students?* 新しい生徒に対する責任はだれにあるのですか．▶定義2 **U** the fact of sth being your fault; blame ～が自分の責任であるという事実；責任→責任，負担，重荷 ‖ *No group has yet admitted responsibility for planting the bomb.* その爆弾を仕掛けたことを認めたグループはまだない．

成句 shift the blame/responsibility (for sth) (onto sb) ⇒ **SHIFT**¹

\***responsible** /rɪspάnsəb(ə)l/ 形 ▶定義1 (名詞の前は不可) responsible (for sb/sth); responsible (for doing sth) having the job or duty of dealing with sb/sth, so that it is your fault if sth goes wrong ～を処理する仕事または義務を持っているので，～がうまくいかない場合は自分の責任であると覚悟を決めて→～に責任がある，責任を負うべき ‖ *The school is responsible for the safety of the children in school hours.* 学校は，学校にいる間の子供たちの安全について責任を負っている．*The manager is responsible for making sure the shop is run properly.* 経営者は店がきちんと経営されているかどうかを確認する責任がある．▶定義2 (名詞の前は不可) responsible (for sth) being the person whose fault sth is ～の非がその人の過失によるものであるような→(～の)原因である，(～を)招いた ‖ *Who was responsible for the accident?* だれにその事故の責任があったのですか．▶定義3 (名詞の前は不可) responsible (to sb/sth) having to report to sb/sth with authority, or to sb who you are working for, about what you are doing 権威を持つ～または仕えている…に，自分のしている事を報告しなければならない→(～に)報告する義務がある，(～の)監督下にある ‖ *Members of Parliament are responsible to the electors.* 国会議員は有権者に報告する義務がある．▶定義4 (used about a person) that you can trust to behave well and in a sensible way (人について)その人が行儀良く，思慮深く振る舞うことを確信できる→信頼できる，頼りになる，任せられる，義務履行能力のある，賢明な，分別のある ‖ *Marisa is responsible enough to take her little sister to school.* メリサには小さな妹を学校に連れていくのを十分任せられる．⇔ **irresponsible** ▶定義5 (used about a job) that is important and that should be done by a person who can be trusted (仕事について)重要である，また信頼される人によって行われるべきであるような→責任の重い，責任のある，責任を伴う

▶語法

**those responsible と a responsible man の違い**

present people(現代の人々)と people present(出席者)のように，形容詞を前置するか後置するかによって明確に意味が異なる場合があります．responsible の場合も同様です．a responsible man は「責任感の強い

人」のように人の性質を表し, a man responsible は「責任者」のようにその人の置かれた状況を表します. those responsible も同様で, 場合によっては「(悪事などの) 責任を負うべき者 = 犯人」の意味にもなります.

\***responsibly** /rɪspánsəb(ə)li/ 副 ▶定義 (used about sb's way of behaving) that you can trust; sensible (〜の行動の仕方について) 信頼できるほどに; 良識を持って→**責任を持って, 確実に**

**responsive** /rɪspánsɪv/ 形 ▶定義 paying attention to sb/sth and reacting in a suitable or positive way 〜に注意を払っており, 適切にまたは積極的に反応している→**〜に敏感な, 感じやすい, 答える, 反応の早い, よく反応する** ‖ *By being responsive to changes in the market, the company has had great success.* 市場の変化に敏感に反応することにより, その会社は大成功を収めた.

\***rest**[1] /rest/ 動 ▶定義 1 (自) to relax, sleep or stop after a period of activity or because of illness; to not use a part of your body for a period of time ある活動期間の後, または病気が原因で, くつろぐ, 眠る, あるいは中断する; ある期間, 体の一部分を使わない→**休む, 休憩する, 休息する, 眠る** ‖ *We've been walking for hours. Let's rest here for a while.* 私たちは何時間も歩きました. ここでしばらく休みましょう. ▶定義 2 (他) to not use a part of your body for a period of time because it is tired or painful 疲れている, または痛みがあるため, ある期間, 体の一部分を使わない→**〜を休ませる, 休養させる, 休息させる** ‖ *Your knee will get better as long as you rest it as much as you can.* できるだけ長く休ませなさい. あなたのひざは良くなるでしょう. ▶定義 3 (自) (他) rest (sth) on/against sth to place sth in a position where it is supported by sth else; to be in such a position ほかの〜によって支えられている位置に〜を置く; そのような位置にある→**〜を…に置く, 載せておく, 寄り掛からせる, もたせかける, 〜に置かれている, 載せてある, 寄り掛かる, 支えられている, もたれ掛かる** ‖ *She rested her head on his shoulder and went to sleep.* 彼女は彼の肩に頭をもたせかけて眠った.

成句 **let sth rest** ▶定義 to not talk about sth any longer 〜についてもうこれ以上話さない→**〜をこの辺でやめる, そのままにしておく, もう蒸**

し返さない

句動詞 **rest on sb/sth** ▶定義 to depend on sb/sth or be based on sth 〜に頼る, または…に基づいている→**〜に頼る, 当てにする, 希望をかける, 懸かっている, 基づく** ‖ *The whole theory rests on a very simple idea.* その理論全体は非常に単純な発想に基づいている.

\***rest**[2] /rest/ 名 ▶定義 1 (C)(U) a period of relaxing, sleeping or doing nothing くつろぐ, 眠る, または何もしない期間→**休息, 休憩, 休養, 静養, 睡眠** ‖ *I can't walk any further! I need a rest.* もうこれ以上は歩けません. 休憩が必要です. *I'm going upstairs to* **have a rest** *before we go out.* 私は出掛ける前に一休みしたいので上の階に行ってきます. *Try not to worry now.* **Get some rest** *and think about it again tomorrow.* 今は思い悩まないようにしなさい. 少し休んで明日また考えましょう. *I sat down to* **give** *my bad leg* **a rest**. 私は座って悪い方の足を休めた. ▶定義 2 [単数扱い, 単数または複数形の動詞と共に] **the rest (of sb/sth)** the part that is left; the ones that are left 残った部分; 残された複数の人々→**(〜の) 残り, 残余, そのほかの人々, そのほかの物** ‖ *We had lunch and spent the rest of the day on the beach.* 私たちは昼食を取り, その日の残りの時間はビーチで過ごした. *She takes no interest in what happens in the rest of the world.* 彼女は世界のほかの地域で何が起こっているか全く関心がない. *They were the first people to arrive. The rest came later.* 彼らが最初に到着しました. そのほかの人々は後から来ました. *The rest of our bags are still in the car.* 私たちの残りのバッグはまだ車の中にあります.

成句 **at rest** ▶定義 not moving 動いていない→**止まって, 静止して** ‖ *Do not open the door until the vehicle is at rest.* 車が停止するまでドアを開けてはいけない.

**come to rest** ▶定義 to stop moving 動くことをやめる→**停止する, 静止する, (自然に) 止まる** ‖ *The car crashed through a wall and came to rest in a field.* その車は塀を突き抜けて畑で止まった.

**put/set your/sb's mind at rest** ⇒ **MIND**[1]

\***restaurant** /rést(ə)rənt, -rɑ̀ːnt, -tərnt; rést(ə)rɔːŋ, -rɔ̀ːnt/ 名 (C) ▶定義 a place where you can buy and eat a meal お金を払って食事を取ることができる場所➜**レストラン, 料理店, 飲食店, 食堂** ‖ *a fast food/hamburger restaurant* ファーストフード店・ハンバーガーショップ *a Chinese/an Italian/a Thai restaurant* 中華料理店・イタリア料理店・タイ料理店 ☛参 **cafe, takeaway**

**restful** /réstfʊl, -f(ə)l/ [形] ▶定義 giving a relaxed, peaceful feeling くつろいだ平和な雰囲気を与える➜**休息・安らぎを与える, 安らかな, 平穏な, 落ち着いた, 静かな, 平和な** ‖ *I find this piece of music very restful.* 私はこの音楽に非常に安らぎを覚える.

**restless** /réstləs/ [形] ▶定義1 unable to relax or be still because you are bored, nervous or impatient 退屈している, 緊張している, またはいらいらしているため, くつろぐことやじっと静かにしていることができない➜**落ち着かない, 不安な, そわそわした** ‖ *The children always get restless on long journeys.* その子供たちは長旅のときはいつも落ち着かない. ▶定義2 (used about a period of time) without sleep or rest (ある期間について) 睡眠を取っていないまたは休息を取っていない➜**眠れない, 休めない** — restlessly [副] ➜**落ち着きがなく, そわそわと, せわしなく, 休まずに**

**restoration** /rèstəréɪʃ(ə)n/ [名] ▶定義1 [C] [U] the return of sth to its original condition; the things that are done to achieve this 〜が元の状態に戻ること; そのようにするために行われる物事➜**回復, 復旧, 復活, 復帰, 復職** ‖ *The house is in need of restoration.* その家は修繕する必要がある. ▶定義2 [U] the return of sth to its original owner 〜を元の持ち主に返すこと➜**返還, 返却** ‖ *the restoration of stolen property to its owner* 盗難品の持ち主への返還

***restore** /rɪstɔ́ːr/ [動][他] restore sb/sth (to sb/sth) ▶定義1 to put sb/sth back into his/her/its former condition or position 〜を前の状態または位置に戻す➜**〜を回復させる, 復旧する, 復帰させる, 修復する** ‖ *She restores old furniture as a hobby.* 彼女は趣味で古い家具を修復している. *In the recent elections, the former president was restored to power.* 最近の選挙で, 前大統領が権力の座に復帰した. ▶定義2 [正式] restore sth to sb to give sth that was lost or stolen back to sb 失われた, または盗まれた〜を人に返す➜**〜を…に戻す, 返却する, 返還する**

**restrain** /rɪstréɪn/ [動][他] ▶定義 restrain sb/sth (from sth/doing sth) to keep sb or sth under control; to prevent sb or sth from doing sth 〜または…を支配下に置く; 〜または…が〜をするのを妨げる➜**〜を制限する, 抑える, 制止する, 防止する** ‖ *I had to restrain myself from saying something rude.* 私は暴言を吐かぬよう自制する必要があった.

**restrained** /rɪstréɪnd/ [形] ▶定義 not showing strong feelings 強い感情を示さない➜**節度のある, 控えめな, 冷静な, 自制した**

**restraint** /rɪstréɪnt/ [名] ▶定義1 [U] the quality of behaving in a calm or controlled way 穏やかに, または抑制して行動する性質➜**遠慮, 慎み, 節度, 控えめ, 冷静さ** ‖ *It took a lot of restraint on my part not to hit him.* 彼を殴らないでいるためには私の側にかなりの自制心が必要だった. *Soldiers have to exercise **self-restraint** even when provoked.* 兵士はかっとなっても自制心を働かせなければならない. ▶定義2 [C] a restraint (on sb/sth) a limit or control on sth 〜に対する制限または規制➜**制止, 禁止, 拘束, 制約, 制限** ‖ *Are there any restraints on what the newspapers are allowed to publish?* 新聞が掲載してもよいとされている内容には何か制約があるのですか.

**restrict** /rɪstríkt/ [動][他] ▶定義 restrict sb/sth (to sth/doing sth) to put a limit on sb/sth 〜に制限を設ける➜**〜を(…に)限る, 制限する, 限定する** ‖ *There is a plan to restrict the use of cars in the city centre.* 都心部での車の使用を制限する計画がある.

**restricted** /rɪstríktəd/ [形] ▶定義 controlled or limited 規制された, または制限された➜**制限された, 限られた, 限定された** ‖ *There is only restricted parking available.* 駐車制限区域しか利用できません.

**restriction** /rɪstríkʃ(ə)n/ [名] restriction (on sth) ▶定義1 [C] something (sometimes a rule or law) that limits the number, amount, size, freedom, etc of sb/sth 〜の数, 量, 大きさ, 自由などを制限するもの (規則や法律の場合もある) ➜**制限・限定するもの, (〜に対する)制限条件, 制限規定, 規則, 規定** ‖ *parking restrictions in the city centre* 都心部における駐車制限 *The government is to **impose** tighter **restrictions** on the* *number of immigrants permitted to settle in this country.* 政府はこの国に定住することを許可する移民の数に, より厳しい制限規定を設ける予定だ. ▶定義 2 [U]the action of limiting the freedom of sb/sth ～の自由を制限する行為➜**制限, 限定, 制約** ‖ *This ticket permits you to travel anywhere, without restriction.* この切符でどこへでも, つまり無制限に旅行できます.

**restrictive** /rɪstríktɪv/ [形]▶定義 limiting; preventing people from doing what they want 制限している; 人が望む事をするのを妨げている➜**制限する, 限定する, 拘束力のある, 締め付ける**

**rest room** [名] [C] [米] ▶定義 a public toilet in a hotel, shop, restaurant, etc ホテル, 店, レストランなどにある公衆トイレ➜**トイレ, 洗面所, 休憩室, 化粧室** ☛参 **toilet** の注

***result**[1] /rɪzʌ́lt/ [名] ▶定義 1 [C]something that happens because of sth else; the final situation at the end of a series of actions ほかの～が原因で起こるもの; 一連の活動が終わった時点での最終的な状況➜**結果, 結末, 成り行き** ‖ *The traffic was very heavy and **as a result** I arrived late.* 交通量が大変多く, 結果的に私は遅れて着いた. *This wasn't really the result that I was expecting.* これは全く予想外の結果でした. ▶定義 2 [C][U]a good effect of an action ある行動の良い結果➜**成果, 効果, 好結果, 業績** ‖ *He has tried very hard to find a job, until now without result.* 彼は仕事を見つけようと大変な努力をしたが, 今まで何の成果も上がっていない. *The treatment is beginning to show results.* その治療法は効果を見せ始めている. ▶定義 3 [C]the score at the end of a game, competition or election 試合, 競技, または選挙が終わった時点での得点➜**最終得点, 成績, 成績一覧表, スコア, 投票結果** ‖ *Do you know today's football results?* 今日のサッカーの試合結果を知っていますか. *The results of this week's competition will be published next week.* 今週の競技の結果は来週公表されるでしょう. *The result of the by-election was a win for the Liberal Democrats.* 補欠選挙の結果は自由民主党の勝利だった. ▶定義 4 [[C], 通常は複数] the mark given for an exam or test 試験またはテストに与えられた点数➜**成績, 結果** ‖ *When do you **get** your exam **results**?* あなたの試験の結果はいつ分かりますか. ▶定義 5 [C]something that is discovered by a medical test 診療により発見されたこと➜**検査結果** ‖ *I'm still waiting for the result of my X-ray.* 私はレントゲン検査の結果をまだ待っているところです. *The result of the test was negative.* 検査の結果は陰性だった.

**result**[2] /rɪzʌ́lt/ [動][自] ▶定義 **result (from sth)** to happen or exist because of sth ～が原因で起こる, または存在する➜**(～から) 結果として生ずる, (～に) 起因する, 由来する** ‖ *Ninety per cent of the deaths resulted from injuries to the head.* 死亡者の90パーセントは頭部の損傷が原因だった.

[句動詞] **result in sth** ▶定義 to cause sth to happen; to produce as an effect ～を引き起こす; 結果として生じる➜**～に終わる, ～という結果になる, 帰着する** ‖ *There has been an accident on the motorway, resulting in long delays.* 高速道路で事故があり, 長時間の遅れが生じてしまった.

**resume** /rɪz(j)úːm/ [動][自][他] ▶定義 to begin again or continue after a pause or interruption 休止または中断の後, 再び始める, あるいは続ける➜**再開する; ～を再び始める, 再び続ける** ‖ *Normal service will resume as soon as possible.* できるだけ早期に通常の業務が再開されるでしょう.

**resumé** /réz(j)ʊmèɪ, réɪ-/ [米] = **CV**

**resumption** /rɪzʌ́m(p)ʃ(ə)n/ [名] [単数扱い, [U]] (文) ▶定義 beginning again or continuing after a pause or interruption 休止または中断の後に再び始めること, または続けること➜**再開, 続行**

**resurrect** /rèzərékt/ [動][他] ▶定義 to bring back sth that has not been used or has not existed for a long time 長い間使われなかった, または存在しなかった～を復活させる➜**～を復活させる, よみがえらせる, 生き返らせる** ‖ *From time to time they resurrect old programmes and show them again on television.* 時折, 昔の番組が復活してテレビで再放送される.

**resurrection** /rèzərékʃ(ə)n/ [名] ▶定義 1 [U]bringing back sth that has not existed or not been used for a long time 長い間存在しなかった, または使われなかった～を復活させること➜**よみがえり, 復興, 再生, 再流行** ▶定義 2 **the Resurrection** [単数扱い] (in the Christian religion) the return to life of Jesus Christ (キリスト教で) イエス キリストの復活➜**キリスト復活**

**resuscitate** /rɪsʌ́sətèɪt/ [動][他] ▶定義 to bring sb

R

who has stopped breathing back to life 呼吸が停止した～を生き返らせる→～を生き返らせる, 蘇生(そせい)させる, ～の意識を回復させる ‖ *Unfortunately, all efforts to resuscitate the patient failed.* 残念ながらその患者を蘇生させるための努力はすべて失敗に終わった. — resuscitation /rɪsʌ̀sətéɪʃ(ə)n/ 名 Ｕ→蘇生術, 蘇生, 意識の回復 ‖ *mouth-to-mouth resuscitation* 口移し式人工呼吸

**retail** /ríːteɪl/ 名 Ｕ ▶定義 the selling of goods to the public in shops, etc 店などで一般の人々に品物を販売すること→小売り ☛参 **wholesale**

**retailer** /ríːteɪlər/ 名 Ｃ ▶定義 a person or company who sells goods to the public in a shop 店で一般の人々に品物を販売する人または会社→小売り業者, 小売り商人

**retain** /rɪtéɪn/ 動 他 正式 ▶定義 to keep or continue to have sth; not to lose ～を保持する, または持ち続ける; 失わない→～を保つ, 保持する, 保有する, 持ち続ける, 維持する ‖ *Despite all her problems, she has managed to retain a sense of humour.* あらゆる難題にもくじけずに, 彼女は何とかユーモアのセンスを持ち続けてきた. ☛ 名 **retention**

**retaliate** /rɪtǽlieɪt/ 動 自 ▶定義 retaliate (against sb/sth) to react to sth unpleasant that sb does to you by doing sth unpleasant in return ～が自分に向けて行う不愉快な…に対して, 仕返しに不愉快な～を行うことによって反応する→(～に)報復する, 復讐(ふくしゅう)する, 仕返しする ‖ *They have announced that they will retaliate against anyone who attacks their country.* 彼らは, 祖国を攻撃する者にはそれがだれであろうと報復すると発表した. — retaliation /rɪtæ̀liéɪʃ(ə)n/ 名 Ｕ retaliation (against sb/sth) (for sth)→仕返し, 報復 ‖ *The terrorist group said that the shooting was in retaliation for the murder of one of its members.* テロリストのグループは, その銃撃は仲間の1人を殺害したことへの報復だと述べた.

**retarded** /rɪtáːrdəd/ 形 ▶定義 slower to develop than normal 普通よりも発達するのが遅い→発達の遅い, 知能の遅れた

**retention** /rɪténʃ(ə)n/ 名 Ｕ ▶定義 the action of keeping sth or of being kept ～を保持する, または保持される行為→維持(力), 保持(力), 保有, 保存 ☛ 動 **retain**

**rethink** /riːθíŋk, rɪ-/ 動 他 (過, 過分 **rethought** /-θɔ́ːt/) ▶定義 to think about sth again because you probably need to change it おそらく変更する必要があるので, ～についてもう一度考える→～を再考する, 考え直す ‖ *The government has been forced to rethink its economic policy.* 政府は経済政策の再考を強いられてきた.

***retire** /rɪtáɪər/ 動 自 ▶定義1 retire (from sth) to leave your job and stop working usually because you have reached a certain age 通常はある年齢になったことを理由に, 仕事を辞める, および働くことをやめる→(～を)退職する, 引退する ‖ *Injury forced her to retire from professional athletics.* けがのために, 彼女はプロの陸上選手を引退せざるを得なかった. ▶定義2 正式 to leave and go to a quiet or private place 静かな, または人目に付かない場所に赴く→身を引く, 退く, 隠居する, 引きこもる

***retired** /rɪtáɪərd/ 形 ▶定義 having stopped work permanently 働くことを永久にやめている→退職した, 引退した, 退役した ‖ *a retired teacher* 退職した教師

***retirement** /rɪtáɪərmənt/ 名 ▶定義1 Ｃ Ｕ the act of stopping working permanently 働くことを永久にやめる行為→退職, 引退, 退役, 定年 ‖ *She has decided to* ***take early retirement****.* 彼女は定年前に退職することにした. *The former world champion has announced his retirement from the sport.* 元世界チャンピオンはその競技からの引退を発表した. ▶定義2 [単数扱い, Ｕ] the situation or period after retiring from work 退職した後の状況または期間→隠居, 退職後の生活, 余生, 定年後の人生 ‖ *We all wish you a long and happy retirement.* 私たちは皆, あなたが長く幸せな余生を送ることを願っています.

▶ pension(年金)は, 退職した人が定期的に受け取る金のことである. その財源は政府, 元の雇い主, またはその両方である. pensioner(年金受給者)または old-age pensioner(老齢年金受給者)は定年で退職した人を指す.

**retiring** /rɪtáɪərɪŋ/ 形 ▶定義 (used about a person) shy and quiet(人について) 人見知りで物静かな→内気な, 引っ込み思案な, 遠慮深い, 恥ずかしがる

**retort** /rɪtɔ́ːrt/ 動 他 ▶定義 to reply quickly to

**retort** what sb says, in an angry or amusing way ～が言うことに対し,怒って,またはおどけて,素早く答える→～と言い返す,逆襲する,切り返す,反ばくする ‖ *'Who asked you for your opinion?' she retorted.*「だれもあなたに意見など聞いていません」と彼女はやり返した. — retort 名 ⓒ→口答え,当意即妙の返答,逆襲,反ばく ‖ *an angry retort* 怒りの反ばく

**retrace** /riːtréɪs, rɪ-/ 動 他 ▶定義 to repeat a past journey, series of events, etc 過去の道程,一連の出来事などを繰り返す→～を引き返す,たどり直す,回想する,振り返る ‖ *If you retrace your steps, you might see where you dropped the ticket.* もと来た道を引き返したら,どこで切符を落としたか分かるかもしれません.

**retract** /rɪtrǽkt/ 動 自 他 正式 ▶定義 to say that sth you have said is not true 自分の言った～は本当ではないと言う→～を撤回する,取り消す ‖ *When he appeared in court, he retracted the confession he had made to the police.* 彼は法廷に姿を見せた時,警察に自白していた内容を撤回した.

**retreat¹** /rɪtríːt/ 動 自 ▶定義 1 (used about an army, etc) to move backwards in order to leave a battle or in order not to become involved in a battle (軍隊などについて) 戦いから退くために,または戦いに巻き込まれないようにするために,後方に移動する→退却する,撤退する ‖ *The order was given to retreat.* 撤退するようにとの命令が出された. ⇔ **advance** ▶定義 2 to move backwards; to go to a safe or private place 後方に移動する; 安全な,または人目に付かない場所に行く→退く,引退する,隠とんする,逃げ込む ‖ (比喩) *She seems to retreat into a world of her own sometimes.* 彼女は時に自分だけの世界に引きこもっているように見える.

**retreat²** /rɪtríːt/ 名 ▶定義 1 ⓒ ⓤ the action of moving backwards, away from a difficult or dangerous situation 困難な,または危険な状況から離れて後方に移動する行為→退却,後退,撤退 ‖ *The invading forces are now in retreat.* 侵略部隊は,現在,退却中である. ⇔ **advance** ▶定義 2 ⓒ a private place where you can go when you want to be quiet or to rest 静かにしていたい,または休養を取りたいときに行くことができる,人目に付かない場所→隠れ家,避難所,保養所,療養所 ‖ *a religious retreat* 静修の場所

**retribution** /ˌretrəbjúːʃ(ə)n/ 名 ⓤ (文) ▶定義 retribution (for sth) punishment for a crime 犯罪に対する処罰→(～に対する)報い,懲罰,報復,返報,天罰

**retrieve** /rɪtríːv/ 動 他 ▶定義 1 retrieve sth (from sb/sth) to get sth back from the place where it was left or lost 残された,または失われた場所からその～を取り戻す→～を(…から)取り戻す,回収する ‖ *Police divers retrieved the body from the canal.* 警察のダイバーは運河から遺体を回収した. ▶定義 2 (computing) to find information that has been stored (コンピューター) 保存されている情報を見つける→～を検索する,引き出す ‖ *The computer can retrieve all the data about a particular customer.* コンピューターで特定の顧客に関するすべてのデータを検索することができる. ▶定義 3 to make a bad situation or a mistake better; to put sth right 悪い状況または間違いを改善する;～を正す→～を回復する,復旧する,ばん回する,埋め合わせる ‖ *The team was losing two-nil at half-time but they managed to retrieve the situation in the second half.* そのチームはハーフタイムでは2対0で負けていたが,後半に何とかばん回した. — retrieval /rɪtríːv(ə)l/ 名 ⓤ→回復,復旧,ばん回,埋め合わせ

**retrospect** /rétrəspèkt/ 名
成句 **in retrospect** ▶定義 thinking about sth that happened in the past, often seeing it differently from the way you saw it at the time 過去に起こった～について考えること,しばしば,その当時とは異なった見方でそれを見ること→回想して,回顧すると,振り返ってみて ‖ *In retrospect, I can see what a stupid mistake it was.* 振り返ってみると,それが何とばかげた誤りだったかが分かる.

**retrospective** /ˌretrəspéktɪv/ 形 ▶定義 1 looking again at the past 過去に再び目を向けている→回想の,回顧的な,レトロの,過去を振り返る,追想にふける,後ろ向きの ‖ *a retrospective analysis of historical events* 歴史的事実の回顧的な分析 ▶定義 2 (used about laws, decisions, payments, etc) intended to take effect from a date in the past (法律,決定,支払いなどについて) 過去のある日から効力を有することが意図されて

## 1382 return

いる→さかのぼる、そ及的な ‖ *Is this new tax law retrospective?* この新しい税法は過去にさかのぼりますか. — **retrospectively** 副 →**過去を振り返ってみて、回顧すると、さかのぼって、そ及して**

★**return**[1] /rɪtə́ːm/ 動 ▶定義1 ⓐ **return (to/from...)** to come or go back to a place ある場所に戻る、または帰る→**(〜から・〜に)戻る、帰る、(〜を)再訪する** ‖ *I leave on the 10th July and return on the 25th.* 私は7月10日に出発して25日に戻ります. *I shall be returning to this country in six months.* 6か月後にこの国に戻ることになっている. *When did you return from Italy?* いつイタリアから戻ったのですか. *He left his home town when he was 18 and never returned.* 彼は18歳の時に郷里を離れたきり二度と帰らなかった. ▶定義2 ⓐ **return (to sth/doing sth)** to go back to the former or usual activity, situation, condition, etc 以前の、または通常の活動、状況、状態などに戻る→**(〜に)戻る、帰る、復帰する** ‖ *The strike is over and they will return to work on Monday.* ストライキが終わったので、彼らは月曜日に仕事に戻るでしょう. *It is hoped that train services will return to normal soon.* 列車の運行は間もなく正常に戻るものと期待されている. ▶定義3 ⓐ to come back; to happen again 戻ってくる；再び起こる→**再びやって来る、巡ってくる、再発する、回復する** ‖ *If the pain returns, make another appointment to see me.* 痛みが再発したら、もう一度予約を取って来院してください. ▶定義4 ⓑ **return sth (to sb/sth)** to give, send, put or take sth back 〜を返す、送り返す、元に戻す、または持ち帰る→**〜を(…に)戻す、返す、返却する** ‖ *I've stopped lending him things because he never returns them.* 彼は私が貸した物を返したためしがないので、私はもう彼に貸さないことにした. *Application forms must be returned by 14 March.* 申込書は3月14日までに返送すること. ▶定義5 ⓐ to react to sth that sb does, says or feels by doing, saying, or feeling sth similar 〜が行う、言う、または感じる〜に対し、同じような〜を行う、言う、または感じることによって反応する→**〜で返す、応じる、〜に報いる** ‖ *I've phoned them several times and left messages but they haven't returned any of my calls.* 私は彼らに数回電話し、伝言も残したのに、彼らからの電話が1つもかかってきていません. *We'll be happy to return your hospitality if you ever come to our country.* あなたが私たちの国にいらっしゃったときには、私たちが受けた親切なもてなしのお返しを喜んでしたいと思います. ▶定義6 ⓐ (in sport) to hit or throw the ball back (スポーツで)球を打ち返す、または投げ返す→**〜を打ち返す、返球する、投げ返す、リターンする**

★**return**[2] /rɪtə́ːm/ 名 ▶定義1 [単数扱い] ⓐ **return (to/from...)** coming or going back to a place or to a previous activity, situation or condition ある場所、または元の活動、状況、状態に戻ること、あるいは帰ること→**(〜に・〜から)戻ること、帰ること、復帰、回復、再発** ‖ *I'll contact you on my return from holiday.* 休暇から戻ったら連絡します. *He has recently made a return to form (= started playing well again).* 彼は最近、調子を回復した(＝再びいいプレーをし始めた). ▶定義2 ⓤ giving, sending, putting or taking sth back 〜を返す、送り返す、元に戻す、または持ち帰ること→**返却、返送、返品、返還、還付** ‖ *I demand the immediate return of my passport.* 私はパスポートを即刻返却するよう要求した. ▶定義3 ⓒ (in sport) the act of hitting or throwing the ball back (スポーツで)球を打ち返す、または投げ返す行為→**返球、打ち返し、リターン** ‖ *She hit a brilliant return.* 彼女は見事に打ち返した. ▶定義4 ⓒ ⓤ (a) **return (on sth)** the profit from a business, etc 事業などによる利益→**(〜の)利益、収益、収入、総売上高** ‖ *This account offers high returns on all investments.* この計算書はすべての投資で高収益を上げることを示しています. ▶定義5 ⓒ (または 英 **return ticket**, 米 **round trip; round trip ticket**) a ticket to travel to a place and back again ある場所に移動してから再び戻るための切符→**帰りの切符、往復切符** ‖ *A day return to Oxford, please.* オックスフォードへの日帰りの切符を1枚ください. *Is the return fare cheaper than two singles?* 片道切符2枚よりも往復運賃の方が安いですか. ⇨ **single, one-way** ▶定義6 (または **the return key**) [単数扱い] the button on a computer that you press when you reach the end of a line or of an instruction 行末または指示の最後に来たときに押すコンピューターのボタン→**リターンキー、改行復帰キー**

**成句** by return (of post) 英 ▶定義 immediately; by the next post 即座に; 次の郵便で→至急(に), 折り返し

in return (for sth) ▶定義 as payment or in exchange (for sth); as a reaction to sth (〜に対する) 支払いまたは引き換えとして; 〜に対する反応として→(〜の)お返しに, 返礼として, 返報に, 代わりに ‖ *Please accept this present in return for all your help.* いろいろと助けてくださったことへのお礼としてこの贈り物を受け取ってください.

**returnable** /rɪtˈɜːnəb(ə)l/ 形 ▶定義 that can or must be given or taken back 返す, または取り戻すことができるような, またはそうしなければならないような→返却できる, 回収される, 報告すべき, 返還すべき ‖ *a non-returnable deposit* 返却できない保証金

**reunion** /riːjúːnjən, rɪ-/ 名 ▶定義 1 ⓒ a party or occasion when friends or people who worked together meet again after they have not seen each other for a long time 一緒に勉強・仕事をした友達または人々が, 長い間互いに会わなかった後で再び会う集まりや機会→再会の集い, 同窓会, クラス会 ‖ *The college holds an annual reunion for former students.* その大学は卒業生のために年1回の同窓会を開いている. ▶定義 2 ⓒⓊ a reunion (with sb/between A and B) coming together again after being apart 離れ離れになった後で再び集まること→再結合すること, 再合同すること, 再会 ‖ *The released hostages had an emotional reunion with their families at the airport.* 解放された人質たちは空港で家族と感激の再会をした.

**reunite** /rìːjuːnáɪt, rɪ̀-/ 動 ⓘⓣ ▶定義 reunite (A with/and B) to come together again; to join two or more people, groups, etc together again 再び集まる; 複数の人, グループなどを再び一緒にする→再結合する, 再会する, (AをBと)再結合させる, 再会させる ‖ *The missing child was found by the police and reunited with his parents.* 行方不明になっていた子供が警察により発見され, 両親の元に戻された.

**Rev** 略 Reverend→〜師

**rev**¹ /rev/ 動 ⓘⓣ (**revving**; **revved**) ▶定義 rev (sth) (up) when an engine revs or when you rev it, it turns quickly and noisily エンジンが回転速度を上げるとき, またはエンジンの回転速度を上げるとき, エンジンが素早く, 騒々しく回転する→回転数・回転速度を上げる, アクセルを数回踏んで加速する, 吹かす

**rev**² /rev/ 名 ⓒ 略式 ▶定義 (used when talking about an engine's speed) one complete turn (エンジンの速度について話すときに用いて) 1回の完全な回転→回転 ‖ *4000 revs per minute* 毎分4000回転 →参 **revolution**

*****reveal** /rɪvíːl/ 動 ⓣ ▶定義 1 reveal sth (to sb) to make sth known that was secret or unknown before 以前は秘密だった, または知られていなかった〜を知られるようにする→〜を(…に)明らかにする, 示す, 漏らす, 暴露する, 暴く ‖ *He refused to reveal any names to the police.* 彼はだれの名前も警察に明かさなかった. ▶定義 2 to show sth that was hidden before 以前は隠されていた〜を示す→〜を示す, 明らかにする, 見せる, 現す ‖ *The X-ray revealed a tiny fracture in her right hand.* X線撮影により, 彼女の右手の骨に小さなひびが入っていることが分かった.

**revealing** /rɪvíːlɪŋ/ 形 ▶定義 1 allowing sth to be known that was secret or unknown before 以前は秘密だった, または知られていなかった〜が知られることを許している→明らかにする, 暴露する, 赤裸々な ‖ *This book provides a revealing insight into the world of politics.* この本は政界の内情を暴露しています. ▶定義 2 allowing sth to be seen that is usually hidden, especially sb's body 通常は隠されている〜, 特に〜の体が, 見られることを許している→透けている, 肌を露出する ‖ *a very revealing swimsuit* 露出度の高い水着

**revel** /rév(ə)l/ 動 (**revelling**; **revelled**: 米 **reveling**; **reveled**)
**句動詞** revel in sth/doing sth ▶定義 to enjoy sth very much 〜を大いに楽しむ→〜を大いに喜ぶ, 〜に夢中になる, ふける ‖ *He likes being famous and revels in the attention he gets.* 彼は有名であることが好きなので, 注目を集めて大いに喜んでいる.

**revelation** /rèvəléɪʃ(ə)n/ 名 ▶定義 1 ⓒ something that is made known, that was secret or unknown before, especially sth surprising 以前は秘密だった, または知られていなかったが, 今は知られている物事, 特に驚くべき事→意外な

## 1384 revenge

新事実, 暴露された事実, 新発見, 思い掛けないこと ‖ *This magazine is full of revelations about the private lives of the stars.* この雑誌にはスターの私生活に関する暴露された事実がたくさん載っている. ▶定義2 ［単数扱い］a thing or a person that surprises you and makes you change your opinion about sb/sth 驚かせるような, また何かについての意見を変えさせるような物事または人→思い掛けない事, 驚くべき事実, 思い掛けない人

**revenge** /rɪvéndʒ/ 名 U ▶定義 revenge (on sb) (for sth) something that you do to punish sb who has hurt you, made you suffer, etc 傷付けたり, 困らせたりなどした~を懲らしめるために行うこと→(~への・~に対する)復讐(ふくしゅう), 仕返し, 報復, 返報, 遺恨 ‖ *He made a fool of me and now I want to get my revenge.* 彼が私をばかにしたので, 今は復讐したいと思っている. *He wants to take revenge on the judge who sent him to prison.* 彼は自分を刑務所に送った裁判官に仕返しをしたいと思っている. *The shooting was in revenge for an attack by the nationalists.* その銃撃は, 国粋主義者たちによる攻撃への報復措置として行われた. ☞参 **vengeance** —revenge 動 ⦿ revenge yourself on sb→~に復讐する, 報復する, 恨みを晴らす ‖ *She revenged herself on her enemy.* 彼女は敵に復讐した. ☞参 avenge

**revenue** /révən(j)ùː/ 名 [U, 複数扱い] ▶定義 money regularly received by a government, company, etc 政府, 会社などが定期的に受け取る金→歳入, 総利益, 総収益(金) ‖ *Revenue from income tax rose last year.* 昨年は所得税による歳入が増加した.

**reverence** /révərəns/ 名 U 正式 ▶定義 reverence (for sb/sth) a feeling of great respect 大いに尊敬する気持ち→(~への)尊敬, 崇敬, 敬愛, 敬意

**Reverend** (または **reverend**) /révərənd/ 形 (略 Rev) ▶定義 the title of a Christian priest キリスト教の司祭の敬称→敬愛なる, ~(尊)師

**reverent** /révərənt/ 形 正式 ▶定義 showing respect 敬意を表している→敬虔(けいけん)な, 恭しい

**reversal** /rɪvə́ːrs(ə)l/ 名 U C ▶定義 the action of changing sth to the opposite of what it was before; an occasion when this happens ~を以前の状態の反対へと変える行為; そのような事が起こる機会→反転, 逆転, どんでん返し, 取り消し, 撤回 ‖ *The government insists that there will be no reversal of policy.* 政府は政策の撤回はあり得ないと主張している. *The decision taken yesterday was a complete reversal of last week's decision.* 昨日なされた決定は, 先週決定された事をすっかり覆すものだった.

*****reverse**¹ /rɪvə́ːrs/ 動 ▶定義1 ⦿ to put sth in the opposite position to normal or to how it was before ~をいつもとは反対の位置に, または以前の状態に置く→~を逆にする, ひっくり返す, 裏返す, 逆転させる ‖ *Today's results have reversed the order of the top two teams.* 今日の試合の結果により上位2チームの順位が逆転した. ▶定義2 ⦿ to exchange the positions or functions of two things or people 2つの物事または2人の人の位置あるいは機能を入れ替える→~を反対にする, 変える, 置き換える, 入れ替える ‖ *Jane and her husband have reversed roles - he stays at home now and she goes to work.* ジェーンと夫は役割を替えた － 今は彼が家にいて, 彼女が働きに出ている. ▶定義3 ⦿⦿ to go backwards in a car, etc; to make a car go backwards 車などで後進する; 車を後退させる→後退する, 逆進する;~を後退させる, 逆進させる ‖ *It will probably be easier to reverse into that parking space.* あの駐車スペースには, おそらくバックの方が入りやすいでしょう. *He reversed his brand new car into a wall.* 彼は新車をバックさせて塀にぶつけた.

成句 reverse (the) charges 英 ▶定義 to make a telephone call that will be paid for by the person who receives it 電話を受ける側が料金を支払う形で電話をかける→料金受取人払いで電話をかける, コレクトコールをする ‖ *Phone us when you get there, and reverse the charges.* そこへ着いたら私たちに電話をしなさい. 料金は受取人払いにしなさい. *a reverse charge call* 料金受取人払い通話

▶アメリカ英語での表現は call collect.

*****reverse**² /rɪvə́ːrs/ 名 ▶定義1 ［単数扱い］the reverse (of sth) the complete opposite of what was said just before, or of what is expected たった今言われた事, または予想されている事とは

正反対のもの→**逆, 反対, 裏返し, 逆転** ‖ *Of course I don't dislike you - quite the reverse (= I like you very much).* もちろんあなたのことは嫌いではありません – 全く逆です(= あなたのことが大好きです). *This course is the exact reverse of what I was expecting.* このコースは私の期待していたものと正反対だ. ▶定義2 (または **reverse gear**) [U] the control in a car, etc that allows it to move backwards 車などに付いている後進を可能にする制御装置→**バックギア, 後退装置** ‖ *Leave the car **in reverse** while it's parked on this hill.* 車をこの坂道に駐車している間はギアをバックに入れておきなさい. *Where's reverse in this car?* この車のバックギアはどこですか.

[成句] **in reverse** ▶定義 in the opposite order, starting at the end and going backwards to the beginning 反対の順序で, つまり最後から始めて最初まで逆戻りしている→**反対に, 逆さまに, 逆に**

***reverse**[3] /rɪvɜ́ːrs/ [形] ▶定義 opposite to what is expected or has just been described 予想される, またはたった今述べられた事と反対の→**逆の, 反対の, あべこべの**

[成句] **in/into reverse order** ▶定義 starting with the last one and going backwards to the first one 最後のものから始めて最初のものまで逆戻りしている→**逆の順に, 逆に** ‖ *The results will be announced in reverse order.* 成績は逆の順に発表されるでしょう.

**reversible** /rɪvɜ́ːrsəb(ə)l/ [形] ▶定義 (used about clothes) that can be worn with either side on the outside (衣服について)どちら側を表にしても着ることができるような→**裏返しても使える, 両面仕立ての, リバーシブルの** ‖ *a reversible coat* リバーシブルのコート

**revert** /rɪvɜ́ːrt/ [動][自] ▶定義 **revert (to sth)** to return to a former state or activity 元の状態または活動に戻る→**(〜に)戻る, 立ち返る, 再発する** ‖ *The land will soon revert to jungle if it is not farmed.* この土地は耕作しないでいるとすぐジャングルに逆戻りしてしまうでしょう. *If the experiment is unsuccessful we will revert to the old system.* その試みがうまくいかなかったら古い制度に戻りましょう.

***review**[1] /rɪvjúː/ [名] ▶定義1 [C][U] the examining or considering again of sth in order to decide if changes are necessary 変更が必要であるかどうかを判断するために, 〜を再び調査または考慮すること→**再調査, 再吟味, 再検討, 再考** ‖ *There will be a review of your contract after the first six months.* 最初の6か月が過ぎた時点で契約の見直しがあるでしょう. *The system is in need of review.* その制度は再検討する必要があります. ▶定義2 [C] a look back at sth in order to check, remember, or be clear about sth 〜を調べる, 思い出す, または明確にするために, その〜を振り返ること→**検査, 検閲, 回顧, 反省, 復習** ‖ *a review of the major events of the year* その年の主な出来事の回顧 ▶定義3 [C] a newspaper or magazine article, or an item on television or radio, in which sb gives an opinion on a new book, film, play, etc 〜が新しく出た本や映画, 演劇などに関して意見を述べている新聞または雑誌の記事, あるいはテレビまたはラジオ番組の1コマ→**批評, 論評, 評論** ‖ *The film got bad reviews.* その映画は悪評を得た.

**review**[2] /rɪvjúː/ [動][他] ▶定義1 to examine or consider sth again in order to decide if changes are necessary 変更が必要であるかどうかを判断するために, 〜を再び調査または考慮する→**〜を再調査する, 再検討する, 再吟味する, 再考する** ‖ *Your salary will be reviewed after one year.* あなたの給料は1年後に見直しされるでしょう. ▶定義2 to look at or think about sth again to make sure that you understand it 理解したことを確認するために〜を見直す, または考え直す→**〜を復習する** ‖ *Let's review what we've done in class this week.* 今週授業で習った事を復習しましょう. ▶定義3 to write an article or to talk on television or radio, giving an opinion on a new book, film, play, etc 新しく出た本や映画, 演劇などについて記事を書く, あるいはテレビやラジオで話す→**〜を批評する, 論評する, 書評を書く** ‖ *In this week's edition our film critic reviews the latest films.* 今週号では, 本誌の映画評論家が最新の映画を批評している.

**reviewer** /rɪvjúːər/ [名][C] ▶定義 a person who writes about new books, films, etc 新しく出た本や映画などについて著述する人→**評者, 評論家, 批評家, 批評する人**

***revise** /rɪváɪz/ [動] ▶定義1 [他] to make changes to sth in order to correct or improve it 訂正する,

または改善するために、～に変更を加える→**～を改訂する, 校訂する, 修正する, 改正する** ‖ *The book has been revised for this new edition.* その本は今回の新しい版で改訂された. *I revised my opinion of him when I found out that he had lied.* 私は彼がうそをついていたと知った時, 彼に対する見方を変えた. ▶定義2 🔵🔴 医 revise (for sth) to read or study again sth that you have learnt, especially when preparing for an exam 特に試験に備えるために, 学習した～を読み直す, または勉強し直す→**(～に備えて)…を復習する** ‖ *I can't come out tonight. I'm revising for my exam.* 私は今夜, 外出することができません. 試験に備えて復習しています. *None of the things I had revised came up in the exam.* 私が復習した事柄は何1つ試験に出ませんでした.

**revision** /rɪvíʒ(ə)n/ 名 ▶定義1 🔵🔴 the changing of sth in order to correct or improve it 訂正する, または改善するために～を変更すること→**訂正, 修正, 改訂, 見直し, 改正** ‖ *It has been suggested that the whole system is in need of revision.* 制度全体を改正する必要があることはずっと提案されてきた. ▶定義2 🔴 医 the work of reading or studying again sth you have learnt, especially when preparing for an exam 特に試験に備えるために, 学習した～を読み直す, または勉強し直す作業→**復習** ‖ *I'm going to have to do a lot of revision for History.* 私は今から歴史の授業の復習をみっちりする必要があるのです.

**revival** /rɪváɪv(ə)l/ 名 ▶定義1 🔵🔴 the act of becoming or making sth strong or popular again ～が再び元気になる, または～を再び元気にする, あるいは～が再び流行する, または～を再び流行させる行為→**蘇生(そせい), 回復, 生き返ること, 復活, 復興, 再興** ‖ *economic revival* 経済復興 *a revival of interest in traditional farming methods* 伝統的な農耕方法に再び関心が高まること ▶定義2 🔵 a new performance of a play that has not been performed for some time しばらく上演されていない演劇を新たに上演すること→**再演, 再上演, リバイバル** ‖ *a revival of the musical 'The Sound of Music'* ミュージカル「サウンド オブ ミュージック」の再演

**revive** /rɪváɪv/ 動 🔵🔴 ▶定義1 to become or to make sb/sth strong or healthy again; to come or to bring sb back to life or consciousness ～が再び元気になる, または健康になる, あるいはそのようにする; ～が生き返る, または意識をよみがえらせる→**回復する, 生き返る; ～を生き返らせる** ‖ *Hopes have revived for an early end to the fighting.* その戦いが早期に終結する望みがわいてきた. *I'm very tired but I'm sure a cup of coffee will revive me.* 私は大変疲れていますが, コーヒーを1杯飲めばきっと元気を取り戻せます. *Attempts were made to revive him but he was already dead.* 蘇生(そせい)させようと試みたが, 彼は既に死亡していた. ▶定義2 to become or to make sth popular again; to begin to do or use sth again ～が再び流行する, または～を再び流行させる; ～を再びし始める, または再び使い始める→**復活する, 復興する; ～を復活させる, 復興させる** ‖ *Public interest in athletics has revived now that the national team is doing well.* 今や国の代表チームが健闘しているので, 陸上競技に対する大衆の興味関心が戻ってきた. *to revive an old custom* 昔の習慣を復活させる

**revolt** /rɪvóult/ 動 ▶定義1 🔵 revolt (again sb/sth) to protest in a group, often violently, against the person or people in power 権力を持つ人または人々に対して, 集団で, しばしば暴力的に抗議する→**(～に)背く, (～に対して)反乱を起こす, 反逆する, 反抗する** ‖ *A group of generals revolted against the government.* 将軍たちは一団となって政府に反旗をひるがえした. ▶定義2 🔵 to make sb feel disgusted or ill ～をうんざりさせる, または気分を悪くさせる→**～をむかつかせる, 反感を抱かせる, 不快にさせる** ‖ *The sight and smell of the meat revolted him.* 肉を目にし, においをかいで彼は気分が悪くなった. ☛ 名 revulsion — revolt 名 🔵🔴→**反乱, 反逆, 反抗, 反感, 嫌悪** ‖ *The people rose in revolt against the corrupt government.* 民衆は腐敗した政府に対して立ち上がった.

**revolting** /rɪvóultɪŋ/ 形 ▶定義 extremely unpleasant; disgusting 極度に不愉快な; 嫌悪を感じさせるような→**不快な, むかつかせる, 実に嫌な, 胸が悪くなる** ‖ *What a revolting colour/smell!* 何て嫌な色・においだ.

*****revolution** /rèvəlúːʃ(ə)n/ 名 ▶定義1 🔵🔴 action taken by a large group of people to try to change the government of a country, especially by violent action 一国の政府を変えようとして

人々の大規模な集団によって起こされる行動, 特に暴力的な行動→革命 ‖ *the French Revolution of 1789* 1789年のフランス革命 *a country on the brink of revolution* 革命寸前の国 ▶定義2 ⓒa revolution (in sth) a complete change in methods, opinions, etc, often as a result of progress しばしば進歩の結果として, 方法, 意見などが完全に変わること→革命, 大変革, 革命的な出来事 ‖ *the Industrial Revolution* 産業革命 ▶定義3 ⓒⓤa movement around sth; one complete turn around a central point (for example in a car engine) ～の周りを回ること; 中心点の周りをぐるっと1回転すること(例えば車のエンジンで)→回転, 旋回(運動) ‖ *400 revolutions per minute* 毎分400回転 ☜参 **rev²**

**revolutionary¹** /rèvəlúːʃ(ə)nəri, -nèri/ 形 ▶定義1 connected with or supporting political revolution 政治的な革命に関係した, またはそれを支持している→革命の ‖ *the revolutionary leaders* 革命指導者たち ▶定義2 producing great changes; very new and different 大きな変化を生み出している; 非常に新しく, 今までと大いに異なっている→変革的な, 革命的な, 画期的な ‖ *a revolutionary new scheme to ban cars from the city centre* 都心で車を禁止するという画期的な新しい計画

**revolutionary²** /rèvəlúːʃ(ə)nəri, -nèri/ 名 ⓒ (複 **revolutionaries**) ▶定義 a person who starts or supports action to try to change the government of a country, especially by using violent action 特に暴力的行動を取ることにより, 一国の政府を変えようとする活動を開始する, または支持する人→革命家, 革命支持者, 革命主義者, 革命論者

**revolutionize** (または **-ise**) /rèvəlúːʃ(ə)naiz/ 動⓽ ▶定義 to change sth completely, usually improving it ～を完全に変える, 大抵の場合改善に向かう→～を大改革する, 劇的に変える, 根本から変える, ～に革命をもたらす ‖ *a discovery that could revolutionize the treatment of mental illness* 精神疾患の治療法を根本から変えるかもしれない発見

**revolve** /rɪválv/ 動ⓘ ▶定義 to move in a circle around a central point 中心点の周りを円を描いて動く→回転する, ぐるぐる回る ‖ *The earth revolves around the sun.* 地球は太陽の周りを回っている.

**句動詞** revolve around sb/sth ▶定義 to have sb/sth as the most important part ～を最も重要な部分として持つ→～を中心にして回る, 動く, 営まれる, 展開する ‖ *Her life revolves around the family.* 彼女の生活は家族中心に回っている.

**revolver** /rɪválvər/ 名 ⓒ ▶定義 a type of small gun with a container for bullets that turns round 銃弾を込める部分が回転するような小型銃の一種→リボルバー, 回転式連発けん銃, 連発ピストル

**revolving** /rɪválvɪŋ/ 形 ▶定義 that goes round in a circle 円を描いて回るような→回転する, 回転式の, 旋回する ‖ *revolving doors* 回転式ドア

**revulsion** /rɪvʌ́lʃ(ə)n/ 名 ⓤ ▶定義 a feeling of disgust (because sth is extremely unpleasant) (～が極めて不愉快であるために)胸の悪くなるような気分→反感, 嫌悪, 憎悪, 極度の不快感 ☜動 revolt

*★**reward¹** /rɪwɔ́ːrd/ 名 reward (for sth/doing sth) ▶定義1 ⓒⓤsomething that you are given because you have done sth good, worked hard, etc 良い事をした, 熱心に働いたなどの理由で与えられるもの→報酬, 報奨, 報い, 褒美, お礼 ‖ *Winning the match was just reward for all the effort.* その試合に勝ったことは, これまでの努力に対する当然の報酬だった. ▶定義2 ⓒan amount of money that is given in exchange for helping the police, returning sth that was lost, etc 警察に協力したり, 拾得物を届けることなどに対して与えられる金→謝礼金, 報奨金, 懸賞金 ‖ *Police are offering a reward for information leading to a conviction.* 警察は犯罪の立証につながる情報に報奨金を出している.

**reward²** /rɪwɔ́ːrd/ 動⓽ ▶定義 reward sb (for sth/for doing sth) (しばしば受動態で) to give sth to sb because he/she has done sth good, worked hard, etc 良い～をした, 熱心に働いたなどの理由で～に…を与える→(～に対して)…に報いる, 報酬を与える ‖ *Eventually her efforts were rewarded and she got a job.* ついに彼女は努力が報われて職を得た.

**rewarding** /rɪwɔ́ːrdɪŋ/ 形 ▶定義 (used about an activity, job, etc) giving satisfaction; making you happy because you think it is important, useful, etc (活動, 仕事などについて) 満足を与えてくれる; それが重要である, 役立っているな

どと思うことにより，うれしいと感じさせてくれる →やりがいのある，満足のいく，価値のある，有益な

**rewind** /rìːwáɪnd, rɪ-/ 動 他 (過, 過分 **rewound**) ▶定義 to make a video or cassette tape go backwards ビデオテープまたはカセットテープを逆戻りさせる →~を巻き戻す ‖ *Please rewind the tape at the end of the film.* 映画が終わったらテープを巻き戻してください． — rewind 名 Ｕ →巻き戻し ☛参 **fast forward**

**rewrite** /rìːráɪt, rɪ-/ 動 他 (過 **rewrote** /-róʊt/; 過分 **rewritten** /-rítn/) ▶定義 to write sth again in a different or better way ～を異なった風に，またはより良く書き直す →~を書き直す，書き換える

**rhetoric** /rétərɪk/ 名 Ｕ 正式 ▶定義 a way of speaking or writing that is intended to impress or influence people but is not always sincere 人々に印象づける，または影響を与えることが意図されているが，必ずしも本心からではないような，話し方あるいは書き方 →修辞学，修辞法，特別な効果をねらった言語表現，レトリック — rhetorical /rɪtɔ́ːrɪk(ə)l/ 形 →修辞法の，修辞学の，修辞法を用いた，表現が凝った — rhetorically /rɪtɔ́ːrɪk(ə)li/ 副 →修辞的に，誇張して，おおげさに

**rhetorical question** 名 Ｃ ▶定義 a question that does not expect an answer 答えを期待していない質問 →修辞疑問

**rheumatism** /rúːmətɪz(ə)m/ 名 Ｕ ▶定義 an illness that causes pain in muscles and where your bones join together (the joints) 筋肉や骨が結合している場所(関節)に痛みを引き起こす病気 →リューマチ，リューマチ性関節炎

**rhino** /ráɪnoʊ/ (複 **rhinos**) 略式 =RHINOCEROS

**rhinoceros** /raɪnɑ́s(ə)rəs, rə-/ 名 Ｃ (複 **rhinoceros** または **rhinoceroses**) ▶定義 a large animal from Africa or Asia, with a thick skin and with one or two horns on its nose 厚い皮で覆われ，鼻の上に1本か2本の角を持つ，アフリカまたはアジア産の大型動物 →サイ

**rhubarb** /rúːbɑːrb/ 名 Ｕ ▶定義 a plant with long red parts (stalks) that can be cooked and eaten as fruit 加熱処理され，果実として食用にできる赤色の長い部分(葉柄)を持つ植物 →マルバダイオウ，食用ダイオウ，ルバーブ

**rhyme**¹ /ráɪm/ 名 ▶定義 1 Ｃ a word that has the same sound as another ほかの語と同じ音を持つ語 →同韻語 ▶定義 2 Ｃ a short piece of writing, or something spoken, in which the word at the end of each line sounds the same as the word at the end of the line before it 各行の終わりの語が前の行の終わりの語と同じ音を持つような短い書き物，または話されたもの →押韻詩，詩歌，韻文 ☛参 **nursery rhyme** ▶定義 3 Ｕ the use of words in a poem or song that have the same sound, especially at the ends of lines 同じ音を持つ語を詩または歌の中に使うこと，特に行の終わりに →韻を踏むこと，押韻，脚韻 ‖ *All of his poetry was written in rhyme.* 彼の詩はすべて韻を踏んで書かれていた．

**rhyme**² /ráɪm/ 動 ▶定義 1 自 rhyme (with sth) to have the same sound as another word; to contain lines that end with words that sound the same ほかの語と同じ音を持つ；同じ音を持つ語で終わる行を含む →(~と)韻を踏む，韻が合う ‖ *'Tough' rhymes with 'stuff'.* tough は stuff と韻を踏んでいる． ▶定義 2 他 rhyme sth (with sth) to put together words that have the same sound 同じ音を持つ語を組み合わせる →~を(…と)韻を踏ませる，押韻させる

***rhythm** /ríð(ə)m/ 名 Ｃ Ｕ ▶定義 a regular repeated pattern of sound or movement 音または動作が規則的に繰り返されるパターン →リズム，調子，律動，韻律 ‖ *I'm not keen on the tune but I love the rhythm.* そのメロディーはそれほどでもないが，リズムは大好きだ． *He's a terrible dancer because he has no sense of rhythm.* 彼はリズム感がないのでダンスがひどく下手だ． *He tapped his foot in rhythm with the music.* 彼はその音楽に合わせて足で拍子を取った． — rhythmic /ríðmɪk/ (または rhythmical /ríðmɪk(ə)l/) 形 →律動的な，きちんと韻を踏んだ，リズミカルな，調子のいい ‖ *the rhythmic qualities of African music* アフリカ音楽の律動性 — rhythmically /-k(ə)li/ 副 →律動的に，きちんと韻を踏んで，リズミカルに，規則正しく

**rib** /rɪb/ 名 Ｃ ▶定義 one of the curved bones that go round your chest 肺を囲んでいる湾曲した骨の1つ1つ →肋骨(ろっこつ)，あばら骨 ‖ *He's so thin that you can see his ribs.* 彼は大変やせているのであばら骨が分かるほどだ． ☛ C5 ページのさし絵

**ribbon** /ríb(ə)n/ 名 ❍ Ⓤ ▶定義 a long, thin piece of material that is used for tying or decorating sth ～を結ぶ, または飾るために使われる, 長く薄い生地 →リボン, リボン生地 ‖ *a present wrapped in a blue ribbon* 青いリボンが掛けられたプレゼント ☛ **hat, wrap** のさし絵

\***rice** /ráɪs/ 名 Ⓤ ▶定義 short, thin, white or brown grain from a plant that grows on wet land in hot countries. We cook and eat rice. 気温の高い国々の湿地に育つ植物からとれる, 白または茶色の短く細い穀粒. 加熱処理して食べる →米, 米粒 ‖ *boiled/fried/steamed rice* 炊いた・いためた・蒸したご飯 ☛ **cereal** のさし絵

> ▶日本語 vs 英語
>
> rice と「ご飯」
>
> rice は1語で日本語の「もみ, 稲苗, 稲, 米, 飯」に相当し, イネの生育の各段階, および調理後まで表します. 他方, 日本語の「牛肉」に相当する語は英語では beef ですが, さらに牛の部位によって, chuck, brisket, fillet, plate, flank, rib, sirloin, shank, round などと呼ばれます. これは本来日本は農耕に基づく米食中心, 英米は狩猟に基づく肉食中心の食文化が言葉に反映しているのです.

\***rich** /rɪtʃ/ 形 ▶定義1 having a lot of money or property; not poor 多額のお金または財産を持っている; 貧しくない →裕福な, 金持ちの, 富んだ ‖ *a rich family/country* 裕福な家庭・国 ‖ *one of the richest women in the world* 世界で最も裕福な女性の1人 ☛参 **wealthy** ⇔ **poor** ▶定義2 **the rich** 名 [複数扱い] people with a lot of money or property 多額のお金または財産を持つ人々 →金持ちの人々 ▶定義3 **rich in sth** containing a lot of sth たくさんの～を含んでいる →～に富んでいる, 恵まれた, ～で満ちている, ～が豊富な, 豊かな ‖ *Oranges are rich in vitamin C.* オレンジはビタミンCが豊富です. ▶定義4 (used about food) containing a lot of fat, oil, sugar or cream and making you feel full quickly (食べ物について) たくさんの脂肪, 油, 砂糖またはクリーム (乳脂肪) を含んでおり, またすぐに満腹感を感じさせてくれる →栄養価の高い, カロリーの高い, 濃厚な, こくのある ‖ *a rich chocolate cake* こってりしたチョコレートケーキ ▶定義5 (used about soil) containing the substances that make it good for growing plants in (土壌について) 植物を育てるのに良い物質を含んでいる →肥えた, 肥沃 (ひよく) な ▶定義6 (used about colours, sounds or smells) strong and deep (色, 音, においについて) 強くて濃い →濃い, 鮮明な, 朗々とした, 豊かで太い — **richness** 名 Ⓤ →豊富であること, 豊かさ, 肥沃, 高価

**riches** /rítʃəz/ 名 [複数扱い] 正式 ▶定義 a lot of money or property 多額のお金または財産 →富, 財産 ☛類 **wealth**

**richly** /rítʃli/ 副 ▶定義1 in a generous way 気前良く →ぜいたくに, 豪華に, 豊富に, 豊かに ‖ *She was richly rewarded for her hard work.* 彼女の懸命な仕事は十分に報われた. ▶定義2 in a way that people think is right 人々が当然であると思うほどに →十分に, 完全に, 当然に ‖ *His promotion was richly deserved.* 彼の昇進は極めて当然だった.

**rickety** /ríkəti/ 形 ▶定義 likely to break; not strongly made 壊れそうな; 頑丈に作られていない →ぐらぐらする, がたがたする, がたつく, よぼよぼの ‖ *a rickety old fence* ぐらぐらしている古い柵 (さく) *rickety furniture* ぐらついた家具

**ricochet** /ríkəʃèɪ/ 動 自 (過, 過分 **ricocheted** /-ʃèɪd/) ▶定義 **ricochet (off sth)** (used about a moving object) to fly away from a surface after hitting it (動いている物体について) ある面にぶつかってから飛び去る →(～に当たって) 跳ね返る ‖ *The bullet ricocheted off the wall and grazed his shoulder.* 銃弾は壁に当たって跳ね返り, 彼の肩をかすめた.

\***rid** /rɪd/ 動 他 (現分 **ridding**; 過, 過分 **rid**) 正式 ▶定義 **rid yourself/sb/sth of sb/sth** to make yourself/sb/sth free from sb/sth that is unpleasant or not wanted 自分や～を不愉快なまたは望まない…から自由にする →～を…から除去する, 取り除く, ～を免れる, ～から解放される ‖ *He was unable to rid himself of his fears and suspicions.* 彼は恐怖や疑念から抜け出すことができなかった. 関 *He was a nuisance and we're **well rid** of him (= it will be much better without him).* 彼は厄介者だったので, 私たちは彼がいなくなってやれやれと思っています (= 彼のいない方がずっとうまくいくことでしょう).

成句 **get rid of sb/sth** ▶定義 to make yourself

## 1390 riddance

free of sb/sth that is annoying you or that you do not want; to throw sth away 困らせている、または望まない～から自分を自由にする；～を捨てる➔～から抜け出す，～を免れる，～を片付ける，取り除く，追い払う‖ *Let's get rid of that old chair and buy a new one.* あの古いいすを捨てて新しいのを買おう．

**riddance** /rídns/ 名
成句 **good riddance (to sb/sth)**（口語）▶定義 used for expressing pleasure or satisfaction that sb/sth that you do not like has gone 好きではない～が去った喜びや満足感を表現するために用いて➔（～が）いなくなってやれやれだ，いい厄介払いできてよかった

**ridden**[1] **RIDE**[1] の過去分詞

**ridden**[2] /rídn/ 形 正式（通常は複合形容詞で）
▶定義 full of ～で一杯の➔～が多い，一杯ある‖ *She was guilt-ridden.* 彼女は罪の意識に取り付かれていた．*She was ridden with guilt.* 彼女は罪の意識に悩まされていた．

**riddle** /rídl/ 名 C ▶定義1 a difficult question that you ask people for fun that has a clever or amusing answer 楽しみで人に聞いてみる，巧妙なまたは面白い答えを持つ難しい問題➔なぞなぞ，判じ物 ▶定義2 a person, thing or event that you cannot understand or explain 理解する，または説明することができない人，物，または出来事➔なぞ，なぞの人，不可解な人・物・出来事

**riddled** /rídld/ 形 ▶定義 **riddled with sth** full of sth, especially sth unpleasant ～で特に不愉快な～で一杯の➔～で一杯の，～に満ちた‖ *This essay is riddled with mistakes.* この小論は間違いだらけです．

★**ride**[1] /ráid/ 動（過 **rode** /róud/; 過分 **ridden** /rídn/）
▶定義1 自 他 to sit on a horse and control it as it moves 馬に乗り，その動きを操る➔馬に乗る，馬を乗りこなす，乗馬をする，馬を御する‖ *We rode through the woods and over the moor.* 私たちは馬に乗って森を抜け，荒野を走った．*Which horse is Dettori riding in the next race?* デトリは次のレースでどの馬に乗るのですか．
●イギリス英語では，楽しみで馬に乗ることを **go riding** と表現するのが一般的である．*She goes riding every weekend.* 彼女は毎週末，乗馬に出掛ける．アメリカ英語では **go horseback riding** が使われる．▶定義2 自 他 to sit on a bicycle, motorbike, etc and control it as it moves 自転車，オートバイなどに乗り，その動きを操る➔～に乗る‖ *She jumped onto her motorbike and rode off (= went away).* 彼女は自分のオートバイに飛び乗って走り去った(= 去っていった)．*Can John ride a bicycle yet?* ジョンはもう自転車に乗れますか．▶定義3 自 他 特に 困 to travel as a passenger in a bus, car, etc バス，車などで乗客として移動する➔～に乗っていく — **rider** 名 C ➔乗り手，ライダー，騎手

★**ride**[2] /ráid/ 名 C ▶定義1 a short journey on a horse or bicycle, or in a car, bus, etc 馬または自転車に乗って，または車，バスなどで，短距離の移動をすること➔～に乗ること，乗せること，乗り物による旅行‖ *It's only a short bus/train ride into Warwick.* ウォリックまではバス・列車に乗ってすぐです．*We went for a bike ride on Saturday.* 私たちは土曜日に自転車で出掛けた．
▶定義2 used to describe what a journey or trip is like 旅程または旅行がどのような様子であるかを説明するために用いて➔乗り心地，乗り具合‖ *a smooth/bumpy/comfortable ride* 滑るような・がたごと揺れる・快適な乗り心地 ▶定義3 a large machine at an amusement park which you pay to go on for amusement or excitement; an occasion when you go on one of these 楽しみで，または刺激を求めて金を払って乗る，遊園地にある機械で動く大きな乗り物; それらの1つに乗る機会➔乗り物‖ *My favourite fairground ride is the roller coaster.* 移動遊園地で私のお気に入りの乗り物はジェットコースターです．

成句 **take sb for a ride** 略式 ▶定義 to cheat or trick sb➔～をからかう，だます

**ridge** /rídʒ/ 名 C ▶定義1 a long, narrow piece of high land along the top of hills or mountains 丘または山の一番高い所に沿った細長い高地➔山の背，尾根，稜線（りょうせん），分水れい ▶定義2 a line where two surfaces meet at an angle 2つの面がある角度を成して接する線➔細長い隆起部，背，峰，棟

**ridicule** /rídəkjùːl/ 名 U ▶定義 unkind laughter or behaviour that is intended to make sb/sth appear silly ～がばかげて見えるようにしようとする，意地の悪い笑い，または振る舞い➔嘲笑（ちょうしょう），あざけり，からかい，冷やかし‖ *He* had become an object of ridicule. 彼は嘲笑の的になっていた. — ridicule 動 他 →~を嘲笑する, あざける, 冷やかす, ばかにする ‖ The idea was ridiculed by everybody present. その考えは, そこに居合わせた全員からばかにされた.

*ridiculous /rədíkjələs/ 形 ▶定義 very silly or unreasonable 非常にばかげた, または不合理な→ばかげた, ばかばかしい, こっけいな, おかしな, 途方もない, とんでもない ‖ They're asking a ridiculous (= very high) price for that house. 彼らはその家に対して法外な(= 非常に高い)価格を要求している. — ridiculously 副 →ばかばかしいほど, こっけいに, 途方もなく

riding /ráidɪŋ/ (米 horseback riding) 名 ❶ ▶定義 the sport or hobby of riding a horse 馬に乗るスポーツまたは趣味→乗馬 ‖ riding boots 乗馬用ブーツ a riding school 乗馬学校

rife /ráif/ 形 (名詞の前は不可) 正式 ▶定義 (used especially about bad things) very common (特に悪いものについて)非常に一般的な→広まって, 流行して, 蔓延(まんえん)して, ~に満ちて ‖ Rumours are rife that his wife has left him. 彼の元妻が去ったといううわさが広まっている.

rifle¹ /ráif(ə)l/ 名 ❺ ▶定義 a long gun that you hold against your shoulder to shoot with 肩に当てて構えて撃つ長い銃→ライフル銃, 施条(しじょう)銃, 小銃 ☛ ライフル銃を load (装填(そうてん)する), aim (ねらいをつける), fire (発砲する)と言う.

rifle² /ráif(ə)l/ 動 自 他 ▶定義 rifle (through) sth to search sth usually in order to steal from it 大抵の場合, 盗む目的で, その~を探す→荒らす, 盗む目的で荒らす; ~をかき回して探す, くまなく探す ‖ I caught him rifling through the papers on my desk. 私は彼が私の机の上にある書類を荒らしているところを捕らえた.

rift /ríft/ 名 ❺ ▶定義 1 a serious disagreement between friends, groups, etc that stops their relationship from continuing 関係を続けていくのを妨げるような, 友達, 集団などの間での深刻な意見の相違→亀裂(きれつ), ひび, 不和, 対立 ‖ a growing rift between the brothers ますます深刻なっていく兄弟間の不和 ▶定義 2 a very large crack or opening in the ground, a rock, etc 地面, 岩などにある, 非常に大きなひび割れ, または開口部→断層, 亀裂, 切れ目, 裂け目, 割れ目

rig /ríg/ 動 他 (rigging; rigged) ▶定義 to arrange or control an event, etc in an unfair way, in order to get the result you want 自分が望む結果を得るために, 不正なやり方で, 催しなどを手配する, または統制する→~を不正手段で操る, 自分に有利に工作する, 操作する, ~に八百長をする ‖ They claimed that the competition had been rigged. 彼らはその競技は八百長だったと抗議した.

句動詞 rig sth up ▶定義 to make sth quickly, using any materials you can find 見つけられる材料を何でも使って~を素早く作る→~を間に合わせに作る, 急ごしらえする ‖ We tried to rig up a shelter using our coats. 私たちは上着を使って間に合わせのテントを作ろうとした.

rig² /ríg/ = OIL RIG

rigging /rígɪŋ/ 名 ❶ ▶定義 the ropes, etc that support a ship's sails 船の帆を支えるロープなど→索具

*right¹ /ráit/ 形 ▶定義 1 correct; true 正しい; 真実の→適当な, 当を得た, 間違いのない, 正確な, 合っている, 本当の ‖ I'm afraid that's not the right answer. 残念ですがそれは正解ではありません. Have you got the right time? 正確な時間が分かりますか. You're quite right - the film does start at 7 o'clock. 全くあなたの言う通りです - その映画は確かに7時に始まります. You were right about the weather - it did rain. あなたの言う通りの天気になりました - 本当に雨が降りました. 'You're Chinese, aren't you?' 'Yes, that's right.'「あなたは中国人ですね」「ええ, その通りです」 ▶定義 2 right (for sb/sth) best; most suitable 最高の; 最適な→適切な, ふさわしい, 好都合な, 申し分のない ‖ I hope I've made the right decision. 私の下した判断が適切であったことを望んでおります. I am sure we've chosen the right person for the job. 私には, 私たちがその仕事に打って付けの人を選んだという自信がある. I would help you to wash the car, but I'm not wearing the right clothes. 私はあなたが洗車するのを手伝いたいと思っていますが, それに適した服装をしていません.

▶定義 3 (used about behaviour, actions, etc) fair; morally and socially correct (振る舞い, 行動などについて)公平な; 道徳的および社会的に正しい→正しい, 正当な, 当然の, 正義の ‖ It's not

## right²

right to pay people so badly. そんなに低い賃金を支払うのは正当ではない. *What do you think is* **the right thing** *to do?* 何をすべきだと思いますか. ⇨ 定義 1〜3 **wrong** ▶定義4 healthy or normal; as it should be 健康な, または正常な, あるべき姿で→健康な, 体の調子が良い, 健全な, 正常な ‖ *The car exhaust doesn't sound right - it's making a funny noise.* その車の排気管には異常がありそうです — 変な音が出ています. *I don't know what it is, but something's just not right.* それが何であるか分かりませんが, 何か普通ではありません. ▶定義5 on or of the side of the body that faces east when a person is facing north 人が北に向いているときに東に向く身体の側に, または身体の側の→右の, 右側の, 右方への, 右向きの ‖ *Most people write with their right hand.* ほとんどの人は右手で書く. *He's blind in his right eye.* 彼は右目が不自由です. ⇨ **left** ▶定義6 因 (口語) (used for emphasizing sth bad) real or complete (悪い〜を強調するために用いて) 本物の, または完全な→正真正銘の, 本当の, ごまかしでない ‖ *I'll look a right idiot in that hat!* 私があの帽子をかぶったら正真正銘のばかに見えるでしょう. — **rightness** 名 ❶ →正しさ, 公正, 正義, 正当性, 高潔

成句 get/start off on the right/wrong foot (with sb) ⇨ **FOOT**¹

get on the right/wrong side of sb ⇨ **SIDE**¹

on the right/wrong track ⇨ **TRACK**¹

put/set sth right ▶定義 to correct sth or deal with a problem 〜を正す, または問題を処理する→〜を正常(な状態)に戻す, 時計の時間を合わせる, 思い違いを訂正する, 整理する ‖ *There's something wrong with the lawnmower. Do you think you'll be able to put it right?* その芝刈り機はどこかおかしい所があります. あなたはそれを修理できると思いますか.

right (you are)! (口語) ▶定義 yes, I will or yes, I agree; OK はい, やりましょう, はい承知しました; 分かりました→よろしい, 承知した, ごもっとも, その通り ‖ *'See you later!' 'Right you are!'* 「じゃあまたね」「またね」

(as) right as rain ▶定義 completely healthy and normal 完全に健康で正常な→すっかり健康を回復して, 全く正常で

## *right² /ráɪt/ 副 ▶定義1 exactly; directly 正確に; 直接に→正しく, 正確に, 間違いなく, まともに, すぐに, 直接に ‖ *The train was right on time.* その列車は定刻だった. *He was sitting right beside me.* 彼は私のすぐそばに座っていた. ▶定義2 correctly; in the way that it should happen or should be done 正しく; 起こるべき, または行われるべき方法で→正しく, 公正に, 正確に, 適切に, ふさわしく ‖ *Have I spelt your name right?* 私はあなたの名前を正しくつづっていますか. *Nothing seems to be going right for me at the moment.* 今のところ, 私には何1つうまくいっていないように思える. ⇨ **wrong** ▶定義3 all the way; completely ずっと; 完全に→はるばると, すっかり, 全く ‖ *Did you watch the film right to the end?* あなたはその映画を最後までずっと見ましたか. *There's a high wall that goes right round the house.* その家の周囲をぐるりと巡る高い壁がある. ▶定義4 to the right side 右側に→右に[へ], 右手に, 右側に[へ] ‖ *Turn right at the traffic lights.* その信号を右折しなさい. ⇨ **left** ▶定義5 immediately 即座に→すぐに, 直ちに ‖ *Wait here a minute - I'll be right back.* ここでちょっと待っていてください — すぐに戻ります. ▶定義6 (口語) (used for preparing sb for sth that is about to happen) get ready; listen (〜が今にも起こりそうな…に備えることに用いて) →準備はいいかい, よし, それでは ‖ *Have you got your seat belts on? Right, off we go.* シートベルトを締めましたか. それでは, さあ出発です.

成句 right/straight away ⇨ **AWAY**

right now ▶定義 at this moment; exactly now 今の時点で; ちょうど今→ただ今は, 今のところは, 今すぐ ‖ *We can't discuss this right now.* 私たちは今の時点ではこの事について議論できない.

serve sb right ⇨ **SERVE**

## *right³ /ráɪt/ 名 ▶定義1 ❶ what is morally good and fair 道徳的に正しく公平なこと→正しいこと, 公正, 正しい・正当な行い, 公平な扱い ‖ *Does a child of ten really understand the difference between right and wrong?* 10歳の子供に善悪の違いが本当に分かるだろうか. *You **did right** to tell me what happened.* 起こった事を話してくれるとは, あなたは正しい事をしました. ⇨ **wrong** ▶定義2 [単数扱い] the right side or direction 右側または右の方向→右, 右側, 右方, 右

手 ‖ *We live in the first house **on the right**.* 私たちは右側の1軒目の家に住んでいる. *Take the first right and then the second left.* 1本目の道を右折, 次を左折しなさい. ⇔ **left** ▶定義3 [U][C]

the right (to sth/to do sth) a thing that you are allowed to do according to the law; a moral authority to do sth 法律によって行うことが許されていること; ～を行う道徳上の権限➜**(～に対する･～する)権利** ‖ *Freedom of speech is one of the basic **human rights**.* 言論の自由は基本的人権の1つである. ***civil rights*** *(= the rights each person has to political and religious freedom, etc)* 市民権(= 各人が持っている, 政治や宗教の自由などの権利) *animal rights campaigners* 動物の権利の活動家 *Everyone has the right to a fair trial.* すべての人は公正な裁判を受ける権利がある. *You have no right to tell me what to do.* あなたには私に指図する権利はない.

▶定義4 **the Right** [単数扱い, 単数または複数形の動詞と共に] the people or political parties who are against social change 社会の変化に反対する人々または政党➜**右翼, 右派, 保守派, 保守党**

[成句] be in the right ▶定義 to be doing what is correct and fair 正しく公平な事をしている➜**正しい, 道理がある, (～するのも)もっともで** ‖ *You don't need to apologize. You were in the right and he was in the wrong.* あなたが謝る必要はありません. あなたの言った事はもっともなことで, 彼が間違っていたのです.

by rights ▶定義 according to what is fair or correct 公正な, または正しい事に従って➜**当然(の権利によって), 本来は, 正しくは** ‖ *By rights, half the profit should be mine.* 本来なら, その利益の半分は私のものになるはずです.

in your own right ▶定義 because of what you are yourself and not because of other people 他人によるものではなく, 自分が自分自身であることのために➜**自己の権利で, 生得の権利で, 本来の資質･価値で, 独力で**

within your rights (to do sth) ▶定義 acting in a reasonable or legal way 合理的に, または合法的に行動する➜**～する権利･権限がある** ‖ *You are quite within your rights to demand to see your lawyer.* あなたには当然, 弁護士との面会を要求する権利がある.

**right**[4] /ráɪt/ [動][他] ▶定義 to put sb/sth/yourself back into a normal position ～や自分自身を正常な位置に戻す➜**～をまっすぐにする, 建て直す, 起こす, 元通りにする, 本来の状態にする** ‖ *The boat tipped over and then righted itself again.* そのボートは転覆してから自然に元に戻った.

[成句] right a wrong ▶定義 to do sth to correct an unfair situation or sth bad that you have done 不正な状況または自分がしでかした悪い～を正すために…を行う➜**不正を正す**

right angle [名] [C] ▶定義 an angle of 90° 90度の角度➜**直角** ‖ *A square has four right angles.* 正方形には直角が4つあります.

**righteous** /ráɪtʃəs/ [形][正式] ▶定義 that you think is morally good or fair 道徳的に良いまたは公平であると思うような➜**正しい, 正義の, 正しい事をする, 高潔な, もっともな** ‖ *righteous anger/indignation* 無理もない怒り･憤り ☛参 **self-righteous**

**rightful** /ráɪtfʊl, -f(ə)l/ [形](名詞の前だけ) [正式] ▶定義 legally or morally correct; fair 法的に, または道徳的に正しい; 公正な➜**正当な権利を持っている, 合法的な, 正統の, 正当な** — rightfully /ráɪtfʊli, -f(ə)li/ [副] ➜**正しく, 正当に, 合法的に, 公正に**

**right-hand** [形](名詞の前だけ) ▶定義 of or on the right of sb/sth ～の右の, または右に➜**右の, 右側の, 右の方への, 右手の** ‖ *The postbox is on the right-hand side of the road.* 郵便ポストは道路の右側にあります. *in the top right-hand corner of the screen* 画面の右上の角

**right-handed** [形] ▶定義 using the right hand for writing, etc and not the left 書くときなどに左手ではなく右手を使っている➜**右利きの, 右手による, 右手用の**

**right-hand man** [名][単数扱い] ▶定義 the person you depend on most to help and support you in your work 仕事上で自分を補佐し, 後ろ盾となってくれる最も頼りになる人➜**右腕となる人, 信頼のおける補佐, 腹心の人物** ‖ *the President's right-hand man* 大統領の腹心

**rightly** /ráɪtli/ [副] ▶定義 correctly or fairly 正しく, または適切に➜**公正に; 当然に** ‖ *He's been sacked and **quite rightly**, I believe.* 彼は首になったが, 極めて当然のことだと思う.

**right of way** [名]([複] **rights of way**) ▶定義1 [C]

R

特に 英 a path across private land that the public may use; legal permission to go into or through another person's land 一般の人々の利用が認められている，私有地を通る小道；ほかの人の土地の中に入る，または通り抜ける法的な許可→通行権が設定された道; 通行権 ‖ *Walkers have right of way through the farmer's field.* 歩行者にはその農場主の畑を通り抜ける通行権がある. ▶定義2 ❶ (used in road traffic) the fact that a vehicle in a particular position is allowed to drive into or across a road before another vehicle in a different position（道路交通について）ある特定の位置にある車両が，ほかの位置の別の車両に優先して道路に進入または横断することが許されていること→優先通行権 ‖ *He should have stopped - I had the right of way.* 彼は止まるべきだった － 私の方に優先通行権があった.

**right wing** 名 [単数扱い，単数または複数形の動詞と共に] ▶定義 the people in a political party who are against social change 社会の変化に反対する政党に属する人々→右翼，右派，保守派 ― right-wing 形 →右翼の，右派の，右翼的な，保守的な ‖ *a right-wing government* 右翼政権 ⇔ **left-wing**

**rigid** /rídʒəd/ 形 ▶定義1 not able or not wanting to change or be changed 変化できない，または変化を望んでいない→頑固な，柔軟性のない，融通が利かない ▶定義2 difficult to bend; stiff 曲げにくい，硬い→硬くて曲がらない；こわばった，硬直した ‖ *a rucksack with a rigid frame* 硬いフレームの付いたリュックサック *She was rigid with fear.* 彼女の体は恐怖で硬直していた. ― **rigidity** 名 ❶→堅いこと，硬直，厳格，厳密 ― **rigidly** 副→堅く，頑丈に，厳格に ‖ *The speed limit must be rigidly enforced.* 速度制限は厳格に遵守されなければならない.

**rigorous** /rígərəs/ 形 ▶定義 done very carefully and with great attention to detail 非常に入念に，細部にまで多大な注意を払って行われた→厳格な，厳しい，厳密な，正確な ‖ *Rigorous tests are carried out on the drinking water.* 飲用水には厳密な検査が行われている. ― **rigorously** 副 →厳格に，厳しく；厳密に，正確に

**rigour** (米 **rigor**) /rígər/ 名 正式 ▶定義1 ❶ doing sth carefully with great attention to detail 入念に，細部にまで多大な注意を払って〜を行うこと→厳密，精密，正確 ‖ *The tests were carried out with rigour.* その検査は厳密に行われた. ▶定義2 ❶ the quality of being strict 厳格であるという特性→厳格，厳しさ，精密さ ‖ *the full rigour of the law* 最大限に厳格な法律の適用 ▶定義3 [❻，通常は複数] difficult conditions 困難な状況→(天候・環境の)厳しさ，苦しさ，過酷さ

**rim** /rím/ 名 ❻ ▶定義 an edge at the top or outside of sth that is round 円い物の縁，(茶わんなどの場合) てっぺんの縁，(メガネなどの場合) 外側の縁→縁，へり ‖ *the rim of a cup* カップの縁 ☞ **cup** のさし絵

**rind** /ráɪnd/ 名 ❻ ❶ ▶定義 the thick hard skin on the outside of some fruits, some types of cheese, meat etc 一部の果実，ある種のチーズ，肉などの外側を覆う，厚く硬い皮→皮, 外皮 ▶レモンやオレンジの皮は rind または peel と呼ばれる. バナナやトマトのようにもっと柔らかい外皮は skin と言う.

★**ring** /rɪŋ/ 名 ▶定義1 ❻ a piece of jewellery that you wear on your finger 指にはめる宝飾品→指輪 ‖ *a gold/diamond/wedding ring* 金の指輪・ダイヤの指輪・結婚指輪 *an engagement ring* 婚約指輪 ☞ **jewellery** のさし絵 ▶定義2 ❻ (通常は複合名詞で) a round object of any material with a hole in the middle 素材のいかんを問わず，中央に穴の開いた輪形のもの→輪，環 ‖ *curtain rings* カーテンリング *a key ring (= for holding keys)* 環状のキーホルダー (= かぎをまとめておくための物) ▶定義3 ❻ a round mark or shape 円形の跡または円形→円い跡，輪形 ‖ *The coffee cup left a ring on the table top.* テーブルの上にコーヒーカップの円い跡が残った. *Stand in a ring and hold hands.* 輪になって立ち，手をつなぎなさい. ▶定義4 ❻ the space with seats all around it where a performance, boxing match, etc takes place 座席がステージを囲むように設けられている，公演，ボクシングの試合などが行われる場所→(サーカスなどの)円形演技場，競技場，競馬場，ボクシングのリング ‖ *a circus/boxing ring* サーカス・ボクシングのリング ▶定義5 (米 **burner**) ❻ one of the round parts on the top of an electric or gas cooker on which you can put pans 電気・ガスこんろの表側に付いた円形の部品．この上になべを載せることができる→熱

環 ▶定義6 ❻a number of people who are involved in sth that is secret or not legal together 秘密または非合法的な事にかかわりを持つ何人かの人々→徒党, 一味, 一団 ‖ *a spy/drugs ring* スパイ団・麻薬組織 ▶定義7 ❸ the sound made by a bell; the action of ringing a bell ベルの音; ベルを鳴らす行為→(ベルなどの)鳴る音,(鐘・ベルなどを)鳴らすこと ‖ *There was a ring at the door.* 玄関のベルが鳴った. ▶定義8 ［単数扱い］a ring of sth a particular quality that words or sounds have 言葉または音が持つ一種独特の性質→響き, 調子, 感じ ‖ *What the man said had a ring of truth about it (= sounded true).* その男の話には真実味があった(= 真実であるように聞こえた).

成句 give sb a ring 英略式 ▶定義 to telephone sb→~に電話をかける ‖ *I'll give you a ring in the morning.* 午前中にお電話します.

★**ring**² /rɪŋ/ 動 (過 **rang** /ræŋ/; 過分 **rung** /rʌŋ/) ▶定義1 ❸⓲ (特に 米 **call**) ring (sb/sth) (up) to telephone sb/sth→(~に)電話をかける ‖ *What time will you ring tomorrow?* 明日何時に電話をくださいますか. *I rang up yesterday and booked the hotel.* 昨日電話をかけてホテルを予約した. *Ring the station and ask what time the next train leaves.* 駅に電話して次の列車が何時に出るか尋ねなさい. ☛類 phone ▶定義2 ❸⓲to make a sound like a bell or to cause sth to make this sound ベルのような音を立てる, または~にそのような音を出させる→鳴る;(鐘・ベル)を鳴らす ‖ *Is that the phone ringing?* あれは電話の鳴っている音ですか. *We rang the door bell but nobody answered.* 私たちは玄関のベルを鳴らしたが, だれも出てこなかった. ▶定義3 ❸ring (for sb/sth) to ring a bell in order to call sb, ask for sth, etc ~を呼んだり, …を頼んだりするためにベルを鳴らす→(鐘・ベルを鳴らして)(~を)呼ぶ, 求める,(合図のために)ベルを鳴らす ‖ *'Did you ring, sir?' asked the stewardess.* 「お呼びでしょうか」とスチュワーデスは尋ねた. *Could you ring for a taxi, please?* 電話でタクシーを呼んでくださいませんか. ▶定義4 ❸ (used about words or sounds) to have a certain effect when you hear them (言葉または音について) 聞いたときにある印象を与える→(心・耳に)響く, 残る, ～らしく聞こえる ‖ *Her words didn't ring true (= you felt that you could not*

# rink 1395

*believe what she said).* 彼女の言葉には真実味が感じられなかった(= 彼女の言った事は信用できないと感じた). ▶定義5 ❸ring (with sth) to be filled with loud sounds 大きな音で満たされる→(~で)鳴り響く, 鳴る ‖ *The music was so loud it made my ears ring.* 音楽はあまりにも騒々しかったので耳ががんがんした. ▶定義6 ⓲ (過, 過分 **ringed**)(しばしば受動態で)to surround sb/sth ~を囲む→~を円く取り囲む ▶定義7 ⓲ (米 **circle**)(過, 過分 **ringed**) to draw a circle around sth ~の周りに円を書く→~を丸で囲む

成句 ring a bell ▶定義 to sound familiar or to remind you, not very clearly, of sb/sth 聞き慣れた音がする, またはあまりはっきりとではないが~を思い出させる→聞き覚えがある; 記憶を呼び起こす ‖ *'Do you know Chris Oliver?' 'Well, the name rings a bell.'*「クリス オリバーを知っていますか」「さて, 名前には聞き覚えがありますが」

句動詞 ring (sb) back 英 ▶定義 to telephone sb again or to telephone sb who has telephoned you ~に再び電話する, または電話をくれた人に電話する→~に電話をかけ直す, 折り返し電話をする ‖ *I can't talk now - can I ring you back?* 今話ができませんか - かけ直してもいいですか.

ring in 英 ▶定義 to telephone a television or radio show, or the place where you work テレビ・ラジオのショー, または自分の勤め先に電話する→(会社などに)電話を入れる, 電話で伝える ‖ *Mandy rang in sick this morning.* マンディーは今朝, 勤め先に電話を入れて病気だと伝えた.

ring out ▶定義 to sound loudly and clearly 大きくはっきりと鳴り響く→(声などが)響き渡る

**ringleader** /ˈrɪŋliːdər/ 名 ❻ ▶定義 a person who leads others in crime or in causing trouble 犯罪や, 問題を起こす人々の先頭に立って采配を振るう人→首謀者, リーダー ‖ *The ringleaders were jailed for 15 years.* 首謀者たちは15年間刑務所に入っていた.

**ring road** 名 ❻ 英 ▶定義 a road that is built all around a town so that traffic does not have to go into the town centre 車が町の中心に入らなくて済むように, 町の周りをぐるっと囲むように建設された道路→環状道路 ☛参 **bypass**¹

**rink** /rɪŋk/ = SKATING RINK

**rinse** /rɪns/ 動他 ▶定義 to wash sth in water in order to remove soap or dirt せっけんや汚れを落とすために、~を水で洗う→~をゆすぐ, (汚れなど)すすぎ落とす ‖ *Rinse your hair thoroughly after each shampoo.* シャンプーする度に髪をよくすすぎなさい. ― rinse 名 C→ゆすぎ, すすぎ

**riot** /rάɪət/ 名 C ▶定義 a situation in which a group of people behave in a violent way in a public place, often as a protest 一団の人々が, しばしば抗議として, 公共の場所で暴力的に振る舞う状況→暴動, 騒動, 一揆(いっき) ‖ *Further riots have broken out in Manchester.* マンチェスターでさらなる暴動が起きた. ― riot 動 自→暴動を起こす, 騒ぐ ‖ *There is a danger that the prisoners will riot if conditions do not improve.* もし状況が改善しなければ, 囚人たちが暴動を起こす危険性がある. ― rioter 名 C→暴徒, 暴動者

成句 **run riot** ▶定義 1 to behave in a wild way without any control 何の抑制もなく, 乱暴に振る舞う→奔放に振る舞う, 騒ぎ回る, 暴れ回る ‖ *At the end of the football match, the crowd ran riot.* サッカーの試合の後で, 群衆は大騒ぎした. ▶定義 2 (used about your imagination, feelings, etc) to allow sth to develop and continue without trying to control it (想像力, 感情などについて)(想像力や感情などを)抑制しようとしないで, 際限なく出るに任せる→(想像などが)とどまることがない

**riotous** /rάɪətəs/ 形 ▶定義 1 wild or violent; lacking in control 手に負えない, または暴力的な; 抑制を欠いている→暴動的な; 奔放な, 羽目を外した ▶定義 2 wild and full of fun 熱狂的でにぎにぎしい→騒々しい, にぎやかな

**RIP** /ὰːr aɪ píː/ 略 ▶定義 (used on graves) rest in peace→(墓石に用いて)安らかに眠れ

**rip**¹ /rɪp/ 動 (**ripping**; **ripped**) ▶定義 1 自他 to tear or be torn quickly and suddenly 急にビリッと裂ける, または引き裂かれる→裂ける, 破れる; ~を引き裂く, 破る ‖ *Oh no! My dress has ripped!* まあ大変. ドレスが破けてしまった. *He ripped the letter in half/two and threw it in the bin.* 彼はその手紙を2つに引き裂いて, ごみ箱に投げ捨てた. *The blast of the bomb ripped the house apart.* 爆風でその家はばらばらに崩壊した. ▶定義 2 他 to remove sth quickly and violently often by pulling it しばしば引っ張って, ~を素早く乱取に取り除く→~をもぎ取る, はぎ取る, ひったくる ‖ *He ripped the poster from the wall.* 彼は壁からポスターを引きはがした.

句動詞 **rip through sth** ▶定義 to move very quickly and violently through sth あっと言う間にものすごい勢いで~を通り抜ける→~をすごい勢いで通り抜ける ‖ *The house was badly damaged when fire ripped through the first floor.* 火の手がすごい勢いで2階を通り抜けた時に, その家はひどい損傷を被った.

**rip sb off** 略式 ▶定義 to cheat sb by charging too much money for sth 何かに対し法外な代金を請求して~をだます→人に高値を吹っ掛ける, ~をだます

**rip sth up** ▶定義 to tear sth into small pieces ~を細かく引き裂く→~をずたずたに切り裂く

**rip**² /rɪp/ 名 C ▶定義 a long tear (in material, etc) (生地などの)長い裂け目→裂け目, ほころび

★**ripe** /rάɪp/ 形 ▶定義 1 (used about fruit, grain, etc) ready to be picked and eaten(果実, 穀物などについて)すぐにも収穫して食べられる→熟した, 実った ▶定義 2 **ripe (for sth)** ready for sth or in a suitable state for sth ~の準備ができた, または~に適した状態の→(~の)機が熟した, 準備の整った ― ripen /-(ə)n/ 動自他→熟す, 実る; ~を熟させる, 実らせる

**rip-off** 名 C 略式 ▶定義 something that costs a lot more than it should 不当に高くかかるもの→法外に高いもの, 代金の吹っ掛け, いんちき ‖ *The food in that restaurant is a complete rip-off!* あのレストランの食事は全くべらぼうに高い.

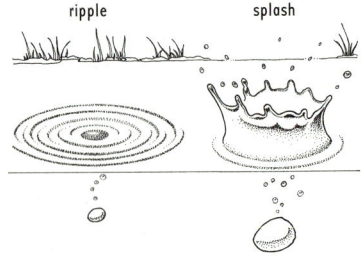

ripple        splash

**ripple** /rɪ́p(ə)l/ 名 C ▶定義 1 a very small wave or movement on the surface of water 水面の非

常に小さな波または動き→**さざなみ, 波紋** ▶定義2 [通常は単数] *a ripple (of sth)* a sound that gradually becomes louder and then quieter again; a feeling that gradually spreads through a person or a group of people だんだん大きくなり,それから再び静かになっていく音; 個人または集団にだんだん広がっていく感情→**さざなみのような音, さざめき; 感情の伝播(でんぱ), 波紋** ‖ *a ripple of laughter* さざめく笑い声 — **ripple** 動 自 他 →さざなみが立つ, さざめく, (感情などが)波紋のように広がる; 〜にさざなみを立てる

★**rise**¹ /ráɪz/ 名 ▶定義1 **C** *a rise (in sth)* an increase in an amount, a number or a level 量, 数の増加や程度の上昇→**増加, 上昇** ‖ *There has been a* ***sharp rise*** *in the number of people out of work.* 失業者の数が急増している. ⇔ **drop, fall** ▶定義2 **C** (困**raise**) an increase in the money you are paid for the work you do 行った仕事に対し支払われる金額が増えること→**昇給, 賃上げ** ‖ *I'm hoping to* ***get a rise*** *next April.* 今度の4月に昇給があることを期待している. *a 10%* ***pay rise*** 10パーセントの昇給 ▶定義3 [単数扱い] *the rise (of sth)* the process of becoming more powerful or important より強力に, または重要になっていく過程→**出世, 昇進, 向上, 興隆** ‖ *The rise of fascism in Europe.* ヨーロッパにおけるファシズムの台頭. *her meteoric* ***rise to fame/power*** 彼女が名声・権力をあっと言う間に華々しく手にすること

成句 **give rise to sth** 正式 ▶定義 to cause sth to happen or exist 〜を引き起こす,または発生させる→**(好ましくない事)を引き起こす, 生じる**

★**rise**² /ráɪz/ 動 自 ( 過 **rose** /róʊz/; 過分 **risen** /ríz(ə)n/) ▶定義1 to move upwards, to become higher, stronger or to increase→**上がる, 高くなる, 強くなる, 増す** ‖ *Smoke was rising from the chimney.* 煙突から煙が立ち昇っていた. *The temperature has risen to nearly forty degrees.* 気温は40度近くまで上がった. ⇔ **fall** ▶定義2 (文) to get up from a chair, bed, etc いすなどから立ち上がる, ベッドから起き上がる→**立ち上がる, 起き上がる, 起立する, 起床する** ‖ *The audience rose and applauded the singers.* 聴衆は立ち上がって歌手たちに拍手を送った. ▶定義3 (used about the sun, moon, etc) to appear above the horizon (太陽, 月などについて) 地平線の上に現れる→**出る, 昇る** ‖ *The sun rises in the east and sets in the west.* 太陽は東から昇り,西に沈む. ⇔ **set** ▶定義4 to become more successful, powerful, important, etc 地位・権限・重要性などがさらに高まる→**地位が上がる, 出世する, 昇進する** ‖ *He rose through the ranks to become managing director.* 彼はさまざまな地位を経て社長になった. *She* ***rose to power*** *in the 90s.* 彼女は90年代に権力の座に就いた. ▶定義5 to be seen above or higher than sth else ほかの〜よりも上に,または高い所に見える→**(山, 建物などが)そびえ立つ** ▶定義6 to come from 〜から生じる→**(川が)〜に源を発する, 始まる; (物事が)〜のせいで起こる, 生ずる; (音声などが)〜から聞こえてくる, 上がる** ‖ *Shouts of protest rose from the crowd.* 抗議の叫び声が群衆から上がった. ▶定義7 *rise (up) (against sb/sth)* to start fighting against your ruler, government, etc 支配者,政府などに反抗して戦いを始める→**反乱を起こす, 反抗する** — **rising** 形 →**増加する, 新進の, 上り坂の, (太陽・月などが)昇りかけている** ‖ *the rising cost of living* 高騰する生活費 *a rising young rock star* 新進の若いロックスター

成句 **rise to the occasion, challenge, task, etc** ▶定義 to show that you are able to deal with a problem, etc successfully 問題などをうまく処理できることを示す→**臨機応変の処理をする**

★**risk**¹ /rɪsk/ 名 ▶定義1 **C U** *(a) risk (of sth/ that...); (a) risk (to sb/sth)* a possibility of sth dangerous or unpleasant happening; a situation that could be dangerous or have a bad result 危険な,または好ましくない事が起こる可能性; 危険な,または悪い結果になりかねない状況→**危険(性), おそれ, リスク** ‖ *Don't* ***take*** *any* ***risks*** *when you're driving.* 運転中は危ない事は一切してはいけません. *You could drive a car without insurance, but it's* ***not worth the risk***. 保険に入らないで車を運転することも可能だが,それは危険を冒してまですることではない. *Scientists say these pesticides* ***pose a risk*** *to wildlife.* 科学者は,これらの殺虫剤は野生生物に害を及ぼす危険性があると言っている. *If we don't leave early enough we* ***run the risk*** *of missing the plane.* 十分余裕を見て出発しない

と,飛行機に乗り損なうような危険を冒すことになる. *Small children are most* ***at risk*** *from the disease.* 幼い子供たちがこの病気の危険に最もさらされている. ▶定義2 [単数扱い] a person or thing that might cause danger 危険を招く可能性のある人物または物事➜**要注意人物,危険な物,危険な事** ‖ *If he knows your real name he's a security risk.* もし彼があなたの本名を知っていたら,国の安全を危くするような危険人物です.

[成句] at your own risk ▶定義 having the responsibility for whatever may happen 起こるかもしれない事すべてに対して責任を持って➜**自分の責任において** ‖ *This building is in a dangerous condition - enter at your own risk.* この建物は危険な状態にあります − 自分の責任において入りなさい(入っては危険です).

at the risk (of sth/doing sth) ▶定義 even though there could be a bad effect たとえ悪い影響があるとしても➜**〜を懸けて,〜の危険を冒して,(〜することを)覚悟で** ‖ *He rescued the girl at the risk of his own life.* 彼は命懸けでその女の子を救った.

***risk**² /rɪsk/ [動][他] ▶定義1 to take the chance of sth unpleasant happening 好ましくない事が起きる危険を冒してやる➜**〜を覚悟でやる,あえてする** ‖ *If you don't work hard now you risk failing your exams.* 今,一生懸命勉強しなければ試験に失敗しかねませんよ. ▶定義2 to put sth or yourself in a dangerous position 自分自身または〜を危険な状況に置く➜**〜を危険にさらす,懸ける** ‖ *The man had to* ***risk*** *his* ***life*** *to save the little boy.* その男性は,小さな男の子を助けるために自分の命を危険にさらさなければならなかった.

**risky** /rÍski/ [形] (**riskier**; **riskiest**) ▶定義 involving the possibility of sth bad happening; dangerous 悪い事が起こる可能性を含んでいる; 危険な➜**(行動などが)危険な,冒険的な**

**ritual** /rítʃuəl/ [名][C][U] ▶定義 an action, ceremony or process which is always done the same way いつも同じやり方で行われる行動,儀式,または過程➜**儀式,仕来り** ‖ *(a) religious ritual* 宗教儀式 — ritual [形]➜**儀式の,儀礼的な** — ritually [副]➜**儀式として**

**rival**¹ /ráɪv(ə)l/ [名][C] ▶定義 a person or thing that is competing with you 自分と競っている人または物➜**競争相手,好敵手,ライバル** ‖ *It seems that we're rivals for the sales manager's job.* 僕たちは販売部長のポストをねらうライバル同士のようだね.

**rival**² /ráɪv(ə)l/ [動][他] (**rivalling**; **rivalled**: [米] **rivaling**; **rivaled**) ▶定義 rival sb/sth (for/in sth) to be as good as sb/sth 〜と同じくらい優れている➜**(〜の点で)(人・物)に匹敵する,肩を並べる** ‖ *Nothing rivals skiing for sheer excitement.* ぞくぞくするような興奮という点でスキーに匹敵するものはない.

**rivalry** /ráɪv(ə)lri/ [名][C][U] ([複] **rivalries**) ▶定義 rivalry (with sb); rivalry (between A and B) competition between people, groups, etc 人々,集団などの間の競争➜**(〜との・〜の間の)競争,対抗** ‖ *There was a lot of rivalry between the sisters.* 姉妹の間にはかなりの対抗意識があった.

***river** /rívər/ [名][C] ▶定義 a large, natural flow of water that goes across land and into the sea 陸地を横切り海に流れ込む,大規模な自然の水路➜**川** ‖ *the River Nile* ナイル川 *He sat down on the bank of the river to fish.* 彼は川岸に腰を下ろして魚釣りをした.

> ➤ river(川)が海に流れ込むということを, flow into the sea と言う. 川が海と出合う所,すなわち河口は river mouth, ボートが川の上を走るという場合は sail on the river, 歩いていくにせよ,船で行くにせよ,川上の方向を目指す場合は(walk, sail) up river, 川下へ向かう場合は, down river となる.

**riverside** /rívərsàɪd/ [名] [単数扱い] ▶定義 the land next to a river 川に隣接した陸地➜**河畔,川辺** ‖ *a riverside hotel* 河畔のホテル

**rivet**¹ /rívət/ [名][C] ▶定義 a metal pin for fastening two pieces of metal together 2個の金属片を留めるための金属のピン➜**リベット,びょう**

**rivet**² /rívət/ [動][他] (通常は受動態で) ▶定義 to keep sb very interested 〜の興味を強く引き付けておく➜**〜を(…に)集中させる,くぎ付けにする,引き付ける** ‖ *I was riveted by her story.* 私は彼女の話にすっかり引き付けられてしまった. — riveting [形]➜**強く興味を引く,面白い**

**rm** [略] room➜**部屋**

**roach** /róutʃ/ [米] = COCKROACH

***road** /róud/ [名] ▶定義1 [C] a way between places, with a hard surface which cars, buses, etc can drive along 場所と場所の間のルート.

車, バスなどが通れるよう路面が硬いのが特徴→**道路, 道, 車道** ‖ *Turn left off the main (= important) road.* 幹線(= 重要な)道路を出て左折しなさい. *road signs* 道路標識

▶ road(匧highway)は町や村を結ぶ: *a road map of Slovakia* (スロバキアの道路地図). 道端に建物の建つ町・市・村のroad(道路)は, しばしばstreet(通り)と呼ばれる. 町の外にある道路にはstreetは使われない: *a street map of London* (ロンドンの市街地図). 道沿いにしばしば木々や建物が立ち並ぶ広い通りはavenue(並木道)と呼ばれる. motorway(匧freeway/expressways; 高速自動車道路)は, carriageway(車道)が2本ある道路で, それぞれに2, 3本のlane(車線)があり, 車が市街地を避けて高速で長距離を移動するために建設されている. A-roadとは, 町と町を結ぶ大きな主要幹線道路のことで, B-roadは, より小規模の田舎の道路を指す. 地図上のMはmotorwayを表す.

▶定義2 **Road** (略**Rd**) [単数扱い] used in names of roads, especially in towns 特に都市の道路の名前に用いて→**〜街, 〜街道** ‖ *60 Marylebone Road, London* ロンドン市メリルボーン街60番
成句 **by road** ▶定義 in a car, bus, etc 車, バスなどで→**(鉄道でなく)道路を通って, 陸路で** ‖ *It's going to be a terrible journey by road - let's take the train.* 車で行くと過酷な旅になりそうだ - 列車で行こう.
**on the road** ▶定義 travelling 移動している→**(車に乗って)旅行して, (劇団などが)地方巡業中で, (野球チームなどが)ロードに出て** ‖ *We were on the road for 14 hours.* 私たちは14時間車で移動していました.

**roadblock** /róʊdblɑ̀k/ 名 C ▶定義 a barrier put across a road by the police or army to stop traffic 交通を遮断するために, 警察または軍隊によって道路をふさぐ形で設置された柵(さく)→**バリケード, 道路封鎖物**

**roadside** /róʊdsàɪd/ 名 [C, 通常は単数] ▶定義 the edge of a road 道路の端→**道端, 路傍** ‖ *a roadside cafe* 道端の喫茶店

**road tax** 名 C U 匧 ▶定義 a tax which the owner of a vehicle has to pay to be allowed to drive it on public roads 車両の所有者が, 公道を利用させてもらうために支払わなければならない税金→**(道路の)通行税**

# roaring 1399

**the roadway** /róʊdweɪ/ 名 [単数扱い] ▶定義 the part of the road used by cars, etc; not the side of the road 車などが使用する道路の部分; 道路わきではない→**車道**

**roadworks** /róʊdwɜ̀ːrks/ 名 [複数扱い] ▶定義 work that involves repairing or building roads 道路の修理または建設にかかわる作業→**道路工事**

**roadworthy** /róʊdwɜ̀ːrði/ 形 ▶定義 in good enough condition to be driven on the road 路上で運転しても大丈夫な状態の→**(車が)路上走行に適した**

**roam** /róʊm/ 動 自 他 ▶定義 to walk or travel with no particular plan or aim 特別な計画や目的を持たないで歩く, または旅行する→**(〜を)歩き回る, ぶらつく, 放浪する** ‖ *Gangs of youths were roaming the streets looking for trouble.* 非行少年グループがひともんちゃく起こそうと通りをぶらついていた.

**roar** /rɔːr/ 動 ▶定義1 自 to make a loud, deep sound 低い大きな音を出す→**ほえる, ごうごうと音を立てる, 大笑いする** ‖ *She roared with laughter* at the joke. 彼女はその冗談に声を上げて笑った. *The lion opened its huge mouth and roared.* ライオンが大きな口を開けてほえた.
▶定義2 自 他 to shout sth very loudly 大声で叫ぶ→**わめく, どなる; 〜を大声で言う・歌う**
▶定義3 自 roar along, down, past, etc to move in the direction mentioned, making a loud, deep sound 低い大きな音を立てながら, 言及された方向に進む→**(車・飛行機などが)ごう音を立ててどんどん進む, (中心地点から)離れた方向へと進む, 前を通り過ぎていく** ‖ *A motorbike roared past us.* オートバイがごう音を立てて私たちの前を通り過ぎていった. — **roar** 名 C U →**(獣の)ほえる声, うなり声; 叫び声, 怒号, 大きな笑い声; ごう音** ‖ *the roar of heavy traffic on the motorway* 高速道路の激しい交通騒音 *roars of laughter* 大笑い

**roaring** /rɔ́ːrɪŋ/ 形 ▶定義1 making a very loud noise 非常に大きな音を立てている→**ほえる, 騒々しい** ▶定義2 (used about a fire) burning very well (火について)非常によく燃えている→**ごうごうと燃え盛る** ▶定義3 very great 大変すばらしい→**盛んな, 活気ある, 大繁盛の** ‖ *a roaring success* 大成功

**roast¹** /róust/ 動 ▶定義1 圓他 to cook or be cooked in an oven or over a fire オーブンまたは直火で調理する，または調理される→焼ける；～を焼く，あぶる ‖ *a smell of roasting meat* 肉を焼いているにおい *to roast a chicken* 鶏肉を焼く ☞参 **cook**の注 ▶定義2 他 to heat and dry sth ～を熱して乾燥させる→～(豆など)をいる ‖ *roasted peanuts* いったピーナツ ― **roast** 形 (名詞の前だけ)→焼けた，あぶった，いった ‖ *roast beef/potatoes/chestnuts* ローストビーフ・焼きジャガイモ・焼きぐり

**roast²** /róust/ 名 ▶定義1 C a piece of meat that has been cooked in an oven オーブンで調理された肉→焼き肉，ロースト ▶定義2 C 特に 米 an outdoor meal at which food is cooked over a fire 食べ物を直火で調理する，戸外での食事→野外の焼き肉パーティー ☞参 **barbecue**

***rob** /rάb/ 動他 (**robbing**; **robbed**) rob sb/sth (of sth) ▶定義1 to take money, property, etc from a person or place illegally 金銭，所有物などを人または場所から非合法的に取る→～から(…を)奪う，強奪する，(場所など)を襲う ‖ *to rob a bank* 銀行強盗をする ☞参 **steal**の注 ▶定義2 rob sb/sth (of sth) to take sth away from sb/sth that he/she/it should have ～が当然手にすべきものをその手から奪う→～から(…を)奪う，失わせる ‖ *His illness robbed him of the chance to play for his country.* 病気のために彼は国のためにプレーする機会を失った.

***robber** /rάbər/ 名 C ▶定義 a person who steals from a place or a person, especially using violence or threats 特に暴力または脅しを使って，場所または人から物を盗む人→強盗，泥棒 ☞参 **thief**の注

**robbery** /rάbəri/ 名 C U (複 **robberies**) ▶定義 the crime of stealing from a place or a person, especially using violence or threats 特に暴力または脅しを使って，場所または人から物を盗むという犯罪→強盗，盗難，強奪 ‖ *They were found guilty of armed robbery (= using a weapon).* 彼らは武装強盗罪(=武器を使って)で有罪となった.

**robe** /róub/ 名 C ▶定義1 a long, loose piece of clothing, especially one worn at ceremonies 特に儀式で着用される丈の長いゆったりとした衣服→ローブ，礼服，式服，法服 ▶定義2 米 = **DRESSING GOWN**

**robin** /rάbən/ 名 C ▶定義 a small brown bird with a bright red chest 真っ赤な胸をした茶色の小さな鳥→コマドリ，ロビン

**robot** /róubàt, -bət/ 名 C ▶定義 a machine that works automatically and can do some tasks that a human can do 自動的に動き，人にできる仕事の一部を行うことができる機械→ロボット ‖ *These cars are built by robots.* これらの車はロボットによって組み立てられている.

**robust** /roubΛ́st, róubəst/ 形 ▶定義 strong and healthy 頑健で健康な→強健な，たくましい

***rock¹** /rάk/ 名 ▶定義1 U the hard, solid material that forms part of the surface of the earth 地表の一部を成す，硬い固形物質→岩，岩石，岩盤，岩壁 ‖ *layers of rock formed over millions of years* 何百万年もの間に形成された岩の層 ▶定義2 [C, 通常は複数] a large mass of rock that sticks out of the sea or the ground 海または地面から突き出ている大きな岩の塊→暗礁，岩礁 ‖ *The ship hit the rocks and started to sink.* 船は暗礁にぶつかって沈み始めた. ▶定義3 C a single large piece of rock 1個の大きな岩石→1つの岩石 ‖ *The beach was covered with rocks that had broken away from the cliffs.* その砂浜は，崖(がけ)から崩れ落ちた岩石で覆われていた.
▶定義4 C 米 a small piece of rock that can be picked up; a stone 拾い上げることができる小さな岩石；石→小石 ‖ *The boy threw a rock at the dog.* 少年は犬に向かって石を投げた.
▶定義5 (または **rock music**) U a type of pop music with a very strong beat, played on electric guitars, etc エレキギターなどで演奏される，非常に強いビートのポップスの一種→ロック，ロックミュージック ‖ *I prefer jazz to rock.* 私はロックよりジャズの方が好きです. *a rock singer/band* ロック歌手・バンド ☞参 **classical**, **jazz**, **pop** ▶定義6 U 英 a type of hard sweet made in long, round sticks 長くて丸い棒状の硬いキャンデーの一種→棒あめ，棒状の砂糖菓子

成句 **on the rocks** ▶定義1 (used about a marriage, business, etc) having problems and likely to fail (結婚，事業などについて)問題を抱えていて，今にも駄目になりそうな→破産寸前で，(結婚が)破たんしかかって ▶定義2 (used about drinks) served with ice but no water (飲み物につ

いて)氷だけで, 水で割らずに出される➔オンザロックで ‖ whisky on the rocks ウイスキーのオンザロック

**rock**[2] /rɑk/ 動 ▶定義1 ⾃ 他 to move backwards and forwards or from side to side; to make sb/sth do this 前後または左右に動く; 〜をそのように動かす➔揺れる; 〜を揺り動かす, 揺らす ‖ boats rocking gently on the waves 波の上で静かに揺れるボート He rocked the baby in his arms to get her to sleep. 彼は赤ん坊を抱いて静かに揺すって寝かし付けた. ▶定義2 他 to shake sth violently 〜を激しく揺さぶる➔(爆発・地震などが) 〜を (激しく) 振動させる ‖ The city was rocked by a bomb blast. 爆風によって町は激しく揺れた. ▶定義3 他 to shock sb 〜を動揺させる➔〜を動転させる, 震かんさせる

成句 **rock the boat** ▶定義 to do sth that causes problems or upsets people 問題を引き起こす, または人々を動揺させるような事をする➔波風を立てる, 秩序を乱す ‖ They employ mainly quiet people who won't complain and rock the boat. 彼らは, 主として不平を言ったり秩序を乱したりしないようなおとなしい人々を雇った.

**rock and roll** (または **rock 'n' roll**) 名 U ▶定義 a type of music with a strong beat that was most popular in the 1950s 1950年代に最も人気があった, 強いビートの音楽の一種➔ロックンロール

**rock bottom** 名 U ▶定義 the lowest point (限界の) 最低点➔どん底, 最低ライン ‖ He **hit rock bottom** when he lost his job and his wife left him. 彼は職を失い, 妻に出ていかれ, どん底に落ちた. rock-bottom prices 最安価格

**rock climbing** 名 U ▶定義 the sport of climbing rocks and mountains with ropes, etc ロープなどを使って岩や山を登るスポーツ➔ロッククライミング, 岩登り

**rocket**[1] /rɑkət/ 名 C ▶定義1 a vehicle that is used for travel into space 宇宙に行くのに使われる乗り物➔ロケット ‖ a space rocket 宇宙ロケット to launch a rocket ロケットを打ち上げる ▶定義2 a weapon that travels through the air and that carries a bomb 空中を爆弾を運んで進む武器➔ロケット推進ミサイル ☛類 **missile** ▶定義3 an object that shoots high into the air and explodes in a beautiful way when you light it with a flame 点火すると空高く飛んでいき, 美しく爆発する物➔打ち上げ花火, ロケット花火 ☛ **firework** のさし絵

**rocket**[2] /rɑkət/ 動 ⾃ ▶定義 to increase or rise very quickly 急速に増加または上昇する➔(量・価格などが) 急に上がる, 高騰する ‖ Prices have rocketed recently. 最近, 物価が急騰した.

**rocky** /rɑ́ki/ 形 ▶定義 covered with or made of rocks 岩で覆われた, または岩でできた➔岩の多い, ごつごつした, 岩でできた ‖ a rocky road/coastline 岩だらけの道・岩の多いごつごつした海岸線

**rod** /rɑd/ 名 C (しばしば複合語で) ▶定義 a thin straight piece of wood, metal, etc 木・金属などでできた細長い直線状の物➔棒, さお ‖ a fishing rod 釣りざお

**rode** RIDE[1] の過去形

**rodent** /róʊdnt/ 名 C ▶定義 a type of small animal, such as a rat, a rabbit, a mouse, etc, which has strong sharp front teeth ネズミ, ウサギ, ハツカネズミなどのように, 丈夫で鋭い前歯を持つ小さな動物の一種➔げっ歯類の動物

**rodeo** /róʊdioʊ, rədéɪoʊ/ 名 C ( 複 **rodeos**) ▶定義 a competition or performance in which people show their skill in riding wild horses, catching cows, etc 荒馬を乗りこなす技, 牛を捕まえる技などを見せる競技会または興行➔ロデオ

**roe** /róʊ/ 名 U ▶定義 the eggs of a fish that we eat 食用の魚の卵➔魚の卵, はららご, 魚精, しらこ

**rogue** /róʊg/ 形 ▶定義 behaving differently from other similar people or things, often causing damage 同類のほかの人々または物とは異なる行動を示し, しばしば被害を他に及ぼす➔(動物が) 群れから離れて狂暴な, (人が) 一匹狼 (おおかみ) の, はみ出し者の; 異常な, 欠陥のある ‖ a rogue gene/program 変異遺伝子・ローグプログラム (ウイルス入りのコンピュータプログラム)

\***role** /róʊl/ 名 C ▶定義1 the position or function of sb/sth in a particular situation 特定の状況における〜の立場または役目➔役割, 任務, 機能 ‖ Parents **play** a vital **role** in their children's education. 親は子供の教育に極めて重要な役割を果たしている. ▶定義2 a person's part in a play, film, etc 演劇, 映画などで人が演じる役➔役 ‖ She was chosen to **play the role** of Cleopatra. 彼女はクレオパトラの役に選ばれた. a **leading** *role* in the film 映画の主役

**role play** 🈩 ⓒ ⓤ ▶定義 an activity, used especially in teaching, in which a person acts a part 授業で特に使われる,人がある役割を演じる活動→(語学学習での)役割演技

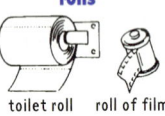
rolls
toilet roll　roll of film

**\*roll**¹ /róul/ 🈩 ⓒ ▶定義 1 something made into the shape of a tube by turning it round and round itself 円形にくるくると巻いた物→巻いた物,一巻き,巻物 ‖ *a roll of film/wallpaper* フィルム1本・壁紙一巻き ▶定義 2 bread baked in a round shape for one person to eat 1人前用に焼いてある丸型のパン→ロールパン ☛ **bread** のさし絵 ▶定義 3 moving or making sth move by turning over and over 何回も転がっていくこと,またはそのようにして~を動かすこと→転がり,回転 ‖ *Everything depended on one roll of the dice.* すべてはさいころの目にかかっていた. ▶定義 4 an official list of names 公式の氏名一覧表→名簿,出席簿 ‖ *the electoral roll (= the list of people who can vote in an election)* 選挙人名簿(= 選挙で投票することができる人の一覧) ▶定義 5 a long, low sound 長く続く低い音→とどろき,(太鼓の)連打音 ‖ *a roll of drums* 太鼓の連打 ▶定義 6 a movement from side to side 左右に揺れる動き→(飛行機や船の)横揺れ,ローリング

**roll**² /róul/ 🈔 ▶定義 1 🈊 ⓘ to move by turning over and over; to make sth move in this way 何回も転がっていく;そのようにして~を動かす→転がる,転がっていく;~を転がす ‖ *The apples fell out of the bag and rolled everywhere.* リンゴが袋から落ちて,あちこちに転がった. *He tried to roll the rock up the hill.* 彼は岩を坂の上まで転がして運ぼうとした. ▶定義 2 🈊 to move smoothly, often on wheels しばしば車輪付きで滑らかに進む→(車が)滑らかに進む,(汗,涙などが)流れ落ちる ‖ *The car began to roll back down the hill.* その車は後ろ向きにずるずると坂を滑り落ち始めた. *Tears were rolling down her cheeks.* 涙が彼女のほおを伝って落ちていた. ▶定義 3 🈊 ⓘ roll (sth) (over) to turn over and over; to make sth do this 何回も転がる;~を何回も転がす→(人・動物が)転がる,転げ回る;~を転がす,倒す,ひっくり返す ‖ *The horse was rolling in the dirt.* 馬は泥の中で転げ回っていた. *The car rolled over in the crash.* その車は衝突してグルグルッと横転した. *We rolled the log over to see what was underneath.* 私たちは下に何があるか見ようとして,丸太をひっくり返した. ▶定義 4 🈊 ⓘ roll (sth) (up) to make sth into the shape of a ball or tube ~を球形または円筒形にする→丸くなる,丸まる;~を巻く,丸める ‖ *He was rolling himself a cigarette.* 彼は自分用にたばこを巻いていた. *The insect rolled up when I touched it.* 虫は私が触ると丸まった. ⇔ **unroll** ▶定義 5 ⓘ roll sth (out) to make sth become flat by moving sth heavy over it 上に載せた重い物を動かして,~を平らにする→(地面を)(ローラーで)ならす,(金属・練り粉など)を伸ばす ‖ *Roll out the pastry thinly.* ペーストリーの生地を薄く伸ばしてください. ▶定義 6 🈊 to move from side to side 左右に揺れ動く→(船が)横揺れする,揺れる,(人が)よろよろと歩く ‖ *The ship began to roll in the storm.* 船はあらしで横揺れし始めた.

成句 **be rolling in money/in it** (俗語) ▶定義 to have a lot of money 多額のお金を持っている→金をうなるほど持っている

句動詞 **roll in** 略式 ▶定義 to arrive in large numbers or amounts 多数または多量に到着する→(注文などが)殺到する,たくさん来る ‖ *Offers of help have been rolling in.* 援助の申し出が殺到している.

**roll up** 略式 ▶定義 (used about a person or a vehicle) to arrive, especially late (人または乗り物について)特に遅れて,到着する→(人が)(車で)到着する,乗り入れる,遅れて現れる

**roller** /róulər/ 🈩 ⓒ ▶定義 1 a piece of equipment or part of a machine that is shaped like a tube and used, for example, to make sth flat or to help sth move 円筒形をした装置,または機械の一部.~を平らにしたり,…の移動の補助に使われる→(運搬用)ころ,足車,キャスター ‖ *a roller blind on a window* 窓の巻き上げ式ブラインド ▶定義 2 [通常は複数] small plastic tubes that are used to make sb's hair curly 頭髪をカールするのに使うプラスチック製の小さな円筒形の器具→ヘアカーラー

**Rollerblade**™ /róulərbleid/ 🈩 ⓒ ▶定義 a boot

with one row of narrow wheels on the bottom 底に幅の狭い車輪が一列に付いたブーツ→ローラーブレード(商標名) ‖ *a pair of Rollerblades* 1足のローラーブレード ☞ **skate**のさし絵 — **rollerblade** 動→ローラーブレードで滑る ☞ go rollerblading は, 遊びでローラーブレードで滑ることを表す一般的な言い方である. *We go rollerblading every weekend.* 私たちは毎週末にローラーブレードで滑りに行く.

**roller coaster** 名 C ▶定義 a narrow metal track that goes up and down and round tight bends, and that people ride on in a special vehicle for fun 上り下り, 急カーブのある幅の狭いレール. その上を人々は楽しみに特別の車両に乗って走る→ジェットコースター

**roller skate** (または **skate**) 名 C ▶定義 a type of shoe with small wheels on the bottom 底に小さな車輪が付いた靴の一種→ローラースケート靴 ‖ *a pair of roller skates* ローラースケート靴1足 ☞ **skate**のさし絵 — **roller skate** 動自→ローラースケートをする — **roller skating** 名 U→ローラースケート, ローラースケートで滑ること

**rolling pin** 名 C ▶定義 a piece of wood, etc in the shape of a tube, that you use for making pastry flat and thin before cooking ペーストリーを焼く前に, 生地を平らに薄く伸ばすのに使う円筒形の木製器具→めん棒, のし棒 ☞**kitchen**のさし絵

**Roman** /róumən/ 形 ▶定義 1 connected with ancient Rome or the Roman Empire 古代ローマまたはローマ帝国に関連した→古代ローマの, ローマ人の, ローマ帝国の ‖ *Roman coins* 古代ローマ時代の硬貨 *the Roman invasion of Britain* ローマ帝国の英国侵攻 ▶定義 2 connected with the modern city of Rome 現代のローマに関連した→現代ローマの, 現代ローマ市民の — **Roman** 名 C→(古代)ローマ人, (現代)ローマ市民

**the Roman alphabet** 名 [単数扱い] ▶定義 the letters A to Z, used especially in Western European languages 特に西欧の言語で使われている, AからZまでの文字→ローマ字

**Roman Catholic** (または **Catholic**) 名 C 形 ▶定義 (a member) of the Christian Church which has the Pope as its head 教皇を長とするキリスト教の教会の(信者)→ローマカトリック教会の, ローマカトリック教徒, カトリック信者 ‖ *She's (a) Roman Catholic.* 彼女はカトリック信者です. ☞参 **Protestant**

**Roman Catholicism** (または **Catholicism**) 名 U ▶定義 the beliefs of the Roman Catholic Church ローマカトリック教会の信条→(ローマ)カトリック教, (ローマ)カトリック教の教義・制度・儀式

**romance** /rouméns, rə-/ 名 ▶定義 1 C a love affair 恋愛関係→恋愛, ロマンス, 情事 ‖ *The film was about a teenage romance.* その映画はティーンエージャーの恋愛についてのものだった. ▶定義 2 U a feeling or atmosphere of love or of sth new, special and exciting 恋愛感情, また何か新鮮で特別な胸躍る気持ち・雰囲気→ロマンチックな気分・雰囲気, 恋愛感情 ▶定義 3 C a novel about a love affair→恋愛小説, ロマンス ‖ *historical romances* 歴史恋愛小説

**Roman numerals** 名 [複数扱い] ▶定義 the letters used by the ancient Romans as numbers 古代ローマ人が数字として使っていた文字→ローマ数字
▶ IV(= 4), X(=10)などのローマ数字は, 今でも時々使われている. 例えば本のページや章の番号付け, または一部の時計に見られる.

★**romantic**¹ /rouméntik/ 形 ▶定義 1 having a quality that strongly affects your emotions or makes you think about love; showing feelings of love 感情に強く影響を及ぼす, または愛について考えさせる性質を持った; 愛情を表している→ロマンチックな, わくわくするような ‖ *a romantic candlelit dinner* ろうそくをともしたロマンチックなディナー *He isn't very romantic - he never says he loves me.* 彼はあまりロマンチックではない — 私に愛していると言ったためしがない. ▶定義 2 involving a love affair 恋愛にかかわる→恋愛に関する, 恋愛の ‖ *Reports of a romantic relationship between the two film stars have been strongly denied.* その2人の映画スターが恋愛関係にあるという報道は強く否定されている. ▶定義 3 having or showing ideas about life that are emotional rather than real or practical 人生について, 現実的または実際的というよりむしろ情緒的な考えを持っている, または表している→非現実的な, 現実離れした, 空想的な ‖ *He has a romantic idea that he'd like to live on a*

*farm in Scotland.* 彼はスコットランドの農園で暮らしたいという非現実的な考えを持っている.
— romantically /-k(ə)li/ 圖 ▶空想的に, ロマンチックに

**romantic**[2] /roʊmǽntɪk/ 图 ❻ ▶定義 a person who has ideas that are not based on real life or that are not very practical 実生活に基づいていない, またはあまり実際的でない考えを持つ人→**空想家, 現実離れした人, ロマンチスト**

**romanticize** (または **-ise**) /roʊmǽntəsàɪz/ 動 ⊜ ⊕ ▶定義 to make sth seem more interesting, exciting, etc than it really is 〜を実際よりも面白く, 胸がときめくように思わせる→**(〜を)ロマンチックに扱う; ロマンチックな考えをする**

**romp** /rɑmp/ 動 ⊜ ▶定義 (used about children and animals) to play in a happy and noisy way (子供または動物について)楽しくにぎやかに遊ぶ→**跳ね回る, 飛び跳ねて騒ぐ** — romp 图 ❻→**騒々しい遊び, はしゃぎ回ること**

成句 **romp home/to victory** ▶定義 to win easily→**楽々と勝つ, 楽勝する** ∥ *United romped to a 4-0 victory over Juventus.* ユナイテッドは4－0でユベントスに楽勝した.

★**roof** /ruːf, rʊf/ 图 ❻ ( 複 **roofs**) ▶定義 **1** the part of a building, vehicle, etc which covers the top of it 建物, 車両などの最上部を覆う部分→**屋根, ルーフ** ∥ *a flat/sloping/tiled roof* 平屋根・勾配(こうばい)のある屋根・かわら屋根 *the roof of a car* 車の屋根 *The library and the sports hall are **under one roof** (= in the same building).* 図書館と屋内競技場は1つ屋根の下に(= 同じ建物の中に)ある. ☞ C7ページのさし絵 ▶定義 **2** the highest point of the inside of sth 〜の内部の一番高い部分→**(洞穴・通路などの)天井, 一番高い所** ∥ *The roof of the cave had collapsed.* 洞窟(どうくつ)の天井は崩れ落ちていた. *The soup burned the roof of my mouth.* 熱いスープで上あごをやけどしてしまった.

成句 **a roof over your head** ▶定義 somewhere to live→**住む所** ∥ *I might not have any money, but at least I've got a roof over my head.* お金はないかもしれないが, 少なくとも住む家はある.

**roof rack** 图 ❻ ▶定義 a structure that you fix to the roof of a car and use for carrying luggage or other large objects 荷物やほかの大きな物を運ぶために, 車の上に取り付ける台→**ルーフラック** ☞ **rack**のさし絵

**rooftop** /rúːftɒp, rɒ́f-/ 图 [ ❻, 通常 は 複 数 ] ▶定義 the outside of the roofs of buildings 建物の屋根の外側→**屋根, 屋上** ∥ *From the tower we looked down over the rooftops of the city.* 私たちは塔からその都市の屋根を見下ろした.

★**room** /ruːm, rʊm/ 图 ▶定義 **1** ❻a part of a house or building that has its own walls, floor and ceiling 家または建物で, 壁・床・天井のある一画→**部屋, 室** ∥ *a sitting/dining/living room* 医 居間・食堂・困 居間 *I sat down in the waiting room until the doctor called me.* 私は医者に呼ばれるまで待ち合い室に腰掛けていた. *I'd like to book a double room for two nights next month.* 来月, 2人部屋を2泊予約したいのですが. ▶定義 **2** ⓤ **room (for sb/sth); room (to do sth)** space; enough space 空間; 必要なだけの空間→**(〜のための・〜するための)空間, 場所** ∥ *These chairs **take up** too much **room**.* これらのいすは場所を取りすぎる. *I threw away my old clothes to **make room** in the wardrobe for some new ones.* 洋服だんすに新しい服を数着入れる場所を空けるために古い服を捨てた. *There were so many people that there wasn't any room to move.* あまりにも大勢の人がいたので, 身動きするすきまもなかった. ☞参 **space**と**place**[1]の注 ▶定義 **3** ⓤ**room for sth** the opportunity or need for sth 〜の機会または必要性→**(〜の・〜する)機会, 余地, 余裕, 可能性** ∥ *There's **room for improvement** in your work (= it could be much better).* あなたの作品にはまだ改善の余地があります(= ずっと良くなる可能性がある). *The lack of time gives us very little **room for manoeuvre**.* 時間が足りなくて駆け引きをする余裕はほとんどない.

**roomful** /rúːmfʊl, -f(ə)l, rʊ́m-/ 图 ❻ ▶定義 a large number of people or things in a room 部屋の中の多数の人々または物→**部屋一杯(の〜)**

**room-mate** 图 ❻ ▶定義 a person that you share a room with in a flat, etc アパートなどの部屋を共有する人→**ルームメイト, 同室者, 同居人**

**roomy** /rúːmi, rʊ́mi/ 形 (**roomier; roomiest**) ▶定義 having plenty of space 十分なスペースがある→**(部屋・車などが)広い, 広々とした, ゆったりした** ∥ *a roomy house/car* 広々とした家・ゆったりとした車

**roost** /ru:st/ 名 C ▶定義 a place where birds rest or sleep 鳥が休む,または眠る場所➡(鳥の)止まり木,ねぐら ― roost 動 自 ➡止まり木に止まる,ねぐらにつく

**rooster**¹ /rú:stər/ 米 = COCK¹(1)

★**root**¹ /ru:t/ 名 C ▶定義 1 C the part of a plant that grows under the ground and takes in water and food from the soil 地下に伸びて土壌から水分や養分を取り込む植物の部分➡根 ‖ *The deep roots of these trees can cause damage to buildings.* 地下深く伸びたこれらの木の根が,建物に被害を与える可能性がある. *root vegetables such as carrots and parsnips* ニンジンやパースニップのような根菜 ☛ C2 ページのさし絵
▶定義 2 C the part of a hair or tooth that is under the skin and that attaches it to the rest of the body 毛髪・歯の一部.皮膚の中にあって,毛髪・歯を根付かせている➡(歯・毛髪などの)付け根
▶定義 3 **roots** [複数扱い] the place where you feel that you belong, because you grew up there, live there or your relatives once lived there 自分が育ち,現在暮らしている所,または親戚(しんせき)がかつて住んでいた所,などの理由で帰属意識を持つことのできる場所➡ルーツ,心のふるさと ▶定義 4 C the basic cause or origin of sth ～の基本的な原因または起源➡根本,根源 ‖ *Let's try and get to the root of the problem.* その問題の根本に迫ってみましょう.
☛参 **square root**

**root**² /ru:t/ 動
句動詞 **root about/around (for sth)** ▶定義 to search for sth by moving things 物を動かして～を探す➡(豚などが)(食べ物を求めて)鼻で地面を掘る,(人が)(～を探して)そこらをひっかき回す ‖ *What are you rooting around in my desk for?* 私の机をひっかき回して一体何を探しているのですか.

**root for sb** ▶定義 to give support to sb who is in a competition, etc 競技などに出ている人を支援する➡～を応援する,声援する

**root sth out** ▶定義 to find and destroy sth bad completely 悪い事を見つけて完全に打ち砕く➡～を根絶する,根こそぎにする

★**rope**¹ /róʊp/ 名 C U ▶定義 very thick, strong string that is used for tying or lifting heavy things, climbing up, etc 重い物を縛る,持ち上げる,またはそれを使って登る,などのために使われる非常に太くて丈夫なひも➡ロープ,綱,縄 ‖ *We need some rope to tie up the boat with.* 私たちはボートをくくり付けておくのにロープが必要です. ☛ **cable** のさし絵

成句 **show sb/know/learn the ropes** ▶定義 to show sb/know/learn how a job should be done ある仕事がどのように行われるべきかを,～に教える・知っている・習う➡～にこつを教える,こつを知っている,こつを覚える,仕方を学ぶ

**rope**² /róʊp/ 動 他 ▶定義 **rope A to B/A and B together** to tie sb/sth with a rope ～をロープで縛る➡～を…に縛り付ける,～をロープで縛り合わせる

句動詞 **rope sb in (to do sth)** 略式 ▶定義 to persuade sb to help in an activity, especially when he/she does not want to ～が特にそう望んでいないときに,その人を説得してある活動を手伝わせる➡～を誘い込む,引き入れる ‖ *I've been roped in to help at the school play.* 学校の演劇を手伝うよう誘い込まれてしまった.

**rope sth off** ▶定義 to put ropes round or across an area in order to keep people out of it 中に人が入らないように,ある場所をロープで囲む,またはロープを渡す➡(ある区域を)ロープで仕切る,囲う

**rosary** /róʊz(ə)ri/ 名 C (複 **rosaries**) ▶定義 a string of small round pieces of wood, etc used for counting prayers 祈りを数えるときに用いられる,木製などの小さい珠(たま)をひもに通したもの➡ロザリオ,数珠

**rose**¹ /róʊzeɪ, -/ 名 U ▶定義 pink wine ピンク色のワイン➡ロゼワイン,ロゼ

**rose**¹ **RISE**² の過去形

★**rose**² /róʊz/ 名 C ▶定義 a flower with a sweet smell, that grows on a bush that usually has sharp points (**thorns**) growing on it 通常先のとがったもの(とげ)のある低木に咲く,甘い香りのする花➡バラ,バラの花 ☛ C2 ページのさし絵

**rosette** /roʊzét/ 名 C ▶定義 a decoration made from long pieces of coloured material (**ribbons**) that you wear on your clothes. Rosettes are given as prizes or worn to show that sb supports a particular political party. 衣服に付ける飾り.色の付いた細長い生地(リボン)でできており,賞品として与えられたり,ある特定の政党を

支持していることを表すために身に着けたりする→バラ飾り, バラ結び ☛ medal のさし絵

**roster** /rástər/ 特に 米 = ROTA

**rostrum** /rástrəm/ 名 ◉ ▶定義 a platform that sb stands on to make a public speech, etc 演説などをする人が立つ壇 →演壇, 説教壇

**rosy** /róυzi/ 形 (**rosier**; **rosiest**) ▶定義 1 pink and pleasant in appearance ピンク色で見た目が感じの良い →健康そうな, 血色の良い ‖ *rosy cheeks* 赤いほお ▶定義 2 full of good possibilities 望ましい可能性に満ちた →ばら色の, (前途などが)明るい ‖ *The future was looking rosy.* 未来はばら色に見えていた.

**rot** /rɑt/ 動 ⊜ ⊕ (**rotting**; **rotted**) ▶定義 to go bad or make sth go bad as part of a natural process 自然の作用で悪くなる, または～を悪くする →腐る, 腐敗する; ～を腐らせる, 腐敗させる ‖ *Too many sweets will rot your teeth!* 甘い物を食べすぎると歯が悪くなりますよ. ☛ 類 **decay** ― **rot** 名 ⓤ →腐敗, 堕落, 腐敗物

**rota** /róυtə/ ◉ (米 または **roster**) 名 ▶定義 a list of people who share a certain job or task and the times that they are each going to do it ある仕事または作業を分担で行う人々の名前と, その時間表 →職務表, 当番表 ‖ *We organize the cleaning on a rota.* 私たちは掃除を当番制にしている.

**rotary** /róυtəri/ 形 ▶定義 moving in circles round a central point 中心点の周囲をぐるぐる回る →回転する, (機械)が回転式の

**rotate** /róυteɪt, -ˊ-/ 動 ⊜ ⊕ ▶定義 1 to turn in circles round a central point; to make sth do this 中心点の周囲をぐるぐる回る; ～をそのように回転させる →回転する, 自転する; ～を回転させる ‖ *The earth rotates on its axis.* 地球は地軸を中心に回転している. ▶定義 2 to happen in turn or in a particular order; to make sth do this 交替で, またはある順番に起こる; ～にそのような事をさせる →交替する, 交替でする; ～を交替させる, (仕事)を輪番でする ‖ *We rotate the duties so that nobody is stuck with a job they don't like.* 嫌な仕事をいつまでも押し付けられることがないように, 私たちは職務を交替で行っている.

**rotation** /roυteɪʃ(ə)n/ 名 ◉ ⓤ ▶定義 1 movement in circles around a central point 中心点の周囲をぐるぐる回る動き →回転, 回転運動 ‖ *one rotation every 24 hours* 24 時間ごとに 1 回転 ▶定義 2 happening or making things happen in a particular order ある順番で起こること, または～をそのようにようにすること →交替, 輪番, ローテーション ‖ *The company is chaired by all the members in rotation.* その会社は社員全員が交替で社長を務めている.

**rotor** /róυtər/ 名 ◉ ▶定義 a part of a machine that turns round, for example the long metal parts (**blades**) that go round on top of a type of aircraft (**a helicopter**) 機械の回転部分. 例えば, ある種の航空機(ヘリコプター)の屋根で回転する長い金属部分(回転翼) →ローター, (モーターなどの)回転部

**rotten** /rɑ́tn/ 形 ▶定義 1 (used about food and other substances) old and not fresh enough or good enough to use (食べ物およびそのほかの物質について) 使用するには古くて鮮度に欠ける, または良くない →腐った, 朽ちた ‖ *rotten vegetables* 腐った野菜 ▶定義 2 略式 very unpleasant 非常に不快な →ひどい, 最低の ‖ *That was a rotten thing to say!* よくもそんなひどい事, 言えたものね. ▶定義 3 (口語) used to emphasize that you are angry 腹を立てていることを強調するのに用いて →駄目な, 嫌な ‖ *You can keep your rotten job!* そんなひどい仕事なんか要らないよ.

**rouge** /ruːʒ/ 名 ⓤ (古) ▶定義 a red powder or cream used for giving more colour to the cheeks 顔色を良くするためにほおに付ける赤い粉またはクリーム →ほお紅

★**rough**¹ /rʌf/ 形 ▶定義 1 not smooth or level 滑らかでない, または平らでない →(表面が)ざらざらした; でこぼこの ‖ *rough ground* でこぼこした地面 ⇔ **smooth**, **soft** ▶定義 2 violent; not calm or gentle 乱暴な; 落ち着いていない, または物静かでない →手荒な, 粗暴な, 荒っぽい ‖ *You can hold the baby, but don't be rough with him.* 赤ちゃんを抱いても構わないけど, 乱暴に扱わないでね. *The sea was rough and half the people on the boat were seasick.* 海が荒れて, 船に乗っていた人の半数は船酔いしていた. ⇔ **calm** ▶定義 3 made or done quickly or without much care; approximate 素早く, またはあまり注意を払わないで作られる, あるいは行われる; おおよその →大雑把な; 大まかな, 大体の ‖ *a rough esti-*

mate 概算 *Can you give me a rough idea of what time you'll be arriving?* 大体何時ころ到着する予定なのかを教えてくれませんか. ▶定義 4

書式 looking or feeling ill 気分が悪そうに見える,または気分が悪い➡気分が悪い,やつれた ‖ *You look a bit rough - are you feeling all right?* 少し気分が悪そうですね － 大丈夫ですか. — roughness 名 ❶➡定義 粗いこと,ざらざら・でこぼこしている所,乱暴,不作法

成句 **be rough (on sb)** ▶定義 be unpleasant or bad luck for sb 〜にとって好ましくない,または不運な➡(事が)(〜にとって)酷である,不運である

**rough²** /rʌf/ 名

成句 **in rough** ▶定義 done quickly without worrying about mistakes, as a preparation for the finished piece of work or drawing 完成品または完成図に向けての準備として,間違いを気にしないで素早く行われた➡ざっと,下書きで

**take the rough with the smooth** ▶定義 to accept difficult or unpleasant things in addition to pleasant things 楽しい事に加えて,困難な事や好ましくない事も受け入れる➡人生の幸不幸[運不運]を共に受け入れる

**rough³** /rʌf/ 副 ▶定義 in a rough way➡乱暴に,荒っぽく ‖ *One of the boys was told off for playing rough.* 男の子たちの中の1人は荒っぽいプレーをしてしかられた.

成句 **live/sleep rough** ▶定義 to live or sleep outdoors, usually because you have no home or money 通常家またはお金がないため,戸外に住む,または寝る➡浮浪生活をする,野宿する

**rough⁴** /rʌf/ 動

成句 **rough it** ▶定義 to live without all the comfortable things that you usually have 普段使いつけている快適なものを全く使わないで生活する➡不便を忍ぶ,不自由な生活をする ‖ *You have to rough it a bit when you go camping.* キャンプに行ったときは,少し不便な生活をしなければならない.

**roughage** /ˈrʌfɪdʒ/ 名 ❶ ▶定義 the types or parts of food (fibre) which help your stomach to deal with other foods 胃腸の消化機能を促進するタイプの食物またはその部分(繊維)➡食物繊維(質)

**roughen** /ˈrʌf(ə)n/ 動 他 ▶定義 to make sth less smooth or soft 〜の滑らかさ,または柔らかさを減らす➡〜をざらざらにする,粗くする

\***roughly** /ˈrʌfli/ 副 ▶定義 1 in a violent way; not gently 乱暴に; 穏やかにではなく➡乱暴に,手荒に ‖ *He grabbed her roughly by her arm.* 彼は彼女の腕を乱暴につかんだ. ▶定義 2 not exactly; approximately 正確にではなく; おおよそ➡大体,おおよそ ‖ *It took roughly three hours, I suppose.* おおよそ3時間かかったと思う.

**roulette** /ruːˈlet/ 名 ❶ ▶定義 a game in which a ball is dropped onto a moving wheel that has holes with numbers on them. The players bet on which number hole the ball will be in when the wheel stops. 数字を記したくぼみがいくつもある回転円盤に球を投げ入れるゲーム. 参加者は,回転盤が止まった時にその球がどの数字のくぼみに入るかをかける➡ルーレット

\***round¹** /raʊnd/ 形 ▶定義 having the shape of a circle or a ball 円形または球形をした➡円い,円形の,球状の ‖ *a round table* 丸テーブル

成句 **in round figures/numbers** ▶定義 given to the nearest 10, 100, 1000, etc; not given in exact numbers 10,100,1000 などに最も近い数で表される; 正確な数字では示されていない➡端数のない数で; 概算で,概数で

\***round²** /raʊnd/ 副 前

▶ come round, get round, go round などのように,さまざまな動詞を伴った特別の用法については,その動詞の項を参照.

▶定義 1 in a circle or curve; on all sides of sth 円形には曲線を描いて; 〜の四方に➡(〜を)回って,(〜の)周りに,(〜を)囲んで ‖ *He had a bandage right round his head.* 彼は頭にぐるぐる包帯を巻いていた. *We sat round the table, talking late into the night.* 私たちはテーブルを囲んで座り,夜遅くまでしゃべっていた. *We were just talking about Ravi and he came **round the corner**.* 私たちがちょうどラビのことを話していたら,彼が角を曲がってやって来た. *How long would it take to walk round the world?* 徒歩で世界一周するにはどれくらいかかるでしょうか.(比喩)*It wasn't easy to see a way round the problem (= a way of solving it).* その問題の解決策(＝ 解決する方法)を見つけるのは簡単ではなかった. ▶定義 2 in a full circle 一周して➡(〜を)一回りして,(〜の)周りを回って ‖ *The wheels spun **round and round***

but the car wouldn't move. 車輪はぐるぐる回ったが車は動こうとしなかった. ▶定義3 turning to look or go in the opposite direction 反対の方向を見るために、または反対の方向に進むために、向きを変えて→(〜を)ぐるりと回って、(向きを変えて)反対に ‖ Don't look round but the teacher's just come in. きょろきょろ見回すんじゃないぞ、でも今先生が入ってきたところだ. She turned the car round and drove off. 彼女は車の向きをぐるりと変えて走り去った. ▶定義4 from one place, person, etc to another ある場所・人などから別の場所・人などに→(人々に)回して、行き渡るように ‖ Pass the photographs round for everyone to see. 全員が見られるようにその写真を回してください.
I've been rushing round all day. 私は一日中忙しく走り回っていた. ▶定義5 in or to a particular area or place ある特定の地域・場所において、またはある特定の地域・場所の方へ→(〜の)近くに、辺りに；ある場所へ、出向いて ‖ Do you live round here? あなたはこの近くにお住まいですか. I'll come round to see you at about 8 o'clock. 私は8時ころ、あなたに会いにそちらへ伺います. ▶定義6 in or to many parts of sth 〜の多くの部分に、または多くの部分へ→(〜の)あちこちに、あちこちを、(〜の)方々に、方々を ‖ Let me show you round the house. 家の中をご案内しましょう. He spent six months travelling round Europe. 彼は6か月かけてヨーロッパ中を旅した.

成句 round about (sth) ▶定義 in the area near a place; approximately ある場所に近い所に；およそ→(〜の)近くに、辺りに；約〜、およそ〜、〜ころ ‖ We hope to arrive round about 6. 私たちは6時ころに到着したいと思っている.

the other way round ▶定義 in the opposite way or order 反対の方向または順序で→あべこべに、逆さまに ‖ My appointment's at 3 and Lella's is at 3.15 - or was it the other way round? 私の予約が3時でレラが3時15分です − それともその逆だったかしら.

▶ aroundはroundと同じ意味を持ち、アメリカ英語ではroundよりも一般的.

\*round³ /ráund/ 名 ❻ ▶定義1 a number or series of events, etc いくつかの、または一連の出来事など→繰り返し、連続、(仕事・交渉などの)一区切り ‖ a further round of talks with other European countries ほかのヨーロッパ諸国と今後さらに行う一連の会談 ▶定義2 a regular series of visits, etc, often as part of a job しばしば仕事の一部として、定期的に行う一連の訪問など→巡回、巡視、一回り、一巡 ‖ The postman's round takes him about three hours. 郵便集配人が配達区域を一巡するのに約3時間かかる. Dr Adamou is on his daily round of the wards. アダモ先生は日課となっている病棟の回診に出ているところです.
▶定義3 a number of drinks (one for all the people in a group) 何杯かの飲み物(グループ全員に1杯ずつ)→(飲み物などの)一渡り(分) ‖ It's my round (= it's my turn to buy the drinks). 今度は私がおごる番だ(= 私がその飲み物代を払う番だ). ▶定義4 one part of a game or competition 試合または競技の一部分→1試合、一勝負、1番、1ラウンド、一回り ‖ Parma will play Real Madrid in the next round. パルマは次の試合でレアルマドリッドと対戦する予定だ. ▶定義5 (in golf) one game, usually of 18 holes (ゴルフで)通常は18ホールの、1試合→1ラウンド ‖ to play a round of golf ゴルフを1ラウンドプレーする ▶定義6 a bullet or a number of bullets, fired from a gun 銃から発射された1発または数発の弾丸→(銃などの)1発、一斉射撃 ‖ He fired several rounds at us. 彼は私たちに向け数発発砲した. ▶定義7 a short, sudden period of loud noise 大きな音が突然鳴り出す短い期間→(歓声などの)一しきり ‖ The last speaker got the biggest round of applause. 最後の演説者が最も大きな拍手喝さいを浴びた.

**round⁴** /ráund/ 動 ⓗ ▶定義 to go round sth 〜を回っていく→〜を回る、曲がる ‖ The police car rounded the corner at high speed. パトカーが猛スピードで角を曲がった.

句動詞 round sth off ▶定義 to do sth that completes a job or an activity 仕事または活動の仕上げとなる〜をする→〜を(…で)仕上げる、完成させる、締めくくる ‖ We rounded off the meal with coffee and chocolates. 私たちはコーヒーとチョコレートで食事を締めくくった.

round sb/sth up ▶定義 to bring sb/sth together in one place 〜を1箇所に連れてくる→〜を駆り集める、寄せ集める ‖ The teacher rounded up the children. 先生は子供たちを集めた.

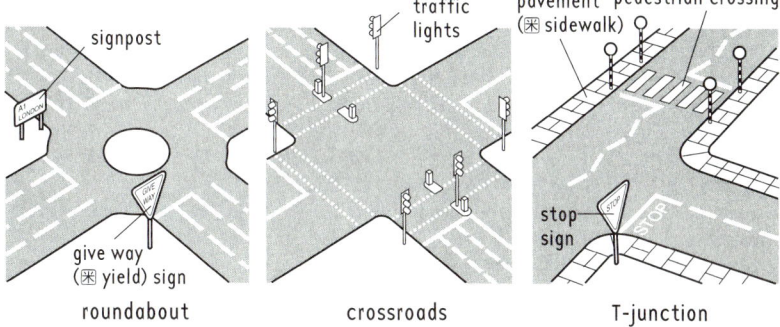

roundabout　　　　　crossroads　　　　　T-junction

**round sth up/down** ▶定義 to increase/decrease a number, price, etc to the nearest whole number 数，価格などを増減して，最も近い整数にする→(端数のない数に)〜を切り上げる，切り捨てる

**roundabout¹** /ráʊndəbàʊt/ 名 ● ▶定義 1 a circle where several roads meet, that all the traffic has to go round in the same direction 数本の道路が出会い，通行車のすべてが同じ方向に回らなければならない環状道路→環状交差路，ロータリー ▶定義 2 a round platform made for children to play on. They sit or stand on it and sb pushes it round. 子供が乗って遊ぶために作られた円い台．子供がその上に座るか立つかし，人が押して回す→球形の回転式遊具 ☛ swing のさし絵 ▶定義 3 = MERRY-GO-ROUND

**roundabout²** /ráʊndəbàʊt/ 形 ▶定義 longer than is necessary or usual; not direct 必要以上に，または通常よりも長い；率直でない→回り道の，遠回りの；(言葉が)遠回しの，えん曲な，間接の ‖ We got lost and came by rather a roundabout route. 私たちは道に迷い，かなり回り道をしてやって来ました．

**rounders** /ráʊndərz/ 名 ⓤ ▶定義 a British game that is similar to baseball 野球に似た英国のゲーム→ラウンダーズ

**round trip** 名 ● ▶定義 1 a journey to a place and back again ある場所に行きまた元の所へ戻る旅→往復旅行 ‖ It's a four-mile round trip to the centre of town. その町の中心までは往復4マイルの道のりです． ▶定義 2 米 = RETURN²(5)

**rouse** /ráʊz/ 動 ⓣ ▶定義 1 正式 to make sb wake up→〜を目覚めさせる，起こす ‖ She was sleeping so soundly that I couldn't rouse her. 彼女はあまりにもぐっすりと眠っていたので起こすことができなかった． ▶定義 2 to make sb/sth very angry, excited, interested, etc 〜を非常に怒らせる，興奮させる，関心をかき立てるなど→〜を怒らせる，刺激する，奮起させる，かき立てる

**rousing** /ráʊzɪŋ/ 形 ▶定義 exciting and powerful 人の心をわくわくさせて，力強い→奮起させる，鼓舞する ‖ a rousing speech 心を奮い立たせる演説

*****rout** /ráʊt/ 動 ⓣ ▶定義 to defeat sb completely 〜を完全に負かす→〜を完全に打ち負かす，総崩れにする ― rout 名 ● →壊滅的敗走，大敗北，総崩れ

**route** /ruːt, ráʊt/ 名 ● ▶定義 1 a route (from A) (to B) a way from one place to another ある場所から別の場所への道→(〜からの・〜への)道，道筋，ルート，航路，路線 ‖ What is the most direct route from Bordeaux to Lyon? ボルドーからリヨンへの最短ルートはどれですか． I got a leaflet about the bus routes from the information office. 案内所でバスの路線図を手に入れた． ▶定義 2 a route to sth a way of achieving sth 〜を達成する方法→(ある目的・結果への)道，手段 ‖ Hard work is the only route to success. 勤勉こそ成功への唯一の道です．

**★routine¹** /ruːtíːn/ 名 ▶定義 1 ⓒ ⓤ the usual order and way in which you regularly do things 物事をいつも通りにやる場合の手順と方法→いつもの手順, 決まり切った仕方 ‖ *Make exercise part of your daily routine.* 運動を日課の1つにしなさい. ▶定義 2 ⓤ tasks that have to be done again and again and so are boring 何度もしなければならず, そのために退屈な仕事→決まり切った仕事, マンネリ化した仕事 ▶定義 3 ⓒ a series of movements, jokes, etc that are part of a performance 演技・興行の一部を成す, 一連の動き, 冗談など→(演技などで)決まり切った所作, 一連の決まり文句, 決まった出し物 ‖ *a dance/comedy routine* 決まり切ったダンスのステップ・コメディーの出し物

**routine²** /ruːtíːn/ 形 ▶定義 1 normal and regular; not unusual or special 標準で正規の; 異常または特別ではない→いつもの, 日常の; 規定通りの, 型通りの, 決まり切った ‖ *The police would like to ask you some routine questions.* 警察はあなたに型通りの質問をしたがっています.

▶定義 2 boring; not exciting 退屈な; わくわくさせない→ありふれた, 月並みな, 代わり映えのしない, マンネリの ‖ *It's a very routine job, really.* それは実に決まり切った仕事なんです, 本当に.

**routinely** /ruːtíːnli/ 副 ▶定義 regularly; as part of a routine 定期的に; 慣例の一部として→いつものように, 日常的に; 規定通りに ‖ *The machines are routinely checked every two months.* 機械は定期的に2か月ごとに点検される.

**★row¹** /róu/ 名 ⓒ ▶定義 1 a line of people or things 人または物の列→列, 並び ‖ *a row of books* 一列に並んだ本 *The children were all standing in a row at the front of the class.* 子供たちは教室の最前部に一列に並んで立っていた. ▶定義 2 a line of seats in a theatre, cinema, etc 劇場, 映画館などの座席の列→座席の列 ‖ *Our seats were in the back row.* 私たちの座席は一番後ろの列だった. *a front-row seat* 最前列の座席

成句 **in a row** ▶定義 one after another; without a break 次から次へ; 間断なく→連続して, 立て続けに ‖ *It rained solidly for four days in a row.* 4日間立て続けに間断なく雨が降り続いた.

**row²** /róu/ 動 ▶定義 1 ⊜ ⓤ to move a boat through the water using long thin pieces of wood with flat parts at the end (oars) 先端部分が平らな細長い木(オール)を使って, 水上でボートを走らせる→ボートをこぐ; ~をこぐ ‖ *We often go rowing on the lake.* 私たちはよく湖にボートをこぎに行きます. ▶定義 2 ⓤ to carry sb/sth in a boat that you row→~をこいで運ぶ ‖ *Could you row us over to the island?* 私たちをあの島までボートで連れていってくれませんか. ☛参 **paddle** — **row** 名 [単数扱い]→オールでこぐこと, ボート遊び

**★row³** /ráu/ 名 ▶定義 1 ⓒ a row (about/over sth) a noisy argument or serious disagreement between two or more people, groups, etc 2人またはそれ以上の人々, 集団などの間の, 騒々しい口論あるいは深刻な意見の不一致→(~のことでの)(騒々しい)けんか, 口論, 論争 ‖ *When I have a row with my girlfriend, I always try to make up as soon as possible.* ガールフレンドと大げんかをしたときは, いつもできるだけ早く仲直りしようとします. *A row has broken out between the main parties over education.* 教育をめぐって2大政党の間で激しい論争が巻き起こった. ▶定義 2 [単数扱い] a loud noise 騒々しい物音→騒音, 騒動, 騒ぎ ‖ *What a row! Could you be a bit quieter?* 何という騒ぎなんでしょう. もう少し静かにできませんか. — **row** 動 ⊜ row (with sb) (about/over sth)→(~と…のことで)けんかする, 口論する ‖ *Pete and I are always rowing about money!* ピートと私はいつもお金のことでけんかばかりしている.

**rowdy** /ráudi/ 形 ▶定義 noisy and likely to cause trouble 騒々しくて問題を起こしそうな→騒々しい, 乱暴な, けんか好きの ‖ *a rowdy group of football fans* 騒々しいサッカーファンの集団 *rowdy behaviour* 粗暴な振る舞い — **rowdily** 副 →騒々しく, 乱暴に — **rowdiness** 名 ⓤ →騒々しさ, 乱暴な行為, 騒ぎ

**rowing boat** ( 米 **rowboat** /róubòut/) 名 ⓒ ▶定義 a small boat that you move through the water using long thin pieces of wood with flat parts at the end (oars) 先端部分が平らな細長い木(オール)を使って水上を進ませる小さなボート→(オールでこぐ)ボート ☛ **boat** のさし絵

**★royal** /rɔ́ɪ(ə)l/ 形 ▶定義 1 connected with a king or queen or a member of their family 王または女王, あるいはその家族の一員に関連した→国

王の, 女王の, 王室の ‖ *the royal family* 王室 ▶定義2 (used in the names of organizations) supported by a member of the royal family（組織の名前に用いて）王室の一員の支援を受けている→王立の, 勅許の ― royal 名 ●略式→王室の一員 ‖ *the Queen, the Princes and other royals* 女王, 皇太子, およびそのほかの王室の人々

**Royal Highness** 名 ● ▶定義 used when you are speaking to or about a member of the royal family 王室の人に話し掛けたり, または彼らに言及するときに用いて→殿下, 妃殿下

**royalty** /rɔ́ɪ(ə)lti/ (複 **royalties**) ▶定義1 ❶ members of the royal family 王室の人々→王族, 王室の人 ▶定義2 ❷ an amount of money that is paid to the person who wrote a book, piece of music, etc every time his/her work is sold or performed 本, 曲などを書いた人に対し, その作品が販売または演奏される度に支払われる金→（著作・作曲などの）印税；（戯曲の）上演料 ‖ *The author earns a 2% royalty on each copy sold.* その作家は本が1冊売れることに2パーセントの印税が入る.

**rpm** /ɑ́ːr piː ém/ 略 revolutions per minute→毎分回転数, 毎分〜回転 ‖ *engine speed 2500 rpm* エンジン速度毎分2500回転

**RSI** /ɑ́ːr es áɪ/ 名 ❶ ▶定義 repetitive strain injury; pain and swelling, especially in the wrists and hands, caused by doing the same movement many times in a job or an activity 仕事または活動中に同じ動きを何度も行うために起きる, 特に手首および手の痛みやはれ→けんしょう炎, 反復運動（過多）損傷

**RSVP** /ɑ́ːr es viː píː/ 略 ▶定義 (used on invitations) please reply（招待状に用いて）→お返事をお願いします

**Rt Hon** 略 Right Honourable ▶定義 a title for Cabinet ministers in the government and some other people in important positions 閣僚および重要な地位にあるほかの人々に対する敬称→閣下

\***rub** /rʌb/ 動 (**rubbing**; **rubbed**) ▶定義1 ❶❷ to move your hand, a cloth, etc backwards and forwards on the surface of sth while pressing firmly 手や布などを何かの表面に強く押し付けるようにして前後に動かす→（表面を）こする, 摩擦する; 〜を(…に)こすり付ける ‖ *Ralph rubbed his hands together to keep them warm.* ラルフ

# rub 1411

は手が冷たくならないように両手をこすり合わせた. *The cat rubbed against my leg.* その猫は私の足に体をすり付けた. ▶定義2 ❷ rub sth in (to sth) to put a cream, liquid, etc onto a surface by rubbing こすって表面にクリーム, 液体などを塗る→〜を(…に)塗る, すり込む ‖ *Apply a little of the lotion and rub it into the skin.* ローションを少し付けて肌にすり込みます. ▶定義3 ❶❷ rub (on/against sth) to press on/against sth, often causing pain or damage 〜に押し付け, しばしば痛みまたは損傷を引き起こす→(〜に)擦れる, こすれ合う ‖ *These new shoes are rubbing my heels.* この新しい靴はかかとに当ってこすれて痛い. ― rub 名 ●→こすること, 磨くこと, 障害, 困難, 難点

成句 rub salt into the wound/sb's wounds ▶定義 to make a situation that makes sb feel bad even worse 〜の気分を悪くさせるような状況を, さらに悪化させる→〜の気持ちをさらに傷付ける, 〜を一層苦しめる

**rub shoulders with sb** ▶定義 to meet and spend time with famous people 有名な人々と会い, 共に時間を過ごす→(有名人・金持ちと)交際する, 付き合う ‖ *As a journalist you rub shoulders with the rich and famous.* ジャーナリストとして, あなたは金持ちや有名人と付き合いがあるでしょう.

句動詞 **rub it/sth in** ▶定義 to keep reminding sb of sth embarrassing that he/she wants to forget 忘れたがっているきまりの悪い〜を, …にいつまでも思い出させる→嫌な事をしつこく言う, 当てこする ‖ *I know it was a stupid mistake, but there's no need to rub it in!* 私だってそれがばかな間違いだったことは分かっている, でもそれをしつこく言わなくたっていいじゃないか.

**rub off (on/onto sb)** ▶定義 (used about a good quality) to be passed from one person to another（良い性質について）ある人から別の人へ伝えられる→(〜に)移る, 受け継がれる, 影響する ‖ *Let's hope some of her enthusiasm rubs off onto her brother.* 彼女とのかかわりの中で, その熱心さがいくらかでも弟に伝わることを願いましょう.

**rub sth off (sth)** ▶定義 to remove sth from a surface by rubbing こすって〜を表面から取り

除く→～をこすり落とす、こすって消す‖ He rubbed the dirt off his boots. 彼はブーツの泥をこすり落とした.

rub sth out ▶定義 to remove the marks made by a pencil, chalk, etc using a rubber, cloth, etc 鉛筆、チョークなどでできた跡を、消しゴム、布などで消す→(文字など)を消しゴムで消す‖ That answer is wrong. Rub it out. その答えは間違っています。消しゴムで消しなさい.

***rubber** /rʌ́bər/ 名 ▶定義1 ❶ a strong substance that can be stretched and does not allow water to pass through it, used for making tyres, boots, etc. Rubber is made from the juice of a tropical tree or is produced using chemicals. 引き伸ばすことが可能で、水を通さない丈夫な物質。これを使ってタイヤや長靴などが作られる。熱帯地方のある植物の樹液、または化学物質を原料として製造される→ゴム、天然ゴム、合成ゴム‖ a rubber ball ゴムボール rubber gloves ゴム手袋 foam rubber 気泡ゴム ▶定義2 ❷(特に 米 **eraser**) a small piece of rubber that you use for removing pencil marks from paper; soft material used for removing chalk marks or pen marks from a board 鉛筆の跡を紙の上から消すのに使う小さなゴム; チョークまたはペンの跡を黒板から消すのに使われる柔らかい布→消しゴム、消すもの、黒板ふき

**rubber band**(または **elastic band**) 名 ❷ ▶定義 a thin circular piece of rubber that is used for holding things together 物を１つにまとめるために使われる、細い輪状のゴム→輪ゴム、ゴムバンド‖ Her hair was tied back with a rubber band. 彼女の髪はゴムバンドで後ろに束ねてあった. ☞ S4 ページのさし絵

**rubber stamp** 名 ❷ ▶定義 a person or group who gives official approval to sth without thinking about it first ～について先に考えることもせず、正式な認可を与えてしまう人または集団→機械的に承認する人・組織 ☞ S4 ページのさし絵 — rubber-stamp 動 他 ～を考えなしに承認する‖ The committee have no real power - they just rubber-stamp the chairman's ideas. その委員たちには実権がありません − 彼らはただ委員長の考えを形式的に承認しているだけです.

**rubbery** /rʌ́b(ə)ri/ 形 ▶定義 like rubber→ゴムのような‖ This meat is rubbery. この肉は硬い.

***rubbish** /rʌ́bɪʃ/ (米 **garbage**; **trash**) 名 ❶ ▶定義1 things that you do not want any more; waste material もう要らない物; 廃棄物→ごみ、くず、廃棄物、がらくた‖ The dustmen collect the rubbish every Monday. ごみ収集人たちは毎週月曜日にごみを集める. a rubbish bin ごみ入れ It's only rubbish - throw it away. それはただのがらくたです − 捨てなさい. ☞参 waste ☞ **bin** のさし絵 ▶定義2 something that you think is bad, silly or wrong 悪い、ばかげている、または間違っていると思うもの→くず、下らないもの、ばかげた考え‖ I thought that film was absolute rubbish. その映画は実に下らないと思った. Don't talk such rubbish. そんなばかげた事を言うな.

**rubbish tip** = TIP¹(4)

**rubble** /rʌ́b(ə)l/ 名 ❶ ▶定義 pieces of broken brick, stone, etc, especially from a damaged building 特に壊れた建物から出た、レンガ、石などの破片→破片、がれき

**rubella** /ruːbélə/ = GERMAN MEASLES

**ruby** /rúːbi/ 名 ❷ (複 **rubies**) ▶定義 a type of precious stone that is red 赤い宝石の一種→ルビー、紅玉

**rucksack** /rʌ́ksæk, rúk-/ 名 ❷ 英 ▶定義 a bag that you use for carrying things on your back 物を背負って運ぶのに使う袋→リュックサック ☞類 backpack, pack ☞ **bag** のさし絵

**rudder** /rʌ́dər/ 名 ❷ ▶定義 a piece of wood or metal that is used for controlling the direction of a boat or plane 船または飛行機の方向を制御するのに使う、木製または金属製のもの→(船の)かじ、(飛行機の)方向舵

***rude** /ruːd/ 形 ▶定義1 rude (to sb) (about sb/sth) not polite 礼儀正しくない→(～に対して) (…について) 失礼な、無礼な、不作法な、ぶしつけな‖ She was very rude to me about my new jacket. 彼女は私の新しい上着のことで大変失礼な事を言った. It's rude to interrupt when people are speaking. 人が話しているときに遮るのは失礼です. I think it was rude of them not to phone and say that they weren't coming. 彼らが電話で来られないと連絡してこなかったのは失礼だと思う. ☞参 impolite ▶定義2 connected with sex, using the toilet, etc in a way that might offend people 性や、人に不快感を与えるような

排せつ行為に関連した➔**みだらな, 下品な, わいせつな** ‖ *a rude joke/word/gesture* 下品な冗談・言葉・身振り ▶定義3 sudden and unpleasant 突然で不愉快な➔**突然の, 出し抜けの, 激しい, 乱暴な, 荒々しい** ‖ *If you're expecting any help from him, you're in for a rude shock.* 彼からの援助を期待しているとしたら, ひどいショックを受けることになるよ. — **rudely** 副➔無礼に, 不作法に; 粗雑に, 大雑把に; 突然に, 荒々しく — **rudeness** 名 **U**➔失礼, 無礼, 無作法

**rudimentary** /ruːdəmént(ə)ri/ 形 ▶定義 very basic or simple 非常に基本的または単純な➔**初歩的な, 基本的な**

**ruffle** /rʌ́f(ə)l/ 動他 ▶定義1 ruffle sth (up) to make sth untidy or no longer smooth 〜を乱雑に散らかす, または平らでなくする➔**(水面)を波立たせる, (髪など)をくしゃくしゃにする** ‖ *to ruffle sb's hair* 〜の髪をくしゃくしゃにする ▶定義2 (しばしば受動態で) to make sb annoyed or confused 〜をいらいらさせる, または混乱させる➔**〜をいら立たせる, 動揺させる**

**rug** /rʌɡ/ 名 **C** ▶定義1 a piece of thick material that covers a small part of a floor 床のわずかな部分を覆う厚い布➔**(小型の)敷物, じゅうたん**
➤ carpet, mat と比較.
☛ C7ページのさし絵 ▶定義2 a large piece of thick cloth that you put over your legs or around your shoulders to keep warm, especially when travelling 特に旅行中, 冷えないように足または肩に掛ける大きな厚い布➔**ひざ掛け**

**rugby** /rʌ́ɡbi/ 名 **U** ▶定義 a form of football that is played by two teams of 13 or 15 players with a roundish ball that can be carried, kicked or thrown 各々13名または15名から成る2つのチームが, 丸を帯びた球を持ったり, けったり, 投げるなどして競うフットボールの一種➔**ラグビー**
➤ Rugby League (ラグビーリーグ) は1チーム13人, Rugby Union (ラグビーユニオン) は15人で行う.
☛参 league

**rugged** /rʌ́ɡəd/ 形 ▶定義1 (used about land) rough, with a lot of rocks and not many plants (土地について)岩も多く, 植物もあまり生えていない, でこぼこの➔**でこぼこの, ごつごつした, 起伏の多い, 岩だらけの** ▶定義2 (used about a man) strong and attractive (人について)強く魅力的な➔**(顔などが)(好ましく)粗削りの, いかつい** ▶定義3 strong and made for difficult conditions 頑強で, 困難な状況に向いている➔**頑丈な, 丈夫な, たくましい**

*★**ruin**¹ /rúːən, -ìn/ 動他 ▶定義1 to damage sth so badly that it loses all its value, pleasure, etc 持っている価値・喜びなど, すべてが失われるほど, 〜をひどく駄目にする➔**〜を破滅させる, 崩壊させる, 荒廃させる, 台なしにする** ‖ *a ruined building* 荒廃した建物 *The bad news ruined my week.* 悪い知らせで私の1週間は台なしになった. *That one mistake ruined my chances of getting the job.* あの1つの間違いで私はその仕事をつかむ機会をふいにしてしまった. ▶定義2 to cause sb to lose all his/her money, hope of being successful, etc 〜に全財産, 成功の望みなどを失わせる➔**〜を没落させる, 零落させる, 破産させる** ‖ *The cost of the court case nearly ruined them.* 裁判の費用で彼らは破産したと言ってもいいくらいだ.

*★**ruin**² /rúːən, -ìn/ 名 ▶定義1 **U** the state of being destroyed or very badly damaged 破壊された, またはひどい損傷を受けた状態➔**荒廃, 崩壊, 壊滅状態** ‖ *The city was in a state of ruin.* その都市は壊滅状態だった. ▶定義2 **U** the cause or state of having lost all your money, hope of being successful, etc 全財産, 成功の望みなどを失った原因, または失った状態➔**破滅の原因, 破滅, 破産** ‖ *Many small companies are facing financial ruin.* 多くの小さな会社が財政的破たんに直面している. ▶定義3 **C** the parts of a building that are left standing after it has been destroyed or badly damaged 破壊された, またはひどい損傷を受けた後, そのまま残っている建物の部分➔**廃虚, 遺跡, 残骸(ざんがい)** ‖ *the ruins of the ancient city of Pompeii* 古代都市ポンペイの遺跡

**成句 go to rack and ruin** ⇒ **RACK**¹
**in ruin(s)** ▶定義 badly damaged or destroyed ひどく損傷を受けた, または破壊された➔**(建物など)廃虚となって, 荒廃して, 崩壊して; (計画・希望など)駄目になって** ‖ *After the accident her life seemed to be in ruins.* その事故の後, 彼女の人生はめちゃくちゃになってしまったようだ.

**ruinous** /rúːənəs, -sənəs/ 形 ▶定義 causing serious problems, especially with money 特に金銭的な深刻な問題をもたらす➡破産のもとになるような、破産を招く

\***rule**¹ /ruːl/ 名 ▶定義1 ❻an official statement that tells you what you must or must not do in a particular situation or when playing a game ある特定の状況において、またはゲームをしているときにしなければならない事、あるいはしてはならない事を公式に示したもの➡規則、規程、規約、ルール、決まり ‖ to **obey/break a rule** 規則を守る・破る *Do you know the rules of chess?* チェスのルールを知っていますか. *It's **against the rules** to smoke in this area.* この区画で喫煙するのは規則違反です. *The company have strict **rules and regulations** governing employees' dress.* その会社には、従業員の服装を規制する厳格な、細かい規則がある.

▶ law (法) の方が強い意味を持つ. 破った場合には、公式に罰せられることがある.

▶定義2 ❻a piece of advice about what you should do in a particular situation ある特定の状況でどうすべきかについての助言➡定則、通則 ‖ *When you run a marathon, the **golden rule** is: don't start too fast.* マラソンを走るときの大原則: スタートから飛ばしすぎてはならない. ▶定義3 [単数扱い] what is usual 通例であること➡習慣、習わし;普通のこと、常態 ‖ *Large families are the exception rather than the rule nowadays.* 大家族は最近では普通というよりむしろ例外です. *As a general rule, women live longer than men.* 一般に女性は男性よりも長生きする. *I don't read much as a rule.* 私は概してあまり読書をしません. ▶定義4 ❻(in a language) a description of what is usual or correct (言語で) 慣用的または規範的な事を記述したもの➡規則 ‖ *What is the rule for forming the past tense?* 過去形にするときの規則はどのようなものですか. ▶定義5 ❶government; control➡統治;支配 ‖ *The country is **under military rule**.* その国は軍の支配下にある.

成句 bend the rule ⇒ **BEND**¹

a rule of thumb ▶定義 a simple piece of practical advice, not involving exact details or figures 正確な細目または数字を含んでいない、簡潔で実際的な助言➡経験則、経験的にまず間違いのないやり方・知恵

work to rule ▶定義 to follow the rules of your job in a very strict way in order to cause delay, as a form of protest against your employer or your working conditions 雇用者または労働環境に抗議する1つの方法として、業務を遅滞させるために、業務規則を非常に厳密に守る➡順法闘争を行う

\***rule**² /ruːl/ 動 自 他 ▶定義1 rule (over sb/sth) to have the power over a country, group of people, etc 国、団体などを支配する➡支配する、統治する;〜を支配する、統治する ‖ *Julius Caesar ruled over a vast empire.* ジュリアス シーザーは広大な帝国を支配した. (比喩) *His whole life was ruled by his ambition to become President.* 彼の全人生は、大統領になりたいという野望に支配されていた. ▶定義2 rule (on sth); rule (in favour of/against sb/sth) to make an official decision 公式判断を下す➡(〜に関し;〜に有利・不利に)裁決する、裁定を下す判決を下す;〜を裁決する、裁定する、〜であると決定する ‖ *The judge will rule on whether or not the case can go ahead.* 裁判官はその訴訟が審理に値するものか決めるだろう.

句動詞 rule sb/sth out ▶定義 to say that sb/sth is not possible, cannot do sth, etc; to prevent sth 〜は可能ではない、〜をすることはできないなどと言う;〜を阻止する➡(可能性など)を否定する、不可能にする;妨げる ‖ *The government has ruled out further increases in train fares next year.* 政府は、来年列車の運賃をさらに値上げすることを認めないとした.

**ruler** /ˈruːlər/ 名 ❻ ▶定義1 a person who rules a country, etc 国などを治める人➡支配者、統治者 ▶定義2 a straight piece of wood, plastic, etc marked with centimetres, that you use for measuring sth or for drawing straight lines 〜の長さを計る、または直線を引くために用いる、センチメートル単位の目盛りの付いた木製、プラスチック製などの直線形の道具➡定規、物差し ☞ S4 ページのさし絵

**ruling**¹ /ˈruːlɪŋ/ 形 (名詞の前だけ) ▶定義 with the most power in an organization, country, etc 組織、国などで最も権力を持っている➡支配する、有力な ‖ *the ruling political party* 与党

**ruling**² /ˈruːlɪŋ/ 名 ❻ ▶定義 an official decision➡判決、裁決

**rum** /rʌm/ 名 U C ▶定義 a strong alcoholic drink that is made from the juice of a plant from which sugar is made (sugar cane) 砂糖の原料となる植物(サトウキビ)の汁から作られた，アルコール度の高い飲み物→ラム酒

**rumble** /rʌ́mb(ə)l/ 動 自 ▶定義 to make a deep heavy sound 低く重苦しい音を立てる→ゴロゴロ鳴る，とどろく ‖ *I was so hungry that my stomach was rumbling.* あまりにも空腹だったのでおなかがグーグー鳴っていた． — **rumble** 名 [単数扱い]→ゴロゴロ，低い雑音 ‖ *a rumble of thunder* 雷がゴロゴロと鳴る音

**rummage** /rʌ́mɪdʒ/ 動 自 ▶定義 to move things and make them untidy while you are looking for sth ～を探す間に，物を動かして散らかす→かき回して探す，探し回る ‖ *Nina rummaged through the drawer looking for the tin-opener.* ニナは引き出しをかき回して缶切りを探した．

★**rumour**(米 **rumor**) /rúːmər/ 名 C U ▶定義 (a) rumour (about/of sb/sth) (a piece of) news or information that many people are talking about but that is possibly not true 大勢の人が話しているが，ことによると真実ではないかもしれない消息，または情報→(～についての)うわさ，風評，流言 ‖ *I didn't start the rumour about Barry's operation.* バリーの手術のことでうわさを立てたのは私ではありません． ***Rumour has it*** (= people are saying) *that Lena has resigned.* うわさによると(= 人々が言っている)リナは辞めたらしい． *to confirm/deny a rumour* (= to say that it is true/not true) うわさを肯定する・否定する(= それが本当である・本当ではないと言う)．

**rumoured** (米 **rumored**) /rúːmərd/ 形 ▶定義 reported or said, but perhaps not true 報告されている，または言われているが，おそらく真実ではない→うわさされている，うわさの ‖ *They are rumoured to be getting divorced.* 彼らは離婚するだろうとうわさされている．

**rump** /rʌmp/ 名 C ▶定義 the back end of an animal 動物のしりの部分→(動物の)しり ‖ *rump steak* (= meat from the rump) ランプステーキ(= しり肉)

★**run**¹ /rʌn/ 動 自 他 (現分 **running**; 過 **ran** /ræn/; 過分 **run**) ▶定義1 自 他 to move using your legs, going faster than a walk 足を使って，歩くよりも速く動く→走る，駆ける；(ある距離)を走っていく ‖ *I had to run to catch the bus.* バスに間に合うように走らなければならなかった． *I often **go running** in the evenings* (= as a hobby). 夜によくランニングに出掛ける(= 趣味として)． *I ran nearly ten kilometres this morning.* 今朝10キロ近く走った． ▶定義2 自 他 to move, or move sth, quickly in a particular direction ある方向に素早く移動する，または～を動かす→急いでいく，駆け付ける；(手・指など)を(…に)さっと走らせる ‖ *I've been running around after the kids all day.* 一日中，子供の後をあちこち追い掛け回していた． *The car ran off the road and hit a tree.* その車は道路から誤って外れ木にぶつかった． *She ran her finger down the list of passengers.* 彼女は乗客リストをさっと指でたどった． ▶定義3 自 to lead from one place to another; to be in a particular position ある場所から別の場所に至る；特定の位置にある→(線路・道路などが)通じている，走っている ‖ *The road runs along the side of a lake.* その道路は湖沿いに延びている． ▶定義4 他 to organize or be in charge of sth; to provide a service ～を組織する，または～の責任を持つ；サービスを提供する→(店・会社など)を経営する，(会など)を運営する；(講座・サービスなど)を行う ‖ *She runs a restaurant.* 彼女はレストランを経営している． *They run English courses all the year round.* 彼らは一年中，英語の講座を開いている． ▶定義5 自 他 to operate or function; to make sth do this 作動する，または機能する；～を作動・機能させる→(機械などが)動く，作動する；～を動かす，操作する ‖ *The engine is running very smoothly now.* 今，エンジンは非常に円滑に作動している． *We're running a new computer program today.* 今日，新しいコンピュータープログラムを操作する予定だ． ▶定義6 自 to operate at a particular time 特定の時間に運行する→(車・船などが)走る，(バス・列車などが)定期的に運行する，通っている ‖ *All the trains are **running late** this morning.* 今朝はすべての列車の運行が遅れています． *We'd better hurry up - we're **running behind schedule**.* 私たちは急いだ方がいい ― 予定より遅れている． ▶定義7 他 to use and pay for a vehicle 車を使い，その費用を支払う→(車など)を維持する，所有する ‖ *It costs a lot to*

## 1416 run¹

*run a car.* 車を持つのはお金がひどくかかる. ▶定義8 ⓔ to continue for a time しばらくの間,継続する→続く,及ぶ,(劇などが)続演される ‖ *My contract has two months left to run.* 私の契約はあと2か月有効です. *The play ran for nearly two years in a London theatre.* その演劇はロンドンの劇場で2年間近く上演された. ▶定義9 ⓔ ⓐ (used about water or other liquid) to flow; to make water flow (水またはそのほかの液体について) 流れる; 水を流す→流れる,滴る; 〜を流す,放出する ‖ *When it's really cold, my nose runs.* 本当に寒いと鼻水が出る. *I can hear a tap running somewhere.* どこかの蛇口から水が出ているのが聞こえる. *to run a bath/a tap* ふろに水を張る・水道の蛇口から水を出す ▶定義10 ⓔ run with sth to be covered with flowing water 流れる液体に覆われる→(体の一部などが)液体を流す,出す ‖ *My face was running with sweat.* 私の顔は汗まみれになっていた. ▶定義11 ⓔ (used about the colour in material, etc) to spread, for example when the material is washed (生地などの色について) 例えば生地が洗われたときに色が広がる→落ちる,にじむ ‖ *Don't put that red shirt in the washing machine. It might run.* その赤いシャツを洗濯機に入れてはいけません.色落ちするかもしれません. ▶定義12 ⓔ run (for sth) to be one of the people hoping to be chosen (a candidate) in an election 選挙で当選を望んでいる人(候補者)の1人である→(〜に)立候補する,出馬する ‖ *He's running for president.* 彼は大統領戦に出馬している. ▶定義13 ⓐ to publish sth in a newspaper or magazine 新聞または雑誌に〜を掲載する→(広告・記事など)を掲載する ‖ *'The Independent' is running a series of articles on pollution.* 『インディペンデント』紙は汚染に関する記事を連載している. ▶定義14 ⓐ run a test/check (on sth) to do a test or check on sth 〜に関してテストまたは調査を行う→〜を行う,実施する ‖ *They're running checks on the power supply to see what the problem is.* 当局は,問題が何であるか知るために,電力供給に関する調査を行っている.

成句 be running at ▶定義 to be at a certain level ある水準にある→(大きさ・数量などが)(平均して)〜である

run for it ▶定義 to run in order to escape 逃げるために走る→(特に命令文で)急いで逃げる

▶ runを含むこのほかの成句については,名詞,形容詞などの項を参照.例えば run in the family は family の項にある.

句動詞 run across sb/sth ▶定義 to meet or find sb/sth by chance→〜に偶然出会う,〜を偶然見つける

run after sb/sth ▶定義 to try to catch sb/sth 〜を捕まえようとする→〜を追い掛ける,追跡する

run away ▶定義 to escape from somewhere ある場所から逃げる→(〜から)逃げる,逃げ出す,家出する,駆け落ちする ‖ *He's run away from home.* 彼は家出した.

run sb/sth down ▶定義1 to hit a person or an animal with your vehicle 車で人または動物にぶつかる→(車・運転者が)(人など)を跳ねる,ひく ‖ *She was run down by a bus.* 彼女はバスにひかれた. ▶定義2 to criticize sb/sth 〜を批判する→〜をけなす,こき下ろす ‖ *He's always running her down in front of other people.* 彼はいつも人前で彼女をけなしてばかりいる.

run (sth) down ▶定義 to stop functioning gradually; to make sth do this 次第に機能しなくなる; 〜をそのようにする→(時計などが)止まる,(電池などが)切れる; 〜を弱らせる,(規模など)を縮小する ‖ *Turn the lights off or you'll run the battery down.* 明かりを消しなさい.さもないとバッテリーが上がってしまうでしょう.

run into sb ▶定義 to meet sb by chance→〜に偶然出会う,ばったり出会う

run into sth ▶定義 to have difficulties or a problem 困難または問題を抱える→(問題)にぶつかる,(困難など)に陥る ‖ *If you run into any problems, just let me know.* 何か問題にぶつかったら,すぐ私に知らせなさい.

run (sth) into sb/sth ▶定義 to hit sb/sth with a car, etc 車で〜にぶつかる→〜にぶつかる,衝突する ‖ *He ran his car into a brick wall.* 彼は車をれんが塀にぶつけた.

run sth off ▶定義 to copy sth, using a machine 機械を使ってコピーする→〜を印刷する,コピーする

run off with sth ▶定義 to take or steal sth 〜を取る,または盗む→〜を持ち去る,持ち逃げする

**run out (of sth)** ▶定義 to finish your supply of sth; to come to an end ～の蓄えを使い果たす; 終わる➡～を使い果たす,切らす;(在庫品などが) なくなる, 尽きる,(期限などが)切れる ‖ *We've run out of coffee.* 私たちはコーヒーを切らしてしまった. *Time is running out.* もう少しで時間切れになる. *My passport runs out next month.* 私のパスポートは来月切れる.

**run sb/sth over** ▶定義 to hit a person or an animal with your vehicle 車で人または動物にぶつかる➡～をひく, 跳ねる ‖ *The child was run over as he was crossing the road.* 子供は道路を横断中に車にひかれた.

**run through sth** ▶定義 to discuss or read sth quickly ～についてざっと話し合う, ～をざっと読む➡～をざっと調べる, ～にざっと目を通す, ～を(さっと)読み返す ‖ *She ran through the names on the list.* 彼女は名簿にざっと目を通した.

★**run**² /rʌn/ 名 ▶定義 1 ●an act of running on foot 足を使って走る行為➡走ること, 一走り, 競走 ‖ *I go for a three-mile run every morning.* 私は毎朝3マイル走りに行く. *The prisoner tried to **make a run for it** (= to escape on foot).* 囚人は急いで逃げようとした(= 走って逃げようとした). ▶定義 2 ●a journey by car, train, etc 車, 列車などの道程➡運行, 路線 ‖ *The bus driver was picking up kids on the school run.* バスの運転手は通学路線で子供たちを拾っていた. ▶定義 3 [単数扱い] a series of similar events or sth that continues for a very long time 一連の類似した出来事または非常に長い間続く～➡(ある状況・事態の)連続,(劇・映画などの)連続公演[上映] ‖ *We've had a run of bad luck recently.* 私たちはこのところ不運続きです. ▶定義 4 [単数扱い] **a run on sth** a sudden great demand for sth ～に対する突然の大きな需要➡大需要, 注文殺到, 大売れ行き ▶定義 5 ●a point in the games of baseball and cricket 野球・クリケットの試合の得点➡得点, 1点

成句 **in the long run** ⇒ **LONG**¹

**on the run** ▶定義 hiding or trying to escape from sb/sth ～から隠れて, または逃げようとして➡逃走中の, 退却中の ‖ *The escaped prisoner is still on the run.* 脱獄囚はまだ逃走中です.

**runaway**¹ /rʌ́nəwèɪ/ 形 ▶定義 1 out of control➡制御できない, 手に負えない ‖ *a runaway horse/car/train* 放れ馬・暴走車・暴走列車 ▶定義 2 happening very easily あっさりと起こって➡あっと言う間に起こった, たやすい,(勝利などが)楽々と得られた ‖ *a runaway victory* 圧勝

**runaway**² /rʌ́nəwèɪ/ 名 ● ▶定義 a person, especially a child, who has left or escaped from somewhere どこかから出ていった, または逃げ出した人, 特に子供➡家出人[少年・少女], 逃亡者, 脱走者

**run-down** 形 ▶定義 1 (used about a building or place) in bad condition (建物または場所について)悪い状態で➡荒廃した, 衰退した, 活気のない ‖ *a run-down block of flats* 荒廃したフラット式の共同住宅 ▶定義 2 very tired and not healthy 非常に疲れて健康でない➡疲れ切った, 健康を害した

**rung**¹ /rʌŋ/ 名 ● ▶定義 one of the bars that form the steps of a ladder はしごに足掛かりとして付いているいくつもの横木の1つ➡はしごの段 ☞ **ladder** のさし絵

**rung**² **RING**² の過去分詞形

**runner** /rʌ́nər/ 名 ● ▶定義 1 a person or animal that runs, especially in a race 特に競走で, 走る人または動物➡走る人, 走る動物, (競技の)走者, ランナー, 出走馬 ‖ *a long-distance runner* 長距離走者 ▶定義 2 a person who takes guns, drugs, etc illegally from one country to another 銃, 麻薬などを違法にある国から別の国に運ぶ人➡密輸業者

**runner-up** 名 ● (複 **runners-up**) ▶定義 the person or team that finished second in a race or competition 競技・競争で2位になった個人またはチーム➡次点者・チーム, 2着の者・チーム

★**running**¹ /rʌ́nɪŋ/ 名 ● ▶定義 1 the action or sport of running 走る行為またはスポーツ➡走ること, ランニング, 競走 ‖ *How often do you **go running**?* あなたはどのくらい走りに行くのですか. *running shoes* ランニングシューズ ▶定義 2 the process of managing a business or other organization 事業またはそのほかの組織を経営すること➡経営, 管理, 運転 ‖ *She's not involved in the day-to-day running of the office.* 彼女は事務所の日々の運営にはかかわっていません. *the **running costs** of a car (= petrol, insurance, repairs, etc)* 車の維持費(= ガソリ

ン, 保険, 修理など)

**成句 in/out of the running (for sth)** 略式 ▶定義 having/not having a good chance of getting or winning sth 〜に勝つ, 〜を獲得する見込みがかなりある・ない→(競技などで)**勝ち目があって・なくて**

\***running**² /rʌ́nɪŋ/ 形 ▶定義 1 used after a number and a noun to say that sth has happened a number of times in the same way without a change 〜が同じように変わることなく何回か起こった事を表すために, 数字や名詞の後に使われて→**連続する, 繰り返される** || *Our school has won the competition for four years running.* 私たちの学校はその競技に4年連続優勝している. ▶定義 2 (名詞の前だけ) flowing or available from a tap (used about water) (水について) 流れている, 蛇口をひねればいつでも使える→(水などが)**流れている** || *There is no running water in the cottage.* その小屋には水道がない. ▶定義 3 (名詞の前だけ) not stopping; continuous 止まっていない; 切れ目なく続いて→(長期的に)**続いている** || *a running battle between two rival gangs* 2つの敵対する暴力団同士の間断のない戦い

**running commentary** 名 C ▶定義 a spoken description of sth while it is happening 〜について, 同時進行的に口頭で行う説明→**実況放送**

**runny** /rʌ́ni/ 形 略式 ▶定義 1 containing more liquid than is usual or than you expected 通常よりも, または予想よりも多くの液体を含んでいる→(固まり方が)**緩い, 水っぽい** || *runny jam* 柔らかすぎるジャム ▶定義 2 (used about your eyes or nose) producing too much liquid (目・鼻について) 分泌液が多すぎる→**涙の出る, 鼻水の出る** || *Their children always seem to have runny noses.* 彼らの子供たちはいつも鼻水を垂らしているようだ.

**run-up** 名 [単数扱い] ▶定義 1 the period of time before a certain event ある出来事の前の期間→**準備期間** || *the run-up to the election* 選挙へ向けての準備期間 ▶定義 2 (in sport) a run that people do in order to be going fast enough to do an action (スポーツで)ある動作に必要な速度を十分に付けるためにする走り→**助走**

**runway** /rʌ́nweɪ/ 名 C ▶定義 a long piece of ground with a hard surface where aircraft take off and land at an airport 空港で航空機が離着陸する, 表面の硬い帯状の地面→**滑走路**

**rupture** /rʌ́ptʃər/ 名 C U ▶定義 1 a sudden bursting or breaking 突然の破壊→**破裂; (内臓器官の)破裂** ▶定義 2 正式 the sudden ending of good relations between two people or groups 2人または2つのグループの間の良好な関係が突然終わること→**決裂, 破たん** ― rupture 動 自 他 →**破裂する, 裂ける; 〜を破裂させる, 裂く** || *Her appendix ruptured and she had to have emergency surgery.* 彼女は盲腸が破裂し緊急手術を受けねばならなかった.

**rural** /rúːrəl/ 形 ▶定義 connected with the country, not the town 町ではなく田舎に関係した→**田舎の, 田園の, 農村の** ☞参 urban, rustic

**ruse** /ruːz/ 名 C ▶定義 a trick or clever plan 策略または巧妙な計画→**策略, 計画**

\***rush**¹ /rʌʃ/ 動 ▶定義 1 自 他 to move or do sth with great speed, often too fast 大変な速度で, しばしば過度の速度で移動する, または〜を行う→**大急ぎで行く; 〜を急いでやる** || *I rushed back home when I got the news.* その知らせを聞いて大急ぎで家に戻った. *Don't rush off - I want to talk to you.* 急いで行かないでください ― 話があるんだから. *The public rushed to buy shares in the new company.* 人々はその新会社の株を買いに走った. ▶定義 2 他 to take sb/sth to a place very quickly→〜を(…へ)大急ぎで運ぶ || *He suffered a heart attack and **was rushed to hospital**.* 彼は心臓まひに見舞われて病院に急送された. ▶定義 3 自 他 rush (sb) (into sth/into doing sth) to do sth or make sb do sth without thinking about it first 先に考えることをしないで大急ぎで行動する, または〜に…を急いでさせる→**(〜を)せっかちにする, 急いでする; 〜をせき立てて…させる** || *Don't let yourself be rushed into marriage.* 慌てて結婚しないことです. *Don't rush me - I'm thinking!* 私をせかさないで ― 考えている最中なのだから.

**成句 be rushed/run off your feet** ⇒ **FOOT**¹

\***rush**² /rʌʃ/ 名 ▶定義 1 [単数扱い] a sudden quick movement 突然の素早い動き→**突進, 突撃** || *At the end of the match there was a rush for the exits.* 試合が終了すると皆が出口に殺到した. *I was so nervous, all my words came out* *in a rush*. とても緊張していたので，すべての言葉がわーっと一気に出てしまった．▶定義2 [単数扱い，**U**] a situation in which you are in a hurry and need to do things quickly 急いでいて，物事を急いでしなければならない状況→**慌ただしさ，急ぐこと，急ぎ** ‖ *I can't stop now. I'm in a terrible rush.* 今立ち止まってはいられません．ひどく急いでいますから．*Don't hurry your meal. There's no rush.* 慌てて食事をしなくても大丈夫です．急いでいませんから．▶定義3 [単数扱い] a rush (on sth) a time when many people try to get sth 大勢の人が～を得ようとするとき→**(人などの)殺到，(需要・注文などの)急増** ‖ *There's been a rush to buy petrol before the price goes up.* 値上がりする前に石油を買おうと人々が殺到した．▶定義4 [単数扱い] a time when there is a lot of activity and people are very busy 多くの活動があって，人々が多忙なとき→**目まぐるしさ，混雑，ラッシュ** ‖ *We'll leave early to avoid the rush.* 混雑を避けるため早めに出発しましょう．▶定義5 **C** a type of tall grass that grows near water 水辺に生える背の高い草の一種→**イグサ，トウシンソウ** ☞ C2 ページのさし絵

**rush hour** 名 **C** ▶定義 the times each day when there is a lot of traffic because people are travelling to or from work 1日のうち，通勤する人々で交通量の多い時間→**混雑時間，ラッシュアワー** ‖ *rush-hour traffic* ラッシュアワーの交通量

**rust** /rʌst/ 名 **U** ▶定義 a reddish-brown substance that forms on the surface of iron, etc, caused by the action of air and water 空気と水の作用で鉄などの表面に形成される赤茶色の物質→**さび** — rust 動自他→**さびる，さびつく；～をさびさせる** ‖ *Some parts of the car had rusted.* 車の一部の部品はさびてしまっていた．

**rustic** /ˈrʌstɪk/ 形 ▶定義 typical of the country or of country people; simple 田舎または田舎の人に典型的な；素朴な→**田舎の，田園の，素朴な** ‖ *The whole area is full of rustic charm.* その地域全体が田舎の魅力にあふれている．☞参 **rural**, **urban**

**rustle** /ˈrʌs(ə)l/ 動自他 ▶定義 to make a sound like dry leaves or paper moving 枯れ葉や紙が動くときのような音を立てる→**サラサラと音を立てる，サラサラ・カサカサいう；～をサラサラと音**

を立てさせる ‖ *There was a rustling noise in the bushes.* 茂みでカサカサと音がした．— rustle 名 [単数扱い]→**サラサラ・カサカサという音，衣(きぬ)擦れの音**

句動詞 rustle sb/sth up 略式 ▶定義 to find sb or prepare sth in a short time 短期間に～を見つける，または…を準備する→**(人・物を)かき集める，(食事など)を(有り合わせの物で)急いでこしらえる** ‖ *to rustle up a quick snack* 有り合わせの食事を急いでこしらえる

\*rusty /ˈrʌsti/ 形 ▶定義1 (used about metal objects) covered with a brownish substance (rust) as a result of being in contact with water and air (金属の物体について) 水と空気に接触する結果，茶色がかった物質(さび)で覆われた→**さびた，さびついた** ‖ *rusty tins* さびついたブリキの缶 ▶定義2 (used about a skill) not as good as it was because you have not used it for a long time (技能について) 長い間使っていなかったため以前ほど優れていない→**鈍った，衰えた，下手になった** ‖ *My French is rather rusty.* 私のフランス語はかなりさびついている．

**rut** /rʌt/ 名 **C** ▶定義 a deep track that a wheel makes in soft ground 車輪が柔らかい地面に付ける深い跡→**わだち，車の跡**

成句 be in a rut ▶定義 to have a boring way of life that is difficult to change 変えることが難しい退屈な生き方をする→**型にはまっている，マンネリに陥っている**

**ruthless** /ˈruːθləs/ 形 ▶定義 (used about people and their behaviour) hard and cruel; determined to get what you want and showing no pity to others (人またはその行動について) 厳しく残酷な；断固として欲しいものは手に入れ，他人に対して情け容赦もない→**無慈悲な，冷酷な，情け容赦のない** ‖ *a ruthless dictator* 冷酷な独裁者 — ruthlessly 副→**無慈悲に，冷酷に** — ruthlesness 名 **U**→**無慈悲さ，冷酷さ**

**rye** /raɪ/ 名 **U** ▶定義 a plant that is grown in colder countries for its grain, which is used to make flour and also an alcoholic drink (whisky) 小麦粉およびアルコール飲料(ウイスキー)の原料になる，寒い方の国で穀物として栽培される植物→**ライムギ，クロムギ** ☞ **cereal** のさし絵

# S s

**S, s¹** /es/ 名 C (複 **S's; s's**) ▶定義 the nineteenth letter of the English alphabet 英語アルファベットの第19文字 → s (S) が表す音, s (S) の文字, s (S) の字形のもの ‖ *'School' begins with (an) 'S'.* School はSで始まる.

**S²** 略 ▶定義1 small (size) → S (サイズ) ▶定義2 (米 **So**) south(ern) → 南, 南の ‖ *S Yorkshire* 南ヨークシャー

**sabbath** /sǽbəθ/ (または **the Sabbath**) 名 [単数扱い] ▶定義 the day of the week for rest and prayer in certain religions (Sunday for Christians, Saturday for Jews) ある特定の宗教における安息と祈りの曜日 (キリスト教では日曜日, ユダヤ教では土曜日) → 安息日

**sabotage** /sǽbətɑ̀ːʒ/ 名 U ▶定義 damage that is done on purpose and secretly in order to prevent an enemy or competitor being successful, for example by destroying machinery, roads, bridges, etc 敵対または競争する相手の成功を阻止するために, 例えば, 機械, 道路, 橋などの破壊工作を通して, 故意かつ秘密に行う破壊行為 → サボタージュ, 妨害行為 ‖ *industrial/economic/military sabotage* 産業・経済・軍事面に対する破壊活動 ― **sabotage** 動 他 → ～に破壊行為を行う, ～を妨害する

**saccharin** /sǽk(ə)rən/ 名 U ▶定義 a very sweet substance that can be used instead of sugar 砂糖の代用となる甘味料 → サッカリン

**sachet** /sǽʃeɪ, -/ 名 C ▶定義 a small plastic or paper packet that contains a small amount of liquid or powder 少量の液体や粉末を入れるプラスチックまたは紙の小袋 → 袋 ‖ *a sachet of shampoo/sugar/coffee* (1回分の) シャンプー・砂糖・コーヒーの入った小袋 ☞ **container** のさし絵

**sack¹** /sæk/ 名 C ▶定義 a large bag made from a rough heavy material, paper or plastic, used for carrying or storing things 物の運搬または貯蔵に使われる, 丈夫で厚手の布, 紙またはプラスチック製の大きな袋 → (大) 袋, ずだ袋 ‖ *sacks of flour/potatoes* 小麦粉・ジャガイモの入った袋

成句 **get the sack** 英 ▶定義 to be told by your employer that you can no longer continue working for him/her (usually because you have done sth wrong) (通常, 過ちを犯したため) 雇い主から解雇を言い渡される → 首になる, 解雇される ‖ *Tony got the sack for poor work.* トニーは働きが悪かったので首になった.

**give sb the sack** 英 ▶定義 to tell an employee that he/she can no longer continue working for you (because of bad work, behaviour, etc) (仕事振り, 態度などが悪いため) 従業員に解雇を告げる → ～を首にする, 解雇する ‖ *Tony's work wasn't good enough and he was given the sack.* トニーは働きが良いとは言えなかったので, 首を言い渡された.

**sack²** /sæk/ (特に 米 **fire**) 動 他 ▶定義 to tell an employee that he/she can no longer work for you (because of bad work, bad behaviour, etc) (仕事振り, 態度などが悪いため) 従業員に解雇を告げる → ～を首にする, 解雇する ‖ *Her boss has threatened to sack her if she's late again.* 上司は彼女にもう一度遅刻したら首だと脅した.

**sacred** /séɪkrəd/ 形 ▶定義1 connected with God, a god or religion 神や宗教に関連した → 宗教的な, 神聖な ‖ *The Koran is the sacred book of Muslims.* コーランはイスラム教の聖典だ. ▶定義2 too important and special to be changed or harmed 変更したり侵してはならないほど重要で特殊な → 侵し難い, 尊重すべき ‖ *a sacred tradition* 侵し難い伝統

**sacrifice¹** /sǽkrəfàɪs/ 名 U C ▶定義1 giving up sth that is important or valuable to you in order to get or do sth that seems more important; sth that you give up in this way より重要に思われるものを得たり実行するため, 自分にとって重要または価値のあるものをあきらめること; そのようにしてあきらめたもの → 犠牲 ‖ *If we're going to have a holiday this year, we'll have to make some sacrifices.* 今年休暇を取るつもりならば, 私たちは何か (を) 犠牲にしなければならないでしょう. ▶定義2 **sacrifice (to sb)** the act of offering sth to a god, especially an animal that has been killed in a special way; an animal, etc that is offered in this way 神への供物として, 特に特殊な方法で殺した動物をささげること; そのようにしてささげられた動物など → (～に) いけにえをささげること; いけにえ

**sacrifice²** /sǽkrəfàɪs/ 動 他 ▶定義1 **sacrifice sth (for sb/sth)** to give up sth that is important or valuable to you in order to get or do sth that seems more important より重要に思われるものを得たり実行するため, 自分にとって重要または価値のあるものをあきらめる→〜を(…のために)犠牲にする ‖ *She is not willing to sacrifice her career in order to have children.* 彼女は子供を産むために自分の仕事を犠牲にしたいとは思わない. ▶定義2 🔵 🔴 to kill an animal and offer it to a god, in order to please the god 神を喜ばせるため, 動物を殺してささげる→いけにえをささげる; 〜をいけにえとしてささげる

**sacrilege** /sǽkrəlɪdʒ/ 🔵 [🔴, 単数扱い] ▶定義 treating a religious object or place without the respect that it deserves 当然払うべき敬意も示さずに, 宗教的事物や場所を扱うこと→神聖なもの[場所]を汚すこと, 冒涜(ぼうとく)

★**sad** /sæd/ 🔷 (**sadder; saddest**) ▶定義1 **sad (to do sth); sad (that...)** unhappy or causing sb to feel unhappy 不幸せな, 〜を悲しい気持ちにさせる→悲しい, 悲しませる ‖ *We are very sad to hear that you are leaving.* あなたがここを去ると聞いて, 私たちは本当に悲しく思います. *I'm very sad that you don't trust me.* あなたが私を信用してくれないことはとても残念だ. *That's one of the saddest stories I've ever heard!* これは今まで聞いた中で最も悲しい話の1つだ. *a sad poem/song/film* 悲しい詩・歌・映画 ▶定義2 bad or unacceptable 悪い, 受け入れられない→嘆かわしい, 惨めな ‖ *It's a sad state of affairs when your best friend doesn't trust you.* 親友があなたを信用していないとしたら, それは嘆かわしい状況だ. — **sadden** /sǽdn/ 🔶 🔵 〜を悲しませる ‖ *The news of your father's death saddened me greatly.* あなたのお父上のふ報は私をひどく悲しませました. — **sadness** 🔵 🔴 →悲しみ, 悲嘆

**saddle** /sǽdl/ 🔵 🔴 ▶定義1 a seat, usually made of leather, that you put on a horse so that you can ride it 乗馬する際に馬の背に載せる, 通常皮でできた座部→くら ☛ **horse** のさし絵 ▶定義2 a seat on a bicycle or motorbike 自転車やオートバイの座席→サドル ☛ S7ページのさし絵 — **saddle** 🔶 〜(馬など)にくらを置く 句動詞 **saddle sb with sth** ▶定義 to give sb a responsibility or task that he/she does not want 望んでいない責任や仕事を〜に与える→〜に(重荷・責任などを)負わせる

**sadism** /séɪdɪz(ə)m, sǽd-/ 🔵 🔴 ▶定義 getting pleasure, especially sexual pleasure, from hurting other people 他人を傷付けることで快楽, 特に性的な快楽を得ること→サディズム, 加虐性愛 ➤ **masochism** と比較.

**sadist** /séɪdɪst, sǽd-/ 🔵 🔴 ▶定義 a person who gets pleasure, especially sexual pleasure, from hurting other people 他人を傷付けることで快楽, 特に性的な快楽を得る人→サディスト — **sadistic** /sədístɪk, sæ-/ 🔷 →サディスティックな — **sadistically** /-k(ə)li/ 🔶 →サディスティックに, 嗜虐(しぎゃく)的に

**sadly** /sǽdli/ 🔶 ▶定義1 unfortunately 不幸にも→悲しいことに, 残念なことに ‖ *Sadly, after eight years of marriage they had grown apart.* 悲しいことに, 8年の結婚生活の後, 彼らは夫婦と言える関係でなくなってしまっていた. ▶定義2 in a way that shows unhappiness 不幸そうな様子で→悲しそうに ▶定義3 in a way that is wrong 誤って, 不適切に→嘆かわしいほど ‖ *If you think that I've forgotten what you did, you're **sadly mistaken**.* 君がした事を僕が忘れているとでも思っているなら, 君は完全に思い違いしているよ.

**sae, SAE** /ès eɪ íː/ 🔶 stamped addressed envelope →返信用封筒

**safari** /səfɑ́ːri, -fǽri/ 🔵 🔴 🔘 (複 **safaris**) ▶定義 a trip to see or hunt wild animals, especially in East Africa 特に東アフリカで野生動物を見たり狩猟したりする旅行→サファリ, (東アフリカでの)狩猟旅行 ‖ *to be/go **on safari*** サファリ旅行に出ている・サファリ旅行に出掛ける

★**safe**¹ /séɪf/ 🔷 ▶定義1 (名詞の前は不可) **safe (from sb/sth)** free from danger; not able to be hurt 危険のない; 危害を加えられることのない→(〜から)安全な, (〜の)危険のない ‖ *She didn't feel **safe** in the house on her own.* 家の中に1人でいると, 彼女は安心できなかった. *Do you think my car will be safe in this street?* この通りに私の車を置いても安全だと思いますか. *Keep the papers where they will be safe from fire.* 火事の危険のない, 安全な場所に書類を保管しなさい. ▶定義2 **safe (to do sth); safe (for sb)** not likely to cause danger, harm or risk 危険, 危害, 損害の恐れのない→(〜しても)安全な; (〜に対して)安全で ‖ *Don't sit on that chair, it isn't safe.* そ

## 1422　safe²

のいすに座ってはいけません危ないから. *I left my suitcase in a **safe place** and went for a cup of coffee.* 私はスーツケースを安全な場所に置いて，コーヒーを1杯飲みに行った. *Is this drug safe for children?* この薬は子供に飲ませても大丈夫ですか. *She's a very safe driver.* 彼女は非常に安全な運転をする人だ. *It's not safe to walk alone in the streets at night here.* この辺りの通りを夜間，1人で歩くのは危険だ. *Is it safe to drink the water here?* ここの水を飲んでも大丈夫ですか. *I think **it's safe to say** that the situation is unlikely to change for some time.* しばらくの間，状況は変わりそうにないと言っても差し支えないと思う. ▶定義3（名詞の前は不可）not hurt, damaged or lost 危害を加えられていない，被害を受けていない，行方不明になっていない→**安全な，無事な** ‖ *After the accident he checked that all the passengers were safe.* 事故後，彼は乗客全員が無事かどうかを確認した. *After five days the child was found, **safe and sound**.* 5日後，その子供はけがもなく無事発見された.— safely 副→**安全に，無事に** ‖ *I rang my parents to tell them I had arrived safely.* 両親に電話をして，無事に到着したことを伝えた.

成句 in safe hands ▶定義 with sb who will take good care of you よく面倒を見てくれる人と一緒に→**確かな人に預けられて**

on the safe side ▶定義 not taking risks; being very careful 危険を冒さずに；非常に慎重に→**大事をとって**

**safe²** /séɪf/ 图 Ｃ ▶定義 a strong metal box or cupboard with a special lock that is used for keeping money, jewellery, documents, etc in 貨幣，宝石，書類などの保管に用いる，特殊なかぎの付いた丈夫な金属製の箱や棚→**金庫**

**safeguard** /séɪfgɑːrd/ 图 Ｃ ▶定義 a safeguard (against sb/sth) something that protects against possible dangers 起こり得る危険から保護するもの→**（危険・損失に対する）保護，防衛（手段），安全装置**— safeguard 動 他→**～を保護する，守る** ‖ *to safeguard sb's interests/rights/privacy* ～の利益・権利・プライバシーを守る

***safety** /séɪfti/ 图 Ｕ ▶定義 the state of being safe; not being dangerous or in danger 安全な状態；危険でないこと，危険な状態にないこと→**安全** ‖ *In the interests of safety, smoking is forbidden.* 安全のため，喫煙は禁止されています. *road safety* (= the prevention of road accidents) 交通安全(= 交通事故防止) *New safety measures have been introduced on trains.* 列車に新しい安全対策が導入された.

**safety belt** = SEAT BELT

**safety net** 图 Ｃ ▶定義1 a net that is placed to catch sb who is performing high above the ground if he/she falls 高所で芸をする人の落下に備えて置かれたネット→**安全ネット，転落防止網** ▶定義2 an arrangement that helps to prevent disaster (usually with money) if sth goes wrong 事がうまくいかなくなった場合，最悪の事態を回避する一助として，（通常財政的に）講じられる措置→**セーフティーネット，救済策**

**safety pin** 图 Ｃ ▶定義 a metal pin with a point that is bent back towards the head, which is covered so that it cannot be dangerous. 危なくないように覆いを付けた上端部の方向に，ピンの先が折り返されている金属製のピン→**安全ピン** ☛ pin のさし絵

**safety valve** 图 Ｃ ▶定義 a device in a machine that allows steam, gas, etc to escape if the pressure becomes too great 圧力が高くなりすぎた場合に蒸気・ガスなどを逃がす機械内の装置→**安全弁**

**sag** /sæɡ/ 動 自 (**sagging**; **sagged**) ▶定義 to hang or to bend down, especially in the middle 特に中央部が垂れる，折れ曲がる →**（橋，天井，板などが）たわむ，（皮膚などが）たるむ**

**saga** /sáːɡə/ 图 Ｃ ▶定義 a very long story; a long series of events 非常に長い物語；長期にわたる一連の出来事→**大河小説，長編冒険物語，（長々と続く）経験談**

**Sagittarius** /sædʒətéəriəs/ 图 Ｃ Ｕ ▶定義 the ninth sign of the zodiac, the Archer 黄道十二宮の9番目である射手(いて)座→**射手座，人馬宮**

**said** SAY¹ の過去・過去分詞形

*sail¹ /séɪl/ 動 ▶定義1 自 (used about a boat or ship and the people on it) to travel on water in a ship or boat of any type (大型・小型の船，および乗船者について) あらゆるタイプの大小の船で水上を移動する→**航海する，航行する** ‖ *I stood at the window and watched the ships sailing by.* 私は窓際に立ち，船が航行するのを眺めた. *to sail round the world* 船で世界一周する ▶定義2

🔁 ⓥⓘ to travel in and control a boat with sails, especially as a sport 特にスポーツとして帆船を制御しながら走る➔(ボートなどを)操縦する,帆走する ‖ *My father is teaching me to sail.* 今父がらヨットの操縦の仕方を教えてもらっているところだ. *I've never sailed this kind of yacht before.* 今までこのようなヨットを走らせたことはない. ☛ ヨットを走らせて余暇を過ごすときは, go sailing という言い方をする. *We often go sailing at weekends.* 私たちはしばしば週末セーリングに出掛ける. ▶定義3 ⓥⓘ to begin a journey on water 水路の旅に出る➔**出航する, 出帆する** ‖ *When does the ship sail?* その船はいつ出航しますか. *We sail for Santander at six o'clock tomorrow morning.* 私たちは, 明日の朝6時にサンタンデルに向けて出航します. ▶定義4 ⓥⓘ to move somewhere quickly in a smooth or proud way 滑るように, または堂々と素早く進む➔**滑るように進む, (人が)さっそうと歩く** ‖ *The ball sailed over the fence and into the neighbour's garden.* ボールはフェンスをさっと越えて, 隣の庭に入った. *Mary sailed into the room, completely ignoring all of us.* メアリーは, 私たち全員を完全に無視しながら, さっそうと部屋に入ってきた.

成句 sail through (sth) ▶定義 to pass a test or exam easily テスト, 試験に楽々と合格する➔**(試験などに)悠々と通る, (〜に)楽に成功する**

**sail**² /séɪl/ ⓝ ▶定義1 ⓒ a large piece of strong material that is fixed onto a ship or boat. The wind blows against the sail and moves the ship along. 大小の船に取り付けられた, 大きくて丈夫な素材でできた船具の1つ. これに風が吹き付けることで船が進む➔**帆** ▶定義2 [単数扱い] a trip on water in a ship or boat with a sail 大小の帆船での船旅➔**帆走, 航行, 航海** ▶定義3 ⓒ any of the long parts that the wind moves round that are attached to a building (windmill) 建造物(風車)に取り付けられた, 風を受けて回る長い部品➔**風車の翼板** ☛ windmill のさし絵

成句 set sail ⇒ SET¹

**sailboard** /séɪlbɔːrd/ = WINDSURFER(1)
**sailing** /séɪlɪŋ/ ⓝ ⓤ ▶定義 the sport of being in, and controlling, small boats with sails 小型の帆船に乗り込んで操縦するスポーツ➔**セーリング, 帆走[ヨット]競技**
**sailing boat** (米 **sailboat**) ⓝ ⓒ ▶定義 a boat with a sail or sails 帆の付いた小型船➔**帆船**

\***sailor** /séɪlər/ ⓝ ▶定義 a person who works on a ship or a person who sails a boat 大型船で働く人または小型船を操縦する人➔**船員, 船乗り**

\***saint** /séɪnt/ ⓝ ⓒ ▶定義1 a very good or religious person who is given special respect after death by the Christian church キリスト教会から死後特別な敬意を示される, 非常に徳の高い, または信仰の厚い人物➔**聖人, 聖徒**
▶ 称号として用いられる場合, saint は大文字で書き始める: *Saint Patrick* (聖パトリック). 地名, 教会名などでは, 通常, 省略形の St が用いられる: *St Andrew's Church* (聖アンドリュー教会). 名詞の前に置かれた saint は /snt/ と発音される. patron saint を参照.
▶定義2 a very good, kind person 非常に善良で親切な人➔**聖人のような人**

**sake** /séɪk/ ⓝ ⓒ
成句 for Christ's/God's/goodness'/Heaven's/pity's, etc sake(口語) ▶定義 used to emphasize that it is important to do sth or to show that you are annoyed 〜を是非ともしなければならないことを強調したり, 迷惑していることを示すのに用いて➔**お願いだから, 後生だから, 一体全体** ‖ *For goodness' sake, hurry up!* お願いだから, 急いで. *Why have you taken so long, for God's sake?* 一体全体, どうしてそんなに長くかかったのですか. ☛ for God's sake と特に for Christ's sake はより強い表現なので, 人によっては気分を害することがある.

for the sake of sb/sth; for sb's/sth's sake ▶定義 in order to help sb/sth 〜を助けるために➔**〜のために** ‖ *Don't go to any trouble for my sake.* 私のために手間をかけないでください. *They only stayed together for the sake of their children/for their children's sake.* 彼らはただ子供たちのために離婚しないでいた.

for the sake of sth/of doing sth ▶定義 in order to get or keep sth; for the purpose of sth 〜を手に入れるまたは保有するために; 〜の目的のために➔**〜のために, 〜をするために** ‖ *She gave up her job for the sake of her health.* 彼女は健康のために仕事を辞めた.

\***salad** /sæləd/ ⓝ ⓒⓤ ▶定義 a mixture of vegetables, usually not cooked, that you often eat together with other foods ほかの料理と一緒によく食する，主として生の野菜を混ぜ合わせたもの→**サラダ** ‖ *All main courses are served with chips or salad.* すべてのメインコースには，フライドポテトかサラダが一緒に付いてきます． ☛ C4 ページのさし絵

\***salary** /sǽl(ə)ri/ 名 C U (複 **salaries**) ▶定義 the money that a person receives (usually every month) for the work he/she has done 行った仕事に対して(通常は毎月)受け取る金銭→**給料，給与** ‖ *My salary is paid directly into my bank account.* 私の給料は銀行口座に直接振り込まれる． *a high/low salary* 高給・薄給 ☛参 **pay**² の注

\***sale** /séɪl/ 名 ▶定義**1** C U the action of selling or being sold; the occasion when sth is sold 売る行為または売られる行為；物が売られる機会→**販売，売却** ‖ *The sale of alcohol to anyone under the age of 18 is forbidden.* 18歳未満の人へのアルコール飲料の販売は禁止されている． *a sale of used toys* 使用済みおもちゃの販売 ▶定義**2** **sales**［複数扱い］the number of items sold 売れた商品の数→**売上高** ‖ *Sales of personal computers have increased rapidly.* パソコンの売り上げは急速に上昇している． *The company reported excellent sales figures.* その会社は高い販売数を報告した． ▶定義**3** **sales** U (または **sales department**) the part of a company that deals with selling its products 会社の製品の販売に携わる部署→**販売部(門)，営業(部)** ‖ *Jodie works in sales/in the sales department.* ジョディーは営業部で働いている． *a sales representative/sales rep* 販売の外交員，セールスマン ▶定義**4** C a time when shops sell things at prices that are lower than usual 店が通常よりも低い価格で商品を販売する時期→**バーゲンセール，(大)安売り，特売** ‖ *The sale starts on December 28th.* セールは12月28日に始まる． *I got several bargains* **in the sales**. 私はセールでいくつか掘り出し物を手に入れた． ☛参 **car boot sale, jumble sale**

威句 **for sale** ▶定義 offered for sb to buy 人が買えるように売りに出された→**売り物** ‖ *This painting is not for sale.* この絵画は売り物ではありません． *I see our neighbours have* **put their house** **up for sale**. 見たところ隣人は家を売りに出しているようだ．

**on sale** ▶定義**1** available for sb to buy, especially in shops 特に店頭で買えるようになっている→**売りに出されて，販売されて** ‖ *This week's edition is on sale now at your local newsagents.* 今週号は地元の新聞・雑誌販売店で現在売り出し中である． ▶定義**2** 米 offered at a lower price than usual 通常より安い価格で売りに出された→**特売中で，特価で**

**sales clerk** (または **clerk**) 米 = SHOP ASSISTANT

**salesman** /séɪlzmən/ 名 C (複 **-men** /-mən/) ▶定義 a man whose job is selling things to people 商品販売を仕事とする男性 →**(男性の)店員，販売係；外交員，セールスマン**

**salesperson** /séɪlzpɚrs(ə)n/ 名 C (複 **salespeople** /séɪlzpìːp(ə)l/) ▶定義 a person whose job is selling things to people, especially in a shop 特に店などで商品を売ることを仕事とする人→**店員，販売係**

**saleswoman** /séɪlzwùmən/ 名 C (複 **-women** /-wìmən/) ▶定義 a woman whose job is selling things to people 商品販売を仕事とする女性→**(女)店員，(女性の)販売係；外交員，セールスレディー**

**salient** /séɪliənt/ 形 (名詞の前だけ) ▶定義 most important or noticeable 最も重大な，最も注目すべき→**顕著な，目立つ**

**saliva** /səláɪvə/ 名 U ▶定義 the liquid that is produced in the mouth 口の中で分泌される液体→**だ液，つば** ☛参 **spit**

**salmon** /sǽmən/ 名 C U (複 **salmon**) ▶定義 a large fish with silver skin and pink meat that we eat 皮が銀色で肉がピンク色の大きな食用魚→**鮭(さけ)，鮭の肉** ‖ *smoked salmon* スモークサーモン

**salmonella** /sælmənélə/ 名 U ▶定義 a type of bacteria that causes food poisoning 食中毒の原因となるバクテリアの一種→**サルモネラ菌**

**salon** /sǽlɒn, sǽlən; sɪlɔ́n/ 名 C ▶定義 a shop where you can have beauty or hair treatment or where you can buy expensive clothes 美顔術や髪の手入れをしてもらう店，または高価な衣服が買える店→**(美容・服飾等の)店**

**saloon** /səlúːn/ (米 **sedan**) 名 C ▶定義 a car with a fixed roof and a separate area (**boot**) for luggage 固定された屋根と独立した荷物入れ(トラ

ンク)のある自動車➜セダン ☛ car のさし絵

*__salt__[1] /sɔːlt/ [名] [U] ▶定義 a common white substance that is found in sea water and the earth. Salt is used in cooking for flavouring food. 海水や地中にあるごく一般的な白い物質. 食物の味付けのために料理に使われる➜**塩, 食塩** ‖ *Season with **salt and pepper**.* 塩コショウで味付けをする. *Add a pinch (= a small amount) of salt.* 塩を一つまみ(= 少量)加える. ― salt [形]➜**塩を含んだ, 塩気のある** ‖ *salt water* 塩水

[成句] rub salt into the wound/sb's wounds ⇒ RUB

take sth with a pinch of salt ⇒ PINCH[2]

__salt__[2] /sɔːlt/ [動][他](通常は受動態で) ▶定義 to put salt on or in sth ～に塩を掛ける, ～に塩を入れる➜**～に塩を振る, 塩味を付ける** ‖ *salted peanuts* 塩味の付いたピーナッツ

__salt water__ [形] ▶定義 living in the sea 海に住む➜**海水の, 塩水の, 海産の** ‖ *a salt water fish* 海水魚

➤河川に住む魚は freshwater fish (淡水魚) と言う.

__salty__ /sɔ́ːlti/ [形] ▶定義 having the taste of or containing salt 塩味のする, 塩を含んだ➜**塩味の, 塩気のある** ‖ *I didn't like the meat, it was too salty.* その肉料理はおいしくなかった, 塩気が強すぎたからだ.

__salute__ /səlúːt/ [名] [C] ▶定義1 an action that a soldier, etc does to show respect, by holding his/her hand to the forehead 軍人などが敬意を示すために手を額に当てること➜**敬礼** ‖ *to give a salute* 敬礼する ▶定義2 something that shows respect for sb➜**人に敬意を示すもの, 敬意** ‖ *The next programme is **a salute to** one of the world's greatest film stars.* 世界で最も偉大な映画スターの1人に敬意を表して次のプログラムをささげます. ― salute [動][自][他] ➜**(～に)敬礼する, 敬意を表す** ‖ *The soldiers saluted as they marched past the general.* 兵士たちは将軍の前を行進する際に敬礼した.

__salvage__[1] /sǽlvɪdʒ/ [名] [U] ▶定義 saving things that have been or are likely to be lost or damaged, especially in an accident or a disaster; the things that are saved 特に事故や災害で損失・損傷したもの, あるいはしそうなものを救い出すこと; 救出された物➜**救助, 海難救助, (沈没船の)引き揚げ(作業), サルベージ; 救出された貨物** ‖ *a salvage operation/company/team* (沈没船などの)引き揚げ作業・海難救助会社・救助隊

__salvage__[2] /sǽlvɪdʒ/ [動][他] ▶定義 salvage sth (from sth) to manage to rescue sth from being lost or damaged; to rescue sth or a situation from disaster ～が損失・損傷されかかっているところをどうにか救い出す; 物または状況を災害から救い出す➜**～を(…から)救出する, 救助する** ‖ *They salvaged as much as they could from the house after the fire.* 火災の後, 彼らはできるだけたくさんの物を家屋の中から回収した.

__salvation__ /sælvéɪʃ(ə)n/ [名] ▶定義1 [U] (in the Christian religion) being saved from the power of evil (キリスト教で) 悪の力から救われること➜**救い, 救済** ▶定義2 [U, 単数扱い] a thing or person that rescues sb/sth from danger, disaster, etc ～を危険, 災害などから救う物または人➜**救済者, (人にとって)救いとなる物・手段**

*__same__ /séɪm/ [形][副][代] ▶定義1 the same... (as sb/sth); the same...that... not different, not another or other; exactly the one or ones that you have mentioned before 異ならない, 別物でない; 先に言及したまさにそのもの➜**～と同じ, 同一の; 同じ[同一の]物・事** ‖ *My brother and I had the same teacher at school.* 兄と私は学校で同じ先生に教わった. *They both said the same thing.* 彼らは2人とも同じ事を言った. *I'm going to wear the same clothes as/that I wore yesterday.* 私は昨日着たのと同じ服を着るつもりだ. *This one looks **exactly the same** as that one.* これはあれと全く同じ物に見える. ▶定義2 the same... (as sb/sth); the same...that... exactly like the one already mentioned 先に言及したものと全く同じような[に]➜**(～と)同じような[に]** ‖ *I wouldn't buy the same car again (= the same model of car).* 二度と同じ車(= 同じ型の車)を買わないつもりだ. *We treat all the children in the class the same.* 私たちはそのクラスの子供たち全員を同じように扱う. *I had the same experience as you some time ago.* しばらく前に, あなたと同じような経験をした. *All small babies look the same.* 小さい赤ん坊は皆同じに見える. *Is there another word that means the same as this?* これと同じ意味を持つ別の単語はありますか.

S

## sample 1426

▶「同じ種類の〜」という場合, a same... とは言えず, the same sort of... を用いる: *I'd like the same sort of job as my father.* (私は父と同じような仕事に就きたい.)

成句 **all/just the same** ▶定義 in spite of this/that; anyway それにもかかわらず; とにかく→**それでも, やはり** ‖ *I understand what you're saying. All the same, I don't agree with you.* あなたの言っている事は分かりますが, それでもやはり, 同意しかねます. *I don't need to borrow any money but thanks all the same for offering.* 金を借りる必要はありませんが, とにかく申し出をありがとう.

**at the same time** ▶定義1 together; at one time 一緒に, 一斉に→**同時に** ‖ *I can't think about more than one thing at the same time.* 私は一度に2つ以上の事を考えることができない.

▶定義2 on the other hand; however 他方; しかしながら→**それでもやはり** ‖ *It's a very good idea but at the same time it's rather risky.* それはとてもいい考えだが, それでもやはり相当危険.

**much the same** ⇒ **MUCH**

**on the same wavelength** ▶定義 able to understand sb because you have similar ideas and opinions 自分と同じような考えや意見を持っているため, 〜を理解できる→**波長が合って, 考え方・好みが合って, 気が合って**

**(the) same again**(口語) ▶定義 a request to be served or given the same drink as before 前と同じ飲み物をついでくれという要求→**もう1杯**

**same here**(口語) ▶定義 the same thing is also true for me 同じ事が自分にも当てはまる→**私も同じだ, 同感だ** ‖ *'I'm bored.' 'Same here.'*「退屈だなあ」「同感だ」

**(the) same to you**(口語) ▶定義 used as an answer when sb says sth rude to you or wishes you sth 人が失礼な事を言ったり, あいさつしてくれたときの返答として用いて→**お互いにね, 君もね, ご同様に** ‖ *'You idiot!' 'Same to you!'*「大ばか者」「お前こそ」 *'Have a good weekend.' 'The same to you.'*「良い週末を」「あなたも」

**sample** /sáːmp(ə)l; sǽm-/ 名 **C** ▶定義 a small number or amount of sb/sth that is looked at, tested, examined, etc to find what the rest is like 全体がどのようなものかを調べるため, 考察・テスト・調査などを行う, その中の限られた数量の物または人→**標本, サンプル** ‖ *The interviews were given to a **random sample** of shoppers.* 無作為に抽出された買い物客に対してインタビューが行われた. *to take a blood sample* 血液サンプルを採る *a free sample of shampoo* シャンプーの無料試供品 ☛類 **specimen** ― **sample** 動 他 ▶〜の標本・サンプルを抽出する, 味を見る ‖ *You are welcome to sample any of our wines before making a purchase.* 購入される前に私たちのワインを是非試飲してください.

**sanatorium** /sæ̀nətɔ́ːriəm/ (米 **sanitarium** /sæ̀nətéəriəm/) 名 **C** ▶定義 a type of hospital where patients who need a long period of treatment for an illness can stay 病気に対する長期治療が必要な患者が滞在することのできる病院→**サナトリウム, 療養所**

**sanction**¹ /sǽŋkʃ(ə)n/ 名 ▶定義1 [**C**, 通常は複数]sanctions (against sb) an official order that limits business, contact, etc with a particular country, in order to make it do sth, such as obeying international law 国際法の遵守など, 一定の行為をさせるために, 特定の国との通商, 関係などを制限する公式命令→**(〜に対する)制裁(措置)** ‖ *The sanctions against those countries have now been lifted.* それらの国々に対する制裁は現在解除されている. ▶定義2 **U** 正式 official permission to do or change sth 〜をしたり, 変えたりしてよいという公式の許可→**許可, 認可** ▶定義3 **C** a punishment for breaking a rule or law 規約や法律違反に対する処罰→**処罰, 刑罰**

**sanction**² /sǽŋkʃ(ə)n/ 動 他 ▶定義 to give official permission for sth 〜に対して公式の許可を与える→**〜を許可する, 認可する**

**sanctuary** /sǽŋktjuəri; -tʃuèri/ 名 (複 **sanctuaries**) ▶定義1 **C** a place where birds or animals are protected from being hunted 鳥や動物を狩猟から守る場所→**鳥獣保護区, サンクチュアリ** ▶定義2 **C U** a place where sb can be safe from enemies, the police, etc 〜が敵や警察などから免れていられる場所→**聖域, 避難所, (亡命者などの)逃げ込み場**

*★**sand** /sænd/ 名 ▶定義1 **U** a powder consisting of very small grains of rock, found in deserts and on beaches 砂漠や水辺に見られる, 岩石の微小な粒子→**砂** ☛ C8ページのさし絵 ▶定義2 **the sands**[複数扱い]a large area of sand 砂の

広い地域→砂地,砂浜,砂漠

**sandal** /sǽndl/ 名 C ▶定義 a type of light, open shoe that people wear when the weather is warm 暑いときに履く, 軽くて, 足を覆い包まない靴→サンダル ☞ shoe のさし絵

**sandcastle** /sǽndkɑ̀ːs(ə)l; -kæ̀s(ə)l/ 名 C ▶定義 a pile of sand that looks like a castle, made by children playing on a beach 海岸で遊ぶ子供たちが作る城のように見える砂の山→砂の城

**sand dune** = DUNE

**sandpaper** /sǽndpèɪpər/ 名 U ▶定義 strong paper with sand on it that is used for rubbing surfaces in order to make them smooth 表面をこすって滑らかにするために使用される, 砂粒の付いた丈夫な紙→紙やすり, サンドペーパー

*__sandwich__¹ /sǽn(d)wɪdʒ; sǽnwɪtʃ/ 名 C ▶定義 two slices of bread with food between them 間に食べ物が挟んである2枚のパン→サンドイッチ ‖ *a ham/cheese sandwich* ハム・チーズサンド ☞ C4 ページのさし絵

**sandwich**² /sǽn(d)wɪdʒ; sǽnwɪtʃ/ 動 他 ▶定義 *sandwich sb/sth (between sb/sth)* to place sb/sth in a very narrow space between two other things or people ほかの2つの物や人の間の狭いすきまに~を置く・入れる→~を(…の間に)挟む, 詰め込む

**sandy** /sǽndi/ 形 ▶定義 covered with or full of sand 砂で覆われた, 砂に満ちた→砂だらけの

**sane** /séɪn/ 形 ▶定義 1 (used about a person) mentally normal; not crazy (人について) 精神的に正常な; 気が狂っていない→正気の ‖ *No sane person would do anything like that.* 正気の人間ならばそんな事はしないだろう. ▶定義 2 (used about a person or an idea, a decision, etc) sensible; showing good judgement (人や考え, 決定などについて) 良識ある; 良い判断を示す→分別ある, 健全な ⇔ insane ☞ 名 sanity

**sang** SING の過去形

**sanitarium** 米 = SANATORIUM

**sanitary** /sǽnət(ə)ri; -tèri/ 形 ▶定義 connected with the protection of health, for example how human waste is removed 例えば人間の排せつ物の処理方法など, 健康の保護に関する→衛生の, 衛生上の ‖ *Sanitary conditions in the refugee camps were terrible.* 難民キャンプの衛生状態はひどかった. ☞参 insanitary

**sanitary towel** (米 **sanitary napkin**) 名 C ▶定義 a thick piece of soft material that women use to absorb blood lost during their period (3)女性が生理中の出血の吸収用に使う, 柔らかい素材でできた厚手のもの→生理用ナプキン ☞参 tampon

**sanitation** /sæ̀nətéɪʃ(ə)n/ 名 U ▶定義 the equipment and systems that keep places clean, especially by removing human waste 特に排せつ物を処理して場所を清潔に保つ器具や装置→衛生設備

**sanity** /sǽnəti/ 名 U ▶定義 1 the state of having a normal healthy mind 正常の健全な精神を持っている状態→正気 ▶定義 2 the state of being sensible and reasonable 良識や思慮分別のある状態→(行動・思想などの)健全 ⇔ insanity ☞ 形 sane

**sank** SINK¹ の過去形

**Santa Claus** /sǽntə klɔ̀ːz/ =FATHER CHRISTMAS

**sap**¹ /sæp/ 名 U ▶定義 the liquid in a plant or tree 植物や樹木の内部の液体→樹液

**sap**² /sæp/ 動 他 (**sapping**; **sapped**) ▶定義 *sap (sb of) sth* to make sb/sth weaker; to destroy sth gradually ~を弱らせる, ~を徐々に滅ぼす→(人から)(気力など)を奪う, (勢力・体力など)を徐々に失わせる ‖ *Years of failure have sapped (him of) his confidence.* 長年の失敗で彼は次第に自信を失っていった.

**sapling** /sǽplɪŋ/ 名 C ▶定義 a young tree 若い木→苗木 ☞ C2 ページのさし絵

**sapphire** /sǽfàɪər/ 名 C U ▶定義 a bright blue precious stone 明るい青色の宝石→サファイア

**sarcasm** /sɑ́ːrkæ̀z(ə)m/ 名 U ▶定義 the use of words or expressions to mean the opposite of what they actually say. People use sarcasm in order to criticize other people or to make them look silly. 実際に述べている事と反対の意味になるように, 語や表現を使うこと. 他人を批判したり, おとしめたりするために用いる→皮肉, 嫌味 ☞参 ironic — **sarcastic** /sɑːrkǽstɪk/ 形 →皮肉な, 嫌味な ‖ *a sarcastic comment* 皮肉たっぷりな批評 — **sarcastically** /-k(ə)li/ 副 →皮肉に, 嫌味に

**sardine** /sɑːrdíːn/ 名 C ▶定義 a type of very small silver-coloured fish that we cook and eat

調理して食するごく小さな銀色の魚→イワシ ‖ *a tin of sardines* イワシの缶詰

**sari** /sάːri/ 图 C ▶定義 a dress that consists of a long piece of shiny cloth (silk) or cotton that women, particularly Indian women, wear around their bodies 光沢のある布(絹)や綿布の長い一枚布から成る衣服.女性,特にインドの女性が身にまとう→サリー ☞ C6 ページのさし絵

**sash** /sǽʃ/ 图 C ▶定義 a long piece of material that is worn round the waist or over the shoulder, often as part of a uniform 腰に巻いたり,肩に掛けたりする長い布地.しばしば制服の一部として着用される→サッシュ,飾り帯

**Sat** 略 Saturday→土曜日 ‖ *Sat 2 May* 5月2日土曜日

**sat** SIT の過去・過去分詞形

**Satan** /séɪtn/ 图 [単数扱い] ▶定義 a name for the Devil 悪魔の名称→サタン ☞参 **devil**

**satchel** /sǽtʃ(ə)l/ 图 C ▶定義 a bag, often carried over the shoulder, used by schoolchildren for taking books to and from school かばんの一種.学童が学校の往復に本を入れるのに使用する.肩に掛けるものが多い→学生かばん,肩掛けかばん

**satellite** /sǽt(ə)làɪt/ 图 C ▶定義1 an electronic device that is sent into space and moves around the earth or another planet for a particular purpose ある目的のために,宇宙に打ち上げられ,地球などの惑星の周囲を回る電子装置→人工衛星 ‖ *a weather/communications satellite* 気象・通信衛星 ▶定義2 a natural object that moves round a bigger object in space 宇宙空間で,より大きな物体の周りを回る,自然に存在する物体→衛星

**satellite dish** (または **dish**) 图 C ▶定義 a large, circular piece of equipment that people have on the outside of their houses, that receives signals from a satellite(1) so that they can receive satellite television 衛星放送テレビ番組が受信できるように屋外に取り付ける,人工衛星からの信号をキャッチする大きな円形の装置→衛星受信アンテナ

**satellite television** (または **satellite TV**) 图 U ▶定義 television programmes that are broadcast using a satellite(1) 人工衛星を使って放送されるテレビ番組→衛星放送テレビ番組

**satin** /sǽt(ə)n/ 图 U ▶定義 a type of cloth that is smooth and shiny 滑らかで光沢のある布→サテン,しゅす ‖ *a satin dress/ribbon* サテンの衣服・リボン

**satire** /sǽtàɪər/ 图 ▶定義1 ❶ the use of humour to attack a person, an idea or behaviour that you think is bad or silly 不快に,または愚かに思われる人物,考え,行動などを攻撃するためにユーモアを用いること→風刺,皮肉 ▶定義2 ❷ *a satire (on sb/sth)* a piece of writing or a play, film, etc that uses satire 風刺を用いた文書,戯曲,映画など→風刺文[劇・詩・小説・映画] ‖ *a satire on political life* 政治生活についての風刺文 ― **satirical** /sətírɪk(ə)l/ 形 →風刺的な,皮肉っぽい ‖ *a satirical magazine* 風刺雑誌 ― **satirically** /-k(ə)li/ 副 →風刺的に,皮肉っぽく

*****satisfaction** /sæ̀tɪsfǽkʃ(ə)n/ 图 U C ▶定義 the feeling of pleasure that you have when you have done, got or achieved what you wanted; sth that gives you this feeling やりたい事をしたり,手に入れたり,成し遂げたときに抱く喜びの感情;そのような感情を抱かせるもの→満足(感),満足を抱かせるもの ‖ *Roshni stood back and looked at her work with a sense of satisfaction.* ロシュニは後ろに下がって,満足げに自分の作品を眺めた. *We finally found a solution that was **to** everyone's **satisfaction**.* 私たちはとうとう,だれもが満足する解決策を見つけた. *She was about to **have the satisfaction of** seeing her book in print.* 彼女は自分の著作が活字になるのを見るという満足感を今にも味わおうとしているところだった. ⇔ **dissatisfaction**

*****satisfactory** /sæ̀tɪsfǽkt(ə)ri/ 形 ▶定義 good enough for a particular purpose; acceptable ある特定の目的に対して十分な;意にかなう→満足のいく,なかなか良い ‖ *This piece of work is not satisfactory. Please do it again.* この作品は満足のいく出来ではありません.やり直してください. ⇔ **unsatisfactory** ― **satisfactorily** /-t(ə)rɪli/ 副 →満足できるほどに,十分に ‖ *Work is progressing satisfactorily.* 作業は思い通りに進行している.

**satisfied** /sǽtɪsfàɪd/ 形 ▶定義 *satisfied (with sb/sth)* pleased because you have had or done what you wanted 望むものを手に入れた,またはやりたい事をしたので満足して →(〜に)

満足して,納得して ‖ *a satisfied smile* 満ち足りた微笑 *a satisfied customer* 満足した顧客 ⇔ **dissatisfied**

\***satisfy** /sǽtəsfài/ 動他 (現分 **satisfying**; 三単現 **satisfies**; 過, 過分 **satisfied**) ▶定義 1 to make sb pleased by doing or giving him/her what he/she wants 〜が望む事を行ったり与えたりして,〜を喜ばせる→**〜を満足させる** ‖ *No matter how hard I try, my piano teacher is never satisfied.* 私がどんなに努力しても,私のピアノの先生は決して満足しない. ▶定義 2 to have or do what is necessary for sth 〜に対して必要なものを所有している・必要な事を行う →**(条件など)を満たす** ‖ *Make sure you satisfy the entry requirements before you apply to the university.* 大学に出願する前に,入学条件を満たしているか確認しなさい. *I had a quick look inside the parcel just to satisfy my curiosity.* ただ好奇心を満たすため,小包の中をちらっとのぞいた. ▶定義 3 satisfy sb (that...) to show or give proof to sb that sth is true or has been done 〜が正しいこと,または遂行されたことを〜に示す・立証する→**〜を(…だと)納得させる,確信させる** ‖ *Once the police were satisfied that they were telling the truth, they were allowed to go.* 真実を話していると警察がひとたび確信すると,彼らは釈放された.

**satisfying** /sǽtəsfàiŋ/ 形 ▶定義 pleasing, giving satisfaction 喜ばしい,満足を与える→**満足のいく,十分な** ‖ *I find it satisfying to see people enjoying something I've cooked.* 自分の料理したものを,人が喜んで食べているのを見るのは気持ちのいいものだ.

**satsuma** /sætsúːmə, sǽtsʊmàː/ 名 C ▶定義 a type of small orange 小さなオレンジの一種→**温州(うんしゅう)ミカン**

**saturate** /sǽtʃ(ə)rèit/ 動他 ▶定義 1 to make sth extremely wet 〜を極端に湿らせる→**〜をぐっしょりぬらす** ‖ *Her clothes were completely saturated.* 彼女の服はびしょぬれだった. ▶定義 2 to fill sth so completely that it is impossible to add any more これ以上加えることができないほど〜を満たす→**〜を飽和状態にする** ‖ *The market is saturated with cheap imports.* 市場は安い輸入品で満ちあふれている. — **saturation** /sætʃəréiʃ(ə)n/ 名 U ▶定義 浸透, 飽和

\***Saturday** /sǽtərdèi, -di/ 名 C U (略 **Sat**) ▶定義 the day of the week after Friday 金曜日の次の曜日→**土曜日**

▶曜日は最初の文字を必ず大文字で書く. 文中での曜日の使い方の例については, **Monday** を参照.

**Saturn** /sǽtəm/ 名 [単数扱い] ▶定義 the planet that is sixth in order from the sun and that has rings around it 太陽から6番目に位置する惑星. 周りに環(わ)を持つ→**土星**

\***sauce** /sɔːs/ 名 C U ▶定義 a thick hot or cold liquid that you eat on or with food 食べ物に掛けたり,一緒に食したりする,熱い,または冷たいどろっとした液体→**ソース** ‖ *The chicken was served in a delicious sauce.* チキンはおいしいソースを添えて出された. *ice cream with chocolate sauce* チョコレートソースを掛けたアイスクリーム ☞ C4 ページのさし絵 ☞参 **gravy**

\***saucepan** /sɔ́ːspən; -pæn/ 名 C ▶定義 a round metal pot with a handle that is used for cooking things on top of a cooker こんろの上で調理するときに用いる,取っ手の付いた円い金属製のなべ→**ソースパン** ☞参 **pan**

\***saucer** /sɔ́ːsər/ 名 C ▶定義 a small round plate that you put under a cup カップの下に置く小さな円い皿→**ソーサー, 受け皿** ☞ **cup** のさし絵

**sauna** /sɔ́ːnə, sáʊ-/ 名 C ▶定義 1 a type of bath where you sit in a room that is very hot ふろの一種. 非常に高温の部屋の中に座って入る→**サウナ, 蒸しぶろ** ‖ *to have a sauna* サウナぶろに入る ▶定義 2 the room that you sit in to have a sauna サウナを楽しむために入って座る部屋→**サウナ(浴場)**

**saunter** /sɔ́ːntər, sáːn-/ 動自 ▶定義 to walk without hurrying 急がずに歩く→**ぶらつく, 散歩する**

\***sausage** /sɔ́ːsɪdʒ/ 名 C U ▶定義 a mixture of meat cut into very small pieces, spices, etc that is made into a long thin shape. Some sausage is eaten cold in slices; other types are cooked and then served whole. ひき肉, 香辛料などを混ぜ合わせた, 細長い形をした食品. 薄切りにして冷たいまま食するものや, 加熱してそのまま食卓に供されるものがある→**ソーセージ, 腸詰め** ‖ *garlic/liver sausage* ニンニク・レバー入りソーセージ *We had sausages and chips for lunch.*

## 1430 savage

私たちは昼食にソーセージとフライドポテトを食べた. ☞ C4 ページのさし絵

**savage**¹ /sǽvɪdʒ/ 形 ▶定義 very cruel or violent ひどく残酷な, 暴力的な➔ **どう猛な, 残忍な, 凶暴な; 猛烈な** ‖ *He was the victim of a savage attack.* 彼は残忍な暴行の被害者だった. *The book received savage criticism.* その本は酷評を受けた. — savage 動 ⊕➔**〜を猛攻撃する, 〜に襲い掛かる** ‖ *The boy died after being savaged by a dog.* その少年は犬に襲われて死亡した. — savagely 副➔**残忍に, 凶暴に** — savagery /sǽvɪdʒri/ 名 ❶➔**残忍, 凶暴**

**★save**¹ /séɪv/ 動 ▶定義 1 ⊕ save sb/sth (from sth/from doing sth) to keep sb/sth safe from death, harm, loss, etc 〜を死亡, 危害, 損失などから守る➔**〜を(…から)救う, 救助する** ‖ *to save sb's life* 〜の生命を救う *to save sb from drowning* おぼれかけている人を助ける *We are trying to save the school from closure.* 私たちはその学校が閉校にならないよう努力している. ▶定義 2 ⊜⊕ save (sth) (up) (for sth) to keep or not spend money so that you can use it later 後で使えるように金を取っておく・使わない➔**(〜のために)貯金する; 〜を蓄える** ‖ *I'm saving up for a new bike.* 私は新しいバイクを購入するため貯金している. *Do you manage to save any of your wages?* 給料の一部をやりくりして貯蓄していますか. ▶定義 3 ⊕ to keep sth for future use 後で使うために〜を取っておく➔**〜を取っておく** ‖ *I'll be home late so please save me some dinner.* 帰りが遅くなるから, 夕食を取っておいてください. *Save that box. It might come in useful.* その箱を取っておきなさい. 後で使えるかもしれないから. *If you get there first, please save me a seat.* もしあなたが先に着いたら, 私の席を取っておいてください. ▶定義 4 ⊜⊕ save (sb) (sth) (on) sth to avoid wasting time, money, etc 時間, 金などの浪費を省く➔**(〜を)節約する, (〜を)省く** ‖ *It will save you twenty minutes on the journey if you take the express train.* 急行列車に乗れば, 20 分節約できる. *You can save on petrol by getting a smaller car.* もっと小さな車を買えば, ガソリンが節約できる. *This car will save you a lot on petrol.* この車なら多量のガソリンが節約できる. ▶定義 5 ⊕ save (sb) sth/doing sth to avoid, or make sb able to avoid, doing sth unpleasant or difficult 不愉快な・困難な〜をしなくて済む, または〜がそのような…をしなくて済むようにする➔**〜を省く, 〜を省かせる, 人が〜しなくて済むようにする** ‖ *If you make an appointment it will save you waiting.* 予約なされば, 待たずに済みます. ▶定義 6 ⊕ to store information in a computer by giving it a special instruction 特定の指示を入力して, データをコンピューターに記憶させる➔**〜を保存する** ‖ *Don't forget to save the file before you close it.* ファイルを閉じる前に保存するのを忘れないでください. ▶定義 7 ⊕ to stop a goal being scored in sports such as football, hockey, etc サッカー, ホッケーなどのスポーツでゴールを決められるのを阻止する➔**(シュート・得点など)を防ぐ, (勝利)を守る**

成句 keep/save sth for a rainy day ⇨ **RAINY**
save face ▶定義 to prevent yourself losing the respect of other people 他人からの尊敬を失わないようにする➔**面目を保つ**

**save**² /séɪv/ 名 ❻ ▶定義 (in football, etc) the action of preventing a goal from being scored (サッカーなどで)ゴールを決められないよう阻止する動作➔**(敵の得点の)阻止, 守備** ‖ *The goalkeeper made a great save.* ゴールキーパーは見事に得点を阻止した.

**saver** /séɪvər/ 名 ❻ ▶定義 1 a person who saves money for future use 将来使うために貯金する人➔**貯蓄家, 預金者** ‖ *The rise in interest rates is good news for savers.* 利率の上昇は預金者にとって良いニュースだ. ▶定義 2 (しばしば複合語で)a thing that helps you save time, money, or the thing mentioned 時間, 金, または言及された物を節約するのに役立つもの➔**〜を節約するもの, 節約装置**

**saving** /séɪvɪŋ/ 名 ▶定義 1 ❻ a saving (of sth) (on sth) an amount of time, money, etc that you do not have to use or spend 使わずに済む時間, 金などの量 ➔**(〜の)節約(量)** ‖ *The sale price represents a saving of 25% on the usual price.* 特価価格は通常価格の 25 パーセント引きだ. ▶定義 2 **savings**[複数扱い] money that you have saved for future use 将来使うために貯蓄した金➔**貯金** ‖ *All our savings are in the bank.* 私たちの貯金はすべて銀行に預けてある.

**saviour** (米 **savior**) /séɪvjər/ 名 ❻ ▶定義 a person who rescues or saves sb/sth from danger, loss, death, etc 〜を危険, 損失, 死亡などから救出する人➡救助者, 救済者

**savoury** (米**savory**) /séɪv(ə)ri/ 形 ▶定義 (used about food) having a taste that is not sweet(食べ物について)味が甘くない➡塩味の効いた, 辛口の ☛参 **sweet**

**saw**[1] SEE の過去形

★**saw**[2] /sɔː/ 名 C ▶定義 a tool that is used for cutting wood, etc. A saw has a long flat metal part (a blade) with sharp teeth on it, and a handle at one or both ends. 木などを切るために用いる道具. 鋭い歯の付いた長い平らな金属部分を持ち, 一方または両方の端に取っ手が付いている➡のこぎり ☛ **tool** のさし絵 ― saw 動自他 (過 sawed; 過分 sawn /sɔːn/) ➡(〜を)のこぎりで切る, のこぎりをひく ‖ *to saw through the trunk of a tree* 木の幹をのこぎりでひく *He sawed the log up into small pieces.* 彼は丸太をのこぎりでひいて, 小さくした.

▶アメリカ英語では, 過去分詞は sawed となる.

**sawdust** /sɔ́ːdʌst/ 名 U ▶定義 very small pieces of wood that fall like powder when you are cutting a large piece of wood 大きな木材を切断する際に出る粉状になった木片➡おがくず

**sax** /sæks/ 略式 = SAXOPHONE

**saxophone** /sǽksəfòʊn/ (または 略式 **sax**) 名 C ▶定義 a metal musical instrument that you play by blowing into it. Saxophones are especially used for playing modern music, for example jazz. 息を吹き込んで演奏する金属製の管楽器. 特にジャズなどの現代音楽を演奏する際に用いられる➡サクソフォーン ‖ *This track features Dexter Gordon on sax.* この曲はデクスター・ゴードンのサックス演奏を売り物にしている.

☛参 **piano** の注 ☛ **music** のさし絵

★**say**[1] /seɪ/ 動他 (三単現 **says** /sez, (弱) səz/; 過・過分 **said** /sed, (弱) səd/) ▶定義 **1** say sth (to sb); say that...; say sth (about sb) to speak or tell sb sth, using words 言葉を用いて〜に…を話す, 伝える ➡(〜に)…と言う, (〜に)…を話す; 〜と言う; (〜について)…と言う ‖ *'Please come back,' she said.*「どうぞ戻ってきて」と彼女は言った. *The teacher said we should hand in our essays on Friday.* 先生は, 小論を金曜日に提出するようにと言った. *I said goodbye to her at the station.* 私は駅で彼女に別れを告げた. *We can ask him, but I'm sure he'll say no.* 彼に尋ねてもいいが, きっと「ノー」と言うだろう. *He said to his mother that he would phone back later.* 彼は母親に後で電話をかけ直すと言った. *They just sat there without saying anything.* 彼らは何も言わずにただそこに座っていた. *'This isn't going to be easy,' she said to herself (= she thought).*「これは簡単にはいかないわ」と彼女は考えた (= 彼女は思った). *'What time is she coming?' 'I don't know - she didn't say.'*「彼女は何時に来るの」「さあ ― 彼女は何も言わなかったわ」 *It is said that cats can sense the presence of ghosts.* 猫は幽霊の存在を感じることができると言われている.

▶ say と tell の違いについて. say はしばしば実際に話された言葉と共に, または間接話法での that の前で用いられる: *'I'll catch the 9 o'clock train,' he said.*(「私は9時の列車に乗ります」と彼は言った.) *He said that he would catch the 9 o'clock train.* (彼は9時の列車に乗ると言った.) また say では say sth to sb という表現を用いることができる: *He said to me that he would catch the 9 o'clock train.* (彼は私に9時の列車に乗ると言った.) tell の後には話している相手を表す名詞または代名詞が必ず来ることに注意: *He told me that he would catch the 9 o'clock train.* (彼は私に9時の列車に乗ると言った.) また, tell は命令や忠告を与える場合にも使える (say は使えない): *I told them to hurry up.* (私は彼らに急ぐように言った.) *She's always telling me what I ought to do.* (彼女はいつも私にどうすべきか指図してばかりいる.)

▶定義 **2** to express an opinion on sth 〜について意見を述べる➡〜と言う, 言明する, 述べる, 主張する ‖ *I wouldn't say she's unfriendly - just shy.* 私は彼女をよそよそしいとは思わない ― 単に内気なのだ. *What is the artist trying to say in this painting?* 画家はこの絵で何を言おうとしているのか. *Well, what do you say? Do you think it's a good idea?* それで, あなたはどう思いますか. 良い考えだと思いますか. *It's hard to say what I like about the book.* その本のどこが気に入ったのかを言葉にするのは難しい.

## say²

*'When will it be finished?' **'I couldn't say** (= I don't know).'* 「それはいつ終わりますか」「さあ, 何とも言えません(= 分かりません)」 ▶定義3 (used about a book, notice, etc) to give information (本, 掲示などについて)情報を与える→ **〜と書いてある, 伝える, 〜を示す** ‖ *What time does it say on that clock?* その時計は何時を指していますか. *The map says the hotel is just past the railway bridge.* 地図にはそのホテルが鉄橋のすぐ先にあると出ています. *The sign clearly says 'No dogs'.* その掲示板には「犬お断り」とはっきり書いてある. ▶定義4 **say sth (to sb)** to show a feeling, a situation, etc without using words 言葉を用いずに感情, 状況などを示す→ **(〜に) …を表す** ‖ *His angry look said everything about the way he felt.* 彼の怒った顔が, どのように彼が感じているかをすべて物語っていた. ▶定義5 to imagine or guess sth about a situation; to suppose ある状況について〜を想像, または推測する; 仮定する→ **仮に〜だとすると, (例示するものの前に用いて) 例えば** ‖ *We will need, say, £5000 for a new car.* 新車を購入するのには, まあ5000ポンドは要るだろう. *Say you don't get a place at university, what will you do then?* 仮に大学に入れなかったら, どうしますか.

成句 **go without saying** ▶定義 to be clear, so that you do not need to say it はっきりしていて, それについて言う必要がない→**言うまでもない** ‖ *It goes without saying that the children will be well looked after at all times.* 子供たちが常によく面倒を見てもらえる事は言うまでもない.

**have a lot, nothing, etc to say for yourself** ▶定義 to have a lot, nothing, etc to say in a particular situation ある特定の状況で言い分がたくさんある, 何もない…→**言いたい事がある, ない…** ‖ *Late again! What have you got to say for yourself?* また遅刻しましたね. どんな言い訳をするつもりですか.

**I must say**(口語) ▶定義 used to emphasize your opinion 意見を強調するのに用いて→**全く, 本当のところ** ‖ *I must say, I didn't believe him at first.* 本当のところ, 私は当初彼を信用していなかった.

**I wouldn't say no**(口語) ▶定義 used to say that you would like sth 〜が欲しいという場合に用いて→**喜んで頂きます** ‖ *'Coffee?' 'I wouldn't say no.'* 「コーヒーはいかが」「喜んで頂きます」

**Say when**(口語) ▶定義 used to tell sb to say when you have poured enough drink in his/her glass or put enough food on his/her plate グラスに飲み物が十分に注がれたり, 皿に料理が十分盛られたとき言ってくれと相手に頼むのに用いて→**十分な量になったら言ってください, よくなったら言ってください**

**that is to say…** ▶定義 which means… それは〜を意味する→**(挿入語句として) すなわち, 言い換えれば** ‖ *We're leaving on Friday, that's to say in a week's time.* 私たちは金曜日に, つまり1週間後に出発します.

**say²** /séɪ/ 名[単数扱い, **U**] ▶定義 **(a) say (in sth)** the authority or right to decide sth ある事を決定する権限や権利→**(〜について)発言の機会, 発言権, 決定権** ‖ *I'd like to have some say in the arrangements for the party.* 私はパーティーの準備について少し言わせてもらいたい事がある.

成句 **have your say** ▶定義 to express your opinion 自分の意見を述べる→**言い分を述べる** ‖ *Thank you for your comments. Now let somebody else have their say.* ご意見ありがとうございました. それでは, ほかの人に発言していただきましょう.

**saying** /séɪɪŋ/ 名 **C** ▶定義 a well-known phrase that gives advice about sth or says sth that many people believe is true 〜に関して忠告を与えたり, 多くの人々が真実であると思う事を表現する, よく知られた言い回し→**ことわざ, 格言** ‖ *'Love is blind' is an old saying.* 「恋は盲目」は古いことわざだ. ☞参 **proverb**

**scab** /skæb/ 名 **C U** ▶定義 a mass of dried blood that forms over a part of the body where the skin has been cut or broken 切ったり傷付けたりした皮膚にできる, 乾いた血の塊→**かさぶた** ☞参 **scar**

**scaffold** /skǽfəld, -foʊld/ 名 **C** ▶定義 a platform on which criminals were killed in past times by hanging 昔, 罪人を縛り首にした台→**絞首台**

**scaffolding** /skǽfəldɪŋ/ 名 **U** ▶定義 long metal poles and wooden boards that form a structure which is put next to a building so that people who are building, painting, etc can stand and work on it 金属製の支柱と木製の板でできた構

造物. 建物に近接して置かれ, 建築・塗装などをする人がその上に立って作業をすることができる→足場

**scald** /skɔːld/ 動⑯ ▶定義 to burn sb/sth with very hot liquid 非常に高温の液体で～をやけどさせる →(熱湯・蒸気などで)～をやけどさせる ‖ *I scalded my arm badly when I was cooking.* 料理をしているときに, 腕をひどくやけどしてしまった. — scald 名 ⓒ →やけど — scalding 形 →やけどするほど熱い ‖ *scalding hot water* やけどするほど熱い湯

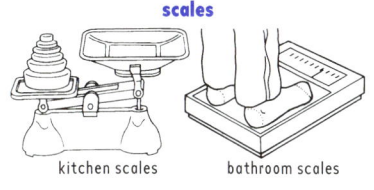

kitchen scales　bathroom scales

*****scale**[1] /skeɪl/ 名 ▶定義 1 ⓒⓊ the size of sth, especially when compared to other things ～の規模, 特にほかの物と比較した場合→規模, 程度, スケール ‖ *We shall be making the product **on a large scale** next year.* 我々は来年, この製品を大規模に生産するつもりだ. *At this stage it is impossible to estimate **the full scale of** the disaster.* 現段階では, 災害の規模全体を推定することは不可能だ. ▶定義 2 ⓒ a series of marks on a tool or piece of equipment that you use for measuring sth ～の測定に使う道具や器具に付いている一連の印→目盛り, 度盛り ‖ *The ruler has one scale in centimetres and one scale in inches.* 定規にはセンチの目盛りとインチの目盛りが付いている. ▶定義 3 ⓒ a series of numbers, amounts, etc that are used for measuring or fixing the level of sth ～の程度を測定または確定するのに使われる一連の数, 量など→等級, 段階, 等級表 ‖ *The earthquake measured 6.5 on the Richter scale.* その地震はリヒタースケールでマグニチュード 6.5 を記録した. *the new pay scale for nurses* 看護婦の新しい給与表 ▶定義 4 ⓒ the relationship between the actual size of sth and its size on a map or plan ～の実際の大きさと地図や設計図上の大きさとの関係→縮尺 ‖ *The map has a scale of one centimetre to a kilometre.* その地図は 1 キロメートルを 1 センチメートルに縮尺したものだ. *a scale of 1: 50000 (= one to fifty thousand)* 5 万分の 1 の縮尺 *We need a map with a larger scale.* もっと大きな縮尺の地図が必要だ. *a scale model* 縮尺模型 ▶定義 5 scales[複数扱い] a piece of equipment that is used for weighing sb/sth ～の重さを量るのに用いる器具→はかり, 体重計 ‖ *I weighed it on the kitchen scales.* 私は台所用のはかりでその重さを量った. ▶定義 6 ⓒ a series of musical notes which go up or down in a fixed order. People play or sing scales to improve their technical ability. 一定の順序で上下する一連の音符. 技術を向上させるため, これに沿って演奏したり歌ったりする→音階 ‖ *the scale of C major* ハ長調音階 ▶定義 7 ⓒ one of the small flat pieces of hard material that cover the body of some fish and animals 一部の魚や動物の体を覆っている, 小さくて平らな硬い物→うろこ ‖ *the scales of a snake* 蛇のうろこ ☛ C1 ページのさし絵

**scale**[2] /skeɪl/ 動⑯ ▶定義 to climb up a high wall, steep cliff, etc 高い壁, 険しい崖(がけ)などによじ登る→(塀など)によじ登る, (山など)に登る 句動詞 scale sth up/down ▶定義 to increase/decrease the size, number, importance, etc of sth 物の大きさ, 数量, 重要性などを増す・減らす→～の規模を拡大・縮小する ‖ *Police have scaled up their search for the missing boy.* 警察は行方不明の少年の捜索範囲を拡大した.

**scalp** /skælp/ 名 ⓒ ▶定義 the skin on the top of your head that is under your hair 頭髪の下にある皮膚→頭皮

**scalpel** /ˈskælp(ə)l/ 名 ⓒ ▶定義 a small knife that is used by doctors (surgeons) when they are doing operations 医者(外科医)が手術をする際に用いる小刀→メス

**scamper** /ˈskæmpər/ 動⑲ ▶定義 (used especially about a child or small animal) to run quickly (特に子供や小動物について)素早く走る→すばしこく走る, 駆け回る, 跳ね回る

**scan** /skæn/ 動⑯ (**scanning**; **scanned**) ▶定義 1 to look at or read every part of sth quickly until you find what you are looking for 探している物を見つけるまで, ある物の各部分を素早く見る, または読む→～をざっと見る・読む, ～に急いで目を通す ‖ *Vic scanned the list until he found his*

## 1434 scandal

*own name*. ヴィックはリストにざっと目を通して、自分の名前を見つけた. ▶定義2 (used about a machine) to examine what is inside a person's body or inside an object such as a suitcase (機械について)人の体内や、スーツケースのような物の内部に何があるか検査する→〜を調べる、走査する、スキャンする ‖ *Machines scan all the luggage for bombs and guns.* 爆弾や銃がないか機械ですべての荷物を調べる. — scan 名 ⒞→走査、検査 ‖ *The scan showed the baby was in the normal position.* 検査で赤ん坊が正常の位置にあることが分かった.

**scandal** /skǽnd(ə)l/ 名 ▶定義1 ⒞ⓤ an action, a situation or behaviour that shocks people; the public feeling that is caused by such behaviour 人々にショックを与える行動、状況または振舞い; そのような振舞いによって引き起こされる世間の感情→スキャンダル、醜聞、不祥事、汚職事件; 騒ぎ、物議 ‖ *The chairman resigned after being involved in a financial scandal.* 財政上のスキャンダルに巻き込まれた結果、議長は辞任した. *There was no suggestion of scandal in his private life.* 彼の私生活にはスキャンダルを思わせるものは何もなかった. *The poor state of school buildings is a real scandal.* 校舎のひどい有り様は言語道断だ. ▶定義2 ⓤ talk about sth bad or wrong that sb has or may have done 人が行った、または行った可能性のある悪い事や間違った事についてのうわさ→中傷、悪評、陰口 ‖ *to spread scandal about sb* 〜についての中傷をまき散らす

**scandalize** (または **-ise**) /skǽnd(ə)làɪz/ 動 他 ▶定義 to cause sb to feel shocked by doing sth that he/she thinks is bad or wrong 〜が良くない、間違っていると考えている…をやって、その人をあきれさせる→〜を憤慨させる、あきれさせる、〜のまゆをひそめさせる

**scandalous** /skǽnd(ə)ləs/ 形 ▶定義 very shocking or wrong 大変衝撃的な、誤った→けしからん、ひどい ‖ *It is scandalous that so much money is wasted.* これほど多額の金が無駄にされているのはけしからん事だ.

**Scandinavia** /skæ̀ndənéɪviə/ 名 [単数扱い] ▶定義 the group of countries in northern Europe that consists of Denmark, Norway and Sweden. Sometimes Finland and Iceland are also said to be part of Scandinavia. デンマーク、ノルウェー、スウェーデンから成る北ヨーロッパの国々. フィンランド、アイスランドを含むこともある→スカンジナビア、北欧 — **Scandinavian** 形→スカンジナビア(人・語)の、北欧(人・語)の

**scanner** /skǽnər/ 名 ⒞ ▶定義 an electronic machine that can look at, record or send images or electronic information 画像や電子データを検索、記録、送信する電子機械→走査器、スキャナー ‖ *The scanner can detect cancer at an early stage.* スキャナーは初期のがんを見つけることができる. *I used the scanner to send the document by e-mail.* 書類を電子メールで送信するのにスキャナーを用いた.

**scant** /skænt/ 形 (名詞の前だけ) ▶定義 not very much; not as much as necessary あまり多くない; 必要なほどたくさんない→乏しい、不足気味の

**scanty** /skǽnti/ 形 ▶定義 too small in size or amount 大きさや量が小さすぎる→乏しい、不十分な ‖ *We didn't learn much from the scanty information they gave us.* 彼らがくれた乏しい情報から、我々が得るところはほとんどなかった. — **scantily** 副→乏しく、不足して ‖ *I realized I was too scantily dressed for the cold weather.* この寒い陽気に自分があまりにも薄着だと気が付いた.

**scapegoat** /skéɪpgòʊt/ 名 ⒞ ▶定義 a person who is punished for things that are not his/her fault 自分の過ちでない事で罰を受ける人→スケープゴート、(他人の罪の)身代わり ‖ *When Alison was sacked she felt she had been **made a scapegoat** for all the company's problems.* 首になった時、アリソンは自分が会社のすべての問題の責任を取らされたと感じた.

*****scar** /skɑːr/ 名 ⒞ ▶定義 a mark on the skin that is caused by a cut that skin has grown over 切り傷の跡に皮膚が新たにかぶさって生じた傷跡→傷跡 ‖ *The operation didn't leave a very big scar.* 手術で大きな傷跡は残らなかった. ☛参 scab — scar 動 自 他 (scarring; scarred)→傷跡が残る; 〜に傷跡を付ける ‖ *William's face was **scarred for life** in the accident.* 事故でウィリアムの顔に生涯傷跡が残った.

*****scarce** /skeərs/ 形 ▶定義 not existing in large quantities; hard to find 多量にはない; 見つけに

くい→乏しい, 不足の, 少ない; まれな ‖ *Food for birds and animals is scarce in the winter.* 鳥や動物の食糧は冬には不足する. ⇔ **plentiful** — **scarcity** /skéəs(ə)ti/ 名 ◉ Ⓤ (複 **scarcities**) ▶定義 不足, 欠乏 ‖ *(a) scarcity of food/jobs/resources* 食料不足・就職難・資源不足

**scarcely** /skéəsli/ 副 ▶定義 **1** only just; almost not→辛うじて; ほとんど~ない ‖ *There was scarcely a car in sight.* 車はほとんど1台も見当たらなかった. *She's not a friend of mine. I scarcely know her.* 彼女は私の友人ではない. 私は彼女をほとんど知らない. ☞参 **hardly** ▶定義 **2** used to suggest that sth is not reasonable or likely ~が理にかなわない, またはありそうにないことを示唆するのに用いて→まさか~(し)ない, とても~ない ‖ *You can scarcely expect me to believe that after all you said before.* あなたがあんな事を言った後で, まさか私がそんな事を信じるなんて思っていないでしょうね.

***scare**¹ /skeər/ 動 ▶定義 **1** Ⓗ to make a person or an animal frightened 人や動物を怖がらせる→ ~を怖がらせる, おびえさせる ‖ *The sudden noise scared us all.* 突然の音で私たちは皆おびえた. *It scares me to think what might happen.* 何が起きるのだろうと考えると怖くなる. ▶定義 **2** Ⓘ to become frightened 怖くなる→おびえる ‖ *I don't scare easily, but when I saw the gun I was terrified.* 私は容易には怖からない方だが, 銃を見た時には恐怖を覚えた.

句動詞 scare sb/sth away/off ▶定義 to make a person or animal leave or stay away by frightening them 人や動物を怖がらせて去らせる・近付けさせない →(人や動物)を脅かして追い払う ‖ *Don't make any noise or you'll scare the birds away.* 音を立てないでください, さもないと鳥が逃げてしまいます.

**scare**² /skeər/ 名 ◉ ▶定義 **1** a feeling of being frightened おびえの情感→**恐怖, おびえ, 不安** ‖ *It wasn't a serious heart attack but it gave him a scare.* それは大事に至る心臓発作ではなかったが, 彼をどきっとさせた. ▶定義 **2** a situation where many people are afraid or worried about sth ~について多くの人たちが恐れたり心配している状況 →**(社会的)不安, 恐慌状態** ‖ *Last night there was a bomb scare in the city centre.* 昨夜, 市の中心街で爆弾騒ぎがあった.

---

scatter 1435

**scarecrow** /skéərkroʊ/ 名 ◉ ▶定義 a very simple model of a person that is put in a field to frighten away the birds 鳥を驚かせて追い払うために田畑に置かれた, 非常に簡単な人の模型→**かかし**

*scared /skeərd/ 形 ▶定義 **scared (of sb/sth); scared (of doing sth/to do sth)** frightened → (~を)怖がる, (~に)おびえる ‖ *Are you scared of the dark?* あなたは暗闇(やみ)が怖いですか. *She's scared of walking home alone.* 彼女は1人で歩いて帰宅するのを怖がっている. *Everyone was too scared to move.* だれもが恐怖のあまり動けなかった.

**scarf** /skɑːrf/ 名 ◉ (複 **scarfs** /skɑːrfs/ または **scarves** /skɑːrvz/) ▶定義 **1** a long thin piece of cloth, usually made of wool, that you wear around your neck to keep warm 保温のため首の回りに巻く薄くて長い, 通常ウール地の布→**マフラー, えり巻き** ☞ C6 ページのさし絵 ▶定義 **2** a square piece of cloth that women wear around their neck or shoulders or over their heads to keep warm or for decoration 保温やおしゃれのため女性が首や肩の周りに巻いたり, 頭にかぶったりする四角い布→**スカーフ**

**scarlet** /skɑːrlət/ 形 名 Ⓤ ▶定義 (of a bright red colour 明るい赤色(の) → **緋(ひ)色(の), 深紅(の)**

**scary** /skéəri/ 形 (**scarier; scariest**) 略式 ▶定義 frightening→**怖い, 恐ろしい** ‖ *a scary ghost story* 恐ろしい幽霊の話 *It was a bit scary driving in the mountains at night.* 夜間に山中を運転するのは少し怖かった.

**scathing** /skéɪðɪŋ/ 形 ▶定義 expressing a very strong negative opinion about sb/sth; very critical ~に対して非常に強い否定的な意見を表した; 非常に批判的な→**辛辣(しんらつ)な, 痛烈な** ‖ *a scathing attack on the new leader* 新しい指導者への容赦のない批判 *scathing criticism* 酷評

**scatter** /skǽtər/ 動 ▶定義 **1** Ⓘ (used about a group of people or animals) to move away quickly in different directions (人や動物の集団について)さまざまな方向に素早く散る→**散り散りになる, 分散する** ▶定義 **2** Ⓗ to drop or throw things in different directions over a wide area 広い範囲にわたってさまざまな方向に物を落とす・投げる → **~をまき散らす** ‖ *The wind scat-*

## 1436 scattered

*tered the papers all over the room.* 風で紙が部屋に散らばった.

**scattered** /skǽtərd/ 形 ▶定義 spread over a large area or happening several times during a period of time 広い範囲に広がった, 一定の時間内に何度も起こる➔**散らばった, 点在する, まばらな, 時折の** ‖ *There will be sunny intervals with scattered showers today.* 今日は晴れ間の合間に, 時々にわか雨があるでしょう.

**scavenge** /skǽvəndʒ, -vɪndʒ/ 動自他 ▶定義 to look for food, etc among waste and rubbish 廃棄物やごみの中から食べ物などを探す➔(～を)あさる — **scavenger** 名 C➔**死体をあさる動物, 清掃動物** ‖ *Scavengers steal the food that the lion has killed.* 清掃動物はライオンが殺した動物の肉を盗む.

**SCE** /ès siː íː/ 略 Scottish Certificate of Education ▶定義 Pupils in Scotland take the SCE at Standard grade at the age of about 16 and at Higher grade at about 17. スコットランドでは, 生徒は16歳くらいのときに標準レベル (Standard grade), 17歳くらいのときに上位レベル (Higher grade) の SCE を取得する➔**スコットランド中等教育終了試験**

**scenario** /sənáːrioʊ/ 名 C (複 **scenarios**) ▶定義 1 one way that things may happen in the future 将来物事がこう起こるかもしれないという1つの在り方➔**筋書き, シナリオ** ‖ *A likely scenario is that the company will get rid of some staff.* 会社が人員を何名か解雇することはありそうな筋書きだ. ▶定義 2 a description of what happens in a play or film 演劇や映画での出来事を書いたもの➔**台本, 脚本, シナリオ**

*****scene** /síːn/ 名 ▶定義 1 C the place where sth happened ～が起こった場所➔**場所, 現場** ‖ *the scene of a crime/an accident* 犯罪・事故現場 *An ambulance was on the scene in minutes.* 救急車は数分で現場に到着した. ▶定義 2 C an occasion when sb expresses great anger or another strong emotion in public ～が激しい怒りなどの強い感情を人前で表す場面➔**大騒ぎ, 醜態** ‖ *There was quite a scene when she refused to pay the bill.* 彼女が料金の支払いを拒んだ時はかなりの大騒ぎになった. ▶定義 3 C one part of a book, play, film, etc in which the events happen in one place 出来事の起こる場所が1箇所で構成される, 本, 劇, 映画などの一部➔**場面, シーン** ‖ *The first scene of 'Hamlet' takes place on the castle walls.*「ハムレット」の冒頭の場面は城壁が舞台になっている. ▶定義 4 C U what you see around you in a particular place ある場所で自分の周囲に見えるもの➔**眺め, 光景, 景色, 風景** ‖ *Her new job was no better, but at least it would be a change of scene.* 彼女の新しい仕事は前よりも良くはなかったが, 少なくとも環境の変化にはなるだろう. ▶定義 5 **the scene** [単数扱い] the way of life or the present situation in a particular area of activity 生活様式, 特定の活動領域における現在の状況➔**～界, 情勢, 事態** ‖ *The political scene in Eastern Europe is very confused.* 東欧の政治情勢は非常に混とんとしている. *the fashion scene* ファッション界

**scenery** /síːn(ə)ri/ 名 U ▶定義 1 the natural beauty that you see around you in the country 地方で周囲一面に見られる自然の美しさ➔**風景, 景観, 景色** ‖ *The scenery is superb in the mountains.* 山々に囲まれた景観は壮大だ. ▶定義 2 the furniture, painted cloth, boards, etc that are used on the stage in a theatre 劇場の舞台で用いられる家具, 彩色された布, 板など➔**舞台装置, 舞台背景** ‖ *The scenery is changed during the interval.* 舞台装置は幕間(まくあい)に入れ替えられる.

▶ 田園の一地帯の眺めが美しいとき, beautiful scenery (美しい景色) を用いて表す. ある地域の特色が配列された様子には landscape が使われる: *Trees and hedges are a typical feature of the British landscape.* (樹木や生け垣はイギリスの風景の典型的な特徴だ.) *an urban landscape* (= in a city or town) (都市の (= 市や町の) 景観). 窓から外をのぞいたり, 高い所から見下ろしたときに見えるものを表現する場合, view を用いる: *There was a marvellous view of the sea from our hotel room.* (私たちのホテルの部屋からすばらしい海の眺めが広がっていた.) country(3) の注を参照.

**scenic** /síːnɪk, sén-/ 形 ▶定義 having beautiful scenery 美しい景観を持つ➔**景色・眺めの良い, 風光明媚(めいび)な**

**scent** /sént/ 名 ▶定義 1 C U a pleasant smell 好

ましいにおい➔香り,芳香 ‖ *This flower has no scent.* この花は香りがない. ▶定義2 ⓒⓊthe smell that an animal leaves behind and that some other animals can follow ある動物が残し,ほかの動物がその跡をたどることができるにおい➔(獣の)遺臭 ▶定義3 Ⓤ 特に 医 a liquid with a pleasant smell that you wear on your skin to make it smell nice; perfume 良い香りがするように皮膚に付ける,好ましい香りを持つ液体; 香水➔香水 ▶定義4 [単数扱い] the feeling that sth is going to happen ある事が起きるだろうという感じ➔勘,気配 ‖ *The scent of victory was in the air.* 勝利の予感がした. — scent 動Ⓣ➔(犬などが)〜をかぎ付ける ‖ *The dog scented a rabbit and shot off.* その犬はウサギのにおいをかぎ出し,鉄砲玉のように飛び出していった. — scented 形➔良い香りのする,(〜の)香りのする

**sceptic** (米 **skeptic**) /sképtɪk/ 名 Ⓒ ▶定義 a person who doubts that sth is true, right, etc 〜の真実,正しさなどを疑う人→懐疑論者,疑い深い人 — sceptical(米 skeptical)/-k(ə)l/ 形 ▶定義 sceptical (of/about sth)➔疑い深い,(〜について)懐疑的な ‖ *Many doctors are sceptical about the value of alternative medicine.* 多くの医者は代替医療の価値について懐疑的だ.

**scepticism** (米 **skepticism**) /sképtəsìz(ə)m/ 名 Ⓤ ▶定義 a general feeling of doubt about sth; a feeling that you are not likely to believe sth 〜に対する一般的な懐疑心; 〜を信じそうにもないという感じ➔懐疑

**schedule**[1] /ʃédjuːl, skédʒuːl/ 名 ▶定義1 ⒸⓊa plan of things that will happen or of work that must be done これから起きる出来事や,しなければならない仕事に関する計画➔予定,計画,スケジュール ‖ *Max has a busy schedule for the next few days.* マックスは次の数日間,予定が詰まっている. *to be ahead of/behind schedule (= to have done more/less than was planned)* 予定よりも早い・遅い(= 成し遂げた事が計画よりも多い・少ない) ▶定義2 米 = TIMETABLE

**schedule**[2] /ʃédjuːl, skédʒuːl/ 動Ⓣ ▶定義 schedule sth (for sth) to arrange for sth to happen or be done at a particular time 〜を特定の時に起こるように,または行われるように手はずを整える➔〜を(…に)予定する ‖ *We've scheduled the meeting for Monday morning.* 我々は月曜日の午前中に会議を予定している. *The train was scheduled to arrive at 10.07.* その列車は10時7分に到着することになっていた.

**scheme**[1] /skiːm/ 名 Ⓒ ▶定義1 a scheme (to do sth/for doing sth) an official plan or system for doing or organizing sth 〜を行ったり組織したりするための公式の計画や体制➔(〜しようとする・〜の)計画,案; 組織,機構 ‖ *a new scheme to provide houses in the area* その地域に住宅を供給する新しい計画 *a local scheme for recycling newspapers* 新聞紙再利用のための地域計画 ▶定義2 a clever plan to do sth 〜を行うための巧妙な計画➔計略,策略,たくらみ ‖ *He's thought of a new scheme for making money fast.* 彼は手っ取り早く金を稼ぐ新しいもくろみを思い付いた. ☛参 **colour scheme**

**scheme**[2] /skiːm/ 動ⒾⓉ ▶定義 to make a secret or dishonest plan 秘密の,または不正な計画を立てる➔(〜を)たくらむ ‖ *She felt that everyone was scheming to get rid of her.* 彼女はみんなが自分を追い払おうとたくらんでいると感じた.

**schizophrenia** /skìtsoʊfríːniə/ 名 Ⓤ ▶定義 a serious mental illness in which a person confuses the real world and the world of the imagination and often behaves in strange and unexpected ways 現実の世界と空想の世界を混同し,しばしば奇妙で突飛な行動をする,重度の精神病➔精神分裂症 — schizophrenic /skìtsoʊfrénɪk/ 形 Ⓒ➔精神分裂症の,精神分裂症患者

**scholar** /skálər/ 名 Ⓒ ▶定義1 a person who studies and has a lot of knowledge about a particular subject 特定の学問上のテーマについて研究し,多くの知識を持っている人➔学者 ▶定義2 a person who has passed an exam or won a competition and has been given some money (a scholarship) to help pay for his/her studies 試験に合格,コンクールに優勝などし,学費の助けになる金(奨学金)を授与された人➔奨学金受給者,奨学生,給費生 ‖ *a British Council scholar* ブリティッシュカウンシル給費生 ☛参 **student**

**scholarship** /skálərʃɪp/ 名 ▶定義1 Ⓒan amount of money that is given to a person who has passed an exam or won a competition, in order

## 1438　school

to help pay for his/her studies 試験に合格, コンクールに優勝などした人に授与される学資助成金→**奨学金** ‖ *to win a scholarship to Yale* エール大学へ入る奨学金を獲得する　▶定義2　❶ serious study of an academic subject ある学問分野の本格的な研究→**学問, 学識**

\*school /skuːl/ 🔊　▶定義1　Ⓒ the place where children go to be educated 子供たちが教育を受けに通う場所→**(建物・施設としての)学校, 校舎** ‖ *Where did you go to school?* あなたはどこの学校に通われましたか. *They're building a new school in our area.* 私たちの地域で今新しい学校が建築中だ. *Do you have to wear school uniform?* 学校に制服を着ていかなければならないのですか. *Was your school co-educational (= for boys and girls) or single-sex?* 君の学校は共学(＝男女両方のための学校)でしたか, それとも男子[女子]校でしたか.　▶定義2　Ⓤ the time you spend at a school; the process of being educated in a school 学校で過ごす時期; 学校で教育を受ける過程 →**(制度としての)学校(教育), 授業, 学業** ‖ *Their children are still at school.* 彼らの子供たちはまだ在学中だ. *Children start school at 5 years old in Britain and can leave school at 16.* イギリスでは, 子供たちは5歳で学校に通い始め, 16歳でやめることができる. *School starts at 9 o'clock and finishes at about 3.30.* 学校は9時に始まり, 3時30分ころ終わる. *After school we usually have homework to do.* 放課後, 私たちには大抵やらなければならない宿題がある.

▶学校に通常の理由で(つまり生徒または先生として)行くことを言う場合, school の前に冠詞 (the) を付けない: *Where do your children go to school?* (お子さんたちはどちらの学校に通っていますか.) *I enjoyed being at school.* (私は学校生活を楽しんだ.) *Do you walk to school?* (歩いて通学しているのですか.) 別の理由で(例えば, 親として)学校に行くというときには, school の前に the を付ける: *I have to go to the school on Thursday to talk to John's teacher.* (ジョンの担任と話をするため, 木曜日に学校に行かなければならない.) また, 学校についてより詳しい情報を与える場合にも, a または the を用いなければならない: *Rani goes to the school in the next village.* (ラニは隣村の学校に通っている.) *She teaches at a school for children with learning difficulties.* (彼女は学習が困難な子供たちを対象とする学校で教えている.)

▶定義3　[単数扱い, 単数または複数形の動詞と共に] all the pupils and teachers in a school 学校にいる生徒と先生全員→**(教職員を含む)全校, 全校生徒** ‖ *The whole school cheered the winner.* 全校が優勝者に喝采した.　▶定義4　(複合語を作るために用いて) connected with school 学校に関する→**学校の, 学校教育に関する** ‖ *children of school age* 学齢に達した子供たち *The bus was full of schoolchildren.* バスは学童で込み合っていた. *It is getting increasingly difficult for school-leavers to find jobs.* 中途退学者が仕事を見つけるのはますます困難になってきている. *Schoolteachers have been awarded a 2% pay rise.* 教員に(対し)2パーセントの賃上げが認められた. *I don't have many good memories of my schooldays.* 私には学校時代のいい思い出がほとんどない.　▶定義5　Ⓒ a place where you go to learn a particular subject ある特定の科目を学ぶために通う場所→**教習所, 訓練所, 専門学校** ‖ *a language/driving/drama/business school* 語学学校・自動車教習所・演劇専門学校・ビジネススクール　▶定義6　Ⓒ 困 a college or university→**単科大学, 総合大学**　▶定義7　Ⓒ a department of a university that teaches a particular subject ある特定の学科を教える大学の学部→**学部** ‖ *the school of geography at Leeds University* リーズ大学地理学部　▶定義8　Ⓒ a group of writers, painters, etc who have the same ideas or style 思想や様式が同じ作家, 画家などの集まり→**流派, 学派, ～派** ‖ *the Flemish school of painting* フランドル派絵画　▶定義9　Ⓒ a large group of fish swimming together 一緒に遊泳している魚の大きな群れ →**(魚の)群れ**

> ▶社会・文化 🌐
>
> **学校のいろいろ**
>
> アメリカは日本のように6-3-3制が多く見られます. 小学校は elementary school (primary school), 中学校が junior high school, 高等学校が senior high school, 大学は university (college) となります.

イギリスの制度はもう少し複雑で4年制の小学校(junior school)と大学(university, college)の間に7年制の総合中等学校(comprehensive school)やグラマースクール(grammar school)などがあります。一方、最初から進学を目指すため、これとは別のコースを進む生徒もいます。私立小学校(preparatory school)、パブリックスクール(public school)を経て大学に行くというもので、上流階級の子供に多く見られます。

イギリスでは、public school というと大学進学を目指す生徒が通う全寮制の私立学校で Eton(イートン校)とか Rugby(ラグビー校、ラグビー発祥の学校)などが有名です。しかし、アメリカで public school というと日本と同じく「公立学校」で、private school が「私立学校」を指します。

**成句 a school of thought** ▶定義 the ideas or opinions that one group of people share 1つのグループが共有する思想や意見→**学派, 学説, 考え方** ‖ *There are various schools of thought on this matter.* この問題についてはさまざまな学説がある.

**schooling** /skúːlɪŋ/ 名 Ⓤ ▶定義 the time that you spend at school; your education 学校で過ごす年月; 教育→**学校教育(を受けること)**

*****science** /sáɪəns/ 名 ▶定義 1 Ⓤ the study of and knowledge about the physical world and natural laws 自然界や自然の法則の研究とそれらに関する知識→**科学, 自然科学, 科学的知識** ‖ *Modern science has discovered a lot about the origin of life.* 現代の科学は生命の起源について多くの事を発見している. *Fewer young people are studying science at university.* 大学で自然科学を学ぶ若い人が少なくなりつつある.
▶定義 2 Ⓒ one of the subjects into which science can be divided 科学が分類される各分野の1つ →**(学問の分野としての)科学** ‖ *Biology, chemistry and physics are all sciences.* 生物学, 化学, 物理学はすべて科学である.
▶人と社会の研究は social science (社会科学) と言う.

**science fiction** 名 Ⓤ ▶定義 books, films, etc about events that take place in the future, often involving travel in space しばしば宇宙旅行を含む, 未来に起こる出来事を描いた本, 映画など→空想科学小説, SF

*****scientific** /ˌsaɪənˈtɪfɪk/ 形 ▶定義 1 connected with or involving science 科学に関する, 科学に関連のある→**科学の** ‖ *We need more funding for scientific research.* 我々は科学研究のためにより多くの資金を必要としている. *scientific instruments* 科学器械 ▶定義 2 (used about a way of thinking or of doing sth) careful and logical (考え方や〜のやり方について)周到で論理的な→**科学的な** ‖ *a scientific study of the way people use language* 言語の用い方に関する科学的な研究 — **scientifically** /-k(ə)li/ 副→**科学的に** ‖ *Sorting out the files won't take long if we do it scientifically.* 科学的に行えば, ファイルの分類にそんなに時間はかからないだろう.

*****scientist** /sáɪəntɪst/ 名 Ⓒ ▶定義 a person who studies or teaches science, especially biology, chemistry or physics 科学, 特に生物学, 化学, 物理学を研究, または教える人→**科学者**

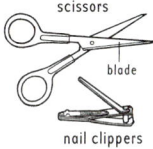

*****scissors** /sízərz/ 名 [複数扱い] ▶定義 a tool for cutting things that consists of two long, flat, sharp pieces of metal that are joined together 2本の長く平らな鋭い金属片が接合された, 物を切るための道具→**はさみ** ☞ scissors は複数名詞である. *These scissors are blunt.* (このはさみは切れ味が悪い.) 1丁のはさみを表す場合, a scissors とは言えず, a pair of scissors と言わなければならない.

**scoff** /skɑf/ 動 ▶定義 1 Ⓘ **scoff (at sb/sth)** to speak about sb/sth in a way that shows you think that he/she/it is stupid or ridiculous 〜が愚かだ, ばかばかしいと思っていることをあからさまにした話し方をする→**(〜を)あざける, あざ笑う**
▶定義 2 Ⓣ 英略式 to eat a lot of sth quickly たくさんの量を素早く食べる →**(〜を)がつがつ食う**

**scold** /skóʊld/ 動 Ⓣ ▶定義 **scold sb (for sth/for doing sth)** to speak angrily to sb because he/she has done something bad or wrong 悪い事または誤った事をしたという理由で, 〜に対して怒った口調で話す→**〜をしかる** ☞ tell off の方が一般的である.

**scone** /skóʊn, skɑ́n/ 名 Ⓒ ▶定義 a small, simple

cake, usually eaten with butter on 小さい素朴なケーキ.普通バターを付けて食べる→スコーン,ビスケット

**scoop**[1] /skuːp/ 名 ◉ ▶定義1 a tool like a spoon used for picking up ice cream, flour, grain, etc スプーンのような道具.アイスクリーム,小麦粉,穀物などをすくい取るのに用いる→大さじ,ひしゃく ▶定義2 the amount that one scoop contains 1回にすくえる量→(アイスクリームなどの)一すくい,一盛り ▶定義3 an exciting piece of news that is reported by one newspaper, television or radio station before it is reported anywhere else ほかの新聞,テレビ,ラジオなどで報道される前に独占的に報道される,人の好奇心をそそるニュース→特ダネ,スクープ

**scoop**[2] /skuːp/ 動 ◉ ▶定義1 scoop sth(out/ up) to make a hole in sth or to take sth out by using a scoop or sth similar すくい取る道具を用いて〜に穴を掘る,〜を取り除く→(穴など)を掘る,えぐる ‖ *Scoop out the middle of the pineapple.* パイナップルの芯(しん)を取り出しなさい. ▶定義2 scoop sb/sth (up) to move or lift sb/sth using a continuous action 連続的な動作で〜を動かす,持ち上げる→〜を抱き上げる,〜をすくい上げる ‖ *He scooped up the child and ran.* 彼は子供をすくい上げて,走った. ▶定義3 to win a big or important prize 大きな・重要な賞を勝ち取る→(賞)をさらう ‖ *The film has scooped all the awards this year.* 今年はその映画が賞を総なめにした. ▶定義4 to get a story before all other newspapers, TV stations, etc ほかのすべての新聞社,テレビ局などの前に新聞種を入手する→(他社)を特ダネで出し抜く

**scooter** /skúːtər/ 名 ◉ ▶定義1 a light motorbike with a small engine 小型エンジンを搭載した小型オートバイ→スクーター ☞ **motorbike** のさし絵 ▶定義2 a child's toy with two wheels that you stand on and move by pushing one foot against the ground 子供の遊び道具.車が2つ付いていて,その上に乗って,片足で地面をけって動かす→(子供用の)スクーター

**scope** /skóup/ 名 ▶定義1 ⓤ scope (for sth/to do sth) the chance or opportunity to do sth 〜を行う好機,機会→(能力などを示す)機会,(活動などの)余地 ‖ *The job offers plenty of scope for creativity.* その仕事は創造性を働かせる余地が豊富にある. ▶定義2 [単数扱い] the variety of subjects that are being discussed or considered 目下議論・検討中の題目の広がり→範囲,領域 ‖ *The government was unwilling to extend the scope of the inquiry.* 政府はその調査の範囲を広げることに消極的だった.

**scorch** /skɔːrtʃ/ 動 ⊕ ▶定義 to burn sth so that its colour changes but it is not destroyed 色は変わるが,破壊しない程度に〜を焼き焦がす→〜を焦がす ‖ *I scorched my blouse when I was ironing it.* 私はアイロンがけの最中に自分のブラウスを焦がしてしまった.

**scorching** /skɔ́ːrtʃɪŋ/ 形 ▶定義 very hot 非常に暑い→焼けるような,じりじりと暑い ‖ *It was absolutely scorching on Tuesday.* 火曜日はまさに焼き付くような暑さだった.

*****score**[1] /skɔːr/ 名 ▶定義1 ⓒ the number of points, goals, etc that sb/sth gets in a game, competition, exam, etc 試合,競技,試験などで〜が獲得する点数,得点など→点数,得点,成績,スコア ‖ *What was the final score?* 最終得点は何点でしたか. *The score is 3-2 to Liverpool.* スコアは3対2で,リバプールの勝利です. *The top score in the test was 80%.* その試験の最高得点は 80 点だった. ▶定義2 **scores**[複数扱い] very many→多数,たくさん ‖ *Scores of people have written to offer their support.* 大勢の人々が手紙で援助を申し出た. ▶定義3 ⓒ the written form of a piece of music 楽曲を書き表したもの→楽譜,譜面
**成句 on that score** ▶定義 as far as that is concerned それに関する限り→その点に関しては ‖ *Lan will be well looked after. Don't worry on that score.* ランはきちんと面倒を見てもらえますよ.その点に関しては心配しなくてもいいです.

*****score**[2] /skɔːr/ 動 ⊜ ⊕ ▶定義 to get points, goals, etc in a game, competition, exam, etc 試合,競技,試験などで点数,得点などを獲得する→(〜を)得点する ‖ *The team still hadn't scored by half-time.* そのチームは前半が終了してもまだ1点も取っていなかった. *Louise scored the highest marks in the exam.* ルイーズは試験で最高点を取った.

**scoreboard** /skɔ́ːrbɔːrd/ 名 ⓒ ▶定義 a large board that shows the score during a game, competition, etc 試合,競技などの間,得点を表示する大きな板→得点掲示板,スコアボード

**scorn¹** /skɔːrn/ 名 U ▶定義 scorn (for sb/sth) the strong feeling that you have when you do not respect sb/sth ～を尊敬［尊重］しないときに抱く強い感情→軽べつ,さげすみ

**scorn²** /skɔːrn/ 動他 ▶定義 1 to feel or show a complete lack of respect for sb/sth ～に対して尊敬［尊重］を全く欠いた気持ちを抱く・態度を示す→～を軽べつする,さげすむ‖ *The President scorned his critics.* 大統領は自分を批判する者たちを一笑に付した. ▶定義 2 to refuse to accept help or advice, especially because you are too proud 特に自尊心が強すぎて,手助けや忠告を拒む→～を(軽べつして)はねつける,拒絶する‖ *The old lady scorned all offers of help.* 老婦人は一切の援助の申し出をはねつけた. ― scornful /-fʊl, -f(ə)l/ 形→軽べつに満ちた,さげすんだ‖ *a scornful look/smile/remark* 軽べつに満ちた表情・嘲笑(ちょうしょう)・冷ややかな言葉 ― scornfully /-fʊli, -f(ə)li/ 副→軽べつして,さげすんで

**Scorpio** /skɔ́ːrpioʊ/ 名 (複 **Scorpios**) C U ▶定義 the eighth sign of the zodiac, the Scorpion 黄道十二宮の8番目であるさそり座→さそり座,天蠍(かつ)宮

**scorpion** /skɔ́ːrpiən/ 名 C ▶定義 a creature which looks like a large insect and lives in hot countries. A scorpion has a long curved tail with a poisonous sting in it. 大きな昆虫に似た,暑い国々に生息する生き物.長い曲がった尾の中に毒針を持つ→さそり

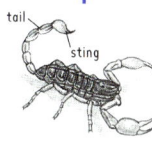
scorpion
tail
sting

**Scot** /skɑt/ 名 C ▶定義 a person who comes from Scotland スコットランド出身の人→スコットランド人

**Scotch** /skɑtʃ/ 名 U C ▶定義 a strong alcoholic drink (whisky) that is made in Scotland; a glass of this スコットランドで造られるアルコール度数の高い飲み物(ウイスキー);この飲み物1杯→スコッチウイスキー,スコッチウイスキー1杯 ☛参 **Scottish** の注

**Scots** /skɑts/ 形 ▶定義 of or connected with people from Scotland スコットランド出身の人の・に関する→スコットランド人の ☛参 **Scottish** の注

**Scotsman** /skɑ́tsmən/ 名 C ▶定義 a man who comes from Scotland スコットランド出身の男性 →(男性の)スコットランド人

***Scottish** /skɑ́tɪʃ/ 形 ▶定義 of or connected with Scotland, its people, culture, etc スコットランド,スコットランド人,スコットランド文化などの・に関する→スコットランドの,スコットランド人［語］の

▶ Scots は通常,スコットランド人についてのみ用いる: *a Scots piper*((スコットランド人の)バグパイプ奏者). Scottish はスコットランドと,スコットランド出身の人にも物にも用いる: *Scottish law/dancing/music*(スコットランドの法律・舞踊・音楽) *She speaks with a strong Scottish accent.* (彼女は強いスコットランドなまりで話す.) *the Scottish Highlands* (スコットランド高地地方). Scotch は,人ではなく,ウイスキーや一部の食べ物に対して用いられる.

**scoundrel** /skáʊndrəl/ 名 C (古) ▶定義 a man who behaves very badly towards other people, especially by being dishonest 他人に対し,粗暴な,特に不正な振る舞いをする男性→悪漢,悪党

**scour** /skáʊər/ 動他 ▶定義 1 to clean sth by rubbing it hard with sth rough 表面がざらざらした物で強くこすって～をきれいにする→～を磨く,(汚れなど)をこすり取る‖ *to scour a dirty pan* 汚れたなべを磨く ▶定義 2 to search a place very carefully because you are looking for sb/sth ～を探し求めて,ある場所を非常に入念に探す→～を探し回る

**scourge** /skəːrdʒ/ 名 C ▶定義 a person or thing that causes a lot of trouble or suffering 多大な困難や苦労をもたらす人や物→悩みの種‖ *Raul was the scourge of the United defence.* ラウルはユナイテッド(イギリスのサッカークラブの名前)のディフェンスの頭痛の種だった.

**scout** /skáʊt/ 名 C ▶定義 1 **Scout** (または **Boy Scout**) a member of an organization (the Scouts) that teaches boys how to look after themselves and encourages them to help others. Scouts do sport, learn useful skills, go camping, etc. 少年たちに自分の面倒を自分で見る方法を教え,人助けを奨励する団体(ボーイスカウト)の一員.団員はスポーツをしたり,役に立つ技術を学習したり,キャンプに行ったりする→

## 1442 scowl

ボーイスカウト ☛参Guide ▶定義2 a soldier who is sent on in front of the rest of the group to find out where the enemy is or which is the best route to take 敵の居どころや最適な進路を探るために,所属部隊に先駆けて前方に遣わされる兵士→**斥候(せっこう)(兵),偵察兵**

**scowl** /skáʊl/ 名動 ▶定義 a look on your face that shows you are angry or in a bad mood 怒っている,または不機嫌であることを示す表情→**しかめっ面,仏頂面** ☛参 frown — scowl 動自→**顔をしかめる,仏頂面をする**

**scrabble** /skrǽb(ə)l/ 動自 ▶定義 to move your fingers or feet around quickly, trying to find sth or get hold of sth ～を見つけたり,つかもうとして,指や足を素早く動き回す→**かき回して探す** ‖ *She scrabbled about in her purse for some coins.* 彼女は小銭を探して財布の中をかき回した.

**scramble** /skrǽmb(ə)l/ 動自 ▶定義1 to climb quickly up or over sth using your hands to help you; to move somewhere quickly 手を使って素早く～によじ登る;素早くどこかに移動する→**よじ登る,乗り越える;素早く～に移る** ‖ *He scrambled up the hill and over the wall.* 彼は急いで小山によじ登り,次いで塀を乗り越えた. *He scrambled to his feet* (= off the ground) *and ran off into the trees.* 彼は慌てて立ち上がると,木立の中へと走り去った. *The children scrambled into the car.* 子供たちは急いで車に乗り込んだ. ▶定義2 scramble (for sth/to do sth) to fight or move quickly to get sth which a lot of people want 大勢の人が望む～を手に入れるために争う,素早く移動する→**奪い合う,先を争って～する** ‖ *People stood up and began scrambling for the exits.* 人々は立ち上がると,出口を目掛けて殺到し始めた. *Everyone was scrambling to get the best bargains.* だれもが先を争って一番の掘り出し物を手に入れようとしていた. — scramble 名 [単数扱い]→**よじ登ること,争奪**

**scrambled egg** 名 U ▶定義 eggs mixed together with milk and then cooked in a pan 牛乳と混ぜ合わせてから,フライパンで加熱調理した卵→**いり卵,スクランブルエッグ**

**scrap**¹ /skræp/ 名 ▶定義1 C a small piece of sth ～の小片→**破片,小片,切れ端** ‖ *a scrap of paper/cloth* 紙・布切れ *scraps of food* いくらかの食べ物,食べ残し ▶定義2 U something that you do not want any more but that is made of material that can be used again 不用になったが,再利用できる素材で作られた物→**スクラップ,廃物,くず鉄** ‖ *The old car was sold for scrap.* その古い車はスクラップとして売られた. *scrap paper* (再生用の)紙くず,古紙 ▶定義3 C 略式 a short fight or argument ごく一時的なけんか,口論 →**(一時的な)いさかい,言い争い**

**scrap**² /skræp/ 動他 (**scrapping; scrapped**) ▶定義 to get rid of sth that you do not want any more 不用になった～を捨てる→**～を廃棄する,処分する** ‖ *I think we should scrap that idea.* 我々はその考えを捨てるべきだと思う.

**scrapbook** /skrǽpbʊk/ 名 C ▶定義 a large book with empty pages that you can stick pictures, newspaper articles, etc in 写真,新聞記事などをはり付けることができるようにページが空白になっている大判の本→**スクラップブック,切り抜き帳**

**scrape**¹ /skréɪp/ 動他 ▶定義1 scrape sth (down/out/off) to remove sth from a surface by moving a sharp edge across it firmly 鋭い刃を強く押し付けるように動かして,表面から～を取り除く→**～をこすり落とす,～をこすって汚れを取る** ‖ *Scrape all the mud off your boots before you come in.* 入る前に靴の泥を全部こすり落としなさい. ▶定義2 scrape sth (against/along/on sth) to damage or hurt sth by rubbing it against sth rough or hard 表面のざらざらした物,または硬い物にこすり付けることにより,～を傷める,傷付ける→**～をこする,～に擦り傷を付ける,擦りむく** ‖ *Mark fell and scraped his knee.* マークは転んで,ひざを擦りむいた. *Sunita scraped the car against the wall.* サニタは塀に車をこすって傷付けた. ▶定義3 自 scrape (sth) against/along/on sth to rub (sth) against sth and make a sharp unpleasant noise ～が…にこすれて,または～を…にこすり付けて,鋭い不快な音を立てる→**～にきしみ音を立てさせる;(～を)こすってきしみ音を立てる** ‖ *The branches scraped against the window.* 枝が窓に当たって嫌な音を立てた. ▶定義4 他 to manage to get or win sth with difficulty 苦労して何とか～を手に入れる,獲得する→**どうにか～を手に入れる** ‖ *I just* scraped a pass in the maths exam. 私は数学の試験に何とか合格した.

**句動詞** scrape by **定義** to manage to live on the money you have, but with difficulty 持っている金で何とか苦労して生活する→**どうにか食べていく** ‖ We can just scrape by on my salary. 私たちは私の給料で何とか生活できている.

scrape through (sth) **定義** to succeed in doing sth with difficulty 〜をすることにやっとのことで成功する→**(試験などに)辛うじて通る** ‖ to scrape through an exam (= just manage to pass it) 辛うじて試験に通る(= どうにか試験に合格する)

scrape sth together/up **定義** to get or collect sth together with difficulty 何とか苦労して〜を手に入れる,集める→**(金,人質など)をかき集める**

**scrape**² /skréɪp/ 图 **C 定義1** the action or unpleasant sound of one thing rubbing hard against another ある物を別の物に強くこする動作,またはその際に発する不快な音→**こすること,きしむ音,ぎーぎーという音** **定義2** damage or an injury caused by rubbing against sth rough ざらざらした表面に当たって擦れたことが原因でできた損傷,けが→**こすった跡,擦り傷** ‖ I got a nasty scrape on my knee. 私はひざをひどく擦りむいた. **定義3 略式** a difficult situation that was caused by your own stupid behaviour 自分自身の愚かな振る舞いによって生じた困難な状況→**窮地,苦境**

**scrap heap** 图 **C 定義** a large pile of objects, especially metal, that are no longer wanted 不用になった物,特に金属,の山→**(くず鉄などの)廃物の山,ごみの山**

**成句** on the scrap heap **定義** not wanted any more 不用になる→**お払い箱になる** ‖ Many of the unemployed feel that they are on the scrap heap. 失業者の多くは自分が不用になって捨てられたと感じている.

**scrappy** /skrǽpi/ 形 **定義** not organized or tidy and so not pleasant to see まとまりがない,あるいは整然としていないので,見るのが不快な→**まとまりのない,断片的な** ‖ a scrappy essay/football match まとまりのない小論文・サッカーの試合

\*scratch¹ /skrætʃ/ 動 **定義1 自 他** scratch(at sth) to rub your skin with your nails, especially because it is irritating you (itching) 特に不快な(かゆい)ため,皮膚をつめでこする→**(〜を)かく** ‖ Don't scratch at your insect bites or they'll get worse. 虫に刺された所をかかないでください.さもないともっとひどくなりますよ. Could you scratch my back for me? 私の背中をかいてくれませんか. She sat and scratched her head as she thought about the problem. 彼女は座って頭をかきながら,問題について考えた. **定義2 自 他** to make a mark on a surface or a slight cut on a person's skin with sth sharp 鋭い〜で表面に印を付ける,人の皮膚に軽い切り傷を付ける→**(〜を)ひっかく,(〜に)かき傷を付ける** ‖ The cat will scratch if you annoy it. 猫をいら立たせると,ひっかきますよ. The table was badly scratched. テーブルはひどいかき傷が付いていた. **定義3 自** to make a sound by rubbing a surface with sth sharp 鋭い〜で表面をこすって音を出す→**ひっかいて音を出す,がりがりいう** ‖ The dog was scratching at the door to go outside. 犬は外に出たいとドアをひっかいていた. **定義4 他** to use sth sharp to make or remove a mark 先のとがった〜を用いて印を付ける・印を取り除く→**(印,名前など)をひっかいて描く・書く,削り取る** ‖ He scratched his name on the top of his desk. 彼は自分の机の上に名前を刻み付けた. I tried to scratch the paint off the table. 私はテーブルからペンキを削り取ろうとした.

\*scratch² /skrætʃ/ 图 **定義1 C** a cut, mark or sound that was made by sb/sth sharp rubbing a surface 人または鋭い物が表面をこすってできた傷,跡,その時出る音→**かき傷,かき跡,ひっかく・きしむ音** ‖ There's a scratch on the car door. 自動車のドアに1箇所かすり傷がある. ☛ **blob** のさし絵 **定義2** [単数扱い] an act of scratching part of the body because it is irritating you (itching) 不快な(かゆい)ため体をかく動作→**(かゆい所などを)かくこと,ひっかくこと** ‖ The dog had a good scratch. 犬はかゆい所を気持ち良さそうにひっかいた.

**成句** from scratch **定義** from the very beginning→**最初から,ゼロから** ‖ I'm learning Spanish from scratch. 私はゼロからスペイン語を習っている.

(be/come) up to scratch **略式 定義** to be/become good enough そこそこに良い, 良くな

る➜良い状態で, ある基準に達して

**scrawl** /skrɔːl/ [動][自][他] ▶定義 to write sth quickly in an untidy and careless way ぞんざいでいいかげんに素早く書く➜(〜を)**走り書きする, なぐり書きする** ‖ *He scrawled his name across the top of the paper.* 彼は紙の上端に自分の名前を走り書きした. — scrawl [名] [単数扱い] ➜ **走り書き, なぐり書き** ‖ *Her signature was just a scrawl.* 彼女の署名は単なるなぐり書きにすぎなかった. ☛参 **scribble**

***scream**[1] /skriːm/ [動][自][他] ▶定義 scream(sth) (out) (at sb) to cry out loudly in a high voice because you are afraid, excited, angry, in pain, etc 恐怖, 興奮, 怒り, 痛みなどを感じて, 高い大きな声で叫ぶ ➜(〜を)**大声で叫ぶ, 金切り声で言う, 悲鳴を上げる** ‖ *She saw a rat and screamed out.* 彼女はネズミを見て悲鳴を上げた. *'Don't touch that,' he screamed.* 「それに触るな」と彼は大声で叫んだ. *She screamed at the children to stop.* 彼女は子供たちに止まれと大声で叫んだ. *He screamed with pain.* 彼は苦痛に悲鳴を上げた. *He clung to the edge of the cliff, screaming for help.* 彼は崖(がけ)っぷちにしがみ付いて, 大声で助けを求めた. ☛参 **shout**

**scream**[2] /skriːm/ [名] ▶定義1 [C] a loud cry in a high voice 高い大きな叫び声➜**叫び声, 絶叫, 悲鳴** ‖ *a scream of pain* 苦痛の悲鳴 ▶定義2 [単数扱い] [略式] a person or thing that is very funny とてもおかしな人または出来事➜**こっけいな人・物・事, お笑い草** ‖ *Sharon's a real scream.* シャロンは実に傑作な人だ.

**screech** /skriːtʃ/ [動][自][他] ▶定義 to make an unpleasant loud, high sound 不快で, 高く大きな音, または声を出す ➜(〜を)**金切り声で言う; (ブレーキなどが)鋭い音を立てる** ‖ *'Get out of here,' she screeched at him.* 「ここから出てって」と彼女は彼に向かって金切り声を上げた. ☛参 **shriek** — screech [名] [単数扱い] ➜ **金切り声, 鋭い音** ‖ *the screech of brakes* ブレーキのキーという音

***screen**[1] /skriːn/ [名] ▶定義1 [C] a flat vertical surface that is used for dividing a room or keeping sb/sth out of sight 部屋を仕切ったり, 〜の目隠しに用いる垂直な平面体➜**仕切り, ついたて** ‖ *The nurse pulled the screen round the bed.* 看護婦は仕切りをベッドの周りに引いた. ▶定義2 [C] the glass surface of a television or computer where the picture or information appears 画像や情報が表示されるテレビ, コンピューターのガラス面➜**画面, スクリーン** ☛ S5 ページのさし絵 ▶定義3 [C] the large flat surface on which films are shown 映画を映し出す大型の平面➜**スクリーン, 映写幕** ▶定義4 [[U], 単数扱い] films and television 映画・テレビ全体➜**映画・テレビ(界)** ‖ *Some actors look better in real life than on screen.* 俳優の中には映画やテレビで見るよりも実物の方が良く見える人がいる.

**screen**[2] /skriːn/ [動][他] ▶定義1 screen sb/sth (off) (from sb/sth) to hide or protect sb/sth from sb/sth else 〜をほかの…から隠す・保護する➜**〜を(…から)遮る, 覆い隠す, かくまう, 守る** ‖ *The bed was screened off while the doctor examined him.* 医師が彼を診察している間, ベッドは目隠しされていた. *to screen your eyes from the sun* 目を太陽から守る ▶定義2 screen sb (for sth) to examine or test sb to find out if he/she has a particular disease or if he/she is suitable for a particular job 〜が特定の病気にかかっているかどうか, または〜が特定の仕事に向いているかどうかを見るために検査・審査を行う➜**〜を(…について)検査する; 審査する, 選抜・選考する** ‖ *All women over 50 should be screened for breast cancer.* 50 歳以上のすべての女性は乳がんの検診を受けるべきだ. *The Ministry of Defence screens all job applicants.* 国防省はすべての求職者たちを審査する. ▶定義3 to show sth on television or in a cinema ある物をテレビや映画館で見せる➜**〜を放映する, 上映する**

**screen saver** [名] [C] ▶定義 a computer program that replaces what is on the screen with a moving image if the computer is not used for certain amount of time コンピューターが一定時間使用されない場合, 画面の映像に代わって動く画像を表示するコンピュータープログラム➜**スクリーンセーバー**

***screw**[1] /skruː/ [名] [C] ▶定義 a thin pointed piece of metal used for fixing two things, for example pieces of wood, together. You turn a screw with a special tool (a screwdriver). 先が細くとがった金属製の物. 2つの物, 例えば木片などを合わせて固定するために用いる. 専用の道具(ねじ回

S

**screw**² /skruː/ 動 ▶定義1 他 screw sth (on, down, etc) to fasten sth with a screw or screws→～をねじで留める‖ *The bookcase is screwed to the wall.* 本棚はねじで壁に固定されている. *The lid is screwed down so you can't remove it.* ふたは外れないようにねじで留められている. ▶定義2 自他 to fasten sth, or to be fastened, by turning ～をねじって固定する, ねじって固定される→ねじって締める;～をねじって締める‖ *The legs screw into holes in the underside of the seat.* いすの脚は座面の裏の穴にねじってはまるようになっている. *Make sure that you screw the top of the jar on tightly.* びんのふたを必ずきっちりと閉めなさい. ▶定義3 screw sth (up) (into sth) to squeeze sth, especially a piece of paper, into a tight ball ～を, 特に紙などを押しつぶして硬い球にする→～を丸める, 丸めて～にする‖ *He screwed the letter up into a ball and threw it away.* 彼はその手紙を丸めて投げ捨てた.

句動詞 screw (sth) up (俗語) ▶定義 to make a mistake and cause sth to fail 誤りを犯して, ～を失敗させる→～を台なしにする, めちゃくちゃにする‖ *You'd better not screw up this deal.* へまをしてこの取り引きを台なしにしないようにしなさい.

screw your eyes, face, etc up ▶定義 to change the expression on your face by nearly closing your eyes, in pain or because the light is strong 苦痛や光が強いため, 目をぎゅっと細めて顔の表情を変える→目を細める, 顔をしかめる

*__screwdriver__ /skrúːdraɪvər/ 名 C ▶定義 a tool that you use for turning screws ねじを回すのに使用する道具→ねじ回し, ドライバー ☞ **tool** のさし絵

**scribble** /skríb(ə)l/ 動 自他 ▶定義1 to write sth quickly and carelessly 素早くぞんざいに～を書く→(～を)走り書きする, なぐり書きする‖ *to scribble a note down on a pad* メモ帳にメモを走り書きする ☞参 **scrawl** ▶定義2 to make marks with a pen or pencil that are not letters or pictures ペンや鉛筆で文字でも絵でもないものを書く→いたずら書きする, 落書きする‖ *The children had scribbled all over the walls.* 子供たちは壁に落書きした. ― scribble 名 C U →

走り書き, なぐり書き, 落書き

**script** /skrɪpt/ 名 ▶定義1 C the written form of a play, film, speech, etc 演劇, 映画, 演説などを書き記したもの→台本, 脚本, 原稿‖ *Who wrote the script for the movie?* だれがその映画の脚本を書いたのですか. ▶定義2 C U a system of writing 文字体系→表記法, 文字, 書体‖ *Arabic/Cyrillic/Roman script* アラビア文字・キリル文字・ローマ[ラテン]文字

**scripture** /skríptʃər/ 名 U (または **the scriptures** [複数扱い]) ▶定義 the holy books of religion, such as the Bible 聖書など宗教の聖典→聖書, 聖典, 経典

**scroll**¹ /skróʊl/ 名 C ▶定義 a long roll of paper with writing on it 文字が書かれている長い巻紙→巻物

**scroll**² /skróʊl/ 動 自 ▶定義 scroll (up/down) to move text up and down or left and right on a computer screen コンピューターの画面でテキストを上下または左右に動かす→スクロールする

**scrollbar** /skróʊlbɑːr/ 名 C ▶定義 a tool on a computer screen that you use to move the text up and down or left and right テキストを上下または左右に動かすのに用いる, コンピューター画面上のツール→スクロールバー ☞ S5 ページのさし絵

**scrounge** /skráʊndʒ/ 動 自他 略式 ▶定義 scrounge (sth) (from/off sb) to get sth by asking another person to give it to you instead of making an effort to get it for yourself 自分で努力しないで人頼みで～を手に入れる→(～を…から)ねだる, せびる, せしめる‖ *Lucy is always scrounging money off her friends.* ルーシーはしょっちゅう友人に金をせびっている.

**scrub**¹ /skrʌb/ 動 自他 (**scrubbing**; **scrubbed**) ▶定義1 scrub (sth) (down/out) to clean sth with soap and water by rubbing it hard, often with a brush しばしばブラシを用いて, ～をせっけんと水で強くこすってきれいにする→(床・壁などを)ごしごし洗う, ごしごしこする‖ *to scrub (down) the floor/walls* 床・壁をごしごしこする ▶定義2 scrub (sth) (off/out); scrub (sth) (off sth/out of sth) to remove sth or be removed by scrubbing ごしごしこすって～を取り除く;こすって取れる→～をこすって洗い落と

## 1446 scrub²

す; ごしごしこすってきれいになる || *to scrub the dirt off the walls* 壁の汚れをこすり落とす | *I hope these coffee stains will scrub out.* このコーヒーの染みがこすってきれいに落ちればいいが.

**scrub²** /skrʌb/ 名 ▶定義1 [単数扱い] an act of cleaning sth by rubbing it hard, often with a brush しばしばブラシを用いて, ～を強くこすって洗う動作→ごしごしこすって洗うこと || *This floor needs a good scrub.* この床はよくこすってきれいにする必要がある. ▶定義2 Ⓤ small trees and bushes that grow in an area that has very little rain 雨がほとんど降らない地域に生育する小さな木や低木→やぶ, 低木林

**scruff** /skrʌf/ 名
成句 **by the scruff (of the/your neck)** ▶定義 by the back of the/your neck 首の後ろの所を→えり首を

**scruffy** /skrʌfi/ 形 ▶定義 dirty and untidy 不潔でだらしがない→薄汚い, みすぼらしい || *He always looks so scruffy.* 彼はいつも非常にだらしなく見える. *scruffy jeans* 薄汚れたジーンズ

**scrum** /skrʌm/ 名 Ⓒ ▶定義 the part of a game of rugby when several players put their heads down in a circle and push against each other to try to get the ball ラグビーの試合の一部. 数人の選手が頭を下にして円形になり, 互いに押し合ってボールを得ようとするところ→スクラム

**scruples** /skrú:p(ə)lz/ 名 [複数扱い] ▶定義 a feeling that stops you from doing sth that you think is morally wrong 道徳的に間違っていると思うことをしないように呼び止める感情→良心のとがめ, ためらい || *I've got no scruples about asking them for money (= I don't think it's wrong).* 私は彼らに金を無心するのに何のためらいもない (= それが悪い事だとは思わない).

**scrupulous** /skrú:pjələs/ 形 ▶定義1 very careful or paying great attention to detail 非常に慎重な, 細かい点にもよく注意して→綿密な, 慎重な, 周到な, 細心の || *a scrupulous investigation into the causes of the disaster* 災害の原因の綿密な調査 ▶定義2 careful to do what is right or honest 正しい, またはうそ偽りのない行動をするように気を遣って→良心的な, 誠実な ⇔ **unscrupulous** — **scrupulously** 副→綿密に, 周到に, 良心的に || *scrupulously clean/honest/tidy* 徹底的に清潔な・真っ正直な・異常なほどにきれい好きな

**scrutinize** (または **-ise**) /skrú:t(ə)nàɪz/ 動 他
▶定義 to look at or examine sth carefully→～を綿密に調べる, 吟味する || *The customs official scrutinized every page of my passport.* 税関員は私のパスポートを1枚ずつ綿密に調べた.
— **scrutiny** /skrú:t(ə)ni/ 名 Ⓤ→綿密な調査, 吟味 || *The police kept all the suspects **under close scrutiny**.* 警察は容疑者全員を周到な監視下に置いた.

**scuba-diving** /sk(j)ú:bə dáɪvɪŋ, skú:-/ 名 Ⓤ
▶定義 swimming under water using special equipment for breathing 呼吸用の特別の器具を用いて水中を泳ぐこと→スキューバダイビング || *to go scuba-diving* スキューバダイビングに出掛ける ☛ **dive** のさし絵

**scuff** /skʌf/ 動 他 ▶定義 to make a mark on your shoes or with your shoes, for example by kicking sth or by rubbing your feet along the ground 例えば物をけったり, 足を地面にこすり付けることによって, 靴に, または靴で, 跡を付ける→(靴・床など)をすり減らす, こする, (靴・床など)に傷を付ける

**scuffle** /skʌ́f(ə)l/ 名 Ⓒ ▶定義 a short, not very violent fight あまり暴力的でない短いけんか→取っ組み合い, つかみ合い

**sculptor** /skʌ́lptər/ 名 Ⓒ ▶定義 a person who makes figures or objects (**sculptures**) from stone, wood, etc 石, 木などから人物像や物像を作成する人→彫刻家

**sculpture** /skʌ́lptʃər/ 名 ▶定義1 Ⓤ the art of making figures or objects from stone, wood, clay, etc 石, 木, 粘土などから人物像や物像を作成する技術→彫刻(術) ▶定義2 Ⓒ Ⓤ a work or works of art that were made in this way このようにして生み出された芸術作品→彫刻(品)

**scum** /skʌm/ 名 ▶定義1 Ⓤ a dirty or unpleasant substance on the surface of a liquid 液体の表面に浮かぶ汚い・不快な物質→浮きかす, (水面の)あか, (料理の)あく ▶定義2 (俗語) an insulting word for people that you have no respect for 何の敬意も感じられない人に対して用いる侮辱的な言葉→人間のくず || *Drug dealers are scum.* 麻薬の売人は人間のくずだ.

**scurry** /skʌ́ri, skə́:ri/ 動 自 (現分 **scurrying**; 三単現 **scurries**; 過, 過分 **scurried**) ▶定義 to run quickly with short steps; to hurry 短い歩幅で素早く走る; 急ぐ➡️**小走りする, 急いで走る**

**scuttle** /skʌ́tl/ 動 ❶ ▶定義 to run quickly with short steps or with the body close to the ground 短い歩幅で, あるいは胴体が地面に触れるばかりの低い姿勢で素早く走る➡️**急いで走る, 慌てて走る** ‖ *The spider scuttled away when I tried to catch it.* 私が捕まえようとすると, クモは急いで逃げていった.

**scythe** /sáɪð/ 名 ❻ ▶定義 a tool with a long handle and a long, curved piece of metal with a very sharp edge (a blade). You use a scythe to cut long grass, corn etc. 非常に鋭い刃先(刃)を持った長い湾曲形の金属片に長い木の柄を取り付けた道具. 長く伸びた草, 穀物(小麦)などを切るのに用いる➡️**大がま, 草刈りがま**

**SE** 略 south-east(ern)➡️**南東(の), 東南(の)** ‖ *SE Asia* 東南アジア

*__sea__ /síː/ 名 ▶定義 **1** (しばしば **the sea**) ❶ the salt water that covers large parts of the surface of the earth 地球の表面の大部分を覆う塩水➡️**海, 海洋** ‖ *The sea is quite calm/rough today.* 今日の海はとても穏やかだ・荒れている. *Do you live by the sea?* あなたは海の近くに住んでいるのですか. *to travel by sea* 海路で旅行する *There were several people swimming in the sea.* 数人が海で泳いでいた. ☞ C8 ページのさし絵 ▶定義 **2** (しばしば **Sea**) ❻ a particular large area of salt water. A sea may be part of the ocean or may be surrounded by land. ある特定の広大な塩水の地域. 海洋の一部, または陸地で囲まれている場合もある➡️**〜海, 内海** ‖ *the Mediterranean Sea* 地中海 *the Black Sea* 黒海 ☞参 **ocean** ▶定義 **3** [単数扱い] (または **seas**[複数扱い]) the state or movement of the waves of the sea 海の波の状態または動き➡️**波, うねり, 荒波, (ある状態の)海** ‖ *The boat sank in heavy (= rough) seas off the Scottish coast.* その船はスコットランド沖で荒海(= 荒波)に沈んだ. ▶定義 **4** [単数扱い] a large amount of sb/sth close together 寄り集まったたくさんの〜➡️**たくさんの〜, 多量の〜, 〜の海**

成句 **at sea** ▶定義 **1** sailing in a ship 船で航海している➡️**航海中で, 海上で** ‖ *They spent about three weeks at sea.* 彼らは約3週間を洋上で過ごした. ▶定義 **2** not understanding or not knowing what to do 何をすべきか分かっていない・知らない➡️**途方に暮れて, 困って, どうしたらよいか分からなくて**

**the seabed** 名 [単数扱い] ▶定義 the floor of the sea 海の床➡️**海底**

**seafood** /síːfùːd/ 名 ❶ ▶定義 fish and shellfish from the sea that we eat 海で捕れる食用の魚貝類➡️**海産物, シーフード**

**the sea front** [単数扱い] ▶定義 the part of a town facing the sea 都会の海に面した区域➡️**臨海地区, 海岸通り, シーフロント** ‖ *The hotel is right on the sea front.* そのホテルはちょうど海に面した所にある. *to walk along the sea front* 海岸通りを散歩する ☞ C8 ページのさし絵

**seagull** /síːɡʌ̀l/ = **GULL**

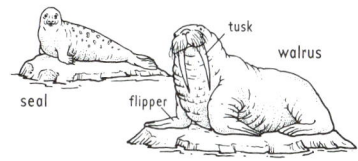

**seal**¹ /síːl/ 名 ❻ ▶定義 **1** a grey animal with short fur that lives in and near the sea and that eats fish. Seals have no legs and swim with the help of short flat arms (flippers). 海中や海辺に生息し, 魚を食べる, 毛の短い灰色の動物. 足がなく, 短く平たい腕(ひれ足)を使って泳ぐ➡️**アザラシ; アシカ, オットセイ** ▶定義 **2** an official design or mark that is put on a document, an envelope, etc to show that it is genuine or that it has not been opened 本物であること, 開封されていないことなどを示すために文書, 封筒などに付される公式の図案や印➡️**印, 印章, 紋章** ▶定義 **3** a small piece of paper, metal, plastic, etc on a packet, bottle, etc that you must break before you can open it 小包, びんなどにはられた, 開ける前に破らなければならない紙片, 金属片, プラスチック片など➡️**封印, 封緘(ふうかん), 封, シール** ▶定義 **4** something that stops air or liquid from getting in or out of something 空気や液体の流入, 流出を防ぐためのもの➡️**封, 封印物, 密封材** ‖ *The seal has worn and oil is escaping.* 封が摩耗して, 油が漏れ出している.

**seal**² /síːl/ 動 他 ▶定義 **1** **seal sth (up/down)** to close or fasten a package, envelope, etc 小包,

## 1448　sea level

封筒などを閉じる・閉める→~を封印する, ~に封をする ‖ *The parcel was sealed with tape.* 包みはテープで封がしてあった. *to seal (down) an envelope* 封筒の封をする ▶定義2 **seal sth (up)** to fill a hole or cover sth so that air or liquid does not get in or out 空気や液体が流入, 流出しないように穴をふさぐ, ~に覆いをする→~を密封する, 密閉する, ~に封をする ‖ *The food is packed in sealed bags to keep it fresh.* 食品は新鮮さを保つため, 密封された袋に詰めてある. ▶定義3 正式 to make sth sure, so that it cannot be changed or argued about 変更されたり言い争われたりすることがないように~を確実にする→~を確実にする; ~に調印する ‖ *to seal an agreement* 協定に調印する

句動詞 **seal sth off** ▶定義 to stop any person or thing from entering or leaving an area or building ~が領域や建物に出入りできないようにする→(地域など)を封鎖する, ~を立ち入り禁止にする ‖ *The building was sealed off by the police.* その建物は警察によって封鎖された.

**sea level** 名 U ▶定義 the average level of the sea, used for measuring the height of places on land 海面の平均の高さ. 陸の高さを測定するのに用いる→平均海面 ‖ *The town is 500 metres above sea level.* その町は海抜500メートルの所にある.

**sea lion** 名 C ▶定義 a type of large animal that lives in the sea and on land and uses two flat arms (**flippers**) to move through the water 海中と陸上に生息し, 2本の平たい腕(ひれ足)を使って水中を移動する大型の動物→アシカ, トド

**seam** /siːm/ 名 C ▶定義1 the line where two pieces of cloth are sewn together 2枚の布を縫い合わせた線→縫い目, とじ目 ● C6ページのさし絵 ▶定義2 a layer of coal under the ground 地下にある石炭の層→石炭層, 鉱脈

**seaman** /ˈsiːmən/ 名 C (複) **-men** /-mən/) ▶定義 a sailor→船員, 船乗り

**seance** (または **séance**) /ˈseɪɑːns/ 名 C ▶定義 a meeting at which people try to talk to the spirits of dead people 死者の霊魂と話をしようとする集会→交霊術の会, 交霊会

*****search** /sɜːtʃ/ 動 自他 ▶定義 search (sb/sth) (for sb/sth); search (through sth) (for sth) to examine sb/sth carefully because you are looking for something; to look for sth that is missing ある物を捜しているため, ~を念入りに調べる; 紛失した~を捜す (~はないかと)(場所・人の身体などを)調べる, 捜す, (~はないかと)(~を徹底的に)捜す ‖ *The men were arrested and searched for drugs.* 男たちが逮捕され, 麻薬を所持していないか身体検査された. *Were your bags searched at the airport?* あなたの荷物は空港で調べられましたか. *They are still searching for the missing child.* 彼らは今でも行方不明の子供を捜索している. *She searched through the papers on the desk, looking for the letter.* 彼女は手紙を捜し出そうと机の上にあるすべての書類をくまなく調べた. — **search** 名 C U ▶探索, 捜索, 調査, 検査 ‖ *the search for the missing boy* 行方不明の少年の捜索 *She walked round for hours **in search of** her missing dog.* 彼女は行方不明の犬を捜して, 何時間も歩き回った.

**searcher** /ˈsɜːtʃər/ 名 C ▶定義1 a person who is looking for sb/sth ~を探している人→探索者, 調査官 ▶定義2 a program that allows you to look for particular information on a computer コンピューターで特定の情報を探すことのできるプログラム→サーチャー, 検索プログラム

**searching** /ˈsɜːtʃɪŋ/ 形 ▶定義 (used about a look, question, etc) trying to find out the truth (目付き, 質問などについて)真実を求めようとする→探るような, (検査・探索が)厳しい, (目付きなどが)鋭い ‖ *The customs officers asked a lot of searching questions about our trip.* 税関職員は私たちの旅行について鋭い質問をたくさんした.

**search party** 名 C ▶定義 a group of people who look for sb who is lost or missing 道に迷ったり行方不明の人を捜す一団→捜索隊

**search warrant** 名 C ▶定義 an official piece of paper that gives the police the right to search a building, etc 警察に建物などを捜索する権利を与える公式の書類→(家宅)捜索令状

**seashell** /ˈsiːʃel/ 名 C ▶定義 the empty shell of a small animal that lives in the sea 海に生息する小さな動物の空き殻→貝殻, 貝

**seashore** /ˈsiːʃɔːr/ (通常は **the seashore**) 名 U ▶定義 the part of the land that is next to the sea 海に隣接した陸地の部分→海岸, 海辺 ‖ *We were looking for shells **on the seashore**.* 私たちは海岸で貝殻を探した.

**seasick** /síːsìk/ 形 ▶定義 feeling sick or vomiting because of the movement of a boat or ship 船の揺れによって気分が悪くて,あるいはおう吐して→**船に酔った,船酔いの** ‖ *to feel/get/be seasick* 船酔いする・船酔いしている ☞参 **airsick, carsick, travel-sick**

**seaside** /síːsàid/ (しばしば **the seaside**) 名[単数扱い] ▶定義 an area on the coast, especially one where people go on holiday 沿岸の地域,特に人々が休暇で出掛ける所→**海辺,海岸** ‖ *to go to the seaside* 海岸に出掛ける *a seaside town* 海辺の町

★**season**¹ /síːz(ə)n/ 名 **C** ▶定義 **1** one of the periods of different weather into which the year is divided 季節ごとに年を区切った中の1期間→**季節,四季の1つ** ‖ *In cool countries, the four seasons are spring, summer, autumn and winter.* 気温の低い国々では,春,夏,秋,冬の4つの季節がある. *the dry/rainy season* 乾季・雨季 ▶定義 **2** the period of the year when sth is common or popular or when sth usually happens or is done 1年で〜が一般的になる,または広まる時期,〜が一般的に起こる,または行われる時期→**時期,季節,シーズン** ‖ *the holiday/football season* 休暇のシーズン・サッカーシーズン
成句 **in season** ▶定義 **1** (used about fresh foods) available in large quantities (生鮮食品について) 多量に入手可能になる→**旬で,出回って,食べごろで** ▶定義 **2** (used about a female animal) ready to have sex (雌の動物について) 交尾可能な→**盛りがついて,交尾期にあって**
**out of season** ▶定義 **1** (used about fresh foods) not available in large quantities (生鮮食品について) 多量に入手できない→**旬を過ぎて,季節外れで** ▶定義 **2** (used about a place where people go on holiday) at the time of year when it is least popular with tourists (行楽地について) 1年で旅行者が最も少なくなる時期→**シーズンオフで,閑散期で**

**season**² /síːz(ə)n/ 動 他 ▶定義 to add salt, pepper, spices, etc to food in order to make it taste better 食物の味を良くするために塩,コショウ,香辛料などを加える→**〜を味付けする,〜に味を付ける** — **seasoning** 名 **C U** →**調味料,味付け** ‖ *Add seasoning to the soup and serve with bread.* スープに調味料を加え,パンを添えて食卓に出しなさい.

**seasonal** /síːz(ə)n(ə)l/ 形 ▶定義 happening or existing at a particular time of the year 1年のある特定の時期に起こる・存在する→**季節の,季節的な** ‖ *There are a lot of seasonal jobs in the summer.* 夏季にはこの季節だけの仕事がたくさんある.

**seasoned** /síːz(ə)nd/ 形 ▶定義 having a lot of experience of sth 〜の経験が豊富な→**熟練した,慣れた** ‖ *a seasoned traveller* 旅慣れた人

**season ticket** 名 **C** ▶定義 a ticket that allows you to make a particular journey by bus, train, etc or to go to a theatre or watch a sports team as often as you like for a fixed period of time 一定期間,好きな回数だけバス,電車などである特定の旅行ができたり,好きな回数だけ観劇や競技の観戦ができるチケット→**定期乗車券,定期入場券,シーズンチケット**

★**seat**¹ /siːt/ 名 **C** ▶定義 **1** something that you sit on 腰掛けるもの→**座席,席,いす** ‖ *Please take a seat (= sit down).* どうぞ着席してください(=お座りください). *the back/driving/passenger seat of a car* 自動車の後部座席・運転席・助手席 ☞ **motorbike**, S7ページのさし絵 ▶定義 **2** the part of a chair, etc that you sit on いすなどの腰掛ける部分→**座部,座** ▶定義 **3** a place in a theatre, on a plane, etc where you pay to sit 劇場,飛行機など,料金を支払って座る場所→**観客席,座席,シート** ‖ *There are no seats left on that flight.* その便は満席だ. ▶定義 **4** a place on a council or in a parliament that you win in an election 選挙で勝ち取った評議会や議会の席→**議席,議員・委員の地位** ‖ *to win/lose a seat* 議席を獲得する・失う
成句 **be in the driving seat** ▶定義 to be the person, group, etc that has the most powerful position in a particular situation ある状況で最も影響力のある立場の人物・集団である→**責任ある立場にいる,主導権を握っている**
**take a back seat** ⇒ **BACK**²

**seat**² /siːt/ 動 他 ▶定義 **1** (しばしば受動態で) 正式 to sit down 腰掛ける→**〜を座らせる,着席させる** ‖ *Please be seated.* どうぞお座りください. ▶定義 **2** to have seats or chairs for a particular number of people 特定の人数分の座席またはいすがある →**(〜人)を収容する,(〜人分)の座**

## 1450 seat belt

席がある

**seat belt** (または **safety belt**) 名 C ▶定義 a strap that is fixed to the seat in a car or plane and that you wear around your body so that you are not thrown forward if there is an accident 自動車や飛行機の座席に固定され,事故が起こったときに前に投げ出されないよう,体に装着する帯➡シートベルト,安全ベルト ‖ *to fasten/unfasten your seat belt* シートベルトを締める・外す ☞参 belt ☞ S7 ページのさし絵

**seating** /síːtɪŋ/ 名 U ▶定義 the seats or chairs in a place or the way that they are arranged ある場所における座席,またはいす,座席の配列の仕方➡座席,収容力,座席の配列 ‖ *The conference hall has seating for 500 people.* 会議室には500人分の座席がある.

**seaweed** /síːwiːd/ 名 U ▶定義 a plant that grows in the sea. There are many different types of seaweed. 海中に生育する植物.数多くの種類がある➡海草

**sec** /sek/ 名 C 略式 = SECOND²(2)

**secluded** /sɪklúːdəd/ 形 ▶定義 far away from other people, roads, etc; very quiet 人々や道路などから遠く離れた; 非常に静かな➡人里離れた,人目に付かない; 静かな ‖ *a secluded beach/garden* 人里離れた海岸・人目に付かないひっそりした庭 — **seclusion** /sɪklúːʒ(ə)n/ 名 U ➡隔離,隠遁(いんとん)

*****second**¹ /sék(ə)nd/ 代形副名 ▶定義 2nd➡2番目(の,に),第2(の,に) ‖ *We are going on holiday in the second week in July.* 私たちは7月の第2週に休暇を取って出掛ける予定だ. *Birmingham is the second largest city in Britain after London.* バーミンガムはイギリスでロンドンに次ぐ第2の大都市だ. *She poured herself a second cup of coffee.* 彼女は自分用にもう1杯コーヒーをついだ. *Our team finished second.* 我々のチームは2位だった. *I came second in the competition.* 私はコンクールで2位になった. *Queen Elizabeth the Second* 女王エリザベス2世 *the second of January* 1月2日 *January the second* 1月2日

成句 **second nature (to sb)** ▶定義 something that has become a habit or that you can do easily because you have done it so many times 何度も行ったため習慣になったもの,または簡単にできるもの➡第2の天性,習慣,習性,習癖 ‖ *With practice, typing becomes second nature.* 練習すれば,タイプは何も考えずに打てるようになる.

**second thoughts** ▶定義 a change of mind or opinion about sth; doubts that you have when you are not sure if you have made the right decision 〜についての考えや意見を変えること; 正しい決断を下したか自信がないときに抱く疑念➡再考,考え直すこと ‖ *On second thoughts, let's go today, not tomorrow.* 考え直して,明日ではなく今日出掛けることにしよう. *I'm starting to* ***have second thoughts*** *about accepting their offer.* 彼らの申し出を受け入れることについて,考え直し始めている.

*****second**² /sék(ə)nd/ 名 ▶定義 **1** C one of the 60 parts into which a minute is divided 1分を60に割ったうちの1つ➡秒 ▶定義 **2** (または 略式 **sec**) C a short time 短い時間➡少しの・ちょっとの間,瞬間 ‖ *Wait a second, please.* どうぞ少しお待ちください. ▶定義 **3** U the second of the four or five speeds (gears) that a car can move forward in 自動車が前進する4または5段階の速度(ギア)のうちの2番目➡第2速,セカンド ‖ *Once the car's moving, put it* ***in second****.* 自動車が動き出したら,ギアをセカンドに入れなさい. ▶定義 **4** [C, 通常は複数]something that has a small fault and that is sold at a lower price 若干の欠陥があり,値引きして売られる物➡二級・二流品,傷物,特価商品 ‖ *The clothes are all seconds.* その衣服は全て特価商品だ. ▶定義 **5** C 正式 **a second (in sth)** the second-best result in a British university degree イギリスの大学の学位で2番目に良い成績➡第2級(の成績) ‖ *to get an upper/lower second in physics* 物理学で上位2級・下位2級を得る

**second**³ /sék(ə)nd/ 動 他 ▶定義 to support sb's suggestion or idea at a meeting so that it can then be discussed and voted on 討議し,採決できるよう,会議である人の提案や意見を支持する ➡(提案,動議など)を支持する,採択することに賛成する

*****secondary** /sék(ə)nd(ə)ri; -dèri/ 形 ▶定義 **1** less important than sth else 〜ほど重要でない➡(重要さにおいて)二次的な,第2の,2番目の ‖ *Other people's opinions are secondary - it's my opinion that counts.* 他人の意見は問題ではない —

私の意見こそが重要なのだ. ▶定義2 caused by or developing from sth else 〜によって生じた, 〜から発達した➔**副次的な, 派生的な**

**secondary school** 名 C 英 ▶定義 a school for children aged from eleven to eighteen 11歳から18歳までの子供が通う学校➔**中等学校**

**second-best¹** 形 ▶定義 not quite the best but the next one after the best 最良ではないが, その次に来る➔**2番目に良い, 次善の** ‖ *the second-best time in the 100 metres race* 100メートル競走で2番目に良いタイム ☛参 best

**second-best²** 名 U ▶定義 something that is not as good as the best, or not as good as you would like 最良のものほど良くはないもの, 望んでいるほど良くないもの➔**2番目に良いもの, 次善のもの** ‖ *I'm not prepared to accept second-best.* 私は次善に甘んじるつもりはない.

**second class¹** 名 U ▶定義1 (または **standard class**) ordinary accommodation in a train, boat, plane, etc 列車, 船, 飛行機などの普通座席・客室➔**(乗り物の)2等** ▶定義2 the way of sending letters, etc that is cheaper but that takes longer than first class 料金は安いが, 第1種よりも時間がかかる手紙などの郵送方法➔**第2種郵便, 普通郵便** — second-class 副 ➔**2等で, 第2種郵便で, 普通郵便で** ‖ *to travel second-class* 2等で旅行する *to send a letter second-class* 手紙を普通郵便で出す

**second-class²** 形 ▶定義1 (または **standard class**) used about ordinary accommodation in a train, plane, etc 列車, 飛行機などの普通座席について➔**2等の** ‖ *a second-class ticket* 2等乗車券 *a second-class compartment* 2等客室 ▶定義2 (used about a university degree) of the level that is next after first-class (大学の学位について)**第1級の次のレベルの**➔**第2級の** ‖ *a second-class honours degree in geography* 地理学の第2級優等学位 ▶定義3 of little importance 重要性がほとんどない➔**あまり重要でない, 第2級の** ‖ *Old people should not be treated as second-class citizens.* 老人を二流市民として扱うべきではない.

**second cousin** 名 C ▶定義 the child of your mother's or father's cousin 母親または父親のいとこの子供➔**またいとこ, はとこ**

**second floor** 名 C ▶定義 the floor in a building that is two floors above the lowest floor 建物

---

# secrecy 1451

の一番下の階から2つ上にある階➔**3階** ‖ *I live on the second floor.* 私は3階に住んでいる. *a second-floor flat* 3階建てのアパート

▶アメリカ英語では, second floor は一番下の階から1つ上にある階(2階)を指す.

**the second hand** 名 C ▶定義 the hand on some clocks and watches that shows seconds 一部の置き時計や腕時計に付いている, 秒を示す針➔**秒針**

**second-hand** 形 副 ▶定義1 already used or owned by sb else ほかの人が既に使用, または所有している➔**中古の[で]** ‖ *a second-hand car* 中古車 *I bought this camera second-hand.* 私はこのカメラを中古で買った. ☛参 old ▶定義2 (used about news or information) that you heard from sb else, and did not see or experience yourself(ニュースや情報について)ほかの人から聞き, 自分自身では見たり経験したりしていない➔**又聞きの[で], 間接的な[に]** ☛参 hand

**second language** 名 C ▶定義 a language that is not your native language but which you learn because it is used, often for official purposes, in your country 母語ではないが, 自国でしばしば公的な目的で用いられるため学ぶ言語➔**第2言語, (母語以外の)公用語** ‖ *French is the second language of several countries in Africa.* フランス語はアフリカのいくつかの国で第2言語になっている.

**secondly** /sék(ə)ndli/ 副 ▶定義 (used when you are giving your second reason or opinion) also (2番目の理由や意見を述べるときに用いて)**また, 第2に, 次に** ‖ *Firstly, I think it's too expensive and secondly, we don't really need it.* まず第1にそれは高すぎると思います. そして第2に私たちが本当に必要とするものではありません.

**second-rate** 形 ▶定義 of poor quality 質の悪い➔**二流の, 2等の, 2級の** ‖ *a second-rate poet* 二流詩人

**secrecy** /síːkrəsi/ 名 U ▶定義 being secret or keeping sth secret 秘密になっていること, 〜を秘密にしておくこと➔**秘密, 内密, 内緒** ‖ *I must stress the importance of secrecy in this matter.* この件について, 秘密厳守を是非とも強調しておかなければならない.

**★secret**[1] /síːkrət/ 名 ▶定義 **1** ⓒ something that is not or must not be known by other people 他人に知られていない、または知られてはならない物・事→**秘密,機密,内緒事** ‖ *to keep a secret* 秘密を守る *to let sb in on/tell sb a secret* ～に秘密を打ち明ける・話す *I can't tell you where we're going - it's a secret.* 私たちがどこに行くのか教えられません － 秘密なんです. ***It's no secret that*** *they don't like each other (= everybody knows).* 彼らがお互いに好意を持っていないことは秘密でも何でもない(= だれもが知っている). ▶定義 **2** (単数扱い) *the secret (of/to sth/doing sth)* the only way or the best way of doing or achieving sth ～を行ったり達成するための唯一の方法または最善策 →**(～の)秘けつ,極意,こつ** ‖ *What is the secret of your success (= how did you become so successful)?* あなたが成功した秘けつは何ですか(= どのようにしてあなたはそんなに成功したのですか).

成句 **in secret** ▶定義 without other people knowing 他人に知られないで→**秘密に,ひそかに,内緒で** ‖ *to meet in secret* こっそり会う

**secret**[2] /síːkrət/ 形 ▶定義 **1** *secret (from sb)* that is not or must not be known by other people 他人に知られていない、または知られてはならない →**(～に)秘密の,内密の,内緒の** ‖ *We have to keep the party secret from Carmen.* 私たちはカーメンにそのパーティーの事は内緒にしておかなければならない. *a secret address* 秘密の住所 *a secret love affair* 秘密の情事 ▶定義 **2** used to describe actions that you do not tell anyone about だれにも話さない行動を述べるのに用いて→**ひそかな,隠れた** ‖ *a secret drinker* 隠れてこっそり酒を飲む人 *She's got a secret admirer.* 彼女には、ひそかに崇拝してくれる人がいる. ― **secretly** 副 →**秘密に,内密で,ひそかに** ‖ *The government secretly agreed to pay the kidnappers.* 政府は誘拐犯に金を支払うことを極秘裏に合意した.

**secret agent** (または **agent**) 名 ⓒ ▶定義 a person who tries to find out secret information especially about the government of another country 秘密情報,特に他国の政府に関する極秘情報を探ろうとする人→**諜報(ちょうほう)部員,スパイ** ☛参 **spy**

**secretarial** /sèkrətéəriəl/ 形 ▶定義 involving or connected with the work that a secretary does 秘書や書記官がする仕事にかかわる→**秘書の** ‖ *secretarial skills/work* 秘書の技能・仕事

**★secretary** /sékrətri; -tèri/ 名 ⓒ (複 **secretaries**) ▶定義 **1** a person who works in an office. A secretary types letters, answers the telephone, keeps records, etc. 事務所で働く人. 手紙をタイプで打つ、電話に出る、記録をつけるなどの仕事をする→**秘書** ‖ *the director's personal secretary* 取締役の個人秘書 ▶定義 **2** an official of a club or society who is responsible for keeping records, writing letters, etc 記録をとるまたは手紙を書くなどの仕事を担当するクラブや団体の職員→**秘書,書記,事務員** ▶定義 **3** 米 the head of a government department, chosen by the President 大統領によって選ばれる連邦政府の省の長→**長官** ▶定義 **4** 英 = **SECRETARY OF STATE(1)**

**Secretary of State** 名 ⓒ ▶定義 **1** (または **Secretary**) (in Britain) the head of one of the main government departments (英国で)政府の主要な省の１つの長官→**(国務)大臣** ‖ *the Secretary of State for Defence* 国防大臣 ▶定義 **2** (in the US) the head of the government department that deals with foreign affairs (米国で)外交問題を扱う連邦政府の省の長官→**国務長官**

**secrete** /sɪkríːt/ 動 他 ▶定義 **1** (used about a part of a plant, animal or person) to produce a liquid (植物,動物,人間の一部分について)液体を出す→**～を分泌する** ▶定義 **2** 正式 to hide sth in a secret place 物を秘密の場所に隠す→**～を隠す,人目に付かないようにする**

**secretion** /sɪkríːʃ(ə)n/ 名 正式 ⓒ ⓤ ▶定義 a liquid that is produced by a plant or an animal; the process by which the liquid is produced 植物や動物が出す液体; 液体が生み出される過程→**分泌液,分泌(作用)** ‖ *The frog covers itself in a poisonous secretion for protection.* そのカエルは身を守るため有毒の分泌液で体を覆う.

**secretive** /síːkrətɪv/ 形 ▶定義 liking to keep things secret from other people ほかの人に知られないように物事を秘密にしたがる→**隠し立てする,秘密主義の** ‖ *Wendy is very secretive about her private life.* ウエンディーは自分の個人生活についてひどく隠し立てをする. ― **secretively**

副 →隠し立てして ― **secretiveness** 名 Ⓤ →隠し立て

**the secret service** 名 [単数扱い] ▶定義 the government department that tries to find out secret information about other countries and governments 他国や他国の政府に関する極秘情報を探ろうとする部局 → **秘密諜報(ちょうほう)機関, 諜報部**

**sect** /sekt/ 名 Ⓒ ▶定義 a group of people who have a particular set of religious or political beliefs. A sect has often broken away from a larger group. 特定の信仰や政治的な信念を持つ人々の集まり. より大きなグループから分離したものが多い → **分派, 派閥, セクト**

\***section** /sékʃ(ə)n/ 名 Ⓒ ▶定義 1 one of the parts into which something is divided ある物を分けた部分の1つ → **部分, 区分, (新聞などの)欄, 部門** ‖ *the string section of an orchestra* オーケストラの弦楽器部 *the financial section of a newspaper* 新聞の財政欄 *The library has an excellent reference section.* その図書館の参考図書部門はすばらしい. ▶定義 2 a view or drawing of sth as if it was cut from the top to the bottom so that you can see the inside 内側がよく見えるように, ~を上から下へ切断したと仮定した場合の面, またはそれを描いた図 → **断面図, 切断面** ‖ *The illustration shows a section through a leaf.* イラストには葉の断面図が描かれている.

**sector** /séktər/ 名 Ⓒ ▶定義 1 a part of the business activity of a country 一国の企業活動の一部分 → **部門, 分野** ‖ *The manufacturing sector has declined in recent years.* 製造部門は近年衰退している. *the public/private sector* 公共・民間部門 ▶定義 2 a part of an area or of a large group of people ある地域またはある大きな集団の一部 → **地区, 区域** ‖ *the Christian sector of the city* その都市のキリスト教徒の居住地区

**secular** /sékjələr/ 形 ▶定義 not concerned with religion or the church 宗教や教会に関係しない → **世俗の, 非宗教的な**

**secure**[1] /sɪkjúər/ 形 ▶定義 1 free from worry or doubt; confident 不安や疑いのない; 自信に満ちた → **安全な, 心配のない; 自信を持って, 安心した** ‖ *Children need to* **feel secure**. 子供たちには安心感が必要だ. *to be financially secure* 金銭的に不安のない ⇔ **insecure** ▶定義 2 not likely to be lost; safe 失われそうにない; 安全な → **安定した, 確実な, 確かな** ‖ *Business is good so his job is secure.* 事業が好調なので, 彼の仕事は安定している. *a secure investment* 確実な投資 ▶定義 3 not likely to fall or be broken; firmly fixed 倒れたり壊れたりしそうにない; しっかりと固定された → **(土台などが)しっかりした, 丈夫な** ‖ *That ladder doesn't look very secure.* そのはしごは不安定に見える. ▶定義 4 secure (against/from sth) well locked or protected → **きちんと戸締りされた, 厳重に保管された** ‖ *Make sure the house is secure before you go to bed.* 就寝前にきちんと戸締りしなさい. ― **securely** 副 → **安全に, 確実に, しっかりと** ‖ *All doors and windows must be securely fastened.* すべての戸と窓はしっかりと締めておかなければならない.

**secure**[2] /sɪkjúər/ 動 Ⓣ ▶定義 1 secure sth (to sth) to fix or lock sth firmly ~をしっかりと固定する, ~にかぎをかける → **~を(…に)固定する, しっかりと締める** ‖ *The load was secured with ropes.* 荷はロープでしっかりと固定された. *Secure the rope to a tree or a rock.* ロープを木か岩にしっかりとくくり付けなさい. ▶定義 2 secure sth (against/ from sth) to make sth safe ~を安全にする → **~を安全にする, ~を(…の危険から)守る** ‖ *The sea wall needs strengthening to secure the town against flooding.* 町を洪水から守るため, 護岸堤を強化する必要がある. ▶定義 3 to obtain or achieve sth, especially by having to make a big effort 特に大変な努力をして, ~を得る, または達成する → **~を確保する, 手に入れる** ‖ *The company has secured a contract to build ten planes.* その会社は苦労して10機の飛行機を建造する契約を手にした.

\***security** /sɪkjúərəti/ 名 ( 複 **securities**) ▶定義 1 Ⓤ the state of feeling safe and being free from worry; protection against the difficulties of life 安全で, 心配・不安のない状態; 生活上の難しい問題から守られていること → **安全, 無事, 安心感** ‖ *Children need the security of a stable home environment.* 子供たちには安定した家庭環境という不安のない状態が必要なのだ. *financial/job security* 財政上の保証・雇用保証 ⇔ **insecurity** ▶定義 2 Ⓤ things that you do to protect sb/sth from attack, danger, thieves, etc ~を攻撃, 危険, 泥棒などから守るためにすること → **防護, 警**

備, 安全確保 ‖ *Security was tightened at the airport before the president arrived.* 大統領が到着する前に, 空港の警備は一層厳重になった. *The robbers were caught on the bank's **security cameras**.* 泥棒たちは銀行の監視カメラに捕えられた. ▶定義3 Ⓤ the section of a large company or organization that deals with the protection of buildings, equipment and staff 建物, 器具, 職員などの保護を担当する大企業や組織の部署→警備部門, 警備組織 ‖ *If you see a suspicious bag, contact airport security immediately.* 不審な荷物を見つけたら, すぐに空港の警備部門に連絡しなさい. ▶定義4 ⒸⓊ something of value that you use when you borrow money. If you cannot pay the money back then you lose the thing you gave as security. 借金の際に利用する高価な物. 借金を返済することができなければ, 担保として預けた物を失うことになる→担保, 抵当, 担保物件

**sedan** /sɪdǽn/ 名 Ⓒ 米 = SALOON

**sedate**¹ /sɪdéɪt/ 形 ▶定義 quiet, calm and well-behaved 物静かで落ち着いており, 行儀の良い→穏やかな, おとなしい, 落ち着いた

**sedate**² /sɪdéɪt/ 動 Ⓗ ▶定義 to give sb a drug or medicine to make him/her feel calm or want to sleep ～を落ち着かせたり, 眠気を催させるために, 薬を投与する→～に鎮静剤を投与する, ～を(鎮静剤で)落ち着かせる, 眠くする ‖ *The lion was sedated and treated by a vet.* ライオンは獣医に鎮静剤を投与されてから治療を受けた. — sedation /sɪdéɪʃ(ə)n/ 名 Ⓤ→鎮静剤による治療, 鎮静状態 ‖ *The doctor put her **under sedation**.* 医者は彼女に鎮静剤を投与した.

**sedative** /sédətɪv/ 名 Ⓒ ▶定義 a drug or medicine that makes you feel calm or want to sleep 感情を落ち着かせ, 眠気を感じさせる薬または薬剤→鎮静剤 ➡参 tranquillizer

**sedentary** /sédnt(ə)ri; -tèri/ 形 ▶定義 involving a lot of sitting down; not active 座っていることの多い; 活動的でない→(運動しないで)ほとんど座っている ‖ *a sedentary lifestyle/job* 一日中座って過ごしがちな生活様式・座業

**sediment** /sédəmənt/ 名 ⒸⓊ ▶定義 a thick substance that forms at the bottom of a liquid 液体の底にたまったどろどろした物質→沈殿物, お

り, かす

**seduce** /sɪd(j)úːs/ 動 Ⓗ ▶定義1 seduce sb (into sth/ doing sth) to persuade sb to do sth he/she would not usually agree to do ～を説きつけて普通は承知しないことをさせる→～を(…するよう)そそのかす, 誘惑する ‖ *Special offers seduce customers into spending their money.* 特別提供は顧客の心を巧みに引き付けて金を使わせる. ▶定義2 to persuade sb to have sex with you 自分と肉体関係を持つよう～を説得する→～を誘惑する, 口説く — seduction /sɪdʌ́kʃ(ə)n/ 名 ⒸⓊ→誘惑, そそのかし

**seductive** /sɪdʌ́ktɪv/ 形 ▶定義1 sexually attractive 性的に魅力的な→魅惑的な, 人を引き付ける ‖ *a seductive smile* 魅惑的な微笑 ▶定義2 attractive in a way that makes you want to have or do sth ～を手に入れたい, やりたいと思わせるような魅力を持った→誘惑的な, 人の気をそそる ‖ *a seductive argument/opinion* (= one which you are tempted to agree with) それなりに魅力的な議論・意見 (= 同意したい気持ちにさせる議論・意見)

*see /síː/ 動 (過 saw /sɔː/; 過分 seen /síːn/) ▶定義1 ⒾⒽ to become conscious of sth, using your eyes; to use the power of sight 自分の目で～を知覚する; 視覚を働かせる→(～が)見える, (～を)見る, (～が)目に入る ‖ *It was so dark that we couldn't see.* とても暗くて私たちには何も見えなかった. *On a clear day you can see for miles.* 晴れた日には, 何マイルも見渡すことができる. *Have you seen my wallet anywhere?* どこかで私の財布を見掛けませんでしたか. *I've seen a mouse run under the cooker.* たった今, ネズミがこんろの下を走るのを見た. *He looked for her but couldn't see her in the crowd.* 彼は彼女を捜したが, 群集の中に彼女を見つけることはできなかった. ➡参 look¹の注 ▶定義2 Ⓗ to look at or watch a film, play, television programme, etc 映画, 演劇, テレビ番組などを見る→(見ようとして)～を見る, 見物する ‖ *Did you see that programme on sharks last night?* 昨晩あのサメの番組を見ましたか. *Have you seen Spielberg's latest film?* スピルバーグの最新映画を見ましたか. ▶定義3 Ⓗ to find out sth by looking, asking or waiting 見たり, 聞いたり, 待つなどして, ～を探り出す→～を調べる, 確かめる, ～を見て知る ‖ *Go and see if the postman* *has been yet.* 郵便配達がもう来たかどうか行って見てきてちょうだい. *We'll **wait and see** what happens before making any decisions.* 決定を下す前に何が起こるかしばらく様子を見てみよう. *'Can we go swimming today, Dad?' 'I'll see.'*「パパ, 今日皆で泳ぎに行ける」「考えておこう」 *I saw in the paper that they're building a new theatre.* 私は新聞で新しい劇場が建設中だということを知った. ▶定義4 ⓗ to spend time with sb; to visit sb ～と時間を過ごす; ～を訪問する→～に会う, ～を訪ねる, (医者など)に診てもらう ‖ *I saw Alan at the weekend; we had dinner together.* 週末, 私はアランに会い, 一緒に夕食を取った. *You should see a doctor about that cough.* そのせきは医者に診てもらうべきだ. ▶定義5 ⓔⓗ to understand sth; to realize sth ～を理解する; ～を知る→理解する, 知る, 分かる ‖ *Do you **see what I mean**?* 私の言う事が分かりますか. *She doesn't **see the point in** spending so much money on a car.* 車にそんなに多額の金を費やす意味が彼女には分からない. *'You have to key in your password first.' 'Oh, I see.'*「最初にパスワードを入力なさらないと」「あ, 分かりました」 ▶定義6 ⓗ to have an opinion about sth ～について意見を持つ→～と考える, 見なす ‖ *How do you see the situation developing?* 状況がどのように展開していくとお考えですか. ▶定義7 ⓗ to imagine sth as a future possibility ～が将来起こり得る事として想像する→～を想像する, 予想する, 心に思い浮かべる ‖ *I can't see her changing her mind.* 彼女が考えを変えるとは想像できない. ▶定義8 ⓗ to do what is necessary in a situation; to make sure that sb does sth ある状況で必要な事をする; ～が…を必ずするようにする→～であるように取り計らう, 配慮する ‖ *I'll see that he gets the letter.* 彼が必ず手紙を受け取れるように手配しましょう. ▶定義9ⓗ to go with sb, for example to help or protect him/her ～を助けたり守ったりするために一緒に行く→～を(…まで)送っていく, ～に付き添う, ～を案内する ‖ *He asked me if he could see me home, but I said no.* 彼は家まで送っていこうかと言ってくれたが, 私は断った. *I'll see you to the door.* ドアの所までお送りしましょう. ▶定義10ⓗ to be the time when an event happens ある出来事が起きる時期である →(ある時代が)(事件など)に遭遇する, ～を経験する ‖ *Last year saw huge changes in the education system.* 昨年は教育制度が大幅に変更された.

> ▶語法
>
> see と look の違い
>
> see は「(自然と)目に入る」で, look は「視線を向ける」です. look は必ずしも物が見えることを意味しません. 例えば, I looked carefully, but I couldn't see anything. (注意深く目を凝らしたが何も見えなかった)というようなことがあり得ます. また「(何かを求めて)視線を動かす」というときには, I looked for my key. のように for を用います.

成句 as far as I can see ⇒ **FAR**²
as far as the eye can see ⇒ **FAR**²
let me see; let's see ⇒ **LET**
see eye to eye (with sb) ▶定義 to agree with sb; to have the same opinion as sb ～に同意する; ～と同じ意見を持つ→意見が一致する, 同調する ‖ *We don't always see eye to eye on political matters.* 私たちは政治問題でいつも意見が一致するわけではない.
see if... ▶定義 to try to do sth ～をしようとする→～かどうか確かめる, 調べる ‖ *I'll see if I can find time to do it.* それをする時間があるかどうか確かめてみます. *See if you can undo this knot.* この結び目をほどくことができるかどうか見てください.
see you around 略式 ▶定義 used for saying goodbye to sb you have made no arrangement to see again 再会の取り決めをしていない人にさようならを言うのに用いて→じゃあ(また)ね
see you (later) ▶定義 used for saying goodbye to sb you expect to see soon or later that day すぐに, またはその日のうちに会うつもりでいる人にさようならを言うのに用いて→それじゃあ(また), バイバイ
you see ▶定義 used for giving a reason 理由を述べるのに用いて→知っての通り, ほら, ねえ ‖ *She's very unhappy. He was her first real boyfriend, you see.* 彼女はとても不幸だ. 何しろ彼が初めての真の恋人だったのだから.

句動詞 see about sth/doing sth ▶定義 to deal with sth ～を処理する→～を手配する, ～をする

よう取り計らう ‖ *I've got to go to the bank to see about my traveller's cheques.* 私は銀行に行って、トラベラーズチェックを手配しなければならない.

see sb off ▶定義 to go with sb to the railway station, the airport, etc in order to say goodbye to him/her さようならを言うために～と一緒に駅,空港などに行く→**～を見送る**

see through sb/sth ▶定義 to be able to see that sb/sth is not what he/she/it appears ～が見掛け通りでないことが分かる→**～の本質を見抜く,見破る** ‖ *The police immediately saw through his story.* 警察はすぐに彼の作り話を見破った.

see to sb/sth ▶定義 to do what is necessary in a situation; to deal with sb/sth ある状況で必要な事をする；～に対処する→**～を引き受ける,～に対し必要な処置をする** ‖ *I'll see to the travel arrangements and you book the hotel.* 私が旅行の手配を引き受けるから,あなたはホテルを予約してください.

\*seed /síːd/ 名 ▶定義1 ⦿Ⓤ the small hard part of a plant from which a new plant of the same kind can grow 植物の小さくて硬い部分.そこから同じ種類の新しい植物が生長する→**種,種子** ‖ *a packet of sunflower seeds* 1袋のひまわりの種 ☛ C2 と C3 ページのさし絵 ▶定義2 ⦿ the start of a feeling or event that continues to grow 次第に高まる感情,または次第に大きくなる出来事の始まり→**種,根源,もと** ▶定義3 ⦿ a player in a sports competition, especially tennis, who is expected to finish in a high position 特にテニスなどのスポーツの試合で,上位に入賞すると考えられる選手→**シード選手**

seeded /síːdəd/ 形 ▶定義 (used about a player or a team in a sports competition) expected to finish in a high position (スポーツの試合に出場する選手やチームについて)上位に入賞すると考えられる→**シードの**

seedless /síːdləs/ 形 ▶定義 having no seeds→**種のない,種なしの** ‖ *seedless grapes* 種なしブドウ

seedling /síːdlɪŋ/ 名 ⦿ ▶定義 a very young plant or tree that has grown from a seed 種から生長した非常に若い植物または木→**実生(みしょう)の苗木,若木**

seedy /síːdi/ 形 ▶定義 dirty and unpleasant; possibly connected with illegal or immoral activities 汚れていて不快な；違法な,または不道徳な行動にことによると関連している→**みすぼらしい；いかがわしい,怪しげな** ‖ *a seedy hotel/neighbourhood* いかがわしいホテル・うさんくさい界隈(かいわい)

seeing /síːɪŋ/ (または **seeing that**; **seeing as**) 接 略式 ▶定義 because; as ～という理由で；だから→**～であるから,～なので** ‖ *Seeing as we're going the same way, I'll give you a lift.* 同じ方向に行くのですから,車でお送りしましょう.

seek /síːk/ 動⦿ (過, 過分 **sought** /sɔ́ːt/) 正式 ▶定義1 to try to find or get sth ～を見つけようとする,または手に入れようとする→**～を探し求める,得ようとする** ‖ *Politicians are still seeking a peaceful solution.* 政治家たちは平和的な解決をまだ模索している. ▶定義2 seek sth (from sb) to ask sb for sth →**(～に)…を求める,要求する** ‖ *You should seek advice from a solicitor about what to do next.* 次に何をすべきか事務弁護士に助言を求めるべきですよ. ▶定義3 seek (to do sth) to try to do sth ～を行おうとする→**～しようと努める,努力する** ‖ *They are still seeking to find a peaceful solution to the conflict.* 彼らは今もなお紛争の平和的な解決策を見つけようと努力している. ▶定義4 -seeking (複合形容詞を作るために用いて) looking for or trying to get the thing mentioned 言及された事・物を探す,または手に入れようとする→**～を追い求める,追求する** ‖ *attention-seeking behaviour* 人の注意をひこうとする振る舞い *a heat-seeking missile* 熱追尾式ミサイル

\*seem /síːm/ 動⦿ ▶定義 seem (to sb) (to be) sth; seem (like) sth (進行形不可) to give the impression of being or doing sth; to appear ～のような印象,または～をしているような印象を与える；～に見える→**～のように見える,思われる** ‖ *Emma seems (like) a very nice girl.* エマはとてもすてきな少女のようだ. *Emma seems to be a very nice girl.* エマはとてもすてきな少女のようだ. *It seems to me that we have no choice.* 私たちには選択肢がないように思われる. *You seem happy today.* あなたは今日幸せそうに見える. *This machine doesn't seem to work.* この機械は動かないようだ.

## ▶語法

**seem to は断定を避ける助動詞**

He seems to be sick. = It seems (that) he is sick. のような書き換えではなく, seem to を have to, able to と同様に助動詞としてとらえる方が実際的です. 例えば, We seem to have a new member.（新しいメンバーがいるようだね）や I seem to have misplaced my glasses.（眼鏡をどこかに置いてきてしまったようだ）のような場合を見ると, 断定を避ける助動詞として seem to が機能しているのがよく分かります.

**seeming** /síːmɪŋ/ 形（名詞の前だけ）▶定義 appearing to be sth ～のように見える→見せ掛けの, 上辺の, 外見だけの ∥ Despite her seeming enthusiasm, Sandra didn't really help much. 上辺は意気込んでいるようだったが, 実際にはサンドラはあまり役に立たなかった. ― **seemingly** 副→見せ掛けでは, 上辺は, 見たところでは ∥ a seemingly endless list of complaints 尽きることのなさそうな苦情のリスト

**seen** SEE の過去分詞形

**seep** /síːp/ 動自 ▶定義 (used about a liquid) to flow very slowly through sth（液体について）～を通って非常にゆっくりと流れ出す→染み込む, 染み出す, 漏れる ∥ Water started seeping in through small cracks. 小さなひびから水が染み込み始めた.

**see-saw** 名C ▶定義 an outdoor toy for children that consists of a long piece of wood that is balanced in the middle. One child sits on each end of the see-saw and one goes up while the other is down. 中央で釣り合っている長い板でできた子供向けの外遊びの遊具. 子供がシーソーの両端に座り, 一方が上がると, もう一方が下がる→シーソー

**seethe** /síːð/ 動自 ▶定義1 to be very angry 非常に怒る→腹を立てる, 立腹する ∥ I was absolutely seething. 私は心底腹を立てていた.
▶定義2 seethe (with sth) to be very crowded 非常に込み合う →（～で）騒然とする, 混雑する ∥ The streets were seething with people. 通りは人々でごった返していた.

**segment** /ségmənt/ 名C ▶定義1 a section or part of sth ～の一区分, または一部分→部分, 区分, 区切り ∥ I've divided the sheet of paper into three segments. 私はその紙を3つに分けた. a segment of the population 人口の一区分 ▶定義2 one of the parts into which an orange can be divided オレンジの実を分けた一部分→袋 ☛ C3 ページのさし絵

**segregate** /ségrɪgèɪt/ 動他 ▶定義 segregate sb/sth (from sb/sth) to separate one group of people or things from the rest ～の集団を他から分ける→～を(…から)隔離する, 分離する ∥ The two groups of football fans were segregated to avoid trouble. 混乱を避けるため, サッカーファンの2つのグループは互いに引き離されていた. ☛参 integrate ― **segregation** /sègrɪgéɪʃ(ə)n/ 名U →（差別による）隔離, 分離 ∥ racial segregation (= separating people of different races) 人種の分離（政策）(= 異なった人種の人々を分離すること)

**seize** /síːz/ 動他 ▶定義1 to take hold of sth suddenly and firmly; to grab sth ～を突然しっかりとつかむ; ～を握る→～をぐいと握る, つかみ取る ∥ The thief seized her handbag and ran off with it. その泥棒は彼女のかばんを引ったくって, 走り去った.（比喩）to seize a chance/an opportunity チャンス・機会をつかむ ▶定義2 to take control or possession of sb/sth ～の管理権または所有権を手にする→～を押収する, 差し押さえる ∥ The police seized 50 kilos of illegal drugs. 警察は50キロの違法な薬物を押収した. ▶定義3（通常は受動態で）(used about an emotion) to affect sb suddenly and very strongly（感情について）突然, 非常に強く～に影響を及ぼす→～を襲う, 駆り立てる ∥ I felt myself seized by panic. 私はパニックに襲われた.

**句動詞** seize (on/upon) sth ▶定義 to make use of a good and unexpected chance 予期せぬ好機を利用する →（機会を）捕らえる, つかむ, ～に飛び付く ∥ He seized on a mistake by the goalkeeper and scored. 彼はゴールキーパーのミスを捕らえて, 得点を上げた.

**seize up** ▶定義 (used about a machine) to stop working because it is too hot, does not have enough oil, etc（機械について）過熱, またはオイル不足などのために動きが止まる→動かなくなる, 停止する

**seizure** /síːʒər/ 名 ▶定義1 ❶ using force or legal authority to take control or possession of sth ～の管理権または所有権を得るため、実力または法的権限を行使すること→押収,差し押さえ ‖ *the seizure of 30 kilos of heroin by police* 警察による30キロのヘロインの押収 ▶定義2 ❷ a sudden strong attack of an illness, especially one affecting the brain 特に脳に影響を及ぼす突然で激しい病気の発作→発作,卒中

**seldom** /séldəm/ 副 ▶定義 not often; rarely→めったにない,ほとんどない ‖ *There is seldom snow in Athens.* アテネではほとんど雪が降らない. *I very seldom go to the theatre.* 私はめったに劇場に行かない.

**select**¹ /səlékt/ 動他 ▶定義 to choose sb/sth from a number of similar things 数多くの類似したものの中から～を選ぶ→～を選ぶ,選び出す ‖ *The best candidates will be selected for interview.* 最適な候補者が面接に選ばれることになる. ☞ select は choose よりも正式で,決定を下すときに慎重・入念であることを示唆する.

**select**² /səlékt/ 形正式 ▶定義1 carefully chosen as the best of a group ある集団の最良のものとして慎重に選ばれた→選ばれた,選抜された,えり抜きの ‖ *A university education is no longer the privilege of a select few.* 大学教育はもはや選ばれた少数の人たちの特権ではない. ▶定義2 used or owned by rich people 金持ちの人々が用いる,または所有する →(上流階級・金持ちに)会員を限定した,入選の厳しい,高級な

**selection** /səlékʃ(ə)n/ 名 ▶定義1 ❶ choosing or being chosen 選ぶこと,選ばれること→選択,選抜 ‖ *The manager is responsible for team selection.* 監督はチームメンバーの選定に責任を負う. ▶定義2 ❷ a number of people or things that have been chosen 選ばれたいくつかの人々や物→精選,抜粋,選集 ‖ *a selection of hits from the fifties and sixties* 50年代,60年代のヒット曲の選集 ▶定義3 ❷ a number of things from which you can chose 選択できるように用意されたいくつかの物→品ぞろえ,商品,展示品 ‖ *This shop has a very good selection of toys.* この店はおもちゃの品ぞろえがとても豊富だ.

**selective** /səléktɪv/ 形 ▶定義1 careful when choosing 選ぶときに慎重な→えり好みする,入念に選ぶ ‖ *She's very selective about who she invites to her parties.* 彼女はパーティーに招待する人を非常に慎重に選ぶ. ▶定義2 concerning only some people or things; not general 一部の人々や物のみに関する;一般的でない→えり抜きの,選択的な ‖ *selective schools/education* 選抜学校・教育 ― **selectively** 副→えり好みして,選択的に,選抜的に

**self** /self/ 名 ❷ (複 **selves** /selvz/) ▶定義 a person's own nature or qualities その人自身の性質や特性→自己,自我,本質,個性,本性 ‖ *It's good to see you back to your old self again* (= feeling well or happy again). あなたがまた元のあなた (= 体調の良い,または明るく楽しそうな状態) に戻られて,うれしく思います. *Her spiteful remark revealed her true self* (= what she was really like). 彼女の悪意に満ちた批評で彼女の本性 (= 彼女の本当の姿) がさらけ出された.

**self-addressed envelope** = STAMPED ADDRESSED ENVELOPE

**self-assured** 形 = ASSURED ― **self-assurance** 名 = ASSURANCE(2)

**self-catering** 形 英 ▶定義 (used about a holiday or a place to stay) where meals are not provided for you so you cook them yourself (休暇や宿泊施設について) 食事が出ないので自分で調理する →(休暇施設などが)自炊(用)の

**self-centred** (米 **self-centered**) 形 ▶定義 thinking only about yourself and not about other people 自分のことだけで他人のことは考えない→自己中心的な,自己本位の,利己的な ☞参 **selfish**

**self-confessed** 形 ▶定義 admitting that you are sth or do sth that most people consider to be bad 自分は大多数の人が悪人と考えるような人物である,または悪事と考えるような事をしていると,自ら認める →(普通は悪い意味について) 自認する,自称の

**self-confident** 形 ▶定義 feeling sure about your own value and abilities 自分自身の価値や能力について確信している→自信のある ☞参 **confident** ― **self-confidence** 名 ❶→自信 ‖ *Many women lack the self-confidence to apply for senior jobs.* 多くの女性は上級職に応募するだけの自信に欠ける.

**self-conscious** 形 ▶定義 too worried about what other people think about you 他人が自分

をどう思うかについて心配しすぎる➔人目を気にする, 自意識過剰な — self-consciously 副 ➔人目を気にして, 自意識過剰で — self-consciousness 名 Ⓤ➔自意識過剰

**self-contained** 形 困 ▶定義 (used about a flat, etc) having its own private entrance, kitchen and bathroom (アパートなどについて) 専用の玄関, 台所, 浴室がある➔(アパートが) 各戸独立の, 必要な設備を完備した ‖ *a self-contained apartment* 独立式アパート

**self-control** 名 Ⓤ ▶定義 the ability to control your emotions and appear calm even when you are angry, afraid, excited, etc 怒り, 恐怖, 興奮などを感じた場合でも, 自分の感情を抑制して平静に見せる能力➔自制, 克己 ‖ *to lose/keep your self-control* 自制心を失う・保つ

**self-defence** (困 **self defense**) 名 Ⓤ ▶定義 the use of force to protect yourself or your property 自分自身または自分の財産を守るために実力を行使すること➔自己防衛, 自衛, 護身 ‖ *Lee is learning karate for self-defence.* リーは護身のため空手を習っている. *to shoot sb in self-defence* (= *because they are going to attack you*) 自己防衛で (= 〜が自分に襲い掛かろうとしたため)〜を撃つ

**self-destruct** 動 自 ▶定義 to destroy him/her/itself 自分自身を破壊する ➔(ロケット・ミサイルなどが) 自滅する, 自己破壊する — self-destructive 形➔自滅的な, 自己破壊機能を持つ — self-destruction 名 Ⓤ➔自滅, 自己破壊

**self-discipline** 名 Ⓤ ▶定義 the ability to make yourself do sth difficult or unpleasant 困難または不快な〜を自らに課して実行する能力➔自己鍛錬, 自己訓練, 自己修養 ‖ *It takes a lot of self-discipline to give up smoking.* 禁煙するには自己鍛錬が大いに必要だ.

**self-employed** 形 ▶定義 working for yourself and earning money from your own business 自分自身のために働き, 自分自身の事業で金を稼ぐ➔自営の, 自家営業の

**self-esteem** 名 Ⓤ ▶定義 a good opinion of your own character and abilities 自分自身の性格や能力についての良い評価➔自尊心, 自負(心) ‖ *a man with high/low self-esteem* 自尊心の高い・低い男性

**self-evident** 形 ▶定義 that does not need any proof or explanation; clear 証明や説明を必要としない; 明白な➔自明の, 分かりきった

**self-explanatory** 形 ▶定義 clear and easy to understand; not needing to be explained はっきりしていて分かりやすい; 説明を必要としない➔自明の, そのままで明白な, 読め[見れ]ば分かる ‖ *The book's title is self-explanatory.* その本の題名は改めて説明するまでもない.

**self-indulgent** 形 ▶定義 allowing yourself to have or do things you enjoy (sometimes when it would be better to stop yourself) (時にはやめておいた方が良いときに) 好きな物事を気ままに手に入れたり, したりする➔わがままな, 放縦な, 勝手気ままな — self-indulgence 名 Ⓒ Ⓤ➔わがまま, 放縦, したい放題すること

**self-interest** 名 Ⓤ ▶定義 thinking about what is best for yourself rather than for other people 他人のことよりも自分にとって何が最善かを考えること➔私利, 私欲, 利己主義

\*__selfish__ /sélfiʃ/ 形 ▶定義 thinking only about your own needs or wishes and not about other people's 自分のニーズや願望だけを考え, 他人のことは考えない➔利己的な, わがままな, 自分本位の ‖ *a selfish attitude* 身勝手な態度 *I'm sick of your selfish behaviour!* あなたのわがままな振る舞いにもううんざりだ. ⇔ **unselfish**, **selfless** ☛参 **self-centred** — selfishly 副➔利己的に, 自分本位に, わがままに — selfishness 名 Ⓤ➔わがまま, 身勝手

**selfless** /sélfləs/ 形 ▶定義 thinking more about other people's needs or wishes than your own 自分のことよりもむしろ他人のニーズや願望について考える➔無私の, 利己心のない

**self-made** 形 ▶定義 having become rich or successful by your own efforts 自分の努力で裕福になった, または成功した➔独力で成功した, たたき上げの ‖ *a self-made millionaire* 独力で億万長者になった人

**self-pity** /sélf pìti/ 名 Ⓤ ▶定義 the state of thinking too much about your own problems or troubles and feeling sorry for yourself 自分の問題や心配事について考えすぎ, 自分を哀れに思う状態➔自己憐憫(れんびん), 自分自身を哀れむこと

**self-portrait** 名 Ⓒ ▶定義 a picture that you draw or paint of yourself 自分自身を鉛筆や絵の

具を使って描いた絵画→自画像

**self-raising flour** (米 **self-rising flour**) 名 U ▶定義 flour that contains a substance that makes cakes, etc rise during cooking 焼き上がる間にケーキなどを膨らませる物質の入った小麦粉→ベーキングパウダー入りの小麦粉, 膨らし粉入りのパンケーキ用小麦粉 ☞参 plain flour

**self-reliant** 形 ▶定義 not depending on help from anyone else 他人からの助けに頼らない→自力本願の, 独立独歩の ☞参 reliant

**self-respect** 名 U ▶定義 a feeling of confidence and pride in yourself 自分に対する自信や誇らしい気持ち→自尊(心) ‖ Old people need to keep their dignity and self-respect. 老人は威厳や自尊心を保つことが肝要だ. ☞参 respect — **self-respecting** 形 (しばしば否定文で)→自尊心のある, 誇り高い; 本当に~と呼べる(人・物), 真の ‖ No self-respecting language student (= nobody who is serious about learning a language) should be without this book. およそまともな言語学習者(= 真剣に言葉の学習に取り組んでいる者)ならこの本を読むべきだ.

**self-righteous** 形 ▶定義 believing that you are always right and other people are wrong, so that you are better than other people 常に自分が正しく他人は間違っており, 自分の方が他人よりも優れていると信じている→独り善がりの, 独善的な ☞参 righteous — **self-righteously** 副 →独り善がりに, 独善的に — **self-righteousness** 名 U →独り善がり, 独善

**self-sacrifice** 名 U ▶定義 giving up what you need or want, in order to help others 他人を助けるために自分が必要とする, または欲する物事をあきらめる→自己犠牲, 献身(的行為)

**self-service** 形 ▶定義 (used about a shop, petrol station, restaurant, etc) where you serve yourself and then pay at a special desk (a cash desk) (商店, ガソリンスタンド, レストランなどについて) 自分で求める物を得て, 特定の場所(レジ)で代金を支払う→セルフサービスの

**self-sufficient** 形 ▶定義 able to produce or provide everything that you need without help from or having to buy from others 他人から助けてもらったり, 買い入れることもなく, 必要なもののすべてを生産または供給することのできる→自給自足の, 自給自足できる

**\*sell** /sel/ 動 (過, 過分 **sold** /sóuld/) ▶定義1 自他 sell (sb) (sth) (at/for sth); sell (sth) (to sb) (at/for sth) to give sth to sb who pays for it and is then the owner of it ~に対して代金を支払い, その結果, その所有者となった人に, その金を渡す→(人に)(物を)(~の値段で)売る, 売り渡す ‖ We are going to sell our car. 私たちは車を売却する予定だ. I sold my guitar to my neighbour for £200. 私はギターを隣人に200ポンドで売り渡した. Would you sell me your ticket? あなたのチケットを譲っていただけませんか. I offered them a lot of money but they wouldn't sell. 私は彼らに多額の金を払うと申し出たが, 彼らは売ろうとしなかった. ▶定義2 他 to offer sth for people to buy 人に購入者してもらうように~を売りに出す→~を売る, 販売する, 扱う ‖ Excuse me, do you sell stamps? すみません, お宅では切手を扱っていますか. to sell insurance/advertising space 保険のセールスをする・広告を取る ▶定義3 自他 to be bought by people in the way or in the numbers mentioned; to be offered at the price mentioned 言及された方法や数量で人々に買われる; 言及された価格で売りに出される→(~で)売れる, 売られる ‖ These watches sell at £1000 each in the shops but you can have this one for £500. これらの腕時計は小売店では1個1000ポンドで売られていますが, これは500ポンドで買えますよ. Her books sell well abroad. 彼女の著書は外国でよく売れている. This newspaper sells over a million copies a day. この新聞は1日100万部以上売れている. ▶定義4 他 to make people want to buy sth 人々に~を買いたいという気にさせる→~を売り込む, 宣伝する, 販売を促進する ‖ They rely on advertising to sell their products. 彼らは製品の売り込みを宣伝に頼っている. ☞定義1~4 名 sale ▶定義5 他 sell sth/yourself to sb to persuade sb to accept sth; to persuade sb that you are the right person for a job, position, etc ~を説得して…を受け入れさせる; 自分が仕事, 地位などに適切な人物であることを~に納得させる→(人に考えなど)を売り込む, 納得させる;(人に)自分を売り込む ‖ Now we have to try and sell the idea to the management. こうなったら, 経営陣にこの企画を納得してもらうよう努力しなければならない.

**成句** be sold on sth **略式** ▶定義 to be very enthusiastic about sth ~に夢中である, 熱中している

**句動詞** sell sth off ▶定義 to sell sth in order to get rid of it, often at a low price 処分するためにしばしば低価格で~を売る➔~を安く売り払う ‖ *The shops sell their remaining winter clothes off in the spring sales.* 商店は春の大売出しで在庫の冬物の衣服を安く売り払う.

sell out; be sold out ▶定義 (used about tickets for a concert, football game, etc) to be all sold (コンサート, サッカーの試合などのチケットについて)➔売り切れる ‖ *All the tickets sold out within two hours* 2時間以内にすべてのチケットが売り切れた. *The concert was sold out weeks ago.* そのコンサートは何週間も前に売り切れた.

sell out (of sth); be sold out (of sth) ▶定義 to sell all of sth so that no more is/are available to be bought 買える物がなくなるまで~をすべて売り尽くす➔~をすべて売り切る, 全部売り尽くされる ‖ *I'm afraid we've sold out of bread.* すみませんが, パンはみんな売り切れてしまいました.

sell up ▶定義 to sell everything you own, especially your house, your business, etc (in order to start a new life, move to another country, etc) (新しい生活を始めたり, 他国に移住したりするため)特に家屋, 事業などの所有物をすべて売る➔~を売り払う, 処分する

**sell-by date** 名 ⓒ 英 ▶定義 the date printed on food containers, packets, etc after which the food should not be sold 食品の容器, 箱などに印刷された, それ以降販売してはならない日付➔販売 [賞味] 期限 ‖ *This milk is past its sell-by date.* この牛乳は販売期限を過ぎている.

**seller** /sélər/ 名 ⓒ ▶定義 **1** (しばしば複合語で) a person or business that sells 物を売る人または企業➔売り手, 販売人, 販売業者 ‖ *a bookseller* 本屋 *a flower seller* 花屋 ▶定義 **2** something that is sold, especially in the amount or way mentioned 特に言及された数量や方法で売れるもの➔売れ行きが~のもの ‖ *This magazine is a big seller in the 25-40 age group.* この雑誌は25歳から40歳の年齢層でよく売れている. ☞参 **best seller**

**sellotape**™ /séloʊtèɪp/ 名 ⓤ 英 ▶定義 a type of clear tape that is sold in rolls and used for sticking things ~をはるのに用いられる透明テープの一種. 巻き状で販売されている➔セロテープ ☞参 **tape** — sellotape 動 他 ➔~をセロテープではる

**selves** SELF の複数形

**semblance** /sémbləns/ 名 [単数扱い, ⓤ] **正式** ▶定義 (a) semblance of sth the appearance of being sth or of having a certain quality ~のように, または何か特定の性質を持っているように見えること➔~めいたもの, 外見, 外観, 見掛け

**semen** /síːmən; -men/ 名 ⓤ ▶定義 the liquid that is produced by the male sex organs containing the seed (sperm) necessary for producing babies or young 男性または雄の生殖器から作り出される液体. この中に赤ん坊や子を作るために必要な種(精子)が含まれている➔精液

**semi** /sémi/ 名 ⓒ (複 semis /sémiz/) 英 **略式** ▶定義 a house that is joined to another one with a shared wall between them, forming a pair of houses 共有の壁でもう1軒の家に接続し, 2軒で1棟を形成している家の1軒➔2軒連続住宅, 2戸建て家屋

**semicircle** /sémɪsɜ̀ːrk(ə)l/ 名 ⓒ ▶定義 one half of a circle; something that is arranged in this shape 円の半分; 半円形に並べられた物➔半円, 半円形の物 ‖ *I want you all to sit in a semicircle.* 皆, 半円形に座りなさい. ☞参 **circle**

**semicolon** /sémikòʊlən/ 名 ⓒ ▶定義 a mark (;) used in writing for separating parts of a sentence or items in a list 1つの文の中を区切ったり, 一覧表の項目を分けるために用いる句読点(;)➔セミコロン

**semi-detached** 形 ▶定義 (used about a house) joined to another house with a shared wall on one side forming a pair of houses (家屋について)共有の壁でもう1軒の家と接続して, 2軒で1棟を形成する➔2軒1棟の, 仕切り壁で隣家と続いた

**semi-final** /sèmi fáɪnl/ 名 ⓒ ▶定義 one of the two games in a sports competition which decide which players or teams will play each other in the final スポーツ競技で, 決勝戦に出場する選手またはチームを決めるために行う2試合のうちの1つ➔準決勝 ☞参 **quarter-final**, **final** — semi-finalist /-fáɪnlɪst/ 名 ⓒ ➔準決勝出

## 1462 seminar

場選手

**seminar** /sémənɑːr/ 名 ❹ ▶定義1 a class at a university, college, etc in which a small group of students discuss or study a subject with a teacher 少人数の学生が教師とある課題について討論,研究する,大学の授業→ゼミナール,ゼミ,演習 ‖ *I've got a seminar on Goethe this morning.* 今朝はゲーテのゼミがある. ▶定義2 a meeting for business people in which working methods, etc are taught or discussed 作業方式などを学んだり討論したりする,実業家たちの集まり→セミナー, 研究集会, 討論会 ‖ *a one-day management seminar* 1日経営セミナー

**Sen** 略 (in US politics) Senator→(米国の政治で)上院議員

**senate** /sénət/ (しばしば **the Senate**) 名 [❹, 単数または複数形の動詞と共に] ▶定義 one of the two groups of elected politicians who make laws in the government in some countries, for example the US 選挙で選ばれる2つの政治家集団のうちの1つ. アメリカ合衆国など一部の国の政治体制では立法をつかさどる→上院
☛参 Congress, House of Representatives

**senator** /sénətər/ (しばしば **Senator**) 名 ❹ (略 **Sen**) ▶定義 a member of a group of elected politicians (the Senate) who make laws in the government in some countries, for example the US アメリカ合衆国などの一部の国の政治体制において法律を制定する,選挙で選ばれた政治家の集団(上院)の一員→上院議員 ‖ *Senator McCarthy* マッカーシー上院議員

*****send** /send/ 動 ⓗ (過,過分 **sent** /sent/) ▶定義1 **send sth (to sb/sth); send (sb) sth** to make sth go or be taken somewhere, especially by mail, radio, etc 特に郵便,無線などで〜をある所に向かわせる,または届けさせる→〜を(…に)送る, 送信する, 発送する, 届ける ‖ *to send a letter/parcel/message/fax to sb* 〜に手紙・小包・伝言・ファックスを送る *Don't forget to send me a postcard.* 忘れずに私にハガキを送ってくださいね. ▶定義2 to tell sb to go somewhere or to do sth; to arrange for sb to go somewhere 〜にある所に行くよう,または…するよう命じる; 〜がある所に行くよう手配する→〜を行かせる, 派遣する ‖ *My company is sending me on a training course next month.* 会社は来月,トレーニングコースに私を派遣する予定だ. *She sent the children to bed early.* 彼女は子供たちを早く寝かせた. *to send sb to prison* 〜を刑務所に送る *I'll send someone round to collect you at 10.00.* 10時にあなたを迎えに人をやるつもりだ. ▶定義3 to cause sb/sth to move in a particular direction, often quickly or as a reaction that cannot be prevented 〜を,しばしば非常な速さで,または防ぎようのない反動で,特定の方向に動かす→〜を…させる ‖ *I accidentally pushed the table and sent all the drinks flying.* 誤ってテーブルを押してしまい,飲み物を皆四方に散乱させてしまった. ▶定義4 **send sb (to/into sth)** to make sb have a particular feeling or enter a particular state 〜にある特定の感情を抱かせる,またはある特定の状態にする→〜を(…の状態に)する ‖ *The movement of the train sent me to sleep.* 列車の揺れで私は眠ってしまった.

成句 give/send sb your love ⇒ **LOVE**¹
句動詞 **send for sb/sth** ▶定義 to ask for sb to come to you; to ask for sth to be brought or sent to you 自分の所に来るようにと〜を呼びにやる; 〜を自分の所に持ってこさせる,または送らせる→〜を呼びにやる, 〜を取りに行かせる, 〜を取り寄せる ‖ *Quick! Send for an ambulance!* 急いで.救急車を呼びにやりなさい.

**send sth in** ▶定義 to send sth to a place where it will be officially dealt with 公式に処理される場所に〜を送る→〜を送付する, 提出する ‖ *I sent my application in three weeks ago but I still haven't had a reply.* 私は3週間前に願書を提出したが,まだ返事を受け取っていない.

**send off (for sth); send away (to sb) (for sth)** ▶定義 to write to sb and ask for sth to be sent to you 〜に手紙を書いて,…を送らせる→(〜を)郵便で取り寄せる・注文する ‖ *Let's send off for some holiday brochures.* 休暇用のパンフレットをいくつか取り寄せよう.

**send sb off** ▶定義 (used in a sports match) to order a player who has broken a rule to leave the field and not to return (スポーツの試合で用いて)規則を破った選手に競技場を去り,戻らないよう命令する→〜を退場させる ‖ *Beckham was sent off for a foul in the first half.* ベッカムは反則のため,前半で退場させられた.

**send sth off** ▶定義 to post sth 〜を郵送する→

(手紙など)を郵送する,ポストに投かんする‖ *I'll send the information off today.* 今日その情報を送ります.

**send sth out** ▶定義1 to send sth to a lot of different people or places 多数の人たちやさまざまな場所に～を送る →**(通知状など)を発送する,送付する**‖ *We sent out the invitations two months before the wedding.* 私たちは結婚式の2か月前に招待状を発送した. ▶定義2 to produce sth, for example light, heat, sound, etc 光,熱,音などを発する→**～を放つ,発する,出す**

**send sb/sth up** 英略式 ▶定義 to make sb/sth look ridiculous or silly especially by copying him/her/it in a way that is intended to be amusing わざと面白おかしく物まねをして,～をこっけい,またはばかばかしく見せる→**～をまねる,まねてからかう,ちゃかす**

**senile** /síːnaɪl/ 形 ▶定義 behaving in a confused and strange way, and unable to remember things because of old age 老齢のため訳の分からない奇妙な行動をし,物事を覚えていられない→**老衰の,もうろくした,ぼけた**‖ *I think she's going senile.* 彼女がだんだんもうろくしてきたと思う. — senility /sənílət̬i/ 名 Ⓤ ▶定義**老衰,もうろく,老人性痴ほう**

**senior**¹ /síːnjər/ 形 ▶定義1 senior (to sb) having a high or higher position in a company, organization, etc 会社,団体などで(より)高い地位を占める→**上位の,上級の,上司の,先輩の**‖ *a senior lecturer/officer/manager* 上級講師・上官・上級支配人 *He's senior to me.* 彼は私の先輩・上司だ.

▶定義2 (しばしば **Senior**)(略 **Snr, Sr**)特に 米 used after the name of a man who has the same name as his son, to avoid confusion 息子と同じ名前を持つ男性の名前の後に,混乱を避けるために付けて→**父親の,父の方の** ▶定義3 英 (used in schools) older (学校で用いて)→ **年長の,年上の** ▶定義4 米 connected with the final year at high school or college 高等学校や大学の最終学年に関する→**最終学年の,最上級の** ☛参 **junior**¹

**senior**² /síːnjər/ 名 Ⓒ ▶定義1 somebody who is older or of a higher position (than one or more other people) (ほかの人または人々よりも) 年上または上の地位にいる人→**先輩,年長者,上役,上官**‖ *My oldest sister is **ten years my senior**.* 一番上の姉は私より10歳年上だ. *She felt under-*valued, both by her colleagues and her seniors. 彼女は同僚や上司から過小評価されていると感じた. ▶定義2 米 one of the older students at a school 学校で年長の生徒の1人→**上級生** ▶定義3 米 a student in the final year of school, college or university 高校や大学の最終学年の生徒・学生→**最上級生**‖ *high school seniors* 高等学校の最上級生 ☛参 **junior**²

**senior citizen** = OLD-AGE PENSIONER

**seniority** /sɪnjɔ́(ː)rət̬i, -njár-/ 名 Ⓤ ▶定義 the position or importance that a person has in a company, organization, etc in relation to others 人が会社,組織などで占める相対的な地位,重要性→**年功(序列),古参,先任順位**‖ *The names are listed below **in order of seniority**.* 名前は以下に先任順で記載されている.

**sensation** /senséɪʃ(ə)n/ 名 ▶定義1 Ⓒ a feeling that is caused by sth affecting your body or part of your body 体に作用する～によって引き起こされる感じ→**感じ,感覚,気持ち**‖ *a pleasant/unpleasant/tingling sensation* 心地良い・不快・ひりひりする感じ ▶定義2 Ⓤ the ability to feel when touching or being touched 触れたり触れられたりしたときに感じる能力→**感覚,知覚,感覚機能**‖ *For some time after the accident he had no sensation in his legs.* 事故後しばらくの間,彼は足の感覚がなかった. ▶定義3 [Ⓒ, 通常は単数] a general feeling or impression that is difficult to explain 説明し難い全般的な感情や印象→**(～のような)感じ,漠然とした印象**‖ *I had the peculiar sensation that I was floating in the air.* 宙に浮いているような奇妙な感じがした.

▶定義4 [Ⓒ, 通常は単数] great excitement, surprise or interest among a group of people; sb/sth that causes this excitement 一群の人々の間で生じた大きな興奮,驚き,興味; こういった興奮状態を引き起こす人,物事→**大評判,大騒ぎ,物議,センセーション; 大評判の物・事・人,大事件**‖ *The young American **caused a sensation** by beating the top player.* その若いアメリカ人は,一流選手を破ってセンセーションを巻き起こした.

**sensational** /senséɪʃ(ə)n(ə)l/ 形 ▶定義1 causing, or trying to cause, a feeling of great excitement, surprise or interest among people 人々の

# 1464　sense¹

間で大きな興奮, 驚き, 興味を引き起こす, または引き起こそうとする➡**世間をあっと言わせるような, センセーショナルな** ‖ *This magazine specializes in sensational stories about the rich and famous.* この雑誌は金持ちや有名人についての興味本位な記事を売り物にしている.

▶定義2 昭式 extremely good or beautiful; very exciting ものすごく良い, または美しい; とてもわくわくする➡**目覚しい, すばらしい, 見事な, 大評判の** — sensationally 副 ➡ **人騒がせに, センセーショナルに, すばらしく, 見事に**

\*sense¹ /sens/ 名 ▶定義1 ❶ the ability to think or act in a reasonable or sensible way; good judgement 分別, または良識をもって考えたり, 行動したりする能力; 優れた判断力➡**思慮分別, 良識, 道理, 判断力** ‖ *At least he had the sense to stop when he realized he was making a mistake.* 彼には間違っていると気付いたときにともかく中断するだけの分別があった. *I think there's a lot of sense in what you're saying.* あなたのおっしゃる事は大いに道理にかなっていると思います. ☛参 common sense ▶定義2 [❶, 単数扱い] the ability to understand sth; the ability to recognize what sth is or what its value is 〜を理解する能力; 〜が何であるか, またはそれにどんな価値があるかを認識する能力 ➡ **(〜を)理解する力, センス** ‖ *She seems to have lost all sense of reality.* 彼女は現実感をすべて失ってしまったようだ. *I like him - he's got a great sense of humour.* 私は彼が好きだ — 彼にはすばらしいユーモアのセンスがある. *I'm always getting lost. I've got absolutely no sense of direction.* いつも道に迷ってばかりいる. 私には全く方向感覚が欠けている. ▶定義3 ❶ sense (in doing sth) the reason for doing sth; purpose 〜を行う理由; 目的 ➡ **(〜する)意義, 価値; 意図** ‖ *There's no sense in going any further - we're obviously lost.* これ以上進んでも意味がない — 私たちは明らかに道に迷ってしまった. *What's the sense in making things more difficult for yourself?* 自分で事態をより難しくすることにどんな意味があるというのか. ▶定義4 [❶, 単数扱い] a natural ability to do or produce sth well 〜を立派に行う, または生み出す生来の能力➡**感覚, 判断力, センス** ‖ *Good business sense made her a millionaire.* 持ち前の優れた経営センスで彼女は億万長者になった. *He's got absolutely no dress sense (= he dresses very badly).* 彼にはおしゃれ感覚が全くない (= 彼はとてもひどい服装をしている). ▶定義5 [単数扱い] a feeling or consciousness of sth 〜についての感じ, または意識➡**感じ, 感触, 気持ち, 意識** ‖ *I felt a tremendous sense of relief when the exams were finally over.* やっと試験が終わって, ものすごくほっとした. *She only visits her family out of a sense of duty.* 彼女は義務感から家族を訪ねるだけだ. ▶定義6 ❻ one of the five natural physical powers of sight, hearing, smell, taste and touch, that people and animals have 人間や動物に生来備わった視覚, 聴覚, 臭覚, 味覚, 触覚という5つの感覚の1つ➡**感覚, 五感のうちの1つ** ‖ *I've got a cold and I've lost my sense of smell.* 風邪を引いて, 臭覚がなくなってしまった. *Dogs have an acute sense of hearing.* 犬には鋭い聴覚が備わっている.

▶定義7 ❻ (used about a word, phrase, etc) a meaning (単語, 語句などについて)➡**意味, 語義** ‖ *This word has two senses.* この語には2つの意味がある.

成句 come to your senses ▶定義 to finally realize that you should do sth because it is the most sensible thing to do 〜をするのが最も賢明なのだから, それをすべきだとようやく気付く➡**正気を取り戻す, 迷いが覚める**

in a sense ▶定義 in one particular way but not in other ways; partly ほかの意味ではなく, ある1つの意味において; 部分的に➡**ある意味[点]では, いくぶん** ‖ *In a sense you're right, but there's more to the matter than that.* ある意味であなたは正しいが, その問題はそれだけでは済まない.

make sense ▶定義1 to be possible to understand; to have a clear meaning 理解することができる; 明白な意味を持つ➡**理解できる, 意味を成す** ‖ *What does this sentence mean? It doesn't make sense to me.* この文はどういう意味ですか. 私には訳が分かりません. ▶定義2 (used about an action) to be sensible or logical (行動について)理にかなう, 論理的である➡**道理にかなう, もっともだ** ‖ *I think it would make sense to wait for a while before making a decision.* 決定をする前に, しばらく待った方が賢明だと思う.

**make sense of sth** ▶定義 to manage to understand sth that is not clear or is difficult to understand 明白でない、または分かりにくい事をどうにか理解する →～の意味をくみ取る、～を理解する ‖ *I can't make sense of these instructions.* 私にはこれらの指示が理解できない.

**talk sense** ⇒ **TALK**¹(6)

**sense²** /sens/ 動他（進行形は不可）▶定義 to realize or become conscious of sth; to get a feeling about sth even though you cannot see it, hear it, etc ～に気付く、～を意識する；見たり聞いたりなどできなくても～について感知する →～を感じる、感知する、気付く ‖ *I sensed that something was wrong as soon as I went in.* 中に入ってすぐに何か様子がおかしいと感じた.

➤この動詞は進行形では使われないが、現在分詞(= -ing 形)は一般に見られる： *Sensing a scandal, the tabloid photographers rushed to the star's hotel.* (スキャンダルを察知して、ゴシップ紙のカメラマンたちはそのスターのホテルに殺到した.)

**senseless** /sénsləs/ 形 ▶定義 1 having no meaning or purpose 意味や目的を持たない →無意味な ▶定義 2 unconscious 意識のない →意識を失った、感覚のない ‖ *He was beaten senseless.* 彼は殴られて意識を失った.

**sensibility** /sènsəbíləti/ 名（複 **sensibilities**) ▶定義 1 ❶ ❷ the ability to understand and experience deep feelings, for example in art, literature, etc 芸術、文学などにおける、深い感情を理解し感じ取る能力 →（繊細な）感受性、感性、鑑賞能力 ▶定義 2 **sensibilities**[複数扱い] a person's feelings, especially when he/she is easily offended 特に傷付けられやすい感情 →傷付きやすい感情、繊細な感情、多感

*\***sensible** /sénsəb(ə)l/ 形 ▶定義 (used about people and their behaviour) able to make good judgements based on reason and experience; practical (人またはその行動について) 道理や経験に基づいて良い判断をすることができる；実際的な →分別のある、道理にかなった、賢明な；実用的な、役に立つ ‖ *a sensible person/decision/precaution* 良識のある人・賢明な判断・理にかなった予防策 *Stop joking and give me a sensible answer.* 冗談はやめて、まともに答えてください. *I think it would be sensible to leave early, in case there's a lot of traffic.* 交通渋滞に備えて、早めに出発した方が賢明だと思う. ⇔ **silly**, **foolish** — **sensibly** /-əb(ə)li/ 副 →良識的に、賢明に ‖ *Let's sit down and discuss the matter sensibly.* さあ座って、良識をもってこの件について話し合いましょう.

➤ sensible, sensitive と比較. sensible は常識、理にかなった行動、良識的な判断に関連している. sensitive は感情や情緒、あるいは視覚、聴覚、触覚、臭覚、味覚の五感に関連している.

*\***sensitive** /sénsətɪv/ 形 ▶定義 1 sensitive (to sth) showing that you are conscious of and able to understand people's feelings, problems, etc 人々の感情、問題などに気付いており、それらを理解できることを表して →（～に）敏感な ‖ *It wasn't very sensitive of you to keep mentioning her boyfriend. You know they've just split up.* 彼女のボーイフレンドについて話してばかりいて、君も無神経だよ. 知っての通り、彼らは別れたばかりなのだから. *to be sensitive to sb's feelings/wishes* ～の気持ち・願望に敏感である ▶定義 2 sensitive (about/to sth) easily upset, offended or annoyed, especially about a particular subject 特にある特定の話題に対してすぐにうろたえたり、気分を害したり、いらいらする →（～に）敏感に反応する、神経過敏な ‖ *She's still a bit sensitive about her divorce.* 彼女はいまだに自分の離婚のことを気にしている. *He's very sensitive to criticism.* 彼は批評をとても気にする. ⇔ 定義 1, 2 **insensitive** ▶定義 3 (used about a subject, a situation, etc) needing to be dealt with carefully because it is likely to cause anger or trouble (話題、状況などについて) 人を怒らせたり問題を引き起こす可能性があるため、慎重に扱う必要のある →微妙な、慎重な取り扱いを要する、厄介な ‖ *This is a sensitive period in the negotiations between the two countries.* 今が2国間の協議で最も慎重を要する時だ. ▶定義 4 sensitive (to sth) easily hurt or damaged; painful, especially if touched 傷付きやすい、痛みやすい；特に触れられたときに痛む →（～に）弱い、傷付きやすい；痛む ‖ *a new cream for sensitive skin* 敏感肌用の新しいクリーム *My teeth are very sensitive to hot or cold food.* 熱い食べ物や冷たい食べ物を食べると歯がひどく染

みる． ▶定義5 (used about a scientific instrument, a piece of equipment, etc) able to measure very small changes (科学的な装置，器具などについて) 非常にわずかな変化でも測定できる→感度の良い，高感度の ☞参 sensible の注 — sensitively 副 →敏感に，慎重に ‖ *The investigation will need to be handled sensitively.* その調査は慎重に取り扱う必要がある． — sensitivity /sènsətívəti/ 名 ⓤ →敏感さ，感受性，感度 ‖ *I think your comments showed a complete lack of sensitivity.* あなたの意見には思いやりが全く欠けていると思う．

**sensual** /sénjuəl; -sjuəl/ 形 ▶定義 connected with physical or sexual pleasure 肉体的または性的な快楽に関する→官能的な，肉感的な，性欲をそそる ‖ *the sensual rhythms of Latin music* ラテン音楽の官能的なリズム — sensuality /sènʃuǽləti; -sju-/ 名 ⓤ →肉欲にふけること，みだら

**sensuous** /sénjuəs; -sju-/ 形 ▶定義 giving pleasure to the mind or body through the senses 五感を通して心身に喜びを与える→感覚に訴える，(感覚的に) 非常に心地良い，甘美な ‖ *the sensuous feel of pure silk* 100パーセントシルクの快い感触 — sensuously 副 →感覚に訴えるように，美感に訴えて — sensuousness 名 ⓤ →感覚に訴えること，甘美

**sent** SEND の過去・過去分詞形

**\*sentence**[1] /sént(ə)ns/ 名 ⓒ ▶定義1 (文法) a group of words containing a subject and a verb, that expresses a statement, a question, etc. When a sentence is written it begins with a big (capital) letter and ends with a full stop. 主語と動詞を含む単語の集まり．陳述，疑問などを表す．表記する場合，大(頭)文字で書き始め，最後に終止符を付ける→文 ☞参 phrase ▶定義2 the punishment given by a judge to sb who has been found guilty of a crime 有罪判決を受けた人に裁判官が与える刑罰→判決，宣告 ‖ *20 years in prison was a very harsh sentence.* 20年の懲役は非常に厳しい判決だった．

**sentence**[2] /sént(ə)ns/ 動 他 ▶定義 *sentence sb (to sth)* (used about a judge) to tell sb who has been found guilty of a crime what the punishment will be (裁判官について) 有罪と決まった人に対してどのような刑罰かを告げる→〜に判決を下す，〜に(…の刑を)宣告する，〜を刑に処する ‖ *The judge sentenced her to three months in prison for shoplifting.* 判事は彼女に万引きのかどで3か月の懲役を言い渡した．

**sentiment** /séntəmənt/ 名 ▶定義1 ⓒ ⓤ 正式 (しばしば複数形で) an attitude or opinion that is often caused or influenced by emotion しばしば感情に誘発または作用される態度または意見→心情，心証，感情，(感情の混じった)意見 ‖ *His comments expressed my sentiments exactly.* 彼の意見は私の心情を正確に表現していた． ▶定義2 ⓤ feelings such as pity, romantic love, sadness, etc that influence sb's action or behaviour (sometimes in situations where this is not appropriate) 人の行動や態度を(時にはそうあってはならない状況で)左右する，哀れみ，熱愛，悲しみなどの感情→感傷，多感 ‖ *There's no room for sentiment in business.* 商売には感傷の入る余地はない．

**sentimental** /sèntəmént(ə)l/ 形 ▶定義1 producing or connected with emotions such as romantic love, pity, sadness, etc which may be too strong or not appropriate 恋愛感情，同情，悲しみなどの強烈すぎたり，不適切な感情をそそる，またはそのような感情に関する→感傷的な，情にもろい，涙もろい，お涙ちょうだいの ‖ *How can you be sentimental about an old car!* 何だってあなたは古い車に感傷的になるの．*a sentimental love song* 感傷的な恋の歌 ▶定義2 connected with happy memories or feelings of love rather than having any financial value 金銭上の価値があるというよりむしろ，幸せな思い出や恋愛感情に関連した→心情的な，(特別な)思い入れのある ‖ *The jewellery wasn't worth much but it had great sentimental value to me.* その宝石は大した値打ちはなかったが，私には思い入れのある大切なものだった． — sentimentality /sèntəmentǽləti/ 名 ⓤ →涙もろさ，感傷的な事 — sentimentally /-t(ə)li/ 副 →感傷的に，心情的に，懐かしくて

**sentry** /séntri/ 名 ⓒ (複 sentries) ▶定義 a soldier who stands outside a building and guards it 建物の外に立って番をする兵士→番兵，歩哨(ほしょう)，見張り番

**separable** /sép(ə)rəb(ə)l/ 形 ▶定義 able to be separated→分離できる，分けられる ⇔ **inseparable**

**separate**¹ /sép(ə)rət/ 形 ▶定義1 separate (from sth/sb) apart; not together 離れた；一緒でない→離れた，ばらばらの，別々の ‖ *You should always keep your cash and credit cards separate.* 現金とクレジットカードはいつも別々に保管すべきだ． ▶定義2 different; not connected 異なる；つながっていない→別個の，離れた，独立した ‖ *We stayed in separate rooms in the same hotel.* 私たちは同じホテルの別々の部屋に宿泊した．

> ▶音声とつづり字
>
> separate と ate 規則
>
> separate は動詞と形容詞とで発音が異なります．動詞では[sép.ə.rèɪt]，形容詞では[sép.ə.rət]と語尾は短くなります．名詞の場合は candidate, deligate のように，2 通りの発音がある場合もあるので注意が必要です．mediate では [-ɛɪt] と発音され，immediate, immediately のような場合は [-ɪt] と発音されます．-ate は第2アクセントがあり，その前の前の音節に第1アクセントがあります．その例は以下のように多くあります．
>
> apprécie cálculate dessíminate méditate dédicate pérmeate éducate evaluate

**separate**² /sép(ə)rèɪt/ 動 ▶定義1 自他 separate (sb/sth) (from sb/sth) to stop being together; to cause people or things to stop being together 一緒にいることをやめる；人々や物に一緒になっていることをやめさせる→分かれる，(〜を)分離する ‖ *I think we should separate into two groups.* 私たちは2つのグループに分かれるべきだと思う． *The friends separated at the airport.* 友人たちは空港で分かれた． *I got separated from my friends in the crowd.* 私は人込みで友人と離れ離れになってしまった．
▶定義2 他 separate sb/sth (from sb/sth) to keep people or things apart; to be between people or things with the result that they are apart 複数の人や物を分けておく；複数の人や物の間に入り，それらを分ける→〜を分ける，隔てる ‖ *The two sides of the city are separated by the river.* その町は川で二分されている．
▶定義3 自 to stop living together as a couple with your wife, husband or partner 妻・夫・同棲(どうせい)相手とカップルとして一緒に暮らすのをやめる→別居する ‖ *His parents separated when he was still a baby.* 彼の両親は彼がまだ赤ん坊のときに別居した．

**separated** /sép(ə)rèɪtəd/ 形 ▶定義 not living together as a couple any more もはや夫婦として一緒に生活していない→別居中で，別々に暮らして ‖ *My wife and I are separated.* 私と妻は現在別居中だ．

**separately** /sép(ə)rətli/ 副 ▶定義 apart; not together 離れて；一緒ではなく→離れて，ばらばらに，別々に ‖ *Shall we pay separately or all together?* 別々に支払いましょうか，それとも一緒にまとめて支払いましょうか．

**separation** /sèpəréɪʃ(ə)n/ 名 ▶定義1 ⒞ⓤ the action of separating or being separated; a situation or period of being apart 分かれるまたは分けられる動作；離れている状態または期間→分離；別離した状態，別離期間 ▶定義2 ⒞ an agreement where a couple decide not to live together any more カップルがこれ以上一緒に暮らさないという協定・合意→別居 ‖ *a trial separation* 試験的な別居

**Sept** 略 September→9月 ‖ *2 Sept 1920* 1920年9月2日

**September** /septémbər/ 名 ⓤⒸ (略 Sept) ▶定義 the ninth month of the year, coming after August 8月の次に来る，1年の9番目の月→9月 ▶文中での月の表し方については，January の例と注を参照．

**septic** /séptɪk/ 形 ▶定義 infected with poisonous bacteria 毒性のある細菌に感染した →(傷などが)病菌で侵された，腐敗性の，敗血症の ‖ *The wound went septic.* その傷は敗血症になった．

**sequel** /síːkwəl/ 名 ⒞ a sequel (to sth) ▶定義1 a book, film, etc that continues the story of the one before 前回の話を引き継ぐ本，映画など→(〜の)続き，続編，後編 ▶定義2 something that happens after, or is the result of, a previous event 先に起こった出来事の後に起こるもの，または先に起こった出来事の結果 →(〜の)結果，帰着点；後日談

**sequence** /síːkwəns/ 名 ▶定義1 ⒞ a number of things (actions, events, etc) that happen or come one after another 次々と起こる，または出てくるたくさんの物事(動作，出来事など)→連

## 1468 serene

続,連続するもの,続発 ‖ *Complete the following sequence: 1, 4, 8, 13,...* 次の数列を完成させなさい: 1, 4, 8, 13,... ▶定義2 ❶ the order in which a number of things happen or are arranged たくさんの物事が起こる、または並べられた順序 →**順序, 順番, 順序** ‖ *The photographs are in sequence.* その写真は順番に並んでいる.

**serene** /səríːn/ 形 ▶定義 calm and peaceful 穏やかで平和な →**穏やかな, 静かな, 落ち着いた** ‖ *a serene smile* 穏やかな微笑 — **serenely** 副 →**穏やかに, 静かに, 落ち着いて** — **serenity** /sərénəti/ 名 ❶ →**静けさ, 平穏**

**sergeant** /sáːrdʒ(ə)nt/ 名 ❻ (略 **Sgt**) ▶定義1 an officer with a low position in the army or air force 陸軍または空軍における低い地位の士官 →**軍曹** ▶定義2 an officer with a middle position in the police force 警察で中間の地位にいる警官 →**巡査部長**

**serial** /sí(ə)riəl/ 名 ❻ ▶定義 a story in a magazine or on television or radio that is told in a number of parts over a period of time 雑誌,テレビ,ラジオである期間何回かに分けて語られる物語 →**続き物, 連載小説, 連続番組** ‖ *the first part of a six-part drama serial* 6回にわたる連続ドラマの第1回分 ☞参 **series** の注 — **serialize**(または -ise) /-riəlàɪz/ 動 他 →**~を連載する, 連続番組として放送する**

**serial number** 名 ❻ ▶定義 the number marked on sth to identify it and to distinguish it from other things of the same type ~を特定し、同じ種類のほかの物から区別するために付けられた番号 →**通し番号, 認識番号, シリアルナンバー**

\*series /sí(ə)riːz/ 名 ❻ (複 **series**) ▶定義1 a number of things that happen one after another and are of the same type or connected 同じタイプ、または関連性のあるもので、連続的に起きるいくつかのもの →**連続, 一連, 一続き** ‖ *a series of events* 一連の出来事 *There has been a series of burglaries in this district recently.* 最近,この地区では強盗が連続発生している. ▶定義2 a number of programmes on radio or television which have the same main characters and each tell a complete story 複数のラジオ・テレビ番組で、主な登場人物が変わらず、一話完結のもの →**(一話完結の)続き物, 連続物, シリーズ物**

► series, serial と比較. series の場合,各回の主な登場人物が同じで,一話完結になっている. 一方, serial の場合には,同じ話が何回かに分けて継続的に語られる.

\***serious** /sí(ə)riəs/ 形 ▶定義1 bad or dangerous 悪い, 危険な →**重大な, 深刻な, ゆゆしい** ‖ *a serious accident/illness/offence* 大事故・重病・重罪 *Pollution is a very serious problem.* 公害は非常に深刻な問題だ. *Her condition is serious and she's likely to be in hospital for some time.* 彼女の病状は重く、しばらくの間入院していることになりそうだ. ▶定義2 needing to be treated as important, not just for fun 冗談ではなく重要なものとして取り扱う必要のある →**まじめな, 重要な, 厳粛な** ‖ *Don't laugh, it's a serious matter.* 笑わないで、これはまじめな問題なのだから. *a serious discussion* 真剣な議論 ▶定義3 **serious (about sth/about doing sth)** (used about a person) not joking; thoughtful (人について)ふざけていない; 考え込んだ →**(~について)本気な, まじめな, 真剣な** ‖ *Are you serious about starting your own business (= are you really going to do it)?* 事業を起こすことを本気で考えているのですか(= あなたは本当に事業を起こすつもりなのか). *He's terribly serious. I don't think I've ever seen him laugh.* 彼はひどくまじめだ. 今まで彼が笑うのを見たことがないと思う. *You're looking very serious. Was it bad news?* とても深刻そうな顔付きをしていますね. 悪い知らせだったのですか. — **seriousness** 名 ❶ →**ゆゆしさ, まじめ, 真剣, 深刻**

\***seriously** /sí(ə)riəsli/ 副 ▶定義1 in a serious way 重く, 真剣に →**重大に, ひどく; 真剣に, まじめに** ‖ *Three people were seriously injured in the accident.* その事故で3人が重傷を負った. *My mother is seriously ill.* 母は重病だ. *It's time you started to think seriously about the future.* あなたも将来についてそろそろ真剣に考えるべき時だ. ▶定義2 used at the beginning of a sentence for showing that you are not joking or that you really mean what you are saying 文の始めに用いて, 冗談を言っていない, すべて本気であるということを示す →**まじめな話だが, 冗談はさておき** ‖ *Seriously, I do appreciate all your help.* 本当の話, あなたの手助けをとても感謝しています. *Seriously, you've got nothing to worry about.* 冗談は抜きにして, あなたには心配すべ

き事は何もない. ▶定義3 used for expressing surprise at what sb has said and asking if it is really true 〜が言った事に対する驚きを表現し, それが本当の事なのかを質問するのに用いて→本当ですか, 本気ですか ‖ *I'm 40 today.' 'Seriously? You look a lot younger.'*「私は今日で40歳になります」「本当ですか. ずっと若く見えますよ」

成句 **take sb/sth seriously** ▶定義 to treat sb or sth as important 〜を重要なものとして取り扱う→〜を重要と見なす, 真に受ける, 深刻に受け止める ‖ *You take everything too seriously! Relax and enjoy yourself.* 君はすべてをまじめに受け止めすぎるよ. リラックスして楽しみなさい.

**sermon** /sə́:mən/ 名 ● ▶定義 a speech on a religious or moral subject that is given as part of a service in church 教会で礼拝の一部として行われる宗教的または道徳的な主題に関する演説→説教, 説法

**serrated** /səréitəd, séreitəd/ 形 ▶定義 having a row of points in V-shapes along the edge 刃の縁に V 字形の先端が並んでいる→のこぎり(歯)状の, ぎざぎざの, 刻みのある ‖ *a knife with a serrated edge* のこぎり歯の小刀

**servant** /sə́:rv(ə)nt/ 名 ● ▶定義 a person who is paid to work in sb's house, doing work such as cooking, cleaning, etc 人の家で料理, 掃除などの仕事を行って収入を得る人→召使い, 使用人
☛参 civil servant

*****serve** /sə:rv/ 動 ▶定義1 ⓗ to give food or drink to sb during a meal; to take an order and then bring food or drink to sb in a restaurant, bar, etc 食事中に〜に飲み物を出す; レストラン, バーなどで注文を取り, 〜に飲み物を運ぶ →(飲食物)を出す; (客)の注文を取る ‖ *Breakfast is served from 7.30 to 9.00 am.* 朝食は午前 7 時30分から 9 時の間に出される. ▶定義2 ⓗ (used about an amount of food) to be enough for a certain number of people (食事の量について) ある特定の人数に対して十分にある →(料理などが)〜人分ある ‖ *According to the recipe, this dish serves four.* 調理法によれば, この料理は 4 人分です. ▶定義3 ⓔ ⓗ (in a shop) to take a customer's order; to give help, sell goods, etc (店で)客の注文を取る; 客の手助けをしたり, 商品を売るなどする →(店で)客の注文を聞く; (客)に応対する, (客)の注文を聞く, (客)の用を承る, (客)に品物を見せる ‖ *There was a long queue of people waiting to be served.* 店員の対応を待つ人たちの長い列ができていた. ▶定義4 ⓔ ⓗ to be useful or suitable for a particular purpose ある目的に役立つ, 向いた→役立つ, 間に合う; 〜の役に立つ, (目的)にかなう ‖ *The judge said the punishment would serve as a warning to others.* 判事は刑罰がほかの人々への警告になるだろうと言った. *It's an old car but it will* **serve** *our* **purpose** *for a few months.* 古い車だが, 2, 3 か月は間に合うだろう. ▶定義5 ⓔ ⓗ to perform a duty or provide a service for the public or for an organization 一般の人々のためや組織のために職務を果たす, または奉仕する→(〜に)仕える, (職務を)務める, 働く, 勤務する, 奉仕する ‖ *During the war, he served in the Army.* 戦時中, 彼は陸軍に勤務した. *She became a nurse because she wanted to serve the community.* 彼女は社会に奉仕したかったので看護婦になった. ▶定義6 ⓗ to spend a period of time in prison as punishment 刑罰として一定期間を刑務所で過ごす →(刑期など)を務める ‖ *He is currently* **serving** *a ten-year* **sentence** *for fraud.* 彼は現在, 詐欺罪で 10 年の刑に服役中だ. ▶定義7 ⓔ ⓗ (in tennis and similar sports) to start play by hitting the ball (テニスや同種の競技で)球を打って競技を開始する→(ボールを)サーブする

成句 **first come, first served** ⇒ **FIRST**²
**serve sb right** ▶定義 used when sth unpleasant happens to sb and you do not feel sorry for him/her because you think it is his/her own fault ある人に不快な事が起こっても, 自業自得だからと気の毒に思わない場合に用いて→(〜に)当然の報いである, 自業自得である ‖ *'I feel sick.' 'It serves you right for eating so much.'*「吐き気がする」「あれほど食べたのだから自業自得さ」

**server** /sə́:rvər/ 名 ● ▶定義 a computer that stores information that a number of computers can share 複数のコンピューターが共有することのできる情報をしまっておくコンピューター→サーバー ☛参 client

*****service**¹ /sə́:rvəs/ 名 ▶定義1 ● a system or organization that provides the public with sth

## 1470 service[2]

that it needs; the job that an organization does 必要な～を社会に提供する制度や組織; 組織が行う仕事 →(郵便・電信・電話などの)公共事業, (ガス・水道・電気などの)供給, 施設 ‖ *There is a regular bus service to the airport.* その空港へはバスの定期便がある. *the postal service* 郵便事業 *the National Health Service* 国家医療制度 *We offer a number of financial services.* 我々は数々の投資情報サービスを提供している. ☞参 **Civil Service** ▶定義2 ❶(または **the services**) [複数扱い] the armed forces; the army, navy or air force; the work done by the people in them 軍隊; 陸軍, 海軍, 空軍; 軍人が行う仕事 →**陸・海・空)軍; 軍務, 兵役** ‖ *They both joined the services when they left school.* 学校卒業後, 彼らは2人とも兵役に服した. *Do you have to do military service in your country?* あなたの国に兵役の義務はありますか. ▶定義3 ❶Ⓒ work done for sb; help given to sb ～のために行われる仕事; ～への手助け →**勤務, 尽力** ‖ *He left the police force after thirty years' service.* 彼は30年間勤めた後, 警察を退いた. ▶定義4 ❶ the work or the quality of work done by sb when serving a customer 客に応対する仕事またはその仕事振り →**接客, 客扱い, サービス** ‖ *I enjoyed the meal but the service was terrible.* 食事はおいしかったが, サービスはひどかった. *Is service included in the bill?* 勘定書にはサービス料は含まれていますか. ▶定義5 Ⓒ the checks, repairs, etc that are necessary to make sure that a machine is working properly 確実に機械が正しく作動するために必要な点検, 修理など →**(製品に対する)アフターサービス, 点検修理, 整備** ‖ *We take our car for a service every six months.* 私たちは6か月ごとに車を整備に出す. ▶定義6 ❻ a religious ceremony, usually including prayers, singing, etc 通常, 祈祷(きとう), 声楽などを含む宗教的な儀式 →**礼拝, 儀式** ‖ *a funeral service* 葬式 ▶定義7 Ⓒ (in tennis and similar sports) the first hit of the ball at the start of play; a player's turn to serve(7) (テニスや同種の競技で)競技の開始時に最初に球を打つこと; 競技者のサーブの順番 →**サーブ; サーブの順番** ▶定義8 **services** [複数扱い] a place at the side of a motorway where there is a petrol station, a shop, toilets, a restaurant, etc 高速道路のわきの, ガソリンスタンド, 店, 便所, レストランなどがある場所 →**休憩所, サービスエリア**

### ▶社会・文化

**morning service**

「モーニングサービス」と聞くと喫茶店の朝食メニューを思い浮かべる人もいるかもしれません. しかし, 英語で morning service と言えば教会で司式される朝のミサ(礼拝)のことです.

ミサのことは通例 service(カトリックでは Mass)と言います. 多くの教会は毎週日曜日にミサを開きます.

**service**[2] /sə́ːrvəs/ 動 Ⓖ ▶定義 to examine and, if necessary, repair a car, machine, etc 自動車, 機械などを検査し, 必要に応じて修理する →**～を点検する, 修理する, 整備する, ～のアフターサービスをする** ‖ *All cars should be serviced at regular intervals.* すべての自動車は定期的に整備されるべきだ.

**service station** = SERVICE[1](8)

**serviette** /sə̀ːrviét/ 名 Ⓒ ▶定義 a square of cloth or paper that you use when you are eating to keep your clothes clean and to clean your mouth or hands on 物を食べているとき, 衣服が汚れないように, また口や手をふくために用いる四角い布や紙 →**(テーブル用)ナプキン** ☞類 **napkin**

**session** /séʃ(ə)n/ 名 ▶定義1 Ⓒ a period of doing a particular activity ある特定の活動を行う期間 →**会期, 開廷期間, 授業(時間), (大学の)学期** ‖ *The whole tape was recorded in one session.* 1回の録音どりで, そのテープ全部の録音ができた. *She has a session at the gym every week.* 彼女は週に1回ジムのクラスに出ている. ▶定義2 ⒸⓊ a formal meeting or series of meetings of a court of law, parliament, etc 裁判所, 議会などの1回の公式の会議, または何回か継続して開催される一連の会議 →**会議, 会合, 開会, 開廷**

★**set**[1] /set/ 動 (現分 **setting**; 過, 過分 **set**) ▶定義1 ⓣ to put sb/sth in a particular place or position ～をある特定の場所・位置に置く →**～を置く, 載せる** ‖ *I set the box down carefully on the floor.* 私はその箱を慎重に床の上に置い

た. ▶定義2 ⓣ (しばしば受動態で) to make the action of a book, play, film, etc take place in a particular time, situation, etc 本, 劇, 映画などの出来事をある特定の時間, 状況下で起こるようにする➔(舞台)を設定する ‖ *The film is set in 16th century Spain*. その映画は16世紀のスペインを舞台にしている. ▶定義3 ⓣ to cause a particular state or event; to start sth happening ある特定の状況や出来事を引き起こす; 〜を始めさせる➔〜を…させる, 〜を…の状態にする ‖ *The new government set the prisoners free*. 新政府は受刑者たちを釈放した. *The rioters set a number of cars on fire*. 暴徒たちは何台もの車に火をつけた. ▶定義4 ⓣ to prepare or arrange sth for a particular purpose 〜をある特定の目的のために準備・手配する➔〜を準備する, 整える; 〜を(…に)調整する, 合わせる ‖ *I set my alarm for 6.30*. 目覚まし時計を6時30分に合わせた. *to set the table (= put the plates, knives, forks, etc on it)* 食卓の用意をする (= 食卓の上に皿, ナイフ, フォークなどを置く) ▶定義5 ⓣ to decide or arrange sth ～を決定, または手配する➔〜を設定する, 決定する, 指定する ‖ *Can we set a limit of two hours for the meeting?* 会議に2時間の時間制限を設けることはできませんか. *They haven't set the date for their wedding yet*. 彼らはまだ結婚式の日取りを決めていない. ▶定義6 ⓣ to do sth good that people have to try to copy or achieve 人々が模倣または達成の努力をなすべき正しい事を行う➔(模範, 基準など)を示す, 作る, 定める, (記録など)打ち立てる ‖ *Try to set a good example to the younger children*. 小さな子供たちに良い手本を示すように努力しなさい. *He has set a new world record*. 彼は世界新記録を樹立した. *They set high standards of customer service*. 彼らはほかに先駆けて高い顧客サービス基準を示した. ▶定義7 ⓣ to give sb a piece of work or a task 〜に仕事や作業を与える➔〜を割り当てる, 与える, 課す ‖ *We've been set a lot of homework this weekend*. この週末はたくさんの宿題が出ている. *I've set myself a target of four hours' study every evening*. 私は毎晩4時間勉強するという目標を自分に課した. ▶定義8 ⓘ to become firm or hard 硬くなる, 固くなる➔固まる, 凝固する ‖ *The concrete will set solid/hard in just a few hours*. コンクリートはわずか数時間でしっかりと固まる. ▶定義9 ⓣ to fix a precious stone, etc in a piece of jewellery 宝石などを装身具に固定する➔〜をはめ込む, ちりばめる ▶定義10 ⓣ to fix a broken bone in the correct position so that it can get better 骨折が治るように折れた骨を正しい位置に固定する➔(骨折・脱臼(だっきゅう)した骨)を元に戻す, つぐ ‖ *The doctor set her broken leg*. 医者は彼女の骨折した脚の骨をついだ. ▶定義11 ⓘ (used about the sun) to go down below the horizon in the evening (太陽について) 夕方, 水平線・地平線の下に沈む➔沈む, 没する ⇔ **rise**

成句 **set foot (in/on sth)** ▶定義 to visit, enter or arrive at/in a place ある場所を訪問する, 中に入る, 到着する➔(〜に)足を踏み入れる, 立ち入る ‖ *No woman has ever set foot in the temple*. これまで女性がその寺院に足を踏み入れたことはない.

**put/set sth right** ⇒ **RIGHT**[1]

**set sail** ▶定義 to begin a journey by sea 航海を開始する➔出帆する, 出航する ‖ *Columbus set sail for India*. コロンブスはインドに向けて出帆した.

**set your heart on sth; have your heart set on sth** ⇒ **HEART**

**put/set your/sb's mind at rest** ⇒ **MIND**[1]

**set eyes on sb/sth** ▶定義 to see sb/sth 〜を見る➔〜を見る, 会う ‖ *He loved the house the moment he set eyes on it*. 彼はその家を一目見て気に入った.

句動詞 **set about sth** ▶定義 to start doing sth, especially dealing with a problem or task 特に問題や仕事の処理など, 〜を開始する➔〜に取り掛かる, 〜に着手する, 〜を処理する ‖ *How would you set about tackling this problem?* あなたはどのようにこの問題に着手するつもりですか.

**set sth aside** ▶定義 ⓣ to keep sth to use later 後で使うために〜を取っておく➔〜を取っておく ‖ *I try to set aside part of my wages every week*. 私は毎週, 給料の一部を取っておこうと努力している.

**set sb/sth back** ▶定義 to delay sb/sth➔〜を遅らせる ‖ *The bad weather has set our plans back six weeks*. 悪天候のため, 我々の計画は6週間遅れた.

set forth 正式 ▶定義 to start a journey 旅行を開始する→出発する

set sth forth 正式 ▶定義 to show or tell sth to sb or to make sth known ～に…示す、または教える、～を知らせる→(意見など)を明確に述べる、発表する; ～を展示する

set in ▶定義 to arrive and remain for a period of time 到来し、その後一定期間とどまる →(季節・天候が)到来する、始まる;(好ましくないことが)広がる、定着する ‖ *I'm afraid that the bad weather has set in.* 悪天候が到来し、しばらく居座るのではないかと案じています.

set off ▶定義 to leave on a journey→旅行に出る、出発する ‖ *We set off at 3 o'clock this morning.* 私たちは今朝3時に出発した.

set sth off ▶定義 to do sth which starts a reaction 反動を伴う事を行う→～を引き起こす、誘発する、始めさせる ‖ *When this door is opened, it sets off an alarm.* このドアを開けると警報が鳴る.

set out ▶定義 to leave on a journey 旅行に出掛ける→旅行に出る、出発する

set out to do sth ▶定義 to decide to achieve sth ～を達成しようと心に決める→～することを目指す、企てる、～することに取り掛かる ‖ *He set out to prove that his theory was right.* 彼は自分の理論の正しさの証明に取り掛かった.

set (sth) up ▶定義 to start a business, organization, system, etc 事業、会社、制度などを始める→～を始める、創設する、設立する、制定する ‖ *The company has set up a new branch in Wales.* その会社はウェールズに新しい支店を構えた.

★**set**² /set/ 名 C ▶定義1 a number of things that belong together 一組になっている複数のもの→一式、一そろい、一組 ‖ *a set of kitchen knives* 包丁一式 *In the first set of questions, you have to fill in the gap.* 最初の一連の質問では空所を埋めなくてはなりません. *a set of instructions* 一連の指示 *a spare set of keys* 予備のかぎ一組 *a chess set* チェスのセット ▶定義2 a piece of equipment for receiving television or radio signals テレビや無線信号を受信する装置→受信機、受像機 ‖ *a television set* テレビ ▶定義3 the scenery that is made for a play or film 演劇や映画のために作られた舞台装置→舞台装置、セット、大道具 ▶定義4 (in tennis) a group of games forming part of a match (テニスで)試合の一部を構成する一連のゲーム→セット ‖ *China won the volleyball final by three sets to one.* 中国がセット3対1でバレーボールの決勝戦に勝った.

**set**³ /set/ 形 ▶定義1 placed in a particular position ある特定の位置に置かれた→置かれた、位置した ‖ *deep-set eyes* 深くくぼんだ目 *Our house is quite set back from the road.* 私たちの家は道からかなり引っ込んだ所にある.

▶定義2 fixed and not changing; firm 決まっていて変わらない; 断固とした→所定の決まった、意を決した、頑固な ‖ *There are no set hours in my job.* 私の仕事には決まった勤務時間がない. *I'll have the set menu (= with a fixed price and limited choice of dishes).* 私はコース料理(=値段が決まっていて献立の選択肢が限定されている)を頂きます. ▶定義3 (used about a book, text, etc) that everyone must study for an exam (本、教科書などについて)試験のために全員が勉強しなければならない→指定された、必須(ひっす)の、課題の ‖ *We have to study three set texts for French.* 私たちはフランス語の指定教科書を3冊勉強しなければならない. ▶定義4 set (for sth); set (to do sth) ready, prepared or likely to do sth ～を行う用意・準備が整った、～をやりそうな →(～の)準備ができて、用意が整った、～しそうな ‖ *Okay, I'm set - let's go!* よろしい、用意ができた — さあ、出掛けよう. *I was all set to leave when the phone rang.* 電話が鳴った時、私は出掛ける準備をすっかり整えていた. *The Swiss team look set for victory.* スイスチームは勝利に向けて万全を期しているようだ.

成句 be set against sth/doing sth ▶定義 to be determined that sth will not happen or that you will not do sth ～は決して起きない、～を決してしない、と固く決心している→～に断固反対している

be set on sth/doing sth ▶定義 to be determined to do sth ～を行うと固く決心している→～を固く決意している ‖ *She's set on a career in acting.* 彼女は俳優業を志している.

**setback** /sétbæk/ 名 C ▶定義 a difficulty or problem that stops you progressing as fast as you would like 望む速度で前進することを阻む障害や問題➡妨げ, 後退, 挫折(ざせつ), つまずき ‖ *She suffered a major setback when she missed the exams through illness.* 病気のため試験を受けられなかった時, 彼女は大きな挫折を経験した.

**settee** /setí:/ 名 C ▶定義 a long soft seat with a back and arms that more than one person can sit on 複数の人が座ることのできる, 背もたれとひじ掛けの付いた長くて柔らかいいす➡長いす, ソファー ☞類 **sofa**

**setting** /sétɪŋ/ 名 C ▶定義 1 the position sth is in; the place and time in which sth happens 〜がある場所; 〜が起こる場所と時間➡環境, 背景; 設定, 舞台 ‖ *The hotel is in a beautiful setting, close to the sea.* そのホテルは海に近い美しい場所にある. ▶定義 2 one of the positions of the controls of a machine 機械の調整用つまみの位置の1つ➡計器類の調整点, 目盛りの位置 ‖ *Cook it in the oven on a moderate setting.* オーブンの目盛りを「中」にして焼きなさい.

**settle** /sétl/ 動 ▶定義 1 自他 to put an end to an argument or disagreement 論争や争いを終わらせる➡和解する; 〜を解決する, 〜を処理する, 〜にけりを付ける ‖ *They settled the dispute without going to court.* 彼らは裁判に訴えることなく争いを解決した. *They settled out of court.* 彼らは示談で和解した. *We didn't speak to each other for years, but we've settled our differences now.* 私たちは長年お互いに口をきいていなかったが, 今は和解している. ▶定義 2 他 to decide or arrange sth finally 〜を最終的に決定する, 取り決める➡〜を決定する, 〜に決める, 確定する ‖ *Everything's settled. We leave on the nine o'clock flight on Friday.* すべてが取り決められた. 私たちは金曜日の9時の便で出発する. ▶定義 3 自 to go and live permanently in a new country, area, town, etc 新しい国, 地域, 町などに行き, 永住する➡定住する, 移民する, 移り住む ‖ *A great many immigrants have settled in this country.* 非常に多くの移民がこの国に移り住んだ. ▶定義 4 自他 to put yourself or sb else into a comfortable position 自分自身またはほかの人を楽な場所に落ち着かせる➡〜を(いすなどに)座らせる, くつろがせる; 腰を下ろす, くつろぐ ‖ *I settled in front of the television for the evening.* その晩はずっとテレビの前でくつろいでいた. *She settled herself beside him on the sofa.* 彼女はソファーの彼の隣にゆったりと腰を落ち着けた. ▶定義 5 自他 to become or to make sb/sth calm or relaxed 落ち着く, くつろぐ, 〜を落ち着かせる, 〜をくつろがせる➡落ち着く, 収まる, くつろぐ; 〜を落ち着かせる, 〜を鎮静させる, くつろがせる ‖ *The baby wouldn't settle.* 赤ん坊はぐずついて静かになろうとしなかった. ▶定義 6 他 to pay money that you owe 借りている金を払う➡〜を支払う, 清算する ‖ *to settle a bill/a debt* 勘定・借金を払う ▶定義 7 自 to land on a surface and stop moving 着地して移動をやめる ➡(鳥などが)止まる, 降りる, 着地する ‖ *A flock of birds settled on the roof.* 鳥の群れが屋根に舞い降りた.

**句動詞** **settle down** ▶定義 1 to get into a comfortable position, sitting or lying 座ったり横になったりして, 楽な姿勢になる➡ゆっくりくつろぐ, ゆったりと座る ▶定義 2 to start having a quieter way of life, especially by staying in the same place or getting married 特に同じ場所にとどまる, または結婚するなどして, 前よりも穏やかな生活を始める➡落ち着く, 身を固める, 定住する ‖ *She had a number of jobs abroad before she eventually settled down.* 最終的に身を固めるまで, 彼女は外国でいくつもの職業に就いた. ▶定義 3 to become calm and quiet 落ち着いて静かになる ➡(騒ぎなどが)落ち着く, 静かになる ‖ *Settle down! It's time to start the lesson.* 静かにしなさい. 始業の時間ですよ.

**settle down to sth** ▶定義 to start doing sth which involves all your attention 集中力を必要とする〜をし始める➡〜に本気になる, 没頭する, 身を入れる, 腰を据える ‖ *Before you settle down to your work, could I ask you something?* あなたが本腰で作業を始める前に質問をしてもよろしいですか.

**settle for sth** ▶定義 to accept sth that is not as good as what you wanted 望んでいたほど良くないものを受け入れる ➡(不満足なもの)で我慢する, 手を打つ ‖ *We're going to have to settle for the second prize.* 私たちは2等賞で我慢しなければならないだろう.

**settle in/into sth** ▶定義 to start feeling comfortable in a new home, job, etc 新しい家, 仕事

などで居心地の良さを感じ始める➡落ち着く, (環境)に慣れる, なじむ ‖ *How are the children settling in at their new school?* 子供たちは新しい学校にうまくなじんでいますか.

**settle on sth** ▶定義 to choose or decide sth after considering many different things 多くの物事を考慮した後, 〜を選ぶ, または決める➡〜に決める, 決定する

**settle up (with sb)** ▶定義 to pay money that you owe to sb 〜に借りている金を返す➡(〜に)勘定を支払う, 清算する, 負債を返済する

**settled** /sétld/ 形 ▶定義 1 not changing or not likely to change 変わらない, 変わりそうにない➡定着した, 落ち着いた ‖ *More settled weather is forecast for the next few days.* 予報ではこれから2, 3日間, もう少し安定した天気になりそうだ. ▶定義 2 comfortable; feeling that you belong (in a home, a job, a way of life, etc) 居心地の良い;(家, 仕事, 生活の仕方などに)自分が合っていると感じる➡くつろいだ, なじんだ ‖ *We feel very settled here.* 私たちはここにすっかりなじんでいると感じる.

**settlement** /sétlmənt/ 名 C U ▶定義 1 an official agreement that ends an argument; the act of reaching an agreement 論争を終わらせる公式の合意; 合意に達する行為➡解決, 合意, 決着 ‖ *a divorce settlement* 離婚調停 *the settlement of a dispute* 紛争の解決 ▶定義 2 a place that a group of people have built and live in, where few or no people lived before; the process of people starting to live in a place 以前, 人がほとんど, あるいは全くいなかった所に人々が集団で住み着いて築いた居住地; 人々がある場所に住み始める過程➡入植地; 入植, 定住 ‖ *There is believed to have been a prehistoric settlement on this site.* この場所には有史以前の居住地があったと信じられている. *the settlement of the American West* アメリカ西部の開拓地

**settler** /sétlər/ 名 C ▶定義 a person who goes to live permanently in a place where not many people live あまり人が住んでいない場所に行き, 永住する人➡移民, 開拓者, 入植者 ‖ *the first white settlers in Australia* オーストラリアへの最初の白人移住者

*★**seven** /sév(ə)n/ 数 ▶定義 1 7

▶文中での数詞の使い方については, six の項を参照.

▶定義 2 (複合形容詞を作るために用いて) having seven of the thing mentioned 言及されたものを7つ持つ➡7つの, 7個の ‖ *a seven-sided coin* 七角形の硬貨

*★**seventeen** /sèv(ə)ntíːn, ⁻⁻/ 数 ▶定義 17

▶文中での数詞の使い方については, six の項を参照.

**seventeenth** /sèv(ə)ntíːnθ, ⁻⁻/ 代形副 ▶定義 17th➡17番目(の, に), 第17(の, に) ☞参 sixth の例

**seventh**[1] /sév(ə)nθ/ 名 C ▶定義 the fraction 1/7; one of seven equal parts of sth 7分の1; 〜を7等分したうちの1つ➡7分の1 ☞参 sixth の例

**seventh**[2] /sév(ə)nθ/ 代形副 ▶定義 7th➡7番目(の, に), 第7(の, に) ☞参 sixth の例

**seventieth** /sév(ə)ntiəθ/ 代形副 ▶定義 70th➡70番目(の, に), 第70(の, に) ☞参 sixth の例

*★**seventy** /sév(ə)nti/ 数 ▶定義 70

▶文中での数詞の使い方については, sixty の項を参照.

**sever** /sévər/ 動 他 ▶定義 1 to cut sth into two pieces; to cut sth off 〜を2つに切る; 〜を切断する➡〜を切る, 切断する ‖ *The builders accidentally severed a water pipe.* 建設業者は誤って水道管を切断してしまった. *His hand was almost severed in the accident.* 事故で彼の手は危うく切断されるところだった. ▶定義 2 to end a relationship or communication with sb 〜との関係や交流を終わりにする➡〜との関係を断つ, 断絶する ‖ *He has severed all links with his former friends.* 彼は以前の友人とのすべてのきずなを断ち切った.

*★**several** /sév(ə)rəl/ 代形 ▶定義 more than two but not very many; a few 2つ以上だがあまり多くない; いくつかの➡いくつか(の), 数個(の), 数人(の) ‖ *It took her several days to recover from the shock.* 彼女がショックから立ち直るには数日を要した. *There were lots of applications for the job - several of them from very well-qualified people.* その仕事にはたくさんの応募があった — そのうちのいくつかは非常に優秀な人たちからのものだった. *I don't think it's a good idea for several reasons.* いくつかの理由でそれが良い考えだとは思わない.

**severe** /sɪvíər/ 形 ▶定義 1 causing sb to suffer,

be upset or have difficulties ~に痛手を被らせる，~の気分を害する，困らせる➡**厳しい，過酷な，情け容赦のない** ‖ *Such terrible crimes deserve the severest punishment.* あのような恐ろしい犯罪は厳罰に値する. *I think your criticism of her work was too severe.* 彼女の作品に対するあなたの批評は厳しすぎたと思う. ▶定義2 extremely bad or serious 極度に悪い，深刻な➡**ひどい，深刻な，過酷な** ‖ *The company is in severe financial difficulty.* その会社は深刻な財政難にある. *He suffered severe injuries in the fall.* 彼は転落して重傷を負った. *severe weather conditions* 過酷な気象条件 — **severely** 副➡**厳しく，情け容赦なく，激しく，重く** ‖ *The roof was severely damaged in the storm.* その屋根はあらしでひどく破損した. *The report severely criticizes the Health Service.* その報告書は公共医療を厳しく批判している. — **severity** /səvérəti/ 名 Ｕ➡**厳格，厳しさ，激しさ，重さ** ‖ *I don't think you realize the severity of the problem.* あなたは問題の深刻さに気付いていないようだ.

*__sew__ /sóu/ 動 自 他 (過 **sewed**; 過分 **sewn** /sóun/ または **sewed**) ▶定義 sew (sth) (on) to join pieces of cloth, or to join sth to cloth, using a needle and thread and forming stitches 針と糸を使って縫い目を作りながら布切れをつなぎ合わせる，または~を布に留める➡**縫い物・針仕事をする；~を縫う，縫い合わせる，~を…に縫い付ける** ‖ *I can't sew.* 私は裁縫ができない. *A button's come off my shirt - I'll have to sew it back on* シャツのボタンが取れてしまった － 付け直さなければならない. ☛ **knit** のさし絵

句動詞 sew sth up ▶定義1 to join two things by sewing; to repair sth by sewing two things together 2つの物を縫い合わせる；2つの物を縫い合わせて~を修復する➡**~を縫い合わせる，縫合する** ‖ *The surgeon sewed up the wound.* 外科医は傷口を縫合した. ▶定義2 to arrange sth so that it is certain to happen or be successful 確実に起こるよう，または必ず成功するように~の手はずを整える ➡**(交渉など)をうまくまとめる，(選挙などの)勝利をほぼ確実にする**

**sewage** /súːɪdʒ/ 名 Ｕ ▶定義 the waste material from people's bodies that is carried away from their homes in water in large underground pipes (sewers) 地中に埋設された太い管(下水管)の水で家庭から流し出される，人体からの排せつ物➡**汚水，下水，汚物**

**sewer** /súːər, sóər/ 名 Ｃ ▶定義 an underground pipe that carries human waste to a place where it can be treated 人の排せつ物を処理する場所まで運ぶ，地中に埋設された管➡**下水管，下水道，下水溝**

**sewing** /sóuɪŋ/ 名 Ｕ ▶定義1 using a needle and thread to make or repair things 物を作ったり修理したりするために針と糸を使用すること➡**縫うこと，裁縫，針仕事** ‖ *I always take a sewing kit when I travel.* 旅行するときは私はいつも裁縫用具を持っていく. *a **sewing machine*** ミシン ▶定義2 something that is being sewn 縫いかけの物➡**縫い物**

**sewn** **SEW** の過去分詞形

*__sex__ /seks/ 名 ▶定義1 Ｕ the state of being either male or female 男性，女性のいずれかである状態➡**性，性別** ‖ *Applications are welcome from anyone, regardless of sex or race.* 性別や人種に関係なく，だれでも申し込み自由です. *Do you mind what sex your baby is?* あなたは赤ん坊の性別が気になりますか. ☛類 **gender** ▶定義2 Ｃ one of the two groups consisting of all male people or all female people 全員が男性または女性である2つの集団のうちの一方➡**男[女]性** ‖ *the male/female sex* 男性・女性 *He's always found it difficult to get on with **the opposite sex** (= women).* 異性(= 女性)と親しくするのは苦手だと彼はいつも感じてきた.

▶定義3 (または 正式 **intercourse**; **sexual intercourse**) Ｕ the physical act in which the sexual organs of two people touch and which can result in a woman having a baby 2人の性器が接触し，その結果として女性が妊娠することがある肉体的な行為➡**性交，性交渉，セックス** ‖ *to **have sex** with somebody* ~と性交する *sex education in schools* 学校での性教育

**sexism** /séksɪz(ə)m/ 名 Ｕ ▶定義 the unfair treatment of people, especially women, because of their sex; the attitude that causes this 人々，特に女性をその性のために不当に扱うこと；そのような扱いの原因となる態度➡**性差別，女性蔑視(べっし)，性差別主義** — **sexist** /séksɪst/ 形➡**性差別をする，性差別主義の** ‖ *a sexist attitude to* women 女性に対する性差別的な態度 sexist jokes 性差別的な冗談

\*sexual /sékʃuəl; -sjuəl/ 形 ▶定義 connected with sex 性に関する →性の, 性的な ‖ sexual problems 性的な問題 the sexual organs 性器 a campaign for sexual equality (= to get fair and equal treatment for both men and women) 性的平等を求める(= 男性, 女性双方にとって公正で平等な扱いを獲得する)運動

　▶ sexy と比較.

— sexually /sékʃuəli; -sjuəli/ 副 →性的に, 男女の別によって ‖ to be sexually attracted to sb 性的に～にひかれる

**sexual intercourse** 正式 = SEX(3)

**sexuality** /sèkʃuǽləti; -sju-/ 名 ⓤ ▶定義 the nature of sb's sexual activities or desires ～の性行動や性欲の特質 →性的特質, 性欲, 性能力

**sexy** /séksi/ 形 (**sexier**; **sexiest**) 略式 ▶定義 sexually attractive or exciting 性的に魅力のある, 興奮させる →性的魅力のある, 色っぽい, セクシーな ‖ Do you find the lead singer sexy? あのリードシンガーはセクシーだと思いますか. a sexy dress 挑発的な衣装

**Sgt** 略 sergeant→軍曹

**sh** /ʃ(ː)/ 感嘆詞 ▶定義 used to tell sb to stop making noise 騒ぐのをやめるよう～に注意するのに用いて →しっ, 静かに ‖ Sh! People are trying to sleep in here. しっ. みんな眠ろうとしているのですよ.

**shabby** /ʃǽbi/ 形 ▶定義 1 in bad condition because of having been used or worn too much 頻繁に使用または着用されたために状態が悪い →使い古した, 着古した, 傷んだ ‖ a shabby suit よれよれのスーツ ▶定義 2 (used about people) dressed in an untidy way; wearing clothes that are in bad condition (人について)むさくるしい身なりをした; 傷んだ服を着ている →だらしがない, みすぼらしい, むさくるしい ▶定義 3 (used about the way that sb is treated) unfair; not generous (人の扱い方について)不当な; 寛大でない →卑しい, 卑劣な, 恥ずべき — shabbily 副 →みすぼらしく, だらしなく, 卑劣に ‖ a shabbily-dressed man むさくるしい身なりをした男 She felt she'd been treated shabbily by her employers. 彼女は自分が雇い主から不当な扱いをされてきたと感じた.

**shack** /ʃæk/ 名 ⓒ ▶定義 a small building, usually made of wood or metal, that has not been built well 通常, 木やブリキでできた建て方も粗末な小さな建物→掘っ立て小屋, バラック

\*shade¹ /ʃeɪd/ 名 ▶定義 1 ⓤ an area that is out of direct sunlight and is darker and cooler than areas in the sun 直射日光が当たらず, 日なたよりも暗くて涼しい場所→日陰, 陰, 物陰 ‖ It was so hot that I had to go and sit **in the shade**. とても暑かったので, 私は日陰の所に行って座らなければならなかった. ▶定義 2 ⓒ something that keeps out light or makes it less bright 光を遮ったり暗くするために用いる物→光を遮る物, 日よけ, かさ, シェード ‖ a lampshade ランプのかさ ▶定義 3 **shades**[複数扱い] 略式 = SUNGLASSES ▶定義 4 ⓒ **a shade (of sth)** a type of a particular colour ある特定の色の種類→色合い, 色調, 濃淡の度合い ‖ a shade of green 緑色の色調 ▶定義 5 ⓒ a small difference in the form or nature of sth ～の形態や本質のわずかな違い→わずかな相違, 微妙なあや, ニュアンス ‖ a word with various shades of meaning さまざまなニュアンスの異なる意味を持つ言葉 ▶定義 6 [単数扱い] **a shade** a little bit 少し→ほんの少し, ごくわずか, ～気味

**shade²** /ʃeɪd/ 動 他 ▶定義 1 to protect sth from direct light; to give shade to sth ～を直接の光から守る; ～に陰を作る →～を陰にする, ～に光が当たらないようにする, ～を覆う ‖ The sun was so bright that I had to shade my eyes. 太陽がまぶしかったので, 手をかざして目に光が当たらないようにしなければならなかった. ▶定義 2 **shade sth (in)** to make an area of a drawing darker, for example with a pencil 鉛筆などで, 絵の一部をほかの部分よりも暗くする➔~に陰影を付ける, 明暗・濃淡を付ける ‖ *The trees will look more realistic once you've shaded them in.* 陰影を付けると, 木々はもっと本物らしく見えるようになります.

**＊shadow¹** /ʃǽdoʊ/ 名 ▶定義1 C a dark shape on a surface that is caused by sth being between the light and that surface 光源とある表面との中間に~があることにより, その表面にできる暗い形➔**影, 投影法師** ‖ *The dog was chasing its own shadow.* 犬は自分の影を追い掛けていた. *The shadows lengthened as the sun went down.* 日が傾くにつれて影が長くなった. ☞ shade のさし絵 ▶定義2 U an area that is dark because sth prevents direct light from reaching it ある物に遮られて直射光が届かないために暗くなっている領域➔**陰, 暗がり** ‖ *His face was in shadow.* 彼の顔は陰になっていた. ▶定義3 [単数扱い] a very small amount of sth 非常に少量の~➔**ごくわずか, ~気味, 気配** ‖ *I know without **a shadow of doubt** that he's lying.* 彼がうそをついているといささかの疑いもなく信じている. 成句 cost a shadow (across/over sth) ⇒ CAST¹

**shadow²** /ʃǽdoʊ/ 動他 ▶定義 to follow and watch sb's actions 人の後を付けて行動を監視する➔**~を尾行する, ~の後を付ける** ‖ *The police shadowed the suspect for three days.* 警察は容疑者を3日間尾行した.

**shadow³** /ʃǽdoʊ/ 形 ▶定義 (in British politics) belonging to the biggest political party that is not in power, with special responsibility for a particular subject, for example education or defence. Shadow ministers would probably become government ministers if their party won the next election. (英国の政治で)例えば教育や防衛などの特定の問題に責任を負う, 最大野党に属する. この政党が次の選挙で勝てば, 陰の内閣の大臣たちが大体は政府の閣僚になる➔**影の(内閣の)** ‖ *the shadow Cabinet* 影の内閣

**shadowy** /ʃǽdoʊi/ 形 ▶定義1 dark and full of shadows 暗くて影の多い➔**影の多い, 暗い** ‖ *a shadowy forest* 暗い森 ▶定義2 difficult to see because there is not much light 光が十分でないので見えにくい➔**ぼんやりとした, かすかな, はっきりしない** ‖ *A shadowy figure was coming towards me.* かすかな人影が私に近付いてきた ▶定義3 that not much is known about; mysterious あまり知られていない; なぞめいた➔**なぞめいた, 実体不明の**

**shady** /ʃéɪdi/ 形 ▶定義1 giving shade; giving protection from the sun 日陰を与える; 太陽光線から保護する➔**陰を作る, 陰の多い, 陰になった, 日陰の** ‖ *I found a shady spot under the trees and sat down.* 私は木陰を見つけて腰を下ろした. ▶定義2 略式 not completely honest or legal 完全に信頼できる, 合法的であるとは言い難い➔**うさんくさい, 怪しい, いかがわしい**

**shaft** /ʃɑːft; ʃæft/ 名 C ▶定義1 a long, narrow hole in which sth can go up and down or enter or leave ~がその中で上がり降り, または出入りできる, 長くて狭い穴➔**坑, 管, 通路, シャフト** ‖ *a lift shaft* エレベーターシャフト *a mine shaft* 縦坑 ▶定義2 a bar that connects parts of a machine so that power can pass between them 動力伝達が可能なように機械の部品を相互に連結する棒➔**軸, 心棒, シャフト**

**shaggy** /ʃǽgi/ 形 ▶定義1 (used about hair, material, etc) long, thick and untidy (髪の毛, 服の生地の毛などについて)長く, 密生していて, 乱れている➔**ぼさぼさの, くしゃくしゃの, けばだった, 毛足の長い** ▶定義2 covered with long, thick, untidy hair 密生したぼさぼさの毛に覆われた➔**毛むくじゃらの, 毛深い, もじゃもじゃの** ‖ *a shaggy dog* 毛むくじゃらの犬

**＊shake¹** /ʃéɪk/ 動 (過 **shook** /ʃʊk/; 過分 **shaken** /ʃéɪk(ə)n/) ▶定義1 自他 to move from side to side or up and down with short, quick movements 左右または上下に小刻みに素早く動く➔**揺れる, 揺れ動く, 振動する; ~を揺らす, 揺れ動かす, 振る, 揺さぶる** ‖ *I was so nervous that I was shaking.* 私はびくびくして震えていた. *The whole building shakes when big lorries go past.* 大型トラックが通り過ぎると建物全体が揺れる. (比喩) *His voice shook with emotion as he described the accident.* その事故のことを話す彼の声は興奮で震えていた. *Shake the bottle before taking the medicine.* 薬を飲む前にびんを振りなさい. *She shook him to wake him up.* 彼女は彼を揺すって起こした. ▶定義2 他 to disturb or upset sb/sth ~を混乱させる, 乱す➔

# 1478 shake²

~を乱す,動揺させる,揺るがす ‖ *The scandal has shaken the whole country.* 醜聞は国全体を震かんさせた. ▶定義3 to cause sth to be less certain; to cause doubt about sth ~を以前ほど確かでないものにする;~について疑問を抱かせる→~をぐらつかせる,弱める ‖ *Nothing seems to shake her belief that she was right.* 自分が正しいという彼女の信念は何事にも揺るがないようだ.

### ▶コミュニケーション
**握った手を上下させるのが「握手」**

出会った者同士,日本人がお辞儀するところで,欧米人は握手をします.日本で夫婦・兄弟・恋人同士お辞儀しないように,欧米でも親密な間柄では握手はしません.それは友好的な関係を確認し合う儀礼行動だからです. hand-shake は「握手」と訳されますが,握り合った手を2,3回上下に振る(shake)のが特徴で,その時お互い目を見つめ合うのが礼儀とされます.起源的には,誓約・契約の際に二心ないことを表す誠意の印として始まったと言われます.

**成句** shake sb's hand/shake hands (with sb)/shake sb by the hand ▶定義 to take sb's hand and move it up and down (when you meet sb, to show that you have agreed on sth, etc)(~に会ったとき,または~に同意したことを示すためなどに)~の手を取り,上下に動かす→~と握手をする ☞ S6 ページのさし絵

shake your head ▶定義 to move your head from side to side, as a way of saying no 「ノー」という１つの方法として,頭を左右に振る→首を横に振る,かぶりを振る ☞ S6 ページのさし絵

**句動詞** shake sb/sth off ▶定義 to get rid of sb/sth; to remove sth by shaking ~を追い払う;振り動かして~を取り除く→~を振り落とす,払いのける;(病気・悪習など)を直す,断ち切る ‖ *I don't seem to be able to shake off this cold.* この風邪はなかなか治らないようだ. *Shake the crumbs off the tablecloth.* テーブルクロスからパンくずを払い落としなさい.

**shake²** /ʃéɪk/ 名 C ▶定義 the action of shaking sth or being shaken ~を振ったり,~が振られたりする動き→振ること,振り,揺れ,振動,動揺

**shake-up** 名 C ▶定義 a complete change in the structure or organization of sth ~の構造や組織の完全な変化→大改革,大刷新,再編成

**shaky** /ʃéɪki/ 形 (**shakier**; **shakiest**) ▶定義 shaking or feeling weak because you are frightened or ill 恐怖のあまり,または体の具合が悪いために震えている,または脱力感を覚える→震える,ふらつく,よろよろする ▶定義2 not firm; weak or not very good しっかりしていない;もろいまたは弱々しい,状態があまり良くない→揺れる,ぐらつく;不安定な,心もとない ‖ *The table's a bit shaky so don't put anything heavy on it.* そのテーブルは少しぐらぐらしているので,重い物を載せないでください. *They've had a **shaky start** to the season losing most of their games.* 彼らは今季ほとんどの試合に負けるという不安定なスタートを切った.— shakily 副→震えて,よろよろして

★**shall** /ʃ(ə)l, 強形 ʃæl/ 法助動詞(否定形 **shall not**; 短縮形 **shan't** /ʃɑ(ː)nt; ʃænt/) ▶定義1 used for asking for information or advice 情報や助言を求めるのに用いて→~でしょうか,~したらいいでしょうか ‖ *What time shall I come?* 何時に来ればよろしいですか. *Where shall we go for our holiday?* 休暇にどこへ行きましょうか. ▶定義2 used for offering to do sth ~をしようと申し出るのに用いて→~しましょうか ‖ *Shall I help you carry that box?* その箱を運ぶのを手伝いましょうか. *Shall we drive you home?* お宅まで車で送りましょうか. ▶定義3 **shall we** used for suggesting that you do sth with the person or people that you are talking to 話している相手と一緒に~をしようと提案するのに用いて→~しませんか ‖ *Shall we go out for a meal this evening?* 今夜食事に出掛けませんか.

▶法助動詞についての説明は,巻末の「文法早見表」を参照.

▶定義4 正式 used with 'I' and 'we' in future tenses, instead of 'will' 未来時制でwillの代わりにIやweと用いて→~でしょう,だろう ‖ *I shall be very happy to see him again.* 彼にまたお目に掛かれたらとてもうれしく思います. *We shan't be arriving until ten o'clock.* 私たちは10時まで到着しないでしょう. *At the end of this year, I shall have been working here for five years.* 今年の終わりにはここに５年間勤務していること

になります. ▶定義5 [正式] used for saying that sth must happen or will definitely happen 〜が起こらなければならない,または確実に起きるであろうと言うのに用いて➡〜するものとする,すべきである,こととする ‖ *In the rules it says that a player shall be sent off for using bad language.* 規則では,下品な言葉を使った選手は退場させるべきものとしている.

> ▶語法
>
> 法令文の shall と意志
>
> shall は主語よりも「一段上の権威の意志」と考えると,いろいろな用法が整理できます.例えば,You shall have my answer next week.(来週答えよう)では,主語に力関係で勝る権威(= 話し手)の意志を表します.また,Students shall use this parking lot.(学生はこの駐車場を使うこと)は,学生より上の権威(= 大学当局)の意志を表します.この権威は為政者・神などにもなります.

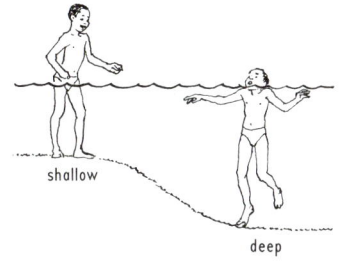

**shallow/deep**

shallow

deep

\***shallow** /ʃǽlou/ 形 ▶定義 **1** not deep; with not much distance between top and bottom 深くない;上から下までの距離があまりない➡浅い ‖ *The sea is very shallow here.* ここは浅瀬になっている. *a shallow dish* 浅い皿 ▶定義 **2** not having or showing serious or deep thought 真剣さまたは思慮深さに富んだ考えを持っていない,または表していない➡浅はかな,浅薄な,薄っぺらな ‖ *a shallow person/book* 薄っぺらな人・内容のない本 ⇔ 両方の定義 **deep** — **shallowness** 名 ⓤ➡浅いこと;浅はかなこと,浅薄

\***shame**¹ /ʃéim/ 名 ▶定義 **1** ⓤ the unpleasant feeling of guilt and embarrassment that you get when you have done sth stupid or morally wrong; the ability to have this feeling 愚かな事や道徳に反する事をしたときに抱く,罪や困惑の不快な感情; そのような感情を抱く能力➡恥,恥ずかしい思い,恥辱,しゅう恥心 ‖ *She was **filled with shame** at the thought of how she had lied to her mother.* 母親にうそをついたことを考えると,彼女は恥ずかしさで一杯になった. *His actions have **brought shame on** his whole family.* 彼の行為は家族全員に恥をかかせた. *He doesn't care how he behaves in public. He's got **no shame**!* 彼は人前でどう振る舞うかなど意に介さない.彼には全くしゅう恥心がない. ☛ 形 **ashamed** ▶定義 **2 a shame** [単数扱い] a fact or situation that makes you feel disappointed がっかりさせられる事実または状況➡残念なこと,遺憾なこと ‖ *It's a shame about Adam failing his exams, isn't it?* アダムが試験に落ちたのは残念ですね. *What a shame you have to leave so soon.* あなたがこんなに早く出発しなければならないなんて,本当に残念です. *It would be a shame to miss an opportunity like this.* このような機会を逃すとしたら残念なことだ.

**shame**² /ʃéim/ 動 ⓣ ▶定義 to make sb feel shame for sth bad that he/she has done 〜に己の犯した悪い事を恥ずかしいと思わせる➡〜を恥じさせる,恥じ入らせる

**shameful** /ʃéimfəl, -f(ə)l/ 形 ▶定義 which sb should feel bad about; shocking 〜が悪いと感じるべき; 衝撃的な➡恥ずべき,不面目な,けしからぬ ‖ *a shameful waste of public money* 恥ずべき公金の無駄遣い — **shamefully** 副➡恥ずかしく,いかがわしく

**shameless** /ʃéimləs/ 形 ▶定義 not feeling embarrassed about doing sth bad; having no shame 悪い事をしても恥ずかしいと感じない;しゅう恥心を持たない➡恥知らずの,しゅう恥心のない,ずうずうしい ‖ *a shameless display of greed and bad manners* 強欲と無作法をおくめんもなく丸出しにした行動 — **shamelessly** 副➡破廉恥に,ずうずうしく

\***shampoo** /ʃæmpúː/ 名 ▶定義 **1** ⓒ ⓤ a liquid that you use for washing your hair; a similar liquid for cleaning carpets, cars, etc 洗髪に用いる液体;じゅうたんや車などの汚れを取るのに用いる同種の液体➡シャンプー; 液体の洗剤 ‖ *shampoo for greasy/dry/normal hair* 脂性用・乾

燥用・普通髪用シャンプー ▶定義2 [C] the action of washing sth with shampoo ～をシャンプーで洗う動作➜**洗髪, (じゅうたんなどを)洗剤で洗うこと** — shampoo [動][他] (現分 shampooing; 三単現 shampoos; 過, 過分 shampooed) ➜ **～をシャンプーで洗う, 洗髪する**

**shamrock** /ʃǽmrɑ̀k/ [名] [C][U] ▶定義 a plant with three leaves, which is the national symbol of Ireland 三つ葉の植物. アイルランドの国花➜**コメツブツメクサ, シロツメクサ, オランダレンゲ**

**shandy** /ʃǽndi/ [名] [C][U] ([複] **shandies**) ▶定義 a drink that is a mixture of beer and a sweet, colourless, non-alcoholic drink with bubbles (lemonade) ビールと, アルコールを含まない甘い無色の炭酸飲料(レモネード)を混ぜ合わせた飲み物➜**シャンディー**

**shan't** SHALL NOT の短縮形

**shanty town** /ʃǽntitàʊn/ [名] [C] ▶定義 an area, usually on the edge of a big city, where poor people live in bad conditions in buildings that they have made themselves 通常, 大都市の外れにある, 貧しい人たちが自分で建てた建物にひどい状態で住んでいる地域➜**貧民窟(くつ), スラム街**

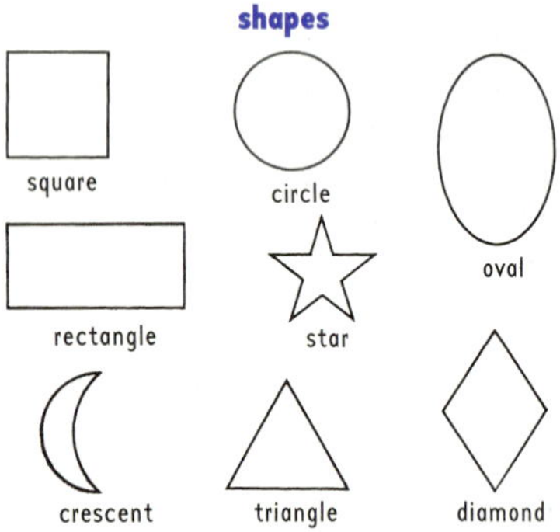
shapes
square
circle
oval
rectangle
star
crescent
triangle
diamond

***shape**[1] /ʃéɪp/ [名] ▶定義1 [C][U] the form of the outer edges or surfaces of sth; an example of sth that has a particular form ～の外縁や表面の形; ある特定の形をした～の一例➜**形, 形状, 外形, 形態** ‖ *a round/square/rectangular shape* 円形・正方形・長方形 *a cake **in the shape of** a heart* ハート形のケーキ *clothes to fit people of **all shapes and sizes*** あらゆる体形, サイズの人に合う衣服 *Squares, circles and triangles are all different shapes.* 四角形, 円形, 三角形は皆形が異なる. *I could just make out a dark shape in the distance.* 遠くに黒っぽい形がどうやら見分けられた. *The country is roughly square **in shape**.* その国の形はほぼ四角形である. ▶定義2 **-shaped**(複合形容詞を作るために用いて) having the shape mentioned 言及された形をした➜**～のような形をした, ～形の** ‖ *an L-shaped room* L字型の部屋 ▶定義3 [U] the physical condition of sb/sth; the good or bad state of sb/sth ～の健康状態, ～の物理的な状態; ～の良し悪しの状態➜**状態; 調子, 具合** ‖ *She was **in** such bad **shape** (= so ill) that she had to be taken to hospital.* 彼女は非常に具合が悪かったので, 病院に連れていかなければならなかった. *I go swimming regularly to keep **in shape**.* 私は健康を維持するため, 定期的に泳ぎに行く. ▶定義4 [単数扱い] the shape (of sth) the organization, form or structure of sth ～の構成, 形状または構造➜**形態, 様態**

[成句] out of shape ▶定義1 not in the usual or correct shape いつもの, または正しい状態にない➜**形が崩れて, 形が整わないで, 不格好な** ‖ *My sweater's gone out of shape now that I've washed it.* 洗濯したら私のセーターの形が崩れてしまった. ▶定義2 not physically fit 体の調子が良くない ➜**(健康などが)不調で** ‖ *You're out of shape. You should get more exercise.* 体調があまり良くありませんね. もっと運動しなくてはいけませんよ.

take shape ▶定義 to start to develop well うまく展開し始める➜**形になる, 具体化する, 実現する, 目鼻がつく** ‖ *Plans to expand the company are beginning to take shape.* 会社の拡張計画が具体化し始めている.

***shape**[2] /ʃéɪp/ [動][他] ▶定義1 shape sth (into sth) to make sth into a particular form ～をある特定の形にする➜**～を(…に)形づくる, ～の形にする** ‖ *Shape the mixture into small balls.* 混ぜ合わせた物を小さなボールの形にしなさい. ▶定義2 to influence the way in which sth develops; to cause sth to have a particular form or nature ～の展開の行方に影響を及ぼす; ～がある特定の形状や性質を持つようにする➜**～に重要な影響を与える, ～を決定する; ～を方向づける, 形成する** ‖ *His political ideas were shaped* by his upbringing. 彼の政治思想は幼少期の教育によって形づくられた.

**shapeless** /ʃéɪpləs/ [形] ▶定義 not having a clear shape はっきりとした形のない➜**定形のない, まとまりのない, 不格好な** ‖ *a shapeless dress* ずんどう型のドレス

***share**[1] /ʃeər/ [動] ▶定義 1 [他] share sth (out) to divide sth between two or more people 2人以上で～を分ける➜**～を分ける, 分け合う, 分配する** ‖ *We shared the pizza out between the four of us.* 私たちは4人でピザを分けた. ▶定義 2 [自][他] share (sth) (with sb) to have, use, do or pay sth together with another person or other people ほかの人または人々と一緒に～を所有する, 使用する, 行う, 支払う ➜**(～を)(…と)共有する, 分担する, 共同で行う, 分かち合う** ‖ *I share a flat with four other people.* 私はほかの4人とアパートを共同で使用している. *I shared my sandwiches with Jim.* 私のサンドイッチをジムと分け合って食べた. *We share the same interests.* 私たちは同じ趣味を持っている. ▶定義 3 [他] share sth (with sb) to tell sb about sth; to allow sb to know sth ～に…について話す; ～に…を知らせる➜**～を(人に)話す, 伝える** ‖ *Sometimes it helps to share your problems.* 自分の問題を聞いてもらうと時には楽になることがある.

***share**[2] /ʃeər/ [名] ▶定義 1 [単数扱い] share (of sth) a part or amount of sth that has been divided between several people 複数の人たちの間で分けられた～の一部または量➜**分け前, 取り分, 分担, 割り当て** ‖ *We each pay a share of the household bills.* 私たちはそれぞれ家計費の負担分を支払っている. *I'm willing to **take** my **share** of the blame.* (問題に対する)責任の一端を潔く負うつもりだ. ▶定義 2 [[C], 通常は複数] shares (in sth) one of many equal parts into which the value of a company is divided, that can be sold to people who want to own part of the company 会社の価値を均等に分けた部分の1つ. 会社の一部を所有したい人に売ることができる➜**株, 株式**

[成句] (more than) your fair share of sth ⇒ FAIR[1]

**shareholder** /ʃéərhòʊldər/ [名] [C] ▶定義 an owner of shares in a company 会社の株式の所有者➜**株主**

shark

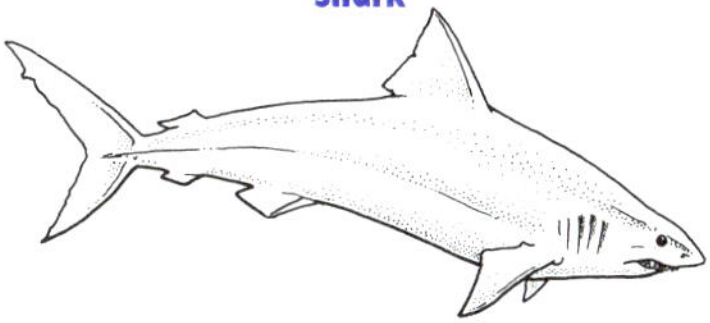

**shark** /ʃɑːrk/ [名] [C] ([複] **sharks** または **shark**) ▶定義 a large, often dangerous, sea fish that has a lot of sharp teeth 鋭い歯を多数持ち, しばしば人に危害を与える大きな海水魚➜**サメ, フカ**

***sharp**[1] /ʃɑːrp/ [形] ▶定義 1 having a very thin but strong edge or point; that can cut or make a hole in sth easily 非常に薄いが鋭い縁や先を持つ; 簡単に～を切断したり穴を開けたりすることのできる➜**鋭い, 鋭利な, (先の)とがった; よく切れる** ‖ *a sharp knife* よく切れるナイフ *sharp teeth* 鋭い歯 ⇔ **blunt** ▶定義 2 (used about a change of direction or level) very great and sudden (方向や高さの変化について)非常に大きくて突然な ➜**(変化などが)急な, 急激な, (カーブなどが)急な, 切り立った** ‖ *a sharp rise/fall in inflation* インフレーションの急激な上昇・減速 *This is a sharp bend so slow down.* ここは急カーブだから速度を落としなさい. ▶定義 3 clear and definite はっきりしていて明白な➜**はっきりした, くっきりした, 鮮明な** ‖ *the sharp outline of the hills* 丘陵のくっきりとした稜線(りょうせん) *a sharp contrast between the lives of the rich and the poor* 富者と貧者の生活の著しい相違 ▶定義 4 able to think, act, understand, see or hear quickly 素早く考え, 行動し, 理解し, 見たり聞いたりすることのできる➜**頭の切れる, 鋭い, 鋭敏な** ‖ *a sharp mind* 非常によく切れる頭 *You must have sharp eyes if you can read that sign from here.* ここからあの標識を読み取ることができるとしたら, あなたはよほどいい目をしているに違いない. ▶定義 5 (used about actions or movements) quick and sudden (動作や動きについて)素早くて突然の➜**機敏な, 迅速な, 活発な** ‖ *One short sharp blow was enough to end the fight.* 素早い一撃でけんかの片がついた. ▶定義 6 (used about words, comments, etc) said in an angry way; intended to upset sb or be critical (言葉, 意見などについて)怒った調子

で言った; ～を狼狽(ろうばい)させたり批判がましくすることを意図した→**厳しい, 辛辣(しんらつ)な, 痛烈な** ▶定義7 (used about pain) very strong and sudden(痛みについて)非常に強くて突然の→**激しい, 鋭い** ‖ *a sharp pain in the chest* 胸の激痛 ⇔ **dull** ▶定義8 (used about sth that affects the senses) strong; not mild or gentle, often causing an unpleasant feeling(感覚に影響を及ぼす～について)強い, 穏やかさ, まろやかさに欠け, しばしば不快感を招く→**刺激の強い, 鋭い, 強烈な** ‖ *a sharp taste* 舌を刺すような味 *a sharp wind* 身を切るような風 ▶定義9 (記号 #) (in music) half a note higher than the stated note (音楽で)楽譜で指定された音よりも半音高い→**半音高い, 嬰(えい)音の, シャープ記号の付いた** ‖ *in the key of C sharp minor* 嬰ハ短調で ☞参 **flat¹(5)** ▶定義10 (in music) slightly higher than the correct note (音楽で)→**正しい音よりも高い, ピッチが高い** ‖ *That last note was sharp. Can you sing it again?* 最後の音が高すぎましたよ. もう一度歌ってみてくれますか. ☞参 **flat¹(6)**
— **sharply** /ʃɑ́ərpli/ 副 ▶定義 **鋭く, 厳しく, 急に, はっきりと, 鋭敏に** ‖ *The road bends sharply to the left.* その道は左に急カーブしている. *Share prices fell sharply this morning.* 今朝, 株価が急落した. — **sharpness** 名 **U**→**鋭さ, 機敏, 鋭敏**

**sharp²** /ʃɑːrp/ 副 ▶定義1 (used about a time) exactly, punctually(時間について)正確に, 時間通りに→**きっかりに, ちょうど** ‖ *Be here at three o'clock sharp.* 3時きっかりにここにいなさい. ▶定義2 turning suddenly 突然曲がる→**急に, 突然, 鋭く** ‖ *Go to the traffic lights and turn sharp right.* あの信号の所まで行って, 右に急角度で曲がりなさい. ▶定義3 (in music) slightly higher than the correct note (音楽で)正しい音よりも少し高く→**正しい音よりも高く, ピッチが高く** ☞参 **flat¹(6)**

**sharp³** /ʃɑːrp/ 名 **C** (記号 #) ▶定義 (in music) a note that is half a note higher than the note with the same letter (音楽で)同じ記号で書かれた音よりも半音高い音→**嬰(えい)音, 嬰記号, シャープ** ☞参 **flat²(2)**

**sharpen** /ʃɑ́ːrp(ə)n/ 動 自他 ▶定義 to become or to make sth sharp or sharper (より)鋭くなる; ～を(より)鋭くする→**鋭くなる, ～を鋭くする, とがらせる** ‖ *to sharpen a knife* ナイフを研ぐ *This knife won't sharpen.* このナイフは鋭くならない.

**sharpener** /ʃɑ́ːrp(ə)nər/ 名 **C** ▶定義 an object or tool that is used for making sth sharp ～を鋭くするために用いる物または道具→**研ぐ道具, 削る道具** ‖ *a pencil/knife sharpener* 鉛筆削り器・包丁研ぎ器

**shatter** /ʃǽtər/ 動 ▶定義1 自他 (used about glass, etc) to break into very small pieces (ガラスなどについて) 壊れて小さな破片になる→**粉々にする[なる]; ～を粉みじんにする, 粉砕する** ‖ *I dropped the glass and it shattered on the floor.* グラスを落としたら, 床の上で粉々に割れてしまった. *The force of the explosion shattered the windows.* 爆発の勢いで窓が粉みじんになった. ▶定義2 他 to destroy sth completely ～を完全に破壊する→**～を打ち砕く, くじく, 台なしにする** ‖ *Her hopes were shattered by the news.* 彼女の希望はその知らせで完全に打ち砕かれた.

**shattered** /ʃǽtəd/ 形 ▶定義1 very shocked and upset 大きな衝撃を受けて動揺した→**取り乱した, おろおろした** ▶定義2 略式 very tired とても疲れた→**ぐったりした, 疲れた** ‖ *I'm absolutely shattered.* 全くくたくただ.

★**shave¹** /ʃéɪv/ 動 自他 ▶定義 shave (sth) (off) to remove hair from the face or another part of the body with an extremely sharp piece of metal (a razor) 非常に鋭い金属製の物(かみそり)で顔やそのほかの体の部分から毛を取り除く→**～をそる, そり落とす; ひげをそる** ‖ *I cut myself shaving this morning.* 今朝, ひげそり中に顔を切ってしまった. *When did you shave off your moustache?* あなたはいつ口ひげをそり落としたのですか. *to shave your legs* 足の毛をそる

**句動詞 shave sth off (sth)** ▶定義 to cut a very small amount from sth 非常に少ない量を～から切り取る→**～を薄く削る, (かんななどで)削り取る** ‖ *We'll have to shave a bit off the door to make it close properly.* きちんと閉まるようにするには, ドアを少し削る必要があるだろう.

**shave²** /ʃéɪv/ 名 [ **C**, 通常は単数 ] ▶定義 the action of shaving ひげをそる動作→**ひげをそること, ひげそり** ‖ *to have a shave* ひげをそる *I need a shave.* ひげをそらなくては.

**成句 a close shave/thing** ⇒ **CLOSE³**

**shaven** /ʃéɪv(ə)n/ 形 ▶定義 having been shaved

→ひげ・髪をそった ‖ clean-shaven (= not having a beard or moustache) ひげをきれいにそった(= あごひげや口ひげのない)

**shaver** /ʃéɪvər/(または **electric razor**) 名 C ▶定義 an electric tool that is used for removing hair from the face or another part of the body 顔やそのほかの体の部分から毛を取り除くのに用いられる電気器具 → **電気かみそり, シェーバー**

**shawl** /ʃɔːl/ 名 C ▶定義 a large piece of cloth that is worn by a woman round her shoulders or head or that is put round a baby 女性が肩や頭に掛けて着用したり, 赤ん坊をくるんだりする大きな布 → **肩掛け, ショール**

*__she__ /ʃi, ʃɪ, 強形 ʃiː/ 代 (動詞の主語) ▶定義 the female person who has already been mentioned 既に言及されている女の人 → **彼女は, 彼女が, あの女性は, あの女性が** ‖ *'What does your sister do?' 'She's a dentist.'* 「あなたのお姉さんの職業は何ですか」「彼女は歯医者をしています」/ *I asked her a question but she didn't answer.* 彼女に質問をしたが, 彼女は答えなかった.

**shear** /ʃɪər/ 動 他 (過 **sheared**; 過分 **sheared** または **shorn**) ▶定義 to cut the wool off a sheep 羊の毛を刈り取る → **(羊の毛)を刈る**

**shears** /ʃɪərz/ 名 [複数扱い] ▶定義 a tool that is like a very large pair of scissors and that is used for cutting things in the garden 庭園内の物を切るのに使われる大きなはさみの形をした道具 → **大ばさみ, 植木ばさみ** ‖ *a pair of shears* 大ばさみ一丁 ☞ **garden** のさし絵

**sheath** /ʃiːθ/ 名 C (複 **sheaths** /ʃiːðz, ʃiːθs/) ▶定義 a cover for a knife or other sharp weapon ナイフやそのほかの先のとがった武器用の覆い → **さや, 覆い, ケース** ☞ **spear** のさし絵

**she'd** /ʃɪd, 強形 ʃiːd/ **SHE HAD, SHE WOULD** の短縮形

**shed**¹ /ʃed/ 名 C ▶定義 a small building that is used for keeping things or animals in 物や動物を入れておくための小さな建物 → **物置, 小屋** ‖ *a garden shed* 園芸用具置き場 *a bicycle shed* 自転車置き場 *a cattle shed* 牛小屋 ☞ C7ページのさし絵

**shed**² /ʃed/ 動 他 (現分 **shedding**; 過, 過分 **shed**) ▶定義 **1** to lose sth because it falls off 抜け落ちたために〜を失う → **(植物が)(葉など)を落とす, (動物が)(皮・毛・羽など)を脱ぐ, 脱ぎ捨てる** ‖ *This snake sheds its skin every year.* この蛇は毎年脱皮する. *Autumn is coming and the trees are beginning to shed their leaves.* 秋が訪れ, 木々は葉を落とし始めている. ▶定義 **2** to get rid of or remove sth that is not wanted 必要でない〜を取り除く, 除去する → **〜を取り除く, 捨てる**

成句 shed blood (文) ▶定義 to kill or injure people 人々を殺害する, 傷付ける → **血を流す, 流血の惨事を起こす**

**shed light on sth** ▶定義 to make sth clear and easy to understand 〜を明確にし, 理解しやすくする → **〜を明確にする, 解明する, 〜に光を当てる**

**shed tears** ▶定義 to cry 泣く → **涙を流す, 泣く**

*__sheep__ /ʃiːp/ 名 C (複 **sheep**) ▶定義 an animal that is kept on farms and used for its wool or meat 農場で飼育され, 毛や肉をとるために用いられる動物 → **羊, メンヨウ**
▶ 雄の羊は ram, 雌の羊は ewe, 子羊は lamb と言う. 羊が鳴くときには bleat を用いる. 鳴き声は baa と表記される. 羊肉は lamb または mutton と言う. meat の注を参照.

☞ **goat** のさし絵

**sheepdog** /ʃiːpdɒ(ː)g, -dɑ̀g/ 名 C ▶定義 a dog that has been trained to control sheep 羊のまとめ役用に訓練された犬 → **牧羊犬, 羊の番犬**

**sheepish** /ʃiːpɪʃ/ 形 ▶定義 feeling or showing embarrassment because you have done sth silly 愚かな事をしたために, きまり悪い思いをして, またはそのような素振りを見せて → **ばつの悪そうな, きまり悪げな, おどおどした** ‖ *a sheepish grin* ばつの悪そうな(にやっとした)笑い —
sheepishly 副 → **きまり悪そうに, おどおどして**

**sheepskin** /ʃiːpskɪ̀n/ 名 U ▶定義 the skin of a sheep, including the wool, from which coats, etc are made 毛の付いた羊の皮, コートなどに使われる → **羊皮, 羊のなめし皮** ‖ *a sheepskin rug/jacket* 羊皮の敷物・上着

**sheer** /ʃɪər/ 形 ▶定義 **1** (名詞の前だけ) used to emphasize the size, degree or amount of sth 〜の大きさ, 程度, 量を強調するのに用いて → **全くの** ‖ *It's sheer stupidity to drink and drive.* 飲酒運転するなど愚の骨頂だ. *It was **sheer luck** that I happened to be in the right place at the right time.* 私がちょうどいい時, いいところに, たまたま居合わせたのは全くの幸運だった. *Her success is due to sheer hard work.* 彼女の成功はひ

とえに大変な努力のたまものだ. *I only agreed out of sheer desperation.* 私はただ苦し紛れに同意しただけだ. ▶定義2 very steep; almost vertical 非常に傾斜の急な; ほとんど垂直の→切り立った, 険しい ‖ *Don't walk near the edge. It's a **sheer** drop to the sea.* 端の方を歩かないでください,海まで全くの断崖(だんがい)絶壁ですから.

\*sheet /fi:t/ 名 C ▶定義1 a large piece of material used on a bed ベッドの上に使う大きな布→敷き布, シーツ ☞ bed のさし絵 ▶定義2 a piece of paper that is used for writing, printing, etc on 書いたり印刷したりするのに用いる紙1枚→1枚の紙 ‖ *a sheet of notepaper* 便せん1枚 *Write each answer on a separate sheet.* 答えは皆別紙に記入しなさい. ☞参 balance sheet ▶定義3 a flat, thin piece of any material, especially a square or rectangular one 特に正方形または長方形をした薄い平板の物 →(薄い物の)1枚, 薄板 ‖ *a sheet of metal/glass* 1枚の金属板・ガラス板 ▶定義4 a wide, flat area of sth 幅広い平らな空間→広がり, 一面の〜 ‖ *The road was covered with **a sheet of** ice.* その道路は一面氷で覆われていた.

sheikh(または sheik) /ʃi:k, ʃeɪk/ 名 C ▶定義 an Arab ruler アラブの支配者→首長, 族長, 家長

\*shelf /ʃelf/ 名 C ( 複 shelves /ʃelvz/) ▶定義 a long flat piece of wood, glass, etc that is fixed to a wall or in a cupboard, used for putting things on 壁や食器棚に固定して物を載せるために使う長くて平らな木板, ガラス板など→棚, 棚板 ‖ *I put up a shelf in the kitchen.* 台所に棚を取り付けた. *I reached up and took down the book from the top shelf.* 手を伸ばして, 一番上の棚からその本を取った. *a bookshelf* 本棚 ☞ C7ページのさし絵

she'll /ʃil, ʃəl, 強形 ʃi:l/ SHE WILL の短縮形

\*shell¹ /ʃel/ 名 ▶定義1 C U a hard covering that protects eggs, nuts and some animals 卵, 木の実, 一部の動物などを保護する硬い覆い→殻, 皮, 甲羅, 貝殻 ‖ *Some children were collecting shells on the beach.* 数人の子供たちが浜辺で貝殻を集めていた. *a piece of eggshell* 卵の殻のかけら *Tortoises have a hard shell.* 亀には硬い甲羅がある. ☞ nut, shellfish, snail のさし絵 ▶定義2 C the walls or hard outer structure of sth 〜の壁または外側の硬い構造体 →(建物などの)骨組み, 外郭 ‖ *The body shell of the car is made in another factory.* 車体は別の工場で製造されている. ▶定義3 C a metal container that explodes when it is fired from a large gun 大型の銃砲から発射されるとさく裂する金属製の容器→砲弾

成句 **come out of your shell** ▶定義 to become less shy and more confident when talking to other people 人と話をするときに前ほど恥ずかしがらずに自信を持つようになる→打ち解ける, 胸襟を開く

**go, retreat, etc into your shell** ▶定義 to suddenly become shy and stop talking 突然恥ずかしくなって話すのをやめる→自分の殻に閉じこもる, 無口になる

shell² /ʃel/ 動 ▶定義1 to take the hard outer layer (shell) off a nut or other kind of food 木の実やほかの食物の硬い外皮(殻)をむく→〜の殻をむく, 皮を取る ‖ *to shell peas* えんどう豆のさやを取る ▶定義2 to fire metal containers (shells) full of explosives from a large gun 爆薬を詰めた金属製の容器(砲弾)を大型の火器から発砲する→〜に弾丸を浴びせる, 〜を砲撃する, 爆撃する

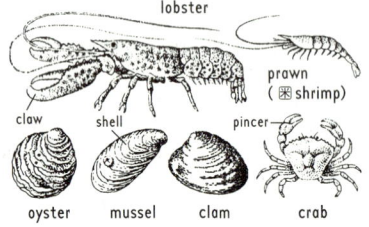
shellfish
lobster
prawn (米 shrimp)
claw
shell
oyster
mussel
clam
pincer
crab

shellfish /ʃelfɪʃ/ 名 ( 複 shellfish) ▶定義1 a type of animal that lives in water and has a shell 水中に生息する, 殻を持った動物→貝, 甲殻類(カニ・エビなど) ▶定義2 U these animals eaten as food 食用にするこれらの生物→食用貝, カニ, エビ

\*shelter¹ /ʃeltər/ 名 ▶定義1 U shelter (from sth) protection from danger or bad weather 危険や悪天候からの保護→保護, 避難, かくまうこと ‖ *to give somebody food and shelter* 〜に食料と住まいを提供する *We looked around for* *somewhere to **take shelter** from the storm.* あらしを避けていられる所がどこかないか辺りを見回した. ▶定義2 ❸ a small building that gives protection, for example from bad weather or attack 例えば悪天候や攻撃などから守ってくれる小さな建物→避難所, 隠れ家, 収容施設, 雨宿り場所, 防空壕(ごう) ‖ *a bus shelter* (屋根や囲い付き)バス停 *an air-raid shelter* 防空壕

**shelter**[2] /ʃéltər/ 動 ▶定義1 ⾃ shelter (from sth) to find protection or a safe place 防護やや安全な場所を見つける→避難する, 隠れる, よける ‖ *Let's shelter from the rain under that tree.* あの木の下で雨宿りをしよう. ▶定義2 ⽤ shelter sb/sth (from sb/sth) to protect sb/sth; to provide a safe place away from harm or danger ～を守る; 危害や危険から守られた安全な場所を提供する→～を(…から)保護する, 庇護(ひご)する, かくまう ‖ *The trees shelter the house from the wind.* 木々がその家の風よけになっている.

**sheltered** /ʃéltərd/ 形 ▶定義1 (used about a place) protected from bad weather (場所について)悪天候から守られた →(雨・風などから)守られた ▶定義2 protected from unpleasant things in your life 暮らしの中の嫌な事から守られた→(人生の労苦から)庇護(ひご)された, 世間から隔離された, 保護された, 過保護の ‖ *We had a sheltered childhood, living in the country.* 私たちは田舎に暮らしていたので, 世間の波風から庇護された子供時代を過ごした.

**shelve** /ʃelv/ 動⽤ ▶定義 to decide not to continue with a plan, etc, either for a short time or permanently 計画などの続行を短期間中止, または無期延期することを決定する→～を棚上げする, 先送りにする, 無期延期にする ‖ *Plans for a new motorway have been shelved.* 新しい自動車道路の計画は先送りにされている.

**shelves** /ʃelvz/ **SHELF** の複数形

**shelving** /ʃélvɪŋ/ 名 U ▶定義 a set of shelves 一そろいの棚→棚, 棚数, 棚材

**shepherd**[1] /ʃépərd/ 名 ❸ ▶定義 a person whose job is to look after sheep 羊の世話を仕事とする人→羊飼い, 牧羊者

**shepherd**[2] /ʃépərd/ 動⽤ ▶定義 to guide and look after people so that they do not get lost 道に迷ったりしないように人々を案内し, 世話をする→～を案内する, 導く, 付き添う

**sheriff** /ʃérəf/ 名 ❸ ▶定義 an officer of the law in a US county アメリカで郡の法をつかさどる官吏→郡保安官, シェリフ

**sherry** /ʃéri/ 名 ❸ U (復 **sherries**) ▶定義 a type of strong Spanish wine; a glass of this wine スペイン産の強いブドウ酒の一種; グラス1杯のこの酒→シェリー酒(アルコール度の高い白ワイン)

**she's** /ʃiz, ʃɪz, 強形 ʃiːz/ **SHE IS**, **SHE HAS** の短縮形

**shield**[1] /ʃiːld/ 名 ❸ ▶定義1 (in past times) a large piece of metal or wood that soldiers carried to protect themselves (昔)兵士が自分を守るために持ち歩いた大きな金属の板または木の板→盾 ▶定義2 **riot shield** a piece of equipment made of strong plastic, that the police use to protect themselves from angry crowds 警察官が怒った群集から身を守るために用いる, 強化プラスチックでできた器具→暴動鎮圧用盾, シールド ▶定義3 a person or thing that is used to protect sb/sth especially by forming a barrier 特に障壁を作って～を守るために用いられる人または物→保護者, 防護物, 後ろ盾 ‖ *The metal door acted as a shield against the explosion.* 金属製のドアが爆発に対する防護役を果たした. ▶定義4 an object or drawing in the shape of a shield, sometimes used as a prize in a sports competition 時にスポーツ競技の賞品として用いられる, 盾の形をした物または図形→優勝盾, 盾形の記章 ☞ **medal** のさし絵

**shield**[2] /ʃiːld/ 動⽤ ▶定義 shield sb/sth (against/from sb/sth) to protect sb/sth from danger or damage ～を危険や損傷から保護する→～を(…から)保護する, 庇護(ひご)する, 守る ‖ *I shielded my eyes from the bright light with my hand.* 私は片手で強い日差しから目を守った.

**shift**[1] /ʃɪft/ 動⾃⽤ ▶定義1 to move or be moved from one position or place to another ある位置・場所からほかの位置・場所に移動する, または移動される→移る, 位置を変える; (位置など)を変える, ～を移す ‖ *She shifted uncomfortably in her chair.* 彼女はいすに座って落ち着かぬ様子でもぞもぞしていた. *He shifted his desk closer to the window.* 彼は自分の机をもっと窓の近くに移した. ▶定義2 to change your opinion of or attitude towards sth ～に対する意見や態度を変

える➜**変わる; 〜を変える, 変更する** ‖ *Public attitudes towards marriage have shifted over the years.* 長い間に結婚に対する人々の態度は変わってきている.

[成句] **shift the blame/responsibility (for sth) (onto sb)** ▶定義 to make sb else responsible for sth you should do or for sth bad you have done 自分がしなければならない事, または自分がしてしまった悪い事に対する責任を, 他人に押し付ける ➜**(〜の)責任を(…に)転嫁する, 責任をなすり付ける**

**shift²** /ʃɪft/ [名] ▶定義 1 [C] **a shift (in sth)** a change in your opinion of or attitude towards sth 〜に対する意見や態度の変化 ➜**(〜の)変化, 変更, 転換** ‖ *There has been a shift in public opinion away from war.* 世論は戦争から離反する方向に転換してきている. ▶定義 2 [[C], 単数または複数形の動詞と共に] (in a factory, etc) one of the periods that the working day is divided into; the group who work during this period (工場などで) 1日の労働時間を分割したものの1つ; その時間就労する人たち➜**(勤務の)交替, 交替勤務時間; 交替勤務者, 交替組** ‖ *The night shift has/have just gone off duty.* たった今夜勤の人たちが仕事を終えたところだ. *to work* ***in shifts*** 交替制で働く *shift work/workers* 交替勤務・交替勤務者 *to be on the day/night shift* 日勤・夜勤である ▶定義 3 [単数扱い] one of the keys that you use for writing on a computer, etc, that allows you to write a big (capital) letter コンピューターなどで文を書くときに用いる, 大(頭)文字を入力することのできるキー➜**シフト** ‖ *the shift key* シフトキー

**shifty** /ʃɪ́fti/ [形] ▶定義 (used about a person or his/her appearance) giving the impression that you cannot trust him/her (人物やその人の外見について) 信用できない印象を与える➜**こそこそした, 狡猾(こうかつ)な, ずるい** ‖ *shifty eyes* うさんくさい目付き

**shilling** /ʃɪ́lɪŋ/ [名] [C] ▶定義 1 the basic unit of money in some countries, for example Kenya ケニヤなど, いくつかの国で用いられている通貨単位➜**シリング** ▶定義 2 a British coin worth five pence that was used in past times イギリスで過去に使用されていた5ペンス相当の硬貨➜**シリング**

**shimmer** /ʃɪ́mər/ [動][自] ▶定義 to shine with a soft light that seems to be moving 揺れ動くように見える柔らかい光に輝く➜**かすかに光る, ちらちら光る, 揺らめく** ‖ *Moonlight shimmered on the sea.* 月光が海に揺らめいていた.

**shin** /ʃɪn/ [名] [C] ▶定義 the bone down the front part of your leg from your knee to your foot ひざから足までの脚の前面の骨➜**脛骨(けいこつ), 向こうずね** ☛ C5 ページのさし絵

***shine¹** /ʃáɪn/ [動] (過, 過分 **shone** /ʃóʊn; ʃɔn/) ▶定義 1 [自] to send out or to reflect light; to be bright 光を発するまたは反射する; 輝いている➜**光る, 輝く, 照る** ‖ *I could see a light shining in the distance.* 遠くに一筋の光が輝いているのが見えた. *The sea shone in the light of the moon.* 海が月明かりに照らされて光っていた. ▶定義 2 [他] to direct a light at sb/sth 〜に光を向ける ➜**(光線など)を(〜に)向ける, 〜を照らす** ‖ *The policeman shone a torch on the stranger's face.* 警官はその見知らぬ人物の顔を懐中電灯で照らした.

**shine²** /ʃáɪn/ [名] [単数扱い] ▶定義 1 a bright effect caused by light hitting a polished surface 磨かれた表面に光が当たって生じるきらきらした明るい現象➜**輝き, 光沢, つや** ▶定義 2 the act of polishing sth so that it shines 光沢が出るように〜を磨く動作➜**磨くこと, つや出し**

**shingle** /ʃɪ́ŋg(ə)l/ [名] [U] ▶定義 small pieces of stone lying in a mass on a beach 海岸に大量にある小さな石➜**小石, 砂利**

**shin pad** [名] [C] ▶定義 a thick piece of material used to protect the shin when playing some sports ある競技をするとき, 向こうずねを守るために用いる厚い素材でできた物➜**すね当て**

**shiny** /ʃáɪni/ [形] (**shinier**; **shiniest**) ▶定義 causing a bright effect when in the sun or in light 日光や光に当たるときらきらと光沢を生み出す➜**輝く, 光る, 光沢のある** ‖ *The shampoo leaves your hair soft and shiny.* そのシャンプーを使うと髪が柔らかくなり光沢が出ます. *a shiny new car* ぴかぴかの新車

***ship¹** /ʃɪp/ [名] [C] ▶定義 a large boat used for carrying passengers or cargo by sea 乗客や貨物の海上輸送に用いられる大型の船 ➜**(大型の)船, 艦** ‖ *to travel* ***by ship*** 船旅をする *to launch a ship* 船を進水させる

S

➤ boat は ship よりも小さい. voyage（乗客を運ぶ距離が長い場合）には liner を, crossing（短い場合）には ferry を用いる.

**ship**² /ʃɪp/ 動他 (**shipping**; **shipped**) ▶定義 to send or carry sth by ship or by another type of transport 船やほかの輸送手段によって〜を送る・運ぶ→**(貨物)を船で送る, 輸送する, 発送する, 出荷する**

**shipbuilder** /ʃípbìldər/ 名 C ▶定義 a person or company who makes or builds ships 船を作る・建造する人または会社→**造船業者, 造船技師**
— shipbuilding 名 U →造船, 造船業, 造船術

**shipment** /ʃípmənt/ 名 ▶定義 1 U the carrying of goods from one place to another ある場所から別の場所に商品を運ぶこと→**船積み, 発送, 出荷** ▶定義 2 C a quantity of goods that are sent from one place to another ある場所から別の場所に送られる商品の量→**積み荷, 船荷**

**shipping** /ʃípɪŋ/ 名 U ▶定義 1 ships in general or considered as a group 船一般, または1つの集合体としてとらえられた場合の船→**船舶** ▶定義 2 the carrying of goods from one place to another ある場所から別の場所に商品を運ぶこと→**船舶輸送, 船積み** ‖ *a shipping company* 船会社

**shipwreck** /ʃíprèk/ 名 C U ▶定義 an accident at sea in which a ship is destroyed by a storm, rocks, etc and sinks 大しけ, 岩礁などで船が破壊され, 沈没する海の事故→**難破, 沈没** ☞ このような事故に遭った人や船を be shipwrecked（難破する）と表現したりする.

**shipyard** /ʃípjɑ̀ːrd/ 名 C ▶定義 a place where ships are repaired or built 船を修理または建造したりする場所→**造船所**

**shirk** /ʃəːrk/ 動自他 ▶定義 to avoid doing sth that is difficult or unpleasant, especially because you are too lazy 特に怠慢さから, 困難または不快な〜を回避する→**(責任などを)逃れる, (仕事などを)サボる, おこたる** ‖ *to shirk your responsibilities* 責任を逃れる

★**shirt** /ʃəːrt/ 名 C ▶定義 a piece of clothing made of cotton, etc, worn on the upper part of the body 木綿などで作られた, 上半身に着用する衣類→**シャツ, ワイシャツ, 肌着**
➤ 通常, shirt には首の部分に collar（えり）, 長いまたは短い sleeves（そで）, 前部に buttons（ボタン）が付いている.

shock² 1487

☛ C6 ページのさし絵

**shiver** /ʃívər/ 動自 ▶定義 to shake slightly, especially because you are cold or frightened 特に寒さ・恐怖のため, 少し震える→**ぶるぶる震える, おののく** ‖ *shivering with cold/fright* 寒さ・恐怖でぶるぶる震えて — shiver 名 C →**震え, 寒気, 身震い, おののき** ‖ *The thought sent a shiver down my spine.* その事を考えると背筋が寒くなった.

**shoal** /ʃóʊl/ 名 C ▶定義 a large group of fish that swim and feed together 連れ立ってえさを食べ泳ぐ魚の大群→**群れ, 魚群**

★**shock**¹ /ʃɑk/ 名 ▶定義 1 C U the feeling that you get when sth unpleasant happens suddenly; the situation that causes this feeling 不愉快な事が突然起きたときに抱く感情; この感情を引き起こす状況→**動揺, (精神的)打撃; 衝撃的な出来事** ‖ *The sudden noise gave him a shock.* 突然の物音に彼は驚いた. *The bad news came as a shock to her.* その悪い知らせは彼女にはショックだった. *I'm still suffering from shock at the news.* 私はいまだにその知らせを受けた時の衝撃から立ち直っていない. *His mother is in a state of shock.* 彼の母親はショックを受けている. ▶定義 2 U a serious medical condition of extreme weakness caused by damage to the body 身体的な痛手によって生じた医学的に憂慮すべき極度の衰弱状態→**ショック(症)** ‖ *He was in/went into shock after the accident.* 彼は事故後ショック症状だった・ショック症状に陥った. ▶定義 3 C a violent shaking movement (caused by a crash, explosion, etc) （衝突, 爆発などによって引き起こされる）激しい揺れ→**衝撃, 激動, 振動, ショック** ▶定義 4 C = **ELECTRIC SHOCK**

★**shock**² /ʃɑk/ 動 ▶定義 1 他 to cause an unpleasant feeling of surprise in sb 〜に不快な驚きの感情を抱かせる→**〜をぎょっとさせる, ぎくりとさせる, 〜に衝撃を与える** ‖ *We were shocked by his death.* 私たちは彼の死に衝撃を受けた. *I'm sorry, I didn't mean to shock you when I came in.* ごめんなさい. ここに入るのに, 別にあなたを驚かせるつもりはなかったのです. ▶定義 2 自他 to make sb feel disgusted or offended 〜をむかつかす, 〜の気分を害する→**〜を憤慨させる; あ**

# 1488 shocking

きれさせる ‖ *These films deliberately set out to shock.* これらの映画は始めからわざと人をぎょっとさせることをねらって作られている． ― **shocked** 形 →ぎょっとした，ぎくりとした，憤慨した，あきれた ‖ *a shocked expression/look* ぎょっとした表情・様子

**shocking** /ʃákɪŋ/ 形 ▶定義1 that offends or upsets people; that is morally wrong 人々の気分を害する，人々を動揺させる；道徳的に間違った →衝撃的な，ぎょっとさせる，あきれた ‖ *a shocking accident* 衝撃的な事故 *shocking behaviour/news* あきれた振る舞い・衝撃的な知らせ ▶定義2 特に 英略式 very bad とても悪い →ひどい，話にならない

**shod** SHOE² の過去・過去分詞形

**shoddy** /ʃádi/ 形 ▶定義1 made carelessly or with poor quality materials ぞんざいに，または品質の悪い材料で作られた →安物の，粗悪な ‖ *shoddy goods* 粗悪品 ▶定義2 dishonest or unfair 不正直な，不公正な →卑劣な，下劣な ― **shoddily** 副 →卑劣に，下劣に

**\*shoe¹** /ʃuː/ 名 C ▶定義1 a type of covering for the foot, usually made of leather or plastic 通常，皮や合成皮革で作られた足を覆う物の一種 →靴 ‖ *a pair of shoes* 靴1足 *running shoes* ランニングシューズ *What size are your shoes/What is your shoe size?* あなたの靴のサイズはいくつですか． あなたの靴のサイズは何ですか． *I tried on a nice pair of shoes but they didn't fit.* 良さそうな靴を試しに履いてみたが，サイズが合わなかった． ▶定義2 = HORSESHOE

成句 in my, your, etc place/shoes ⇒ PLACE¹

> ▶社会・文化
> 
> 靴は衣類の一部
> 
> 靴は欧米では衣服(clothes)の一部とされています．自分の家でも，原則として寝るとき衣服を寝巻きに着替えるときに靴を脱ぐまで，靴を履いたままで過ごします．したがって，靴を脱ぐというのは，人目を避けて行うべきプライベートな行為と考えられています．

**shoe²** /ʃuː/ 動 他 (過，過分 **shod** /ʃɑd/) ▶定義 to fit a shoe on a horse →馬に蹄(てい)鉄を打つ

**shoelace** /ʃúːleɪs/ (特に 米 **shoestring**) 名 C ▶定義 a long thin piece of material like string used to fasten a shoe 靴を締めるために使うひも状の細長い素材 →靴ひも ‖ *to tie/untie a shoelace* 靴ひもを結ぶ・ほどく

**shoestring** /ʃúːstrɪŋ/ 特に 米 = SHOELACE

成句 **on a shoestring** ▶定義 using very little money ごくわずかな金を使って →わずかな金・資金・元手で ‖ *to live on a shoestring* 細々と暮らす

**shone** SHINE¹ の過去・過去分詞形

**shoo** /ʃuː/ 間 ▶定義 (usually said to animals or small children) Go away! (通常は動物や小さな子供に対して言う) あっちへ行け →シッ，シッシッ ― **shoo** 動 他 (過，過分 **shooed**) ▶定義 **shoo sb/sth away, off, out, etc** to make sb/sth go away by saying 'shoo' and waving your hands 「シッ」と言って手を振りながら～を立ち去らせる →シッと言って～を追い払う，立ち去らせる

**shook** SHAKE¹ の過去形

**\*shoot¹** /ʃuːt/ 動 (過，過分 **shot** /ʃɑt/) ▶定義1 自他 **shoot (sth) (at sb/sth)** to fire a gun or another weapon 銃などの武器を発射する →(弓矢を)射る，(銃を)発射する，撃つ ‖ *Don't shoot!* 撃つな． *She shot an arrow at the target, but missed it.* 彼女は的に向け矢を放ったが，当たらなかった． ▶定義2 他 to injure or kill sb/sth with a gun 銃で～をけがさせる・殺害する →(人などを)撃つ，撃ち殺す，射殺する ‖ *The policeman was shot in the arm.* その警察官は腕を撃たれた． *The soldier was shot dead.* その兵士は撃ち殺された． ▶定義3 自他 to hunt and kill birds and animals with a gun as a sport スポーツとして鳥や動物

を追って銃で殺す→狩猟する, ~を射止める ‖ *He goes shooting at the weekends.* 週末, 彼は狩猟に出掛ける. ☞参 hunting ▶定義4 🔵🔴 to move somewhere quickly and suddenly; to make sth move in this way 素早く突然にどこかに動く; そのように~を動かす→素早く動く, 急に動く; ~をさっと動かす ‖ *The car shot past me at 100 miles per hour.* 車は時速100マイルで私のそばをさっと走りすぎた. ▶定義5 🔵 (of pain) to go very suddenly along part of your body (痛みが)突然体の一部を走る→走る ‖ *The pain shot up my leg.* 私の脚に痛みが走った. *shooting pains in the chest* 胸を走る痛み ▶定義6 🔵🔴 to make a film or photograph of sth ~の映画や写真を撮る→映画を撮影する, 写真を撮る; ~を撮影する ‖ *They shot the scene ten times.* 彼らはその場面を10回撮影した. ▶定義7 🔵 shoot (at sth) (in football, etc) to try to kick or hit the ball into the goal(サッカーなどで)ボールをゴールに向けてける, または打とうとする→シュートする ‖ *He should have shot instead of passing.* 彼はパスではなくシュートすべきだった. ☞名 shoot

句動詞 shoot sb/sth down ▶定義 to make sb/sth fall to the ground by shooting him/her/it ~を地面に撃ち落とす→~を撃ち殺す, ~を撃ち落とす ‖ *The helicopter was shot down by a missile.* ヘリコプターはミサイルで撃墜された.

shoot up ▶定義 to increase by a large amount; to grow very quickly 大量に増える; 急に大きくなる→急増する, 急成長する ‖ *Prices have shot up in the past year.* 昨年は物価が急上昇した.

**shoot**² /ʃuːt/ 名 🔴 ▶定義 a new part of a plant or tree 植物や木の新しい部分→新芽, 若い枝

**shooting star** 名 🔴 ▶定義 a piece of rock that burns with a bright light as it travels through space 宇宙を通り過ぎる際に, 明るい光を放って燃える石→流れ星, 流星

*★**shop**¹ /ʃɒp/ (米**store**) 名 🔴 ▶定義 a building or part of a building where things are bought and sold 物が売買される建物または建物の一部→店, 商店 ‖ *a cake/shoe shop* ケーキ屋・靴屋 *a corner shop (= a local shop, usually at the corner of a street)*(スーパーなどに対して)小商店(=通常街角にある地元の商店) *When do the shops open?* 店はいつ開くのですか. *a butcher's/baker's shop* 肉屋・パン屋

---

# shopping 1489

➤ 「肉屋で」などと言うとき, 通常, at the butcher's shop ではなく at the butcher's と表現する.

成句 talk shop ⇒ **TALK**¹

*★**shop**² /ʃɒp/ 動 🔵 (**shopping**; **shopped**) ▶定義 shop (for sth) to go to a shop or shops in order to buy things 買い物をするために店に行く→買い物に出掛ける, 買い物をする ‖ *He's shopping for some new clothes.* 彼は新しい服を買いに来ているところだ.

➤ shop よりも go shopping の方がより一般的である : *We go shopping every Saturday.* (私たちは毎週土曜日に買い物に出掛ける.)

— **shopper** 名 🔴→買い物客

句動詞 shop around (for sth) ▶定義 to look at the price and quality of an item in different shops before you decide where to buy it どこで買うか決める前にさまざまな店で品物の価格や品質をチェックする→商店を見て回る

**shop assistant** (米**sales clerk**; **clerk**) 名 🔴 ▶定義 a person who works in a shop 店で働く人→店員, 売子

**shop floor** 名 [単数扱い] 米 ▶定義 an area of a factory where things are made; the people who make things in a factory 工場で物が作られる場所; 工場で物を作る人→(工場などの)作業現場; (経営側に対して)現場の作業員, 工場労働者

**shopkeeper** /ʃɒpkiːpər/ ( 米 **storekeeper**) 名 🔴 ▶定義 a person who owns or manages a small shop 小さな店を所有または管理する人→小売店経営者, 小売店主, 店長

**shoplifter** /ʃɒplɪftər/ 名 🔴 ▶定義 a person who steals sth from a shop while pretending to be a customer 客の振りをして店の~を盗む人→万引きをする人 ☞参 thief の注

**shoplifting** /ʃɒplɪftɪŋ/ 名 🔵 ▶定義 the crime of stealing goods from a shop while pretending to be a customer 客の振りをして店から品物を盗む犯罪→万引き ‖ *He was arrested for shoplifting.* 彼は万引きのかどで逮捕された. ☞参 lift¹ (6)

*★**shopping** /ʃɒpɪŋ/ 名 🔵 ▶定義1 the activity of going to the shops and buying things 店に行って物を買う行為→買い物, ショッピング ‖ *We always do the shopping on a Friday night.* 私たちはいつも金曜日の夜に買い物をする. *a shop-*

*ping basket/bag/trolley* 買い物かご・袋・ワゴン ▶定義2 特に 医 the things that you have bought in a shop 店で買った品物→買った品物

**shopping centre** (医 **shopping mall; mall**) 名 ⓒ ▶定義 a place where there are many shops, either outside or in a covered building たくさんの店がある場所. 1つの建物に入っている場合も、屋外に並んでいる場合もある→ショッピングセンター, 商店街 ☞ C8 ページのさし絵

\*shore /ʃɔːr/ 名 ⓒ Ⓤ ▶定義 the land at the edge of a sea or lake 海や湖の水際にある陸地→岸, 海岸, 湖畔, 河岸

➤ ashore は on shore (岸へ, 上陸して) と同義である.

**shorn** SHEAR の過去分詞形

\*short¹ /ʃɔːrt/ 形容 ▶定義1 not measuring much from one end to the other 端から端までの長さがあまりない→短い ‖ *a short line/distance/dress* 短い線・距離・ドレス *This essay is rather short.* このエッセーはやや短い. *short hair* 短い髪 ⇔ **long** ☞ 動 **shorten** ▶定義2 less than the average height 平均的な身長よりも低い→背の低い ‖ *a short, fat man* 背の低い太った男 ⇔ **tall** ▶定義3 not lasting a long time; brief 長時間続かない; 短い→短時間の, 短い, 長続きしない ‖ *a short visit/film* 短い滞在・短編映画 *She left a short time ago.* 彼女は少し前に出ていった. *to have a short memory* (= *to only remember things that have happened recently*) 物忘れしやすい (= 最近起こった事しか覚えていない) ⇔ **long** ☞ 動 **shorten** ▶定義4 **short (of/on sth)** not having enough of what is needed 必要な物が十分にない→ (～が) 不足している, 足りない ‖ *Because of illness, the team is two players short.* そのチームは選手が病気のため, 2人足りない. *Good secretaries are **in short supply** (= there are not enough of them).* 優れた秘書が不足している (= 人数が十分でない). *We're a bit short of money at the moment.* 私たちは今, 少々金欠だ. *Your essay is a bit short on detail.* 君のエッセーはやや詳細に欠ける. ☞ 名 **shortage** ▶定義5 suddenly 突然に→急に, 不意に ‖ *She stopped short when she saw the accident.* 事故を目撃して彼女は突然立ち止まった. ▶定義6 **short for sth** used as a shorter way of saying sth or as an abbreviation ～を短く表現したり省略したりする場合に用いて→～を略して, ～の省略形で, 短縮形で ‖ *'Bill' is short for 'William'.* 「ビル」は「ウィリアム」の略称だ.

▶定義7 **short (with sb)** (used about a person) speaking in an impatient and angry way to sb (人について) ～に対していらいらと怒った口調で話す→(～に対して) ぶっきらぼうな, 無愛想な, 素っ気ない ☞ 副 **shortly**

成句 **cut sth/sb short** ▶定義 to not allow sb to finish speaking; to interrupt ～に最後まで話させない; ～を遮る→～を中断する, ～を遮る, 話の腰を折る

**fall short (of sth)** ▶定義 to not be enough; to not reach sth 十分でない; ～に達しない→ (～に) 不足する; (目標などに) 達しない ‖ *The pay rise fell short of the workers' demands.* 賃上げは労働者の要求に達しなかった.

**for short** ▶定義 as a short form 省略形として→略して, 短く言って ‖ *She's called 'Diana', or 'Di' for short.* 彼女は「ダイアナ」あるいは略して「ダイ」と呼ばれている.

**go short (of sth)** ▶定義 to be without enough (of sth) (～が) 十分にないままでいる→ (～に) 不自由する, 足りないままやっていく ‖ *He made sure his family never went short of food.* 彼は自分の家族が決して食べる物に不自由することがないようにした.

**in the long/short term** ⇒ **TERM¹**

**in short** ▶定義 in a few words; briefly 数語で; 簡潔に→要約すると, 短く言うと, 要するに

**run short (of sth)** ▶定義 to have used up most of sth so there is not much left ～を大部分使ってしまったためほとんど残っていない→ (～が) 不足する, (～を) 切らす, 使いきる ‖ *We're running short of coffee.* コーヒーがもうじき切れそうだ.

**short of sth/doing sth** ▶定義 apart from; except for ～を別として; ～以外は→～を除いて, ～を別として, ～以外は ‖ *Nothing short of a miracle will save the business now.* 奇跡以外に現在の経営状態を救うものはない.

**stop short of sth/doing sth** ⇒ **STOP¹**

**short²** /ʃɔːrt/ 名 ⓒ ▶定義1 略式 = SHORT CIRCUIT ▶定義2 特に 医 a small strong alcoholic drink 少量の強い酒→強い酒 (ウイスキー, ブランデー, ジンなど), ストレートの酒 ‖ *I prefer wine to shorts.* 私は強い酒よりもワインの方が好きだ.

**shortage** /ʃɔːrtɪdʒ/ 名 C ▶定義 a situation where there is not enough of sth 〜が十分にない状況 ➡不足, 欠乏 ‖ *a food/housing/water shortage* 食料·住宅·水不足 *a shortage of trained teachers* ベテラン教師の不足

**short circuit**（または 略式 **short**）名 C ▶定義 a bad electrical connection that causes a machine to stop working 機械の作動停止の原因となる具合の悪い電気の接続 ➡短絡, ショート — **short-circuit** 動 自他 ➡短絡する, ショートする; 〜を短絡させる, ショートさせる ‖ *The lights short-circuited.* 照明がショートした.

**shortcoming** /ʃɔːrtkʌmɪŋ/ 名 [C, 通常は複数] ▶定義 a fault or weakness 欠点, 弱点 ➡欠点, 短所, 欠陥

**short cut** 名 C ▶定義 a quicker, easier or more direct way to get somewhere or to do sth ある場所に行くまたは〜を行うための, より迅速·簡単·直接的な方法 ➡近道, 手っ取り早い方法 ‖ *He took a short cut to school through the park.* 彼は学校まで公園を通って近道をした.

**shorten** /ʃɔːrtn/ 動 自他 ▶定義 to become shorter or to make sth shorter 短くなる, 〜を短くする ➡短くなる, 縮む; 〜を短くする, 縮める

**shortfall** /ʃɔːrtfɔːl/ 名 C ▶定義 shortfall (in sth) the amount by which sth is less than you need or expect 必要とする, または期待するよりも少ない量 ➡（〜の）不足

**shorthand** /ʃɔːrthænd/ 名 U ▶定義 a method of writing quickly that uses signs or short forms of words 記号や単語の省略形を使って素早く筆記する方法 ➡速記 ‖ *to write in shorthand* 速記で書く *a shorthand typist* 速記者

**shortlist** /ʃɔːrtlɪst/ 名 [C, 通常は単数] ▶定義 a list of the best people for a job, etc who have been chosen from all the people who want the job 仕事などを求めるすべての人々から選抜された最適任者の一覧表 ➡（最終審査用の）候補者名簿, 選抜候補者リスト ‖ *She's one of the four people on the shortlist.* 彼女は最終候補者名簿に載った4人のうちの1人だ. — **shortlist** 動 ▶最終候補者名簿に載せる, 選抜候補者リストに入れる ‖ *Six candidates were shortlisted for the post.* 6人の候補者がその役職の最終候補者名簿に載せられた.

**short-lived** /ʃɔːrtlɪvd/ 形 ▶定義 lasting only for a short time 短時間しか続かない ➡短命の, はかない, 長

---

# short-term 1491

続きしない

**shortly** /ʃɔːrtli/ 副 ▶定義1 soon; not long すぐに; 長くたたずに ➡すぐに, 間もなく ‖ *The manager will see you shortly.* 部長がすぐにお会いいたします. ▶定義2 in an impatient, angry way いらいらと怒っているように ➡ぶっきらぼうに, 無愛想に, 素っ気なく

\***shorts** /ʃɔːrts/ 名 [複数扱い] ▶定義1 a type of short trousers ending above the knee that you wear in hot weather, while playing sports, etc ひざ上丈の短いズボン. 暑い天気のとき, スポーツをしているときなどに着用する ➡ショートパンツ, 半ズボン ☛ C6ページのさし絵 ▶定義2 米 a piece of loose clothing that men wear under their trousers ズボンの下に着用するゆったりした衣服 ➡男性用の下着, パンツ ‖ *boxer shorts* ボクサーショーツ
▶ shortsは複数形なので, 例えば「新しいショートパンツ」のことをa new shortとは言えない. 次のような言い方が可能: *I need to get some new shorts.*（新しいショートパンツが何枚か必要だ.）*I need to get a new pair of shorts.*（新しいショートパンツが1枚必要だ.）

**short-sighted** 形 ▶定義1 （特に 米 **near-sighted**） able to see things clearly only when they are very close to you 非常に近くにある物だけをはっきり見ることができる ➡近視の, 近眼の ‖ *I have to wear glasses because I'm short-sighted.* 私は近視なので眼鏡を掛けなければならない. ⇔ **long-sighted** ▶定義2 not considering what will probably happen in the future 将来起こるかもしれない事について考慮しない ➡近視眼的な, 先見の明がない ‖ *a short-sighted attitude/policy* 近視眼的な態度·政策

**short-staffed** 形 ▶定義 (used about an office, a shop, etc) not having enough people to do the work (事務所, 店などについて) 働く人の数が十分でない ➡人手不足の, 職員不足の

**short story** 名 C ▶定義 a piece of writing that is shorter than a novel 長編小説よりも短い作品 ➡短編小説

**short-term** 形 ▶定義 lasting for a short period of time from the present 現時点から短期間存続する ➡短期の, 短期間の ‖ *short-term plans/memory* 短期計画·記憶

## 1492 shot¹

**\*shot¹** /ʃɑt/ 名 C ▶定義1 a shot (at sb/sth) an act of firing a gun, etc, or the noise that this makes 銃などを撃つ行為, またはそれによって生じる音→**発射, 発砲, 銃声** ‖ *to take **a shot** at the target* 的をねらって撃つ *The policeman fired **a warning shot** into the air.* 警察官は空に向けて警告の一発を撃った. ▶定義2 (in sport) the action of kicking, throwing or hitting a ball in order to score a point or a goal (競技で)点を取る・ゴールを決めるためにボールをける・投げる・打つ行為→**シュート, ショット** ‖ *Owen scored with a low shot into the corner of the net.* オーエンはネットのコーナーに低いシュートを決めた. *Good shot!* ナイスショット. ▶定義3 a photograph or a picture in a film 写真, 映画のコマ→**写真, 映画の一場面, ワンカット** ‖ *I got some good shots of the runners as they crossed the line.* 走者たちが決勝点に達したときのいい写真を何枚か撮った. ▶定義4 [通常は単数] 略式 a shot (at sth/at doing sth) a try at doing sth; an attempt 〜を試しにやってみようとすること; 試み→**試み, 企て** ‖ *Let me **have a shot** at it (= let me try to do it).* 試しに私にそれをやらせてください(= 私に試させてください). *Just **give it your best shot** (= try as hard as you can).* ただ最善を尽くせばいい(= できるだけ一生懸命やってみなさい). ▶定義5 a small amount of a drug that is put into your body using a needle 針を使って体内に注入する少量の薬→**注射** ▶定義6 (しばしば **the shot**) a heavy metal ball that is thrown as a sport (the shot-put) 競技として投げる重い金属製の球(砲丸)→**砲丸**

成句 a long shot ⇒ **LONG¹**
call the shots/tune ⇒ **CALL¹**
like a shot 略式 ▶定義 very quickly; without stopping to think about it 非常に素早く; 立ち止まって考えずに→**弾丸のように早く; すかさず, すぐさま, 即座に** ‖ *If someone invited me on a free holiday, I'd go like a shot.* もしだれかがただの休暇に私を招待してくれたら, 二つ返事で行くのだが.

**shot²** SHOOT¹ の過去・過去分詞形
**shotgun** /ʃɑtgʌn/ 名 C ▶定義 a long gun that is used for shooting small animals and birds 小動物や鳥を撃つのに用いられる銃身の長い銃→**猟銃, 散弾銃, ショットガン**

**\*should** /ʃəd, ʃʊd, 強形 ʃʊd/ 法助動詞 (否定形 **should not**; 短縮形 **shouldn't** /ʃʊdnt/) ▶定義1 (used for saying that it is right or appropriate for sb to do sth, or for sth to happen) ought to (〜がある行為をする, あるいは〜が起こることが当然または適切であると表現するのに用いて)→**〜すべきである, するのが当然だ** ‖ *The police should do something about street crime in this area.* 警察はその地域の街頭での犯罪に対して何とかすべきだ. *Children shouldn't be left on their own.* 子供たちだけにしておいてはならない. *I'm tired. I shouldn't have gone to bed so late/I should have gone to bed earlier.* ああ疲れた. あんなに夜遅くまで起きているのではなかった・もっと早く寝るべきだった. ▶定義2 used for giving or for asking for advice 助言を与えたり求めたりするのに用いて→**〜したらよい, することが望ましい** ‖ *You should try that new restaurant.* あの新しいレストランに行ってみるといいですよ. *Do you think I should phone him?* 彼に電話した方がいいと思いますか. *What should I do?* 私はどうしたらよいのだろう. ▶定義3 used for saying that you expect sth is true or will happen 〜は本当のはず, または起こるはずといった見込みを表すのに用いて→**〜のはずだ, だろう, 多分〜だ** ‖ *It's 4.30. They should be in New York by now.* 4時30分だ. 彼らは今ごろニューヨークのはずだ. *It should stop raining soon.* 雨はきっとすぐにやむだろう. ▶定義4 因 正式 used with 'I/we' instead of 'would' in 'if' sentences if 節(仮定法)の帰結節で would の代わりに I や we と用いて→**〜だろう, するだろうに** ‖ *I should be most grateful if you could send me...* 私に〜を送っていただけたら本当に有り難いのですが. ▶定義5 正式 used after 'if' and 'in case' to refer to a possible event or situation 起こり得る出来事や状況について述べるのに if や in case の後に用いて→**万一〜ならば, たとえ〜でも** ‖ *If you should decide to accept, please phone us.* 万一引き受けることに決められたら, 私どもの方にお電話ください. *Should you decide to accept...* 万一引き受けることに決められたら〜(if が省略された倒置文) ▶定義6 used as the past tense of 'shall' when we report what sb says 〜が言った事を報告するときに shall の過去形として用いて→**〜する**

だろう; 〜しましょうか ‖ He asked me if he should come today (= he asked 'Shall I come today?'). 彼は私に今日伺いましょうかと尋ねた(= 彼は「今日, 伺いましょうか」と尋ねた).
▶定義7 **I should imagine, say, think etc** used to give opinions that you are not certain about 確信の持てない意見を述べるのに用いて→(私(ども)としては)〜なのですが, …でしょう

▶法助動詞についての説明は, 巻末の「文法早見表」を参照.

\***shoulder**¹ /ʃóʊldər/ 名 ▶定義1 ❸the part of your body between your neck and the top of your arm 首と上腕の付け根との間にある体の一部分→肩, 肩部 ‖ I asked him why he'd done it but he just **shrugged his shoulders** (= raised his shoulders to show that he did not know or care). 彼になぜそんな事をしたのか尋ねたが, 彼はただ肩をすくめただけだった(= 知らないまたは気にしていないことを示すために肩を上げた). She fell asleep with her head on his shoulder. 彼女は彼の肩に頭を乗せたまま眠ってしまった. ☞ C5 ページのさし絵 ▶定義2 **-shouldered** (複合形容詞を作るために用いて) having the type of shoulders mentioned 言及したタイプの肩を持っている→〜の肩をした, 肩が〜の ‖ a broad-shouldered man 肩幅の広い男性 ▶定義3 ❸ a part of a dress, coat, etc that covers the shoulders 衣服, コートなどの肩を覆う部分→肩の部分
☞参 **hard shoulder**

---

▶**日本語 vs 英語**

「肩凝り」日英比較

根を詰めた仕事や人間関係のストレスから来る肩の筋肉痛(aching shoulder muscles)は, 日本では国民的疾患と言えるほど一般的ですが, 英米では肩凝りを訴える声はほとんど聞かれません.「肩凝り」に該当する英語表現を見つけることさえ難しいのです. 彼らは同じような凝りを肩よりもむしろ首の後ろ側(the back of one's neck)に感じ, 疲れたとき「肩をたたく」代わりに「首をこする」(rub (the back of) one's neck)ことが多いです.

---

成句 **a shoulder to cry on** ▶定義 used to describe a person who listens to your problems and understands how you feel 悩みを聞いて気持ちを理解してくれる人を表現するのに用いて→悩みを聞いてくれる人, 悩みを打ち明けられる人, 困ったときに頼りになる人
**have a chip on your shoulder** ⇒ **CHIP**¹
**rub shoulders with sb** ⇒ **RUB**

**shoulder**² /ʃóʊldər/ 動 他 ▶定義1 to accept the responsibility for sth 〜に対する責任を引き受ける→〜を引き受ける, 担う, 負う ‖ to **shoulder the blame/responsibility** for sth 〜に対する責め・責任を負う ▶定義2 to push sb/sth with your shoulder 肩で〜を押す→〜を肩で押す, 肩で押し分ける

**shoulder bag** 名 ❸ ▶定義 a type of bag that you carry over one shoulder with a long strap 長いひもで片方の肩に掛けて持ち運ぶタイプのかばん→ショルダーバッグ, 肩掛けかばん ☞類 **handbag**

**shoulder blade** 名 ❸ ▶定義 either of the two large flat bones on each side of your back, below your shoulders 肩の下, 背中の左右に1つずつある大きくて平らな骨→肩甲骨 ☞ C5 ページのさし絵

\***shout** /ʃáʊt/ 動 ▶定義1 ❸shout (at/to sb); **shout out** to speak or cry out in a very loud voice 非常に大きな声で話す, 叫ぶ→(〜に向かって)叫ぶ, 大声で言う, どなる ‖ There's no need to shout - I can hear you. 大声を出さなくてもいいですよ − あなたの声はちゃんと聞こえていますから. The teacher shouted angrily at the boys. 教師は怒って少年たちにどなり散らした. to shout out in pain/excitement 痛さで・興奮して叫ぶ ▶定義2 他 shout sth (at/to sb); **shout sth out** to say sth in a loud voice 〜を大きな声で言う→(〜に向かって)…を叫ぶ, 大声で言う ‖ 'Careful,' she shouted. 「気を付けて」と彼女は叫んだ. The students kept shouting out the answers, so we stopped playing in the end. 生徒たちが答えを大声で言い続けるので, ついに一同ゲーム(クイズゲーム)を中止した. The captain shouted instructions to his team. 主将はチームに向かって大声で指示を出した. ☞参 **scream** ― **shout** 名 ❸→叫び, 叫び声, 大声
句動詞 **shout sb down** ▶定義 to shout so that sb who is speaking cannot be heard 話している〜の声が聞こえなくなるように大声を出す→

## 1494　shove

どなって(〜を)黙らせる, 大声で言い負かす ‖ *The speaker was shouted down by a group of protesters.* 演説者は抗議者の一団に大声でやじり倒された.

**shove** /ʃʌv/ 動自他 略式 ▶定義 to push with a sudden, rough movement 出し抜けに荒々しく押す → 〜を手荒く押す, 突く, 押しのける ‖ *Everybody in the crowd was **pushing and shoving**.* 群集が押し合いへし合いしていた. *The policeman shoved the thief into the back of the police car.* 警察官は泥棒をパトカーの後部座席に押し込んだ. — shove 名 [C, 通常は単数] → 一押し, 一突き ‖ *to give sb/sth a shove* 〜をぐいと押す

**shovel** /ʃʌv(ə)l/ 名 C ▶定義 a tool used for picking up and moving earth, snow, sand, etc 土, 雪, 砂などをすくい上げて移すのに用いる道具 → シャベル, スコップ ☞参 spade ☞ garden のさし絵 — shovel 動自他 (shovelling; shovelled: 米 shoveling; shoveled) → シャベルを使う, 〜をシャベルですくう

***show**¹ /ʃoʊ/ 動 (過 **showed**; 過分 **shown** /ʃoʊn/ または **showed**) ▶定義1 ⓦ show sb/sth (to sb); show sb (sth) to let sb see sb/sth 〜に…を見せる → (〜に)…を見せる, 示す ‖ *I showed the letter to him.* 私は手紙を彼に見せた. *I showed him the letter.* 私は彼に手紙を見せた. *She showed me what she had bought.* 彼女は買った物を私に見せた. *They're showing his latest film at our local cinema.* 彼の最新作の映画は地元の映画館で上映中だ. *She was showing signs of stress.* 彼女はストレスの兆候を示していた. *This white T-shirt really shows the dirt.* この白いTシャツは本当に汚れが目立つ. *The picture showed him arguing with a photographer.* その写真には, 彼がカメラマンと口論しているところが写っていた. ▶定義2 ⓦ to make sth clear; to give information about sth 〜を明らかにする; 〜について情報を与える → 〜を示す, 表す, 明らかにする ‖ *Research shows that most people get too little exercise.* 調査は大多数の人の運動量があまりにも少ないことを示している. *This graph shows how prices have gone up in the last few years.* このグラフはここ2, 3年間でどのように物価が上昇したかを示している. ▶定義3 自 to be able to be seen; to appear 見て取ることができる; 現れる → 見える, 表に出る, 現れる ‖ *I tried not to let my disappointment show.* 私は失望が顔に出ないように努めた. ▶定義4 ⓦ to help sb to do sth by doing it yourself; to explain sth 自分でやってみせて〜が…を行うのを助ける; 〜を説明する → (方法など)を示す, 教える; 〜を説明する ‖ *Can you show me how to put the disk in the computer?* コンピューターにディスクを入れる方法を教えていただけますか. ▶定義5 ⓦ to lead sb to or round a place; to explain how to go to a place 人をある場所まで, またはある場所の周辺を案内する; ある場所への行き方を説明する → 〜を案内する; (道などを)教える ‖ *I'll come with you and show you the way.* 一緒に行って道をお教えしましょう. *Shall I show you to your room?* お部屋までご案内しましょうか. *A guide showed us round the museum.* ガイドが美術館を案内してくれた.

句動詞 show (sth) off 略式 ▶定義 to try to impress people by showing them how clever you are or by showing them sth that you are proud of 自分がいかに賢いかを誇示することで, または誇りに思っている〜を見せ付けることで, 人々に強く印象づけようとする → (〜を)見せびらかす, ひけらかす, 誇示する ‖ *John was showing off by driving his new car very fast.* ジョンは新車をすごく速く走らせて見せびらかしていた.

show up 略式 ▶定義 to arrive, especially when sb is expecting you 特に〜が待ち受けているときに到着する → 現れる, 到着する, 顔を出す ‖ *I thought you'd never show up.* 君は絶対来ないと思ったよ.

show (sth) up ▶定義 to allow sth to be seen 〜を見えるようにする → 〜を目立たせる, あらわにする, 暴く ‖ *The sunlight shows up those dirty marks on the window.* 太陽光であの窓の汚れが目立つ.

show sb up 略式 ▶定義 to make sb embarrassed about your behaviour or appearance 自分の振る舞いや外見で〜に恥ずかしい思いをさせる → 〜に恥をかかせる ‖ *He showed her up by shouting at the waiter.* 彼はウエーターをどなりつけて彼女に恥をかかせた.

***show**² /ʃoʊ/ 名 ▶定義1 C a type of entertainment performed for an audience 観客のために行われる娯楽の一種 → 見せ物, 出し物, ショー, 映

画,演劇,番組 ‖ *a TV comedy show* テレビのコメディー番組 *a quiz show* クイズ番組 ▶定義2 ◐◑ an occasion when a collection of things are brought together for people to look at 人々に見せるために物を一堂に集めた催し→展示会,展覧会,品評会 ‖ *a dog show* 犬の品評会 *a fashion show* ファッションショー *Paintings by local children will be **on show** at the town hall next week.* 地域の子供たちのかいた絵が来週公会堂で展示される予定だ. ▶定義3 ◐◑ something that a person does or has in order to make people believe sth that is not true 本物でない〜を人々に本物と思わせるために人がする,または有する何か→見せ掛け,振り ‖ *Although she hated him, she **put on a show of** politeness.* 彼女は彼を嫌っていたが,礼儀正しさを装った. *His bravery is **all show** (=he is not as brave as he pretends to be).* 彼の勇敢さは全くの見せ掛けだ(=彼は見せ掛けているほど勇敢ではない). ▶定義4 [単数扱い] an occasion when you let sb see sth 〜に…を見せること→見せること,示すこと,表示,表明 ‖ *a show of emotion/gratitude/temper* 感激・感謝・怒りを表すこと

**show business** (または 略式 **showbiz**) /ʃóʊbɪz/ 图 ⓤ ▶定義 the business of entertaining people, in the theatre, in films, on television, etc 演劇,映画,テレビなどで人を楽しませる産業→娯楽産業,ショービジネス,芸能界 ‖ *He's been **in show business** since he was five years old.* 彼は5歳のときから芸能界にいる.

**showdown** /ʃóʊdaʊn/ 图 ⓒ ▶定義 a final argument, meeting or fight at the end of a long disagreement 長い不和の末の最後の論争,話し合い,勝負→土壇場,大詰め,決着 ‖ *The management are preparing for a showdown with the union.* 経営陣は組合との最終対決に備えている.

\***shower**¹ /ʃáʊər/ 图 ⓒ ▶定義1 a piece of equipment that produces a spray of water that you stand under to wash; the small room or part of a room that contains a shower 水しぶきを出す装置,その下に立って体を洗う; シャワーのある小さな部屋または部屋の一部→シャワー,シャワー室 ‖ *The shower doesn't work.* シャワーが故障している. *She's in the shower.* 彼女はシャワーを浴びているところだ. *I'd like a room with a shower, please.* シャワー付きの部屋をお願いします. ☛ C7 ページのさし絵 ▶定義2 an act of

# show-off 1495

washing yourself by standing under a shower シャワーの下に立って体を洗う行為→シャワーを浴びること ‖ *I'll just **have a** quick **shower** then we can go out.* 急いでシャワーを浴びてくるから,その後一緒に出掛けよう. ▶定義3 a short period of rain 短時間の雨→にわか雨,短時間の雨,驟雨(しゅうう) ☛参 **rain**, **acid rain** ▶定義4 a lot of very small objects that fall or fly through the air together 一斉に空中から落下,または空中を飛翔(ひしょう)するたくさんの微小な物体→(〜の)雨,多量(の),(〜の)洪水 ‖ *a shower of sparks/broken glass* 降り注ぐ火の粉・ガラスの破片の雨

**shower**² /ʃáʊər/ 動 ▶定義1 ⓘ ⓣ **shower (down) on sb/sth; shower sb with sth** to cover sb/sth with a lot of small falling objects たくさんの小さな落下物で〜を覆う→雨のように注ぐ; 〜に…を雨のように与える・ばらまく・浴びせる ‖ *Ash from the volcano showered down on the town.* 火山灰が街に雨のように降り注いだ. *People suffered cuts after being showered with broken glass.* 人々はガラスの破片を浴びて切り傷を負った. ▶定義2 ⓘ to wash yourself under a shower シャワーで体を洗う→シャワーを浴びる ‖ *I came back from my run, showered and got changed.* ジョギングの後帰宅し,シャワーを浴びて服を着替えた.

**showing** /ʃóʊɪŋ/ 图 ▶定義1 ⓒ an act of showing a film, etc 映画などを見せる行為→上映,上演,展示 ‖ *The second showing of the film begins at 8 o'clock.* その映画の第2回目の上映は8時に始まる. ▶定義2 [単数扱い] how sb/sth behaves; how successful sb/sth is 〜の働き具合; 〜の出来栄え→情勢,出来栄え,成績 ‖ *On its present showing, the party should win the election.* 現状からすると,その政党は選挙に勝つはずだ.

**showjumping** /ʃóʊdʒʌmpɪŋ/ 图 ⓤ ▶定義 a competition in which a person rides a horse over a series of fences (jumps) 人が馬に乗って一連の柵(さく)(障害物)を越える競技→障害飛越(ひえつ)馬術競技

**shown** SHOW¹ の過去分詞形

**show-off** /ʃóʊ(ː)f/ 图 ⓒ ▶定義 a person who tries to impress others by showing them how clever he/she is, or by showing them sth he/she is proud of 自分がいかに賢いかを誇示したり,自慢の～を見せ付けたりして,人々に強く印象づけようとする人➡見せびらかす人,自慢屋,目立ちたがり ‖ *She's such a show-off, always boasting about how good she is at this and that.* 彼女は大変な目立ちたがり屋で,自分が何やかやといかに有能か,いつも自慢ばかりしている.

**showroom** /ʃóʊrùːm, -ròm/ 名 **C** ▶定義 a type of large shop where customers can look at goods such as cars, furniture and electrical items that are on sale 客が自動車,家具,電気製品などの商品を見ることのできる大型店舗➡商品陳列室,展示室,ショールーム

**shrank** SHRINK の過去形

**shrapnel** /ʃræpnl/ 名 **U** ▶定義 small pieces of metal that fly around when a bomb explodes 爆弾が爆発したときに飛び散る小さな金属片➡榴散(りゅうさん)弾・爆弾・地雷の破片

**shred**¹ /ʃred/ 名 ▶定義 **1 C** a small thin piece of material that has been cut or torn off 切り落とされたり引きちぎられたりした小さな薄い断片➡切れ端,破片,断片 ‖ *His clothes were torn to shreds by the rose bushes.* バラの茂みで彼の服はビリビリに引き裂かれた. ▶定義 **2** a shred of sth [単数扱い] (否定文で) a very small amount of sth 非常に少量の～➡わずか,少量,ほんの少し ‖ *There wasn't a shred of truth in her story.* 彼女の話には真実のかけらもなかった.

**shred**² /ʃred/ 動 **他** (**shredding**; **shredded**) ▶定義 to tear or cut sth into shreds ～をずたずたに引き裂く・切り刻む➡～をずたずたにする,断片に切る,シュレッダーにかける ‖ *shredded cabbage* キャベツの千切り

**shrewd** /ʃruːd/ 形 ▶定義 able to make good decisions because you understand a situation well 状況をよく理解して正しい決定を下すことのできる➡洞察力のある,鋭い,賢い,頭の切れる,抜け目のない ‖ *a shrewd thinker/decision* 洞察力に富んだ思想家・賢い決定 — shrewdly 副➡鋭く,そつなく,如才なく

**shriek** /ʃriːk/ 動 ▶定義 **1 自** to make a short, loud, noise in a high voice 甲高い声で短く大きな音を出す➡悲鳴を上げる,金切り声を出す,甲高い声を出す ‖ *She shrieked in fright.* 彼女は恐怖のため悲鳴を上げた. *The children were shrieking with laughter.* 子供たちはけたたましく笑っていた. ▶定義 **2 他** to say sth loudly in a high voice 甲高い声で～を大声で言う➡～を甲高い声で言う,金切り声で言う ‖ *'Stop it!' she shrieked.*「やめて」と彼女は金切り声で言った. ☛参 screech — shriek 名 **C** ➡悲鳴,金切り声,甲高い声

**shrill** /ʃrɪl/ 形 ▶定義 (used about a sound) high and unpleasant (音について) 高くて不快な➡甲高い,金切り声の,鋭い ‖ *a shrill cry* 甲高い叫び声

**shrimp** /ʃrɪmp/ 名 **C** ▶定義 a small sea creature with a shell and a lot of legs that turns pink when you cook it 火を通すとピンク色に変わる,殻と多数の足を持った小さな海の生物➡小エビ,エビ

➤ shrimp は prawn よりも小さい.

☛ shellfish のさし絵

**shrine** /ʃraɪn/ 名 **C** ▶定義 a place that is important to a particular person or group of people for religious reasons or because it is connected with a special person 宗教的な理由から,または特定の人物との結び付きのために,ある人または人々の集団にとって重要な場所➡聖堂,聖廟(びよう),聖地

'Oh no! My T-shirt has **shrunk**!'

'Oh no! My T-shirt has **stretched**!'

**shrink** /ʃrɪŋk/ (過去 **shrank** /ʃræŋk/ または **shrunk** /ʃrʌŋk/; 過分 **shrunk**) ▶動 ▶定義1 ⾃他 to become smaller or make sth smaller 小さくなる; ～を小さくする→**小さくなる, 縮む; ～を小さくする, 縮ませる** ‖ *My T-shirt shrank in the wash.* 洗濯で T シャツが縮んでしまった. *Television has shrunk the world.* テレビのお陰で世界が小さくなった. *The rate of inflation has shrunk to 4%.* インフレ率が4パーセントに縮小している.

▶定義2 ⾃ to move back because you are frightened or shocked 恐怖や衝撃を受けたために後ろに下がる→**後ずさりする, たじろぐ, ひるむ** ‖ *We shrank back against the wall when the dog appeared.* 犬が出てきたので, 私たちは後ずさりして壁に身を押し付けた.

**句動詞** shrink from sth/doing sth ▶定義 to not want to do sth because you find it unpleasant 不快な事なのでやりたくない→**～を避ける, しりごみする;(～すること)を嫌がる**

**shrivel** /ʃrɪ́v(ə)l/ 動⾃他 ( **shrivelling**; **shrivelled**; 米 **shriveling**; **shriveled**) ▶定義 shrivel (sth) (up) to become smaller, especially because of dry conditions 特に乾燥した状況のために小さくなる→**しなびる, しぼむ, 縮む; ～をしなびさせる** ‖ *The plants shrivelled up and died in the hot weather.* 暑さで植物がしなびて枯れた.

**shroud**¹ /ʃraʊd/ 名 C ▶定義 a cloth or sheet that is put round a dead body before it is buried 埋葬の前に, 遺体に巻き付ける布やシーツ→**死体を包む布, 屍衣(しい)**

**shroud**² /ʃraʊd/ 動他 ▶定義 shroud sth (in sth) (通常は受動態で) to cover or hide sth ～を覆う, 隠す→**～を(…で)覆う, 覆い隠す**

**Shrove Tuesday** /ʃroʊv t(j)uːzdi, -deɪ/ 名 C ▶定義 the day before a period of forty days (Lent) during which some Christians do not eat certain foods 一部のキリスト教徒が特定の食べ物を口にしない40日間(四旬節)の始まる前日→**告解火曜日, ざんげ火曜日**

▶一部の国では, 告解火曜日の前の期間を carnival (カーニバル) として祝う. イギリスでは, 多くの人たちがこの日に pancakes (パンケーキ) を食べる.

**shrub** /ʃrʌb/ 名 C ▶定義 a small bush 小さな潅木(かんぼく)→**潅木, 低木**

**shrubbery** /ʃrʌ́b(ə)ri/ 名 C ( 複 **shrubberies**) ▶定義 an area where a lot of small bushes have been planted たくさんの低木が植えられている場所→**低木の林, 低木の植え込み**

**shrug** /ʃrʌɡ/ 動⾃他 ( **shrugging**; **shrugged**) ▶定義 to lift your shoulders as a way of showing that you do not know sth or are not interested ～を知らない, または～に興味がないことを示す方法として肩を持ち上げる→**(肩を)すくめる** ‖ *'Who knows?' he said and shrugged.*「そんな事だれが知るかい(= だれも知らない)」と言って彼は肩をすくめた. *'It doesn't matter to me,' he said, shrugging his shoulders.*「僕には関係ないさ」と彼は肩をすくめながら言った.

☛ S6 ページのさし絵 - shrug 名 C ▶**肩をすくめること** ‖ *I asked him if he was sorry and he just answered with a shrug.* 後悔しているのかと尋ねると, 彼はただ肩をすくめて見せた.

---

▶コミュニケーション

「すくめた肩」は無関心・無力のしぐさ

shrug one's shoulder(s): 両腕または片方の肩をすくめて,「仕方ない」(I can't help it)「どうでもよい」(I don't care)「分からない」(I don't know)など, 無関心, 無力, あきらめを表す動作. 肩をすくめるとき, 同時にてのひらを相手側に広げます. このてのひらを上向きに示す動作は, 英米では自分の立場の弱さを認めるしぐさとされ,「これこの通り」と無防備な自分をさらけ出しているのがこの動作の特徴です. 日本人の, 無力で「肩身が狭い」といった「縮み」感覚からは出てこないしぐさでしょう.

---

**句動詞** shrug sth off ▶定義 to not allow sth to affect you in a bad way ～が自分に悪影響を及ぼさないようにする→**～をあっさりと片付ける, 無視する, 軽視する** ‖ *An actor has to learn to shrug off criticism.* 俳優は批判を受け流すすべを学ばなければならない.

**shrunk** ⇒ SHRINK

**shudder** /ʃʌ́dər/ 動⾃ ▶定義 to suddenly shake hard, especially because of an unpleasant feeling or thought 特に不快な感情や考えによって突然激しく震える→**震える, 身震いする, ぞっとする, 身の毛がよだつ** ‖ *Just to think about the acci-*

dent makes me shudder. その事故のことを考えるだけでぞっとする. *The engine shuddered violently and then stopped.* エンジンが激しく震動して止まった. — shudder 名 C →身震い, 戦慄(せんりつ), 震え, 震動

**shuffle**[1] /ʃʌf(ə)l/ 動 ▶定義1 自 to walk by sliding your feet along instead of lifting them off the ground 地面から足を持ち上げずに引きずって歩く →足を引きずって歩く ‖ *The child shuffled past, wearing her mother's shoes.* 子供は母親の靴を履いて, 引きずるように歩きながら通り過ぎていった. ▶定義2 自他 to move your body or feet around because you are uncomfortable or nervous 居心地が悪いまたは神経質になっているため, 体や足をもぞもぞ動かす →もぞもぞ動く; ~をもぞもぞ動かす ‖ *The audience were so bored that they began to shuffle in their seats.* 聴衆は退屈のあまり座席でもぞもぞし始めた. ▶定義3 自他 to mix a pack of playing cards before a game ゲームを始める前にトランプを切る →(トランプを)切る, シャッフルする ‖ *It's your turn to shuffle.* あなたがトランプを切る番ですよ. *She shuffled the cards carefully.* 彼女は慎重にトランプを切った.

**shuffle**[2] /ʃʌf(ə)l/ 名 [C, 通常は単数] ▶定義1 a way of walking without lifting your feet off the ground 地面から足を持ち上げない歩き方 →足を引きずって歩くこと ▶定義2 an act of shuffling cards トランプを切る行為 →トランプを切ること, シャッフル

**shun** /ʃʌn/ 動 他 (**shunning**; **shunned**) (文) ▶定義 to avoid sb/sth; to keep away from sb/sth ~を避ける; ~に近寄らない →~を避ける, 遠ざける ‖ *She was shunned by her family when she married him.* 彼と結婚して, 彼女は家族から疎外されてしまった.

*__shut__[1] /ʃʌt/ 動 (現分 **shutting**; 過, 過分 **shut**) ▶定義1 自他 to make sth closed; to become closed ~を閉める; 閉まる →閉まる, 閉じる; ~を閉める, 閉じる ‖ *Could you shut the door, please?* ドアを閉めていただけませんか. *I can't shut my suitcase.* スーツケースが閉まらないのよ. *Shut your books, please.* 本を閉じてください. *He shut his eyes and tried to go to sleep.* 彼は目を閉じて眠ろうとした. *This window won't shut properly.* この窓はきちんと閉まらない. *The doors open and shut automatically.* ドアは自動的に開閉します. ▶定義2 自他 (used about a shop, restaurant, etc) to stop doing business for the day; to close (店, レストランなどについて)1日の業務を終了する; 閉める →(店などを)閉店する, 営業をやめる ‖ *What time do the shops shut on Saturday?* 商店は土曜日には何時に閉店するのですか. ▶定義3 他 to prevent sb/sth from leaving a place; to close a door on sth ~がある場所を出ていけないようにする; ~の上に戸を閉める →~を閉じ込める, 締め出す; ~を(…に)挟む ‖ *She shut herself in her room and refused to come out.* 彼女は部屋に閉じこもり, 出てくることを拒んだ. *Tony shut his fingers in the door of the car.* トニーは車のドアに指を挟んだ.

**句動詞** **shut sb/sth away** ▶定義 to keep sb/sth in a place where people cannot find or see him/her/it 人に見つからない場所に~を置く →~を閉じ込める, 隔離する

**shut (sth) down** ▶定義 (used about a factory, etc) to close for a long time or for ever (工場などについて)長期間または永久に閉める →(店などを)閉店する, 閉鎖する, 廃業する ‖ *Financial problems forced the business to shut down.* 財政難で, 会社は閉鎖に追い込まれた.

**shut sb/sth off (from sth)** ▶定義 to keep sb/sth apart from sth ~を…から遠ざける →~を(…から)切り離す, 隔離する, 隔絶する ‖ *He shuts himself off from the rest of the world.* 彼は世間から遠ざかっている.

**shut sb/sth out** ▶定義 to keep sb/sth out ~を締め出す →~を締め出す, 追い出す, 排除する ‖ *He tried to shut out all thoughts of the accident.* 彼は事故のことは一切考えまいとした.

**shut (sb) up** 略式 ▶定義1 to stop talking; to be quiet 話すのをやめる; 静かにする →黙る, 沈黙する ‖ *I wish you'd shut up!* 静かにしてください. ▶定義2 to make sb stop talking ~に話をやめさせる →~を黙らせる

**shut sb/sth up (in sth)** ▶定義 to put sb/sth somewhere and stop him/her leaving ~をどこかに入れてそこから離れないようにする →~を(…に)閉じ込める, 監禁する ‖ *He was shut up in prison for nearly ten years.* 彼は10年近くも刑務所に入れられていた.

**shut**² /ʃʌt/ 形 (名詞の前は不可) ▶定義1 in a closed position 閉まった状態の→**閉じた, 閉まっている** ‖ *Make sure the door is shut properly before you leave.* 出る前にドアがきちんと閉まっているか確認しなさい.

► closed は名詞の前で使用する (a closed door = 閉まっているドア) ことができるが, shut はできない.

▶定義2 not open to the public 一般に公開されていない→**開いていない** ‖ *The restaurant was shut so we went to one round the corner.* そのレストランは閉まっていたので, 私たちは角のレストランに行った.

成句 keep your mouth shut ⇒ **MOUTH**¹

**shutter** /ʃʌtər/ 名 C ▶定義1 a wooden or metal cover that is fixed outside a window and that can be opened or shut. A shop's shutter usually slides down from the top of the shop window. 窓の外側に固定され, 開閉することのできる木製または金属製の覆い. 通常, 店のシャッターはショーウインドーの上から下にスライドする→**よろい戸, 雨戸, シャッター** ☛ **curtain** のさし絵 ▶定義2 the part at the front of a camera that opens for a very short time to let light in so that a photograph can be taken カメラの正面にある部品. ここが短時間開いて光が入り, 写真が撮れるようになっている→**シャッター**

**shuttle** /ʃʌtl/ 名 C ▶定義 a plane, bus or train that travels regularly between two places 2地点間を定期的に運行する飛行機, バス, 列車→**定期往復便, 折り返し運転**

**shuttlecock** /ʃʌtlkɑ̀k/ 名 C ▶定義 (in the sport of badminton) the small, light object that is hit over the net (バドミントンの競技で) ネット越しに打つ小さな軽い物体→**バドミントンの羽根, シャトルコック** ☛ S1 ページのさし絵

*****shy**¹ /ʃaɪ/ 形 ▶定義1 nervous and uncomfortable about meeting and speaking to people; showing that sb feels like this 人に会ったり話したりすることに神経質で不安な; このように感じることを見せている→**恥ずかしがりの, 内気な, 引っ込み思案の; 恥ずかしそうな** ‖ *She's very shy with strangers.* 彼女は知らない人にひどく人見知りする. *a shy smile* はにかんだ笑い ▶定義2 shy (of/about sth/doing sth) frightened to do sth or to become involved in sth ～をしたり, ～に巻き込まれることを恐れる→**(～を・～すること**を)ためらう, (～を)したがらない ‖ *She's not shy of telling people what she thinks.* 彼女は自分の考えをおくさずに人に言う. — **shyly** 副 →**恥ずかしそうに, はにかんで** — **shyness** 名 U →**内気, はにかみ, おくびょう** ‖ *He didn't overcome his shyness till he had left school.* 彼は学校を出るまで内気な性格を克服できなかった.

**shy**² /ʃaɪ/ 動 (現分 **shying**; 三単現 **shies**; 過, 過分 **shied**) 自 ▶定義 (used about a horse) to suddenly move back or sideways in fear (馬について) 恐怖のため突然後ろにがったり横に移動する→**後ずさりする**

句動詞 shy away from sth/from doing sth ▶定義 to avoid doing sth because you are afraid 恐れて～するのを避ける→**～を避ける, ～にしりごみする, おじけづく**

**sibling** /sɪ́blɪŋ/ 名 C 正式 ▶定義 a brother or a sister 兄, 弟, 姉, 妹→**兄弟, 兄弟姉妹** ☛ 普通の表現では brother(s) and sister(s) を用いる. *Have you got any brothers and sisters?* 兄弟はいますか.

*****sick**¹ /sɪk/ 形 ▶定義1 not well; ill 健康でない; 病気の→**具合が悪い; 病気の** ‖ *a sick child* 病気の子供 *Do you get paid for days when you're off sick (= from work)?* 病気で (= 仕事を) 休んでいる期間も, 給料は払われるのですか. *You're too ill to work today - you should phone in sick.* 今日あなたはとても具合が悪くて仕事は無理ですよ － 病欠の電話を入れるべきだ.

► イギリス英語では be sick は通常「食べた物を吐く, ～を吐する」を意味する.

▶定義2 the sick 名 [複数扱い] people who are ill 病気の人々→**病人** ▶定義3 feeling ill in your stomach so that you may bring up food through your mouth (**vomit**) 食べ物を吐く (おう吐する) そうなほど胃にむかつきを感じる→**むかついて, 吐き気がして, 気持ちが悪い** ‖ *I feel sick - I think it was that fish I ate.* 吐き気がする － 食べた魚のせいではないかと思う. *Don't eat any more or you'll make yourself sick.* これ以上食べると気分が悪くなりますよ. ☛参 **nausea**, **travel-sick**, **seasick**, **airsick**, **carsick** ▶定義4 sick of sb/sth feeling bored or annoyed because you have had too much of sb/sth ～とあまりに多くかかわったため, うん

# 1500 sick²

ざりしたり、嫌気が差して→～に飽き飽きして、うんざりして、嫌気がして ‖ *I'm sick of my job.* 自分の仕事に嫌気が差している. *I'm sick of tidying up your mess!* あなたの散らかした後を片付けるのにはもううんざりだ. ▶定義5 **sick (at/about sth)** very annoyed or disgusted by sth →にいらいらして、気分を害して、嫌気が差して→**うんざりして、嫌気がして** ‖ *He felt sick at the sight of so much waste.* 彼はあまりの浪費を目の当たりにしてうんざりした. ▶定義6 略式 mentioning disease, suffering, death, etc in a cruel or disgusting way 病気、苦しみ、死などについてむごい、またはひどい口のきき方をして→**病的な、不健全な、悪趣味の** ‖ *He offended everyone with a sick joke about blind people.* 彼は盲人について趣味の悪い冗談を言って皆の気分を害した.

成句 **be sick** ▶定義 to bring up food from the stomach; vomit 胃から食べ物を戻す; おう吐する→**吐く、おう吐する、戻す** ‖ *It's common for women to be sick in the first months of pregnancy.* 妊娠初期の数か月間に女性が吐いたりするのはよくある事だ.

**make sb sick** ▶定義 to make sb very angry ～を非常に怒らせる→**～を怒らせる、むかつかせる、不快にする** ‖ *Oh, stop complaining. You make me sick!* もう不平はやめて. あなたにはもううんざりよ.

**sick to death of sb/sth** ▶定義 feeling tired of or annoyed by sb/sth ～に飽き飽きする、うんざりする→**～に嫌気が差す、すっかり嫌になる** ‖ *I'm sick to death of his grumbling.* 彼の不平不満に全くうんざりしている.

**sick²** /sík/ 名 Ⓤ ▶定義 food that sb has brought up from his/her stomach; vomit 人が胃から吐き戻した食べ物; ヘド→**吐いた物、吐しゃ物、おう吐** ‖ *There was sick all over the car seat.* 吐いた物が車の座席一面に広がっていた.

**sicken** /síkən/ 動 Ⓣ ▶定義 to make sb feel disgusted ～を嫌な気分にさせる→**～をうんざりさせる、～に吐き気を催させる** ‖ *The sight of people fighting sickens me.* 人々がけんかしているのを見ると、むかむかする. — **sickening** 形→**吐き気を催させる、むかつくような; 腹の立つ** ‖ *His head made a sickening sound as it hit the road.* 彼の頭は道路に打ち付けられて胸が悪くなるような嫌な音を立てた.

**sick leave** 名 Ⓤ ▶定義 a period spent away from work, etc because of illness 病気のため仕事などから離れている期間→**病気休暇(期間)** ‖ *Mike's been off on sick leave since March.* マイクは3月から病気で休んでいる.

**sickly** /síkli/ 形 ▶定義1 (used about a person) weak and often ill (人について)弱くて病気がちの→**病弱な、病気がちの、病身の** ‖ *a sickly child* 病弱な子供 ▶定義2 unpleasant; causing you to feel ill 不快な; 気分を悪くさせる→**不快な、吐き気を催させる、むかつく** ‖ *the sickly smell of rotten fruit* 腐った果物の嫌なにおい

**sickness** /síknəs/ 名 ▶定義1 Ⓤthe state of being ill 病気の状態→**病気、不健康** ‖ *A lot of workers are absent because of sickness.* 病気のため多くの作業員が欠勤している. ▶定義2 Ⓤa feeling in your stomach that may make you bring up food through your mouth 食べ物を戻してしまいそうな胃の感じ→**吐き気、むかつき** ‖ *Symptoms of the disease include sickness and diarrhoea.* その病気の症状には吐き気と下痢がある. ▶定義3 ⒸⓊa particular type of illness ある特定の種類の病気→**病気、～病** ‖ *pills for seasickness* 船酔いのための薬 *Sleeping sickness is carried by the tsetse fly.* 眠り病はツェツェバエによって媒介される.

★**side¹** /sáid/ 名 Ⓒ ▶定義1 one of the flat outer surfaces of sth 〜の外郭を成す平面の1つ→**面** ‖ *A cube has six sides.* 立方体には面が6つある. ▶定義2 **-sided**(複合形容詞を作るために用いて) having the number of sides mentioned 言及された数の面を持つ→**〜面の、〜面体の、〜辺の、〜側の** ‖ *a six-sided coin* 六角形の硬貨 ▶定義3 one of the surfaces of sth except the top, bottom, front or back 〜の上下、または前後以外の面の1つ→**側面、わき、側** ‖ *I went round to the side of the building.* 私は建物のわきに回った. *The side of the car was damaged.* 車の側面が破損した. ▶定義4 the edge of sth, away from the middle 〜の中心から離れた端の部分→**わき、端、縁** ‖ *Make sure you stay at the side of the road when you're cycling.* 自転車に乗っているときは道路わきから離れないようにしなさい. *We moved to one side to let the doctor get past.* 私たちは医者が通れるようにわきに寄っ

た. ▶定義5 the area to the left or right of sth; the area in front of or behind sth 〜の左または右側; 〜の前または後側 →側, 部分, 地域 ‖ We live (on) **the other side** of the main road. 私たちは本通りの向こう側に住んでいる. It's more expensive to live on the north side of town. 街の北側の方が生活費は高い. In Japan they drive on **the left-hand side** of the road. 日本では車は左側通行だ. She sat at the side of his bed/at his bedside. 彼女は彼のベッドの傍らに腰掛けた. ▶定義6 either of the two flat surfaces of sth thin 薄い〜の2つの平らな表面のうちの1つ→**面, 表, 裏** ‖ Write on both sides of the paper. 書類の両面に記入しなさい. ▶定義7 the right or the left part of your body, especially from under your arm to the top of your leg 特にわきの下から太ももの付け根までの体の左右いずれかの側面 →わき腹, 横腹 ‖ She lay on her side. 彼女は横向きに寝た. The soldier stood with his hands by his sides. その兵士は手を両わきに付けて立っていた. ▶定義8 either of two or more people or groups who are fighting, playing, arguing, etc against each other 互いに戦闘・競技・論争などをしている2人以上の人または集団のいずれか一方 →**側, 派, 組, チーム** ‖ The two sides agreed to stop fighting. 双方は停戦することに合意した. the winning/losing side 勝った側・負けた側 Whose side are you on? (= Who do you want to win?) あなたはどちらの味方ですか(=だれに勝ってもらいたいのか). ▶定義9 what is said by one person or group that is different from what is said by another ほかの人・集団と異なる言い分 →**面, 側, 局面** ‖ I don't know whose **side of the story** to believe. どちらの側の話を信じたらよいのか分からない. ▶定義10 your mother's or your father's family 母方または父方の家族 →〜方(かた), 〜系, 系統 ‖ There is no history of illness **on his mother's side**. 彼の母方には病歴はない.

成句 get on the right/wrong side of sb ▶定義 to please/annoy sb 〜を喜ばせる・いら立たせる →〜に気に入られる, 好かれる・〜に嫌われる, 〜の不興を買う ‖ He tried to get on the right side of his new boss. 彼は新しい上司に気に入られようと努めた.

look on the bright side ⇒ **LOOK**¹

on/from all sides; on/from every side ▶定義 in/from all directions あらゆる方向に[から] →四方八方に[から], 至る所に[から]

on the big, small, high, etc side 略式 ▶定義 slightly too big, small, high, etc 少し大きすぎる, 小さすぎる, 高すぎるなど →いくぶん〜で, 〜気味で

on the safe side ⇒ **SAFE**¹

put sth on/to one side; leave sth on one side ▶定義 to leave or keep sth so that you can use it or deal with it later 後で利用・対処できるように〜を残しておく, 取っておく →〜を傍らによけておく, 取っておく, 〜を棚上げにする ‖ You should put some money to one side for the future. あなたは将来のために金をいくらか取っておくべきだ.

side by side ▶定義 next to each other; close together 互いに隣り合って, 互いに接近して →**並んで, 平行して, 一緒に** ‖ They walked side by side along the road. 彼らは横に並んで道を歩いた.

take sides (with sb) ▶定義 to show that you support one person rather than another in an argument 議論で一方の側を支援することを示す →**一方を支持する, 〜の側に立つ, (〜に)味方する** ‖ Parents should never take sides when their children are quarrelling. 子供たちのけんかで, 親は絶対に一方の味方をすべきではない.

**side**² /sáid/ 動

句動詞 side with sb (against sb) ▶定義 to support sb in an argument 議論で〜を支持する →〜の側に立つ, 〜の味方をする

**sideboard** /sáidbɔːrd/ 名 C ▶定義 a type of low cupboard about as high as a table, that is used for storing plates, etc in a room that is used for eating (dining room) 食卓とほぼ同じ高さの丈の低い食器棚. 食事する部屋(食堂)で皿などの収納に使われる →食器棚, 食器台, サイドボード ☛ C7 ページのさし絵

**sideburns** /sáidbɜːrnz/ 名 [複数扱い] ▶定義 hair that grows down a man's face in front of his ears 男性の耳の前からほおにかけて生えている毛 →短いほおひげ; もみあげ

**side effect** 名 C ▶定義1 the unpleasant effect that a drug may have in addition to its useful effects 薬の有益な作用に加えて, 起きることの

**1502 sideline**

ある好ましくない作用→**副作用** ‖ *Side effects of the drug include nausea and dizziness.* その薬の副作用には吐き気とめまいがある. ▶定義2 an unexpected effect of sth that happens in addition to the intended effect 意図した通りの結果とは別に生じ得る予期しない結果→**思わぬ結果, 副産物** ‖ *One of the side effects when the chemical factory closed was that fish returned to the river.* その化学工場が閉鎖されたときの思わぬ結果の1つは, 川に魚が戻ったことだった.

**sideline** /sáɪdlàɪn/ 名 ▶定義1 C something that you do in addition to your regular job, especially to earn extra money 特に余分な収入を得るため, 本業のほかに行う仕事→**副業, アルバイト, 内職** ‖ *He's an engineer, but he repairs cars as a sideline.* 彼は技術者だが, 副業として自動車を修理している. ▶定義2 **sidelines** [複数扱い] the lines that mark the two long sides of the area used for playing sports such as football, tennis, etc; the area behind this フットボール, テニスなどの競技区画の両わきを示す2本の線; この線の外側の領域→**サイドライン; サイドラインの外側**
成句 **on the sidelines** ▶定義 not involved in an activity; not taking part in sth 活動に携わっていない; 〜に参加していない→**傍観して, 試合に出ないで**

**sidelong** /sáɪdlɔ̀(ː)ŋ, -làn/ 形 ▶定義 directed from the side; sideways 横から向けられた; 横向きの→**横の, 横に向けた, 斜めの** ‖ *a sidelong glance* 横目

**side road** 名 C ▶定義 a small road which joins a bigger main road より大きな本線に合流する小さな道路→**わき道, 間道**

**side street** 名 C ▶定義 a narrow or less important street near a main street 本通りのそばにある狭い, またはあまり重要でない通り→**横丁, わき道, 横通り**

**sidetrack** /sáɪdtræk/ 動他 (通常は受動態で) ▶定義 to make sb forget what he/she is doing or talking about and start doing or talking about sth less important 今している事や話している事を〜に忘れさせ, より重要でない…をしたり, 話し始めさせたりする→**(人の話・活動)をわき道にそらす, 脱線させる**

**sidewalk** /sáɪdwɔ̀ːk/ 米 = **PAVEMENT**

**sideways** /sáɪdweɪz/ 副形 ▶定義1 to, towards or from one side 一方の側へ(向けて), または一方の側から→**横の, 横に, 横へ, 横から, 斜めの, 斜めに** ‖ *He jumped sideways to avoid being hit.* 彼は殴られまいと横に跳びのいた. ▶定義2 with one of the sides at the top 片側を上にして→**片側を上に向けて, 横に向けて, 横ざまに** ‖ *We'll have to turn the sofa sideways to get it through the door.* このドアからソファーを出すには横に倒さなければならないだろう.

**sidle** /sáɪdl/ 動自 ▶定義 **sidle up/over (to sb/sth)** to move towards sb/sth in a nervous way, as if you do not want anyone to notice you だれにも気付かれたくないかのようにびくびくしながら〜の方に進む→**こそこそ歩く, 忍び寄る**

**siege** /siːdʒ/ 名 C U ▶定義 a situation in which an army surrounds a town for a long time or the police surround a building so that nobody can get in or out だれも出入りできないように軍隊が長期間町を囲む, または警察が建物を囲む状況→**(警察による建物の)包囲; 包囲攻撃, 包囲期間**

**siesta** /siéstə/ 名 C ▶定義 a short sleep or rest that people take in the afternoon, especially in hot countries 特に暑い国で人々が午後に取る短い睡眠や休憩→**シエスタ, 昼寝, 午睡, 昼休み** ‖ *to have/take a siesta* シエスタを取る

**sieve** /sɪv/ 名 C ▶定義 a type of kitchen tool that has a metal or plastic net, used for separating solids from liquids or very small pieces of food from large pieces 金属製またはプラスチック製の網の付いた台所用具. 固体と液体とを分離したり, 食物を非常に細かい物と大きな物とに分離するのに使われる→**ふるい, こし器, 裏ごし器, ざる** ‖ *Pour the soup through a sieve to get rid of any lumps.* 塊を取り除くため, スープをこし器にかけてください. ☞ **kitchen** のさし絵 — sieve 動他 〜をふるいにかける, こす, 裏ごしする ‖ *to sieve flour* 小麦粉をふるう

**sift** /sɪft/ 動 ▶定義1 他 to pass flour, sugar or a similar substance through a kitchen tool (a sieve) in order to remove any lumps 塊を取り除くため小麦粉や砂糖などを台所用具(ふるい)に通す→**〜をふるう, ふるいにかける, ふるい分ける** ‖ *to sift flour/sugar* 小麦粉・砂糖をふるう
▶定義2 自他 **sift (through) sth** to examine sth very carefully 非常に慎重に〜を検査する→

(証拠など)を厳密に調べる; 精査する ‖ *It took weeks to sift through all the evidence.* すべての証拠を厳密に調べるのに何週間もかかった.

\***sigh** /sái/ 動 ▶定義1 📵 to let out a long, deep breath that shows you are tired, sad, disappointed, etc 疲労, 悲嘆, 失望などを示す長くて深い息をつく→ため息をつく, 吐息をつく ‖ *She sighed with disappointment at the news.* 彼女はその知らせに失望してため息をついた. ▶定義2 📵 to say sth with a sigh ため息をつきながら~を言う→~をため息混じりに言う, 嘆息して語る ‖ *'I'm so tired,' he sighed.* 「とても疲れた」と彼はため息混じりに言った. ▶定義3 📵 to make a long sound like a sigh ため息のような長い音を出す→(風などが)そよぐ, ため息のような音を立てる ― sigh 名 📵→ため息, 吐息

成句 heave a sigh ⇒ **HEAVE**[1]

\***sight**[1] /sáit/ 名 ▶定義1 🅄 the ability to see 見る能力→視力, 視覚 ‖ *He lost his sight in the war (= he became blind).* 彼は戦争で視力を失った (= 失明した). *My grandmother has very poor sight.* 私の祖母は目がひどく悪い. ▶定義2 **-sighted**(複合形容詞を作るために用いて)having eyes that are weak in a particular way ある特定の点で弱い目をした→視力が~の ‖ *I'm short-sighted/long-sighted.* 私は近視・遠視だ.

▶定義3 [単数扱い] **the sight of sb/sth** the act of seeing sb/sth ~を見る行為→~を見ること, ~が見えること ‖ *I feel ill **at the sight of** blood.* 私は血を見ると気分が悪くなる. ▶定義4 🅄 a position where sb/sth can be seen ~が見える所→視界, 視野, 見える範囲 ‖ *They waited until the plane was **in/within sight** and then fired.* 彼らは飛行機が視界に入るまで待って, それから発砲した. *When we get over this hill the town should **come into sight.*** この丘を越えれば街が見えるはずだ. *She didn't let the child **out of** her **sight.*** 彼女は子供から目を離さなかった. ▶定義5 📵something that you see 見える~→景色, 光景, 眺め ‖ *The burned-out building was a terrible sight.* 焼き尽くされた建物は悲惨な光景だった. ▶定義6 **sights**[複数扱い] places of interest that are often visited by tourists 観光客がよく訪れる名所→名所, 観光地 ‖ *When you come to New York I'll show you the sights.* ニューヨークにいらしたときには, 名所にご案内しましょう. ▶定義7 **a sight**[単数扱い] 略式 a per-

---

sign[1] 1503

son or thing that looks strange or amusing 様子の奇妙な, おかしな~→見物, 物笑いの種 ▶定義8 [📵, 通常は複数]the part of a gun that you look through in order to aim it ねらいを定めるためにのぞく銃の部分→照準器, 照準, ねらい

成句 at first glance/sight ⇒ **FIRST**[1]
catch sight/a glimpse of sb/sth ⇒ **CATCH**[1]
in sight ▶定義 likely to happen or come soon すぐに起こりそうで, 来そうで→(結末などが)近付いて, 間近で ‖ *A peace settlement is in sight.* 平和的解決は間近だ.
lose sight of sb/sth ⇒ **LOSE**
on sight ▶定義 as soon as you see sb/sth ~を見るとすぐに→見てすぐ, 即座に ‖ *The soldiers were ordered to shoot the enemy on sight.* 兵士たちは敵を見たらすぐに撃つように命令された.

**sight**[2] /sáit/ 動 他 ▶定義 to see sb/sth, especially after looking out for him/her/it 特に探した結果, ~を見つける→~を見つける, 認める

**sighting** /sáitɪŋ/ 名 📵 ▶定義 an occasion when sb/sth is seen ~が見られる特別な出来事→目撃, 観測 ‖ *the first sighting of a new star* 新星の初観測

**sightseeing** /sáitsìːɪŋ/ 名 🅄 ▶定義 visiting the sights of a city, etc as a tourist 観光客として都市などの観光地を訪れること→観光, 見物, 遊覧 ‖ *We did some sightseeing in Rome.* 私たちはローマで観光をした.

**sightseer** /sáitsìːər/ 名 📵 ▶定義 a person who visits the sights of a city, etc as a tourist 観光客として都市などの観光地を訪れる人→観光客 ➤ 参 **tourist**

\***sign**[1] /sáin/ 名 📵 ▶定義1 **sign (of sth)** something that shows that sb/sth is present, exists or may happen ~が存在する, または起こる可能性があることを示す~→~の印, 表れ, 証拠, 兆候 ‖ *The patient was **showing** some **signs** of improvement.* その患者は回復の兆しを見せていた. *As we drove into the village there wasn't a sign of life anywhere (= we couldn't see anyone).* 私たちがその村に入ったとき, 生き物の気配がどこにもなかった(= だれも見掛けることができなかった). ▶定義2 a piece of wood, paper, etc that has writing or a picture on it that gives you a piece of information, an instruction or a warning 情報, 指示, または警告を示す文字や絵のある木片, 紙など➜**標識, 表示, 看板** ‖ *What does that sign say?* あの標識には何と書いてありますか. *a road sign* 道路標識 *Follow the signs to Banbury.* バンベリーまで標識に従っていきなさい. ☛ **roundabout** のさし絵 ▶定義3 a movement that you make with your head, hands or arms that has a particular meaning 頭, 手, 腕などで行う, 特定の意味を持った動作➜**身振り, 手まね, 合図, 信号** ‖ *I **made a sign** for him to follow me.* 付いてくるように彼に合図をした. *I'll **give** you **a sign** when it's time for you to speak.* あなたの話す番が来たら, こちらから合図をします(= 私が合図をします). ▶定義4 a type of shape, mark or symbol that has a particular meaning ある特定の意味を持つ形, 印, 記号➜**印, 記号, 符号** ‖ *In mathematics, a cross is a plus sign.* 数学では + はプラスの記号だ. ▶定義5 (または **sign of the zodiac**) one of the twelve divisions or symbols of the zodiac 黄道帯を12に分けた区分や記号のうちの1つ➜**宮, 星座** ‖ *I'm a Leo. What sign are you?* 私は獅子(しし)座です. あなたは何座ですか.

**➤日本語 vs 英語**

**「サイン」の2つの意味**

クレジットカードで買い物をする人が増えて,「サインをする」という言い方は日常的になりました. この場合の「サイン」は英語では動詞なので, sign a document となります. ちなみに名詞形は signature です. 英語には全く意味の違う sign という名詞があるので, 混同しないようにする必要があります. こちらは,「道路標識」「記号」「兆候」「気配」「合図」などの意味. 野球の監督が「サインを送る」の「サイン」はこちらです.

***sign²** /sáɪn/ [動][自][他] ▶定義1 to write your name on a letter, document, etc to show that you have written it or that you agree with what it says 自分が書いたものであること, または内容に同意したことを示すために手紙, 書類などに自分の名前を書く➜**(〜に)署名する** ‖ *'Could you sign here, please?'* 「ここに署名していただけますか」 *I forgot to sign the cheque.* 小切手に署名するのを忘れた. *The two presidents signed the treaty.* 2人の大統領はその条約に署名した. ☛ [名] signature ▶定義2 [他] sign sb (up) to get sb to sign a contract to work for you 〜に自分のために働くという契約にサインさせる➜**〜と雇用契約をする** ‖ *Real Madrid have signed two new players.* レアルマドリッドは2人の新しい選手と契約した. ▶定義3 [自] to communicate using sign language 手話を用いて会話する➜**手話で話す, 手話で伝える**

[句動詞] sign in/out ▶定義 to write your name to show you have arrived at or left a hotel, club, etc ホテル, クラブなどへの出入りを示すために名前を書く➜**署名して到着·外出を記録する**

sign up (for sth) ▶定義 to agree formally to do sth 〜をすることに正式に同意する➜**(〜に)参加する, 登録する** ‖ *I've signed up for evening classes.* 私は夜間授業に申し込んだ.

***signal** /sígnl/ [名] [C] ▶定義1 a sign, action or sound that sends a particular message ある特定のメッセージを送る記号, 動作, 音➜**合図, 信号, シグナル** ‖ *When I give (you) the signal, run!* 合図したら走りなさい. ▶定義2 an event, action or fact that shows that sth exists or is likely to happen 〜が存在する, または起こりそうだということを示す出来事, 行動, 事実➜**印, 表れ, 証拠, 兆候** ‖ *The fall in unemployment is a clear signal that the economy is improving.* 失業率の低下は景気が回復していることの明らかな兆しだ. ▶定義3 a set of lights used to give information to train drivers 列車の運転手に情報を与えるために用いられる発光体一式➜**信号, シグナル** ▶定義4 a series of radio waves, etc that are sent out or received 送受信される一連の電波など➜**信号, 信号波** ‖ *a signal from a satellite* 衛星からの電波 — signal [動][自][他] (signalling; signalled: [米] signaling; signaled) ➜**(〜に)合図する, 信号を送る, (〜を)信号で伝える** ‖ *She was signalling wildly that something was wrong.* 彼女は何かがおかしいと激しく合図していた.

**signatory** /sígnət(ə)ri; -tɔ̀ːri/ [名] [C] ([複] **signatories**) ▶定義 signatory (to sth) one of the people or countries that sign an agreement, etc 合意書などに署名した人たちまたは国々の1つ➜**署名者, 調印者, 調印国, 加盟国**

***signature** /sígnətʃər/ [名] [C] ▶定義 a person's

name, written by that person and always written in the same way 常に一定の書体で書かれる自筆の名前➔**署名, サイン** ‖ *I couldn't read his signature.* 私には彼の署名が読めなかった. ☛ 動 sign

**significance** /sɪgnífɪkəns/ 名 ① ▶定義 the importance or meaning of sth 〜の重要性, 意味➔**重要性, 重大さ, 意味, 意義** ‖ *Few people realized the significance of the discovery.* その発見の重要性に気付いた人はほとんどいなかった.

*__significant__ /sɪgnífɪkənt/ 形 ▶定義1 important or large enough to be noticed 注目に値するほど重大な, または多い➔**重要な, 重大な, (数量が)かなりの** ‖ *Police said that the time of the murder was extremely significant.* 殺人の犯行時刻が非常に重要だと警察は語った. *There has been a significant improvement in your work.* あなたの研究に著しい進歩が見られる. ▶定義2 having a particular meaning ある特定の意味を持つ➔**意味のある, 意味ありげな, 意味深長な** ‖ *It could be significant that he took out life insurance shortly before he died.* 死亡する少し前に彼が生命保険を掛けたことに何か意味がありそうだ. — significantly 副 ➔**著しく, 意味深く, 意味ありげに** ‖ *Attitudes have changed significantly since the 1960s.* 1960年代以降, 考え方が著しく変化している.

**signify** /sígnəfàɪ/ 動 他 (現分 **signifying**; 三単現 **signifies**; 過, 過分 **signified**) 正式 ▶定義1 to be a sign of sth; to mean 〜の印である; 〜を意味する➔**〜を意味する, 表す, 示す** ‖ *What do those lights signify?* あの光は何を意味しているのですか. ▶定義2 to express or indicate sth 〜を表現する, 示す➔**〜を表明する, 示す, 知らせる** ‖ *They signified their agreement by raising their hands.* 彼らは挙手をして同意を示した.

**sign language** 名 ① ▶定義 a language used especially by people who cannot hear or speak, using the hands to make signs instead of spoken words 話し言葉の代わりに手を使って合図する, 耳または口の不自由な人が特に使う言葉➔**手話**

**signpost** /sáɪnpòʊst/ 名 ⓒ ▶定義 a sign at the side of a road that gives information about directions and distances to towns 街への方向や距離についての情報を与える道路わきの標識➔**標識, 道路標識, 道標** ☛ **roundabout** のさし絵

**Sikh** /siːk/ 名 ⓒ ▶定義 a member of one of the religions of India (**Sikhism**) that developed from Hinduism but teaches that there is only one god シク教 (インドにおける宗教の1つ) の信者. ヒンズー教から派生し, 神は唯一であると説く➔**シク教徒** — **Sikhism** /síːkɪz(ə)m/ 名 ① ➔**シク教**

*__silence__ /sáɪləns/ 名 ▶定義1 ① no noise or sound at all 全く雑音や音がしないこと➔**物音がしないこと, 静寂, 静けさ** ‖ *There must be silence during examinations.* 試験中は静粛でなければならない. ▶定義2 ⓒ ① a period when nobody speaks or makes a noise だれも話したり音を立てたりしない間➔**沈黙の期間, 無言** ‖ *My question was met with an awkward silence.* 私の質問に対して気まずい沈黙が流れた. *We ate in silence.* 私たちは無言で食事をした. ▶定義3 ① not making any comments about sth 〜について何も意見を言わないこと➔**黙殺, 沈黙** — silence 動 他 ➔**〜を静かにさせる; (意見など)を封じる**

**silencer** /sáɪlənsər/ (米 **muffler**) 名 ⓒ ▶定義1 a device which is fixed to the long tube under a vehicle (exhaust pipe) to reduce the noise made by the engine 車両下の長い管 (排気管) に取り付けられた, エンジンの騒音を減らすための装置➔**消音器, マフラー** ☛ **motorbike** のさし絵 ▶定義2 the part of a gun that reduces the noise when it is fired 銃の発射音を減らす部品➔**消音装置, サイレンサー**

*__silent__ /sáɪlənt/ 形 ▶定義1 where there is no noise; making no noise; very quiet 騒音のない; 音を立てない; 非常に静かな➔**物音がしない; 音を立てない; 静まり返った** ‖ *The house was empty and silent.* その家は人気がなく, 静まり返っていた. ▶定義2 **silent (on/about sth)** refusing to speak about sth 〜について話すのを拒む➔**(〜について)言及をしない, 黙っている, 沈黙した** ‖ *The policeman told her she had the right to remain silent.* 警察官は彼女に黙秘権があることを伝えた. ▶定義3 not using spoken words 話し言葉を用いない➔**無言の, 声を出さない, 寡黙な** ‖ *a silent prayer/protest* 黙祷 (もくとう) ・無言の抗議 ▶定義4 (of a letter) not pronounced

(文字について)→発音されない,黙音の‖ The 'b' in 'comb' is silent. combのbは発音されない.— **silently** 副→静かに,黙って,無言で

**silhouette** /sìluét/ 名 C ▶定義 the dark solid shape of sb/sth seen against a light background 明るさを背景にして見える真っ黒な〜の形→シルエット,影絵,輪郭 — **silhouetted** 形→シルエットで描かれた

**silicon chip** /sílıkən tʃıp, -ləkən/ 名 C ▶定義 (computing) a piece of a chemical element (silicon) that is used in computers, etc コンピューター(シリコン)の1断片→シリコンチップ

**silk** /sɪlk/ 名 U ▶定義 the soft smooth cloth that is made from threads produced by an insect (a silkworm) 虫(蚕)が生み出す糸で作られた柔らかく滑らかな布→絹,絹布,シルク‖ a silk shirt/dress 絹のワイシャツ・ドレス

**silky** /sílki/ 形 ▶定義 smooth, soft and shiny; like silk 滑らかで柔らかく光沢のある;絹のような→滑らかな,柔らかな,つやのある,絹のような‖ silky hair 柔らかくつやのある髪

**sill** /sɪl/ 名 C ▶定義 a shelf that is at the bottom of a window, either inside or outside 窓下の内外いずれか一方にある棚→窓の下枠,窓敷き居‖ a window sill 窓台

★**silly** /síli/ (**sillier**; **silliest**) ▶定義 1 not showing thought or understanding; foolish 思考力や理解力のない;愚かな→思慮のない,ばかな,愚かな‖ a silly mistake ばかげた間違い Don't be so silly! そんなばかげた事をするな[言うな]. ⇔ **sensible** ▶定義 2 appearing ridiculous, so that people will laugh with you 人々が笑うような→ばかげた,いかれた,こっけいな‖ I'm not wearing that hat - I'd look silly in it. その帽子はかぶらないわ－かぶるとばかみたいに見えるから. — **silliness** 名 U →ばかなこと,思慮のないこと,ばかげた行為

**silt** /sɪlt/ 名 U ▶定義 sand, soil or mud that collects at the sides or on the bottom of a river 川の両岸や底に集まる砂,土,泥→沈泥,微砂,シルト

★**silver**[1] /sílvər/ 名 U ▶定義 1 (元素記号 **Ag**) a valuable grey-white metal that is used for making jewellery, coins, etc 宝石,硬貨などを作るのに用いる高価な灰色がかった白色の金属→銀‖ a silver spoon/necklace 銀のスプーン・首飾り That's a nice ring. Is it silver? すてきな指輪ですね.それは銀製ですか. ▶定義 2 coins made from silver or sth that looks like silver 銀で作られた硬貨,銀のように見える〜→銀貨,銀めっき,銀製品 ▶定義 3 objects that are made of silver, for example knives, forks, spoons, dishes ナイフ,フォーク,スプーン,皿など銀で作られた物→銀器,銀食器‖ The thieves stole some jewellery and some valuable silver. 泥棒たちはいくつかの宝石と高価な銀器を盗んだ.

成句 every cloud has a silver lining ⇒ **CLOUD**[1]

★**silver**[2] /sílvər/ 形 ▶定義 1 having the colour of silver 銀色をした→銀の,銀色の,銀白の‖ a silver sports car 銀色のスポーツカー ▶定義 2 celebrating the 25th anniversary of sth 〜の25周年を祝う→25年目の,25周年の‖ They're celebrating their silver wedding this year. 彼らは今年銀婚式を迎える. ☞参 **diamond, golden**

**silver medal** (または **silver**) 名 C ▶定義 a small flat round piece of silver that is given to the person or team that comes second in a sports competition 競技で準優勝した個人やチームに与えられる小型の皿状の銀製品→銀メダル,銀賞‖ to win a silver medal at the Olympic Games オリンピック大会で銀メダルを獲得する ☞参 **gold medal, bronze medal** — **silver medallist** 名 C →銀メダル受賞者,銀メダリスト

**silver wedding** 名 C ▶定義 the 25th anniversary of a wedding→結婚25周年,銀婚式 ☞参 **golden wedding, diamond wedding**

**silvery** /sílvəri/ 形 ▶定義 having the appearance or colour of silver 外観や色が銀色の→銀白の‖ an old lady with silvery hair 銀髪をした老婦人

★**similar** /sím(ə)lər/ 形 ▶定義 similar (to sb/sth); similar (in sth) like sb/sth but not exactly the same 〜に似ているが,同一ではない→似ている,類似の,同類の‖ Our houses are very similar in size. 私たちの家は大きさがほとんど同じだ. Your handwriting is very similar to mine. あなたの筆跡は私のとよく似ている. ⇔ **different, dissimilar** — **similarly** 副→類似して,同様に,同じように‖ The plural of 'shelf' is 'shelves'. Similarly, the plural of 'wolf' is 'wolves'. shelf の複数形は shelves だ.同様に wolf の複数形は

wolves だ.

**similarity** /sìməlǽrəti/ 名 (複 **similarities**)
▶定義1 [❶, 単数扱い] similarity (to sb/sth); similarity (in sth) the state of being like sb/sth but not exactly the same 〜に似ているが, 同一ではない状態➡**類似, 同類, 相似** ‖ *She bears a remarkable/striking **similarity** to her mother.* 彼女は驚くほど母親似だ. ▶定義2 ❷ a similarity (between A and B); a similarity (in/of sth) a characteristic that people or things have which makes them similar 人や物がお互いを似通うものにしている特徴➡**類似性, 類似点, 相似点, 共通点** ‖ *Although there are some similarities between the two towns, there are a lot of differences too.* 2つの街はいくつか類似点があるが, 相違点も多い. *similarities in/of style* 文体の類似性

**simmer** /símər/ 動 ❶ ❶ ▶定義 to cook gently in a liquid that is almost boiling 沸騰寸前の温度の液体でゆっくり調理する➡**(とろ火で)ぐつぐつ煮える; 〜をとろ火で煮る, ことこと煮る**

*****simple** /símp(ə)l/ 形 ▶定義1 easy to understand, do or use; not difficult or complicated 理解しやすい, 実行しやすい, 使いやすい; 難しくない, 複雑でない➡**簡単な, 平易な, 単純な, 簡潔な** ‖ *This dictionary is written in simple English.* この辞書は平易な英語で書かれている. *a simple task/method/solution* 簡単な仕事・方法・解決策 / *I can't just leave the job. It's not as simple as that.* ただ仕事を辞めるというわけにはいかない. 事はそれほど簡単ではない. ▶定義2 without decoration or unnecessary extra things; plain and basic 装飾や不必要な余計なものがない; 飾り気がなく必要最小限の➡**簡素な, 質素な, 飾り気のない** ‖ *a simple black dress* 飾り気のない黒いドレス *The food is simple but perfectly cooked.* 食材は質素だが, 調理は見事だ. ▶定義3 (used about a person or a way of life) natural and not complicated (人や生活様式について) 自然で複雑でない➡**気取らない, 素朴な, 簡素な, つましい** ‖ *a simple life in the country* 田舎での簡素な暮らし ▶定義4 not intelligent; slow to understand 頭が良くない; 理解が遅い➡**愚かな, 頭が弱い** ▶定義5 used for saying that the thing you are talking about is the only thing that is important or true 自分の話している事が, 唯一重要・真実な事なのだと言うのに用いて➡**全くの, 純然たる,** 純粋な, 単なる ‖ *I'm not going to buy it **for the simple reason that** (= only because) I haven't got enough money.* お金が十分にないというただそれだけの理由で(= のために)それを買わないつもりだ.

**simplicity** /sɪmplísəti/ 名 ❶ ▶定義1 the quality of being easy to understand, do or use 理解しやすい, 実行しやすい, 使いやすいという特色➡**簡単, 平易, 単純** ‖ *We all admired the simplicity of the plan.* 私たちは皆その計画の単純明快さに感嘆した. ▶定義2 the quality of having no decoration or unnecessary extra things; being natural and not complicated 装飾がない, または余分なものがないという特色; 自然で複雑でないこと➡**質素, 簡素, 地味** ‖ *I like the simplicity of her paintings.* 私は彼女の絵画の飾り気のなさが好きだ.

**simplify** /símpləfàɪ/ 動 ❶ (現分 **simplifying**; 三単現 **simplifies**; 過, 過分 **simplified**) ▶定義 to make sth easier to do or understand; to make sth less complicated 〜をもっと実行・理解しやすくする; 〜をもっと複雑でないものにする➡**〜を簡単にする, 平易にする, 単純化する** ‖ *The process of applying for visas has been simplified.* ビザの申請手続きが簡略化された. ― simplification /sìmpləfəkéɪʃ(ə)n/ 名 ❷ ❶ ➡**簡易化, 簡素化, 単純化**

**simplistic** /sɪmplístɪk/ 形 ▶定義 making a problem, situation, etc seem less difficult and complicated than it really is 問題, 状況などを実際よりも易しく簡単に見せた➡**単純に割り切った, 短絡的な, 極度に単純化された**

**simply** /símpli/ 副 ▶定義1 used to emphasize how easy or basic sth is 〜がいかに簡単か, または初歩的かを強調するのに用いて➡**ただ, 単に** ‖ *Simply add hot water and stir.* ただ湯を注いでかき混ぜなさい. ▶定義2 (形容詞を強調して) completely; absolutely 完全に; 絶対に➡**全く, 実に, とても** ‖ *That meal was simply excellent.* その食事は全くすばらしかった. ▶定義3 in a way that makes sth easy to understand 〜を理解しやすくするように➡**簡単に, 平易に, 分かりやすく** ‖ *Could you explain it more simply?* もっと易しく説明していただけませんか. ▶定義4 in a simple, basic way; without decoration or unnecessary extra things 簡素に、必要最小限に；装飾や余分なものなしに→**質素に、簡素に、地味に** ‖ *They live simply, with very few luxuries.* 彼らはぜいたく品などほとんどないつましい生活を送っている. ▶定義5 only; just→**ただ、単に、単純に** ‖ *There's no need to get angry. The whole problem is simply a misunderstanding.* 怒る必要はない．問題のすべては単なる誤解だ．

**simulate** /símjəlèɪt/ 動他 ▶定義 to create certain conditions that exist in real life using computers, models, etc, usually for study or training purposes 通常，研究や訓練のために，コンピューター，模型などを用いて実生活に実在する一定の状況を作り出す→**〜の模擬実験をする、模擬的に実現する、〜をシミュレーションする** ‖ *The astronauts trained in a machine that simulates conditions in space.* 宇宙飛行士は宇宙と同じ状況を模擬的に実現した(機械)装置の中で訓練を受けた. ― simulation /sìmjəléɪ(ə)n/ 名 ⒞⒰→**模擬実験、シミュレーション** ‖ *a computer simulation of a nuclear attack* コンピューターによる核攻撃の模擬実験

**simultaneous** /sàɪməltéɪniəs, -njəs, sìm-/ 形 ▶定義 happening or done at exactly the same time as sth else ほかの〜ときっかり同時に起こるまたは行われる→**同時の、同時に起こる、同時に行われる** ― simultaneously 副→**同時に、一斉に**

**sin** /sɪn/ 名 ⒞⒰ ▶定義 an action or way of behaving that is not allowed by a religion 宗教で許されていない行為や行動様式→**(道徳・宗教上の)罪、罪悪** ‖ *He believes it is a sin for two people to live together without being married.* 2人が結婚しないで一緒に暮らすことは罪だと彼は信じている. ― sin 動⒤ (sinning; sinned)→**罪を犯す** ― sinner 名 ⒞→**罪人、不信心者**

*****since** /sɪns/ 副接前 ▶定義1 from a particular time in the past until a later time in the past or until now 過去のある特定の時点から、それより後の過去のある時点まで、あるいは現在まで→**それ以来、〜(して)以来、〜(して)以降** ‖ *My parents bought this house in 1975 and we've been living here ever since.* 両親は1975年にこの家を購入し，それ以来私たちはここに住んでいる. *I've been working in a bank ever since I left school.* 私は学校を卒業してからずっと銀行に勤めている. *It was the first time they'd won since 1974.* 彼らが勝ったのは1974年以来初めてのことだった. *I haven't seen him since last Tuesday.* 先週の火曜日以降，彼に会っていない. *She has had a number of jobs since leaving university.* 彼女は大学を卒業してから今日までいくつもの職に就いている.

▶物事が起こっている期間について話す場合には、sinceとforの両方が用いられる．その期間の始まりの時点を表すにはsinceを、その期間の長さを表すにはforを用いる：*I've known her since 1997.*（彼女とは1997年以来の知り合いだ.）*I've known her for three years.*（彼女と知り合って3年になる.）

▶定義2 at a time after a particular time in the past 過去のある特定の時点以降のある時に→**その後** ‖ *We were divorced two years ago and she has since married someone else.* 私たちは2年前に離婚したが、その後，彼女はほかの人と結婚した. ▶定義3 because; as→**〜だから；〜なので** ‖ *Since they've obviously forgotten to phone me, I'll have to phone them.* どうみても彼らは私に電話するのを忘れているようなので，こちらから電話しなければならないだろう.

*****sincere** /sɪnsíər/ 形 ▶定義1 (used about a person) really meaning or believing what you say; not pretending (人について)本気で言っている、自分の発言に信念を持っている；見せ掛けでない→**誠実な、まじめな** ‖ *Do you think she was being sincere when she said she admired me?* 彼女が私のことを尊敬すると言った時，本心だったと思いますか. ▶定義2 (used about a person's feelings, beliefs or behaviour) true; showing what you really mean or feel (人の感情，信念，振る舞いなどについて)本当の；自分が本当に言おうとしている事、または感じている事を表す→**本心からの、真実の、偽りのない、率直な** ‖ *Please accept our sincere thanks/apologies.* 私たちの心からの感謝・謝罪を受け入れてください. ⇔ **insincere** ― sincerely 副→**心から、誠実に、真心込めて** ‖ *I am sincerely grateful to you for all your help.* あなたのご援助に心から感謝いたします. *Yours sincerely, ...* (= at the end of a formal letter) 敬具 (= 正式な手紙の終わりに添えて) ― sincerity /sɪnsérəti, -síər-/ 名 ⒰→**誠実、誠意、率直さ** ⇔ **insincerity**

**sinful** /sínfʊl, -f(ə)l/ 形 ▶定義 breaking a religious law; immoral 宗教上の戒律を破る; 不道徳な→罪深い, 邪悪な, 罰当たりな

*__sing__ /síŋ/ 動自他 (過 __sang__ /sæŋ/; 過分 __sung__ /sʌŋ/) ▶定義 to make musical sounds with your voice 声で音楽的な音を出す→歌う; ~を歌う, さえずる ‖ *He always sings when he's in the bath.* 彼はふろの中でいつも歌っている. *The birds were singing outside my window.* 私の部屋の窓の外で鳥たちがさえずっていた. *She sang all her most popular songs at the concert.* 彼女は音楽会で彼女の持ち歌で最も人気のあるものをすべて歌った. ― __singing__ 名 **U** →歌うこと, 歌唱, 声楽 ‖ *singing lessons* 声楽の授業

**singe** /sɪndʒ/ 動自他 (現分 __singeing__) ▶定義 to burn the surface of sth slightly, usually by accident; to be burned in this way ~の表面を通常誤って少し焼く; そのように焼かれる→表面が焼ける, 焦げる; ~の表面を焼く, ~を焦がす

**singer** /síŋər/ 名 **C** ▶定義 a person who sings, or whose job is singing, especially in public 歌う人, または特に人前で歌うことを仕事にしている人→歌う人, 歌手, 声楽家 ‖ *an opera singer* オペラ歌手

*__single__¹ /síŋg(ə)l/ 形 ▶定義 **1** (名詞の前だけ) only one ただ 1 つの→たった 1 つの, たった 1 人の, 唯一の, 単一の ‖ *He gave her a single red rose.* 彼は彼女に 1 本の赤いバラを贈った. *I managed to finish the whole job in a single afternoon.* 私はたった半日で全部の仕事を何とか片付けた. *I went to a **single-sex** (= for boys only or girls only) school.* 私は男女別学の (= 男子または女子のみの) 学校に通った. ▶定義 **2** (名詞の前だけ) used to emphasize that you are talking about each individual item of a group or series あるグループまたは一連のもののうち個々の項目について話している事を強調するのに用いて→1 つ 1 つの, 各々の, 個々の ‖ *You answered **every single** question correctly. Well done!* あなたは 1 つ 1 つの質問に正しく答えました. よくできました. ▶定義 **3** not married 結婚していない→独身の, 未婚の ‖ *Are you married or single?* あなたは結婚していますか, それとも独身ですか. *a single man/woman* 未婚の男性・女性 ▶定義 **4** (名詞の前だけ) for the use of only one person 1 人だけで使用する→1 人用の, シングルの ‖ *I'd like to book a single room, please.* 1 人部屋を予約したいのですが. ☞参 **bed**¹ の注 ▶定義 **5** (または **one-way**) (名詞の前だけ) (used about a ticket or the price of a ticket) for a journey to a particular place, but not back again (切符や切符の価格について) ある特定の場所への往路用で, 復路を含まない→片道の ‖ *How much is the single fare to Rome?* ローマまでの片道料金はいくらですか. ☞参 **return**²(5)

**成句** in single file ⇒ **FILE**¹

**single**² /síŋg(ə)l/ 名 ▶定義 **1** **C** a ticket for a journey to a particular place, but not back again ある特定の場所までの往路用の切符. 帰りは含まない→片道切符 ‖ *Two singles to Hull, please.* ハルまでの片道切符を 2 枚下さい. ☞参 **return**²(5) ▶定義 **2** **C** a CD, tape, etc that has only one song on each side; the main song on this tape or CD 片面に 1 曲しか入っていない CD, テープなど; このようなテープや CD のメインソング→シングル, シングル盤 ‖ *Catatonia's new single* カタトニアのニューシングル ☞参 **album** ▶定義 **3** **C** a bedroom for one person in a hotel, etc ホテルなどの 1 人用の寝室→1 人部屋, シングルルーム ☞参 **double**³(5) ▶定義 **4** **singles** [複数扱い] people who are not married and do not have a romantic relationship with sb else 独身で, ほかのだれとも恋愛関係にない人々→独身者, 未婚者 ▶定義 **5** **singles** [複数扱い] a game of tennis, etc in which one player plays against one other player テニスなどで選手 1 人対 1 人の試合→シングルス ☞参 **doubles**

**single**³ /síŋg(ə)l/ 動

**句動詞** single sb/sth out (for sth) ▶定義 to give special attention or treatment to one person or thing from a group ある集合体から人 1 人だけ, または物 1 つだけを特に注目したり, 特別扱いする→~を選び出す, 選抜する ‖ *She was singled out for criticism.* 彼女だけが名指しで批判を浴びた.

**single-handed** 形 副 ▶定義 on your own with nobody helping you だれの手助けもなく自分 1 人で→独力の, 独力で, 1 人で

**single-minded** 形 ▶定義 having one clear aim or goal which you are determined to achieve どうしても成し遂げると心に決めた 1 つの明白な目的・目標を持った→1 つの目的を持つ

た, ひたむきな, 専念した — **single-mindedness** 图 Ⓤ → ひたむきさ, 専念, いちず

**single parent** 图 Ⓒ ▶定義 a person who looks after his/her child or children without a husband, wife or partner 夫, 妻, 同棲(どうせい)相手なしで自分の子供(たち)の世話をする人→**1人で子供を育てる親, 片親** ‖ *a single-parent family* 片親の家庭

**singly** /síŋ(g)li/ 副 ▶定義 one at a time; individually 一度に1つずつ; 個々に→**1つ1つ, 個々に, 単独で** ‖ *You can buy the tapes either singly or in packs of three.* テープは1本ずつでも3本パックでも購入できます.

**singular** /síŋgjələr/ 形 ▶定義**1**(文法) in the form that is used for talking about one person or thing only 単一の人や事物について述べる場合に用いられる形態の→**単数の, 単数形の** ‖ *'Table' is a singular noun; 'tables' is a plural noun.* table は単数名詞で, tables は複数名詞である. ☞参 **plural** ▶定義**2**(文)unusual 普通でない→**非凡な, 並外れた, まれに見る** — **singular** 图 [単数扱い](文法)→**単数, 単数形** ‖ *The word 'clothes' has no singular.* clothes という語には単数形がない. *What's the singular of 'people'?* people の単数形は何ですか.

**sinister** /sínəstər/ 形 ▶定義 seeming evil or dangerous; making you feel that sth bad will happen 邪悪または危険に見える; 何か悪い事が起こると感じさせる→**邪悪な, 悪意のある, 不吉な, 縁起の悪い** ‖ *There's something sinister about him. He frightens me.* 彼は何か底意地の悪そうな感じがする. 私は彼が怖い.

*****sink**¹ /sɪŋk/ 動 (過 **sank** /sæŋk/; 過分 **sunk** /sʌŋk/) ▶定義**1** 自他 to go down or make sth go down under the surface of liquid or a soft substance 液体の表面または軟質の物体の表面より下へ下がる, または〜を下へ行くようにする→**沈む, 沈没する, 埋まる; 〜を沈める, 埋める** ‖ *If you throw a stone into water, it sinks.* 水に石を投げると石は沈む. *My feet sank into the mud.* 足が泥の中にズブズブと沈んでしまった. ☞ **float** のさし絵 ▶定義**2** 自 (used about a person) to move downwards, usually by falling or sitting down (人について)通常倒れたり座ったりすることで, 体が下方に動く→**倒れる, (ぐったりと)座り込む** ‖ *I came home and sank into a chair, exhausted.* 私は帰宅すると, 疲れてぐったりといすに座り込んだ. ▶定義**3** 自 to get lower; to fall to a lower position or level 低くなる; 低い位置・水準まで落ちる→**下がる; 沈下する, 傾く** ‖ *We watched the sun sink slowly below the horizon.* 私たちは太陽がゆっくりと水平線の下に沈んでいくのを眺めた. ▶定義**4** 自 to decrease in value, number, amount, strength, etc 価値, 数, 量, 強さなどが減少する→**下落する, 低くなる, 減る, 弱まる**

成句 **your heart sinks** ⇒ **HEART**
句動詞 **sink in** ▶定義 (used about information, an event, an experience, etc) to be completely understood or realized (情報, 出来事, 経験などについて)完全に理解される, 認識される→**十分に理解される, 身に染みる** ‖ *It took a long time for the terrible news to sink in.* その恐ろしい知らせを十分にのみ込むまで長い時間を要した.

**sink in; sink into sth** ▶定義 (used about a liquid) to go into sth solid; to be absorbed (液体について)固い〜の中に入り込む; 吸収される→**(〜に)染み込む**

*****sink**² /sɪŋk/ 图 Ⓒ ▶定義 a large open container in a kitchen, with taps to supply water, where you wash things 台所にある大きなふたのない容器. 水を供給する蛇口が付いており, 物を洗うのに用いる→**流し, シンク** ☞ C7 ページのさし絵 ☞参 **washbasin**

**sinus** /sáɪnəs/ 图 Ⓒ (しばしば複数形で) ▶定義 one of the spaces in the bones of your face that are connected to your nose 鼻につながっている, 顔の骨の中の空洞の1つ→**副鼻腔(こう), 副鼻洞(とう), 静脈洞** ‖ *I've got a terrible cold and my sinuses are blocked.* ひどい風邪を引いて, 鼻が詰まっている. *a sinus infection* 鼻炎

**sip** /sɪp/ 動 自他 (**sipping; sipped**) ▶定義 to drink, taking only a very small amount of liquid into your mouth at a time 一度にごく少量の液体を口に入れて飲む→**(〜を)すする, ちびちび飲む, 少しずつ飲む** ‖ *We sat in the sun, sipping lemonade.* 私たちはレモネードを少しずつ飲みながら日なたで座っていた. — **sip** 图 Ⓒ →**ちびちび飲むこと, ーすすり, 一口**

**siphon** (または **syphon**) /sáɪf(ə)n/ 動 他 ▶定義**1** **siphon sth into/out of sth; siphon sth off/out** to remove a liquid from a container, often into another container, through a tube 容器から管を通して液体を取り除き, しばしば別の容器に移し変える→〜をサイフォンで(…に・…から)吸い上げる, 移す ▶定義2 **siphon sth off; siphon sth (from/out of sb/sth)** to take money from a company illegally over a period of time ある期間にわたって企業から不法に金を取る→(利益など)を(〜から)吸い上げる, しぼり取る, 流用する

\***sir** /sər,sə́ːr/ 名 ▶定義1 [単数扱い] used as a polite way of speaking to a man whose name you do not know, for example in a shop or restaurant, or to show respect 例えば店やレストランなどで, 名前が分からない男性に対する丁寧な呼び掛け, または敬意表現として用いて→お客さん, だんな ‖ *I'm afraid we haven't got your size, sir.* 申し訳ございませんが, お客様のサイズはございません. ☞参 **madam** ▶定義2 used at the beginning of a formal letter to a male person or male people 男性にあてた正式な手紙の初めに用いて→拝啓, 各位 ‖ *Dear Sir...* 拝啓 *Dear Sirs...* 各位 ☞参 **Madam** ▶定義3 /sər/ [単数扱い] the title that is used in front of the name of a man who has received one of the highest British honours イギリスの最高位の称号の1つを受けた男性の名前の前に用いる敬称→サー, 〜卿

**siren** /sáiərən/ 名 ▶定義 a device that makes a long, loud sound as a warning or signal 警告や信号として長い大きな音を出す装置→サイレン, 警笛 ‖ *an air-raid siren* 空襲警報のサイレン *Three fire engines raced past, sirens wailing.* サイレンの不吉な音が鳴り響く中3台の消防自動車が走り去った.

\***sister** /sístər/ 名 ▶定義1 a girl or woman who has the same parents as another person 両親を同じくする少女または女の人→姉, 妹 ‖ *I've got one brother and two sisters.* 私には兄[弟]が1人と姉[妹]2人いる. *We're sisters.* 私たちは姉妹だ. ☞参 **half-sister, stepsister**. 英語には「兄弟姉妹」を意味する一般的な語はない. *Have you got any brothers and sisters?* (あなたには兄弟姉妹がいますか.) sibling は非常に改まった語である. ▶定義2 (しばしば **Sister**) 英 a female hospital nurse in a high position 高い地位にいる看護婦→看護婦長, 看護主任 ▶定義3 **Sister** a member of certain female religious groups; a nun 女性の宗教団体の一員; 尼僧→シスター, 修道女 ▶定義4 (通常は形容詞として用いて) a thing that belongs to the same type or group as sth else ほかの〜と同じ種類やグループに属するもの→姉妹のような関係にある, 姉妹〜 ‖ *We have a sister company in Japan.* 我が社には日本に姉妹会社がある. ▶定義5 略式 a woman who you feel close to because she is a member of the same society, group, etc as you 自分と同じ団体, グループなどに属しているため親しみを感じる女性→女の友人・仲間・同志, (女性の)会員仲間

**sister-in-law** 名 ⓒ (複 **sisters-in-law**) ▶定義1 the sister of your husband or wife 夫や妻の姉・妹→義理の姉・妹 ▶定義2 the wife of your brother 兄・弟の妻→義理の姉・妹

\***sit** /sɪt/ 動 (現分 **sitting**; 過, 過分 **sat** /sæt/) ▶定義1 ⓘ to rest your weight on your bottom, for example in a chair 例えばいすなどの上で, 腰に体重を掛ける→座る, 腰を下ろす, 着席する, 座っている ‖ *We sat in the garden all afternoon.* 私たちは午後中庭に出て座っていた. *She was sitting on the sofa, talking to her mother.* 彼女はソファーに腰掛けて, 母親と話していた. ▶定義2 **sit sb (down)** to put sb into a sitting position; make sb sit down 〜を座る姿勢にさせる; 〜を座らせる→〜を座らせる, 着席させる ‖ *He picked up his daughter and sat her down on a chair.* 彼は娘を抱き上げていすに腰掛けさせた. *She sat me down and offered me a cup of tea.* 彼女は私を座らせて, 1杯の紅茶を勧めた. ▶定義3 ⓘ to be in a particular place or position ある特定の場所や位置にいる→位置する, ある, 動かない ‖ *The letter sat on the table for several days before anybody opened it.* その手紙はだれも開封しないまま何日間もテーブルの上に置いてあった. ▶定義4 他 英 to take an exam 試験を受ける→〜を受ける, 受験する ‖ *If I fail, will I be able to* **sit the exam** *again?* もし落ちたら, 試験はもう一度受けられますか. ▶定義5 ⓘ 正式 (used about an official group of people) to have a meeting or series of meetings (公式の集団について) 一連の会議を催す→(議会, 法廷などが) 開かれる

成句 **sit on the fence** ▶定義 to avoid saying which side of an argument you support 議論の

## 1512 sitcom

どちら側を支持するか、明言を避ける→**態度をはっきりさせない、形勢を見る、日和見的な態度を取る**

**句動詞** **sit about/around** 略式 ▶定義 to spend time doing nothing active or useful 活動的な事や有益な事を何もせずに時を過ごす→**ぶらぶらする、のらくらする、ぼけっと座っている** ‖ *We just sat around chatting all afternoon.* 私たちは午後中何もせずにただ座っておしゃべりして過ごした.

**sit back** ▶定義 to relax and not take an active part in what other people are doing くつろいで、ほかの人たちが行っている事に積極的に参加しない→**傍観する、手を出さない、くつろぐ** ‖ *Sit back and take it easy while I make dinner.* 私が夕食を作る間、ゆっくりとくつろいでいてください.

**sit down** ▶定義 to lower your body into a sitting position 腰を落として座った姿勢を取る→**座る、着席する、腰掛ける** ‖ *He sat down in an armchair.* 彼はひじ掛けいすに腰を下ろした.

**sit sth out** ▶定義 **1** to stay in a place and wait for sth unpleasant or boring to finish ある場所にとどまって、不快または退屈な〜が終わるのを待つ→**(我慢して)〜の間中座っている、〜の終わりまでいる** ▶定義 **2** to not take part in a dance, game, etc 踊り、試合などに参加しない→**〜に加わらない、参加しない**

**sit through sth** ▶定義 to stay in your seat until sth boring or long has finished 退屈なまたは長い〜が終わるまで自分の席にとどまる→**〜の終わりまでいる、じっとしている**

**sit up** ▶定義 **1** to move into a sitting position when you have been lying down or to make your back straight 横になった状態から座る姿勢に変わる、あるいは背筋を伸ばす→**起き上がる、起き直る、背筋をきちんと伸ばして座る** ‖ *Sit up straight and concentrate!* 姿勢を正して集中しなさい. ▶定義 **2** to not go to bed although it is very late 非常に遅い時間でも就寝しない→**夜更かしする、寝ずに起きている、徹夜する** ‖ *We sat up all night talking.* 私たちは夜通し語り明かした.

**sitcom** /sítkɑm/ (または 正式 **situation comedy**) 名 C U ▶定義 a funny programme on television that shows the same characters in different amusing situations each week 同じ登場人物を週ごとに異なるおかしな状況に置いて見せるテレビのお笑い番組→**連続ホームコメディー、シチュエーションコメディー**

**site** /sáɪt/ 名 C ▶定義 **1** a piece of land where a building was, is or will be situated 建物がかつてあった・現にある・将来建つ予定の場所→**場所、位置、敷地、用地、建設予定地** ‖ *a building/construction site* 建築用地・建設現場 *The company is looking for a site for its new offices.* その会社は新しい事務所の建設用地を探している. ▶定義 **2** a place where sth has happened or that is used for sth 〜が起こった場所、または〜のために使われる場所→**現場、跡** ‖ *the site of a famous battle* 有名な戦闘の跡 — **site** 動 他 (文)〜の用地を定める、〜を置く

**sitting** /sítɪŋ/ 名 C ▶定義 **1** a period of time during which a court of law or a parliament meets and does its work 法廷や議会が開かれ、その職務が遂行される期間→**開廷期間、開会期間、会期** ▶定義 **2** a time when a meal is served in a school, hotel, etc to a number of people at the same time 学校、ホテルなどで同時に大勢の人に食事を出す時間→**食事時間** ‖ *Dinner will be in two sittings.* 夕食は2回に分かれています.

**sitting room** 英 = LIVING ROOM

**situated** /sítʃueɪtɪd/ 形 ▶定義 in a particular place or position ある特定の場所または位置にあって→**位置している、ある、〜の状態に置かれた** ‖ *The hotel is conveniently situated close to the beach.* そのホテルは海岸に近い便利な場所にある.

**\*situation** /sìtʃuéɪʃ(ə)n/ 名 C ▶定義 **1** the things that are happening in a particular place or at a particular time ある特定の場所またはある特定の時間に起こっていること→**状況、情勢、事態、状態、立場** ‖ *The situation in the north of the country is extremely serious.* その国の北部の状況は極めて深刻だ. *Tim is **in a difficult situation** at the moment.* ティムは現在難しい立場にある. *the economic/financial/political situation* 経済情勢・金融情勢・政局 ▶定義 **2** (文) the position of a building, town, etc in relation to the area around it 建物、街などが周りの地域との関連で占める位置→**位置、場所、敷地、用地** ▶定義 **3** (文・古) a job 職→**職、勤め口** ‖ *Situations Vacant (=*

*the part of a newspaper where jobs are advertised*) 求人(= 新聞の求人欄の出ている箇所)

**sit-up** 名 ⓒ ▶定義 an exercise for the stomach muscles in which you lie on your back with your legs bent, then lift the top half of your body from the floor ひざを折り曲げてあおむけに寝て,上半身を床から持ち上げる,腹筋運動→**(寝ている姿勢からの)起き上がり腹筋運動, シットアップ** ‖ to **do sit-ups** 腹筋運動をする ☛ S1 ページのさし絵

\***six** /síks/ 数 ▶定義 1 6 ‖ *The answers are on page six.* 答えは6ページに出ている. *There are six of us for dinner tonight.* 私たちで今夜一緒に食事をするのは6人です. *They have six cats.* 彼らは猫を6匹飼っている. *My son is six (years old) next month.* うちの息子は来月で6歳になる. *She lives at 6 Elm Drive.* 彼女はエルムドライブ6番地に住んでいる. *a birthday card with a big six on it* 大きく6と書かれたバースデーカード ▶定義 2 **six-**(複合語で) having six of the thing mentioned 言及のものを6つ持つ→**6の, 6つの, 6個の, 6人の** ‖ *She works a six-day week.* 彼女は週6日働いている.

▶日付,測定値,価格などの数についての説明は,巻末の数についての特別項目を参照.

\***sixteen** /sìkstíːn, ⌒/ 数 ▶定義 16

▶文中での数詞の使い方については,six の項を参照.

**sixteenth** /sìkstíːnθ, ⌒/ 代形副 ▶定義 16th→16 番目(の,に), 第16(の,に) ☛参 sixth の例

**sixth**¹ /síksθ/ 代形副 ▶定義 6th→6番目(の,に), 第6(の,に) ‖ *I've had five cups of tea already, so this is my sixth.* もう紅茶を5杯飲んでいるので,これが6杯目になる. *This is the sixth time I've tried to phone him.* 彼に電話をしようとしたのはこれで6回目だ.

▶日付,測定値,価格などの数についての説明は,巻末の数についての特別項目を参照.

**sixth**² /síksθ/ 名 ⓒ ▶定義 the fraction 1/6; one of six equal parts of sth 6分の1;〜を6等分したうちの1つ→**6分の1**

**sixth form** 名 [ⓒ, 通常は単数, 単数または複数形の動詞と共に] 英 ▶定義 the final two years at secondary school for students from the age of 16 to 18 who are studying for A level exams A レベル試験に向けて勉強している16歳から18歳までの生徒たちが通う中等学校の最後の2年間→**第6学年,最上級学年** — **sixth-former** 名 ⓒ →**6年生, 最上級生**

**sixtieth** /síkstiəθ/ 代形副 ▶定義 60th→60番目(の,に), 第60(の,に) ☛参 sixth の例

\***sixty** /síksti/ 数 ▶定義 1 60 ‖ *Sixty people went to the meeting.* 60人が会議に出席した. *There are sixty pages in the book.* その本は60ページある. *He retired at sixty.* 彼は60歳で退職した.

▶文中での数詞の使い方については, six の項を参照.

▶定義 2 **the sixties**[複数扱い] the numbers, years or temperatures between 60 and 69; the 60s 60から69までの数, 年, 温度→**60台, 60年代, 60代, 60度台** ‖ *I don't know the exact number of members, but it's in the sixties.* 会員の正確な人数は知らないが, 60人台だ. *The most famous pop group of the sixties was The Beatles.* 60年代で最も人気のあったポップグループはビートルズだった. *The temperature tomorrow will be in the high sixties.* 明日の気温は60度台後半になるだろう.

句同 **in your sixties** ▶定義 between the age of 60 and 69 60歳から69歳の間の→**60歳台の, 60代の** ‖ *I'm not sure how old she is but I should think she's in her sixties.* 彼女の年齢は正確には分からないが,60代だと思う. *in your early/mid/late sixties* 60代前半・半ば・後半で

▶日付,測定値,価格などの数についての説明は,巻末の数についての特別項目を参照.

\***size**¹ /sáɪz/ 名 ▶定義 1 Ⓤ how big or small sth is 〜の大小→**大きさ, 寸法, サイズ** ‖ *I was surprised at the size of the hotel. It was enormous!* そのホテルの大きさに驚いた. けた外れの大きさだった. *The planet Uranus is about four times the size of (= as big as) Earth.* 天王星は地球の約4倍の大きさがある(= 4倍程度大きい).

▶物の大きさを尋ねるとき, 通常は How big...? と言う: *How big is your house?*(あなたの家はどのくらいの大きさですか.)いくつかの決まった寸法で製造される物の大きさを尋ねるときには, What size...? と言う: ***What size shoes do you take?***(いくつのサイズの靴をお履きですか.) *What size are you? (= when buying clothes)*(あなたは何サイズですか.)(= 衣服を購入するときに)

### size²

▶定義2 ❻ one of a number of fixed measurements in which sth is made 〜を作る場合のいくつか決まった寸法の1つ→**サイズ,号数,型,番,判** ‖ *Have you got this dress in a bigger size?* もっと大きなサイズでこれと同じ服がありますか. *I'm a size 12.* 私のサイズは12番です. *What size pizza would you like? Medium or large?* どのサイズのピザがよろしいですか. Mですか,それともLですか. ▶定義3 **-sized**(または**-size**) (複合形容詞を作るために用いて) of the size mentioned 言及された大きさの→**〜の大きさの,サイズの,型の** ‖ *a medium-sized flat* 中くらいの大きさのアパート *a king-size bed* キングサイズのベッド

### size² /sáɪz/ 動

**句動詞** size sb/sth up ▶定義 to form an opinion or judgement about sb/sth 〜について考え方をまとめる,または判断を下す→**〜を評価する,判断する,見定める**

### sizeable(または sizable) /sáɪzəb(ə)l/ 形 ▶定義
quite large→**かなり大きい,相当大きい** ‖ *a sizeable sum of money* 相当な金額

### sizzle /síz(ə)l/ 動 ▶定義 to make the sound of food frying in hot fat 熱い油で食べ物が揚げられている音を立てる→**ジュージューいう音を立てる,ジュージューいう**

Rollerblade™  roller skate  skateboard  ice skate

### skate¹ /skeɪt/ 名 ❻ ▶定義1 (または **ice skate**) a boot with a thin sharp metal part on the bottom that is used for moving on ice 氷の上を移行するのに使われる,底に薄くて鋭い金具の付いた編み上げ靴→**スケート靴,アイススケート靴** ▶定義2 = **ROLLER SKATE** ▶定義3 a large flat sea fish that can be eaten 食用の大型で平らな海の魚→**ガンギエイ**

### skate² /skeɪt/ 動 ❺ ▶定義1 (または **ice-skate**) to move on ice wearing special boots (ice skates) 専用の編み上げ靴(スケート靴)を履いて氷の上を移動する→**スケートをする,スケートで滑る** ‖ *Can you skate?* スケートができますか. *They skated across the frozen lake.* 彼らは凍った湖をスケートで渡った. ☛ 娯楽としてのスケートの話をする場合には go skating が一般的に用いられる. ▶定義2 = **ROLLER SKATE** — skater 名 ❻→**スケートをする人,スケーター,スケートの選手**

### skateboard /skéɪtbɔːrd/ 名 ❻ ▶定義 a short narrow board with small wheels at each end that you can stand on and ride as a sport 狭く短い板の両端に小さい車輪の付いたスポーツ用具.その上に立って乗る→**スケートボード** ☛ skate のさし絵 — skateboarding 名 ❶ スケートボード遊び,スケートボードをすること ‖ *When we were children we used to go skateboarding in the park.* 子供のころ,私たちは公園へスケートボードをしに出掛けたものだ.

### skating /skéɪtɪŋ/ 名 ▶定義1 (または **ice skating**) ❶ the activity or sport of moving on ice wearing special boots 専用の編み上げ靴を履いて氷の上を移動する行為または競技→**スケート,スケート遊び** ‖ *Would you like to go skating this weekend?* 今週末,スケートに出掛けませんか. ▶定義2 = **ROLLER SKATING**

### skating rink (または **ice rink; rink**) 名 ❻ ▶定義 a large area of ice, or a building containing a large area of ice, that is used for skating on スケート用の氷の広場,またはこれを収容した建物→**スケート場,スケートリンク**

### *skeleton¹ /skélət(ə)n/ 名 ❻ ▶定義 the structure formed by all the bones in a human or animal body 人間や動物の体内にあるすべての骨によって組み立てられたもの→**骨格,骸骨(がいこつ),骨組み** ‖ *the human skeleton* 人間の骸骨 *a dinosaur skeleton* 恐竜の骨格

### skeleton² /skélət(ə)n/ 形 ▶定義 (used about an organization, a service, etc) having the smallest number of people that is necessary for it to operate (組織,サービスなどについて)機能するのに必要な最小限の人数で→**必要最小限の,最低限の**

### skeptic, skeptical, skepticism 困 = SCEPTIC, SCEPTICAL, SCEPTICISM

**sketch** /sketʃ/ 名 C ▶定義1 a simple, quick drawing without many details 細部を省いて手早くかいた素描→スケッチ, 下絵, 素描 ‖ *He drew a rough sketch of the new building on the back of an envelope.* 彼は封筒の裏に新しい建物の簡単な下絵をかいた. ▶定義2 a short funny scene on television, in the theatre, etc テレビ, 演劇などでの短いこっけいな場面→寸劇 ‖ *The drama group did a sketch about a couple buying a new house.* その劇団は新しい家を買う夫婦のことを寸劇にして見せた. ▶定義3 a short description without any details 細かい説明のない短い記述→概略, 概要, 大要 ― sketch 動 自 他 →(〜を)スケッチする, 写生する, (〜の)概略を説明する ‖ *I sat on the grass and sketched the castle.* 私は芝生の上に座って, 城のスケッチをした.

**sketchy** /skétʃi/ 形 ▶定義 not having many or enough details 詳細に乏しい, または詳細が不十分な→概略だけの, 大まかな, 不備な

**ski**¹ /skiː/ 動 自 (現分 **skiing**; 過, 過分 **skied**) ▶定義 to move over snow on skis スキーを履いて雪の上を移動する→スキーをする, スキーで滑る ‖ *When did you learn to ski?* いつスキーを習ったのですか. *They go skiing every year.* 彼らは毎年スキーに出掛ける. ― ski 形 →スキーの, スキー用の ‖ *a ski resort/instructor/slope/suit* スキーリゾート・スキーのインストラクター・スキースロープ・スキーウェア ― skiing 名 U →スキー, スキーをすること, スキーで滑ること ‖ *alpine/downhill/cross-country skiing* アルペン・滑降・クロスカントリースキー

**ski**² /skiː/ 名 C ▶定義 one of a pair of long, flat, narrow pieces of wood or plastic that are fastened to boots and used for sliding over snow 一組の木製またはプラスチック製の長く平らな細い板の1つ. 編み上げ靴に固定し, 雪の上を滑るために用いる→スキー, スキー板 ‖ *a pair of skis* 一組のスキー

**skid** /skɪd/ 動 自 (**skidding**; **skidded**) ▶定義 (usually used about a vehicle) to suddenly slide forwards or sideways without any control (通常は車両について)制御を失って突然前または横に滑る→横滑りする, スリップする ‖ *I skidded on a patch of ice and hit a tree.* 凍った所で滑って木にぶつかった. ― skid 名 C →横滑り, スリップ ‖ *The car went into a skid and came off the road.* その車はスリップして道路から飛び出した.

**skier** /skíːər/ 名 C ▶定義 a person who skis→スキーをする人, スキーヤー ‖ *Mina's a good skier.* マイナはスキーが上手だ.

*****skilful** (米 **skillful**) /skílfəl/ 形 ▶定義1 (used about a person) very good at doing sth (人について)〜をするのがとてもうまい→上手な, 熟練した, 腕利きの ‖ *a skilful painter/politician* 腕のいい画家・敏腕の政治家 *He's very skilful with his hands.* 彼は手先がとても器用だ. ▶定義2 done very well とてもうまくできた→巧みな, すばらしい ‖ *skilful guitar playing* すばらしいギターの演奏 ― skilfully /-fəli/ 副 →上手に, 熟練して, 巧みに

*****skill** /skɪl/ 名 ▶定義1 U the ability to do sth well, especially because of training, practice, etc 特に訓練, 練習などによって〜を巧みにこなす能力→腕前, 熟練, 技量 ‖ *It takes great skill to make such beautiful jewellery.* このような美しい宝飾品を作るには大変な技量がいる. *This is an easy game to play. No skill is required.* これは簡単なゲームだ. 何の技量も必要ない. ▶定義2 C an ability that you need in order to do a job, an activity, etc well 仕事, 活動などを上手にこなすために必要な能力→技能, 技術, 技(わざ) ‖ *The course will help you to develop your reading and listening skills.* その講座は読解力や聴解力を伸ばすのに役立つ. *management skills* 管理能力 *Typing is a skill I have never mastered.* タイプの技術は私が十分に習得しなかったものだ.

**skilled** /skɪld/ 形 ▶定義1 (used about a person) having skill; skilful (人について)技能のあ

る; 熟練した➜(特殊の)技量を持った, 腕の良い ‖ *a skilled worker* 熟練工 ▶定義 2 (used about work, a job etc) needing skill or skills; done by people who have been trained (仕事, 職業などについて) 技量や技能を必要とする; 訓練を受けた人たちによって行われる➜**熟練を要する, 特殊技能を要する** ‖ *a highly skilled job* 非常に熟練を要する仕事 *Skilled work is difficult to find in this area.* この地域[領域]では特殊技能を要する仕事を探すのは難しい. ⇔ **unskilled**

**skim** /skɪm/ [動] (**skimming**; **skimmed**) ▶定義 1 [他] skim sth (off/from sth) to remove sth from the surface of a liquid ～を液体の表面から取り除く➜**～を(…から)すくい取る, すくい上げる** ‖ *to skim the cream off the milk* 牛乳から乳脂をすくい取る ▶定義 2 [自][他] to move quickly over or past sth, almost touching it or touching it slightly 触れるか触れないかの近さで, ～の上を素早く移動する, または～の前を通り過ぎる➜**すれすれに動く, (～を)かすめる, 滑るように進む** ‖ *The plane flew very low, skimming the tops of the buildings.* 飛行機は建物のてっぺんをすれすれに低空飛行をした. ▶定義 3 [自][他] skim (through/over) sth to read sth quickly in order to get the main idea, without paying attention to the details and without reading every word 細部には注意を払わず, 一語一語読まずに主旨を理解するために～をざっと読む➜**(～に)ざっと目を通す, 拾い読みする, 飛ばし読みする** ‖ *I usually just skim through the newspaper in the morning.* 普段朝は, 新聞にざっと目を通すだけだ.

**skimmed milk** [名] [U] ▶定義 milk from which the cream has been removed 乳脂を取り除いた牛乳➜**脱脂乳, スキムミルク**

**skimp** /skɪmp/ [動][自] ▶定義 skimp (on sth) to use or provide less of sth than is necessary 必要な数量以下しか使わない, また与えない➜**けちる, 出し惜しみする, 節約する**

**skimpy** /skímpi/ [形] ▶定義 using or having less than is necessary; too small or few 必要な数量以下しか使わない, またはそれだけしかない; 小さすぎる, 少なすぎる➜**不十分な, 貧弱な; 乏しい**

***skin**[1] /skɪn/ [名] [C] [U] ▶定義 1 the natural outer covering of a human or animal body 人間や動物の体を覆う天然の外皮➜**皮膚, 肌, 皮** ‖ *to have (a) fair/dark/sensitive skin* 肌が白い・黒い・敏感だ *skin cancer* 皮膚がん ▶定義 2 **-skinned** (複合形容詞を作るために用いて) having the type of skin mentioned 言及された種類の肌を持つ➜**～の肌をした, ～の皮膚をした** ‖ *My sister's very dark-skinned.* 私の姉はとても黒い肌をしている. ▶定義 3 (しばしば複合語で) the skin of a dead animal, with or without its fur, used for making things 加工用の有毛・無毛の死んだ動物の皮➜**皮, 皮革, 獣皮** ‖ *a sheepskin jacket* 羊の皮の上着 *a bag made of crocodile skin* ワニ皮製のかばん ▶定義 4 the natural outer covering of some fruits or vegetables; the outer covering of a sausage 果物や野菜を覆う天然の外皮; ソーセージの外皮➜**皮, 表皮** ‖ *(a) banana/tomato skin* バナナ・トマトの皮 ☛参 **rind** の注 ☛ C3 ページのさし絵 ▶定義 5 the thin solid surface that can form on a liquid 液体の表面にできる薄い固体➜**膜** ‖ *A skin had formed on top of the milk.* 牛乳の表面に膜が張っていた.

[成句] by the skin of your teeth [略式] ▶定義 (used to show that sb almost failed to do sth) only just (～が…をやり損ないそうになったことを示すために用いて) 辛うじて➜**辛うじて, 際どいところで, 間一髪で** ‖ *I ran into the airport and caught the plane by the skin of my teeth.* 私は空港に駆け込み, 間一髪で飛行機に間に合った.

have a thick skin ⇒ **THICK**[1]

skin-deep ▶定義 (used about a feeling or an attitude) not as important or as strongly felt as it appears to be; superficial (感情や態度について) 見掛けほど重要でない, または痛切に感じていない; 上辺だけの➜**表面だけの, 上っ面の, 上辺だけの** ‖ *I knew his concern about me was only skin-deep.* 私に対する彼の関心は上辺だけにすぎないことを私は知っていた.

**skin**[2] /skɪn/ [動][他] (**skinning**; **skinned**) ▶定義 to remove the skin from sth ～から皮を取り除く➜**～の皮をむく, 皮をはぐ**

[成句] keep your eyes peeled/skinned (for sb/sth) ⇒ **EYE**[1]

**skinny** /skíni/ [形] ▶定義 (used about a person) too thin (人について) やせすぎた➜**やせこけた, 骨と皮ばかりの, やせ衰えた** ☛参 **thin** の注

**skintight** [形] ▶定義 (used about a piece of clothing) fitting very tightly and showing the shape of the body (衣類について) 体にぴったり

と合っていて体の線があらわな→体にぴったりの, 体にぴったり付いた

**skip**¹ /skɪp/ 動 (**skipping**; **skipped**) ▶定義1 ⾃ to move along quickly and lightly in a way that is similar to dancing, with little jumps and steps, from one foot to the other 躍るように小さく跳ねては前に足を出して, 片足ずつ交互に素早く軽やかに移動する→軽く飛ぶ, 飛び跳ねる, 跳ね回る, スキップする‖ *A little girl came skipping along the road.* 小さな女の子が道をスキップしながらやって来た. *Lambs were skipping about in the field.* 小羊たちが野原を跳ね回っていた.
▶定義2 ⾃ to jump over a rope that you or two other people hold at each end, turning it round and round over the head and under the feet 自分でロープの両端を持つなり, 2人に片端ずつ持たせるなりして, 上下にグルグルとロープを回しながらそれを跳びくぐる→縄跳びをする‖ *Some girls were skipping in the playground.* 数人の少女たちが遊び場で縄跳びをしていた.
▶定義3 ⾃ to not do sth that you usually do or should do 普段している, またはすべき事をしない→を省く, 抜かす, 飛ばす, 省略する‖ *I got up rather late, so I skipped breakfast.* かなり遅く起きてしまったので, 朝食を抜いた. ▶定義4 ⾃ to miss the next thing that you would normally read, do, etc 通常ならば次に読んだりしたりするはずの事をし損なう→を飛ばす, 抜かす‖ *I accidentally skipped one of the questions in the test.* 私はうっかり試験の問題を1つ抜かしてしまった.

**skip**² /skɪp/ 名 C ▶定義1 a small jumping movement 小さく飛び跳ねる動き→軽く跳ぶこと, 飛び跳ねること, スキップ ▶定義2 a large, open metal container for rubbish, often used during building work しばしば建設作業中に用いられる, 大型のふたのない金属製の廃棄物用容器→(廃棄物を運ぶ)大型容器

**skipper** /skípər/ 名 C 略式 ▶定義 the captain of a boat or ship, or of a sports team 大型・小型の船の船長, スポーツチームの主将→船長, 機長, 主将

**skipping rope** 名 C ▶定義 a rope, often with handles at each end, that you turn over your head and then jump over, for fun or for exercise 両端に取っ手の付いたロープ. 遊びまたは運動用にこれを頭越しに回して飛びくぐる→縄跳びの縄

## sky 1517

**skirmish** /skə́ːrmɪʃ/ 名 C ▶定義 a short fight between groups of people 人間の集団同士の小戦→小競り合い, 衝突

★**skirt**¹ /skə́ːrt/ 名 C ▶定義 a piece of clothing that is worn by women and girls and that hangs down from the waist 下半身を覆う婦人・少女用衣服→スカート ☞参 **culottes** ☞ C6ページのさし絵

**skirt**² /skə́ːrt/ 動 ⾃他 ▶定義 to go around the edge of sth ～の縁を回る→(～の)へりに沿って行く, (～の)端を通る, (～に沿って)ある
句動詞 skirt round sth ▶定義 to avoid talking about sth in a direct way ～について直接話すことを避ける→(問題)を避ける, 回避する‖ *The manager skirted round the subject of our pay increase.* 経営者は我々の賃上げ問題への言及を避けた.

**skittles** /skɪ́tlz/ 名 U ▶定義 a game in which players try to knock down as many bottle-shaped objects (**skittles**) as possible by throwing or rolling a ball at them 競技者が球を投げたり転がしたりして, びんの形をした物体(九柱戯用のピン)をできるだけ数多く倒そうとするゲーム→九柱戯, スキトルズ

**skive** /skáɪv/ 動 ⾃ 英略式 ▶定義 skive (off) to not work when you should 働くべきときに働かない→仕事をサボる, ずる休みをする, ずらかる

**skulk** /skʌlk/ 動 ⾃ ▶定義 to stay somewhere quietly and secretly, hoping that nobody will notice you, especially because you are planning to do sth bad 特に悪い事をたくらんでいるため, だれにも気付かれないように, どこかにひっそりと隠れている→こそこそする, こそこそ隠れる, 潜む

★**skull** /skʌl/ 名 C ▶定義 the bone structure of a human or animal head 人間や動物の頭の骨格→頭蓋(ずがい)骨, 頭骨‖ *She suffered a fractured skull in the fall.* 彼女は転落して頭蓋骨を骨折した. ☞ C5ページのさし絵

★**sky** /skáɪ/ 名 [C, 通常は単数, U] (複 **skies**) ▶定義 the space that you can see when you look up from the earth, and where you can see the sun, moon and stars 地上から見上げたときに見える空間. そこに太陽, 月, 星を見ることができる→空, 大空, 天空, 上空‖ *a cloudless/clear* *blue sky* 雲一つない・澄み切った青い空 ‖ *I saw a bit of blue sky between the clouds.* 雲の間から青い空がのぞいているのが見えた. ‖ *I saw a plane high up **in the sky**.* 空高く飛行機が飛んでいるのが見えた.

**sky-high** 形副 ▶定義 very high 非常に高い・高く → 天高い, 空高く, 非常に高い・高く, 法外に

**skyline** /skáɪlàɪn/ 名 C ▶定義 the shape that is made by tall buildings, etc against the sky 空を背景に高い建物などが画する輪郭 → **空を背景とした輪郭, スカイライン** ‖ *the Manhattan skyline* マンハッタンのスカイライン

**skyscraper** /skáɪskrèɪpər/ 名 C ▶定義 an extremely tall building 非常に高い建物 → **超高層ビル, 摩天楼, 高層建築**

> ▶語法
>
> 空をこする(scrape)摩天楼
>
> 超高層ビルを摩天楼と呼びますが、これはskyscraperの翻訳です. 壁紙をはがす道具のこともスクレーパーと呼びます. 天・空をこするような高い建物の意味なので「魔」ではなく摩擦の「摩」の字が用いられているのです. 摩天楼の代表格と言えば今でもニューヨークのEmpire State Buildingの名前が挙がります.

**slab** /slæb/ 名 C ▶定義 a thick, flat piece of sth 〜の厚く平らな一片 → **(木・石の)平板(ひらいた), (パン・菓子などの)平たく厚い1切れ** ‖ *huge concrete slabs* 分厚いコンクリートの平板 ☞ C7ページのさし絵

**slack** /slæk/ 形 ▶定義1 loose; not tightly stretched 緩い; ぴんと張っていない → **緩い; 締まっていない, たるんだ** ‖ *Leave the rope slack.* 縄をたるませておきなさい. ▶定義2 (used about a period of business) not busy; not having many customers (業務時間について)忙しくない; 客が少ない → **忙しくない, 活気のない, 閑散とした, 不景気な** ‖ *Trade is very slack here in winter.* ここでは冬になると商売がとても暇になる. ▶定義3 not carefully or properly done 慎重にまたはきちんと行われていない → **不注意な, 怠慢な, いいかげんな** ‖ *Slack security made terrorist attacks possible.* 警備の不備がテロリストの攻撃を許した. ▶定義4 (used about a person) not doing your work carefully or properly (人について)仕事を慎重にまたはきちんと行っていない → **物臭な, 無精な, のろい** ‖ *You've been rather slack about your homework lately.* あなたは最近, 宿題のやり方がいいかげんですね.

**slacken** /slǽk(ə)n/ 動 自 他 ▶定義1 to become or make sth less tight 緩くなる; 〜を緩める → **緩む, たるむ; 〜を緩める, 緩和する** ‖ *The rope slackened and he pulled his hand free.* 縄が緩んだので, 彼は(縛られていた)手を引き抜いた. ▶定義2 slacken (sth) (off) to become or make sth slower or less active 遅くなるまたは活発でなくなる; 〜を遅くするまたは不活発にする → **(速度が)のろくなる, (商売などが)不活発になる; 〜を不活発にする, 減じる, 〜を弱める** ‖ *He slackened off his pace towards the end of the race.* 彼はレースの終盤近くになって速度を落とした.

**slacks** /slæks/ 名 [複数扱い] ▶定義 trousers (especially not very formal ones) (特にあまり正装用でない)ズボン → **スラックス, 普段用のズボン** ‖ *a pair of slacks* 1本のスラックス

**slag**¹ /slæg/ 動

句動詞 slag sb off 略式 ▶定義 to say cruel or critical things about sb 〜についてひどいまたは辛辣(しんらつ)な事を言う → **〜をぼろくそに言う, こき下ろす, けなす**

**slag**² /slæg/ 名 U ▶定義 the waste material that is left after metal has been removed from rock 鉱石から金属を取り除いた後に残る廃棄物 → **スラグ, 鉱滓(こうさい), 溶滓(ようし)**

**slag heap** 名 C ▶定義 a hill made of slag スラグでできた小山 → **ぼた山**

**slain** SLAYの過去分詞形

**slalom** /slάːləm/ 名 C ▶定義 (in skiing, canoeing, etc) a race along a course on which competitors have to move from side to side between poles (スキー, カヌーなどで)競技者がポールの間を左右に縫って移動しなければならないコースで行われるレース → **スラローム, 回転滑降, 回転競技**

**slam** /slæm/ 動 (**slamming**; **slammed**) ▶定義1 自 他 to shut or make sth shut very loudly and with great force 非常に大きな音を立て, すごい勢いで閉まる; または〜を閉める → **バタンと閉まる; 〜をバタンと閉める, 乱暴に閉める** ‖ *I heard* the front door slam. 玄関のドアがバタンと閉まる音を聞いた. *She slammed her book shut and rushed out of the room.* 彼女は本を乱暴に閉じると, 部屋から飛び出した. ▶定義2 ⓑ to put sth somewhere very quickly and with great force ～をある所に非常に素早く勢いよく置く→～をドシンと置く, 荒っぽく投げ付ける, たたき付ける ‖ *He slammed the book down on the table and stormed out.* 彼はテーブルに本をたたき付けると怒って飛び出した. ☞参 **grand slam**

**slander** /slǽndər, slɑ́ːn-/ 名 ⓒⓤ ▶定義 a spoken statement about sb that is not true and that is intended to damage the good opinion that other people have of him/her; the legal offence of making this kind of statement ある人物に対する信用・評価を落とすことを意図した口頭による虚偽の陳述; このような陳述を行う違法行為→誹謗(ひぼう), 中傷, 悪口, 名誉毀損(きそん) ― **slander** 動 ⓣ→～を誹謗する, 中傷する, ～の名誉を傷付ける ― **slanderous** /-dərəs/ 形 →中傷的な, 名誉を傷付ける

\***slang** /slǽŋ/ 名 ⓤ ▶定義 very informal words and expressions that are more common in spoken language. Slang is sometimes used only by a particular group of people (for example students, young people, criminals) and often stays in fashion for a short time. Some slang is not polite. 話し言葉の中でより多く使われる非常にくだけた単語や言い回し. 時にはある特定の集団(例えば学生, 若者, 犯罪者)でのみ用いられ, しばしば短期間流行する. 丁寧でない表現もある→俗語, スラング ‖ *'Fag' is slang for 'cigarette' in British English.* イギリス英語では fag は cigarette(たばこ)の俗語だ.

**slant**¹ /slɑːnt; slǽnt/ 動 ▶定義1 ⓘ to be at an angle, not vertical or horizontal 垂直, 水平ではなく傾いている→傾斜する, 傾く, 斜めになる ‖ *My handwriting slants backwards.* 私の手書きの文字は左の方(普通とは逆方向)に傾く. *That picture isn't straight - it's slanting to the right.* その絵はまっすぐでない ― 右に傾いている. ▶定義2 (通常は受動態で)to describe information, events, etc in a way that supports a particular group or opinion 情報, 出来事などをある特定の集団や意見を支持するような書き方をする→～を歪曲(わいきょく)する, 曲げる, ゆがめて伝える ― **slanting** 形 →傾いた, 斜めの ‖ *She has beautiful slanting eyes.* 彼女は目じりの上がった美しい目をしている.

**slant**² /slɑːnt; slǽnt/ 名 ▶定義1 [単数扱い] a position at an angle, not horizontal or vertical 水平でも垂直でもなく斜めに傾いた位置→傾斜, 傾き, 斜め, 勾配(こうばい) ‖ *The sunlight fell on the table at a slant.* 日差しがテーブルの上に斜めに差し込んでいた. ▶定義2 ⓒ a way of thinking, writing, etc about sth, that sees things from a particular point of view ～についてある特定の視点から物事を見た考え方・書き方など→(特殊な)見方, 見解

**slap**¹ /slǽp/ 動 ⓣ (**slapping**; **slapped**) ▶定義1 to hit sb/sth with the inside of your hand when it is flat ～を平手で打つ→～を平手打ちする, ピシャリと打つ, びんたする ‖ *She slapped him across the face.* 彼女は彼の横つ面をピシャッとはたいた. *People slapped him on the back and congratulated him on winning.* 人々は彼の背中をぽんとたたいて, 勝利を祝した. ☞ S6 ページのさし絵 ▶定義2 to put sth onto a surface quickly and carelessly ～を素早くぞんざいに物の表面に置く→～を無造作に置く, (～に)パタンと置く ― **slap** 名 ⓒ→平手打ち, ピシャリと打つこと, びんた ‖ *I gave him a slap across the face.* 私は彼の顔に平手打ちを食らわした.

**slap**² /slǽp/ (または **slap bang**) 副 略式 ▶定義 used to show that sth happens accidentally at a bad time or place 具合の悪い時や場所で偶然～が起こることを示すのに用いて→出し抜けに, まともに, もろに ‖ *I hurried round the corner and walked slap into someone coming the other way.* 急いで角を曲がったら, 反対側からやって来た人ともろにぶつかってしまった.

**slapdash** /slǽpdæʃ/ 形 ▶定義 careless, or done quickly and carelessly いいかげんな, または急いでぞんざいにした→いいかげんな, ぞんざいな ‖ *slapdash building methods* ぞんざいな建築工法 *He's a bit slapdash about doing his homework on time.* 彼は時間通りに宿題をするということに, 少しいいかげんなところがある.

**slapstick** /slǽpstɪk/ 名 ⓤ ▶定義 a type of humour that is based on simple physical jokes, for example people falling over or hitting each other 互いにつまずいて転んだり, 殴り合いをす

るなど，単純でこっけいな体の動きを中心にした喜劇→どたばた喜劇，スラップスティック

**slap-up** 形 略式 ▶定義 (used about a meal) very large and very good (食事について)分量が非常に多く満足できる→飛び切り上等の，豪勢な，豪華な

**slash** /slæʃ/ 動 ▶定義1 他自 slash (at) sb/sth to make or try to make a long cut in sth with a violent movement ～を乱暴に長めに切り付けるまたは切り付けようとする→(～を)さっと切る，めった切りにする，切り付ける ▶定義2 他 to reduce an amount of money, etc very much 金額などを大幅に減らす→～を大幅に切り下げる，削減する ‖ *The price of coffee has been slashed by 20%.* コーヒーの値段は20パーセントも切り下げられた.

**slat** /slæt/ 名 C ▶定義 one of a series of long, narrow pieces of wood, metal or plastic, used in furniture, fences etc 木，金属，プラスチックの細長い一連の板の1枚. 家具，柵(さく)などに用いられる→細長い薄板，小割板，(ブラインドの)羽根板，横木

**slate** /sleɪt/ 名 ▶定義1 Ⓤ a type of dark grey rock that can easily be split into thin flat pieces 薄い板状に簡単に割り裂くことのできる濃い灰色の岩石→粘板岩 ▶定義2 C one of the thin flat pieces of slate that are used for covering roofs 屋根をふくのに用いられる粘板岩の薄板→(屋根ぶき用の)スレート

**slaughter** /ˈslɔːtər/ 動 他 ▶定義1 to kill an animal, usually for food 動物を通常食肉用に殺す→～を殺す，屠殺(とさつ)する ▶定義2 to kill a large number of people at one time, especially in a cruel way 大勢の人を特に残酷な方法で一度に殺す→～を虐殺する，大量に殺す ‖ *Men, women and children were slaughtered and whole villages destroyed.* 男女子供が大量虐殺され，村全体が破壊された. ☞参 **kill** の注 ― **slaughter** 名 Ⓤ→蓄殺，虐殺，大量殺人

**slaughterhouse** /ˈslɔːtərhaʊs/ (または 医 **abattoir**) 名 C ▶定義 a place where animals are killed for food 動物が食肉用に殺される場所→食肉処理場，屠殺(とさつ)場

**slave**¹ /sleɪv/ 名 C ▶定義 (in past time) a person who was owned by another person and had to work for him/her (昔)ほかの人に所有され，その人のために働かされた人→奴隷 ― **slavery** 名 Ⓤ→奴隷制度，奴隷であること，奴隷の身分 ‖ *the abolition of slavery in America* 米国における奴隷制度の廃止

**slave**² /sleɪv/ 動 自 ▶定義 slave (away) to work very hard ひたすらに一生懸命働く→奴隷のように働く，あくせく働く

**slay** /sleɪ/ 動 他 (過 **slew** /sluː/; 過分 **slain** /sleɪn/) (古) ▶定義 to kill violently; to murder 暴力的に殺す; 殺害する→～を殺す，殺害する，惨殺する

**sleazy** /ˈsliːzi, sleɪ-/ 形 ▶定義 (used about a place or a person) unpleasant and probably connected with criminal activities (場所や人について)不快で，犯罪行為に関係していそうな→みすぼらしい，安っぽい，いかがわしい ‖ *a sleazy nightclub* 安っぽいナイトクラブ

**sledge** /sledʒ/ (米 または = **sled** /sled/) 名 C ▶定義 a vehicle without wheels that is used for travelling on snow. Large sledges are often pulled by dogs, and smaller ones are used for going down hills, for fun or as a sport. 雪の上を移動するのに用いる車輪のない乗り物. 大型のものはしばしば犬が引っ張って動かし，小型のものは娯楽やスポーツとして坂道を下るのに用いられる→大型そり，(小型)そり，犬ぞり ☞参 **bobsleigh**, **toboggan** ☞ **sleigh** のさし絵 ― **sledge** 動 自→そりに乗る，そりで行く

**sleek** /sliːk/ 形 ▶定義1 (used about hair or fur) smooth and shiny because it is healthy (毛髪や獣毛について)健康なため滑らかで光沢のある→滑らかな，つやのある，すべすべした ▶定義2 (used about a vehicle) having an elegant, smooth shape (自動車について)形が優雅ですらりとした→格好のいい，スマートな，優美な ‖ *a sleek new sports car* スマートな新しいスポーツカー

★**sleep**¹ /sliːp/ 名 ▶定義1 Ⓤ the natural condition of rest when your eyes are closed and your mind and body are not active or conscious 目は閉じ，心身共に活動していないまたは意識していない，自然な休息の状態→眠り，睡眠 ‖ *Most people need at least seven hours' sleep every night.* ほとんどの人は毎晩最低7時間の睡眠を必要とする. *I didn't get much sleep last night.* 昨晩あまり眠れなかった. *Do you ever talk in your sleep?* あなたは寝言を言うことがありますか. *I couldn't get to sleep last night.* 昨晩寝つ

けなかった. ▶定義2 ［単数扱い］a period of sleep→睡眠時間, 一眠り‖ *You'll feel better after a good night's sleep.* 一晩ぐっすり眠れば, 気分が良くなりますよ. *I sometimes have a short sleep in the afternoon.* 時々午後に一眠りする.

成句 go to sleep ▶定義1 to start sleeping 眠り始める→眠る, 寝入る‖ *He got into bed and soon went to sleep.* 彼は寝床に入るとすぐに眠った. ▶定義2 (used about an arm, leg, etc) to lose the sense of feeling in it (腕, 足などについて)感覚を失う→しびれる, まひする

put (an animal) to sleep ▶定義 to kill an animal that is ill or injured because you want to stop it suffering 病気やけがの動物を苦しみから解放してやりたいために動物を殺す→(動物を)眠らす, 殺す

\***sleep**² /sliːp/ 動 (過, 過分 **slept** /slept/) ▶定義1 🅐 to rest with your eyes closed and your mind and body not active 目を閉じ, 心身を活動させずに休息する→眠る, 睡眠を取る, 寝る‖ *Did you sleep well?* よく眠りましたか. *I only slept for a couple of hours last night.* 昨晩2時間くらいしか眠らなかった. *I slept solidly from 10 last night till 11 this morning.* 昨晩10時から今朝11時まで熟睡した.

▶ asleepは通常, 眠っている人のことを描写するのに用いる: *The baby's asleep.* (赤ん坊は眠っている.) go to sleepは「眠り始める」という意味で用いる動詞である: *I was reading in bed last night, and I didn't go to sleep until about one o'clock.* (私は昨晩ベッドで本を読んでいて, 1時くらいまで眠りにつかなかった.)

▶定義2 🅑 (used about a place) to have enough beds for a particular number of people (場所について)ある特定の人数分だけベッドがある→〜人分の宿泊設備がある, 〜人分の寝床がある

成句 sleep/live rough ⇒ **ROUGH**³

句動 sleep in ▶定義 to sleep until later than usual in the morning because you do not have to get up 起きる必要がないので通常よりも遅くまで寝ている→朝寝坊する

▶ oversleepと比較.

sleep together; sleep with sb ▶定義 to have sex with sb (usually when you are not married to or living with that person) (相手と主として結婚していないまたは同棲(どうせい)していない場合に)〜と性交渉を持つ→寝る, ベッドを共にする

**sleeper** /slíːpər/ 名 🅒 ▶定義1 (形容詞と共に) a person who sleeps in a particular way. If you are a light sleeper you wake up easily. 特定の眠り方をする人. a light sleeperは眠りが浅い人すぐに目が覚める人を言う→眠る人, 眠りが〜な人‖ *a light/heavy sleeper* 眠りの浅い人・熟睡する人 ▶定義2 a bed on a train; a train with beds 列車の寝台; 寝台付き列車→寝台車の寝台, 寝台車

**sleeping bag** 名 🅒 ▶定義 a large soft bag that you use for sleeping in when you go camping, etc キャンプなどに出掛けた際, 中に入って眠るための大きな柔らかい袋→寝袋

**sleeping pill** 名 🅒 ▶定義 a medicine in solid form that you swallow to help you sleep 眠れるようにするために飲む錠剤→睡眠薬‖ *to take a sleeping pill* 睡眠薬を飲む

**sleepless** /slíːpləs/ 形 ▶定義 (used about a period, usually the night) without sleep (ある時間帯, 通常夜間について) 眠りのない→眠れない, 不眠の ― sleeplessness 名 🅤 →眠れないこと, 不眠 ☞ 参 insomnia

**sleepwalk** /slíːpwɔːk/ 動 🅐 ▶定義 to walk around while you are asleep 眠りながら歩き回る→夢遊状態で歩く, 夢中歩行する

**sleepy** /slíːpi/ 形 ▶定義1 tired and ready to go to sleep 疲れてすぐにでも眠れる→眠い, 眠たい, 眠そうな‖ *These pills might make you feel a bit sleepy.* これらの薬を飲むと少し眠くなるかもしれない. ▶定義2 (used about a place) very quiet and not having much activity (場所について)非常に静かであまり活気がない→眠っているような, 活気のない ― sleepily 副 →眠たくて, 眠そうに

**sleet** /sliːt/ 名 🅤 ▶定義 a mixture of rain and snow 雨と雪が混ざった物→みぞれ ☞ 参 **weather** の注

\***sleeve** /sliːv/ 名 🅒 ▶定義1 one of the two parts of a piece of clothing that cover the arms or part of the arms 両腕または両腕の一部を覆う衣類の2つの部分のうちの1つ→そで, たもと‖ *a blouse with long sleeves* 長そでのブラウス ☞ C6ページのさし絵 ▶定義2 **-sleeved** (複合形容詞を作るために用いて) with sleeves of a particular kind ある特定の種類のそでの付いた→〜そ

での, 〜のそでの付いた ‖ *a short-sleeved shirt* 半そでのシャツ

**sleeveless** /slíːvləs/ 形 ▶定義 without sleeves そでの付いていない→そでのない, そでなしの ‖ *a sleeveless sweater* そでなしのセーター

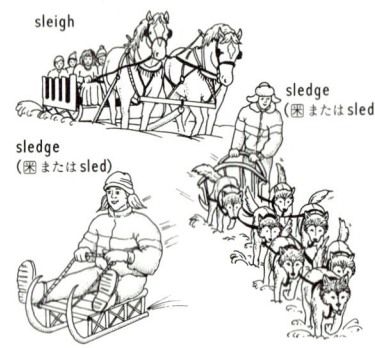

**sleigh** /sléɪ/ 名 C ▶定義 a vehicle without wheels that is used for travelling on snow and that is usually pulled by horses 雪の上を移動するのに用いる車輪のない乗り物. 通常は馬が引いて走る→馬車ぞり, そり ☞参 bobsleigh

**slender** /sléndər/ 形 ▶定義1 (used about a person or part of sb's body) thin in an attractive way (人や人の体の部分について) 魅力的に細い→ほっそりとした, すらりとした ‖ *long slender fingers* 長くほっそりとした指 ▶定義2 smaller in amount or size than you would like 望んでいるよりも量が少ない, 規模が小さい→**(資力・可能性などが) わずかな, 乏しい** ‖ *My chances of winning are very slender.* 私が勝つ可能性はごくわずかだ.

**slept** SLEEP¹ の過去・過去分詞形

**slew** SLAY の過去形

*****slice**¹ /sláɪs/ 名 C ▶定義1 a flat piece of food that is cut from a larger piece より大きな一塊の食べ物から切り取られた平たい一片→**1切れ, 薄切り, スライス** ‖ *a thick/thin slice of bread* 厚切り・薄切りのパン1枚 *Cut the meat into thin slices.* 肉を薄切りにしなさい. ☞ bread のさし絵 ☞ cake のさし絵 ▶定義2 a part of sth 〜の一部分→**一部, 部分, 分け前** ‖ *The directors have taken a large slice of the profits.* 重役たちは利益

の相当分をふところに収めた.

*****slice**² /sláɪs/ 動 ▶定義1 ⊕ to cut into thin flat pieces 薄い平らな片に切る→**〜を薄く切る, スライスする** ‖ *Peel and slice the apples.* リンゴの皮をむいて薄く切りなさい. *a loaf of sliced bread* 薄切りにしたパン1斤 ▶定義2 ⊜⊕ to cut sth easily with sth sharp 〜を鋭い物でさっと切る→**(〜を) 切る, 切り取る** ‖ *He sliced through the rope with a knife.* 彼はナイフでロープをすぱっと切った. *The glass sliced into her hand.* ガラスで彼女の手がパクッと切れた. ▶定義3 ⊕ (in ball sports) to hit the ball on the bottom or side so that it does not travel in a straight line (球技で) まっすぐ進まないように球の底や側面を打つ→**(ボール) をスライスさせる**

**slick**¹ /slɪk/ 形 ▶定義1 done smoothly and well, and seeming to be done without any effort 難なくうまく行われ, 骨を折った様子が見えない→**やすやすとやってのけた, 見事な, 鮮やかな** ▶定義2 clever at persuading people but perhaps not completely honest 人々を説得するのはうまいが, おそらく完全に正直とは言えない→**口のうまい, 如才ない**

**slick**² /slɪk/ = OIL SLICK

*****slide**¹ /sláɪd/ 動 (過, 過分 slid /slɪd/) ▶定義1 ⊜⊕ to move or make sth move smoothly along a surface 表面を滑らかに移動する; または〜を滑らかに移動させる→**滑らかに滑る, 滑走する; 〜を滑らせる, 〜を滑走させる** ‖ *She fell over and slid along the ice.* 彼女は転んで氷沿いに滑った. *The doors slide open automatically.* ドアが自動的にすうっと開く. ▶定義2 ⊜⊕ to move or make sth move quietly without being noticed 気付かれないで静かに移動する; または〜をそのように移動させる→**そっと移動する, こっそり歩く; 〜をそっと動かす, 滑り込ませる** ‖ *I slid out of the room when nobody was looking.* だれも見ていないときに部屋をそっと抜け出した. *She slid her hand into her pocket and took out a gun.* 彼女はポケットに手を滑り込ませ, 銃を取り出した. ▶定義3 ⊜ (used about prices, values, etc) to go down slowly and continuously (価格, 価値などについて) ゆっくりと継続的に下がる→**徐々に下がる, 減少する, 下落する** ▶定義4 ⊜ to move gradually towards a worse situation 徐々に悪い状況に移行する→**次第に陥る, 染まる, はまる** ‖ *The company slid into debt* *and eventually closed.* その企業は赤字に陥り，とうとう倒産した．

**\*slide**² /sláɪd/ 图 ⓒ ▶定義1 a small piece of glass that you put sth on when you want to examine it under a piece of equipment that makes things appear much bigger (a microscope) 物を拡大して見せる装置(顕微鏡)で，調べたいと思う物を載せる小さなガラス片→載物ガラス, スライド ▶定義2 a large toy consisting of a ladder and a long piece of metal, plastic, etc. Children climb up the ladder then slide down the other part. はしごと，金属，プラスチック製などの長い板でできた大型の遊戯具．子供たちははしごを登ってから板の部分を滑り降りる→滑り台 ☞ swing のさし絵 ▶定義3 a continuous slow fall, for example of prices, values, levels, etc 例えば物価，価値，水準などが連続してゆっくりと下がること→減少, 下落, 低下 ▶定義4 a small piece of photographic film in a plastic or cardboard frame プラスチックや厚紙の枠が付いた写真用の小さなフィルム→スライド ☞参 transparency

**\*slight** /sláɪt/ 形 ▶定義1 very small; not important or serious 非常に小さな；重要でない，重大でない→わずかな, かすかな, 取るに足りない ∥ *I've got a slight problem, but it's nothing to get worried about.* ちょっとした問題を抱えていますが，心配するほどのことはありません． *a slight change/difference/increase/improvement* わずかな変化・違い・増加・改善 *I haven't the slightest idea (= no idea at all) what you're talking about.* あなたが何について話をしているのかさっぱり(＝全く)分からない． ▶定義2 (used about a person's body) thin and light (人の体について) 細くて軽い→ほっそりした, やせた, きゃしゃな ∥ *His slight frame is perfect for a long-distance runner.* 彼のほっそりした体型は長距離走者に打って付けだ．

成句 **not in the slightest** ▶定義 not at all 全く～ない→少しも～ない, これっぽっちも～でない ∥ '*Are you angry with me?' 'Not in the slightest.*' 「私のことを怒っていますか」「ちっとも」

**\*slightly** /sláɪtli/ 副 ▶定義1 a little 少し→いささか, わずかに, かすかに ∥ *I'm slightly older than her.* 私は彼女より少しばかり年上だ． ▶定義2 a slightly-built person is small and thin 小さくて細い→ほっそりと, きゃしゃで

slink 1523

**\*slim**¹ /slɪm/ 形 (**slimmer; slimmest**) ▶定義1 thin in an attractive way 魅力的に細い→ほっそりとした, すらりとした, スリムな ∥ *a tall, slim woman* 背の高いすらりとした女性 ☞参 thin の注 ▶定義2 not as big as you would like 望んでいるほど大きくない→わずかな, 不十分な, 貧弱な ∥ *Her chances of success are very slim.* 彼女が成功する可能性はごくわずかだ．

**slim**² /slɪm/ 動 ⓘ (**slimming; slimmed**) ▶定義 to become or try to become thinner and lighter by eating less food, taking exercise, etc 減食・運動などでやせて体重が軽くなるまたはそうなろうとする→やせる, 細くなる, 体重を減らす ☞参 diet

**slime** /slaɪm/ 图 Ⓤ ▶定義 a thick unpleasant liquid どろっとした不快な液体→どろどろ(ねばねば)した物, 粘液, 粘着物, 泥砂, ヘドロ ∥ *The pond was covered with slime and had a horrible smell.* その池は汚泥だらけで，ひどいにおいを放っていた．

**slimy** /sláɪmi/ 形 ▶定義1 covered with slime→汚泥だらけの, ぬるぬるした ▶定義2 (used about a person) pretending to be friendly, in a way that you do not trust or like (人について) 信用できないまたは好ましくないやり方でも親しげな振りをする→いやらしい, 取り入ろうとする, ぺこぺこする

**sling**¹ /slɪŋ/ 图 ⓒ ▶定義 a piece of cloth that you put under your arm and tie around your neck to support a broken arm, wrist, etc 骨折した腕，手首などを支えるために腕を通して首の所で結ぶ布切れ→三角巾, つり包帯 ☞ **bandage** のさし絵

**sling**² /slɪŋ/ 動 ⓗ (過, 過分 **slung**) ▶定義1 to put or throw sth somewhere in a rough or careless way ～を乱暴にまたは無造作に，ある所に置くまたは投げる→～を投げる, ほうる, ほうり出す ▶定義2 to put sth into a position where it hangs loosely ～をだらりと垂れ下がる状態に置く→～をつるす, 掛ける, つり下げる

**slingshot** /slíŋʃɑ̀t/ 米 = **CATAPULT**¹

**slink** /slɪŋk/ 動 ⓘ (過, 過分 **slunk**) ▶定義 to move somewhere slowly and quietly because you do not want anyone to see you, often when you feel guilty or embarrassed しばしばやましかったり，きまり悪い時，だれにも見られたくないた

めに,ゆっくりと静かに移動する➜**こそこそ歩く,こそこそ逃げる,こっそり動く**

***slip**[1] /slɪp/ [動] (**slipping**; **slipped**) ▶定義1 [自] slip (over); slip (on sth) to slide accidentally and fall or nearly fall 誤って滑って転ぶ,転びそうになる➜**滑る,滑って転ぶ,ずり落ちる** ‖ *She slipped over on the wet floor.* 彼女はぬれた床で滑って転んだ. *His foot slipped on the top step and he fell down the stairs.* 彼は階段の一番上の段で足を滑らせて,下まで転げ落ちた. ▶定義2 [自] to slide accidentally out of the correct position or out of your hand 誤って正しい位置から,または手から滑り落ちる➜**滑り落ちる,外れる,抜ける** ‖ *This hat's too big. It keeps slipping down over my eyes.* この帽子は大きすぎる.私の目の上辺りまでずり落ちてきてしまう. *The glass slipped out of my hand and smashed on the floor.* 手からグラスが滑り落ちて床の上で粉々になった. ▶定義3 [自] to move or go somewhere quietly, quickly, and often without being noticed 静かに素早く,しばしば人に気付かれずに,ある場所に移る,または行く➜**滑るように動く,そっと移動する,こっそり動く** ‖ *While everyone was dancing we slipped away and went home.* 皆が踊っている間に私たちはそっと抜け出して帰宅した. ▶定義4 [他] slip sth (to sb); slip (sb) sth to put sth somewhere or give sth to sb quietly and often without being noticed ～を静かに,しばしば気付かれずにある場所に置く,または…に与える➜**～をそっと置く,～を(…に)こっそり手渡す** ‖ *She picked up the money and slipped it into her pocket.* 彼女は金を拾い上げると,そっとポケットに滑り込ませた. ▶定義5 [自][他] slip into/out of sth; slip sth on/off to put on or take off a piece of clothing quickly and easily 素早くさっと服を着るまたは脱ぐ➜**～をさっと着る・脱ぐ,まとう,履く,はめる,外す** ‖ *I slipped off my shoes.* 私はさっと靴を脱いだ. ▶定義6 [自] to fall a little in value, level, etc 価値,水準などが少し下がる➜**下がる,低下する,悪化する**

[成句] let sth slip ⇒ **LET**

slip your mind ▶定義 to be forgotten 忘れられる➜**(物事が)記憶・関心から去る,落ちる** ‖ *I'm sorry, the meeting completely slipped my mind.* すみません,会議のことをすっかり忘れていました.

[句動詞] slip out ▶定義 to accidentally say sth or tell sb sth ～をうっかり言う,または～に…をうっかり話す➜**口を滑らせる,うっかり口をつく,失言する** ‖ *I didn't intend to tell them. It just slipped out.* 私は彼らに話すつもりはなかった.つい口が滑ってしまったのだ.

slip up [略式] ▶定義 to make a mistake 間違いをする➜**間違う,誤る,へまをする**

**slip**[2] /slɪp/ [名] [C] ▶定義1 a small mistake, usually made by being careless or not paying attention 主として,軽率,不注意による小さな誤り➜**(ちょっとした)間違い,失敗,しくじり** ‖ *to make a slip* ちょっとした間違いを犯す ▶定義2 a small piece of paper 小さな紙切れ➜**紙片,メモ用紙** ‖ *I made a note of her name on **a slip of paper**.* 私は彼女の名前を紙切れに書き留めた. [英] *There seems to be a mistake on my **payslip** (= the piece of paper from your employer each month showing how much money you have been paid and how much tax, etc has been taken off).* 私の給料明細表(= 毎月雇用者から与えられる,支払い額や税金の天引き額などを記載した紙)に間違いがあるようだ. ▶定義3 an act of sliding accidentally and falling or nearly falling 誤って滑って転ぶまたは転びそうになる動作➜**滑ること,滑って転ぶこと,つまずき** ▶定義4 a thin piece of clothing that is worn by a woman under a dress or skirt 女性がドレスやスカートの下に着用する薄い衣類➜**スリップ,ペチコート**

[成句] give sb the slip [略式] ▶定義 to escape from sb who is following or trying to catch you 後を付けている人,または捕まえようとしている人から逃れる➜**～からまんまと逃れる,～をまく,～の目をくらまして逃げる**

a slip of the tongue ▶定義 something that you say that you did not mean to say 言うつもりはなくて言ってしまった事➜**失言,言い誤り,口を滑らせること**

**slipped disc** [名] [C] ▶定義 a painful injury caused when one of the flat things (discs) between the bones in your back (spine) moves out of its correct position 背中の骨(背骨)の間にある平らな物(椎間板)が正常な位置からずれたときに生じる痛みのある損傷➜**椎間板(ついかんばん)ヘルニア,ぎっくり腰**

**slipper** /slípər/ [名] [C] ▶定義 a light soft shoe that

S

is worn inside the house 家の中で履く軽くて柔らかい靴→部屋履き, 上履き, スリッパ ‖ *a pair of slippers* 1足のスリッパ ☛ **shoe** のさし絵

**slippery** /slíp(ə)ri/ (または略式 **slippy**) 形 ▶定義 (used about a surface or an object) difficult to walk on or hold because it is smooth, wet, etc (表面や物体について)つるつるしたり, ぬれたりしているために歩きにくいまたはつかみにくい→つるつる滑る, 滑りやすい, つかみにくい ‖ *a slippery floor* 滑りやすい床

**slip road** (米 **entrance/exit ramp**) 名 C ▶定義 a road that leads onto or off a motorway 高速道路に入ったり出たりする道路→高速道路への出入り道路, 進入路, 退出路

**slit**¹ /slít/ 名 C ▶定義 a long narrow cut or opening 細長い切り込みや開口部→切り込み, 切り口, 細長いすきま, 裂け目, スリット ‖ *a long skirt with a slit up the back* 後ろにスリットの入ったロングスカート

**slit**² /slít/ 動他 (**slitting**; 過, 過分 **slit**) ▶定義 to make a long narrow cut in sth ～に細長い切り込みを入れる→～を細長く切る, 裂く, 切り開く, ～にスリットを入れる ‖ *She slit the envelope open with a knife.* 彼女はナイフで封筒を切り開いた.

**slither** /slíðər/ 動自 ▶定義 to move by sliding from side to side along the ground like a snake 蛇のように地面をジグザグに滑りながら移動する→ずるずる滑る, 滑るように行く, 滑るように進む ‖ *I saw a snake slithering down a rock.* 1匹の蛇が岩をずるずると滑り降りていくのを見た.

**slob** /slɑ́b/ 名 C 略式 ▶定義 (used as an insult) a very lazy or untidy person (侮辱として用いて)非常な無精者またはだらしのない人→無精者, だらしのない人, 野暮天, 間抜け

**slog**¹ /slɑ́g/ 動自 (**slogging**; **slogged**) ▶定義 1 略式 slog (away) (at sth); slog (through sth) to work hard for a long period at sth difficult or boring 長時間, 困難または退屈な事に一生懸命励む→骨を折って働く, こつこつ働く, 精を出す, 頑張って(～を)やる ‖ *I've been slogging away at this homework for hours.* 私は何時間もこの宿題を頑張ってやっている. ▶定義 2 slog down, up, along, etc to walk or move in a certain direction with a lot of effort やっとのことである方向に歩くまたは移動する→重い足取りで下っていく, 上っていく, 進む

**slog**² /slɑ́g/ 名 [単数扱い] ▶定義 a period of long, hard, boring work or a long, tiring journey 長時間のきつい退屈な仕事, 長くて退屈な行程→つらい仕事, 骨の折れる仕事, 苦闘, 苦しい道のり, 強行軍

**slogan** /slóʊɡən/ 名 C ▶定義 a short phrase that is easy to remember and that is used in politics or advertising 政治や広告で用いられる覚えやすい短い文句→標語, スローガン, モットー, キャッチフレーズ ‖ *Anti-government slogans had been painted all over the walls.* 反政府のスローガンが壁一面にペンキで書かれていた. *an advertising slogan* 広告のキャッチフレーズ

**slop** /slɑ́p/ 動自他 (**slopping**; **slopped**) ▶定義 (used about a liquid) to pour over the edge of its container; to make a liquid do this (液体について)容器の縁からあふれる, またはあふれさせる→こぼれる; ～をこぼす ‖ *He filled his glass too full and beer slopped onto the table.* 彼はグラスを一杯に満たしすぎたので, ビールがテーブルの上にこぼれた.

\***slope** /slóʊp/ 名 ▶定義 1 C a surface or piece of land that goes up or down 上方または下方に傾いている地面または土地→坂, 斜面, 丘 ‖ *The village is built on a slope.* その村は傾斜地にある. *a steep/gentle slope* 急な・なだらかな坂 *The best ski slopes are in the Alps.* 最高のスキーのゲレンデはアルプスにある. ▶定義 2 [単数扱い] the amount that a surface is not level; the fact of not being level 表面が平たんでない度合い; 平たんでないこと→勾配(こうばい), 傾斜, 傾斜度 — slope 動自 ▶定義 傾斜する, 傾く, 坂になる ‖ *The road slopes down to the river.* その道路は川に向かって下り坂になっている. *a sloping roof* 勾配のある屋根

**sloppy** /slɑ́pi/ 形 ▶定義 1 that shows lack of care, thought or effort; untidy 気配り, 思慮, または努力の不足を示す; だらしのない→ずさんな, いいかげんな, だらしのない ‖ *a sloppy worker/writer/dresser* いいかげんな仕事をする人・雑な文章を書く人・服装のだらしない人 *a sloppy piece of work* ずさんな仕事 ▶定義 2 (used about clothes) not tight and without much shape (服装について)体にぴったりせずあまり形のない→だらしのない, ぶかぶかの, だぶだぶの ▶定義 3 英 略式 showing emotions in a silly embarrassing way 感情の表し方が愚かで恥ずかしい➡**感傷的な,めめしい,めそめそした** ‖ *I can't stand sloppy love songs.* 感傷的なラブソングには耐えられない. ☛ より正式な語は sentimental.

**slosh** /slɑʃ/ 動自式 ▶定義1 自 (used about a liquid) to move around noisily inside a container (液体について) 容器の中を音を立てながら動き回る➡**(水などが)バシャバシャ跳ねる,揺れ動く,跳ねる** ▶定義2 他 to pour or drop liquid somewhere in a careless way 不注意に液体をつぐまたはこぼす➡**〜を不器用につぐ,バシャッと跳ね飛ばす**

**sloshed** /slɑʃt/ 形 (俗語) ▶定義 drunk➡**酔っ払った,酒に酔った**

**slot**¹ /slɑt/ 名 C ▶定義1 a straight narrow opening in a machine, etc 機械などのまっすぐな細い開口部➡**細長い穴,溝,硬貨投入口,料金差し入れ口** ‖ *Put your money into the slot and take the ticket.* 金を投入口に入れて切符を取りなさい. ☛ telephone のさし絵 ▶定義2 a place in a list, system, organization, etc 一覧表,機構,組織などに占める場所➡**地位,位置,場所** ‖ *The single has occupied the Number One slot for the past two weeks.* そのシングル盤はここ 2 週間第 1 位を占めている.

**slot**² /slɑt/ 動他自 (**slotting; slotted**) ▶定義 to put sth into a particular space that is designed for it; to fit into such a space 〜を専用に設計された特定の空間に入れる; 特定の空間にぴったりはまる➡**〜をはめ込む,入れる; 入る,うまくはまる** ‖ *He slotted a tape into the VCR.* 彼はビデオデッキにテープを差し込んだ. *The video slotted in easily.* そのビデオは簡単に納まった.

成句 **fall/slot into place** ⇒ **PLACE**¹

**slot machine** 名 C ▶定義 a machine with an opening for coins that sells drinks, cigarettes, etc or on which you can play games 飲み物,たばこなどの販売,またはゲームのできる,硬貨の投入口が付いた機械➡**自動販売機,スロットマシン**

**slouch** /slaʊtʃ/ 動自 ▶定義 to sit, stand or walk in a lazy way, with your head and shoulders hanging down 肩を落とし,うなだれて,だらしなく座る・立つ・歩く➡**前かがみにだらしなく座る・立つ・歩く**

**slovenly** /slʌv(ə)nli/ 形 (古) ▶定義 lazy, careless and untidy 無精で不注意でだらしない➡**無精な,だらしのない,いいかげんな**

**★slow**¹ /sloʊ/ 形 副 ▶定義1 moving, doing sth or happening without much speed; not fast あまり速度を出さずに動く,〜をする,〜が起こる; 速くない➡**(速度・動作などが)遅い,のろい,ゆっくりとした; 遅く,のろく,ゆっくりと** ‖ *The traffic is always very slow in the city centre.* 市の中心部ではいつも車の流れが非常に遅い. *Haven't you finished your homework yet? You're being very slow!* まだ宿題を終えていないのですか.いつになくぐずぐずしてますね. *Progress was slower than expected.* 進行は期待していたよりも遅かった. *a slow driver/walker/reader* ゆっくりと運転する人・足ののろい人・読むのが遅い人 ⇔ **fast** ▶ slow を副詞として用いることはできるが,slowly の方がはるかに一般的である.ただし,slow はしばしば複合語で用いられる: *slow-moving traffic* (のろのろ進む車の流れ) 比較級 slower と more slowly はいずれもよく使われる: *Could you drive a bit slower/more slowly, please?* (もう少しゆっくり運転していただけませんか.)

▶定義2 **slow to do sth; slow (in/about) doing sth** not doing sth immediately 〜をすぐにしない➡**〜するのが遅い,〜するのに手間取る,なかなか〜しない** ‖ *She was rather slow to realize what was going on.* 彼女は何が起こっているのかなかなか理解しなかった. *They've been rather slow in replying to my letter!* 彼らは私の手紙になかなか返事をくれない. ▶定義3 not quick to learn or understand 物覚えまたは物分かりが悪い➡**物覚えの悪い,理解の遅い,のみ込みが悪い** ‖ *He's the slowest student in the class.* 彼はクラスで一番物覚えの悪い生徒だ. ▶定義4 not very busy; with little action あまり忙しくない; ほとんど活気のない➡**不景気な,不振の,活気のない** ‖ *Business is very slow at the moment.* ちょうど今商売は大変不景気だ. ▶定義5 (名詞の前は不可) (used about watches and clocks) showing a time that is earlier than the real time (腕時計や時計について) 実際の時間よりも前の時刻を示す➡**遅れている** ‖ *That clock is five minutes slow (= it says it is 8.55 when the correct time is 9.00).* その時計は5分遅れている (= 正しい時刻が9時のときに8時55分を示している). —

slowness 名 ⓤ →遅いこと, 緩慢

成句 quick/slow on the uptake ⇒ UPTAKE

***slow**² /slóu/ 動 自他 ▶定義 to start to move, do sth or happen at a slower speed; to cause sth to do this よりゆっくりした速度で動き出す, 〜をし出すまたは〜が起こり出す; 〜をそのようにさせる→**速度が落ちる, 遅くなる; 〜を遅くする** ‖ *He slowed his pace a little.* 彼は少し歩調を緩めた.

句動詞 **slow (sb/sth) down/up** ▶定義 to start to move, do sth or happen at a slower speed; to cause sb/sth to do this よりゆっくりした速度で動き出す, 〜をし出すまたは〜が起こり出す; 〜をそのようにさせる→**速度が落ちる; 〜の速度を落とす** ‖ *Can't you slow down a bit? You're driving much too fast.* もう少し速度を落とせませんか. スピードを出しすぎていますよ. *These problems have slowed up the whole process.* これらの問題が全体の進行を遅らせている.

***slowly** /slóuli/ 副 ▶定義 at a slow speed; not quickly ゆっくりとした速度で; 速くなく→**遅く, ゆっくりと, のろく** ‖ *He walked slowly along the street.* 彼はゆっくりと通りを歩いていた.

**slow motion** 名 ⓤ ▶定義 (in a film or on television) a method of making action appear much slower than in real life (映画やテレビで)動きを現実よりもずっとゆっくりと見せる方法→**高速度撮影による動き, スローモーション** ‖ *They showed the winning goal again, this time in slow motion.* 彼らは, 今度はスローモーションで, もう一度決勝のゴールを見せた.

**sludge** /slʌdʒ/ 名 ⓤ ▶定義 a thick, soft unpleasant substance; mud どろどろとした柔らかい不快な物質; 泥→**泥, ぬかるみ, 軟泥, ヘドロ**

**slug** /slʌg/ 名 ⓒ ▶定義 a small black or brown animal with a soft body and no legs, that moves slowly along the ground and eats garden plants 柔らかい体をした足のない小さな黒または茶色の動物. 地面をゆっくりと移動し, 庭の植物を食べる→**ナメクジ** ☛ snail のさし絵

**sluggish** /slʌ́gɪʃ/ 形 ▶定義 moving or working more slowly than normal in a way that seems lazy 無精に見えるくらい通常よりもゆっくりと動くまたは働く→**のろい, (動作などが) 鈍い, 緩慢な**

**slum** /slʌm/ 名 ⓒ ▶定義 an area of a city where living conditions are extremely bad, and where the buildings are dirty and have not been repaired for a long time 生活状態が極端に悪く, 建物が汚れていて長い間修復されていない都市の一区域→**スラム街, 貧民街, 貧民窟(くつ)**

**slump**¹ /slʌmp/ 動 自 ▶定義 **1** (used about economic activity, prices, etc) to fall suddenly and by a large amount (経済活動, 価格などについて)突然大幅に下落する→**暴落する, 落ち込む, 不振となる** ‖ *Shares in BP slumped 33p to 181p yesterday.* 英国石油会社の株価は昨日 33 ペンス下がって 181 ペンスに大きく落ち込んだ. *The newspaper's circulation has slumped by 30%.* その新聞の発行部数は 30 パーセント落ち込んでいる. ▶定義 **2** to fall or sit down suddenly when your body feels heavy and weak, usually because you are tired or ill 主として疲れや病気のため, 体が重苦しく弱く感じられて突然倒れるまたは座り込む→**バタンと倒れる, 崩れるように座る**

**slump**² /slʌmp/ 名 ⓒ ▶定義 **1 a slump (in sth)** a sudden large fall in sales, prices, the value of sth, etc 〜の販売量, 価格, 価値などの急な大下落→**暴落, 落ち込み** ‖ *a slump in house prices* 住宅価格の急落 ▶定義 **2** a period when a country's economy is doing very badly and a lot of people do not have jobs 国の経済状態が非常に悪く, 多数の人が失業している時期→**不況, 不景気, 景気の不振** ‖ *The British car industry is in a slump.* イギリスの自動車業界は景気が悪い.

**slung** SLING² の過去・過去分詞形
**slunk** SLINK の過去・過去分詞形

**slur**¹ /sləːr/ 動 自他 (**slurring**; **slurred**) ▶定義 to pronounce words in a way that is not clear, often because you are drunk しばしば酔っているため, 不明瞭(めいりょう)に語を発音する→**〜を不明瞭に発音する, 不明瞭に言う**

**slur**² /sləːr/ 名 ⓒ ▶定義 **a slur (on sb/sth)** an unfair comment or an insult that could damage people's opinion of sb/sth 〜に対する評判を損ないかねない不当な意見や侮辱→**中傷, 非難, 悪口, 侮辱**

**slurp** /sləːrp/ 動 自他 略式 ▶定義 to drink noisily 音を立てて飲む→**(〜を)ずるずる[ちゅーちゅー]と音を立てて飲む, すすりながら飲む**

**slush** /slʌʃ/ 名 ⓤ ▶定義 **1** snow that has been on the ground for a time and that is now a dirty mixture of ice and water 地面にしばらく残っていた雪が、今は氷と水の混じったぬかるみ状態になったもの→**半解けの雪、解けかけた雪、ぬかるみ** ▶定義2 略式 films, books, feelings, etc that are considered to be silly because they are too romantic and emotional あまりにロマンチックで感傷的すぎて下らないと思われる映画,本,感情など→**感傷的で安っぽい読み物,映画** — slushy 形→**雪解けの、ぬかるみの、感傷的な**

**sly** /slaɪ/ 形 ▶定義1 (used about a person) acting or done in a secret or dishonest way, often intending to trick people (人について) しばしば人々をだますことを意図して、内緒でまたは不正直に行動する、またはそのような形で行われる→**こそこそした、陰険な、ずるい** ☞類 cunning ▶定義2 (used about an action) suggesting that you know sth secret (行動について) 何か秘密を知っているとほのめかす→**秘密を知っていると言いたげな、訳知り顔の、意味ありげな** ‖ a sly smile/look 意味ありげな笑い・訳知り顔 — slyly 副→**ずるく、悪賢く**

**smack** /smæk/ 動他 ▶定義 to hit sb with the inside of your hand when it is flat, especially as a punishment 特に罰として平手でたたく→**〜をピシャリと打つ、たたく** ‖ I never smack my children. 私は決して自分の子供たちに手を上げない。— smack 名 ⓒ→**平手打ち、ピシャリと打つ音** ‖ You're going to get a smack if you don't do as I say! 私の言った通りにしないと、平手打ちを食うことになるよ.

句動詞 smack of sth ▶定義 to make you think that sb/sth has an unpleasant attitude or quality 〜に不快な態度・特性があると思わせる→**〜の気味がある、〜染みたところがある、〜めいたところがある**

*****small** /smɔːl/ 形副 ▶定義1 not large in size, number, amount, etc 大きさ、数、量などが大きくない→**小さい、狭い、少ない、小型の、小さく、少なく** ‖ a small car/flat/town 小型車・狭いアパート・小さな町 a small group of people 小人数のグループ a small amount of money 小額の金 She's painted the picture far too small. 彼女はその絵を小さくかきすぎてしまった. That dress is too small for you. その洋服はあなたには小さすぎる. ▶定義2 young 若い→**若い、幼い** ‖ He has a wife and three small children. 彼には妻と3人の幼い子供がいる. When I was small we lived in a big old house. 幼いころ、私たちは大きな古い家に住んでいた. ▶定義3 not important or serious; slight 重要でない、重大でない;下らない→**取るに足らない、ささいな** ‖ Don't worry. It's only a small problem. 心配しなさんな. ささいな問題だ.
➤ small は big や large の最も一般的な反意語である. little は小ささの概念を表すだけでなく、ある種の感情を表すために別の形容詞と一緒に用いられる: a horrible little man (恐ろしい小男) a lovely little girl (かわいらしい小さな女の子) a nice little house (すてきな小さい家) 比較級、最上級 smaller, smallest もよく使われる. small は rather, quite, very などの語としばしば一緒に用いられる: My flat is smaller than yours. (私のアパートはあなたのよりも小さい.) The village is quite small. (その村はとても小さい.) a very small car (大変小さな自動車) little はあまり rather, quite, very などの語と一緒には用いられない. 通常比較級、最上級がない.

成句 in a big/small way ⇒ WAY¹

**small ad** 英 略式 = CLASSIFIED ADVERTISEMENT

**small change** 名 Ⓤ ▶定義 coins that have a low value 小額の硬貨→**小銭**

**the small hours** 名 [複数扱い] ▶定義 the early morning hours soon after midnight 真夜中直後の午前が始まる最初の2,3時間→**真夜中過ぎ(午前0時から3時ころまでを言う)**

**smallpox** /ˈsmɔːlpɒks/ 名 Ⓤ ▶定義 a serious infectious disease that causes a high temperature and leaves marks on the skin. In past times many people died from smallpox. 高熱を出し、皮膚に跡が残る重い伝染病. 昔は大勢の人々が死亡した→**天然痘、疱瘡(ほうそう)**

**the small print** (米 the fine print) 名 Ⓤ ▶定義 the important details of a legal document, contract, etc that are usually printed in small type and are therefore easy to miss 法律文書・契約書などの重要な細目. 通常小さな活字で印刷されていて見落としやすい→**細目、細字部分** ‖ Make sure you read the small print before you sign anything. どんな書類でも署名をする前に必ず細字部分を読みなさい.

**small-scale** 形 ▶定義 (used about an organization or activity) not large; limited in what it does (組織や活動について) 大きくない; することが限られた➔**小規模の**

**small talk** 🈂 🈫 ▶定義 polite conversation, for example at a party, about unimportant things パーティーなどであまり重要でない事について話す儀礼的な会話➔**世間話, おしゃべり, 雑談** ‖ *We had to **make small talk** for half an hour.* 私たちは (儀礼上) 世間話を半時間ほどしなければならなかった.

★**smart**¹ /smɑːrt/ 形 ▶定義1 特に 英 (used about a person) having a clean and tidy appearance (人について) 清潔で整った外見をした➔**身なりのきちんとした, 洗練された** ‖ *You look smart. Are you going somewhere special?* 決まってますね. どこか特別な所にお出掛けですか. ▶定義2 特に 英 (used about a piece of clothing, etc) good enough to wear on a formal occasion (衣服などについて) 正式な場所に着ていけるほどの➔**しゃれた, きちんとした, 洗練された** ‖ *a smart suit* しゃれた服 ▶定義3 clever; intelligent 賢い, 知的な➔**頭の切れる, 利口な, 賢明な** ‖ *He's not smart enough to be a politician.* 彼は政治家になれるほど明敏でない. ▶定義4 特に 英 fashionable and usually expensive 上流の人たち向きの通常高価な➔**高級な, 流行の** ‖ *a smart restaurant/hotel* 高級レストラン・ホテル ▶定義5 (used about a movement or action) quick and usually done with force (動きや動作について) 素早く, 通常は勢いよく行われる➔**機敏な, 活発な, きびきびした** ― **smartly** 副 ➔**スマートに, こぎれいに, 利口に, 素早く, 激しく, 強く** ‖ *She's always smartly dressed.* 彼女はいつもしゃれた格好をしている.

---

**▶日本語 vs 英語**

**smart は「頭が良い」**

「あの人はスマートだ」と言うと, ほっそりしているという意味ですが, 英語の smart にはそのような意味は全くありません.「やせている」は英語では slim です. smart は「頭が良い」とか「身なりが良い」とか「格好が良い」という意味で使われます. 洋服を格好良く着こなすためには, やせていた方が良いとされたことから,「やせている」=「スマートだ」という和製英語ができたようです.

---

**smart**² /smɑːrt/ 動 ▶定義1 smart (from sth) to feel a stinging pain in your body 体に刺すような痛みを感じる➔**うずく, ずきずき痛む, ひりひりする** ▶定義2 smart (from/over sth) to feel upset or offended because of a criticism, failure, etc 批判, 失敗などのため困惑するまたは気分を害する➔**(〜で)感情を害する, 怒る, 憤慨する**

**smart card** 🈂 🄲 ▶定義 a plastic card, for example a credit card, on which information can be stored in electronic form 情報を電子的に記憶させることのできる, クレジットカードなどのプラスチック製カード➔**スマートカード**

**smarten** /ˈsmɑːrt(ə)n/ 特に 英
**何動詞** smarten (yourself/sb/sth) up ▶定義 to make yourself/sb/sth look tidy and more attractive 自分自身や〜をきれいに, より魅力的に見せる➔**きれいになる, めかす; 〜をきれいにする, 粋(いき)にする**

★**smash**¹ /smæʃ/ 動 ▶定義1 自他 to break sth, or to be broken violently and noisily into many pieces 〜を乱暴に騒々しく粉々に壊す; 激しく音を立てて〜が粉々になる➔**粉々になる; 〜を粉々にする, 粉砕する** ‖ *The glass smashed into a thousand pieces.* グラスが無数の破片に砕け散った. *The police had to smash the door open.* 警察はドアをたたき壊して開けなければならなかった. ▶定義2 自他 smash (sth) against, into, through, etc to move with great force in a particular direction; to hit sth very hard ある特定の方向にものすごい勢いで移動する; 〜を強く打つ➔**(〜に)激突する, 衝突する, (〜を)ぶち抜く, 〜を強くぶつける** ‖ *The car smashed into a tree.* 車は木に激突した. *He smashed his fist through the window.* 彼はこぶしで窓をぶち割った. ▶定義3 他 smash sth (up) to crash a vehicle, usually causing a lot of damage 通常大きな破損を招くほど車などを衝突させる ➔ **〜をぶつつける, 衝突させる** ▶定義4 他 (in tennis) to hit a ball that is high in the air downwards very hard over the net (テニスで) 空中に高く上がったボールをネットの向こう側に強く打ち下ろす➔**〜をスマッシュする**

**smash**² /smæʃ/ 🈂 ▶定義1 [単数扱い] the action or the noise of sth breaking violently 〜が激しく壊れる動作または音➔**粉砕, 粉砕する音, ガチャ**

## 1530 smear¹

ンという音, 激突, 強打 ▶定義2 ❻ (in tennis, etc) a way of hitting a ball that is high in the air downwards and very hard over the net (テニスなどで)空中に高く上がったボールをネットの向こう側に強く打ち下ろす方法 →スマッシュ ▶定義3 (または **smash hit**) ❻略式 a song, play, film, etc that is very successful 非常に成功した歌, 劇, 映画など →**大当たり, 大ヒット, 大成功**

**smear¹** /smɪər/ 動 ❻ ▶定義 smear sth on/over sth/sb; smear sth/sb with sth to spread a sticky substance across sth/sb ~にベタベタした物を塗る →(べとつくものなどを)~に塗り付ける, ~に…を塗って汚す ‖ *Her face was smeared with blood.* 彼女の顔は血だらけになっていた.

**smear²** /smɪər/ 名 ❻ ▶定義1 a dirty mark made by spreading a substance across sth ~にある物質を塗ってできた汚れ →**汚れ, 染み, 汚点** ▶定義2 something that is not true that is said or written about an important person and that is intended to damage people's opinion about him/her, especially in politics 特に政界で重要人物の世間的評価を傷付けることを意図して, 虚偽の事を言ったり書いたりすること →**中傷, 誹謗(ひぼう), 名誉毀損(きそん)** ‖ *He was the victim of a smear campaign.* 彼は組織的な中傷攻撃の被害者だった.

★**smell¹** /smel/ 動(過, 過分 **smelt** /smelt/ または **smelled** /smeld/) ▶定義1 ❸ smell (of sth) to have a particular smell ある特定のにおいがする →**におう, 香る, (~の)においがする** ‖ *Dinner smells good!* 夕食のいいにおいがする. *This perfume smells of roses.* この香水はバラの香りがする. *His breath smelt of whisky.* 彼の息はウイスキーのにおいがした. ▶定義2 ❸ to have a bad smell →**嫌なにおいがする, 悪臭を放つ, 臭い** ‖ *Your feet smell.* あなたの足はにおう. ▶定義3 ❻ to notice or recognize sb/sth by using your nose 鼻で~に気付くまたは識別する →**~のにおいがする, ~のにおいで気付く, ~のにおいが分かる** ‖ *He could smell something burning.* 彼には何かが焦げるにおいがした. *Can you smell gas?* ガスのにおいがしますか. *I could still smell her perfume in the room.* その部屋で彼女の香水の残り香がまだしていた.

▶ smellなど感覚, 例えばtaste(味覚), see(視覚), hear(聴覚)に関する動詞は進行形では使われない. その代わり例えばcanを使う: *I can smell smoke.*(たばこのにおいがする.)

▶定義4 ❻ to put your nose near sth and breathe in so that you can discover or identify its smell においをかいだりにおいの正体を見極めるために~に鼻を近付けて息を吸う →**~のにおいをかぐ, かいでみる** ‖ *I smelt the milk to see if it had gone off.* 牛乳が駄目になっていないかにおいをかいでみた. ▶定義5 ❸ to be able to smell においをかぐことができる →**においをかぐ力がある, 臭覚がある, 鼻が利く** ‖ *I can't smell properly because I've got a cold.* 風邪を引いたので鼻が利かない.

★**smell²** /smel/ 名 ▶定義1 ❻ the impression that you get of sth by using your nose; the thing that you smell 鼻で感じ取った~の印象; においをかいだもの →**におい, 香り** ‖ *What's that smell?* そのにおいは何ですか. *a sweet/musty/fresh/sickly smell* 甘い香り・かび臭いにおい・さわやかな香り・むかつくにおい *a strong/faint smell of garlic* ニンニクの強烈な・かすかなにおい ▶定義2 [単数扱い]an unpleasant smell 不快なにおい →**悪臭** ‖ *Ugh! What's that smell?* うっ. あの悪臭は何ですか.

▶ stink, stench, odour, pongはすべて不快なにおいに対して用いられる語である. aroma, fragrance, perfume, scentは心地良い香りを指す.

▶定義3 ❶ the ability to sense things with the nose 鼻で物をかぎ取る能力 →**臭覚** ‖ *Dogs have a very good sense of smell.* 犬は非常に鼻が利く. ▶定義4 ❻ the action of putting your nose near sth to smell it においをかぐために鼻を~に近付ける動作 →**においをかぐこと, 一かぎ** ‖ *Have a smell of this milk; is it all right?* この牛乳のにおいをかいでみてください. 大丈夫ですか.

**smelly** /ˈsmeli/ 形略式 ▶定義 having a bad smell →**嫌なにおいのする** ‖ *smelly feet* 臭い足

★**smile¹** /smaɪl/ 名 ❻ ▶定義 an expression on your face in which the corners of your mouth turn up, showing happiness, pleasure, etc 口の両端を上げて幸せ, 喜びなどを表している顔の表情 →**笑い, 微笑, ほほえみ** ‖ *to have a smile on your face* 顔に笑みをたたえる *'It's nice to see you,' he said with a smile.* 「あなたにお会いでき

てうれしいです」と彼はにこっとしながら言った. ☛参 **beam**, **grin**, **smirk**

**\*smile²** /smáɪl/ 動 ▶定義1 📵 smile (at sb/sth) to make a smile appear on your face 顔に笑いを浮かべせる➔(〜に)微笑する, ほほえむ, にっこりする ‖ *to smile sweetly/faintly/broadly* 愛らしく・かすかに・にこやかに笑う *She smiled at the camera.* 彼女はカメラに向かってほほえんだ.
▶定義2 📵 to say or express sth with a smile 笑いながら〜を言うまたは表現する➔ほほえんで〜を示す, 微笑して〜を表現する ‖ *I smiled a greeting to them.* 私は彼らににっこり笑ってあいさつした.

**smirk** /smɜːrk/ 名 ⓒ ▶定義 an unpleasant smile which you have when you are pleased with yourself or think you are very clever 自分自身に満足したり, 自分がとても賢いと思ったりしたときに浮かべる不愉快な笑い➔にやにや笑い ― smirk 動 📵 ➔にやにや笑う

**smog** /smɔ(ː)g, smag/ 名 ⓤ ▶定義 dirty, poisonous air that can cover a whole city 街全体を覆うことがある汚れた有毒の空気➔スモッグ, 煙霧

**\*smoke¹** /smóʊk/ 名 ▶定義1 ⓤ the grey, white or black gas that you can see in the air when something is burning 何かが燃えているときに空中に見える灰色・白・黒色のガス➔煙, 噴煙, 煤煙(ばいえん) ‖ *Thick smoke poured from the chimney.* 濃い煙が煙突から吐き出されていた. *a room full of cigarette smoke* たばこの煙が充満した部屋 ▶定義2 [ⓒ, 通常は単数] an action of smoking a cigarette, etc たばこなどを吸う動作➔一服, 喫煙

**\*smoke²** /smóʊk/ 動 ▶定義1 📵📵 to breathe in smoke through a cigarette, etc and let it out again; to use cigarettes, etc in this way, as a habit たばこなどから煙を吸い込み, 再び吐き出す; 習慣としてたばこなどをこのように吸う➔(たばこを)吸う; 喫煙する ‖ *Do you mind if I smoke?* たばこを吸っても構いませんか. *I used to smoke 20 cigarettes a day.* 私はかつて日に20本のたばこを吸っていた. ▶定義2 📵 to send out smoke➔煙を出す ‖ *The oil in the pan started to smoke.* なべの油が煙を出し始めた.
― smoker 名 ⓒ ➔たばこを吸う人, 喫煙者 ‖ *She's a* **chain smoker** *(= she finishes one cigarette and then immediately lights another).* 彼女はチェーンスモーカーだ(= 彼女はたばこを吸い終わるとすぐに別のに火をつける). ⇔ **non-smoker** ― smoking 名 ⓤ ➔たばこを吸うこと, 喫煙 ‖ *My doctor has advised me to give up smoking.* 医者は私に禁煙するよう忠告した. *Would you like a table in the smoking or non-smoking section?* お席は喫煙席と禁煙席のどちらがよろしいですか.

**smoked** /smóʊkt/ 形 ▶定義 (used of certain types of food) given a special taste by being hung for a period of time in smoke from wood fires (ある種の食べ物に用いて) 木を燃やした煙の中に一定時間つるして独特の風味を付けた➔薫製(くんせい)にした, 薫製の ‖ *smoked salmon/ham/cheese* 薫製の鮭・ハム・チーズ

**smoky** /smóʊki/ 形 ▶定義1 full of smoke; producing a lot of smoke 煙に満ちた; 多量の煙を出す➔煙だらけの, 煙が立ち込めた, 煙の多い, 煙った ‖ *a smoky room/fire* 煙い部屋・くすぶった火 ▶定義2 with the smell, taste or appearance of smoke 煙のにおい・味・外見をした➔煙のにおい・味のする, すすけた, (色などが)くすんだ

**smolder** 米 = SMOULDER

**\*smooth¹** /smuːð/ 形 ▶定義1 having a completely flat surface with no lumps or holes or rough areas こぶ, 穴, ざらざらした所のない完全に平らな表面を持つ➔滑らかな, すべすべした, 凹凸のない ‖ *smooth skin* 滑らかな肌 *a smooth piece of wood* すべすべした木片 ⇔ **rough** ▶定義2 (of a liquid mixture) without lumps (液体の混合物について) 塊のない➔むらのない, よく混ざった, 均一な ‖ *Stir the sauce until it is smooth.* むらがなくなるまでソースをかき混ぜなさい. ⇔ **lumpy** ▶定義3 without difficulties 困難を伴わない➔順調な, 円滑に進む, 障害のない ‖ *The transition from the old method to the new has been very smooth.* 古い方式から新しい方式への移行はとても順調に行われている.
▶定義4 (of a journey in a car, etc) with an even, comfortable movement (自動車などでの旅行について) 調子の良い快適な動きの➔快調な, 円滑に動く, きしらない ‖ *You get a very smooth ride in this car.* この車はとても乗り心地がいい. ⇔ **bumpy** ▶定義5 too pleasant or polite to be trusted 愛想が良すぎてまたは丁寧すぎて信用できない➔お世辞のうまい, 口先のう

ますぎる, 如才ない ☞ 通常は男性について批判的に用いる. *I don't like him. He's far too smooth.* 彼のことは好きになれない. あまりに口がうますぎる. ― **smoothness** 名 ⓤ →滑らかさ, 平たん, 口当たりの良さ, 流ちょう, 口先上手

成句 **take the rough with the smooth** ⇒ **ROUGH**²

**smooth**² /smuːð/ 動 他 ▶定義 smooth sth (away, back, down, out, etc) to move your hands in the direction mentioned over a surface to make it smooth 言及された方向に手を動かして表面を平らにする → 〜を滑らかにする, 平らにする, ならす, なで付ける

**smoothly** /smúːðli/ 副 ▶定義 without any difficulty 困難なしに → 順調に, 円滑に, よどみなく ‖ *My work has been going quite smoothly.* 私の仕事は極めて順調に進んでいる.

**smother** /smʌ́ðər/ 動 他 ▶定義 1 smother sb (with sth) to kill sb by covering his/her face so that he/she cannot breathe 呼吸ができないように顔を覆って〜を殺す → 〜を(…で)窒息死させる, 窒息させる, 〜の息を止める ‖ *She was smothered with a pillow.* 彼女はまくらで窒息死した. ▶定義 2 smother sth/sb in/with sth to cover sth/sb with too much of sth 有り余るほどの〜で…を覆う → 〜を…で厚く包む, 〜に…をあふれるほど与える ▶定義 3 to stop a feeling, etc from being expressed 感情などを表現するのをやめる → (感情など)を抑える, こらえる, 押し殺す ▶定義 4 to stop sth burning by covering it 〜を覆って燃焼を止める → 〜を覆って消す ‖ *to smother the flames with a blanket* 毛布で覆って火を消す

**smoulder** (米 **smolder**) /smóuldər/ 動 自 ▶定義 to burn slowly without a flame 炎を出さずにゆっくりと燃える → いぶる, くすぶる ‖ *a cigarette smouldering in an ashtray* 灰皿でくすぶっているたばこ

**smudge** /smʌdʒ/ 動 ▶定義 1 他 to make sth dirty or untidy by touching it 触って〜を汚すまたは汚くする → 〜をこすって汚す, 〜に染みを付ける ‖ *Leave your painting to dry or you'll smudge it.* 絵を乾かしておかないとこすって汚してしまいますよ. ▶定義 2 自 to become untidy, without a clean line around it 周りのすっきりした輪郭がなくなってだらしなくなる → にじむ, 崩れる ‖ *Her lipstick smudged when she kissed him.* 彼にキスをして彼女の口紅が崩れてしまった. ― **smudge** 名 Ⓒ →汚れ, 染み, 汚点

**smug** /smʌg/ 形 ▶定義 too pleased with yourself 自分自身に満足しすぎた → 独り善がりの, うぬぼれた, 自己満足した ‖ *Don't look so smug.* そういい気な顔するのはやめろよ. ☞ この語は批判的に用いられる. ― **smugly** 副 → うぬぼれて, 自己満足して, 気取って ‖ *He smiled smugly as the results were announced.* 結果が発表されると, 彼はいかにも満足げにほほえんだ. ― **smugness** 名 ⓤ → うぬぼれ, きざ

**smuggle** /smʌ́g(ə)l/ 動 他 ▶定義 to take things into or out of a country secretly in a way that is not allowed by the law; to take a person or a thing secretly into or out of a place 〜を法律で認められていない方法で秘密裏に国内に持ち込むまたは国外に持ち出す; 〜をこっそりとある場所に運び込むまたは運び出す → 〜を密輸する, こっそり持ち込む, 持ち出す, 〜をこっそり連れ込む, 連れ出す ‖ *The drugs had been smuggled through customs.* それらの麻薬は税関を通って密輸された. ― **smuggler** 名 Ⓒ → 密輸業者, 密輸船 ‖ *a drug smuggler* 麻薬密輸業者

\*snack /snæk/ 名 Ⓒ ▶定義 food that you eat quickly between main meals 主要な食事の間に軽く口にする食べ物 → 軽食, 間食, スナック ‖ *I had a snack on the train.* 私は列車で軽い食事を取った. ― **snack** 動 自 略式 snack on sth → 〜の軽食を取る

**snack bar** 名 Ⓒ ▶定義 a type of small cafe where you can buy a small quick meal like a sandwich サンドイッチのような手軽な軽食を買うことのできる小さな軽食堂 → 軽食堂, スナックバー

**snag**¹ /snæg/ 名 Ⓒ ▶定義 a small difficulty or disadvantage that is often unexpected or hidden 主として思い掛けないまたは隠されたささいな難点, 不利な点 → 思わぬ障害, 困難, 欠点 ‖ *His offer is very generous - are you sure there isn't a snag?* 彼の申し出はとても寛大だ ― 本当に思いも掛けない難点はないのだろうか.

**snag**² /snæg/ 動 他 (**snagging**; **snagged**) ▶定義 to catch a piece of clothing, etc on sth sharp and tear it 鋭い物に服などを引っ掛けて裂く → 〜を引っ掛ける, 引っ掛けてかき裂きにする

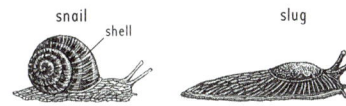

snail　shell　slug

**snail** /snéɪl/ 名 C ▶定義 a type of animal with a soft body and no legs that is covered by a shell. Snails move very slowly. 殻で覆われた柔らかい体をした足のない動物.非常にゆっくりと動む→カタツムリ

**snail mail** 名 U 略式 ▶定義 used by people who use e-mail to describe the system of sending letters by ordinary post 電子メールを使用している人たちが,普通の郵便で手紙を送る仕組みを表現するのに用いて→スネールメール,普通郵便,カタツムリ郵便

★**snake**¹ /snéɪk/ 名 C ▶定義 a type of long thin animal with no legs that slides along the ground by moving its body from side to side 体を左右にくねらして地面を滑るように進む,足のない細長い動物→蛇

**snake**² /snéɪk/ 動 自 (文) ▶定義 to move like a snake in long curves from side to side 蛇のように左右に長い曲線を描きながら移動する→くねる,うねる,蛇行する

★**snap**¹ /snǽp/ 動 (**snapping**; **snapped**) ▶定義1 自他 to break or be broken suddenly, usually with a sharp noise 主として鋭い音を立てて突然壊れるまたは壊される→ポキンと折れる,プツンと切れる;～をポキンと折る,～をプツンと切る ‖ *The top has snapped off my pen.* ペンのキャップがポキンと取れてしまった. *The branch snapped.* 枝がポキッと折れた. *I snapped my shoelace when I was tying it.* 靴ひもを結んでいる最中にプツンと切ってしまった. ▶定義2 自他 to move or be moved into a particular position, especially with a sharp noise 特に鋭い音を立てて特定の位置へと移動するまたは移される→バタンと閉まる,カチッと開く;～をバタンと閉める,～をカチッと開ける ‖ *She snapped the bag shut and walked out.* 彼女はハンドバッグをカチッと閉めると突然出ていった. ▶定義3 自他 snap (sth) (at sb) to speak or say sth in a quick angry way ～を早口で怒った口調で話すまたは言う→(人に)がみがみ言う,かみ付くように言う;～を鋭い口調で言う ‖ *Why do you always snap at me?* どうしていつも私にがみがみ言うのです

か. ▶定義4 自 to try to bite sb/sth ～をかもうとする→かみ付く,かみ付こうとする ‖ *The dog snapped at the child's hand.* 犬が子供の手にかみ付いた. ▶定義5 自他 略式 to take a quick photograph of sb/sth 素早く～の写真を撮る→(～の)スナップ写真を撮る ‖ *A tourist snapped the plane as it crashed.* 観光客は飛行機が墜落するところを写真に撮った. ▶定義6 自 to suddenly be unable to control your feelings any longer 突然感情を制御することができなくなる→取り乱す,かっとなる,切れる ‖ *Suddenly something just snapped and I lost my temper with him.* 突然何かがプツンと切れて,私は彼にかんしゃくを破裂させてしまった.

> ▶コミュニケーション
>
> どんなとき「指を鳴らす」か
>
> snap one's fingers: 指をパチンと鳴らすしぐさ.「そうだ！」と何かを思い付いたとき,「しまった」「畜生」と悔しがるとき,音楽のリズムに合わせて拍子を取るときなど,日英で共通の意味に使われることが多くあります.英米人独特の使い方としては,「こんな具合に簡単」と,指をポンと鳴らして見せるしぐさがあります.これは in a snap of one's fingers（瞬時に）, with a snap of one's fingers（やすやすと）といった慣用句に投影されています.

成句 **snap your fingers** ▶定義 to make a sharp noise by moving your middle finger quickly against your thumb, especially when you want to attract sb's attention 特に～の注意をひきたいときに中指を親指に素早くこすって鋭い音を立てる→指をぱちんと鳴らす

句動詞 **snap sth up** ▶定義 to buy or take sth quickly, especially because it is very cheap 特に非常に安いので～を急いで買うまたは手に入れる→～に飛び付く,先を争って買う,我勝ちに取る

**snap**² /snǽp/ 名 ▶定義1 C a sudden sharp sound of sth breaking ～が壊れる突然の鋭い音→ポキンと折れる音,プツンと切れる音 ▶定義2 (または **snapshot**) C a photograph that is taken quickly and in an informal way 素早く構えず撮った写真→スナップ写真 ‖ *I showed*

## 1534 snap³

them some holiday snaps. 私は彼らに休日のスナップ写真を見せた. ▶定義3 **❶英** a card game where players call out 'Snap' when two cards that are the same are put down by different players 異なるプレーヤーが同じカード2枚を下に置いたときにプレーヤーたちが「スナップ」と宣言するトランプのゲーム→スナップ

**snap³** /snæp/ **形略式**（名詞の前だけ）▶定義 done quickly and suddenly, often without any careful thought しばしば慎重に考えずに急いで突然行われる→急な,即座の,軽々しい‖ *a snap decision/judgement* 早急な決定・判断

**snare** /sneər/ **图❻** ▶定義 a device (trap) used to catch birds or small animals 鳥や小動物を捕まえるのに用いる器具（わな）→わな — snare **動他**→〜をわなに掛ける

**snarl** /snɑːrl/ **動自他** ▶定義 snarl (sth) (at sb) (used about an animal) to make an angry sound while showing the teeth（動物について）歯を見せながら怒った声を出す→歯をむいてうなる,うなり声を出す‖ *The dog snarled at the stranger.* その犬は見知らぬ人に向かってうなった. — snarl **图**[**❻**, 通常は単数]→ うなること

**snatch¹** /snætʃ/ **動** ▶定義1 **自他** to take sth with a quick rough movement 〜を素早い乱暴な動作で取る→（〜を）引ったくる, 奪い取る; 引ったくろうとする‖ *A boy snatched her handbag and ran off.* 少年は彼女の手提げかばんを引ったくる走って逃げた. ☛類 **grab**. 意味は同じである. ▶定義2 **他** to take or get sth quickly using the only time or chance that you have 今ある唯一の時間や好機を利用して素早く〜を取るまたは手に入れる→〜を急いで取る, 運良く得る, 素早くつかむ‖ *I managed to snatch some sleep on the train.* 私はどうにか列車で少し眠ることができた.

**句動詞** snatch at sth ▶定義 to try to take hold of sth suddenly 〜を突然つかもうとする→〜を引ったくろうとする, 引ったくろうと〜に手を伸ばす‖ *The man snatched at my wallet but I didn't let go of it.* 男が私の財布を引ったくろうとしたが, 私は財布を離さなかった.

**snatch²** /snætʃ/ **图** ▶定義1 [単数扱い]a sudden movement that sb makes when trying to take hold of sth 〜をつかもうとするときに…がする突然の動作→引ったくろうとすること, 引ったくり ▶定義2 [**❻**, 通常は複数] a short part or period of something 〜の短い一部, 短い期間→断片, 一片, 一節, 一時, 一働き, 一休み‖ *I heard snatches of conversation from the next room.* 隣の部屋から会話がとぎれとぎれに聞こえた.

**sneak¹** /sniːk/ **動** ▶定義1 **自** sneak into, out of, past, etc sth; sneak in, out, away, etc to go very quietly in the direction mentioned, so that no one can see or hear you だれにも見られたり聞かれたりしないように, 言及された方向にそっと行く→〜にこっそり入る, 〜からこっそり出る, 〜の前をこっそり通り過ぎる; こっそり入る・出る・去る‖ *The prisoner sneaked past the guards.* 囚人はこそこそと看守の前を通り過ぎた. *Instead of working, he sneaked out to play football.* 彼は勉強しないでサッカーをしにこっそり抜け出した. ▶定義2 **他略式** to do or take sth secretly→〜をこっそりする, こっそり取る‖ *I tried to sneak a look at the test results in the teacher's bag.* 私は先生のかばんの中にあった試験結果をこっそり見ようとした.

**句動詞** sneak up (on sb/sth) ▶定義 to go near sb very quietly, especially so that you can surprise him/her 特にびっくりさせようとして非常に静かに〜に近付く→（〜に）忍び寄る, こっそり近付く

**sneak²** /sniːk/ **图❻略式** ▶定義 a person, especially a child, who tells sb about the bad things sb has done 〜がした悪い事について…に告げ口する人, 特に子供→告げ口する人, 教師に告げ口する生徒, 密告者 ☛ この語は批判的に用いられる.

**sneaker** /sníːkər/ **米** = **PLIMSOLL**, **TRAINER(1)**

**sneaking** /sníːkɪŋ/ **形** ▶定義 (used about feelings) not expressed; secret（感情について）表現されない; 秘密の→ひそかな, 口には出さない, 内緒の‖ *I've a sneaking suspicion that he's lying.* 私は彼がうそをついているのではないかというひそかな疑いを抱いている.

**sneer** /snɪər/ **動自** ▶定義 sneer (at sb/sth) to show that you have no respect for sb/sth by the expression on your face or the way that you speak 顔の表情や話し振りで〜に対して敬意を持っていないことを示す→あざ笑う, 冷笑する, あざける‖ *She sneered at his attempts to speak French.* 彼女は彼がフランス語を話そうとする

のをあざ笑った. — sneer 名 C → 冷笑, あざけり, 軽べつ

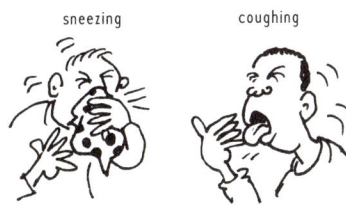
sneezing  coughing
He's blowing his nose.

**sneeze** /sníːz/ 動自 ▶定義 to make air come out of your nose suddenly and noisily in a way that you cannot control, for example because you have a cold 風邪などのために, 突然抑えが利かなくなったように, 鼻から騒々しく息を出す→くしゃみをする ‖ *Dust makes me sneeze.* ほこりで私はくしゃみが出る. — sneeze 名 C → くしゃみ

**snide** /snáɪd/ 形 ▶定義 (used about an expression or comment) critical in an unpleasant way (表現や批評について) 意地悪く非難がましい→**嫌味な, とげのある, 悪意に満ちた**

**sniff** /snɪf/ 動 ▶定義 1 自 to breathe air in through the nose in a way that makes a sound, especially because you have a cold or you are crying 特に風邪を引いていたり泣いていたりするため, 音を立てて鼻から息を吸い込む→鼻をすする, すすり泣く ‖ *Stop sniffing and blow your nose.* すするのをやめて鼻をかみなさい.
▶定義 2 自他 sniff (at) sth to smell sth by sniffing 鼻をすすってにおいをかぐ→(～を)くんくんかぐ, (～の)においをかぐ ‖ *'I can smell gas,' he said, sniffing the air.*「ガスのにおいがする」と彼は空気をかぎながら言った. *The dog sniffed at the bone.* 犬はくんくん骨のにおいをかいだ. — sniff 名 C → 鼻をすすること, 鼻をすする音, においをかぐこと ‖ *Have a sniff of this milk and tell me if it's still OK.* この牛乳のにおいをかいで, まだ大丈夫かどうか教えてください.

**sniffle** /snɪf(ə)l/ 動自 ▶定義 to make noises by breathing air suddenly up your nose, especially because you have a cold or you are crying 特に風邪を引いていたり泣いていたりするため, 突然鼻から息を吸って音を出す→鼻をすする, すすり泣く

**snigger** /snígər/ 動自 ▶定義 snigger (at sb/sth) to laugh quietly and secretly in an unpleasant way 嫌味に声も出さずにひそかに笑う→忍び笑いする, くすくす笑う — snigger 名 C → 忍び笑い, くすくす笑い

**snip**¹ /snɪp/ 動自他 (**snipping**; **snipped**) ▶定義 snip (sth) (off, out, in, etc) to cut using scissors, with a short quick action 素早くチョキンとはさみで切る→(～を)はさみでチョキンと切る ‖ *He sewed on the button and snipped off the ends of the cotton.* 彼はボタンを縫い付けて, 木綿糸の両端をはさみでチョキンと切った. *to snip a hole in sth* ～を(はさみで)チョキンと切って穴を開ける

**snip**² /snɪp/ 名 C ▶定義 1 a small cut made with scissors はさみで作った小さな切り口→切り口, 切れ目 ‖ *She made a small snip in the cloth.* 彼女は布に小さな切れ目を入れた. ▶定義 2 英 略式 something that is much cheaper than expected 予期していたよりはるかに安い物→お買い得品

**snippet** /snípət/ 名 C ▶定義 a small piece of sth, especially information or news 特に情報やニュースなどのわずかな一片→断片, 抜粋, 引用

**snivel** /snív(ə)l/ 動自 (**snivelling**; **snivelled**: 米 **sniveling**; **sniveled**) ▶定義 to keep crying quietly in a way that is annoying じれったくいつまでも声を出さずに泣き続ける→すすり泣く, めそめそ泣く, 泣きじゃくる

**snob** /snɑb/ 名 C ▶定義 a person who thinks he/she is better than sb of a lower social class and who admires people who have a high social position 社会階級の低い人に対しては自分の方が優れていると考え, 社会階級の高い人に対しては崇拝をする人→俗物, 上流気取りの人, スノッブ ‖ *He's such a snob - he wears his Oxford University tie all the time.* 彼はすごい俗物だ － いつでもオックスフォード大学のネクタイをしている. — snobbish → 俗物の, 上流気取りの, お高く留まった— snobbishly 副 → 上流気取りで, お高く留まって— snobbishness 名 U → 俗物根性, 上流気取り

**snobbery** /snɑ́b(ə)ri/ 名 U ▶定義 behaviour or attitudes typical of people who think they are better than other people in society, for example because they have more money, better education, etc ほかの人々よりも金や高い教育などがあるから自分の方が優れていると考える人たちの典型的な振る舞い・態度 →俗物根性,上流気取り,いやらしい上流崇拝,俗物的言動 ‖ *To say that 'all pop music is rubbish' is just snobbery.*「ポップミュージックはすべて下らない」と言うことは単なる俗物的言動だ.

**snog** /snɑg/ 動⾃略式 ▶定義 (used about a couple) to kiss each other for a long period of time (一組の男女について) 長い間キスする →(～と)キスする,愛撫(ぶ)する — snog 名 [単数扱い] → キス,愛撫

**snooker** /snúːkər, snʊ́-/ 名Ⓤ ▶定義 a game in which two players try to hit a number of coloured balls into pockets at the edges of a large table using a long stick (cue) 2人のプレーヤーが長い棒(キュー)を使って色の付いた多数の球を大きな卓の端にある穴に向かって打ち込む遊戯 →スヌーカー ‖ *to play snooker* スヌーカーをする ☛参 **billiards**, **pool**

**snoop** /snuːp/ 動⾃ ▶定義 snoop (around); snoop (on sb) to look around secretly and without permission in order to find out information, etc 情報などを探し出すために内緒で許可なく見て回る →詮索(せんさく)する,ひそかにかぎ回る,こそこそうろつく ‖ *She suspected that her neighbours visited just to snoop on her.* 彼女は隣人が彼女のことをただ詮索しにやって来たのではと疑った.

**snooty** /snúːti/ 形略式 ▶定義 acting in a rude way because you think you are better than other people 他人よりも優れていると考えているために無作法に振る舞う →横柄な,ごう慢な,人をさげすんだ

**snooze** /snuːz/ 動⾃略式 ▶定義 to have a short sleep, especially during the day 特に日中に短い睡眠を取る →居眠りする,うたた寝する — snooze 名 [Ⓒ, 通常は単数] →居眠り,うたた寝 ‖ *I had a bit of a snooze on the train.* 列車で少しうとうとと居眠りをした. ☛参 **nap**

**snore** /snɔːr/ 動⾃ ▶定義 to breathe noisily through your nose and mouth while you are asleep 寝ている間に鼻と口とで騒々しく息をする →いびきをかく ‖ *She heard her father snoring in the next room.* 彼女には父親が隣の部屋でいびきをかいているのが聞こえた. — snore 名Ⓒ →いびき ‖ *He's got the loudest snore I've ever heard.* 彼は私が今まで聞いた中で一番大きないびきをかく.

**snorkel** /snɔ́ːrk(ə)l/ 名Ⓒ ▶定義 a short tube that a person swimming just below the surface of the water can use to breathe through 水面のすぐ下を泳いでいる人が息をするために用いる短い管 →シュノーケル,スノーケル
▶このような泳ぎについて話すとき,go snokelling (シュノーケルで潜水に出掛ける) という表現を用いる.
☛ **dive** のさし絵

**snort** /snɔːrt/ 動⾃ ▶定義 **1** (used about animals) to make a noise by blowing air through the nose and mouth (動物について) 鼻と口から息を出して音を立てる →鼻を鳴らす,鼻息を荒くする ▶定義 **2** (used about people) to blow out air noisily as a way of showing that you do not like sth, or that you are impatient (人について) ～が気に入らないことやいらいらしていることを示す方法として騒々しく息を吐く →鼻を鳴らす,鼻を鳴らして言う — snort 名Ⓒ →鼻を鳴らすこと,荒い鼻息

**snot** /snɑt/ 名Ⓤ略式 ▶定義 the liquid produced by the nose 鼻から出る液体 →鼻水,鼻汁

**snout** /snaʊt/ 名Ⓒ ▶定義 the long nose of certain animals 一部の動物の高い鼻 →(豚などの)鼻,突き出た鼻 ‖ *a pig's snout* 豚の鼻 ☛ **badger** のさし絵

*****snow**¹ /snoʊ/ 名Ⓤ ▶定義 small, soft, white pieces of frozen water that fall from the sky in cold weather 寒い季節に空から降ってくる小さく柔らかい水の白い氷結片 →雪,降雪 ‖ *Three inches of snow fell during the night.* 夜の間に雪が3インチ降った. *The snow melted before it could settle (= stay on the ground).* 雪は積もる(= 地面に堆積(たいせき)する)前に解けた.
☛参 **weather** の注

*****snow**² /snoʊ/ 動⾃ ▶定義 (used about snow) to fall from the sky (雪について) 空から降る →雪が降る ‖ *It snowed all night.* 一晩中雪が降った.

**snowball**¹ /snoʊbɔːl/ 名Ⓒ ▶定義 a lump of snow that is pressed into the shape of a ball and used by children for playing ボールの形に押し固めた雪の塊.子供たちが遊びに用いる →雪玉,雪つぶて

**snowball²** /snóubɔːl/ 動自 ▶定義 to quickly grow bigger and bigger or more and more important 急速にどんどん大きくなるまたは重要になる→雪だるま式に増える,加速度的に拡大する

**snowboard** /snóubɔːrd/ 名C ▶定義 a type of board that you fasten to both your feet and use for moving down mountains that are covered with snow 両足に固定して,雪で覆われた山を降りるのに用いる板→スノーボード— **snowboarding** 名U→スノーボードをすること,スノーボード ❶→Have you ever been snowboarding? 今までにスノーボードをしたことがありますか. ☞ ski のさし絵

**snowdrift** /snóudrìft/ 名C ▶定義 a deep pile of snow that has been made by the wind 風で作られる大きな雪の山→雪の吹きだまり ‖ The car got stuck in a snowdrift. 車は雪の吹きだまりにはまって立ち往生した.

**snowdrop** /snóudrɑ̀p/ 名C ▶定義 a type of small white flower that appears at the end of winter 冬の終わりに現れる小さな白い花の一種→スノードロップ,ユキノハナ,マツユキソウ ☞ C2 ページのさし絵

**snowed in** 形 ▶定義 not able to leave home or travel because the snow is too deep 雪が深すぎて家から出ることができない,または移動することができない→雪で閉じ込められる,雪で身動きができなくなる

**snowed under** 形 ▶定義 with more work, etc than you can deal with 処理能力を超えた仕事があって→圧倒される,多忙な

**snowfall** /snóufɔ̀ːl/ 名 ▶定義1 Cthe snow that falls on one occasion 一度に降る雪→(1回の)降雪 ‖ heavy snowfalls 大雪 ▶定義2 Uthe amount of snow that falls in a particular place ある1箇所に降る雪の量→降雪量

**snowflake** /snóuflèik/ 名C ▶定義 one of the small, soft, white pieces of frozen water that fall together as snow 雪として一斉に降る小さな柔らかい白い氷結片の1つ→雪片,雪のひら

**snowman** /snóumæ̀n/ 名C (複 **-men** /-mèn/) ▶定義 the figure of a person made out of snow 雪で作られた人の像→雪だるま,雪人形

**snowplough**(米 **snowplow**) /snóuplàu/ 名C ▶定義 a vehicle that is used to clear snow away from roads or railways 道路や線路から雪を取り除くのに用いる車→除雪車,除雪機 ☞参 plough

**snowy** /snóui/ 形 ▶定義 with a lot of snow 雪の多い→雪の多い,雪の降る,雪の積もった ‖ snowy weather 雪の天気 a snowy scene 雪景色

**Snr**(または **Sr**) 略 特に 米 Senior→父親の,父の方の

**snub** /snʌb/ 動他 (**snubbing**; **snubbed**) ▶定義 to treat sb rudely, for example by refusing to look at or speak to him/her 顔を見ようともしない,話し掛けようともしないなど,人を無作法にあしらう→〜を鼻であしらう,わざと無視する,侮辱する,相手にしない — **snub** 名C→すげない振る舞い,冷遇,侮辱 ‖ When they weren't invited to the party, they felt it was a snub. 彼らはパーティーに招待されなかったことを侮辱だと感じた.

**snuff** /snʌf/ 名U ▶定義 (especially in past times) tobacco which people breathe up into the nose in the form of a powder(特に昔)鼻から吸う粉状のたばこ→かぎたばこ

**snuffle** /snʌ́f(ə)l/ 動自 ▶定義 (used about people and animals) to make a noise through your nose(人や動物について)鼻から音を出す→鼻を鳴らす,鼻をくんくんさせる ‖ The dog snuffled around the lamp post. その犬は街灯柱の周りで鼻をクンクンさせた.

**snug** /snʌg/ ▶定義1 warm and comfortable 暖かく心地いい→快適な,気持ちのいい,(暖かく)居心地の良い ‖ a snug little room 居心地の良い小さな部屋 The children were snug in bed. 子供たちは寝床でぬくぬくしていた. ▶定義2 fitting sb/sth closely→(体などに)ぴったり合う ‖ Adjust the safety belt to give a snug fit. 体にぴったり合うようにシートベルトを調整しなさい. — **snugly** 副→快適に,心地良く,ぴったりと,きちんと

**snuggle** /snʌ́g(ə)l/ 動自 ▶定義 snuggle (up to sb); snuggle (up/down) to get into a position that makes you feel safe, warm and comfortable, usually next to another person 通常はだれかのすぐそばで,安全で,暖かく快適な気分でいられる姿勢を取る→寄り添う,擦り寄る;(子供など)を抱き寄せる,(心地良い所に)〜を擦り寄せる ‖ She snuggled up to her mother. 彼女は母親の所に擦り寄った. I snuggled down under the blanket to get warm. 私は暖まるため毛布の下に

ゆったりと横になった.

**so¹** /sóu/ 副 ▶定義1 used to emphasize an adjective or adverb, especially when this produces a particular result 特に形容詞・副詞で描写されている状況がある特定の結果を生み出す場合, それを強調するのに用いて→**そんなに, そんなに, 非常に, とても** ∥ *She's so ill (that) she can't get out of bed.* 彼女はとても具合が悪くて起き上がることができない. *He was driving so fast that he couldn't stop.* 彼はものすごく速く車を走らせていたので停車することができなかった. *You've been so kind. How can I thank you?* ほんとにご親切にしてくださって. どうお礼を申し上げて良いやら分かりません. ☞参 **such** の注 ▶定義2 used in negative sentences for comparing people or things 人や物を比較する場合の否定文で用いて→**それほど, そんなに** ∥ *She's not so clever as we thought.* 彼女は私たちが考えていたほど利口ではない. ▶定義3 used in place of something that has been said already, to avoid repeating it 繰り返しを避けるため, 既に言及した内容の代わりに用いて→**そのように, そのようで, そう** ∥ *Are you coming by plane? If so, (= if you are coming by plane) I can meet you at the airport.* 飛行機で来られる予定ですか. もしそうなら(= もしあなたが飛行機で来るのならば)空港に迎えに行きますよ. *'I failed, didn't I?' 'I'm afraid so.'*「私は落第したんですね」「残念ながらそうです」

▶正式な英語では, 既に話に出た動作に言及する場合, 代名詞do + soの形をとることもある: *He asked me to write to him and I did so (= I wrote to him).* (彼は私に手紙をくれるように頼んだのでそうした(= 私は彼に手紙を書いた).)

▶定義4 (動詞の否定形と用いない) also, too ~もまた, ~も→**~もまたそうで, 同じように, 同様に** ∥ *He's a teacher and so is his wife.* 彼は教師だが, 彼の妻もそうだ. *'I've been to New York.' 'So have I.'*「私はニューヨークに行ったことがある」「私も」 *I like singing and so does Helen.* 私は歌うのが好きだが, ヘレンもそうだ.

▶否定文に関しては, neitherを参照.

▶定義5 used to show that you agree that sth is true, especially when you are surprised 特に驚いたとき, その通りだと同意を示すのに用いて→**本当で, その通りで** ∥ *'It's getting late.' 'So it is. We'd better go.'*「遅くなってきましたね」「そうですね. もう行きましょう」 ▶定義6 正式 (used when you are showing sb sth) in this way; like this (~に…を示すときに用いて)こんな風に; このように→**このような, こんな風に** ∥ *It was a black insect, about so big (= using your hands to show the size).* それは黒い昆虫で, このくらいの(= 両手を使って大きさを示しながら)大きさだった. *Fold the paper in two diagonally, like so.* 対角線に沿って紙を2つに折ってください, こんな風に.

成句 **and so on (and so forth)** ▶定義 used at the end of a list to show that it continues in the same way 一連の物が同じように続いていることを示すため, 一番最後に用いて→**~など, その他** ∥ *They sell pens, pencils, paper and so on.* その店ではペン, 鉛筆, 用紙などを売っている.

**I told you so** ▶定義 used to tell sb that he/she should have listened to your advice 自分の忠告に耳を傾けるべきだったと相手に伝えるのに用いて→**だからそう言ったでしょう, だから言わないことではない** ∥ *'I missed the bus.' 'I told you so. I said you needed to leave earlier.'*「バスに乗り損ねてしまった」「だから言ったでしょう. もっと早く家を出なさいって」

**it (just) so happens** ▶定義 (used to introduce a surprising fact) by chance (驚くべき事実を話し始めるために用いて)偶然→**偶然, たまたま, 運良く, あいにく** ∥ *It just so happened that we were going the same way, so he gave me a lift.* たまたま方向が同じだったので, 彼は私を車で送ってくれた.

**just so** ⇒ **JUST¹**

**or so** ▶定義 (used to show that a number, time, etc is not exact) approximately; about (数字, 時間などが正確でないことを示すために用いて)おおよそ; 約→**大体, ~ほど, ~くらい** ∥ *A hundred or so people came to the meeting.* 100人かこらの人たちが集会にやって来た.

**so as to do sth** ▶定義 with the intention of doing sth; in order to do sth ~をするつもりで; ~をするために→**~をするように, ~をするために**

**so much for** ▶定義 used for saying that sth was not helpful or successful ~が役に立たなかったまたは成功しなかったことを言うのに用い

て→～のことはそれだけ、～のことはそれまで、～はそんなもの ‖ *So much for that diet! I didn't lose any weight at all.* あのダイエットはこれでおしまい。全く減量できなかった。

**that is so** 正式 ▶定義 that is true それは本当だ→**その通りだ。本当だ。そうだ。**

\***so**² /sóu/ 接 ▶定義1 with the result that; therefore ～という結果になって; したがって→**だから、それで、その結果** ‖ *She felt very tired so she went to bed early.* 彼女はとても疲れていたので、早く就寝した。 ▶定義2 so (that) with the purpose that; in order that ～の目的で; ～するために→**～するために、～するように** ‖ *She wore dark glasses so (that) nobody would recognize her.* だれにも気付かれないように彼女は色の濃いサングラスをしていた。 ▶定義3 used to show how one part of a story follows another 話の一部分がどのように次へとつながるかを示すのに用いて→**それで、それから** ‖ *So what happened next?* それで次に何が起きたのですか。

成句 **so what?** 略式 ▶定義 (showing that you think sth is not important) Who cares? (～が重要でないと考えていることを示して)だれが構うものか→**それがどうしたというのか、だからどうだというのか** ‖ *'It's late.' 'So what? We don't have to go to school tomorrow.'* 「もう遅いですよ」「だからどうだっていうの。明日は学校に行かなくていいんだから」

**soak** /sóuk/ 動 ▶定義1 自 他 to become or make sth completely wet すっかりぬれる、～を完全にぬらす→**つかる、浸る; ～を液体につける、浸す、ずぶぬれにする** ‖ *Leave the dishes to soak for a while.* しばらくの間、皿を水につけておきなさい。 *The dog came out of the river and shook itself, soaking everyone.* 犬が川から上がってブルブルッと体を揺すったので、みんなずぶぬれになった。 ▶定義2 自 **soak into/through sth; soak in** (used about a liquid) to pass into or through sth (液体について)～に染み通る、～を通り抜ける→**～に染み込む・通る; 染み通る** ‖ *Blood had soaked through the bandage.* 血が包帯ににじんでいた。

句動詞 **soak sth up** ▶定義 to take sth in (especially a liquid) ～を(特に液体を)吸収する→**～を吸い取る、吸い込む、吸収する** ‖ *I soaked the water up with a cloth.* 私は布で水を吸い取った。

**soaked** /sóukt/ 形 (名詞の前は不可) ▶定義 extremely wet 非常にぬれた→**ずぶぬれの、びしょぬれの** ‖ *I got soaked waiting for my bus in the rain.* 私は雨の中バスを待っていてずぶぬれになった。

**soaking** /sóukɪŋ/ (または **soaking wet**) 形 ▶定義 extremely wet 非常にぬれた→**ずぶぬれの、びしょぬれの、ずぶぬれにする**

**so-and-so** 名 C (複 **so-and-so's**) 略式 ▶定義1 a person who is not named 名指しされていない人→**だれそれ、なにがし、だれだれ** ‖ *Imagine a Mrs So-and-so telephones. What would you say?* 夫人が電話をかけてきたと想定してください。あなたなら何と言いますか。 ▶定義2 a person that you do not like 好きでない人→**嫌なやつ、嫌われ者、あいつ** ‖ *He's a bad-tempered old so-and-so.* 彼は気難しいろくでもない老人だ。

\***soap** /sóup/ 名 U ▶定義 a substance that you use for washing and cleaning 洗濯・清掃に用いる物質→**せっけん** ‖ *He washed his hands with soap.* 彼はせっけんで手を洗った。 *a bar of soap* 棒状の固形せっけん *soap powder* (= for washing clothes) 粉せっけん (= 衣服の洗濯用) — **soapy** 形→**せっけんだらけの、せっけんを含んだ、せっけんのような**

**soap opera** (または 略式 **soap**) 名 C ▶定義 参 a story about the lives and problems of a group of people which continues several times a week on television or radio テレビまたはラジオで週に数回連続で放送される、ある人たちの生活または問題についての物語→**連続ドラマ、連続メロドラマ** ☛参 opera

**soar** /sɔːr/ 動 自 ▶定義1 to fly high in the air 空中を高く飛ぶ→**空高く飛ぶ、舞い上がる** ▶定義2 to rise very fast 急速に上がる→**(物価・温度などが)急上昇する、急騰する** ‖ *Prices are soaring because of inflation.* インフレのため物価が急騰している。

**sob** /sɑb/ 動 自 (**sobbing**; **sobbed**) ▶定義 to cry while taking in sudden, sharp breaths; to speak while you are crying 突然激しく息を吸いながら泣く; 泣きながら話す→**すすり泣く、むせび泣く、泣きじゃくる、むせび泣きながら話す** ‖ *The child was sobbing because he'd lost his toy.* 子供はおもちゃをなくしてしまったので泣きじゃくっていた。— sob 名 C→**すすり[むせび]泣き、むせ**

び泣く声 ‖ *It was heartbreaking to listen to her sobs.* 彼女のすすり泣きを聞いて胸が張り裂けそうだった.

**sober**¹ /sóubər/ 形 ▶定義 1 (of a person) not affected by alcohol (人について) アルコールの影響を受けていない→酒に酔っていない, しらふの ‖ *He'd been drunk the first time he'd met her, but this time he was **stone-cold sober**.* 初めて彼女に会った時彼は酔っ払っていたが, 今回は全くのしらふだった. ▶定義 2 not funny; serious おかしなところがない; まじめな→まじめな, 謹厳な ‖ *a sober expression* まじめな顔付き *Her death is a sober reminder of just how dangerous drugs can be.* 彼女の死は麻薬がいかに危険かを粛然と想起させるものだ. ▶定義 3 (of a colour) not bright or likely to be noticed (色について) 明るくない, 人目に付きそうにない→地味な, 落ち着いた, 控えめな ‖ *a sober grey suit* 地味なグレーのスーツ

**sober**² /sóubər/ 動
句動詞 sober (sb) up ▶定義 to become or make sb become normal again after being affected by alcohol 酔っ払った後に平静の状態に戻る; 酔っ払った〜を平静の状態に戻す→酔いが覚める; 〜の酔いを覚ます ‖ *I need a cup of black coffee to sober me up.* 酔いを覚ますには, 1杯のブラックコーヒーが必要だ. *There's no point talking to him until he's sobered up.* 酔いが覚めるまで, 彼に話しても無駄だ.

**sobering** /sóubəriŋ/ 形 ▶定義 making you feel serious 人をまじめな気持ちにさせる→人をまじめにさせる, (人の)頭を冷やすような, 考えさせる ‖ *It is **a sobering thought** that over 25 million people have been killed in car accidents.* 自動車事故で2500万人以上の人が死亡していることを考えると深刻な気持ちになる.

**Soc** 略 Society→協会, 会 ‖ *Amateur Dramatic Soc* 演劇愛好会

**so-called** 形 ▶定義 1 used to show that the words you describe sb/sth with are not correct 〜を言い表す言葉が正しくないことを示すのに用いて→いわゆる, 俗に言う, 名ばかりの ‖ *Her so-called friends only wanted her money.* 彼女の友人とやら言われる人たちは彼女のお金が欲しいだけだった. ▶定義 2 used to show that a special name has been given to sb/sth 〜に別の名前が付けられていることを示すのに用いて→いわゆる

**soccer** /sákər/ 特に 米 = FOOTBALL(1)

**sociable** /sóuʃəb(ə)l/ 形 ▶定義 enjoying being with other people; friendly 人と一緒にいることを楽しむ; 親しみやすい→社交的な, 人付き合いの良い, 愛想の良い

*★**social** /sóuʃ(ə)l/ 形 ▶定義 1 connected with society and the way it is organized 社会または社会の組織の仕方に関する→社会の, 社会に関する, 社会的な ‖ *social problems/issues/reforms* 社会問題・問題・改革 ▶定義 2 concerning the position of people in society 社会での人の地位に関する→社会的地位に関する, 社会における, 社会的な ‖ *We share the same social background.* 私たちは育ちや家柄など社会的バックを共有している. ▶定義 3 connected with meeting people and enjoying yourself 人に会って楽しむことに関する→社交の, 親睦(しんぼく)の(ための), 社交的な ‖ *a social club* 社交クラブ *She has a busy social life.* 彼女は忙しい社交生活を送っている. *Children have to develop their **social skills** when they start school.* 学校へ上がると子供たちは人との付き合い方を身に付けていかなければならない. ▶定義 4 (used about animals) living in groups (動物について) 集団で生活する→社会性のある, 群居性のある — **socially** /-ʃ(ə)li/ 副 →社会的に, 社交的に, 打ち解けて ‖ *We work together but I don't know him socially.* 彼とは一緒に働いてはいるが, 職場の外では付き合いがない.

**socialism** /sóuʃ(ə)lìz(ə)m/ 名 Ⓤ ▶定義 the political idea that is based on the belief that all people are equal and that money and property should be equally divided すべての人々は平等であり, 財産はすべて平等に分配されなければならないという信念に基づいた政治思想→社会主義 参 communism, Marxism, capitalism — **socialist** 形 名 Ⓒ →社会主義の, 社会主義的な, 社会主義者 ‖ *socialist beliefs/policies/writers* 社会主義の考え・政策・作家 *Tony was a socialist when he was younger.* トニーは若い時社会主義者だった.

**social science** 名 Ⓒ Ⓤ ▶定義 the study of people in society 社会における人間に関する研究→社会科学

**social security** (米 **welfare**) 名 Ⓤ ▶定義 money

paid regularly by the government to people who are poor, old, ill, or who have no job 貧しい人・老人・病人・失業者に対して政府が定期的に支払う金➡社会福祉手当, 生活保護 ‖ *to live on social security* 生活保護を受けて生活する

**social services** [複数扱い] ▶定義 a group of services organized by local government to help people who have money or family problems 金銭または家族問題を抱える人たちを支援するために地方自治体によって組織された一連の事業➡社会福祉事業, 社会事業

**social work** ▶定義 work that involves giving help and advice to people with money or family problems 金銭または家族問題を抱える人たちに対して援助または助言を与えることに関する仕事➡ソーシャルワーク, 社会福祉事業 — social worker ➡ソーシャルワーカー, 社会事業相談員, 民生委員

*__society__ /səsáɪəti/ (複 societies) ▶定義 1 the people in a country or area, thought of as a group, who have shared customs and laws 慣習・おきてを共有し, 1つの集団を形成していると見なされる一国または一地域内の人々➡社会, 共同体 ‖ *a civilized society* 文明社会 *Society's attitude to women has changed considerably this century.* 今世紀, 女性に対する社会の考えは大きく変化している. *The role of men in society is changing.* 社会における男性の役割は変わりつつある. ▶定義 2 an organization of people who share a particular interest or purpose; a club ある特定の趣味または目的を共有する人たちの団体; クラブ➡協会, 会, 団体, クラブ ‖ *a drama society* 演劇愛好会

**sociologist** /sòʊsiálədʒɪst, -ʃi-/ ▶定義 a student of or an expert in sociology 社会学を研究する人, またはその分野の専門家➡社会学者

**sociology** /sòʊsiálədʒi, -ʃi-/ ▶定義 the study of human societies and social behaviour 人間の社会または社会行動に関する研究➡社会学 — sociological /sòʊsiəládʒɪk(ə)l, -ʃiiə-/ ➡社会学の, 社会学に関する, 社会学的な

*__sock__ /sɑk/ ▶定義 a piece of clothing that you wear on your foot and lower leg, inside your shoe 足または脚の下部, 靴の内側に着用する衣類➡(短い)靴下, ソックス ‖ *a pair of socks* 靴下1足 ☛ C6 ページのさし絵

成句 **pull your socks up** 英 ▶定義 to start working harder or better than before 前よりも一生懸命にまたはさらによく働き始める➡気を引き締めてかかる, 頑張る, しっかりやる

**socket** /sákət/ ▶定義 1 (または **power point, plug**) a place in a wall where a piece of electrical equipment can be connected to the electricity supply 電気器具が電源に接続される壁の場所➡差し込み口, コンセント ☛ **plug** のさし絵 ▶定義 2 a hole in a piece of electrical equipment where another piece of equipment can be connected 別の電気器具の接続を可能にする電気器具の穴➡ソケット, 穴, 受け口, 軸受け ▶定義 3 a hole that sth fits into 〜が納まる穴➡窩(か), 槽(そう) ‖ *your eye socket* 眼窩(がんか)

**soda** /sóʊdə/ ▶定義 1 (または **soda water**) water that has bubbles in it and is usually used for mixing with other drinks 通常ほかの飲料と混ぜ合わすのに用いられる気泡性の水➡炭酸水, ソーダ水 ‖ *a whisky and soda* ウイスキーのソーダ水割り ▶定義 2 米 = FIZZY DRINK

**sofa** /sóʊfə/ ▶定義 a comfortable seat with a back and arms for two or more people to sit on 背もたれとひじ掛けの付いた2人以上の人が座れる座り心地の良い腰掛け➡ソファー, 長いす ‖ *a sofa bed (= a sofa that you can open out to make a bed)* ソファーベッド(= 広げてベッドにすることのできるソファー) ☛類 **settee** ☛ C7 ページのさし絵

*__soft__ /sɔ(ː)ft, sɑft/ ▶定義 1 not hard or firm 固くない, 硬くない➡柔らかい, 軟らかい ‖ *a soft bed/seat* 柔らかいベッド・座席 *The ground is very soft after all that rain.* あれだけの量の雨で地面がとても柔らかくなっている. ⇔ **hard** ▶定義 2 smooth and pleasant to touch; not rough 滑らかで触り心地が良い; ざらざらしていない➡手触りの柔らかな, 滑らかな, すべすべした ‖ *soft skin/hands* すべすべの肌・手 *a soft towel* 手触りの柔らかなタオル ⇔ **rough** ▶定義 3 (used about sounds, voices, words, etc) quiet or gentle; not loud or angry(音, 声, 語などについて)静かな, 穏やかな; 大声でない, 怒っていない➡静かな, 穏やかな, 低い, 優しい, ソフトな ‖ *She spoke in a soft whisper.* 彼女は静かなささやき声で話した. ⇔ **loud, harsh** ▶定義 4 (used about light, colours etc) gentle and pleasant(光, 色などに

ついて)穏やかで好ましい➡穏やかな,柔らかい,落ち着いた ‖ *The room was decorated in soft pinks and greens.* その部屋は落ち着いたピンク色と緑色で装飾されていた. ⇔ **bright** ▶定義5 (used about people) kind and gentle, sometimes too much so (人について)時には過度に優しくて穏やかな➡優しい,柔和な,寛大な,甘い ‖ *A good manager can't afford to be too soft.* 良い管理者は人に甘すぎてはいられない. ⇔ **hard**, **strict** ▶定義6 (used about illegal drugs) less dangerous and serious than the type of illegal drugs which can kill people (麻薬について)死に至るような麻薬よりも危険や問題が少ない➡弱い,常用性の低い

▶ hard drug と比較.

— softly 副 ➡柔らかく,静かに,優しく,寛大に ‖ *He closed the door softly behind him.* 彼は入ってきた[出ていった]後静かにドアを閉めた. — softness 图 Ⓤ➡柔らかさ,穏やかさ,優しさ

成句 **have a soft spot for sb/sth** 略式 ▶定義 to have good or loving feelings towards sb/sth ～に対して好感またはいとしい気持ちを抱く➡～に好感を持つ,弱い,甘い

**soft drink** 图 Ⓒ ▶定義 a cold drink that contains no alcohol アルコールを含まない冷たい飲み物➡清涼飲料,炭酸飲料,ソフトドリンク

**soften** /sɔ́(:)f(ə)n, sǽf-/ 動 ▶定義1 🟦 🔵 to become softer or gentler; to make sb/sth softer or gentler より柔らかくなるまたは穏やかになる;～を柔らかくするまたは穏やかにする➡柔らかくなる;～を柔らかくする,温和にする,柔軟にする ‖ *a lotion to soften the skin* 肌を柔らかくする化粧水 ▶定義2 🔵 to make sth less shocking and unpleasant ～をより衝撃的・不快でないものにする➡～を和らげる,穏やかにする ‖ *Her letter sounded too angry so she softened the language.* 書いた手紙が怒気を含みすぎているように思われたので,彼女は表現を和らげた. *The air bag softened the impact of the crash.* エアバッグは衝突時の衝撃を和らげた.

**soft-hearted** 形 ▶定義 kind and good at understanding other people's feelings 優しくて他人の感情をよく理解する➡心の優しい,情け深い ⇔ **hard-hearted**

**soft option** 图 Ⓒ ▶定義 the easier thing to do of two or more possibilities, but not the best one 2つ以上ある選択肢の中で最善ではないがほかよりもやりやすいもの➡より楽な選択肢,楽な方法,安易な道 ‖ *The government has taken the soft option of agreeing to their demands.* 政府は彼らの要求に応じるという安易な方法を選んだ.

**soft-spoken** 形 ▶定義 having a gentle, quiet voice 穏やかで静かな声をした➡穏やかな口調の,優しい声の,(言葉など)物柔らかな ‖ *He was a kind, soft-spoken man.* 彼は優しく穏やかに話をする人だ.

**software** /sɔ́(:)ftwèər, sǽft-/ 图 Ⓤ ▶定義 (computing) the programs and other operating information used by a computer (コンピューター)コンピューターで用いられるプログラムおよびそのほかの操作に関する情報➡ソフトウェア ‖ *There's a lot of new educational software available now.* 現在,数多くの新しい教育ソフトが利用できる. ☛参 **hardware**

**soggy** /sɔ́(:)gi, sági/ 形 ▶定義 very wet and soft and so unpleasant 非常にぬれていて柔らかく不快➡水浸しの,びしょぬれの,じめじめした,べちゃっとした

***soil**¹ /sɔ́il/ 图 ▶定義1 Ⓒ Ⓤ the substance that plants, trees, etc grow in; earth 植物,樹木などが生育する物質;土➡土,土壌 ‖ *poor/dry/acid/sandy soil* やせた・乾いた・酸性の・砂の多い土 ☛参 **ground**¹の注 ☛ C2ページのさし絵 ▶定義2 Ⓤ (文) the land that is part of a country 国土の一部➡土地,国土

**soil**² /sɔ́il/ 動 ⓗ 正式 (しばしば受動態で) ▶定義 to make sth dirty ～を汚す➡～を汚す,汚損する,～に染みを付ける

**solace** /sáləs/ 图 [ Ⓤ, 単数扱い ] (文) ▶定義 **solace (in sth)** a person or thing that makes you feel better or happier when you are sad or disappointed 悲しいとき,失望しているときに気持ちを引き立て明るくしてくれる人または物➡慰め,慰安,慰めになるもの ‖ *to find/seek solace in sb/sth* ～に慰めを見いだす・求める

**solar** /sóulər/ 形 (名詞の前だけ) ▶定義1 connected with the sun 太陽に関する➡太陽の,太陽に関する ‖ *a solar eclipse (= when the sun is blocked by the moon)* 日食 (= 太陽が月で遮られる状態) ▶定義2 using the sun's energy 太陽のエネルギーを利用した➡太陽光線[熱]を利用

した ‖ solar heating/power 太陽熱暖房・太陽熱

**the solar system** 名 [単数扱い] ▶定義 the sun and the planets that move around it 太陽とその周りを巡る惑星→**太陽系**

**sold** SELL の過去・過去分詞形

***soldier** /sóʊldʒɚr/ 名 ❻ ▶定義 a member of an army 陸軍の一員→**兵士, 兵隊, 軍人** ‖ The soldiers marched past. 兵隊が行進して通り過ぎた.

**sole**¹ /sóʊl/ 形 (名詞の前だけ) ▶定義 1 only; single 唯一の, たった1つの→**唯一の, たった1つの, 1人の** ‖ His sole interest is football. 彼の唯一の興味はサッカーだ. ▶定義 2 belonging to one person only; not shared ただ1人だけに属する; 共有されていない→**独占的な, 単独の** — **solely** 副→**ただ1人で, 単独で, 単に, 専ら** ‖ I agreed to come solely because of your mother. ただあなたのお母さんのために, 私はここに来ることに同意したのだ.

**sole**² /sóʊl/ 名 ▶定義 1 ❻ the bottom surface of your foot 足の裏側→**足の裏** ☞ C5 ページのさし絵 ▶定義 2 ❻ the part of a shoe or sock that covers the bottom surface of your foot 靴または靴下の一部で足の裏側を覆う部分→**靴底, 底** ☞ shoe のさし絵 ▶定義 3 ❻ ❶ (複 sole) a flat sea fish that we eat 平らな形をした食用の海水魚→**シタビラメ, シタガレイ; その肉**

**solemn** /sɑ́ləm/ 形 ▶定義 1 (used about a person) very serious; not happy or smiling (人について) 非常にまじめな; 楽しそうでない, にこにこしていない→**まじめな, 謹厳な, 重々しい** ‖ Her solemn face told them that the news was bad. 彼女の重々しい顔付きで, その知らせが悪いものであることが彼らに分かった. ▶定義 2 sincere; done or said in a formal way 真摯(しんし)な; 改まって行われたまたは述べられた→**厳粛な, 荘厳な, 厳かな, 正式の, 公式の** ‖ to make a solemn promise 厳かな誓約を行う — **solemnity** /səlémnəti/ 名 ❶→**厳粛, 荘厳, まじめさ, 荘厳な儀式** — **solemnly** 副→**厳粛に, 厳かに, まじめに, 正式に** ‖ 'I have something very important to tell you,' she began solemnly. 「あなたにとても大切な話があります」と彼女は改まった口調で話し始めた.

**solicit** /səlísət/ 動 ▶定義 1 ❻ 正式 to ask sb for money, help, support, etc ～に金銭, 援助, 支援などを求める→**～を請い求める, 懇願する** ‖ They tried to solicit support for the proposal. 彼らはその提案に対する支持を求めようとした. ▶定義 2 ❶ ⑯ (used about a woman who has sex for money) to go to sb, especially in a public place, and offer sex in return for money (金のためにセックスをする女性について) 特に公共の場所で～に近付き金と引き換えに性交渉を申し出る→**(売春婦が)(客)を引く; 客を誘う**

**solicitor** /səlísə(r)ɚr/ 名 ❻ 英 ▶定義 a lawyer whose job is to give legal advice, prepare legal documents and arrange the buying and selling of land, etc 法的な助言, 法律書類の作成, 土地の売買の手配などを行うことを業務とする弁護士→**事務弁護士** ☞参 lawyer の注

***solid**¹ /sɑ́ləd/ 形 ▶定義 1 hard and firm; not in the form of liquid or gas 固くて強固な; 液体または気体でない→**固い; 固体の, 固形の** ‖ It was so cold that the village pond had **frozen solid**. とても寒かったので村の池がカチカチに凍ってしまった. ▶定義 2 having no holes or empty spaces inside; not hollow 内に穴またはすきまがない; 中空でない→**すきまのない, うつろでない** ‖ a solid mass of rock 硬い岩の塊 ▶定義 3 strong, firm and well-made 強く, 頑丈で, 作りの良い→**頑丈な, 堅固な, がっしりした** ‖ a solid little car 頑丈な小型車(比喩) They built up a solid friendship over the years. 彼らは長年にわたって確固たる友情を築いた. ▶定義 4 of good enough quality; that you can trust それなりに良質の; 信頼できる→**信用できる, 堅実な, 確実な** ‖ The police cannot make an arrest without solid evidence. 警察は確実な証拠なしに逮捕してはならない. ▶定義 5 (名詞の前だけ) made completely of one substance, both on the inside and outside 内側も外側も1つの素材だけで作られた→**純粋の, 混じり物のない** ‖ a solid gold chain 純金の首飾り ▶定義 6 (口語) without a break or pause 中断またはとぎれのない→**間断のない, 連続した, 切れ目なしの** ‖ I was so tired that I slept for twelve solid hours/twelve hours solid. 非常に疲れていたので12時間ぶっ通しで眠った. — **solidity** /səlídəti/ 名 ❶→**固いこと, 充実, 堅固, 堅実さ**

**solid**² /sɑ́ləd/ 名 ❻ ▶定義 1 a substance or object that is hard; not a liquid or gas 固い物質または物体; 液体または気体でない物→**固体, 固**

形物‖ *Liquids become solids when frozen.* 液体が凍ると固体になる. *The baby is not yet on solids (= solid food).* 赤ん坊はまだ固形食を始めていない. ▶定義2 an object that has length, width and height, not a flat shape 平面形ではなく, 長さ, 幅, 高さを持つ物体 →立体‖ *A cube is a solid.* 立方体は立体である.

**solidarity** /sɑ̀lədǽrəti/ 名 U ▶定義 solidarity (with sb) the support of one group of people for another, because they agree with their aims 目的が一致しているため, ある集団が別の集団に対して与える支持 →結束, 団結, 連帯‖ *Many local people expressed solidarity with the strikers.* 地元の人たちの多くがストライキ参加者たちに連帯を表明した.

**solidify** /səlídəfàɪ/ 動自 (現分 **solidifying**; 三単現 **solidifies**, 過, 過分 **solidified**) ▶定義 to become hard or solid 固くなる, 固体になる →凝固する, 固体化する, 強固になる

**solidly** /sɑ́lədli/ 副 ▶定義1 strongly 強く →頑丈に, 堅固に, 強固に‖ *a solidly built house* 頑丈に建てられた家 ▶定義2 without stopping 中断せずに →連続して, 切れ目なく, ぶっ通しで‖ *It rained solidly all day.* 一日中ぶっ通しで雨が降った.

**solitaire** /sɑ́lətèər, -́--́/ 名 U ▶定義1 a game for one person in which you remove pieces from a special board by moving other pieces over them until you have only one piece left 駒(こま)を飛び越しながら, 最後に1つ残るまで専用の盤から駒を取り除いていく, 1人用の遊び →ソリテール ▶定義2 英 = PATIENCE(2)

**solitary** /sɑ́lətèri, -tèri/ 形 ▶定義1 done alone, without other people ほかの人たちと一緒でなく単独で行われた →1人だけの, 単独の, 孤独な‖ *Writing novels is a solitary occupation.* 小説の執筆は孤独な仕事だ. ▶定義2 (used about a person or an animal) enjoying being alone; frequently spending time alone (人または動物について)1人でいることを楽しむ; しばしば1人だけで時を過ごす →孤独な, 孤独好きな, 独りぼっちの, 独居性の‖ *She was always a solitary child.* 彼女はいつも独りでいるのが好きな子供だった. ▶定義3 one on its/his/her own with no others around (名詞の前だけ)近くにほかの人・物もなく, ただその人・物だけの →人里離れた, 孤立した, 独りの, 寂しい‖ *a solitary figure walking up the hillside* 丘陵の斜面を歩くぽつんとした人影 ●類 **lone** ▶定義4 (名詞の前だけ)(通常は否定文または疑問文で) only one; single 唯一の; たった1つの →唯一の, たった1つの, たった1人の‖ *I can't think of a solitary example (= not even one).* たった1つの例も (= 1つの例さえも)考え付かない.

**solitary confinement** 名 U ▶定義 a punishment in which a person in prison is kept completely alone in a separate cell away from the other prisoners 刑務所にいる囚人がほかの囚人と離れた別個の個室に完全に独りで収容される処罰 →独房監禁

**solitude** /sɑ́lət(j)ùːd/ 名 U ▶定義 the state of being alone, especially when you find this pleasant 特に心地良い1人の状態 →孤独, 独居, 1人でいること‖ *She longed for peace and solitude.* 彼女は平穏と孤独を求めていた.
▶ **loneliness, isolation** と比較.

**solo¹** /sóʊloʊ/ 名 C (複 **solos**) ▶定義 a piece of music for only one person to play or sing 1人で演奏する, または歌う音楽 →独唱, 独奏, ソロ ●参 **duet** ─ **soloist** 名 C →独唱者, 独奏者, 独演者, ソリスト

**solo²** /sóʊloʊ/ 形副 ▶定義1 (done) alone; by yourself 1人で(行われた); 独力で →1人で(する), 単独の[で]‖ *a solo flight* 単独飛行 *to fly solo* 単独で飛行する ▶定義2 connected with or played as a musical solo ソロに関する, ソロで演奏された →独唱の[で], 独奏の[で], ソロの[で]‖ *a solo artist (= a singer who is not part of a group)* ソロアーティスト(= グループの1人でない歌手)

**soluble** /sɑ́ljəb(ə)l/ 形 ▶定義1 soluble (in sth) that will dissolve in liquid 液体に溶ける →溶ける, 溶けやすい, 溶解できる‖ *These tablets are soluble in water.* これらの錠剤は水に溶ける.
▶定義2 正式 (used about a problem, etc) that has an answer; that can be solved (問題などについて)答えのある, 解くことのできる →解決できる, 解答できる ⇔ **insoluble**

*__**solution** /səlúːʃ(ə)n/ 名 ▶定義1 C a solution (to sth) a way of solving a problem, dealing with a difficult situation, etc 問題の解決法, 困難な状況の対処法など →(~の)解決, 解決策, 解決法‖ *a solution to the problem of unemployment 失業問題の解決策 ▶定義2 ❸the solution (to sth) the answer (to a game, competition etc)（ゲーム，コンテストなどの）唯一の答え→(〜の)正解 ‖ *The solution to the quiz will be published next week.* そのクイズの正解は来週発表される. ▶定義3 ❸Ⓤ(a) liquid in which sth solid has been dissolved 固体が溶けている液体→**溶液** ‖ *sailne solution* 食塩水

*__solve__ /sɒlv/ 動他 ▶定義1 to find a way of dealing with a problem or difficult situation 問題または困難な状況に対処する方法を見つける→**〜を解決する，解く，打開する** ‖ *The government is trying to solve the problem of inflation.* 政府はインフレ問題を打開しようとしている. *The police have not managed to solve the crime.* 警察はまだその犯罪を解決できないでいる. *to solve a mystery* 不可解ななぞを解き明かす ▶定義2 to find the correct answer to a competition, a problem in mathematics, a series of questions, etc 競技，数学の問題，一連の質問などの正解を見つける→**〜を解く，解答する，解明する** ‖ *to solve a puzzle/equation/riddle* パズル・方程式・なぞを解く ☛ solution ☛ 形 soluble

__solvent__ /ˈsɒlv(ə)nt/ 名 ❸Ⓤ ▶定義 a liquid that can dissolve another substance ほかの物質を溶かすことのできる液体→**溶剤，溶媒**

__sombre__(困**somber**)/ˈsɒmbər/ 形 ▶定義1 dark in colour; dull 色が暗い; 鈍い→**地味な，くすんだ，黒ずんだ** ▶定義2 sad and serious 悲しくて重々しい→**憂鬱(ゆううつ)な，陰気な，ふさいだ** ― **sombrely** 副→**暗く，地味に，陰気に**

*__some__ /s(ə)m, 強形 sʌm/ 形代 ▶定義1 (不可算名詞，および複数形の可算名詞の前で)a certain amount of or a number of 一定量の，一定数の→**いくらかの，いくつかの，多少の，少しの** ‖ *We need some butter and some potatoes.* バターとジャガイモがいくらか要る. *I don't need any more money - I've still got some.* これ以上の金は要らない ― まだ少し持っているから.

▶ 否定文または疑問文では some の代わりに any を使用する: *Do we need any butter?*（バターは要りますか.）*I need some more money. I haven't got any.*（もう少し金が必要だ.持ち合わせが全然ない.）疑問文で some の使われる例は次を参照.

▶定義2 used in questions when you expect or want the answer 'yes' 肯定の答えを期待または望んでいるときの疑問文に用いて→**多少(の)，いくらか(の)，いくつか(の)** ‖ *Would you like some more cake?* もう少しケーキはいかがですか. *Can I take some of this paper?* この紙を少し持っていってもいいですか. ▶定義3 some (of sb/sth) used when you are referring to certain members of a group or certain types of a thing, but not all of them ある集団の全員ではなく，一定の成員，あるもののすべてではなく，一定のタイプに言及するときに用いて→**一部(の)，いくらか(の)，いくつか(の)，いく人か(の)** ‖ *Some pupils enjoy this kind of work, some don't.* この種の作業を楽しむ生徒もいれば，そうでない生徒もいる. *Some of his books are very exciting.* 彼の本の中には面白くて胸がわくわくするようなものがある. *Some of us are going to the park.* 私たちの中の何人かは公園に出掛ける予定だ. ▶定義4 used with singular countable nouns for talking about a person or thing without saying any details 詳細に触れずに人・物について話すとき，可算名詞の単数形と用いて→**ある，何かの，だれかの，どこかの，いつかの** ‖ *I'll see you again some time, I expect.* またいつかお会いすることでしょう. *There must be some mistake.* 何か間違いがあるに違いない. *I read about it in some newspaper or other.* はっきりしないがどこかの新聞でそれについて読んだ.

__somebody__ /ˈsʌmbədi, -bɒdi/（または**someone**）代 ▶定義 a person who is not known or not mentioned by name 名前を知らない人または名前を挙げないでいる人→**ある人，だれか** ‖ *How are you? Somebody said that you'd been ill.* お元気ですか. だれかがあなたは病気だと言っていました. *She's getting married to someone she met at work.* 彼女は職場で会った人と結婚する予定だ. *There's somebody at the door.* 戸口にだれかがいる. *I think you should talk to **someone else** (= another person) about this problem.* この問題についてだれかほかの人(=別の人)と話し合うべきだと思う.

▶ somebody, anybody, everybody は動詞の単数形と共に用いられるが，複数の代名詞で受けることが多い(ただし正式な英語では his/her または him/her を用いなければならな

# 1546 some day

い): *Somebody* has left **their** coat behind. (だれかがコートを置いていった.) *Has anyone not brought **their** books?* (本を持ってきていない人はいますか.) *I'll see everybody concerned and tell **them** the news.* (私は関係者全員に会ってその知らせを伝えるつもりだ.) somebody と anybody の違いは some と any の違いと同じである. some の注を参照.

**some day** 副 (または **someday**) ▶定義 at a time in the future that is not yet known まだ分からない未来のある時に→いつか,そのうち,他日 ∥ *I hope you'll come and visit me some day.* いつかあなたが私の所に訪ねてきてくださることを願っています.

*****somehow** /sámhàʊ/ 副 ▶定義1 in a way that is not known or certain 知られていないまたははっきりしていない方法で→何らかの方法で,何とかして,どうにか ∥ *The car's broken down but I'll get to work somehow.* 車は故障してしまったが,何とかして仕事に行くつもりだ. *Somehow we had got completely lost.* 知らないうちに完全に道に迷ってしまった. ▶定義2 for a reason you do not know or understand 自分でも知らないまたは分からない理由で→どういう訳か,なぜか,どうも,何となく ∥ *I somehow get the feeling that I've been here before.* どうも前にここに来た気がする.

**someone** /sámwÀn, -wən/ = SOMEBODY
**someplace** /sámplèɪs/ 米 = SOMEWHERE
**somersault** /sáməsɔ̀ːlt/ 名 ● ▶定義 a movement in which you roll right over with your feet going over your head 頭の上方に足が来るように体を回転させる動き→宙返り,とんぼ返り,回転

*****something** /sámθɪŋ/ 代 ▶定義1 a thing that is not known or not named 何か分からないもの,または名前で示されていないもの→あるもの,ある事,何か ∥ *I've got something in my eye.* 私の目に何かが入った. *Wait a minute - I've forgotten something.* ちょっと待って - 何か忘れ物をしてしまった. *Would you like **something else** (= another thing) to drink?* 何かほかの飲み物(= 別の飲み物)をお望みですか.

➤ something と anything の違いは some と any の違いと同じである. some の注を参照.

▶定義2 a thing that is important, useful or worth considering 重要なもの,役に立つもの,考慮に値するもの→重要な物・人,大した物・人,結構なこと,(いくらかの)真理 ∥ *There's **something in** what your mother says.* あなたの母親の言うことには一理ある. *I think you've got something there - I like that idea.* なるほど君もなかなかいい事を言う - その考えが気に入ったよ.

▶定義3 略式 used to show that a description, an amount, etc is not exact 描写,量などが正確でないことを示すのに用いて→～と何とか,～かいくらか ∥ *a new comedy series aimed at **thirty-somethings** (= people between thirty and forty years old).* 30代(= 30歳から40歳までの人たち)を対象にした新しい連続コメディー

> ►コミュニケーション
>
> 「とか何とか」に当たる英語表現
>
> くだけた会話で,名前・年数などよく覚えていないとき *Her name is Lisa something* (彼女の名前はリサ何とか)といった具合に something を使うことがあります. また or something を使って,日本語の「とか何とか」に似た大まかな言い方もします. 例えば,青い顔をした友人に, *Did you see a ghost or something?* (幽霊か何か見たの?) と言ったり,珍しく勉強している友人に, *Do you have a test or something?* (テストか何かあるの?) と言うこともあります.

成句 **or something** 略式 ▶定義 used for showing that you are not sure about what you have just said 今言った事について確信がないことを示すのに用いて→～か何か ∥ *'What's his job?' 'I think he's a plumber, or something.'* 「彼の仕事は何ですか」「配管工か何かだと思います」

**something like** ▶定義 similar to ～に似ている→多少～に似ている,いくぶん～のような ∥ *A loganberry is something like a raspberry.* ローガンベリーは何かラズベリーのようなものだ.

**something to do with** ▶定義 connected or involved with ～に関する,～に関連した→～に関するもの,～に関連したもの ∥ *The programme's something to do with the environment.* その番組は環境に関連したものだ.

*****sometime** (または **some time**) /sámtàɪm/ 副 ▶定義 at a time that you do not know exactly or have not yet decided 正確には分からない、またはまだ決定していない時に→**いつか、そのうち、いずれ、近々** ‖ *I'll phone you sometime this evening.* 今夜いつか君に電話するよ. *I must go and see her sometime.* いずれ近いうちに彼女に会いに行かなければならない.

**\*sometimes** /sʌ́mtàɪmz, s(ə)mtáɪmz/ 副 ▶定義 on some occasions; now and then 時折; 時々→**時折、時々、時には** ‖ *Sometimes I drive to work and sometimes I go by bus.* 私は車で仕事に出掛けるときもあれば、バスで出掛けるときもある. *I sometimes watch television in the evenings.* 晩に時々テレビを見る.

**somewhat** /sʌ́m(h)wʌ̀t, -(h)wət/ 副 ▶定義 rather; to some degree いくぶん、多少→**いくぶん、少し、多少、やや** ‖ *We missed the train, which was somewhat unfortunate.* 私たちは列車に乗り損ねてしまった - やや不運なことだったが.

**\*somewhere** /sʌ́m(h)wèər/ (困 または **someplace**) 副 ▶定義1 at, in, or to a place that you do not know or do not mention by name 名前を知らない、または言及されていない場所で、場所に、場所へ→**ある場所で[に・へ]、どこかに、どこかへ** ‖ *I've seen your glasses somewhere downstairs.* あなたの眼鏡を階下のどこかで見掛けた. *'Have they gone to France?' 'No, I think they've gone somewhere else (= to another place) this year.'* 「彼らはフランスに行ったのですか?」「いいえ、今年はどこかほかの場所(= 別の場所)に行ったのだと思います」

➤ somewhere と anywhere の違いは some と any の違いと同じである. some の注を参照.

▶定義2 used when you do not know an exact time, number, etc 正確な時間、数などを知らないときに用いて→**およそ〜のころ、およそ〜くらい** ‖ *Your ideal weight should probably be somewhere around 70 kilos.* あなたの理想の体重はおよそ70キロくらいだろう.

**\*son** /sʌn/ 名 C ▶定義 a male child 男の子供→**息子、せがれ** ☞参 **daughter**

**sonata** /sənɑ́ːtə/ 名 C ▶定義 a piece of music written for the piano, or for another instrument together with the piano ピアノまたはピアノと共に演奏されるほかの楽器のために作られた曲→**ソナタ、奏鳴曲**

**\*song** /sɔ́(ː)ŋ, sɑŋ/ 名 ▶定義1 C a piece of music with words that you sing 歌詞の付いた曲→**歌、歌曲** ‖ *a folk/love/pop song* フォークソング、ラブソング、ポップソング ▶定義2 U songs in general; music for singing 歌一般; 歌唱用の音楽→**歌うこと、歌唱、声楽** ‖ *to burst/break into song (= to suddenly start singing)* 急に歌い出す (= 突然歌い始める) ▶定義3 U C the musical sounds that birds make 鳥の音楽的な鳴き音→**鳴き声、さえずり** ‖ *birdsong* 鳥のさえずり

**songwriter** /sɔ́(ː)ŋràɪtər, sɑ́ŋ-/ 名 C ▶定義 a person whose job is to write songs 歌を書くことを職業とする人→**ソングライター(ポピュラーな曲の作詞・作曲、またはその両方をする人)**

**sonic** /sɑ́nɪk/ 形 (専門用語) ▶定義 connected with sound waves 音波に関する→**音波の、音の、音速の**

**son-in-law** 名 C (複 **sons-in-law**) ▶定義 the husband of your daughter 娘の夫→**娘婿、義理の息子**

**\*soon** /suːn/ 副 ▶定義1 in a short time from now; a short time after sth else has happened 今から短時間の間に; ほかの〜が起こってから少したって→**すぐに、間もなく、もうすぐ** ‖ *It will soon be dark.* もうすぐ暗くなる. *He left soon after me.* 彼は私のすぐ後に出ていった. *We should arrive at your house soon after twelve.* 私たちは12時ちょっと過ぎにあなたの家に到着するはずです. (口語) *See you soon.* じゃあまたね.

▶定義2 early; quickly 早く; 素早く→**早く、早めに、速やかに** ‖ *Don't leave so soon. Stay for tea.* そんなに早々と帰らないでください. お茶を飲んでいってください. *How soon can you get here?* あとのどのくらいでここに来ることができますか.

成句 **as soon as** ▶定義 at the moment (that); when 〜するちょうどその時; 〜する時に→**〜するとすぐに、〜や否や** ‖ *Phone me as soon as you hear some news.* 何か知らせを聞いたらすぐに私に電話しなさい. *I'd like your reply as soon as possible (= at the earliest possible moment).* できるだけ早く(= 可能な限り早い機会に)返事してください.

**no sooner...than** (文) ▶定義 immediately when or after 〜するとすぐに、〜した直後に→**〜するとすぐに、〜するや否や** ‖ *No sooner had I shut the door than I realized I'd left my keys inside.*

ドアを閉めるや否や私は中にかぎを置き忘れたことに気が付いた.

➤語順に注意. no soonerのすぐ後に動詞が続き, その後に主語が来る.

sooner or later ▶定義 at some time in the future; one day 未来のある時に; いつか➜**遅かれ早かれ, いつか, そのうち**

**soot** /sʊt/ [名] [U] ▶定義 black powder that comes from burning things and collects in chimneys 物を燃やすと生じ, 煙突内にたまる黒い粉➜**すす, 煤煙(ばいえん)**

**soothe** /suːð/ [動][他] ▶定義1 to make sb calmer or less upset; to comfort sb ～を落ち着かせる, 取り乱した～の気持ちを静める; ～を慰める➜**～を落ち着かせる, 慰める, なだめる** ▶定義2 to make a part of the body or a feeling less painful 体の一部または心の痛みを少なくする➜**～を和らげる, 楽にする, 軽くする** ‖ *The doctor gave me some skin cream to soothe the irritation.* 医者はひりひりする痛みを和らげるスキンクリームをくれた. — soothing [形]➜**気持ちを落ち着かせる, 痛みを和らげる** ‖ *soothing music* 心が和む音楽 *a soothing massage* 痛みを和らげるマッサージ —soothingly [副]➜**なだめるように, 気持ちを落ち着かせるように, 和らげるように**

**sophisticated** /səfístəkèɪtəd/ [形] ▶定義1 having or showing a lot of experience of the world and social situations; knowing about fashion, culture, etc 豊富な世間的経験を持ち, 社会の場数を多く踏んだ, またはそうした経験の豊かさを示す; ファッション, 文化などについてよく知っている➜**世慣れた, 如才ない; 洗練された, あか抜けた, 教養のある** ▶定義2 (used about machines, systems, etc) advanced and complicated (機械, システムなどについて) 高度で複雑な➜**精巧な, 高度な, 高性能の, 非常に複雑な** ▶定義3 able to understand difficult or complicated things 難しいまたは複雑な事が理解できる➜**見識のある, 目の肥えた** ‖ *Voters are much more sophisticated these days.* 有権者は近ごろずっと目が肥えている. — sophistication /səfìstəkéɪʃ(ə)n/ [名] [U]➜**世間慣れ, 洗練, 精巧**

**soppy** /sápi/ [形][略式] ▶定義 full of unnecessary emotion; silly 無用な感情に満ちた; 愚かな➜**ひどく感傷的な, めそめそした, ばかばかしい** ‖ *a soppy romantic film* ひどくセンチメンタルな恋愛映画

**soprano** /səpráːnoʊ, -prǽ-/ [名] [C] ([複] **sopranos** /-noʊz/) ▶定義 the highest singing voice; a woman, girl, or boy with this voice 最も高い歌声; この音域の声を持つ女性, 少女, 少年➜**ソプラノ, 最高音域, ソプラノ歌手**

**sordid** /sɔːrdəd/ [形] ▶定義1 unpleasant; not honest or moral 不快な; 正直でないまたは道徳的でない➜**下劣な, 卑しい, 浅ましい, 強欲な** ‖ *We discovered the truth about his sordid past.* 私たちは彼の卑劣な過去についての真相を突き止めた. ▶定義2 very dirty and unpleasant 非常に汚れていて不快な➜**汚い, 不潔な, みすぼらしい**

***sore**[1] /sɔ́ːr/ [形] ▶定義 (used about a part of the body) painful, especially when touched (体の部分について) 特に触れられたときに痛む➜**(触れると)痛い, ひりひりする, ずきずきする, 炎症を起こして痛い** ‖ *to have a sore throat* のどが痛む *My feet were sore from walking so far.* あんなに遠くまで歩いたため足が痛んだ. — soreness [名] [U]➜**痛み, 苦痛, 痛さ** ‖ *a cream to reduce soreness and swelling* 痛みとはれを和らげるクリーム

[成句] a sore point ▶定義 a subject that is likely to make sb upset or angry when mentioned 話に出せば～を動揺させたり怒らせそうな話題➜**触れてほしくない話題, 人の感情を害するような問題, 痛い所, 弱点**

stand/stick out like a sore thumb ▶定義 to be extremely obvious, especially in a negative way 特に否定的な意味で非常に目立つ➜**ひどく目立つ, 目障りである, 場違いである** ‖ *A big new office block would stand out like a sore thumb in the old part of town.* 大きな新しいオフィスビルは旧市街ではひどく場違いで目に付く.

**sore**[2] /sɔːr/ [名] [C] ▶定義 a painful, often red place on your body where the skin is cut or infected 切り傷·炎症により皮膚がしばしば赤くなって痛む箇所➜**触れると痛い所, 擦り傷, はれ物, ただれ**

**sorely** /sɔ́ːrli/ [副][正式] ▶定義 very much; seriously➜**非常に, ひどく** ‖ *You'll be **sorely missed** when you leave.* あなたがいなくなるとひどく寂しくなるでしょう.

**sorrow** /sɔ́ːroʊ, sá-/ [名][正式] ▶定義1 [U] a feeling of great sadness because sth bad has happened 不運な～が起こったために感じる深い悲しみ➜**悲しみ, 悲哀, 悲痛** ▶定義2 [C] a very sad event or situation 非常に悲しい出来事または状況 → 悲しいこと,不幸,難儀 — sorrowful 形 → 悲しんでいる,悲嘆に暮れている,悲しげな,哀れな — sorrowfully 副 → 悲しそうに,悲しんで,悲嘆に暮れて

\*sorry¹ /sɔ́ːri, sɑ́ri/ 形 (sorrier; sorriest) ▶定義1 (名詞の前は不可) sorry (to see, hear, etc); sorry that... sad or disappointed 悲しんで,失望して → 気の毒で,気の毒に思って,かわいそうで,残念で ‖ *I was sorry to hear that you've been ill.* お病気だったとはお気の毒でした. *I am sorry that we have to leave so soon.* こんなにすぐにここを出ていかなければならないなんて残念です. *'Simon's mother died last week.' 'Oh, I am sorry.'* 「サイモンのお母様が先週亡くなられました」「まあ,それはお気の毒に」 ▶定義2 (名詞の前は不可) sorry (for/about sth); sorry (to do sth/that...) used for excusing yourself for sth that you have done 自分がした〜をわびるのに用いて → すまなく思って,後悔して,遺憾で ‖ *I'm awfully sorry for spilling that coffee.* コーヒーをこぼしてしまって本当にすみません. *I'm sorry I've kept you all waiting.* 皆さんをお待たせしてすみません. *I'm sorry to disturb you so late in the evening, but I wonder if you can help me.* こんなに夜遅くお邪魔して申し訳ありませんが,助けていただけないでしょうか. ▶定義3 (名詞の前は不可) used for politely saying 'no' to sth, disagreeing with sth or introducing bad news 丁寧な断り,不賛成の表明,悪い知らせの伝達などに用いて → 残念で,残念ながら〜で,悪いが〜で ‖ *'Would you like to come to dinner on Friday?' 'I'm sorry, I'm busy that evening.'* 「金曜日に夕食にいらっしゃいませんか」「残念ですがその夜は忙しいので」 *I'm sorry, I don't agree with you. I think we should accept the offer.* 悪いけれど,あなたの意見には賛成できません.私たちはその申し出を受けるべきだと思います. *I'm sorry to tell you that your application has been unsuccessful.* あなたにご応募いただきましたが,残念ながら不採用となりました. ▶定義4 (名詞の前だけ) very bad とても悪い → ひどい,お粗末な,情けない,惨めな ‖ *The house was in a **sorry state** when we first moved in.* 私たちが引っ越した当初,この家はひどい状態だった. *They were a **sorry sight** when they finally got home.* 彼らがようやく帰宅した時,見るも哀れな姿だった.

## sorry² 1549

成句 be/feel sorry for sb ▶定義 to feel sadness or pity for sb 〜に対して悲しみまたは同情を抱く → 〜を気の毒に思う,かわいそうに思う,〜に対してすまないと思う ‖ *I feel very sorry for the families of the victims.* 犠牲者の家族が気の毒だ. *Stop feeling sorry for yourself!* 我が身を嘆くのはやめなさい.

\*sorry² /sɔ́ːri, sɑ́ri/ 間 ▶定義1 used for making excuses, apologizing, etc 言い訳・謝罪などする場合に用いて → すみません,申し訳ありません,ごめんなさい ‖ *Sorry, I didn't see you standing behind me.* すみません,あなたが私の後ろに立っているのに気付きませんでした. *Sorry I'm late - the bus didn't come on time.* 遅れてごめんなさい — バスが定刻通りに来なかったのです. *He didn't even **say sorry** (= apologize)!* 彼はごめんとも言わなかった (= 彼は謝罪をしなかった). ▶定義2 特に 英 (used for asking sb to repeat sth that you have not heard correctly) (正しく聞き取れなかった〜を繰り返すよう…に頼むために用いて) → すみませんがもう一度,何とおっしゃいましたか. ‖ *'My name's Dave Harries.' 'Sorry? Dave who?'* 「私の名前はデーブハリーズです」「すみません.デーブ何とおっしゃいましたか」 ▶定義3 (used for correcting yourself when you have said sth wrong) (間違った事を言ったときに訂正するために用いて) → すみません,間違えました ‖ *Take the second turning, sorry, the third turning on the right.* 2番目の角を,失礼,3番目の角を右に曲がってください.

> ▶コミュニケーション
> 
> 「すみません」と thank you
> 
> 日本語ではお礼の意味で「すみません」と言うことがあります.特にわざわざ自分のために何かしてくれたときなど,手間をかけて申し訳なかったという気持ちが働くために「すみません」となるのでしょう.英語はこの場合 Thank you (very much) となり,本当に迷惑を掛けない限り,I'm sorry (to have caused you so much trouble) と言ったりはしません.すまないという気持ちより,相手の好意に感謝の気持ちを表すのが礼儀とされるのです.

## 1550 sort¹

**sort¹** /sɔːrt/ 名 **定義1** ❶ a sort of sb/sth a type or kind → 型, 種類, タイプ ‖ *What sort of music do you like?* あなたはどんな種類の音楽が好きですか. *She's got **all sorts of** problems at the moment.* 彼女は目下あらゆる種類の問題を抱えている. *There were snacks - peanuts, olives, **that sort of thing**.* おつまみが出ていたよ — ピーナッツとか, オリーブとか, そういったものが. **定義2** [単数扱い] 特に 医 a particular type of character; a person 特定の性格; 人 → (性質などが)〜な人, 〜のタイプの人 ☞類 kind

成句 a sort of sth 略式 **定義** a type of sth; sth that is similar to sth 〜の一種, 〜に似たもの → 一種の〜, 〜のようなもの ‖ *Can you hear a sort of ticking noise?* カチカチいうような音が聞こえませんか.

sort of (口語) **定義** rather; in a way 多少, ある意味で → 多少, いくらか, 何だか〜のようだ[するようだ] ‖ *'Do you see what I mean?' 'Sort of.'* 「僕の言っている事が分かるかい」「まあね」*I'd sort of like to go, but I'm not sure.* 何だか行きたい気もするが, まだよく分からない.

**sort²** /sɔːrt/ 動 **定義1** sort sth (into sth) to put things into different groups or places, according to their type, etc; to separate things of one type from others 〜をタイプなどに従って異なるグループ・場所に分ける, または別々の場所に置く; あるタイプの〜を他から区別する → 〜を(…に)分類する, 区分けする, 分ける, 仕分ける, 区別する ‖ *I'm just sorting these papers into the correct files.* ちょうど今これらの書類を正しいファイルに分類しているところだ. **定義2** 特に 医 略式 (しばしば受動態で) to find an answer to a problem or difficult situation; to organize sth/sb 問題または困難な状況に対する答えを見いだす; 〜をまとめる → 〜を解決する, 片付ける; まとめる ‖ *I'll have more time when I've **got things sorted** at home.* 家庭でのいろいろな事が片付けば, もっと時間が持てるようになるでしょう.

句動詞 sort sth out **定義1** to find an answer to a problem; to organize sth 問題に対する答えを見いだす; 〜をまとめる → 〜を処理する, 解決する; 整とんする ‖ *I haven't found a flat yet but I hope to sort something out soon.* まだアパートは見つかっていないが, 直に何とかなればと思っている. **定義2** to tidy or organize sth 〜を整とんする, まとめる → 〜を整える, 整理する, まとめる ‖ *The toy cupboard needs sorting out.* おもちゃの棚を整理する必要がある.

sort through sth **定義** to look through a number of things, in order to find sth that you are looking for or to put them in order 〜を探すため, または整理するために, 多くの…に目を通す → 〜を仕分ける, 区分けする, 整理する

**so-so** /sòu sóu, ⌃ ⌃/ 形副 略式 **定義** all right but not particularly good/well 一応いいが, 特に良くない[良くもなく] → まあまあ(の), まずまず(の), 可もなく不可もない[く] ‖ *'How are you?' 'So-so.'* 「調子はどうかい」「まあまあだね」

**souffle** /súːfleɪ, ⌃ ⌃/ 名 ❻ ❶ **定義** a type of food made mainly from egg whites, flour and milk, beaten together and baked until it rises 卵の白身, 小麦粉, 牛乳を主たる材料とし, これらをかき混ぜて膨らむまで焼いた食べ物 → スフレ

**sought** SEEK の過去・過去分詞形
**sought after** 形 **定義** that people want very much, because it is of high quality or rare 品質が高い, または珍しいため人々が非常に求めている → 人気のある, 需要の多い, 珍重されている, 引っ張りだこの

**soul** /sóul/ 名 **定義1** ❻ the spiritual part of a person that is believed to continue to exist after the body is dead 肉体が死んだ後も存在し続けると信じられている人の霊的部分 → 魂, 霊魂, 霊 **定義2** ❻ ❶ the inner part of a person containing his/her deepest thoughts and feelings 最も深い思考や感情を含む人間の内面 → 精神, 心; 心の奥底 ‖ *There was a feeling of restlessness deep in her soul.* 彼女の心の奥深くにはじっとしていられない気持ちがあった. ☞参 spirit **定義3** ❻ (古) (形容詞と用いて) a particular type of person あるタイプの人 → 〜な人 **定義4** [単数扱い] (否定文で) a person → 人, 人間 ‖ *There wasn't a soul in sight (= there was nobody).* 人っ子一人見えなかった (= だれもいなかった). *Promise me you won't tell a soul.* だれにも話さないと約束してください. **定義5** (または **soul music**) ❶ a type of popular African American music アフリカ系アメリカ人の大衆音楽の一種 → ソウルミュージック ‖ *a soul singer* ソウルシンガー

成句 heart and soul ⇒ HEART

**soulful** /sóulful, -f(ə)l/ 形 ▶定義 having or showing deep feeling 深い感情を抱くまたは示す→**感情・魂のこもった, 情感豊かな** ‖ *a soulful expression* 感情に満ちた表現

**soulless** /sóulləs/ 形 ▶定義 without feeling, warmth or interest 感情,温かみまたは面白みのない→**感情を欠いた, 魂のこもっていない, 退屈な** ‖ *soulless industrial towns* 人間味のない工業都市

★**sound**¹ /sáund/ 名 ▶定義 1 ❻ ❶ something that you hear or that can be heard 自分に聞こえてくるもの, または一般に聞こえるもの→**音, 音響, 響き** ‖ *the sound of voices* 人声 *a clicking/buzzing/scratching sound* カチッ・ブンブン・ガリガリという音 *After that, he didn't **make a sound**.* その後,彼は物音一つ立てなかった. *She opened the door without a sound.* 彼女は音を立てずに戸を開けた. *Light travels faster than sound.* 光は音よりも速く進む. *sound waves* 音波 ▶定義 2 ❶ what you can hear coming from a television, radio, etc テレビ,ラジオなどから聞こえるもの→**音, 音量** ‖ *Can you turn the sound up/down?* 音量を上げて・下げてくれませんか.

成句 **by the sound of it/things** ▶定義 judging from what sb has said or what you have read about sb/sth 〜が言ったり,自分が〜について読んだりした事から判断して→**うわさによると, 聞いた感じからすると** ‖ *She must be an interesting person, by the sound of it.* 聞いた感じでは[話からすると],彼女は面白い人に違いない.

★**sound**² /sáund/ 動 ▶定義 1 ⊜(通常は進行形では使われない) to give a particular impression when heard or read about; to seem 聞いたり読んだりしたときにある特定の印象を抱かせる; 〜と思われる→**〜に聞こえる, 〜に思われる, 〜の印象を与える** ‖ *That **sounds like** a child crying.* あれは子供の泣き声のように聞こえる. *She sounded upset and angry on the phone.* 電話での彼女は動揺して怒っているようだった. *You sound like your father when you say things like that!* そんな事を言うとき,あなたはお父さんそっくりの口振りだ. *He sounds a very nice person from his letter.* 手紙から察すると彼は非常に感じの良い人のようだ. *Does she sound like the right person for the job?* 彼女はその仕事にふさわしい人のように思われますか. *It doesn't sound as if/though he's very reliable.* 彼はあま

り信頼できるような人には思われない. ☛ 口語,特に米口語では as if または as though の代わりにしばしば like が用いられるが,イギリス英語の文語では正しくないと考えられている.

▶定義 2 **-sounding** (複合形容詞を作るために用いて) seeming to be of the type mentioned, from what you have heard or read これまで聞いたり読んだりした事から察すると,言及されたタイプのように思われる→**〜な音がする, 〜に聞こえる, 〜のような印象を与える** ‖ *a Spanish-sounding surname* スペイン人のような名字

▶定義 3 ⊕ to cause sth to make a sound; to give a signal by making a sound 〜に音を出させる; 音を出して合図する→**〜を鳴らす, 吹く, 発する;(音で)〜を知らせる, 合図する** ‖ *to sound the horn of your car* 車のクラクションを鳴らす *A student on one of the upper floors **sounded the alarm**.* 上の階の生徒が非常警報を鳴らした.

句動詞 **sound sb out (about sth)** ▶定義 to ask sb questions in order to find out what he/she thinks or intends 人が何を考えているか,どんなつもりであるかを知るために〜に質問する→**(〜について)…の本心を探る, 〜の意見を打診する, 〜の見解を確かめる**

★**sound**³ /sáund/ 形副 ▶定義 1 sensible; that you can depend on and that will probably give good results 分別のある; 信頼できて良い結果を多分もたらすような→**(判断など)妥当な, 堅実な, 信頼のおける, 安全な** ‖ *sound advice* 適切な助言 *a sound investment* 安全な投資 ▶定義 2 healthy and strong; in good condition 健康で丈夫な; 良い状態の→**(心身が)健全な; 欠陥のない,(基盤などが)堅固な** ‖ *The structure of the bridge is basically sound.* その橋の構造は基本的にしっかりしている. ⇔ **unsound** — **soundness** 名 ❶ →**健全, 堅実, 妥当**

成句 **be sound asleep** ▶定義 to be deeply asleep→**ぐっすり眠っている, 熟睡している**

**sound effect** 名 [ ❻, 通常は複数 ] ▶定義 a sound that is made artificially, for example the sound of the wind, and used in a play, film or computer game to make it more realistic 例えば風の音など,人工的に作り出される音.演劇,映画,コンピューターゲームなどでより現実味を出すために使われる→**音響効果, 擬音**

**soundly** /sáundli/ 副 ▶定義 completely or deeply 徹底的に, 深く→十分に, 徹底的に, しっかりと ‖ *The children were sleeping soundly.* 子供たちはぐっすりと眠っていた.

**soundproof** /sáundprùːf/ 形 ▶定義 made so that no sound can get in or out 音が外から入ったり, 外へ漏れたりしないように作られた→防音の, 防音装置を施した ‖ *a soundproof room* 防音装置を施した部屋

**soundtrack** /sáundtræk/ 名 C ▶定義 the recorded sound and music from a film or computer game 映画またはコンピューターゲームから録音された音または音楽→サウンドトラック, 録音帯, サウンドトラック音楽, サントラ録音 ☞参 **track**

*__soup__ /suːp/ 名 U C ▶定義 liquid food made by cooking meat, vegetables, etc in water 肉, 野菜などを水の中で煮て作る流動体食物→スープ ‖ *a tin of chicken soup* チキンスープの缶詰 ☞ C4 ページのさし絵

*__sour__ /sáuər/ 形 ▶定義1 having a sharp taste like that of a lemon レモンのように酸っぱい味のする→酸っぱい, 酸味のある ‖ *This sauce is quite sour.* このソースは酸味が強い. ▶定義2 (used especially about milk) tasting or smelling unpleasant because it is no longer fresh (特に牛乳について用いて) 新鮮でなくなったため嫌な味またはにおいのする→(腐敗して)酸っぱくなった, すえた ‖ *This cream has gone sour.* このクリームは酸っぱくなってしまっている. ▶定義3 (used about people) angry and unpleasant (人について) 怒っていて不快な→不機嫌な, 気難しい, 不快な, 意地の悪い ‖ *a sour expression* 不機嫌な表情 *a sour-faced old woman* 気難しい顔付きをした老女— **sour** 動 他 正式 ~をまずくする, 駄目にする, こじれさせる ‖ *The disagreement over trade tariffs has soured relations between the two countries.* 関税をめぐる意見の対立で両国間の関係がこじれてしまった. — **sourly** 副→不機嫌に, 気難しく — **sourness** 名 U→酸味, 不機嫌

成句 **go/turn sour** to stop being pleasant or friendly 楽しくなくなる, または友好的でなくなる→(物事が)うまくいかなくなる, まずくなる, 悪くなる ‖ *Their relationship turned sour after a few months.* 数か月後, 彼らの関係が悪化した.

**sour grapes** ▶定義 pretending to not want sth that is hard you secretly want, because you cannot have it 本当はひそかに欲しいものを手に入らないので欲しくない振りをすること→負け惜しみ

*__source__ /sɔːrs/ 名 C ▶定義 a place, person or thing where sth comes or starts from or where sth is obtained ~の発生・起点となる, または~を入手する所, 人, 物→(情報などの)出所, 出典; (川などの)源; (物事の)原因, 起こり ‖ *Britain's oil reserves are an important source of income.* イギリスに埋蔵されている石油は重要な財源だ. *This word has its source in Greek.* この言葉はギリシャ語が元になっている. *The television is a great source of entertainment.* テレビは娯楽の大きな供給源だ. *Police have refused to reveal the source of their information.* 警察は情報源を明らかにすることを拒んだ.

*__south__¹ /sáuθ/ (または **the south**) 名 [単数扱い] (略 S) ▶定義1 the direction that is on your right when you watch the sun rise; one of the four main directions that we give names to (**the points of the compass**) 日の出を見ているときの右の方向; 名称が付けられている4つの主な方位(コンパス上の点)の1つ→南, 南方, 南部 ‖ *warm winds from the south* 南からの暖かい風 *Which way is south?* 南はどちらですか. *We live to the south of (= further south than) London.* 私たちはロンドンの南方に(ロンドンから南の所に)住んでいる. ☞ **north** のさし絵 ▶定義2 **the South** the southern part of any country, city, region or the world 国, 都市, 地域, 世界の南部→南部, 南部地方, 南半球, 南極地方 ‖ *Nice is in the South of France.* ニースはフランス南部地方にある. ☞参 **north, east, west**

**south**² /sáuθ/ 形 副 ▶定義1 (または **South**)(名詞の前だけ) in the south 南にある→南の, 南方の, 南部の ‖ *the south coast of Cornwall* コーンウォールの南海岸 ▶定義2 to or towards the south 南へ, 南に向かって→南へ, 南に, 南方へ ‖ *The house faces south.* その家は南向きだ. *We live just south of Birmingham.* 私たちはバーミンガムの真南に住んでいる. ▶定義3 (used about a wind) coming from the south (風について) 南から来る→南から吹く, 南からの

**southbound** /sáuθbàund/ 形 ▶定義 travelling or

leading towards the south 南に向かって進む, 南へ通じる→南へ向かう, 南行きの, 南回りの

**south-east**¹ (または **the South-East**) 名 [単数扱い] (略 **SE**) ▶定義 the direction or a region that is halfway between south and east 南と東の中間の方向または地域→南東, 南東部, 南東地方 ☛ **north** のさし絵

> ▶音声とつづり字
> 
> South-east は South と east とどちらが強い?
> 
> 現代英語では, 一般に終わりの方が強くなる性質があり, アクセントは左下の例のようになります. しかし, その後に, Asia が来ると, 右下の例のように South のほうが強くなります.
> 
> ○ ◎　　　　◎ ○ ○
> South-east　　South-east Asia

**south-east**² 形副 ▶定義 in, from or to the south-east of a place or country ある場所または国の南東に[の], 南東から(の), 南東へ→南東の, 南東へ, 南東に, 南東から(の) ‖ *the south-east coast of Spain* スペインの南東沿岸

**south-easterly** 形 ▶定義 towards the south-east 南東の, 南東への ‖ *in a south-easterly direction* 南東方向に ▶定義 2 (used about a wind) coming from the south-east (風について)南東から来る→南東から吹く, 南東からの

**south-eastern** 形 (名詞の前だけ) ▶定義 connected with the south-east of a place or country ある場所または国の南東部に関する→南東の, 南東部の ‖ *the south-eastern states of the US* アメリカ南東部の州

**south-eastward(s)** 副 ▶定義 towards the south-east 南東に向かって→南東へ, 南東に

**southerly** /sʌ́ðəli/ 形 ▶定義 1 to, towards or in the south 南へ(の), 南に向かっての, 南の→南の, 南への, 南寄りの ‖ *Keep going in a southerly direction.* 南方向にずっと進みなさい. ▶定義 2 (used about a wind) coming from the south (風について)南から来る→南から吹く, 南からの

*****southern** (または **Southern**) /sʌ́ðən/ 形 ▶定義 of, in or from the south of a place ある地域の南の, 南での, 南からの→南の, 南方の, 南部の, 南からの, 南への ‖ *a man with a southern accent* 南部地方のなまりのある男性 *Greece is in Southern Europe.* ギリシャは南ヨーロッパにある.

**southerner** (または **Southerner**) /sʌ́ðənə/ 名 C ▶定義 a person who was born in or lives in the southern part of a country ある国の南部生まれ, または南部在住の人→南部の人, 南部出身者, 南部生まれの人 ⇔ **northerner**

**the South Pole** 名 [単数扱い] ▶定義 the point on the Earth's surface which is furthest south 地表で一番南にある地点→南極 ☛ **earth** のさし絵

**southward** /sáuθwəd, (海) sʌ́ðəd/ (または **southwards**) 形副 ▶定義 towards the south 南に向かって[いる]→南の方へ(の), 南に向かって・向かう, 南向きに[の]

**south-west**¹ (または **the South-West**) 名 [単数扱い] (略 **SW**) ▶定義 the direction or region halfway between south and west 南と西の中間の方向または地域→南西, 南西部, 南西地方 ☛ **north** のさし絵

**south-west**² 形副 ▶定義 in, from or to the south-west of a place or country ある場所または国の南西で(の), 南西から(の), 南西へ(の)→南西の, 南西にある, 南西からの, 南西へ[に・から] ‖ *the south-west coast of France* フランスの南西海岸 *Our garden faces south-west.* うちの庭は南西向きだ.

**south-westerly** 形 ▶定義 1 towards the south-west 南西に向かっての→南西の, 南西への ‖ *in a south-westerly direction* 南西方向に ▶定義 2 (used about a wind) coming from the south-west (風について)南西から来る→南西から吹く, 南西からの

**south-western** 形 (名詞の前だけ) ▶定義 connected with the south-west of a place or country ある場所または国の南西部に関する→南西の, 南西部の

**south-westward(s)** 副 ▶定義 towards the south-west 南西に向かって→南西へ, 南西に ‖ *Follow the B409 south-westward for twenty miles.* ハイウエーB409を南西方向に20マイル進みなさい.

**souvenir** /sùːvəníə, ⌢⌢/ 名 C ▶定義 something that you keep to remind you of somewhere you have been on holiday or of a special event 休暇で出掛けたことのある場所, または特別の出来

事を思い出すために取っておく物→記念品, 土産, 思い出の品, 形見 ‖ *I brought back a menu as a souvenir of my trip.* 私は旅行の記念としてメニューを持ち帰った.

**sovereign**[1] /sάv(ə)rən, sΛ́v-, -vəm-/ 名 C ▶定義
a king or queen 国王または女王→**君主, 主権者, 統治者, 元首**

**sovereign**[2] /sάv(ə)rən, sΛ́v-, -vəm-/ 形 ▶定義 **1**
(used about a country) not controlled by any other country; independent (国について) 他国に支配されていない; 独立した→**独立の, 自主の, 主権を有する** ▶定義 **2** having the highest possible authority 最高の権力を持つ→**主権を有する, (権力が)最高の, 絶対の, 至上の**

**sovereignty** /sάv(ə)rənti, sΛ́v-, -vəm-/ 名 U
▶定義 the power that a country has to control its own government 国家が保有する, 自国の政治を支配する権力→**主権, 統治権**

**sow**[1] /sάʊ/ 名 C ▶定義 an adult female pig 大人の雌の豚→**雌豚** ☛参 **pig** の注

**sow**[2] /sóʊ/ 動他 (過 **sowed**; 過分 **sown** /sóʊn/ または **sowed**) ▶定義 sow A (in B); sow B (with A) to plant seeds in the ground 種を地面にまく→**(種を)(畑などに)まく, ~に(…の)種をまく** ‖ *to sow seeds in pots* 植木鉢に種をまく *to sow a field with wheat* 畑に麦を作付けする

**soya bean** /sɔ́ɪəbìːn/ (米 **soy bean** /sɔ́ɪbìːn/) 名 C
▶定義 a type of bean that can be cooked and eaten or used to make many different kinds of food, for example flour, oil and a sort of milk 調理して食べたり, 粉, 油, ミルクの一種など, さまざまの多くの種類の食品を作ることのできる豆→**大豆**

**soy sauce** (または **soya sauce**) 名 U ▶定義 a dark brown sauce that is made from soya beans and that you add to food to make it taste better 大豆から作り, 味を良くするために食べ物に加えたりする濃い茶色のソース→**しょうゆ**

**spa** /spάː/ 名 C ▶定義 a place where mineral water comes out of the ground and where people go to drink this water because it is considered to be healthy 地中から鉱水がわき, この鉱水が健康に良いとされるために人々が飲みに来る場所→**鉱泉, 温泉, 温泉場, 保養地**

*****space**[1] /spéɪs/ 名 ▶定義 **1** C U space (for sb/sth) (to do sth) an place or area that is empty or not used 空っぽで何もないまたは使用されていない場所または区域→**空間, 空き地, 余地, 余白** ‖ *Is there enough space for me to park the car there?* そこに駐車するスペースが十分ありますか. *Shelves would take up less space than a cupboard.* 棚の方が食器棚よりも場所を取らないだろう. *a parking space* 駐車場 *We're short of space.* 私たちにはスペースが少々足りない. *There's a space here for you to write your name.* ここに氏名を書き入れる空欄があります. *Leave a space after the comma.* コンマの後にスペースを空けなさい. ☛参 **room** と **place**[1] の注 ▶定義 **2** U (または **outer space**) (しばしば複合名詞を作るために用いて) the area which surrounds the planet Earth and the other planets and stars 地球やほかの惑星や星を取りまく領域→**宇宙, 宇宙空間** ‖ *space travel* 宇宙旅行 *a spaceman/spacewoman* (= *a person who travels in space*) 男性・女性宇宙飛行士 (= 宇宙を旅行する人) *a spacecraft/spaceship* 宇宙船 ▶定義 **3** [C, 通常は単数] a period of time 一定の期間→**時間, 期間, しばらくの間, 短時間** ‖ *Priti had been ill three times in/within the space of four months.* プリティーは4か月の間に3回病気した. *He's achieved a lot in a short space of time.* 彼は短時間でさまざまな事を成し遂げている. ▶定義 **4** U time and freedom to think and do what you want 考えたり自分の欲することをする時間と自由→**場, 自由, 不干渉, 機会** ‖ *I need some space to think.* しばらく考える自由な時間が欲しい.

**space**[2] /spéɪs/ 動他 ▶定義 space sth (out) to arrange things so that there are empty spaces between them 間に何もない空間ができるように~を配置する→**~を一定の間隔で置く, 間隔を置いて配置する, ~の間に間隔を置く**

**spacious** /spéɪʃəs/ 形 ▶定義 having a lot of space; large in size 大きな空間を持つ; 広大な→**広々とした, 広い, ゆったりとした, 広大な** ─ **spaciousness** 名 U →広々としていること, 広大

**spade** /spéɪd/ 名 ▶定義 **1** C a tool that you use for digging 土を掘り返すのに用いる道具→**すき, 鍬(くわ)** ☛ **dig, garden** のさし絵 ☛参 **shovel** ▶定義 **2 spades** [複数扱い] the group (suit) of playing cards with pointed black symbols on them 先のとがった黒い記号の付いたト

ランプの組(組札)→**スペードの組札** ‖ *the king of spades* スペードのキング ☛参 **card** の注とさし絵 ▶定義3 ❸ one of the cards from this suit スペードの組のカードの1枚→**スペード, スペードのカード** ‖ *Have you got a spade?* あなたはスペードを持っていますか.

**spaghetti** /spəgéti/ 名 ⓤ ▶定義 a type of Italian food (pasta) made from flour and water that looks like long strings 小麦粉と水で作られた, 長いひものように見えるイタリアの食べ物(パスタ)→**スパゲッティ** ‖ *How long does spaghetti take to cook?* スパゲッティの調理時間はどのくらいですか. ☛ C4 ページのさし絵

**span**¹ /spæn/ 名 ⓒ ▶定義1 the length of sth from one end to the other 〜の端から端までの長さ→**全長, 差し渡し, 範囲, 長さ, 距離** ‖ *the wingspan of a bird* 鳥の翼長 ▶定義2 the length of time that sth lasts or continues 〜が持続・継続する時間の長さ→**全期間, 継続・持続時間** ‖ *Young children have a short attention span.* 幼い子供が注意力を持続できる時間は短い.

**span**² /spæn/ 動 ⓣ (**spanning; spanned**) ▶定義1 to form a bridge over sth 〜の上に橋を架ける→**(川)に橋を架ける, (橋が)(川)に架かる** ▶定義2 to last or continue for a particular period of time ある特定の期間持続・継続する→**〜に及ぶ, 広がる, わたる, またがる**

**spank** /spæŋk/ 動 ⓣ ▶定義 to hit a child on his/her bottom with an open hand as a punishment 罰として平手で子供のしりをたたく→**〜のしりを平手でたたく, ピシャリと打つ**

> ▶社会・文化
> **子供への仕置き**
> 親は感情的にならずに子供を罰すべきだという考え方から, 英米には「儀式化された制裁」(ritualized punishment)がいろいろな形で古くから存在します. spanking は幼児向きのそうした仕置きの1つです. さあ覚悟しなさいと, 子供をひざの上にうつぶせに寝かせ, 裸のしり(a bare bottom)を通常は平手, 時にはヘアブラシの裏, 部屋履きの裏などで打ちます.

\***spanner** /spǽnər/ ( 米 **wrench**) 名 ⓒ ▶定義 a metal tool with an end shaped for turning small metal rings (nuts) and pins (bolts) that are used for holding things together 片端が物を固定するのに使われる小型の金属輪(ナット)と留金(ボルト)を回転させるのに適した作りとなっている金属製の工具→**スパナ, レンチ** ☛ **tool** のさし絵

\***spare**¹ /speər/ 形 ▶定義1 not needed now but kept because it may be needed in the future 現在必要ではないが, 将来必要になるかもしれないので取ってある→**予備の, 余分の** ‖ *The spare tyre is kept in the boot.* スペアタイヤがトランクに入れてある. *a spare room* (来客用などの)予備の部屋 ▶定義2 not used for work 仕事に使われない→**空いた, 手すきの, 暇な** ‖ *What do you do in your spare time?* 暇な時間に何をなさいますか. ▶定義3 not being used; free 使用されていない; 空いている→**空いている, 空席の** ‖ *There were no seats spare so we had to stand.* 空いている座席がなかったので, 私たちは立っていなければならなかった. — spare 名 ⓒ →**予備品, 予備部品, スペア** ‖ *The fuse has blown. Where do you keep your spares?* ヒューズが飛んでしまった. スペアはどこに置いてありますか.

**spare**² /speər/ 動 ⓣ ▶定義1 spare sth (for sb); spare (sb) sth to be able to give sth to sb 〜に…を与えることができる→**(〜に)(時間・金など)を取っておく, 分ける, 割く** ‖ *I suppose I can spare you a few minutes.* あなたに2, 3分なら割けると思います. ▶定義2 spare sb (from) sth/doing sth to save sb from having an unpleasant experience 〜に不愉快な経験をさせない→**(〜に)(面倒など)を掛けないようにする, 〜に(不快な思い)を味わわせないようにする** ‖ *You could spare yourself waiting if you book in advance.* 前もって予約しておけば, お待ちにならなくても済むでしょう. ▶定義3 spare no effort, expense, etc to do sth as well as possible without limiting the money, time, etc involved 当然必要となる金銭, 時間などを制限せずに〜をできる限り十分に行う→**(努力・費用など)を惜しまない, 使い惜しみしない, けちけちしない** ‖ *No expense was spared at the wedding.* 結婚式には費用を惜しまなかった. *He spared no effort in trying to find a job.* 彼は仕事を探すのに努力を惜しまなかった. ▶定義4 spare sb/sth (from sth) to not hurt or damage sb/sth ～を傷付けたり損害を与えたりしない➡～に(苦痛・害など)を与えない, 免じてやる

成句 **to spare** ▶定義 more than is needed 必要以上の➡余分の, 余っている ‖ *There's no time to spare. We must leave straight away.* もう時間がない. 今すぐ出発しなければならない.

**spare part** 名 **C** ▶定義 a part for a machine, engine, etc that you can use to replace an old part which is damaged or broken 機械, エンジンなどの傷んだまたは壊れた古い部品を交換するのに用いることのできる部品➡予備部品, 交換用部品

**sparing** /spéərɪŋ/ 形 正式 ▶定義 using only a little of sth; careful ～をほんのわずかしか使用しない; 金に細かい➡質素な, 節約する, 倹約する, (使い方が)控えめの — sparingly 副➡節約して, 控えめに

**spark**¹ /spɑːrk/ 名 ▶定義 1 **C** a very small bright piece of burning material 燃えている物質の非常に微小なきらきらした一片➡火花, 火の粉 ‖ *A spark set fire to the carpet.* 火花でカーペットに火がついた. ▶定義 2 **C** a flash of light that is caused by electricity 電気によって生じる一瞬の光➡閃光(せんこう), 電気火花, スパーク ‖ *A spark ignites the fuel in a car engine.* スパークによって自動車のエンジンの燃料が点火される.

▶定義 3 **C U** an exciting quality that sb/sth has ～が持つ活気に満ちた性質➡活気, 生気, 刺激, 才気, ひらめき

**spark**² /spɑːrk/ 動

句動詞 spark sth off ▶定義 to cause sth ～を引き起こす➡～の口火を切る, ～の引き金になる, ～を誘発する ‖ *Eric's comments sparked off a tremendous argument.* エリックの意見は激しい議論を引き起こした.

**sparkle** /spɑːrk(ə)l/ 動 自 ▶定義 to shine with many small points of light たくさんの小さな閃光(せんこう)を発しながら光る➡きらきら光る, 輝く, きらめく ‖ *The river sparkled in the sunlight.* 川は日の光を受けてきらきらと輝いていた. — sparkle 名 **C U**➡火花, 輝き, きらめき, 光沢

**sparkling** /spɑːrk(ə)lɪŋ/ 形 ▶定義 1 shining with many small points of light たくさんの小さな閃光(せんこう)を発しながら光る➡輝く, きらめく, 光る ‖ *sparkling blue eyes* きらきらとした青い目 ▶定義 2 (used about a drink) containing bubbles of gas (飲み物について)気泡を含む➡発泡性の ‖ *sparkling wine/mineral water* 発泡ブドウ酒・ソーダ水 ☛ bubble のさし絵

**spark plug** 名 **C** ▶定義 a small piece of equipment in an engine that produces a bright flash of electricity (a spark) to make the fuel burn and start the engine 燃料を燃やしてエンジンを始動させるため, きらきらした電気の閃光(せんこう)(電気火花)を作り出す, エンジン内の小さな装置➡点火プラグ

**sparrow** /spǽroʊ/ 名 **C** ▶定義 a small brown and grey bird that is common in many parts of the world 世界の多くの地域で一般的に見られる小さな茶色と灰色の鳥➡スズメ

**sparse** /spɑːrs/ 形 ▶定義 small in quantity or amount 数量・量の少ない➡まばらな, 少ない, (毛髪などが)薄い ‖ *a sparse crowd* まばらな人の群れ *He just had a few sparse hairs on his head.* 彼の頭には薄い毛がほんのわずかあるだけだ. — sparsely 副➡まばらに, 散在して ‖ *a sparsely populated area* 人口過疎地域 — sparseness 名 **U**➡まばら

**spartan** /spɑːrtən/ 形 正式 ▶定義 very simple and not comfortable 非常に質素で快適でない➡質実剛健な, 質素で厳しい ‖ *spartan living conditions* 質素で厳しい生活状態

**spasm** /spǽz(ə)m/ 名 **C U** ▶定義 a sudden movement of a muscle that you cannot control 自分では制御できない発作的な筋肉の動き➡けいれん, 引き付け, 発作 ‖ *He had painful muscular spasms in his leg.* 彼は足に痛みの激しい筋肉のけいれんを感じた.

**spat** SPIT¹ の過去・過去分詞形

**spate** /speɪt/ 名 [単数扱い] ▶定義 a large number or amount of sth happening at one time 一度に多数または多量発生する～➡多数, 大量, 続発 ‖ *There has been a spate of burglaries in the area recently.* 最近その地域では押し込み強盗が多発している.

**spatial** /spéɪʃ(ə)l/ 形 正式 ▶定義 connected with the size or position of sth ～の大きさまたは位置に関する➡空間の, 空間的な

**spatter** /spǽtər/ 動 他 ▶定義 spatter sb/sth (with sth); spatter sth (on sb/sth) to cover sb/sth with small drops of sth wet ぬれた～の細

かい水滴を…に浴びせる➔～に(…を)跳ね掛ける,～を(…に)跳ね散らす

**spatula** /spǽtʃələ/ 名 ●定義 a tool with a wide flat part used in cooking for mixing and spreading things 物を混ぜたり塗ったりするのに使う幅の広い平らな部分のある料理道具➔へら★kitchen のさし絵

**★speak** /spíːk/ 動 (過 **spoke** /spóuk/; 過分 **spoken** /spóukən/) ▶定義1 ●speak (to sb) (about sb/sth); speak (of sth) to talk or say things 話す, ものを言う➔(人に)(～について)話す, ものを言う ‖ *I'd like to speak to the manager, please.* 支配人に話がしたいのですが. *Could you speak more slowly?* もっとゆっくり話していただけませんか. *I was so angry I could hardly speak.* ひどく腹を立てていたのでほとんど口がきけなかった.

➤ speakとtalkは意味がほぼ同じだが, talkの方がよりくだけた形で使われ, 複数の人が会話をしているのを示す. 一方, speakは特に改まった状況でただ1人だけで話をしているのを示すのに使われる: *I'd like to speak to the manager, please.* (支配人に話がしたいのですが.) *We talked all night.* (私たちは一晩中話をした.) *The head teacher spoke to the class about university courses.* (校長はそのクラスの生徒たちに大学の教育課程について話をした.)

▶定義2 ● (進行形は不可) to know and be able to use a language 言語を知っていて使うことができる➔(ある言語)を話す, 使う, (言語)を使う能力がある ‖ *Does anyone here speak German?* だれかドイツ語を話せる人はここにいますか. *She speaks (in) Greek to her parents.* 彼女は両親に対してギリシャ語を[で]話す. *a French-speaking guide* フランス語を話すガイド

▶定義3 ●speak (on/about sth) to make a speech to a group of people 一団の人に向かって演説を行う➔(～について)演説する, 講演する

▶定義4 ● 略式 be speaking (to sb) to be friendly with sb again after an argument 口論の後再び～と親しくなる➔(会って)口をきく, 言葉を交わす, 話をする

成句 be on speaking terms (with sb) ▶定義 to be friendly with sb again after an argument 口論の後再び～と親しい間柄である➔(～とは)口をきく間柄である, 言葉を交わす間柄である ‖ *Thankfully they are back on speaking terms again.* 有り難いことに彼らは再び言葉を交わす間柄に戻っている.

so to speak ▶定義 used when you are describing sth in a way that sounds strange 一風変わった表現で～を説明するときに用いて➔いわば, 言ってみれば ‖ *She turned green, so to speak, after watching a television programme about the environment.* 環境についてのテレビ番組を見た後, 彼女はいわば緑に染まってしまった(本来の意味は「顔が青ざめる」だが, ここでは「環境保護に関心のある」の意味に使われている).

speak for itself ▶定義 to be very clear so that no other explanation is needed ほかの説明が不要なほど非常にはっきりとしている➔はっきりと証明している, 自明の事である ‖ *The statistics speak for themselves.* 統計がおのずと物語っている.

speak/talk of the devil ⇒ **DEVIL**

speak your mind ▶定義 to say exactly what you think, even though you might offend sb 万一～を怒らせるような事があっても, 自分が考えている事を正確に言う➔率直な気持ちを話す, 考えている事をはっきり言う

句動詞 speak for sb ▶定義 to express the thoughts or opinions of sb else ほかの人の考えまたは意見を述べる➔～を代弁する, ～に代わって意見を述べる, ～を代表して話をする

speak out (against sth) ▶定義 to say publicly that you think sth is bad or wrong ～が悪いまたは間違っていると思うと公言する➔思い切って意見を言う, 率直に意見を述べる, (～に反対だと)遠慮なく言う

speak up ▶定義 to speak louder もっと大きな声で話す➔大声で話す, はっきり話す

**speaker** /spíːkər/ 名 ●定義1 a person who makes a speech to a group of people 一団の人々に対して演説を行う人➔演説者, 講演者 ‖ *Tonight's speaker is a well-known writer and journalist.* 今夜の講演者は有名な作家兼ジャーナリストだ. ▶定義2 a person who speaks a particular language ある特定の言語を話す人➔話す人, 話者 ‖ *She's a fluent Russian speaker.* 彼女は流ちょうにロシア語を話す. ▶定義3 = **LOUDSPEAKER(1)**

## 1558 spear

*sheath, dagger, sword, spear*

**spear** /spɪər/ 名 C ▶定義 a long pole with a sharp point at one end, used for hunting or fighting 狩猟または戦闘に用いられる,片方の先端がとがった細長い棒→やり,投げやり,やす

**spearhead** /spíərhèd/ 名 [ C, 通常は単数 ] ▶定義 a person or group that begins or leads an attack 攻撃の開始・先導を務める人または集団→先頭,先鋒(せんぽう),率先者,一番やり — spearhead 動 →〜の先頭に立つ,先頭に立って行動する,先鋒を務める

**spearmint** /spíərmìnt, -mənt/ 名 U ▶定義 a type of leaf with a strong fresh taste that is used in sweets, etc 菓子などに使われる強いさわやかな味のする葉→オランダハッカ, ミドリハッカ, スペアミント ‖ *spearmint chewing gum* スペアミントのチューインガム ⇒参 **peppermint**

★**special**¹ /spéʃ(ə)l/ 形 ▶定義1 not usual or ordinary; important for some particular reason 普通・通常でない;ある特定の理由で重要な→特別な,特殊な,特異な,格別の ‖ *a special occasion* 特別な機会 *Please take special care of it.* それには特に気を付けてください. *Are you doing anything special tonight?* 今夜何か特別な事をする予定ですか. ▶定義2 (名詞の前だけ) for a particular purpose ある特定の目的のための→専用の,特殊な,専門の ‖ *Andy goes to a special school for the deaf.* アンディーは聴覚障害者のための特殊学校に通っている. *There's a special tool for doing that.* それをするための特殊な用具がある.

**special**² /spéʃ(ə)l/ 名 C ▶定義 something that is not of the usual or ordinary type 普通・通常でないもの→特別のもの,臨時のもの,臨時列車,特別番組,号外 ‖ *an all-night election special on TV* テレビの終夜選挙特報 *I'm going to cook one of my specials tonight.* 今夜は私の得意特別料理の1つを作るつもりだ.

**specialist** /spéʃ(ə)lɪst/ 名 C ▶定義 a person with special or deep knowledge of a particular subject 特定の問題について専門知識のある人,または深く精通している人→専門家;専門医 ‖ *She's a specialist in diseases of cattle.* 彼女は家畜の病気の専門家だ. *I have to see a heart specialist.* 私は心臓の専門医の診察を受けなければならない. *to give specialist advice* 専門家としての助言を与える

**speciality** /spèʃiǽləti/ 名 C (複 **specialities**) (米 **specialty** /spéʃ(ə)lti/; 複 **specialties**) ▶定義1 an area of study or a subject that you know a lot about その人が豊富な知識を持っている学問分野または主題→専門,専攻,得意(なもの) ▶定義2 something made by a person, place, business, etc that is very good and that he/she/it is known for 個人,地域,企業などによって作られる非常に優れたもので,その作り手または産地を有名にしている物→名物,特産品,特製品,自慢の料理 ‖ *The cheese is a speciality of the region.* チーズはその地方の特産品だ.

**specialize** (または **-ise**) /spéʃ(ə)làɪz/ 動 自 ▶定義 specialize (in sth) to give most of your attention to one subject, type of product, etc 1つの研究主題,1種類の製品などに専念する→(〜を)専門にする,専門に取り扱う,専門に勉強する,専攻する ‖ *This shop specializes in clothes for taller men.* この店は背の高い男性用の服を専門に取り扱っている. — **specialization** (または **-isation**) /spèʃ(ə)laɪzéɪʃ(ə)n; -lə-/ 名 U →専門化,特殊化;限定

**specialized** (または **-ised**) /spéʃ(ə)làɪzd/ 形 ▶定義1 to be used for a particular purpose ある特定の目的に使われる→専用の,特殊な ‖ *a specialized system* 特殊なシステム ▶定義2 having or needing deep or special knowledge of a particular subject ある特定分野に対して深い知識または専門知識を持っているまたは要する→専門の,専門化した ‖ *We have specialized staff to help you with any problems.* 当社ではどんな問題でも皆様にご協力できる専門のスタッフをそろえております.

**specially** /spéʃ(ə)li/ (または **especially**) 副 ▶定義1 for a particular purpose or reason ある特定の目的または理由のために→特別の目的のため,わざわざ ‖ *I made this specially for you.* 特別あなたのためにこれを作りました. ▶定義2 particularly; very; more than usual 特に;非常に,通

常よりももっと➡️格別の目的のために, とりわけ ‖ *The restaurant has a great atmosphere but the food is not specially good.* そのレストランは雰囲気はとても良いが, 食事は特においしいわけではない. *It's not an especially difficult exam.* それはとりわけ難しい試験ではない.

**specialty** 米 = SPECIALITY

★**species** /spíːʃiːz/ 名 C (複 **species**) ▶定義 a group of plants or animals that are all the same and that can breed together 全く同じ種類で, 交配可能な植物または動物の集まり➡️種(しゅ), 種類 ‖ *This conservation group aims to protect endangered species.* この自然保護団体は絶滅寸前の種の保護を目的としている. *a rare species of frog* 珍しい種類のカエル

★**specific** /spɪsífɪk/ 形 ▶定義 **1** specific (about sth) detailed or exact 詳細な, 正確な➡️明確な, 明細な, 細かく具体的な, はっきりとした ‖ *You must give the class specific instructions on what they have to do.* クラスの人たちに何をしなければならないかはっきりとした指示を与えなければいけませんよ. *Can you be more specific about what the man was wearing?* その男性が着ていた物についてもっと具体的に話していただけませんか. ▶定義 **2** particular; not general 特定の, 一般的でない➡️特定の, 一定の, 固有の ‖ *Everyone has been given a specific job to do.* 皆それぞれやるべき特定の仕事を与えられている. ― specifically /-k(ə)li/ 副 ➡️特に, とりわけ; 具体的に言えば, はっきり限定して ‖ *a play written specifically for radio* 特にラジオのために書かれた戯曲

**specification** /spès(ə)fəkéɪʃ(ə)n/ 名 C U ▶定義 detailed information about how sth is or should be built or made 〜がどのように組み立て・作製されるか, またはされるべきかについての詳細な情報➡️仕様, 明細; 仕様書, 明細書, 設計書

**specify** /spésəfàɪ/ 動 他 (現分 **specifying**; 三単現 **specifies**; 過, 過分 **specified**) ▶定義 to say or name sth clearly or in detail 〜をはっきりとまたは詳細に言う, あるいは指定する➡️〜を明細に述べる・記す, 特定する, はっきり指定する ‖ *The fire regulations specify the maximum number of people allowed in.* 火災防止規定には収容することのできる最大人数が明記されている.

**specimen** /spés(ə)mən/ 名 C ▶定義 **1** an example of a particular type of thing, especially intended to be studied by experts or scientists 特に専門家または科学者の研究の対象にされる, ある特定のタイプの物の代表例➡️標本, 見本, 実例, 典型 ▶定義 **2** a small amount of sth that is tested for medical or scientific purposes 医学または科学上の目的で検査される少量の〜➡️標本, 試料, 試験片, 検体 ‖ *Specimens of the patient's blood were tested in the hospital laboratory.* その患者の血液の検査試料は病院の試験室で検査された. ☛類 sample

**speck** /spek/ 名 C ▶定義 a very small spot or mark 非常に小さな汚れまたは染み➡️斑点(はんてん), 小さな傷, 汚点, 微小片 ‖ *a speck of dust/dirt* 一片のほこり・一点の汚れ

**specs** /speks/ 略式 = GLASSES

**spectacle** /spéktək(ə)l/ 名 C ▶定義 something that is impressive or shocking to look at 見て強く印象づけられたりショッキングに感じたりするもの➡️壮観, (壮大な)見せ物, 見物, スペクタクル, 美観, 光景

**spectacles** /spéktək(ə)lz/ 正式 = GLASSES

**spectacular** /spektǽkjələr/ 形 ▶定義 very impressive to see 見て強く印象づけられる➡️目を見張る, 壮観な, 見ごたえのある, あっと言わせる ‖ *The view from the top of the hill is quite spectacular.* 丘の頂上からの眺めはとても壮大だ. ― spectacularly 副 ➡️壮観で, 見物で

★**spectator** /spektéɪtər/ 名 C ▶定義 a person who is watching an event, especially a sporting event 特にスポーツなどのイベントを見ている人➡️観客, 観衆, 見物人

**spectre** (米 **specter**) /spéktər/ 名 C ▶定義 **1** something unpleasant that people are afraid might happen in the future 将来ひょっとして起こるのではないかと人々が恐れている不快なもの➡️恐ろしいもの, 不安のもと ‖ *the spectre of unemployment* 失業の不安・影 ▶定義 **2** (古) = GHOST

**spectrum** /spéktrəm/ 名 [C, 通常は単数] (複 **spectra** /spéktrə/) ▶定義 **1** the set of seven colours into which white light can be separated 白色光が分かれてできる7つの色➡️スペクトル, 分光 ‖ *You can see the colours of the spectrum in a rainbow.* スペクトルの7色は虹の中に見ることができる. ▶定義 **2** all the possible varieties

## 1560　speculate

of sth ～のありとあらゆる変種→(変動するものの)範囲,幅,連続体 ‖ *The speakers represented the whole spectrum of political opinions.* 演説者たちはあらゆる政治意見を述べた.

**speculate** /spékjəlèɪt/ 動 ▶定義1 自他 speculate (about/on sth); speculate that... to make a guess about sth ～について推測する→(～について)(…だと)推測する,～をあれこれ思索する ‖ *to speculate about the result of the next election* 次の選挙の結果について推測する ▶定義2 自 to buy and sell with the aim of making money but with the risk of losing it 損をする危険を冒しながら,金もうけを目的として売買する→投機する,思惑買い・売りをする ‖ *to speculate on the stock market* 株式市場で投機をする ― **speculation** /spèkjəlét(ə)n/ 名 ❶❶→推測,憶測; 投機 ― **speculator** 名 ❷→思索家,理論家,投機家,投資家,相場師

**sped** SPEED² の過去・過去分詞形

*****speech** /spiːtʃ/ 名 ▶定義1 ❷ a formal talk that you give to a group of people 集まった人々に対して行う改まった話→演説,講演,話,談話 ‖ *The Chancellor is going to **make a speech** to city businessmen.* 大臣は都市部の事業者に対して講演をする予定だ. ▶定義2 ❶ the ability to speak 話す能力→話す能力,言語能力,話すこと ‖ *He lost the **power of speech** after the accident.* 事故後,彼は口がきけなくなった. *freedom of speech (= being allowed to express your opinions openly)* 言論の自由(=自分の意見を公然と表現することが認められていること) ▶定義3 ❶ 関連 the particular way of speaking of a person or group of people ある人または人々の集団に特有の話し方→話し方,話し振り,話し言葉,方言 ‖ *She's doing a study of children's speech.* 彼女は子供の話し言葉の研究を行っている.
▶定義4 ❷ a group of words that one person must say in a play 劇中で人が言わなければならない一連の言葉→台詞(せりふ)

**speechless** /spíːtʃləs/ 形 ▶定義 not able to speak, for example because you are shocked, angry, etc ショックまたは怒りなどのため,口がきけない→口もきけない(ほどの),あぜんとして,言語を絶する

*****speed**¹ /spiːd/ 名 ▶定義1 ❶ fast movement 速い動き→速いこと,速さ,迅速,スピード ‖ *I intend to start the race slowly and gradually **pick up speed**.* レースの出だしでゆっくりと走り,徐々にスピードを上げるつもりだ. *The bus was travelling **at speed** when it hit the wall.* バスが壁に衝突した時,スピードを出して走っていた. ▶定義2 ❷❶ the rate at which sb/sth moves or travels ～が動くまたは進む速度→速度,速力,速さ,スピード ‖ *The car was travelling **at a speed of 140 kilometres an hour**.* その車は時速140キロメートルで走行していた. *to travel **at top/high/full/maximum speed*** 最高速度・高速・全速力・最大速度で進む

**speed**² /spiːd/ 動 (過,過分 **sped** /sped/) ▶定義1 to go or move very quickly 非常に速く進むまたは動く→急ぐ,疾走する ‖ *He sped round the corner on his bicycle.* 彼は自転車であっと言う間に角を曲がった. ▶定義2 (進行形だけ) to drive a car, etc faster than the legal speed limit 法定速度よりも速く自動車などを運転する→違反速度で走る,制限速度以上のスピードで走る,スピード違反をする ‖ *The police said she had been speeding.* 警官は彼女はスピード違反をしていたと言った.

句動詞 **speed (sth) up** (過,過分 speeded) ▶定義 to go or make sth go faster より速く進む; ～をより速く進ませる→スピードを上げる,加速する; ～を急がせる,促進させる ‖ *The new computer system should speed up production in the factory.* 新しいコンピューターシステムは工場の生産速度を速めるはずだ.

**speedboat** /spíːdbòʊt/ 名 ❷ ▶定義 a small fast boat with an engine エンジンを搭載した高速の小型ボート→高速モーターボート,快速モーターボート

**speeding** /spíːdɪŋ/ 名 ❶ ▶定義 driving a car, etc faster than the legal speed limit 法定速度よりも速く自動車などを運転すること→速度違反,スピード違反

**speed limit** 名 [❷, 通常は単数] ▶定義 the highest speed that you may drive without breaking the law on a particular road ある特定の道路で法律に違反せずに運転することのできる最高速度→制限速度,最高速度 ‖ *He was going way **over the speed limit** when the police stopped him.* 警官が制止した時,彼は制限速度をはるかに超えて走っていた.

**speedometer** /spɪdάmətər/ 名 C ▶定義 a piece of equipment in a vehicle that tells you how fast you are travelling 走行中の速度を示す車内の装置→速度計,走行距離計 ☞ S7 ページのさし絵

**speedway** /spíːdweɪ/ 名 U ▶定義 the sport of racing motorbikes around a roundish track 円形のコースを走るオートバイ競技→(スピードウェーでの)オートバイレース

**speedy** /spíːdi/ 形 ▶定義 fast; quick 速い; 素早い,迅速な,即席の ‖ *a speedy response/reply* 素早い応答・回答 — **speedily** 副 ▶→速く,直ちに,迅速に,即座に — **speediness** 名 U →速いこと,高速,迅速

*__spell__¹ /spel/ 動 (過, 過分 **spelled** /speld/ または **spelt** /spelt/) ▶定義1 自他 to write or say the letters of a word in the correct order 正しい順序で単語の文字を書くまたは言う→~をつづる, (~の)つづりを言う,つづりを書く ‖ *I could never spell very well at school.* 私は在学中つづりがからっきし駄目だった. *How do you spell your surname?* あなたの名字はどうつづるのですか. *His name is spelt P-H-I-L-I-P.* 彼の名前のつづりは P-H-I-L-I-P です. ▶定義2 他 (used about a set of letters) to form a particular word (一組の文字について)ある特定の単語になる→つづると~という語になる,つづって~と読む ‖ *If you add an 'e' to 'car' it spells 'care'.* car に e を足すと care という語になる. ▶定義3 他 to mean sth; to have sth as a result ~を意味する; 結果として~になる→~を意味する,~になる,~の結果をもたらす ‖ *Another poor harvest would spell disaster for the region.* もう一度凶作になればその地域は大変なことになるだろう.

句動詞 **spell sth out** ▶定義1 to write or say the letters of a word or name in the correct order 正しい順序で単語または名前の文字を書くまたは言う→~の文字を略さずにつづる,1字1字丹念に読む・書く ‖ *I have an unusual name, so I always have to spell it out to people.* 私の名前は珍しいので,いつも人に1字1字つづって見せなければならない. ▶定義2 to express sth in a very clear and direct way ~を非常に明確かつ直接的に述べる→~をはっきり説明する,詳細に述べる

**spell**² /spel/ 名 C ▶定義1 a short period of time 短期間→しばらくの間,一時,一続き ‖ *a spell of cold weather* 寒さ続き ▶定義2 (especially in stories) magic words or actions that cause sb to be in a particular state or condition (特に物語で)~をある特定の状態にしてしまう魔法の言葉または動作→魔法,魔力,呪文,まじない

**spelling** /spélɪŋ/ 名 ▶定義1 C U the way that letters are arranged to make a word 単語を構成する文字の配列の仕方→(語の)つづり,スペリング,綴字(ていじ)法 ‖ *'Center' is the American spelling of 'centre'.* center は centre のアメリカ式のつづりだ. ▶定義2 U the ability to write the letters of a word correctly 単語の文字を正しく書く能力→語をつづる能力,スペリング能力 ‖ *Roger is very poor at spelling.* ロジャーは単語のつづりが大の苦手だ.

**spelt** SPELL¹ の過去・過去分詞形

*__spend__ /spend/ 動 (過, 過分 **spent** /spent/) ▶定義1 自他 spend (sth) (on sth) to give or pay money for sth ~に対して金を出すまたは支払う→(~に)(…の額の金を)支払う,費やす,金を使う ‖ *How much do you spend on food each week?* あなたは毎週食費にいくら使いますか. *You shouldn't go on spending like that.* そんな風にお金をどんどん使ってはいけませんよ. ▶定義2 他 spend sth (on sth/doing sth) to pass time 時間を過ごす→~を(…に・…して)費やす,過ごす,送る ‖ *I spent a whole evening writing letters.* その夜ずっと手紙を書いて過ごした. *I'm spending the weekend at my parents' house.* 週末を両親の所で過ごすつもりだ. *He spent two years in Rome.* 彼は2年間ローマで暮らした. *I don't want to spend too much time on this project.* その計画にあまり多くの時間を費やしたくない.

**spending** /spéndɪŋ/ 名 U ▶定義 the amount of money that is spent by a government or an organization 政府または組織が費やした金額→支出,支出額,費用

**sperm** /spəːm/ 名 ▶定義1 C (複 sperm または sperms) a cell that is produced in the sex organs of a male and that can join with a female egg to produce young 男性の性器で作られ,女性の卵子と結合して子を作ることのできる細胞→精子 ▶定義2 U the liquid that contains sperms 精子を含む液体→精液

**sphere** /sfɪər/ 名 C ▶定義1 any round object shaped like a ball ボールのような形をした丸い

1562 spice¹

物体→球,球体,球形,球面 ☞ **cube** のさし絵 ▶定義2 an area of interest or activity 興味または活動の領域→**範囲,領域,分野,本領**— spherical /sférɪk(ə)l, sfíːər-/ 形→球の,球状の,丸い

**spice**¹ /spáɪs/ 名 ▶定義1 ⓒⓊ a substance, especially a powder, that is made from a plant and used to give flavour to food 植物から作られ,食べ物の味付けに使われる,特に粉状の物→**香辛料,薬味,スパイス** ‖ I use a lot of herbs and spices in my cooking. 私は料理にたくさんのハーブやスパイスを使う. Pepper and paprika are two common spices. コショウとパプリカは2大香辛料だ. ☞参 **herb** ▶定義2 Ⓤ excitement and interest 刺激または面白み→**趣,情趣,面白み,ピリッとしたところ** ‖ to **add spice** to a situation 場面に趣を加える — spicy 形→香辛料を入れた,スパイスの効いた,趣のある ‖ Do you like spicy food? 香辛料の効いた食べ物がお好きですか.

**spice**² /spáɪs/ 動他 spice sth (up) (with sth) ▶定義1 to add spice to food 食べ物に香辛料を加える→**~に香辛料を加える,(香辛料で)味を付ける** ‖ He always spices his cooking with lots of chilli powder. 彼はいつも料理にたくさんのチリパウダーを加える. ▶定義2 to add excitement to sth ~に刺激を加える→**~に面白みを加える,興を添える**

**spider** /spáɪdər/ 名 ⓒ ▶定義 a type of small animal like an insect with eight legs. Spiders make (spin) special nets (webs) to catch insects for food. 8本の足を持つ昆虫のような小動物.昆虫をえさとして捕まえるため,特殊な網(クモの巣)を作る(かける)→**クモ**

**spike** /spáɪk/ 名 ⓒ ▶定義 a piece of metal, wood, etc that has a sharp point at one end 片方の先端がとがっている金属片,木片など→**大くぎ,(塀の上に付ける)忍び返し,スパイク**

**spill**

He's **spilled** his milk.

*spill /spɪl/ 動自他 (過,過分 spilt /spɪlt/ または spilled) ▶定義1 (used especially about a liquid) to accidentally come out of a container; to make a liquid, etc do this (特に液体について)としたはずみで容器から出る;液体などをこのように容器から出す→**こぼれる,あふれる;~をこぼす,まき散らす** ‖ The bag split, and sugar spilled everywhere. 袋が破れて砂糖があちらこちらにこぼれてしまった. Some water had spilled out of the bucket onto the floor. 水がバケツから床にこぼれていた. I've spilt some coffee on the desk. 私はコーヒーを机の上にこぼしてしまった. ▶定義2 自 spill out, over, into, etc to come out of a place suddenly and go in different directions 突然ある場所から出てきて,さまざまな方向に行く→**こぼれ出る,あふれ出る,~の中へこぼれ込む** ‖ The train stopped and everyone spilled out. 列車が停止し,人々がどっと降りてきた. — spill 名 ⓒ→**こぼれること,あふれること,流出,こぼれた物** ‖ Many seabirds died as a result of the oil spill. 石油の流出によってたくさんの海鳥が死んだ.

成句 spill the beans 略式 ▶定義 to tell a person about sth that should be a secret 秘密にすべき~を人に告げる→**秘密を漏らす,口を滑らす**

*spin¹ /spɪn/ 動 (spinning; 過,過分 spun /spʌn/) ▶定義1 自他 spin (sth) (round) to turn or to make sth turn round quickly 素早く回転する,~を素早く回転させる→**回る,回転する;~を回す** ‖ Mary spun round when she heard someone call her name. メアリーはだれかが自分の名前を呼ぶのを聞いてさっと振り返った. to spin a ball/coin/wheel ボールにスピンをかける,硬貨を(指ではじいて)回す,車輪を回す ▶定義2 自他 to make thread from a mass of wool, cotton, etc 羊毛,綿などの塊から糸を作る→**(糸などを)紡ぐ,(綿・羊毛などで)(糸を)紡ぐ;(くもが)(糸を)吐く,(巣を)作る** ‖ A spider spins a web. クモは巣をかける. ▶定義3 他 to remove water from clothes that have just been washed in a washing machine by turning them round and round very fast 高速で何度も回転させて,洗濯機で洗った衣服から水分を取り除く→**~を脱水する,脱水機にかける,脱水乾燥する**

句動詞 spin sth out ▶定義 to make sth last as long as possible ~をできるだけ長く続けさせる→**(議論など)を長引かせる,引き伸ばす,(金銭**

などを)長く保たせる

**spin**² /spín/ 名 C U ▶定義1 an act of making sth spin ～を回転させる動作→回転, ひねり, スピン ‖ *She put a lot of spin on the ball.* 彼女はボールにものすごいスピンをかけた. ▶定義2 (especially in politics) a way of talking publicly about a difficult situation, a mistake, etc that makes it sound positive for you (特に政治で)困難な状況, 誤りなどについて肯定的に聞こえるように公に話す方法→情報操作

成句 **go/take sb for a spin** ▶定義 to go/take sb out in a car or other vehicle 車などで出掛ける, または～を車などに乗せて出掛ける→(～と一緒に)ドライブする, ドライブに出掛ける

**spinach** /spínɪtʃ, -dʒ/ 名 U ▶定義 a plant with large dark green leaves that can be cooked and eaten as a vegetable 野菜として調理して食べられる大きな濃い緑色の葉をした植物→ホウレンソウ ☛ C3 ページのさし絵

**spinal** /spáɪnl/ 形 ▶定義 connected with the bones of your back (the spine) 背中の骨(背骨)に関する→背骨の, 脊柱の, 脊髄の ☛類 **backbone**

**spin doctor** 名 C ▶定義 (especially in politics) a person who finds ways of talking about difficult situations, mistakes, etc in a positive way (特に政治で)困難な状況, 誤りなどを肯定的に話す方法を見つける人→(特に政治家の)報道対策アドバイザー, 対メディアスポークスマン

**spin dryer** 名 C 英 ▶定義 a machine that removes water from wet clothes by turning them round and round very fast 高速で何度もぬれた衣類を回転させて, 水分を取り除く機械→(遠心分離式)脱水機 ─ **spin-dry** 動 他 →～を脱水機にかける, 遠心力で脱水する

**spine** /spáɪn/ 名 C ▶定義1 the bones of the back of a person or animal; the backbone 人間または動物の背中の骨; 背骨→背骨, 脊柱, 脊椎 ▶定義2 one of the sharp points like needles, on some plants and animals 一部の植物または動物に付いている, 針のようにとがった突起の1つ→とげ, 針, 突起 ‖ *Porcupines use their spines to protect themselves.* ヤマアラシは身を守るために針を使う. ☛参 **prickle** ▶定義3 the narrow part of the cover of a book that you can see when it is on a shelf 本の表紙で棚に置いたときに見える本の表紙の幅の狭い部分→(本の)背

**spineless** /spáɪnləs/ 形 ▶定義 weak and easily frightened 弱くて怖がりやすい→意気地のない, 勇気のない, 根性のない, ひ弱な

**spin-off** 名 C ▶定義 a **spin-off (from/of sth)** something unexpected and useful that develops from sth else ほかの～から派生した予期せぬ有益なもの→(～の)副産物, 副次的効果, 波及効果

**spinster** /spínstər/ 名 C (古) ▶定義 a woman, especially an older woman, who has never been married 結婚したことのない, 特に年配の女性→(婚期を過ぎた)独身女性, オールドミス ➤ 今日では, 結婚していない男女を指すのに single が最も一般的に使われる.
☛参 **bachelor**

**spiral** /spáɪərəl/ 名 C ▶定義 a long curved line that moves round and round away from a central point ぐるぐる回りながら中心点から遠ざかっていく長い曲線→渦巻き線, らせん, らせん状の物 ─ **spiral** 形 →渦巻き形の, らせん形の, コイル状の ‖ *a spiral staircase* らせん階段 ─ **spiral** 動 自 (spiralling; spiralled: 米 spiraling; spiraled)→らせん形になる, らせん状に動く, らせんを描く

**spire** /spáɪər/ 名 C ▶定義 a tall pointed tower on the top of a church 教会の最上部にある先のとがった高い塔→尖塔(せんとう), とがり屋根, 尖頂(せんちょう)

★**spirit**¹ /spírət/ 名 ▶定義1 [単数扱い] the part of a person that is not physical; your thoughts and feelings, not your body 人間の肉体でない部分, 思考と感情であり, 肉体ではない→精神, 心 ‖ *the power of the human spirit to overcome difficulties* 困難に打ち勝つ人間の精神力 ▶定義2 C the part of a person that many people believe still exists after his/her body is dead; a ghost or a being without a body 肉体が死んだ後も存在し続けると多くの人が信じている人間の部分; 幽霊, 肉体のない存在→魂, 霊魂, 霊 ‖ *It was believed that people could be possessed by evil spirits.* 人は悪霊に取り付かれることがあると信じられていた. ☛参 **soul** ▶定義3 C the mood, attitude or state of mind of sb/sth ～の気分, 態度, 心の状態→気分, 精神状態, 機嫌, 元気 ‖ *to be in high/low spirits (= in a happy/sad* mood) 意気軒昂（けんこう）・意気消沈で（= 幸せ・悲しい気分で）ある ▶定義4 -spirited（複合形容詞を作るために用いて）having the mood or attitude of mind mentioned 言及された気分または態度の→～の精神を持つ, 気分が～の, 元気が～の ‖ *a group of high-spirited teenagers* 元気のいいティーンエージャーの一団 ▶定義5 spirits [複数扱い] 特に 医 strong alcoholic drinks, for example whisky and vodka 例えばウイスキーやウオッカなど, アルコール成分の強い飲み物→強い酒 ▶定義6 Ⓤ energy, strength of mind or determination 気力, 精神力, 気概→意気込み, 気迫, 勇気 ‖ *The group had plenty of team spirit.* そのグループは団結心に満ちていた. ▶定義7 [単数扱い] the typical or most important quality of sth ～の典型的なまたは最も重要な特質→精神, 特質 ‖ *the pioneer spirit* 開拓者精神 *The painting perfectly captures the spirit of the times.* その絵は時代の精神を完ぺきに捕らえている.

**spirit**[2] /spírət/ 動
句動詞 spirit sb/sth away/off ▶定義 to take sb/sth away secretly ～をひそかに連れ[持ち]去る→～をこっそり連れ去る, 誘拐する, ～を内緒で持ち去る

**spirited** /spírətəd/ 形 ▶定義 full of energy, determination and courage エネルギーと気概と勇気に満ちた→元気のいい, 意気盛んな, 勇気のある, 活発な

**spiritual** /spírɪtʃuəl/ 形 ▶定義1 concerning deep thoughts, feelings or emotions rather than the body or physical things 肉体または物質的なものよりむしろ, 深い思想, 感情, 情緒に関する→精神的な, 精神の, 霊的な, 魂の ‖ *spiritual development/growth/needs* 精神的な発達・成長・欲求 ☞参 **material** ▶定義2 concerning the Church or religion 教会または宗教に関する→宗教的な, 神聖な, 教会の ‖ *a spiritual leader* 精神的指導者 — **spiritually** /-tʃuəli/ 副→精神的に, 霊的に, 宗教的に

**spiritualism** /spírɪtʃuəlìz(ə)m/ 名 Ⓤ ▶定義 the belief that people who have died can get messages to living people, usually through a special person (**a medium**) 通常は特殊な人（霊媒）を通じて死者が生者にメッセージを伝えることができるという信仰→心霊信仰, 神霊主義; 降神術, 交霊術 — **spiritualist** 名 Ⓒ →心霊主義者, 降神術者

**spit**[1] /spɪt/ 動 圓 他 (**spitting**; 過, 過分 **spat** /spæt/)
►アメリカ英語では過去・過去分詞形を spit とすることもある.
▶定義 **spit (sth) (out)** to force liquid, food, etc out from your mouth 口から液体, 食べ物などを無理に出す→(～を)吐く, 吐き出す ‖ *He took one sip of the wine and spat it out.* 彼はワインを一口飲むと吐き出した.

**spit**[2] /spɪt/ 名 ▶定義1 Ⓤ 略式 the liquid in your mouth 口内の液体→つば, だ液 ☞参 **saliva** ▶定義2 Ⓒ a long, thin piece of land that sticks out into the sea, a lake, etc 海, 湖などに突き出た細長い陸地→岬, 砂州, 出州 ▶定義3 Ⓒ a long thin metal stick that you put through meat to hold it when you cook it over a fire 肉を火の上で料理するときに持っていられるように肉に突き刺す細長い金属製の棒→くし, 焼きぐし, 鉄ぐし ‖ *chicken roasted on a spit* 鶏肉のくし焼き

★**spite** /spaɪt/ 名 Ⓤ ▶定義 the desire to hurt or annoy sb ～を傷付けたいまたは困らせたいという欲望→悪意, 意地悪 ‖ *He stole her letters out of spite.* 彼は腹いせに彼女の手紙を盗んだ. — **spite** 動 他→～に意地悪をする, ～をいじめる, 困らせる

成句 **in spite of** ▶定義 used to show that sth happened although you did not expect it 予期していなかった～が起きたことを示すのに用いて→～にもかかわらず ‖ *In spite of all her hard work, Sue failed her exam.* 一生懸命勉強したにもかかわらず, スーは試験に落ちた. ☞類 **despite**

**spiteful** /spáɪtfʊl, -f(ə)l/ 形 ▶定義 behaving in a cruel or unkind way in order to hurt or upset sb ～を傷付けたり困らせたりするために残酷, または意地悪に振る舞って→悪意に満ちた, 意地の悪い ‖ *He's been saying a lot of spiteful things about his ex-girlfriend.* 彼は自分の元恋人についてあれこれひどい事を言っている. — **spitefully** /-fʊli, -f(ə)li-/ 副→意地悪く

★**splash**[1] /splæʃ/ 動 圓 他 ▶定義 (used about a liquid) to fall or to make liquid fall noisily or fly in drops onto a person or thing（液体について）人または物の上に大きな音を立てて落ちる, または液体を落とす; ～にしぶきとなって降り懸かるまたは降り掛ける→跳ねる, 飛び散る; ～を跳ね

掛ける, 飛び散らす ‖ *Rain splashed against the windows.* 雨が音を立てて窓に跳ね返った. *The children were splashing each other with water.* 子供たちが互いに水を掛け合っていた. *Be careful not to splash paint onto the floor.* 床にペンキが飛び散らないように気を付けなさい.
句動 splash out (on sth) 英略式 ▶定義 to spend money on sth that is expensive and that you do not really need 高価で本当は必要ない物に金を使う→(~に)金を派手に使う, 金をまき散らす, 散財する

**splash**² /splæʃ/ 名 C ▶定義 1 the sound of liquid hitting sth or of sth hitting liquid 液体が~にぶつかるかまたは~が液体にぶつかる音→跳ねる音, バシャン, ザブン, ザブザブ, バシャバシャ ‖ *Paul jumped into the pool with a big splash.* ポールはザブンという大きな音を立ててプールに飛び込んだ. ▶定義 2 a small amount of liquid that falls onto sth ~の上に落ちた少量の液体→跳ね, しぶき, 染み ‖ *splashes of oil on the cooker* レンジの上に跳ねた油 ☞ ripple のさし絵 ▶定義 3 a small bright area of colour 明るい彩りの小空間→(明るい)色の斑点(はんてん) ‖ *Flowers add a splash of colour to a room.* 花を飾ると部屋に明るい彩りが加わる.

**splatter** /splǽtər/ 動 自 他 ▶定義 (used about a liquid) to fly about in large drops and hit sb/sth noisily (液体について) 大粒の滴となって飛び散り, ~に騒々しく当たる→(水などが)バシャッと飛び散る, ~をバシャッと飛び散らかす ‖ *The paint was splattered all over the floor.* ペンキが床中に飛び散っていた. *Heavy rain splattered on the roof.* 大雨が大きな音を立てて屋根を打った.

**splay** /spleɪ/ 動 自 他 ▶定義 splay (sth) (out) (to cause sth) to spread out or become wide apart at one end 広がる, ~を広げる; 一方の端で大きく広がる, ~をそのように広げる→広がる, ~を広げる; 外へ斜めに広がる, ~を外へ斜めに広げる ‖ *splayed fingers* 広げられた指

**splendid** /spléndəd/ 形 ▶定義 1 very good; excellent 非常に良い; 優れた→すてきな, すばらしい, 申し分のない ‖ *What a splendid idea!* 何てすばらしい考えでしょう. ▶定義 2 very impressive 非常に印象的な→豪華な, 華麗な, 際立った, 立派な ‖ *the splendid royal palace* 壮麗な宮殿 — splendidly 副 →すばらしく, 申し分なく, 立派に

**splendour** (米 **splendor**) /spléndər/ 名 U ▶定義 very impressive beauty 非常に印象深い美しさ→豪華さ, 壮麗, 立派

**splint** /splɪnt/ 名 C ▶定義 a piece of wood or metal that is tied to a broken arm or leg to keep it in the right position 骨折した腕または足を正しい位置に固定するために縛り付ける木製または金属製の物→添え木, 副木, 当て木

**splinter** /splɪ́ntər/ 名 C ▶定義 a small thin sharp piece of wood, metal or glass that has broken off a larger piece 木・金属・ガラス製の物の一部が割れ落ちた薄くとがった小片→破片, かけら, 切れ端, とげ ‖ *I've got a splinter in my finger.* 指にとげが刺さってしまった. — splinter 動 自 他 →破片になる, 粉々になる; ~を裂く, ばらばらにする

*__split__¹ /splɪt/ 動 (現分 **splitting**; 過, 過分 **split**) ▶定義 1 自 他 split (sb) (up) (into sth) to divide or to make a group of people divide into smaller groups より小さなグループに分かれる; 人々の集団をより小さなグループに分ける→分かれる, 分裂する; ~を(…に)分ける, 分離させる ‖ *Let's split into two groups.* 2つのグループに分かれましょう. ▶定義 2 他 split sth (between sb/sth); split sth (with sb) to divide or share sth ~を分けるまたは共有する→~を(…の間で)分配する, 分ける, (~と)分け合う, 分かち合う ‖ *We split the cost of the meal between the six of us.* 私たちは食事代を6人で割り勘にした.
▶定義 3 自 他 split (sth) (open) to break or make sth break along a straight line 直線に沿って割れるまたは~をそのように割る→裂ける, 割れる; ~を(縦に)裂く, 割る ‖ *My jeans have split.* 私のジーンズが裂けてしまった.
感句 split the difference ▶定義 (used when agreeing on a price) to agree on an amount or figure that is halfway between the two amounts or figures already mentioned (価格に合意するときに用いて) 既に言及された2つの量または数字の中間の量または数字で合意する→(条件・値段などの)中間を取る, 歩み寄る, 半分ずつ負担する
split hairs ▶定義 to pay too much attention in an argument to details that are very small and not important 議論で, 大変ささいで重要でない細部に過剰の注意を払う→必要以上に細かい区

別立てをする、ささいな事にこだわる、重箱の隅をつつく ☛ 通常は批判的に用いられる.
**句動詞** split up (with sb) ▶定義 to end a marriage or relationship 結婚または関係を終わりにする→(恋人・夫婦などが)別れる,(〜と)仲たがいする ‖ *He's split up with his girlfriend.* 彼は彼女と別れた.

**split**² /splít/ 名 C ▶定義1 a disagreement that divides a group of people 人々を仲間割れにする意見の相違→**分裂, 仲間割れ, 不和** ▶定義2 a long cut or hole in sth 〜の長く裂けた箇所または穴→**裂け目, 割れ目, ひび割れ**

**split-second** C ▶定義 a very short period of time 非常に短い期間→**ほんの一瞬, 瞬間, 一瞬間**

**splutter** /splʌ́tər/ 動 ▶定義1 自 他 to speak with difficulty for example because you are very angry or embarrassed 非常に怒っていたり当惑しているためにうまく話せない→(〜を)しどろもどろで言う, せき込んで話す ▶定義2 自 to make a series of sounds like a person coughing 人がせき込んでいるような音を立てる→**ブツブツ・パチパチという音を出す** ― splutter 名 C→**しどろもどろに話すこと,(せき込んだ話し手などの)騒音, ぶつぶつ言う声, パチパチという音**

★**spoil** /spɔ́il/ 動 他 (過, 過分 **spoilt** /spɔ́ilt/ または **spoiled** /spɔ́ild/) ▶定義1 to change sth good into sth bad, unpleasant, useless, etc; to ruin sth 良い物事を悪い、嫌なまたは役に立たないものなどに変える; 〜を台なしにする→**〜を駄目にする, 損なう, 使えなくする, 台なしにする** ‖ *The new office block will spoil the view.* その新しいオフィスビルのお陰で見晴らしは損なわれるだろう. *Our holiday was spoilt by bad weather.* 私たちの休日は悪天候のため台なしになった. *Eating between meals will spoil your appetite.* 間食すると食欲がなくなる. ▶定義2 to do too much for sb, especially a child, so that you have a bad effect on his/her character 人のため、特に子供のためにいろいろやりすぎて、性格に悪影響を及ぼす→**〜を甘やかして駄目にする, わがままな性格にする** ‖ *a spoilt child* 駄々っ子 ▶定義3 spoil sb/yourself to do sth special or nice to make sb/yourself happy 自分自身やだれかを満ち足りた気持ちにするために、何か特別な事、楽しい事をする→**(客など)を大切に扱う, 〜にサービスを尽くす; (自分が)ぜいたくをする, (お金をかけて)大いに楽しむ**

**spoils** /spɔ́ilz/ 名 [複数扱い] (文) ▶定義 things that have been stolen by thieves, or taken in a war or battle 泥棒に盗まれた物、または戦争で奪い取られた物→**盗品, 略奪品, 戦利品** ‖ *the spoils of war* 戦利品

**spoilsport** /spɔ́ilspɔ̀ːrt/ 名 C 略式 ▶定義 a person who tries to stop other people enjoying themselves, for example by not taking part in an activity 活動への不参加などにより、ほかの人たちが楽しんでいるのをやめさせようとする人→**他人の楽しみを台なしにする人, 他人の興をそぐ人, 座を白けさせる人**

**spoke**¹ /spóuk/ 名 C ▶定義 one of the thin pieces of metal that connect the centre of a wheel (the hub) to the outside edge (the rim) 車輪の中央(ハブ)を外側の縁(外輪)に連結する薄い金属製の物→**スポーク, 輻(や)** ☛ S7 ページのさし絵

**spoke**² SPEAK の過去形
**spoken** SPEAK の過去分詞形
**spokesman** /spóuksmən/ 名 C (複 -men /-mən/) ▶定義 a person who is chosen to speak for a group or organization ある集団または組織の代弁者に選ばれた人→**スポークスマン, 代弁者, 代表者**

★**spokesperson** /spóukspə̀ːrs(ə)n/ 名 C (複) **spokespersons** または **spokespeople** /spóukspìːp(ə)l/ ▶定義 a person who is chosen to speak for a group or organization ある集団または組織の代弁者に選ばれた人→**代弁者, 代表者** ☛ spokesperson は男性、女性のいずれに対しても用いることができるため、今日ではしばしば spokesman または spokeswoman よりも好まれる.

**spokeswoman** /spóukswùmən/ 名 C (複 **-women** /-wìmən/) ▶定義 a woman who is chosen to speak for a group or organization ある集団または組織の代弁者に選ばれた女性→**スポークスウーマン, 代弁者, 代表者**

**sponge**¹ /spʌ́ndʒ/ 名 C U ▶定義1 a piece of artificial or natural material that is soft and light and full of holes and can hold water easily, used for washing yourself or cleaning sth 柔らかで軽く、穴がたくさん開いていて水分を簡単に

含むことのできる人造または天然素材でできた物.体や物を清潔にするのに使われる➡スポンジ, 海綿, 海綿状の物 ☞ **bucket** のさし絵 ▶定義2 = **SPONGE CAKE**

**sponge**[2] /spʌndʒ/ 動他 ▶定義 to remove or clean sth with a wet sponge[1](1) or cloth ぬれたスポンジまたは布で, ~を取り除くまたはきれいにする➡~を洗う, ふく, ぬぐう

句動詞 **sponge off sb** 略式 ▶定義 to get money, food, etc from sb without paying or doing anything in return 金を払つて見返りに何かをすることなく, 人から金, 食料などを得る➡(~から)(…を)せびり取る, せしめる, (人に)たかる

**sponge bag** (または **toilet bag**) 名 C 英 ▶定義 a small bag in which you put soap, toothpaste, etc (toiletries) when you are travelling 旅行中のせつけん, 練り歯磨きなど(洗面用品)を入れる小さなバッグ➡携帯洗面用具入れ, 化粧品入れ, 洗面用具入れ

**sponge cake** (または **sponge**) 名 C U ▶定義 a light cake made with eggs, flour and sugar, and usually no fat 卵, 小麦粉, 砂糖で作られた, 通常脂肪分の入つていない軽いケーキ➡スポンジケーキ

**sponsor** /spánsər/ 名 C ▶定義1 a person or an organization that helps to pay for a special sports event, etc (usually so that it can advertise its products) (通常は製品の広告を兼ねて)特別なスポーツの試合などに対して資金を援助する人または団体➡スポンサー, 広告主, 番組提供者 ☞参 **patron** ▶定義2 a person who agrees to pay money to a charity if sb else completes a particular activity だれかが特定の活動をやり遂げることを条件に, 慈善のために出資することに同意する人➡後援者, 出資者 — **sponsor** 動他 ➡~のスポンサーを務める, ~を主催する, 後援する ‖ *a sponsored walk to raise money for children in need* 困つている子供たちを対象にした慈善事業の資金集めのためのクロスカントリー競歩 — **sponsorship** 名 U ➡スポンサーであること, 後援, 資金援助 ‖ *Many theatres depend on industry for sponsorship.* 劇場の多くは産業界に資金援助を頼つている.

**spontaneous** /spɑntéɪniəs/ 形 ▶定義 done or happening suddenly; not planned 突然行われる, または起こる; 計画されていない➡自然に起こる, 自発的な, 無意識の, 自然な ‖ *a spontaneous burst of applause* 期せずしてどっとわき上がつた拍手 — **spontaneously** 副 ➡自然に, 自発的に, 無意識に — **spontaneity** /spɑ̀nt(ə)níːəti, -néɪə-/ 名 U ➡自発性, 自然さ

**spooky** /spúːki/ 形 略式 ▶定義 strange and frightening 異様で恐ろしい➡気味の悪い, 恐ろしい, 幽霊の出そうな ‖ *It's spooky being in the house alone at night.* 夜 1 人きりで家にいるのは気味が悪い.

**spool** /spuːl/ 名 C ▶定義 a round object which thread, film, wire, etc are put around 糸, フィルム, ワイヤーなどを巻き付けておく丸い物➡糸巻き, 巻き枠, リール, スプール ☞参 **reel**

★**spoon** /spuːn/ 名 C ▶定義 an object with a round end and a long handle that you use for eating, mixing or serving food 物を食べたり食べ物を混ぜたりよそったりするのに用いる, 先が丸くて長い取っ手の付いた物➡さじ, スプーン ‖ *Give each person a knife, fork and spoon.* 1 人 1 人にナイフ, フォーク, スプーンを上げてください. *a wooden spoon for cooking* 調理用の木製のさじ ☞ **kitchen** のさし絵 — **spoon** 動他 ➡~をスプーンですくう, よそう

**spoonful** /spúːnfʊl/ 名 C ▶定義 the amount that one spoon can hold 1つのさじですくえる量➡スプーン1杯分, 1さじ分, 少量 ‖ *Add two spoonfuls of sugar.* 砂糖を2さじ加えなさい.

**sporadic** /spərǽdɪk/ 形 ▶定義 not done or happening regularly 定期的に行われない, または起こらない➡時折の, 散発的な, 散在する, ばらばらの — **sporadically** /-k(ə)li/ 副 ➡時折, あちこち, ばらばらに

★**sport** /spɔːrt/ 名 ▶定義1 U a physical game or activity that you do for exercise or because you enjoy it 運動または楽しみのために行う体を使った遊びまたは活動➡運動, スポーツ ‖ *John did a lot of sport when he was at school.* ジョンは学生時代に大いにスポーツをした. *Do you like sport?* スポーツはお好きですか. ▶定義2 C a particular game or type of sport ある特定のスポーツの試合または特定のスポーツ➡運動, スポーツ, 競技, 競技種目 ‖ *What's your favourite sport?* 好きなスポーツは何ですか. *winter sports* (= *skiing, skating, etc*) ウインタースポーツ (= スキ

ー、スケートなど）— **sporting** 形 →運動(用)の、スポーツ(用)の、運動・スポーツ好きな ‖ *a major sporting event* 大きなスポーツイベント

**sports car** 名 C ▶定義 a low, fast car often with a roof that you can open 背の低い高速車．屋根が開閉できるものが多い →スポーツカー

**sportsman** /spɔ́ːrtsmən/ 名 C (複 **-men** /-mən/) ▶定義 a man who does a lot of sport or who is good at sport 運動をよくする男性または運動が得意な男性 →スポーツマン、スポーツ愛好家 ‖ *a keen sportsman* スポーツに熱心な人

**sportsmanlike** /spɔ́ːrtsmənlàɪk/ ▶定義 behaving in a fair, generous and polite way when you are playing a game or doing sport 試合またはスポーツをしているときに公正、寛大かつ礼儀正しく振る舞って →スポーツマンらしい、正々堂々とした、公正な

**sportsmanship** /spɔ́ːrtsmənʃìp/ 名 U ▶定義 the quality of being fair, generous and polite when you are playing a game or doing sport 試合またはスポーツをしているときに公正、寛大かつ礼儀正しくあるという特質 →スポーツマンシップ、スポーツマン精神、スポーツマンにふさわしい行動、正々堂々とした態度

**sportswoman** /spɔ́ːrtswùmən/ 名 C (複 **-women** /-wìmən/) ▶定義 a woman who does a lot of sport or who is good at sport 運動をよくする女性または運動が得意な女性 →スポーツウーマン、スポーツ愛好家

***spot**¹ /spɑt/ 名 C ▶定義 1 a small round mark on a surface 表面の小さな点 →斑点(はんてん)、まだら、ぶち、水玉模様 ‖ *Leopards have dark spots.* ヒョウには黒点がある． *a blue skirt with red spots on it* 青地に赤い水玉のスカート ☛ 形 **spotted** ▶定義 2 a small dirty mark on sth 〜の上に付いた小さな汚れ →汚れ、染み、汚点、傷 ‖ *grease/rust spots* 油の染み・さびの汚れ ▶定義 3 a small red or yellow lump that appears on your skin 皮膚にできる小さな赤または黄色のはれ物 →吹き出物、発疹(はっしん)、にきび、おでき ‖ *Many teenagers get spots.* ティーンエージャーの多くはにきびができる． ☛ 形 **spotty** ▶定義 4 a particular place or area 特定の場所または地域 →場所、地点、箇所、スポット ‖ *a quiet/lonely/secluded spot* 静かな・人里離れた・人目に付かない場所 ▶定義 5 [通常は単数] a **spot of sth** 英略式 a small amount of sth 少量の〜 →少量の、少しの、1滴の、1口の ▶定義 6 = **SPOTLIGHT(1)**

成句 **have a soft spot for sb/sth** ⇒ **SOFT**

**on the spot** ▶定義 1 immediately すぐに →直ちに、即座に、その場で ‖ *Paul was caught stealing money and was dismissed on the spot.* ポールは金を盗んでいるところを捕まり、すぐさま解雇された． ▶定義 2 at the place where sth happened or where sb/sth is needed 〜が起こった場所で、または〜が必要とされる場所で →その場で、現場で ‖ *The fire brigade were on the spot within five minutes.* 消防団は5分以内に現場に到着していた．

**put sb on the spot** ▶定義 to make sb answer a difficult question or make a difficult decision without having much time to think 〜に考える時間をあまり与えずに難しい質問への回答を求めたり難しい決断を迫る →〜を窮地に陥れる、立ち往生させる、〜に即答・即決を迫る

***spot**² /spɑt/ 動 他 (**spotting**; **spotted**) (進行形は不可) ▶定義 to see or notice sb/sth, especially suddenly or when it is not easy to do 特に突然に、または見つけにくいときに〜を見つける、またはそれに気付く →〜を見つける、発見する、見抜く、(場所など)を突き止める ‖ *I've spotted a couple of spelling mistakes.* 2つのスペリングの誤りを見つけた．

▶この動詞は進行形では使われないが、現在分詞(= -ing 形)は一般に見られる: *Spotting a familiar face in the crowd, he began to push his way towards her.* (群衆の中に見慣れた顔を見つけると、彼は人を押しのけながら彼女の方に押し進んでいった．)

**spot check** 名 C ▶定義 a check that is made suddenly and without warning on a few things or people chosen from a group 集団から選んだ2、3の物や人に突然予告なしに行う検査 →抜き打ち検査、無作為抽出検査、抜き取り検査

**spotless** /spɑ́tləs/ 形 ▶定義 perfectly clean 完全に清潔な →染みのない、汚れのない、清潔な

**spotlight** /spɑ́tlàɪt/ 名 ▶定義 1 (または **spot**) C a lamp that can send a single ray of bright light onto a small area. Spotlights are often used in theatres. 狭い箇所に一筋の明るい光を送ることのできる照明．しばしば劇場で用いられる →スポ

ットライト, 舞台用集中照明器具 ☞ **light** のさし絵 ▶定義2 **the spotlight** [単数扱い] the centre of public attention or interest 世間の注目または関心の中心→世間の注目, 注視, 脚光 ‖ *to be in **the spotlight*** 世間の注目を集めて(いる)

**spot on** 形 医略式 (名詞の前は不可) ▶定義 exactly right 全く正確な→正確な, ぴったりの ‖ *Your estimate was spot on.* あなたの見積もりはどんぴしゃだった.

**spotted** /spɑ́təd/ 形 ▶定義 (used about clothes, cloth, etc) covered with round shapes of a different colour (衣服, 布などについて)地と違う色の円形模様を散らした→水玉模様の, 斑点(はんてん)のある, ぶちの ‖ *a spotted blouse* 水玉模様のブラウス

**spotty** /spɑ́ti/ 形 ▶定義 having small red or yellow lumps on your skin 皮膚に小さな赤, または黄色のはれ物のある→吹き出物のある, 発疹(はっしん)のある, にきびのある

**spouse** /spáʊs, -z/ 名 **C** (文) ▶定義 your husband or wife 夫または妻→配偶者 ☞ spouse は所定の書き込み用紙・文書などで用いられる改まったまたは公式の語である.

**spout**¹ /spáʊt/ 名 **C** ▶定義 a tube or pipe through which liquid comes out 液体が流れ出る管またはパイプ→(やかん・ポットなどの)口, (ポンプなどの)噴出口 ‖ *the spout of a teapot* ティーポットの注ぎ口

**spout**² /spáʊt/ 動 **自** 他 ▶定義1 to send out a liquid with great force; to make a liquid do this 勢いよく液体を送り出す; 液体をこのように流出させる→吹き出る, ほとばしり出る; (液体など)を吹き出す, 噴出する ▶定義2 略式 **spout (on/off) (about sth)** to say sth, using a lot of words, in a way that is boring or annoying 言葉を使いまくって, 人をうんざりさせる, またはいら立たせるような言い方をする→(～について)ぺらぺらしゃべる, まくしたてる

**sprain** /spréɪn/ 動 他 ▶定義 to injure part of your body, especially your wrist or the thinnest part of your leg (**ankle**), by suddenly bending or turning it 体の一部, 特に手首, 足首を急に曲げたり, ひねったりして痛める→～をくじく, 捻挫(ねんざ)する ‖ *to sprain your ankle* 足首を捻挫する — sprain 名 **C** ▶くじくこと, 捻挫

**sprang** **SPRING**² の過去形

**sprawl** /sprɔ́ːl/ 動 **自** ▶定義1 to sit or lie with your arms and legs spread out in an untidy way だらしなく腕または足を広げて座るまたは横たわる→手足を伸ばす, 手足を投げ出して座る, 大の字に寝そべる ‖ *People lay sprawled out in the sun.* 人々は日なたで手足を伸ばして寝転んでいた. ▶定義2 to cover a large area of land 土地を広く占める→不規則に広がる, だらだらと延びる, 無秩序に広がる — sprawling 形→大の字に寝ている, 不規則に広がる, まとまりのない ‖ *the sprawling city suburbs* 無計画に広がった都市の郊外

**spray**¹ /spréɪ/ 名 ▶定義1 **U** liquid in very small drops that is sent through the air 空中に送り出される非常に細かい滴状の液体→しぶき, 水煙 ‖ *clouds of spray from the waves* 波しぶき ▶定義2 **C** **U** liquid in a special container (**an aerosol**) that is forced out under pressure when you push a button ボタンを押すと圧力で飛び出す専用の容器(エアゾール)に入った液体→スプレー, 噴霧, 噴霧器, 霧吹き ‖ *hairspray* ヘアスプレー ☞ **container** のさし絵

**spray**² /spréɪ/ 動 **自** 他 ▶定義 (used about a liquid) to be forced out of a container or sent through the air in very small drops; to send a liquid out in this way (液体について)容器から押し出される, または非常に細かい滴状で空中へ送られる; 液体をそのような状態で送り出す→(液体などが)しぶきになる, 飛散する; ～を吹き掛ける, 散布する ‖ *The crops are regularly sprayed with pesticide.* 作物に定期的に殺虫剤を散布する.

\***spread**¹ /spréd/ 動 (過, 過分 **spread**) ▶定義1 **自** 他 to affect a larger area or a bigger group of people; to make sth do this より広い範囲または人々のより大きな集団に影響を及ぼす; ～にそのような影響を及ぼさせる→広がる, 及ぶ, (病気などが)蔓延(まんえん)する; ～を広める, ばらまく, 蔓延させる ‖ *The fire spread rapidly because of the strong wind.* 強い風のために火があっと言う間に広がった. *Rats and flies **spread disease**.* ネズミとハエは病気を蔓延させる. *to **spread rumours** about sb* ～についてのうわさを流す ▶定義2 **他** **spread sth (out) (on/over sth)** to open sth that has been folded so that it covers a larger area; to move things so that they cover a larger area より大きな面積を覆うために折り畳んであったものを開く; より大きな面積を覆うために～を動かす➜**(毛布·テーブル掛けなど)を(～に)掛ける, 一面に広げる, 伸ばす, 開く** ‖ *Spread the map out on the table so we can all see it!* 私たち全員が見られるようにテーブルの上に地図を広げなさい. ▶定義3 [他] spread A on/over B; spread B with A to cover a surface with a layer of a soft substance 表面一面に柔らかい物を塗る➜**～を…の上に塗る, ～に…を塗る** ‖ *to spread jam on bread* ジャムをパンに塗る *to spread bread with jam* パンにジャムを塗る ▶定義4 [他] spread sth (out) (over sth) to separate sth into parts and divide them between different times or people ～を部分に分け, その分けたものをそれぞれ異なる時期や人々に配分する➜**(仕事·金など)を分配する, (支払いなど)を(～に)わたって行う, 分散させる** ‖ *You can spread your repayments over a period of three years.* 返済を3年間の分割払いにすることができます.

[句動詞] spread (sb/yourself) out ▶定義 to move away from the others in a group of people in order to cover a larger area より大きな区域をカバーするために, 集団のほかの人から離れてよそに移動する➜**(人が)分散する; 人を分散させる** ‖ *The police spread out to search the whole area.* 警察は全域を捜索するために方々に散らばった.

**spread²** /spred/ [名] ▶定義1 [U] an increase in the amount or number of sth that there is, or in the area that is affected by sth 今あるものが量または数の上で増加すること, 何かに侵された範囲が拡大すること➜**広まり, 普及, 流布, 蔓延(まんえん)** ‖ *Dirty drinking water encourages **the spread of disease**.* 汚染された飲み水は病気の蔓延を増長する. ▶定義2 [C][U] a soft food that you put on bread パンに塗る柔らかい食べ物➜**パンに塗る物, ジャム, バター** ▶定義3 [C] a newspaper or magazine article that covers one or more pages 1ページ, またはそれ以上のページにわたる新聞または雑誌の記事➜**(新聞·雑誌の)大見出し記事, 見開き広告** ‖ *a double-page spread* 2ページにわたる記事

**spreadsheet** /sprédʃiːt/ [名] [C] ▶定義 (computing) a computer program for working with rows of numbers, used especially for doing accounts (コンピューター)何列もの数字を処理する, 特に会計事務の計算に使われる, コンピュータープログラム➜**スプレッドシート, 表計算ソフト, 財務会計ソフト**

**spree** /spriː/ [名] [C][略式] ▶定義 a short time that you spend doing sth you enjoy, often doing too much of it しばしば過度に, 楽しい～をして過ごす短い時間➜**ばか騒ぎ, どんちゃん騒ぎ, ふざけ** ‖ *to **go on a** shopping/spending **spree*** 派手に買い物をしまくる·金に糸目を付けずに使いまくる

**sprig** /sprɪg/ [名] [C] ▶定義 a small piece of a plant with leaves on it 葉の付いた草木の小さな部分➜**小枝, 若枝**

***spring¹** /sprɪŋ/ [名] ▶定義1 [C][U] the season of the year between winter and summer when the weather gets warmer and plants begin to grow 天候が次第に暖かくなり植物が生長し始める, 冬と夏の間の季節➜**春, 春季** ‖ *Daffodils bloom **in spring**.* ラッパスイセンは春に開花する. ▶定義2 [C] a long piece of thin metal or wire that is bent round and round. After you push or pull a spring it goes back to its original shape and size. 円状にぐるぐる巻いてある細長い金属片または針金. 押したり引っ張ったりしても, 元の形と大きさに戻る➜**ばね, ぜんまい, スプリング** ‖ *bed springs* ベッドスプリング ☛ **coil**のさし絵 ▶定義3 [C] a place where water comes up naturally from under the ground 水が地下から自然にわき出てくる場所➜**泉, 水源, 源泉** ‖ *a hot spring* 温泉 ▶定義4 [C] a sudden jump upwards or forwards 上方または前方に突然跳ぶこと➜**跳ぶこと, 跳ねること, 跳躍, 飛躍**

**➤音声とつづり字**

Spring has come. の言い方

「春が来た」に当たる英語の表現は, 春が来て夏になったという過去の出来事としてとらえるにはSpring came. と過去形で表現し, 春が来て今が春であるという現在に過去から結果が及ぶ場合は現在完了で表します. hasは普通, 弱形で発音しますので, comeの前で, 無声化し, Spring has come. [sprɪŋ s kʰʌ́m スプインッスカム]のようになります.

**spring**² /sprɪŋ/ 動⾃ (過 **sprang** /spræn/; 過分 **sprung** /sprʌn/) ▶定義 1 to jump or move quickly 素早く跳ぶまたは移動する→跳ぶ,跳ねる,跳躍する,さっと動く ‖ *When the alarm went off, Ray sprang out of bed.* アラームが鳴り出した途端、レイは寝床から飛び出した. *to spring to your feet (= stand up suddenly)* さっと立ち上がる(= 突然起立する)(比喩)*to spring to sb's defence/assistance (= to quickly defend or help sb)* いち早く~を擁護・援助する(= 素早く~を弁護・手助けする) ▶定義 2 (used about an object) to move suddenly and violently (物について)突然激しく動く→急にはじける,跳ね返る,パッと~する ‖ *The branch sprang back and hit him in the face.* 枝が突然跳ね返って彼の顔にぶつかった. ▶定義 3 to appear or come somewhere suddenly ある場所に突然現れるまたはやって来る→突然現れる,急に起こる,わき起こる ‖ *Tears sprang to her eyes.* 彼女の目に突然涙が浮かんだ. *Where did you just spring from?* 君は一体どこから現れたの.

成句 come/spring to mind ⇒ **MIND**¹

句動詞 **spring from sth** (文) ▶定義 to be the result of ~の結果である→~から生じる,~に由来する ‖ *The idea for the book sprang from an experience she had while travelling in India.* その本の着想はインド旅行中に彼女が得た経験から来ている.

**spring sth on sb** 格式 ▶定義 to do or say sth that sb is not expecting ~の予期していない…を行うまたは言う→突然~で…を驚かす,(話など)を~に急に持ち出す

**spring up** ▶定義 to appear or develop quickly or suddenly 素早くまたは突然現れるまたは展開する→ひょっこり現れる,急に起こる,わき起こる ‖ *Play areas for children are springing up everywhere.* 子供の遊び場があちらこちらにできている.

**springboard** /spríŋbɔːrd/ 名 C ▶定義 1 a low board that bends and that helps you jump higher, for example before you jump into a swimming pool 水泳プールに飛び込むときなど、板のたわみでより高く飛ぶのを助ける,丈の低い台板→飛び込み板,跳躍台,踏み切り板 ▶定義 2 **a springboard (for/to sth)** something that helps you start an activity, especially by giving you ideas 特に人に何かを思い付くきっかけを与えて事に着手する糸口となる~→踏み台,出発点,飛躍のための足掛かり

**spring-clean** 動他 ▶定義 to clean a house, room, etc very well, including the parts that you do not usually clean 通常は掃除しない部分も含めて家,部屋などをよく掃除する→~の大掃除をする,春の大掃除をする

**spring onion** 名 C U ▶定義 a type of small onion with a long green central part and leaves 長い緑色の茎と葉を持つ小さなタマネギ→春タマネギ ☞ C3 ページのさし絵

**springtime** /spríŋtàim/ 名 U (文) ▶定義 the season of spring 春の季節→春,春季

**springy** /spríŋi/ 形 ▶定義 going quickly back to its original shape or size after being pushed, pulled, etc 押したり引っ張ったりしても素早く元の形または大きさに戻る→ばねのある,弾力性のある,よく弾む,軽快な ‖ *soft springy grass* 柔らかく弾力のある草

**sprinkle** /spríŋk(ə)l/ 動他 ▶定義 **sprinkle A (on/onto/over B); sprinkle B (with A)** to throw drops of water or small pieces of sth over a surface 表面に水滴または細かな~を投げる→(水・香辛料など)を(~に)振り掛ける,まき散らす,(場所)に(~を)まく,振り掛ける ‖ *to sprinkle sugar on a cake* 砂糖をケーキに振り掛ける *to sprinkle a cake with sugar* ケーキに砂糖を振り掛ける

**sprinkler** /spríŋk(ə)lər/ 名 C ▶定義 a device with holes in it that sends out water in small drops. Sprinklers are used in gardens, to keep the grass green, and in buildings, to stop fires from spreading. 水が細かい水滴になって出る穴の付いた装置.芝生を青く保たせるために庭内で,火事の延焼を防ぐために屋内で用いられたりする→水まき機,散水装置,散水車,スプリンクラー

**sprint** /sprɪnt/ 動自他 ▶定義 to run a short distance as fast as you can 短距離を全速力で走る→(短距離を)全速力で走る,全力疾走する ─ sprint 名 C ▶定義 短距離競争,全力疾走,スプリント

**sprout**¹ /spráʊt/ 動自他 ▶定義 (used about a plant) to begin to grow or to produce new leaves (植物について)生育し始める,新しい葉を出す→芽吹く,発芽する,生え始める; ~を発芽させる ‖ *The seeds are sprouting.* 種が発芽している.

**sprout²** /spráʊt/ 名 C ▶定義1 = BRUSSELS SPROUT ▶定義2 a new part that has grown on a plant 植物に新しく生えた部分 ➡芽, 新芽

**spruce** /spru:s/ 動
句動詞 spruce (sb/yourself) up ▶定義 to make sb/ yourself clean and tidy 〜や自分自身をきれいに整える ➡(〜の)身なりを整える, (〜を)こぎれいにする, めかす

**sprung** SPRING²の過去分詞形

**spud** /spʌd/ 名 C 略式 ▶定義 a potato ➡ジャガイモ

**spun** SPIN¹の過去分詞形

**spur¹** /spɜːr/ 名 C ▶定義1 a piece of metal that a rider wears on the back of his/her boots to encourage the horse to go faster 馬に気合を入れてより速く走らせるために乗り手が長靴のかかとに付ける金具 ➡拍車 ☛ horse のさし絵 ▶定義2 a spur (to sth) something that encourages you to do sth or that makes sth happen more quickly 何かをするように人に励みを与える事物, または〜がより速やかに起こるようにする事物 ➡拍車, 刺激 ‖ *My poor exam results acted as a spur to make me study harder.* 試験の結果が悪かったことに発奮して, 私はもっと一生懸命勉強する気になった.
成句 on the spur of the moment ▶定義 without planning; suddenly 計画なく; 突然に ➡その時の弾みで, 衝動的に, とっさの思い付きで

**spur²** /spɜːr/ 動 他 (**spurring, spurred**) ▶定義 spur sb/sth (on/onto sth) to encourage sb or make him/her work harder or faster 〜を励ます, または〜をより一生懸命またはより速く働かせる ➡〜を駆り立てる, 激励する, 鼓舞する ‖ *The letter spurred me into action.* 手紙は私を行動に駆り立てた. *We were spurred on by the positive feedback from customers.* 私たちは客からの好意的な反応に激励された.

**spurn** /spɜːn/ 動 他 正式 ▶定義 to refuse sth that sb has offered to you 〜が申し出た…を拒む ➡〜(申し出など)をはねつける, 拒否する, 拒絶する ‖ *to spurn an offer of friendship* 友達になろうという申し出を断る

**spurt** /spɜːt/ 動 ▶定義1 自 他 (used about a liquid) to come out quickly with great force; to make a liquid do this (液体について)すさまじい勢いで素早く出てくる; 液体をこのように流出させる ➡吹き出る, 噴出する, ほとばしる; 〜を噴出させる ‖ *Blood spurted from the wound.* 傷口から血が吹き出した. ▶定義2 自 to suddenly increase your speed or effort 突然速度を上げるまたは一層の努力をする ➡力走する, 大奮闘する, スパートをかける — spurt 名 C ➡噴出, ほとばしり; スパート, 激発

**spy¹** /spáɪ/ 名 C (複 **spies**) ▶定義 a person who tries to get secret information about another country, person or organization ほかの国, 人, 組織に関する秘密の情報を得ようとする人 ➡スパイ, 間諜(かんちょう), 密偵

**spy²** /spáɪ/ 動 (現分 **spying**; 三単現 **spies**; 過, 過分 **spied**) ▶定義1 自 to try to get secret information about sb/sth 〜に関して秘密の情報を得ようとする ➡スパイする, 詮索(せんさく)する, 探偵する, ひそかに探る ☛参 espionage ▶定義2 他 正式 to see 見る ➡(遠くの[隠れた]もの)を発見する
成句 spy on sb/sth ▶定義 to watch sb/sth secretly 〜をひそかに見張る ➡〜をひそかに監視する, 探る ‖ *The man next door is spying on us.* 隣家の男性が私たちをこっそり見張っている.

**spyhole** /spáɪhòʊl/ 名 C ▶定義 a small hole in a door for looking at the person on the other side before deciding to let him/her in 扉の向こうにいる人を中に入れると決める前に, 様子を見るのに使う扉に付いた小さな穴 ➡のぞき穴

**Sq** 略 ▶定義1 = SQUARE²(6) ‖ *10 sq cm* 10平方センチメートル ▶定義2 **Sq** = SQUARE¹(2) ‖ *6 Hanover Sq* ハノーバー広場6番地

**squabble** /skwɑ́b(ə)l/ 動 自 ▶定義 squabble (over/about sth) to argue in a noisy way about sth that is not very important あまり大事でない〜について騒々しく言い争う ➡(つまらぬ事で)口論[けんか]する, 言い合う, 言い争う — squabble 名 C ➡口論, 口げんか, 小競り合い

**squad** /skwɑd/ 名 [C, 単数または複数形の動詞と共に] ▶定義 a group of people who work as a team チームとして働く人たちの集団 ➡チーム, 班, 隊, 団 ‖ *He's a policeman with the drugs squad.* 彼は麻薬特捜班所属の警察官だ.

**squadron** /skwɑ́drən/ 名 [C, 単数または複数形の動詞と共に] ▶定義 a group of military aircraft or ships 戦闘機または戦艦の一団 ➡(米空軍の)飛行大隊, (英空軍の)飛行中隊, 小艦隊

**squalid** /skwάləd/ 形 ▶定義 very dirty, untidy and unpleasant 非常に不潔でだらしなく、その上不快な→**不潔な、むさくるしい、ごみごみした** ‖ *squalid housing conditions* むさくるしい住宅事情

**squall** /skwɔːl/ 名 C ▶定義 a sudden storm with strong winds 強風を伴った突然のあらし→**突風、疾風、スコール**

**squalor** /skwάlər/ 名 U ▶定義 the state of being very dirty, untidy or unpleasant 非常に不潔な、だらしないまたは不快な状態→**不潔、むさくるしさ、みすぼらしさ** ‖ *to live in squalor* 不潔なひどい状況で暮らしている

**squander** /skwάndər/ 動他 ▶定義 squander sth (on sth) to waste time, money, etc 時間、金などを浪費する→**…を(…に)浪費する、空費する、無駄遣いする** ‖ *He squanders his time on TV and computer games.* 彼はテレビとコンピューターゲームで時間を浪費している.

\***square**¹ /skweər/ 名 C ▶定義 **1** a shape that has four sides of the same length and four angles of 90 degrees (right angles) 同じ長さの4つの辺と90度(直角)の4つの角を持つ形→**正方形、四角** ‖ *There are 64 squares on a chess board.* チェスの盤には64個のマスがある. ☞ **shape** のさし絵 ▶定義 **2** (または **Square**) (略 **Sq**) an open space in a town or city that has buildings all around it 町または都市の中で、四方を建物に囲まれた広々とした空間→**(四角い)広場、スクエア** ‖ *Protesters gathered in the town square.* 抗議者たちが町の広場に集結した. *Trafalgar Square* トラファルガー広場 ☞ C8 ページのさし絵 ▶定義 **3** the number that you get when you multiply another number by itself ある数を同一の数と掛けた時に得られる値→**二乗、二乗した数、平方** ‖ *Four is the square of two.* 4は2の二乗だ. ☞参 **square root**

\***square**² /skweər/ 形副 ▶定義 **1** having four straight sides of the same length and corners of 90° 同じ長さのまっすぐな4つの辺と4つの90度の角度を持っている→**正方形の、四角い[に]** ‖ *a square tablecloth* 四角いテーブルクロス ▶定義 **2** shaped like a square or forming an angle of about 90° 正方形のような形をした、角度が約90度の→**角張った、がっしりした** ‖ *a square face* 角張った顔 *square shoulders* がっしりした肩 ▶定義 **3** (名詞の前は不可) not owing any money 借金のない→**貸し借りのない、勘定済みの、清算した** ‖ *Here is the money I owe you. Now we're (all) square.* ここにお借りしていた金があります. これで貸し借りなしですね. ▶定義 **4** (名詞の前は不可) having equal points (in a game, etc) (ゲームなどで)得点が同じ→**同点の、互角の、五分五分の** ‖ *The teams were all square at half-time.* 前半、両チームはタイだった. ▶定義 **5** fair or honest, especially in business matters 特に取り引きに関して公正なまたは正直な→**まっとうな、公明正大な[に]、正直な[に]** ‖ *a square deal* 公正な取り引き ▶定義 **6** (略 **sq**) used for talking about the area of sth ～の面積について話をするのに用いて→**平方の、二乗の** ‖ *If a room is 5 metres long and 4 metres wide, its area is 20 square metres.* 縦5メートル、横4メートルの部屋ならば、面積は20平方メートルになる. ▶定義 **7** (used about sth that is square in shape) having sides of a particular length (正方形の～について) ある特定の長さの辺を持つ→**～平方の、～四方の** ‖ *The picture is twenty centimetres square (= each side is twenty centimetres long).* その絵画は20センチメートル四方ある(= 各辺の長さが20センチメートルある). ▶定義 **8** (または **squarely**) in an obvious and direct way まともに直接的に→**まともに、まっすぐに** ‖ *to look sb square in the eye* まっすぐに～の目を見る *I think the blame falls squarely on her.* 責任はずばり彼女にあると思う.

成句 **a square meal** ▶定義 a good meal that makes you feel satisfied 満足のいく十分な食事→**充実した食事、ちゃんとした食事、しっかりとした食事**

**square**³ /skweər/ 動自他 ▶定義 square(sth) with sb/sth to agree with sth; to make sure that sb/sth agrees with sth ～と合致する、～を(…と)必ず一致させるようにする→**～と一致する; ～を(…と)一致させる、～を(…に)了解[同意]させる** ‖ *Your conclusion doesn't really square with the facts.* あなたの結論は事実とあまり合致していない. *If you want time off you'll have to square it with the boss.* 休みが欲しいのならば、上司と話をつけなければいけませんよ.

句動詞 **square up (with sb)** ▶定義 to pay sb the money that you owe him/her 借りている金

を～に支払う→支払いを済ませる,清算する,けりを付ける

**squared** /skweəd/ 形 ▶定義 (used about a number) multiplied by itself(数について)同数の数を掛けた→二乗の,平方の‖ *Four squared is sixteen.* 4の二乗は16になる. ☞参 **square root**

**square root** 名 C ▶定義 a number that produces another particular number when it is multiplied by itself ある数を同一の数と掛けたときに得られる数の元の数→平方根,二乗根‖ *The square root of sixteen is four.* 16の平方根は4である. ☞参 **square**, **squared**, **root**

**squash**¹ /skwɒʃ/ 動 ▶定義 1 ⓤ to press sth so that it is damaged, changes shape or becomes flat ～が壊れたり,変形したり,ぺちゃんこになるほど強く押す→～を押しつぶす,踏みつぶす,ぺちゃんこにする‖ *The fruit at the bottom of the bag will get squashed.* 袋の底の果物はつぶれてしまいますよ. *Move up - you're squashing me!* 前に進んでください－つぶされそうです. ☞ **squeeze**のさし絵 ▶定義 2 ⓤ ⓤ to go into a place, or move sb/sth to a place, where there is not much space 空きがあまりない所に入り込む,～をそういう所に入れ込む→ぎゅうぎゅう詰める,割り込む;～を押し込める,詰め込む‖ *We all squashed into the back of the car.* 私たちは皆自動車の後部座席にぎゅうぎゅう詰めて入った.

▶定義 3 ⓤ to destroy sth because it is a problem ～が問題であるために打ち壊す→～(案など)を退ける,拒絶する,(暴動など)を鎮圧する,つぶす‖ *to squash sb's suggestion/plan/idea* ～の提案・計画・発案を退ける

**squash**² /skwɒʃ/ 名 ▶定義 1 [C,通常は単数] a lot of people in a small space 狭い所にいる大勢の人→群集,雑踏,殺到,ぎゅうぎゅう詰め‖ *We can get ten people around the table, but it's a bit of a squash.* テーブルの周りに10人を座らすことはできるが,少々窮屈だ. ▶定義 2 ⓤ C 英 a drink that is made from fruit juice and sugar. You add water to squash before you drink it. 果汁と砂糖で作られた飲み物. 水を加えてから飲む→スカッシュ(普通は無炭酸果汁飲料)‖ *orange squash* オレンジスカッシュ ▶定義 3 ⓤ a game for two people, played in a special room (court). You play squash by hitting a small rubber ball against any one of the walls of the room. 専用の部屋(コート)で行う2人用の競技.部屋の壁面のいずれかに小さなゴムボールを当てて行う→スカッシュ,スカッシュテニス‖ *a squash racket* スカッシュ用のラケット

**squat**¹ /skwɒt/ 動 ⓤ (**squatting**; **squatted**) ▶定義 1 to rest with your weight on your feet, your knees bent and your bottom just above the ground 体重を両足にかけ,ひざを折り,腰を地面のすれすれに落とした状態で休む→しゃがむ,うずくまる,座る ☞ **kneel**のさし絵 ▶定義 2 to go and live in an empty building without permission from the owner 所有者の許可なく人の住んでいない建物に入って生活する→無断で住み着く,不法占拠する

> ▶日本語 vs 英語
>
> いろいろな座り方
>
> しゃがんだり,正座したりすることを squat と言いますが,床にひざを付ける正座のような座り方は,kneel と言った方が誤解されません.床におしりを付いて座るのは sit on the floor,「あぐらをかく」は sit cross-legged.「足を組んで座る」は sit with one's legs crossed と言います.

**squat**² /skwɒt/ 形 ▶定義 short and fat or thick 背が低くて太っている,低くてずんぐりした→ずんどうの,ずんぐりとした‖ *a squat ugly building* ずんぐりとした不格好な建物

**squatter** /skwɒtər/ 名 C ▶定義 a person who is living in an empty building without the owner's permission 所有者の許可なく人の住んでいない建物で生活している人→無断居住者,不法占拠者

**squawk** /skwɔːk/ 動 ⓤ ▶定義 (used especially about a bird) to make a loud unpleasant noise (特に鳥について)大きくて不快な音を出す→ガーガー鳴く,ギャーギャー泣く — **squawk** 名 C ガーガー鳴く声,ギャーギャー泣く声

**squeak** /skwiːk/ 名 C ▶定義 a short high noise that is not very loud あまり大きくない短い高い音→チューチュー鳴く声,キーキーきしむ音,ギャーギャー泣く声,甲高い声‖ *the squeak of a mouse* ネズミの鳴き声 *She gave a little squeak of surprise.* 彼女は驚いて小さな叫び声を上げた. — **squeak** 動 ⓤ ⓤ→チューチュー鳴く,キー

キーきしむ, ギャーギャー泣く; ～をキーキー声で言う ― **squeaky** 形 →チューチュー鳴く, キーキーきしむ, ギャーギャー泣く, キーキー声の ‖ *a squeaky floorboard* ミシミシきしむ床板 *a squeaky voice* 金切り声

**squeal** /skwiːl/ 動自他 ▶定義 to make a loud high noise because of pain, fear or enjoyment 痛み, 恐れまたは喜びから大きな高い音を出す→**悲鳴を上げる, 歓声を上げる, キーキー言う** ‖ *The baby squealed in delight at the new toy.* 赤ん坊は新しいおもちゃに大喜びしてキャッキャッと声を上げた. ― **squeal** 名 C→**甲高い声, 悲鳴, 歓声, キーキー言う音**

  ▶ squeal は squeak よりも大きくて長いが, scream ほど大きくはない.

**squeamish** /skwíːmɪʃ/ 形 ▶定義 easily upset by unpleasant sights, especially blood 特に血などの不快なものを見てすぐに動揺する→**吐き気を催しやすい, すぐ気分が悪くなる, 神経質の**

squeeze  crush
squash  press

***squeeze**¹ /skwiːz/ 動 ▶定義1 他 squeeze sth (out); squeeze sth (from/out of sth) to press sth hard for a particular purpose ある特定の目的のため～を強く押す→**～をぎゅっと押す, 絞る, (～から)しぼり取る** ‖ *She squeezed his hand as a sign of affection.* 彼女は愛情の印として彼の手をぎゅっと握った. *to squeeze a tube of toothpaste* 練り歯磨きのチューブを絞る *Squeeze a lemon/the juice of a lemon into a glass.* レモン・レモンの汁をグラスにしぼり出しなさい. *I squeezed the water out of the cloth.* 布から水気を絞り出した. ▶定義2 自他 squeeze (sb/sth) into, through, etc sth; squeeze (sb/sth) through, in, past, etc to force sb/sth into or through a small space ～を小さな狭い所に押し込むまたは無理に通させる→**～の中に割り込む, ～の中を無理に通る, 無理に通り過ぎる; ～を…の中に押し込む, 詰め込む, (予定などに～を)割り込ませる, ～を無理に通させる** ‖ *We can squeeze another person into the back of the car.* 車の後部座席にもう1人押し込むことができる. *There was just room for the bus to squeeze past.* バスがやっと通れる余地しかなかった.

**squeeze**² /skwiːz/ 名 ▶定義1 C an act of pressing sth firmly ～をぎゅっと押す行為→**絞ること, 握りしめること, 握手をすること, 抱き締めること** ‖ *He gave her hand a squeeze and told her he loved her.* 彼は彼女の手をぎゅっと握りながら愛していると言った. ▶定義2 C the amount of liquid that you get from squeezing an orange, a lemon, etc オレンジ, レモンなどをしぼったときに得られる液体の量→**しぼったもの, (少量の)しぼり汁, 一しぼりの分量** ‖ *a squeeze of lemon* 一しぼりのレモン汁 ▶定義3 [単数扱い] a situation where there is not much space あまりスペースのない状況→**ぎっしり詰まっていること, 押し合い, 雑踏, すし詰め** ‖ *It was a tight squeeze to get everybody around the table.* 皆にテーブルを囲んで座ってもらうのは相当窮屈だった. ▶定義4 [C, 通常は単数] an effort to use less money, time, etc, especially with the result that there is not enough 結果的に不足の状態のままだが, 金・時間などの節約に努めること→**(経済上の)苦境, 困難な状況, (金融の)引き締め**

**squelch** /skweltʃ/ 動自 ▶定義 to make the sound your feet make when you are walking in deep wet mud 深いぬかるみの中を歩くときに出る音を出す→**ピシャピシャ音を立てる, 音を立てて歩く, グチャグチャ音を立てる, クチャクチャ音を立てる**

**squid** /skwɪd/ 名 C U (複 squid または squids) ▶定義 a sea animal that we eat with a long soft body and ten long parts (tentacles) 長くて柔らかい体をした10本の触腕を持つ食用の海生動物→**イカ** ☛ **octopus** のさし絵

**squiggle** /skwíɡ(ə)l/ 名 C略式 ▶定義 a quickly drawn line that goes in all directions 急いで書いたためにあちこちうねり回っている線→**(文字などの)くねった線, 走り書き, なぐり書き**

**squint** /skwɪnt/ 動自 ▶定義1 squint (at sth) to look at sth with your eyes almost closed 〜をほとんど目を閉じるようにして見る→目を細めて見る, 横目で見る ‖ to squint in bright sunlight 明るい日の光に目を細める ▶定義2 to have eyes that appear to look in different directions at the same time 同時に別々の方向を見ているように見える眼をしている→斜視である — squint 名 C →細目で見ること; 斜視

**squirm** /skwɜːm/ 動自 ▶定義 to move around in your chair because you are nervous, uncomfortable, etc 不安, 居心地の悪さなどのためいすの中であちこち体位を変える→もじもじする, もぞもぞする, 身もだえする

**squirrel** /skwɜːrəl/ 名 C ▶定義 a small red or grey animal with a long thick tail that lives in trees and eats nuts 樹上で生活し, 木の実を食べる小動物. 尾は長くて太く, 毛は赤または灰色をしている→リス

**squirt** /skwɜːrt/ 動自他 ▶定義 If a liquid squirts or if you squirt it, it is suddenly forced out of sth in a particular direction. 液体が〜から特定の方向にほとばしり出る, 液体を〜から特定の方向にほとばしらせる→噴出する, ほとばしる; 〜を噴出させる, (噴出させて)〜に吹き掛ける ‖ I cut the orange and juice squirted out. オレンジを切ると, 果汁がほとばしり出た. She squirted water on the flames. 彼女は炎目掛けて水を浴びせた. He squirted me with water. 彼は私に水を浴びせた. — squirt 名 C →噴出, ほとばしり, しぶき ‖ a squirt of lemon juice レモン果汁のしぶき

**Sr** 略 = SNR

**St** 略 ▶定義1 = SAINT ‖ St Peter 聖ペトロ ▶定義2 = STREET ‖ 20 Swan St スワン街20番地 ▶定義3 st 英 stone; a measure of weight ストーン; 重量の単位→ストーン

**stab**¹ /stæb/ 動他 (**stabbing**; **stabbed**) ▶定義 to push a knife or other pointed object into sb/sth 小刀などの先のとがった物を〜に押し込む→〜を刺す, 突き刺す, ひどく傷付ける ‖ The man had been stabbed in the back. その男性は背中を刺されていた. He stabbed a potato with his fork. 彼はフォークでジャガイモを突き刺した.

**stab**² /stæb/ 名 C ▶定義1 an injury that was caused by a knife, etc 小刀などで付けられた傷→刺し傷, 突き傷 ‖ He received stab wounds to his neck and back. 彼は首と背中に刺し傷を受けた. ▶定義2 a sudden sharp pain 突然の鋭い痛み→刺すような痛み, 激痛

成句 have a stab at sth/doing sth 略式 ▶定義 to try to do sth 〜をしてみようとする→〜を企てる, 試しにやってみる, ちょっと手を出してみる

**stabbing**¹ /stæbɪŋ/ 名 C ▶定義 an occasion when sb is injured or killed with a knife or other sharp object 小刀などの先のとがった物で負傷したり殺害されたりする事件→刺すこと, 刺し殺すこと, 刺殺(事件)

**stabbing**² /stæbɪŋ/ 形 (名詞の前だけ) ▶定義 (used about a pain) sudden and strong (痛みについて)突然の強い→刺すような

**stability** /stəbɪləti/ 名 U ▶定義 the state or quality of being steady and not changing 安定していて変化しない状態または性質→安定, 安定性, 安定度, 確固 ‖ After so much change we now need a period of stability. あれだけの大きな変革の後, 今安定期間を必要としている. The ladder is slightly wider at the bottom for greater stability. はしごは安定性を増すために, 底の部分が若干広くなっている. ⇔ **instability** ☛ 形 stable

**stabilize** (または **-ise**) /stéɪbəlaɪz/ 動自他 ▶定義 to become or to make sth firm, steady and unlikely to change しっかりと安定して変化しそうもない状態になる; 〜をそのような状態にする→安定する, 固定する; 〜を安定させる, 固定させる ‖ The patient's condition has stabilized. 患者の容態は安定したところだ. ☛参 destabilize

**stable**¹ /stéɪb(ə)l/ 形 ▶定義 steady, firm and unlikely to change 安定した, しっかりして, 変化しそうにない→安定した, びくともしない, 一定の, 不変の ‖ This ladder doesn't seem very stable. このはしごはあまり安定しているようには見えない. The patient is **in a stable condition**. その患者は安定した状態にある. ⇔ **unstable** ☛ 名 stability

**stable**² /stéɪb(ə)l/ 名 C ▶定義 a building where horses are kept 馬を飼っておく建物→馬小屋, 馬屋, 厩舎(きゅうしゃ)

**stack**¹ /stæk/ 名 C ▶定義1 a tidy pile of sth きちんと積み重ねられた〜→積み重ねた山, 山 ‖ a stack of plates/books/chairs 山積みにされた

皿・本・いす ▶定義2 略式 (しばしば複数形で) a lot of sth たくさんの〜→**多量, 多数, たくさん** ‖ *I've still got stacks of work to do.* まだしなければならない仕事が山ほどある.

**stack**² /stæk/ 動他 ▶定義 stock sth (up) to put sth into a tidy pile 〜をきちんとした山にする→**〜を積み重ねる[上げる], 山積みにする** ‖ *Could you stack those chairs for me?* 私のためにここにあるいすを積み重ねていただけませんか.

**stacked** /stækt/ 形 ▶定義 full of piles of things 積み上げた〜で一杯の→**山積みの** ‖ *The room was stacked high with books.* その部屋には本がうず高く積み上げられていた.

*****stadium** /stéɪdiəm/ 名 C ( 複 **stadiums** または **stadia** /-diə/) ▶定義 a large structure, usually with no roof, where people can sit and watch sport 人が座ってスポーツを観戦することのできる, 通常は屋根のない大きな建物→**(野外)競技場, 野球場, スタジアム**

*****staff** /stɑːf; stæf/ 名 [C, 通常は単数, U] ▶定義 the group of people who work for a particular organization ある特定の団体のために働く人たちの集団→**社員, 職員, 部員, 局員, スタッフ** ‖ *hotel/library/medical staff* ホテルの従業員・図書館の職員・医療スタッフ *Two **members of staff** will accompany the students on the school trip.* 職員のうち2人が修学旅行で生徒に付き添う予定だ. *The hotel has over 200 people **on its staff**.* そのホテルは200人以上の従業員を抱えている. *full-time/part-time staff* 常勤・非常勤職員 *a staffroom (= in a school)* (学校の) 職員室 ● staff は通常は単数形で用いられるが, 動詞は複数形を使う. *The staff all speak good English.* 職員は皆英語を上手に話す. — **staff** 動他 (通常は受動態で) → **〜に職員を配置・配属する** ‖ *The office is staffed 24 hours a day.* その事務所は24時間職員が配置されている.

**stag** /stæg/ 名 C ▶定義 the male of a type of large wild animal that eats grass (deer) 草を食べる大型の野生動物 (シカ) の雄→**雄ジカ** ● deer のさし絵

*****stage**¹ /stéɪdʒ/ 名 ▶定義1 C one part of the progress or development of sth 〜の経過または進展の一部→**段階, 時期, 局面** ‖ *The first stage of the course lasts for three weeks.* そのコースの第1段階は3週間続く. *I suggest we do the journey **in two stages**.* 旅行を2段階に分けてしてはどうだろうか. ***At this stage** it's too early to say what will happen.* 今の段階でこれから何が起こるかを言うのは早すぎる. ▶定義2 C a platform in a theatre, concert hall, etc on which actors, musicians, etc perform 劇場, コンサートホールなどで, 俳優, 音楽家らが演技, 演奏する一段高くなった場所→**舞台, 演壇, ステージ** ▶定義3 [単数扱い, U] the world of theatre; the profession of acting 演劇界; 俳優業→**演劇; 舞台活動, 俳優業, 演劇関係の仕事** ‖ *Her parents didn't want her to **go on the stage**.* 彼女の両親は彼女を役者にしたくなかった. *an actor of stage and screen* 舞台兼映画俳優

**stage**² /stéɪdʒ/ 動他 ▶定義1 to organize a performance of a play, concert, etc for the public 演劇, コンサートなどの公演を計画して催す→**〜を上演する, 公に催す** ▶定義2 to organize an event 行事を準備・主催する→**〜を企てる, 計画する, (華々しく)実現する** ‖ *They have decided to stage a 24-hour strike.* 彼らは24時間ストライキを行うことを決定した.

**stage manager** 名 C ▶定義 the person who is responsible for the stage, lights, scenery, etc during a theatre performance 芝居の上演中舞台, 照明, 舞台面などに責任を持つ人→**舞台監督, 舞台主任**

**stagger** /stǽgər/ 動自 ▶定義 to walk with short steps as if you could fall at any moment, for example because you are ill, drunk or carrying sth heavy 病気, 酩酊(めいてい), 重い荷物の運搬などのために, 狭い歩幅で今にも倒れそうに歩く→**ふらつく, よろめく, よろよろ歩く, 千鳥足で歩く** ‖ *He staggered across the finishing line and collapsed.* 彼はふらつきながらゴールインすると倒れてしまった.

**staggered** /stǽgərd/ 形 ▶定義1 略式 very surprised 非常に驚いた→**びっくりした, あぜんとした, 仰天した** ‖ *I was absolutely staggered when I heard the news.* 私はその知らせを聞いてびっくり仰天した. ▶定義2 (used about a set of times, payments, etc) arranged so that they do not all happen at the same time (一連の時間, 支払いなどについて) すべてが同時に起こらないように手配された→**互い違いに並んだ, ずらした, 時差別の** ‖ *staggered working hours (= when* people start and finish work at different times) 時差出勤 (= 人々が別々の時間に仕事を始め終えること)

**staggering** /stǽɡərɪŋ/ 形 ▶定義 that you find difficult to believe→信じ難い, 驚異的な — **staggeringly** 副 →驚くほど, 信じ難いほど

**stagnant** /stǽɡnənt/ 形 ▶定義1 (used about water) not flowing and therefore dirty and having an unpleasant smell (水について) 流れていないため汚れて嫌なにおいのする→よどんだ, 悪臭を放つ, 濁った ▶定義2 (used about business, etc) not active; not developing (景気などについて) 活発でない; 発展していない→停滞した, 沈滞した, 不活発な, 不景気な ‖ a stagnant economy 停滞した経済

**stagnate** /stæɡnéɪt, -´-/ 動 ⾃ ▶定義1 to stop developing, changing or being active 発展したり変化したり活動的であることをやめる→停滞する, 沈滞する, 不活発になる ‖ a stagnating economy 停滞している経済 ▶定義2 (used about water) to be or become stagnant (水について) よどんでいる, よどんだ状態になる→よどむ, 濁る, 流れない — **stagnation** /stæɡnéɪʃ(ə)n/ 名 Ⓤ →停滞, 沈滞, 不況, 不景気, よどみ

**stag night** (または **stag party**) 名 Ⓒ ▶定義 a party for men only that is given for a man just before his wedding day 結婚する男性のために式の前日開かれる男性だけのパーティー→結婚式前夜の男だけのパーティー, スタッグパーティー

▶ hen party と比較.

**staid** /stéɪd/ 形 ▶定義 serious, old-fashioned and rather boring まじめで旧式でやや退屈な→(人の中身・外見・趣味などが)(き)まじめな, 落ち着いた, 古風な, 謹厳な

*****stain** /stéɪn/ 動 ⾃ ⾃他 ▶定義 to leave a coloured mark that is difficult to remove 色の付いた取りにくい汚れを残す→染みが付く, 汚れる; ~に染みを付ける, ~を汚す ‖ Don't spill any of that red wine - it'll stain the carpet. その赤ワインを一滴もこぼさないでね - カーペットに染みが付くから. — **stain** 名 Ⓒ→染み, 汚れ, 汚点 ‖ The blood had left a stain on his shirt. その血は彼のシャツに染みを残していた. ☞ **blob** のさし絵

**stained glass** 名 Ⓤ ▶定義 pieces of coloured glass that are used in church windows, etc 教会の窓などに用いられる色の付いたガラス→ステンドグラス ‖ a stained-glass window ステンドグラスの窓

**stainless steel** 名 Ⓤ ▶定義 a type of steel that does not change colour or get damaged by water (rust) 変色したり水によって傷んだりしない(さびない)種類の鋼鉄→ステンレス, ステンレス鋼, ステンレススチール ‖ a stainless steel pan ステンレス製のなべ

*****stair** /stéər/ 名 ▶定義1 **stairs** [複数扱い] a series of steps inside a building that lead from one level to another 建物内の1つの階から次の階へと通じる連続した段→階段 ‖ a flight of stairs 一続きの階段 I heard somebody coming **down the stairs**. だれかが階段を下りていく音が聞こえた. She ran **up the stairs**. 彼女は階段を駆け上った. ☞参 **downstairs**, **upstairs**

▶ stair, step と比較. stairs, flights of stairs は通常は建物の内側にある階段を指す. steps は通常は建物の外側にあり, 石またはコンクリートで作られた階段を指す.

☞ C7 ページのさし絵 ▶定義2 Ⓒ one of the steps in a series inside a building 建物内の階段のうちの1段→階段の段, 1段

**staircase** /stéərkèɪs/ (または **stairway**) 名 Ⓒ
▶定義 a set of stairs with rails on each side that you can hold on to つかまることのできる横棒が両側に付いた一続きの階段→(手すり付きの)階段, はしご段; 階段室 ☞参 **escalator** ☞ C7 ページのさし絵

**stake**¹ /stéɪk/ 名 ▶定義1 Ⓒ a wooden or metal pole with a point at one end that you push into the ground 地面に突き刺して用いる一方の先がとがった木製または金属製の棒→くい, 棒, 支柱 ▶定義2 Ⓒ a part of a company, etc that you own, usually because you have put money into it 通常会社などに出資したことによるその会社における自己保有分→(事業への)出資分, 株, 利害(関係) ‖ Foreign investors now **have a** 20% **stake in** the company. 外国投資家たちは現在この会社の株の20パーセントを持っている.

▶定義3 **stakes** [複数扱い] the things that you might win or lose in a game or in a particular situation 勝負事またはある特定の状況で勝ち取ったり失ったりする物→かけ金, かけられたもの, 賞金 ‖ We play cards for money, but never for *very high stakes.* 私たちは金をかけてトランプをするが、決して高いかけ金で勝負することはない. **成句 at stake** ▶定義 in danger of being lost; at risk 負ける恐れがある;危険で➡**危険にさらされて,危うくなって** ‖ *He thought very carefully about the decision because he knew his future was at stake.* 彼は自分の将来が懸かっていることを知っていたため、その決定について非常に慎重に考えた.

**stake**² /stéɪk/ 動 他 ▶定義 **stake sth (on sth)** to put your future, etc in danger by doing sth, because you hope that it will bring you a good result 自分のする事は好結果をもたらすと信じて、それを実行して自らの将来などを危険にさらす➡**~を(…に)懸ける** ‖ *He is staking his political reputation on this issue.* 彼はこの問題に政治家としての名声を懸けている.

**成句 stake a/your claim (to sth)** ▶定義 to say that you have a right to have sth 自分は~を所有する権利があると言う➡**(~の)所有権を主張する,(~に対する)権利を主張する**

**句動詞 stake sth out** ▶定義**1** to clearly mark an area of land that you are going to use 使用しようとする土地の範囲にはっきりと印を付ける➡**~をくいで囲む,仕切る** ▶定義**2** to make your position, opinion, etc clear to everyone すべての人に自分の立場、意見などを明らかにする➡**~をはっきりさせる,明らかにする,明言する** ‖ *In his speech, the President staked out his position on tax reform.* 大統領は演説で税制改革に対する彼の立場を明らかにした. ▶定義**3** to watch a place secretly for a period of time ある一定時間ひそかにある場所を見続ける➡**~を見張る,張り込ませる** ‖ *The police had been staking out the house for months.* 警察は何か月もその家に張り込んでいた.

*★**stale** /stéɪl/ 形 ▶定義**1** (used about food or air) old and not fresh any more (食べ物または空気について)古くなり、もはや新鮮でない➡**古くて,新鮮でない,腐りかけた,気の抜けた,かび臭い,むっとする** ‖ *The bread will **go stale** if you don't put it away.* しまっておかないとそのパンは古くなってしまいますよ. ▶定義**2** not interesting or exciting any more 面白くなくなった、好奇心をそそらなくなった➡**新鮮さを失った,陳腐な,使い古された** ☛参 **fresh**

**stalemate** /stéɪlmèɪt/ 名 [単数扱い, U]

▶定義**1** a situation in an argument in which neither side can win or make any progress 議論でどちらの側も勝利または進展できない状態➡**こう着状態,行き詰まり,窮地** ▶定義**2** (in chess) a position in which a game ends without a winner because neither side can move (チェス)どちらの側も駒を動かすことができないため勝者なしにゲームを終える状態➡**ステールメート,手詰り**

**stalk**¹ /stɔːk/ 名 C ▶定義 one of the long thin parts of a plant which the flowers, leaves or fruit grow on 植物の細長い部分. そこに花・葉がついたり、果物がなる➡**茎,柄,幹** ☛ C3 ページのさし絵

**stalk**² /stɔːk/ 動 ▶定義**1** 他 to move slowly and quietly towards an animal in order to catch or kill it 捕まえる、殺すなどの目的で動物に向かってゆっくりとひそかに進んでいく➡**~に忍び寄る,~の後をそっと追う** ‖ *a lion stalking its prey* 獲物にそっと忍び寄るライオン ▶定義**2** 他 to follow a person over a period of time in a frightening or annoying way 人が怖がったり、迷惑がったりするような付きまとい方を一定期間する➡**そっと~の後を付ける,~にしつこく近付く** ‖ *The actress claimed the man had been stalking her for two years.* 女優はその男が2年間彼女に付きまとっていたと主張した. ▶定義**3** 自 to walk in an angry way 怒ったように歩く➡**怒った足取りで歩く,大またで歩く,闊歩(かっぽ)する**

**stall**¹ /stɔːl/ 名 ▶定義**1** C a small shop with an open front or a table with things for sale 店先または台の上に売り物を並べた小さな店➡**露店,屋台,売店** ‖ *a market stall* 市場の露店 *a bookstall at the station* 駅の本屋 ☛ C8 ページのさし絵 ▶定義**2 stalls** [複数扱い] the seats nearest the front in a theatre or cinema 劇場または映画館の最前部に最も近い座席➡**最前列の特別席,1階正面席** ▶定義**3** [C, 通常は単数] a situation in which a vehicle's engine suddenly stops because it is not receiving enough power 乗り物のエンジンが動力不足のため不意に作動しなくなる状態➡**エンスト,(航空機の)失速** ‖ *The plane went into a stall and almost crashed.* 飛行機が失速し、もう少しで墜落するところだった.

**stall**² /stɔːl/ 動 自 他 ▶定義**1** (used about a vehicle) to stop suddenly because the engine is not receiving enough power; to make a vehicle do this accidentally (乗り物について) エンジンに動力が十分回らないため不意に作動を停止する; 誤って乗り物をそのような状態にする **エンストする, 立ち往生する, 失速する; ～を立ち往生させる, エンストさせる, 失速させる** ‖ *The bus often stalls on this hill.* この丘ではしばしばバスがエンストする. *I kept stalling the car.* エンストを起こしてばかりいた. ▶定義2 to avoid doing sth or to try to stop sth happening until a later time 後まで～をしないでおく, または～が起こらないようにする→**(言い訳などをして, 時間などを) 稼ぐ, 言い逃れする; ～を待たせる, 遅らせる, 引き延ばす**

**stallion** /stǽljən/ 名 C ▶定義 an adult male horse, especially one that is kept for breeding 特に繁殖・改良用に飼われている大人の雄の馬→**種馬** ●参 horse の注

**stalwart** /stɔ́:lwərt/ 形 ▶定義 always loyal to the same organization, team, etc 常に同じ団体, チームなどに忠実な→**忠実な, 愛党心の強い, 信念の固い** ‖ *a stalwart supporter of the club* そのクラブ一筋の応援者 — **stalwart** 名 C→**愛党心の強い人, 信念の固い人**

**stamina** /stǽmənə/ 名 U ▶定義 the ability to do sth that involves a lot of physical or mental effort for a long time 長時間にわたって肉体的または知的努力を多く必要とする～を行う能力→**根気, 気力, 体力, 耐久力, スタミナ** ‖ *You need a lot of stamina to run long distances.* 長距離を走るにはものすごいスタミナがいる.

**stammer** /stǽmər/ 動 自 他 ▶定義 to speak with difficulty, repeating sounds and pausing before saying things correctly 正確に物を言う前に音を繰り返したりつかえたりして, 話しにくそうに話す→**どもる; ～をどもりながら言う, 口ごもる** ‖ *He stammered an apology and left quickly.* 彼は口ごもりながらわびを言うと素早く立ち去った. — **stammer** 名 [単数扱い]→**どもること, どもり, 口ごもり** ‖ *to have a stammer* どもる

★**stamp**¹ /stæmp/ 名 C ▶定義1 (または **postage stamp**) a small piece of paper that you stick onto a letter or package to show that you have paid for it to be posted 郵送費用が支払い済みであることを示すために手紙または小包にはり付ける小さな紙→**郵便切手, 印紙, 証紙** ‖ *a first-class/second-class stamp* 第1種・第2種郵便切手 *Barry's hobby is collecting stamps.* バリーの趣味は切手集めだ.

▶英国の郵便制度では, 国内のほかの区域に手紙などを郵送するための切手には first-class(第1種郵便)切手と second-class(第2種郵便)切手の2種類ある. 第1種郵便切手をはった手紙は費用がよりかかるが, より迅速に届く.

▶定義2 a small object that prints some words, a design, the date, etc when you press it onto a surface 押し付けると, 言葉, 模様, 日付などが印刷される小さな物→**印, 刻印機, 押し型, 打ち型, スタンプ** ‖ *a date stamp* 日付印 ▶定義3 the mark made by stamping sth onto a surface ～を強く押してできた印→**印, 刻印, 消印, スタンプ** ‖ *Have you got any visa stamps in your passport?* パスポートにビザの証印がありますか. (比喩) *The government has given the project its stamp of approval.* 政府はその事業に対して認可のお墨付きを与えた. ▶定義4 **the stamp of sth** [通常は単数] something that shows a particular quality or that sth was done by a particular person ある特質を示す, またはある特定の人がしたものであることを示す～**特徴, 特質, 印, 痕跡(こんせき)**

**stamp**² /stæmp/ 動 ▶定義1 自 他 **stamp (on sth)** to put your foot down very heavily and noisily 片足を激しくドスンと踏み下ろす→**(～を)踏み付ける, 踏み鳴らす, 踏んで～の状態にする** ‖ *He stamped on the spider and squashed it.* 彼はクモを踏み付けてぺちゃんこにした. *It was so cold that I had to stamp my feet to keep warm.* とても寒かったので, 足踏みして体を暖めなければならなかった. *She stamped her foot in anger.* 彼女は怒って片足で床をバンと踏み鳴らした. ▶定義2 自 to walk with loud heavy steps 大きな足音を立てて荒々しく歩く→**足を踏み鳴らして歩く, ドシンドシンと歩く** ‖ *She stamped around the room, shouting angrily.* 彼女は怒って声を張り上げながら, 足を踏み鳴らして部屋を歩き回った. ▶定義3 他 **stamp A (on B); stamp B (with A)** to print some words, a design, the date, etc by pressing a small object (a stamp) onto a surface 小さな物(スタンプ)を押し付けて言葉, 模様, 日付などを印刷する→(～

に)(…)の印を押す,～に(…の)印を押す,刻印する,検印を押す ‖ *to stamp a passport* パスポートに証印を押す

**stamp sth out** ▶定義 to put an end to sth completely ～を完全に終わらせる→**～を鎮圧する,撲滅する** ‖ *The police are trying to stamp out this kind of crime.* 警察はこの種の犯罪を撲滅しようとしている.

**stamped addressed envelope** (または **self-addressed envelope**) 名 C (略 sae) ▶定義 an empty envelope with your own name and address and a stamp on it that you send to a company, etc when you want sth sent back to you ～を返送してほしいときに会社などに郵送する,本人の氏名,住所を記入し切手をはった空の封筒→**返信用封筒**

**stampede** /stæmpíːd/ 名 C ▶定義 a situation in which a large number of animals or people start running in the same direction, for example because they are frightened or excited 恐怖または興奮などのため,多数の動物・人間が一斉に同じ方向に走り始める状況→**驚いてどっと逃げ出すこと,殺到** ― **stampede** 動→**どっと逃げ出す,殺到する**

**stance** /stæns/ 名 C, 通常は単数 ▶定義1 **stance (on sth)** the opinions sb expresses publicly about sth ～について…が公式に表明した意見→**(公にした)立場,態度,意見** ‖ *the Prime Minister's stance on foreign affairs* 外交問題に対する首相の態度 ▶定義2 the position in which somebody stands, especially when playing a sport 特にスポーツをするときの立つ位置→**構え,(立った)姿勢,(ゴルフ・野球の打者の)足の位置,スタンス**

★**stand**¹ /stænd/ 動 自 他 (過,過分 **stood** /stʊd/) ▶定義1 自 to be on your feet, not sitting or lying down; to be upright 座らず,横にならずに立っている;まっすぐに立っている→**立っている** ‖ *He was standing near the window.* 彼は窓辺に立っていた. ***Stand still - I'm trying to draw you!*** じっと立っていて － あなたを描こうとしているところだから. *Only a few houses were left standing after the earthquake.* 地震の後,崩れずに残っていた家はわずか数軒だった. ▶定義2 自 **stand (up)** to rise to your feet from another position 別の体位から立ち上がる→**立ち上がる,起立する** ‖ *He stood up when I entered the room.* 私が部屋に入ると,彼は立ち上がった. ▶定義3 to put sb/sth in a particular place or position ～をある特定の場所または位置に置く→**～を立てる,立て掛ける,立てて置く** ‖ *We stood the mirror against the wall while we decided where to hang it.* どこに掛けるか決めている間,とりあえず私たちは鏡を壁に立て掛けて置いた. ▶定義4 自 to be or to stay in a particular position or situation ある特定の位置または状況にあるまたはとどまる→**(～の)状態にある,～のままでいる,(～に)ある** ‖ *The castle stands on a hill.* その城は丘の上にある. *The house has stood empty for ten years.* その家は10年間空き家のままだ. ▶定義5 自 (used about an offer, a decision, etc) to stay the same as before, without being changed (提案,決定などについて) 変更されずに前と同じままである→**そのままである,変わらないでいる,有効である** ‖ *Does your decision still stand?* あなたの決定は依然として生きているのですか. *The world record has stood for ten years.* その世界記録は10年間塗り替えられていない. ▶定義6 自 **stand (at) sth** to be of a particular height, level, amount, etc ある特定の高さ,水準,量などである→**(人・建物などの)高さが～である,(温度計が)～度を示す** ‖ *The world record stands at 6.59 metres.* その世界記録は6メートル59だ. *The building stands nearly 60 metres high.* その建物は高さが60メートル近くある. ▶定義7 自 **stand (on sth)** to have an opinion or view about sth ～について意見または見解を持つ→**(～に)(賛成・反対の)立場を取る** ▶定義8 自 **stand to do sth** to be in a situation where you are likely to do sth ～をしそうな状況にある→**～しそうである,～する可能性がある** ‖ *If he has to sell the company, he stands to lose a lot of money.* 会社を売却しなければならないとしたら,彼は多額の金を失うことになりそうだ. ▶定義9 自 **stand (for/as sth)** to be one of the people hoping to be chosen in an election (*a candidate*) 選挙で当選したいと願う人たちの1人(候補者)になる→**(～に)立候補する,出馬する** ‖ *She's standing for the European Parliament.* 彼女は欧州議会に立候補している. ▶定義10 他 (否定文,疑問文で can, could と共に)to not

## 1582 stand²

like sb/sth at all; to hate sb/sth ～を全く好まない; ～を嫌う→～を我慢する, 辛抱する, 耐える‖ I can't stand that woman - she's so rude. 私はあの女に我慢がならない － 彼女は非常に無礼な人だ. I couldn't **stand the thought of** waiting another two hours so I went home. あと２時間待つなんて考えたくもなかったので家に帰った.

▶定義11 🔵(特に can, could と用いて)to be able to survive difficult conditions 困難な状況で生き抜くことができる→～に耐える, 持ちこたえる, 立ち向かう‖ Camels can stand extremely hot and cold temperatures. ラクダは極寒, 極暑に耐えられる. ☞類 **bear, take**

**句動詞** stand around ▶定義 to stand somewhere not doing anything 何もせずにある場所に立っている→何もしないで突っ立っている, じっとしている‖ A lot of people were just standing around outside. 大勢の人たちが外で何もせずに突っ立っていた.

stand aside ▶定義 to move to one side わきに移動する→わきへ寄る‖ People stood aside to let the police pass. 警察官を通すため, 人々はわきへ寄った.

stand back ▶定義 to move back 後ろに移動する→後ろへ下がる, 引っ込む, 身を引く‖ The policeman told everybody to stand back. 警察官は皆に後ろへ下がるように言った.

stand by ▶定義1 to be present, but do nothing in a situation ある状況に身を置くが何もしない→何もしないで見ている, 傍観する, 傍らにいる‖ How can you stand by and let them treat their animals like that? どうしてあなた方は, ただ黙って彼らに動物をあんな風に扱わせておけるのですか. ▶定義2 to be ready to act いつでも行動できる→待機する, 出番に備える, スタンバイする‖ The police are standing by in case there's trouble. 警察は問題が起きた場合に備えて待機している.

stand for sth ▶定義1 to be a short form of sth ～を省略した形である→～の略である, ～を表す, 意味する, 象徴する‖ What does BBC stand for? BBC は何の略ですか. ▶定義2 to support sth (such as an idea or opinion) (考えまたは意見など)～を支持する→～を支持する, ～の味方をする, ～に賛成する‖ I hate everything that the party stands for. その党が支持する事はすべて嫌いだ.

stand in (for sb) ▶定義 to take sb's place for a short time 短い期間～の代わりをする→(～の)代理を務める, 代役となる

stand out ▶定義 to be easily seen or noticed 見やすい, 気付きやすい→目立つ, 際立つ, 突出する

stand up ▶定義 to be or become vertical 直立しているまたは直立する→立っている, 立つ‖ You'll look taller if you stand up straight. まっすぐ立てばもっと背が高く見えるでしょう.

stand sb up 略式 ▶定義 to not appear when you have arranged to meet sb, especially a boyfriend or girlfriend 特に恋人など人に会う約束をしたのに現れない→～に待ちぼうけを食らわす, ～とのデートをすっぽかす, 約束を破る

stand up for sb/sth ▶定義 to say or do sth which shows that you support sb/sth ～の支持を表す事を言う, または行動をする→～を支持する, 擁護する, ～のために立ち上がる‖ I admire him. He really stands up for his rights. 彼には敬服する. 彼は自分の権利を守るために本当に立ち上がるからだ.

stand up to sb/sth ▶定義 to defend yourself against sb/sth who is stronger or more powerful より強いまたは権力のある～に立ち向かって自分自身を守る→～を恐れずに立ち向かう, ～に敢然と立ち向かう, ～に勇敢に対抗する

★**stand²** /stænd/ 🔵 ▶定義1 a table or object that holds or supports sth, often so that people can buy it or look at it 人が買ったり見たりすることができるように, ～を載せておく台→～立て, ～置き, ～掛け, 露店, 屋台‖ a newspaper/hamburger stand 新聞の売店・ハンバーガースタンド a company stand at a trade fair 見本市の企業の展示場 ▶定義2 a large structure where people can watch sport from seats arranged in rows that are low near the front and high near the back スポーツ観戦ができる大きな建造物. 座席は前列が低く, 後列が高くなるように配列されている→(野球場・競馬場などの)観覧席, スタンド ▶定義3 a **stand(on/against sth)** a strong effort to defend yourself or sth that you have a strong opinion about 自分自身または自分が確固とした考えを持っている～を守ろうとするたくましい努力→(～に対する・～に反対の)立場, 態度, 考え方, 見解‖ The workers have decided to **take/make a stand** against further job losses.

労働者たちはこれ以上の失業に反対の立場を取ることを決めた.

**★standard¹** /stǽndərd/ 名 C ▶定義1 a level of quality 質のレベル→**水準, 標準, 基準** ‖ *We complained about the low standard of service in the hotel.* 私たちはホテルのサービスの程度の低さについて苦情を言った. *This work is not **up to** your usual **standard**.* この作品はあなたのいつもの水準に達していない. ▶定義2 a level of quality that you compare sth else with 他との比較での質のレベル→**基準, 尺度, 規範** ‖ *By European **standards** this is a very expensive city.* ヨーロッパの基準ではこの都市は非常に物価が高い. *He is a brilliant player **by any standard**.* どの尺度から見ても彼はすばらしい選手だ. ▶定義3［通常は複数］a level of behaviour that is morally acceptable 道徳的に容認できる行動の基準→**基準, 手本, 模範, 道徳的規範** ‖ *Many people are worried about falling standards in modern society.* 大勢の人が現代社会のモラルの低下を心配している.

**standard²** /stǽndərd/ 形 ▶定義1 normal or average; not special or unusual 普通の, 平均的な; 特別でない, 異常でない→**標準の, 標準的な, 普通の, 並みの, 一般的な** ‖ *He's got long arms, so standard sizes of shirt don't fit him.* 彼は腕が長いので, 標準的なサイズのシャツは合わない. ▶定義2 that people generally accept as normal and correct 人々が一般的に普通で正しいと認める→**標準の, 基準となる, 容認できる** ‖ *standard English* 標準英語

**standardize**（または**-ise**）/stǽndərdàɪz/ 動他 ▶定義 to make things that are different the same 異なる～を同じにする→**～を規格化する, 標準化する** ‖ *Safety tests on old cars have been standardized throughout Europe.* 古い車の安全検査はヨーロッパ全体で標準化されている. ― standardization（または standardisation）/stændərdaɪzéɪʃ(ə)n; -dəzéɪ-/ 名 U →**規格化, 標準化, 画一化**

**standard of living** 名 C ▶定義 the amount of money and level of comfort that a particular person or group has ある特定の人または集団が有する金額または快適さの程度→**生活水準** ‖ *There is a higher standard of living in the north than in the south.* 北部の方が南部よりも生活水準が高い.

---

## standpoint 1583

▶同義の表現に living standards がある. この表現は複数形で用いられる: *Living standards have improved.*（生活水準が向上した.）

**standby** /stǽndbàɪ/ 名 ▶定義1（複 **standbys**) a thing or person that can be used if needed, for example if sb/sth is not available or in an emergency 人・物が求めに応じられない場合, または緊急の際など, 必要に応じて利用可能な人・物→**交代要員, 代役, 控え, 代替品, 予備** ‖ *We always keep candles **as a standby** in case there is a power cut.* 私たちは万一の送電停止に備えてろうそくをいつも予備に置いている. ▶定義2 U the state of being ready to do sth immediately if needed or if a ticket becomes available 必要に応じて, または券が手に入るようになった場合すぐに対応できる状態→**待機状態, キャンセル待ち** ‖ *Ambulances were **on standby** along the route of the marathon.* 救急車がマラソンのコースに沿って待機していた. *We were **put on standby** for the flight to Rome.* 私たちはローマ行きの飛行機のキャンセル待ちになった. ― standby 形（名詞の前だけ）→ **代役の, 控えの, 待機の, キャンセル待ちの** ‖ *a standby ticket/passenger* キャンセルで生じた券・キャンセル待ちの乗客

**standing¹** /stǽndɪŋ/ 名 U ▶定義1 the position that sb/sth has, or how people think of him/her/it ～が占める位置, また～に対する人々の評価→**立場, 地位, 身分, 評判** ‖ *The agreement has no legal standing.* その合意には法律的な有効性はない. ☛類 **status** ▶定義2 the amount of time during which sth has continued to exist ～が存在し続ける期間→**存続・持続期間, 継続**

**standing²** /stǽndɪŋ/ 形 ▶定義 that always exists; permanent 常に存在する; 恒久的な→**常置の, 常備の, 永続的な, 絶え間なく続く, 相変わらずの**

**standing order** 名 C ▶定義 an instruction to your bank to make a regular payment to sb from your account 銀行に対して自分の口座から～に定期的な支払いを行わせる指示→**自動振替依頼, 定期的支払い命令**

**standpoint** /stǽndpɔ̀ɪnt/ 名 C ▶定義 a particular way of thinking about sth ～についてのある特定の考え方→**見地, 立場, 観点, 見方** ☛類 **point of view**

## 1584 standstill

**standstill** /stǽndstɪl/ 名 [単数扱い] ▶定義 a situation when there is no movement, progress or activity 動き, 進展または活動が何もない状況→**停止, 休止, 行き詰まり, 足踏み状態** ‖ *The traffic is at/has come to a complete standstill.* 交通は完全に止まっている・止まった.

成句 grind to a halt/standstill ⇒ **GRIND**¹

**stank** STINK の過去形

**staple** /stéɪp(ə)l/ 名 C ▶定義 a small thin piece of bent wire that you push through pieces of paper using a special tool in order to fasten them together (stapler) 複数の紙をとじ合わすために, 特殊な道具(ホチキス)を使って紙に通す小さくて細い折り曲げられた針金→**ホチキスの針, とじ金** ☞ S4ページのさし絵 ― staple 動 他 →~をホチキスで留める, とじる ‖ *Staple the letter to the application form.* 申込書に手紙をホチキスで留めなさい. ― stapler 名 C→**ホチキス, 紙とじ機**

**staple diet** 名 [C, 通常は単数] ▶定義 the main food that a person or animal normally eats 人または動物が通常食べている主な食べ物→**主食, 基本食品** ‖ *a staple diet of rice and fish* 米と魚を主体とする常食

\*__star__¹ /stɑːr/ 名 ▶定義 1 a large ball of burning gas in outer space that you see as a small point of light in the sky at night 夜空に小さな光の点として見ることのできる, 大気圏外空間で燃えている大きなガスの球→**星, 恒星** ‖ *It was a clear night and the stars were shining brightly.* その夜は雲一つなく, 星が明るく輝いていた. ▶定義 2 C a shape, decoration, mark, etc with five or six points sticking out in a regular pattern 5つまたは6つの突起が規則正しく付いている形, 模様, 印など→**星形, 星章, 星印** ‖ *I've marked the possible candidates on the list with a star.* リストに載っている有力候補に星印を付けた. ☞ shape のさし絵 ▶定義 3 C a mark that represents a star that is used for telling you how good sth is, especially a hotel or restaurant 特にホテルまたはレストランなどの等級を示すのに用いられる星印→**星, 星印** ‖ *a five-star hotel* 5つ星のホテル ▶定義 4 C a famous person in acting, music or sport 演劇, 音楽, スポーツで有名な人→**花形, 人気者, スター** ‖ *a pop/rock/film/ movie star* ポップ・ロック・映画スター *a football/ tennis star* サッカー・テニスの花形選手 ▶定義 5 **stars** [複数扱い] = **HOROSCOPE**

**star**² /stɑːr/ 動 (**starring**; **starred**) ▶定義 1 自 **star (in sth)** to be one of the main actors in a play, film, etc 演劇, 映画などの主役の1人である→**(~で)主役を務める, (~に)主演する** ‖ *Gwyneth Paltrow is to star in a new romantic comedy.* グウィネス パルトロウは新しいロマンチックコメディーで主演することになっている.

▶定義 2 他 to have sb as a star→**~を主役にする, 主演させる** ‖ *The film stars Kate Winslett.* その映画はケート ウィンスレットが主演している.

**starboard** /stɑ́ːrbɔ̀ːrd, -bərd/ 名 U ▶定義 the side of a ship that is on the right when you are facing towards the front of it 船首に向かって船の右側の側面→**右舷(うげん), 右側** ⇔ **port**

**starch** /stɑːrtʃ/ 名 C U ▶定義 1 a white substance that is found in foods such as potatoes, rice and bread ジャガイモ, 米, パンなどの食物にある白い物質→**でんぷん, でんぷん食品** ▶定義 2 a substance that is used for making cloth rigid 布を固くするのに用いられる物質→**(洗濯用)のり**

**stardom** /stɑ́ːrdəm/ 名 U ▶定義 the state of being a famous person in acting, music or sport 演劇, 音楽, スポーツで有名人であるという状態→**スターの地位, スターの身分, スターダム** ‖ *She shot to stardom in a Broadway musical.* 彼女は一躍ブロードウェーミュージカルのスターの地位に踊り出た.

\*__stare__ /steər/ 動 自 ▶定義 **stare (at sb/sth)** to look at sb or sth for a long time because you are surprised, shocked, etc 驚きまたは衝撃などのために, ~を長い間見る→**(~を)見詰める, じっと見る, 凝視する** ‖ *Everybody stared at his hat.* だれもが彼の帽子をじろじろ眺めた. *He didn't reply, he just stared into the distance.* 彼は答えずに遠くをじっと見詰めるだけだった.

**stark**¹ /stɑːrk/ 形 ▶定義 1 very empty and without decoration and therefore not attractive 非常にがらんとして, 装飾がなく, そのため魅力的でない→**空っぽの, がらんとした, 飾りのない寒々とした** ‖ *a stark landscape* 荒涼とした景色 ▶定義 2 unpleasant and impossible to avoid 不愉快で避けることのできない→**容赦のない, どうしようもない, 動かしようのない** ‖ *He now faces*

the **stark reality** of life in prison. 彼は今,刑務所暮らしという逃れられない現実に直面している.
▶定義3 very different to sth in a way that is easy to see 容易に見て取れるほど〜と大きく異なる➡**くっきりとした,あからさまな,赤裸々な,(対照が)際立った**

**stark**² /stɑːrk/ 副 ▶定義 completely; extremely 完全に;極端に➡**全く,完全に** ‖ *stark naked* 丸裸の *Have you gone stark raving mad?* 完全に気でも狂ったのか.

**starlight** /stάːrlaɪt/ 名 Ⓤ ▶定義 the light that is sent out by stars in the sky 空の星が放つ光➡**星の光,星明かり**

**starry** /stάːri/ 形 ▶定義 full of stars 星が一杯の➡**星の多い,星の光に照らされた,星明かりの** ‖ *a starry night* 星の降る夜

\***start**¹ /stɑːrt/ 動 ▶定義1 🗎 ⓘ **start (sth/to do sth/doing sth)** to begin doing sth 〜をし始める➡**始まる;〜を始める,開始する** ‖ *Turn over your exam papers and start now.* 試験用紙を裏返して始めなさい. *We'll have to start (= leave) early if we want to be in Dover by 10.00.* 10時までにドーバーに着いていたいのならば,私たちは早く出発しなければ(=たたなければ)ならない. *Prices start at £5.* お値段は5ポンドからございます. *After waiting for an hour, the customers started to complain.* 客は1時間待った後,苦情を言い始めた. *She started playing the piano when she was six.* 彼女は6歳の時にピアノを弾き始めた. *What time do you have to* **start work** *in the morning?* 朝何時に仕事を始めなければならないのですか. ▶定義2 🗎 ⓘ to begin or to make sth begin to happen 始まる;〜を始めさせる➡**始まる;〜に始めさせる,〜を始める** ‖ *What time does the concert start?* コンサートは何時に始まりますか. *I'd like to start the meeting now.* それでは会議を始めたいと思います. *The police think a young woman may have started the fire.* 警察は若い女がその火事を起こしたのかもしれないと考えている. ☛参 **begin** の注 ▶定義3 🗎 ⓘ **start (sth) (up)** (used about a machine, etc) to begin to work; to make an engine, a car, etc begin to work (機械などについて)作動し始める;エンジン,自動車などを始動する➡**動き始める;(〜を)始動させる** ‖ *The car won't start.* 車がどうしても動かない. *We heard an engine starting up in the street.* 私たちは通りでエンジンがかかる音を聞いた. *He got onto his motor bike, started the engine and rode away.* 彼はオートバイに乗り,エンジンをかけ,走り去った. ▶定義4 🗎 ⓘ **start (sth) (up)** to create a company, an organization, etc; to begin to exist 会社,組織などを新しく作る;存在し始める➡**〜を起こす,設立する;現れる,生じる,起こる** ‖ *They've decided to start their own business.* 彼らは自分たちの事業を起こすことを決心した. *There are a lot of new companies starting up in that area now.* 現在,その領域で多くの新しい企業が登場している. ▶定義5 ⓘ to make a sudden, quick movement because you are surprised or afraid 驚きまたは不安からいきなり急な動きをする➡**ぎくっとする,はっとする,びくっと動く,飛び上がる** ‖ *A loud noise outside made me start.* 外で大きな音がして私はびくっとした.

**成句** get/start off on the right/wrong foot (with sb) ⇒ **FOOT**¹

**to start (off) with** ▶定義1 used for giving your first reason for sth 〜に対する第1の理由を述べるのに用いて➡**まず第1に,そもそも** ‖ *'Why are you so angry?' 'Well, to start off with, you're late, and secondly you've lied to me.'* 「なんでそんなに怒っているのか」「ええと,まずは君が遅刻したから,次に君が僕にうそをついたから」▶定義2 in the beginning; at first➡**初めは,最初は** ‖ *Everything was fine to start with, but the marriage quickly deteriorated.* 初めはすべてが順調だったが,結婚生活はすぐにまずくなってしまった.

**set/start the ball rolling** ⇒ **BALL**

**句動詞** **start off** ▶定義 to begin in a particular way ある特定の方法で始める➡**(〜で)始める,活動し始める** ‖ *I'd like to start off by welcoming you all to Leeds.* 皆さんリーズへようこそと歓迎の言葉で私のあいさつを始めたいと思います.

**start on sth** ▶定義 to begin doing sth that needs to be done する必要のある〜をし始める➡**(〜を)始める,(〜に)着手する,取り掛かる**

**start out** ▶定義 to begin your life, career, etc in a particular way that changed later 人生,職歴などを後で変化することになる特定の方法で始める➡**人生を始める,仕事を始める,社会に出る** ‖

## 1586 start²

*She started out as a teacher in Glasgow.* 彼女はグラスゴーで教師として出発した.

start over 米 ▶定義 to begin again 再び開始する→**再出発する, やり直す**

★**start²** /stɑːrt/ 名 ▶定義 1 [C, 通常は単数] the point at which sth begins ～が始まる時点→**始まり, 開始, 出発点, 出だし** ‖ *The chairman made a short speech at the start of the meeting.* 会議の初めに議長が短い演説を行った. *I told you it was a bad idea from the start.* 最初からそれは悪い考えだとあなたに言ったでしょう. ▶定義 2 [C, 通常は単数] the action or process of starting ～を始めるという行為または過程→**始まり, 開始, 着手, 始動** ‖ *to make a fresh start (= do sth again in a different way)* 新規まき直しをする (= 別の方法でもう一度～を行う) ▶定義 3 **the start** [単数扱い] the place where a race begins 競争が始まる地点→**スタート地点, スタートライン** ‖ *The athletes are now lining up at the start.* 選手たちは今スタートラインに一直線に並んでいる. ▶定義 4 [C, 通常は単数] an amount of time or distance that you give to a weaker person at the beginning of a race, game, etc 競争, ゲームなどの初めに, 弱い者に与えられる時間または距離→**先発権; 有利な立場**

▶ head start と比較.

▶定義 5 [C, 通常は単数] a sudden quick movement that your body makes because you are surprised or afraid 驚きまたは不安から体がいきなり急な動きをすること→**ぎくっとすること, はっとすること, びくっという動き, 飛び上がり** ‖ *She woke up with a start.* 彼女ははっとして目を覚ました.

成句 **for a start** (口語) ▶定義 (used to emphasize your first reason for sth) (～に対する第1の理由を強調するために用いて)→**第1に, まず, 手始めに** ‖ *'Why can't we go on holiday?' 'Well, for a start we can't afford it...'* 「なんでうちは休暇に出掛けられないの」「ええと, 第1に, うちにはそんな余裕がないからよ」

get off to a good, bad, etc start ▶定義 to start well, badly, etc うまい, 下手な, 出だしをする→**好調な・不調なスタートを切る, 調子良く・悪く始める**

get off to a flying start ⇒ **FLYING**

**starter** /stɑːrtər/ (米 通常は **appetizer**) 名 C ▶定義 a small amount of food that is served before the main course of a meal 食事のメインコースの前に出される少量の食べ物→**最初に出る料理, 前菜**

**starting point** 名 C starting point (for sth) ▶定義 1 an idea or topic that you use to begin a discussion with 議論の出発点となる考えまたはトピック→**出発点, 起点** ▶定義 2 the place where you begin a journey 旅行を始める場所→**出発点, 出発地**

**startle** /stɑːrtl/ 動 他 ▶定義 to surprise sb/sth in a way that slightly shocks or frightens him/her/it ～に多少の衝撃や恐怖を与えるような驚かせ方をする→**～をびっくりさせる, ギョッとさせる, 仰天させる** ‖ *The gunshot startled the horses.* 銃声に馬たちが飛び上がった. — **startled** 形→**びっくりする, 仰天する, 驚く** — **startling** /stɑːrtlɪŋ/ 形→**びっくりさせるような, 驚くべき**

**starvation** /stɑːrˈveɪʃ(ə)n/ 名 U ▶定義 suffering or death because there is not enough food 食料が不十分なために苦しむこと, または死ぬこと→**飢餓, 餓死, 窮乏, 欠乏** ‖ *to die of starvation* 餓死する

★**starve** /stɑːrv/ 動 自 他 ▶定義 to suffer or die because you do not have enough food to eat; to make sb/sth suffer or die in this way 食料不足で苦しむ, または死ぬ; ～をそのようにして苦しめるまたは死なせる→**飢える, 飢えに苦しむ, 餓死する; ～を飢えさせる, 餓死させる** ‖ *Millions of people are starving in the poorer countries of the world.* 世界中の貧しい国々では何百万人という人が飢餓に苦しんでいる. *That winter many aminals starved to death.* その冬, 数多くの動物が餓死した.

成句 **be starved of sth** ▶定義 to suffer because you are not getting enough of sth that you need 必要な～を十分得ていないため苦しむ→**～に飢えている, ～が不足している** ‖ *The children had been starved of love and affection for years.* 子供たちは長い間愛情に飢えていた.

**be starving** 略式 ▶定義 to be extremely hungry→**とても空腹である, はらぺこである**

★**state¹** /steɪt/ 名 ▶定義 1 C the mental, emotional or physical condition that sb/sth is in at a particular time ある特定の時点での～の, 精神

的,感情的または物理的な状態➔**状態,様子,有り様,事態,形勢,状況** ‖ *the state of the economy* 経済状態 *He is in a state of shock.* 彼はショック状態にある. *The house is in a terrible state.* その家はひどい有り様だ. ▶定義**2**（または **State**）**C** a country considered as an organized political community controlled by one government 1つの政府で統制されている組織化された政治的共同体と見なされる国➔**国,国家** ‖ *Pakistan has been an independent state since 1947.* パキスタンは1947年以来独立国家となっている. ☛参 **country** の注 ▶定義**3**（特に **the State**）**U** the government of a country 国の政府➔**政府** ‖ *affairs/matters of state* 国事 *the relationship between the Church and the State* 教会と国家の関係 *a state-owned company* 国有企業 *She went to a state school.* 彼女は公立学校に通った. *heads of State (= government leaders)* 国家元首（= 政府指導者）▶定義**4**（または **State**）**C** an organized political community forming part of a country 国の一部を構成する組織的政治共同体➔**州** ‖ *the southern States of the US* アメリカ南部の州

➤ **county**, **province** と比較.

▶定義**5** **U** the formal ceremonies connected with high levels of government or with the leaders of countries 政府の上層部または国の指導者たちに関する正式な儀式➔**公式,儀式** ‖ *The Queen is going on a state visit to China.* 女王が中国に公式訪問する予定だ. ▶定義**6 the States** [複数扱い] 略式 the United States of America アメリカ合衆国➔**アメリカ,米国** ‖ *We lived in the States for about five years.* 私たちは5年ほどアメリカで暮らしていた.

成句 **be in/get into a state** 特に 英 略式 ▶定義 to be or become very nervous or upset 非常にいらいらしている・いらいらする,非常に動揺している・動揺する➔**取り乱している・取り乱す,いらいらしている・いらいらする** ‖ *Now don't get into a state! I'm sure everything will be all right.* おいおい,がたがたするのはやめろよ. すべてうまくいくこと,請け合いだよ.

**state of affairs** ▶定義 a situation 状況➔**状況,状態,事態** ‖ *This state of affairs must not be allowed to continue.* この事態をこのまま存続させるわけにはいかない.

**state of mind** ▶定義 mental condition 精神状態➔**精神状態,心理状態** ‖ *She's in a very confused state of mind.* 彼女は非常に混乱した精神状態にある.

*****state**[2] /stéɪt/ 動他 ▶定義 to say or write sth, especially formally ～を特に正式に言うまたは書く➔**(正式に)述べる,言明する,表明する** ‖ *Your letter states that you sent the goods on 31 March, but we have never received them.* 手紙には商品は3月31日に発送したと書かれていますが,こちらではまだ受け取っておりません.

**stately** /stéɪtli/ 形 ▶定義 formal and impressive 格式高く印象的な➔**威厳のある,堂々とした,荘厳な** ‖ *a stately old building* 風格のある古い建物

**stately home** 名 **C** 英 ▶定義 a large old house that has historical interest and can be visited by the public 一般の人が訪れることのできる歴史的な重要性を持つ大きな古い家➔**(一般公開されている田舎の)大邸宅,カントリーハウス,館(やかた)**

*****statement** /stéɪtmənt/ 名 **C** ▶定義**1** something that you say or write, especially formally 特に正式に口頭または書面で述べられたもの➔**声明(書),言明,申し立て** ‖ *The Prime Minister will **make a statement** about the defence cuts today.* 総理大臣は本日防衛費の削減について声明を発表する予定だ. ▶定義**2** = **BANK STATEMENT**

**statesman** /stéɪtsmən/ 名 **C**（複 **-men** /-mən/）▶定義 an important and experienced politician who has earned public respect 一般大衆の尊敬を得ている有力で経験豊富な政治家➔**政治家**

**static**[1] /stætɪk/ 形 ▶定義 not moving, changing or developing 動かない,変わらない,進展しない➔**静止状態の,固定状態の,動きのない,活気のない** ‖ *House prices are static.* 住宅価格には動きがない.

**static**[2] /stætɪk/ 名 **U** ▶定義**1** sudden noises that disturb radio or television signals, caused by electricity in the atmosphere 大気中の電気によって生じる,ラジオまたはテレビの信号を妨害する突然の雑音➔**空電,空電による雑音,空電障害** ▶定義**2**（または **static electricity**）electricity that collects on a surface 表面にたまっている電気➔**静電気** ‖ *My hair gets full of static when I brush it.* ブラシをかけると私の髪に静電気が一

杯起きる.

**＊station¹** /stéɪʃ(ə)n/ 名 C ▶定義1 (または **railway station**) a building on a railway line where trains stop so that passengers can get on and off 乗客が乗り降りできるように列車が停車する鉄道の建物→**駅,鉄道駅,停車駅** ▶定義2 (通常は複合名詞で) a building from which buses begin and end journeys バスの発着用建物→**バス発着所,停留所** ▶定義3 (通常は複合名詞で) a building where a particular service or activity is based ある特定のサービスまたは活動の拠点となる場所→**署,局,所,事業所,本部** || *a police/fire station* 警察署・消防署 *a petrol station* ガソリンスタンド *a power station (= where electricity is generated)* 発電所 (= 電力を発生させる場所) ▶定義4 (しばしば複合名詞で) a radio or television company and the programmes it sends out ラジオ・テレビ局とそこから,送信される番組→**ラジオ局,テレビ局,ラジオ番組,テレビ番組** || *a local radio/TV station* 地元のラジオ局・テレビ局 *He tuned in to another station.* 彼は別の局にチャンネルを合わせた. ☞ 参 channel

**station²** /stéɪʃ(ə)n/ 動 (しばしば受動態で) ▶定義 to send sb, especially members of the armed forces, to work in a place for a period of time 特に軍の要員など,〜を一定期間ある場所で働かすため送り出す→**〜を部署に就かせる,配置する,駐在させる,駐屯させる**

**stationary** /stéɪʃ(ə)nəri, -èri/ 形 ▶定義 not moving 動いていない→**動かない,静止した,止まっている,変化のない,固定の** || *He crashed into the back of a stationary vehicle.* 彼は停車中の車両の後ろに衝突した.

**stationer's** /stéɪʃ(ə)nərz/ 名 [単数扱い] ▶定義 a shop that sells writing equipment, such as paper, pens, envelopes, etc 紙,ペン,封筒などの筆記用具を販売する店→**文具店,文房具店**

**＊stationery** /stéɪʃ(ə)n(ə)ri, -nèri/ 名 U ▶定義 writing equipment, for example pens, pencils, paper, envelopes ペン,鉛筆,紙,封筒などの筆記用具→**筆記用具,文具,文房具,事務用品** ☞ S4ページのさし絵

**station wagon** 米 = ESTATE CAR

**statistics** /stətístɪks/ 名 ▶定義1 [複数扱い] numbers that have been collected in order to provide information about sth 〜について情報を提供するために収集された数字→**統計,統計データ,統計表** || *Statistics indicate that 90% of homes in this country have a television.* 統計によればこの国の家庭の90パーセントがテレビを所有している. *crime statistics* 犯罪統計 ▶定義2 U the science of collecting and studying these numbers これらの数字を収集して研究する学問→**統計学** ― **statistical** /stətístɪk(ə)l/ 形→**統計の,統計的な,統計上の,統計学に基づく** || *statistical information* 統計データ ― **statistically** /-k(ə)li/ 副→**統計的に,統計上,統計学に基づいて**

**＊statue** /stǽtʃuː/ 名 C ▶定義 a figure of a person or animal that is made of stone or metal and usually put in a public place 石または金属でできた,通常は公共の場所に置かれる人または動物の像→**像,石像,銅像** ☞ column のさし絵

**stature** /stǽtʃər/ 名 U (文) ▶定義1 the importance and respect that sb has because people have a high opinion of his/her skill or of what he/she has done 技量,業績などに対する世間の高い評価によって得られる威信・信望→**名声,威信,偉大さ** ▶定義2 the height of a person 人の背の高さ→**身長,背丈,背** || *He's quite small in stature.* 彼はかなり背が低い.

**status** /stéɪtəs, stǽt-/ 名 ▶定義1 U the legal position of a person, group or country 人,集団または国の法的な地位→**(法)身分** || *Please indicate your name, age and marital status (= whether you are married or single).* 氏名,年齢,配偶関係 (= 結婚しているか独身か) を述べてください. *They were granted refugee status.* 彼らには難民の身分が認められた. ▶定義2 [単数扱い] your social or professional position in relation to other people 他と比較した場合の自分の社会的または職業的地位→**地位,身分,資格** || *Teachers don't have a very high status in this country.* この国では教師の地位はあまり高くない. ☞ 類 standing ▶定義3 U a high social position→**高い社会的地位,高い身分,ステータス,信望** || *The new job gave him much more status.* 新しい仕事に就いて,彼の社会的信用ははるかに高まった.

**the status quo** /stèɪtəs kwóʊ/ 名 [単数扱い] ▶定義 the situation as it is now, or as it was before a recent change 現にある状態,または最近の変化以前にかつてあった状態→**現状**

**status symbol** 名 C ▶定義 something that a person owns that shows that he/she has a high position in society and a lot of money 高い社会的地位と金をたくさん持っていることを示す所有物➡**地位の象徴, 身分の象徴, ステータスシンボル**

**statute** /stǽtʃuːt/ 名 C 正式 ▶定義 a law or a rule 法律, 規則➡**法令, 法規, 成文法**

**statutory** /stǽtʃət(ə)ri, -tɔːri/ 形 正式 ▶定義 decided by law 法律で定められた➡**制定法の, 制定法上の, 制定令によって定められた** ‖ *a statutory right* 法定の権利

**staunch** /stɔːntʃ/ 形 ▶定義 believing in sb/sth or supporting sb/sth very strongly; loyal ～を非常に強く信じるまたは支持する; 忠実な➡**信頼できる, 頼りになる, 堅実な, 忠実な**

**stave** /stéɪv/ 動
句動詞 **stave sth off** ▶定義 to stop sth unpleasant from happening now, although it may happen at a later time; to delay sth 後で起こるかもしれないが, 不快な～が今起きないようにする; ～を遅らせる➡**～(危険・破滅など)を(一時的に)食い止める; 遅らせる** ‖ *to stave off hunger/illness/inflation/bankruptcy* 飢え・病気・インフレ・倒産を食い止める

*★**stay**¹ /stéɪ/ 動 自 ▶定義1 to continue to be somewhere and not go away ある場所にずっといて, どこへも行かない➡**とどまる, じっとしている, いる** ‖ *Patrick stayed in bed until 11 o'clock.* パトリックは11時まで寝ていた. *I can't stay long.* 長くとどまっていられない. *Stay on this road until you get to Wells.* ウェルズに着くまでこの道をずっと進んでいきなさい. *Pete's staying late at the office tonight.* ピートは今夜遅くまで事務所にいる予定だ. ▶定義2 to continue to be in a particular state or situation without change 変化せずに依然としてある特定の状態または状況のままでいる・ある➡**～のままでいる, ～のままである, ～の状態を保つ** ‖ *I can't stay awake any longer.* もうこれ以上目を開けていられない. *I don't know why they stay together (= continue to be married or in a relationship).* どうして彼らがずっと一緒にいるのか(= ずっと結婚し続けている, または恋愛[性的]関係を続けているのか)分からない.

▶ remainとstayは意味が似ているが, remainの方が改まった表現である.

▶定義3 to live in a place temporarily as a visitor or guest 訪問者または客として一時的にある場所に住む➡**滞在する, 泊まる, 住む** ‖ *We stayed with friends in France.* 私たちはフランスで友人たちの家に泊まった. *Which hotel are you staying at?* どこのホテルに泊まっていらっしゃるのですか. *Can you stay for lunch?* お昼ご飯を食べていきませんか. *Why don't you stay the night?* 今夜泊まっていきませんか.

成句 **stay put** 略式 ▶定義 to continue in one place; to not leave ある1つの場所にとどまる; 立ち去らない➡**動かないでいる, そのままでいる**

句動詞 **stay behind** ▶定義 to not leave a place after other people have gone ほかの人たちが行った後もある場所を立ち去らない➡**居残る, 残る, 後に残る** ‖ *I'll stay behind and help you wash up.* 残って後片付けを手伝いますよ.

**stay in** ▶定義 to remain at home and not go out 家にとどまって出掛けない➡**家にいる, 外出しない, 居残る** ‖ *I'm going to stay in and watch TV.* 家にいてテレビを見るつもりだ.

**stay on (at...)** ▶定義 to continue studying, working, etc somewhere for longer than expected or after other people have left 予期していたよりも長く, またはほかの人たちが立ち去った後もある場所で勉強, 仕事などを続ける➡**(任務・年限などの後も)(～に)居続ける, 留任する**

**stay out** ▶定義 to continue to be away from your house, especially late at night 特に夜遅くずっと家から出たままでいる➡**外に出ている, 家に帰らない, 外出したままである**

**stay up** ▶定義 to go to bed later than usual 通常よりも遅く就寝する➡**遅くまで起きている, 寝ずに起きている, 寝ないでいる** ‖ *I'm going to stay up to watch the late film.* 深夜映画を見るために寝ないで起きているつもりだ.

**stay**² /stéɪ/ 名 C ▶定義 a period of time that you spend somewhere as a visitor or guest 訪問者または客としてある場所で過ごす期間➡**滞在期間, 滞在, 逗留(とうりゅう)** ‖ *Did you enjoy your stay in Crete?* クレタ島での滞在は楽しかったですか.

**STD** /ès tiː díː/ 略 ▶定義1 英 subscriber trunk dialling; the system by which you can make long-distance telephone calls direct 直接長距離

1590 steady

電話をかけることのできるシステム→加入者長距離直通方式, 局外直接ダイヤル方式
▶定義2 sexually transmitted disease→性行為で感染する病気, 性行為感染症, 性病

\*steady¹ /stédi/ 形 (steadier; steadiest)
▶定義1 developing, growing or happening gradually and at a regular rate 徐々に, かつ一定の速度で進展, 成長または発生する→一定の, 一様の, むらのない, 間断のない, 規則的な ‖ a steady increase/decline 着実な増加・減少
▶定義2 staying the same; not changing and therefore safe 同じ状態のままである; 変わらないので安全な→不変の, 安定した, 決まった, 定まった ‖ a steady job/income 定職・定収入
▶定義3 firmly fixed, supported or balanced; not shaking or likely to fall down しっかり固定された, 支えられたまたはバランスの取れた; 揺れていない, 落ちそうにない→安定した, ぐらつかない, 不動の, 確固とした ‖ You need a **steady hand** to take good photographs. 良い写真を撮るには手ぶれしないようにしなくてはならない. He held the ladder steady as she climbed up it. 彼女がはしごを上る時, 彼ははしごがぐらつかないように押さえた. — **steadily** 副 →着々と, 着実に, 絶え間なく, しっかりと ‖ Unemployment has risen steadily since April 1998. 1998年4月以降, 失業率がどんどん上昇している.

steady² /stédi/ 動 自他 (現分 steadying; 三単現 steadies; 過, 過分 steadied) ▶定義 to stop yourself/sb/sth from moving, shaking or falling; to stop moving, shaking or falling 自分自身, またはほかの~が動いたり, 揺れたり, 倒れたりしないようにする; 動き, 揺れ, 転落を止める→安定する, 落ち着く; ~を安定させる, 落ち着かせる, 固定する ‖ She thought she was going to fall, so she put out a hand to steady herself. 彼女は自分が転びそうだと思ったので転ぶまいと(何かにつかまるため)手を伸ばした. He had to **steady his nerves/voice** before beginning his speech. 演説を始める前に彼は神経・声を落ち着かせなければならなかった.

steak /stéɪk/ 名 C U ▶定義 a thick flat piece of meat or fish 肉または魚の厚くて平らな切り身→ステーキ, 牛肉・魚肉の厚い切り身 ‖ a piece of steak 1枚のステーキ a cod/salmon steak タラ・サケのステーキ ☛参 **chop²** ☛ C4ページのさし絵

\*steal /stíːl/ 動 (過 stole /stóʊl/; 過分 stolen /stóʊlən/) ▶定義1 自他 steal (sth) (from sb/sth) to take sth from a person, shop, etc without permission and without intending to return it or pay for it 許可を得ず, 返すまたは代金を支払うつもりもなしに人, 店などから~を取る→(~を)(…から)盗む, こっそり取る, 盗みをする ‖ The terrorists were driving a stolen car. テロリストたちは盗難車を運転していた. We found out she had been stealing from us for years. 私たちは彼女が長年にわたって私たちからこっそり盗んでいたことを知った.

▶物を盗む場合にはsteal, 人や場所から物を強奪する場合にはrobを用いる: My camera has been stolen! (私のカメラが盗まれた.) I've been robbed! (私は強盗に襲われた.) to rob a bank (銀行強盗を働く)

☛参 **thief** の注 ▶定義2 自 steal away, in, out, etc to move somewhere secretly and quietly ひそかに静かにある場所に移動する→そっと立ち去る, 忍び込む, ひそかに抜け出る

stealth /stélθ/ 名 U 正式 ▶定義 behaviour that is secret or quiet 秘密の, または静かな行動→こっそりすること, ひそかなやり方, 内密 — stealthy 形 →人目を盗んだ, ひそかな ‖ a stealthy approach/movement 人目を忍んだ接近・行動 — stealthily 副 →ひそかに, こっそりと

\*steam¹ /stíːm/ 名 U ▶定義 the hot gas that is produced by boiling water 水を沸騰させるときに出る熱い気体→蒸気, 水蒸気, 湯気, スチーム ‖ Steam was rising from the coffee. 湯気がコーヒーから立ち上っていた. a steam engine (= that uses the power of steam) 蒸気機関(= 蒸気の力を用いるエンジン)

成句 **let off steam** 略式 ▶定義 to get rid of energy or express strong feeling by behaving in a noisy or wild way 騒々しく, または荒々しく振る舞って, 精力または強い感情を発散させる→精力を発散する, うっぷんを晴らす

**run out of steam** ▶定義 to gradually lose energy or enthusiasm 徐々に気力または情熱を失う→息切れする, 活力を失う, (活動などが)弱まる

steam² /stíːm/ 動 ▶定義1 自 to send out steam 蒸気を出す→蒸気を出す, 湯気を立てる ‖ a bowl *of steaming hot soup* 湯気の立つ熱いスープ1杯 ▶定義 2 [他] to place food over boiling water so that it cooks in the steam; to cook in this way 湯気で熱が通るように, 食べ物を沸騰した物の上に載せる; このような方法で調理する ➜ **～を蒸気で料理する, 蒸す, ふかす** ‖ *steamed vegetables/fish* 蒸した野菜・魚 *Leave the potatoes to steam for 30 minutes.* ジャガイモを30分間ふかしなさい.

[成句] be/get steamed up [略式] ▶定義 to be or become very angry or worried about sth ～について非常に怒っているまたは心配している, ～について非常に怒るまたは心配する ➜ **怒る, 激怒する, いらいらする**

[句動詞] steam (sth) up ▶定義 to cover sth or become covered with steam ～を蒸気で覆う, 蒸気で覆われる ➜ **曇る; ～を曇らせる** ‖ *My glasses have steamed up.* 私の眼鏡が曇った.

**steamroller** /stíːmròʊlər/ [名] [C] ▶定義 a big heavy vehicle with wide heavy wheels that is used for making the surface of a road flat 道路の表面を平らにするために用いられる, 幅の広い重たい車輪の付いた頑強な大型の車 ➜ **蒸気ローラー, スチームローラー**

***steel**[1] /stiːl/ [名] [U] ▶定義 a very strong metal that is made from iron mixed with another substance (carbon). Steel is used for making knives, tools, machines, etc. 鉄に別の物質(炭素)を混ぜて作る非常に強い金属. ナイフ, 工具, 機械などを作るのに用いられる ➜ **鋼鉄, はがね, スチール**

**steel**[2] /stiːl/ [動] [他] ▶定義 steel yourself to prepare yourself to deal with sth difficult or unpleasant 困難な, または不快な～に対処する覚悟をする ➜ **決心する, 決意を固める** ‖ *Steel yourself for a shock.* ショックに動じないように気持ちをしっかり持ちなさい.

**steelworks** /stíːlwə̀ːrks/ [名] [[C], 単数または複数形の動詞と共に] ([複] **steelworks**) ▶定義 a factory where steel is made 鋼鉄が作られる工場 ➜ **製鋼所, 製鉄工場**

***steep** /stiːp/ [形] ▶定義 1 (used about a hill, mountain, street, etc) rising or falling quickly; at a sharp angle (丘, 山, 通りなどについて)急な上りの, または下りの; 急な角度の ➜ **険しい, 急な, 切り立った, 急勾配(こうばい)の** ‖ *I don't think I can cycle up that hill. It's too steep.* 自転車であの丘は上れないと思う. あまりに急だから. ▶定義 2 (used about an increase or fall in sth) very big (～の上昇または下落について)とても大きい ➜ **急激な, 途方もない, 極端な** ▶定義 3 [略式] too expensive あまりに高価な ➜ **不当に高い, 法外な** — steeply [副] ➜ **急勾配(こうばい)で, 急で[に]** ‖ *House prices have risen steeply this year.* 今年は住宅の価格が急上昇した. — steepness [名] [U] ➜ **険しいこと, 急勾配**

**steeped** /stiːpt/ [形] ▶定義 steeped in sth having a lot of; full of sth ～をたくさん持っている; ～に満ちている ➜ **～で満ちている, ～に包まれた, 深く浸った** ‖ *a city steeped in history* 歴史に満ちあふれた都市

**steeple** /stíːp(ə)l/ [名] [C] ▶定義 a tower on the roof of a church, often with a pointed top (spire) 教会の屋根の上の塔. しばしばてっぺんがとがっていることが多い ➜ **尖塔(せんとう), とがり屋根**

***steer** /stɪər/ [動] ▶定義 1 [自][他] to control the direction that a vehicle is going in 乗り物の進む方向を制御する ➜ **(～の)かじを取る, ハンドルを切る, (～を)操縦する, 運転する** ‖ *Can you push the car while I steer?* 私がハンドルを切りますからその間車を押してくれませんか. *to steer a boat/ship/bicycle/motorbike* ボート・船のかじを取る, 自転車・オートバイを操縦する

➤ steerは乗り物の方向を制御することを意味する. ride(自転車・オートバイに乗る), sail(小型の船を走らせる)という場合, steerと同時に, ほかの事すべての制御が含まれる.

▶定義 2 [他] to take control of a situation and try to influence the way it develops 状況の主導権を握って, 進展の仕方に影響を及ぼそうとする ➜ **～を(ある方向に)向ける, 導く, 支配する** ‖ *She tried to steer the conversation away from the subject of money.* 彼女は金の話題から会話をそらそうとした.

[成句] keep/stay/steer clear (of sb/sth) ⇒ CLEAR[2]

**steering** /stíərɪŋ/ [名] [U] ▶定義 the parts of a vehicle that control the direction that it moves in 乗り物の動く方向を制御する部品 ➜ **ハンドル, ステアリング, かじ** ‖ *a car with power steering* パワーステアリングを装備した自動車

S

## 1592　steering wheel

**steering wheel** (または **wheel**) 名 C ▶定義 the wheel that the driver turns in a vehicle to control the direction that it moves in 動く方向を制御するために乗り物内で操縦者が回すハンドル→ハンドル, ステアリングホイール, 操舵輪(そうだりん) ☛ S7 ページのさし絵

★**stem**¹ /stem/ 名 C ▶定義1 the main long thin part of a plant above the ground from which the leaves or flowers grow 地上に伸びて, 葉や花をつける, 植物の細長い主要部分→茎, 幹 ☛ C2 ページのさし絵 ▶定義2 (文法) the main part of a word onto which other parts are added ほかの要素が追加される語の基幹部→語幹 ‖ *'Writ-' is the stem of the words 'write', 'writing', 'written' and 'writer'.* writ- は write, writing, written, writer の語幹である.

**stem**² /stem/ 動 他 (**stemming**; **stemmed**) ▶定義 to stop sth that is increasing or spreading 増加・蔓延(まんえん)しているものを止める→～を止める, 抑える, 食い止める

句動詞 **stem from sth** (進行形は不可) ▶定義 to be the result of sth ～に由来する→～に起因する, ～から生じる, 起こる

▶この動詞は進行形では使われないが, 現在分詞(= -ing 形)は一般に見られる: *He was treated for depression stemming from his domestic and business difficulties.* (彼は家庭や商売上のトラブルが原因でなったうつ病の治療を受けた.)

**stench** /stentʃ/ 名 [C, 単数扱い] ▶定義 a very unpleasant smell 非常に不快なにおい→嫌なにおい, 悪臭, 異臭

★**step**¹ /step/ 名 C ▶定義1 the action of lifting one foot and putting it down in a different place 片足を持ち上げて別の所に下ろす動作→歩み, 1歩, 歩幅 ‖ *Nick took a step forward and then stopped.* ニックは1歩前に出ると立ち止まった. *I heard steps outside the window.* 窓の外で足音が聞こえた. *We were obviously lost so we decided to retrace our steps (= go back the way we had come).* 私たちは明らかに道に迷ってしまったので, 来た道を戻ることにした. ▶定義2 one action in a series of actions that you take in order to achieve sth ～を達成するために取る一連の行動の1つ→処置, 手段, 方法 ‖ *This will not solve the problem completely, but it is a step in the right direction.* これで問題が完全に解決するわけではないが, 正しい方向への1歩である. ▶定義3 one of the surfaces on which you put your foot when you are going up or down stairs 階段を上るまたは降りるときに足を乗せる面の1つ→段, 階段 ‖ *on the top/bottom step* 一番上・下の段 ☛参 stair の注

成句 **in/out of step (with sb/sth)** ▶定義 moving/not moving your feet at the same time as other people when you are marching, dancing, etc 行進, 踊りなどしているときにほかの人たちと同時に足を動かす・動かさない→足並みをそろえて・乱して, 歩調を合わせて・乱して

**step by step** ▶定義 (used for talking about a series of actions) moving slowly and gradually from one action or stage to the next (一連の動作について話すために用いて) 1つの動作または段階から次へゆっくりと徐々に移動して→一歩一歩(の), ゆっくりと(した), 段階的に[な] ‖ *clear step-by-step instructions* 分かりやすい段階的な指示

**take steps to do sth** ▶定義 to take action in order to achieve sth ～を達成するために行動を取る→～するための処置をとる, 方法を講じる, 行動を起こす, ～する手を打つ

**watch your step** ▶定義1 to be careful about where you are walking 歩いている所に気を付ける→足元に気を付ける, 注意して歩く ▶定義2 to be careful about how you behave 振る舞いに気を付ける→言動に気を付ける

★**step**² /step/ 動 自 (**stepping**; **stepped**) ▶定義 to lift one foot and put it down in a different place when you are walking 歩いているときに片足を持ち上げて別の所に下ろす→足を上げて踏み出す, (一歩一歩)歩く, 歩を進める ‖ *Be careful! Don't step in the mud.* 気を付けなさい. 泥に足を踏み入れないようにしなさい. *to step forward/back* 前進・後退する *Ouch! You stepped on my foot!* 痛い. 私の足を踏みましたよ. ▶定義2 to move a short distance; to go somewhere 短い距離を移動する; ある場所へ行く→(短い距離を)歩いていく, 出掛ける, 立ち去る ‖ *Could you step out of the car please, sir?* 車から降りていただけませんか. *I stepped outside for a minute to get some air.* 外気に当たるためにちょっと外に出た.

**句動詞** step down ▶定義 to leave an important job or position and let sb else take your place 重要な仕事または地位から退いてほかの〜に譲る➡**辞任する, 辞職する, 退陣する**

step in ▶定義 to help sb in a difficult situation or to become involved in a dispute 困難な状況に陥っている〜を助ける, 争いに巻き込まれる➡**介入する, 干渉する, 乗り出す, 首を突っ込む**

step sth up ▶定義 to increase the amount, speed, etc of sth の量, 速度などを増す〜を**増加させる, 上げる, 高める** ‖ *The Army has decided to step up its security arrangements.* 陸軍は防衛準備を増強することを決定した.

**step-** /step/ (複合名詞で用いて) ▶定義 related as a result of one parent marrying again 片親が再婚した結果縁続きになった➡**継(けい)〜, まま〜, 義理の**

**stepbrother** /stépbrʌðər/ 名 **C** ▶定義 the son from an earlier marriage of sb who has married your mother or father 母, または父と結婚した人の前の結婚相手との間にできた息子➡**継父・継母の(連れ子である)息子, まま兄弟**
➤ half-brother と比較.

**stepchild** /stéptʃaɪld/ 名 **C** (複 **stepchildren**) ▶定義 the child from an earlier marriage of your husband or wife 夫または妻の前の結婚相手との間にできた子供➡**連れ子, まま子**

**stepdaughter** /stépdɔːtər/ 名 **C** ▶定義 the daughter from an earlier marriage of your husband or wife 夫または妻の前の結婚相手との間にできた娘➡**まま娘, (女の)まま子**

**stepfather** /stépfɑːðər/ 名 **C** ▶定義 the man who has married your mother when your parents are divorced or your father is dead 両親の離婚, または父親の死亡後に母親と結婚した男性➡**継父(けいふ), まま父**

**stepladder** /stéplædər/ 名 **C** ▶定義 a short ladder with two parts, one with steps, that are joined together at the top so that it can stand on its own and be folded up when you are not using it. 片側に踏み台の付いた2つの部分から成る短いはしご. これらは最上部でつながっているため, 立て掛けずに使え, 使わないときは折り畳むこともできる➡**段ばしご, 脚立(きゃたつ), 踏み台**

**stepmother** /stépmʌðər/ 名 **C** ▶定義 the woman who has married your father when your parents are divorced or your mother is dead 両親の離婚, または母親の死亡後に父親と結婚した女性➡**継母(けいぼ), まま母**

**stepping stone** 名 **C** ▶定義 **1** one of a line of flat stones that you can step on in order to cross a river 川を渡るために伝い歩きできる, 一列に並べられた平らな石の1つ➡**踏み石, 飛び石**
▶定義 **2** something that allows you to make progress or helps you to achieve sth 前進を可能にするもの, または〜を達成する手助けとなるもの➡**踏み台, 足掛かり, 手段, 方法**

**stepsister** /stépsɪstər/ 名 **C** ▶定義 the daughter from an earlier marriage of sb who has married your mother or father 母, または父と結婚した人の前の結婚相手との間にできた娘➡**継父・継母の(連れ子である)娘, まま姉妹**
➤ half-sister と比較.

**stepson** /stépsʌn/ 名 **C** ▶定義 the son from an earlier marriage of your husband or wife 夫または妻の前の結婚相手との間にできた息子➡**まま息子, (男の)まま子**

**stereo** /stériòʊ, stíər-/ (複 **stereos**) 名 ▶定義 **1** (または **stereo system**) **C** a machine that plays CDs or cassettes, or a radio that has two boxes (speakers) so that you hear separate sounds from each 2個の箱(スピーカー)からそれぞれ別の音が聞こえる仕組みになっているCD・カセット再生機, またはラジオ➡**ステレオ, ステレオ再生装置** ‖ *a car/personal stereo* カーステレオ・携帯用カセットプレーヤー(ウォークマン) ☛ S7ページのさし絵 ▶定義 **2** **U** the system for playing recorded music, speech etc in which the sound is divided in two parts 録音された音楽, 談話などを再生するためのシステムで, 音が2つの部分に分けられている➡**ステレオ方式, 立体音響** ‖ *This programme is broadcast in stereo.* この番組はステレオで放送されている.
☛参 mono — stereo 形➡**ステレオの, ステレオ方式の, 立体音響の** ‖ *a stereo television* ステレオテレビ

**stereotype** /stérioʊtàɪp, stíər-/ 名 **C** ▶定義 a fixed idea about a particular type of person or thing, which is often not true in reality ある特定の種類の人・物についての固定した考え. 実際には本当でないことが多い➡**固定観念, 既成概念,**

通念, ステレオタイプ ― **stereotype** 動他→～を決まりきった型にはめる, 定型化する, 固定観念に当てはめる ‖ *In advertisements, women are often stereotyped as housewives.* 広告では女性はしばしば主婦として類型化されている.

**sterile** /stérəɪl, -əl/ 形 ▶定義1 not able to produce young animals or babies 動物または人間が子供を作ることができない→子ができない, 繁殖力のない, 生殖力のない, 不妊の ▶定義2 completely clean and free from bacteria 完全に清潔で無菌の→無菌の, 滅菌した, 殺菌した ‖ *All equipment used during a medical operation must be sterile.* 手術で用いられるすべての器具は滅菌したものでなければならない. ▶定義3 not producing any useful result 有益な結果を生み出さない→不毛の, 効果のない, 無益な ‖ *a sterile discussion/argument* 実りのない議論・論争 ― **sterility** /stəríləti, ste-/ 名 U→繁殖不能, 生殖不能, 不妊, (土地の)不毛, 滅菌状態 ― **sterilization** (または **sterilisation**) /stèrəlaɪzéɪʃ(ə)n/ 名 U→不妊にすること, 避妊手術, 殺菌, 消毒

**sterilize** (または **-ise**) /stérəlaɪz/ 動他 ▶定義1 to make sb/sth completely clean and free from bacteria ～を完全に清潔にして無菌状態にする→～を滅菌する, 殺菌する, 消毒する ▶定義2 (通常は受動態で) to perform an operation on a person or an animal so that they cannot have babies 子供ができないように人または動物に手術をする→～を不妊にする, ～に不妊手術をする

**sterling**¹ /stə́ːrlɪŋ/ 名 U ▶定義 the system of money that is used in Britain, that uses the pound as its basic unit イギリスで用いられているポンドを基本単位とする通貨体系→英貨

**sterling**² /stə́ːrlɪŋ/ 形 ▶定義 of very high quality 非常に品質の高い→優れた, 立派な ‖ *sterling work* 一流の仕事

**stern**¹ /stəːrn/ 形 ▶定義 very serious; not smiling 非常に真剣な; 笑っていない→厳しい, 険しい, 厳格な, 過酷な ‖ *a stern expression/warning* いかめしい表情・厳しい警告 ― **sternly** 副→厳格に, 厳しく

**stern**² /stəːrn/ 名 C ▶定義 the back end of a ship or boat 船またはボートの後ろ端→船尾, とも, 後部 ☛参 **bow**³

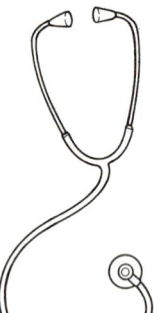

stethoscope

**stethoscope** /stéθəskòʊp, -θə-/ 名 C ▶定義 the piece of equipment that a doctor uses for listening to your breathing and heart 呼吸または心音を聞くために医者が用いる器具→聴診器

**stew** /st(j)uː/ 名 C U ▶定義 a type of food that you make by cooking meat and/or vegetables in liquid for a long time 肉と・または野菜を液体に入れて長時間加熱して作る食べ物→煮込み料理, シチュー ― **stew** 動自他→とろ火で煮える; ～をとろ火で煮込む, シチューにする

**steward** /st(j)úːərd, st(j)óərd/ 名 C ▶定義1 a man whose job is to look after passengers on an aircraft, a ship or a train 飛行機, 船, 列車の乗客の面倒を見ることを仕事とする男性→スチュワード, 男性客室乗務員, 船室係, 給仕, ボーイ ▶定義2 英 a person who helps to organize a large public event, for example a race レースなどの大きな公的行事の計画・開催を手伝う人→幹事, 世話人, 世話役

**stewardess** /st(j)úərdəs, st(j)úːərd-, -ɪs/ 名 C ▶定義1 a woman whose job is to look after passengers on an aircraft 飛行機の乗客の面倒を見ることを仕事にしている女性→スチュワーデス, 女性客室乗務員 ☛類 **air hostess** ▶定義2 a woman who looks after the passengers on a ship or train 船または列車の乗客の面倒を見る女性→船室係, 乗客係, 給仕

**\*stick**¹ /stɪk/ 動 (過, 過分 **stuck** /stʌk/) ▶定義1 自他 stick (sth) in/into (sth) to push a pointed object into sth; to be pushed into sth 先のとがった物を～に刺し込む; ～に押し込まれる→(～に)刺さる, 突き刺さる; ～を(…に)刺す, 突き刺す, 突き立てる ‖ *Stick a fork into the meat to see if it's ready.* もういいかどうか見るため, 肉にフォークを刺してみなさい. ▶定義2 自他 to fix sth to sth else by using a special substance (**glue**); to become fixed to sth else 特別の物質

(のり)を用いて～と…とを接着させる; ほかの～に固定される➡くっつく; ～をくっつける, はる, はり付ける ‖ *I stuck a stamp on an envelope.* 封筒に切手をはった. ▶定義3 ⦿略式 to put sth somewhere, especially quickly or carelessly ～を特に急いで, または無造作にある場所に置く➡**～を無造作に置く, ひょいと置く, 突っ込む, 突き出す** ‖ *Stick your bags in the bedroom.* かばんを寝室に置きなさい. *Just at that moment James stuck his head round the door.* ちょうどその時, ジェームズがドアの所に顔を出した. ▶定義4 ⦿ **stick (in sth)** (used about sth that can usually be moved) to become fixed in one position so that it cannot be moved (通常は動かせる～について)動かすことができなくなるように1箇所に固定される➡**(～に)はまり込む, 動かなくなる, 引っ掛かる, 行き詰まる** ‖ *The car was stuck in the mud.* 車がぬかるみにはまって動けなくなった. *This drawer keeps sticking.* この引き出しはしょっちゅう引っ掛かって動かなくなる. ▶定義5 ⦿略式 (しばしば否定文, 疑問文で) to stay in a difficult or unpleasant situation 困難な, または不快な状況にとどまる➡**～を我慢する, 辛抱する, ～に耐える** ‖ *I can't stick this job much longer.* 私はもうこの仕事に我慢できない.

成句 poke/stick your nose into sth ⇒ **NOSE**¹

stick/put your tongue out ⇒ **TONGUE**

句動詞 **stick around** 略式 ▶定義 to stay somewhere, waiting for sth to happen or for sb to arrive ～が起こるまたは…が到着するのを待ちながらある場所にとどまる➡**(期待して)そこら辺にいる, 近くで待つ, そこらで待つ**

**stick at sth** 略式 ▶定義 to continue working at sth even when it is difficult そうするのが難しいときでも, ～に取り組み続ける➡**～をこつこつ(まじめに)やる, 一生懸命続ける, ～に精を出す**

**stick by sb** 略式 ▶定義 to continue to give sb help and support even in difficult times 困難なときでも～に手助けまたは支援を与え続ける➡**～に忠実である, ～を見捨てない, ～を支持する**

**stick out** 略式 ▶定義 to be very noticeable and easily seen 非常に人目をひき, 容易に目に付く➡**目立つ, 人目に付く** ‖ *The new office block really sticks out from the older buildings around it.* 新しいオフィスビルは周囲の古い建物から際立って見える.

**stick (sth) out** ▶定義 to be further out than sth else; to push sth further out than sth else ほかの～よりも外に飛び出ている; ～をほかの…よりも遠くに押し出す➡**突き出る, 飛び出る, はみ出す; ～を突き出す** ‖ *The boy's head was sticking out of the window.* 少年の顔は窓から出ていた.

**stick it/sth out** 略式 ▶定義 to stay in a difficult or unpleasant situation until the end 最後まで困難または不快な状況にとどまる➡**やり抜く, 終わりまで我慢する, 最後まで頑張る**

**stick to sth** 略式 ▶定義 to continue with sth and not change to anything else ～をし続け, それ以外の～に変更したりしない➡**～に執着する, 固執する, 忠実である**

**stick together** 略式 ▶定義 (used about a group of people) to stay friendly and loyal to each other (集団について)仲良く互いに忠実であり続ける➡**協力し合う, 団結する**

**stick up** ▶定義 to point upwards 上を向いている➡**突き出る, 突っ立つ** ‖ *You look funny. Your hair's sticking up!* 何かこっけいな感じだな. 髪の毛が突っ立ってるよ.

**stick up for yourself/sb/sth** 略式 ▶定義 to support or defend yourself/sb/sth 自分自身や～を支持するまたは弁護する➡**～を(あくまで)支持する, (あくまで)弁護する, (権利など)を擁護する** ‖ *Don't worry. I'll stick up for you if there's any trouble.* 心配しないで. 何か問題があれば私があなたをあくまで守るから.

★**stick**² /stɪk/ 名 C ▶定義1 a small thin piece of wood from a tree 樹木から落ちたり切り取られたりした小さな薄い木片➡**木切れ, 棒切れ, 小枝** ▶定義2 特に 英 = **WALKING STICK** ▶定義3 (in hockey and some other sports) a long thin piece of wood that you use for hitting the ball (ホッケーなどのスポーツで)球を打つのに用いる細長い木➡**スティック, (ゴルフの)クラブ, (スキーの)ストック** ‖ *a hockey stick* ホッケー用のスティック ●参 **bat**², **club**²(2), **racket**¹ ☞ S1ページのさし絵 ▶定義4 a long thin piece of sth 細長い～➡**棒状の物, 棒, (野菜の)茎, 軸** ‖ *a stick of celery/dynamite* セロリの茎・ダイナマイト1本

**sticker** /stíkər/ 名 C ▶定義 a piece of paper with writing or a picture on one side that you can stick onto sth ～にはり付けることのでき

る，片面に文字または絵を書いた紙→ステッカー，のり付きラベル，ポスター

**\*sticky** /stíki/ 形 (**stickier**; **stickiest**) ▶定義1 used for describing a substance that easily becomes joined to things that it touches, or sth that is covered with this kind of substance 触れた～に簡単にくっつく物質，またはこの種の物質で覆われた～を表すのに用いて→**くっつく，粘着性の，ねばねばした** ‖ *These sweets are very sticky.* これらのキャンデーはとてもべとべとしている．*sticky tape* 粘着テープ ▶定義2 略式 (used about a situation) difficult or unpleasant (状況について) 困難な，不快な→**厄介な，困難な，面倒な**

**\*stiff**¹ /stíf/ 形 ▶定義1 (used about material, paper, etc) firm and difficult to bend or move (紙そのほかの物の材質などについて) 硬くて曲げにくいまたは動かしにくい→**硬い，曲がりにくい，曲がらない，動きの悪い** ‖ *My new shoes feel rather stiff.* 私の新しい靴はかなり硬く感じる．*The door handle is stiff and I can't turn it.* 戸の取っ手が硬くて回すことができない．▶定義2 (used about parts of the body) not easy to move (体の部分について) 動かしにくい→**よく動かない，こわばった，凝った** ‖ *My arm feels really stiff after playing tennis yesterday.* 昨日テニスをしてから，腕を動かすとすごく痛い．▶定義3 (used about a liquid) very thick; almost solid (液体について) 非常に濃い；ほとんど固体の→**固い，固練りの，粘りのある** ‖ *Beat the egg whites until they are stiff.* 固くなるまで卵の白身を泡立てなさい．▶定義4 more difficult or stronger than usual 通常よりも困難なまたは強力な→**難しい，厳しい，厄介な，手ごわい，強い** ‖ *The firm faces stiff competition from its rivals.* その会社はライバル企業からの厳しい競争に遭っている．*a stiff breeze/wind* 強い風 ▶定義5 (used about sb's behaviour) not relaxed or friendly; formal (人の振る舞いについて) くつろいでいない，打ち解けていない，形式張った→**よそよそしい，ぎこちない，堅苦しい** ▶定義6 (used about an alcoholic drink) strong (アルコール飲料について) 強い→**アルコール分の多い，(アルコールの)強い** ‖ *a stiff whisky* 強いウイスキー ― stiffness 名 ⓤ→**固いこと，堅苦しさ，頑固さ，剛性**

**stiff**² /stíf/ 副 略式 ▶定義 extremely 極度に→**ひどく，途方もなく，すごく** ‖ *to be bored/frozen/scared/worried stiff* ひどく退屈する，凍ってカチカチになる，ひどくおびえる・心配する

**stiffen** /stíf(ə)n/ 動 ▶定義1 ⓘ (used about a person) to suddenly stop moving and hold your body very straight, usually because you are afraid or angry (人について) 通常恐怖または怒りのために突然立ち止まり体をこわばらせる→**こわばる，硬直する，固くなる** ▶定義2 ⓘⓣ to become rigid; to make sth rigid so that it will not bend 硬くなる；～が折り曲がらないように…を固くする→**固まる，凝固する；～を固める**

**stiffly** /stífli/ 副 ▶定義 in an unfriendly formal way 打ち解けない形式張った様子で→**堅苦しく，よそよそしく，ぎこちなく** ‖ *He smiled stiffly.* 彼はぎこちなく笑った．

**stifle** /stáɪf(ə)l/ 動 ▶定義1 ⓣ to stop sth happening, developing or continuing ～の発生・進展・継続を妨げる→**～を抑える，抑圧する，押し殺す** ‖ *Her strict education had stifled her natural creativity.* 厳格な教育で彼女の生来の創造性は抑えられてしまっていた．*to stifle a yawn/cry/giggle* あくびをかみ殺す，涙・くすくす笑いを抑える ▶定義2 ⓘⓣ to be or to make sb unable to breathe because it is very hot and/or there is no fresh air 非常に暑く，新鮮な空気がないため，またはただ新鮮な空気がないため，息ができなくなる，または～を息苦しくさせる→**息苦しくなる，窒息する；～を息苦しくする，窒息させる，息の根を止める** ‖ *Richard was almost stifled by the smoke.* リチャードは煙で窒息しそうになった． ― stifling /stáɪf(ə)lɪŋ/ 形→**息苦しい，息が詰まるほど暑い，重苦しい，窮屈な** ‖ *The heat was stifling.* 暑さは息苦しかった．

**stigma** /stígmə/ 名 ⓒⓤ ▶定義 bad and often unfair feelings that people in general have about a particular illness, way of behaving, etc 一般の人たちがある特定の病気，振る舞い方などについて抱いているしばしば不当な悪感情→**汚名，恥辱，不名誉** ‖ *There is still a lot of stigma attached to being unemployed.* 失業に対してはいまだに恥ずべき事という考えが根強くある．

**\*still**¹ /stíl/ 副 ▶定義1 continuing until now or until the time you are talking about and not finishing 今までまたは話題にしている時点まで続いていて終わらない→**まだ，相変わらず，今もなお，今でも** ‖ *Do you still live in London?* まだロ

ンドンに住んでいるのですか. *It's still raining.* まだ雨が降っている. *I've eaten all the food but I'm still hungry.* 食べる物すべて食べてしまったが, まだ空腹だ. *In 1997 Zoran was still a student.* 1997年, ゾランはまだ学生だった. ◗定義2 in addition; more 加えて; もっと➜**さらに, それに加えて, その上に** ‖ *There are still ten days to go until my holiday.* 休暇までまだあと10日もある. ◗定義3 in spite of what has just been said 直前に言及した事にもかかわらず➜**それにもかかわらず, それでも, それでもやはり** ‖ *He had a bad headache but he still went to the party.* 彼は頭痛がひどかったが, それでもパーティーに出掛けた. ◗定義4 used for making a comparative adjective stronger 比較級を強調するのに用いて➜**なお一層, さらに** ‖ *It was very cold yesterday, but today it's colder still.* 昨日は非常に寒かったが, 今日はもっと寒い. *There was still more bad news to come.* やがて届くべきもっと悪い知らせがあった.

> **➤語法**
>
> still と yet の違い
>
> 日本語では共に「まだ」に相当するので使い分けに注意が必要です. yet は通例, 否定文や疑問文に用いられ「まだ～ない」「もう～?」の意味になります. 一方, stillの原義はstill life (静物画), Stand still. (じっと立っていろ) のように「静止した, 動かない」です. したがってIs it still raining? (まだ降ってる?) では「依然として, 相も変わらず」の意味になります.

***still**[2] /stɪl/ [形][副] ◗定義1 not moving 動かない➜**静止した, 動かない, じっとしている** ‖ *Stand still! I want to take a photograph!* 動かないで. 写真を撮りたいのだから. *Children find it hard to **keep/stay still** for long periods.* 子供たちは長時間じっとしているのがつらいようだ. ◗定義2 quiet or calm 静かな, 穏やかな➜**静かな, しんとした, 穏やかな, 平穏な, 落ち着いた** ‖ *The water was perfectly still.* 水面は完全に静まり返っていた. ◗定義3 (used about a drink) not containing gas (飲み物について) 気泡の入っていない➜**発泡性でない, 炭酸入りでない** ‖ *still mineral water* 炭酸の入っていない鉱水 ☛参 **fizzy**, **sparkling** ☛ **bubble** のさし絵 — stillness [名] [U] ➜**静止, 静寂, 静けさ**

**still**[3] /stɪl/ [名] [C] ◗定義 a single photograph that is taken from a film or video 映画またはビデオから取った1枚の写真➜**スチール写真, 静止画, 静止画像**

**stillborn** /stílbɔ̀ːrn/ [形] ◗定義 (used about a baby) dead when it is born (赤ん坊について) 生まれた時に死んでいる➜**死産の**

**stilt** /stɪlt/ [名] [C] ◗定義1 one of two long pieces of wood, with places to rest your feet on, on which you can walk above the ground 足を載せる場所の付いた2本一組の長い木の棒のうちの1本. これを使って地上高く歩くことができる➜**竹馬, 高足** ‖ *Have you tried walking **on stilts**?* あなたは竹馬に乗って歩いてみたことがありますか. ◗定義2 one of a set of poles that support a building above the ground or water 地上または水上に建つ建物を支える柱のうちの1本➜**支柱, 脚柱**

**stilted** /stíltəd/ [形] ◗定義 (used about a way of speaking or writing) not natural or relaxed; too formal (話し方または書き方について) 自然でない, 緊張を緩めていない; あまりに形式張った➜**堅苦しい, おおげさな, 誇張した, 不自然な, ぎこちない**

**stimulant** /stímjələnt/ [名] [C] ◗定義 a drug or medicine that makes you feel more active 人をより活動的に感じさせる薬➜**興奮剤, 刺激剤**

**stimulate** /stímjəlèɪt/ [動][他] ◗定義1 to make sth active or more active ～を (より) 活動的にする➜**～を刺激する, 活気づける** ‖ *Exercise stimulates the blood circulation.* 運動は血液の循環を活発にする. *The government has decided to cut taxes in order to stimulate the economy.* 政府は景気を刺激するために減税を行うことを決定した. ◗定義2 to make sb feel interested and excited about sth ～について…に面白さや興奮を覚えさせる➜**～を刺激する, 興奮させる** ‖ *The lessons don't really stimulate him.* それらの授業は彼の興味をあまりかき立てない. — stimulation /stìmjəléɪʃ(ə)n/ [名] [U] ➜**刺激, 興奮, 鼓舞, 激励**

**stimulating** /stímjəlèɪtɪŋ/ [形] ◗定義 interesting and exciting 興味深くて, わくわくする➜**刺激する, 励ましとなる, 非常に興味のある** ‖ *a stimulating discussion* 刺激的な議論

**stimulus** /stímjələs/ [名] [C][U] ([複] **stimuli** /-làɪ, -lìː/) ◗定義 something that causes activity,

S

★**sting**¹ /stɪŋ/ 動自他 (過, 過分 **stung** /stʌŋ/)
▶定義 1 (used about an insect, plant, etc) to make a person or animal feel a sudden pain by pushing sth sharp into his/her skin and sending poison into him/her (昆虫, 植物などについて) とがった物で皮膚を刺し毒を送り込んで人または動物に突然の痛みを感じさせる→(〜を)針で刺す, とげで刺す ‖ *Ow! I've been stung by a bee!* アイタッ. ハチに刺されてしまった. *Be careful. Those plants sting.* 気を付けなさい. これらの植物にはとげがあります. ▶定義 2 to make sb/sth feel a sudden, sharp pain 〜に突然の鋭い痛みを感じさせる→〜に刺すような刺激を与える, 〜をずきずきさせる, ピリッと刺激する ‖ *Soap stings if it gets in your eyes.* せっけんは目に入るとひりひりする. ▶定義 3 to make sb feel very hurt and upset because of sth you say 自分の言った事で〜をひどく傷付けて動揺させる→〜を傷付ける, 悩ます, 苦しめる

★**sting**² /stɪŋ/ 名 C ▶定義 1 the sharp pointed part of some insects and animals that is used for pushing into the skin of a person or an animal and putting in poison 一部の昆虫・動物が, 人または動物の皮膚を刺して毒を注入するために使う先の鋭くとがった部分→針, とげ, 毒牙(どくが) ☞ scorpion のさし絵 ▶定義 2 the pain that you feel when an animal or insect pushes its sting into you 動物または昆虫に刺されたときに感じる痛み→刺された痛み, 刺し傷, 刺すこと ‖ *I got a wasp sting on the leg.* ハチに足を刺された. ▶定義 3 a sharp pain that feels like a sting 刺されたときのような鋭い痛み→刺すような痛み, 激痛

**stink** /stɪŋk/ 動自 (過 **stank** /stæŋk/ または **stunk** /stʌŋk/; 過分 **stunk**) 語式 stink (of sth) ▶定義 1 to have a very strong and unpleasant smell 非常に強く不快なにおいがする→悪臭を放つ, 〜のにおいがする, におう ‖ *It stinks in here - open a window!* ここはにおう － 窓を開けなさい. *to stink of fish* 魚臭い ▶定義 2 to seem to be very bad, unpleasant or dishonest ひどく悪そう, 不愉快そうにまたは不正直そうに見える→評判が悪い, 鼻持ちならない ‖ *The whole business stinks of corruption.* この件はすべて腐敗まみれで鼻持ちならない. ― **stink** 名 C ▶悪臭, 嫌なにおい, 悪評, 物議

**stint** /stɪnt/ 名 C ▶定義 a fixed period of time that you spend doing sth 〜をして過ごす一定の期間→任期, 勤務期間, 割り当て期間 ‖ *He did a brief stint in the army after leaving school.* 学校卒業後, 彼は短期間軍隊に勤務した.

**stipulate** /ˈstɪpjəleɪt/ 動他 正式 ▶定義 to say exactly and officially what must be done しなければならない事を厳密かつ正式に述べる→〜を規定する, 明記する, 明文化する ‖ *The law stipulates that all schools must be inspected every three years.* 法律には, すべての学校が3年ごとに査察を受けなければならないことが明記されている. ― **stipulation** /ˌstɪpjəˈleɪʃ(ə)n/ 名 C U → 規定, 明記, 約定, 契約

★**stir**¹ /stɜːr/ 動 (**stirring**; **stirred**) ▶定義 1 他 to move a liquid, etc round and round, using a spoon, etc さじなどを使って液体などを何度もかき回す→〜をかき回す, かき混ぜる ‖ *She stirred her coffee with a teaspoon.* 彼女はティースプーンでコーヒーをかき回した. ▶定義 2 自他 to move or make sb/sth move slightly わずかに動く; 〜を軽く動かす→わずかに動く, 身動きする, 動き出す; 〜を動かす ‖ *She heard the baby stir in the next room.* 彼女は赤ん坊が隣の部屋でもぞもぞ動く音を聞いた. ▶定義 3 他 to make sb feel a strong emotion 〜に強い感情を抱かせる→〜の心をかき立てる, 〜を奮起させる, 感動させる ‖ *The story stirred Carol's imagination.* その物語はキャロルの想像力をかき立てた. *a stirring speech* 感動的な演説

句動詞 **stir sth up** ▶定義 to cause problems, or to make people feel strong emotions 問題を引き起こす, または人々に強い感情を抱かせる→〜を引き起こす, そそのかす, かき立てる ‖ *He's always trying to stir up trouble.* 彼はいつもトラブルを起こそうとしてばかりいる. *The article stirred up a lot of anger among local residents.* その記事は地元住民の間で大きな怒りをかき立てた.

**stir**² /stɜːr/ 名 ▶定義 1 C the action of stirring かき回す動作→かき回すこと, かき混ぜること ‖ *Give the soup a stir.* スープをかき回しなさい.

▶定義2 [単数扱い] something exciting or shocking that everyone talks about 皆が話題にする面白いまたは衝撃的な物→騒ぎ,物議,混乱,評判

**stirrup** /stírəp, stír-, stɔ́:r-/ 图 ● ▶定義 one of the two metal objects that you put your feet in when you are riding a horse 馬に乗るときに足を踏み掛ける2つの金属製の器具の1つ→あぶみ,あぶみがね ☞ horse のさし絵

*****stitch**¹ /stítʃ/ 图 ● ▶定義1 one of the small lines of thread that you can see on a piece of material after it has been sewn 縫った後の縫い物の上に見える小さな糸の目→縫い目,針目,一針,一縫い,一かがり ☞ knit のさし絵 ▶定義2 one of the small pieces of thread that a doctor uses to sew your skin together if you cut yourself very badly, or after an operation 大けがをしたときまたは手術の後皮膚を縫い合わせるために医者が用いる糸の小さな目→一針 ‖ *How many stitches did you have in your leg?* 足を何針縫いましたか. ▶定義3 one of the small circles of wool that you put round a needle when you are knitting 編物をするときに針に巻き付ける毛糸の小さな環→網目,一編み ▶定義4 [通常は単数] a sudden pain that you get in the side of your body when you are running 走っているときにわき腹に感じる鋭い痛み→わき腹の激痛,さしこみ

成句 **in stitches** 略式 ▶定義 laughing so much that you cannot stop 止まらないほどに笑いこけて→笑いが止まらなくて,笑いこける,おなかがよじれるほど笑って

**stitch**² /stítʃ/ 動 ⊕ ⊕ ▶定義 to sew 縫う→(~を)縫う,縫い付ける,とじる,縫合する

*****stock**¹ /stɑk/ 图 ▶定義1 Ⓤ Ⓒ the supply of things that a shop, etc has for sale 店などが所有する商品の在庫→在庫(品),仕入れ(品),ストック ‖ *We'll have to order extra stock if we sell a lot more this week.* 今週もっと多く売れば,追加のストックを注文しなければならない. *I'm afraid that book's **out of stock** at the moment. Shall I order it for you?* 残念ながら現在その本は品切れです.注文いたしましょうか. *I'll see if we have your size **in stock**.* お客様のサイズが在庫にあるかどうか見て参ります. ▶定義2 Ⓒ an amount of sth that has been kept ready to be used いつでも使えるように用意してある物の量→貯蔵(品),蓄え,蓄積,備蓄 ‖ *Food stocks in the village were very low.* その村の食料の蓄えは非常に少なかった. ▶定義3 Ⓒ Ⓤ a share that sb has bought in a company, or the value of a company's shares ~が購入した会社の株の持ち分,会社の株の価値→株,株式,株券;公債,債券,資本金 ‖ *to invest in stocks and shares* 公債や株に投資する ▶定義4 Ⓒ Ⓤ a liquid that made by boiling meat, bones, vegetables, etc in water, used especially for making soups and sauces 肉,骨,野菜などを水に入れて沸騰させて作る,特にスープ・ソースに利用される液体→煮出し汁,スープストック

成句 **take stock (of sth)** ▶定義 to think about sth very carefully before deciding what to do next 次に何をするか決める前に~について非常に慎重に考える→(~を)吟味する,調査する,慎重に検討する,よく考える

**stock**² /stɑk/ 動 ⊕ ▶定義1 (usually used about a shop) to have a supply of sth (通常は店について) 在庫として~を持っている→(商品)を店に置く,貯蔵する,在庫にしておく ‖ *They stock food from all over the world.* あの店は世界中の食料を置いている. ▶定義2 to fill a place with sth ある場所を~で満たす→~を(…で)一杯にする,~をそろえる ‖ *a well-stocked library* 本のよくそろった図書館

句動詞 **stock up (on/with sth)** ▶定義 to collect a large supply of sth for future use 将来使用するために多量の~を集める→(~を)仕入れる,買い込む,買いだめする,蓄え込む ‖ *to stock up with food for the winter* 冬に備えて食料を買い込む

**stock**³ /stɑk/ 形 (名詞の前だけ) ▶定義 (used for describing sth that sb says) used so often that it does not have much meaning (~が言う…を表現するために用いて) 使い古されてあまり意味がない→使い古された,ありふれた,陳腐な ‖ *He always gives the same stock answers.* 彼はいつも同じ決まりきった答えをする.

**stockbroker** /stɑ́kbròukər/ (または **broker**) 图 ● ▶定義 a person whose job it is to buy and sell shares in companies for other people 他人のために会社の株を売買することを仕事にしている人→株式仲買人

**stock exchange** 图 ● ▶定義1 a place where

shares in companies are bought and sold 会社の株が売買される場所→**証券取引所,株式取引所** ‖ *the Tokyo Stock Exchange* 東京証券取引所 ▶定義2（または **stock market**）the business or activity of buying and selling shares in companies 会社の株式を売買する業務または活動→**証券取引,株式取引** ☞参 **exchange**

**stocking** /stákɪŋ/ 名 C ▶定義 one of a pair of thin pieces of clothing that fit tightly over a woman's feet and legs 女性の足・脚にぴったりと合う, 薄地の衣類一対のうちの1つ→**長靴下, ストッキング** ‖ *a pair of stockings* 1足のストッキング ☞参 **tights** ☞ C6ページのさし絵

**stockist** /stákɪst/ 名 C ▶定義 a shop that sells goods made by a particular company ある特定の会社の商品を売る店→**(特定の商品の)取扱店**

**stocktaking** /stáktèɪkɪŋ/ 名 U ▶定義 the activity of counting the total supply of things that a shop or business has at a particular time 商店・会社が在庫の全商品の数をある特定の時期に確認する作業→**在庫調べ, 棚卸し** ‖ *They close for an hour a month to do the stocktaking.* 彼らは棚卸しのため, 毎月1時間店を閉める.

**stocky** /stáki/ 形 ▶定義 (used about a person's body) short but strong and heavy（人の体について）背が低いが頑丈で肉付きの良い→**がっしりとした, ずんぐりとした, 頑丈な**

**stoic** /stóʊɪk/（または **stoical** /-k(ə)l/）形 正式 ▶定義 suffering pain or difficulty without complaining 不平を言わずに痛みまたは困難に耐える→**自制的な, 禁欲的な, 冷静な, ストイックな** — **stoically** /-k(ə)li/ 副 →**自制的に, 禁欲的に, 冷静に, 平然として** — **stoicism** /stóʊəsɪz(ə)m/ 名 U →**禁欲, 自制心, 冷静, 平然**

**stole** STEAL の過去形

**stolen** STEAL の過去分詞形

**stolid** /stálǝd/ 形 ▶定義 (used about a person) showing very little emotion or excitement（人について）喜怒哀楽の感情または興奮をほとんど示さない→**何の感情[興味] も示さない, 鈍感な, ぼんやりした** — **stolidly** 副 →**無感動で, 鈍感で, ぼんやりして**

*****stomach**¹ /stámək/（または略式 **tummy**）名 C ▶定義1 the organ in your body where food goes after you have eaten it 食べた物が送られる体内の器官→**胃** ‖ *He went to the doctor with stomach pains.* 彼は胃痛で医者にかかった. ☞ C5ページのさし絵 ▶定義2 the front part of your body below your chest and above your legs 胸の下から脚の上までの体の正面部分→**腹, 腹部, 下腹** ‖ *She turned over onto her stomach.* 彼女は腹ばいになった. ☞ C5ページのさし絵

**stomach**² /stámək/ 動 他 略式（通常は否定文または疑問文で）▶定義 to be able to watch, listen to, accept, etc sth that you think is unpleasant 不快だと思う～を見る, 聞くまたは受け入れることができる→**～に耐える, ～を我慢する** ‖ *I can't stomach too much violence in films.* 映画の中での暴力のあまりの多さに我慢がならない.

**stomach-ache** 名 C U ▶定義 a pain in your stomach 胃の痛み→**胃痛, 腹痛** ‖ *I've got terrible stomach-ache.* ひどく胃が痛む. ☞参 **ache** の注

**stomp** /stamp/ 動 自 略式 ▶定義 to walk with heavy steps ドシンドシンと歩く→**(怒って)ドシンドシンと歩く, 足を踏み鳴らして歩く**

*****stone** /stóʊn/ 名 ▶定義1 U a hard solid substance that is found in the ground 地中にある硬い固形物→**(物質・材質としての)石, 石材, 岩** ‖ *The house was built of grey stone.* その家は灰色の石で造られていた. *a stone wall* 石壁 ▶定義2 C a small piece of rock 岩の小片→**(個々の)石, 小石, 石ころ** ‖ *The boy picked up a stone and threw it into the river.* 少年は石を拾い上げて川の中に投げた. ▶定義3 C →**PRECIOUS STONE** ▶定義4 C the hard seed inside some fruits, for example peaches, plums, cherries and olives 例えばモモ, スモモ, サクランボ, オリーブなどの果物の中にある硬い種→**種, 核** ▶定義5 C （複 **stone**）a measure of weight; 6.35 kilograms. There are 14 pounds in a stone. 重量の単位; 6.35キログラム. 1ストーンは14ポンド→**ストーン** ‖ *I weigh eleven stone two (= 2 pounds).* 私の体重は11ストーン2ポンドだ.

**stoned** /stóʊnd/ 形（俗語）▶定義 not behaving or thinking normally because of drugs or alcohol 薬またはアルコールのため振る舞い方や考え方が正常でない→**(酒に)酔いつぶれた; (麻薬で)恍惚(こうこつ)となった**

**stony** /stóʊni/ 形 ▶定義1 (used about the ground) having a lot of stones in it, or covered with stones（地面について）地中にたくさんの石のある, 石で覆われている→**石の, 石の多い, 石だ**

らけの ▶定義2 not friendly 和やかでない→冷酷な,冷ややかな,冷たい,無表情の ‖ *There was a stony silence as he walked into the room.* 彼が部屋に入ると冷ややかな沈黙があった.

**stood** STAND¹の過去・過去分詞形

*****stool** /stuːl/ 名 C ▶定義 a seat that does not have a back or arms 背もたれ・ひじ掛けがないいす→腰掛け,スツール ‖ *a piano stool* ピアノ用のいす

**stoop** /stuːp/ 動 自 ▶定義 to bend your head and shoulders forwards and downwards 頭と肩を前にかがめる→かがむ,前かがみになる,身をかがめる ‖ *He had to stoop to get through the low doorway.* 彼は低い戸口を通り抜けるために身をかがめなければならなかった. ― stoop 名 [単数扱い]→ 身をかがめること,前かがみ,猫背 ‖ *to walk with a stoop* 前かがみになって歩く

句動詞 stoop to sth/doing sth ▶定義 to do sth bad or wrong that you would normally not do 通常ではしないような悪い,または誤った〜をする→〜に身を落とす,品位を落として〜をする,恥を忍んで〜をする

*****stop**¹ /stɑp/ 動 (**stopping**; **stopped**) ▶定義1 自他 to finish moving or make sth finish moving 動き終わる;〜の動きを終えさせる→止まる,立ち止まる,停止する;〜を止める,停止させる ‖ *He walked along the road for a bit, and then stopped.* 彼はしばらく道路沿いに歩いてから立ち止まった. *Does this train stop at Didcot?* この列車はディドコットで停車しますか. *My watch has stopped.* 腕時計が止まってしまった. *I stopped someone in the street to ask the way to the station.* 私は通りで人を呼び止め,駅への道を尋ねた. ▶定義2 自他 to no longer continue or make sth not continue これ以上続かない;〜を続かなくする→やめる,やむ;〜をやめさせる,中断する,中止する ‖ *I think the rain has stopped.* 雨はやんだと思う. *It's stopped raining now.* 今雨がやんだところだ. *Stop making that terrible noise!* その嫌な音を出すのをやめなさい. *The bus service stops at midnight.* バスの運行は真夜中に止まる. *We tied a bandage round his arm to stop the bleeding.* 私たちは出血を止めるために彼の腕に包帯を巻いた.

▶ある事をするために止まる場合にはstop to do sthと言う: *On the way home I stopped to buy a newspaper.* (帰宅途中で私は新聞を買うために立ち止まった.) これ以上ある事を行わない場合にはstop doing sthと言う: *Stop talking and listen to me!* (話すのをやめて私の言うことを聞きなさい.)

▶定義3 他 stop sb/sth (from) doing sth to make sb/sth end or finish an activity; prevent sb/sth from doing sth 〜に活動をやめさせるまたは終了させる;〜が…をするのを妨げる→〜が…するのをやめさせる,中止させる,妨げる,押しとどめる ‖ *They've built a fence to stop the dog getting out.* 彼らは犬が出ないように柵(さく)を立てた. *I'm going to go and you can't stop me.* 私は行くつもりだから,止めようとしても駄目です. ▶定義4 自他 stop (for sth); stop (and do/to do sth) to end an activity for a short time in order to do sth 〜を行うために短い間活動を止める→中断する,(仕事などを)中断して〜する,休憩する,手を休める ‖ *Shall we stop for lunch now?* ここで昼休みにしませんか. *Let's stop and look at the map.* 立ち止まって地図を見よう. *We stopped work for half an hour to have a cup of coffee.* 私たちは30分間作業を中断して1杯のコーヒーを飲んだ.

成句 stop at nothing ▶定義 to do anything to get what you want, even if it is wrong or dangerous たとえ誤っていようと危険であろうと,欲しい物を手に入れるために何でもする→どんな事でもする,何でもやりかねない,何事にも躊躇(ちゅうちょ)しない

stop short of sth/doing sth ▶定義 to almost do sth, but then decide not to do it at the last minute 〜をやりそうになるが,土壇場でやらないことに決める→〜を・〜するのを思いとどまる,〜までには至らない,〜の手前で思いとどまる

句動詞 stop off (at/in...) ▶定義 to stop during a journey to do sth 〜をするために旅行中に立ち寄る→(〜に)立ち寄る,途中下車する,短期間滞在する

stop over (at/in...) ▶定義 to stay somewhere for a short time during a long journey 長期の旅行中にしばらくの間ある場所にとどまる→(〜に)しばらく滞在する,旅の途中で〜に泊まる,途中下車する

*****stop**² /stɑp/ 名 C ▶定義1 an act of stopping or state of being stopped 止まる動作,止まってい

る状態➡**止まること,停止,中止,休止,停車,立ち寄り,滞在** ‖ *Our first stop will be in Edinburgh.* 私たちの最初の立ち寄り先はエディンバラになる予定だ. *Production at the factory will* **come to a stop** *at midnight tonight.* 工場の生産は今日の真夜中に停止することになっている. *I managed to* **bring** *the car* **to a stop** *just in time.* どうにか間に合って車を止めることができた. ▶定義2 the place where a bus, train, etc stops so that people can get on and off 人々が乗り降りできるように,バス,列車などが止まる場所➡**停留所,停車駅,停泊所** ‖ *a bus stop* バス停 *I'm getting off at the next stop.* 次の停留所で降ります.
成句 **pull out all the stops** ⇒ **PULL**¹
**put a stop to sth** ▶定義 to prevent sth bad or unpleasant from continuing 悪い事または不快な事が続くのを阻止する➡**~をやめさせる,中止させる,終わらせる**

**stopgap** /stápgæp/ 图 ❻ ▶定義 a person or a thing that does a job for a short time until sb/sth permanent can be found 常任の要員,恒久的な物が見つかるまで短期間代わりをする人・物➡**臨時の人,間に合わせ(の人・物),その場しのぎ**

**stopover** /stápòʊvər/ 图 ❻ ▶定義 a short stop in a journey 旅行中の短い立ち寄り➡**立ち寄り,途中下車,短期滞在**

**stoppage** /stápɪdʒ/ 图 ❻ ▶定義1 a situation in which people stop working as part of a protest 抗議の一部として人々が働くのを止める状況➡**作業中止,休業,罷業(ひぎょう),ストライキ** ▶定義2 (in sport) an interruption in a game for a particular reason (スポーツで)ある特定の理由による試合の中断➡**試合の中断**

**stopper** /stápər/ 图 ❻ ▶定義 an object that you put into the top of a bottle in order to close it びんの口をふさぐために挿入する物➡**栓,詰め,詰め物**

**stopwatch** /stápwàtʃ/ 图 ❻ ▶定義 a watch which can be started and stopped by pressing a button, so that you can measure exactly how long sth takes 所要時間を正確に測定できる時計.ボタン1つでスタートさせたり,止めたりすることができる➡**ストップウォッチ**

**storage** /stɔ́ːrɪdʒ/ 图 ❶ ▶定義 the keeping of things until they are needed; the place where they are kept ~が必要になるまで保管すること; ~を保管する場所➡**保管,貯蔵,収納; 貯蔵庫,倉庫** ‖ *This room is being used for storage at the moment.* 今のところ,この部屋は保管場所として用いられている.

★**store**¹ /stɔːr/ 图 ❻ ▶定義1 a large shop 大型の店➡**店,百貨店,デパート** ‖ *She's a sales assistant in a large department store.* 彼女は大きなデパートの店員だ. *a furniture store* 家具店 ☞参 **chain store** ▶定義2 囲 = **SHOP**¹(1) ▶定義3 a supply of sth that you keep for future use; the place where it is kept 後で使用するために保管しておく~の蓄え; ~を保管する場所➡**蓄え,貯蔵,倉庫,貯蔵庫** ‖ *a good store of food for the winter* 冬に備えて蓄えられた十分な食料 *Police discovered a weapons store in the house.* 警察はその家で貯蔵された武器を発見した.
成句 **in store (for sb/sth)** ▶定義 going to happen in the future 将来起こる予定の➡**(運命・出来事などが)(~に)起ころうとして,降り懸かろうとして,待ち構えて** ‖ *There's a surprise in store for you when you get home!* 家に帰ったら,あなたがびっくりするようなことが待っていますよ.
**set...store by sth** ▶定義 to consider sth to be important ~を重要だと考える➡**~を重んじる,重視する,大切にする** ‖ *Nick sets great store by his mother's opinion.* ニックは母親の意見をとても大切にしている.

★**store**² /stɔːr/ 動 ⓗ ▶定義 to keep sth or a supply of sth for future use ~または…の蓄えを後日使用するために保管する➡**~を保管する,貯蔵する,蓄える,取っておく** ‖ *to store information on a computer* 情報をコンピュータに保存する

**storekeeper** /stɔ́ːrkìːpər/ 囲 =**SHOPKEEPER**

**storeroom** /stɔ́ːruːm, -rùm/ 图 ❻ ▶定義 a room where things are kept until they are needed ~が必要になるまで保管しておく部屋➡**貯蔵室,収納室,物置**

**storey** (囲 **story**) /stɔ́ːri/ 图 ❻ (複 **storeys**: 囲 **stories**) ▶定義 one floor or level of a building 建物の1つの階➡**階,階層** ‖ *The building will be five storeys high.* その建物は5階建てになる予定だ. *a two-storey house* 2階建ての家 *a multi-storey car park* 多層式・立体駐車場

**stork** /stɔːrk/ 图 ❻ ▶定義 a large white bird with a long beak, neck and legs. Storks often make their homes (**nests**) on the top of buildings. く

ちばし, 首, 足の長い大きな白い鳥. しばしば建物の最上部に住みか(巣)を作る→コウノトリ

*  **storm**¹ /stɔːm/ 名 C ▶定義 very bad weather, with a lot of rain, strong winds, etc 多量の雨, 強風などを伴う非常な悪天候→**あらし, 暴風, 暴風雨** ‖ *Look at those black clouds. I think there's going to be a storm.* あの黒い雲を見てごらん. あらしが来ると思う. *a hailstorm/snowstorm/sandstorm/thunderstorm* ひょう(あられ)のあらし・吹雪・砂あらし・雷雨
   ➤ storm は非常な悪天候を表す一般的な語である. 非常に強い風は gale(強風), 暴風を伴うあらしは hurricane(ハリケーン)と言う. 強烈な渦巻く風を伴うあらしは cyclone(サイクロン), tornado(竜巻), typhoon(台風), whirlwind(つむじ風)などと呼ばれる. 非常にひどい吹雪は blizzard(猛吹雪)と言う.

**storm**² /stɔːm/ 動 ▶定義1 自 to enter or leave somewhere in a very angry and noisy way 非常に怒って騒々しくある場所に入るまたは出る→**怒って飛び込む・飛び出る, 激しい勢いで突進する, 荒々しく乱入する** ‖ *He threw down the book and stormed out of the room.* 彼は本を投げ捨てて荒々しく部屋から飛び出した. ▶定義2 他 to attack a building, town, etc suddenly and violently in order to take control of it 建物・町などの支配権を得るために突然猛攻撃する→**～を急襲する, 襲撃する, 猛攻する**

**stormy** /stɔːmi/ 形 ▶定義1 used for talking about very bad weather, with strong winds, heavy rain, etc 強風, 豪雨などを伴う大変な悪天候について話すのに用いて→**あらしの, 暴風の, 暴風雨の** ‖ *a stormy night* あらしの夜 *stormy weather* 荒天 ▶定義2 involving a lot of angry argument and strong feeling 怒りをぶつけ合うような口論と激情を多く伴う→**激しい, 荒れた, 乱暴な, 波乱に富んだ** ‖ *a stormy relationship* 波乱に富んだ関係

*  **story** /stɔːri/ 名 C (複 **stories**) ▶定義1 *a story (about sb/sth)* a description of people and events that are not real 実在しない人々または事実でない出来事の記述→**話, 物語, 童話, 昔話, (短編)小説** ‖ *I'll tell you a story about the animals that live in that forest.* 君にあの森に住んでいる動物たちの話をしてあげよう. *I always read the children a bedtime story.* 私はいつも子供たちに寝る前に物語を読んで聞かせてやる. *a detective/fairy/ghost/love story* 推理小説・おとぎ話・怪談・恋愛小説 ▶定義2 an account, especially a spoken one, of sth that has happened 起こった～についての特に口頭による説明→**話, 報告, 陳述, 説明, 申し立て** ‖ *The police didn't believe his story.* 警察は彼の供述を信じなかった. ▶定義3 a description of true events that happened in the past 過去に起こった本当の出来事の記述→**逸話, 挿話, 伝記, 身の上話** ‖ *He's writing his life story.* 彼は自伝を書いている. ▶定義4 an article or report in a newspaper or magazine 新聞または雑誌の記事または報道→**記事, 新聞種, ニュース** ‖ *The plane crash was the front-page story in most newspapers.* その飛行機の墜落事故はほとんどの新聞で 1 面記事になった. ▶定義5 米 = STOREY

**stout** /staʊt/ 形 ▶定義1 (used about a person) rather fat (人について)かなり太っている→**太った, 肥えた, ずんぐりとした** ▶定義2 strong and thick 頑丈で分厚い→**強い, 頑丈な, しっかりした** ‖ *stout walking boots* 丈夫な散歩用のブーツ

**stove** /stoʊv/ 名 C ▶定義1 the top part of a cooker that has gas or electric rings ガスこんろまたは電気こんろのある調理器の最上部→**レンジ, こんろ** ‖ *He put a pan of water to boil on the stove.* 彼は湯を沸かすためにこんろの上になべを置いた. ▶定義2 a closed metal box in which you burn wood, coal, etc for heating 暖房のためにまき, 石炭などを燃やす金属製の箱状のもの→**ストーブ, 暖炉** ‖ *a wood-burning stove* まきストーブ

**stow** /stoʊ/ 動 他 ▶定義 *stow sth (away)* to put sth away in a particular place until it is needed 必要になるまで～をある場所にしまい込む→**～をしまい込む, 詰め込む**

**stowaway** /stóʊəwèɪ/ 名 C ▶定義 a person who hides in a ship or plane so that he/she can travel without paying 運賃を払わずに旅行できるように船または飛行機の中に隠れている人→**密航者, 無賃搭乗[乗船]客**

**straddle** /strǽdl/ 動 他 ▶定義1 (used about a person) to sit or stand with your legs on each side of sth (人について)～の両側に足を置いて座るまたは立つ→**～をまたぐ, ～にまたがる, ～をまたいで立つ・座る** ‖ *to straddle a chair* いすにま

## 1604 straggle

たがる ▶定義2 (used about a building, bridge, etc) to be on both sides of sth (建物, 橋などについて) 〜の両側にある➔〜にまたがる, (境界など)の両側に及んでいる

**straggle** /strǽg(ə)l/ 動自 ▶定義1 to walk, etc more slowly than the rest of the group 集団のほかの人たちよりもゆっくりと歩いたりする➔はぐれる, 落伍(らくご)する, だらだらと歩く ‖ *The children straggled along behind their parents.* 子供たちは両親の後ろをだらだらと歩いていた. ▶定義2 to grow, spread or move in an untidy way or in different directions 乱雑に, またはさまざまな方向に伸びる, 広がるまたは動く➔(列なども)ばらばらになる; だらしなく広がる ‖ *Her wet hair straggled across her forehead.* ぬれた髪が彼女の額全体にほつれて広がっていた. ― straggler 名 C ➔落伍者, はぐれた人・鳥, 迷い出た枝 ― straggly 形 ➔ばらばらの, (髪が)ほつれた ‖ *long straggly hair* 長いほつれ毛

**\*straight¹** /stréɪt/ 形 ▶定義1 with no bends or curves; going in one direction only 折れ曲がりのない; 1つの方向だけに延びる➔直線の, まっすぐな, 一直線の, 直行の ‖ *a straight line* 直線 *He's got dark, straight hair.* 彼は黒いまっすぐな髪をしている. *Keep your back straight!* 背中をまっすぐ伸ばしていなさい. *He was so tired he couldn't walk in a straight line.* 彼はひどく疲れていたのでまっすぐに歩くことができなかった. ☛ **hair, line** のさし絵 ▶定義2 (名詞の前は不可) in an exactly horizontal or vertical position 全く水平または垂直の位置にある➔水平な, 垂直な, 直立の, 傾いていない ‖ *That picture isn't straight.* その絵はまっすぐでない. ▶定義3 honest and direct 正直で単刀直入の➔正直な, 率直な, 誠実な, きっぱりとした ‖ *Politicians never give a straight answer.* 政治家は絶対にまともな回答をしない. *Are you being straight with me?* あなたは私に何か隠していませんか.

▶定義4 tidy or organized as it should be きちんと整理・整とんされた➔きちんとした, 整とんされた, 整理した ‖ *It took ages to put the room straight after we'd decorated it.* 模様替えをした後, 部屋を片付けるのに長い時間かかった.

▶定義5 略式 attracted to people of the opposite sex; heterosexual 異性に引き付けられる; 異性愛の➔異性愛の, 同性愛でない, ホモでない, まともな ⇔ **gay** ▶定義6 略式 used to describe a person who you think is too serious and boring まじめすぎて退屈と思う人を表現するのに用いて➔まじめな, まじめくさった

成句 **get sth straight** ▶定義 to make sure that you understand sth completely 〜を必ず完全に理解するようにする➔〜を(状況など)をはっきりさせる, 正しく理解する

**keep a straight face** ▶定義 to stop yourself from smiling or laughing にっこりしたり, 声を立てて笑ったりしないようにする➔(笑いをこらえて)まじめくさった顔をしている, 真顔でいる

**put/set the record straight** ⇒ **RECORD**¹

**\*straight²** /stréɪt/ 副 ▶定義1 not in a curve or at an angle; in a straight line 曲がりも傾きもしないで; 直線で➔一直線に, まっすぐに ‖ *Go straight on for about two miles until you come to some traffic lights.* 信号の所まで2マイルほど直進しなさい. *He was looking straight ahead.* 彼はまっすぐ前方を見ていた. *to sit up straight (= with a straight back)* 姿勢を正して (= 背中を伸ばして)座る ▶定義2 without stopping; directly 止まらずに; 直接➔続けて, とぎれずに, じかに ‖ *I took the children straight home after school.* 学校が終わった後私は子供たちを家にまっすぐに連れ帰った. *to walk straight past sb/sth* 歩いて〜をさっと通り越す *I'm going straight to bed when I get home.* 家に帰ったらまっすぐ床に就くつもりだ. *He joined the army straight from school.* 彼は卒業後すぐに陸軍に入隊した. ▶定義3 in an honest and direct way 正直で率直に➔正直に, 率直に, 包み隠さずに ‖ *Tell me straight, doctor – is it serious?* 先生, 正直に話してください － 病気は重いのですか.

成句 **go straight** ▶定義 to become honest after being a criminal 罪を犯した後にまっとうになる➔まっとうになる, まじめに暮らす, 堅気になる

**right/straight away** ⇒ **AWAY**

**straight out** ▶定義 in an honest and direct way 正直で率直に➔正直に, 率直に, 包み隠さずに ‖ *I told Asif straight out that I didn't want to see him any more.* 私はアシフにもう会いたくないと率直に話した.

**straighten** /stréɪt(ə)n/ 動自他 ▶定義 **straighten (sth) (up/out)** to become straight or to make sth straight まっすぐになる；〜をまっすぐにする➡まっすぐになる，きちんとなる；〜をまっすぐにする，きちんとする ‖ *The road straightens out at the bottom of the hill.* その道は丘のふもとで直線になる． *to straighten your tie* ネクタイをまっすぐにする

**句動詞** straighten sth out ▶定義 to remove the confusion or difficulties from a situation 状況から混乱または困難を取り除く➡〜を正す，解決する，きちんとする

straighten up ▶定義 to make your body straight and vertical 背筋をまっすぐに伸ばす➡(姿勢が)まっすぐになる，姿勢を正す

**straightforward** /strèɪtfɔ́ːrwərd, ⌢-/ 形 ▶定義 1 easy to do or understand; simple 簡単にできる，理解しやすい；簡単な➡分かりやすい，簡単な，単純な ‖ *straightforward instructions* 分かりやすい指示 ▶定義 2 honest and open 正直で包み隠しのない➡正直な，率直な，単刀直入な ‖ *a straightforward person* 竹を割ったような人

**strain**¹ /stréɪn/ 名 ▶定義 1 Ⓤ pressure that is put on sth when it is pulled or pushed by a physical force 物理的な力で引っ張ったり押すときに〜にかかる圧力➡ぴんと張ること，引っ張る力，張力 ‖ *Running downhill puts strain on the knees.* 下り坂を走るとひざに負担がかかる． *The rope finally broke **under the strain**.* 無理に引っ張りすぎてついにロープが切れた． ▶定義 2 ⒸⓊ worry or pressure caused by having too much to deal with 処理すべき事がありすぎて生じた心配または圧迫感➡重圧，重荷，緊張，ストレス，無理，過労 ‖ *to be **under a lot of strain** at work* 仕事中は非常に緊張している ▶定義 3 Ⓒ something that makes you feel worried and tense 心配させ，緊張させるもの➡不安のもと，緊張のもと，骨の折れる仕事，負担 ‖ *I always find exams a terrible strain.* 私はいつも試験を大きな負担に感じる． ▶定義 4 ⒸⓊ an injury to part of your body that is caused by using it too much 使いすぎによって体の部分に生じた損傷➡体を痛めること，筋違い ▶定義 5 Ⓒ one type of animal, plant or disease that is slightly different from the other types ほかの種類と多少異なる動物，植物または病気の変種➡変種，亜種，品種

**strain**² /stréɪn/ 動 ▶定義 1 自他 to make a great effort to do sth 〜を行うのに多大な努力をする➡全力を発揮する，懸命に努力する，骨折る；〜を最大限に働かせる，精一杯使う ‖ *I was straining to see what was happening.* 何が起きているのか見ようと私は目を凝らしていた． *Bend down as far as you can without straining.* 無理しないでできるだけ体を折り曲げなさい． ▶定義 2 他 to injure a part of your body by using it too much 使いすぎて体の一部を痛める➡〜を痛める，弱める，悪くする ‖ *Don't read in the dark. You'll strain your eyes.* 暗い所で読むのはやめなさい．目を悪くしますよ． *I think I've strained a muscle in my neck.* 私は首筋を違えたようだ． ▶定義 3 他 to put a lot of pressure on sth 〜にかなりの圧力をかける➡〜を引っ張る，〜を損なう，悪くする，壊す ‖ *Money problems have strained their relationship.* 金銭問題で彼らの関係にひびが入ってしまった． ▶定義 4 他 to separate a solid and a liquid by pouring them into a special container with small holes in it 小さな穴のある特殊な容器に入れて固体と液体を分離する➡〜をこす，〜をこして取り除く，〜の水気を切る ‖ *to strain tea/vegetables/spaghetti* 紅茶をこす，野菜・スパゲッティの水気を切る

**strained** /stréɪnd/ 形 ▶定義 1 not natural or friendly 自然でない，友好的でない➡不自然な，緊迫した ‖ *Relations between the two countries are strained.* 2つの国の関係は緊迫している． ▶定義 2 worried because of having too much to deal with 処理すべきことがありすぎて悩んでいる➡疲れた，不安な，緊張した ‖ *Martin looked tired and strained.* マーティンは疲れて参っているように見えた．

**strait** /stréɪt/ 名 ▶定義 1 [Ⓒ, 通常は複数] a narrow piece of sea that joins two larger seas 2つのより大きな海を結ぶ狭い海➡海峡，水路 ‖ *the straits of Gibraltar* ジブラルタル海峡 ▶定義 2 **straits** [複数扱い] a very difficult situation, especially one caused by having no money 特に金がないために生じる非常に困難な状況➡苦境，困窮，難局，困難 ‖ *The company is in financial straits.* その会社は財政的苦境にある．

**成句** be in dire straits ⇒ **DIRE**

**straitjacket**(または **straightjacket**) /stréɪtdʒækət/ 名 Ⓒ ▶定義 a piece of clothing like a jacket with long arms which is put on people who are considered dangerous to prevent them from behaving violently 危険と思われる人物に着せる暴力的な振る舞いを阻止するための、長そでのジャケットのような衣服→拘束服, 拘束衣

**strand** /strænd/ 名 C ▶定義1 a single piece of cotton, wool, hair, etc 1本の木綿糸, 毛糸, 髪の毛など→単糸, (1本の)糸, (1本の)髪の毛 ▶定義2 one part of a story, situation or idea 話, 状況または考えの一部分→集まって全体を成す構成要素, (話などの)筋道

**stranded** /strǽndəd/ 形 ▶定義 left in a place that you cannot get away from 出られない場所に置き去りにされた→取り残された, 立ち往生した, 途方に暮れた ‖ *We were left stranded when our car broke down in the mountains.* 山中で車が故障し, にっちもさっちもいかなくなってしまった.

*★**strange** /stréɪndʒ/ 形 ▶定義1 unusual or unexpected 普通でない, 予期していない→変な, 不思議な, 奇妙な, 変わった, 予想外の ‖ *A very strange thing happened to me on the way home.* 帰り道, とても妙な事が私の身に起きた. *a strange noise* 異常な音 ▶定義2 that you have not seen, visited, met, etc before 以前に見たり訪ねたり会ったことのない→未知の, 見知らぬ, 不案内な, 不慣れな, なじみのない ‖ *a strange town* 初めての町 *My mother told me not to talk to strange men.* 母は私に見知らぬ男の人に話し掛けてはならないと言った.

▶よその国から来た人・物について話すときにはstrangeは使わない. foreignを参照.

— **strangely** 副 →奇妙なことに; 奇妙に, 変に ‖ *The streets were strangely quiet.* 通りは奇妙なほど静かだった. *Tim's behaving very strangely at the moment.* ティムは今, とても妙な振る舞い方をしている. — **strangeness** 名 U →未知, 奇妙さ, 不思議

*★**stranger** /stréɪndʒər/ 名 C ▶定義1 a person that you do not know 知らない人→見知らぬ人, よその人 ‖ *I had to ask a **complete stranger** to help me with my suitcase.* 見ず知らずの人にスーツケースを持ってくれと頼まなければならなかった.

▶よその国から来た人について話すときにはstrangerは使わない. foreignを参照.

▶定義2 a person who is in a place that he/she does not know 知らない場所にいる人→(ある場所に)初めての人, 不案内な人 ‖ *I'm a stranger to this part of the country.* 私はこの地方は初めてだ.

**strangle** /strǽŋɡ(ə)l/ 動 他 ▶定義1 to kill sb by squeezing his/her neck or throat with your hands, a rope, etc 手, ひもなどで首または のどを絞めて〜を殺す→〜を絞め殺す, 絞殺する, 窒息させる ☛類 **throttle** ☛参 **choke** ▶定義2 to prevent sth from developing 〜が発展・成長するのを妨げる→〜を締め付ける, 抑え付ける

*★**strap** /stræp/ 名 C ▶定義 a long narrow piece of leather, cloth, plastic, etc that you use for carrying sth or for keeping sth in position 〜を運ぶ, または固定するのに用いる細長い皮, 布, プラスチックなど→ひも, 帯, 革ひも, 肩ひも, つり革 ‖ *I managed to fasten my watch strap but now I can't undo it.* どうにか腕時計のバンドを留めたが, 今度は外すことができない. ☛ **bag, binoculars, clock**のさし絵 — **strap** 動 他 (**strapping; strapped**)→〜をひもで縛る, くくる, (〜で)(動かないように)…を固定する ‖ *The racing driver was securely strapped into the car.* レーシングドライバーは車にしっかりとシートベルトで固定されていた.

**strategic** /strətíːdʒɪk/ (または **strategical**) 形 ▶定義1 helping you to achieve a plan; giving you an advantage 計画を成就するために役立つ; 優位にする→戦略に基づく, 戦略的な, 戦略上有利な ‖ *They made a strategic decision to sell off part of the company.* 彼らは会社の一部を売却する戦略的な決定を下した. ▶定義2 connected with a country's plans to achieve success in a war or in its defence system 戦争または防衛体制に成果を上げるための国家計画に関連した→戦略の, 戦略上重要な(不可欠の) ▶定義3 (used about bombs and other weapons) intended to be fired at the enemy's country rather than be used in battle (爆弾などの武器について)戦闘で使用するより, 敵国に向けて発射することを意図した→敵の本土をねらった, 敵の軍事・経済的枢要をねらった — **strategically** /-k(ə)li/ 副 →戦略上, 戦略に基づいて, 戦略的に ‖ *The island is strategically important.* その島は戦略上重要だ.

**strategy** /strǽtədʒi/ 名 (複 **strategies**) ▶定義1 C a plan that you use in order to achieve sth 〜

を達成するために用いる計画→(**具体的な**)**戦術, 戦法, 手段** ‖ *What's your strategy for this exam?* この試験に対するあなたの作戦は何ですか. ▶定義2 ❶ the action of planning how to do or achieve sth ～をどのように行うかまたは達成するかを計画すること→(**全体的な**)**戦略,(全体の)作戦, 計画** ‖ *military strategy* 軍事戦略

\*__straw__ /strɔː/ 名 ▶定義1 ❶ the long, straight, central parts (stems) of plants, for example wheat, that are dried and then used for animals to sleep on or for making baskets, covering a roof, etc 小麦などの植物の茎を乾かしたもの.動物の寝床に敷いたり,かごを作ったり,屋根をふくのに使われる→ **わら, 麦わら** ‖ *a straw hat* 麦わら帽子 ☛ C4 ページのさし絵 ▶定義2 ❸ one piece of straw 1 本のわら→**わら1本, 麦わら1本** ▶定義3 ❸ a long plastic or paper tube that you can use for drinking through 飲み物を飲むのに使うプラスチック,または紙製の細長い管→**ストロー** ☛ container のさし絵

成句 __the last/final straw__ ▶定義 the last in a series of bad things that happen to you and that makes you decide that you cannot accept the situation any longer 自分の身に起きる一連の悪い事の中で,これ以上事態を容認できないと決心させる最後の出来事→**忍耐の限界を超えさせるもの, 我慢の限度を超えさせるもの, 破滅などの引き金になる最後の一小事**

__strawberry__ /ˈstrɔːb(ə)ri; -bèri/ 名 ❸ (複 __strawberries__) ▶定義 a small soft red fruit with small white seeds on it 小さな白い種が表面に付いた柔らかい小さな赤い果物→**イチゴ** ‖ *strawberries and cream* ストロベリークリーム

__stray__¹ /stréɪ/ 動 ⓐ ▶定義1 to go away from the place where you should be いるべき場所から離れる→(**仲間に**)**はぐれる, 道に迷う** ‖ *The sheep had strayed onto the road.* 羊が道路に迷い込んだ. ▶定義2 to not keep to the subject you should be thinking about or discussing 考えるべき,または議論すべき課題からそれる→**それる, 外れる, 脱線する** ‖ *My thoughts strayed for a few moments.* 私はわずかの間ぼんやりと上の空の状態だった.

__stray__² /stréɪ/ 名 ❸ ▶定義 a dog, cat, etc that does not have a home 家を持たない犬,猫など→**野良犬, 野良猫, 迷い出た家畜** — __stray__ 形 (名詞の前だけで)→ **はぐれた, 迷い込んだ, 他から別れ**た ‖ *a stray dog* 野良犬

__streak__¹ /striːk/ 名 ❸ ▶定義1 __streak (of sth)__ a thin line or mark 細い線,または印→**線, 筋, しま** ‖ *The cat had brown fur with streaks of white in it.* その猫は茶色の毛に白いしまがあった. ▶定義2 a part of a person's character that sometimes shows in the way he/she behaves 振る舞い方に時々現れる人の性格の一部→**気味, 兆候, 傾向, 要素** ‖ *Vesna's a very caring girl, but she does have a selfish streak.* ヴェスナはとても面倒見の良い少女だが,自分勝手なところがある. ▶定義3 a continuous period of bad or good luck in a game of sport スポーツの試合の不運・幸運の続く期間→(**勝ち・負けなどの**)**一続き, 連続** ‖ *The team is __on a losing/winning streak__ at the moment.* 目下チームは負け・勝ち続けている.

__streak__² /striːk/ 動 ⓐ 略式 ▶定義 to run fast 速く走る→**疾走する, 全速力で走る**

__streaked__ /striːkt/ 形 ▶定義 __streaked (with sth)__ having lines of a different colour 何条かの異なる色の付いた→**しまのある, 筋のある, 筋状の** ‖ *black hair streaked with grey* 白髪混じりの黒髪

\*__stream__¹ /striːm/ 名 ❸ ▶定義1 a small river 小さな川→**小川, 流水, 流れ** ‖ *I waded across the shallow stream.* 私は浅い小川を歩いて渡った. ▶定義2 the continuous movement of a liquid or gas 液体または気体の連続的な移動→**流れ, 水流, 潮流, 気流** ‖ *a stream of blood* 間断のない血液の流れ ▶定義3 a continuous movement of people or things 人・物の連続的な移動→**流れ, 連続** ‖ *a stream of traffic* とぎれのない車の流れ ▶定義4 a large number of things which happen one after another 次々と起こる多数のもの→**流れ, 連続** ‖ *a stream of letters/telephone calls/questions* ひっきりなしの手紙・電話・質問

__stream__² /striːm/ 動 ⓐ ▶定義1 (used about a liquid, gas or light) to flow in large amounts (液体,気体,光について)多量に流れる→**どっと流れる, 流れ込む,(光が)差し込む** ‖ *Tears were streaming down his face.* 涙が彼の顔を伝って流れていた. *Sunlight was streaming in through the windows.* 日光が窓から差し込んでいた. ▶定義2 (used about people or things) to move somewhere in a continuous flow (人・物について)ど

## 1608 streamer

こかに次々と流れるように移動する➡流れるように動く,とめどなく続く,ひっきりなしに動く‖ *People were streaming out of the station.* 人々が駅からぞろぞろと出てきていた.

**streamer** /stríːmər/ 名 C ▶定義 a long piece of coloured paper that you use for decorating a room before a party, etc パーティーなどの前に部屋を飾り付けるのに用いる色の付いた細長い紙➡飾りリボン,吹き流し,長旗,テープ

**streamline** /stríːmlaɪn/ 動 他 ▶定義1 to give a vehicle, etc a long smooth shape so that it will move easily through air or water 水中・空中の移動が容易なように,乗り物などの形を縦長の滑らかなものにする ➡ ～を流線型にする ▶定義2 to make an organization, process, etc work better by making it simpler 組織,工程などを簡素化してより良く機能するようにする➡～を合理化する,能率的にする,簡素化する — **streamlined** 形➡流線型の,簡素化された,簡潔な,すっきりとした

★**street** /stríːt/ 名 C ▶定義1 a road in a town, village or city that has shops, houses, etc on one or both sides 商店・住宅などが片側または両側に並ぶ,町・村・都市の道路➡通り,街,街路‖ *to walk along/down the street* 通りを歩く *to cross the street* 通りを横切る *I met Karen in the street this morning.* 私は今朝,通りでカレンに会った. *a narrow street* 狭い通り *a street map of Rome* ローマの市街地図 ➡参 **road** の注 ▶定義2 **Street**(略式 **St**) [単数扱い] used in the names of streets Street 通りの名前に用いて➡～通り,～街‖ *64 High Street* 本通り 64 番地 *The post office is in Sheep Street.* 郵便局はシープ通りにある.

### ▶語法

**on/in the street の英米差**

アメリカ英語では on the street を,イギリス英語では in the street を使うのが一般的です. on の場合は street を平面(二次元)ととらえ,in の場合は空間(三次元)ととらえているのでしょう.

ニューヨークでは,東西に走る通りを street, 南北に走る通りを avenue と区別して呼んでいます.京都に例えると street が「三条」などの「条」に avenue が「丸太町通り」などの「通り」に相当します.

成句 **the man in the street** ⇒ **MAN**¹
**streets ahead (of sb/sth)** 略式 ▶定義 much better than sb/sth➡(～より)ずっと良い,格段に優れている
**(right) up your street** 略式 ▶定義 (used about an activity, subject, etc) exactly right for you because you know a lot about it, like it very much, etc(活動,話題などについて)それについての知識が豊富である,または非常に好きであるなどの理由でその人にまさに打って付けで➡～に打って付けで,お手のもので,～の専門・得意で

★**strength** /streŋ(k)θ/ 名 ▶定義1 U the quality of being physically strong; the amount of this quality that you have 肉体的に強いこと;肉体的頑健さの度合い➡強さ,力,体力‖ *He pulled with all his strength but the rock would not move.* 彼は力一杯引っ張ったが,岩はびくともしなかった. *I didn't have the strength to walk any further.* 私にはこれ以上歩く体力がなかった. ▶定義2 U the ability of an object to hold heavy weights or not to break or be damaged easily 重い物を持ちこたえる,または簡単に破壊・損傷しない物体の能力➡強さ,強度,耐久力‖ *All our suitcases are tested for strength before they leave the factory.* 当社のスーツケースはすべて工場から出荷される前に強度の検査が行われる. ▶定義3 U the power and influence that sb has ～の持つ力または影響力➡勢力,威力,権力,影響力‖ *Germany's economic strength* ドイツの経済力 ▶定義4 U how strong a feeling or opinion is 感情または意見の強さの度合い➡力,強烈[熱烈]さ,効果,(議論などの)説得力 ▶定義5 C U a good quality or ability that sb/sth has ～が所有している優れた性質または能力➡強み,長所,よりどころ,支え‖ *His greatest strength is his ability to communicate with people.* 彼の最も大きな強みは人と意志疎通を図る能力だ. *the strengths and weaknesses of a plan* 計画の長所と短所 ⇒ **weakness**
成句 **at full strength** ▶定義 (used about a group) having all the people it needs or usually has(集団について)必要とする,または通常有するすべての人員がそろっている➡勢ぞろいして,全員そろって,全員こぞって‖ *Nobody is injured,*

so the team will be at full strength for the game. だれもけがをしていないので、チームは全員そろって臨むことになる.

**below strength** ▶定義 (used about a group) not having the number of people it needs or usually has (集団について) 必要とする、または通常有する人員がそろっていない→**定員以下で，定員未満で，定員に達していない**

**on the strength of** ▶定義 as a result of information, advice, etc 情報，忠告などの結果として→**～の力を得て，～のお陰で，～を頼りに，根拠にして**

**strengthen** /stréŋ(k)θ(ə)n/ 動自他 ▶定義 to become stronger or to make sth stronger より強くなる；～をより強くする→**強くなる；～を強くする，強化する，増強する** ‖ exercises to strengthen your muscles 筋肉を強くする運動 ⇔ **weaken**

**strenuous** /strénjuəs/ 形 ▶定義 needing or using a lot of effort or energy 多大な努力またはエネルギーを必要とする、または用いる→**多大な努力を要する，骨の折れる，精力的な，活発な，猛烈な** ‖ Don't do **strenuous** exercise after eating. 食後は激しい運動をしてはいけない. She's making a **strenuous effort** to be on time every day. 彼女は毎日時間を守ろうと奮闘している.
— strenuously 副 →**精力的に，活発に，猛烈に**

★**stress**¹ /stres/ 名 ▶定義 1 ©Ⓤ worry and pressure that is caused by having too much to deal with あまりにも処理すべきことが多すぎるための心労・重圧→**重圧，緊張，ストレス** ‖ He's been **under** a lot of **stress** since his wife went into hospital. 彼は妻が入院してから多大なストレスにさらされている. ☛参 **trauma** ▶定義 2 Ⓤ stress (on sth) the special attention that you give to sth because you think it is important 重要だと考えるため～に払う特別な注意→**強調，力説，重点，重み** ‖ We should **put** more **stress** on preventing crime. 私たちは犯罪の防止にもっと重点を置くべきだ. ▶定義 3 ©Ⓤ (a) stress (on sth) the force that you put on a particular word or part of a word when you speak 話すときに特定の語または語の一部に置く強勢→**強勢，語勢，ストレス，アクセント** ‖ In the word 'dictionary' the stress is on the first syllable, 'dic'. dictionary という語では強勢は第 1 音節の dic にある. ▶定義 4 ©Ⓤ a physical force that may cause sth to bend or break 物が曲がったり壊れたりする原因となり得る物理的な力→**圧力，重圧** ‖ Heavy lorries **put** too much **stress** on this bridge. 重量のあるトラックが渡るとこの橋に過度の圧力がかかる.

**stress**² /stres/ 動他 ▶定義 to give sth special force or attention because it is important 重要なため～に特別に力を入れるまたは注目する→**～を強調する，力説する，～に重点を置く** ‖ The minister stressed the need for a peaceful solution. 大臣は平和的な解決の必要性を強調した. Which syllable is stressed in this word? この語ではどの音節に強勢が置かれるのですか. ☛類 **emphasize**

**stressful** /strésfʊl, -f(ə)l/ 形 ▶定義 causing worry and pressure 心労または圧迫感の原因となる→**重圧のかかる，緊張を要する，ストレスの多い** ‖ a stressful job ストレスの多い仕事

★**stretch**¹ /stretʃ/ 動 ▶定義 1 自他 to pull sth so that it becomes longer or wider; to become longer or wider in this way ～がより長くまたは広くなるように引っ張る；このように引っ張られてより長くまたは広くなる→**伸びる，広がる；～を伸ばす，広げる** ‖ The artist stretched the canvas tightly over the frame. 画家は額縁にカンバスをぴんと張った. My T-shirt stretched when I washed it. 洗濯をしたら私の T シャツが伸びてしまった. ☛ **shrink** のさし絵 ▶定義 2 自他 stretch (sth) (out) to push out your arms, legs, etc as far as possible 腕，足などをできるだけ遠くにぐっと出す→**手足を伸ばす，～を一杯に伸ばす，広げる** ‖ He switched off the alarm clock, yawned and stretched. 彼は目覚まし時計のスイッチを切り，あくびをして伸びをした. She stretched out on the sofa and fell asleep. 彼女はソファーに大の字になると眠ってしまった. She stretched out her arm to take the book. 彼女は本を取るために腕を伸ばした. ☛ S1 ページのさし絵 ▶定義 3 自 to cover a large area of land or a long period of time 広大な地域に及ぶ，長期にわたる→**広がる，延びる，続く，及ぶ，わたる** ‖ The long white beaches stretch for miles along the coast. 長い白い砂浜が海岸沿いに何マイルも広がっている. ▶定義 4 他 to make use of all the money, ability, time, etc that sb has available for use ～が使用できる金,能力,時間などをすべて利用する➔～を最大限に働かせる,使いきる ‖ *The test has been designed to really stretch students' knowledge.* その試験は生徒たちの知識を実際に最大限働かせるように作成されている.

成句 **stretch your legs** ▶定義 to go for a walk after sitting down for a long time 長い間座っていた後に散歩に出掛ける➔足を伸ばす,立ち上がって歩く,足をほぐす

**stretch**² /strétʃ/ 名 C ▶定義 1 a stretch (of sth) an area of land or water 陸地または水の広がり➔広がり,一続き,範囲,限度 ‖ *a dangerous stretch of road* 道路の危険区域 ▶定義 2 [通常は単数]the action of making the muscles in your arms, legs, back, etc as long as possible 腕,足,背中などの筋肉をできるだけ長く伸ばす動作➔伸ばすこと,伸びること,ストレッチ ‖ *Stand up, everybody, and have a good stretch.* 皆さん,立ち上がって手足を思い切り伸ばしてください.

成句 **at a stretch** ▶定義 without stopping 止まらずに➔一気に,一息に,立て続けに ‖ *We travelled for six hours at a stretch.* 私たちは一気に6時間(車両で)走り続けた.

**at full stretch** ⇒ **FULL**¹

**stretcher** /strétʃər/ 名 C ▶定義 a piece of cloth supported by two poles that is used for carrying a person who has been injured けがをした人を運ぶのに用いられる,2つの棒で支えられた布➔担架,担架車,ストレッチャー

*strict /stríkt/ 形 ▶定義 1 not allowing people to break rules or behave badly 規則違反や行儀の悪さを許さない➔厳格な,厳しい ‖ *Samir's very strict with his children.* サミールは子供たちにとても厳しい. *I went to a very strict school.* 私は非常に厳格な学校に通った. ▶定義 2 that must be obeyed completely 完全に従わなければならない➔厳しい,絶対的な ‖ *I gave her strict instructions to be home before 9.00.* 私は彼女に9時前に帰宅するように厳しく指示した. ▶定義 3 exactly correct; accurate 全く正しい; 正確な➔厳密な,精密な,正確な ‖ *a strict interpretation of the law* 法律の厳密な解釈

**strictly** /stríktli/ 副 ▶定義 in a strict way 厳しく➔厳しく,厳格に,絶対に,厳密に,精密に ‖ *Smoking is strictly forbidden.* 喫煙は厳禁されている.

成句 **strictly speaking** ▶定義 to be exactly correct or accurate 全く間違いなく,正確であるためには➔厳密に言えば,厳密には ‖ *Strictly speaking, the tomato is not a vegetable. It's a fruit.* 厳密に言えばトマトは野菜ではなく果物だ.

**stride**¹ /stráid/ 動 自 (過 **strode** /stróud/; 過分 **stridden** /strídn/) ▶定義 to walk with long steps, often because you feel very confident or determined しばしば非常に自信がある,または決意が固いために大きな歩幅で歩く➔大またで歩く,闊歩(かっぽ)する ‖ *He strode up to the house and knocked on the door.* 彼はその家の方へ大またで歩いていき戸をたたいた.

**stride**² /stráid/ 名 C ▶定義 a long step 大きな歩幅➔大また,一またぎ,闊歩(かっぽ)

成句 **get into your stride** ▶定義 to start to do sth in a confident way and well after an uncertain beginning 心もとない不安定な出だしの後,～を自信を持って立派にやり始める➔調子が出る,本調子になる,本来の調子を取り戻す

**make great strides** ▶定義 to make very quick progress 非常に早く進歩する➔急速に進歩する,長足の進歩を遂げる

**take sth in your stride** ▶定義 to deal with a new or difficult situation easily and without worrying 新たなまたは困難な状況にやすやすと苦もなく対処する➔～を難なく切り抜ける,楽々と処理する,うまくこなす

**strident** /stráidnt/ 形 ▶定義 (used about a voice or a sound) loud and unpleasant (声または音について)大きくて不快な➔耳障りな,甲高い,キーキー言う

**strife** /stráif/ 名 U (文) ▶定義 trouble or fighting between people or groups 人々または集団の間のトラブルまたは争い➔争い,不和,紛争,もめ事

*strike¹ /stráik/ 名 C ▶定義 1 a period of time when people refuse to go to work, usually because they want more money or better working conditions 通常,より多くの賃金またはより良い労働条件を求めて人々が働くことを拒否する期間➔ストライキ,スト ‖ *a one-day strike* 1日スト *Union members voted to go on strike.* 労働組合員たちはストに入ることを票決した.

▶定義 2 a sudden military attack, especially by aircraft 特に飛行機による突然の軍事攻撃➔空

襲, 攻撃, 集中攻撃

\*strike² /stráik/ 動 (過, 過分 struck /strʌ́k/)
▶定義1 他 正式 to hit sb/sth 〜をたたく→〜をたたく, 打つ, 殴る, ぶつける ‖ *The stone struck her on the head.* 石が彼女の頭に当たった. *The boat struck a rock and began to sink.* ボートが岩にぶつかって沈み始めた.

➤ hit の方がより一般的である: *The stone hit her on the head.* (石が彼女の頭に当たった.)

▶定義2 自他 to attack and harm sb/sth suddenly 不意に〜を襲って害を与える→(〜を)攻撃する, 襲う, 襲撃する ‖ *The earthquake struck Kobe in 1995.* 1995年に地震が神戸を襲った. *The building had been **struck by lightning**.* その建物に雷が落ちた. ▶定義3 自 to stop work as a protest 抗議として働くのをやめる→ストライキをする, ストをする ‖ *The workers voted to strike for more money.* 労働者たちは賃上げを求めてストライキを票決した. ▶定義4 他 **strike sb (as sth)** to give sb a particular impression ある特定の印象を〜に与える→〜に印象づける, 〜の心を打つ, 〜に…だと思わせる・感じさせる ‖ *Does anything here strike you as unusual?* ここで何かが異常だと感じますか. *He strikes me as a very caring man.* 彼はとても思いやりのある男性のように思う. ▶定義5 他 (used about a thought or an idea) to come suddenly into sb's mind (考えまたは思い付きについて) 心に不意に浮かぶ→〜の心に浮かぶ, 〜に思い当たる, 思い付く ‖ *It suddenly struck me that she would be the ideal person for the job.* 彼女はその仕事に打って付けの人物だろうということが突然私の頭にひらめいた. ▶定義6 他 to produce fire by rubbing sth, especially a match, on a surface 特にマッチなど, 何かの表面にこすり付けて火をつける→〜を擦る, つける, こする ‖ *She struck a match and lit her cigarette.* 彼女はマッチを擦ってたばこに火をつけた. ▶定義7 自他 (used about a clock) to ring a bell so that people know what time it is (時計について) 何時か分かるようにベルを鳴らす→時を打つ, 鳴って知らせる, 合図する; (時計が) (時)を打つ, 報じる ▶定義8 他 to discover gold, oil, etc in the ground 地中の金, 石油などを発見する→〜を掘り当てる, 見つける

成句 **strike a balance (between A and B)** ▶定義 to find a middle way between two extremes 両極端の中間を見つける→(両者の)バランスを取る, 釣り合いを取る, うまく両立させる

**strike a bargain (with sb)** ▶定義 to make an agreement with sb 〜と協定を結ぶ→(〜と) 取り引きする, 協定する, 契約する

**within striking distance** ▶定義 near enough to be reached or attacked easily 簡単に届く, または攻撃できるほど近い→ごく近い所に, 至近距離に

句動詞 **strike back** ▶定義 to attack sb/sth that has attacked you 攻撃した〜を攻撃する→打ち返す, 殴り返す

**strike up sth (with sb)** ▶定義 to start a conversation or friendship with sb 〜と会話または友好関係を始める→(〜と)(会話・交際)を始める, 結ぶ

**striker** /stráikər/ 名 C ▶定義1 a person who has stopped working as a protest 抗議として働くことをやめている人→ストライキをする人, ストライキ参加者 ▶定義2 (in football) a player whose job is to score goals (サッカーで) 得点することが役目の選手→センターフォワード, ストライカー

**striking** /stráikiŋ/ 形 ▶定義 very noticeable; making a strong impression 非常に目立つ; 強烈な印象を与える→人目をひく, 印象的な, 顕著な, (人が)すばらしく魅力的な ‖ *There was a striking similarity between the two men.* 2人の男性には際立った類似点があった. — **strikingly** 副 →著しく, 際立って

\*string¹ /strɪŋ/ 名 ▶定義1 C U a piece of long, strong material like very thin rope, that you use for tying things 物を結ぶのに用いる, 長くて丈夫な極細のロープのようなもの→ひも, 細ひも, 糸, ひも状の物 ‖ *a ball/piece/length of string* 1巻き・1本・1本のひも *The key is hanging on a string.* かぎはひもにつるしてある. ☛ **cable** のさし絵 ▶定義2 C one of the pieces of thin wire, etc that produce the sound on some musical instruments 一部の楽器に付いている, 音を出す細い金属線などの1本→弦 ‖ *A guitar has six strings.* ギターには弦が6本ある. ☛ **music** のさし絵 ▶定義3 C one of the pieces of thin material that is stretched across the thing (racket) that you use to hit the ball in tennis and other sports テニスなどのスポーツで球を

打つ具(ラケット)に張ってある何条かの細い素材の１つ➜**ガット,つる** ▶定義4 **the strings**[複数扱い] the instruments in an orchestra that have strings オーケストラの弦を持つ楽器➜**弦楽器(部)** ▶定義5 [C] **a string of sth** a line of things that are joined together on the same piece of thread 同じ糸で一列につないだ物➜**ひもに通した物,数珠つなぎにしたもの** ‖ *a string of beads* 一連のビーズ ▶定義6 [C] **a string of sth** a series of people, things or events that follow one after another 次から次へと続く一続きの人·物·出来事➜**一続きの～,一列,行列,連続,連発** ‖ *a string of visitors* 訪問者の列

[成句] **(with) no strings attached; without strings** ▶定義 with no special conditions 特別な条件なしに➜**条件を付けずに,付帯条件なしに,ひも付きでない**

**pull strings** ⇒ **PULL**¹

**string**² /strɪŋ/ [動][他](過,過分 **strung** /strʌŋ/) ▶定義 **string sth (up)** to hang up a line of things with a piece of string, etc ひもなどで一連の～をつるす➜**～にひも·糸を通す,数珠つなぎにする,～をひも·糸でつなぐ,ひも·糸でつるす**

[句動詞] **string sb/sth out** ▶定義 to make people or things form a line with spaces between each person or thing ～を間隔をおいて一列に並ばせる➜**～を一列に並べる,配列する**

**string sth together** ▶定義 to put words or phrases together to make a sentence, speech, etc 文,話などを作るために語または語句を組み合わせる➜**(言葉など)をつなぎ合わせる,どうにかつないで意味のある文にする**

S

**stringent** /stríndʒ(ə)nt/ [形] ▶定義 (used about a law, rule, etc) very strict (法律,規則などについて)➜ **厳しい,厳格な**

***strip**¹ /strɪp/ [名] [C] ▶定義 a long narrow piece of sth➜**細長い一片,切れ** ‖ *a strip of paper* 細長い紙切れ

**strip**² /strɪp/ [動] (**stripping**; **stripped**) ▶定義1 [自][他] **strip (sth) (off)** to take off your clothes; to take off sb else's clothes 自分の服を脱ぐ; ほかの～の服をはぐ➜**裸になる,衣服を脱ぐ; ～を裸にする,衣服をはぎ取る** ‖ *The doctor asked him to strip to the waist.* 医者は彼に上半身裸になるよう言った. *I was stripped and searched at the airport by two customs officers.* 私は空港で２人の税関職員に服を脱がされて検査された. ▶定義2 [他] **strip sb/sth (of sth)** to take sth away from sb/sth ～から…を取り除く➜**～から(…を)はぐ,奪う,剥奪(はくだつ)する,取り去る** ‖ *They stripped the house of all its furniture.* 彼らは家からすべての家具を持ち出した. ▶定義3 [他] **strip sth (off)** to remove sth that is covering a surface 表面を覆う～を取り除く➜**～をむく,はがす,取り除く** ‖ *to strip the paint off a door* 扉のペンキをはがす *to strip wallpaper* 壁紙をはがす

***stripe** /stráɪp/ [名] [C] ▶定義 a long narrow line of colour 細長い色の線➜**しま,しま模様,ストライプ** ‖ *Zebras have black and white stripes.* しま馬には黒と白のしま模様がある. — **striped** /stráɪpt/ [形]➜**しまのある,しま模様の,ストライプの** ‖ *a red and white striped dress* 赤と白のしま模様の服

**stripper** /strípər/ [名] [C] ▶定義 a person whose job is to take off his/her clothes in order to entertain people 人々を楽しませるために服を脱ぐことを仕事にしている人➜**ストリッパー**

**striptease** /strípti:z/ [名] [C] [U] ▶定義 entertainment in which sb takes off his/her clothes, usually to music 通常は音楽に合わせて人が服を脱いでみせる娯楽➜**ストリップショー**

**strive** /stráɪv/ [動][自](過 **strove** /stróʊv/; 過分 **striven** /strív(ə)n/) [正式] ▶定義 **strive (for sth/to do sth)** to try very hard to do or get sth ～をしよう,または手に入れようと懸命に努力する➜**(～を目指して·～しようと)努力する,骨折る,励む** ‖ *to strive for perfection* 完ぺきを目指して努力する

**strode** **STRIDE**¹ の過去形

***stroke**¹ /stróʊk/ [名] ▶定義1 [C] one of the movements that you make when you are writing or painting 文字を書くまたは絵をかくときに行う動きの１つ➜**一筆,一画,筆の運び,筆使い** ‖ *a brush stroke* はけ[筆]遣い ▶定義2 [C] one of the movements that you make when you are swimming, rowing, playing golf, etc 水泳·漕艇(そうてい),ゴルフなどの動きの１つ➜**一かき,一こぎ,一振り,一打ち** ‖ *Woods won by three strokes (= hits of the ball in golf).* ウッズは３打(＝ゴルフで球を打つ数)差で勝利した. ▶定義3 [C] [U] (複合語で用いて) one of the styles of swimming 泳ぎの型の１つ➜**泳ぎの型,泳法** ‖

*I can do backstroke and breaststroke, but not front crawl.* 私は背泳ぎと平泳ぎはできるが、クロールは駄目だ. ●参 **crawl** ▶定義4 ● a sudden illness which attacks the brain and can leave a person unable to move part of his/her body, speak clearly, etc 脳を襲う突然の病気. 身体の一部が利かなくなったり、はっきりと口がきけなくなるなどの障害が残ることがある→脳卒中,卒中;発作 ‖ *to have a stroke* (脳)卒中を起こす ▶定義5 [単数扱い] **a stroke of sth** a sudden successful action or event 思いも掛けない上首尾の行動または出来事→突然の事,思い掛けない事,偶然の巡り合わせ ‖ *It was a stroke of luck finding your ring on the beach, wasn't it?* 海岸で指輪が見つかったのは思い掛けない幸運だったね.

成句 **at a/one stroke** ▶定義 with a single action 1つの動作で→一撃で,一挙に,たちまち,あっと言う間に

**not do a stroke (of work)** ▶定義 to not do any work at all 全く働かない→一働きもしない,少しも仕事をしない

**stroke**² /stróuk/ 動他 ▶定義1 to move your hand gently over sb/sth ～の上で優しく手を動かす→～をなでる、なで付ける、さする ‖ *She stroked his hair affectionately.* 彼女は愛情を込めて彼の髪をなでた. *to stroke a dog* 犬をなでる ▶定義2 to move sth somewhere with a smooth movement ～を滑らかな動きである場所に移動する→(ボール)を巧みに打つ

**stroll** /stróul/ 名 ● ▶定義 a slow walk for pleasure 楽しみのためにゆっくり歩くこと→ぶらぶら歩き,散歩,散策 ‖ *to go for a stroll* along the beach 海岸を散歩する ─ **stroll** 動自→ぶらつく,散歩する,散策する

*__strong__ /strɔ(:)ŋ, strɒŋ/ 形 ▶定義1 (used about a person) physically powerful; able to lift or carry heavy things (人について)肉体的に力のある;重い物を持ち上げたり運ぶことができる→強い,力強い,丈夫な,たくましい ‖ *I need someone strong to help me move this bookcase.* この本棚を運ぶのを手伝ってくれるだれか力のある人が必要だ. *to have strong arms/muscles* たくましい腕・筋肉を持つ ▶定義2 (used about an object) not easily broken or damaged (物について)たやすく壊れないまたは損傷しない→丈夫な,頑丈な,強固な,しっかりとした ‖ *That chair isn't strong enough for you to stand on.* そのいすはあなたがその上に立っても大丈夫なほど頑丈ではない. ▶定義3 (used about a natural force) powerful (自然の力について)強力な→強い,激しい,強烈な ‖ *strong winds/currents/sunlight* 強風・激しい潮流・太陽の強烈な光 ▶定義4 having a big effect on the mind, body or senses 心・体・感覚に大きな影響を持つ→(影響力が)強い,(酒が)強い,(色・光・香りなどが)強烈な,濃い ‖ *a strong smell of garlic* ニンニクの強烈なにおい *strong coffee* 濃いコーヒー *a strong drink* (= with a lot of alcohol in it) 強い酒(＝アルコールが多く含まれている飲み物) *I have the strong impression that they don't like us.* 私は彼らが私たちを嫌っているという強い印象を抱いている. ▶定義5 (used about opinions and beliefs) very firm; difficult to fight against (意見または信念について)非常に強固な;逆らって戦いにくい→強い,強固な,熱烈な,ぐらつかない ‖ *There was strong opposition to the idea.* そのアイデアには強硬な反対があった.

*strong support for the government's plan* 政府の計画に対する力強い支援 ▶定義6 powerful and likely to succeed 力強く成功しそうな→有力な,優勢な,力量のある ‖ *She's a strong candidate for the job.* 彼女はその仕事の有力な候補者だ. *a strong team* 実力のあるチーム ▶定義7 (名詞の後で)having a particular number of people ある特定の数の人がいる→総勢～の,人員・兵員が～の ● すべての定義 名 **strength** ― **strongly** 副→頑丈に,強固に,強硬に,猛烈に,熱心に ‖ *The directors are strongly opposed to the idea.* 重役たちはその考えに猛反対している. *to feel very strongly about sth* ～について非常に強い関心を持っている

成句 **going strong** 略式 ▶定義 continuing, even after a long time 長い時間が経過した後も続いている→相変わらず好調で,繁盛して,うまくいって,達者で,元気で ‖ *The company was formed in 1851 and is still going strong.* その会社は1851年に設立されたが今なお好調を続けている.

**sb's strong point** ▶定義 something that a person is good at ～が得意な…→得意,長所,利点 ‖ *Maths is not my strong point.* 数学は私の得意科目ではない.

**strong-minded** 形 ▶定義 having firm ideas

or beliefs 強固な考えまたは信念を持っている→**意志の強い,決然とした,果断な,決断力に富む**

**stroppy** /strɑ́pi/ 形 医(俗語) ▶定義 (used about a person) easily annoyed and difficult to deal with (人について) すぐに腹を立てて扱いにくい→**怒りっぽい,気難しい,手のかかる**

**strove** STRIVE の過去形

**struck** STRIKE² の過去・過去分詞形

★**structure**¹ /strʌ́ktʃər/ 名 ▶定義 1 C U the way that the parts of sth are put together or organized ～の部分の組み立て方または組織のされ方→**構造,組織,組み立て,仕組み** ‖ *the political and social structure of a country* 国の政治・社会構造 *the grammatical structures of a language* ある言語の文法構造 ▶定義 2 C a building or sth that has been built or made from a number of parts 建物または数多くの部分から組み立てられたり作られたりした物→**建物,建造物,建築物** ‖ *The old office block had been replaced by a modern glass structure.* 古いオフィスビル街は現代的なガラスの建築物に取って代わられた.
— **structural** /strʌ́ktʃərəl/ 形 →**構造(上)の,構造的な,組織の**

**structure**² /strʌ́ktʃər/ 動 他 ▶定義 to arrange sth in an organized way ～を系統立てて整える→**～を組み立てる,体系化する** ‖ *a carefully-structured English course* 入念に組み立てられた英語のコース[課程]

★**struggle**¹ /strʌ́g(ə)l/ 動 自 ▶定義 1 struggle (with sth/for sth/to do sth) to try very hard to do sth, especially when it is difficult 特に何かをするのが大変なとき,それをしようと懸命に努力する→**(～と)格闘する,(～を得ようと・～しようと)奮闘する,努力する,取り組む** ‖ *We struggled up the stairs with our heavy suitcases.* 私たちは重いスーツケースを持ってやっとのことで階段を上った. *Maria was struggling with her English homework.* マリアは英語の宿題と格闘していた. *The country is struggling for independence.* その国は独立のために戦っている. ▶定義 2 struggle (with sb/sth); struggle (against sth) to fight in order to prevent sth or to escape from sb ～を未然に防ぐ,または～から逃れるために戦う→**もがく,あがく,(～と)戦う,取っ組み合う** ‖ *He shouted and struggled but he couldn't get free.* 彼は叫んでもがいたが逃れることはできなかった. *A passer-by was struggling with one of the robbers on the ground.* 1人の通行人が路上で泥棒たちの1人ともみ合っていた. *He has been struggling against cancer for years.* 彼は何年もがんと闘っている.

**句動詞** **struggle on** ▶定義 to continue to do sth although it is difficult 困難にもかかわらず～をし続ける→**苦労して続ける,どうにかやっていく・暮らしていく** ‖ *I felt terrible but managed to struggle on to the end of the day.* 気分がひどく悪かったが,どうにかその日の終わりまで頑張り通した.

**struggle**² /strʌ́g(ə)l/ 名 C ▶定義 1 a fight in which sb tries to do or get sth when this is difficult ～をする,または手に入れることが困難なときに,それをしようと努力する戦い→**闘争,苦闘,(必死の)努力,もがき,取り組み** ‖ *All countries should join together in the struggle against terrorism.* すべての国が一致してテロ行為に対する戦いに加わるべきだ. *He will not give up the presidency without a struggle.* 彼は戦わずに大統領の地位をあきらめはしないだろう. *a struggle for independence* 独立のための戦い ▶定義 2 [通常は単数] sth that is difficult to achieve 達成が困難な～→**非常な努力を要する仕事,困難な作業,苦労** ‖ *It will be a struggle to get there on time.* 時間通りにそこに到着するのは一苦労だろう.

**strum** /strʌm/ 動 自 他 (**strumming**; **strummed**) ▶定義 to play a guitar by moving your hand up and down over the strings 弦の上で手を上下に動かしてギターを演奏する→**(～を)かき鳴らす,つま弾いて演奏する,軽く弾く**

**strung** STRING² の過去・過去分詞形

**strut** /strʌt/ 動 自 (**strutting**; **strutted**) ▶定義 to walk in a proud way 得意げに歩く→**そり返って歩く,威張って歩く,気取って歩く**

**stub** /stʌb/ 名 C ▶定義 the short piece of a cigarette or pencil that is left after the rest of it has been used たばこ・鉛筆を使った後のわずかな残り→**吸殻,短い吸差し,(鉛筆の)使い残り**

**stubble** /stʌ́b(ə)l/ 名 U ▶定義 1 the short parts of corn, wheat, etc that are left standing after the rest has been cut 穀物・小麦などを刈り取った後切り倒されないで短く残った部分→**刈り株,切り株** ▶定義 2 the short hairs that grow on a man's face when he has not shaved for some time しばらくそらないうちに短く伸びた男性の顔ひげ➡無精ひげ,短く伸びたひげ ☛ **hair** のさし絵

**stubborn** /stʌ́bərn/ 形 ▶定義 not wanting to do what other people want you to do; refusing to change your plans or decisions ほかの人たちがしてほしいと思っている事をしたがらない;自分の計画または決定を変更することを拒む➡頑固な,強情な,意固地な ‖ *She's too stubborn to apologize.* 彼女は強情でなかなか謝ったりしない. ☛類 **obstinate** ☛参 **pig-headed** — **stubbornly** 副 ▶頑固に,頑強に,断固として ‖ *He stubbornly refused to apologize so he was sacked.* 彼は断固として謝罪することを拒んだので解雇された. — **stubbornness** 名 Ｕ ▶頑固さ,強情,不屈

**stuck**¹ **STICK**² の過去・過去分詞形

**stuck**² /stʌk/ 形 ▶定義 1 not able to move 動くことができない➡動けなくて,はまり込んで,引っ掛かって ‖ *This drawer's stuck. I can't open it at all.* この引き出しは引っ掛かっている. 全く開けることができない. *We were stuck in traffic for over two hours.* 私たちは交通渋滞に遭って2時間以上身動きできなかった. ▶定義 2 not able to continue with an exercise, etc because it is too difficult あまりに難しすぎるため練習問題などを続けることができない➡行き詰まって,困りきって,つっかえて ‖ *If you get stuck, ask your teacher for help.* 困ったら先生に助けを求めなさい.

**stud** /stʌd/ 名 ▶定義 1 Ｃ a small piece of metal that sticks out from the rest of the surface that it is fixed to 表面から出っ張って取り付けられた小さな金属片➡びょう,くぎ,飾りボタン ‖ *a black leather jacket with studs all over it* びょうがちりばめられた黒い革のジャケット ▶定義 2 Ｃ a small, round, solid piece of metal that you wear through a hole in your ear or other part of the body 耳や体のほかの部分に穴を開けて身に着ける小さな丸い硬い金属片➡スタッド,ピアス ▶定義 3 Ｃ one of the pieces of plastic or metal that stick out from the bottom of football, etc boots and that help you stand up on wet ground サッカーなどで履く靴底から突き出たプラスチックまたは金属製の物. これがあればぬれたグランドでも立っていられる➡靴底のびょう,スパイク ▶定義 4 Ｃ Ｕ a number of high quality horses or other animals that are kept for breeding young animals; the place where these horses, etc are kept 繁殖用に飼われる優秀な馬またはそのほかの動物の一群; これらの馬などを飼う場所➡繁殖用の馬・動物,種馬; 種馬の飼育場,繁殖場 ‖ *a stud farm* 種馬飼育場

**studded** /stʌ́dəd/ 形 ▶定義 1 covered or decorated with small pieces of metal that stick out from the rest of the surface 表面から突き出た小さな金属片で覆われたまたは飾られた➡びょうで覆われた,飾りボタンのちりばめられた,飾りびょうで飾られた ▶定義 2 studded (with sth) containing a lot of sth 〜をたくさん含んでいる➡(〜を)たくさん付けた,(〜で)一杯の

*****student** /st(j)úːd(ə)nt/ 名 Ｃ ▶定義 a person who is studying at a college or university 大学で勉強している人➡学生,大学生 ‖ *Paola is a medical student at Bristol University.* パオラはブリストル大学の医学生だ. *a full-time/part-time student* 全日制・定時制の学生 *a postgraduate/research student* 大学院生・研究生

▶ **pupil** と比較. **scholar**, **graduate**, **undergraduate** を参照.

> ▶音声とつづり字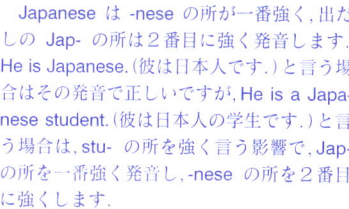
>
> Japanese のアクセント位置
>
> Japanese は -nese の所が一番強く,出だしの Jap- の所は2番目に強く発音します. *He is Japanese.*(彼は日本人です.)と言う場合はその発音で正しいですが,*He is a Japanese student.*(彼は日本人の学生です.)と言う場合は,stu- の所を強く言う影響で,Jap- の所を一番強く発音し,-nese の所を2番目に強くします.

**studied** /stʌ́dɪd/ 形 正式 ▶定義 carefully planned or done, especially when you are trying to give a particular impression 特にある特定の印象を与えようとしているときに慎重に計画されたまたは行われた➡慎重に考え抜いた; わざとらしい,故意の,不自然な

*****studio** /st(j)úːdiòʊ/ 名 Ｃ ( 複 **studios**) ▶定義 1 a room where an artist or photographer works 芸術家または写真家が仕事をする部屋➡仕事場,アトリエ,工房 ▶定義 2 a room or building where films or television programmes are

## 1616 studious

made, or where music, radio programmes, etc are recorded 映画またはテレビ番組の作成,あるいは音楽,ラジオ番組などの録音をする部屋または建物→**スタジオ,撮影所,録音室,放送室** ‖ *a film/TV/recording studio* 映画・テレビの録音スタジオ

**studious** /stjúːdiəs/ 形 ▶定義 (used about a person) spending a lot of time studying(人について)多くの時間を勉強して過ごす→**よく勉強する,勉強好きな,学問に励む**

**studiously** /stjúːdiəsli/ 副 ▶定義 with great care 多大な注意を払って→**慎重に,熱心に,念入りに**

\*__study__¹ /stʌ́di/ 名 (複 **studies**) ▶定義 1 ❶the activity of learning about sth 〜についての学習活動→**勉強,勉学,学習,研究** ‖ *One hour every afternoon is left free for individual study.* 毎日午後の1時間は自習のために空けてある. *Physiology is the study of how living things work.* 生理学は生体の機能に関する学問である. ▶定義 2 **studies** [複数扱い] the subjects that you study 研究している主題→**研究科目,(特定分野の)研究** ‖ *business/media/Japanese studies* 経営・マスメディア・日本研究 ▶定義 3 ❸ a piece of research that examines a question or a subject in detail 1つの問題または主題を精査する研究→**研究,調査** ‖ *They are doing a study of the causes of heart disease.* 彼らは心臓病の原因について研究を行っている. ▶定義 4 ❸ a room in a house where you go to read, write or study 家の中で読書,書き物,勉強をするために使う部屋→**書斎,勉強部屋**

\*__study__² /stʌ́di/ 動 (現分 **studying**; 三単現 **studies**; 過,過分 **studied**) ▶定義 1 ❶❷ study (sth/for sth) to spend time learning about sth 〜を学んで時間を過ごす→**(〜を)勉強する,学ぶ,学習する,研究する** ‖ *to study French at university* 大学でフランス語を学ぶ *Leon has been studying hard for his exams.* レオンは試験に向けて一生懸命勉強している. ▶定義 2 ❷ to look at sth very carefully 〜を非常に慎重に見る→**〜を詳しく調べる,注意深く観察する,注視する,じっと見る** ‖ *to study a map* 地図を詳しく調べる

\*__stuff__¹ /stʌf/ 名 ❶ 略式 ▶定義 1 used to refer to sth without using its name 名前を使わずに〜に言及するのに用いて→**物,代物(しろもの)** ‖ *What's that green stuff at the bottom of the bottle?* びんの底にある緑色の物は何ですか. *The shop was burgled and a lot of stuff was stolen.* 店に泥棒が入り,たくさんの物が盗まれた. *They sell stationery and stuff (like that).* 彼らは文房具やそういった物を売っている. *I'll put the swimming stuff in this bag.* 水泳用具をこのかばんに入れるつもりだ. ▶定義 2 used to refer in general to things that people do, say, think, etc 人々がする事,言う事または考える事を一般的に示すのに用いて→**物事,事,振る舞い,(しばしば下らない)話,考え事** ‖ *I've got lots of stuff to do tomorrow so I'm going to get up early.* 明日する事がたくさんあるので早く起きるつもりだ. *I don't believe all that stuff about him being robbed.* 彼が強盗に遭ったなんていうばかげた話は一切信用しない. *I like reading and stuff.* 私は読書やそういったたぐいの事が好きだ.

**stuff**² /stʌf/ 動 ▶定義 1 ❹ stuff sth (with sth) to fill sth with sth 〜を…で満たす→**物に(〜を)詰める,詰め込む** ‖ *The pillow was stuffed with feathers.* まくらには羽毛が詰めてあった. *red peppers stuffed with rice* 米の詰め物をした赤トウガラシ ▶定義 2 ❹ 略式 stuff sth into sth to put sth into sth else quickly or carelessly 急いで,または無造作に〜をほかの…に入れる→**〜を…に押し込む,突っ込む** ‖ *He quickly stuffed a few clothes into a suitcase.* 彼は急いで服を2,3着スーツケースに詰め込んだ. ▶定義 3 ❹ 略式 stuff sb/yourself (with sth) to eat too much of sth 〜を食べすぎる→**〜にたらふく(…を)食べさせる,(〜を)腹一杯食べる** ‖ *Barry just sat there stuffing himself with sandwiches.* バリーはただそこに腰掛けてサンドイッチを腹一杯食べていた. ▶定義 4 ❹ to fill the body of a dead bird or animal with special material so that it looks as if it is alive 生きているように見せるために死んだ鳥または動物に特殊な物を詰める→**〜を剥製(はくせい)にする,剥製にするために〜に詰め物をする** ‖ *They've got a stuffed crocodile in the museum.* 美術館には剥製のワニがある.

**stuffing** /stʌ́fɪŋ/ 名 ❹ ▶定義 1 a mixture of small pieces of food that you put inside a chicken, vegetable, etc before you cook it 加熱する前に鶏,野菜などの中に入れる細かい食べ物を混ぜ合わせたもの→**詰め物** ▶定義 2 the material that you put inside cushions, soft toys, etc クッション, 柔らかいおもちゃなどの中に入れる→~詰め物, 綿, 羽毛, わら

**stuffy** /stʌfi/ 形 ▶定義1 (used about a room) too warm and having no fresh air(部屋について)暖かすぎて新鮮な空気がない→むっとする, 風通しの悪い, 息の詰まる ▶定義2 略式 (used about a person) formal and old-fashioned(人について)堅苦しく古風な→堅苦しい, 古臭い, 保守的な, 融通の利かない

**stumble** /stʌmb(ə)l/ 動自 ▶定義1 stumble (over/on sth) to hit your foot against sth when you are walking or running and almost fall over 歩いたり走ったりしているとき, 足を物にぶつけて転びそうになる→(~に)つまずく, よろける, ぶつかる ▶定義2 stumble (over/through sth) to make a mistake when you are speaking, playing music, etc 話または演奏の途中で間違いをする→(~で)とちる, 間違える, (~を)つかえながら言い終える ‖ *The newsreader stumbled over the name of the Russian tennis player.* ニュースキャスターはロシア人のテニス選手の名前でつかえた. 句動詞 stumble across/on sb/sth ▶定義 to meet or find sb/sth by chance ~に偶然会う, または~を偶然見つける→~に偶然出くわす, ~を偶然見つける

**stumbling block** 名 C ▶定義 something that causes trouble or a difficulty, so that you cannot achieve what you want 結果的に望むことが達成できなくなるようなトラブル・困難を引き起こすもの→つまずかせるもの, 邪魔物, 障害, ネック ‖ *Money is still the stumbling block to settling the dispute.* 金のことがいまだに紛争解決の障害になっている.

**stump**¹ /stʌmp/ 名 C ▶定義 the part that is left after sth has been cut down, broken off, etc ~が切り落とされたり折られたりなどした後に残った部分→切り株, (折れた)歯の根, (手足などが切断された後の)残りの部分, 吸差し ‖ *a tree stump* 木の切り株

**stump**² /stʌmp/ 動他 略式 ▶定義 to cause sb to be unable to answer a question or find a solution for a problem ~に, 質問に答えるまたは問題の解決策を見つけることをできなくさせる→~を困らせる, 途方に暮れさせる, 立ち往生させる ‖ *I was completely stumped by question 14.* 私は第14問で全く答えに詰まってしまった.

# stupendous 1617

**stun** /stʌn/ 動他 (**stunning**; **stunned**) ▶定義1 to make a person or animal unconscious or confused by hitting him/her/it on the head 脳天をたたいて人または動物の意識を失わせる, または混乱させる→~を気絶させる, 失神させる, ~の気を失わせる ▶定義2 to make a person very surprised by telling him/her some unexpected news 思い掛けない知らせを伝えて人を非常に驚かせる→~をたまげさせる, あぜんとさせる, 動転させる, 当惑させる ‖ *His sudden death stunned his friends and colleagues.* 彼の突然の死に友人や同僚はぼう然とした. — stunned 形→気絶した, 失神した, 動転した, 当惑した, 酔っ払った

**stung** STING¹ の過去・過去分詞形
**stunk** STINK の過去分詞形

**stunning** /stʌnɪŋ/ 形 略式 ▶定義 very attractive, impressive or surprising とても魅力的な, 印象的なまたは意外な→びっくりさせる, はっとする, 目の覚めるような, すてきな, すばらしい ‖ *a stunning view* すばらしい眺め

**stunt**¹ /stʌnt/ 名 C ▶定義1 something that you do to get people's attention 人の注意をひくために行う事→人目をひくための行為, 目立つ行為, 人気取り ‖ *a publicity stunt* 人目をひく宣伝行為 ▶定義2 a very difficult or dangerous thing that sb does to entertain people or as part of a film 人々を楽しませるため, または映画の一部として行われる非常に難しい, または危険な行為→曲芸, 離れ業, 見事な演技, スタント ‖ *Some actors do their own stunts, others use a stunt man.* 俳優の中には自分でスタントを演じる者もいればスタントマンを使う者もいる.

**stunt**² /stʌnt/ 動他 ▶定義 to stop sb/sth growing or developing properly ~の順調な発育または成長を妨げる→~を妨げる, ~の成長を妨げる, ~の発育を遅らせる ‖ *A poor diet can stunt a child's growth.* 粗悪な食事は子供の成育を妨げることがある.

**stuntman** /stʌntmæn/ 名 C ( 複 **-men** /-mən/) ▶定義 a person who does sth dangerous in a film in the place of an actor 映画で俳優の代わりに危険な~をする人→スタントマン

**stupendous** /st(j)uːpéndəs/ 形 ▶定義 very large or impressive 非常に大きい, または印象的な→とてつもない, 途方もない, ずば抜けた, 巨大な ‖ *a*

### 1618　stupid

*stupendous achievement* 偉業

**★stupid** /stˈ(j)úːpəd/ 形 ▶定義1 not intelligent or sensible 頭が良くない,分別のない→ばかな,愚かな,ばかげた,下らない,非常識な,無分別な ‖ *Don't be so stupid, of course I'll help you!* ばかな事は言わないで,もちろん助けてあげますよ. *He was stupid to trust her.* 彼女を信用するなんて彼も愚かだった. *a stupid mistake/suggestion/question* 愚かな間違い・下らない提案・ばかげた質問 ▶定義2 (名詞の前だけ) 略式 used to show that you are angry or do not like sb/sth 怒っていることまたは～が気に入らないことを示すのに用いて→いまいましい,むかつく,腹の立つ,ひどくつまらない ‖ *I'm tired of hearing about his stupid car.* 私は彼の下らない車の話を聞くのにもううんざりだ. ― **stupidity** /stˌ(j)uːpídəti/ 名 ❶→愚かさ,愚鈍,愚行,愚考 ― **stupidly** 副→愚かに(も),ばかみたいに

**stupor** /stˈ(j)úːpər/ 名 [単数扱い, ❶] ▶定義 the state of being nearly unconscious or being unable to think properly ほとんど意識のない,またはまともに考えることのできない状態→意識混濁,人事不省,ぼう然自失,ぼうっとすること

**sturdy** /stˈəːrdi/ 形 (**sturdier**; **sturdiest**) ▶定義 strong and healthy; that will not break easily 頑丈で健康な; 壊れにくい→たくましい,屈強な,頑丈な,しっかりとした,断固とした ‖ *sturdy legs* がっしりとした足 *sturdy shoes* 丈夫な靴 ― **sturdily** 副→丈夫に,頑強に ― **sturdiness** 名 ❶→屈強,頑丈,断固

**stutter** /stˈʌtər/ 動 自 他 ▶定義 to have difficulty when you speak, so that you keep repeating the first sound of a word 話をするとき言葉がすらすらと出ず,単語の最初の音を繰り返す→(～を)どもる,詰まる,口ごもる,どもりながら言う ― **stutter** 名 ❸→どもること,どもり,吃(きつ) ‖ *to have a stutter* どもる

**sty** (または **stye**) /stάɪ/ 名 ❶ ( 複 **sties** または **styes**) ▶定義1 a painful spot on the skin that covers the eye (the eyelid) まぶたにできる痛いおでき→物もらい,麦粒腫(ばくりゅうしゅ) ▶定義2 = PIGSTY

**★style** /stάɪl/ 名 ▶定義1 ❶ ❶ the way that sth is done, built, etc ～のやり方,建て方など→やり方,方法,形式,流儀,スタイル ‖ *a new style of architecture* 建築の新しい様式 *The writer's style is very clear and simple.* その作家の文体は非常に明快で分かりやすい. *an American-style education system* アメリカ流の教育制度 ▶定義2 ❸ ❶ the fashion, shape or design of sth ～の流行,型またはデザイン→型,スタイル,流行型,格好 ‖ *We stock all the latest styles.* 当店は最新流行型のすべてを取りそろえている. *I like your new hairstyle.* あなたの新しいヘアスタイルが好きだ. ▶定義3 ❶ the ability to do things in a way that other people admire 人が感嘆するようなやり方で物事を行う能力→品・格好の良さ,気品,風格・洗練 ‖ *He's got no sense of style.* 彼はおしゃれ感覚が全くない.

> **▶日本語 vs 英語**
>
> **style は「型」のこと**
>
> 体の均整が取れているという意味で「スタイルが良い」と言いますが,英語では have a good figure と言います. style には体の均整という意味はありません. style は,洋服の着方,書き方,話し方,庭の造り方,音楽,芸術など,様々なものの「様式」という意味で使われます.「フォーマル」は formal style,「カジュアル」は casual style. その点 hair style は日本語でも,まさに「髪」の「型」です.

**stylish** /stάɪlɪʃ/ 形 ▶定義 fashionable and attractive おしゃれで魅力的な→流行に合った,当世風の,上品な,スマートな ‖ *She's a stylish dresser.* 彼女は着こなしがうまい.

**suave** /swɑːv/ 形 ▶定義 (usually used about a man) confident, elegant and polite, sometimes in a way that does not seem sincere (通常は男性について) 時には上辺だけのように見えるが,自信に満ち,上品で,丁寧な→温和な,物柔らかな,洗練された,丁寧な,慇懃(いんぎん)な

**subconscious** /sˌʌbkάnʃəs/(または **unconscious**) 名 [単数扱い, ❶] ▶定義 **the subconscious** the hidden part of your mind that can affect the way that you behave without you realizing 気付かないうちに行動の仕方に影響を及ぼすことのある心の隠れた部分→潜在意識 ― **subconscious** 形→潜在意識の,意識下の ‖ *the subconscious mind* 潜在意識 *Many advertisements work at a subconscious level.* 広告の多くは意識下レベルで作用する. ― **subconsciously** 副→

半ば無意識で, 潜在意識で, 意識下で

**subdivide** /sʌ̀bdəváɪd/ [動][自][他] [定義] to divide or be divided into smaller parts より小さな部分に分けるまたは分かれる ➜**細分する; ～を細分する, 小分けする, 細別する** — subdivision /sʌ̀bdəvíʒ(ə)n/ [名] [C][U] ➜**細分, 小分け, (細分された)区画**

**subdue** /səbd(j)úː/ [動][他] [定義] to defeat sb/sth or bring sb/sth under control ～を打ち負かす, ～を支配下に置く ➜**～を征服する, 支配する, (反乱など)を鎮圧する**

**subdued** /səbd(j)úːd/ [形] [定義] 1 (used about a person) quieter and with less energy than usual (人について)いつもより静かで活動的でない➜**(いつになく)おとなしい, 控えめな, 沈んだ** [定義] 2 not very loud or bright 音があまり大きくない, または色があまり鮮やかでない➜**(声·光·感情などが)抑えられた, 弱められた, 和らげられた** ‖ *subdued laughter/lighting* 押し殺した笑い·柔らかい照明

***subject**[1] /sʌ́bdʒɪkt/ [名] [C] [定義] 1 a person or thing that is being considered, shown or talked about 考察·提示·話の対象となっている人·物➜**(研究などの)主題, 題目, 話題, テーマ** ‖ *What subject is the lecture on?* その講義の演題は何ですか. *What are your views on this subject?* この問題に対するあなたの見解は何ですか. *I've tried several times to **bring up**/**raise the subject** of money.* 私は何度か金の話題を持ち出そうとした. [定義] 2 an area of knowledge that you study at school, university, etc 学校, 大学などで学ぶ学問の領域➜**教科, 学科, 科目** ‖ *My favourite subjects at school are Biology and French.* 学校で好きな教科は生物学とフランス語だ. [定義] 3 (文法) the person or thing that does the action described by the verb in a sentence 文中において動詞が表す動作をする人·物➜**主語, 主部** ‖ *In the sentence 'The cat sat on the mat', 'the cat' is the subject.* The cat sat on the mat という文では the cat が主語になる. ☛参 **object** [定義] 4 a person from a particular country, especially one with a king or queen; a citizen 特に王または女王の統治する特定の国の出身者; 国民➜**臣民, 国民** ‖ *a British subject* イギリス国民

[成句] change the subject ⇒ **CHANGE**[1]

**subject**[2] /səbdʒékt/ [動]

[句動詞] subject sb/sth to sth [定義] to make sb/sth experience sth unpleasant ～に嫌な…を経験させる ➜**～を(嫌な目など)にさらす, ～に(嫌な事)を経験させる** ‖ *He was subjected to verbal and physical abuse from the other boys.* 彼はほかの少年たちから暴言や暴行を受けた.

**subject**[3] /sʌ́bdʒɪkt/ [形] subject to sth [定義] 1 likely to be affected by sth ～の影響を受けやすい➜**～を受けやすい, 被りやすい, ～にかかりやすい, 左右されやすい** ‖ *The area is subject to regular flooding.* その地域は定期的に洪水に見舞われやすい. *Smokers are more subject to heart attacks than non-smokers.* たばこを吸う人はたばこを吸わない人よりも心臓発作を起こしやすい. [定義] 2 depending on sth as a condition 条件として～次第の➜**～を条件とする, ～を受ける必要がある, ～次第である** ‖ *The plan for new housing is still subject to approval by the minister.* 新しい住宅供給計画はまだ大臣の承認を必要とする. [定義] 3 controlled by or having to obey sb/sth ～に支配された, または従わなければならない➜**～に支配されている, 従属している, 服従している**

**subjective** /səbdʒéktɪv/ [形] [定義] based on your own tastes and opinions instead of on facts 事実よりも自分自身の好みまたは意見に基づいた➜**主観の, 主観的な, 個人的な** ‖ *Try not to be so subjective in your essays.* エッセーではあまり主観的にならないようにしなさい. ⇔ **objective** — subjectively [副] ➜**主観的に, 主観で**

**subject matter** [名] [U] [定義] the ideas or information contained in a book, speech, painting, etc 書物, 演説, 絵画などの中にある考えまたは情報➜**主題, 内容, 題材**

**subjunctive** /səbdʒʌ́ŋktɪv/ [名] [単数扱い] [定義] the form of a verb in certain languages that expresses doubt, possibility, a wish, etc ある特定の言語で, 疑念, 可能性, 願望などを表す動詞の形➜**仮定法, 叙想法** — subjunctive [形] ➜**仮定法の, 叙想法の**

**sublime** /səbláɪm/ [形][正式] [定義] of extremely high quality that makes you admire sth very much 感嘆せずにはいられないほど高い質の➜**荘厳な, 崇高な, 雄大な, 気高い, すばらしい** — sublimely [副] ➜**荘厳な, ものすごく, ひどく**

**submarine** /sʌ́bməriːn, ˌ--ˈ-/ [名] [C] [定義] a type

S

of ship that can travel under the water as well as on the surface 水上だけでなく水中も進むことのできる船→潜水艦,潜水艇

**submerge** /səbmə́ːrdʒ/ 動@他 ▶定義 to go or make sth go under water 水面下に沈む;～を水面下に沈ませる→潜水する,水没する;～を水中に入れる(沈める),水浸しにする,水没させる ‖ *The fields were submerged by the floods.* 洪水で田畑が冠水した. ― submerged 形→水没した,浸水した,水中の

**submission** /səbmíʃ(ə)n/ 名 ▶定義1 Ⓤ the accepting of sb else's power or control because he/she has defeated you 負けたために,打ち負かした人の権力または支配を受け入れること→服従,屈服,降服 ▶定義2 ⓊⒸ the action of giving a plan, document, etc to an official organization so that it can be studied and considered; the plan, document, etc that you send 計画書・書類などを検討し考慮してもらえるように公的機関に提出すること;送った計画書,書類など→提出,提示;提出物

**submissive** /səbmísɪv/ 形 ▶定義 ready to obey other people and do whatever they want 人に服従し,その人の欲する事を何でもすぐしがちな→従順な,服従的な,言いなりになる

**submit** /səbmít/ 動 (**submitting**; **submitted**) ▶定義1 他 submit sth (to sb/sth) to give a plan, document, etc to an official organization so that it can be studied and considered 計画書,書類などを検討し考慮してもらえるように公的機関に提出する→～を(…に)提出する,提示する ‖ *to submit an application/complaint/claim* 申込書・苦情申し立て書・請求を提出する ▶定義2 自 submit (to sb/sth) to accept sb/sth's power or control because he/she has defeated you 負けたために,打ち負かした～の権力または支配を受け入れる→(～に)服従する,屈服する,降服する

**subordinate**¹ /səbɔ́ːrd(ə)nət/ 形 ▶定義 subordinate (to sb/sth) having less power or authority than sb else; less important than sth else ～よりも権力または権限が小さい;～よりも重要でない→(～の)下位の,(～に)従属する,副次的な,補助的な ― subordinate 名 Ⓒ→従属物,従業員,部下 ‖ *the relationship between superiors and their subordinates* 上司と部下の関係

**subordinate**² /səbɔ́ːrd(ə)nət/ 動@他 ▶定義 to treat one person or thing as less important than another ある人・物を他よりも軽視して扱う→～を(…の)下位に置く,～を(…に)従わせる,従属させる,軽視する

**subordinate clause** 名 Ⓒ (文法) ▶定義 a group of words that is not a sentence but that adds information to the main part of the sentence 文ではないが,文の主要部分に情報を付け加える語群→従属節 ‖ *In the sentence 'We left early because it was raining', 'because it was raining' is the subordinate clause.* We left early because it was raining という文では because it was raining が従属節である.

**subscribe** /səbskráɪb/ 動@ ▶定義1 subscribe (to sth) to pay for a newspaper or magazine to be sent to you regularly 新聞または雑誌が定期的に手元に送られるよう代金を支払う→(～を)予約購読する,購読契約をする,予約する,購読する ▶定義2 正式 subscribe to sth to agree with an idea, belief, etc 考え,信念などに同意する→～に同意する,賛成する,承諾する ‖ *I don't subscribe to the view that all war is wrong.* 戦争はすべて悪いという見方には賛成しない.

**subscriber** /səbskráɪbər/ 名 Ⓒ ▶定義 a person who pays to receive a newspaper or magazine regularly or to use a particular service 定期的に新聞または雑誌を受け取るため,または特定のサービスを利用するために,代金を支払う人→購読者,予約者,(ケーブルテレビなどの)加入者 ‖ *subscribers to satellite and cable television* 衛星・ケーブルテレビの加入者

**subscription** /səbskrípʃ(ə)n/ 名 Ⓒ ▶定義 an amount of money that you pay, usually once a year, to receive a newspaper or magazine regularly or to belong to an organization 定期的に新聞または雑誌を受け取るため,またはある団体に所属するために,通常年に1度支払う金額→購読料,予約金,会費

**subsequent** /sʌ́bsɪkwənt/ 形 正式 (名詞の前だけ) ▶定義 coming after or later (順序・時間的に)後から来る→後の,その後の,それに続く ‖ *I thought that was the end of the matter but subsequent events proved me wrong.* それでこの件は終わりだと思ったが,続いて起こった出来事で私が間違っていたことが分かった. ― subsequently 副→その後,後に,それに続いて ‖ *The rumours were subsequently found to be untrue.* うわさはその後うそだと分かった.

**subservient** /səbsə́ːrviənt/ 形 ▶定義1 subservient (to sb/sth) too ready to obey other people むやみに人に服従しがちな→(〜の)言いなりになる,(〜に)追従的な,卑屈な ▶定義2 正式 subservient (to sth) considered to be less important than sb/sth else ほかの人・物ほど重要でないと見なされる→重要度の劣る,(〜に)従属的な — subservience 名 Ⓤ→卑屈,追従,おべっか,従属

**subside** /səbsáɪd/ 動自 ▶定義1 to become calmer or quieter より穏やかまたは静かになる→(あらし・騒ぎ・感情などが)収まる,引く,静まる ‖ *The storm seems to be subsiding.* あらしが収まってきているようだ. ▶定義2 (used about land, a building, etc) to sink down into the ground(土地,建物などについて)地中に沈む→沈下する,落ち込む,沈む — subsidence /səbsáɪd(ə)ns, sʌ́bsə-/ 名 Ⓤ→沈下,陥没

**subsidiary**[1] /səbsídiəri, -dièri/ 形 ▶定義 connected with sth but less important than it 〜に関係しているがそれよりも重要度が劣る→補助的な,副次的な,従属する,付随する

**subsidiary**[2] /səbsídiəri, -dièri/ 名 Ⓒ (複 **subsidiaries**) ▶定義 a business company that belongs to and is controlled by another larger company より大きな別の会社に属し統制されている会社→子会社,系列会社

**subsidize** (または **-ise**) /sʌ́bsədàɪz, -zə-/ 動他 ▶定義 (used about a government, etc) to give money in order to keep the cost of a service low (政府などについて)公共事業の経費を低く抑えるために金を出す→〜に助成金を与える,補助金を出す ‖ *Public transport should be subsidized.* 公共輸送機関は助成金を支給されるべきだ.

**subsidy** /sʌ́bsədi, -zə-/ 名 Ⓒ Ⓤ (複 **subsidies**) ▶定義 money that the government, etc pays to help an organization or to keep the cost of a service low 団体を支援するため,または公共事業の経費を低く抑えるために政府などが支払う金→助成金,補助金,奨励金 ‖ *agricultural/state/ housing subsidies* 農業・国の・住宅助成金

**subsist** /səbsíst/ 動自 正式 ▶定義 subsist (on sth) to manage to live with very little food or money 食糧または金がほとんどないまま何とか生活する→(〜によって)何とか生きていく,やっと生活する — subsistence 名 Ⓤ→何とか生きていくこと,ぎりぎりの生活・生計,生存

★**substance** /sʌ́bst(ə)ns/ 名 ▶定義1 Ⓒ a solid or liquid material 固体,液体→物質,物 ‖ *poisonous substances* 毒物 *The cloth is coated in a new waterproof substance.* その布は新しい防水材でコーティングされている. ▶定義2 Ⓤ importance, value or truth 意義,価値,真実→実質,中身,本質,実体,真実 ‖ *The commissioner's report gives substance to these allegations.* その委員の報告書はこれらの主張を裏付けている. ▶定義3 Ⓤ the most important or main part of sth 〜の最も重要なまたは主要な部分→真意,要旨,大意 ‖ *What was the substance of his argument?* 彼の主張の要旨は何だったのか.

**substandard** /sʌ̀bstǽndərd/ 形 ▶定義 of poor quality; not as good as usual or as it should be 品質の悪い;いつもほどまたは本来あるべき品質ほど良くない→標準以下の,通常以下の,基準に達しない

**substantial** /səbstǽnʃ(ə)l/ 形 ▶定義1 large in amount 量の多い→たくさんの,かなりの,相当な,十分な ‖ *The storms caused substantial damage.* あらしによってかなりの損害がもたらされた. *a substantial sum of money* 相当な金額 ▶定義2 large or strong 大きくて強い→しっかりした,丈夫な,強固な ⇔ **insubstantial**

**substantially** /səbstǽnʃ(ə)li/ 副 ▶定義1 very much; greatly 非常に;大いに→十分に,かなり,相当 ‖ *House prices have fallen substantially.* 住宅価格はかなり下落している. ▶定義2 generally; in most points 一般的に;ほとんどの点で→大体において,実質上,おおむね

**substitute** /sʌ́bstət(j)ùːt/ 名 Ⓒ ▶定義 a substitute (for sb/sth) a person or thing that takes the place of sb/sth else 〜に代わる人・物→(〜の)代わり,代理人,代役,補欠,(〜の)代用品 ‖ *One player was injured so the substitute was sent on to play.* 1人の選手が負傷したので補欠を試合に出場させた. — substitute 動他 substitute sb/sth (for sb/sth)→〜を(…の)代わりに使う,代用する ‖ *You can substitute margarine for butter.* バターの代わりにマーガリンを使ってもよい. — substitution /sʌ̀bstət(j)úːʃ(ə)n/ 名 Ⓒ Ⓤ→代理,代

用; 取り替え、交替

**subtitle** /sʌ́btàɪtl/ 名 [C, 通常は複数] ▶定義 the words at the bottom of the picture on television or at the cinema. The subtitles translate the words of a foreign film or programme or show the words that are spoken, to help people with hearing problems. テレビまたは映画の画面の下に出る語句. 外国映画または外国の番組の台詞(せりふ)を翻訳したもの、または耳の不自由な人のために音声の言葉を示したもの→**字幕, スーパー**

**subtle** /sʌ́tl/ 形 ▶定義 1 not very noticeable; not very strong or bright あまり目立たない; あまり強くないまたは明るくない→**微妙な, かすかな, ほのかな** ‖ subtle colours 微妙な色合い / I noticed a subtle difference in her. 彼女のかすかな違いに気が付いた. ▶定義 2 very clever; and using indirect methods to achieve sth 非常に巧妙な; ~を達成するために間接的な方法を用いる→**精巧な, 手の込んだ, 巧妙な, 狡猾(こうかつ)な** ‖ Advertisements persuade us to buy things in very subtle ways. 広告は実に巧妙な手で私たちを説き伏せて物を買わせる. — subtlety /sʌ́tlti/ 名 C U (複 subtleties) → 微妙さ, 巧妙さ, 緻密, 精巧; (しばしば複数形で)かすかな違い, 微妙な点 — subtly /sʌ́tli/ 副 →微妙に, 巧妙に, それとなく

*****subtract** /səbtrǽkt/ 動 他 ▶定義 subtract sth (from sth) to take one number or quantity away from another 別の数量からある数量を取り去る→**~を(…から)引く, 減じる, 控除する** ‖ If you subtract five from nine you get four. 9から5を引くと4になる. ⇔ **add** — subtraction /səbtrǽkʃ(ə)n/ 名 C U →差し引くこと, 引き算, 減法

*****suburb** /sʌ́bə:rb/ 名 C ▶定義 an area where people live that is outside the central part of a town or city 町または都市の中心部の外にある, 人の住む地域→**郊外, 近郊, 都市周辺部** ‖ Most people live in the suburbs and work in the centre of town. 人々のほとんどは郊外に住み, 町の中心部で働いている. — suburban /səbə́:rb(ə)n/ 形 →郊外の, 近郊の, 郊外に住む ☜ しばしば郊外の生活は退屈だと考えられるため, suburban は「退屈で面白くない」という意味で用いられることがある. — suburbia /səbə́:rbiə/ 名 U →(しばしば軽べつ的)郊外, 郊外居住者, 郊外特有の生活様

式・考え方

**subversive** /səbvə́:rsɪv/ 形 ▶定義 trying to destroy or damage a government, religion or political system by attacking it secretly and in an indirect way ひそかな間接的な攻撃法で政府・宗教・政治体制を破壊したり, 打撃を与えようとする→**(体制などを)破壊しようとする, 打倒・転覆をもくろむ** ‖ subversive literature/activities (転覆をねらった)危険文書・破壊活動 — subversive 名 C →破壊活動分子, 危険分子, 転覆計画者 — subversion /səbvə́:rʒ(ə)n, -ʃ(ə)n; -ʃ(ə)n/ 名 U →転覆, 破壊, 打倒

**subvert** /səbvə́:rt/ 動 他 ▶定義 to try to destroy or damage a government, religion or political system by attacking it secretly and in an indirect way ひそかな間接的な攻撃法で政府・宗教・政治体制を破壊したり, 打撃を与えようとする→**~を覆す, 打倒する, 転覆する**

**subway** /sʌ́bwèɪ/ 名 C ▶定義 1 a tunnel under a busy road or railway that is for people who are walking (**pedestrians**) 交通量の多い道路または線路の下にある, 歩行者のための通路→**地下道** ▶定義 2 英 = **UNDERGROUND**³

*****succeed** /səksí:d/ 動 ▶定義 1 自 succeed (in sth/doing sth) to manage to achieve what you want; to do well どうにかして望みを達成する; うまくいく→**(~に・~するのに)成功する, うまくいく, 合格する, 成し遂げる, 思い通りの結果を得る** ‖ Our plan succeeded. 私たちの計画はうまくいった. A good education will help you succeed in life. 良い教育は出世の手助けになる. to succeed in passing an exam 試験に合格する⇔ **fail** ▶定義 2 自他 to have a job or important position after sb else ~の後を継いで職または重要な地位に就く→**引き継ぐ, 継承する, ~の後任になる, ~の後を継ぐ** ‖ Tony Blair succeeded John Major as Prime Minister in 1997. トニー ブレアはジョン メージャーの後を継いで1997年に首相になった.

*****success** /səksés/ 名 ▶定義 1 U the fact that you have achieved what you want; doing well and becoming famous, rich, etc 望みを達成したということ; 立派にやって有名・裕福などになること→**成功, 合格, 成就, 出世** ‖ Hard work is **the key to success**. 勤勉は成功のかぎだ. Her attempts to get a job for the summer have not **met with** much **success** (= she hasn't managed to do it).

夏の間の仕事を得ようと彼女はいろいろやってみているがあまり成功していない(=うまくいっていない). *What's the secret of your success?* あなたの成功の秘けつは何ですか. ▶定義2 **⊙** the thing that you achieve; sth that becomes very popular 成し遂げるもの;非常に評判になるもの→**成功したもの,大当たり,大ヒット** ‖ *He really tried to **make a success of** the business.* 彼は事業を成功させようと本気で努力した. *The film 'Titanic' was a huge success.*「タイタニック」の映画は大当たりした. ⇔ **failure**

*  **successful** /səksésfʊl, -f(ə)l/ 形 ▶定義 having achieved what you wanted; having become popular, rich, etc 望んでいた事を達成した;評判または裕福になった→**成功した,うまくいった,合格した,出世した,大当たりの** ‖ *a successful attempt to climb Mount Everest* うまくいったエベレスト山登頂の試み *a successful actor* 成功した俳優 — **successfully** /-fʊli, -f(ə)li/ 副 →**首尾良く,成功して,出世して,大当たりして**

**succession** /səkséʃ(ə)n/ 名 ▶定義1 **⊙** a number of people or things that follow each other in time or order; a series 時間・順序に従って次々と続く多数の人・物;一続き→**連続(する物)** ‖ *a succession of events/problems/visitors* 一連の出来事・相次ぐ問題・ひっきりなしの訪問者 ▶定義2 **⓿** the right to have an important position after sb else ほかの~に続いて重要な地位を得る権利→**継承権,相続権,相続**

成句 **in succession** ▶定義 following one after another 次々に続く→**連続して,引き続いて,相次いで** ‖ *There have been three deaths in the family in quick succession.* 矢継ぎ早にその家族に3つの不幸があった.

**successor** /səksésər/ 名 **⊙** ▶定義 a person or thing that comes after sb/sth else and takes his/her/its place ほかの~の後を継いで,…に取って代わる人または物→**後継者,継承者,後任,後に続くもの** ☞参 **predecessor**

**succinct** /səksíŋkt/ 形 ▶定義 said clearly, in a few words 言葉少なにはっきりと述べた→**簡潔な,ずばりの,手短な** — **succinctly** 副 →**簡潔に,ずばり,手短に**

**succulent** /sʌ́kjələnt/ 形 ▶定義 (used about fruit, vegetables and meat) containing a lot of juice and tasting very good(果物,野菜,肉について)汁をたっぷり含んでとてもおいしい→**汁の多い,水気の多い,みずみずしい,肉汁の多い**

**succumb** /səkʌ́m/ 動 自 正式 ▶定義 **succumb (to sth)** to stop fighting against sth ~に対する戦いをやめる→**(~に)負ける,屈する,圧倒される**

* **such** /sʌtʃ, sətʃ/ 形 ▶定義1 (used for referring to sb/sth that you mentioned earlier) of this or that type (先に述べた~に言及するために用いて)この種の,その種の→**そのような,こういう,こんな,そんな,同様の;そのような人・物・事** ‖ *I don't believe in ghosts. There's **no such thing**.* 私は幽霊を信じない.そんなものは存在しない. *The economic situation is such that we all have less money to spend.* 皆使える金があまりないような経済状況だ. ▶定義2 used for emphasizing the degree of sth ~の程度を強調するのに用いて→**そんなに[こんなに]~な,とても~な,非常に~な,これほどの,それほどの** ‖ *It was such a fascinating book that I couldn't put it down.* とても面白い本だったので下に置く[読むのをやめる]ことができなかった. *It seems such a long time since we last met.* 私たちが最後に会ってからとても長い時間がたったように思われる.

▶ such は名詞の前または前に形容詞を従えた名詞の前で使われる:*Simon is such a bore!*(サイモンはとても退屈なやつだ.) *Susan is such a boring woman.*(スーザンはとても退屈な女性だ.) 名詞なしで使われる形容詞の前では so が使われる:*Don't be so boring.*(うんざりするような話はもうよせん.) 比較:*It was so cold we stayed at home.*(とても寒かったので私たちはずっと家にいた.) *It was such a cold night that we stayed at home.*(とても寒い夜だったので私たちはずっと家にいた.)

▶定義3 used to describe the result of sth ~の結果を述べるのに用いて→**~のような具合に,~のようなやり方で** ‖ *The statement was worded **in such a way that** it did not upset anyone.* その声明はだれも動揺させないように書かれていた.

成句 **as such** ▶定義 as the word is usually understood; exactly 言葉が通常理解される通りに;正確に→**(通常は否定文で)それ自体で(は),厳密な意味では** ‖ *It's not a promotion as such, but it will mean more money.* それは正確には昇進ではなく,賃金が上がるということだ.

**such as** ▶定義 for example 例えば→**~などの,**

## 1624 suck

〜のような，例えば〜のような ‖ *Fatty foods such as chips are bad for you.* フライドポテトのような油の多い食事は体に悪い．

*suck /sʌk/ 動 ▶定義1 🔵🔴 to pull a liquid into your mouth 口の中に液体を吸い込む→(〜を)吸う，(〜を)すする，吸い込む ‖ *to suck milk up through a straw* ストローでミルクを吸う ☛ blow のさし絵 ▶定義2 🔵🔴 to have sth in your mouth and keep touching it with your tongue 〜を口に入れて舌で触り続ける→(〜を)しゃぶる，なめる ‖ *He was noisily sucking (on) a sweet.* 彼は音を立てながらあめをなめていた．

▶定義3 🔴 to pull sth in a particular direction, using force 〜を特定の方向へ勢いよく引き寄せる→〜を吸い込む，吸い上げる，吸い出す ‖ *Vacuum cleaners suck up the dirt.* 掃除機はほこりを吸い上げる．

**sucker** /sʌ́kər/ 名 © ▶定義1 略式 a person who believes everything that you tell him/her and who is easy to trick or persuade to do sth 聞いた事をすべて信じて簡単にだまされたり，勧められたりして何かをしてしまう人→だまされやすい人，すぐに引っ掛かる人，いいカモ ▶定義2 a part of some plants, animals or insects that is used for helping them stick onto a surface 一部の動植物，昆虫が何かの表面に張り付くのに使う体の一部→吸根，吸盤

**suction** /sʌ́kʃ(ə)n/ 名 Ⓤ ▶定義 the action of removing air or liquid from a space or container so that sth else can be pulled into it or so that two surfaces can stick together ほかの〜が中に吸い込まれるように，または2面が互いにくっつき合うようにすきままたは容器から気体・液体を取り除く動作→吸うこと，吸い上げ，吸引，吸引力 ‖ *A vacuum cleaner works by suction.* 掃除機は吸引力で動く．

*sudden /sʌ́dn/ 形 ▶定義 done or happening quickly, or when you do not expect it 素早く，または予期しない時に行われたまたは起きた→突然の，急な，思い掛けない ‖ *a sudden decision/change* 急な決定・変更 — suddenly 副 →突然，急に，思い掛けなく，不意に ‖ *Suddenly, everybody started shouting.* 突然皆が叫び始めた．— suddenness 名 Ⓤ →突然，急，不意

成句 **all of a sudden** ▶定義 quickly and unexpectedly 急に思い掛けなく→突然，急に，不意に ‖ *All of a sudden the lights went out.* 突然明かりが消えた．

**sudden death** ▶定義 a way of deciding who wins a game where the score is equal by playing one more point or game スポーツ競技で同点の場合，もう1点得点するまで，またはもう1回試合をして，勝敗を決める方法→サドンデス，決勝の1回勝負

**suds** /sʌdz/ 名 [複数扱い] ▶定義 the bubbles that you get when you mix soap and water せっけんと水を混ぜ合わせたときにできる泡→せっけんの泡，せっけん水

**sue** /s(j)uː, suː/ 動 🔵🔴 ▶定義 **sue (sb) (for sth)** to go to a court of law and ask for money from sb because he/she has done sth bad to you, or said sth bad about you 人にひどい事をされた，または言われたために裁判所に訴えて，その人から金を請求する→訴訟を起こす，(〜を)(…のかどで…を求めて)告訴する，訴える ‖ *to sue sb for libel/breach of contract/damages* 名誉毀損(きそん)で・契約不履行で・損害賠償を請求して〜を訴える

**suede** /sweɪd/ 名 Ⓤ ▶定義 a type of soft leather which does not have a smooth surface and feels a little like cloth 表面がつるつるしておらず，布のような触り心地のする柔らかい革→スエード，スエード革，スエード調の生地

**suet** /s(j)úːət, súː-/ 名 Ⓤ ▶定義 a type of hard animal fat that is used in cooking 調理で用いられる動物性の硬い脂肪→スエット(牛・羊などの腎臓(じんぞう)付近の脂肪)

*suffer /sʌ́fər/ 動 ▶定義1 🔵🔴 suffer (from sth); suffer (for sth) to experience sth unpleasant, for example pain, sadness, difficulty, etc 痛み，悲しみ，困難などの不快な〜を経験する→(〜で)苦しむ，(〜の)病気にかかる，〜を被る，受ける，経験する ‖ *Mary often suffers from severe headaches.* メアリーはよくひどい頭痛に悩まされる．*Our troops suffered heavy losses.* 我々の軍からおびただしい死傷者が出た．*He made a rash decision and now he's suffering for it.* 彼は軽率な決断をして，今その報いを受けている．▶定義2 🔵 to become worse in quality 質が悪くなる→悪くなる，駄目になる，悪化する ‖ *My work is suffering as a result of problems at home.* 家庭のごたごたで私の仕事も悪

影響を受けている. — **sufferer** 名 ❻→苦しむ人,病人,患者 ‖ *asthma sufferers* ぜん息患者 — **suffering** 名 ❶→苦痛,苦労,受難

**sufficient** /səfíʃ(ə)nt/ 形 正式 ▶定義 as much as is necessary; enough 必要なだけある;十分な→**十分な, 足りる** ‖ *We have sufficient oil reserves to last for three months.* 私たちの所には3か月持つのに十分な量の石油の備蓄がある. ⇔ **insufficient** — **sufficiently** 副 →十分に,たっぷりと,足りるほど

**suffix** /sʌ́fɪks/ 名 ❻ (文法) ▶定義 a letter or group of letters that you add at the end of a word, and that changes the meaning of the word or the way it is used 語の末尾に付けて,その語の意味または,その語の使われ方を変える文字→**接尾辞** ‖ *To form the noun from the adjective 'sad', add the suffix 'ness'.* 形容詞の sad から名詞を作るには接尾辞の ness を付けなさい. ☞参 **prefix**

**suffocate** /sʌ́fəkèɪt/ 動 自他 ▶定義 to die because there is no air to breathe; to kill sb in this way 呼吸する空気がないために死ぬ; 呼吸する空気をなくして~を殺す→**窒息(死)する, 息苦しくなる; ~を窒息(死)させる, ~の息を詰まらせる** — **suffocating** 形 →息苦しくなる(ほどの), 息が詰まりそうな — **suffocation** /sʌ̀fəkéɪʃ(ə)n/ 名 ❶→窒息, 窒息死

***sugar** /ʃúgər/ 名 ▶定義**1** ❶ a sweet substance that you get from certain plants 特定の植物からとれる甘い物質→**砂糖, 糖, 糖質** ‖ *Do you take sugar in tea?* 紅茶に砂糖を入れますか. ☞C4 ページのさし絵 ▶定義**2** ❻ (in a cup of tea, coffee, etc) the amount of sugar that a small spoon can hold; a lump of sugar (1杯の紅茶, コーヒーなどの中で) 小さなスプーンに盛ることのできる砂糖の量; 角砂糖1個→**砂糖一さじ, 角砂糖1個**

**sugary** /ʃúgəri/ 形 ▶定義 very sweet とても甘い→**甘い, 砂糖のような, 砂糖でできた**

***suggest** /sədʒést; sə(g)dʒést/ 動 他 ▶定義**1** suggest sth (to sb); suggest doing sth; suggest that... to mention a plan or an idea that you have for sb to discuss or consider ~に議論または検討してほしい計画またはアイデアを話に出す→**~を(人に)提案する, ~してはどうかと言う, ~することを提案する, 提唱する, 持ち出す** ‖ *Can anybody suggest ways of raising more money?* もっと資金が調達できる方法についてだれか提案してくれませんか. *Tony suggested going out for a walk.* トニーは散歩に出掛けたらどうかと言い出した. *Tony suggested (that) we go out for a walk.* トニーは散歩に出掛けたらどうかと言った. *Tony suggested a walk.* トニーは散歩を提案した. ▶定義**2** suggest sb/sth (for/as sth) to say that a person, thing or place is suitable 人,物または場所が適切であると言う→**~を(…に)勧める, 推す** ‖ *Who would you suggest for the job?* あなたはその仕事にだれを推しますか.

➤ suggest sb sth の形をとることはできない.

☞参 **recommend** ▶定義**3** to say or show sth in an indirect way ~を間接的に言うまたは示す→**~をほのめかす, 示唆する, 暗に示す** ‖ *Are you suggesting the accident was my fault?* その事故が私の責任だとおっしゃりたいのですか.

***suggestion** /sədʒést∫(ə)n; sə(g)dʒés-/ 名 ▶定義**1** ❻ a plan or idea that sb mentions for sb else to discuss and consider ~がほかの…に議論または検討してもらうために述べる計画またはアイデア→**提案, 提唱** ‖ *May I make a suggestion?* 1つ提案してもいいですか. *Has anyone got any suggestions for how to solve this problem?* この問題の解決法について案のある方いませんか. ▶定義**2** ❶ putting an idea into a person's mind; giving advice about what to do, etc 人の心に考えを吹き込むこと; 何をすべきか忠告を与えること→**提案(すること), 発案, 示唆, 暗示, ほのめかし** ▶定義**3** [単数扱い] a slight amount or sign of sth ~のわずかな量, ~の兆候→**気配, 気味, 様子, かすかな印**

**suggestive** /sədʒéstɪv; sə(g)dʒés-/ 形 ▶定義**1** suggestive (of sth) making you think of sth; being a sign of sth ~を人に思い出させる; ~の兆候である→**(~を)連想させる, 示唆に富む, 暗示的な** ‖ *Your symptoms are more suggestive of an allergy than a virus.* これはウイルスよりもむしろアレルギーを思わせる症状です. ▶定義**2** making you think about sex 性について考えさせる→**思わせ振りな, 挑発的な, 際どい, いかがわしい** ‖ *a suggestive dance/remark/posture* 挑発的な踊り・言葉・姿態 — **suggestively** 副 →暗示的に, 思わせ振りに, 挑発的に

## suicidal

**suicidal** /s(j)ù:əsáɪdl; sù:ɪ-/ 形 ▶定義1 (used about a person) wanting to kill himself/herself (人について)自殺を望んでいる→自殺の,自殺したがっている,自殺の恐れのある‖ *to be/feel suicidal* 自殺しそうである・自殺したい気分である ▶定義2 likely to have a very bad result; extremely dangerous 非常に悪い結果をもたらしそうな; 非常に危険な→自滅的な,向こう見ずな,自暴自棄な

*__suicide__ /s(j)ú:əsaɪd; sú:ɪ-/ 名 ❶ ⓒ ▶定義 the act of killing yourself deliberately 故意に自らの命を絶つ行為→自殺,自殺行為・事件‖ *Ben has tried to **commit suicide** several times.* ベンは何度か自殺を試みたことがある. *There have been three suicides by university students this year.* 今年は大学生による自殺が3件発生している.

*__suit__¹ /s(j)u:t; su:t/ 名 ⓒ ▶定義1 a formal set of clothes that are made of the same material, consisting of a jacket and either trousers or a skirt 同じ生地で作られた,上着とズボンまたはスカートから成る正式の衣服→スーツ,一そろい,一式‖ *He always wears a suit and tie to work.* 彼は会社にはいつもスーツとネクタイを着ていく. ☞ C6 ページのさし絵 ▶定義2 an article of clothing or set of clothes that you wear for a particular activity ある特定の活動のために着用する衣服1点または一式→~服,~着‖ *a tracksuit/swimsuit* トラックスーツ・水着 ▶定義3 one of the four sets of thirteen playing cards (hearts, clubs, diamonds and spades) that form a pack トランプを構成する各13枚ずつのカード4組(ハート,クラブ,ダイヤ,スペード)のうちの一組→組,組札 ☞参 card の注とさし絵 成句 follow suit ⇒ FOLLOW

*__suit__² /s(j)u:t; su:t/ 動 ⓗ (進行形は不可) ▶定義1 to be convenient or useful for sb/sth ~にとって便利または有用である→~に好都合である,適する,合う‖ *Would Thursday at 9.30 suit you?* 木曜日の9時30分でご都合はよろしいですか. *He will help around the house, but only when it suits him.* 彼は家の手伝いをするが,自分に都合が良い時だけだ. ▶定義2 (used about clothes, colours, etc) to make you look attractive (衣服,色などについて)人を魅力的に見せる→~に似合う‖ *That dress really suits you.* そのドレスはあなたに実によく似合っている.

*__suitable__ /s(j)ú:təb(ə)l; sú:t-/ 形 ▶定義 suitable (for sb/sth); suitable (to do sth) right or appropriate for sb/sth ~にとってふさわしいまたは適切な(~に・~するのに)適した,ふさわしい,~向きの‖ *The film isn't suitable for children.* その映画は子供向きではない. *I've got nothing suitable to wear for a wedding.* 私は結婚式に着るのにふさわしい服を何も持っていない. ⇔ unsuitable — suitability /s(j)ù:təbíləti; sú:t-/ 名 ❶→適切,適合,ふさわしいこと,似合うこと — suitably 副→適切に,ふさわしく,うまく

*__suitcase__ /s(j)ú:tkeɪs; sú:t-/ (または case) 名 ⓒ ▶定義 a box with a handle that you use for carrying your clothes, etc in when you are travelling 旅行中に衣類などを持ち運ぶのに使う取っ手の付いた箱→スーツケース,旅行かばん ☞ bag のさし絵

**suite** /swi:t/ 名 ⓒ ▶定義1 a set of rooms, especially in a hotel 特にホテルの一続きの部屋→一続きの部屋,スイート(ルーム)‖ *the honeymoon/penthouse suite* 新婚カップル用のスイートルーム・屋上高級アパートの続き部屋 *a suite of rooms/offices* 一続きの部屋・(数個の)事務所の続き部屋 ☞参 en suite ▶定義2 a set of two or more pieces of furniture of the same style or covered in the same material 同じ様式または同じ素材で張った2点以上の家具セット→一式の家具,一そろいの家具‖ *a three-piece suite (= a sofa and two armchairs)* 3点セット (= ソファーと2脚のひじ掛けいす)

**suited** /s(j)ú:təd; sú:t-/ 形 ▶定義 suited (for/to sb/sth) appropriate or right for sb/sth ~に適切なまたはふさわしい→(~に)適した,ふさわしい,~向きの

**sulfur** 米 = SULPHUR

**sulk** /sʌlk/ 動 ⓘ ▶定義 to refuse to speak or smile because you want people to know that you are angry about sth 何かに腹を立てていることを知ってもらいたいため,口をきこうとしない,または笑おうとしない→むくれる,すねる,むっつりする — sulky 形→むくれた,すねた,むっつりした,不機嫌な — sulkily /-ili/ 副→むくれて,すねて,むっつりして,不機嫌に

**sullen** /sʌ́lən/ 形 ▶定義 looking bad-tempered and not wanting to speak to people 見るからに機嫌が悪そうで人に話したがらない→むくれた,

すねた, むっつりした, 不機嫌な ‖ *a sullen face/expression/glare* 仏頂面・不機嫌な表情・むっとにらんだ目付き — **sullenly** 副 ➡ **むくれて, すねて, むっつりして, 不機嫌に**

**sulphur** (米**sulfur**) /sʌ́lfər/ 名 Ⓤ (元素記号 **S**)
▶定義 a natural yellow substance with a strong unpleasant smell 強い不快なにおいのする黄色い天然の物質 ➡ 硫黄

**sultan** (または **Sultan**) /sʌ́lt(ə)n/ 名 Ⓒ ▶定義 the ruler in some Muslim countries 一部のイスラム教の国の支配者 ➡ サルタン, スルタン, イスラム教国君主

**sultana** /sʌltɑ́ːnə, -tǽnə/ 名 Ⓒ ▶定義 a dried grape with no seeds in it that is used in cooking 調理で用いられる種なし干しブドウ ➡ スルタナ, 種なし干しブドウ ☛参 raisin

**sultry** /sʌ́ltri/ 形 ▶定義 **1** (used about the weather) hot and uncomfortable (天候について) 暑くて不快な ➡ **蒸し暑い, 暑苦しい, うだるように暑い** ▶定義 **2** (used about a woman) behaving in a way that makes her sexually attractive (女性について) 性的に魅力的に見えるように振る舞う ➡ **官能的な, 扇情的な, なまめかしい**

*★**sum**¹ /sʌm/ 名 Ⓒ ▶定義 **1** an amount of money ➡ **金額** ‖ *The industry has spent huge **sums of money*** *modernizing its equipment.* 産業界は設備の近代化に膨大な額の金を費やしている.
▶定義 **2** [通常は単数] **the sum (of sth)** the amount that you get when you add two or more numbers together 2つ以上の数字を足して得られる値 ➡ **合計, 和, 総計, 総和, 総額** ‖ *The sum of two and five is seven.* 2と5の合計は7である.
▶定義 **3** a simple problem that involves calculating numbers 計算を伴う単純な問題 ➡ **算数問題, 計算問題, 計算** ‖ *to **do sums** in your head* 暗算する

**sum**² /sʌm/ 動 (**summing; summed**)
句動詞 **sum (sth) up** ▶定義 to describe in a few words the main ideas of what sb has said or written 話・文章の主要なポイントを少ない語数で表す ➡ **(～を)要約する, 概説する; ～の要点を述べる, ～をかいつまんで話す** ‖ ***To sum up**, there are three options here...* 要するにここに選択肢が3つあるということだ.

**sum sb/sth up** ▶定義 to form an opinion about sb/sth ～についての考えをまとめる ➡ **(人物・情勢など)をさっと見定める, 一目で評価する, 即座に判断する** ‖ *He summed the situation up immediately.* 彼は状況を即座に判断した.

**summary**¹ /sʌ́məri/ 名 Ⓒ (複 **summaries**)
▶定義 a short description of the main ideas or points of sth but without any details ～についての詳細を省いた, 中心的な見解または要点の短い記述 ➡ **要約, 概略, 大要** ‖ *A brief summary of the experiment is given at the beginning of the report.* その実験の簡単な大要がレポートの最初に記載されている. ●類 **precis** — **summarize** (または **-ise**) /sʌ́məraɪz/ 動 他 ～を要約する, 手短に述べる, かいつまんで言う ‖ *Could you summarize the story so far?* これまでの話を手短に話していただけませんか.

**summary**² /sʌ́məri/ 形 正式 ▶定義 done quickly and without taking time to think about whether it is the right thing to do or following the right process やっていい事かどうか時間をかけて考えずに, または正しい手順を踏まずに, 急いで行われた ➡ **(処置などが)即決の, 略式の, 深く考えない** ‖ *a summary judgment* (法)略式の(正式民事審理を経ないでなされる)判決

*★**summer** /sʌ́mər/ 名 Ⓒ Ⓤ ▶定義 one of the four seasons of the year, after spring and before autumn. Summer is the warmest season of the year. 四季のうち, 春と秋の間の季節. 1年で最も暑い季節 ➡ **夏, 夏季** ‖ *Is it very hot here in summer?* ここは夏はとても暑いですか. *a summer's day* 夏の日 — **summery** 形 ➡ **夏の, 夏季の, 夏のような, 夏のように暑い** ‖ *summery weather* 夏のような天気 *a summery dress* 夏向きの服

**summertime** /sʌ́mərtàɪm/ 名 Ⓤ ▶定義 the season of summer 夏の季節 ➡ **夏, 夏季** ‖ *It's busy here in the summertime.* ここは夏季は忙しい.

**summing-up** 名 Ⓒ (複 **summings-up**) ▶定義 a speech in which a judge gives a short description (**summary**) of what has been said in a court of law before a decision (**verdict**) is reached 裁判官が法廷で話された事を, 決定(評決)の前に手短に説明(要約)する演説 ➡ **(裁判官による)事件概要の説明**

**summit** /sʌ́mət/ 名 Ⓒ ▶定義 **1** the top of a mountain 山の頂上 ➡ **山頂, 頂** ▶定義 **2** an important meeting or series of meetings between the leaders of two or more countries 2か国以上の

## 1628 summon

首脳が行う重要な一連の会議→首脳会議, サミット

**summon** /sʌ́mən/ 動他 ▶定義1 正式 to order a person to come to a place ある場所に来るように人に命令する→〜を呼び出す, 召還する, (裁判所へ)出頭を命じる, (議会などを)召集する ‖ *The boys were summoned to the head teacher's office.* 男子生徒たちは校長室に呼び出された. ▶定義2 summon sth (up) to find strength, courage or some other quality that you need even though it is difficult to do so たとえ困難でも必要な力, 勇気などを見いだす→〜を奮い立たせる, 奮い起こす ‖ *She couldn't summon up the courage to leave him.* 彼女は彼と別れる勇気を奮い起こすことができなかった.

**summons** /sʌ́mənz/ 名 C (複 summonses) ▶定義 an order to appear in a court of law 裁判所に出頭を求める命令書→(裁判所への)召喚状, 呼び出し状

**Sun** 略 Sunday→日曜日 ‖ *Sun 5 April* 4月5日日曜日

*__sun__¹ /sʌn/ 名 ▶定義1 the sun [単数扱い] the star that shines in the sky during the day and that gives the earth heat and light 昼間空に輝いて地球に熱と光を与える天体→太陽, 日 ‖ *The sun rises in the east and sets in the west.* 太陽は東から昇り西に沈む. *the rays of the sun* 太陽光線 ▶定義2 [単数扱い, U] light and heat from the sun 太陽からの光と熱→日光, 日なた ‖ *Don't sit in the sun too long.* 日なたにあまり長く座り続けないように. *Too much sun can be harmful.* 日光に当たりすぎると害になることがある. 成句 catch the sun ⇒ **CATCH**¹

**sun**² /sʌn/ 動他 (**sunning**; **sunned**) ▶定義 sun yourself sit or lie outside when the sun is shining in order to enjoy the heat 暖かさを満喫するために太陽が輝いているときに外で座ったり横になったりする→日光浴をする, 日なたぼっこをする

**sunbathe** /sʌ́nbeɪð/ 動自 ▶定義 to take off most of your clothes and sit or lie in the sun in order to make your skin go darker (get a tan) 肌を濃い色にする(日焼けする)ために衣服のほとんどを脱いで日なたに座ったり横わたったりする→日光浴をする, 日なたぼっこをする ☞ C8 ページのさし絵 ☞参 bathe

**sunbeam** /sʌ́nbiːm/ 名 C ▶定義 a line (ray) of sunlight 日光の線(光線)→太陽光線, 日光

**sunburn** /sʌ́nbɜːn/ 名 U ▶定義 red painful skin caused by spending too long in the sun 日なたであまりに長時間過ごしたため生じた赤くひりひり痛む皮膚→日焼け, 日焼けによる炎症 — sunburned (または sunburnt) 形→(ひりひりと)日焼けした, 日に焼けた

*__Sunday__ /sʌ́ndi, -deɪ/ 名 C U (略 Sun) ▶定義 the day of the week after Saturday 土曜日の次の曜日→日曜日

▶曜日は最初の文字を必ず大文字で書く. 文中での曜日の使い方の例については Monday を参照.

**sundial** /sʌ́ndaɪ(ə)l/ 名 C ▶定義 a type of clock used in past times that uses the shadow of a pointed piece of metal to show what the time is 先のとがった金属片の影の具合で今何時かを示す昔使われた時計→日時計

**sundry** /sʌ́ndri/ 形 (名詞の前だけ) ▶定義 of various kinds that are not important enough to be named separately それぞれ名前を挙げるほど重要でないさまざまな種類の→雑多な, 種々さまざまな, いろいろな

成句 all and sundry 略式 ▶定義 everyone みんな→だれもかれも皆, どれもこれも皆

**sunflower** /sʌ́nflaʊər/ 名 C ▶定義 a very tall plant with large yellow flowers, often grown for its seeds and their oil, which is used in cooking しばしば種と油を採るために栽培される, 大きな黄色い花を咲かせる非常に背の高い植物. 種からとった油は料理に使われる→ヒマワリ

**sung** SING の過去分詞形

**sunglasses** /sʌ́nglɑːsəz, -glæs-/ (または **dark glasses**, 略式 **shades**) 名 [複数扱い] ▶定義 a pair of glasses with dark glass in them to protect your eyes from bright sunlight まぶしい日光から目を保護するための色の濃いガラスを用いた眼鏡→サングラス

**sunk** SINK¹ の過去分詞形

**sunken** /sʌ́ŋk(ə)n/ 形 ▶定義1 below the water 水面下の→水中の, 海底の, 沈没した ‖ *a sunken ship* 沈没船 ▶定義2 (used about cheeks or eyes) very far into the face as a result of illness or age (ほおまたは目について)病気または年のため顔面の奥に引っ込んだ→落ちくぼんだ, こけた ▶定義3 at a lower level than the surrounding area 周囲より一段低くなった➜**一段低い所にある,少し下がった所の** ‖ *a sunken bath/garden* 床より低くしつらえた浴槽・沈庭園

**sunlight** /sʌ́nlàɪt/ [名] [U] ▶定義 the light from the sun 太陽の明かり➜**日光,陽光,太陽光**

**sunlit** /sʌ́nlɪ̀t/ [形] ▶定義 having bright light from the sun 日光の当たる➜**太陽に照らされた,日に当たっている,明るい** ‖ *a sunlit terrace* 日の当たるテラス

**sunny** /sʌ́ni/ [形] (**sunnier**; **sunniest**) ▶定義 having a lot of light from the sun 日光がよく当たる➜**明るく日が射す,日当たりの良い,陽光にあふれた,明るい** ‖ *a sunny garden* 日当たりの良い庭 *a sunny day* よく晴れた日

**sunrise** /sʌ́nràɪz/ [名] [U] ▶定義 the time when the sun comes up in the morning 朝太陽が昇る時間➜**日の出(の時刻),暁** ‖ *to get up* ***at sunrise*** 日の出と共に起きる ☛参 **dawn**, **sunset**

**sunset** /sʌ́nsèt/ [名] [C] [U] ▶定義 the time when the sun goes down in the evening 夕方太陽が沈む時間➜**日の入り(の時刻),日没,日暮れ** ‖ *The park closes* ***at sunset****.* その公園は日没時に閉鎖される. *a beautiful sunset* 美しい入り日

**sunshine** /sʌ́nʃàɪn/ [名] [U] ▶定義 heat and light from the sun 太陽の熱と光➜**日光,太陽の光線,日差し,日なた** ‖ *We sat down* ***in the sunshine*** *and had lunch.* 私たちは日なたに腰を下ろし昼食を取った.

**sunstroke** /sʌ́nstròʊk/ [名] [U] ▶定義 an illness that is caused by spending too much time in very hot, strong sunlight 非常に強く暑い日差しの下で長時間過ごしたために起こる病気➜**日射病** ‖ *Keep your head covered or you'll* ***get sunstroke****.* 帽子をかぶらないと日射病になりますよ.

**suntan** /sʌ́ntæ̀n/ (または **tan**) [名] [C] ▶定義 when you have a suntan, your skin is darker than usual because you have spent time in the sun 日なたで過ごしたため通常よりも肌の色が濃くなること➜**(健康的な)日焼け** ‖ *to have/get a suntan* 日焼けしている・する *suntan oil* (きれいに日焼けするための)日焼け用オイル — **suntanned** (または **tanned**) [形] ➜**日焼けした,日に焼けた**

***super** /s(j)úːpər, súː-/ [形] [略式] ▶定義 **1** (しばしば複合語を作るために用いて) bigger, better, stronger than other things of the same type 同じ種類のほかの物より大きい,良い,強い➜**巨大な,最高級の,強力な,高性能の,超～** ‖ *a new super computer* 新型のスーパーコンピューター *superglue* 強力接着剤 ▶定義 **2** (古) very good; wonderful 非常に良い;すばらしい➜**優れた,すばらしい,極上の** ‖ *We had a super time.* 私たちはすてきな時間を過ごした.

**superb** /s(j)ʊpə́ːrb, sə-; sʊ-/ [形] ▶定義 extremely good, excellent 非常に良い,すばらしい➜**すばらしい,見事な,最高の,極上の** — **superbly** [副] ➜**すばらしく,見事に**

**supercilious** /s(j)ùːpərsɪ́liəs; sùː-/ [形] ▶定義 showing that you think that you are better than other people ほかの人たちよりも自分の方が優れていると思っていることを示して➜**ごう慢な,横柄な,人を見下す** ‖ *a supercilious smile* 人を小ばかにした笑い — **superciliously** [副] ➜**ごう慢で,横柄に,人を見下して**

**superficial** /s(j)ùːpərfɪ́ʃ(ə)l; sùː-/ [形] ▶定義 **1** not studying or thinking about sth in a deep or complete way ～について深くまたは徹底的に学んでいないまたは考えていない➜**表面的な,浅薄な,皮相な** ‖ *a superficial knowledge of the subject* その問題についての浅薄な知識 ▶定義 **2** only on the surface, not deep 表面だけの,深くない➜**表面にある,表面近くの,浅い** ‖ *a superficial wound/cut/burn* 浅いけが・切り傷・軽いやけど ▶定義 **3** (used about people) not caring about serious or important things (人について)重大な事・大事なものについて関心がない➜**浅はかな,薄っぺらな,中身のない,つまらない** ‖ *He's a very superficial sort of person.* 彼はとても薄っぺらな人間だ. — **superficiality** /s(j)ùːpərfɪ̀ʃiǽləti; sùː-/ [名] [U] ➜**表面的なこと,皮相,浅薄** — **superficially** /-ʃ(ə)li/ [副] ➜**表面的に,見掛けは,浅薄に**

**superfluous** /s(j)uːpə́ːrfluəs; suː-/ [形] ▶定義 more than is wanted; not needed 求めていたよりも多い;必要でない➜**余分な,余計な,有り余る,不必要な**

**superhuman** /s(j)ùːpərhjúːmən; sùː-/ [形] ▶定義 greater than is usual for human beings 人間の通常の域を超えた➜**超人的な,人間の域を超えた,神業の** ‖ *superhuman strength* 超人的な強さ

**superimpose** /s(j)ùːpərɪmpóʊz; sùː-/ [動] [他] ▶定義 **superimpose sth (on sth)** to put sth on top of sth else so that what is underneath can

S

still be seen 下に置いた物が見えるような形で〜をほかの…の上に置く→〜を(…の上に)重ねる, 重ね合わせる, 重ね焼きする ‖ *The old street plan was superimposed on a map of the modern city.* 昔の市街図が今の市内地図の上に重ね合わされた.

**superintendent** /s(j)ùːpɹɪnténd(ə)nt; sùː-/ 名 C 定義1 a police officer with a high position 地位の高い警察官→困 警察署長, 因 警視 ‖ *Detective Superintendent Waters* ウォーターズ刑事部長 定義2 a person who looks after a large building 大きな建物を管理する人→管理人, 管理者, 監督者

*****superior**[1] /s(j)uːpíəriər, sʊ-/ 形 定義1 superior (to sb/sth) better than usual or than sb/sth else 通常より良い, ほかの〜よりも良い→(〜より)優れた, (〜に)勝る, 上等な, 優秀な ‖ *He is clearly superior to all the other candidates.* 彼は明らかにほかのすべての候補者より優れている. ⇔ **inferior** 定義2 superior (to sb) having a more important position より重要な地位を持つ→(〜より)上位の, 上級の, 上官の, 上役の ‖ *a superior officer* 上官 定義3 thinking that you are better than other people 自分がほかの人たちよりも優れていると考える→思い上がった, ごう慢な, 高慢な, 人を見下すような — **superiority** /s(j)uːpìəriɔ́(ː)rəti, -ár-; sʊ-/ 名 U → 優れていること, 優越, 卓越, 優勢, 優位; 優越感

**superior**[2] /s(j)uːpíəriər, sʊ-/ 名 C 定義 a person of higher position より高い地位にいる人→上司, 上官, 上役 ‖ *Report any accidents to your superior.* 何か事故があったら上司に報告しなさい. ⇔ **inferior**

**superlative** /s(j)uːpə́ːrlətɪv, sʊ-/ 名 C 定義 the form of an adjective or adverb that expresses its highest degree 最も高い程度を表す形容詞または副詞の形→最上級 ‖ *'Most beautiful', 'best' and 'fastest' are all superlatives.* most beautiful, best, fastest はすべて最上級だ.

*****supermarket** /súːpərmàːrkət, s(j)úː-/ 名 C 定義 a very large shop that sells food, drink, goods used in the home, etc 食品, 飲み物, 家庭用品などを販売している非常に大きい店→スーパーマーケット, スーパー

**supernatural** /s(j)ùːpərnǽtʃ(ə)rəl, sùː-/ 定義1 that cannot be explained by the laws of science 科学法則で説明できない→超自然の, 不可思議な, 超常の, 神秘的な ‖ *a creature with supernatural powers* 超能力を持った生物 定義2 the **supernatural** 名[単数扱い] events, forces or powers that cannot be explained by the laws of science 科学法則で説明できない出来事, 威力または能力→超常現象, 超自然の力, 超自然のもの ‖ *I don't believe in the supernatural.* 私は超自然的な存在を信じない.

**supersede** /s(j)ùːpərsíːd; sùː-/ 動 他 定義 to take the place of sb/sth which existed or was used before and which has become old-fashioned 以前存在したり, 利用されたりしたが現在では時代後れになった〜の代わりをする→〜に取って代わる, 〜の地位を奪う, 座を奪う, 後を継ぐ ‖ *Steam trains were gradually superseded by electric trains.* 蒸気機関車は徐々に電気機関車に取って代わられた.

**supersonic** /s(j)ùːpərsɑ́nɪk; sùː-/ 形 定義 faster than the speed of sound 音速よりも速い→超音速の

**superstar** /s(j)úːpərstàːr, súː-/ 名 C 定義 a singer, film star, etc who is very famous and popular 非常に有名で人気の高い歌手, 映画スターなど→大スター, スーパースター

**superstition** /s(j)ùːpərstíʃ(ə)n; sùː-/ 名 C U 定義 a belief that cannot be explained by reason or science 理性または科学で説明できないものを信じること→迷信, 迷信に基づく習慣・行為 ‖ *According to superstition, it's unlucky to walk under a ladder.* 迷信でははしごの下を歩くのは縁起が悪いとされる. — **superstitious** /s(j)ùːpərstíʃəs; sùː-/ 形 → 迷信の, 迷信的な, 迷信を信じる ‖ *I never do anything important on Friday the 13th - I'm superstitious.* 私は 13 日の金曜日には大事な事は何もしない ― 迷信深いから.

> ►社会・文化
>
> 英米の迷信
>
> 　迷信で一番有名なのが Friday the thirteenth (13日の金曜日) でしょう. キリストが十字架に付けられて亡くなったのが金曜日だったことと, その前日にキリストが開いた最後の晩餐 (ばんさん) の席にいたのが13人だったからです. ほかに有名なのは black cat (黒猫) です. ただし, アメリカでは縁起の

悪いものとされる黒猫も,イギリスでは幸運をもたらすものとされています.一方,縁起の良いものの代表例は four-leaf clover (四つ葉のクローバー) でしょう.いずれにせよこれらには科学的根拠がなく,それゆえ迷信 (superstition) と言われるのです.

**superstore** /s(j)ú:pərstɔ:r, sú:-/ 名 ❶ ▶定義 a very large shop that sells food or a wide variety of one particular type of goods 食料品またはある特定の1種類の商品を品数を豊富にそろえて販売する非常に大きな店→スーパーストア

**supervise** /s(j)ú:pərvàɪz; sú:-/ 動 ⾃ ⾃他 ▶定義 to watch sb/sth to make sure that work is being done properly or that people are behaving correctly 必ず作業がきちんと行われるように,または人が正しく機能しているように,人・物を監督する→(~を)監督する,管理する,指揮する,指図する ‖ *Your job is to supervise the building work.* あなたの仕事は建設作業を監督することだ. — **supervision** /sù:pərvíʒ(ə)n; s(j)ù:-/ 名 ❶→監督,管理,指揮 ‖ *Children should not play here without supervision.* 子供は大人の監督なしにここで遊んではならない. — **supervisor** 名 ❶→監督者,管理者,指揮者

**supper** /sʌ́pər/ 名 ❶ ❶ (古) ▶定義 the last meal of the day, either the main meal of the evening or a small meal that you eat quite late, not long before you go to bed 1日の最後の食事.夜の主要な食事か,就寝早い前に食べる軽食のいずれか→夕食,晩ご飯,(軽い)夜食

**supple** /sʌ́pl/ 形 ▶定義 that bends or moves easily; not stiff 簡単に曲がるまたは動く;堅くない→曲げやすい,しなやかな,柔軟な ‖ *Children are generally far more supple than adults.* 一般的に子供は大人よりもずっと体が柔らかい. — **suppleness** 名 ❶→柔軟性,しなやかさ

**supplement** /sʌ́pləmənt/ 名 ❶ ▶定義 something that is added to sth else ほかの〜に加えられた…→補足,補充(物),付録,増刊号,追加料金 ‖ *You have to pay a small supplement if you travel on a Saturday.* 土曜日に旅行する場合には多少の追加料金を支払わなければならない. — **supplement** 動 ⾃他 supplement sth (with sth)→〜を(…で)補う,補足する ‖ *to supplement your diet with vitamins* 食事をビタミンで補う — **supplementary** /sʌ̀pləmént(ə)ri/ 形 →補充の,追加の,付録の ‖ *supplementary exercises at the back of the book* 本の後ろにある補充問題

**supplier** /səplάɪər/ 名 ❶ ▶定義 a person or company that supplies goods 商品を提供する人または会社→供給者,供給業者,(原料)供給国

★**supply**¹ /səplάɪ/ 動 ⾃他 (現分 **supplying**; 三単現 **supplies**, 過, 過分 **supplied**) ▶定義 supply sth (to sb); supply sb (with sth) to give or provide sth 〜を与える,提供する→(人に)物を供給する,〜に(物を)あてがう,支給する,提供する ‖ *The farmer supplies eggs to the surrounding villages.* その農夫は卵を周辺の村に供給している. *He supplies the surrounding villages with eggs.* 彼は周辺の村に卵を供給している.

**supply**² /səplάɪ/ 名 (複 **supplies**) ❶ ▶定義 a store or amount of sth that is provided or available to be used 供給される物またはすぐに使用できる物の蓄えまたは量→(使用可能な)量,蓄え,在庫品,供給(量) ‖ *The water supply was contaminated.* 上水道が汚染された. *Food supplies were dropped by helicopter.* 食糧がヘリコプターで投下された. *In many parts of the country water is* ***in short supply*** *(= there is not much of it).* その国の多くの地域で水の供給が不足している(= 水があまりない).

★**support**¹ /səpɔ́:rt/ 動 ⾃他 ▶定義 **1** to help sb by saying that you agree with him/her/it, and sometimes giving practical help such as money 同意を表明したり,時には実際に役立つ金銭的な援助を与えて,人を助ける→〜を支持する,支援する,後援する,支える,財政的に援助する ‖ *Several large companies are supporting the project.* いくつかの大きな会社がそのプロジェクトを支援している. *Which political party do you support?* あなたはどの政党を支持していますか. ▶定義 **2** to give sb the money he/she needs for food, clothes, etc 食糧,衣服などに必要な金を〜に与える→〜を養う,扶養する ‖ *Jim has to support two children from his previous marriage.* ジムは先の結婚で生まれた2人の子供を養わなければならない. ▶定義 **3** to carry the weight of sb/sth 〜の重さを支える→〜を支える,〜の支えになる,〜に耐える ‖ *Large columns support the roof.* 大きな柱が屋根を支えている. ▶定義 **4** to show that sth is true or correct 〜が

## 1632 support²

真実または正しいことを示す→〜を裏付ける, 立証する, 論拠を与える ‖ *What evidence do you have to support what you say?* あなたは自分の発言を裏付けるどのような証拠をお持ちですか. ▶定義5 to have a particular sports team as your favourite ひいきのチームとしてある特定のスポーツチームを持っている→〜を応援する,〜のファンである ‖ *Which football team do you support?* あなたはどのサッカーチームを応援していますか.

**\*support²** /səpɔ́ːrt/ 名 ▶定義1 ❶ support (for sb/sth) help and encouragement that you give to a person or thing 〜に与える援助または激励→支持, 支援, 応援 ‖ *public support for the campaign* その運動に対する大衆の支持 *Steve spoke in support of the proposal.* スティーヴはその提案を支持する発言をした. ▶定義2 ❸❶ something that carries the weight of sb/sth or holds sth firmly in place 人・物の重さに耐える, または〜をしっかりと固定する物→支え, 支柱, 土台 ‖ *a roof support* 屋根の支柱 *She held on to his arm for support.* 彼女は体を支えるために彼の腕にしがみ付いた. ▶定義3 ❶ money to buy food, clothes, etc 食糧, 衣服などを買うための金→生活費, 生活の糧 ‖ *She has no job, no home and no means of support.* 彼女は仕事も家も生活手段もない.

成句 moral support ⇒ **MORAL¹**

**supporter** /səpɔ́ːrtər/ 名 ❸ ▶定義 a person who supports a political party, sports team, etc 政党, スポーツチームなどを支持または応援する人→支持者, 後援者, ファン, サポーター ‖ *football supporters* サッカーファン

**supportive** /səpɔ́ːrtɪv/ 形 ▶定義 giving help or support to sb in a difficult situation 困難な状況にある人に援助または支援を与える→支えとなる, 支援的な ‖ *Everyone was very supportive when I lost my job.* 私が失業した時, 皆がとても励ましてくれた.

**\*suppose** /səpóʊz/ 動他 ▶定義1 to think that sth is probable 〜があり得ると考える→〜ではないかと思う, 考える, 想像する, 推測する ‖ *What do you suppose could have happened?* あなたは何が起きたのだと推測しますか. *I don't suppose that they're coming now.* 彼らはおそらくまだ来ないと思う. ▶定義2 to pretend that sth will happen or is true 何かが起こる, または真実であると仮定する→〜であるとする, 〜だとする ‖ *Suppose you won the lottery. What would you do?* 宝くじを当てたとしたら, あなたは何をしますか. ▶定義3 used to make a suggestion, request or statement less strong 提案, 要請, 主張などを和らげるのに用いて→〜してはどうですか, 〜していただけませんか, 〜だと思う ‖ *I don't suppose you'd lend me your car tonight, would you?* 今夜車を貸していただけませんかね. ▶定義4 used when you agree with sth, but are not very happy about it 何かに同意するが, あまり喜んでいないときに用いて→〜だと思う, 〜でしょうね ‖ *'Can we give Andy a lift?' 'Yes, I suppose so, if we must.'* 「アンディーを同乗させてあげませんか」「ええ, まあいいでしょう. どうしてもと言うならば」

成句 be supposed to do sth ▶定義1 to be expected to do sth or to have to do sth 〜すると期待されている, 〜しなければならない→〜することになっている, 〜するはずである ‖ *The train was supposed to arrive ten minutes ago.* その列車は10分前に到着するはずだった. *This is secret and I'm not supposed to talk about it.* これは秘密であり, 私はその事について話してはならないことになっている. ▶定義2 略式 to be considered or thought to be sth→〜であると考えられている, 思われている ‖ *This is supposed to be the oldest building in the city.* これはこの市で最も古い建物だと考えられている.

**supposedly** /səpóʊz(ə)dli/ 副 ▶定義 according to what many people believe 多くの人が信じているところでは→思われるところでは, 多分, 推定上

**supposing** /səpóʊzɪŋ/ 接 ▶定義 if sth happens or is true; what if 何かが起きるまたは真実であるとすると; もしも〜だとしたら→〜と仮定すると, もし〜ならば ‖ *Supposing the plan goes wrong, what will we do then?* 計画が思い通りにいかないとしたら, その時はどうすればよいのだろう.

**supposition** /sʌ̀pəzɪ́ʃ(ə)n/ 名 ❸❶ ▶定義 an idea that a person thinks is true but which has not been shown to be true 人が真実だと考えているが, 真実だと立証されていない考え→仮説, 仮定, 推測

**suppress** /səprés/ 動他 ▶定義1 to stop sth by

using force 力を用いて~を止める➡~を静める, 抑える, 鎮圧する ▶定義2 to stop sth from being seen or known ~が見られるまたは知られるのを止めさせる➡~を隠す, 伏せる, 削除する ‖ *to suppress the truth* 真実を伏せる ▶定義3 to stop yourself from expressing your feelings, etc 自分の感情などを表現するのを止める➡~を抑える, こらえる, 止める ‖ *to suppress laughter/a yawn* 笑い・あくびをかみ殺す — suppression /səpréʃ(ə)n/ 名 ❶・❷ 抑圧, 鎮圧, 削除

**supremacy** /səprémǝsi, s(j)uː-, s(j)ʊ-/ 名 ❶ ▶定義 supremacy (over sb/sth) the state of being the most powerful 最も有力である状態➡**優位, 優越, 覇権**

**supreme** /səpríːm, s(j)uː-, s(j)ʊ-/ 形 ▶定義 the highest or greatest possible 可能な限り最も高いまたは大きい➡**最高の, 最大の, 最上の, この上ない**

**supremely** /səpríːmli, s(j)uː-, s(j)ʊ-/ 副 ▶定義 extremely 極めて➡**この上なく, 最高に**

**surcharge** /sə́ːrtʃɑːrdʒ/ 名 ❻ ▶定義 an extra amount of money that you have to pay for sth 何かに対して支払わなければならない割り増しの金➡**追加料金, 追徴金**

\*__sure__ /ʃʊər, ʃɔːr/ 形 副 ▶定義1 (名詞の前は不可) having no doubt about sth; certain 何かについて疑いを持っていない; 確信している➡**確かであると思う, 自信がある** ‖ *You must be sure of your facts before you make an accusation.* 非難する前に (自分の語る) 事実を確信していなければならない. *I'm not sure what to do next.* 次に何をしたらよいのかよく分からない. *Craig was sure that he'd made the right decision.* クレイグは自分が正しい決断をしたと確信していた. *I think I had my bag when I got off the bus but I'm not sure.* 私はバスを降りた時にかばんを持っていたと思うが, 自信がない.

▶ sureとcertainは意味がとてもよく似ている. しかし, 使い方が多少異なる. 比較: *It is certain that there will be an election next year.* (来年はきっと選挙がある.) *There is sure to be an election next year.*

▶定義2 (名詞の前は不可) sure of sth; sure to do sth that you will definitely get or do, or that will definitely happen 確実に手に入れるまたは行うような, あるいは確実に起こるような➡**きっと~をする, ~を行うのは確実である** ‖ *If you go and see them you can be sure of a warm welcome.* 彼らに会いに行けば, きっと温かい歓迎を受けるでしょう. *If you work hard you are sure to pass the exam.* 一生懸命勉強すれば, 必ず試験に合格することでしょう. ⇔ **unsure**

▶定義3 that you can be certain of 確信できるような➡**確かな, 間違いのない, 確実な, 当てになる** ‖ *A noise like that is a sure sign of engine trouble.* あのような雑音はエンジントラブルの確かな兆候だ. ▶定義4 略式 used to say 'yes' to sb 人に「はい」と言うときに用いて➡**もちろん, いいとも, その通り** ‖ '*Can I have a look at your newspaper?*' '*Sure.*'「新聞を見せてもらってもいいですか」「もちろん」

成句 Be sure to do sth ▶定義 Don't forget to do sth 忘れずに~しなさい➡**必ず~しなさい** ‖ *Be sure to write and tell me what happens.* どうなるか必ず手紙を書いて知らせてください.

for sure ▶定義 without doubt 疑いなく➡**確かに, 確実に, きっと** ‖ *Nobody knows for sure what happened.* 何が起きたのか, だれもはっきりとは知らない.

make sure ▶定義1 to find out whether sth is in a particular state or has been done 物事がある特定の状態にあるかどうか, または行われたかどうかを確かめる➡**確認する, 念を入れる** ‖ *I must go back and make sure I closed the window.* 私は戻って, 窓を閉めたことを確認しなければならない. ▶定義2 to take the action that is necessary 必要な行動を取る➡**必ず~する, 確実に~する** ‖ *Make sure you are back home by 11 o'clock.* 11時までに必ず家に帰りなさい.

sure enough ▶定義 as was expected 予期されていた通りに➡**思った通り, 確かに, 案の定** ‖ *I expected him to be early, and sure enough he arrived five minutes before the others.* 私は彼が早く来ると思っていたが, 案の定ほかの人たちよりも5分早く到着した.

sure of yourself ▶定義 confident about your opinions, or about what you can do 自分の意見またはできる事に確信がある➡**自信がある, 自信過剰である**

sure (thing) 米 略式 ▶定義 yes はい➡**もちろん, いいとも** ‖ '*Can I borrow this book?*' '*Sure thing.*'「この本を借りてもいいですか」「もちろん」

## surely

### ▶語法

**sure と certain**

両者の微妙な意味の差異を気にするよりも、頻度の高いパターンをまず身に付けましょう。sure は He is sure to come.(彼は必ず来ます)のように「人が主語」でよく用いられます。一方 certain は One thing is certain.(確かなことが1つある)のように「物が主語」でよく用いられます。

また、Be sure to lock the door.(ドアに必ずかぎをかけなさい)の場合と異なり、Make sure that you arrive in time.(必ず間に合うように来なさい)の場合は、that SV となります。

---

★**surely** /ʃúəli, ʃɔ́:r-/ 副 ▶定義1 without doubt 疑いなく→**確かに、必ず、きっと** ‖ *This will surely cause problems.* これは間違いなく問題を引き起こすだろう。 ▶定義2 used for expressing surprise at sb else's opinions, plans, actions, etc ほかの人の意見、計画、行動などに対する驚きを表すのに用いられて→**本当に、まさか、よもや** ‖ *Surely you're not going to walk home in this rain?* まさかこの雨の中を歩いて帰宅するつもりではないでしょうね。 *'Meena's looking for another job.' 'Surely not.'* 「ミーナは別の仕事を探しています」「まさかそんなはずはないでしょう」 ▶定義3 困 略式 yes; of course はい;もちろん→**いいとも、どうぞ**

**surf**¹ /sə:rf/ 名 Ⓤ ▶定義 the white part on the top of waves in the sea 海の波の一番高い所にある白い部分→**波しぶき、白い波**

**surf**² /sə:rf/ 動 自 ▶定義 to stand or lie on a special board (**a surfboard**) and ride on a wave towards the shore 専用の板(サーフボード)の上に立ってまたは横になって、海岸に向かって波に乗る→**波乗りをする、サーフィンをする**

成句 **surf the net** ▶定義 to use the Internet インターネットを使う→**ネットサーフィンをする、あちこちのサイトを見て回る**

★**surface**¹ /sə́:rfəs/ 名 ▶定義1 Ⓒthe outside part of sth 物の外側の部分→**表面、表、外面** ‖ *the earth's surface* 地球の表面 *Teeth have a hard surface called enamel.* 歯にはエナメル質と呼ばれる硬い外面がある。 *This tennis court has a very uneven surface.* このテニスコートの表面はとてもでこぼこしている。 ▶定義2 **the surface** [単数扱い]the top part of an area of water 水域の一番上の部分→**水面** ‖ *leaves floating on the surface of a pond* 池の水面に浮かんでいる葉 ▶定義3 Ⓒthe flat top part of a piece of furniture, used for working on 作業するために用いられる、家具の一番上の平らな部分→**台** ‖ *a work surface* 作業台 *kitchen surfaces* 調理台 ▶定義4 [単数扱い]the qualities of sb/sth that you see or notice, that are not hidden 隠されていない、見えるまたは目に留まる人や物の性質→**外見、外観、見掛け、上辺** ‖ *Everybody seems very friendly but there are a lot of tensions below/beneath the surface.* 皆はとても親しげに見えるが、水面下ではかなり緊迫した関係にある。

**surface**² /sə́:rfəs/ 動 ▶定義1 自 to come up to the surface of water 水の表面に上がってくる→**浮上する** ▶定義2 自 to appear again 再び現れる→**姿を現す、表面化する、明るみに出る** ‖ *All the old arguments surfaced again in the discussion.* 昔の論争のすべてが、その討論で再び表面化した。 ▶定義3 他 to cover the surface of sth ～の表面を覆う→**～の表面を仕上げる、舗装する**

**surface mail** 名 Ⓤ ▶定義 letters, packages, etc that go by road, rail or sea, not by air 航空機ではなく、車、鉄道、または船で届く手紙、小包など→**普通郵便** ⇒参 airmail

**surfeit** /sə́:rfət/ 名 [単数扱い](文) ▶定義 **a surfeit (of sth)** too much of sth 多すぎる～→**過度の～、～の過多**

**surfer** /sə́:rfər/ 名 Ⓒ ▶定義 a person who rides on waves standing on a special board 専用の板の上に立って波に乗る人→**サーファー、サーフィンをする人**

**surge** /sə:rdʒ/ 名 [Ⓒ,通常は単数]**a surge (of/in sth)** ▶定義1 a sudden strong movement in a particular direction by a large number of people or things 多数の人や物がある特定の方向へ突然勢いよく動くこと→**殺到、高まり、急増、うねり** ‖ *a surge forward* 前の方に殺到すること *a surge (= an increase) in the demand for electricity* 電気の需要の高まり(= 増加) ▶定義2 a sudden strong feeling 突然の激しい感情→**激昂(げっこう)、動揺** — **surge** 動 自 →**殺到する、高騰する、急**

増する, 込み上げる ‖ *The crowd surged forward.* 群集が前の方に殺到した.

**surgeon** /sə́ːrdʒ(ə)n/ 名 C ▶定義 a doctor who performs medical operations (surgery) 手術(外科手術)を行う医者➡**外科医** ‖ *a brain surgeon* 脳外科医

**surgery** /sə́ːrdʒ(ə)ri/ 名 (複 **surgeries**) ▶定義 1 ❶ medical treatment in which your body is cut open so that part of it can be removed or repaired 体の一部を除去または治すことができるように, 体を切り開く医療行為➡**手術, 外科手術** ‖ *to undergo surgery* 手術を受ける ☞参 **plastic surgery, operation** ▶定義 2 C U the place or time when a doctor or dentist sees patients 医者または歯医者が患者を診る場所または時間➡**医院, 診療所, 診察室, 診療時間** ‖ *Surgery hours are from 9.00 to 11.30.* 診療時間は9時から11時30分です.

**surgical** /sə́ːrdʒɪk(ə)l/ 形 ▶定義 connected with medical operations 手術に関する➡**外科手術の, 外科的な, 外科用の** ‖ *surgical instruments* 外科用具 ― surgically /-k(ə)li/ 副➡**外科的に, 手術によって**

**surly** /sə́ːrli/ 形 ▶定義 unfriendly and rude 友好的でなく無礼な➡**不機嫌な, むっつりとした, 無愛想な** ‖ *a surly expression* ぶっきらぼうな表現

**surmount** /sərmáʊnt/ 動 他 ▶定義 to deal successfully with a problem or difficulty 問題または困難をうまく処理する➡**〜を乗り越える, 克服する, 〜に打ち勝つ** ☞参 **insurmountable**

\***surname** /sə́ːrnèɪm/ (または **last name**) 名 C ▶定義 the name that you share with other people in your family 家族のほかの人たちと共有する名前➡**姓, 名字** ‖ *'What's your surname?' 'Jones.'* 「あなたの名字は何ですか」「ジョーンズです」☞参 **name**の注

**surpass** /sərpǽs; -páes/ 動 他 正式 ▶定義 to do sth better than sb/sth else or better than expected ほかの〜よりも, または予期されていたよりも, うまく物事を行う➡**〜をしのぐ, 超える, 〜に勝る** ‖ *The success of the film surpassed all expectations.* その映画の成功はあらゆる予想を上回っていた.

**surplus** /sə́ːrpləs, -plʌ̀s/ 名 C U ▶定義 an amount that is extra or more than you need 追加のまたは必要以上の量➡**余剰, 過剰** ‖ *the food surplus in Western Europe* 西欧の余剰食糧 ―

surplus 形➡**余剰の, 過剰な** ‖ *They sell their surplus grain to other countries.* 彼らは余った穀物を他国に売っている.

\***surprise**[1] /sərpráɪz/ 名 ▶定義 1 ❶ the feeling that you have when sth happens that you do not expect 予期していない物事が起きたときに抱く感情➡**驚き, 驚嘆, びっくり** ‖ *They looked up in surprise when she walked in.* 彼女が入ってくると, 彼らは驚いて顔を上げた. *To my surprise they all agreed with me.* 驚いたことに, 彼らは皆, 私に賛成した. ▶定義 2 C something that you did not expect or know about 予期しなかったまたは知らなかった物事➡**驚くべき事, 意外な物, 思い掛けない出来事** ‖ *What a pleasant surprise to see you again!* あなたに再会できるとは何とうれしい驚きでしょう. *The news came as a complete surprise.* その知らせは全く意外だった. *a surprise visit/attack/ party* 不意の訪問・奇襲・びっくりパーティー

成句 **take sb by surprise** ▶定義 to happen or do sth when sb is not expecting it 〜が予期していない時に起きるまたは何かを行う➡**〜を驚かせる, びっくりさせる, 〜の不意を突く**

**surprise**[2] /sərpráɪz/ 動 他 ▶定義 1 to make sb feel surprised 〜を驚かせる➡**〜をびっくりさせる, 仰天させる** ‖ *It wouldn't surprise me if you get the job.* あなたがその仕事を得たとしても私は驚かないだろう. ▶定義 2 to attack or find sb suddenly and unexpectedly 突然, 不意に〜を攻撃するまたは見つける➡**〜の不意を襲う, 虚を突く, 〜を奇襲する**

\***surprised** /sərpráɪzd/ 形 ▶定義 feeling or showing surprise 驚きを感じているまたは表している➡**驚いた, びっくりした, 仰天した** ‖ *I was very surprised to see Cara there. I thought she was still abroad.* 私はあそこでキャラに会ってとてもびっくりした. まだ外国にいると思っていた.

\***surprising** /sərpráɪzɪŋ/ 形 ▶定義 that causes surprise 驚きを引き起こすような➡**驚くべき, 驚かせるような, 意外な** ‖ *It's surprising how many adults can't read or write.* こんなにも多くの大人が読み書きできないとは驚きだ. ― surprisingly 副➡**驚いたことに, びっくりしたことに, 意外にも** ‖ *Surprisingly few people got the* *correct answer.* 意外なことに，正しい答えを出せた人はほとんどいなかった.

**surreal** /səríəl, -ríː(ə)l/ (または **surrealistic** /sərìːəlístɪk, -rìə-/) 形 ▶定義 very strange; with images mixed together in a strange way like in a dream とても奇妙な; 夢の中のように像が奇妙に混ぜ合わされた→超現実的な, シュールレアリスムの, シュールな ‖ *a surreal film/painting/situation* 幻想的な映画・シュールレアリスムの絵画・非現実的な状態

**surrender** /səréndər/ 動 ▶定義**1** 自他 surrender (to sb) to stop fighting and admit that you have lost 戦うのをやめて自分が負けたことを認める→降伏する ☞類 **yield** ▶定義**2** 他 正式 surrender sb/sth (to sb) to give sb/sth to sb else ～をほかの…に与える→～を(…に)明け渡す, 引き渡す, 譲り渡す ‖ *The police ordered them to surrender their weapons.* 警察は彼らに武器を引き渡すよう命じた.— surrender 名 C U →降伏, 降参, 引き渡し, 明け渡し

**surreptitious** /sʌ̀ːrəptíʃəs, sʌ̀r-/ 形 ▶定義 done secretly ひそかに行われた→内密の, 秘密の, 隠密の ‖ *I had a surreptitious look at what she was writing.* 私は彼女が書いている物をこっそり見た.— surreptitiously 副 →内密に, 秘密に, ひそかに

**surrogate** /sʌ́ːrəgèɪt, -gət; sʌ́rəgɪt/ 名 C 形 ▶定義 (a person or thing) that takes the place of sb/sth else ほかの人や物の代わりになる(人または物)→代理人, 代行者, 代用品; 代理の, 代わりの ‖ *a surrogate mother (= a woman who has a baby and gives it to another woman who cannot have children)* 代理母(= 赤ん坊を出産し, 子供を持つことのできない別の女性に与える女性)

*****surround** /səráʊnd/ 動 他 ▶定義 surround sb/sth (by/with sth) to be or go all around sb/sth (～で)…を取り巻く, 一周する→～を包囲する, 取り巻く ‖ *The garden is surrounded by a high wall.* その庭は高い塀で囲まれている. *Troops have surrounded the parliament building.* 軍隊が国会議事堂を取り囲んだ.

**surrounding** /səráʊndɪŋ/ 形 (名詞の前だけ) ▶定義 that is near or around sth 物のそばまたは周りにある→付近の, 周囲の, 取り囲んでいる

**surroundings** /səráʊndɪŋz/ 名 [複数扱い] ▶定義 everything that is near or around you; the place where you live 自分のそばまたは周りにあるすべての物; 住んでいる場所→環境, 境遇, 周囲の状況 ‖ *to live in pleasant surroundings* 快適な環境で暮らす *animals living in their natural surroundings (= not in zoos)* 自然環境(= 動物園ではない)に生息する動物 ☞参 **environment**

**surveillance** /sərvéɪləns/ 名 U ▶定義 the careful watching of sb who may have done sth wrong 悪いことを行ったかもしれない人を注意深く見張ること→監視, 見張り ‖ *The building is protected by surveillance cameras.* その建物は監視カメラで守られている.

**survey**¹ /sʌ́ːrveɪ, sərveɪ/ 名 C ▶定義**1** a study of the opinions, behaviour, etc of a group of people ある集団の人々の意見, 行動などを調べること→調査, 標本調査 ‖ *Surveys have shown that more and more people are getting into debt.* 調査によれば, 借金をする人がますます増えている. *to carry out/conduct/do a survey* 調査を(実施)する ▶定義**2** the action of examining an area of land and making a map of it ある地域を調査して地図を作ること→測量, 測地 ▶定義**3** the action of examining a building in order to find out if it is in good condition 状態が良いかどうかを確かめるために建物を調べること→査定, 検分

**survey**² /sərvéɪ, sʌ́ːrveɪ/ 動 他 ▶定義**1** to look carefully at the whole of sth ～の全体を注意深く見る→～を観察する, 見渡す, ～の全体を眺める ‖ *We stood at the top of the hill and surveyed the countryside.* 私たちは丘の頂上に立って田園地帯を見晴らした. ▶定義**2** to carefully measure and make a map of an area of land ある地域を慎重に測定して地図を作る→～を測量する, 測地する ▶定義**3** to examine a building carefully in order to find out if it is in good condition 状態が良いかどうかを確かめるために建物を調べる→査定する, 検分する

*****survive** /sərváɪv/ 動 ▶定義**1** 自他 to continue to live or exist in or after a difficult or dangerous situation 困難なまたは危険な状況の中で, あるいはその後で, 生き続けるまたは存在し続ける→生き残る, 存続する ‖ *More than a hundred people were killed in the crash and only five passengers survived.* その衝突[墜落]事故で

100人以上が死亡し, たった5人の乗客だけが助かった. *How can she survive on such a small salary?* あんなに少ない給料で一体どうやって彼女はやっていけるのだろうか. *to survive a plane crash* 飛行機の墜落事故で生き残る *Not many buildings survived the bombing.* その爆撃を免れた建物は多くなかった. ▶定義2 ⓬ to live longer than sb/sth → ~よりも長く生きる ― survival /sərváɪv(ə)l/ 名 ⓾ ➡生き残ること, 生き延びること, 生存, 残存, 存続 ‖ *A heart transplant was his only chance of survival.* 心臓移植しか彼が助かる道はなかった. ― survivor 名 ⓒ ➡生存者, 残された人 ‖ *There were five survivors of the crash.* その衝突・墜落事故の生存者は5人だった.

**susceptible** /səséptəb(ə)l/ 形 (名詞の前は不可) ▶定義 susceptible to sb/sth easily influenced, damaged or affected by sb/sth ~に簡単に影響される, 傷付けられる, または侵される → **~に影響されやすい, すぐ左右される, 感染しやすい** ‖ *People in a new country are highly susceptible to illness.* 人は新しい土地に行くと非常に病気にかかりやすくなる.

**★suspect**[1] /səspékt/ 動 ⓬ ▶定義1 to believe that sth may happen or be true, especially sth bad ~, 特に悪い~が起こるまたは真実であるかもしれないと信じる → **どうも~らしいと思う** ‖ *The situation is worse than we first suspected.* 状況は私たちが最初に想像していたよりも悪い. *Nobody suspected that she was thinking of leaving.* 彼女が退職することを考えていたとはだれも思わなかった. ☛参 **unsuspecting** ▶定義2 to not be sure that you can trust sb or believe sth ~を信頼したり, または物事を信じたりすることができると確信していない → **~を疑う, 怪しむ, 信用しない** ‖ *I rather suspect his motives for offering to help.* 手伝おうと申し出た彼の動機を, 私はかなり怪しいと思っている. ▶定義3 suspect sb (of sth/of doing sth) to believe that sb is guilty of sth ~が…について罪があると信じる → **~に…の嫌疑をかける, ~が…をしたのではないかと疑う** ‖ *I suspect Laura of taking the money.* 私はローラがその金を取ったのではないかと疑っている. *She strongly suspected that he was lying.* 彼女は彼がうそをついていると強く疑った. ☛ 名 **suspicion**

**suspect**[2] /sʌ́spekt/ 名 ⓒ ▶定義 a person who is thought to be guilty of a crime 犯罪に罪があると考えられている人 → **容疑者, 被疑者** ‖ *The suspects are being questioned by police.* 容疑者たちは警察の尋問を受けている.

**suspect**[3] /sʌ́spekt, səspékt/ 形 ▶定義 possibly not true or not to be trusted おそらく真実でない, または信頼できない → **疑わしい, 怪しい, うさんくさい** ‖ *to have suspect motives* 疑わしい動機を持つ *a suspect parcel* (= that may contain a bomb) 怪しい小包 (= 爆弾が入っているかもしれない)

**suspend** /səspénd/ 動 ⓬ ▶定義1 suspend sth (from sth) (by/on sth) to hang sth from sth else ~をほかの…からつり下げる → **~を…から掛ける, つり下げる, ぶら下げる** ‖ *The huge skeleton is suspended from the museum's ceiling on chains.* 巨大な骸骨 (がいこつ) が博物館の天井から鎖でつり下げられている. ▶定義2 to stop or delay sth for a time しばらくの間, ~を停止するまたは遅らせる → **~を一時停止にする, 一時中止する, 見合わせる, 保留する** ‖ *Some rail services were suspended during the strike.* ストライキの間, 一部の列車の運行が中止された. *The young man was given a **suspended sentence*** (= he will not go to prison unless he commits another crime). その若い男性に執行猶予付きの判決が下された (= 別の罪を犯さない限り刑務所に入らない). ▶定義3 suspend sb (from sth) to send sb away from his/her school, job, position, etc for a period of time, usually as a punishment 通常は罰として, ある期間, 学校, 仕事, 地位などから~を追いやる → **~を停学にする, 停職にする, 休職にする, 営業・出場停止にする** ‖ *He was suspended from school for a week for stealing.* 彼は窃盗のため1週間停学になった. ☛ 名 **suspension**

**suspender** /səspéndər/ 名 ▶定義1 英 [ⓒ, 通常は複数] a short piece of elastic that women use to hold up the thin pieces of clothing that fit closely over a woman's legs and feet (**stockings**) 女性が足にぴったりする薄い衣類 (ストッキング) を固定するのに用いる短いゴムひも → **ガーター, 靴下留め** ▶定義2 **suspenders** [複数扱い] 米 = **BRACE**[1] (2)

**suspense** /səspéns/ 名 ⓾ ▶定義 the feeling of

excitement or worry that you have when you feel sth is going to happen, when you are waiting for news, etc 物事が起きそうであると感じるときや知らせを待っているときなどに抱く動揺または不安感→**気懸かり, 懸念, 緊張感** ‖ *Don't keep us in suspense. Tell us what happened.* 気をもませないで. 何が起きたのか私たちに話してください.

**suspension** /səspénʃ(ə)n/ 名 ▶定義1 **C U** not being allowed to do your job or go to school for a period of time, usually as a punishment 通常は罰として, ある期間, 仕事をしたり通学したりすることが許されないこと→**停職, 停学, 営業停止, 出場停止** ‖ *suspension on full pay* 有給自宅待機 ▶定義2 **U** delaying sth for a period of time ある期間, 物事を遅らせること→**延期, 保留** ☛ 動 suspend ▶定義3 **the suspension U** the parts that are connected to the wheels of a car, etc that make it more comfortable to ride in 自動車の車輪などに接続されている, 乗り心地をより快適にする部品→**車体懸架装置, サスペンション**

*****suspicion** /səspíʃ(ə)n/ 名 ▶定義1 **C U** a feeling or belief that sth is wrong or that sb has done sth wrong 何かが不正である, または人が悪い事を行ったと感じること, あるいは信じること→**疑い, 疑念, 嫌疑, 容疑** ‖ *I always treat smiling politicians with suspicion.* 私は笑みを浮かべている政治家を常に疑いの目で見る. *She was arrested on suspicion of murder.* 彼女は殺人の容疑で逮捕された. *He is under suspicion of being involved in drug smuggling.* 彼には麻薬の密輸にかかわった疑いがかけられている. ▶定義2 **C** a feeling that sth may happen or be true 何かが起きるかもしれないまたは真実であるかもしれないという感じ→**~ではないかと思うこと, ~らしいという感じ, ~と踏むこと** ‖ *I have a suspicion that he's forgotten he invited us.* 私は, 彼が私たちを招待したのを忘れているのではないかと踏んでいる. ☛ 動 suspect

**suspicious** /səspíʃəs/ 形 ▶定義1 suspicious (of/about sb/sth) feeling that sb has done sth wrong, dishonest or illegal だれかが悪い, 不正な, あるいは違法な事を行ったと感じている→**疑っている, 疑念を持っている** ‖ *We became suspicious of his behaviour and alerted the police.* 私たちは彼の行動に疑いを抱き, 警察に通報した. ▶定義2 that makes you feel that sth is wrong, dishonest or illegal 何かが悪い, 不正である, あるいは違法であると思わせるような→**疑わしい, 怪しい, 不審な** ‖ *The old man died in suspicious circumstances.* その老人は不審な状況下で死んだ. *It's very suspicious that she was not at home on the evening of the murder.* 殺人のあった夜に彼女が家にいなかったことは, 非常に疑わしい. *a suspicious-looking person* うさんくさく見える人 — suspiciously 副 ▶疑い深く, 疑わしげに, 怪しそうに, うさんくさそうに, 怪しいことに ‖ *to behave suspiciously* 不審な態度で振る舞う

**sustain** /səstéɪn/ 動 他 ▶定義1 to keep sb/sth alive or healthy ~を生かしておく, または健康に保つ→**~を維持する, 扶養する** ‖ *Oxygen sustains life.* 酸素は生命を維持する. ▶定義2 to make sth continue for a long period of time without becoming less ~を長い間, 減少させずに続けさせる→**~を持続させる, 維持する, 継続する** ‖ *It's hard to sustain interest for such a long time.* そんなに長い間, 興味を持続させるのは大変だ. ▶定義3 正式 to experience sth bad 好ましくない事を経験する→**~を被る, 受ける, 経験する** ‖ *to sustain damage/an injury/a defeat* 損害を被る・けがを負う・敗北する

**SW** 略 south-west(ern)→**南西(の)** ‖ *SW Australia* オーストラリア南西部

**swagger** /swǽɡər/ 動 自 ▶定義 to walk in a way that shows that you are too confident or proud 自信過剰または高慢であることを表すように歩く→**ふんぞり返って歩く, 威張って歩く** — swagger 名 [単数扱い]→**威張った歩き方, 尊大な態度**

*****swallow** /swάloʊ/ 動 ▶定義1 他 to make food, drink, etc go down your throat to your stomach 食べ物, 飲み物などをのどから胃に移動させる→**~を飲み込む, 飲み下す** ‖ *It's easier to swallow pills if you take them with water.* 錠剤は水と一緒に飲む方が飲みやすい. ☛ lick のさし絵 ▶定義2 自 to make a movement in your throat, often because you are afraid or surprised, etc しばしば不安または驚きのために, のどを動かす→**のどをごくりとさせる, つばを飲む** ‖ *She swallowed hard and tried to speak, but nothing came out.* 彼女はぐっとつばを飲み込んで話そうとしたが, 言葉が出てこなかった. ▶定義3 他

to accept or believe sth too easily 〜をあまりにも簡単に受け入れるまたは信じる→〜をうのみにする, 真に受ける ‖ *You shouldn't swallow everything they tell you!* 彼らが話すことを何でも真に受けてはいけません. ▶定義4 ⓜto accept an insult, etc without complaining 不平を言わずに侮辱などを受け入れる→〜を甘受する, 我慢する, 〜に耐える ‖ *I find her criticisms very hard to swallow.* 私には彼女の批判はとても受け入れ難い. ▶定義5 ⓜswallow sth (up) to use all of sth, especially money 〜を, 特に金をすべて使う→〜を使い果たす, 平らげる ‖ *The rent swallows up most of our monthly income.* 家賃で私たちの月収のほとんどが消えてしまう. — swallow 名 C→飲み込むこと, 一飲み

成句 hard to swallow ⇒ **HARD**¹

**swam** SWIM の過去形

**swamp**¹ /swɑmp/ 名 C ⓜ ▶定義 an area of soft wet land 柔らかく湿った土地→沼地, 湿地, 湿原

**swamp**² /swɑmp/ 動 ⓜ ▶定義1 to cover or fill sth with water 〜を水で覆うまたは満たす→〜を水浸しにする ‖ *The fishing boat was swamped by enormous waves.* その釣り船は巨大な波によって浸水した. ▶定義2 swamp sb/sth (with sth) (通常は受動態で) to give sb so much of sth that he/she cannot deal with it 処理できないほど多量の〜を…に与える→〜を(…で)圧倒する; 〜に殺到する, 押し寄せる ‖ *We've been swamped with applications for the job.* 私たちの所にはその仕事への応募が殺到している.
☛類 **inundate**

**swan** /swɑn/ 名 C ▶定義 a large, usually white, bird with a very long neck that lives on lakes and rivers 湖または川に生息し, とても長い首を持つ, 大きくて通常は白い鳥→白鳥 ☛ **duck** のさし絵

*****swap** (または **swop**) /swɑp/ 動 T ⓜ (**swapping**; **swapped**) ▶定義 swap (sth) (with sb); swap A for B to give sth for sth else; to exchange ほかの〜に対して…を与える; 交換する→〜を…と取り替える, 交換する, やり取りする ‖ *When we finish these books shall we swap (= you have my book and I'll have yours)?* これらの本を読み終わったら交換しましょうか(= あなたが私の本を, 私があなたの本を取る). *Would you swap seats with me?* 私と席を替わってくれませんか. *I'd swap my job for hers any day.* 私はいつでも自分の仕事と彼女の仕事を交換するつもりだ. — swap 名 [単数扱い]→交換, 取り替え ‖ *Let's do a swap.* 交換しよう.

成句 change/swap places (with sb) ⇒ **PLACE**¹

**swarm**¹ /swɔːm/ 名 C ▶定義1 a large group of insects, especially bees, moving around together 一緒に動き回っている昆虫, 特にハチの大きな集団→群れ, 大群 ‖ *a swarm of bees/locusts/flies* ハチ・バッタ・ハエの群れ ▶定義2 a large number of people together 一緒にいる多数の人々→群衆, 大勢

**swarm**² /swɔːm/ 動 I ▶定義 to fly or move in large numbers 多数で飛ぶまたは移動する→群れを成して飛ぶ, 動く

何動詞 swarm with sb/sth ▶定義 to be too crowded or full あまりにも混雑した, または一杯になる→〜で埋まる, あふれる

**swat** /swɑt/ 動 T (**swatting**; **swatted**) ▶定義 to hit sth, especially an insect, with sth flat→〜を, 特に昆虫を, 平らな物でたたく

**sway** /sweɪ/ 動 ▶定義1 Ⓘto move slowly from side to side 左右にゆっくりと動く→揺れ動く ‖ *The trees were swaying in the wind.* 風で木が揺れ動いていた. ▶定義2 ⓜto influence sb 〜に影響を与える→〜を動かす, 左右する ‖ *Many people were swayed by his convincing arguments.* 多くの人たちが彼の説得力ある主張に感化された.

*****swear** /sweər/ 動 (過 **swore** /swɔːr/; 過分 **sworn** /swɔːrn/) ▶定義1 Ⓘswear (at sb/sth) to use rude or bad language 無礼なまたは汚い言葉を使う→ののしる, 毒づく, 悪態をつく ‖ *He hit his thumb with the hammer and swore loudly.* 彼は金づちで親指を打ち, 大声でののしった. *There's no point in swearing at the car just because it won't start!* 始動しないというだけで車をののしっても意味がないよ. ☛参 **curse**
▶定義2 Ⓘ ⓜswear (to do sth); swear that... to make a serious promise 真剣な約束をする→(〜と)誓う, 宣誓する ‖ *When you give evidence in court you have to swear to tell the truth.* 法廷で証言するときは真実を述べることを宣誓しなければならない. *Will you swear not to tell anyone?* だれにも話さないと誓いますか.

## 1640 swear word

**句動詞** swear by sth ▶定義 to believe completely in the value of sth ～の価値を完全に信じる→～を信じきる, ～を当てにする

swear sb in (通常は受動態で) ▶定義 to make sb say officially that he/she will accept the responsibility of a new position ～に新しい地位の責任を受け入れることを公式に言わせる→～を宣誓就任させる‖ *The President will be sworn in next week.* 大統領は,来週宣誓就任することになっている.

**swear word** (または(古) **oath**) 名 C ▶定義 a word that is considered rude or bad and that may offend people 無礼または汚いと考えられていて, 人の気分を害する可能性のある語→ののしりの言葉, 口汚い言葉

★**sweat** /swet/ 動 自 ▶定義1 to produce liquid through your skin because you are hot, ill or afraid 暑いため, 病気のため, あるいは不安のために皮膚から液体を出す→汗をかく, 汗ばむ, 発汗する ▶定義2 sweat (over sth) to work hard 一生懸命に働く→汗水たらして働く, 精を出す‖ *I've been sweating over that problem all day.* 私は一日中その問題に熱心に取り組んでいる.— sweat 名 C U ▶汗, 発汗‖ *He stopped digging and wiped the sweat from his forehead.* 彼は掘るのをやめて額の汗をぬぐった. *He woke up in a sweat.* 彼は汗びっしょりで目が覚めた ☛参 perspiration

**成句** work/sweat your guts out ⇒ **GUT**¹

★**sweater** /swétər/ 名 C ▶定義 a warm piece of clothing with long sleeves, often made of wool, which you wear on the top half of your body 長そでの暖かい衣服で, しばしば羊毛でできており, 上半身に着用する→セーター

▶ sweater, jumper, pullover, jerseyはどれも同じ衣服を指す語である. しばしば羊毛または似たような素材で作られる. sweatshirt (スエットシャツ) は通常は木綿で作られており, 非公式の場でまたは運動用に着用される. cardigan (カーディガン) は前面で縦に留める.

☛ C6ページのさし絵

**sweatshirt** /swétʃɜːrt/ 名 C ▶定義 a warm piece of cotton clothing with long sleeves, which you wear on the top half of your body 長そでの暖かい木綿の衣服で, 上半身に着用する→スエットシャツ, トレーナー ☛ C6ページの

さし絵

**sweaty** /swéti/ 形 ▶定義1 wet with sweat 汗でぬれた→汗をかいた, 汗まみれの‖ *I was hot and sweaty after the match and needed a shower.* 私は, 試合後暑くて汗をかいたので, シャワーを浴びなければならなかった. ▶定義2 causing you to sweat 汗が出る→暑くて汗の出る, 骨の折れる‖ *a hot sweaty day* 暑くて汗の出る日

**swede** /swiːd/ 名 C U ▶定義 a large, round, yellow vegetable that grows under the ground 地中で生長する, 大きくて丸い黄色の野菜→スウェーデンカブ, カブハボタン ☛ C3ページのさし絵

★**sweep**¹ /swiːp/ 動/(過, 過分 **swept** /swept/) ▶定義1 自他 to clean the floor, etc by moving dust, dirt, etc away with a brush ほうきでちり, ほこりなどを移動させることによって, 床などをきれいにする→掃き掃除をする; ～を掃く, 清掃する‖ *to sweep the floor* 床を掃く *I'm going to sweep the leaves off the path.* 私は歩道の葉を掃除するつもりだ. ☛参 clean² の注 ▶定義2 他 to remove sth from a surface using your hand, etc 手などを用いて表面から～を取り除く→～を払う, 払いのける‖ *He swept the books angrily off the table.* 彼は怒ってテーブルから本を払いのけた. ▶定義3 自他 to move quickly and smoothly over the area or in the direction mentioned 指示された範囲全体または方向に素早く滑らかに移動する→(～を)さっと通る, 吹き抜ける, (～に)瞬く間に広まる‖ *Fire swept through the building.* 火があっと言う間にその建物全体に広がった. ▶定義4 他 to move or push sb/sth with a lot of force 大きな力で～を動かすまたは押す→～を押し流す, 吹き飛ばす, 洗い流す‖ *The huge waves swept her overboard.* 巨大な波が彼女を船外にほうり出した. *He was swept along by the huge crowd.* 彼は大群集に押されて進んだ. ▶定義5 自 to move in a way that impresses or is intended to impress people 人々に印象づけるようにまたは印象づけることが意図されているように移動する→さっそうと歩く, 悠々と歩く, 堂々と進む‖ *Five big black Mercedes swept past us.* 大きな黒いベンツが5台悠々と私たちを追い越した. ▶定義6 自他 to move over an area, especially in order to look for sth 特に～を探すために, ある領域全体を移動する→(～を)見渡す, 見回る‖ *The army were sweeping the fields for mines.* 軍隊は戦場

をしらみつぶしにして地雷を探していた. *His eyes swept quickly over the page.* 彼はさっとそのページ全体に目を走らせた.

句動詞 sweep (sb/sth) aside ▶定義 to not allow sb/sth to affect your progress or plans ～に進行または計画への影響を与えさせない➡～を一蹴(いっしゅう)する, 退ける, わきに押しやる

sweep sth out ▶定義 to remove dirt and dust from the floor of a room or building using a brush ほうきを使って部屋または建物の床から, ちりとほこりを取り除く➡～を掃き出す

sweep over sb ▶定義 (used about a feeling) to suddenly affect sb very strongly (感情について) 突然～に非常に強く影響を与える➡～の心をさらう

sweep (sth) up ▶定義 to remove dirt, dust, leaves, etc using a brush ほうきを使ってちり, ほこり, 葉などを取り除く➡～を掃く, 掃いて片付ける

**sweep**[2] /swiːp/ 名 C ▶定義 1 [通常は単数] the action of moving dirt and dust from a floor or surface using a brush ほうきを使って床または表面からちりとほこりを移動させること➡(掃き)掃除, 清掃 ∥ *I'd better give the floor a sweep.* 床を掃かなくては. ▶定義 2 a long, curving shape or movement 長く湾曲している形または動き➡弧を描く流れるような動き ∥ *He showed us which way to go with a sweep of his arm.* 彼は腕をさっと振って, 進むべき方向を私たちに示した. ▶定義 3 a movement over an area, especially in order to look for sth 特に何かを探すため, ある領域全体を移動すること➡広範な捜索, しらみつぶしの捜索 ▶定義 4 = CHIMNEY SWEEP

成句 a clean sweep ⇒ CLEAN[1]

**sweeper** /swíːpər/ 名 C ▶定義 1 a person or thing that cleans surfaces with a brush ほうきで表面をきれいにする人または物➡掃除人, 掃除機 ∥ *He's a road sweeper.* 彼は道路の清掃作業員だ. *Do you sell carpet sweepers?* カーペット用の掃除機を売っていますか. ▶定義 2 (in football) the defending player who plays behind the other defending players (サッカーで) ほかの守備の選手たちの後ろでプレーする守備の選手➡スイーパー

**sweeping** /swíːpɪŋ/ 形 ▶定義 1 (used about statements, etc) too general and not accurate enough (発言などについて) 漠然としすぎていて, あまり正確ではない➡大雑把な, 大まかな, 無差別の ∥ *He made a sweeping statement about all politicians being dishonest.* 彼はすべての政治家が不正直だと十把一からげに述べた. ▶定義 2 having a great and important effect 大きくて重大な影響力を持っている➡大々的な, 徹底的な, 全面的な ∥ *sweeping reforms* 抜本的な改革

*****sweet**[1] /swiːt/ 形 ▶定義 1 containing, or tasting as if it contains, a lot of sugar たくさんの砂糖が含まれている, または含んでいるような味のする➡甘い, 甘口の, 砂糖入りの ∥ *Children usually like sweet things.* 子供は大抵甘いものが好きだ. *This cake's too sweet.* このケーキは甘すぎる. ☛参 savoury ▶定義 2 (used especially about children and small things) attractive; cute (特に子供または小さな物について用いて) 魅力的な; かわいい➡愛らしい ∥ *a sweet little kitten* かわいい子猫 *Isn't that little girl sweet?* その少女は愛らしいですよね. ▶定義 3 having or showing a kind character 優しい性格を持っている, または表している➡優しい, 親切な, 思いやりのある ∥ *a sweet smile* 優しいほほえみ *It's very sweet of you to remember my birthday!* 私の誕生日を忘れないでいてくれて, とてもうれしいわ. ▶定義 4 (used about a smell or a sound) pleasant (香りまたは音について) 心地良い➡香りの良い, かぐわしい, 良い声の, 美声の — sweetness 名 U➡甘さ, 甘味, 美味, 愛らしさ, 優しさ

成句 have a sweet tooth ▶定義 to like eating sweet things 甘い物を食べるのを好む➡甘党である, 甘い物に目がない

*****sweet**[2] /swiːt/ 名 ▶定義 1 [C, 通常は複数] (米 candy U) a small piece of boiled sugar, chocolate, etc, often sold in a packet しばしば小さな包みで売られている, 煮詰めた少量の砂糖, チョコレートなど➡キャンデー, あめ, 砂糖菓子 ∥ *He was sucking a sweet.* 彼はキャンデーをなめていた. *a sweet shop* 菓子屋 ▶定義 2 C U sweet food served at the end of a meal 食事の最後に出される甘い食べ物➡食後の甘い物, デザート ☛参 pudding, dessert

**sweet corn** 名 U ▶定義 yellow grains from a tall plant (maize) that taste sweet and are eaten as a vegetable 甘い味がして, 野菜として食され

る, 背の高い植物(トウモロコシ)からとれる黄色い穀物→**トウモロコシ, スイートコーン** ☛ C3 ペ ージのさし絵

**sweeten** /swíːt(ə)n/ 動他 ▶定義 to make sth sweet by adding sugar, etc→**砂糖などを加えて～を甘くする**

**sweetener** /swíːt(ə)nər/ 名 C U ▶定義 a substance used instead of sugar for making food or drink sweet 食べ物または飲み物を甘くするために, 砂糖の代わりに用いられる物質→**甘味料** ‖ *artificial sweeteners* 人工甘味料

**sweetheart** /swíːthɑ̀ːrt/ 名 C ▶定義 1 used when speaking to sb, especially a child, in a very friendly way 人, 特に子供に対して, 非常に親しげに話し掛けるときに用いられる→**ねえ君, あなた** ‖ *Do you want a drink, sweetheart?* ねえ, 君は飲み物が欲しいかい. ▶定義 2 (古) a boyfriend or girlfriend ボーイフレンドまたはガールフレンド→**恋人, 愛人**

**sweetly** /swíːtli/ 副 ▶定義 in an attractive, kind or pleasant way 魅力的に, 親切に, あるいは心地良く→**甘く, 優しく, 愛らしく** ‖ *She smiled sweetly.* 彼女はにこやかにほほえんだ. *sweetly-scented flowers* 甘い香りのする花

*__swell__[1] /swel/ 動 (過 **swelled** /sweld/; 過分 **swollen** /swóul(ə)n/ または **swelled**) ▶定義 1 自他 swell (up) to become or to make sth bigger, fuller or thicker 大きく, 一杯に, あるいは厚くなる, または～をそのようにする→**膨らむ, はれる, ～を膨らませる, 大きくする** ‖ *After the fall her ankle began to swell up.* 転倒した後, 彼女の足首がはれ上がってきた. *Heavy rain had swollen the rivers.* 激しい雨で川が増水した. ▶定義 2 自他 to increase or make sth increase in number or size 数が増える, 大きくなる, または～の数や大きさを増やす→**増加する, 増大する, ～を増す, 高める** ‖ *The crowd swelled to 600 by the end of the evening.* その晩の終わりまでに群衆は600人に膨れ上がった. ▶定義 3 自 (文) (used about feelings or sound) to suddenly become stronger or louder (感情または音について)突然強くまたは大きくなる→**高まる, 胸が一杯になる** ‖ *Hatred swelled inside him.* 憎しみが彼の胸に込み上げた.

**swell**[2] /swel/ 名 [単数扱い] ▶定義 the slow movement up and down of the surface of the sea 海の表面がゆっくりと上下に移動すること→**うねり, 大波**

*__swelling__ /swélɪŋ/ 名 ▶定義 1 C a place on your body that is bigger or fatter than usual because of an injury or illness けがまたは病気のために通常よりも大きく, または太くなっている体の部分→**はれ物, こぶ** ‖ *I've got a nasty swelling under my eye.* 目の下にひどいはれ物ができている. ▶定義 2 U the process of becoming swollen はれていく過程→**はれ** ‖ *The disease often causes swelling of the ankles and knees.* その病気は足首またはひざのはれを引き起こすことが多い.

**sweltering** /swéltərɪŋ/ 形 略式 ▶定義 much too hot あまりにも暑すぎる→**うだるように暑い, 蒸し暑い** ‖ *It was sweltering in the office today.* 今日は事務所の中がうだるように暑かった.

**swept** SWEEP[1] の過去・過去分詞形

**swerve** /swəːrv/ 動 自 ▶定義 to change direction suddenly 突然向きを変える→**それる, 外れる, 曲がる** ‖ *The car swerved to avoid the child.* その車は子供をよけるために急にハンドルを切った. — swerve 名 C →**急に向きを変えること, それること, 外れること, 曲がること**

**swift** /swɪft/ 形 ▶定義 happening without delay; quick 遅れることなく起こっている; 素早い→**迅速な, 速やかな, 即座の, 早慶の** ‖ *a swift reaction/decision/movement* 素早い反応・即決・迅速な動き *a swift runner* 走るのが速い人 — swiftly 副→**素早く, 迅速に, 速やかに, 即座に**

**swig** /swɪɡ/ 動 自 他 (**swigging**; **swigged**) 略式 ▶定義 to take a quick drink of sth, especially alcohol ～を, 特にアルコールを, 素早く飲む→**～をぐいっと飲む** — swig 名 C →**ぐいっと飲むこと, 一飲み**

**swill** /swɪl/ 動他 ▶定義 swill sth (out/down) to wash sth by pouring large amounts of water, etc into, over or through it 多量の水などを注いで, 上に掛けて, あるいは中に通して, ～を洗う→**～をすすぐ, 水洗いする, 洗い流す**

*__swim__ /swɪm/ 動 (現分 **swimming**; 過 **swam** /swæm/; 過分 **swum** /swʌm/) ▶定義 1 自他 to move your body through water 水中で体を移動させる→**(～を)泳ぐ, 水泳する; 泳いで渡る** ‖ *How far can you swim?* あなたはどのくらい泳ぐことができますか. *Hundreds of tiny fish swam past.* 何百もの小さな魚が泳いでいった.

➤娯楽で泳ぐことについて話す場合にはgo swimmingが一般的に用いられる: *We go swimming every Saturday.*（私たちは毎週土曜日に泳ぎに行く.）ある特定の場合について話しているときはgo for a swimと言うこともできる: *I went for a swim this morning.*（私は今朝,泳ぎに出掛けた.）

● S1ページのさし絵 ▶定義2 ⓐ be swimming (in/with sth) to be covered with a lot of liquid 多量の液体で覆われている→～であふれる,～につかる,浸る ‖ *The salad was swimming in oil.* そのサラダには油がたくさん掛かっていた. ▶定義3 ⓐ to seem to be moving or turning 動いているまたは回転しているように見える→ぐるぐる回るように見える ‖ *The floor began to swim before my eyes and I fainted.* 床が目の前でぐるぐる回り始め,私は失神した. ▶定義4 ⓐ (used about your head) to feel confused（頭について）混乱する→ふらふらする,めまいがする ‖ *My head was swimming with so much new information.* 私の頭は新しい情報であふれ返っていた. — swim [単数扱い]→水泳,泳ぐこと,一泳ぎ ‖ *to go for/have a swim* 泳ぎに行く・泳ぐ — swimmer 名 ⓒ →泳ぐ人,泳ぎ手 ‖ *a strong/weak swimmer* 泳ぎの得意な人・苦手な人

**swimming bath** 名 ⓒ（または **swimming baths**[複数扱い] ▶定義 a public swimming pool, usually indoors 通常は屋内にある,公共の水泳プール→屋内水泳プール

*__swimming pool__（または **pool**）名 ⓒ ▶定義 a pool that is built especially for people to swim in 特に人が中に入って泳ぐために造られたプール→（水泳）プール ‖ *an indoor/outdoor/open-air swimming pool* 屋内・屋外・野外プール

**swimming trunks** 名 [複数扱い] ▶定義 a piece of clothing like shorts that a man wears to go swimming 男性が泳ぐときに着用する,短パンのような衣服→水泳パンツ,海水パンツ ‖ *a pair of swimming trunks* 水泳パンツ1着 ☛ C6 ページのさし絵

**swimsuit** /swíms(j)ùːt/（または **swimming costume**）名 ⓒ ▶定義 a piece of clothing that a woman wears to go swimming 女性が泳ぐときに着用する衣服→水着,ワンピース型水着 ☛参 bikini ☛ C6ページのさし絵

**swindle** /swíndl/ 動 ⓗ ▶定義 swindle sb/sth (out of sth) to trick sb in order to get money, etc 金などを得るために～をだます→ペテンにかける,だまし取る,詐取する — swindle 名 ⓒ →詐取,詐欺,ペテン ‖ *a tax swindle* 税金のごまかし

**swine** /swáin/ 名 ▶定義1 ⓒ 略式 a very unpleasant person 非常に不愉快な人→嫌なやつ,卑劣・下品なやつ ▶定義2 [複数扱い]（古）pigs→豚

*__swing__¹ /swíŋ/ 動 (過,過分 **swung** /swʌŋ/) ▶定義1 ⓐ ⓗ to move backwards and forwards or from side to side while hanging from sth; to make sb/sth move in this way 何かからぶら下がりながら,前後または左右に動く; ～をそのように動かす→揺れる,ぶらぶらする; ～を揺らす,振る ‖ *The rope was swinging from a branch.* その縄は枝にぶら下がって揺れていた. *She sat on the wall, swinging her legs.* 彼女は足をぶらぶらさせながら,塀の上に座っていた. ▶定義2 ⓐ ⓗ to move or make sb/sth move in a curve 曲線を描いて動く,または～をそのように動かす→弧を描くように動く[かす],回る[す],曲がる[げる] ‖ *The door swung open and Rudi walked in.* ドアが勢いよく開いてルディが入ってきた. *He swung the child up onto his shoulders.* 彼はその子をひょいと肩の上に乗せた. ▶定義3 ⓐ to move or change from one position or situation towards the opposite one ある位置または状況から反対の位置または状況の方向に移動するあるいは変わる→向きを変える,方向転換する ‖ *She swung round when she heard the door open.* 彼女はドアの開く音を聞いて振り返った. *His moods swing from one extreme to the other.* 彼の気分は極端から極端に変わる. ▶定義4 ⓐ ⓗ swing (at sb/sth) to try to hit sb/sth ～を打とうとする→一発食らわせる,～に殴り掛かる,スイングする

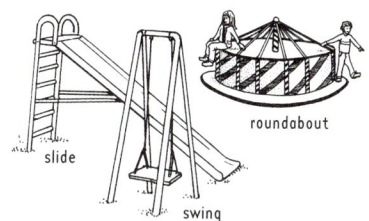

roundabout / slide / swing

*__swing__² /swíŋ/ 名 ▶定義1 [単数扱い] a swinging movement or rhythm 揺れているリズムまたは

## 1644 swipe

動き➔揺れ,揺らし,殴ること,打つこと ‖ *He took a swing at the ball.* 彼は球を力一杯打った. ▶定義2 ❻a seat, a piece of rope, etc that is hung from above so that you can swing backwards and forwards on it 乗って前後に揺らすことのできるように上からつり下げられた座席,縄など➔ぶらんこ ‖ *Some children were playing on the swings.* 数人の子供たちがぶらんこに乗って遊んでいた. ▶定義3 ❻a change from one position or situation towards the opposite one ある位置または状況から反対の位置または状況の方向に変わること➔ぐるっと回ること,振り返ること,方向転換,変動

成句 in full swing ⇒ **FULL**¹

**swipe** /swaɪp/ 動 ▶定義1 他 略式 swipe (at) sb/sth to hit or try to hit sb/sth by moving your arm in a curve 曲線を描くように腕を動かして〜を打つまたは打とうとする➔〜を強打する,強打しようとする,大振りで打つ ‖ *He swiped at the wasp with a newspaper but missed.* 彼は新聞紙でスズメバチをたたこうとしたが失敗した. ▶定義2 略式 to steal sth 〜を盗む➔〜をかっ払う,くすねる ▶定義3 他 to pass the part of a plastic card on which information is stored through a special machine for reading it 情報を読み取るために,プラスチック製のカードの情報保存部分を専用の機械に通す➔〜を機械で読み取る,読み取り機に通す ‖ *The receptionist swiped my credit card and handed me the slip to sign.* 受付係は私のクレジットカードを読み取り機に通し,私に伝票を渡してサインを求めた. — swipe 名 ❻➔強打,大振りの一撃 ‖ *She took a swipe at him with her handbag.* 彼女はハンドバッグで彼を殴ろうとした.

**swipe card** 名 ❻ ▶定義 a small plastic card on which information is stored which can be read by an electronic machine 電子的な機械で読み取ることのできる,情報が保存された小さなプラスチック製カード➔スワイプカード

**swirl** /swɜːrl/ 動 ▶定義 to make or cause sth to make fast circular movements 速く円形に動く,または〜をそのようにさせる➔渦を巻く,旋回する;〜に渦を巻かせる ‖ *Her long skirt swirled round her legs as she danced.* 彼女が踊っている間,長いスカートが彼女の足の周りをくるくる舞った. *He swirled some water round in his mouth and spat it out.* 彼は水で口をすすぎ,その水を吐き出した. — swirl 名 ❻➔渦(巻き),ぐるぐる回ること

★**switch**¹ /swɪtʃ/ 名 ❻ ▶定義1 a small button or sth similar that you press up or down in order to turn on electricity 電流を通すために押し上げるまたは押し下げる小さなボタン,あるいは似たような物➔スイッチ,開閉器 ‖ *a light switch* 電灯のスイッチ ▶定義2 a sudden change 突然の変化➔変更,切り替え ‖ *a switch in policy* 政策の転換

★**switch**² /swɪtʃ/ 動 自 他 ▶定義1 switch (sth) (over) (to sth); switch (between A and B) to change or be changed from one thing to another ある〜から別の…に変わる,または変える➔切り替わる,転じる,移す,切り替える,転換する ‖ *I'm fed up with my glasses - I'm thinking of switching over to contact lenses.* 私は眼鏡が嫌になった — コンタクトレンズに替えようと思っている. *Press these two keys to switch between documents on screen.* 画面の文書を切り替えるには,これらの2つのキーを押しなさい. *The match has been switched from Saturday to Sunday.* その試合は土曜日から日曜日に変更された. ▶定義2 switch (sth) (with sb/sth); switch (sth) (over/round) to exchange positions, activities, etc 位置,活動などを交換する➔交替する・させる,交換する,取り替える ‖ *This week you can have the car and I'll go on the bus, and next week we'll switch over.* 今週はあなたが車を使って私がバスで行き,来週は交替しよう. *Someone switched the signs round and everyone went the wrong way.* だれかが標識を入れ替えたので,みんなが間違った方向に行った.

句動詞 switch (sth) off/on ▶定義 to press a switch in order to start/stop electric power 電力を始動または停止するために(〜の)スイッチを押す➔(〜の)スイッチを切る・入れる ‖ *Don't forget to switch off the cooker.* レンジのスイッチを切るのを忘れないように.

switch (sth) over ▶定義 to change to a different television programme 別のテレビ番組に変える➔(テレビの)チャンネルを切り替える

**switchboard** /swɪtʃbɔːrd/ 名 ❻ ▶定義 the place in a large company, etc where all the telephone calls are connected 大きな会社などの中で,すべての通話が接続される場所→電話交換台,電話交換機

**swivel** /swív(ə)l/ 動 自 他 (swivelling; swivelled; 困 swiveling; swiveled) ▶定義 swivel (sth) (round) to turn around a central point; to make sth do this 中心の周りを回る; 〜をそのようにする→旋回する,回転する; 〜を旋回させる,回転させる ‖ She swivelled round to face me. 彼女はくるりと振り返って私の方を向いた. He swivelled his chair towards the door. 彼はドアの方向にいすを回した.

**swollen**¹ SWELL¹ の過去分詞形

**swollen**² /swóul(ə)n/ 形 ▶定義 thicker or wider than usual 通常よりも厚い,または幅広い→膨れた,はれた ‖ Her leg was badly swollen after the accident. 事故の後,彼女の足はひどくはれ上がった.

**swoop** /swu:p/ 動 自 ▶定義 1 to fly or move down suddenly 突然下に向かって飛ぶまたは移動する→急降下する,舞い降りる ‖ The bird swooped down on its prey. その鳥は,突然獲物に襲い掛かった. ▶定義 2 (used especially about the police or the army) to visit or capture sb/sth without warning (特に警察または軍隊について用いて)警告なしに〜を訪れるまたは捕まえる→急襲する,奇襲する ‖ Police swooped at dawn and arrested the man. 警察は明け方に踏み込んで,その男を逮捕した. ― swoop 名 C a swoop (on sb/sth)→急降下,急襲,手入れ

**swop** =SWAP

**sword** /sɔːrd/ 名 C ▶定義 a long, very sharp metal weapon, like a large knife 大きなナイフのような,長くて非常に鋭い金属製の武器→剣,刀 ☞ spear のさし絵

**swore** SWEAR の過去形

**sworn** SWEAR の過去分詞形

**swot**¹ /swɑt/ 動 自 他 (swotting; swotted) ▶定義 swot (up) (for/on sth); swot sth up to study sth very hard, especially to prepare for an exam 特に試験の準備をするために,〜を一生懸命に勉強する→(〜を)猛勉強する,詰め込む ‖ She's swotting for her final exams. 彼女は最終試験に向けて猛勉強中だ.

**swot**² /swɑt/ 名 C 略式 ▶定義 a person who studies too hard 一生懸命に勉強しすぎる人→がり勉屋,がり勉

**swum** SWIM の過去分詞形

**swung** SWING¹ の過去・過去分詞形

**syllable** /síləb(ə)l/ 名 C ▶定義 a word or part of a word which contains one vowel sound 母音を1つ含む単語,または母音のそのような部分→音節,シラブル ‖ 'Mat' has one syllable and 'mattress' has two syllables. mat には1つ, mattress には2つの音節がある. The stress in 'international' is on the third syllable. international の強勢は第3音節にある.

**syllabus** /síləbəs/ 名 C (複 syllabuses) ▶定義 a list of subjects, etc that are included in a course of study 学習課程に含まれている学習項目などの一覧表→教授細目,講義概要 ☞参 curriculum

★**symbol** /símb(ə)l/ 名 C ▶定義 1 a symbol (of sth) a sign, object, etc which represents sth 何かを代表する記号,物など→象徴,表象,シンボル ‖ The cross is the symbol of Christianity. 十字架はキリスト教の象徴である. ▶定義 2 a symbol (for sth) a letter, number or sign that has a particular meaning ある特定の意味を持つ文字,数字,あるいは記号→記号,符号 ‖ O is the symbol for oxygen. O は酸素を表す記号である.

**symbolic** /sɪmbɑ́lɪk/ (または **symbolical** /-k(ə)l/) 形 ▶定義 used or seen to represent sth 何かを代表するために用いられる,またはそう見られる→象徴的な,〜を象徴する ‖ The white dove is symbolic of peace. 白いハトは平和の象徴だ. ― symbolically /-k(ə)li/ 副 →象徴的に,象徴して,記号で

**symbolism** /símb(ə)lɪz(ə)m/ 名 U ▶定義 the use of symbols to represent things, especially in art and literature 特に美術または文学で,物事を象徴する記号を用いること→象徴化,象徴的表現,象徴主義

**symbolize** (または **-ise**) /símb(ə)laɪz/ 動 他 ▶定義 to represent sth 〜を代表する→〜を表す,象徴する,〜の象徴である,〜を象徴化する,記号で表す ‖ The deepest notes in music are often used to symbolize danger or despair. 音楽の最も低い音は,しばしば危険または絶望を象徴するために用いられる.

**symmetric** /səmétrɪk/ (または **symmetrical** /-rɪk(ə)l/) 形 ▶定義 having two halves that match each other exactly in size, shape, etc 大きさ,形

## 1646 symmetry

などが互いに全く同じである半分を2つ持っている→左右・上下対称の, シンメトリーな — symmetrically /-k(ə)li/ 副 →左右・上下対称に, 釣り合って

**symmetry** /símətri/ 名 ❶ ▶定義 the state of having two halves that match each other exactly in size, shape, etc 大きさ, 形などが互いに全く同じである半分を2つ持っている状態→左右・上下対称, シンメトリー, 釣り合い

★**sympathetic** /sìmpəθétɪk/ 形 ▶定義1 sympathetic (to/towards sb) showing that you understand other people's feelings, especially their problems ほかの人の気持ち, 特にその人の問題を理解していることを示している→同情的な, 共感的な, 思いやりのある ‖ When Suki was ill, everyone was very sympathetic. スキが病気だった時, 皆がとても同情した. I felt very sympathetic towards him. 私は彼に非常に同情した.

▶英語では, sympatheticは「親しみやすく感じが良い」という意味ではない. この意味を表現したい場合には, niceを用いる: I met Alex's sister yesterday. She's very nice. (私は昨日アレックスの妹に会った. 彼女はとてもすてきだ.)

▶定義2 sympathetic (to sb/sth) being in agreement with or supporting sb/sth ～に賛成しているまたは支持している→～に賛成の, 支持する, 共感して ‖ I explained our ideas but she wasn't sympathetic to them. 私は自分たちの考えを説明したが, 彼女は賛意を示してくれなかった. — sympathetically /-k(ə)li/ 副 →同情して, 支持して, 共感して

**sympathize** (または **-ise**) /símpəθàɪz/ 動 ⾃ sympathize (with sb/sth) ▶定義1 to feel sorry for sb; to show that you understand sb's problems ～を気の毒に思う; ～の問題を理解していることを示す→(～に)同情する ‖ I sympathize with her, but I don't know what I can do to help. 私は彼女に同情するが, どうしたら助けになれるのか分からない. ▶定義2 to support sb/sth ～を支持する→～に共感する, 共鳴する, 賛同する ‖ I find it difficult to sympathize with his opinions. 私は彼の意見に同意し難い.

**sympathizer** /símpəθàɪzər/ 名 ⓒ ▶定義 a person who agrees with and supports an idea or aim ある考えまたは目的に同意し支持する人→賛同者, 共鳴者, 同調者, シンパ

★**sympathy** /símpəθi/ 名 (複 **sympathies**) ▶定義1 ⓤ sympathy (for/towards sb) an understanding of other people's feelings, especially their problems ほかの人の気持ち, 特にその人の問題を理解していること→同情, 思いやり ‖ Everyone feels great sympathy for the victims of the attack. 皆がその攻撃の犠牲者たちにとても同情している. I don't expect any sympathy from you. あなたに同情してもらおうとは思っていない. I have no sympathy for Mark - it's his own fault. 私はマークが気の毒とは全く思わない — あれは彼自身の責任だ.

▶定義2 **sympathies** [複数扱い] feelings of support or agreement 支持または同意の気持ち→共感, 共鳴, 同感, 賛同

**成句** in sympathy (with sb/sth) ▶定義 in agreement, showing that you support or approve of sb/sth 同意して, ～を支持または賛同することを示している→(～に)賛同して, 共感して, (～を)支持して ‖ Taxi drivers stopped work in sympathy with the striking bus drivers. タクシーの運転手たちは, ストライキ中のバスの運転手に賛同して働くのをやめた.

**symphony** /símfəni/ 名 ⓒ (複 **symphonies**) ▶定義 a long piece of music written for a large orchestra 大きなオーケストラのために書かれた長い楽曲→交響曲, シンフォニー

**symptom** /sím(p)təm/ 名 ⓒ ▶定義1 a change in your body that is a sign of illness 病気の兆候となる体の変化→症状, 兆候 ‖ The symptoms of flu include a headache, a high temperature and aches in the body. インフルエンザの症状には頭痛, 高熱, 体の痛みが含まれる. ▶定義2 a sign (that sth bad is happening or exists) (悪い事が起きつつある, または存在するという)印→前兆, 兆し, 兆候 — symptomatic /sìm(p)təmǽtɪk/ 形 →症状の, 兆候を示す, 前兆となる

**synagogue** /sínəgɔ̀g, -gɔ̀ːg/ 名 ⓒ ▶定義 a building where Jewish people go to pray or to study their religion ユダヤ人が祈るためまたは自分たちの宗教を学ぶために行く建物→ユダヤ教の礼拝堂, シナゴーグ

**synchronize** (または **-ise**) /síŋkrənàɪz, sín-/ 動 ⓣ ▶定義 to make sth happen or work at the same time or speed ～を同じ時または同じ速度

で起こすあるいは働かせる→〜を同期させる,〜を同時に起こす,動かす,同時進行させる ‖ *We synchronized our watches to make sure we agreed what the time was.* 私たちは確実に時刻を一致させるために,腕時計を合わせた.

**syndicate** /síndɪkət/ 名 C ▶定義 a group of people or companies that work together in order to achieve a particular aim ある特定の目標を達成するために一緒に働く人々または会社の集団→シンジケート,企業連合

**syndrome** /síndròʊm/ 名 C ▶定義 1 a group of signs or changes in the body that are typical of an illness ある病気に典型的に現れる体の諸症状または諸変化→症候群,シンドローム ‖ *Down's syndrome* ダウン症候群 *Acquired Immune Deficiency Syndrome (Aids)* 後天性免疫不全症候群（エイズ） ▶定義 2 a set of opinions or a way of behaving that is typical of a particular type of person, attitude or social problem あるタイプの人,態度,あるいは社会問題に典型的な一連の意見または振る舞い方→兆候,現象,行動様式

**synonym** /sínənìm/ 名 C ▶定義 a word or phrase that has the same meaning as another word or phrase in the same language 同じ言語内でほかの語や句と同じ意味を持つ語や句→同義語,同意語,類義語 ‖ *'Big' and 'large' are synonyms.* big と large は同義語である. — **synonymous** /sənɑ́nəməs/ 形（比喩）**synonymous (with sth)**→〜と同意の,同義の,類似の

**syntax** /síntæks/ 名 U ▶定義 the system of rules for the structure of a sentence in a language ある言語における文の構造に関する規則体系→統語論,統辞法,構文法

**synthesizer**（または **-iser**）/sínθəsàɪzər/ 名 C ▶定義 an electronic musical instrument that can produce a wide variety of different sounds 幅広いさまざまな音を作り出すことができる電子楽器→シンセサイザー

**synthetic** /sɪnθétɪk/ 形 ▶定義 made by a chemical process; not natural 化学的に製造された; 天然ではない→合成の,人造の,人工の ‖ *synthetic materials/fibres* 合成物質・繊維 — **synthetically** /-k(ə)li/ 副 →合成的に,人工的に

**syphon** = SIPHON

**syringe** /sərínʤ, sírɪnʤ/ 名 C ▶定義 a plastic or glass tube with a needle that is used for taking a small amount of blood out of the body or for

# systematic 1647

putting drugs into the body 体から少量の血液を取り出すためまたは体内に薬を入れるために用いられる,針の付いたプラスチックあるいはガラス製の管→注射器

**syrup** /sírəp/ 名 U ▶定義 a thick sweet liquid, often made by boiling sugar with water or fruit juice しばしば水または果汁で砂糖を煮詰めて作られる,濃い甘い液体→シロップ,砂糖水,(糖)みつ ‖ *peaches in syrup* シロップ漬けのモモ ☞参 **treacle**

★**system** /sístəm/ 名 ▶定義 1 ❶ a set of ideas or rules for organizing sth; a particular way of doing sth 物事を組織するための一連の概念または規則; 物事を行うある特定の方法→制度,組織,体系,仕組み,システム,方式,手順 ‖ *We have a new computerized system in the library.* 私たちは図書館に新しくコンピューター化されたシステムを導入している. *The government is planning to reform the education system.* 政府は教育制度を改革することを計画している. ▶定義 2 ❶ a group of things or parts that work together 共に作動する一群の物または部品→装置,機構,系統,システム ‖ *a central heating system* 集中暖房装置 *a transport system* 輸送システム ▶定義 3 ❶ the body of a person or animal; parts of the body that work together 人間または動物の体; 共に機能する体の部分→系統,系,組織,器官,機能 ‖ *the central nervous system* 中枢神経系 ▶定義 4 **the system**［単数扱い］略式 the traditional methods and rules of a society 社会の伝統的な秩序または規則→体制,社会秩序 ‖ *You can't beat the system* (= you must accept these rules). 体制を打破することはできない(= 規則を受け入れなければならない).
成句 **get sth out of your system** 略式 ▶定義 to do sth to free yourself of a strong feeling or emotion 強い気持ちまたは感情を取り除くために物事を行う→〜を頭から追い払う,捨て去る,忘れようとする,〜から自由になる

**systematic** /sìstəmǽtɪk/ 形 ▶定義 done using a fixed plan or method ある一定の計画または方法を用いて行われた→組織的な,系統立った,体系的な,整然とした ‖ *a systematic search* 系統立った捜査 — **systematically** /-k(ə)li/ 副 →組織的に,系統的に,体系的に,整然と

# T t

**T, t¹** /tiː/ 名 C (複 **T's; t's**) ▶定義 the twentieth letter of the English alphabet 英語アルファベットの第20文字, t (T) が表す音, t (T) の文字, t (T) の字形のもの ‖ *'Table' begins with (a) 'T'*. Table は T で始まる.

**t²** (略 **tn**) 略 ton(s), tonne(s) → トン, メートルトン ‖ *5t coal* 5トンの石炭

**ta** /tɑː/ 間 英 略式 ▶定義 thank you → ありがとう

**tab** /tæb/ 名 C ▶定義 **1** a small piece of cloth, metal or paper that is fixed to the edge of sth to help you open, hold or identify it ～の端に固着されている布, 金属, または紙の小片で, その～を開ける, つかむ, あるいはほかと区別することを容易にするもの → つまみ, プルタブ, 耳, 付け札 ‖ *You open the tin by pulling the metal tab.* その缶は金属のつまみを引いて開けます. ▶定義 **2** the money that you owe for food, drink, etc in a bar, cafe or restaurant; the bill バー, カフェ, レストランで食べ物や飲み物などに対して支払うべき金額; 勘定書 → 請求書, 伝票

成句 **keep tabs on sb/sth** 略式 ▶定義 to watch sb/sth carefully; to check sth ～を注意深く見る; ～を調査する, ～を見張る, 監視する

*****table** /ˈteɪb(ə)l/ 名 C ▶定義 **1** a piece of furniture with a flat top supported by legs 平らな表面が数本の脚で支えられてできている家具 → テーブル, 食卓, 台 ‖ *a dining/bedside/coffee/kitchen table* 食卓・ナイトテーブル・コーヒーテーブル・台所用のテーブル *Could you **lay/set the table** for lunch? (= put the knives, forks, plates, etc on it)* 昼食のために食卓の用意をしていただけませんか (= ナイフ, フォーク, 皿などを食卓に並べる). *Let me help you **clear the table** (= remove the dirty plates, etc at the end of a meal).* 食卓を片付けるのをお手伝いしましょう (= 食事の後で汚れた皿などを片付ける).

▶食卓に物を置くことは put things on the table, 人が食卓に着く (= 食卓を囲む) ことは sit at the table (= around the table) と表現する.

☛ C7 ページのさし絵 ▶定義 **2** a list of facts or figures, usually arranged in rows and columns down a page 通常, 行と列の形式でページ上に順番に並べられた, 事実または数字の一覧 → 表, 一覧表 ‖ *Table 3 shows the results.* 表3がその結果を表している.

**tablecloth** /ˈteɪb(ə)lklɒ(ː)θ, -klɔːθ/ 名 C ▶定義 a piece of cloth that you use for covering a table, especially when having a meal 特に食事をするときに, 食卓に掛けるのに使う布 → テーブルクロス, テーブル掛け

**table manners** 名 [複数扱い] ▶定義 behaviour that is considered correct while you are having a meal at a table with other people 他人と一緒に食事をしているときの, 正しいと見なされる行儀 → テーブルマナー, 食事作法

**tablespoon** /ˈteɪb(ə)lspuːn/ 名 C ▶定義 **1** a large spoon used for serving or measuring food 料理を取り分けるまたは分量を計るために使われる大きなスプーン → テーブルスプーン, 大さじ ▶定義 **2** (または **tablespoonful**) the amount that a tablespoon holds 大さじ1杯に入る量 → 大さじ1杯分 ‖ *Add two tablespoons of sugar.* 大さじ2杯の砂糖を入れなさい.

*****tablet** /ˈtæblət/ 名 C ▶定義 a small amount of medicine in solid form that you swallow 飲み込むことができる固形の小さな薬剤 → 錠剤 ‖ *Take two **tablets** every four hours.* 4時間おきに2錠服用しなさい. ☛ **bandage** のさし絵

**table tennis** (または 略式 **ping-pong**) 名 U ▶定義 a game with rules like tennis in which you hit a light plastic ball across a table with a small round bat テニスに似たルールで, プラスチック製の軽い球を円形の小さなラケットで台越しに打ち合う競技 → 卓球, ピンポン

**tabloid** /ˈtæblɔɪd/ 名 C ▶定義 a newspaper with small pages, a lot of pictures and short articles, especially about famous people 紙面が小さく, 特に有名人に関する写真や短い記事が多い新聞 → タブロイド版新聞

**taboo** /təˈbuː, tæ-/ 名 C (複 **taboos**) ▶定義 something that you must not say or do because it might shock, offend or embarrass people 人に衝撃を与え, 怒らせ, 当惑させるかもしれないため, 言ったり行ったりしてはならないこと → タブー, 禁忌 ― **taboo** 形 → タブーの, 禁忌の ‖ *a taboo subject/word* タブーの話題・禁句

**tacit** /ˈtæsɪt/ 形 正式 ▶定義 understood but not actually said 理解されているが実際には口に出して言われていない → 暗黙の, 無言の ― **tacitly**

[副] ➜暗黙のうちに, それとなく

**tack**[1] /tæk/ [名] ▶定義1 [単数扱い] a way of dealing with a particular situation ある特定の状況に対処する方法➜**方針, やり方** ‖ *If people won't listen we'll have to try a different tack.* 人が耳を貸そうとしないのなら, 私たちは別のやり方でやってみなければならないだろう. ▶定義2 [C] a small nail with a sharp point and a flat head とがった先端と平たい頭を持つ小さなくぎ➜**びょう, 留めびょう**

**tack**[2] /tæk/ [動][他] ▶定義1 to fasten sth in place with tacks[1](2) ➜**～をびょうでしっかり固定する** ▶定義2 to fasten cloth together temporarily with long stitches that can be removed easily 簡単に取り外せるような大きな縫い目で布を一時的に縫い合わせる➜**～を仮縫いする**

[句動詞] **tack sth on (to sth)** ▶定義 to add sth extra on the end of sth ～の終わりに余分な…を付け加える➜**～を付け足す, 添える**

***tackle**[1] /tǽk(ə)l/ [動] ▶定義1 [他] to make an effort to deal with a difficult situation or problem 困難な状況や問題に対処するために努力する➜**～に取り組む** ‖ *The government must tackle the problem of rising unemployment.* 政府は失業率の上昇という問題に取り組まなければならない. *Firemen were brought in to tackle the blaze.* その火炎に対処するために消防士が派遣された. ▶定義2 [自][他] (used in football, etc) to try to take the ball from sb in the other team (ラクビーなどについて) 相手チームの～からボールを奪い取ろうとする➜**(～に) タックルする** ▶定義3 [他] to stop sb running away by pulling him/her down ～を引き倒して, その人が逃げ出すのを妨げる➜**～に組み付く, 捕捉(ほそく)する** ▶定義4 [他] **tackle sb about sth** to speak to sb about a difficult subject 難しい問題について～と話をする➜**～と渡り合う, やり合う** ‖ *I'm going to tackle him about the money he owes me.* 彼が私にしている借金について, 私は彼とやり合うつもりだ.

**tackle**[2] /tǽk(ə)l/ [名] ▶定義1 [C] the action of trying to get the ball from another player in football, etc ラグビーなどでほかの選手からボールを奪い取ろうとする行為➜**タックル** ▶定義2 [U] the equipment you use in some sports, especially fishing ある種のスポーツ, 特に釣りで使う用具➜**用具(一式)** ‖ *fishing tackle* 釣り道具

**tacky** /tǽki/ [形][略式] ▶定義1 cheap and of poor quality and/or not in good taste 安価で質が悪く, 品の良くない➜**安っぽい, 野暮ったい** ‖ *a shop selling tacky souvenirs* 安っぽい土産物を売っている店 ▶定義2 (used about paint, etc) not quite dry; sticky (ペンキなどについて) 完全には乾いていない; べとつく➜**生乾きの, 粘着性の**

**tact** /tækt/ [名][U] ▶定義 the ability to deal with people without offending or upsetting them 人を怒らせたり気分を害させたりしないで対応することができる能力➜**如才なさ** ‖ *She handled the situation with great tact and diplomacy.* 彼女は如才なさと駆け引きのうまさを十分に発揮して, その状況に対処した.

**tactful** /tǽktfʊl, -f(ə)l/ [形] ▶定義 careful not to say or do things that could offend people 人を怒らせるかもしれないような事を言ったり行ったりしないように注意している➜**如才ない, 機転の利く** — **tactfully** /-fʊli, -f(ə)li/ [副] ➜**如才なく, そつなく**

***tactic** /tǽktɪk/ [名] ▶定義1 [[C], 通常は複数] the particular method you use to achieve sth 何かを達成するために用いる特定の方法➜**方法, 方策, 作戦** ‖ *We must decide what our tactics are going to be at the next meeting.* 次の会議ではどの方策を取ることにするのか決めなければならない. *I don't think this tactic will work.* 私はこの方法ではうまくいかないと思う. ▶定義2 **tactics** [複数扱い] the skilful arrangement and use of military forces in order to win a battle 戦闘に勝つための, 軍隊の巧みな配置や使い方➜**戦術, 兵法**

**tactical** /tǽktɪk(ə)l/ [形] ▶定義1 connected with the particular method you use to achieve sth ～を達成するために用いる特定の方法に関連している➜**戦術の, 戦術上の** ‖ *a tactical error* 戦術上の誤り *tactical discussions/planning* 戦術上の議論・計画 ▶定義2 designed to bring a future advantage 将来有利に働くよう計画された➜**駆け引きのうまい, 抜け目のない** ‖ *a tactical decision* 抜け目のない決定 — **tactically** /-k(ə)li/ [副] ➜**戦術的に, 駆け引き上**

**tactless** /tǽktləs/ [形] ▶定義 saying and doing things that are likely to offend and upset other

T

people 他人を怒らせ気分を害させるであろう事を言ったり行ったりしている→気の利かない, 無神経な ‖ It was rather tactless of you to ask her how old she was. あなたが彼女に年齢を聞いたのはちょっと無神経だった. — tactlessly 副 → 気が利かずに, 無神経に

**tadpole** /tædpòul/ 名 ⓒ ▶定義 a young form of a greenish animal that can live in water and on land (a frog) when it has a large black head and a long tail 水中でも陸上でも生活できる緑色がかった動物 (カエル) の幼生で, 黒くて大きい頭と長い尾を持っているもの→オタマジャクシ ☞ frog のさし絵

**tag**¹ /tæg/ 名 ⓒ ▶定義 1 (しばしば複合名詞を作るために用いて) a small piece of card, material, etc fastened to sth to give information about it; a label 〜についての情報を表示するために取り付けられる小さなカード, 材質など; ラベル→付け札, 荷札, 付せん ‖ How much is this dress? There isn't a price tag on it. このドレスはいくらですか. 値札が付いていないのですが. ☞ label のさし絵 ▶定義 2 (文法) = **QUESTION TAG**

**tag**² /tæg/ 動他 (**tagging**; **tagged**) ▶定義 to fasten a tag onto sb/sth→札を〜に取り付ける

句動詞 tag along ▶定義 to follow or go somewhere with sb, especially when you have not been invited 特に誘われていないときに, 〜の後に付いていく, または一緒にどこかへ行く→付いていく, 付きまとう

\***tail**¹ /téɪl/ 名 ▶定義 1 ⓒ the part at the end of the body of an animal, bird, fish, etc 動物, 鳥, 魚などの体の末端にある部分→尾, しっぽ ‖ The dog barked and wagged its tail. その犬はほえながらしっぽを振った. ☞ horse, otter, scorpion のさし絵 ▶定義 2 ⓒ the back part of an aircraft, spacecraft, etc 航空機, 宇宙船などの後部→尾部, 尾翼 ▶定義 3 **tails** [複数扱い] a man's formal coat that is short at the front but with a long, divided piece at the back, worn especially at weddings 男性の正式な上着で, 前面は短いが後ろは分かれていて長く, 特に結婚式のときに着用するもの→燕尾 (えんび) 服 ▶定義 4 **tails** [複数扱い] the side of a coin that does not have the head of a person on it 硬貨の, 表面に人の頭像がない方の面→硬貨の裏面 ‖ 'We'll toss a coin to decide,' said my father. '**Heads or tails?**'「コインを投げて決めよう」と父が言った.「表か裏か」 ▶定義 5 ⓒ 略式 a person who is sent to follow sb secretly to get information about him/her 〜についての情報を得るためにひそかにその〜の後を付けるように仕向けられる人→尾行者

成句 make head or tail of sth ⇒ **HEAD**¹

**tail**² /téɪl/ 動他 ▶定義 to follow sb closely, especially to watch where he/she goes 特に〜がどこへ行くのかを見守るために, その〜の後にぴったりと付いていく→〜の後を付ける, 尾行する

句動詞 tail away/off 特に 英 ▶定義 to become smaller and weaker より小さく弱くなる→次第に小さくなる, 薄くなる

**tailor**¹ /téɪlər/ 名 ⓒ ▶定義 a person whose job is to make clothes, especially for men 洋服, 特に紳士服を作ることを仕事としている人→仕立て屋, 洋服屋

**tailor**² /téɪlər/ 動他 (通常は受動態で) ▶定義 1 tailor sth to/for sb/sth to make or design sth for a particular person or purpose ある人や目的のために〜を作る, または設計する→〜に合わせて作る ‖ programmes tailored to the needs of specific groups 特定のグループのニーズに合わせて作られたプログラム ▶定義 2 to make clothes 洋服を作る→〜を仕立てる ‖ a well-tailored coat 仕立ての良い上着

**tailor-made** 形 ▶定義 tailor-made(for sb/sth) made for a particular person or purpose and therefore very suitable ある特定の人や目的のために作られており, そのためにとても合っている→(〜に) 合わせて作った, おあつらえ向きの, ぴったりの

**taint** /téɪnt/ 名 [通常は単数] 正式 ▶定義 the effect of sth bad or unpleasant that spoils the quality of sb/sth 〜の性質を損なうような悪い, または不快なことの結果→痕跡 (こんせき), 悪点 ‖ the taint of corruption 腐敗の痕跡 — taint 動他 (通常は受動態で) →〜を汚す, 傷付ける ‖ Her reputation was tainted by the scandal. 彼女の評判はそのスキャンダルによって傷付けられた.

\***take** /téɪk/ 動他 (過 **took** /tʊk/; 過分 **taken** /téɪk(ə)n/) ▶定義 1 to carry or move sb/sth; to go with sb from one place to another 〜を運ぶ,

または移動する；〜と一緒にある場所からほかの場所へ行く ➡ **〜を持っていく, 連れていく, 運ぶ** ‖ *Take your coat with you - it's cold.* 上着を持っていきなさい — 寒いですから. *Could you take this letter home to your parents?* この手紙を持って帰って, ご両親に渡していただけませんか. *The ambulance took him to hospital.* 救急車が彼を病院へ運んでいった. *I'm taking the children swimming this afternoon.* 私は今日の午後, 子供たちを泳ぎに連れていくつもりです. ☞ **borrow** のさし絵  ▶定義 **2** to put your hand round sth and hold it (and move it towards you) 〜の周りに手を置いて握る (そして自分の方に動かす) ➡ **〜を手に取る, つかむ** ‖ *She held out the keys, and I took them.* 彼女がかぎを差し出し, 私はそれを手に取った. *He took a sweater out of the drawer.* 彼は引き出しからセーターを取り出した. *She took my hand/me by the hand.* 彼女は私の手を取った.  ▶定義 **3** to remove sth from a place or a person, often without permission しばしば許可がないのに, 〜をある場所または人から取り去る ➡ **〜を持ち去る, 盗む** ‖ *Who's taken my pen?* 私のペンを取ったのはだれですか. *My name had been taken off the list.* 私の名前はそのリストから外されていた. *The burglars took all my jewellery.* その強盗たちは私の宝石類をすべて盗んだ.  ▶定義 **4** to accept or receive sth 〜を受け入れる, または受け取る ‖ *If you take my advice you'll forget all about him.* 私の忠告に従えば, 彼のことはすべて忘れられるでしょう. *Do you take credit cards?* クレジットカードは使えますか. *What coins does the machine take?* この機械にはどのコインが使えますか. *I'm not going to take the blame for the accident.* 私はその事故の責任を取るつもりはない. *She's not going to take the job.* 彼女にはその仕事を引き受けるつもりがない.  ▶定義 **5** to capture a place by force; to get control of sb/sth ある場所を力ずくで占領する；〜の支配権を手に入れる ➡ **〜を奪取する, 占領する** ‖ *The state will take control of the company.* 国家がその企業を支配するだろう.  ▶定義 **6** to understand sth or react to sth in a particular way 〜を理解する, または〜に対してある特定のやり方で反応する ➡ **〜を (…と) 理解する, 見なす, 受け止める** ‖ *She took what he said as a compliment.* 彼女は彼が言った事を褒め言葉と受け取った. *I wish you would take things more seriously.* あなたが物事をもっと真剣に受け止めてくれたらいいのに.  ▶定義 **7** to get a particular feeling from sth 〜からある特定の感情を持つ ➡ **〜を抱く, 感じる** ‖ *He takes great pleasure in his grandchildren.* 彼は孫に大きな喜びを感じている. *When she failed the exam she took comfort from the fact that it was only by a few marks.* 彼女は試験に失敗した時, それがわずかな点数の差だったことに慰めを得た.  ▶定義 **8** to be able to deal with sth difficult or unpleasant 困難な, または不快な〜に対処することができる ➡ **〜に耐える** ‖ *I can't take much more of this heat.* 私はこれ以上の暑さに耐えられない. ☞類 **stand** ▶定義 **9** to need sth/sb 〜を必要とする ➡ **〜がかかる, 〜を要する** ‖ *It took three people to move the piano.* そのピアノを動かすのは 3 人がかりだった. *How long did the journey take?* その旅行にどのくらい時間がかかりましたか. *It took a lot of courage to say that.* それを言うには大変な勇気が要った.  ▶定義 **10** to swallow sth 〜を飲み込む ➡ **〜を飲む, 服用する** ‖ *Take two tablets four times a day.* 1 日 4 回 2 錠ずつ飲みなさい. *Do you take sugar in tea?* 紅茶に砂糖を入れますか.  ▶定義 **11** to write or record sth 〜を書く, または記録する ➡ **〜を書き留める** ‖ *She took notes during the lecture.* 彼女は講義の間, ノートを取っていた. *The police officer took my name and address.* その警官は私の名前と住所を書き留めた.  ▶定義 **12** to photograph sth ➡ **〜を (写真に) 撮る** ‖ *I took some nice photos of the wedding.* 結婚式の写真が数枚良く撮れていた.  ▶定義 **13** to measure sth 〜を測定する ➡ **〜を計る, 測る** ‖ *The doctor took my temperature/pulse/blood pressure.* その医者は私の体温・脈拍・血圧を計った.  ▶定義 **14** (進行形は不可) to have a certain size of shoes or clothes 靴や衣服がある特定のサイズである ➡ **〜が合う, サイズが〜である, 〜を身に着ける** ‖ *What size shoes do you take?* 靴のサイズはどれくらいですか.  ▶定義 **15** (進行形は不可) to have enough space for sb/sth 〜に十分な場所がある ➡ **〜が収容できる** ‖ *How many passengers can this bus take?* このバスには何人の乗客が乗れますか.  ▶定義 **16** used with nouns to say that sb is performing an action ～がある動作をしていることを表すために名詞と共に用いて→～をする ‖ **Take a look** at this article (= look at it). この記事を見なさい(= この記事を読みなさい). We have to **take a decision** (= decide). 私たちは決断をする(= 決断する)必要がある. ▶定義 17 to study a subject for an exam; to do an exam 試験のためにある科目を勉強する; 試験をする→～を受ける, 学ぶ, 履修する ‖ I'm **taking** the advanced exam this summer. 私は今年の夏に上級の試験を受けるつもりだ.

▶定義 18 **take sb (for sth)** to give lessons to sb→～に科目を教える ‖ Who **takes** you for History? (= who is your teacher) だれがあなたに歴史を教えていますか(= だれがあなたの先生ですか). ▶定義 19 to use a form of transport; to use a particular route ある交通機関を利用する; ある特定の路線を利用する→～に乗っていく, 利用する ‖ I always **take** the train to York. 私はいつも列車でヨークへ行く. Which road do you **take** to Hove? ホーヴへはどの道を行きますか. **Take** the second turning on the right. 右側にある2番目の曲がり角を曲がりなさい. ▶定義 20 (進行形不可)(文法) to have or need a word to go with it in a sentence or other structure 文やその他の構造の中で一緒に使う単語を持つまたは必要とする→(補語, 目的語など)をとる, 要する ‖ The verb 'depend' **takes** the preposition 'on'. 動詞 depend は前置詞 on をとる.

成句 **be taken with sb/sth** ▶定義 to find sb/sth attractive or interesting ～を魅力的または面白いと感じる→～に心を引き付けられる, 心を奪われる

**I take it (that...)** ▶定義 (used to show that you understand sth from a situation, even though you have not been told) I suppose (たとえ知らされていなくても, 状況から～を理解していることを表すために用いて) 私は...だと推測する→...と理解する, 思っている ‖ I **take** it that you're not coming? あなたは来ないということですね.

**take it from me** ▶定義 believe me 私を信じなさい→きっと～だ

**take a lot out of sb** ▶定義 to make sb very tired ～をとても疲れさせる→～をくたくたにする

**take a lot of/some doing** ▶定義 to need a lot of work or effort 多くの仕事または努力を必要とする→たくさん～する必要がある

▶ take を含むこのほかの成句については, 名詞, 形容詞などの項を参照. 例えば take place は place¹ の項にある.

句動詞 **take sb aback** ▶定義 to surprise or shock sb ～を驚かせる, または～に衝撃を与える→～の不意を打つ, ～をぎょっとさせる

**take after sb** (進行形不可) ▶定義 to look or behave like an older member of your family, especially a parent 家族の中の年長の者, 特に親に似ている, またはそのように振る舞う→(顔付きや動作が)～に似ている

**take sth apart** ▶定義 to separate sth into the different parts it is made of ～を, それを構成する別々の部分に分ける→～を分解する, ばらばらにする

**take sth away** ▶定義1 to cause a feeling, etc to disappear ある感情などを消失させる→～を取り除く, 取り去る ‖ These aspirins will **take** the pain **away**. このアスピリンが痛みを取り除くだろう. ▶定義2 to buy cooked food at a restaurant, etc and carry it out to eat somewhere else, for example at home 調理された食べ物をレストランなどで買い, 家などのほかの場所へ持ち出して食べる→～を買って持ち帰る, テイクアウトする ☛ 名 takeaway

**take sb/sth away (from sb)** ▶定義 to remove sb/sth ～を取り除く→(～から)...を取り上げる ‖ She **took** the scissors **away** from the child. 彼女は子供からはさみを取り上げた.

**take sth back** ▶定義1 to return sth to the place that you got it from ～を, それを手に入れた場所に戻す→～を返す ▶定義2 to admit that sth you said was wrong 自分が言った～が間違っていたと認める→～を取り消す, 撤回する

**take sth down** ▶定義1 to remove a structure by separating it into the pieces it is made of ある構造物を, それを構成する部分に分けることによって除去する→～を取り壊す, 解体する ‖ They **took** the tent **down** and started the journey home. 彼らはテントを解体し, 帰途に就いた.

▶定義2 to write down sth that is said 言われた～を書き留める→～を書き留める, 記録する

**take sb in** ▶定義1 to make sb believe sth that is not true ～に真実ではないことを信じさせ

る➔~をだます, 担ぐ ‖ *I was completely taken in by her story.* 私は彼女の話にすっかりだまされた. ▶定義2 to invite sb who has no home to live with you 家のない~に自分と同居するように招く➔~を泊める, 受け入れる

**take sth in** ▶定義 to understand what you see, hear or read 見たり聞いたり読んだりしたものを理解する➔~を理解する, ~が分かる ‖ *There was too much in the museum to take in at one go.* その博物館には一遍には理解しきれないほどたくさんのものがあった.

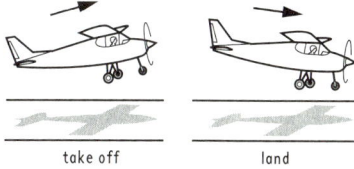
take off　　　　　　land

**take off** ▶定義1 (used about an aircraft) to leave the ground and start flying (航空機について) 地面から離れて飛行を始める➔離陸する, 飛び立つ ⇔ **land** ▶定義2 (used about an idea, a product, etc) to become successful or popular very quickly or suddenly (考えや製品などについて) 非常に速く, または突然に, 成功したり人気が出たりする➔軌道に乗る, うまくいく, よく売れ出す

**take sb off** ▶定義 to copy the way sb speaks or behaves in an amusing way ~の話し方または動作を面白おかしくまねる➔~の物まねをする

**take sth off** ▶定義1 to remove sth, especially clothes ~, 特に衣服を取り除く➔~を脱ぐ, 外す ‖ *Come in and take your coat off.* 中に入って上着を脱ぎなさい. ▶定義2 to have the period of time mentioned as a holiday 示された期間を休暇とする➔~を休暇として取る, ~の間仕事を休む ‖ *I'm going to take a week off.* 私は1週間の休暇を取るつもりだ.

**take on** ▶定義 to start to employ sb ~を雇用し始める➔~を雇い入れる, 採用する ‖ *The firm is taking on new staff.* その会社は新しい社員を雇い始めている.

**take sth on** ▶定義 to accept a responsibility or decide to do sth 責任を負う, または~を行うことを決める➔~を引き受ける ‖ *He's taken on a lot of extra work.* 彼は余分な仕事をたくさん引き受けている.

# take 1653

**take sb out** ▶定義 to go out with sb (for a social occasion) (社交のために) ~と一緒に出掛ける➔~を連れていく, 連れ出す ‖ *I'm taking Sarah out for a meal tonight.* 私は今晩, サラを食事に連れ出すつもりだ.

**take sth out** ▶定義 to remove sth from inside your body 体の中から~を取り除く➔~を抜く, 摘出する ‖ *He's having two teeth taken out.* 彼は歯を2本抜いてもらうことになっている.

**take sth out (of sth)** ▶定義 to remove sth from sth ~から…を取り除く➔(~から)…を取り出す, 引き出す ‖ *He took a notebook out of his pocket.* 彼はポケットからノートを取り出した. *I need to take some money out of the bank.* 私は銀行からお金を少し引き出す必要がある.

**take it out on sb** ▶定義 to behave badly towards sb because you are angry or upset about sth, even though it is not this person's fault たとえ~のせいではなくても, 何かに怒っていたり腹を立てたりしているために, その~に対して悪く振る舞う➔~に八つ当たりする, 当たり散らす

**take (sth) over** ▶定義 to get control of sth or responsibility for sth ~の支配権を得る, または~に対する責任を負う➔~を引き継ぐ, 乗っ取る, 接収する ‖ *The firm is being taken over by a large company.* その会社はある大会社に乗っ取られている. *Who's going to take over as assistant when Tim leaves?* ティムが辞めたらだれが代わって助手を務めるのですか.

**take to sb/sth** ▶定義 to start liking sb/sth ~を好きになり始める➔~が気に入る, ~になじむ, 懐く

**take to sth/doing sth** ▶定義 to begin doing sth regularly as a habit ~を習慣として定期的にするようになる➔~が習慣になる, ~に熱中する

**take sth up** ▶定義 to start doing sth regularly (for example as a hobby) (例えば趣味として) ~を定期的にやるようになる➔~を趣味として始める ‖ *I've taken up yoga recently.* 私は最近ヨガを始めた.

**take up sth** ▶定義 to use or fill an amount of time or space ある時間または空間を利用する, または満たす➔~を占める, ふさぐ ‖ *All her time is taken up looking after the new baby.* 彼女の時

間はすべて、生まれたばかりの赤ん坊の世話に取られている. ☛類 **occupy**

**take sb up on sth** ▶定義1 to say that you disagree with sth that sb has just said, and ask him/her to explain it ～が言ったばかりの事に同意しないと言い、その～にその事の説明を求める→～に…の説明を求める ‖ *I must take you up on that last point.* 私はあなたにその最後の点について説明してもらいたい. ▶定義2 俗式 to accept an offer that sb has made ～が行った申し出を受け入れる→～の…に応じる

**take sth up with sb** ▶定義 to ask or complain about sth ～について…に尋ねる、または不満を言う→～との間で…を取り上げる、持ち出す ‖ *I'll take the matter up with my MP.* その問題を国会議員（下院議員）に相談します.

**takeaway** /téɪkəwèɪ/ (米 **takeout**; **carryout**) 名 C ▶定義1 a restaurant that sells food that you can eat somewhere else ほかの所でも食べることのできる食べ物を売る飲食店→持ち帰り用料理を売る店 ▶定義2 the food that such a restaurant sells そのような飲食店が売る食べ物→持ち帰り用料理 ‖ *Let's have a takeaway.* テイクアウトにしよう.

**take-off** 名 U C ▶定義 the moment when an aircraft leaves the ground and starts to fly 航空機が地面を離れて飛行を始める瞬間→離陸 ‖ *The plane is ready for take-off.* その飛行機は離陸の準備ができている. ⇔ **landing**

**takeover** /téɪkòʊvər/ 名 C ▶定義 the act of taking control of sth ～の支配権を得ること→接収、引き継ぎ、乗っ取り ‖ *They made a takeover bid for the company.* 彼らはその会社を乗っ取ろうと企てた. *a military takeover of the government* 軍部による政府乗っ取り

**takings** /téɪkɪŋz/ 名［複数扱い］▶定義 the amount of money that a shop, theatre, etc gets from selling goods, tickets, etc 店、劇場などが商品やチケットなどを販売することによって得る金額→売上、収益

**talcum powder** /tǽlkəm pàʊdər/（または **talc** /tǽlk/）名 U ▶定義 a soft powder which smells nice. People often put it on their skin after a bath. いい香りのする、滑らかなパウダー. 入浴後に肌に付けることが多い→タルカムパウダー、滑石粉

**tale** /téɪl/ 名 C ▶定義1 a story about events that are not real 現実ではない出来事についての話→話、物語 ‖ *fairy tales* おとぎ話 ▶定義2 a report or description of sb/sth that may not be true ～についての真実ではないかもしれない報告または記述→うそ、作り話 ‖ *I've heard tales of people seeing ghosts in that house.* あの家で幽霊を見た人がいるという話を聞いたことがある.

\***talent** /tǽlənt/ 名 C U ▶定義 (a) talent (for sth) a natural skill or ability 生まれながらの技能や能力→才能、天分 ‖ *She has a talent for painting.* 彼女には絵の才能がある. *His work shows great talent.* 彼の作品はすばらしい才能を示している. — **talented** 形 →（生まれつき）才能のある、有能な ‖ *a talented musician* 才能のある音楽家

\***talk**¹ /tɔːk/ 動 ▶定義1 自 talk (to/with sb) (about/of sb/sth) to say things; to speak in order to give information or to express feelings, ideas, etc ものを言う; 情報を与える、または感情、考えなどを表すために話す→話す、口をきく、しゃべる ‖ *I could hear them talking downstairs.* 彼らが階下でしゃべっているのが聞こえた. *Can I talk to you for a minute?* ちょっとお話してもよろしいですか. *Nasreen is not an easy person to talk to.* ナスリーンは話し掛けやすい人ではない. *We need to talk about the plans for the weekend.* 私たちは週末の計画について相談する必要がある. *He's been talking of going to Australia for some time now.* 彼はオーストラリアに行くことを、ここのところずっとしゃべっている. *Dr Hollis will be talking about Japanese Art in her lecture.* ホリス博士は講義で日本の美術について話をすることになっている. ☛参 **speak** の注 ▶定義2 自他 to discuss sth serious or important 重大な、または重要な～について議論する→話し合う、語り合う、相談する ‖ *We can't go on like this. We need to talk.* 私たちはこんな風にやっていくことはできない. 話し合う必要がある. *Could we talk business after dinner?* 夕食後、仕事の話し合いをしましょうか. ▶定義3 自 to discuss people's private lives 人の私生活を話題にする→うわさ話をする、陰口をきく ‖ *His strange lifestyle started the local people talking.* 彼の奇妙な生活様式が、地元民がうわさ話をするきっかけとなった. ☛類

**gossip** ▶定義4 🇪 to give information to sb, especially when you do not want to 特に自分が望まないときに、〜に情報を与える→(しぶしぶ)**情報を漏らす, 口を割る, 白状する**

**成句** **know what you are talking about** ⇒ **KNOW**¹

**talk sense** ▶定義 to say things that are correct or sensible 適切または相応な事を言う→**もっともな事を言う, 筋の通った話をする** ‖ *He's the only politician who talks any sense.* 彼は筋の通った話をする唯一の政治家だ.

**talk/speak of the devil** ⇒ **DEVIL**

**talk shop** ▶定義 to talk about your work with the people you work with, outside working hours→**共に働いている人と就業時間外に仕事の話をする**

**句動詞** **talk down to sb** ▶定義 to talk to sb as if he/she is less intelligent or important than you 〜が自分ほど聡明(そうめい)ではない、または地位が高くないかのように、その〜に対して話す→**〜を見下して話をする, (話の)レベルを落として話す, 見くびった態度で話す**

**talk sb into/out of doing sth** ▶定義 to persuade sb to do/not to do sth 〜をするように・しないように…を説得する→**〜に話をして…にする, 〜を説得して…させる, 〜を説得して…をやめさせる, 思いとどまらせる** ‖ *She tried to talk him into buying a new car.* 彼女は彼を説得して新車を購入させようとした.

**talk sth over (with sb)** ▶定義 to discuss sth with sb, especially in order to reach an agreement or make a decision 特に合意に達する、または決断をするために、〜について…と話し合う→**〜について相談する, 議論する, よく話し合う, 語り合う**

*****talk**² /tɔːk/ 图 ▶定義1 🇨 a **talk (with sb) (about sth)** a conversation or discussion 会話または議論→**話, 談話, 会話, 相談, 話し合い** ‖ *Tim and I had a long talk about the problem.* ティムと私はその問題についてゆっくり話をした.

▶定義2 **talks** [複数扱い] formal discussions between governments 政府間の正式な話し合い→**会談, 協議, 交渉** ‖ *The Foreign Ministers of the two countries will meet for talks next week.* 両国の外務大臣が来週会談することになっている. *arms/pay/peace talks* 軍縮会談・賃金交渉・和平会談 ▶定義3 🇨 a **talk (on sth)** a formal speech on a particular subject; a lecture ある特定のテーマについての正式な演説; 講義→**講演, 演説, 講話** ‖ *He's giving a talk on 'Our changing world'.* 彼は「変わり行く現代の世界」について話している. ▶定義4 🇺 略式 things that people say that are not based on facts or reality 人が言っている、事実や現実に基づいていない事→**うわさ, 世評, 話の種, 話題, 風説** ‖ *He says he's going to resign but it's just talk.* 彼は辞任すると言っているが、それは単なる話の種だ. ☛参 **small talk**

**talkative** /tɔːkətɪv/ 形 ▶定義 liking to talk a lot よく話をするのが好きである→**話し好きな, おしゃべりな, 口数の多い**

*****tall** /tɔːl/ 形 ▶定義1 (used about people or things) of more than average height; not short (人または物について)平均以上の高さがある; 背の低くない→**背の高い, (幅に比べて高さが)高い** ‖ *a tall young man* 背の高い若者 *a tall tree/tower/chimney* 高い木・塔・煙突 *Nick is taller than his brother.* ニックはお兄さんよりも背が高い. ⇔ **short** ▶定義2 used to describe the height of sb/sth 〜の高さを述べるために用いて→**身長が〜ある, 高さが〜ある** ‖ *Claire is five feet tall.* クレアは身長が5フィートあります. *How tall are you?* あなたの身長はどのくらいありますか. ☛参 **height**

▶ tall と high には同じような意味がある. tall は, 人や木などの細長いものの高さを述べるときに用いる: *He is six foot three inches tall.* (彼は身長が6フィート3インチあります.) *A tall oak tree stands in the garden.* (背の高いナラの木が庭に立っている.) *the tall skyscrapers of Manhattan* (マンハッタンの超高層ビル). high は, 〜の寸法や地面からの隔たりを述べるときに用いる: *The fence is two metres high.* (その垣根は高さが2メートルある.) *a room with high ceilings* (天井の高い部屋)

**tambourine** /ˌtæmbəˈriːn/ 图 🇨 ▶定義 a musical instrument that has a circular frame covered with plastic or skin, with metal discs round the edge. To play it, you hit it or shake it with your hand. 円形の枠にプラスチックまたは皮が張られ、縁に金属の円盤が付いている楽器. 手でたたいたり振ったりして演奏する→**タンバリン** ☛

# 1656 tame¹

**music** のさし絵

**tame¹** /téɪm/ 形 ▶定義 **1** (used about animals or birds) not wild or afraid of people (動物や鳥について) 野生ではない，または人を怖がらない→飼いならされた，なれた ‖ *The birds are so tame they will eat from your hand.* その鳥は人によくなれているので，あなたの手からでもえさを食べる． ▶定義 **2** boring; not interesting or exciting 退屈な；面白くない，またはわくわくしない→退屈な，つまらない，精彩を欠く，単調な ‖ *After the big city, you must find village life very tame.* 大都市にいた後には，村の生活がとても単調に思えるに違いない．

**tame²** /téɪm/ 動他 ▶定義 to bring sth wild under your control; to make sth tame 野生の～を支配下に置く；～を飼いならす→～を飼いならす

**tamper** /tǽmpər/ 動
句動詞 tamper with sth ▶定義 to make changes to sth without permission, especially in order to damage it 特に～に損害を与えるため，許可なしにその～に変更を加える→～をいじくる，みだりに変更する，勝手に書き換える

**tampon** /tǽmpɑn/ 名 C ▶定義 a tightly-rolled piece of cotton material that a woman puts inside her body to absorb the blood that she loses once a month 女性が月に1回排出する血液を吸収させるために体内に入れる，円筒形にしっかりと巻いた綿製品→タンポン ☞参 **sanitary towel**

**tan¹** /tæn/ 名 ▶定義 **1** C = SUNTAN ▶定義 **2** ❶ a colour between yellow and brown 黄色と茶色の中間の色→黄褐色 ― tan 形→黄褐色の，日焼けした，皮なめし（用）の

**tan²** /tæn/ 動自他 (**tanning**; **tanned**) ▶定義 (used about a person's skin) to become brown as a result of spending time in the sun (人の肌について) 太陽の下で過ごした結果，褐色になる→肌が日に焼ける；～を日焼けさせる ‖ *Do you tan easily?* あなたは日焼けしやすいですか． ― tanned 形→日に焼けた ‖ *You're looking very tanned - have you been on holiday?* よく日焼けしているようですね ― 休暇を取っていたのですか．

**tandem** /tǽndəm/ 名 C ▶定義 a bicycle with seats for two people, one behind the other 2人分のサドルが付いている自転車．1人の後ろにもう1人が乗る→2人乗り自転車，タンデム式自転車

成句 **in tandem (with sb/sth)** ▶定義 working together with sth/sb else; happening at the same time as sth else ほかの～と一緒に働いている；ほかの～と同じ時に起きている→～と協力して，一緒に，提携して，～と相前後して

**tangent** /tǽndʒ(ə)nt/ 名 C ▶定義 a straight line that touches a curve but does not cross it 曲線に接するが交わらない直線→接線，タンジェント，正接

成句 **go off at a tangent**; 米 **go off on a tangent** ▶定義 to suddenly start saying or doing sth that seems to have no connection with what has gone before 前に済んだ事とは何の関連もないように見える～を突然言い始める，またはやり始める→突然見当違いの事を言い出す，本題から脱線する，方針・考えを急に変える

**tangerine** /tǽndʒəríːn, ⌣/ 名 ▶定義 **1** C a fruit like a small sweet orange with a skin that is easy to take off むきやすい皮の付いた，小さくて甘いオレンジのような果物→タンジェリン
▶定義 **2** U 形 (of) a deep orange colour 濃いオレンジ色 (の)→ミカン色，オレンジ色，赤味の強いオレンジ色，タンジェリン色の

**tangible** /tǽndʒəb(ə)l/ 形 ▶定義 that can be clearly seen to exist 存在していることがはっきりと見えるような→現実の，具体的な，実体的な，明白な，確実な ‖ *There are tangible benefits in the new system.* 新しいシステムには実体的な利益がある． ⇔ **intangible**

**tangle** /tǽŋg(ə)l/ 名 C ▶定義 a confused mass, especially of threads, hair, branches, etc that cannot easily be separated from each other 特に糸，毛，枝などの，互いを簡単に分離することができないような混乱した塊→もつれ，絡まり，混乱 ‖ *My hair's full of tangles.* 私の髪はもつれきっている．*This string's in a tangle.* このひもはもつれている． ― tangled 形→もつれた，ややこしい，混乱した，極めて複雑に入り組んだ ‖ *The wool was all tangled up.* その毛糸はすっかりもつれていた．

*****tank** /tǽŋk/ 名 C ▶定義 **1** a container for holding liquids or gas; the amount that a tank will hold 液体や気体を入れるための容器；タンクに入る量→タンク，水槽，タンク1杯分の量 ‖ a *water/fuel/petrol/fish* **tank** 水槽・燃料タンク・ガソリンタンク・魚類用の水槽 *We drove there and back on one tank of petrol.* 私たちはタンク１杯のガソリンでそこまで行って帰ってきた. ☛ **dive**, **motorbike** のさし絵 ▶定義2 a large, heavy military vehicle covered with strong metal and armed with guns, that moves on special wheels 強固な金属で覆われ砲を装備した, 特殊な車輪で動く大型で重量のある軍隊の乗り物→タンク, 戦車

**tanker** /tǽŋkər/ 图 © ▶定義 a ship or lorry that carries oil, petrol, etc in large amounts 石油, ガソリンなどを大量に運ぶ船またはトラック→タンカー, 油輸送船, タンクローリー, タンク車 ‖ *an oil tanker* 油槽船

**tannoy** /tǽnɔɪ/ 图 © ▶定義 a system used for giving spoken information in a public place 公共の場所で音声による情報を与えるために用いられる装置→タノイ, タンノイ, スピーカーシステム, 拡声器 ‖ *They announced over the tannoy that our flight was delayed.* 私たちの乗る便が遅れることが場内アナウンスで放送された.

**tantalizing** (または **tantalising**) /tǽntlaɪzɪŋ/ 形 ▶定義 making you want sth that you cannot have or do; tempting 所有したりすることができないものを欲しいと思わせている; 気持ちをそそる→じらすような, 欲望・興味をそそる, じれったがらせる ‖ *A tantalizing aroma of cooking was coming from the kitchen.* 食欲をそそる料理の香りが台所から漂ってきていた. ― **tantalizingly** (または **tantalisingly**) 副 →じらすように, じれったいほど

**tantrum** /tǽntrəm/ 图 © ▶定義 a sudden explosion of anger, especially by a child 特に子供によって, 怒りが突然爆発すること→かんしゃく, 怒りの爆発, 不機嫌

\***tap**¹ /tǽp/ 動 (**tapping**; **tapped**) ▶定義1 圓 他 **tap (at/on sth); tap sb/sth (on/with sth)** to touch or hit sb/sth quickly and lightly ～に素早く軽く触れる, またはたたく→(～を)軽くたたく, たたいて拍子を取る, コツコツたたく ‖ *Their feet were tapping in time to the music.* 彼らの足はその音楽に合わせて拍子を取っていた. *She tapped me on the shoulder.* 彼女は私の肩をポンとたたいた. ☛ S6 ページのさし絵 ▶定義2 圓 他 **tap (into) sth** to make use of a source of energy, knowledge, etc that already exists 既に存在しているエネルギー源, 知識などを利用する→～を開発する, 利用する, 開拓する ‖ *to tap the skills of young people* 若者の技能を利用する ▶定義3 他 to fit a device to sb's telephone so that his/her calls can be listened to secretly ～の通話をひそかに聞くことができるように, その～の電話機にある装置を備え付ける→～を盗聴する, (電話線・電信線に)タップを付けて傍受・盗聴する

---

▶コミュニケーション

頭がおかしい人を表す身振りの日英比較

**tap one's temple**: 人差し指で片方のこめかみをトントンとたたいて, 頭の出来不出来を示すしぐさ. 通常は「ここがイカレてる」と, 頭の具合がおかしいことを表します. 英米では, 頭がおかしい人は, 体本体に頭がしっかり取り付けられていないため, 肝心なねじが緩んだため(He has a screw loose; He hasn't got his head screwed on right)といった俗説があり, 欠陥工事の所在をこのしぐさで示します.

---

\***tap**² /tǽp/ 图 © ▶定義1 (米 **faucet**) a type of handle that you turn to let water, gas, etc out of a pipe or container 水や気体などを管や容器から出すためにひねる取っ手の一種→蛇口, コック, 栓 ‖ *Turn the hot/cold tap on/off.* お湯・水の出る方の蛇口を開けなさい・閉めなさい. ☛ **plug** のさし絵 ▶定義2 a light hit with your hand or fingers 手または指で軽くたたくこと→コツコツたたくこと ▶定義3 a device that is fitted to sb's telephone so that his/her calls can be listened to secretly ～の通話をひそかに聞くことができるように, その～の電話機に備え付けられている装置→盗聴器, 隠しマイク

**tap dance** 图 © ▶定義 a style of dancing in which you tap the rhythm of the music with your feet, wearing special shoes with pieces of metal on them 金属の付いた特殊な靴を履き, 足で音楽のリズムを取るダンスの一種→タップダンス ― **tap-dance** 動 圓 →タップダンスを踊る

\***tape**¹ /téɪp/ 图 ▶定義1 ❶a thin band of plastic material used for recording sound, pictures or information 音声, 映像, 情報などを記録するた

めに使われるプラスチック製の薄い帯状の物→**磁気テープ** || *I've got the whole concert **on tape** (= recorded).* 私はそのコンサート全体をテープに録った(=録画した). ▶定義2 ❻a cassette which is used for recording or playing music, videos, etc 音楽やビデオなどを録音または再生するために使われるカセット→**(録音・録画用の)テープ** || *a blank tape (= a tape which is empty)* 何も録音されていないテープ(=空いているテープ) *to rewind a tape* テープを巻き戻す ▶定義3 ❶a long narrow band of plastic, etc with a sticky substance on one side that is used for sticking things together, covering electric wires, etc 物をくっつけ合わせたり電線を包んだりするために使われる, 片方の面に粘着性の物質が付いた, プラスチックなどでできている細長い帯状の物→**テープ** || *sticky/adhesive tape* 粘着テープ・ばんそうこう ☛参 **Sellotape** ▶定義4 ❻❶a narrow piece of cloth that is used for tying things together or as a label 物を結び合わせるために, または札として使われる細長い布切れ→**ひも, 平ひも, テープ, リボン** ☛参 **red tape** ▶定義5 ❻a piece of material stretched across a race track to mark where the race finishes 競走の終わる所を表すために, 走路に渡して張られた物→**(ゴールの)テープ**

**tape**² /teɪp/ 動❶ ▶定義1 to record sound, music, television programmes, etc using a cassette カセットを使って音声, 音楽, テレビ番組などを録る→**～をテープに録音・録画する** ▶定義2 *tape sth (up)* to fasten sth by sticking or tying sth with tape¹(3) ～をtape¹(3)でくっつけ合わせたり結び合わせたりしてしっかり固定する→**～にテープを巻く, テープで縛る, テープをはる**

**tape measure**(または **measuring tape**) 名❻ ▶定義 a long thin piece of plastic, cloth or metal with centimetres, etc marked on it. It is used for measuring things. 1センチごとなどの目盛りが付いている, プラスチック, 布, または金属でできている薄くて長い物. 物の寸法を測るために用いられる→**巻き尺** ☛参 **tape**

**tape recorder** 名❻ ▶定義 a machine that is used for recording and playing sounds on tape テープに音声を録音したり再生したりするために用いられる機器→**テープレコーダー**

**tapestry** /ˈtæpəstri/ 名❻Ⓤ (複 **tapestries**) ▶定義 a piece of heavy cloth with pictures or designs sewn on it in coloured thread 色の付いた糸で絵や図柄を縫い付けた, 大きな1枚の布→**つづれ織り, タペストリー**

**tap water** 名❻ ▶定義 water that comes through pipes and out of taps, not water sold in bottles ボトルで売られている水ではなく, 管と蛇口から出てくる水→**生水, 水道水**

**tar** /tɑːr/ 名Ⓤ ▶定義1 a thick black sticky liquid that becomes hard when it is cold. Tar is obtained from coal and is used for making roads, etc. 冷えると固くなる, 黒い濃くて粘着性のある液体. 石炭からとれ, 道路などを造るために使われる→**タール** ☛参 **Tarmac** ▶定義2 a similar substance formed by burning tobacco たばこを燃やすことによって作られる同じような物質→**(たばこの)タール, やに** || *low-tar cigarettes* タールの含有量が少ないたばこ

★**target**¹ /ˈtɑːrɡət/ 名❻ ▶定義1 a result that you try to achieve 達成しようとする目標→**到達目標, 達成目標, 対象, 目標額** || *Our target is to finish the job by Friday.* 私たちの目標は, その仕事を金曜日までに終わらせることだ. *So far we're right on target (= making the progress we expected).* 私たちは今のところは順調である(=期待していた進捗(しんちょく)を見せている). *a target area/audience/group (= the particular area, audience, etc that a product, programme, etc is aimed at)* 対象となる地域・聞き手・集団(=ある製品やプログラムなどがねらい定めた特定の地域, 聞き手など) ▶定義2 a person, place or thing that you try to hit when shooting or attacking 射撃または攻撃するときに命中させようとする人, 場所, または物→**攻撃目標** || *Doors and windows are an easy target for burglars.* 戸と窓は強盗にとってねらいやすい攻撃目標である. ▶定義3 a person or thing that people criticize, laugh at, etc 人々が批判や嘲笑(ちょうしょう)などをする対象の人または物→**的, 種, 対象** || *The education system has been the target of heavy criticism.* 教育制度は強い批判の的となっている. ▶定義4 an object, often a round board with circles on it, that you try to hit in shooting practice 射撃練習で命中させようとする目標. 円がいくつか書かれている

円い板であることが多い→的, 標的 ‖ to aim at/hit/miss a target 的をねらう・的に当たる・的を外れる

**target**² /tá:rgət/ 動 ⑯ (通常は受動態で) ▶定義 target sb/sth; target sth at/on sb/sth to try to have an effect on a particular group of people; to try to attack sb/sth ある特定の集団の人々に影響を与えようとする; 〜を攻撃しようとする→〜を的・目標にする, 〜を…に向ける, 〜の対象を…にする, 〜を攻撃目標にする ‖ *The product is targeted at teenagers.* その製品は10代を対象としている.

**tariff** /tǽrəf/ 名 ⓒ ▶定義1 a tax that has to be paid on goods coming into a country 国に入ってくる商品に対して支払われなければならない税金→関税 ▶定義2 a list of prices, especially in a hotel 特にホテルにあるような価格表→料金表, 運賃表

**Tarmac**™ /tá:mæk/ 名 ▶定義1 ⓒ Ⓤ a black material used for making the surfaces of roads 道路の表面を作るために使われる黒い物質→タールマク ☛参 tar ▶定義2 the tarmac [単数扱い] an area covered with a Tarmac surface, especially at an airport 特に空港にあるような, タールマクで舗装された区域→タールマクで舗装された道路, 滑走路, エプロン

**tarnish** /tá:nɪʃ/ 動 ▶定義1 ⓐ ⓘ (used about metal, etc) to become or to make sth less bright and shiny (金属などについて) 〜の輝きや光が弱くなる, または弱くする→曇る, 光沢・つやを失う; 〜を曇らせる, 光沢・つやを失わせる ▶定義2 ⓣ to spoil the good opinion people have of sb/sth 〜に対して人がしている良い評価を損なう→〜を汚す, 傷付ける, 〜の質・価値を低下させる

**tarpaulin** /tá:pɔːlɪn, -pə-/ 名 ⓒ Ⓤ ▶定義 strong material that water cannot pass through, which is used for covering things to protect them from the rain 水を通すことができない丈夫な素材で, 雨から守るために物に掛けるときに使われるもの→防水シート, 防水布

**tart**¹ /tɑːt/ 名 ▶定義1 ⓒ Ⓤ an open pie filled with sweet food such as fruit or jam 果物やジャムのような甘い食べ物を中に詰めた, 中身の見えるパイ→タルト ☛ C4 ページのさし絵 ▶定義2 ⓒ 英略式 a woman who dresses or behaves in a way that people think is immoral

人が不道徳であると考えるような服の着方や振る舞い方をする女性→ふしだらな女, 売春婦, 不身持ちな女

**tart**² /tɑːt/ 動
句動詞 tart sb/sth up 英略式 ▶定義 to decorate and improve the appearance of sb/sth 〜の見掛けを飾って良くする→〜をけばけばしく・ごてごて飾り立てる, 安っぽく着飾る

**tartan** /tá:tn/ 名 Ⓤ ⓒ ▶定義1 a traditional Scottish pattern of coloured squares and lines that cross each other 互いに交差している色の付いた四角と線から成る, スコットランドの伝統的な図柄→タータン(チェック), 格子柄 ▶定義2 material made from wool with this pattern on it そのような図柄の毛織物→タータン, 格子柄の毛織物(の衣服)

*__task__ /tɑːsk; tæsk/ 名 ⓒ ▶定義 a piece of work that has to be done, especially an unpleasant or difficult one なされなければならない仕事で, 特に不愉快な, または困難なもの→仕事, 職務, 務め, (骨の折れる)作業, 任務 ‖ *Your first task will be to type these letters.* あなたの最初の仕事は, これらの手紙をタイプすることでしょう. *to perform/carry out/undertake a task* 任務を遂行する

*__taste__¹ /teɪst/ 名 ▶定義1 [単数扱い] the particular quality of different foods or drinks that allows you to recognize them when you put them in your mouth; flavour 口に入れたときにそれが何であるかを認識させるような, さまざまな食べ物や飲み物の特定の性質; 風味→味, 風味 ‖ *I don't like the taste of this coffee.* 私はこのコーヒーの味は好きではない. *a sweet/bitter/sour/salty taste* 甘い・苦い・酸っぱい・塩辛い味 ▶定義2 Ⓤ the ability to recognize the flavour of food or drink 食べ物や飲み物の風味を認識できる能力→味覚 ‖ *I've got such a bad cold that I seem to have lost my sense of taste.* 私はこんなにひどい風邪を引いているので, 味覚がなくなったような気がする. ▶定義3 [ⓒ, 通常は単数] a taste (of sth) a small amount of sth to eat or drink that you have in order to see what it is like それがどのようなものかを知るために食べる, または飲む少量の〜→〜の一口, 少量, 試食, 味見 ‖ *Have a taste of this cheese to*

## 1660 taste²

see if you like it. このチーズがお好みかどうか、一口食べてみてください。 ▶定義4 [単数扱い] a short experience of sth ～の短い経験→ちょっとした経験，味 ‖ *That was my **first taste** of success.* あれは私が初めて成功した経験だった。 ▶定義5 ❶the ability to decide if things are suitable, of good quality, etc 物事が適しているかどうか，良質であるかどうかなどを決めることができる能力→鑑賞力，審美眼，センス，品，判断力 ‖ *He has excellent **taste** in music.* 彼は音楽のセンスが抜群だ。 ▶定義6 [単数扱い] a taste (for sth) what a person likes or prefers 人が好きである，または好んでいるもの→趣味，好み，嗜好（しこう）‖ *She has developed a **taste** for modern art.* 彼女は現代美術が好きになった。

成句 (be) in bad, poor, etc taste ▶定義 (used about sb's behaviour) (to be) unpleasant and not suitable （～の行動について）不快でありふさわしくない→悪趣味で，下品で，儀礼に反した ‖ *Some of his comments were in very bad **taste**.* 彼のコメントの一部はとても品がないものだった。

★**taste²** /téɪst/ 動 ▶定義1 ⊜ taste (of sth) to have a particular flavour ある特定の風味を持っている→～の味がする ‖ *The pudding **tasted** of oranges.* このプディングはオレンジの味がした。 *to **taste** sour/sweet/delicious* 酸っぱい・甘い・いい味がする ▶定義2 ⊕ to notice or recognize the flavour of food or drink 食べ物や飲み物の風味に気付く，または認識する→～の味を感じる，味が分かる ‖ *Can you **taste** the garlic in this soup?* このスープはガーリックの味がするのが分かりますか。 ▶定義3 ⊕ to try a small amount of food and drink; to test the flavour of sth 少量の食べ物や飲み物を試食・試飲する；～の風味を試してみる→～を味見する ‖ *Can I **taste** a piece of that cheese to see what it's like?* あのチーズがどんな味がするのか、1切れ食べてみてもいいですか。

**tasteful** /téɪstful, -f(ə)l/ 形 ▶定義 (used especially about clothes, furniture, decorations, etc) attractive and well-chosen （特に衣服，家具，装飾などについて）魅力的で精選された→趣味の良い，センスの良い，上品な，審美眼のある，風流な ‖ *tasteful furniture* 趣味の良い家具 ⇔ tasteless — tastefully /-fʊli, -f(ə)li/ 副 →趣味良く，上品に

**tasteless** /téɪstləs/ 形 ▶定義1 having little or no flavour ほとんど、または全く味のない→味のない、まずい ‖ *This sauce is rather **tasteless**.* このソースはかなりまずい。 ⇔ tasty ▶定義2 likely to offend people 人を怒らせそうである→品のない、下品な、卑俗な ‖ *His joke about the funeral was particularly **tasteless**.* その葬儀についての彼の冗談は特に品がなかった。 ▶定義3 (used especially about clothes, furniture, decorations, etc) unattractive; not well-chosen （特に衣服，家具，装飾などについて）魅力のない；精選されていない→趣味の悪い、悪趣味な、無風流な ⇔ tasteful

**tasty** /téɪsti/ 形 (**tastier**; **tastiest**) ▶定義 having a good flavour おいしい味がしている→おいしい、美味な、風味のきいた、うまい ‖ *spaghetti with a **tasty** mushroom sauce* おいしいマッシュルームソースが掛かったスパゲッティ

**tattered** /tǽtərd/ 形 ▶定義 old and torn; in bad condition 古くて裂けている；ひどい状態である→ぼろぼろの、壊れた ‖ *a **tattered** coat* ぼろぼろの上着

**tatters** /tǽtərz/ 名

成句 in tatters ▶定義 badly torn or damaged; ruined ひどく裂けている、または損傷している；台なしになった→ぼろぼろで、ずたずたで ‖ *Her dress was in **tatters**.* 彼女のドレスはぼろぼろだった。

**tattoo** /tætúː/ 名 ⓒ (複 **tattoos**) ▶定義 a picture or pattern that is marked permanently on sb's skin ～の肌に永久的に付けられている絵または図柄→入れ墨，彫り物 — tattoo 動 ⓗ (tattooing; tattooed)→～に入れ墨をする，～の（模様の）入れ墨をする ‖ *She had his name **tattooed** on her left hand.* 彼女は左手に彼の名前の入れ墨をしていた。

**tatty** /tǽti/ 形 略式 ▶定義 in bad condition ひどい状態で→みすぼらしい、薄汚い、ぼろの、お粗末な ‖ *tatty old clothes* みすぼらしい古着

**taught** TEACH の過去・過去分詞形

**taunt** /tɔːnt/ 動 ⓗ ▶定義 to try to make sb angry or upset by saying unpleasant or cruel things 不快な事やむごい事を言って、～を怒らせたり腹を立てさせようとしたりする→～を…のことであざける、ののしる、責める — taunt 名 ⓒ →あ

ざけり, ののしり, 侮辱的・挑発的な言葉, 痛烈な皮肉

**Taurus** /tɔ́ːrəs/ 名 C U ▶定義 the second sign of the zodiac, the Bull 黄道十二宮の2番目である牡牛座➡**牡牛座, 金牛宮**

**taut** /tɔːt/ 形 ▶定義 (used about rope, wire, etc) stretched very tight; not loose (綱, 針金などについて) しっかりぴんと張った; 緩んでいない➡**ぴんと張った**

**tavern** /tǽvəm/ 名 C (古) ▶定義 a pub パブ➡**酒場, 居酒屋, バー, 飲み屋**

*__tax__ /tæks/ 名 C U ▶定義 (a) tax (on sth) the money that you have to pay to the government so that it can provide public services 政府が公共事業を行うことができるように人々が支払わなければならない金➡**税金, 税** ‖ *income tax* 所得税 *There used to be a tax on windows.* かつては窓にも税金がかかっていた. ― tax 動 他 (しばしば受動態で)  **〜に税金をかける, 課税する** ‖ *Alcohol, cigarettes and petrol are heavily taxed.* 酒, たばこ, ガソリンには重税が課せられている.

**taxable** /tǽksəb(ə)l/ 形 ▶定義 on which you have to pay tax 税金を支払わなければならない対象である➡**課税対象となる, 課税できる, 有税の** ‖ *taxable income* 課税対象となる所得

**taxation** /tækséiʃ(ə)n/ 名 U ▶定義 1 the system by which a government takes money from people so that it can pay for public services 公共事業に対して支払うことができるように, 政府が人々からお金を徴収する制度➡**課税, 徴税, 税制** ‖ *direct/indirect taxation* 直接税・間接税 ▶定義 2 the amount of money that people have to pay in tax 人々が税として支払わなければならない金額➡**税金, 税金額** ‖ *to increase/reduce taxation* 増税する・減税する *high/low taxation* 高額の税金・低額の税金

**tax-free** 形 ▶定義 on which you do not have to pay tax 税金を支払う必要のない対象である➡ **免税の, 非課税の, 税引きの, 無税の**

*__taxi__ /tǽksi/ (または **taxicab** 特に 米 **cab**) 名 C ▶定義 a car with a driver whose job is to take you somewhere in exchange for money 対価を得て人をどこかへ連れていくことを仕事とする運転手のいる車➡**タクシー** ‖ *Shall we go by bus or get/take a taxi?* バスで行きましょうか, それともタクシーで行きましょうか.

tea 1661

▶支払わなければならない金額 (fare (運賃)) は meter (メーター) に表示されている.

**taxi²** /tǽksi/ 動 自 ▶定義 (used about an aircraft) to move slowly along the ground before or after flying (航空機について) 飛行する前または後に地面に沿ってゆっくり移動する➡**誘導路を滑走する, ゆっくり滑走路を移動する**

**taxing** /tǽksɪŋ/ 形 ▶定義 difficult; needing a lot of effort 困難な; 多大な努力を必要としている➡**荷が重い, 厄介な, 負担の重い, 苦労の多い, 面倒な** ‖ *a taxing exam* 負担の大きい試験

**taxi rank** 名 C ▶定義 a place where taxis park while they are waiting to be hired タクシーが乗客を待っている間に駐車している場所➡**タクシー乗り場, 客待ちタクシー用待機所**

**TB** /tíː bíː/ 略 tuberculosis ➡**結核**

**tbsp** 略 tablespoonful(s)➡**大さじ1杯** ‖ *Add 3 tbsp sugar.* 大さじ3杯の砂糖を加えてください.

*__tea__ /tiː/ 名 ▶定義 1 ❶ a hot drink made by pouring boiling water onto the dried leaves of the tea plant or of some other plants; a cup of this drink 沸騰している湯を茶の木の葉, またはそのほかの植物の葉を乾燥させたものに注いでできる温かい飲み物; そのような1杯の飲み物 ➡**茶, 紅茶** ‖ *a cup/pot of tea* 1杯のお茶・ポット1杯のお茶 *weak/strong tea* 薄いお茶・濃いお茶 *herb/mint/camomile tea* ハーブティー・ミントティー・カモミールティー *Two teas and one coffee, please.* 紅茶を2つとコーヒーを1つ下さい. ☞ C4 ページのさし絵 ▶定義 2 ❶ the dried leaves that are used for making tea お茶をいれるために使われる乾燥した葉➡**茶の葉** ‖ *a packet of tea* 1袋のお茶 ▶定義 3 C U 特に 英 a small afternoon meal of sandwiches, cakes, etc and tea to drink, or a cooked meal eaten at 5 or 6 o'clock サンドイッチ, ケーキなどと紅茶による午後の軽食, または5時か6時に取る料理➡**午後のお茶 (の時間), ティー** ‖ *The kids have their tea as soon as they get home from school.* その子供たちは, 学校から帰るとすぐにお茶にする.

---

▶音声とつづり字

tea の出だしの帯気音

日本語では「ティー」のように言いますが,

## 1662 tea bag

英語では出だしの t を言うとき,強く息を同時に出して[t<sup>h</sup>i:]のように言います.これを帯気音(aspiration)と名付けています.p, t, k が出だしのとき,また音節の頭に来るときにすべて帯気音が伴います.ただし,sp, st, sk 場合は帯気音は伴いません.

### ▶社会・文化

**英国のティータイム**

「紅茶」は red tea ではなく black tea と言います.「ミルクティー」「レモンティー」は和製英語で,英語ではそれぞれ tea with milk in it, tea with lemon in it が正しい表現です.ところで,tea は「軽食」という意味でも使われます.英国の上流階級では,遅い夕食の前に,午後4時ごろ紅茶とサンドイッチなどで軽食(afternoon tea)を取るからです.

---

成句 (not) sb's cup of tea ⇒ **CUP¹**

**tea bag** 图 ❻ ▶定義 a small paper bag with tea leaves in it, that you use for making tea お茶をいれるために使う,お茶の葉が入っている小さな紙の袋→ティーバッグ ☜ C4ページのさし絵

**\*teach** /tiːtʃ/ 動 (過, 過分 **taught** /tɔːt/) ▶定義1
❸❻ teach sb (sth/to do sth); teach sth (to sb) to give sb lessons or instructions so that he/she knows how to do sth ～が…を行う方法が分かるように～に教える→～に…を教える, 教授する ‖ *My mother taught me to play the piano.* 私の母は私にピアノの弾き方を教えてくれた. *Jeremy is teaching us how to use the computer.* ジェレミーは私たちにコンピューターの使い方を教えているところだ. *He teaches English to foreign students.* 彼は外国人の学生に英語を教えている. *I teach in a primary school.* 私は小学校で教えている. ▶定義2 ❻ to make sb believe sth or behave in a certain way ～に…を信じさせる,またはある様式で振る舞わせる→～だと教える, 悟らせる ‖ *The story teaches us that history often repeats itself.* その話は,歴史がしばしば繰り返すものであることを私たちに教えている. *My parents taught me always to tell the truth.* 両親はいつも私に真実を話すよう教えた. ▶定義3 ❻ to make sb have a bad experience so that he/she is careful not to do the thing that caused it again ～がそれを引き起こす物事を再びしないよう注意深くなるように,その～にひどい経験をさせる→～に(…すべきでないと)思い知らせる, (～すると)ひどい目に遭うと警告する, 教え込む ‖ *A week in prison? That'll teach him to drink and drive!* 刑務所に1週間だって？それなら,飲酒運転をしたらそういう目に遭うと彼に思い知らせることができるだろう.

成句 teach sb a lesson ▶定義 to make sb have a bad experience so that he/she will not do the thing that caused it again ～がそれを引き起こす物事を再びしなくなるように,その～にひどい経験をさせる→～に教訓を与える, ～を訓戒する

**\*teacher** /tiːtʃər/ 图 ❻ ▶定義 a person whose job is to teach, especially in a school or college 特に学校や大学で,教えることを仕事としている人→先生, 教師, 教員 ‖ *He's a teacher at a primary school.* 彼は小学校の先生だ. *a maths/chemistry/music teacher* 数学の先生・化学の先生・音楽の先生 ☞参 **head¹(6)**

### ▶社会・文化

**先生のいろいろ**

学校の先生は普通 teacher, school teacher と言います.校長先生のことは principal とか headmaster(女性は headmistress)と呼ばれます.

アメリカの大学では,教授を professor, 准教授(教授と助教授の間のポスト)を associate professor, 助教授を assistant professor, 専任講師を instructor, そして非常勤講師を lecturer と呼びます.イギリスの大学では,教授を professor, 助教授を reader, 専任講師を senior lecturer と言っています.なお,学長は president です.

---

**teaching** /tiːtʃɪŋ/ 图 ▶定義1 ❶the work of a teacher 教師の仕事→教授, 授業, 教職 ‖ *My son went into teaching and my daughter became a doctor.* 私の息子は教職に進み,娘は医者になった. *teaching methods* 教授法 ▶定義2 [❻, 通常は複数] ideas and beliefs that are taught by sb/sth ～によって教えられる思想や信条→教義,

教え, 教訓 ‖ the teachings of Gandhi ガンジーの教え

**tea cloth** 英 = TEA TOWEL

**teacup** /tíːkÀp/ 名 C ▶定義 a cup that you drink tea from お茶を飲むカップ→紅茶茶わん, 湯飲み茶わん, ティーカップ

**tea leaves** 名 [複数扱い] ▶定義 the small leaves that are left in a cup after you have drunk the tea お茶を飲んだ後にカップに残っている小さな葉→紅茶の出がらし, 茶殻

*__team__¹ /tíːm/ 名 C ▶定義 1 a group of people who play a sport or game together against another group もう一方の集団に対抗してスポーツやゲームを共にする人々の集団→チーム, 団, 組 ‖ a football team サッカーのチーム Are you __in__/__on__ the team? あなたはそのチームの一員ですか. ▶定義 2 a group of people who work together 共に仕事をする人々の集団→仲間, 一団 ‖ a team of doctors 医師団

▶ team が単数形で用いられる場合, その後に続くのは単数形の動詞でも複数形の動詞でもよい: The team play/plays two matches every week. (そのチームは毎週2回試合をしている.)

**team**² /tíːm/ 動

[句動詞] team up (with sb) ▶定義 to join sb in order to do sth together ~を一緒に行うために…に加わる→~と協力する, 協同する ‖ I teamed up with Elena to plan the project. 私はそのプロジェクトの計画を立てるためにエレナと協力した.

**teamwork** /tíːmwə̀ːrk/ 名 U ▶定義 the ability of people to work together 人々の共に仕事をする能力→チームワーク, 協同作業, 協力 ‖ Teamwork is a key feature of the training programme. チームワークは, そのトレーニングプログラムの主な特色である.

**teapot** /tíːpɒt/ 名 C ▶定義 a container that you use for making tea in and for serving it お茶を中に入れてつぐために使う容器→ティーポット, きゅうす, 茶びん ☛ C4 ページのさし絵

*__tear__¹ /tíər/ 名 [C, 通常は複数] ▶定義 a drop of water that comes from your eye when you are crying, etc 泣いているときなどに目からこぼれる一滴の滴→涙 ‖ I was __in tears__ (= crying) at the end of the film. 私はその映画が終わった時に涙を浮かべていた (= 泣いていた). The little girl __burst into tears__ (= suddenly started to cry). その少女はわっと泣き出した (= 突然泣き始めた).

[成句] shed tears ⇒ SHED²

tear

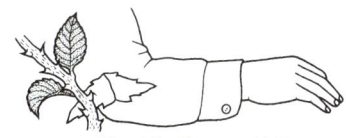

'Oh no! I've **torn** my shirt!'

She **tore up** the letter.

*__tear__² /téər/ 動 (過 tore /tɔːr/; 過分 torn /tɔːrn/) ▶定義 1 自他 to damage sth by pulling it apart or into pieces; to become damaged in this way ~を引っ張ってばらばらにしたり, ずたずたに破ったりして, 損害を与える; このようにして傷が付く→(~を)裂く, 引き裂く, 破る, ちぎる ‖ I tore my shirt on that nail. 私はシャツをあのくぎに引っ掛けて破った. She tore the letter in half. 彼女はその手紙を2つに裂いた. I tore a page out of my notebook. 私はノートから1ページちぎった. This material doesn't tear easily. この生地は簡単には引き裂けない. ▶定義 2 他 to remove sth by pulling violently and quickly ~を乱暴に, 素早く引っ張って取り去る→~を…から引きはがす, はぎ取る, もぎ取る, 引き離す ‖ Paul tore the poster down from the wall. ポールは壁からポスターをはぎ取った. He tore the bag out of her hands. 彼は彼女の手からバッグをもぎ取った. ▶定義 3 他 to make a hole in sth by force ~に力ずくで穴を開ける→~を引き裂いて (穴などを) 作る ▶定義 4 自 tear along, up, down, past, etc to move very quickly in a particular direction ある方向に非常に速く移動する→突進する, 疾走する, 猛烈な勢

## 1664 tearful

いで動く ‖ *An ambulance went tearing past.* 救急車が猛烈な勢いで通り過ぎていった. —**tear** 名 ⓒ→ 裂け目, 割れ目, 破れ, ほころび, 突進, 大急ぎ ‖ *You've got a tear in the back of your trousers.* あなたのズボンの後ろが破れていますよ.

成句 **wear and tear** ⇒ **WEAR²**

句動詞 **tear sth apart** ▶定義1 to pull sth violently into pieces ～を乱暴に引っ張ってずたずたにする → ～を裂いて分ける, ばらばらにする ▶定義2 to destroy sth completely ～を完全に破壊する → ～を分裂させる ‖ *The country has been torn apart by the war.* その国は戦争によって分裂させられている.

**tear yourself away (from sb/sth)** ▶定義 to make yourself leave sb/sth or stop doing sth ～から自分を離れさせる, または～をするのをやめる → ～を…から引き離す, 去らせる, しぶしぶ離れる

**be torn between A and B** ▶定義 to find it difficult to choose between two things or people 2つの物事または2人の人の間で選ぶのが難しいことが分かる → ～のどちらを選択すべきか迷う, ～の間で板挟みになっている

**tear sth down** ▶定義 (used about a building) to destroy it (建物について) それを破壊する → ～を取り壊す, 倒壊させる, 解体する ‖ *They tore down the old houses and built a shopping centre.* 彼らはそれらの古い家を取り壊し, ショッピングセンターを建設した.

**tear sth up** ▶定義 to pull sth into pieces, especially sth made of paper ～, 特に紙でできている～を引っ張ってずたずたにする → ～をずたずたに引き裂く ‖ *'I hate this photograph,' she said, tearing it up.* 「この写真は嫌いだわ」と彼女は言って, びりびりに引き裂いた.

**tearful** /tíərfʊl, -f(ə)l/ 形 ▶定義 crying or nearly crying 泣いている, またはほとんど泣きそうである → 涙ぐんだ, 涙で一杯の, 泣いている, 涙ながらの, 泣きそうな

**tear gas** 名 Ⓤ ▶定義 a type of gas that hurts the eyes and throat, and is used by the police, etc to control large groups of people 目やのどに痛みを与える気体の一種で, 大集団の人々を制圧するために警察などによって用いられるもの → 催涙ガス

**tease** /tíːz/ 動 自 他 ▶定義 to laugh at sb either in a friendly way or in order to upset him/her ～のことを好意的に, または怒らせるために笑う → (～を)からかう, いじめる, 冗談を言う, ふざける, 冷やかす ‖ *Don't pay any attention to those boys. They're only teasing.* あの少年たちに注意を払わないで. 彼らはふざけているだけですから. *They teased her about being fat.* 彼らは彼女を太っているとからかった.

**teaspoon** /tíːspuːn/ 名 Ⓒ ▶定義1 a small spoon used for putting sugar in tea, coffee, etc 紅茶, コーヒーなどに砂糖を入れるために使われる小さなスプーン → 茶さじ, ティースプーン ▶定義2 (または **teaspoonful** /-fʊl/) the amount that a teaspoon can hold 茶さじですくうことのできる量 → 茶さじ1杯(分)

**tea towel** (または **tea cloth**) 名 Ⓒ ▶定義 a small towel that is used for drying plates, knives, forks, etc 皿, ナイフ, フォークなどをふくために使われる小さなタオル → ふきん

*****technical** /téknɪk(ə)l/ 形 ▶定義1 connected with the practical use of machines, methods, etc in science and industry 科学や産業で機械, 方法などの実際的な利用に関連している → 技術の, 技術的な, 工業技術の, 機械技術の, 応用科学の ‖ *The train was delayed due to a technical problem.* その電車は, 技術上の問題のために遅れた. ▶定義2 connected with the skills involved in a particular activity or subject ある特定の活動または学科に関する技術に関連している → 専門の, 専門的な, 専門用語を使った ‖ *This computer magazine is too technical for me.* このコンピューター雑誌は私には専門的すぎる.

**technicality** /tèknəkǽləti/ 名 Ⓒ (複 **technicalities**) ▶定義 one of the details of a particular subject or activity ある特定の活動または学科の細目の1つ → 専門的な事項・問題・方法, 専門用語

**technically** /téknɪk(ə)li/ 副 ▶定義1 according to the exact meaning, facts, etc 正確な意味, 事実などによると → 原則的には, 厳密には, 正式には ‖ *Technically, you should pay by May 1st, but it doesn't matter if it's a few days late.* 原則的には5月1日までに支払うべきだが, 2, 3日遅れても問題はない・構わない. ▶定義2 in a way that involves detailed knowledge of the machines, etc that are used in industry or science 産業や科学で利用される機械などについての, 詳細な知識にかかわる方法で→**技術的に** ‖ *The country is technically not very advanced.* その国は技術的にあまり進んでいない.

▶**定義3** used about sb's practical ability in a particular activity 〜の, ある特定の活動における実際的な能力について→**専門的に** ‖ *He's a technically brilliant dancer.* 彼は才能豊かなダンサーだ.

**technician** /teknɪʃ(ə)n/ 名 **C** ▶定義 a person whose work involves practical skills, especially in industry or science 特に産業または科学, 実際的な技術にかかわる仕事をしている人→**(ある分野の)専門家, (専門)技術者** ‖ *a laboratory technician* 実験技術者

\***technique** /tekníːk/ 名 ▶定義1 **C** a particular way of doing sth 〜を行う, ある特定の方法→**技術, 技巧, 技法, 手法, テクニック** ‖ *new techniques for teaching languages* 言語教育の新しい手法 *marketing/management techniques* マーケティングの技術・経営技術 ▶定義2 **U** the practical skill that sb has in a particular activity 〜がある特定の活動で持っている実際的な技術→**技量, 手腕, 腕前, こつ** ‖ *He's a naturally talented runner, but he needs to work on his technique.* 彼は生まれつきの才能のある走者だが, 技術に取り組む必要がある.

\***technology** /teknɑ́lədʒi/ 名 **C U** ( 複 **technologies**) ▶定義 the scientific knowledge and/or equipment that is needed for a particular industry, etc ある特定の産業などで必要とされる, 科学的な知識・機器→**科学技術, テクノロジー, 工業技術, 工学, 応用科学, 技術** ‖ *developments in computer technology* コンピューター技術の発展 — **technological** /tèknəlɑ́dʒɪk(ə)l/ 形→**科学技術の, 工業上の, 工学の** ‖ *technological developments* 科学技術の発展 — **technologist** /teknɑ́lədʒɪst/ 名 **C**→**科学技術者** ‖ *Technologists are developing a computer that can perform surgery.* 科学技術者たちは, 手術を行うことのできるコンピューターを開発している.

**teddy** /tédi/ (または **teddy bear**) 名 **C** ( 複 **teddies**) ▶定義 a toy for children that looks like a bear クマに似ている, 子供のおもちゃ→**テディーベア (クマのぬいぐるみ)**

**tedious** /tíːdiəs/ 形 ▶定義 boring and lasting for a long time 退屈で長い時間続いている→**単調で退屈な, 長たらしくて飽き飽きする, うんざりする** ‖ *a tedious train journey* 単調で退屈な列車の旅

**teem** /tiːm/ 動 **自** ▶定義 **teem with sth** (used about a place) to have a lot of people or things moving about in it (場所について) その中で動き回っている人または物がたくさんある→**〜で一杯である, 満ちている** ‖ *The streets were teeming with people.* その通りは人で一杯だった.

**teenage** /tíːnèɪdʒ/ 形 ( 名 詞 の 前 だ け ) ▶定義1 between 13 and 19 years old 13歳から19歳の間の→**10代の, 13歳から19歳の人々の** ‖ *teenage children* ティーンエージャーの子供たち ▶定義2 typical of or suitable for people between 13 and 19 years old 13歳から19歳の間の人々に特有の, または適している→**ティーンエージャー特有の, ティーンエージャー向けの** ‖ *teenage magazines/fashion* ティーンエージャー向けの雑誌・ティーンエージャー特有のファッション

**teenager** /tíːnèɪdʒər/ 名 **C** ▶定義 a person aged between 13 and 19 years old 13歳から19歳の間の年齢の人→**ティーンエージャー** ‖ *Her music is very popular with teenagers.* 彼女の音楽はティーンエージャーに大変人気がある.

☞参 **adolescent**

**teens** /tiːnz/ 名 [複数扱い] ▶定義 the period of a person's life between the ages of 13 and 19 人の一生における13歳から19歳までの期間→**10代, 少年・少女時代** ‖ *to be **in your** early/late **teens*** ローティーンである・ハイティーンである

**teeshirt** /tíːʃɜːrt/ 名 = **T-SHIRT**

**teeth** **TOOTH** の複数形

**teethe** /tiːð/ 動 **自** (通常 -ing 形で) ▶定義 (used about a baby) to start growing its first teeth (赤ん坊について) 1本目の歯が生え始める→**歯が生える**

**teething troubles** (または **teething problems**) 名 [複数扱い] ▶定義 the problems that can develop when a person, system, etc is new 人, 制度などが不慣れなときに現れることのあ

る問題→(事業などの)初期の障害,初めの苦労,初期の困難,発足時の苦労 ‖ *We've just installed this new software and are having a few teething troubles with it.* 私たちはこの新しいソフト(ウェア)をインストールしたばかりで、初期の障害がいくつか起きている.

**teetotal** /ˌtiːˈtóʊtl, ⌣⌣/ 形 (名詞の前は不可)
▶定義 (used about a person) never drinking alcohol (人について)アルコール飲料を全く飲まない→絶対禁酒(主義)の ー **teetotaller** (困 **teetotaler**) /-tlər/ 名 ❻→絶対禁酒(主義)者

**TEFL** /téfəl/ 略 Teaching English as a Foreign Language→外国語としての英語教授法

**tel** 略 telephone (number)→電話(番号) ‖ *tel 01865 56767* 電話 01865 56767

**telecommunications** /ˌtèləkəmjuːnəkéɪʃ(ə)nz/ 名 [複数扱い] ▶定義 the technology of sending signals, images and messages over long distances by radio, telephone, television, etc 信号,画像,メッセージを,ラジオ,電話,テレビなどによって遠距離に送る技術→遠隔通信,電気通信,遠距離通信

**telegram** /téləɡræm/ 名 ❻ ▶定義 a message that is sent by a system (telegraph) that uses electrical signals and that is then printed and given to sb 電気信号を用いる方式(電信)で送られ,印刷されて~に渡されるメッセージ→電報,電文

**telegraph** /téləɡrɑːf; -ɡræf/ 名 ❶ ▶定義 a method of sending messages over long distances, using wires that carry electrical signals 電気信号を伝送する電線を使ってメッセージを遠距離に送る方法→電信,電報

**telegraph pole** 名 ❻ ▶定義 a tall wooden pole that is used for supporting telephone wires 電話線を支えるために使われる,木製の背の高い柱→電信柱,電柱

**telemarketing** /téləmɑ̀ːrkətɪŋ/ = TELESALES

**telepathy** /təlépəθi/ 名 ❶ ▶定義 the communication of thoughts between people's minds without using speech, writing or other normal methods 言葉,文字,そのほかの通常の方法を使わずに,人々の心と心の間での伝達→テレパシー,精神感応,以心伝心

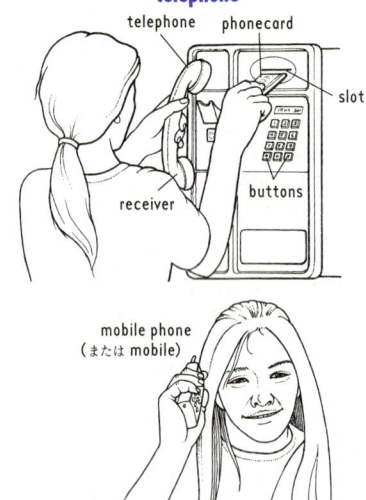

telephone
telephone phonecard
slot
receiver buttons

mobile phone
(または mobile)

*__telephone__ /téləfòʊn/ (または 略式 phone) 名
▶定義 1 ❶ an electrical system for talking to sb in another place by speaking into a special piece of equipment 特殊な機器に向かって話すことにより,別の場所にいる~に話すための電気的なシステム→電話 ‖ *Can I contact you by telephone?* 電話で連絡を取ってもいいですか. *to make a phone call* 電話をかける *What's your telephone number?* あなたの電話番号は何番ですか. ☛ 特に話しているときには,telephone よりも phone を使う方が一般的である. ▶定義 2 ❻ the piece of equipment that you use when you talk to sb by telephone 電話で~に話すときに使う機器→電話,電話機 ‖ *Could I use your telephone?* 電話をお借りしてよろしいでしょうか. *a mobile phone (= one that you can carry around)* 携帯電話(= 持ち歩くことができる電話) *a public telephone* 公衆電話

▶電話をかけるときには,まず最初に電話番号の dial (ダイヤル) を回す. 電話が鳴ることを ring, 相手が出ることを answer と言う. 相手が既に電話を使っている場合は,電話は engaged (話し中) である. 話し終えたら,電話を hang up (切る) か put the phone down (受話器を置く) 必要がある. ほかの地域や国にかける場合に電話番号の前にダイヤルを回す番号は,それぞれ code (市外局番,国番号) と呼

ばれる: 'What's the code for Spain?'（「スペインの国番号は何番ですか」）
— telephone（または phone）動 自 他 → ~に電話をかける, 電話する, 電話で話す ‖ *Sarah phoned. She's going to be late.* サラは電話で話していた. 彼女は遅刻するだろう. *I'll phone you later.* 後で電話します.
成句 on the phone/telephone ⇒ **PHONE**

**telephone box**（または **phone box**; **call box**） 名 C 定義 a small covered place in a street, etc that contains a telephone for public use 公共利用のための電話を備えた, 通りなどにある覆いのある狭い場所→**公衆電話ボックス**

**telephone directory**（または 略式 **phone book**） 名 C 定義 a book that gives a list of the names, addresses and telephone numbers of the people in a particular area ある特定の地域の人々の名前, 住所, 電話番号の一覧を掲載している本→**電話帳**

**telephone exchange**（または **exchange**） 名 C 定義 a place belonging to a telephone company where telephone lines are connected to each other 電話会社が所有している, 電話線が相互に接続されている場所→**電話交換局, 電話交換室**

**telesales** /téləseɪlz/（または **telemarketing**） 名 U 定義 a method of selling things by telephone 電話で物を売る方法→**テレホンセールス, 電話での売り込み** ‖ *He works in telesales.* 彼はテレホンセールスの仕事をしている.

**telescope** /téləskòʊp/ 名 C 定義 an instrument in the shape of a tube with special glass inside it. You look through it to make things that are far away appear bigger and nearer. 内側に特殊なガラスが入っている, 管の形をした器具. それを通して見ると, 遠く離れた所にある物がより大きく近くに見える→**望遠鏡** ☞ **binoculars** のさし絵

**teletext** /télətèkst/ 名 U 定義 a service that provides news and other information in written form on television ニュースやそのほかの情報をテレビ上に文字で提供する事業→**文字(多重)放送, テレテクスト**

**televise** /téləvàɪz/ 動 他 定義 to show sth on television テレビで~を見せる→**~をテレビで放送する** ‖ *a televised concert* テレビ放送された音楽会

tell 1667

***television** /téləvìʒ(ə)n, ˌ--ˈ-/（または **TV**, 英 略式 **telly**）名 定義1（または **television set**） C a piece of electrical equipment in the shape of a box. It has a glass screen which shows programmes with moving pictures and sounds. 箱の形をした電気機器. 動画や音声で番組を表示するガラス製の画面が付いている→**テレビ(受像機)** ‖ *to turn the television on/off* テレビをつける・消す ☞ C7 ページのさし絵 定義2 U the programmes that are shown on a television set テレビに表示される番組→**テレビ, テレビ番組** ‖ *Paul's watching television.* ポールはテレビを見ている. 定義3 U the electrical system and business of sending out programmes so that people can watch them on their television sets 人々がテレビで見られるように, 番組を送り出す電気的なシステムおよび事業→**テレビ放送, テレビ業界** ‖ *a television presenter/series/documentary* テレビ番組の司会者・テレビ番組のシリーズ・テレビのドキュメンタリー *cable/satellite/terrestrial/digital television* ケーブルテレビ放送・衛星放送・地上波放送・デジタル放送 *She works in television.* 彼女はテレビ業界で働いている.
成句 on television 定義 being shown by television; appearing in a television programme テレビによって表示されている; テレビ番組として現れている→**テレビに, テレビで, テレビ放送している** ‖ *What's on television tonight?* 今夜, テレビで何をやっていますか.

*tell /tel/ 動（過, 過分 told /toʊld/）定義1 他 tell sb (sth/that...); tell sb (about sth); tell sth to sb to give information to sb by speaking or writing 話すこと, または書くことによって~に情報を与える→**~に…を話す, 語る, 言う, 知らせる, 告げる, 教える** ‖ *She told me her address but I've forgotten it.* 彼女は住所を教えてくれたが, 私はそれを忘れてしまった. *He wrote to tell me that his mother had died.* 彼はお母さんが亡くなったことを知らせる手紙をくれた. *Tell us about your holiday.* 休日について話してください. *to* **tell the truth/a lie** 本当の事を言う・うそを言う *to* **tell a story** 話をする *Excuse me, could you tell me where the station is?* すみませんが, 駅はどこにあるのか教えてくださいませ

## 1668 telling

んか. *He tells that story to everyone he sees.* 彼はあの話を会う人みんなにしている. ☛参 **say** の注 ▶定義2 🔵 ⓑ **tell sb to do sth** to order or advise sb to do sth ～をするよう…に命令する, または勧める➡〜にしなさいと言う, 命じる, 指示する, 助言する ‖ *The policewoman told us to get out of the car.* その婦人警官は私たちに車から降りなさいと命じた. ▶定義3 🔵 ⓑ to know, see or judge (sth) correctly (〜を) 正確に知る, 理解する, または判断する➡〜だとはっきりと分かる, 確信を持つ, 〜を見分ける, 〜を…と区別できる ‖ *'What do you think Jenny will do next?' 'It's hard to tell.'*「ジェニーは次に何をすると思う」「それはなかなか分からないね」 *I could tell that he had enjoyed the evening.* 私には彼が楽しい晩を過ごしたことが分かるよ. ***You can never tell*** *what he's going to say next.* 彼が次に何を言うか全く分からない. *I can't **tell the difference between** Dan's sisters.* 私にはダンの姉妹を見分けることができない. ▶定義4 ⓑ (used about a thing) to give information to sb (物について) 情報を〜に与える➡〜を教える, 示す, 表す, 物語る ‖ *This book will tell you all you need to know.* この本はあなたが知っておく必要のあることがすべて書いてある. ▶定義5 🔵 to not keep a secret 秘密を守らない➡〜のことを言い付ける, 口外する ‖ *Promise you won't tell!* 口外しないと約束しなさい. ▶定義6 🔵 tell (on sb/sth) to have a noticeable effect 著しい効果がある➡(〜に) こたえる, 影響する, 効く, ものを言う, 効き目がある ‖ *I can't run as fast as I could - my age is beginning to tell!* かつて走れた速さと同じ速さで走ることができない ー 年齢のせいだろう.

成句 **all told** ▶定義 with everybody or everything counted and included すべての人あるいは物が数えられた, または含められた➡全部で, 合計で, 全体として

**(I'll) tell you what** 略式 ▶定義 used to introduce a suggestion 提案を導入するために用いて➡いい考えがある, ねえちょっと (聞いてよ), 実はこうなんだ, じゃこうしよう ‖ *I'll tell you what - let's ask Diane to take us.* そうだいい考えがある ー ダイアンに私たちを連れていってくれるよう頼んでみよう.

**I told you (so)** 略式 ▶定義 I warned you that this would happen. 私はこれが起きるだろうとあなたに警告した➡ほらごらん, だから言っただろう

**tell A and B apart** ⇒ **APART**
**tell the time** ▶定義 to read the time from a clock or watch 時計から時刻を読み取る➡時計を見て時刻が分かる, 時計の見方を知っている

句動詞 **tell sb off (for sth/for doing sth)** ▶定義 to speak to sb angrily because he/she has done sth wrong 〜が悪い…したので, その〜に対して怒って話し掛ける➡〜を…のことでしかりつける ‖ *The teacher told me off for not doing my homework.* その先生は宿題をしてこなかったことで私をしかりつけた.

**tell on sb** ▶定義 to tell a parent, teacher, etc about sth bad that sb has done 親, 先生などに, 〜がやった悪い…について話す➡〜のことを言い付ける, 〜の告げ口をする

**telling** /télɪŋ/ 形 ▶定義1 showing, without intending to, what sb/sth is really like 〜が実際にどんな感じであるか, 見せようとしなくても現れている➡心の内を表す, 本心を漏らす, おのずと表す ‖ *The number of homeless people is a telling comment on today's society.* ホームレスの人々の数は今日の社会を如実に表している.
▶定義2 having a great effect 多大な効果がある➡効き目のある, 効果的な, 手ごたえのある, 有効な ‖ *That's quite a telling argument.* あれは実に有効な議論だ.

**tell-tale** 形 ▶定義 giving information about sth secret or private 秘密の, または個人的な〜についての情報を与えている➡暴露する, 露見させる, 明るみに出す ‖ *He said he was fine, but there were tell-tale signs of worry on his face.* 彼は元気だと言ったが, 顔には明らかに心配そうな表情が浮かんでいた.

**telly** /téli/ (複 **tellies**) 英 略式 =TELEVISION
**temp**¹ /temp/ 名 ⓒ 略式 ▶定義 a temporary employee, especially in an office, who works somewhere for a short period of time when sb else is ill or on holiday 特に事務所で, ほかの〜が病気または休暇のときの短期間にどこかで働く, 臨時の従業員➡臨時雇い(の人), パートタイマー, 臨時職員 —temp 動 🔵➡臨時雇いとして働く

**temp**² /temp/ 略 temperature➡温度, 気温 ‖

temp 15°C 気温摂氏15度

**temper** /témpər/ 图 ▶定義1 ❻ ❶ if you have a temper you get angry very easily. temperを持っていれば, すぐに怒る→かんしゃく, 短気, 不機嫌, 腹立ち ‖ *Be careful of Paul. He's got quite a temper!* ポールに気を付けて. ひどいかんしゃく持ちだから. *You must learn to control your temper.* あなたはかんしゃくを抑えるようにしなければなりませんよ. ▶定義2 ❻ the way you are feeling at a particular time ある特定の時での感じ方→気分, 機嫌 ‖ *It's no use talking to him when he's in a bad temper.* 彼の機嫌が悪いときに話し掛けても無駄だ. ☛類 **mood**

成句 **in a temper** ▶定義 feeling very angry and not controlling your behaviour とても怒っていて, 自分の行動を抑制できない→かんしゃくを起こしている, 機嫌が悪い

**keep/lose your temper** ▶定義 to stay calm/to become angry 冷静な状態である・怒る→かんしゃくを抑える, 平静を保つ, 我慢する, 腹を立てる, 平静を失う, 堪忍袋の緒が切れる ☛参 **bad-tempered**

**temperament** /témp(ə)rəmənt/ 图 ❻ ❶ ▶定義 a person's character, especially as it affects the way he/she behaves and feels 特に振る舞い方や感じ方に影響を及ぼすような, 人の性質→気性, 気質 ‖ *to have an artistic/a fiery/a calm temperament* 芸術的気質・激しやすい気質・冷静な気質を持っている

**temperamental** /tèmp(ə)rəméntl/ 形 ▶定義 often and suddenly changing the way you behave or feel 振る舞い方や感じ方がしばしば, 急に変わっている→移り気な, 気まぐれな, 気性の激しい, 神経質な

**temperate** /témp(ə)rət/ 形 ▶定義 (used about a climate) not very hot and not very cold (気候について) あまり暑くなく, あまり寒くない→温暖な, 温和な, 穏やかな

\***temperature** /témp(ə)rətʃər/ 图 ▶定義1 ❻ ❶ how hot or cold sth is 〜がどのくらい熱い [暑い], または冷たい [寒い] かということ→温度, 気温 ‖ *Heat the oven to a temperature of 200°C.* オーブンを摂氏200度に熱しなさい. *a high/low temperature* 高温・低温 *an increase in temperature* 気温の上昇 ▶定義2 ❻ how hot or cold a person's body is 人の体がどのくらい熱いか, または冷たいかということ→体温

---

### temporary 1669

▶社会・文化

摂氏と華氏

英語の天気予報で「最高気温(the highest temperature)が86度」と言ったりするのを聞いても驚いてはいけません. 英語圏では通例, 華氏(°F)で表し, 摂氏(°C)よりもはるかに多く使います. 86°Fは30°Cのことです. 両者の換算は次の通りです.

°C = (°F − 32) × 5/9

°F = °C × 9/5 + 32

なお, 摂氏と華氏はそれぞれ, Celsius(セルシウス)というスウェーデンの天文学者(摂氏温度計を考え出した人), Fahrenheit(ファーレンハイト)というドイツの物理学者の名から付けられました.

---

成句 **have a temperature** ▶定義 (used about a person) to be hotter than normal because you are ill (人について) 病気のため体温が平熱よりも高い→熱がある

**take sb's temperature** ▶定義 to measure the temperature of sb's body with a special instrument (a thermometer) 特別な計器 (体温計) で〜の体の温度を計る→〜の体温を計る

**temple** /témp(ə)l/ 图 ❻ ▶定義1 a building where people pray to a god or gods 人々が神または神々に祈る建物→神殿, 寺, 寺院, 聖堂, 教会堂 ‖ *a Buddhist/Hindu temple* 仏教の寺・ヒンズー教の寺院 ▶定義2 one of the flat parts on each side of your forehead 額の両側にある平い部分の一方→こめかみ ☛ C5 ページのさし絵

**tempo** /témpoʊ/ 图 ( 複 **tempos** /témpoʊz/) ▶定義1 [単数扱い, ❶] the speed of an activity or event 活動または出来事の速さ→テンポ, 速さ, 速度 ▶定義2 ❻ ❶ the speed of a piece of music 1曲の速度→テンポ, 速度 ‖ *a fast/slow tempo* アップテンポ・スローテンポ

\***temporary** /témp(ə)rəri; -pərèri/ 形 ▶定義 lasting for a short time; not permanent 短い間, 続いている; 永久的ではない→一時的な, つかの間の, はかない, 仮の, 臨時の, 間に合わせの ‖ *a temporary job* 臨時の仕事 *This arrangement is only temporary.* この協定は仮のものにすぎない. — **temporarily** /témp(ə)rərɪli;

tèmpərérəli, ﹍﹍/ [副] ➜一時的に, 仮に, つかの間, 臨時に

***tempt** /tem(p)t/ [動][他] ▶定義 tempt sb (into sth/into doing sth); tempt sb (to do sth) to try to persuade or attract sb to do sth, even if it is wrong たとえ不正な事であっても～をするよう…を説得する, または引き付ける ➜～を誘惑する, そそのかす, ～をそそのかして…する気にさせる ‖ *His dream of riches had tempted him into a life of crime.* 金持ちになりたいという夢が彼を悪の道にそそのかした. *She was tempted to stay in bed all morning.* 彼女は午前中ずっと寝ていたいという誘惑に駆られた.

**temptation** /tem(p)téɪʃ(ə)n/ [名] ▶定義1 [U] a feeling that you want to do sth, even if you know that it is wrong たとえ不正な事だと分かっていても, ～をしたいという気持ち ➜誘惑, 衝動 ‖ *I managed to **resist the temptation** to tell him what I really thought.* 私は本当に思っていることを彼に伝えたいという誘惑に何とか耐えた. *She wanted a cigarette badly, but didn't **give in to temptation**.* 彼女はたばこがとても吸いたかったが, 誘惑に負けなかった. ▶定義2 [C] a thing that attracts you to do sth wrong or silly 不正な, またはばかげた～をさせるよう引き付けるもの ➜誘惑するもの, 心をひくもの ‖ *All that money is certainly a big temptation.* あれほどの金額は確かに誘惑が大きい.

**tempting** /tém(p)tɪŋ/ [形] ▶定義 attractive in a way that makes you want to do or have sth ～をしたい, または所有したいと思わせるほど魅力的な ➜気持ちをそそる, 心を惑わす, 魅力的な, うっとりさせる ‖ *a tempting offer* 魅力的な申し出

***ten** /ten/ [数] ▶定義 10

➤文中での数詞の使い方については, six の項を参照.

**tenacious** /tənéɪʃəs/ [副] ▶定義 not likely to give up or let sth go; determined あきらめたり～をそのままにすることをしそうにない; 決然とした ➜粘り強い, 意志の固い, 不屈な, 断固とした, 頑強な — tenacity /tənǽsəti/ [名] [U] ➜意志の固さ, 固持, 固執, 頑強, 粘り強さ

**tenancy** /ténənsi/ [名] [C] [U] ([複] **tenancies**) ▶定義 the use of a room, flat, building or piece of land, for which you pay rent to the owner 所有者に賃料を支払って部屋, アパート, 建物, 土地を利用すること ➜賃借り, 借用 ‖ *a six-month tenancy* 6か月の借用期間 *It says in the tenancy agreement that you can't keep pets.* ペットを飼うことはできないと賃貸契約にある.

**tenant** /ténənt/ [名] [C] ▶定義 a person who pays money (rent) to the owner of a room, flat, building or piece of land so that he/she can live in it or use it 居住または利用することができるように, 部屋, アパート, 建物, 土地の所有者に金 (賃料) を支払う人 ➜賃借人, 入居者, 借用者, 賃貸権保有者, テナント

➤所有者は landlord (男の家主, 地主) または landlady (女の家主, 地主) と呼ばれる.

***tend** /tend/ [動] ▶定義1 [自] tend to do sth to usually do or be sth 大抵～をする, または～である ➜～する傾向がある, ～しがちだ, よく～する ‖ *Women tend to live longer than men.* 女性は男性よりも長生きする傾向がある. *There tends to be a lot of heavy traffic on that road.* あの道路は大抵交通が激しい. *My brother tends to talk a lot when he's nervous.* 私の兄は不安になるとよくしゃべる傾向がある. ▶定義2 [自] used for giving your opinion in a polite way 自分の意見を丁寧に述べるために用いて ➜私としては～するのですが ‖ ***I tend to think** that we shouldn't interfere.* 私たちが干渉するべきではないと思いますが. ▶定義3 [自][他][正式] tend (to) sb/sth to look after sb/sth ～の世話をする ➜～の世話をする, ～に注意する, 気を配る ‖ *Paramedics tended (to) the injured.* 救急隊員たちはそのけが人を介抱した.

**tendency** /téndənsi/ [名] [C] ([複] **tendencies**) ▶定義 a tendency (to do sth/towards sth) something that a person or thing usually does; a way of behaving 人または物が大抵するということ; 振る舞い方 ➜傾向, 風潮, 気配, 性向, 性癖 ‖ *They both **have a tendency** to be late for appointments.* 彼らは2人とも約束に遅れて来る傾向がある. *The dog began to show vicious tendencies.* その犬は凶暴なたちであるところを見せ始めた. *She seems to have a tendency towards depression.* 彼女にはうつ病の傾向があるようだ.

**tender**[1] /téndər/ [形] ▶定義1 kind and loving 優しくて愛情に満ちた ➜優しい, 思いやりのある, 愛情のこもった, 哀れみ深い ‖ *tender words/*

T

*looks/kisses* 愛情のこもった言葉・まなざし・キス ▶定義2 (used about food) soft and easy to cut or bite; not tough (食べ物について) 柔らかくて切ったりかんだりしやすい; 固くない→**柔らかい, かみやすい** ‖ *The meat should be nice and tender.* その肉はおいしくて柔らかいはずだ. ▶定義3 (used about a part of the body) painful when you touch it (体の一部分について) そこに触ると痛みを感じる→**触ると痛い, 敏感な**

成句 *at a tender age; at the tender age of...* ▶定義 when still young and without much experience まだ若くて経験があまりない時に→**幼い年齢で, 年端もいかないで** ‖ *She went to live in London at the tender age of 15.* 彼女はわずか15歳の時にロンドンに移り住んだ. ―**tenderly** 副→優しく, 親切に, 穏やかに, そっと, 愛情を込めて ―**tenderness** 名 **Ⓤ**→優しさ, 思いやり, 愛情, 柔らかさ, ひ弱さ, もろさ

**tender**² /téndər/ 動 自他 (文) ▶定義 to offer or give sth formally ～を正式に申し出る, または与える→**～を申し出る, 提供する, 提出する, 差し出す** ‖ *After the scandal the Foreign Minister was forced to tender her resignation.* そのスキャンダルの後, 外務大臣は辞表を提出せざるを得なかった. ―**tender** (または **bid**) 名 **Ⓒ**→申し出, 提出, 提供, 入札, 見積もり ‖ *Several firms submitted a tender for the catering contract.* 複数の会社がその仕出しの契約に対して見積書を提出した.

**tendon** /téndən/ 名 **Ⓒ** ▶定義 a strong, thin part inside your body that joins a muscle to a bone 筋肉を骨につなぐ, 体内の細く強じんな部分→**腱 (けん)**

**tenement** /ténəmənt/ 名 **Ⓒ** ▶定義 a large building that is divided into small flats, especially in a poor area of a city 特に都会の貧しい地域で, 狭いアパートに分かれている大きな建物→**(大都市のスラム街にある) 安アパート, 共同住宅**

★**tennis** /ténəs/ 名 **Ⓤ** ▶定義 a game for two or four players who hit a ball over a net using a piece of equipment (**a racket**) that is held in one hand 片手で持った道具 (ラケット) を使ってネット越しにボールを打つ, 2人または4人で行う競技→**テニス, 庭球** ‖ *Let's play tennis.* テニスをしよう. *to have a game of tennis* テニスをする *a tennis match* テニスの試合

**tense**¹ 1671

▶テニスは, singles (シングルス) (2人の間で行う試合) または doubles (ダブルス) (1チーム2人から成る2チーム間で行う試合) でできる.

>**音声とつづり字**
>
>テニスを英語らしく発音しよう
>
>tennis を, 詳しい発音記号では [tʰén.ɪs] または [tʰén.ɪs] と表記しています. [tʰen-] は息 (帯気音) を同時に出すことが必要です. 次に [-nɪs] の所は「ニス」ではなく,「ニィスまたはナス」と発音します. 前舌を口蓋 (こうがい) からできるだけ離して発音すると良いでしょう.

**tenor** /ténər/ 名 **Ⓒ** ▶定義1 a fairly high singing voice for a man; a man with this voice 男性のかなり高い歌声; そのような声を持った男性→**テノール, テナー (の声の人), テナー歌手** ‖ *Pavarotti is a famous Italian tenor.* パヴァロッティは有名なイタリア人テナー歌手だ.

▶テナーは, alto (アルト) と baritone (バリトン) の中間である.

▶定義2 a musical instrument that plays notes within the same limits as a tenor voice テナーの声と同じ範囲内の音を出す楽器→**テナー・テノール楽器** ‖ *a tenor saxophone* テナーサックス

**tenpin bowling** /ténpɪn bòʊlɪŋ/ 名 **Ⓤ** ▶定義 a game in which you roll a heavy ball towards ten objects (**tenpins**) and try to knock them down 重いボールを10本の目標物 (テンピンズ) に向かって転がして倒そうとする遊び→**(英国の球技) テンピンズ, 十柱戯**

★**tense**¹ /tens/ 形 ▶定義1 (used about a person) not able to relax because you are worried or nervous (人について) 心配であったり不安であったりするために, くつろぐことができない→**緊張した, 張り詰めた, ぴりぴりした** ‖ *She looked pale and tense.* 彼女は顔色が悪く, 緊張しているように見えた. ▶定義2 (used about a muscle or a part of the body) tight; not relaxed (筋肉や体の一部分について) 硬い; ほぐれていない→**張った** ▶定義3 (used about an atmosphere or situation) in which people feel worried and not relaxed (雰囲気や状況について) 人々が心配していて, くつろいでいないような→**緊迫**

## 1672 tense²

した, 堅苦しい

**tense²** /tens/ 動自他 ▶定義 tense (up) to have muscles that have become hard and not relaxed 固くなり, ほぐれていない筋肉がある→**緊張する; ～を緊張させる**

**＊tense³** /tens/ 名 C U (文法) ▶定義 a form of a verb that shows if sth happens in the past, present or future ～が過去, 現在, または未来のいずれに起きるかを表す動詞の形態→**時制, テンス**
▶動詞の時制についての説明は, 巻末の「文法早見表」を参照.

**tension** /ténʃ(ə)n/ 名 ▶定義1 C U the condition of not being able to relax because you are worried or nervous 心配であったり不安であったりするためにくつろぐことができない状態→**緊張, 不安** ‖ *I could hear the tension in her voice as she spoke.* 彼女の話している時, その声から緊張している様子が聞き取れた.
▶定義2 C U bad feeling and lack of trust between people, countries, etc 人, 国などの間の悪い感情, 信頼の欠如→**緊張, 緊迫, 緊迫状態, 対立** ‖ *There are signs of growing tensions between the two countries.* その2国間の緊張が高まっている兆しがある. ▶定義3 U (used about a rope, muscle, etc) the state of being stretched tight; how tightly sth is stretched (綱, 筋肉などについて) ぴんと張っている状態; ～がどのくらいぴんと張っているかということ→**ぴんと張ること, 伸張, 引っ張り, 張った状態** ‖ *The massage relieved the tension in my neck.* マッサージで首の張りが取れた.

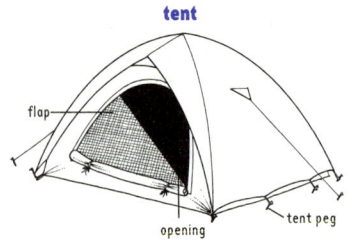

tent
flap
opening
tent peg

**＊tent** /tent/ 名 C ▶定義 a small structure made of cloth that is held up by poles and ropes. You use a tent to sleep in when you go camping. 柱とロープで支えられた布製の小さな建造物. キャンプに行ったときに中で寝るために使う→**テント, 天幕** ‖ *to put up/take down a tent* テントを張る・畳む

**tentacle** /téntɪk(ə)l/ 名 C ▶定義 one of the long thin soft parts like legs that some sea animals have 海に住む動物の一部が持っている, 足のような細長く柔らかい部分の1つ→**触手, 触角, 触腕** ‖ *An octopus has eight tentacles.* タコには8本の触腕がある. ☞ **octopus** のさし絵

**tentative** /téntətɪv/ 形 ▶定義1 (used about plans, etc) uncertain; not definite (計画などについて) 不確実な; 明確ではない→**仮の, 試験的な, とりあえずの, 確定的でない** ▶定義2 (used about a person or his/her behaviour) not confident about what you are saying or doing (人やその振る舞いについて) 自分が言ったり行ったりしていることに自信がない→**ためらいがちの, おずおずした, 自信のなさそうな** ‖ *a tentative smile/suggestion* ためらいがちな笑み・提案 ― **tentatively** 副 ▶**仮に, とりあえず, 試験的に, 一応, ためらいがちに**

**tenterhooks** /téntərhʊks/ 名 [複数扱い]
成句 **(be) on tenterhooks** ▶定義 to be in a very nervous or excited state because you are waiting to find out what is going to happen これから何が起きるのかが分かるのを待っているため, 非常に不安である, または興奮している→**やきもきしている, 気をもんでいる, いても立ってもいられない**

**＊tenth¹** /tenθ/ 代形副 ▶定義 10th→**10番目(の, に), 第10(の, に)** ☞参 **sixth** の例

**＊tenth²** /tenθ/ 名 C ▶定義 the fraction 1/10; one of ten equal parts of sth 分数の1/10; ～の均等な10個の部分の1つ→**10分の1** ☞参 **sixth** の例

**tenuous** /ténjuəs/ 形 ▶定義 very weak or uncertain 非常に弱い, または不安定である→**非常に薄い, もろい, 貧弱な, 薄弱な** ‖ *The connection between Joe's story and what actually happened was tenuous.* ジョーの話と実際に起きた事との関係は非常に薄い.

**tenure** /ténjər, -njʊər/ 名 U ▶定義 a legal right to live in a place, hold a job, use land, etc for a certain time ある一定の時期にある場所に住む, 職を持つ, 土地を利用するなどできる法的な権利→**保有権, 在職権, (終身)在職権 (米国大学教員の権利)**

**tepid** /tépəd/ 形 ▶定義 (used about liquids) only slightly warm (液体について) ほんのわずかだけ暖かい→**生ぬるい、微温の**

★**term**¹ /tə:m/ 名 ▶定義 **1** ❻ a word or group of words with a particular meaning ある特定の意味を持った言葉、または語群→**専門用語、学術用語、術語、用語** ‖ *What exactly do you mean by the term 'racist'?* 一体どのようなつもりで racist という用語を使っているのですか. *a technical term in computing* コンピューターの専門用語 ▶定義 **2** **terms** [複数扱い] **in terms of...; in...terms** used for showing which particular way you are thinking about sth or from which point of view 〜について特にどのように考えているか、またはどの視点から考えているかを表すために用いて→**〜の点から、〜に関して、〜によって、〜に置き換えて** ‖ *The flat would be ideal in terms of size, but it is very expensive.* そのアパートは広さの点では申し分ないが、とても高くつく. ▶定義 **3** **terms** [複数扱い] the conditions of an agreement 協定の条件→**条件、条項** ‖ *Under the terms of the contract you must give a week's notice.* その契約の条件に従い、1週間前に解約の予告を出さなければならない. *Both sides agreed to the peace terms.* 両者はその平和条約に同意した. ▶定義 **4** ❻ a period of time into which a school or university year is divided 学校または大学の学年が分けられている期間→**学期** ‖ *the autumn/spring/summer term* 秋学期・春学期・夏学期 *an end-of-term test* 学期末試験 ▶定義 **5** ❻ a period of time for which sth lasts 〜が続く期間→**期間、期限、任期** ‖ *The US President is now in his second term of office.* 米国の大統領は現在2期目の任期中である.

成句 **be on equal terms (with sb)** ⇒ **EQUAL**¹
**be on good, friendly, etc terms (with sb)** ▶定義 to have a friendly relationship with sb 〜と友好的な関係を持っている→**〜とうまくやっている、仲の良い間柄である、親しい関係である**
**come to terms with sth** ▶定義 to accept sth unpleasant or difficult 不快な、または困難な〜を受け入れる→**困難などに耐えてやっていく、〜をあきらめて受け入れる、甘受する**
**in the long/short term** ▶定義 over a long/short period of time in the future 未来の長い・短い期間にわたって→**長期的には、長い目で見れば、短**

期的には、短期的に見れば

★**term**² /tə:m/ 動 他 ▶定義 to describe sb/sth by using a particular word or expression ある特定の言葉または表現を用いて〜を表す→**〜を…と呼ぶ、称する、名付ける** ‖ *the period of history that is often termed the 'Dark Ages'* しばしば「暗黒時代」と呼ばれる歴史上の時代

**terminal**¹ /tə́:mən(ə)l/ 形 ▶定義 (used about an illness) slowly causing death (病気について) ゆっくりと死に至っている→**末期の、死に至る、不治の** ‖ *terminal cancer* 末期がん — **terminally** /-n(ə)li/ 副 →**終末に、末端に、末期的に、致命的に、期末に** ‖ *a terminally ill patient* 末期症状の患者

**terminal**² /tə́:mən(ə)l/ 名 ❻ ▶定義 **1** a large railway station, bus station or building at an airport where journeys begin and end 旅行が始まるまたは終わるような大きな鉄道の駅、バスの発着場、あるいは空港の建物→**始発駅、終着地、ターミナル、ターミナルビル、発着ロビー** ‖ *the bus terminal* バスターミナル *Which terminal are you flying from?* どの発着ロビーから離陸するのですか. ▶定義 **2** the computer that one person uses for getting information from a central computer or for putting information into it 1人の人が中央のコンピューターから情報を得るために、またはそれに情報を入力するために使うコンピューター→**端末、ターミナル**

**terminate** /tə́:mənent/ 動 自 他 正式 ▶定義 to end or to make sth end 終わる、または〜を終わらせる→**〜の終わりに来る、終わる、終了する；〜を終わらせる、終結させる** ‖ *to terminate a contract/an agreement* 契約・協定を解除する — **termination** 名 Ü →**終了、終結、終末、終点、結末**

**terminology** /tə̀:mənálədʒi/ 名 Ü ▶定義 the special words and expressions that are used in a particular profession, subject or activity ある特定の職業、学科、あるいは活動で使われる特別な言葉や表現→**術語、専門用語**

**terminus** /tə́:mənəs/ 名 ❻ (複 **terminuses** /-nəsəz, -ɪz/) ▶定義 the last stop or station at the end of a bus route or railway line バスの路線、または鉄道の路線の終わりにある、最終の停留所または駅→**終着駅、終点、ターミナル**

**terrace** /térəs/ 名 ▶定義 **1** ❻ a flat area of stone next to a restaurant or large house where people can have meals, sit in the sun, etc 人が食事をしたりするまたは日光浴をする，レストランや大きな家に隣接する石でできた平たんな場所→**テラス，壇** ●参 **patio, veranda, balcony** ▶定義2 ●医 a line of similar houses that are all joined together 全体がつながっている同じような家の並び→**テラスハウス，連続住宅，住宅棟** ▶定義3 [●, 通常は複数] one of a series of steps that are cut into the side of a hill so that crops can be grown there 作物が育てられるように丘の斜面に切り開かれた段々の1つ→**台地，高台，段丘** ▶定義4 **terraces**[複数扱い] the wide steps that people stand on to watch a football match 人がサッカーの試合を観戦するために乗る，幅の広い段→**立ち見席**

**terraced** /térəst/ 形 ▶定義1 医 (used about a house) forming part of a line of similar houses that are all joined together (家について) 全体がつながっている同じような家の並びを構成している→**テラスハウスの，連続住宅の** ▶定義2 (used about a hill) having steps cut out of it so that crops can be grown there (丘について) 作物が育てられるように丘の斜面に切り開かれた段々がある→**斜面がテラス状の，階段状に切り開かれた**

**terrain** /təréɪn/ 名 ⓤ ▶定義 land of the type mentioned 言及されている種類の土地→**地形，地勢** ∥ *mountainous/steep/rocky terrain* 山地・険しい地形・岩の多い地形

*****terrible** /térəb(ə)l/ 形 ▶定義1 very unpleasant; causing great shock or injury 非常に不快な; 強い打撃や大きなけがを引き起こしている→**恐ろしい，怖い，ものすごい** ∥ *a terrible accident* ものすごい事故 *terrible news* 恐ろしいニュース *What a terrible thing to do!* 何て怖いことをするのだろう. ▶定義2 ill or very upset 気分が悪い，またはとても動揺している→**極めて不快な，つらい** ∥ *I feel terrible. I think I'm going to be sick.* とても気分が悪い. 病気ではないかと思う. *He felt terrible when he realized what he had done.* 彼は自分がしたことに気付いた時，大変すまないと思った. ▶定義3 very bad; of poor quality 非常に悪い; 質の悪い→**ひどい，大変な，甚だしい，下手な，ひどく悪い** ∥ *a terrible hotel/book/memory/driver* とんでもないホテル・ひどい本・嫌な記憶・下手な運転手 ▶定義4 (名詞の前だけ) used to emphasize how bad sth is ～がいかに悪いかを強調するために用いて→**猛烈な，ひどい，大変な，すごい** ∥ *in terrible pain/trouble* ひどい痛み・大変な苦労 *The room was in a terrible mess.* その部屋はすごく散らかっていた.

*****terribly** /térəbli/ 副 ▶定義1 very 非常に→**非常に，とても，ひどく** ∥ *I'm terribly sorry.* 大変申し訳ありません. ▶定義2 very badly 非常に悪く→**恐ろしく，ものすごく，すごく下手に，ひどく悪く** ∥ *I played terribly.* 私はひどい演奏をした. *The experiment went terribly wrong.* その実験はひどい失敗に終わった.

**terrier** /tériər/ 名 ● ▶定義 a type of small dog 小犬の一種 → **テリア**

**terrific** /tərífɪk/ 形 ▶定義1 略式 extremely nice or good; excellent 非常にすばらしい，または良い; 非常に優れた→**すばらしい，すごくいい，すてきな** ∥ *You're doing a terrific job!* あなたはすごくいい仕事をしていますね. ▶定義2 (名詞の前だけ) very great とても大きな→**ものすごい，猛烈な，とてつもない** ∥ *I've got a terrific amount of work to do.* 私はとてつもない分量の仕事を抱えている. ― **terrifically** /-k(ə)li/ 副 →**とても，ものすごく** ∥ *terrifically expensive* ものすごく高価な

*****terrified** /térəfàɪd/ 形 ▶定義 terrified (of sb/sth) very afraid とても怖い→**～を怖がった，～におびえた，ぞっとする** ∥ *I'm absolutely terrified of snakes.* 私は蛇が断然怖い. *What's the matter? You look terrified.* どうしたのですか. おびえているように見えますが.

**terrify** /térəfàɪ/ 動 ● (現分 **terrifying**; 三単現 **terrifies**; 過, 過分 **terrified**) ▶定義 to frighten sb very much ～を非常に怖がらせる→**～を恐れさせる，おびえさせる，怖がらせる**

**territorial** /tèrətɔ́ːriəl/ 形 (名詞の前だけ) ▶定義 connected with the land or area of sea that belongs to a country ある国に属する土地または海域に関連している→**領土の，領地の，特定領域の** ∥ *territorial waters* 領海

**territory** /térət(ə)ri/ -tò:ri/ 名 (複 **territories**) ▶定義1 ● ⓤ an area of land that belongs to one country ある国に属する土地の範囲→**領土，領地** ∥ *to fly over enemy territory* 敵の領土の上を飛行する ▶定義2 ● ⓤ an area that an animal has as its own 動物が自分のものとして持って

いる領域→縄張り, テリトリー ▶定義3 ❶an area of knowledge or responsibility 知識または責任の範囲→領域, 分野 ‖ *Computer programming is Frank's territory.* コンピューターのプログラミングはフランクの専門だ.

**terror** /térər/ 名 ▶定義1 ❶very great fear 非常に大きな恐怖→恐怖, 恐ろしさ ‖ *He screamed in terror as the rats came towards him.* 彼はネズミが向かってきた時, 恐ろしさのあまり叫んだ. ▶定義2 ❻a person or thing that makes you feel afraid 人を怖がらせる人または物→恐怖の種, 恐ろしい物, 恐ろしい人, 脅威 ‖ *the terrors of the night* 夜の恐怖 ▶定義3 ❶ violence and the killing of ordinary people for political purposes 政治的な目的のための暴力や一般の人を殺すこと→テロ(行為) ‖ *a campaign of terror* テロ活動 ▶定義4 ❻a person or animal, especially a child, that is difficult to control 支配しにくい人または動物, 特に子供→厄介な人, 手に負えない子供, 利かん坊 ‖ *Joey's a little terror.* ジョーイはちょっと厄介な人だ.

**terrorism** /térərɪz(ə)m/ 名 ❶ ▶定義 the killing of ordinary people for political purposes 政治的な目的で普通の人を殺すこと→テロリズム, テロ行為 ‖ *an act of terrorism* テロ行為 — **terrorist** /térərɪst/ 名 ❻形→テロリスト, 暴力革命主義者, テロ行為者

**terrorize** (または **-ise**) /térərὰɪz/ 動 ⓗ ▶定義 to make sb feel frightened by using or threatening to use violence against him/her ~に暴力を働いて, または暴力を働くと脅かしてその~を怖がらせる→~を恐れおののかせる, 恐怖に陥れる, 恐れさせる, テロ手段で脅迫する ‖ *The gang has terrorized the neighbourhood for months.* その一味は何か月もの間, 近所の人々を恐怖に陥れている.

**terse** /tɔːrs/ 形 ▶定義 said in few words and in a not very friendly way わずかな言葉で, あまり好意的ではない言い方をされた→ぶっきらぼうな, 素っ気ない, 簡潔な ‖ *a terse reply* 素っ気ない返事

**tertiary** /tɔ́ːrʃəri, -ʃièri/ 形 ▶定義 (used about education) at university or college level (教育について) 大学レベルで→第3位の, 高等の ‖ *a tertiary college* 高等専門学校

**TESL** /tés(ə)l/ 略 Teaching English as a Second Language → 第2言語としての英語教授法

test² 1675

*****test**¹ /test/ 名 ❻ ▶定義1 a short exam to measure sb's knowledge or skill in sth ~における…の知識や技術を測る簡単な試験→テスト, 試験, 考査, 検査 ‖ *We have a spelling test every Friday.* 私たちは毎週金曜日にスペルテストがある.

▶テストを take (受ける) と, それに pass (受かる)(合格) か fail (失敗する)(不合格) かする.

▶定義2 a short medical examination of a part of your body 身体のある部分についての簡単な健康診断→検査 ‖ *to have an eye test* 目の検査を受ける ▶定義3 an experiment to find out if sth works or to find out more information about it ~が機能しているかどうかを調べる, または~についてさらに多くの情報を見つけ出すための実験→実験, 試験, 分析 ‖ *Tests show that the new drug is safe and effective.* 実験から新薬が安全で効果があることが分かる. *to carry out/perform/do a test* 実験を行う ▶定義4 a situation or event that shows how good, strong, etc sb/sth is ~がどのくらい良いか, 強いかなどを示している状態または出来事→試練, 試すための手段, 試金石

成句 **put sb/sth to the test** ▶定義 to do sth to find out how good, strong, etc sb/sth is ~がどのくらい良いか, 強いかなどを調べるために…をする→~を試す, 試験する, 吟味する

*****test**² /test/ 動 ⓗ ▶定義1 **test sb/sth (for sth); test sth (on sb/sth)** to try, use or examine sth carefully to find out if it is working properly or what it is like ~が適切に機能しているかどうか, または~がどのようなものであるかを調べるために, その~を試す, 使う, 試験する→~をテストする, 試験する, 試す ‖ *These cars have all been tested for safety.* これらの車についてすべて安全性がテストされた. *Do you think drugs should be tested on animals?* 薬品は動物で試すべきだと思いますか. ▶定義2 to examine a part of the body to find out if it is healthy 健康であるかどうかを調べるために体のある部分を検査する→~を検査する ‖ *to have your eyes tested* 目の検査を受ける ▶定義3 **test sb (on sth)** to examine sb's knowledge or skill in sth ~における…の知識や技術を試す→~を試験する, テストする ‖ *We're being tested on irregular* *verbs this morning.* 私たちは今朝, 不規則動詞のテストを受けています.

**testament** /téstəmənt/ 图 [ⓒ, 通常は単数] (文) ▶定義 a testament (to sth) something that shows that sth exists or is true ～が存在していること, または真実であることを示すもの→あかし, 証明, 証明するもの, 証拠

**testicle** /téstɪk(ə)l/ 图 ⓒ ▶定義 one of the two roundish male sex organs that produce the male cells (sperm) that are needed for making young 子を作るために必要とされる雄の細胞 (精子) を作る, 男性の丸みを帯びた 2 つの生殖器のうちの 1 つ→睾丸 (こうがん)

**testify** /téstəfaɪ/ 動 ⓘ ⓣ (現分 **testifying**; 三単現 **testifies**; 過, 過分 **testified**) ▶定義 to make a formal statement that sth is true, especially in a court of law 特に法廷で, ～が真実であると正式な申し立てをする→～であると証言をする, ～の証人となる, ～を証明する

**testimony** /téstəməni; -mòʊni/ 图 (複 **testimonies**) ▶定義 1 ⓒ ⓤ a formal statement that sth is true, especially one that is made in a court of law ～が真実であるという正式な申し立てで, 特に法廷でなされるもの→証言 ▶定義 2 [ⓤ, 単数扱い] 正式 something that shows that sth else exists or is true ほかの～が存在していること, または真実であることを示すもの→証拠, 証明, 現れ, 印

**test tube** 图 ⓒ ▶定義 a thin glass tube that is used in chemical experiments 化学の実験で使われる細長いガラス製品→試験管

**tetanus** /tét(ə)nəs/ 图 ⓤ ▶定義 a serious disease that makes your muscles, especially the muscles of your face, hard and impossible to move. You can get tetanus by cutting yourself on sth dirty. 筋肉, 特に顔の筋肉を固くして動かすことができないようにする重病. 不潔な～でけがをするとなる可能性がある→破傷風

**tether**[1] /téðər/ 動 ⓣ ▶定義 to tie an animal to sth with a rope, etc 動物を綱などで～に結び付ける→～をつなぎ綱でつなぐ, つなぎ留める

**tether**[2] /téðər/ 图 ⓒ
成句 at the end of your tether ⇒ **END**[1]

*****text** /tekst/ 图 ▶定義 1 ⓤ the main written part of a book, newspaper, etc (not the pictures, notes, index, etc) 本, 新聞などの書かれた主要な部分 (写真, 注釈, 索引などではない) →本文 ▶定義 2 ⓒ the written form of a speech, interview, etc 演説, インタビューなどの書かれたもの→原文, 原典, 話した通りの言葉 ‖ *The newspaper printed the complete text of the interview.* その新聞はインタビューの全文を掲載した. ▶定義 3 ⓒ a book or a short piece of writing that people study as part of a literature or language course 文学や語学の課程の一部として勉強する本, または短い文章→文献, 指定図書 ‖ *a set text (= one that has to be studied for an examination)* 指定された本 (= 試験のために勉強しなければならない本)

**textbook** /tékstbʊk/ 图 ⓒ ▶定義 a book that teaches a particular subject and that is used especially in schools 特定の科目を教え, 特に学校で使われる本→教科書, テキスト, 教本 ‖ *a history textbook* 歴史の教科書

**textile** /tékstaɪl, -tl/ 图 ⓒ ▶定義 any cloth made in a factory 工場で作られた布地→織物, 布地 ‖ *cotton textiles* 綿織物 *the textile industry* 織物産業

**texture** /tékstʃər/ 图 ⓒ ⓤ ▶定義 the way that sth feels when you touch it 触れたときに, ～が感じさせる方法→手触り, 肌触り, 肌合い, きめ ‖ *a rough/smooth/coarse texture* ざらざらした・滑らかな・ごわごわした手触り *This cheese has a very creamy texture.* このチーズはとても滑らかで柔らかい.

*****than** /ð(ə)n, 強形 ðæn/ 接 前 ▶定義 1 used when you are comparing two things 2 つのものを比べるときに用いて→～よりも, ～に比べて ‖ *He's taller than me.* 彼は私より背が高い. *He's taller than I am.* 彼は私よりも背が高い. *London is more expensive than Madrid.* ロンドンはマドリードよりも (生活費が) 高い. *You speak French much better than she does/than her.* あなたは彼女よりも上手にフランス語を話しますね.

▶定義 2 used with 'more' and 'less' before numbers, expressions of time, distance, etc 数, 時間や距離などを表す語句の前で more や less と用いて→～よりも, ～に比べて ‖ *I've worked here for more than three years.* 私はここで 3 年以上働いている. ▶定義 3 used after 'would rather' to say that you prefer one thing to another 一方よりももう一方の方が好きである

ことを述べるためにwould ratherの後に用いて∥～するよりはむしろ、～するくらいならいっそ∥ I'd rather play tennis than football. 私はサッカーをするよりもテニスをする方がいい.

\***thank** /θæŋk/ 動⑪ ▶定義 thank sb (for sth/for doing sth) to tell sb that you are grateful ～に有り難く思っていると言う→～に感謝する, 礼を述べる, 謝意を表す ∥ I'm writing to thank you for the present you sent me. あなたがくれたプレゼントに対するお礼の手紙を書いているところです. I'll go and thank him for offering to help. 私は彼の所に行き, 援助を申し出てくれたことに対してお礼を言うつもりだ.

▶ thank you と thanks はどちらも, 何かに対して有り難く思っているとだれかに言うために用いられる. thanks の方が口語的である: Thank you very much for your letter. (お手紙をどうもありがとう.) 'How are you, Rachel?' 'Much better, thanks.' (「レイチェル, 調子はどう」「大分良くなったよ, ありがとう」) thank you と thanks は, だれかが申し出てくれたことを受け入れるためにも用いることができる: 'Stay for dinner.' 'Thank you. That would be nice.' (「食事をしていって」「ありがとう. それはうれしいです」) ものを断りたい場合は, no, thank you または no, thanks と言えばよい: 'Would you like some more tea?' 'No, thanks.' (「お茶をもう少しいかがですか」「いえ, 結構です」)

成句thank God/goodness/heavens ▶定義 used for expressing happiness that sth unpleasant has stopped or will not happen 不快な～が止まった, またはもう起こらないという喜びを表すために用いて→やれやれ, 有り難い, ああ助かった, しめた ∥ Thank goodness it's stopped raining. 有り難い, 雨がやんだわ.

**thankful** /θæŋkfʊl, -f(ə)l/ 形 ▶定義 thankful (for sth/to do sth/that...) (名詞の前は不可) pleased and grateful うれしく, 有り難く思っている→～を感謝している, 非常にうれしい, 有り難く思う ∥ I was thankful to hear that you got home safely. あなたが無事に帰宅したと聞いて私は非常にうれしかった. I was thankful for my thick coat when it started to snow. 雪が降り始めた時, 厚手の上着を着ていて有り難く思った.

**thankfully** /-fʊli, -f(ə)li/ 副 ▶定義 1 used for expressing happiness that sth unpleasant did not or will not happen 不快な～が止まった, またはもう起こらないという喜びを表すために用いて→有り難いことに, 幸いにも ●類 **fortunately** ∥ Thankfully, no one was injured in the accident. 幸いにもその事故でけが人は出なかった. ▶定義 2 in a pleased or grateful way うれしく, または有り難く→感謝して, 有り難く ∥ I accepted her offer thankfully. 私は彼女の申し出を有り難く受け入れた.

**thankless** /θæŋkləs/ 形 ▶定義 involving hard work that other people do not notice or thank you for ほかの人が気付かない, または感謝をしない大変な仕事に関して→報われない, 割に合わない, 感謝されない

\***thanks** /θæŋks/ 名 [複数扱い] ▶定義 words which show that you are grateful 有り難いと思っていることを表す言葉→感謝(の言葉), 謝意, 謝辞 ∥ I'd like to express my thanks to all of you for coming here today. 今日ここに来てくださったことに対し, 皆様にお礼を申し上げたい.

成句 thanks to sb/sth ▶定義 because of sb/sth ～の理由で→～のお陰で, ～のせいで, ～のために ∥ We're late, thanks to you! あなたのお陰で私たちは遅れたのです.

a vote of thanks ⇒ **VOTE**¹

**Thanksgiving(Day)** /θæŋksgívɪŋ deɪ; ~-/ 名 Ⓤ Ⓒ ▶定義 a public holiday in the US and in Canada 米国とカナダの公的な祝日→感謝祭 ▶感謝祭は, 米国では11月の第4木曜日, カナダでは10月の第2月曜日である. もともと, 収穫を神に感謝する日であった.

**thank you** 名 Ⓒ ▶定義 an expression of thanks 感謝を表す表現→ありがとう, どうも

\***that** /ðæt/ 形代接副 ▶定義 1 (複 **those** /ðóʊz/) used to refer to a person or thing, especially when he/she/it is not near the person speaking 特に人または物が話し手の近くにいない場合, その人または物に言及するために用いて→あれ, それ, あの, その ∥ I like that house over there. 私は向こうのあの家が気に入っている. What's that in the road? 道路にあるあれは何ですか. 'Could you pass me the book?' 'This one?' 'No, that one over there.' 「その本を取ってくださいませんか」「これですか」「いいえ, 向こうにある, あれです」 ▶定義 2 (複 **those**

# 1678　thatched

/ðóuz/) used for talking about a person or thing already known or mentioned 既に知られている，または言及された人または物について話すために用いて →**例の，あの，あの事，その事，あの時，その時** ‖ *That was the year we went to Spain, wasn't it?* あれは私たちがスペインに行った年でしたよね．*Can you give me back that money I lent you last week?* 先週あなたに貸したあの金を返してくれませんか．▶定義 3 /ðət, 強形 ðæt/ （関係節を導くために用いて）the person or thing already mentioned 既に言及された人または物 →**～であるところの，～をする** ‖ *I'm reading the book that won the Booker prize.* 私はブッカー賞を受賞した本を読んでいる．*The people that live next door are French.* 隣に住んでいる人々はフランス人だ．

▶ that が関係節において動詞の目的語である場合，しばしば省略される: *I want to see the doctor (that) I saw last week.*（私は先週診てもらった医者に診てもらいたい．）*I wore the dress (that) I bought in Paris.*（私はパリで買ったドレスを着た．）

▶定義 4 /ðət, 強形 ðæt/ used after certain verbs, nouns and adjectives to introduce a new part of the sentence 文の新しい部分を導くために，ある動詞，名詞，形容詞の後に用いて →**～ということ** ‖ *She told me that she was leaving.* 彼女はこれから出発すると私に言った．*I hope that you feel better soon.* あなたの気分がすぐに良くなるといいのですが．*I'm certain that he will come.* 私は彼が来ると確信している．*It's funny that you should say that.* あなたがあの事を言うなんて変ですね．

▶次のような文では that は省略されることが多い: *I thought you would like it.*（あなたはそれが気に入るだろうと思っていた．）

▶定義 5（形容詞，副詞と用いて）as much as that それと同じくらい →**それほど，そんなに，あんなに** ‖ *30 miles? I can't walk that far.* 30マイルだって．私はそんなに遠くまで歩けないよ．

成句 **that is (to say)** ▶定義 used when you are giving more information about sb/sth ～についてさらに多くの情報を与えているときに用いて →**すなわち，言い換えると，もっと正確に言うと，つまり** ‖ *I'm on holiday next week. That's to say, from Tuesday.* 私は来週，つまり火曜日から休暇を取ります．

**that's that** ▶定義 there is nothing more to say or do 言う事，またはする事がもうない →**それで終わりだ，それで決まりだ，さあ済んだぞ，それ以上話しても無駄だ** ‖ *I'm not going and that's that.* 行かないと言ったら行かないんだ．

**thatched** /θætʃt/ 形 ▶定義 (used about a building) having a roof made of dried grass (**straw**)（建物について）干し草（わら）でできた屋根がある →**わらぶきの，かやぶきの**

**thaw** /θɔː/ 動 自 他 ▶定義 **thaw (sth) (out)** to become or to make sth become soft or liquid again after freezing 凍った後で柔らかくなる，または再び液体になる，あるいは～をそのようにする →**解ける，解けて元に戻る；～を解かす，解凍する** ‖ *Is the snow thawing?* 雪が解けていますか．*Always thaw chicken thoroughly before you cook it.* 鶏肉は必ず調理する前に完全に解凍してください．● 参 **melt** — **thaw** 名［C，通常は単数］→ **雪解け，解氷，雪解けの暖かさ，緊張緩和**

＊**the** /（子音の前）ðə,（母音の前）ði, 強形 ðiː/ 冠詞 ▶定義 1 used for talking about a person or thing that is already known or that has already been mentioned 既に知られている，または言及された人または物について話すために用いて →**その，あの，この，例の，問題の** ‖ *I took the children to the dentist.* 私はその子供たちを歯医者に連れていった．*We met the man who bought your house.* 私たちはあなたの家を買った男性に会った．*The milk is in the fridge.* 例の牛乳は冷蔵庫に入っている．▶定義 2 used when there is only one of sth ～がただ1つしかないときに用いて ‖ *The sun is very strong today.* 今日は日差しがとても強い．*Who won the World Cup?* ワールドカップで優勝したのはだれですか．*the government* 政府 ▶定義 3 used with numbers and dates 数や日付と共に用いて ‖ *This is the third time I've seen this film.* この映画を見たのはこれで3回目です．*Friday the thirteenth* 13日の金曜日 *I grew up in the sixties.* 私は60年代に育った．▶定義 4 used with adjectives to name a group of people ある人々の集団の名前を言うために，形容詞と共に用いて →**～な[の]人たち** ‖ *the French* フランス人 *the poor* 貧しい人々 ▶定義 5 正式 used with a singular noun when you are talking generally about sth 〜について一般的に話しているときに,単数の名詞と共に用いて→〜というもの ‖ *The dolphin is an intelligent animal.* イルカは賢い動物である. ▶定義 6 with units of measurement, meaning 'every' 単位と共に用い,「〜ごとに」という意味を表して→〜に付き,〜単位で ‖ *Our car does forty miles to the gallon.* 私たちの車は1ガロンで40マイル走る. ▶定義 7 with musical instruments 楽器と共に ‖ *Do you play the piano?* あなたはピアノを弾きますか. ▶定義 8 the well-known or important one よく知られた,または重要なもの→あの有名な,最も重要な,あの,かの,例の ‖ *'My best friend at school was Tony Blair.' 'You mean the Tony Blair?'* 「私の在学中の親友はトニー ブレアでした」「あのトニー ブレアのことですか」

➤この意味の場合,the は /ðiː/ と発音される.

▶定義 9 the...the... used for saying that the way in which two things change is connected 2つの物の変化の仕方が関連していることを述べるために用いて→〜すればするほどますます〜,〜すればするだけ ‖ *The more you eat, the fatter you get.* 食べれば食べるほどますます太る.
➤冠詞についての説明は,巻末の「文法早見表」を参照.

\*__theatre__ /θíətər, θíː-/ (米 **theater**) 名 ▶定義 1 **C** a building where you go to see plays, shows, etc 演劇,ショーなどを見に行く建物→劇場 ‖ *How often do you go to the theatre?* 劇場にはどのくらいよく行きますか. ▶定義 2 **U** plays in general; drama 演劇一般;ドラマ→演劇,劇文学,劇作品 ‖ *He's studying modern Russian theatre.* 彼はロシアの現代演劇を勉強している. ▶定義 3 [単数扱い, **U**] the work of acting in or producing plays 演劇を演じる,または作り出す仕事→演劇界,劇団 ‖ *He's worked in (the) theatre for thirty years.* 彼は(その)劇団で30年仕事をしている. ▶定義 4 **U** = OPERATING THEATRE

__theatrical__ /θiætrɪk(ə)l/ 形 ▶定義 1 (名詞の前だけ) connected with the theatre 演劇・劇場と関連して→演劇の,演劇に関する,劇的な,演劇のための,劇場の ▶定義 2 (used about behaviour) dramatic and exaggerated because you want people to notice it (振る舞いについて)人々に気付いてほしいために,芝居染みていておおげさ

theme 1679

な→芝居がかった,おおげさな,わざとらしい

__theft__ /θeft/ 名 **C U** ▶定義 the crime of stealing sth 〜を盗むという犯罪→盗み,窃盗,窃盗罪 ‖ *There have been a lot of thefts in this area recently.* この地域では最近,窃盗が多発している. *The woman was arrested for theft.* その女性は窃盗罪で逮捕された. ☛参 __thief__ の注

\*__their__ /ðeər, 弱形 ðər/ 代 ▶定義 1 of or belonging to them 彼らの,または彼らに属している→彼らの,彼女らの,それらの ‖ *The children picked up their books and walked to the door.* その子供たちは自分の本を手に取り,ドアまで歩いていった. ▶定義 2 略式 used instead of his or her his または her の代わりに用いて→(その)人の ‖ *Has everyone got their book?* 皆さん,自分の本を持ちましたか.

\*__theirs__ /ðeərz/ 代 ▶定義 of or belonging to them 彼らの,または彼らに属している→彼らのもの,彼女らのもの,それらのもの ‖ *Our flat isn't as big as theirs.* 私たちのアパートは彼らのものほど広くない.

\*__them__ /ðəm, 強形 ðem/ 代 (動詞または前置詞の目的語) ▶定義 1 the people or things mentioned earlier 前に言及された人々または物→彼らを,彼らに,彼女らを,彼女らに,それらを,それらに ‖ *I'll phone them now.* 今,彼らに電話しましょう. *'I've got the keys here.' 'Oh good. Give them to me.'* 「ここにかぎを手に入れました」「ああよかった.それらを私に下さい」 *We have students from several countries but **most of them** are Italian.* 私たちは数か国から学生を受け入れていますが,そのほとんどはイタリア人です. *They asked for your address so I gave it to them.* 彼らがあなたの住所を尋ねてきたので,教えました.

➤ them は,くだけた言い方で言われていることを表すために 'em と書かれることもある.

▶定義 2 略式 him or her 彼または彼女→(その)人を,(その)人に ‖ *If anyone phones, tell them I'm busy.* だれかから電話があったら,私は忙しいと言ってくれ.

__theme__ /θiːm/ 名 **C** ▶定義 the subject of a talk, a piece of writing or a work of art 話,文章,芸術作品の主題→テーマ,主題,題目,論題,話題 ‖ *The theme of today's discussion will be 'Our chang-*

ing cities'. 今日の話し合いのテーマは「変わり行く都市」についてでしょう.

**theme park** 🔹🔹▶定義 a park with a lot of things to do, see, ride on, etc, which are all based on a single idea ある1つの考えにすべて基づいて構成されている、する事、見る物、乗り物がたくさんある公園 →テーマパーク

*****themselves** /ð(ə)msélvz, ðem-/ 🔹 ▶定義1 used when the people or things who do an action are also affected by it ある行動をする人々または物が、その行動によって影響を受けるときに用いて→彼ら自身を、彼ら自身に、彼女ら自身を、彼女ら自身に、それら自体を、それら自体に ‖ *Helen and Sarah seem to be enjoying themselves.* ヘレンとサラは楽しんでいるようだ. *People often talk to themselves when they are worried.* 人は不安なときによく独り言を言う. ▶定義2 used to emphasize 'they' they を強調するために用いて→彼ら自身, 彼女ら自身, それ自体 ‖ *They themselves say that the situation cannot continue.* その状態は続かないだろうと彼ら自身が言っている. *Did they paint the house themselves? (= or did sb else do it for them?)* 彼らは自分たちで家にペンキを塗ったのですか(= それともほかのだれかが彼らのためにそれをしてくれたのですか).

成句 (all) by themselves ▶定義1 alone 単独で→自分たちだけで ‖ *The boys are too young to go out by themselves.* その少年たちは自分たちだけで外出するには幼すぎる. ☞参 alone の注 ▶定義2 without help 助けを得ないで→独力で ‖ *The children cooked the dinner all by themselves.* その子供たちは自分たちだけで夕食を作った.

*****then** /ðen/ 副 ▶定義1 (at) that time あの時(に) →その時, あの時, その当時, そのころ ‖ *In 1990? I was at university then.* 1990年かい. 私はそのころ大学に在学中だったよ. *I spoke to him on Wednesday, but I haven't seen him since then.* 私は水曜日に彼と話したが、その時からずっと会っていない. *They met in 1941 and remained close friends from then on.* 彼らは1941年に出会い、それ以来ずっと親友でいた. *I'm going tomorrow. Can you wait until then?* 私は明日行きます. それまで待てますか. *Phone me tomorrow - I will have decided by then.* 明日電話をください－それまでに決めておきますから. ▶定義2 next; after that 次に; その後に→それから, その次に, 今度は ‖ *I'll have a shower and get changed, then we'll go out.* 私がシャワーを浴びて着替えてから出掛けましょう. *There was silence for a minute. Then he replied.* 少しの間、沈黙があった. それから彼は返事をした.

▶定義3 used to show the logical result of a statement or situation ある陳述や状況の論理的な結果を示すために用いて→それなら, それでは, そういうことなら, そうすれば ‖ *'I don't feel at all well.' 'Why don't you go to the doctor then?'* 「私は気分がとても悪いです」「それなら医者に行ったらどうですか」 *If you don't do any work then you'll fail the exam.* 全く勉強しないのならば試験に落ちるでしょうね. ▶定義4 (口語) (used after words like now, okay, right, etc to show the beginning or end of a conversation or statement) (会話や陳述の初め、または終わりを表すために, now, okay, right などの言葉の後に用いて)→それでは、では, さて ‖ *Now then, are we all ready to go?* さて、出掛ける準備はできましたか. *Right then, I'll see you tomorrow.* それでは明日お会いしましょう.

成句 then/there again ⇒ AGAIN
there and then; then and there ⇒ THERE

**thence** /ðens/ 副 (古) ▶定義 from there →そこから

**theology** /θiάlədʒi/ 🔹🔹 ▶定義 the study of religion 宗教についての学問→神学 — **theological** /θi:ələdʒik(ə)l/ 形 →神学の, 神学上の, 神学的な

**theoretical** /θi:ərétik(ə)l/ 形 ▶定義1 based on ideas and principles, not on practical experience 実際的な経験ではなく、考えや原理に基づいている→理論の, 理論的な, 理論に基づいた ‖ *A lot of university courses are still too theoretical these days.* 大学の課程の多くは、今日でもいまだに理論に偏りすぎている. ▶定義2 that may possibly exist or happen, although it is unlikely ありそうではないが、ひょっとすると存在する、または起こるかもしれない→理論上の, 仮説の, 理論の上だけで存在する ‖ *There is a theoretical possibility that the world will end tomorrow.* 世界が明日終わりになるという可能性は理論上ある. ☞参 practical — **theoretically** /-k(ə)li/

副 →理論上は, 名目上は

**theory** /θíəri/ 名 (複 **theories**) ▶定義1 ⓒ an idea or set of ideas that try to explain sth 〜を説明しようとするある考え方, または一連の考え方 → **学説, 〜論, 理論, 学理, 仮説** ‖ *the theory about how life on earth began* 地球上の生命がどのように始まったかについての学説 ▶定義2 ⓤ the general idea or principles of a particular subject ある主題についての一般的な考え方, または原理 → **理論, 原理** ‖ *political theory* 政治理論 *the theory and practice of language teaching* 言語教育についての理論と実際 ▶定義3 ⓒ an opinion or a belief that has not been shown to be true 正しいということがまだ示されていない意見または信念 → **推測, 憶測, 意見, 持論**

成句 **in theory** ▶定義 as a general idea which may not be true in reality 実際は正しくないかもしれない, 一般的な考えとして → **理論上は, 理論的には, 理屈では** ‖ *Your plan sounds fine in theory, but I don't know if it'll work in practice.* あなたの計画は理論的には良くできているが, それが実際にうまくいくかどうかは分からない.

**therapeutic** /θèrəpjúːtɪk/ 形 ▶定義1 helping you to relax and feel better くつろぎ, 気分が良くなるのを促している → **治療効果のある, 治癒力のある, 健康維持に役立つ** ‖ *I find listening to music very therapeutic.* 音楽を聴くことはとても治療効果があると思う. ▶定義2 helping to cure an illness 病気を治療するのに役立つ → **治療の, 治療に関する, 治療できる** ‖ *therapeutic drugs* 治療薬

**therapy** /θérəpi/ 名 ⓤ ▶定義 treatment to help or cure a mental or physical illness, usually without drugs or medical operations 精神的または肉体的な病気を, 通常は薬や医療手術によらないで和らげたり治療したりする方法 → **治療, 療法** ‖ *to have/undergo therapy* 治療を受ける・行う ― **therapist** /θérəpɪst/ 名 ⓒ → **セラピスト, 治療専門家, 療法士** ‖ *a speech therapist* 言語療法士

**\*there** /ðeər, 弱形 ðər/ 副 代 ▶定義1 used as the subject of 'be', 'seem', 'appear', etc to say that sth exists 〜が存在することを述べるために be, seem, appear などの主語として用いて → **〜がある, 〜がいる** ‖ *Is there a god?* 神様はいますか. *There's a man at the door.* 戸口に男が1人いる. *There wasn't much to eat.* 食べる物があまりなかった. *There's somebody singing outside.* だれか外で歌を歌っている人がいる. *There seems to be a mistake here.* ここに間違いがあるようだ. ▶定義2 in, at or to that place その場所で, その場所へ → **そこに, そこで, そこへ** ‖ *Could you put the table there, please?* テーブルをそこに置いてくださいませんか. *I like Milan. My husband and I met there.* 私はミラノが好きです. 主人と私はそこで出会ったので. *Have you been to Bonn? We're going there next week.* ボンに行ったことがありますか. 私たちはそこへ来週行く予定です. *Have you looked under there?* そこの下を見ましたか.

▶定義3 used for calling attention to sth 〜に注意を促すために用いて → **ほら, そら, さあ** ‖ *Oh look, there's Kate!* 見てごらん, ほら, ケートだ. *Hello there! Can anyone hear me?* やあ, 元気かい. みんな私の声が聞こえますか.

▶定義4 at that point (in a conversation, story, etc) その点で (会話, 話などの中で) → **その点で, その箇所で, そこで** ‖ *Could I interrupt you there for a minute?* そこでちょっとお話の邪魔をしてもよろしいでしょうか. ▶定義5 available if needed 必要があれば利用できる → **すぐに助けてくれる** ‖ *Her parents are always there if she needs help.* 彼女の両親は, 彼女が助けを必要とすれば, いつでもすぐに助けてくれる.

成句 **be there for sb** ▶定義 to be available to help and support sb when he/she has a problem 〜が問題を抱えているときに, 助けたり支えたりすることができる → **すぐに助けてくれる** ‖ *Whenever I'm in trouble, my sister is always there for me.* 私が困っているときにはいつでもすぐに姉が助けてくれる.

**then/there again** ⇒ **AGAIN**

**there and then; then and there** ▶定義 immediately; at that time and place 直ちに; その時間と場所で → **即刻, その時その場で, すぐその場で, 直ちに**

**there you are** ▶定義1 used when you give sth to sb 〜を…に渡すときに用いて → **はいどうぞ, さあどうぞ** ‖ *There you are. I've bought you a newspaper.* はいどうぞ. 新聞を買ってきました. ▶定義2 used when you are explaining sth to sb ~に…を説明しているときに用いて→**ほらごらん, 言った通りだろう** ‖ *Just press the switch and there you are!* ただそのスイッチを押せばいいのですよ. ほら言った通りでしょう.

**thereabouts** /ðéərəbàuts/ （困 **thereabout** /ðéərəbàut/) 副（通常 or の後で）▶定義 somewhere near a number, time or place ある数字, 時刻, 場所などに近いどこかで→**その辺りに, そのころ, それくらい, その前後に, およそ** ‖ *There are 100 students, or thereabouts.* 100人かそこらの生徒がいる. *She lives in Sydney, or thereabouts.* 彼女はシドニーかその辺りに住んでいる.

**thereafter** /ðeərǽːftər, -ǽf-/ 副（文）▶定義 after that その後で →**その後は, それ以来, それから先**

**thereby** /ðèərbái/ 副（文）in that way その方法で→**それによって, その方法によって**

**therefore** /ðéərfɔ̀ːr/ 副 ▶定義 for that reason その理由のために→**それゆえに, したがって, その結果, だから** ‖ *The new trains have more powerful engines and are therefore faster.* その新しい電車はより強力なエンジンがある. だからもっと速く走る. ☛類 **thus**

**therein** /ðèərín/ 副（文）▶定義 because of sth that has just been mentioned 言及されたばかりの~のために→**その中に, その点に, そこに**

**thereupon** /ðéərəpɔ̀(ː)n, -əpɑ̀n/ 副（文）▶定義 immediately after that and often as the result of sth その直後に, しばしば~の結果として→**その結果, そのすぐ後で, そこで早速**

**thermal**¹ /θɔ́ːrm(ə)l/ 形 ▶定義1 connected with heat 熱に関連している→**熱の, 温度の** ‖ *thermal energy* 熱エネルギー ▶定義2 (used about clothes) made to keep you warm in cold weather (衣服について) 寒い天候のときに暖かさを保つように作られている→**保温用の, 防寒用の** ‖ *thermal underwear* 防寒用の下着

**thermal**² /θɔ́ːrm(ə)l/ 名 ▶定義1 **thermals** [複数扱い] clothes, especially underwear, made to keep you warm in cold weather 寒い天候のときに暖かさを保つように作られている衣服, 特に下着→**防寒着** ▶定義2 **C** a flow of rising warm air 上昇する暖かい空気の流れ→**上昇温暖気流**

*****thermometer** /θəmάmətər/ 名 **C** ▶定義 an instrument for measuring the temperature of sb's body or of a room ~の体や部屋の温度を計測するための器具→**温度計, 寒暖計, 体温計**

**Thermos**™ /θɔ́ːrməs/ （または **Thermos flask**) 名 **C** ▶定義 a type of container used for keeping a liquid hot or cold 液体を暖かく, または冷たく保つために使われる容器の一種→**サーモス, 魔法びん, ポット**

**thermostat** /θɔ́ːrməstæ̀t/ 名 **C** ▶定義 a device that controls the temperature in a house or machine by switching the heat on and off as necessary 家の中や機械の温度を, 必要に応じて温度のスイッチを切り替えることによって調整する装置→**自動温度調節装置, サーモスタット**

**thesaurus** /θɪsɔ́ːrəs/ 名 **C** （複 **thesauruses**) a book that contains lists of words and phrases with similar meanings 類似した意味の単語や句を掲載している本→**類義語辞典, 分類語彙（ごい）辞典, シソーラス**

**these** ⇒ **THIS**

**thesis** /θíːsəs/ 名 **C** （複 **theses** /θíːsìːz/) ▶定義1 a long piece of writing on a particular subject that you do as part of a university degree 大学の学位の一部として取り組む, ある特定のテーマについての長い文章→**学位請求論文, 卒業論文** ‖ *He did his thesis on Japanese investment in Europe.* 彼は日本のヨーロッパへの投資について卒業論文を書いた. ☛参 **dissertation**
▶定義2 an idea that is discussed and presented with evidence in order to show that it is true それが正しいことを示すために議論され, 証拠と共に提示されるある考え→**命題, 定立, テーゼ**

*****they** /ðéɪ, (特に母音の前) ðe/ 代（動詞の主語）
▶定義1 the people or things that have been mentioned 既に言及されている人々または複数の物→**彼らは, 彼女らは, それらは** ‖ *We've got two children. They're both boys.* 私たちには子供が2人いる. 彼らは2人とも男の子だ. *'Have you seen my keys?' 'Yes, they're on the table.'* 「私のかぎを見掛けましたか」「ええ, それらはテーブルの上にありますよ」 ▶定義2 people in general or people whose identity is not known or stated 一般の人々, または身元が知られていない, あるいは述べられていない人々→**人々は, 世の人は, みんなは** ‖ *They say it's going to be a mild winter.* 暖冬になるという話だ. ▶定義3 略式 used instead of he or she he または she の

代わりに用いて➔**彼らは, 彼女らは, その人は** ‖ *Somebody phoned for you but they didn't leave their name.* だれかがあなたに電話をかけてきたが, その人は名前を言わなかった.

**they'd** /ðéɪd/ THEY HAD, THEY WOULD の短縮形

**they'll** /ðéɪl/ THEY WILL の短縮形

**they're** /ðéər/ THEY ARE の短縮形

**they've** /ðéɪv/ THEY HAVE の短縮形

★**thick**¹ /θɪk/ 形 ▶定義1 (used about sth solid) having a large distance between its opposite sides; not thin (固体の〜について)反対側との間に大きな隔たりがある; 薄くない➔**厚い, 厚みのある, 太い, 肉太の** ‖ *a thick black line* 黒い太線 *a thick coat/book* 厚手の上着・分厚い本 *These walls are very thick.* これらの壁はとても厚みがある. ▶定義2 used for saying what the distance is between the two opposite sides of something ある物の反対に位置する2つの面がどのくらい離れているか, を述べるために用いて➔**厚さが〜の, 太さが〜の** ‖ *The ice was six centimetres thick.* その氷は厚さが6センチあった. ▶定義3 having a lot of things close together たくさんの物が密集している➔**密な, 込み合った, 密集した, 茂った, 濃い** ‖ *a thick forest* 密林 *thick hair* 濃い髪 ▶定義4 (used about a liquid) that does not flow easily (液体について)滑らかに流れないような➔**どろっとした, 濃厚な, 濃密な, 濃い, 濁った** ‖ *thick cream* 濃いクリーム *This paint is too thick.* このペンキは濃すぎる. ⇔ 定義1〜4 thin ▶定義5 (used about fog, smoke, etc) difficult to see through (霧, 煙などについて)見通すのが難しい➔**濃い, どんよりした, 深い, 曇った, よどんだ** ‖ *There'll be a thick fog tonight.* 今晩は濃い霧が出るだろう. *thick clouds of smoke* もうもうとした煙 ▶定義6 **thick (with sth)** containing a lot of sth/sb close together たくさんの〜が密集して入っている➔**〜で一杯の, 〜で覆われた** ‖ *The air was thick with dust.* 空気はほこりで一杯だった. *The streets were thick with shoppers.* 通りは買い物客であふれていた. ▶定義7 (used about sb's accent) very strong (〜のなまりについて)とても強い➔**ひどくなまった** ▶定義8 略式 slow to learn or understand; stupid 学んだり理解したりするのが遅い; 愚かな➔**頭の回転が悪い, 鈍い, 愚鈍な** ― **thick** 副 ➔**厚く, 太く, 濃く**

に ‖ *Snow lay thick on the ground.* 雪が地面に厚く積もった. ― **thickly** 副 ➔**厚く, 太く, 濃く, 密集して** ‖ *Spread the butter thickly.* バターを厚く塗ってください. *a thickly wooded area* 木がうっそうと茂った地域

成句 **have a thick skin** ▶定義 to be not easily upset or worried by what people say about you 人が自分について言った言葉によって, すぐに腹を立てたり悩んだりしない➔(批評・非難に)**傷付かない, 鈍感だ**

**thick**² /θɪk/ 名

成句 **in the thick of sth** ▶定義 in the most active or crowded part of sth; very involved in sth 〜において最も活発な, または詰まった部分に; 〜に深くかかわっている➔**〜のまっただ中に**

**through thick and thin** ▶定義 through difficult times and situations 困難な時期や状況を経て➔**困難に負けずに, どんな事があっても, 万難を排して**

**thicken** /θɪk(ə)n/ 動 自 他 ▶定義 to become or to make sth thicker より厚く・太く・濃くなる, または〜をより厚く・太く・濃くする➔**厚くなる, 太くなる, 濃密になる, 〜を厚くする, 太くする, 濃密にする**

**thickness** /θɪknəs/ 名 C U ▶定義 the quality of being thick or how thick sth is 厚い・太い・濃いという性質, または〜がどのくらい厚い・太い・濃いかということ➔**厚いこと, 太いこと, 濃いこと, 厚さ, 太さ, 濃さ**

**thick-skinned** 形 ▶定義 not easily worried or upset by what other people say about you 他人が自分について言った言葉によって, すぐに悩んだり腹を立てたりしない➔(批評・侮辱などに対して)**鈍感な, 無神経な, 面の皮の厚い, 厚顔な** ‖ *Politicians have to be thick-skinned.* 政治家は厚顔でなければならない.

★**thief** /θiːf/ 名 C (複 **thieves** /θiːvz/) ▶定義 a person who steals things from another person ほかの人から物を盗む人➔**泥棒, こそ泥, かっ払い**

▶ thief は, 通常, 暴力を働かないでこっそりと物を盗む人に対する一般的な語である. そのような犯罪は theft (窃盗) という. robber は, 銀行や店などから盗みを働き, 暴力または脅迫をすることが多い. burglar は, 多くは夜

に，家や店などに侵入して物を盗む，shoplifter は，店が開いているときに押し入り，金を払わないで物を持っていく．mugger は，路上で人から盗みを働き，暴力または脅迫をする．steal の注を参照．

**thigh** /θáɪ/ 名 ● 定義 the top part of your leg, above your knee ひざより上の, 足の一番上の部分 → **太もも, 大腿（だいたい）部** ☞ C5 ページのさし絵

**thimble** /θímb(ə)l/ 名 ● 定義 a small metal or plastic object that you wear on the end of your finger to protect it when you are sewing 裁縫をしているときに指先を保護するために付ける, 金属またはプラスチック製の小さな物 → **指ぬき**

★**thin**¹ /θín/ 形 (**thinner**; **thinnest**) ▶定義 1 (used about sth solid) having a small distance between the opposite sides; not thick (固体の〜について) 反対側との間の小さな隔たりがある; 厚くない → **薄い, 細い, 細長い, 肉細の** ‖ *a thin book/shirt* 薄い本・シャツ *a thin slice of meat* 1 切れの薄切り肉 ▶定義 2 having very little fat on the body; not fat 体にほんのわずかの脂肪しか付いていない; 太っていない → **やせた, ほっそりした, 細い** ‖ *You need to eat more. You're too thin!* あなたはもっと食べる必要がありますよ. やせすぎですよ.

▶ thin, skinny, slim, underweight はどれも同じような意味を持っている. thin は, 体に肉がほんのわずかしか付いていない人を描写するための, 最も一般的な語である. slim は, 魅力的にやせている人を描写するときに用いられる: *You're so slim! How do you do it?* (あなたはとてもすらっとしていますね. どうやってそのようになったのですか.) 〜が skinny であると言う場合は, その〜がやせすぎていて魅力的ではないことを意味している. underweight はかなり改まった語で, 医学的にやせすぎている人を表すために用いられることが多い: *The doctor says I'm underweight.* (その医者は私がやせすぎであると言っている.)

▶定義 3 (used about a liquid) that flows easily; not thick (液体について) 滑らかに流れるような; どろっとしていない → **薄い, 水っぽい, 弱い** ‖ *a thin sauce* 薄いソース ▶定義 4 (used about mist, smoke, etc) not difficult to see through (霧, 煙などについて) 見通すのが難しくない → **希薄な** ▶定義 5 having only a few people or things with a lot of space between them ほんのわずかの人または物しかなく, それらの間に大きな間隔がある → **まばらな, 薄い, 少ない** ‖ *The population is rather thin in this part of the country.* その国のこの地域では, 人口がかなり少ない. ⇔ 定義 1, 3, 4 **thick** — **thin** 副 → **薄く, 細く, まばらに** ‖ *Don't slice the onion too thin.* タマネギをあまり薄く切らないでください. — thinly 副 → **薄く, 細く, まばらに, 貧弱に** ‖ *thinly sliced bread* 薄切りのパン *thinly populated areas* 人口の少ない地域

成句 thin on the ground ⇒ **GROUND**¹
through thick and thin ⇒ **THICK**²
vanish, etc into thin air ▶定義 to disappear completely 完全に消える → **跡形もなく消える**
wear thin ⇒ **WEAR**¹

★**thin**² /θín/ 動 自 他 (**thinning**; **thinned**) ▶定義 thin (sth) (out) to become thinner or fewer in number; to make sth thinner より薄くなる, または数が少なくなる; 〜をより薄くする → **薄くなる, 減る; 〜を薄くする, 減らす, まばらにする** ‖ *The trees thin out towards the edge of the forest.* 木は森の外れへ行くほどまばらになる. *Thin the sauce by adding milk.* 牛乳を加えてソースを薄めてください.

★**thing** /θíŋ/ 名 ▶定義 1 ● an object that is not named 名前の挙げられていない物 → **物, 物体** ‖ *What's that red thing on the table?* テーブルの上にあるあの赤い物は何ですか. *A pen is a thing you use for writing with.* ペンは, 書くために使う物だ. *I need to get a few things at the shops.* 店でいくつかの物を買う必要がある. ▶定義 2 ● a quality or state 質または状態 → **(形のない) もの** ‖ *There's **no such thing as** a ghost (= it doesn't exist).* 幽霊のようなものなどない (= 存在しない). *The best thing about my job is the way it changes all the time.* 私の仕事について最も良い点は, 常に変化があることです. ▶定義 3 ● an action, event or statement → **活動, 出来事, 陳述** ‖ *When I get home the first thing I do is have a cup of tea.* 家に帰って私が最初にすることは, お茶を 1 杯飲むことだ. *A strange thing happened to me yesterday.* 奇妙な事が昨日私に起こった. *What a nice thing to say!* 何てすてきな

言葉でしょう. ▶定義4 ❻a fact, subject, etc 事実, 主題など ➡言いたい事, 話, 考え, 意見, 問題, 情報 ‖ *He told me a few things that I didn't know before.* 彼は, 私が前に知らなかった事実をいくつか話してくれた. ▶定義5 **things**[複数扱い] clothes or tools that belong to sb or are used for a particular purpose ~に属している, またはある目的で使われる衣服や道具 ➡持ち物, 所持品, 衣服, 着物, 道具, 用具 ‖ *I'll just go and pack my things.* ちょっと行って身の回りの物を荷造りしよう. *We keep all the cooking things in this cupboard.* 私たちはすべての調理用具をこの食器棚に入れています. ▶定義6 **things**[複数扱い] the situation or conditions of your life 生活の状態または状況 ➡事態, 状況, 状態, 形勢 ‖ *How are things with you?* 調子はいかがですか.

▶定義7 ❻used for expressing how you feel about a person or an animal ある人または動物についてどのように感じているかを表すために用いて ➡人, やつ ‖ *You've broken your finger? You poor thing!* 指を折ってしまったの. かわいそうに. ▶定義8 **the thing** [単数扱い] exactly what is wanted or needed 正確に求められている, または必要とされていること ➡正しいこと, 当を得たこと, 重要なこと ‖ *That's just the thing I was looking for!* それこそが私の探していたものです.

成句 a close shave/thing ⇒ **CLOSE**³
be a good thing (that) ▶定義 to be lucky that ~とは運がいい ➡~とは幸運だ, ~でよかった ‖ *It's a good thing you remembered your umbrella.* あなたが自分の傘のことを思い出してくれてよかった.

do your own thing ▶定義 to do what you want to do, independently of other people 他人とは無関係に, 自分のしたいことをする ➡自分勝手に振る舞う, 好きな事をする, 自分のしたい通りにする
first/last thing ▶定義 as early/late as possible できるだけ早く・遅く ➡何はさておき, 真っ先に; 最後に ‖ *I'll telephone her first thing tomorrow morning.* 私は明日の朝一番に彼女に電話をしよう. *I saw him last thing on Friday evening.* 私は金曜日の晩の終わりに彼を見た.
for one thing ▶定義 used for introducing a reason for something ある事の理由を導入するために用いて ➡1つには, 第1には ‖ *I think we should go by train. For one thing it's cheaper.* 私たちは電車で行くべきだと思います. 1つには, その方が安いからです.

have a thing about sb/sth 語式 ▶定義 to have strong feelings about sb/sth ~について熱心な気持ちを持っている ➡~が大好きである, ~に取り付かれている, ~を毛嫌いする, 恐れている
to make matters/things worse ⇒ **WORSE**
take it/things easy ⇒ **EASY**²

\*think /θɪŋk/ 勔 ( 過, 過分 thought /θɔːt/)
▶定義1 ❺⑭ think (sth) (of/about sb/sth); think that... to have a particular idea or opinion about sth/sb; to believe ~についてある考え, または意見を持っている; 信じる ➡~と思う, 考える, 信じる ‖ *'Do you think (that) we'll win?' 'No, I don't think so.'* 「あなたは私たちが勝つと思いますか」「いいえ, そうは思いません」 *'Sue's coming tomorrow, isn't she?' 'Yes, I think so.'* 「スーは明日, 来ますよね」「ええ, そう思います」 *I think (that) they've moved to York but I'm not sure.* 私は彼らがヨークに引っ越したと思うが, 確かではない. *What did you think of the film?* その映画についてどう思いましたか. *What do you think about going out tonight?* 今晩出掛けるのはどうですか. *Gary's on holiday, I think.* ゲーリーは休暇を取っていると思います.

▶定義2 ❺ think (about sth) to use your mind to consider sth or to form connected ideas 頭を使って~を熟慮する, または関連する考えをまとめる ➡考える, 熟考する, 検討する ‖ *Think before you speak.* 話す前によく考えなさい. *What are you thinking about?* 何について考えているのですか. *He had to think hard (= a lot) about the question.* 彼はその質問について一生懸命(= よく)考えなければならなかった.

▶定義3 ❺ think of/about doing sth; think that... to intend or plan to do sth ~をするつもりである, または計画している ➡~のつもりになる, ~しようかと考えている ‖ *We're thinking of moving house.* 私たちは引っ越しをしようかと考えている. *I think I'll go for a swim.* 私は泳ぎに行こうと思います. ▶定義4 ❺to form an idea of sth; to imagine sth ~についての考えをまとめる; ~を想像する ➡考え付く, 想像がつく ‖ *Just think what we could do with all that money!* その金全部で一体何ができるか, ちょっ

と考えてごらん. ▶定義5 ⓔ think about/of sb to consider the feelings of sb else ほかの〜の気持ちを考慮に入れる➔考える, 思い巡らす, 考慮する, 思いやる ‖ *She never thinks about anyone but herself.* 彼女は決して自分以外の人について思いやることはない. ▶定義6 ⓜ to remember sth; to have sth come into your mind 〜を覚えている; 〜を心に浮かばせる➔〜を思い出す, 〜を覚えている ‖ *Can you think where you left the keys?* かぎをどこに置いてきたか思い出せますか. *I didn't think to ask him his name.* 私は彼に名前を尋ねるのを忘れていた. ▶定義7 ⓜ to expect sth 〜を予想する➔〜だと予期する, 予想する ‖ *The job took longer than we thought.* その仕事は私たちが予想していたよりも長くかかった. ▶定義8 ⓔ to think in a particular way ある方法で考える➔〜な考え方をする ‖ *If you want to be successful, you have to* ***think big.*** 成功したいと思うのならば, 大きな事を考えなさい. *We've got to* ***think positive.*** 前向きに考えなければならない. — think 图 [単数扱い] ➔ 考えること, 一考, 思考, 考え, 見解 ‖ *I'm not sure. I'll have to* ***have a think*** *about it.* 私には分かりません. それについて考えなければなりません.

成句 think better of (doing) sth ▶定義 to decide not to do sth; to change your mind 〜をしないことに決める; 考えを変える➔〜を見直す, 考え直してやめる

think highly, a lot, not much, etc of sb/sth ▶定義 to have a good, bad, etc opinion of sb/sth 〜について良い, 悪いなどの意見を持つ➔〜を高く評価する, 重んじる, 良いと思う; 軽べつする, 軽んじる ‖ *I didn't think much of that film.* 私はその映画があまりいいとは思わなかった.

think the world of sb ▶定義 to love and admire sb very much 〜をとても愛し, 賞賛する➔〜をとても大切に思っている, 〜が大好きである, 最高に重んじる, 高く買う

句動詞 think of sth ▶定義 to create an idea in your imagination 想像してある考えを生み出す➔〜を思い付く, 考え付く, 考え出す, 案出する ‖ *Who first thought of the plan?* だれが最初にその計画を思い付いたのですか.

think sth out ▶定義 to consider carefully all the details of a plan, idea, etc ある計画, 考えなどの詳細のすべてを入念に検討する➔〜を考え抜く, 慎重に検討する ‖ *a well-thought-out scheme* よく考え抜かれた計画

think sth over ▶定義 to consider sth carefully 〜を慎重に検討する➔〜をじっくりと考える, 熟考する, よく考える ‖ *I'll think your offer over and let you know tomorrow.* あなたの申し出をじっくり考えて, 明日お知らせします.

think sth through ▶定義 to consider every detail of sth carefully 〜のあらゆる詳細を入念に検討する➔〜をよく考える, 考え抜く, 篤と考える ‖ *He made a bad decision because he didn't think it through.* 彼はそれについてよく考えなかったため, 不適切な決定をした.

think sth up ▶定義 to create sth in your mind; to invent 心の中で〜を生み出す; 考案する➔〜を考え出す, 思い付く, 発明する, 案出する ‖ *to think up a new advertising slogan* 広告の新しいキャッチフレーズを考え出す

**thinker** /θíŋkər/ 图 ⓒ ▶定義1 a person who thinks about serious and important subjects 重大な, または重要なテーマについて考える人➔思索家, 思想家 ▶定義2 a person who thinks in a particular way あるやり方で考える人➔考え方が〜の人, 〜な考え方をする人 ‖ *a quick/creative/clear thinker* 素早く・独創的に・明せきにものを考える人

**thinking**¹ /θíŋkɪŋ/ 图 ⓤ ▶定義1 using your mind to think about sth 頭を使って〜について考えること➔思考, 思索, 考え事 ‖ *We're going to have to do some quick thinking.* 私たちはすぐに考えてみなければならないだろう. ▶定義2 ideas or opinions about sth 〜についての考え, または意見➔考え, 判断, 意見, 見解 ‖ *This accident will make them change their thinking on safety matters.* この事故は, 安全の問題についての彼らの考えを変えるだろう. ☛参 **wishful thinking**

**thinking**² /θíŋkɪŋ/ 厖 ▶定義 intelligent and using your mind to think about important subjects 賢明で, 頭を使って重要なテーマについて考えている➔知的な, 知性のある, 思考力のある, 分別のある

★**third**¹ /θɚːrd/ 代形副 ▶定義 3rd➔3番目 (の, に), 第3 (の, に) ☛参 **sixth** の例

**third**² /θɚːrd/ 图 ⓒ ▶定義1 the fraction 1/3; one

of three equal parts of sth 分数の1/3; 〜の均等な3個の部分の1つ→**3分の1** ▶定義2 医a result in final university exams, below first and second class degrees 大学の最終試験での結果で, 第1級, 第2級の下→**最下位の成績, 第3級**

**thirdly** /θə́ːrdli/ ▶定義 used to introduce the third point in a list 一覧表において3つ目の点を導入するために用いて→**第3に, 3番目に** ‖ *We have made savings in three areas: firstly, defence, secondly, education and thirdly, health.* 私たちは次の3つの分野で蓄えをした. 第1に防衛, 第2に教育, 第3に医療である.

**third party** 名 ⓒ ▶定義 a person who is involved in a situation in addition to the two main people involved 主な関係者2人に加えて, ある状況にかかわっている人→**第三者, 第三当事者**

**the Third World** 名 [単数扱い] ▶定義 the poorer countries of Asia, Africa and South America アジア, アフリカ, 南アメリカの中の貧しい国々→**第三世界**

**thirst** /θəːrst/ 名 ▶定義1 [Ⓤ, 単数扱い] the feeling that you have when you want or need a drink 飲み物が欲しいとき, または必要なときに抱く気持ち→**のどの渇き** ‖ *Cold tea really quenches your thirst.* 冷たいお茶は実にのどの渇きをいやしてくれる. *to die of thirst* 脱水症で死ぬ ▶定義2 [単数扱い] **a thirst for sth** a strong desire for sth 〜への強い欲望→**〜への渇望, 熱望, 切望** ☛参 **hunger**

*****thirsty** /θə́ːrsti/ 形 (**thirstier**; **thirstiest**) ▶定義 wanting or needing a drink 飲み物を欲している, または必要としている→**のどが渇いた** ‖ *I'm thirsty. Can I have a drink of water, please?* のどが渇いているのですが, 水を1杯頂けませんか.
☛参 **hungry** ― **thirstily** 副 →**のどが渇いて**

*****thirteen** /θə̀ːrtíːn/ 名/形 ▶定義 13
▶文中での数詞の使い方については, **six** の項を参照.

**thirteenth** /θə̀ːrtíːnθ, -/ 代/形/副 ▶定義 13th →**13番目(の, に), 第13(の, に)** ☛参 **sixth** の例

**thirtieth** /θə́ːrtiəθ/ 代/形/副 ▶定義 30th→**30番目(の, に), 第30(の, に)** ☛参 **sixth** の例

*****thirty** /θə́ːrti/ 名/形 ▶定義 30
▶文中での数詞の使い方については, **six** の項を参照.

# this 1687

*****this** /ðɪs/ 形/代 (複 **these** /ðiːz/) ▶定義1 used for talking about sb/sth that is close to you in time or space 時間的または空間的に自分に近い〜について話すために用いて→**これ, この, ここの, こちらの** ‖ *Have a look at this photo.* この写真を見てください. *These boots are really comfortable. My old ones weren't.* これらのブーツはとても履き心地が良い. 私の古いブーツはそうではなかった. *Is this the book you asked for?* これがあなたが求めていた本ですか. *These are the letters to be filed, not those over there.* これらがファイルしておく手紙です. あちらにある手紙ではありません. *This chair's softer than that one, so I'll sit here.* このいすはあれよりも柔らかいから, 私はこっちに座ろう.

▶定義2 used for talking about sth that was mentioned or talked about earlier 前に言及された, または話題になった〜について話すために用いて→**これ, この事** ‖ *Where did you hear about this?* この事についてあなたはどこで聞いたのですか. ▶定義3 used for introducing sb or showing sb sth 〜を紹介する, または〜に…を見せるために用いて→**この人, この物, これ** ‖ *This is my wife, Claudia, and these are our children, David and Vicky.* これが妻のクローディアで, こちらが私たちの子供のデーヴィッドとヴィッキーです. *It's easier if you do it like this.* こうしたら, もっと簡単だ. ▶定義4 (used with days of the week or periods of time) of today or the present week, year, etc (曜日または期間と共に用いて) 今日の, または現在の週, 年などの→**今の, 今日の, 現在の, 今度の, この次の** ‖ *Are you busy this afternoon?* あなたは今日の午後は忙しいですか. *this Friday (= the Friday of this week)* この金曜日 (=今週の金曜日) ▶定義5 略式 (used when you are telling a story) a certain (物語を聞かせているときに用いて) ある→**ある1人の, ある1つの** ‖ *Then this woman said...* それからある女の人がこう言いました. ― **this** 副 →**こんなに, これほど, これだけ** ‖ *The road is not usually this busy.* その道路はいつもこれほど車が多くはない.

成句 **this and that; this, that and the other**
▶定義 various things さまざまなもの→**あれやこれや, あれこれ, いろいろな事, あらゆる種類の**

もの ‖ We chatted about this and that. 私たちはあれやこれやとおしゃべりした.

**thistle** /θísəl/ 名 C ▶定義 a wild plant with purple flowers and sharp points (prickles) on its leaves 紫色の花をつけ, 葉にとがった部分(とげ)がある野草 →アザミ ☞ C2 ページのさし絵

**thong** /θɔː(ː)ŋ, θɑŋ/ 米 = FLIP-FLOP

**thorn** /θɔːrn/ 名 C ▶定義 one of the hard sharp points on some plants and bushes, for example on rose bushes 例えばバラの茂みなどの植物や低木にある, 固くてとがった部分の1つ →とげ ☞ C2 ページのさし絵

**thorny** /θɔ́ːrni/ 形 ▶定義1 causing difficulty or disagreement 困難または不一致を引き起こしている →厄介な, 面倒な, 扱いにくい, 困難な ‖ a thorny problem/question 面倒な問題・厄介な質問 ▶定義2 having thorns とげを持っている →とげのある, とげの多い, とげだらけの, とげのような

*__thorough__ /θə́ːrə; θə́ːroʊ/ 形 ▶定義1 careful and complete 入念で完全な →徹底的な, 完ぺきな, 完全な ‖ The police made a thorough search of the house. 警察はその家を徹底的に捜索した.

▶定義2 doing things in a very careful way, making sure that you look at every detail 物事を非常に慎重に行い, 必ず細部まですべて見ている →非常に注意深い, きちょうめんな, 細心な, 周到な ‖ Pam is slow but she is very thorough. パムは反応が遅いけれども非常にきちょうめんだ. — thoroughness 名 U →完全, 徹底

**thoroughly** /θə́ːrəli; θə́ːroʊ-/ 副 ▶定義1 in a careful and complete way 入念で完全に →徹底的に, 完全に, 入念に, 綿密に ‖ to study a subject thoroughly あるテーマを綿密に研究する

▶定義2 completely; very much すっかり; 非常に →全く, 存分に, すっかり ‖ We thoroughly enjoyed our holiday. 私たちは休日を存分に楽しんだ.

**those** THAT(1,2) の複数形

*__though__ /ðoʊ/ 接 副 ▶定義1 in spite of the fact that; although 〜という事実にもかかわらず; 〜であるけれども →〜だけれども, 〜にもかかわらず, たとえ〜でも ‖ Though he had very little money, Alex always managed to dress smartly. アレックスは金をほとんど持っていなくても, いつもこぎれいな身なりでいようとした. She still loved him even though he had treated her so badly. 彼は彼女に対してとてもひどい扱いをしたが, 彼女は彼のことをまだ愛していた.

▶定義2 but しかし →〜とは言うものの, 〜であるが, もっとも〜ではあるが ‖ I'll come as soon as I can, though I can't promise to be on time. できるだけ早く来ます. とは言っても, 時間通りにという約束はできませんが. ▶定義3 略式 however しかしながら →でも, しかし, やっぱり, けれど, もっとも ‖ I quite like him. I don't like his wife, though. 私は彼のことがとても気に入っている. でも彼の奥さんは好きではない. ☞ 参 although の注

成句 as if ⇒ AS

as though ⇒ AS

**thought¹** THINK の過去・過去分詞形

*__thought²__ /θɔːt/ 名 ▶定義1 C an idea or opinion 考え, または意見 →考え, 意見, 思い付き, アイデア ‖ What are your thoughts on this subject? このテーマについてのあなたの考えはどのようなものですか. The thought of living alone filled her with fear. 1人で生活すると考えただけでも, 彼女は不安で一杯になった. I've just had a thought (= an idea). 考え (= アイデア) が1つ浮かんだ. ▶定義2 U the power or process of thinking 考える力, または過程 →考えること, 熟考, 思案, 思考(力) ‖ I need to give this problem some thought. この問題をもう少し考える必要がある. ▶定義3 thoughts [複数扱い] a person's mind and all the ideas that are in it 人の心, およびそこに浮かぶすべての考え →考え ‖ You are always in my thoughts. あなたは私の考えの中にいつも入っている. ▶定義4 [単数扱い] a feeling of care or worry 心配または不安という気持ち →思いやり, 心遣い, 配慮 ‖ They sent me flowers. What a kind thought! 彼らは私に花を送ってくれた. 何と優しい心遣いだろうか.

▶定義5 U particular ideas or a particular way of thinking 特定の考え, またはある特定の考え方 →思想, 思潮 ‖ a change in medical thought on the subject そのテーマについての医学的見解の変化

成句 deep in thought/conversation ⇒ DEEP¹

a school of thought ⇒ SCHOOL

second thoughts ⇒ SECOND¹

**thoughtful** /θɔ́ːtfʊl, -f(ə)l/ 形 ▶定義1 thinking deeply 深く考えている→考え込んだ, 物思いにふけった ‖ *a thoughtful expression* 物思いにふけっている顔付き ▶定義2 thinking about what other people want or need 他人が望む, または必要としていることについて考えている→思いやりがある, 親切な, 情け深い ‖ *It was very thoughtful of you to send her some flowers.* 彼女に花を送ったとは, あなたはとても優しい心を持つ方でしたね. — thoughtfully /-fʊli, -f(ə)li/ 副→考え込んで, 物思いにふけって, 親切に, 注意深く — thoughtfulness 名 ❶→思慮深さ, 思いやり, 親切

**thoughtless** /θɔ́ːtləs/ 形 ▶定義 not thinking about what other people want or need or what the result of your actions will be 他人が望む, または必要としていることや, 自分の行動の結果がどうなるかについて考えていない→軽率な, 不注意な, 思いやりのない, 心ない, 思慮を欠く ☞類 inconsiderate — thoughtlessly 副→軽率に, 思いやりなく — thoughtlessness 名 ❶→軽率さ, 思いやりのなさ, 不親切, 思慮のないこと

***thousand** /θáʊz(ə)n(d)/ 数 ▶定義 1000
▶数について話しているときは, thousand を単数で用いることに注意.「たくさん」を意味する場合は, thousands を用いる: *There were over 70000 spectators at the match.* (その試合には7万人以上の観客が集まった.) *Thousands of people attended the meeting.* (何千人もの人々がその会議に出席した.)
文中での数詞の使い方については, six の項を参照. 数についての説明は, 巻末の数についての特別項目を参照.

**thousandth**¹ /θáʊz(ə)n(d)θ/ 形 ▶定義 1000th 1000番目の→第1000の, 1000番目の

**thousandth**² /θáʊz(ə)n(d)θ/ 名 ❶ ▶定義 the fraction 1/1000; one of a thousand equal parts of sth 分数の1/1000;～の均等な1000個の部分の1つ→1000分の1

**thrash** /θræʃ/ 動 ▶定義1 ❶to hit sb/sth many times with a stick, etc as a punishment ～を罰としてむちなどで何度もたたく→～を打ち据える, 散々に打つ, 打って懲らしめる ▶定義2 自❶ thrash (sth) (about/around) to move or make sth move wildly without any control 勝手に激しく動く, または～を動かす→のたうちまわる, 手足をばたばたさせる, ～を激しく振り動かす ▶定義3 ❶ to defeat sb easily in a game, competition, etc 試合や競争などで～を簡単に負かす→～をたたきのめす, 完敗させる, 打ち負かす

**句動詞** thrash sth out ▶定義 to talk about sth with sb until you reach an agreement 合意に達するまで～について…と話をする→～を合意に至るまで徹底的に論じる, 議論して練り上げる

**thrashing** /θræʃɪŋ/ 名 ❶ ▶定義1 the action of hitting sb/sth many times with a stick, etc as a punishment ～を罰としてむちなどで何度もたたくこと→むちで打つこと, むち打ち ▶定義2 略式 a bad defeat in a game 試合でのひどい敗北→大敗

***thread**¹ /θred/ 名 ▶定義1 ❶❶a long thin piece of cotton, wool, etc that you use for sewing or making cloth 布を縫う, または作るために使う, 綿, 毛などでできた1本の細長いもの→糸, 縫い糸 ‖ *a needle and thread* 針と糸 ☞ cable のさし絵 ▶定義2 ❶the connection between ideas, the parts of a story, etc 考えと考え, 話の部分と部分などの間のつながり→筋道, 脈絡, 続き ‖ *I've lost the thread of this argument.* この議論の筋道が分からなくなった.

**thread**² /θred/ 動 ❶ ▶定義1 to put sth long and thin, especially thread, through a narrow opening or hole 長く細い～, 特に糸を, 狭いすきま, または穴に通す→～に糸を通す, ～を突き通す ‖ *to thread a needle* 針に糸を通す *He threaded the belt through the loops on the trousers.* 彼はズボンのベルト通しにベルトを通した. ▶定義2 to join things together by putting them onto a string, etc 物をひもなどに通して一緒にする→～を糸を通してつなぐ, ～に糸を通す

**成句** thread your way through sth ▶定義 to move through sth with difficulty, going around things or people that are in your way 行く手をふさいでいる物や人々の周りを行きながら, ～をやっとのことで通り抜ける→～を縫うようにして進む

**threadbare** /θrédbèər/ 形 ▶定義 (used about material or clothes) old and very thin (物や衣服について) 古く, とても薄い→擦り切れた, 着古した

***threat** /θret/ 名 ▶定義1 ❶a warning that sb may hurt, kill or punish you if you do not do

**1690　threaten**

what he/she wants ～の望む事をしなければ、その～があなたを傷付ける、殺す、または罰するかもしれないという警告→**脅迫, 脅し, 脅威, 威嚇** ‖ to **make threats** against sb ～を脅す *He keeps saying he'll resign, but he won't **carry out** his **threat**.* 彼は辞職すると言い続けているが、その脅しを実行することはないだろう. ▶定義2 [**U**, 単数扱い] the possibility of trouble or danger 困難または危険の可能性→**兆し, おそれ, 前兆** ‖ *The forest is **under threat** from building developments.* その森でビルが開発されるおそれがある. ▶定義3 **C** a person or thing that may damage sth or hurt sb; something that indicates future danger ～に損害を与える、あるいは～を傷付けるかもしれない人または物; 将来の危険性を示す物→**～にとって脅かしになる人・物, 脅威を与える人・物**

★**threaten** /θrét(ə)n/ 動 ▶定義1 他 threaten sb (with sth); threaten (to do sth) to warn that you may hurt, kill or punish sb if he/she does not do what you want 自分の望むことをしなければ～を傷付ける、殺す、または罰するかもしれないと警告する→**～を脅す, 脅迫する, ～すると脅す** ‖ *The boy threatened him with a knife.* その少年はナイフで彼を脅した. *She was threatened with dismissal.* 彼女は解雇するぞと脅された. *The man threatened to kill her if she didn't tell him where the money was.* その男は金がどこにあるのか言わなければ殺すと言って彼女を脅した. ▶定義2 自他 to seem likely to do sth unpleasant 不快な～をしそうに見える→**～が迫っている; ～するおそれがある, ～を脅かす** ‖ *The wind was threatening to destroy the bridge.* 風でその橋が壊れるおそれがあった. — threatening 形 →**脅すような, 脅迫する, 威嚇的な** — threateningly 副 →**脅すように, 威嚇的に, 脅迫的に, 荒れ模様で**

★**three** /θriː/ 数 ▶定義1 3 ▶定義2 [複合形容詞を作るために用いて] having three of the thing mentioned 言及されたものが3つある → **3つの, 3個の, 3人の** ‖ *a three-legged stool* 3本足の腰掛け ☞参 **third**

▶文中での数詞の使い方については, six の項を参照.

**three-dimensional** (または **3-D**) 形 ▶定義 having length, width and height 長さ, 幅, 高さがある→**三次元の, 立体の, 立体的に見える, 3-D の** ‖ *a three-dimensional model* 三次元の模型

**threshold** /θréʃ(h)ðʊld/ 名 **C** ▶定義1 the ground at the entrance to a room or building 部屋または建物への入り口の地面→**敷き居** ▶定義2 the level at which sth starts to happen ～が起こり始める段階→**(変化が起こる) 限界点, 境界** ‖ *Young children have a low boredom threshold.* 幼い子供たちは物事に飽きやすい. ▶定義3 the time when you are just about to start sth or find sth ～をまさに始めようとする、または見つけうとする時→**出発点, 取っ掛かり, 始め, 発端** ‖ *We could be **on the threshold of** a scientific breakthrough.* 私たちは科学の大躍進の始まりにいるのかもしれない.

**threw** **THROW** の過去形

**thrift** /θrɪft/ 名 **U** ▶定義 the quality of being careful not to spend too much money 金をあまり多く使いすぎないように気を付けているという性質→**倹約, 節約, 質素** — thrifty 形 → **倹約する, 節約する, つましい, やりくり上手な, 質素な**

**thrill** /θrɪl/ 名 **C** ▶定義 a sudden strong feeling of pleasure or excitement 突然起きる強い喜び、または興奮の気持ち→**ぞくぞくする感じ, スリル, 身震い** — thrill 動 →**～をぞくぞくさせる, わくわくさせる, 感動させる, 興奮させる** ‖ *His singing thrilled the audience.* 彼の歌唱は聴衆を感動させた. — thrilled 形 →**感動した, 感激した, わくわくした** ‖ *He was absolutely thrilled with my present.* 彼は私のプレゼントにすっかり感激していた. — thrilling 形 →**ぞくぞくさせる, スリル満点の, スリリングな, 身の毛のよだつ**

**thriller** /θrɪlər/ 名 **C** ▶定義 a play, film, book, etc with a very exciting story, often about a crime しばしば犯罪についての、とてもぞくぞくさせるような話の演劇, 映画, 本など→**スリラー物**

**thrive** /θráɪv/ 動 自 (過 **thrived** または **throve** /θróʊv/; 過分 **thrived**) ▶定義 to grow or develop well よく成長する、または発展する→**栄える, 成功する, すくすくと育つ, 成長する, 生い茂る** — thriving 形 →**成功した, 繁栄している, 繁茂する** ‖ *a thriving industry* 繁栄している産業

★**throat** /θróʊt/ 名 **C** ▶定義1 the front part of your neck 首の前部→**のど, のど首** ‖ *The attacker grabbed the man by the throat.* 襲撃者

はその男性ののど首をつかんだ. ☞ C5 ページのさし絵 ▶定義2 the back part of your mouth and the passage down your neck through which air and food pass 口の奥の部分で, 首の下方向に空気や食べ物が通る管→のど, 咽喉(いんこう) ‖ *She got a piece of bread stuck in her throat.* 彼女はのどに1切れのパンをつかえさせた. *I've got a sore throat.* 私はのどが痛い. ☞ C5 ページのさし絵
成句 clear your throat ⇒ **CLEAR**³
have/feel a lump in your throat ⇒ **LUMP**¹

**throb** /θrɑb/ 動⾃ (**throbbing**; **throbbed**) ▶定義 to make strong regular movements or noises; to beat strongly 周期的な力強い動きをする, または音を立てる; 力強く鼓動する→鼓動する, 脈打つ, どきどきする, 振動する, ずきずき痛む ‖ *Her finger throbbed with pain.* 彼女の指は痛みでずきずきした. — throb 名 ⓒ→鼓動, 脈打つこと, 振動, ずきずき痛むこと

**throne** /θróʊn/ 名 ▶定義1 ⓒ the special chair where a king or queen sits 王または女王が座る特別ないす→王座, 玉座 ▶定義2 **the throne** [単数扱い] the position of being king or queen 王または女王である地位→王権, 君主の地位, 王位

**throng**¹ /θrɔ(ː)ŋ, θrɑŋ/ 名 ⓒ (文) ▶定義 a large crowd of people 非常に多くの人々→群衆, 人だかり, 大勢, 多数

**throng**² /θrɔ(ː)ŋ, θrɑŋ/ 動⾃他 (文) ▶定義 (used about a crowd of people) to move into or fill a particular place (多くの人々について) ある特定の場所へ入っていく, またはある特定の場所を一杯に占める→群がる, 押し寄せる; 〜を一杯にする

**throttle**¹ /θrɑ́tl/ 動他 ▶定義 to hold sb tightly by the throat and stop him/her breathing 〜ののどをきつくつかみ, その〜の呼吸を止める→〜ののどを絞める, 〜を窒息させる ☞類 **strangle**

**throttle**² /θrɑ́tl/ 名 ⓒ ▶定義 the part in a vehicle that controls the speed by controlling how much fuel goes into the engine 乗り物で, エンジンにどのくらいの燃料を送るかを制御することによってスピードを調整する部分→スロットル, 絞り弁

\*through /θruː/ 前 副 ▶定義1 from one end or side of sth to the other 〜の一方の端または側からもう一方へ→〜を通り抜けて, 貫いて, 通して ‖ *We drove through the centre of London.* 私たちはロンドンの中心を車で通り抜けた. *to look through a telescope* 望遠鏡で見る *She cut through the rope.* 彼女はロープを切り離した. *to push through a crowd of people* 群衆を押し分けて進む ▶定義2 from the beginning to the end of sth 〜の始めから終わりまで→〜の始めから終わりまで, 〜の間中, ずっと ‖ *Food supplies will not last through the winter.* 食糧の供給は冬の間中は続かないだろう. *We're halfway through the book.* 私たちはその本をまだ半分ぐらいしか読んでいない. *He read the letter through and handed it back.* 彼はその手紙を読み終えてから返した. ▶定義3 past a limit, stage or test 限界, 段階, あるいは試験を過ぎて→〜を経て, 完了して, 首尾良く終えて, 切り抜けて ‖ *He lifted the rope to let us through.* 彼は私たちを通すためにそのロープを持ち上げた. *She didn't get through the first interview.* 彼女は最初の面接に合格できなかった. ▶定義4 because of; with the help of 〜の理由で; 〜を活用して→〜のために, 〜によって, 〜を通じて, 〜のお陰で ‖ *Errors were made through bad organization.* 組織上の問題のために間違いが起きた. *David got the job through his uncle.* デーヴィッドはおじさんを通じて職を得た. ▶定義5 (または **thru**) 米 until, and including 〜までで, 〜を含んでいる→〜まで, 〜の終わりまで ‖ *They are staying Monday through Friday.* 彼らは月曜日から金曜日まで滞在する予定だ. ▶定義6 英 connected by telephone 電話でつながっている→電話がつながって, 通じて ‖ *Can you put me through to extension 5678, please?* 内線 5678 につないでくれませんか.

句動詞 **be through (with sb/sth)** ▶定義 to have finished with sb/sth 〜と終わる, 〜を終える→〜と別れる, 縁を切る, 〜との関係を断つ, 〜を終える, 仕上げる, 用済みにする

**throughout** /θruːáʊt/ 動 前 ▶定義1 in every part of sth 〜のあらゆる部分で→〜の至る所に, 〜の隅から隅まで, 〜中くまなく ‖ *The house is beautifully decorated throughout.* その家は隅から隅まで美しく飾り付けされている. *The match can be watched live on television throughout the world.* その試合は世界のどこでもテレビ中継で見られる. ▶定義2 from the

## 1692 throve

beginning to the end of sth 〜の始めから終わりまで→〜中ずっと，〜の始めから終わりまで ‖ *We didn't enjoy the holiday because it rained throughout.* ずっと雨が降っていたため，私たちは休暇を楽しめなかった．

**throve** THRIVE の過去形

**＊throw** /θróu/ 動（過 **threw** /θruː/；過分 **thrown** /θróun/） ▶定義1 ⓗ throw (sth) (to/at sb); throw sb sth to send sth from your hand through the air by moving your hand or arm quickly 手または腕を素早く動かして，手から〜を空中を通して送る→（〜を）投げる，ほうる，投げて渡す ‖ *How far can you throw?* どのくらい遠くまで投げられますか． *Throw the ball to me.* そのボールを私の方に投げなさい． *Throw me the ball.* そのボールを私の方に投げなさい． *Don't throw stones at people.* 石を人に目掛けて投げてはいけません． ▶定義2 ⓗ to put sth somewhere quickly or carelessly 〜をどこかに素早く，またはぞんざいに置く→〜をほうり投げる，引っ掛ける，さっと着る ‖ *He threw his bag down in a corner.* 彼は隅にかばんをほうり投げた． *She threw on a sweater and ran out of the door.* 彼女はセーターをさっと着て，戸口から走り出ていった． ▶定義3 ⓗ to move your body or part of it quickly or suddenly 体またはその一部を素早く，あるいは急に動かす→〜を急に動かす，さっと向ける，投げる ‖ *Jenny threw herself onto the bed and sobbed.* ジェニーはベッドに身を投げ出して泣きじゃくった． *Lee threw back his head and roared with laughter.* リーは頭を急にのけぞらせて大笑いした． ▶定義4 ⓗ to cause sb to fall down quickly or violently 〜を素早く，または乱暴に倒れさせる→〜を投げ飛ばす，投げ倒す，投げ出す ‖ *The bus braked and we were thrown to the floor.* バスがブレーキをかけたため，私たちは床に投げ出された．

▶定義5 ⓗ to put sb in a particular (usually unpleasant) situation 〜をある状態（通常は不快な）に置く→〜を…に投げ込む，投げ入れる，陥れる ‖ *We were thrown into confusion by the news.* 私たちはその知らせを聞いて混乱状態になった． ▶定義6 ⓗ 略式 to make sb feel upset, confused or surprised 〜を動揺させる，混乱させる，あるいは驚かせる→〜を当惑させる，動揺

させる ‖ *The question threw me and I didn't know what to reply.* その質問は私をうろたえさせ，私は何と答えたらよいか分からなかった．

▶定義7 ⓗ to send light or shade onto sth 〜に光または影を落とす→〜を投げ掛ける，浴びせる，向ける ‖ *The tree threw a long shadow across the lawn.* その木は芝生に長い影を落としていた． ―throw 名 ⓒ▶投げること，投球，投げて届く距離，射程 ‖ *It's your throw (= it's your turn to throw the dice in a board game, etc).* 今度はあなたの番ですよ（＝盤上のゲームなどで，あなたがさいころを振る順番だ）． *a throw of 97 metres* 射程距離97メートル

**句動詞** throw sth away ▶定義1（または throw sth out）to get rid of rubbish or sth that you do not want がらくたや必要としていない〜を片付ける→〜を捨てる，投げ捨てる ‖ *I threw his letters away.* 私は彼の手紙を処分した． ▶定義2 to waste or not use sth useful 役に立つ〜を無駄にする，または使わない→〜を浪費する，無駄に費やす，逃す，逸する ‖ *to throw away a good opportunity* いい機会を逃す

throw sth in 略式 ▶定義 to include sth extra without increasing the price 余分な〜を値段を上げないで含める→〜を（商品に）添える，おまけに付ける，サービスする

throw sb out ▶定義 to force sb to leave a place 〜にある場所を離れるよう強制する→〜を…から追い出す，ほうり出す

throw sth out ▶定義1 to decide not to accept sb's idea or suggestion 〜の考えや提案を受け入れないことに決定する→〜を否決する，拒否する ▶定義2 ＝ THROW STH AWAY(1)

throw up 略式 ▶定義 to vomit; to be sick 吐く；病気である→食べ物を吐く，戻す

throw sth up ▶定義1 to vomit food 食べ物を吐く→〜を吐く，戻す ▶定義2 to produce or show sth 〜を生み出す，または見せる→〜を生み出す，目立たせる ▶定義3 to leave your job, career, studies, etc 職，仕事，研究などをやめる→〜を突然やめる，辞す，辞職する，放棄する

**thru** 米 ＝ THROUGH(5)

**thrust**[1] /θrʌst/ 動 ⓘ ⓗ（過，過分 **thrust**）
▶定義1 to push sb/sth suddenly or violently; to move quickly and suddenly in a particular direction 〜を突然，または乱暴に押す；ある方向に素早く，急に動く→（〜を）強く急に押す，ぐい

と押す, 押しやる, 突く ‖ *The man thrust his hands deeper into his pockets.* その男は両手をポケットに深く突っ込んだ. *She thrust past him and ran out of the room.* 彼女は彼を押しのけ, その部屋から逃げ出した. ▶定義2 to make a sudden forward movement with a knife, etc ナイフなどを持って急に前進する→〜を…に突き刺す, 突きかかる

句動詞 thrust sb/sth upon sb ▶定義 to force sb to accept or deal with sb/sth 〜を受け入れる, または対応するよう…に強制する→〜に…を押し付ける, 強制する

**thrust**² /θrʌst/ 名 ▶定義1 the thrust [単数扱い] the main part or point of an argument, policy, etc 議論, 政策などの主要な部分または点→要点, 論点, 骨子, 趣旨 ▶定義2 ● a sudden strong movement forward 急で力強い前進→強い押し, 突き

**thud** /θʌd/ 名 ● ▶定義 the low sound that is made when a heavy object hits sth else 重い物がほかの〜にぶつかったときに生じる低い音→ドスン, ズシン, ドサッという音 ‖ *Her head hit the floor with a dull thud.* 彼女の頭は鈍い音を立てて床にぶつかった. ― thud 動 (thudding; thudded) →ドスン, ズシン, ドサッという音を立てる, ドスンと落ちる

**thug** /θʌɡ/ 名 ● ▶定義 a violent person who may harm other people 他人を傷付けるかもしれないような乱暴な人→凶漢, 悪漢, 凶悪犯, 暴漢, 悪党

\***thumb**¹ /θʌm/ 名 ● ▶定義1 the short thick finger at the side of each hand それぞれの手の横に付いている, 太く短い指→親指 ☞ C5 ページのさし絵 ▶定義2 the part of a glove, etc that covers your thumb(1) 手袋などで thumb(1) を覆う部分→(手袋の) 親指

成句 a rule of thumb ⇒ **RULE**¹

stand/stick out like a sore thumb ⇒ **SORE**¹

the thumbs up/down ▶定義 a sign or an expression that shows approval/disapproval 承認・不承認を示す身振り, または表現→賛同・満足を表す身振り・合図; 不賛同・非難・不満を表す身振り・合図

under sb's thumb ▶定義 (used about a person) completely controlled by sb (人について) 〜に完全に支配されている→〜の言いなりになって, 影響を受けて, 圧力を受けて ‖ *She's got him under her thumb.* 彼女は彼を自分の支配下に置いた.

**thumb**² /θʌm/ 動 ● ▶定義 thumb (through) sth to turn the pages of a book, etc quickly 本などのページを素早くめくる→ぱらぱらとめくる, ざっと目を通す, 飛ばし読みする

成句 thumb a lift ▶定義 to hold out your thumb to cars going past, to ask sb to give you a free ride 通り過ぎていく車に向かって親指を突き出し, ただで車に乗せてくれるよう〜に頼む→車に乗せてくれるよう頼む ☞参 **hitchhike** の注

**thumbtack** /θʌ́mtæk/ 米 = **DRAWING PIN**

**thump** /θʌmp/ 動 ▶定義1 ● to hit sb/sth hard with sth, usually your closed hand (fist) 〜を…, 通常は閉じた手 (こぶし) で, 強くたたく→〜を強く音を立てて打つ, 〜を強く殴る ‖ *He started coughing and Jo thumped him on the back.* 彼がせき込み始めたので, ジョーは背中を強くたたいてやった. ▶定義2 ● to make a loud sound by hitting sth or by beating hard 〜をたたいて, または強く打って大きな音を立てる→〜をぶつける, 打ち鳴らす, ドキンドキンと打つ ‖ *His heart was thumping with excitement.* 彼の心臓は興奮でドキンドキンと打っていた. ― thump 名 ● →強打, ゴツンとたたく音, 強く殴ること

**thunder**¹ /θʌ́ndər/ 名 ● ▶定義 the loud noise in the sky that you can hear when there is a storm あらしのときに聞こえる, 空で起きる大きな音→雷鳴, 雷 ‖ *a clap/crash/roll of thunder* 雷鳴 ▶ thunder は, 大抵 lightning (稲光) の後に聞こえる.

**thunder**² /θʌ́ndər/ 動 ▶定義1 (it と用いて) to make a loud noise in the sky during a storm あらしの間に空で大きな音を立てる→雷が鳴る ‖ *The rain poured down and it started to thunder.* 雨が激しく降り, 雷が鳴り出した. ▶定義2 to make a loud deep noise like thunder 雷のように低く大きい音を立てる→大きな音を立てて通る, ごう音を立てて走る, とどろく ‖ *Traffic thundered across the bridge.* 往来の車がごう音を立てて橋を渡った.

**thunderstorm** /θʌ́ndərstɔːrm/ 名 ● ▶定義 a storm with loud noises and flashes of light in the sky (thunder and lightning) 空に起こる大きな音と光のひらめき (雷鳴と稲光) を伴ったあらし➔激しい雷雨

**Thur** (または **Thurs**) 略 Thursday➔木曜日 ‖ *Thurs 26 June* 6月26日木曜日

*__Thursday__ /θə́ːrzdeɪ, -di/ 名 ❻ ❶ ( 略 **Thur**; **Thurs**) ▶定義 the day of the week after Wednesday 水曜日の次の曜日➔**木曜日**
▶曜日は最初の文字を必ず大文字で書く. 文中での曜日の使い方の例については, Monday を参照.

*__thus__ /ðʌs/ 副 正式 ▶定義1 like this; in this way このように; この方法で➔**このように, そのように** ‖ *Thus began the series of incidents which changed her life.* このようにして, 彼女の人生を変える一連の出来事が始まった. ▶定義2 because of or as a result of this このために, またはこの結果として➔**したがって, だから** ☛類 therefore

__thwart__ /θwɔːrt/ 動 他 ▶定義 thwart sth; thwart sb (in sth) to stop sb doing what he/she planned to do; to prevent sth happening 〜がしようと計画していることをやめさせる; 〜が起こるのを妨げる➔**〜の計画を駄目にする, 邪魔をする, 〜を挫折 (ざせつ) させる, くじく** ‖ *to thwart sb's plans/ambitions/efforts* 〜の計画・大望・努力を挫折させる *She was thwarted in her attempt to gain control.* 支配権を獲得しようとする彼女の企ては頓挫 (とんざ) した.

__thyme__ /taɪm/ 名 ❶ ▶定義 a plant that is used in cooking (a herb) and has small leaves and a sweet smell 料理で使われる植物 (ハーブ) で, 小さな葉がつき, 甘い香りがするもの➔**タイム, タチジャコウソウ**

__tic__ /tɪk/ 名 ❻ ▶定義 a sudden quick movement of a muscle, especially in your face or head, that you cannot control 自分では抑えることのできない, 特に顔や頭の筋肉の素早く急な動き➔**顔のけいれん, チック** ‖ *He has a nervous tic.* 彼には神経性のチックがある.

__tick__¹ /tɪk/ 動 ▶定義1 自 (used about a clock or watch) to make regular short sounds (時計について) 規則的な小さい音を立てる➔**カチカチ音を立てる, チクタクと鳴る** ▶定義2 (米 **check**) 他 to put a mark (√) next to a name, an item on a list, etc to show that sth has been dealt with or chosen 〜が処理された, または選択されたことを表すために, 印(√)を名前, 一覧表の項目などの横に付ける➔**〜に照合済みの印を記入する, 印を付ける, 〜をチェックする** ‖ *Please tick the appropriate box.* 適切なボックスにチェックをしてください.
▶イギリス英語では, correct(正しい)答え, 文章などに正しい印(√)を付け, 間違っている物にはクロス(X)を付ける. アメリカ英語では, 何かが wrong(間違っている)ことを示すためにチェックの印(√)を付ける.

成句 **what makes sb/sth tick** ▶定義 the reasons why sb behaves or sth works in the way he/she/it does 〜がそのように振る舞う理由, または〜がそのように動く理由➔**〜がそうする理由, 動機, 何が〜を動かしているのか** ‖ *He has a strong interest in people and what makes them tick.* 彼は, 人々と人々を動かすものに強い関心を持っている.

句動詞 **tick away/by** ▶定義 (used about time) to pass (時間について) 過ぎる➔**刻々と経過する, 過ぎ去る**

**tick sb/sth off** ▶定義 to put a mark (√) next to a name an item on a list, etc to show that sth has been done or sb has been dealt with 〜がなされた, または処理されたことを表すために, 印(√)を名前, 一覧表の項目などの横に付ける➔**〜をチェックする, 〜に印を付ける**

**tick over** 略式 (通常, 進行形で用いて) ▶定義1 (used about an engine) to run slowly while the vehicle is not moving (エンジンについて) その車が動いていない間, ゆっくり走る➔**低速で空転する, アイドリングする** ▶定義2 to keep working slowly without producing or achieving very much 非常にたくさん生産したり達成したりしないで, ゆっくりと動き続ける➔**どうにかやっていく, まあまあの状態を続ける, 平穏に進んでいる**

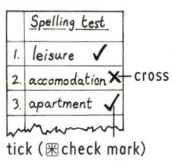

tick (米check mark)

__tick__² /tɪk/ 名 ❻ ▶定義1 (米 **check mark**; **check**) a mark (√) next to an item on a list that shows that sth has been done or next to an answer to show that it is either correct or wrong 一覧表の

項目の横にあって, ～が行われたことを示す, あるいは回答の横にあって, 正しいか間違っているかを示す印 (✓) → 照合済みの印, チェック ‖ *Put a tick after each correct answer.* それぞれの正解の後ろにチェックを入れなさい.

▶アメリカ英語では, 記載されている回答などの横に付いているチェックの印は, 何かが wrong (間違っている) ことを示す. イギリス英語では, その印は correct (正しい) ことを示し, 誤りを示すためにはクロス (✗) が使われる.

▶定義2 (または **ticking**) the regular short sound that a watch or clock makes when it is working 時計が動いているときに立てる, 規則的な短い音 → カチカチという音, チクタクという音 ▶定義3 医 略式 a moment 瞬間 → 一瞬, ちょっと

\*ticket /tíkət/ 名 C ▶定義1 a ticket (for/to sth) a piece of paper or card that shows you have paid for a journey, or allows you to enter a theatre, cinema, etc 旅行に対して支払いが済んでいることを示す, または劇場, 映画館などに入ることを許可する, 一片の紙やカード → 切符, 券, 乗車券, 入場券, チケット ‖ *two tickets for the Cup Final* 優勝杯を争う決勝戦のチケット2枚 *a single/return ticket to London* ロンドンまでの片道切符・往復切符 *a ticket office/machine/collector* 切符売り場・券売機・集札係 ☞参 **season ticket** ▶定義2 a piece of paper or a label in a shop that shows the price, size, etc of sth that is for sale 店で, 売りに出ている～の値段, 大きさなどを示す一片の紙または札 → 値札, 正札, 札, ラベル ☞ **label** のさし絵 ▶定義3 an official piece of paper that you get when you have parked illegally or driven too fast telling you that you must pay money as a punishment (a fine) 不法に駐車したり高速で運転したときに受け取るもので, 罰として金を払わなければならない (罰金) と書いてある公式の書類 → 駐車違反切符, 交通違反切符, チケット, 呼び出し状 ‖ *a parking ticket* 駐車違反の切符

### ▶社会・文化

切符の種類

列車の乗車券はアメリカではrailroad ticket, イギリスでは railway ticket と呼びます. またアメリカ・イギリスで片道切符はそれぞれ one-way ticket, single ticket, 往復切符が round-trip ticket, return ticket です. また定期券は米英でそれぞれ commuter's ticket (commuter's pass), season ticket と呼びます.

熟句 just the job/ticket ⇒ **JOB**

**tickle** /tík(ə)l/ 動 ▶定義1 他 to touch sb lightly with your fingers or with sth soft so that he/she laughs ～が笑うように, その～に指または柔らかい…で軽く触れる → ～をくすぐる ‖ *She tickled the baby's toes.* 彼女はその赤ん坊のつま先をくすぐった. ▶定義2 自他 to produce or to have an uncomfortable feeling in a part of your body 体の一部分に不快な感じを生じさせる, またはそのような感じがある → ちくちくする, むずむずする; ちくちくさせる, むずむずさせる ‖ *My nose tickles/is tickling.* 鼻がむずむずする・むずむずしている. *The woollen scarf tickled her neck.* そのウールのスカーフは彼女の首をちくちくと刺激した. ▶定義3 他 略式 to amuse and interest sb ～を楽しませる, または興味を持たせる → ～を喜ばせる, 楽しませる, 笑わせる ‖ *That joke really tickled me.* あの冗談は本当に笑わせてくれた. ― **tickle** 名 C → くすぐり, くすぐったい感じ, むずがゆさ

**ticklish** /tíklɪʃ/ 形 ▶定義 if a person is ticklish, he/she laughs when sb touches him/her in a sensitive place. ある人がticklishであれば, ～がその人の敏感な所に触れたら笑う → くすぐったがりの ‖ *Are you ticklish?* あなたはくすぐったがりですか.

**tidal** /táɪdl/ 形 ▶定義 connected with the regular rise and fall of the sea (tides) 海 (潮) の規則的な満ち干に関連している → 潮の, 潮の作用による, 潮の干満のある

**tidal wave** 名 C ▶定義 a very large wave in the sea which destroys things when it reaches the land, and is often caused by movements under the surface of the earth (an earthquake) 海で, 陸に達すると物を破壊し, しばしば地球の表面下の動き (地震) によって引き起こされる, 非常に大きな波 → 津波, 高波, 高潮

**tide**¹ /táɪd/ 名 C ▶定義1 the regular change in the level of the sea caused by the moon and the sun. At high tide the sea is closer to the land, at low tide it is farther away and more of the beach can be seen. 月と太陽によって引き起こされる, 海抜の規則的な変化. 満潮のときには海が陸に近くなり, 干潮のときには海が遠ざかって浜辺がより多く見えるようになる→**潮, 潮の干満, 潮汐 (ちょうせき)** || *The tide is coming in/going out.* 潮が満ちてきた・引いていった. **●参 ebb** ▶定義**2** [通常は単数] the way that most people think or feel about sth at a particular time ～に対するある時の大半の人々の考え方, または感じ方→**風潮, 形勢, 傾向, 時流** || *It appears that* ***the tide has turned*** *in the government's favour.* 形勢は政府に有利になったようだ.

**tide**² /táid/ 動
句動詞 **tide sb over** ▶定義 to give sb sth to help him/her through a difficult time ～が困難な時期を乗り越えるのを助けるため, その～に…を与える→**～に困難・危機を乗り切らせる, 切り抜けさせる**

*****tidy**¹ /táidi/ 形 (**tidier**; **tidiest**) ▶定義**1** 特に 医 arranged with everything in good order; neat すべてがきちんと整理されている; 小ぎれいな→**きちんと片付いた, 小ぎれいな, 整然とした** || *If you keep your room tidy it is easier to find things.* 部屋をきれいにしておけば, 物を見つけやすい. ▶定義**2** (used about a person) liking to keep things in good order; neat (人について) 物をきちんとしておくのが好きな; 小ぎれいな→**きれい好きな, きちょうめんな** || *Mark is a very tidy boy.* マークはとてもきれい好きな少年だ. ⇔ **untidy** — **tidily** 副→**きちんと, 整然と** — **tidiness** 名 **Ü**→**きちんとしていること, 整然さ**

*****tidy**² /táidi/ 動 自 他 (現分 **tidying**; 三単現 **tidies**; 過, 過分 **tidied**) ▶定義 **tidy (sb/sth/yourself) (up)** to make sb/sth/yourself look in order and well arranged ～・自分を整然と見えるようにし, きちんと整える→**(～を) きちんとする, 整とんする, 片付ける** || *We must tidy this room up before the visitors arrive.* 私たちは, 来客が到着する前に, この部屋を片付けなければならない.
句動詞 **tidy sth away** ▶定義 to put sth into the drawer, cupboard, etc where it is kept so that it cannot be seen ～を, 見えないようにするために, いつも入れてある引き出し, 戸棚などに入れる→**～を片付ける, しまう**

*****tie**¹ /tái/ 名 **C** ▶定義**1** (医 または **necktie**) a long thin piece of cloth worn round the neck, especially by men, with a knot at the front. A tie is usually worn with a shirt. 特に男性が首の回りに巻く, 正面に結び目がある 1 枚の細長い布. 通常はワイシャツと共に着用する→**ネクタイ** || *a striped silk tie* シルクのストライプのネクタイ **●参 bow tie ●** C6 ページのさし絵 ▶定義**2** [通常は複数] a strong connection between people or organizations 人と人, または組織と組織の間の強いつながり→**結び付き, つながり, きずな, 縁, 関係** || *personal/emotional ties* 個人的な・感情的な結び付き *family ties* 家族のきずな ▶定義**3** something that limits your freedom 自由を制限するもの→**束縛するもの, 足手まとい, 重荷, 拘束** ▶定義**4** a situation in a game or competition in which two or more teams or players get the same score 試合や競争で, 2 つ以上のチーム, または 2 人以上の選手が同じ得点数を上げている状況→**同点, タイ, 引き分け** || *There was a tie for first place.* 第 1 位は同点だった.

*****tie**² /tái/ 動 (現分 **tying**; 三単現 **ties**; 過, 過分 **tied**) ▶定義**1** 他 to fasten sb/sth or fix sb/sth in position with rope, string, etc; to make a knot in sth 綱, ひもなどで～をしっかり固定する, または～を適所に取り付ける; ～に結び目を作る→**～を結ぶ, くくる, 縛る, つなぐ, 結び付ける, 縛り付ける** || *The prisoner was tied to a chair.* その囚人はいすに縛り付けられいた. *Kay tied her hair back with a ribbon.* ケイは髪を後ろでリボンで結んだ. *to tie sth in a knot* ～に結び目を作る *to tie your shoelaces* 靴ひもを結ぶ ⇔ **untie** ▶定義**2** 他 **tie sb (to sth/to doing sth)** (通常は受動態で) to limit sb's freedom and make him/her unable to do everything he/she wants to ～の自由を制限し, その～のしたい事が何もできないようにする→**～を縛り付ける, 束縛する, 拘束する** || *I don't want to be tied to staying in this country permanently.* 私は永久にこの国にいることを義務付けられたくない. ▶定義**3** 自 **tie (with sb) (for sth)** to have the same number of points as another player or team at the end of a game or competition 試合または競争が終わった時点で, ほかの選手やチームと同じ得点数を上げている→**同点になる, 引き分ける, タイになる** || *England tied with Italy for third place.* イングランドはイタリアと 3 位を分け合った.

成句 your hands are tied ⇒ **HAND**¹

句動詞 tie sb/yourself down ▶定義 to limit sb's/your freedom 〜・自分の自由を制限する➔〜を束縛する, 拘束する, 縛り付ける ‖ *Having young children really ties you down.* 幼い子供がいると本当に縛り付けられる.

tie in (with sth) ▶定義 to agree with other facts or information that you have; to match ほかの事実や持っている情報に同意する; 調和する➔〜に結び付く, 一致する ‖ *The new evidence seems to tie in with your theory.* その新しい証拠は, あなたの理論と一致するようだ.

tie sb/sth up ▶定義 1 to fix sb/sth in position with rope, string, etc 綱, ひもなどで〜を適所に取り付ける➔〜を結ぶ, 縛り上げる, 結び付ける ‖ *The dog was tied up in the back garden.* その犬は裏庭につながれた. ▶定義 2 (通常は受動態で) to keep sb busy 〜を忙しくさせておく➔〜で忙しい, 〜をくぎ付けにする, 忙殺する ‖ *Mr Jones is tied up in a meeting.* ジョーンズ氏は会議で忙殺されている.

**tier** /tɪər/ 名 C ▶定義 one of a number of levels いくつかの段階のうちの1つ➔列, 段, 層, 階, 段階, 階層

**tiger** /ˈtaɪɡər/ 名 C ▶定義 a large wild cat that has yellow fur with black lines (stripes). Tigers live in parts of Asia. 黒い線(しま)のある黄色い毛皮を持った, 野生の大型のネコ科の動物. アジアの一部に生息している➔トラ

▶ 雌のトラはtigress, 子供はcubと呼ばれる.
☞ lion のさし絵

\***tight** /taɪt/ 形 副 ▶定義 1 fixed firmly in position and difficult to move or unfasten しっかりと適所に固定され, 動かしたり取り外したりするのが難しい➔きつい, 堅い, しっかり締まった, 堅く結んだ ‖ *a tight knot* 堅い結び目 *Keep a **tight grip/hold** on this rope.* このロープにしっかりとつかまっていなさい. ***Hold tight** so that you don't fall off.* 落ちないようにしっかりとつかまっていなさい.

▶ 過去分詞の前では, tight ではなく tightly が用いられる: *The van was packed tight with boxes.* (そのバンには箱がぎっしりと詰め込んであった.) *The van was tightly packed with boxes.* (そのバンには箱がぎっしりと詰め込んであった.)

▶定義 2 (used about clothes) fitting very closely in a way that is often uncomfortable (衣服について) しばしば着心地の良くないほど, とてもぴったりと体に合っている➔きつい, 窮屈な, ぴったりした ‖ *These shoes hurt. They're too tight.* この靴は痛い. きつすぎます. *a tight-fitting skirt* ぴったり合ったスカート ⇔ **loose** ▶定義 3 controlled very strictly and firmly 非常に厳密に, 堅固に規制されている➔厳しい, 厳格な, 厳重な ‖ *Security is very tight at the airport.* 空港の警戒はとても厳重である. ▶定義 4 stretched or pulled hard so that it cannot be stretched further さらに伸ばせないように, 強く伸ばされている, または引っ張られている➔ぴんと張った, 緩みのない ‖ *The rope was stretched tight.* そのロープはぴんと張られていた. ▶定義 5 not having much free time or space 自由な時間や空間をあまり持っていない➔きっしり詰まった, 余裕のない, 身動きできない, 狭い ‖ *My schedule this week is very tight.* 今週の私の予定は, ぎっしり詰まっている. ▶定義 6 **-tight** (複合形容詞を作るために用いて) not allowing sth to get in or out 〜が入ったり出たりするのを許していない➔〜の漏らない, 防〜 ‖ *an airtight/watertight container* 気密の・耐水の容器 — **tightly** 副 ‖ しっかりと, きつく, 堅く, ぴんと張って ‖ *Screw the lid on tightly.* ふたを回してしっかり閉めなさい. *She kept her eyes tightly closed.* 彼女は目をしっかりと閉じていた. — **tightness** 名 U➔堅く締まっていること, 窮屈さ, 堅固, 緊張, 金詰まり

**tighten** /ˈtaɪtn/ 動 自 他 ▶定義 tighten (sth) (up) to become or to make sth tight or tighter きつく, またはよりきつくなる, あるいは〜をきつく, またはよりきつくする ➔ しっかり締まる, 厳重になる; 〜をしっかり締める, ぴんと張る, 堅くする, 強化する ‖ *His grip on her arm tightened.* 彼女の腕をつかんでいた彼の手に力が入った. *He tightened the screws as far as they would go.* 彼はねじを締められるところまでしっかり締め付けた.

成句 tighten your belt ▶定義 to spend less money because you have less than usual available いつも使える金額よりも少ない額しか持っていないため, より少ない金を使う➔倹約する, 耐乏生活をする

## 1698　tightrope

**句動詞** tighten up (on) sth ▶定義 to cause sth to become stricter 〜をより厳密になるようにさせる→〜を厳しくする，厳重にする，強化する ‖ to tighten up security/a law 警備・法を強化する

**tightrope** /táɪtròʊp/ 名 C ▶定義 a rope or wire that is stretched high above the ground on which people walk, especially as a form of entertainment 特に催し物の一種として，地上に高く張られ，人がその上を歩く綱または針金→綱渡りの張り綱

**tights** /táɪts/ (米 **pantyhose**) 名 [複数扱い] ▶定義 a piece of thin clothing, usually worn by women, that fits tightly from the waist over the legs and feet 通常は女性が履く，腰から足全体にぴったりと沿った薄い衣料→タイツ，パンティーストッキング ‖ a pair of tights 1足のタイツ ☞参 stocking ☞ C6 ページのさし絵

★**tile** /táɪl/ 名 C ▶定義 one of the flat, square objects that are arranged in rows to cover roofs, floors, bathroom walls, etc 屋根，床，浴室の壁などを覆うために何列にもわたって並べられる，四角く平たい物の1つ→タイル，かわら ☞ C7 ページのさし絵 ― tile 動他 〜にタイルを張る，〜をかわらでふく ‖ a tiled bathroom タイル張りの浴室

**till**¹ /tɪl/ 略式 = UNTIL

**till**² /tɪl/ (または **cash register**) 名 C ▶定義 the machine or drawer where money is kept in a shop, etc 店や店などで金が常時置いてある機械，または引き出し→レジ(スター)，金銭登録機，現金箱，現金入れの引き出し ‖ Please pay at the till. レジでお支払いください．

**tilt** /tɪlt/ 動 自 他 ▶定義 to move, or make sth move, into a position with one end or side higher than the other 一方の端または側が他方より高い位置に移動する，または〜を動かす→傾く；〜を傾ける，かしげる，倒す ‖ The front seats of the car tilt forward. 車の前の座席は前に倒れる． She tilted her head to one side. 彼女は首を片方にかしげた． ― tilt 名 [単数扱い]→傾けること，傾き，傾斜，かしげること

**timber** /tímbər/ 名 ▶定義1 (特に 米 **lumber**) U wood that is going to be used for building 建築に使われる予定の材木→材木，木材，板材 ▶定義2 C a large piece of wood 1本の大きな材木→横木，はり，肋材(ろくざい) ‖ roof timbers 屋根のはり

★**time**¹ /táɪm/ 名 ▶定義1 [U, 単数扱い] a period of minutes, hours, days, etc 数分，数時間，数日などの間→時，時間，歳月，時の経過，期間 ‖ As time passed and there was still no news, we got more worried. 時がたち，まだ何の知らせもないので，私たちはますます心配になった． You're **wasting time** - get on with your work! あなたは時間を無駄にしていますよ－仕事をしなさい． I'll go by car to **save time**. 私は時間を浮かせるために車で行くつもりだ． free/spare time 自由な時間・空いている時間 We haven't got time to stop now. 私たちには今，立ち止まっている時間はありません． I've been waiting **a long time**. 私は長い間ずっと待っている． Learning a language **takes time**. 言語を学ぶには時間がかかる． ▶定義2 U C time (to do sth); time (for sth) the time in hours and minutes shown on a clock; the moment when sth happens or should happen 時計に表示されている，時間と分で表す時；〜が起こる，または起こるべき瞬間→時刻，時間，〜すべき時，時機 ‖ What's the time?/What time is it? 今何時ですか． Can you tell me the times of trains to Bristol, please? ブリストル行きの列車の時刻を教えてくれませんか． It's time to go home. もう帰る時間ですよ． **By the time** I get home, Alex will have cooked the dinner. 私が家に着く時間までに，アレックスは夕食を作っておいてくれるだろう． **This time tomorrow** I'll be on the plane. 明日のこの時間は私は飛行機の中だ． It's time for lunch. お昼の時間だ． ▶定義3 [単数扱い] a system for measuring time in a particular part of the world 世界のある特定の地域での時刻を示すための体系→標準時 ‖ eleven o'clock local time 現地時間の11時 ▶定義4 C an occasion when you do sth or when sth happens 〜をする，または〜が起こる時→〜回，〜度，〜する時 ‖ I phoned them three times. 私は彼らに3回電話をかけた． I'll do it better **next time**. 次回はそれをもっとうまくやります． **Last time** I saw him, he looked ill. 私が彼に最後に会った時，彼は具合が悪そうに見えた． **How many times** have I told you not to touch that? それに触らないようにと何回言えばわかるの． ▶定義5 C an event or an occasion that you experience in a certain way ある特定の

状況で経験する出来事,または時→**期間,時期,一時** ‖ ***Have a good time*** tonight. 今晩楽しんでおいでね. *We had a terrible time at the hospital.* 私たちは病院で極めて不快な思いをした.

▶**定義 6** ❻a period in the past; a part of history 過去のある期間; 歴史の一部→**時代,時世,年代** ‖ *In Shakespeare's times, few people could read.* シェークスピアの時代には,文字を読める人がほとんどいなかった. *The 19th century was a time of great industrial change.* 19世紀は産業に大きな変化があった時代だ. ▶**定義 7** ❻Ⓤthe number of minutes, etc, taken to complete a race or an event 競走や競技を完了させるのにかかる,分などの単位で計った時間→**タイム,所要時間,計測時間** ‖ *What was his time in the hundred metres?* 彼の100メートルのタイムはどれくらいでしたか.

成句 (and) about time (too); (and) not before time(口語)▶定義 used to say that sth should already have happened ~が既に起こっているべきだと言うために用いて→**やっとだね,遅すぎるくらいだ,もっと早くてもいいくらいだ**

ahead of your time ⇒ **AHEAD**

all the time/the whole time ▶定義 during the period that sb was doing sth or that sth was happening ~が…をしている,または~が起きている期間に→**その間ずっと,~している間中** ‖ *I searched everywhere for my keys and they were in the door all the time.* 私はかぎを見つけようと辺りをくまなく探したが,その間中かぎはドアに付いたままだった.

at the same time ⇒ **SAME**

at a time ▶定義 on each occasion それぞれの時に→**一度に,一遍に,続け様に** ‖ *The lift can hold six people at a time.* そのエレベーターには一度に6人まで乗ることができる. *She ran down the stairs two at a time.* 彼女は階段を一度に2段ずつ駆け下りた.

at one time ▶定義 in the past; previously 過去に; 以前に→**かつては,ひところは,昔は**

at the time ▶定義 at a particular moment or period in the past; then 過去のある特定の時,または期間に; その当時→**その時,その当時** ‖ *I agreed at the time but later changed my mind.* 私はその時同意したが,後で考えを変えた.

at times ▶定義 sometimes; occasionally 時々; 時折→**時々,時折,たまに** ‖ *At times I wish we'd never moved house.* もう二度と引っ越すことがなければいいのにと私は時々思う.

before your time ▶定義 before you were born 生まれる前に→**~が生まれる前に,まだその時にならないうちに**

behind the times ▶定義 not modern or fashionable 現代的でも流行を追ってもいない→**時代後れで,時勢に後れて,流行後れで,旧式で**

bide your time ⇒ **BIDE**

buy time ⇒ **BUY**¹

for the time being ▶定義 just for the present; not for long ちょうど今のところ; 長い間ではなく→**当分の間,差し当たって,当座は,当面は**

from time to time ▶定義 sometimes; not often 時々; 度々ではない→**時々,折々,時折,時あるごとに**

give sb a hard time ⇒ **HARD**¹

have a hard time doing sth ⇒ **HARD**¹

have no time for sb/sth ▶定義 to not like sb/sth ~を好きではない→**~を軽べつする,嫌う,~に我慢がならない** ‖ *I have no time for lazy people.* 私は怠け者が嫌いだ.

have the time of your life ▶定義 to enjoy yourself very much 非常に楽しむ→**これまでにないほど楽しい思いをする**

in the course of time ⇒ **COURSE**

in good time ▶定義 early; at the right time 早く; 適切な時に→**~に十分間に合うように早く,予定より早く,余裕を残して,時間通りに,ちょうどいい時に**

in the nick of time ⇒ **NICK**¹

in time (for sth/to do sth) ▶定義 not late; with enough time to be able to do sth 遅れていない; ~をすることができるだけの十分な時間がある→**間に合って,遅れずに,ちょうどいい時に** ‖ *Don't worry. We'll get to the station in time for your train.* 心配しないで. あなたの電車に間に合うように私たちは駅に行きますから.

It's about/high time(口語)▶定義 used to say that you think sb should do sth very soon ~が…を直ちにするべきであると言うために用いて→**もうそろそろ~してもいいころ,機の熟したとき,とっくに~すべき時刻,潮時** ‖ *It's about time you told him what's going on.* 何が起きているのか,そろそろ彼に話してもいいころだ.

kill time, an hour, etc ⇒ **KILL**[1]
once upon a time ⇒ **ONCE**
on time ▶定義 not too late or too early; punctual 遅すぎても早すぎてもいない; 時間を守る➜**時間通りに, 定刻に, 遅れずに** ‖ *The train left the station on time.* その電車は駅を定刻に出た.
one at a time ⇒ **ONE**[1]
take your time ▶定義 to do sth without hurrying 急がないで～をする➜**のんびりとやる, ゆっくりとする**
tell the time ⇒ **TELL**
time after time; time and (time) again ▶定義 again and again; repeatedly 何度も何度も; 繰り返して➜**何度も何度も, しばしば, いく度も**

**time**[2] /táɪm/ [動][他] ▶定義**1**（しばしば受動態で）to arrange to do sth or arrange for sth to happen at a particular time ある特定の時間に～をするように, または～が起こるように手はずを整える➜**～に良い時機を選ぶ, ～に時刻を合わせる, ～するように時間が決められている** ‖ *Their request was badly timed (= it came at the wrong time).* 彼らの要請はタイミングが悪かった(= ふさわしくない時に起こった). *She timed her arrival for shortly after three.* 彼女は３時少し過ぎに到着するよう調整した. ▶定義**2** to measure how long sb/sth takes ～がどのくらい時間がかかるかを計る➜**～の時間・速度を計る** ‖ *Try timing yourself when you write your essay.* 論文を書くときに時間を計ってみなさい.

T

**time-consuming** [形] ▶定義 that takes or needs a lot of time たくさんの時間がかかる, または必要となるような➜**時間のかかる, 時間を食う, 手間暇のかかる**

**time lag** = **LAG**[2]

**timeless** /táɪmləs/ [形][正式] ▶定義 that does not seem to be changed by time or affected by changes in fashion 時間によって変化を受けたり, 流行の変化に影響されたりすることのないように見える➜**時間を超越した, 時代に左右されない, 不朽の**

**time limit** [名] [C] ▶定義 a time during which sth must be done その間に～がなされなければならないという時間➜**期限, タイムリミット, 時限, 制限時間** ‖ *We have to* ***set a time limit*** *for the work.* 私たちはその仕事の締め切りを決めなければならない.

**timely** /táɪmli/ [形] ▶定義 happening at exactly the right time ちょうど適切な時に起こっている➜**時を得た, 折の良い, タイムリーな**

**timer** /táɪmər/ [名] [C] ▶定義 a person or machine that measures time 時間を計る人または機器➜**時計係, 計時係, ストップウオッチ, タイマー, タイムスイッチ** ‖ *an oven timer* オーブンのタイマー

**times**[1] /táɪmz/ [前]（記号×）▶定義 used when you are multiplying one figure by another ある数にほかの数を掛けるときに用いて➜**～倍した** ‖ *Three times four is twelve.* ３掛ける４は12.

**times**[2] /táɪmz/ [名]［複数扱い］▶定義 used for comparing things ものを比較するために用いて➜**～倍** ‖ *Tea is* ***three times as/more*** *expensive in Spain than in England.* スペインでの紅茶の値段はイングランドの３倍する.

**timetable** /táɪmtèɪb(ə)l/（[米]**schedule**）[名] [C] ▶定義 a list that shows the times at which sth happens ～が起こる時を示している一覧表➜**予定表, 計画表, 時間割り, 時刻表, 運行予定表** ‖ *a bus/train/school timetable* バスの時刻表・電車の時刻表・学校の時間割り

**timid** /tímәd/ [形] ▶定義 easily frightened; shy and nervous すぐにぎょっとする; 内気で神経過敏な➜**おくびょうな, 気の小さい, 物おじする, おどおどした, 内気な** — timidity [名] [U]➜**おくびょう, 小心, 内気** — timidly [副]➜**おくびょうに, おずおずと, 恐る恐る, 怖々**

**timing** /táɪmɪŋ/ [名] [U] ▶定義**1** the time when sth is planned to happen ～が起こるように計画されている時➜**タイミング, 好機の選択, 時間調整** ‖ *The manager was very careful about the timing of his announcement.* その経営者は発表のタイミングにとても注意を払っていた. ▶定義**2** the skill of doing sth at exactly the right time ～をちょうど良い時にする技術➜**間合い, 間の取り方** ‖ *The timing of her speech was perfect.* 彼女のスピーチの間の取り方は完ぺきだった.

***tin** /tɪn/ [名] ▶定義**1** [U]（元素記号**Sn**）a soft silver-white metal that is often mixed with other metals しばしばほかの金属と混ぜられる, 銀白色の柔らかい金属➜**スズ, ブリキ** ▶定義**2**（または**tin can**; 特に [米]**can**）[C] a closed metal container in which food, paint, etc is stored and sold; the contents of one of these containers 食べ物, ペ

ンキなどが保存され売られる,閉じた金属の容器;そのような容器の1つの中身→缶詰の缶,缶詰の中身 ‖ *a tin of peas/beans/soup* エンドウ・豆・スープの缶詰 *a tin of paint/varnish* ペンキ・ニスの缶 ☞ **container** のさし絵 ▶定義3 **C** a metal container with a lid for keeping food in 中に食べ物を入れておくための,ふたの付いた金属の容器→ブリキ製の容器 ‖ *a biscuit/cake tin* ビスケット・(パン)ケーキの缶 — tinned 形→缶詰の,缶詰にした ‖ *tinned peaches/peas/soup* モモ・エンドウ・スープの缶詰

**tinfoil** /tínfɔɪl/ = **FOIL**¹

**tinge** /tɪndʒ/ 名 [C, 通常は単数] ▶定義 a small amount of a colour or a feeling 少しの色または気持ち→色,薄い色合い,~気味,かすかな~,~染みたところ ‖ *a tinge of sadness* そこはかとない物悲しさ — tinged 形 tinged (with sth)→~が混じった ‖ *Her joy at leaving was tinged with regret.* 彼女の出発するときの喜びには後悔が入り交じっていた.

**tingle** /tíŋg(ə)l/ 動 自 ▶定義 (used about a part of the body) to feel as if a lot of small sharp points are pushing into it (体の一部分について) ぴりっとする小さな点が体内に押し入ってくるように感じる → ちくちくする,ひりひりする,うずく,刺す痛みを感じさせる ‖ *His cheeks tingled as he came in from the cold.* 寒い所から入ってくると,彼のほおはひりひりした. — tingle 名 [通常は単数]→ちくちくすること,ひりひりすること,うずき,ぞくぞくする感じ ‖ *a tingle of excitement/anticipation/fear* ぞくぞくする興奮・期待・恐怖

**tinker** /tíŋkər/ 動 自 ▶定義 tinker (with sth) to try to repair or improve sth without having the proper skill or knowledge 適切な技術や知識を持たないで,~を修理または改良しようとする→(~を)いじくり回す,(~に)下手に手を加える

**tinkle** /tíŋk(ə)l/ 動 自 ▶定義 to make a light high ringing sound, like that of a small bell 小さな鈴のように,軽やかで高い音が鳴る→リンリンと鳴る,チリンと鳴る — tinkle 名 [C, 通常は単数]→リンリンと鳴る音,チリンと鳴る音

**tin-opener** (特に 困 **can-opener**) 名 **C** ▶定義 a tool that you use for opening a tin of food 食品の缶詰を開けるときに使う道具→缶切り

**tinsel** /tíns(ə)l/ 名 **U** ▶定義 long strings of shiny coloured paper, used as a decoration to hang on a Christmas tree クリスマスツリーにつるす飾りとして使われる,色が付いてぴかぴか光った長い紙→ぴかぴか光る紙の薄紗・糸,ティンセル

**tint** /tɪnt/ 名 **C** ▶定義 a shade or a small amount of a colour 陰,またはほのかな色→淡い色,ほのかな色 ‖ *white paint with a pinkish tint* ピンクがかった白のペンキ — tint 動 他 →~に淡い色を付ける,色合いを添える,陰影を付ける,~を染める ‖ *tinted glasses* 淡い色の付いた眼鏡 *She had her hair tinted.* 彼女は髪を染めてもらった.

*★**tiny** /táɪni/ 形 (**tinier**; **tiniest**) ▶定義 very small とても小さい→ごく小さい,ちっちゃな,ごくわずかの ‖ *the baby's tiny fingers* 赤ん坊のちっちゃな指

*★**tip**¹ /tɪp/ 名 **C** ▶定義1 the thin or pointed end of sth ~の細長い,またはとがった先端→先,先端,頂点,頂上,先端部 ‖ *the tips of your toes/fingers* つま先・指先 *the tip of your nose* 鼻の先 *the southernmost tip of South America* 南米の最南端 ▶定義2 **a tip (on/for sth/doing sth)** a small piece of useful advice about sth practical 実用的な~についての,役に立つちょっとした助言→~についての内報,情報,助言,警告,秘けつ,示唆 ‖ *useful tips on how to save money* 金をためる方法についての役に立つ情報 ▶定義3 a small amount of extra money that you give to sb who serves you, for example in a restaurant レストランなどで,サービスを提供してくれた人に渡す,特別な少額の金→チップ,心付け,祝儀 ‖ *to leave a tip for the waiter* ウエーターにチップを置いていく *I gave the porter a $5 tip.* 私はポーターに5ドルのチップをやった. ▶定義4 英 (または **rubbish tip**) a place where you can take rubbish and leave it ごみを持っていって置いておく場所→ごみ捨て場 ☞類 **dump** ▶定義5 英略式 a place that is very dirty or untidy とても汚い,または散らかっている場所→汚い場所,散らかった部屋

成句 (have sth) on the tip of your tongue ▶定義 to be sure you know sth but to be unable to remember it for the moment ~を確かに知っているが,今すぐには思い出すことができない→~がのどまで出かかって,思い出しかかって,思い出しそうで思い出せない

## 1702 tip²

**the tip of the iceberg** ▶定義 only a small part of a much larger problem かなり大きな問題の中のほんの小さな部分→氷山の一角, ほんの一部分

**tip²** /típ/ 動 (**tipping; tipped**) ▶定義1 自他 tip (sth) (up) to move so that one side is higher than the other; to make sth move in this way 片側がもう一方の側よりも高くなるように動く; ～をそのように動かす→傾く; ～を傾ける, かしげる ‖ *When I stood up, the bench tipped up and the person on the other end fell off.* 私が立ち上がるとベンチが傾き, 向こうの端に座っていた人が落ちた. ▶定義2 他 to make sth come out of a container by holding or lifting it at an angle 容器をある角度に持ってまたは持ち上げて, ～をその中から出す→～をひっくり返す, 捨てる, ほうり出す ‖ *Tip the dirty water down the drain.* 汚い水は排水溝に捨てなさい. *The child tipped all the toys onto the floor.* その子はおもちゃを全部, 床にほうり出した. ▶定義3 自他 to give a waiter, etc a small amount of extra money (in addition to the normal charge) to thank him/her 感謝の意を表すため, ウエーターなどに (通常の料金とは別に) 特別な少額の金を渡す→(～に) チップをやる ‖ *She tipped the taxi driver generously.* 彼女はタクシーの運転手に気前良くチップをやった. ▶定義4 他 tip sb/sth (as sth/to do sth) to think or say that sb/sth is likely to do sth ～が…をしそうであると思う, または言う→～に内報する, ～を予想する ‖ *This horse is tipped to win the race.* この馬がレースに勝つだろうと予想されている. *He is widely tipped as the next Prime Minister.* 彼は次期首相と広く目されている.

句動詞 **tip sb off** ▶定義 to give sb secret information ～に秘密情報を教える→～に内報する, 警告する, 密告する, こっそり知らせる

**tip (sth) up/over** ▶定義 to fall or turn over; to make sth do this 落ちる, またはひっくり返る; ～をそのようにする→転覆する, ひっくり返る, ～をひっくり返す ‖ *An enormous wave crashed into the little boat and it tipped over.* 巨大な波が小舟に襲い掛かり, その船は転覆した.

**tip-off** 名 C ▶定義 secret information that sb gives, for example to the police, about an illegal activity that is going to happen ～が警察などに教える, これから起こりそうである違法な出来事についての秘密情報→秘密情報, 内報, 警告 ‖ *Acting on a tip-off, the police raided the house.* 警察は, 秘密情報に基づいて行動し, その家を手入れした.

**tiptoe¹** /típtòʊ/ 名

成句 **on tiptoe** ▶定義 standing or walking on the ends of your toes with your heels off the ground, in order not to make any noise or to reach sth high up 音を立てないように, または高い所にある～に背伸びするため, かかとを地面から離し, つま先で立ったり歩いたりしている→つま先立ちで, 抜き足差し足で

**tiptoe²** /típtòʊ/ 動 自 ▶定義 to walk on your toes with your heels off the ground かかとを地面から離し, つま先で歩く→つま先立ちで (そっと) 歩く, 忍び足で歩く

**tire¹** /táɪər/ 動 自他 ▶定義 to feel that you need to rest or sleep; to make sb feel like this 休んだり眠ったりする必要があると感じる; ～にそのように感じさせる→疲れる, 飽きる; ～を疲れさせる, くたびれさせる, うんざりさせる

句動詞 **tire of sth/sb** ▶定義 to become bored or not interested in sth/sb any more うんざりする, または～にもはや興味がなくなる→～に飽きる, うんざりする

**tire sb/yourself out** ▶定義 to make sb/yourself very tired; to exhaust sb/yourself ～・自分をとても疲れさせる; ～・自分を疲れ果てさせる→～を疲労困憊 (こんぱい) させる ‖ *The long walk tired us all out.* 長く歩いたので私たちは皆くたくたになった.

**tire²** 米 = TYRE

★**tired** /táɪərd/ 形 ▶定義 feeling that you need to rest or sleep 休んだり眠ったりする必要があると感じている→疲れた, 飽きた, うんざりした, 嫌になった ‖ *She was tired after a hard day's work.* 彼女は日中, 一生懸命に働いて疲れた. *I was completely **tired out** (= exhausted) after all that.* それがすべて済むと, 私は心底疲れた (= 疲れ果てた). — tiredness 名 U →疲れ, 疲労, 倦怠 (けんたい)

成句 **be tired of sb/sth/doing sth** ▶定義 to be bored with or annoyed by sb/sth/doing sth ～に, または…をすることにうんざりする, またはいらいらする→～に飽きて, ～が嫌になって ‖ *I'm* *tired of this game. Let's play something else.* このゲームには飽きた. ほかの事をしようよ. *I'm **sick and tired** of listening to the same thing again and again.* 同じ事を何度も何度も聞くのには飽き飽きしている.

**tireless** /táɪərləs/ 形 ▶定義 putting a lot of hard work and energy into sth over a long period of time without stopping or losing interest やめたり興味をなくしたりせずに, 長時間にわたって多くの作業と労力を~に注いでいる➡疲れを知らない, 飽きることのない, 根気強い, たゆみない, 不断の

**tiresome** /táɪərsəm/ 形 正式 ▶定義 that makes you angry or bored; annoying 怒らせたり, うんざりさせたりするような; いらいらさせている➡厄介な, 面倒な, 煩わしい, うんざりさせる, 退屈な

**tiring** /táɪərɪŋ/ 形 ▶定義 making you want to rest or sleep 休んだり眠ったりしたいと思わせている➡疲れさせる, 骨の折れる, 退屈な ‖ *a tiring journey/job* 退屈な旅・骨の折れる仕事

**tissue** /tíʃuː, -ʃuː/ 名 ▶定義1 [ ❶, 複数扱い] the mass of cells that form the bodies of humans, animals and plants 人, 動物, 植物の生体を形づくる細胞の集まり➡組織 ‖ *muscle/brain/nerve/scar tissue* 筋肉組織・脳組織・神経組織・瘢痕(はんこん)組織 *Radiation can destroy the body's tissues.* 放射能は体の組織を破壊してしまう. ▶定義2 ❶ a thin piece of soft paper that you use to clean your nose and throw away after you have used it 鼻をかむために使い, 使った後は捨てる, 薄くて柔らかい紙➡ティッシュペーパー ‖ *a box of tissues* ティッシュペーパーの箱 ▶定義3 (または **tissue paper**) ❶ thin soft paper that you use for putting around things that may break 壊れそうな物を包むために使う, 薄くて柔らかい紙➡薄様紙

**tit** /tɪt/ 名 ❶ (俗語) ▶定義 a woman's breast 女性の胸➡女性の乳房(複数形), 乳首(単数形) ☛ この言葉を不快に思う人もいる.
成句 **tit for tat** ▶定義 something unpleasant that you do to sb because he/she has done sth to you ~が自分に対して…をしたため, 自分がその人に対してする不快な事➡仕返し, しっぺ返し, 報復, 目には目を歯には歯を, 売り言葉に買い言葉

**titbit** /títbɪt/ (米 **tidbit**) 名 ❶ ▶定義1 a small but very nice piece of food 少量だがとてもおいしい食べ物➡少量のおいしい食べ物, 一口の珍味 ▶定義2 an interesting piece of information 面白い情報➡取って置きの話, 面白い話

*****title** /táɪtl/ 名 ❶ ▶定義1 the name of a book, play, film, picture, etc 本, 演劇, 映画, 絵画などの名前➡題, 表題, 題名, 書名, 見出し ‖ *I know the author's name but I can't remember the title of the book.* 著者の名前は分かるのだが, その本の題名が思い出せない. ▶定義2 a word that shows a person's position, profession, etc ある人の地位や職業などを表す言葉➡称号, 敬称, 肩書き ‖ *'Lord', 'Doctor', 'Reverend', 'Mrs' and 'General' are all titles.* Lord, Doctor, Reverend, Mrs, General はどれも敬称や肩書きである. ▶定義3 the position of being the winner of a competition, especially a sports competition 競技, 特にスポーツの競技の勝者であるという地位➡選手権, タイトル ‖ *Sue is playing this match to defend her title (= to remain champion).* スーはタイトルを防衛する(= 選手権保持者であり続ける)ためにこの試合をしている.

**titled** /táɪtld/ 形 ▶定義 having a word, for example 'Duke', 'Lady', etc before your name that shows that your family has an important position in society 名前の前に, 一族が社会で重要な地位にあることを示す, Duke, Lady などの言葉が付いている➡称号・爵位を持っている, 肩書きのある

**title-holder** 名 ❶ ▶定義 the person or team who won a sports competition the last time it took place; the current champion この前行われたスポーツ競技で優勝した人またはチーム; 現在の選手権保持者➡タイトル保持者・チーム, 選手権保持者・チーム

**title role** 名 ❶ ▶定義 the main character in a film, book, etc whose name is the same as the title 映画や本などで, その題名と同じ名前の中心人物➡主題役, タイトルロール

**titter** /títər/ 動 ❶ ▶定義 to laugh quietly, especially in an embarrassed or nervous way 特に当惑してまたは神経質に, 声を立てないで笑う➡くすくす笑う, 忍び笑いをする — **titter** 名 ❶ ➡くすくす笑い, 忍び笑い

**T-junction** 名 ❶ ▶定義 a place where two roads join to form the shape of a T 2本の道路が交差してT字型になっている所➡T字路, T字

# 1704 to

形三差路 ☞ roundabout のさし絵

\*to /(子音の前) tə, (母音の前) tu, (文または節の終わり) tu/ 前 副 ▶定義1 in the direction of; as far as 〜の方向に; 〜まで→〜へ, 〜に, 〜まで, 〜に向かって ‖ *She's going to London.* 彼女はロンドンに行くことになっている. *Turn to the left.* 左に曲がりなさい. *Pisa is to the west of Florence.* ピサはフィレンツェの西にある. *He has gone to school.* 彼は学校へ行ったところだ. ▶定義2 used to show the end or limit of a series of things or period of time 一連の事またはある期間の, 終わりや限界を表すために用いて→〜まで, 〜に至るまで ‖ *from Monday to Friday* 月曜から金曜まで *from beginning to end* 始めから終わりまで ▶定義3 used to show the person or thing that receives sth 〜を受け取る人または物を表すために用いて→〜に, 〜に対して ‖ *Give that to me.* それを私によこしなさい. *I am very grateful to my parents.* 私は両親に大変感謝している. *What have you done to your hair?* 髪をどうしたのですか. *Sorry, I didn't realize you were talking to me.* ごめんなさい. あなたが私に話し掛けているのに気付きませんでした. ▶定義4 (nearly) touching sth; directed towards sth 〜に (ほとんど) 触れている; 〜の方に向けられている→〜に, 〜へ, 〜に接して, 〜について ‖ *He put his hands to his ears.* 彼は耳に手をやった. *They sat back to back.* 彼らは背中合わせに座った. *She made no reference to her personal problems.* 彼女は自分の個人的な問題については触れなかった. ▶定義5 reaching a particular state ある状態に達している→〜になるまで, 〜になるように ‖ *The meat was cooked to perfection.* その肉は完全に火が通っていた. *His speech reduced her to tears (= made her cry).* 彼のスピーチを聴いて, 彼女は感動のあまり涙を流した (= 彼女に涙を流させた). ▶定義6 used to introduce the second part of a comparison 比較の対象を導入するために用いて→〜よりも, 〜と比較して ‖ *I prefer theatre to opera.* 私はオペラよりも芝居の方が好きだ. ▶定義7 (used for expressing quantity) for each unit of money, measurement, etc (数量を表すために用いて) 金, 計測などの単位に対して→〜ごとに, 〜当たり, 〜に付き ‖ *How many dollars are there to the euro?* 1ユーロは何ドルになりますか. ▶定義8 (used to say what time it is) before→(何時かを言うために用いて) 前に ‖ *It's ten to three (= ten minutes before three o'clock).* 3時10分前です (= 3時までに10分ある). ▶定義9 used to express sb's opinion or feeling about sth 〜についての…の意見や気持ちを表すために用いて→〜にとって, 〜に ‖ *To me, it was the wrong decision.* 私にとって, それは間違った決断だった. *It sounded like a good idea to me.* それは私には良い考えのように聞こえた. *I don't think our friendship means anything to him.* 私たちの友情が彼にとっては何も意味を持たないものだと思う. ▶定義10 used for expressing a reaction or attitude to sth 〜に対する反応や態度を表すために用いて→〜したことには, 〜にも ‖ *To my surprise, I saw two strangers coming out of my house.* 驚いたことに, 私は自分の家から知らない人が2人出てくるのを見た. *His paintings aren't really to my taste.* 彼の絵はあまり私の好みではない. ▶定義11 used with verbs to form the infinitive 不定詞を構成するために, 動詞と用いて→〜すること, 〜であること ‖ *I want to go home now.* 私は今, 家に帰りたい. *Don't forget to write.* 手紙を書くのを忘れないように. *I didn't know what to do.* 私は何をすべきか分からなかった. ▶定義12 /tuə/ (used about a door) in or into a closed position (戸について) 閉じた状態で, または閉じた状態になって→閉まった状態に, 閉まって ‖ *Push the door to.* ドアを閉めなさい. 成句 **to and fro** ▶定義 backwards and forwards 後ろや前に→あちこち, 行ったり来たり

**toad** /tóud/ 名 C ▶定義 a small cold-blooded animal that has a rough skin and lives both on land and in water ざらざらした皮膚を持ち, 陸上でも水中でも生活する, 小さな冷血動物→ヒキガエル, ガマ ☞ **frog** のさし絵

**toadstool** /tóudstùːl/ 名 C ▶定義 a type of small wild plant (a fungus) that is usually poisonous, with a round top and a thin supporting part 通常は毒があり, 先が円形で, それを支える部分が細長い, 野生の小さな植物 (菌類) の一種→食用でないキノコ, 毒キノコ ☞参 **mushroom**, **fungus**

**toast** /tóust/ 名 ▶定義1 ❶a thin piece of bread that is heated on both sides to make it brown

両面を熱してこんがり焼いた薄いパン→**トースト** ‖ *a piece/slice of toast* トースト1枚 ▶定義2 ❻ a toast (to sb/sth) an occasion at which a group of people wish sb happiness, success, etc, by drinking a glass of wine, etc at the same time 集団の人々が,1杯のワインなどを同時に飲んで~の幸福,成功などを祈る機会→**乾杯,祝杯** ‖ *I'd like to propose a toast to the bride and groom.* 新郎と新婦のために乾杯をしたいと思います. ☛参 drink ― toast 動他→**~をこんがり焼く,火であぶる,~のために乾杯する,~を祝して乾杯する**

**toaster** /tóʊstər/ 名 ❻ ▶定義 an electrical machine for making bread turn brown by heating it on both sides パンの両面を熱してこんがり焼くための電気製品→**トースター**

**tobacco** /təbǽkoʊ/ 名 ❼ ▶定義 the substance that people smoke in cigarettes and pipes (the dried leaves of the tobacco plant) 紙巻きたばこやパイプに詰めて吸う物(乾燥したたばこの葉)→**刻みたばこ**

**tobacconist** /təbǽkənɪst/ 名 ▶定義1 ❻a person who sells cigarettes, matches, etc 紙巻きたばこやマッチなどを売る人 → **たばこ商人,たばこ小売商** ▶定義2 (または **the tobacconist's**)[単数扱い] a shop where you can buy cigarettes, matches, etc 紙巻きたばこやマッチなどを買える店 → **たばこ屋**

**toboggan** /təbɑ́g(ə)n/ 名 ❻ ▶定義 a type of flat board with flat pieces of metal underneath, that people use for travelling down hills on snow for fun 遊びで雪の積もった斜面を降りるために使う,下面に平たい金属が付いている平らな板→**トボガン,リュージュ,ローデル**

  ▶ toboggan は小型の sledge(そり)である. bob-sleigh を参照.

★**today** /tədéɪ/ 名 ❼ 副 ▶定義1 (on) this day この日(に)→**今日(は),本日は** ‖ *Today is Monday.* 今日は月曜日です. *What shall we do today?* 今日は何をしましょうか. *School ends a week today* (= on this day next week). 学校は来週の今日(= 来週のこの日)でおしまいだ. *Where is today's paper?* 今日の新聞はどこにありますか. ▶定義2 (in) the present age; these days 今の時代(に);近ごろ→**現代,今日(では),現在(では)** ‖ *Young people today have far more freedom.* 現代の若者の方がはるかに自由である. ☛類 nowadays

**toddle** /tɑ́dl/ 動 ❾ ▶定義1 to walk with short steps like a very young child 非常に幼い子供のように,短い歩幅で歩く→**よちよち歩く,ちょこちょこ歩く** ▶定義2 略式 to walk or go somewhere どこかへ散歩する,または行く→**散歩する,ぶらぶら歩く**

**toddler** /tɑ́dlər/ 名 ❻ ▶定義 a young child who has only just learnt to walk 歩くことをちょうど覚えたばかりの幼い子供→**よちよち歩きを始めた幼児,歩き始めの子**

★**toe**¹ /tóʊ/ 名 ❻ ▶定義1 one of the small parts like fingers at the end of each foot 足の先にある,手の指のような小さな部分の1つ→**足の指,つま先** ☛ C1, C5ページのさし絵 ▶定義2 the part of a sock, shoe, etc that covers your toes 靴下や靴などで,つま先を覆っている部分→**つま先**

**toe**² /tóʊ/ 動 (現分 **toeing**; 過, 過分 **toed**)
成句 **toe the (party) line** ▶定義 to do what sb in authority tells you to do, even if you do not agree with him/her たとえ権力のある~に同意していなくても,その~がやれと命令する事をする→**規則に従う,慣習に従う,言われた通りにする,人の考えに従う**

**TOEFL** /tóʊfəl/ 略 Test of English as a Foreign Language ▶定義 the examination for foreign students who want to study at an American university 米国の大学で学ぶことを希望する外国人の学生のための試験→**トーフル**

**toenail** /tóʊnèɪl/ 名 ❻ ▶定義 one of the hard flat parts that cover the end of your toes 足の指の先を覆っている,平たく堅い部分の1つ→**足の指のつめ** ☛ C5 ページのさし絵

**toffee** /tɑ́fi/ 名 ❻ ❼ ▶定義 a hard sticky sweet that is made by cooking sugar and butter together 砂糖とバターを一緒に煮て作った,べとべとの硬い菓子→**タフィー**

★**together**¹ /təgéðər/ 副 ▶定義1 with or near each other 共に,互いのそばに→**一緒に,共に,連れ立って,1箇所に** ‖ *Can we have lunch together?* 一緒にお昼を食べませんか. *They walked home together.* 彼らは一緒に歩いて帰宅した. *I'll get all my things together tonight because I want to leave early.* 早く出発したいの

## together[2]

で, 今夜, 身の回りの物を全部まとめるつもりです. *Stand with your feet together.* 足をそろえて立ちなさい. ▶定義2 so that two or more things are mixed or joined to each other 2つ以上のものが混ざる, または互いにくっつくように→**合わせて, 一緒にして** ‖ *Mix the butter and sugar together.* バターと砂糖を混ぜ合わせなさい. *Tie the two ends together.* 端と端とを結び合わせなさい. *Add these numbers together to find the total.* これらの数を足して合計を出しなさい. ▶定義3 at the same time 同時に→**同時に, 一斉に** ‖ *Don't all talk together.* 皆が同時にしゃべってはいけません.

成句 get your act together ⇒ ACT[2]

**together with** ▶定義 in addition to; as well as 〜に加えて; 〜だけではなく→**〜と共に, 〜と一緒に, 〜に加えて** ‖ *I enclose my order together with a cheque for £15.* 15ポンドの小切手と一緒に注文書を同封します.

**together**[2] /təɡéðər/ 形略式 ▶定義 (used about a person) organized, capable (人について) きちんとした, 有能な→**冷静な, 落ち着いた, しっかりした** ‖ *I'm not very together this morning.* 今朝の私は, あまり落ち着いていない.

**togetherness** /təɡéðərnəs/ 名 U ▶定義 a feeling of friendship 親しい気持ち→**一体感, 連帯感**

**toil** /tɔ́il/ 動 自 正式 ▶定義 to work very hard or for a long time at sth とても熱心に または長い時間, 〜の仕事をする→**〜に骨を折ってせっせと働く, 精を出して働く** ― **toil** 名 U →**苦労, 骨折り, 骨の折れる仕事, 苦役**

*** toilet** /tɔ́ilət/ 名 C ▶定義 a large bowl with a seat, connected to a water pipe, that you use when you need to get rid of waste material from your body; the room containing this 体から老廃物を取り除く必要があるときに使う, 送水管につながっていて台座の付いた大きな鉢状の物; それが入っている部屋→**便器, 便所, トイレ, 洗面所, 化粧室** ‖ *I need to go to the toilet* (= use the toilet). トイレに行きたい (= トイレを使いたい).

▶家では通常, toiletまたはくだけた言い方でlooと呼ぶ. lavatoryとWCは, 改まった古典的な語である. 公共の場では, Ladies (女性用) またはGents (男性用) と呼ばれる. アメリカ英語の場合, 家ではbathroom, 公共の場ではrestroom, ladies' room (女性用), men's room (男性用) などと言う.

☛ C7ページのさし絵

**toilet bag** (または **sponge bag**) 名 C ▶定義 a bag that you use when travelling to carry things such as soap, toothpaste, etc (toiletries) 旅行するときにせっけんや練り歯磨き粉など (洗面用具) を持ち運ぶために使う袋→**(旅行用)洗面用具入れ**

**toilet paper** (または **toilet tissue**) 名 U ▶定義 soft, thin paper that you use to clean yourself after going to the toilet トイレに行った後, 自分を清潔にするために使う, 薄くて柔らかい紙→**トイレットペーパー**

**toiletries** /tɔ́ilətriz/ 名 [複数扱い] ▶定義 things such as soap or toothpaste that you use for washing, cleaning your teeth, etc 洗ったり歯を磨いたりするためなどに使う, せっけんや練り歯磨き粉のような物→**洗面用品, 化粧用品**

▶旅行するときには, 通常, 洗面用品をsponge bagまたはtoilet bag (洗面用具入れ) に入れて持ち運ぶ.

**toilet roll** 名 C ▶定義 a long piece of toilet paper rolled round a tube 筒に巻き付けられた, 長いトイレットペーパー→**一巻きのトイレットペーパー, トイレットペーパーのロール** ☛ roll のさし絵

**token**[1] /tóukən/ 名 C ▶定義1 a round piece of metal, plastic, etc that you use instead of money to operate some machines or as a form of payment ある機械を操作するために, または支払いの方法として, 金の代わりに使う金属やプラスチックなどでできた円いもの→**代用貨幣, 代用硬貨, トークン** ▶定義2 英 a piece of paper that you can use to buy sth of a certain value in a particular shop. Tokens are often given as presents. 特定の店である価値のある金額の〜を買うために使うことのできる, 1枚の紙片. プレゼントとして贈られることが多い→**商品(引換)券** ‖ *a £10 book/CD/gift token* 10ポンドの図書券・CD券・ギフト券 ☛参 voucher

▶定義3 something that represents or is a symbol of sth 〜を表す, または〜の象徴であるもの→**〜の印, 象徴, 証拠, 兆候** ‖ *Please accept this gift as a token of our gratitude.* 私たちの感

謝の印としてこの贈り物をお受け取りください.

**token**² /tóukən/ 形 (名詞の前だけ) ▶定義1 done, chosen, etc in a very small quantity, and only in order not to be criticized 批判されないようにするだけのために、ほんのわずかな数量でなされたまたは選ばれたなどの→**形だけの、名目上の、名ばかりの、ほんのわずかな** ‖ *There is a token woman on the board of directors.* 重役会には申し訳程度の人数の女性しかいない. ▶定義2 small, but done or given to show that you are serious about sth and will keep a promise or an agreement 小さいが、～について真剣であり、約束や契約を守ることを示すためになされた、または与えられた→**保証の、証拠として与えられた・なされた** ‖ *a token payment* 内金

**told** TELL の過去・過去分詞形

**tolerable** /tál(ə)rəb(ə)l/ 形 ▶定義1 quite good, but not of the best quality かなり良いが最高級ではない→**まずまずの、なかなかの、悪くない** ▶定義2 of a level that you can accept or deal with, although unpleasant or painful 不快または痛みを伴うものであるが、受け入れたり対処できたりする程度である→**耐えられる、我慢のできる、許容できる** ‖ *Drugs can reduce the pain to a tolerable level.* 薬は痛みを我慢のできる程度にまで和らげることができる. ⇔ **intolerable**

**tolerant** /tál(ə)r(ə)nt/ 形 ▶定義 tolerant (of/towards sb/sth) the ability to allow or accept sth that you do not like or agree with 好きではない、または同意していない～を認めたり受け入れたりする能力→**寛容な、寛大な、～を容認する、許容する、辛抱強い** ⇔ **intolerant** — **tolerance** 名 U tolerance (of/for sb/sth)→**寛容、寛大さ、容認、許容、忍耐、我慢(強さ)** ‖ *religious/racial tolerance* 宗教的寛容・人種的寛容 ⇔ **intolerance**

**tolerate** /tálərèit/ 動 他 ▶定義1 to allow or accept sth that you do not like or agree with 好きではない、または同意していない～を認めたり受け入れたりする→**～を許容する、黙認する、大目に見る** ‖ *In a democracy we must tolerate opinions that are different from our own.* 民主主義では、自分たちとは異なる意見を許容しなければならない. ▶定義2 to accept or be able to deal with sb/sth unpleasant without complaining 不快な～を、不平を言わずに受け入れるまたは対処できる→**～を我慢する、耐える、堪え忍ぶ** ‖ *The* 

*noise was more than she could tolerate.* その音は彼女の我慢できる限度を超えていた. — **toleration** /tàləréiʃ(ə)n/ = **TOLERANCE**

**toll** /tóul/ 名 ▶定義1 C money that you pay to use a road or bridge 道路または橋を利用するために支払う金→**通行料(金)、使用料(金)** ‖ *motorway tolls* 高速道路の通行料 *a toll bridge* 有料橋 ▶定義2 [C, 通常は単数] the amount of damage done or the number of people who were killed or injured by sth ～によって受けた損害全体、または殺されたり負傷したりした人の数→**犠牲、損失、損害、被害、死傷者数** ‖ *The official death toll has now reached 5000.* 公式の死者の数は既に5000人にも上った.

成句 **take a heavy toll/take its toll (on sth)** ▶定義 to cause great loss, damage, suffering, etc 大規模な損失、損害、被害などをもたらす→**～に悪影響を及ぼす、～を大量に失わせる**

*★**tomato** /təmá:tou, -mei-/ 名 C (複 **tomatoes**) ▶定義 a soft red fruit that is often eaten without being cooked in salads, or cooked as a vegetable 調理せずにサラダに入れたり、野菜として調理したりして食べられることの多い、赤くて柔らかい果物→**トマト** ‖ *tomato juice/soup/sauce* トマトジュース・トマトスープ・トマトソース ☞ C3 ページのさし絵

**tomb** /tu:m/ 名 C ▶定義 a large place, usually built of stone under the ground, where the body of an important person is buried 通常は地下が石造りになっており、重要な地位にある人の遺体が埋葬されている広い場所→**墓、墓穴、納骨所、納骨堂、霊廟(びょう)** ‖ *the tombs of the Pharaohs* ファラオの墓 ☞参 **grave**

**tomboy** /támbɔi/ 名 C ▶定義 a young girl who likes the same games and activities that are traditionally considered to be for boys 従来、男の子向けであると考えられているものと同じ遊びや活動を好む幼い女の子→**おてんば娘、おきゃん、男の子のような女の子**

**tombstone** /tú:mstòun/ 名 C ▶定義 a large flat stone that lies on or stands at one end of the place where a person is buried (a grave) and shows the name, dates, etc of the dead person 人が埋葬されている場所(墓)の上に置かれている、またはその一方の端に立っている、死者の名

前や日付などを示した平たい大きな石→**墓石, 墓碑** ☞参 **gravestone**, **headstone**

**tomcat** /tɑ́mkæt/（または **tom**）图 C ▶定義 a male cat 雄の猫→**雄猫** ⇔ **taddy**

*__tomorrow__ /təmɔ́ːrou, -mɑ́r-/ 副 U 形 ▶定義 1 (on) the day after today 今日の次の日(に)→**明日(は)** ‖ *Today is Friday so tomorrow is Saturday.* 今日は金曜日だから明日は土曜日だ. *See you tomorrow.* 明日お会いしましょう. *I'm going to bed. I've got to get up early tomorrow morning.* 私はもう寝ます. 明日は朝早く起きなければならないので. *a week tomorrow (= a week from tomorrow)* 来週の明日(= 明日から1週間後)

▶注意. tomorrow morning, tomorrow afternoonなどという言い方はするが, tomorrow in the morningなどとは言わない. morningの注を参照.

▶定義 2 the future 未来→**未来, 将来, 明日, いずれ** ‖ *The schoolchildren of today are tomorrow's workers.* 今の学童たちは未来の担い手である.

**ton** /tʌn/ 图 ▶定義 1 C a measure of weight; 2240 pounds 重量の単位; 2240ポンド→**トン** ▶tonとtonneとを混同しないようにする. 1トンは1,016メートルトンに等しい. アメリカ英語では1トンが2000ポンドである.

▶定義 2 **tons** [複数扱い] 略式 a lot たくさん→**大量, 多量, 多数** ‖ *I've got tons of homework to do.* やらねばならない宿題が大量にある.

**tone**¹ /tóun/ 图 ▶定義 1 C U the quality of a sound or of sb's voice, especially expressing a particular emotion 音または〜の声の質, 特にある感情を表している声の質→**音色, 音調, 調子, 語調, 口調, 語気** ‖ *'Do you know each other?' she asked in a casual tone of voice.* 「お互いに知り合いなの」と, 彼女は打ち解けた口調で尋ねた.

▶定義 2 [単数扱い] the general quality or style of sth 〜の一般的な性質または様式→**気風, 風格, 風潮, 傾向, 雰囲気** ‖ *The tone of the meeting was optimistic.* その会議の雰囲気は楽観的なものだった. ▶定義 3 C a shade of a colour 色の濃淡→**色調, 色合い, 濃淡, 明暗** ‖ *warm tones of red and orange* 赤とオレンジの暖かい色調

▶定義 4 C a sound that you hear on the telephone 受話器から聞こえる音→**発信音** ‖ *Please speak after the tone (= an instruction on an answering machine).* 発信音の後にお話しください(= 留守番電話での指示).

**tone**² /tóun/ 動 他 ▶定義 **tone sth (up)** to make your muscles, skin, etc firmer, especially by doing exercise 筋肉, 皮膚などを, 特に運動することによって, より引き締める→**〜の体を強くする, 健康にする**

句動詞 **tone sth down** ▶定義 to change sth that you have said, written, etc, to make it less likely to offend 不快感をあまり与えないようにするために, 言ったり書いたりなどした〜を変更する→**〜を和らげる**

**tone-deaf** 形 ▶定義 not able to sing or hear the difference between notes in music 音楽で, 音の違いを歌ったり聞き分けたりすることができない→**音痴の**

**tongs** /tɔ(ː)ŋz, tɑŋz/ 图 [複数扱い] ▶定義 a tool that looks like a pair of scissors but that you use for holding or picking things up はさみのような, 物をつかんだり拾い上げたりするために使う道具→**つかみばさみ, やっとこ, 火ばし** ☞ **kitchen**のさし絵

*__tongue__ /tʌŋ/ 图 ▶定義 1 C U the soft part inside your mouth that you can move. You use your tongue for speaking, tasting things, etc. 口の中で動かすことのできる, 柔らかい部分. 話したり物を味わったりするために使う→**舌** ☞ C5ページのさし絵 ▶定義 2 C U the tongue of some animals, cooked and eaten 一部の動物の, 調理されて食用になる舌→**舌肉, タン** ▶定義 3 C 正式 a language 言語→**言語, 国語** ‖ *your mother tongue (= the language you learned as a child)* 母国語(= 子供の時に身に付けた言語)

成句 **on the tip of your tongue** ⇒ **TIP**¹
**put/stick your tongue out** ▶定義 to put your tongue outside your mouth as a rude sign to sb 〜に対する失礼なしぐさとして, 舌を口の外に出す→**人に向かって舌を出す, あかんべえをする**
**a slip of the tongue** ⇒ **SLIP**²
**(with) tongue in cheek** ▶定義 done or said as a joke; not intended seriously 冗談としてなされた, または言われた; 本気で意図されたのではない→**不まじめに, 冗談で, 皮肉に, 冷やかされた, 本心とは裏腹に**

**tongue-tied** 形 ▶定義 not saying anything

because you are shy or nervous 恥ずかしかったりおくびょうであるために、何も言っていない→口のきけない、黙りこくった、口ごもる、ものを言いたがらない

**tongue-twister** 名 C ▶定義 a phrase or sentence with many similar sounds that is difficult to say correctly when you are speaking quickly 早く話しているときに正確に言うのが難しい、似たような音がたくさん含まれている句や文→早口言葉、舌のもつれるような語句

**tonic** /tánɪk/ 名 ▶定義 1 (または **tonic water**) ● U a type of water with bubbles in it and a rather bitter taste that is often added to alcoholic drinks しばしばアルコール飲料に加えられる、中に泡が立ち、やや苦味のある水の一種→トニックウォーター ‖ *a gin and tonic* ジントニック ▶定義 2 ● U a medicine or sth you do that makes you feel stronger, healthier, etc, especially when you are very tired 特に非常に疲れているときに、より丈夫である、より健康であるなどと感じさせる薬または人がする何か→強壮剤、滋養剤、元気を回復させるもの、活力を与えるもの ‖ *A relaxing holiday is a wonderful tonic.* くつろげる休日は大いに元気を回復させてくれる.

*****tonight** /tənáɪt/ 名 U 副 ▶定義 (on) the evening or night of today 今日の晩または夜(に)→今夜(は)、今晩 ‖ *Tonight is the last night of our holiday.* 今夜が私たちの休暇の最後の夜だ. *What's on TV tonight?* 今夜はテレビで何がありますか. *We are staying with friends tonight and travelling home tomorrow.* 私たちは今晩、友達の家に泊まり、明日帰宅する予定です.

**tonne** /tʌn/ 名 C ▶定義 a measure of weight; 1000 kilograms 重量の単位; 1000キロ→メートルトン ☞参 ton

**tonsil** /táns(ə)l/ 名 C ▶定義 one of the two soft lumps in your throat at the back of your mouth 口の奥ののどにある、2つの柔らかい肉塊のうちの1つ→扁桃腺(へんとうせん) ‖ *She had to have her tonsils out* (= removed in a medical operation). 彼女は扁桃腺を切ってもらわなければならなかった(= 手術で除去する).

**tonsillitis** /tànsəláɪtəs/ 名 U ▶定義 an illness in which the tonsils become very sore and swollen 扁桃腺(へんとうせん)が非常に痛くなり、はれ上がる病気→扁桃腺炎

### too/enough

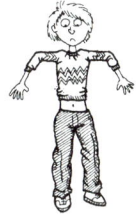 

Tom's sweater is **not** big **enough**.　Kevin's sweater is **too** big.

*****too** /tuː/ 副 ▶定義 1 (形容詞や副詞の前で用いて) more than is good, allowed, possible, etc 良い、許容されている、可能であるなどという状態を超えている→あまりに〜すぎる、必要以上に〜、〜にとって…すぎる、〜するには…すぎる ‖ *These boots are too small.* このブーツは小さすぎる. *It's far too cold to go out without a coat.* 上着を着ないで外出するにはかなり寒すぎる. *It's too long a journey for you to make alone.* あなたが1人で行くには長すぎる旅だ.

▶注意. It's a too long journeyとは言わない.

▶定義 2 (否定文と用いない) in addition; also さらに; 〜もまた→〜もまた、同様に ‖ *Red is my favourite colour but I like blue, too.* 赤は私の好きな色だが、青も好きだ. *Phil thinks you're right and I do too.* フィルはあなたが正しいと思っており、私もそう思う.

▶注意. 節の最後に、肯定文への同意を表すにはtooを、否定文への同意を表すにはeitherを用いる: *I like eating out and Rakesh does too.* (私は外食が好きだが、ラケシュもまた外食が好きだ.) *I don't like cooking and Rakesh doesn't either.* (私は料理が好きではないが、ラケシュも同じく料理が好きではない.)

▶定義 3 used to add sth which makes a situation even worse 状況をさらに悪化させる事を追加するために用いて→その上、しかも ‖ *Her purse was stolen. And on her birthday too.* 彼女の財布が盗まれた. しかも彼女の誕生日に.

▶定義 4 (通常、否定文で用いて) very→あまり ‖ *The weather is not too bad today.* 今日は天気がそれほど悪くない.

**took** TAKE の過去形

1710　tool

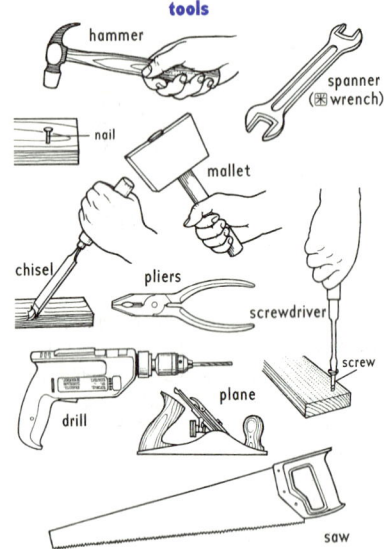

tools
hammer
spanner (米wrench)
nail
mallet
chisel
pliers
screwdriver
screw
plane
drill
saw

**★tool** /túːl/ 名 C ▶定義 a piece of equipment such as a hammer, that you hold in your hand(s) and use to do a particular job 手に持ち,ある特定の仕事をするために使う,金づちなどの器具→道具,工具,工作機械 ‖ *Hammers, screwdrivers and saws are all carpenter's tools.* 金づち,ねじ回し,のこぎりはすべて大工道具である. *garden tools* 園芸用品 *a tool kit (= a set of tools in a box or a bag)* 工具一式(= 箱または袋に入った工具のセット)

▶tool は通常,スパナや金づちなどのように,手に持つ物である. implement は,農業や園芸などの場合のように,戸外で用いられることが多い. machine には稼働する部品があり,電力やエンジンなどで動く. instrument は,技術的な,または精密な作業によく用いられる: *a dentist's instruments*(歯科用器械). device は,便利であると見なされ,ある特定の作業をするために作られた道具を表す,より一般的な語である: *The machine has a safety device which switches the power off if there is a fault.*(その機械には,欠陥があった場合には電源を切る安全装置が付いている.)

**toolbar** /túːlbɑ̀ːr/ 名 C ▶定義 a row of symbols on a computer screen that show the different things that the computer can do コンピューターの画面上にある,そのコンピューターが実行できるさまざまな事を示している記号の列→ツールバー ☛ S5 ページのさし絵

**toot** /túːt/ 名 C ▶定義 the short high sound that a car horn makes クラクションが立てる高く短い音→ブーブーいう音,警笛を鳴らす音 ─ **toot** 動 自 他 →ブーブー鳴る; ～をブーブー鳴らす,警笛を鳴らす ‖ *Toot your horn to let them know we're here.* 私たちがここにいることを彼らに知らせるために警笛を鳴らしなさい.

**★tooth** /túːθ/ 名 C (複 **teeth** /tíːθ/) ▶定義 **1** one of the hard white things in your mouth that you use for biting 口の中にあり,物をかむために使う白く硬い物の1つ1つ→歯 ‖ *She's got beautiful teeth.* 彼女はきれいな歯をしている.

▶食べ物の小片を取り除くために歯を磨くことを brush/clean と言う. decayed(虫歯になる)と,歯医者がその歯を fill(詰める)あるいは extract/take out(抜く)ことになる. 歯をすべて抜いてしまった場合は,false teeth(入れ歯)や dentures(義歯)を入れることがある.

☛ C5 ページのさし絵　☛参 **wisdom tooth**
▶定義 **2** one of the long narrow pointed parts of an object such as a comb くしのような物にある,先のとがった細長い部分の1つ→歯状のもの,歯,(のこぎり・やすりなどの)目

**成句** by the skin of your teeth ⇒ **SKIN**¹
gnash your teeth ⇒ **GNASH**
grit your teeth ⇒ **GRIT**²
have a sweet tooth ⇒ **SWEET**¹

**toothache** /túːθèɪk/ 名 [ U C, 通常は単数 ]
▶定義 a pain in your tooth or teeth 1本または複数の歯の痛み→歯痛　☛参 **ache** の注

**toothbrush** /túːθbrʌ̀ʃ/ 名 C ▶定義 a small brush with a handle that you use for cleaning your teeth 歯を磨くために使う,柄の付いた小さなブラシ→歯ブラシ ☛ **brush** のさし絵

**toothpaste** /túːθpèɪst/ 名 U ▶定義 a substance that you put on your toothbrush and use for cleaning your teeth 歯ブラシに付け,歯を磨くために使う物→練り歯磨き粉

**toothpick** /túːθpìk/ 名 C ▶定義 a short pointed piece of wood that you use for getting pieces of food out from between your teeth 歯の間から食

べ物の小片を取り出すために使う, 短く先のとがった木製の物→**つまようじ**

★**top**¹ /tɑp/ 图 ▶定義1 ● the highest part or point of sth 〜の最も高い部分または点→**最上部, 頂上, 頂, てっぺん, 先端, 頭** ‖ *The flat is **at the top of the stairs**.* そのアパートは階段を上り詰めた所にある. *Snow was falling on the mountain tops.* 雪は山の頂上に降っていた. *Start reading at the top of the page.* そのページの一番上から読みなさい. ⇔ **foot** ▶定義2 ● the flat upper surface of sth 〜の上側の平たい表面→**表面, 上部, 上面** ‖ *a desk/table/bench top* 机・テーブル・ベンチの表面 ▶定義3 [単数扱い] the top (of sth) the highest or most important position 最も高い, または重要な地位→**最高位, 首位, 首席, トップ, 上座, 上席** ‖ *to be at the top of your profession* その職業で最高位にある ▶定義4 ● the cover that you put onto sth in order to close it 閉じるために〜に掛ける覆い→**ふた, 栓, キャップ, 屋根, 幌 (ほろ)** ‖ *Put the tops back on the pens or they will dry out.* ペンのキャップを元に戻してください. そうしないと乾いてしまいますから.

▶ top や cap は小さくて円形である場合が多い. しばしば, 回して取り外す: *a bottle top* (びんのふた) *Unscrew cap to open.* (キャップを外すと開きます.) lid は大きい. 引き上げて取る: *a saucepan lid* (ソースパンのふた) *Put the lid back on the box.* (その箱にふたを戻しなさい.)

☛ **container** のさし絵 ▶定義5 ● a piece of clothing that you wear on the upper part of your body 上半身に着る衣服→**(ツーピースの)上半身, 上着, トップ** ‖ *a tracksuit/bikini/pyjama top* トラックスーツの上着・ビキニのトップ・パジャマの上着 *I need a top to match my new skirt.* 新しいスカートに合う上着が必要です. ☛ C6 ページのさし絵 ▶定義6 ● a child's toy that turns round very quickly on a point 一点で非常に速く回転する, 子供のおもちゃ→**こま**

成句 **at the top of your voice** ▶定義 as loudly as possible できるだけ大きな声で→**声を限りに, 大声で**

**get on top of sb** 略式 ▶定義 to be too much for sb to manage or deal with 管理したり対処したりするのが〜の手に負えない→**〜の手に負えなくなる, 〜を悩ます** ‖ *I've got so much work to do. It's really getting on top of me.* 私にはやるべき仕事があまりにもたくさんある. 本当に手に負えなくなってきている.

**off the top of your head** 略式 ▶定義 just guessing or using your memory without preparing or thinking about sth first 〜について初めに準備するまたは考えることをしないで, 推測するまたは記憶を頼ることをしている→**準備なしに, 即席で, あまりよく考えずに, ふと思い付くままに**

**on top** ▶定義1 on or onto the highest point 最も高い点の上に, またはその点の方へ→**上に, 上方に, 最上部に, 頭のてっぺんで** ‖ *a mountain with snow on top* 頂上に雪をかぶった山 ▶定義2 in control; in a leading position 支配して; 第1位の地位に→**支配して, 高い地位に, 最上位で, 優位に立って** ‖ *Josie always seems to come out on top.* ジョージーはいつも勝利を収めているようだ.

**on top of sb/sth** ▶定義1 on, over or covering sb/sth else ほかの〜の上に, 上方に, または覆って→**〜の上に** ‖ *Books were piled on top of one another.* 本が次々に積み重ねられていた. *The remote control is on top of the TV.* リモコンはテレビの上にある. ▶定義2 in addition to sb/sth else ほかの〜に加えて→**〜に加えて** ‖ *On top of everything else, the car's broken down.* なおその上に, 車が故障した. ▶定義3 略式 very close to sb/sth 〜に非常に近い→**〜のすぐそばに, 〜に接するように, 〜に迫って** ‖ *We were all living on top of each other in that tiny flat.* 私たちは皆, あの小さなアパートに身を寄せ合って住んでいた.

**over the top; OTT** 特に 英 略式 ▶定義 exaggerated or done with too much effort 誇張された, または多大すぎる労力を費やして行われた→**過度に, 目標・規定以上に**

★**top**² /tɑp/ 形 ▶定義 highest in position or degree 位置や程度が最も高い→**一番上の, 首席の, 最上位の, 最高の, 最大の, 一流の** ‖ *one of Britain's top businessmen* 英国で最高の実業家の1人 *at top speed* 最高速度で *the top floor of the building* その建物の最上階 *She got top marks for her essay.* 彼女は論文で最高点を取った.

**top**³ /tɑp/ 動 ⓒ (**topping**; **topped**) ▶定義1 to be higher or greater than a particular amount ある数量よりも高い, または大きい→**〜を超す, 上回**

る、〜より勝る ▶定義2 to be in the highest position on a list because you are the most important, successful, etc 最も重要である、または最も成功しているなどという理由から一覧表の一番高い位置にある→〜の先頭にある、トップに載っている、首位を占める ▶定義3 top sth (with sth) (通常は受動態で) to put sth on the top of sth 〜を…の上に置く→〜の頂上を…で覆う、〜で…にふたをする ‖ *cauliflower topped with cheese sauce* チーズソースが上に掛かったカリフラワー

**句動詞** top (sth) up ▶定義 to fill sth that is partly empty 一部分が空の〜を満たす→つぎ足して〜を一杯にする、〜をなみなみとつぐ、補給する

**top hat** 名 C ▶定義 the tall black or grey hat that a man wears on formal occasions 男性が正式な場でかぶる、黒または灰色で背の高い帽子→シルクハット ☛ hat のさし絵

**top-heavy** 形 ▶定義 heavier at the top than the bottom and likely to fall over 一番下よりも一番上の方が重く、倒れそうである→頭部が重すぎる、頭でっかちの、不安定な

★**topic** /tápɪk/ 名 C ▶定義 a subject that you talk, write or learn about 話す、書くまたは学ぶ対象のテーマ→話題、論題、題目、主題、トピック

**topical** /tápɪk(ə)l/ 形 ▶定義 connected with sth that is happening now; that people are interested in at the present time 今起こっている〜と関連している；現在、人々が興味を持っているような → 現下の、話題の、時局的な、時事問題の、今関心を集めている

**topless** /tápləs/ 形副 ▶定義 (used about a woman) not wearing any clothes on the upper part of the body so that her breasts are not covered (女性について)上半身に何も衣服を着けていないため、胸が覆い隠されていない→トップレスの、上半身を露出した

**topmost** /tápmòʊst/ 形 (名詞の前だけ) ▶定義 highest 最も高い→一番上の、てっぺんの、最高の ‖ *the topmost branches of the tree* その木の一番上の枝

**topping** /tápɪŋ/ 名 C U ▶定義 something such as cream or a sauce that is put on the top of food to decorate it or make it taste nicer 飾りを付けるために、またはよりおいしくするために食べ物の上に掛けられる、クリームやソースのようなもの→トッピング、上飾り

**topple** /tápl/ 動 ▶定義1 自 topple (over) to become less steady and fall down 安定しなくなり倒れる → ぐらついて倒れる、ひっくり返る ‖ *Don't add another book to the pile or it will topple over.* その本の山にもう1冊乗せないで。乗せたらひっくり返るでしょうから。▶定義2 他 to cause a leader of a country, etc to lose his/her position of power or authority 国などの長から、権力や権限のある地位を失わせる → 〜を地位から没落させる、〜を転覆する、倒す、崩壊させる

**top secret** 形 ▶定義 that must be kept very secret, especially from other governments 特にほかの政府から、極めて内密にしておかねばならないような→極秘の、最高機密の、国家機密の

★**torch** /tɔːrtʃ/ 名 C ▶定義1 (米 **flashlight**) a small electric light that you carry in your hand 手で持ち運ぶ、電気でつく小さな明かり→懐中電灯 ‖ *Shine the torch under the sofa and see if you can find my ring.* ソファーの下を懐中電灯で照らして、私の指輪が見つかるかどうか見てください。☛ light のさし絵 ▶定義2 a long piece of wood with burning material at the end that you carry to give light 明るくするために持ち運ぶ、端に燃料を付けた長い木の棒→たいまつ、トーチ ‖ *the Olympic torch* オリンピックの聖火

**tore** TEAR² の過去形

**torment** /tɔ́ːment/ 名 U C ▶定義 great pain and suffering in your mind or body; sb/sth that causes this 心または体の大きな痛みや苦しみ；それの原因となる人・物→苦痛、激痛、苦悩、苦痛・苦悩の原因、悩みの種 ‖ *to be in torment* 苦しんでいる — torment /tɔːmént, ≂/ 動 他 ▶〜をひどく苦しめる、痛め付ける、虐待する、悩ます、困らす

**torn** TEAR² の過去分詞形

**tornado** /tɔːméɪdoʊ/ 名 C (複 **tornadoes**) ▶定義 a violent storm with a very strong wind that blows in a circle 渦を巻いている、非常に強い風を伴った激しいあらし→大竜巻、トルネード、大旋風 ☛参 storm の注

**torpedo** /tɔːrpíːdoʊ/ 名 C (複 **torpedoes**) ▶定義 a bomb, shaped like a long narrow tube, that is fired from a type of ship that travels under the water (a submarine) and explodes when it hits another ship 水中を進む船(潜水艦)から発射され、ほかの船に命中すると爆発する、細長い管のような形をした爆弾→魚雷

**torrent** /tɔ́(ː)r(ə)nt, tár-/ 名 C ▶定義 a strong fast flow of sth, especially water 〜の, 特に水の, 速くて強い流れ→急流, 奔流, 激流, ほとばしり ‖ *The rain was coming down **in torrents**.* 雨は土砂降りだった.

**torrential** /tɔːrénʃ(ə)l, tə-/ 形 ▶定義 (used about rain) very great in amount (雨について) 量がとても多い→滝のような, 激しい, 急流のような

**torso** /tɔ́ːrsoʊ/ 名 C (複 **torsos**) ▶定義 the main part of your body, not your head, arms and legs 頭や腕や足ではない, 身体の主要な部分→胴, 胴部

tortoise ( 米 turtle)

**tortoise** /tɔ́ːrtəs/ (米 **turtle**) 名 C ▶定義 a small animal with a hard shell that moves very slowly. A tortoise can pull its head and legs into its shell to protect them. 非常にゆっくり動く, 硬い甲羅を持った小さな動物. 頭と足を保護するために甲羅の中に引っ込めることができる→カメ

**tortuous** /tɔ́ːrtʃuəs/ 形 ▶定義 1 complicated, not clear and simple 込み入っていて, 明瞭(めいりょう)・簡潔ではない→回りくどい, 持って回った, 込み入って分かりにくい, 遠回しの ▶定義 2 (used about a road, etc) with many bends (道路などについて) カーブの多い→曲がりくねった, ねじれた

**torture** /tɔ́ːrtʃər/ 名 U C ▶定義 1 the action of causing sb great pain either as a punishment or to make him/her say or do sth 罰として, または〜を言わせるまたはさせるために, 〜に大きな苦痛を与える行為→拷問, 虐待 ‖ *His confession was extracted **under torture**.* 彼の自白は拷問によって引き出された. ▶定義 2 mental or physical suffering 精神的な, または肉体的な苦痛→苦痛, 苦悩, 激痛 ‖ *It's torture having to sit here and listen to him complaining for hours.* ここに座って彼の愚痴を何時間も聞かなければならないのは苦痛だ. — torture 動 ⊕ →〜を拷問にかける, 〜を拷問で引き出す, 〜をひどく苦しめる, 悩ます ‖ *Most of the prisoners were tortured into making a confession.* 囚人の大半は拷問に遭って自白した. *She was tortured by the thought that the accident was her fault.* 彼女は, その事故の責任は自分にあったという考えにひどく苦しめられた. — torturer 名 C →拷問する人, 苦しめる人, 悩ませるもの

**Tory** /tɔ́ːri/ 名 C 形 (複 **Tories**) ▶定義 a member or supporter of the British Conservative Party; connected with this party 英国の保守党の一員または支持者; その政党に関連している→英国の保守党員, 保守党支持者, 保守党の ‖ *the Tory Party conference* 保守党会議 ☞参 **party** の注

**toss** /tɔ(ː)s, tɑs/ 動 ▶定義 1 ⊕ to throw sth lightly and carelessly 〜を軽く, ぞんざいに投げる→〜をほうり投げる, ほうる, 軽く投げる ‖ *Bob opened the letter and tossed the envelope into the bin.* ボブは手紙を開封し, 封筒をごみ箱にポイと投げ捨てた. ▶定義 2 ⊜ ⊕ to move, or make sb/sth move up and down or from side to side 上下または左右に動く, または〜を動かす→上下に動く, 揺れる; 〜を激しく揺さぶる, 振り動かす ‖ *He lay **tossing and turning** in bed, unable to sleep.* 彼は眠ることができず, ベッドで横になって寝返りを打っていた. *The ship was tossed about by huge waves.* その船は大波にもまれて激しく揺れた. ▶定義 3 ⊕ to move your head back quickly especially to show you are annoyed or impatient 特にいらいらしている, または我慢できないことを示すために, 頭を後ろへ素早く動かす→〜を急にぐいと上げる, つんとそらす ‖ *I tried to apologise but she just **tossed** her **head** and walked away.* 私は謝ろうとしたが, 彼女は頭をつんと後ろにそらして歩き去った. ▶定義 4 ⊜ ⊕ toss (up) (for sth) to throw a coin into the air in order to decide sth, by guessing which side of the coin will land facing upwards 硬貨のどちらの面が上を向いて落ちるかを当てて〜を決めるために, 硬貨を空中に

## 1714　tot¹

投げる→(硬貨)を投げる; (〜を)硬貨を投げて決める ‖ *to toss a coin* コインを投げる ☛参 **heads, tails**. これらは硬貨のそれぞれの面の言い方で, どちらの面が上を向いているかを当てるときに heads or tails? (表か裏か)と言う.
— toss 名 C →ほうり投げること, 投げ上げ, トス, 揺れ, 急に動かすこと, 硬貨投げ

成句 win/lose the toss ▶定義 to guess correctly/wrongly which side of a coin will face upwards when it lands コインが落ちたときにどちらの面が上を向いているかを正しく・間違って推定する→硬貨投げで勝つ・負ける ‖ *Ms Hingis won the toss and chose to serve first.* ヒンギスさんは硬貨投げで勝ち, 先にサーブする方を選んだ.

**tot¹** /tɒt/ 名 C ▶定義 1 略式 a very small child とても幼い子供→幼児, 小児, ちびっこ ▶定義 2 特に 英 a small glass of a strong alcoholic drink アルコールの強い飲み物のほんの一口→一口, 1杯, 少量

**tot²** /tɒt/ 動 (totting; totted)
句動詞 **tot (sth) up** 略式 ▶定義 to add numbers together to form a total 数をすべて足して合計を出す→締めて〜になる, 〜を合計する

*****total¹** /tóʊtl/ 形 ▶定義 being the amount after everyone or everything is counted or added together; complete すべての人または物が数えられた, またはその合計を出された後の数量である; 完全な→全体の, 全部の, 合計の, 総計の, 完全な, 全くの ‖ *What was the total number of people there?* そこにいる人の総人数は何でしたか. *a total failure* 完全な失敗 *They ate in total silence.* 彼らは全くしゃべらずに食事をした.

**total²** /tóʊtl/ 名 C ▶定義 the number that you get when you add two or more numbers or amounts together 2つ以上の数や量をすべて足すと得られる数→総計, 合計, 総額, 総量, 全体 — total 動 (totalling; totalled: 米 totaling; totaled)→〜を総計する, 合計する, 合計〜になる ‖ *His debts totalled more than £10000.* 彼の負債は合計で1万ポンド以上になった.

成句 in total ▶定義 when you add two or more numbers or amounts together 2つ以上の数や量をすべて足すと→全部で, 全体で, 合計で, 総計で ‖ *The appeal raised £4 million in total.* その訴えによって全部で400万ポンド集まった.

*****totally** /tóʊtli/ 副 ▶定義 completely 完全に→全く, すっかり ‖ *I totally agree with you.* 私はあなたに全面的に同意している.

**totter** /tɒtər/ 動 自 ▶定義 to stand or move in a way that is not steady, as if you are going to fall, especially because you are drunk, ill or weak 特に酔っている, 病気であるまたは弱っているために, まるで倒れてしまうかのように安定していない状態で立つ, または動く→よろめく, よろよろ・ふらふら歩く, ぐらつく

*****touch¹** /tʌtʃ/ 動 ▶定義 1 他 to put your hand or fingers onto sb/sth 〜の上に手または指を乗せる→〜に触れる, 〜を触る ‖ *It's very delicate so don't touch.* それはとても壊れやすいですから触らないでください. *He touched her gently on the cheek.* 彼は彼女のほおに優しく触れた. *The police asked us not to touch anything.* 警察は私たちに何にも触らないようにと頼んだ. ▶定義 2 自 他 (used about two or more things, surfaces, etc) to be or move so close together that there is no space between them (2つ以上の物や表面などについて)それらの間にすきまが全くないほど近くにあるまたは動く→(〜に)届く, 達する, 接触する, 隣接する ‖ *They were sitting so close that their shoulders touched.* 彼らは肩が触れ合うほどくっついて座っていた. *This bicycle is too big. My feet don't touch the ground.* この自転車は大きすぎる. 私の足が地面に届かない. ▶定義 3 他 to make sb feel sad, sorry for sb, grateful, etc 〜を悲しませる, 〜のことを気の毒に思わせるまたは感謝させるなどする→〜を感動させる, 〜に同情させる, 〜の心を動かす ☛参 形 **touched** ▶定義 4 他 (否定文で) to be as good as sb/sth in skill, quality, etc 〜の技術や質などと同じくらい良い→〜に匹敵する, かなう, 比肩する ‖ *He's a much better player than all the others. No one else can touch him.* 彼はほかのだれよりもはるかに優れた選手だ. 彼にかなう者はほかにいない.

成句 touch wood; knock on wood ⇒ **WOOD**
句動詞 **touch down** ▶定義 (used about an aircraft) to land (航空機について)→着陸する
**touch on/upon sth** ▶定義 to mention or refer to a subject for only a short time ほんの短い時間だけあるテーマに触れる, または言及する→〜に簡単に言及する, 触れる

*****touch²** /tʌtʃ/ 名 ▶定義 1 [C, 通常は単数] the

action of putting your hands or fingers onto sb/sth ～の上に手または指を乗せる行為→接触, 触ること, 触れること ‖ *I felt the touch of her hand on my arm.* 私は腕に彼女の手が触れるのを感じた. ▶定義2 ❶ the way sth feels when you touch it ～に触れたときにその～が持っている感触→触感, 感触, 手触り ‖ *Marble is cold to the touch.* 大理石は手触りが冷たい. ▶定義3 ❶ one of the five senses; the ability to feel things and know what they are like by putting your hands or fingers on them 五感の中の1つ. 物に手や指を乗せることによって, その物を感じ, どのようなものであるかが分かる感覚→触覚 ‖ *The sense of touch is very important to blind people.* 触覚は目の見えない人にとってとても重要なものである. ▶定義4 ❹ a small detail that is added to improve sth ～をより良くするために加えられた細部→加筆, 一筆, 仕上げ ‖ *The flowers in our room were a nice touch.* 私たちの部屋にある花は良いアクセントになっていた. *She's just putting the finishing touches to the cake.* 彼女はちょうどそのケーキに最後の仕上げをしているところだ. ▶定義5 [単数扱い] a way or style of doing sth ～をする方法または様式→手法, 筆致, タッチ, 演奏振り, ～流 ‖ *She prefers to write her letters by hand for a more personal touch.* 彼女は, その人らしさがより感じられるため, 手紙を手書きする方を好んでいる. ▶定義6 [単数扱い] **a touch (of sth)** a small amount of sth 少量の～→～の気味, 少量の～, ちょっと, 少し

成句 **in/out of touch (with sb)** ▶定義 being/not being in contact with sb by speaking or writing to him/her 話をしたり手紙を書いたりして～との連絡がある・ない→～と連絡を取っている・取っていない, ～と連絡して・連絡が途絶えて ‖ *During the year she was abroad, they kept in touch by letter.* 彼女が海外にいる間, 彼らは手紙で連絡を取っていた.

**in/out of touch with sth** ▶定義 having/not having recent information about sth ～についての最新の情報を持っている・持っていない→～の事情に通じている・通じていない, ～についての理解がある・ない ‖ *We're out of touch with what's going on.* 私たちは何が起きているのか分かっていない.

**lose touch** ⇒ **LOSE**

**lose your touch** ⇒ **LOSE**

**touched** /tʌtʃt/ 形 (名詞の前は不可) ▶定義 **touched (by sth); touched that...** made to feel sad, sorry for sb, grateful, etc 悲しむ, ～のことを気の毒に思うまたは感謝するなどさせられている → 感動して, 心を動かされて ‖ *We were very touched by the plight of the refugees.* 私たちはその難民の苦境に大変心を動かされた. *I was touched that he offered to help.* 私は彼が援助を申し出てくれたことに感動した.

**touching** /ˈtʌtʃɪŋ/ 形 ▶定義 that makes you feel sad, sorry for sb, grateful, etc 悲しむ, ～のことを気の毒に思うまたは感謝するなどするような→感動的な, 心を打つ, 涙ぐましい, 痛ましい, 胸を打つ

**touch screen** 名 ❹ ▶定義 (computing) a computer screen which shows information when you touch it (コンピューター) 触れると情報を表示するコンピューターの画面→タッチスクリーン ‖ *touch screen technology* タッチスクリーン技術

**touchy** /ˈtʌtʃi/ 形 ▶定義1 **touchy (about sth)** easily upset or made angry すぐにうろたえたり怒ったりする→怒りっぽい, 短気な, 神経質な, 敏感な, 感じやすい ‖ *He's a bit touchy about his weight.* 彼は自分の体重のことにちょっと神経質だ. ▶定義2 (used about a subject, situation, etc) that may easily upset people or make them angry (ある問題や状況などについて) 人々をすぐにうろたえさせるまたは怒らせるかもしれないような→厄介な, 扱いにくい, 慎重な配慮を要する, 際どい ‖ *Don't mention the exam. It's a very touchy subject.* その試験のことには触れないでください. とても微妙な問題ですから.

\***tough** /tʌf/ 形 ▶定義1 difficult; having or causing problems 困難な; 問題を持っているまたは起こしている→困難な, 厄介な, 骨の折れる, 難しい ‖ *It will be a tough decision to make.* それは難しい決断だろう. *He's had a tough time of it (= a lot of problems) recently.* 彼は最近, 困難な状況にある (= たくさんの問題を抱えている).

▶定義2 **tough (on/with sb/sth)** strict; not feeling sorry for anyone 厳しい; だれに対しても気の毒に思っていない→～に対して厳しい, 強硬な, 非情な, 冷酷な ‖ *The government plans to*

**get tough with** people who drink and drive. 政府は飲酒運転をした者に対して厳しく対処するつもりである. *Don't be too tough on them - they were only trying to help.* 彼らにあまり厳しすぎないようにしてください－彼らはただ助けようとしていただけなのですから. ▶定義3 strong enough to deal with difficult conditions or situations 困難な状態や状況に対処できるほど十分強い→強い, 丈夫な, たくましい, タフな, 強じんな ‖ *You need to be tough to go climbing in winter.* 冬登山に行くには強健でなければならない. ▶定義4 (used especially about meat) difficult to cut and eat (特に肉について)切って食べるのが難しい→硬い, 切れにくい, かみにくい, かみ切れない ▶定義5 not easily broken, torn or cut; very strong 簡単に壊れる, 破れるまたは切れることがない; 非常に強い→強い, 硬い, 頑丈な, 破れにくい, 切れにくい ‖ *a tough pair of boots* 丈夫なブーツ ▶定義6 略式 **tough (on sb)** unfortunate for sb in a way that seems unfair 不公平に見えて～にとって不運な→不運な, 不幸な, ～にとってひどい, つらい ‖ *It's tough on her that she lost her job.* 彼女にとって職を失ったのはつらいことである. — **toughness** 名 Ｕ ▶定義 不屈さ, 強さ, 堅さ, 頑強さ, 難しさ

**toughen** /tʌ́f(ə)n/ 動 自他 ▶定義 **toughen (sb/sth) (up)** to make sb/sth tough ～を強くする→硬くなる, 頑丈になる, たくましくなる, 困難になる; ～を硬くする, 頑丈にする, たくましくする, 困難にする

*****tour** /tʊər/ 名 ▶定義1 Ｃ **a tour (of/round/around sth)** a journey that you make for pleasure during which you visit many places 楽しみで行い, その間にいくつもの場所を訪れるような旅→旅行, 周遊旅行, ツアー ‖ *to go on a ten-day coach tour of/around Scotland* バスによる10日間のスコットランド周遊に出掛ける *a sightseeing tour* 観光旅行 *a tour operator (= a person or company that organizes tours)* ツアーオペレーター(＝旅行を手配する人または会社) ☛参 **travel** の注 ▶定義2 Ｃ a short visit around a city, famous building, etc 街や有名な建物などの短時間での見学→見物, 見学, 視察 ‖ *a guided tour round St Paul's Cathedral* セントポール大聖堂のガイド付きツアー ▶定義3 Ｃ Ｕ an official series of visits that singers, musicians, sports players, etc make to different places to perform, play, etc 歌手, 音楽家, スポーツ選手などが演奏するまたは試合をするために行う, さまざまな場所への一連の公式訪問→巡業, 巡演, 遠征旅行, ツアー ‖ *The band is currently on tour in America.* そのバンドは現在, アメリカをツアー中である. *a concert/cricket tour* コンサートツアー・クリケットのツアー — **tour** 動 自他 →(～を)旅行する, 見学する, 周遊する, 巡業する, 遠征する ‖ *We toured southern Spain for three weeks.* 私たちはスペイン南部を3週間かけて回った.

**tourism** /túərɪz(ə)m/ 名 Ｕ ▶定義 the business of providing and arranging holidays and services for people who are visiting a place ある場所を訪れる人々に休暇とサービスを提供し, 手配する事業→観光事業 ‖ *The country's economy relies heavily on tourism.* その国の経済は観光事業に大幅に依存している.

**tourist** /túərɪst/ 名 Ｃ ▶定義 a person who visits a place for pleasure ある場所に楽しみで訪れる人→旅行者, 観光客 ☛参 **sightseer**

**tournament** /tɔ́ːməm(ə)nt; tɑ́ːr-, túər-/ 名 Ｃ ▶定義 a competition in which many players or teams play games against each other 多くの選手やチームが互いに試合をするような競技会→トーナメント, 勝ち抜き試合, 選手権大会

**tousled** /táʊz(ə)ld/ 形 ▶定義 (used about hair) untidy, often in an attractive way (髪について)しばしば人の気をひくような, 乱れ方をしている→くしゃくしゃの, だらしない格好の

**tow** /tóʊ/ 動 他 ▶定義 to pull a car or boat behind another vehicle, using a rope or chain ほかの乗り物の後ろに, 綱や鎖を使って車または船を引っ張る→～を綱・鎖で引く, けん引する ‖ *My car was towed away by the police.* 私の車は警察にけん引された. — **tow** 名 [単数扱い] →綱・鎖で引くこと, 引かれること, けん引, 引かれていく車・船, 引く車・船
成句 **in tow** 略式 ▶定義 following closely behind 後ろにぴったりと付いている→引き連れて, 従えて ‖ *He arrived with his wife and five children in tow.* 彼は妻と5人の子供を連れて到着した.

*****towards** /tɔːrdz, təwɔ́ːrdz/ (または **toward** /tɔːrd, təwɔ́ːrd/) 前 ▶定義1 in the direction of sb/sth ～

の方向に➡〜の方へ,〜に向かって,向いて,面して ‖ *I saw Ken walking towards the station.* 私はケンが駅に向かって歩いているのを見た. *She had her back towards me.* 彼女は私に背を向けていた. *a first step towards world peace* 世界平和への第一歩 ▶定義2 near or nearer a time or date ある時間や日に近い,またはより近くなる ➡〜ころ,〜くらい ‖ *It gets cool towards evening.* 夕方近くには涼しくなる. *The shops get very busy towards Christmas.* クリスマスのころは店がとても忙しくなる. ▶定義3 (used when you are talking about your feelings about sb/sth) in relation to (〜について自分の気持ちを話しているときに用いて)〜に関して➡〜に対して,〜について ‖ *Patti felt very protective towards her younger brother.* パッティは弟に対して強いいたわりの気持ちを感じた. *What is your attitude towards this government?* 現在の政府に対してあなたはどう思いますか. ▶定義4 as part of the payment for sth 〜に対する支払いの一部として➡〜のために,足しに,一助に ‖ *The money will go towards the cost of a new minibus.* その金は新しいマイクロバスの費用の足しになるだろう.

*towel /táu(ə)l/ 名 C ▶定義 a piece of cloth or paper that you use for drying sb/sth/yourself 〜・自分自身を乾かすために使う布または紙➡タオル,手ぬぐい,手ふき ‖ *a bath/hand/beach towel* バスタオル・ハンドタオル・ビーチタオル *kitchen/paper towels* キッチンタオル・ペーパータオル ☛参 **sanitary towel**, **tea towel**

*tower /táuər/ 名 C ▶定義 a tall narrow building or part of a building such as a church or castle 細くて背の高い建物,または教会や城などの建物の一部➡塔,タワー ‖ *the Eiffel Tower* エッフェル塔 *a church tower* 教会の塔

**tower block** 名 C 英 ▶定義 a very tall building consisting of flats or offices 複数のアパートや事務所から成っている,非常に背の高い建物➡高層ビル,高層住宅

*town /táun/ 名 ▶定義1 C a place with many streets and buildings. A town is larger than a village but smaller than a city. 多くの街路や建物がある場所. 村より大きいが,都市よりは小さい➡町,街 ‖ *Romsey is a small market town.* ラムジーは市の立つ小さな町である. *After ten years away, she decided to move back to her home town (= the town where she was born and spent her childhood).* 10年離れていたが,彼女は故郷(= 生まれ,子供時代を過ごした町)に戻ることにした. ▶定義2 **the town**[単数扱い] all the people who live in a town ある町に住んでいるすべての人々➡町の住民,市民 ‖ *The whole town is talking about it.* 町中の者がそれについてうわさをしている. ▶定義3 U the main part of a town, where the shops, etc are 店などがある,町の主要な部分➡都市の中心部,商業地区,繁華街 ‖ *I've got to go into town this afternoon.* 今日の午後は町へ行かなくてはならない. 成句 **go to town (on sth)** 略式 ▶定義 to do sth with a lot of energy and enthusiasm; to spend a lot of money on sth たくさんの労力と熱心さで〜をする; 〜にたくさんの金を費やす➡〜を徹底的にやる,思い切りやる,〜を大金を投じて派手にやる

**(out) on the town** 略式 ▶定義 going to restaurants, theatres, clubs, etc, for entertainment, especially at night 特に夜に,気晴らしにレストラン,劇場,クラブなどへ行っている➡夜遊びして,町に遊興に出掛けて

**town council** 名 C 英 ▶定義 a group of people who are responsible for the local government of a town ある町の地方自治に責任を負っている人々の集団➡町議会

**town hall** 名 C ▶定義 a large building that contains the local government offices and often a large room for public meetings, concerts, etc 地方自治体の事務所のほかに,しばしば公的な会議やコンサートなどのための広い部屋も入っている大きな建物➡町役場,市役所,町政庁舎,公会堂 ☛参 **hall**

**toxic** /tɑ́ksɪk/ 形 ▶定義 poisonous 有毒な➡毒性のある,有毒な

*toy¹ /tɔ́ɪ/ 名 C ▶定義 an object for a child to play with 子供が遊ぶ対象の物➡おもちゃ,がん具 ‖ *The little boy continued playing with his toy cars.* その小さな男の子はおもちゃの車で遊び続けた. *a toy soldier/farm* おもちゃの兵隊・農場 *a toyshop* おもちゃ屋

**toy²** /tɔ́ɪ/ 動
句動詞 **toy with sth** ▶定義1 to think about doing sth, perhaps not very seriously 〜をする

1718　trace¹

ことについて,あまり真剣にではないだろうが,考える→〜を漠然と持つ,少し考えてみる ‖ *She's **toying with the idea of** going abroad for a year.* 彼女は海外に1年行こうかと漠然と考えている. ▶定義2 to move sth about without thinking about what you are doing, often because you are nervous or upset しばしば不安であったりうろたえたりしているため,自分が何をしているかを考えないで〜を動かす→〜をいじくる,おもちゃにする,もてあそぶ ‖ *He toyed with his food but hardly ate any of it.* 彼は食べ物をおもちゃにしていて,ほとんどどれも食べなかった.

**trace¹** /treɪs/ 動他 ▶定義1 trace sb/sth (to sth) to find out where sb/sth is by following marks, signs or other information 印や記号やそのほかの情報に従うことによって,〜がどこにあるかを調べる→〜をたどる,捜し出す,追跡する ‖ *The wanted man was traced to an address in Amsterdam.* 指名手配中のその男は,アムステルダムの住所まで追跡されて捜し出された. ▶定義2 trace sth (back) (to sth) to find out where sth came from or what caused it; to describe the development of sth 〜がどこから来たか,または〜の原因となったものが何かを調べる;〜の進展について述べる→〜をさかのぼって調べる,〜の原因を突き止める,〜を明らかにする ‖ *She traced her family tree back to the 16th century.* 彼女は,自分の家系図をさかのぼっていくと16世紀までたどり着いた. ▶定義3 to make a copy of a map, plan, etc by placing a piece of transparent paper (tracing paper) over it and drawing over the lines 地図,図面などの上に透き通った紙(トレーシングペーパー)を置き,線を上からなぞることによって,複写を作る→〜を敷き写す,トレースする

★**trace²** /treɪs/ 名 ▶定義1 C U a mark, an object or a sign that shows that sb/sth existed or happened 〜が存在した,または起こったことを表す印,物,あるいは形跡→跡,足跡,痕跡(こんせき),形跡,名残,跡形 ‖ *traces of an earlier civilization* 初期の文明の跡 *The man **disappeared**/**vanished without trace**.* その男は跡形もなく消え去った. ▶定義2 C a trace (of sth) a very small amount of sth ごくわずかの量の〜→ほんのわずかの〜,少しの〜,微量の ‖ *Traces of blood were found under her fingernails.* 彼女の指のつめの中から微量の血液が検出された.

★**track¹** /træk/ 名 ▶定義1 C a natural path or rough road 自然のままの小道,またはでこぼこした道→(踏みならされてできた)小道,道 ‖ *Follow the dirt track through the wood.* 舗装されていない道をたどって森を通り抜けなさい. ☞C8ページのさし絵 ▶定義2 [C,通常は複数] marks that are left on the ground by a person, an animal or a moving vehicle 人,動物,動いている乗り物などによって地面に残された印→通った跡,足跡,わだち ‖ *The hunter followed the tracks of a deer.* そのハンターはシカの足跡をたどっていった. *tyre tracks* タイヤの跡 ☞参 **footprint** ▶定義3 C U the two metal rails on which a train runs その上を電車が走る,金属の2本のレール→鉄道線路 ‖ *The train stopped because there was a tree across the track.* 線路上に木が倒れていたため,その電車は止まった. ▶定義4 C a piece of ground, often in a circle, for people, cars, etc to have races on 人や車などがそこで競走するための,多くは円形の敷地→トラック,走路 ‖ *a running track* 競走路 ▶定義5 C one song or piece of music on a cassette, CD or record カセット,CD,レコードなどに入っている1曲の歌または楽曲→トラック,1曲録音帯,録音された曲 ‖ *the first track from her latest album* 彼女の最新アルバムの1曲目 ☞参 **soundtrack**

成句 **keep/lose track of sb/sth** ▶定義 to have/not have information about what is happening or where sb/sth is 何が起こっているか,または〜がどこにあるかについての情報を持っている・持っていない→〜の跡をたどる・見失う,〜を見失わない・分からなくなる

**off the beaten track** ⇒ **BEAT¹**
**on the right/wrong track** ▶定義 having the right/wrong idea about sth 〜について正しい・間違った考えを持っている→〜が正しく・間違って ‖ *That's not the answer but you're on the right track.* それは正解ではありませんが,考え方は合っています.

**track²** /træk/ 動他 ▶定義 to follow the movements of sb/sth 〜の動きに付いていく→〜の跡を追う,〜を突き止める,追跡する,探知する ‖ *to track enemy planes on a radar screen* レーダーの画面上で敵機を追跡する

句動詞 **track sb/sth down** ▶定義 to find sb/sth

after searching for him/her/it ～を捜した結果，見つける➔～を捜し出す，やっと見つけ出す，追い詰めて捕まえる

**track event** 名 C ▶定義 a sports event that consists of running round a track in a race, rather than throwing sth or jumping ～を投げたり跳躍したりするのではなく，競走でトラックの周りを走ることから成る運動競技➔**トラック種目，トラック競技** ☛参 field event

**track record** 名 [単数扱い] ▶定義 all the past successes or failures of a person or organization ある人または組織の，過去におけるすべての成功や失敗➔**実績，業績**

**tracksuit** /træks(j)ùːt, -sùːt/ 名 C ▶定義 a warm pair of soft trousers and a matching jacket that you wear for sports practice 運動するときに着用する，柔らかくて暖かいズボンと，それに合った上着➔**トラックスーツ**

**tractor** /træktər/ 名 C ▶定義 a large vehicle that is used on farms for pulling heavy pieces of machinery 農場で重い機械類を引っ張るために使われる大型の乗り物➔**トラクター，けん引車**

★**trade**¹ /tréɪd/ 名 ▶定義 1 U the buying or selling of goods or services between people or countries 人と人，または国と国との間で商品やサービスを売買すること➔**貿易，通商，商売，商業，取り引き** ‖ an international trade agreement 国際通商協定 Trade is not very good (= not many goods are sold) at this time of year. 1年の中でこの時期は商売があまり繁盛しない(= 商品があまりたくさん売れない). ▶定義 2 C a particular type of business ある特定の種類の事業➔**～の商売，～業，～業界** ‖ the tourist/building/retail trade 観光業・建築業・小売り業 ▶定義 3 C U a job for which you need special skill, especially with your hands 特に手先を使った，特殊な技術を必要とする仕事➔**職業，仕事，手職業，手仕事** ‖ Jeff is a plumber **by trade**. ジェフの職業は配管工だ. to learn a trade 商売を覚える ☛参 work の注

★**trade**² /tréɪd/ 動 ▶定義 1 I trade (in sth) (with sb) to buy or sell goods or services 商品やサービスを売買する➔**～と貿易する，取り引きする，売買する，商う** ‖ We no longer trade with that country. 私たちはもうあの国とは貿易をしていない. to trade in luxury goods 高級品を商う to trade in stocks and shares 株と債券を売買す

## tradition 1719

る ▶定義 2 他 trade sth (for sth) to exchange sth for sth else ～をほかの…と交換する➔**～を…と交換する** ‖ He traded his CD player for his friend's bicycle. 彼は自分の CD プレーヤーを友人の自転車と交換した. ― trading 名 U ➔**貿易，通商**

句動詞 trade sth in (for sth) ▶定義 to give sth old in part payment for sth new or newer 新しい，またはより新しい…に対する支払いの一部として古い…を渡す➔**～を…のために下取りに出す** ‖ We traded in our old car for a van. 私たちは古い車を下取りに出してバンを買った.

**trademark** /tréɪdmɑːrk/ 名 C (略 TM) ▶定義 a special symbol, design or name that a company puts on its products and that cannot be used by any other company 企業が自社の製品に付け, 他社に使われることのない特別な記号, デザイン, 名前など➔**(登録)商標，トレードマーク**

**trader** /tréɪdər/ 名 C ▶定義 a person who buys and sells things, especially goods in a market or company shares 物を，特に市場の商品や企業の株を，売買する人➔**貿易業者，商人，売買人** ☛C8 ページのさし絵

**tradesman** /tréɪdzmən/ C (複 -men /-mən/) ▶定義 a person who brings goods to people's homes to sell them or who has a shop 人の家へ商品を持っていって売る人，または店を持っている人➔**商品配達人，商人，小売店主**

**trade union** (または **trades union**; **union**) 名 C ▶定義 an organization for people who all do the same type of work. Trade unions try to get better pay and working conditions for their members. 同じ種類の仕事をしている人のための団体. 構成員の賃金の値上げや労働条件の改善を求めようとする➔**労働組合**

★**tradition** /trədíʃ(ə)n/ 名 C U ▶定義 a custom, belief or way of doing sth that has continued from the past to the present 過去から現在まで続いてきた風習，信仰，～のやり方など➔**伝統, 慣習, 仕来り, 儀礼, 因習** ‖ religious/cultural/literary traditions 宗教的・文化的・文学的な慣習 **By tradition**, the bride's family pays the costs of the wedding. 伝統的に花嫁の家族が結婚式の費用を支払う. ― traditional /-ʃ(ə)n(ə)l/ 形 ➔**伝統的な, 慣習に従った, 伝統を守る, 保守的な, 従来の** ‖

*It is traditional in Britain to eat turkey at Christmas.* 英国ではクリスマスに七面鳥を食べるのが伝統だ. — **traditionally** /-ʃ(ə)n(ə)li/ 副 ➡ 伝統的に, 伝統に従って

\***traffic** /ˈtræfɪk/ 名 **U** ▶定義1 all the vehicles that are on a road at a particular time ある特定の時間に路上にある, すべての乗り物 ➡ **往来, 交通, 交通量** ‖ *heavy/light traffic* 交通量が多い・少ない *We got stuck **in traffic** and were late for the meeting.* 私たちは交通渋滞で動けなくなったため, その会議に遅れた. ▶定義2 the movement of ships, aircraft, etc 船, 航空機などの動き ➡ **交通, 交通運輸, 交通量** ‖ *air traffic control* 航空交通管制 ▶定義3 *traffic (in sth)* the illegal buying and selling of sth 〜の違法な売買 ➡ **不正な商品取り引き, 貿易, 売買** ‖ *the traffic in drugs/firearms* 麻薬取り引き・小火器の取り引き — **traffic** 動 自 (現分 **trafficking**; 過, 過分 **trafficked**) *traffic (in sth)* ➡ 〜と…の密売買をする, 不正取り引きをする ‖ *He was arrested for trafficking in drugs.* 彼は麻薬取り引きで逮捕された.

**traffic island** (または **island**) 名 **C** ▶定義 a higher area in the middle of the road, where you can stand and wait for the traffic to pass when you want to cross 道の中央にある高くなっている区域で, 渡りたいときにそこに立って車が通り過ぎるのを待つことができる所 ➡ **(道路の) 安全地帯, 交通島**

**traffic jam** 名 **C** ▶定義 a long line of cars, etc that cannot move or that can only move very slowly 動くことができない, または非常にゆっくりとしか動けない, 車などの長い列 ➡ **交通渋滞, 交通まひ** ‖ *to be stuck in a traffic jam* 交通渋滞で動けない

**traffic light** 名 [**C**, 通常は複数] ▶定義 a sign with three coloured lights (red, amber and green) that is used for controlling the traffic where two or more roads meet 2本以上の道路が交わる所の交通を規制するために用いられる, 3色(赤, 黄, 青)の明かりが付いた標識 ➡ **交通信号(灯)** ☛ **roundabout** のさし絵

**traffic warden** 名 **C** 英 ▶定義 a person whose job is to check that cars are not parked in the wrong place or for longer than is allowed 車が, 不適切な場所に, または許可されている時間よりも長く駐車されていないかどうかを調べることを仕事とする人 ➡ **交通監視員, 交通監視官**

**tragedy** /ˈtrædʒədi/ 名 (複 **tragedies**) ▶定義1 **C U** a very sad event or situation, especially one that involves death 特に死にかかわるような, とても悲しい出来事や状態 ➡ **悲劇的な事, 惨事, 悲しい事件** ‖ *It's a tragedy that he died so young.* 彼がそんなに若くして亡くなったのは悲しいことだ. ▶定義2 **C** a serious play that has a sad ending 悲しい結末となる堅い演劇 ➡ **悲劇** ‖ *Shakespeare's 'King Lear' is a tragedy.* シェークスピアの「リア王」は悲劇である.
☛ **comedy**

**tragic** /ˈtrædʒɪk/ 形 ▶定義1 that makes you very sad, especially because it involves death 特に死にかかわるために, とても悲しい思いをさせるような ➡ **悲劇的な, 悲惨な, 痛ましい** ‖ *It's tragic that she lost her only child.* 彼女が一人っ子を失ったのは痛ましいことだ. *a tragic accident* 悲惨な事故 ▶定義2 (文) (名詞の前だけ) (used about literature) in the style of tragedy (文学について) 悲劇の様式で ➡ **悲劇の, 悲劇的な** ‖ *a tragic actor/hero* 悲劇俳優・悲劇的な英雄 — **tragically** /-k(ə)li/ 副 ➡ 悲劇的に, 悲惨にも, 痛ましいことに

**trail**[1] /treɪl/ 名 **C** ▶定義1 a series of marks in a long line that is left by sb/sth as he/she/it moves 〜が移動するときに残された, 長い線状の一連の印 ➡ **通った跡, 足跡** ‖ *a trail of blood/footprints* 血痕(けっこん)・足跡 ▶定義2 a track, sign or smell that is left behind and that you follow when you are hunting sb/sth 後に残され, 〜を追っているときにたどる跡, 印, においなど ➡ **跡, 臭跡, 手掛かり, 形跡** ‖ *The dogs ran off **on the trail of** the fox.* 犬はキツネの跡を追って走り去った. ▶定義3 a path through the country 田舎の小道 ➡ **小道, 獣道** ☛ C8 ページのさし絵

**trail**[2] /treɪl/ 動 ▶定義1 自 他 to pull or be pulled along behind sb/sth 〜の後ろについて引く, または引かれる ➡ **(〜を) 引きずる, 引きずっていく** ‖ *The skirt was too long and trailed along the ground.* そのスカートは長すぎたため, 地面を引きずっていた. ▶定義2 自 to move or walk slowly behind sb/sth else, usually because you are tired or bored 通常, 疲れているまたはうんざりしているため, ほかの〜の後ろをゆっくりと

移動する, または歩く➡足を引きずる, 疲れてのろのろ歩く, だらだら付いていく ‖ *It was impossible to do any shopping with the kids trailing around after me.* 私の後を付いて回る子供たちがいると, 買い物をすることなど全くできなかった. ▶定義3 ⓘ ⓘ trail (by/in sth)(通常, 進行形で用いて)to be in the process of losing a game or a competition 試合や競争に負けているところである➡リードされる; 〜に後れを取る, 負けている, 〜の後を走る ‖ *At half-time Liverpool were trailing by two goals to three.* ハーフタイムの時点で, リバプールが2対3で負けていた.
▶定義4 ⓘ (used about plants or sth long and thin) to grow over sth and hang downwards; to lie across a surface(植物や細長い〜について)…を越えて生長し垂れ下がる; 表面を横切っている➡はう, 伸びる ‖ *Computer wires trailed across the floor.* コンピュータのケーブルが床の上をはっていた.
句動詞 trail away/off ▶定義 (used about sb's voice) to gradually become quieter and then stop(〜の声について)次第に静かになってやむ➡次第に弱くなる, だんだん聞こえなくなる

**trailer** /tréɪlər/ 🔊 ⓒ ▶定義1 a type of container with wheels that is pulled by vehicle 乗り物によって引っ張られる, 車輪の付いたコンテナの一種➡トレーラー, 付属車 ‖ *a car towing a trailer with a boat on it* ボートを載せたトレーラーを引っ張っている車 ▶定義2 匚匚 = CARAVAN(1)
▶定義3 特に 匚匚 a series of short pieces taken from a film and used to advertise it 映画から選んで集められ, 宣伝するために使われる一連の短い場面➡予告編 ☞参 clip

*train¹ /treɪn/ 🔊 ⓒ ▶定義1 a type of transport that is pulled by an engine along a railway line. A train is divided into sections for people (carriages and coaches) and for goods (wagons). エンジンによって鉄道線路に沿って引っ張られる交通手段の一種. 人を運ぶもの(客車)と貨物を運ぶもの(貨車)に分かれている➡列車, 電車, 汽車 ‖ *a passenger/goods/freight train* 旅客車・貨物列車・貨物列車 *a fast/slow/express train* 急行列車・鈍行列車・急行列車 *to catch/take/get the train to London* ロンドン行きの列車に間に合う・乗る・間に合う *the 12 o'clock train to Bristol* 12時発ブリストル行きの列車 *to get on/off a train* 電車に乗る・電車から降りる *Hurry up or we'll miss the train.* 急ぎなさい. そうしないとその電車に間に合いませんよ. *You have to change trains at Reading.* レディングで列車を乗り換えなければなりません.
➤注意. 一般的な話をする場合は by train と言う. 列車によるある特定の移動の間を意味するときは on the train と言う: *Miranda travels to work by train.* (ミランダは電車で通勤している.) *Yesterday she fell asleep on the train and missed her station.* (昨日, 彼女は電車で寝入ったため降りる駅を乗り過ごしてしまった.)
▶定義2 [通常は単数]a series of thoughts or events that are connected 関連している一連の考え, または出来事➡連続, つながり ‖ *A knock at the door interrupted my train of thought.* 戸をノックする音で思考の流れが中断された.

*train² /treɪn/ 🔊 ▶定義1 ⓘ train sb (as sth/to do sth) to teach a person to do sth which is difficult or which needs practice 困難な, または練習が必要な事をすることを人に教える➡〜を訓練する, 教育する, 養成する, しつける, 仕込む, 調教する ‖ *The organization trains guide dogs for the blind.* その団体は目の見えない人のための盲導犬を訓練している. *There is a shortage of trained teachers.* 熟練した教員が不足している. ▶定義2 ⓘ train (as/in sth) (to do sth) to learn how to do a job ある仕事のやり方を習う➡訓練される, 訓練を受ける, 練習する ‖ *She trained as an engineer.* 彼女は技師としての教育を受けた. *He's not trained in anything.* 彼は何の訓練も受けていない. *He's training to be a doctor.* 彼は医者になる教育を受けている.
▶定義3 ⓘ ⓘ train (for sth) to prepare yourself, especially for a sports event, by practising; to help a person or an animal to do this 特にスポーツ競技に備えて, 練習して準備する; 人または動物がそれをするのを助ける➡〜に備えて…を訓練する, 体調を整える, 調整する ‖ *I'm training for the London Marathon.* 私はロンドンマラソンに向けてトレーニング中です. *to train racehorses* 競走馬を訓練する
▶定義4 ⓘ train sth (at/on sb/sth) to point a gun, camera, etc at sb/sth 銃, カメラなどを〜に向ける➡〜を…に向ける, 照準する ー training 🔊 ⓤ➡訓練, 教育, 養成, 調教, トレーニ

ング, コンディショニング ‖ to be **in training** for the Olympics オリンピックに向けてトレーニング中である.

**trainee** /treɪníː/ 名 C ▶定義 a person who is being taught how to do a particular job ある仕事のやり方を教わっている人→訓練を受けている人, 実習生, 研修生, 訓練生

**trainer** /tréɪnər/ 名 C ▶定義 1 (米 **sneaker**) [通常は複数]a shoe that you wear for doing sport or as informal clothing 運動をするため, または普段着として履く靴→運動靴, トレーニングシューズ, スニーカー ☞参 plimsoll ☞ shoe, S1ページのさし絵 ▶定義 2 a person who teaches people or animals how to do a particular job or skill well, or to do a particular sport ある仕事や技の正しいやり方, またはある運動競技の仕方を人や動物に教える人→訓練する人, トレーナー, コーチ, 調教師 ‖ teacher trainers 教師養成者 a racehorse trainer 競走馬の調教師

**trainspotter** /tréɪnspɑ̀tər/ 名 C 英 ▶定義 1 a person who collects the numbers of railway engines as a hobby 鉄道の機関車の番号を趣味として集めている人→機関車マニア, 機関車の番号を記録する人 ▶定義 2 a person who has a boring hobby or who is interested in the details of a subject that other people find boring うんざりするような趣味を持っている人, または他人がうんざりするテーマの細部に興味がある人→(熱狂的)マニア ― trainspotting 名 U →監視人

**trait** /tréɪ; tréɪt/ 名 C ▶定義 a quality that forms part of your character or personality 人の性格や個性の一部を形づくっている性質 → 特徴, 特質, 特性, 特色

**traitor** /tréɪtər/ 名 C ▶定義 a traitor (to sb/sth) a person who is not loyal to his/her country, friends, etc 自分の国や友人などに対して忠実ではない人→裏切り者, 背信者, 反逆者
▶ traitor(裏切り者)は自分の友人や国などをbetray(裏切る)と言い, 自国に対する犯罪はtreason(反逆罪)と呼ばれる.

**tram** /trǽm/ (米 **streetcar**; **trolley**) 名 C ▶定義 a type of bus that works by electricity and that moves along special rails in the road carrying passengers 電力で動き, 乗客を運びながら道路にある特別な線路に沿って移動する一種のバス→路面電車, 市街電車, 市電

**tramp**[1] /trǽmp/ 名 ▶定義 1 C a person who has no home or job and who moves from place to place 家や仕事がなく, あちこちに移動する人→浮浪者, 放浪者, 無宿者 ▶定義 2 [単数扱い]the sound of people walking with heavy or noisy steps 重い, または騒がしい足取りで歩いている人の音→重い足音

**tramp**[2] /trǽmp/ 動 自 他 ▶定義 to walk with slow heavy steps, especially for a long time 特に長い時間, ゆっくりと重い足取りで歩く→ドシンドシンと歩く, 重い足取りで歩く

**trample** /trǽmp(ə)l/ 動 自 他 ▶定義 **trample on/over sb/sth** to walk on sb/sth and damage or hurt him/her/it 〜の上を歩き, それに損害を与えるまたはけがをさせる→(〜を)踏み付ける, 踏みつぶす ‖ The boys trampled on the flowers. その少年たちは花を踏み付けた.

**trampoline** /trǽmpəlìːn, -lən/ 名 C ▶定義 a piece of equipment for jumping up and down on, made of a piece of strong material fixed to a metal frame by springs 金属の骨組みにばねで取り付けられた丈夫な生地でできており, その上で上下に飛び跳ねるための用具→トランポリン

**trance** /trɑːns; trǽns/ 名 C ▶定義 a mental state in which you do not notice what is going on around you 自分の周りで起こっていることに気付かないような精神状態→催眠状態, 恍惚(こうこつ), 夢中 ‖ to go/fall into a trance 失神する

**tranquil** /trǽŋkwəl/ 形 正式 ▶定義 calm and quiet 穏やかで静かな→静かな, 穏やかな, 平穏な, 落ち着いた

**tranquillizer** (または **-iser**) 英 または **tranquilizer**) /trǽŋkwəlàɪzər/ 名 C ▶定義 a drug that is used for making people feel calm or to help them sleep 人を穏やかな気分にさせるため, または眠るのを助けるために使われる薬 → 精神安定剤, トランキライザー ☞参 sedative

**transaction** /trænzǽkʃ(ə)n/ 名 C ▶定義 a piece of business that is done between people 人と人との間で行われる取り引きの1つ→業務, 取り引き, 売買 ‖ financial transactions 金融取引

**transatlantic** /trænzətlǽntɪk/ 形 ▶定義 to or from the other side of the Atlantic Ocean; across the Atlantic 大西洋のもう一方の側へ, ま

たはもう一方の側から；大西洋を横断して➡**大西洋横断の, 大西洋両岸を結ぶ** ‖ *a transatlantic flight/voyage* 大西洋横断飛行・大西洋横断航海

**transcend** /trænsénd/ 動 正式 ▶定義 to go further than the usual limits of sth 〜の普通の限度よりもさらに先に進む➡**限界・範囲を超える, 超越する**

**transcript** /trǽnskrìpt/（または **transcription**）名 C ▶定義 a written or printed copy of what sb has said 〜が言ったことを筆記した, または印刷した写し➡**書写, 転写, 文字に書き換えたもの, 筆記録** ‖ *a transcript of the interview/trial* インタビュー・裁判の筆記録

**transfer**¹ /trænsfə́ːr/ 動（**transferring**; **transferred**）▶定義1 自他 transfer (sb/sth) (from...) (to...) to move, or to make sb/sth move, from one place to another ある場所からほかの場所へ移動する, または〜を移動させる➡**移る；〜を移す, 動かす, 運ぶ** ‖ *He's transferring to our Tokyo branch next month.* 彼は来月, 私たちの東京支社に転勤になる. *I'd like to transfer £1000 from my deposit account (= in a bank).* 私は預金口座から（= 銀行で）1000ポンド振り込みたい. *Transfer the data onto a disk.* そのデータをディスクに移し替えなさい. ▶定義2 他 to officially arrange for sth to belong to, or be controlled by, sb else 〜がほかの…の所有になるように, またはほかの〜に管理されるように公式に手配する➡**〜を譲る, 移譲する, 譲渡する** ‖ *She transferred the property to her son.* 彼女は財産を息子に譲渡した. — transferable /-fə́ːrəb(ə)l/ 形➡**移せる, 譲渡できる, 転写できる** ‖ *This ticket is not transferable (= may only be used by the person who bought it).* この券は譲渡できない（= それを買った人しか使うことができない）.

**transfer**² /trǽnsfər/ 名 ▶定義1 C U moving or being moved from one place, job or state to another ある場所, 仕事, 国から他へ移動すること, または移動させられること➡**移動, 移転, 転任, 移籍** ‖ *Paul is not happy here and has asked for a transfer.* ポールはここで満足していないので, 異動を願い出た. ▶定義2 U changing to a different vehicle or route during a journey 旅程の途中で別の乗り物や路線に乗り換えること➡**乗り換え, 乗り継ぎ** ‖ *Transfer from the airport to the hotel is included.* 空港からホテルまでの乗り継ぎが含まれている. ▶定義3 C 困 a ticket that allows you to continue your journey on another bus or train 別のバスや電車で旅を続けることを許可する切符➡**乗り換え切符, 乗り継ぎ切符** ▶定義4 C 特に 英 a piece of paper with a picture or writing on it that you can stick onto another surface by pressing or heating it 押しまたは熱することによってほかの表面にはり付けられる, 絵や文字の付いた紙➡**転写のための絵・図案, 写し絵**

**transform** /trænsfɔ́ːm/ 動 他 ▶定義 transform sb/sth (from sth) (into sth) to change sb/sth completely, especially in a way which improves sb/sth 特に〜を良くするようにして, その〜をすっかり変える➡**〜を変える, 変形させる, 変質させる, 変換する** — transformation /trænsfəméɪʃ(ə)n/ 名 C U ➡**変化, 変形, 変質, 変換, 転換**

**transfusion** /trænsfjúːʒ(ə)n/ 名 C ▶定義 the action of putting new blood into a person's body instead of his/her own because he/she is ill 人が病気であるため, 本人のものではなく新しい血液をその人の体内に注入すること➡**輸血** ‖ *a blood transfusion* 輸血

**transistor** /trænzístər/ 名 C ▶定義 a small piece of electronic equipment that is used in computers, radios, televisions, etc コンピューター, ラジオ, テレビなどで使われている小さな電子機器➡**トランジスター**

---

▶**音声とつづり字**

transistor はどこを強く読む？

transistorを単独に言うと, -sis- の所が強くなりますが, radioがその後に付くと強勢移動の現象が起こり,

○ ○ － ◎ --
transistor radio

のようになります. しかし, その前にgoodが付くと, 強勢移動がなくなり,

○ ○ ○ － ◎ --
good transistor radio

のようになります. なお, 特に性能が良いことを強調したいときは, 当然 goodが最も強くなります.

**transit** /trǽnsət/ 名 ᴜ ▶定義 1 the act of being moved or carried from one place to another ある場所からほかの場所へ動かされる,または運ばれること→輸送, 移送, 運搬, 運送 ‖ *The goods had been damaged in transit.* その商品は輸送中に傷んだ. ▶定義 2 going through a place on the way to somewhere else ほかのどこかへ行く途中にある場所を通り抜けること→通過, 通行

**transition** /trænzíʃ(ə)n, -síz(ə)n/ 名 ᴄ ᴜ ▶定義 (a) transition (from sth) (to sth) a change from one state or form to another ある状態や形からほかの状態や形への変化→移行, 移り変わり, 変遷, 推移 ‖ *the transition from childhood to adolescence* 子供時代から青年期への移り変わり — **transitional** /-f(ə)n(ə)l/ 形 →移り変わる, 過渡的な, 過渡期の ‖ *a transitional stage/period* 過渡期の段階・移り変わる時期

**transitive** /trǽnsətɪv/ 形（文法）▶定義 (used about a verb) that has a direct object (動詞について) 直接目的語をとるような → 他動詞の ‖ *In this dictionary transitive verbs are marked '[T]'.* この辞書では,他動詞には他の印が付いている.
⇔ **intransitive**
▶他動詞についての説明は,巻末の「文法早見表」を参照.

*****translate** /trænzléɪt, træns-/ 動 自 他 ▶定義 translate (sth) (from sth) (into sth) to change sth written or spoken from one language to another 書かれた,または話された～をある言語から別の言語に変える→～を…から～に翻訳する,通訳する,訳す ‖ *This book has been translated from Czech into English.* この本はチェコ語から英語に翻訳された. ☞参 **interpret** — **translation** /trænzléɪʃ(ə)n, trænz-, tra:ns-/ 名 ᴄ ᴜ→翻訳, 翻訳されたもの, 翻訳書, 訳文 ‖ *a word-for-word translation* 逐語訳 *an error in translation* 翻訳の中の誤り

**translator** /trænzléɪtər, træns-/ 名 ᴄ ▶定義 a person who changes sth that has been written or spoken from one language to another 書かれた,または話された～をある言語から別の言語に変える人→翻訳家, 翻訳者, 通訳 ☞参 **interpreter**

**transmission** /trænzmíʃ(ə)n, træns-/ 名 ▶定義 1 ᴜ sending sth out or passing sth on from one person, place or thing to another ある人,場所,物から他へ～を送り出したり回したりすること→伝送, 伝達, 伝染 ‖ *the transmission of television pictures by satellite* 人工衛星によるテレビ画面の伝送 *the transmission of a disease/virus* 病気・ウイルスの伝染 ▶定義 2 ᴄ a TV or radio programme テレビまたはラジオの番組→テレビ番組, ラジオ番組 ▶定義 3 ᴜ ᴄ the system in a car, etc by which power is passed from the engine to the wheels 車などで,それによって動力がエンジンから車輪に受け渡される装置→変速機, トランスミッション, 伝動装置

**transmit** /trænzmít, træns-/ 動 他 (**transmitting**; **transmitted**) ▶定義 1 to send out television or radio programmes, electronic signals, etc テレビやラジオの番組,電子信号などを送り出す→～を送信する,発信する,放送する ‖ *The match was transmitted live all over the world.* その試合は世界中に生放送された. ▶定義 2 to send or pass sth from one person or place to another ～をある人や場所からほかの人や場所へ送る,または回す→～を移す,送る,知らせる,伝える,伝染させる ‖ *a sexually transmitted disease* 性感染症

**transmitter** /trænzmítər, træns-/ 名 ᴄ ▶定義 a piece of equipment that sends out electronic signals, television or radio programmes, etc 電子信号,テレビ番組,ラジオ番組などを発送する機器→送信機, 発信器

**transparency** /trænspǽr(ə)nsi, -péər-/ 名 ᴄ (複 **transparencies**) ▶定義 a piece of plastic on which you can write or draw or that has a picture, etc on it that you look at by putting it on a special machine (**projector**) and shining light through it その上に文字を書くまたは絵をかくことができる,または専用の機器（プロジェクター）の上に載せ,光を透過させて見る写真などがある,1枚のプラスチック製品→OHP用フィルム, スライド ‖ *a transparency for the overhead projector* OHP用のフィルム ☞参 **slide²(4)**

*****transparent** /trænspǽr(ə)nt, -péər-/ 形 ▶定義 that you can see through 透かして見ることができるような→透明な,透けて見える,透き通った ‖ *Glass is transparent.* ガラスは透明である. ⇔ **opaque**

**transplant¹** /trænsplá:nt; -plǽnt/ 動 他 ▶定義 1

to take out an organ or other part of sb's body and put it into another person's body 〜の身体のある器官、またはそのほかの部分を取り出し、それをほかの人の体内に入れる➡〜を移植する ▶定義2 to move a growing plant and plant it somewhere else 生長している植物を移動させ、ほかの場所に植える➡〜を植え替える, 移植する ● 参 graft

**transplant**² /trænsplá:nt; -plænt/ 名 C ▶定義 a medical operation in which an organ, etc is taken out of sb's body and put into another person's body ある器官などが〜の身体から取り出され、ほかの人の体内に入れられる医療手術➡移植, 移植手術 ‖ *to have a heart/liver/kidney transplant* 心臓移植・肝臓移植・腎臓（じんぞう）移植を受ける.

★**transport**¹ /trǽnspɔ:rt/（特に 米 **transportation**）名 U ▶定義1 the action of carrying or taking people or goods from one place to another 人または荷物をある場所からほかの場所へ運ぶまたは持っていくこと➡輸送, 運送, 運搬 ‖ *road/rail/sea transport* 陸上輸送・鉄道輸送・海上輸送 ▶定義2 vehicles that you travel in; a method of travel それに乗って移動する乗り物; 移動の方法➡輸送手段, 交通機関,（移動のための）乗り物, 足 ‖ *Do you have your own transport (for example a car)?* 自分の交通手段（例えば車）がありますか. *I travel to school by **public transport**.* 私は公共の交通機関を使って通学している. *His bike is his only means of transport.* 彼の自転車は単なる交通手段にすぎない. — **transport** /trænspɔ́:rt/ 動 他 ➡〜を運ぶ, 輸送する, 運送する

**transvestite** /trænzvéstait/ 名 C ▶定義 a person, especially a man, who enjoys dressing like a member of the opposite sex 異性の人のような服装をすることを楽しむ人, 特に男性➡服装倒錯者

★**trap**¹ /træp/ 名 C ▶定義1 a piece of equipment that you use for catching animals 動物を捕まえるために使う装置➡わな, 落とし穴, 〜捕り器 ‖ *a mousetrap* ネズミ捕り *The rabbit's leg was caught in the trap.* ウサギの足がわなに掛かった. ▶定義2 a clever plan that is designed to trick sb 〜をだますためにもくろまれた巧妙な計画➡わな, 計略, 策略 ‖ *She **walked straight into the trap**.* 彼女はまともにわなに陥った. ▶定義3 an unpleasant situation from which it is hard to escape そこから逃れることが難しい不快な状況➡窮境

★**trap**² /træp/ 動 他 (**trapping**; **trapped**) ▶定義1（しばしば受動態で）to keep sb in a dangerous place or a bad situation from which he/she cannot escape 〜を, そこから逃れることのできないような危険な場所やひどい状況に置いておく➡〜を閉じ込める, 置く ‖ *The door closed behind them and they were trapped.* 彼らの後ろで戸が閉まり, 彼らは閉じ込められた. *Many people are trapped in low-paid jobs.* 多くの人々が低賃金の仕事に追いやられている. ▶定義2 to catch and keep or store sth 〜を捕まえて, そのままにする, または取っておく➡〜の流れを止める, 〜をトラップで遮る, トラップ装置を施す ‖ *Special glass panels trap heat from the sun.* 特殊ガラスパネルが太陽の熱を遮る. ▶定義3 to force sb/sth into a place or situation from which he/she/it cannot escape 〜を, そこから逃れることのできないような場所や状況に押し込む➡〜を窮屈な所に閉じ込める, 困難な立場に追い込む ‖ *Police believe this new evidence could help trap the killer.* 警察はこの新しい証拠が殺人犯を追い詰めるのに役立つと信じている. ▶定義4 to catch an animal, etc in a trap わなで動物などを捕まえる➡〜をわなで捕らえる ▶定義5 **trap sb (into sth/into doing sth)** to make sb do sth by tricking him/her 〜をだまして…をさせる➡〜をわなに掛ける, だまして〜させる, 陥れる ‖ *She had been trapped into revealing her true identity.* 彼女はだまされて自分の本当の身元を明かしてしまった.

**trapdoor** /trǽpdɔ̀:r/ 名 C ▶定義 a small door in a floor or ceiling 床または天井にある小さな戸➡跳ね上げ戸, 落とし戸, 上げぶた

**trapeze** /træpí:z; trə-/ 名 C ▶定義 a wooden or metal bar hanging from two ropes high above the ground, used by entertainers (**acrobats**) 芸人（曲芸師）によって使われる, 地面から高い所で2本のロープからぶら下がっている木製または金属製の棒➡（空中）ぶらんこ

**trappings** /trǽpiŋz/ [複数扱い] ▶定義 clothes, possessions, etc which are signs of a particular social position ある特定の社会的地位の印である衣服,所持品など→**装飾,衣装,式服,礼服,装具,飾り物**

**trash** /træʃ/ 米 = **RUBBISH**

**trash can** 米 = **DUSTBIN**

**trashy** /trǽʃi/ 形 ▶定義 of poor quality 品質の悪い→**下らない,価値のない,つまらない,ばかばかしい** ‖ trashy novels つまらない小説

**trauma** /trɔ́ːmə, tráʊ-/ 名 © Ⓤ ▶定義 (an event that causes) a state of great shock or sadness 大きな打撃または悲しみの状態(の原因となる出来事)→**心的外傷,トラウマ** ‖ the trauma of losing your parents 両親を失ったことによるトラウマ ☛参 stress — **traumatic** /trɔːmǽtɪk, trə-, traʊ-/ 形→**心的外傷を残す,忘れられないくらい衝撃的な,深く傷付いた**

★**travel**¹ /trǽv(ə)l/ 動 (**travelling**; **travelled**: 米 **traveling**; **traveled**) ▶定義 **1** 圓 to go from one place to another, especially over a long distance 特に長距離にわたって,ある場所からほかの場所へ行く→**旅行する,旅をする,行く,通う** ‖ Charles travels a lot on business. チャールズは商用でよく旅行する. to travel abroad 海外旅行をする to travel by sea/air/car 海路・空路・車で旅行する to travel to work 通勤する travelling expenses 旅行費用 ▶定義 **2** 他 to make a journey of a particular distance ある距離を旅行する→**〜を旅行する,移動する** ‖ They travelled 60 kilometres to come and see us. 彼らは私たちに会いに来るために60キロ移動した.

成句 **travel light** ▶定義 to take very few things with you when you travel 旅行するときにごくわずかな物しか持っていかない→**身軽に旅行する,軽装で旅する**

★**travel**² /trǽv(ə)l/ 名 ▶定義 **1** Ⓤ the action of going from one place to another ある場所からほかの場所へ行くこと→**旅行,旅** ‖ air/rail/space travel 空の旅・鉄道旅行・宇宙旅行 a travel bag/clock/iron (= designed to be used when travelling) 旅行かばん・旅行用小型時計・旅行用アイロン (= 旅行時に使うように作られた) ▶定義 **2** **travels** [複数扱い] time spent travelling, especially to places that are far away 旅行,特に遠く離れた所への旅行に費やされた時間→**長期の旅行,外国旅行**

▶ travel は数えられない単語で,一般的にあちこちへ移動することについて述べる場合にのみ使える: Foreign travel is very popular these days. (このごろは海外旅行がとても人気がある.) ある特定の場所からほかの場所へ行くことを言う場合は journey を用いる. journey は長い移動にも使える: the journey across Canada (カナダ横断の旅). あるいは短いが繰り返されるものにも使える: the journey to work (通勤). tour は,数箇所を訪ねるような周遊旅行や巡り歩きのことである. 国,都市,名所などを巡る旅を指す: a three-week tour around Italy (3週間のイタリア周遊の旅) a guided tour of the castle (その城のガイド付きツアー). trip は,旅行全体(ある場所への滞在やそこまでの道中も含む)について考えているときに使うことが多い: They're just back from a trip to Japan. They had a wonderful time. (彼らは日本への旅から戻ったばかりだ. 彼らにとってすばらしい旅だった.) しかし: 'How was the journey back?' 'Awful - the plane was delayed!' (「帰りはどうだった」「ひどかったよ － 飛行機が遅れたからね」) trip は短い場合もある: a day trip (日帰り旅行). あるいは長い場合もある: a trip round the world (世界一周旅行). 商用と遊びのどちらにも使える: How about a shopping trip to London this weekend? (今度の週末にロンドンへ買い物旅行に行きませんか.) He's on a business trip to New York to meet a client. (彼は顧客に会うためにニューヨークへ出張中です.) excursion は,集団の人々と一緒に出掛ける,手配された短い旅行のことである: The holiday includes a full-day excursion by coach to the capital. (休暇旅行にはバスによる首都への1日遠足が含まれている.) go on a journey/tour/trip/excursion という言い方をする.

**travel agency** 名 © (複 **travel agencies**) ▶定義 a company that makes travel arrangements for people (booking tickets, flights, hotels, etc) 人のために旅行の手配(切符,飛行機の便,ホテルなどの予約)をする会社→**旅行代理店,旅行社**

**travel agent** 名 ▶定義 **1** © a person whose job is to make travel arrangements for people 人のために旅行の手配をすることを仕事とする

人→旅行代理業者, 旅行業者 ▶定義2 **the travel agent's** [単数扱い] the shop where you can go to make travel arrangements, buy tickets, etc そこへ行って旅行の手配, 切符の購入などができる店→旅行代理店

**traveller** (米 **traveler**) /trǽv(ə)lər/ 名 C ▶定義1 a person who is travelling or who often travels 旅行中の人, またはよく旅行する人→旅行者, 旅人, 旅行家 ▶定義2 英 a person who travels around the country in a large vehicle and does not have a permanent home anywhere 大きな乗り物で国内を旅して回り, 定住する家をどこにも持たない人→ジプシー, 漂泊者 ☞参 **gypsy**

**traveller's cheque** (米 **traveler's check**) 名 C ▶定義 a cheque that you can change into foreign money when you are travelling in other countries ほかの国を旅行しているときに外貨に換えることのできる小切手→トラベラーズチェック, 旅行者用小切手

**travel-sick** 形 ▶定義 feeling sick or vomiting because of the movement of the vehicle you are travelling in 移動しているときに乗っている乗り物の動きのために, 気分が悪くなるまたは戻している→乗り物酔いした, 乗り物に酔った ☞参 **airsick**, **carsick**, **seasick**

\***tray** /treɪ/ 名 C ▶定義1 a flat piece of wood, plastic, metal, etc with slightly higher edges that you use for carrying food, drink, etc on 食べ物や飲み物などを載せて運ぶために使う, 縁がわずかに高くなっている, 木, プラスチック, 金属などの平たい物→盆, トレー, 浅い盛り皿 ▶定義2 a flat container with low edges in which you put papers, etc on a desk 机の上に置いて書類などを入れておく, 縁の浅い平たい入れ物→整理箱, 事務書類整理箱

**treacherous** /trétʃ(ə)rəs/ 形 ▶定義1 (used about a person) that you cannot trust and who may do sth to harm you (人について) 信用することができず, 人を傷付ける~をするかもしれないような→不誠実な, 裏切りの, 背く, 油断のならない ‖ *He was weak, cowardly and treacherous.* 彼は弱くておくびょうで不誠実だった. ▶定義2 dangerous, although seeming safe 安全そうに見えるが危険な→危険な, 当てにならない, 油断できない, 頼りにならない

**treachery** /trétʃ(ə)ri/ 名 U ▶定義 the act of causing harm to sb who trusts you 自分を信じてくれている~に損害をもたらすこと→裏切り, 背信行為, 不信, 反逆

**treacle** /tríːk(ə)l/ (米 **molasses**) 名 U ▶定義 a thick, dark, sticky liquid that is made from sugar 砂糖から作られた, 濃厚で黒っぽくべとべとした液体→糖みつ ☞参 **syrup**

**tread**[1] /tred/ 動 (過 **trod** /trɒd/; 過分 **trodden** /trɒdn/) ▶定義1 I **tread (on/in/over sb/sth)** to put your foot down while you are walking 歩いているときに足を下ろす→踏む, 踏み付ける, 足が踏み下ろされる ‖ *Don't tread in the puddle!* 水たまりに入らないように. *He trod on my foot and didn't even say sorry!* 彼は私の足を踏んだが謝りもしなかった. ▶定義2 他 **tread sth (in/into/down)** to press down on sth with your foot 足で~を踏み付ける→~を踏む, 踏み付ける, 踏んで作る, 踏み固める ‖ *This wine is still made by treading grapes in the traditional way.* このワインは今も伝統的にブドウを踏みつぶして作られている.

**tread**[2] /tred/ 名 ▶定義1 [単数扱い] the sound you make when you walk; the way you walk 歩くときに立てる音; 歩き方→足音, 足取り, 歩き振り ▶定義2 C U the pattern on the surface of a tyre on a vehicle which is slightly higher than the rest of the surface 乗り物のタイヤの表面にある, 表面の残りの部分よりもわずかに高くなっている模様→トレッドの模様, 溝形模様, トレッドパターン

**treason** /tríːz(ə)n/ 名 U ▶定義 the criminal act of causing harm to your country, for example by helping its enemies 例えば敵を助けるなどして, 自分の国に損害をもたらす犯罪行為→反逆罪 ☞参 **traitor** の注

\***treasure**[1] /tréʒər/ 名 ▶定義1 U a collection of very valuable objects, for example gold, silver, jewellery, etc 例えば金, 銀, 宝石などのような非常に価値の高い物の集まり→宝, 宝物, 財宝, 財産, 富 ‖ *to find buried treasure* 埋もれた宝を見つける ▶定義2 C something that is very valuable 非常に価値の高いもの→貴重品, 重要なもの, 重要品

**treasure**[2] /tréʒər/ 動 他 ▶定義 to consider sb/sth to be very special or valuable ~を非常に

特別である,または価値があると見なす→〜を大切にする,重んじる,尊ぶ ‖ I will treasure those memories forever. それらの思い出をいつまでも大切に心にしまっておきます.

**treasure hunt** 名 C ▶定義 a game in which people try to find a hidden prize by following special signs (clues) which have been left in different places さまざまな場所に残されている特別な印(手掛かり)をたどって,隠されている賞品を見つけようとするゲーム→宝探し

**treasurer** /tréʒərər/ 名 C ▶定義 the person who looks after the money and accounts of a club or an organization クラブや企業の金と会計簿の管理をする人→会計担当者,会計係,出納係,出納官,財務官

**the Treasury** /tréʒ(ə)ri/ 名[単数扱い,単数または複数形の動詞と共に] ▶定義 the government department that controls public money 公金を管理する政府の省 → 財務省,大蔵省

\***treat**¹ /triːt/ 動 他 ▶定義 **1** treat sb/sth (with/as/like sth) to act or behave towards sb/sth in a particular way 〜に対してある態度で行動する,または振る舞う→〜を扱う,取り扱う,〜に接する,〜を…として扱う,待遇する ‖ Teenagers hate being treated like children. 10代は子供扱いされるのを嫌がる.(口語)They **treat** their workers **like dirt** (= very badly). 彼らは社員をないがしろに(= とてもひどい扱いを)している. You should treat older people with respect. 年長者には敬意を持って接するべきだ. to treat sb badly/fairly/well 〜を虐待する・公平に扱う・〜に良くする ▶定義 **2** treat sth as sth to consider sth in a particular way 〜をある観点でとらえる→〜を…と見なす,考える,処理する ‖ I decided to treat his comment as a joke. 私は彼の言葉を冗談と見なすことにした. ▶定義 **3** to deal with or discuss sth in a particular way 〜にある方法で対処する,または話し合う→〜を論じる,扱う,〜について述べる ‖ The article treats this question in great detail. その記事はこの問題を詳しく論じている. ▶定義 **4** treat sb/sth (for sth) to use medicine or medical care to try to make a sick or injured person well again 病人やけが人を再び元気にしようとするために,薬を使うまたは治療を施す→〜を治療する,手当てする ‖ The boy was treated for burns at the hospital. その男の子は病院でやけどの治療を受けた. ▶定義 **5** treat sth (with sth) to put a chemical substance onto sth in order to protect it from damage, clean it, etc 損傷から守るまたは清潔にするなどのために,〜に化学物質を掛ける→〜を処理する,加工する ▶定義 **6** treat sb/yourself (to sth) to pay for sth or give sb/yourself sth that is very special or enjoyable 非常に特別な,または楽しい〜の代金を支払う,またはそのような〜を…・自分に与える→(〜を)…におごる,ごちそうする,もてなす,歓待する ‖ Clare treated the children to an ice cream (= she paid for them). クレアはその子供たちにアイスクリームをごちそうした(= 彼女がその代金を支払った).

**treat**² /triːt/ 名 C ▶定義 something special or enjoyable that you pay for or give to sb/yourself 自分が代金を支払う,あるいは〜・自分に与える特別な,または楽しいもの→楽しみ,喜び,ごちそう,おごり ‖ I've brought some cream cakes as a treat. 私はクリームケーキをごちそうに買ってきた. It's a real treat for me to stay in bed late. 遅くまで寝ているのは実に楽しい.

成句 trick or treat ⇒ **TRICK**

\***treatment** /tríːtmənt/ 名 ▶定義 **1** U C treatment (for sth) the use of medicine or medical care to cure an illness or injury; sth that is done to make sb feel and look good 病気やけがを治すための薬の使用や治療; 〜の気分を良くするまたは健康にするためになされる事→治療,処置,手当て,治療法 ‖ to require hospital/medical treatment 入院治療・医療を必要とする ▶定義 **2** U the way that you behave towards sb or deal with sth 〜に対する振る舞い方,または〜に対処する方法→取り扱い,扱い方,待遇,処理 ‖ The treatment of the prisoners of war was very harsh. 捕虜に対する扱いはとても残酷だった. ▶定義 **3** U C treatment (for sth) a process by which sth is cleaned, protected from damage, etc 〜が清潔にされるまたは損傷から守られるなどの過程→処理

**treaty** /tríːti/ 名 C (複 **treaties**) ▶定義 a written agreement between two or more countries 2国以上の間で交わされた書面による協定→条約,協定,盟約,条約文書 ‖ to sign a peace treaty 平和条約に調印する

**treble**[1] /trébəl/ 動自他 ▶定義 to become or to make sth three times bigger 3倍の大きさになる、または～を3倍の大きさにする→3倍になる; ～を3倍にする ‖ *Prices have trebled in the past ten years.* 過去10年で物価は3倍になった. — treble 形 ▶3倍の, 3重の ‖ *This figure is treble the number five years ago.* この数字は5年前の数字の3倍である.

**treble**[2] /trébəl/ 名 C ▶定義1 a high singing voice, especially that of a young boy 特に幼い男の子の, 高い歌声→最高声(部), 高音域, ソプラノ, ボーイソプラノ ▶定義2 a boy who has a high singing voice 高い歌声を持つ男の子→ボーイソプラノ

*★**tree** /triː/ 名 C ▶定義 a tall plant that can live for a long time. Trees have a thick wooden central part from which branches grow. 長い間生き続けることができる背の高い植物. 中心を成す太い木の部分があり, そこから枝が伸びる→木, 樹木, 高木, 立ち木 ‖ *an oak/apple/elm tree* オークの木・リンゴの木・ニレの木 ☞ C2 ページのさし絵

**trek** /trek/ 名 C ▶定義1 a long hard walk, lasting several days or weeks, usually in the mountains 通常は山の中で, 数日間または数週間続く長くつらい歩行→(つらい)(徒歩)旅行, (長くてつらい)旅, 苦難に満ちた旅・移動 ▶定義2 略式 a long walk 長く歩くこと→徒歩による小旅行, 徒歩の短い旅 — trek 動自 (trekking; trekked)→徒歩で旅行する, ゆっくり(難儀して)旅行する, のろのろと(苦難に耐えつつ)旅をする

▶長距離を楽しみで歩くことを述べる場合は go trekking を用いる.

**tremble** /trémbəl/ 動自 ▶定義 tremble (with sth) to shake, for example because you are cold, frightened, etc 例えば寒さのためまたはぎょっとするなどのために震える→(～で)震える, 身震いする, おののく, わななく ‖ *She was pale and trembling with shock.* 彼女は顔色が悪く, ショックでぶるぶる震えていた. *His hand was trembling as he picked up his pen to sign.* 署名するためにペンを取った時, 彼の手は震えていた. — tremble 名 C→震え, おののき, 身震い, 振動, 揺れ

**tremendous** /triméndəs/ 形 ▶定義1 very large or great とても大きい, または多い→非常に大きい, 巨大な, ばく大な, おびただしい, 甚だしい ‖ *a tremendous amount of work* おびただしい量の仕事 ▶定義2 略式 very good とても良い→すばらしい, すてきな, なかなかの ‖ *It was a tremendous experience.* それはすばらしい経験だった.

**tremendously** /triméndəsli/ 副 ▶定義 very; very much 非常に; とても多くの→とてつもなく, 非常に, 猛烈に ‖ *tremendously exciting* とてもわくわくするような *Prices vary tremendously from one shop to another.* 価格は店によって大幅に変わる.

**tremor** /trémər/ 名 C ▶定義 a slight shaking movement わずかに揺れる動き→微震, 軽い揺れ, 震え, 身震い, 微動 ‖ *There was a tremor in his voice.* 彼の声は震えていた.

**trench** /trentʃ/ 名 C ▶定義1 a long narrow hole dug in the ground for water to flow along それに沿って水が流れるように地面に掘られた細長い穴→溝, 堀, くぼみ ▶定義2 a long deep hole dug in the ground for soldiers to hide in during enemy attacks 兵隊が敵の攻撃の間に隠れるために地面に掘られた深く長い穴→塹壕(ざんごう), 壕(ごう)

**trend** /trend/ 名 C ▶定義 a trend (towards sth) a general change or development 全体的な変化または発展→傾向, 趨勢(すうせい), 動向, 風潮, トレンド, 流行 ‖ *The current trend is towards smaller families.* 現在は人数の少ない家族に向かう傾向にある. *He always followed the latest trends in fashion.* 彼はいつも流行の最先端を追っていた.

> ▶語法
> trend that SV は不可, trend of 名詞 ...ing を使う
>
> 同格の that が使えない典型的な名詞です. このような場合には「名詞 + of (+ 意味上の主語) + 動名詞」のパターンを用います. したがって「日本人旅行者が海外で休暇を過ごす傾向」は the trend of Japanese tourists spending holidays abroad となります. ここでは tourists と spending の間に意味上の「主語 + 動詞」の関係があります.

成句 **set a/the trend** ▶定義 to start a new style or fashion 新しい様式や流行を起こす→流

## 1730 trendy

行させる, 流行を作り出す

**trendy** /tréndi/ 形略式 ▶定義 fashionable 流行の➡流行の先端を行く, 流行を追う, トレンディーな

**trespass** /tréspəs/ 動自 ▶定義 to go onto sb's land or property without permission 許可なしに〜の土地や不動産の中に入る➡〜に不法侵入する — **trespasser** 名 C ➡不法侵入者, 侵害者

*__trial__ /tráɪ(ə)l/ 名 C U ▶定義 1 the process in a court of law where a judge, etc listens to evidence and decides if sb is guilty of a crime or not 法廷で裁判官などが証言を聴き, 〜がある罪を犯したかどうかを決める手順➡裁判, 公判, 審理 ‖ *a fair trial* 公正な審理 *He was on trial for murder.* 彼は殺人の容疑で裁判にかけられた. ▶定義 2 an act of testing sb/sth 〜を試すこと➡試み, 試用, 試運転, 試行 ‖ *New drugs must go through extensive trials.* 新薬は広範囲にわたる試験に合格しなければならない. *a trial period of three months* 3か月の試用期間

成句 **trial and error** ▶定義 trying different ways of doing sth until you find the best one 最良の方法を見つけるまで, 〜を行う方法をいろいろとやってみること➡試行錯誤, 手探り

**trial run** 名 C ▶定義 an occasion when you practise doing sth in order to make sure you can do it correctly later on 後で正確にできることを確認するために, 〜をする練習をする機会➡試行, 実験, 試運転, 試乗

*__triangle__ /tráɪæŋg(ə)l/ 名 C ▶定義 1 a shape that has three straight sides 直線の辺が3つある形➡三角形 ‖ *a right-angled triangle* 直角三角形 ☛ **shape** のさし絵 ▶定義 2 a metal musical instrument in the shape of a triangle that you play by hitting it with a metal stick 金属の棒でたたいて音を出す, 三角形の形をした金属製の楽器➡トライアングル ☛ **music** のさし絵

**triangular** /traɪæŋɡjələr/ 形 ▶定義 shaped like a triangle 三角形のような形をした➡三角の, 三角形の

**tribe** /tráɪb/ 名 C ▶定義 a group of people that have the same language and customs and that have a leader (*a chief*) 同じ言語と慣習を持ち, 統率者(長)がいる人々の集団➡部族, 種族, 一族, 〜族 ‖ *tribes living in the Amazonian rainforest* アマゾン川流域の熱帯雨林に住む部族 — **tribal** /tráɪb(ə)l/ 形 ➡部族の, 種族の ‖ *tribal art* 部族の芸術

**tribunal** /traɪbjúːnl, trɪ-/ 名 C ▶定義 a type of court with the authority to decide who is right in particular types of dispute or disagreement ある特定の種類の紛争や論争においてだれが正しいかを決める権限を持つ法廷➡裁判所, 法廷 ‖ *an industrial tribunal* 産業裁判所

**tributary** /tríbjətəri; -teri/ 名 C (複 **tributaries**) ▶定義 a small river that flows into a larger river より大きな川に流れ込んでいる小さな川➡支流

**tribute** /tríbjuːt, -bjət/ 名 ▶定義 1 C U **tribute (to sb)** something that you say or do to show that you respect or admire sb/sth, especially sb who has died 〜を, 特に亡くなった〜を尊敬または賞賛していることを示すために, 言うまたは行うこと➡賞賛・尊敬・感謝の印, 賛辞, 謝辞 ‖ *A special concert was held as a tribute to the composer.* その作曲家をたたえて特別演奏会が開かれた. ▶定義 2 [単数扱い] **a tribute (to sb/sth)** a sign of how good sb/sth is 〜がいかにすばらしいかの表れ➡〜の価値を証明するもの, 証拠, あかし ‖ *The success of the festival is a tribute to the organizers.* その祭りの成功は主催者の力量を証明するものである.

成句 **pay tribute to sb/sth** ⇒ **PAY**¹

*__trick__ /trɪk/ 名 C ▶定義 1 something that you do to make sb believe sth that is not true or a joke that you play to annoy sb 真実ではないことを〜に信じさせるためにすること, または〜を困らせるためにする悪ふざけ➡たくらみ, 計略, 策略, ごまかし, いたずら, 悪さ, 悪ふざけ ‖ *The thieves used a trick to get past the security guards.* その泥棒たちは警備員の前を通り過ぎるために策略を使った. ▶定義 2 something that confuses you so that you see, remember, understand, etc things in the wrong way 物事を間違って見る, 覚えるまたは理解するなどするように困惑させるもの➡引っ掛け, 落とし穴 ‖ *It was a trick question* (= one in which the answer looks easy, but actually is not) それは引っ掛け問題(= 答えが簡単そうに見えるが実際はそうではない問題)だった. ▶定義 3 an action that uses special skills to make people believe sth which is not true or real as a form of entertainment 余興として, 特殊な技を使い, 本

当または本物ではない～を人々に信じさせる活動➜**手品, トリック, 奇術** ‖ *The magician **performed a trick** in which he made a rabbit disappear.* その手品師はウサギの姿を消してしまう手品をした. *a card trick* トランプの手品 ▶定義4 [通常は単数] a clever or the best way of doing sth ～を行う賢明な, または最良の方法➜**うまいやり方, こつ, 秘けつ, 要領** — trick [動][他]➜**～をだます, 担ぐ** ‖ *I'd been tricked and I felt like a fool.* 私はだまされて, ばかみたいな気がした.

[成句] do the job/trick ⇒ **JOB**

play a joke/trick on sb ⇒ **JOKE**[1]

trick or treat 特に [米] ▶定義 a tradition in which children dressed as ghosts, etc go to people's houses on the evening of October 31st (Hallowe'en) and threaten to do sth bad to them if they do not give them sweets, etc 10月31日(ハロウィーン)の晩に, 子供たちがお化けなどのふん装をして人々の家に行き, お菓子などをくれなければ悪い事をすると脅かすという慣習➜**お菓子をくれないといたずらするぞ** ‖ *to go trick or treating* お菓子をねだりに行く

[句動詞] trick sb into sth/doing sth ▶定義 to persuade sb to do sth by making him/her believe sth that is not true ～に真実ではない…を信じさせて, その…をするよう説得する➜**～をだまして…させる** ‖ *He tricked me into lending him money.* 私は彼にだまされて金を貸してしまった.

trick sb out of sth ▶定義 to get sth from sb by making him/her believe sth that is not true 真実ではない事を信じさせて, ～から…を手に入れる➜**～をだまして…を奪う** ‖ *Stella was tricked out of her share of the money.* ステラはだまされて取り分の金を奪われた.

**trickery** /trík(ə)ri/ [名] [U] ▶定義 the use of dishonest methods to trick sb in order to get what you want 自分の望むものを手に入れるために, ～をだますような不正な方法を使うこと➜**ごまかし, ペテン, 詐欺**

**trickle** /trík(ə)l/ [動][自] ▶定義1 (used about a liquid) to flow in a thin line (液体について) 細い線で流れる➜**少しずつ流れる, 滴り落ちる, ポタポタ落ちる** ‖ *Raindrops trickled down the window.* 雨の滴が窓を伝った. ▶定義2 to go somewhere slowly and gradually ゆっくり少しずつどこかに行く➜**少しずつ来る·行く·進む·動く** — trickle [名] [[C], 通常は単数]➜**細い流れ, 滴り, 滴, ぽつぽつ来る·行くこと, ゆっくりとした動き·流れ** ‖ *a trickle of water* 水の滴り

**tricky** /tríki/ [形] (**trickier**; **trickiest**) ▶定義 difficult to do or deal with 行うまたは対処するのが難しい➜**扱いにくい, 難儀な, 落とし穴のある, こつのいる** ‖ *a tricky situation* 扱いにくい状況

**tricycle** /tráɪsɪk(ə)l/ [名] [C] ▶定義 a bicycle that has one wheel at the front and two at the back 車輪が前に1つ, 後ろに2つある自転車➜**三輪車**

**trifle** /tráɪf(ə)l/ [名] ▶定義1 **a trifle** [単数扱い] [正式] slightly; rather わずかに; やや➜**少し** ▶定義2 [C] something that is of little value or importance 価値や重要性がほとんどないもの➜**つまらない事, 下らない物, ささいな事** ▶定義3 [C][U] [英] a type of cold sweet food (dessert) made from cake and fruit covered with a sweet yellow sauce (custard) and cream ケーキと果物でできており, 黄色い甘いソース(カスタード)とクリームが掛かった甘くて冷たい食べ物(デザート)➜**トライフル**

**trifling** /tráɪf(ə)lɪŋ/ [形] ▶定義 very small or unimportant とても小さい, またはあまり重要ではない➜**わずかな, 少しの, 瑣末(さまつ)な, 取るに足りない, 下らない, つまらない**

**trigger**[1] /trígər/ [名] [C] ▶定義1 the part of a gun that you press to fire it 銃で, 押して発射する部分➜**引き金** ‖ *to pull the trigger* 引き金を引く ▶定義2 the cause of a particular reaction or event, especially a bad one ある反応や出来事の, 特に悪いものの原因➜**きっかけ, 誘因, 引き金, 刺激**

**trigger**[2] /trígər/ [動][他] ▶定義 trigger sth (off) to make sth happen suddenly ～を突然起こす➜**～を引き起こす, ～のきっかけとなる, ～を誘発する** ‖ *Her cigarette smoke had triggered off the fire alarm.* 彼女のたばこの煙で火災報知機が鳴った.

**trillion** /tríljən/ [数] ▶定義 one million million➜**1兆**

➤文中での数詞の使い方については, six の項を参照. 数についての説明は, 巻末の数についての特別項目を参照.

T

**trilogy** /trílədʒi/ 名 C (複 **trilogies**) ▶定義 a group of three novels, plays, etc that form a set 3つで一組となる小説, 演劇など→**三部作, 三部曲**

**trim**¹ /trɪm/ 動他 (**trimming**; **trimmed**) ▶定義1 to cut a small amount off sth so that it is tidy こぎれいになるように〜を少し切り落とす→**〜を刈り込む, きれいに手入れする, 整える** || *to trim your hair/fringe/beard* 整髪する・前髪を切りそろえる・あごひげを整える *The hedge needs trimming.* 生け垣を刈り込む必要がある. ▶定義2 trim sth (off sth) to cut sth off because you do not need it 〜を必要としないため切り落とす→**〜から減らす, 削る, 削減する, 刈り取る, 切り取る** || *Trim the fat off the meat.* 肉の脂身を切り落としてください. ▶定義3 trim sth (with sth) to decorate the edge of sth with sth 〜の縁を…で飾る→**〜を…で飾る, 飾り付ける** — trim 名 C, 通常は単数→**刈り込み, 手入れ, 調髪, 装飾, 飾り付け** || *My hair needs a trim.* 私の髪は調髪してもらう必要がある.

**trim**² /trɪm/ 形 ▶定義1 (used about a person) looking thin, healthy and attractive (人について) やせていて健康的で魅力的に見えている→**すらりとした** ▶定義2 well cared for; tidy よく手入れされた; 整然とした→**きちんとした, 整った, 整備された, こぎれいな**

**trimming** /trímɪŋ/ 名 ▶定義1 trimmings [複数扱い] extra things which you add to sth to improve its appearance, taste, etc 〜の外見, 味などを良くするために加える特別なもの→**飾り, 装飾, 最後の仕上げに装飾的に付け加えるもの, 付け合わせ** ▶定義2 C U material that you use for decorating the edge of sth 〜の縁を飾るために使う物→**へり飾り**

**trio** /tríːoʊ/ 名 (複 **trios**) ▶定義1 [C, 単数または複数形の動詞と共に] a group of three people who play music or sing together 一緒に音楽を演奏する, または歌う3人のグループ→**トリオ, 三重奏団, 三重唱団** ▶定義2 C a piece of music for three people to play or sing 3人で演奏する, または歌う楽曲→**トリオ, 三重奏曲, 三重唱曲**

★**trip**¹ /trɪp/ 名 C ▶定義 a journey to a place and back again, either for pleasure or for a particular purpose 楽しみで, または特定の目的で, ある場所へ行ってまた戻る旅→**旅行, 旅, 外出, 通うこと** || *How was your trip to Turkey?* トルコへの旅はいかがでしたか. *We had to make several trips to move all the furniture.* 私たちはすべての家具を動かすために何度も通わなければならなかった. *to go on a business/shopping trip* 出張する・買い物旅行に出掛ける ☛参 travel の注 — **tripper** 名 C→**(日帰りの)旅行者, 観光客** || *Brighton was full of* **day trippers** *(= people on trips that last for one day) from London.* ブライトンはロンドンからの日帰りの観光客(=1日の旅行に出ている人々)で一杯だった.

★**trip**² /trɪp/ 動 (**tripping**; **tripped**) ▶定義1 自 trip (over/up); trip (over/on sth) to catch your foot on sth when you are walking and fall or nearly fall 歩いているときに, 足を〜に引っ掛け, 転ぶ, または転びそうになる→**〜につまずく, よろめく, 踏み外す, つまずいて倒れる, よろける** || *Don't leave your bag on the floor. Someone might trip over it.* 床にかばんを置かないで. つまずく人がいるかもしれないから. *She tripped up on a loose paving stone* 彼女は浮き上がった敷石につまずいて転んだ. ▶定義2 他 trip sb (up) to catch sb's foot and make him/her fall or nearly fall 〜の足を引っ掛けて転ばせる, または転びそうにする→**〜をつまずかせる, よろめかせる, 転ばせる** || *Linda stuck out her foot and tripped Barry up.* リンダは足を突き出してバリーをつまずかせた.

句動詞 **trip (sb) up** ▶定義 to make a mistake; to make sb say sth that he/she did not want to say 間違える; 〜に言いたがらない…を言わせる→**間違える, 失敗する; 〜を失敗させる, 〜の揚げ足を取る** || *The journalist asked a difficult question to try to trip the politician up.* 記者は, その政治家の揚げ足を取るために難しい質問をした.

**triple** /trípəl/ 形 (名詞の前だけ) ▶定義 having three parts, happening three times or containing three times as much as usual 3つの部分から成っている, 3回起きている, あるいはいつもの3倍を含んでいる → **3部から成る, 3つの部分から成る, 3回繰り返された, 三重の, 3倍の** || *You'll receive triple pay if you work over the New Year.* 新年に働いたら3倍の給料がもらえますよ. — **triple** 動 自 他→**3倍[三重]になる; 〜を3倍[三重]にする**

**triplet** /tríplət/ 名 C ▶定義 one of three children or animals that are born to one mother at the same time 1人の母親から同時に生まれた3人の子供のうちの1人, または3匹の動物のうちの1匹→3つ子の1人, (複数形)3つ子 ☞参 **twin**

**tripod** /tráɪpɒd/ 名 C ▶定義 a piece of equipment with three legs that you use for putting a camera, etc on その上にカメラなどを載せるために使う, 3本の脚のある装置→三脚 ☞ **camera** のさし絵

\***triumph**[1] /tráɪəmf/ 名 C U ▶定義 a great success or victory; the feeling of happiness that you have because of this 大成功または大勝利; そのために感じる満足感→大勝利, 大成功, 功績, 勝利感, 勝利の喜び, 成功の喜び, 歓喜 ∥ *The team returned home in triumph.* そのチームは意気揚々と帰った. *The new programme was a triumph with the public.* その新しいプログラムは一般の人々にとって大勝利だった.

**triumph**[2] /tráɪəmf/ 動 自 ▶定義 triumph (over sb/sth) to achieve success; to defeat sb/sth 成功する; ～を負かす→大勝利を収める, 成功する, (～を)打ち負かす, 克服する ∥ *France triumphed over Brazil in the final.* フランスは決勝戦でブラジルを打ち負かした.

**triumphant** /traɪʌ́mfənt/ 形 ▶定義 feeling or showing great happiness because you have won or succeeded at sth ～に勝った, または成功したので大きな満足感を感じている, あるいは表している→勝ち誇った, 意気揚々とした, 大得意の ∥ *a triumphant cheer* 勝ち誇って上げた歓声 — triumphantly 副 →勝ち誇って, 意気揚々として, 大得意で

**trivial** /tríviəl/ 形 ▶定義 of little importance; not worth considering 重要性がほとんどない; 考慮する価値がない→つまらない, ささいな, 重要でない, ありふれた, 平凡な ∥ *a trivial detail/problem* 重要でない細部・ささいな問題 — triviality /trìviǽləti/ 名 C U (複 trivialities)→つまらないこと, 平凡さ, つまらないもの

**trivialize** (または -ise) /tríviəlàɪz/ 動 他 ▶定義 to make sth seem less important, serious, etc than it really is ～を実際よりも重要ではない, 重大ではないなどのように見せる→～をつまらぬものとして扱う, わい小化する, 平凡化する

**trod** **TREAD**[1] の過去形
**trodden** **TREAD**[1] の過去分詞形

**trolleys**

luggage trolley
(米 luggage cart)

shopping trolley
(米 shopping cart)

**trolley** /trɒ́li/ 名 C ▶定義1 (米 cart) a piece of equipment on wheels that you use for carrying things 物を運ぶために使う, 車輪の付いた装置→カート, 手押し車, トロッコ ∥ *a supermarket/shopping/luggage trolley* スーパーマーケットのカート・ショッピングカート・手荷物用のカート ▶定義2 英 a small table with wheels that is used for carrying or serving food and drinks 食べ物や飲み物を運ぶまたは出すために使われる, キャスターの付いた小さなテーブル→ワゴン ∥ *a tea/sweet/drinks trolley* お茶用ワゴン・お菓子用ワゴン・飲み物用ワゴン ▶定義3 米 = **TRAM**

**trombone** /trɒmbóʊn/ 名 C ▶定義 a large metal (brass) musical instrument that you play by blowing into it and moving a long tube backwards and forwards その中に息を吹き込み, 長い管を前後に動かして演奏する, 金属製の(真鍮(しんちゅう)の)大きな楽器→トロンボーン ☞参 **piano** の注 ☞ **music** のさし絵

**troop** /tru:p/ 名 ▶定義1 troops [複数扱い] soldiers 兵士たち→軍隊, 軍勢 ▶定義2 C a large group of people or animals 人々または動物の大きな集団→集団, 群れ, 一団 — troop 動 自 →集団でぞろぞろと歩く, 群がる, 集まる ∥ *When the bell rang everyone trooped into the hall.* ベルが鳴ると皆がホールへぞろぞろと歩いていった.

**trophy** /tróʊfi/ 名 C (複 trophies) ▶定義 a large silver cup, etc that you get for winning a competition or race 競技や競争に勝つともらう, 銀製の大きな賞杯→優勝記念品, トロフィー ☞ **medal** のさし絵

**tropic** /trɒ́pɪk/ 名 ▶定義1 [ C, 通常は単数] one of the two lines around the earth that are 23°27' north (the Tropic of Cancer) and south (the Tropic of Capricorn) of the line around the middle of the earth (the equator) 地球の中央線(赤道)の南北23度27分(南回帰線・北回帰線)で, 地球を回る2本の線のうちの1本→回帰線 ☛ **earth** のさし絵 ▶定義 2 **the tropics** [複数扱い] the part of the world that is between these two lines, where the climate is hot and wet 世界の中でそのような2本の線の間にあり, 気候は暑く雨が多い地域→熱帯地方 — tropical /-k(ə)l/ 形 →熱帯の, 熱帯地方の, 熱帯性の, 熱帯産の ‖ *tropical fruit* 熱帯地方の果物

**trot**[1] /trɑt/ 動 (**trotting**; **trotted**) 自 ▶定義 1 (used about a horse and its rider) to move forward at a speed that is faster than a walk (馬やその乗り手について)並足よりも速い速度で前進する→速足で駆ける, だく足を踏む, トロットで駆ける ☛参 **canter, gallop** ▶定義 2 (used about a person or an animal) to walk fast, taking short quick steps (人や動物について)短い歩幅と素早い足取りで速く歩く→早足で行く, 小走りする, 急ぎ足で行く

句動詞 **trot sth out** 略式 ▶定義 to repeat an old idea rather than thinking of sth new to say 新しい何かを言うことを考えないで, 古い考えを繰り返して言う→(言い古された話・言い訳などを)口にする, (既によく知られた事を)口にする ‖ *to trot out the same old story* 昔の同じ話を持ち出してしゃべる

**trot**[2] /trɑt/ 名 [単数扱い] ▶定義 a speed that is faster than a walk 並足よりも速い速度→速足, だく足

成句 **on the trot** 略式 ▶定義 one after another; without stopping 次から次へと; 止まらずに→連続して, 絶えず活動して, 忙しくしている ‖ *We worked for six hours on the trot.* 私たちは連続6時間働いた.

**★trouble**[1] /trʌ́b(ə)l/ 名 ▶定義 1 ⓤⓒ **trouble** (with sb/sth) (a situation that causes) a problem, difficulty or worry 問題, 困難, 悩み (を引き起こすような状態)→困難, 苦労, 心配事, 災難, 不幸, 危険 ‖ *If I don't get home by 11 o'clock I'll be in trouble.* 11時までに家に帰らなければ私は厄介なことになるだろう. *I'm having trouble getting the car started.* 私はその車を発車させるのに苦労している. *I'm having trouble with my car.* 自分の車のことで困っている. *financial troubles* 財政難 *Marie is clever. The trouble is she's very lazy.* マリーは賢いが, 困ったことに彼女はとても怠け者だ. ▶定義 2 ⓤ extra work or effort 余分な仕事や労力→厄介, 面倒, 迷惑, 骨折り, 不便 ‖ *Let's eat out tonight. It will save you the trouble of cooking.* 今晩は外食しよう. そうすれば料理する手間が省けるから. *Why don't you stay the night with us. It's no trouble.* その夜は私たちの家に泊まったらどうですか. 全然迷惑ではありませんよ. *I'm sorry to put you to so much trouble.* 大変ご迷惑をお掛けして申し訳ありません. ▶定義 3 ⓒ ⓤ a situation where people are fighting or arguing with each other 人が互いに戦っている, または言い争っている状態→争い事, もめ事, 混乱, 騒乱, トラブル, 紛争 ‖ *There's often trouble in town on Saturday night after the bars have closed.* 街では土曜の夜にバーが閉まった後, 争い事がよくある. ▶定義 4 ⓤ illness or pain 病気や苦痛→病気, 患い, 障害 ‖ *back/heart trouble* 背中の痛み・心臓病

成句 **ask for trouble** ⇒ **ASK**

**get into trouble** ▶定義 to get into a situation which is dangerous or in which you may be punished 危険な, または罰せられるかもしれないような状態に陥る→困ったことになる, 面倒を起こす, ごたごたを起こす, 処罰される, しかられる

**go to a lot of trouble (to do sth)** ▶定義 to put a lot of work or effort into sth 多大な仕事や労力を〜に投入する→〜するのに手間をかける, 骨を折る, 尽力する ‖ *They went to a lot of trouble to make us feel welcome.* 彼らは私たちを温かく迎えるために大変骨を折ってくれた.

**take trouble over/with sth; take trouble to do sth/doing sth** ▶定義 to do sth with care 注意深く〜をする→苦労する, 〜するよう骨折る, 尽力する

**take the trouble to do sth** ▶定義 to do sth even though it means extra work or effort たとえそれが余分な仕事や労力を要することでも〜をする→労を惜しまず〜する, わざわざ〜する

**trouble**[2] /trʌ́b(ə)l/ 動 他 ▶定義 1 to make sb worried, upset, etc 〜を心配させる, うろたえさせるなどする→〜を困らせる, 悩ます, 心配させる, 苦しめる ‖ *Is there something troubling you?* 何か困っていることがありますか. ▶定義 2 正式 **trouble sb (for sth)** (used when you are politely asking sb for sth or to do sth) to disturb sb（〜に…を、または〜をしてくれるよう丁寧に頼むときに用いて）〜に迷惑を掛ける→**〜に面倒を掛ける，迷惑を掛ける，迷惑を顧みずに頼む，〜の手を煩わせる** ‖ *Sorry to trouble you, but would you mind answering a few questions?* 申し訳ありませんが、2、3の質問に答えてくださいませんか。 ☛類 **bother**

**troublemaker** /trʌ́b(ə)lmèikər/ 名 C ▶定義 a person who often deliberately causes trouble しばしば故意に問題を引き起こす人→**いつももんちゃくを起こす人，ごたごたを起こす人，トラブルメーカー**

**troublesome** /trʌ́b(ə)lsəm/ 形 ▶定義 causing trouble, pain, etc over a long period of time 長い期間にわたって問題，苦痛などの原因となっている→**厄介な，面倒な，手の掛かる，うるさい，骨の折れる，難しい**

**trough** /trɔ(ː)f, trɑf/ 名 C ▶定義 1 a long narrow container from which farm animals eat or drink 飼育場の動物がそこから食べたり飲んだりする細長い容器→**飼い葉おけ，水入れ，えさ入れ** ▶定義 2 a low area or point, between two higher areas 2つの高い区域の間にある低い区域または点→**くぼみ，谷，気圧の谷，景気の谷間**

★**trousers** /tráuzərz/（米 **pants**）名 [複数扱い] ▶定義 a piece of clothing that covers the whole of both your legs 両足全体を覆う衣服→**ズボン**
　▶注意. trousersは複数形の単語なので、例えばa new trouserとは言えない。次のような言い方はできる: *I need some new trousers.*（新しいズボンが何本か必要だ。）*I need a new pair of trousers.*（新しいズボンが1本必要だ。）ほかの名詞の前では、trouser という語形で用いられる: *a trouser suit (= a woman's suit consisting of a jacket and trousers)*（トラウザースーツ（= 上着とズボンから成る女性用のスーツ））

☛ C6ページのさし絵

**trout** /tráut/ 名 C U (複 trout) ▶定義 a type of fish that lives in rivers and that we eat 川に住み、人が食べる魚の一種→**マス，ニジマス**

**truant** /trúːənt/ 名 C ▶定義 a child who stays away from school without permission 許可なしに学校を休む子供→**ずる休みする生徒，無断欠席の生徒** — **truancy** /-ənsi/ 名 U ▶定義 ずる休み，無断欠席

成句 **play truant**; 米 **play hooky** ▶定義 to stay away from school without permission 許可なしに学校を休む→**学校をずる休みする，サボる**

**truce** /trúːs/ 名 C ▶定義 an agreement to stop fighting for a period of time ある期間、戦うことをやめるという協定→**休戦，停戦，休戦協定**
☛参 **ceasefire**

★**truck** /trʌ́k/ 名 C ▶定義 1 特に 米 = **LORRY** ‖ *a truck driver* トラックの運転手 ☛ **vehicle** のさし絵 ▶定義 2 英 an section of a train that is used for carrying goods or animals 列車の中で、貨物や動物を運ぶために使われる部分→**屋根のない貨車，無蓋(むがい)貨車** ‖ *a cattle truck* 家畜輸送車

**trudge** /trʌ́dʒ/ 動 自 ▶定義 to walk with slow, heavy steps, for example because you are very tired とても疲れているなどのため、ゆっくりと重い足取りで歩く→**重い足取りでとぼとぼ歩く**

★**true** /trúː/ 形 ▶定義 1 right or correct 正しい、または正確な→**本当の，真実の，正確な，間違いのない，実物そのままの** ‖ *Is it true that Adam is leaving?* アダムが辞めるというのは本当ですか. *I didn't think the film was at all **true to life** (= it didn't show life as it really is).* その映画が真に迫っているとは全く思えなかった（= 実際の生活のように表現していなかった）. *Read the statements and decide if they are true or false.* その申し立てを読んで、真実であるか虚偽であるかを判断しなさい. ⇔ **untrue, false** ▶定義 2 real or genuine, often when this is different from how sth seems しばしば〜が見えている様子と違うときに、本当の、または真の→**本当の，真実の** ‖ *The novel was based on **a true story**.* その小説は実話が元になっていた. ⇔ **false** ▶定義 3 having all the typical qualities of the thing mentioned 言及されているものの典型的な性質をすべて持っている→**本物の，正真正銘の，純粋な** ‖ *How do you know when you have found **true love**?* 真実の愛をいつ見つけたかなんてどうやって分かるでしょう. ▶定義 4 **true (to sb/sth)** behaving as expected or as promised 期待された通りに、または約束した通りに振る舞っている→**〜に誠実な，忠実な，当てになる，確かな** ‖ *He was **true to his word** (= he did what he had* *promised).* 彼は約束を守った（= 彼は自分が約束したことをした）. *She has been a true friend to me.* 彼女はずっと私にとって誠実な友人である. ☛图 **truth**

成句 **come true** ▶定義 to happen in the way you hoped or dreamed 望んでいた、または夢見ていた通りに起こる→**実現する, 本当になる, 事実となる** ‖ *My dream has come true!* 私の夢が実現したわ.

**too good to be true** ▶定義 used to say that you cannot believe that sth/sb is as good as it/he/she seems 〜が見えている様子と同じであるとは信じられないと言うときに用いて→**にわかには信じられない, 信じ難い**

**true to form** ▶定義 typical; as usual 典型的な; いつものように→**例によって, 思った通り, いつも通りに**

**truly** /trúːli/ 副 ▶定義 1 (used to emphasize a feeling, statement) really; completely（気持ち, 陳述を強調するために用いて）本当に; すっかり→**本当に, 全く, 誠実に, 心から** ‖ *We are truly grateful to you for your help.* あなたが助けてくださったことに私たちは心から感謝しています.

▶定義 2 used to emphasize that sth is correct or accurate 〜が正しいあるいは正確であることを強調するために用いて→**真実に, 偽りなく, 事実の通りに, 正確に** ‖ *I cannot truly say that I was surprised at the news.* その知らせに驚いたとはとても言えない.

➤ Yours truly は改まった手紙の末尾によく用いられる.

成句 **well and truly** ⇒ **WELL**¹

**trump** /trʌmp/ 名 ⓒ ▶定義 (in some card games) a card of the chosen set (suit) that has a higher value than cards of the other three sets during a particular game （トランプゲームで）あるゲームのときにほかの3つの組のカード（組み札）よりも高い価値のある, 選ばれた組のカード→**切り札** ‖ *Spades are trumps.* スペードが切り札だ.

**trump card** 名 ⓒ ▶定義 a special advantage you have over other people that you keep secret until you can surprise them with it それを使ってほかの人を驚かせるまで秘密にしておく, その人たちよりも特に有利な点→**切り札, 奥の手, 最後の手段** ‖ *It was time for her to play her trump card.* 彼女が奥の手を使う番だった.

**trumpet** /trʌ́mpət/ 名 ⓒ ▶定義 a metal (brass) musical instrument that you play by blowing into it. There are three buttons on it which you press to make different notes. その中に息を吹き込んで演奏する金属製の（真鍮（しんちゅう）の）楽器. 3つのボタンが付いており, それを押して異なる音を出す→**トランペット, ラッパ** ☛参 **piano** の注 ⓜ **music** のさし絵

**truncheon** /trʌ́ntʃ(ə)n/ 英（または **baton**）名 ⓒ （古）▶定義 a short thick stick that a police officer carries as a weapon 警官が武器として携えている太く短い棒→**警棒**

**trundle** /trʌ́ndl/ 動 ⓘ ⓣ ▶定義 to move, or make sth heavy move, slowly and noisily ゆっくり騒々しく動く, またはそのように重い〜を動かす→**転がる, 動いていく, 走る; 〜を転がす, ごろごろ押していく, 引いていく** ‖ *A lorry trundled down the hill.* トラックが坂道をがたがたと下っていった.

**trunk** /trʌŋk/ 名 ▶定義 1 ⓒ the thick central part of a tree that the branches grow from そこから枝が伸びている, 木の中心を成す太い部分→**幹, 樹幹** ☛ C2 ページのさし絵 ▶定義 2 ⓒ 米 = **BOOT**¹(2) ▶定義 3 ⓒ an elephant's long nose 象の長い鼻→**象の鼻** ☛ **elephant** のさし絵 ▶定義 4 **trunks** [複数扱い] = **SWIMMING TRUNKS** ▶定義 5 ⓒ a large box that you use for storing or transporting things 物を保管するまたは運ぶために使う大きな箱→**トランク, 大型旅行かばん** ▶定義 6 [通常は単数] the main part of your body (not including your head, arms and legs) 身体の主要な部分（頭, 腕, 足は含まない）→**胴, 胴体, 体幹**

*****trust** /trʌst/ 名 ▶定義 1 ⓤ trust (in sb/sth) the belief that sb is good, honest, sincere, etc and will not try to harm or trick you 〜が善良, 正直, 誠実, などであり, 人を傷付けようまたはだまそうとはしないだろうと信じること→**信頼, 信用, 信任** ‖ *Our marriage is based on love and trust.* 私たちの結婚は愛情と信頼の上に成り立っている. *I should never have put my trust in him.* 私は彼を信用すべきではなかった. ☛参 **distrust, mistrust** ▶定義 2 ⓒ ⓤ a legal arrangement by which a person or organization looks after money and property for sb else until that person is old enough to control it ほかの～が金や財産を管理できる年齢になるまで, 人または組織がその人に代わってそれらを管理するという法的な取り決め→**信託**

**成句** take sth on trust ▶定義 to believe what sb says without having proof that it is true ～の言うこと, それが正しいという証拠がないのに信じる→**～をうのみにする, 確かめずに～を信用する** || *I can't prove it. You must take it on trust.* 私にはそれを証明することができません. だからあなたはそのまま信用するしかありません.

★**trust**[2] /trʌst/ **動 他** ▶定義 trust sb (to do sth); trust sb (with sth) to believe that sb is good, sincere, honest, etc and that he/she will not trick you or try to harm you ～が善良, 正直, 誠実などであり, 人をだまそうとしたり傷付けたりはしないだろうと信じる→**～を信頼する, 信用する, 信任する, 当てにする, 頼りにする** || *He said the car was safe but I just don't trust him.* 彼はその車が安全だと言ったが, 私は彼を全く信用していない. *You can't trust her with money.* 彼女にはお金を預けられない. *I don't trust that dog. It looks dangerous.* 私にはあの犬は安心できない. 危害を加えそうに見えるから. ☛参 mistrust, distrust

**成句** Trust sb (to do sth) (口語) ▶定義 it is typical of sb to do sth ～をするのはその人らしい→**～ならきっと…する** || *Trust Alice to be late. She's never on time!* アリスならきっと遅れるよ. 時間通りに来たためしがないのだから.

**trustee** /trʌstíː/ **名 C** ▶定義 a person who looks after money or property for sb else ほかの～に代わって金や財産を管理する人→**受託者, 被信託者, 保管人, 管財人**

**trusting** /trʌ́stɪŋ/ **形** ▶定義 believing that other people are good, sincere, honest, etc 他人が善良, 正直, 誠実などであると信じている→**信頼の念に満ちた, 人を信じやすい, 人を疑わない**

**trustworthy** /trʌ́stwɜːrði/ **形** ▶定義 that you can depend on to be good, sincere, honest, etc 善良, 正直, 誠実などであることを当てにできる→**信頼できる, 信用できる, 当てになる, 頼りになる**

★**truth** /truːθ/ **名** ( 複 ) truths /truːðz, truːθs/)

▶定義**1** the truth [単数扱い] what is true; the facts 真実であるもの; 事実→**真実, 事実, 真相** || *Please tell me the truth.* 本当のことを話してください. *Are you telling me the whole truth about what happened?* 起こった事について事実をすべて話してくれていますか. *The truth is, we can't afford to live here any more.* 実は私たちはもうここに住むだけの余裕がないのです.

▶定義**2** ● the state or quality of being true 真実であるという状態たる性質→**真実であること, 本当であること, 真実性, 真実味** || *There's a lot of truth in what she says.* 彼女の言うことには多分に真実味がある. ▶定義**3** ● a fact or idea that is believed by most people to be true ほとんどの人々に真実であると信じられている事実や考え→**真理, 原理, 立証された事実** || *scientific/universal truths* 科学的事実・普遍的な真理 ☛形 true

**truthful** /trúːθfʊl, -f(ə)l/ **形** ▶定義**1** truthful (about sth) (used about a person) who tells the truth; honest (人について) 真実を語るような; 正直な→**うそを言わない, 正直な, 誠実な** || *I don't think you're being truthful with me.* あなたは私に対して誠実ではないと思う. ▶定義**2** (used about a statement) true or correct (陳述について) 真実の, または正確な→**真実の, 正しい, 事実に即した, 本当の** || *a truthful account* 事実に即した報告 — truthfully /-fʊli, -f(ə)li/ **副** →**誠実に, 正直に, 正しく, 事実に即して, 正直に言えば, 本当のところ**

★**try**[1] /traɪ/ **動** (現分 trying; 三単現 tries; 過, 過分 tried) ▶定義**1** **自** try (to do sth) to make an effort to do sth ～をしようと努力する→**～しようと努める, 努力する, 挑戦する** || *I tried to phone you but I couldn't get through.* 私はあなたに電話しようとしましたが通じませんでした. *She was trying hard not to laugh.* 彼女は笑わないよう懸命に努めていた. *She'll try her best to help you.* 彼女はあなたを助けようと最善を尽くしてくれるでしょう. *I'm sure you can do it if you try.* それはやってみたらきっとできると思いますよ.

➤ try and は try to よりも口語的である. 過去時制で使うことはできない: *I'll try and get there on time.* (そこに時間通りに着くようにします.) *I tried to get there on time, but I was too late.* (私はそこに時間通りに着くよう努力したが遅れてしまった.)

▶定義**2** **他** try (doing) sth to do, use or test

# 1738　try²

sth in order to see how good or successful it is ~がどれほど適しているか、またはうまくいくかを見てみるために、それをする、使う、あるいは試す→~を試してみる、試用する、試食する ‖ *I've tried everything but I can't get the baby to sleep.' 'Have you tried taking her out in the car?'* 「あらゆる事をやってみましたが、赤ん坊を眠らせることができないんです」「車で外に連れ出してみましたか」 *Have you ever tried raw fish?* 生の魚を食べてみたことがありますか. *We tried the door but it was locked.* 私たちはその戸を開けようとしてみたが、かぎがかかっていた.

▶定義3 ⓤ **try sb (for sth)** to examine sb in a court of law in order to decide if he/she is guilty of a crime or not ~が有罪かどうかを決めるために、法廷でその人を尋問する→~を裁く、裁判する、審問する、審理する ‖ *He was tried for murder.* 彼は殺人容疑で裁判にかけられた.

成句 **try your hand at sth** ▶定義 to do sth such as an activity or a sport for the first time ある活動やスポーツのような~を初めてする→~に挑戦する、腕試しに~をやってみる

句動詞 **try sth on** ▶定義 to put on a piece of clothing to see if it fits you propely 衣服が自分の体にぴったり合っているかどうかを見てみるために、それを身に着ける→~を試しに着てみる、試着する ‖ *Can I try these jeans on, please?* このジーンズを履いてみていいでしょうか.

**try sb/sth out** ▶定義 to test sb/sth to find out if he/she/it is good enough ~が適しているかどうかを調べるために、それを試す→~を厳密にテストする、十分に試してみる、実地試験する、試しに使ってみる

**try²** /tráɪ/ 名 ⓒ (複 **tries**) ▶定義 an occasion when you try to do sth; an attempt ~をやってみる機会；試み→試み、試し、努力 ‖ *I don't know if I can move it by myself, but I'll give it a try.* それを自分で動かせるかどうか分からないが、やってみようと思う.

**trying** /tráɪɪŋ/ 形 ▶定義 that makes you tired or angry 疲れさせる、または怒らせるような→つらい、苦しい、~にこたえる、骨の折れる、腹立たしい、しゃくにさわる、厄介な ‖ *a trying journey* 苦しい旅

**T-shirt** (または **teeshirt**) 名 ⓒ ▶定義 a shirt with short sleeves and without buttons or a collar そでが短く、ボタンやえりのないシャツ→Tシャツ ☞ C6 ページのさし絵

**tsp** 略 teaspoonful(s) =茶さじ ‖ *Add 1 tsp salt.* 茶さじ1杯の塩を加えてください.

**tub** /tʌb/ 名 ⓒ ▶定義1 a large round container 円い大きな容器→おけ、たらい、鉢 ▶定義2 a small plastic container with a lid that is used for holding food 食べ物を入れるために使われる、ふたのあるプラスチック製の小さな容器→円い容器、入れ物 ‖ *a tub of margarine/ice cream* マーガリン・アイスクリームの容器 ☞ **container** のさし絵

**tuba** /t(j)úːbə/ 名 ⓒ ▶定義 a large metal (brass) musical instrument that makes a low sound 低い音が鳴る金属製の（真鍮（しんちゅう））の大きな楽器→チューバ ☞参 piano の注 ☞ **music** のさし絵

★**tube** /t(j)uːb/ 名 ▶定義1 ⓒ a long empty pipe 空洞になっている長い管→管、筒、チューブ ‖ *Blood flowed along the tube into the bottle.* 血が管を通ってびんに流れ込んだ. *the inner tube of a bicycle tyre* 自転車のタイヤのチューブ ☞参 **test tube** ▶定義2 ⓒ **a tube (of sth)** a long thin container with a lid at one end made of soft plastic or metal. Tubes are used for holding thick liquids that can be squeezed out of them. 柔らかいプラスチックまたは金属でできている、一方の端にふたの付いた細長い容器. それから絞り出される濃厚な液体を入れるために使われる→チューブ ‖ *a tube of toothpaste* チューブ入り歯磨き粉 ☞ **container** のさし絵 ▶定義3 **the tube**［単数扱い］英略式 = UNDERGROUND³

**tuberculosis** /t(j)ʊbə:rkjəlóʊsəs/ 名 ⓤ (略 **TB**) ▶定義 a serious disease that affects the lungs 肺を侵す重い病気→結核

**tubing** /t(j)úːbɪŋ/ 名 ⓤ ▶定義 a long piece of metal, rubber, etc in the shape of a tube 管の形をした金属、ゴムなどの長いもの→管、パイプ

**TUC** /tíː juː síː/ 略 the Trades Union Congress ▶定義 the association of British trades unions 英国の労働組合の協会→労働組合会議

**tuck** /tʌk/ 動 ⓒ ▶定義1 **tuck sth in, under, round, etc (sth)** to put or fold the ends or edges of sth into or round sth else so that it looks tidy きちんとして見えるように、~の端や

縁をほかの…の中や回りに入れる, あるいは折り込む→~にタックを取る, ひだを寄せる, ~の端を押し込む, 挟み込む, たくし込む, くるむ ‖ *Tuck your shirt in - it looks untidy like that.* シャツのすそを中に入れなさい - あのようにだらしなく見えますよ. ▶定義2 **tuck sth (away)** to put sth into a small space, especially to hide it or to keep it safe 特に隠すためは安全に保管するために, ~を狭い所に入れる→~を押し込む, しまい込む, 隠す ‖ *The letter was tucked behind a pile of books.* その手紙は積み上げられた本の山の後ろに隠されていた.

句動詞 **tuck sth away** ▶定義1 (受動態で)to be situated in a quiet place; to be hidden 静かな場所に置かれている; 隠されている→~を人目に付かない所に置く・建てる ‖ *The house was tucked away among the trees.* その家は森の中の人目に付かない所に建っていた. ▶定義2 to hide sth somewhere; to keep sth in a safe place ~をどこかに隠す; ~を安全な場所に保管する→~を隠す, しまい込む ‖ *He tucked his wallet away in his inside pocket.* 彼は財布を内ポケットにしまい込んだ.

**tuck sb in/up** ▶定義 to make sb feel comfortable in bed by pulling the covers up around him/her ~に寝具を掛けて, ベッドで寝心地良くする→~を…でくるむ, シーツ・毛布などを掛ける

**tuck in; tuck into sth** 特に 英(口語) ▶定義 to eat with pleasure 喜んで食べる→~をがつがつ食べる, たらふく食う, かき込む

**Tue** (または **Tues**) 略 Tuesday→火曜日 ‖ *Tues 9 March* 3月9日火曜日

\***Tuesday** /t(j)úːzdeɪ, -di/ 名 C U (略**Tue**; **Tues**)
▶定義 the day of the week after Monday 月曜日の次の曜日→火曜日
▶曜日は最初の文字を必ず大文字で書く. 文中での曜日の使い方の例については, Monday を参照.

**tuft** /tʌft/ 名 C ▶定義 a small amount of hair, grass, etc growing together 一緒に生えている少量の髪, 草など→房, 束

**tug**¹ /tʌg/ 動 自 他 (**tugging**; **tugged**) ▶定義 **tug (at/on sth)** to pull sth hard and quickly, often several times ~を強く素早く引く, 大抵は何度も→(~を)強く引っ張る, ぐいと引く, 引っ張って動かす, 引きずり出す ‖ *The little boy tugged at his father's trouser leg.* その小さな男の子はお父さんのズボンの足を強く引っ張った.

**tug**² /tʌg/ 名 C ▶定義1 a sudden hard pull 急に強く引くこと→強く引っ張ること, カー杯引くこと ‖ *She gave the rope a tug.* 彼女はその綱を強く引っ張った. ▶定義2 (または **tugboat**) a small powerful boat that is used for pulling ships into a port, etc 船を港などに引っ張って入れるために使われる, 強力な小型ボート→引き船, タグボート

**tuition** /t(j)uːíʃ(ə)n/ 名 U ▶定義 **tuition (in sth)** teaching, especially to a small group of people 特に少人数の人に, 教えること→教授, 教育, 指導, 授業 ‖ *private tuition in Italian* イタリア語の個人指導 *tuition fees* (= the money that you pay to be taught, especially in a college or university) 授業料 (= 特に大学で, 教わるために支払う金)

**tulip** /t(j)úːlɪp/ 名 C ▶定義 a brightly-coloured flower, shaped like a cup, that grows in the spring 春に育つ, カップのような形をした鮮やかな色の花→チューリップ ☞ C2 ページのさし絵

**tumble** /tʌmb(ə)l/ 動 自 ▶定義1 to fall down suddenly but without serious injury 急に, しかし大きな傷を受けることなく倒れる→転ぶ, 倒れる, 転げ落ちる, 転落する ‖ *He tripped and tumbled all the way down the steps.* 彼はつまずいて階段を下までで転げ落ちた. ▶定義2 to fall suddenly in value or amount 価値や総額が突然低くなる→急落する, 暴落する, 下落する ‖ *House prices have tumbled.* 住宅の価格が急落した. ▶定義3 to move in a particular direction in an untidy way 無秩序にある方向へ動く→慌てて来る・行く, 動く, 転がり込む, 転ぶように飛び出す ‖ *She opened her suitcase and all her things tumbled out of it.* 彼女がスーツケースを開けると, 中の物が全部転がり出てしまった. — **tumble** 名 C →転倒, 転落, 落下, 急落, 混乱状態, 無秩序, 乱雑

句動詞 **tumble down** ▶定義 to fall down; to collapse 倒れ落ちる; 崩壊する→崩れ落ちる, 転落する, 崩壊する ‖ *The walls of the old house were tumbling down.* その古い家の壁は崩れ落ちていた.

**tumble-dryer** (または **tumble-drier**) 名 C 英 定義 a machine that dries clothes by moving them about in hot air 温風の中で衣服を移動させて乾かす機器→回転式乾燥機

**tumbler** /tʌ́mblər/ 名 C 定義 a tall glass for drinking out of with straight sides and no handle 側面が曲がっておらず取っ手のない, 飲み物を飲むための背の高いコップ→タンブラー

**tummy** /tʌ́mi/ 名 C (複 **tummies**) 略式 = **STOMACH**¹

**tumour** (米 **tumor**) /t(j)úːmər/ 名 C 定義 a mass of cells that are not growing normally in the body as the result of a disease 病気の結果, 体内で正常に育っていない細胞の塊→腫瘍(しゅよう), はれ物, 出来物 ‖ *a brain tumour* 脳腫瘍

**tumultuous** /t(j)umʌ́ltʃuəs/ 形 定義 very noisy, because people are excited 人々が興奮しているためにとてもうるさい→騒然とした, 騒がしい, 騒々しい ‖ *tumultuous applause* 万雷の拍手

**tuna** /t(j)úːnə/ (または **tuna fish**) 名 C U (複 **tuna**) 定義 a large sea fish that we eat 人が食べる大型の海水魚→マグロ ‖ *a tin of tuna* ツナの缶詰

★**tune**¹ /t(j)uːn/ 名 C U 定義 a series of musical notes that are sung or played to form a piece of music 1つの楽曲を形づくるために歌われる, または演奏される一連の音符→曲, 歌曲, 旋律, 節, メロディー ‖ *The children **played** us **a tune** on their recorders.* その子供たちは私たちにリコーダーで1曲演奏してくれた.

成句 call the shots/tune ⇒ **CALL**¹
change your tune ⇒ **CHANGE**¹
in/out of tune 定義1 at/not at the correct musical level (pitch) 正確な音の高さ(ピッチ)である・ない→音の調子が合って・音の調子が外れて ‖ *You're singing out of tune.* 歌の調子が外れていますよ. 定義2 having/not having the same opinions, interests, feelings, etc as sb/sth 〜と同じ意見, 関心, 気持ちなどを持っている・持っていない→〜と調和して・しないで, 仲が良く・悪く

**tune**² /t(j)uːn/ 動 定義1 他 to make small changes to the sound a musical instrument makes so that it is at the correct musical level (pitch) 正確な音の高さ(ピッチ)になるように, 楽器の出す音に少し変更を加える→〜を調律する, 〜の音を合わせる ‖ *to tune a piano/guitar* ピアノを調律する・ギターを調弦する 定義2 他 to make small changes to an engine so that it runs well よく走るように, エンジンに少し変更を加える→〜を調整する, チューンする 定義3 自 tune (in) to sth to listen to a particular radio station ある特定のラジオ局を聴く→〜を…に合わせる ‖ ***Stay tuned*** *to this station for the latest news.* チャンネルはこのままで最新ニュースをお聞きください.

句動詞 tune in (to sth) 定義 to move the controls of a radio or television so that you can listen to or watch a particular station ある特定の放送局が聴ける, または見られるようにするために, ラジオあるいはテレビのダイヤルやチャンネルを動かす→〜に周波数を合わせる, チャンネルを合わせる

tune up 定義 to make small changes to a group of musical instruments so that they sound pleasant when played together 一緒に演奏されたときに心地良い音がするように, 楽器群に少し変更を加える→〜の調子を合わせる, 調律する

**tuneful** /t(j)úːnfʊl, -f(ə)l/ 形 定義 (used about music) pleasant to listen to (音楽について) 聴いて心地良い→調子の良い, 旋律の豊かな, 調べの美しい, いい音を出す, 音楽的な

**tunic** /t(j)úːnɪk/ 名 C 定義1 a piece of women's clothing, usually without sleeves, that is long and not tight 長くてぴったりとしておらず, 通常はそでがない, 女性の衣服→女性用オーバーブラウス, 短いコート, 短いオーバースカート 定義2 米 the jacket that is part of the uniform of a policeman, soldier, etc 警察官, 兵隊などの制服の一部である上着→制服の上着

★**tunnel** /tʌ́nl/ 名 C 定義 a passage under the ground 地下の通路→トンネル, 地下道, 坑道 ‖ *The train disappeared into a tunnel.* その電車はトンネルに姿を消した. — tunnel 動 自 他 (**tunnelling; tunnelled**: 米 **tunneling; tunneled**)→〜にトンネルを掘る, トンネルを掘って〜を作る, トンネルを掘って〜を進む

**turban** /tə́ːrb(ə)n/ 名 C 定義 a covering for the head worn especially by Sikh and Muslim men. A turban is made by folding a long piece of cloth around the head. 特にシーク教徒とイスラム教徒の男性が着用する,頭を覆うもの.長い布を頭に巻き付けてできる→**ターバン** ☛ C6ページのさし絵

**turbulent** /tə́ːrbjələnt/ 形 ▶定義1 in which there is a lot of change, disorder and disagreement, and sometimes violence 多くの変動,騒動,不一致があり,時には暴力もあるような→**乱暴な,不穏な,動乱の,騒々しい,騒然とした** ▶定義2 (used about water or air) moving in a violent way(水や空気について)激しく動いている→**荒い,荒れ狂う** — turbulence 名 🅤→**大荒れ,動乱,騒乱,乱流,乱気流**

**turf**¹ /təːrf/ 名 🅤 🅒 ▶定義 (a piece of) short thick grass and the layer of soil underneath it 密生している短い草とその下にある土の層(の一片)→**芝,芝土,芝生,芝地**

**turf**² /təːrf/ 動 🅣 ▶定義 to cover ground with turf 地面を芝で覆う→**～を芝で覆う,～に芝を張る,芝を植え付ける**

**句動詞** turf sb out (of sth) 英略式 ▶定義 to force sb to leave a place ～をある場所から無理やり立ち退かせる→**～を追い出す,締め出す,追い払う,ほうり出す**

**turkey** /tə́ːrki/ 名 🅒 🅤 ▶定義 a large bird that is kept on farms. Turkeys are usually eaten at Christmas in Britain and at Thanksgiving in the US. 農場で飼育される大きな鳥.通常,英国ではクリスマスに,米国では感謝祭のときに食べられる→**七面鳥**

**成句** cold turkey ⇒ **COLD**¹

**turmoil** /tə́ːrmɔil/ 名 [🅤,単数扱い] ▶定義 a state of great noise or confusion 大きな騒音や混乱のある状態→**騒ぎ,騒動,混乱,混迷,動揺** ‖ *His mind was **in (a) turmoil**.* 彼の心は動揺していた.

★**turn**¹ /təːrn/ 動 ▶定義1 🅘 🅣 to move or make sth move round a fixed central point 一定の中心点の周りを動く,または～を動かす→**回る,回転する;～を回す,回転させる,ひねる** ‖ *The wheels turned faster and faster.* 車輪はだんだん速く回転した. *She turned the key in the lock.* 彼女はかぎを錠に差し込んで回した. *Turn the steering wheel to the right.* 車のハンドルを右に切りなさい. ▶定義2 🅘 🅣 to move your body, or part of your body, so that you are facing in a different direction 違う方向に向くように,体または体の一部分を動かす→**振り向く;～を向ける** ‖ *He turned round when he heard my voice.* 彼は私の声が聞こえると振り向いた. *She turned her back on me (= she deliberately moved her body to face away from me).* 彼女は私に背中を向けた(= 彼女は私から顔を背けるために故意に体を動かした). ▶定義3 🅘 🅣 to change the position of sth ～の位置を変える→**ひっくり返る,裏返しになる;～をひっくり返す,裏返す,めくる,折り返す** ‖ *I turned the box upside down.* 私はその箱をひっくり返した. *He turned the page and started the next chapter.* 彼はページをめくり,次の章に取り掛かった. *Turn to page 33 in your books.* 本の33ページを開きなさい. ▶定義4 🅣 to point or aim sth in a particular direction ～をある方向に向ける,または向かせる→**～を向ける,変える,そらす,傾ける,専心させる** ‖ *She turned her attention back to the television.* 彼女はテレビに注意を戻した. ▶定義5 🅘 🅣 to change direction when you are moving 移動しているときに方向を変える→**方向を変える;～を曲がる,～へ向かう** ‖ *Go straight on and **turn left** at the church.* まっすぐ進み,教会の所を左へ曲がりなさい. *The car **turned the corner**.* その車はその角を曲がった. ▶定義6 🅘 🅣 (to cause) to become ～にな(らせ)る→**～になる,変わる,転じる,色付く,腐る;～を…に変える,変化させる** ‖ *He turned very red when I asked him about the money.* 私がその金について尋ねると,彼は真っ赤になった. *These caterpillars will turn into butterflies.* これらの毛虫はチョウになるだろう. ▶定義7 🅣(進行形は不可) to reach or pass a particular age or time ある年齢または時間に達する,あるいは過ぎる→**～に達する,なる,～を越す,過ぎる,超える** ‖ *It's turned midnight.* 真夜中になった.

▶ turnを含む成句については,名詞,形容詞などの項を参照.例えばturn a blind eyeはblindの項にある.

**句動詞** turn (sth) around/round ▶定義 to change position or direction in order to face the opposite way, or to return the way you came 反対の方向を向くために,または来た道を帰るために,位置や向きを変える→**～に向きを変える,振り向く,～の向きを変える,振り向かせる** ‖ *This*

## 1742 turn¹

road is a dead end. We'll have to turn round and go back to the main road. この道は行き止まりだ，向きを変えて大通りに戻らなければならないだろう. He turned the car around and drove off. 彼は車の向きを変えて走り去った．

**turn away** ▶定義 to stop looking at sb/sth ～を見るのをやめる➔～から顔を背ける，避ける‖ She turned away in horror at the sight of the blood. 彼女は血を見て怖くなり顔を背けた．

**turn sb away** ▶定義 to refuse to allow a person to go into a place 人が特定の場所に入るのを認めようとしない➔～を…から退ける，追い払う，入場を断る，追い返す，引き返させる

**turn back** ▶定義 to return the same way that you came 来た道と同じ道を帰る➔引き返す‖ We've come so far already, we can't turn back now. 私たちはもう随分遠くまで来てしまったから，今から戻ることはできない．

**turn sb/sth down** ▶定義 to refuse an offer, etc or the person who makes it 申し出などを，またはそれをした人を断る➔～を拒絶する，断る，はねつける，却下する‖ Why did you turn that job down? なぜその仕事を断ったのですか. He asked her to marry him, but she turned him down. 彼は彼女に求婚したが断られた．

**turn sth down** ▶定義 to reduce the sound or heat that sth produces ～が発する音や熱を弱める➔～を小さくする，弱める，下げる，低くする‖ Turn the television down! テレビの音量を小さくしなさい．

**turn off (sth)** ▶定義 to leave one road and go on another ある道を離れてほかの道を行く➔わき道へ入る，横道にそれる，～からわき道に入る

**turn sth off** ▶定義 to stop the flow of electricity, water, etc by moving a switch, tap, etc スイッチ，蛇口などを動かして，電気，水道などの流れを止める➔～を消す，止める，締める，～のスイッチを切る‖ He turned the TV off. 彼はテレビを消した．

**turn sth on** ▶定義 to start the flow of electricity, water, etc by moving a switch, tap, etc スイッチ，蛇口などを動かして，電気，水道などを流す➔～をつける，出す，開く，～のスイッチを入れる‖ to turn the lights on 明かりをつける

**turn out (for sth)** ▶定義 to be present at an event ある催しに出席する➔～に繰り出す，出掛ける，出席する，集まる

**turn out (to be sth)** ▶定義 to be in the end 最後に～である➔結局～となる，～と判明する，終わる‖ The weather turned out fine. 結局お天気になった. The house that they had promised us turned out to be a tiny flat. 彼らが私たちに約束した家は小さなアパートであることが判明した．

**turn sth out** ▶定義 to move the switch, etc on a light or a source of heat to stop it 明かりや熱源のスイッチなどを消すために動かす➔～を消す，スイッチを切る‖ Turn the lights out before you go to bed. 寝る前に明かりを消しなさい．

**turn over** ▶定義1 to change position so that the other side is facing out or upwards ほかの面が外または上を向くように位置を変える➔ひっくり返る，寝返る，寝返りを打つ‖ He turned over and went back to sleep. 彼は寝返りを打ち，また眠った. ▶定義2 (used about an engine) to start or to continue to run（エンジンについて）動き始める，または動き続ける➔始動する，回転する，かかる ▶定義3 英 to change to another programme when you are watching television テレビを見ているときにほかの番組に変える➔チャンネルを変える

**turn sth over** ▶定義1 to make sth change position so that the other side is facing out or upwards ほかの面が外または上を向くように～の位置を変える➔～をひっくり返す，裏返す，掘り起こす，めくる‖ You may now turn over your exam papers and begin. 試験問題の用紙を表に返して始めなさい. ▶定義2 to keep thinking about sth carefully ～について入念に考え続ける➔～を熟考する，じっくり考える‖ She kept turning over what he'd said in her mind. 彼女は彼が言ったことを心の中でじっくり考え続けた．

**turn to sb/sth** ▶定義 to go to sb/sth to get help, advice, etc 助けや助言などを得るために～の所へ行く➔～に頼る，問い合わせる，救い・助言を求める，～を参照する，調べる

**turn up** ▶定義1 to arrive; to appear 到着する；現れる➔現れる，姿を現す，到着する，訪れる，出席する，姿を見せる‖ What time did they finally turn up? 彼らは結局，何時に現れたのですか．

▶定義2 to be found, especially by chance 特に偶然に，見つかる➔見つかる，出てくる‖ I lost my glasses a week ago and they haven't turned up *yet.* 私は1週間前に眼鏡をなくしたが、まだ出てこない。

**turn sth up** ▶定義 to increase the sound or heat that sth produces ～が発する音や熱を強める→**～を上げる, 強める, 大きくする** ‖ *Turn the heating up - I'm cold.* 暖房を強くしてください — 寒いので.

★**turn**² /tə́:m/ 图 C ▶定義 **1** the action of turning sb/sth round ～を回すこと→**回転, 旋回, 回すこと** ‖ *Give the screw another couple of turns to make sure it is really tight.* そのねじをもう何回か回して, しっかり締めなさい. ▶定義 **2** a change of direction in a vehicle 乗り物の向きを変えること→**方向転換, 曲がること, 折り返し, ターン** ‖ *to make a **left/right turn*** 左折・右折する *a U-turn (= when you turn round in a vehicle and go back in the opposite direction)* Uターン (= 車の向きを変え, 反対の方向に戻ること) ▶定義 **3** (医 **turning**) a bend or corner in a road, river, etc 道路, 川などのカーブや角→**曲がり角, 曲がり目, コーナー, 折り返し地点, 湾曲部** ‖ *Take the next turn on the left.* 次の角を左に曲がりなさい. ▶定義 **4** [通常は単数] the time when sb in a group of people should or is allowed to do sth 人々の集まりの中の～が…をすべきである, または…することを許可される時→**順番, 順, 番, 機会** ‖ *Please wait in the queue until it is your turn.* 自分の順番が来るまで一列に並んでお待ちください. *Whose turn is it to do the cleaning?* だれが掃除をする番ですか. ☞類 **go** ▶定義 **5** an unusual or unexpected change 普通でない, または予期しない変化→**変化, 展開, 転換, 変わり目, 転換期** ‖ *The patient's condition has **taken a turn for the worse** (= suddenly got worse).* その患者の状態は悪化した (= 急に悪くなった).

成句 **(do sb) a good turn** ▶定義 to do sth helpful for sb ～のために役立つ…をする→**～に親切にする, 優しくする**

**in turn** ▶定義 one after the other 順々に→**交替で, 代わる代わる, 次々に, 順に** ‖ *I spoke to each of the children in turn.* 私はその子たちに順番に話し掛けた.

**take turns (at sth)** ▶定義 to do sth one after the other to make sure it is fair 公平になるように～を順に行う→**交替で～をする**

---

turnstile 1743

**the turn of the century/year** ▶定義 the time when a new century/year starts 新しい世紀・年が始まる時→**世紀の変わり目, 年の変わり目**

**wait your turn** ⇒ **WAIT**¹

**turning** /tə́:nɪŋ/ 圏 (または **turn**) 图 C ▶定義 a place where one road leads off from another 道がほかの道から始まる所→**曲がり角, 曲がり目, 分岐点, 分かれ道** ‖ *We must have taken a wrong turning.* 私たちは曲がる角を間違えたに違いない.

**turning point** 图 C ▶定義 **a turning point (in sth)** a time when an important change happens, usually a good one 通常は望ましい, 重大な変化が起こる時→**転換期, 転換点, 変わり目, 節目, 転機, 峠**

**turnip** /tə́:nɪp/ 图 C U ▶定義 a round white vegetable that grows under the ground 地下で生長する, 球形の白い野菜→**カブ, カブラ ☞ C3** ページのさし絵

**turn-off** 图 C ▶定義 the place where a road leads away from a larger or more important road 道が, 大きな, または主要な道から始まる所→**分岐点, 岐路** ‖ *This is the turn-off for York.* ここはヨークへの岐路である.

**turnout** /tə́:maʊt/ 图 [C, 通常は単数] ▶定義 the number of people who go to a meeting, sports event, etc 会議, スポーツ, 催しなどに出掛ける人の数→**人手, 出席, 出席者数, 動員, 投票者数**

**turnover** /tə́:nòʊvər/ 图 [単数扱い] ▶定義 **1** a **turnover (of sth)** the amount of business that a company does in a particular period of time ある期間に企業が行う仕事の量→**営業上の総取引高, 総売上高** ‖ *The firm has an annual turnover of $50 million.* その会社の年間総取引高は5000万ドルである. ▶定義 **2** the rate at which workers leave a company and are replaced by new ones 社員が会社を辞め, ほかの新しい社員と入れ替わる割合→**労働移動率, 雇用率, 転職率** ‖ *a high turnover of staff* 高い転職率

**turnstile** /tə́:nstaɪl/ 图 C ▶定義 a metal gate that moves round in a circle when it is pushed, and allows one person at a time to enter a place 押されると回転し, 一度に1人ずつある場

所に入らせる金属製の出入り口→回転式出入り口［木戸・改札口］

**turpentine** /tɚ́ːrp(ə)ntàɪn/ 名 Ｕ ▶定義 a clear liquid with a strong smell that you use for removing paint or for making paint thinner ペンキを落とすまたは薄めるために使う、強いにおいのする透明な液体 → テレビン油、テレピン、テレペンチン、松ヤニ

**turquoise** /tɚ́ːrk(w)ɔɪz/ 形 ▶定義1 Ｃ Ｕ a blue or greenish-blue precious stone 青色、または緑がかった青色をした高価な石→トルコ石、トルコ玉 ▶定義2 Ｕ (of) a greenish-blue colour 緑がかった青色（の）→青緑色

**turret** /tɚ́ːrət; tɔ́ːr-/ 名 Ｃ ▶定義 a small tower on the top of a large building 大きな建物の上にある小さな塔→小塔、タレット

**turtle** /tɚ́ːrtl/ 名 Ｃ ▶定義1 a reptile with a thick shell that lives in the sea 海に住む、硬い甲羅を持ったは虫類の動物 → カメ、ウミガメ ▶定義2 米 = TORTOISE ☞ tortoise のさし絵

**tusk** /tʌsk/ 名 Ｃ ▶定義 one of the two very long pointed teeth of an elephant, etc. Elephants' tusks are made of a hard, white substance like bone (ivory). 象などの先のとがったとても長い2本の歯の1つ。象のtusksは骨のように硬くて白い物質（象牙（ぞうげ））でできている→きば ☞ elephant, seal のさし絵

**tussle** /tʌ́s(ə)l/ 名 Ｃ 略式 ▶定義 a tussle (for/over sth) a fight, for example between two or more people who want to have the same thing 例えば1つの物を欲しいと願う2人以上の間で起こるような戦い→取っ組み合い、組み打ち、格闘、乱闘

**tut** /tʌt/ （または **tut-tut**) 間 ▶定義 the way of writing the sound that people make to show disapproval of sb/sth ～への不満を示すために人が立てる音の表し方→ちぇっ、ちょっ、ちっ

**tutor** /t(j)úːtər/ 名 Ｃ ▶定義1 a private teacher who teaches one person or a very small group 1人または非常に人数の少ないグループを教える個人教師→個人教師、家庭教師 ▶定義2 医 a teacher who is responsible for a small group of students at school, college or university. A tutor advises students on their work or helps them if they have problems in their private life. 学校、大学などで少人数の学生に対して責任を持つ教師。勉強について助言する、または学生の私生活に問題がある場合は支援する→チューター、個人指導教師、個別指導教員

**tutorial** /t(j)uːtɔ́ːriəl/ 名 Ｃ ▶定義 a lesson at a college or university for an individual student or a small group of students 個人または少人数の学生に対する大学での授業→個別指導(時間)

**tuxedo** /tʌksíːdoʊ/ (米) **tuxedos** /-doʊz/) (または 略式 **tux** 米 = DINNER JACKET

★**TV** /tìː víː/ 略 = TELEVISION

**twang** /twæŋ/ 名 Ｃ ▶定義 the sound that is made when you pull a tight piece of string, wire or elastic and then let it go suddenly ぴんと張った弦、針金、ゴムひもなどを引っ張り、急にそれを離したときに鳴る音→ビーン・ブーンと鳴る音 ― **twang** 動 自 他 ▶ビーン・ブーンと鳴る、〜をかき鳴らす、つま弾く、ビーン・ブーンと鳴らす

**tweed** /twiːd/ 名 Ｕ ▶定義 thick woollen cloth with a rough surface used for making clothes 衣服を作るために使われる、目が粗く厚みのある毛織物地→ツイード

**tweezers** /twíːzərz/ 名 [複数扱い] ▶定義 a small tool consisting of two pieces of metal that are joined at one end. You use tweezers for picking up or pulling out very small things. 2つの金属が一方の端でつながっている小さな道具。非常に小さな物を持ち上げるまたは取り出すために使う→毛抜き、ピンセット ‖ a pair of tweezers 1本のピンセット

★**twelfth** /twelfθ/ 代形副 ▶定義 12th→12番目(の、に)、第12(の、に) ☞参 sixth の例

★**twelve** /twelv/ 数 ▶定義 12 ☞参 dozen
▶文中での数詞の使い方については、six の項を参照。

★**twentieth** /twéntiəθ/ 代形副 ▶定義 20th→20番目(の、に)、第20(の、に) ☞参 sixth の例

★**twenty** /twénti/ 数 ▶定義 20
▶文中での数詞の使い方については、six の項を参照。

★**twice** /twaɪs/ 副 ▶定義 two times 2回→2度、2回、2倍 ‖ *I've been to Egypt twice - once last year and once in 1994.* 私はエジプトに2回行ったことがある － 1回は去年、もう1回は1994年だ。*The film will be shown twice daily.* その映画は1日2回上映されるだろう。*Take the medicine twice a day.* その薬を1日2回飲みなさ

い. *Prices have risen twice as fast in this country as in Japan.* この国の物価は日本の２倍の速さで上昇した.

**twiddle** /twídl/ 動⾃他 英 ▶定義 twiddle (with) sth to keep turning or moving sth with your fingers, often because you are nervous or bored しばしば不安であるまたは退屈しているために, ～を指でずっと回している, または動かしている→いじり回す, くるくる回る; ～をいじる, もてあそぶ, くるくる回す

**twig** /twɪɡ/ 名 C ▶定義 a small thin branch on a tree or bush 高木や低木の細く短い枝→**小枝, 細枝** ☞ C2 ページのさし絵

**twilight** /twáɪlàɪt/ 名 U ▶定義 the time after the sun has set and before it gets completely dark 太陽が沈んだ後の, 真っ暗になるまでの時→**薄明かり, たそがれ(時), 薄暮** ☞参 dusk

★**twin** /twɪn/ 名 C ▶定義 1 one of two children or animals that are born to one mother at the same time １人の母親から同時に生まれた２人の子供のうちの１人, または２匹の動物のうちの１匹→**双子の一方** ‖ *They're very alike. Are they twins?* 彼らはよく似ていますね. 双子ですか. *a twin brother/sister* 双子の兄[弟・姉・妹] *identical twins* 一卵性双生児 ☞参 triplet
▶定義 2 one of a pair of things that are the same or very similar 同じ, またはよく似ている一組の物のうちの１つ→**形が同じ２つの物の１つ, よく似ている２つの物の１つ** ‖ *twin engines* 双発 *twin beds* ツインベッド ☞参 bed¹の注

**twinge** /twɪndʒ/ 名 C ▶定義 1 a sudden short pain 突然の短い痛み→**鋭い痛み, 刺すような痛み, うずき** ‖ *He suddenly felt a twinge in his back.* 彼は急に背中に鋭い痛みを感じた.
▶定義 2 a twinge (of sth) a sudden short feeling of an unpleasant emotion 突然の短い不快感情→**心の痛み, 心痛, 苦しみ, 苦悩**

**twinkle** /twíŋk(ə)l/ 動⾃ ▶定義 1 to shine with a light that seems to go on and off ついたり消えたりするように見える光で輝く→**ぴかぴか光る, きらきら光る, ちらちら光る, きらめく, 輝く** ‖ *Stars twinkled in the night sky.* 星が夜空にきらめいていた. ▶定義 2 (used about your eyes) to look bright because you are happy (人の目について)うれしいために輝いて見える→**輝く, きらきら光る** — twinkle 名 [単数扱い]→**きらめき, 目の輝き**

# twist¹ 1745

**twin town** 名 C ▶定義 one of two towns in different countries that have a special relationship 特別な関係を持っている, 別々の国にある２つの都市のうちの１つ→**姉妹都市** ‖ *Grenoble is Oxford's twin town.* グルノーブルはオックスフォードの姉妹都市である.

**twirl** /twɜːrl/ 動⾃他 ▶定義 twirl (sb/sth) (around/round) to turn round and round quickly; to make sb/sth do this 素早くぐるぐる回る; ～をそのようにする→**急速に回る; ～を急速に回す, 振り回す**

★**twist**¹ /twɪst/ 動 ▶定義 1 ⾃他 to bend or turn sth into a particular shape, often one it does not go in naturally; to be bent in this way ～をある形に, しばしば自然にはそうならないような形に, 曲げる, または変える; そのように曲げられる→**ねじれる, よれる, ゆがむ; ～をねじる, ひねる, ゆがめる** ‖ *She twisted her long hair into a knot.* 彼女は長い髪をねじって結び目を作った. *Her face twisted in anger.* 彼女の顔は怒りでゆがんだ. *He twisted his ankle while he was playing squash.* 彼はスカッシュをしている時に足首をひねった. ▶定義 2 ⾃他 to turn a part of your body while the rest stays still 体の一部の向きを, ほかの部分はそのままにして変える→**身をよじる, 体をくねらせる; ～をひねる, よじらせる** ‖ *She twisted round to see where the noise was coming from.* 彼女はその物音がどこでしているのかを知るために体をねじった. *He kept twisting his head from side to side.* 彼は首を左右にひねり続けていた. ▶定義 3 他 to turn sth around in a circle with your hand ～を手で回転させる→**～を回転させる, 回す, ひねって向きを変える** ‖ *She twisted the ring on her finger nervously.* 彼女は指輪を不安そうに回してはめた. *Most containers have twist-off caps.* ほとんどの容器には, ひねって取るふたが付いている.
▶定義 4 ⾃ (used about a road, etc) to change direction often (道などについて)方向をよく変える→**縫うように進む, 蛇行する, 曲がりくねる** ‖ *a narrow twisting lane* 曲がりくねった細い小道 *The road twists and turns along the coast.* その道路は海岸に沿って曲がりくねっている.
▶定義 5 ⾃他 twist (sth) (round/around sth) to put sth round another object; to be round

## 1746 twist²

another object ～をほかの物の周りに置く；ほかの物の周りにある➡～に巻き付く, 絡み付く, ～を…に巻き付ける, 巻く, 絡ませる ‖ *The telephone wire has **got twisted** round the table leg.* 電話のコードがテーブルの脚に絡み付いてしまっている. ▶定義6 ⓜ to change the meaning of what sb has said ～が言ったことの意味を変える➡～を曲解する, ゆがめる, でっち上げる, こじつける ‖ *Journalists often **twist** your words.* 記者はしばしば人の言葉を曲解する.

成句 **twist sb's arm** 略式 ▶定義 to force or persuade sb to do sth ～に…を無理やりさせる, またはするように説得する➡～に無理に頼み込む, 圧力をかける, 強いる

**twist²** /twɪst/ 名 Ⓒ ▶定義1 the action of turning sth with your hand, or of turning part of your body ～を手で回すこと, または体の一部の向きを変えること➡ねじり, ひねり ‖ *She killed the chicken with one **twist** of its neck.* 彼女はその鶏の首を一ひねりして殺した. ▶定義2 an unexpected change or development in a story or situation ある話や状態における予期しない変化, あるいは進展➡急変, 意外な展開, 予想外の進展 ▶定義3 a place where a road, river, etc bends or changes direction 道路, 川などがカーブしている, または向きを変えている所➡カーブ, 曲がり, 湾曲 ‖ *the **twists and turns** of the river* 川の曲がりくねり ▶定義4 something that has become or been bent into a particular shape ある形に曲がった, または曲げられたもの➡ゆがみ, 絡み, もつれ, よじれ, ねじれ ‖ *Straighten out the wire so that there are no **twists** in it.* その針金をよじれがないようにまっすぐに伸ばしなさい.

**twit** /twɪt/ 名 Ⓒ 旧式 ▶定義 a stupid person 愚かな人➡ばか者, 間抜け

**twitch** /twɪtʃ/ 動 自他 ⓜ ▶定義 to make a quick sudden movement, often one that you cannot control; to cause sth to make a sudden movement しばしば自分で抑えられないような, 突然の素早い動きをする；～を突然動かす➡ぐいと引っ張る, ぴくっと動く, 引きつる；～を急に引く, ぴくっと動かす, 引きつらせる ‖ *The rabbit twitched and then lay still.* そのウサギはぴくっとけいれんした後, 動かなくなった. *He twitched his nose.* 彼は鼻をぴくつかせた. ― **twitch** 名 Ⓒ➡ぐいと引っ張ること, 引きつり, けいれん, 激しい痛み, うずき ‖ *He has a nervous twitch.* 彼は緊張するとけいれんを起こす.

**twitter** /ˈtwɪtə(r)/ 動 自 ▶定義 (used about birds) to make a series of short high sounds (鳥について)連続した短い高い声を出す➡さえずる

*__two__ /tuː/ 数 ▶定義1 2 ☞参 **second**
▶文中での数詞の使い方については, **six** の項を参照.
▶定義2 **two-**(複合形容詞を作るために用いて) having two of the thing mentioned 言及された物が2つある➡2の, 2個の, 2人の ‖ *a two-week holiday* 2週間の休暇

成句 **be in two minds (about sth/about doing sth)** ⇒ **MIND¹**

**in two** ▶定義 in or into two pieces 2つに, または2つになって➡2つに, 真っ二つに ‖ *The plate fell on the floor and broke in two.* その皿は床に落ちて2つに割れた.

**tycoon** /taɪˈkuːn/ 名 Ⓒ ▶定義 a person who is very successful in business or industry and who has become rich and powerful 事業または業界で大変成功し, 裕福に, そして影響力が強くなった人➡巨頭, 大物, 実力者, ボス

*__type__¹ /taɪp/ 名 ▶定義1 Ⓒ **a type (of sth)** a group of people or things that share certain qualities and that are part of a larger group; a kind or sort ある一定の性質を共有し, 大きな集まりの一部である人々または物の集まり；種類または部類➡型, タイプ, 類型, 種類 ‖ *Which type of paint should you use on metal?* 金属にはどのタイプのペンキを使えばいいのですか. *Spaniels are a type of dog.* スパニエルは犬の一種である. *You meet all types of people in this job.* この仕事ではあらゆるタイプの人に出会えます. *the first building of its type in the world* その型としては世界初の建物 *I love this type/these types of movie.* 私はこの・これらの種類の映画が大好きだ. ▶定義2 Ⓒ a person of a particular kind ある性質の人➡～タイプの人 ‖ *He's the careful type.* 彼は注意深いタイプだ. *She's **not the type to** do anything silly.* 彼女はばかげた事をするような人ではない. ☞参 **typical** ▶定義3 **-type**(複合形容詞を作るために用いて) having the qualities, etc of the group, person or thing mentioned 言及された

集まり，人，あるいは物の性質などを持っている→～型の，～形式の，～版の，～式の，～タイプの ‖ *a ceramic-type material* セラミックタイプの原料 *a police-type badge* 警察式の記章 ▶定義4 ❶ letters that are printed or typed 印刷された，またはタイプされた文字→**活字，文字，字体**

\***type**² /táɪp/ 動 ⓘ ⓣ ▶定義 to write sth by pressing keys on a machine that have letters on 活字の付いた機械のキーを押して～を書く→**タイプを打つ；～をワープロで打つ，活字にする** ‖ *Can you type?* タイプが打てますか． *to type a letter* 手紙をワープロで打つ ― typing 名 ⓤ →**タイプライター・ワープロを打つこと，タイピング** ‖ *typing skills* タイピングの技術

**typewriter** /táɪpràɪtər/ 名 ⓒ ▶定義 a machine that you use for writing in print 活字でものを書くために使う機械→**タイプライター**

**typewritten** /táɪprìtn/ 形 ▶定義 written using a typewriter or computer タイプライターまたはコンピューターを使って書かれた→**タイプライターで打った，ワープロで打った**

**typhoid** /táɪfɔɪd/ 名 ⓤ ▶定義 a serious disease that can cause death. People get typhoid from bad food or water. 死因となる可能性のある重い病気．悪くなった食べ物や水から感染する→**腸チフス**

**typhoon** /taɪfúːn/ 名 ⓒ ▶定義 a violent tropical storm with very strong winds 非常に強い風を伴う，熱帯性の激しいあらし→**台風** ☞参 storm の注

\***typical** /típɪk(ə)l/ 形 typical (of sb/sth) ▶定義1 having or showing the usual qualities of a particular person, thing or type ある特定の人，物，あるいは型の通常の性質を持っている，または表している → **典型的な，代表的な，～を代表している，象徴する** ‖ *a typical Italian village* 典型的なイタリアの村 *There's no such thing as a typical American (= they are all different).* 典型的なアメリカ人と言えるものはない (= アメリカ人は皆異なっている)．⇔ untypical, atypical
▶定義2 behaving in the way you expect 期待した通りに行動している → **～に特有の，有りがちな，独特な，～の特徴を示している** ‖ *It was absolutely typical of him not to reply to my letter.* 私の手紙に返事を書かないのはいかにも彼らしかった．

---

tyre 1747

\***typically** /típɪk(ə)li/ 副 ▶定義1 in a typical case; that usually happens in this way 典型的な場合に；通常，そのように起こるように → **例によって，一般的に，大体は** ‖ *Typically it is the girls who offer to help, not the boys.* 一般的に援助を申し出るのは女の子であって，男の子ではない．▶定義2 in a way that shows the usual qualities of a particular person, type or thing ある特定の人，型，あるいは物の通常の性質を表しているように→**典型的に，独特に，象徴的に** ‖ *typically British humour* 典型的なイギリス流ユーモア

**typify** /típəfàɪ/ 動 ⓣ (現分 **typifying**; 三単現 **typifies**; 過, 過分 **typified**) ▶定義 to be a typical mark or example of sb/sth ～の典型的な印，または例である→**～の典型となる，特徴を表す，～を代表する，象徴する** ‖ *This film typified the Hollywood westerns of that time.* この映画は当時のハリウッド西部劇を代表するものだった．

**typist** /táɪpɪst/ 名 ⓒ ▶定義 a person who works in an office typing letters, etc 職場で手紙などをタイプすることを仕事とする人→**タイピスト**

**tyranny** /tírəni/ 名 ⓤ ▶定義 the cruel and unfair use of power by a person or small group to control a country or state 1つの国または州を治めるために，1人あるいは1つの小さな集団が権力を冷酷かつ不公平に行使すること→**専制政治，独裁政治，暴政，圧制，虐政** ― tyrannical /təránɪk(ə)l, taɪ-/ 形 → **暴君的な，専制的な，圧制的な，暴虐な，非道な** ‖ *a tyrannical ruler* 専制的な支配者 ― tyrannize (または -ise) /tírənàɪz/ 動 ⓘ ⓣ→**暴政を行う；～に暴威を振るう，～を虐げる**

**tyrant** /táɪ(ə)rənt/ 名 ⓒ ▶定義 a cruel ruler who has complete power over the people in his/her country 自国の国民に対して全面的な力を持った冷酷な支配者→**暴君，圧制者，専制君主，独裁者** ☞参 dictator

\***tyre** (米 tire) /táɪər/ 名 ⓒ ▶定義 the thick rubber ring that fits around the outside of a wheel 車輪の外周にはまっている厚いゴムの輪→**タイヤ** ‖ *a flat tyre (= a tyre with no air in it)* パンクしたタイヤ (= 中に空気が入っていないタイヤ)
☞ S7ページのさし絵

# U u

**U, u¹** /juː/ 名 C (複 **U's; u's** /-z/) ▶定義 the twenty-first letter of the English alphabet 英語アルファベットの第21文字→u(U)が表す音, u(U)の文字, u(U)の字形のもの ‖ *'Ulcer' begins with (a) 'U'.* Ulcer はUで始まる.

**U²** /juː/ 略 因 ▶定義 (used about films that are suitable for anyone, including children) universal (映画について, 子供を含めだれでも見られる映画) ユニバーサル→一般向き(の), 万人向き(の)

**udder** /ʌ́dər/ 名 C ▶定義 the part of a female cow, etc that hangs under its body and produces milk 雌牛などの体から垂れ下がった部分で乳が出る所→(牛・ヤギなどの)乳房

**UEFA** /juéɪfə/ 略 the Union of European Football Associations→ヨーロッパサッカー協会連合 ‖ *the UEFA cup* UEFA 杯

**UFO** (または **ufo**) /júː èf óʊ, júːfoʊ/ 略 an unidentified flying object→未確認飛行物体 ☞参 **flying saucer**

**ugh** /uːx, ʌx, ʌg/ 間 ▶定義 used in writing to express the sound that you make when you think sth is disgusting 何かを実に嫌だと思うときに発する声を表記するのに用いて→うっ, うえっ, おえっ

★**ugly** /ʌ́gli/ 形 (**uglier; ugliest**) ▶定義 **1** unpleasant to look at or listen to; unattractive 見てまたは聞いて不快な; 魅力がない→醜い, 見苦しい, 嫌な ‖ *The burn left an ugly scar on her face.* そのやけどは彼女の顔に醜い傷跡を残した. *an ugly modern office block* 不格好な近代的オフィス街 ▶定義 **2** (used about a situation) dangerous or threatening (状況について) 危険なまたは脅かす→物騒な, 厄介な, 荒れた ━ **ugliness** 名 U→醜いこと, 醜悪

**UHT** /jùː eɪtʃ tíː/ 略 ▶定義 used about foods such as milk that are treated to last longer 日持ちするよう処理された牛乳のような食品について→超高温処理された ‖ *UHT milk* 超高温殺菌牛乳

**UK** /jùː kéɪ/ 略 the United Kingdom ▶定義 England, Scotland, Wales and N Ireland イングランド, スコットランド, ウェールズおよび北アイルランド→連合王国, 英国 ‖ *a UK citizen* 英国国民

**ulcer** /ʌ́lsər/ 名 C ▶定義 a painful area on your skin or inside your body. Ulcers may produce a poisonous substance and sometimes bleed. 皮膚または体内の痛む所. 組織を破壊する物質を分泌することもあり, 時として出血することもある→潰瘍 ‖ *a mouth/stomach ulcer* 口内炎・胃潰瘍

**ulterior** /ʌltíəriər/ 形 ▶定義 that you keep hidden or secret 隠してある, 秘密にしてある→言外の, 隠された ‖ *Why is he suddenly being so nice to me? He must have an **ulterior** motive.* 彼はなぜ急に私に親切にするのだろうか. 魂胆があるに違いない.

**ultimate¹** /ʌ́ltəmət/ 形 (名詞の前だけ) ▶定義 **1** being or happening at the end; last or final 最後にあるまたは起きる; 最後または最終の→究極の ‖ *Our ultimate goal is complete independence.* 私たちの最終目標は完全な独立です. ▶定義 **2** the greatest, best or worst→最大の, 最高の, 最悪の

**ultimate²** /ʌ́ltəmət/ 名 [単数扱い] 略式 ▶定義 **the ultimate (in sth)** the greatest or best 最大または最高のもの→究極のもの, 最終結果, 最高段階 ‖ *This new car is the ultimate in comfort.* この新車は快適性では最高だ.

**ultimately** /ʌ́ltəmtli/ 副 ▶定義 **1** in the end 最後に→最終的に, 結局 ‖ *Ultimately, the decision is yours.* 最終的には, あなたが決めることです. ▶定義 **2** at the most basic level; most importantly 最も基本的な段階では; 最も重要なことには→根本的には, 究極的には

**ultimatum** /ʌ̀ltəméɪtəm/ 名 C (複 **ultimatums**) ▶定義 a final warning to sb that, if he/she does not do what you ask, you will use force or take action against him/her 人への最終警告で, 依頼した事をその人がやらない場合は, その人に対し実力行使に出るまたは何か行動を起こすという警告→最後通牒(つうちょう), 最終条件 ‖ *I gave him an ultimatum - either he paid his rent or he was out.* 私は彼に最後通牒を渡した ― 家賃を支払うかそれとも出ていくかのどちらかだった.

**ultra-** /ʌ́ltrə/ (複合語で) ▶定義 extremely 極端に→範囲を超えた, 超～ ‖ *ultra-modern* 超近代的な

**ultraviolet** /ʌ̀ltrəváɪələt/ 形 ▶定義 of a type of light that causes your skin to turn darker and that can be dangerous in large amounts 皮膚の

色を濃くする,また多量だと危険なこともある光線の一種→紫外(線)の,紫外線を利用した

**umbilical cord** /ˌʌmbílɪk(ə)l kɔ́ːrd/ 图 ❻ ▶定義 the tube that connects a baby to its mother before it is born 生まれるまで赤ん坊を母親に結び付けている管→へその緒,せい帯

\***umbrella** /ʌmbrélə/ 图 ❻ ▶定義 an object that you open and hold over your head to keep yourself dry when it is raining 開いて頭の上に差し掛けて使うもの,雨が降っているときぬれないようにする→(こうもり)傘,雨傘 ‖ to put an umbrella up/down 傘を差す・閉じる

**umpire** /ʌ́mpàɪər/ 图 ❻ ▶定義 a person who watches a game such as tennis or cricket to make sure that the players obey the rules テニスまたはクリケットのような試合で選手がルールを守っていることを確認するため監視する人→審判員,アンパイア ☞参 referee — umpire 動 圁 ⓗ →審判をする,仲裁者となる

**umpteen** /ˌʌm(p)tíːn, ˈ-ˌ-/ 代形瞎氓 ▶定義 very many; a lot→非常にたくさん;多数 — **umpteenth** /ˌʌm(p)tíːnθ, ˈ-ˌ-/ 代形→数えきれないほど多数番目の,何度目の ‖ For the umpteenth time - phone if you're going to be late! 何度も言ったでしょう — 遅刻するときは電話しなさい.

**UN** /júː én/ 略 the United Nations Organization→国際連合,国連

\***unable** /ʌnéɪb(ə)l/ 形 ▶定義 unable to do sth not having the time, knowledge, skill, etc to do sth; not able to do sth→~をする時間,知識,技量などがない;~をすることができない ‖ She lay there, unable to move. 彼女は動くこともできずにそこに横たわっていた. ☞ inability

**unacceptable** /ˌʌnəkséptəb(ə)l/ 形 ▶定義 that you cannot accept or allow 受け入れるまたは許すことができない→容認できない ⇔ **acceptable** — **unacceptably** /-bli/ 副 →受け入れられずに,容認できずに

**unaccompanied** /ˌʌnəkʌ́mp(ə)nɪd/ 形 ▶定義 alone, without sb/sth else with you 1 人で,ほかの人や物を伴わないで→同伴者なしの,連れのない ‖ Unaccompanied children are not allowed in the bar. 同伴者のいない子供だけでバーに入ることを禁じます.

**unaffected** /ˌʌnəféktəd/ 形 ▶定義 1 not changed by sth ほかの物により変化されない→影響されない,変わらない,心を動かされない ▶定義 2 behaving in a natural way without trying to impress anyone だれかに印象づけようとすることなく自然に振る舞う→気取らない,有りのままの ⇔ **affected**

**unaided** /ʌnéɪdəd/ 副 ▶定義 without any help 何の援助もなく→援助なしの,自力の

**unanimous** /juːnǽnəməs, jʊ-/ 形 ▶定義 1 (used about a group of people) all agreeing about sth (人の集団について) ~について全員が同意して→全員一致の,満場一致の ‖ The judges were unanimous in their decision. 全裁判官が一致して裁決を下した. ▶定義 2 (used about a decision, etc) agreed by everyone (決定などについて) 全員が賛成した→満場一致の,全員一致の ‖ The jury reached a unanimous verdict of guilty. 陪審員団は全員一致で有罪評決を下した. — **unanimously** 副 →(満場)一致で

**unarmed** /ʌnɑ́ːrmd/ 形 ▶定義 having no guns, knives, etc; not armed 銃,ナイフなどを持たずに;武装しないで→非武装の,無防備の,丸腰の ⇔ **armed**

**unashamed** /ˌʌnəʃéɪmd/ 形 ▶定義 not feeling sorry or embarrassed about sth bad that you have done 自分が行った悪い事に関して後悔の念または恥ずかしさを感じない→恥じない,恥を知らない,ずうずうしい ⇔ **ashamed** — **unashamedly** /-ʃéɪmədli/ 副 →恥を知らないで,ずうずうしく,平然と

**unassuming** /ˌʌnəsjúːmɪŋ; -əsúːm-/ 形 ▶定義 not wanting people to notice how good, important, etc you are 自分がいかに優れているか,重要であるかなどを人に認めてもらいたいと思わない→気取らない,謙そんな,控えめな

**unattached** /ˌʌnətǽtʃt/ 形 ▶定義 1 not connected to sb/sth else ほかの人や物と連結していない→くっついていない,離れている,無所属の,中立の ▶定義 2 not married; without a regular partner 結婚していない;決まったパートナーがいない→未婚の,フリーの

**unattended** /ˌʌnəténdəd/ 形 ▶定義 not watched or looked after 見られていない,または面倒を見られていない→付き添いのない,係の者が付いていない,放置された ‖ Do not leave children unattended. 子供をほったらかしにしておくな.

**unauthorized** /ʌnɔ́ːθəraɪzd/ 形 ▶定義 done

without permission 許可なく行われた➡️認可されていない,権限のない,独断の

**unavoidable** /ˌʌnəvɔ́ɪdəb(ə)l/ 形 ▶定義 that cannot be avoided or prevented 避けるまたは防ぐことができない➡️避けられない,やむを得ない ⇔ **avoidable** — unavoidably /-əbli/ 副 ➡️やむを得ず

**unaware** /ˌʌnəwéər/ 形 (名詞の前は不可) ▶定義 unaware (of sb/sth) not knowing about or not noticing sb/sth➡️(〜について)知らない,または気付かない ‖ *She seemed unaware of all the trouble she had caused.* 彼女は自分が引き起こしたすべての問題に気付いていないようだった. ⇔ **aware**

**unawares** /ˌʌnəwéərz/ 副 ▶定義 by surprise; without expecting sth or being prepared for it 不意に; 物事を予期しないで,または心構えができていないで➡️出し抜けに,不意に,思い掛けなく ‖ *I was taken completely unawares by his suggestion.* 私は彼の提案にすっかり面食らった.

**unbalanced** /ˌʌnbǽlənst/ 形 ▶定義 1 (used about a person) slightly crazy (人について)少し狂っている➡️気の変な ▶定義 2 not fair to all ideas or sides of an argument 議論ですべての考えまたは当事者に公平というわけではない➡️偏った,釣り合いの取れない,不公平な ⇔ **balanced**

**unbearable** /ˌʌnbéərəb(ə)l/ 形 ▶定義 too unpleasant, painful, etc for you to accept あまりの不愉快,苦痛などのため受け入れることができない➡️(人に)耐えられない,我慢できない ☛類 **intolerable** ⇔ **bearable** — unbearably /-əbli/ 副 ➡️我慢できないほどに,耐えられないほどに ‖ *It was unbearably hot.* 耐えられないほど暑かった.

**unbeatable** /ˌʌnbíːtəb(ə)l/ 形 ▶定義 that cannot be defeated or improved on 打ち負かすまたはそれに勝ることができない➡️卓越した ‖ *unbeatable prices* どこにも負けない価格

**unbeaten** /ˌʌnbíːtn/ 形 ▶定義 that has not been beaten or improved on 打ち負かされたことがない,またはそれに勝るものがない➡️無敵の

**unbelievable** /ˌʌnbəlíːvəb(ə)l/ 形 ▶定義 very surprising; difficult to believe 非常に驚かされる; 信じ難い➡️驚くべき ⇔ **believable** ☛参 **incredible** — unbelievably /-əbli/ 副 ➡️信じられないほど ‖ *His work was unbelievably bad.* 彼の仕事は信じられないほど出来が悪かった.

**unblemished** /ˌʌnblémɪʃt/ 形 ▶定義 not spoiled, damaged or marked in any way 汚れ,傷または跡が何も付いていない➡️汚点のない,潔白な ‖ *The new party leader has an unblemished reputation.* 新しい党首は汚点一つない名声の持ち主だ.

**unborn** /ˌʌnbɔ́ːn/ 形 ▶定義 not yet born まだ生まれていない➡️将来の

**unbroken** /ˌʌnbróuk(ə)n/ 形 ▶定義 1 continuous; not interrupted 継続的な; 中断されない➡️とぎれない,連続した ‖ *a period of unbroken silence* 完全な沈黙の間 ▶定義 2 that has not been beaten 打ち負かされていない➡️(記録が)破られていない ‖ *His record for the 1500 metres remains unbroken.* 1500メートル競技における彼の記録は破られていない.

**uncalled-for** /ˌʌnkɔ́ːld fɔːr/ 形 ▶定義 (used about behaviour or comments) not fair and not appropriate (行為または言動について)公平でなく,適当でない➡️不適当な,的外れな,余計な ‖ *That comment was quite uncalled-for.* そのコメントは不適当極まりなかった.

**uncanny** /ˌʌnkǽni/ 形 ▶定義 very strange; that you cannot easily explain 非常に奇妙な; 簡単に説明することができない➡️異様な,神秘的な ‖ *an uncanny coincidence* 気味が悪いほどの偶然の一致

*__uncertain__ /ʌnsə́ːrtn/ 形 ▶定義 1 uncertain (about/of sth) not sure; not able to decide 不確かな; 決定することができない➡️確信がない,自信がない ‖ *She was still uncertain of his true feelings for her.* 彼女は自分に対する彼の本当の気持ちにまだ確信が持てなかった. ▶定義 2 not known exactly or not decided 正確に分かっていない,または決められていない➡️はっきりしない,疑わしい ‖ *He's lost his job and his future seems very uncertain.* 彼は職を失い,将来が全く見えない. ⇔ **certain** — uncertainly 副 ➡️不確実で,自信がなく,頼りなく — uncertainty 名 ❻ ❿ (複 uncertainties)➡️不確かさ,半信半疑 ‖ *Today's decision will put an end to all the uncertainty.* 今日の決定はもろもろの不確かな状況に終止符を打つだろう. ⇔ **certainty**

**unchanged** /ˌʌntʃéɪndʒd/ 形 ▶定義 staying the

same; not changed 同じ状態にとどまる；変化しない➡無変化の,元のままの

**uncharacteristic** /ˌʌnkærɪktərístɪk/ 形 ▶定義
not typical or usual 典型的ではない，または通常ではない➡らしくない,特色を表していない ⇔ **characteristic** — **uncharacteristically** /-k(ə)li/ 副 ➡特徴的ではなく,珍しいことに

\***uncle** /ʌ́ŋk(ə)l/ 名 **C** ▶定義 the brother of your father or mother; the husband of your aunt 自分の父または母の兄弟；伯母・叔母の夫➡**伯父・叔父** ‖ Uncle Steven スティーヴンおじさん

\***uncomfortable** /ʌnkʌ́mfərtəb(ə)l/ 形 ▶定義1 not pleasant to wear, sit in, lie on, etc 着る・座る・横になるなどするのに快適でない➡心地良くない,不快な ‖ uncomfortable shoes 履き心地の悪い靴 ▶定義2 not able to sit, lie, etc in a position that is pleasant 快適な姿勢で座る・横になるなどすることができない➡窮屈な,楽でない ▶定義3 feeling or causing worry or embarrassment 心配または居心地悪さを感じるまたは引き起こす➡落ち着かない,気詰まりな ‖ I felt very uncomfortable when they started arguing in front of me. 彼らが私の前で口論を始めたので,非常に気詰まりに感じた. ⇔ **comfortable** — **uncomfortably** /-əbli/ 副 ➡不快に,心地悪く,落ち着かずに

**uncommon** /ʌnkʌ́mən/ 形 ▶定義 unusual 普通でない➡まれな,異常な,著しい ⇔ **common**

**uncompromising** /ʌnkʌ́mprəmaɪzɪŋ/ 形 ▶定義
refusing to discuss or change a decision 決まったことを議論したり変更するのを拒む➡妥協のない,不屈の,断固たる

**unconcerned** /ˌʌnkənsə́ːrnd/ 形 ▶定義
unconcerned (about/by/with sth) not interested in sth or not worried about it (〜に)興味がない，または(〜を)心配していない➡無関心な ⇔ **concerned**

**unconditional** /ˌʌnkəndíʃ(ə)n(ə)l/ 形 ▶定義
without limits or conditions 制限または条件のない➡無制限の,無条件の,絶対的な ‖ an unconditional surrender 無条件降伏 ⇔ **conditional** — **unconditionally** /-ʃ(ə)n(ə)li/ 副 ➡無制限に,無条件に

\***unconscious** /ʌnkʌ́nʃəs/ 形 ▶定義1 in a state that is like sleep, for example because of injury or illness 例えばけがまたは病気が原因で眠っているような状態になっている➡意識を失った,気絶した,無意識の ‖ He was found lying unconscious on the kitchen floor. 彼は台所の床の上で意識を失って倒れているところを発見された. ▶定義2 unconscious of sb/sth not knowing or aware of sb/sth 〜を知らずにまたは気付かずに➡〜を意識していない ▶定義3 done, spoken, etc without you thinking about it or realizing it それについて考えることなく，または気付くことなく行われた,話されたなど➡無自覚の,意図していない ‖ The article was full of unconscious humour. その記事は何気ないユーモアにあふれていた. ⇔ **conscious** ▶定義4 **the unconscious** 名 [単数扱い] = **SUBCONSCIOUS** — **unconsciously** 副 ➡知らず知らずに,無意識のうちに — **unconsciousness** 名 **U** ➡無意識

**uncontrollable** /ˌʌnkəntróʊləb(ə)l/ 形 ▶定義
that you cannot control 自分で制御することができない➡制御できない,抑制できない,手に負えない ‖ I suddenly had an uncontrollable urge to laugh. 私は突然笑い出したい抑え難い衝動に駆られた. — **uncontrollably** /-əbli/ 副 ➡制御できずに,抑制できずに,手に負えずに

**uncountable** /ʌnkáʊntəb(ə)l/ 形 (文法) ▶定義
an uncountable noun cannot be counted and so does not have a plural. In this dictionary uncountable nouns are marked '[U]'. 不可算名詞は数えることができない,だから複数形を持たない.この辞書で不可算名詞は **U** で表示してある➡不可算の,数えることができない ⇔ **countable**

▶不可算名詞についての説明は,巻末の「文法早見表」を参照.

**uncover** /ʌnkʌ́vər/ 動 **H** ▶定義1 to remove the cover from sth 〜の覆いを取る➡〜の覆いをはがす,ふたを取る ⇔ **cover** ▶定義2 to find out or discover sth 〜を見つけ出すまたは発見する➡(秘密)を暴露する,明らかにする,摘発する ‖ Police have uncovered a plot to murder a top politician. 警察は政界トップ殺害の陰謀を摘発した.

**undecided** /ˌʌndɪsáɪdəd/ 形 ▶定義1 not having made a decision 決定していない➡決心のつかない,優柔不断の ‖ I'm still undecided about whether to take the job or not. 私はまだその仕事に就くか否か決めかねている. ▶定義2 without any result or decision 何の結果または決定もなく→未定の,未決着の ⇔ **decided**

**undeniable** /ˌʌndɪnáɪəb(ə)l/ 形 ▶定義 clear, true or certain 明確な,本当のまたは確実な→否定できない,明白な,紛れもない — **undeniably** /-əbli/ 副 →明白に,確かに

***under** /ʌ́ndər/ 前 副 ▶定義1 in or to a position that is below sth→~より下の位置に[へ] ‖ *We found him hiding under the table.* 私たちは彼がテーブルの下に隠れているのを見つけた. *The dog crawled under the gate and ran into the road.* その犬は門の下をくぐり抜けて道路に飛び出した.

▶比較 under, below, beneath, underneath. 1つの物がもう1つの物のすぐ下にあると言うのにunderを用いる.その2つの物の間には空間があってもよい: *The cat is asleep under the table.*(猫はテーブルの下で眠っている.)または1つの物がもう1つの物に触れているまたは覆われている場合もある: *I think your letter is under that book.*(あなたの手紙はその本の下にあると思います.)1つの物がもう1つの物より低い位置にあると言うのにはbelowを使うことができる: *They live on the floor below us.*(彼らは私たちの下の階に住んでいます.) *The skirt comes down to just below the knee.*(そのスカート丈はちょうどひざ下まである.)ある物の片側からもう一方の側への動きについて述べるときはbelowではなくunderを使う: *We swam under the bridge.*(私たちは橋の下を泳いだ.)正式に書くときは,beneathを使って,ある物がもう1つの物の真下にあると言うことができるが,underの方がより一般的である.ある物が別の物に覆われているまたは隠されていることを強調するときにはunderの代わりにunderneathを使うことができる: *Have you looked underneath the sofa as well as behind it?*(ソファーの後ろだけでなく下も見ましたか.)

▶定義2 below the surface of sth; covered by sth ~の表面下に;~に覆われて→~の内側に,~をかぶって ‖ *Most of an iceberg is under the water.* 氷河のほとんどの部分は水面下にある. *He was wearing a vest under his shirt.* 彼はシャツの下に肌着を着ていた. ▶定義3 less than a certain number; younger than a certain age ある数より少ない;ある年齢より若い→~未満で[の] ‖ *People working under 20 hours a week will pay no extra tax.* 労働時間が週20時間未満の人は余分の税を払わなくてよい. *Nobody under eighteen is allowed to buy alcohol.* 18歳未満の人のアルコール飲料購入は禁じられている. ▶定義4 governed or controlled by sb/sth ~に統治された,または支配された→~の下に,~の影響を受けて ‖ *The country is now under martial law.* その国は現在,戒厳令が敷かれている. ▶定義5 according to a law, agreement, system, etc 法律,契約,組織などによって→~に基づいて,~に従って ‖ *Under English law you are innocent until you are proved guilty.* イギリスの法律では有罪が証明されるまでは無罪です. ▶定義6 experiencing a particular feeling, process or effect 特定の感情,過程または影響を経験して→~(の影響)の下で,~中で[の] ‖ *He was jailed for driving under the influence of alcohol.* 彼は飲酒運転により拘置された. *a building under construction* 建設中の建物 *The manager is **under pressure** to resign.* その支配人は辞任するように圧力をかけられている. *I was **under the impression that** Bill was not very happy there.* 私は,ビルがそこであまり幸せではないと感じました. ▶定義7 using a particular name 特定の名前を使って→~を名乗って,~という名前で ‖ *to travel under a false name* 偽名を使って旅行する ▶定義8 found in a particular part of a book, list, etc 本,リストなどの特定部分に見られる→~の(項目)中に ‖ *You'll find some information on rugby under 'team sports'.* team sportsの項目を見ればラグビーに関する情報が得られるでしょう.

**under-** /ʌ́ndər/ (複合語で) ▶定義1 lower in level or position 水準または位置がより低い→下(位)の,従属した ‖ *an under-secretary* 次官 ▶定義2 not enough 不十分な[に]→(標準より)少なく ‖ *undercooked food* 調理不十分な食物

**underclothes** /ʌ́ndərklòu(ð)z/ 名[複数扱い]= **UNDERWEAR**

**undercover** /ˌʌndərkʌ́vər, ⌐/ 形 ▶定義 working or happening secretly 内密で働いている,または起こっている→秘密に行う,秘密の ‖ *an undercover reporter/detective* 覆面記者・秘密探偵

**undercut** /ˌʌndərkʌ́t, ⌐/ 動 他 (現分 **undercut-**

**ting**; 過, 過分 **undercut**) ▶定義 to sell sth at a lower price than other shops, etc ほかの店などより低価格で〜を売る➔**より安く売る**

**underdog** /ˈʌndə(r)ˌdɒg, -ˌdɔːg/ 名 ⓒ ▶定義 a person, team, etc who is weaker than others, and not expected to be successful 他よりも弱く, 活躍が期待されていない人, チームなど➔**負けそうな人, 負け犬** ∥ *San Marino were the underdogs, but managed to win the game 2-1.* サンマリノは試合で負けが予想されていたが, 2対1で何とか勝った.

**underestimate** /ˌʌndərˈestəmeɪt/ 動他 ▶定義 1 to guess that the amount, etc of sth will be less than it really is 〜の量などが実際より少ないだろうと推測する➔**〜を少なく見積もりすぎる** ▶定義 2 to think that sb/sth is not as strong, good, etc as he/she/it really is 〜が実際より強くない, 優れていないなどと考える➔**〜を過小評価する, 見くびる** ∥ *Don't underestimate your opponent. He's a really good player.* 敵を見くびってはいけない. 彼は実に優れた選手だ. ⇔ **overestimate** ─ underestimate /-mət, -mèɪt/ 名 ⓒ➔**少なすぎる見積もり, 過小評価**

**underfoot** /ˌʌndərˈfʊt/ 副 ▶定義 under your feet; where you are walking 足の下に; 歩いている場所に➔**足の下に, 踏み付けて, 地面に** ∥ *It's very wet underfoot.* 足元が水浸しだ.

**undergo** /ˌʌndərˈɡoʊ/ 動他 (過 **underwent** /-ˈwent/; 過分 **undergone** /-ˈɡɔːn, -ˈɡɑːn/) ▶定義 to have a difficult or unpleasant experience 苦しいまたは不愉快な経験を持つ➔**〜を経験する, 〜に耐える, 経る, 被る** ∥ *She underwent a five-hour operation.* 彼女は5時間に及ぶ手術に耐えた.

**undergraduate** /ˌʌndərˈɡrædʒuət, -eɪt/ 名 ⓒ ▶定義 a university student who has not yet taken his/her first degree 最初の学位をまだ取得していない大学生➔**学部学生** ☞参 **graduate**, **postgraduate**

*★**underground**[1] /ˈʌndərɡraʊnd/ 形 ▶定義 1 under the surface of the ground 地面の下の➔**地下の** ∥ *an underground car park* 地下駐車場 ▶定義 2 secret or illegal 秘密または違法の➔**秘密の, 地下組織の** ∥ *an underground radio station* アングラジオ放送局

*★**underground**[2] /ˌʌndərˈɡraʊnd/ 副 ▶定義 1 under the surface of the ground 地面の下に➔**地下に[で]** ∥ *The cables all run underground.* ケーブルはすべて地下を走っている. ▶定義 2 into a secret place 秘密の場所に➔**隠れて, 潜んで** ∥ *She went underground to escape from the police.* 彼女は警察から逃れるため地下に身を潜めた.

*★**underground**[3] /ˈʌndərɡraʊnd/ (米 **subway**) 名 [単数扱い] ▶定義 a railway system under the ground 地下の鉄道システム➔**地下鉄**
▶ロンドンでは地下鉄を the underground または the tube と呼ぶ.

**undergrowth** /ˈʌndərɡroʊθ/ 名 Ⓤ ▶定義 bushes and plants that grow around and under trees 木々の周りまたは下に生育する潅木(かんぼく)や植物➔**下生え, やぶ**

**underhand** /ˌʌndərˈhænd/ 形 ▶定義 secret or not honest 秘密のまたは正直でない➔**不正な, 公明正大でない**

*★**underline** /ˌʌndərˈlaɪn, ˈ--/ 動他 ▶定義 1 to draw a line under a word, etc 言葉などの下に線を引く➔**〜に下線を引く** ▶定義 2 to show sth clearly or to emphasize sth➔**〜をはっきりと示す, または〜を強調する** ∥ *This accident underlines the need for greater care.* この事故はより細心の注意を払う必要性を明白に示している.

**underlying** /ˌʌndərˈlaɪɪŋ/ 形 ▶定義 important but hidden 重要だが隠された➔**内在する, 潜在的な** ∥ *the underlying causes of the disaster* その大惨事の隠された原因

**undermine** /ˌʌndərˈmaɪn/ 動他 ▶定義 to make sth weaker 〜を弱める➔**(健康など)を徐々に衰えさせる, 蝕(むしば)む, (名声)をひそかに傷付ける** ∥ *The public's confidence in the government has been undermined by the crisis.* 政府に対する民衆の信頼は, その危機によって弱くなった.

*★**underneath** /ˌʌndərˈniːθ/ 前 副 ▶定義 under; below➔**(〜の)真下に; 下に** ∥ *The coin rolled underneath the chair.* その硬貨はいすの下に転がった. ☞参 **under** の注

**the underneath** /ˌʌndərˈniːθ/ 名 [単数扱い] ▶定義 the bottom or lowest part of something ある物の底または最も低い部分➔**下部, 下側, 底** ∥ *There is a lot of rust on the underneath of the car.* その車の底の部分にはかなりのさびが生じている.

**underpants** /ˈʌndərpænts/ (英 または **pants**) 名

## 1754　underpass

[複数扱い] ▶定義 a piece of clothing that men or boys wear under their trousers 男性または男の子がズボンの下に履く衣類→ズボン下, パンツ

**underpass** /ˈʌndərpæs, -pɑːs/ 名 ● ▶定義 a road or path that goes under another road, railway, etc 道路, 鉄道などの下をくぐる別の道路または小道→ガード下道路, 地下道, (小さな)トンネル

**underpay** /ˌʌndərˈpeɪ/ 動 他 (過, 過分 **underpaid**) ▶定義 to pay sb too little ～に過少な支払いをする→～に(給料を)十分に支払わない ⇔ overpay

**underprivileged** /ˌʌndərˈprɪv(ə)lɪdʒd/ 形 ▶定義 having less money, rights, opportunities, etc than other people in society 社会において金, 権利, 機会などがほかの人よりも少ない→(社会的・経済的に)恵まれない ⇔ privileged

**underrate** /ˌʌndərˈreɪt/ 動 他 ▶定義 to think that sb/sth is less clever, important, good, etc than he/she/it really is ～の賢さ, 重要性, 質などが実際より劣っていると考える→～を過小評価する ⇔ overrate

**undershirt** /ˈʌndərʃɜːrt/ 米 = VEST(1)

*understand** /ˌʌndərˈstænd/ 動 (過, 過分 **understood** /-ˈstʊd/) ▶定義 1 自他 to know or realize the meaning of sth ～の意味を知るまたは認識する→(～を)理解する・している, (～の)意味が分かる ‖ I'm not sure that I really understand. 私は本当に理解できているとの自信がない. I didn't understand the instructions. 用法の説明を理解していませんでした. Please speak more slowly. I can't understand you. もっとゆっくり話してください. おっしゃることが理解できません. Do you understand what I'm asking you? 私があなたに頼んでいる事が分かりますか. ▶定義 2 他 to know how or why sth happens or why it is important ～がどのようにまたはなぜ起きるのか, またはなぜそれが重要なのかが分かる→(過程・原因・性質)を理解する, 了解する ‖ I can't understand why the engine won't start. なぜエンジンがかからないのか分からない. As far as I understand it, the changes won't affect us. 私の知る限りでは, その変更は私たちに影響ないでしょう. ▶定義 3 他 to know sb's character and why he/she behaves in a particular way ～の特徴を知る, またなぜその人が特定の振る舞い方をするのかが分かる→～の気持ち・性質・扱い方が分かる ‖ It's easy to understand why she felt so angry. 彼女がなぜあんなに腹を立てたのかは容易に理解できる. ▶定義 4 他 正式 to have heard or been told sth ～を聞いたことがある, または話に聞いている→～と聞き及ぶ

成句 **give sb to believe/understand (that)** ⇒ **BELIEVE**

**make yourself understood** ▶定義 to make your meaning clear 言いたいことを明白にする→自分の考え・話を人に分からせる ‖ I can just about make myself understood in Russian. 私はロシア語で大体自分の考えを人に理解してもらうことができる.

**understandable** /ˌʌndərˈstændəb(ə)l/ 形 ▶定義 that you can understand→理解可能な — **understandably** /-əbli/ 副→もっともなことに, ～であることは理解できる ‖ She was understandably angry at the decision. 彼女は, 当然のことながら, その決定に腹を立てていた.

*understanding¹** /ˌʌndərˈstændɪŋ/ 名 ▶定義 1 [U, 単数扱い] the knowledge that sb has of a particular subject or situation 人が特定の課題または状況に関して持っている知識→理解, 見解 ‖ A basic understanding of physics is necessary for this course. この講座(を受講する)には, 物理の基本知識が必要です. He has little understanding of how computers work. 彼は, コンピューターがどうやって動くかほとんど理解していない. ▶定義 2 [C, 通常は単数] an informal agreement 略式の合意→取り決め ‖ I'm sure we can **come to/reach an understanding** about the money I owe him. 私が彼に借りているお金に関して, 私たちは話をまとめられると思う. ▶定義 3 U the ability to know why people behave in a particular way and to forgive them if they do sth wrong or bad 人々がなぜ特定の振る舞い方をするのかを理解し, 間違ったまたは悪い物事をしても許せる能力→理解力, 思いやり ▶定義 4 U the way in which you think sth is meant 何かの意図を解すること→解釈 ‖ My understanding of the arrangement is that he will only phone if there is a problem. 彼は問題がある場合にのみ電話してくる手はずになっていると私は理解している.

成句 **on the understanding that...** ▶定義 only if...; because it was agreed that... ～である場合のみ; ～という合意がなされているので→～とい

う条件で、〜という理解の上で ‖ We let them stay in our house on the understanding that it was only for a short period. 私たちは、短期間だけだという条件で彼らを家に滞在させた.

**\*understanding²** /ʌ̀ndərstǽndɪŋ/ 形 ▶定義 showing kind feelings towards sb; sympathetic 人に親切心を示す; 同情的な→**理解力のある, 思いやりのある**

**understate** /ʌ̀ndərstéɪt/ 動他 ▶定義 to say that sth is smaller or less important than it really is 〜が実際よりも小さいまたは重要でないという→**〜を控えめに述べる,(数)を少なく言う** ⇔ **overstate** — understatement 名 ❻▶**控えめに言うこと, 控えめな表現** ‖ *'Is she pleased?' 'That's an understatement. She's delighted.'*「彼女は喜んでいますか」「それどころか！彼女は大喜びしていますよ」

**understudy** /ʌ́ndərstʌ̀di/ 名 ❻ (複 **understudies**) ▶定義 an actor who learns the role of another actor and replaces him/her if he/she is ill 別の俳優の役を習得して, その俳優が病気のとき代役を務める俳優→**代役**

**undertake** /ʌ̀ndərtéɪk/ 動他 (過 **undertook**; /-túk/ 過分 **undertaken** /-téɪk(ə)n/) ▶定義 1 to decide to do sth and start doing it 〜を行うことを決めて, やり始める→**〜に着手する** ‖ *The company is undertaking a major programme of modernization.* その会社は大掛かりな近代化計画に取り組み始めている. ▶定義 2 to agree or promise to do sth 〜を行うことを合意する, または約束する→**〜を引き受ける**

**undertaker** /ʌ́ndərtèɪkər/ (または **funeral director**; 米 または **mortician**) 名 ❻ ▶定義 a person whose job is to prepare dead bodies to be buried and to arrange funerals 死体を埋葬する準備と葬儀の手配を仕事とする人→**葬儀屋**

**undertaking** /ʌ̀ndərtéɪkɪŋ, -́--/ 名 [❻, 通常は単数] ▶定義 1 a piece of work or business 1つの仕事または事業→**事業, 企て** ‖ *Buying the company would be a risky undertaking.* その会社の買収は危険をはらんだ仕事だろう. ▶定義 2 undertaking (that.../to do sth) a formal or legal promise to do sth 〜を行う正式なまたは法的約束→**約束, 保証**

**undertone** /ʌ́ndərtòʊn/ 名 ❻ ▶定義 a feeling, quality or meaning that is not expressed in a direct way 直接には表現されない感情, 性質または意味→**言外の響き, 潜在的要素, 底流**
成句 **in an undertone; in undertones** ▶定義 in a quiet voice 静かな声で→**小声で**

**undervalue** /ʌ̀ndərvǽljuː/ 動他 ▶定義 to place too low a value on sb/sth 〜の価値を低く見積もりすぎる→**〜を過小評価する, 〜を軽視する**

**underwater** /ʌ̀ndərwɔ́ːtər/ 形副 ▶定義 existing, happening or used below the surface of water 水面下で存在する, 起こるまたは使われる→**水面下の[で], 水中(用)の[で]** ‖ *underwater exploration* 水中探索 *an underwater camera* 水中カメラ *Can you swim underwater?* 潜水で泳ぐことができますか.

**\*underwear** /ʌ́ndərwèər/ 名 Ⓤ ▶定義 clothing that is worn next to the skin under other clothes ほかの洋服の下に, 素肌に直接着る衣類→**下着類, 肌着類**
➤ underclothes は同じ意味を持つ複数名詞.

**underweight** /ʌ̀ndərwéɪt/ 形 ▶定義 weighing less than is normal or correct 通常または正しい重量に足りない→**重量不足の** ☞参 **thin** の注 ⇔ **overweight**

**the underworld** /ʌ́ndərwə̀ːrld/ 名 [単数扱い] ▶定義 people who are involved in organized crime 組織的犯罪にかかわっている人々→**暗黒街, やくざの世界**

**undesirable** /ʌ̀ndɪzáɪərəb(ə)l/ 形 ▶定義 unpleasant or not wanted; likely to cause problems 不愉快な, または欲されていない; 問題を起こしそうな→**不快な, 望ましくない** ⇔ **desirable**

**undid** **UNDO**の過去形

**undignified** /ʌ̀ndígnɪfaɪd/ 形 ▶定義 causing you to look foolish and to lose the respect of other people 自分を愚かに見せるような, また他人からの尊敬を失わせるような→**品位のない, みっともない** ⇔ **dignified**

**undivided** /ʌ̀ndəváɪdəd/ 形
成句 **get/have sb's undivided attention** ▶定義 to receive all sb's attention→**〜の完全な注目を集める**

**give your undivided attention (to sb/sth)** ▶定義 to give all your attention to sb/sth 〜に完全な関心を向ける→**〜にわき目も振らずに専心する**

**\*undo** /ʌndúː/ 動他 (三単現 **undoes**; 過 **undid**; 過分 **undone**) ▶定義 1 to open sth that was tied or fastened 結ばれたまたは締められた〜を開く→(ひも)をほどく、(包み)を開く、(ボタン)を外す｜ to undo a knot/zip/button 結び目をほどく・ファスナーを開く・ボタンを外す ▶定義2 to destroy the effect of sth that has already happened 既に起きた〜の効果を打ち消しにする→〜を元に戻す, 取り消す, 無効にする ‖ *His mistake has undone all our good work.* 彼の間違いのため、私たちのよくできた仕事がすべて台なしになった.

**undone** /ʌndʌ́n/ 形 ▶定義1 open; not fastened or tied 開いている；締めたり結んだりしていない→開いている、ほどけている ‖ *I realized that my zip was undone.* 私は自分のファスナーが開いているのに気付いた. ▶定義2 not done 行われていない→なされていない、未完遂の ‖ *I left the housework undone.* 私は家事をやり残したままにした.

**undoubted** /ʌndáʊtəd/ 形 ▶定義 definite; accepted as being true 確定的な；真実として受け入れられた→疑問の余地のない、確かな — undoubtedly 副 →疑問の余地なく、明らかに

*****undress** /ʌndrés/ 動 ▶定義1 ⦿to take off your clothes→衣服を脱ぐ ☛ get undressed の方が undress より一般的に使われる. ‖ *He got undressed and had a shower.* 彼は服を脱いでシャワーを浴びた. ▶定義2 ⦿to take off sb's clothes→〜の服を脱がせる ⇔ dress — undressed 形 →衣服を脱いだ、裸の

**undue** /ʌnd(j)úː/ 形 ▶定義 more than is necessary or reasonable 必要以上または理にかなっている以上の→不当な、過度の ‖ *The police try not to use undue force when arresting a person.* 警察は人を逮捕する際に不当な力を行使しないよう努めている. — unduly 副 →不当に、過度に ‖ *She didn't seem unduly worried by their unexpected arrival.* 彼女は予期せぬ彼らの到来にもそれほど当惑した様子はなかった.

**unearth** /ʌnə́ːrθ/ 動 ⦿ ▶定義 to dig sth up out of the ground; to discover sth that was hidden 〜を地面から掘り出す；隠されていた〜を発見する→〜を掘り出す、発掘する、〜を明るみに出す ‖ *Archaeologists have unearthed a Roman tomb.* 考古学者たちは古代ローマの墓を発掘した.

**unearthly** /ʌnə́ːrθli/ 形 ▶定義 strange or frightening 奇妙なまたは恐ろしい→この世のものとは思われない、気味の悪い ‖ *an unearthly scream* ぞっとするような叫び声

成句 **at an unearthly hour** 略式 ▶定義 extremely early in the morning 朝極端に早く→非常識な早い時刻に、とんでもない早朝に

**unease** /ʌníːz/ (または **uneasiness**) 名 ⦾ ▶定義 a worried or uncomfortable feeling 心配なまたは居心地の悪い気持ち→不安、心配、心痛

**uneasy** /ʌníːzi/ 形 ▶定義1 **uneasy** (about sth/doing sth) worried; not feeling relaxed or comfortable 心配な；安心できないまたは居心地の悪い気持ちで→不安な、落ち着かない ▶定義2 not settled; unlikely to last 確定しない；継続しそうにない→(状態が)不安定な、人を不安にする ‖ *an uneasy compromise* 安心できない妥協 — uneasily 副 →不安そうに、心配して、落ち着かず

**uneconomic** /ʌnekənɑ́mɪk, -iːkə-/ 形 ▶定義 (used about a company, etc) not making or likely to make a profit; unprofitable (会社などについて)利益を生んでいないまたは生みそうにない；利益のない→非経済的な ⇔ economic

**uneconomical** /ʌnekənɑ́mɪk(ə)l, -iːkə-/ 形 ▶定義 wasting money, time, materials, etc お金、時間、材料などを無駄に使う→不経済な、無駄の多い ⇔ economical — uneconomically /-k(ə)li/ 副 →不経済に、無駄に

*****unemployed** /ʌnɪmplɔ́ɪd, -em-/ 形 ▶定義1 not able to find a job; out of work 仕事を見つけられない；仕事のない→失業中の ‖ *She has been unemployed for over a year.* 彼女は1年以上失業している. ☛類 **jobless** ⇔ **employed** ▶定義2 **the unemployed** 名 [複数扱い] people who cannot find a job 仕事を見つけられない人々→失業者

*****unemployment** /ʌnɪmplɔ́ɪmənt, -em-/ 名 ⦾ ▶定義1 the situation of not being able to find a job 仕事を見つけられない状態→失業(状態) ‖ *The number of people claiming **unemployment benefit** (= money given by the state) has gone up.* 失業手当(=国から支給されるお金)を請求する人の数が増加した. ⇔ **employment** ▶定義2 the number of people who are unemployed 雇用されていない人の数→失業者数、失業率 ‖ *The economy is doing very badly and unemployment is rising.* 経済状態が非常に悪く、失業者数が増加している. ☛類 **joblessness**

☛参 **the dole**

**unending** /ʌnéndɪŋ/ [形] ▶定義 having or seeming to have no end 終わりのない，またはないように思える ➜**果てしない，何度も繰り返される**

**unequal** /ʌníːkw(ə)l/ [形] ▶定義**1** not fair or balanced 公平または均衡でない ➜**不公平な，不釣り合いな** ‖ *an unequal distribution of power* 不均等な力の配分 ▶定義**2** different in size, amount, level, etc 大きさ，量，水準などが異なる ➜**等しくない，同等でない** ⇔ **equal** — unequally [副] ➜**不均等に，等しくなく**

**uneven** /ʌníːv(ə)n/ [形] ▶定義**1** not completely smooth, level or regular 完全に滑らか，平ら，または規則的ではない ➜**でこぼこした，ふぞろいな，不規則な** ‖ *The sign was painted in rather uneven letters.* その標識にはペンキでかなりふぞろいな文字が書かれていた．⇔ **even** ▶定義**2** not always of the same level or quality いつも同じ水準または質であるわけではない ➜**むらのある，一様でない，等質でない** — unevenly [副] ➜**不均衡に，不規則に** ‖ *The country's wealth is unevenly distributed.* その国の富は不公平に配分されている．

***unexpected** /ʌnɪkspéktəd/ [形] ▶定義 not expected and therefore causing surprise 予期していないので驚かされる ➜**思い掛けない，不意の** — unexpectedly [副] ➜**思い掛けなく，突然に，意外なことに** ‖ *I got there late because I was unexpectedly delayed.* 私は思い掛けないことで手間取り，そこに着くのが遅れた．

***unfair** /ʌnféər/ [形] ▶定義**1** unfair (on/to sb) not dealing with people as they deserve; not treating each person equally 人々にふさわしい扱いをしない;各々の人を公平に扱わない ➜**不当な，不公平な，偏った** ‖ *This law is unfair to women.* この法律は女性にとって不公平である．*The tax is unfair on people with low incomes.* その税金は低所得者に不公平だ．▶定義**2** not following the rules and therefore giving an advantage to one person, team, etc 規則にのっとっていない，したがってある人またはチームなどに有利な ➜**規則に反した，公正でない** ⇔ **fair** — unfairly [副] ➜**不公平に，不当に** — unfairness [名] [U] ➜**不正，不公平**

**unfaithful** /ʌnféɪθfʊl, -f(ə)l/ [形] ▶定義 unfaithful (to sb/sth) having a sexual relationship with sb who is not your husband, wife or partner 夫，妻または決まったパートナーでない～と性的関係を持つ ➜**不貞な，不倫している，不誠実な** ⇔ **faithful** — unfaithfulness [名] [U] ➜**不貞，不倫，不誠実**

**unfamiliar** /ʌnfəmíljər/ [形] ▶定義**1** unfamiliar (to sb) that you do not know well 自分がよく知らない ➜**未知の，なじみの薄い** ‖ *an unfamiliar part of town* 町のまだ知らない場所 ▶定義**2** unfamiliar (with sth) not having knowledge or experience of sth ～の知識または経験を持たない ➜**(～に)精通していない，慣れていない，親しくない** ‖ *I'm unfamiliar with this author.* 私はこの著者についてよく知らない．⇔ **familiar**

**unfashionable** /ʌnfǽʃ(ə)nəb(ə)l/ [形] ▶定義 not popular at a particular time 特定の時において人気がない ➜**流行に合わない，野暮な** ‖ *unfashionable ideas/clothes* 流行に合わない考え·洋服 ⇔ **fashionable** ☛参 **old-fashioned**

**unfavourable** ([米] **unfavorable**) /ʌnféɪvərəb(ə)l/ [形] ▶定義**1** showing that you do not like or approve of sb/sth ～を好まないまたは認めないことを示す ➜**好意的でない，否定的な** ▶定義**2** not good and likely to cause problems or make sth difficult 良くない，また問題を起こしそうな，または何かを難しくしそうな ➜**不都合な，不利な** ⇔ **favourable** ☛参 **adverse**

**unfit** /ʌnfít/ [形] ▶定義**1** unfit (for sth/to do sth) not suitable or not good enough for sth ～に適していない，または良くない ➜**(～に)不向きな，(～の)資格·能力に欠ける** ‖ *His criminal past makes him unfit to be a politician.* 彼は過去に犯罪を犯しているので，政治家になる資格がない．▶定義**2** not in good physical health, especially because you do not get enough exercise 特に運動不足により肉体的に健康でない ➜**不健康な，体の弱い** ⇔ **fit**

**unfold** /ʌnfóʊld/ [動][自][他] ▶定義**1** to open out and become flat; to open out sth that was folded 広がって平らになる; 折り畳んである～を広げる ➜**(つぼみが)開く;(折り畳んだ紙·布)を広げる，開く** ‖ *The sofa unfolds into a spare bed.* そのソファーは広げると予備のベッドになります．*I unfolded the letter and read it.* 私は手紙を広げて読んだ．⇔ **fold (up)** ▶定義**2** to become known, or to allow sth to become

U

known a little at a time 少しずつ知られる、または~を少しずつ明らかにする→はっきりしてくる; 打ち明ける

**unforeseen** /ˌʌnfɔːrˈsíːn/ 形 ▶定義 not expected 予想していない→予期しない, 思い掛けない ‖ *an unforeseen problem* 思い掛けない問題

**unforgettable** /ˌʌnfərˈɡétəb(ə)l/ 形 ▶定義 making such a strong impression that you cannot forget it 強い印象を受けて忘れることができない→忘れられない, いつまでも記憶に残る

*****unfortunate** /ʌnˈfɔːrtʃ(ə)nət/ 形 ▶定義 1 not lucky 不運な→不幸な, 不幸をもたらす ⇔ **fortunate** ▶定義 2 that you feel sorry about それについて残念に思う→遺憾な, 残念な — **unfortunately** 副 →不運にも, あいにく, 不幸にして ‖ *I'd like to help you but unfortunately there's nothing I can do.* あなたの力になりたいのだが, あいにく私にできる事は何もない.

**unfounded** /ʌnˈfáʊndəd/ 形 ▶定義 not based on or supported by facts 事実に基づいていない, または事実の裏付けがない→根拠・理由のない ‖ *unfounded allegations* 事実無根の申し立て

*****unfriendly** /ʌnˈfréndli/ 形 ▶定義 unfriendly (to/toward sb) unpleasant or not polite to sb ~に不親切な, または礼儀正しくない→(~に)友好的でない, 優しくない ⇔ **friendly**

**ungainly** /ʌnˈɡéɪnli/ 形 ▶定義 moving in a way that is not smooth or elegant 滑らかまたは優雅ではない動き方をする→見苦しい, ぎこちない

**ungrateful** /ʌnˈɡréɪtfʊl, -f(ə)l/ 形 ▶定義 not feeling or showing thanks to sb 人に感謝の気持ちがない、または感謝を示さない→感謝しない, 恩知らずの ⇔ **grateful** — **ungratefully** /-fʊli, -f(ə)li/ 副 →感謝しないで, 恩知らずに

**unguarded** /ʌnˈɡɑːrdəd/ 形 ▶定義 1 not protected or guarded 保護または警戒されていない→守られていない, 無防備の ▶定義 2 saying more than you wanted to 言うつもり以上のことまで言う→軽率な, 不注意な ⇔ **guarded**

**unhappily** /ʌnˈhæpɪli/ 副 ▶定義 1 sadly 悲しく→不幸に, 惨めに ▶定義 2 unfortunately 不運にも→不運にして, あいにく ⇔ **happily**

*****unhappy** /ʌnˈhæpi/ 形 (**unhappier**; **unhappiest**) ▶定義 1 unhappy (about sth) sad 悲しい→不幸な ‖ *She's terribly unhappy about losing her job.* 彼女は仕事を失ってひどく悲しんでいる. *He had a very unhappy childhood.* 彼は非常に不幸な子供時代を送った. ▶定義 2 unhappy (about/at/with sth) not satisfied or pleased; worried 不満足または不愉快で; 心配で→不満な ‖ *They're unhappy at having to accept a pay cut.* 彼らは賃金カットを受け入れざるを得ないことに不満を抱いている. ⇔ **happy** — **unhappiness** 名 U →不幸, 不運, 悲哀

**unhealthy** /ʌnˈhélθi/ 形 ▶定義 1 not having or showing good health 健康でない, または健康を表さない→健康でない, 病弱な ‖ *He looks pale and unhealthy.* 彼は顔色が悪く病弱に見える. ▶定義 2 likely to cause illness or poor health 病気または不健康の原因になりそうな→健康に良くない, 体に悪い, 有害な ‖ *unhealthy conditions* 不健康な状態 ▶定義 3 not natural 不自然な→不健全な, 病的な ‖ *an unhealthy interest in death* 死に対する病的な興味 ⇔ **healthy**

**unheard** /ʌnˈhɜːrd/ 形 (名詞の前は不可) ▶定義 not listened to or given any attention 聞いてもらえない, 何の注意も払われない→聞く耳を持たれない ‖ *My suggestions went unheard.* 私の提案は聞き入れられなかった.

**unheard-of** 形 ▶定義 not known; never having happened before 知られていない; 今まで起こったことがない→聞いたことがない, 前代未聞の

**unicorn** /ˈjúːnəkɔːrn/ 名 C ▶定義 an animal that only exists in stories, that looks like a white horse with one horn growing out of its forehead 物語の中にだけ存在する動物で, 額から1本の角が生えている白い馬のように見える→一角獣

**unidentified** /ˌʌnaɪˈdéntəfàɪd/ 形 ▶定義 whose identity is not known 身元が分からない→未確認の, 正体不明の ‖ *An unidentified body has been found in the river.* 川で身元不明の死体が見つかった.

*****uniform**[1] /ˈjúːnəfɔːrm/ 名 C U ▶定義 the set of clothes worn at work by the members of certain organizations or groups and by some schoolchildren ある組織または集団の構成員が就業中に着用する, また一部の学童が着用する一そろいの衣服→制服, ユニフォーム ‖ *I didn't know he was a policeman because he wasn't in uniform.* 彼が制服を着用していなかったので, 警官だと分からなかった. — **uniformed** 形 →制服を

着た
**uniform**[2] /júːnəfɔːrm/ 形 ▶定義 not varying; the same in all cases or at all times 変化していない; どんな場合でもまたはいつ何時でも同じの 同形の, 一律の, 均一の, 画一的な — **uniformity** /jùːnəfɔːrməti/ 名 ❶ 一律, 均一性, 画一性

**unify** /júːnəfài/ 動 ❶ (現分 **unifying**; 三単現 **unifies**; 過, 過分 **unified**) ▶定義 to join separate parts together to make one unit, or to make them similar to each other 互いに分かれた部分を結合して1つの物を作る, またはそれらの部分を互いに似たものにする→ 〜を統合する, 一体化する, (〜に)統一する — **unification** /jùːnəfəkéɪʃ(ə)n/ 名 ❶ 統合, 一体化, 統一

**unilateral** /jùːnɪlǽt(ə)r(ə)l, -nə-/ 形 ▶定義 done or made by one person who is involved in sth without the agreement of the other person or people ほかの人または人々の同意を得ることなく, 物事にかかわる1人の人によってなされたまたは作られた→一方的な, 片務的な ‖ *a unilateral declaration of independence* 一方的独立宣言 ☛参 **multilateral** — **unilaterally** /-r(ə)li/ 副 → 一方的に, 片側だけで

**uninhabitable** /ʌ̀nɪnhǽbətəb(ə)l/ 形 ▶定義 not possible to live in そこに住むことができない→ 居住に適しない ⇔ **habitable**

**uninhabited** /ʌ̀nɪnhǽbətəd/ 形 ▶定義 (used about a place or a building) with nobody living in it (場所または建物について)だれもそこに住んでいない→無人の ⇔ **inhabited**

**uninhibited** /ʌ̀nɪnhíbətəd/ 形 ▶定義 behaving in a free and natural way, without worrying what other people think of you 他人にどう思われるか気に掛けず, 自由に自然な振る舞いをしている→気兼ねをしない, 自由な, 思うままの ⇔ **inhibited**

**unintelligible** /ʌ̀nɪntélədʒəb(ə)l/ 形 ▶定義 impossible to understand 理解することが不可能な→ 理解できない, 分かりにくい, 判読できない ⇔ **intelligible**

**uninterested** /ʌ̀nínt(ə)rəstəd, -t(ə)rest-/ 形 ▶定義 *uninterested (in sb/sth)* having or showing no interest in sb/sth 〜に興味を持たない, または示さない→ 無関心の, むとんちゃくな ‖ *She seemed uninterested in anything I had to say.* 彼女は, 私の言おうとする何事にも関心がないように見えた. ⇔ **interested**

---

unit 1759

➤ disinterested と比較. disinterested は別の意味になる.

***union** /júːnjən/ 名 ▶定義 **1** [❶, 単数扱い] the action of joining or the situation of being joined 結合する行為, または結合している状態→結合, 合併, 団結 ▶定義 **2** ❸ a group of states or countries that have joined together to form one country or group 複数の州または国が集結して1つの国または集合体を構成したもの→連合, 連邦, 連合国家 ‖ *the European Union* 欧州連合 ▶定義 **3** = **TRADE UNION** ▶定義 **4** ❸ an organization for a particular group of people 特定の人の集団のための組織→同盟, 連盟 ‖ *the Athletics Union* 陸上競技連盟

**the Union Jack** 名 ❸ ▶定義 the national flag of the United Kingdom, with red and white crosses on a dark blue background 英国の国旗で, 紺色のバックに紅白の十字が入っている→ 英国国旗, ユニオンジャック

***unique** /juníːk/ 形 ▶定義 **1** not like anything else; being the only one of its type ほかの何にも似ていない; その種における唯一の→類のない, 無比の, 無二の ‖ *Shakespeare made a unique contribution to the world of literature.* シェークスピアは文学の世界に類のない貢献をした. ▶定義 **2** *unique to sb/sth* connected with only one place, person or thing ある場所, 人または物にだけ関連する→〜に特有の, 固有の, 独特の ‖ *This dance is unique to this region.* この踊りは当地特有のものです. ▶定義 **3** very unusual 非常に珍しい→珍しい, 風変わりな, ユニークな

**unisex** /júːnɪsèks, -nə-/ 形 ▶定義 designed for and used by both sexes 男女両用にデザインされた, また使用される→男女兼用の, 男女両用の ‖ *unisex fashions* 男女兼用のファッション

**unison** /júːnəs(ə)n, -z(ə)n/ 名
成句 *in unison* ▶定義 saying, singing or doing the same thing at the same time as sb else ほかの人と同時に同じものを言う, 歌う, または行う→異口同音に, 斉唱で, 一致して ‖ *'No, thank you,' they said in unison.* 「いいえ結構です」と彼らは口をそろえて言った.

***unit** /júːnət/ 名 ❸ ▶定義 **1** a single thing which is complete in itself, although it can be part of sth larger より大きな物の一部ともなり得るが, それ

## 1760 unite

自体で完全な1つの物→**1つのまとまり, 構成単位, 一団** ‖ *The book is divided into ten units.* その本は10単元に分かれている. ▶定義2 a fixed amount or number used as a standard of measurement 計量の基準として使われる決まった量または数→**単位** ‖ *a unit of currency* 通貨単位 ▶定義3 a group of people who perform a certain function within a larger organization より大きな組織の中である機能を果たす人々の集まり→**部署, 部門, 班** ‖ *the intensive care unit of a hospital* 病院の集中治療部門 ▶定義4 a small machine that performs a particular task or that is part of a larger machine 特定の働きをする小さな機械, またはさらに大きな機械の一部を成す小さな機械→**装置, 部品** ‖ *The heart of a computer is the central processing unit.* コンピューターの心臓部は中央処理装置です. ▶定義5 a piece of furniture that fits with other pieces of furniture and has a particular use 1個の家具で, ほかの家具に合わせられ, 特定の用途を持つもの→**ユニット家具** ‖ *matching kitchen units* 調和するキッチンユニット ☛ C7ページのさし絵

**unite** /juːnáɪt/ 動 ▶定義1 自他 to join together and act in agreement; to make this happen 団結し, 合意の下で活動する; またそのようにさせる→**結合する・させる, 一体になる; ~を接着する, 合体させる, 接合する, 結び付ける** ‖ *Unless we unite, our enemies will defeat us.* 私たちが一致団結しないと, 敵に打ち負かされるだろう.
▶定義2 自 unite (in sth/in doing sth) to join together for a particular purpose 特定の目的で団結する→**協力して(~する)** ‖ *We should all unite in seeking a solution to this terrible problem.* 私たちは全員が協力してこの難問の解決策を見いだすべきだ.

**united** /juːnáɪtɪd/ 形 ▶定義 joined together by a common feeling or aim 共通の感情または目的により結び付いた→**連合した, 団結した, 結束した**

**the United Kingdom** 名 [単数扱い] (略UK)
▶定義 England, Scotland, Wales and Northern Ireland イングランド, スコットランド, ウェールズおよび北アイルランド→**連合王国, 英国**
▶ the UKはイングランド, スコットランド, ウェールズおよび北アイルランドを含むが, アイルランド共和国(エール)は別の国で英国には含まれない. Great Britain(グレイトブリテン)はイングランド, スコットランド, ウェールズのみを含む. the British Isles(イギリス諸島)はイングランド, スコットランド, ウェールズ, 北アイルランドおよびアイルランド共和国を含む.

**the United Nations** 名 [単数扱い, 単数または複数形の動詞と共に] (略**UN**) ▶定義 the organization formed to encourage peace in the world and to deal with problems between countries 世界の平和を強め, 各国間の問題を処理するための組織→**国際連合**

**the United States (of America)** 名 [単数扱い, 単数または複数形の動詞と共に] (略**US; USA**) ▶定義 a large country in North America made up of 50 states and the District of Columbia 北アメリカの大国で, 50の州とコロンビア特別区から成る→**アメリカ合衆国, 米国**

**unity** /júːnəti/ 名 U ▶定義 the situation in which people are in agreement and working together 人々が合意の下で共に働いている状態→**統一性, 統一体, 結束性, 調和**

*****universal** /jùːnəvɜ́ːrs(ə)l/ 形 ▶定義 connected with, done by or affecting everyone in the world or everyone in a particular group 全世界あるいは特定の集団のすべての人と関係がある, それらの人により行われる, またはそれらの人に影響を及ぼす→**全世界の, 人類共通の, 普遍的な** ‖ *The environment is a universal issue.* 環境は全世界共通の問題だ. — universally /-s(ə)li/ 副 →**普遍的に, 全世界に, 例外なく**

**the universe** /júːnəvɜ̀ːrs/ 名 [単数扱い] ▶定義 everything that exists, including the planets, stars, space, etc 惑星, 恒星, 宇宙などを含む, 存在するすべてのもの→**宇宙(全体), 森羅(しんら)万象**

*****university** /jùːnəvɜ́ːrs(ə)ti/ 名 C (複**universities**) ▶定義 an institution that provides the highest level of education, in which students study for degrees and in which academic research is done 最高水準の教育を施す機関で, そこでは学生が学位取得のために学び, また学術的研究が行われる→**(総合)大学** ‖ *Which university did you go to?* あなたはどの大学に行きましたか. *I did History at university.* 私は大学で歴史を学んだ. *a university lecturer* 大学の講師

➤学生として大学に通うことを意味するときは, at university また go to university など, やthe を伴わない表現を用いる: *He's hoping to go to university next year.*(彼は来年大学に行くことを希望している.)しかしほかの目的で大学に行く場合には, a や the を伴う: *I'm going to a conference at the university in July.*(私は7月に大学で行われる会議に出席を予定している.)

\*unkind /ʌnkáɪnd/ 形 ▶定義 unpleasant and not friendly 不快で非友好的な➡不親切な, 冷酷な ‖ *That was an unkind thing to say.* そんな事を言うのは思いやりに欠けていた. *The zoo was accused of being unkind to its animals.* その動物園は動物を冷酷に扱っていることで非難された. ⇔ kind — unkindly 副➡不親切に, 冷酷に, 思いやりなく — unkindness 名 ❻ ❶ ➡不親切, 不人情, 冷酷

**unknown**[1] /ʌnnóʊn/ 形 ▶定義1 unknown (to sb) that sb does not know; without sb knowing 〜が知らない; 〜に知られていない➡未知の, 未確認の, 不明の ‖ *Unknown to the boss, she went home early.* 上司に知られることなく, 彼女は早く帰宅した. ▶定義2 not famous or familiar to other people 有名でない, または他人に知られていない➡無名の, 未知の ‖ *an unknown actress* 無名の女優 ⇔ well-known, famous

成句 an unknown quantity ▶定義 a person or thing that you know very little about ほとんど知られていない人または物➡未知数, (能力が)未知数の人, (性能が)未知の物

**unknown**[2] /ʌnnóʊn/ 名 ▶定義1 通常 は the unknown [単数扱い] a place or thing that you know nothing about 全く知らない場所または物➡未知の場所・物, 未知の世界 ‖ *a fear of the unknown* 未知の世界の恐怖 ▶定義2 ❻ a person who is not well known よく知られていない人➡無名の人

**unleaded** /ʌnlédəd/ 形 ▶定義 not containing lead 鉛を含まない➡無鉛の ‖ *unleaded petrol* 無鉛ガソリン

\*unless /ənlés, ʌn-/ 接 ▶定義 if...not; except if もし〜でなければ; 〜である場合を除いて➡〜でない限り ‖ *I was told that unless my work improved, I would lose the job.* 私は業績を改善できなければ仕事を失うことになると言われた. *'Would you like a cup of coffee?' 'Not unless you've already made some.'* 「コーヒーを1杯いかがですか」「まだいれていただいてなければ, 結構です」 *Unless anyone has anything else to say, the meeting is closed.* ほかに発言がなければ, 会議を終了します. *Don't switch that on unless I'm here.* 私がここにいる場合を除いて, そのスイッチを入れてはならない.

\*unlike /ʌnláɪk/ 形前 ▶定義1 in contrast to; different from 〜と対照的に; 〜と違って➡(〜に)似ていない, (〜と)異なって ‖ *She's unlike anyone else I've ever met.* 彼女は今まで会ったことのあるどの人とも全く違う. *He's extremely ambitious, unlike me.* 彼は私と違って極めて野心的な人だ. *This is an exciting place to live, unlike my home town.* ここは私の故郷と違って住むのに刺激的な場所です. ▶定義2 not typical of; unusual for 〜に典型的でない; 〜にしては通常と違う➡〜に似つかわしくない ‖ *It's unlike him to be so rude - he's usually very polite.* あれほど不作法なのは彼らしくない — いつもは非常に礼儀正しい人だ.

\*unlikely /ʌnláɪkli/ 形 (unlikelier; unlikeliest) ▶定義1 unlikely (to do sth/that...) not likely to happen; not expected; not probable 起こりそうもない; 予測されない; 可能性の低い➡ありそうにない, 〜しそうにない, 見込みのない ‖ *I suppose she might win but I think it's very unlikely.* 彼女は勝つかもしれないが, 私が思うに, ほとんど見込みがない. *It's **highly** unlikely that I'll have any free time next week.* 私は来週自由になる時間をまず持てそうにない. ⇔ likely ▶定義2 difficult to believe 信じ難い➡まゆつば物の ‖ *an unlikely excuse* まゆつば物の言い訳 ☛類 improbable

**unlimited** /ʌnlímətəd/ 形 ▶定義 without limit; as much or as great as you want 制限のない; 望むだけ多くのまたは大きな➡無制限の, 際限のない ⇔ limited

\*unload /ʌnlóʊd/ 動 ▶定義1 ❸ ❶ unload (sth) (from sth) to take things that have been transported off or out of a vehicle 輸送された物を車両から降ろすまたは取り出す➡(積み荷を)(〜から)降ろす ‖ *We unloaded the boxes from the back of the van.* 私たちはバンの後部から箱を降ろした. ▶定義2 ❸ ❶ (used about a vehicle) to have the things removed that have been transported (車両について) 輸送したものを降ろしてもらう ➡ (積み荷を) 降ろす ‖ *Parking here is restricted to vehicles that are loading or unloading.* ここでの駐車は, 荷物の積み降ろしをする車のみに限定されている. ⇔ **load** ▶定義3 略式 unload sb/sth (on/onto sb) to get rid of sth you do not want or to pass it to sb else 要らない〜を処分する, またはほかの…に渡す ➡ (負担になる〜) を片付ける, 押し付ける ‖ *He shouldn't try and unload the responsibility onto you.* 彼はあなたに責任を押し付けるべきではない.

**unlock** /ʌnlák/ 動 自 他 ▶定義 to open the lock on sth using a key; to be opened with a key かぎを使って〜の錠を開ける; かぎで開けられる ➡ 〜の錠を開ける; 錠が開く ‖ *I can't unlock this door.* 私はこのドアの錠を開けることができない. *This door won't unlock.* この扉は錠が開かない. ⇔ **lock**

*****unlucky** /ʌnláki/ 形 (**unluckier; unluckiest**) ▶定義 having or causing bad luck 不運なまたは不運を招く ➡ 運が悪い, ついていない, 不吉な ‖ *They were unlucky to lose because they played so well.* 彼らは, あれほど健闘したのに負けたはついていなかった. *Thirteen is often thought to be an unlucky number.* 13は時として不吉な数と思われる. ⇔ **lucky** — **unluckily** 副 ➡ 不運に (も), あいにく, 残念なことに

**unmarried** /ʌnmǽrɪd/ 形 ▶定義 not married; single ➡ 未婚の; 独身の ⇔ **married**

**unmistakable** /ʌ̀nməstéɪkəb(ə)l/ 形 ▶定義 that cannot be confused with anything else; easy to recognize ほかの何とも混同される可能性のない; 容易に認識できる ➡ 間違いようのない, 紛れもない ‖ *She had an unmistakable French accent.* 彼女は明らかにフランス語なまりがあった. — **unmistakably** /-əbli/ 副 ➡ 間違いようもなく, 紛れもなく

**unmoved** /ʌnmúːvd/ 形 ▶定義 not affected emotionally 感情的に影響を受けない ➡ 心を動かされない, 冷静な ‖ *The judge was unmoved by the boy's sad story, and sent him to jail.* 判事は, その少年の悲しい身の上話に哀れみを示すことなく, 彼を少年院に送った.

**unnatural** /ʌnnǽtʃ(ə)rəl/ 形 ▶定義 different from what is normal or expected 正常なまたは予想されていたものと異なる ➡ 不自然な, 異常な, わざとらしい ⇔ **natural** — **unnaturally** /-rəli/ 副 ➡ 不自然に, 異常に ‖ *It's unnaturally quiet in here.* この辺りは異常に静かだ.

*****unnecessary** /ʌnnésəs(ə)ri, -nésəsèri/ 形 ▶定義 more than is needed or acceptable 必要以上の, または受け入れられる以上の ➡ 不必要な, 余計な ‖ *We should try to avoid all unnecessary expense.* 我々は余計な出費を避けるよう努めるべきだ. ☞参 **needless** は別の意味になる. ⇔ **necessary** — **unnecessarily** /ʌnnésəs(ə)r(ə)li; -nesəsérəli/ 副 ➡ 不必要に, 無駄に, 余計に ‖ *His explanation was unnecessarily complicated.* 彼の説明は必要以上に複雑だった.

**unnoticed** /ʌnnóʊtəst/ 形 ▶定義 not noticed or seen 気付かれない, または見られない ➡ 見落とされた, 人目に付かない ‖ *He didn't want his hard work to go unnoticed.* 彼は一生懸命働いたことを見落とされたくなかった.

**unobtrusive** /ʌ̀nəbtrúːsɪv/ 形 ▶定義 avoiding being noticed; not attracting attention 気付かれないようにする; 注目を集めない ➡ 遠慮がちな, 控えめの — **unobtrusively** 副 ➡ 遠慮がちに, 控えめに ‖ *He tried to leave as unobtrusively as possible.* 彼はできるだけ人目に付かぬよう立ち去ろうとした.

**unofficial** /ʌ̀nəfíʃ(ə)l/ 形 ▶定義 not accepted or approved by a person in authority 権限を持っている人に受け入れられていないまたは承認されていない ➡ 非公式の, 私的な, 非公認の ‖ *an unofficial strike* 山猫スト *Unofficial reports say that four people died in the explosion.* 非公式の報道によると, その爆発で4人が死亡した. ⇔ **official** — **unofficially** /-ʃ(ə)li/ 副 ➡ 非公式に, 私的に, 非公認で

**unorthodox** /ʌnɔ́ːrθədɑks/ 形 ▶定義 different from what is generally accepted, usual or traditional 一般に受け入れられていない, 通常または伝統的なものと異なる ➡ 正統でない, 異端の ⇔ **orthodox**

**unpack** /ʌnpǽk/ 動 自 他 ▶定義 to take out the things that were in a bag, suitcase, etc かばん, スーツケースなどに入っているものを取り出す ➡ (包み) を解く, 荷を解く; (かばんから) 〜を取り出す ‖ *When we arrived at the hotel we unpacked and went to the beach.* 私たちはホテ

ルに到着すると, 荷を解いて浜辺に行った. ⇔ **pack**

**unpaid** /ʌnpéɪd/ 形 ▶定義1 not yet paid まだ支払いが済んでいない➡未払いの, 未納の ‖ *an unpaid bill* 未払い請求書 ▶定義2 not receiving money for work done 仕事をしたことに対し報酬を受け取らない➡無報酬の ‖ *an unpaid assistant* 無報酬のアシスタント ▶定義3 (used about work) done without payment (仕事について) 支払いを受けずに行う➡無給の ‖ *unpaid overtime* 手当ての付かない残業, サービス残業

*__unpleasant__ /ʌnplézənt/ 形 ▶定義1 causing you to have a bad feeling; not nice 嫌な気持ちにさせる; 不親切な➡不快な, 嫌な ‖ *This news has come as an unpleasant surprise.* この知らせにより, 思い掛けず嫌な気持ちになった. ⇔ **pleasant** ▶定義2 unfriendly; impolite 非友好的な; 不作法な➡思いやりのない, 失礼な ‖ *There's no need to get unpleasant, we can discuss this in a friendly way.* いがみ合う必要はない, 私たちはこの件について友好的に話し合うことができる. — unpleasantly 副➡不愉快に, 感じが悪く, 非友好的に

**unplug** /ʌnplʌ́g/ 動 (unplugging; unplugged) ▶定義 to remove a piece of electrical equipment from the electricity supply 電源から電気機器を外す➡〜のコンセント・プラグを抜く ‖ *Could you unplug the cassette recorder, please?* すみませんが, そのカセットレコーダーのプラグを抜いてくれますか. ⇔ plug sth in

**unpopular** /ʌnpɑ́pjələr/ 形 ▶定義 unpopular (with sb) not liked by many people 多くの人に好まれない➡人気がない, 不評の, はやらない ‖ *Her methods made her very unpopular with the staff.* 彼女のやり方はスタッフの間で大変な不評を買った. ⇔ **popular** — unpopularity /ʌnpɑpjəlǽrəti/ 名 ▶不人気, 不評

**unprecedented** /ʌnprésədəntəd/ 形 ▶定義 never having happened or existed before 今までに起こったことがない, または存在したことがない➡先例のない ☞参 precedent

**unprovoked** /ʌnprəvóʊkt/ 形 ▶定義 (used especially about an attack) not caused by anything the person who is attacked has said or done (特に攻撃について) 攻撃された人が言ったことまたはした事が原因ではない➡こちらから挑発したものでない, 正当な理由のない ⇔ provoked

**unqualified** /ʌnkwɑ́ləfaɪd/ 形 ▶定義1 not having the knowledge or not having passed the exams that you need for sth 何かのために必要な知識を持たない, またはそれに要求される試験に受かっていない➡無資格の, 適任でない ‖ *I'm unqualified to offer an opinion on this matter.* 私はこの件について意見を述べる資格がない. ⇔ qualified ▶定義2 complete; absolute 完全な; 絶対的な➡制限されない, 無条件の ‖ *an unqualified success* 完全な勝利

**unquestionable** /ʌnkwéstʃənəbl/ 形 ▶定義 certain; that cannot be doubted 確かな; 疑うことのできない➡疑う余地のない, 議論の余地のない, 申し分のない ⇔ questionable — unquestionably /-əbli/ 副➡疑いなく, 明らかに ‖ *She is unquestionably the most famous opera singer in the world.* 彼女は疑いなく世界で最も有名なオペラ歌手だ.

**unravel** /ʌnrǽvəl/ 動 (unravelling; unravelled: 米 unraveling; unraveled) 自他 ▶定義1 to unfasten or remove the knots from a piece of string, thread, etc; to come unfastened in this way 糸, ひもなどをほどく, または結び目を解く; そのようにしてほどける➡〜をほどく, ほぐす; ほどける, ほぐれる ‖ *I unravelled the tangled string and wound it into a ball.* 私はもつれた糸をほどいて, 糸玉に巻いた. ▶定義2 (used about a complicated story, etc) to become or to make sth become clear (複雑な話などについて) 明白になる, または〜を明らかにする➡(難問)を解明する, 解く

**unreal** /ʌnríəl, -rí:(ə)l/ 形 ▶定義1 very strange and seeming more like a dream than reality 非常に奇妙な, また現実というより夢のように思える➡実在しない, 夢のような ‖ *Her voice had an unreal quality about it* 彼女の声には信じられないような音色があった. ▶定義2 not connected with reality 現実と結び付いていない➡非現実的な ‖ *Some people have unreal expectations of marriage.* ある人は結婚に対して非現実的な期待を抱いている.

**unreasonable** /ʌnríːznəb(ə)l/ 形 ▶定義 unfair; expecting too much 不当な; 期待が過ぎる➡理性的でない, 道理を外れた; 法外な, 過度の ‖ *I think* *she is being totally unreasonable.* 私は、彼女が全く道理をわきまえていないと思う. *He makes unreasonable demands on his staff.* 彼は部下に過度な要求をしている. ⇔ **reasonable** — unreasonably /-əbli/ 副 ➡**無分別に, 不合理に, 法外に**

**unrelenting** /ʌnrɪléntɪŋ/ 形 ▶定義 continuously strong, not becoming weaker or stopping 継続的に強く, 弱まることまたは止まることがない ➡**容赦しない, 緩むことのない**

**unreserved** /ʌnrɪzə́ːrvd/ 形 ▶定義1 (used about seats in a theatre, etc) not kept for the use of a particular person (劇場などの座席について) 特定の人が使用するよう取ってはいない ➡**予約していない** ⇔ **reserved** ▶定義2 without limit; complete 制限のない; 完全な ➡**無条件の, 全面的な** ‖ *The government's action received the unreserved support of all parties.* 政府の取った措置はすべての政党から全面的に支持された. — unreservedly /ʌnrɪzə́ːrvdli/ 副 ➡**制限なく, 無条件に**

**unrest** /ʌnrést/ 名 ❶ ▶定義 a situation in which people are angry or not happy and likely to protest or fight 人々が腹を立てているまたは不満で, 抗議または争いを起こしそうな状況 ➡**社会的不安, 動揺, 不穏** ‖ *social unrest* 社会不安

**unrivalled** (米 **unrivaled**) /ʌnráɪv(ə)ld/ 形 ▶定義 much better than any other of the same type 同じ種類の中で他よりもずっと良い ➡**無敵の, 無比の, 抜群の** ‖ *His knowledge of Greek theology is unrivalled.* ギリシャ神学の知識にかけては彼の右に出るものはない.

**unroll** /ʌnróʊl/ 動 ⾃ ⾷ ▶定義 to open from a rolled position ➡**〜が巻いた状態から開く・広がる; 巻いた〜をほどく・広げる** ‖ *He unrolled the poster and stuck it on the wall.* 彼は丸めたポスターを広げて壁に張った. ⇔ **roll up**

**unruly** /ʌnrúːli/ 形 ▶定義 difficult to control; without discipline 制御するのが難しい; 規律のない ➡**手に負えない, 無法な** ‖ *an unruly crowd* 暴走する群衆 — unruliness 名 ❶ ➡**無秩序, 気まま**

**unsavoury** (米 **unsavory**) /ʌnséɪv(ə)ri/ 形 ▶定義 unpleasant; not morally acceptable 不愉快な; 道徳的に受け入れられない ➡**不快な; いかがわしい** ‖ *His friends are all unsavoury characters.* 彼の友人は芳しくない人物ばかりだ.

**unscathed** /ʌnskéɪðd/ 形 ▶定義 not hurt, without injury 傷がない, けがのない ➡**無傷の** ‖ *He came out of the fight unscathed.* 彼は戦いから無傷で帰還した.

**unscrew** /ʌnskrúː/ 動 ⾷ ▶定義1 to remove the screws from sth 〜からねじを外す ➡**〜のねじを抜く** ▶定義2 to open or remove sth by turning it 〜を回して開けるまたは取り外す ➡**〜を回して抜く** ‖ *Could you unscrew the top of this bottle for me?* このびんの栓を開けてくれませんか.

**unscrupulous** /ʌnskrúːpjələs/ 形 ▶定義 being dishonest, cruel or unfair in order to get what you want 欲しいものを手に入れるために不正直, 残酷または不正な事をする ➡**恥知らずな, 無節操な** ⇔ **scrupulous**

**unsightly** /ʌnsáɪtli/ 形 ▶定義 very unpleasant to look at; ugly 見て非常に不愉快な; 醜い ➡**見苦しい, 目障りな** ‖ *an unsightly new building* 目障りな新築建物

**unskilled** /ʌnskíld/ 形 ▶定義 not having or needing special skill or training 特別の技術を持たないまたは訓練を受けていない, またはそれらを必要としない ➡**(人が) 熟練していない, 非熟練の, (仕事が) 熟練を要しない** ‖ *an unskilled job/worker* 熟練を要しない仕事, 非熟練工 ⇔ **skilled**

**unsolicited** /ʌnsəlísɪtəd/ 形 ▶定義 not asked for 頼まれていない ➡**余計なお世話の** ‖ *unsolicited praise/advice* お節介な褒め言葉・助言

**unsound** /ʌnsáʊnd/ 形 ▶定義1 in poor condition; weak 劣った状態の; 弱い ➡**堅固でない; 健全でない** ‖ *The building is structurally unsound.* その建物は構造的に弱い. ▶定義2 based on wrong ideas and therefore mistaken 誤った考えに基づいているので間違っている ➡**根拠のない, 頼りにならない** ⇔ **sound**

**unstable** /ʌnstéɪb(ə)l/ 形 ▶定義1 likely to fall down or move; not firmly fixed 落ちそうなまたは動きそうな; しっかり固定されていない ➡**不安定な, ぐらつく, 動きやすい** ▶定義2 likely to change or fail 変わりそうなまたは失敗しそうな ➡**変わりやすい, 崩れそうな** ‖ *a period of unstable government* 不安定な政治の時期 ▶定義3 (used about a person's moods or behaviour) likely to change suddenly or often (人の気分または振る舞いについて) 突然またはしばしば変わ

りそうな➔**気まぐれな, 情緒不安定な** ⇔ **stable** ☛ 名 instability

**unstuck** /ʌnstʌ́k/ 形 ▶定義 no longer stuck together or stuck down もはや一緒にくっついていない, またははり付いていない➔**はがれた** ‖ *The label on the parcel is about to come unstuck.* その小包のラベルは今にもはがれそうだ. 成句 come unstuck ▶定義 to fail badly; to be unsuccessful ひどく失敗する; 不成功に終わる➔**駄目になる, しくじる** ‖ *His plan came unstuck when he realized he didn't have enough money.* 資金が十分ないことに気が付き, 彼の計画が駄目になった.

**unsuitable** /ʌns(j)úːtəb(ə)l/ 形 ▶定義 not right or appropriate for sb/sth 人・物に適切でないまたはふさわしくない➔**適していない, 似合わない** ‖ *This film is unsuitable for children under 12.* この映画は12歳未満の子供には向かない. ⇔ **suitable**

**unsure** /ʌnʃúər, -ʃɔ́ːr/ 形 ▶定義1 unsure of yourself not feeling confident about yourself➔**自分に自信がない** ‖ *He's young and still quite unsure of himself.* 彼は若く, まだ自分に大した自信もない. ▶定義2 unsure (about/of sth) not certain; having doubts➔**確信がない; 疑念がある** ‖ *I didn't argue because I was unsure of the facts.* 私はその事実に確信がなかったので主張しなかった. ⇔ **sure, certain**

**unsuspecting** /ʌnsəspéktɪŋ/ 形 ▶定義 not realizing that there is danger 危険の存在に気付かない➔**怪しまない, 気付かない** ☛参 **suspect, suspicious**

**untangle** /ʌntǽŋg(ə)l/ 動他 ▶定義 to separate threads which have become tied together in a confused way 複雑に結ばれた糸を分離する➔**〜をほどく** ‖ *The wires got mixed up and it took me ages to untangle them.* ワイヤーが絡まっていて, ほどくのにものすごく時間がかかった.

**unthinkable** /ʌnθíŋkəb(ə)l/ 形 ▶定義 impossible to imagine or accept 想像したり受け入れたりできない➔**考えられない, あり得ない** ‖ *It was unthinkable that he would never see her again.* 彼がもう二度と彼女に会わないとは想像もつかなかった.

**unthinking** /ʌnθíŋkɪŋ/ 形 ▶定義 done, said, etc without thinking carefully 注意深く考えないで行われた, 言われたなど➔**思慮のない, 軽率な** — unthinkingly 副 ➔軽率に, 無分別に

\***untidy** /ʌntáɪdi/ 形 ▶定義1 not tidy or well arranged きちんとしていない, またはよく整とんされていない➔**散らかった, 乱雑な** ‖ *an untidy bedroom* 散らかった寝室 *untidy hair* だらしのない髪 ▶定義2 (used about a person) not keeping things tidy or in good order (人について) 物事をきちんとしない, または整理整とんしない➔**だらしない** ‖ *My flatmate is so untidy!* 私のアパートの同居人はものすごくだらしない. ⇔ **tidy, neat** — untidily 副 ➔乱雑に, だらしなく — untidiness 名 U➔無精, ずさん

**untie** /ʌntáɪ/ 動他 (現分 untying; 三単現 unties; 過, 過分 untied) ▶定義 to remove a knot; to free sb/sth that is tied by a rope, etc 結び目をほどく; ロープなどで縛った〜を自由にする➔**(結び目を)ほどく; 解く** ⇔ **tie up, fasten**

**until** /əntíl/ (または **till**) 前接 ▶定義 up to the time or the event mentioned 示された時間または出来事まで➔**〜まで(ずっと)** ‖ *The restaurant is open until midnight.* そのレストランは夜12時まで開いている. *Until that moment she had been happy.* その時点まで彼女はずっと幸せだった. *She waited until he had finished.* 彼女は, 彼が終わるまでずっと待っていた. *We won't leave until the police get here (= we won't leave before they come).* 私たちは警察が来るまでここを離れるつもりはない(= 私たちは彼らが来る前にここを離れるつもりはない).

▶注意. until は英語で正式・略式どちらにおいても使うことができる. till は略式英語でより一般的だが, 普通文章では使われない. till/until は時間に関してのみ使うこと. 距離については as far as を使う: *I walked as far as the shops.* (私は商店街まで歩いた.) 数については up to を使う: *You can take up to 20 kilos of luggage.* (荷物は20キロまで携帯できます.)

**untold** /ʌntóʊld/ 形 ▶定義 very great; so big, etc that you cannot count or measure it 非常に大きい; とても大きいなどの理由で数えたり計ったりできない➔**無数の, 言い表せない** ‖ *untold suffering* 言い表せないほどの苦悩

**untoward** /ʌntəwɔ́ːrd, ʌntɔ́ːrd/ 形 ▶定義 (used about an event, etc) unexpected and unpleasant (出来事などについて) 予期しておらず不愉快

な →運の悪い、困った ‖ *The security guard noticed nothing untoward.* 警備員は何らの異常にも気付かなかった.

**untruth** /ʌ́ntrúːθ/ 名 ● (複 **untruths** /-trúːðz, -trúːθs/) (文) ▶定義 something that is not true; a lie 本当ではないもの；うそ →偽り、虚言 — untruthful /-fʊl, -f(ə)l/ 形 →真実でない、偽りの

**untypical** /ʌ̀ntípɪk(ə)l/ 形 ▶定義 not typical or usual →典型的でない、または普通ではない ‖ *an untypical example* 通常と違う例 ⇔ typical ☞比 atypical

**unused**¹ /ʌ̀njúːzd/ 形 ▶定義 that has not been used 使われたことがない →未使用の

**unused**² /ʌ̀njúːst/ 形 ▶定義 unused to sth/to doing sth not having any experience of sth 〜の経験が全くない →〜したことがない ‖ *She was unused to getting such a lot of attention.* 彼女は、このように多大な注目を浴びるのは初めてだった.

*\***unusual** /ʌ̀njúːʒuəl, -ʒəl/ 形 ▶定義 1 not expected or normal 予期しない、または正常でない →異常な、まれな ‖ *It's unusual for Joe to be late.* ジョーが遅れるなんて珍しい. ⇔ usual ▶定義 2 interesting because it is different 変わっているので面白い →独特の、珍しい ‖ *What an unusual hat!* 何て変わった帽子なんだ.

**unusually** /ʌ̀njúːʒuəli, -ʒəl-/ 副 ▶定義 1 in a way that is not normal or typical of sb/sth 人・物に正常または普通でないやり方で →いつもと違って、異常に ‖ *Unusually for her, she forgot his birthday.* 彼女は、珍しく彼の誕生日を忘れていた. ⇔ usually ▶定義 2 more than is common; extremely 普通以上に；極めて →並外れて、著しく

**unveil** /ʌ̀nvéɪl/ 動 他 ▶定義 to show sth new to the public for the first time 新しい〜を初めて公開する →〜のベールを取る、〜を初公開する ‖ *The President unveiled a memorial to those who died in the war.* 大統領はその戦争で亡くなった人々の記念碑の除幕を行った.

**unwanted** /ʌ̀nwɔ́(ː)ntəd, -wɑ́nt-/ 形 ▶定義 not wanted 望まれない →不必要な、余計な ‖ *an unwanted gift* 不必要な贈答品

**unwarranted** /ʌ̀nwɔ́(ː)rəntəd, -wɑ́r-/ 形 ▶定義 that is not deserved or for which there is no good reason 当然と見なされない、または正当な理由のない →不当な ‖ *unwarranted criticism* 不当な批判

**unwell** /ʌ̀nwél/ 形 (名詞の前は不可) ▶定義 ill; sick 病気の；気分が悪い →具合が悪い ‖ *to feel unwell* 気分が優れない

**unwieldy** /ʌ̀nwíːldi/ 形 ▶定義 difficult to move or carry because it is too big, heavy, etc 大きすぎる、重すぎるなどのため、動かしたり運んだりしにくい →手に負えない

**unwilling** /ʌ̀nwílɪŋ/ 形 ▶定義 not wanting to do sth but often forced to do it by other people 〜をやりたくないのに、しばしば他人から強制される →気の進まない、嫌々ながらの ⇔ willing

**unwind** /ʌ̀nwáɪnd/ 動 (過, 過分 **unwound** /-wáʊnd/) ▶定義 1 自 他 if you unwind sth or if sth unwinds, it comes away from sth that it had been put round それが巻き付けられている物から解ける →ほどく、ほどける ‖ *The bandage had unwound.* 包帯が解けた. ▶定義 2 自 略式 to relax, especially after working hard →特に一生懸命働いた後でくつろぐ ‖ *After a busy day, it takes me a while to unwind.* 忙しい1日を終えた後は、緊張が解けるまでに少し時間がかかる. ☞参 wind³

**unwise** /ʌ̀nwáɪz/ 形 ▶定義 showing a lack of good judgement; foolish 正しい判断ができないことを示す；愚かな →浅はかな ‖ *It would be unwise to tell anyone about our plan yet.* 私たちの計画について人に話すのはまだ得策ではなかろう. ⇔ wise — **unwisely** 副 →愚かにも、浅はかにも

**unwitting** /ʌ̀nwítɪŋ/ 形 ▶定義 not realizing sth; not intending to do sth 何かに気付かない；何かを行う意志がない →知らず知らずの、身に覚えのない ‖ *an unwitting accomplice to the crime* その犯罪に知らず知らず加担してしまった共犯者 — **unwittingly** 副 →意識せずに、知らず知らずに

**unwrap** /ʌ̀nrǽp/ 動 他 (**unwrapping**; **unreapped**) ▶定義 to take off the paper, etc that covers or protects sth 〜を覆うまたは保護する紙などを取り除く →(包み)を開ける

**unzip** /ʌ̀nzíp/ 動 自 他 (**unzipping**; **unzipped**) ▶定義 if a bag, piece of clothing, etc unzips, or you unzip it, you open it by pulling on the device that fastens the opening (the zip) 開口部を閉じている装置(チャック)を引っ張ることにより開ける →(ジッパー)が開く、〜のジッパー

を開ける ⇔ **zip (up)**

\***up** /ʌp/ 前副

➤ 多くの動詞を伴った特別な用法, 例えば pick sth up については, 動詞の見出し語を参照のこと.

▶定義 **1** at or to a high or higher level or position 高いまたはより高い水準または場所に[へ]→**上へ, 上方へ** ‖ The monkey **climbed up** the tree. 猿が木の上に登った. I carried her suitcase up to the third floor. 私は彼女のスーツケースを4階まで運んだ. **Put** your **hand up** if you know the answer. 答えが分かる人は手を上げなさい. I walked up the hill. 私は丘を歩いて登った. ▶定義 **2** in or into a vertical position 垂直の姿勢で[に]→**直立して** ‖ **Stand up**, please. 立ってください. Is he up (= out of bed) yet? 彼は起きましたか(= ベッドから出ましたか). ▶定義 **3** used for showing an increase in sth 何かが増加したことを示すのに用いて→**高まって, 増して** ‖ Prices have **gone up**. 物価は上昇した. Turn the volume up. 音量を上げなさい. ▶定義 **4** used with verbs of closing or covering 閉じるまたは覆う意味の動詞と用いて→**閉じた・固定した状態に** ‖ **Do up** your coat. It's cold. コートのボタンを掛けなさい. 寒いですよ. She tied the parcel up with string. 彼女は小包をひもでしっかりと縛った. I found some wood to **cover up** the hole. 私はその穴をきっちりふさぐための木切れを見つけた. ▶定義 **5** to the place where sb/sth is 人・物がいる・ある場所に→**〜の方まで, 〜に向かって** ‖ She ran up to her mother and kissed her. 彼女は母親に走り寄ってキスした. A car drove up and two men got out. 車が近付いてきて, 2人の男が降りた. ▶定義 **6** coming or being put together 一緒になる, または一緒にされる→**合計して, 寄せ集めて** ‖ The teacher collected up our exam papers. 先生は私たちの答案用紙を集めた. Asif and Joe teamed up in the doubles competition. アシフとジョーはダブルスの試合でチームを組んだ. ▶定義 **7** (used about a period of time) finished (ある期間について)終了した→**時間が尽きて, 閉会で** ‖ Stop writing. Your time's up. 書くのをやめなさい. 時間切れです. ▶定義 **8** into pieces→**ばらばらに** ‖ We chopped the old table up and used it for firewood. 私たちは古いテーブルをおのでばらばらに切って薪として使った. She **tore up** the letter and threw it away. 彼女は手紙を細かく破いて, 投げ捨てた. ▶定義 **9** used for showing that an action continues until it is completed ある行為が終わるまで続くことを示すのに用いて→**完全に, すっかり** ‖ **Eat up**, everybody, I want you to finish everything on the table. 皆さん, 全部食べてください, テーブルの上のものすべてを平らげてほしいのです. Can you help me **clean up** the kitchen? 台所の片付けを手伝ってくれますか. ▶定義 **10** in a particular direction→**特定の方向に** ‖ I live just **up the road**. 私はその道を上った所に住んでいます. **Move up** a little and let me sit down. 少し詰めて私を座らせてください. ▶定義 **11** in or to the north→**北へ** ‖ My parents have just moved **up north**. 私の両親は北の方に引っ越したばかりです. When are you going up to Scotland? いつスコットランドに行く予定ですか. ▶定義 **12** (used about computers) working; in operation→**(コンピューターについて)作動している; 機能している** ‖ Are the computers back up yet? コンピューターはもう回復していますか. ▶定義 **13** 略式 used for showing that sth is spoiled 何かが台なしになったことを示すのに用いて→**損なわれて** ‖ I really messed up when I told the interviewer I liked sleeping. 面接官に眠ることが好きだと言ってしまい, 本当に失敗だった.

成句 be up for sth ▶定義 **1** to be available to be bought or chosen 買うまたは選ぶことができる→**売りに出されて, 立候補して** ‖ That house is up for sale. その家は売りに出されている. How many candidates are up for election? 選挙には何人の人が立候補していますか. ▶定義 **2** 略式 to be enthusiastic about doing sth 何かをするのに熱中して→**意気込んで** ‖ Is anyone up for a swim? だれか一泳ぎしたい人はいますか.

be up to sb ▶定義 to be sb's responsibility 〜の責任において→**〜の責任で, 次第で** ‖ I can't take the decision. It's not up to me. 私には, 決定を下すことができない. それは私の責任ではないから.

not up to much 略式 ▶定義 not very good あまり良くない→**大したことはない** ‖ The programme wasn't up to much. その出し物は大したことはなかった.

up against sth/sb ▶定義 facing sth/sb that

## 1768 upbringing

causes problems 問題の原因になっている~に相対して➡~に直面して

**up and down** ▶定義 backwards and forwards, or rising and falling 前後の方向に，または上がったり下がったりして➡**前後に，上下に** ‖ *He was nervously walking up and down outside the interview room.* 彼は緊張して面接室の外を行ったり来たりしていた.

**up and running** ▶定義 (used about sth new) working well➡**(新しい物について) うまく作動している**

**up to sth** ▶定義1 as much/many as ~の量・数まで➡**最高~まで** ‖ *We're expecting up to 100 people at the meeting.* 私たちはその会議に100名までの出席者を予想している. ▶定義2 as far as now 今まで➡**~に至るまで** ‖ *Up to now, things have been easy.* 今までは事は簡単だった. ▶定義3 capable of sth➡**~をすることができる** ‖ *I don't feel up to cooking this evening. I'm too tired.* 私は今晩は料理をする気になれません. 疲れきってしまいました. ▶定義4 doing sth secret and perhaps bad 秘密でおそらく善からぬ~をする➡**~をしてかそうとして** ‖ *What are the children up to? Go and see.* 子供たちは何をしでかすつもりなんだろうか. 行って見てきなさい.

**what's up?** 略式 ▶定義 what's the matter?➡**どうしたのか**

**upbringing** /ˈʌpbrɪŋɪŋ/ 名 [単数扱い] ▶定義 the way a child is treated and taught how to behave by his/her parents 両親の子供の扱い方，また振る舞いの教え方➡**養育，しつけ** ‖ *a strict upbringing* 厳しいしつけ

**update** /ʌpdéɪt/ 動 他 ▶定義1 to make sth more modern ~をより近代的にする➡**~を最新式にする** ▶定義2 to put the latest information into sth; to give sb the latest information ~に最新情報を入力する; ~に最新の情報を与える➡**データを更新する** ‖ *Our database of addresses is updated regularly.* 我が社の住所データベースは定期的に更新されています. ― update /ʌpdéɪt/ 名 C ➡**最新化，最新情報，最新版** ‖ *an update on a news story (= the latest information)* 報道記事の最新版 (= 最新の情報)

**upgrade** /ʌpgréɪd, ʌpgréɪd/ 動 他 ▶定義 to change sth so that it is of a higher standard ~をより高水準になるよう変更する➡**~を格上げする** ‖ *Upgrading your computer software can be expensive.* あなたのコンピュータのソフトウェアをアップグレードするのは高くつくかもしれない. ― upgrade /ʌpgréɪd/ 名 C ➡**性能・質の向上，格上げ**

**upheaval** /ʌphíːv(ə)l/ 名 C U ▶定義 a sudden big change, especially one that causes a lot of trouble 突然の大きな変化，特に多くの問題を引き起こすもの➡**大変動，激変**

**uphill** /ʌphíl/ 形 副 ▶定義1 going towards the top of a hill 坂の一番上に向かう➡**登りの，上へ向かって** ⇔ **downhill** ▶定義2 needing a lot of effort 多大な努力を要する➡**困難な，骨の折れる** ‖ *It was an uphill struggle to find a job.* 仕事を探すのはかなりの努力を必要とした.

**uphold** /ʌphóʊld/ 動 他 (過，過分 **upheld** /-héld/) ▶定義 to support a decision, etc especially when other people are against it 特に他人が反対しているとき，決定などを支持する➡**~を擁護する**

**upholstered** /ʌphóʊlstərd/ 形 ▶定義 (used about a chair, etc) covered with a soft thick material (いすなどについて) 柔らかく厚い素材で覆われた➡**布・革張りをした**

**upholstery** /ʌphóʊlstəri/ 名 U ▶定義 the thick soft materials used to cover chairs, car seats, etc いす，車の座席などを覆うのに使われる厚くて柔らかい素材➡**いす張り用品**

**upkeep** /ʌpkiːp/ 名 U ▶定義1 the cost or process of keeping sth in a good condition 何かを良い状態に保つための費用またはその過程➡**管理(費)，維持(費)，営繕(費)** ‖ *The landlord pays for the upkeep of the building.* 家主は建物の維持に必要な費用を支払う. ▶定義2 the cost or process of providing children or animals with what they need to live 子供または動物が生きていくのに必要な費用またはその過程➡**養育・飼育 (費用)**

**upland** /ʌplənd/ 形 ▶定義 consisting of hills and mountains 丘や山から成る➡**高地の，山地の** ― upland 名 [C, 通常は複数] ➡**高地，山地**

**uplifting** /ʌplíftɪŋ/ 形 ▶定義 producing a feeling of hope and happiness 希望や喜びの気持ちがわいてくる➡**精神的・感情的高揚を招く，意気を盛んにする** ‖ *an uplifting speech* 精神を高揚させる演説

**upon** /əpɔ́(ː)n, əpán/ 前 正式 = ON

**＊upper** /ʌ́pər/ 形 ▶定義 in a higher position than sth else; situated above sth ほかの物よりも高い位置にある; 何かの真上に位置する→上(位)の ‖ *He had a cut on his upper lip.* 彼は上唇に切り傷を負った. ⇔ **lower**

成句 get, have, etc the upper hand ▶定義 to get into a stronger position than another person; to gain control over sb ほかの人よりも強い地位に就く; 人の支配権を掌握する→優勢となる

**upper case** 名 Ⓤ ▶定義 letters that are written or printed in their large form; capital letters→大文字で書かれたまたは印刷された文字; 大文字 ‖ *'BBC' is written in upper case.* 'BBC' は大文字で書かれている. ⇔ **lower case**

**uppermost** /ʌ́pərmòust/ 形 ▶定義 in the highest or most important position 最高のまたは最重要な位置にある→最高の, 最上の, 最も有力な ‖ *Concern for her family was **uppermost in her mind**.* 家族に対する心配が彼女の心の中で最も重要な位置を占めていました.

**＊upright** /ʌ́praɪt, -/ 形副 ▶定義1 in or into a vertical position 垂直の姿勢で[に]→直立した ‖ *I was so tired I could hardly stay upright.* 私はあまりにも疲れきって, まっすぐに立っていられないほどだった. ☛類 **erect** ▶定義2 honest and responsible→正直で責任感の強い

成句 bolt upright = **BOLT**³

**uprising** /ʌ́praɪzɪŋ/ 名 Ⓒ ▶定義 a situation in which a group of people start to fight against the people in power in their country 人々が集団を成して自国の権力者たちと戦いを始める状態→反乱, 暴動

**uproar** /ʌ́prɔːr/ 名 [Ⓤ, 単数扱い] ▶定義 a lot of noisy, confusion, anger, etc; an angry discussion about sth たくさんの雑音, 混乱, 怒りなど; 何かに関する論争→大騒ぎ, 騒動 ‖ *The meeting ended **in uproar**.* 会議は大騒ぎのうちに幕を閉じた.

**uproot** /ʌprúːt/ 動 他 ▶定義 to pull up a plant by the roots→(植物)を根こそぎ抜く ‖ *Strong winds had uprooted the tree.* 強風のため, 木は根こそぎにやられた.

**ups** /ʌps/ 名

成句 ups and downs ▶定義 both good times and bad times いい時も悪い時も→浮き沈み, 栄枯盛衰 ‖ *We're happy together but we've had our ups and downs.* 私たちは一緒になって幸せだが, いい時も悪い時も経験した.

# upshot 1769

**＊upset**¹ /ʌpsét/ 動 他 (現分 **upsetting**; 過, 過分 **upset**) ▶定義1 to make sb worry or feel unhappy ～を心配させるまた不安を感じさせる→～の心を乱す, 狼狽(ろうばい)させる, かき乱す ‖ *The pictures of starving children upset her.* 餓えている子供たちの写真を見て, 彼女は悲しんだ. ▶定義2 to make sth go wrong ～をうまくいかなくする→～を駄目にする, 狂わす ‖ *to upset someone's plans* 人の計画を狂わす ▶定義3 to knock sth over ～をひっくり返す→～を転覆させる, こぼす, 散乱させる ‖ *I upset a cup of tea all over the tablecloth.* 私はカップに入ったお茶をテーブルクロス一面にひっくり返してしまった. ▶定義4 to make sb ill in the stomach ～の胃を気持ち悪くさせる→～をむかむかさせる

**＊upset**² /ʌpsét/ 形 ▶定義1 worried and unhappy 心配で不安な→心を乱した, 狼狽(ろうばい)した ‖ *She was looking very upset about something.* 彼女は, 何かをとても悩んでいるようだった. ▶定義2 slightly ill 少し具合が悪い→体調が狂った ‖ *I've got **an upset stomach**.* 私は胃の調子が悪い.

▶注意. この形容詞は文中で, 名詞の前では /ʌ́pset/ と発音され, それ以外の位置に来たときは /ʌpsét/ と発音される.

**upset**³ /ʌ́psèt/ 名 ▶定義1 Ⓒ Ⓤ a situation in which there are unexpected problems or difficulties 予期しない問題または困難がある状況→混乱, 乱れ, 意外な結果 ‖ *The company survived the recent upset in share prices.* その会社は, 最近の株価の混乱を切り抜けた. ▶定義2 Ⓒ a slight illness in your stomach 胃の調子がわずかに悪いこと→不調 ‖ *a stomach upset* 胃の不調 ▶定義3 Ⓒ Ⓤ a situation that causes worry and sadness 心配や悲しみを引き起こす状況→狼狽(ろうばい), 動転 ‖ *She's had a few upsets recently.* 彼女は最近ショックな出来事が 2, 3 あった. *It had been the cause of much emotional upset.* その事は非常に気がもめる原因だった.

**upshot** /ʌ́pʃɑ̀t/ 名 [単数扱い] ▶定義 the upshot (of sth) the final result, especially of a conversation or an event 特に会話または出来事の最終結果→結末, 結論

**＊upside down** /ʌpsaɪd dáʊn/ 副 ▶定義1 with the top part turned to the bottom 一番上の部分が底に来て→逆さまに, あべこべに ‖ *You're holding the picture upside down.* あなたは絵を逆さまに持っていますよ. ☞ **back**のさし絵 ▶定義2 略式 in or into a very untidy state 非常に乱雑な状態に[へ]→混乱して, ごたごたと ‖ *I had to* ***turn the house upside down*** *looking for my keys.* 私はかぎを探すのに家中をひっかき回さなければならなかった.

**＊upstairs** /ʌpstéərz/ 副 ▶定義 to or on a higher floor of a building 建物の上の階へ[で]→階上へ[で] ‖ *to go upstairs* 上の階へ行く *She's sleeping upstairs.* 彼女は上の階で眠っている. ⇔ **downstairs** — upstairs /ʌpstéərz/ 形 →階上の ‖ *an upstairs window* 上の階の窓 — the upstairs 名 略式 →上の階 ‖ *We're going to paint the upstairs.* 私たちは上の階の部屋にペンキを塗るつもりだ.

**upstream** /ʌpstríːm/ 副形 ▶定義 in the direction that a river flows from 川が流れてくる方向→上流へ[で・の] ‖ *He found it hard work swimming upstream.* 彼は川上へ向かって泳ぐのは大変だと分かった. ⇔ **downstream**

**upsurge** /ʌ́psɜːrdʒ/ 名 [C, 通常は単数] ▶定義 an upsurge (in sth) a sudden increase of sth 〜の突然の増加→急騰, 急増, 高揚

**uptake** /ʌ́pteɪk/ 名 成句 quick/slow on the uptake ▶定義 quick/slow to understand the meaning of sth ものの意味を理解するのが速い・遅い→理解が速い・遅い ‖ *I gave him a hint but he's slow on the uptake.* 私は彼にヒントを与えたが, 彼はのみ込みが遅い.

**uptight** /ʌptáɪt, ˋ/ 形 略式 ▶定義 nervous and not relaxed 神経質で, くつろいでいない→緊張した, 怒った ‖ *He gets uptight before an exam.* 彼は, 試験の前は緊張する.

**＊up-to-date** 形 ▶定義1 modern 現代的な→時代に後れない, 当世風の ▶定義2 having the most recent information 最新の情報を持つ→最新(式)の

**up-to-the-minute** 形 ▶定義 having the most recent information possible できる限り最新の情報を持つ→極めて最新の

**upturn** /ʌ́ptɜːrn/ 名 C ▶定義 an upturn (in sth) an improvement in sth 〜の改善→向上, 好転 ‖ *an upturn in support for the government* 政府の支持率上昇 ⇔ **downturn**

**upturned** /ʌptɜ́ːrnd/ 形 ▶定義1 pointing upwards→先が上を向いた ‖ *an upturned nose* 天井を向いた鼻 ▶定義2 turned upside down 上下逆さになった→ひっくり返った

**＊upward** /ʌ́pwərd/ 形 ▶定義 moving or directed towards a higher place より高い場所に向かって動いている, またはそこへ向けられた→上向きの, 上位の ‖ *an upward trend in exports (= an increase)* 輸出の上向き傾向(= 増加) ⇔ **downward** — upward (または upwards /-wərdz/) 副 →上の方へ, 上向きに, 上位へ

**upwards of** 前 ▶定義 more than the number mentioned 示された数より多くの→〜を超える ‖ *They've invited upwards of a hundred guests.* 彼らは100名を超える客を招待した.

**uranium** /jʊəréɪniəm/ 名 U (元素記号 U) ▶定義 a metal that can be used to produce nuclear energy 核エネルギーを生み出すのに使用可能な金属→ウラニウム, ウラン ‖ *Uranium is highly radioactive.* ウラニウムは放射性が高い.

**Uranus** /júərənəs, jʊəréɪnəs/ 名 [単数扱い] ▶定義 the planet that is seventh in order from the sun 太陽から7番目の惑星→天王星

**＊urban** /ɜ́ːrbən/ 形 ▶定義 connected with a town or city 街または都市に関連した→都市の, 都会の ‖ *urban development* 都市開発 ☞参 **rural**

**＊urge**¹ /ɜːrdʒ/ 動 他 ▶定義1 urge sb (to do sth); urge sth to advise or try hard to persuade sb to do sth 〜に…をするよう助言する, または強く説得してそうさせようとする→〜するよう説得する, 催促する, 強く迫る ‖ *I urged him to fight the decision.* 私は彼にその決定に立ち向かうよう説得した. *Drivers are urged to take care on icy roads.* 運転者は凍結した道路では注意していただきたい. *Police urge caution on the icy roads.* 警察は, 道路が凍結しているので注意するよう警告している. ▶定義2 to force sb/sth to go in a certain direction 〜を強制してある方向に行かせる→〜をせき立てる, 駆り立てる, 推進する ‖ *He urged his horse over the fence.* 彼は柵(さく)を越えるよう馬を駆り立てた.

**句動詞 urge sb on** ▶定義 to encourage sb 〜を励ます→〜を力づける ‖ *The captain urged his team on.* キャプテンはチームを激励した.

**urge²** /ɜːrdʒ/ 名 C ▶定義 a strong need or desire 強い必要性または欲望→欲求,衝動 ‖ *sexual/creative urges* 性的欲望・創造への衝動

**\*urgent** /ˈɜːrdʒ(ə)nt/ 形 ▶定義 needing immediate attention 即座の注意を要する→急を要する,緊急の ‖ *an urgent message* 緊急連絡 — **urgency** /-dʒ(ə)nsi/ 名 U→緊急(性),切迫 ‖ *a matter of the greatest urgency* 最も急を要する問題 — **urgently** 副→差し迫って,緊急に ‖ *I must see you urgently.* あなたに緊急に会わなければならない.

**urinate** /ˈjʊərəneɪt/ 動 自 正式 ▶定義 to pass urine from the body 身体から尿を排出する→排尿する

**urine** /ˈjʊərən/ 名 U ▶定義 the yellowish liquid that is passed from your body when you go to the toilet トイレに行ったとき身体から排出される黄色っぽい液体→尿,小便

**urn** /ɜːrn/ 名 C ▶定義1 a special container, used especially to hold the powder (ashes) that is left when a dead person has been burnt (cremated) 特に亡くなった人が焼かれて(火葬),残った粉(灰)を入れておくのに使われる特別な容器→骨つぼ ▶定義2 a large metal container used for making a large quantity of tea or coffee and for keeping it hot 大きな金属製の容器で,多量の紅茶またはコーヒーを沸かし,保温するのに使われる→コーヒー・紅茶沸かし器

**US** /jùː és/ 略 the United States (of America)→(アメリカ)合衆国

**\*us** /əs, s, 強形 ʌs/ 代(動詞の目的語として,またはbe動詞の後に用いて) ▶定義 me and another person or other people; me and you 自分とほかの人または人々; 自分とあなた→私たちを[に],我々を[に] ‖ *Come with us.* 私たちに付いてきなさい. *Leave us alone.* 私たちをほっておいてください. *Will you write to us?* 私たちに手紙をくれますか.

**USA** /jùː es éɪ/ 略 the United States of America→アメリカ合衆国

**usable** /ˈjuːzəb(ə)l/ 形 ▶定義 that can be used 使うことができる→使用できる,使用に適した

**usage** /ˈjuːsɪdʒ, -zɪdʒ/ 名 ▶定義1 U the way that sth is used; the amount that sth is used ものの使われ方; ものが使われる量→使い方,扱い(方),使用量 ▶定義2 C U the way that words are normally used in a language ある言語における単語の標準的使われ方→語法,慣用法 ‖ *a guide to English grammar and usage* 英語文法および語法の手引き

**\*use¹** /juːz/ 動 他 (現分 **using**; 過,過分 **used** /juːzd/) ▶定義1 use sth (as/for sth); use sth (to do sth) to do sth with a machine, an object, a method, etc for a particular purpose 特定の目的のために機械,物,方法などで何かを行う→〜を(…として・…のために・…するために)使う,用いる,使用する,利用する ‖ *Could I use your phone?* 電話を使わせていただけますか. *The building was used as a shelter for homeless people.* その建物は,ホームレスの人々の避難場所として使われていた. *A gun is used for shooting with.* 銃は射撃に使われる. *What's this used for?* これは何に使うものですか. *We used the money to buy a house.* 私たちは,家を購入するのにそのお金を使った. *Use your imagination!* 想像力を働かせなさい. *That's a word I never use.* それは,私が決して使わない言葉だ. ▶定義2 to need or to take sth 〜を必要とする,または使う→〜を消費する ‖ *Don't use all the milk.* ミルクを使いきってはいけません. ▶定義3 to treat sb/sth in an unfair way in order to get sth that you want 自分が欲しいものを手に入れるために〜を不公平に扱う→〜を悪用する,利用する

**句動詞 use sth up** ▶定義 to use sth until no more is left 〜がなくなるまで使う→〜を使い尽くす,使いきる

**\*use²** /juːs/ 名 ▶定義1 U the action of using sth or of being used ものを使う行為または使われる行為→使用,利用 ‖ *The use of computers is now widespread.* コンピューターの使用が現在広がっている. *She kept the money for use in an emergency.* 彼女はそのお金を万一に備えて取っておいた. ▶定義2 C U the purpose for which sth is used ものが使われる目的→用途,使用目的 ‖ *This machine has many uses.* この機械にはたくさんの用途がある. ▶定義3 U the ability or permission to use sth ものを使う能力または許可→機能 ‖ *He lost the use of his*

## 1772 used

hand after the accident. 彼は事故の後, 手が使えなくなった. *She offered them the use of her car.* 彼女は彼らに自分の車を使ってもよいと申し出た. ▶定義4 **❶**the advantage of sth; how useful sth is ものの利点; ものがいかに役立つか →**効用, 有用性** ∥ *It's no use studying for an exam at the last minute.* ぎりぎりになって試験勉強をしても無駄だ. *What's the use of trying?* やってみることが何の役に立つのですか. *Will this jumper be of use to you or should I get rid of it?* このセーターはあなたの役に立つでしょうか, それとももう処分すべきですか.

成句 **come into/go out of use** ▶定義 to start/stop being used regularly or by a lot of people 通常にまたは大勢の人に使われ始める・なくなる →**使われ始める, すたれる** ∥ *E-mail came into widespread use in the 1990s.* 1990年代に電子メールが使われ始めた.

**make use of sth/sb** ▶定義 to use sth/sb in a way that will give you an advantage 〜を自分に有利になるように使う →**〜を利用する**

*****used** /juːzd/ 形 ▶定義1 that has had another owner before 以前別の所有者がいた →**中古の, 使用済みの** ∥ *a garage selling used cars* 中古車を販売する自動車整備場 ☛ 同じ意味を持つ別の単語は second-hand. ▶定義2 /juːs(t)/ **used to sth/to doing sth** familiar with sth; accustomed to sth 〜に通じている; 〜に慣れている ∥ *He's used to the heat.* 彼はその暑さには慣れている. *I'll never get used to getting up so early.* 私は, こんなに早く起きるのには決して慣れないだろう.

*****used to** /juːs(t) tə, (母音の前) -tu, (文または節の終わり) -tuː/ 法助動詞 ▶定義 for talking about sth that happened often or continuously in the past or about a situation which existed in the past 過去に頻繁にまたは継続的に起きた事柄, または過去に存在した状況について言い表すのに用いる →**(以前は)よく〜したものだ, (かつては)〜だった** ∥ *She used to live with her parents (= but she doesn't now).* 彼女は, かつては両親と暮らしていた(= しかし, 今は暮らしていない). *You used to live in Glasgow, didn't you?* あなたは, 以前グラスゴーに住んでいたことがありますよね. *Did you use to smoke?* あなたは, 以前は喫煙していましたか. *He didn't use to speak to me.* 彼は, 以前は私と口をきかなかったものだ.

▶ use to を否定形や疑問文にするには通常 did を用いる: *I didn't use to like jazz.* (私は, 昔ジャズが好きではなかった.) *Did she use to be in your class?* (彼女は, 以前あなたのクラスにいましたか.) 過去の事のみを述べる「used to + 不定詞」と, 過去・現在または未来の事を述べられる「be used to (doing) sth」を混同しないよう注意. 比較: *I used to live on my own (= but now I don't).* (私は以前は1人で住んでいた(= だが, 今はそうではない).) *I'm used to living on my own (= I am accustomed to it).* (私は1人で住むのに慣れている.)

*****useful** /júːsfəl/ 形 ▶定義 having some practical use; helpful 何らかの実際的用途を持つ; 役に立つ →**有益な** ∥ *a useful tool* 便利な道具 *useful advice* 役立つ助言 — **usefully** /-fəli/ 副 →**有益に** — **usefulness** 名 **❶** →**有益性**

成句 **come in useful** ▶定義 to be of practical help in a certain situation ある状況において実際に役立つ →**役立つようになる** ∥ *Don't throw that box away - it might come in useful for something.* その箱を捨てるんじゃない - 何かの役に立つかもしれない.

*****useless** /júːsləs/ 形 ▶定義1 that does not work well, that does not achieve anything うまく動かない, 何も成し遂げることができない →**無用な, 無益な, 無駄な** ∥ *This new machine is useless.* この新しい機械は使い物にならない. *It's useless complaining/to complain - you won't get your money back.* 文句を言っても無駄です - お金は戻ってこないでしょう. ▶定義2 略式 **useless (at sth/at doing sth)** (used about a person) weak or not successful at sth (人について)〜が下手または うまくいかない →**役に立たない** ∥ *I'm useless at sport.* 私はスポーツは苦手です. — **uselessly** 副 →**無駄に, 無益に** — **uselessness** 名 **❶** →**無駄, 無益**

*****user** /júːzər/ 名 **❻** (しばしば複合語で) ▶定義 a person who uses a service, machine, place, etc サービス, 機械, 場所などを使う人 →**使用者, 利用者** ∥ *users of public transport* 公共輸送機関の利用者 *drug users* 麻薬使用者

**user-friendly** 形 ▶定義 (used about computers, books, machines, etc) easy to understand and use（コンピューター，本，機械などについて）理解しやすく使いやすい➡**分かりやすい，易しい**

**usher**[1] /ʌ́ʃər/ 名 ◉ ▶定義 a person who shows people to their seats in a theatre, church, etc 劇場，教会などにおいて人々を座席に案内する人➡**案内係**

**usher**[2] /ʌ́ʃər/ 動 他 ▶定義 to take or show sb where to go 〜を行くべき場所へ連れていく，またはその場所を指し示す➡**〜を案内する，誘導する** ‖ *I was ushered into an office.* 私は事務所に案内された．

句動詞 usher sth in ▶定義 to be the beginning of sth new or to make sth new begin 新しい〜の先駆けとなる，または新しい〜を始める➡**〜の先駆けとなる，到来を告げる** ‖ *The agreement ushered in a new period of peace for the two countries.* その条約は，2か国間に新しい平和の時代の到来を告げた．

\***usual** /júːʒuəl, -ʒəl-/ 形 ▶定義 usual (for sb/sth) (to do sth) happening or used most often 最も頻繁に起こる，または使われている➡**いつもの，通常の** ‖ *It's usual for her to work at weekends.* 彼女が週末働くのは，よくあることだ．*He got home later than usual.* 彼はいつもより遅く帰宅した．*I sat in my usual seat.* 私はいつもの自分の席に座った．⇔ **unusual**

成句 as usual ▶定義 in the way that has often happened before これまで頻繁に起きたやり方で➡**いつものように，例によって** ‖ *Here's Dylan, late as usual!* ほらディランが来た，いつものように遅刻してね．

**usually** /júːʒuəli, -ʒəl-/ 副 ▶定義 in the way that is usual; most often 通常のやり方で；最も頻繁に➡**通常，いつもは** ‖ *She's usually home by six.* 彼女は普通は6時までに家に帰っている．*Usually, we go out on Saturdays.* いつもなら私たちは土曜日に出掛ける．

**utensil** /juténsəl/ 名 ◉ ▶定義 a type of tool that is used in the home 家で使われる道具の一種➡**(日用)道具** ‖ *kitchen/cooking utensils* 台所用品・調理器具 ☛ **kitchen**のさし絵

**uterus** /júːt(ə)rəs/ 名 ◉ (複 **uteruses**; 学術用語では **uteri** /-raɪ/) 正式 ▶定義 the part of a woman or female animal where a baby develops before it is born 女性または動物の雌の器官で，産まれる前に赤子が育つ場所➡**子宮**
➤より略式な語はwomb．

**utility** /juːtíləti/ 名 (複 **utilities**) ▶定義 1 ◉ 特に 米 a service provided for the public, such as a water, gas or electricity supply 水道，ガスまたは電気のように，公共に供給されるサービス➡**公共サービス** ‖ *the administration of public utilities* 公共事業の運営 ▶定義 2 Ⓤ 正式 the quality of being useful 役立つ資質➡**有用性，有益性，実用性** ▶定義 3 ◉ (computing) a program or part of a program that does a particular task（コンピューター）特定のタスクを実行するプログラムまたはプログラムの一部➡**ユーティリティープログラム** ‖ *a utility program* ユーティリティープログラム（ユーザーの処理の支援を目的とするソフトウェア）

**utility room** 名 ◉ ▶定義 a small room in some houses, often next to the kitchen, where people keep large pieces of kitchen equipment, such as a washing machine 一部の家にある小さな部屋で，台所に隣接することが多く，例えば洗濯機のような大型の台所器具を置いておく場所➡**ユーティリティールーム**

**utilize**（または **-ise**）/júːt(ə)laɪz/ 動 他 正式 ▶定義 to make use of sth 〜を利用する➡**〜を役立たせる，活用する** ‖ *to utilize natural resources* 天然資源を利用する

**utmost**[1] /ʌ́tməʊst, -məst/ 形 正式 (名詞の前だけ) ▶定義 greatest➡**最大の，最高の** ‖ *a message of the utmost importance* 最重要な連絡事項

**utmost**[2] /ʌ́tməʊst, -məst/ 名 [単数扱い] ▶定義 the greatest amount possible 可能な限り最大の量➡**最大限，極限** ‖ *Resources have been exploited to the utmost.* 資源は最大限に開発されてきた．*I will do my utmost (= try as hard as possible) to help.* 私は最善を尽くして（= できるだけ頑張って）お手伝いします．

**Utopia**（または **utopia**）/juːtóʊpiə, juː-/ 名 ◉ Ⓤ ▶定義 a place or state that exists only in the imagination, where everything is perfect 想像上でのみ存在する場所または国家で，そこではすべてが完璧である➡**ユートピア，理想郷** ― **Utopian**（または **utopian**）/-pi(ə)n/ 形➡**理想郷の，空想的な，夢物語の**

**utter**[1] /ʌ́tər/ 形 (名詞の前だけ) ▶定義 complete;

total 完全な; 全面的な →**全くの, 徹底的な** ‖ He felt an utter fool. 彼は(自分が)よくよくのばかだと気付いた. — utterly 副 →**全く, すっかり, 完全に** ‖ It's utterly impossible. それは全くあり得ないことだ.

**utter²** /ʌ́tər/ 動他 ▶定義 to say sth or make a sound with your voice 〜を言う, または声を発する→**〜を言葉で述べる, 〜を発する, 口に出す** ‖ She did not utter a word (= she did not say anything) in the meeting. 彼女は会議で一言も発言しなかった(= 彼女は何も言わなかった). — utterance /ʌ́t(ə)rəns/ 名 C 正式 →**発言**

**U-turn** /júː tə̀ːrn/ 名 C ▶定義1 a type of movement where a car, etc turns round so that it goes back in the direction it came from 車などが来た方向に戻るためにぐるっと向きを変える動きの一種→**Uターン** ▶定義2 略式 a sudden change from one plan or policy to a completely different or opposite one 1つの計画または政策から全く異なったまたは正反対のものに突然変わること→**180度の転換, 方向転換** ☛参 about turn

# V v

**V, v¹** /víː/ 名 C (複 V's; v's) ▶定義1 the twenty-second letter of the English alphabet 英語アルファベットの第22文字→**v(V)が表す音, v(V)の文字, v(V)の字形のもの** ‖ 'Velvet' begins with (a) 'V'. VelvetはVで始まる. ▶定義2 the shape of a V Vの形→**V字型のもの** ‖ a V-neck sweater Vネックのセーター

**v²** 略 ▶定義1 (または **vs**) versus; against 〜に対して→**〜対…** ‖ Liverpool vs Everton リバプール対エヴァートン ▶定義2 V volt(s)→**ボルト** ‖ a 9V battery 9ボルトのバッテリー ▶定義3 verse→**韻文, 詩節** ▶定義4 略式 very→**とても** ‖ v good 非常に良い

**vacancy** /véɪk(ə)nsi/ 名 C (複 vacancies) ▶定義1 a vacancy (for sb/sth) a job that is available for sb to do だれかが行うために空いている仕事→**空席, 欠員** ‖ We have a vacancy for a secretary in our office. 私たちの事務所で秘書に1人

欠員がある. ▶定義2 a room in a hotel, etc that is available ホテルなどの部屋で, 利用可能なもの→**空室** ‖ The sign outside the hotel said 'No Vacancies'. ホテルの外の掲示には, 「満室」とあった.

**★vacant** /véɪk(ə)nt/ 形 ▶定義1 (used about a house, hotel room, seat, etc) not being used; empty (家, ホテルの部屋, 席などについて)→**使用されていない; 空いている** ▶定義2 (used about a job in a company, etc) that is available for sb to take (会社などでの仕事について) 人が就くことが可能な→**空席の, 欠員未補充の** ‖ the 'Situations Vacant' page (= the page of a British newspaper where jobs are advertised) 「求人」のページ(= 英国の新聞で求人広告を載せているページ) ▶定義3 showing no sign of intelligence or understanding 知力や理解力の気配が見られない→**(頭が)空っぽな, (表情が)うつろな** ‖ a vacant expression うつろな表情 — vacantly 副 →**うつろに, ぼんやりと** ‖ She stared at him vacantly. 彼女はうつろな表情で彼をじっと見詰めた.

**vacate** /véɪkèɪt, -́-; vəkéɪt/ 動他 正式 ▶定義 to leave a building, a seat, a job, etc so that it is available for sb else 建物, 席または職などを去り, ほかの人が利用できるようにする→**〜を明け渡す, 退く**

**vacation** /vəkéɪʃ(ə)n, veɪ-/ 名 ▶定義1 C 英 any of the periods of time when universities or courts of law are closed 大学または法廷が閉じられている期間→**(定期)休暇, 休廷期** ‖ the Christmas/Easter vacation クリスマス休暇・イースター休暇 ▶定義2 C U 米 (a) holiday→**休暇** ‖ The boss is on vacation. 上司は休暇中です. ☛参 holidayの注

**vaccinate** /vǽksənèɪt/ 動他 ▶定義 vaccinate sb (against sth)(しばしば受動態で)to protect a person or an animal against a disease by giving him/her/it a mild form of the disease with a needle which is put under the skin (an injection) 人間または動物を病気から守るために, 病原体を弱くしたものを皮膚の下に入れた針で人間または動物に与える(注射する)→**〜に予防接種をする** ‖ Were you vaccinated against measles as a child? 子供の時に麻疹(はしか)の予防接種をしましたか. ☛ immunizeおよびinoculateも同様の意味を持つ. — vaccination

/vǽksənéɪʃ(ə)n/ 名 ❻ Ⓤ →予防接種

**vaccine** /vǽksi:n, ⌃; vækśi:n, -sɪn/ 名 ❻
▶定義 a mild form of a disease that is put into a person or an animal's blood using a needle (an injection) in order to protect the body against that disease 病原体を弱くしたもので、その病気から身体を守るために針を使って（注射）人間または動物の血液に入れられる →ワクチン

**vacuum**[1] /vǽkjum, -kjəm, -kjʊəm/ 名 ❻
▶定義 1 a space that is completely empty of all substances, including air or other gases 空気またはほかの気体も含めて、あらゆる物質が全く入っていない空間 →真空, 真空状態 ‖ *vacuum-packed foods* (= *in a pack from which most of the air has been removed*) 真空パックの食品（= 空気がほとんど取り去られたパックに入っている）▶定義 2 [通常は単数] a situation from which sth is missing or lacking 何かが欠けているまたは不足している状態 →空虚, 空白

▶定義 3 略式 =VACUUM CLEANER

**vacuum**[2] /vǽkjum, -kjəm, -kjʊəm/ 動 ⊕ ❻
▶定義 to clean sth using a vacuum cleaner 電気掃除機を使って～を掃除する →(～に)電気掃除機をかける

vacuum cleaner

**vacuum cleaner**（または 略式 **vacuum**）名 ❻
▶定義 an electric machine that cleans carpets, etc by sucking up dirt ごみを吸い込むことによってじゅうたんなどを掃除する電気機械 →電気掃除機 ☛参 **cleaner**

**vagina** /vədʒáɪnə/ 名 ❻ ▶定義 the passage in the body of a woman or female animal that connects the outer sex organs to the part where a baby grows (womb) 女性または動物の雌の体内にある通路の部分で、外性器と赤ん坊が生育する場所（子宮）をつなぐ所 →膣（ちつ）

**vagrant** /véɪɡrənt/ 名 ❻ ▶定義 a person who has no home and no job, especially one who asks people for money 家も仕事もない人で、特に人々にお金を請う人 →浮浪者, 物ごい

**vague** /véɪɡ/ 形 ▶定義 1 not clear or definite 明瞭（めいりょう）でないまたは明確でない →ぼんやりした, はっきりしない ‖ *He was very vague about how much money he'd spent.* 彼は自分がどのくらいお金を使ったのか、全くあいまいだった. *a vague shape in the distance* 遠くのぼんやりとした形 ▶定義 2 (used about a person) not thinking or understanding clearly（人について）明確に考えていないまたは理解していない →あいまいな, 漠然とした ‖ *She looked vague when I tried to explain.* 私が説明しようとした時, 彼女は理解していないようだった. — **vagueness** 名 Ⓤ →あいまいさ, 漠然

**vaguely** /véɪɡli/ 副 ▶定義 1 in a way that is not clear; slightly 明瞭（めいりょう）でないやり方で; わずかに →漠然と; 少し ‖ *Her name is vaguely familiar.* 彼女の名前は何となく聞き覚えがある. ▶定義 2 without thinking about what is happening 起こっている事について考えることなく →上の空で ‖ *He smiled vaguely and walked away.* 彼は上の空ではほえみ、そして歩き去った.

***vain** /véɪn/ 形 ▶定義 1 useless; failing to produce the result you want 無益な; 願っていた結果を生み出せない →無駄な, 実りのない ‖ *She turned away in a vain attempt to hide her tears.* 彼女は涙を見せまいとして顔を背けたが、無駄だった. ▶定義 2 (used about a person) too proud of your own appearance, abilities, etc（人について）自分の容貌（ようぼう）・能力などについて自信過剰な →うぬぼれた, 虚栄心の強い ‖ *He's so vain - he looks in every mirror he passes.* 彼はとてもうぬぼれが強い ― 通り過ぎる鏡を全部見る. — **vainly** 副 →無駄に, むなしく ☛名 **vanity**

成句 **in vain** ▶定義 without success 成功せずに →無駄に, むなしく, 無意味に ‖ *The firemen tried in vain to put out the fire.* 消防士は火を消そうとしたが、無駄だった.

**valentine** /vǽləntàɪn/ 名 ❻ ▶定義 1（または **valentine card**）a card that you send, usually without putting your name on it, to sb you love 愛する人に送るカードで、通常は名前を記さないもの →バレンタインカード

▶このカードを St Valentine's Day（聖バレンタインデー）（2月14日）に送る習慣がある.

▶定義 2 the person you send this card to →このカードを送る相手

## 1776 valiant

**▶社会・文化**

バレンタインデー

ヨーロッパでは古くから2月14日から小鳥が発情すると言われ,これが愛の告白日となり,キリスト教殉教者 St. Valentine を記念する日と結び付いたのが起源とされます.日本では女性が男性にチョコレートを渡して愛を告白する日になっていますが,欧米では男性からも女性にプレゼントやカードを贈ることが普通に行われます.

日本では,プレゼントをもらった男性が1か月後にお礼をするホワイトデーがありますが,これも比較的最近始まった日本独自の習慣です.

**valiant** /vǽljənt/ 形 正式 ▶定義 full of courage and not afraid 勇気にあふれ,恐れていない→**勇猛果敢な,断固とした** — **valiantly** 副 →勇敢に,雄々しく

★**valid** /vǽləd/ 形 ▶定義1 valid (for sth) that is legally or officially acceptable 法律的または公式に受け入れられる→**有効な,法的効力のある** ‖ *This passport is valid for one year only.* このパスポートは,1年間に限り有効だ. ▶定義2 based on what is logical or true; acceptable 論理的な事または本当の事に基づいた;受け入れられる→**正当な,妥当な** ‖ *I could raise no valid objections to the plan.* 私はその計画に対して,根拠のある異議は唱えられなかった. *Jeff's making a perfectly valid point.* ジェフは,完ぺきに正当な主張を唱えている. ⇔ **invalid** — **validity** /vəlídəti/ 名 Ü→**妥当(性),有効(性)**

★**valley** /vǽli/ 名 C ▶定義 the low land between two mountains or hills, which often has a river flowing through it 2つの山または丘の間の低地で,しばしばその中を川が流れている→**谷,渓谷,流域** ☞ C8ページのさし絵

★**valuable** /vǽlj(u)əb(ə)l/ 形 ▶定義1 worth a lot of money 多額のお金に値する→**高価な** ‖ *Is this ring valuable?* この指輪は高価なものですか. ▶定義2 very useful 非常に役に立つ→**有益な** ‖ *a valuable piece of information* 有益な情報 ⇔ **valueless, worthless**. 注意. invaluable の意味は「非常に有益な」である.

**valuables** /vǽlj(u)əb(ə)lz/ 名 [複数扱い] ▶定義 the small things that you own that are worth a lot of money, such as jewellery, etc 例えば宝石などのように,小さいが高価な所有物→**貴重品** ‖ *Please put your valuables in the hotel safe.* ホテルの金庫に貴重品を入れてください.

**valuation** /væ̀ljuéɪʃ(ə)n/ 名 C ▶定義 a professional judgement about how much money sth is worth 物にいくらの値打ちがあるかについての専門家による判定→**評価,査定**

★**value**¹ /vǽljuː/ 名 ▶定義1 ❶ C the amount of money that sth is worth 何かが値する金額→**価値,値打ち** ‖ *The thieves stole goods with a total value of $10000.* 泥棒は総額1万ドルに相当する商品を盗んだ. *to go up/down in value* 価格が上がる・下がる ☞参 face value ▶定義2 ❶ Ü how much sth is worth compared with its price 物がその価格に比較してどれくらいの価値があるか→**値打ち** ‖ *The hotel was good/excellent value* (= *well worth the money it cost*). ホテルは金額に十分見合う(=かかった費用に十分値する)ものだった. *Package holidays give the best value for money.* パック旅行が値段的には最も買い得だ. ▶定義3 ❶ the importance of sth 物事の重要性→**価値** ‖ *to be of great/little/no value to sb* ~にとって,非常に価値がある・ほとんど価値がない・全く価値がない *This bracelet is of great sentimental value to me.* このブレスレットは,私にとって心情的に高い価値がある. ▶定義4 **values** [複数扱い] beliefs about what is the right and wrong way for people to behave; moral principles 人の行いについて,どのようなものが正しくどのようなものが間違っているかという信念;道徳的基準→**価値観,価値基準** ‖ *a return to traditional values* 伝統的価値観への回帰 *Young people have a different set of values and expectations.* 若者は異なった価値基準と期待を持っている.

**value**² /vǽljuː/ 動 他 (現分 **valuing**) ▶定義1 value sb/sth (as sth) to think sb/sth is very important ~が非常に重要であると考える→**~を高く評価する,~を尊重する** ‖ *Sandra has always valued her independence.* サンドラは常に自立を重んじてきた. *I really value her as a friend.* 私は彼女を友人として本当に高く評価している. ▶定義2 (通常は受動態で) value sth (at sth) to decide the amount of money that sth is worth ~にいくらの

価値があるかを決める→～を評価する,査定する ‖ *The house was valued at $150000.* 家は15万ドルと見積もられた.

**valueless** /vǽljuːləs/ 形 ▶定義 without value or use; worthless 価値や用途がない;値打ちのない→**無価値の,つまらない**⇔valuable ☞参 **invaluable**. この語は異なる意味を持つ

**valve** /vælv/ 名 ● ▶定義 a device in a pipe or tube which controls the flow of air, liquid or gas, letting it move in one direction only パイプまたは管に付いている装置で,空気,液体または気体の流れを制御して一方向にのみ通すもの→**バルブ,弁** ‖ *a radiator valve* ラジエーターのバルブ *the valve on a bicycle tyre* 自転車タイヤのバルブ ☞ S7ページのさし絵

**vampire** /vǽmpàɪər/ 名 ● ▶定義 (in horror stories) a dead person who comes out at night and drinks the blood of living people (恐怖小説の中で) 夜になると現れ,生きている人の血を吸う死人→**吸血鬼**

\***van** /væn/ 名 ● ▶定義 a road vehicle that is used for transporting things 物の輸送に使われる自動車→**バン,ワンボックス車** ☞ van(バン) は,lorry(トラック) より小さく,有蓋(ゆうがい) 車である.☞ **vehicle** のさし絵

**vandal** /vǽndl/ 名 ● ▶定義 a person who damages sb else's property intentionally and for no purpose 他人の所有物を,故意に何の目的もなく破壊する人→**破壊行為者** — **vandalism** /-dĭz(ə)m/ 名 ⓤ →(故意の)破壊,蛮行 ‖ *acts of vandalism* 破壊活動 — **vandalize**(または-ise) /vǽndlàɪz/ 動 ⓣ (通常は受動態で) →～を(故意に)破壊・損傷する ‖ *All the phone boxes in this area have been vandalized.* この地域の電話ボックスはすべて破壊された.

**vanilla** /vənílə/ 名 ⓤ ▶定義 a substance from a plant that is used for giving flavour to sweet food 甘い食べ物に風味を付けるために用いられる,植物からとれる物質の1つ→**バニラ** ‖ *vanilla ice cream* バニラアイスクリーム

\***vanish** /vǽnɪʃ/ 動 ⓘ ▶定義 1 to disappear suddenly or in a way that you cannot explain 突然に,または説明のつかない方法で姿を消す→**消失する** ‖ *When he turned round, the two men had vanished without trace.* 彼が振り返ると,2人の男は跡形もなく消えていた. ▶定義 2 to stop existing 存在しなくなる→**なくなる,絶滅する** ‖

*This species of plant is vanishing from our countryside.* この植物の種は,この国の田舎から絶滅しかかっている.

**vanity** /vǽnəti/ 名 ⓤ ▶定義 the quality of being too proud of your appearance or abilities 自分の容姿または能力に誇りを持ちすぎる性質→**うぬぼれ,虚栄心,見え** ☞ 形 **vain**

**vantage point** /vάːntɪdʒ pɔ̀ɪnt; vǽn-/ 名 ● ▶定義 a place from which you have a good view of sth 物の眺めが良い場所→**見晴らしの利く位置** ‖ (比喩) *From our modern vantage point, we can see why the Roman Empire collapsed.* 現代の観点から見ると,ローマ帝国が崩壊した理由が分かる.

**vapour** (米**vapor**) /véɪpər/ 名 ● ⓤ ▶定義 a mass of very small drops of liquid in the air, for example steam 例えば水蒸気のように,液体の非常に小さな滴が空気中に集まったもの→**蒸気,かすみ** ‖ *water vapour* 水蒸気

**variable** /véəriəb(ə)l/ 形 ▶定義 not staying the same; often changing 同じままでいない;しばしば変化する→**変わりやすい,不定な** — **variability** /vèəriəbíləti/ 名 ⓤ →**変わりやすさ,流動性**

**variant** /véəriənt/ 名 ● ▶定義 a slightly different form or type of sth 何かの形または型のわずかに違うもの→**異形体,変異**

\***variation** /vèəriéɪʃ(ə)n/ 名 ▶定義 1 ● ⓤ (a) variation (in sth) a change or difference in the amount or level of sth 何かの数量または水準の変化,または差異→**変化,変動** ‖ *There was a lot of variation in the examination results.* 試験の結果には大きな差異があった. *There may be a slight variation in price from shop to shop.* お店によって,値段に若干の違いがあるかもしれない. ▶定義 2 ● a variation (on/of sth) a thing that is slightly different from another thing in the same general group 同一の集団の中で,ほかの個体とわずかに違うもの→**異体,異形** ‖ *All her films are just variations on a basic theme.* 彼女の映画はすべて,1つの基本テーマをいろいろな形に変えたものにすぎない.

**varied** /véərid/ 形 ▶定義 having many different kinds of things or activities 多様な種類の物や活動を持っている→**変化に富んだ,種々雑多な** ‖ *I* try to make my classes as varied as possible. 私は授業をできるだけ変化に富んだものにしようと努めている.

***variety** /vərάɪəti/ 名 (複 **varieties**) ▶定義1 [単数扱い] a variety (of sth) a number of different types of the same thing 同じ物のさまざまな種類→**いろいろ(の～)** ‖ There is a **wide variety** of dishes to choose from. 幅広い種類の料理から選べる. ▶定義2 ❶the quality of not being or doing the same all the time 常に同じではないまたは同じ事をしないという性質→**変化, 多様性** ‖ There's so much variety in my new job. I do something different every day! 私の新しい仕事は, とても変化に富んでいる. 毎日何かしら違った事をしている. ▶定義3 ❸a variety (of sth) a type of sth (～の) 種類→**品種, 変種** ‖ a new variety of apple called 'Perfection' Perfectionと名付けられたリンゴの新種

***various** /véəriəs/ 形 ▶定義 several different いくつかの異なった→**いろいろな, さまざまな** ‖ I decided to leave London for various reasons. 私はいろいろな理由により, ロンドンを去る決心をした.

**varnish** /vά:nɪʃ/ 名 U ▶定義 a clear liquid that you paint onto hard surfaces, especially wood, to protect them and make them shine 硬い表面(特に木面)に塗る透明の液体で, 表面を保護し光沢を付けるもの→**ニス, ワニス** ☞参 nail varnish — varnish 動 他 →**～にニスを塗る**

***vary** /véəri/ 動 (現分 **varying**; 三単現 **varies**; 過, 過分 **varied**) ▶定義1 自 vary (in sth) (used about a group of similar things) to be different from each other (同類のものの集合について) 互いに異なる→**(～において)さまざまである, 異なる** ‖ The hotel bedrooms vary in size from medium to very large. 当ホテルの寝室は, 広さが中くらいから特大までいろいろある. ▶定義2 自 vary (from...to...) to be different or to change according to the situation, etc→**(状況などに応じて)異なるまたは変化する** ‖ The price of the holiday varies from £500 to £1200, depending on the time of year. 行楽旅行の値段は, 季節によって500ポンドから1200ポンドの間で変動する. ▶定義3 他 to make sth different by changing it often in some way ある方法で頻繁に変えることにより, ～を違ったものにする→**～に変化を付ける** ‖ I try to vary my work as much as possible so I don't get bored. 私は, 飽きないように, できるだけ仕事に変化を付けるように努めている.

***vase** /vɑ:z, véɪs, -z/ 名 C ▶定義 a container that is used for holding cut flowers 切り花を入れておくために使われる容器→**花びん**

**vasectomy** /væséktəmi, veɪzék-/ 名 C (複 **vasectomies**) ▶定義 (medical) a medical operation to stop a man being able to have children (医学)医療手術で, 男性に子供が作れないようにするもの→**精管切除, パイプカット**

***vast** /vɑ:st; væst/ 形 ▶定義 extremely big 極めて大きい→**広大な, ばく大な** ‖ a vast sum of money ばく大な額のお金 a vast country 広大な国 — vastly 副→**非常に, 大いに** ‖ a vastly improved traffic system 大きく改善された交通システム

**VAT** /vì: eɪ tí:, væt/ (または **Vat**) 略 value added tax→**付加価値税** ‖ prices include VAT 価格は付加価値税を含む

**vault**¹ /vɔ:lt/ 名 C ▶定義1 a room with a strong door and thick walls in a bank, etc that is used for keeping money and other valuable things safe 銀行などにある強固な扉と厚い壁を備えた部屋で, お金およびそのほかの貴重品を安全に保管しておくために使用されるもの→**金庫室, 貴重品保管室** ▶定義2 a room under a church where dead people are buried 教会の地下にある部屋で死んだ人々が埋葬される所→**地下納体堂** ‖ a family vault 家族用埋葬室 ▶定義3 a high roof or ceiling in a church, etc, made from a number of arches joined together at the top 教会などの高い屋根または天井で, 多数のアーチが頂点で接合されているもの→**丸天井**

**vault**² /vɔ:lt/ 動 自 他 ▶定義 vault (over) sth to jump over or onto sth in one movement, using your hands or a pole to help you→**手またはポールの助けを借りて一気に～を飛び越える; ～に飛び乗る** ‖ The boy vaulted over the wall. 少年は塀を飛び越えた.

**VCR** /vì: si: ά:r/ 略 video cassette recorder→**ビデオカセットレコーダー, ビデオ装置**

**VDU** /vì: di: jú:/ 名 C ▶定義 visual display unit; a screen on which you can see information from a computer コンピューターからの情報が見られ

る画面→ディスプレー装置

**veal** /vi:l/ 名 U ▶定義 the meat from a young cow (calf)→若い牛(子牛)の肉 ☞参 meatの注

**veer** /vɪər/ 動 自 ▶定義 (used about vehicles) to change direction suddenly (乗り物について)突然方向を変える→**突然曲がる,それる** ‖ *The car veered across the road and hit a tree.* 車は,向きを変えて道路を横に突っ切り,木に衝突した.

**veg**[1] /vedʒ/ 名 U 英 略式 ▶定義 vegetables→野菜,青物 ‖ *a fruit and veg stall* 果物と野菜の屋台

**veg**[2] /vedʒ/ 動 英 (俗語)
句動詞 veg out ▶定義 to relax and do nothing that needs thought or effort リラックスして,思考や努力を要する事を何もしない→**のんびりする** ‖ *I'm just going to go home and veg out in front of the telly.* 私はちょうど家に帰ってテレビの前でのんびり過ごそうとしているところだ.

**vegan** /ví:g(ə)n/ 名 C ▶定義 a person who does not eat meat or any other animal products at all 肉またはそのほかの畜産製品を一切食べない人→**絶対菜食主義者,完全菜食主義者** ☞参 **vegetarian** — vegan 形→絶対菜食主義の,完全菜食主義の

***vegetable** /védʒ(ə)təb(ə)l/ (または 略式 **veg**; **veggie**) 名 C ▶定義 a plant or part of a plant that we eat. Potatoes, beans and onions are vegetables. 食用の植物または植物の一部. ジャガイモ,豆そしてタマネギはvegetablesである→**野菜,青物** ‖ *vegetable soup* 野菜スープ

**vegetarian** /vèdʒətéəriən/ ( 英 略式 **veggie**) 名 C ▶定義 a person who does not eat meat or fish 肉または魚を食べない人→**菜食主義者** ☞参 **vegan** — vegetarian 形→菜食主義の,野菜だけの ‖ *a vegetarian cookery book* 菜食主義者用の料理法の本

**vegetation** /vèdʒətéɪʃ(ə)n/ 名 U 正式 ▶定義 plants in general; all the plants that are found in a particular place 植物一般; ある特定の場所で見られるすべての植物→**植物,草木,植生** ‖ *tropical vegetation* 熱帯植物

**veggie** /védʒi/ 名 C 略式 ▶定義 1 英 = VEGETARIAN ▶定義 2 = VEGETABLE — veggie 形→菜食主義の ‖ *a veggie burger* 菜食主義者用ハンバーガー

**vehement** /ví:əmənt/ 形 ▶定義 showing very strong (often negative) feelings, especially anger 非常に強い(しばしば否定的な)感情,特に怒り,を表している→**激昂(げっこう)した,強烈な** ‖ *a vehement attack on the government* 政府に対する激しい攻撃

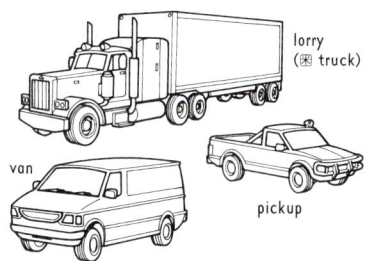

lorry (米 truck)
van
pickup

***vehicle** /ví:ək(ə)l, ví:hɪ-/ 名 C ▶定義 1 something which transports people or things from place to place, especially on land, for example cars, bicycles, lorries and buses 人または物をある場所から別の場所へ運ぶもので,特に陸路のもの. 例えば自動車,自転車,トラック,バス→**乗り物,車,輸送機関** ‖ *Are you the owner of this vehicle?* あなたがこの車の所有者ですか. ▶定義 2 something which is used for communicating particular ideas or opinions 特定の考えや意見を伝えるのに使われるもの→**伝達手段,媒体** ‖ *This newspaper has become a vehicle for Conservative opinion.* この新聞は保守党の見解の伝達手段となってしまった.

**veil** /veɪl/ 名 C ▶定義 a piece of thin material for covering the head and face of a woman 女性の頭と顔を覆うための薄い布地→**ベール** ‖ *a bridal veil* 花嫁のベール

**vein** /veɪn/ 名 ▶定義 1 C one of the tubes which carry blood from all parts of your body to your heart 身体のあらゆる部位から心臓に血液を送る管→**静脈** ☞参 **artery** ▶定義 2 [単数扱い, U] a particular style or quality 特定の様式または性質→**特質,気質** ‖ *After a humorous beginning, the programme continued in a more serious vein.* ユーモラスな出だしの後,番組はよりまじめな調子で続いた.

**Velcro**™ /vélkrou/ 名 U ▶定義 a material for fastening parts of clothes together. Velcro is made of a man-made material (nylon) and is used in small pieces, one rough and one smooth, that can stick together and be pulled apart. 衣服の部分を留めるための物.合成繊維の素材(ナイロン)で作られ,一方はざらざらしてもう一方はすべすべした小片が用いられ,それ同士をくっつけたり引き離したりできるもの→**マジックテープ, ベルクロ**

**velocity** /vəlásəti/ 名 U (専門用語) ▶定義 the speed at which sth moves 〜が動く速さ→**速度**

**velvet** /vélvət/ 名 U ▶定義 a kind of cloth made of cotton or other material, with a soft thick surface on one side only 綿そのほかの素材でできた布地の一種で,片面だけが柔らかで厚手になっているもの→**ビロード,ベルベット,別珍(べっちん)** ‖ *black velvet trousers* 黒いビロードのズボン

**vendetta** /vendétə/ 名 C ▶定義 a serious argument or dispute between two people or groups which lasts for a long time 2人または2つの集団の間の真剣な議論または争議で,長い間続くもの→**抗争**

**vending machine** 名 C ▶定義 a machine from which you can buy drinks, cigarettes, etc by putting coins in it 硬貨を入れて,飲料またはたばこなどを買うことができる機械→**自動販売機** ● C8ページのさし絵

**vendor** /véndər, véndɔːr/ 名 C 正式 ▶定義 a person who is selling sth 物を売っている人→**販売員,売り主,行商人** ● 参 **purchaser** ● C8ページのさし絵

**veneer** /vəníər/ 名 ▶定義 1 C U a thin layer of wood or plastic that is stuck onto the surface of a cheaper material, especially wood, to give it a better appearance 木またはプラスチックの薄い層で,安い素材,特に木,の表面に張って外見をより良く見せるためのもの→**化粧板,ベニヤ板の表面** ▶定義 2 [単数扱い] 正式 **a veneer (of sth)** a part of sb's behaviour or of a situation which hides what it is really like underneath 人の行為や状況の一部で,それが本当はどのようなものであるかを下に隠しているもの→**上辺,見せ掛け** ‖ *a thin veneer of politeness* 上辺だけの見え透いた丁寧さ

**venetian blind** /vəníːʃ(ə)n bláɪnd/ 名 C ▶定義 a covering for a window that is made of horizontal pieces of flat plastic, etc which can be turned to let in as much light as you want 平たんな水平のプラスチック板などでできた窓の覆いで,角度を変えて好みの量の光を入れることができるもの→**ブラインド,板すだれ**

**vengeance** /véndʒ(ə)ns/ 名 U (文) ▶定義 **vengeance (on sb)** the act of punishing or harming sb in return for sth bad he/she has done to you, your friends or family 自分,友人または家族に対してなされた悪い事のお返しに,それをした人に懲罰を与えるまたは危害を加える行為→**復讐(ふくしゅう),仕返し** ‖ *He felt a terrible desire for vengeance on the people who had destroyed his career.* 彼は自分の人生を破滅させた人々に対して復讐をしたいという恐ろしい欲求を感じた. ● 参 **revenge**

成句 **with a vengeance** ▶定義 to a greater degree than is expected or usual 予想または普通よりも程度が強く→**予想外に,並外れて** ‖ *After a week of good weather winter returned with a vengeance.* 1週間良い天気が続いた後に,厳しい冬が戻ってきた.

**venison** /vénəs(ə)n, -z(ə)n/ 名 U ▶定義 the meat from a large wild animal (deer)→**大型の野生動物(シカ)の肉**

**venom** /vénəm/ 名 U ▶定義 1 the poisonous liquid that some snakes, spiders, etc produce when they bite or sting you 毒を含む液体で,ある種の蛇,クモなどがかむまたは刺すときに出すもの→**毒液** ▶定義 2 extreme anger or hatred and a desire to hurt sb 非常に激しい怒りや憎しみおよび人を傷付けたいという願望→**憎悪の念** ‖ *She shot him a look of pure venom.* 彼女は彼に,憎悪そのもののまなざしを向けた. ―
**venomous** /vénəməs/ 形→**毒腺を持つ,憎悪に満ちた**

**vent** /vent/ 名 C ▶定義 an opening in the wall of a room or machine which allows air to come in, and smoke, steam or smells to go out 部屋や機械の壁にある開口部で,空気を中に入れて煙,水蒸気またはにおいを外に出すもの→**換気孔** ‖ *an air vent* 通気孔 *a heating vent* 暖気孔

**ventilate** /vént(ə)lèɪt/ 動 他 ▶定義 to allow air to move freely in and out of a room or building 部屋または建物に空気を自由に出入りさせる→**〜を換気する** ‖ *The office is badly ventilated.* この事務所は換気が悪い. ― **ventilation** /vènt(ə)léɪʃ(ə)n/ 名 U →**通気, 換気** ‖ There was *no ventilation in the room except for one tiny window.* ちっぽけな窓が1つある以外, その部屋には換気設備が何もなかった.

**venture**¹ /véntʃər/ 名 C ▶定義 a project which is new and possibly dangerous, because you cannot be sure that it will succeed 成功するかどうか確信が持てないために, 危険かもしれない新事業→**冒険, 試み, 冒険的事業** ‖ *a business venture* 投機的事業

**venture**² /véntʃər/ 動 自 ▶定義 to do sth or go somewhere new and dangerous, when you are not sure what will happen 何が起きるか確かではないときに, 新しく危険な事をするまたは新しく危険な場所に行く→**危険を冒してする, 思い切ってする** ‖ *He ventured out into the storm to look for the lost child.* 彼は行方不明の子供を捜すために, あらしの中を思い切って出掛けた. *The company has decided to venture into computer production as well as design.* 会社は, コンピューターの設計だけでなく製造にも乗り出すことに決めた.

**venue** /vénjuː/ 名 C ▶定義 the place where people meet for an organized event, for example a concert or a sporting event 例えば音楽会またはスポーツ競技のような催し物のために人々が集まる場所→**開催場所, 開催予定地**

**Venus** /víːnəs/ 名 [単数扱い] ▶定義 the planet that is second in order from the sun and nearest to the earth 太陽からの順番が2番目で, 地球に一番近い惑星→**金星**

**veranda**(または**verandah**) /vərǽndə/ (米 または **porch**) 名 C ▶定義 a platform joined to the side of a house, with a roof and floor but no outside wall 家の側面に取り付けられた台で, 屋根と床はあるが外壁はない→**ベランダ, 縁側**
☞参 **balcony, patio, terrace**

*****verb** /vɜːrb/ 名 C (文法) ▶定義 a word or group of words that is used to indicate that sth happens or exists, for example bring, happen, be, do. 物事が起きるまたは存在することを示す語または語群, 例えば bring, happen, be, do→**動詞** ☞参 **phrasal verb**

**verbal** /vɜːrb(ə)l/ 形 正式 ▶定義 **1** connected with words, or the use of words 言葉または言葉の使い方に関する→**言葉の, 言葉による** ‖ *verbal skills* 言葉遣い ▶定義 **2** spoken, not written→**書かれたものでなく, 口頭の** ‖ *a verbal agree-*

*ment/warning* 口約束・口頭での警告 — **verbally** /vɜːrb(ə)li/ 副 →**言葉で, 口頭で**

*****verdict** /vɜːrdɪkt/ 名 C ▶定義 **1** the decision that is made by a specially chosen group of people (the jury) in a court of law, which states if a person is guilty of a crime or not 特別に選ばれた人々の集団 (陪審員団) が法廷で下した決定で, 人が犯罪行為で有罪か否かを申し立てるもの→**評決, 答申** ‖ *The jury **returned a verdict** of 'not guilty'.* 陪審員団は, 「無罪」の評決を下した. *Has the jury **reached a verdict**?* 陪審員団は評決に達しましたか. ▶定義 **2** **a verdict (on sb/sth)** a decision that you make or an opinion that you give after testing sth or considering sth carefully 〜を慎重に考査または熟考した後に下した決定または意見→**(〜についての)判断, 意見, 結論** ‖ *The general verdict was that the restaurant was too expensive.* 大方の意見では, そのレストランは高すぎた.

**verge**¹ /vɜːrdʒ/ 名 C 英 ▶定義 the narrow piece of land at the side of a road, railway line, etc that is usually covered in grass 道路, 鉄道線路などの端の幅の狭い土地で, 通常は草で覆われている→**縁, へり**
成句 **on the verge of sth/doing sth** ▶定義 very near to doing sth, or to sth happening もう少しで〜をするところで, またはもう少しで〜が起きるところで→**〜寸前の, 今にも〜しようとして** ‖ *He was on the verge of a nervous breakdown.* 彼はノイローゼ寸前だった. *Scientists are on the verge of discovering a cure.* 科学者たちは今にも治療法を発見しようとしている.

**verge**² /vɜːrdʒ/ 動
句動詞 **verge on sth** ▶定義 to be very close to an extreme state or condition 極限の状態または情勢に非常に近いところにある→**ほとんど〜しかけている, 〜寸前である** ‖ *What they are doing verges on the illegal.* 彼らがしている事は違法に近い.

**verify** /vérəfaɪ/ 動 他 (現分 **verifying**; 三単現 **verifies**; 過, 過分 **verified**) 正式 ▶定義 to check or state that sth is true 〜が本当であるかを確かめる, またはそうであると言明する ‖ *to verify a statement* 声明文に間違いがないことを確かめる — **verification** /vèrəfəkéɪʃ(ə)n/ 名 U →**証明,**

## 1782 vermin

確認

**vermin** /vɜ́ːmən/ 名[複数扱い] ▶定義 small wild animals (for example rats) that carry disease and destroy plants and food 小型の野生動物(例えばネズミ)で、病気を伝染させ、植物または食物を台なしにするもの→害虫,害獣,害鳥

**versatile** /vɜ́ːrsətàɪl; -t(ə)l/ 形 ▶定義1 (used about an object) having many different uses(物について)多様な用途を持っている→多用途の,万能の ‖ a versatile tool that drills, cuts or polishes 穴を開けたり,切ったり磨いたりできる多用途の道具 ▶定義2 (used about a person) able to do many different things(人について)多くの異なった事を行うことができる→何でもこなす,多才な ‖ She's so versatile! She can dance, sing, act and play the guitar! 彼女は何て多才なんだ.踊り,歌,演技にギターも弾ける.

*****verse** /vɜːrs/ 名 ▶定義1 ❶writing arranged in lines which have a definite rhythm and often finish with the same sound (rhyme) 行を整えて書かれたもので,各行が一定の韻律を持ち,同じ音で終わっている(押韻)ことが多い→韻文 ‖ He wrote his valentine's message in verse. 彼はバレンタインのメッセージを韻文で書いた.

▶定義2 ❷a group of lines which form one part of a song or poem 歌詞または詩の一部を成す,行の集まり→節,連 ‖ This song has five verses. この歌詞は5節から成る.

*****version** /vɜ́ːrʒ(ə)n, -ʃ(ə)/ 名 ❷ ▶定義1 a thing which has the same basic content as sth else but which is presented in a different way ほかのものと基本的な内容は同じであるが,別の形で提示されているもの→版,〜化したもの,バージョン ‖ Have you heard the live version of this song? この歌のライブ版を聴いたことがありますか. ▶定義2 a person's description of sth that has happened 起きた事に関する,ある人なりの説明→意見,見解,話 ‖ The two drivers gave very different versions of the accident. 2人の運転手は,事故について非常に異なる説明をした.

**versus** /vɜ́ːrsəs/ 前 ▶定義1 (略 v, vs) used in sport for showing that two teams or people are playing against each other スポーツ競技で用いられ,2チームまたは2人が対戦中であることを示す→〜対…,〜に対して ‖ England versus Argentina イングランド対アルゼンチン ▶定義2 used for showing that two ideas or things that are opposite to each other, especially when you are trying to choose one of them 2つの考えまたは事柄がお互いに正反対であることを示し、特にそのうちの1つを選ぼうとしているときに用いて→〜か…か ‖ It's a question of quality versus price. これは品質か値段かの問題だ.

*****vertical** /vɜ́ːrtɪk(ə)l/ 形 ▶定義 going straight up at an angle of 90° from the ground 地面に対して90度の角度でまっすぐに伸びた→鉛直の,縦方向の ‖ a vertical line 鉛直線 The cliff was almost vertical. その崖はほとんど垂直だった.

➤ horizontal, perpendicularと比較.

☞ **line**のさし絵 — **vertically** /-k(ə)li/ 副 →鉛直に,縦に

*****very** /véri/ 副形 ▶定義1 used with an adjective or adverb to make it stronger 形容詞または副詞と用いて,その意味を強調する→とても,非常に,大変 ‖ very small 非常に小さい very slowly とてもゆっくりと I don't like milk very much. 私は牛乳がそれほど好きではありません. 'Are you hungry?' 'Not very.'「おなかがすいていますか」「いや,そんなには」

➤ veryは形容詞の最上級と共に用いる: very best, youngest, etc (まさに最良の,全く若い,など).しかし形容詞の比較級にはmuchまたはvery muchを使う: much better; very much younger (はるかに良い;ずっと若い)

▶定義2 used to emphasize a noun 名詞を強調するのに用いて→まさにその,ちょうどその ‖ We climbed to the very top of the mountain (= right to the top). 私たちは山のまさに頂上まで(= まさしく頂上まで)登った. You're the very person I wanted to talk to (= exactly the right person). あなたこそ私が話したかった人だ(= まさにその人だ).

**vessel** /vés(ə)l/ 名 ❷ ▶定義1 (文) a ship or large boat→船,大型船 ▶定義2 (古) a container for liquids, for example a bottle, cup or bowl→液体を入れる容器,びん,カップ,ボウル ‖ ancient drinking vessels 古代の飲用の器

*****vest** /vest/ 名 ❷ ▶定義1 (米 **undershirt**) a piece of clothing that you wear under your other clothes, on the top part of your body ほかの衣服の下に着用する衣類で,上半身用の

もの→**肌着, アンダーシャツ** ▶定義2 米=WAISTCOAT

**vested interest** /vèstəd ínt(ə)rest; -t(ə)rèst/ 名 C ▶定義 a strong and often secret reason for doing sth that will bring you an advantage of some kind, for example more money or power 何かを行う強い理由または多くは秘密の理由で, それにより人にある種の利益, 例えばお金や権力, をもたらすもの→**利害関係, 強い関心**

**vestige** /véstɪdʒ/ 名 C ▶定義 a small part of sth that is left after the rest of it has gone あるものの, ほかの部分がなくなってしまった後に残っているわずかな部分→**痕跡(こんせき), 名残, 残片** ‖ *the last vestige of the old system* 古い制度の最後の痕跡 ☛類 trace

*****vet**[1] /vet/ ( または 正式 **veterinary surgeon** 米 **veterinarian**) 名 C ▶定義 a doctor for animals 動物を診る医者→**獣医** ‖ *We took the cat to the vet/to the vet's.* 私たちは猫を獣医・動物病院に連れていった.

**vet**[2] /vet/ 動 他 (**vetting**; **vetted**) ▶定義 to do careful and secret checks before deciding if sb/sth can be accepted or not 〜を受け入れるか否かを決める前に, 慎重かつ秘密裏に調査を行う→**〜を吟味する, 〜を審査する** ‖ *All new employees at the Ministry of Defence are carefully vetted (= somebody examines the details of their past lives).* 国防省に新たに雇用される職員はすべて慎重に身元調査をされる (= 過去の履歴を詳しく調査される).

**veteran** /vét(ə)rən/ 名 C ▶定義1 a person who has served in the army, navy or air force, especially during a war 陸軍, 海軍または空軍で, 特に戦争中に軍務に服したことのある人→**退役軍人, 復員軍人** ▶定義2 a person who has very long experience of a particular job or activity 特定の仕事または活動で非常に長い経験を持つ人→**熟練家, ベテラン**

**veterinary** /vét(ə)rən(ə)ri; -nèri/ 形 ▶定義 connected with the medical treatment of sick or injured animals 病気またはけがをした動物の医療に関した→**獣医(学)の** ‖ *a veterinary practice* 獣医の仕事 ☛参 vet

**veto** /víːtou/ 動 他 (現分 **vetoing**; 三単現 **vetoes**; 過, 過分 **vetoed**) ▶定義 to refuse to give official permission for an action or plan, when other people have agreed to it ほかの人が賛成しているときに, その活動または計画に対して正式な許可を与えることを拒む→**〜を拒否する, 〜に拒否権を行使する** ‖ *The Prime Minister vetoed the proposal to reduce taxation.* 首相は減税案に対して拒否権を行使した. ― veto 名 C U (複 vetoes) →**拒否, 拒否権行使, 禁止** ‖ *the right of veto* 拒否権

**vexed** /vekst/ 形 ▶定義 causing difficulty, worry, and a lot of discussion 困難, 心痛や多くの議論を引き起こす→**困った, 厄介な, 面倒な** ‖ *the vexed question of our growing prison population* 囚人の増加という難題

**via** /váɪə/ 前 ▶定義1 going through a place ある場所を通っていって→**〜経由で** ‖ *We flew from Paris to Sydney via Bangkok.* 私たちはパリからシドニーへ, バンコク経由で飛行した. ▶定義2 by means of sth; using sth 〜を手段として; 〜を使って→**〜によって, 〜を媒介として** ‖ *These pictures come to you via our satellite link.* これらの写真は衛星回線によってお届けしています.

**viable** /váɪəb(ə)l/ 形 ▶定義 that can be done; that will be successful 行われることができる; 成功するであろう→**実行可能な, ものになる** ‖ *I'm afraid your idea is just not commercially viable.* 残念ながらあなたの案は, 採算的に全く実現不可能です. ― viability /vàɪəbíləti/ 名 U →**実行可能性**

**viaduct** /váɪədʌkt/ 名 C ▶定義 a long, high bridge which carries a railway or road across a valley 谷に架かった線路または道路を支える, 長くて高い橋→**高架橋**

**vibrant** /váɪbr(ə)nt/ 形 ▶定義1 full of life and energy; exciting 活気と活力に満ちた; 刺激的な→**躍動的な, 活気あふれる** ‖ *a vibrant city/atmosphere/personality* 活気に満ちた都市・雰囲気・性格 ▶定義2 (used about colours) bright and strong (色について)→**鮮やかで強烈な**

**vibrate** /váɪbreɪt; -/ 動 自 ▶定義 to make continuous very small and fast movements from side to side 非常に小さくそして速い左右の動きをし続ける→**小刻みに揺れる, 振動する** ‖ *When a guitar string vibrates it makes a sound.* ギターの弦が振動すると, 音を出す. ― vibration /vaɪbréɪʃ(ə)n/ 名 C U →**振動**

## vicar

**vicar** /víkər/ 名 C ▶定義 a priest of the Church of England. A vicar looks after a church and the people in the surrounding area (parish). 英国国教会の聖職者. 教会とその周辺地域(教区)の人々を受け持つ→**教区牧師** ☛参 minister

**vicarage** /víkərɪdʒ/ 名 C ▶定義 the house where a vicar lives 教区牧師が住む家→**牧師館**

**vice** /váɪs/ 名 ▶定義1 U criminal activities involving sex or drugs 性または薬物関係の犯罪行為→**不道徳行為** ▶定義2 C a moral weakness or bad habit 道徳的欠陥または悪習慣→**悪癖** ‖ *Greed and envy are terrible vices.* 強欲としっとはひどい悪徳だ. *My only vice is smoking.* 私の唯一の悪習慣は喫煙だ. ☛参 virtue ▶定義3 (米 vise) a tool that you use to hold a piece of wood, metal, etc firmly while you are working on it 作業をしている間, 木片, 金属片などをしっかりと固定させるのに使う道具→**万力** ‖ (比喩)*He held my arm in a vice-like (= very firm) grip.* 彼は私の腕を万力のように(= 非常にしっかりと)つかんだ.

**vice-** /váɪs/ (複合名詞を作るために用いて) ▶定義 having a position second in importance to the position mentioned 示された地位に次いで重要な地位にいる→**副~** ‖ *Vice-President* 副大統領 *the vice-captain* 団長, 副主将

**vice versa** /vàɪs(i) və́ːrsə/ 副 ▶定義 in the opposite way to what has just been said すぐ前に言われた事とは反対に→**逆に, 反対に, 逆もまたしかり** ‖ *Anna ordered fish and Maria chicken - or was it vice versa?* アンナは魚を, マリアはチキンを注文しました - いや逆でしたか.

**vicinity** /vəsínəti/ 名

成句 **in the vicinity (of sth)** 正式 ▶定義 in the surrounding area 取り巻く地域に→**近所に, 付近に, 周辺に** ‖ *There's no bank in the immediate vicinity.* すぐ近くに銀行がない.

**vicious** /víʃəs/ 形 ▶定義1 cruel; done in order to hurt sb/sth 残酷な; 人・物を傷付けるためになされた→**悪意に満ちた, 意地の悪い** ‖ *a vicious attack* 悪意に満ちた攻撃 ▶定義2 (used about an animal) dangerous; likely to hurt sb (動物について)危険な; 人を傷付けるような→**凶暴な** — **viciously** 副 →**悪意を持って, 残忍に**

成句 **a vicious circle** ▶定義 a situation in which one problem leads to another and the new problem makes the first problem worse 1つの問題が次の問題を引き起こし, その新しい問題が最初の問題をさらに悪化させる状況→**悪循環**

*****victim** /víktəm/ 名 C ▶定義 a person or animal that is injured, killed or hurt by sb/sth 人・物によって傷付けられた, 殺されたまたは痛められた人または動物→**犠牲者, 被害者, 被災者** ‖ *a murder victim* 殺人の被害者 *The children are often the innocent victims of a divorce.* 子供たちはしばしば離婚によって罪のない犠牲者となる.

**victimize** (または **-ise**) /víktəmàɪz/ 動 他 ▶定義 to punish or make sb suffer unfairly ~を不当に罰するまたは苦しめる→**~を犠牲にする, 苦痛を与える** — **victimization** (または **-isation**) /vìktəmaɪzéɪʃ(ə)n; -mə-/ 名 U →**犠牲にすること**

**victor** /víktər/ 名 C 正式 ▶定義 the person who wins a game, competition, battle, etc 試合, 競争または戦いなどに勝つ人→**勝利者, 勝者**

**Victorian** /víktɔ́ːriən/ 形 ▶定義1 connected with the time of the British queen Victoria (1837-1901) 英国のビクトリア女王の時代 (1837〜1901年)に関連した→**ビクトリア朝(時代)の** ‖ *Victorian houses* ビクトリア朝様式の家 ▶定義2 having attitudes that were typical in the time of Queen Victoria ビクトリア時代に典型的な考え方を持つ→**昔風の, 厳格な** — **Victorian** 名 C →**ビクトリア時代(風)の人**

*****victory** /víkt(ə)ri/ 名 C U (複 **victories**) ▶定義 success in winning a battle, game, competition, etc 戦い, 試合または競争などに勝利を収めること→**勝利, 戦勝, 優勝** ‖ *Keane led his team to victory in the final.* キーンは決勝戦でチームを優勝に導いた. — **victorious** /víktɔ́ːriəs/ 形 →**勝利を収めた, 勝った** ‖ *the victorious team* 勝利チーム

成句 **romp home/to victory** ⇒ **ROMP**

*****video** /vídiòu/ 名 (複 **videos**) ▶定義1 U the system of recording moving pictures and sound by using a camera, and showing them using a machine (**a video recorder**) connected to a television カメラを使って動画と音声を録画し, テレビに接続した機器(ビデオレコーダー)を用いてそれを写すシステム→**ビデオ(装置)** ‖ *We recorded the wedding on video.* 私たちはその結婚式をビデオに録画した. *The film is coming out on video in May.* その映画は5月にビデオが

出る. ▶定義2 (または **video cassette**) ❻ a tape or cassette on which you record moving pictures and sound or on which a film or television programme has been recorded テープまたはカセットで, 動画および音声を録画したもの, あるいは映画またはテレビ番組が録画されたもの→ビデオテープ, ビデオソフト ‖ *Would you like to see the video we made on holiday?* 私たちが休暇で撮ったビデオを見ませんか. *to rent a video* ビデオを貸す ▶定義3 =VIDEO RECORDER — video 動他 (三単現 videos; 現分 videoing; 過, 過分 videoed)→〜をビデオに録画する ‖ *We hired a camera to video the school play.* 私たちは学芸会をビデオに録画するためにカメラを借りた.

**video recorder** (または **video**; **video cassette recorder**) 名 ❻ (略 VCR) ▶定義 a machine that is connected to a television on which you can record or play back a film or television programme 映画またはテレビ番組の録画または再生ができる, テレビに接続された機械→ビデオ (装置)

**videotape** /vídiouteɪp/ 名 ❻ = VIDEO(2) — videotape 動他 = VIDEO ‖ *a videotaped interview* ビデオに収録された会見

*\***view**[1] /vjuː/ ▶定義1 ❻ a view (about/on sth) an opinion or a particular way of thinking about sth 〜についての意見またはある特定の考え方→見解, 考え, 見方 ‖ *He expressed the view that standards were falling.* 彼は, 水準が下がっているという意見を述べた. *In my view, she has done nothing wrong.* 私の見解では, 彼女は何も悪い事はしていない. *She has* **strong views** *on the subject.* 彼女はその問題について断固とした考えを持っている. ▶定義2 ❶ the ability to see sth or to be seen from a particular place ある特定の場所から物を見るまたは見られる能力→視界, 視野, 視力 ‖ *The garden was hidden from view behind a high wall.* その庭は高い塀の陰で視界から隠れていた. *to come into view* 視界に入る *to disappear from view* 視界から消える ▶定義3 ❻ what you can see from a particular place, especially beautiful natural scenery ある特定の場所から見ることができるもの, 特に美しい自然の景色→眺め, 風景 ‖ *There are* **breathtaking views** *from the top of the mountain.* その山の頂上からは, 息をのむような眺めだ. *a room with* **a sea view** 海の見える部屋 ☛参 **scenery** の注

成句 have, etc sth in view 正式 ▶定義 to have sth as a plan or idea in your mind 心の中に計画または案として〜を持つ→〜を心に抱く

in full view (of sb/sth) ⇒ FULL[1]

in view of sth ▶定義 because of sth; as a result of sth 〜が理由で; 〜の結果として→〜を考慮して, 〜のために ‖ *In view of her apology we decided to take no further action.* 彼女の謝罪を考慮して, 私たちはこれ以上の措置を取らないことに決めた.

a point of view ⇒ POINT[1]

with a view to doing sth 正式 ▶定義 with the aim or intention of doing sth→〜する目的または意図で

*\***view**[2] /vjuː/ 動他 正式 ▶定義1 view sth (as sth) to think about sth in a particular way 〜についてある風に考える→〜を (…と) 考える ‖ *She viewed holidays as a waste of time.* 彼女は休暇を時間の無駄と見なしていた. ▶定義2 to watch or look at sth 〜を凝視するまたは見る→〜を眺める ‖ *Viewed from this angle, the building looks much taller than it really is.* この角度から眺めると, その建物は実際よりもずっと高く見える.

**viewer** /vjúːər/ 名 ❻ ▶定義 a person who watches television テレビ番組を見る人→視聴者

**viewpoint** /vjúːpɔɪnt/ 名 ❻ ▶定義 a way of looking at a situation; an opinion 状況の見方; 意見→観点, 見地 ‖ *Let's look at this problem from the customer's viewpoint.* この問題を顧客の観点から見てみよう. ☛類 **point of view**

**vigil** /vídʒəl/ 名 ❻ ❶ ▶定義 a period when you stay awake all night for a special purpose 特別な目的のために一晩中起きている時間→徹夜 ‖ *All night she* **kept vigil** *over the sick child.* 彼女は病気の子供を徹夜で看病した.

**vigilant** /vídʒələnt/ 形 正式 ▶定義 careful and looking out for danger 注意し, 危険を警戒する→警戒をおこたらない — vigilance /-əns/ 名 ❶→警戒, 用心

**vigilante** /vídʒəlænti/ 名 ❻ ▶定義 a member of a group of people who try to prevent crime or punish criminals in a community, especially because they believe the police are not doing this 地域共同体で犯罪を防ぐまたは犯罪者を罰しようとする人々の集団の一員で,特に警官がこの事を行わないと確信しているので行う→自警団員

**vigour** (困 **vigor**) /vígər/ 名 ❶ ▶定義 strength or energy 力強さまたは活力→元気, 精力 ‖ *After the break we started work again with renewed vigour.* 休憩の後,私たちは元気を回復して再び働き始めた.— **vigorous** /vígərəs/ 形 →活発な,元気な ‖ *vigorous exercise* 激しい運動 — **vigorously** 副 →精力的に,力強く

**vile** /váɪl/ 形 ▶定義 very bad or unpleasant 非常に悪いまたは不快な→不愉快な, ひどい ‖ *She's in a vile mood.* 彼女は機嫌が悪い. *a vile smell* 嫌なにおい

**villa** /vílə/ 名 C ▶定義 **1** a house that people rent and stay in on holiday 人々が休暇に借りて滞在する家→別荘 ▶定義 **2** a large house in the country, especially in Southern Europe 特に南欧の,田舎にある大きな家→郊外の大邸宅

\***village** /vílɪdʒ/ 名 C ▶定義 **1** ❶ a group of houses with other buildings, for example a shop, school, etc, in a country area. A village is smaller than a town. 田園地域にある家々の集まりで,例えば店,学校などほかの建物もある. town (街) よりも小さい→村, 村落 ‖ *a small fishing village* 小さな漁村 *the village shop* 村の商店 ▶定義 **2** [単数扱い, 単数または複数形の動詞と共に] all the people who live in a village 村に住むすべての人々→村人, 村民 ‖ *All the village is/are taking part in the carnival.* 村全体が謝肉祭に参加している.

**villager** /vílɪdʒər/ 名 C ▶定義 a person who lives in a village 村に住む人→村人, 村民

**villain** /vílən/ 名 C ▶定義 **1** an evil person, especially in a book or play 特に本または劇の中の,悪人→悪役 ‖ *In most of his films he has played villains, but in this one he's a good guy.* 出演した映画のほとんどで彼は悪役を演じたが,この映画では善人の役だ. ☛参 **hero** ▶定義 **2** 略式 a criminal 犯罪者→悪党 ‖ *The police caught the villains who robbed the bank.* 警官は銀行強盗をした悪党を捕まえた.

**vindictive** /vɪndíktɪv/ 形 ▶定義 wanting or trying to hurt sb without good reason 正当な理由なしに,人を傷付けたがるまたは傷付けようとする→復讐 (ふくしゅう) 心のある, 恨みを忘れない ‖ *a vindictive comment/person* 悪意に満ちた批評・人 — **vindictiveness** 名 ❶ →悪意, 遺恨

**vine** /váɪn/ 名 C ▶定義 the plant that grapes grow on ブドウがなる植物→ブドウ (の木)

**vinegar** /vínɪɡər/ 名 ❶ ▶定義 a liquid with a strong sharp taste that is made from wine. Vinegar is often mixed with oil and put onto salads. 果実酒から作られる,強い酸味のある液体. しばしば油と混ぜてサラダに掛けられる→食用酢, ビネガー

**vineyard** /vínjərd/ 名 C ▶定義 a piece of land where grapes are grown ブドウが生育する地所→ブドウ園, ブドウ畑

**vintage**¹ /víntɪdʒ/ 名 C ▶定義 the wine that was made in a particular year→ある特定の年に作られたワイン ‖ *1999 was an excellent vintage.* 1999年は極上ワインの年だった.

**vintage**² /víntɪdʒ/ 形 ▶定義 **1** (used about wine) that was produced in a particular year and district (ワインについて) →ある特定の年に特定の場所で作られた ‖ *a bottle of vintage champagne* 特定の年および地域のシャンパン1本 ▶定義 **2** of very high quality 非常に高い品質の→第1級の, 代表的な ‖ *a vintage performance by Robert De Niro* ロバート デニーロによる第1級の演技

**vinyl** /váɪn(ə)l/ 名 C ❶ ▶定義 a strong plastic that can bend easily and is used for making wall, floor and furniture coverings, book covers, etc 丈夫なプラスチックで,簡単に曲げることができて,壁・床・家具の覆い,本の表紙などを作るのに用いられる→ビニール

**viola** /vióʊlə/ 名 C ▶定義 a musical instrument with strings, that you hold under your chin and play with a long thin object (*a bow*) made of wood and hair 弦楽器の1つで,あごの下で支え,木と毛でできた細長い物 (弓) で弾く→ビオラ ‖ *A viola is like a large violin.* ビオラは大型のバイオリンのようなものだ. ☛参 **piano** の注

**violate** /váɪəleɪt/ 動 他 正式 ▶定義 **1** to break a rule, an agreement, etc 規則, 協定などを破る→~に違反する ‖ *to violate a peace treaty* 平和条約に違反する ▶定義 **2** to not respect sth; to spoil or damage sth ~に敬意を払わない; ~を

駄目にするまたは害する➔〜を侵害する, 妨げる ‖ to violate sb's privacy/rights 〜のプライバシー・権利を侵害する — violation /vàiəléiʃ(ə)n/ 名 ⒞⒰➔違反, 侵害 ‖ violation of human rights 人権侵害

**\*violence** /váiələns/ 名 ⒰ ▶定義1 behaviour which harms or damages sb/sth physically 人・物を物理的に傷付けるまたは害する行為➔暴力, 暴行 ‖ They threatened to **use violence** if we didn't give them the money. 彼らは、お金を出さないと暴力を使うと(私たちを)脅した. **an act of violence** 暴力行為 ▶定義2 great force or energy 巨大な力または勢い➔激しさ, すさまじさ ‖ the violence of the storm あらしの猛威

**\*violent** /váiələnt/ 形 ▶定義1 using physical strength to hurt or kill sb; caused by this behaviour 人を傷付けるまたは殺すために物理的な力を使って; この行為によって引き起こされた➔暴力的な, 暴力による ‖ The demonstration started peacefully but later turned violent. デモは平穏に始まったが、後になって暴力的なものに変わった. a violent death 非業の死 violent crime 凶悪な犯罪 ▶定義2 very strong and impossible to control 非常に強くて制御できない➔激しい, 激情的な ‖ He has a violent temper. 彼は気性が激しい. a violent storm/collision 激しいあらし・衝突 — violently 副➔激しく, 乱暴に ‖ The ground shook violently and buildings collapsed in the earthquake. 地震で地面が激しく揺れ、建物が崩壊した.

**violet** /váiələt/ 名 ▶定義1 ⒞a small plant that grows wild or in gardens and has purple or white flowers and a pleasant smell 野生または庭園に生育し、紫または白の花を咲かせ良い香りがする小さな植物➔スミレ(の花) ☛ C2ページのさし絵 ▶定義2 ⒰a bluish purple colour 青みを帯びた紫色➔スミレ色 — violet 形➔スミレ色の

**\*violin** /vàiəlín/ 名 ⒞ ▶定義 a musical instrument with strings, that you hold under your chin and play with a long thin object (a bow) made of wood and hair 弦楽器の1つで、あごの下で支え、木と毛でできた細長い物(弓)で弾く➔バイオリン ☛参 pianoの注. 略式の英語では、fiddleと呼ばれることもある. ☛ musicのさし絵

**VIP** /ví: ai pí:/ 名 略式 very important person➔要人, 重要人物 ‖ the VIP lounge at the airport 空港

の要人用の休憩室 give someone the VIP treatment (= treat sb especially well) 人を要人としてもてなす(= 人を特に丁寧にもてなす)

**virgin**¹ /vɜ́:rdʒən/ 名 ⒞ ▶定義 a person who has never had sex 一度も性交渉を持ったことがない人➔処女, 童貞

**virgin**² /vɜ́:rdʒən/ 形 ▶定義 that has not yet been used, touched, damaged, etc まだ使われたことがない、触れられたことがない、傷付けられたことがないなど➔人の手の入っていない ‖ virgin forest 原始林

**virginity** /vərdʒínəti/ 名 ⒰ ▶定義 the state of never having had sex 一度も性交渉を持ったことがない状態➔処女・童貞であること, 処女・童貞性 ‖ to lose your virginity 処女・童貞を失う

**Virgo** /vɜ́:rgou, víər-/ 名 ⒞⒰ ▶定義 the sixth sign of the zodiac, the Virgin 黄道十二宮の6番目である乙女座➔乙女座, 処女宮

**virile** /vírail, vírəl, váirəil/ ▶定義 (used about a man) strong and having great sexual energy (男性について)力強くて、絶大な性的精力を持っている➔男らしい, 力強い, りりしい

**virility** /vəríləti, var-/ 名 ⒰ ▶定義 a man's sexual power and energy 男性の性的な力強さと精力➔男らしさ, りりしさ

**virtual** /vɜ́:rtʃuəl/ 形 (名詞の前だけ) ▶定義1 being almost or nearly sth ほとんどまたはもう少しで、〜である➔実質的な, 事実上の ‖ The country is in a state of virtual civil war. その国は事実上の内戦状態にある. ▶定義2 made to appear to exist by computer コンピューターにより、実在しているように見える➔仮想の ‖ virtual reality 仮想現実 — virtually /-tʃuəli/ 副➔実質的には, 事実上は ‖ The building is virtually finished. その建物は実質的には完成している.

**\*virtue** /vɜ́:rtʃu:/ 名 ▶定義1 ⒰behaviour which shows high moral standards 高い道徳水準を示す振る舞い➔道徳的態度, 善行 ‖ to lead a life of virtue 徳のある人生を送る ☛類 goodness ▶定義2 ⒞a good quality or habit 良い性質または習慣➔徳, 美徳, 道徳 ‖ Patience is a great virtue. 忍耐はすばらしい美徳だ. ☛参 vice ▶定義3 ⒞⒰ the virtue (of sth/of being/doing sth) an advantage or a useful quality of sth 〜の利点または有益な性質➔長所, 良いところ ‖

*This new material **has the virtue** of being strong as well as very light.* この新しい素材は、非常に軽いだけではなく強いという利点も持っている.

成句 **by virtue of** 正式 ▶定義 by means of sth or because of sth ～の手段によって、または～の理由によって→～のお陰で、～が理由で

**virtuoso** /vɜːrtʃuˈóusou, -zou/ 名 C (複 **virtuosos** または **virtuosi**) ▶定義 a person who is extremely skilful at sth, especially playing a musical instrument 何かに非常に熟練した人で、特に楽器を演奏する人→名人, 名手, 達人, 巨匠

**virtuous** /vɜ́ːrtʃuəs/ 形 ▶定義 behaving in a morally good way 道徳的に正しく振る舞っている→徳の高い, 高潔な

**virulent** /vír(j)ələnt/ 形 ▶定義 1 (used about a poison or a disease) very strong and dangerous （毒または病気について）非常に強くて危険な→有毒な, 悪性の ‖ *a particularly virulent form of influenza* ことに悪性の種類の流行性感冒 ▶定義 2 正式 very strong and full of anger 非常に強いそして怒りに満ちた→敵意に満ちた, 憎悪を持った ‖ *a virulent attack on the leader* 指導者に対する敵意に満ちた攻撃

\***virus** /váiərəs/ 名 C (複 **viruses**) ▶定義 1 a living thing, too small to be seen without a special instrument (microscope), that causes disease in people, animals and plants 非常に小さいために特別な器具（顕微鏡）がなければ見えない生命体で、人間, 動物また植物の病気の原因となるもの→ウイルス ‖ *HIV, the virus that is thought to cause Aids* HIV, すなわちエイズの原因と考えられているウイルス *to catch a virus* ウイルスに感染する ☞参 **bacteria**, **germ** ▶定義 2 (computing) instructions that are put into a computer program in order to stop it working properly and destroy information（コンピューター）プログラムが正常に働くのを停止させ情報を破壊するために, コンピュータープログラムの中に送り込まれた命令→コンピューターウイルス

**visa** /víːzə, -sə/ 名 C ▶定義 an official mark or piece of paper that shows you are allowed to enter, leave or travel through a country 公式の印または書類で, ある国を入国, 出国または通過する許可を示したもの→入国査証, ビザ ‖ *His passport was full of visa stamps.* 彼のパスポートは, 入国査証のスタンプで一杯だった. *a tourist/work/student visa* 観光・労働・学生ビザ

**vise** 米 = **VICE(3)**

**visibility** /vìzəbíləti/ 名 U ▶定義 the distance that you can see in particular light or weather conditions 特定の光または気象状況の下で見ることができる距離→視界, 視距離 ‖ *In the fog visibility was down to 50 metres.* 霧の中で視界は50メートルに低下していた. *poor/good visibility* 視界の悪さ・良さ

\***visible** /vízəb(ə)l/ 形 ▶定義 that can be seen or noticed 見えるまたは気付くことのできる→目に見える, 視認可能な ‖ *The church tower was visible from the other side of the valley.* 教会の塔は谷のもう一方の側からも見えた. *a visible improvement in his work* 彼の仕事での目に見えて明らかな上達 ⇔ **invisible** — **visibly** /-(ə)li/ 副 →明らかに, 目に見えて ‖ *Rosa was visibly upset.* ローザは明らかに気分を害していた.

\***vision** /víʒ(ə)n/ 名 ▶定義 1 U the ability to see; sight 見る能力, 視覚→視力 ‖ *to have good/poor/normal/perfect vision* 視力が良い・弱い・普通である・完ぺきである ▶定義 2 C a picture in your imagination 想像の中に描かれたもの→空想, 理想像 ‖ *They have a vision of a world without weapons.* 彼らは武器のない世界という理想像を抱いている. *I had visions of being left behind, but in fact the others had waited for me.* 私は置き去りにされるものと想像したが, 実際にはほかの人たちは私を待ってくれていた. ▶定義 3 C a dream or similar experience often connected with religion しばしば宗教に関係する, 夢または同様の経験→幻, 幻覚, 幻影 ▶定義 4 U the ability to make great plans for the future 将来に向けて壮大な計画を立てる能力→予見力, 先見(の明) ‖ *a leader of great vision* 偉大な先見の明を持つ指導者 ▶定義 5 U the picture on a television or cinema screen テレビ画面または映画のスクリーンに描かれるもの→映像, 画像 ‖ *a temporary loss of vision* 映像の一時的な中断

**visionary** /víʒ(ə)nəri; -èri/ 形 ▶定義 having great plans for the future 将来に向けて壮大な計画を持っている→先見の明のある, 予見力のある ‖ *a visionary leader* 先見の明のある指導者 — **visionary** 名 C →先見の明のある人, 空想家, 理想

主義者

**\*visit** /vízət/ 動自他 ▶定義 to go to see a person or place for a period of time 人または場所を一定期間訪ねていく→(〜を)訪問する, 訪ねる ‖ *I don't live here. I'm just visiting.* 私はここに住んでいません. ただ滞在しているだけです. *We often visit relatives at the weekend.* 私たちは週末にしばしば親戚(しんせき)を訪れる. *She's going to visit her son in hospital.* 彼女は病院に息子の見舞いに行くところです. *When you go to London you must visit the Science Museum.* ロンドンに行ったら, 科学博物館に行かなければなりません. — visit 名 C→訪問 ‖ *The Prime Minister is on a visit to Germany.* 首相はドイツを訪問している. *We had a flying (= very short) visit from Richard on Sunday.* 私たちは日曜日にリチャードの慌ただしい(= 非常に短時間の)訪問を受けた.

**\*visitor** /vízətər/ 名 C ▶定義 a person who visits sb/sth 人・物を訪ねる人→訪問客, 来客, 観光客 ‖ *visitors to London from overseas* 海外からのロンドン観光客

**visor** /váizər/ 名 C ▶定義 1 the part of a hard hat (a helmet) that you can pull down to protect your eyes or face 堅固な帽子(ヘルメット)の一部分で, 下に引き下げて目または顔を保護するためのもの→面頬(めんぼお), 風防 ▶定義 2 a piece of plastic, cloth, etc on a hat or in a car, which stops the sun shining into your eyes 帽子または車にあるプラスチック, 布などで, 日差しが目に入るのを防ぐもの→ひさし, 日よけ板 ☞ hatのさし絵

**\*visual** /víʒuəl/ 形 ▶定義 connected with seeing 視覚に関する→視覚の ‖ *the visual arts (= painting, sculpture, cinema, etc)* 視覚芸術(= 絵画, 彫刻, 映画など) — **visually** /víʒuəli/ 副 →視覚の面で, 視覚的に ‖ *The film is visually stunning.* その映画は視覚的に驚くほど美しい.

**visual aid** 名 C ▶定義 a picture, film, map, etc that helps a pupil to learn sth 絵, 映画, 地図など, 生徒が何かを学習する助けになるもの→視覚教材

**visualize** (または **-ise**) /víʒuəlàiz/ 動他 ▶定義 to imagine or have a picture in your mind of sb/sth 〜のイメージを想像するまたは心に抱く→〜を思い描く ‖ *It's hard to visualize what this place looked like before the factory was built.* 工場が建設される前のこの場所がどのような様子だったのかを想像するのは難しい.

**\*vital** /váɪtl/ 形 ▶定義 1 very important or necessary 非常に重要または必要な→極めて重要な, 不可欠な ‖ *Practice is vital if you want to speak a language well.* ある言語を上手に話したいならば, 練習が不可欠だ. *vital information* 極めて重要な情報 ▶定義 2 full of energy; lively 活力に満ちた; 活発な→活気のある, 元気の良い — **vitally** /váɪtli/ 副 →極めて, 決定的に ‖ *vitally important* 極めて重要な

**vitality** /vaɪtǽləti/ 名 U ▶定義 the state of being full of energy 活力に満ちた状態→活気, 躍動感

**\*vitamin** /vítəmən; váɪt-/ 名 C ▶定義 one of several substances that are found in certain types of food and that are important for growth and good health ある種の食物に含まれるいくつかの物質の1つで, 成長および健康のために重要なもの→ビタミン ‖ *Oranges are rich in vitamin C.* オレンジはビタミンCが豊富です.

**vivacious** /vəvéɪʃəs, vaɪ-/ 形 ▶定義 (used about a person, usually a woman) full of energy; lively and happy (人, 通常は女性について)活力に満ちた; 活発で幸福な→生き生きした, はつらつとした

**vivid** /vívəd/ 形 ▶定義 1 having or producing a strong, clear picture in your mind 心の中に強烈で鮮明なイメージを抱くまたは作り出す→生き生きとした, 迫真の, 鮮やかな ‖ *vivid dreams/memories* 鮮明な夢・生々しい記憶 ▶定義 2 (used about light or a colour) strong and very bright (光または色について)強烈で非常に明るい→鮮やかな ‖ *the vivid reds and yellows of the flowers* 花々の鮮明な赤と黄色 — **vividly** 副 →鮮やかに, 鮮明に

**vivisection** /vìvəsékʃ(ə)n/ 名 U ▶定義 doing scientific experiments on live animals 生きている動物で科学実験を行うこと→(動物の)生体実験

**vixen** /víks(ə)n/ 名 C ▶定義 the female of a type of reddish wild dog (fox) 赤みを帯びた野生のイヌ科の動物(キツネ)の雌→雌ギツネ

**viz** /vɪz, néɪmli/ 略 (しばしばnamelyと読まれる) ▶定義 that is to say; in other words ということは; 言い換えれば→すなわち, つまり

**vocabulary** /vouk&ébjəl(ə)ri, və-; -lèri/ 名 (複 **vocabularies**) ▶定義1 ❸⓾ all the words that sb knows or that are used in a particular book, subject, etc 人が知っている、またはある特定の書物、主題などで用いられる、すべての語→**語彙（ごい）** ‖ He has an amazing vocabulary for a five-year-old. 彼は5歳にしては驚くべき語彙を持っている. There are many ways to increase your English vocabulary. 英語の語彙を増やすには多くの方法がある. ▶定義2 [単数扱い] all the words in a language ある言語に含まれるすべての語→**語彙総体** ‖ New words are always coming into the vocabulary. 常に新しい語句がその言語の語彙に加わっている.

**vocal** /vóuk(ə)l/ 形 ▶定義1 (名詞の前だけ) connected with the voice 声に関する→**声の, 音声の** ‖ **vocal cords** (= the muscles in the back of your throat that move to produce the voice) 声帯 (= 声を作り出すために動く, のどの後ろにある筋肉) ▶定義2 expressing your ideas or opinions loudly or freely 考えまたは意見を, 声高にまたは自由に述べる→**はっきりものを言う, 強硬な** ‖ a small but vocal group of protesters 小人数だが強硬な抗議団体

**vocalist** /vóuk(ə)lɪst/ 名 ❸ ▶定義 a singer, especially in a band 特にバンドでの, 歌い手→**歌手, ボーカリスト** ‖ a lead/backing vocalist リードボーカリスト・伴奏歌手

**vocation** /voukéɪʃ(ə)n/ 名 ❸⓾ ▶定義 a type of work or a way of life that you believe to be especially suitable for you 自分に特に適していると信じている種類の仕事または生き方→**天職** ‖ Peter has finally found his vocation in life. ピーターはついに人生の天職を見つけた.

**vocational** /voukéɪʃ(ə)n(ə)l/ 形 ▶定義 connected with the skills, knowledge, etc that you need to do a particular job ある特定の仕事をする上で必要な技能, 知識などに関する→**職業の, 職業に関する** ‖ vocational training 職業訓練

**vociferous** /vousíf(ə)rəs/ 形 正式 ▶定義 expressing your opinions or feelings in a loud and confident way 声高で無遠慮に意見または感情を述べる→**わめき立てる, 声高な** — **vociferously** 副→**やかましく, 声高に**

**vodka** /vádkə/ 名 ⓾ ▶定義 a strong clear alcoholic drink originally from Russia アルコール度が高く透明な酒で, 元はロシア産のもの→**ウオッカ**

**vogue** /vóug/ 名 ❸⓾ ▶定義 a vogue (for sth) a fashion for sth 物の流行→**(〜の) はやり** ‖ a vogue for large cars 大型車の流行 That hairstyle is **in vogue** at the moment. 今あの髪形がはやっている.

**voice**¹ /vɔ́ɪs/ 名 ▶定義1 ❸ the sounds that you make when you speak or sing; the ability to make these sounds 話すまたは歌うときに出す音; これらの音を出す能力→**声, 声を出す力** ‖ He had a bad cold and **lost** his **voice** (= could not speak for a period of time). 彼はひどい風邪を引いて, 声が出なかった (= 一定期間, 話すことができなかった). to speak in a loud/soft/low/hoarse voice 大声・小声・低い声・しわがれ声で話す to lower/raise your voice (= speak more quietly/loudly) 声を落とす・声を大きくする (= より静かに・より大声で話す) Shh! **Keep your voice down!** しっ. 静かに話してください. Alan is 13 and his **voice is breaking** (= becoming deep and low like a man's). アランは13歳で, 変声期を迎えている (= 成年男子のように, 太く低い声になる). ▶定義2 **-voiced** (複合形容詞を作るために用いて) having a voice of the type mentioned 示された種類の声を持つ→**〜声の** ‖ husky-voiced ハスキーな声の ▶定義3 [単数扱い] **a voice (in sth)** (the right to express) your ideas or opinions 自分の考えまたは意見 (を述べる権利)→**発言権** ‖ The workers want more of a voice in the running of the company. 従業員たちは, 会社の経営についてより強い発言権を要求している. ▶定義4 ❸ a particular feeling, attitude or opinion that you have or express 人が抱くまたは表明する特定の感情, 態度または意見→**意見, 声** ‖ You should listen to the voice of reason and apologise. あなたは理性の声を聞いて謝るべきだ. ▶定義5 [単数扱い] (文法) the form of a verb that shows if a sentence is active or passive 文が能動であるか受動であるかを示す動詞の形態→**態** ‖ 'Keats wrote this poem' is in the **active voice**. 「キーツがこの詩を書いた」という文は能動態である. 'This poem was written by Keats' is in the **passive voice**. 「この詩はキーツによって書かれた」という文は受動態である.

▶受動態についての説明は,巻末の「文法早見表」を参照.

成句 at the top of your voice ⇒ TOP¹

**voice²** /vɔ́ɪs/ 動他 ▶定義 to express your opinions or feelings 意見または感情を述べる→意見を口に出す ‖ *to voice complaints/criticisms* 不満・批判を口にする

**void¹** /vɔ́ɪd/ 名[C, 通常は単数] 正式 ▶定義 a large empty space 広くて空っぽの空間→真空, 虚無感 ‖ *Her death left a void in their lives.* 彼女の死は彼らの人生に喪失感を残した.

**void²** /vɔ́ɪd/ 形 ▶定義1 (used about a ticket, contract, decision, etc) that can no longer be accepted or used (切符,契約,決定などについて)もはや受け入れられないまたは使用できない→無効の ‖ *The agreement was declared void.* その協定は無効であると宣言された. ▶定義2 正式 void (of sth) completely lacking sth 〜を完全に欠いた→〜のない ‖ *This book is totally void of interest for me.* この本は私には全く興味に欠ける.

**vol** 略 ▶定義1 (複 vols) volume (of a book)→(本の)1巻, 1冊 ‖ *The Complete Works of Byron, Vol 2* バイロン全著作集の第2巻 ▶定義2 volume→容積,体積 ‖ *vol 333 ml* 容量は333ミリリットル

**volatile** /vάlətàɪl; -t(ə)l/ 形 ▶定義1 that can change suddenly and unexpectedly 突然,不意に変わり得る→変わりやすい,不安定な ‖ *a highly volatile situation which could easily develop into rioting* すぐに暴動に発展しそうな,極めて不安定な状況 *a volatile personality* 気まぐれな性格 ▶定義2 (used about a liquid) that can easily change into a gas (液体について)気体になりやすい→揮発性の, 爆発しやすい

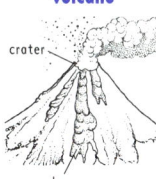

volcano

crater

lava

**volcano** /vɑlkéɪnoʊ/ 名 C (複 volcanoes; volcanos) ▶定義 a mountain with a hole (crater) at the top through which steam, hot melted rock (lava), fire, etc sometimes come out 頂上にくぼみ(噴火口)のある山で,水蒸気,熱く溶けた岩(溶岩),火などがそこから噴出することがある→火山 ‖ *an active/dormant/extinct volcano* 活火山・休火山・死火山 *When did the volcano last erupt?* 火山が最後に噴火したのはいつですか. — **volcanic** /vɑlkǽnɪk/ 形→火山性の ‖ *volcanic rock/ash* 火成岩・火山灰

*****volley** /vάli/ 名 C ▶定義1 (in tennis, etc) a hit or kick of the ball before it touches the ground (テニスなどで)球が地面に触れる前に打つまたはけること→ボレー ‖ *a forehand/backhand volley* フォアハンド・バックハンドボレー ▶定義2 a number of stones, bullets, etc that are thrown or shot at the same time 一度に投げられるまたは撃たれる,石または弾丸など→一斉射撃,雨あられ ‖ *The soldiers fired a volley over the heads of the crowd.* 兵士たちは群集の頭上に一斉射撃をした. ▶定義3 a lot of questions, insults, etc that are directed at one person very quickly, one after the other 1人の人に矢継ぎ早に向けられる,多数の質問,侮辱的言動など→連発 ‖ *a volley of abuse* 矢継ぎ早の罵詈雑言(ばりぞうごん) — **volley** 動 自 他 (〜を)ボレーで返す,ボレーをする ‖ *Rios volleyed the ball into the net.* ライオスはネットの中に球をボレーで返した.

**volleyball** /vάlibɔ̀ːl/ 名 U ▶定義 a game in which two teams of six players hit a ball over a high net with their hands while trying not to let the ball touch the ground on their own side 自陣の床にボールが触れないようにしながら,6人から成る2チームが高いネット越しにボールを手で打つ競技→バレーボール

**volt** /vóʊlt/ 名 C (略 v) ▶定義 a unit for measuring electrical force 電圧を計る単位→ボルト

**voltage** /vóʊltɪdʒ/ 名 形 C ▶定義 an electrical force measured in units (volts)→単位(ボルト)で表された電圧

*****volume** /vάljuːm, -jəm/ 名 ▶定義1 C U the amount of space that sth contains or fills 何かが内に含むまたは満たす空間の量→容積,体積 ‖ *What is the volume of this sphere?* この球体の容積はいくつですか. ☛参 **area(2)** ▶定義2 C U the large quantity or amount of sth 多量のまたは多数の物→大量,多量 ‖ *the sheer volume (= the large amount) of traffic on the roads* 路上の,驚くほど多い(= かなりの量の)交通量 *I've got volumes of work to get through.* 私にはやってしまうべき仕事が山のようにある. ▶定義3 [U, 単数扱い] how loud a sound is

## 1792 voluntary

音の大きさ→**音量, ボリューム** ‖ *to turn the volume on a radio up/down* ラジオのボリュームを上げる・下げる *a low/high volume* 小さい・大きい音量 ▶定義4 **C**(略**vol**) a book, especially one of a set or series 特に全集またはシリーズものの中の, 1冊の本→**巻** ‖ *The dictionary comes in three volumes.* その辞書は全3巻になっている.

★**voluntary** /válənt(ə)ri; -tèri/ 形 ▶定義1 done or given because you want to do it, not because you have to do it それをしなければならないからではなく, それをしたいために行われるまたは与えられる→**自発的な, 自由意志による** ‖ *He took voluntary redundancy and left the firm last year.* 彼は昨年自主退職に応じ, 会社を辞めた. ⇔ **compulsory** ▶定義2 done or working without payment 報酬なしでなされたまたは報酬なしで働く→**善意による, 無償の** ‖ *She does some voluntary work at the hospital.* 彼女は病院で無償奉仕をしている. ▶定義3 (used about movements of the body) that you can control (体の動きについて)制御できる→**随意の** ⇔ **involuntary** — **voluntarily** /válənt(ə)rəli; -tèr-, ╌╌╌/ 副 →**自発的に, 自主的に** ‖ *She left the job voluntarily, she wasn't sacked.* 彼女は自分から仕事を辞めたのであり, 首になったのではなかった.

★**volunteer**¹ /vàləntíər/ 名 **C** ▶定義1 a person who offers or agrees to do sth without being forced or paid to do it 強制されたり報酬を受けることなく, 何かをすることを申し出るまたはそうすることに同意する人→**ボランティア, 志願者, 有志** ‖ *Are there any volunteers to do the washing up?* だれか食器洗いをしてくれる人はいませんか. ▶定義2 a person who joins the armed forces without being ordered to 命令されることなく, 軍隊に入隊する人 →**志願兵, 義勇兵** ☞参 **conscript**²

★**volunteer**² /vàləntíər/ 動 ▶定義1 **自他** volunteer (sth); volunteer (to do sth) to offer sth or to do sth which you do not have to do or for which you will not be paid しなくてもよいまたは報酬を得られない〜を差し出すまたは行う→(進んで〜に)当たる ‖ *They volunteered their services free.* 彼らは進んで無料奉仕した. *She frequently volunteers for extra work because she really likes her job.* 彼女は本当に仕事が好きなので, しばしば自発的に残業する. *One of my friends volunteered to take us all in his car.* 友人の1人が, 私たち全員を彼の車で連れていくことを買って出た. ▶定義2 **自** volunteer (for sth) to join the armed forces without being ordered 命令されることなく, 軍隊に入隊する → (〜の) 志願兵になる, 義勇兵になる ▶定義3 **他** to give information, etc or to make a comment or suggestion without being asked to→**求められることなしに, 情報などを提供する, 批評・助言をする** ‖ *I volunteered a few helpful suggestions.* 私はいくつかの役に立つ助言を進んで与えた.

**vomit** /vámət/ 動 **自他** ▶定義 to bring food, etc up from the stomach and out of the mouth 食べ物などを胃から逆流させ, 口の外に出す→(〜を)**吐く, 戻す** ☛ イギリス英語の日常会話では, be sick と言う. — vomit 名 **U** →**吐くこと, おう吐**

★**vote**¹ /vóut/ 名 ▶定義1 **C** a vote (for/against sb/sth) a formal choice in an election or at a meeting, which you show by holding up your hand or writing on a piece of paper 選挙法は会議での正式な選択行為で, 挙手または用紙に記すことによって意思表示するもの→**投票** ‖ *The votes are still being counted.* 投票用紙はまだ集計中だ. *There were 10 votes for, and 25 against the motion.* その動議に対する賛成は10票, 反対は25票だった. ▶定義2 **C** a vote (on sth) a method of deciding sth by asking people to express their choice and finding out what most people want 人々に選択を示すように求め, 最も多くの人々が望んでいる事を見つけ出すことによって, 物事を決定する方法→**票決, 採決** ‖ *The democratic way to decide this would be to take a vote.* これを決めるための民主的な方法は, 投票で選ぶことだろう. *Let's have a vote/put it to the vote.* 投票で決めましょう・採決しましょう. ▶定義3 **the vote** [単数扱い] the total number of votes in an election 選挙における全体の投票数→**投票総数** ‖ *She obtained 30% of the vote.* 彼女は投票総数の30パーセントを獲得した. ▶定義4 **the vote** [単数扱い] the legal right to vote in political elections 政治の選挙で投票する法的権利→**選挙権, 参政権** ‖ *Women did* *not get the vote in this country until the 1920s.* この国では, 女性は 1920 年代まで選挙権を得られなかった.

**成句** cast a/your vote ⇒ **CAST**¹
a vote of thanks ▶定義 a short speech to thank sb, usually a guest at a meeting, dinner, etc 人に謝意を表すための短い演説で, 通常は会議または晩餐(ばんさん)会などの来賓のために行う→**感謝の辞** ‖ *The club secretary proposed a vote of thanks to the guest speaker.* クラブの幹事はゲスト講演者に対する感謝の辞を述べた(感謝決議を提案した).

*****vote**² /vóʊt/ 動 ▶定義1 自他 vote (for/against sb/sth); vote (on sth); vote to do sth to show formally a choice or opinion by marking a piece of paper or by holding up your hand 用紙に記すまたは挙手することによって, 選択または意見を公式に示す→**(〜に賛成・反対して)投票する; (〜を)採決する** ‖ *Who did you vote for in the last general election?* この前の総選挙では, あなたはだれに投票しましたか. *46% voted in favour of (= for) the proposed change.* 46 パーセントが, 提案された変更を支持する(= 賛成の)投票をした. *Very few MPs voted against the new law.* 新しい法律に反対の票を投じた下院議員はほとんどいなかった. *After the debate we'll vote on the motion.* 討論の後, 私たちはその動議を採決に付す予定だ. *They voted to change the rules of the club.* 彼らはクラブの規則を変更するように票決した. *I voted Liberal Democrat.* 私は自由民主党に投票した. ▶定義2 他 (通常は受動態で) to choose sb for a particular position or prize→**ある特定の地位・賞に〜を選ぶ** ‖ *He was voted best actor at the Oscars.* 彼はオスカーの最優秀主演男優賞に選ばれた. — voter 名 ⓒ→**投票者, 有権者**

**vouch** /vaʊtʃ/ 動自 ▶定義 vouch for sb/sth to say that a person is honest or good or that sth is true or genuine 〜が正直であるまたは優れていると言う, あるいは〜が本当であるまたは本物であると言う→**(〜を)請け合う, 保証する, 太鼓判を押す**

**voucher** /váʊtʃər/ 名 ⓒ 英 ▶定義 a piece of paper that you can use instead of money to pay for all or part of sth 物の全額または一部の支払いができる, お金の代わりに使える紙片→**引換券, クーポン** ↜参 token

**vow** /vaʊ/ 名 ⓒ ▶定義 a formal and serious promise (especially in a religious ceremony) 正式で厳粛な約束(特に宗教儀式において)→**誓い, 誓約** ‖ *to keep/break your marriage vow* 結婚に際しての誓いを守る・破る — vow 動 他 〜を誓う, 誓約する ‖ *We vowed never to discuss the subject again.* 私たちはこの問題について二度と再び議論しないことを誓った.

*****vowel** /váʊ(ə)l/ 名 ⓒ ▶定義 any of the sounds represented in English by the letters a, e, i, o or u 英語で a, e, i, o, u の文字で表される音のいずれか→**母音** ↜参 consonant

**voyage** /vɔ́ɪɪdʒ/ 名 ⓒ ▶定義 a long journey by sea or in space 船上または宇宙での長い旅→**航海, 宇宙旅行** ‖ *a voyage to Jupiter* 木星への宇宙旅行 — voyager 名 ⓒ→**航海者, 旅行者**

**VSO** /ˌviː es óʊ/ 略 医 Voluntary Service Overseas ▶定義 a scheme for people to go to work in developing countries 発展途上国に働きに行く人々のための事業→**海外協力隊**

**vulgar** /vʌ́lɡər/ 形 ▶定義1 not having or showing good judgement about what is attractive or appropriate; not polite or well-behaved 何が魅力的あるいは適切であるかについて, 適正な判断を持たないまたは示さない; 礼儀正しくないまたは行儀が良くない→**悪趣味な, 下品な** ‖ *vulgar furnishings* 悪趣味な調度品 *a vulgar man/woman* 下品な男・女 ▶定義2 rude or likely to offend people 無礼な, 人の気に障りそうな→**わいせつな, 野卑な** ‖ *a vulgar joke* 卑わいな冗談 — vulgarity /vʌlɡǽrəti/ 名 ⓒ Ⓤ (複 vulgarities)→**下品, 粗野, わいせつ, 悪趣味**

**vulnerable** /vʌ́ln(ə)rəb(ə)l/ 形 ▶定義 vulnerable (to sth/sb) weak and easy to hurt physically or emotionally 身体的または感情的に弱く, 傷付きやすい→**か弱い, 攻撃されやすい** ‖ *Poor organization left the troops vulnerable to enemy attack.* 貧弱な編制のため, 軍隊は敵の攻撃に対して無防備な状態に置かれた. ⇔ **invulnerable** — vulnerability /vʌ̀ln(ə)rəbíləti/ 名 Ⓤ→**傷付きやすいこと, 無防備**

**vulture** /vʌ́ltʃər/ 名 ⓒ ▶定義 a large bird with no feathers on its head or neck that eats dead animals 死んだ動物を食べる, 頭部または首に羽毛のない大型の鳥→**ハゲタカ, コンドル**

# W w

**W, w**¹ /dʌ́b(ə)ljuː/ 名 C (複 **W's**; **w's**) ▶定義 the twenty-third letter of the English alphabet 英語アルファベットの第23文字 →w(W)が表す音, w(W)の文字, w(W)の字形のもの ∥ *'Water' begins with (a) 'W'.* WaterはWで始まる.

**W**² 略 ▶定義 **1** watt(s)→ワット ∥ *a 60W light bulb* 60ワットの電球 ▶定義 **2** west(ern)→西(の) ∥ *W Cumbria* 西カンブリア地方(イングランド北西部)

**wacky** (または **whacky**) /wǽki/ 形 略式 ▶定義 amusing or funny in a slightly crazy way 少々狂気染みて, 面白い, こっけいな →風変わりな, おどけた

**wad** /wɑd/ 名 C ▶定義 **1** a large number of papers, paper money, etc folded or rolled together 一緒に折り畳んだ, あるいは巻いた多量の紙, 紙幣など→束, 札束 ∥ *He pulled a wad of £20 notes out of his pocket.* 彼は20ポンド紙幣の札束をポケットから取り出した. ▶定義 **2** a mass of soft material that is used for blocking sth or keeping sth in place 〜をふさいだり, 〜をその場所に固定するための柔らかい素材の塊→詰め物, (紙・綿・ぼろ切れなどによる)押さえ ∥ *The nurse used a wad of cotton wool to stop the bleeding.* 看護婦は, 止血用に丸めた脱脂綿を使った.

**waddle** /wɑ́dl/ 動自 ▶定義 to walk with short steps, moving the weight of your body from one side to the other, like a duck アヒルのように体を左右に振りながら短い歩幅で歩く→よちよち歩く, よたよた歩く

**wade** /wéid/ 動自 ▶定義 to walk with difficulty through fairly deep water, mud, etc ある程度深みのある水やぬかるみなどの中を苦労して歩く→やっと歩く, 苦労して歩く

句動詞 **wade through sth** ▶定義 to deal with or read sth that is boring and takes a long time 退屈で時間のかかる〜に取り組む, あるいは読み通す →〜を苦労して進む, やり通す, やっと切り抜ける

**wafer** /wéifər/ 名 C ▶定義 a very thin, dry biscuit often eaten with ice cream 薄くて乾燥したビスケットの一種で, よくアイスクリームと共に食べる→ウエファース, ウエハース

**waffle**¹ /wɑ́f(ə)l, wɔ́ː-/ 名 ▶定義 **1** C a flat cake with a pattern of squares on it that is often eaten warm with a sweet sauce (syrup) 格子模様の付いた平たいケーキで, しばしば温かいまま甘いソース(シロップ)を掛けて食べる →ワッフル ▶定義 **2** U 英 略式 language that uses a lot of words but that does not say anything important or interesting 言葉を多く用いるが, 内容が重要でないまたは興味をかき立てない話や文章 →無駄口, つまらない話 ∥ *The last two paragraphs of your essay are just waffle.* あなたの小論文の最後の2段落は, まさに駄文だ.

**waffle**² /wɑ́f(ə)l, wɔ́ː-/ 動自 英 略式 ▶定義 **waffle (on) (about sth)** to talk or write for much longer than necessary without saying anything important or interesting 重要な事や興味深い事を何も含まず, 必要以上に長く話したり記述する→無駄口をたたく, 駄文を書く

**waft** /wɑːft, wɑft, wæft/ 動自他 ▶定義 to move, or make sth move, gently through the air 空気中を穏やかに動く, あるいは〜を動かす→漂う, 漂わせる ∥ *The smell of her perfume wafted across the room.* 彼女の香水の香りが部屋中に漂っていた.

**wag** /wǽg/ 動自他 (**wagging**; **wagged**) ▶定義 to shake up and down or move from side to side; to make sth do this 上下に揺れる, または左右に振れる; 〜にそのような動きをさせる→揺れる; 〜を振る, 振り動かす ∥ *The dog wagged its tail.* その犬はしっぽを振った.

★**wage**¹ /wéidʒ/ 名 [単数扱い] (または **wages** [複数扱い]) ▶定義 the regular amount of money that you earn for a week's work 1週間の労働で稼ぐ一定金額→(特に肉体労働による)賃金, 給料, 週給 ∥ *a weekly wage of £200* 週給200ポンド *What's the national minimum wage (= the lowest wage that an employer is allowed to pay by law)?* 国定の最低賃金(= 法律により, 雇用者が支払うことを認められている最低の賃金)はいくらですか.

▶単数形wageは主に, 支払われた金額について, あるいはwage packet(給料袋), wage rise(賃上げ)などのようにほかの単語と組み合わせて用いられる. 複数形wagesはその金自体を表す: *I have to pay the rent out of my wages.* (私は給料の中から賃貸料を支払わなければならない.) pay²の注を参照.

**wage²** /wéɪdʒ/ 動他 ▶定義 wage sth (against/on sb/sth) to begin and then continue a war, battle, etc 戦争, 戦闘を始め, 継続する→(戦争・戦闘などを)遂行する, 行う ‖ *to wage war on your enemy* 敵に戦争を仕掛ける

**waggle** /wǽg(ə)l/ 動自他 略式 ▶定義 to move up and down or from side to side with quick, short movements; to make sth do this 上下または左右に素早く短く動く; ～をそのようにさせる→揺れる; ～を揺らす, ～を振る

**wagon** /wǽgən/ 名 C (米 **freight car**) ▶定義 an open railway truck used for carrying goods or animals 荷物や動物を輸送するのに使う屋根のない貨車→無蓋(むがい)貨車 ‖ *coal transported in goods wagons* 貨車で輸送された石炭

**waif** /wéɪf/ 名 C ▶定義 a small thin person, usually a child, who seems to have nowhere to live 見たところ住む所がない小さなやせた人で, 通常は子供→浮浪児, 浮浪者

**wail** /wéɪl/ 動 ▶定義1 自他 to cry or complain in a loud, high voice, especially because you are sad or in pain 悲しさや痛さのあまり, 大きな甲高い声で泣く, あるいは訴える→嘆き悲しむ, 泣き叫ぶ ▶定義2 自 (used about things) to make a sound like this (物について)そのような音を出す→(風・サイレンなどが)泣くような音を出す ‖ *sirens wailing in the streets outside* 外の通りで物悲しく響くサイレン — **wail** 名 C ▶悲痛の泣き声, 叫び声 ‖ *a wail of anguish/despair/distress* 苦悩・絶望・悲しみの叫び *the wail of sirens* サイレンの物悲しい音

*****waist** /wéɪst/ 名 [ C, 通常は単数 ] ▶定義1 the narrowest part around the middle of your body 身体の中央の最も細い部分→腰, ウエスト ‖ *She put her arms around his waist.* 彼女は彼の腰に両腕を回した. ☞ C5ページのさし絵 ▶定義2 the part of a piece of clothing that goes round the waist 衣服の腰回り→胴部, ウエスト ‖ *The trousers are too baggy round the waist.* そのズボンはウエストがぶかぶかだ.

**waistband** /wéɪstbæ̀nd/ 名 C ▶定義 the narrow piece of material at the waist of a piece of clothing, especially trousers or a skirt 衣服の, 特にズボンやスカートのウエスト部分に着ける細長いもの→ベルト, 腰ひも, 腰帯 ☞ C6ページのさし絵

**waistcoat** /wéɪstkòʊt/ ( 米 **vest**) 名 C ▶定義 a piece of clothing with buttons down the front and no sleeves that is often worn over a shirt and under a jacket as part of a man's suit 前のボタンが縦に並んだそでのない衣服で男性用スーツの一部として, しばしばシャツの上, ジャケットの下に着用される→ベスト, チョッキ ☞ C6ページのさし絵

**waistline** /wéɪstlàɪn/ 名 [ C, 通常は単数 ] ▶定義1 (used to talk about how fat or thin a person is) the measurement or size of the body around the waist (人が太っているかやせているかについて)胴回りの寸法, または大きさ→腰のくびれ, 腰線 ▶定義2 the place on a piece of clothing where your waist is 衣服のウエスト部分→胴回り, ウエストライン

*****wait¹** /wéɪt/ 動自 ▶定義1 wait (for sb/sth) (to do sth) to stay in a particular place, and not do anything until sb/sth arrives or until sth happens ～が到着するまで, または～が起こるまで, 何もせずにある特定の場所にとどまる→待つ, 待ち受ける, 待機する ‖ *Wait here. I'll be back in a few minutes.* ここでお待ちください. 数分で戻ります. *Have you been waiting long?* 長いことお待ちになりましたか. *If I'm a bit late, can you wait for me?* もし私が少し遅れても, 待ってくれますか. *I'm waiting to see the doctor.* 私は医者に診てもらうため, 順番待ちをしている.

▶ wait, expect と比較: *I was expecting him to be there at 7.30 but at 8 I was still waiting.* (私は7時30分に彼がそこに今来るかと待っていたが, 8時になってもまだ待っている状態だった.) *I'm waiting for the exam results but I'm not expecting to pass.* (私は試験結果を待ち受けているが, 合格すると期待してはいない.) ～が起こる, または～が到着するまで, 何もせずに1箇所にとどまって時間を過ごす場合に wait を用いる: *I waited outside the theatre until they arrived.* (彼らが到着するまで, 私は劇場の外で待っていた.) 何かが起こる可能性が高いと考え, または信じて, それが起こるまでほかの事をして時間を過ごす場合に expect を用いる: *I'm expecting you to get a good grade in your exam.* (あなたが試験で良い成績を取ると私は期待しています.)

## 1796 wait[2]

▶定義2 to be left or delayed until a later time もっと後までほうっておかれる,または先延ばしされる→**放置される,延期される** ‖ *Is this matter urgent or* **can** *it* **wait**? この件は緊急ですか,それとも後回しにできますか.

成句 **can't wait/can hardly wait** ▶定義 used when you are emphasizing that sb is very excited and enthusiastic about doing sth ～が…をすることについて非常に興奮し,また熱狂していることを強調するのに用いて→**～したくて待ちきれない,～が待ち遠しい** ‖ *The kids can't wait to see their father again.* 子供たちは父に再会するのが待ち遠しくてたまらない.

**keep sb waiting** ▶定義 to make sb wait or be delayed, especially because you arrive late 遅れて到着するので,～を待たせる,あるいは遅延させる→**～を待たせる,～を待たせておく** ‖ *I'm sorry if I've kept you waiting.* お待たせしたとしたら,ごめんなさい.

**wait and see** ▶定義 to be patient and find out what will happen later (perhaps before deciding to do sth) (行動を決定する前に) 辛抱強く,後に起きるであろう事を突き止める→**成り行きを見守る,静観する** ‖ *We'll just have to wait and see - there's nothing more we can do.* 私たちはただ静観するしかありません － 私たちにできる事はもう何もありませんから.

**wait your turn** ▶定義 to wait until the time when you are allowed to do sth ～をすることが許される時まで待つ→**時機を待つ,順番を待つ**

句動詞 **wait behind** ▶定義 to stay in a place after others have left it ほかの人々が去った後もある場所にとどまる→**居残る,残って待つ** ‖ *She waited behind after class to speak to her teacher.* 彼女は授業の後,先生と話をするために居残った.

**wait in** ▶定義 to stay at home because you are expecting sb to come or sth to happen ～が来る,または～が起こるのを期待しているので,家にとどまる→**自宅待機する**

**wait on sb** ▶定義 to serve food, drink etc to sb, usually in a restaurant 通常はレストランで～に食事や飲み物などを給仕する→**給仕をする**

**wait up (for sb)** ▶定義 to not go to bed because you are waiting for sb to come home ～が帰ってくるのを待っているので,寝ないでおく→**寝ないで待つ,起きて待つ**

★**wait**[2] /wéɪt/ 名 [C, 通常は単数] ▶定義 **a wait (for sth/sb)** a period of time when you wait 待っている時間→**待ち時間**

成句 **lie in wait (for sb)** ⇒ LIE[2]

★**waiter** /wéɪtər/ 名 C ▶定義 a man whose job is to serve customers at their tables in a restaurant, etc レストランなどで,食卓で客たちに給仕することが仕事の男性→**給仕,ウエーター**

**waiting list** 名 C ▶定義 a list of people who are waiting for sth, for example a service or medical treatment, that will be available in the future ～を待っている人々の名簿で,例えばサービスや治療を後で受けられるようにしておくもの→**順番待ち名簿,(病院の)受付簿** ‖ *to put your name* **on a waiting list** 氏名を受付簿に記入する

**waiting room** 名 C ▶定義 a room where people can sit while they are waiting, for example for a train, or to see a doctor or dentist 列車や医者,歯医者の治療などを待っている間,人々が座っていられる部屋→**待ち合い室**

★**waitress** /wéɪtrəs, -ɪs/ 名 C ▶定義 a woman whose job is to serve customers at their tables in a restaurant, etc レストランなどで,食卓で客たちに給仕することが仕事の女性→**女性の給仕,ウエートレス**

**waive** /wéɪv/ 動 他 正式 ▶定義 to say officially that a rule, etc need not be obeyed; to say officially that you no longer have a right to sth ある規則などに従う必要のないことを正式に述べる;人が～への権利をもはや持っていないことを正式に述べる→**～を免除する,～を放棄する** ‖ *In your case, we will waive your tuition fees.* あなたの場合,授業料が免除されるでしょう.

★**wake**[1] /wéɪk/ 動 自 他 (過 **woke** /wóʊk/; 過分 **woken** /wóʊk(ə)n/) ▶定義 **wake (sb) (up)** to stop sleeping; to make sb stop sleeping 眠っているのをやめる;～が眠っているのをやめさせる→**起きる;～を起こす** ‖ *I woke early in the morning and got straight out of bed.* 私は朝早く目を覚まし,すぐに起床した. *Wake up! It's nearly 8 o'clock!* 起きなさい.もうすぐ8時ですよ. *Could you wake me at 7.30, please?* 7時30分に私を起こしていただけませんか.

☛ 形 **awake**

句動詞 **wake sb up** ▶定義 to make sb become more active or full of energy ～をより活発に、または元気一杯になるようにする➡～を活気づかせる, 奮起させる ‖ *She always has a coffee to wake her up when she gets to work.* 彼女は仕事に取り掛かるとき、いつもコーヒーを飲んで自分をシャキッとさせる.

**wake up to sth** ▶定義 to realize sth; to notice sth ～に気付く; ～を認識する➡～に目覚める, ～に気付く

**wake**² /wéɪk/ 名 C ▶定義 **1** an occasion before a funeral when people meet to remember the dead person, traditionally held at night to watch over the body before it is buried 人々が死者を追悼するために集まる葬式の前の儀式で、伝統的に、夜間、埋葬される前の死者を見守るために行われる➡通夜 ▶定義 **2** the track that a moving ship leaves behind on the surface of the water 走行している船が水面に残す跡➡航跡

成句 **in the wake of sb/sth** ▶定義 following or coming after sb/sth ～の後に付いてくる、または続いてくる➡～の跡を追って, ～の直後に, ～の結果として ‖ *The earthquake left a trail of destruction in its wake.* 地震はその後に破壊のつめ跡を残した.

**waken** /wéɪk(ə)n/ 動 自 他 正式 (古) ▶定義 to stop sleeping or to make sb/sth stop sleeping 眠っているのをやめる、または～が眠っているのをやめさせる➡起きる; ～を起こす ‖ *She wakened from a deep sleep.* 彼女は深い眠りから目を覚ました.

★**walk**¹ /wɔːk/ 動 ▶定義 **1** 自 to move or go somewhere by putting one foot in front of the other on the ground, but without running 地面の上で、一方の足をもう片方の前に置いて移動する、あるいはどこかへ行く、ただし走らない➡歩く, 歩行する ‖ *The door opened and Billy walked in.* ドアが開き、ビリーが中へ入ってきた. *I walk to work every day.* 私は毎日歩いて出勤している. *He walks with a limp.* 彼は足を引きずって歩く. *Are the shops **within walking distance** (= near enough to walk to)?* それらの店は歩いていける距離にありますか(= 歩いていけるほど近いですか). ▶定義 **2** 自 to move in this way for exercise or pleasure➡運動や楽しみのために歩く ☛ 楽しみのために長時間歩くことを言い表すとき、しばしば go walking (散歩する, ぶらぶら

歩く, 徒歩旅行をする)を用いる. *We often go walking in the Alps in the summer.* 私たちは、夏にしばしばアルプスで山歩きをする. **walk**²の注を参照. ▶定義 **3** 他 to go somewhere with sb/sth on foot, especially to make sure he/she gets there safely 特に～がある場所に安全にたどり着くことを確かめるため、その～と一緒に歩いて出掛ける➡～に付き添って歩く, ～を送る ‖ *I'll **walk** you home if you don't want to go on your own.* 1人で帰りたくないのなら、私があなたを家まで送りましょう. *He walked me to my car.* 彼は私の車の所まで付き添ってくれた. ▶定義 **4** 他 to take a dog out for exercise 運動のために犬を外へ連れ出す➡(犬)を散歩させる ‖ *I'm just going to **walk the dog**.* 私はちょうど犬を散歩に連れていくところだ. — **walker** 名 C ➡歩く人, 散歩好きな人 ‖ *She's a fast walker.* 彼女は歩くのが速い. *This area is very popular with walkers.* この地域は散歩好きな人々に非常に人気がある.

句動詞 **walk off with sth** ▶定義 **1** to win sth easily ～をたやすく勝ち取る➡(賞など)をさらっていく, (試合など)に楽に勝つ ‖ *She walked off with all the prizes.* 彼女はすべての賞をさらっていった. ▶定義 **2** to steal sth; to take sth that does not belong to you by mistake ～を盗む; 誤って自分のものでない～を取る➡～を盗む, ～を誤って持っていく ‖ *When I got home I realized that I had walked off with her pen.* 家に着いた時、私は誤って彼女のペンを持ってきてしまったことに気付いた.

**walk out (of sth)** ▶定義 to leave suddenly and angrily 突然、怒って立ち去る➡突然出ていく, 立腹して出ていく ‖ *She walked out of the meeting in disgust.* 彼女は嫌気が差して会議を突然退席した.

**walk out on sb** 略式 ▶定義 to leave sb for ever 永久に～を見捨てる➡～を見捨てる, 見限る ‖ *He walked out on his wife and children after 15 years of marriage.* 彼は15年の結婚生活の後、妻と子供たちを捨てて出ていった.

**walk (all) over sb** 略式 ▶定義 **1** to treat sb badly, without considering his/her needs or feelings ～の要望や感情を考えずに、その～にひどい扱いをする➡～を虐待する, ～を虐げる ‖ I

# walk²

don't know why she lets her husband walk all over her like that. 自分の夫がそのように彼女を虐待することを、なぜ彼女が許すのか、私には分からない。▶定義 2 to defeat sb completely ～を完全に打ち負かす→～に完勝する‖ He played brilliantly and walked all over his opponent. 彼はすばらしい試合をして、対戦相手を打ち負かした。

**walk up (to sb/sth)** ▶定義 to walk towards sb/sth, especially in a confident way 特に自信に満ちた様子で、～に向かって歩く→～に歩み寄る、近寄る

★**walk²** /wɔːk/ 名 ▶定義 1 ❶ going somewhere on foot for pleasure, exercise, etc 楽しみや運動などのために徒歩でどこかへ行くこと→散歩、徒歩旅行‖ We went for a walk in the country. 私たちは田舎を散歩した。I'm just going to take the dog for a walk. 私はちょうど犬を散歩に連れていくところだ。The beach is five minutes' walk/a five-minute walk from the hotel. 浜辺はそのホテルから歩いて5分の所にある。

▶楽しみのために短時間歩くことを述べるときは、go for a walkを用いる。数時間または数日間続くかもしれないような、長時間歩くことを述べるときは、go walkingを用いる。

▶定義 2 ❷ a path or route for walking for pleasure 楽しみのために歩く小道または道筋→散歩道、遊歩道‖ From here there's a lovely walk through the woods. ここから森を抜けるすてきな散歩道があります。▶定義 3 [単数扱い]a way or style of walking→歩き方、歩き振り‖ He has a funny walk. 彼はおかしな歩き方をする。

▶定義 4 [単数扱い]the speed of walking→歩く速度‖ She slowed to a walk. 彼女は歩く速度を緩めた。

成句 **a walk of life** ▶定義 a person's job or position in society 人の職業、または社会における地位→職業分野、社会的階層‖ She has friends from all walks of life. 彼女にはあらゆる職種および社会的地位の友人がいる。

**walkie-talkie** /ˌwɔːki ˈtɔːki, ˌ- ˈ-/ 名 ❷ 略式
▶定義 a small radio that you can carry with you to send or receive messages メッセージを送受信するための、持ち運び可能な小型無線機→携帯用無線通話機、ウォーキートーキー

**walking stick**(または **stick**) 名 ❷ ▶定義 a stick that you carry and use as a support to help you walk 歩行を助けるための支えとして持ち運んで使用する棒→つえ、ステッキ

▶ crutchと比較

☞ **bandage**のさし絵

**walkover** /ˈwɔːkˌoʊvər/ 名 ❷ ▶定義 an easy win or victory in a game or competition 試合や競争で楽々と勝つこと、あるいは勝利すること→楽勝、不戦勝

★**wall** /wɔːl/ 名 ❷ ▶定義 1 a solid, vertical structure made of stone, brick, etc that is built round an area of land to protect it or to divide it 石やれんがなどで作られた固く垂直な構造物で、ある広さの土地を守るまたは区分するために、その周りに建てられている→塀、防壁‖ There is a high wall all around the prison. 刑務所の周りはすべて高い塀で囲まれている。▶定義 2 one of the sides of a room or building joining the ceiling and the floor 天井と床をつないでいる、部屋や建物の側面の1つ→壁、内壁、仕切り壁‖ He put the picture up on the wall. 彼はその絵を壁に掛けた。

成句 **up the wall** 略式 ▶定義 crazy or angry 気が狂って、怒って→頭にきて、腹を立てて、いらいらして‖ That noise is driving me up the wall. あの騒音のせいで私は気が変になりそうだ。

**walled** /wɔːld/ 形 ▶定義 surrounded by a wall 壁に囲まれた→壁のある、塀を巡らした

★**wallet** /ˈwɒlɪt, ˈwɔːl-/ (米 **billfold**) 名 ❷ ▶定義 a small, flat, folding case in which you keep paper money, plastic cards, etc 紙幣、プラスチック製カードなどを入れておく、小さく平らな折り畳み式の入れ物→札入れ、財布 ☞参 **purse**

**wallop** /ˈwɒləp/ 動他 略式 ▶定義 to hit sb/sth very hard ～を非常に強くたたく→～を打ちのめす、強打する

**wallow** /ˈwɒloʊ/ 動自 **wallow (in sth)** ▶定義 1 (used about people and large animals) to lie and roll around in water, etc in order to keep cool or for pleasure (人や大きな動物について)涼をとるあるいは楽しむ目的で、水などに横たわり、転げ回る→ごろごろする、寝そべる‖ I spent an hour wallowing in the bath. 私は1時間ふろにつかっていた。▶定義 2 to take great pleasure in sth (a feeling, situation, etc) ～(感情、状況など)を大いに楽しむ→(～に)ふける、おぼれる‖ to *wallow in self-pity* (= *to think about your unhappiness all the time and seem to be enjoying it*) 自己憐憫(れんびん)にふける(= 四六時中自分の不幸ばかりを考えているが,それを楽しんでいるように見える)

**wallpaper** /wɔ́ːlpèɪpər/ 名 U ▶定義 paper that you stick to the walls of a room to decorate or cover them 飾るまたは覆うために,部屋の壁に張り付ける紙→壁紙 — wallpaper 動 自 他 →～に壁紙を張る

**wall-to-wall** 形(名詞の前だけ) ▶定義 (used especially about a carpet) covering the floor of a room completely (特にじゅうたんについて)部屋の床を完全に覆った→床一面の,壁から壁まで敷き詰められた

**wally** /wéɪli/ 名 C (複 **wallies**) 英 (俗語) ▶定義 a silly person; a fool ばかな人; ばか→うすのろ,間抜け

**walnut** /wɔ́ːlnʌt, -nət/ 名 ▶定義1 C a nut that we eat, with a hard brown shell that is in two halves 2つに分かれる堅い茶色の殻の付いた,食用の木の実→クルミ ☞ **nut**のさし絵 ▶定義2 (または **walnut tree**) C the tree on which these nuts grow クルミがなる木→クルミの木 ▶定義3 U the wood of the walnut tree, used in making furniture 家具を作るときに使用されるクルミの木の材木→クルミ材

**walrus** /wɔ́ː(ː)lrəs, wɑ́l-/ 名 C ▶定義 a large animal that lives in or near the sea in Arctic regions. It is similar to another sea animal (**seal**) but the walrus has two long outer teeth (**tusks**). 北極地方の海中またはその周辺に住む大型の動物.別の海洋動物(アザラシ)に似ているが,walrus は2本の長い,外に突き出した歯(きば)を持っている→セイウチ(海象) ☞ **seal**のさし絵

**waltz**¹ /wɔː(ː)l(t)s/ 名 C ▶定義 an elegant dance that you do with a partner, to music which has a rhythm of three beats; the music for this dance 3拍子のリズムの音楽に合わせてパートナーと一緒に踊る優雅なダンス; このダンスのための音楽→ワルツ,円舞曲 ‖ *a Strauss waltz* シュトラウスの円舞曲

**waltz**² /wɔː(ː)l(t)s/ 動 ▶定義1 自 他 to dance a waltz→ワルツを踊る ‖ *They waltzed around the floor.* 彼らはフロアのあちこちでワルツを踊り回った. *He waltzed her round the room.* 彼女と部屋中でワルツを踊り回った. ▶定義2 自 略式 to go somewhere in a confident way 自信に満ちた様子でどこかへ行く→素早く動く,軽快に歩く ‖ *You can't just waltz in and expect your meal to be ready for you.* 自分の食事の支度ができていると期待して悠然と部屋に入ってきても,それはありませんよ.

**wan** /wɑn/ 形 ▶定義 looking pale and ill or tired 青白くて,病気または疲れているように見える→青ざめた,血色の悪い,やつれた

**wand** /wɑnd/ 名 C ▶定義 a thin stick that people hold when they are doing magic tricks 手品[魔術]をするときに,手品[魔術]師が手に持つ細いつえ→魔法のつえ,手品のつえ ‖ *I wish I could* **wave a magic wand** *and make everything better.* 魔法のつえを一振りして,すべてが良くなればいいな.

*★**wander** /wɑ́ndər/ 動 ▶定義1 自 他 to walk somewhere slowly with no particular sense of direction or purpose 特定の方向または目的を意識せずに,ゆっくり辺りを歩く→歩き回る,ぶらつく,さまよい歩く ‖ *We spent a pleasant day wandering around the town.* 私たちは町をあちこちぶらついて,楽しい1日を過ごした. *He was found in a confused state, wandering the streets.* 彼は街をさまよって途方に暮れているところを発見された. ▶定義2 自 *wander (away/off) (from sb/sth)* to walk away from a place where you ought to be or the people you were with いるべき場所からあるいは一緒にいた人たちから歩いて離れる→はぐれる,迷う,迷子になる ‖ *We must stay together while visiting the town so I don't want anybody to wander off.* 町に滞在中,だれも迷子にならないように私たちは一緒にいなければなりません. *Don't wander away from the main road.* 幹線道路から外れないでください. ▶定義3 自 (used about sb's mind, thoughts, etc) to stop paying attention to sth; to be unable to stay on one subject(～の心中,思考などについて)…に注意を払うのをやめる; 1つの話題にとどまることができない→(考えなどが)取り留めがなくなる,(話などが)脱線する,それる ‖ *The lecture was so boring that my attention began to wander.* 講義がとても退屈だったので,私は注意力が散漫になった.

## 1800 wane¹

**wane¹** /wéɪn/ 動自 ▶定義1 (文) to become gradually weaker or less important 次第に弱くなる、または重要でなくなる→**弱まる, 衰える** ‖ *My enthusiasm was waning rapidly.* 私の情熱は急速に冷めていった. ▶定義2 (used about the moon) to appear slightly smaller each day after being full and round (月について) 満月の後、毎日少しずつ小さくなって現れる→**(月が)欠ける**

**wane²** /wéɪn/ 名
成句 **on the wane** (文) ▶定義 becoming smaller, less important or less common 次第に小さくなる、重要でなくなる、あるいは一般的でなくなる→**衰えかけて, 落ち目になって** ‖ *The singer's popularity seems to be on the wane these days.* このごろ、その歌手の人気は衰えてきているようだ.

**wangle** /wǽŋɡ(ə)l/ 動他 略式 ▶定義 to get sth that you want by persuading sb or by having a clever plan 〜を説き伏せて、または策略を巡らせて、自分の欲しい…を獲得する→**〜をせしめる, 〜をうまく手に入れる** ‖ *Somehow he wangled a day off to meet me.* 彼は私に会うために何とか1日の休暇を手に入れた.

**wanna** /wɑ́nə/ ▶定義 a way of writing 'want to' or 'want a', which is considered to be bad style, to show that sb is speaking in an informal way want toやwant aのつづり方の1つで、好ましくない口調と見なされているが、打ち解けた態度で話していることを示す→want to, want a の略式 ‖ *I wanna go home now.* 私は今すぐ家に帰りたい. ☞参 **gonna** の注

★**want¹** /wɔ́(ː)nt, wɑ́nt/ 動他 (進行形は不可)
▶定義1 **want sth (for sth); want (sb) to do sth; want sth (to be) done** to have a desire or a wish for sth 〜に対して欲望や願望を持つ→**〜が欲しい, 〜を望む; (人に)〜をしてもらいたいと思う, 〜させたい, (自分が)〜したいと思う; 〜に…であってもらいたいと思う** ‖ *He wants a new bike.* 彼は新しい自転車を欲しがっている. *What do they want for breakfast?* 彼らは朝食に何を食べたがっていますか. *I don't want to discuss it now.* 私は今、それを議論したくない. *I want you to stop worrying about it.* 私はあなたにそれについて心配するのをやめてほしいのです. *The boss wants this letter typed.* 上司はこの手紙をタイプしてほしいと思っている. *I don't want Emma going out on her own at night.* 私はエマに、夜1人で外出して欲しくないと思っている. *They want Bhanot as captain.* 彼らはバノットを主将に望んでいる.

▶ want と would like は意味の点では似ているが、would like の方がより丁寧である: *'I want a drink!' screamed the child.* (「飲み物ちょうだい」とその子供は叫んだ.) *'Would you like some more tea, Mrs Atwal?'* (「もう少しお茶をいかがですか、アトワル夫人」)

▶定義2 略式 used to say that sth needs to be done 〜がなされる必要があることを伝えるときに用いて→**〜が必要である, 〜が要る** ‖ *The button on my shirt wants sewing on.* 私のシャツのボタンは縫い付ける必要がある. *The house wants a new coat of paint.* その家は新しくペンキを塗る必要がある. ▶定義3 略式 (used to give advice to sb) should or ought to (〜に忠告するために用いて) 〜すべきである, 〜するのが当然である→**〜しなければならない, 〜した方が良い** ‖ *He wants to be more careful about what he tells people.* 彼は人々に話す事柄についてもっと気を付けるべきである. ▶定義4 (通常は受動態で) to need sb to be in a particular place or for a particular reason 〜が特定の場所にいることを求められている、または特定の理由で必要とされている→**〜に用がある, 〜を呼ぶ** ‖ *Mrs Lewis, you are wanted on the phone.* ルイス夫人、電話ですよ. *She is **wanted by the police** (= the police are looking for her because she is suspected of committing a crime).* 彼女は警察のお尋ね者になっている (= 彼女に犯罪の容疑がかかっているため、警察が彼女を捜している). ▶定義5 to feel sexual desire for sb 〜に対して性的欲望を感じる→**人を(性的に)求める**

▶ この動詞は進行形では用いられないが、現在分詞 (= -ing 形) では (分詞構文では) 頻繁に見られる: *She kept her head down, not wanting to attract attention.* (彼女は注意をひきたくなかったので、頭を下げ続けた.)

★**want²** /wɔ́(ː)nt, wɑ́nt/ 名 正式 ▶定義1 **wants** [複数扱い] sth you need or want 必要なあるいは欲しい〜→**必要なもの, 欲しいもの** ‖ *All our wants were satisfied.* 私たちに必要なもののすべてが十分にあった. ▶定義2 [単数扱い] a lack of sth 〜の欠乏→**不足** ‖ *He's suffering due to a want of* *care.* 彼は十分な手当てが受けられないために苦しんでいる.

成句 for (the) want of sth ▶定義 because of a lack of sth; because sth is not available 〜が不足しているため；〜が手に入らないため→〜の不足のために，〜がなくて ‖ *I took the job for want of a better offer.* より良い申し出がなかったため，私はその仕事を引き受けた.

**wanting** /wɔ́(:)ntɪŋ, wɑ́ntɪŋ/ 形正式 wanting (in sth)（名詞の前は不可）▶定義1 not having enough of sth; lacking 〜を十分に持っていない；不足している→足りない，欠けている ‖ *The children were certainly not wanting in enthusiasm.* 子供たちは，間違いなく意気込みに欠けてはいなかった. ▶定義2 not good enough 十分に良い状態ではない→(標準・必要などに)不十分な，達していない ‖ *The new system was found wanting.* 新しいシステムは不十分であることが判明した.

**wanton** /wɔ́(:)nt(ə)n, wɑ́n-/ 形正式 ▶定義 (used about an action) done in order to hurt sb or damage sth for no good reason（動作について）正当な理由のためでなく，〜を傷付けるため，あるいは〜を壊すために行われた→いわれのない，悪意のある，理不尽な ‖ *wanton vandalism* 非道な破壊的行為

\***war** /wɔːr/ 图 ▶定義1 Ⓤ Ⓒ a state of fighting between different countries or groups within countries using armies and weapons 異なる国々または国内の集団同士の間で軍隊と武器を用いて戦っている状態→戦い，戦争，戦争状態 ‖ *The Prime Minister announced that the country was at war.* 首相は，国が戦争状態にあることを公表した. *to declare war on another country (= announce that a war has started)* 別の国に対して宣戦布告する (= 戦争が始まったことを公表する) *When war broke out (= started), thousands of men volunteered for the army.* 戦争が勃発（ぼっぱつ）した(= 始まった)とき，何千もの男たちが軍隊に志願した. *a civil war (= fighting between different groups in one country)* 内戦(= 国内の異なる集団同士の戦い) *to go to war against sb* 〜(人・国)に対して戦いを始める *to fight a war* 戦争を遂行する ▶定義2 Ⓒ Ⓤ very aggressive competition between groups of people, companies, countries, etc 異なる人々の集団，企業，国などの間の非常に激しい競争→激しい競争，闘争 ‖ *a price war among oil companies* 石油会社間の激しい価格競争 ▶定義3 [Ⓤ, 単数扱い] war (against/on sb/sth) efforts to end or get rid of sth 〜を終わらせる，または取り除くための努力→争い，闘い ‖ *We seem to be winning the war against organized crime.* 我々は，組織犯罪撲滅の闘いに勝利を収めつつあるようだ.

**war crime** 图 Ⓒ ▶定義 a cruel act that is committed during a war and that is against the international rules of war 戦争中に行われる残虐な行為で，戦争に関する国際法に違反している行為→戦争犯罪

\***ward**¹ /wɔːrd/ 图 Ⓒ ▶定義1 a separate part or room in a hospital for patients with the same kind of medical condition 同じ種類の病状にある患者のための，病院内の区切られた部分または部屋→病棟，病室 ‖ *the maternity/psychiatric/surgical ward* 産科・精神科・外科病棟 ▶定義2 医 one of the sections into which a town is divided for elections 選挙のために分けられた町の区域の1つ→区，選挙区 ▶定義3 a child who is under the protection of a court of law; a child whose parents are dead and who is cared for by another adult (**guardian**) 裁判所の保護下にある子供；両親が死亡し，別の大人(後見人)から世話を受けている子供→被後見人，被保護者 ‖ *The child was made a ward of court.* その子供は被後見人とされた.

**ward**² /wɔːrd/ 動

句動詞 ward sb/sth off ▶定義 to protect or defend yourself against danger, illness, attack, etc 危険，病気，攻撃などから身を守る，防御する→〜から身をかわす，避ける

**warden** /wɔ́ːrdn/ 图 Ⓒ ▶定義1 a person whose job is to check that rules are obeyed or to look after the people in a particular place ある特定の場所で，規則が守られているかを点検する，または人々の世話をすることを仕事とする人→監視人，管理人 ‖ *a traffic warden (= a person who checks that cars are not parked in the wrong place)* 交通監視員(= 車が誤った場所に止められていないことを点検する人) ▶定義2 特に 米 the person in charge of a prison 刑務所を任されている人→刑務所長

**warder** /wɔ́ːrdər/ 名 C 英 ▶定義 a person whose job is to guard prisoners 囚人を見張ることを仕事とする人→看守 ☞参 guard

**wardrobe** /wɔ́ːrdròub/ 名 C ▶定義1 a large cupboard in which you can hang your clothes 中に衣服をつるすことができる大型の戸棚→衣装だんす, 洋服だんす ☞ C7ページのさし絵 ▶定義2 a person's collection of clothes 人が持っているすべての衣装→持ち衣装, 衣装‖ I need a whole new summer wardrobe. 私は新しい夏服が一式必要だ.

**ware** /weər/ 名 ▶定義1 Ⓤ (複合語で用いて) made from a particular type of material or suitable for a particular use ある特定の材料から作られた, または特定の使用目的向きの→～製品, ～用品‖ glassware ガラス製品 kitchenware 台所用品 ▶定義2 wares [複数扱い] (古) goods offered for sale 売却用に提供される品物→商品, 売り物

**warehouse** /wéərhàus/ 名 C ▶定義 a building where large quantities of goods are stored before being sent to shops 販売店に送られる前の大量の商品が保管される建物→倉庫, 保管所, 貯蔵所

**warfare** /wɔ́ːrfèər/ 名 U ▶定義 methods of fighting a war; types of war 戦争の戦い方; 戦いの種類→戦法, 戦術‖ guerrilla warfare ゲリラ戦術

**warily, wariness** ⇒ WARY

**warlike** /wɔ́ːrlàik/ 形 ▶定義 liking to fight or good at fighting 戦うことが好きな, または戦いの上手な→好戦的な, 挑戦的な‖ a warlike nation 好戦的な民族

***warm**¹ /wɔːm/ 形 ▶定義1 having a pleasant temperature that is fairly high, between cool and hot 低温と高温の中間でやや高目の気持ちのいい温度を持っている→暖かい, 温暖な‖ It's quite warm in the sunshine. 日なたはかなり暖かい. I jumped up and down to keep my feet warm. 私は足が冷えないように上下に飛び跳ねた. ☞参 cold¹ の注 ▶定義2 (used about clothes) preventing you from getting cold (衣服について) 冷えるのを防いでいる→暖かい, 保温性の‖ Take plenty of warm clothes. 暖かい服をたくさん持っていきなさい. ▶定義3 friendly, kind and pleasant 好意的で, 親切で感じの良い→(心の) 温かい, 思いやりのある‖ I was given a very warm welcome. 私はとても温かい歓迎を受けた. ▶定義4 creating a pleasant, comfortable feeling 楽しい, 気持ちの安らぐ感情を生み出す→暖かい‖ warm colours 暖色 ─ the warm [単数扱い]→暖かい場所, 暖かい状態‖ It's awfully cold out here - I want to go back into the warm. ここは戸外でとても寒い ─ 中の暖かい場所に戻りたいな. ─ warmly 副→暖かく, 温かく, 心を込めて‖ warmly dressed 暖かい服装をした She thanked him warmly for his help. 彼女は彼の手助けに心から感謝した.

***warm**² /wɔːm/ 動 自 他 ▶定義 warm (sb/sth) (up) to become or to make sb/sth become warm or warmer ～が暖まる, または～を暖かくする→暖まる; ～を暖める‖ It was cold earlier but it's beginning to warm up now. さっきは寒かったが, 今は暖かくなり始めている. I sat in front of the fire to warm up. 私は体を暖めるために暖炉の前に座った.

句動詞 warm to/towards sb ▶定義 to begin to like sb that you did not like at first 初めは好きでなかった～を好きになり始める→～に好意を持つ, 好意を抱く

warm to sth ▶定義 to become more interested in sth →～への興味が深まる→～に(より)熱心になる, ～に(もっと)興味を持つ

warm up ▶定義 to prepare to do an activity or sport by practising gently 穏やかに行うことによって, 活動または運動の準備をする→準備運動をする, ウォーミングアップをする‖ The team warmed up before the match. そのチームは, 試合の前に準備運動をした.

**warm-hearted** 形 ▶定義 kind and friendly 親切で友好的な→心温まる, 思いやりのある

**warmth** /wɔːrmθ/ 名 U ▶定義1 a fairly high temperature or the effect created by this, especially when it is pleasant 比較的高い温度, または特にその温度が心地良いときに生み出される効果→暖かさ, 温暖さ‖ She felt the warmth of the sun on her face. 彼女は顔に太陽の暖かさを感じた. ▶定義2 the quality of being kind and friendly 親切で友好的な性質→(心の) 温かさ, 思いやり‖ I was touched by the warmth of their welcome. 私は彼らの歓迎の温かさに感動した.

\***warn** /wɔːn/ 動 中 ▶定義1 warn sb (of sth); warn sb (about sb/sth) to tell sb about sth unpleasant or dangerous that exists or might happen, so that he/she can avoid it 現存するあるいは予測される不愉快または危険な〜について…に伝える。その人がそれを避けられるようにするのが目的である〜に注意する,警告する ‖ *When I saw the car coming I tried to warn him, but it was too late.* その車がこちらへ来るのを見た時,私は彼に注意しようとしたが,手後れだった. *The government is warning the public of possible terrorist attacks.* 政府は,テロリストによる攻撃の可能性を国民に警告している. *He warned me about the danger of walking home alone at night.* 彼は私に,夜1人で歩いて帰宅することの危険性について注意した. ▶定義2 warn (sb) against doing sth; warn sb (not to do sth) to advise sb not to do sth 〜に…をしないよう忠告する〜→に注意する,警告する ‖ *The radio warned people against going out during the storm.* あらしの間は外出しないようにラジオで警告された. *I warned you not to trust him.* 私はあなたに彼を信用しないよう忠告した.

**warning** /wɔːnɪŋ/ 名 C U ▶定義 something that tells you to be careful or tells you about sth, usually sth bad, before it happens 注意するように伝えること,あるいは通常は悪い〜が起こる前に,それについて伝えること→**警告, 予告** ‖ *Your employers can't dismiss you **without warning**.* 雇い主は予告なしに人を解雇することはできない. *You could have given me some warning that your parents were coming to visit.* あなたの両親が訪ねてくることを,私に一言いってくれてもよかったのに.

**warp** /wɔːp/ 動 ▶定義1 自 他 to become bent into the wrong shape, for example as a result of getting hot or wet; to make sth become like this 例えば暑さや湿気の結果として,おかしな形に折れ曲がった状態になる; 〜をそのような状態にする→反る,ゆがむ,折れ曲がる; 〜を反らせる,ゆがませる,折れ曲げる ‖ *The window frame was badly warped and wouldn't shut.* 窓枠がひどくゆがみ,閉まらなくなった. ▶定義2 他 to influence sb so that he/she starts behaving in an unusual or shocking way 〜に影響を与え,奇妙なまたはぞっとする振る舞いをさせる→**(心や判断など)をゆがめる** ‖ *His experiences in the war had warped him.* 戦争体験が彼の心をゆがめた. — warped 形→曲がった,ゆがんだ

**warpath** /wɔːpɑːθ; wɔːrpæθ/ 名 慣用 (be/go) on the warpath 慣用式 ▶定義 to be very angry and want to fight or punish sb 激怒し,〜と争いたい,あるいは罰したいと思う→激怒する,けんか腰になる,気負い立つ

**warrant**¹ /wɔ(ː)rənt, wɑ́r-/ 名 C ▶定義 an official written statement that gives sb permission to do sth 〜に…を行う許可を与える公式の書面→**許可証, 証明書** ‖ *a search warrant* (= a document that allows the police to search a house) 捜査令状 (= 警察が家宅捜索することを許可した文書)

**warrant**² /wɔ(ː)rənt, wɑ́r-/ 動 他 正式 ▶定義 to make sth seem right or necessary; to deserve sth 〜を正しい,または必要であるようにさせる; 〜に値する〜→**を正当とする,是認する; 〜は当然のことである, 〜に値する** ‖ *I don't think her behaviour warrants such criticism.* 私は,彼女の振る舞いがそのような批判に値するとは思わない.

**warranty** /wɔ́(ː)rənti, wɑ́r-/ 名 C U (複 **warranties**) ▶定義 a written statement that you get when you buy sth, which promises to repair or replace it if it is broken or does not work 〜を買ったときに入手する書面で,その物が壊れるまたは動かない場合に,修理または交換することを約束するもの→**保証書** ‖ *Fortunately my stereo is still **under warranty**.* 幸運にも,私のステレオはまだ保証期間中だ.
☛参 guarantee

**warrior** /wɔ́(ː)riər, wɑ́r-/ 名 C (古) ▶定義 a person who fights in a battle; a soldier 戦闘で戦う人; 兵士→**戦士, 武士, 武人**

**warship** /wɔ́ːʃɪp/ 名 C ▶定義 a ship for use in war 戦争で使用される船→**軍艦**

**wart** /wɔːrt/ 名 C ▶定義 a small hard dry lump that sometimes grows on the face or body 時々顔や体にできる小さな堅い乾燥したはれ物→**いぼ**

**wartime** /wɔ́ːrtaɪm/ 名 U ▶定義 a period of time during which there is a war 戦争が行われている期間→**戦時**

## 1804 wary

**wary** /wéəri/ 形 ▶定義 wary (of sb/sth) careful because you are uncertain or afraid of sb/sth 〜に対し確信が持てないまたは〜を恐れているために，用心する →**用心深い，慎重な** ‖ *Since becoming famous, she has grown wary of journalists.* 有名になってから，彼女はジャーナリストに対して用心深くなった．— **warily** /-rəli/ 副 →用心深く，慎重に

**was** ⇒ BE

*****wash**[1] /wɔ(ː)ʃ, wɑʃ/ 動 ▶定義1 自他 to clean sb/sth/yourself with water and often soap 水としばしばせっけんを使って，〜・自分自身をきれいにする →**(〜を) 洗う，洗浄する，洗濯する** ‖ *to wash your hands/face/hair* 手・顔・髪を洗う *That shirt needs washing.* あのシャツは洗濯する必要がある． *Wash and dress quickly or you'll be late!* 急いで顔を洗って着替えないと，遅刻するわよ． *I'll wash (= wash the dishes), you dry.* 私が洗う (= 皿を洗う) から，あなたはふいて． ☛参 **clean**[2] の注 ▶定義2 自他 (used about water) to flow or carry sth/sb in the direction mentioned (水について) 言及された方向に流れる，あるいは〜を運ぶ→**〜を押し流す，流す，さらっていく** ‖ *I let the waves wash over my feet.* 私は足を波に洗われるのに任せた． *The current washed the ball out to sea.* 潮流がボールを外洋まで押し流した． ▶定義3 自 to be able to be washed without being damaged 損なわれずに洗われることができる→**洗濯が利く，洗濯しても色落ちしない** ‖ *Does this material wash well, or does the colour come out?* この生地は洗濯しても大丈夫ですか，それとも色落ちしますか．

成句 **wash your hands of sb/sth** ▶定義 to refuse to be responsible for sb/sth any longer もはや〜に対して責務を負うことを拒否する→**〜と縁を切る** ‖ *They washed their hands of their son when he was sent to prison.* 息子が刑務所に送られた時，両親は彼と縁を切った．

句動詞 **wash sb/sth away** ▶定義 (used about water) to carry sb/sth away (水について) 〜を運び去る→**押し流す，さらっていく** ‖ *The floods had washed away the path.* 洪水がその小道を押し流した．

**wash (sth) off** ▶定義 to (make sth) disappear by washing 〜を洗って消滅させる，消滅する→洗い流す，洗い落とす ‖ *The writing has washed off and now I can't read it.* 文字が洗い流されてしまって，今では判読できない． *Go and wash that make-up off!* その化粧を洗い落としてきなさい．

**wash out** ▶定義 to be removed from a material by washing 洗うことで，生地から取り除かれる→**洗い落ちる** ‖ *These grease marks won't wash out.* これらの油染みは洗い落とせない．

**wash sth out** ▶定義 to wash sth or the inside of sth in order to remove dirt 汚れを取り除くために，〜または〜の内部を洗浄する→**洗い流す** ‖ *I'll just wash out this bowl and then we can use it.* ちょっとこの鉢の中をきれいに洗ってきましょう，そうすればまた使えますよ．

**wash (sth) up** ▶定義1 英 to wash the plates, knives, forks, etc after a meal 食事の後，皿，ナイフ，フォークなどを洗う→**(食器類) を洗って片付ける** ‖ *Whose turn is it to wash up?* 食後の片付けは，だれの番ですか． ▶定義2 米 to wash your face and hands→**顔と手を洗う** ‖ *Go and wash up quickly and put on some clean clothes.* 急いで顔と手を洗って，清潔な服を着なさい． ▶定義3 (しばしば受動態で) (used about water) to carry sth to land and leave it there (水について) 〜を陸地に運び，そこに置き去りにする→**(漂流物・動物など) を打ち上げる** ‖ *Police found the girl's body washed up on the beach.* 警察は少女の死体が浜に打ち上げられているのを発見した．

*****wash**[2] /wɔ(ː)ʃ, wɑʃ/ 名 ▶定義1 [C, 通常は単数] an act of cleaning or being cleaned with water 水で洗う，または洗われる行為→**洗浄，洗濯** ‖ *I'd better go and have a wash before we go out.* 一緒に出掛ける前に，ふろ場に行って顔や手 (や体) を洗った方がいいと思う． ▶定義2 [単数扱い] the waves caused by the movement of a ship through water 船が水面を進むことによって引き起こされる波→**白波，航跡**

成句 **in the wash** ▶定義 (used about clothes) being washed (衣服について) 洗濯される→**洗濯中の，洗濯物の中に** ‖ *'Where's my red T-shirt?' 'It's in the wash.'* 「私の赤いTシャツはどこ」「洗濯中よ」

**washable** /wɔ́(ː)ʃəb(ə)l, wɑ́ʃəb(ə)l/ 形 ▶定義 that can be washed without being damaged 損なわれることなく洗われることのできる→**洗濯の**

利く

**washbasin** /wɔ́(:)ʃbèɪsn, wɑ́ʃbèɪsn/(または **basin**) 名 C ▶定義 a large bowl for water that has taps and is fixed to a wall, in a bathroom, etc 水のための大きな鉢で、蛇口が付いていて浴室などの壁に固定されているもの→洗面台 ☛参 sink ☛ plug のさし絵

**washed out** 形 ▶定義 tired and pale 疲労して青ざめた∥つかれた, 元気のない‖ They arrived looking washed out after their long journey. 彼らは長旅の後、疲れきった様子で到着した.

*__washing__ /wɔ́(:)ʃɪŋ, wɑ́ʃɪŋ/ 名 U ▶定義1 clothes that need to be washed or are being washed 洗濯することが必要な、または洗濯されようとしている衣服→洗濯物‖ Could you put the washing in the machine? 洗濯物を洗濯機に入れていただけませんか. a pile of dirty washing 汚れた洗濯物の山 ▶定義2 the act of cleaning clothes, etc with water 水で衣服などを洗う行為→洗濯‖ I usually **do the washing** on Mondays. 私は普通、毎週月曜日に洗濯をする.

**washing machine** 名 C ▶定義 an electric machine for washing clothes 衣服を洗うための電気機器→洗濯機 ☛ C7 ページのさし絵

**washing powder** 名 U ▶定義 soap in the form of powder for washing clothes 衣服を洗うための粉状のせっけん→粉せっけん, 粉末洗剤

**washing-up** 名 U ▶定義1 the work of washing the plates, knives, forks, etc after a meal 食事の後、皿、ナイフ、フォークなどを洗う仕事→食器洗い, 食後の後片付け‖ I'll **do the washing-up**. 後片付けは私がしますよ. **washing-up liquid** 洗剤液 ▶定義2 plates, etc that need washing after a meal 食事の後、洗わなければならない皿など→使った食器, 汚れた食器‖ Put the washing-up next to the sink. 汚れた食器を流しの隣に置きなさい.

**washout** /wɔ́(:)ʃaʊt, wɑ́ʃaʊt/ 名 C 略式 ▶定義 an event that is a complete failure, especially because of rain 特に雨のために, 完全な失敗となった催し物→大失敗

**washroom** /wɔ́(:)ʃruːm, wɑ́ʃ-, -rùm/ 名 C 米 ▶定義 a toilet, especially in a public building 特に公共の建物にあるトイレ→公衆トイレ

**wasn't** WAS NOT の短縮形

**wasp** /wɑsp, wɔ(:)sp/ 名 C ▶定義 a small black and yellow flying insect that can sting 刺すこと

のある、小さな黒と黄色の飛ぶ昆虫→(スズメバチ科、ジガバチ科の)ハチ ☛ insect のさし絵

**wastage** /wéɪstɪdʒ/ 名 U 正式 ▶定義 using too much of sth in a careless way; the amount of sth that is wasted 不注意なやり方で〜を使用しすぎること; 無駄に使われた〜の量→浪費, 損失, 損失量, 消耗量

*__waste__¹ /wéɪst/ 動他 ▶定義1 waste sth (on sb/sth); waste sth (in doing sth) to use or spend sth in a careless way or for sth that is not necessary 不注意なやり方で、あるいは必要でない〜のために、…を使うまたは費やす→〜を浪費する, 無駄に使う‖ She wastes a lot of money on cigarettes. 彼女は多額の金をたばこに浪費している. He wasted his time at university because he didn't work hard. 彼は一生懸命勉強しなかったので、大学での時間を無駄にした. She wasted no time in decorating her new room (= she did it immediately). 彼女は時間を無駄にせずに新しい部屋を飾り付けた（= すぐにそうした）. ▶定義2 (通常は受動態で)to give sth to sb who does not value it 〜を、その価値を評価しない…に与える→〜を無駄にする, もったいないことをする‖ Expensive wine is wasted on me. I don't even like it. 高いワインは私にはもったいない. ちっとも好きではないから.

*__waste__² /wéɪst/ 名 ▶定義1 [単数扱い] a waste (of sth) using sth in a careless and unnecessary way 不注意かつ不要に〜を使うこと→浪費, 無駄遣い‖ The seminar was **a waste of time** - I'd heard it all before. 講座は時間の無駄だった — すべて以前に聞いていたから. It seems a waste to throw away all these old newspapers. 古新聞を全部捨ててしまうのはもったいないと思う. ▶定義2 U material, food, etc that is not needed and is therefore thrown away 必要でないので捨てられる資材, 食物など→廃棄物, ごみ, くず‖ nuclear waste 核廃棄物 A lot of household waste can be recycled and reused. 家庭のごみの多くはリサイクルして再利用できる. ☛参 rubbish ▶定義3 **wastes** [複数扱い] 正式 large areas of land that are not lived in and not used だれも住み着いていなくて, 使われていない広い土地→荒地, 荒野, 原野‖ the wastes of the Sahara desert 荒涼としたサハラ砂漠

[成句] go to waste ▶定義 to not be used and so thrown away and wasted 使われずに捨てられて無駄になる➜**無駄になる** ‖ *I can't bear to see good food going to waste!* 私はまだ食べられる物が無駄にされてしまうことには耐えられない.

**waste**[3] /wéɪst/ [形] (名詞の前だけ) ▶定義1 (used about land) not used or not suitable for use; not looked after (土地について) 使用されていない, 使用に適さない; 省みられない➜**不毛の, 荒れ果てた** ‖ *There's an area of waste ground outside the town where people dump their rubbish.* 人々がごみを投げ捨てる荒れ地が町外れにある. ▶定義2 no longer useful; that is thrown away もはや役に立たない; 捨てられる➜**不用の, 廃物の, くずの, ごみになった** ‖ *waste paper* 紙くず *waste material* 廃棄物

**wasted** /wéɪstəd/ [形] ▶定義1 not necessary or successful 不要な, 失敗した➜**無駄にした, 役に立たない** ‖ *a wasted journey* 無駄な旅行 ▶定義2 very thin, especially because of illness 特に病気のために, とてもやせ細った➜**やつれた, 衰弱した** ▶定義3 (俗語) suffering from the effects of drugs or alcohol 薬物またはアルコールの影響を受けている➜**薬物中毒の, アルコール依存症の, 酔った**

**wasteful** /wéɪstfʊl, -f(ə)l/ [形] ▶定義 using more of sth than necessary; causing waste 必要以上の～を使う; 無駄を引き起こす➜**無駄遣いする, 浪費的な**

**waste-paper basket** [名] [C] ▶定義 a basket, etc in which you put paper, etc which is to be thrown away 捨てるべき紙などを入れるかごなど➜**くずかご, ごみ入れ** ☛ **bin** のさし絵

***watch**[1] /wɑtʃ/ [動] ▶定義1 [自][他] to look at sb/sth for a time, paying attention to what happens 何が起こるか注目しながら, しばらく～を見る➜ **(～の動きを) じっと見る, 見守る, 注視する** ‖ *I **watched in horror** as the car swerved and crashed.* 私は, その車が急にそれて衝突するのをぞっとしながら見ていた. *I'm watching to see how you do it.* 私は, あなたがそれをいかにこなすか見ていますよ. *We **watch television** most evenings.* 私たちはほとんど毎晩テレビを見る. *Watch what she does next.* 彼女が次に何をするかよく見なさい. *I watched him open the door and walk away.* 私は, 彼がドアを開けて立ち去るのを見た. ▶定義2 [他] to take care of sth for a short time しばらくの間～の面倒を見る➜ **～を見守る, ～の世話をする, 看護する** ‖ *Could you watch my bag for a second while I go and get a drink?* 私が飲み物を買いに行っている少しの間, かばんを見ていてくださいませんか. ▶定義3 [他] watch sb/sth (for sth) to be careful about sb/sth; to pay careful attention to sth/sb ～に気を配る; ～に注意を払う➜**～に気を付ける, ～を注意して見る** ‖ *You'd better **watch what you say** to her. She gets upset very easily.* あなたは彼女に対する言葉遣いに気を付けた方がいい. 彼女は怒りやすい人だから. *Watch those two boys - they're acting suspiciously.* あの2人の少年を見張っていなさい － 疑わしい行動を取っているから.

[成句] watch your step ⇒ **STEP**[1]

[句動詞] watch out ▶定義 to be careful because of possible danger or trouble 危険や災難の可能性があるため, 注意する➜**注意する, 用心する, 警戒する** ‖ *Watch out! There's a car coming.* 気を付けて. 車が近付いてくるよ. *If you don't watch out you'll lose your job.* 用心していないと, 仕事を失いますよ.

watch out for sb/sth ▶定義 to look carefully and be ready for sb/sth 注意深く見て, ～に備えている➜**～を見張る, 警戒する, ～に用心する** ‖ *Watch out for snakes if you walk through the fields.* 野原を通り抜けるときは, 蛇に用心しなさい.

watch over sb/sth ▶定義 to look after or protect sb/sth ～の面倒を見るまたは守る➜**～を世話する, 看護する** ‖ *For two weeks she watched over the sick child.* 彼女は2週間, 病気の子供を看病した.

***watch**[2] /wɑtʃ/ [名] ▶定義1 [C] a type of small clock that you usually wear around your wrist 小さい時計の一型式で, 普通手首の回りに着ける➜**腕時計** ‖ *a digital watch* デジタル式腕時計 *My watch is a bit fast/slow (= shows a time that is later/earlier than the correct time).* 私の時計は少し進んでいる・遅れている (= 正しい時間よりも未来の・過去の時間を示す). ☛参 **clock** ▶定義2 [単数扱い, [U]] the action of watching sb/sth in case of possible danger or problems 危険や問題が発生する可能性に備えて～を観察する動作➜**監視, 注視, 警戒, 用心** ‖ *Tour com-*

W

panies have to **keep a close watch on** the political situation in the region. 旅行会社は、その地域の政治状況を注意深く見守らなければならない.

**watchdog** /wɑ́tʃdɔ̀(ː)g, -dɑ̀g/ 名 C 定義 a person or group whose job is to make sure that large companies respect people's rights 大企業が人々の権利を尊重しているかを確認することを仕事とする人または団体➡**監視人, 監視役** || *a consumer watchdog* 消費者監視団体

**watchful** /wɑ́tʃfʊl, -f(ə)l/ 形 定義 careful to notice things 物事に気付くように注意して➡**用心深い, 注意深い, 油断のない**

★**water**¹ /wɔ́ːtər, wɑ́t-/ 名 定義 1 ❶ the clear liquid that falls as rain and is in rivers, seas and lakes 雨となって降り、川や海、湖にたまっている透明な液体➡**水** || *a glass of water* コップ1杯の水 *All the rooms have hot and cold running water.* すべての部屋に温水と冷水の水道が設備されている. *drinking water* 飲み水 *tap water* 水道水

➤ water (水) は100℃に温められると、boil (沸騰する) と言い、steam (蒸気) となると言う. 蒸気が冷たい物の表面に触れると、condense (結露する) と言い、再び水になる. 水が0℃以下に冷やされると、freeze (凍る) と表し、ice (氷) になると言う.

定義 2 ❶ a large amount of water, especially the water in a lake, river or sea 大量の水、特に湖や川、海の水➡**池, 湖, 川, 海** || *Don't go too near the edge or you'll fall in the water!* 水辺に近付きすぎると、水の中に落ちてしまうよ. *After the heavy rain several fields were under water.* 豪雨の後、いくつかの野原が浸水した. 定義 3 ❶ the surface of an area of water 水域の表面➡**水面** || *Can you swim under water?* あなたは水中を泳ぐことができますか. *I can see my reflection in the water.* 私の姿が水面に映っているのが見える. 定義 4 **waters** [複数扱い] the water in a particular sea, lake, etc or near a particular country ある特定の海・湖などの水、またはある特定の国の周辺の水➡**水域, 海域, 領海, 近海** || *The ship was still in British waters.* その船はまだイギリスの領海内にいた.

成句 keep your head above water ⇒ **HEAD**¹
pass water ⇒ **PASS**¹

**water**² /wɔ́ːtər, wɑ́t-/ 動 定義 1 ⓤ to give water to plants 植物に水を与える➡**～に水をやる** 定義 2 ⓤ (used about the eyes or mouth) to fill with liquid (目または口について) 液体で満たす➡**涙が出る, よだれが出る** || *The smoke in the room was starting to make my eyes water.* 室内の煙のせいで、涙が出始めた. *These menus will really make your mouth water.* これらのメニューを見ただけで、よだれが出てきますよ.

句動詞 water sth down 定義 1 to add water to a liquid in order to make it weaker 液体を薄めるために水を加える➡**～を水で薄める, 水で割る** 定義 2 to change a statement, report, etc so that the meaning is less strong or direct 声明や報告書などを変更し、その真意の強さや直接性を薄める➡**～の表現を和らげる, ～の効果を弱める**

**watercolour** /wɔ́ːtərkʌ̀lər, wɑ́t-/ 名 定義 1 **watercolours** [複数扱い] paints that are mixed with water, not oil 油ではなく水と混ぜられる塗料➡**水彩絵の具** 定義 2 ❶ a picture that has been painted with watercolours 水彩絵の具でかかれた絵➡**水彩画**

**watercress** /wɔ́ːtərkrès; wɑ́t-/ 名 U 定義 a type of plant with small round green leaves which have a strong taste and are often eaten in salads 風味の強い、小さな丸い緑色の葉を付けた植物の一種類で、サラダにして食べることが多い➡**オランダガラシ, ミズガラシ, クレソン**

**waterfall** /wɔ́ːtərfɔ̀ːl; wɑ́t-/ 名 C 定義 a river that falls down from a cliff, rock, etc 断崖 (だんがい) や岩などから落ちる川➡**滝** ☛ C8ページのさし絵

**watering can** 名 C 定義 a container with a long tube on one side which is used for pouring water on plants 植物に水をやるために用いられる、片側に長い管の付いた容器➡**じょうろ** ☛ **garden** のさし絵

**waterlogged** /wɔ́ːtərlɔ̀(ː)gd; wɑ́t-/ 形 定義 1 (used about the ground) extremely wet (地面について) 極端にぬれた➡**水浸しの, 水の染み込んだ** || *Our boots sank into the waterlogged ground.* 私たちの長靴が水浸しの地面に埋まった. 定義 2 (used about a boat) full of water and likely to sink (ボートについて) 水が満ちて沈みそうな➡**浸水した**

**watermelon** /wɔ́ːtərmèlən; wát-/ 名 C U
▶定義 a large, round fruit with a thick, green skin. It is pink or red inside with a lot of black seeds. 厚い緑色の皮を持つ,大きくて丸い果物. 中はピンクまたは赤色で,たくさんの黒い種がある→すいか ☜ C3ページのさし絵

**waterproof** /wɔ́ːtərprùːf; wát-/ 形 ▶定義 that does not let water go through 水を通さない→防水の,耐水の ‖ *a waterproof jacket* 防水ジャケット

**watershed** /wɔ́ːtərʃèd; wát-/ 名 C ▶定義 an event or time which is important because it marks the beginning of sth new or different 新しい,または異なった〜の始まりをはっきりと示すために重要な出来事または時期→分岐点,転機

**waterski** /wɔ́ːtərskìː; wát-/ 動 自 ▶定義 to move across the surface of water standing on narrow boards (**waterskis**) and being pulled by a boat 細い板(水上スキー板)に立ち,ボートに引っ張られながら水面を進む→水上スキーをする ☜ C8ページのさし絵

**watertight** /wɔ́ːtərtàɪt; wát-/ 形 ▶定義**1** made so that water cannot get in or out 水が出入りできないよう作られた→水を通さない,防水の ‖ *a watertight container* 防水密封容器 ▶定義**2** (used about an excuse, opinion, etc) impossible to prove wrong; without any faults (言い訳,意見などについて)間違っていると証明することが不可能な; 何の落ち度もない→水も漏らさない,すきのない,完ぺきな ‖ *His alibi was absolutely watertight.* 彼のアリバイは実に完ぺきだった.

**waterway** /wɔ́ːtərwèɪ; wát-/ 名 C ▶定義 a canal, river, etc along which boats can travel 船が航行できる運河,川など→運河,水路,航路

**watery** /wɔ́ːtəri; wát-/ 形 ▶定義**1** containing mostly water 大部分水を含んでいる→水を過度に含んだ,水っぽい ‖ *watery soup* 薄くて味のないスープ *A watery liquid came out of the wound.* 水のような液体が傷口から出てきた. ▶定義**2** weak and pale 弱くて薄い→(色などが)薄い,淡い,青白い ‖ *watery sunshine* 淡い日差し *a watery smile* 微笑

**watt** /wɑt/ 名 C ▶定義 a unit of electrical power 電力の単位→ワット ‖ *a 60-watt light bulb* 60ワットの電球

*****wave**[1] /weɪv/ 名 C ▶定義**1** a line of water moving across the surface of water, especially the sea, that is higher than the rest of the surface 特に海で,ほかの水面よりも高い水面上を横切って動いている水の列→波 ‖ *We watched the waves roll in and break on the shore.* 私たちは波がうねり,海岸で砕けるのを見ていた. ☜参 **tidal wave** ☜ C8ページのさし絵 ▶定義**2** a sudden increase or spread of a feeling or type of behaviour 感情,またはある種の行動が突然増加あるいは広がること→(感情・行動などの)波,高まり,急増 ‖ *There has been a wave of sympathy for the refugees.* 難民に対する同情が高まっている. *a crime wave* 犯罪の急増 *The pain came in waves.* 痛みは,波のように襲ってきた. ☜参 **heatwave** ▶定義**3** a large number of people or things suddenly moving or appearing somewhere 突然ある場所で動き出すまたは現れる大勢の人々あるいはたくさんのもの→殺到する人々,激増するもの ‖ *There is normally a wave of tourists in August.* 8月はいつも大勢の観光客が殺到する. ▶定義**4** a movement of sth, especially your hand, from side to side in the air 物,特に人の手が空中で左右に動くこと→手を振ること ‖ *With a wave of his hand, he said goodbye and left.* 手を振りながら,彼はさよならを言って去った. ▶定義**5** the form that some types of energy such as sound, light, heat, etc take when they move ある種のエネルギー,例えば音,光,熱などが移動するときにとる形→波,波動 ‖ *sound waves* 音波 *shock waves from the earthquake* 地震の衝撃波 ☜参 **long wave**, **medium wave**, **short wave** ▶定義**6** a gentle curve in your hair 髪の緩やかな曲線→ウエーブ,縮れ ☜参 **perm**

*****wave**[2] /weɪv/ 動 ▶定義**1** 自 他 to move your hand from side to side in the air, usually to attract sb's attention or as you meet or leave sb 通常,〜の注意をひくために,あるいは〜と会うまたは別れるときに,手を空中で左右に動かす→手を振る,手を振ってあいさつする ‖ *She waved to me as the train left the station.* 列車が駅を離れる時,彼女は私に手を振った. *I leant out of the window and waved goodbye to my friends.* 私は窓の外へ身を乗り出して,友人たちに手を振

って別れのあいさつをした. ☛ S6 ページのさし絵 ▶定義2 ⓫ **wave sth (at sb); wave sth (about)** to hold sth in the air and move it from side to side ～に対し…を空中に保って, それを左右に動かす (手や旗など) を振る, 揺り動かす, 振り回す ‖ *The crowd waved flags as the President came out.* 大統領が現れると, 群衆は旗を振った. *She was talking excitedly and waving her arms about.* 彼女は興奮して両腕を振り回しながら話していた. ▶定義3 ⓫ **wave sb/sth away, on, through, etc** to move your hand in a particular direction to show sb/sth which way to go ～がどの方向に進むべきかを示すために, 特定の方向に手を動かす➔～に手を振って合図する ‖ *There was a policeman in the middle of the road, waving us on.* 道路の中央に警察官がいて, 私たちに進むよう手を振って合図した. ▶定義4 ⓮ to move gently up and down or from side to side 上下または左右に穏やかに動く➔そよぐ, 揺らぐ ‖ *The branches of the trees waved gently in the breeze.* 木々の枝がそよ風にゆったりとそよいだ.

**句動詞** **wave sth aside** ▶定義 to decide not to pay attention to sb/sth because you think he/she/it is not important 重要でないと判断して, ～に注意を払わないことにする➔(人など)を払いのける, (提案など) を退ける

**wave sb off** ▶定義 to wave to sb who is leaving 去っていく～に手を振る➔～に手を振って送り出す

**waveband** /wéɪvbænd/ 名 ⓒ ▶定義 a set of radio waves of similar length 類似した波長を持つ一組の電波➔(テレビ・ラジオの) 周波数帯

**wavelength** /wéɪvleŋ(k)θ/ 名 ⓒ ▶定義1 the distance between two sound waves 2 つの音波間の距離➔波長 ▶定義2 the length of wave on which a radio station sends out its programmes ラジオ局が番組を送信する波の長さ➔周波数

**成句** **on the same wavelength** ⇒ **SAME**

**waver** /wéɪvər/ 動 ⓘ ▶定義1 to become weak or uncertain, especially when making a decision or choice 特に決断または選択を行うときに, 気が弱くなる, または不確かになる➔(決心・判断などに) 迷う, ためらう ‖ *He never wavered in his support for her.* 彼は, 彼女を支えることを決してためらわなかった. ▶定義2 to move in a way that is not firm or steady しっかりしていない, あるいは着実でない様子で動く➔ふらつく, よろける, 震える ‖ *His hand wavered as he reached for the gun.* 彼は銃に手を伸ばすと手が震えた.

**wavy** /wéɪvi/ 形 ▶定義 having curves; not straight 曲線のある; まっすぐでない➔波状の, 波形の, (髪が) ウェーブをかけた ‖ *wavy hair* ウェーブのかかった髪 *a wavy line* 波線 ☛ **hair**, **line** のさし絵

**wax** /wæks/ 名 ⓤ ▶定義1 a substance made from fat or oil that melts easily and is used for making candles, polish, etc 脂肪または油から作られた物質で, 簡単に溶け, ろうそくやつや出し剤などを作るために使われる➔ろう, ワックス ☛ **candle** のさし絵 ▶定義2 a yellow substance that is found in your ears 耳の中にある黄色い物質➔耳あか

★**way**¹ /wéɪ/ 名 ▶定義1 ⓒ **a way (to do sth/of doing sth)** a particular method, style or manner of doing sth ～を行う特定の方法, 様式, または流儀➔方法, やり方 ‖ *What is* **the best way** *to learn a language?* 言語を習得するための一番良い方法はどのようなものですか. *I've discovered a brilliant way of saving paper!* 私は紙を節約するすばらしい方法を発見した. *They'll have to find the money* **one way or another**. 彼らはどうにかして, その金を見つけなければならないだろう. *He always* **does things** *his* **own way**. 彼はいつも我を通す. *She smiled* **in a friendly way**. 彼女は優しくほほえんだ. ▶定義2 [ⓒ, 通常は単数] the route you take to reach somewhere; the route you would take if nothing were stopping you ある場所に行き着くためにたどる道筋; 行く手を妨げられなければ取るであろう道筋➔～へ行く道, 道筋, 通り道 ‖ *Can you tell me* **the way to** *James Street?* ジェームズ通りへ行く道を教えてくれませんか. *Which way should I go to get to the town centre?* 中心街へは, どちらの方へ行けばいいですか. *If you* **lose** *your* **way**, *phone me*. 道に迷ったら, 私に電話しなさい. *We stopped* **on the way to** *Leeds for a meal*. 私たちはリーズに行く途中で, 食事に立ち寄った. *Can I drive you home? It's* **on my way**. あなたの家まで車で送りましょうか ― 私の通り道ですから. *Get out of my way!* 道を空けてくだ

## 1810　way²

さい. *Can you move that box - it's **in my/the way**.* その箱を移動してくれませんか － 邪魔になります. ▶定義3 [単数扱い] a direction or position 方向または位置➡**方向, 方角** ‖ *Look this way!* こちらの方を見て. *That painting is **the wrong way up** (= with the wrong edge at the top).* その絵は上下逆さまだ(= 間違ったへりが上になっている). *Shouldn't you be wearing that hat **the other way round**? (= facing in the other direction)* その帽子は逆に(= 反対方向に向けて)かぶった方が良いのではないでしょうか. *He thought I was older than my sister but in fact it's **the other way round** (= the opposite of what he thought).* 彼は私が姉よりも年上だと思っていたが, 実際には逆(= 彼が考えていたことの反対)だ. ☛参 **back to front** ▶定義4 ●a path, road, route, etc that you can travel along その上を移動できる小道, 道路, 通路など➡**小道, 道路, 通路, 軌道** ☛参 **highway, motorway, railway** ▶定義5 [単数扱い] a distance in space or time 空間または時間の隔たり➡**道のり, 距離** ‖ *It's **a long way** from London to Edinburgh.* ロンドンからエディンバラへはかなりの距離だ. *The exams are still **a long way off**.* 試験はまだずっと先の事だ. *We came **all this way** to see him and he's not at home!* 私たちは彼に会うためにはるばるやって来たのに, その彼が家にいないなんて.

成句 be set in your ways ▶定義 to be unable to change your habits, attitudes, etc 自分の習慣, 態度などを変えられない➡**自分の流儀に固執する**

by the way ▶定義 (used for adding sth to the conversation) on a new subject (会話で~を追加するために用いて) 新しい話題について➡**ところで, ついでながら** ‖ *Oh, by the way, I saw Mario in town yesterday.* ああ, ところで, 昨日街でマリオを見掛けたよ.

change your ways ⇒ **CHANGE**¹

get/have your own way ▶定義 to get or do what you want, although others may want sth else ほかの人たちは別の~を望んでいるかもしれないが, 自分の欲しい物を手に入れる, または自分のしたい事をする➡**自分の思い通りにする, 我が道を行く**

give way ▶定義 to break or fall down 壊れる, 倒れる➡**崩れる, 崩壊する** ‖ *The branch of the tree suddenly gave way and he fell.* 木の枝が突然折れてきて, 彼は落ちた.

give way (to sb/sth) ▶定義1 to stop or to allow sb/sth to go first 止まる, あるいは~が先に行くのを許す➡**~に取って代わられる, ~に道を譲る** ‖ *Give way to traffic coming from the right.* 右側から来た車に道を譲りなさい. ☛ **roundabout** のさし絵 ▶定義2 to allow sb to have what he/she wants although you did not at first agree with it 最初は賛成していなかったが, ~が欲しがるものを手に入れることを許す➡**(力・主張などに)屈する, 譲歩する** ‖ *We shall not give way to the terrorists' demands.* 我々はテロリストの要求には決して屈しないぞ.

go a long way ⇒ **LONG**¹

go out of your way (to do sth) ▶定義 to make a special effort to do sth ~を行うために特別な努力をする➡**わざわざ~をする**

have a long way to go ⇒ **LONG**¹

the hard way ⇒ **HARD**¹

in a/one/any way; in some ways ▶定義 to a certain degree but not completely 完全ではないが, ある程度まで➡**ある点では, ある意味では, ある程度は** ‖ *In some ways I prefer working in a small office.* ある意味では, 私は小さな事務所で働く方が好きだ.

in a big/small way ▶定義 used for expressing the size or importance of an activity ある活動の規模や重要性を表現するために用いて➡**大規模・小規模に, 大々的・ささやかに** ‖ '*Have you done any acting before?*' '*Yes, but in a very small way (= not very much).*' 「これまでに芝居の経験がありますか」「ええ, でも少しだけ(= 大した量の経験ではありません)」

in the way ▶定義1 blocking the road or path 道路または通路をふさいで➡**行く手をふさいで, 通りの妨げになって** ‖ *I can't get past. There's a big lorry in the way.* 私は通り抜けられない. 行く手を大型のトラックがふさいでいる. ▶定義2 not needed or wanted 必要とされていない, あるいは望まれていない➡**邪魔になって** ‖ *I felt rather in the way at my daughter's party.* 娘のパーティーで, 私はかなり邪魔者になっているように感じた.

learn the hard way ⇒ **LEARN**

no way 略式 ▶定義 definitely not 絶対に~ない

→とんでもない, 駄目だ, 無理だ ‖ 'Can I borrow your car?' 'No way!'「あなたの車, 借りられる」「とんでもない」

under way ▶定義 having started and making progress 既に始まって進行中で→(計画などが)進行中で, (船が)航行中で ‖ Discussions between the two sides are now under way. 双方の協議が現在進行中だ.

a/sb's way of life ▶定義 the behaviour and customs that are typical of a person or group of people 個人または集団の典型的な振る舞いと慣習→生活様式

**way**² /wéɪ/ 副 略式 ▶定義 very far; very much とても遠くに, とてもたくさん→はるかに, ずっと ‖ I finally found his name way down at the bottom of the list. 私はその一覧表のずっと下の最後の部分でとうとう彼の名前を見つけた. Matt's got way more experience than me. マットは私よりもずっと経験が豊富だ.

**WC** /dʌb(ə)lju: síː/ 略 toilet→トイレ (water closet (水洗便所)の略語)

*****we** /wɪ, wi, wiː/ 代 ▶定義 the subject of a verb; used for talking about the speaker and one or more other people 動詞の主語; 話し手ともう1人またはそれ以上の人々を指す→私たち, 僕たち, 我々 ‖ We're going to the cinema. 私たちは映画館へ行くところです. We are both very pleased with the house. 私たちは2人ともその家にとても満足している.

*****weak** /wiːk/ 形 ▶定義 1 (used about the body) having little strength or energy; not strong (身体について) 体力や活力がほとんどない; 強くない→弱い, 弱々しい, 無力な ‖ The child was weak with hunger. その子供は空腹で衰弱していた. Her legs felt weak. 彼女は両足に力が入らなかった. ▶定義 2 that cannot support a lot of weight; likely to break 多量の重さを支えられない; 壊れてしまいそうな→弱い, 壊れやすい, もろい ‖ That bridge is too weak to take heavy traffic. その橋はもろすぎて激しい交通量に耐えられない. ▶定義 3 not having economic success 経済的な成功を収めていない→弱い, 競争力のない, 低迷する, 活気のない ‖ a weak currency/ economy/market 競争力のない通貨・低迷している経済・弱気の市場 ▶定義 4 easy to influence; not firm or powerful 影響されやすい; 堅固ではない, 強力でない→(性格・意志などが)弱い, 薄弱な ‖ He is too weak to be a good leader. 彼は軟弱すぎて良い指導者にはなれない. a weak character 意志の弱い性格 ▶定義 5 (used about an argument, excuse, etc) not easy to believe (口論, 言い訳などについて) 容易には信じられない→(論拠などが)不十分な, 説得力に欠ける, 下手な ‖ She made some weak excuse about washing her hair tonight. 今夜髪を洗うことについて, 彼女は下手な言い訳をした. ▶定義 6 not easy to see or hear; not definite or strong 見えにくい, 聞き取りづらい; 明確でない, 強くない→はっきりしない, 弱々しい, ぼんやりとした, かすかな ‖ a weak voice 弱々しい声 She gave a weak smile. 彼女はかすかにほほえんだ. ▶定義 7 (used about liquids) containing a lot of water, not strong in taste (液体について) 多量の水を含んでいて風味が強くない→薄い, 水っぽい ‖ weak coffee 薄いコーヒー I like my tea quite weak. 私は紅茶はかなり薄いのが好きだ. ▶定義 8 **weak (at/in/on sth)** not very good at sth ～があまり得意でない→苦手な, 不得意な, 弱い ‖ He's weak at Maths. 彼は数学が苦手だ. His maths is weak. 彼は数学の計算に弱い. a weak team 弱いチーム ⇔ すべての定義 **strong** — **weakly** 副→弱く, 弱々しく, 優柔不断に

*****weaken** /wíːk(ə)n/ 動 自 他 ▶定義 1 to become less strong; to make sb/sth less strong より強くなくなる; ～をより強くなくさせる→弱る, 衰弱する; ～を弱らせる, 衰弱させる ‖ The illness had left her weakened. その病気で彼女は衰弱した. The building had been weakened by the earthquake. その建物は地震でもろくなっていた. ⇔ **strengthen** ▶定義 2 to become less certain or firm about sth ～についての確信, または厳格さがより薄れる→(考え, 決心などが)ぐらつく, 弱気になる; (考え, 決心など)をぐらつかせる, 弱気にさせる ‖ She eventually weakened and allowed him to stay. 彼女は, 最後には軟化して, 彼がとどまることを許した.

**weak form** 名 C ▶定義 a way of pronouncing a word when it is not emphasized 強調されないときの単語の発音方法→弱形

*****weakness** /wíːknəs/ 名 ▶定義 1 U the state of being weak 弱い状態→弱さ, 弱いこと, 薄弱 ‖ He

thought that crying was a sign of weakness. 彼は,泣き叫ぶことは弱さの表れだと思った.
▶定義2 ❸a fault or lack of strength, especially in a person's character 特に人の性格において,短所または長所の不足→**短所,弱点,欠点,弱み,あら** ‖ It's important to know your own strengths and weaknesses. 自分の長所と短所を知ることは重要だ. ⇔ 定義1, 2 **strength** ▶定義3 [❸, 通常は単数] a weakness for sth/sb a particular and often foolish liking for sth/sb 格別にしかもしばしば愚かなほど～を好むこと→**～がむやみに好きであること,～に目がないこと** ‖ I have a weakness for chocolate. 私はチョコレートに目がない.

*wealth /welθ/ 図 ▶定義1 ❶a lot of money, property, etc that sb owns; the state of being rich ～が所有する多額の金や財産など;裕福である状態→**富,(大きな)財産;裕福** ‖ They were a family of enormous wealth. 彼らはばく大な財産を所有する一家だった. ☛類 **riches** ▶定義2 [単数扱い] a wealth of sth a large number or amount of sth 多数の～,大量の～**豊富な** ‖ a wealth of information/experience/talent 豊富な情報・経験・才能

*wealthy /wélθi/ 形 (**wealthier, wealthiest**) ▶定義 having a lot of money, property, etc; rich 多額の金や財産などを所有している;裕福な→**富んだ;豊富な**

wean /wiːn/ 動 ❹ ▶定義 to gradually stop feeding a baby or young animal with its mother's milk and start giving it solid food 赤ん坊や幼い動物にその母親の乳を与えるのを徐々にやめて,固形食を与え始める→**～を離乳させる**

*weapon /wépən/ 図 ❸ ▶定義 an object which is used for fighting or for killing people, such as a gun, knife, bomb, etc 人々と戦うあるいは殺すために使われるもの,例えば銃,短刀,爆弾など→**武器,兵器**

*wear¹ /weər/ 動 (過 **wore** /wɔːr/;過分 **worn** /wɔːrn/) ▶定義1 ❹ to have clothes, jewellery, etc on your body 衣服,装身具などを身に着けている→**～を着ている,履いている,かぶっている** ‖ He was wearing a suit and tie. 彼はスーツを着て,ネクタイを締めていた. I wear glasses for reading. 私は読書のときは眼鏡を掛ける.

▶定義2 ❹ to have a certain look on your face ある様子を顔に浮かべている→**(表情)を表している,示している,浮かべている** ‖ His face wore a puzzled look. 彼は困惑した表情を浮かべていた.
▶定義3 ❹ ❹ to become or make sth become thinner, smoother or weaker because of being used or rubbed a lot 何度も使われまたはこすられたことで,～がより薄く,滑らかに,または弱くなる,あるいは～をそのようにさせる→**すり減る;～をすり減らす,使い古す** ‖ These tyres are badly worn. これらのタイヤはひどくすり減っている. The soles of his shoes had worn smooth. 彼の靴底はツルツルにすり減っていた. ▶定義4 ❹ to make a hole, path, etc in sth by rubbing, walking, etc こすること,歩くことなどによって,～に穴,通り道などを作る→**(穴,溝など)を掘る,開ける,(土地)を浸食する** ‖ Put some slippers on or you'll wear a hole in your socks! スリッパを履きなさい.そうしないとソックスに穴が開いてしまいますよ. ▶定義5 ❹ to last for a long time without becoming thinner or damaged 薄くならないで,または破損しないで長い間持つ→**使用に耐える,持つ,長持ちする** ‖ This material wears well. この素材はとても長持ちする.

成句 wear thin ▶定義 to have less effect because of being used too much 使われすぎたので,効果が薄れている→**(言葉,冗談などが)新鮮味を失う,(言葉,冗談などの)効果が薄れる** ‖ We've heard that excuse so often that it's beginning to wear thin. 私たちはその言い訳をあまりに頻繁に聞いていたので,見え透いたものになり始めている.

句動詞 wear (sth) away ▶定義 to damage sth or to make it disappear over a period of time, by using or touching it a lot; to disappear or become damaged in this way 長期間にわたって何度も使ったり触れたりして,～に損害を与える,または消滅させる;そのようにして消滅する,または傷付く→**～をすり減らす;すり減る,擦り切れる** ‖ The wind had worn the soil away. 風によって少しずつ土がなくなった.

wear (sth) down ▶定義 to become or to make sth smaller or smoother ～がより小さく,またはより滑らかになる,あるいは～をそのようにさせる→**すり減る;～をすり減らす** ‖ The heels on these shoes have worn right down. この靴のかかとはすっかりすり減っていた.

wear sb/sth down ▶定義 to make sb/sth weaker by attacking, persuading, etc 攻撃, 説得などにより〜を弱らせる→〜を参らせる, (抵抗, 反対など)を弱らせる(敵, 人, 議論など)に勝つ ‖ *They wore him down with constant arguments until he changed his mind.* 彼らは, 彼が考えを変えるまで, 繰り返し議論して打ち負かした.

wear off ▶定義 to become less strong or to disappear completely 強くなくなる, または完全に消える→消滅する ‖ *The effects of the drug wore off after a few hours.* その薬の効き目は数時間で消えた.

wear (sth) out ▶定義 to become too thin or damaged to use any more; to cause sth to do this もう使えないほどに薄くなる, または駄目になる→すり減る; 〜をすり減らす, (もう使えないほど)使い古す, 駄目にする ‖ *Children's shoes wear out very quickly.* 子供たちの靴はあっと言う間に駄目になる.

wear sb out ▶定義 to make sb very tired 〜を非常に疲れさせる→〜を参らせる ‖ *She wore herself out walking home with the heavy bags.* 彼女は重いかばんをいくつか持って家まで歩き, すっかり疲れきってしまった. ☞参 worn-out

**★wear**² /weər/ 名 ❶ ▶定義 **1** wearing or being worn; use as clothing 身に着けていること, または着られていること; 衣類として使うこと→着用; 使用 ‖ *You'll need jeans and jumpers for everyday wear.* 普段着として, ジーンズとセーターが必要になります. ▶定義 **2** (通常は複合語で) used especially in shops to describe clothes for a particular purpose or occasion 特に小売店で, 特定の目的または機会のための衣服を表現するために用いて→(ある目的のための)衣装, 〜着 ‖ *casual/evening/sports wear* 普段着・夜会服・運動着 *children's wear* 子供服 ▶定義 **3** long use which damages the quality or appearance of sth 〜の品質または外観を損なう長期間の使用→消耗, 摩滅, 擦り切れ, 着古し ‖ *The engine is checked regularly for signs of wear.* エンジンは, 摩耗の兆候がないかを見るため, 定期的に点検される.

成句 wear and tear ▶定義 the damage caused by ordinary use 通常の使用による損傷→傷み, 擦り切れ, 消耗

the worse for wear ⇒ **WORSE**

**weary** /wíəri/ 形 ▶定義 very tired, especially after you have been doing sth for a long time 特に長い時間〜をし続けた後, 非常に疲れた→疲れ果てた, 飽き飽きした, うんざりした ‖ *He gave a weary smile.* 彼はうんざりした笑いを浮かべた.
— wearily /wíərəli/ 副 →疲れて, 飽き飽きして, 退屈して — weariness 名 ❶ →疲労, 退屈

**★weather**¹ /wéðər/ 名 ❶ ▶定義 the climate at a certain place and time, how much wind, rain, sun, etc there is and how hot or cold it is ある特定の場所と時間での気候のことで, 風量, 雨量, 日照具合などがどの程度で, 暑さや寒さがどのくらいかということ→天気, 天候, 気象 ‖ *What's the weather like where you are?* そちらの天気はどうですか. *hot/warm/sunny/fine weather* 暑い・暖かい・晴れた・良い天気 *cold/wet/windy/wintry weather* 寒い・雨の・風の強い・冬らしい天気 *I'm not going for a run in this weather!* こんな天気では, 私は走りに行かないよ.

▶ rain (雨)は, 雲から落ちる水滴である. snow (雪)は, 凍った雨である. 柔らかく白色で, しばしば地面に積もる. sleet (みぞれ)は, 完全には凍っていない雨である. hail (あられ・ひょう)は, 凍って氷になった雨である. とても弱く雨が降っているのは drizzling (霧雨・こぬか雨)である. 雨が非常に激しく降っているときは pouring (土砂降り)である. fog (霧)は, 地上レベルの雲のようなもので, 遠くを見渡しにくくする. mist (もや)は, 薄い霧である. storm も参照.

成句 make heavy weather of sth ⇒ **HEAVY**
under the weather 略式 ▶定義 not very well あまり良くない→調子が悪い, 元気がない

**weather**² /wéðər/ 動 ▶定義 **1** 自他 to change or make sth change in appearance because of the effect of the sun, air or wind 太陽, 空気または風の影響により〜の外観が変わる, または〜の外観を変える→(岩石などが)風化する; (岩石など)を風化させる ‖ *The farmer's face was weathered by the sun.* その農夫の顔は, 日焼けして変化していた. (陽にさらされ続けて, 深いしわが刻み込まれていた.) ▶定義 **2** 他 to come safely through a difficult time or experience 困難な時期または体験を安全に切り抜ける→〜をしのぐ ‖ *Their company managed to weather the recession and recover.* 彼らの会社は, 何とか不況を乗り切って回復した.

**weather-beaten** 形 ▶定義 (used especially about a person's face or skin) made rough and damaged by the sun and wind (特に人の顔や皮膚について)太陽と風によってざらつき傷んだ→**日に焼けた,風雨にさらされた**

**weather forecast** (または **forecast**) 名 C ▶定義 a description of the weather that is expected for the next day or next few days 翌日または次の数日間に予測される天気の記述→**天気予報** ☞参 weather

**weave** /wiːv/ 動 自 他 (過 **wove** /wóuv/ または定義2 **weaved**; 過分 **woven** /wóuv(ə)n/ または定義2 **weaved**) ▶定義1 to make cloth, etc by passing threads under and over a set of threads that is fixed to a frame (**loom**) 枠(機(はた))に固定された一組の織り糸に,別の織り糸を上下に通して布などを作る→**織る,機織(はたおり)をする; ~を織る, 織って~を作る** ‖ *woven cloth* 織布 ▶定義2 to change direction often when you are moving so that you are not stopped by anything 移動中に,何物にも止められないように,しばしば方向を変える→**(~を)縫うように進む・通る, (~を)すり抜ける** ‖ *The cyclist weaved in and out of the traffic.* その自転車に乗った人は,車の間を縫うように進んだ.

**web** /web/ 名 C ▶定義 a type of fine net that a spider makes in order to catch small insects 小さな昆虫を捕まえるためにクモが作る,細かい網の一種→**クモの巣** ‖ *A spider spins webs.* クモが巣をかける. ☞参 cobweb

**Wed** Wednesday→**水曜日** ‖ *Wed 4 May* 5月4日水曜日

**we'd** /wɪd, wiːd/ **WE HAD, WE WOULD**の短縮形

*****wedding** /wédɪŋ/ 名 C ▶定義 a marriage ceremony and often the meal or party that follows it (**the reception**) 結婚の儀式で,しばしばその後に食事やパーティー(披露宴)が行われる→**結婚式,婚礼** ‖ *I've been invited to their wedding.* 私は彼らの結婚式に招待された. *a wedding dress/guest/present* ウエディングドレス・結婚式の招待客・結婚の贈り物 *a wedding ring (= one that is worn on the third finger to show that a person is married)* 結婚指輪(= 薬指にはめられて,結婚していることを示す指輪)

▶ marriage(結婚)とは,だれかと結婚している状態を表す語である.marriageは, weddingと同様に,「結婚式」の意味で使われることもある.結婚する男性は bridegroom(花婿),女性は bride(花嫁)である.そのほか,結婚式で重要な人々には best man(新郎の付き添い人)と bridesmaids(花嫁の付き添い人たち)がいる.結婚式は, church wedding(教会結婚式)または registry office(登記所)で行うことができる.25年間結婚している夫婦は silver wedding(銀婚式)を祝い,50周年では golden wedding(金婚式),60周年では diamond wedding(ダイヤモンド婚)を祝う.

**wedge**¹ /wedʒ/ 名 C ▶定義 a piece of wood, etc with one thick and one thin pointed end that you can push into a small space, for example to keep things apart 例えば物と物を離しておくために,すきまに押し込める,一方の端が厚く,もう一方の端が薄くとがっている木片など→**くさび** ‖ *The door was kept open with a wedge.* そのドアは,くさびによって開いたままにされていた.

**wedge**² /wedʒ/ 動 他 ▶定義1 to force sth apart or to prevent sth from moving by using a wedge くさびを使って~を無理やり離しておく,または~が動かないようにする→**~をくさびで留める, ~にくさびを挟む** ‖ *to wedge a door open* ドアにくさびを挟んで開いたままにしておく ▶定義2 to force sth/sb to fit into a small space ~を無理やり小さな空間に収める→**~を無理に押し込む, 詰め込む** ‖ *The cupboard was wedged between the table and the door.* 食器棚は,テーブルとドアの間に押し込まれていた.

*****Wednesday** /wénzdeɪ, -di/ 名 C U (略**Wed**) ▶定義 the day of the week after Tuesday 火曜日の次の曜日→**水曜日**

▶曜日は最初の文字を必ず大文字で書く.文中での曜日の使い方の例については, Mondayを参照.

**wee** /wiː/ (または **wee-wee**) 名 C U 略式 ▶定義 (used by young children or when you are talking to them) water that you pass from your body; urine (幼児が,または幼児に向かって話すときに用いて)体から流れ出る水; 尿→**おしっこ** — **wee** 動 自 →**おしっこをする**

**weed**¹ /wiːd/ 名 ▶定義1 ❶ a wild plant that is not wanted in a garden because it prevents

other plants from growing properly ほかの植物がきちんと生長するのを妨げるので,庭に生えてほしくないと思われている野生植物→雑草
▶定義2 ❶a mass of very small green plants that floats on the surface of an area of water 水の表面に多量に浮かんでいる非常に小さな緑色の植物の塊→藻,水草,海草

**weed**² /wiːd/ 動自他 ▶定義 to remove weeds from a piece of ground, etc 一区画の地面などから雑草を取り除く→(〜の)雑草を抜く・除く
句動詞 weed sth/sb out ▶定義 to remove the things or people that you do not think are good enough 十分に良いと思っていない物または人々を取り除く→取り除く,排除する,根絶する‖ He weeded out all the letters with spelling mistakes in them. 彼はつづりの間違いがある手紙をすべて取り除いた.

**weedy** /wíːdi/ 形略式 ▶定義 small and weak 小さくて弱い→ひょろひょろした,ひ弱そうな,貧弱な‖ a small weedy man 小柄でひ弱そうな男

*week /wiːk/ 名 C ▶定義1 a period of seven days, especially from Monday to Sunday or from Sunday to Saturday 7日間,特に月曜日から日曜日,または日曜日から土曜日まで→1週間‖ We arrived **last week**. 私たちは先週到着した. He left two weeks ago. 彼は2週間前に去った. I haven't seen her for a week. 私は1週間彼女を見掛けていない. I go there twice a week. 私は週に2度そこへ行く. They'll be back in a week/in a week's time. 彼らは1週間後に戻るだろう.
▶イギリス英語では通常,2週間をfortnightと言う.
▶定義2 the part of the week when people go to work, etc, usually from Monday to Friday 1週間のうち人々が仕事などに行く部分で,普通月曜日から金曜日まで→平日‖ She works hard during the week so that she can enjoy herself at the weekend. 彼女は週末を楽しく過ごすことができるよう,平日は一生懸命に働く. I work a 40-hour week. 私は週40時間勤務である.
成句 today, tomorrow, Monday, etc week ▶定義 seven days after today, tomorrow, Monday, etc 今日,明日,月曜日などから7日後→1週間後の今日,明日,月曜日など
week in, week out ▶定義 every week without a rest or change 休みまたは変更がなく毎週→毎週毎週,来る週も来る週も‖ He's played for the same team week in, week out for 20 years. 彼が毎週毎週同じチームでプレーして20年になる.
a week yesterday, last Monday, etc ▶定義 seven days before yesterday, Monday, etc 昨日,月曜日などから7日前→先週の昨日,先週の月曜日など

*weekday /wíːkdèi/ 名 C ▶定義 any day except Saturday or Sunday 土曜日,日曜日以外の日→週日,平日,ウイークデー‖ I only work on weekdays. 私は平日しか働かない.

*weekend /wìːkénd/ ⌒| 名 C ▶定義 Saturday and Sunday 土曜日と日曜日→週末,ウイークエンド‖ What are you doing **at the weekend**? 週末にあなたは何をしますか.☛「週末に」の意味のat the weekendはイギリス英語で使われる.アメリカ英語ではon the weekendと言う.

*weekly¹ /wíːkli/ 形副 ▶定義 happening or appearing once a week or every week 週に1度または毎週起こる,あるいは現れる→週1回(の),毎週(の),週刊の‖ a weekly report 週報 We are paid weekly. 私たちは週給をもらっている.

**weekly**² /wíːkli/ 名 C (複 **weeklies**) ▶定義 a newspaper or magazine that is published every week 毎週1回発行される新聞や雑誌→週刊紙,週刊誌

**weep** /wiːp/ 動自他 (過,過分 **wept** /wept/) 正式 ▶定義 to let tears fall because of strong emotion; to cry 激しい感情のため涙を流す;泣く→嘆き悲しむ;(涙を)流す‖ She wept at the news of his death. 彼女は彼の死の知らせに涙を流した.

*weigh /wéi/ 動 ▶定義1 他to measure how heavy sth is, especially by using a machine (scales) 特に器械(はかり)を使って,〜の重さを測定する→〜の重さを量る‖ I weigh myself every week. 私は毎週体重を測定する. Can you weigh this parcel for me, please? この小包の重さを量ってくれませんか. ▶定義2 他to have or show a certain weight ある重さを持つ,または示す→(〜の)目方がある‖ I weigh 56 kilos. 私は体重が56キロある. How much does this weigh? これはどのくらいの重さですか.
▶定義3 他weigh sth (up) to consider sth carefully 〜を慎重に考える→〜をよく考える,評価す

る, 査定する ‖ *You need to weigh up your chances of success.* あなたは成功する可能性をじっくり検討する必要がある. ▶定義4 ⓤ **weigh sth (against sb/sth)** to consider if one thing is better, more important, etc than another or not ある物がほかの物・人より, 優れているのか否か, 重要であるのか否かなどを熟考する→〜を比較してよく考える, 〜を比較検討する ‖ *We shall weigh the advantages of the plan against the risks.* その計画のメリットをリスクと対比して検討しよう. ▶定義5 ⓘ **weigh against (sb/sth)** to be considered as a disadvantage when sb/sth is being judged 〜の評価において, 欠点と見なされる→(〜に)不利に働く, 不利となる ‖ *She didn't get the job because her lack of experience weighed against her.* 経験不足が不利に働いて, 彼女はその職を得られなかった.

**句動詞 weigh sb down** ▶定義 to make sb feel worried and sad 〜を心配させ, 悲しませる→〜をふさぎ込ませる, 気をめいらせる ‖ *He felt weighed down by all his responsibilities.* 彼はすべての責務によって打ちひしがれた思いだった.

**weigh sb/sth down** ▶定義 to make it difficult for sb/sth to move (by being heavy) (重みによって)〜を動きにくくさせる→〜を重みで動きにくくする ‖ *I was weighed down by heavy shopping.* たくさん買い物をしたため, 歩きにくかった.

**weigh on sb/sth** ▶定義 to make sb worry 〜を心配させる→〜の重荷となる, 圧迫する

▶ weigh on sb's mindとも言う: *That problem has been weighing on my mind for a long time.* (あの問題は, 長い間私の重荷となっていた.)

**weigh sb/sth up** ▶定義 to consider sb/sth carefully and form an opinion 〜を慎重に考えて, 見解をまとめる→〜を評価する, 査定する, 値踏みする ‖ *I weighed up my chances and decided it was worth applying.* 私は自分の可能性をよく考えて, 応募する価値があると判断した.

★**weight**¹ /wéɪt/ 名 ▶定義1 ❶ how heavy sth/sb is; the fact of being heavy 〜がどのくらい重いか; 実際に重さがあること→重さ, 重量, 目方, 体重 ‖ *The doctor advised him to lose weight (= become thinner and less heavy).* 医者は彼に減量する(= やせて軽くなる)よう忠告した. *He's put on weight (= got fatter).* 彼は体重が増えた(= 太った). *The weight of the snow broke the branch.* 雪の重みで枝が折れた. ▶定義2 ❷ a heavy object 重い物→重量のある物 ‖ *The doctor has told me not to lift heavy weights.* 医者は私に, 重い物を持ち上げないようにと言った. ▶定義3 ❷ a piece of metal that weighs a known amount that can be used to measure an amount of sth, or that can be lifted as a form of exercise 既知の重さの金属の塊で, 〜の量を計るために使われる, または運動の一形態として持ち上げられる→おもり, 分銅, (重量挙げの)ウエート ‖ *a 500-gram weight* 500グラムのおもり *She lifts weights in the gym as part of her daily training.* 彼女は日々のトレーニングの一環として, ジムでウエートを持ち上げる. ☛ S1ページのさし絵 ▶定義4 [単数扱い] something that you are worried about 自分が心配している物事→(心の)重荷, 重圧, 負担 ‖ *Telling her the truth took a weight off his mind.* 彼女に真実を告げたことで, 彼は肩の荷が下りた.

**成句 carry weight** ⇒ **CARRY**
**pull your weight** ⇒ **PULL**¹

**weight**² /wéɪt/ 動 ⓤ ▶定義1 **weight sth (down) (with sth)** to hold sth down with a heavy object or objects 重い物で〜を押さえ付ける→〜に重みを加える, 〜をおもりで押さえる ‖ *to weight down a fishing net* 魚獲用の網におもりを付ける ▶定義2 (通常は受動態で) to organize sth so that a particular person or group has an advantage/disadvantage 特定の人または集団が利益・不利益を得るように, 〜を組織する→〜を(ある方向に)偏らせる, 傾かせる ‖ *The system is weighted in favour of/against people with children.* その制度は子供を持つ人々に有利・不利になっている.

**weightless** /wéɪtləs/ 形 ▶定義 having no weight, for example when travelling in space 例えば宇宙を旅行しているときのように, 重量がない→無重力の — **weightlessness** 名 ⓤ →無重量, 無重力, 無重力状態

**weightlifting** /wéɪtlɪftɪŋ/ 名 ⓤ ▶定義 a sport in which heavy metal objects are lifted 重い金属製の物体を持ち上げる競技→重量挙げ

**weight training** 名 Ｕ ▶定義 the activity of lifting heavy objects (weights) as a form of exercise 運動の一形態として重い物(ウエート)を持ち上げる活動→**重量挙げ, ウエートトレーニング** ‖ *I do weight training to keep fit.* 私は健康を維持するためにウエートトレーニングを行っている.

**weighty** /wéɪti/ 形 (**weightier**; **weightiest**) ▶定義 serious and important 深刻で重要な→**(問題などの)重要な, 重大な, 深刻な** ‖ *a weighty question* 重大な疑問

**weir** /wɪər/ 名 Ｃ ▶定義 a type of wall that is built across a river to stop or change the direction of the flow of water 水の流れを止めるまたは方向を変えるために河川を横切って建設された壁の一種→**せき, ダム**

**weird** /wɪərd/ 形 ▶定義 strange and unusual 奇妙で普通でない→**異様な, 気味の悪い, 風変わりな** ‖ *a weird noise/experience* ぞっとする音・経験
— **weirdly** 副 →異様に, 気味悪く

\***welcome**¹ /wélkəm/ 動 他 ▶定義 **1** to be friendly to sb when he/she arrives somewhere ～がどこかに到着したときに, その人に好意的である→**～を歓迎する, 歓待する** ‖ *Everyone came to the door to welcome us.* みんな, 私たちを歓迎するためにドアまで来てくれた. ▶定義 **2** to be pleased to receive or accept sth 喜んで～を受け取る, または受け入れる→**(意見など)を喜んで受け入れる** ‖ *I've no idea what to do next, so I'd welcome any suggestions.* 次に何をするか全く思い付かないので, 私はどんな提案でも喜んでお受けします. — **welcome** 名 Ｃ→**歓迎, 歓待** ‖ *Let's give a warm welcome to our next guest.* 次のお客様を暖かく迎えましょう.

\***welcome**² /wélkəm/ 形 ▶定義 **1** received with pleasure; giving pleasure 喜んで受け入れられる; 喜びを与える→**歓迎される, 喜ばれる** ‖ *You're always welcome here.* ここではあなたをいつでも歓迎しますよ. *welcome news* 吉報 ▶定義 **2** welcome to sth/to do sth allowed to do sth ～をすることを許す→**自由に～をしてよい** ‖ *You're welcome to use my bicycle.* ご自由に私の自転車を使ってください. ▶定義 **3** used to say that sb can have sth that you do not want yourself 自分が欲しくない～を…が取ってもよいと伝えるために用いて→**～を勝手にしてよい** ‖ *Take the car if you want. You're welcome to it. It's always breaking down.* よければその車をもらってください. ご自由にしてもらって結構です. いつも故障ばかりしていますが. — **welcome** 間→**ようこそ, いらっしゃい** ‖ *Welcome to London!* ロンドンへようこそ. *Welcome home!* おかえりなさい.

**成句 make sb welcome** ▶定義 to receive sb in a friendly way ～を好意的なやり方で受け入れる→**～を歓迎する, 歓待する**

**you're welcome** (口語) ▶定義 you don't need to thank me あなたは私にお礼を言う必要はありません→**どういたしまして** ‖ *'Thank you for your help.' 'You're welcome.'* 「手伝ってくれて, ありがとう」「どういたしまして」

**weld** /weld/ 動 自 他 ▶定義 to join pieces of metal by heating them and pressing them together 複数の金属片を加熱し互いに押し付けることによって, 接合する→**(～を)溶接する**

\***welfare** /wélfeər/ 名 Ｕ ▶定義 **1** the general health, happiness of a person, an animal or a group 人や動物, あるいはそれらの集団の一般的な健康, 幸福→**幸福, 福祉, 福利, 厚生** ‖ *The doctor is concerned about the child's welfare.* 医者はその子供の健康を気に掛けている. ▶定義 **2** the help and care that is given to people who have problems with health, money, etc 健康, 金銭などの問題を抱える人々に与えられる援助と保護→**福祉援助, 生活保護** ‖ *education and welfare services* 教育および福祉事業 ▶定義 **3** 米 = SOCIAL SECURITY

**welfare state** 名 [単数扱い] ▶定義 a system organized by a government to provide free services and money for people who have no job, who are ill, etc; a country that has this system 政府が組織する制度で, 失業中または病気の人々へ, 無料のサービスや金銭を提供するもの; このような制度を持つ国→**社会保障制度; 福祉国家**

**we'll** /wɪl, wil/ **WE SHALL, WE WILL** の短縮形

\***well**¹ /wel/ 副 (**better**; **best**) ▶定義 **1** in a good way 良い風に→**良く, うまく, 上手に** ‖ *You speak English very well.* あなたはとても上手に英語を話しますね. *I hope your work is going well.* 私はあなたの仕事が順調であることを望んでいます. *You passed your exam! Well done!* 君は試験に合格したよ. でかした. *He took it well when*

## 1818 well²

*I told him he wasn't on the team.* チームに入れないと私が告げたとき,彼はそれを冷静に聞き入れた. ⇨ **badly** ▶定義2 completely or fully 完全に,または十分に→**よく,たっぷりと** ‖ *Shake the bottle well before opening.* 開ける前にびんをよく振りなさい. *How well do you know Henry?* あなたはヘンリーとどの程度知り合いなのですか.
▶定義3 very much かなり→**相当に,はるかに,優に** ‖ *They arrived home well past midnight.* 彼らは夜中の12時をかなり過ぎたころに帰宅した. *She says she's 32 but I'm sure she's well over 40.* 彼女は32歳だと言っているが,優に40歳を過ぎていると私は確信している. *This book is **well** worth reading.* この本は読む価値が十分ある. ▶定義4 (can, could, may, あるいは might と用いて) probably or possibly おそらく,またはことによると→**多分,もしかすると** ‖ *He might well be right.* 多分彼が正しいのだろう. ▶定義5 (can, could, may, あるいは might と用いて) with good reason 正当な理由があって→**正当に,もっともで,道理にかなって** ‖ *I can't very well refuse to help them after all they've done for me.* 彼らが私のためにあれやこれやとやってくれた後で,彼らの手伝いを拒む道理などない.
'*Where's Bill?*' '*You may **well** ask!* (= I don't know either)' 「ビルはどこ」「聞くのももっともだ.(= 私も知らない)」
成句 **as well (as sb/sth)** ▶定義 in addition to sb/sth →**その上へ~も,~もまた,~だけでなく…も,~もまた,~と同様に…も** ‖ *Can I come as well?* 私も一緒に行っていいですか. *He's worked in Japan as well as Italy.* 彼はイタリアだけでなく日本でも働いたことがある. ☞参 **also** の注
**augur well/ill for sb/sth** ⇒ **AUGUR**
**bode well/ill (for sb/sth)** ⇒ **BODE**
**do well** ▶定義1 to be successful 成功する→**成功する,うまくいく** ‖ *Their daughter has done well at university.* 彼らの娘は大学で良い成績を収めた. ▶定義2 to be getting better after an illness 病気の後,良くなっていく→**だんだん回復している** ‖ *Mr Singh is doing well after his operation.* シン氏は手術後,だんだん回復している.
**do well to do sth** ▶定義 used to say that sth is the right and sensible thing to do ~を行うことが適切で,妥当であると言うために用いて→**~するのが良い** ‖ *He would do well to check the facts before accusing people.* 人々を非難する前に,彼は事実を確認した方がいい.
**may/might (just) as well** ▶定義 used for saying that sth is the best thing you can do in the situation, even though you may not want to do it そうしたくはないかもしれないが,そうするのがその状況で行える最善の~であると言うときに用いて→**~した方が良い,~してもよかろう** ‖ *I may as well tell you the truth - you'll find out anyway.* あなたに真実を告げてしまった方がいいかもしれないね — どのみち分かってしまうのだから.
**mean well** ⇒ **MEAN**¹
**well and truly** ▶定義 completely 完全に→**全く,すっかり** ‖ *We were well and truly lost.* 私たちはすっかり迷子になってしまった.
**well/badly off** ⇒ **OFF**¹

★**well²** /wel/ 形 (**better** /bétər/, **best** /best/) (名詞の前は不可) ▶定義1 in good health 健康で→**元気で** ‖ '*How are you?*' '*I'm very well, thanks.*' 「お元気ですか」「元気です,ありがとう」 *This medicine will make you **feel better**.* この薬を飲めば気分が良くなりますよ. ***Get well soon*** (= written in a card that you send to somebody who is ill). 早く良くなってください(= 病気にかかっている人へ送るカードに書かれる言葉) ▶定義2 in a good state 良い状態で→**良い,申し分ない,満足な** ‖ *I hope all is well with you.* 万事順調でありますように.
成句 **all very well (for sb)** 略式 ▶定義 used for showing that you are not happy or do not agree with sth 自分は幸せでない,あるいは~に賛成しないことを示すために用いて→**(~にとっては)もっともだ,結構なことだ** ‖ *It's all very well for her to criticize* (= it's easy for her to criticize) *but it doesn't help the situation.* 批判することは彼女にとっては結構なことだ(= 彼女が批判するのは簡単だ)が,それでは状況の改善に役立たない.
**(just) as well (to do sth)** ▶定義 sensible; a good idea 思慮分別のある;良い考え→**好都合である,賢明である** ‖ *It would be just as well to ask his permission.* 彼に許可を得ることが賢明だろう(彼に許可を得た方が良い). ☞参 **just** の **it is just as well (that)**

★**well³** /wel/ 間 ▶定義1 used for showing surprise 驚きを示すために用いて→**まあ, おや, えっ** ‖ *Well, thank goodness you've arrived.* まあ, あなたが無事に着いてよかった. ▶定義2 used for expressing uncertainty 不確定さを表現するために用いて→**さあ, はあ** ‖ *'Do you like it?' 'Well, I'm not really sure.'* 「それは好きですか」「うーん, よく分かりません」 ▶定義3 used when you begin the next part of a story or when you are thinking about what to say next 話の続きを始めるとき, あるいは次に何を言うか考えているときに用いて→**ええと, そして, さて, それでは, うーん** ‖ *Well, the next thing that happened was...* さて, 次に起こった出来事は… *Well now, let me see...* ええと, そうですね… ▶定義4 used to show that you are waiting for sb to say sth ～が…を言うのを待っていることを示すために用いて→**それで, それから, どうなの** ‖ *Well? Are you going to tell us what happened?* それで. その話の続きを言ってくれるの. ▶定義5 used to show that you want to finish a conversation 会話を終わらせたいことを示すために用いて→**では, それでは** ‖ *Well, it's been nice talking to you.* では, あなたとお話しできて楽しかったですよ. ▶定義6 (または **oh well**) used for showing that you know there is nothing you can do to change a situation 状況を変えるために自分にできる事は何もないことが分かっていることを示すために用いて→**仕方がない, まあ, まあいいさ, やれやれ** ‖ *Oh well, there's nothing we can do about it.* やれやれ, それについては私たちにはなすすべがありませんね.

**well**⁴ /wel/ 名 C ▶定義1 a deep hole in the ground from which water is obtained 水を得るための地中の深い穴→**井戸** ‖ *to draw water from a well* 井戸から水をくむ ▶定義2 = OIL WELL

**well**⁵ /wel/ 動 自 ▶定義 well (out/up) (used about a liquid) to come to the surface (液体について) 表に出る→**わき出る** ‖ *Tears welled up in her eyes* 彼女の目に涙があふれた.

**well-balanced** 形 ▶定義1 (used about a person) calm and sensible (人について) 穏やかで分別のある→**良識のある** ▶定義2 (used about a meal, etc) containing enough of the healthy types of food your body needs (食事などについて) 身体が必要とする健康的な食物を十分に含んでいる→**バランスの取れた** ‖ *a well-balanced*

## well-meaning

*diet* バランスの取れた食事

**well-behaved** 形 ▶定義 behaving in a way that most people think is correct ほとんどの人たちが正しいと考えるやり方で振る舞っている→**行儀の良い**

**well-being** 名 U ▶定義 a state of being healthy and happy 健康で幸せな状態→**幸福, 健康**

**well done** 形 ▶定義 (used about meat, etc) cooked for a long time (肉などについて) 長時間加熱した→**よく火を通した, 十分に焼けた**
▶ rare, medium と比較.

**well-dressed** 形 ▶定義 wearing attractive and fashionable clothes 魅力的で流行の衣服を着ている→**身なりの良い**

**well-earned** 形 ▶定義 that you deserve, especially because you have been working hard 特に一生懸命に働き続けたために, 価値のある→**(つぎ込んだ労力に)見合う, 与えられて当然の, 受けるに値する** ‖ *a well-earned holiday* 与えられて当然の休日

**well-fed** 形 ▶定義 having good food regularly 良い食事を定期的に取っている→**栄養の十分な, 太った**

**well-informed** 形 ▶定義 knowing a lot about one or several subjects 1つまたはいくつかの主題についてよく知っている→**博識の, 見聞の広い, (ある分野に)精通した**

**wellington** /wélɪŋtn/ (または 略式 **welly** /wéli/) 名 C ( 複 **wellingtons**; **wellies**) 英 ▶定義 one of a pair of long rubber boots that you wear to keep your feet and the lower part of your legs dry 脚のひざから下と足の部分をぬれないように保つために履く, 長いゴム製の靴の片方→**ゴム長靴, ウエリントンブーツ** ‖ *a pair of wellingtons* ウエリントンブーツ1足

**well-kept** 形 ▶定義 looked after very carefully so that it has a tidy appearance 整った外観を保てるよう, とても注意深く世話された→**手入れの行き届いた, よく管理された** ‖ *a well-kept garden* 手入れの行き届いた庭

**well-known** 形 ▶定義 known by a lot of people; famous 多くの人たちに知られている; 有名な→**有名な, よく知られた** ⇔ **unknown**

**well-meaning** 形 ▶定義 (used about a person) wanting to be kind or helpful, but often not having this effect (人について) 親切であるまたは役立つことを望んでいるが、しばしば不首尾に終わる ➡ 善意の, 善意を持った, 好意を持った

**well-meant** 形 ▶定義 intended to be kind or helpful but not having this result 親切であるまたは役立つことを望んでいるが、そのような結果にならない ➡ (結果はともかく)善意から出た

**well-to-do** 形 ▶定義 having a lot of money, property, etc; rich 多額の金、財産などを所有している; 裕福な ➡ 富裕な

**well-wisher** 名 C ▶定義 somebody who hopes that a person or thing will be successful 人や物事が成功するよう願っている人 ➡ 支持者, 応援者 ‖ *She received lots of letters from well-wishers before the competition.* 競技前、彼女は応援者たちからたくさんの手紙を受け取った。

★**Welsh** /welʃ/ 形 ▶定義 from Wales ウェールズからの ➡ ウェールズの, ウェールズ人・語の ☞ 巻末の地名の項を参照.

**went** GO¹ の過去形

**wept** WEEP の過去・過去分詞形

**we're** /wɪər, wiːər/ WE ARE の短縮形

**were** ⇒ BE

★**west** /west/ 名 [単数扱い] (略 W) ▶定義 1 (または **the west**) the direction you look towards in order to see the sun go down; one of the four main directions that we give names to (**the points of the compass**) 太陽が沈むのを見るために向く方向; 名付けられた4つの主な方角の1つ(コンパスの方位) ➡ 西, 西方 ‖ *Which way is west?* どちらの方向が西ですか。 *Rain is spreading from the west.* 雨が西から広がってきている。 *There's a road to the west of here.* ここから西方に向かう道がある。 ☞ **north** のさし絵 ▶定義 2 **the west**; **the West** the part of any country, city, etc that is further to the west than other parts 国、市などの地域でほかの地域よりも西にある部分 ➡ 西部, 西部地方 ‖ *I live in the west of Scotland.* 私はスコットランド西部に住んでいる。 *The climate in the West is much wetter than the East.* 西部の気候は東部よりもずっと雨が多い。 ▶定義 3 **the West** [単数扱い] the countries of North America and Western Europe 北米および西欧の国々 ➡ 西側諸国, 欧米 — **west** 形副 ▶定義 in, to or towards the west 西の, 西へ, 西に向かって ➡ 西にある, 西部の, 西へ, 西方へ ‖ *The island is five miles west of here.* その島はここから5マイル西にある。 *to travel west* 西に向かって旅行する *West London* 西ロンドン、ロンドン西部

**westbound** /wéstbàʊnd/ 形 ▶定義 travelling or leading towards the west 西へ向かう, 西に通じている ➡ 西行きの ‖ *the westbound carriageway of the motorway* 高速道路の西行きの車線

**westerly** /wéstərli/ 形 ▶定義 1 to, towards or in the west 西への, 西に向かっての, 西にある ➡ 西の, 西寄りの ‖ *in a westerly direction* 西の方向にある ▶定義 2 (used about winds) coming from the west (風について) 西から来る ➡ (風が)西からの

★**western**¹ (または **Western**) /wéstərn/ 形 ▶定義 1 in or of the west 西にある, 西の ➡ 西部の ‖ *western France* 西フランス ▶定義 2 from or connected with the western part of the world, especially Europe or North America 世界の西部, 特にヨーロッパまたは北米からの, または関係のある ➡ 西洋の, 欧米の, 西側の

**western**² /wéstərn/ 名 C ▶定義 a film or book about life in the past in the west of the United States アメリカ合衆国西部の昔の生活についての映画または本 ➡ 西部劇, ウエスタン, 西部もの

**westerner** /wéstərnər/ 名 C ▶定義 a person who was born or who lives in the western part of the world, especially Europe or North America 世界の西部, 特にヨーロッパまたは北米に生まれた人, またはそこに住む人 ➡ 西洋人, 欧米人 ‖ *Westerners arriving in China usually experience culture shock.* 中国を訪れる西洋人は、大抵カルチャーショックを体験する。

**westernize** (または **-ise**) /wéstərnaɪz/ 動 他 (通常は受動態で) ▶定義 to make a country or people more like Europe and North America 国や人々をもっとヨーロッパや北米のようにする ➡ 西洋化する, 欧米化する ‖ *Young people in our country are becoming westernized through watching American television programmes.* 我が国の若者はアメリカのテレビ番組を見て欧米化してきている。

**the West Indies** 名 [複数扱い, 単数または複数形の動詞と共に] ▶定義 a group of islands in the Caribbean Sea that consists of the Bahamas, the Antilles and the Leeward and Windward Islands カリブ海にある諸島で，バハマ諸島，アンティル諸島，リーワード諸島，ウィンドワード諸島から成る➡西インド諸島 — West Indian 形 ➡西インド諸島の人 ‖ *The West Indians won their match against Australia.* 西インド諸島は，試合でオーストラリアに勝った． — West Indian 形➡西インド諸島の

**westward** /wés(t)wərd/ 形 ▶定義 towards the west 西に向かっての➡西方への，西に向かう，西向きの ‖ *in a westward direction* 西の方角に — westward(またはwestwards)副 ➡西の方へ，西に向かって，西向きに ‖ *to fly westwards* 西に向かって飛ぶ

\***wet**¹ /wet/ 形 (**wetter**; **wettest**) ▶定義1 covered in a liquid, especially water 液体，特に水で覆われた➡ぬれた ‖ *wet clothes/hair/grass/roads* ぬれた衣服・髪・芝生・道路 *Don't get your feet wet.* 足をぬらさないようにしなさい．

➤ moistは，「少しぬれた」を意味する．dampは，少しぬれていて，そのために不快に感じる物を描写するのに用いられる: *Don't sit on the grass. It's damp.*（芝生に座らないで．じめじめしてるから．）

▶定義2 (used about the weather, etc) with a lot of rain（天候などについて）雨の多い➡雨降りの，雨がちの ‖ *a wet day* 雨の日 ▶定義3 (used about paint, etc) not yet dry or hard（塗料などについて）まだ乾いていない，または固まっていない➡塗り立ての ‖ *The ink is still wet.* そのインクはまだ乾いていない． ⇔ 定義 1，2，3 **dry** ▶定義4 (used about a person) without energy or enthusiasm（人について）活力または情熱のない➡気の弱い，意気地のない ― **the wet** 名 [単数扱い]➡雨，雨降り，雨天 ‖ *Come in out of the wet (= the rainy weather).* 雨宿りに，中にお入りなさい． 成句 **a wet blanket** 略式 ▶定義 a person who spoils other people's fun, especially because he or she refuses to take part in sth 特に行事に参加することを断って，ほかの人たちの楽しみを台なしにする人➡楽しみに水を差す人，座を白けさせる人

**wet through** ▶定義 extremely wet すっかりぬれた➡びしょぬれになって，ずぶぬれで

**wet**² /wet/ 動 他 (現分 **wetting**; 過, 過分 **wet** または **wetted**) ▶定義1 to make sth wet➡〜をぬらす ▶定義2 (used especially of young children) to make yourself or your bed, clothes, etc wet by letting a yellowish liquid (**urine**) escape from your body（特に幼児について）体から黄色い液体(尿)を漏らすことによって，自分自身，ベッド，または衣類などをぬらす➡おねしょをする，おもらしをする

**wet suit** 名 C ▶定義 a rubber suit that covers the whole of the body, used by people doing sports in the water or swimming under the water 身体全体を覆うゴム製のスーツで水中でスポーツをしたり水中を泳ぐ人たちが使用する➡ウエットスーツ

**we've** /wɪv, wiːv/ **WE HAVE**の短縮形

**whack** /(h)wæk/ 動 他 略式 ▶定義 to hit sb/sth hard 〜を強くたたく➡(つえなどで)〜をぴしゃりと打つ

whale

**whale** /(h)weɪl/ 名 C ▶定義 a very large animal that lives in the sea and looks like a very large fish 海に生息する非常に大きな動物で，非常に大きな魚のように見える➡鯨

**whaling** /(h)wéɪlɪŋ/ 名 U ▶定義 the hunting of whales 鯨の捕獲➡捕鯨

**wharf** /(h)wɔːrf/ 名 C (複 **wharves** /(h)wɔːrvz/) ▶定義 a platform made of stone or wood at the side of a river where ships and boats can be tied up 石または木で造られた川岸にある壇で，そこに船やボートを係留できる➡波止場，埠頭（ふとう）

\***what** /(h)wɑt/ 形代 ▶定義1 used for asking for information about sb/sth 〜についての情報を問うために用いて➡何，どんな物，どんな事，何をする人，どんな人，何者 ‖ *What time is it?* 今，何時ですか． *What kind of music do you like?* どんな種類の音楽が好きですか． *She asked him what he was doing.* 彼女は彼に何をしているのか尋ねた． *What's their phone number?* 彼らの電話番号は何番ですか． ☛参 **which**の注 ▶定義2 the thing or things that have been mentioned or

## whatever

said 話に出た、または言われた物事→〜である物・事、〜する物・事‖ *What he says is true.* 彼の言っている事は真実だ. *I haven't got much, but you can borrow what money I have.* たくさんはないけれど、私が持っているだけのお金を貸してもいいですよ. ▶定義3 used for emphasizing sth 〜を強調するために用いて→何という、何て‖ *What strange eyes she's got!* 彼女は何て不思議な目をしているのだろう. *What a kind thing to do!* 何て、思いやりのあることをするのでしょう. ▶定義4 used to express surprise or to tell sb to say or repeat sth 驚きを表現する、あるいは人に何かを言うように、または繰り返すように伝えるために用いて→えっ、何、何だって‖ *'I've asked Alice to marry me.' 'What!'*「アリスに私と結婚してくれるよう頼んだんだ」「何だって」

成句 how/what about...? ⇒ **ABOUT**²

**what for** ▶定義 for what purpose or reason どんな目的または理由で→何のために、どんなつもりで、なぜ‖ *What's this little switch for?* この小さなスイッチは何のためのものですか. *What did you say that for (= why did you say that)?* どういうつもりでそんな事を言ったのか.

**what if...?** ▶定義 what would happen if...? もし〜なら何が起こるのか→(もし)〜だったらどうなるだろうか、(もし)〜だったらどうしようか‖ *What if the car breaks down?* もし車が故障したらどうしようか.

> ▶語法
>
> How far is it? と What is the distance?
>
> 具体物でなく、抽象的な名詞を主語にして what を用いることがよくあります. この場合は、What is the distance? (距離はどれくらいですか?) のように主語が何らかの尺度 (この場合は距離) を表す名詞です. *How far is the distance? とは言えないので注意しましょう. 同様の例として What is the diametre? (半径はどれくらい?), What is the population? (人口はどれくらい?), What is the price? (値段はどれくらい?), What is your height? (身長はどれくらい?) があり、これらの名詞を主語にすると「how + 形容詞」は使えません.

---

\***whatever** /(h)watévər/ 形副代 ▶定義1 any or every; anything or everything いずれの、またはすべての; どんな物事も、またはあらゆる物事が→〜する物・事は何でも、何であれ‖ *You can say whatever you like.* 言いたい事は何でも言って構いません. *He took whatever help he could get.* 彼は、得られる手助けはすべて受け入れた. ▶定義2 used to say that it does not matter what happens or what sb does, because the result will be the same 結果が同じになるため、何が起ころうと、あるいは何をしようと重要ではないことを言うために用いて→たとえ何が〜でも、いかに〜でも、何を〜でも‖ *I still love you, whatever you may think.* あなたがどう思っても、私は今でもあなたを愛しています. *Whatever she says, she doesn't really mean it.* 彼女が何を言おうと、本気で言ってはいない. ▶定義3 (used for expressing surprise or worry) what (驚きや心配を表現するために用いて)→一体何が、一体何を‖ *Whatever could have happened to them?* 一体全体彼らに何が起こったというのだ.

▶定義4 (または **whatsoever**) at all→少しも、少しの〜も‖ *I've no reason whatever to doubt him.* 私が彼を疑う理由は何もない. *'Any questions?' 'None whatsoever.'*「何か質問は」「何もありません」

成句 **or whatever** 略式 ▶定義 or any other or others of a similar kind または何かほかの似たようなもの→〜とか何かそんな物・人、〜など‖ *You don't need to wear anything smart - jeans and a sweater or whatever.* しゃれた服装をする必要はないですよ − ジーンズとセーターとかそのような服装で結構です.

**whatever you do** ▶定義 used to emphasize that sb must not do sth 人が何かをしてはいけないことを強調するために用いて→どんな事があっても、絶対に、とにかく、いずれにせよ‖ *Don't touch the red switch, whatever you do.* 絶対に赤いスイッチには触れてはいけません.

\***wheat** /(h)wiːt/ 名 ❶ ▶定義1 a type of grain which can be made into flour 小麦粉に加工できる穀粒の一種→小麦の実 ▶定義2 the plant which produces this grain この穀物を実らせる植物→小麦‖ *a field of wheat* 小麦畑 ☞ **cereal** のさし絵

\***wheel**¹ /(h)wiːl/ 名 ▶定義1 ❻ one of the circular objects under a car, bicycle, etc that turns when it moves 自動車,自転車などの下に取り付けられており,動くときに回転する丸い物体の1つ→**車輪** ‖ *His favourite toy is a dog on wheels.* 彼のお気に入りのおもちゃは車輪付きの犬だ. *By law, you have to carry a spare wheel in your car.* 法律によって,車にスペアの車輪を積んでいなければならない.▶定義2［通常は単数］= **STEERING WHEEL** ‖ *Her husband was **at the wheel** (= he was driving) when the accident happened.* 事故が起きたとき,彼女の夫がハンドルを握っていた(= 運転していた). ☞ S7 ページのさし絵

**wheel**² /(h)wiːl/ 動 ▶定義1 ⓗ to push along an object that has wheels; to move sb about in/on a vehicle with wheels 車輪の付いた物をどんどん押し進める;車輪の付いた乗り物に乗せて〜を移動させる→〜**を動かす; 運ぶ** ‖ *He wheeled his bicycle up the hill.* 彼はその坂道を自転車を押して登った. *She was wheeled back to her bed on a trolley.* 彼女は手押し車でベッドへ戻された.▶定義2 ⓘ to fly round in circles 円を描いて飛ぶ→**旋回する,輪を描いて飛ぶ** ‖ *Birds wheeled above the ship.* 船の上を鳥がぐるぐる回りながら飛んだ.▶定義3 ⓘ to turn round suddenly→**突然向きを変える** ‖ *Eleanor wheeled round, with a look of horror on her face.* エレナーは恐怖の表情を浮かべて,ぐるりと向きを変えた.

**wheelbarrow** /(h)wíːlbæroʊ/ (または **barrow**) 名 ⓒ ▶定義 a type of small open container with one wheel and two handles that you use outside for carrying things 戸外で物を持ち運ぶときに使用する,1つの車輪と2つの持ち手が付いた,覆いのない小型容器の一種→**手押しの一輪車** ☞ **garden** のさし絵

**wheelchair** /(h)wíːltʃèər/ 名 ⓒ ▶定義 a chair with large wheels that a person who cannot walk can move or be pushed about in 歩けない人が自分で移動したり,押してもらって移動することのできる,大きな車輪の付いたいす→**車いす**

**wheel clamp** 英 = **CLAMP**¹(2)

**wheeze** /(h)wiːz/ 動 ⓘ ▶定義 to breathe noisily, for example if you have a chest illness うるさい音を立てて呼吸する,例えば,胸の病気にかかっているときなど→**ゼイゼイいう,ゼイゼイ息を切らす**

*****when** /(h)wen/ 副 接 ▶定義1 at what time いかなる時に→**いつ** ‖ *When did she arrive?* 彼女はいつ到着したの. *I don't know when she arrived.* 彼女がいつ到着したのか私は知らない.▶定義2 used for talking about the time at which sth happens or happened 〜が起こるときまたは起こったときについて用いて→〜**するとき** ‖ *Sunday is the day when I can relax.* 日曜日はくつろげる日だ. *I last saw her in May, when she was in London.* 私が最後に彼女に会ったのは5月で,その時彼女はロンドンにいた. *He jumped up when the phone rang.* 電話が鳴った時,彼は(驚いて)飛び上がった.

▶未来について述べるとき,whenの後に現在時制を使うことに注意: *I'll call you when I'm ready.*(用意ができたら,声を掛けますよ.)

▶定義3 since; as; considering that →〜**だから; 〜ので; 〜を考慮すると** ‖ *Why do you want more money when you've got enough already?* 既に十分お金があるのに,どうしてもっと欲しいのですか.

▶ when は,起こると思う,または起こると分かっている物事について話すのに用いられるが,起こるかどうか確信のない物事についてはifが用いられる.次の2例を比較: *I'll ask her when she comes (= you are sure that she will come).*(彼女が来た時に尋ねることにしよう(= 彼女が来ることに確信がある).) *I'll ask her if she comes (= you are not sure whether she will come or not).*(もし彼女が来れば尋ねるつもりだ(= 彼女が来るのか来ないのか確信がない).)

*****whenever** /(h)wenévər/ 接 副 ▶定義1 at any time; no matter when いつでも; たとえいつでも→**いかなる時でも** ‖ *You can borrow my car whenever you want.* お好きなとき,いつでも私の車を借りていいですよ. *Don't worry. You can give it back the next time you see me, or whenever.* 心配しないで.次に会うときか,ほかのときにでも返してくれればいいですよ.▶定義2 (used when you are showing that you are surprised or impatient) when(驚いている,またはしびれを切らしていることを表すために用いて)→**一体いつ** ‖ *Whenever did you find time to do all that cooking?* 君は,この料理を全部作る時間を一体いつ見つけたの.

*****where** /(h)weər/ 副 接 ▶定義1 in or to what

place or position どの場所・位置で，またはどの場所・位置へ→**どこで，どこへ** ‖ *Where can I buy a newspaper?* 新聞はどこで買えますか． *I asked him where he lived.* 私は彼にどこに住んでいるのか尋ねた． ▶定義**2** in or to the place or situation mentioned 話に出た場所または所在地で[へ]→**～する・～であるところの[で・へ]** ‖ *the town where you were born* あなたが生まれた町 *She ran to where they were standing.* 彼女は，彼らが立っている所へ走った． *Where possible, you should travel by bus, not taxi.* 可能ならば，タクシーではなくバスで移動すべきだ． *We came to a village, where we stopped for lunch.* 私たちはある村に着き，そこで昼食を取った． *Where maths is concerned, I'm hopeless.* 数学ということになると，私は苦手だ．

**whereabouts**¹ /(h)wéərəbàuts/ 副 ▶定義 where; in or near what place どこに[で]; どの場所に[で・の近くに]→**どこで，どこに，どの辺りで** ‖ *Whereabouts did you lose your purse?* あなたはどの辺りで財布をなくしたのですか．

**whereabouts**² /(h)wéərəbàuts/ 名 [複数扱い] ▶定義 the place where sb/sth is 人がいる場所，物がある場所→**所在，在りか，行方** ‖ *The whereabouts of the stolen painting are unknown.* 盗まれた絵の所在は不明だ．

**whereas** /(h)weərǽz/ 接 ▶定義 used for showing a fact that is different 異なる事実を示すのに用いて→**ところが～，他方では～，～であるのに対して** ‖ *He eats meat, whereas she's a vegetarian.* 彼は肉を食べるが彼女は菜食主義者だ．
▪類 while

**whereby** /(h)weərbái/ 副 (文) ▶定義 by which; because of which→**それによって～するところの; そのために～するところの** ‖ *These countries have an agreement whereby foreign visitors can have free medical care.* それらの国々には，外国からの訪問者が無料で治療を受けられるという取り決めがある．

**whereupon** /(h)wèərəpɔ́(:)n, -əpán/ 接 (文) ▶定義 after which その後→**そこで，その時点で** ‖ *He fell asleep, whereupon she walked quietly from the room.* 彼が眠りに就くと彼女は静かに部屋から出ていった．

*****wherever** /(h)weərévər/ 接 副 ▶定義**1** in or to

any place どの場所でも[へも]→**～する所ならどこへ[に]でも，どこであろうとも** ‖ *You can sit wherever you like.* どこでもお好きな所に座ってください． *She comes from Desio, wherever that is (= I don't know where it is).* 彼女はデシオの出身だ．それがどこにあるとしても(= それがどこかは知らない)． ▶定義**2** everywhere, in all places that go to すべての場所で→**～する所はどこに[で]でも** ‖ *Wherever I go, he goes.* 私が行く所はどこでも，彼も行く． ▶定義**3** used for showing surprise 驚きを表すのに用いて→**一体どこへ[で]** ‖ *Wherever did you learn to cook like that?* あなたは，一体どこであんな料理の仕方を習ったの．

成句 **or wherever** ▶定義 or any other place またはほかのいかなる場所でも→**～またはそのような所に[で]** ‖ *The students might be from Sweden, Denmark or wherever.* 学生たちはスウェーデン，デンマークか，あるいはその辺りの出身かもしれない．

**whet** /(h)wet/ 動 (**whetting**; **whetted**)
成句 **whet sb's appetite** ▶定義 to make sb want more of sth ～に物をもっと欲しがらせる→**～の食欲・欲望をそそる** ‖ *Our short stay in Dublin whetted our appetite to spend more time there.* 短期間ダブリンに滞在しただけだが，私たちはもっといたいと思った．

*****whether** /(h)wéðər/ 接 ▶定義**1** ( ask, doubt, know などの動詞の後に用いて) if→**～かどうか** ‖ *He asked me whether he would be coming to the party.* 彼は，私たちがパーティーに来るのかどうか私に尋ねた． ▶定義**2** used for expressing a choice or doubt between two or more possibilities 2つ以上の可能性から選択または疑いを表すために用いて→**～かどうか** ‖ *I can't make up my mind **whether** to go **or not**.* 私は行こうかどうしようか，決心がつかない．

▶定義1の意味では，whetherとifの両方が用いられる．「to + 動詞」の前では，whetherのみが用いられる: *Have you decided whether to accept the offer yet?*(その申し出を受け入れるかどうか，もう決めましたか．) 前置詞の後には，whetherだけが用いられる: *the problem of whether to accept the offer*(その申し出を受け入れるべきかどうかという問題)

成句 **whether or not** ▶定義 used to say that sth will be true in either of the situations that are mentioned 話で触れられた状況のいずれの場合でも当てはまることを言うのに用いて➡**~であろうとなかろうと, いずれにしても** ‖ *We shall play on Saturday whether it rains or not.* 私たちは, 雨が降っても降らなくても土曜日に試合をします. *Whether or not it rains, we shall play on Saturday.* 雨が降っても降らなくても, 私たちは土曜日に試合をします.

\***which** /(h)wɪtʃ/ 形代 ▶定義**1** used in questions to ask sb to be exact, when there are a number of people or things to choose from 選択できる人々や物が複数あるとき, だれ・どれかを尋ねる質問の中で用いて➡**どの, どれ, どちら(の)** ‖ *Which hand do you write with?* どちらの手で書きますか. *Which is your bag?* どれがあなたのかばんですか. *She asked me which book I preferred.* 彼女は私に, どちらの本の方が好きなのか尋ねた. *I can't remember which of the boys is the older.* 私はどちらの少年が年長なのか思い出せない.

▶ which と what について. 選択の対象となる集団または数が限られているときには which を用いる: *Which car is yours? The Ford or the Volvo (= there are only two cars there)?* (どの車があなたのですか. フォードですか, それともボルボですか (= そこには2台の車しかない).) 選択の対象が限られていないときに, what を用いる: *What car would you choose (= of all the makes of the car that exist), if you could have any one you wanted?* (好きな車を所有できるとしたら, どの車を選びますか (= 存在するすべての車種の中で).) *What is your name?* (あなたの名前は何ですか.)

▶定義**2** used for saying exactly what thing or things you are talking about 話の対象がどの物事であるのかを正確に言うために用いて➡**である…, ~する…** ‖ *Cars which use unleaded petrol are more eco-friendly.* 無鉛ガソリンを使用する自動車は, より環境に優しい. 正式 *The situation in which he found himself was very difficult.* 彼が置かれた状況は非常に困難なものだった.

▶あまり形式張らない英語では, *The situation which he found himself in was very difficult.* となる. この例では, which はしばしば省略される: *The situation he found himself in...*

▶定義**3** used for giving more information about a thing or animal 物や動物について, より多くの情報を与えるのに用いて➡**そしてそれは~だ(が)** ‖ *My first car, which I bought as a student, was a Renault.* 私の最初の車は, 学生の時に買ったもので, ルノーでした. ☛ which の前と which に続く節の終わりに, コンマがあることに注意.

▶定義**4** used for making a comment on what has just been said 今, 言ったばかりの内容に, 意見を述べるのに用いて➡**それは, その事は** ‖ *We had to wait 16 hours for our plane, which was really annoying.* 私たちは飛行機を16時間も待たなければならなかったが, それには本当にうんざりした. ☛ which の前にコンマがあることに注意.

\*whichever /(h)wɪtʃévər/ 代 ▶定義**1** any person or thing; it does not matter which one you choose いずれの人も, いずれの物も; どちらを選んでも構わない➡**~するものはどちらでも, ~であるものはどちらでも, どれでも** ‖ *You can choose whichever book you want.* どれでも, お好きな本をお選びください. ▶定義**2** (used for expressing surprise) which (驚きを表現するために用いて) どっち➡**一体どっちが[を]** ‖ *You're very late. Whichever way did you come?* ひどい遅刻だよ. 一体どういうふうに来たの.

**whiff** /(h)wɪf/ 名 [通常は単数] ▶定義 **a whiff (of sth)** a smell, especially one which only lasts for a short time におい, 特にほんの短い時間しか続かないもの➡**かすかな香り・におい** ‖ *He caught a whiff of her perfume.* 彼は彼女の香水のかすかな香りに気付いた.

\*while¹ /(h)wáɪl/ (または正式 whilst /(h)wáɪlst/) 接 ▶定義**1** during the time that; when➡**~する間(に); ~する時(に)** ‖ *He always phones while we're having lunch.* 私たちが昼食を取っている間, 彼はいつも電話をする. ▶定義**2** at the same time as ~すると同時に➡**~しながら** ‖ *He always listens to the radio while he's driving to work.* 彼は職場へ向かって運転しながら, いつもラジオを聴いている. ▶定義**3** 正式 used when you are contrasting two ideas 2つの概念を対比するのに用いて➡**その一方では~, ~であるのに対し, (他方では)さらに~** ‖ *Some countries are rich, while others are extremely poor.* 豊か

# 1826　while[2]

な国もあれば,極端に貧しい国もある. ☞類 **whereas**

★**while**[2] /(h)wáɪl/ 名 [単数扱い] ▶定義 a (usually short) period of time (通常, 短い) ある期間➔(し ばらくの)間, (少しの)時間 ‖ *Let's sit down here for a while.* しばらくここに座りましょう.
成句 once in a while ⇒ **ONCE**
worth sb's while ⇒ **WORTH**[1]

**while**[3] /(h)wáɪl/ 動
句動詞 while sth away ▶定義 to pass time in a lazy or relaxed way ぶらぶらして, またはゆった りして時間を過ごす➔(時を)ぶらぶら・気ままに 過ごす, (暇)をつぶす ‖ *We whiled away the evening chatting and listening to music.* 私たち は, おしゃべりしたり音楽を聴いたりして, その 晩をゆったりと過ごした.

**whim** /(h)wɪm/ 名 ⓒ ▶定義 a sudden idea or desire to do sth (often sth that is unusual or not necessary) (しばしば普通でない, または必要で ない)~をしようという突然の考えまたは欲望➔ **気まぐれ, 思い付き** ‖ *We bought the house on a whim.* 私たちは, ふとした気まぐれでその家を 買った.

**whimper** /(h)wímpər/ 動 自 ▶定義 to cry softly, especially with fear or pain 特に恐怖または痛み で, 弱々しく泣く➔(子供が)しくしく・めそめそ泣 く, (犬が)くんくん鳴く — whimper 名 ⓒ➔すす り泣き, しくしく, めそめそとした泣き声, くんくん と鳴く声

**whine** /(h)wáɪn/ 動 ▶定義1 自 ⓘ to complain about sth in an annoying, crying voice いら立た しい泣き声で~について不平を言う➔**愚痴をこ ぼす, 泣き言を言う** ‖ *The children were whining all afternoon.* 子供たちは午後の間ずっと泣き言 を言っていた. ▶定義2 自 to make a long high unpleasant sound because you are in pain or unhappy 痛み, または悲しみのため, 高い長い不 快な音を出す➔(子供が)むずかって泣く, (犬が) 悲しげにくんくん鳴く, 鼻を鳴らす ‖ *The dog is whining to go out.* その犬は外へ出たいとくんく ん鳴いている. — whine 名 ⓒ➔鼻を鳴らす声, す すり泣き, 愚痴, 泣き言

**whip**[1] /(h)wɪp/ 名 ⓒ ▶定義1 a long thin piece of leather, etc with a handle, that is used for mak-ing animals go faster and for hitting people as a punishment 握りの付いた, 細長い革ひもで, 動 物をより速く移動させるために, また罰として人 をたたくために用いられる➔**むち** ‖ *He cracked the whip and the horse leapt forward.* 彼がむち をびしっと鳴らすと, 馬は前へ飛び跳ねた. ▶定義2 (in British and the US) an official of a political party who makes sure that all mem-bers vote on important matters (英国, 米国で)重 要議題にすべての党員が投票するように図る政 党の担当者➔**院内党幹事**

**whip**[2] /(h)wɪp/ 動 (whipping; whipped) ▶定義1 他 to hit a person or an animal hard with a whip, as a punishment or to make him/her/it go faster or work harder 罰として, あるいはより速く移動 させるために, またはより一生懸命働かせるため に, 人や動物をむちで強くたたく➔**~をむち打つ, ~にむちを当てる** ▶定義2 自 略式 to move quickly, suddenly or violently 素早く, 突然に, ま たは激しく動く➔**さっと動く, 急に動く, 突進する** ‖ *She whipped round to see what had made the noise behind her.* 彼女は, 背後で何が音を立 てたのか確かめるため, さっと振り向いた. ▶定義3 他 to remove or pull sth quickly and suddenly ~を素早く急に取り除く, または引っ 張る➔**~を急に動かす, 引ったくる** ‖ *He whipped out a pen and made a note of the number.* 彼は ペンをさっと取り出すと, その番号を書き留め た. ▶定義4 他 whip sth (up) to mix the white part of an egg, cream, etc until it is light and thick 卵の白身やクリームなどを白くとろっとす るまで混ぜる➔**~を強くかき回して泡立てる** ‖ *whipped cream* ホイップクリーム ▶定義5 他 英 略式 to steal sth➔**~を盗む, 引ったくる** ‖ *Who's whipped my pen?* 私のペンを取ったのはだれで すか.

句動詞 whip through sth 略式 ▶定義 to do or finish sth very quickly ~を素早く行う, または終 える➔**(仕事)を素早く片付ける**

whip sb/sth up ▶定義 to deliberately try to make people excited or feel strongly about sth 物事について人々を興奮させる, または強く感 じさせるように故意に試みる➔**(感情など)をかき 立てる, 興奮させる, (興味など)を刺激する** ‖ *to whip up excitement* 興奮をかき立てる

whip sth up 略式 ▶定義 to prepare food quickly 手早く食事の支度をする➔**(食事)をさっ と作る, 手早く作る, 大急ぎで作る** ‖ *to whip up a*

*quick snack* 軽食をさっと作る

**whir** 特に 米 = **WHIRR**

**whirl**¹ /(h)wəːrl/ 動自他 ▶定義 to move, or to make sb/sth move, round and round very quickly in a circle 円を描きながら素早く動き回る、あるいは～をそのようにさせる➡旋回する、ぐるぐる回る、渦巻く;～を旋回させる、ぐるぐる回す、渦巻かせる ‖ *The dancers whirled round the room.* ダンサーたちは部屋中をぐるぐると回った. (比喩) *I couldn't sleep. My mind was whirling after all the excitement.* 私は眠れなかった. あの大騒ぎの後、私は取り留めもなくいろいろな事を考えていた.

**whirl**² /(h)wəːrl/ 名[単数扱い] ▶定義 1 the action or sound of sth moving round and round very quickly 物が円を描きながら素早く動き回る行為または音➡旋回(音), 回転(音) ‖ *the whirl of the helicopter's blades* ヘリコプターの回転翼の旋回(音) ▶定義 2 a state of confusion or excitement 混乱または興奮状態➡(頭・心の)混乱, 乱れ, 興奮 ‖ *My head's **in a whirl** - I'm so excited.* 頭がくらくらする － すごく興奮している. ▶定義 3 a number of events or activities happening one after the other 次から次に起こる一連の出来事または活動➡(出来事・会合などの)せわしなさ, 慌ただしさ, 目まぐるしさ ‖ *The next few days passed in a whirl of activity.* その次の数日間は目まぐるしく過ぎた.

成句 give sth a whirl 略式 ▶定義 to try sth to see if you like it or can do it 気に入るかどうか、またはできるかどうかを見るために～を試す➡試しに～してみる、～を試してみる

**whirlpool** /(h)wə́ːrlpùːl/ 名 C ▶定義 a place in a river or the sea where currents in the water move very quickly round in a circle 川や海の中で、水の流れが円を描いて素早く回っている場所➡渦, 渦巻き

**whirlwind** /(h)wə́ːrlwìnd/ 名 C ▶定義 a very strong circular wind that forms a tall column of air moving round and round in a circle as it travels across the land or the sea 円状に吹く非常に強い風で、高い空気の柱を形成し、陸地や海を横切りながら円を描くように移動するもの➡旋風, つむじ風 ☞参 **storm** の注

**whirr** (特に 米 **whir**) /(h)wəːr/ 動自 ▶定義 to make a continuous low sound like the parts of a machine moving 機械が動いているときのような, 連続した低い音を出す➡(機械・昆虫・鳥などが)ブンブン音を立てて動く・飛ぶ ‖ *The noise of the fan whirring kept me awake.* 扇風機の立てるブーンという音で, 私は眠れなかった. — **whirr** (特に 米 **whir**) 名 [C, 通常は単数] ➡ブンブンいう音

**whisk**¹ /(h)wɪsk/ 名 C ▶定義 a tool that you use for beating eggs, cream, etc very fast 卵, クリームなどを素早くかき混ぜるために使う道具➡泡立て器 ☞ **kitchen** のさし絵

**whisk**² /(h)wɪsk/ 動他 ▶定義 1 to beat or mix eggs, cream, etc very fast using a fork or a whisk フォークや泡立て器を使って素早く卵, クリームなどを撹拌(かくはん)する, または混ぜる➡～を泡立てる, かき混ぜる ‖ *Whisk the egg whites until stiff.* 卵白を固くなるまで泡立てます. ▶定義 2 to take sb/sth somewhere very quickly ～を素早くどこかへ連れていく➡～をさっと払いのける, 取り払う, 連れ去る ‖ *The prince was whisked away in a black limousine.* 王子は黒いリムジンで急に連れ去られた.

**whisker** /(h)wɪ́skər/ 名 C ▶定義 one of the long thick hairs that grow near the mouth of some animals such as a mouse, cat, etc ネズミ, 猫など, 一部の動物の口の辺りに生える長くて太い毛の1本➡ひげ ☞ C1 ページのさし絵

**whisky** /(h)wɪ́ski/ 名 (複 **whiskies**)
▶米国とアイルランドでは, つづりは whiskey である.
▶定義 1 ❶ a strong alcoholic drink that is made from grain and is sometimes drunk with water and/or ice 穀物から作られる強いアルコール飲料で, 水または氷または両方と共に飲むことがある➡ウイスキー ‖ *Scotch whisky* スコッチウイスキー ▶定義 2 ❷ a glass of whisky ➡ 1 杯のウイスキー

*****whisper** /(h)wɪ́spər/ 動自他 ▶定義 to speak very quietly into sb's ear, so that other people cannot hear what you are saying ～の耳に非常に静かな声で話す, 何を言っているのかほかの人には聞こえないように➡ささやく, そっと話す;～をささやく, 小声で言う — **whisper** 名 C ➡ささやき, 小声, 低い声 ‖ *to speak **in a whisper*** 小声で話す

*****whistle**¹ /(h)wɪ́s(ə)l/ 名 C ▶定義 1 a small metal

or plastic tube that you blow into to make a long high sound or music 長く高い音または音楽を鳴らすために吹く, 小さな金属製あるいはプラスチック製の管→ホイッスル,笛 ‖ *The referee blew his whistle to stop the game.* 試合を中断するために, 審判がホイッスルを吹いた. ▶定義2 the sound made by blowing a whistle or by blowing air out between your lips 笛を吹く, または唇から息を吹き出すことで鳴る音→ピューという音, 口笛 ‖ *United scored just moments before the final whistle.* 終了のホイッスルが鳴る直前にユナイテッドが点を入れた. *He gave a low whistle of surprise.* 彼は驚いて低くヒューと口笛を吹いた.

★**whistle**² /(h)wís(ə)l/ 動 ▶定義1 自他 to make a musical or a high sound by forcing air out between your lips or by blowing a whistle 唇から強く息を吹き出す, または笛を吹くことによって, 音楽または高い音を鳴らす→口笛を吹く, ホイッスルを鳴らす ‖ *He whistled a tune to himself.* 彼は口笛でメロディーを吹いた. ▶定義2 自 to move somewhere quickly making a sound like a whistle 笛のような音を鳴らしながら素早くどこかへ移動する→(弾丸・矢が)ひゅーと飛ぶ, (風が)ぴゅーっと鳴る ‖ *A bullet whistled past his head.* 弾丸がヒューと飛んできて彼の頭をかすめた.

★**white**¹ /(h)wáıt/ 形 ▶定義1 of the very light colour of fresh snow or milk 新雪や牛乳のように非常に明るい色の→白色の, 純白の ‖ *a white shirt* 白いスカート *white coffee (= with milk)* ミルク入りコーヒー (= ミルクの入った) ▶定義2 (used about a person) belonging to or connected with a race of people who have pale skin (人について) 色の薄い肌をした人種に属している, あるいは関係のある→白人の, 白人種の ▶定義3 white (with sth) (used about a person) very pale because you are ill, afraid, etc (人について) 病気または恐怖のために非常に青ざめている→青ざめた, 血の気のない, 青白い ‖ *to be white with shock/anger/fear* 衝撃・怒り・恐怖で青ざめる *She went white as a sheet when they told her.* 彼らが彼女に話をすると, 彼女は蒼白(そうはく)になった.
成句 black and white ⇒ **BLACK**¹

★**white**² /(h)wáıt/ 名 ▶定義1 U the very light colour of fresh snow or milk 新雪や牛乳のような非常に明るい色→白, 白色 ‖ *She was dressed in white.* 彼女は白い服を着ていた. ▶定義2 [C, 通常は複数] a member of a race of people with pale skin 色の薄い肌をした人種の一員→白人 ▶定義3 C U the part of an egg that surrounds the yellow part (yolk) and that becomes white when it is cooked 卵の黄色い部分(卵黄)の周りにあり, 加熱されると白くなる部分→卵白, 白身 ‖ *Beat the whites of four eggs.* 卵の白身4個分を泡立てます. ☞ **egg**のさし絵 ▶定義4 C the white part of the eye 目の白い部分→白目
成句 in black and white ⇒ **BLACK**²

**white-collar** 形 ▶定義 (used about work) done in an office not a factory; (used about people) who work in an office (仕事について) 工場ではなく事務所で行われる; (人について) 事務所で働いている→事務労働の, 事務職の; ホワイトカラーの, サラリーマンの ☞参 **blue-collar**

**white elephant** 名 [単数扱い] ▶定義 something that you no longer need and that is not useful any more, although it cost a lot of money 多額の費用がかかったが, もはや必要がなく, 今後役立つこともないもの→無用の長物

**the White House** 名 [単数扱い] ▶定義1 the large house in Washington D.C. where the US president lives and works 米国の大統領が住み, 仕事をしている, ワシントンD.C.にある大邸宅→ホワイトハウス, 大統領官邸 ▶定義2 used to refer to the US president and the other people in the government who work with him/her アメリカ合衆国の大統領と, 大統領と共に働く政府関係者に言及するために用いて→米国政府

**white lie** 名 C ▶定義 a lie that is not very harmful or serious, especially one that you tell because the truth would hurt sb ほとんど害のない, または深刻でないうそ, 特に真実が〜を傷付けるかもしれないときに言う→罪のないうそ, 善意のうそ

**whitewash**¹ /(h)wáıtwɔ(ː)ʃ, -wɒʃ/ 名 U ▶定義1 a white liquid that you use for painting walls 壁を塗るために使う白い液体→しっくい, 水性白色塗料, 水性石灰塗料 ▶定義2 [単数扱い] trying to hide unpleasant facts about sb/sth 人・物事につ

いての不快な事実を隠そうとすること➜**ごまかし,隠蔽(いんぺい)** ‖ *The opposition claimed the report was a whitewash.* 反対派はその報告書がごまかしであると主張した.

**whitewash**[2] /(h)wáɪtwɔ̀(ː)ʃ, -wɑ̀ʃ/ [動][他] ◗定義1 to paint whitewash onto a wall➜**(壁)にしっくいを塗る** ◗定義2 to try to hide sth bad or wrong that you have done 自分の行ってしまった悪いまたは間違った～を隠そうとする➜**～をごまかす,取り繕う**

**white-water rafting** [名] ◗定義 the sport of travelling down a fast rough section of a river, lake, etc in a rubber boat ゴム製ボートで,川,湖などの流れの急な所を下る競技➜**急流下り**

**whizz**[1] (特に [米]**whiz**) /(h)wɪz/ [動][自][略式] ◗定義 to move very quickly, often making a high continuous sound しばしば高い連続的な音を出しながら,素早く移動する➜**ビュンと音を立てる,風を切って進む** ‖ *The racing cars went whizzing by.* レーシングカーがビュンビュン音を立てて通り過ぎた.

**whizz**[2] (特に [米]**whiz**) /(h)wɪz/ [名][単数扱い] ◗定義 a person who is very good and successful at sth 何かが非常に得意で成功した人➜**名人,達人** ‖ *She's a whizz at crosswords.* 彼女はクロスワードの達人だ. *He's our new marketing **whizz-kid** (= a young person who is very good at sth).* 彼は,マーケティング部門の新しい天才少年(= 何かが非常に得意な若者)だ.

***who** /huː/ [代] ◗定義1 used in questions to ask sb's name, identity, position, etc 人の名前,身元,地位などを尋ねる質問の中で用いて➜**だれ,どういう人** ‖ *Who was on the phone?* 電話の相手はだれでしたか. *Who's that woman in the grey suit?* グレーのスーツを着たあの女性はだれですか. *She wondered who he was.* 彼女は彼がだれだったかしらと思った. ◗定義2 used for saying exactly which person or what kind of person you are talking about 話の対象がどの人またはどのような人であるのか,正確に言うために用いて➜**～する…,～である…** ‖ *I like people who say what they think.* 私は自分の思っている事を言う人が好きだ. *That's the man who I met at Ann's party.* あの人は,私がアンのパーティーで会った男の人です. *The woman who I work for is very nice.* 私が部下として働いている女性は[私の上司である女性は]非常に感じが良い.

➤上の２つの例(= whoが目的語となっている例と,前置詞を付けて用いている例)では,who を省略できる: *That's the man I met at Ann's party.* (あの人は,私がアンのパーティーで会った男の人です.) *The woman I work for is very nice.* (私が部下として働いている女性は[私の上司である女性は]非常に感じが良い.)

◗定義3 used for giving extra information about sb 人について補足情報を与えるために用いて➜**そしてその人(たち)は,するとその人(たち)は** ‖ *My mother, who's over 80, still drives a car.* 私の母は,80歳を過ぎているのですが,今でも車を運転しています. ☛ 与える補足情報がコンマで主節から区切られていることに注意. ☛参 **whom** の注

**who'd** /huːd, hud, hʊd/ **WHO HAD, WHO WOULD** の短縮形

***whoever** /huːévər/ [代] ◗定義1 the person or people who; any person who ～する·である人または人々; ～する·であるだれでも➜**～する·である人はだれでも** ‖ *I want to speak to whoever is in charge.* 私はだれでもいいから担当者と話がしたい. ◗定義2 it does not matter who だれであっても構わない➜**だれでも** ‖ *I don't want to see anybody - whoever it is.* 私はだれとも会いたくない − その人がだれであっても. ◗定義3 (used for expressing surprise) who (驚きを表現するために用いて)だれが➜**一体だれが** ‖ *Whoever could have done that?* 一体だれがあんな事をしでかしたんだろう.

***whole**[1] /hóʊl/ [形] ◗定義1 complete; full 全部の; 十分な➜**すべての,全体の,～全部,全～** ‖ *I drank a whole bottle of water.* 私はびんの水を全部飲んだ. *Let's just forget **the whole thing**.* すべてを忘れることにしましょう. *She wasn't telling me the **whole truth**.* 彼女は私にすべての真実を伝えてはいなかった. ◗定義2 not broken or cut 壊されていない,または削られていない➜**完全な,無傷の,そっくりそのままの,丸ごとの** ‖ *Snakes swallow their prey whole (= in one piece).* 蛇は獲物を丸ごと(= かみ切らないで)飲み込む. ☛ [副] wholly

**whole**[2] /hóʊl/ [名][単数扱い] ◗定義1 a thing that is complete or full in itself それ自身だけで完全または十分であるもの➜**完全なもの,統一体** ‖

W

*Two halves make a whole.* 半分が2つで完全なものになる. ▶定義2 **the whole of sth** all that there is of sth ～すべて→**(物)全体, 全部** ‖ *I spent the whole of the morning cooking.* 私は午前中ずっと料理をして過ごした.

成句 **as a whole** ▶定義 as one complete thing or unit and not as separate parts 部分に分かれていない1つの完全なものまたは単位として→**全体として(の)** ‖ *This is true in Britain, but also in Europe as a whole.* それはイギリスだけでなく, ヨーロッパ全般においても事実だ.

**on the whole** ▶定義 generally, but not true in every case 一般に, しかし個々の場合において事実でないこともある→**概して, 大体において, 全体から見て** ‖ *On the whole I think it's a very good idea.* 大体において, それはとても良い考えだと思う.

**wholefood** /hóʊlfùːd/ 名 U ▶定義 **wholefoods** [複数扱い] food that is considered healthy because it does not contain artificial substances and is produced as naturally as possible 人工的な物質を含んでおらずできるだけ自然に生産されているため, 健康に良いと考えられている食物→**自然食品, 無添加食物**

**wholehearted** /hòʊlhάːrtəd/ 形 ▶定義 complete and enthusiastic 完全なかつ熱狂的な→**心からの, 熱烈な, 誠心誠意の** ‖ *to give sb your wholehearted support* ～を心から支持する ― **wholeheartedly** 副 →**心から, 心を込めて**

**wholemeal** /hóʊlmìːl/ 副 形 (または **wholewheat**) 形 名 ▶定義 (made from) flour that contains all the grain including the outside layer (husk) 外側の層(殻)を含む穀物全体が入っている小麦粉(から作られた)→**全粒小麦粉の, 全麦の, 全粒粉で作った** ‖ *wholemeal bread/flour* 全粒粉で作ったパン・全粒小麦粉

**wholesale** /hóʊlsèɪl/ 副形 (形容詞のとき, 名詞の前のみ) ▶定義1 connected with buying and selling goods in large quantities, especially in order to sell them again and make a profit 大量の商品の売買に関連した, 特に再販売して利益を上げるための→**卸売りの, 卸売りで** ‖ *They get all their building materials wholesale.* 彼らはすべての建築資材を卸売りで買う. *wholesale goods/prices* 卸売り商品・価格 ☞参 **retail**

▶定義2 (usually about sth bad) very great; on a very large scale (通常, 好ましくない物事について)非常に大きい; 大規模な→**大量の[に], 大規模な[に]** ‖ *the wholesale slaughter of wildlife* 野生動物の大量虐殺

**wholesome** /hóʊlsəm/ 形 ▶定義1 good for your health 健康に良い→**健康的, 衛生的な** ‖ *simple wholesome food* 質素で健康的な食事 ▶定義2 having a moral effect that is good 道徳的に善い影響を持つ→**(道徳的・精神的に)ためになる, 健全な, 有益な** ‖ *clean wholesome fun* みだらでない健全な娯楽

**who'll** /hul, hul, huːl/ **WHO WILL** の短縮形

**wholly** /hóʊ(l)li/ 副 ▶定義 completely; fully 完全に; 十分に→**すっかり, 全く** ‖ *George is not wholly to blame for the situation.* その状況は, すべてがジョージのせいというわけではない.

★**whom** /(疑問詞) huːm, (関係詞) (h)um/ 代 正式 ▶定義 used instead of 'who' as the object of a verb or preposition 動詞または前置詞の目的語として, who の代わりに用いて→**だれを, だれに** ‖ *Whom did you meet there?* あなたはそこでだれに会ったのですか. *He asked me whom I had met.* 彼は私がだれに会ったのか尋ねた. *To whom am I speaking?* (電話で)どちら様でしょうか.

➤ who の代わりに whom を使うのは, 非常に格式張っている. 例えば *He asked me with whom I had discussed it.* (彼は, 私がだれとその相談をしたのかと尋ねた.)という文は, 通常, *He asked me who I had discussed it with.* と表現する. (前置詞の位置が文の最後になることに注意.)

**whooping cough** /húːpɪŋ kɒ̀(ː)f, hóʊpɪŋ-, (h)wúːpɪŋ-, (h)wóʊpɪŋ-, -kɑ̀ːf/ 名 U ▶定義 a serious disease, especially of children, which makes them cough loudly and not be able to breathe easily 特に子供がかかる重い病気で, これにかかると大きなせきをし, 呼吸が楽にはできなくなる→**百日ぜき**

**whoops** /(h)ʊps, (h)wuːps/ 間 ▶定義 used when you have, or nearly have, a small accident ちょっとした災難に遭ったとき, または遭いそうになったときに用いて→**おっと, えっ** ‖ *Whoops! I nearly dropped the cup.* おっと. あやうくカップを落とすところだった.

**whoosh** /(h)wuːʃ, (h)wʊʃ/ ▶定義 the sudden

movement and sound of air or water going past very fast 空気または水が非常に速く通り過ぎるときの,突然の動きと音➔ヒュー,シュー ― whoosh 動(自)➔ヒュー・シューと音を立てる,ヒュー・シューと音を立てて動く

**who're** /huːər, huər/ WHO AREの短縮形

**who's** /huːz/ WHO IS, WHO HASの短縮形

*****whose** /(h)uːz, huz/ 形代 ▶定義1 (used in questions to ask who sth belongs to) of whom (だれのものなのか尋ねる質問の中で用いて) ➔だれの ‖ *Whose car is that?* あれはだれの車ですか. *Whose is that car?* あの車はだれのものですか. *Those are nice shoes ― I wonder whose they are.* すてきな靴だ ― だれの靴かしら. ▶定義2 (used to say exactly which person or thing you mean, or to give extra information about a person or thing) of whom; of which (自分が意味しているものがどの人または物であるか正確に言うために,あるいは人または物について補足情報を与えるために用いて) ➔その人の,その物の ‖ *That's the boy whose mother I met.* あれは,私がその母親に会った少年です. *My neighbours, whose house is up for sale, are splitting up.* いま家が売りに出されている私の隣人たちは,離婚しようとしている. ☛ 人や物について補足情報を与えるためにwhoseを使うとき,その節をコンマで主節から分けなければならない.

**who've** /huːv/ WHO HAVEの短縮形

*****why** /(h)wáɪ/ 副 ▶定義1 for what reason 何の理由で➔なぜ,どうして ‖ *Why was she so late?* なぜ彼女はそんなに遅れたのか. *I wonder why they went.* 私はなぜ彼らが行ったのかと思う. *'I'm not staying any longer.' 'Why not?'* 「もういとましなくては」「どうしてですか」 ▶定義2 used for giving or talking about a reason for sth 物事についての理由を与える,または理由について話すのに用いて➔~する・である理由,訳 ‖ *The reason why I'm leaving you is obvious.* 私があなたと別れる理由は明らかです. *I'm tired and that's why I'm in such a bad mood.* 私は疲れている,だからこんなに機嫌が悪いのだ.

成句 **why ever** ▶定義 used to show that you are surprised or angry 驚き,または怒りを示すのに用いて➔一体なぜ,一体どうして ‖ *Why ever didn't you phone?* 一体なぜあなたは電話をしなかったのか.

**why not?** ▶定義 used for making or agreeing to a suggestion 提案をする,または提案に賛成するのに用いて➔~しませんか,そうしましょう ‖ *Why not phone her tonight?* 今夜彼女に電話したらどうですか. *'Shall we go out tonight?' 'Yes, why not?'* 「今夜出掛けませんか」「ええ,いいですよ」

**wick** /wɪk/ 名 Ⓒ ▶定義 the piece of string that burns in the middle of a candle ろうそくの中央で燃えるひも状の物➔(ろうそくの)芯(しん),灯心 ☛ **candle**のさし絵

*****wicked** /wíkəd/ ▶定義1 morally bad; evil 道徳的に悪い;邪悪な➔不道徳な,悪意のある,意地悪な ▶定義2 略式 slightly bad but in a way that is amusing and/or attractive 少々邪悪だが,面白いか魅力的または両方の➔いたずらな,腕白な ‖ *a wicked sense of humour* いたずらっぽいユーモアのセンス ― **wickedly** 副➔不道徳に,意地悪く ― **wickedness** 名 Ⓤ➔不道徳,悪意

*****wide**¹ /wáɪd/ 形 ▶定義1 measuring a lot from one side to the other 一方の側からもう一方の側までずい分と幅のある➔横幅のある,幅の広い ‖ *The road was not wide enough for two cars to pass.* その道路は2台の車が通れるほど幅広くなかった. *a wide river* 川幅の広い川 ⇔ **narrow** ☛ **width** ☛参 **broad**の注 ▶定義2 measuring a particular distance from one side to the other 一方の側からもう一方の側まで特定の距離がある➔幅が~ある,幅が~で[の] ‖ *The box was only 20 centimetres wide.* その箱は,幅がわずか20センチしかなかった. *How wide is the river?* その川はどのくらいの幅がありますか. ▶定義3 including a large number or variety of different people or things; covering a large area 多数のまたは多様な人々または物を含む;広範囲にわたる➔(範囲・知識が)広い,多方面にわたる,(見方などが)偏らない ‖ *You're the nicest person in **the whole wide world**!* あなたはこの広い世界の中で一番すてきな人です. *a **wide range/choice/variety** of goods* 豊富な商品群 *a manager with wide experience of industry* 業界経験の豊富な経営者 ▶定義4 fully open 十分に開いた➔(目・戸が)大きく開いた ‖ *The children's eyes were wide with excitement.* 子供たちは,興奮で目を大きく見開いていた. ▶定義5 not near what you wanted to touch or hit 触れたいまたは

当てたいと思った所に近くない→(的から)外れた, それた, 離れた, 見当違いの ‖ *His first serve was wide (for example in tennis).* 彼の最初のサーヴは大きくそれた(例えば, テニスで). — **widely** 副 ▶幅広く, 広範囲に, 大いに ‖ *Their opinions differ widely.* 彼らの意見は大きく食い違っている. *Steve travelled widely in his youth.* スティーブは若いころ, あちらこちらを旅行した.

★**wide**² /wáid/ 副 ▶定義 as far or as much as possible; completely できるだけ遠くまたは多く; 完全に→広く, (目・戸を)大きく開いて, 一杯に ‖ *Open your mouth wide.* 口を大きく開けなさい. *It was late but she was still wide awake.* 遅い時間だったが, 彼女はまだしっかり目が覚めていた. *The front door was wide open.* 玄関の戸は開け放たれていた.

**widen** /wáidn/ 動自他 ▶定義 to become wider; to make sth wider→より広くなる; ~をより広くする ‖ *The road widens just up ahead.* その道はすぐその先で広くなっている.

**wide-ranging** 形 ▶定義 covering a large area or many subjects 広範囲または数多くの主題を網羅する→広範な ‖ *a wide-ranging discussion* 広範囲にわたる議論

**widespread** /wáidsprèd/ 形 ▶定義 found or happening over a large area; affecting a large number of people 広範囲で見られるまたは起こる; 大勢の人々に影響する→広く行き渡った, 普及した, はびこった ‖ *The storm has caused widespread damage.* そのあらしは広範囲に及ぶ被害をもたらした.

**widow** /wídou/ 名 C ▶定義 a woman whose husband has died and who has not married again 夫が死亡し, 再婚していない女性→未亡人, 寡婦, 後家, やもめ — **widowed** /wídoud/ 形 →未亡人となった ‖ *She's been widowed for ten years now.* 彼女が夫を亡くして10年になる.

**widower** /wídouər/ 名 C ▶定義 a man whose wife has died and who has not married again 妻が死亡し, 再婚していない男性→男やもめ

★**width** /wídθ, wí(t)θ/ 名 U ▶定義 1 U the amount that sth measures from one side or edge to the other 物の片側・片端からもう片側・片端までを測った量→(横)幅, 広さ, 間口 ‖ *The room is eight metres in width.* その部屋は幅が8メートルある. *The carpet is available in two different widths.* そのカーペットは2種類の幅が用意されている. ☞ 形 **wide** ● **length** のさし絵 ▶定義 2 C the distance from one side of a swimming pool to the other 水泳プールの片側からもう片側までの距離→幅 ☞参 **length, breadth**

**wield** /wi:ld/ 動他 ▶定義 1 to have and use power, authority, etc 権力, 権限などを持ち, それを使う→(権力)を振るう, 行使する ‖ *She wields enormous power in the company.* 彼女は会社で絶大な権力を振るっている. ▶定義 2 to hold and be ready to use a weapon 武器を保持し, 使う準備を整えている→(武器・武力)を振るう ‖ *Some of the men were wielding knives.* 男たちの何人かは刃物を振り回していた.

**wiener** /wí:nər/ 米 = **FRANKFURTER**

★**wife** /wáif/ 名 C ( 複 **wives** /wáivz/) ▶定義 the woman to whom a man is married 男性が結婚している相手の女性→妻, 奥さん

**wig** /wíg/ 名 C ▶定義 a covering made of real or false hair that you wear on your head 頭に着用する, 本物またはにせの髪の毛で作られた覆い→かつら

**wiggle** /wíg(ə)l/ 動自他 略式 ▶定義 to move from side to side with small quick movements; to make sb do this 小刻みに素早く左右に動く; ~をそのように動かす→小刻みに・ぴくぴく動く; ~を動かす ‖ *You have to wiggle your hips in time to the music.* あなたは音楽に合わせて腰を小刻みに揺らさなければならない. — **wiggle** 名 C →小刻みな身の動き, ぴくぴく動く・動かすこと

**wigwam** /wígwàm, -wɔ̀:m; -wæm/ 名 C ▶定義 a type of tent that was used by some Native Americans in past times 昔, 一部の先住アメリカ人に使われていたテントの一種→北米インディアンのテント小屋

★**wild**¹ /wáild/ 形 ▶定義 1 (used about animals or plants) living or growing in natural conditions, not looked after by people (動植物について) 人の世話にならないで, 自然な状態で生息または成長する→野生の ‖ *wild animals/flowers/strawberries* 野生動物・野の花・野いちご ▶定義 2 (used about an area of land) in its natural state; not changed by people (ある範囲の土地について) 自然な状態の; 人の手の入っていない→自然のままの, 荒れ果てた; 未開の, 人の住まない ‖ *the* *wild plains of Siberia* シベリアの未開の大平原 ▶定義3 (used about a person or his/her behaviour or emotions) without control or discipline; slightly crazy(人, 人の振る舞い, 人の感情について)抑制や規律のない; 少々気違い染みた→**乱暴な, 無法な; 狂気染みた, 熱狂的な** ‖ *The crowd went wild with excitement.* 群衆は興奮して狂乱した. *They let their children run wild* (= behave in an uncontrolled way). 彼らは子供たちを好き勝手にさせている(= 勝手気ままに振る舞う). ▶定義4 not carefully planned; not sensible or accurate 慎重には計画されていない; 賢明なは正確でない→**大雑把な; 無謀な** ‖ *She made a wild guess.* 彼女はでたらめな推測をした. *wild accusations/rumours* 見当違いの非難・うわさ ▶定義5 形式 **wild (about sb/sth)** liking sb/sth very much 〜が非常に好きな→**〜に夢中の, 熱中した** ‖ *I'm not wild about their new house.* 私は彼らの新しい家がそれほど好きというわけではない. ▶定義6 (used about the weather) with strong winds; stormy(天候について)強い風を伴う; あらしのような→**荒れた** ‖ *It was a wild night last night.* 昨日はあらしの一夜だった. ― wildly 副 →乱暴に, 無法に狂気染みて, でたらめに ― wildness 名 ❶→荒れ果てた様, 荒々しさ, 激しさ, 途方もなさ

**wild**² /wáɪld/ 名 ▶定義1 **the wild**[単数扱い] a natural environment that is not controlled by people 人によって管理されていない自然環境→**自然, 野生** ‖ *the thrill of seeing elephants in the wild* 荒野で象を見ることのスリル ▶定義2 **the wilds**[複数扱い] places that are far away from towns, where few people live 市街地からははるかに遠く, ほとんど人が住んでいない所→**未開地, 荒れ地, 原野** ‖ *They live somewhere out in the wilds.* 彼らは原野のどこかに住んでいる.

**wilderness** /wíldənəs/ 名[**C**, 通常は単数] ▶定義1 a large area of land that has never been used for building on or for growing things 何かを建てたり栽培するために使われたことが一度もない広大な土地→**未開地, 荒れ地, 原野** ‖ *The Antarctic is the world's last great wilderness.* 南極は世界中で最後に残された広大な未開地だ. ▶定義2 a place that people do not take care of or control 人が世話や管理をしていない場所→**荒れるままの所, 無秩序な場所** ‖ *Their garden is a wilderness.* 彼らの庭は荒れ放題になっている.

**wildlife** /wáɪldlàɪf/ 名 ❶ ▶定義 birds, plants, animals, etc that are wild and live in a natural environment 自然環境に生息する野生の鳥, 植物, 動物など→**野生生物**

**wilful** (困 または **willful**) /wílfəl/ 形 ▶定義1 done deliberately although the person doing it knows that it is wrong 悪いことだと知っていながら, 故意に行われた→**故意の, わざとした** ‖ *wilful damage/neglect* わざと傷付けること・故意に無視すること ▶定義2 doing exactly what you want, no matter what other people think or say 他人がどう思おうと言おうと関係なく, 自分のしたい通りにする→**わがままな, 強情な, 頑固な** ‖ *a wilful child* わがままな子供 ― **wilfully** /-fəli/ 副 →故意に, わざと, わがままに, 頑固に

★**will**¹ /l, (w)əl, wɪl/ 助助動詞(短縮形 **'ll**; 否定形 **will not**; 短縮形 **won't** /wóʊnt/) ▶定義1 used in forming the future tenses 未来時制を作るときに用いて→**〜でしょう, 〜だろう, 〜する・なるでしょう** ‖ *He'll be here soon.* 彼はすぐここに来るでしょう. *I'm sure you'll pass your exam.* あなたが試験に合格することを確信しています. *I'll be sitting on the beach this time next week.* 来週のこの時間, 私は海辺に座っていることだろう. *Next Sunday, they'll have been in England for a year.* 次の日曜日で, 彼らは1年間イギリスにいたことになる. ▶定義2 used for showing that sb is offering sth or wants to do sth, or that sth is able to do sth 人が何かを申し出ているまたはしたいと思っている, あるいは物が何かをすることができることを示すのに用いて→**〜するつもりである, 〜しようと思う** ‖ '*We need some more milk.*' '*OK, I'll get it.*' 「もう少し牛乳が必要だ」「分かった, 私が買ってきましょう」 *Why won't you tell me where you were last night?* 昨夜どこにいたのかなぜ教えてくれないの. *My car won't start* 私の車はエンジンがかからない. ▶定義3 used for asking sb to do sth 人に何かをするように頼むのに用いて→**〜してくれませんか, 〜しませんか** ‖ *Will you sit down, please?* どうぞお座りください. ▶定義4 used for ordering sb to do sth 人に何かをするよう命じるのに用いて→**〜しなさい** ‖ *Will you all be quiet!* 皆さん, お静かに. ▶定義5 used for saying

# 1834　will²

that you think sth is probably true 何かがおそらく事実であると思うと言うのに用いて→~だろう, ~であろう ‖ *That'll be the postman at the door.* 玄関に来たのは郵便配達員だろう. *He'll have left work by now, I suppose.* 彼はこの時間までには退社していると思うよ. ▶定義6 (肯定文でのみ) used for talking about sth annoying that sb always or very often does 人がいつもまたは非常に頻繁に行う迷惑な物事について話すのに用いて→いつも~する, よく~する

▶迷惑していることを示したいときは, willに強勢を置かなくてはならない. また短縮形は用いられない: *He will keep interrupting me when I'm trying to work.* (私が仕事をしようとすると, 彼はいつも邪魔し続ける.) 法助動詞についての説明は, 巻末の「文法早見表」を参照.

*★**will**² /wɪl/ 名 ▶定義1 ❻ Ⓤ the power of the mind to choose what to do; a feeling of strong determination 何をすべきかを選択する意志の力; 強い決意の感情→意志, 意欲, 決意 ‖ *Both her children have got very strong wills.* 彼女の子供は2人ともとても強い意志を持っている. *My father seems to have lost **the will to live**.* 私の父は生きる意欲を失ってしまったようだ. ▶定義2 **-willed** (複合形容詞を作るために用いて) having the type of will mentioned 示された種類の意志を持っている→~の意志 ‖ *a strong-willed/weak-willed person* 意志の強い・意志の弱い人 ▶定義3 [単数扱い] what sb wants to happen in a particular situation ある特定の状況で人が起きてほしいと思っていること→(~の)望み, 願い ‖ *My mother doesn't want to sell the house and I don't want to **go against** her **will**.* 母は家を売りたくないと思っている, そして私は母の希望に反したくない. ▶定義4 ❻ a legal document in which you write down who should have your money and property after your death 自分の死後, お金や財産をだれが所有すべきかを記載した法律に基づく文書→遺言書 ‖ *You really ought to **make a will**.* あなたは本当に遺言書を作成すべきです. *Gran left us some money **in her will**.* おばあちゃんは遺言書で多少のお金を私たちに残した.

成句 **of your own free will** ⇒ **FREE**¹

**will**³ /wɪl/ 動 ⑲ ▶定義 to use the power of your mind to do sth or to make sth happen 何かをするためにまたは起こらせるために自分の意志の力を活用する→~を意志の力で…させる, ~を成し遂げる ‖ *He willed himself to carry on to the end of the race.* 彼は意志の力でレースの最後まで持ちこたえた.

*★**willing** /wɪlɪŋ/ 形 ▶定義1 willing (to do sth) (名詞の前は不可) happy to do sth; having no reason for not doing sth 喜んで~をする; ~をしない理由がない→~するのをいとわない, ~しても構わない ‖ *Are you willing to help us?* 私たちを手伝っていただけますか. *She's **perfectly willing** to lend me her car.* 彼女は私に車を貸すことを全くいとわない. *I'm not willing to take any risks.* 私はどんな危険も冒したくない. ▶定義2 ready or pleased to help and not needing to be persuaded; enthusiastic 進んでまたは喜んで手助けをし, 説得される必要はない; 熱心な→自発的な, 快い, 乗り気の, 心からの ‖ *a willing helper/volunteer* 自発的な援助者・志願者 ⇔ **unwilling** — **willingly** 副 →喜んで, 快く, 進んで — **willingness** 名 [Ⓤ, 単数扱い] →進んでする気持ち, 喜んでする心持ち, 乗り気

**willow** /wɪloʊ/ (または **willow tree**) 名 ❻ ▶定義 a tree with long thin branches that hang down which grows near water 水の近くで生長し, 垂れ下がった長くて細い枝を持つ木→柳, 柳の木

**will power** 名 Ⓤ ▶定義 determination to do sth; strength of mind 何かをする決意; 意志の力→意志力, 根性 ‖ *It takes a lot of will power to give up smoking.* 禁煙するには強い意志力が必要だ.

**willy** /wɪli/ 名 ❻ (複 **willies**) 略式 ▶定義 a word used to refer to the male sex organ (**penis**) 男性の性器 (陰茎) に言及するために用いる語→ペニス

**willy-nilly** /wɪli nɪli/ 副 ▶定義1 in a careless way without planning 計画的でなくいいかげんに→無計画に, 乱雑に, 手当たり次第 ‖ *Don't spend your money willy-nilly.* 無計画にお金を使ってはいけませんよ. ▶定義2 if you want to or not 望もうと望むまいと→否応なしに, どのみち, 好むと好まざるとにかかわらず

**wilt** /wɪlt/ 動 ⓐ ▶定義 (used about a plant or flower) to bend and start to die, because of heat or a lack of water (植物, または花について) 暑さや水不足のために, 折れ曲がり死にかける→

しぼむ, しおれる

**wily** /wáɪli/ 形 ▶定義 clever at getting what you want 自分の欲しいものを手に入れることに賢い→策をろうする, 狡猾(こうかつ)な, ずる賢い ☞類 **cunning**

**wimp** /wɪmp/ 名 C 略式 ▶定義 a weak person who has no courage or confidence 勇気または自信のない弱い人→意気地なし, 弱虫 — **wimpish** 形→意気地なしの, 弱虫の

*****win** /wɪn/ 動 (現分 **winning**; 過, 過分 **won** /wʌn/) ▶定義1 自他 to be the best, first or strongest in a race, game, competition, etc 競走, 競技, 試合などで最高, 最速, または最強になる→勝利する; ～で勝つ ‖ *to win a game/match/championship* 競争・試合・優勝決定戦に勝つ *I never win at table tennis.* 私は卓球で一度も勝つことがない. *Which party do you think will win the next election?* あなたは次の選挙でどの党が勝つと思いますか. ▶定義2 他 to get money, a prize, etc as a result of success in a competition, race, etc 試合, 競走などで成功した結果として賞金, 賞などを得る→～を勝ち取る, ～を獲得する ‖ *We won a trip to Australia.* 私たちはオーストラリア旅行を勝ち取った. *Who won the gold medal?* だれが金メダルを獲得しましたか. *He won the jackpot in the lottery.* 彼は宝くじで大金を獲得した.

▶「仕事で金を稼ぐ」の「稼ぐ」は win ではなくて earn であることに注意: *I earn £15000 a year.*(私は年間15000ポンドを稼ぐ.)

▶定義3 他 (to make sb) to get sth by hard work, great effort, etc 激しい労働, 多大な努力などによって物を得る, 人に物を得させる→(名声・賞賛・人気など)を勝ち取る, 得る, 獲得する; 勝ち取らせる, 獲得させる ‖ *Her brilliant performance won her a great deal of praise.* 彼女のすばらしい演技は多くの賞賛を勝ち取った. *to win support for a plan* 計画への支援を得る — **win** 名 C→勝利, 成功 ‖ *We have had two wins and a draw so far this season.* 今シーズン, これまでのところ私たちは2勝1引き分けだ. — **winning** 形→勝利を収めた, 勝った, 当たりの ‖ *The winning ticket is number 65.* 当たり札は65番だ.

成句 **win/lose the toss** ⇒ **TOSS**

**you can't win** 略式 ▶定義 there is no way of being completely successful or of pleasing everyone 完全に成功したり皆を喜ばせる方法はない→思い通りにはいかない, どうにもならない ‖ *Whatever you do you will upset somebody. You can't win.* 何をどうしたところで, 必ずだれかを怒らせてしまうでしょう. どうにもならないよ.

句動詞 **win sb over/round (to sth)** ▶定義 to persuade sb to support or agree with you 自分を支持するように, または自分に合意するように, ～を説得する→～を(味方に)引き入れる, ～を説得する, 説得して～の考えにさせる ‖ *They're against the proposal at the moment, but I'm sure we can win them over.* 彼らは今はその提案に反対しているが, 我々が彼らを説き伏せることができると私は確信している.

**wince** /wɪns/ 動 自 ▶定義 to make a sudden quick movement (usually with a part of your face) to show you are feeling pain or embarrassment 痛みや当惑を感じていることを示すために, (通常は顔の一部を)突然素早く動かす→びくっとする, 顔をしかめる

**winch** /wɪntʃ/ 名 C ▶定義 a machine that lifts or pulls heavy objects using a thick chain, rope, etc がっしりした鎖, ロープなどで重い物を持ち上げるまたは引っ張る機械→巻き上げ機, ウインチ — **winch** 動 他→～をウインチで巻き上げる ‖ *The injured climber was winched up into a helicopter.* けがを負った登山者はウインチでヘリコプターに引き上げ, 収容された.

*****wind**[1] /wɪnd, (詩) wáɪnd/ 名 ▶定義1 C U air that is moving across the surface of the earth 地球の表面を移動している空気→風 ‖ *There was a strong wind blowing.* 強い風が吹いていた. *A gust of wind blew his hat off.* 一陣の風に, 彼の帽子が吹き飛ばされた. *gale-force/strong/high winds* 強風 ▶定義2 U the breath that you need for doing exercise or playing a musical instrument 運動をしたり楽器を演奏したりするために必要な息→息, 呼吸, 肺活量 ‖ *She stopped running to get her wind back.* 彼女は呼吸を整えるため, 走るのをやめた. ▶定義3 U gas that is formed in your stomach 胃に形成されるガス→ガス ‖ *The baby cries when he has wind.* その赤ん坊はおなかにガスがたまると泣く. ▶定義4 U the group of instruments in an orchestra that you blow into to produce the

## 1836　wind²

sound オーケストラの楽器のうち, 息を吹き込んで音を鳴らすグループ➡管楽器部

成句 get wind of sth ▶定義 to hear about sth that is secret 秘密である～について耳にする➡～かぎ付ける, ～に感付く

**wind²** /wɪnd/ 動 他 ▶定義1 to cause sb to have difficulty in breathing ～が呼吸するのを困難にさせる➡～の息を切らす, 気絶させる ‖ *The punch in the stomach winded her.* 腹部への一撃で, 彼女は息ができなくなった. ▶定義2 to help a baby get rid of painful gas in the stomach by rubbing or gently hitting its back 赤ん坊の背中をこすったりそっとたたくことによって, 胃にたまっている苦しいガスを排出させる➡げっぷをさせる

★**wind³** /wáɪnd/ 動 (過, 過分 **wound** /wáʊnd/) ▶定義1 (used about a road, path, etc) to have a lot of bends or curves in it (道路, 小道などについて)カーブがたくさんある➡曲がりくねる ‖ *The path winds down the cliff to the sea.* その小道は, 崖(がけ)を曲がりくねりながら海まで続いている. ▶定義2 他 to put sth long round sth else several times 長い～をほかの物の回りに数回巻く➡～を巻き付ける ‖ *She wound the bandage around his arm.* 彼女は彼の腕に包帯を巻いた. ▶定義3 他 to make sth work or move by turning a key, handle, etc➡かぎ, 取っ手などを回して～を作動させる, または移動させる ‖ *He wound the car window down.* 彼は, 取っ手を回して自動車の窓を開けた. *Wind the tape on a bit to the next song.* 次の曲までテープを少し進めなさい.

句動詞 wind down ▶定義 (about a person) to rest and relax after a period of hard work, worry, etc (人について)激しい労働, 悩みなどの後, 休養してのんびりする➡リラックスする, くつろぐ, 落ち着く ☞参 unwind

wind up ▶定義 to find yourself in a place or situation that you did not intend to be in 自分が意図していなかった場所や状況にいることが分かる➡～のはめになる, 結局～する ‖ *We got lost and wound up in a dangerous-looking part of town.* 私たちは道に迷い, 街の危険そうな地域に入り込むはめになった.

wind sb up ▶定義 to annoy sb until he/she becomes angry ～が怒り出すまで悩ます➡～をいら立たせる, 怒らせる

wind sth up ▶定義 to finish, stop or close sth ～を終了する, やめる, 閉める➡(話・会合を)終える, (店・会社を)畳む, 解散する ‖ *The company was losing money and was soon wound up.* その会社は損失を出しており, まもなく解散した.

**windfall** /wíndfɔːl/ 名 C ▶定義 an amount of money that you win or receive unexpectedly 思い掛けず勝ち取ったり受け取った金➡意外な授かりもの, 転がり込んだ大金, 棚ぼた

**winding** /wáɪndɪŋ/ 形 ▶定義 with bends or curves in it カーブの多い➡曲がりくねった ‖ *a winding road through the hills* 山々を通り抜ける曲がりくねった道

**wind instrument** 名 C ▶定義 a musical instrument that you play by blowing through it 息を吹き込んで演奏する楽器➡管楽器, 吹奏楽器

**windmill** /wín(d)mìl/ 名

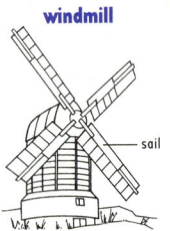
windmill
sail

C ▶定義 a tall building or structure with long parts (sails) that turn in the wind. In past times windmills were used for making flour from grain, but now they are used mainly for producing electricity. 風に吹かれて回転する長い部分(風車の翼)の付いた高い建物または建造物. 昔, 穀類を粉にひくために使われていたが, 今では主に電気を起こすのに用いている➡風車, 風車小屋

★**window** /wíndoʊ/ 名 C ▶定義1 the opening in a building, car, etc that you can see through and that lets light in. A window usually has glass in it. 見通しになっていて中に光が差し込む建物や自動車などの開口部で, 普通ガラスがはめられている➡窓 ‖ *Open the window. It's hot in here.* 窓を開けなさい. ここは暑いですよ. *a shop window* ショーウインドー *These windows need cleaning.* これらの窓はきれいにする必要がある. ☞ C7ページのさし絵 ▶定義2 an area on a computer screen that has a particular type of information in it ある特定の種類の情報が表示されているコンピューター画面の1領域➡ウインドー ☞ C7ページのさし絵 ▶定義3 a time when you have not arranged to do anything and so are free to meet sb, etc 何も予定していない時間で,そのため自由に人と会うなどできる→**自由時間, 空き時間** ‖ *I'm busy all Tuesday morning, but I've got a window from 2 until 3.* 私は火曜日の午前中はずっと忙しいが,2時から3時までは空いている.

**windowpane** /wíndoupèin/ 名 C ▶定義 one piece of glass in a window 窓にはめられている1枚のガラス→**窓ガラス**

**window-shopping** 名 U ▶定義 looking at things in shop windows without intending to buy anything 何を買うつもりもなく,ショーウインドーに展示された商品を見ること→**ウインドーショッピング**

**window sill** (または **window ledge**) 名 C ▶定義 the narrow shelf at the bottom of a window, either inside or outside 窓の内側または外側で下部にある細長い棚→**窓の下枠, 窓敷き居** ☞ **curtain** のさし絵

**windpipe** /wíndpàip/ 名 C ▶定義 the tube that takes air from the throat to the lungs のどから肺まで空気を通す管→**気管**

**windscreen** /wíndskrì:n/ (米 **windshield** /wíndʃì:ld/) 名 C ▶定義 the window in the front of a vehicle 乗り物の前部にある窓→**フロントガラス, 風よけ, 風防** ☞ S7ページのさし絵

**windscreen wiper** (または **wiper** 米 **windshield wiper**) 名 C ▶定義 one of the two moving arms (**blades**) that remove water, snow, etc from the front window of a car (the windscreen) 自動車の前にある窓(フロントガラス)から水滴,雪などを取り除く,2本の動く腕状のもの(羽根)の1本→**ワイパー** ☞ S7ページのさし絵

**windsurf** /wíndsə̀ːrf/ 動 自 ▶定義 to move over water standing on a special board with a sail 帆の付いた専用ボードに立ったまま水面を移動する→**ウインドサーフィンをする** ☞ 通常は go windsurfing (ウインドサーフィンをしに行く)と言う. *Have you ever been windsurfing?* あなたはウインドサーフィンをしたことがありますか. — windsurfing 名 U→**ウインドサーフィン**

**windsurfer** /wíndsə̀ːrfər/ 名 C ▶定義 1 (または **sailboard**) a board with a sail that you stand on as it moves over the surface of the water, pushed by the wind 風に吹かれて水面を移動するときにその上に立つ,帆の付いたボード→**ウイ**ンドサーフィン用ボード ▶定義 2 a person who rides on a board like this このようなボードに乗る人→**ウインドサーフィンをする人**

**windswept** /wíndswèpt/ 形 ▶定義 1 (used about a place) that often has strong winds (場所について)しばしば強い風が吹く→**風に吹きさらされた, 吹きさらしの** ‖ *a windswept coastline* 吹きさらしの海岸線 ▶定義 2 looking untidy because you have been in a strong wind 強い風の中にいたためにだらしなく見える→(髪・服が)**風で乱れた** ‖ *windswept hair* 風で乱れた髪

**windy** /wíndi/ 形 (**windier**; **windiest**) ▶定義 with a lot of wind たくさんの風のある→**風の強い** ‖ *a windy day* 風の強い日

\***wine** /wáin/ 名 C U ▶定義 an alcoholic drink that is made from grapes, or sometimes other fruit ブドウや時にはほかの果実から作られるアルコール飲料→**ワイン, ブドウ酒** ‖ *sweet/dry wine* 甘口・辛口ワイン *German wines* ドイツ製ワイン

▶ワインには red (赤), white (白), rosé (ロゼ)の3色がある.

\***wing** /wíŋ/ 名 ▶定義 1 Ⓒ one of the two parts that a bird, insect, etc uses for flying 鳥,昆虫などが飛ぶときに使う2つの部分の1つ→**羽, 翼** ‖ *The chicken ran around flapping its wings.* その鶏は羽を羽ばたかせながら走り回った. ☞ **insect** のさし絵 ▶定義 2 Ⓒ one of the two long parts that stick out from the side of a plane and support it in the air 飛行機の側面から突き出ていて,空中で飛行機を支えている2つの長い部分の1つ→**主翼** ▶定義 3 Ⓒ a part of a building that sticks out from the main part or that was added on to the main part 建物の主要部分から突き出ている,または主要部分に付加された部分→**翼(よく), そで, ウイング** ‖ *the maternity wing of the hospital* 病院の産科病棟 ▶定義 4 (米 **fender**) Ⓒ the part of the outside of a car that covers the top of the wheels 自動車の外側の一部で,車輪の上部を覆う所→**泥よけ, フェンダー** ▶定義 5 [Ⓒ, 通常は単数] a group of people in a political party that have particular beliefs or opinions 政党内の,ある特定の信念や意見を持つ人々の集団→**党派,(右翼・左翼などの)翼** ‖ *the right wing of the Conservative Party* 保守党の右

派 ☛参 **left-wing**, **right-wing** ▶定義6 ⓒ(in football, etc) the part at each side of the area where the game is played(サッカーなどで)試合が行われる領域のそれぞれの側の部分→**ウイング** ‖ *to play on the wing* ウイングでプレーする ▶定義7 (または **winger**) (in football, etc) a person who plays in an attacking position at one of the sides of the field(サッカーなどで)フィールドのどちらかの側の攻撃ポジションでプレーする人→**ウイングの選手** ▶定義8 **the wings** [複数扱い](in a theatre) the area at the sides of the stage where you cannot be seen by the audience(劇場で)舞台の両側にある,観客から見られない領域→**舞台わき,舞台のそで**

成句 **take sb under your wing** ▶定義 to take care of and help sb who has less experience than you 自分より経験の少ない〜の面倒を見て助ける→**〜をかばう,〜を庇護(ひご)する,〜を保護する**

**wink** /wíŋk/ 動 ⓘ ▶定義 **wink (at sb)** to close and open one eye very quickly, usually as a signal to sb 通常は〜への合図として,片目を素早く閉じて開く→**まばたきする,目くばせする** ☛参 **blink** — **wink** 名 ⓒ→**まばたき,目くばせ,一瞬** ‖ *He smiled and gave the little girl a wink.* 彼はにっこりと笑い,その少女にウインクした. *I didn't sleep a wink (= not at all).* 私は一睡もしなかった(= 全くしなかった).

成句 **forty winks** ⇒ **FORTY**

*****winner** /wínər/ 名 ⓒ ▶定義1 a person or animal that wins a competition, game, race, etc 試合,競技,競走などに勝利する人または動物→**勝利者,優勝者,勝ち馬** ‖ *The winner of the competition will be announced next week.* そのコンテストの優勝者は来週発表される. ▶定義2 略式 something that is likely to be successful→**成功しそうなもの** ‖ *I think your idea is a winner.* あなたの着想は成功すると私は思います. ▶定義3 (in sport) a goal that wins a match, a hit that wins a point, etc(スポーツで)試合に勝つゴール,点を獲得するヒットなど→**勝ち越しの1点,決勝の1点** ‖ *Anelka scored the winner in the last minute.* アネルカは土壇場で勝ち越しの1点を入れた.

**winning** ⇒ **WIN**

*****winter** /wíntər/ 名 ⓒ ⓤ ▶定義 the coldest season of the year between autumn and spring 秋と春の間の,1年で最も寒い季節→**冬,冬季** ‖ *It snows a lot here in winter.* ここでは冬にたくさん雪が降る. *a cold winter's day* 寒い冬の日 *We went skiing in France last winter.* 去年の冬,私たちはフランスへスキーに行った. — **wintry** /wíntri/ 形→**冬の,冬らしい,冬のような** ‖ *wintry weather* 冬の天気

**winter sports** 名 [複数扱い] ▶定義 sports which take place on snow or ice, for example skiing and skating 雪や氷の上で行われるスポーツ,例えばスキーやスケート→**ウインタースポーツ**

**wintertime** /wíntərtàim/ 名 ⓤ ▶定義 the period or season of winter 冬の期間または冬の季節→**冬,冬季**

*****wipe**¹ /wáip/ 動 ⓣ ▶定義1 to clean or dry sth by rubbing it with a cloth, etc 布などでこすって〜をきれいにする,または乾かす→**ふく,ぬぐう** ‖ *She stopped crying and wiped her eyes with a tissue.* 彼女は泣くのをやめて,ティッシュで目をぬぐった. *Could you wipe the table, please?* テーブルをふいていただけませんか. ☛参 **clean**² の注 ▶定義2 **wipe sth from/off sth; wipe sth away/off/up** to remove sth by rubbing it こすって〜から…を取り除く→**ふき取る,ぬぐい去る** ‖ *He wiped the sweat from his forehead.* 彼は額の汗をぬぐった. *Wipe up the milk you spilled.* こぼした牛乳をふき取りなさい. ▶定義3 **wipe sth (off) (sth)** to remove sound, information or images from sth 〜から音,情報,画像を取り除く→**(録音・録画したもの)を消す,消去する,(経験)を忘れ去る,ぬぐい去る** ‖ *I accidentally wiped the tape.* 私は誤ってテープを消去してしまった. *I tried to wipe the memory from my mind.* 私は心の内から記憶をぬぐい去ろうとした.

句動詞 **wipe sth out** ▶定義 to destroy sth completely 〜を完全に破壊する→**〜を一掃する,絶滅させる,全滅させる** ‖ *Whole villages were wiped out in the bombing raids.* 村々全体が爆撃による急襲で壊滅した.

**wipe**² /wáip/ 名 ⓒ ▶定義1 the action of wiping ふく動作→**ふくこと,ぬぐうこと,一ふき** ‖ *He gave the table a quick wipe.* 彼はテーブルをさっと一ふきした. ▶定義2 a piece of paper or thin cloth that has been made wet with a special liquid and is used for cleaning sth 特別な液体で湿らされていて,物をきれいにするために使われる紙または薄い布➜(抗菌剤などの入った)ウエットティッシュ,布 ‖ *a box of baby wipes* 赤ちゃん用ウエットティッシュ1箱

**wiper** /wáɪpər/ = WINDSCREEN WIPER

***wire**[1] /wáɪər/ [名] [C] [U] ▶定義1 metal in the form of thin thread; a piece of this 細い糸状の金属;その1本➜針金,金属線,ワイヤー ‖ *a piece of wire* 1本の針金 *Twist those two wires together.* この2本の針金をより合わせなさい. *a wire fence* 金網の囲い ▶定義2 a piece of wire that is used to carry electricity 電力を供給するのに使われる1本の金属線➜電線 ‖ *telephone wires* 電話線 ☛ **cable** のさし絵

**wire**[2] /wáɪər/ [動][他] ▶定義1 wire sth (up) (to sth) to connect sth to a supply of electricity or to a piece of electrical equipment by using wires 電線を使って〜を電源または電気器具に接続する➜〜に電線をつなぐ,〜に配線する ‖ *to wire a plug* プラグに配線する *The microphone was wired up to a loudspeaker.* そのマイクはスピーカーに接続されていた. ▶定義2 wire sth (to sb); wire sb sth to send money to sb's bank account using an electronic system コンピューターシステムを使って〜の銀行口座へお金を送る➜(お金を)電信為替で送る,電送する ‖ *The bank's going to wire me the money.* 銀行が私に電信送金することになっている. ▶定義3 to join two things together using wire 針金を使って2つの物を結び付ける➜針金で縛って留める,針金で結び付ける

**wiring** /wáɪərɪŋ/ [名] [U] ▶定義 the system of wires that supplies electricity to rooms in a building 建物内の部屋へ電力を供給する金属線のシステム➜配線システム,配線

**wiry** /wáɪəri/ [形] ▶定義 (used about a person) small and thin but strong (人について)小柄でやせているが強い➜筋肉質の,筋金入りの

**wisdom** /wízdəm/ [名] [U] ▶定義 the ability to make sensible decisions and judgements because of your knowledge or experience 知識または経験によって,賢明な決定と判断をする能力➜英知,賢明さ,知恵,分別 ‖ *I don't see the wisdom of this plan (= I do not think that it is a good idea).* 私には,この計画の賢明さが分からない(= 私はそれが良い考えだとは思わない).
☛ [形] wise

**wisdom tooth** [名] [C] ▶定義 one of the four teeth at the back of your mouth that appear when you are about 20 years old 20歳のころに口の奥に生えてくる4本の歯の1本➜親知らず ☛参 **tooth** の注

***wise** /wáɪz/ [形] ▶定義 having the knowledge or experience to make good and sensible decisions and judgements 優れた,賢明な決定と判断を行うための知識や経験を備えた➜賢明な,分別のある,聡明(そうめい)な ‖ *a wise choice* 賢明な選択 *It would be wiser to wait for a few days.* 2,3日待つ方が賢明だろう. — wisely [副] ➜賢明に,思慮深く,抜け目なく

***wish**[1] /wɪʃ/ [動] ▶定義1 [他] wish (that)(しばしば過去時制の動詞と共に)to want sth that cannot now happen or that probably will not happen 今は起こらない,または将来起こりそうにない物事が欲しい➜〜であればよいのにと思う,〜できればよいのにと思う ‖ *I wish I had listened more carefully.* もっと注意深く聞いていたらよかったのになあ. *I wish that I knew what was going to happen.* 何が起こるか分かっているならなあ. *I wish I was taller.* もっと背が高ければなあ. *I wish I could help you.* あなたを助けることができればよいところですが.

➤注意. 正式な英語では, I, he, she に対して was の代わりに were を使う: *I wish I were rich.* (金持ちであればいいのにと思う.) *She wishes she were in a different class.* (彼女は別のクラスに入っていればいいのにと思う.)

▶定義2 [自] wish for sth to say to yourself that you want sth that can only happen by good luck or chance 幸運または偶然でのみ起こり得る〜が欲しいと心の中で考える➜〜を望む,願う ‖ *She wished for her mother to get better.* 彼女は母親の回復を願った. ▶定義3 [他] [正式] wish (to do sth) to want to do sth➜〜をしたいと思う,願う ‖ *I wish to make a complaint about one of the doctors.* 医者の1人について苦情を言いたいと思っています. ▶定義4 [他] to say that you hope sb will have sth 〜が…を所有できるようにと望んでいることを言葉にする➜(幸運・成功など)を祈る ‖ *I rang him up to* ***wish*** *him* ***a happy birthday.*** 私は誕生日のお祝いを伝えよ

W

## 1840　wish²

うと彼に電話した. *We **wish** you **all the best** for your future career.* 私たちは、あなたのお仕事でのご成功をお祈りします.

**★wish²** /wɪʃ/ 名 ▶定義1 ❶a feeling that you want to have sth or that sth should happen 何かを所有したい、または何かが起こってほしいという感情→願望,望み,願い,希望 ‖ *I have no **wish** to see her ever again.* 私は二度と彼女に会いたくないと思っている. *Doctors should respect the patient's **wishes**.* 医者は患者の希望を尊重すべきだ. ▶定義2 ❶a try at making sth happen by thinking hard about it, especially in stories when it often happens by magic 物事について深く念じることによって、それを起こそうとする試み、特に物語の中ではしばしば魔法によって起こるもの→望み事,願い事 ‖ *Throw a coin into the fountain and **make a wish**.* その泉に硬貨を投げ入れて、願いを掛けなさい. *My **wish** came true (= I got what I asked for).* 私の望みが実現した(=自分が願っていたものを手に入れた). ▶定義3 **wishes** [複数扱い] a hope that sb will be happy or have good luck 人に幸せになってほしい、または幸運を手に入れてほしいという望み→(幸福・成功を)祈る言葉 ‖ *Please give your parents my **best wishes**.* あなたのご両親によろしくお伝えください. *Best Wishes (= at the end of a letter)* ご多幸・ご成功を祈って(=手紙の結びの言葉)

**wishful thinking** 名 ❶ ▶定義 ideas that are based on what you would like, not on facts 事実ではなく、自分の望みに基づく考え→希望的観測,甘い考え ☛参 thinking

**wisp** /wɪsp/ 名 ❶ ▶定義1 a few pieces of hair that are together 一緒になっている少量の髪の毛→(毛髪の)房 ▶定義2 a small amount of smoke 少量の煙→一筋 ─ **wispy** 形→薄い,まばらな

**wistful** /wɪ́stfəl/ 形 ▶定義 feeling or showing sadness because you cannot have what you want 望んでいるものが手に入らないために悲しみを感じているまたは示している→物欲しそうな,物足りなさそうな ‖ *a **wistful** sigh* 物欲しそうなため息 ─ **wistfully** /-fəli/ 副→物欲しそうに

**wit** /wɪt/ 名 ❶ ▶定義1 the ability to use words in a clever and amusing way 気が利いて人を楽しませるように言葉を使う能力→機知,ウイット,機転 形 witty ▶定義2 **-witted** (複合形容詞を作るために用いて) having a particular type of intelligence→ある特定の種類の知性を持っている ‖ *quick-**witted*** 頭の回転の速い *slow-**witted*** 頭の回転の遅い ▶定義3 (または **wits** [複数扱い]) the fact of being clever; intelligence 賢明であること;知性→賢明さ,分別,知性 ‖ *The game of chess is essentially **a battle of wits**.* チェスの試合は本質的に知性の戦いだ.

成句 **at your wits' end** ▶定義 not knowing what to do or say because you are very worried 心配のあまり、何をすべきかまたは何を言うべきかが分からない→途方に暮れて

**keep your wits about you** ▶定義 to be ready to act in a difficult situation 困難な状況で行動する用意ができている→冷静さを保つ,分別を失わない

**witch** /wɪtʃ/ 名 ❶ ▶定義 (in past times and in stories) a woman who is thought to have magic powers (昔、および物語で)魔力を持っていると考えられる女性→魔女 ☛参 wizard

**witchcraft** /wɪ́tʃkrɑ̀:ft, -kræ̀ft/ 名 ❶ ▶定義 the use of magic powers, especially evil ones 特に邪悪な魔力の使用→魔法,魔術,妖術(ようじゅつ)

**★with** /wɪð, wɪθ/ 前 ▶定義1 in the company of sb/sth; in or to the same place as sb/sth 〜と一緒に;〜と同じ場所に、または同じ場所へ→〜と(一緒に),〜と共に ‖ *I live **with** my parents.* 私は両親と住んでいる. *Are you coming **with** us?* あなたは私たちと一緒に来ますか. *I talked about the problem **with** my tutor.* 私は教師とその問題について話し合った. ▶定義2 having or carrying sth →〜を持っているまたは持ち歩いている→〜が付いている,〜のある ‖ *a girl **with** red hair* 赤毛の少女 *a house **with** a garden* 庭付きの家 *the man **with** the suitcase* そのスーツケースを持った男性 ▶定義3 using sth→〜を使って,〜で ‖ *Cut it **with** a knife.* それをナイフで切りなさい. *I did it **with** his help.* 私は彼に手伝ってもらってそれをした. ▶定義4 used for saying what fills, covers, etc sth 満たすまたは覆うなどする物を表すのに用いて→〜で(作る,覆う),〜を(供給する,提供する) ‖ *Fill the bowl **with** water.* そのボールを水で一杯にしなさい. *His hands were covered **with** oil.* 彼の手は油にまみれていた.

▶定義5 in competition with sb/sth; against sb/sth 〜と競争して; 〜に逆らって➔〜と, 〜を相手に ‖ *He's always arguing with his brother.* 彼はいつも兄[弟]と言い争いをしている. *I usually play tennis with my sister.* 私は大抵姉[妹]とテニスをする. ▶定義6 towards, concerning or compared with sb/sth➔〜に向かって, 〜に関連して, 〜と比較して ‖ *Is he angry with us?* 彼は私たちに(対して)腹を立てていますか. *There's a problem with my visa.* 私のビザに問題がある. *Compared with Canada, England has mild winters.* カナダと比較すれば, イギリスの冬は穏やかだ. ▶定義7 including sth➔〜を含んで ‖ *The price is for two people with all meals.* その値段は2人分で, すべての食事を含んでいる. ▶定義8 used to say how sth happens or is done 物事がどのように起こるかまたはなされるかを表すのに用いて➔〜して, 〜したままで ‖ *Open this parcel with care.* この小包を注意して開けなさい. *to greet sb with a smile* 人に笑顔であいさつをする ▶定義9 because of sth; as a result of sth➔〜のために; 〜の結果として ‖ *We were shivering with cold.* 私たちは寒さで震えていた. *With all the problems we've got, we're not going to finish on time.* 抱えているすべての問題のために[多くの問題を抱えているので], 時間通りに終えられそうにない. ▶定義10 in the care of sb➔〜の手元に, 〜の所に ‖ *We left the keys with the neighbours.* 私たちは隣人にかぎを預けた. ▶定義11 agreeing with or supporting sb/sth 〜に合意して, 支持して➔〜の味方で ‖ *We've got everybody with us on this issue.* この問題ではみんなの賛成を取り付けている. ⇔**against** ▶定義12 at the same time as sth➔〜と同時に, 〜と共に ‖ *I can't concentrate with you watching me all the time.* あなたがずっと私を見ていると, 集中できません.

成句 **be with sb** ▶定義 to be able to follow what sb is saying 〜が言っている事に付いていくことができる➔〜の言う事を理解している ‖ *I'm not quite with you. Say it again.* あなたの言っている事がよく分かりません. もう一度言ってください.

\***withdraw** /wɪðdrɔ́ː, wɪθ-/ 動 ( 過 **withdrew** /-drúː/; 過分 **withdrawn** /-drɔ́ːn/) ▶定義1 🅑🅜 withdraw (sb/sth) (from sth) to move or order sb to move back or away from a place ある場所から移動する, 後退する, 立ち退く, あるいは〜に命令する➔(〜から)退く, 撤退する; (〜に…から)退かせる, 撤退させる ‖ *The troops withdrew from the town.* 軍隊はその街から撤退した. ▶定義2 🅜 to remove sth or take sth away 〜を取り除くまたは片付ける➔〜を取り下げる, 撤回する ‖ *to withdraw an offer/a statement* 申し出・声明を撤回する ▶定義3 🅜 to take money out of a bank account 銀行口座から金を引き出す➔〜を引き出す, 下ろす ‖ *How much would you like to withdraw?* いくら引き出されますか. ☛参 **deposit** ▶定義4 🅘 to decide not to take part in sth 〜に参加しないことを決心する➔身を引く, 脱落する, 引き下がる ‖ *Jackson withdrew from the race at the last minute.* ジャクソンは土壇場になってレースへの参加をやめた.

**withdrawal** /wɪðdrɔ́ː(ə)l, wɪθ-/ 名 ▶定義1 🅒🅤 moving or being moved back or away from a place ある場所から後退・立ち退きをすること, またはそうさせられること➔撤退 ‖ *the withdrawal of troops from the war zone* 交戦地帯からの軍の撤退 ▶定義2 🅒 taking money out of your bank account; the amount of money that you take out 銀行口座から金を引き出すこと; 引き出した金額➔引き出し, 払い戻し金額 ‖ *to **make a withdrawal*** 預金を引き出す ▶定義3 🅤 the act of stopping doing sth, especially taking a drug 何かをすることをやめる行為, 特に麻薬の摂取をやめること➔使用中止(の段階) ‖ *When he gave up alcohol he suffered severe **withdrawal symptoms**.* アルコールをやめた時, 彼はひどい禁断症状に襲われた.

**withdrawn** /wɪðdrɔ́ːn, wɪθ-/ 形 ▶定義 (used about a person) very quiet and not wanting to talk to other people (人について)非常に静かで, ほかの人たちと話したがらない➔引っ込み思案の, 内向的な

**wither** /wíðər/ 動 ▶定義1 🅘🅜 wither (sth) (away) (used about plants) to become dry and die; to make a plant do this (植物について)しおれて死ぬ; 植物をそのようにする➔枯れる, しぼむ; 〜を枯らす, しぼませる ‖ *The plants withered in the hot sun.* 強い日差しで植物が枯れた.
▶定義2 🅜 wither (away) to become weaker

then disappear 弱くなって消える→衰える,衰退する ‖ *This type of industry will wither away in the years to come.* この業種は数年もすれば衰退するだろう.

**withering** /wíðərɪŋ/ 形 ▶定義 done to make sb feel silly or embarrassed ～に間抜けな思いをさせるような,あるいはばつの悪い思いをさせるような→人をどぎまぎさせる,赤面させる ‖ *a withering look* どぎまぎした様子

**withhold** /wɪðhóʊld, wɪθ-/ 動他 (過,過分 **withheld** /-hèld/) 正式 ▶定義 withhold sth (from sb/sth) to refuse to give sth to sb ～に…を上げるのを拒む→(許可・許諾)を保留する,(情報・権利)を与えずにおく ‖ *to withhold information from the police* 警察に情報を知らせない

*__within__ /wɪðín, wɪθ-/ 前 副 ▶定義1 in a period not longer than a particular length of time ある特定の時間の長さよりも長くない期間内に→～以内で,以内に ‖ *I'll be back within an hour.* 私は1時間以内に戻ります. *She got married, found a job and moved house, all within a week.* 彼女は結婚し,仕事を見つけ,引っ越しをしたが,それらはすべて1週間内の出来事だった. ▶定義2 within sth (of sth) not further than a particular distance from sth ～からある特定の距離よりも遠くない→(～から)…以内の(所)に ‖ *The house is within a kilometre of the station.* その家は駅から1キロ以内の所にある. ▶定義3 not outside the limits of sb/sth ～の限界の外側にない→～の範囲内で,～を超えずに ‖ *Each department must keep within its budget.* 各部はそれぞれの予算枠を守らなければならない. ▶定義4 正式 inside sb/sth ～の内側の→内に,中に,内部に ‖ *The anger was still there deep within him.* 彼の心の奥底にはまだ怒りが潜んでいた.

*__without__ /wɪðáʊt, wɪθ-/ 前 副 ▶定義1 not having or showing sth ～を持っていない,または示していない→～のない,付いていない,欠けた ‖ *Don't go out without a coat on.* コートを着ないで外出してはいけません. *He spoke without much enthusiasm.* 彼はあまり熱意なく話した. *If there's no salt we'll have to manage without.* もし塩がなければ,塩なしでどうにかしなければならないだろう. ▶定義2 not using or being with sb/sth ～を使わないで,～と共にいないで→～を持たずに,～を連れないで,～なしで,～を使わないで,～の助力なしに ‖ *I drink my coffee without milk.* 私は牛乳を入れずにコーヒーを飲む. *Can you see without your glasses?* あなたは眼鏡なしで見えますか. *Don't leave without me.* 私を置いていかないで. ▶定義3 used with a verb in the -ing form to mean 'not' 否定の意味で,動詞の-ing形と共に用いて→～しないで,～せずに ‖ *She left without saying goodbye.* 彼女はさよならを言わずに立ち去った. *I used her phone without her knowing.* 私は彼女に内緒で彼女の電話を使った.

**withstand** /wɪðstǽnd, wɪθ-/ 動他 (過,過分 **withstood** /-stód/) 正式 ▶定義 to be strong enough not to break, give up, be damaged, etc 壊れたりあきらめたり傷付けられることなどがないほど十分に強い→～によく耐える,～に抵抗する,逆らう ‖ *These animals can withstand very high temperatures.* これらの動物はとても高い温度に耐えられる.

*__witness__¹ /wítnəs/ 名 C ▶定義1 (または **eyewitness**) a witness (to sth) a person who sees sth happen and who can tell other people about it later ～が起こったのを見ていて,後でそれについてほかの人たちに伝えることのできる人→目撃者 ‖ *There were two witnesses to the accident.* その事故には2人の目撃者がいた. ▶定義2 a person who appears in a court of law to say what he/she has seen or what he/she knows about sb/sth 裁判所に出廷して,見たことまたは何かについて知っている事を述べる人→証人,参考人 ‖ *a witness for the defence/prosecution* 弁護側・検察側の証人 ▶定義3 a person who sees sb sign an official document and who then signs it himself/herself 人が公式文書に署名するのを見届けて,次に自分自身がそれに署名する人→連署人,保証人

成句 bear witness (to sth) ⇒ **BEAR**²

**witness**² /wítnəs/ 動他 ▶定義1 to see sth happen and be able to tell other people about it later ～が起こるのを見ていて,後でそれについてほかの人たちに伝えることができる→～を目撃する ‖ *to witness a murder* 殺人を目撃する ▶定義2 to see sb sign an official document and then sign it yourself 人が公式文書に署名す

るのを見届けて, 次に自分自身がそれに署名する → (連署人, 保証人として) 〜に署名する, 連署する ‖ *to witness a will* 遺言書に証人として署名する

**witness box** (米 **witness-stand**) 名 C ▶定義 the place in a court of law where a witness stands when he/she is giving evidence 証人が証言をするときに立つ裁判所内の場所 → 証言席

**witty** /wíti/ 形 (**wittier**; **wittiest**) ▶定義 clever and amusing; using words in a clever way 気が利いていて, 人を楽しませる; 気の利いた言葉の使い方をする → 機知に富んだ, 才気のある ‖ *a very witty speech* とても機知に富んだ演説 ☛ 名 wit

**wives** WIFE の複数形

**wizard** /wízərd/ 名 C ▶定義 (in stories) a man who is believed to have magic powers (物語の中で) 魔力を持っていると信じられている男性 → 魔法使い ☛ 参 witch, magician

**wk** 略 (複 **wks**) week → 週

**wobble** /wɑ́b(ə)l/ 動 自 他 ▶定義 to move from side to side in a way that is not steady; to make sb/sth do this 安定していない様子で左右に移動する; 〜をそのようにする → よろめく, ぐらぐらする, 揺れる; 〜をぐらつかせる, 揺らす ‖ *Put something under the leg of the table. It's wobbling.* テーブルの脚の下に何か置いて. ぐらぐらしているから. *Stop wobbling the desk. I can't write.* 机を揺らすのはやめて. 書けないでしょ.
— **wobbly** /wɑ́b(ə)li/ 形 → (物が) ぐらぐらする, 不安定な, (人が) ふらふらする

**woe** /wóu/ 名 成句 ▶定義 1 **woes** [複数扱い] the problems that sb has 人が抱えている問題 → 災難, 災い, 不幸 ▶定義 2 U (古) great unhappiness 大きな悲しみ → 悲哀, 悲嘆, 苦悩

成句 **woe betide sb** ▶定義 used as a warning that there will be trouble if sb does/does not do a particular thing もし人がある特定の事をしたりしなかったりすると問題が起こるという警告として用いて → 〜に災いあれ ‖ *Woe betide anyone who yawns while the boss is talking.* 上司が話している間にあくびをする人に災いあれ.

**wok** /wɑk/ 名 C ▶定義 a large pan that is shaped like a bowl and used for cooking Chinese food ボウルのような形をした, 中国料理を調理するために使う大きいなべ → 中華なべ ☛ **pan** のさし絵

**woke** WAKE¹ の過去形
**woken** WAKE¹ の過去分詞形

**wolf** /wʊlf/ 名 C (複 **wolves** /wʊlvz/) ▶定義 a wild animal that looks like a dog and that lives and hunts in a group (pack) 犬のような姿をし, 集団 (群) で生活し狩りをする野生動物 → オオカミ

*****woman** /wʊ́mən/ 名 C (複 **women** /wímən/) ▶定義 1 an adult female person 大人の女性 → 女性, 女の人 ‖ *men, women and children* 男性たち, 女性たちおよび子供たち *Would you prefer to see a woman doctor?* 女医に診てもらった方がよろしいですか. ▶定義 2 **-woman** (複合語で) a woman who does a particular activity ある特定の活動をしている女性 → 〜に従事・関係する女性, 女性〜家 ‖ *a businesswoman* 女性実業家

**womanhood** /wʊ́mənhʊd/ 名 U ▶定義 the state of being a woman 女性である状態 → (成人した) 女であること

**womanly** /wʊ́mənli/ 形 ▶定義 having qualities considered typical of a woman 女性の特徴をよく示すと考えられている性質を持っている → 女性らしい, 女性的な, 女性にふさわしい

**womb** /wu:m/ 名 C ▶定義 the part of a woman or female animal where a baby grows before it is born 女性または動物の雌の体の一部で, 誕生前の赤ん坊がそこで成長する → 子宮 ☛ より正式な語は uterus である.

**won** WIN の過去・過去分詞形

*****wonder**¹ /wʌ́ndər/ 動 ▶定義 1 自 他 **wonder (about sth)** to want to know sth; to ask yourself questions about sth 〜を知りたいと思う; 〜について自問する → 〜ではないかと思う, 〜かしらと思う ‖ *I wonder what the new teacher will be like.* 新しい先生はどんな先生なのだろうか. *Vesna's been gone a long time - I wonder if she's all right.* ヴェスナは長いこと行ったきりだ — 彼女は元気でやっているだろうか. *It was something that she had been wondering about for a long time.* それは彼女が長い間思いを巡らせていたことだった.

▶定義 2 他 used as a polite way of asking a question or of asking sb to do sth 質問する, ま

## 1844 wonder²

たは人に何かをするよう頼む丁寧な言い方として用いて→~してよろしいでしょうか，~していただけるでしょうか，~しませんか ‖ *I wonder if you could help me.* お手伝いしていただけるでしょうか. *I was wondering if you'd like to come to dinner at our house.* 私たちの家へ夕食を食べにいらっしゃいませんか. ▶定義3 🔵🔴 wonder (at sth) to feel great surprise or admiration 大きな驚きまたは賞賛を感じる→（~を）不思議に思う，（~に）驚く ‖ *We wondered at the speed with which he worked.* 私たちは彼が作業する速さに驚いた. *'She was very angry.' 'I don't wonder (= I'm not surprised). She had a right to be.'*「彼女はとても怒っていたよ」「不思議ではない（= 私は驚かない）. 彼女は怒って当然だった」

★**wonder²** /wʌ́ndər/ 名 ▶定義1 🔵a feeling of surprise and admiration 驚きと賞賛の感情→驚き, 驚嘆, 不思議 ‖ *The children just stared in wonder at the acrobats.* 子供たちはその曲芸に驚いて，ただただじっと見ていた. ▶定義2 🔴something that causes you to feel surprise or admiration 驚きや賞賛を感じさせる何か→驚異的な物・人・出来事, 奇跡, 奇観 ‖ *the wonders of modern technology* 現代技術の驚異

成句 do wonders (for sb/sth) ▶定義 to have a very good effect on sb/sth ~に非常に良い影響を持つ→奇跡を起こす, 驚くほどよく効く ‖ *Working in Mexico did wonders for my Spanish.* メキシコでの勤務で, 私のスペイン語は驚異的に上達した.

it's a wonder (that)... ▶定義 it's surprising that... ....は驚きだ→よく~できたものだ ‖ *It's a wonder we managed to get here on time, with all the traffic.* あの渋滞の中, 何とか時間通りにここに到着できたのは驚きだ.

no wonder ▶定義 it is not surprising 驚くことではない→不思議ではない, 当たり前だ, 道理で ‖ *You've been out every evening this week. No wonder you're tired.* あなたは, 今週毎晩外出している. 疲れているのは当たり前だ.

★**wonderful** /wʌ́ndərfəl/ 形 ▶定義 extremely good; fantastic 非常に良い; すばらしい→すてきな ‖ *What wonderful weather!* 何てすばらしい天気なんでしょう. *It's wonderful to see you again.* また君に会えてとてもうれしい. — **wonderfully** /-fəli/ 副 →すばらしく, すてきに

**won't** WILL NOT の短縮形

★**wood** /wʊd/ 名 ▶定義1 🔵🔴the hard substance that trees are made of 樹木が作られている硬い物質→木材, 材木 ‖ *He chopped some wood for the fire.* 彼は火にくべるためにいくつかまきを割った. *Pine is a soft wood.* 松は軟材である. ☞ C2ページのさし絵 ▶定義2 🔴（しばしば複数形で) an area of land that is covered with trees. A wood is smaller than a forest. 木々で覆われた土地. 森は大森林よりも小さい→森, 林 ‖ *a walk in the woods* 森の中の散歩

成句 touch wood; 米knock on wood ▶定義 an expression that people use (often while touching a piece of wood) to prevent bad luck 悪い運を避けるために人々が（しばしば木をたたきながら) 用いる表現→嫌な事が起こりませんように, うまくいくように, くわばらくわばら ‖ *I've been driving here for 20 years and I haven't had an accident yet - touch wood!* 私はここで20年間運転しているが, まだ一度も事故を起こしたことはないよ － これからもそうでありますように.

**wooded** /wʊ́dəd/ 形 ▶定義 (used about an area of land) having a lot of trees growing on it (土地について) そこに多くの木々が生えている→木の生い茂った, 樹木に覆われた

**wooden** /wʊ́dn/ 形 ▶定義 made of wood 木材で作られた→木製の, 木でできた

**woodland** /wʊ́dlænd, -lənd; -lənd/ 名 🔵🔴 ▶定義 land that has a lot of trees growing on it 多くの木々が生えている土地→森林地帯, 森林 ‖ *The village is surrounded by woodland.* その村は森林に囲まれている. *woodland birds* 森林地帯の鳥

**woodwind** /wʊ́dwìnd/ 名 [単数扱い, 単数または複数形の動詞と共に] ▶定義 the set of musical instruments that you play by blowing into them 息を吹き込んで演奏する一群の楽器→木管楽器

**woodwork** /wʊ́dwɜːrk/ 名 🔴 ▶定義1 the parts of a building that are made of wood such as the doors, stairs, etc ドア, 階段など, 建物の木製の部分→木造部 ▶定義2 the activity or skill of making things out of wood 木で物を作る活動またはその技術→木工, 木工技術

**woof** /wʊf, wuːf/ 名 C略式 ▶定義 used for describing the sound (a bark) that a dog makes 犬が発する声（ほえ声）を表現するのに用いて➡ウー，ワン

*****wool** /wʊl/ 名 U ▶定義 1 the soft thick hair of sheep 羊の柔らかく厚い毛➡羊毛 ▶定義 2 thick thread or cloth that is made from wool 羊毛から作られた太い糸または織物➡毛糸，毛織物，ウール ‖ *The sweater is 50% wool and 50% acrylic.* そのセーターは羊毛 50 パーセント，アクリル 50 パーセントだ． ☞参 **cotton wool** ☞ **knit** のさし絵

**woollen** (米 **woolen**) /wúlən/ 形 ▶定義 made of wool 羊毛でできた➡羊毛製の，毛織物の，ウールの ‖ *a warm woollen jumper* 暖かい毛織物のセーター

**woolly** (米 **wooly**) /wúli/ 形 ▶定義 like wool or made of wool 羊毛のような，羊毛でできた➡羊毛のような，ふんわりした羊毛製の ‖ *The dog had a thick woolly coat.* その犬はふさふさと毛が生えていた．*long woolly socks* 長いウールの靴下

*****word**¹ /wɜːrd/ 名 ▶定義 1 C a sound or letter or group of sounds or letters that expresses a particular meaning ある特定の意味を表す音または文字，あるいはそれらのまとまったもの➡語，単語，言葉 ‖ *What's the Greek word for 'mouth'?*「口」を表すギリシャ語は何ですか．*What does this word mean?* この単語の意味は何ですか． ▶定義 2 C a thing that you say; a short statement or comment 口に出して言うこと；短い声明または論評➡一言，ちょっとした話，発言 ‖ *Could I have a word with you in private?* 内密にちょっと話があるのですが．*Don't say a word about this to anyone.* この事はだれにも一言も言うな． ▶定義 3 ［単数扱い］a promise➡約束，誓言 ‖ *I give you my word* that I won't tell anyone. 私はだれにも言わないと，あなたに約束します．*I'll keep my word* to her and lend her the money. 私は彼女との約束を守って，彼女にお金を貸すつもりです．*You'll just have to trust him not to go back on his word.* あなたは，約束を破らないと言う彼の言葉を信じるしかない．

成句 a dirty word ⇒ **DIRTY**¹
not breathe a word (of/about sth) (to sb) ⇒ **BREATHE**
not get a word in edgeways ▶定義 to not be able to interrupt when sb else is talking so that you can say sth yourself 自分が何かを言おうとしても，ほかの人が話をしていて割り込むことができない➡話に割り込めない，口を挟めない，横から口を出せない
have, etc the last word ⇒ **LAST**¹
in other words ⇒ **OTHER**
lost for words ⇒ **LOST**²
put in a (good) word for sb ▶定義 to say sth good about sb to sb else ～について良い事をほかの人に言う➡～のために口添えをする，～を推挙する ‖ *If you could put in a good word for me I might stand a better chance of getting the job.* あなたが私のために口添えをしてくれれば，就職できる見込みがさらに増すかもしれない．
take sb's word for it ▶定義 to believe what sb says without any proof ～が言った事を証拠なしに信じる➡～の言う事を真に受ける，うのみにする
word for word ▶定義 1 repeating sth exactly 言葉を正確に繰り返して➡一言一句正確に，そっくり同じ言葉で ‖ *Sharon repeated word for word what he had told her.* シャロンは，彼が彼女に語った事を一言一句正確に繰り返した． ▶定義 2 translating each word separately, not looking at the general meaning 全体的な意味を考えずに，単語ごとに分けて翻訳して➡一語一語，逐語的に ‖ *a word-for-word translation* 逐語訳，直訳

**word**² /wɜːrd/ 動 他（しばしば受身態で）▶定義 to choose carefully the words that you use to express sth ～を表現するのに使う言葉を慎重に選ぶ➡～を言葉で言い表す ‖ *The statement was carefully worded so that nobody would be offended by it.* だれも気を悪くすることのないよう，その声明は慎重に表現されていた．

**wording** /wɜ́ːrdɪŋ/ 名［単数扱い］▶定義 the words that you use to express sth 何かを表現するために使う言葉➡言葉遣い，語法，言い回し ‖ *The wording of the contract was vague.* その契約書の表現はあいまいだった．

**word-perfect** 形 ▶定義 able to say sth that you have learnt from memory, without making a mistake 習得した記憶を頼りに，誤りなく何か

## 1846　word processor

を言える→(台詞(せりふ)を)完全に覚えている

**word processor** 名 C ▶定義 a type of small computer that you can use for writing letters, reports, etc. You can correct or change what you have written before you print it out. 手紙, 報告書などを書くために使える小型コンピューターの一種. 書いた内容を, 印刷する前に修正または変更することができる→ワードプロセッサー, ワープロ — word processing 名 U →(コンピューター上で行う)文書作成, 文書処理

**wore** WEAR¹の過去形

*****work**¹ /wəːrk/ 動 ▶定義1 自 他 work (as sth) (for sb); work (at/on sth); work (to do sth) to do sth which needs physical or mental effort, in order to earn money or to achieve sth お金を稼ぐためまたは何かを達成するために, 身体的または精神的な努力を必要とすることを行う→働く, 仕事をする, 勉強する ‖ *She's working for a large firm in Glasgow.* 彼女はグラスゴーの大企業で働いている. *I'd like to work as a newspaper reporter.* 私は, 新聞記者として働きたい. *Doctors often work extremely long hours.* 医者は, しばしば極めて長時間働く. *My teacher said that I wouldn't pass the exam unless I worked harder.* もっとしっかり勉強しないと私は試験に合格できないだろうと先生は言った. *I hear she's working on a new novel.* 私は, 彼女が新しい小説に取り組んでいると聞いている. *I'm going to stay in tonight and work at my project.* 私は今夜外出しないで, 自分の研究課題に取り組むつもりだ. ▶定義2 他 to make yourself/sb work, especially very hard 自分自身・他人を, 特にとても厳しく働かせる→〜をこき使う, 勉強させる ‖ *The coach works the players very hard in training.* そのコーチは選手たちを厳しく練習させる. ▶定義3 自 他 (used about a machine, etc) to function; to make sth function; to operate (機械などについて)機能する; 〜を機能させる, 操作する→作動する, 働く; 〜を使う, 運転する ‖ *Our telephone hasn't been working for several days.* 私たちの電話はこの数日間壊れている. *We still don't really understand how the brain works.* 脳がどのように機能するのか, 我々はまだ本当には理解していない. *Can you show me how to work the photocopier?* コピー機の使い方を教えてくれませんか. ▶定義4 自 to have the result or effect that you want; to be successful 自分の望んでいる結果または効果を得る; 成功する→(計画が)うまくいく, (薬が)効く, 作用する ‖ *Your idea sounds good but I don't think it will really work.* あなたの着想はすばらしく聞こえるが, それが本当にうまくいくとは思わない. *The heat today could work in favour of the African runners.* 今日の暑さはアフリカ出身のランナーには好都合かもしれない. ▶定義5 自 他 to move gradually to a new position or state 新しい位置または状態へ徐々に進行する→徐々に進む, 次第に〜になる; 〜を少しずつ進ませる ‖ *Engineers check the plane daily, because nuts and screws can work loose.* ナットやねじが次第に緩んでくることがあるので, 技師たちが毎日飛行機の点検をしている. *I watched the snail work its way up the wall.* 私はカタツムリがゆっくりと壁を上っていくのを見た. ▶定義6 自 他 to use materials to make a model, a picture, etc 模型, 絵などを作成するために材料を用いる→〜を加工する, (粘土)を練る ‖ *He worked the clay into the shape of a horse.* 彼は粘土を馬の形に作り上げた. *She usually works in/with oils or acrylics.* 彼女は大抵油絵の具かアクリル絵の具でかく.

成句 work/perform miracles ⇒ **MIRACLE**
work/sweat your guts out ⇒ **GUT**¹
work to rule ⇒ **RULE**¹

句動詞 **work out** ▶定義1 to develop or progress, especially in a good way 特に良い方向で展開または進展する→うまくいく ‖ *I hope things work out for you.* ご成功を祈ります. ▶定義2 to do physical exercises in order to keep your body fit 健康を維持するために運動をする→運動をする, 体操する ‖ *We work out to music at my exercise class.* 私の体操のクラスでは, 私たちは音楽に合わせて運動する.

**work out (at)** ▶定義 to come to a particular result or total after everything has been calculated すべてを計算・考慮した後に, 特定の結果または合計になる→(費用が)計算の結果〜となる, 最終的に〜となる ‖ *If we divide the work between us it'll work out at about four hours each.* もし私たちの間で仕事を分けるなら, それぞれ4時間程度という計算になる.

**work sb out** ▶定義 to understand sb→～を理解する, 推し量る, 知る ‖ *I've never been able to work her out.* 私はずっと彼女を理解できないでいる.

**work sth out** ▶定義1 to find the answer to sth; to solve sth ～の答えを見つける; ～を解決する→**解く** ‖ *I can't work out how to do this.* 私はこれのやり方が分からない. ▶定義2 to calculate sth→**～を計算する, 算定する** ‖ *I worked out the total cost.* 私は総費用を算定した. ▶定義3 to plan sth ～を計画する→**練り上げる** ‖ *Have you worked out the route through France?* あなたはフランス経由のルートを案出しましたか.

**work up to sth** ▶定義 to develop or progress to sth ～まで展開または進展する→**～へ徐々に向かう** ‖ *Start with 15 minutes' exercise and gradually work up to 30.* 最初は15分間の運動から始めて, 徐々に30分まで延ばしなさい.

**work sth up** ▶定義 to develop or improve sth with effort 努力して～を展開または改善する→**～に手を加える, 仕上げる** ‖ *I'm trying to work up the energy to go out.* 私は外出する気力を奮い立たせようとしている.

**work sb/yourself up (into sth)** ▶定義 to make sb/yourself become angry, excited, upset, etc 人・自分自身を怒らせる, 興奮させる, 悩ませるなど→**～を(ある状態へ)あおり立てる, 盛り上げる** ‖ *He had worked himself up into a state of anxiety about his interview.* 彼は面接について不安を募らせていた.

★**work**² /wəːrk/ 🔊 ▶定義1 ❶the job that you do, especially in order to earn money; the place where you do your job 特にお金を稼ぐために行う仕事; 仕事を行う場所→**仕事, 勤め口, 商売, 事業; 職場, 会社** ‖ *It is very difficult to find work in this city.* この町で仕事を見つけることはとても難しい. *He's been out of work (= without a job) for six months.* 彼は6か月間失業している (= 仕事がない). *When do you start work?* あなたはいつ仕事を始めるのですか. *I'll ask if I can leave work early today.* 私は今日仕事を早退できるか聞くつもりだ. *I go to work at 8 o'clock.* 私は8時に出勤する. *The people at work gave me some flowers for my birthday.* 職場の人たちが私の誕生日に花束をくれた. *Police work is not as exciting as it looks on TV.* 警察の仕事はテレビで見るほど刺激的ではない.

# work² 1847

➤ workは, 不可算名詞である. 文脈によってはjobが用いられなければならない: *I've found work at the hospital.* (私は病院で仕事を見つけた.) *I've got a new job at the hospital.* (私は病院で新しい職を得た.) employmentは, 金銭が支払われる仕事に就いている状態であり, workやjobよりも正式かつ公式的である: *Many married women are in part-time employment.* (結婚している女性の多くがパートタイム勤務だ.) occupationは, 身分や職業を尋ねるために書類上で用いられる語である: *Occupation: student* (職業: 学生), *Occupation: bus driver* (職業: バス運転手). professionは, 特別な訓練と高等教育を必要とする職業である: *the medical profession* (医業). tradeは, 自分の手を使い, 特別な技能を必要とする職業である: *He's a carpenter by trade.* (彼の職業は大工だ.)

▶定義2 ❶something that requires physical or mental effort that you do in order to achieve sth 何かを達成するために, 身体的または精神的な努力を要求するもの→**仕事, 作業, 労働, 勉強, 研究** ‖ *Her success is due to sheer hard work.* 彼女の成功は, 一心不乱に仕事したことによる. *I've got a lot of work to do today.* 私は今日しなければならない仕事がたくさんある. *We hope to start work on the project next week.* 我々は来週からその計画に取り掛かろうと思っている. ▶定義3 ❶something that you are working on or have produced いま取り掛かり中, または作り出したもの→**作品, 成績, 製作, 製品** ‖ *a piece of written work* 一編の作文 *The teacher marked their work.* 教師は彼らの成績を採点した. *Is this all your own work?* これはすべてあなた自身でやったものですか.

▶定義4 ❷a book, painting, piece of music, etc 書物, 絵画, 楽曲など→**(芸術の)作品, 著作** ‖ *an early work by Picasso* ピカソの初期の作品 *the complete works of Shakespeare* シェークスピアの全作品 ▶定義5 **works** [複数扱い]the act of building or repairing sth 何かを組み立てたり改修する行為→**工事, 事業** ‖ *The roadworks are causing long traffic jams.* 道路工事が長い交通渋滞を引き起こしている. ▶定義6 **works** [❷, 単数または複数形の動詞と共に](しばし

ば複合語で) a factory→**工場, 製作所** ‖ *The steelworks is/are closing down.* その製鋼所は現在閉鎖されようとしている.

**成句 get/go/set to work (on sth)** ▶定義 to begin; to make a start (on sth) 始める;(～を)始動する→**取り掛かる**

**workable** /wə́ːrkəb(ə)l/ 形 ▶定義 that can be used successfully; practical うまく用いられる;実用的な→**(機械・道具が)動く,使える,(計画が)実行可能な,(材料が)加工できる** ‖ *a workable plan/solution* 実行できる計画・解決策

**workaholic** /ˌwəːrkəhɔ́(ː)lɪk, -hɑ́l-/ 名 C ▶定義 a person who loves work and does too much of it 仕事が大好きで,やりすぎる人→**仕事中毒の人,仕事の虫**

**workbook** /wə́ːrkbʊ̀k/ 名 C ▶定義 a book with questions and exercises in it that you use when you are studying sth 何かを勉強するときに使う,質問や練習問題が書かれている本→**学習帳,練習帳,ワークブック**

★**worker** /wə́ːrkər/ 名 C ▶定義 1 (しばしば複合語で) a person who works, especially one who does a particular kind of work 働く人,特にある特定の種類の仕事をしている人→**労働者,勤労者,作業員** ‖ *factory/office/farm workers* 工場・内勤・農場労働者 *skilled/manual workers* 熟練・肉体労働者 ▶定義 2 a person who is employed to do physical work rather than organizing things or managing people 物事を組織したりまたは人々を管理するというより,むしろ身体的な仕事をするために雇われている人→**肉体労働者,職工,労働者階級の人** ‖ *Workers' representatives will meet management today to discuss the pay dispute.* 賃金争議について議論するために,労働者の代表が今日,経営陣と会う. ▶定義 3 a person who works in a particular way→**ある特定のやり方で働く人** ‖ *a slow/fast worker* のろのろと・てきぱきと働く人

**workforce** /wə́ːrkfɔ̀ːrs/ 名 [C,単数または複形の動詞と共に] ▶定義 1 the total number of people who work in a company, factory, etc 1つの企業,工場などで働いている人々の総数→**従業員数,労働力** ▶定義 2 the total number of people in a country who are able to work ある国で働ける人々の総数→**労働人口** ‖ *Ten per cent of the workforce is/are unemployed.* 労働人口の10パーセントが失業している.

★**working** /wə́ːrkɪŋ/ 形 (名詞の前だけ) ▶定義 1 employed; having a job 雇われている;仕事を得ている→**働いている,就労中の,仕事に従事している** ‖ *the problems of childcare for working mothers* 働く母親にとっての子育ての問題 ▶定義 2 connected with your job 仕事に関係した→**仕事上の,労働に関する** ‖ *He stayed with the same company for the whole of his working life.* 彼は全労働期間をその会社に勤務して過ごした. *The company offers excellent working conditions.* その会社はすばらしい労働条件を提供している. ▶定義 3 good enough to be used, although it could be improved 改善の余地はあるかもしれないが使用するに足りる→**実際に役立つ,実用的な** ‖ *We are looking for someone with a working knowledge of French.* 我々は実務的なフランス語の知識を持っている人を探している.

**成句 in working order** ⇒ **ORDER**¹

**workings** /wə́ːrkɪŋz/ 名 [複数扱い] ▶定義 the way in which a machine, an organization, etc operates 機械,組織などが機能する方法→**仕組み,(機械の)動かし方,(機構などの)働き** ‖ *It's very difficult to understand the workings of the legal system.* 法律制度の仕組みを理解することは,とても難しい.

**workload** /wə́ːrklòʊd/ 名 C ▶定義 the amount of work that you have to do しなければならない仕事の量→**仕事量,作業量,ノルマ** ‖ *She often gets home late when she has a heavy workload.* 仕事の量が多いとき,彼女はしばしば帰宅が遅くなる.

**workman** /wə́ːrkmən/ 名 C (複 **-men** /-mən/) ▶定義 a man who works with his hands, especially at building or making things 自分の手を使って仕事をする人で,特に物を組み立てたり作ったりする人→**職人,職工**

**workmanlike** /wə́ːrkmənlàɪk/ 形 ▶定義 done, made, etc very well, but not original or exciting とても上手になされていたり作られていたりするが,独創的または刺激的とは言えない→**巧みな,腕の良い,職人芸の** ‖ *The leading actor gave a workmanlike performance.* その主演男優は巧みな演技をした.

**workmanship** /wə́ːrkmənʃɪp/ 名 U ▶定義 the

skill with which sth is made 何かを作る技能→(職人の)手並み, 腕, 技量

**work of art** 名 C (複 **works of art**) ▶定義 a very good painting, book, piece of music, etc 非常に優れた絵画, 書物, 楽曲など→**芸術作品** ☛参 art

**workout** /wə́ːrkàʊt/ 名 C ▶定義 a period of physical exercise, for example when you are training for a sport or keeping fit 例えばスポーツに備えてまたは健康を保つためにトレーニングしている, 運動の時間→**練習, トレーニング** ‖ *She does a twenty-minute workout every morning.* 彼女は毎朝20分間のトレーニングを行う.

**worksheet** /wə́ːrkʃìːt/ 名 C ▶定義 a piece of paper with questions or exercises on it that you use when you are studying sth 何かを勉強しているときに使う, 質問や練習問題が書かれている1枚の紙→**練習問題用紙**

**workshop** /wə́ːrkʃɑ̀p/ 名 C ▶定義 1 a place where things are made or repaired 物が作られたり修理される場所→**作業場, 工作室** ▶定義 2 a period of discussion and practical work on a particular subject, when people share their knowledge and experience 特定の課題について議論と実際の作業を行う時間で, 人々が知識や経験を共有する→**勉強会, 研修会, 講習会** ‖ *a drama/writing workshop* 戯曲研究会・書き方講習会

**worktop** /wə́ːrktɑ̀p/ (または **work surface**) 名 C ▶定義 a flat surface in a kitchen, etc that you use for preparing food, etc on 食事を支度するときなどに使う, 台所などの平らな面→**調理台, 作業台** ☛ C7ページのさし絵

*****world** /wəːrld/ 名 C ▶定義 1 **the world** [単数扱い] the earth with all its countries and people すべての国々と人々を含む地球→**世界** ‖ *a map of the world* 世界地図 *the most beautiful place in the world* 世界中で最も美しい場所 *I took a year off work to travel round the world.* 私は世界中を旅するために, 1年間の休暇を取った. *She is famous all over the world.* 彼女は世界中で有名だ. ▶定義 2 [単数扱い] a particular part of the earth or group of countries 地球上のある特定の部分, またはある特定の国々→**世界, 圏** ‖ *the western world* 西側世界 *the Arab world* アラブ世界 *the Third World* 第三世界 ▶定義 3 [単数扱い] the life and activities of people; their experience 人々の生活と活動; 人々の経験→**世の中, 世間, 俗世** ‖ *It's time you learned something about the real world!* あなたは世間のことを分かってもいいころだ. *the modern world* 近代社会 ▶定義 4 C (しばしば複合語で) a particular area of activity or group of people or things 特定の範囲の活動, あるいは人々または物の集団→**〜界, 〜の世界, 〜の社会** ‖ *the world of sport/fashion/politics* スポーツ界・ファッション界・政界 *the medical/business/animal/natural world* 医学界・実業界・動物の世界・自然界 ▶定義 5 [単数扱い] the people in the world 世界中の人々→**人類, 人間** ‖ ***The whole world** seemed to know the news before me!* 世界中の人々が私よりも早くそのニュースを知っていたようだ. (私だけが知らされていなかったなんて, あんまりだ.) ▶定義 6 C a planet with life on it 生命体のいる惑星→**(生物の存在しそうな)天体, 星** ‖ *Do you believe there are other worlds out there, like ours?* あなたは, 宇宙に地球のように生物の住む星があると信じますか.

成句 **do sb a/the world of good** 略式 ▶定義 to have a very good effect on sb 〜にとても良い影響を持つ, もたらす→**大いに〜の役に立つ** ‖ *The holiday has done her the world of good.* 休暇は彼女に良い影響をもたらした.

**in the world** ▶定義 used to emphasize what you are saying 自分が言っている事を強調するために用いて→**一体全体, (否定を強調して)決して〜ない** ‖ *Everyone else is stressed but he doesn't seem to have a care in the world.* ほかのだれもが緊張しているが, 彼は全く不安がっているようには見えない. *There's no need to rush - we've got all the time in the world.* 急ぐ必要はないよ − 私たちには時間がたっぷりあるのだから. *What in the world are you doing?* 一体全体あなたは何をしているのですか.

**the outside world** ⇒ **OUTSIDE**[2]
**think the world of sb/sth** ⇒ **THINK**

**world-famous** 形 ▶定義 known all over the world 世界中で知られている→**世界的に有名な, 世界に名高い**

**worldly** /wə́ːrldli/ 形 ▶定義 1 connected with ordinary life, not with the spirit 霊魂にではな

く, 普通の生活に関係した➜**現世の, この世の, 世間の** ‖ *He left all his worldly possessions to his nephew.* 彼は財産をすべて甥(おい)に残した. ▶定義**2** having a lot of experience and knowledge of life and people 人生と人々について多くの経験や知識を持っている➜**世慣れた, 世知にたけた, 世渡りのうまい** ‖ *a sophisticated and worldly man* 洗練され世知にたけた男

**world war** [名] [C] ▶定義 a war that involves a lot of different countries 多くのさまざまな国を巻き込む戦争➜**世界大戦** ‖ *the Second World War* 第２次世界大戦 *World War One* 第１次世界大戦

**worldwide** /wə̀ːrldwáɪd/ [形][副] ▶定義 (happening) in the whole world 全世界で(の)➜**世界中に広まった, 世界中の[に]** ‖ *The product will be marketed worldwide.* その製品は世界中の市場に出されることになっている. *The situation has caused worldwide concern.* その状況は世界的な関心を呼んでいる.

**the World Wide Web** (または**the Web**) [名] [単数扱い] ([略]**WWW**) ▶定義 the international system of computers that makes it possible for you to see information from around the world on your computer 世界中からの情報を自分のコンピューター上で見られるようにする国際的なコンピューターの組織➜**ワールドワイドウェブ** ‖ *web pages* ウェブページ *a web site (= where a company, an organization, etc has information about itself on the Web)* ウェブサイト(= 企業, 団体などがウェブ上に所有している, それ自身についての情報のある所) ☛参 **the Internet**

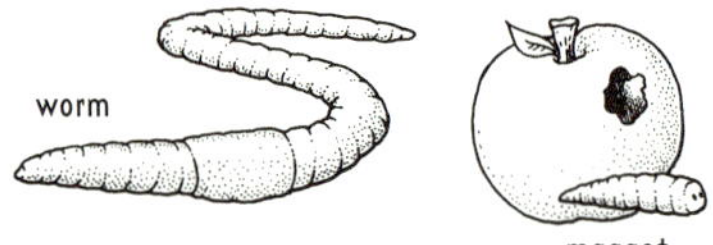


**worm**[1] /wəːrm/ [名] [C] ▶定義**1** a small animal with a long thin body and no eyes, bones or legs 細長い体で, 目や骨, 脚のない小さな動物➜**虫, 蠕虫(せんちゅう)** ‖ *an earthworm* みみず ▶定義**2** **worms** [複数扱い] one or more worms that live inside a person or an animal and may cause disease 人や動物の体内に住み, 病気の原因になることもある虫➜**寄生虫** ‖ *He's got worms.* 彼の体内には寄生虫がいる.

**worm**[2] /wəːrm/ [動][他] ▶定義 worm your way/yourself along, through, etc to move slowly or with difficulty in the direction mentioned 示された方向にゆっくりとまたは困難を伴いながら移動する➜**～をのろのろと進む, 徐々に前進する** ‖ *I managed to worm my way through the crowd.* 私は群衆の間をはうように何とか進んだ.

[句動詞] worm your way/yourself into sth ▶定義 to make sb like you or trust you, in order to dishonestly gain an advantage for yourself 自分自身の利益を不正に得るため, 人に自分を気に入らせたり信用させる➜**～に巧妙に取り入る**

**worn** WEAR[1] の過去分詞形

**worn-out** [形] ▶定義**1** too old or damaged to use any more これ以上使用できないほど古くなったり駄目になった➜**使い古した, 擦り切れた** ‖ *My shoes are completely worn-out.* 私の靴はすっかり擦り切れてしまっている. ▶定義**2** extremely tired 極度に疲れた➜**疲れきった, 疲労困憊(こんぱい)の** ‖ *I'm absolutely worn-out. I think I'll go to bed early.* 私はすっかり疲れきっている. 早く寝ることにしよう. ☛参 **wear**

***worried** /wʌ́rid; wə́ːrid/ [形] ▶定義 worried (about sb/sth); worried (that...) thinking that sth bad might happen or has happened 悪い物事が起きるのではないか, または起きているのではないかと考えて➜**心配している, 不安な** ‖ *Don't look so worried. Everything will be all right.* そんなにくよくよした顔付きをしないで. すべてうまくいくよ. *I'm **worried sick** about the exam.* 私は試験のことがひどく心配だ. *We were **worried stiff** (= extremely worried) that you might have had an accident.* あなたが事故に遭ったのかもしれないと, 私たちはとても心配した(= 極度に心配した).

***worry**[1] /wʌ́ri; wə́ːri/ [動] (現分**worrying**; 三単現**worries**; 過, 過分**worried**) ▶定義**1** [自] worry (about sb/sth) to think that sth bad might happen or has happened 悪い物事が起きるのではないか, または起きているのではないかと考える➜**心配する, 気に病む, 悩む** ‖ *Don't worry - I'm sure everything will be all right.* くよくよしないで ― きっとすべてうまくいくよ. *There's*

W

*nothing to worry about.* 心配することは何もない. *He worries if I don't phone every weekend.* 私が毎週末電話しないと, 彼は心配する. ▶定義2 [他] worry sb/yourself (about sb/sth) to make sb/yourself think that sth bad might happen or has happened 悪い物事が起きるのではないか, または起きているのではないかと, 人や自分自身に思わせる➜**心配する, 気をもむ; ～を心配させる, ～の気をもませる** ‖ *What worries me is how are we going to get home?* 私が気をもんでいる事は, 私たちがどうやって家に帰るかということだ. *She worried herself sick when he was away in the army.* 彼が入隊していた時, 彼女は病気になるほど心配した. ▶定義3 [他] worry sb (with sth) to disturb sb; to bother sb ～を悩ませる; ～を困らせる➜**～を心配させる, 苦しめる** ‖ *I'm sorry to worry you with my problems but I really do need some advice.* 私の問題であなたを悩ませてごめんなさい. けれども本当に助言が必要なのです.

[成句] not to worry ▶定義 it is not important; it doesn't matter 重要ではない; 問題ではない➜**くよくよするな, 心配するな**

***worry**[2] /wʌ́ri; wə́ːri/ [名] ([複] **worries**) ▶定義1 [U] the state of worrying about sth 何かについて心配している状態➜**心配, 不安, 悩み, 苦労** ‖ *His son has caused him a lot of worry recently.* 最近, 彼は息子が悩みの種となっている. ▶定義2 [C] something that makes you worry; a problem 心配させるもの, 問題➜**心配事, 苦労の種** ‖ *Crime is a real worry for old people.* 犯罪は老人にとって本当に心配の種だ. *financial worries* 金銭上の心配事 — worrying [形]➜**(事態が)気をもませる, 気懸かりな** ‖ *a worrying situation* 気懸かりな状況

***worse** /wəːrs/ [形][副] (bad, badly の比較級) ▶定義1 not as good or as well as sth else ほかの～と比べて良くない, または良くなく➜**より悪い[く], より劣った[て], もっとひどい[く]** ‖ *My exam results were **far**/**much** worse than I thought they would be.* 試験結果は私が思っていたよりも, はるかに・ずっと悪かった. *She speaks German **even worse** than I do.* 彼女はドイツ語を話すのが私よりもさらに下手だ. ▶定義2 (名詞の前は不可) more ill; less well より不健康で; より優れない➜**(体の具合が)より悪い, もっと(気分が)優れない** ‖ *If you **get** any **worse** we'll call the doctor.* あなたの体調がもっと悪くなったら, 医者を呼びますよ. — worse [名] [U]➜**一層悪い事・物** ‖ *The situation was already bad but there was worse to come.* 状況は既に悪かったが, さらに悪化することが予想された.

[成句] to make matters/things worse ▶定義 to make a situation, problem, etc even more difficult or dangerous than before➜**状況, 問題などを以前よりもっと困難または危険にする**

none the wiser/worse ⇒ **NONE**[2]

the worse for wear [略式] ▶定義 damaged; not in good condition 損害を受けた; 良い状態にない➜**(長期の使用で)古くなっている, 傷んでいる, くたびれている** ‖ *This suitcase looks a bit the worse for wear.* このスーツケースは少し傷んでいるように見える.

worse luck! (口語) ▶定義 unfortunately 不運にも➜**ついてないなあ, 運の悪いことに** ‖ *The dentist says I need three fillings, worse luck!* 歯医者は, 3箇所詰める必要があると言っている. ついてないなあ.

**worsen** /wə́ːrs(ə)n/ [動][自][他] ▶定義 to become worse or to make sth worse 悪くなる; ～を悪くさせる➜**悪化する; ～を悪化させる** ‖ *Relations between the two countries have worsened.* その2国の関係は悪化した.

**worship** /wə́ːrʃəp/ [動] (**worshipping**; **worshipped**: [米] **worshiping**; **worshiped**) ▶定義1 [自][他] to pray to and show respect for God or a god 神に祈り, 敬意を示す➜**(神を)崇拝する, 礼拝する** ‖ *People travel from all over the world to worship at this shrine.* この聖堂で祈りをささげるために, 世界中から人々がはるばるとやって来る. ▶定義2 [他] to love or admire sb/sth very much ～を強く愛するまたは賞賛する➜**～を熱愛する, 大切にする, 賛美する** ‖ *She worshipped her husband.* 彼女は夫を熱愛していた. — worship [名] [U]➜**礼拝, 崇拝, 賛美, 礼賛, 熱愛** ‖ *Different religions have different forms of worship.* 宗教によって礼拝の形式が異なる. — worshipper [名] [C]➜**崇拝者**

***worst**[1] /wəːrst/ [形][副] (bad, badly の最上級) ▶定義 the least pleasant or suitable; the least

W

well 最も心地良くない、または最も適切でない; 最も良くない→**最も悪い; 最も悪く** ‖ *It's been the worst winter that I can remember.* 覚えている限りでは、この冬が最悪だ. *A lot of the children behaved badly but my son behaved worst of all!* 多くの子供たちの行儀は悪かったが、中でも私の息子は一番ひどかった.

**worst**² /wəːrst/ 图 [単数扱い] ▶定義 something that is as bad as it can be 可能な限り悪いもの→**最も悪い事[物・人], 最悪(の事態)** ‖ *My parents always expect the worst if I'm late.* 私の両親は、私が遅くなるといつも最悪の事態を予想する.

成句 **at (the) worst** ▶定義 if the worst happens or if you consider sb/sth in the worst way もしも最悪の事態が起きたら[起きても], またはだれか・何かを最悪に考えるとしたら[しても]→**最悪の場合でも, せいぜい** ‖ *The problem doesn't look too serious. At worst we'll have to make a few small changes.* その問題はそれほど深刻には見えない. 最悪の場合でも、いくつかの小さな変更をしなければならない程度だろう.

**if the worst comes to the worst** ▶定義 if the worst possible situation happens もしも考えられる最悪の事態が発生したら→**最悪の事態が訪れたら, 万一の場合には**

***worth**¹ /wəːrθ/ 形 ▶定義 **1** having a particular value (in money) ある特定の(金銭的)価値を持つ→**〜の価値がある, 値打ちがある** ‖ *How much do you think that house is worth?* あの家はいくらの価値があると思いますか. ▶定義 **2** worth doing, etc used as a way of recommending or advising 推薦する, または助言するときの方法として用いる→**〜する価値がある, 〜するに値する** ‖ *That museum's well worth visiting if you have time.* その博物館は、時間があれば訪れる価値が十分にある. *The library closes in 5 minutes - it's not worth going in.* その図書館はあと5分で閉館だ — 入ってもしょうがないよ.

▶「その車を修理する価値はない」と言うとき、*It isn't worth repairing the car.* と *The car isn't worth repairing.* のどちらも用いることができる.

▶定義 **3** enjoyable or useful to do or have, even if it means extra cost, effort, etc 費用, 労力などが余計にかかるとしても、する, または持つことが楽しい, 有益な→**(時間や労力をかける)価値がある** ‖ *It takes a long time to walk to the top of the hill but it's worth the effort.* 丘の上まで歩くには長時間かかるが、その労力に値する. *Don't bother cooking a big meal. It isn't worth it - we're not hungry.* わざわざごちそうを作らなくていいですよ — そんな必要はありません、私たちはおなかがすいていませんから.

成句 **get your money's worth** ⇒**MONEY**

**worth sb's while** ▶定義 helpful, useful or interesting to sb 〜にとって役立つ, 有益な, 面白い→**(人が)やってみるだけの価値のある**

**worth**² /wəːrθ/ 图 **U** ▶定義 **1** the value of sb/sth; how useful sb/sth is は 〜の価値; どれほど〜が有益であるか→**価値, 値打ち; 有用さ** ‖ *She has proved her worth as a member of the team.* 彼女はチームメンバーとしての自分の価値を証明した. ▶定義 **2** the amount of sth that the money mentioned will buy 示された金額で買える物の量→**(〜だけの)分量, 〜相当量** ‖ *ten pounds' worth of petrol* 10ポンド相当のガソリン ▶定義 **3** the amount of sth that will last for the time mentioned 示された期間続く物の量→**(〜だけの)分量, 〜相当量** ‖ *two days' worth of food* 2日分の食料

**worthless** /wə́ːrθləs/ 形 ▶定義 **1** having no value or use 価値や用途がない→**無価値の, 値打ちのない, 役に立たない** ‖ *It's worthless - it's only a bit of plastic!* これは価値がない — ただのプラスチック片だ. ▶定義 **2** (used about a person) having bad qualities (人について)悪い性格を持っている→**役立たずの, 無能な, 下らない**

☞参 **priceless, valuable, invaluable**

**worthwhile** /wə̀ːrθ(h)wáɪl/ 形 ▶定義 enjoyable, useful or satisfying enough to be worth the cost or effort 費用や労力に値するほど楽しい, 有益な, 満足する→**やりがいがある, 価値がある** ‖ *Working for so little money just isn't worthwhile.* そんなに少ない金のために働くことは、ちっとも価値がない.

***worthy** /wə́ːrði/ 形 (**worthier; worthiest**) ▶定義 **1** worthy of sth/to do sth good enough for sth or to have sth 〜に足る良さがある, 〜を持つに足る良さがある→**〜に値する, 〜するに足る, ふさわしい** ‖ *He felt he was not worthy to accept such responsibility.* 自分はそのような責任を引き受けるには値しないと、彼は感じた. ▶定義 **2**

國that should receive respect, support or attention 尊敬を受ける,支援される,または注目されるべき→尊敬すべき,賞賛すべき,立派な,相応の,ふさわしい ‖ *a worthy leader* 立派な指導者 *a worthy cause* 立派な目的

\***would** /wəd, (ə)d 強形 wʊd/ 法助動詞(短縮形 **'d**; 否定形 **would not**; 短縮形 **wouldn't** /wʊdnt/)
▶定義1 used when talking about the result of an event that you imagine 想像する出来事の結果について話すときに用いて→～でしょう,～だろう ‖ *He would be delighted if you went to see him.* あなたが会いに行けば,彼はきっと喜ぶでしょう. *She'd be stupid not to accept.* 彼女がそれを受け入れないなら,ばかだね. *I would have done more, if I'd had the time.* 私に時間があれば,もっとできたのに. ▶定義2 used for asking sb politely to do sth 人に何かをするよう丁寧に頼むために用いて→～していただけますか ‖ *Would you come this way, please?* こちらに来ていただけますか. ▶定義3 used with 'like' or 'love' as a way of asking or saying what sb wants 人が何が欲しいかを尋ねるまたは言う方法として,like または love と用いて→～したいと思う,～が頂きたい ‖ *Would you like to come with us?* 私たちと一緒に行きませんか. *I'd love a piece of cake.* (私は)ケーキ(の注文)をお願いします. ▶定義4 to agree or be ready to do sth 何かをすることに同意する,または進んでする→～するつもりである,～する意志がある ‖ *She just wouldn't do what I asked her.* 彼女は私が頼んだことをする気が全くない. ▶定義5 used as the past form of 'will' when you report what sb says or thinks 人が話すこと,または考えていることを報告するときに,willの過去形として用いて→～するつもりだ,～しよう,～することになる ‖ *They said that they would help us.* 彼らは,私たちを手伝いましょうと言った. *She didn't think that he would do a thing like that.* 彼女は,彼がそのような事をする(つもりだ)とは思わなかった. ▶定義6 used after 'wish' wish の後に用いて→～してくれれば ‖ *I wish the sun would come out.* 太陽が出てくれればなあ. ▶定義7 used for talking about things that often happened in the past 過去にしばしば起きた事について話すのに用いて→よく～したものだ,～するのが常だった ‖ *When he was young he would often walk in these woods.* 若いころ,彼はよくこの森を散歩したものだ. ▶定義8 used for commenting on behaviour that is typical of sb ある人に典型的な振る舞いについて意見を言うのに用いて→いつも・決まって～する ‖ *You would say that. You always support him.* あなたならそう言うでしょう.いつも彼の味方だから. ▶定義9 used when you are giving your opinion but are not certain that you are right 自分の見解を述べたいが,正しいかどうかはっきりしないときに用いて→おそらく～でしょう ‖ *I'd say she's about 40.* 彼女はおそらく40歳くらいでしょう.
▶法助動詞についての説明は,巻末の「文法早見表」を参照.

> ▶語法
>
> 過去の習慣の would は状態動詞をとらない
>
> would も used to も使える場合の微妙な意味の違いを考える前に,used to は使えても would が使えない動詞があることに注意しましょう. would の後には動作動詞しか来ません.したがって,「子供のころはチョコが好きだった」の意味で *I would like chocolate when I was a little boy.* と言うことはできません.この場合は,I used to like chocolate... としなければいけません. used to は動作動詞・状態動詞の両方と一緒に使うことができるからです. *There used to be a castle here.* とは言えますが, \**There would be a castle here.* とは言えないのです.

\***wound**¹ /wuːnd, ( 古 ・ 詩 ) wáond/ 名 C
▶定義 an injury to part of your body, especially a cut, often one received in fighting 体の部分の傷,特に切り傷,多くは争っているときに受けたもの→傷,外傷,けが ‖ *a bullet wound* 弾傷
成句 rub salt into the wound/sb's wounds ⇒ **RUB**

**wound**² /wuːnd/ 動他(通常は受動態で)
▶定義1 to injure sb's body with a weapon ～の体を武器で傷付ける→～を傷付ける,負傷させる ‖ *He was wounded in the leg during the war.* 彼は戦争中に足を負傷した. ☛参 hurt の注
▶定義2 正式 to hurt sb's feelings deeply 人の感情を深く傷付ける→傷付ける,害する ‖ *I was*

wounded by his criticism. 私は彼の批判に深く傷付けられた. — wounded /wúːndəd/ 形 →傷付いた, 負傷した, (感情が) 傷付けられた ‖ a wounded soldier 負傷兵 — the wounded 名 [複数扱い] →負傷者(たち) ‖ Paramedics tended to the wounded at the scene of the explosion. 救命救急隊は, 爆発の現場にいる負傷者を助けに向かった.

**wound³** /wáund/ WIND³ の過去・過去分詞形
**wove** WEAVE の過去形
**woven** WEAVE の過去分詞形
**wow** /wáu/ 間 略式 ▶定義 used for expressing that you are very impressed and surprised by sth 何かにとても感銘している, または驚いていることを表現するのに用いて→わあ, おやまあ ‖ Wow! What a fantastic boat! わあ. 何てすてきなボートだ.

**WP** 略 word processing; word processor→文書処理; ワードプロセッサー

**wrangle** /ræŋɡ(ə)l/ 名 C ▶定義 a noisy or complicated argument やかましいまたは込み入った論争→口論, 論争, 言い争い ‖ The company is involved in **a legal wrangle** over copyrights. その会社は著作権に関する法的な論争に巻き込まれている. — wrangle 動 自 →口論・論争する, 言い争う

**wrap**

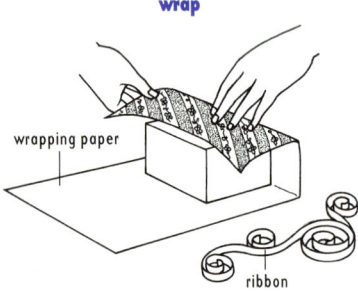

wrapping paper

ribbon

*__wrap__ /ræp/ 動 他 (**wrapping**; **wrapped**) ▶定義 1 wrap sb/sth (up) (in sth) to put paper or cloth around sb/sth as a cover 覆いとして～に紙または布を巻く→～を(…で)包む, くるむ ‖ to wrap up a present 贈り物を包む The baby was found wrapped in a blanket. その赤ん坊は毛布でくるまれて発見された. ▶定義 2 wrap sth round/around sb/sth to tie sth such as paper or cloth around an object or a part of the body 物または体の一部に, 例えば紙または布を巻く→～を…に巻き付ける ‖ The man had a bandage wrapped round his head. その男は頭に包帯を巻いていた.

成句 be wrapped up in sb/sth ▶定義 to be very involved and interested in sb/sth ～に深くかかわり合って興味がある→～に没頭している, ～に夢中になっている ‖ They were completely wrapped up in each other. They didn't notice I was there. 彼らはすっかりお互いに心を奪われていて, 私がそこにいるのに気が付かなかった.

句動 wrap (sb/yourself) up ▶定義 to put warm clothes on sb/yourself 人・自分自身に暖かい衣服を着せる, 着る→～をくるめる, くるまる

**wrapper** /rǽpər/ 名 C ▶定義 the piece of paper or plastic which covers sth when you buy it ～を買うときに, それを覆う1枚の紙またはプラスチック→包装紙, 包み紙 ‖ a sweet/chocolate wrapper 菓子・チョコレートの包み紙

**wrapping** /rǽpɪŋ/ 名 C U ▶定義 paper, plastic, etc that is used for covering sth in order to protect it ～を保護するために覆いに使われる紙, プラスチックなど→包装用材料, 包装紙 ‖ Remove the wrapping before heating the pie. パイを温める前に包装紙を外しなさい.

**wrapping paper** 名 U ▶定義 paper which is used for putting round presents 贈り物をくるむために使われる紙→包装紙 ☞ wrap のさし絵

**wrath** /rɔ(ː)θ; ræθ, rɑːð/ 名 U (文) ▶定義 very great anger とても強い怒り→激怒, 憤怒

**wreak** /riːk/ 動 他 正式 ▶定義 wreak sth (on sb/sth) to cause great damage or harm to sb/sth ～へ大きな損害または傷害を引き起こす→(～に)(怒り)を浴びせる, (危害・罰)を加える, (復讐(ふくしゅう))をする ‖ Fierce storms **wreak havoc** at this time of year. この季節にはすさまじいあらしが荒れ狂う.

**wreath** /riːθ/ 名 C (複 **wreaths** /riːðz, -θs/)
▶定義 a circle of flowers and leaves, especially one that you give to the family of sb who has died 花と葉の輪, 特に亡くなった人の家族へ与えるもの→花輪

**wreck** /rek/ 名 ▶定義 1 C a ship that has sunk or been badly damaged at sea 海に沈んだ, または海上でひどく破壊された船→難破船, 難破物

の残骸(ざんがい) ‖ *Divers searched the wreck.* ダイバーたちがその難破船を捜索した. ▶定義2 ●a car, plane, etc which has been badly damaged, especially in an accident 特に事故で, ひどく破壊された車, 飛行機など→**事故の残骸, 破損車** ‖ *The car was a wreck but the lorry escaped almost without damage.* その車はひどく破壊されたが, トラックはほとんど損害がなかった. ▶定義3 [●, 通常は単数] 略式 a person or thing that is in a very bad condition とてもひどい状態にある人または物→**(病気で)やせ衰えた人, 弱った人, 打ちひしがれた人** ‖ *He drove so badly I was **a nervous wreck** when we got there.* 彼がひどい運転をしたので, そこへ着いた時, 私は神経が参っていた.— wreck 動他→**～を大破させる, 破壊する, (計画)をぶち壊す, (体を)損ねる** ‖ *Vandals had wrecked the school hall.* 心ない破壊者たちがその学校の講堂を破壊した. *The strike wrecked all our holiday plans.* そのストライキは, 私たちの休暇の計画をすべて駄目にした.

**wreckage** /rékɪdʒ/ 名 ① ▶定義 the broken pieces of sth that has been destroyed 破壊された物の破片→**残骸(ざんがい), 名残** ‖ *Investigators searched the wreckage of the plane for evidence.* 捜査官が証拠を求めて飛行機の残骸を捜索した.

**wrench**¹ /rentʃ/ 動他 ▶定義1 wrench sb/sth (away, off, etc) to pull or turn sb/sth strongly and suddenly ～を強く突然引っ張る, または向きを変える→**～をねじる, ひねる** ‖ *They had to wrench the door off the car to get the driver out.* 運転手を救出するために, 彼らは車のドアをこじ開け, 取り外さなければならなかった. (比喩) *The film was so exciting that I could hardly wrench myself away.* その映画は非常に面白かったので, 私は全く席を立てなかった.
▶定義2 to injure part of your body by turning it suddenly 体を突然ねじってその一部を傷付ける→**～を捻挫(ねんざ)する, ～の筋を違える**

**wrench**² /rentʃ/ 名 ▶定義1 ●a sudden, violent pull or turn 急激に激しく引く[引かれる]こと, または向きを変える[変えられる]こと→**ねじり, ひねり, 捻挫(ねんざ), 筋違い** ‖ *With a wrench I managed to open the door.* 無理やりひねって, 私は何とかドアを開けた. ▶定義2 [単数扱い] the sadness you feel because you have to leave sb/sth 人から去らなければならない, または物を捨てなければならないために感じる悲しみ→**(別れの)悲しみ, 悲痛, 苦痛** ▶定義3 ● 米 = SPANNER

**wrestle** /résəl/ 動圓 ▶定義1 wrestle (with) sb to fight by trying to get hold of your opponent's body and throw him/her to the ground. People wrestle as a sport. 相手の体をつかみ, 地面へ投げ飛ばそうとして戦う. 人々はスポーツとしてレスリングをする→**レスリングをする, 相撲を取る, 格闘する** ‖ *He managed to wrestle the man to the ground and take the knife from him.* 彼は何とかその男を地面に組み伏せて, その手からナイフを奪った. ▶定義2 wrestle (with sth) to try hard to deal with sth that is difficult 難しい～を処理しようと熱心に試みる→**(問題に)取り組む, 全力を尽くす, (誘惑と)戦う**

**wrestling** /résəlɪŋ/ 名 ① ▶定義 a sport in which two people fight and try to throw each other to the ground 2人が戦って, お互いを地面に投げ飛ばそうとする競技→**レスリング, 相撲** ‖ *a wrestling match* レスリングの試合 — wrestler 名 ●→**レスリングの選手, レスラー, 力士**

**wretch** /retʃ/ 名 ●(古) ▶定義 a poor, unhappy person 貧しく不幸な人→**哀れな人, 惨めな人** ‖ *The poor wretch was clearly starving.* その哀れな人は明らかに飢えていた.

**wretched** /rétʃəd/ 形 ▶定義1 very unhappy 非常に不幸な→**惨めな, 悲惨な, 哀れな** ▶定義2 略式 used for expressing anger 怒りを表現するのに用いて→**いまいましい, ろくでもない** ‖ *That wretched dog has chewed up my slippers again!* あのいまいましい犬がまた私のスリッパをかんでしまった.

**wriggle** /rígəl/ 動圓他 ▶定義1 wriggle (about/ around) to move about, or to move a part of your body, with short, quick movements, especially from side to side 動き回る, あるいは体の一部を短く素早く, 特に左右に動かす→**(みみずが)のたくる, (人が)身をよじる, 体をくねらせる** ‖ *The baby was wriggling around on my lap.* 赤ん坊が私のひざの上でもがいていた. *She wriggled her fingers about in the hot sand.* 彼女は熱い砂の中で指をくねらせた. ▶定義2 to move in the direction mentioned by making quick turning movements 素早く回転して、示された方向へ移動する➡体をくねらせて進む∥ *The worm wriggled back into the soil.* その虫はのたくりながら土の中へ戻っていった.

句動詞 wriggle out of sth/doing sth 略式 ▶定義 to avoid sth by making clever excuses うまい言い訳をして～を避ける➡(困難)を切り抜ける,(仕事)を逃れる,しないで済ます∥ *It's your turn to wash up - you can't wriggle out of it this time!* あなたが食器を洗う番ですよ － 今度は逃れられませんよ.

**wring** /rɪŋ/ 動⊕(過, 過分 **wrung** /rʌŋ/) ▶定義 wring sth (out) to press and squeeze sth in order to remove water from it 水を取り除くために～を押しつぶす➡(衣類)を絞る

**wrinkle**¹ /rɪ́ŋk(ə)l/ 名 C ▶定義 a small line in sth, especially one on the skin of your face which you get as you grow older 物にある小さな線,特に年を取るにつれて顔の皮膚にできるもの➡しわ∥ *She's got fine wrinkles around her eyes.* 彼女は目の回りに小じわがある. *Smooth out the wrinkles in the fabric.* 布地のしわを伸ばしなさい. ☞参 furrow — wrinkled /rɪ́ŋk(ə)ld/ 形▶しわの寄った,しわだらけの

**wrinkle**² /rɪ́ŋk(ə)l/ 動⊜⊕ ▶定義 wrinkle (sth) (up) to form small lines and folds in sth ～に小さな線や折り目を形づくる➡しわが寄る;～にしわを寄せる,∥ *She wrinkled her nose at the nasty smell.* 彼女は不快なにおいに鼻にしわを寄せた. *My skirt had wrinkled up on the journey.* 私のスカートが旅行中にしわになっていた.

★**wrist** /rɪst/ 名 C ▶定義 the narrow part at the end of your arm where it joins your hand 手とつながる腕の端の狭い部分➡手首 ☞ C5ページのさし絵

**wristwatch** /rɪ́stwɒtʃ, -wɔ́ːtʃ/ 名 C ▶定義 a watch on a strap which you wear round your arm near your hand 腕の,手に近い部分の回りにはめる,ベルトに付いている時計➡腕時計

**writ** /rɪt/ 名 C ▶定義 a legal order to do or not to do sth, given by a court of law ～をする、またはしないようにと裁判所から与えられる法的な命令➡令状

★**write** /raɪt/ 動(過 **wrote** /roʊt/; 過分 **written** /rɪ́tn/) ▶定義1 自⊕ to make words, letters, etc, especially on paper using a pen or pencil 言葉や文字などを,特にペンまたは鉛筆を使って紙に書く➡書く,記入する;～を書く,～を記入する∥ *I can't write with this pen.* 私はこのペンでは書けません. *Write your name and address on the form.* その用紙にあなたの氏名と住所を記入しなさい. ▶定義2 ⊕ to create a book, story, song, etc in written form for people to read or use 人々が読むまたは使うために、書物,物語,歌などを文書の形で創作する➡～を書く,執筆する,～を作詞・作曲する∥ *Tolstoy wrote 'War and Peace'.* トルストイは『戦争と平和』を執筆した. *He wrote his wife a poem.* 彼は妻に詩を書いた. *Who wrote the music for that film?* あの映画の音楽を作曲したのはだれですか.

▶定義3 自⊕ write (sth) (to sb); write (sb) sth to write and send a letter, etc to sb ～にあてて手紙などを書いて送る➡手紙を書く;(人に)(手紙など)を書く,出す∥ *I've written a letter to my son./I've written my son a letter.* 私は息子あてに手紙を書いた. *I've written to him.* 私は彼に手紙を書いた.

▶アメリカ英語では、I've written him. とも言える.

*She wrote that they were all well and would be home soon.* 彼女は,彼らが皆元気ですぐに家に戻ると手紙を書いた. *She phones every week and writes occasionally.* 彼女は毎週電話をし,時々手紙を書く. ▶定義4 ⊕ write sth (out) (for sb) to fill or complete a form, cheque, document, etc with the necessary information 人のために用紙,小切手,文書などに必要な情報を記入するまたは仕上げる➡必要事項を記入する,～に書き入れる∥ *I wrote out a cheque for £10.* 私は10ポンドの小切手を切った.

句動詞 write back (to sb) ▶定義 to send a reply to sb ～に返事を送る➡(～に)手紙の返事を書く

write sth down ▶定義 to write sth on paper, especially so that you can remember it 特に後で思い出すことができるよう,紙に～を書く➡～を書き留める,書き記す∥ *Did you write down Jon's address?* あなたはジョンの住所を書き留めましたか.

write in (to sb/sth) (for sth) ▶定義 to write a letter to an organization, etc to ask for sth, give an opinion, etc 物を頼む,意見を述べるなどの

ために団体などに手紙を書き送る➔投書する, (〜を)手紙で請求・注文する

write off/away (to sb/sth) (for sth) ▶定義 to write a letter to an organization, etc to order sth or ask for sth 〜を注文するまたは頼むために団体などに手紙を書き送る➔請求・注文の手紙を出す

write sb/sth off ▶定義 to accept or decide that sb/sth will not be successful or useful 〜が成功しないまたは役に立たないことを受け入れる, あるいは決断する➔〜をなかったものとする, 〜をあきらめる ‖ *Don't write him off yet. He could still win.* まだ彼を見捨てないで. 彼はまだ勝てるかもしれない.

write sth off ▶定義 to accept that you will not get back an amount of money you have lost or spent 失ったまたは費やした金額が戻らないことを受け入れる➔〜を帳消しにする ‖ *to write off a debt* 負債を帳消しにする

write sth out ▶定義 to write the whole of sth on paper 紙に〜のすべてを書く➔〜を略さずに書く, 〜を書き上げる ‖ *Can you write out that recipe for me?* 私のために, あの料理の作り方を詳しく書いてくれませんか.

write sth up ▶定義 to write sth in a complete and final form, often using notes that you have made しばしば書き留めたメモを用いて, 〜を完全で最終的な形に書く➔〜を清書する, 最終稿にまとめる ‖ *to write up lecture notes* 講義録を清書する

**write-off** 名 C ▶定義 a thing, especially a vehicle, that is so badly damaged that it is not worth repairing ひどく壊れているので修理に値しない物, 特に乗り物➔(大破した車など)廃棄処分にするしかない物

\***writer** /ráɪtər/ 名 C ▶定義 a person who writes, especially one whose job is to write books, stories, etc 書く人, 特に書物, 物語などを書くことを仕事にしている人➔作家, 著述家, ライター, 記者

**writhe** /ráɪð/ 動 自 ▶定義 to turn and roll your body about 自分の体をくねらせて転がる➔身をよじる, 身もだえする ‖ *She was writhing in pain.* 彼女は痛みでもがき苦しんでいた.

\***writing** /ráɪtɪŋ/ 名 U ▶定義 1 words that have been written or printed; the way a person writes 書かれた, または印刷された言葉; 人が書く方法➔書き物; 筆跡, 書法, 書き方 ‖ *This card's got no writing inside. You can put your own message.* このカードの内側には何も書かれていません. ですから, あなた自身のメッセージを書き込むことができます. *I can't read your writing, it's too small.* 私はあなたの書いた文字が読めません. 文字が小さすぎます. ▶定義 2 the skill or activity of writing words 言葉を書く技能または行為➔書くこと, 習字 ‖ *He had problems with his reading and writing at school.* 彼は学校での読み書きに問題があった. ▶定義 3 the activity or job of writing books, etc 本などを書く行為または仕事➔執筆, 文筆(業), 著述(業) ‖ *It's difficult to earn much money from writing.* 執筆で多額の金を稼ぐのは難しい. ▶定義 4 the books, etc that sb has written or the style in which sb writes 人が書いた書物など, または人が書く形式➔著作, 作品, 文体 ‖ *Love is a common theme in his early writing.* 「愛」が彼の初期作品に共通のテーマだ.

成句 in writing ▶定義 in written form 書かれた形状で➔書面で, 文書にして ‖ *I'll confirm the offer in writing next week.* 私は来週申し出を書面で確認します.

**writing paper** 名 U ▶定義 paper for writing letters on 手紙を書くための紙➔便せん

**written**[1] **WRITE**の過去分詞形

**written**[2] /rítn/ 形 ▶定義 expressed on paper; not just spoken 紙の上に表現された; 単に話されただけではない➔書いた, 筆記の, 書面の ‖ *a written agreement* 合意書

\***wrong**[1] /rɔːŋ, rɑŋ/ 形 副 ▶定義 1 not correct; in a way that is not correct 正しくない方法で➔間違った, 誤った ‖ *the wrong answer* 正しくない答え *I always pronounce that word wrong.* 私はいつもあの単語を誤って発音してしまう. *You've got the wrong number (= on the telephone).* (=電話で)あなたは間違った番号にかけていますよ. *I think you're wrong about Nicola - she's not lazy.* あなたはニコラを誤解していると思う - 彼女は怠け者ではないよ. ⇔ **right** ▶定義 2 not the best; not suitable 最善ではない; 適切でない➔不適当な, 不適切な ‖ *That's the wrong way to hold the bat.* そのバットの握り方は良くない. *I think she married the wrong man.* 彼女

はふさわしくない男と結婚したと、私は思う. *I like him - I just think he's wrong for the job.* 私は彼が好きだ ― ただ彼がその仕事に合わないと思っているだけだ. ▶定義3 (名詞の前は不可) wrong (with sb/sth) causing problems or difficulties; not as it should be 問題や困難を引き起こしている；あるべき状態ではない→具合が悪い、おかしい、(機械が)故障で ‖ *You look upset. Is something wrong?* あなたは調子が悪そうだ. どうかしましたか. ***What's wrong** with the car this time?* 今度はその車のどこが故障しているのですか. *She's got something **wrong** with her leg.* 彼女は足の調子が悪い. ▶定義4 wrong (to do sth) not morally right or honest 道徳的に正しくない、または正直でない→悪い、不正な ‖ *It's **wrong** to tell lies.* うそをつくのは悪い事だ. *The man said that he had done nothing **wrong**.* その男は、自分は何も悪い事はしていないと言った.

成句 get on the right/wrong side of sb ⇒ SIDE¹

get sb wrong 略式 ▶定義 to not understand sb ~を理解しない→~を誤解する ‖ *Don't get me **wrong**! I don't dislike him.* 私を誤解しないで. 私は彼が嫌いではありません.

go wrong ▶定義1 to make a mistake 間違いをする→道を間違える、失敗する、ミスをする ‖ *I'm afraid we've gone **wrong**. We should have taken the other road.* 私たちは道を間違えたようだ. もう一方の道を行くべきだった. ▶定義2 to stop working properly or to stop developing well 適切に動作しなくなる、またはうまく発展しなくなる→(機械が)故障する ‖ *My computer's gone **wrong** and I've lost all my work.* 私のコンピューターが故障して、作業データがすべて失われてしまった.

get/start off on the right/wrong foot (with sb) ⇒ FOOT¹
on the right/wrong track ⇒ TRACK¹

**wrong**² /rɔːŋ, rɒŋ/ 名 ▶定義1 ❶things that are morally bad or dishonest 道徳的に悪いまたは不正直なこと→悪、不正、悪い事 ‖ *Children quickly learn the difference between **right** and **wrong**.* 子供たちはすぐに善と悪の違いを学ぶ. ▶定義2 ❷an action or situation which is not fair 公正ではない行為または状況→不正行為、悪行、不当な扱い ‖ *A terrible **wrong** has been done. Those men should never have gone to prison.* ひどい不正行為が行われていた. あの男たちは決して刑務所に送られるべきではなかった.

成句 in the wrong ▶定義 (used about a person) having made a mistake; whose fault sth is (人について)誤りを犯している；責任のある→(行動が)正しくない、間違っている

**wrong**³ /rɔːŋ, rɒŋ/ 動他 ▶定義 to do sth to sb which is bad or unfair ~に対して悪いまたは不正な事をする→~を不当に扱う、~にぬれぎぬを着せる ‖ *I **wronged** her when I said she was lying.* 私は彼女がうそをついていると言って、彼女を中傷した.

**wrongful** /rɔ́ːŋfʊl, rɒ́ŋ-, -f(ə)l/ 形 正式 (名詞の前だけ) ▶定義 not fair, not legal or not moral 公正でない、法律に沿っていない、または道徳的でない→不正な、違法な、不当な ‖ *He sued the company for **wrongful** dismissal.* 彼は不当解雇で会社を訴えた.

**wrongly** /rɔ́ːŋli, rɒ́ŋli/ 副 ▶定義 in a wrong or mistaken way 悪いまたは間違った方法で→不正に、違法に、不当に ‖ *He was **wrongly** accused of stealing money.* 彼は金を盗んだと不当に非難された.

▶副詞としてのwrongは、特に会話の中では、動詞または動詞の目的語の後に用いられる: *He's spelt my name **wrong**.* (彼は私の名前を間違ってつづった.) 副詞のwronglyは、特に過去分詞または動詞の前で用いられる: *My name's been **wrongly** spelt.* (私の名前は間違ってつづられた.)

**wrote** WRITE の過去形
**wrung** WRING の過去・過去分詞形

**wry** /rái/ 形 ▶定義 expressing both disappointment and amusement 失望と愉快さの両方を表している→(顔が)苦々しい、(顔を)しかめた ‖ *'Never mind,' she said with a **wry** grin. 'At least we got one vote.'* 「気にしないで」と彼女は苦笑いをしながら言った. 「少なくとも私たちは1票を得られたのだから」― **wryly** 副 (顔を)しかめて

**wt** 略 weight→重量 ‖ *net wt 500g* 正味重量500グラム

**WWW** /dʌ́b(ə)ljuː dʌ́b(ə)ljuː dʌ́b(ə)ljuː/ 略 the World Wide Web→ワールドワイドウェブ

# X x

**X, x** /eks/ 名 C ( 複 X's; x's) ▶定義 the twenty-fourth letter of the English alphabet 英語アルファベットの第24文字→x(X)が表す音, x(X)の文字, x(X)の字形のもの ‖ *'Xylophone' begins with (an) 'X'*. XylophoneはXで始まる.
▶ 解答が間違っていることを示す場合, 教師はXを付ける. また, 人の名前の代わりにも使われ, その人の名前を知らないまたは言いたくない場合に用いる: *Mr and Mrs X* (某氏, 某夫人). 手紙の最後では, Xはキスを表す: *Lots of love, Mary XX* (たくさんの愛を込めて, メアリー キスキス)

**xenophobia** /zènoʊfóʊbiə, -nə-/ 名 U ▶定義 a fear or hatred of foreign people and cultures 外国の人・文化に対する恐怖心, 強い嫌悪→外国(人)嫌い, 外国(人)恐怖症 — **xenophobic** 形→外国(人)嫌いの, 外国(人)恐怖症の

**Xerox**™ /zíərɑks/ 名 C ▶定義 1 a machine that produces copies of letters, documents, etc 手紙, 書類などのコピーを取る機械→ゼロックス, 乾式コピー機 ▶定義 2 a copy produced by such a machine この機械で取ったコピー→ゼロックスでコピーした文書 ☛類 **photocopy** — **xerox** 動他→〜をゼロックスでコピーする, 〜をゼロックスで複写する

**XL** 略 extra large (size)→特大(サイズ)

**Xmas** /krísməs, éksməs/ 名 C U 略式 ▶定義 (文章で短縮形として用いて) Christmas→クリスマス ‖ *Happy Xmas (= written message in a Christmas card)* メリークリスマス (= クリスマスカードに書かれるメッセージ)

**X-ray** 名 C ▶定義 1 [通常は複数] a kind of light that makes it possible to see inside solid objects, for example the human body, so that they can be examined and a photograph of them can be made 固形物, 例えば人体の内部を見ることを可能にする光線の一種で, それにより対象物を検査することができ, またそれらの写真をとることが可能になる→エックス線, レントゲン ▶定義 2 a photograph that is made with an X-ray machine エックス線機器で撮影した写真→エックス線写真, レントゲン写真 ‖ *The X-ray showed that the bone was not broken.* レントゲン写真は, 骨折していないことを示していた. ☛参 **ray** — **X-ray** 動他→〜のレントゲン写真を撮る, 〜をエックス線検査する ‖ *She had her chest X-rayed.* 彼女は胸部のレントゲン写真を撮ってもらった.

**xylophone** /záɪloʊfòʊn, -lə-/ 名 C ▶定義 a musical instrument that consists of a row of wooden bars of different lengths. You play it by hitting these bars with a small hammer. 違う長さの木製の棒が並んでできている楽器. 小さなばちでそれらの棒をたたいて演奏する→木琴, シロフォン ☛参 **piano**の注 ☛ **music**のさし絵

# Y y

**Y, y** /wáɪ/ 名 C ( 複 Y's; y's) ▶定義 the twenty-fifth letter of the English alphabet 英語アルファベットの第25文字→y(Y)が表す音, y(Y)の文字, y(Y)の字形のもの ‖ *'Yawn, begins with (a) 'Y'*. YawnはYで始まる.

**yacht** /jɑt/ 名 C ▶定義 1 a boat with sails used for pleasure 楽しみのために帆走に使われる小さな船→スポーツ用小型帆船, ヨット ‖ *a yacht race* ヨットレース ▶定義 2 a large boat with a motor, used for pleasure 楽しみのために使われるモーターの付いた大きな船→大型ヨット, 快速船, クルーザー ☛参 **dinghy**

**yachting** /jɑtɪŋ/ 名 U ▶定義 the activity or sport of sailing or racing yachts ヨットに乗ること, スポーツとしてあるいは競技としての帆走→ヨット遊び, ヨット競争

**yachtsman** /jɑtsmən/ 名 C ( 複 **-men** /-mən/) ▶定義 a person who sails a yacht in races or for pleasure→レースであるいは楽しみのためにヨットを操縦する人(男性)

**yachtswoman** /jɑtswùmən/ 名 C ( 複 **-women** /-wìmən/) ▶定義 a woman who sails a yacht in races or for pleasure→レースであるいは楽しみのためにヨットを操縦する女性

**yank** /jæŋk/ 動 自 他 略式 ▶定義 to pull sth suddenly, quickly and hard 〜を急に, 素早く, 強い力で引く→(〜を)ぐいと引っ張る ‖ *She yanked at the door handle.* 彼女はドアのノブを

ぐいと引いた. — **yank** 名 ⓒ → 物をぐいと引っ張ること

**yap** /jæp/ 動 自 (**yapping**; **yapped**) ▶定義 (used about dogs, especially small ones) to make short, loud noises in an excited way (犬, 特に小さな犬について) 興奮した様子で短く, 耳障りな音を立てる →キャンキャンほえ立てる

\***yard** /jɑːrd/ 名 ⓒ ▶定義1 医 an area outside a building, usually with a hard surface and a wall or fence around it 建物の外側の区域で, 通常は表面が硬く, その周囲に塀または垣根を巡らせている →庭, 中庭 ‖ *a school/prison yard* 校庭・刑務所の中庭 ⟵参 **courtyard**, **churchyard**
▶定義2 米 = GARDEN¹(1) ▶定義3 (通常は複合語で) an area, usually without a roof, used for a particular type of work or purpose 多くは屋根のない, 特定の作業や目的のために使われる区域 →作業場, 製造場, 置き場 ‖ *a shipyard/boatyard* 造船所・艇庫 *a builder's yard* 建築業者の作業場

▶イギリス英語では, 家に付属した土地は, 芝生や花々などがある部分を garden, コンクリートや石で舗装されている部分を yard と呼ぶ. アメリカ英語では, 芝生の有無にかかわらず, yard と呼ぶ. C7ページのさし絵を参照.

▶定義4 (略式 **yd**) a measure of length; 0.914 of a metre. There are 3 feet in a yard. 長さの単位; 0.914メートルに相当する. 1ヤードは3フィート →ヤード, ヤール ‖ *Our house is 100 yards from the supermarket.* 私たちの家はスーパーマーケットから100ヤード(の所に)ある.

**yardstick** /jɑ́ːrdstìk/ 名 ⓒ ▶定義 a standard with which things can be compared 物事が比較されるときの基準 →判断・比較の基準, 尺度, 物差し ‖ *Exam results should not be the only yardstick by which pupils are judged.* 試験の結果だけで生徒を評価するべきではない.

**yarn** /jɑːrn/ 名 ▶定義1 Ⓤ thread (usually of wool or cotton) that has been prepared (**spun**) and is used for knitting, etc 準備されて (紡がれて), 編み物などに使われる糸 (通常はウールまたは綿) →編み物・織物用糸, 毛糸 ▶定義2 ⓒ 略式 a long story that sb tells, especially one that is invented or exaggerated 人が聞かせる長い話, 特にでっち上げた話やおおげさな話 →長話, ほら話

\***yawn** /jɔːn/ 動 自 ▶定義 to open your mouth wide and breathe in deeply, especially when you are tired or bored 特に疲れているときや退屈しているときに, 口を大きく開いて深く息を吸い込む →あくびをする ‖ *I kept yawning all through the lecture.* 講演の間, あくびばかりしていた. — **yawn** 名 ⓒ →あくび ‖ *'How much longer will it take?' he said with a yawn.*「さらにどのくらい時間がかかるの」と彼はあくびをしながら言った.

**yd** (複 **yds**) 略 yard ▶定義 a measure of length 長さの単位 →ヤード

**yeah** /jeə, jæə/ 間 略式 ▶定義 yes →ええ, うん, そう

\***year** /jɪər, jəːr/ 名 ▶定義1 ⓒ (または **calendar year**) the period from 1 January to 31 December, 365 or 366 days divided into 12 months or 52 weeks 1月1日から12月31日までの365日または366日の期間で, 12か月または52週に区切られている →(暦の上の)年 ‖ *last year/this year/next year* 去年・今年・来年 *The population of the country will be 70 million by the year 2010.* その国の人口は, 2010年までに7000万人になるだろう. *Interest is paid on this account once a year.* この口座の利息は, 年に1回支払われる. *a leap year* (= one that has 366 days) うるう年 (= 366日ある年) *the New Year* (= the first days of January) 新年 (= 1月初めの数日間) ▶定義2 any period of 12 months, measured from any date 任意の日から数えられた12か月間 →(12か月から成る)年, 1年間 ‖ *She worked here for twenty years.* 彼女はここで20年働いた. *He left school just over a year ago.* 彼はちょうど1年前に退学 [卒業] した. *In a year's time, you'll be old enough to vote.* 1年したら, あなたも投票できる年齢になる.
▶定義3 ⓒ a period of 12 months in connection with schools, the business world, etc 学校や実業界などに関連した12か月間 →学年, 年度 ‖ *the academic/school year* 大学・学校の学年度 *the tax/financial year* 課税年度, 会計年度 ▶定義4 ⓒ 主に 医 (used in schools, universities, etc) the level that a particular student is at (学校や大学などについて) ある特定の学生が学んでいるレベル →〜年生 ‖ *My son is in year ten now.* 私の息子は現在高校1年生だ. *The first-years* (= stu-

*dents in their first year at school/university, etc) do French as a compulsory subject.* 1年生(=学校・大学などに入って1年目の学生)ではフランス語が必修科目になっている. *He was a year below me at school.* 彼は, 学校では私よりも1年下だった. ▶定義5 [**C**, 通常は複数] (used in connection with the age of sb/sth) a period of 12 months (人や物の年に関連して用いて) 12 か月間 ➔ ~歳, ~年 ‖ *He's ten years old today.* 彼は今日で10歳だ. *a six-year-old daughter* 6歳の娘 *This car is nearly five years old.* この車は, 製造されてからもう少しで5年になる. *The company is now in its fifth year.* その会社は5年目に入っている.

➤ He's ten. または He's ten years old. という言い方はするが, He's ten years. や a ten-years-old boy とは言わない. age の注を参照.

▶定義 **6 years** [複数扱い] a long time 長い間 ➔ 長年, 何年もの間 ‖ *It happened years ago.* それは何年も前に起きた. *I haven't seen him for years.* 彼には長い間会っていない.

成句 **all year round** ▶定義 for the whole year 1年の間ずっと ➔ 一年中

**donkey's years** ⇒ **DONKEY**

**year after year; year in year out** ▶定義 every year for many years 長年にわたって毎年 ➔ 来る年も来る年も, 毎年必ず, 年々歳々

\***yearly** /jíəɹli, jáːɹli/ 形副 ▶定義 (happening) every year or once a year 毎年, または1年に1回(起こる) ➔ 年1回(の), 例年(の) ‖ *The conference is held yearly.* その会議は毎年開催される.

**yearn** /jəːɹn/ 動自 (文) ▶定義 yearn (for sb/sth); yearn (to do sth) to want sb/sth very much, especially sth that you cannot have ~を, 特に自分が所有できない~を強く欲しがる ➔ ~にあこがれる, 切望する, 切に~したがる ― **yearning** 名 **C U** ➔ 切望, 強い思い, 熱望

**yeast** /jiːst/ 名 **U** ▶定義 a substance used for making bread rise and for making beer, wine, etc パンを膨らませたり, ビールやワインを醸造したりするために使う物質 ➔ イースト, 酵母(菌)

**yell** /jel/ 動自他 ▶定義 yell (out) (sth); yell (sth) (at sb/sth) to shout very loudly, often because you are angry, excited or in pain とても大きな声で叫ぶ, 大抵は怒っている, 興奮している, あるいは痛みを感じているため ➔ **大声を上げる, どなる; ~を大声で言う, ~を叫んで言う** ‖ *She yelled out his name.* 彼女は彼の名前を叫んだ. *There's no need to yell at me, I can hear you perfectly well.* 大きな声を出さなくてもいいよ, 君の声はちゃんと聞こえているから. ― **yell** 名 **C** ➔ 叫び声, わめき声

\***yellow** /jélou/ 名 **C U** 形 ▶定義 (of) the colour of lemons or butter レモンやバターのような色(をした) ➔ 黄色, 黄色の ‖ *a pale/light yellow dress* 淡い・明るい黄色の服 *a bright shade of yellow* 鮮やかな黄色 *the yellows and browns of the autumn leaves* 黄色や茶色に色付いた秋の木の葉

**yellow card** 名 **C** ▶定義 (used in football) a card that is shown to a player as a warning that he/she will be sent off the field if he/she behaves badly again (サッカーについて) 警告として選手に示されるカードで, 再び不当に振る舞った場合, 退場させられる ➔ イエローカード
☛参 **red card**

**yellowish** /jélouɪʃ/ 形 (または **yellowy** /jélouɪ/)
▶定義 slightly yellow in colour やや黄色を帯びた ➔ 黄色っぽい, 黄色がかった

**yellow line** 名 **C** 英 ▶定義 a yellow line at the side of a road to show that you can only park there for a limited time 道路の端の黄色い線で, 限られた時間だけ駐車できることを示す ➔ イエローライン ‖ *double yellow lines* (= you must not park there at all) ダブルイエローライン (= そこには駐車してはならない)

**the Yellow Pages**™ 名 [複数扱い] ▶定義 a telephone book (on yellow paper) that lists all the business companies, etc in a certain area in sections according to the goods or services they provide ある地域のすべての企業などを, その取り扱っている商品やサービスに従った業種別に, 一覧表示した (黄色い紙の) 電話帳 ➔ 職業別電話帳, イエローページ

**yelp** /jelp/ 動自 ▶定義 to give a sudden short cry, especially of pain 特に苦痛によって, 突然の短い叫び声を上げる ➔ 叫ぶ, 悲鳴を上げる ― **yelp** 名 **C** ➔ 叫び声, 悲鳴

\***yes** /jes/ 間 ▶定義1 used to give a positive answer to a question, for saying that sth is true

# 1862　yesterday

or correct or for saying that you want sth ある事が事実であるまたは正しい、あるいは何かを望んでいると伝えるために、質問に対して肯定的な返事をするときに用いて→**はい, そうです** ‖ '*Are you having a good time?*' '*Yes, thank you.*'「楽しんでいますか」「はい, ありがとう」 '*You're married, aren't you?*' '*Yes, I am.*'「あなたは結婚していますよね」「はい, しています」 '*May I sit here?*' '*Yes, of course.*'「ここに座ってもいいですか」「はい, もちろんです」 '*More coffee?*' '*Yes, please.*'「コーヒーをもう少しいかがですか」「ええ, お願いします」 ▶定義2 used for showing you have heard sb or will do what he/she asks 人からの呼び掛けが聞こえたことを、あるいは人からの依頼に答えることを表すのに用いて→**はい** ‖ '*Waiter!*' '*Yes, madam.*'「ボーイさん」「はい, 何でしょうか」 ▶定義3 used when saying that a negative statement that sb has made is not true 人が言った否定的な言葉が事実ではないときに用いて→**いいえ, いや** ‖ '*You don't care about anyone but yourself.*' '*Yes I do.*'「君は自分以外の人には関心がないんだね」「いいえ, そんな事はありません」⇔ **no** — **yes** 名 **C** (複 **yeses** /jésəz, -ɪz/) →「はい」という返事 ‖ *Was that a yes or a no?* それはイエス, ノーのどちらでしたか.

### ▶音声とつづり字

**Yes や No の言い方とそれぞれの意味**

英語ではイントネーションの違いにより、違った印象を与えます. 下がり口調で言うと、伝達が終わったという印象を相手は受けますが, 上がり調子だと, 何かがさらに続く印象を受けます. 例えば, 道を聞く人が Yes を上昇調で言うと, 相手に説明を続けてほしいことを示します. また, Have you seen David? という質問に対し, No と下がり口調で答えると, 質問した人は相手が会話を続ける意思がないと思います. また, Yes を下降上昇調で言うと, 部分的に賛成することを表すので, 相手はその理由を聞きたいという意思を含んでいます.

*★**yesterday** /jéstərdèɪ, -di/ 副 名 **C U** ▶定義 (on) the day before today 今日の1日前の日 (に)→**昨日 (は)** ‖ *Did you watch the film on TV yesterday?* 昨日, その映画をテレビで見ましたか. *yesterday morning/afternoon/evening* 昨日の午前・午後・晩 *I posted the form **the day before yesterday** (= if I am speaking on Wednesday, I posted it on Monday).* 私はその書類をおととい投かんした (= これを水曜日に言っているとすると, 投かんしたのは月曜日). *Have you still got yesterday's paper?* 昨日の新聞をまだ持っていますか. *I spent the whole of yesterday walking round the shops.* 昨日は一日中, あちこちの店を見て歩いた.

*★**yet** /jet/ 副 接 ▶定義1 used with negative verbs or in questions for talking about sth that has not happened but that you expect to happen 動詞の否定形と共に, あるいは疑問文の中で, まだ起きていないが起きると期待している物事について話すのに用いて→**まだ (～ない), 今までのところは (～ない), もう, 既に** ‖ *Has it stopped raining yet?* もう雨はやみましたか. *I haven't seen that film yet.* その映画はまだ見たことがない.

▶アメリカ英語では次のようにも言う: *I didn't see that film yet.*

▶定義2 (動詞の否定形と共に) now; as early as this 今; 今の時点では→**(今は) まだ, 今すぐには** ‖ *You don't have to leave yet - your train isn't for another hour.* まだ出発しなくていい — 君が乗る電車はまだ1時間は来ないから. ▶定義3 from now until the period of time mentioned has passed 今から, 述べられた期間が経過するまで→**さらに, まだ** ‖ *She isn't that old, she'll live for years yet.* 彼女はそれほど年を取っているわけではない, まだ何年も生きるだろう. ▶定義4 (特に may または might と用いて) at some time in the future 未来のある時点で→**やがて, いつか, そのうち** ‖ *With a bit of luck, they may yet win.* ほんの少し運があれば, 彼らはそのうち勝てるかもしれない. ▶定義5 (最上級と用いて) until now/until then; so far 今まで・その時まで; これまでで→**今までに, これまでに** ‖ *This is her best film yet.* これは今までの彼女の映画の中で最高傑作だ. ▶定義6 used with comparatives to emphasize an increase in the degree of sth 比較級と用いて, 物事の程度の増加を強調する→**さらに, 一層, その上** ‖ *a recent and yet more improbable theory* 最新で, しかもありそうもない理論 ▶定義7 but; in spite of that しかし; それ

にもかかわらず➡けれども ‖ *He seems pleasant, yet there's something about him I don't like.* 彼は感じが良さそうに見えるが，それでも私には気に入らないところがある．

成句 as yet ▶定義 until now 今まで➡今のところ ‖ *As yet little is known about the disease.* その病気のことは，今のところ，ほとんど分かっていない．

yet again ▶定義 (used for expressing surprise or anger that sth happens again) once more; another time (物事が再び起きたことへの驚き，または怒りを表すために用いて) もう一度; また➡またしても ‖ *I found out that he had lied to me yet again.* 彼がまたもや私にうそをついていたことが判明した．

yet another ▶定義 used for expressing surprise that there is one more of sth 物がもう1つあることへの驚きを表すのに用いて➡また1つ ‖ *They're opening yet another fast food restaurant in the square.* その区域にファーストフードの店がまた1軒オープンしようとしている．

yet to do, etc ▶定義 that has not been done and is still to do in the future まだ行われていないが，将来行われる予定である➡まだ～していない ‖ *The final decision has yet to be made.* 最終的な決定はまだされていない．

**YHA** /ˌwaɪ eɪtʃ ˈeɪ/ 略 英 Youth Hostels Association➡ユースホステル協会

**yield**¹ /jiːld/ 動 ▶定義 1 他 to produce or provide crops, profits or results 作物，利益，または成果を産出あるいは供給する➡～を産み出す，生じる，もたらす ‖ *How much wheat does each field yield?* それぞれの畑では，どのくらいの小麦が収穫されますか．*Did the experiment yield any new information?* その実験の結果，何か新しい事が分かりましたか．▶定義 2 自 正式 yield (to sb/sth) to stop refusing to do sth or to obey sb 物事をするのを拒んだり人に従うのを拒んだりするのをやめる➡屈服する，負ける，応じる ‖ *The government refused to yield to the hostage takers' demands.* 政府は，人質を取っている者たちの要求に応じることを拒否した．☛ give in の方がより略式．▶定義 3 他 yield sb/sth (up) (to sb/sth) to allow sb to have control of sth that you were controlling 自分が統制していた～の権限を…に持たせる➡～を与える，譲渡する ‖ *The army has yielded power to the rebels.* 軍は反乱者たちに権限を譲った．▶定義 4 自 正式 to move, bend or break because of pressure 圧力に屈して動く，曲がる，壊れる➡たわむ，屈する ‖ *The dam finally yielded under the weight of the water.* そのダムは，水の重みでとうとう決壊した．☛ give way の方がより略式．▶定義 5 自 米 yield (to sb/sth) to allow other vehicles on a bigger road to go first 広い道路で，ほかの車両を先に行かせる➡道を譲る ‖ *You have to yield to traffic from the left here.* ここでは左側から来た車両に道を譲らなければいけない．☛ イギリス英語では give way が用いられる．

句動詞 yield to sth 正式 ▶定義 to be replaced by sth, especially sth newer 特に新しい～に取って代わられる➡～に取って代わられる ‖ *Old-fashioned methods have yielded to new technology.* 昔ながらの方法が新しい技術に取って代わられた．☛ give way の方がより略式．

**yield**² /jiːld/ 名 C ▶定義 the amount that is produced 産出される量➡産出高，収穫量，収益，利回り ‖ *Wheat yields were down 5% this year.* 今年は，小麦の収穫高が5パーセント減った．*This investment has an annual yield of 12%.* この投資の利回りは年12パーセントだ．

**yo** /joʊ/ 間 特に 米 (俗語) ▶定義 used by some people when they see a friend; hello 友達に会ったときに，ある種の人々によって用いて; やあ➡よう，おっす，おい

**yob** /jɒb/ 名 C 英 (俗語) ▶定義 a boy or young man who is rude, loud and sometimes violent or aggressive 不作法で騒がしく，時には暴力的または攻撃的な少年あるいは若い男➡よた者，チンピラ ☛参 lout, hooligan

**yoga** /ˈjoʊɡə/ 名 U ▶定義 a system of exercises for the body that helps you control and relax both your mind and your body 精神と肉体の両方を自ら制御し，緊張をほぐすことに役立つ，身体のための体系的な運動➡ヨガ

**yoghurt** (または **yogurt**) /ˈjɒɡət; ˈjoʊɡərt/ 名 C U ▶定義 a slightly sour, thick liquid food made from milk 牛乳から作られ，少し酸味のある，濃厚な液状食品➡ヨーグルト ‖ *plain/banana/strawberry yoghurt* プレーンヨーグルト・バナナヨーグルト・ストロベリーヨーグルト ☛ C4ページのさし絵

**yoke** /jóʊk/ 名 ▶定義1 ❶a long piece of wood fixed across the necks of two animals so that they can pull heavy loads together 2頭の動物の首に渡して固定された長い木の棒.そうすることでその2頭が一緒に重い積み荷を引くことができる→**くびき** ▶定義2 ［単数扱い］something that restricts your freedom and makes your life difficult 人の自由を束縛し,その生活を困難にさせるもの→**束縛, 支配** ‖ *the yoke of parental control* 親の支配による束縛

**yolk** /jóʊ(l)k/ 名 ❶❶ ▶定義 the yellow part in the middle of an egg 卵の中央にある黄色い部分→**黄身, 卵黄** ☞ **egg** のさし絵

**yonks** /jɑŋks/ 名 ❶ (俗語) ▶定義 a very long time とても長い間→**長い間** ‖ *I haven't been to the theatre for yonks.* 長い間芝居を見に行っていない.

*****you** /ju, jə, juː/ 代 ▶定義1 used as the subject or object of a verb, or after a preposition to refer to the person or people being spoken or written to 動詞の主語や目的語として用いて, あるいは前置詞の後ろに置いて, 話の相手または手紙の相手となる人または人々を指す→**あなた(たち)は, あなた(たち)が, あなた(たち)を, あなた(たち)に** ‖ *You can play the guitar, can't you?* あなたはギターが弾けますよね. *I've told you about this before.* この事は,以前,あなたにお話ししました. *Bring your photos with you.* あなたの写真を持参してください. ▶定義2 used with a noun, adjective or phrase when calling sb sth 人を何らかと呼ぶときに,名詞,形容詞,句と共に用いて→**お前(たち), そこの人** ‖ *You idiot! What do you think you're doing?* このばか.自分が何をしていると思っているんだ. ▶定義3 used for referring to people in general 一般的に「人々」を指すのに用いて→**人は, だれでも** ‖ *The more you earn, the more tax you pay.* (だれでも)収入が増えれば税金も増える. ☞ 次の例文のように one を使って同じ意味を表すことができるが,you に比べて改まった表現であり,今では古風な用法になりつつある. *The more one earns, the more tax one pays.*

**you'd** /jəd, jʊd, juːd/ **YOU HAD** または **YOU WOULD** の短縮形

**you'll** /jəl, jʊl, juːl/ **YOU WILL** の短縮形

*****young**¹ /jʌŋ/ 形 (**younger** /jʌŋɡər/, **youngest** /jʌŋɡəst/) ▶定義 not having lived or existed for very long; not old 生まれてから,または現れてから,あまり時間がたっていない; 年を取っていない,古くない→**若い, 幼い, 年少の, 新しい, 新興の** ‖ *They have two young children.* 彼らには幼い子供が2人いる. *I'm a year younger than her.* 私は彼女より1つ年下です. *My father was the youngest of eight children.* 私の父は8人兄弟の一番下だった. *my younger brothers* 私の弟たち ⇔ **old**

成句 **young at heart** ▶定義 behaving or thinking like a young person, although you are old 年を取ってはいるけれど,若者のような振る舞いまたは考え方をする→**気が若い**

**young**² /jʌŋ/ 名 ［複数扱い］ ▶定義1 young animals 動物の子たち→**(動物・鳥の)子供, ひな** ‖ *Swans will attack to protect their young.* 白鳥はひな鳥を守るために攻撃するだろう. ▶定義2 **the young** young people considered as a group 1つの集団と見なされる若い人々→**若者たち** ‖ *The young of today are more ambitious than their parents.* 今時の若者たちは,親の世代よりも野心を持っている.

**youngish** /jʌŋɪʃ/ 形 ▶定義 quite young なかなか若い→**若々しい**

**youngster** /jʌŋstər/ 名 ❶ ▶定義 a young person 若い人→**若者** ‖ *There is very little entertainment for youngsters in this town.* この街には若者向けの娯楽がほとんどない.

*****your** /jər, jʊər, jɔːr/ 代 ▶定義1 of or belonging to the person or people being spoken to 話の相手となっている人または人々の,あるいはそういう人または人々の所有する→**あなた(たち)の, 君(たち)の** ‖ *What's your flat like?* あなたのアパート［マンション］はどんな作りですか. *Thanks for all your help.* ありがとう,とても助かりました. *How old are your children now?* あなたのお子さんたちは今いくつになりましたか. ▶定義2 belonging to or connected with people in general 一般的に人々の所有する,または人々に関係のある→**人の** ‖ *When your life is as busy as mine, you have little time to relax.* (人は一般に)私と同じくらい忙しい生活をしていれば,くつろぐ時間はほとんどない. ▶定義3 話式 used for saying that sth is well-known to people in general 一般的に物事が人々によく知られている事

を言うために用いて➔いわゆる,例の,くだんの,言うところの ‖ *So this is your typical English pub, is it?* それで,これが言うところの典型的なイングリッシュパブかね. ▶定義4 (または **Your**) used in some titles ある種の称号で用いて ‖ *your Highness* 殿下,あるいは妃殿下

**you're** /jər, juər, jɔːr/ **YOU ARE** の短縮形

\***yours** /jóərz, jɔːrz/ ▶定義1 of or belonging to you あなた(たち)のもの,またはあなた(たち)の所有であるもの➔あなた(たち)のもの,君(たち)のもの ‖ *Is this bag yours or mine?* このバッグは君のですか,僕のですか. *I was talking to a friend of yours the other day.* 私は,先日あなたの友達と話をしました. ▶定義2 **Yours** used at the end of a letter 手紙の結びに用いて➔敬具,かしこ ‖ *Yours sincerely.../faithfully...* 敬具,敬白 (主に 英)*Yours...* 草々

\***yourself** /juərsélf, jɔːr-, jər-/ (複 **yourselves** /-sélvz/) ▶定義1 used when the person or people being spoken to both do an action and are also affected by it 話の相手となっている人または人々がある行為を行い,その影響も受ける場合に用いて➔(あなたが)自分自身を,(あなたが)自分自身に ‖ *Be careful or you'll hurt yourself.* 気を付けないと,けがをしますよ. *Here's some money. Buy yourselves a present.* ここにお金があるから,自分たちへのプレゼントを買いなさい. *You're always talking about yourself!* 君はいつも自分のことばかり話しているね. ▶定義2 used for emphasis 強調するために用いて➔(あなたが)自分で,あなた自身(で) ‖ *You yourself told me there was a problem last week.* 先週,問題があると言ったのは君自身だよ. *Did you repair the car yourselves? (= or did sb else do it for you?)* その車は君たちが自分で直したのですか(= それともだれかほかの人が代わりに直してくれたのですか). ▶定義3 you➔あなた ‖ *'How are you?' 'Fine, thanks. And yourself?'* 「元気ですか」「ええ,ありがとう.あなたは」 ▶定義4 in your normal state; healthy あなたの普通の状態;健康な状態➔いつものあなた,本来の君 ‖ *You don't look yourself today.* 今日はいつもの君らしくないね.

成句 (**all**) **by yourself/yourselves** ▶定義1 alone 1人で➔独りぼっちで ‖ *Do you live by yourself?* あなたは1人で暮らしているのですか. ☞参 **alone** の注 ▶定義2 without help 援助

なしで➔独力で,1人で ‖ *You can't cook dinner for ten people by yourself.* あなた1人では,10人分の夕食を作れない.

\***youth** /juːθ/ 名 (複 **youths** /juːðz, -θs; -ðs/) ▶定義1 ❶the period of your life when you are young, especially the time before a child becomes an adult 人生における若い時代,特に子供が大人になる前の時期➔青春時代,青年期,若いころ ‖ *He was quite a good sportsman in his youth.* 彼は若いころ,とても優れたスポーツマンだった. ▶定義2 ❶the fact or state of being young 若いという事実または状態➔若さ,元気,未熟さ ‖ *I think that her youth will be a disadvantage in this job.* 彼女の若さは,この仕事では不利になると思う. ▶定義3 ❸a young person (usually a young man, and often one that you do not have a good opinion of) 若い人(普通は若い男性で,しばしば自分が高く評価していない男性)➔若者,若造,若い連中 ‖ *a gang of youths* 若造の一団 ▶定義4 **the youth** ❶young people considered as a group 1つの集団として見なされた若い人々➔若い人たち,青年層,青年男女 ‖ *the youth of today* 今時の若者たち ☞参 **age, old age**

**youthful** /júːθfʊl, -f(ə)l/ 形 ▶定義1 typical of young people 若い人に典型的な➔若者らしい,少壮の ‖ *youthful enthusiasm* 若者らしい熱っぽさ ▶定義2 seeming younger than you are 実際の年齢よりも若く見える➔若々しい,元気な ‖ *She's a youthful fifty-year-old.* 彼女ははつらつとした50歳だ.

**youth hostel** 名 ❸ ▶定義 a cheap and simple place to stay, especially for young people, when they are travelling 特に旅行中の若い人々のための,安価で簡素な宿泊施設➔ユースホステル

**you've** /jʊv, juːv, jəv/ **YOU HAVE** の短縮形

**Yo Yo**™ (または **yo-yo**) 名 ❸ (複 **Yo Yos, yo-yos**) ▶定義 a toy which is a round piece of wood or plastic with a string round the middle. You put the string round your finger and can make the yo-yo go up and down it. 円い形をした木片またはプラスチックのおもちゃで,中心の回りにひもを巻き付けてある.そのひもを指に巻き,上下させて遊ぶ➔ヨーヨー

**yr** (複 **yrs**) 略 year➔年

**yuck** /jʌk/ 間 略式 ▶定義 used for saying that you think sth is disgusting or very unpleasant 物に対してむかむかする、非常に不快であると思っていることを伝えるのに用いて→おえっ、うえっ、げつ ‖ *It's filthy! Yuck!* うわっ、汚い、げっ、— **yucky** 形 →嫌な、まずい ‖ *What a yucky colour!* 何て嫌な色なんだ.

**yummy** /jʌ́mi/ 形 略式 ▶定義 tasting very good; delicious とても良い味のする；美味な→おいしい ‖ *a yummy cake* おいしいケーキ

**yuppie** (または **yuppy**) /jʌ́pi/ 名 C (複 **yuppies**) ▶定義 a successful young professional person who lives in a city, earns a lot of money and spends it on fashionable things 都会に住み、大金を稼ぎ、その収入を流行のものに消費する、成功した若い専門職の人→ヤッピー

# Z z

**Z, z** /zed, ziː/ 名 C ( 複 **Z's; z's**) ▶定義 the twenty-sixth letter of the English alphabet 英語アルファベットの第 26 文字→z(Z)が表す音、z(Z)の文字、z(Z)の字形のもの ‖ *'Zero' begins with (a) 'Z'.* Zero は Z で始まる.

**zany** /zéɪni/ 形 ▶定義 funny in an unusual and crazy way 並外れた、途方もない様子でこっけいな→奇想天外な、突拍子もない ‖ *a zany comedian* 奇想天外なコメディアン

**zap** /zæp/ 動 (**zapping; zapped**) 略式 ▶定義 1 © **zap sb/sth (with sth)** to destroy, hit or kill sb, usually with a gun or other weapon 通常は銃またはほかの武器で〜を徹底的にやっつける、殴るまたは殺す→〜を殺す、撃ち殺す、気絶させる ‖ *It's a computer game where you have to zap aliens with a laser.* それは、レーザーで宇宙人を殺さなければならないコンピューターゲームだ. ▶定義 2 🖳 to change television programmes very quickly using an electronic device (**remote control**) 電子装置(リモコン)を使ってテレビ番組を非常に速く切り替える→(テレビのチャンネルを)リモコンで次々に替える

**zeal** /ziːl/ 名 U (文) ▶定義 great energy or enthusiasm 大きな精力または熱心さ→熱意、熱狂、熱中 ‖ *religious zeal* 宗教的熱意

**zealous** /zéləs/ 形 ▶定義 using great energy and enthusiasm 大きな精力または熱心さを用いた→熱心な、熱狂的な — **zealously** 副 →熱心に、熱狂的に

zebra

**zebra** /zíːbrə, zéb-/ 名 C ( 複 **zebra** または **zebras**) ▶定義 an African wild animal that looks like a horse, with black and white lines (**stripes**) all over its body 馬に似ているアフリカの野生動物で、身体全体に白と黒の線(しま)がある→しま馬、ゼブラ

**zebra crossing** 名 C 英 ▶定義 a place where the road is marked with black and white lines and people can cross safely because cars must stop to let them do this 道路上に白黒のしま模様が印されている場所で、ここでは歩行者を渡らせるために車が止まらなければならないので、歩行者は安全に渡ることができる→(白黒のしま模様の)横断歩道 ☛参 **pedestrian crossing**

★**zero** /zíərəʊ/ 名 ▶定義 1 C 0→(数字の) 0、ゼロ、零

► 文中での数詞の使い方については、six の項を参照.

▶定義 2 ❶ freezing point; 0°C 氷点；0°C→(温度計の)零度 ‖ *The temperature is likely to fall to five degrees below zero (= -5°C).* 気温は氷点下 5°C(= -5°C)まで下がりそうだ. ▶定義 3 ❶ the lowest possible amount or level; nothing at all 起こり得る最低の量または水準；全く何もない→無、最低、どん底 ‖ *zero growth/inflation/profit* ゼロ成長・インフレ率ゼロ・ゼロ収益

►イギリス英語では、数字の 0 にはさまざまな呼び方がある. zero は科学的または専門的文脈では最も一般的である. nil はスポーツ、特にサッカーの得点では最もよく用いられる(しゃべる場合). nought は数字の 0 が大きな数字の部分であることを示す場合に使われる： *a million is one followed by six noughts.*(百万は、1 の後に 0 が 6 つ並ぶ.) O (オー)は電話番号または飛行機の便名などの数字を言う場合に最もよく用いられる.

**zest** /zest/ 名[ U, 単数扱い ] ▶定義 zest (for sth) a feeling of enjoyment, excitement and enthusiasm 喜び, 興奮または熱狂の感情 →**熱意, 熱情, 強い喜び** ‖ *She has a great **zest** for life.* 彼女は人生に強い喜びを持っている.

**zigzag** /zígzæg/ 名 C 形 ▶定義 (consisting of) a line with left and right turns, like a lot of letter W's, one after the other W の字が多数続いているような, 左右交互に折れ曲がっている線(でできている) →**ジグザグの, 稲妻形(の)** ‖ *The skier came down the slope in a series of zigzags.* スキーヤーはジグザグを描きながら滑走斜面を降りてきた. *a zigzag pattern/line* ジグザグ模様・線 ☞ **line**のさし絵 — zigzag 動 自 (zigzagging; zigzagged) →(人が)ジグザグに進む, (道が)ジグザグに延びている

**zinc** /zɪŋk/ 名 U ▶定義 a whitish metal, often put on the surface of iron and steel as protection against water 白っぽい金属で, しばしば鉄または鋼鉄の表面を覆い水から保護する →**亜鉛**

*★**zip** /zɪp/ (米 **zipper**) 名 C ▶定義 a device for fastening clothes, bags, etc 服, かばんなどを閉めるための器具 →**ファスナー, チャック** ‖ *to do up/undo a zip* チャックを閉める・開ける ☞ **button**のさし絵 — zip 動 他 (zipping; zipped) zip sth (up) ~をファスナー[チャック]で閉める・開ける ‖ *There was so much in the bag that it was difficult to zip it up.* かばんの中にたくさん詰め込んであったので, ファスナーを閉めるのに一苦労だった. ⇔ **unzip**

**ZIP code** (または **zip code**) 米 = POSTCODE

**the zodiac** /zóudiæk/ 名 [単数扱い] ▶定義 a diagram of the positions of the sun, moon and planets, which is divided into twelve equal parts, each with a special name and symbol (the signs of the zodiac) 太陽, 月, または惑星の位置図で, 12 等分され, 各々に特別な名称と象徴(黄道十二宮)が付けられている →**黄道十二宮, 黄道帯, 獣帯**

▶ 黄道十二宮は新聞, 雑誌のastrology (占星術)およびholoscopes (星占い)で用いられる(しばしばthe stars (星回り)と呼ばれる). 人々は星座と, それが人の性格および将来に及ぼすと考えられる影響について, しばしば口にする: *Which sign (of the zodiac) are you?* (あなたの星座は(黄道十二宮の)何ですか.)

**zone** /zoʊn/ 名 C ▶定義 an area that is different from those around it for example because sth special happens there 例えば特別な事がそこで起こるなどのため, 周りとは異なった1つの区域 →**地帯, 地域** ‖ *a war zone* 戦争地帯

**zoo** /zu:/ 名 C (複 **zoos**) ▶定義 a park where many kinds of wild animals are kept so that people can look at them and where they are bred, studied and protected 多くの種類の野生動物が飼われている公園で, 人々が動物を観察でき, また動物を繁殖させ, 調査し, 保護する所 →**動物園**

**zoology** /zoʊɑ́lədʒi, zu:-/ 名 U ▶定義 the scientific study of animals 動物の科学的研究 →**動物学** ☞参 **botany, biology** — zoological /zòʊəlɑ́dʒɪk(ə)l/ 形 →**動物学(上)の, 動物に関する** — zoologist /zoʊɑ́lədʒɪst, zu:-/ 名 C →**動物学者**

**zoom** /zu:m/ 動 自 ▶定義 to move or go somewhere very fast ある場所へ非常に速く動くまたは行く →**猛スピードで行く, 急に動く** ‖ *Traffic zoomed past us.* 車が私たちのそばを猛スピードで通り過ぎていった.

句動詞 zoom in (on sb/sth) ▶定義 (used in photography) to give a closer view of the object/person being photographed by fixing a special device to the camera (a zoom lens) (写真で用いて)カメラに特別の器具(ズームレンズ)を取り付けることにより, 写真を撮られている物・人のより接近した像を提供する →**(カメラが)(~を)ズームレンズで大写しにする, ズームインする** ‖ *The camera zoomed in on the actor's face.* カメラはその俳優の顔を大写しにした. ☞ **camera**のさし絵

**zoom lens** 名 C ▶定義 a device on a camera that can make an object being photographed appear gradually bigger or smaller so that it seems to be getting closer or further away 撮られている物を徐々に大きくまたは小さく見えるようにすることができるカメラの器具で, それによりその物が接近するようにまたは遠ざかるように感じられる →**ズームレンズ**

**zucchini** /zuki:ni/ (複 **zucchini** または **zucchinis**) 特に 米 = COURGETTE

# Animals C1

## Animals

muzzle, ear, fur, tail, whiskers, fangs, paw, claw, pad, hind or back legs, front legs, antlers, horn, tusk, hoof, toes, trunk

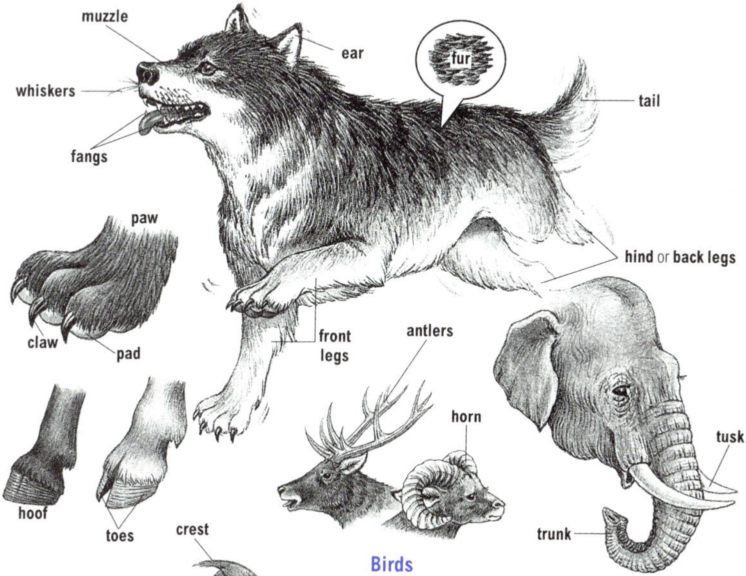

## Birds

crest, wing, beak, chick, shell, bill, tail, breast, feather, leg, claw, nest, egg, webbed foot

## Fish

tail, fin, scales, gills

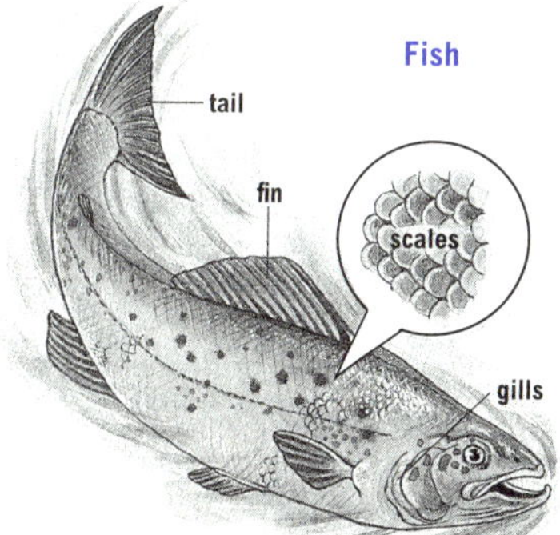

## Insects

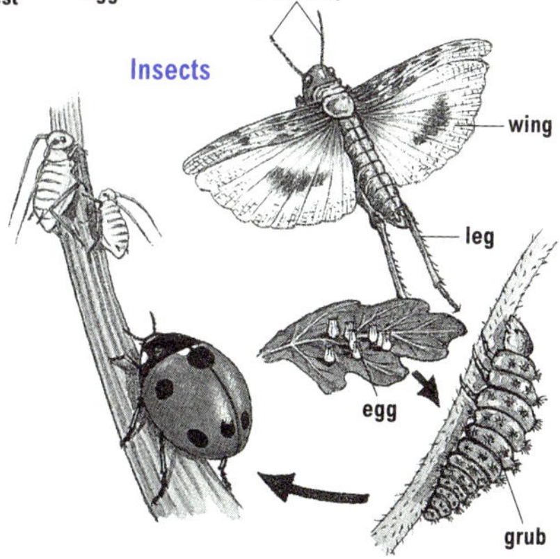

antennae, wing, leg, egg, grub

# C2 Plants

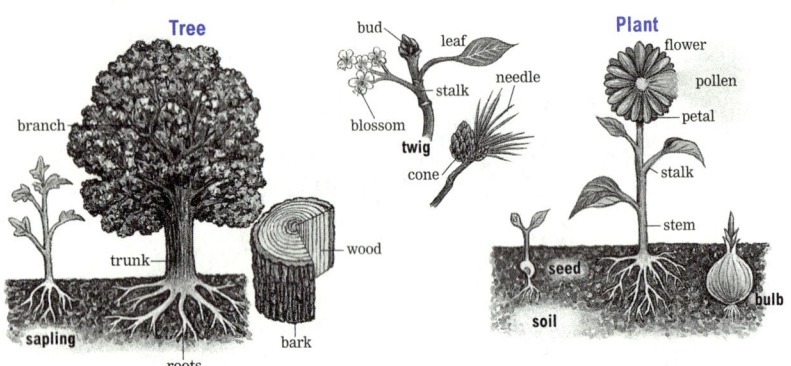

## Types of plants and flower

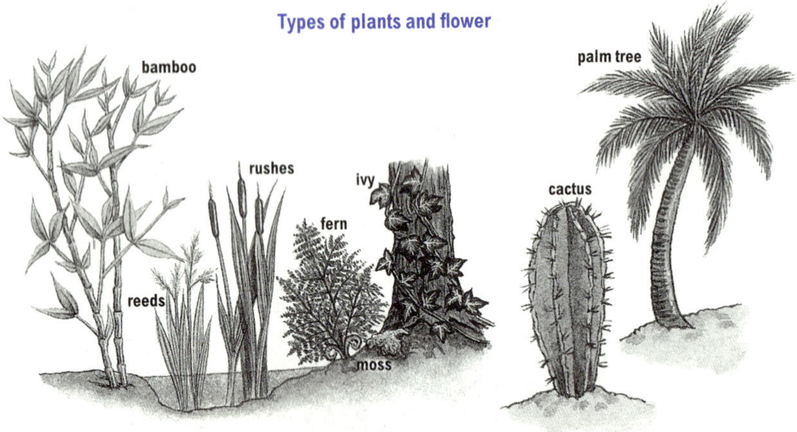

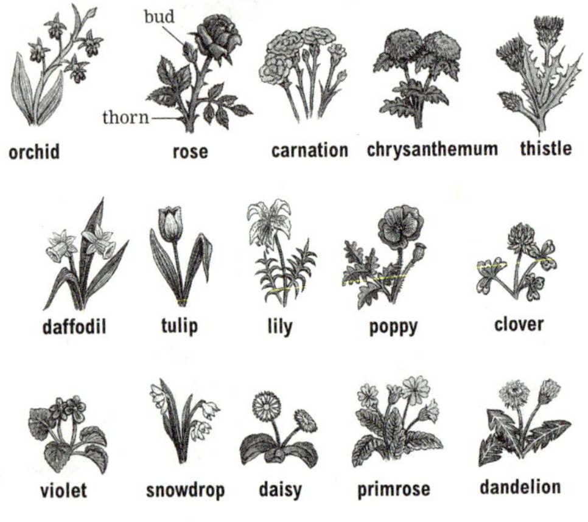

# Fruit and Vegetables

# Food and Drink

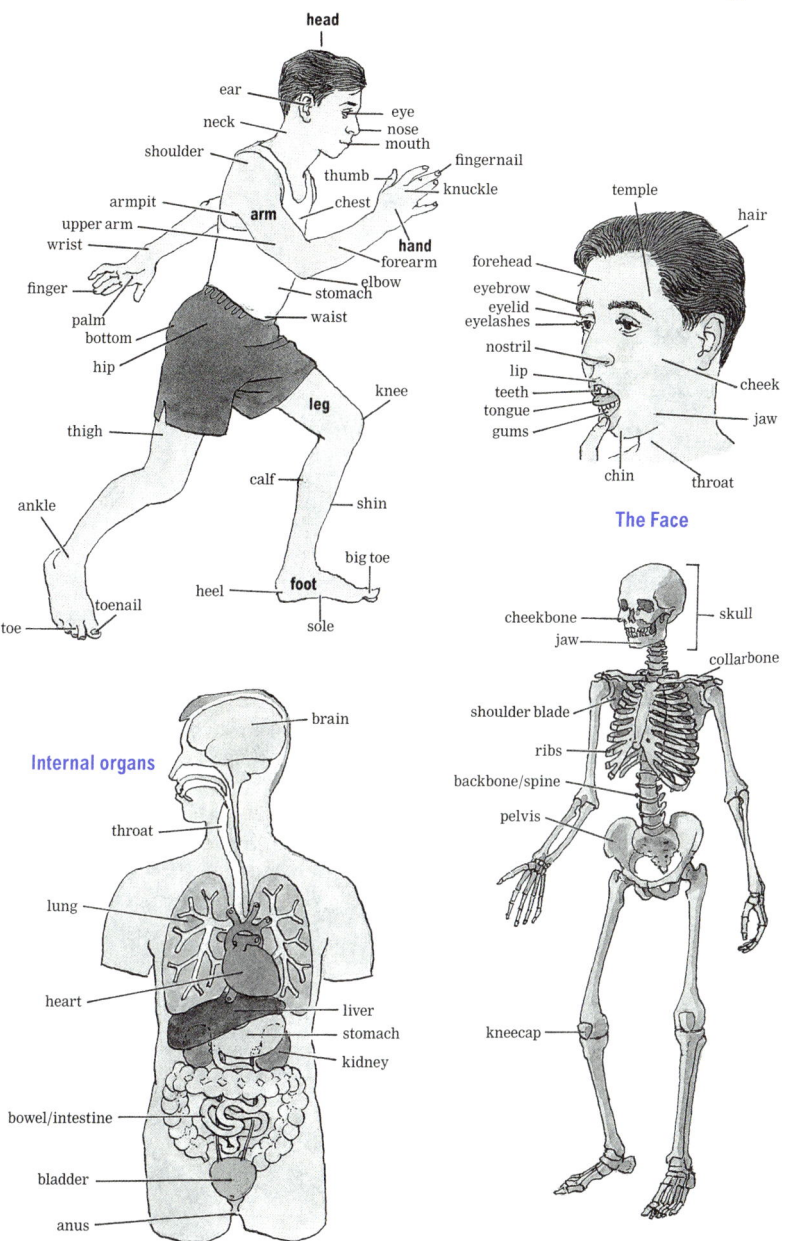

# The Human Body

**The Face**

**Internal organs**

**The Skeleton**

# Clothes

turban
jacket
tie
suit
trousers
(米 pants)
sari
bow tie
shirt
waistcoat
(米 vest)
trousers
(米 pants)
T-shirt
dungarees
(米 overalls)
scarf
dress

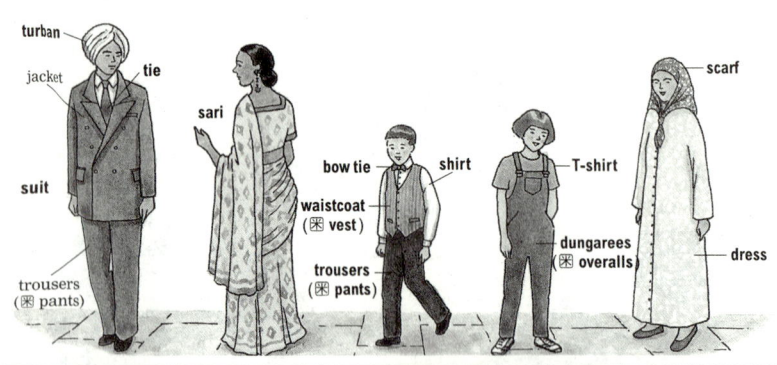

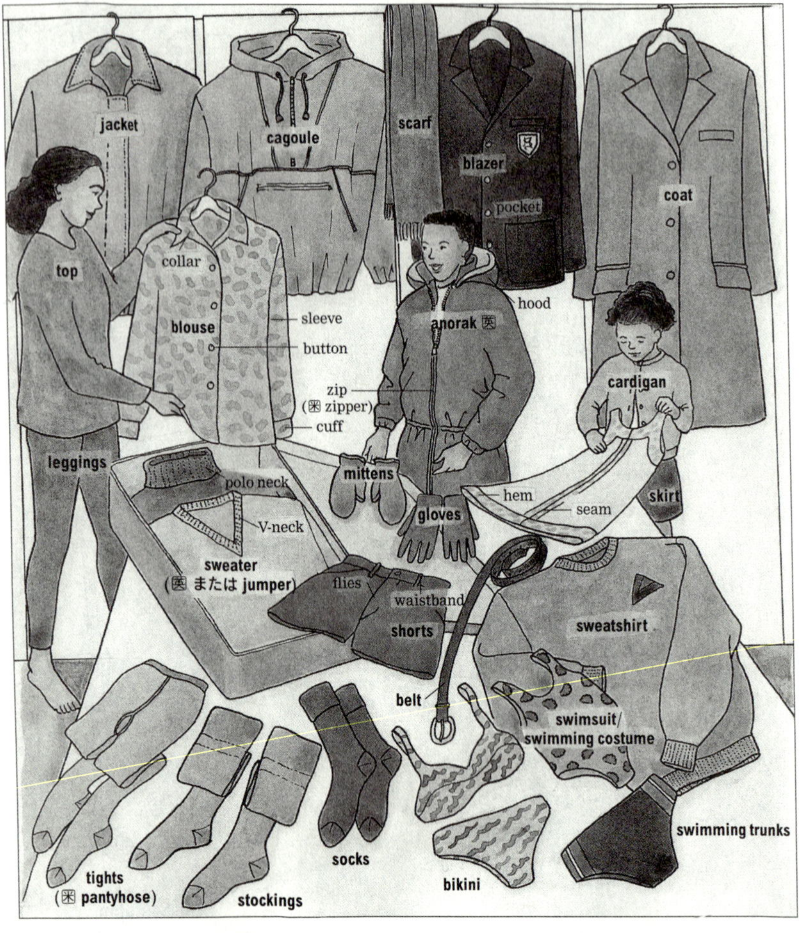
jacket
cagoule
scarf
blazer
pocket
coat
top
collar
blouse
sleeve
button
zip
(米 zipper)
cuff
anorak 英
hood
cardigan
leggings
mittens
polo neck
V-neck
gloves
hem
seam
skirt
sweater
(英 または jumper)
flies
waistband
shorts
sweatshirt
belt
swimsuit/
swimming costume
swimming trunks
tights
(米 pantyhose)
stockings
socks
bikini

# The House C7

# C8 Postcards

## Seaside

Dear Penny
Having a great time at the seaside. Yesterday we went to the beach. I paddled but the kids were brave enough to swim (the sea was freezing!). Had an ice cream on the pier then walked along the harbour's promenade. The promenade's very pretty – might go for a boat trip tomorrow.
See you soon,
love Kate & family

## Mountains

Hi Linda
Been hiking up Bear Mountain. From the top you could see for miles. The lake looked tiny from up there. Had lunch in a log cabin then caught the cable car back down – couldn't walk another step. I'd love to go skiing here in the winter. Bet you wish you were here!
Barry

## City

Dear All

I'm exhausted. Spent this morning in the Natural History Museum then went shopping. Found a great market with loads of interesting stalls. Right now I'm sitting at a cafe in the main square watching the world go by. Don't want to come home!

best wishes
Rachel

# 文法早見表 目次

## Verbs

| | |
|---|---|
| The tenses of regular verbs | G2 |
| Talking about the present | G4 |
| Talking about the past | G5 |
| Talking about the future | G6 |
| Transitive and intransitive verbs | G8 |
| Conditionals | G8 |
| Reported speech | G9 |
| The passive | G10 |
| Modal verbs | G10 |

## Nouns

| | |
|---|---|
| Countable and uncountable nouns | G12 |
| Articles | G12 |
| The possessive with 's | G13 |
| Much, many, alot, a little, a few | G14 |

## Adjectives

| | |
|---|---|
| Comparatives and superlatives | G14 |
| Adjectives with nouns | G15 |

## Relative clauses

G16

# G2 Verbs: the tenses of regular verbs
(動詞：規則動詞の時制)

## The Simple Tenses (単純時制)

➤ I, you, we, および they では同じ形の動詞を使用します．
また，he, she および it では同じ形の動詞を使用します．

### The present simple (単純現在形)

| | | |
|---|---|---|
| I look | *do I look?* | I do not look (**don't look**) |
| he looks | *does he look?* | he does not look (**doesn't look**) |

### The simple past (単純過去形)

| | | |
|---|---|---|
| I looked | *did I look?* | I did not look (**didn't look**) |
| he looked | *did he look?* | he did not look (**didn't look**) |

### The present perfect (現在完了形)

| | | |
|---|---|---|
| I have looked (**I've looked**) | *have I looked?* | I have not looked (**haven't looked**) |
| he has looked (**he's looked**) | *has he looked?* | he has not looked (**hasn't looked**) |

### The past perfect (pluperfect) (過去完了形)

| | | |
|---|---|---|
| I had looked (**I'd looked**) | *had I looked?* | I had not looked (**hadn't looked**) |
| he had looked (**he'd looked**) | *had he looked?* | he had not looked (**hadn't looked**) |

### The future simple (単純未来形)

| | | |
|---|---|---|
| I will look (**I'll look**) | *will I look?* | I will not look (**won't look**) |
| he will look (**he'll look**) | *will he look?* | he will not look (**won't look**) |

### The future perfect (未来完了形)

| | | |
|---|---|---|
| I will have looked (**I'll have looked**) | *will I have looked?* | I will not have looked (**won't have looked**) |
| he will have looked (**he'll have looked**) | *will he have looked?* | he will not have looked (**won't have looked**) |

### The conditional (条件文)

| | | |
|---|---|---|
| I would look (**I'd look**) | *would I look?* | I would not look (**wouldn't look**) |
| he would look (**he'd look**) | *would he look?* | he would not look (**wouldn't look**) |

### The conditional perfect (条件文完了形)

| | | |
|---|---|---|
| I would have looked (**would've looked**) | *would I have looked?* | I would not have looked (**wouldn't have looked**) |
| he would have looked (**would've looked**) | *would he have looked?* | he would not have looked (**wouldn't have looked**) |

# Verbs: the tenses of regular verbs G3
## （動詞：規則動詞の時制）

## The Continuous Tenses（継続相の時制）

▶ 継続相の時制は進行形とも呼ばれます. **I**, **you**, **we** および **they** では同じ形の動詞を使用します. ただし, **you** に対してのみ異なる形が使われる動詞もあります. **he**, **she** および **it** では同じ形の動詞を使用します.

### The present continuous（現在進行形）

| | | |
|---|---|---|
| I am looking (**I'm looking**) | am I looking? | I am not looking (**I'm not looking**) |
| you are looking (**you're looking**) | are you looking? | you are not looking (**aren't looking**) |
| he is looking (**he's looking**) | is he looking? | he is not looking (**isn't looking**) |

### The past continuous（過去進行形）

| | | |
|---|---|---|
| I was looking | was I looking? | I was not looking (**wasn't looking**) |
| you were looking | were you looking? | you were not looking (**weren't looking**) |
| he was looking | was he looking? | he was not looking (**wasn't looking**) |

### The present perfect continuous（現在完了進行形）

| | | |
|---|---|---|
| I have been looking (**I've been looking**) | have I been looking? | I have not been looking (**haven't been looking**) |
| you have been looking (**you've been looking**) | have you been looking? | you have not been looking (**haven't been looking**) |
| he has been looking (**he's been looking**) | has he been looking? | he has not been looking (**hasn't been looking**) |

### The past perfect continuous（過去完了進行形）

| | | |
|---|---|---|
| I had been looking (**I'd been looking**) | had I been looking? | I had not been looking (**hadn't been looking**) |
| he had been looking (**he'd been looking**) | had he been looking? | he had not been looking (**hadn't been looking**) |

### The future continuous（未来進行形）

| | | |
|---|---|---|
| I will be looking (**I'll be looking**) | will I be looking? | I will not be looking (**won't be looking**) |
| he will be looking (**he'll be looking**) | will he be looking? | he will not be looking (**won't be looking**) |

### The future perfect continuous（未来完了進行形）

| | | |
|---|---|---|
| I will have been looking (**I'll have been looking**) | will I have been looking? | I will not have been looking (**won't have been looking**) |
| he will have been looking (**he'll have been looking**) | will he have been looking? | he will not have been looking (**won't have been looking**) |

### The conditional continuous（条件文進行形）

| | | |
|---|---|---|
| I would be looking (**I'd be looking**) | would I be looking? | I would not be looking (**wouldn't be looking**) |
| he would be looking (**he'd be looking**) | would he be looking? | he would not be looking (**wouldn't be looking**) |

### The conditional perfect continuous（条件文完了進行形）

| | | |
|---|---|---|
| I would have been looking (**would've been looking**) | would I have been looking? | I would not have been looking (**wouldn't have been looking**) |
| he would have been looking (**would've been looking**) | would he have been looking? | he would not have been looking (**wouldn't have been looking**) |

# Verbs (動詞)

## Talking about the present (現在についての表現)

| | |
|---|---|
| ▶ 現在行っている動作を説明するには, **present continuous**(現在進行形)を使用します. | We're just **having** breakfast.<br>What **are** you **reading**?<br>She's not **listening** to me. |
| また, まだ完了していない事柄を説明するときにも, 現在進行形を使用します. 話す時点でその動作を行っていなくても現在進行形を使用できます. | I'm **learning** Japanese.<br>She's **writing** a book about snails. |
| 頻繁に起こり, 迷惑だと感じている事柄を説明するには, 現在進行形と共に **always** を使用します. | He's always **asking** silly questions.<br>They're always **coming** round here to borrow something. |
| 継続相の時制で使用できない動詞もあります. need, want, know はその一例です.<br>▶ promise, agree, seem, appear, understand, appreciate の項も参照してください. これらは動作ではなく状態を説明する動詞です. | I **need** some new shoes.<br>She **hates** her job.<br>They **love** Mexican food.<br>He **wants** to go home.<br>**Do** you **know** Tania Smith? |
| その他の動詞では, 動作を説明するときは現在進行形, 状態を説明するときは単純現在形を使用します. | He's **tasting** the soup.<br>The soup **tastes** salty.<br>She's **being** difficult again.<br>She's a difficult child.<br>What **are** you **thinking** about?<br>Do you **think** I should leave? |

| | |
|---|---|
| ▶ 不変の事実を説明するには, **present simple**(単純現在形)を使用します. | Whales **are** mammals.<br>Rice **doesn't grow** in this climate.<br>He **lives** in Spain.<br>What temperature **does** water **boil** at? |
| 定期的に起こる事柄を説明するときも単純現在形を使用します. | She **leaves** for school at 8 o'clock.<br>**Does** he **work** in a factory?<br>We **don't** often **go** out for a meal. |

# Verbs(動詞) G5

## Talking about the past(過去についての表現)

| | |
|---|---|
| ▶過去に完了した動作を説明するときは,**past simple**(単純過去形)を使用します. | He **got** up, **paid** the bill, and **left**.<br>I **didn't read** the letter, I just **gave** it to Lee.<br>What **did** you **say** to him? |
| 一般に,特定の期間について話すときに使用します. | **Did** you **speak** to Amy yesterday? |
| **過去の一定の時間に継続していたが現在は終了している状態**を説明するときも,単純過去形を使用します. | I **went** to school in Scotland.<br>**Did** she really **work** there for ten years?<br>He **didn't grow** up in Canada – he went there as an adult. |
| また,過去,定期的に行っていた動作を説明するときも単純過去形を使用します. | I often **played** tennis with her. She always **won**.<br>They never **went** to the cinema when they **lived** in the country. |

| | |
|---|---|
| ▶過去に始まり現在も継続している状態を説明するときは,**present perfect**(現在完了形)を使用します. | They **have lived** here for ten years, and they don't want to move.<br>I've **worked** here since 1998.<br>I've **known** Caroline for years. |
| 時間について述べないとき,または時間がそれほど重要でないときは,一般に,現在完了形を使用します. | He's **written** a book.<br>We've **bought** a new computer. |
| 動作は過去に完了しているが現在もその動作の影響が残っているときも,現在完了形を使用します. | **He's lost** his calculator (and he still hasn't found it). |
| 動作や状態が現在まで継続している期間を示すには,現在完了形と共に **since** および **for** を使用します. | I **have known** about it since Christmas.<br>How long **have** you **known**?<br>She **hasn't bought** any new clothes for years. |
| イギリス英語では,現在完了形と共に **just**, **ever**, **already**, **yet** をよく使用します. | I've just **arrived**.<br>**Have** you ever **been** here before?<br>He's already **packed** his suitcases.<br>**Haven't** you **finished** yet? |
| ある期間に起こって現在もまだ完了していない事柄を説明するときも,現在完了形を使用します. | The train **has been** late three times this week.<br>He still **hasn't visited** her. |

# G6 Verbs（動詞）

| | |
|---|---|
| ▶ 過去に始まり現在も継続している動作，または完了したばかりで影響や成果を明確に認識できる動作について説明するには，**present perfect continuous**（現在完了進行形）を使用します． | I**'ve been working** since eight o'clock – can I have a break now?<br>My hands are dirty because I**'ve been gardening**.<br>They **haven't been learning** English very long. |
| ▶ 何らかの動作を行った時点で既に進行していた事柄を説明するには，**past continuous**（過去進行形）を使用します． | It **was raining** when I left the house.<br>**Was** he **cooking** dinner when you got home?<br>I **wasn't wearing** a coat and I got very wet. |
| 現在進行形と同様，過去進行形は「状態」を説明する動詞には使用できません． | The fresh bread **smelled** wonderful (not ~~was smelling~~) |
| ▶ 過去に行った動作を述べ，それより前に起こった事柄を説明するには，**past perfect**（過去完了形）を使用します． | When I got to the station, the train **had left**.<br>I **had** never **met** Ed before he came to Bath.<br>They **had moved** into the flat three months before Joe lost his job. |
| ▶ 過去のある期間よりもさらにさかのぼった時間に行った動作を説明するには，**past perfect continuous**（過去完了進行形）を使用します． | My hands were dirty because I **had been gardening**.<br>She **hadn't been working** at the shop very long when they sacked her. |

## Talking about the future（未来についての表現）

future（未来形）と呼ばれる時制以外にも，未来について説明する方法がいくつかあります．

| | |
|---|---|
| ▶ 具体的な時間と共に今後の計画について説明するには，**present continuous**（現在進行形）を使用します． | He**'s flying** to Japan in August.<br>What **are** you **doing** this evening?<br>I**'m not starting** my new job till next Monday. |
| ▶ 今後行う予定だがまだ準備していない事柄について説明するには，**be going to** を使用します． | I**'m going to phone** Michael tonight.<br>What **are** you **going to do** when you leave school?<br>I**'m not going to be** as strict with my children as my parents were with me. |

# Verbs(動詞) G7

| | |
|---|---|
| ▶ 話している最中に決定した意思について説明するには，**will** と不定詞を使用します． | I can't do this. I**'ll ask** the teacher.<br>I**'ll take** the blue one.<br>We**'ll have** the salad, please. |
| ▶ （話者の意思や計画とは無関係に）将来に起こると知っているまたは考えている事柄について説明するときは，**will** と不定詞を使用します． | It **will be** 25° tomorrow.<br>She**'ll be** in the office on Monday.<br>**Will** he **pass** the exam, do you think?<br>This job **won't take** long. |
| **when**, **as soon as**, **before**, **until**などの節で将来的な事柄を述べるときは，**present simple**（単純現在形）を使用します． | Ring me as soon as you **hear** any news.<br>I'll look after Jo until you **get** back.<br>You'll recognize the street when you **see** it. |
| ▶ 要求，約束，提案などを述べるときも，**will** と不定詞を使用します． | **Will** you **buy** some bread on your way home?<br>We**'ll be** back early, don't worry.<br>I**'ll help** you with your maths. |
| ▶ 次の瞬間にも起こり得る近い将来の事柄について説明するには，**about to** と不定詞を使用します． | Go and ask him quickly. He's **about to go** out. |
| ▶ 将来の一定期間に継続する予定の動作について説明するには，**future continuous**（未来進行形）を使用します． | I**'ll be waiting** near the ticket office. I**'ll be wearing** a green hat.<br>This time next week you**'ll be relaxing** in the sun! |
| ▶ だれかの計画や意思について質問するには，**will be + -ing** を使用します． | How many nights **will** you **be staying**?<br>**Will** you **be flying** back or going by train? |
| ▶ 将来の特定の時間に完了する予定の事柄について説明するには，**future perfect**（未来完了形）を使用します． | I **will have finished** this work by 3 o'clock.<br>They**'ll have lived** here for four years in May. |
| ▶ 正式な準備が完了している将来の計画（時間割やプログラムなど）について説明するには，**present simple**（単純現在形）を使用します． | We **leave** Palma at 10 and **arrive** in Luton at 12.30.<br>School **starts** on 9 September. |

# G8 Verbs（動詞）

## Transitive and intransitive verbs（他動詞と自動詞）

**⓪** 直接目的語をとる動詞を **transitive verbs**（他動詞）と呼び，本書では，⓪と表します．例えば，**include**という動詞を参照してください．
　He included four new names on the list.
この動詞を以下のように使用することはできません．
　~~He included.~~

**⓪** 直接目的語をとることができない動詞を **intransitive verbs**（自動詞）と呼び，本書では，⓪と表します．例えば，**arrive**という動詞を参照してください．
　We arrived very late at the hotel.
この動詞を以下のように使用することはできません．
　~~We arrived the hotel.~~

**⓪⓪** 多くの動詞は自動詞と他動詞のどちらにでも使用することができ，本書では，⓪⓪と表します．
　⓪ He spoke for two hours.　　　　　　⓪ Do you speak Japanese?
　⓪ This door only locks from the outside.　⓪ Have you locked the door?

間接目的語と直接目的語の2つをとることができる動詞もあります．
**give**という動詞に記載されている構造を参照してください．
　**give sb sth; give sth to sb**
この場合，
　He gave his mother the CDs.　または　He gave the CDs to his mother.
の2通りの構造を使用できます．
片方または両方の目的語に代名詞を使用できます．
　He gave her the CDs.　　　　　　　　He gave her them.
　He gave the CDs to her.　　　　　　　He gave them to her.
　He gave them to his mother.

## Conditionals（条件文）

**if**を使った文章は可能性を表しています．**if**を使った文章構造は，大きく分けて3種類あります．

1. If I **write** my essay this afternoon, I **will have** time to go out tonight.
   (It is still morning, and it is probable that I will do this – **if**節は **present tense**（現在形），主節は **future tense**（未来形）.)

2. If I **wrote** my essay this afternoon, I **would have** time to go out tonight.
   (It is still morning, but I think it is less likely that I will do this – **if**節は **simple past**（単純過去形），主節は **conditional tense**（条件文）.)

3. If I **had written** my essay this afternoon, I **would have had** time to go out tonight.
   (It is now evening, and I haven't written my essay: it is now impossible for me to go out – **if**節は **past perfect**（過去完了形），主節は **conditional perfect**（条件文完了形）.)

**if**節には，以下のように，不変の事実，または過去に不変であった事柄を説明する用法があります．

If you **mix** blue and red, you **get** purple.
　(どちらの節も **present simple**（単純現在形）.)

If I **asked** her to come with us, she always **said** no.
　(どちらの節も **simple past**（単純過去形）.)

# Verbs: Reported speech(動詞: 間接話法) G9

## Direct speech to reported speech(直接話法から間接話法への変換)
Jeff: 'I'm coming home.' → Jeff said he was coming home.

話者が **said**, **asked** などの単語を使って自分以外の人の言葉を伝達するとき、通常、時制を1段階過去に戻します。

'I **don't know** whether Jane **wants** to come.' → He said he **didn't know** whether Jane **wanted** to come.

'She **is thinking** of staying at home tomorrow.' → He said she **was thinking** of staying at home the following day.

'**Have** you **booked** your ticket?' → She asked whether he **had booked** his ticket.

'I **finished** my exams yesterday.' → He said he **had finished** his exams the day before.

'I'**ll ring** from the station.' → He told me he **would ring** from the station.

**should**, **would**, **might**, **could**, **must**, および **ought** の法助動詞の場合は、通常、時制を変更しません。

'We might go to the cinema.' → They said they might go to the cinema.

**say**, **ask**などの伝達動詞を現在形または現在完了形で使用するときは、通常、後に続く節の時制を変更しません。

'I'm going home.' → Barry says he's going home.
Barry's just told me he's going home.

## Reporting requests and commands(要求と命令の伝達)
要求や命令を伝達するとき、通常、不定詞構文を使用します。

'Please will you do the dishes?' → She **asked me to do** the dishes.
'Don't touch the stove!' → She **told** the children **not to touch** the stove.

## Reporting questions(質問の伝達)
「はい」と「いいえ」で答える質問を伝達するには、**if**または**whether**を使用します。

'Are you ready?' → She asked **if/whether I was ready**.

**wh-**で始まる単語の質問を伝達するには、従属節に **wh-**の単語を使用します。

'When are you leaving?' → She asked me **when I was leaving**.

この文章では、平叙文と同じ語順を使用します。疑問文の語順にはなりません。

'Did you see them?' → He asked me **if I had seen** them.

## Reporting verbs(伝達動詞)
以下に、その他の **reporting verbs**(伝達動詞)を使った間接話法の例を挙げます。

'Will you come with me?' 'All right.' → She **agreed** to come with me.
'Sorry I didn't phone you.' → She **apologized** for not phoning me.
'Did you steal the money?' 'Yes, I did.' → He **admitted** (to) stealing the money.
→ He **admitted** that he'd stolen the money.
'Shall we take a break now' → He **suggested** taking a break.
'You should have a holiday.' → He **advised** me to have a holiday.
'I'm freezing!' → He **complained** that he was freezing.

# G10 Verbs: The passive（動詞: 受動態）

**active sentence（能動態）**の文章では，動作主である人や物が主語になります．
　**Masked thieves** stole a valuable painting from the museum last night.

この文章を**passive sentence（受動態）**に変換すると，動詞の目的語が主語になります．
　**A valuable painting** was stolen from the museum last night.

受動態は，動作主が不明であるときや動作主が重要でないときに使用します．科学論文などの形式的な文書では一般的に使用される文章構造です．
　The liquid was heated to 60° and then filtered.

動作主について述べるときは，文末に**by**を付けて付加します．
　The painting was stolen **by masked thieves**.

新しい情報を文章の最後に述べて強調したいときも，受動態を使用します．
　The picture was painted **by Constable**.

受動態は，**be**動詞と **past participle（過去分詞）**を使って作られます．
- The painting **is valued** by experts at 2 million dollars.
- The theft **is being investigated** by the police.
- Other museums **have been warned** to take extra care.
- The painting **was kept** in a special room.
- The lock **had been broken** and the cameras **had been switched off**.
- This morning everything possible **was being done** to find the thieves.
- Staff at the museum **will be questioned** tomorrow.
- An international search **is to be started**.
- The theft must **have been planned** with the help of someone inside the museum.

目的語を2つとる文章でも受動態を使用できます．
　An American millionaire gave **the museum the painting**.
　→**The museum** was given **the painting** by an American millionaire.
　The director told **the staff the news** this morning.
　→**The staff** were told **the news** this morning by the director.

# Verbs: Modal verbs （動詞:法動詞）

### Ability（能力）　can　could　be able to
　**Can** he swim?
　My brother **could** swim when he was two.
　I **couldn't** find my keys this morning.
　I **could have** run faster, but I didn't want the others to get tired.
　She **has** not **been able to** walk since the accident.
　He **was able to** speak to Ann before she left.
　Will people **be able to** live on the moon one day?

▶ could と managed to の違いについては，**could** の注を参照してください．

# Verbs: Modal verbs（動詞：法動詞） G11

### Possibility（可能性） could may might
**Could/Might** you have lost it on the way home?
She **may/might/could** be ill. I'll phone her.
I **may have/might have** left my purse in the shop.
Amy **might/may** know the answer.
I **might/may** not go if I'm tired.
He **might have** enjoyed the party if he'd gone.

### Permission（許可） can could may may not must not
**Can** we come in?
You **can't** get up until you're better.
**Could** we possibly stay at your flat?
(*written*) Staff **may** take their break between 12 and 2.
(*formal*) **May** I sit here?
(*written*) Crockery **may not** be taken out of the canteen.
(*formal*) You **must not** begin until I tell you.

### Obligation（義務） ought to/should（弱意） have (got) to/must（強意）
I **ought to/should** go on a diet.
I **ought to have/should have** asked her first.
(*written*) All visitors **must** report to reception on arrival.
I **must** get that report finished today.
Do you **have to** write your name on the form?
She **had to** throw the burnt cake away.
You **will have to** wait, I'm afraid.

### Advice（助言） ought to should
**Ought** I **to/Should** I write and thank him?
She **ought to/should** go out more often.
You **ought to have/should have** gone to bed earlier.
You **shouldn't** borrow the car without asking.

### No necessity（必要性の否定） don't have to shouldn't have didn't need to needn't have
You **don't have to** pick us up, we can take a taxi.
They **didn't have to** go through customs.
You **shouldn't have** bothered making lunch, we could have bought a sandwich.
He **didn't need to** have any fillings at the dentist's.
They **needn't have** waited.

▶ didn't need to と needn't have の違いについては，**need²** の注を参照してください．

### Requests（要求） can could will would
**Can** you pass me the dictionary?　　**Will** you buy me an ice cream, Mum?
**Could** you help me with my translation?　　**Would** you type this letter for me, please?

▶ Could と would の方が can, will より形式張った表現です．

### Offers and suggestions（申し出と提案） shall will
**Shall** I do the washing-up?　　I'**ll** take you to the airport.
**Shall** we go now?

# G12 Nouns(名詞)

## Countable and uncountable nouns(可算名詞と不可算名詞)

**C**    **Countable noun**(可算名詞)は，単数形でも複数形でも使用できます．
a friend/two friends      one book/five books
本書では，可算名詞を**C**と表します．

**U**    **Uncountable noun**(不可算名詞)は複数形で使用できないだけでなく，**a/an**が前に付加されることもありません．不可算名詞は数えられないものを表す名詞です．本書では，**U**と表します．例として，
**rice**, **money**, **water**, **information**, **advice**, **furniture**を参照してください．
**some rice**と言うことはできますが，a riceや two ricesと言うことはできません．**importance**, **luck**, **happiness**などの抽象名詞もほとんどが不可算名詞です．

**C U**    名詞の中には，可算と不可算の両方の意味を持つものがあります．
本書では，そのような名詞を**C U**や**U C**と表します．
例として，**cheese**, **coffee**, **paper**, **friendship**を参照してください．
- **U** ▶ Have some cheese!
- **C**   They sell a variety of cheeses. (= types of cheese)
- **U** ▶ I don't drink much coffee.
- **C**   She ordered too many coffees. (=cups of coffee)
- **U** ▶ I haven't got any more paper.
- **C**   Can you buy me a paper? (= a newspaper)
- **U** ▶ Friendship is more important than wealth.
- **C**   None of these were lasting friendships. (= relationships)

[単数扱い]    常に単数形で使用する名詞もあります．本書ではそのような名詞を[単数扱い]と表します．例として，**aftermath**, **dearth**, **brink** を参照してください．
このような名詞には複数形を使用できませんが，**a/an**や**the**を前に付加することはできます．
in the aftermath of the earthquake
There was a dearth of fresh food.
We are on the brink of disaster.

[複数扱い]    常に複数形で使用する名詞もあります．例として **jeans**, **sunglasses**, **scissors**を参照してください．本書ではそのような名詞を[複数扱い]と表します．
a sunglasses のように使用することはできません．
単体の品目について述べるには，**a pair**を使用します．
**a pair of sunglasses**            **two pairs of sunglasses.**
**headphones**, **clothes**, および **goods**などの単語は常に複数形で使用します．
I need to buy some new clothes.
**the poor**などのように人のグループを叙述する名詞は，複数形で受けます．
The poor are getting poorer and the rich are getting richer.

## Articles(冠詞)

### The definite article(定冠詞)

**definite article**(定冠詞)**the**は，話者が述べる人や物を相手が知っているときに使用します．

Thank you for **the** flowers (= the ones that you brought me).
**The** teacher said my essay was the best (= our teacher).

# Nouns(名詞) G13

川や諸島の名前の前には the が付きます.
    Which is longer, **the** Rhine or **the** Danube?
    Where are **the** Seychelles?
    Menorca is one of **the** Balearic Islands.

## The indefinite article(不定冠詞)

**indefinite article**(不定冠詞)**a**(母音の前は**an**)は,話者が述べる人や物を相手が知らないときや,特定でない人や物について述べるときに使用します.
    He's got **a** new bike. (I haven't mentioned it before.)
    Could you bring me **a** knife? (Any knife will be okay.)

人や物の種類や分類について述べるときも a/an を使用します.例えば,職業の前には a/an が付きます.
    She's **an** accountant.

価格や速度などにも a/an を使用します.
    $100 **a** day                    50 cents **a** pack
    70 kilometres **an** hour        three times **a** week

## No article(冠詞なし)

概念を述べるときは article(冠詞)を付けません.
    I love flowers (all flowers).
    Honey is sweet (all honey).
    Are nurses well paid here? (nurses in general)

国,郡,州,道路,湖などの名前には,ほとんどの場合,the を付けません.
    I'm going to Turkey.            a house in Walton Street
    She's from Yorkshire.           Lake Louise
    They live in Iowa.

人物の名前を肩書きと並べて述べるときは,肩書きの前に the を付けません.
    President Kennedy             **the** President of the United States.

> ▶ 冠詞の詳しい使用法については,**school**, **university**, **college**, **hospital**, **prison**, および **piano** を参照してください.

## The possessive with 's (所有の 's)

単語や人の名前に **'s** を付けて,所有を表すことができます.ほとんどの場合,人,国,動物を表す単語の後に付けられます.
    Ann**'s** job                       the children**'s** clothes
    the manager**'s** secretary      the dog**'s** basket
    my brother**'s** computer      Spain**'s** beaches

複数形の s で終わる単語の場合,s の後にアポストロフィーのみを付けます.
    the boys**'** rooms              the Smiths**'** house

## G14 Nouns(名詞)

### much, many, a lot, a little, a few

much は通常, 否定文や疑問文で uncountable nouns(不可算名詞)と共に使用します.
I haven't got much money left.
Did you watch much television?

肯定文で much を使用すると, 非常に形式張った表現になります.
There will be much discussion before a decision is made.

many は通常, 否定文や疑問文で countable nouns(可算名詞)と共に使用します.
There aren't many tourists here in December.
Are there many opportunities for young people?
肯定文では, a lot of より形式張った表現にするときに使用します.
Many people prefer to stay at home

a lot of や 略式 lots of は, 可算名詞と不可算名詞のどちらとも使用できます.
A lot of tourists visit the castle.   He's been here lots of times.
I've spent a lot of money.    You need lots of patience to make model aircraft.

a little は uncountable nouns(不可算名詞)と共に使用します.
Add a little vinegar.

a few は countable nouns(可算名詞)と共に使用します.
I've got a few letters to write.

> ▶ このような文章では, a littleや a fewは肯定的な意味を持ちます. aを取って fewや littleとすると, 否定的な意味になります.
> Few people have ever seen these animals in the wild.
> There is now little hope that they can win the championship.

# Adjectives(形容詞)

## Comparatives and Superlatives(比較級と最上級)

以下に, 比較級と最上級を使用した文章を示します.
Temperatures yesterday were **highest** in the south-east. The **sunniest** place was Brighton, and the **wettest** was Glasgow. Tomorrow will be **cooler** than today, but in Scotland it will be a **drier** day. **Better** weather is expected for the weekend, but it will become **more changeable** again next week.

### 形容詞を比較級や最上級にする方法
1音節の形容詞の場合, 末尾に **-er**, **-est**を付加します.
| cool | cooler | coolest |
| high | higher | highest |

# Adjectives(形容詞) G15

-eで終わる形容詞には, **-r**, **-st** のみを付加します.
nice            nicer                   nicest

以下のような単語では, 最後の文字を繰り返してから **-e**, **-er** を付加します.
wet             wetter                  wettest
big             bigger                  biggest

3音節以上の形容詞には, **more**, **most** を使用します.
changeable      more changeable         most changeable
interesting     more interesting        most interesting

2音節語で特に **-er**, **-y**, **-ly** で終わる単語は, 以下のように **cool** と同じように活用します.
clever          cleverer                cleverest

**-y** で終わる単語は, **-y** を **-i** に変更します.
sunny           sunnier                 sunniest
friendly        friendlier              friendliest

一部の2音節語は以下のように **interesting** と同じように活用します.
harmful         more harmful            most harmful

**irregular forms**(不規則変化形)を持つ形容詞もあります.
good            better                  best
bad             worse                   worst

## Adjectives with nouns(名詞を修飾する形容詞)

大部分の形容詞は, 修飾する名詞の**前**か, 関連する動詞の**後**に置かれます.
**I need a new bike.**                **This bike isn't new.**
**It's an interesting book.**         **She said the film sounded interesting.**

ただし, 名詞の**前に置けない**形容詞もあります. 本辞典では（名詞の前は不可）と記載しています. **asleep** の用法を参照してください. つまり, **Don't wake him – he's asleep.** と言うことはできますが, ~~an asleep child~~ と言うことはできません.

> ▶ **afraid**, **alive**, **ashamed**, **certain**, および **pleased** の項も参照してください.

常に名詞の前に置かれる形容詞もあります. 本辞典では（名詞の前だけ）と記載しています. 形容詞 **chief** の用法を参照してください. つまり, That was the **chief** disadvantage. と言うことはできますが, ~~This disadvantage was chief.~~ と言うことはできません.

> ▶ **downright**, **flagrant**, **former**, および **main** の項も参照してください.

## G16 Relative clauses（関係詞節）

### Defining relative clauses（制限的関係詞節）

制限的関係詞節では、話者が述べる人や物を **define**（定義）または **identify**（特定）します．

Which of them is the boss?　　　　The man **who came in late** is the boss.

> ▶ 制限的関係詞節の前にはコンマを入れません．代名詞には，**who**, **whom**, **that**, および **which** を使用します．

**subject**（主語）が人のとき
　　the man **who** came in late　or　the man **that** came in late

**object**（目的語）が人のとき
　　the girl **that** I saw　or　the girl I saw　or　the girl **whom** I saw (正式)

**subject**（主語）が物のとき
　　the chair **that** is in the corner　or　the chair **which** is in the corner (正式)

**object**（目的語）が物のとき
　　the book **that** I'm reading　or　the book I'm reading　or
　　the book **which** I'm reading (正式)

> ▶ 目的語のとき，**that**, **who**, **which** を省略できます．

**whose** は人の**所有**を表します．
　　the woman **whose** car broke down　the people **whose** house was burgled

**whose** は通常，物の説明には使用されません．
　　the chair ~~whose~~ leg is broken

物を説明する場合は，以下のような表現が一般的です．
　　the chair with the broken leg

### Non-defining relative clauses（非制限的関係詞節）

非制限的関係詞節では，省略しても文章が成り立つように途中に句を挿入し，述べている人や物の**情報を付け足します**．挿入句の前後にはコンマを入れて，主節と区切ります．

　　The film, which was shot in Mexico, has won an Oscar.

非制限的関係詞節における関係代名詞は，人について述べるときは **who**，物について述べるときは **which**，所有を表すときは **whose** を使用します．

　　My sister, who is a vegetarian, ordered a cheese salad.
　　The tickets, which can be bought at the station, are valid for one day.
　　Lucy, whose car had broken down, arrived by bus.

# MEMO

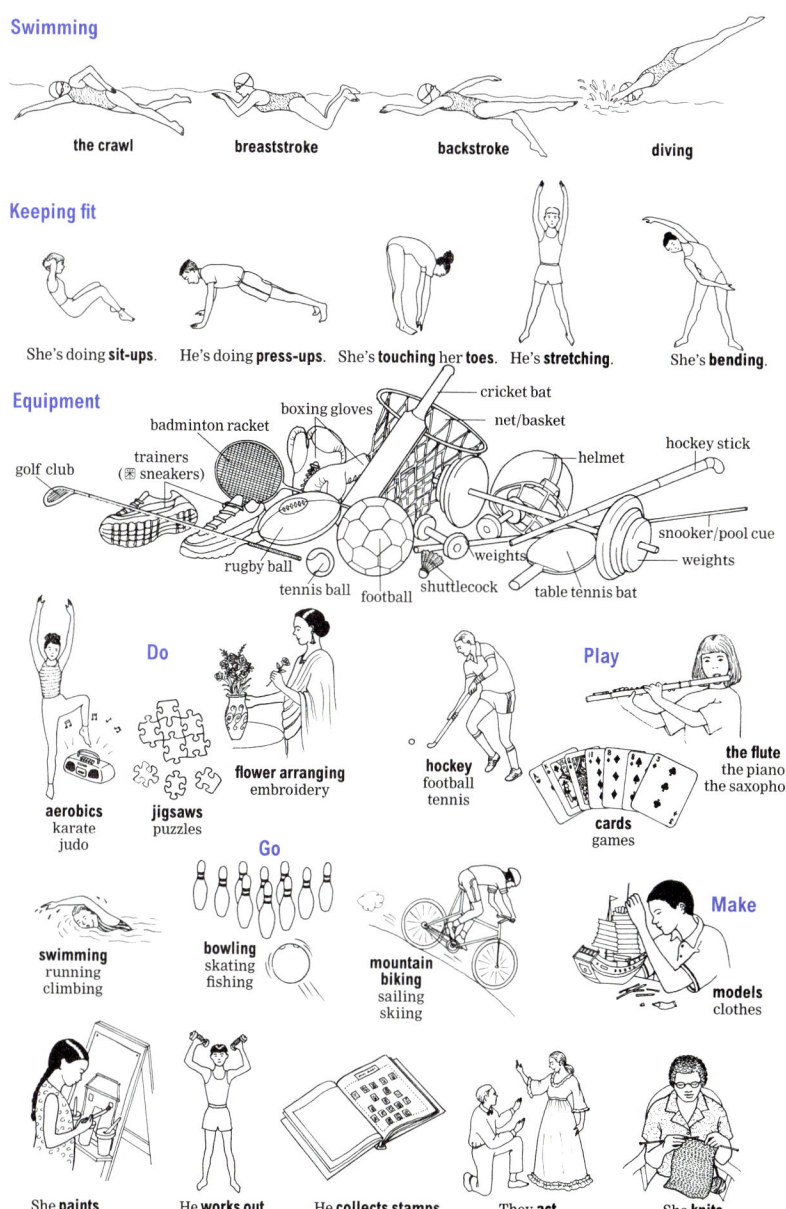

## S2 The Environment(環境)

食物, 物資, およびエネルギーを成長, 増大させるために, 環境に有害な影響が多く与えられてきました.

Gases produced by cars, power stations and factories cause **acid rain**①(酸性雨), which kills trees and fish and damages buildings. By using more **environmentally-friendly forms of transport**②(環境に優しい交通手段), we help reduce this form of pollution.

A layer of carbon dioxide and other gases traps heat and keeps the earth at the right temperature. This is called **the greenhouse effect**③(温室効果). By burning **fossil fuels**(化石燃料) (oil, coal, petrol, etc) we are producing too much carbon dioxide, which is causing temperatures to rise gradually. This **global warming**④(地球温暖化) could lead to dramatic changes in climate.

A layer of a gas called ozone protects the earth from harmful ultraviolet radiation. Certain chemicals used in industry, such as **CFCs**(フロン(ガス)), have caused a hole to develop in **the ozone layer**⑤(オゾン層). The increased levels of ultraviolet radiation damage plants and sea life, and increase the risk of skin cancer.

Most of the energy we use to heat and light buildings, run machines, etc is made by burning fossil fuels. These will eventually run out, so we need to use more **alternative sources of energy**⑥(代替エネルギー), such as **wind** and **solar power**(風力および太陽エネルギー), that are renewable and do not pollute the air. We should also avoid wasting energy by using less electricity and water and insulating our houses.

We are destroying our forests, which produce oxygen and provide habitats for animals and birds. **Deforestation**⑦(森林伐採) also allows rain to wash away the soil, making the land useless for growing things.

We pollute water by dumping waste ⑧ from factories and houses, and by accidentally spilling chemicals and oil. **Chemical fertilizers**⑨(化学肥料) damage rivers and lakes by causing a layer of tiny plants, called algae, to cover the surface of the water ⑩. **Organic farming**⑪(有機農法) does not harm the water supply.

Burying rubbish in **landfills**⑫((ごみの)埋め立て地) can let harmful chemicals leak through the ground into rivers, and it uses a lot of land. Burning rubbish ⑬ adds to global warming. By sorting our rubbish for **recycling** ⑭(再利用), we can cut down on waste.

**harmful**(有害)   **helpful**(有益)

## S4 The Office(オフィス)

# Computers(コンピューター)

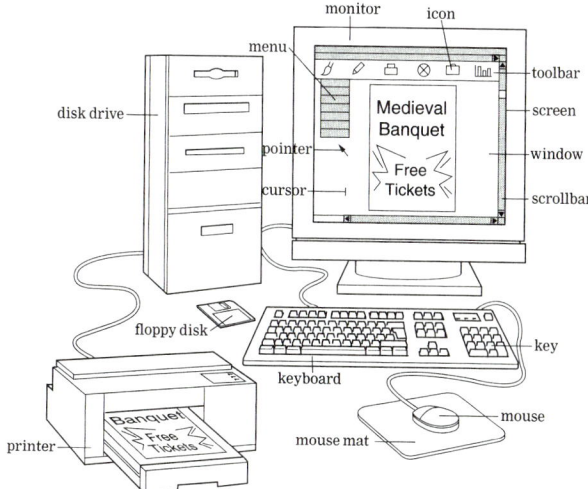

A computer can **store**(保存する) and **process**(処理する) information. This information is called **data**(データ) and can be words, numbers or **graphics**(図表) (pictures/images). To process data, the computer uses a **program**(プログラム), which is a set of instructions stored on the computer's **hard drive**(ハードドライブ).

To **input**(入力する) data, you can **enter** it using the **keyboard**(キーボード). If you want to store this data, you **save**(保存する) it in the computer's **memory**(記憶装置) or onto a **floppy disk**(フロッピーディスク). Large amounts of information, such as books, can be stored on a **CD-ROM**.

On the screen, **icons**(アイコン) (special symbols), which are arranged in a row on a **toolbar**(ツールバー) or on the **desktop**(デスクトップ), and menus show you what programs and data are stored on the computer and what jobs the computer can do. You use the **mouse**(マウス) to **click on**(クリックする) an icon and tell the computer what job you want it to do and to move to the part of the screen you want to work on. A small marker called a **cursor**(カーソル) shows your position on the screen.

Computers can be connected to other computers to form a **network**(ネットワーク). This allows different people to have access to the same information and to communicate with each other using **e-mail**(電子メール) (electronic mail). To communicate with someone using e-mail, you send your message to their **e-mail address**(電子メールアドレス). For example, **john.jones@aol.com** is a typical e-mail address. To say this address, you say 'John dot Jones at A O L dot com'.

**The Internet**(インターネット) or **the Net** is an enormous network that covers the world. People who want to make information available to the whole world can pay for their own space on the Internet. This is called a **web site**. **The Web**(ウェブ) or **the World Wide Web** (**WWW**) is the system which lets you **download**(ダウンロードする) (look at) information on the Internet. You can enter a subject and find all the web sites that have information about it. This is called **surfing**(サーフィン) the Net. **Online**(オンラインの) services are ones that are available on the Internet.

## S6 Action verbs（行為を示す動詞）

# The Car and bike (車と自転車) S7

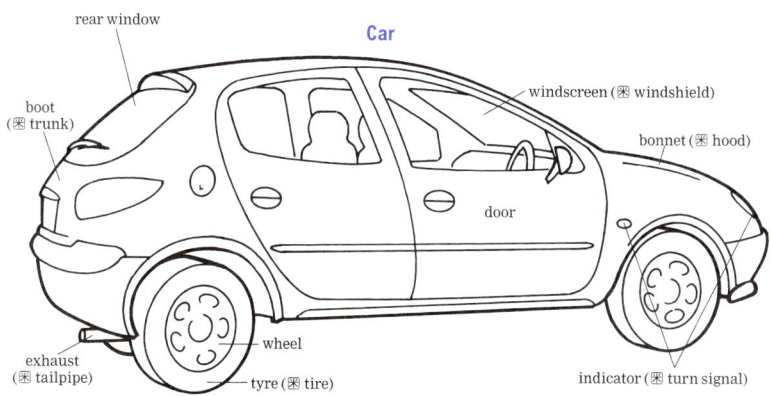

**Car**

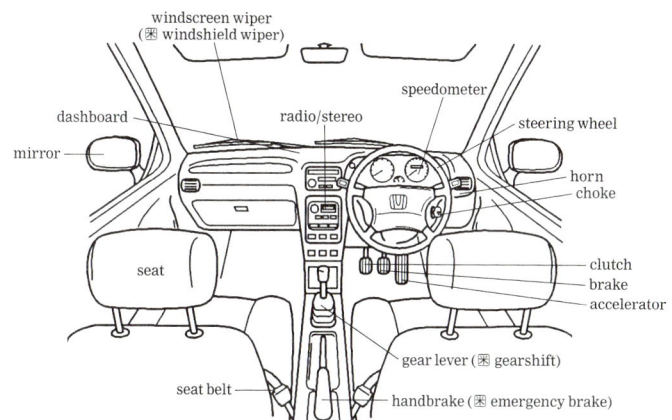

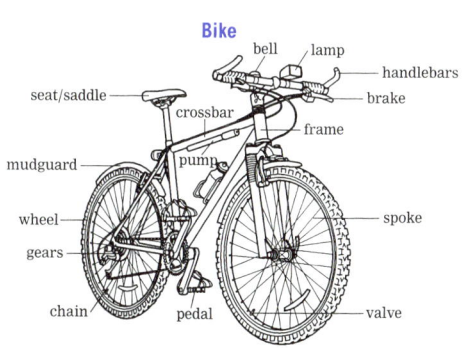

**Bike**

# Letter writing(手紙の書き方)

## The Layout of a letter(手紙のレイアウト)

**Formal letter(正式の手紙)**
- **never** write your name at the top of a letter
- write your own address on the right-hand side **and** write the address and name or position of the person you are writing to below that on the left-hand side
- write the date in full underneath your own address

**Informal letter(略式の手紙)**
- **never** write your name at the top of a letter
- write your own address above the date but **not** the address of the person you are writing to
- the date can be abbreviated and goes under your address

## Style(スタイル)

**In formal letters you...(正式の手紙の場合)**
- use Sir or Madam, or the person's title + surname
- use the passive
- do not use contractions or abbreviations
- use single-word verbs, formal linking words and phrases
- use long sentences, impersonal style
- sign with your full name and print it afterwards

**In informal letters you...(略式の手紙の場合)**
- use first names only
- use I/we
- can use contractions and abbreviations
- can use phrasal verbs, idioms and colloquial language
- use short sentences, omit pronouns, etc
- sign with your first name only

### 導入部と終結部

**Formal 1(正式の手紙1)**
(相手の名前を知らない場合)

    Dear Sir or Madam,
    Yours faithfully,
    Gwen Hollis

**Formal 2(正式の手紙2)**
(相手の名前を知っている場合)

    Dear Ms/Mr Marzec,
    Yours sincerely,
    Gwen Hollis

**Informal(略式の手紙)**

    Dear Jania,
    Yours/Love from/Best Wishes
    Gwen

### 段落分け

手紙の情報を系統立てて整理するために段落を使います.

1st Your reason for writing the letter
2nd Dates, facts and further details
3rd A request for action, information, etc
4th Ending/conclusion

## Important phrases(重要な表現)

以下は,正式または略式の手紙で使用される表現です.正式の手紙の表現1は,略式の手紙ではaに相当します.

**Formal(正式の手紙)**
1. I would be grateful if you could …
2. I look forward to hearing from you
3. I am writing to …
4. I regret to inform you …
5. You will be informed of …
6. I enclose a cheque for …
7. I would be happy to attend an interview at your convenience
8. 
9. Further to my letter of September 8th …
10. Please do not hesitate to contact me should you require any further information
11. Please give my regards to …

**Informal(略式の手紙)**
a. I'd love to come and see you
b. We'll let you know about …
c. Hope you got my last letter
d. Do you think you could …?
e. Just a note to say …
f. Write back soon/Keep in touch
g. when you can make it
h. I'm really sorry to say …
i. Give my love to …
j. Here's the money for …
k. Just give me a ring if you need to know anything else

# Letter writing (手紙の書き方)

## Informal and formal letters (正式の手紙と略式の手紙)

### ▶ Informal

> 10, Park Road,
> Birmingham,
> B15 4BU.
>
> 3/6/00
>
> Dear Morag,
>
> Sorry I haven't been in touch for ages but I hope you're all well. I'm actually writing to ask you a favour.
> On July 16th, I'm coming to Scotland with 5 of my students here, who are really keen to visit as much of Britain as possible. I thought it would be really nice if we could all stay in your B&B in Nairn for a few nights. I'm sure they'd all appreciate your huge breakfasts and general hospitality! We'd come for 3 nights from 17th to 19th July, and we'd need something like two single and two twin-bedded rooms (the latter preferably with en-suite bathrooms). Can you let me know if you can fit us in, and how much you charge now?
> I really hope to see you soon. Write back or ring me asap so I can book the trip. Could you also tell me how much deposit you'd need? Thanks a lot. Give my love to Duncan and the kids.
>
> Love from,
> Alison
>
> PS I'm getting one of the students to write a formal letter to you as well, to give her a chance to practise her letter writing.

### ▶ Formal

> 10, Park Road,
> Birmingham,
> B15 4BU
> 3rd June, 2000
>
> Mrs M. Maclennan,
> 12 St Helen's Road,
> Nairn NV12 4E2
>
> Dear Mrs. Maclennan,
> Your guest house was recommended to us by our English teacher, and I am writing to enquire whether you have any rooms available this July.
>
> There are six of us in the group: five students and our teacher. We are planning a trip to Scotland this summer and would be interested in reserving two twin-bedded rooms and two single rooms for three nights, from July 17th to July 19th.
>
> If you should have rooms available for those dates, I would be grateful if you could tell me the price of bed and breakfast per person and whether any of the rooms have en-suite bathrooms. I would also need to know whether a deposit is required in advance. I look forward to hearing from you.
>
> Yours sincerely
> Sandra Garcia

# S10 Essay writing（小論文の書き方）

小論文を書くときは，自分の考えを理路整然と，かつ形式的な書き方で表現しなければなりません．ここでは，一般的な主題である「メリットとデメリット」に関する小論文の構成を例に挙げ，接続語の使用法や句読法を説明します．

---

*Discuss the advantages and disadvantages of having a car.*

Nowadays, as roads are becoming more and more crowded, people are considering both the advantages and the disadvantages of having a car before they buy one.

The main advantage of the car is that it gives the freedom to travel when and where you want, without being limited to fixed routes and timetables. **What is more**, you can carry several passengers and as much luggage as you like, at no extra cost. **In addition to this**, you can travel in comfort in a car, with a seat to yourself and the possibility of comforts such as a music system and air conditioning.

**On the other hand**, owning a car is very expensive. As well as the price of the car, the cost of tax, insurance, petrol and repairs must also be considered before buying. **Moreover**, the increase in traffic means that drivers are spending more and more time stuck in traffic jams. Perhaps the major disadvantage of cars in general is the huge damage that they do to human life and to the environment, and all motorists must accept that they are making a small contribution to this.

**To sum up**, provided you have access to an efficient public transport system, then buying and running your own car could be considered an expensive luxury.

---

序文では，提起する問題が重要である理由，または関心を持った理由を簡潔に述べます．

小論文では，バランスが重要です．この場合，メリットとデメリットを同じ数だけ列挙します．

新しい段落を始めるときは，5文字分空けます．

結論では，主題について個人的見解を述べます．

**太字**で記されたような接続語を使って，考えをまとめます．

# Prepositions（前置詞）

使用する前置詞を誤ると文章が論理的でなくなることが多いため、注意する必要があります。以下のように、前置詞のリストを自分で作成し、活用してください。リストを手元において毎日前置詞を追加していくと、習得に役立ちます。

|  | **in** | **on** | **at** |
|---|---|---|---|
| 場所 | **in** a queue<br>**in** France/Rome<br>**in** the street | **on** the first floor<br>**on** the list<br>**on** the street | **at** the top/the bottom<br>**at** the cinema/the station<br>**at** work/school |
| 時間 | **in** the morning<br>**in** two weeks<br>*in 2001* | **on** Friday/my birthday<br>**on** time | **at** 3 o'clock<br>**at** the weekend<br>**at** first |
| 方法 | **in** the car/a taxi<br>**in** a hurry<br>**in** English | **on** your own | **at** your first attempt<br>one **at** a time |
| 成句 | **in** general<br>**in** theory/in practice | **on** paper<br>**on** the whole<br>*on a diet* |  |
| 動詞, 名詞,<br>形容詞の後 | I'm not interested **in** politics. | He had a bet **on** the race. | I was surprised **at** his reaction.<br>Stop laughing **at** me! |

# Prefixes and suffixes(接頭辞と接尾辞)

## Prefixes(接頭辞)

**a-** not: **atypical**

**ante-** before: **antenatal** (= before birth)

**anti-** against: **anti-American**, **antisocial**

**auto-** self: **autobiography** (the story of the writer's own life)

**bi-** two: **bicycle**, **bilingual** (using two languages), **bimonthly** (twice a month or every two months)

**cent-, centi-** hundred: **centenary** (= the hundredth anniversary), **centimetre** (= one hundredth of a metre)

**circum-** around: **circumnavigate** (= sail around)

**co-** with; together: **co-pilot**, **coexist**, **cooperation**

**con-** with; together: **context** (the words or sentences that come before and after a particular word or sentence)

**contra-** against; opposite: **contradict** (say the opposite)

**counter-** against; opposite: **counterrevolution**, **counterproductive** (producing the opposite of the desired effect)

**de-** taking sth away; the opposite: **defrost** (removing the layers of ice from a fridge, etc), **decentralize**

**deca-** ten: **decathlon** (a competition involving ten different sports)

**deci-** one tenth: **decilitre**

**dis-** reverse or opposite: **displeasure**, **disembark**, **discomfort**

**ex-** former: **ex-wife**, **ex-president**

**extra-** 1 very; more than usual: **extra-thin**, **extra-special** 2 outside; beyond: **extraordinary**, **extraterrestrial** (coming from somewhere beyond the earth)

**fore-** 1 before; in advance: **foreword** (= at the beginning of a book) 2 front: **foreground** (= the front part of a picture), **forehead**

**hexa-** six; **hexagon** (a shape with six sides)

**in-, il-, im-, ir-** not: **incorrect**, **invalid**, **illegal**, **illegible**, **immoral**, **impatient**, **impossible**, **irregular**, **irrelevant**

**inter-** between; from one to another: **international**, **interracial**

**kilo-** thousand: **kilogram**, **kilowatt**

**maxi-** most; very large: **maximum**

**mega-** million; very large: **megabyte**, **megabucks** (= a lot of money)

**micro-** very small: **microchip**

**mid-** in the middle of: **mid-afternoon**, **midair**

**milli-** thousandth: **millisecond**, **millimetre**

**mini-** small: **miniskirt**, **mini-series**

**mis-** bad or wrong; not: **misbehave**, **miscalculate**, **misunderstand**

**mono-** one; single: **monolingual** (= using one language), **monorail**

**multi-** many: **multinational** (= involving many countries)

**non-** not: **non-alcoholic**, **nonsense**, **non-smoker**, **non-stop**

**nona-** nine: **nonagon** (a shape with nine sides)

**octa-** eight: **octagon** (a shape with eight sides)

**out-** more; to a greater degree: **outdo**, **outrun** (= run faster or better than sb)

**over-** more than normal; too much: **overeat**, **oversleep** (= sleep too long)

**penta-** five: **pentagon** (a shape with five sides), **pentathlon** (a competition involving five different sports)

**post-** after: **post-war**

**pre-** before: **prepay**, **preview**

**pro-** for; in favour of: **pro-democracy**, **pro-hunting**

**quad-** four: **quadruple** (= multiply by four), **quadruplet** (= one of four babies born at the same time)

**re-** again: **rewrite**, **rebuild**

**semi-** half: **semicircle**, **semiconscious**

**septa-** seven: **septagon** (a shape with seven sides)

**sub-** 1 below; less than: **subzero** 2 under: **subway**, **subtitles** (= translations under the pictures of a film)

**super-** extremely; more than: **superhuman** (= having greater power than humans normally have), **supersonic** (= faster than the speed of sound)

**tele-** far; over a long distance: **telecommunications**, **telephoto lens**

**trans-** across; through: **transatlantic**, **transcontinental**

**tri-** three: **triangle**, **tricycle**

**ultra-** extremely; beyond a certain limit: **ultramodern**

**un-** not; opposite; taking sth away: **uncertain**, **uncomfortable**, **unsure**, **undo**, **undress**

**uni-** one; single: **uniform** (= having the same form)

# Prefixes and suffixes(接頭辞と接尾辞) S13

## Suffixes(接尾辞)

**-able, -ible,-ble** (to make adjectives) possible to: **acceptable, noticeable, convertible, divisible** (= possible to divide), **irresistible** (= that you cannot resist)

**-age** (to make nouns) a process or state: **storage, shortage**

**-al** (to make adjectives) connected with: **experimental, accidental, environmental**

**-ance, -ence, -ancy, -ency** (to make nouns) an action, process or state: **appearance, performance, existence, intelligence, pregnancy, efficiency**

**-ant, -ent** (to make nouns) a person who does sth: **assistant, immigrant, student**

**-ation** (to make nouns) a state or action: **examination, imagination, organization**

**-ble** → **-able**

**-ed** (to make adjectives) having a particular state or quality: **bored, patterned**

**-ee** (to make nouns) a person to whom sth is done: **employee** (= sb who is employed), **trainee** (= sb who is being trained)

**-en** (to make verbs) to give sth a particular quality; to make sth more ~: **shorten, widen, blacken, sharpen, loosen,** (but note: **lengthen**)

**-ence (-ency)** → **-ance**

**-ent** → **-ant**

**-er** (to make nouns) a person who does sth: **rider, painter, banker, driver, teacher**

**-ese** (to make adjectives) from a place: **Japanese, Chinese, Viennese**

**-ess** (to make nouns) a woman who does sth as a job: **waitress, actress**

**-ful** (to make adjectives) having a particular quality: **helpful, useful, beautiful**

**-hood** (to make nouns) **1** a state, often during a particular period of time: **childhood, motherhood 2** a group with sth in common: **sisterhood, neighbourhood**

**-ian** (to make nouns) a person who does sth as a job or hobby: **historian, comedian, politician**

**-ible** → **-able**

**-ical** (to make adjectives from nouns ending in -y or -ics) connected with: **economical, mathematical, physical**

**-ify** (to make verbs) to produce a state or quality: **beautify, simplify, purify**

**-ing** (to make adjectives) producing a particular state or effect: **interesting**

**-ish** (to make adjectives) **1** describing nationality or language: **English, Swedish, Polish 2** like sth: **babyish, foolish 3** fairly, sort of: **longish, youngish, brownish**

**-ist** (to make nouns) **1** a person who has studied sth or does sth as a job: **artist, scientist, economist 2** a person who believes in sth or belongs to a particular group: **capitalist, pacifist, feminist**

**-ion** (to make nouns) a state or process: **action, connection, exhibition**

**-ive** (to make adjectives) having a particular quality: **attractive, effective**

**-ize, -ise** (to make verbs) producing a particular state: **magnetize, standardize, modernize, generalize**

**-less** (to make adjectives) not having sth: **hopeless, friendless**

**-like** (to make adjectives) similar to: **childlike**

**-ly** (to make adverbs) in a particular way: **badly, beautifully, completely**

**-ment** (to make nouns) a state, action or quality: **development, arrangement, excitement, achievement**

**-ness** (to make nouns) a state or quality: **kindness, happiness, weakness**

**-ology** (to make nouns) the study of a subject: **biology, psychology, zoology**

**-or** (to make nouns) a person who does sth, often as a job: **actor, conductor, sailor**

**-ous** (to make adjectives) having a particular quality: **dangerous, religious, ambitious**

**-ship** (to make nouns) showing status: **friendship, membership, citizenship**

**-ward, -wards** (to make adverbs) in a particular direction: **backward, upwards**

**-wise** (to make adverbs) in a particular way: **clockwise, edgewise**

**-y** (to make adjectives) having the quality of the thing mentioned: **cloudy, rainy, fatty, thirsty**

# S14 Irregular verbs（不規則動詞）

以下のリストは，動詞の不定形，past tense（過去形）および past participle（過去分詞形）を示したものです．2種類の形式が記載されている場合は，本文でその動詞の項を参照し，意味の違いを理解してください．

| Infinitive 不定形 | Past Tense 過去形 | Past Participle 過去分詞形 | Infinitive 不定形 | Past Tense 過去形 | Past Participle 過去分詞形 |
|---|---|---|---|---|---|
| arise | arose | arisen | dream | dreamt, dreamed | dreamt, dreamed |
| awake | awoke | awoken | drink | drank | drunk |
| be | was/were | been | drive | drove | driven |
| bear | bore | borne | dwell | dwelt, dwelled | dwelt, dwelled |
| beat | beat | beaten | eat | ate | eaten |
| become | became | become | fall | fell | fallen |
| befall | befell | befallen | feed | fed | fed |
| begin | began | begun | feel | felt | felt |
| bend | bent | bent | fight | fought | fought |
| beset | beset | beset | find | found | found |
| bet | bet, betted | bet, betted | flee | fled | fled |
| bid | bid | bid | fling | flung | flung |
| bind | bound | bound | fly | flew | flown |
| bite | bit | bitten | forbid | forbade, forbad | forbidden |
| bleed | bled | bled | forecast | forecast | forecast |
| blow | blew | blown | foresee | foresaw | foreseen |
| break | broke | broken | forget | forgot | forgotten |
| breed | bred | bred | forgive | forgave | forgiven |
| bring | brought | brought | forgo | forwent | forgone |
| broadcast | broadcast | broadcast | forsake | forsook | forsaken |
| build | built | built | freeze | froze | frozen |
| burn | burnt, burned | burnt, burned | get | got | got; 米 gotten |
| burst | burst | burst | give | gave | given |
| bust | bust, busted | bust, busted | go | went | gone |
| buy | bought | bought | grind | ground | ground |
| cast | cast | cast | grow | grew | grown |
| catch | caught | caught | hang | hung, hanged | hung, hanged |
| choose | chose | chosen | have | had | had |
| cling | clung | clung | hear | heard | heard |
| come | came | come | hide | hid | hidden |
| cost | cost | cost | hit | hit | hit |
| creep | crept | crept | hold | held | held |
| cut | cut | cut | hurt | hurt | hurt |
| deal | dealt | dealt | input | input, inputted | input, inputted |
| dig | dug | dug | | | |
| dive | dived; 米 dove | dived | | | |
| do | did | done | keep | kept | kept |
| draw | drew | drawn | | | |

# Irregular verbs(不規則動詞)

| Infinitive 不定形 | Past Tense 過去形 | Past Participle 過去分詞形 | Infinitive 不定形 | Past Tense 過去形 | Past Participle 過去分詞形 |
|---|---|---|---|---|---|
| kneel | knelt; 特に米 kneeled | knelt; 特に米 kneeled | put | put | put |
| know | knew | known | quit | quit | quit |
| lay | laid | laid | read | read | read |
| lead | led | led | rebuild | rebuilt | rebuilt |
| lean | leant, leaned | leant, leaned | repay | repaid | repaid |
| leap | leapt, leaped | leapt, leaped | rethink | rethought | rethought |
| learn | learnt, learned | learnt, learned | rewind | rewound | rewound |
| leave | left | left | rewrite | rewrote | rewritten |
| lend | lent | lent | rid | rid | rid |
| let | let | let | ride | rode | ridden |
| lie | lay | lain | ring | rang | rung |
| light | lighted, lit | lighted, lit | rise | rose | risen |
| lose | lost | lost | run | ran | run |
| make | made | made | saw | sawed | sawn; 米 sawed |
| mean | meant | meant | say | said | said |
| meet | met | met | see | saw | seen |
| mislay | mislaid | mislaid | seek | sought | sought |
| mislead | misled | misled | sell | sold | sold |
| misread | misread | misread | send | sent | sent |
| misspell | misspelt, misspelled | misspelt, misspelled | set | set | set |
| mistake | mistook | mistaken | sew | sewed | sewn, sewed |
| misunderstand | misunderstood | misunderstood | shake | shook | shaken |
| mow | mowed | mown, mowed | shear | sheared | shorn, sheared |
| outdo | outdid | outdone | shed | shed | shed |
| outgrow | outgrew | outgrown | shine | shone | shone |
| overcome | overcame | overcome | shoe | shod | shod |
| overdo | overdid | overdone | shoot | shot | shot |
| overhang | overhung | overhung | show | showed | shown, showed |
| overhear | overheard | overheard | shrink | shrank, shrunk | shrunk |
| overpay | overpaid | overpaid | shut | shut | shut |
| override | overrode | overridden | sing | sang | sung |
| overrun | overran | overrun | sink | sank | sunk |
| oversee | oversaw | overseen | sit | sat | sat |
| oversleep | overslept | overslept | slay | slew | slain |
| overtake | overtook | overtaken | sleep | slept | slept |
| overthrow | overthrew | overthrown | slide | slid | slid |
| pay | paid | paid | sling | slung | slung |
| prove | proved | proved; 米 proven | slink | slunk | slunk |
| | | | slit | slit | slit |

# Irregular verbs(不規則動詞)

| Infinitive 不定形 | Past Tense 過去形 | Past Participle 過去分詞形 | Infinitive 不定形 | Past Tense 過去形 | Past Participle 過去分詞形 |
|---|---|---|---|---|---|
| smell | smelt, smelled | smelt, smelled | take | took | taken |
| sow | sowed | sown, sowed | teach | taught | taught |
| speak | spoke | spoken | tear | tore | torn |
| speed | sped, speeded | sped, speeded | tell | told | told |
| | | | think | thought | thought |
| spell | spelt, spelled | spelt, spelled | thrive | thrived, throve | thrived |
| spend | spent | spent | throw | threw | thrown |
| spill | spilt, spilled | spilt, spilled | thrust | thrust | thrust |
| spin | spun | spun | tread | trod | trodden |
| spit | spat; 米または spit | spat; 米または spit | undercut | undercut | undercut |
| | | | undergo | underwent | undergone |
| | | | underpay | underpaid | underpaid |
| split | split | split | understand | understood | understood |
| spoil | spoilt, spoiled | spoilt, spoiled | undertake | undertook | undertaken |
| spread | spread | spread | undo | undid | undone |
| spring | sprang | sprung | unwind | unwound | unwound |
| stand | stood | stood | uphold | upheld | upheld |
| steal | stole | stolen | upset | upset | upset |
| stick | stuck | stuck | wake | woke | woken |
| sting | stung | stung | wear | wore | worn |
| stink | stank, stunk | stunk | weave | wove, weaved | woven, weaved |
| stride | strode | stridden | | | |
| strike | struck | struck | weep | wept | wept |
| string | strung | strung | wet | wet, wetted | wet, wetted |
| strive | strove | striven | win | won | won |
| swear | swore | sworn | wind | wound | wound |
| sweep | swept | swept | withdraw | withdrew | withdrawn |
| swell | swelled | swollen, swelled | withhold | withheld | withheld |
| | | | withstand | withstood | withstood |
| swim | swam | swum | wring | wrung | wrung |
| swing | swung | swung | write | wrote | written |

# Expressions using numbers
## (数字を使った表現)

### The Numbers(数字)

| | | | |
|---|---|---|---|
| 1 | one | 1st | first |
| 2 | two | 2nd | second |
| 3 | three | 3rd | third |
| 4 | four | 4th | fourth |
| 5 | five | 5th | fifth |
| 6 | six | 6th | sixth |
| 7 | seven | 7th | seventh |
| 8 | eight | 8th | eighth |
| 9 | nine | 9th | ninth |
| 10 | ten | 10th | tenth |
| 11 | eleven | 11th | eleventh |
| 12 | twelve | 12th | twelfth |
| 13 | thirteen | 13th | thirteenth |
| 14 | fourteen | 14th | fourteenth |
| 15 | fifteen | 15th | fifteenth |
| 16 | sixteen | 16th | sixteenth |
| 17 | seventeen | 17th | seventeenth |
| 18 | eighteen | 18th | eighteenth |
| 19 | nineteen | 19th | nineteenth |
| 20 | twenty | 20th | twentieth |
| 21 | twenty-one | 21st | twenty-first |
| 22 | twenty-two | 22nd | twenty-second |
| 30 | thirty | 30th | thirtieth |
| 40 | forty | 40th | fortieth |
| 50 | fifty | 50th | fiftieth |
| 60 | sixty | 60th | sixtieth |
| 70 | seventy | 70th | seventieth |
| 80 | eighty | 80th | eightieth |
| 90 | ninety | 90th | ninetieth |
| 100 | a/one hundred* | 100th | hundredth |
| 101 | a/one hundred and one* | 101st | hundred and first |
| 200 | two hundred | 200th | two hundredth |
| 1 000 | a/one thousand* | 1 000th | thousandth |
| 10 000 | ten thousand | 10 000th | ten thousandth |
| 100 000 | a/one hundred thousand* | 100 000th | hundred thousandth |
| 1 000 000 | a/one million* | 1 000 000th | millionth |

**Examples**  697: six hundred and ninety-seven
3 402: three thousand, four hundred and two
80 534: eighty thousand, five hundred and thirty-four

\* 1という数字を強調したいときは、**a hundred**, **a thousand**の代わりに **one hundred**, **one thousand**を使用します.

### Telephone Numbers(電話番号)

電話番号を言うときは、数字を1つずつ述べます. 通常、2, 3けたの後に間をおきます.
 509236  five o nine – two three six
**66** という番号の場合, **six six** または **double six** と言います.
 02166  o two one – six six or o two one – double six.

市外に電話をかけるときは、電話番号の前に **area code**(市外局番)を付けなければなりません. 01865は Oxfordの市外局番です.
また、大企業に電話をかけるときは、**extension number**(内線番号)を使用できます. (01865) 56767 x 4840 (extension 4840)

# S18 Expressions using numbers
(数字を使った表現)

## Fractions and Decimals (分数と小数)

| | | | |
|---|---|---|---|
| ½ | a half | ⅓ | a/one third |
| ¼ | a quarter | ⅖ | two fifths |
| ⅛ | an/one eighth | 7/12 | seven twelfths |
| 1/10 | a/one tenth | 1 ½ | one and a half |
| 1/16 | a/one sixteenth | 2 ⅜ | two and three eighths |

| | | | |
|---|---|---|---|
| **0.1** | (nought) point one | **1.75** | one point seven five |
| **0.25** | (nought) point two five | **3.976** | three point nine seven six |
| **0.33** | (nought) point three three | | |

## Percentages and Proportions (百分率と比率)

**90%** of all households have a television.
**Nine out of ten** households have a television.
**Nine tenths of** all households have a television.

## Mathematical Expressions (計算式の記号)

- **+** plus
- **-** minus
- **x** times or multiplied by
- **÷** divided by
- **=** equals
- **%** per cent
- **3²** three squared
- **5³** five cubed
- **6¹⁰** six to the power of ten

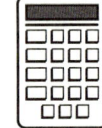

**Examples**
- **7+6=13** seven plus six equals (or is) thirteen
- **5x8=40** five times eight equals forty
  or five eights are forty
  or five multiplied by eight is forty

## Temperature (温度)

イギリス英語では,通常,**degrees Celsius**(摂氏度)で温度を表します.ただし,イギリス人の間では現在も **Fahrenheit**(華氏)での表現が主流です.アメリカでは,科学分野での表現を除き,**Fahrenheit**(華氏)が使用されています.
**Fahrenheit**(華氏)を **Celsius**(摂氏)に変換するには,
華氏温度から32を引き,5を掛けて9で割ります.

```
      68°F −
      32
=     36 x
       5
=     180 ÷ 9
=     20°C
```

# Expressions using numbers S19
(数字を使った表現)

### Examples
Water freezes at 32°F and boils at 212°F.
The maximum temperature this afternoon will be 15°, and the minimum tonight may reach –5° (minus five).
She was running a temperature of 102° last night, and it's still above normal.

## Weight (重量)

| | **GB** | **Metric** |
|---|---|---|
| | 1 ounce (oz) | = 28.35 grams (g) |
| 16 ounces | = 1 pound (lb) | = 0.454 kilogram (kg) |
| 14 pounds | = 1 stone (st) | = 6.356 kilograms |
| 112 pounds | = 1 hundredweight (cwt) | = 50.8 kilograms |
| 20 hundredweight | = 1 ton (t) | = 1.016 tonnes |

### Examples
The baby weighed 8 lb 2oz (eight pounds two ounces).
For this recipe you need 750g (seven hundred and fifty grams) of flour.

> ▶ メモ: アメリカでは, 1 hundredweightは 100 pounds, 1 tonは 2000 lbまたは 0.907 tonne と同等です. アメリカ英語ではstoneを使用しないため, 重量を表現するときはpoundで述べます. *He weighs 180 pounds.*

## Length (長さ)

| | **GB** | **Metric** |
|---|---|---|
| | 1 inch (in) | = 25.4 millimetres (mm) |
| 12 inches | = 1 foot (ft) | = 30.48 centimetres (cm) |
| 3 feet | = 1 yard (yd) | = 0.914 metre (m) |
| 1 760 yards | = 1 mile | = 1.609 kilometres (km) |

### Examples
300 dots per inch
flying at 7000 feet
The speed limit is 30 mph (thirty miles per hour).
The room is 11'x 9'6" (eleven feet by nine feet six *or* eleven foot by nine foot six).

## Area (面積)

| | **GB** | **Metric** |
|---|---|---|
| | 1 square inch (sq in) | = 6.452 square centimetres |
| 144 square inches | = 1 square foot (sq ft) | = 929.03 square centimetres |
| 9 square feet | = 1 square yard (sq yd) | = 0.836 square metre |
| 4840 square yards | = 1 acre | = 0.405 hectare |
| 640 acres | = 1 square mile | = 2.59 square kilometres or 259 hectares |

### Examples
an 80-acre country park
160 000 square miles of the jungle have been destroyed.

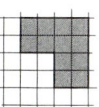

# S20 Expressions using numbers
(数字を使った表現)

## Cubic Measure (体積度量法)

|  | **GB** | **Metric** |
|---|---|---|
|  | 1 cubic inch (cu in) | = 16 39 cubic centimetres (cc) |
| 1728 cubic inches | = 1 cubic foot (cu ft) | = 0.028 cubic metre |
| 27 cubic feet | = 1 cubic yard | = 0.765 cubic metre |

**Example**
a car with a 1500 cc engine

## Capacity (容積)

|  | **GB** | **US** | **Metric** |
|---|---|---|---|
| 20 fluid ounces (fl oz) | = 1 pint (pt) | = 1.201 pints | = 0.568 litre (l) |
| 2 pints | = 1 quart (qt) | = 1.201 quarts | = 1.136 litres |
| 4 quarts | = 1 gallon (gall) | = 1.201 gallons | = 4.546 litres |

**Examples**
I drink a litre of water a day.   a quart of orange juice

## Times (時刻)

|  | **In Conversation** | **In official language** |
|---|---|---|
| 06.00 | six o'clock | (o) six hundred (hours) |
| 06.05 | five past six | (o) six o five |
| 06.10 | ten past six | (o) six ten |
| 06.15 | (a) quarter past six | (o) six fifteen |
| 06.20 | twenty past six | (o) six twenty |
| 06.30 | half past six | (o) six thirty |
| 06.35 | twenty-five to seven | (o) six thirty-five |
| 06.40 | twenty to seven | (o) six forty |
| 06.45 | (a) quarter to seven | (o) six forty-five |
| 06.50 | ten to seven | (o) six fifty |
| 06.55 | five to seven | (o) six fifty-five |
| 10.12 | twelve minutes past ten | ten twelve |
| 13.10 | ten past one | thirteen ten |
| 19.56 | four minutes to eight | nineteen fifty-six |

アメリカ英語では, past の代わりに **after**, to の代わりに **of** を使用します.

► **メモ**: 公式の場では, 24 時間制で時間を表現します. *The next train is the 07.02 to Marlow. (o seven o two)* 会話では次のように述べます. *I left at seven in the morning/two in the afternoon/eight in the evening/eleven at night.* やや形式的な表現では, **a.m.**(午前) および **p.m.**(午後) が使用されます. *School starts at 9 a.m.*

## Dates (日付)

日付は, 数字のみ, または数字と文字で表記します.
  15/4/01 (米 4/15/01)  15 April 2001  April 15th, 2001 (**特に**米)
以下のようにも述べられます.
April the fifteenth, two thousand and one  or  the fifteenth of April, two thousand and one (米 April fifteenth, two thousand and one)

**Example**
She was born on 4 May (May the fourth/the fourth of May).

# Map of Britain and Ireland
（イギリスとアイルランドの地図）

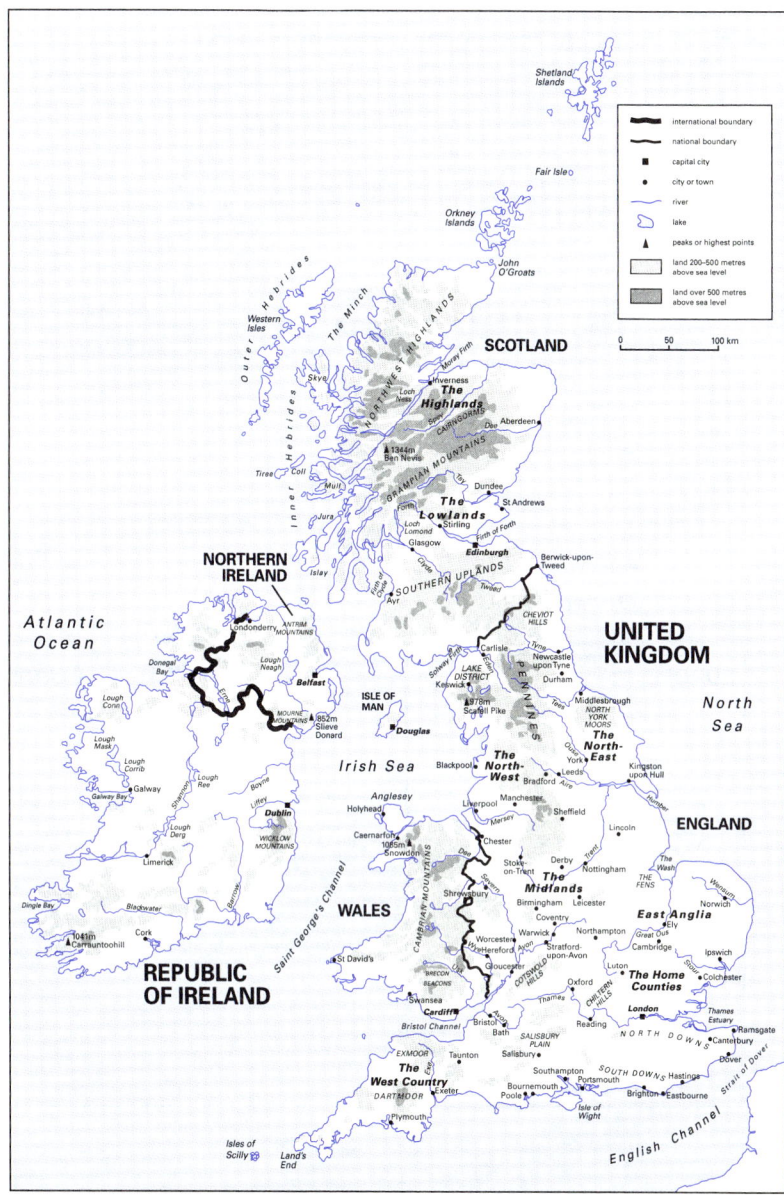

# World map showing capital cities
（世界各国の首都）

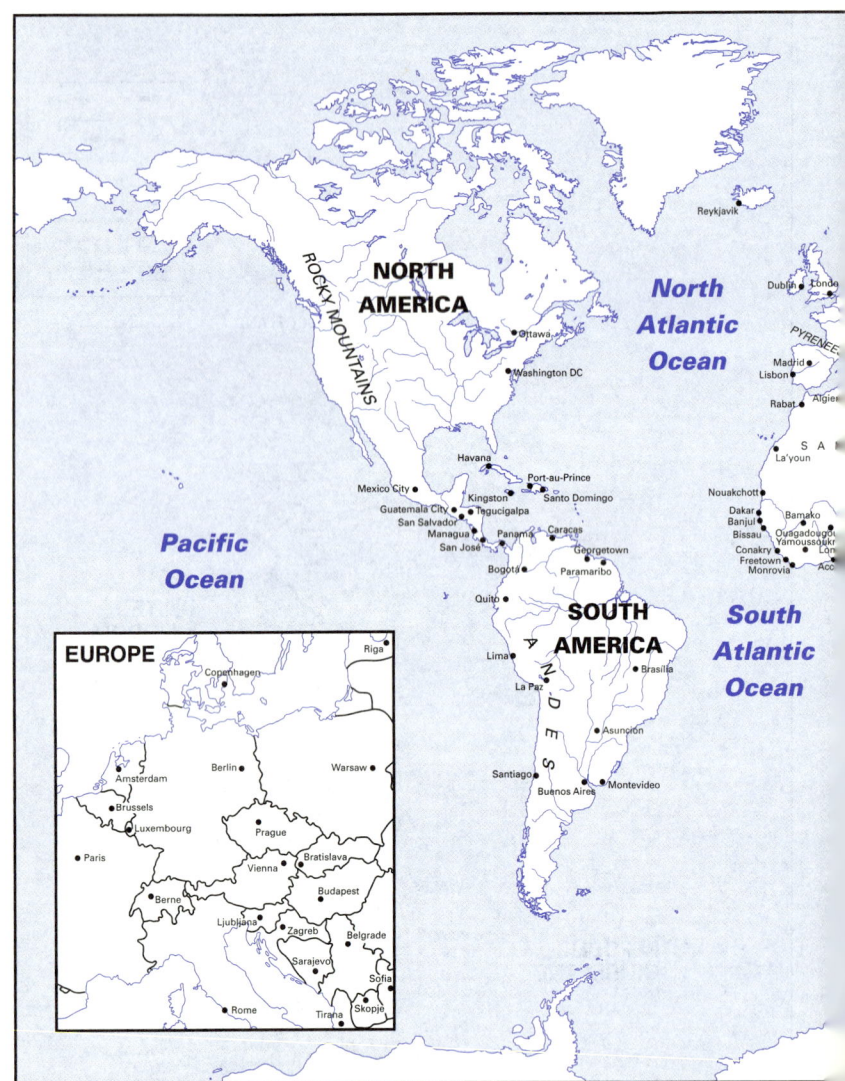

# World map showing capital cities
（世界各国の首都）

# Geographical names（地名）

以下のリストは，世界の国名とその形容詞形，首都を示したものです．
一般的に，国民について述べる場合，「形容詞＋people」の形を使います．

**Moroccan people, French people, Israeli people, Japanese people**

形容詞に **-s** を付けて表すこともできます．

**Moroccans, Israelis**

ただし，形容詞の語末が /s/ /z/ /ʃ/ の音で終わる場合は，**the** を使い，**-s** を使うことはできません．

**the Swiss, the Chinese, the French**

複数の国民について述べる場合は，形容詞形に **-s** を付けます（ただし，語末が /s/ /z/ /ʃ/ の音で終わる場合は除きます）．

**two Germans, some Pakistanis, a group of Japanese, a few Swiss**

上記の規則以外で，特殊な単語で表される国民もあります（下記のリストでは，Adjective の欄で形容詞の後ろに掲載しています）．例：**Denmark: Danish, a Dane**

**two Danes, several Turks, a roomful of Dutchwomen**

\* のマークを付けた地名はスペースの都合上，S22, S23の地図に掲載することができませんでした．

| Country | Adjective | Capital |
|---|---|---|
| Afghanistan アフガニスタン | Afghan | Kabul |
| Africa アフリカ | African | — |
| Albania アルバニア | Albanian | Tirana |
| Algeria アルジェリア | Algerian | Algiers |
| America アメリカ | →(the) United States of America | |
| Angola アンゴラ | Angolan | Luanda |
| Antarctica 南極大陸 | Antarctic | — |
| Antigua and Barbuda アンティグアバーブーダ | Antiguan, Barbudan | St John's\* |
| (the) Arctic 北極 | Arctic | — |
| Argentina アルゼンチン | Argentine, Argentinian | Buenos Aires |
| Armenia アルメニア | Armenian | Yerevan |
| Asia アジア | Asian | — |
| Australia オーストラリア | Australian | Canberra |
| Austria オーストリア | Austrian | Vienna |
| Azerbaijan アゼルバイジャン | Azerbaijani, an Azeri | Baku |
| (the) Bahamas バハマ | Bahamian | Nassau\* |
| Bahrain バーレーン | Bahraini | Manama |
| Bangladesh バングラデシュ | Bangladeshi | Dhaka |
| Barbados バルバドス | Barbadian | Bridgetown\* |
| Belarus ベラルーシ | Belorussian | Minsk |
| Belgium ベルギー | Belgian | Brussels |
| Benin ベニン | Beninese | Porto Novo |
| Bhutan ブータン | Bhutanese | Thimphu |
| Bolivia ボリビア | Bolivian | La Paz |
| Bosnia-Herzegovina ボスニアヘルツェゴビナ | Bosnian | Sarajevo |
| Botswana ボツワナ | Botswanan, person: Motswana people: Batswana | Gaborone |
| Brazil ブラジル | Brazilian | Brasilia |

# Geographical names（地名） S25

| Country | Adjective | Capital |
|---|---|---|
| **Brunei Darussalam** ブルネイダルサラーム | Brunei, Bruneian | Bandar Seri Begawan |
| **Bulgaria** ブルガリア | Bulgarian | Sofia |
| **Burkina** ブルキナ | Burkinese | Ouagadougou |
| **Burma** ミャンマー（旧ビルマ） | Burmese | Yangon |
| **Burundi** ブルンジ | Burundian | Bujumbura |
| **Cambodia** カンボジア | Cambodian | Phnom Penh |
| **Cameroon** カメルーン | Cameroonian | Yaoundé |
| **Canada** カナダ | Canadian | Ottawa |
| **Cape Verde** カボベルデ | Cape Verden | Praia* |
| **(the) Central African Republic** 中央アフリカ共和国 | Central African | Bangui |
| **Chad** チャド | Chadian | N'Djamena |
| **Chile** チリ | Chilean | Santiago |
| **China** 中国 | Chinese | Beijing |
| **Colombia** コロンビア | Colombian | Bogotá |
| **Comoros** コモロ | Comoran | Moroni* |
| **Congo** コンゴ | Congolese | Brazzaville |
| **Costa Rica** コスタリカ | Costa Rican | San José |
| **Côte d'Ivoire** コートジボワール | →(the) Ivory Coast | |
| **Croatia** クロアチア | Croatian | Zagreb |
| **Cuba** キューバ | Cuban | Havana |
| **Cyprus** キプロス | Cypriot | Nicosia |
| **(the) Czech Republic** チェコ共和国 | Czech | Prague |
| **(the) Democratic Republic of the Congo** コンゴ民主共和国 | Congolese | Kinshasa |
| **Denmark** デンマーク | Danish, a Dane | Copenhagen |
| **Djibouti** ジブチ | Djiboutian | Djibouti |
| **Dominica** ドミニカ | Dominican | Roseau |
| **(the) Dominican Republic** ドミニカ共和国 | Dominican | Santo Domingo |
| **Ecuador** エクアドル | Ecuadorian | Quito |
| **Egypt** エジプト | Egyptian | Cairo |
| **El Salvador** エルサルバドル | Salvadorean | San Salvador |
| **England** イングランド | English, an Englishman an Englishwoman | London |
| **Equatorial Guinea** 赤道ギニア | Equatorial Guinean | Malabo |
| **Eritrea** エリトリア | Eritrean | Asmera |
| **Estonia** エストニア | Estonian | Tallinn |
| **Ethiopia** エチオピア | Ethiopian | Addis Ababa |
| **Europe** ヨーロッパ | European | — |
| **Fiji** フィジー | Fijian | Suva* |
| **Finland** フィンランド | Finnish, a Finn | Helsinki |
| **France** フランス | French, a Frenchman a Frenchwoman | Paris |
| **(the) FYROM** マケドニア | Macedonian | Skopje |
| **Gabon** ガボン | Gabonese | Libreville |
| **(the) Gambia** ガンビア | Gambian | Banjul |
| **Georgia** グルジア | Georgian | Tbilisi |
| **Germany** ドイツ | German | Berlin |
| **Ghana** ガーナ | Ghanian | Accra |
| **Great Britain** 英国 | British, a Briton | London |

# Geographical names (地名)

| Country | Adjective | Capital |
|---|---|---|
| Greece ギリシャ | Greek | Athens |
| Grenada グレナダ | Grenadian | St George's* |
| Guatemala グアテマラ | Guatemalan | Guatemala City |
| Guinea ギニア | Guinean | Conakry |
| Guinea-Bissau ギニアビサウ | Guinean | Bissau |
| Guyana ガイアナ | Guyanese | Georgetown |
| Haiti ハイチ | Haitian | Port-au-Prince |
| Holland オランダ | → (the) Netherlands | |
| Honduras ホンジュラス | Honduran | Tegucigalpa |
| Hungary ハンガリー | Hungarian | Budapest |
| Iceland アイスランド | Icelandic | Reykjavik |
| India インド | Indian | New Delhi |
| Indonesia インドネシア | Indonesian | Jakarta |
| Iran イラン | Iranian | Tehran |
| Iraq イラク | Iraqi | Baghdad |
| Ireland アイルランド | Irish, an Irishman, an Irishwoman | Dublin |
| Israel イスラエル | Israeli | Jerusalem |
| Italy イタリア | Italian | Rome |
| (the) Ivory Coast コートジボワール | Ivorian | Yamoussoukro |
| Jamaica ジャマイカ | Jamaican | Kingston |
| Japan 日本 | Japanese | Tokyo |
| Jordan ヨルダン | Jordanian | Amman |
| Kazakhstan カザフスタン | Kazakh | Akmola |
| Kenya ケニア | Kenyan | Nairobi |
| Kiribati キリバス | Kiribati | Tarawa* |
| Korea, North 北朝鮮 | North Korean | Pyongyang |
| Korea, South 韓国 | South Korean | Seoul |
| Kuwait クウェート | Kuwaiti | Kuwait City |
| Kyrgyzstan キルギスタン | Kyrgyz | Bishkek |
| Laos ラオス | Laotian | Vientiane |
| Latvia ラトビア | Latvian | Riga |
| Lebanon レバノン | Lebanese | Beirut |
| Lesotho レソト | Sotho, person: Mosotho people: Basotho | Maseru |
| Liberia リベリア | Liberian | Monrovia |
| Libya リビア | Libyan | Tripoli |
| Liechtenstein リヒテンシュタイン | Liechtenstein, a Liechtensteiner | Vaduz* |
| Lithuania リトアニア | Lithuanian | Vilnius |
| Luxembourg ルクセンブルク | Luxembourg, a Luxembourger | Luxembourg |
| Madagascar マダガスカル | Madagascan, a Malagasy | Antananarivo |
| Malawi マラウイ | Malawian | Lilongwe |
| Malaysia マレーシア | Malaysian | Kuala Lumpur |
| (the) Maldives モルディブ | Maldivian | Male* |
| Mali マリ | Malian | Bamako |
| Malta マルタ | Maltese | Valletta* |
| Mauritania モーリタニア | Mauritanian | Nouakchott |
| Mauritius モーリシャス | Mauritian | Port Louis* |
| Mexico メキシコ | Mexican | Mexico City |
| Moldova モルドバ | Moldovian | Chişinău |
| Mongolia モンゴル | Mongolian, a Mongol | Ulan Bator |

# Geographical names(地名)

| Country | Adjective | Capital |
|---|---|---|
| Montserrat モントセラト | Montserratian | Plymouth* |
| Morocco モロッコ | Moroccan | Rabat |
| Mozambique モザンビーク | Mozambiquean | Maputo |
| Myanmar ミャンマー | →Burma | |
| Namibia ナミビア | Namibian | Windhoek |
| Nauru ナウル | Nauruan | Nauru* |
| Nepal ネパール | Nepalese | Kathmandu |
| (the) Netherlands オランダ | Dutch, a Dutchman, a Dutchwoman | Amsterdam |
| New Zealand ニュージーランド | New Zealand, a New Zealander | Wellington |
| Nicaragua ニカラグア | Nicaraguan | Managua |
| Niger ニジェール | Nigerian | Niamey |
| Nigeria ナイジェリア | Nigerian | Abuja |
| Northern Ireland 北アイルランド | Northern Irish | Belfast* |
| Norway ノルウェー | Norwegian | Oslo |
| Oman オマーン | Omani | Muscat |
| Pakistan パキスタン | Pakistani | Islamabad |
| Panama パナマ | Panamanian | Panama |
| Papua New Guinea パプアニューギニア | Papuan | Port Moresby |
| Paraguay パラグアイ | Paraguayan | Asunción |
| Peru ペルー | Peruvian | Lima |
| (the) Philippines フィリピン | Philippine, a Filipino | Manila |
| Poland ポーランド | Polish, a Pole | Warsaw |
| Portugal ポルトガル | Portuguese | Lisbon |
| Qatar カタール | Qatari | Doha |
| Romania ルーマニア | Romanian | Bucharest |
| Russia ロシア | Russian | Moscow |
| Rwanda ルワンダ | Rwandan | Kigali |
| San Marino サンマリノ | San Marinese | San Marino* |
| São Tomé and Principe サントメプリンシペ | São Tomean | São Tomé* |
| Saudi Arabia サウジアラビア | Saudi, Saudi Arabian | Riyadh |
| Scotland スコットランド | Scottish, Scots, a Scot a Scotsman, a Scotswoman | Edinburgh* |
| Senegal セネガル | Senegalese | Dakar |
| (the) Seychelles セーシェル | Seychellois | Victoria* |
| Sierra Leone シエラレオネ | Sierra Leonean | Freetown |
| Singapore シンガポール | Singaporean | Singapore |
| Slovakia スロバキア | Slovak | Bratislava |
| Slovenia スロベニア | Slovene, Slovenian | Ljubljana |
| (the) Solomon Islands ソロモン諸島 | Solomon Islander | Honiara* |
| Somalia ソマリア | Somali | Mogadishu |
| South Africa 南アフリカ | South African | Pretoria |
| Spain スペイン | Spanish, a Spaniard | Madrid |
| Sri Lanka スリランカ | Sri Lankan | Colombo |
| St Kitts and Nevis セントクリストファーネビス | Kittitian, Nevisian | Basseterre* |
| St Lucia セントルシア | St Lucian | Castries* |
| St Vincent and the Grenadines セントビンセントグレナディーン | Vincentian | Kingstown* |

# Geographical names（地名）

| Country | Adjective | Capital |
|---|---|---|
| Sudan スーダン | Sudanese | Khartoum |
| Suriname スリナム | Surinamese | Paramaribo |
| Swaziland スワジランド | Swazi | Mbabane |
| Sweden スウェーデン | Swedish, a Swede | Stockholm |
| Switzerland スイス | Swiss | Berne |
| Syria シリア | Syrian | Damascus |
| Taiwan 台湾 | Taiwanese | Taipei |
| Tajikistan タジキスタン | Tajik | Dushanbe |
| Tanzania タンザニア | Tanzanian | Dodoma |
| Thailand タイ | Thai | Bangkok |
| Tibet チベット | Tibetan | Lhasa* |
| Togo トーゴ | Togolese | Lomé |
| Tonga トンガ | Tongan | Nuku'alofa* |
| Trinidad and Tobago トリニダードトバゴ | Trinidadian, Tobagonian | Port-of-Spain* |
| Tunisia チュニジア | Tunisian | Tunis |
| Turkey トルコ | Turkish, a Turk | Ankara |
| Turkmenistan トルクメニスタン | Turkmen | Ashgabat |
| Tuvalu ツバル | Tuvaluan | Funafuti* |
| Uganda ウガンダ | Ugandan | Kampala |
| Ukraine ウクライナ | Ukrainian | Kiev |
| (the) United Arab Emirates アラブ首長国連邦 | Emirian | Abu Dhabi |
| (the) United Kingdom 連合王国 | British, a Briton | London |
| (the) United States of America アメリカ合衆国 | American | Washington DC |
| Uruguay ウルグアイ | Uruguayan | Montevideo |
| Uzbekistan ウズベキスタン | Uzbek | Tashkent |
| Vanuatu バヌアツ | Vanuatan | Vila* |
| Venezuela ベネズエラ | Venezuelan | Caracas |
| Vietnam ベトナム | Vietnamese | Hanoi |
| Wales ウェールズ | Welsh, a Welshman, a Welshwoman | Cardiff* |
| (the) West Indies 西インド諸島 | West Indian | — |
| Western Sahara 西サハラ | Sahrawian, Sahrawi | Laâyoune |
| Western Samoa 西サモア | Samoan | Apia* |
| (the) Yemen Republic イエメン共和国 | Yemeni | Sana'a |
| Yugoslavia ユーゴスラビア | Yugoslavian | Belgrade |
| Zambia ザンビア | Zambian | Lusaka |
| Zimbabwe ジンバブエ | Zimbabwean | Harare |

# MEMO

## ワードパワー英英和辞典

初版第1刷発行　2002年2月20日
初版第4刷発行　2003年3月10日

◎編集主幹◎
島岡 丘

◎発行人◎
藤井史昭

◎発行◎
株式会社 増進会出版社
ホームページ http://www.zkai.co.jp/

◎編集人◎
石原 明

◎企画編集◎
株式会社 Z会出版
〒411-0944　静岡県駿東郡長泉町竹原383-9
(055) 973-7117

◎発売◎
BSS株式会社
〒112-0011　東京都文京区千石4-37-4
(03) 3946-7181

◎書容設計◎
羽良多平吉 & 株式会社エディックス

◎印刷・製本◎
図書印刷株式会社

定価は箱に表示してあります.
乱丁・落丁はお取り替えいたします.
ISBN 4-939149-58-7 C7582
Printed in Japan